TOTAL BASEBALL

THIRD EDITION

EDITED BY

John Thorn and Pete Palmer

with Michael Gershman

HarperPerennial

A Division of HarperCollinsPublishers

Total Baseball Staff
Third Edition

Editors
John Thorn   *Pete Palmer*

Project Consultants
Michael Gershman   *David Reuther*

Associate Editor
David Pietrusza

Assistant Editor
Susan Ray

Book Design
Marc Cheshire
Jacquie Roland

Typographer
Starkey & Henricks
Peter Bird, President

HarperCollins Publishers
Maron L. Waxman, Editorial Director, Harper Reference
Carol Cohen, Vice President and Publisher, Harper Reference

TOTAL BASEBALL (Third Edition). Copyright © 1993 by Total Baseball.
Copyright © 1989, 1991 by Professional Ink, Inc.
"Casey at the Bat" by Donald Hall, published by David R. Godine,
Publisher, Inc., copyright © 1988 by Donald Hall.
All rights reserved. Printed in the United States of America.
No part of this book may be used or
reproduced in any manner whatsoever
without written permission
except in the case of brief quotations embodied in critical articles and reviews.
For information address HarperCollins Publishers, Inc., 10 East 53rd Street, New York, NY 10022.

HarperCollins books may be purchased for educational, business, or sales promotional use. For information, please write: Special Markets
Department, HarperCollins Publishers, Inc., 10 East 53rd Street, New York, NY 10022.

Library of Congress Cataloging-in-Publication Data
    Total Baseball / edited by John Thorn and Pete Palmer—3rd ed.
        p.   cm.
    ISBN 0-06-273189-0
1. Baseball—United States—History.   I. Thorn, John, 1947-
II. Palmer, Pete.   III. Michael Gershman
GV863.A1T68   1993
    796.357'0973—dc20   92-45555

93 94 95 CW 10 9 8 7 6 5 4 3 2 1

Contents

PART TWO

The Registers, Leaders, and Rosters

Appendixes

Acknowledgments

This third edition of *Total Baseball* could not have been published without the assistance of a legion of writers, researchers, and editorial/production staff. The principal contributors in these areas are credited on the preceding staff page and table of contents; others may be acknowledged within the text or in the separate introductions to the various sections of Part 2. Still others provided vital inspiration, investigative tips, and production help, yet go unmentioned in the body of the book; this page is for them, especially those who took part in the launch of the book back in 1989.

Michael Gershman joined us for *Total Baseball III*, bringing his varied talents to every aspect of the book and the new production company that has developed from it. Mike believed we could open up *Total Baseball* to a wider audience without abandoning the features that have endeared us to specialists; several of the changes on display in this edition reflect his fresh views.

David Pietrusza had provided invaluable fact checking to the second edition, as well as a fine piece on the business of baseball (with Steve Mann). This time around his involvement was greater: in addition to fact checking and additional writing assignments, Dave undertook the updating and midnight-oil burning that in the second edition had been the province of Richard Puff. Susan Ray, another veteran of the second edition, was of vital help in the book's final weeks.

Marc Cheshire's splendid design for the first edition has stood the test of time. Jacquie Roland supplied some additional refinements, notably for the title page and part-titles. She also assisted in the project coordination, earning the *croix de guerre* that in earlier editions had been won by Marc Cheshire and Gypsy da Silva.

Peter Bird, president of Starkey & Henricks, has supervised the mammoth job of setting *Total Baseball* in all its editions. We thank him and his extraordinary staff for going the extra mile for us, especially in the final weeks of production.

Without the commitment of HarperCollins to publishing this book in a paperbound, reasonably priced new edition, this very costly project might have seen its readership dwindle. Agent Jay Acton introduced us to the good folks at HarperCollins, beginning with Nick Bakelar and Carol Cohen and culminating with Maron Waxman. For Maron particularly—with whom we have worked on so many other books through the years but never before one of this scope and complexity—we extend deep appreciation for making this edition of *Total Baseball* the best yet. To others at Harper Reference, a tip of the cap to Kathy McKitty, Joana Jebsen, Craig Herman, and Nancy Dickinson.

Thanks as well to Eric Pozzo and all the brainy types out at CMC (Creative Multimedia Corporation) who thought to bring *Total Baseball* to the public in electronic form, through CD-ROM technology. We still can't quite believe that a compact disc weighing an ounce or so contains everything in this book, but is so.

We are indebted to David Reuther, our friend and associate in many other books. His contributions to the editorial, production, and business aspects of *Total Baseball*—both the original and second editions—were truly indispensable.

For research help, particularly into the years before 1920, we extend heartfelt thanks to (alphabetically) SABR colleagues Bill Carle, Bob McConnell, David Neft, Bob Tiemann, and Frank Williams. Bill Carle helped us with biographical data, especially debut dates. Bob McConnell lent his personal expertise and his knowledge of the John Tattersall research collection to clear up a variety of perplexing areas. David Neft supplied us with heretofore unknown RBI data for the National League of 1880–1885 and inspired us by his example, as the man who headed the Information Concepts, Inc., team that produced *The Baseball Encyclopedia* of 1969. Bob Tiemann provided game scores and sites for a host of pre-1900 games that were most helpful in deriving, for the first time, home-road stats for the nineteenth century; he also headed the SABR research project that yielded the National Association data described below. And Frank Williams continued his remarkable efforts in correcting pitcher won-lost records before 1920.

A veritable legion of readers took us up on our invitation to write with their corrections and suggestions, from the mathematical to the typographical; we thank them in the aggregate here and list them by name in the Notes on Contributors near the end of the book.

And last, we thank some giants of baseball research whose work informs these pages but who are no longer with us to receive the tribute: in no particular order, Ernie Lanigan, John Tattersall, S. C. Thompson, Alex Haas, Preston D. Orem, Len Gettelson, Lee Allen, and Harold Seymour.

This book is dedicated to the great pioneers
of baseball, the ones who made
the game as we know and love it,

Henry Chadwick

Harry Wright

John M. Ward

Babe Ruth

Branch Rickey

Jackie Robinson

area and in other towns and cities of antebellum America. In the 1850s the rise of baseball clubs and team competition helped to meet the recreational needs of Americans who were caught up in an increasingly urban and industrial society. By the 1860s one of every six Americans lived in towns or cities, and by then newspapers were covering games and noting the booming popularity of baseball. Mostly a northern and midwestern phenomenon, baseball fever ran highest in the New York City area, where in the 1850s games were being played "on every available green plot within a ten-mile circuit of the city." Spearheading the baseball boom were formally organized clubs with officers, clubhouses and playing grounds. Among the many clubs, the Knickerbockers sought to rule the game by posing as arbiters of play, rules, and decorum. Since no leagues or playing schedules existed, formal games in the 1850s were arranged by correspondence between club secretaries. The lordly Knickerbockers resisted such overtures, preferring to play among themselves, yet insisting on their preeminence over all other clubs. But the dynamic American game was not to be bound by gentlemanly monopolists or by arbitrary codes of amateurism. By the end of the 1850s, victories and the prospect of gate receipts were becoming more important factors. As more clubs embraced these goals, greater emphasis was placed on obtaining good players at whatever affronts to amateur standards.

In 1858 the Knickerbockers were dethroned as would-be overlords of baseball by the newly organized National Association of Base Ball Players. That year, representatives of twenty-five clubs formed the Association for the ostensible purpose of codifying rules and establishing guidelines for organized clubs and team competition. But the Association speedily established itself as the new arbiter of the game. Among its early rulings were the establishment of a pitcher's box and the standardization of the nine-inning game. The Association also approved the practice of charging paid admissions at games and that year saw 1,500 spectators pay 50¢ each to watch a game played between Brooklyn and New York "all-star" teams. Although the Association established no league or formal playing schedules, its authority was accepted and it lasted until 1871, when it was replaced by a lame organization called the National Association of Amateur Base Ball Players—to differentiate it from the newly founded National Association of Professional Base Ball Players. Meanwhile, by 1860 some sixty clubs had joined the first National Association; mostly they came from the East and Midwest, but a sprinkling of college teams was included. Mounting hostilities between the North and South account for the absence of southern clubs.

American baseball's popularity was at high tide when the Civil War broke out, but the South was excluded from major league baseball competition for many years. Indeed, one of the smaller legacies of the war between the states was major league baseball's east-west alignment of its franchises. And yet the war, which claimed 600,000 American lives, also popularized the game in all sections of the country, as soldiers in both armies played the game in camps and in prison compounds. This infusion of interest in the game set the stage for an even greater baseball boom which swept the North in the immediate postwar era.

Meanwhile, as the war raged toward its conclusion, baseball's popularity diminished for a time on the northern home front. Still, strong teams like the Brooklyn Excelsiors, the Brooklyn Eckfords, and the Brooklyn Atlantics delighted fans by their spirited competition. At the time, pitcher Jim Creighton of the Excelsiors became a popular hero by leading his team on a victorious eastern tour in 1860. In 1862 and 1863 the Eckfords laid claim to being America's best team, and the Brooklyn Atlantics, led by Dickey Pearce, boasted consecutive unbeaten seasons in 1864 and 1865.

The game's popularity among returning soldiers helped to inspire a major baseball boom in post–Civil War America. By 1865 the game was widely touted as America's "national game," and its growing popularity was evidenced by the proliferation of organized clubs. In 1865, ninety-one clubs had joined the Association; the following year membership swelled to nearly two hundred; and 1867 saw more than three hundred clubs enrolled, including more than a hundred from midwestern towns and cities. At their own expense, the powerful Washington Nationals embarked on an unprecedented midwestern tour in 1867; they were beaten in one game by the previously unheralded Rockford (Illinois) Forest City nine. Although the Nationals' tour suggested that some type of organized competition was needed, it failed to produce such reforms as an organized league or a fixed playing schedule. However, editor Frank Queen of the *New York Clipper*, a popular sporting journal, hit upon the idea of giving gold awards annually to the best team and the nine best players. But such judgments were arbitrary and inadequate. Meanwhile, the style of play continued to improve in the late 1860s. Pitchers became more than passive servers as one of them, Arthur "Candy" Cummings, popularized a wrist-twisting, curved-ball delivery. Moreover, fielders became more mobile, baserunners took to sliding to avoid fielders' tags, and a rule change outlawed the one-bounce-and-out catch.

But baseball's dynamic postwar growth also confronted the shaky National Association with vexing problems. Rampant commercialism was one of them. As more clubs charged admission to games, many took to dividing receipts among the players. This trend swelled the ranks of "professional" players, whose presence posed a serious threat to the Association's amateur code. In 1863 Association leaders debated the problem, but vacillated by grudgingly allowing professionals to retain their memberships. The following year the Association defined a professional player as one who "plays base ball for money, place, or emolument." The definition embraced many players, some of whom drew straight salaries, or shared gate receipts, or occupied jobs that were awarded as a subterfuge to conceal their ball-playing activities. What's more, some of the professionals were jumping their contracts for better offers from other clubs. Dubbed "revolvers," they posed a major threat to the shaky authority of the National Association.

The Cincinnati Reds of 1869

By the late 1860s baseball was becoming more of a business, and playing competitive baseball was becoming a recognized career. As baseball writer Henry Chadwick

observed in 1868, a new rank ordering among ball players was evidenced by the makeup of the Brooklyn Atlantics club. At the top was the club's elite professional team, followed by the club's amateur nine, with the lowly "muffins," or third-rate players, at the bottom. As baseball clubs came to be dominated by professional interests, some clubs financed their operations by selling stock shares and becoming joint stock companies, while others, which depended on shared gate receipts, operated as "co-operative nines."

Until 1869 the professional movement in baseball was mainly a covert trend, but in that year the Cincinnati Red Stocking club boldly announced its intention of fielding an all-salaried team which would compete against the top teams in the land. This forthright move was the brainchild of club president Aaron B. Champion, a Cincinnati businessman and local booster. The Reds were not the first professional team, nor the first all-salaried team, nor the first team to go undefeated over a season. But as the first openly announced all-salaried team, the Reds, led by player-manager Harry Wright, who became known as the "Father of Professional Baseball," toured the country in 1869, winning some 60 games without a loss. The following year, the well-drilled Reds won another 24 before losing in June to the host Brooklyn Atlantics by an 8–7 score in eleven innings. Although the Reds' effort was financially unremunerative to its stockholders, who voted to return to amateur play after the 1870 season, the experiment inspired an enduring myth that professional baseball in America arose out of this episode. In truth the professional movement was already strongly entrenched. But the Reds' example inspired imitators and brought the smouldering amateur-professional controversy to a head. Thus when the National Association, at its annual meeting in 1870, sought to curb the professional movement, the professional delegates withdrew and formed their own organization in March 1871. This successful coup stunned the amateur National Association, which never recovered and died in 1874. It also marked the beginning of major league baseball in America. From 1871 to the present day, most changes in American baseball rules and style of play would be inspired by the professional major leagues.

The First Major League: The National Association of Professional Base Ball Players

America's first professional baseball league, the National Association of Professional Base Ball Players, was also the first major league. In its ranks were the strongest teams and the best players. The players controlled the league and enjoyed full freedom of contract and movement. Financial support came to those clubs whose stockholders or investors derived more prestige than monetary rewards from their sponsorship. And in this artist-patron relationship, player salaries had a higher priority than investor profits.

The National Association was created by a single evening's work on March 17, 1871. Structurally the league resembled the old amateur National Association, whose constitution was modified to serve professional interests and whose playing rules were adopted. Admission to the professional league required the payment of a ten-dollar

entry fee, in stark contrast to the multimillion-dollar price tag now placed on a major league franchise. Like its predecessor, the professional National Association lacked a fixed schedule of games; each team was expected to play each rival five times in a season, with playing dates to be arranged by secretarial correspondence. The championship pennant was awarded to the team with the most victories, and a championship committee was empowered to rule on any disputed claims.

Although the National Association dominated organized baseball in 1871–1875, its structural defects portended its coming demise. The player-run organization wielded little control over players or teams. The easy admission policy made for a chronic dropout problem as disenchanted teams found it easy to turn their backs on ten dollars. Because of the absence of a fixed playing schedule, few contending teams played their required quota of games. Disputes over officiating stemmed from a reliance on volunteer umpires. Teams also quarreled over ticket pricing and the division of gate receipts. Indeed, most teams lost money, and such losses fueled the tension between players and investors. Critics accused the player-controlled league of failing to discipline players, especially the contract jumpers, drunkards, and alleged game fixers. Unresolved problems like these sowed the seeds of the league's eventual collapse, but while it lasted, the National Association also provided spectators with a sprightly brand of baseball.

Campaigns of the National Association, 1871–1875

The Association's 1871 campaign featured an exciting three-way battle between the Chicago White Stockings, Philadelphia Athletics, and Harry Wright's Boston Red Stockings. The Chicago team, which was housed in a new 7,000-seat wooden park and which boasted a $4,500 salaried star among its players, set a fast pace until the city's tragic fire destroyed the park. Forced to play their remaining games on the road, the White Stockings finished third and dropped out of the league until 1874. At the season's end, the Athletics and Red Stockings each had won 22 games, but the championship committee awarded the pennant to the Athletics, who had fewer losses. Harry Wright's plea that his Boston Reds had come closer to meeting their scheduled obligations was disallowed. Thus in spite of continuing controversy and a devastating fire, the National Association enjoyed an auspicious debut. Most clubs profited, and only one dropped out of the race. At the Association's annual meeting, the professionals tightened their hold on the league by electing one of their own, Bob Ferguson of the Brooklyn Atlantics, to serve as president.

Eleven clubs entered the lists for the 1872 campaign, but hopes for a wide-open race were crushed by Harry Wright's powerful Boston team, which rolled to the championship on a 39–8 record. Stocked with stars like pitcher Al Spalding, infielder Ross Barnes (whose bunting prowess permitted him to take maximum advantage of the then-prevailing fair-foul hitting rule), and shortstop George Wright, the Red Stockings won the first of four consecutive pennants. They were the first of many powerful major league dynasties to come—a phenomenon which, over the course of major league baseball history,

consistently made a mockery of the idea of competitive balance.

With nine teams competing in 1873, the Reds won a second pennant by staging a late-season drive to overtake the front-running Philadelphia "Phillies," or "Whites." Two Boston newcomers, catcher Jim White and outfielder Jim O'Rourke, contributed to the Reds' 43–16 winning gait. Although overall league revenues were disappointing, only one club dropped from contention during the course of the season.

In 1874, Wright's Reds posted a 52–18 record, to lap the New York Mutuals by 7½ games. That year Wright's team was the only one to play its full schedule of games, an impressive feat considering that Wright's team, in company with the Philadelphia Athletics, embarked upon a six-week baseball tour of Britain in hopes of persuading English sportsmen to adopt America's "national game." Like this first baseball mission, the Association's 1874 season was a financial bust. Although only one club dropped out of the race, accusations of gambling and fixed games clouded the league's reputation.

The 1875 season was the last campaign of the National Association. Thirteen teams entered the fray, but Boston's juggernaut, headed by Spalding, Barnes, O'Rourke, White, and George Wright, buried all rivals. With four Boston men topping the league's hitters, the Reds posted a 71–8 record to finish 15 games up on their nearest pursuers. Of the thirteen contenders, seven failed to finish the 1875 season.

Now in full disarray, the sullied National Association reeled under problems of competitive imbalance, financial losses, and excessive player freedom. The time was ripe for a reformist coup, and a new breed of club directors, headed by William A. Hulbert of the Chicago White Stockings, moved to raise a rival major league that would better serve the interests of the club owners.

But the pioneering National Association was by no means a failure. For all its weaknesses, the Association had popularized professional baseball. Supporters like Henry Chadwick, the innovative sportswriter who now wore the title of "Father of Base Ball," publicized the league by his coverage of games and by his statistics-laden guidebooks. Chadwick's game coverage provided detailed accounts of games with box scores, including a lasting version which he devised in 1876. Such coverage enhanced the game's popularity and inspired widespread coverage by leading newspapers. Chadwick also served on the Association's rules committee, which approved a pitching change that allowed the underhanded pitchers to utilize wrist-snapping curveballs. But Chadwick's quixotic proposal to make baseball a ten-man game failed.

The Association's most solid innovator was Harry Wright, who set high standards for professional promotion. Wright's Boston payroll was baseball's highest until the early 1880s. As Boston's manager, Wright presided over a $35,000 annual budget and dealt creatively with such problems as proper groundskeeping, equipment design and procurement, advertising, and the recruiting and training of players. Wright's mastery paid off in his team's astonishing success. He was honored in these years as the "Father of Professional Base Ball," and his envious colleagues also referred to the National Association as "Harry Wright's League."

The First Stable Major League:
The National League, 1876–1879

President William A. Hulbert of the Chicago White Stockings was the driving force behind the coup that dethroned the National Association. Determined to field a strong team in Chicago, Hulbert in 1875 signed Boston pitcher Al Spalding to play with Chicago the following season, along with three other Boston stars: Ross Barnes, Jim White, and Cal McVey. Hulbert also signed Adrian Anson of the Athletics, who later became Chicago's long-time player-manager and the first major league hitter to notch over 3,000 hits.

Fearing possible reprisals from the player-run National Association, Hulbert moved to create a new league run by business-minded club investors. Backed by representatives from the St. Louis, Louisville, and Cincinnati clubs, Hulbert met with representatives of several eastern clubs—New York, Philadelphia, Boston, and Hartford—in February 1876. Out of this meeting came the National League of Professional Base Ball Clubs. The first permanent major league embraced Hulbert's thirteen-point plan of organization. In keeping with its title, the league emphasized the interests of member clubs over those of the players. Admitted as members were well-financed, joint-stock company clubs, each of which paid annual dues of $100 which were used to finance the league administrative body's handling of disputes, recordkeeping, and officiating fees. The latter expense went for a staff of umpires, each to be paid $5 a game.

The eight charter clubs of the new National League were aligned on an east-west basis, and each team was granted a monopoly over its territory. For the 1876 season, each team agreed to play each rival ten times, with expulsion from the league the penalty for failing to do so. Adopting a high moral stance, NL leaders ordered member clubs to ban gambling, liquor sales, and Sunday games, and to draw up tightly written contracts aimed at preventing players from "revolving." For the players this was tough medicine, but with the strongest teams enrolled in the new league, there was little to do but submit. Indeed, the National Association never survived the NL coup and collapsed in 1876.

As the "Father of the National League," Hulbert presided over its fortunes from 1877 until his death in 1882. However, this most powerful of NL presidents to date owed much to his chief lieutenant, Al Spalding, who retired from the field to become the NL's most powerful advocate and defender. As a reward for his loyal support, Spalding's fledgling sporting goods company received the contract to supply the league's balls and to publish its annual guidebook. Beginning in 1877, Chadwick became the perennial editor of the league's official *Spalding Guide.*

Although its debut was auspicious, the NL's first four campaigns were marred by flagging profits, a major scandal, and opposition from a strong rival in the International Association. In 1876 Spalding pitched and managed the Chicago White Stockings to a 52–14 record, topping their closest pursuer by six games. Because of this runaway, attendance tailed off, prompting two teams, the Philadelphia Athletics and New York Mutuals, to forgo playing their final games in the west. For this breach of rules,

Hulbert expelled the pair, thereby depriving the NL of franchises in the populous Philadelphia and New York areas until 1883.

However, Hulbert made no effort to replace the two; hence only six teams took the field in 1877, the year the NL adopted a formal schedule of games. Spalding's decision to quit pitching that year dashed Chicago's hopes, but Louisville's hopes ran high until late in the season, when Wright's Boston Reds overtook them and won by seven games. But revelations that gamblers had bribed four Louisville players to lose key games marred Boston's victory. Faced with a major crisis, Hulbert responded by banishing the four players (Jim Devlin, George Hall, William Craver, and Al Nichols) for life. In the wake of the scandal, Louisville dropped from the league, followed by Hartford and St. Louis. To replace them, Indianapolis, Milwaukee, and Providence clubs joined the league. Meanwhile the NL also faced strong competition from the rival International Association. A loose league of mostly cooperative (gate-receipt-sharing) teams, the International Association threat prompted NL leaders to form a "League Alliance" of independent teams. By paying fees of ten dollars a year, League Alliance teams won the right to play exhibitions with NL teams, and the NL also pledged to honor their territorial rights and player contracts.

The hard-pressed NL suffered another profitless season in 1878, with Boston winning a second pennant by four games over Cincinnati. Still challenged by the International Association, the NL retaliated by raiding the circuit's teams and playing rosters. Over the winter of 1878–1879, Syracuse and Buffalo were persuaded to quit the Association for memberships in the NL, while Milwaukee and Indianapolis were dropped from the NL. Troy and Cleveland were also admitted to bring the number of NL teams back to its original eight. Such tactics undermined the International Association, which fielded an enfeebled minor league called the National Association in 1879.

In returning to an eight-team format in 1879, NL teams imposed rigid austerity measures. Among them, salaries were slashed and players compelled to buy their own uniforms and share the costs of meals. Moreover, player mobility was limited by the adherence to a reserve clause in player contracts. Limited to five players per team in 1879, by 1883 the reserve system was applied to most player contracts. Thereafter the reserve clause became a major bone of contention between owners and players. Meanwhile Providence won the 1879 pennant race; managed by George Wright and paced by John M. Ward's pitching, the Providence Grays won by 5 games over Wright's Boston Reds.

Major League Baseball's Golden Age, 1880–1889

As the decade of the 1880s dawned, major league baseball was only a pale reflection of the enormously popular spectacle that it would soon become. In 1880 the NL reigned supreme, but the league's financial performance was dismal. Thus far no NL club had matched the profits of Wright's 1875 Boston Reds, player salaries barely exceeded those of the 1869 Cincinnati Reds, annual membership changes underscored the league's instability, and the NL was unrepresented in the populous New York and Philadelphia areas.

At this point, however, a powerful stimulus came from the nation's booming economic and urban growth, and professional baseball expanded vigorously. The first to prosper was the NL, but its rising fortunes inspired rivals like the American Association (AA), which was recognized as a major league under the 1883 National Agreement. The following year another rival, the Union Association, vied for major league status, but the NL and AA joined forces to crush the pretender and maintain the dual major league system. The dual major league system lasted from 1883 to 1891, when it was replaced by a single major league. But in its heyday the dual major league system, with its annual World Series competition between the two leagues, proved to be popular and profitable. By 1889 leading clubs from both circuits counted annual profits of over $100,000. While most of the profits went to club owners, player salaries increased, averaging $2,000 a season, with a few stars getting as much as $5,000. Such gains by players were modest enough, but club owners still sought to limit player salaries. In opposing salary ceilings, players banded together under the Brotherhood of Professional Base Ball Players, which also opposed the unwritten reserve clause, unreasonable fines, and the sale of players from one club to another. In this decade the NL's Chicago White Stockings received $10,000 apiece from the sale of "King" Kelly and John Clarkson to the Boston club.

The prosperity of the major league game was further evidenced by the expanded seasonal playing schedule. From 84 games a season in 1880 the NL increased its schedule to 132 games by 1889, while the AA upped its seasonal schedule to 140 games in 1889. To accommodate growing numbers of fans, including the 2 million who attended major league games in 1889, clubs erected new wooden parks with double-decked stands. To serve them, concessionaire Harry M. Stevens introduced the now classic baseball lunch of hot dogs, soda pop, and peanuts. And to sate the public's hunger for baseball news, daily newspapers expanded their coverage of games, and two weekly journals devoted to baseball—*Sporting Life* and *The Sporting News*—sprang to vigorous life in this decade. Moreover, at the peak of baseball's popularity, Spalding dispatched, in 1888–1889, two major league squads on a world tour in hopes of spreading the American game to other lands.

If Spalding's mission fell short of its goal abroad, at home the professional game was spreading to all corners of the land. In 1889 some 15 minor leagues were operating. Under the National Agreement of 1883, and its subsequent revisions, minor leagues were recognized as a part of organized baseball. Territorial rights and player rosters of such teams were protected by the major leagues. But black players and teams were increasingly excluded from organized baseball. In the past, gentlemen's agreements barred black teams from the amateur National Association and the professional National Association. At this time a few blacks played briefly in the major AA and in some minor leagues, but the presence of the segregated Negro league in Pennsylvania, in 1889, plus the existence of all-black independent professional teams, signaled the

trend toward segregation of black players from organized baseball. Not until 1946 would the color barrier be lifted.

In this dynamic golden age, professional baseball's maturation as a field sport was speeded by a rash of rule changes. In 1881 the pitching distance was extended to fifty feet; in 1884 overhand pitching was legalized; in 1887 a uniform strike zone was established; in 1888 the three-strikes rule and in 1889 the four-balls rule were permanently adopted. These and other changes in playing rules resulted from pragmatic experiments by major league rules committees, whose constant tinkerings kept the game in a state of flux. Some short-lived changes, like the 1887 rule scoring bases on balls as hits and employing a modified four-strike rule, aimed at correcting the pitching-batting imbalance. But these quixotic rules inflated batting averages and produced sixteen .400 hitters before they were discarded at the close of the 1887 season.

NL Campaigns of the 1880s

As the sole major league in 1880, the NL saw its fortunes rise with those of the Chicago dynasty. Winners of three consecutive pennants over the years 1880–1882, the Chicago team was led by player-manager Cap Anson, a popular hero and the leading hitter of the nineteenth century. Fielding a nucleus of stars, including colorful Mike "King" Kelly, pitchers Larry Corcoran and Fred Goldsmith, and catcher Frank "Silver" Flint, Chicago topped Providence by 15 games in 1880, by nine games in 1881, and by three games in 1882. In an unofficial postseason encounter with the rival American Association's Cincinnati champs, the two teams split a pair of games before AA officials canceled this 1882 harbinger of the World Series.

The rise of the AA threatened the dominant NL, which was left leaderless by Hulbert's death in 1882. At Spalding's suggestion, A. G. Mills was elected president. That fall the NL strengthened its position by dropping Troy and Worcester and planting teams in New York and Philadelphia. The NL playing schedule was increased to 98 games.

In the hotly contested 1883 race, Boston ended Chicago's reign by edging Anson's team by four games. That fall Mills ended the AA war by negotiating the National Agreement of 1883, which conceded major league status to the rival AA. Under the agreement, the AA adopted the reserve clause, the two leagues ceased raiding each other's players, and postseason World Series play between the two leagues was accepted. The agreement provided for major league control over lower levels of professional baseball by recognizing the territorial rights of minor league signatories. With frequent changes, this National Agreement remained in force until the American Association war of 1891.

In 1884 the two major leagues faced competition from another major league aspirant. To combat this Union Association incursion, the NL and AA extended reserve coverage to all players and upped their playing schedules to 112 games. The surfeit of major league games contributed to lower attendance for all three embattled leagues, but the Union Association suffered more and was driven out. Least damaged was the NL, whose sprightly 1884 campaign saw pitcher Charles "Old Hoss" Radbourn em-

ploy the new rule legalizing overhand pitching with telling effect. Radbourn won 60 games to lead Providence to 10½-game victory over runner-up Boston. And in the first officially sanctioned World Series, Radbourn defeated the AA champion Mets in three straight games.

The following year Anson's White Stockings regained the heights as they won the first of two consecutive pennants. With ace pitcher John Clarkson winning 53 games, Chicago held off the New York Giants by two games to land the 1885 NL pennant. The Giants' surge owed to a piece of skullduggery by its owner. Having acquired a financial interest in the AA New York Mets, the Giants plucked ace pitcher Tim Keefe from them, and Keefe won 32 games for the Giants in 1885. Such trickery by the NL now had AA leaders wary of their rival, but in the World Series of 1885 AA prestige rose when the St. Louis Browns tied the powerful Chicagoans, and it soared further in 1886, when the Browns defeated Chicago in the $15,000 winner-take-all World Series of that year. The loss blighted Chicago's gritty 2½-game victory over Detroit in the 1886 NL campaign. Following the loss, Spalding sold King Kelly to Boston for $10,000. The sale electrified baseball fans, but it also signaled the end of the Chicago dynasty.

In the memorable 1887 campaign, Detroit won the pennant by 3½ games over the Philadelphia Phillies. Wildly inflated batting averages resulted from rule changes that modified the third-strike rule and scored bases on balls as hits. Detroit feasted under the new rules as Sam Thompson and the "big four" of Dan Brouthers, Jack Rowe, Hardie Richardson, and Jim White keyed a league-leading .343 (.299 when adjusted for that year's counting of walks as hits) team batting average. In World Series play, Detroit thrashed the Browns, winning ten of the fifteen games. That fall the rules committee scuttled the average-inflating rules and the NL increased its playing schedule to 132 games.

As Detroit faded, the New York Giants captured the next two NL pennants. Managed by Jim Mutrie and captained by John Ward, the well-balanced Giants defeated Chicago by 9 games and humbled the Browns in the 1888 World Series. The following year the Giants repeated, edging Boston by a single game and then trouncing the Brooklyn Bridegrooms in the World Series.

The profitable 1889 season marked the passing of the first golden age in major baseball history. Over the next two seasons the NL fought two costly interleague wars that overshadowed the pennant races. In 1890, as the NL battled the serious challenge of the Players League, the Brooklyn Bridegrooms, who were enticed to jump the AA for the NL, won by 6½ games over Anson's Chicago Colts. And in 1891, as the NL battled the AA, manager Frank Selee's Boston Beaneaters defeated Chicago by 3½ games. By then the interleague wars had ended with the NL the victor in both frays. Thus as the 1892 season dawned, the NL once again reigned supreme over major league baseball.

Rival Major Leagues of the 1880s:
American and Union Associations and Players League

The NL's most formidable nineteenth-century rival, the American Association of Base Ball Clubs, was organized by promoters who opposed the NL's monopoly. In wooing

prospective clubs, the AA promoters saw an opportunity: New York, Philadelphia, Cincinnati, and St. Louis were good baseball cities that were not represented in the league. They also established a basic 25¢ admission price and allowed member clubs the option of selling booze and playing Sunday games. To entice good players, the AA promoters rejected the NL's reserve clause; and to ensure orderly play, a salaried corps of umpires was hired—an innovation soon imitated by the NL.

In its maiden season of 1882, the AA's six teams (Cincinnati, Louisville, St. Louis, Pittsburgh, Philadelphia, and Baltimore) prospered. All six finished the season, with Cincinnati winning the pennant by 11½ games over Philadelphia. Emergent stars of the AA included pitcher Will White and second baseman Bid McPhee of Cincinnati, first baseman Charles Comiskey of St. Louis, and outfielder Pete Browning and pitcher Tony Mullane of Louisville among the contenders.

In 1883 the AA expanded to eight clubs by adding Columbus and the New York Mets. By opposing the NL's reserve clause, the AA lured a number of disgruntled NL players into its ranks. Thus strengthened, the AA staged another profitable campaign, which saw the Philadelphia Athletics edge the St. Louis Browns by a single game. The AA's sprightly season prompted the NL to accommodate its rival. That fall NL president Mills and AA president Denny McKnight negotiated the National Agreement of 1883, which recognized the AA as a major league and instituted World Series play between the two leagues. For its part, the AA adopted the reserve clause.

The agreement between the NL and AA was barely concluded when a new league made a bid for major league recognition. The rival Union Association of Base Ball Clubs was organized in Pittsburgh in the fall of 1883. To entice players from the established majors, the UA leaders proclaimed their opposition to the reserve clause. A few major league players jumped to the new league, but most remained with the clubs out of fear of blacklisting, or in some cases because they were bought off by salary increases. With mostly unknown players in their ranks, the eight-team UA commenced playing a 128-game schedule in 1884. From the start the league suffered from unbalanced funding and talent distribution. The UA's principal backer, Henry V. Lucas, poured most of his money into his St. Louis Maroons, a team which won its first twenty-one games and made a shambles of the pennant race. Plagued by financial losses, only five charter teams survived the campaign. Nevertheless, the UA drained attendance from the established majors—especially the AA, which unwisely expanded to counter the threat. In the fall of 1884, the UA folded when Lucas accepted an offer to enroll his St. Louis Maroons in the NL.

The collapse of the UA left the dual major league system intact, but relations between the NL and AA were strained. AA leaders accused their NL allies of duplicity for persuading the AA to expand to twelve teams to counter the UA's incursion. As a result the AA suffered heavier financial losses in its 1884 campaign, which the New York Mets won by 6½ games over Columbus. The Mets' victory was soured by their loss to Providence in the first officially sanctioned World Series. But even more damaging to the AA was the revelation that the Mets had come under the ownership of the NL New York Giants. Moreover, AA suspicions of NL duplicity were heightened by the UA peace settlement which brought the St. Louis Maroons into the NL, where they competed directly with the AA's St. Louis Browns.

As it turned out, the Maroons were no match for the Browns, whose profitable formula of cheap baseball, liquor sales, sideshows, Sunday games, and winning baseball was making a folk hero of the Browns' colorful president, Chris Von der Ahe. Beginning in 1885, player-manager Charles Comiskey led his team to four consecutive AA pennants. In 1885 the Browns won by 16 games over Cincinnati; in 1886, by 12 over Pittsburgh; in 1887, by 14 over Cincinnati; and in 1888, by 6½ over a beefed-up Brooklyn team. Star players like infielder Arlie Latham, outfielder Tip O'Neill, and pitchers Dave Foutz and Bob Caruthers paced the Browns to the first three pennants. Then, when Von der Ahe sold Foutz and Caruthers to Brooklyn in 1888, Comiskey came up with pitcher Silver King, whose 45 victories helped land a fourth consecutive pennant. In World Series play the Browns tied Chicago in 1885 and defeated Anson's team in 1886. But the team was drubbed by Detroit in 1887 and by the Giants in 1888.

Bitter rivalry between the Browns and Brooklyn Bridegrooms dominated the 1889 race, which ended with the Bridegrooms on top of the Browns by 2 games. But the Bridegrooms lost to the Giants in World Series play. Over the winter the St. Louis and Brooklyn factions battled over the choice of a new AA president, and in the stormy aftermath Brooklyn and Cincinnati joined the National League. The loss of these clubs, together with the loss of key players to the newly organized Players' League, crippled the AA. Forced to field weak teams in 1890, the AA ran a poor third to the NL and the Players' League. The AA's dismal race was won by Louisville, which only the year before had finished dead last in the AA with a 27–111 record.

The Players League War of 1890

The Players League of 1890 arose out of the long smoldering hostilities between major league players and owners, dating back to the NL seizure of power in 1876. Under NL control, players lost money and freedom of movement, and were subjected to harsh disciplinary codes backed by threats of expulsion and blacklisting. To the list of player grievances was added the reserve clause in player contracts, which players viewed as a device for lowering salaries and a denial of one's right to sell his services to the highest bidder. For their part, owners credited the clause for stabilizing teams and increasing profits. Although legal challenges sustained the players' position, such victories were too limited to overturn the reserve clause. Nor were players helped when rival leagues attacked the clause because the AA soon embraced the clause and the UA was driven out of business. Frustrated on these fronts, in 1885 the players resorted to collective action by forming the Brotherhood of Professional Base Ball Players. Initially organized as a benevolent association, the Brotherhood, under the leadership of star player and lawyer John Ward, became a collective-bargaining agency by 1887. In confronting the major

league owners, the Brotherhood sought redress on such matters as the reserve clause, the sale of players, and the threatened salary ceiling, known as the Brush classification plan.

In 1888 protracted negotiations between the Brotherhood and the owners broke down when the NL owners refused to budge on the salary ceiling issue, which had been accepted by the AA as part of the National Agreement. When the owners rejected Ward's ultimatum on the key issues, the Brotherhood moved to field a rival major league in 1890. With most of the best players in the fold, the Players' League attracted financial backers who accepted Ward's plan of sharing profits and power with the players. In 1890 the eight-team PL opened play with well-stocked teams in every NL city except Cincinnati.

Faced with a head-to-head battle for survival, the NL relied upon its war committee headed by Spalding. Spalding met the PL head-on by scheduling games on the same dates as PL teams, bribing PL players to jump ranks, initiating costly lawsuits over the reserve clause, lowering ticket prices, cajoling press support by threats to withdraw advertising, and raiding the AA and minor league rosters for players. Loyal managers like Anson, Wright, Bill McGunnigle, and Jim Mutrie persuaded good players to stay with the NL. Roster raids on AA teams lured stars like Billy Hamilton and Tommy Tucker; and promising rookies like pitchers Kid Nichols and Cy Young, infielder Bobby Lowe and outfielder Jess Burkett beefed up the NL teams.

Although beaten in the courts and at the turnstiles by the PL, which finished its season with Mike Kelly's Boston team beating out Ward's Brooklyn team by 6½ games, the PL's financial losses were too much for its backers to bear. In the fall of 1890, the disenchanted PL backers broke ranks and sued for peace. Magnanimous in victory, Spalding imposed no reprisals on PL players, but he gave no ground on the key issues. With the NL girding for war with the AA in the upcoming 1891 season, the salary ceiling implementation was delayed until the latest struggle was over.

The collapse of the PL afforded little relief for the stricken AA. In 1891 all-out war erupted between the NL and AA over the return of players and the relocation of franchises. When the AA's weak Cincinnati club folded, its popular manager Mike Kelly joined the Boston AA team, but after a few days he joined the Boston Nationals. With Kelly gone, the Boston AA team won the pennant by 8½ games over the Browns, but Boston fans flocked to watch Kelly captain the Boston Nationals to the NL pennant.

The 1891 season was the last for the AA. That fall four AA clubs, St. Louis, Louisville, Baltimore and Washington, quit the dying circuit to join the expanded twelve-club National League.

The "Big League": The National League, 1892–1899

The defeat of the AA in 1891 saddled the NL with a $130,000 debt, which was incurred by buying out four of the defeated circuit's clubs. The remaining four AA teams—Baltimore, Louisville, St. Louis, and Washing-

ton—were added to the NL to form the twelve-club National League and American Association of Professional Base Ball Clubs. From 1892 to 1899 this monopolistic "big league" represented major league baseball. Enthralled by their newly created baseball "trust," the league's owners styled themselves as magnates presiding over a million-dollar entertainment industry. The magnates fully expected their monopoly league to produce unprecedented cash and glory. But such dreams were dashed by external factors, including a chronic national recession, the 1898 war with Spain, and the league's competitive imbalance. Eight seasons of play under the twelve-club format underscored its imbalance. With Boston, Baltimore, and Brooklyn winning all the races, fans in other cities lost interest. As profits dwindled, owners imposed a $2,400 ceiling on player salaries and battled one another over the division of gate receipts. Lacking strong leadership, each individual owner ran his club like a feudal fiefdom. Indeed, the blustering antics of the owners often upstaged players in newspaper accounts of this time. Some magnates hatched grandiose schemes aimed at making the monopoly league work more efficiently. Thus Andrew Freedman of the Giants advocated the annual pooling and redistribution of players and profits, provided that the "strongest and most lucrative franchises" got the best players. And another, Cincinnati owner John T. Brush, proposed harsh disciplinary measures aimed at curbing rowdy players, while also experimenting with minor league farm systems as a cheap source of talent.

Indeed, owner infighting over these and other issues damaged the big league's image, but the biggest threat to the league's credibility was the "syndicate" issue. The term "syndicatism" used at this time referred to interlocking club ownership schemes. Following bitter debate in 1898, two such interlocking directorates were approved by the owners. One of these schemes permitted owner Frank Robison of the Cleveland and St. Louis teams to transfer his best players to St. Louis; the other allowed owners Ferdinand Abell and Harry Vonderhorst of the Brooklyn and Baltimore teams to stock the Brooklyn team with the pick of those two squads. These operations made a farce of the 1899 pennant race and prompted the NL to return to an eight-club format in 1900; the cutback was accomplished by dropping Cleveland, Baltimore, Washington, and St. Louis from the NL.

The return to the eight-club format ended eight wayward seasons of major league baseball played under one unwieldy league format. Nevertheless, major league baseball continued to mature in the 1890s. Surprisingly enough, there were no franchise changes in these years. In 1898 the 154-game playing schedule was introduced, a format which dominated until 1961. And in 1893 a major change in playing rules fixed the pitching distance at 60'6" from home plate and also replaced the pitching box with a rubber slab atop a mound. This permanent change was introduced that year to correct the pitching-batting imbalance, a desirable goal which to this day remains elusive. The immediate effect of the lengthened pitching distance was not to give a mild boost to batting averages, but to send them soaring.

Thus in 1894 the Phillies posted a .349 team batting average, with the four-man outfield of Ed Delahanty, Sam Thompson, Billy Hamilton, and Tuck Turner combining

for a .400-plus batting average. Sluggers also prospered, as Thompson hit 129 homers in this era, and Washington outfielder Buck Freeman hit 25 homers in 1899; both these records endured for twenty years. (Later recounts gave the career record to Roger Connor and the single season mark to Ned Williamson who had 27 tainted homers in 1884.) It took pitchers several seasons to adapt to the increased distance, but they did so by developing curves, changeups, and ball-doctoring trick deliveries to go with their fastballs. Meanwhile two offensive styles vied for acceptance in this era. For a brief time the "manly slugging" style feasted on pitchers, but the "scientific style" mastered by the Baltimore and Boston teams, which stressed bunting, stealing, sacrificing, and the hit-and-run, became the dominant offensive style of the next twenty years.

At this time other rule changes allowed player substitutions, established the infield fly rule, treated foul bunts as strikes, defined sacrifice flies and bunts, and introduced the pentagon-shaped home plate. On the playing fields, players wore stylized uniforms and most sported gloves, with catchers employing the big "Decker" mitt and wearing masks and chest protectors. When in action, teams played heady ball, using signals to trigger offensive and defensive movements. Defensively, infielders aligned themselves to turn double plays and outfielders coordinated their play by using backups, cutoffs and relays. Offensively, bunting, sacrificing, sliding, stealing, and hit-and-run plays were familiar tactics. But when teams like the Baltimore Orioles and Cleveland Spiders augmented their play with roughhouse tactics like spiking and jostling runners, baiting umpires, and bench jockeying, this "rowdy" brand of ball stirred the ire of reformers like Indianapolis owner John Brush. But hard-nosed baseball survived its critics, as did Sunday baseball. Despite fervent opposition from Sabbatarians, Sunday games were permitted by local option, although eastern cities held out against such games for twenty years. By then, major league clubs had outgrown the wooden parks of this era. A spate of ballpark fires late in this era inspired tougher safety codes that soon prompted the replacement of the vulnerable old wooden parks with concrete-and-steel edifices.

Big League Campaigns: The NL, 1892–1899

During the big league's eight-year existence, pennant monopolizing was the rule as only Boston, Baltimore, and Brooklyn teams won pennants. Managed by Frank Selee, the powerful Boston Beaneaters won back-to-back pennants in 1892–1893 and in 1897–1898. Paced by pitcher Kid Nichols (who won 297 games in this decade), Boston won the 1892 race played under a split-season format. Boston easily won the first half, but lost the second half by 3 games to manager Pat Tebeau's Cleveland Spiders, whose ace pitcher was the great Cy Young. In the postseason playoff, after the two teams played a scoreless tie, Boston swept the rest of the games to land the 1892 pennant.

In 1893 the unprofitable split-season format was dropped and the pitching distance was increased to 60'6". In a campaign marked by heavy hitting, Boston won by 5 games over Pittsburgh. Pittsburgh's Frank Killen won 34

games to lead hurlers, and outfielder Billy Hamilton batted .380. The following year saw Boston fall to the Baltimore Orioles, who rebounded from an eighth-place finish in 1893 to win the first of three consecutive pennants. Although plagued by poor pitching, the offense-minded Orioles batted .343, with every regular topping the .300 mark at the plate. Future Hall of Famers on this star-studded team included Dan Brouthers, Hugh Jennings, John McGraw, Joe Kelley, Willie Keeler, and Wilbert Robinson. The Orioles won the 1894 pennant by 3 games over the Giants, but lost the first postseason Temple Cup Series, played between the first- and second-place finishers. In this inaugural Temple Cup Series, manager John Ward's Giants swept the Orioles in four straight games.

The following year manager Ned Hanlon's Orioles repeated as NL champions by edging the Cleveland Spiders by 3 games. A .324 team batting average and a brilliant 54–14 home won-loss record keyed the 1895 Orioles. But once again the Orioles failed in Temple Cup play, this time falling to the Spiders by four games to one. In 1896 the Orioles won a third consecutive NL pennant by 9½ games over the Spiders and swept their rivals in postseason Temple Cup play.

Bolstered by newcomers Billy Hamilton, Chick Stahl, and Jimmy Collins, Boston regained the heights in 1897–1898. Nichols won 30 games as the 1897 Beaneaters edged the Orioles by 2 games. But the Orioles won the postseason Temple Cup four games to one, the last year of this unremunerative and "shabby spectacle" which, one observer said, no more resembled the old World Series than a "crabapple does . . . a pippin."

Boston repeated in 1898, in a baseball campaign overshadowed by the Spanish-American War, beating the Orioles by 6 games. But by then the unprofitable "big league" was in its last throes. In a race marred by ludicrous syndicate ventures, in 1899 the Brooklyn Superbas won by 8 games over Boston. A syndicate team, the Superbas were managed by Hanlon, who stocked the Brooklyn team with the best players from the Brooklyn and Baltimore rosters. A similar venture that season had Robison's St. Louis-Cleveland syndicate loading the St. Louis team with the pick of these two clubs. But Robison's venture failed miserably as St. Louis finished fifth while the Cleveland team's 20–134 record was the worst by any major league team playing a 154-game schedule.

In the aftermath of the 1899 campaign, the owners scuttled the twelve-club big league and cut back to eight teams. Baltimore, Cleveland, Washington, and Louisville were dropped at a cost of $100,000, a buyout shared by the eight surviving teams. Born in debt, the monopoly big league died in debt, but the dawning twentieth century soon saw major league baseball prospering under a revived dual league format.

Major League Baseball's Silver Age, 1903–1920

The American League War, 1900–1902

The American League's struggle for major league recognition began in 1900, a propitious time for such an incursion. The NL owners had recently shed four teams, which

left many unemployed players and some promising territories. Moreover, NL owners were distracted by an abortive attempt by other outsiders to revive the American Association, and by the NL's prosperous season of 1900. With a hefty boost from the nation's booming economy, most NL teams made money that year. In a close race the Brooklyn Superbas repeated as NL champs by beating a strong Pittsburgh team by 4½ games.

Such distractions favored the cause of the American League schemers. Prior to 1900, the newly proclaimed American League had operated as the Western League, a strong minor league based in the Midwest. Since 1894 the Western League's president, the able, dictatorial, and hard-drinking Byron "Ban" Johnson, had dreamed of making his circuit into a major league. To this end he had battled with NL owners over the drafting of his league's players, a practice which underscored his league's inferior status. Johnson's opportunity to press toward his goal came in 1899, when the NL cut back to eight teams. With the backing of lieutenants like Charles Comiskey and Connie Mack, Johnson renamed his circuit the American League, his clubs snapped up surplus NL players, and Comiskey moved his team to Chicago, where his White Stockings boldly confronted the NL's Cubs. With solid financial backing and a new ballpark, Comiskey's team of major league castoffs and promising youngsters captured the first AL pennant in a profitable campaign.

Emboldened by the AL's successful 1900 campaign, Johnson took note of the expiring National Agreement and unilaterally proclaimed the AL to be a major league. This 1901 declaration formally opened the American League war, and Johnson's promoters commenced hostilities by invading the NL's Philadelphia and Boston territories and occupying the former NL sites of Baltimore, Washington, Cleveland, and Detroit. To stock their teams, Johnson's financiers offered higher salaries to NL players, and in 1901 over a hundred NL players snapped at the bait. The jumpers included a bevy of stars, among them Cy Young, Clark Griffith, Jimmy Collins, and Nap Lajoie. Then, in a hotly contested and profitable pennant race, Comiskey's Chicago team edged Boston by 4 games to capture the 1901 AL pennant.

The timing of the AL's assault was excellent. In 1901–1902 the leaderless NL owners were locked in a bitter struggle over the choice of a league president. Two factions, one headed by owner Andrew Freedman of the Giants and the other by Spalding, battled to a standstill. In 1902 a temporary Control Commission headed the NL, which finally elected Henry Clay Pulliam as its president. In a complicated settlement the controversial Freedman sold his New York Giants interests for $125,000, on the condition that one of his cronies be permitted to plant an AL franchise in New York in 1903. By then, the AL had concluded another profitable season. With more NL players joining AL ranks, Connie Mack's Philadelphia Athletics landed the 1902 AL pennant by beating the Browns by 5 games.

In the fall of 1902, with most war-weary NL owners favoring a return to the dual major league structure, the NL sued for peace with the AL. Early in 1903 Johnson and Comiskey met with Pulliam and Cincinnati owner August "Garry" Herrmann and negotiated the National Agreement of 1903. Under its terms, the NL and AL

would operate as separate but equal major leagues, bound by common playing rules, harmonized playing schedules, and mutually recognized territories and player contracts. The player contract accord restored the reserve clause and ended the AL's roster raids. The agreement also allowed an AL franchise to be located in New York, which Johnson secured by moving the financially shaky Baltimore Orioles to Manhattan, where in time the team prospered as the New York Yankees. Among other points, the Agreement reclassified the minor leagues and set new rules for the drafting of minor league players. Indeed, in this era minor league baseball grew lustily, reaching an all-time peak in 1913, when 46 leagues started the season. But if the National Agreement stimulated the growth of organized baseball, it did little to empower major league players. Major league players were denied representation on the controlling National Commission, and over the years 1902–1913 two attempts by players to organize unions were beaten down. And if the National Agreement included no salary ceiling plank, the Agreement unequivocally embraced the reserve clause and asserted the right of the National Commission to control baseball "by its own decrees . . . enforcing them without the aid of law, and [making it] answerable to no power outside its own."

The power to enforce these baseball laws came via a master stroke when the negotiators created a three-member National Commission charged with enforcing the National Agreement and keeping peace between the rival major leagues. As earlier demonstrated by the uneasy coexistence that marked the dual major league system of the 1880s, some such high-level executive and judicial body was needed to settle disputes between two independent and highly competitive major leagues. It was a challenge that the National Commission successfully met for seventeen years.

Heading the National Commission were league presidents Johnson and Pulliam and Cincinnati magnate Garry Herrmann, who served as the Commission's permanent chairman. On the face of it, this gave the NL two votes, but Johnson and Herrmann were close friends. Together they served during the lifetime of the National Commission, while four relatively weak presidents represented the NL, whose owners feared to empower any president. By contrast Johnson reigned as the most powerful president in major league history. As the AL's entrenched "czar," Johnson used his powers to safeguard his league against any NL treachery. In defending his league, Johnson personally held all AL franchise leases, ruled on ownership changes, fixed playing schedules, set basic admission prices, and imposed his standards on owners and players. Inevitably such powers incurred enmities among AL owners, but until the Black Sox Scandal of 1919, Johnson's domination of the AL held firm.

Over the years 1903–1920, with Herrmann's support, Johnson dominated the National Commission. In those years the Commission functioned as baseball's Supreme Court, settling disputes between clubs (mostly involving rights to player services), supporting the interests of club owners, disciplining players, defending umpires, fending off Federal League interlopers, defusing a players' union threat, and overseeing relations with the minor leagues. But the most important achievement of the National Commission was its profitable administration of the re-

vived World Series. Initially revived in 1903, the World Series got off to a shaky start when the Giants refused to play the AL champion in 1904. But in 1905 the two leagues adopted a new World Series format that placed the conduct of the classic under the control of the National Commission. With 10 percent of World Series revenues set aside for financing National Commission activities, the Commission faced a stern test. By capable administration the Commission met the challenge and the annual World Series became a profitable and permanent part of each major league season. By 1910 profits from World Series games had increased tenfold over those of 1905. But the Commission was responsible for any World Series chicanery; thus the rigged World Series of 1919 precipitated the downfall of the National Commission.

Peace and Prosperity: 1903–1920

By reviving the dual major league system with World Series play, the framers of the National Agreement harked back to the successful format of the golden 1880s. To that profitable format was added a National Commission charged with keeping the peace between the two major leagues. The combination launched the major leagues on a stable course which produced no franchise changes for the next fifty years. In the 1903–1919 era the pattern was set and the two major leagues enjoyed a silver age of popularity and prosperity. In these years the popularity of the national pastime was buoyed by rising attendance, increased media coverage including motion pictures, and the ever-popular song, "Take Me Out to the Ball Game," introduced in 1908. The game's increasing popularity swelled annual profits, but as always these were unevenly distributed. In these years attendance at major league games increased steadily; from 4.7 million in 1903, attendance rose to 10 million in 1911, before falling under the impact of the Federal League incursion and the nation's involvement in the First World War. To house the growing numbers of fans, durable ballparks constructed of concrete and steel were built during the construction boom of 1909–1911. Capable of housing 30,000 or more fans, these parks served until the post–World War Two construction boom. At this time increasing profits boosted player salaries. By 1910 annual salaries ranged from $900 to $12,000, and by 1915 salaries of superstars like Ty Cobb, Tris Speaker, and Walter Johnson approached $20,000.

In this era stability also characterized the style of play. Only a few rule changes were made. Among them, a rule limited the height of pitching mounds to fifteen inches above the baseline level, the infield fly rule was invoked, a foul bunt on a third strike was ruled a strikeout, and earned run averages by pitchers were included in annual records. On the playing fields teams employed the deadball style of play that resembled the "scientific game" of the 1890s. With new balls seldom being introduced into games, pitchers took command, using a variety of deliveries including spitballs and defacing balls with other foreign substances. In this era, earned run averages of 3.00 or below were seasonal norms, and seasonal batting averages, now affected by bigger parks and improved gloves, hovered around the .250 mark. Offensively, teams relied heavily on bunts, hit-and-run tactics, and base steal-

ing to produce a few runs which power pitchers protected. Not surprisingly, pitching masters like Cy Young, Walter Johnson, Christy Mathewson, Grover Cleveland Alexander, Eddie Plank, and spitball artist Ed Walsh sparkled among the leading stars of this era. But pitted against these dominant hurlers were some of the greatest hitters of all time. The masters of the deadball offense included Detroit's Ty Cobb, who won thirteen AL batting titles while scoring runs and stealing bases at unprecedented rates, and Pittsburgh's Honus Wagner, who won eight NL batting titles and stole 722 bases. Other hitting stars included Eddie Collins, Tris Speaker, Nap Lajoie, Sam Crawford, and the ill-fated Joe Jackson. The decline of the "deadball style" was foreshadowed by the 1910 introduction of the cork-centered ball. When widely used later in the era, it ended the conservative style of offensive play. The transformation was signaled in 1919, when Babe Ruth of the Red Sox hit 29 homers to set a new seasonal homer mark.

By 1919 the stability of the silver age had been undermined by a series of disturbing events. In 1913 interlopers launched the Federal League and vied for major league recognition. That fall President James Gilmore lined up enough wealthy backers to plant Federal League teams in Chicago, Baltimore, Buffalo, Pittsburgh, Indianapolis, Brooklyn, St. Louis, and Kansas City. Over the next two seasons, the "Feds" took to raiding major league rosters with offers of higher salaries. The surfeit of games in 1914 and 1915 lowered major league revenues, but the Federal League invaders suffered more. There were two Federal League campaigns; Indianapolis won the 1914 pennant and Chicago took honors in 1915. The 1915 season was the last gasp of the Feds. Staggered by financial losses, the Feds surrendered when the established majors paid $5 million in compensation and awarded major league franchises to two Federal owners. But an antitrust suit pressed by dissident Baltimore owners against the majors eventually reached the U.S. Supreme Court. In 1922, Justice Oliver Wendell Holmes, speaking for a unanimous court, dismissed the suit and judged major league baseball to be mainly a sport and not a commonly accepted form of interstate commerce. But the 1922 decision was not a definitive ruling, and the major leagues would have to defend the reserve clause against future attacks in the courts and in the Congress of the United States. Nevertheless the FL challenge was the last full-scale incursion by a rival major league against the established majors.

Soon after the Federal League war, major league baseball faced another crisis brought on by America's entry into World War One. In supporting the nation's total war effort, dozens of major league players entered the armed services, and clubs staged patriotic displays, donating money and equipment to troops. For all that, in 1918 the provost marshal ruled major league baseball to be nonessential to the war effort, but his ruling permitted the majors to play a shortened 1918 campaign. That year attendance sank to 3 million, prompting tremulous owners to vote to shorten the 1919 playing schedule. However, to their surprise the war ended, and the attenuated 1919 campaign attracted 6.5 million fans. Caught short by this unexpected boom, officials sought to recoup money by upping the World Series schedule to a best-of-nine-games format.

As it turned out the expanded 1919 World Series precipitated the final crisis that ended the commissioner system. Embittered over their low salaries, eight Chicago White Sox players accepted bribes from gamblers to throw the World Series to the NL champion Cincinnati Reds. When revelations of this "Black Sox Scandal" came to light, it destroyed the National Commission and ended the old National Agreement. Chairman Herrmann resigned early in 1920, and that fall Federal Judge Kenesaw M. Landis was named the game's sole commissioner, an action confirmed by the new National Agreement of 1921. As the autocratic Landis defused the Black Sox Scandal by barring the eight accused Chicago players from organized baseball for life, the major league game lurched into a new golden age of cash and glory.

Deadball Dynasties: The American League, 1903–1920

Over the years 1903–1920, Ban Johnson's "great American League" surpassed its NL rival in attendance and also took an enduring lead over its rival in World Series victories. However, such dominance was not a result of the league's competitive balance; indeed, this dream was never realized in any era of major league history until the early 1980s. In this early phase of AL history, four teams—Boston, Philadelphia, Chicago, and Detroit—dominated all AL pennant races.

The first of the AL minidynasties, the Boston Pilgrims relied in 1903 on the pitching of Cy Young, Bill Dineen, and Tom Hughes to trample the Philadelphia Athletics by 14½ games and then go on to win the first modern World Series over Pittsburgh. The following year Boston repeated, winning a close race by 1½ games over the New York Highlanders. That year manager John McGraw of the Giants refused to meet the Pilgrims in World Series play, but the controversy was resolved over the winter of 1904 with the establishment of a permanent World Series format.

In 1905 manager Connie Mack's Philadelphia Athletics got 87 victories from the pitching corps of Rube Waddell, Eddie Plank, Andy Coakley and Chief Bender, to edge the White Sox by 2 games. But with league-leading pitcher Waddell sidelined by an injury, the A's fell to the Giants in the World Series. As the A's faded in 1906, the most impotent of all pennant winners, the weak-hitting Chicago White Sox, won a close race by 3 games over the Highlanders. In winning, the White Sox batted .230 and scored a mere 570 runs. Yet in World Series play against the Cubs, whose 116 victories were the most ever by a team playing a 154-game schedule, the White Sox prevailed, winning four of the six games.

The next three AL pennants were captured by the Detroit Tigers, the league's most formidable dynasty to date. Managed by Hugh Jennings and powered by outfielders Sam Crawford and Ty Cobb, the latter the Georgia sensation who won the first of a record nine consecutive AL batting titles, the 1907 Tigers defeated Mack's Athletics by 1½ games. The following year the Tigers eked out a half-game win over player-manager Nap Lajoie's Cleveland team, and in 1909 the Tigers held off the Athletics by 3½ games. But in World Series action the Tigers resembled kittens. In 1907 and again in 1908 they fell to the Cubs, and in 1909 they lost to the Pirates.

Those three consecutive World Series losses infuriated AL president Johnson, but four straight AL victories over the years 1910–1913 restored the aplomb of the portly czar. In 1910 Mack's revamped Athletics, newly located in Shibe Park, used the pitching of Plank, Bender, Jack Coombs, and Cy Morgan, and the offensive and defensive skills of his "$100,000 infield" of Stuffy McGinnis, Eddie Collins, Jack Barry, and Frank "Home Run" Baker, to lap the Yankees by 14½ games and topple the Cubs in the World Series. The following year the A's repeated; this time they crushed the Tigers by 13½ games and then beat the Giants in World Series play.

Mack's A's faded to third in 1912, but the renamed Boston Red Sox, now playing in their new Fenway Park, breezed to a 14-game win over the Senators. "Smokey Joe" Wood's 34–5 pitching and Tris Speaker's .383 batting led the Red Sox, who followed their league win with a victory over the Giants in the World Series. With this latest Series, the AL took a lead in this fall competition, which they hold to this day.

The Federal League war was beginning when Mack led his resurgent A's to a 6½-game win over the Senators and another victory over the Giants in the 1913 World Series. In 1914 the Mackmen captured their fourth AL pennant in five years as they outran the Red Sox by 8½ games, but then they lost the World Series to the sweeping "miracle" Boston Braves who had come from last place on July 4 to take the NL flag. That fall, racked by heavy financial losses incurred by the Federal League war, Mack sought to recoup by selling some of his stars. As a result, Mack's emasculated A's spent the next seven seasons in the AL cellar.

As the A's collapsed, the Red Sox and White Sox, both strengthened by player purchases from Mack, monopolized the next five AL races. By purchasing Jack Barry from Mack and snapping up minor league pitcher Babe Ruth, whom Mack had passed over, Boston was the first to cash in. The Red Sox won the 1915 pennant by 2½ games over the Tigers and went on to trounce the Phillies in World Series action. In this the last year of the Federal League war, Boston was one of only seven major league clubs to show a profit. But with the Feds out of the way in 1916, prosperity returned to the major leagues. Despite dealing Speaker to Cleveland, where his .386 batting ended Cobb's skein of nine straight AL batting titles, the Red Sox repeated. Ruth's 23 pitching victories led Boston to a 2-game victory over the White Sox and 5-game victory over the Dodgers in the World Series.

America's entry into the First World War in 1917 sent major league attendance plummeting as manager Clarence "Pants" Rowland drove his White Sox to a 9-game win over Boston. Shine-ball pitcher Eddie Cicotte's 28 victories led all AL hurlers, and Eddie Collins, Joe Jackson, and Happy Felsch supplied the power as the White Sox capped their victory with a win over the Giants in the World Series. But major league profits were low in 1917, and they touched rock bottom the following year, when the war effort forced the majors to cut their playing schedules to 128 games. The Red Sox rebounded to win the 1918 campaign by 2½ games over Cleveland. And by drubbing the Cubs in the World Series, the Red Sox notched their fifth World Series title in as many tries. However, at this point the Red Sox fell victim to their

impecunious owner, Harry Frazee, whose player sales soon divested the team of its ablest stars, including Ruth. As the Red Sox faded, so did their record of World Series triumphs. To this day Red Sox fans are still waiting for a sixth World Series victory.

Boston's collapse opened the way for the powerful White Sox to win the shortened 1919 race by 3½ games over the surging Cleveland Indians. In the wake of the White Sox victory came the sordid World Series of 1919, which saw eight Chicago players conspire with gamblers to throw the extended Series to the Cincinnati Reds. In 1920 the much-publicized revelations of that piece of skullduggery forced owner Charles Comiskey to suspend his eight Black Sox players in the last week of the red-hot 1920 pennant campaign.

Stripped of their stars, the White Sox finished second, a game ahead of the Yankees and two games behind the victorious Cleveland Indians. The gritty Indians lost their star shortstop Ray Chapman when he was fatally beaned by pitcher Carl Mays of the Yankees. To the present day, this remains the only fatality in major league history that was the direct result of a playing field accident. In the memorable World Series of 1920, Cleveland and Brooklyn were tied at two games apiece when Indian second-sacker Bill Wambsganss busted a promising Dodger rally by pulling off the first and only unassisted triple play in World Series history. And in that same game Indian outfielder Elmer Smith hit the first World Series grand-slam homerun. Such heroics, plus three pitching victories by Stan Coveleski, boosted the Indians to a five-games-to-two triumph in the 1920 fall classic. Cleveland's victory also ended the Boston, Philadelphia, Chicago pennant monopoly of the AL's deadball era, while Ruth's 59 homers as a Yankee in 1920 heralded the incoming "big-bang" style of play that would characterize the coming decade of the 1920s.

Deadball Dynasties: The National League, 1901–1920

A similar pattern of competitive imbalance also marked the NL campaigns of the silver age. In this era three NL mini-dynasties—those of Pittsburgh, Chicago, and New York — monopolized the first 14 NL campaigns. Moreover, even as outsiders rose up to win three consecutive pennants over the years 1914–1916, the Giants and Cubs came back to win pennants in 1917–1918 before yielding to the Reds and Dodgers in this era's final two campaigns. Of the three monopolists, the Giants were the most dominating team. Under manager John McGraw, "the Napoleonic genius" who jumped the AL in 1902 to skipper the moribund Giants, the New Yorkers won six pennants, finished second eight times, and suffered only one losing season.

In 1901 the first of this dynastic trio, the Pittsburgh Pirates, won the first of three consecutive NL pennants. Pittsburgh's rise began in 1900, the year the NL cut back to eight teams. When his Louisville team was dropped in the NL's cutback, owner Barney Dreyfuss purchased the Pittsburgh club, which he strengthened by adding Louisville stars Fred Clarke and Honus Wagner to his Pirate team. Powered by player-manager Clarke and Wagner, and unscathed by the disastrous roster raids by AL teams that were weakening his opponents, Pittsburgh won the

1901 NL race by 7½ games over the Phillies; they then won the 1902 race by an awesome 27½ games over runner-up Brooklyn, and captured the 1903 flag by 6½ games over the Giants. In each of these campaigns, both Wagner and Clarke topped the .300 mark in batting. Moreover, Wagner's .355 hitting won the 1903 batting title while outfielder Ginger Beaumont's .357 batting won the 1902 batting title. The Pirate pitching staff was fronted by Deacon Phillippe, who won 66 games in these years, and by Jack Chesbro, who won 49 games in two seasons before jumping to the AL in 1903. In postseasonal play, the 1903 Pirates lost the first modern World Series to the Boston Red Sox.

Pittsburgh sank to fourth place in 1904 as the Giants surfaced to win consecutive pennants in 1904–1905. In 1904 the Giants won 106 games to beat the runner-up Chicago Cubs by 13 games. Power pitching by "Ironman" Joe McGinnity (35–8), Christy Mathewson (33–12), and "Dummy" Taylor (21–15) paced the light-hitting Giants to victory. But in the aftermath of the win, manager McGraw refused to meet the AL champion Boston Pilgrims in World Series play. That issue was resolved in 1905, the year McGraw drove his team to a 9-game win over the Pirates and then to an easy conquest of the Philadelphia Athletics in the World Series, with Mathewson tossing three shutouts.

The following year, the Chicago Cubs emerged as the third NL dynasty of the deadball era. Pennant-starved since 1886, the Chicagoans recouped with a vengeance, winning an astonishing 530 games over the years 1906–1910. Such mastery was good enough to land four pennants in those five years. Skippered by player-manager Frank Chance, who, along with fellow infielders Johnny Evers and Joe Tinker, is now immortalized in baseball folklore, the 1906 Cubs won their record 116 games. Powered by Chance and third baseman Harry Steinfeldt, and armed by Mordecai "Three-Finger" Brown's 26–6 pitching, this superb team buried the Giants by 20 games, but lost the World Series to their hometown AL rivals, the "hitless wonder" White Sox.

The Cubs made it three victories in a row by winning in 1907–1908. The 1907 Cubs crushed Pittsburgh by 17 games, and in the unforgettable season of 1908, the Cubs edged the Giants by a single game. With two weeks remaining in the 1908 season, the Giants, Cubs, and Pirates were locked in a close race. Then, in a fateful encounter with the Cubs at the Polo Grounds, Fred Merkle of the Giants blundered by failing to touch second base as his Giants were scoring what looked like the winning run. In the stormy aftermath of this play, Umpire Hank O'Day ruled Merkle out for failing to touch the base and declared the game a tie because the swirling masses of Giant fans on the field made resumption of play impossible. Later NL president Harry Pulliam supported O'Day's decision and ruled that if necessary the game would be replayed at the close of the season. As it turned out, this was necessary because the Cubs and the Giants finished the season in a dead heat. To settle the outcome, the controversial game was replayed on October 8 at the Polo Grounds. The Cubs won the sudden-death game 4–2, as Brown outpitched Mathewson. In baseball folklore the Giant defeat permanently stigmatized "Bonehead" Fred Merkle as the blamesake of the Giants' defeat. As for the

Cubs, they took full advantage of their quirky victory by defeating the Tigers for a second straight time in World Series action.

In 1909 the Cubs won 104 games, with Brown pitching 27 victories. But the Pirates won 110 that year to beat Chance's men by 6½ games. Wagner led the league in hitting, and pitchers Vic Willis and Howie Camnitz combined for 48 wins. In World Series action, the Pirates hung a third straight loss on the AL champion Tigers. But the Cubs rebounded in 1910, winning 104 games for a second straight year. This time it was enough to lap the Giants by 13, but the Cubs then fell to the Athletics in the World Series.

Over the years 1911–1913 the Giants dominated NL play. In winning three consecutive pennants, they piled up 303 victories; pitchers Mathewson and Rube Marquard accounted for 147 of these, while Giant hitters led the NL in batting each year. But in World Series appearances McGraw's men repeatedly swooned, losing to the Philadelphia Athletics in 1911 and 1913 and to the Boston Red Sox in 1912.

Over the years 1914–1916, a whiff of competitive balance settled over the NL as three outsiders wrested pennants from the three dynasty teams. In 1914 the "miracle" Boston Braves stormed from 10 games back in mid-July to win 60 of their last 76 games; the surge was enough to crush the Giants by 10½ games. The following year, the Philadelphia Phillies landed their first NL pennant on the strength of 31 wins by pitcher Grover Cleveland Alexander and 24 homers by Gavvy Cravath. The Phillies beat out the Boston Braves by 7 games. And in 1916, manager Wilbert Robinson's Dodgers got 25 victories from pitcher Ed Pfeffer as they edged the Phillies by 2½ games. But this trio of outsiders produced only one World Series victory, which came when the Braves swept Mack's Athletics to win the 1914 classic. As for the other interlopers, both the Phillies and Dodgers fell to the Boston Red Sox.

Like the AL's, the NL's wartime campaigns of 1917–1918 were plagued by poor attendance which caused some tremulous owners to sell players in hopes of recouping losses. But the pennant monopolists held firm. The Giants won the 1917 race by 10 games over the Phillies, but then fell for a fourth straight time in World Series play as the White Sox prevailed. And in 1918, after winning the attenuated NL race by 10½ games over the Giants, the Cubs bowed to the Red Sox in the World Series.

The deadball era was drawing to a close in 1919, which was the year that manager Pat "Whiskey Face" Moran drove his Cincinnati Reds to their first NL pennant. The Reds won by 9 games over the runner-up Giants as future Hall of Fame outfielder Edd Roush batted .321 to lead the league. The Reds also won the World Series, but the stench of the Black Sox Scandal sullied their victory. As breaking news stories of that scandal overshadowed stories of the 1920 pennant race, in progress when the news broke, the Brooklyn Dodgers went on to defeat the Giants by 7 games. But the Dodgers lost to an inspired Cleveland Indians team in the World Series. In the atmosphere of gloom caused by the Black Sox Scandal revelations, it was also apparent that the deadball era of stylized baseball play was ending. But a new era was unfolding in the

1920s that would launch the major leagues into new uplands of cash and glory.

Baseball's Second Golden Age, 1921–1931

Over the winter of 1920–1921, crestfallen club owners slavishly chose Federal Judge Kenesaw Mountain Landis to be baseball's high commissioner and empowered him to restore the game's scandal-sullied image. At the time few observers could have predicted that major league baseball was moving into another golden age of cash and glory that would be highlighted by the dazzling exploits of Babe Ruth, who already was enthralling fans by his mastery of the new "big-bang" offensive style. But the sparkling turnabout in baseball's fortunes was also buoyed by the optimistic spirit of America's "roaring twenties." This was a decade of booming prosperity, an expanding urban population, declining work hours, and hefty increases in recreational spending by the American people. By 1929, indeed, Americans were annually spending $4.9 billion for recreational pursuits. To be sure, much of this spending was diverted into movies, radios, and automobiles, but major sports like baseball, football, basketball, boxing, golf, and tennis were attracting millions of hero-worshipping fans. Such adulation made demigods of athletes like Red Grange, Jack Dempsey, Bobby Jones, and Bill Tilden, but all of these sporting heroes were overshadowed by Babe Ruth, who now became the most photographed American of the decade.

During baseball's "guilty season" of 1920, it was the fun-loving Ruth, not the stern moralist Commissioner Landis, who diverted the attention of fans from the Black Sox Scandal. In 1920 the Babe accomplished this feat by smacking 54 homers to break his own seasonal mark, which he had set only the year before. Ruth's latest achievement fully justified the astonishing $125,000 which the Yankees shelled out before the 1920 season to obtain the former Red Sox pitching ace, whose batting prowess dictated regular duty as an outfielder.

With the Yankees, the charismatic Ruth bestrode the baseball scene like a young colossus. The very embodiment of the big-bang offensive style, Ruth notched ten AL homer titles over the years 1920–1931. In the last six of those seasons, he smacked 302 homers, including a record 60 blows in 1927. At the close of the 1931 season Ruth's homer output exceeded 600, and when he retired in 1935, he had raised his total to 714, along with a lifetime batting average of .342.

Inspired by Ruth's example, the big-bang style dominated major league baseball offensives of this and all subsequent eras. While no other team matched the consistent power of the Yankees, in this era NL teams outslugged their AL counterparts. And if no player surpasses Ruth's consistent power, sluggers like Cy Williams, Hack Wilson, Chuck Klein, Harry Heilmann, and Rogers Hornsby ably mastered the big-bang style. In 1930 Wilson hit 56 homers to set an NL seasonal mark, but for sheer all-around batting consistency Hornsby and Heilmann had no peers. Over the years 1921–1927 Tiger outfielder Heilmann topped .390 four times, hit 104 homers, and won four AL batting titles.

Incredibly Hornsby bettered this performance. Over

the years 1920–1925, Hornsby won six NL batting titles, topped the .400 mark in batting three times, and won two Triple Crowns. Hornsby's lifetime batting average of .358 is the best of any right-handed batter in major league history.

Such heroics by players of this era were the highlights of all-out seasonal offensives that dwarfed those of the deadball era. In this decade seasonal batting averages in both major leagues topped .280, with NL batters averaging a whopping .303 in 1930. At the same time, league-wide homer production, averaging 540 a season in the NL and 490 in the AL, helped raise per-game scoring to an average of five runs per team, while relegating base stealing to the status of a secondary tactic. Abetting the big-bang offensives of this era were innovations in technology and in pitching rules. Technology provided livelier balls, which were more frequently changed during games; indeed, fans were now permitted to keep balls hit into the stands. Meanwhile, rule changes of 1920–1921 barred the use of spitters and other doctored balls by all pitchers except for a few specified veterans. Such changes made for much battered pitchers with ERAs of 4.00 now regarded as an acceptable level of pitching performance. To cope with the situation, managers now relied more heavily on relief pitchers. Nevertheless, virtuoso starting pitchers like Johnson, Alexander, Grimes, Grove, Pennock, Hoyt, and Vance ranked among the top stars of this decade.

That fans welcomed the new offensive style was evidenced by the record-setting attendance marks of this era. Despite the lurid exposés of the Black Sox Scandal, a record 9.1 million fans attended major league games in 1920. Then, after falling below that mark for three seasons, attendance soared to an average of 9.6 million a season over the years 1924–1929 and peaked at 10.1 million in 1930. Helping to swell attendance in this era were Sunday games, which were legalized in all cities outside of Pennsylvania. Such support boosted revenues by 40 percent over the previous era and raised annual player salaries to an average of $7,000 by 1930. However, such average figures are misleading. In the NL, the Giants, Dodgers, Pirates, and Cardinals got most of the profits, and the AL Yankees alone accounted for 25 percent of that circuit's annual attendance. Player salaries also varied widely, ranging from less than $2,000 for fringe players to Ruth's princely $80,000 for the season of 1930; moreover, in this era the Yankee and Cub payrolls topped those of other teams.

That the Cardinals ranked with the most profitable NL clubs at this time owed to the genius of General Manager Branch Rickey. One of baseball's greatest innovators, Rickey had an impact on the game that extended far beyond this decade. At this time Rickey made a contender out of the impecunious Cardinals by reviving the farm system and using minor league farm clubs to develop and train young players. By purchasing minor league clubs and establishing working agreements with others, and by deploying scouts to sign young players at low costs, Rickey built and stocked a network of minor league farm clubs which supplied the Cardinals with a steady flow of star players. Despite opposition from Landis, Rickey's farm network flourished and was widely imitated. By cornering the market on young talent and selling surplus players to other major league teams, the Cardinals profited despite poor attendance. For his part, Rickey profited by reaping a percentage from each player sale.

As a baseball innovator, Rickey had a much more enduring impact on the game than Commissioner Landis. By banishing the Black Sox, disciplining players, and presiding in watchdog fashion over annual World Series games, Landis contributed to restoring the game's honest image. But Landis's autocratic posturing grated on major league owners, some of whom resented his opposition to farm systems and his conservative approach to the sale of World Series radio broadcasting rights. Landis also stubbornly opposed the racial integration of organized baseball. Thus in this era outcast black players turned to their own leader, Andrew "Rube" Foster, who founded the Negro National League in 1920. In 1923 the Eastern Colored League took to the field as a second black major league, but gave way in 1928 to the Negro American League, which lasted until 1950. Such leagues fielded great black stars like future Hall of Famers Satchel Paige, Pop Lloyd, "Cool Papa" Bell, the slugging Josh Gibson, and Ray Dandridge. In this decade postseason exhibition games played between white and black major leaguers drew attention to the black stars, whose abilities matched and often surpassed those of white major leaguers.

But the limited exposure afforded to black stars contrasted starkly with the broad media coverage now lavished on the white majors. For this golden era of major league baseball history was gilded by newspaper coverage which touted the games and the player-heroes in romanticized style. Moreover, motion pictures and radio coverage opened new dimensions for promoting the game that suspicious owners of the age were slow to exploit. Conservative owners also took a dim view of the night baseball games which pioneer promoters were staging in the minors and in the black leagues. However, when the golden age ended amidst the worst economic depression of this century, such innovations would enable hard-pressed owners to better cope with the austerities of the 1930s.

Golden Age Campaigns: The AL, 1921–1931

In this era dreams of a competitively balanced AL went for naught as three teams—the Yankees, Senators, and Athletics—dominated the eleven pennant races. Foremost among these powers, the lordly Yankees used Ruth's explosive power to win six pennants and three world titles, while outdrawing all other AL teams by a wide margin. Once established, the Yankee dynasty lasted for forty years, during which time no more than three seasons passed by without the Yankees hoisting another AL pennant. In laying the foundations for this awesome domination, Yankee owners Jake Ruppert and Cap Huston repeatedly took advantage of their financially strapped Boston colleague, Harry Frazee, to denude the latter's Boston Red Sox of its ablest stars. In 1919 the Yankees pried pitcher Carl Mays from Frazee, and at the end of that year, the Yankee owners paid Frazee $125,000 up-front money and also a $300,000 loan to snag their biggest catch of all in Babe Ruth. What's more, over the next few years Frazee paid off the loan by sending more players to New York. By then, picking the right Boston players was the job of General Manager Ed Barrow, who left his

former post as Boston field manager to come to the Yankees. After joining the Yankees at the close of the 1920 season, Barrow's dealings with Frazee over the next three seasons made Yankees of such Boston stars as pitchers Waite Hoyt, Sam Jones, Joe Bush, Herb Pennock, and George Pipgras, catcher Wally Schang, and infielders Everett Scott and Joe Dugan.

Over the years 1921–1923, these acquisitions helped to carry the Yankees to three consecutive pennants while burying the once-proud Red Sox. In 1921, with Ruth smashing 59 homers and driving in 171 runs, and Mays pitching 27 victories, the Yankees defeated the Indians by 4½ games. The following year ex–Red Sox players Jones, Bush, and Scott were on hand to help the Yankees edge the Browns by a single game. However, consecutive World Series losses to the rival New York Giants, whose Polo Grounds the Yankees shared as tenants, blighted these victories. But in 1923 the Yankees, now owned outright by Ruppert, moved into their brand-new Yankee Stadium, where Ruth's opening-day homer signaled a coming turnabout. With Ruth batting .393 that season, leading the league in homers, and sharing the lead in RBIs, the Yankees swept to an easy 16-game romp over the runner-up Tigers. And then, after dropping two of the first three games of the 1923 World Series, the Yankees swept the Giants to land their first world title.

This initial display of Yankee dominance ended in 1924, when the team lost to the Washington Senators by two games. It was Washington's first AL pennant. Led by their "boy manager," second baseman Bucky Harris, the Senators went on to down the Giants in a seven-game World Series struggle. Pitching in relief, the veteran Walter Johnson notched the victory in the final game. The following year the Senators repeated, using a powerful .303 batting assault to top the Athletics by 8½ games. But in World Series action the 1925 Senators blew a three-games-to-one lead and lost to the Pirates in seven games.

As the AL's 1926 season began, any likelihood of a Yankee resurgence seemed a remote possibility. Only the year before, the Yankees languished in seventh place, as illness and insubordination tolled on Ruth's performance. But a contrite Ruth came back as strong as ever, and young infielders Lou Gehrig, Tony Lazzeri, and Mark Koenig revitalized the team. In a close race the Yankees edged the Indians by 3 games, but lost to the Cardinals in a memorable seven-game World Series battle. Rebounding from that defeat, the 1927 Yankees mounted one of the most devastating assaults in major league history. In crushing the runner-up Athletics by 19 games, the Yankees batted .307 and led the AL in all major offensive categories. Ruth's 60 homers set a seasonal mark that lasted for 34 years, and Gehrig weighed in with 47 homers and 175 RBIs. In World Series action the Yankees easily dispatched the Pirates in four games. The following year the Yankees repeated, although they were pressed hard by the Athletics, who finished 2½ games behind. Still the 1928 Yankees finished their season in fine fettle by scoring an avenging four-game sweep of the Cardinals in the World Series.

The Yankees' latest stranglehold on the AL ended in 1929, when manager Connie Mack's power-packed Athletics captured the first of three consecutive pennants. The resurrection of the once-powerful Athletic dynasty was a triumph of patient rebuilding by Mack. After the veteran owner-manager broke up his formidable 1914 team, the Athletics spent the next seven years in the AL cellar. After quitting the depths in 1922, the team improved steadily. In 1928 the Athletics came close to dethroning the Yankees, and in 1929 the Mackmen mounted an offensive which rivaled that of the 1927 Yankees as they crushed the New Yorkers by 18 games. The team's .296 batting average was led by outfielder Al Simmons, who batted .365 with 34 homers and a league-leading 157 RBIs, and by first baseman Jimmy Foxx's .354-33-117 performance. The pitching staff, led by Lefty Grove (20–6), George Earnshaw (24–8), and Rube Walberg (18–11), was the league's best. In World Series play the Athletics crushed the Cubs in five games; one of the team's victories included a devastating 10-run outburst that turned an 8–0 deficit into a 10–8 victory.

Over the next two seasons, the Athletics continued their dominance. In 1930 they defeated the Senators by 8 games, and in 1931 they crushed the runner-up Yankees by 13½ games. In postseason action, the Athletics beat the Cardinals in six games to win the 1930 World Series, but in 1931 the team lost a seven-game struggle to the Cardinals. Indeed, the 1931 AL pennant was to be the last for manager Mack and for the Philadelphia Athletics. Financial losses caused by the nation's deepening Depression forced the aging manager to sell star players to weather the storm. In the past such drastic measures had worked, and Mack had been able to rebuild his team. But advancing age and changing baseball fortunes now conspired against Mack.

Golden Age Campaigns: The NL, 1921–1931

Although upstaged by Ruth and the Yankees and bested in six of eleven World Series clashes, NL teams of this era more than held their own against AL rivals. Indeed, NL sluggers outslugged their AL counterparts in nine of these seasons, NL pitchers posted better ERAs than AL hurlers, and in the inflationary 1930 season NL batters outhit and outslugged their rivals by wide margins. That year NL batters averaged .303 to the AL's .288, and NL sluggers powered 892 homers to 673 for the junior circuit.

And yet in this era the NL was no better balanced competitively than the AL. Of the eleven NL campaigns of this era, the Giants and Cardinals each won four, the Pirates won two, and the Cubs won the other. In 1924 manager McGraw's Giants became the first major league team of this century to win four consecutive pennants. This was a feat matched only by Harry Wright's Boston Red Stockings of the 1870s and by Charley Comiskey's St. Louis Browns of the 1880s. For their part, the Giants of this era turned the trick with a potent batting attack; in their four-year sway, Giant hitters averaged better than .300 and smashed 335 homers.

In stocking his first pennant winner, McGraw pulled off astute trades with the moribund Braves and Phillies to obtain pitcher Art Nehf, shortstop Dave Bancroft, and outfielders Irish Meusel and Casey Stengel. These acquisitions joined with future Hall of Famers Frank Frisch and Ross Youngs to lead the Giants to the 1921 pennant. That year the Giants edged the Pirates by 4 games, and in 1922 they repeated, beating the runner-up Reds by 7

games. In both years the Giants met and defeated the Yankees in World Series play. In 1923 the Giants won a third straight flag by edging the Reds by 4½ games, but they lost the World Series to the Yankees. In 1924, with the addition of first baseman and future Hall of Famer Bill Terry, the Giants eked a narrow 1½-game victory over the Dodgers. In World Series play the Giants lost to the Senators in seven games. The 1924 pennant was Mc-Graw's last as the Giants' manager and the last by a Giant team in this era.

As sicknesses took their toll on McGraw, coach Hugh Jennings, and outfielder Ross Youngs, the Pirates ended the Giants' four-year reign with an 8½-game victory over the New Yorkers. Future Hall of Famers—third baseman Harold "Pie" Traynor, and outfielders Max Carey and Hazen "Ki Ki" Cuyler—led the Pirates, who went on to score a dramatic come-from-behind victory over the Senators in the 1925 World Series.

As the squabbling Pirates faded to third place in 1926, the hitherto unsung Cardinals won their first NL pennant. It was the first of four championships in this era by this emergent new dynasty. The rise of the Cardinals was the handiwork of general manager Branch Rickey. From Rickey's expanding farm system came stalwarts like infielders Jim Bottomley and Tom Thevenow and outfielders Chick Hafey and Taylor Douthit. In 1921 player-manager Rogers Hornsby led the team to a 2-game victory over the Cincinnati Reds. And in a classic seven-game struggle, the Cardinals went on to defeat the Yankees in the World Series.

That fall Rickey enraged Cardinal fans by dealing the contentious Hornsby to the Giants for second baseman Frank Frisch. Frisch batted .337 to lead the 1927 Cardinals, while Hornsby batted .361 with the Giants. Nevertheless, both teams came up short, as the Pirates edged the runner-up Cardinals by 1½ games. Pittsburgh's .305 team batting average was sparked by future Hall of Fame outfielders Paul and Lloyd Waner; Paul's .380 clouting led the league, and brother Lloyd batted .355. But the Pirates were crushed by the Yankees in the 1927 World Series.

Under manager Bill McKechnie, the resilient Cardinals rebounded to win the 1928 campaign by 2 games over the Giants. But like the 1927 Pirates, the Cardinals too were swept by the Yankees in the World Series. As the Cardinals slipped to fourth place in 1929, the Cubs won their only pennant of this era. Managed by Joe McCarthy, the Cub revival was powered by a .303 team batting attack. Newly acquired Rogers Hornsby, who was pried loose from the Braves in a mammoth deal, led the Cubs with a .380 batting average. Behind Hornsby the team's power-packed outfield weighed in with Riggs Stephenson hitting .362, Hack Wilson batting .345 and driving in 159 runs, and "Ki Ki" Cuyler batting .360. The assault boosted the Cubs to a 10½-game victory over the Pirates, but the Chicagoans were no match for the rampaging Athletics in the World Series.

As the golden era ended, manager Gabby Street drove the Cardinals to consecutive pennants in 1930–1931. In 1930 the Cardinals struggled to a 2-game victory over the Cubs, who dumped manager McCarthy in the wake of the loss. In this vintage year of NL hitting, the Cardinals batted .314, but were outhit by the Giants, who smote

.319 as a team! Every Cardinal starter in 1930 topped the .300 mark, and in World Series play the Cardinals outhit the Athletics. Nevertheless, the Athletics won the World Series in six games. The following year, as NL batting mirrored the falling national economy by dropping to .277, the Cardinals coasted to a 13-game victory over the Giants. A .286 team batting average and stout pitching by "Wild Bill" Hallahan, Burleigh Grimes, Paul Derringer, and Jess Haines paced the Cardinals, who defeated the Athletics in the World Series, four games to three. But falling attendance caused by the deepening Depression marred the 1931 NL season. Indeed, the decline signaled the end of the latest golden age and the beginning of a long era of austerity in major league baseball.

Austerity Baseball, 1932–1945

In company with most industrialized nations, America during these years suffered the calamitous effects of a lingering economic Depression followed hard after by years of total war. In America the great Depression blighted the 1930s by creating millions of jobless workers, holding wages far below their 1929 level, slowing population growth, and, of course, drastically reducing recreational spending. Although abetted by federal remedial programs, the national economy languished until 1940, when federal defense-spending programs spurred an economic revival. But the following year the nation faced a second ordeal, when it embarked upon four years of total war against the Axis powers.

Major league baseball felt the effects of the gathering Depression in 1931, when the AL suffered losses while the NL barely broke even. Once engulfed by the economic storm, both major leagues were hard hit as attendance fell to 8.1 million in 1932 and hit rock bottom with an overall total of 6.3 million in 1933. Thereafter attendance improved, but not until 1940 did annual attendance totals reach 10 million. A similar sickening decline affected the minor leagues. But the minors recovered strongly after 1933 and zoomed to a record total attendance of 18 million in 1940.

Since major league baseball's fate was at its gates, declining attendance translated into financial losses. In the AL, six previous years of domination by the Yankees and Athletics had the junior circuit trailing the NL in overall revenues. After losing a total of $156,000 in 1931, the AL suffered three desperate years during which overall losses topped $2 million. Slow improvement began with the 1935 season, but as always revenues were unevenly distributed. Strong clubs like the Yankees and Tigers fared far better than the financially battered Athletics, Browns, and Senators. Nor were conditions much better in the NL, which also lost heavily during the years 1932–1934. In that three-year span every NL team suffered at least two seasons of red ink. A turnabout began with the 1935 season, but over the next six seasons annual profits only twice totaled $500,000. Moreover, like those of the AL, NL revenues were unevenly distributed. The Cubs, Giants, Cardinals, and Reds fared far better than did the woebegone Braves and Phillies.

Under such financial pressures, salaries of major league players were slashed. Annual salary spending in the ma-

jors fell from $4 million in 1929 to $3 million in 1933, and as late as 1940 total payrolls still lagged behind the 1929 figure. Such cuts dropped the average player's salary to $6,000 in 1933, and the 1939 average salary of $7,300 still lagged behind the $7,500 figure of 1929. While such pay was good for those desperate times, job insecurity was rife among big league players of this era. Most players of this era needed no reminders that budget-slashing owners could easily find cheap replacements in the minor leagues. But for the time being, the great stars of the black majors, which also suffered from Depression austerities, posed no competitive threat. However, winds of change were stirring against segregated institutions in America, including major league baseball's unwritten color bar.

Of course, owners also faced a survival-of-the-fittest struggle in this depressed decade. Better-located clubs like the Yankees, Tigers, Cubs, and Giants adapted far better than did the owners of the financially strapped Athletics, Senators, Browns, Braves, and Phillies. Caught up in a vicious cycle, these poorer owners were forced to sell players to better-heeled clubs, a policy which had the effect of worsening attendance. However, one club, the Cardinals, managed to sell players to much better advantage. Although plagued by poor attendance, including three seasons which produced an aggregate home attendance total of fewer than 900,000, and one of those a world championship season which attracted only 325,000 fans at home, the Cardinals still managed to hold their own financially. Player sales from Rickey's well-stocked minor league farm system enabled the Cardinals to recoup financially and at the same time field strong teams.

At this time eager purchasers of players included Tom Yawkey, the wealthy new owner of the Red Sox. In this decade Yawkey spent $1 million on players. As a result Red Sox attendance rose while that of his moribund NL rival the Boston Braves worsened. Other bullish owners included the owners of the Cubs, Reds, Tigers, and Dodgers. But the well-financed Yankees emulated Rickey's example and built an efficient farm system of their own. Directed by the ruthlessly efficient George Weiss, the Yankee farms strengthened the Yankees' stranglehold on the AL.

Still, Depression-imposed austerities challenged all clubs of this era to find new ways to beef up revenues. Perhaps the most drastic of these was the plan of the owner of the St. Louis Browns to move the club to the West Coast, a strategy which was aborted by the outbreak of World War Two. But for the most part promoters tried to find ways of wringing more money from ballpark fans. Among these, expanding concession sales, utilizing promotional schemes, and staging night baseball games were tactics borrowed from minor league promoters and the black majors. But night baseball proved to be the wave of the future for the major leagues. When introduced to the majors in 1935 by Cincinnati general manager Larry MacPhail, the popularity of night baseball had most major league clubs following suit by 1940. Yet another source of profits came from the sale of local radio rights to broadcast accounts of games, a scheme which some owners had tried, but most had stubbornly resisted back in the twenties. By 1939 radio income totaled 7.3 percent of club revenues, up from a negligible 0.3 percent in 1930. Similarly, sales of World Series radio rights, a windfall shared by all major league clubs, now fetched higher prices. And at the close of the decade, the new medium of television showed promise, but the onslaught of World War Two delayed its profitable exploitation.

In the near future such innovations would profoundly alter the major league scene, but for now survival dictated sticking to more conservative measures. Thus in this era no privately financed ballparks were constructed (as, indeed, had been the case in the 1920s with the exception of Yankee Stadium), but Cleveland's publicly financed Municipal Stadium foreshadowed a future building boom that would replace most of the aging major league parks with modern facilities financed by public monies. When that day dawned, black players at last would be playing alongside whites in organized baseball. But in this era Commissioner Landis and his supporters continued their stubborn resistance in the face of mounting public support for organized baseball's integration. The breakthrough came, a year after Landis's death in 1945, as the first black player in this century signed a major league contract. Ironically, the integration of the white majors dealt a death blow to the flourishing black major leagues.

However, such impending changes were only dimly perceived by owners of this era. On the whole the 1930s were conservative years, with no significant rule changes invoked. In these years teams continued to master the big-bang style of play, with annual homer barrages, and pitching ERAs surpassing those of the 1920s. And if Ruth's departure in 1935 deprived the game of its most colorful hero of all time, new slugging stars like Hank Greenberg, Ted Williams, and Joe DiMaggio proved to be worthy successors. Their accomplishments and those of this era's teams were lavishly covered by sportswriters and by a new breed of radio sportscasters, whose ranks included some ex-players. Such coverage broadened baseball's appeal. So did the 1939 opening of the Baseball Hall of Fame at Cooperstown, New York, and the annual ritual of electing baseball immortals to the select circle. Indeed, the first annual election conducted in January of 1936 selected Ty Cobb, Babe Ruth, Honus Wagner, Christy Mathewson, and Walter Johnson as the five charter members. Over the years the number of enshrined players swelled to over 200, including stars from the segregated black majors. And so did the numbers of fans who annually made the pilgrimage to the Hall of Fame; from a few thousand a year in this era, the number of visitors now exceeds 250,000 annually.

The Crisis of World War Two

The major leagues were recovering from Depression-imposed austerities when the nation's entry into World War Two posed a second major crisis. From 1942 until the Allied victory in 1945, the nation's total war effort sapped baseball's manpower and threatened to curtail the 1945 playing season. Among the 12 million Americans summoned to military service during the war years were some 500 major league players and 3,500 minor leaguers. This talent drain shrank the minor leagues to nine circuits at one point, while only President Roosevelt's "green light" enabled the major leagues to continue playing throughout the war years.

That the major leagues continued playing the game in

the face of wartime austerities owed to the resilience of its promoters and the continuing support of the fans. Although annual attendance fell from 10 million in 1941 to 8.8 million in 1942 and to a low point of 7.7 million in 1943, the numbers rebounded to 9 million in 1944 and then soared to a record 11.1 million in 1945. Indeed, baseball's continuing popularity won the support of political figures like J. Edgar Hoover and Senator A. B. Chandler, who were convinced that the game was serving the war effort by boosting morale, both on the homefront and among the troops abroad.

Nevertheless, it was no easy task keeping the game of baseball afloat amidst a total war effort. In these years owners were hard-pressed to find ways of coping with a variety of shortages. Among them, a crunching transportation and hotel accommodation shortage forced promoters to cancel spring training programs in the southlands. And in 1945 the same problems forced the cancellation of that year's All-Star Game. Meanwhile a rubber shortage forced the major leagues to go with a dead "balata" ball (with a hard plastic at the core) in 1943, and all during the war a shortage of wood affected the quality of bats. Early in the war the threat of submarine attacks on coastal shipping also curtailed night games in East Coast centers, but by 1944 the restriction was lifted. Indeed, night games came to be welcomed by government officials, who regarded them as good recreation for defense workers.

But the worst shortage of all was in manpower. Indeed, never before nor since did the major leagues face a talent shortage of such proportions as occurred then. As draft boards denuded team rosters of able players, club officials scoured the land for draft rejects and other ineligibles; at this time, overage and underaged players were welcomed along with aliens. In questing after talented alien players, scouts turned up a mother lode in Latin America. Cuba turned out to be especially rich in prospects and at this time some fifty Cuban players were recruited. Indeed, at one point a young minor league promoter and war hero, Bill Veeck, proposed to buy the sickly NL Phillies franchise and stock it with black players from the Negro Leagues. Landis nixed the proposal.

For their part, owners needed stout hearts and a love of the game to keep going in the face of financial losses. In 1943 the majors lost $240,000, with the Cardinals and Tigers faring better than most other clubs. Hardest hit were the owners of the NL Phillies, who declared bankruptcy. The franchise was sold to the NL for $50,000, and after one abortive sale attempt NL officials sold the club to one of the DuPont Company heirs. Thus in the affluent hands of Bob Carpenter, this chronically weak NL franchise was soon revitalized.

At this time each owner was obliged to do his bit for the war effort. In response, clubs staged war bond sales, admitted servicemen free of charge to games, and allowed radio broadcasts of games to be transmitted free of charge to military bases. Although costly, such gestures paid off by increasing baseball's popularity. By 1944 the worst of the financial reverses caused by the war ended, and when the 1945 season returned overall profits of $1.2 million, it was apparent that major league baseball was once again on the upswing.

Such was not the case for the players who took a financial beating in each of these years. A government edict of 1943, which was part of a general effort to halt inflation by stabilizing wages, froze player salaries. The salary freezes came at a time when player salaries, which averaged $6,400 in 1942, were already at a low point. When the freeze on salaries continued through 1946, it stirred strong unionist sentiments among grousing players that erupted in the first postwar season.

Other changes unleashed by the war forced far-reaching changes on major league baseball. Fair employment policies adopted by the federal government and by some states now threatened major league baseball's long-established practice of racial segregation. Sensing the new trend toward racial integration, Branch Rickey in 1945 signed black major leaguer Jackie Robinson to a Dodger contract. Rickey also sent his scouts in search of other promising talent in the black majors. This was a timely move because Judge Landis's death in 1944 had removed a major stumbling block to the integration of the major leagues.

When the war ended in 1945 with a complete victory over the Axis powers, the prospects for major league baseball looked bright. But that year also brought news of the sale of the Yankees to a triumvirate of owners who paid $2.8 million for the club. And as it turned out, the postwar era would usher in yet another phase of Yankee domination.

Austerity Campaigns: The AL, 1932–1945

In the Depression era of 1932–1941, the AL extended its domination over the NL by winning seven of ten World Series encounters and six of the first nine All-Star Games. The annual All-Star Game was instituted in 1933 and quickly became a popular spectacle that marked the midpoint of each seasonal campaign. Meanwhile in the seasonal campaigns of this decade, AL batters topped their NL counterparts in batting average, homers, RBIs, and stolen bases, while NL hurlers posted lower ERAs than did AL pitchers. But there was an illusory quality to this apparent pattern of mastery. This was because the AL's dominance owed most to the powerful Yankees, who captured six of the AL's seven world titles in these years.

After a three-year hiatus, the Yankees recaptured the AL heights in 1932, crushing the Athletics by 13 games. Gehrig and Ruth combined for 75 homers and Yankee hitters batted .286. Under Manager Joe McCarthy, who was destined to become one of baseball's most victorious managers, pitching superiority also became a Yankee hallmark. In 1932, with Lefty Gomez leading the Yankees staff with 24 wins, the Yankee mound corps led the AL in ERA with 3.98. Thus fortified, the versatile Yankees went on to sweep the Cubs in a legendary World Series matchup, highlighted by Ruth's much-debated "called shot" homerun in the third game. And over the winter George Weiss was hired to build a Yankee farm system, a task which Weiss handled effectively. Within a few years the Yankee farm system laid the foundation for an awesome phase of Yankee domination.

Meanwhile, the other AL teams enjoyed a brief respite, as the Yankees fell behind the front-running Senators and Tigers over the next three seasons. As age tolled on Yankee stars like Ruth, the Senators, now skippered by another young player-manager, shorstop Joe Cronin,

defeated the Yankees by 7 games to win the 1933 pennant race. League-leading hitting and sturdy pitching by Al Crowder and Earl Whitehill, who combined for 46 victories, carried the Senators, who went on to lose the World Series in five games to the Giants. Worse yet, in this rock-bottom Depression year, the Senators attracted only 437,000 home fans. Confronted with financial losses, owner Clark Griffith sold outfield star Goose Goslin to the Tigers. Goslin's loss dashed the Senators' hopes for 1934, and when the team slipped to the second division that year, Griffith sold Cronin—his son-in-law—to the Red Sox for $250,000.

As the Senators suffered, the Detroit Tigers prospered. In addition to landing Goslin in 1934, the Tigers also purchased catcher Mickey Cochrane from the Athletics. Installed as the Tigers' player-manager, Cochrane headed a Tiger resurgence that saw the team rise from a fifth-place finish in 1933 to consecutive AL titles in 1934–1935. In 1934 Cochrane and Goslin teamed with Hank Greenberg and Charley Gehringer to spearhead a .300 team batting attack. What's more, pitchers Schoolboy Rowe and Tommy Bridges combined for 46 wins as the Tigers defeated the Yankees by 7 games. The sprightly effort attracted 919,000 home fans, who watched Detroit land its first AL pennant since 1909. Unhappily for the fans, they also saw the Tigers extend their World Series losing streak to four as the Cardinals prevailed in a seven-game struggle. But in 1935 the Tigers repeated as AL champions, edging the runner-up Yankees by 3 games. Greenberg led the team's .290 batting offensive by batting in 170 runs, and the purchase of Crowder from the Senators beefed up the team's pitching staff. Although a late-season injury kept Greenberg out of action in the 1935 World Series, the Tigers downed the Cubs in five games. It was Detroit's first World Series victory since 1887. But as it turned out, this victory was also the last World Series triumph by any AL team but the Yankees until 1945.

The second phase of Yankee domination over the AL began in 1936. The year before, Ruth's departure had removed the club's greatest drawing card, but this year young Joe DiMaggio appeared. Purchasing him from the San Francisco Seals of the Pacific Coast League for $25,000 and five other ballplayers, the Yankees were taking a chance that DiMaggio would be able to play effectively in spite of his injured knee. Indeed, he was, although the outfielder did prove to be injury-prone. But in 1936 the highly touted DiMaggio was an immediate sensation. In his freshman year he hit .323 with 29 homers and 125 RBIs. That year Gehrig's 49 homers led the league and the Yankees batted .300 as a team with 182 homers. The Yankee assault lapped the runner-up Tigers by 19½ games and in World Series action the Yankees downed the Giants in six games. It was the first of four consecutive World Series titles by the Bronx Bombers. During this record-setting streak, Weiss's farm system provided a steady flow of talented replacements. Included were pitchers Spud Chandler, Steve Sundra, Marius Russo, and Atley Donald; outfielders Tommy Henrich and Charley Keller; and second baseman Joe Gordon. In 1937 the Yankees repeated by topping the Tigers by 13 games; in 1938 they beat out the beefed-up Red Sox by 9½ games; and in 1939 the Red Sox trailed the all-con-

quering Yankees by 17 games. In each of these seasons the Yankees blasted at least 166 homers. And in World Series play their mastery of their NL rivals increased steadily; in 1937 the Giants fell in five games, and in 1938 and 1939 the Yankees swept the Cubs and the Reds. Landing four consecutive world titles was an unprecedented achievement, but such domination also kindled an enduring wave of anti-Yankee hostility among fans and rival teams.

Mercifully for the rest of the AL contenders, a year's respite from Yankee domination came in 1940. The year before, Lou Gehrig's tragic illness ended the career of the great first baseman, whose "iron man" record of having played in 2,130 consecutive games still stands. In 1940 Gehrig's absence was keenly felt, and it enabled the Tigers and Indians to battle the Yankees on even terms. Cleveland's fireballing pitching ace, Bob Feller, won 27 games to lead his team's assault, but tensions between the Indian players and manager Oscar Vitt adversely affected the team's morale. Such tensions enabled the hard-hitting Tigers to close the gap. Batting a league-leading .286, the Tigers were paced by future Hall of Famer Hank Greenberg; the big outfielder batted .340 with a league-leading 41 homers and 150 RBIs. First baseman Rudy York weighed in with a .316 batting average, and his 33 homers and 134 RBIs complemented Greenberg's production. Second baseman Charley Gehringer, another destined Hall of Famer, batted .313 and drove in 81 runs, and outfielder Barney McCosky batted .340. To top it off, portly pitcher Bobo Newsom enjoyed a vintage season with a 21–5 record. In the last week of the season the Tigers deadlocked the Indians, and on the last day of the campaign the Tigers defeated the Indians to win the hotly contested race. In the decisive game, won by the Tigers 2–0, rookie Tiger pitcher Floyd Giebell outpitched the great Feller. Ironically it was Giebell's last major league victory. But in World Series action the Tigers lost to the Cincinnati Reds in seven games.

Hard after that defeat, the gathering storm of World War Two dealt the Tigers a crushing blow. After playing 19 games of the 1941 season, slugger Greenberg was drafted into the Army. As the Tigers slumped, the Yankees rebounded and romped to a runaway 17-game victory over the second-place Red Sox. But this last peacetime AL campaign was fraught with memorable events. For one, by hitting safely in 56 consecutive games, Yankee outfielder Joe DiMaggio sparked the Yankee surge and established an enduring major league record. For another, by batting .406 over the season, Boston outfielder Ted Williams became the last major league player to this day to top the .400 mark. And in the unforgettable World Series of 1941, by missing a third strike with two out in the ninth inning, thereby opening the floodgates for a game-winning Yankee rally in the fourth game, Dodger catcher Mickey Owen won enduring notoriety as the blamesake for the latest Yankee victory. The 1941 Series victory was the eighth straight by Yankee teams.

In the wake of the 1941 major league season, the Japanese attack on Pearl Harbor plunged the nation into full-scale war with the Axis powers. Soon thereafter, the military drafts sapped the playing strength of all teams, but the efficient Yankee farm system enabled the Yankees to retain enough able players to land two more pennants in

1942 and 1943. In 1942 the Yankees led the league in homers, fielding, and pitching to defeat the bridesmaid Red Sox by nine games. Yankee pitcher Ernie Bonham led all AL hurlers with a 21–5 mark, while Red Sox outfielder Ted Williams followed his brilliant 1941 season by notching a rare Triple Crown effort; Williams batted .356 with 36 homers and 137 RBIs. However, Yankee hopes of extending their World Series winning streak came a cropper as the Cardinals downed the New Yorkers in five games.

But the resilient Yankees bounced back in 1943. League-leading slugging and pitching, the latter fronted by Spud Chandler's 20–4, 1.64 ERA performance, carried the Yankees to a 13½-game win over the Washington Senators. To top off the victory, in World Series action the Yankees scored an avenging victory over the Cardinals, who were beaten in five games.

In 1944 the military draft finally denuded the Yankees, who fell to third. As the Yankees sagged, the Browns and the Tigers battled for the top position, and the struggle ended with the St. Louis Browns winning their first and only AL pennant. In edging the Tigers by a single game, the Browns' .252 team batting mark ranked near the bottom of the league. But stout pitching by Jack Kramer, Nelson Potter, and reliever George Caster, and shortstop Vern Stephens's league-leading 109 RBIs made the difference. Matched against their hometown rivals in World Series play, the Browns fell to the Cardinals in six games.

In the last wartime campaign, the 1945 Tigers eked a 1½-game victory over the Senators. Although the Tigers were outhit by five other teams, pitcher Hal Newhouser's 25–9, 1.81 ERA pitching and slugger Greenberg's timely return from military service sparked the Tigers. After missing four seasons of play, Greenberg returned to play in 78 games, during which he batted .311 and drove in 60 runs. In World Series play Greenberg's .304 batting and his two homers led the Tigers to victory over the Cubs in seven games, in what has been described as "the worst World Series ever played."

Austerity Campaigns: The NL, 1932–1945

Although offensively outclassed by the AL, the NL boasted the best pitching in these years. Indeed, pitching decided eight of the first ten NL campaigns of this era while also contributing to the senior circuit's better competitive balance. Over the years 1932–1941 the NL campaigns featured nine close races with five different pennant winners. Thus the longest reign of any would-be dynasty was two years, a feat achieved by the New York Giants and the Cincinnati Reds.

In 1932 the Chicago Cubs rose to the top of the NL and continued a quirky pattern, dating back to 1929, of winning a pennant every three years. In August the embattled Cubs replaced manager Rogers Hornsby with first baseman Charlie Grimm, a timely move that rallied the Cubs. Player-manager Grimm, in company with infielder Billy Herman and outfielders Riggs Stephenson and Johnny Moore, led the .278 team batting attack, while pitcher Lon Warneke (22–6) fronted the team's league-leading pitching staff. The Cubs went on to defeat the Pirates by four games, but were swept by the Yankees in the World Series.

As the Cubs swooned in 1933, another player-manager, first baseman Bill Terry, led the Giants to their first NL pennant since 1924. They did it by scoring a five-game victory over the Pirates. Terry batted .322, and outfielder Mel Ott's 23 homers keyed the Giants' league-leading homer assault. The pitching staff, fronted by lefty Carl Hubbell's 23 victories, was the league's best. And in World Series action the Giants beat the Senators in five games.

The following year the Giants again boasted league-leading pitching, but the hard-hitting Cardinals overtook the New Yorkers in the final week to win by 2 games. Dubbed the "Gas House Gang," these Cardinals symbolized the Depression austerities that affected the nation in this worst year of the economic hard times. The Cardinals drew only 325,000 home fans, but player-manager Frank Frisch, in company with Rip Collins, Ernie Orsatti, Joe Medwick, and Spud Davis, topped the .300 mark in batting to pace the team's league-leading .288 batting effort. But the brightest star was pitcher Dizzy Dean, who won 30 games to become the last major league hurler to crack the 30-game barrier for over thirty years; moreover, Dean's brother Paul won 19. In World Series play, the Cardinals rebounded from a 3–2 deficit in games to beat the Tigers.

The folksy Arkansas country boy Dizzy Dean won 28 games in 1935, but the Cubs trumped the Cardinal ace with their league-leading pitching staff. At the close of the campaign, the Cubs led the Cardinals by four games. Heading the Cub hurlers were Lon Warneke and Bill Lee, each a 20-game winner. Five Cub regulars topped the .300 mark, including infielders Stan Hack and Billy Herman, outfielders Frank Demaree and Augie Galan, and catcher Gabby Hartnett, to pace the team's .288 batting offensive. And outfielder Chuck Klein, a timely acquisition from the moribund Phillies, powered 21 homers. But the Cubs were no match for the Tigers in World Series play; the Tigers defeated the Chicagoans in six games.

Over the next two seasons, Cub hitters topped all NL teams in batting, but each time the team finished second behind the Giants. Dominant pitching, paced by Carl Hubbell's 26 wins and Ott's league-leading 33 homers, led the 1936 Giants to a five-game win over the Cubs and Cardinals. In the second half of the campaign, many eyes were on lefty Hubbell, as the Giant hurler finished the season with 16 consecutive victories to threaten the record seasonal streak of 19 owned by Rube Marquard of the old Giants. Hubbell won the opener of the 1936 World Series, but the Yankees beat the lefty in the fourth game and went on to down the Giants in six games.

But postseasonal play was discounted, and Hubbell went on to add another eight victories in 1937. When the ace finally lost one on Memorial Day, his record (over two seasons) of 24 consecutive victories stood as the best by a major league pitcher. But more important to the Giants' cause in 1937, Hubbell went on to win 22 games and rookie Cliff Melton won 20 as the Giants hung on to beat the runner-up Cubs by 3 games. It was the second straight conquest for the Giants, but in World Series action they again fell to the Yankees, this time losing in five games.

For a last time in 1938, the Cubs used their magical three-year formula to land the NL pennant. In an epic campaign that saw Cincinnati Reds' pitcher Johnny Van-

der Meer pitch two consecutive no-hit games, and the front-running Pirates blow a big lead, the Cubs mounted a remarkable September surge to overhaul and topple the Pirates by 2 games. In a decisive game played in late September's gathering darkness at Wrigley Field, player-manager Gabby Hartnett hit his legendary "homer in the gloaming" as part of a three-game Cub sweep of the Pirates. Although the Cubs batted only .269 that year, the team's pitching staff was the best in the league. Nevertheless, the well-armed Cubs were swept by the Yankees in the 1938 World Series.

As the punchless Cubs sank to fourth place in 1939, manager Bill McKechnie drove the Cincinnati Reds to their first NL pennant since 1919. Since that victory, the Reds had been remembered primarily for pioneering night baseball and for Johnny Vander Meer's double no-hit feat. But recently the club had come under the ownership of radio tycoon Powel Crosley, whose player purchases were strengthening the team. Included were a prize pair of pitchers: Paul Derringer, who was purchased from the Cardinals, and Bucky Walters, who came via the Phillies. In 1939 this duo combined for 52 victories and headed the league's best pitching staff. Supported by sturdy hitting from outfielder Ival Goodman, first baseman Frank McCormick, and catcher Ernie Lombardi, the Reds held off the Cardinals to win by 4½ games. However, the Reds suffered the same fate as did the 1938 Cubs when the Yankees swept them in World Series play. Regrouping after this defeat, the Reds repeated in 1940 as they downed the rebuilt Dodgers by 12 games. For the winning Reds, mediocre hitting was overcome by league-leading pitching and fielding. And in the 1940 World Series it was the Reds who outlasted the Tigers in a seven-game struggle.

In the NL's last peacetime campaign before the outbreak of the Second World War, the Reds fell behind the rising Dodgers and the perennially contending Cardinals. In a close race the Dodgers held on to win by 2½ games over the Cardinals. In rebuilding the Dodgers, general manager Larry MacPhail persuaded the club's banker trustees to bankroll the purchases of players from the Phillies and Cardinals. From the Cardinals came pitcher Curt Davis, and outfielders Medwick and young Pete Reiser. Snagging Reiser from the Cardinals' farm system was a real coup as he led the league in batting with a .343 mark. From the Phillies, MacPhail obtained pitcher Kirby Higbe and first baseman Dolph Camilli; and in 1941 Camilli's 34 homers and 120 RBIs led the league. With additional acquisitions, the 1941 Dodgers fielded few home-grown players. Indeed, player-manager Leo Durocher was a former Cardinal hand. But the Dodger assemblage of mercenaries led the NL in pitching and homers and tied with the Cardinals in hitting. During the frenzied campaign, the Dodgers attracted a million home fans, most of whom mourned their "Bums'" heart-breaking loss to the Yankees in the 1941 World Series.

As wartime exigencies riddled NL teams of playing talent, the Cardinals retained enough players to land three consecutive pennants over the years 1942–1944. Although Rickey left the Cardinals in 1942 to join the Dodgers as that team's general manager, his efficient farm system fueled the Cardinals. In dominating the NL, the Cardinals won 316 games in these years, each time lead-ing the league in hitting and pitching. Managed by Billy Southworth, the 1942 Cardinals needed 106 wins to edge the Dodgers by 2 games. The following year 105 victories enabled the Cardinals to romp to an 18-game win over the runner-up Reds. And in 1944 another 105 victories easily carried the Redbirds to a 14½-game win over the second-place Pirates. In World Series play the Cardinals split with the Yankees, winning in five games in 1942 and losing by the same count in 1943. And in 1944 the Cardinals thrashed the Browns in six games. In these years young outfielder Stan Musial emerged as a superstar with the Cardinals, winning the first of what would be seven NL batting titles with a .357 mark in 1943.

It was the loss of Musial to military service in 1945 which helped the Cubs end the Cardinals' pennant monopoly. League-leading batting, fronted by first baseman Phil Cavaretta's major-league-leading .355 batting, and league-leading pitching carried the Cubs to a 3-game victory over the Cardinals. But the victory was soured by defeat at the hands of the Tigers in the 1945 World Series. Worse still, Cub fans to this day are still looking for another NL pennant.

Baseball's Postwar Era, 1946–1961

Victory in World War Two unleashed a host of pent-up changes which altered American society. Among the most welcomed was a steadily expanding economy which increased jobs, wages, and consumer spending. Bolstered by such growth industries as housing, television, and automobile production, the tide of economic prosperity transformed the nation into an affluent society of dynamic abundance. Moreover, most Americans shared in the fruits of this abundance. With plenty of discretionary income, Americans spent ever-increasing amounts for leisure and recreational purposes. From a total of $11 billion spent in 1946 on such pursuits, such spending topped $18 billion by 1960. By then, the most popular leisure activity was television viewing, with nearly 80 percent of American households of 1960 boasting at least one TV set. And the number of American households increased sharply along with the nation's booming population. A postwar marriage boom fueled a fifteen-year-long baby boom to add to the nation's population growth. And in this era, millions of Americans forsook older cities for new suburban homes, a trend that sped the growth of new urban regions.

But postwar America was also faced with disturbing and controversial changes. At home, long-festering opposition to racial discrimination and segregation now saw black Americans using political action movements to batter away at sources of inequality. Similarly, increased union activity by organized workers was aimed at securing bigger shares of the fruits of abundance. And on the international front, the nation found itself thrust into a role as defender of the free world against Communist expansion. At this time a mounting arms race with the Soviet Union had America and the Russians stockpiling nuclear weapons and extending their rivalry into space exploration. This international ideological struggle translated at home into increased federal spending for defense and space programs, a continuation of the military draft,

and a pervasive fear of Communism which spilled over into political campaigns.

At this time most of these forces and others impacted upon major league baseball. For openers, the rising national prosperity boosted attendance and revenues, but shifting population centers now tempted some club owners to abandon old sites for greener pastures elsewhere. By 1958 five such franchise shifts had occurred. In 1953 the NL Braves became the first breakaway franchise when they abandoned their traditional Boston haunts for Milwaukee; in 1954 the penurious AL Browns departed St. Louis for Baltimore, and the following year the equally penurious AL Athletics moved from Philadelphia to Kansas City. Such moves were controversial, for they destroyed a long-standing, fifty-year-old status quo in major league baseball. But the biggest public uproar echoed from Brooklyn and New York City, when fans of the NL Dodgers and Giants saw these teams move to the West Coast, respectively to Los Angeles and San Francisco. Following upon those moves, a rival major league, the Continental League, threatened to plant teams in some abandoned cities, but mostly in new population centers that now hungered for major league baseball. The urgent need to defuse the Continental League threat and the lesser need to assuage bereft New York fans prompted major league owners to expand the major leagues at the end of this era.

Meanwhile, these breakaway franchise movements, while increasing major league attendance and revenues, were weakening the minor leagues by pre-empting some of the strongest minor league territories. At the same time attendance at minor league games was being undermined by the increasing radio and television broadcasts of major league games. For the minor leagues, such blows were crushers. From an all-time peak in 1949, when the minors fielded 59 leagues with over 7,800 players and attracted 40 million fans, the number of minor leagues steadily dwindled. By the early 1960s, the number of minor leagues had shrunk to nineteen, with fewer than 2,500 players and total annual attendance of less than 20 million fans. By then, major league owners were learning that there was a piper to pay; for the decline of the minors confronted the major leagues with a chronic, persistent problem of talent scarcity. To cope with the knotty talent shortage problem, major league clubs engaged in costly bidding wars for the services of promising young players. And in addition to bidding for "bonus babies," major league clubs recruited black players both at home and in Latin America. Since such moves failed to solve the problem of talent scarcity, by the end of this era the majors were challenged to find ways of subsidizing the surviving minor leagues, to prevent these vital nurseries of playing talent from drying up.

But baseball's talent scarcity problem was also aggravated by the television revolution. As television producers soon learned that other sports attracted viewers, they took to subsidizing rival team sports such as professional football and basketball. As these and other sports gained in popularity, young athletes turned to them in increasing numbers. Indeed, at many schools and colleges baseball now ranked as a minor sport. But television bestowed blessings as well as problems upon baseball. In 1950 baseball telecasting provided $2.3 million in new revenues and by 1960 such annual income topped $12 million. As television income enhanced the value of major league franchises, its potential now became a major consideration in the relocation of franchises. For now, as at the present time, owners clung to the policy of negotiating their own local television contracts. But owners of this era worried over television's impact on live attendance at games. In 1946 a record 18.1 million fans attended major league games and in 1948 rising annual attendance peaked at 21.3 million. Thereafter annual attendance sagged, falling below the 20 million mark during the 1950s. For this turnabout, some owners blamed television for making a free show of the games. But aging parks, located in congested and declining center cities whose populations were shifting to suburban areas, also accounted for the decline. In other ways television altered the game. The steadily increasing number of night games now transformed major league baseball into a primarily nocturnal spectacle—except at Wrigley Field in Chicago. Night baseball was a trend encouraged by the televising of games as producers found night games to be more profitable. And by making celebrities of players, television triggered a rise in player salaries which would reach astonishing proportions in later years. Moreover, by scooping newspapers on the coverage of the outcome of games, television forced baseball writers to adopt a new, more probing style of baseball coverage. But such mixed blessings failed to deter owners of this era from reaping revenues from local and national television contracts. However, it is unlikely that any owner of this era could have envisioned a coming time when television revenue would exceed that of ticket sales at games.

Nor could many owners at the dawn of this era envision the revolutionary impact of the racial integration of baseball. Nevertheless, in 1947 major league baseball became a major front in the ongoing battle for racial equality. That year Branch Rickey's "great experiment" introduced Jackie Robinson as the first known black player in this century to play in the major leagues. Playing first base for the Brooklyn Dodgers that year, Robinson endured a trying ordeal of acceptance, but he passed the test magnificently. A .297 batting average sparked a championship season for the Dodgers and won Robinson the Rookie of the Year honors. More important, his success paved the way for other black stars to follow in his footsteps. By 1958 some hundred black Americans and some eighty black Hispanics played in the major leagues, mostly with NL teams, where their feats helped to exalt the NL over the AL. In Robinson's footsteps there followed such future Hall of Famers as Willie Mays, Roy Campanella, Ernie Banks, and Roberto Clemente. However, the opening of doors into the white major leagues doomed the black major leagues to extinction. By 1950 the era of the great black majors was over. As for the white majors, the recruitment of black players only temporarily alleviated the growing talent shortage.

Meanwhile, the postwar surge in labor union activity in the nation at large was exerting its influence on the major leagues. In 1946 a mounting number of grievances against owners prompted major league players to organize under the newly formed American Baseball Guild. Headed by Boston attorney Robert Murphy, this fourth unionizing attempt by major league players now had play-

ers forming chapters on each team, electing player representatives, and demanding higher salaries, fringe benefits, and a pension plan. A strike threat that year was defused when owners conceded a minimum salary of $5,000, some fringe benefits, and a pension plan to be funded by national radio and television income. The latter concession was portentous; not only were owners committed to the pension principle, but an important precedent was set by giving players a share in national media revenue. Such concessions undercut the Guild, which soon died out. But when the owners attempted to abolish the pension system in 1953, player representatives from the sixteen clubs hired New York attorney J. Norman Lewis to represent their cause. Out of this crisis came the Major League Players Association; under Lewis's leadership, the Association fought a successful battle to retain the pension system. But the Association languished after this struggle and late in this era came under the leadership of Robert Cannon, who ran the Association as a company union until 1966. Then, under Marvin Miller's efficient leadership, the Association became a formidable collective-bargaining agency for the players.

Meanwhile, the Mexican League crisis of 1946 added to the growing tensions between players and owners. That year Mexican League promoters enticed a handful of major league players to jump to Mexican League teams with offers of high salaries. When Commissioner A. B. Chandler blacklisted the jumpers, one of them, Danny Gardella, sued in the federal courts. When a Circuit Court of Appeals found for Gardella, the threat to baseball's reserve clause was serious enough to persuade the owners to settle the case out of court. Subsequently, congressional investigations into baseball's monopolistic practices also threatened the reserve clause, but no legislation followed the work of Congressman Emmanuel Celler's probings.

Nevertheless, by creating the Major League Players Association and by linking pension payments to national television revenues, the militant players of this era laid the groundwork for massive salary breakthroughs to be reaped by a future generation of players. But for now the players had to content themselves with salaries which at least topped those of their forebears. During the 1950s, 75 percent of player salaries ranged from $10,000 to $25,000 a season. However, three superstars—Joe DiMaggio, Ted Williams, and Stan Musial—received annual salaries of $100,000 a season.

But if organized players showed signs of gaining wealth and power, the powers of baseball commissioners were waning. Indeed, when Landis died in 1944, it soon became apparent that the owners would not abide another powerful commissioner. Thus Landis's successor, Commissioner Chandler, was denied a second term in 1951. For his part, Chandler blamed his assertive stance on such issues as his support of the pension plan, his opposition to Sunday night ball, and his defense of the rights of minor league players, for his ouster. Be that as it may, the flamboyant Chandler was replaced by Ford Frick, who served for fourteen years as the compliant tool of the owners. At this time the changing ranks of club owners included a new breed of wealthy businessmen who deferred to powerful owners like Walter O'Malley of the Dodgers and Dan Topping of the Yankees. By wielding influence on the owners' powerful executive committee, their powers far exceeded those of the commissioner.

Among the playing rule changes of this era, the 1950 recodification narrowed the strike zone and a 1954 rule permanently restored the sacrifice fly rule. Of important future significance was a 1959 rule which reacted to the designs of new, publicly financed ballparks in Milwaukee, Kansas City, Baltimore, San Francisco, and Los Angeles, and which anticipated the coming new park-building boom. This rule ordained that parks constructed after 1959 must conform to minimum distances of 325 feet from home plate to the right and left field fences.

On the playing fields, improved fielding was attributed to bigger, more flexible gloves. And the homer production of this era owed much to players wielding lighter, more tapered bats, to the required use of batting helmets, and to the frequent replacement of balls. A team now used as many as 12,000 balls in a season. Offensively such changes resulted in unprecedented homer barrages, with NL hitters averaging more than 1,100 homers a season during the 1950s. What's more, NL hitters regularly also bested AL batters in batting averages and stolen bases. Credit for this turnabout went to the greater number of black stars in the NL. Robinson became the first black star to win a Most Valuable Player Award, and after Robinson received that award in 1949, seven black stars, including sluggers Roy Campanella, Ernie Banks, and Willie Mays, won NL MVP awards in the 1950s. But the most celebrated stars of this era were DiMaggio, Williams, and Musial. DiMaggio retired after the 1951 season with a .325 lifetime batting average, while Williams and Musial starred throughout this era. When he retired in 1960, Williams, despite years lost for service in World War Two and the Korean conflict, owned a .344 lifetime batting average, six AL batting titles, 521 homers, and a pair of Triple Crowns. And when Musial retired in 1963, his credentials showed a .331 lifetime batting average, seven NL batting titles, and an NL record of 3,630 lifetime hits, evenly divided at home and on the road.

For the battered pitchers these postwar years were nightmarish. ERAs hovered around 4.00 in the NL and just below that seasonal mark in the AL. To cope with their batting tormentors, pitchers now relied more upon sliders and some clandestinely employed illegal deliveries like the spitball. Managers responded by deploying relief pitchers. At this time "short relievers," capable of dousing late-inning rallies, now became valued specialists whose exploits were measured by saves and honored late in the era with annual "Fireman of the Year" awards. Among the best of this era's "firemen" were Joe Page of the Yankees, Jim Konstanty of the Phillies, Roy Face of the Pirates, and the much-traveled Hoyt Wilhelm. Indeed, the knuckleball-throwing Wilhelm lasted twenty-one seasons. When he retired in 1972, he had appeared in 1,070 games, with 227 saves and a lifetime ERA of 2.52. But able starters were by no means extinct at this time. Among the very best, lefty Warren Spahn of the Braves went on to win 20 or more games in a dozen seasons, and retired with 363 lifetime victories. To honor the outstanding pitchers of each season, in 1956 the annual Cy Young Award was instituted. The first recipient was Don Newcombe, the black pitching ace of the Brooklyn Dodgers. From 1956 through the 1966 season, only one award was

given annually in the major leagues, but thereafter the best pitcher of the year in each league received a Cy Young Award.

Postwar Campaigns: The AL, 1946–1960

In this era the AL lagged behind the NL both in offensive performance and in annual attendance. For this reversal of fortunes, some observers faulted AL owners for taking a back seat to their NL counterparts in the signing of black stars and in the occupation of such choice sites as Los Angeles and San Francisco. But the AL's biggest problem was the overwhelming superiority of its own New York Yankees. By winning eleven of fifteen postwar-era campaigns, the Yankees made a mockery of the concept of competitive balance. Moreover, by their perennial dominance, the New Yorkers attracted the lion's share of AL attendance, to the detriment of their overmatched competitors. Indeed, such was the magnitude of the Yankee oppression that after 1948 no AL team but the Yankees won a World Series until 1966. For their part, the Yankees won nine world titles, thus singlehandedly maintaining the AL's domination in the annual test of strength between the two majors. Nevertheless, by the end of this era, the growing strength of the NL was evidenced by their team's victories in three of the last five World Series encounters and by victories in nine of this era's seventeen All Star Games.

But when each of the first three AL postwar campaigns produced a new champion, prospects for competitive balance looked bright. In 1946 the Boston Red Sox won their first AL pennant since 1918 to help foster this illusion. League-leading hitting by Red Sox batters, fronted by Ted Williams's .342-38-123 stickwork, and 45 wins posted by pitchers Dave "Boo" Ferriss and Tex Hughson, boosted the Red Sox to 104 wins and a 12-game romp over the defending Detroit Tigers. But after the Red Sox lost a hard-fought seven-game World Series battle at the hands of the Cardinals, another two decades would pass by before this club won another AL pennant.

As the Red Sox faded to third in 1947, the Yankees rebounded from a third-place finish to notch their first postwar pennant. DiMaggio batted .315 with 20 homers and 97 RBIs to lead the team's .271 batting assault. Besides leading the league in homers and batting, the Yankees also fielded the league's best pitching staff; Allie Reynolds, newly acquired from Cleveland, won 19, and rookies Specs Shea and Vic Raschi combined for 21 wins. Reliever Joe Page won 14 and tied for league leadership in saves with 17. It was enough to carry manager Bucky Harris's charges to a 12-game win over the second-place Tigers. Then, for a second time, the Yankees downed the Dodgers in World Series play.

The following year the Yankees, Red Sox, and Indians hooked up in a furious pennant struggle that ended in a tie between the Indians and Red Sox. To settle this first seasonal deadlock in AL history, the two teams played a sudden-death playoff game in Boston. By downing the Red Sox 8–3 in that game, Cleveland won the 1948 AL pennant and went on to beat the Boston Braves in the World Series. League-leading team batting (.282), homer production (155), pitching, and fielding powered the Indians, whose home attendance of more than 2 million fans

was unsurpassed in this era. Player-manager Lou Boudreau led the Indians with a .355 average; outfielder Dale Mitchell batted .336, and outfielder Larry Doby, who joined the team in 1947 as the first black player in the AL, hit .301. Pitchers Bob Lemon, Bob Feller, and Gene Bearden accounted for 59 victories, but the pitching staff got an important boost when owner Bill Veeck acquired the legendary and aging Satchel Paige from the black majors. Paige contributed 6 victories and a save to the team's winning cause.

At this point the resurging Yankees dashed all hopes of continuing the league's pattern of competitive balance. Regrouping under manager Casey Stengel, the Yankees snatched ten of the next twelve AL pennants, including a record five in a row beginning with the 1949 conquest. In the torrid 1949 race, the injury-ridden Yankees edged the Red Sox by a game. Needing a pair of victories to overtake and conquer the Red Sox, the Yankees hosted the Bostonians in the closing days of the campaign and won both games. Key performances included relief pitcher Joe Page's 27 saves and 13 victories, and a .346-14-67 offensive effort by the ailing DiMaggio. Though he was sidelined much of the season by injuries, the Yankee Clipper's heroics helped to offset Williams's tremendous performance for the Red Sox. Williams's .343 batting average was barely edged out by George Kell, and his 43 homers and 159 RBIs led all rivals.

Over the next three seasons, the Yankees prevailed in three close races, edging the Tigers by 3 games in 1950, the Indians by 5 games in 1951, and the Indians by 2 games in 1952. Nor did they stop there. In winning for a fifth straight season in 1953, the Yankees enjoyed their only comfortable edge in their record skein as they downed the perennial bridesmaid Indians by 8½ games. In winning a record five consecutive AL pennants, the great Yankee pitching triumvirate of Allie Reynolds, Vic Raschi, and lefty Ed Lopat combined for a sparkling 255–117 won-loss record. That victory total included two no-hitters pitched by Reynolds in the 1951 campaign. In 1950, future Hall of Famer Ed "Whitey" Ford joined the Yankee staff; Ford's 9–1 pitching performance was a decisive factor in the team's winning stretch drive of that season. Offensively, manager Stengel relied on star performers like DiMaggio and catcher Yogi Berra and successfully platooned such able hitters as outfielders Hank Bauer and Gene Woodling. When age tolled on the great DiMaggio, who retired after the 1951 season, or when the Korean War military draft snagged young stars like Ford and Billy Martin, general manager George Weiss summoned rising stars like Mickey Mantle and Gil McDougald from the Yankee farm system. Shrewd trades by Weiss also landed key performers like Johnny Mize, pitcher Ed Lopat, and relief pitcher Bob Kuzava. In World Series action, the relentless Yankees captured five classics in a row. Three times, in 1949, 1952, and 1953, they toppled the Dodgers. In 1950 they swept the "Whiz Kid" Phillies, and in 1951 they defeated the "Miracle Giants" in six games. In two of these encounters, Kuzava's relief pitching was a deciding factor. And at the pinnacle of their success in 1953, the Yankees could boast of having won their last seven World Series encounters.

The following year, the Yankees won 103 games, their best record under Stengel's leadership, but manager Al

Lopez's Cleveland Indians won the 1954 pennant with an AL record-breaking 111 victories. Second baseman Bobby Avila's .341 hitting won the league's batting title, and Larry Doby's league-leading 32 homers and 126 RBIs headed the team's league-leading 156 homer barrage. With a 2.78 ERA the team's pitching staff was unmatched; the starting trio of Early Wynn, Bob Lemon, and Mike Garcia accounted for 65 victories. But like the 1906 Chicago Cubs, who lost the World Series of that year after winning a major league record 116 games, the Indians fell to the New York Giants, who swept to victory in the 1954 World Series.

The 1954 victory was also Cleveland's last AL pennant to this day. What followed was another assertion of Yankee tyranny. Regrouping in 1955, the Yankees went on to win a string of four consecutive AL pennants. By this time most of the heroes of the 1949–1953 Yankees were gone. To replace the great pitching trio of Reynolds, Raschi, and Lopat, Weiss traded for pitchers Bob Turley and Don Larsen and summoned catcher Elston Howard, the first black player to wear a Yankee uniform, from the farm system. In a close race the 1955 Yankees edged the Indians by 3 games, with Berra winning his third MVP award for his latest offensive performance. Berra batted a workmanlike .272, and his 27 homers drove in 108 runs. Outfielder Mantle batted .306, and his league-leading 37 homers were accompanied by 99 RBIs. And Ford's 18 wins led AL hurlers. But in World Series action the Dodgers finally turned on their Yankee tormentors as they won the fall classic in seven games.

In 1956 Mantle's Triple Crown performance (.353-52-130) and Ford's 19 pitching victories paced the Yankees to an 8-game victory over the Indians. In the aftermath of that victory, the Yankees faced the Brooklyn Dodgers for a seventh and last subway World Series. The next time these two rivals met, the breakaway Dodgers would represent the West Coast city of Los Angeles. What followed was an epochal struggle which the Yankees won in seven games. But Larsen's brilliant pitching in the fifth game stamped this World Series with the mark of immortality. With the Series tied at two games, Larsen pitched a perfect game; it was the first no-hitter in World Series history and the first perfect game pitched in the majors in over thirty years. But the stubborn Dodgers carried the Series another two games before succumbing.

Over the next two seasons the Yankees won two more AL pennants. In 1957 the Bronx Bombers wielded league-leading batting and pitching to down the runner-up White Sox by 8 games. Mantle's .365-34-94 performance won the switch-hitting superstar another MVP Award. Rookie shortstop Tony Kubek's .297 hitting won him Rookie of the Year honors, and rookie Tom Sturdivant's 16 victories led the pitching staff. Nevertheless, the 1957 Yankees lost the World Series in seven games to the transplanted Milwaukee Braves. But the 1958 Yankees avenged that loss. Winning easily by 10 games over manager Al Lopez's White Sox, the Yankees led the AL in team batting, homers, and pitching. Turley's 21 victories led AL pitchers and Mantle's 42 homers led the league's sluggers. Then, in a rematch with the Braves, the gritty Yankees overcame a three-games-to-one deficit to win the 1958 World Series in seven games.

The following year slumping performances by Mantle and Turley contributed to the Yankee's third-place finish. The collapse enabled perennial runner-up manager Al Lopez to drive his Chicago White Sox to a 5-game victory over the Indians. The White Sox batted a weak .250, but they led the league in stolen bases, fielding, and pitching. Veteran pitcher Early Wynn, a future Hall of Famer, notched 22 victories in his last great seasonal performance, and relievers Turk Lown and George Staley fronted the league's best bullpen crew. But the White Sox lost the 1959 World Series to the Los Angeles Dodgers.

That fall the decision by AL owners to expand the league to ten teams in 1961 sounded the knell for the league's hallowed eight-club format and 154-game seasons. As the postwar era ended with the 1960 campaign, the Yankees rebounded to win by 8 games over the Baltimore Orioles. Although soon to pass from the Yankee scene, general manager Weiss pulled off another canny deal by obtaining outfielder Roger Maris from the Kansas City Athletics. With Maris leading the league in RBIs, and Mantle in homers, the well-armed Yankees faced the Pirates in the 1960 World Series. Yet despite a World Series record .338 team batting average, which produced three crushing victories over the Pirates, the Yankees lost the classic in seven games. Hard after this defeat, Weiss and manager Stengel were forced into retirement, although the pair soon surfaced in their familiar capacities with the NL's expansion New York Mets. Meanwhile, with the passing of the 1960 season, the AL prepared to enter the dawning era of expansion.

Postwar Campaigns: The NL, 1946–1961

In this era much of the credit for boosting NL stock above that of the AL belonged to Branch Rickey and Walter O'Malley of the Dodgers. Dodger general manager Rickey built the superb farm system which fueled the Dodger dynasty, and it was Rickey too who successfully pulled off the coup of baseball's racial integration. When Jackie Robinson made his successful debut in 1947, Rickey enjoyed a temporary corner on the market of black players whom his scouts recruited from the fading black majors and from Latin American countries. Moreover, when Dodger owner O'Malley engineered Rickey's ouster in 1950, the aging genius joined the Pirates and laid the groundwork for that forlorn team's rise to power. And as a final touch, it was Rickey's presence among the would-be promoters of the rival Continental League movement in 1959 that goaded major league owners into expanding their circuit in order to deflect the threat.

But the 1957 West Coast move of the Brooklyn Dodgers and New York Giants was O'Malley's doing. Indeed, these moves stirred the Continental League movement. And it was O'Malley, the most powerful and influential owner of this era, who persuaded his colleagues to embark upon the expansionist course. Thus while Rickey and O'Malley plied different courses of action, these embattled rivals together forced major league baseball to adapt to a changing American society.

But the rise of the Brooklyn Dodger dynasty in the NL of this era was mostly Rickey's handiwork. And an effective piece of domination it was. Of the sixteen NL campaigns of this era, the Dodgers won seven and narrowly missed winning three others. And yet the Dodgers, who

won only two world titles, were upstaged by an even greater Yankee dynasty. Nevertheless, the Dodgers lorded over other NL teams. In these years the Braves won three pennants and a World Series; the Giants won two pennants and a World Series; and the four one-time winners—the Cardinals, Phillies, Pirates, and Reds—accounted for two World Series victories. At least it made the NL a better-balanced circuit than the Yankee-dominated AL of this era.

As the NL's postwar era unfolded, the outcomes of the first three campaigns produced an illusion of competitive balance similar to that in the AL. Here too the first three races produced three different winners. The 1946 race pitted the Dodgers against a Cardinal team which Rickey had assembled in his previous tenure at St. Louis. In a donnybrook race, the two teams finished the season in a dead heat. To settle the issue of this first true deadlock in NL history, a best-of-three playoff series was set, which the Cardinals won by sweeping the first two games. Overall, the Cardinals used league-leading pitching, batting, and fielding to assert their superiority. Pitcher Howie Pollet's league-leading 21 victories and 2.01 ERA led the pitching staff. And a pair of outfielders powered the Cardinal offensive: Musial's .365 hitting won the league batting crown, and Enos Slaughter's 130 RBIs topped all others. In the World Series the Cardinals toppled the favored Red Sox in seven games.

As it turned out, St. Louis fans would have to wait another seventeen seasons before a Cardinal team again scaled the heights. Meanwhile in 1947 attention of fans everywhere riveted upon the Dodgers and Jackie Robinson's debut as the first black player of the century to play in the majors. When Commissioner Chandler suspended manager Leo Durocher, Burt Shotton took over the reins of the club and stationed Robinson at first base. Advised by Rickey to turn his cheek against racist slurs, which came mostly from the Cardinals and Phillies, Robinson responded stoically and successfully. His .297 batting that year won him NL Rookie of the Year honors, and his example opened the way for more black players to follow. With outfielders Pete Reiser and Dixie Walker topping the .300 mark at bat, and with pitcher Ralph Branca winning a league-leading 21 games and bullpen master Hugh Casey saving a league-leading 18 games, the Dodgers beat the Cardinals by 5 games. That year the Dodgers also had the satisfaction of seeing their hated rivals, the Giants, finish in fourth place despite a record 221-homer barrage. But in World Series play, another local rival, the Yankees, downed the Dodgers in a grueling seven-game struggle.

In 1948 the Dodgers slipped to third as ex-Cardinal manager Billy Southworth drove the Boston Braves to a 6½-game victory over his former Redbird team. It was Boston's first NL pennant since 1914 and its last as a Beantown franchise. Boston's pitching trio of Johnny Sain (whose 24 victories led all NL hurlers), Warren Spahn, and Vern Bickford fronted the NL's most effective staff. And the team's league-leading .275 batting attack was fronted by outfielder Tommy Holmes (.325), and by infielders Al Dark (.322) and Bob Elliott (100 RBIs). But when the Braves met the Indians in World Series play, the Indians dispatched the Braves in five games. Landing the 1948 NL pennant was the last gasp of this faltering

franchise, which five years later would move to more profitable pastures in Milwaukee.

As the Braves faded in 1949, the Dodgers asserted their dynastic power. Over the next five seasons the Dodgers won three NL races and lost two others by heartbreakingly narrow margins. In 1949 Robinson's league-leading .342 hitting helped the Dodgers eke a 1-game victory over the Cardinals. Joining the MVP Award-winning Robinson were black stars Roy Campanella, who batted .287, and pitcher Don Newcombe, whose 17 wins paced the staff. Outfielder Carl Furillo batted .322 and outfielder Duke Snider and first baseman Gil Hodges, who combined for 46 homers and 207 RBIs, paced the team's league-leading homer assault. But then, for a third time, the Dodgers bowed to the Yankees in the World Series.

In 1950 the Dodger "Boys of Summer" lost by 2 games to the Phillies' "Whiz Kids." Phillies' ace Robin Roberts averted a possible deadlock by outpitching Newcombe on the final day of the season. With youngsters Roberts and Curt Simmons combining for 37 wins, and relief ace Jim Konstanty winning 16 and saving 22 for a Most Valuable Player Award performance, the Phillies boasted the league's best pitching. At the plate the team was powered by Del Ennis, who drove in a league-leading 126 runs, and by young Richie Ashburn, who batted .303. But late in the season the team lost pitcher Simmons to the Korean War military draft. His absence tolled on the Phillies, who were swept by the Yankees in the World Series.

Over the winter of 1950, Dodger owner O'Malley forced Rickey out of his general manager post, but Rickey's departure spared him the agonies of the Dodgers' 1951 season. As the fateful campaign unfolded, the Dodgers soared to a 13½-game lead in early August. But in the September stretch, the "miracle" New York Giants rose to deadlock the Dodgers at the season's end. In the unforgettable playoff series between these traditional rivals, the Giants rallied to win the decisive game on outfielder Bobby Thomson's dramatic ninth-inning homer. In baseball folklore, Thomson's winning blast is immortalized as "the shot heard round the world." Indeed, it was a miraculous season as the Dodgers, paced by the hitting of Robinson and Campanella, led Giant hitters by 15 points. But black stars Monte Irvin (who batted .312-24-121) and rookie Willie Mays (who hit 20 homers) powered the Giants, who also got a .303 performance from team leader Al Dark and a .293 performance with 32 homers from the heroic Thomson. Moreover, Giant pitchers Sal Maglie and Larry Jansen each won 23 games, to pace the league-leading Giant pitching staff. However, the Giants' celebrated "Miracle of Coogan's Bluff" was tarnished by defeat at the hands of the Yankees in the 1951 World Series.

But at this point the snakebit Dodgers picked themselves up and went on to capture the next two NL pennants. In 1952 they outlasted the Giants by 4½ games, and the following year they coasted to a 13-game win over the transplanted Milwaukee Braves. In the hard-fought 1952 race the Giants suffered the loss of Mays to the military draft. It was a crushing blow for the Giants, but Dodger crushers led the league in homers. Snider, Hodges, and Campanella combined for 75, and this trio drove in nearly 300 runs. The pitching was shaky. Able starters Preacher Roe, Carl Erskine, and Billy Loes won 38 games, but reliever Joe Black made the difference.

With a 15–4 record and 15 saves, Black enjoyed the best season of his brief career. The following year, Erskine picked up after the slumping Black and posted a 20–6 record to lead the staff. Behind him the mature Boys of Summer beat a hefty tattoo, leading the league in batting (.285) and homers (208). Rebounding from his previous year's slump, Furillo batted .344 to lead the league, and Campanella's .312-41-142 record won him another MVP Award. It added up to a two-year domination of the NL, but in World Series play the Dodger champs twice fell to their Yankee nemesis; in 1952 they lost the Series in seven games, and the following year they fell in six games.

Shortly after the 1953 Series loss, O'Malley picked the little-known Walter Alston to skipper the club. Although Alston would manage the team for twenty-three seasons, a longer skein than any of his managerial colleagues, his 1954 debut was inauspicious. That year the Dodgers lost to the Giants by 5 games. Offensively the Dodgers outbatted and outscored their rivals, but the Giants matched the Dodgers in homer production and fielded the league's best pitching staff. Returning from military service, Willie Mays led the league in hitting with a .345 mark, and his 41 homers and 110 RBIs firmly established his credentials as one of the leading stars of the decade. That year also saw the ex–bonus baby Johnny Antonelli come into his own as a pitcher. His 21 victories and 2.30 ERA paced the Giant pitching staff, which was the league's best. But the Giants were cast as underdogs in the World Series against the powerful Cleveland Indians. However, a sensational fielding play by outfielder Mays doused a promising Indian rally in the first game, and key pinch hits by "Dusty" Rhodes in each of the first three games triggered winning rallies. The result was a four-game sweep of the Indians.

But the Giant victory was also the team's last as long-time residents of New York. Over the next two seasons, the battle-wise Dodgers rebounded to win another pair of back-to-back pennants. Each year it was the Braves who finished second; in 1955 the Dodgers lapped the Milwaukee Braves by 13½ games, and the following year they held off their rivals by a single game. In 1955 outfielders Snider (.309-42-136) and Furillo (.314), and catcher Campanella (.318-32-107) paced the offensive. For his heroics, Campanella won his third MVP Award of the decade. Newcombe's 20 wins headed the dominant pitching staff. In the aftermath of the easy victory, the Dodgers also managed to defeat their Yankee tormentors for the first time, winning the 1955 World Series in seven games.

For the team's fanatical followers, this was to be the first and only world title they would see flying over Ebbets Field. In 1956 the Dodgers repeated, but only by the narrowest margin. League-leading performances by pitcher Newcombe (27 wins) and Clem Labine (19 saves) and a league-leading 43 homers by Duke Snider were needed to atone for the team's .258 batting. And in the aftermath of the grueling 1956 campaign, New York–area fans witnessed the last subway World Series matchup between the Yankees and Dodgers. Although the Dodgers won the first two games, they lost the Series in seven games. What's more, this Dodger team became the victims of the first no-hit game in World Series history when Yankee hurler Don Larsen hurled his perfect game in the fifth game.

As owner O'Malley laid plans for his team's post-seasonal move to Los Angeles in 1957, his Dodger team fell to third. The following season, the team's first in Los Angeles, they fell further, to seventh place. In these years there was no stopping the well-balanced Milwaukee Braves. As the first breakaway franchise to win a major league pennant in this century, the 1957 Braves attracted over 2 million home fans, who saw the team down the Cardinals by 8 games. Outfielder Hank Aaron's 44 homers and 132 RBIs led the league's hitters, and veteran pitcher Spahn's 21 wins led the league's pitchers. Third baseman Ed Mathews supplied additional power with 32 homers and 94 RBIs, and starting pitchers Lew Burdette and Bob Buhl combined for 35 victories. Then in World Series play the underdog Braves treated their fans to Milwaukee's only world title to this date by downing the Yankees in seven games. The following year the Braves repeated, scoring an 8-game victory over the rising Pirates. Spahn's 22 victories again led NL hurlers and Burdette added 20 victories. At the bat Aaron showed the way with .326-30-95 hitting, with Mathews adding 31 homers and first baseman Frank Torre batting .309. But in a World Series rematch with the Yankees, the Braves blew a commanding three-games-to-one lead, and the avenging Yankees won in seven games. To the Yankees went the honor of becoming the first team in over thirty years to rebound from such a deficit in World Series competition.

As the decade of the fifties drew to a close, the transplanted Los Angeles Dodgers recovered from their seventh-place finish of 1958 to end the Braves' two-year reign. In a brilliant September stretch drive, the Dodgers won thirteen of fourteen games to deadlock the Braves at the end of the campaign. And for a change the Dodgers won the playoff series by sweeping the Braves in two games to claim the NL pennant. The Braves outhit, outhomered, and outpitched the Dodgers, but the Dodgers led the league in fielding, and outfielders Duke Snider (.308-23-88) and Wally Moon (.302-19-74) supplied power enough, and the bullpen saved 26 games. In World Series action against the White Sox, the Dodgers won in six games. The Dodgers' victories included a sweep of its three home games, which were played at the Los Angeles Coliseum, where a record 270,000 fans jammed the converted football stadium to witness the triumphs.

But the Dodgers fell to fourth in 1960 as the Pirates, a team constructed by Rickey, beat the Braves by 7 games. Manager Danny Murtaugh's "Bucs" batted a league-leading .276; shortstop Dick Groat's .325 batting led the NL hitters, and future Hall of Fame outfielder Roberto Clemente batted .314. Vern Law's 20 pitching victories led the starters, but reliever Roy Face was the bellwether of the staff. Face appeared in a league-leading 68 games, won 10 and saved 24, and posted an ERA of 2.90. In World Series play the Pirates were thrice battered by the Yankees, but they won the 1960 classic in seven games. Second baseman Bill Mazeroski's tenth-inning homer in the finale at Forbes Field secured Pittsburgh's first world title in thirty-five years.

The AL had already expanded to ten teams in 1961, when the NL played its last season under the traditional eight-club format with its hallowed 154-game schedule. In a close race the 1961 Cincinnati Reds edged the Dodg-

ers by 4 games. Stout pitching, paced by starters Joey Jay, whose 21 wins led NL pitchers, and Jim O'Toole (19 wins), and 40 saves by the relief corps headed by Jim Brosnan and Bill Henry, carried the team. At bat the Reds batted .270, with outfielders Frank Robinson (.323-37-124) and Vada Pinson (.343-16-87) powering the attack. But when the Reds met the Yankees in World Series play, they succumbed in five games.

The Expansion Era Begins, 1961–1968

In this turbulent decade of American history, major league baseball's tradition-breaking expansion ranked as one of the lesser social disturbances. A time of massive social unrest, the strident sixties saw most established institutions targeted by would-be reformers. Sparking the fires of unrest were the assassinations of the Kennedy brothers and Martin Luther King, the great black civil rights leader. In the wake of these tragedies came storms of protest demonstrations supportive of increased freedom for individuals and for oppressed minorities. But as the decade wore on, the major focus of the protests centered on the nation's involvement in the Vietnam War. This country's latest struggle against the spread of international Communism began in the mid-1960s and lasted until 1973. An unpopular war, the Vietnam involvement consumed over 50,000 American soldiers' lives, polarized the nation into factions embattled over the morality of the war, and ended in a political and military defeat. Moreover, the violent protests against the war spilled over into other social institutions. Thus demonstrations and protest movements by black Americans aimed at securing civil rights and economic betterment erupted at times into urban riots. And among other discontented minorites, many women organized into protest movements and demanded economic and political equality. At this time the widespread consciousness-raising appealed to many Americans, who supported such slogans as "Freedom Now" and affected new lifestyles in social relations, speech, clothing, and hairstyles. And by the end of the decade such supporters included numbers of major league ballplayers, who sought relief from long-established paternal controls imposed upon them by baseball law and custom.

Meanwhile, other forces of change were reshaping the nation and its national game. In this decade the nation's population soared past 200 million, with nearly half that number concentrated in some thirteen sprawling urban regions. Thus even as major league owners embarked upon an initial expansion course in 1960–1961, these new demographics portended further expansion of the two leagues along with the possible relocation of teams now situated in deteriorating urban areas.

Nevertheless, amidst all the disturbing changes the nation's economy continued to prosper. Although they were sapped by continuing inflation, the average wages of all workers rose to an annual figure of $8,000 by the end of the decade. As a result, annual spending for recreation rose to $18 billion, with television viewing continuing to reign as the most popular leisure outlet.

The continuing popularity of televised sports programs, now shown in color with ever-improving visual effects, was a boon to professional sports. While baseball profited from this popular medium, so did half a dozen rival sports. Among these, professional football expanded rapidly under the impetus of hefty national TV contracts which clubowners shared equally. By occupying most of the major urban regions, pro football now threatened baseball's pre-eminent position among the nation's favorite team sports. Indeed, in 1967 professional football's Super Bowl outscored the World Series in television ratings.

In stark contrast to pro football's bold expansionist course was major league baseball's limited expansion movement of these years. Baseball's initial expansion took place over the years 1961–1962 and was primarily an attempt to undercut the threat of the rival Continental League. Under this expansion, each major league added two teams and upped its seasonal playing schedule to 162. A significant departure, the addition of eight more games to playing schedules would drastically affect statistical comparisons of seasonal performances. Moreover, each new franchise owner paid $2 million, which was divided among the eight established clubs of each major league, and also participated in an expansion draft, which was used to enable the owners to stock their teams with players. But since established teams were permitted to withhold their best twenty-five players from the pool of eligibles, the new owners were forced to purchase unprotected cullings.

Under these procedures, the AL took the first expansion plunge in 1961. That year the AL added the Los Angeles Angels and a new edition of the Washington Senators. At the request of owner Cal Griffith, the original Senators relocated to Bloomington, Minnesota, where they became the Minnesota Twins. The furor evoked by that breakaway move forced AL owners to admit the new Washington Senators. It was an unwise move, as the franchise languished under weak ownership and poor attendance. In 1972 the Senators moved to Arlington, Texas, where they fared better as the Texas Rangers. Nor did the AL Angels fare well in Los Angeles, where they were upstaged by O'Malley's Dodgers. However, this well-financed team found prosperity when it was moved to nearby Anaheim in 1965.

For its part the NL did better under its 1962 expansion. That year the NL occupied Houston, where the Colt .45s occupied temporary quarters while awaiting the construction of their new all-weather indoor Astrodome Stadium. When the Astrodome opened in 1965, this expansion team took on a new identity as the Houston Astros. Meanwhile, as part of a deal which allowed the AL to occupy the Los Angeles territory, the NL reoccupied the New York area by admitting the New York Mets. Although the Mets lost 120 games in their first season of play, the team was generously supported by suffering fans, who rejoiced in the return of NL baseball to the Gotham area. After playing its first two seasons in the old Polo Grounds, the Mets moved into newly built Shea Stadium, located in Queens.

Thus did the major leagues move into their first phase of expansion. But each passing season underscored the inadequacy of the ten-club format. Like the twelve-club NL of the 1890s, the ten-club array of the 1960s produced too many losers each season. Annual attendance was dis-

appointing. By 1968, overall major league attendance topped that of 1960 by only 3 million admissions. And added to the problems of this phase of expansion were two controversial franchise shifts. In 1966 the NL's Milwaukee Braves abandoned that city for Atlanta, and in 1968 the AL's Athletics departed Kansas City for Oakland, California, where they poached upon the territory of the NL Giants. Each of these breakaway moves aroused protests from fans of the abandoned sites, and each prompted lawsuits which affected future expansion moves.

Meanwhile major league teams continued to face a growing shortage of playing talent. At most schools and colleges, where baseball now ranked as a minor sport, scouts complained that major sports like football and basketball were getting the best athletes. With the minor leagues shrinking alarmingly, major league owners in 1962 adopted a remedial Player Development Plan. Under this scheme, the minor leagues were reclassified, and each major league team agreed to subsidize at least five minor league teams. And to equitably distribute the limited supply of young prospects, the majors in 1965 adopted the radical plan of an annual free agent (rookie) draft. Under its provisions, each major league club in turn picked from a nationwide pool of high school and college prospects. Thus except for prospecting in foreign countries, the annual rookie draft ended the long and colorful era of free-enterprise scouting in America.

Along with the prevailing national mood of liberation for oppressed groups, the chronic player shortage helped to kindle reformist sentiments among this generation of major league players. More pampered and better trained, doctored, and defended than past generations of players, players of this decade demanded improved salaries, pensions, and working conditions. In these years player disdain for traditional authority was rife, and this was candidly spelled out in revelatory books, including bestsellers authored by pitchers Jim Brosnan and Jim Bouton. And in a precedent-shattering move in 1966, Dodger pitchers Sandy Koufax and Don Drysdale, acting on the advice of a lawyer, staged a successful joint holdout for hefty salary increases. That same year, player representatives strengthened the moribund Major League Players Association (MLPA) by successfully engineering the election of Marvin Miller, an experienced labor negotiator, to serve as the Association's executive director. Landing Miller proved to be a master stroke for the players' cause. By rallying the players and by invoking federal labor relations laws, Miller forced the clubowners to recognize and to bargain collectively with the MLPA. During his seventeen years as executive director, Miller negotiated five Basic Agreements, or labor contracts, which wrung from owners unprecedented concessions and benefits. The Basic Agreements of 1966 and 1969 increased pension benefits and raised minimum salaries along with other gains. Thus by 1970 average player salaries, which totaled $17,000 in 1965, rose to $25,000. At the same time some twenty players were being paid annual salaries of at least $100,000 a year. But Miller's greatest coup of this decade was to win the solid support of major league players behind the MLPA. And by the end of this decade, major league umpires also won recognition and bargaining rights under their newly formed Major League Umpires Association.

Among the deserving recipients of increasing salaries were the growing numbers of black players in major league uniforms. By the end of the sixties, well over a hundred black Americans and scores of Latin Americans were playing in the majors. What's more, their offensive production made a reality of the prevailing Afro-American protest slogan that "black is beautiful." In these years black hitters dominated major league offenses. In the NL, black stars won seven homer titles, as many MVP awards, and six batting titles. And in the AL, blacks won three batting titles and three MVP awards. Among the reigning black superstars, Willie Mays of the Giants was voted Player of the Decade by *The Sporting News;* indeed, Mays posted a remote threat to overtake Ruth's lifetime homer mark, and at the end of his career he had powered 660 homers. But by the end of the decade more observers were touting Braves' outfielder Hank Aaron's chances of bettering Ruth. Meanwhile at this time, Frank Robinson became the first player to win an MVP Award in each major league, and outfielder Roberto Clemente of the Pirates won three NL batting titles.

Sparkling alongside such stars were white prodigies like Roger Maris, who blasted 61 homers in 162 games in 1961, to set a new seasonal mark for homer production; or Carl Yastrzemski, who won an AL Triple Crown; or Pete Rose, who broke in as a rookie in 1963 with the Cincinnati Reds and would later break Cobb's lifetime total of 4,191 hits.

Indeed, such offensive performances occurred despite the hitting famine caused by the dominant pitchers of this era. Abetting the hitting famine was the rule that expanded the strike zone for the 1963 season. But improved coaching techniques, improved gloves and defensive strategies, and, above all, the astute deployment of specialized relief pitchers tolled on hitters of the era. As a result, pitching ERAs averaged 3.30 in this era, and in 1968, the notorious "year of the pitcher," hurlers combined to produce an overall ERA of 2.98, which was the lowest earned run mark in nearly forty years. Not surprisingly, the impact of such virtuosity on hitting was traumatic. In 1967 major league hitters averaged .242, and in 1968 batting bottomed to a nadir of .237. It was that puny mark which prompted remedial action by the rules committee, whose members voted to narrow strike zones and lower pitching mounds for the 1969 season. Such medicine broke the hitting famine, but while it lasted star pitchers made the most of their skills. In 1968 Cardinal ace Bob Gibson posted a 1.12 ERA and fanned a record 35 batters in three appearances in the World Series that fall. That same year, Denny McLain of the Tigers became the first hurler in over thirty years to break the 30-game victory barrier with a 31–6 performance; and Don Drysdale of the Dodgers posted a record 58 consecutive shutout innings. Moreover, in this decade fifteen pitchers would go on to join the ranks of the twenty all-time strikeout leaders.

However, many observers blamed the dominant pitching for lowering seasonal attendance marks in these years. From a record of 15 million in 1966, NL attendance slipped to 11.7 million in 1968, "the year of the pitcher." Nevertheless, annual NL attendance consistently bettered that of the AL; overall NL attendance of this era topped that of the AL by 16 million admissions. But a

major factor accounting for NL attendance strength was the greater number of new ballparks in the senior circuit. In this decade, seven of the ten newly constructed parks were occupied by NL teams. Of these, nine were publicly financed, but the privately financed Dodger Stadium now attracted the lion's share of NL attendance.

But rising television revenues dispelled some of the anxieties over falling attendance. By 1967, revenues from local and national television contracts rose to $25 million, with no sign of abating. On the other hand, by urging more night games, by raising the value of major league franchises, by making celebrities of players, and by the presence of television entrepreneurs in the ranks of club owners, television was reshaping the game. To some alarmists television's influence was menacing. In 1964 the sale of the Yankees to the powerful CBS Network fed fears of excessive television influence. However, such fears were allayed by the declining fortunes of the Yankees under CBS management and by the 1973 resale of the team to private interests.

Campaigns of the Sixties: The AL, 1961–1968

By first expanding to ten teams in 1961, the AL led the NL both in attendance and in hitting. But when the NL followed suit in 1962, the AL was annually worsted in both categories. And when the hitting famine ravaged the major leagues late in this era, except for their leadership in homer hitting, AL batters suffered more.

To add to AL woes, the Yankees continued to monopolize pennants and overall attendance. Four more victories over the years 1961–1964 extended the Yankee's latest consecutive string of pennants to five, during which time the New Yorkers attracted 40 percent of the league's attendance. However, the latest Yankee surge was marred by losses in their last two World Series appearances. And in the wake of their loss to the Cardinals in the 1964 World Series, the Yankees collapsed suddenly and ignominiously. Thereafter, another twelve seasons would pass before a Yankee team again rose to the top of the league. But if rival clubs welcomed the tyrant's fall, they also discovered the draining impact of a weakened Yankee club on AL attendance.

In the AL's first expansion campaign, the 1961 Yankees powered their way to an 8-game win over the Tigers. With Roger Maris bashing a new seasonal record of 61 homers and Mantle poling 54, the Yankees unleashed a record seasonal team barrage of 240 homers. Maris also led the league in RBIs with 142, and Mantle knocked in 128. Ace pitcher Whitey Ford's 25 victories led the league's hurlers and reliever Luis Arroyo's 29 saves was tops in the league. While some observers blamed the Yankee power explosion on the expansion draft, which supposedly weakened pitching staffs around the league, the Yankees had no trouble downing the NL champion Reds in six games in the 1961 World Series.

In 1962 the Yankees won again, beating the Twins by 5 games. League-leading .267 batting and pitcher Ralph Terry's league-leading 23 victories spearheaded the attack. The switch-hitting Mantle's .321 batting topped the team, but this time around the Maris-Mantle slugging combination tailed off to a more modest 63 homers and 189 RBIs. Then, in a seven-game struggle that was drawn

out by unprecedented rain delays, the Yankees defeated the Giants in the 1962 World Series. In the dramatic final game, Terry pitched a 1–0 shutout, but second baseman Bobby Richardson gloved a screaming liner by Giant slugger Willie McCovey to save the Yankee victory.

In retrospect the Yankee glory years ended with the 1962 victory. With Mantle sidelined much of the 1963 season, the Yankees batted only .252, but still romped to an easy 10½-game victory over the hard-hitting Twins. Superb pitching by Ford (whose 24 wins led the league) and by Bouton (who won 21 games) sparked the drive. But in World Series play the Yankees were swept by the Dodgers. Still, the Yankees mounted one last winning effort in 1964. Rallying from six games back in the late going, the team overtook the White Sox and Orioles to win by 1 game over the White Sox. Mantle's last great batting effort (.303-35-111) powered the team, and Ford, Bouton, and Al Downing combined for 48 pitching victories. But it took a nine-game winning streak in September, highlighted by the pitching of rookie Mel Stottlemyre, to turn the trick. However, the Yankees again fell in World Series play, this time losing to the Cardinals in seven games.

In the wake of that loss, like the wonderful one-hoss shay, the aging Yankees collapsed "all at once and nothing first." In 1965 the team sank to sixth place and in 1966 they finished last. The suddenness of the team's collapse was reflected in AL attendance figures; in 1965 AL attendance lagged 5 million behind that of the NL. Into the breach left by the faltering Yankees rushed other contenders, but no team held the heights for more than a single season. First to reach the top were the Minnesota Twins, who won the 1965 race by 7 games over the White Sox. Outfielder Tony Oliva topped all hitters with .321 batting and paced the team's league-leading .254 hitting. Aging slugger and future Hall of Famer Harmon Killebrew hit 25 homers. Pitcher Jim "Mudcat" Grant's 21 wins led all pitchers; Jim Kaat won 18, and reliever Al Worthington won 10 and saved 21. But for a third consecutive time the NL prevailed in World Series action, as the Twins lost to the Dodgers in seven games.

The AL ended its string of World Series losses in 1966, and with this victory the league's teams weaned themselves of Yankee dependence. Indeed, over the preceding eighteen seasons no AL team but the Yankees had won a world title. In exorcising that bugaboo, the Baltimore Orioles began by dispatching the Twins by 9 games. Outfielder Frank Robinson keyed the team's .258 batting assault with league-leading .316-49-122 hitting. The performance won Robinson a Triple Crown and placed him in the records as the first player ever to win an MVP Award in both major leagues. Infielders Brooks Robinson and John "Boog" Powell combined to drive in 209 runs, and the Oriole bullpen corps saved 51 games to make life easier for the young starting pitchers. But in the 1966 World Series three of these pitching prodigies—Jim Palmer, Wally Bunker, and Steve Barber—hurled consecutive shutouts as the Orioles swept the favored Dodgers.

The rising Orioles were destined to become the AL's winningest team of the next 20 years, but in 1967 they slumped to sixth place, which opened the door of opportunity to yet another contender. In a close race the Boston Red Sox won their first pennant since 1946 by edging the

Tigers by a game. In winning the Red Sox overcame the loss of promising young outfielder Tony Conigliaro, who suffered a career-threatening beaning; at the time of his accident, Conigliaro had 20 homers and 67 RBIs. But future Hall of Fame outfielder Carl Yastrzemski won a Triple Crown on .326-44-121 batting to front the team's league leadership in batting (.255) and homers (158). Pitcher Jim Lonborg's 22 wins led the league and reliever John Wyatt saved 20 games. But like their forebears of 1946, the 1967 Red Sox lost to the Cardinals in a seven-game World Series encounter.

In the last year of the ten-club format, the AL race produced the weakest seasonal hitting of this century. As the Red Sox faded, the Detroit Tigers won by 12 games over the reviving Orioles. Although batting a mere .235 as a team, the Tigers led the league in homers, paced by outfielder Willie Horton, who slugged 36. And considering that the best hitting team in the league that year, the Oakland Athletics, batted .240, the Tigers' offensive was proportionally respectable. Moreover, the Tigers boasted pitcher Denny McLain, who won 31 games and lost 6 with a 1.96 ERA. Matched against the Cardinals in the 1968 World Series, the Tigers lost three of the first four games. But pitcher Mickey Lolich won two of the next three, to spark the Tigers to a dramatic comeback victory. It was Detroit's first world title since the war year of 1945.

As the year of 1968 ended, the owners voted to join with the NL in expanding the circuit to twelve teams beginning in 1969. Mercifully for beleaguered batters, the owners also accepted a rules committee proposal to penalize pitchers. Thenceforth in both major leagues the strike zone would be narrowed and pitching mounds would be lowered.

Campaigns of the Sixties: The NL, 1962–1968

Although the NL expanded a year after the AL took the first step, the senior circuit was quick to reassert its offensive superiority. In its brief seven-season span as a ten-team circuit, the NL won four of the seven World Series encounters and seven of eight All-Star Games. Moreover, in six of the seven seasons NL batters topped AL batters in hitting and in stolen bases. And although the AL was better-balanced competitively in this era, as the Dodgers and Cardinals were monopolizing six of the seven NL races, attendance at NL games far surpassed AL attendance.

In 1962 the NL opened its first season as an expanded circuit, with most teams drained of their reserve strength by the expansion draft. In the ensuing campaign, the Dodgers and Giants staged a torrid race. But a late September losing streak by the Dodgers enabled the Giants to draw even at the close of the playing season. To settle the issue, the fourth postseason playoff in NL history was scheduled, with the Dodgers astonishingly involved in all of them. And when Dodger relief pitchers blew a 4–2 lead in the ninth inning of the decisive third game, the Dodgers lost a playoff for the third time. For their part, the Dodgers were led that season by pitcher Don Drysdale, whose 25 wins led all pitchers, and by outfielder Tommy Davis, whose .346 batting and 153 RBIs led all NL hitters. But the hard-hitting Giants led the league in batting (.278)

and in homers (204). Superstar Willie Mays led the Giant attack with .304 batting, 141 RBIs, and a league-leading 49 homers. Fellow outfielders Felipe Alou and Harvey Kuenn topped the .300 mark, and first baseman Orlando Cepeda weighed in with .306 batting, 35 homers, and 114 RBIs. Pitcher Jack Sanford won 24 games, and Juan Marichal and Billy O'Dell combined for 37, while reliever Stu Miller saved 19. However, the Giants lost a seven-game World Series duel to the Yankees.

Thereafter the Dodgers and Cardinals divided the remaining six NL championships of this era. In 1963 the Dodgers won by 6 games over the Cardinals. The team batted a modest .251, but Tommy Davis batted .326 to notch his second straight NL batting title, and shortstop Maury Wills batted .302 and led the league in stolen bases with 40. What really counted was the pitching, as the staff's 2.85 ERA was the league's best. That year lefty Sandy Koufax began a four-year skein of mastery that would propel him into the Hall of Fame. The ace's 25 wins and 1.88 ERA topped all hurlers, and reliever Ron Perranoski's 21 saves was the league's second best mark. In the 1963 World Series, the team's dominant pitching limited Yankee batters to a .171 batting average as the Dodgers swept to victory.

Dodger pitching again topped the league in 1964, with Koufax winning 19 and leading all hurlers with a 1.74 ERA, but poor hitting consigned Alston's men to sixth place. In a hotly contested five-team race, the Phillies led the pack by 6½ games with 12 games remaining on the schedule. But ten consecutive losses dropped the Phillies into a second-place tie with the Reds. The Phillies' swoon opened the gate for the Cardinals, who won 28 of their last 30 games. This brilliant stretch drive enabled the Redbirds to eke a one-game victory over the Phillies and Reds. The Cardinals' league-leading .272 batting made the difference. Infielders Bill White and Ken Boyer combined for 45 homers and 221 RBIs, and outfielder Curt Flood batted .311. But the timely acquisition of outfielder Lou Brock from the Cubs was decisive. Brock batted .348 in 103 games for the Cardinals and his 43 stolen bases ranked just behind Wills's total. And starting pitchers Bob Gibson, Ray Sadecki, and Curt Simmons combined to win 57 games. Yet so unexpected was the Cardinal victory that team manager Johnny Keane had signed a midseason pact to manage the Yankees the following year. The situation raised eyebrows when the Cardinals squared off against the Yankees in the 1964 World Series, but lame-duck Keane led the Cardinals to a seven-game victory over the Yankees.

In the wake of Keane's departure, the 1965 Cardinals dropped to seventh place. Into the power vacuum rushed the Dodgers, who gained the high ground and held it for two seasons against determined opposition from the Giants. Each Dodger victory was a near thing; in 1965 the Dodgers edged the Giants by 2 games, and the following year by 1½. In winning the 1965 pennant, the Dodgers batted a skimpy .245, with nary a .300 hitter in the regular lineup. But once again the Dodger pitching was superb; lefty Koufax won 26 on a 2.04 ERA, to top all NL hurlers, and Don Drysdale added 23 wins. And it was Koufax's shutout pitching in the seventh game of the World Series which led the team to victory over the Twins.

Over the winter Koufax and Drysdale staged an unprecedented joint holdout for salaries that were commensurate with their worth to the team. The two aces won salaries in the $100,000 range although these were grudgingly granted by owner O'Malley. But with Dodger home attendance topping the 2 million mark for the past eight seasons, such salaries were affordable. And in the case of Koufax, it was money well spent. In the close race of 1966 the lefty won 27 games with a 1.73 ERA, both league-leading figures. Drysdale slipped to 13–16, but reliever Phil "the Vulture" Regan saved 21 games. Such heroics were needed as the team batted only .256 with only Tommy Davis, in limited duty, topping the .300 mark. And in the 1966 World Series, the team's poor batting tolled as they were swept by the Orioles.

At the close of the 1966 campaign, the chronic arthritis in Koufax's pitching arm forced the ace to retire at the peak of his career. Thus disarmed, the weak-hitting Dodgers fell from contention. Not so the Cardinals, who perched atop the NL for the next two seasons as they twice drubbed the perennial bridesmaid Giants. In 1967 the Cardinals won by 10½ games, and in 1968 they won by 9. With Gibson sidelined for much of the 1967 season, the Cardinal bullpen responded by leading the league in saves. At bat the Cardinals hit .263, with Flood batting .335 and first baseman Orlando Cepeda batting .325 and driving in a league-leading 111 runs. Outfielder Lou Brock weighed in with .299 batting, and his 52 stolen bases led the league. In the 1967 World Series, Brock's .414 batting and seven stolen bases, and Gibson's three pitching wins and 26 strikeouts, highlighted the Cardinals' victory in the seven-game struggle with the Red Sox.

The following year a healthy Gibson won 22 games with a league-leading ERA of 1.12. In support of the black ace, pitchers Nelson Briles, Steve Carlton, and Ray Washburn combined to pitch 46 victories. Offensively, Brock's 62 steals led the league and Flood batted .301. As a team the Cardinals batted only .249, but in this "year of the pitcher," when overall NL batting stood at .243, it was enough. In the 1968 World Series, Gibson fanned a record 35 batters, but Flood's misjudging of Jim Northrup's fly ball in the seventh game allowed the Tigers to break through and complete their memorable come-from-behind victory.

As the curtain descended on the 1968 season, the major league owners now embarked on a second phase of expansion that would usher in a rich era of cash and glory for the major league game.

The Expanding Majors, 1969–1980

As the stormy sixties drew to a close, the nation united in applauding the successful moon landing by American astronauts in the summer of 1969. And if the strident countercultural protests lingered into the new decade, they lost their steam when the Vietnam War ended in 1973. The nation still had to weather a major political storm in 1974, when the Watergate scandal forced the resignation of President Richard Nixon, but the passing of that crisis marked the ending of the era of social turbulence. By then, a conservative reaction was ascendant and

was marked by such themes as religious and patriotic revival and continuing fears of Communist expansionism.

In retrospect, mounting economic problems turned public attention from social protests to the harsh realities of earning a living. In 1973–1974 the nation suffered its worst economic recession since the thirties. A frightening accompaniment to the recession was mounting "stagflation"—a combination of inflation and rising unemployment. Indeed, by the end of the seventies an estimated 24 million Americans were living at or near the poverty level. To cope with the problem, millions of wives and mothers entered the labor force. As a result, the nation's birthrate declined sharply over the years 1973–1979. Nevertheless, abetted by the falling death rate, the population continued to grow; from a level of 204 million in 1970, the population reached 226 million by 1980.

The trend toward dual-income families in this era translated into rising incomes (albeit, inflated dollars) for most Americans. Nor did rising prices for consumer goods dampen the people's ardor for leisure and recreational pursuits. By the end of the decade, annual spending for recreation reached $40 billion. And because watching televised sports maintained its status as one of the most favored leisure outlets, the popularity of major team sports like baseball increased. For major league club owners of this era, this translated into heftier profits from television sources and surging attendance at the turnstiles.

Happily for major league baseball interests, such increasing prosperity followed hard after its latest expansion movement. In 1968 major league owners voted to add two teams to each league, thus increasing the 1969 major league membership to twenty-four teams. Under the new format, which imitated professional football's earlier and successful experiment, each league was realigned into six-team Eastern and Western Divisions. The 162-game seasonal schedule was retained, with each team playing its intradivisional opponents eighteen times and outsiders twelve times. At the close of a season, the new format called for the two divisional winners in each league to meet in a best-of-five-game playoff series to determine the league championship. Afterward, the champions of each league would meet in the usual World Series competition to determine the ultimate winner.

Supporters of this revolutionary new format touted its successful precedent in pro football and its competitive advantage over the recent ten-team system. Proponents also counted on the lure of each season's divisional races to sustain public interest; after all, such races would return four winners each season instead of two. Furthermore, a divisional winning team got to fly a pennant even if it subsequently lost out in the league championship playoffs. Finally, with six teams competing in each division, the worst any team might do was finish a season in sixth place. It was nice sleight-of-hand logic, and it worked.

Events speedily demonstrated the wisdom of such logic. For their part, baseball fans welcomed the new format once they got used to the new teams with their strange-sounding totems, including the presence of a Canadian team, the Montreal Expos, in the major league ranks. In the NL, the Expos joined the Eastern Division along with the Cardinals, Cubs, Mets, Phillies, and Pi-

rates; in the NL's Western Division, the San Diego Padres were grouped with the Astros, Braves, Dodgers, Giants, and Reds. For its part, the AL installed its two new teams in its Western Division. There the newcoming Kansas City Royals and Seattle Pilots vied with the Angels, Athletics, Twins, and White Sox. However, this made for a perennially stronger Eastern Division, where the established Indians, Orioles, Red Sox, Senators, Tigers, and Yankees were now arrayed.

For the privilege of obtaining one of the new franchises, each newly admitted NL owner paid $10 million and each new AL owner paid $5.6 million; these initiation fees were divided as a windfall among the established clubs of each league. To stock the new teams with players, another expansion draft was held in each league. The latest draft allowed the new owners to purchase unprotected cullings from the rosters of established teams. And like the first expansion draft, this latest one placed the newcomers at a competitive disadvantage. In the NL the Expos and Padres long languished in their divisional cellars, and neither entry won a divisional pennant in this era. But such was not the case with the AL's newcoming Kansas City Royals club. In their first campaign the Royals finished fourth, and over the years 1975–1980 the Royals won four divisional races and a league championship. But on the other hand, the AL's new Seattle Pilots turned out to be a financial disaster. After finishing last in the AL West in 1969, the bankrupt club was sold to Milwaukee interests. There the Brewers prospered, but the relocation had the AL pulling NL chestnuts out of a legal fire. For having earlier allowed the Braves to abandon Milwaukee, the NL faced a menacing lawsuit *(State of Wisconsin v. Milwaukee Braves)*, which was quashed by the AL's decision to relocate the Pilots. But in abandoning Seattle, the AL soon incurred a lawsuit by Seattle interests, a threat that the AL deflected by admitting a new Seattle team, the Mariners, in 1977. That year the AL's unilateral expansion move added two new teams, which raised the league's membership to fourteen clubs while that of the NL remained the same. In addition to the newly admitted Mariners, who joined the Western Division, the AL then added the Toronto Blue Jays to its Eastern Division. This precipitous move resulted in an unbalanced major league format which exists to this day; moreover, since 1977 AL teams have annually played a skewed 162-game schedule.

However, this mini-expansion ploy and another bold move of this era enabled the AL to gain parity with its NL rival. Indeed, drastic measures were needed to restore the AL's attendance deficit, which, over the years 1970–1976, lagged some 24 million admissions behind that of the NL. In an early effort to regain parity, AL owners in 1972 allowed the moribund Washington Senators to move to Arlington, Texas, where they played as the Texas Rangers in the league's Western Division. And to balance that move, the Milwaukee Brewers were relocated in the Eastern Division.

But the most controversial of all AL parity measures was the league's 1973 unilateral adoption of the designated hitter rule. An experiment that was successfully pioneered in the minors, the rule allowed a designated hitter to bat in place of a pitcher in a team's lineup. It must be admitted that the designated hitter rule helped to remedy the AL's chronic problem of weak hitting. Only

the year before, overall AL batting had averaged an anemic .239. In 1973, with AL teams playing designated hitters, the seasonal batting average rose to .259. Thenceforth AL batting averages always surpassed seasonal NL figures. But the NL stubbornly resisted the innovation, and over the years 1973–1985 the use of designated hitters in World Series competition was limited to alternate years.

Meanwhile, the AL quest for parity was aided by a spate of new ballparks. Early in this era the NL opened five new parks. Belatedly, the AL followed suit, with four new parks and a major refurbishing of Yankee Stadium completed over the years 1972–1977. A new feature of some of the new parks, which affected fielding and batting, was the use of artificial playing surfaces. At the present time, ten major league parks are equipped with artificial playing surfaces. In the NL, where the Houston Astros pioneered in artificial surfacing in 1965, the Phillies, Pirates, Cardinals, Expos, and Reds now use artificial surfacing. In the AL, the Mariners, Royals, Twins, and Blue Jays now play home games on synthetic turfs.

Along with new parks, other innovations such as promotional giveaways and expanded concession sales and in-park entertainments contributed to soaring attendance at major league games in this era. After holding at 30 million admissions annually over the years 1973–1975, annual attendance at major league games soared to 43 million by 1980. But if rising attendance stimulated rising revenues, so did television. By 1980 income from national and local TV contracts accounted for 30 percent of baseball's $500 million in revenues of that year. Indeed, throughout the decade baseball's income from national network TV (which all clubs shared) increased steadily. From $17.5 million in 1971, such contracts returned $27.5 million in 1980. In 1980 this translated into a $1.8 million annual windfall for each team. And considering that such contracts covered only World Series games, league championship playoff games, the annual All-Star Game, and selected weekly and weekend games, such figures were impressive.

Indeed, major league owners might have wrung much more money from network TV sources had they not hewed to the policy of allowing clubs to contract individually with local TV stations. In 1975 local TV revenue totaled $31 million, and by 1980 this figure had nearly doubled. However, local TV income was unevenly distributed, which tended to favor some clubs over others. Thus clubs situated in more lucrative local television markets got the lion's share of this source of revenue. Still, at the close of this era local TV markets represented the fastest-growing segment of the television industry.

Nor was television income an unalloyed blessing. In this era some critics charged baseball owners with selling out to television interests when they permitted nocturnal broadcasts of World Series games. But the popularity of such games was evinced when an estimated 75 million TV fans witnessed the dramatic seventh game of the 1975 World Series. But if this demonstration of the game's popularity silenced some critics, others inveighed against the medium's impact on other areas of the game. Among such criticisms was the charge that TV was transforming ballplayers into highly paid and pampered celebrity entertainers.

Certainly player salaries in this decade soared to heights undreamed of by past generations of players. Even allowing for the bugaboo of inflation, the spiraling salary trend was dazzling. At the outset of this era, both a $100,000 salaried player and a $1 million total player payroll were exceptional. In 1971 player salaries averaged $34,000. But thereafter the average rose to $52,000 in 1976, to $90,000 in 1978, to $100,000 in 1979, and to an astonishing $185,000 in 1980. By 1980, indeed, payrolls of $10 million were common and were defended by director Marvin Miller of the Players Association, who noted salaries amounted to less than 20 percent of revenues.

Truth to tell, much of the credit for enriching players of this era belonged to Miller. By threatening to lead his united players in a strike in 1969, Miller was able to negotiate a second Basic Agreement, which raised the minimum salary, increased the pension fund, and won for players the right to use agents in bargaining for salaries with owners. Then when this contract expired and negotiations for a new Basic Agreement bogged down in 1972, the Players Association staged a thirteen-day strike which shortened that season's playing schedule by forcing the cancellation of games. In the aftermath of that strike, Miller negotiated a third Basic Agreement, which won for players the right to arbitrate their salary disputes. In retrospect it was this important concession that really fueled the spiraling salary trend.

In 1975 the players scored another major coup, when the Messersmith-McNally case was decided in their favor. That year Dodger pitcher Andy Messersmith refused to sign his 1975 contract and, after playing the season under his former contract, claimed his right to free agency under the existing reserve-clause procedure. Messersmith's appeal (along with that of pitcher Dave McNally, who chose to retire after the 1975 season) went to a three-member arbitration panel which upheld the players' claim by a 2–1 vote. Professional arbiter Peter Seitz joined with Miller in supporting Messersmith's appeal against the negative vote cast by owners' representative John Gaherin. Certainly the implications of this "Seitz decision" were far-reaching. The decision effectively circumvented the long-established reserve clause which had recently been tested by player Curt Flood (Flood v. Kuhn) before the U.S. Supreme Court. At the time, in 1972, the court rejected Flood's appeal by a 5–3 vote, but the court's ruling suggested that the players might overturn the reserve clause by means of collective bargaining or by legislation. The Messersmith decision was the outcome of collective bargaining. And when the owners failed to overturn the Seitz decision on a legal appeal, they staged a lockout of spring training camps in 1976, claiming that the latest Basic Agreement had expired with no new labor contract in place. However, a compromise reached by the embattled players and owners allowed the 1976 playing season to open on time. And over the following summer, negotiations produced a fourth Basic Agreement, which conceded free agency to six-year veterans. The latest Agreement instituted an annual re-entry draft procedure which enabled qualifying players to auction their services anew. As compensation for losing a veteran player in one of the re-entry drafts, an owner received an extra choice in the annual rookie draft. Thus over the years 1976–1980, some owners bid high prices for the services of veteran free agents. And in turn the gains scored by players in these annual drafts helped to boost the salaries granted by players who opted for salary arbitration procedures.

The combination of re-entry draft bids and salary arbitration awards resulted in spiraling salaries and produced a new breed of player plutocrats. In the first re-entry draft of 1976, outfielder Reggie Jackson received a five-year contract worth $2.93 million from Yankee owner George Steinbrenner. In 1979 the Houston Astros plucked pitcher Nolan Ryan from the re-entry draft by giving the hurler a $1 million annual contract. That same year outfielder Dave Parker wrung a five-year pact worth $900,000 annually from his Pittsburgh owners to dissuade him from entering the re-entry draft. Thus it was hardly surprising that when the fourth Basic Agreement expired in 1980 the owners determined to halt the salary spiral. Among their demands, owners wanted a veteran player in compensation for a player lost via the re-entry draft. And when negotiations broke down, the threat of another player strike darkened the 1980 season. But in the nick of time a compromise between the embattled groups postponed the debacle for a season.

Meanwhile, the plutocratic players basked in a suntime of cash and glory. As television celebrities, players of this era stood as a breed apart from those of past generations. More glamorized by television exposure, far more wealthy, and more pampered, some players now indulged in illegal drugs to the point of self-abuse. At this time baseball's growing problem of drug abuse mirrored a national epidemic of drug abuse which was one of the unhappier legacies from that decade of self-involvement, the embattled sixties.

Yet another survival from that feverish era was the hirsute appearance of many players of this decade. In addition to wearing gaudier uniforms, many players now sported long hair, mustaches, and beards in the fashion of nineteenth-century players. Formerly a symbol of social protest in the sixties, such hirsute appearances now became a widespread affectation of American males. Although some clubs opposed the trend, owner Charles Finley of the Oakland Athletics encouraged it by paying his players $300 apiece to grow facial hair. Once established, the trend spread widely among players and continues to this day. But appearances aside, this breed of players was more pampered, better doctored and trained, and more ably defended than any of their forebears. Indeed, lesser-paid managers were now hard pressed to discipline their charges. Moreover, players of the seventies were less easily replaced. In this era the total number of minor leaguers competing for big league jobs averaged about 3,000 in any season.

Continuing the trend of the last two decades, blacks and Hispanics predominated among the splendid performers of these years. In 1974 the number of black major league players peaked at 26 percent, but the figure leveled off at 20 percent by 1979. By then, Hispanic players comprised 10 percent of the major league players. As before, blacks and Hispanics continued to lead the majors in stolen bases, with superstar Lou Brock of the Cardinals setting a new seasonal mark of 118 thefts while en route to shattering Ty Cobb's lifetime total of 892 bases stolen. In 1974, Hank Aaron broke Ruth's lifetime homer mark and went on to set a new lifetime mark of 755 clouts. But in

toppling the Babe's record, Aaron went to bat 3,965 more times than the great Yankee slugger. And when Willie Mays retired in 1973, his lifetime total of 660 homers ranked third on the all-time slugging list; behind Mays in the fourth position was Frank Robinson, who retired with 586. And in this decade, Aaron, Al Kaline, Mays, Brock, and Roberto Clemente joined the 3,000 hit club, while Rod Carew captured seven AL batting titles, including four in a row over the years 1972–1975. Moreover, in these years twelve black and Hispanic stars won MVP Awards, and pitchers Bob Gibson and Juan Marichal hurled their ways into baseball's Hall of Fame. Finally, it was fitting that the leading player celebrity of this era was Reggie Jackson, a slugging outfielder of mixed black and Hispanic parentage. Widely acclaimed for his homer clouting, Jackson's seven homers in two World Series appearances with the Yankees won him the sobriquet of "Mr. October" and a short-lived "Reggie" candy bar was named for him.

Although they were justly rewarded and celebrated for their feats on the playing fields, black players still faced lingering forms of discrimination. At this time studies showed that black players had to be better-than-average players to make it into the majors. Thus there were few marginal black players on team rosters; moreover, teams were fearful of playing too many black players in a game lest it affect attendance. And retired black players seldom found jobs in baseball as field managers or in top administrative posts. However, Frank Robinson became the first black manager to be hired (and fired)—hired by the Cleveland Indians in 1975, fired in 1977—and a few token black umpires also debuted in this era. (Robinson went on to become the first black manager in the NL, in 1981.)

At the end of this era, *The Sporting News* chose the versatile white star Pete Rose as the recipient of its Player of the Decade Award. It was well deserved. In this era, Rose won a pair of NL batting titles and led the league in total hits four times. In 1978 the Cincinnati infielder, who was dubbed "Charlie Hustle," tied the NL's consecutive-game hitting record by batting safely in 44 consecutive games. That same year Rose joined the 3,000-hit club and continued his relentless drive to topple Ty Cobb's lifetime record of 4,191 hits.

White stars also predominated among pitchers of this era. In these years, Gaylord Perry, Tom Seaver, Phil Niekro, Don Sutton, and Steve Carlton hurled themselves to ultimate memberships in the exclusive 300-victory club. Carlton, Seaver, Perry, Sutton, and Nolan Ryan also were compiling strikeout totals that would later eclipse Walter Johnson's all-time mark. But with pitching ERAs now hovering above the 3.50 mark each season, managers continued to rely on specialized relief pitchers to bail out starters. Most prized were rally-busting short relievers like Mike Marshall of the Dodgers. In 1974 Marshall appeared in a record 106 games; by winning 15 and saving 21, Marshall won both the NL's Cy Young and Fireman of the Year awards for his efforts. Other acclaimed short relievers included Rollie Fingers of the Athletics, who won three Fireman of the Year awards, while saving 244 games. Fireballing Goose Gossage thrice led the AL in saves, and in 1978 he fanned 122 batters in his role as Yankee fireman. Sparky Lyle, who pitched for four differ-

ent clubs in this era, saved 230 games. And late in this era, Bruce Sutter saved 133 games in five seasons with the Cubs.

With pitchers now penalized by a narrower strike zone and lowered mounds, such heroics were needed to cope with the batting resurgence. Offensively teams plied the big-bang tactic with gusto. At this time AL teams regained their power advantage and outhomered their NL rivals in eleven of the twelve seasons. Of course, the AL's 1977 mini-expansion made this a foregone conclusion. In the first year of that expansion, AL sluggers hammered a record 2,013 homers. By then, hitters in both leagues were swinging at cowhide-covered balls instead of the traditional horsehide-covered spheres. But this necessary innovation failed to produce the overall batting surge forecast by alarmed pundits. Except for the AL's unilateral adoption of the designated hitter rule, there were no significant rule changes in these years; most rule changes addressed statistical compilations. And at this time the major league policy of subsidizing the minor leagues was working. With each team spending at least $1.5 million a year to finance up to five minor league teams, by 1977 the minor leagues were stabilized at 17 leagues and 121 teams.

Internally the major leagues were mightily affected by the shift in the balance of power toward players and umpires. The powerful Players Association upset the power balance, as did the Major League Umpires Association. Indeed, umpires had long endured poor pay and job insecurity. But umpires of the 1970s had come a long way since the single-umpire system of the nineteenth century. Not until 1911 did both major leagues adopt a dual-umpire system for every game and the 1930s first saw both major leagues employ three-man crews to work regular season games. By the 1969–1980 era, four-man crews worked each seasonal game and crews for postseasonal games numbered six. More important, the Major League Umpires Association (MLUA) now became a powerful bargaining agency. After winning collective-bargaining rights in 1970, the MLUA waged a successful strike in 1979, a walkout that lasted until mid-May. When the strike ended, the umpires could celebrate a major victory. Among the concessions they wrung from owners was a maximum salary of $50,000 for twenty-year veteran umps, hefty increases in expense allowances, safeguards against arbitrary dismissals, guaranteed pay for forty-five days in the event of a player strike, and—wonder of wonders—a two-week paid vacation. How the late Bill Klem, who earlier in this century worked each game behind the plate for thirteen seasons, would have welcomed that concession! What's more, umpire Ron Luciano became a minor celebrity and, in company with others, became the author of books.

Against such power blocs, the owners now deployed their power committees and hired negotiators. As for Commissioner Bowie Kuhn, he continued to occupy what by now was largely a ceremonial post, one mainly responsive to the wishes of the owners. In 1979 Walter O'Malley's death removed a powerful figure from the owners' camp. In passing, O'Malley left his enormously profitable franchise as his chief legacy; by 1977 the Dodgers were valued at $50 million, twice the value of most franchises. Thus as the decade of the 1980s dawned, base-

ball owners were challenged to find a new leader of O'Malley's stripe and new tactics to restore the balance of power in their favor.

Campaigns of the Seventies: the AL, 1969–1980

Upstaged by the NL in the first two expansion moves, the AL was forced to take drastic measures to gain parity with the NL in attendance and offensive performances. To this end such measures as new park construction and franchise shifts contributed, but most decisive were two bold unilateral moves whereby the AL adopted the designated hitter rule in 1973 and undertook its mini-expansion in 1977. By these strokes the AL ensured its perennial domination, both at bat and at the turnstiles.

But if AL leaders expected the new divisional format of the 1969 expansion move to produce competitive balance, they were disillusioned. Indeed, throughout this era pennant monopoly was the rule in both AL divisions. Over the twelve campaigns of 1969–1980, the Orioles and Yankees dominated the Eastern Division, while the Athletics and Royals ruled the West. By winning six Eastern Division races and finishing second four times, the Orioles now reigned as the winningest team in the majors. For their part, the reviving Yankees won four Eastern races, which left but two for outsiders to divide. In the AL West, it was much the same story. There the Oakland Athletics won five races, the Kansas City Royals won four, and the Minnesota Twins won two.

In the first expansion season of 1969, the Baltimore Orioles asserted their balanced power, which made them the most victorious major league team of this era. Under sophomore manager Earl Weaver, the Orioles stormed the Eastern Division, their 109 victories lapping the runner-up Tigers by 19 games. It was the first of three consecutive Eastern titles for the Birds, with top-ranked pitching the key to each success. In 1969 the Oriole staff was the league's best, with Mike Cuellar (23–11) and Dave McNally (20–7) setting the pace. At bat the Orioles were powered by first baseman Boog Powell (.304-37-121) and outfielder Frank Robinson (.308-32-100). In the West, meanwhile, the Twins were winning the first of two consecutive titles. Victors by 9 games over the Athletics that year, the Twins led the league in batting and relief pitching. Offensive standouts included Rod Carew, whose .332 hitting topped the league, and Harmon Killebrew, whose league-leading 49 homers and 140 RBIs won the veteran slugger the MVP Award. But when the divisional titlists squared off in the first American League Championship Series, the Orioles brushed the Twins aside in three games. The sweep gave the Orioles a fourteen-game winning streak to take to the World Series. But after winning the opening game against the New York Mets, the Orioles surprisingly lost the next four.

In 1970 the crestfallen Orioles came back nearly as strong and downed the Yankees by 15 games to repeat as Eastern champs. Once again manager Earl Weaver's pitching corps was the league's best. Starters Mike Cuellar and Dave McNally each won 24 and Jim Palmer won 20. At the plate the Orioles batted .257, with outfielder Merv Rettenmund's .322 leading the team batting, and Powell (35-114) and Frank Robinson (25-78) supplying the power. In the West, the Twins also repeated, again

topping the Athletics by 9 games and again leading the league in hitting and relief pitching. This time the team batted .262, but Killebrew (41-113) again powered the club. An injury to Carew limited his play, but even so the infielder batted .366. Taking up the slack this year were outfielders Tony Oliva (.325-23-107) and Cesar Tovar, who hit .300. However, when the Twins met the Orioles in LCS play, they were again swept. And this time the Orioles went on to score an avenging victory in World Series play. In crushing the Reds in five games, the Orioles blasted fifty hits; the star Oriole performer was future Hall of Famer Brooks Robinson, who batted .429 and dazzled the Reds with his brilliant fielding at third base.

It was a glorious victory for the Orioles, but astonishingly this well-armed team would not win another world title in this era. In 1971 the Orioles captured a third straight Eastern title by thrashing the Tigers by 12 games. It was a vintage season for Baltimore, which could boast league-leading hitting and pitching, including a quartet of 20-game winning pitchers in Cuellar, McNally, Palmer, and Pat Dobson. Offensively, outfielder Rettenmund (.318) fronted the team's .261 batting attack, and Powell, Frank Robinson, and Brooks Robinson powered the assault with a combined 70 homers and 283 RBIs. In the West, the fading Twins now yielded to the surging Oakland Athletics, who notched the first of five consecutive Western titles in 1971. In matching the Orioles' victory total of 101 games, the Athletics crushed the expansion Kansas City Royals by 16 games. For the A's, rookie pitcher Vida Blue won 24 games with a league-leading 1.82 ERA, and Jim "Catfish" Hunter won 21. Hunter's nickname was hung on the hurler by the team's flamboyant owner, Charley Finley, who also tried unsuccessfully to get Blue to change his first name to "True." Offensively, the A's lacked a .300 hitter, but third baseman Sal Bando (24-94) and outfielder Reggie Jackson (32-80) provided power aplenty. But when the Athletics met the Orioles in LCS play, they were swept by the Orioles. It was the third consecutive LCS sweep by the Orioles. However, the Orioles lost a seven-game World Series struggle to the Pittsburgh Pirates, led by MVP Roberto Clemente.

In the wake of that loss, the Orioles fell from the top, and the balance of power now shifted to the West, where the volatile Athletics won the first of three consecutive AL championships. In the strike-shortened season of 1972, the A's won the Western title by 5½ games over the Chicago White Sox. Left fielder Joe Rudi batted .305, and first baseman Mike Epstein and outfielder Reggie Jackson combined for 51 homers as the A's rolled up 93 wins to head the AL. Moreover, the pitching staff was the league's best; Hunter and Ken Holtzman combined for 40 victories, and reliever Rollie Fingers won 11 and saved 21 games. In the East the strike-shortened schedule enabled the Tigers to eke a half-game victory over the runner-up Red Sox by dint of playing and winning one more game than the Bostonians. Manager Billy Martin's Tigers batted a mere .237, with no .300 hitter among the regulars, but lefty Mickey Lolich's 22 wins fronted the league's second-best pitching corps. In LCS play the weak-hitting Tigers held out for five games before succumbing to the A's, who went on to defeat the Reds in a seven-game World Series struggle. With slugger Jackson sidelined by

an injury, unheralded catcher Gene Tenace took up the offensive slack. Tenace batted .348 and won three World Series games with timely hits.

Over the next two seasons, the Athletics continued their winning ways, twice downing the Orioles in LCS play and twice defeating NL contenders in World Series action. In 1973 the garishly clad A's defeated the Royals by 6 games in the West. Jackson's league-leading 32 homers and 117 RBIs powered the team, which also got superb pitching from Hunter (21–5), Holtzman (21–13), Blue (20–9), and reliever Fingers, who saved 22 games with a 1.92 ERA. That year the Orioles returned to the top in the East by downing the Red Sox by 8 games. In this first season under the designated hitter rule, the Orioles were paced by DH Tommy Davis, who batted .306 and drove in 89 runs. Palmer headed the pitching staff, which was the league's best, with a 22–9 mark; Cuellar won 18; and McNally and young Doyle Alexander combined for 29 wins. In the aftermath the Orioles battled the A's in a tense LCS matchup which went the full five games before Hunter's shutout pitching decided the issue. Then, in World Series action against the New York Mets, the Athletics rallied from a 3–2 deficit to land a second world title. Home runs by Reggie Jackson and Bert Campeneris settled the issue in Game Seven.

In 1974 the Athletics won a third consecutive World Series banner, a feat thus far unmatched under the major leagues' divisional format. In winning the Western race by 5 games over the Texas Rangers, the light-hitting (.247) A's were backed by the best pitching corps in the majors. Hunter's league-leading 25 wins and 2.49 ERA led the staff, who also got 19 wins from Holtzman, 17 wins from Blue, and 18 saves from the redoubtable Fingers. Although lacking a .300 hitter, the team was powered by Bando (22-103), Jackson (29-93), and outfielder Joe Rudi (.293-22-99). In the East, the Orioles won a fifth divisional flag by 2 games over the Yankees. League-leading fielding and sturdy pitching from Cuellar (22–10), McNally (16–10), and Ross Grimsley (18–13) carried the Orioles. In LCS competition the A's lost the opening game, but swept the next three to claim the league pennant. Pitted against the Dodgers in the World Series, the bickering Athletics, who squabbled among themselves and with their owner, nevertheless downed the Dodgers in five games. It was the A's third straight World Series victory, and astonishingly the team's bullpen saved or won all twelve of the games won by the Athletics in their remarkable three-season skein.

But the 1974 league championship was the last by an Athletic team until 1988. Years of bickering between the players and owner Charley Finley wore on the team, and the loss of pitcher Hunter to the Yankees was a crushing blow. Hunter's loss was Finley's fault; after Finley reneged on the terms of Hunter's contract, Hunter sought arbitration, and the ruling allowed the pitcher to become a free agent. Nevertheless, in 1975 the A's won the Western title for a fifth straight year as they outlasted the Royals by 7 games. Despite the loss of Hunter, the team's pitching was the league's second best. Blue won 22 games, Holtzman 18, and Fingers won 10 and saved 24. Offensively, outfielder Claudell Washington led the team with .308 batting, and Jackson drove in 104 runs and hit a league-leading 36 homers. However, the league's power

balance now shifted eastward, where the next five AL champions would be crowned. First of the Eastern powers to emerge were the 1975 Red Sox, who defeated the Orioles by 4½ games. The team's pitching was mediocre, but hefty .275 batting bolstered the assault. Rookie outfielder Fred Lynn's .331-21-105 hitting won him both Rookie of the Year and MVP honors, but outfielder Jim Rice (.309-22-102) came close to matching Lynn's production, while DH Cecil Cooper and catcher Carlton Fisk each topped the .300 mark. In the LCS faceoff, the Red Sox ended Oakland's domination with a three-game sweep. But in World Series action, the Red Sox lost an epochal seven-game struggle to the Cincinnati Reds.

Boston slipped to third in 1976, as another power rose in the AL East. After a twelve-year hiatus, the Yankees regained the heights and held the high ground for the next three seasons. For the Yankee renaissance much of the credit belonged to the team's wealthy and erratic owner, George Steinbrenner. After purchasing the team from the CBS Network in 1973, Steinbrenner boldly promised Yankee fans a pennant within three years, and in 1976 his words rang true. Moreover, the timing was propitious. In 1976 the team returned to its newly refurbished Yankee Stadium after spending two seasons at Shea Stadium in Queens. Under equally brash manager Billy Martin, whom Steinbrenner would fire and rehire five times, the Yankees romped over the runner-up Orioles by 10½ games. League-leading pitching, including 53 wins from starters Hunter, Dock Ellis, and Ed Figueroa, and a league-leading 23 saves from reliever Sparky Lyle eased the way. The team's .269 batting effort was led by outfielder Mickey Rivers, who batted .312, catcher Thurman Munson's .302 and 105 RBIs, and third baseman Graig Nettles's league-leading 32 homers. Meanwhile, the surging Kansas City Royals were breaking Oakland's stranglehold in the West. In downing owner Finley's decimated A's by 2½ games, the Royals matched the .269 batting mark of the Yankees. Third baseman George Brett's .333 topped the league's hitters, but DH Hal McRae was only a point behind at .332, and his 73 RBIs bettered Brett's total. The 1976 victory was the first of three straight Western titles by the Royals, who became the first of the AL's 1969 expansion teams to win a divisional pennant. In LCS play the Royals and Yanks battled for five games before first baseman Chris Chambliss won the pennant for the Yankees with a ninth-inning homer in the final game at Yankee Stadium. However, the Yankees were no match for Cincinnati's powerful "Big Red Machine," which swept to a four-game victory in the World Series.

Over the winter Steinbrenner strengthened his team by acquiring slugger Reggie Jackson in the re-entry draft. Jackson responded by batting .286 with 32 homers and 110 RBIs as the Yankees edged the Orioles by 2½ games in the 1977 Eastern race. Overall the team batted .281, with Rivers's .326 batting leading the team, Munson weighing in with .308-18-100 stickwork, and Nettles driving in 107 runs on 37 homers. Young Ron Guidry (16–7) led the starting pitchers, with Figueroa winning 16, newly acquired Don Gullett winning 14, and reliever Lyle saving 26. In the West, meanwhile, the Royals repeated as they downed the Texas Rangers by 8 games. The Royals batted .277, with outfielder Al Cowens (.312-23-112) leading the team, Brett batting .312, and McRae adding 21 ho-

mers and 92 RBIs. The Royal pitching staff was the league's best; Dennis Leonard won 20 games to lead the league, Paul Splittorff won 16, and the bullpen posted a league-leading 42 saves. In another LCS donnybrook, the Yankees edged the Royals in five games to land a second consecutive AL pennant. And in World Series action the Yankees trounced the Dodgers in six games. For the Yankees, the highlight came in the final game at the Stadium, when Jackson slugged three homers. In the afterglow of the victory, a candy bar was named for Jackson, who also wore the sobriquet of "Mr. October" for the remainder of his colorful career.

In an unforgettable encore performance, the Yankees repeated in 1978 after staging one of the most storied comebacks in baseball history. During much of the turbulent campaign, the Yankees trailed the slugging Red Sox. Midway in the campaign Steinbrenner sacked the volatile Martin for insubordination and replaced him with Bob Lemon. Under Lemon, the Yankees recuperated from a spate of injuries and crushed the Red Sox in two series to gain a tie by the season's end. In the sudden-death playoff game for the Eastern title, pitchers Ron Guidry and Goose Gossage held off the Red Sox, while homers by Jackson and shortstop Bucky Dent capped a 5–4 victory at Fenway Park. That year the Yankee pitchers posted a league-leading 3.10 ERA; Guidry's 25 wins (he lost only 3) and 1.74 ERA were the league's best, and Gossage won 10 and saved 27 games. Outfielder Lou Piniella's .314 batting led the team, which was powered by Jackson (27-97), Nettles (27-93), and Chambliss (who drove in 90 runs). Meanwhile, the upstaged Royals were winning a third consecutive Western title, this time by 5 games over the California Angels. With no .300 hitter in the regular lineup, the Royals batted .268; outfielder Amos Otis led the hitters with .298-22-96 batting. Starting pitchers Leonard and Splittorff combined for 40 victories, and reliever Al Hrabosky saved 20 as the Royals compiled the league's second-best pitching record. But the Yankees toppled the Royals in four games in LCS play. When World Series play began, the Yankees lost the first two games to the Dodgers, but then swept the next four games.

Although Steinbrenner continued to spend heavily on free agents, the 1979 Yankees fell to fourth place in the Eastern Division. By winning 102 games, manager Earl Weaver led the Orioles to an 8-game win over the second-place Milwaukee Brewers. League-leading pitching, paced by Mike Flanagan's 23–9 effort, led the Orioles, whose offense was powered by first baseman Eddie Murray (.295-25-99) and outfielder Ken Singleton (.295-35-111). While the Orioles winged to the top in the AL East, the California Angels ended the Royals' Western reign by scoring a 3-game victory. The Angels' victory ended years of frustration for owner Gene Autry, who had spent $15 million on playing talent since 1961. In 1978 two of Autry's recent acquisitions paid off as Rod Carew batted .318 and Don Baylor won the MVP Award for his .296-36-139 production. But the Angels' pitching corps compiled a vulnerable 4.34 ERA, and in LCS play the Orioles dispatched the Angels in four games. But the Orioles now faced their old Pirate tormentors in the World Series. In an eerie repeat of their 1971 matchup, after leading by three games to one in this 1979 encounter, the Orioles lost to the Pirates in seven games.

As the era ended, the Yankees rebounded to edge the Orioles by 3 games in the East. In the close race, Steinbrenner's latest re-entry draft acquisitions, infielder Bob Watson and pitcher Rudy May, made the difference. May won 15 games, and his 2.47 ERA led the league; Tommy John won 22, Guidry won 17, and the fireballing Gossage saved 33 games in relief. Watson's .307 batting led the hitters, but Jackson batted .300 and his 111 RBIs came with a league-leading 41 homers. This year, however, the Yankees were outmatched by the Royals. Rebounding to win the Western Division by 14 games over the Athletics, the Royals batted a league-leading .286. Brett's .390 batting, which included 24 homers and 118 RBIs, was the best batting mark in the majors since 1941. Outfielder Willie Wilson batted .326 and catcher-outfielder John Wathan batted .305. Pitcher Leonard won 20, and a Yankee castoff, lefty Larry Gura, won 18, with relief ace Dan Quisenberry saving 33 games to tie Gossage for the league lead. In LCS play the Royals, who had feasted on the Yankees during the season, swept the New Yorkers. In the wake of that loss, owner Steinbrenner sacked manager Dick Howser, despite the 103 victories the Yankees had compiled under Howser's leadership. By then, the Royals had lost to the Philadelphia Phillies in six games in the 1980 World Series. Thus the era ended with the National League boasting two straight World Series triumphs which the senior circuit would extend to four in the early 1980s.

Campaigns of the Seventies: the NL, 1969–1980

In this era the NL also failed to achieve the competitive balance envisioned by its 1969 expansion. Over the twelve NL campaigns of these years, both divisions were ruled by powerful dynasties. In the East, the Pirates won six races, the Phillies four, and the Mets two. In the West, the Reds won six races, the Dodgers three, with the Braves, Giants, and Astros as single-season winners.

Yet it was one of the league's lesser powers, the New York Mets, who made a rousing success of the first NL campaign under the new divisional format. Like the moonwalking American astronauts of that summer, the Mets also realized an "impossible dream," and their unlikely triumph became the sports story of that memorable year in the nation's history. In a baseball version of Horatio Alger's rags-to-riches yarns, the forlorn Mets shook off the effects of their horrendous 394–737 won-loss record, which the team had painfully compiled over seven zany seasons of NL play, and won the 1969 Eastern Division race by 8 games over a cocky Chicago Cub team. What's more, the Mets turned the trick by winning 38 of their last 49 games, mostly due to good pitching. Young Tom Seaver's league-leading 25 victories and Jerry Koosman's 17 headed a pitching staff whose 2.99 ERA ranked second in the league. However, a puny .242 team batting average, fronted by outfielder Cleon Jones's .340-12-75, afforded little hope against the Western champion Atlanta Braves, winners by 3 games over the Giants. For the Braves, who led the NL in fielding, Hank Aaron's .300-44-97 batting, and Rico Carty's .342-16-58 effort in limited action, excelled. Pitcher Phil Niekro won 23 and Ron Reed won 18 as the staff turned in a 3.53 ERA. But in the NL's first League Championship Series, the impotent

Mets turned tartars; scoring 27 runs in three games, they swept the favored Braves. However, the Mets appeared to be ludicrously mismatched against the versatile Orioles in the following World Series. But after losing the opening game, the Mets swept the Orioles in the next four games to realize their "impossible dream." In the afterglow, an outpouring of "Metomania" swept the country, and a dozen hastily written books celebrating the team's victory were churned out.

But the following year the powerful Pittsburgh Pirates ruthlessly banished any hopes of a continuing competitive balance in the NL East. Over the next six seasons, the Pirates captured five Eastern pennants, including three in a row over the years 1970–1972. In 1970 the Pirates baptized their newly occupied Three Rivers Stadium by downing the Cubs by 5 games and raising their first divisional flag. The Pirates batted .270, with Roberto Clemente hitting .352 and catcher Manny Sanguillen batting .325. With a 3.70 ERA, their pitching was shaky, but reliever Dave Giusti saved 26 games. Coincident with the Pirates' rise, another power moved to the top in the West as the Cincinnati Reds, now ensconced in their new Riverfront Stadium, scored a crushing 14½-game win over the runner-up Dodgers. At the plate the Reds matched the Pirates' batting, while leading the league in homers with 191. Catcher Johnny Bench's 45 homers and 148 RBIs led all sluggers and won him MVP honors. Infielders Pete Rose (.316) and Tony Perez (.317-40-129), and outfielder Bob Tolan (.316) added to the hit parade which was needed to bolster the pitching staff. The team's starting pitchers completed only 32 games, which inspired the bullpen to compile a league-leading 60 saves. And yet the staff's 3.71 ERA was only a point above that of the Pirates. In the LCS that year, the Reds swept the Pirates, but then the Reds fell to the avenging Orioles in the 1970 World Series.

The following year manager Danny Murtaugh led his Pirates to a 7-game win over the Cardinals in the NL East. At the plate the Pirates upped their batting to .274 as Clemente (.341) and Sanguillen (.319) maintained their pace, while outfielder Willie Stargell's league-leading 48 homers powered the team's league-leading 154-homer assault. In the West, poor pitching consigned the Reds to fourth place, leaving the field to the Giants and Dodgers. After leading most of the way, the Giants faltered in the stretch, but hung on to win by a game over the Dodgers. League-leading fielding buoyed the Giants, who batted only .247. Outfielder Bobby Bonds's .288-33-102 was the best effort by a regular. Future Hall of Fame pitcher Juan Marichal and Gaylord Perry combined for 34 victories as the staff's 3.33 ERA came close to matching the Pirates' mark of 3.31. In LCS play the Pirates lost the opening game, but swept to victory. And when matched against the Orioles in the World Series, the Pirates lost the first two games, but then rebounded to win in seven. The Pirate victory triggered a spate of destructive riots in Pittsburgh, but any fears by city fathers of future riots to come were banished by the shortcomings of the Pirate teams.

Although the 1972 Pirates romped to an 11-game victory over the Cubs in the East, another six seasons would pass before the Bucs won another NL pennant. Future Hall of Famer Roberto Clemente batted .312 and notched his 3,000th career hit as the Pirates matched their .274 batting mark of 1971. Outfielder Al Oliver batted .312 and infielder Richie Hebner batted .300, while Stargell powered the attack with 33 homers and 112 RBIs. Led by starting pitcher Steve Blass (19–8) and reliever Giusti (22 saves), the pitching staff posted a 2.81 ERA. In the West, meanwhile, the Reds rebounded to win by 10½ games over the Houston Astros. The acquisition of infielder Joe Morgan strengthened the Reds, who also got another MVP performance from Bench. The catcher's 40 homers and 125 RBIs led the league, and infielder Rose batted .307. But the pitching staff completed only 25 games. The best effort by a starter was Gary Nolan's 15–5 mark, but the bullpen, led by Clay Carroll's league-leading 37 saves, saved 60 games. In LCS action the Reds rallied from a 2–1 deficit to win the league pennant in five games. In the decisive game, played in Cincinnati, the Reds won 4–3. In the ninth inning of that game, Pirate reliever Bob Moose wild-pitched the winning run home. But when the Reds faced a 3–1 deficit in the World Series, their rally fell short as the Athletics hung on to win the world title in seven games.

Over the winter, Clemente's tragic death while on a mercy mission to Nicaragua was a crushing blow to the Pirate cause. Even so, the 1973 Pirates hung close, finishing third in a weak Eastern Division. On the strength of a lackluster 82–79 record, the Mets edged the Cardinals by 1½ games. Offensively the Mets batted a meager .246 with only 85 homers, but Seaver's 19–10 pitching and league-leading 2.08 ERA and reliever Tug McGraw's 25 saves compensated. In the West the Reds outlasted the Dodgers by 3½ games to win the divisional pennant. Led by Rose's league-leading .338 hitting, the Reds batted .254 and hit 137 homers. Perez batted .314-27-101, Morgan batted .290-26-82, and Bench drove in 104 runs. The Reds also led the league in stolen bases and fielding, and the pitching staff ranked fourth, just behind the Mets. Not surprisingly, the Reds were touted as LCS favorites, but the Mets edged them in five games to emerge as the NL's standard bearer in the World Series. Astonishingly the Mets took a 3–2 lead in the first five Series games against the Athletics. Had they hung on to win with their puny seasonal record, it would have gone into the record books as a quirky record. But the A's quashed this prospect by snagging the final two games to win the 1973 World Series.

As the impotent Mets faded in 1974, the Pirates rose again to win the next two Eastern races before yielding to the rising Phillies. Unsurpassed .274 team batting boosted the Pirates to a thin 1½-game win over the Cardinals in the East. Outfielders Richie Zisk (.313-17-100), Al Oliver (.321 and 85 RBIs), and Stargell (.301-25-96) powered the team, whose pitching staff posted a 3.49 ERA. But the league's balance of power was shifting westward, where the Dodgers and Reds would monopolize the next five NL pennants. In the 1974 Western Division race, the Dodgers defeated the Reds by 4 games. Backed by the most durable infield in baseball history, in Steve Garvey, Dave Lopes, Bill Russell, and Ron Cey, the 1974 Dodgers batted .272. First baseman Garvey, who would set an NL record in consecutive games played, led the assault that year with a .312-21-111 performance which won him MVP honors. Outfielder Jim Wynn added 32 homers and

108 RBIs. Pitchers Andy Messersmith and Don Sutton combined for 39 wins to head the league's top-ranked pitching staff, but reliever Mike Marshall won the pitching honors with his 15 victories and 21 saves. What's more, fireman Marshall appeared in a record 106 games. In the LCS playoff the Dodgers dispatched the Pirates in four games, but the Dodgers lost the World Series to the Athletics in five games.

It was the third consecutive Series victory for the Athletics, but the powerful Cincinnati Reds reversed the trend in 1975–1976. Dubbed "the Big Red Machine," the perennially pitching-poor Reds got only 22 complete games from their starters in 1975, but the team's crushing offense buried the runner-up Dodgers by 20 games. Heading the team's .271 batting offensive was second baseman Joe Morgan, who won MVP honors for his .327 batting and 94 RBIs. Third baseman Rose and outfielders Ken Griffey and George Foster topped .300 at bat, and first baseman Tony Perez and catcher Bench drove in a combined 219 runs. In the East the Pirates beat the Phils by 6½ games to win a second straight divisional title. The Pirates batted .263 and led the league in homers. Outfielder Dave Parker (.308-25-101) and first baseman Stargell (.295-22-90) powered the team, and catcher Manny Sanguillen batted .328. And the pitching staff's 3.02 ERA bettered the Reds. But the Reds swept the Pirates in LCS play and went on to beat the Red Sox in a tense seven-game World Series classic. In the final game at Boston the Reds overcame a 3–0 Boston lead. Morgan's single in the ninth inning provided the margin of victory as the Reds won 4–3. The victory was the Reds' first World Series triumph since 1940.

Nor did they stop there. The following year, as the NL celebrated its hundredth anniversary, the all-conquering Reds downed the Dodgers by 10 games in the West on the strength of league leadership in batting, homers, RBIs, stolen bases, and fielding. Morgan's .320-27-111 batting won the infielder a second straight MVP Award, Rose batted .323, and the outfield of Griffey (.336), Cesar Geronimo (.307), and George Foster (.306) all topped the .300 mark. Foster's 121 RBIs led the league, and the bullpen fronted by Rollie Eastwick led the league in saves. In the East it was the Phillies' misfortune to have to face this wrecking crew in LCS play. That year the Phillies finally won an Eastern title, the first of three consecutive victories, all coming at the expense of the Pirates. In 1976 the Phillies trounced the Pirates by 9 games. Slugging third baseman Mike Schmidt led the league in homers with 38 and drove in 107 runs, and the outfield of Jay Johnstone, Garry Maddox, and Greg Luzinski all topped the .300 mark, with Luzinski batting in 95 runs. Steve Carlton (20–7) headed a pitching staff that bettered the mediocre Reds' staff, but otherwise needed the 36 saves posted by the relief corps of Ron Reed, Tug McGraw, and Gene Garber. The LCS matchup between the Reds and the Phillies was a foregone conclusion which the Reds decided with a sweep. The Reds then went on to sweep the Yankees in the World Series to become the first NL team since 1922 to win back-to-back world titles.

But the Big Red Machine blew a gasket in 1977. The loss of ace pitcher Don Gullett to the re-entry draft (and the Yankees) and a dubious trade which sent first baseman Perez to the Expos created weaknesses that not even the mid-season acquisition of pitcher Tom Seaver from the Mets could assuage. Nor could Foster's herculean batting, which produced a league-leading 52 homers and 149 RBIs together with a .320 batting average. As the pitching-poor Reds faltered, the Dodgers brushed them aside to win the Western title by 10 games. League leadership in homers (191) and pitching buoyed the Dodgers. A successful arm operation gave a new life to lefty Tommy John, whose 20 victories led the pitching staff. Offensively, outfielder Reggie Smith's .302-32-87 led the attack, with outfielder Dusty Baker and infielders Garvey and Ron Cey each topping the 30 mark in homers. Meanwhile, the Phillies repeated in the East, their 101 victories leading the league and topping the runner-up Pirates by 5 games. The Phillies led the league in batting at .279. Outfielder Luzinski's .309-30-130 was his best effort, and Schmidt again powered 38 homers while driving in 101 runs. Carlton led the pitchers with 23 victories, and Larry Christenson's 19–6 mark was his best in the majors; moreover, the bullpen's 43 saves topped the league. Still, the Dodgers defeated the Phillies in four games in the LCS. However, the Dodgers got their comeuppance from the Yankees, who won the 1977 World Series in six games.

Although the victory margin for both teams was skimpier, the 1978 divisional races repeated the scenario of the previous year. In the West the Dodgers repeated by edging the Reds by 2½ games. Once again the pitching staff was the league's best (3.12 ERA). Starters Burt Hooton, Tommy John, Don Sutton, and Doug Rau won 66 games, and reliever Terry Foster saved 22. Garvey headed the team's .264 batting attack with .316-21-113 stickwork; and Cey, Reggie Smith, and Rick Monday combined for 71 homers to head the team's league-leading homer barrage. In the East the Phillies won for a third straight year, but by a skimpy 1½-game margin over the Pirates. Luzinski's 35 homers and 101 RBIs paced a weak .258 batting assault; and Carlton (with 16 wins) and Dick Ruthven (with 13 wins), and relievers Ron Reed and McGraw led the Phils' pitching staff, which was the best in the Eastern Division, but a far cry from the Dodgers' mark of 1978. In LCS play the Dodgers again trounced the Phillies in four games, but again the Dodgers fell to their old Yankee nemesis in six games.

As the decade waned, the Pirates returned to power in the East by edging the runner-up Expos by 2 games. It was the sixth Eastern title of this era for the Pirates, who batted a lusty .272 but whose mediocre pitching staff depended heavily on its superb bullpen headed by Kent Tekulve, who appeared in 94 games and saved 31. Third baseman Bill Madlock's .328 batting led the team along with Parker (.310-25-94) and Stargell, whose 32 homers helped drive in 82 runs. At the same time in the West, the Reds also won their sixth divisional title of the era, beating the Astros by 1½ games. With Rose gone by way of the re-entry draft, his replacement Ray Knight batted .318 and, along with outfielders Griffey (.316) and Foster (.302-30-98), paced the team's .264 batting. Seaver's 16 victories led the team's mediocre pitching staff. The two rival dynasties met for a last time to date in LCS play with the Pirates sweeping the Reds. In World Series action the Pirates fell behind the Orioles three games to one, but swept the last three games for a stunning victory.

In 1980 the Phillies ended a thirty-year drought by

winning an NL pennant. Goaded by manager Dallas Green, the Phillies won 21 of their last 28 games to eke a 1-game victory over the Expos in the East. An MVP performance by slugger Schmidt, who hit 48 homers and drove in 121 runs, powered the Phils, who also got .309 batting from outfielder Bake McBride, and .282 batting and inspired leadership from the transplanted Pete Rose. Lefty Carlton's 24 wins led the league and won him the Cy Young Award, and Dick Ruthven won 17, while bull-pen stalwart Tug McGraw saved 20 games. In the West the Dodgers and Astros finished in a dead heat as the front-running Astros lost their last three games to the visiting Dodgers. But in a sudden-death playoff for the Eastern Division title, Joe Niekro pitched the Astros to a 7–1 victory over the Dodgers at Dodger Stadium. The Astros got .309 hitting from outfielder Cesar Cedeno, and the team batted .261, but the punchless offense produced only 75 homers. But the Astros' pitching staff was the league's best. Joe Niekro won 20 games, Nolan Ryan won 11, and Vern Ruhle won 12. Ruhle's pitching compensated for the loss of power pitcher J. R. Richard, who had compiled a 10–4, 1.89 record when he sustained a career-ending stroke. In LCS play the Phils and Astros battled through five games, with the rebounding Phillies scoring two extra-inning victories in Houston to land the pennant. Thus emboldened, the Phillies went on to beat the Royals in a six-game World Series tussle. It was the Phillies' first world championship in the club's ninety-seven-year history as an NL team.

But in the season after Philadelphia's momentous victory, which saw the local police deploying mounted troopers and guard dogs to restrain the delirious Philadelphia fans, the major leagues were staggered by a crippling player strike.

Baseball's Embattled Decade, 1981–1990

The conservative mood that gripped the nation in the late 1970s also held sway during these years and helped to catapult Ronald Reagan to landslide victories in the presidential elections of 1980 and 1984. Indeed, ex–movie actor Reagan was no stranger to baseball fans, many of whom saw him play the role of ex–pitching great Grover Cleveland Alexander on the silver screen. And now, as an avowed conservative, President Reagan sought to divert the nation's economy toward a free-enterprise course by such tactics as cutting federal taxes and reducing federal domestic spending programs. At the same time Reagan advocated a powerful national defense posture aimed at combating the spread of international communism.

But Reagan's first term was darkened by an economic recession which contributed to high unemployment. Especially hard hit by unemployment were minorities and blue-collar workers in declining industries. Among the declining industries were such former bellwether industries as steel and mining, whose sagging production was attributed to foreign competition. However, the American economy in the main continued to shift from its former heavy-industrial base to its present emphasis on high technology and information and services production.

Nevertheless, before Reagan's first term ended, such factors as federal tax cuts and falling inflation and interest rates spurred an economic recovery which continued into 1987. The boomlet reduced unemployment, but for most workers wage increases were small, and some 20 million Americans still remained at or near the poverty level in 1987. Indeed, some critics faulted Reagan's economic policies for favoring the well-to-do, whose ranks by 1987 included a million millionaires and a score of billionaires among a population of 240 million.

But prospects for continuing affluence dimmed as the year 1987 closed amidst fears of an impending recession. In October the nation's burgeoning national debt (estimated at $2.6 trillion) and a chronic foreign-trade imbalance triggered financial panics in domestic and foreign stock markets. Aggravated by the festering Iran-Contra scandal and the naval confrontation with Iran in the Persian Gulf, the economic crisis boded ill for the Reagan Administration and for the nation's future.

Moreover, other menacing problems clouded the nation's future. Among them was the epidemic of drug abuse which defied efforts at punitive control. According to a 1985 estimate, the multibillion-dollar illegal drug industry was being supported by 20 million American consumers. Included were scores of professional athletes who confronted their officials with the knotty problem of disciplining abusers without violating their civil rights.

And yet for all the sobering national problems, most Americans of these years enjoyed moderately prosperous lifestyles. For this accomplishment, the two-paycheck family trend was largely responsible. By 1987 working women, whose ranks included most wives, accounted for more than half of the American labor force. Buoyed by the additional income, most Americans continued to spend lavishly on leisure and recreational activities. According to one report, Americans in 1987 were spending well over $50 billion a year on gambling, sports betting, and physical activities alone. And among the host of available leisure activities, television viewing, especially televised sports programs, maintained a leading position.

Certainly America's continuing infatuation with major sports was a blessing for baseball as revenues from live attendance and television continued to grow at a record-setting pace. At the same time, however, spiraling player salaries pitted players against owners in a series of pitched battles on the labor front.

Indeed, embattled relations between players and owners was a leitmotif of this era. In 1981 the failure of owners and players to agree on a new labor contract triggered a crippling baseball strike—the worst in the history of major league baseball since the 1890 debacle. A major bone of contention was the owners' demand that a club receive a veteran player as compensation for losing a player in one of the annual re-entry drafts. When the deadline for an agreement expired with no compromise, the players struck on June 11, 1981. Once the strike began, it lasted some fifty days and wiped out a third of the season's playing schedule. The strike cost the united players at least $30 million in lost salaries, and the owners lost an estimated $116 million in revenues. However, the owners were partly compensated by $50 million in strike insurance. On the last day of July, a compromise ended the great player strike. The owners won their point on the player compensation issue, but they had to settle for an indirect approach. Thus when a team lost a player in a re-

entry draft, the team got to choose a veteran player from a pool of surplus players provided by all major league teams. For their part, the players also successfully fended off the owners' demand for a ceiling on salaries. Agreement on these and lesser issues produced a fifth Basic Agreement, which ran through the season of 1984. The eleventh-hour agreement saved what was left of the 1981 season, but the salvage format devised by Commissioner Bowie Kuhn drew much criticism. Kuhn's plan called for a split-season campaign, a format which had been tried and discarded as unsatisfactory in 1892. Under Kuhn's scheme, the first-half winners were those teams which led their divisions at the time of the June 11 player walkout. The second-half winners would be the teams that led the divisions at the close of the campaign after the resumption of play in August. By ruling first-half winners ineligible to repeat as champions, Kuhn's plan of scheduling a round of playoffs to decide the divisional championships in each league was assured. Thus a separate best-of-five playoff series was scheduled to settle first the matter of the 1981 divisional championships. Thereafter, the winners engaged in the usual best-of-five game series to determine the champions of each league. Although the format worked as planned, it was faulted for producing lackadaisical play on the part of three of the four first-half winners and for reducing attendance in the second half of what writer Red Smith called "the dishonest season."

Nor did the great strike of 1981 end the tensions between the embattled players and owners. When the fifth Basic Agreement expired at the end of 1984 with no agreement in place, a new strike threat loomed in 1985. With salaries continuing their upward spiral, averaging $363,000 in 1984 with 36 players paid at least a million dollars that year, the owners determined to arrest the trend. Correctly zeroing in on salary arbitration as the cause of runaway salaries, the owners demanded that a player wait more than the current two-year period before becoming eligible for salary arbitration. In addition, the owners renewed their demand for a ceiling on salaries. Naturally the players resisted, and when no agreement was reached, the players struck on August 6, 1985. But this time the walkout lasted only two days; obviously neither side wanted a repeat of the 1981 ordeal. Following the resumption of negotiations, a sixth Basic Agreement was promulgated. The new contract compromised on the major issues. For their part, the owners failed to get a salary ceiling, but the players agreed to wait three years instead of two to become eligible for salary arbitration. The players won increased pension benefits, which now would pay a retired veteran with ten years of major league service an annual pension of $91,000! And the owners also won their demand to increase the popular League Championship Series playoffs to a best-of-seven-games format beginning with the 1985 season.

Still, the new four-year Basic Agreement failed to end the hostilities between players and owners. As salaries continued to soar, the owners unilaterally cut team player rosters to twenty-four men and proceeded to boycott the re-entry drafts of 1985–1987. Despite the presence of veteran stars on the auction blocks in those years, there were no bidders. In retaliation, the Players Association charged collusion and filed separate grievances for each of the two boycotted drafts. In September 1987 arbiter

Thomas Roberts ruled in favor of the players in the first of those suits, that of 1985. Shortly thereafter, arbiter George Nicolau ruled against the owners in the 1986 and 1987 cases of alleged grievances. The rulings awarded damages in the range of $100 million to the players involved. As a result the chastened owners engaged in open bidding in the re-entry markets of 1988 and 1989. But the Players Association insisted on further collusion protection, which became part of the seventh Basic Agreement that was negotiated after the 1990 lockout. A proviso in that agreement imposed triple damages for any repetition of owner collusion in the signing of free agents.

Still, whatever the outcome of this impending struggle, the players of this era were obvious winners on the salary front. In 1982, the year after the great strike, salaries averaged $250,000. Two years later the average salary climbed to $330,000, almost the same as that of the highest-paid manager, Tom Lasorda of the Dodgers. Then in 1986 the average salary peaked at $412,000 before falling slightly to $410,000 in 1987. The decrease was due in part to teams releasing veteran players and calling up minor leaguers, some of whom could be paid the minimum salary of $62,500. But the decrease was a minor one as annual payrolls for major league clubs in 1987 topped $295 million. Of course, payrolls varied from team to team; in 1987 the Yankee payroll of $18.5 million topped all others, while the $5.6 million payroll of the Seattle Mariners was the lowest of the twenty-six teams.

Average figures also failed to tell the full story of player gains of this era. Boosting average salary figures were the growing number of million-dollar-a-year players. In 1984 there were twenty; in 1985, thirty-six; in 1986, fifty-eight; and in 1987, fifty-seven. Among these plutocrats were a number of $2-million-a-year men, including slugger Mike Schmidt of the Phillies. In signing a two-year contract late in 1987, Schmidt successfully bucked the rumored attempt by owners to hold salaries at $2 million. In Schmidt's words, "I wanted the salary to read $2.25 million probably more for negotiating reasons for my fellow players. . . . I want my fellow players to know that's what top dollar is now." Small wonder then that salaries of baseball players now exceeded those of any rival team sports in America.

In defense of these astronomical player salaries, one could cite major league baseball's continuing prosperity. In this era, annual attendance at major league games repeatedly set new records. After the jarring strike of 1981 limited attendance to 22 million, attendance rebounded to a record 45 million the following year. And despite the national recession, that record fell in 1983. And, after falling by a mere 800,000 in 1984, attendance continued upward. In 1986 annual attendance totaled 47,500,000 and in 1987 it topped 52 million. As in every year since its mini-expansion in 1977, the AL led in attendance, and in 1987 the AL outdrew the NL by 2.5 million. But as always, attendance was unevenly distributed among the clubs. Until 1987 only the Dodgers had topped the 3 million mark in annual attendance, which they did on several occasions, but that year the NL Mets and Cardinals also cracked that barrier. Meanwhile, no AL team had broken the 3 million attendance barrier, but in 1987 the Toronto Blue Jays neared the mark, and in 1988 the Twins surpassed it. Moreover, the attendance

picture was brightening for teams located in older cities like Chicago, Boston, New York, San Francisco, Cleveland, St. Louis, and Milwaukee, where demographic reports showed a reversal of population losses.

However, revenues from soaring attendance alone could not have supported the astonishing salaries of this era. What made the difference was television revenue, which some critics blamed for stimulating the trend by casting ballplayers in the company of highly paid TV celebrities. Be that as it may, in 1983 major league officials negotiated a $1.1 billion, six-year network television contract. When the contract took effect in 1984, revenues from network and local TV sources exceeded those of ticket sales. Although revenues from local TV contracts tended to favor teams that were located in the more lucrative local TV markets, the network TV contract in its final year of 1989 promised a hefty $230 million for all clubs to divide. Nevertheless, it was too soon to write *finis* to the old adage that "at the gate is baseball's fate." In 1985 a reported decline in network TV advertising sales raised the specter that the overexposure of televised sports programs would reverse the trend. Should ratings of televised sports programs decline further, the amount of revenue from network TV would be further reduced.

At this time critics blamed drug abuse by players for lessening the popularity of major sports. But surprisingly baseball's popularity was little affected by revelations of drug abuse by players of this era. In 1980 director Ken Moffett of the Players Association admitted that as many as 40 percent of major league players might be drug abusers. In 1983 the problem reached serious proportions when three Kansas City Royals players were sentenced to jail terms as convicted users. That same year a Dodger pitcher was suspended, and in 1985 a San Diego Padres player was traded for similar offenses. And in 1985 baseball's public image was further tarnished by revelations coming from two Pittsburgh court trials of drug sellers. The testimony named seventeen players as drug users. Although these revelations had no discernible impact on the game's popularity, Commissioner Peter Ueberroth chose to treat the matter as a major scandal. But the commissioner's attempt to force all players to submit to periodic drug tests ran afoul of the Players Association, which insisted that the issue be addressed through collective-bargaining procedures. Still, Ueberroth suspended the accused players and, as a condition for reinstatement, forced each player to donate up to 10 percent of his salary to charities and to engage in antidrug campaigns. After ruling on this matter, Ueberroth announced at the opening of the 1986 season that the drug problem in baseball was solved. But this face-saving claim ignored the reality of the national epidemic of drug abuse and was mocked by the failure of President Reagan's vaunted 1986 antidrug crusade. Indeed, it is most unlikely that the game has been purged of drug abuse, and the problem of devising a punitive policy continued to be an unresolved issue facing the game as it entered the decade of the 1990s.

That major league baseball's popularity was so little troubled by drug scandals, strikes, soaring salaries, or even the economic recession owed much to the dazzling style of play. Indeed, fans of this era witnessed the apotheosis of the big-bang offensives. In the AL, where sluggers consistently outhomered NL swingers by wide margins,

homer records fell like sheaves. Over this seven-year span AL sluggers averaged 2,000 homers a year, with record-breaking seasons succeeding each other over the years 1985–1987. In 1985 AL sluggers bashed 2,178; in 1986, 2,240; and in 1987, a gargantuan 2,634 homers were struck. What's more, NL sluggers in 1987 weighed in with 1,824 homers to break their league's 1970 record.

Major league baseball's 1987 cannonade saw twenty-eight players hit 30 or more homers, including twenty American leaguers. Rookie Mark McGwire of the Oakland Athletics led the AL with 49—an all-time seasonal mark by a yearling, the feat won McGwire a unanimous vote for Rookie of the Year honors. Meanwhile, Andre Dawson of the Cubs matched McGwire's output and won the NL MVP Award despite his team's last-place finish in the NL East. Among the most consistent sluggers of this era, Mike Schmidt of the Phillies led NL sluggers four times, while Dale Murphy of the Braves twice topped the league. By the end of the 1988 season, Schmidt's total of 542 homers ranked him with the all-time leading clouters and following his retirement early in the 1989 season, Schmidt was named Player of the Decade by *The Sporting News*. And at the end of the 1987 season, Reggie Jackson retired from the AL wars with a lifetime total of 563 homers. Jackson's passing from the game left a lonesome gap in AL power circles which young Goliaths like McGwire, Pete Incaviglia, Jose Canseco, George Bell, and Jesse Barfield seemed destined to fill.

But if this era's homer production was unprecedented, seasonal batting achievements were ordinary. Thanks to its designated hitter rule, AL batters annually surpassed NL hitters, with seasonal AL averages topping .260 while those of the NL hovered around the .255 mark. In the NL, black stars continued their batting leadership. Black stars won all of the NL batting titles of this era, with veteran Bill Madlock of the Pirates capturing a pair and young Tony Gwynn of the Padres winning three. It was otherwise in the AL, where a single dominating hitter, third baseman Wade Boggs of the Red Sox, captured four batting titles. An ideal leadoff hitter, the lefty-swinging Boggs batted .349 as a rookie in 1982. Over the next five seasons Boggs averaged a Cobbian .368. Moreover, in 1987 Boggs belted 24 homers to triple his best seasonal homer output thus far. In 1989, he became the first AL player to post seven consecutive 200-hit seasons.

Among the memorable batting feats of this era, Pete Rose gained immortality on September 4, 1985, when the Cincinnati player-manager's single off pitcher Eric Show of the Padres broke Cobb's lifetime record of 4,191 hits. To be sure, Rose needed 2,300 more at bats than Cobb did to turn the trick, but the forty-four-year-old sparkplug put his feat into proper perspective when he said, "I might not be the best player, but I got the most hits." Indeed, and when Rose retired from active play at the end of the 1986 season, he had extended the total hit record to 4,256. While nothing touched Rose's accomplishment, the explosive 1987 season saw Don Mattingly of the Yankees match Dale Long's feat of homering in eight consecutive games, while Paul Molitor of the Brewers hit safely in 39 consecutive games, and rookie catcher Benito Santiago of the Padres hit safely in 34. Santiago's feat won for him NL Rookie of the Year honors.

In the offensive category of stolen bases, NL speedsters

perennially topped their AL counterparts. At this time the newly crowned prince of thieves was outfielder Vince Coleman of the Cardinals. In 1985 Coleman set a rookie record with 110 steals, and at the end of the 1987 season he became the first player ever to swipe 100 or more bases in three consecutive seasons. However, Coleman had yet to top the latest seasonal record of 130 thefts, set by outfielder Rickey Henderson of the Oakland Athletics in 1982. Indeed, in 1990 Henderson broke Ty Cobb's AL record for the most steals, zipped by the mark of Sliding Billy Hamilton, and zeroed in on Lou Brock's major league record.

Not surprisingly the offensive pyrotechnics of these years had pundits wondering whatever had happened to pitching. Indeed, seasonal ERAs skyrocketed in both leagues, with the AL average well above 4.00 and that of the NL above 3.70. Of course this meant that the always volatile pitching-batting equilibrium was again out of whack. For the latest imbalance, observers proffered such explanations as livelier balls, narrowed strike zones, pitchers' fears of retaliation if they threw inside to batters, pitchers relying too much on breaking pitches, and managers relying more on their bullpen and demanding too little of their starters. Indeed, the numbers of complete games pitched by starting pitchers declined as managers relied more on specialized relief pitchers. Among the bullpen specialists, the most celebrated continued to be the firemen who were counted to come on late in a game to save a victory. Among the best were Dan Quisenberry, Goose Gossage, Bruce Sutter (all of whom bowed out in 1990), Todd Worrell, Dave Righetti, Gene Garber (who notched his 200th career save in 1987), and Lee Smith, who set a record by recording 30 or more saves in three consecutive seasons.

Still, it seemed evident that more than yeomanlike relief work was needed to restore pitching to a proper balance with hitting. For now, managers complained of poorly trained pitchers, while pitchers blamed prevailing rules for favoring batters. Nor was it surprising that some pitchers were smuggling in illegal scuffed-ball and spitball deliveries.

However, good pitchers were by no means extinct. In this era Nolan Ryan hurled a record-setting fifth no-hitter in 1981. And at the end of the 1988 season, the forty-one-year-old fireballer, who had lost little of his earlier velocity, extended his all-time leading strikeout total to 4,775 whiffs. Indeed, in 1987 Ryan's 270 strikeouts led the NL, and his 2.76 ERA hardly justified his 8–16 won-loss record. In 1989, the forty-two-year-old Ryan fanned 301 batters and topped the 5000 mark in strikeouts. And in 1990 the venerable fireballer hurled a sixth no-hitter to break his earlier record of five. Among the promising younger pitchers, Dwight Gooden of the Mets blazed his way to a 24–4, 1.53 ERA, with 268 strikeouts in 1985. And the following year Roger Clemens of the Red Sox also went 24–4 to become the first starting pitcher in fifteen years to win the AL MVP Award. Naturally Clemens also won the Cy Young Award that year, and when the ace went 20–9 in 1987, despite early-season ineffectiveness caused by his salary holdout, Clemens won a second Cy Young Award. By winning two straight, Clemens joined the select company of Sandy Koufax, Denny McLain, and Jim Palmer as the only pitchers to win back-to-

back Cy Young Awards. And in 1988 Orel Hershiser's performance from August through October was unprecedented.

Recent Campaigns: The AL, 1981–1990

The long unrealized dream of an era of competitive balance now became something of a reality in the AL, as each of the first seven campaigns produced a new league champion. Moreover, eleven different teams won divisional titles in these years. However, in the West the Oakland Athletics won three divisional championships and captured consecutive league championships in 1988–1989. And the Tigers, Royals, Red Sox, and Angels each won a pair of divisional pennants in this era.

The AL's free-for-all pattern began with the singular campaign of 1981. When the long player strike gutted the middle of that season, a split-season format was adopted in hopes of renewing fan support for the arrested campaign. Under this format, the first half of the season ended when the players walked out on June 11, and the second half ran from the resumption of play in mid-August to the end of the regular playing schedule. Because the June 11 strike date had the Yankees leading the Orioles by 2 games in the East, and the Athletics leading the Rangers by 1½ games in the West, these teams were declared the first-half winners of their divisions. But when the split-season plan barred first-half winners from repeating as divisional champs, the Yankees dawdled to a sixth-place finish in the East's second-half race. Thus the Milwaukee Brewers won the second-half Eastern race by 1½ games over the Red Sox. In the West, the Athletics lost the second half to the Royals by 1 game.

At this point, the split-season script called for a best-of-five-games playoff series to determine the divisional championships. In the East the series went the full five games before the Yankees defeated the Brewers, but in the West the scrappy Athletics swept the Royals. Then in the ensuing League Championship Series the Yankees swept the Athletics. Although the Yankees won the 1981 AL pennant, their overall record was bettered by two other teams. The Yankee victory owed to its pitching staff, whose 2.90 ERA led the league; starters Ron Guidry and Dave Righetti combined for 19 wins, and reliever Goose Gossage saved 20 games. As for the Athletics, whose overall record was the AL's best, they led the league in homers. The Athletics were led by outfielder Rickey Henderson, who batted .319 and led the league in stolen bases, and pitcher Steve McCatty, whose 14 wins and 2.32 ERA led the league. As for the Yankees, their comeuppance came in the World Series. Matched against the resilient Dodgers, the Yankees took the first two games, but then were ignominiously swept. And by losing three games in relief, Yankee pitcher George Frazier added his name to the annals of World Series goats.

In the dog-eat-dog competition of the next six AL seasons, the Yankees failed to win another divisional title. In 1982 the Brewers squeaked to a 1-game win over the Orioles in the East. In winning, the Brewers batted .279 and the team's 216 homers topped the majors, with shortstop Robin Yount winning MVP honors for his .331-29-114 batting exploits. Outfielder Gorman Thomas led the league with 39 homers and drove in 112 runs. And infield-

ers Cecil Cooper (.331-32-121) and Paul Molitor (.302-19-71) complemented Yount's stickwork. But the pitching was shaky, except for starters Pete Vuckovich and Mike Caldwell, who combined for 35 victories. Veteran reliever Rollie Fingers saved 29 games, so the late-season injury that sidelined this mustachioed ace was a crusher. In the West, the California Angels won a close race by 3 games over the Royals. A good hitting team, the Angels finished right behind the Brewers in hitting and homers, and their pitching bettered the Brewers. Starter Geoff Zahn's 18 wins led the staff. Offensively, a quartet of expensive recent acquisitions paced the attack, including infielders Rod Carew (.319) and Doug DeCinces (.301-30-97), and outfielders Fred Lynn (.299) and Reggie Jackson (39 homers and 102 RBIs). Jackson's 39 homers tied Thomas for the league leadership, and the veteran drove in 101 runs. When these two well-matched teams met in LCS play, for a time it seemed likely that Angel manager Gene Mauch might win his first pennant. The Angels took the first two games at home, but were swept by the Brewers in Milwaukee. Thus the Brewers became the first major league team to win an LCS after losing the first two games. But in World Series play it was the Cardinals who rebounded from a 3–2 deficit to defeat the Brewers. This latest loss was the fourth in a row by an AL entry.

But over the next three seasons, three different AL teams ended the NL streak by winning world titles. In 1983 the Orioles drove to a 6-game victory over the runner-up Tigers in the Eastern Division. Pitchers Scott McGregor (18–7), Mike Boddicker (16–8), Storm Davis (13–7), and reliever Tippy Martinez (with 21 saves) headed the league's second-best pitching staff. At bat the Orioles hit .269, and the team's 168 homers led the majors. Shortstop Cal Ripken, Jr.'s .318-27-102 batting won him MVP honors, while first baseman Eddie Murray weighed in with .306-33-111 clouting. Meanwhile, in the West the long-dormant Chicago White Sox stormed to a 20-game victory over the Royals. In landing their first divisional title, the White Sox drew 2 million fans, who saw young Ron Kittle win Rookie of the Year honors with his 35 homers and 100 RBIs. Although lacking a .300 hitter, the White Sox got plentiful power from outfielder Harold Baines (20-99), catcher Carlton Fisk (26-86), and DH Greg Luzinski (32-95). What's more, the White Sox boasted a pair of 20-game winners in Cy Young Award winner LaMarr Hoyt (24–10) and Rich Dotson (22–7). Behind Hoyt, the White Sox won the first LCS game, but the Orioles swept the next three games to win the pennant. The Orioles then dropped the opening game of the 1983 World Series at home, but then swept the Phillies to end the AL's humiliating losing streak.

The following year another new champion surfaced in the AL East, which was now being touted as the strongest division in the majors. Riding the momentum of a 35–5 breakaway gait, the Detroit Tigers went on to win 104 games, enough to lap the Toronto Blue Jays by 15 games. It was indeed a vintage year for manager Sparky Anderson's all-conquering Tigers. Offensively the Tigers led the league in hitting (.271) and homers (187). Shortstop Alan Trammell batted .314, and outfielder Kirk Gibson and catcher Lance Parrish combined to produce 60 homers and 189 RBIs. To top it off, the Tigers also fielded the league's best pitching staff. Starters Jack Morris, Dan

Petry, and Milt Wilcox turned in 54 victories and reliever Willie Hernandez, a recent acquisition from the Phillies, saved 32 games. In 32 of his 33 game-saving situations, Hernandez met the test—an achievement that won him both the Cy Young and MVP awards. Meanwhile, in the weaker Western Division the Royals eked a 3-game win over the Angels and Twins, but the Royals won only six more games than they lost. The Royals batted .268, with outfielder Willie Wilson and DH Hal McRae topping the .300 mark. But the pitching was mediocre and the staff depended heavily on reliever Dan Quisenberry, who saved 44 games. When the Tigers and Royals faced off in LCS play, the Tigers won the 1984 AL pennant by dispatching the Royals in three games. And in World Series action, the Tigers easily defeated the San Diego Padres in five games. By skippering the Tigers to victory, Sparky Anderson became the first manager to win World Series titles in both the American and National leagues.

But the Tigers' view from the top was a brief one. In 1985 they fell 15 games off the pace, leaving the Eastern field to the Blue Jays and Yankees. And at the close of the season, the Blue Jays topped the Yankees by 2 games, to win their first divisional title since joining the AL in the mini-expansion of 1977. The rise of the Blue Jays owed much to general manager Pat Gillick, who, by dint of shrewd trades and canny selections in annual surplus-player drafts, swiftly assembled a pennant contender. In 1985 the Blue Jays' pitching staff led the league, and outfielder Jesse Barfield (.289-27-84) powered an offense that produced a .269 team batting average and 158 homers. Pitcher Dave Stieb's 2.48 ERA led the league's pitchers, although his 14–13 record was disappointing. Starters Doyle Alexander and Jimmy Key combined for 31 victories, and Dennis Lamp posted an 11–0 record in relief. In the lightly regarded Western Division, meanwhile, the Royals became the only AL team of this brief era to repeat as divisional champs. In winning by a single game over the Angels, the Royals batted only .252, but powered 154 homers. Third baseman George Brett's .335-30-112 led the hitters, and first baseman Steve Balboni drove in 88 runs and hit 36 homers. The pitching was good. Young Bret Saberhagen's 20–6, 2.87 ERA won him the Cy Young Award, Charlie Leibrandt's 17 wins came on the league's second-best ERA, and reliever Dan Quisenberry saved 37 games. When the Blue Jays and Royals squared off in the newly extended seven-game LCS, the Blue Jays took a 3–1 lead, but the gritty Royals came on to win in seven games, beating the Blue Jays in their home roost the last two games. In the World Series, the resilient Royals staged yet another memorable comeback against the favored Cardinals. After losing the first two games at home, the Royals fell behind 3–1, but rallied to win the next three games. This latest World Series victory extended the AL's winning streak to three.

In another topsy-turvy campaign, the 1986 Red Sox dethroned the Blue Jays in the East. The Red Sox took the lead in June and hung on to win the division pennant by 5½ games over the Yankees. A .271 team batting assault was fronted by batting champ Wade Boggs (.357-8-71) and outfielder Jim Rice (.324-20-110). Boston's overall pitching was mediocre, but starter Roger Clemens led all pitchers with a 24–4, 2.48 effort that won the big righthander both the MVP and Cy Young awards. While

the Red Sox were winning in the East, the Royals faded in the West as arm miseries tolled on young Saberhagen. Thus the Angels won the division by 5 games over the Texas Rangers. Rookie first baseman Wally Joyner, who replaced the great Carew, batted .299-22-100 to head the Angels' weak .255 batting. But Angel pitching ranked second in the AL, with Mike Witt winning 18 on a sparkling 2.84 ERA, Kirk McCaskill and veteran Don Sutton combining for 32 wins, and reliever Donnie Moore saving 21 games. When the Angels took a 3–1 lead over the Red Sox in LCS play, it now appeared as if manager Gene Mauch might win his first pennant in twenty-five years at the helm of major league teams. Indeed, in the fifth game Mauch's Angels were one pitch away from a league title, but the Red Sox rallied to win the game on heroics by Dave Henderson. The Red Sox then took the next two games at home to land the 1986 AL pennant. In the World Series the Red Sox jumped to a 3–2 lead over the Mets and appeared on the verge of winning their first world title since 1918, but the Mets crushed the dream by winning the last two games at Shea Stadium.

As a climax to the eighty-six-year history of the AL, the 1987 season provided a storied campaign. In a frenetic season which saw AL sluggers set yet another homer mark and attendance climb to new heights, both divisional races were fiercely contested. In the East waged an epic struggle that ended in a 2-game victory by the Tigers. With seven games to play, the Blue Jays led by 3½ games, but incredibly they lost all seven, including three vital games to the Tigers in Detroit. Hefty .272 batting and a major-league-leading 225 homer barrage powered the Tigers, whose shaky pitching staff was bolstered by the September acquisition of veteran Doyle Alexander from the Braves. By posting a 5–0 record with the Tigers, Alexander was named Pitcher of the Month by *The Sporting News*. Among the offensive standouts, shortstop Alan Trammell batted .343-28-105, young catcher Matt Nokes, who replaced the departed Parrish, batted .289-32-87, and forty-year-old first baseman Darrell Evans hit 34 homers and drove in 99 runs. With Anderson's Tigers posting the best record in the majors, scant hope was afforded the Western-winning Minnesota Twins, who defeated the Royals by 2 games to win their first divisional title. Indeed, the Twins surrendered more runs (806) than they scored (786). But the Twins batted .261 and poled 196 homers; outfielder Kirby Puckett (.332-28-99) led the hitters, with outfielder Tom Brunansky and infielders Kent Hrbek and Gary Gaetti combining for 97 homers and 284 RBIs. On the other hand, Twins' pitchers allowed a horrendous 4.63 ERA. But the staff's most respectable member, Frank Viola, stood out as the winningest left-handed pitcher in the majors over the past four seasons. In 1986 Viola posted a 17–10, 2.90 ERA, and veteran Bert Blyleven recorded a 15–12 mark.

Matched against the Tigers in LCS play, the Twins were scorned as hometown dependents whose outstanding home record owed to the vagaries of their much-maligned domed stadium. But the Twins thrashed the Tigers in five games to win their first AL pennant in twenty-two years. Moreover, they went on to beat the crippled Cardinals in a seven-game World Series struggle by scoring all of their victories in their cozy "homer dome" before capacity crowds of screaming, hankie-waving fans. Thus the 1987

World Series stood out as the first where all victories were won on home fields. And the Twins were indeed fortunate to have hosted four of the games in their favorite bailiwick.

In 1988 a timely rule change which redefined the strike zone helped to quell the raging homer epidemic. In an anticlimactic season that saw batting and power hitting tail off, the well-balanced Oakland Athletics dominated the AL West from the start. The A's 104 victories topped the majors and lapped the runner-up Minnesota Twins by 13 games. League-leading pitching, paced by Dave Stewart's 21 wins and reliever Dennis Eckersley's 45 saves, carried the A's who were powered by young outfielder Jose Canseco's .307-42-124 batting. Canseco also stole 40 bases to become the first player to notch at least 40 homers and as many stolen bases. Meanwhile the AL East saw the only hotly contested divisional race in the majors, as the Boston Red Sox edged the Detroit Tigers by a single game; only 3½ games separated the Red Sox from the sixth place Yankees. Barely playing .500 ball at the All-Star break, the Red Sox changed managers—from John McNamara to Joe Morgan—and staged an extended winning streak that carried them to the top. Despite a late-season slump, they hung on to win. Leading the Boston attack, perennial batting champ Wade Boggs batted .366 to lead the majors and outfielder Mike Greenwell weighed in with a .325-22-119 performance. Ace pitchers Roger Clemens and Bruce Hurst each won 18 games and newly acquired reliever Lee Smith saved 29; still, the Red Sox needed the timely pitching of Mike Boddicker, who joined the staff from the Orioles late in the season and won seven games for Boston. However, the Red Sox were mismatched against the A's, who stormed to a sweeping victory in LCS play on the strength of Canseco's 3 homers and Eckersley's four saves in relief of the starters. In the World Series the A's were held in check by the Los Angeles Dodgers' pitchers, notably Orel Hershiser—whose three hits in Game 2 exceeded the Series total of Canseco and Mark McGwire combined.

But the resilient A's came back with a vengeance in 1989. Newcomers included outfielder Rickey Henderson, acquired from the Yankees, and veteran pitcher Mike Moore, picked up in the re-entry draft. Moore signed for $1.9 million, which he repaid by winning 19 games with a nifty 2.61 ERA. Moore buttressed a pitching staff headed by Dave Stewart, whose 21 victories marked the third consecutive year he matched or topped 20 wins. Bob Welch added 17 victories and reliever Dennis Eckersley saved 33 games. Offensively, Henderson led the league in stolen bases (72) and tied for the lead in runs scored (113). Henderson's production offset the loss of slugger Canseco, who missed 88 games because of an injury. Returning to action, Canseco hit 17 homers to augment the 33 hit by McGwire, who drove in 95 runs. Manager Tony LaRussa's team batted .261 with 127 homers. Meanwhile in the AL East, Manager Frank Robinson took over the helm of the hapless Orioles, who won but 54 games in 1988, and drove them to within two games of the divisional championship. For this achievement Robinson was voted AL Manager of the Year, thus becoming the first black manager to win the award in both major leagues. But the AL East championship went to the Toronto Blue Jays, who were skippered by Cito Gaston. In 1989 Gaston

took over a 12–24 team and drove them to a 2-game victory over the Orioles, thus becoming the first black manager to land a divisional title. Toronto's pitching staff was the best in the East, but ranked only fourth in the AL. Dave Stieb's 17–8 pitching led the hurlers, while six Blue Jay sluggers, led by AL homer champ Fred McGriff's 36 blows, reached double figures in homer production. But when the Blue Jays faced the A's in LCS play, the A's crushed them in five games. And matched against the NL Giants in the earthquake-ravaged Bay Area World Series, the A's swept to victory. For pitching two of the four victories, Stewart was named the Series MVP.

Early in the year 1990 continuing animosity stalled the latest negotiations between owners and players for a new Basic Agreement. With tensions inflamed by revelations of owner collusion against free agent players over the years 1985–1987, negotiations broke down. Coming as it did on the centennial anniversary of the great player strike of 1890, this latest confrontation evoked a ghostly sense of *déjà vu*. Thus when the sixth Basic Agreement expired with no new one in place, the owners locked the players out of spring training camps.

The owners aimed at imposing revenue sharing and pay-for-performance plans. For their part, the players rejected these and demanded: a return to the two-year requirement for salary arbitration eligibility; the restoration of twenty-five man playing rosters; protection from owner collusion; and increases in the minimum salary and pension plan funding. With the battle lines drawn, the lockout lasted thirty-two days, affected spring training conditioning, and delayed the opening of the championship season. When a settlement was reached on March 19, the new agreement compromised on the salary arbitration issue, hiked the minimum salary to $100,000, increased the owners' contribution to the pension fund, and provided for punitive damages to be paid in the event of any future conspiracies by owners against free agent players. The owners dropped their revenue-sharing and pay-for-performance proposals, and the players approved the expansion of the NL to fourteen clubs in 1993. Following the settlement, an attenuated spring training program began March 20 and the opening of the playing season was delayed a week. But the 162-game schedule was preserved by extending the regular season three days to make up the cancelled early games. This seventh Basic Agreement promised four years of peace, but lingering animosity between players and owners indicated that the struggle would be resumed once this latest pact expired.

With baseball hostilities returning to their natural habitat of the playing fields, fans were treated to a season of unpredictable events and performances. For one, the 1990 season saw a record nine no-hitters tossed by major league pitchers, a total that matched the number produced in some entire decades of this century. Among these, ageless Nolan Ryan's latest masterpiece extended his record total to six. The veteran also boosted his all-time strikeout mark by fanning another 232 batters. And among relief pitchers, Bobby Thigpen of the White Sox posted a new seasonal mark with 57 saves.

In the AL such pitching pyrotechnics reduced the number of .300 batters to six, but slugger Cecil Fielder of the Detroit Tigers, who had played in Japan during the 1989 season, walloped 51 homers to become the first to top the 50 mark since 1977. In 1990, too, perennial league batting champs Wade Boggs and Tony Gwynn faltered, allowing veterans George Brett and Willie McGee to claim titles. On another note, the season saw Commissioner Fay Vincent bar owner George Steinbrenner from running the New York Yankees. The Yanks finished last in the AL East with the worst record in the AL. The New Yorkers also suffered the ignominy of being swept in their 12 encounters with the Oakland A's.

Indeed, in 1990 the talent-rich Oakland A's were heavy favorites to repeat as World Champions. With star pitchers Bob Welch and Dave Stewart winning 27 and 22 games and reliever Dennis Eckersley saving 48, the A's overcame a mediocre .254 team batting average to win 103 games, the best mark in the majors. But the A's were dogged by the Chicago White Sox who, though finishing 9 games back in the division, attracted over 3 million fans while playing their last season in old Comiskey Park.

In the weaker AL East the Boston Red Sox and the Toronto Blue Jays staged the closest race in any major league division, a struggle that ended with Boston on top by two games. The Red Sox were led by pitcher Roger Clemens' 21-6 effort that included a major league leading 1.93 ERA. In LCS play Boston's vulnerable bullpen, the worst in the majors, faltered. In sweeping the Red Sox the A's won a third consecutive pennant. Although heavily favored to win the World Series for a second straight time, the A's were swept by the NL champion Cincinnati Reds.

Recent Campaigns: The NL, 1981–1990

Although less competitively balanced than the AL, the NL campaigns of this era were hotly contested. Each one of the twelve teams won a divisional title in these years. But the Dodgers won four Western titles and captured two league pennants and two world titles, and in the East the Cardinals won three divisional races and three league championships, yet won only one World Series. Dual divisional titles were won by the Mets, Giants, and Cubs, and singletons were won by the Expos, Padres, Phillies, Braves, Astros, Pirates, and Reds.

When the long players' strike of 1981 gutted team playing schedules by an average of 55 games, the split-season format was unveiled upon resumption of play in August in hopes of salvaging the campaign. By dint of their 1½-game lead over the Cardinals on the June 11 strike day, the Phillies were declared first-half winners in the East; and by virtue of a mere half-game lead over the Reds on that fatal date, the Dodgers became the first-half winners in the West. These were close calls to be sure, but no closer than the results of the second-half races. In the NL East, the Montreal Expos finished a half-game up on the luckless Cardinals, while the Houston Astros edged the snakebit Reds by 1½ games in the West. As frustrated runners-up in two close calls, the Cardinals and Reds with the best overall record in the NL received no recognition. However, the defiant Reds later raised their own home-made pennant as a symbol of protest. In the playoffs for the divisional titles, the Expos beat the Phillies in five games to win in the East, and the Dodgers rallied from a 2–1 deficit in games to beat the Astros in the West. The division-winning Expos and Dodgers then met in the usual

League Championship Series, which the Dodgers won. Once again rallying from a 2–1 deficit, manager Lasorda's men edged the Expos. In winning the NL's forlorn 1981 championship, the Dodgers batted .262, led the league in homers with 82, and fielded the league's second-ranked pitching staff. Rookie pitcher Fernando Valenzuela won his first eight games and finished with a 13–7 mark to pace the staff, while outfielders Pedro Guerrero (.300-12-48) and Dusty Baker (.320-9-49) led the batting attack. In World Series play, the Dodgers once again dug themselves a hole by losing the first two games. But once again they rebounded, this time sweeping their old Yankee tormentors to win the 1981 world title.

With the game's image blighted by the "dishonest season" of 1981, the NL sorely needed a dramatic flourish to regain its credibility. Mercifully this was supplied by the extremely close divisional races of 1982. In the NL East a four-team struggle ended with the Cardinals topping the Phillies by 3 games. At bat the Cardinals hit .264, but with scant power (67 homers). Outfielder Lonnie Smith was the only regular to top the .300 mark, but first baseman Keith Hernandez batted .299 and drove in 94 runs, and outfielder George Hendrick powered the team with his .282-19-104 hitting. By way of compensation, the Cardinals led the league in fielding and stolen bases, and owned the league's second-best mound corps. Starters Joaquin Andujar and Bob Forsch each won 15 games, and ace reliever Bruce Sutter won 9 and saved a league-leading 36 games. In the West, meanwhile, the Braves won their first 13 games and hung on for dear life thereafter to edge the Dodgers by a game. Offensively, the Braves batted only .256, but led the league in homers with 146. Outfielder Dale Murphy's 36 homers generated a league-leading 109 RBIs, and third baseman Bob Horner hit 32 homers and drove in 97 runs. Veteran knuckleball hurler Phil Niekro's 17–4 effort headed the pitching staff, which needed every one of reliever Gene Garber's 30 saves. In LCS play the Braves' mediocre pitching tolled as the Cardinals swept to victory. In ensuing World Series play, the Cardinals fell behind the heavy-hitting Brewers 3–2, but rallied to win the final two games at home. This latest World Series victory was the fourth straight for NL contenders.

When the Cardinals succumbed to poor pitching in 1983, the Phillies snatched the Eastern title by 6 games over the Pirates. The Phillies did it with a brilliant stretch drive, winning twenty-one of their last twenty-five games. Offensively, the aging Phillies batted only .249, but third baseman Mike Schmidt's 40 homers led the league, and his 109 RBIs led the team. A sound pitching staff, fronted by John Denny's Cy Young Award-winning 19–6 effort and reliever Al Holland's 25 saves was a decisive factor in the victory. Meanwhile, in the West the Dodgers also mounted a September stretch drive to topple the Braves by 3 games. Like the Phillies, the Dodgers' .250 hitting was lackluster, but the team led the league in homers (146); outfielder Guerrero's 32 homers and 103 RBIs headed the assault. A major factor was the team's pitching staff, whose 3.10 ERA was the league's best. Valenzuela and Bob Welch combined for 30 victories, and reliever Steve Howe saved 18. In LCS play, veteran hurler Steve Carlton's two victories paced the Phillies to victory in four games. However, the Philadelphia

"Wheeze Kids" fell to the Orioles in five games in the 1983 World Series.

As the Phillies sank to fourth place in 1984, the long-suffering Chicago Cubs notched their first pennant of any sort since 1945. In downing the Mets by 6½ games in the East, the Cubs staged a second-half rally, fronted by ex-Phillie infielder Ryne Sandberg's MVP-winning .314 batting. Dodger castoff Ron Cey contributed 25 homers and 97 RBIs, and young first baseman Leon "Bull" Durham weighed in with 23 homers and 96 RBIs. And the pitching staff was bolstered by yet another recent acquisition, Rick Sutcliffe, whose 16–1 record won him the Cy Young Award. Starter Steve Trout chipped in with 13 victories, and reliever Lee Smith won 9 games and saved 33. While the Cubs were winning in the East, another newcomer, the San Diego Padres, easily won the Western title by 12 games over the runner-up Braves. The Padres batted .259, with young outfielder Tony Gwynn leading the league with his .351 batting. The team's modest total of 109 homers was augmented by third baseman Graig Nettles and outfielder Kevin McReynolds, each of whom poled 20. More distinguished was the pitching staff, whose 3.48 ERA ranked third in the league. Able starters Eric Show, Ed Whitson, and Mark Thurmond combined for 43 victories, and veteran reliever Goose Gossage won 10 and saved 25 games. In LCS play the Cubs pounded out a pair of early victories at Wrigley Field, but the surprising Padres swept the next three games at home to become the first NL team ever to win an LCS after losing the first two games. Sad to say, however, the Padres' world title hopes went aglimmering as the Tigers trounced them in five games in the 1984 World Series.

The following year the Cardinals won another NL pennant. In fending off the rising New York Mets by 3 games in the East, the Cardinals relied on league-leading batting and base stealing. Outfielder Willie McGee's league-leading .353 batting won him the MVP Award, and outfielder Vince Coleman won Rookie of the Year honors by stealing 110 bases—a new record for a rookie. Among other stalwarts, second baseman Tom Herr batted .302; first baseman Jack Clark, recently acquired from the Giants, hit 22 homers and drove in 87 runs; and shortstop Ozzie Smith, who won the league's Gold Glove Award for a sixth straight year, batted .276. What's more, Cardinal pitching ranked second in the league, with ex-Pirate John Tudor leading the hurlers with a 21–8, 1.93 ERA performance. Starters Andujar (21 wins) and Danny Cox (18 wins) lent sturdy support, as did relievers Jeff Lahti and Ken Dayley. The pair's 30 saves compensated for the loss of free agent Sutter. As the Cardinals were winning in the East, the Dodgers went on to win the Western title by 5½ games over the Reds. Offensively, the Dodgers' .261 hitting was led by outfielder Guerrero's .320-33-87 hitting. Better still, the Dodger pitching corps led the majors with a 2.96 ERA. The starting quartet of Orel Hershiser, Bob Welch, Jerry Reuss, and Fernando Valenzuela produced 64 wins, and the bullpen saved 31 games. In LCS play, the well-armed Dodgers took the first two games of the newly established seven-game format, but the Cardinals swept the next four to win the NL pennant. Pitted against the underdog Royals in the 1985 World Series, the Cardinals won three of the first four games, including the first two in the Royals' home lair. But the Royals won the

fifth game at St. Louis and the final two games back home. The sixth game was marred by a disputed call at first base that gave the Royals a life of which they took full advantage. The Royals then won the final game in an 11–0 laugher, and their victory extended the recent AL World Series winning streak to three years.

The following year the New York Mets ended the AL's victory flurry with a dramatic win. In dominating the NL East, the 1986 Mets won 108 games to lap the runner-up Phillies by 21½ games. Offensively, the versatile Mets led the league in hitting (.263), poled 148 homers, and stole 118 bases. First baseman Keith Hernandez (.310-13-83) headed the charge, with outfielder Darryl Strawberry and catcher Gary Carter powering a combined 51 homers and 198 RBIs. As icing on their victory cake, the Mets fielded the best pitching staff in the majors. Starters Bob Ojeda (18–5), Dwight Gooden (17–6), Sid Fernandez (16–6) and Ron Darling (15–6) were formidable, as was the bullpen duo of Roger McDowell (14 wins, 22 saves) and Jesse Orosco (8 wins, 21 saves). While the Mets were compiling the best record in the majors, the Houston Astros were winning the Western Division by 10 games over the Reds. Offensively, the Astros batted .255 with 125 homers. Outfielder Kevin Bass batted .311-20-79 to head the hitters, while first baseman Glenn Davis powered 31 homers and drove in 101 runs. Backing the hitters was the league's second-best pitching staff, fronted by Mike Scott's 18–10 hurling, which was accompanied by a league-leading 2.22 ERA. While the outcome of the LCS appeared to be a foregone conclusion, the Astros hung tough before losing in six games to the Mets. The Red Sox also fell to the Mets in World Series play, but not before throwing a scare into manager Davey Johnson's crew. Indeed, the Red Sox took a 3–2 lead in games before the Mets rallied to win the final two games at Shea Stadium.

The following year most observers picked the swaggering Mets to repeat, but the resilient Cardinals took the 1987 Eastern title by 3 games. Although outhit by the league-leading Met batters, the Cardinals mustered .263 hitting, which they backed by stout relief pitching to pull off their victory. Offensively, the Cardinals' 94 homers were the fewest by any major league team this season, but first baseman Jack Clark bashed 35 and drove in 106 runs. Third baseman Terry Pendleton drove in 96 runs, while shortstop Ozzie Smith drove home 75 runs with nary a homer to his credit. But the Cardinals atoned with a sprightly running game led by outfielder Vince Coleman, who topped 100 seasonal steals for the third straight season. Likewise the shaky pitching staff that completed only ten games was backed by a redoubtable relief crew whose ace, Todd Worrell, saved 33 games. Meanwhile in the NL West, the Giants won over the bridesmaid Reds by 6 games. The Giant victory was a dramatic turnabout for a team that in 1985 had finished last in their division with 100 losses. A fine balance of hitting and pitching made the difference in 1987. At the plate the Giants batted .260 with 205 homers and were led by first baseman Will Clark's .308-35-91 pyrotechnics. Moreover, the pitching staff boasted the league's best ERA, even if the Giant starters completed only 28 games. What mattered was that relievers Scott Garrelts and Jeff Robinson combined for 22 wins and 31 saves. When the Giants met the Cardinals in LCS play, injuries to Jack Clark and Pendle-

ton cast the Cardinals as underdogs. But the Cardinals won their third NL title of the era by overcoming a 3–2 deficit in games with a pair of home-field victories. In World Series play, it was the crippled Cardinals who were favored over the unheralded Twins, but the American Leaguers won four games, all of them in their cozy domed stadium, to edge the Cardinals in seven games.

The pitching rule modification that stemmed the homer tide in 1988 wreaked havoc with NL batters in 1988 as only five regulars attained the .300 mark. Although no New York Met batter joined this circle, Darryl Strawberry boomed a league-leading 39 homers and drove in 101 runs and outfield mate Kevin McReynolds produced a .288-27-99; they powered the Mets to 100 victories and an easy 15-game victory over the Pirates in the NL East. With a 2.91 ERA, the Mets also boasted the best pitching staff in the majors. David Cone led the starters at 20-3 and Dwight Gooden and Ron Darling combined for 35 wins. Relievers Randy Myers and Roger McDowell saved 42 games. In the West, meanwhile, the Los Angeles Dodgers took the lead in July and hung on to win by 7 games over the Cincinnati Reds who along the way got a rare perfect-game pitching performance from Tom Browning. But the Dodgers held claim to the best individual pitching performance of the year when their ace, Orel Hershiser, finished the regular season with a new record of 59 scoreless innings. In addition to a 23–8 record Hershiser led all NL pitchers in innings pitched, complete games, and shutouts. Offensively the modest Dodger attack was powered by newly acquired free agent Kirk Gibson (.290-25-76) and veteran outfielder Mike Marshall (.277-20-82). The lightly regarded Dodgers were afforded little chance against the Mets in LCS play. But the Dodgers prevailed in seven games with Hershiser starting three games and relieving in another. And then they upset the Oakland Athletics in the World Series, despite crippling injuries to Gibson, pitcher John Tudor, and catcher Mike Scioscia.

But there was no encore to such heroics, and the 1989 Dodgers fell to fourth place in the NL West. An impotent .240 batting average that included only 89 homers sabotaged the pitching staff's major league-leading 2.95 ERA. Hershiser again led the league in innings pitched and finished second in ERA, but was held to a 15–15 performance. And the workload took its toll on the Dodger ace, who was sidelined by a crippling shoulder injury at the outset of the 1990 season.

As the struggling Dodgers fell from grace, the Giants and the Padres battled for the 1989 Western title. The talent-laden Reds straggled in fifth, as the investigation of their manager, Pete Rose, culminated in his expulsion from the game. San Diego's reliever Mark Davis saved a league-leading 44 games for the Padres. Offensively, Tony Gwynn's league-leading .336 batting and 203 hits and Jack Clark's 26 homers, 94 RBIs, and a major-league-leading 132 walks fronted a Padre attack that fell three games short of their goal. The victory went to manager Roger Craig's Giants, whose pitching staff, headed by Scott Garrelts's league-leading 14–5 winning percentage and 2.28 ERA, ranked third in the league. At bat, outfielder-third baseman Kevin Mitchell won MVP honors by blasting a matchless 47 homers and 125 RBIs. First baseman Will Clark weighed in with a .333 batting mark

and scored 104 runs to lead the league. That the Giants' .250 team-batting average ranked fourth in the league underscored the NL's impotent batting, which averaged .246 and produced only five .300-plus batters. While the Giants eked out a narrow victory in the West, manager Don Zimmer's Chicago Cubs coasted to a six-game victory over the much-touted, but underachieving Mets in the East. A league-leading .261 batting attack, paced by first baseman Mark Grace's .314 hitting and second baseman Ryne Sandberg's .290 batting, compensated for the pitching staff's sixth-place ranking in the league.

In LCS play the Giants downed the Chicagoans in five games, but then were victimized by the Oakland A's, who swept to victory in the World Series of 1989.

If the status quo was the rule in the AL in 1990, it was otherwise in the NL as the teams resumed play after the lockout-delayed start of the season. When the smoke of battle lifted, the reigning divisional winners of 1989 were dethroned by a pair of fifth-place finishers of the previous year. In gaining the heights in the NL East, the Pittsburgh Pirates won by 4 games over the underachieving New York Mets. Outfielder Barry Bonds batted .301-33-114 and stole 52 bases, and first baseman Bobby Bonilla added 32 homers and 120 RBIs to propel the Pirates. A 22-game winner, Doug Drabek, led the staff, which received a 6-2 boost from Zane Smith, acquired from the Montreal Expos in August.

In the NL West the Cincinnati Reds won four fewer games than did the Pirates, but the team's 91-70 log topped the Los Angeles Dodgers by 5 games. In winning the Western title, the Reds took over on day one and after winning their first seven games, they clung to the top all the way to become the first NL team to accomplish this feat since the inauguration of the 162-game schedule in 1962.

Starters Jose Rijo and Tom Browning combined for 29 wins, but the Reds' bullpen crew, the self-styled "nasty boys" Ron Dibble and Randy Myers, saved 42 games. Among the hitters, rookie Hal Morris played in 107 games and batted .340 and regulars Barry Larkin and Mariano Duncan batted .300. Chris Sabo and Eric Davis combined for 49 homers. Manager Lou Piniella, one of many Steinbrenner managerial castoffs, replaced Pete Rose, who watched the Reds' fall exploits from his prison vantage point.

When the Pirates and Reds clashed in LCS play, the Pirates won the opener but fell to the Reds in six games. Given little chance against the Oakland A's, the NL champion Reds opened the World Series by shutting out their rivals 7-0 behind Jose Rijo. Then with Rijo adding another victory and Hatcher smacking 9 hits in 12 at bats for a new World Series batting mark, the Reds swept the A's! This unexpected victory, reminiscent of the 1914 sweep of the Philadelphia A's by the lowly Boston Braves, brightened a season that appeared to be ill-starred at its outset by the bitter labor struggle.

Campaigns of the Nineties: The AL 1991–1992

While AL teams arrayed themselves for the 1991 campaign, the crushing World Series setback preyed on the minds of many players and officials. The AL East had supplied only one league pennant over the past six seasons, and seemed chronically weak. In 1991 Toronto won by seven games over the Tigers and Red Sox, who tied for second with identical 84–78 records, while all others in the East posted losing records.

In landing their third divisional pennant since 1985, the Blue Jays attracted a record 4 million fans to their all-weather Skydome stadium. Combined with record throngs at Chicago's new Comiskey Park, such crowds enabled the AL to set an all-time pro sports attendance mark for 1991 (over 32 million). What Toronto fans saw was a redoubtable pitching staff of solid starters backed by a bullpen that posted the most saves (60) in the league. Offensively Toronto ranked seventh in batting and eighth in homers, but young second baseman Roberto Alomar switch-hit for .259-9-69 and outfielder Joe Carter, like Alomar newly acquired in a trade with San Diego, powered the team with 33 homers and 108 RBIs.

AL prospects for a World Series title were brighter in the strong Western Division where every team played .500 ball, and where fans were treated to such exploits as Rickey Henderson setting a new lifetime stolen base record and Nolan Ryan pitching his record seventh no-hitter. Heavily favored to repeat as division champs were the Oakland A's, but manager Tony LaRussa's shell-shocked team fell to fourth place, 11 games off the pace. Into this power vacuum rushed the Minnesota Twins, who matched their Atlanta Braves counterparts of the NL West by moving from worst to first in a single season, an unprecedented tandem.

The revitalization of the Twins followed canny moves by GM Andy MacPhail (a grandson of the innovative Larry MacPhail) in the free agent market. Among these moves MacPhail landed the aging free agent pitcher Jack Morris, who signed an incentive-laden contract which earned him $3.8 million for the season, and he also enlisted free agent third baseman Mike Pagliarulo. Both moves paid handsomely as Pagliarulo batted .279 in 121 games while Morris pitched 247 innings and posted and 18–12 record. Backing Morris was sophomore Scott Erickson (20–8) and Mets' castoff Kevin Tampani (16–9) while another ex-Met, Rick Aguilera, emerged as the team's ace reliever (42 saves). Offensively, the Twins batted a league-leading .280 and poled 140 homers. Outfielder Kirby Puckett (.319-15-89) keyed the attack with rookie-of-the-year second baseman Chuck Knoblauch, playing his first season out of Texas A&M, batting .281. The Twins outlasted a challenge from the Chicago White Sox to win by eight games.

In the LCS the twins shook off an early loss to the Blue Jays to score a convincing victory in five games behind Puckett's .492-2-6 batting onslaught. The victory set the stage for one of the most dramatic World Series clashes in recent memory. Playing at home in their enclosed Metrodome, the Twins won the first two games, but lost the next three games in the Braves' lair. Returning home, the Twins tied the Series with a 4–3 victory and nailed down the world title the next night on Series MVP Jack Morris's gritty ten-inning 1–0 victory.

The 1992 season began with the Twins giving every indication of repeating their success. Grabbing an early lead in the AL West, they went on to lead the majors in batting (.277), with Puckett's .329 hitting ranking second in the AL. But in late July the resurgent Oakland A's

swept the Twins at the Metrodome and grabbed a lead which they never relinquished. At season's end the A's owned a 96–66 record with the Twins six games back, followed by the White Sox in third place.

Oakland's return to the top was sparked by first baseman Mark McGwire's reversion to form; the big slugger hit 42 homers and led the league in slugging. As a team the A's batted only .258 with 142 homers, but more decisive support came from the pitching staff, which ranked fourth in the league with a 3.73 ERA. Mike Moore (17–12), Dave Stewart (12–10), and Ron Darling (15–10) headed the staff, but the club's greatest asset was their nonpareil relief ace Dennis Eckersley (51 saves, a 1.91 ERA, and the Cy Young Award).

While the A's were upsetting the status quo in the AL West, no eastern team could nudge the Toronto Blue Jays from the top spot. Once again home fans backed their team in numbers above 4 million. And in landing his third AL East title since assuming his post in 1989, manager Cito Gaston saw his men match Oakland's 96–66 winning clip while eking out a four game win over the rising Milwaukee Brewers. Saddling themselves with the third highest payroll in the majors, the Blue Jays signed free agents DH Dave Winfield and pitcher Jack Morris, the hero on the 1990 Twins. Morris emerged as the AL's winningest pitcher at 21–6. Juan Guzman recovered from an injury to go 16–5–2.64, and Todd Stottlemyre won 12 games. Like the A's, the Blue Jays relied heavily on their bullpen with reliever Tom Henke saving 34 games. On offense the fortyish Winfield batted .290–26–108 and outfielder Joe Carter added 34 homers and 119 RBIs. But more help was needed and the Blue Jays landed ace pitcher Dave Cone in a late season trade with the Mets; in the September stretch drive Cone contributed four vital wins.

In LCS play, the Blue Jays shrugged off a first-game loss at the hands of the AL West champion Oakland A's and went on to thrash their rivals by winning four of the next five games. The victory cast the Toronto Blue Jays as the first foreign team ever to win a major league championship and Gaston as the first black manager ever to land a big league pennant.

Capacity crowds packed the Skydome when the Blue Jays came home after splitting the first two games played in Atlanta. By single-run margins the Blue Jays then won the next two games to take a 3–1 lead in the Series. But the Braves pounded Morris, a loser in all four of his postseason appearances, to win the breakaway game and send the Series back to Atlanta. And there, in an 11-inning 4–3 victory with Winfield driving in the winning runs on a double, the Blue Jays became the first foreign-based team to win a World Series.

Campaigns of the Nineties: The NL, 1991–1992

In the decade just past, each NL team managed to win at least one divisional race. But this unprecedented state of affairs came apart in the NL East when the 1991 Pirates coasted to an easy 14 game victory over the runner-up Cardinals while no other Eastern contender played winning baseball. Bobby Bonilla's .302–18–100 and Barry Bonds' .292–25–116 heroics, coupled with lefty John Smiley's 20–8 hurling, handed the Pirates an opportunity

to avenge their loss to the Reds in the 1990 LCS struggle.

While preseason pundits picked the World Champion Reds to repeat in the NL West, key players like Davis and Rijo went down with injuries, fielding lapses consigned the team's defense to eighth place in the league, and the pitching staff also ranked eighth in effectiveness. As a result the Reds finished with a losing record. With the Reds out of contention, the Western race became a dog fight between the Los Angeles Dodgers and the surprising Atlanta Braves. Offensively the Dodgers were bolstered by the acquisition of free agent outfielders Darryl Strawberry and Brett Butler. Thus fortified, the Dodgers battled into the last week of the season before losing by one game to the Braves.

A last place finisher in the 1990 NL West fray, the Braves' metamorphosis from worst to first was buoyed by the acquisition of free agent third baseman Terry Pendleton, who led NL batters with a .319 average. Pendleton's 22 homers and 86 RBIs were augmented by lusty hitting from outfielders Ron Gant and Dave Justice. What's more, the Braves' pitching staff, headed by Tom Glavine (20–8), young Steve Avery (18–8), and John Smoltz (14–13), turned in the league's third best ERA (3.49). In holding off the Dodgers, the Braves overcame the loss of outfielder Otis Nixon, who was suspended for drug usage, and an injury to second baseman Jeff Treadway. In plugging these gaps, outfielder Lonnie Smith and infielder Mark Lemke performed ably during the September struggles.

In the hard fought struggle for the NL championship, lefty Avery emerged as the MVP by notching two victories while Smoltz blanked the Pirates 1–0 in the climactic seventh game played at Pittsburgh.

Matched against the Minnesota Twins in the World Series, the Braves won all three games in their home park and were sparked by Lemke's timely hitting. At these games Atlanta fans incurred the enmity of organized Native American protesters by their ritualized "tomahawk chop" gestures and their orchestrated war whoops. However, the Braves lost all four games at the Minnesota Metrodome, including the final game as Smith's mental error on the basepaths cast him as the Series goat in his team's 1–0 loss.

As the NL team girded for action in 1992, soothsayers eyed the Dodgers and Mets as likely division winners. Each spent lavishly in the free agent marketplace and the two boasted the highest payrolls in the majors at $40-plus million. For their part the Dodgers acquired ailing outfielder Eric Davis in a trade with the Reds and paid him a salary of $3.6 million, and for nearly $4 million they signed free agent Tom Candiotti, a knuckleball pitcher who played with the 1991 Blue Jays. Meanwhile the Mets dealt three key players to the Royals to acquire star hurler Bret Saberhagen and infielder Bill Pecota. And the Mets also snagged free agent Bobby Bonilla, the versatile star of the Pirates, for a five-year contract calling for more than $5 million a season. For added insurance the New Yorkers picked up free agent first-baseman Eddie Murray for a two-year contract worth $7.5 million. But when the dust settled at the end of the 1992 campaign, the Mets and the Dodgers were horrendous losers. Both teams were bested by the low-payroll Astros, who were forced to play the longest road trip in decades because of the pre-empt-

ing presence of the Republican National Convention in Houston. In their 26–game, 28–day jaunt the Astros went 12–14 and finished the season at .500. By contrast the affluent Dodgers finished 63–99 for the majors' worst record while the Mets edged the Phillies by only two games in escaping the NL East cellar. Injuries to Davis and Strawberry, who combined for a mere 10 homers and 57 RBIs, hobbled the Dodgers while Saberhagen's injury racked the Mets.

As these plutocrats faded from contention the end result was *status quo ante bellum* in both NL divisions. In the East the Pirates shook off Bonilla's loss to snatch an early lead and mount a balanced attack that carried them to 96 victories, enough to stave off a September challenges by Montreal, which finished 9 games behind. In repeating as division champs, the Pirates ranked third in both pitching and batting, led in the latter department by catcher Don Slaught (.345–4–37 in limited duty), and able outfielders Andy Van Slyke (.324–14–89) and Barry Bonds (.311–34–103). Van Slyke ranked second among league hitters and Bonds, a demon hitter in the stretch drive, ranked second in homers and also stole 39 bases. Moreover, both outfielders were Gold Glove winning fielders.

In the West meanwhile, Atlanta posted a 98–64 record, the best in the majors. In recording their second straight Western victory, the Braves relied upon the best pitching staff in the league (3.14 ERA). At bat the Braves led the league in homers (138). Third baseman Pendleton (.311–21–105) and outfielder Otis Nixon (.294–2–22, with 41 stolen bases) headed the hitters. Part-time outfielder Deion Sanders (.304–8–28), who doubled in brass as a star defensive back with the National Football League's Atlanta Falcons, emerged as a rising star, but his double duty as a pro athlete raised questions about his future. Indeed, it was a football injury the previous year that ended the career of another promising star, Bo Jackson.

In a hard fought reprise of their 1991 duel for the NL championship, the Braves took a 3–1 lead in games, but then had to fend off a spirited Pirate charge. In the final game at Atlanta, the Braves, down 2–0 in the ninth inning, mounted a historic rally. The winning hit came off the bat of rookie pinch hitter Francisco Cabrera, who in the regular season had batted only ten times. His single with two out in the ninth scored the tying and winning runs and gave the Braves another shot at the World Series crown.

Playing at home, the Braves won the opener, but lost the next night and then dropped the first two games played in Toronto. Those last two losses extended the Braves' skein of indoor World Series losses to six. Down 3 games to 1, the Braves stayed alive as Lonnie Smith, the 1991 Series goat, smashed a grand-slam homer to key a 7–2 victory. That domed stadium victory sent the Braves back to their Atlanta longhouse where "tomahawk-chop" cheering fans tried vainly to inspire a comeback victory. But after staging a ninth-inning rally to stay alive in the sixth game, the Braves lost by a single run in 11 innings, thus becoming the first team to lose consecutive World Series matches since 1978. And for a second straight time, Native Americans were smiling over the result.

Scanning the Future: Storm Clouds Ahead?

As with most seasons, the 1992 campaign had its dazzling moments. Robin Yount of the Brewers and George Brett of the Royals became the 17th and 18th players to join the 3000 hit club; Bert Blyleven joined the California Angels for his 24th season in the majors, and bounced back from shoulder miseries to boost his lifetime pitching victory total to 287 games. Other happenings were more mundane. The 1992 season saw the end of the bumper harvest of no-hitters of the previous two seasons; in 1992 Kevin Gross of the Dodgers pitched the only one. And if no divisional race was close enough to kindle ferverish September excitement among fans, at least the NLCS and the World Series stirred enough interest to force Presidential candidates to skirt these games when scheduling their televised debates.

Other memorable incidents affected the games of 1992. There was the April earthquake in the Los Angeles area that postponed some games and might have contributed to the Dodgers' shell-shocked seasonal performance. Hard after this natural disaster came some man-made ones like the Los Angeles riots and the bus accident, involving a contingent of California Angels, that severly injured Manager Buck Rodgers. But such events were overshadowed by happenings in other reaches of baseball as when the U.S. Olympic baseball team failed to win a medal at Barcelona, or when an American team won the Little League World Series after it was revealed that the "winning" Filipino team had played overage players.

Upbeat and downer events like these go far to explain baseball's enduring, captivating appeal to its fans. And the upcoming 1993 season, with the long awaited NL expansion to 14 teams, will surely attract more fans even if a recent poll (taken during the 1992 football season) showed sports fans perferring the gridiron game by a wide margin.

The owners of the NL's newly enrolled Colorado Rockies and Florida Marlins, respectively based at pro-football stadiums in Denver and Miami, each paid an entry fee of $95 million for their franchises. A welcome windfall for established clubs, this money will be split among teams in both leagues.

But among the dark clouds of uncertainly hovering over the big league game, none is more menacing than the threat of renewed labor strife between owners and players. Although the Basic Agreement does not expire until December 1993, a renewal clause allows either side to reopen negotiations a year earlier. Money, of course, is the burning issue. The latest fix on the player salary spiral showed annual salaries of 1992 averaging nearly $1 million with 269 players getting that much or more.

To arrest this trend, owners voted, 15–13, in December 1992, to reopen negotiations and, if necessary, impose a lockout in 1993. In defending this hard line, embattled owners cited decreased operating profits—down from $143 million in 1990 to $8.7 million in 1991, to a reported breakeven point in 1992. And with network TV ratings of televised games lowering in 1992, owners, who will each receive $15.4 million from this source in 1993 (the last year of the current contract), rightly fear that the next

contract will yield considerably less. Owners also cited the lingering national recession as a clinching argument for reining in player salaries, but recessions of course are cyclical.

In response to such claims, Don Fehr of the Major League Players Association cited the game's resilience in the face of the recession, as measured by generally rising attendance since 1986, and the fact that 1991 player costs of $130 million overall only amounted to 47% of revenues. Thus, whether contract negotiations begin in 1992 or at the end of the 1993 season, owners are likely to push for a revenue-sharing plan with a salary cap. But some owners are urging that wealthier clubs, based in lucrative local TV markets like New York, Chicago, and Los Angeles, share revenues with poorer clubs like Cleveland. Indeed, in 1992 Cleveland, while operating with an $8.1 million payroll, still managed to post a better record than did the affluent Dodgers and Mets. A potentially divisive argument, it threatens to drive a wedge between have and have-not owners and prevent owners from mounting a united front against the players.

Moreover, maintaining a united front requires leadership and owners of 1992 faced a leadership crisis of their own making. In September a cabal of owners forced the resignation of Commissioner Fay Vincent for being overly zealous in pushing NL team realignment and for his excessive use of his power to act "in the best interests of baseball." Thus, Vincent may have been the last of the eight fetish-kings of baseball as the owners seem bent on restructuring the office and installing a Chief Executive Officer who will be responsible to a board of directors chosen from the 28 clubs.

Should the owners resolve their leadership crisis and also come to terms with the powerful Major League Players Association, they must address other vexing problems. Among these the DH issue looms large and continues to distort World Series competition between the two leagues. Although NL purists firmly oppose this rule, it has been a boon to the AL, where attendance has risen 18 percent since 1987 while remaining virtually the same in the NL. That fans have always preferred watching hitting displays over low scoring games is a historical fact.

Another issue centers about the vulnerability of team managers and general managers. Denied organized power, these officials are easy scapegoats for owners. Since 1900 more than 600 team managers have been sacked, including a record 14 in 1991. And if GMs formerly did much of the sacking, their own vulnerability has been exposed; since 1987 more than half of the 26 GMs have walked the plank.

But such issues pale alongside the longstanding problem of ending persisting discrimination against minorities in baseball. Although black and Latino players now reap salaries commensurate with their skills, these minorities still occupy less than 10 percent of managerial and administrative positions in the game. Perhaps manager Cito Gaston's feat of becoming the first black manager to pilot a World Champion will speed the pace of such needed reforms.

As American baseball gropes toward the future, a litany of the game's problems ought not to discourage lovers of the game. On the contrary, engaging in arguments over the problems that beset the game has always been a requirement of being a fan.

## CHAPTER 3

Team Histories

Frederick Ivor-Campbell

When the National League awarded expansion franchises to Denver and Miami in June 1991, the number of major league clubs reached 28 in each league—the most since 1884. As the Colorado Rockies and Florida Marlins begin play in 1993, they bring to 110 the number of clubs (plus those of the Negro major leagues) that have played major league ball at one time or another since baseball's first professional league—the National Association—was organized in 1871. Some of the early teams dropped out after only a few games, but several have played for more than a century, and one—the present Atlanta Braves—has played every season from 1871 to the present. The only existing franchise older than Atlanta's (which originated as the Boston Red Stockings, then became the Boston and Milwaukee Braves before moving to Atlanta) is the Chicago Cubs, which organized in 1870, a year before league play began. The White Stockings (as they were first known) missed two seasons (1872–1873) in the aftermath of the great Chicago fire, but have since then continuously represented the same city longer than any other club in baseball history.

Here are brief histories of the 28 current big-league clubs, arranged alphabetically by city or state. These are followed by summary histories of the 82 other clubs—now defunct—that at one time also represented their cities in the major leagues.

Atlanta Braves

The Atlanta Braves, who first played in 1871 as Boston's Red Stockings, are the only club to field a team every season of professional league baseball. When the game's first openly professional club, the Cincinnati Red Stockings, decided to revert to amateur status, manager/outfielder Harry Wright and three of his teammates took their talents (and club nickname) to Boston, where, with infielders Ross Barnes and Harry Schafer and pitcher Al Spalding, they formed the nucleus of a team that would dominate the five-year history of the first professional league, the National Association. After a close third-place finish in their first year, the Red Stockings won four pennants in convincing fashion, including a 71–8 record in 1875 with an .899 winning percentage that has never since been approached in major league ball.

When the National League replaced the NA in 1876, four of Boston's best players (including Spalding and Barnes) deserted the club for Chicago. But after a fourth-place finish in 1876, the Red Stockings lured pitcher Tommy Bond from Hartford and finished at the top in 1877 and '78. Bond dominated NL pitching, winning 80 games (40 each year), 22 more than his nearest rival. Although he won another 43 in 1879, Boston slipped to second.

In 1880 the Red Stockings suffered their first losing season as they fell to sixth. After another sixth-place finish the next year, Wright left to manage Providence, but Boston rebounded to third in 1882 and surprised everyone in 1883 by outplaying favored Chicago and Providence to capture their seventh pennant.

Providence knocked them out of the race late in 1884, and Boston remained out of contention the next four seasons. In 1889, though, with several players signed from the defunct Detroit Wolverines (including batting champ Dan Brouthers), and 49 wins from pitcher John Clarkson, the Beaneaters (as they were now more commonly known) waged a two-team race for the championship with the New York Giants. Boston won as many games as the Giants, but lost two more and finished a game back.

Frank Selee, who had managed two straight minor league pennant winners, was hired from Omaha along with his star pitcher, Charles "Kid" Nichols. Their arrival in 1890 ushered in Boston's second golden era. Before they left the club twelve years later, the Beaneaters had won five more NL pennants. Nichols won 27 games in his rookie season, but Boston—decimated by defections to the outlaw Players League—finished only fifth. With the return of some of the defectors in 1891, Clarkson won 33 games, Nichols recorded the first of seven consecutive 30-win seasons, and the Beaneaters returned to the top.

When the NL expanded in 1892 from eight teams to twelve, the schedule too was expanded, and the season divided into two halves. Boston won the first half, and the Cleveland Spiders the second. In a World Series to determine the league champion, the Beaneaters (who at 102–48 had the best over-all season record) defeated the Spiders.

The split season was abandoned and the schedule reduced in 1893—and Boston captured its third straight pennant. Center fielder Hugh Duffy hit .363. The next year, when hitters exploded for a league BA of .309, Duffy led the way with a .440 that is still the major-league record. His Beaneaters didn't win the pennant, but they became the first club in a decade (and the last until 1920) to hit over 100 home runs. Five Beaneaters drove in 100 runs or more, and the team set a big league record for runs scored (1,221) that still stands.

Boston dropped out of contention for a couple of years, but bounced back in 1897 to edge Baltimore for the pen-

nant by two games. In the Temple Cup series, though (played between the first- and second-place teams for the world title), the Orioles overwhelmed Boston four games to one. The next year the schedule was expanded again, and again (as in 1892) Boston won 102 games to lead the league, winning their twelfth pennant. But as the league had abandoned the four-year-old Temple Cup play, there was no World Series.

After coming in second in 1899, Boston dropped out of pennant contention for fourteen years, finishing as far back as 66½ games (in 1906) and losing as many as 108 (in 1909). Five times the club finished last, including the four years from 1909 to 1912. The Braves (as they were now known) rose to fifth in 1913 under new manager George Stallings, but seemed through the first half of 1914 to be securing for themselves another bed in the cellar.

In mid-July they stood a last-place eighth in a tight field. Six days and six wins later they were third. By mid-August they had climbed to second; on August 26 they replaced the New York Giants in first. For two weeks they alternated between first and second, then took off to win the pennant by 10½ games.

Boston's heroes were pitchers Dick Rudolph and Bill James, both in only their second full big league seasons. Rudolph won 27 games in 1914 and James won 26; then they added two more each in the Braves' World Series sweep of the heavily favored Philadelphia Athletics. But Rudolph crafted only one more 20-win season, and James won only 5 games in two final major-league campaigns.

Classy fielding kept the Braves competitive the next two years. In 1915 they spurted once again out of the cellar—but only to second place this time. They began their climb earlier the next year, but a seven-game losing streak in early September dropped them out of a tie for first. They rallied, but finished third. It was the Braves' last close race for thirty-two years.

In the twenty-nine years from 1917 through 1945 the Braves finished only three seasons as high as fourth, and only once as close as nine games from the top. With four years in the cellar and eleven in seventh place, the team finished near the bottom of the league more than half the time. In 1935 slugger Wally Berger led the league in home runs and RBIs, but the Braves lost a club-record 115 games in their worst season ever.

In 1946, with dynamic new ownership headed by contractor Lou Perini, a new manager—Billy Southworth, who had led the Cardinals to three pennants and two world championships—and the return of war veterans like pitchers Warren Spahn and John Sain, the Braves neared the end of their long depression with their first winning season in eight years. At the end of the season Boston acquired third baseman Bob Elliott from Pittsburgh. He enjoyed a career year in 1947, powering the Braves to third place. Spahn and Sain won 21 games each.

Spahn dropped to 15 wins in 1948, but Sain won 24. Four veterans—plus rookie shortstop Alvin Dark—hit over .300. With the league's best pitching and hitting, the Braves moved out in front in June, and shook off their last challengers with a September spurt that left them at the end champions by 6½ games.

But from there on, the Braves' path in Boston was downhill. Cleveland beat them in the World Series, and

the club dropped to fourth for the next three years. Southworth resigned part way into the 1951 season. In 1952 the team fell to seventh; home attendance was less than one-fifth what it had been four years earlier. The next spring Perini moved the franchise to Milwaukee in the league's first realignment since 1900.

The move was a spectacular success. Not only did the Braves rebound to second place, but attendance jumped 649 percent over their previous year in Boston to set an NL record of more than 1.8 million. The league's best pitching staff was led by the trio that would anchor Milwaukee's years of greatness: veteran Warren Spahn, sophomore Lew Burdette, and rookie Bob Buhl. Sophomore third baseman Eddie Mathews led the league in home runs; with outfielder Henry Aaron, who came up the next year, Mathews would give the Braves a consistent source of power through their Milwaukee years.

A July-August surge in 1954 pulled the Braves within a few games of the top before they slipped back, but they set another attendance record and became the first NL club to draw more than two million at home in a season. In 1955 the Braves finished a distant second to the Dodgers, but 1956 produced a great three-way race that found the Braves slightly ahead through much of the season until five straight losses in early September brought them even with the surging Dodgers. It was a dogfight the rest of the way, not settled until the final day, when a Dodger victory over Pittsburgh left Milwaukee a game back in second.

The acquisition of veteran second baseman Red Schoendienst from St. Louis in June 1957 steadied the infield and gave the team a frequent baserunner for Mathews and Aaron to drive in. In August the Braves drew away from the pack, and recovered from a September slump to win the pennant by a convincing 8 games over St. Louis. The Yankees took them to seven games in the World Series, but Burdette's shutout in the finale brought the Braves their first world championship in forty-three years.

Milwaukee repeated as league champions just as convincingly in 1958, but in the autumn classic, after taking the first two games from the Yankees, they lost the Series in seven. The race was much tighter in 1959 until the Giants moved away from the Dodgers and Braves in August. But in September the Giants faltered as the others surged past them, and the season ended with the Braves and Dodgers tied. In a best-of-three playoff, the Dodgers took the pennant in two games—but both by only one run and the second only after twelve innings.

A portent for the Braves' future could be seen in the crowd of under 20,000 that attended the first playoff game in Milwaukee. After setting a third NL record in 1957, Milwaukee attendance had gradually declined, dropping below two million in 1958, the club's second pennant year, and even farther in this year of the tight pennant race. As the Braves declined on the field to a more distant second in 1960, then successively to fourth, fifth, and sixth, so too did the decline continue in the stands to well under a million. Perini sold his majority interest in the club. A tighter race in 1964 stirred a little more fan interest, but when attendance dropped in 1965 to a new Milwaukee low of just over half a million, the club pulled up stakes again and moved to Atlanta.

The Braves' won-lost records in 1965 and '66 were

nearly identical. But in Atlanta attendance improved by almost a million. Of the Braves who had brought glory to Milwaukee, most were gone from the club or in decline. But Aaron was still at the height of his powers, and younger players were beginning to make their mark. Reliever Phil Niekro, for example, was converted to a starter in 1967 and responded with the league's best ERA.

After finishing no higher than fifth in their first three seasons in Atlanta, the Braves celebrated 1969, the first year of divisional play, with a late-season drive that carried them out of a tight five-team race to the championship of the West. Veteran Orlando Cepeda, newly acquired from St. Louis, joined Aaron in supplying power, and Niekro won 23 games as the Braves won ten in a row to clinch the title in their next-to-last game. In the league's first Championship Series, though, the "Miracle" Mets of New York swept Atlanta in three games.

Aaron remained a presence in Atlanta for five more years, and Niekro, after a relatively dismal season in 1970, established himself over the years as one of the game's most durable and effective pitchers. But the team went nowhere. When they enjoyed an occasional good season (as in 1974, when they won 88 games), at least two other clubs did much better. Aaron returned to Milwaukee (to the AL Brewers) in 1975, and attendance sank to an Atlanta low. Yachtsman Ted Turner bought the club in 1976 and attendance rose, but the team sank to the bottom of the division for four years.

In 1982, though, with power from outfielder Dale Murphy and third baseman Bob Horner, and exceptional pitching from Niekro (17–4) and reliever Gene Garber (30 saves, a club record), Atlanta grabbed the division lead with a season-opening 13-game winning streak, and recovered from a midsummer collapse to edge Los Angeles by one game for their second divisional crown. But they were swept in the LCS, this time by St. Louis.

For the next two seasons Murphy's league-leading slugging carried the Braves to second place—a close 3 games behind Los Angeles in 1983 (in a race which pushed Atlanta attendance over two million for the first time), and a tie with Houston 12 games behind San Diego the next year. By 1986, though, they had sunk into the division cellar. Murphy boosted them up a notch in 1987 with the most productive season of his career, but as his power at the plate dropped the next year, the Braves sunk to their worst finish in fifty-three years. Fans fell away, and Atlanta became the first big-league club in three seasons to attract fewer than a million spectators to its home games.

Veteran outfielder Lonnie Smith broke out of a five-year slump in 1989, his second Atlanta season, to become one of baseball's most potent hitters, and in 1990 strong seasons by young sluggers Ron Gant and rookie Dave Justice gave Atlanta hope for the future. But Dale Murphy, in the third year of his decline, was traded to Philadelphia in August, and the Braves, mired in the cellar for their third straight season, remained the weakest draw in major league baseball.

With the first bottom-to-top comeback in NL history, the Braves captured the West in 1991. As Atlanta's home attendance zoomed back above 2 million, the Braves won a battle with Los Angeles that saw eleven ties or lead changes in the season's final weeks, then took the city's

first pennant in a seven game playoff against Pittsburgh. Free agent third baseman Terry Pendleton joined Justice and Gant to power Atlanta's offense, while a trio of young pitchers—Tom Glavine, Steve Avery and (in the second half, after a dismal start) John Smoltz—anchored one of the league's best mound staffs.

In the World Series, the Braves moved to a 3–1 edge over Minnesota before falling short by one extra-inning run in each of the final two games.

Nineteen ninety-two was a near-repeat of 1991. Once again the Braves edged Pittsburgh for the pennant, although this time it took a come-from-behind win in the final at bat of Game Seven to do it. And once again they faltered in the World Series, this time succumbing to Toronto in six games.

Baltimore Orioles

The history of major league baseball in Baltimore dates back to 1872, to the Lord Baltimores of the National Association, and includes the great National League Orioles of the 1890s. The city was also represented in the American League's first big league seasons, 1901–1902. But when those Orioles moved to New York in 1903 and became the Highlanders (later the Yankees), Baltimore was left without a big league club for more than half a century, until the transfer of the Browns from St. Louis in 1954.

The current Orioles didn't get their start in St. Louis, though. Their first home was Milwaukee, where they finished in the AL cellar in 1901. When they moved to St. Louis the next year, they lured several valuable players from the city's NL Cardinals—including 1901 batting champ Jesse Burkett, star shortstop Bobby Wallace, and the Cards' three best pitchers. They also took on the Cardinals' discarded nickname, becoming the new St. Louis Browns.

The Browns finished a strong second to the Philadelphia Athletics in their first St. Louis season, but fell to sixth the next year and, except for a fourth-place finish in 1908 (thanks to the pitching of newly acquired veteran Rube Waddell), remained mired in the second division until 1920. Late in the 1913 season a young Branch Rickey was hired to manage the Browns. In his two full seasons he was unable to lift the club out of the second division, but he did sign college star George Sisler (whom he had coached at the University of Michigan), who became, as the Browns' first baseman, one of the game's all-time greats.

In 1916, his first full season, Sisler led the Browns in hitting as they caught fire in August to record their first winning season in eight years. Pitcher Urban Shocker was obtained from the Yankees two years later and by 1920 had developed into a 20-game winner. Also in 1920, Sisler connected for what is still a major league record 257 hits and batted .407 to help move the Browns up to fourth, their first finish that high since 1908 (though their won-lost record of 76–77 remained on the losing side). The next year Shocker's 27 victories brought them a winning season and third place. And in 1922 the team recorded its finest record ever in St. Louis: 93 wins and a .604 winning percentage.

The 1922 Browns, led by Sisler's sizzling .420 BA, hit .313 as a team to lead the league. Left fielder Ken Williams ran away with the RBI title and beat out Babe Ruth and Tilly Walker for the home run crown. (Ruth, to be honest, did miss nearly a third of the season that year.) Sisler and Williams even finished one-two in AL stolen bases. And though Shocker slipped a bit to 24 wins, he led a pitching staff that recorded the league's lowest ERA. The team led the league in the standings throughout July and into August before the Yankees nudged ahead of them. The Browns hung close, but didn't regain the lead, remaining second, a heartbreaking single game back, at season's end.

Falling back to fifth the next year, as Sisler missed the whole season with a sinus infection, the Browns remained out of contention for the next twenty-one years, dropping to their lowest point in 1939, 64½ games out of first, with 111 losses. They recovered for three winning seasons in the war years 1942–1945, finishing a distant third in 1942, and capturing their only St. Louis pennant in 1944, edging the Detroit Tigers on the final day after trailing them through most of September. The World Series—an all-St. Louis affair—proved anticlimactic for the Browns as they lost to the Cardinals in six games.

The Browns finished third in 1945 before sinking back into the second division. Even the club's purchase by the dynamic Bill Veeck in July 1951 couldn't rouse them out of the depths. (A month after buying the Browns, Veeck made his best-remembered move, bringing in midget Eddie Gaedel for one plate appearance—he walked.)

Unable to earn either victories or money in St. Louis, Veeck in September 1953 sold the club to a Baltimore group, who moved the Browns and renamed them the Orioles. The new owners hired the brilliant Paul Richards to rebuild the team as manager, both in the front office and on the field. It took him (and Lee MacPhail, who became general manager and president in 1958) several years to move the Orioles above .500, but in 1960, young third baseman Brooks Robinson found he could hit as well as field, and rookie Jim Gentile drove in 98 runs; the team made its first run for the pennant since 1944. In first place in early September, they finished second when the Yanks won fifteen straight to pass them by.

The next year the O's did even better, winning six more games than they had in 1960 as Gentile hit 46 home runs and drove in 141. But it was an even better year for New York and Detroit, and Baltimore finished a distant third.

When Hank Bauer was brought in to manage the Orioles in 1964, the team entered its golden decades—twenty years which saw them win seven division titles, six pennants, and three world championships, with only two finishes below third. With Robinson driving in runs and left fielder Boog Powell slugging at a league-leading pace, the O's finished 1964 with wins in seven of their final eight games. But the White Sox won their last nine and the Yankees put together an eleven-game streak near the end to take the flag and leave Baltimore third, two games back.

After another third-place finish in 1965, the Orioles acquired slugging Frank Robinson from Cincinnati and moved second-year pitcher Jim Palmer into the starting rotation. Palmer won 15 to lead a balanced staff, and Frank Robinson captured the Triple Crown. With both Robinsons and Powell driving in 100 runs or more, the O's romped to their first Baltimore pennant. They continued the romp in the World Series, holding Los Angeles to a total of just two runs as they swept to their first world title.

A drop in offensive production and the loss of Palmer to injuries for most of the season plunged Baltimore into a tie for sixth in 1967. Palmer was out the next year, too, but pitchers Dave McNally and Jim Hardin burst to the forefront with fine seasons to lift the club back to second.

Baltimore coach Earl Weaver, a pennant-winning manager in the O's farm system, replaced Hank Bauer at the Orioles' helm in mid-1968 to begin what became one of the longest and most successful managerial tenures of recent times. In fourteen full seasons Weaver led his club to six Eastern Division titles and six second-place finishes, with one season each in third and fourth. His teams featured fine hitters and fielders, but it is the pitching that stands out above the rest. In seven of the fourteen years the Oriole staff compiled the league's lowest ERA, including five consecutive seasons (1969-1973). Oriole pitchers put together in those fourteen years twenty-one 20-win seasons (eight of them by Jim Palmer), and garnered six Cy Young Awards.

In the first three years of divisional play (1969-71) Baltimore ran away with the East championship and swept to the pennant each time in the League Championship Series. The 1969 team (despite an embarrassingly easy loss to the New York Mets in the World Series) is often ranked among the greatest of all time. With overwhelming pitching and fielding, the Orioles took the division crown by 19 games, winning a club-record 109. In fielding, seven percentage points separated the AL's second-best team from the worst; the Orioles fielded three points better than the second-best team. And Oriole pitchers gave up nearly a run less per game than the league average.

Baltimore's performance in 1970 was nearly as impressive. Mike Cuellar and Dave McNally won 24 games each, and Jim Palmer contributed 20 more wins to the O's total of 108. This year they won the World Series as well as the pennant, rolling over Cincinnati in five games.

In the 1971 World Series, though, Pittsburgh came back from losses in the first two games to defeat the Orioles by a run in game seven. The O's captured divisional titles in 1973 and '74, but it was 1979 before they again triumphed in the LCS. Once again, however, they faced the Pittsburgh Pirates in the World Series, and once again took the Series lead, only to fall again in the seventh game.

The 1979 pennant was Weaver's last, as late-season Oriole surges in 1980 and '82 fell just short. But in 1983 the O's—paced by the pitching of veteran Scott McGregor and rookie Mike Boddicker, and the hitting and fielding of Cal Ripken, Jr., and Eddie Murray at short and first—made new manager Joe Altobelli look good. After a comfortable divisional win, they trounced Chicago's White Sox in the LCS and the Philadelphia Phillies in the World Series.

Declining after 1983 despite the return of Earl Weaver in 1985–1986, the Orioles finished last in the East in 1986. Though they rose to sixth in 1987, their .414 winning percentage was their lowest in thirty-two years. Then in 1988 they hit rock bottom, not only finishing last but

also beginning the season with an AL record-setting twenty-one consecutive defeats.

Baltimore's rebound was even more startling than its plummet. Under manager Frank Robinson (who had been handed the hapless O's early in the 1988 season) the 1989 Orioles took over first place in late April, held the lead through August, and stayed within the reach of the division title until Toronto defeated them in the season's penultimate game to clinch the crown. The newly potent bat of catcher Mickey Tettleton and splendid relief from rookie Gregg Olson highlighted the Baltimore resurgence. Olson remained effective in 1990, but the offense faltered, and an August-September slide dropped the Orioles out of the race.

The O's began slowly in 1991, and manager Robinson was replaced by coach Johnny Oates in May, with the club in last place. Although Cal Ripken put together an MVP season, the O's never caught fire, and finished sixth, 24 games out. In 1992, however, playing in the packed new Orioles Park at Camden Yards, Baltimore snapped back to challenge Toronto through much of the season before slipping to third, 7 games out.

Boston Red Sox

Since the end of World War Two, the Red Sox have won the American League pennant four times, only to lose the World Series each time in the seventh game. It was not always thus. In their first two decades they were the league's most successful club, winners of six pennants and five world championships. (No World Series was played the year of their second pennant.)

Organized in 1901 as one of four new eastern clubs in Ban Johnson's newly major league AL, Boston's Americans (or Pilgrims, Puritans, Plymouth Rocks, or Somersets, as they were variously called) quickly established themselves as one of the game's strongest teams. Star third baseman Jimmy Collins was lured from Boston's NL club to manage the new Americans, and he assembled a team that included such former NL standouts as slugger Buck Freeman and pitcher Cy Young. Finishing a strong second in the AL's inaugural major league season, the Pilgrims quickly supplanted their mediocre NL counterparts in the hearts and wallets of Boston fans.

After a third-place finish in 1902, the Pilgrims ran away from the rest of the league in 1903 to take their first pennant by 14½ games over Philadelphia. Young led the league in victories for the third straight season, Freeman took titles in home runs, total bases, and RBIs, and second-year outfielder Patsy Dougherty finished first in hits and runs scored. In the first modern World Series, Boston overcame Pittsburgh's favored Pirates, thereby confirming the AL's claim to major league status.

Boston repeated as pennant winners in 1904, but by a much narrower margin, after a struggle with New York's Highlanders that wasn't settled until the next-to-last day of the season. The NL Giants refused to play Boston in a World Series that year.

Over the next few years, as the Pilgrims dropped into the league cellar, new owner John I. Taylor (whose father, *Boston Globe* publisher Charles Taylor, was said to have bought the club for his son to give him something useful to

do) rid the team of many of the players who had brought it glory. Eventually Taylor was himself maneuvered out of the club presidency, but it turned out he had not been a wanton destroyer. In driving out the old guard he had been making room for new young players: pitcher Joe Wood, for example, and a sprightly outfield of Tris Speaker, Harry Hooper, and Duffy Lewis. The club—now known as the Red Sox—rose out of its depths in the final years of Taylor's presidency, even challenging the league leaders through much of 1909 before dropping away in late August. In 1911, in one of the last acts of his presidency, Taylor had, with his father, purchased land in Boston's Fenway section and built a new ballpark.

Sparked by the spectacular pitching of Joe Wood and Speaker's play at the bat and in center field, the Red Sox of 1912 took the league lead in early June and were never headed, finishing with a club-record 105 victories. In the World Series they edged John McGraw's Giants and Christy Mathewson in one of the most exciting Series ever, four games to three, with one tie. Three years later, with a staff that boasted the AL's four top pitchers in winning percentage (including rookie Babe Ruth), the Sox captured their fourth pennant, staving off a late-season surge by Detroit to finish 2½ games in front. After a first-game loss to the Phillies in the World Series, Boston recovered to sweep the next four by one run apiece.

Joe Wood's ailing arm finally gave out, and Tris Speaker was traded to Cleveland at the start of the 1916 season following a salary dispute. But with Ruth winning 23 games to lead the team, the Sox slid past the White Sox and Tigers in mid-September to take their fifth flag, and waltzed over Brooklyn in the Series.

Incipient disaster struck the Red Sox that December when New York theatrical entrepreneurs Hugh Ward and Harry Frazee bought the club. They put little cash into the deal, counting on future profits to pay the bulk of the purchase price. Ward sailed for Australia, leaving Frazee to run the club. For a while the future looked bright. After a second-place finish in 1917, Frazee hired minor league executive Ed Barrow as manager, and when many of the team's regulars left for military service in World War One, Frazee bought and traded for worthy replacements. In a season shortened a month because of the war, the Sox edged Cleveland for their sixth pennant and defeated the Chicago Cubs for their fifth world championship.

Frazee's theater losses put him in a financial bind and gradually forced him to sell off the best of his players— mostly to the Yankees, who had plenty of money, and an office just a short hop from Frazee's New York theater. Though the Sox fell to sixth place in 1919, Babe Ruth kept attention fixed on the team as he went to the outfield and startled the baseball world with a record 29 home runs. But that winter Frazee sold Ruth to the Yankees for $100,000 and a $300,000 mortgage on Fenway Park.

The Red Sox were embarked on a fifteen-year sojourn in the second division that even a 1923 change in ownership was powerless to end. In the eleven years from 1922 through 1932 the Sox emerged from last place only twice. In 1932 they reached their nadir, losing 111 games and finishing 64 games out of first.

But in 1933, young, wealthy Tom Yawkey bought the club and promptly began what would be a lifetime effort to restore Boston to its former glory. His first efforts to buy

success ready-made with such established stars as Lefty Grove, Jimmie Foxx, and Joe Cronin pulled the club out of the cellar but failed to lift it into pennant contention. But as general manager Eddie Collins began turning up young players to join the veterans, the Sox' fortunes rose. The emergence between 1938 and 1942 of players like Bobby Doerr, Ted Williams, and pitcher Tex Hughson brought Boston a level of success not seen since 1918. In four of the five years they finished second to the Yankees, achieving in 1942 their highest winning percentage since 1915.

The loss of most of these newcomers to military service in World War Two delayed further progress. But with the arrival of rookie pitching sensation Dave Ferriss in 1945, and the acquisition of slugging first baseman Rudy York that winter, the club was prepared for its returning war veterans to join in bringing Boston its greatest season since 1912. With 104 victories, the 1946 Sox won their long-delayed seventh pennant by 12 games over second-place Detroit. Only in the World Series was there disappointment as the heavily favored Sox bowed in Game Seven by one run.

The Yankees ran away from the pack in 1947, but the three years that followed saw the Red Sox three times in the throes of pennant fever. In 1948, after falling back a bit in late September, the Sox won four at the very end to tie Cleveland for first—but lost the one-game playoff. The next year they were 12 games behind the Yankees on July 4, but pulled up gradually to take a one-game lead into the final two-game series in New York. One Sox win would give them the flag, but the Yankees took both games. In 1950 Boston played the league's best ball through July and August, to pull within a game of the Yankees on September 18, but then lost four in a row and all hope of the pennant.

In 1951 the Sox collapsed at season's end to finish third, 11 games back. They came no closer for the next fifteen years, finishing with eight consecutive losing seasons from 1959 through 1966, when they suffered their second successive ninth-place finish in a league now expanded to ten teams.

In 1967 the Sox awakened from their long slumber. A ten-game win streak in mid-July shot them out of mediocrity into the midst of a four-team race for the pennant that was not settled until Boston beat Minnesota and Detroit split a doubleheader on the final day, leaving the Sox on top. Carl Yastrzemski, who had replaced Ted Williams in left field seven years earlier, replaced him now in the fans' awe as he clinched the Triple Crown with a game-winning home run and six other hits in the final two must-win games. But Boston lost the World Series to St. Louis in seven games.

It was eight years before the Red Sox won another pennant, but they came close in 1972, losing the AL East crown by half a game to Detroit in the season's final series. They led the division two years later from mid-July through early September, then fell apart and finished third. But the next year, 1975, they maintained to the end the lead they first took in May, and swept Oakland in the League Championship Series for their ninth pennant. Television viewers will long remember Carlton Fisk's home run that won Game Six of the World Series from Cincinnati. But Red Sox fans also remember that the Sox lost Game Seven the next day, 4–3. Owner Tom Yawkey died

the following July without the world championship he had sought for more than forty years.

Boston contended seriously in 1977 in a tight three-way race, pulling ahead for a time in June and again in August, but ultimately falling 2½ games short. The next year, though, the Sox pulled off another amazing finish. After blowing a 7½-game late-August lead to fall 3⅓ games behind New York in mid-September, they won their final eight scheduled games to tie the Yankees. But in the playoff, Yankee Bucky Dent's three-run pop-fly homer over Fenway's cozy left field wall proved Boston's ruin. The Sox rallied in the eighth to draw within a run, but with two out and a man on third in the ninth, Yastrzemski popped up and the season was history.

Yaz retired in 1983, full of years and honor, but outfielders Jim Rice and Dwight Evans remained from the 1975 champions. Joined by a new generation that included, in Wade Boggs, baseball's most consistent hitter since Ted Williams, and, in Roger Clemens, Boston's most exciting pitcher since Joe Wood, the Sox in 1986 won their tenth pennant, with an amazing comeback over California from a 3–1 deficit in the League Championship Series. In Game Six of the World Series they were within one pitch of capturing their first world title in 68 years. But they lost the game, and in Game Seven—once again—the Series.

When a pitching decline dropped the Sox to fifth place in 1987, and the All-Star break the next year found them barely above .500, manager John McNamara was replaced by coach Joe Morgan. The Sox responded with nineteen wins in their next twenty games and, despite a slump at season's end, took the title in the AL East by one game. In the LCS, though, Oakland swept to the pennant in four games.

In 1989 Boston moved to within half a game of the division lead in August before slipping back to third, but in 1990, with pitcher Clemens back in peak form after a season and a half below par, the Sox arrived at midseason in first place. After trading the lead back and forth with Toronto, they captured the crown of the East on the season's final day. But in the LCS Oakland again swept past them to the pennant.

Roger Clemens won his third Cy Young award in 1991 and the Sox came from 11½ games back in August to within half a game of first-place Toronto in September. But they dropped eleven of their remaining fourteen games to finish in a second-place tie with Detroit. Manager Joe Morgan was replaced by Butch Hobson for 1992, but the downhill slide continued. Dreadful hitting and fielding added insult to a season haunted by injury, and plunged the Sox into the AL East cellar for the first time since the advent of divisional play.

California Angels

Of the ten teams added to the major leagues in the 1960s and '70s, the Angels were quickest to put together a winning season, finishing third in the American League in only their second year of play.

Former cowboy actor and singer Gene Autry brought the club into being as the Los Angeles Angels in December 1960. Playing their first season, 1961, in Los Angeles's

Wrigley Field, a former minor league park with power alleys only five feet deeper than the foul poles, five Angels hit 20 or more home runs. Though the team finished seventh in the standings, they were second in homers only to the mighty Yankees.

What the Angels lost in home runs in 1962 (when they moved out of Wrigley Field into the L.A. Dodgers' new stadium), they more than made up in pitching. Paced by rookie Dean Chance, the Angels nearly doubled their wins on the road, and as late as mid-August stood in second place, within striking distance of New York. Though they tailed off in September, they finished a respectable third, 10 games back.

The team collapsed to ninth the next year, but in 1964 Chance's pitching and splendid relief by rookie Bob Lee overcame the Angels' continuing inertia at the bat to lift them back into the first division. Among Chance's league-leading 11 shutouts were six 1–0 victories.

Los Angeles became the California Angels in 1965 in anticipation of their move south to a new stadium in Anaheim the following year, but neither the name change nor the new location stirred them out of the second division. In 1967, though, with below-average run production but the league's third-best pitching, the Angels in mid-season shot up from ninth to third before leveling off to fifth. After dismal seasons in 1968–1969, career years in 1970 by pitcher Clyde Wright (22 wins, including a no-hitter) and newly acquired left fielder Alex Johnson (202 hits and a league-high .329 BA) helped the Angels snap back with an 86–76 record that matched their previous best (1962).

The seven losing seasons which followed 1970 were somewhat redeemed by the arrival in 1972 of pitcher Nolan Ryan, who burst into superstardom as an Angel, setting a modern record of 383 strikeouts in 1973 and hurling four no-hitters in three years (1973–1975). Ryan's effectiveness dipped in 1978, but the club as a whole came to life, contending closely for the Western Division title all season until Kansas City shot ahead in September.

In 1979 Don Baylor became the first (and, so far, only) DH to be named league MVP, as a renewed offense powered California to its first division title. Baltimore stopped the Angels in the LCS, though. The team's run production dropped off dramatically the next year and the club followed up its best season with its worst.

After another losing season in 1981 (during which Jim Fregosi was replaced as manager by twenty-year veteran Gene Mauch), California lured free-agent slugger Reggie Jackson from the Yankees. With Jackson leading a resurgent offense and Geoff Zahn headlining the league's second-best pitching staff, the Angels rebounded to a new team high of 93 wins in 1982, and their second division title. They defeated Milwaukee in the first two games of the LCS, but lost the next three. A disappointed manager Mauch retired.

Again, in 1983, the Angels followed a championship with a poor season—not quite as bad as 1980, but still their third worst ever. In 1984 they rebounded to .500, good enough for second in a weak division. As a foretaste of continuing improvement, pitcher Mike Witt concluded his rise to staff ace with a perfect game on the season's last day.

Gene Mauch came out of retirement to manage the

Angels again in 1985. With pitching that featured splendid relief from newly acquired Donnie Moore (31 saves; 1.92 ERA), the team led the division much of the season, but lost three games of four to Kansas City in the final week to fall a game behind the Royals into second.

With Witt's 18 wins and 2.84 ERA pacing the staff and rookie first baseman Wally Joyner leading a revitalized offense, California won the 1986 division crown with ease. In the LCS against Boston, the Angels took three of the first four games, and in Game Five were within one pitch of capturing their first pennant. But the Boston Red Sox rallied to win.

In 1987 California for the third time followed up their division championship with a losing season, this time dropping the season finale to tie for last place in the AL West. Manager Mauch retired again, this time for good. After another losing season brought them home a distant fourth in 1988, the Angels signed Doug Rader to manage the club. They also acquired a veteran pitcher—Bert Blyleven—who led a resurgence of Angel pitching that lifted the club to its third best won-lost record ever. But as the West was now the stronger AL division, the team's 91 wins carried them only into third place, eight games back. In 1990 they dropped just one place in the standings, but finished again below .500, 23 games out of first.

The Angels began strong in 1991, even moving into into the division lead on July 3. But seven straight losses plunged them to fifth, and although they finished at .500 for the season, just 14 games out of first, they wound up in the division cellar. They rose in the standings in 1992, finishing in a fifth-place tie with Kansas City, but their won-lost record of 72–90 was their worst in nine years.

Chicago Cubs

The Chicago Cubs have represented the same city in the major leagues longer than any other club. Organized in 1870 to provide a professional challenge to Cincinnati's Red Stockings, the White Stockings (as they were originally known) were one of the founding members of the game's first professional league—the National Association—the next year.

Despite the great Chicago fire, which destroyed their ballpark, uniforms, and club business records late in the 1871 season, the White Stockings completed their schedule, finishing a close second to the Athletics of Philadelphia. But they dropped out of the NA for the next two years because of the fire's devastation. In 1875, in the midst of a second losing season following their return, the club arranged for four of champion Boston's best players to jump to Chicago for the 1876 season. That winter, White Stocking president William A. Hulbert and pitcher/manager Al Spalding (one of the jumpers) led in forming a new league to replace the NA.

Sparked by its Boston players and infielder Adrian "Cap" Anson (lured from the Athletics), the White Stockings in 1876 outscored their opponents by more than five runs per game and handily won the first championship of the new National League. The next year, though, when Spalding (whose pitching had brought Chicago 47 of its 52 victories in 1876) switched over to first base, the club fell off to fifth.

Spalding retired from the field in 1878 to attend to his young sporting goods firm (though he returned as club president from 1882 through 1891). In 1879 Anson was named to manage the team. Leading the league in batting, he restored the White Stockings to their winning ways, and in 1880 led them back to the top.

For twelve years the White Stockings ranked among baseball's best, garnering five pennants (1880–1882, 1885–1886) and four second-place finishes. Anson's stern morality and strict discipline did not make him popular with his often rowdy teammates, but his consistency as a player set an example, and his innovative management made the most of his players' drive and aggressiveness. Anson's forcefulness, however, contributed to baseball's most grievous setback: his adamant refusal in the mid-1880s to take the field against black players prevented the racial integration of the major leagues that had up to then seemed imminent.

After a close finish behind Boston in 1891, the White Stockings' first era as a National League power ended. In each of the next eleven seasons they fell at least 15 games short of the top. The team's youthful ineptitude was reflected in the nicknames that succeeded "White Stockings": the "Colts," the "Orphans" (in 1898, after Anson—by then known as "Pop"—was fired after nineteen years at the helm), and finally, the "Cubs."

When Frank Selee (who had led Boston to greatness in the 1890s) was hired to manage the Cubs in 1902, he inherited a team that had ended the 1901 season 37 games out, its worst finish up to then. By 1903 he had turned catcher/outfielder Frank Chance into a first baseman, moved Joe Tinker from third to short, and brought up Johnny Evers from Troy to play second. The new double-play combination flourished not only in the field but at the bat. The Cubs finished third in 1903 with their best record in a dozen years.

That winter Selee traded for pitcher Mordecai "Three Finger" Brown, and in 1905 signed rookie hurler Ed Reulbach. After leading the Cubs to second place in 1904, Selee, ill with tuberculosis, took a leave of absence in the middle of the 1905 season. Chance took his place and brought the team to third.

Selee never returned, but he had gone a long way toward building a championship team. Trades for outfielder Jimmy Sheckard and third baseman Harry Steinfeldt, the signing of rookie pitcher Jack Pfiester, and the acquisition during the 1906 season of pitchers Orval Overall and Jack Taylor completed one of the greatest teams of all time. The Cubs passed the Giants to take the lead early in May and kept on rising. New York and Pittsburgh made a race of it through July, but the Cubs won 55 of their final 65 games to finish with a record 116 victories, 20 games ahead of second-place New York. The hitting of Steinfeldt and Chance led the Cubs to the top of the league in batting and slugging, and the club topped all others in fielding. But it was the Cub pitching that stood out most. Brown's 1.04 ERA was the league's best, with those of Pfiester and Reulbach second and third. The team ERA of 1.76 was the first below 2.00 since the pitching distance was increased to 60'6" in 1893. Over all, Chicago scored 80 more runs than its nearest rival, and yielded 89 fewer.

But in the World Series, the crosstown "hitless wonder" White Sox matched the Cubs' hitting and pitched twice as effectively to take the crown in six games. It was the third time the Cubs had failed to win the world title: in two of the earliest Series, they had tied the St. Louis Browns by 3–3–1 in 1885, and lost to them the next year, 2–4.

The Cubs' hitting and run production fell off in 1907, but their pitching did not (ERA: 1.73). With 107 wins, they captured their second straight pennant, by 17 games. This time their dominance carried over into the World Series as they swept Detroit after an opening-game tie.

The pennant race of 1908, in sharp contrast to those of the previous two years, was one of the tightest in baseball history. On September 22 the Cubs won two from the Giants to pull into a virtual tie for first (with Pittsburgh third, 1½ games back). The next day the Giants appeared to have beaten the Cubs with an RBI single in the last of the ninth. But young Fred Merkle, on first when the hit was made, seeing the runner on third cross the plate, failed to continue on to second himself and was forced out by alert Cub second baseman Johnny Evers for the third out, which negated the Giant run. Because of increasing darkness and the mood of excited fans on the field, the game was called and ruled a tie. After another week and a half in which all three teams took turns in front, Chicago defeated Pittsburgh to pull ahead by half a game, leaving the Pirates and Giants tied for second. But New York had one more game—and defeated the Boston Braves to pull into a tie with the Cubs. The "Merkle boner" game thus had to be replayed, and this time the Cubs won to take their third straight pennant. In the World Series they again beat Detroit in five games. Their second straight world title was also, to date, their last.

In 1909 the Cubs won 104 games as their pitching staff for the third time in four years recorded an ERA under 2.00, but the club trailed Pittsburgh throughout the season and finished second. In 1910, however, their 104 wins carried them to another pennant, by a comfortable 13 games. It was their last championship of the Chance era. After a World Series loss to the Philadelphia Athletics, and seasons in second and third place, Chance resigned, protesting the unwillingness of owner Charles Murphy to spend money for top players.

The Cubs got a new owner in 1916, and with him a new ballpark. Charles Weeghman, who had owned the Chicago Whales in the short-lived Federal League, purchased the Cubs when the FL went under, and moved them into the park he had built for the Whales. Although there was talk in the 1980s of moving the Cubs out of what is now Wrigley Field, the introduction of night baseball in 1988 assured continuing play in this crown jewel of ballparks.

The team that next carried Chicago to the pennant, in the war-shortened season of 1918, featured only one name familiar to Cubs fans from earlier championship seasons—Fred Merkle. The man whose rookie boner as a Giant had made possible their pennant in 1908 was now their leading run producer. As in earlier pennant-winning seasons, fine pitching predominated, with veteran James "Hippo" Vaughn the league's best pitcher on the league's top staff.

Several years of decline followed the Cubs' World Series loss to the Boston Red Sox. The club hit bottom in 1925 with its first cellar finish in fifty-three years of league

play, but a new era of greatness was at hand. In 1921 wealthy chewing-gum manufacturer William Wrigley had purchased control of the Cubs, with a determination to spend what was needed to produce a winner.

The seeds Wrigley planted eventually bore fruit. In 1926 he hired Joe McCarthy—a successful minor league manager—to lead the club, and drafted outfielder Lewis "Hack" Wilson from Toledo. Wilson immediately became one of the league's leading offensive threats, and the Cubs rebounded to the first division. In 1927 they even led the league through August before dropping back to fourth. A postseason trade brought them outfielder Hazen "Kiki" Cuyler, and a close third-place finish in 1928. Then the Cubs traded with the Braves for second baseman Rogers Hornsby, and in 1929 returned to the top. Led by Wilson's 159 RBIs and Hornsby's 149, five Cubs drove in more than 90 runs each. After battling Pittsburgh for the lead through mid-July, the Cubs hurtled ahead to take the pennant by 10½ games, despite a late-season slump. The slump continued through the World Series, though, as the Athletics humbled the Cubs in five games.

Just four games from the end of the hot pennant race in 1930 (the year Wilson set the major league RBI record with 190), McCarthy—still smarting from criticism arising from the World Series loss—quit as manager. With Hornsby at the helm, the Cubs preserved a second-place finish. They dropped to third the next year, but returned to the top in 1932. Hornsby, near the end of his playing days, was dropped as manager in August, with the Cubs in second, and replaced by first baseman Charlie Grimm. Pitcher Lon Warneke, in his first full season as a starter, led the league in wins and ERA. The club enjoyed a hot streak in August to move out in front of slumping Pittsburgh and hung on to take the flag by four games. The Yankees provided the World Series humiliation this time, a four-game sweep that provided McCarthy (now the Yankee manager) with sweet revenge for the Chicago fans' criticism three years earlier.

It had become a pattern: three years, another pennant. In 1935 a balanced offense (led by catcher "Gabby" Hartnett and second baseman Billy Herman) and the league's best pitching brought the Cubs up from fourth in late June to first in September. They clinched the pennant with three games to go, with their twentieth win of a 21-game streak. In the World Series, Detroit stopped the Cubs in six games.

After two seasons in second, it was time for another pennant. Bill Lee, the Cubs' top pitcher in 1935, was now the league's finest, as was the Cubs' staff. With the club languishing 6½ games back in midseason, Grimm quit as manager and was replaced by catcher Hartnett. In September the Cubs came to life, rising to second early in the month. They overtook Pittsburgh on September 28 with their ninth consecutive win—on Hartnett's homer against the Pirates in the growing darkness with two away in the bottom of the ninth—and clinched the pennant four games later, on the next-to-last day of the season. It was their fourth pennant at three-year intervals—and their sixth straight World Series loss, another Yankee sweep.

In 1940, after fourteen straight winning seasons, the Cubs began a five-year stretch below .500. Jimmie Wilson replaced Hartnett as manager in 1941; then Grimm returned near the start of the 1944 season. The club finished a distant fourth that year, but in 1945, after a middling start, they won twenty-six of thirty midseason games to take a lead they never relinquished. Balanced pitching (sparked by Hank Borowy, who went 11–2 after coming over from the Yankees in July) and the hitting of veteran first baseman Phil Cavarretta (.355) and center fielder Andy Pafko (110 RBIs) held off the pressing St. Louis Cardinals to preserve a sixteenth Cub pennant. But although they battled Detroit through a full seven games in the World Series, they ended up losing again—their ninth defeat in twelve tries.

For the next twenty-three years the Cubs remained out of pennant contention. But in 1969, the first year of divisional play, under the lively management of Leo Durocher, they took an early lead in the NL East. With a potent offense led by veteran sluggers Ron Santo, Ernie Banks, and Billy Williams, the team continued rising through early August. But the New York Mets rose even faster and farther; they didn't pause when Chicago leveled off in late August, and while the Cubs were losing eight straight in September the Mets were winning ten in a row. The Cubs wound up 8 games back.

The next year Chicago started well, slumped in late June, then fought back into the thick of the race in September before fading to another second-place finish. Three years later, in 1973, the Cubs entered July with a substantial lead. Although they fell to fifth by season's end, in the tightly packed division they were only 5 games back. It was to be their closest finish for eleven years.

In 1981 the Wrigley family, no longer able to bankroll a winner, sold the club to the Chicago Tribune Company. Three years later, with a new manager, Jim Frey, and an almost wholly different roster, the new management capped its rebuilding program with the acquisition from Cleveland, in mid-June 1984, of pitcher Rick Sutcliffe. As Sutcliffe fashioned a 16–1 record for his new club, the Cubs moved in front to stay on August 1, and kept on rising to capture their first division title by 6½ games.

Their fall was as rapid as their rise. After winning the first two games of the League Championship Series against San Diego, the pennant was swept out from under them as the Padres took the final three. Four losing seasons followed, in which the Cubs finished no closer than 18½ games behind the division winner.

But in 1989 the team, now managed by Don Zimmer, bounced back to duplicate its 1984 success. With a balanced offense and pitching vastly improved over the previous season, the Cubs took the NL East lead for good on August 7, and finished six games ahead of New York. Once again, though, they were unable to persevere to the pennant, losing the LCS to San Francisco in five games.

Veterans Andre Dawson and Ryne Sandberg enjoyed banner seasons at the bat in 1990. But the pitching faltered and, although the club played well after a poor first half, it took a win on the final day to give the Cubs a tie for fourth place.

As they had done in 1989, Andre Dawson, Mark Grace, and Ryne Sandberg continued to provide offensive clout over the next three years, and in 1992 Cy Young Award winner Greg Maddux and newly acquired Mike Morgan excelled on the mound. But the team could not carve out a winning season, finishing tied for fourth in 1990, and fourth by themselves in 1991 and '92. The Cub

owners snarled when Commissioner Fay Vincent proposed transferring the club from the NL East to the West in 1993 (trading places with Atlanta), a logical move geographically. But the threat passed when Vincent, under pressure from owners dissatisfied with his strong leadership, resigned before the end of the 1992 season.

Chicago White Sox

When minor league owner Charlie Comiskey transferred his club from St. Paul to Chicago as part of the move to upgrade the American League to major league status, he called it the White Stockings, after the Chicago team that dominated the National League in its early years. The new Chicago team revived memories of the old White Stockings, winning the AL championship in 1900, and repeating the triumph in 1901, the league's first major league season. Manager Clark Griffith (who had jumped to the White Stockings from Chicago's NL Cubs) was the team's star pitcher in 1901, winning 24 of 31 decisions as his team took the lead in May and held off the threatening Boston Somersets the rest of the way.

Griffith's effectiveness fell off in 1902, as did the team, (now called the White Sox) which took a sizable lead in July, only to slide back to fourth in August. Griffith left the next year and the White Sox sank to seventh. It would take eighteen years and baseball's greatest scandal for the Sox to finish that low again.

In 1904, after center fielder Fielder Jones replaced left fielder Nixey Callahan as manager, they rose into first place for a moment in August before settling back to third. The next year they made up a seven-game deficit in September to catch the Philadelphia Athletics, but the loss of two games to the A's stalled their drive and left them in second.

Nothing stalled the White Sox drive in 1906. Although they ranked at the very bottom of the league in hitting and entered June five games below .500, their pitching and hustle pulled them through. "Big Ed" Walsh, who had finally mastered the spitball after two years of trying, won 17 games, including a league-high 10 shutouts. Doc White contributed 18 wins with a league-best 1.52 ERA, and Frank Owen and Nick Altrock won 22 and 20, respectively. The Sox shot to the top in August with a 19-game win streak (including 8 shutouts). Early in September, New York's Highlanders passed them, but after the two teams had traded the lead back and forth for a couple of weeks the Sox spurted to take the pennant by 3 games. If the race was close, so were the individual games: the Sox achieved nearly one-third of their victories by the margin of a single run. The "hitless wonders" carried their momentum through the World Series, shocking the mighty crosstown Cubs (who had won a record 116 games that year) four games to two.

In 1907, after leading the league much of the first half, the Sox slipped to third. The next year Walsh pitched in the final seven games on his way to a career-high 40 wins. In a tight finish he pulled the Sox to within a half game of first-place Detroit before they dropped back to third with a loss to the Tigers on the final day.

It was 1915 before the Sox (piloted by rookie manager Clarence H. "Pants" Rowland) next finished that high, and 1916 before they again challenged seriously for the pennant. Comiskey, though accused of pinching pennies in his payment of players, was willing to spend what was needed to acquire them. After the 1914 season he purchased star second baseman Eddie Collins from the A's, and promising young Oscar "Happy" Felsch from minor league Milwaukee. The following August he acquired the great Joe Jackson from Cleveland. Together with the league's best pitching staff, they carried the Sox into the thick of a three-way race and a close second-place finish in 1916, and in 1917 to the pennant with the best winning percentage the club has ever compiled. Ten-year veteran pitcher Eddie Cicotte enjoyed his first 20-win season with a league-high 28 victories, and a league- and career-best 1.53 ERA. After dueling the Boston Red Sox most of the season, Chicago streaked out of reach in late August to finish with 100 wins and a 9-game lead. In the World Series against the New York Giants they captured their second (and, to date, their last) world title, in six games.

With several key players out much of 1918 for military or civilian war service, the White Sox finished out of the running, a dismal sixth. But in 1919, with the team back at full strength, the race once again went to Chicago. If their pitching didn't have quite the depth of the 1917 squad, its best hurlers were in peak form. Cicotte, after an off-year in 1918, attained a career high with 29 wins, as did Lefty Williams with 23 victories. Collins and Jackson enjoyed their best seasons in several years, and infielder Buck Weaver had never been better. Old-time pitcher/second baseman Kid Gleason was a rookie as a big league manager, but his Sox began strong and, after slipping briefly into second in midseason, pulled ahead in July to stay.

When the Sox lost the World Series to underdog Cincinnati, there were rumors of a fix, but nothing came to light for nearly a year. The White Sox looked better than ever in 1920. Though they fell back in May after a hot April, by mid-August they had risen to the thick of a tight three-team race. Felsch, Collins, and Weaver had never played better, Jackson was enjoying one of his very best seasons, and four pitchers were on their way to more than 20 wins. Chicago might not have caught Cleveland's rampaging Indians, but it didn't help that talk of a White Sox scandal revived late in the season, or that the grand jury convened only eight games from the end, or that eight Sox players were indicted and suspended with just three games to play. The teamed finished two games back, in second place.

The indicted players—among whom were Cicotte, Felsch, Jackson, Weaver, and Williams—were acquitted in court when three crucial confessions disappeared, but they were banned for life from organized baseball by commissioner K. M. Landis. The White Sox did not soon recover from the loss. In 1921 they began fifteen years of wandering in the second division, including three seasons in the cellar and one seventh-place finish (in 1932) that, while not the league's most distant, remains the farthest out Chicago has ever finished, 56½ games behind champion New York.

Two of the club's greatest and most durable players arrived during these years: pitcher Ted Lyons (who won 260 games for the Sox over twenty-one years) in 1923, and in 1930 shortstop Luke Appling (who averaged .310 in his twenty years with the club). Owner Comiskey died

in 1931, in the midst of his Sox's most dismal era, but Lyons and Appling were around long enough to enjoy a few fourth- and third-place seasons. But neither saw the Sox contend seriously for the pennant. After his playing career was over, Lyons managed the team for a few years—until 1948, when the Sox lost 101 games and finished last.

That year Frank Lane was lured from the presidency of the American Association to take charge as Chicago's general manager. He began reshaping the team, and after two more losing seasons the White Sox' fortunes began to rise. When Lane hired Paul Richards to manage the club in 1951, the Sox began what became a seventeen-year string of winning seasons.

In 1951, Richards's first season, the Sox spent a month in first place before drifting down to fourth, and the next year began a five-year stopover in third place. In 1954 they won 94 games but were out of the race by August— that was the year Cleveland won 111 and the second-place Yankees 103. Richards moved on to Baltimore, but Marty Marion, who replaced him, kept the Sox in third place. Their 91 wins in 1955 earned them a much tighter race than '54, one that found them in first place at the start of September, until four straight losses dropped them to third.

Frank Lane left at the end of the 1955 season, and young Chuck Comiskey (one of the grandchildren of Charlie Comiskey who now owned the club) took over the front office. A year later Comiskey replaced Marion with Al Lopez, who had piloted the great Cleveland club of 1954 and whose teams, in his six seasons of managing, had never finished below second. Lopez continued his success in Chicago: the Sox moved up to second (though well behind the Yankees) in 1957 and '58. In March 1959, Bill Veeck (who had in previous years owned the Cleveland Indians and the St. Louis Browns) bought a controlling interest in the White Sox from the Comiskey family and stepped into instant success.

With the Yankees suffering an off-year in 1959, Chicago and Cleveland battled for the lead throughout the summer, until the White Sox pulled away in late August. The same 94–60 record that had given them only a distant third in 1954 now carried them to their first pennant in forty years. The close and successful pennant race, and the club's dynamic new ownership, pushed Sox home attendance up more than 78 percent to a new club record.

As they had in 1906, pitching and hustle won the Sox their 1959 pennant. The league's best staff was led by veteran Early Wynn (enjoying his last big season with a league high of 22 wins) and young Bob Shaw (with a career high of 18), and featured the league's top relievers in Gerry Staley and Turk Lown. Shortstop Luis Aparicio, in the midst of a nine-year reign as stolen-base leader, set a personal high in runs scored as the club went 35–15 in one-run games. But in the World Series, Los Angeles stopped Chicago in six games.

The next year the Sox remained competitive until September, but finished third. After dropping to fourth and fifth the next two years (in a league now expanded to ten teams), they returned to second in 1963. The next year the Sox finished a season-long three-way race with nine straight wins, enough to pull them past Baltimore, but a game short of catching the Yankees, whose eleven-game

streak a week earlier had put them out in front. After a third straight second-place finish in 1965, manager Lopez resigned for health reasons.

Under Eddie Stanky—and with the AL's stingiest pitching staff in forty-nine years—the Sox competed into the final week of a hot 1967 race, when five straight losses at the end dropped them to fourth. Only twice in the next thirteen years would they rise above .500; in 1970 they lost a club-record 106 games to finish at the bottom of the AL West. Two years later they took the division lead briefly in late August before dropping back to second, and in 1977 they held the lead through much of the summer before tailing off to third.

Bill Veeck had sold the club and repurchased it in 1976. But in January 1981, after three losing seasons and troubled by poor health and skyrocketing player salaries, he sold the Sox once again, to a group headed by Jerry Reinsdorf and Eddie Einhorn. With Reinsdorf heading the club's baseball operations and lawyer Tony LaRussa piloting the team on the field, the Sox became by 1983 one of the best teams in baseball. With their best record since 1920, the 1983 Sox carried the AL West by 20 games. Rookie slugger Ron Kittle led the attack, backed up by fourth-year outfielder Harold Baines and resurgent old-timers Greg Luzinski and Carlton Fisk. Pitchers La-Marr Hoyt and Rich Dotson attained personal bests to lead the majors in wins (with 24 and 22), and White Sox home attendance for the first time topped two million. In the League Championship Series, though, after a close win over Baltimore in the opener, Chicago lost the next three games and the pennant. The Sox pitching and offense (except for Baines) collapsed the next season, and the team remained out of serious contention for six years.

Most forecasters predicted another dismal season for the Sox in 1990, but as fans watched a new Comiskey Park arise next door, they also saw their club celebrate its final year in the old yard with an astonishing resurgence. With their best start in decades, the Sox stayed close to mighty Oakland through the first half of the season, and even took over first place for brief periods in June and July before Oakland pulled away. Anchoring a strong bullpen, closer Bobby Thigpen shattered the major league record for saves, passing the old record of 46 with a month to go and finishing with 57.

First baseman Frank Thomas, confirming in his first full season the offensive powers he had demonstrated as a rookie in 1990, helped keep the Sox competitive through much of 1991, the inaugural season of their new park. Rookie Wilson Alvarez's August 11 no-hitter capped a seven-game win streak that pulled the team to just a game from the top, but fifteen losses in their next seventeen games stifled their pennant hopes. Thomas continued his awesome offense in 1992, and Jack McDowell showed himself one of the AL's best pitchers, but the team won one game fewer than the year before, and finished third.

Cincinnati Reds

The Red Stockings was the nickname of two pioneering Cincinnati ballclubs—the first avowedly professional team, which was undefeated in 1869, and the charter member club in the National League of 1876–1880. After

a year on the sidelines, the reformed Reds joined the new American Association and captured the 1882 pennant by 11½ games, with a .688 winning percentage that is still the club record. Seven Reds enjoyed career highs in batting, pitcher Will White led the association with 40 wins, and rookie second baseman John "Bid" McPhee proved himself already one of the game's classiest fielders. The Reds even won one of a pair of postseason exhibition games with Chicago's White Stockings, champions of the older and stronger National League.

McPhee remained eighteen years with the Reds and established himself as the finest second baseman of the nineteenth century. But the club would go thirty-seven years before it won another pennant. Twice in their seven remaining years in the AA the Reds finished second, and they enjoyed six winning seasons. Transferring from the AA to the NL in 1890, they finished fourth; at 10½ games out of first, it was their closest finish in the thirty-four years between 1884 and their next pennant-winning season, 1919.

The Reds wound up in the cellar for the first time in 1901. The next year club owner John T. Brush sold out to a group of Cincinnati's political bosses, who in mid-August named August "Garry" Herrmann (formerly head of the water works commission) to run it. Herrmann promptly acquired two outfielders from Baltimore—Cy Seymour and Joe Kelley, who was appointed team manager—who helped pull the Reds up to .500 and to fourth place by season's end. Three winning seasons followed, but then came eleven years in which the Reds finished above .500 only once (and then by only one game). Herrmann, meanwhile had found his calling in baseball administration. He not only remained president of the Reds for twenty-five years, but he also chaired the three-man National Commission that oversaw organized baseball, from its establishment in 1903 until 1920 (when his resignation brought about the commission's demise).

A midseason trade in 1916 brought the Reds Christy Mathewson (at the end of his pitching career) to manage the team, plus outfielder Edd Roush. The next year, with Roush leading the league in batting, the Reds edged above .500 and into fourth place. In 1918 an August spurt boosted the Reds into third place, in a season shortened by a month at the end because of the World War. Roush enjoyed another banner year, but Mathewson left for the Army just before the season ended.

First baseman Hal Chase—suspected of throwing games—was traded away after the season and replaced by veteran Jake Daubert. Southpaw Slim Sallee was purchased from the Giants and righthander Ray Fisher from the Yankees. Pat Moran (who had led the Phillies to a pennant in 1915) was hired to replace Mathewson at the Cincinnati helm. Thus fortified, the Reds in 1919 won their second pennant. Three pitchers—Sallee (21–7), Hod Eller (20–9), and Dutch Ruether (19–7, 1.82 ERA)—reached career peaks, Fisher (14–5) enjoyed one of his best years, Roush won another batting title and finished second in NL RBIs, and three Reds finished in the league's top four in runs scored. The Reds broke quickly at the start, but faltered in May and didn't pass the Giants into first place for good until late July. But from then on, they increased their lead to the end, finishing 9 games in front. Rumors of a White Sox fix to throw

the World Series clouded the Reds' Series triumph—and spoiled it entirely when, a year later, the scandal became public and the truth of the rumors was confirmed.

In 1920 Cincinnati led the league entering September, but Brooklyn spurted and the Reds slumped to a third-place finish, 10½ games out. They dropped to sixth in 1921, but recovered for five years in the first division, including three second-place finishes. But only in 1926 did the Reds contend closely for the flag. After leading the league much of the first half of the season, they found themselves in the second half tangled in a three-way battle with St. Louis and Pittsburgh. But after surging into a narrow lead with seven straight wins in mid-September, they lost their next five games and wound up 2 games back of the Cardinals in second place.

The Reds finished the eleven years after 1926 in the second division, hitting bottom with four straight cellar finishes in 1931–1934. President Herrmann retired after the 1927 season, and within two years a controlling interest in the Reds was sold to a wealthy Cincinnatian, Sidney Weil. But Weil lost his fortune in the stock market crash of 1929 and the Depression that followed. While he continued to run the Reds for four years, his stock in the club was held by the Central Trust Company. In his efforts to turn the club around, Weil acquired catcher Ernie Lombardi from Brooklyn in March 1932, and pitcher Paul Derringer from the St. Louis Cardinals the following May. Derringer lost 25 games in his first Red season and 21 the next, but both remained with the club long enough to star in its return to glory. Owner Weil, however, relinquished his control to the bank in 1933, at the depth of the Depression and of the team's fortunes.

The bank hired Larry MacPhail (who had rescued minor league Columbus by introducing night baseball there) to run the Reds. MacPhail in turn hired Frank Lane to develop a minor league farm system, and persuaded Cincinnati industrialist Powel Crosley, Jr., to invest in the club. On May 24, 1935, Crosley and MacPhail brought night ball to the major leagues (the Reds, with Derringer pitching, beat the Phillies 2–1), and with it a sharp upswing in attendance at Crosley Field. By June 1936, Crosley's increased investment in the Reds had made him the majority owner. The temperamental MacPhail quit suddenly in mid-September 1936, but the Reds replaced him with another successful minor league executive, Warren Giles, who ran the club until his selection in 1952 as president of the NL.

After rising to sixth place in 1935 and fifth the next year, the Reds dropped back into the cellar in 1937. But the following year, under new manager Bill McKechnie, they rose into the first division once again—even holding second place briefly in September before slipping to fourth. Derringer enjoyed the first of three peak seasons, young Johnny Vander Meer contributed 15 wins (including two consecutive no-hitters) and Bucky Walters, after his acquisition from the Phillies in June, compiled his first winning season since converting from third baseman to pitcher in 1935. Catcher Lombardi led the NL in batting, and first baseman Frank McCormick, in his first full season, led the team in RBIs and the league in hits. The stage was set for the club's first back-to-back pennants.

Several Reds reached the apex of their careers in 1939, among them Walters (27–11) and Derringer (25–7), who

between them topped most of the league's pitching stats, and Frank McCormick, who led the league in RBIs and hits and finished second in batting. The club pulled out of the pack to the front before the end of May and held the lead to the end, although St. Louis closed the gap with a late-season surge before slipping 4½ games back.

Cincinnati's sweep by the Yankees in the World Series was something of a shock, but the club had recovered its poise by the next spring. Starting strong and—except for a small dip in August—pushing steadily upward throughout the season, the Reds shook off the persistent Dodgers in midseason and finished 12 games in front with their first 100-win season. McCormick and Lombardi powered the offense, and Walters for the second year in a row took NL crowns in wins and ERA. This time the team's triumph carried through the World Series as Walters and Derringer won two games apiece to edge the Detroit Tigers in seven games.

The Reds' pitching remained strong in 1941, but their hitting and run production fell off and the team struggled to finish third. They remained in the upper division through 1944, but then dropped into an eleven-year trough of losing seasons in which, while they never sank into the cellar, they never rose above fifth.

Ted Kluszewski was in his ninth season as the Reds' slugging first baseman when Cincinnati next offered a serious run for the pennant in 1956 under manager Birdie Tebbetts. Kluszewski led the club in hitting and RBIs, but his 35 home runs were good enough only for third behind rookie Frank Robinson's 38 and Wally Post's 36 on a team that hammered 221 during the season to tie the major league record set nine years earlier by the Giants. The Reds' offense (they led the league in runs scored) kept them in the thick of a three-team race throughout the season, and they finished only 2 games out. That same year, for the first time ever they drew more than a million fans at home.

The Reds dropped out of a tight race in August 1957, and suffered losing seasons the next three years. After the 1960 season, Gabe Paul, who had succeeded Warren Giles as club president and general manager, left to help organize the new Houston club, and the following spring owner Crosley died. Bill DeWitt, who replaced Paul as president (and ultimately purchased control of the club), acquired pitcher Joey Jay from the Milwaukee Braves and third baseman Gene Freese from the White Sox. Jay in 1961 won twelve games more than his previous season high—tying for the league lead with 21, and Freese homered 26 times and drove in 87 runs—both career highs. Most of the team improved on their 1960 stats, and despite a poor start that saw them enter May in last place, the Reds had risen to the top by mid-June. The streaking Dodgers caught them briefly in August, but then fell away as the Reds pushed their pennant-winning margin to 4 games. In the World Series, though, it was the Yankees in five games.

The Reds next threatened in 1964 when, in a wild three-way finish, they won nine straight in late September to take first place for a day before slipping into a tie for second, one game behind St. Louis. In 1965 a young Pete Rose recorded the first of his ten 200-hit seasons as the Reds battled among the leaders through much of the summer before dropping off to fourth.

That December, after a decade of standout offense in Cincinnati, Frank Robinson was traded to Baltimore. The next year, while Robinson won the Triple Crown in assisting his new team to the world championship, the Reds suffered their first losing season in six years and sank to seventh place. That winter, owner DeWitt completed the sale of the team to a group led by Cincinnati newspaper publisher Francis Dale, and including brothers James and William Williams who later acquired a controlling interest in the club.

In 1969, the first year of divisional play, the Reds rose, after a slow start, into the thick of a five-way race in the NL West before stumbling as Atlanta and San Francisco surged in the final three weeks. But the season provided a foretaste of the decade to come as the team captured league crowns in slugging and home runs.

At midseason in 1970 the Reds moved out of Crosley Field—their home for fifty-eight years—into the new Riverfront Stadium. Catcher Johnny Bench and third baseman Tony Perez, with the finest seasons of their long careers, paced an overwhelming Red offense as the team hammered out a new club-high 102 wins to reward rookie manager Sparky Anderson with victory in the NL West by 14½ games, and gain the appelation "Big Red Machine." In the League Championship Series the Reds continued their triumph with a three-game sweep of East winner Pittsburgh. But mighty Baltimore humbled the Reds in the World Series, 4–1.

Cincinnati's hitting and run production fell off sharply the next year, and the club dropped to fourth with their only losing season of the decade. But in 1972—spurred on after a slow start by Johnny Bench's recovery of power, Gary Nolan's finest season on the mound, and the all-around mastery of newly acquired second baseman Joe Morgan—the Reds rebounded after a slow start to take a lead in June and pull away from everyone in July for an easy division win. Victory in the LCS came harder, as powerful Pittsburgh carried the series to the full five games before handing the Reds the pennant with a wild pitch in the last of the ninth inning of the final game. Cincinnati's defeat in the World Series was also close: the Reds won three, and Oakland's four wins were each achieved by a margin of just one run.

The Reds repeated as division titlists in 1973 with a second-half surge from fourth place that carried them past front-runner Los Angeles in September. But the much weaker New York Mets ended Cincinnati's pennant hopes in the LCS, 3–2.

In 1974 the Reds trailed the Dodgers all season and finished 4 games back in second place. But over the next two years the Big Red Machine flattened all opposition. In 1975, after hovering around .500 through mid-May, the Reds began an ascent that carried them to what are still club records: 108 victories and a winning margin of 20 games. The team featured balanced pitching (six starters won ten or more games), a balanced offense in which every regular drove in more than 45 runs (averaging nearly 77 apiece), the best fielding in the majors, and a big NL lead in stolen bases. After a three-game sweep of Pittsburgh in the LCS, the Reds subdued the stubborn Boston Red Sox in seven games for their first world title in thirty-five years, and their third overall.

They won their fourth the next year. Joe Morgan, at the

peak of his career, led the NL in slugging, finished second to teammate George Foster in RBIs, and stole 60 bases. Balanced pitching and offense again put the Reds in front to stay in June, carrying the team to 102 wins and a 10-game lead over Los Angeles at the finish. The LCS produced another sweep—of Philadelphia this time. The World Series was also a sweep as the Reds dispatched the Yankees, outscoring them nearly three to one.

Two years of second-place finishes followed, and the Reds replaced Sparky Anderson at the helm with John McNamara, who led the club back to the top of the NL West in 1979. Pete Rose, after sixteen years in Cincinnati, had signed with the Phillies as a free agent, but Ray Knight (who replaced Rose at third base) minimized the loss with a team-high .318 batting average. Houston led the division much of the summer, but a sustained Reds' surge in August brought them even, then pulled them ahead in early September, where they hung on to take the title by just 1½ games. But that was the end of the Reds' decade of splendor, for Pittsburgh swept past them to the pennant in the LCS.

Joe Morgan left the club after the season, returning as a free agent to Houston, whence he had come eight years earlier. In 1980 the Reds dipped in midseason, recovering to make a race of it in August, only to fade a bit and finish third. The next year, in a season shortened and split in two by a players' strike, the Reds compiled the best overall record in the majors. But they came away empty-handed by finishing half a game behind Los Angeles in the first half-season and 1½ games back of Houston in the second half, losing a chance at postseason play when the powers that be decided to pit the half-season winners against each other for the right to play in the LCS.

As a penurious front office continued to trade away its stars or lose them to free agency, the dispirited Reds dropped to the bottom of the NL West in 1982 with a club-worst 101 losses. Manager McNamara yielded in midseason to coach Russ Nixon, who was himself replaced by Vern Rapp after another last-place finish in 1983. Robert Howsam, Sr., whose shrewd trading as general manager had been instrumental in building the mighty Reds of the 1970s, was called out of semiretirement to restore the club to respectability. Howsam signed free-agent slugger Dave Parker from Pittsburgh, and late in the 1984 season brought Pete Rose back as player-manager. Early in 1985 the NL approved the sale of the Reds to Marge Schott, a Cincinnati automobile dealer. With Parker enjoying his most productive seasons in several years, and newcomers Eric Davis and John Franco developing respectively into one of the league's leading run producers and one of its best relief pitchers, owner Schott's public enthusiasm for her team was rewarded with four straight second-place finishes (and a return in 1987 to a home attendance over two million for the first time in seven years). In 1987 the team even spent two months at the top of the NL West, until an August slump dropped them into a hole from which a late-season rally could not extricate them.

Turmoil ruled the Reds in 1989. Disabling injuries to no fewer than twelve players, including such 1988 standouts as pitcher Danny Jackson (whose 23 wins tied for the league high) and infielders Barry Larkin and Chris Sabo, contributed most to the team's drop to fifth place. But baseball's investigation of manager Pete Rose on charges of gambling on baseball games and other offenses—an investigation which resulted in Rose's lifetime banishment from the game in August—did nothing to bolster Cincinnati's play on the field.

The distress of 1989 was all but forgotten in 1990 as the Reds, under new manager Lou Piniella, leaped to a 9–0 start and, surviving threats from San Francisco in August and Los Angeles in September, held on to first place through the entire season. Larkin and Sabo—whole again—anchored a balanced offense, while pitchers Randy Myers (acquired from the Mets in a trade for John Franco) and Rob Dibble provided All-Star relief to a solid core of starters. In the LCS, the Reds overcame an opening-game loss to capture the pennant from Pittsburgh in six games, then startled Oakland's heavily favored Athletics with a four-game sweep.

The Reds remained in the thick of the 1991 race through midseason, despite a 10-game losing streak in July. But as Atlanta rose to battle early leader Los Angeles, Cincinnati settled into a long decline that at the end left them 20 games back, in fifth place. Barry Larkin and Bip Roberts sparked the league's strongest offense in 1992, as the Reds rebounded to win 90 games. But they let a 6-game mid-season lead get away from them and finished 8 games behind repeat champion Atlanta.

Cleveland Indians

Cleveland is the only club in the American League East without at least one divisional title. Since the advent of divisional play in 1969, the Indians have enjoyed only four winning seasons, finishing last in the East eight times. Their record was not always this dismal. Though no other major league club with their longevity has won as few pennants, the Indians before 1969 ranked consistently among the league's better teams. They finished in the top half of the league nearly 70 percent of the time through their first sixty-eight years, and only once (in 1914) wound up in the cellar.

The Indians (who were at first called the Blues because of the color of their uniforms) succeeded Cleveland's National League Spiders, who in 1899, their final season, lost a major league record 134 games. When the NL dropped the Spiders at the end of the season, Ban Johnson, president of the emerging American League, grasped the opportunity to move into this major market. In 1901, when Johnson proclaimed the AL a major league, Cleveland lured several players from NL clubs and played much better than the Spiders had, but still finished next-to-last in their first big league season. The next year the Bronchos (as they decided to call themselves) languished in last place through June. But during the season they acquired several players through trade and purchase—most notably star second baseman Napoleon "Nap" Lajoie and pitcher Bill Bernhard—who turned the Bronchos around in midseason and lifted them above .500 (and into fifth place) by season's end.

With Lajoie sparkling in the field and dominating the league at the plate, the fans soon settled on another nickname for the club—the Naps—that lasted as long as Lajoie remained in Cleveland. Late in the 1904 season,

Lajoie was named manager. After enjoying moderate success in two of the next three seasons, the Naps in 1908 experienced their best year yet, and one of the team's most exciting finishes ever.

With a ten-game winning streak near the end of the season, they moved from fourth to first, only to be surpassed by Detroit's ten-game streak. Both teams won their season finale, but the Tigers, because they had not made up an earlier rainout, took the pennant by half a game. Cleveland protested that if Detroit had played the missed game and lost, Cleveland would have gained a tie, forcing a playoff that might have brought them the championship. The dispute led to a rules change requiring ties or washouts to be replayed if their outcome could determine the pennant winner.

Poor seasons alternated with good the next few years. Lajoie quit as manager but remained as player. Pitching ace Addie Joss pitched a second no-hitter (he had hurled a perfect game at the height of the 1908 race), but before the start of the 1911 season, Joss was dead of tubercular meningitis. Outfielder Joe Jackson—acquired from the Athletics—hit .408 in his first full big league season. The club reached bottom in 1914 with a last-place finish that found them 18½ games out of *seventh* place, 48½ out of first. After the season Lajoie was waivered to Philadelphia (the fans then voted to rename the club the Indians), and the next August Jackson was sold to the Chicago White Sox as attendance dropped to its lowest level since 1901.

By the time the 1916 season began, though, new ownership had acquired the great Tris Speaker from Boston and brought up from the minors a pair of promising pitchers, Jim Bagby (Sr.) and Stan Coveleski. The club rose only one place that year, to sixth. But they stayed in the pennant fight through July and wound up winning 20 games more than they had the previous year. Attendance more than tripled over 1915.

Sparked by the three newcomers, the Indians rose to third in 1917, and to close second-place finishes the next two years. In 1920 everything came together. Speaker, who had taken over as manager the previous July, hit .388 and enjoyed one of his best years, as did Coveleski with 24 wins. Bagby, in the finest season of his career, led the league with 31 victories, and veteran pitcher Ray Caldwell (picked up from the Boston Red Sox the previous summer) added another 20. Six regulars hit over .300; the club as a whole hit .303.

Involved from mid-June in a close race with the Yankees, joined in August by the White Sox, Cleveland saw its home attendance climb above 900,000 for the first time, to set a club record that would last twenty-six years. The Yankees dropped back a bit in mid-September, but the White Sox hung close until the final week, when eight of their players were indicted and suspended as suspects in the Black Sox scandal of 1919. The Sox lost two of their final three games and all hope of tying Cleveland to force a playoff. The Indians defeated Brooklyn in a World Series that is best remembered for second baseman Bill Wambsganss's unassisted triple play in Game Five.

Cleveland led much of the way in 1921 before a late slump and a New York surge gave the Yankees their first pennant. Through the next quarter century the Indians came close to a pennant only twice. In 1926, with two veteran Georges—pitcher Uhle and first baseman

Burns—enjoying their finest seasons, the Indians came to life in midseason and drew within three games of the Yankees by season's end. Fourteen years later, in 1940, behind the 27 wins of twenty-one-year-old Bob Feller and the inspired play (in the field and at the bat) of second-year shortstop Lou Boudreau, Cleveland made an even closer run for the flag. Throughout the summer the Indians were in or near first place, but six losses in nine games with a resurgent Detroit in late August and September left them a game back at the finish.

Two years later Boudreau, at age twenty-four, was named to manage the Tribe. His team stirred little interest through the war years. But in 1946, with Feller back from military service and pitching his best ever, Cleveland fans boosted home attendance above a million for the first time, even though the team's won-lost record was its worst in eighteen years. The next year, their first full season under new president Bill Veeck, the Indians climbed to fourth. More significantly, Veeck hired the league's first black player, Larry Doby, who became a mainstay of the Indians for the next eight years.

In 1948 the Indians began a nine-year era of excellence with a victory in one of the closest pennant races ever. Through June they ran a three-way race with the Yankees and the surprisingly lively Philadelphia Athletics; in July the Red Sox rose out of nowhere to make it a four-way struggle. In September the A's fell behind, but the three remaining clubs stayed close, and on September 24 found themselves in a three-way tie. Cleveland moved ahead with a four-game win streak, but Boston, after a pair of losses, won their final four (including two to eliminate New York). Cleveland's final-day loss to Detroit left them tied with Boston. In a one-game playoff in Boston the next day (the first playoff in AL history), manager-shortstop Boudreau capped his MVP season with two home runs to help give rookie Gene Bearden his twentieth win and the Tribe their second pennant. The exciting race drew more than 2.6 million Cleveland fans to Municipal Stadium, a new major league record and still Cleveland's season high. By contrast, the World Series against the Boston Braves was anticlimactic—a Cleveland triumph in six games.

By 1951 both owner Veeck and manager Boudreau had moved on, but under new manager Al Lopez the Indians fashioned a six-year stretch in which they finished second to the Yankees five times, and in 1954 they won their third pennant with 111 victories—the most in AL history. The Lopez years, 1951–1956, were punctuated by the power of players like Doby, Luke Easter, Al Rosen, and Vic Wertz. But it was pitching that gave the team its consistency. Bob Lemon and Early Wynn won between 17 and 23 games in every one of the six years, as did Mike Garcia through 1954. As Garcia and Feller (who won 22 in 1951) faded, Art Houtteman was acquired from Detroit for a couple of good years, and Herb Score came along for his two explosive seasons.

The 1954 season—Cleveland's year to break the Yankee grip on the AL—was in fact New York's best season in the eighteen years from 1943 through 1960, a period in which they won twelve pennants. The Yankees kept the race close until early September, and finished with 103 wins. But the Indians won an AL-record 111 games to beat New York by 8. Wynn and Lemon tied for the league lead with 23 wins apiece, and Garcia copped the ERA

crown. Doby led the league in homers and RBIs, and second baseman Bobby Avila took the batting title. Heavily favored to defeat the Giants in the World Series, the Tribe and their fans were shocked when the NL champs swept them in four games.

After Lopez left to manage the White Sox in 1957, the Indians slipped below .500 for the first time in a decade. Rocky Colavito's power and Cal McLish's pitching brought them back in 1959, when they finished second to Lopez's Sox. Their next highest post-Lopez finish came nine years later, in 1968, when Luis Tiant and Sam Mc-Dowell pitched them into third.

From 1969 through 1989 the Indians completed every season in the bottom half of the AL East, rising above .500 in only four seasons while finishing seven years in the division cellar. In 1990, though, with three straight wins at season's end, they passed Baltimore by half a game to wind up a middle-of-the-divison fourth.

The effort proved too much. In July 1991 the Indians dropped into the cellar to stay, spiraling on down to a club-record 105 losses. With nowhere to go but up, the 1992 team, spurred by the offense of Carlos Baerga and Albert Belle, and the impressive pitching of Charles Nagy, played the best ball in the AL after the All Star break, lifting themselves out of the cellar into a fourth-place tie with the Yankees.

Colorado Rockies

Denver was one of two cities awarded a National League franchise in June 1991 (Miami was the other), in the league's first expansion since Montreal and San Diego were added in 1969. The new teams take the field for the first time in 1993, their rosters stocked primarily with players selected from the other major league clubs in a special expansion draft. The Denver franchise, which chose to call itself the Colorado Rockies, will play in Mile High Stadium—home of football's Denver Broncos—until completion of a new ball park, Coors Field, probably in 1995. Former slugger Don Baylor was named to manage the Rockies.

Detroit Tigers

One of the more successful clubs in the American League, the Tigers have enjoyed winning seasons nearly 70 percent of the time. In eighteen of their sixty-one winning seasons, they have remained in contention into the final days, eleven times emerging triumphant as league or division champions. They have finished last in the league or AL East only four times, and have never had more than four losing seasons in a row.

Detroit was one of the clubs from Ban Johnson's Western League that (renamed the American League) raised itself to major league status in 1901 with a talent raid on the long-established National League. In their first six big league seasons, the Tigers displayed little bite, finishing four times in the second division and never threatening for the league lead.

In 1907 all that changed. Sparked by a young right fielder, Ty Cobb (who in his first full big league season led the league in batting, slugging, hits, RBIs, and stolen bases) and led by a dynamic new manager, Hugh "Eeyah" Jennings (who knew enough not to try to tell Cobb how to play the game), the Tigers clawed their way to the pennant in a four-way race. The outcome might have been different if two late-season games with second-place Philadelphia had not been rained out and tied. Today's rules would require that the games be made up.

The 1908 race was even closer, with four teams contending into late September. The race wasn't settled until the final day, when Detroit beat Chicago to edge Cleveland by half a game. Once again the pennant hinged on a rainout that had not been made up. And once again Cobb dominated the league's hitters (though he slipped to fourth in stolen bases).

The Tigers had a slightly easier time of it the next year. It was a three-way race into September, but Detroit then pulled away to finish 3½ games ahead of Philadelphia. Cobb, in his best season yet, took the Triple Crown and returned to the top in stolen bases. But the Tigers were unable to win a World Series. In 1907, after an opening-game tie, the Chicago Cubs swept the next four. The Cubs lost Game Three the next year, but won the other four. And in 1909 Pittsburgh and Detroit alternated victories, with the Pirates emerging world champions in seven games.

Jennings managed Detroit for eleven more seasons; then Cobb took the reins for six years before leaving for Philadelphia. But the Tigers won no more pennants in the Cobb era. Cobb himself continued to dominate the league offensively through 1919. In 1911 he achieved career highs in most offensive categories, including a batting average of .420, but the Tigers managed no better than a distant second to the Athletics. In 1915 they started strong and remained in the race throughout the season. Cobb stole what was for forty-seven years a modern-record 96 bases, and the team's 100 wins proved to be the highest total in their first thirty-three years. But after running neck and neck with the Red Sox through most of August, the Tigers slumped a bit in early September—just enough for the Sox to take the flag by 2½ games. A close third-place finish the next year marked the Tigers' last serious challenge for eighteen years.

In 1934, after six straight years in the second division, and only three years after their most distant finish ever (47 games out), the Tigers turned themselves around to win the pennant with a 101–53 record and a .656 winning percentage, the highest in Tiger history. Two newly acquired veterans—manager/catcher Mickey Cochrane and outfielder Goose Goslin—enjoyed fine seasons at the bat, as did first baseman Hank Greenberg (.339, 139 RBIs) in his first full season, and long-time Tiger second baseman Charlie Gehringer (.356, 127 RBIs). The two other infielders, third baseman Marv Owen and shortstop Billy Rogell enjoyed their finest seasons at the plate for a club whose batting average led the league at .300. It took the Tigers a month to get going, but by mid-July they had shot ahead of the Yankees, pulling farther away through August and September to win by 7 games. But once again, victory in the World Series eluded them as the St. Louis Cardinals blew them away 11–0 in Game Seven.

The Tigers' hitting fell off ten points in 1935, but their slugging jumped eleven points. Paced by Greenberg's 170

RBIs, Detroit—after another slow start—shot up so sharply in July and August that even a September slump gave the Yankees no opportunity to catch them. And finally, in their fifth try, the Tigers won a world championship, overcoming Chicago in six games despite the loss of Greenberg, who broke his wrist in Game Two. Part-owner Frank Navin, who had run the club for three decades, had finally seen his Tigers reach the very top. A month later, after falling from a horse, he suffered a heart attack and died.

Del Baker had replaced Cochrane as manager when Detroit next made a run for the pennant in 1940. In a tight race the Tigers caught up with Cleveland in early September and traded the lead with them for two weeks before pulling ahead to stay with two wins in a three-game series. In the pennant clincher, Detroit's Floyd Giebell outdueled Cleveland great Bob Feller 2–0 for his third—and last—big league victory. In the World Series the Tigers lost once again, as Cincinnati came from behind in Game Seven for a 2–1 win.

Two losing seasons followed, and Steve O'Neill replaced Baker at the helm. In 1944, the wartime Tigers, behind the splendid pitching of workhorses Dizzy Trout and Hal Newhouser (one-two in ERA and innings pitched, and winners of 27 and 29 games), joined the race in late August and found themselves tied with the St. Louis Browns for first going into the last game of the season. But the Browns beat the Yankees and Detroit lost to Washington as Trout failed in his try for a twenty-eighth win.

Hank Greenberg's release from military service in mid-1945 sparked another Tiger run for the pennant. They held the lead from mid-June through August, but in September a surging Washington caught up with them. The race once again went down to the final day, and the final inning, when Greenberg's grand slam overcame a St. Louis lead to give Detroit the flag over the idle Senators. Newhouser, with 25 wins and a 1.81 ERA, was named AL MVP for the second straight year. In the World Series his ERA shot up to 6.10, but he still managed to win two games (including the finale) as the Tigers took the Cubs in seven for their second world title.

In the twenty-three years that passed before their next pennant, the Tigers came close only twice. In 1950 they led the race through the middle of the season, but were caught by the Yankees late in August. After retaking the lead in early September, the two clubs ran neck-and-neck for a while before Detroit fell away to second.

Two years later the Tigers reached their nadir: their first cellar finish, their most losses ever (104), and their lowest winning percentage (.325). After a decade in which they finished no higher than fourth, they rebounded in 1961 as first baseman Norm Cash and left fielder Rocky Colavito both enjoyed the most explosive seasons of their careers. Compiling their best season record since 1934, Detroit led the league through parts of June and July. But this was the year of Maris and Mantle and 109 Yankee victories; when the season ended, the Tigers' 101 wins had earned them only second place.

They came much closer six years later in the great four-way race of 1967 that saw three clubs still contending on the final day, when the Tigers split a doubleheader to tie with Minnesota for second. If 1967 was a scramble, 1968

was all Detroit's. In what is now known as the year of the pitcher, Tiger Denny McLain won 31 games (the last major leaguer to win 30) to lead the team to a 103-win finish, 12 games ahead of Baltimore. Down 1–3 to the Cardinals in the World Series, the pitching of McLain in Game Six and Mickey Lolich in Games Five and Seven brought the Tigers back and gave them their third world championship.

A strike at the start of 1972 contributed to the Tigers' first divisional title, which culminated a four-way race in the AL East. Detroit defeated Boston two games out of three at season's end, to edge the Sox by half a game. But if the strike had not wiped out an unequal number of games, the end of the season could have seen the two clubs tied.

The Tigers lost the pennant to Oakland with a 1–2 loss in the finale of a close League Championship Series, and dropped out of contention for a decade. In 1974 they finished at the bottom of the division, and the next year lost 102 games to post the worst record in the majors.

Finally, after seven seasons in the second division, Detroit put together a strong second half in strike-divided 1981, fading only at the end to tie for second. Three years later the Tigers were back on top with one of their best years. Opening the season with 9 wins, they ended April at 18–2, stretched their mark to 35–5 by late May, and were never headed, finishing a team-record 15 games in front, with 104 wins, their most ever. Their balanced pitching staff led the league in ERA, even though none of their starters finished among the top ten. Tiger newcomer Willie Hernandez (who with Aurelio Lopez compiled a 19–4 record from the bullpen, with 46 saves) earned both Cy Young and MVP awards. After sweeping Kansas City in the LCS, the Tigers took the world championship—their fourth—from San Diego in five games.

In 1987 the Tigers caught Toronto's Blue Jays in the season's final series, tying them for the lead in the first game, moving to the front with a twelve-inning win in the second game, and clinching the division crown in the finale, 1–0. In the LCS, though, Minnesota stopped the favored Tigers, four games to one.

Injuries sidelined veteran keystoners Alan Trammell and Lou Whitaker more than a month each and derailed the season of starter Jeff Robinson in August just as he was emerging as ace of Detroit's pitchers. All the same, the Tigers led the AL East much of the 1988 season before falling back and rallied at season's end to finish second, one game behind Boston.

The next year, though, as new waves of injury broke over an aging lineup, the Tigers dropped into the division cellar in June and kept sinking, finishing with 103 losses and the worst record in the majors. But in 1990 Trammell rebounded from one of his worst seasons with one of his best and, with newly acquired first baseman Cecil Fielder, sparked a Tiger recovery to third place. Fielder, back in the AL after a season in Japan, topped the majors in home runs (with 51, the most in the AL since 1961), slugging percentage, and runs batted in.

The 1991 Tigers clawed their way back from an 8-game deficit in mid-July into a tie with first-place Toronto seven weeks later. But their grip wouldn't hold, and they finished tied for second with Boston. In 1992, for the third year in a row, Detroit led the AL in home runs, but this

time their big bats couldn't lift the club above sixth place.

Florida Marlins

One of two new clubs to join the National League in 1993, the Florida Marlins were formed after the selection, in June 1991, of Miami and Denver as cities for the league's first expansion teams since 1969. The Marlins, headed by entertainment magnate H. Wayne Huizenga, will play in Joe Robbie Stadium, which Huizenga partially owns. Though better known as a football facility, the real-grass stadium also accommodates baseball.

In October 1992 Rene Lachemann, who formerly piloted the Seattle Mariners and Milwaukee Brewers, was named the Marlins' first manager.

Houston Astros

The Colt .45s (as the Astros were originally known) had hoped to begin their history in the Harris County Domed Stadium, but when the start of the vast project was delayed, a temporary outdoor park was built for them next door in time for their 1962 inaugural. Heat, humidity, and giant mosquitoes held Colt home attendance below a million in each of their three outdoor seasons, but when, in 1965, they brought big league baseball indoors for the first time, the fans arrived—more than two million the first year. The original grass under the dome was real, but when the skylight panels were coated over so fielders wouldn't lose sight of high flies, the grass died. In 1966 the club (now known as the Astros) and the stadium (now called the Astrodome) brought to baseball yet another innovation—AstroTurf.

The Houston franchise, conceived as an entry in the abortive Continental League, first took the field instead (along with New York's Mets) in the National League, as part of the league's first expansion since shrinking from twelve teams to eight in 1900. Shrewd player selection by general manager Paul Richards kept the new team from being as bad as the Mets. Although they suffered just as long playing below .500 (seven years), they finished only once below New York in the standings.

When the NL added two more teams in 1969 and split into two divisions, the Astros for the first time made a serious title run. Though they wound up fifth in the West (ahead of only the expansion San Diego Padres), they rose to within two games of the top in August, and again in September, before a six-game losing streak dropped them out of contention. With an 81–81 record, they finished out of the ranks of losers for the first time.

After dropping below .500 again in 1970 and '71, the Astros made their second run for the division title in 1972. At the end of June they were neck and neck with Cincinnati for the lead, but the Reds pulled away over the rest of the season while Houston leveled off for an eventual second-place finish 10½ games back. With a record of 84–69, the Astros had fashioned their first winning season.

In 1975 they endured their worst year ever, losing 97 games to finish at the bottom of the West, 43½ games behind the Reds. But the next year pitcher J. R. Richard, with the first of several fine seasons, brought the club up to third with his 20 wins. By 1979 Richard was the NL's most overwhelming pitcher, leading the league with 313 strikeouts and a 2.71 ERA. His 18 wins and teammate Joe Niekro's 21 sparked a team that spent much of the summer in first place before falling to 1½ games behind Cincinnati at the end.

Houston and Los Angeles battled back and forth for the division lead throughout 1980. Richard began strong and seemed headed for his finest year. With a 10–4 record, he was starting pitcher in the All-Star Game. But shortly after midseason he suffered a stroke that ended his big league career. Led by Joe Niekro and Vern Ruhle (who replaced Richard in the rotation and finished 12–4), the best pitching staff in baseball kept the Astros in the race to season's end, although three straight losses to the Dodgers had left the clubs tied for first. In a one-game playoff, Houston rebounded with a 7–1 win (Niekro's twentieth) to capture the division title. In the League Championship Series, the Astros took the Phillies to the tenth inning of the final game before bowing two games to three.

When a player strike cut the middle out of the 1981 season, intradivisional playoffs were scheduled between the winners of the two halves. Houston, the second-half champion, defeated first-half victor Los Angeles in the first two games, but lost the next three, and with them the division title.

After four years in the middle of the division, the Astros stormed back in 1986 with their best season ever, winning fifteen of their last nineteen games to conquer the West by ten games. Pitcher Mike Scott, who had developed a deceptive split-finger fastball, won 18 to pace a strong Astro staff, leading the league in strikeouts and ERA. On September 25 he clinched the division crown with a no-hitter. In the LCS the Astros lost to the Mets, two games to four—but they held the New Yorkers at bay for fifteen innings of the final game before falling by a run in the sixteenth.

In each of the next three seasons the Astros drew within ½ to 1½ games of first place in August, only to tumble out of the race in the season's final weeks. While the team never challenged for the division lead in 1990, they overcame—with a winning second half—the worst first half in the league to tie for fourth in the NL West.

Rookie first baseman Jeff Bagwell's strong performance at the plate gave Astros fans one of their few reasons to cheer in 1991 as their team plummeted to last place. In 1992 Bagwell's continuing offensive leadership, plus strong relief pitching (especially a career-best season from newly acquired Doug Jones) ignited a fiery final two months that lifted the Astros from sixteen games below .500 to an unexpected 81-81 fourth-place finish.

Kansas City Royals

Two years after the Athletics abandoned Kansas City for the West Coast, patent-medicine millionaire Ewing Kauffman bankrolled an expansion club for the city. Where the A's had been unable in thirteen years to fashion even one winning season, the Royals did it in 1971, their third year (when, ironically, they finished second in

the AL West to the newly invincible Oakland A's). One of the most successful of all expansion clubs, the Royals in their first twenty-two years have finished either first or second in their division fourteen times.

In their fifth season, 1973, the year they moved into new Royals Stadium, the Royals also made their first serious run for the division title. A midsummer spurt carried them into first place in August before they leveled off to another second-place finish behind Oakland.

After a third second-place race with Oakland in 1975 (during which manager Jack McKeon was replaced by Whitey Herzog), the Royals won the division crown in 1976, taking the lead two months into the season and holding it to the end. Third baseman George Brett won his first AL batting championship and carried his hot bat into the League Championship Series, but the Yankees snatched the pennant on Chris Chambliss's home run in the bottom of the ninth inning of the final game.

For two more years the Royals dominated the AL West but failed to stop the Yankees in the LCS. In 1977, with a pitching staff that led the league in ERA and a balanced offense that included four players with more than 20 home runs and 80 RBIs, the Royals compiled a record of 102–60—their finest to date. Though they didn't move into the division lead until mid-August, they were nearly unstoppable the rest of the way. In the LCS they once again battled New York all the way, only to lose the Series and pennant for the second time in the final inning of game five.

The divisional race was a bit tighter in 1978, as California hung close to K.C. through much of August and into September, before the Royals finally pulled away. In the LCS, the Royals tied the Series with a big win in Game Two, but the Yankees came back to take the next two by one run each for their third straight flag.

The Royals slipped to second place in 1979, but the next year (led now by rookie manager Jim Frey) they overwhelmed the rest of a weak division. Despite a month-long decline in September, K.C. finished the season 14 games ahead of Oakland for their fourth divisional title. This was the year Brett chased .400 (ending at .390, the highest major league average since Ted Williams hit .406 in 1941), reliever Dan Quisenberry enjoyed his first big season (12 wins, 33 saves), and starter Dennis Leonard came back from an off-year to record his third 20-win season in four years. It was also the year the Royals finally beat the Yankees to capture their first pennant—with a three-game sweep in the LCS. In the World Series, though, it was Philadelphia in six games.

The player strike of 1981 divided the season into two halves. In the first half the Royals finished fifth, but part way through the second half Dick Howser (who had managed the Yankees to the East title the previous year) replaced Frey as Royals manager and brought the club in first, a game ahead of Oakland. But in the special play-offs, the A's (who had won the first-half race) beat K.C. for the division title with a three-game sweep.

Two more second-place finishes in 1982 (a close race with California) and 1983 (20 games behind the Chicago White Sox) were followed in 1984 by a fifth division championship in a three-way race with California and Minnesota. But Detroit swept away the Royals' pennant hopes in the LCS, in the minimum three games.

For Kansas City, 1985 was a season of catching up. Few picked the Royals to win the West, but with starters Charlie Leibrandt (17–9) and Bret Saberhagen (20–6) finishing two-three in the league ERA race, reliever Quisenberry leading the league in saves for the fourth straight year, and veteran George Brett healthy and enjoying one of his best seasons ever, the Royals chased California throughout the summer and caught them in the final week to take their sixth division crown by a single game. In the LCS against Toronto, K.C. fell behind 1–3, which would have eliminated them in earlier years. But, saved by the expansion of the Series from five games to seven, they came back with three straight wins for their second pennant. Repeating the suspense in the World Series, the Royals again fell behind 1–3, to St. Louis, before rallying once again to win three straight for their first world championship.

During the 1986 season, manager Howser left the club after he was found to have a brain tumor. The Royals dropped below .500 and finished third, their lowest rank in a dozen years. Howser was unable to return to the helm in 1987 as he had hoped and died during the summer. The Royals rallied at season's end to pull themselves above .500 and finish (for the eighth time) runner-up in the West, 2 games behind Minnesota. Although they improved on their 1987 won-lost record in 1988, they finished in third place.

In 1989 Bret Saberhagen, with his most sparkling season yet (23–6, 2.16 ERA), hurled the Royals to their best record since 1980, but their 92 wins earned them only a ninth second-place finish. Confounding predictions of another strong season, following free agent acquisitions Mark Davis and Storm Davis, the Royals in 1990 floundered in the division cellar much of the summer. They wound up in sixth place, 27½ games out. Thirty-seven-year-old George Brett, though, rallied from the worst start of his career (.200 BA in early May) to hit .329 and capture his third AL batting title.

Slugging outfielder Danny Tartabull enjoyed a peak season in 1991 and helped lift K.C. back above .500. But in the strong AL West no club suffered a losing season, so the Royals again had to settle for sixth. When Tartabull left for the Yankees in 1992, the Royals faltered again. But as the West was now the weaker division, the club's 72–90 record was good enough for a fifth-place tie.

Los Angeles Dodgers

When the Dodgers left Brooklyn for Los Angeles, an era ended. From baseball's earliest days Brooklyn had been prominent; the city's Atlantics were the nation's best in the mid-1860s, and since 1884 Brooklyn had been home to major league ball. But before the start of the 1958 season, its link to the big time was severed by an owner who saw greener fields to the west. He was right: the Dodgers in Los Angeles are one of the game's most profitable franchises, regularly attracting more than three million fans per year to Dodger Stadium.

The club's origins were modest. After winning the championship of the minor Inter-State League in 1883, Brooklyn moved up to the major league American Association in 1884 and endured three losing seasons in its first

four years. But in 1888, after signing three regulars from New York's newly defunct Mets and buying pitching/hitting stars Bob Caruthers and Dave Foutz from the AA champion St. Louis Browns, Brooklyn finished second to St. Louis, and the next year dethroned the Browns for their first big league pennant. In a projected ten-game World Series against the National League champion New York Giants, the Bridegrooms (as the Brooklyns had been nicknamed) won three of the first four games, but lost the next five.

Before the start of the 1890 season, Brooklyn transferred from the AA to the more prestigious NL. Many NL clubs performed below par that year, weakened by the loss of players to the outlaw Players League. But Brooklyn held on to most of its players and swept to its second straight pennant. In postseason play, poor weather and lack of fan support caused the World Series against AA winner Louisville to be called off after each team had won three games and tied one. The next year, with other NL teams renewed by players from the failed PL, Brooklyn finished sixth.

When the AA folded after the 1891 season, Brooklyn picked up slugger Dan Brouthers and pitcher George Haddock from pennant-winning Boston, and rebounded in 1892 to finish second and third in the two halves of a divided season. But for the next five years they finished no higher than fifth, and in 1898 sank to tenth in what was now a twelve-team league.

Help was on the way, however—help that today would be prohibited. Longtime Brooklyn president Charles Byrne had died, and the owners of the Baltimore Orioles—Harry Von der Horst and Ned Hanlon—seeing an opportunity to move into the more lucrative Brooklyn market, purchased a half interest in the Bridegrooms. Hanlon retained his Baltimore presidency, but took over as manager in Brooklyn, bringing along with him the core of his Oriole club—shortstop Hughie Jennings and outfielders Joe Kelley and Willie Keeler—plus its two best pitchers, Jim Hughes and Doc McJames.

The infusion of new talent worked wonders, as Brooklyn in 1899 (with a new nickname, the Superbas) took the NL lead in late May, during a twenty-two game winning streak, and held it the rest of the way. That winter, when Baltimore was dropped as the NL cut back from twelve teams to eight, Hanlon moved more Orioles to Brooklyn (including pitcher Joe "Iron Man" McGinnity), and once again led the Superbas to the pennant. That year they also won their first world championship in a series played with second-place Pittsburgh for the elegant Chronicle-Telegraph Cup.

Slow starts in 1901 and '02 kept the Superbas out of pennant contention, although they finished third and second. During this period Charley Ebbets, who had risen from ticket seller to president, took over majority ownership with the purchase of Von der Horst's stock, thereby quashing Hanlon's proposed move back to Baltimore. But Ebbets's clashes with Hanlon hastened the club's decline. In 1903 the team began a twelve-year sojourn in the second division, including a last-place finish in 1905 with their worst record ever (48–104, 56½ games out). Perhaps the most memorable events of these years were the change in nickname to Dodgers, and their move to brand-new Ebbets Field in 1913.

Hanlon was fired as manager after the disastrous 1905 season, but it was not until Wilbert Robinson took over in 1914 that the team began to pull out of its doldrums. Pitcher Jack Pfeffer, in his first full big-league season, won 23 games for the fifth-place Dodgers that year, and two years later led them to the pennant with 25 wins on a sparkling 1.92 ERA.

But the Dodgers lost the World Series to the Boston Red Sox, and in 1917 fell all the way to seventh. After three years in the second division, they bounced back in 1920, turning a three-way race into a rout with sixteen wins in their final eighteen games. After another World Series loss, to Cleveland, the Dodgers returned to the second division for another three years. In 1924 they began slowly, but leaped from twelve games back to an early-September lead, only to slip 1½ games behind the Giants at the finish.

Charley Ebbets died the following April, and Robinson was named to replace him. In his five years as president the club suffered on the field, finishing sixth each year. Fired as president but retained as manager, "Uncle Robbie" saw his Robins (as the Dodgers were now known) lead the league in 1930 most of the time from mid-May to a mid-August decline, then retake the lead for a day in mid-September before tailing off once more to finish fourth. That was Uncle Robbie's last hurrah. When the Robins provided no serious challenge in their fourth-place run the next year, he resigned after eighteen years at the wheel.

A succession of managers followed, but it was not until the Dodgers brought in the free-spending Larry MacPhail as general manager in 1938 that the club began to pull itself back into contention. The highlight of MacPhail's first year with the Dodgers was not the team's finish (seventh) but the introduction of night baseball to Ebbets Field (on June 15, when Cincinnati's Johnny Vander Meer defeated Brooklyn with his second consecutive no-hitter). MacPhail was also looking for new talent, and over the next couple of years he acquired a combination of youngsters and veterans that turned the Dodgers into one of the best teams in the league.

But MacPhail's most brilliant move may have been his conversion of shortstop Leo Durocher into manager Leo Durocher. The loud, driven Durocher alienated many (including MacPhail himself), but provided inspired leadership and a will to win that overcame complaints against him. After a third-place finish in 1939 and second place in 1940, the Dodgers battled the St. Louis Cardinals through all of 1941 before pulling ahead to clinch the pennant with just two games remaining. Veteran first baseman Dolf Camilli led the league in home runs and RBIs, sophomore outfielder Pete Reiser led the league in batting, slugging, and runs scored, and pitchers Kirby Higbe and Whitlow Wyatt tied for the league lead with 22 wins apiece, as the Dodgers for the first time since 1899 won 100 games. Only their loss to the Yankees in the World Series marred their finest season in forty-two years.

In 1942 they played even better, winning 104 games. But a late-season five-game slump dropped them behind the surging Cardinals, and they finished 2 games short of the flag.

MacPhail and many of his players left for the war, and though the club finished third in 1943 and 1945, it was not

until 1946 that the Dodgers again presented a serious challenge. Once again the Cards and Dodgers made a two-team race of it, but this time the race ended in a tie, forcing the first league playoff ever. St. Louis won the pennant with wins in the first two games.

When MacPhail left for the Army, Branch Rickey was hired to run the club. MacPhail had left the club financially sound and a big drawing card; Rickey set about to make it a consistent winner. Famed as the developer of the Cardinal farm system, he was determined at Brooklyn to tap the one source of talent that the major leagues had willfully neglected: black players. He signed Jackie Robinson to Montreal (Brooklyn's leading farm team), and after a year there promoted him to the Dodgers for the 1947 season. Thus began the club's golden Brooklyn decade: ten years in which they won six pennants and—in 1955—a World Series. Two other races went right to the wire; only once did they finish as low as third.

With manager Durocher suspended from baseball for a year for consorting with gamblers, the Dodgers in 1947 were led by grandfatherly Burt Shotton, brought out of his Florida retirement. Robinson's hustle put him at the top of the league in stolen bases and second in runs scored. The team pulled up from fourth in June to first in July, and held the lead to the end. In the World Series they lost to the Yankees in an exciting seven games.

Durocher returned to the helm in 1948, but was replaced by Shotton in midsummer, with the Dodgers in fifth place. Shotton saw the team rise to third that season, then battle back and forth with the Cardinals throughout 1949 before edging them by a game on the final day. Robinson, in his finest season, led the league in hitting and stolen bases, and finished among the leaders in most other offensive categories. Rookie pitcher Don Newcombe led the team in victories with 17, and Preacher Roe led the league in winning percentage. Again the World Series was a loss to the Yankees, this time in only five games.

In 1950 the Dodgers nearly caught the staggering Phillies, losing out only in the tenth inning of the final game. President Rickey left the club for Pittsburgh and was replaced by Walter O'Malley, who replaced manager Shotton with Charlie Dressen. The slugging of catcher Roy Campanella and first baseman Gil Hodges, and 20-win seasons by Roe (22–3) and Newcombe (20–9) kept the Dodgers in front through most of 1951, but New York's surging Giants closed from thirteen games back in August to tie for the lead at the finish. The teams split the first two playoff games. In Game Three the Dodgers were leading by three runs in the last of the ninth when Bobby Thomson's three-run homer gave New York the flag.

The next year, though, the Giants fell short and Brooklyn took the pennant with relative ease. But not the World Series. Although Brooklyn held a 3–2 lead after five games, the Yankees came back to take the final two.

The Dodgers repeated as NL champions in 1953 with their best season ever. Dodger bats overwhelmed the league, hitting 19 points and slugging 63 points above the league average, as the team outscored its nearest rival by more than a run per game. With a club-record 105 wins, the Dodgers cruised to the pennant by 13 games. But again the Yankees took the World Series, in six games.

Dressen wanted a three-year contract and was let go when he turned down another for only one year. Minor

league manager Walter Alston wasn't so demanding, and signed for 1954 the first of a historic string of twenty-three one-year Dodger contracts that would see him into the Hall of Fame. After a second-place finish in Alston's rookie season, the Dodgers in 1955 took the lead from the start and—never challenged—walked away with their eleventh pennant. Outfielder Duke Snider, with one of his most productive seasons, led the league's most powerful squad; Newcombe (20–5) paced the league's best pitching staff.

Once more in the World Series, Brooklyn faced the Yankees, and once more the Series went seven games. But this time there was joy in Brooklyn—Johnny Podres shut out New York in the finale! In an exciting three-way fight in 1956, the Dodgers repeated as pennant-winners, taking their final three games to edge Milwaukee's Braves. Newcombe, in his greatest year, clinched the flag on the final day with his twenty-seventh win. In the World Series, though, it was *déjà vu* time—a sixth Yankee triumph, in seven games. The golden decade was over.

The Dodgers (despite the league's best pitching) vacated the 1957 race in August, finishing third. Before the start of the next season, they had vacated Brooklyn as well, for Los Angeles. Playing in Memorial Coliseum (a converted football stadium) the L.A. Dodgers sank to seventh place in 1958. But the next year the reawakened bats of aging Duke Snider and Gil Hodges, the fiery pitching of young Don Drysdale, and the late-season pitching heroics of Roger Craig (recalled from Spokane) kept the team in the thick of a tight race that found them tied with the Braves at season's end. The Dodgers won the first playoff game in Milwaukee, and captured big league baseball's first West Coast pennant at home the next day, in the twelfth inning. Then they defeated the Chicago White Sox to give the West its first World Series winner.

After finishes of fourth and second, the Dodgers produced record-breaking excitement in 1962 as they moved into brand-new Dodger Stadium in the hills above Los Angeles. Between the new ballpark and the excitement generated on the field, more than 2.75 million fans passed through the turnstiles—a new attendance record that would last until the Dodgers themselves broke it fifteen years later. As pitcher Don Drysdale and left fielder Tommy Davis ignited the league with career-high seasons, and shortstop Maury Wills became the first major leaguer of the century to steal 100 bases, the team locked into a season-long struggle for first place with archrival San Francisco. But after holding a narrow lead much of the season, the Dodgers dropped their last four games to finish in yet another tie—their fourth.

The playoff must have reminded fans of 1951. As they had then, the Giants and Dodgers split the first two games, and the Dodgers once again brought a 4–2 lead into the ninth inning of Game Three. This time, though, it was not a home run that undid them, but a bases-loaded walk.

Sandy Koufax—who had won 14 games in 1962 (and the first of five straight ERA crowns) despite losing half the year with circulation problems in his fingers—rose to dominate the world of pitching the next four years. For three of those years his Dodgers dominated the NL. In 1963 Koufax's 25–5 season carried Los Angeles into the World Series against the Yankees, where two more wins

helped put the New Yorkers away in the minimum four games. The next year Koufax slipped to 19 wins, but the Dodgers fell all the way to a tie for sixth.

They rebounded to the top in 1965. Koufax won 26 and Drysdale 23 in a tight four-team race that saw them fall behind the Giants in early September, only to retake the lead for good later in the month with 13 straight wins. The World Series against Minnesota went to the seventh game before Koufax nailed down another world title with his second shutout in three days.

The race in 1966 was just as close as in '65, with three teams switching leads throughout the season. But the Dodgers, third at the end of August, put together streaks of five and seven wins in September to move to the top, where Koufax clinched the pennant on the final day with his twenty-seventh victory. And then it was all over. After a losing effort in Game Two of the World Series (a Baltimore sweep), Koufax, at age thirty, retired because of arthritis in his pitching elbow. The Dodgers sank to eighth the next year and rose only to seventh in 1968.

In 1969, the first season of divisional play, Los Angeles found itself in the thick of a five-team race in the West until eight straight losses in late September dropped them to fourth. No one challenged Cincinnati in 1970, but the next year the Dodgers closed to within a game of the front-running Giants in September before their drive stalled.

A late-season Dodger slump let Cincinnati get to the top in 1973, but the Dodgers held their lead to the end in 1974. Newly acquired veteran outfielder Jimmy Wynn and first baseman Steve Garvey, in his first full season, led the club offensively; pitcher Mike Marshall set a modern major league record with 106 appearances in relief of a staff that was the league's best (which earned him the Cy Young award). The Dodgers beat Pittsburgh handily in the League Championship Series for their fifth Los Angeles pennant, but lost the World Series to Oakland in five games.

Cincinnati proved untouchable in 1975 and '76, but in 1977 the Dodgers—under new manager Tom Lasorda, who moved up from the coaching staff when Alston retired—jumped to an early lead and held it all the way. Garvey's 33 home runs led a balanced offense in which four players hit 30 or more homers and drove in over 85 runs. Again the Dodgers won the LCS (in four games, against Philadelphia), and again they lost the World Series (to the Yankees, in six games).

Although the divisional race was closer— and the Dodgers broke baseball's three million attendance barrier for the first time—1978 was in most respects a replay of 1977. Garvey again led the club offensively, the Dodgers again beat out Cincinnati in the West and Philadelphia in a four-game LCS, and the Yankees again defeated the Dodgers in a six-game World Series.

A season-long back-and-forth battle with Houston in 1980 ended in a tie for first—the fifth tie for the Dodgers, three more than any other club. In the playoff (reduced from three games to one to bring the NL into line with AL practice), Houston won easily.

When the players went out on strike part way through 1981, the Dodgers, paced by the spectacular pitching of rookie Fernando Valenzuela, found themselves half a game in front of Cincinnati. In a special playoff with poststrike leader Houston, the Dodgers defeated the Astros in five games for the division title, and also went the distance in beating Montreal for the pennant—their twenty-first. Facing the Yankees for the eleventh time in World Series play, they lost the first two games, but swept the next four games to capture their sixth world title.

In 1982, after a poor start, the Dodgers fought back to take the lead in August and again in September before dropping back to second, a game out. More successful drives in 1983 and '85 led to their fifth and sixth division titles, but culminated in defeat in the LCS—to Philadelphia in 1983 and St. Louis two years later. In 1986 and '87 they posted identical 73–89 won-lost records—the team's worst performance in two decades.

But then in 1988, with an infusion of talent from the American League—most notably slugger Kirk Gibson and relief ace Jay Howell—and a spectacular season on the mound from starter Orel Hershiser (who concluded his 23–8 year with a major-league record 59 consecutive scoreless innings), the Dodgers bounced back to the top of the NL West. It took them the full seven games to down the favored Mets in the LCS for their twenty-second pennant, but in the World Series they humbled Oakland's powerful Athletics in just five games for their seventh world crown.

Hershiser (whose 15–15 record belied another strong season on the mound) led a 1989 Dodger pitching staff that yielded the fewest runs in the majors, but with an offense last among major league clubs in *scoring* runs, the Dodgers could finish no better than fourth in the West. Hershiser's 1990 season ended almost as soon as it began when he underwent shoulder surgery in late April, but young Ramon Martinez took up the slack, winning 20 games. With a revived offense that topped the NL West in runs scored, the Dodgers bounced back from a slow first half to draw within 3½ games of Cincinnati in late September and finish second, 5 games out.

From early May to late August 1991, the Dodgers occupied first place in their division, paced by the majors' stingiest pitching staff and the hot bats of free agent signees Brett Butler and Darryl Strawberry. But the team never enjoyed more than a 6-game lead, and with seven straight losses after the All-Star break, began their descent into a great struggle with ascendant Atlanta. From August 21 through season's end the two clubs stayed within two games of each other. With four games to go, Los Angeles held a one-game lead. But they lost their next three games and all hope of the division crown.

In 1992 everything fell apart. Unable to parry the twin blows of injury and inexperience, the Dodgers stumbled to the worst record in the majors, and finished last for only the second time in their 109 years of major league play.

Milwaukee Brewers

When in 1969 the new Seattle Pilots played their home opener in the refurbished minor league Sick's Stadium, 7,000 seats and the left field fence were still unfinished. The Pilots may not have needed the seats. Fewer than 700,000 fans came to see them play—the third worst attendance in the league—as they drifted into the cellar of the American League West with 98 losses. That winter

the Pilots—renamed the Brewers—moved to Milwaukee, where a genuine big league stadium (vacated by the Braves five years earlier) awaited them.

Attendance improved nearly 38 percent in Milwaukee, although the Brewers of 1970 won only one game more than the Pilots had in Seattle. It would be eight more years before they experienced their first winning season. Meanwhile, in 1972, they switched divisions from West to East, trading places with the Washington Senators, who moved West to become the Texas Rangers.

At last—and with power—the Brewers broke their losing pattern in 1978. One key front-office move leading to the turnaround, the signing of free agent Larry Hisle (who the previous year with Minnesota had led the league in RBIs), was also a giant step in the escalation of major league player compensation. With a signing bonus and deferred payments on top of salary, Hisle's six-year contract averaged out to eleven times what he was paid in Minnesota, an annual average figure that would have paid almost 40 percent of the Brewers' player payroll the previous year.

Hisle proved his worth in 1978, leading an offense that sprang to life under rookie manager George Bamberger to top the league in hitting, slugging, homers, and runs scored. On the mound Mike Caldwell won 22 games in the best season of his career. Although the Brewers never threatened the Boston Red Sox or the New York Yankees for the lead, they did rise from below .500 in early June to finish a solid third, 24 games above .500.

A shoulder injury the next April marked the beginning of the end of Hisle's career and perhaps cost Milwaukee the division title. Even without Hisle the team compiled what is still their best winning percentage (.590), as outfielder Gorman Thomas (45 home runs, 123 RBIs) and several other Brewer hitters attained new career peaks of productivity. While they never seriously threatened front-running Baltimore, they rose past Boston in late August to finish second.

Most of the Milwaukee bats remained hot in 1980, but injuries, ragged pitching, and Bamberger's heart attack (which caused him to miss the first part of the season and retire in early September) contributed to a distant third-place finish. In strike-divided 1981, league-leading performances by two newly acquired pitchers—starter Pete Vuckovich (14–4) and reliever Rollie Fingers (28 saves)—helped give the Brewers the best overall record in the AL East, and the second-half championship. But in the special intradivisional playoffs with first-half winner New York, the Yankees captured the division crown three games to two.

The Brewers started slowly in 1982; at the end of May they were two games below .500, near the bottom of the division. A day later Buck Rogers, the Milwaukee coach who had replaced Bamberger as manager two years earlier, was himself replaced by coach Harvey Kuenn. By mid-July the team had risen to first place, and they led the West by more than six games as September neared. But Baltimore had cut the lead to three games by the time Milwaukee arrived for the season's final four games. One win would give the Brewers their first division championship, but they lost the first three games by five, six, and eight runs. Don Sutton, who had been acquired from Houston a month earlier, faced Oriole Jim Palmer in the

season finale: the Brewers made Sutton's job easy, scoring ten runs to Baltimore's two.

Milwaukee's offense—"Harvey's Wallbangers"—had been awesome, scoring more than a run per game above the league average. Just about every offensive category featured one or two Brewers among the league's top three: in hits they took all three top spots. Shortstop Robin Yount, who finished first in slugging, hits, total bases, and doubles, was named major league player of the year.

In postseason play California took a 2–1 lead in the League Championship Series, but Milwaukee came back to take the final two games and the pennant. In the World Series against St. Louis, the Brewers twice took the lead in games, but a Cardinal come-from-behind win in Game Seven ended Brewer hopes.

Milwaukee dropped to fifth in 1983, then to a last-place seventh the next year, 36½ games back—their most distant finish ever. It was not until 1987 that they returned to the winning track, finishing third with 91 victories. Had they remained in the AL West where they started, they would have won the division championship by 6 games.

As veterans Robin Yount and Paul Molitor continued to spark the team's offense, and starter Ted Higuera and reliever Dan Plesac headlined the AL East's best pitching staff, the Brewers in 1988 rose above .500 to stay at the end of August, and finished in a tie for third, just two games behind champion Boston. With Yount and Molitor enjoying even more productive seasons in 1989, and reliever Plesac on a club-record pace for saves, the Brewers drew within half a game of first place in August. But injuries and league-worst fielding took their toll, and the club finished fourth, right at .500. In 1990, as poor fielding led to more than 100 unearned runs, the Brewers dropped to sixth.

Paul Molitor enjoyed a banner season in 1991, and from the first week in August to the finish the Brewers played at a torrid .750 clip. But they had begun their comeback 15 games behind, and too late to raise themselves past fourth, 8 games out. With another sterling season from Molitor in 1992, and another strong finish (after a better first half), Milwaukee drew within 2 games of ultimately victorious Toronto in the season's final week. Still, the Brewers' 92–70 record and second-place finish were their best since their pennant-winning season a decade earlier.

Minnesota Twins

The Twins' beginnings as the Washington Senators were inauspicious. When American League president Ban Johnson established the Senators as part of his move in 1901 to raise the league to major league status, he staffed it with the manager and many of the players from his disbanded Kansas City franchise. Within a decade, four of the eight teams in the new major league had won two or more pennants, and three others had enjoyed at least one season in second place. But the Senators, after sixth-place finishes in their first two seasons, spent the next nine years in seventh or eighth. In 1904, their fourth season, they lost 113 games—still the team worst.

Even the arrival of promising young fireballer Walter Johnson didn't seem to help. By 1909 he was the league's

second-best strikeout artist, but he lost 25 games and the Senators finished farther back than ever—56 games from the top. Johnson turned his record around the next two years, winning 25 games in 1910 and in 1911, but the team rose only to seventh.

When Clark Griffith—a forty-two-year-old former pitching great and one of the founders of the American League—was hired to manage the Senators after the 1911 season, the club's fortunes took an immediate turn for the better. Griffith revamped the lineup—most strikingly in the acquisition of first baseman Chick Gandil from minor league Montreal. The Senators in 1912 won seventeen straight games after Gandil was put into the lineup, and found themselves in the midst of a pennant race. Boston's Red Sox eventually ran away from the field, but the Senators held off Philadelphia for second place. Johnson won 33 games, and his 1.39 ERA led the league.

The next season was Johnson's finest. His league-leading 36 wins, 11 shutouts, and 1.14 ERA were also career bests and enabled Washington to overtake Cleveland late in the season for another second-place finish. But while Johnson continued to top 20 wins per season for several years before beginning to fade, his team was unable to stay competitive, only once in the next decade making a serious run at the pennant (in war-shortened 1918, when they finished 4 games back, in third).

Griffith wanted the Senators to spend more to attract good players; when his demands were rejected, he bought into a controlling interest in the club and named himself president. A year later, in 1921, he retired as field manager. Under a succession of veteran player-managers the team showed some improvement over the next three years, but Griffith's surprise appointment of twenty-seven-year-old second baseman Bucky Harris to manage the team in 1924 worked wonders. Left fielder Goose Goslin drove in more runs than Babe Ruth, and Walter Johnson put together his best season in years to head the league's best pitching staff. A hot streak in June shot the team from fifth to first, and a strong stretch drive in August and September brought them to the finish 2 games ahead of the Yankees. In the World Series a ground ball's lucky bounce over the head of the Giants' third baseman brought the Senators victory in the last of the twelfth inning of the seventh game.

Though the Senators, aided by the acquisition of veteran pitcher Stan Coveleski from Cleveland, fought off the A's to repeat as pennant winners in 1925, they were less successful in postseason play. Once again the Series went the full seven games, but this time Pittsburgh won the world title.

The Senators enjoyed winning seasons in five of the next seven years, as Johnson retired from the mound and replaced Harris as manager. But it was not until 1933, when Johnson was replaced by twenty-six-year-old shortstop Joe Cronin, that the team again pursued the pennant beyond midseason. Two veteran pitchers at the top of their form—Alvin "General" Crowder and Earl Whitehill—and a balanced offense led by Cronin and first baseman Joe Kuhel kept the Senators close to New York through July, and then, as the Yankees leveled off in August, shot the team up out of reach. Although they tailed off a bit at the end, the Senators won the pennant

handily, compiling a .651 winning percentage that is still the club record. The New York Giants, though, took Washington's measure in the World Series and overcame them in five games.

The following October, after a drop from third place in June to a distant seventh at season's end had plunged home attendance nearly 25 percent below the previous year, Griffith—always close to the edge financially—traded Joe Cronin, his manager, star shortstop, and (since September) son-in-law, to the Boston Red Sox for a lesser shortstop and $225,000.

Only twice in their remaining quarter century in Washington did the Senators rise higher than fourth or finish closer than 17 games from the top. In 1943 they placed second, 13½ games behind the runaway Yankees. And two years later, after a poor start, they caught up with frontrunner Detroit in September, only to stall and finish 1½ games out. In their final six Washington seasons, they wound up in the cellar four times.

Calvin Griffith, Clark's adopted son, assumed the club presidency when his father died in 1955. Within three years he was making plans to move the club to Minneapolis. There were threats from Congress and a plea from President Eisenhower not to move the Senators—and at first the league itself opposed the move. But Washington was not a good baseball town even when the Senators were playing well, and in October 1960 a solution was reached. The league would let Griffith move his club to Minnesota, and Washington would be granted a new expansion team.

Players like outfielders Bob Allison and Harmon Killebrew, and pitcher Camilo Pascual, who had enjoyed productive seasons before the move, were even more productive in Minnesota. Other standouts became regulars or joined the club after the move—Zoilo Versalles at shortstop, Rich Rollins at third, Jim Kaat on the mound, and (arriving in 1964) outfielder Tony Oliva and pitcher Jim "Mudcat" Grant. Infielder Rod Carew began his twelve-year stint with the Twins in 1967.

Former outfielder Sam Mele made his major league managerial debut during 1961, and in 1962 saw his Twins come close to catching the Yankees in mid-September, finishing second. The next year they didn't catch fire until August and wound up third. In 1964 they dropped below .500 into a tie for sixth. But after the end of June 1965 no one challenged them as they breezed to their first Minnesota pennant. Oliva led the league in batting for the second straight year, and Versalles (in what was far and away his finest season) led the league in total bases and runs scored. Mudcat Grant led the league with 21 victories (his only 20-win season) and 6 shutouts, and Kaat's 18 wins were the league's third best. In the World Series it took a three-hitter by Los Angeles's Sandy Koufax to stop the Twins in the seventh game.

After a poor start in 1966 that saw them enter July deep in fifth place, the Twins played better than anyone else the rest of the season to sneak ahead of Detroit into second. Killebrew, who had been injured much of the previous year, returned with his old power in '66, and Kaat enjoyed a career-high season with 25 wins.

The Twins began 1967 with another poor start. With the team in disarray and in sixth place, the easygoing Mele was replaced in June by hard-driving Cal Ermer, a

longtime minor league manager. By mid-July the team had risen to second, and a month later (after dropping back to fourth) moved to the top in one of the greatest pennant races ever. Four clubs battled for the title, with three still in the running on the final day. But Boston defeated Minnesota to win the pennant, and Detroit split a doubleheader to tie the Twins for second. The next year Minnesota finished seventh.

Fiery rookie manager Billy Martin replaced Ermer in 1969 and, in this first season of divisional play, piloted the Twins to the championship of the West by a convincing 9 games. Killebrew exploded for the best season of his career (49 home runs, 140 runs driven in), and Carew won the first of his seven batting titles. The first League Championship Series, though, was a disaster for the Twins as Baltimore swept to the pennant in three games. Veteran manager Bill Rigney replaced the difficult Martin at the helm, and piloted Minnesota to an almost identical division crown in 1970, 9 games ahead of Oakland. Pitcher Jim Perry, with 24 victories, enjoyed his second straight 20-win season, and the best of his career. The LCS, though, was another repeat performance—a Baltimore sweep.

For the next thirteen years the Twins remained out of contention, although only in 1981 and '82 did they drop to the bottom of the division. Twice (in 1974 and '76) they recovered from poor starts to make a decent showing, and once (1979) they pushed into first in July before nosediving out of the race. But it was not until the flowering of a new generation of young players in 1984 that a Minnesota title threat could be taken seriously.

The Twins' decline on the field was matched by a decline in attendance, which even their move indoors in 1982 did not significantly redress. The Griffith family, unwilling to risk the high cost of luring proven talent, decided to give up the club after more than sixty years of family ownership. Early in 1984 a buyer was found in Carl Pohlad, a wealthy Minneapolis banker. By the time Pohlad's purchase was completed at the end of July, the Twins' young team had blossomed into the West's front-runner, paced by pitcher Frank Viola's sudden development into a winner, and by the arrival in May of rookie centerfield sparkplug Kirby Puckett. Although the Twins leveled off in August and lost their final six games, to fall to .500 and a tie for second, they had brought the crowds back to the ballpark. The team in 1984 for the first time ever drew more than 1.5 million fans to their home games, and remained well above a million the next two years despite a pair of losing seasons.

In 1987 the Minnesota fans were rewarded for their faithfulness. Although the Twins lost their last five games to finish only eight above .500 (and two ahead of surging Kansas City), their winning record at home was the best in the league, and their title in the West was never in doubt. More surprising was their decisive triumph over favored Detroit in the LCS, four games to one. In the first World Series to feature indoor play, the Twins won the four games played in their Metrodome to capture Minnesota's first world baseball championship in seven games.

Although the Twins in 1988 improved on their 1987 won-lost record—and Frank Viola, Kirby Puckett, and relief ace Jeff Reardon enjoyed career peaks—they finished well back of Oakland in the race for the division

crown. But their home attendance, which had jumped 66 percent in 1987 to top 2 million for the first time, bounded another 45 percent in 1988 to make the Twins the first AL club ever to attract more than 3 million fans in a season.

As the team suffered a general decline in pitching and hitting in 1989, Viola—in the middle of a disappointing season—was traded to the Mets; the Twins finished fifth. Reardon, a free agent, left for Boston after the season. The Twins continued their downhill slide in 1990, slipping from fifth place at midseason to their first cellar finish in eight years.

On May 27, 1991, the Twins stood sixth in the AL West. Three weeks later, after winning eighteen of nineteen games, they were first. There they finished, becoming (like Atlanta in the NL) the first AL team to rise from last place to first in successive seasons. Minnesota's attack featured a balanced offense in which seven players drove in 50 runs or more, and a pitching revival that starred veteran free agent Jack Morris and a pair of young hurlers in their first full seasons, Scott Erickson and Kevin Tapani. In the ALCS, the Twins overcame Toronto in five games, then came back from a 1–3 World Series deficit to defeat Atlanta with a pair of extra-inning victories.

After his single starring season in Minnesota, pitcher Morris moved on to Toronto to hurl the Blue Jays to the championship. The Twins, meanwhile, led the AL West into midseason, before drifting back into a second-place finish behind Oakland.

Montreal Expos

In the spring of 1969, in an unfinished "temporary" ballpark that would be the Expos' home for eight years, major league baseball came to Canada. One of two clubs added to the National League in this first year of divisional play—Montreal in the East and San Diego in the West—the Expos finished 48 games out of first. But although they matched San Diego's 52–110 record and last-place divisional finish, they outdrew the Padres by better than two to one, with a home attendance of more than 1.2 million fans.

After a second last-place (but much improved at 73–89) season in 1970, the Expos moved a notch out of the cellar to fifth in 1971 and '72, and into pennant contention in 1973. Outfielder Ken Singleton became the first Expo to drive in 100 or more runs, rookie pitcher Steve Rogers compiled a sparkling 1.54 ERA (and a 10–5 won-lost record), and reliever Mike Marshall set a new major-league record with 92 pitching appearances (winning 14 games and saving a league-high 31). In the tightest race of the century, all six clubs remained in contention into September, when Philadelphia dropped away. In mid-September Montreal won six straight to catch front-running Pittsburgh, only to lose nine of the next ten and drop back to fifth. Three wins in the final four games lifted them to fourth place, just 3½ games behind the champion New York Mets.

Center fielder Willie Davis (acquired from Los Angeles in a trade for Mike Marshall) led the Expos' offense in another fourth-place season in 1974, but the club sank back to a tie for last in 1975 and sole possession of the

cellar a year later, with a 55–107 record nearly as bad as their first season (and a home attendance little more than half that of 1969).

But with the acquisition of heavy-hitting Tony Perez from Cincinnati, a new manager—the controversial Dick Williams—and strong seasons from catcher Gary Carter, sophomore outfielder Ellis Valentine, and rookie Andre Dawson, the club snapped back in 1977 to win 20 more games than the previous year and rise to fifth. And with their move into the new Olympic Stadium (built for the 1976 Olympics), Expo attendance rebounded from a club low to a new high.

After climbing another notch to fourth in 1978 (as the newly acquired Ross Grimsley became their first—and, to date, only—20-game winner), the Expos put on a run for the title that drove attendance in 1979 to over two million. Third baseman Larry Parrish, with a career-high season, led the club in batting and home runs in a balanced attack that saw five players drive in more than 70 runs. The pitching too was balanced, with six pitchers winning 10 games or more on a staff that compiled the league's lowest ERA. With a fast start in April, the Expos led the East through much of June and into July, when a surging Pittsburgh caught up with them. Both clubs climbed away from the pack to the end of the season. Montreal fell back a bit in August but caught up with the Pirates in September and carried the race to the final day before dropping off to second. The Expos' 95 victories remain the club record to date.

The 1980 race was just as exciting. A three-way struggle with Philadelphia and Pittsburgh through most of the summer narrowed to two teams in September as the Pirates fell away. In a crucial late-September series, the Expos beat the Phillies two games of three to take a half-game lead, but in the final series a week later Philadelphia won two games to clinch the crown.

In a 1981 season divided by a players' strike, Montreal finished the first part of the season in third place, but held off St. Louis to win the second part by half a game. The Expos then won the division championship in a special playoff with first-half winner Philadelphia—their first title—but lost the League Championship Series to Los Angeles.

As the Expos declined gradually over the next five years, most of the regulars left through trade, free agency, or retirement. But in 1987, two 1981 rookies who had remained in Montreal—outfielder Tim Raines and third baseman Tim Wallach—stood out in an Expo comeback that left them in third place, just four games back, with 91 wins and the second-best record in their history.

Strong midsummer surges in 1988 and 1989 propelled the Expos into the thick of the race in the NL East, in 1989 lifting them into the lead for six straight weeks following the acquisition from Seattle of mound ace Mark Langston. But in both years, late-season slumps dropped the club to identical 81–81 finishes. In 1990 strong pitching (despite the loss of free-agents Langston, Bryan Smith, and Pascual Perez) kept the Expos competitive well into September before they fell out of the race.

The collapse of a huge cement beam at Olympic Stadium in September 1991—which forced the Expos to play all their remaining games on the road—was emblematic of the team's collapse into the cellar with their worst record in fifteen years. But the club revived in 1992 under new manager Felipe Alou (who was promoted from coach in late May), rising from fifth place to second behind the pitching of Ken Hill and veteran ace Dennis Martinez, and the offensive leadership of right fielder Larry Walker.

New York Mets

Branch Rickey's projected Continental League never materialized, but its New York and Houston franchises were admitted to the National League, expanding the league to ten clubs in 1962. Few major league teams have been as inept as the New York Mets were in their first season. Despite the presence on the club of such New York favorites as manager Casey Stengel, pitcher Roger Craig, and first baseman Gil Hodges, and of players like outfielders Richie Ashburn and Frank Thomas who were still near peak form, the Mets finished at the bottom of the league in batting, fielding, and pitching. They won only one game in four and suffered a twentieth-century record 120 losses. But New York fans—deprived of National League baseball since the defection of the Dodgers and Giants to the West Coast four years earlier—found their ineptitude lovable. By their third season, having moved out of the old Polo Grounds into brand-new Shea Stadium, the last-place Mets were regularly outdrawing the pennant-bound Yankees.

Former New York Giants catcher Wes Westrum replaced the aging Stengel as manager part way through the 1965 season, and the next year saw the club rise out of the cellar for the first time. But they fell back to tenth in 1967 (despite rookie Tom Seaver's 16 wins—a club record), and Westrum was replaced at the helm by Gil Hodges (who had retired from playing after a few games in 1963). With Jerry Koosman joining Seaver in the starting rotation and setting a new club record with 19 victories, Hodges led the Mets in 1968 back up to ninth place with their first season of more than 70 victories.

In 1969 the majors inaugurated divisional play, but the Mets got off to their usual indifferent start. At the end of May, however, they began to win consistently. By early June they were second in the NL East, though well back of the explosive Chicago Cubs. By September, though, the Cubs were faltering. The "Miracle Mets" caught and passed them with a ten-game winning streak and continued on to take the division title by eight games. Among the many Met heroes, Tom Seaver stands out. He won his last ten starts, sparking the team's final push to triumph and finishing with a league-high 25 wins that still stands as the club record. After a three-game sweep of West champion Atlanta in the league's first Championship Series, the Mets faced the mighty Baltimore Orioles—regarded by many as one of baseball's all-time greatest teams—for the world championship. The Met miracle continued as, after an opening game loss, the New Yorkers humbled the Orioles with four straight wins.

The Mets of 1970 remained competitive into mid-September as they sought to repeat their '69 triumph. But they fell back at the end while Pittsburgh spurted, and finished third. Two more third-place finishes followed in 1971 and '72. Just before the start of the 1972 season, Met coach Yogi Berra moved up to manage the club after

Hodges suffered a fatal heart attack two days before his forty-eighth birthday.

In 1973 the NL East experienced the tightest major league race of the century. Chicago moved out in front of the pack early in the season, but folded in July and August. So did the Mets, who fell from third to a last-place sixth. But although they were last late in August, they were less than seven games out of first. A series of bursts in September, culminating in a seven-game winning streak, shot the Mets through the division into first place by September 21. Although they finished the season only three games above .500, they topped the division by 1½ games. In the LCS they held off the favored Cincinnati Reds to take the pennant in the maximum five games, but lost the World Series when Oakland overcame a 2–3 deficit to win the final two contests.

The Mets then entered a decade-long decline. Though they won as often in 1975 and '76 as they had in 1973, they didn't come close to winning the East, and dropped into a seven-year trough in 1977 which included five seasons in last place. Seaver was traded to Cincinnati in 1977, and Koosman (after two disastrous seasons) was sent to Minnesota in the fall of 1978 (where he won 20 the next year). The heirs of original owner Joan Whitney Payson (who had died in 1975) sold the club to Nelson Doubleday (of the publishing company) and Fred Wilpon in January 1980. In February the new owners hired Frank Cashen as general manager, hoping he could rebuild the Mets as he had the Baltimore Orioles in the late 1960s.

It took a few years to achieve the right blend, but when outfielder Darryl Strawberry was brought up from the minors early in 1983 and first baseman Keith Hernandez was acquired from St. Louis in June, the mix had nearly all the needed ingredients. In 1984, under new manager Davey Johnson, and with rookie pitchers Dwight Gooden and Ron Darling combining for 29 wins, the Mets rebounded to second place with their second-best season record up till then.

The rise continued in 1985. With catcher Gary Carter (newly acquired from Montreal) leading the club in homers and RBIs, and Gooden cementing his superstardom at age twenty with a phenomenal 24–4, 1.53 ERA season, the Mets won 98 games—eight more than the year before—and came within a game of tying St. Louis late in September before slipping 3 games back at the finish.

When the Mets acquired pitcher Bob Ojeda from the Boston Red Sox after the season, many predicted an easy division title for them in 1986. For once, the pundits were right. With Carter, Strawberry, and Hernandez powering the offense, and Ojeda, Darling, and Gooden all placing among the league's top five pitchers in ERA, the Mets won two of every three games (108 in all) to capture the division title by 21½ games.

The postseason battles were tougher. The Mets won the pennant from Houston with a 16-inning victory in Game Six of the LCS, but came within a strike of elimination by the Red Sox in Game Six of the World Series before rallying to take that game and the next for their second world crown.

Strawberry enjoyed his finest season yet in 1987, and pitchers Terry Leach and Rick Aguilera put together a combined won-lost record of 22–4. But Ojeda was lost to injury early in the season, and the Mets, though they hung close and posted 92 wins, lost out—as in 1985—to St. Louis by 3 games.

David Cone (20–3, 2.22 ERA) emerged in 1988 as the ace of the league's best pitching staff, which, with the power of Darryl Strawberry and Kevin McReynolds behind it, carried the Mets back to the top of the NL East, 15 games ahead of runner-up Pittsburgh. But after taking a 3-2 lead in the LCS, they lost the pennant to underdog Los Angeles in seven games.

With co-captains Carter and Hernandez injured and in decline, the Mets floundered through 1989, salvaging a narrow second-place finish over St. Louis with four wins in the season's final three days. The two captains were released after the season. Next May, with the Mets mired 9½ games out, manager Davey Johnson was replaced by coach Bud Harrelson. In June the team—ignited by Strawberry's suddenly hot bat—took off: with a flight that included a club-record eleven-game win streak, the Mets propelled themselves into first place before the end of the month. Through July and August the Mets and Pittsburgh lobbed the division lead back and forth, until the Pirates consigned the New Yorkers to second place for good with a three-game sweep in early September.

Free agent Strawberry signed with Los Angeles for 1991, but the Mets competed strongly into July before tumbling to fifth place with their first losing season in eight years. Manager Harrelson was replaced by Jeff Torborg for 1992, and ex-Pirate star Bobby Bonilla signed with the club as a free agent. But injuries plagued the team throughout the season, and the finish found them once again a distant fifth.

New York Yankees

In its first twenty seasons, the club that became the New York Yankees won no league championship, and finished second only twice. But for the next forty-four years the Yankees dominated the American League, winning nearly two of every three pennants and twenty World Series. After another pennant drought of eleven years, the club in six years won five division titles, four pennants, and their twenty-first and twenty-second World Series. Their current pennant drought, which has lasted eleven years so far, is the third longest in their history.

The Yankees began as the Baltimore Orioles in 1901. But AL president Ban Johnson really wanted a club in New York and, after outmaneuvering the politically influential Giants (who didn't want a competing big league team in their city), Johnson moved the Orioles to the northern end of Manhattan in 1903.

In 1904 the Highlanders (as they were known during their first years in New York because of the high land on which their park was built) chased the Boston Pilgrims through midsummer, catching them in August and trading first place back and forth into October. But after Jack Chesbro defeated Boston 3–2 on October 7 to give New York a half-game lead (it was his forty-first win, a twentieth-century major league record), the Pilgrims came back to win the next two. In the fourth game of the series, with Chesbro again pitching and the score tied 2–2 in the top of the ninth, a wild pitch over the New York catcher's head let in Boston's pennant-clinching run.

The Highlanders again led the league in late September two years later, before tailing off to finish 3 games behind Chicago. But that was the last time they contended seriously for the title for fourteen years. Meanwhile they finished last twice, in 1908 losing a club-worst 103 games, and in 1912 suffering their most distant finish ever—55 games behind pennant-winning Boston.

In 1914 Colonel Jake Ruppert and Tillinghast Huston bought the Yankees, and the next year they purchased pitcher Bob Shawkey from the Philadelphia A's. Shawkey's 24 victories in 1916 led the Yankees to their first winning season in six years, and in 1919, on returning from military service, his 20 wins (plus the 9 of Carl Mays, who came to the club in a controversial midseason deal with the Red Sox) brought the Yankees to third—at 7½ games out, their closest finish in thirteen years.

That winter, on the recommendation of manager Miller Huggins, the Yankees paid a then-record $125,000 (plus a $300,000 loan) to the Red Sox for Babe Ruth. Ruth, with 54 home runs in 1920, obliterated the record of 29 he had set the year before, and Mays and Shawkey together won 46 games in a three-way pennant race that ended with New York a close third.

At season's end Ruppert hired Ed Barrow as Yankee general manager. While managing the Red Sox, Barrow had converted Ruth from a pitcher to outfielder. His December trade with Boston that gave the Yankees pitcher Waite Hoyt and catcher Wally Schang was just the improvement needed to bring the Yankees their first pennant in 1921. Ruth's 59 homers and his career-high 171 RBIs didn't hurt, either.

The prickly Carl Mays, staff ace in 1921 with a 27–9 record, slipped to 13–14 the next year. But the Yankees continued to decimate the Red Sox roster with trades that brought them pitchers "Bullet Joe" Bush and "Sad Sam" Jones, and infielders Everett Scott and Joe Dugan. Bush's 26 wins in 1922 made up for Mays's decline, and the Yankees captured their second straight league championship.

Both races had been tight two-way struggles—with Cleveland in 1921 and the St. Louis Browns in 1922—and both pennants had been followed by a World Series loss to the Giants. But in 1923 the Yankees at last put everything together. After sharing the Giants' Polo Grounds since 1913, they were at home in brand-new Yankee Stadium just across the Harlem River in the Bronx. With the addition of yet another pitcher from the Red Sox—Herb Pennock—and a .393 year from Ruth, they took the lead from the start and built it over the summer to a 16-game margin by the end. For the third time the Yankees faced the Giants in the World Series; this time they beat them, in six games, for their first world championship.

The Yankees lost a close race to Washington in 1924 and collapsed into seventh place in 1925—a year in which Ruth was lost much of the season to surgery and suspension. There were bright spots, though: center fielder Earle Combs, in his first full season, hit .342 to lead Yankee regulars, left fielder Bob Meusel filled Ruth's shoes as AL home run and RBI leader, and first baseman Lou Gehrig arrived to stay. With Ruth's return to full strength in 1926 and the establishment of a new middle infield of Tony Lazzeri and Mark Koenig, the Yankees took their fourth pennant in a race that was not as close as their 3-game

winning margin would suggest. They lost a close World Series to the Cardinals.

Many observers rank the 1927 Yankees as baseball's greatest team ever. Certainly it was the Yankees' greatest team. They won more games (110) than any Yankee team before or since. Ruth hit his 60 home runs, and Gehrig drove in 175. Waite Hoyt led the league in ERA and rookie Wilcy Moore proved the league's premier reliever. As a team the Yankees led the league in hitting (.307) and slugging (.489, still a major league record); their pitchers compiled a 3.20 ERA that was ¾ of a run per game lower than the ERA of the next best team. In the World Series they swept the Pittsburgh Pirates.

The resurgent Athletics made the 1928 race much closer, but New York won three in a row from the A's in mid-September to pull ahead, and held on for their sixth pennant. Another Series sweep (this time against the Cardinals) gave them their third world title.

For three years the A's left the Yankees in the shade. An ill Huggins yielded the club's reins in September 1929 and died before the season had ended. By the time the Yankees returned to the top in 1932, their manager was Joe McCarthy. He had led Chicago's Cubs to the NL pennant in 1929; in fifteen seasons at New York he would lead his club to eight more pennants and seven world championships. Only once would his Yankees finish as low as fourth.

A Yankee pennant and World Series triumph over the Cubs in 1932 was followed by three second-place finishes to Washington (in 1933) and Detroit (in 1934 and 1935). Ruth had retired by the time the Bronx Bombers returned to the top in 1936, but Gehrig was still in top form, catcher Bill Dickey and outfielder George Selkirk developed into formidable sluggers, and Joe DiMaggio arrived to take over center field. New York finished a club-record 19½ games in front and buried the Giants in the World Series.

Three more pennants and three more world titles followed in 1937–1939. Lefty Gomez emerged as the league's premier pitcher in 1937, and DiMaggio picked up the home run and slugging crowns. Again the Giants were vanquished in the World Series. Rookie second baseman Joe Gordon and sophomore outfielder Tommy Henrich joined Dickey, DiMaggio, and a declining Gehrig in leading the slugging Yankees to the 1938 crown and a Series sweep of the Cubs. A balanced attack in 1939 saw seven of the eight starters (including Babe Dahlgren, who replaced the dying Gehrig at first) drive in 80 runs or more as the Yankees won 106 to run away with their eleventh pennant—and eighth World Series, another sweep, with Cincinnati the victim. For the fourth year in a row the offense topped the league in slugging, and overshadowed the steady—if unspectacular—Yankee pitchers, who for the *sixth* consecutive season compiled the league's stingiest ERA.

After catching the leaders with a 19–4 spurt in late summer, the 1940 Yankees fell away to finish a close third. But then came another three convincing pennant wins and a pair of Series triumphs as the nation moved into World War Two. Outfielders DiMaggio and Charlie Keller dominated the Yankee offense in 1941, and rookie shortstop Phil Rizzuto hit .307. Though no Yankee pitcher won more than 15 games, seven won 9 or more (and reliever

Johnny Murphy won 8 while saving a league-high 15). With 101 victories the team was lost from view to the rest of a league in which six of the eight clubs failed to break .500. In the World Series Brooklyn was the loser in five games.

Keller, DiMaggio, and Gordon provided the power, and Tiny Bonham (with 21 wins), Spud Chandler, and rookie Hank Borowy headed the league-leading pitching staff that propelled the Yankees to 103 wins and another easy pennant in 1942. But after winning their previous eight World Series, the Yankees were finally stopped, in five games, by the St. Louis Cardinals.

By 1943 many Yankees were in military service. But pitchers Chandler, Bonham, Borowy, and Murphy were not, and they led the charge to the team's seventh pennant in eight years. In the Series the Yankees reversed the results of the previous year, turning back St. Louis in five.

When Jake Ruppert died in 1939, general manager Barrow succeeded him as president, a position he held until January 1945, when Dan Topping and Del Webb bought the club and installed Larry MacPhail as president, giving him a third of the club and a ten-year contract to run it. The volatile, innovative MacPhail had previously brought new life to Cincinnati and Brooklyn, and did bring night ball to Yankee Stadium. But manager McCarthy, who couldn't get along with MacPhail, quit early in the 1946 season, and the team finished a distant third.

DiMaggio and the others were back from the war by 1946, but it was not until 1947—under new manager Bucky Harris, and with sparkling pitching from Allie Reynolds (acquired from Cleveland), rookie Frank "Spec" Shea, and reliever Joe Page—that the Yankees returned to the top of the heap with an easy pennant win and a narrow World Series triumph over Brooklyn. On the day the Yankees won the Series, though, president MacPhail embarrassed the club and undid himself by brawling in public. Topping and Webb bought out his contract and share of the ownership. Topping took over the presidency, but promoted farm director George Weiss to run the club as general manager.

After the Yankees dropped a pair of season-ending games to the Red Sox to finish third in a tight 1948 race, Weiss replaced manager Harris with Casey Stengel, who in nine years of managing the Braves and Dodgers had only twice seen his club finish as high as fifth. But with Weiss providing a steady stream of talented players via the farm system and canny trades, the Yankees under Stengel proved all but invincible into the '60s.

Stengel's Yankees began by putting together a record string of five world championships. No major league club had ever won five pennants in a row, let alone five World Series, and the Yankees didn't accomplish the feat easily. In 1949, for example, they saw the Red Sox come from 12 games back in midseason to pass them with a three-game series sweep in late September, only to rescue the flag with two close must-win victories over the Sox in the season's final games. In the World Series, Brooklyn was again the victim, in five games.

After losing much of 1949 to injury, DiMaggio returned with power in 1950, shortstop Rizzuto and catcher Yogi Berra enjoyed the finest seasons of their careers, and pitcher Whitey Ford broke into the majors, winning all

nine of his decisions as a starter (he lost one game in relief). But the Yankees struggled even harder for the pennant than the year before, battling three other contenders before finally pulling in front to stay with five straight wins near to the end of the season. Though three of the games in the World Series were decided by just one run, New York took the Phillie "Whiz Kids" without a loss.

No Yankee drove in as many as 90 runs in 1951, and Whitey Ford was drafted for two years of military service. But the remaining pitchers doubled their shutout production and lowered the team ERA by more than half a run per game, enough to propel the club ahead of Cleveland in mid-September. In the World Series the Yankees shook the faith of the "miracle" Giants, four games to two. Cleveland challenged once again in 1952, and again fell just short, as did Brooklyn in carrying the World Series to seven games.

Finally, in 1953, Stengel's Yankees won with relative ease. Ford, back from the Army, won 18 to lead the club to a finish 8½ games up. Once again it was Brooklyn in the World Series, and once again the Yankees beat them.

In 1954 New York won 103 games—the most in Stengel's twelve-year tenure. But Cleveland won an AL-record 111 to take the flag by 8 games. In 1955, though, it was back to second place for Cleveland as New York, with Mickey Mantle now established as one of the game's most productive hitters, settled in for another four pennants. As August passed into September, three teams were within a game of each other at the top. But the Chicago White Sox faltered and fell away, leaving the Yankees and Indians to fight it out. With two weeks left, New York won eight straight to pass Cleveland for good. Facing the Dodgers in the World Series for the sixth time, the Yankees finally lost, as Johnny Podres shut them out in Game Seven to give Brooklyn its first world title since 1900.

From 1956 through 1958 the Yankees seldom found themselves out of first place. Only in 1957, when they leveled off in May before surging to the front in June, were they involved in anything resembling a close race. In postseason play, they went the full seven games all three years, winning twice—from the Dodgers for the sixth time in 1956, and from the Milwaukee Braves in 1958, after losing to them the year before.

In 1959 the Yankees started poorly and never did rise much above .500, finishing a distant third with their worst won-lost record in thirty-four years. After the season, Al Weiss sent an aging Hank Bauer to Kansas City in a trade that brought Roger Maris to New York. In 1960 Maris, with AL titles in slugging and RBIs, won the MVP award. He and Mantle dominated the power stats and led the charge back to the top as the Yankees won their final fifteen games to bury the faltering Orioles.

New York's 1960 pennant was the first in another five-flag streak, but it was the last for Stengel. After Pittsburgh toppled the Yankees in the World Series on Bill Mazeroski's famous home run, president Topping retired both the seventy-year-old Stengel and general manager Weiss, sixty-five, who had been with the club for twenty-eight years.

With the season lengthened by eight games in 1961, Maris broke Ruth's home-run record and rookie manager Ralph Houk led the club to 109 wins, just one off the club

record. Once again Maris and Mantle finished among the best in offensive power, and once again New York took the pennant by 8 games. Ford enjoyed a splendid 25–4 season and celebrated with two more wins in the World Series as the Yankees humbled Cincinnati in five games.

Pitcher Ralph Terry moved out of Ford's shadow in 1962 with 23 wins. Though the Yankees finished just five games ahead of Minnesota, there was little doubt about the outcome from midseason on. In a close World Series with San Francisco, Terry won two, including the clincher with a four-hit shutout.

Though New York won pennants the next two years, the 1962 world title was to be their last until the Steinbrenner era fifteen years later. Despite the loss to injuries of Mantle and Maris for much of 1963, New York dominated the AL, winning by 10½ games with 104 wins. But in postseason play the Yankees were themselves dominated by the Dodgers (now in Los Angeles), who held them to just four runs in a Series sweep.

Yogi Berra replaced Houk as manager for 1964. In a season-long three-way race with the White Sox and Orioles that found the clubs virtually tied in mid-September, only an eleven-game win streak gave the Yankees the space they needed for their final one-game margin of victory. Pitcher Jim Bouton won a pair in the World Series, but the Cardinals took the crown in seven. Berra was fired.

During the 1964 season Topping had sold the Yankees to CBS. The next year the club, which had gone forty years without a losing season, dropped to sixth place, and in 1966 fell to a last-place tenth, their first cellar finish in more than half a century. Even Houk's return as manager in 1967—though it led to some winning seasons—failed to restore the once-proud club to pennant contention, except once, in 1972, when it was mid-September before they fell out of a tight race to finish fourth.

In January 1973 a syndicate headed by Cleveland shipping magnate George Steinbrenner purchased the Yankees from CBS. Although he had vowed not to take a prominent role in running the club, Steinbrenner soon emerged as one of baseball's most active and intrusive owners. Through a series of shrewd trades, offers of big contracts to free agents, and what became a round robin of managerial changes, Steinbrenner's Yankees became competitive again in 1974 (finishing a close second to Baltimore after streaking from last in July to first in September) and returned to the top with three successive pennants and a pair of world championships.

Billy Martin (a former Yankee second baseman) in 1976, his first full season as manager, led the renewed club to a runaway division title. First baseman Chris Chambliss's homer in the last of the ninth of the final game of the League Championship Series gave the Yankees the pennant by the narrowest of margins over the Kansas City Royals. Cincinnati swept New York in the World Series, but the Yankees came back the next year to edge Baltimore and Boston in a three-way race that saw the teams shift back and forth in the standings throughout the season. Slugger Reggie Jackson, signed as a free agent the previous autumn, turned the club's power trio of Chambliss, Graig Nettles, and Thurman Munson into a quartet as the Yankees recorded their first hundred-victory season in fourteen years. After another ninth-inning

win over Kansas City in the LCS finale, New York won the World Series in six games over Los Angeles, and Jackson became "Mr. October" with five home runs—three of them in successive at-bats in the final game.

The 1978 season provided as exciting a race as baseball is likely to see. In mid-July it looked like a Red Sox romp, but the fourth-place Yankees put on a great surge, catching the faltering Sox with a four-game series sweep in early September. Boston dropped 3½ games back, but won their final eight games to catch New York on the final day. In the one-game tiebreaker, Yankee shortstop Bucky Dent lofted a wind-blown three-run homer over Boston's close left field wall in the seventh, and Jackson homered an inning later for New York's final run in the 5–4 win. Again the Royals were the victims in the LCS, as were the Dodgers in the World Series.

After dropping to fourth in 1979, the Yankees held off Baltimore in 1980 to win their fourth division title—but this time Kansas City swept to the pennant in three games. In 1981 the Yankees found themselves in first place when the players struck in June and were thus admitted to an intradivisional playoff with the season's second-half winner, Milwaukee. Narrowly defeating the Brewers for the division title, New York swept Oakland for the pennant in the LCS. But after taking the first two games from Los Angeles in the World Series, they were stopped cold as the Dodgers won the next four.

The Yankees fell below .500 the next year, and although they revived to win 91 games in 1983, they failed to frighten the division leaders until 1985. First baseman Don Mattingly drove in more runs than any American leaguer since 1953 and newcomer (from Oakland) Rickey Henderson scored more often than any major leaguer since 1949—the team remained in the running until Toronto eliminated them with just one game to go.

But Steinbrenner's constant roster manipulation and managerial rotation (Billy Martin alone was hired and fired five times) at last set in motion a steady drop in Yankee effectiveness. While the team remained in the thick of a tight 1988 divisional race until three season-ending losses set them back into fifth place, their won-lost record showed a third straight season of decline. In 1989 the Yankees sank to their worst finish in twenty-two years and in 1990 they dropped to the floor of the AL East with the club's worst record since 1913.

Attempting to gain information damaging to longtime Yankee outfielder Dave Winfield, Steinbrenner dealt with gambler Howard Spira. As his penalty, Steinbrenner was forced to relinquish his controlling interest in the club in August 1990. The team improved a little over the next two years to finish fifth in 1991 and tie for fourth in 1992. But their string of consecutive losing seasons stretched to four, something that hadn't happened to the Yankees in seventy-six years.

Oakland Athletics

The history of the Athletics is a tale of three cities—a story of the best of teams and of the worst of teams. With a thirteen-year sojourn in Kansas City between residence in Philadelphia and Oakland, the A's are the only club to include a stop in Middle America in their trek from the

East Coast to West. They have won fifteen American League pennants (plus four Western Division championships that didn't lead to a pennant), second in the AL only to the incomparable Yankees. But they have also finished last in the league or division twenty-six times, and in sixteen seasons have lost 100 games or more—both AL worsts, by far. A club of extremes, they have been either at the top or at the bottom in nearly one season out of two.

When Ban Johnson in 1901 established four eastern clubs for his American League, he chose Connie Mack to manage the new Philadelphia Athletics and gave him a quarter ownership of the club. Mack, who had been managing the league's Milwaukee franchise, settled in at Philadelphia and set a record for managerial longevity—fifty years—that is unlikely ever to be surpassed.

In his first fourteen years the A's dominated the league, with six pennants and two close second-place finishes. After finishing fourth in 1901, the club won its first pennant the next year, pulling away from the field with spurts in August and September. Rube Waddell led the team with 24 wins, and six regulars hit over .300. The next two years saw the A's fade in August, but in 1905, after forging ahead in early August and hanging on to the lead with two crucial wins over Chicago's surging White Sox in late September, the A's opened October with a five-game winning streak to clinch their second flag. Waddell, with 26 wins, once again led the club (followed closely by Eddie Plank's 25) and compiled a league-leading 1.48 ERA. In the Athletics' first World Series appearance, though, New York's Christy Mathewson provided most of the pitching heroics, shutting out the A's three times in the Giants' 4–1 Series triumph.

Another August decline in 1906 was followed in 1907 by a comeback struggle from fifth place in late May to a 2½-game lead in mid-September. But the loss of a crucial game to Detroit several days later, and the failure to make up a rainout and a tie, left the A's 1½ games behind the Tigers at the finish.

In 1908 the A's suffered their first losing season, but they rebounded in 1909 to chase the Tigers throughout the summer before tailing off to second. In 1910, with a pitching staff that compiled a stunning 1.79 ERA (paced by Jack Coombs, whose 31 wins included 13 shutouts) and with league-leading fielding and hitting, the A's pulled ahead for good in June, increasing their lead through the rest of the season to finish 14½ games in front. In the World Series they continued to dominate, outscoring the Chicago Cubs 35–15 as they took their first world title, in five games. The A's repeated just as convincingly in 1911. With their "$100,000 infield" of Stuffy McInnis, Eddie Collins, Jack Barry, and Frank "Home Run" Baker averaging .323 at the bat, and Jack Coombs winning 28 games to again lead the club (and the league), the A's overtook Detroit in August to win by 13½ games. In the World Series, Baker hit two important home runs against the Giants, and the A's defeated Mathewson twice, avenging their 1905 humiliation with a victory in six games.

A third-place finish in 1912 broke the pennant streak, but the Athletics came back for two more in 1913 and '14, in both seasons pulling away in early June for easy wins. In the 1913 World Series the A's again felled the Giants, this time in just five games, but the next year they were in

turn humiliated by the upstart Boston Braves, who stunned Philadelphia with the first sweep since the renewal of World Series play in 1903.

That winter, Mack began to dismantle his championship club, selling second baseman Collins to the White Sox and releasing pitchers Coombs, Eddie Plank, and Chief Bender. (Third baseman Baker, homesick for the country life, sat out the 1915 season before moving on to the Yankees). Though Mack received $50,000 for Collins, his unconditional release of the three pitchers suggests that he had another reason than financial need for purging his club. (Suspicion of corrupt play in the 1914 World Series has been hinted.)

Whatever Mack's reasons, the changes did not help the club. The A's sank immediately to last place, where they remained for seven years. In 1915 they lost 109 games and finished 58½ games out. The next year they lost 117 games to set a league record for ineptitude that has never been equalled.

It was a decade before Mack was able to restore the club to respectability. In 1924 he brought up Al Simmons, and the next year Jimmie Foxx and pitcher Lefty Grove. Thus renewed, the A's in 1925 battled Washington to the end of August before backing off to second. In 1927 they won 91 games, though their second-place finish was 19 games back of the overwhelming Yankees. In 1928 the A's battled from well back of New York in midseason to overtake them for a day or two in September, only to lose three of four games in a critical Yankee series and slip back to second.

From 1929 through 1931, though, the A's interrupted New York's domination of the AL with three spectacular seasons. In 1929 sophomore pitcher George Earnshaw blossomed into the league's big winner with 24 victories and Grove led the league's stingiest staff with a league-low 2.81 ERA. Six players drove in 79 runs or more (led by Simmons' league-high 157) in powering the A's to 104 wins and an impressive finish 18 games ahead of the second-place Yankees.

After swamping the Cubs in the World Series, the A's repeated as pennant winners in 1930. Simmons led the league in batting (.381), and Grove led its pitchers in just about everything: wins (28), ERA, strikeouts—even saves (9). Again the World Series was no contest as the A's downed the Cardinals in six.

Earnshaw won more than 20 games for his third successive season in 1931, Simmons repeated as batting leader (.390), and Grove enjoyed what would be the finest season of his career (31–4, 2.06 ERA) in carrying the A's to 107 wins—their best record ever. But in Game Seven of the World Series their dominance of the baseball world ended in a Cardinal victory.

Following a second-place finish in 1932, Mack began selling off his stars again. This time the reason was primarily economic. Home attendance—never robust—fell off sharply after 1931, as the Great Depression and the A's decline made their impact felt. By 1935 the Athletics were back in the cellar, where they finished in ten of Mack's final sixteen years as manager.

In 1946 Mack, who since 1940 had been the A's majority stockholder, divided his shares among his three sons, provoking a family squabble over control of the club. In 1950 the two eldest, Roy and Earle, bought out Connie Jr.

and pressured their eighty-seven-year-old father to retire. But with Connie Sr. gone, attendance (which had risen to new highs in the baseball boom that followed World War Two) dropped off again. When in 1954 the A's finished 60 games behind champion Cleveland and attendance dropped to an eighteen-year low, the Macks sold the club to Chicagoan Arnold Johnson, who moved it to Kansas City.

Attendance jumped more than a million the first season in Kansas City (putting the A's over one million for the first time ever), and the team rose a couple of places to sixth. But 1955 was the high point of their thirteen-year stay in the Midwest; the K.C. A's never again rose above seventh, and they finished last six times.

Owner Johnson died in March 1960, and that December his heirs sold the club to the enterprising but abrasive Charles O. Finley. Finley brought in a succession of new managers over the next few years, and in 1965 outfitted his players in new bright green-and-yellow uniforms. But with the league's expansion to ten teams in 1961, the A's had two places lower to sink—and did. After finishing tenth in 1967 for the third time in four years, Finley moved the club to Oakland, California.

Attendance was slow to improve in Oakland—unlike the team. In 1968, their first year on the coast, they put together their first winning season in sixteen years. The next year, with the start of divisional play, the A's took second in the AL West. Reggie Jackson, in only his second full big league season, enjoyed his finest year, with 47 home runs, 118 RBIs, and AL highs in slugging (.608) and runs scored (123).

After another second-place finish in 1970, the A's were ready for a return to glory. In the next five years they won five division titles, winning both the AL pennant and the World Series in the three middle years, 1972–1974. In 1971, with a new manager, Dick Williams, and three pitchers (Vida Blue, Catfish Hunter, and reliever Rollie Fingers) who reached their prime all at once, the A's enjoyed their best season in forty years and won the West by 16 games. Baltimore swept them away in the League Championship Series, but they came back to take the West again the next year. Detroit took them to the limit in the LCS, as did Cincinnati in the World Series, but in both series the A's prevailed in the deciding game by the margin of a single run.

The next year, 1973, Jackson led the league in slugging, homers, and RBIs, Ken Holtzman joined Blue and Hunter in the 20-win column, and home attendance crept over a million (by a few hundred souls) for the first time in Oakland as the A's ran their string of Western Division titles to three. Once again they were pushed to the limit in the postseason—by Baltimore in the LCS and the New York Mets in the World Series—and once again they emerged as world champions.

Manager Williams quit in a dispute with Finley and was replaced by Al Dark, but the outcome in 1974 (except for a drop in attendance to under a million) was the same. Hunter bore more of the pitching load and wound up tied for the AL lead with 25 wins. His 2.49 ERA also led the league, as the staff ended Baltimore's five-year hold on the ERA title. The A's toppled the Orioles in the LCS and (in the first World Series held entirely on the West Coast) won their third consecutive world title in five

closely fought games with Los Angeles.

Free-agent Catfish Hunter deserted to the Yankees, and Baltimore regained the ERA crown in 1975, but pitchers Paul Lindblad and newcomer Dick Bosman combined for a 20–5 record to supplement the efforts of Blue, Holtzman, and Fingers and carry Oakland to an unprecedented fifth straight division title. But there the magic stopped, as Boston swept to the pennant in the LCS.

In the off-season Finley, with moves reminiscent of Connie Mack, tried to sell off his star players: Blue, Jackson, Fingers, Holtzman, and outfielder/first baseman Joe Rudi, one of the team's steadiest hitters. The proposed sales made some sense: the players planned to leave the club at the end of their 1976 option year, and Finley by disposing of them before they played out their option could at least be compensated for his loss. The Jackson and Holtzman deals were approved, but baseball commissioner Bowie Kuhn blocked the sale of the others, citing the "best interests of baseball."

The weakened A's came back from a poor start to close within 2½ games of the Kansas City Royals in 1976, but they dropped to last place the next year. After another last-place finish in 1979, Finley hired fiery Billy Martin to manage the club. Martin brought the A's in second in 1980, and first in the first half of strike-divided 1981. They won the Western Division championship by sweeping Kansas City in the special intradivisional playoffs, but were in turn swept by the Yankees in the LCS.

Finley's sale of the club in 1981 to the folks who bring us Levi's jeans signaled a turn toward normalcy and popularity. Despite a losing season in 1982, the club set a home attendance record as over 1.7 million fans came to watch Ricky Henderson's successful assault on the stolen-base record. In 1987 the A's finished right at .500—for the first time in their history a perfectly average team.

The next season they inaugurated a new multiyear reign as the league's best. Starter Dave Stewart and closer Dennis Eckersley anchored the league's strongest pitching staff and "bash brothers" Jose Canseco and Mark McGwire headlined an awesome offense. In 1988–90 the A's took title to the AL West with the majors' best won-lost record, then sailed past the East champion to the pennant. In 1988 they built a 13-game margin of victory over runner-up Minnesota, winning 104 games and drawing more than 2 million fans to their home games for the first time. They swept Boston in the ALCS, but faltered in the World Series, losing to underdog Los Angeles in five games.

Injuries to several key players—especially Canseco, who missed the first half of the season with a broken wrist—kept the A's from dominating AL play through most of 1989. But the preseason signing of free agent starter Mike Moore had strengthened the pitching, and a June trade that brought Rickey Henderson back after more than four years with the Yankees gave the A's the push they needed to prevail. At full strength by season's end, the A's overwhelmed Toronto in five games for their fourteenth pennant, then swept San Francisco for their world title.

Only Chicago's surprising White Sox challenged Oakland in 1990, and they too fell away in the latter half of the season as the A's walked to the division title with 103 wins. The potent offense was made even more formidable

by the late-season acquisition of Harold Baines from Texas and Willie McGee from St. Louis. But the key to Oakland's dominance was its pitchers, who for the third year in a row compiled the league's lowest earned run average. Bob Welch led the majors with 27 wins, Dave Stewart put together his fourth straight 20-win season, and Dennis Eckersley rebounded from an injury-hampered 1989 with his finest relief year yet. The A's swept over Boston to their third straight pennant, but—shades of 1988!—floundered in the World Series, succumbing in just four games to Cincinnati's aroused Reds.

In 1991 the A's stayed at or near the top into late June before slipping to fourth. Eckersley remained in top form, however, and in 1992 proved almost invincible, with 7 wins and 51 saves. Jose Canseco's trade to Texas late in the season severed the bash brothers' tandem offense, but Mark McGwire enjoyed a banner season at the bat. Despite a wave of injuries that would have sunk most teams, the A's stayed afloat near the front through the first half of the season and held steady in the second half to win their fourth division title in five years. In the LCS the A's fell to Toronto in six games.

Philadelphia Phillies

It took the Phillies thirty-two years to win their first pennant, and ninety-seven to win their first world championship. They have finished last in their league or division twenty-nine times—more than one season in four. In the nine years from 1975 through 1983, though, they were one of the most formidable teams in baseball.

Alfred J. Reach, a sporting goods entrepreneur and former player, and Colonel John Rogers, a Philadelphia lawyer and politician, organized the Phillies in 1883 to bring Philadelphia back into the National League after a six-year absence. In their first season, the Phillies won only 17 of 98 decisions to finish an eighth-place last, as far out of seventh as the seventh-place team was from first. Bad as the Phillies have sometimes been since, their 1883 winning percentage of .173 remains their very worst.

Reach hired the respected Harry Wright to manage the Phillies in 1884, and while Wright failed to lead them to a pennant in his ten years at the helm, he did make them respectable. His fourth-place 1886 team, in fact, compiled a winning percentage of .623 that remained the club's best for ninety years. In 1887 the Phillies, with three pitchers winning more than 20 games, finished second, just 3½ games behind Detroit—their closest finish until their first pennant twenty-eight years later.

The Phillies remained in the upper division twelve of the next fourteen years. For five years—1891–1895—they fielded an outfield of Ed Delahanty, Billy Hamilton, and Sam Thompson—Hall of Famers who rank among the top hitters of all time. In the three heavy-hitting seasons that followed the lengthening of the pitching distance to its present 60'6" in 1893, Delahanty, Hamilton, and Thompson—with help from players like catcher Jack Clements (.394 in 1895) and utility outfielder Tuck Turner (.416 in 1894)—sparked the Phillies to three team batting titles with BAs of over .300. In 1894 the big three joined Turner in batting over .400 and the team hit .349—still the major league club record.

In 1899, with Delahanty's .410 leading the way, the Phillies once again topped .300 to lead the league. Though the team finished third, they won 94 games, a club high they would not surpass for seventy-seven years. President Reach sold his interest in the club after a dispute with co-owner Rogers, and Rogers lost star second baseman Larry Lajoie in a salary dispute to the Athletics (Philadelphia's new entry in the rival American League). But the Phillies chased front-runner Pittsburgh through much of 1901. Though they slumped in August, they recovered to finish second.

It was the end of an era. Delahanty deserted to the AL the next season, and the Phillies dropped to seventh. Rogers sold the club to a syndicate. By 1904 the team was in last place, losing 100 games for the first time.

They rose into the first division the next season, but didn't mount a serious pennant run until 1911, when the pitching of rookie Grover Cleveland Alexander kept them in the thick of the race into midseason. Two years later they enjoyed first place through most of June before fading to a distant second.

In 1915 Alexander brought his ERA down more than a run per game to a league- and career-best of 1.22, hurling 12 shutouts among his 31 wins. Right fielder Gavvy Cravath and first baseman Fred Luderus finished one-two among NL sluggers, and Cravath won home run and RBI crowns. For half a season all eight clubs were in the thick of a tight race, with the Cubs and Phillies at the top of the heap. But in July the Cubs folded, and in August and September the Phillies took off to outdistance the late-surging Boston Braves by 7 games for their first pennant.

The World Series was a Phillies' heartbreak. Four of the five games were decided by a single run—but the runs belonged to the Boston Red Sox, who swept four after the Phillies had taken the opener.

Alexander shut out a record-tying 16 opponents the following year, winning a career-high 33, and teammate Eppa Rixey had his first big year with 22 wins. Through most of the season, the club trailed the leading Dodgers, but caught them in September, only to fall away again in the final week.

After Alexander's 30 wins had brought the Phillies another second-place finish in 1917, the club dealt him to Chicago and embarked on thirty-one years of wandering in the desert. After fourteen losing seasons (eight of them in last place), they climbed to fourth, two games above .500, in 1932, but dropped back the next year into the second division (including nine last-place finishes) for sixteen more years.

Several outstanding players spent time in Philadelphia during these years: Dave Bancroft (a rookie in their pennant season), Cy Williams, Freddy Leach, Chuck Klein, Lefty O'Doul, and Dick Bartell. Of these, only Williams and Klein retired as Phillies. The financially strapped management traded away the others at the height of their careers in deals that included cash as well as players. Even Klein—perhaps the greatest of them all—was sold twice before returning a third time to Philly to end his career.

The Phillies in 1930 produced a season that ranks among the most extraordinary of all time. With Klein and O'Doul leading the way at .386 and .383, every regular hit at least .280, to give the Phillies a team BA of .315. But

Phillie pitchers yielded a record 1199 runs while compiling the worst big league ERA ever—6.71. The club lost 102 games and finished last.

The Phillies' move in 1938 out of tiny, antiquated Baker Bowl into the Athletics' Shibe Park did nothing for attendance—or for performance, as the team strung together a club-record five consecutive last-place finishes from 1938 to 1942, in which they averaged 107 losses per season and finished between 43 and 62½ games out of first.

In February 1943 the league took control of the debt-ridden club and sold it to a group headed by New York sportsman William D. Cox. Cox didn't last long; before the year was out he was barred from baseball for betting on the Phillies. His controlling interest was sold to Robert M. Carpenter, who installed his son, Robert Jr., as president. The younger Carpenter hired former pitcher Herb Pennock as general manager with instructions to build a farm system, and a new era began in the club's history.

Outfielder Del Ennis had come up to hit .313 in 1946, but Pennock died (in January 1948) before he could see the full fruits of his labor. First baseman Dick Sisler would be purchased in March; rookie outfielder Richie Ashburn would lead Phillie batters in 1948 with a .333 BA. Willie Jones wouldn't nail down third base for another year, and rookie pitchers Robin Roberts and Curt Simmons wouldn't overawe the opposition for a couple of seasons yet. But the team that would be dubbed the "Whiz Kids" was gathering. Triple-A manager Eddie Sawyer was brought up in late July.

In 1949, the loss of first baseman Eddie Waitkus (shot in the chest by a crazed young woman) and midseason complacency threatened to strand the Phillies in the second division. But Sawyer fired up his players in a special team meeting, and the Phillies rallied to finish third with the club's best record in thirty-two years.

With new red-pinstripe uniforms and a recovered Eddie Waitkus, the 1950 Phillies pulled away from a tightly bunched first division in July and August, but late in September fell to within two games of onrushing Brooklyn. The Dodgers took the first game of a season-ending two-game series to narrow the gap to one. But in the finale the Phillies' Sisler homered to break a tenth-inning tie. When Brooklyn failed to score in the bottom of the tenth, the Whiz Kids had their pennant.

Curt Simmons, who was called up for military service in September after winning 17 games, missed the World Series. As in 1915, the result for Philadelphia was frustration and heartbreak, as the Phillies were swept by the Yankees—in the first three games by a single run.

Roberts's pitching kept the Phillies in the first division for four of the next five years, but the team made no serious run at another pennant. And when Roberts began to lose his effectiveness the team sank farther, to fifth for two years, then to four years in the cellar, culminating in 1961 with the longest big league losing streak of the century: 23 games.

The club stuck with new manager Gene Mauch, and the 1962 Phillies edged above .500 for the first time in nine years (though finishing seventh in a league newly expanded to ten teams). In 1963 they moved up to fourth with a strong second half. In 1964, with the acquisition of pitcher Jim Bunning from Detroit and infielder Richie

(later Dick) Allen's productive rookie season, Mauch's Phillies moved way out in front in August. But they blew their lead with ten straight losses in late September while Cincinnati was winning nine and St. Louis eight in a row. Only victories in their final two games salvaged a second-place tie.

The Phillies produced winning seasons the next three years but never challenged the leaders. With Mauch replaced as manager during the 1968 campaign, the team embarked on seven straight losing seasons, including three years at the bottom of the NL East.

Pitcher Steve Carlton, acquired from St. Louis in an off-season trade, accounted for nearly half the Phillies' 59 wins in 1972. His 27 victories for the league's worst team gave the club a ray of hope for the future and earned Carlton the Cy Young Award. Carlton lost a league-high 20 games the next year, but as he regained his form over the next three seasons, so too the Phillies gradually rose to the top of the division.

In 1974 sophomore third baseman Mike Schmidt burst to the forefront of the league's power hitters. The Phillies dropped out of contention in August, but wound up third, their best finish since the league split into divisions in 1969. The next year outfielder Greg Luzinski joined Schmidt among the league's top sluggers, and the club rose to second, with their first winning season since 1967.

The Phillies had entered their golden age—nine straight winning seasons (a club record), including five division titles, two pennants, and their first world championship. In 1976 they enjoyed their finest regular season ever. With Schmidt and Luzinski providing the power, Carlton returning to the ranks of 20-game winners and Jim Lonborg climaxing a long comeback with 18 wins, the Phillies took the division lead in May and pulled away, recovering from a late-season dive to finish well ahead of Pittsburgh. Their 101 wins, .6235 winning percentage, and nine-game margin of victory remain club records.

The Phillies were swept by Cincinnati in the League Championship Series, but came back the next season to duplicate their record 101 wins for another comfortable first-place finish. Carlton won 23 (and his second Cy Young Award), and Luzinski enjoyed the best season of his career, driving in 130 runs. After defeating Los Angeles in the LCS opener, though, the Phillies lost the pennant with three straight losses.

In 1978, even though Schmidt and Carlton had off-years, the Phillies led much of the season and captured the division title a third straight time. But it was a tight race, and they barely survived a late-season Pittsburgh surge to finish 1½ games in front. For the third time, their triumph in the East was followed by defeat in the LCS—for the second time at the hands of Los Angeles in four games.

Danny Ozark, in his seventh year as Phillies manager, was replaced by Dallas Green late in a disappointing 1979 season that saw the club stumble after a strong start before rallying in September to finish fourth. But Schmidt was back in top form, and Pete Rose had arrived via free agency to add his bat and hustle.

In a three-way race in 1980 that remained close through August, the Phillies hung tight without being able to move into the lead. But as Pittsburgh folded in late August and early September, the Phillies edged in front

briefly, then battled back and forth with Montreal. Tied with the Expos as the clubs met in Montreal for the season's final three games, Philadelphia took the first 2–1, then—in eleven innings—the second, to clinch their fourth division title in five years. Schmidt, with perhaps his finest season, drove in 121 runs and was named NL MVP; Carlton, with 24 wins, won his third Cy Young Award; and veteran reliever Tug McGraw enjoyed his best season in years.

In an LCS in which four of the five games went into extra innings, the Phillies prevailed over Houston, capturing their first pennant since the Whiz Kids era thirty years earlier. And in the World Series, fortune finally smiled on the team as they overcame Kansas City in six games.

The Phillies won the first half of the strike-divided 1981 season. In the special intradivisional playoff against Montreal, Philadelphia fought back to tie the series after losing the first two games—only to lose the finale.

The Carpenter family—citing the prohibitive cost of running a major league club—sold the team. Manager Dallas Green also left and was replaced by Pat Corrales, who kept the club in the thick of the 1982 race until the final month, when the Phillies slipped 3½ games back, to second. And Steve Carlton did it again: his 23 wins earned him a record fourth Cy Young trophy.

Mike Schmidt again dominated the Phillies' offense in 1983, but Carlton yielded to John Denny as the team's pitching ace. Newly acquired reliever Al Holland emerged as one of the league's best. After general manager Paul Owens took over for Corrales as manager in midseason, the Phillies came alive and took the division title by 6 games. Carlton dominated the LCS with an 0.66 ERA and two wins as the Phillies won their fourth pennant. But their golden age ended in the World Series, when Baltimore triumphed in five games.

The Phillies dropped to .500 and fourth place in 1984, and suffered a losing fifth-place season in 1985. They rebounded to second in 1986 (but 21½ games behind New York), then dropped back below .500 in 1987. Mike Schmidt continued to power the offense—the only member of the 1980 world champions still a Phillie. Despite an impressive lineup of everyday players in 1988, the Phils collapsed, finishing in the division cellar for the first time in fifteen years.

Unable to recover from a shoulder injury, Mike Schmidt retired in May 1989, and despite several midseason trades the Phillies again finished last in the NL East. In 1990, though, the flaming start of one of the players acquired in mid-1989—outfielder Len Dykstra, who was batting above .400 as late as June—lit the Phillies' competitive fires. But as Dykstra cooled off to mere excellence, the Phillies fell out of contention and finished 18 games back, tied for fourth.

A thirteen-game win streak in July–August 1991 came too late to propel the Phillies into the thick of the race, and although they rose to third place in the season's final week, they finished 20 games out. In 1992 they played at the bottom of the NL East much of the season, and finished there for the third time in five years.

Pittsburgh Pirates

Pittsburgh became a big league city in 1882, when its Allegheny baseball club joined with five other teams to form the American Association. Allegheny president H. D. McKnight was named president of the new league, but Allegheny made little stir until the club hired Horace Phillips to manage it and replaced its team in 1885 with players from the defunct Columbus Club, which had finished second in the AA the year before. The new Alleghenys finished a distant third in 1885, but after purchasing Pud Galvin from Buffalo they improved in 1886 to a respectable second behind the invincible St. Louis Browns.

Flushed with success, Allegheny in 1887 became the first club to desert the AA for the older and more highly regarded National League. There they found the competition stiffer and sank back into the second division. In 1890, when most of the team jumped to the rival Pittsburgh Players' League club, Allegheny (known that year as the Innocents) suffered the worst season in Pittsburgh major league history, finishing last, 66½ games out of first place (and 23 out of seventh), with a won-lost record of 23–113.

When the PL folded after just one season, Allegheny merged with its PL counterpart to form the Pittsburgh Athletic Company, thereby retrieving many of its old regulars. The club also hired a second baseman—Lou Bierbaur—whose signing (or theft, as his old club saw it) gave the Innocents a new and more enduring nickname: the Pirates. The renewed club still finished last in 1891, but thirty-six games closer to the top than the year before, and only fractionally out of seventh place.

In 1893 a rules change moved the pitcher 10½ feet farther back from home plate. Of all the NL clubs, the Pirates benefited most from the change: their batting average jumped 63 points—28 more than that of the league as a whole—while their pitchers suffered less than most. The club finished second, with a .628 winning percentage that was their best of the century. Lefty Frank Killen, a twenty-two-year-old pitcher acquired from Washington, led the club's resurgence with a league-leading 34 wins.

Although catcher Connie Mack was called upon to manage the club toward the end of the 1894 season and led them to winning seasons the next two years, the Pirates did not make another serious run for the pennant until 1900. With a team transformed yet again by players from a defunct club—this time the Louisville Colonels—the Pirates battled Brooklyn's Superbas almost to the end of the season before dropping 4½ games back, a solid second. Although they lost the postseason Chronicle-Telegraph Cup games (that year's World Series) to the Superbas, the Pirates were embarked on an era of greatness.

In the merger that brought the Louisville players to Pittsburgh, the Colonels' owner Barney Dreyfuss acquired half ownership of the Pirates. A year later he bought the other half. His perennial hope for the club was a first-division finish; in twenty-six of his thirty-two years of Pirate ownership his hope was rewarded.

Four of the former Louisville players—outfielder-turned-shortstop Honus Wagner, outfielder/manager Fred Clarke, third baseman/outfielder Tommy Leach, and pitcher Deacon Phillippe—and one carryover from the old Pirates, pitcher Sam Leever, remained with Pittsburgh long enough to help lead them to four pennants

and, in 1909, their first world championship. In the sixteen years Clarke managed the Pirates (a club record), they also finished second five times, and slipped out of the first division only in Clarke's final two seasons at the helm.

In contrast to the club's devastation by the Players' League raid of 1890, the Pirates were unaffected in 1901 by raiders from the American League (which that year turned itself into a major league largely by drawing off talent from National League clubs). Only third baseman Jimmy Williams defected to the Americans, and he was ably replaced by Tommy Leach, as the Pirates, with the league's best pitching (Jesse Tannehill and Deacon Phillippe finished one-two in ERA, and Jack Chesbro at 21–10 led in winning percentage), captured their first pennant by a comfortable 7½ games over the Philadelphia Phillies.

The Pirates repeated as pennant winners in 1902 and 1903. The 1902 team was one of the most overwhelming of all time. One Pirate or another led the league in nearly every offensive category: Ginger Beaumont in hits and batting; Tommy Leach in home runs (with 6); and Honus Wagner in slugging, RBIs, runs scored, doubles, and stolen bases. Pitcher Jack Chesbro's 28 wins led the league, and the top five NL pitchers in winning percentage were all Pirates. The club held the lead the whole season, finishing 27½ games ahead of second-place Brooklyn, still a major league record.

Pitchers Chesbro and Tannehill deserted to the AL's New York Highlanders the next season, but their loss merely made Pittsburgh's pennant-winning margin (6½ games) smaller than it might have been. Wagner beat out teammate Fred Clarke for the NL batting crown and finished second to Clarke in slugging. Beaumont took the titles in hits, runs, and total bases. Pitcher Sam Leever, with his finest season, led the club with 25 wins and the league in ERA and winning percentage. Owner Dreyfuss arranged with the AL champion Boston Pilgrims for a best-of-nine World Series—the first between NL and AL champions—but the Pirates lost it in eight games as their tired pitchers at last succumbed to overwork.

Although the Pirates twice finished second over the next four years, they didn't come close to capturing another pennant until 1908, when, in one of the tightest NL races ever, they were edged out by the Chicago Cubs and finished one game back, tied with New York's Giants for second. The following year, though, they moved in June into the new concrete-and-steel Forbes Field and celebrated by returning to the top of the league with a club record 110 wins—holding off the dogged Cubs throughout the season to take the flag by 6½ games. And this time they won the World Series, too, although they needed the full seven games to subdue Detroit's Tigers. Honus Wagner remained the league's dominant offensive force, but aging pitchers Leever and Phillippe were overshadowed by a new crop of standouts: Vic Willis, Howie Camnitz, Nick Maddox, and Lefty Leifield—and the astonishing rookie Babe Adams, who after going 12–3 (with a 1.11 ERA) during the season, won three more games in the World Series.

The Series triumph ended an era. Wagner was past his prime and wound down his long career over the next several seasons as the Pirates dropped out of contention for a dozen years, including four (1914–1917) in the hated

second division. Only Babe Adams remained of the world championship team when Pittsburgh next made a contest of the pennant race in 1921, taking an early lead and holding it most of the summer until an August-September decline dropped them to second place, 4 games back.

Former Pirate infielder Bill McKechnie replaced George Gibson as manager during the following season with the club in fifth place, and saw the Pirates spurt to second before fading to third at the finish. Two more third-place seasons—with the Pirates finishing just 3 games out of first in 1924—paved the way for another pennant in 1925.

The 1925 Pirates fielded several stars: shortstop Glenn Wright, who led the club with 121 RBIs; sophomore right fielder Kiki Cuyler, who led the team in hitting (.357) and the league in runs scored; third baseman Pie Traynor, who shone on the field and at the bat; and Max Carey, who beat out Cuyler for the league stolen base title and enjoyed his finest season (.343) at the plate. The team as a whole hit .307 to lead the league and ran away with the pennant, spurting to catch the front-running Giants in midseason and pushing ahead to an 8½-game lead by season's end. The World Series was tougher, but the Pirates prevailed over the Washington Senators, defeating veteran Walter Johnson in a seventh-game slugfest 9–7. Babe Adams, hero of the 1909 Series and now, at forty-three, nearing the end of his long career, pitched one shutout inning in Game Four.

Rookie outfielder Paul Waner arrived the next season and hit .336, but the team, which had led the race going into August, fell into decline late in the month and finished third, 4½ games out. Max Carey sparked an unsuccessful player uprising against the management and was sold to Brooklyn just before the Pirate collapse in August, and manager McKechnie was replaced after the season by former Washington manager Donie Bush.

In 1927, his first season at the helm, Bush sailed the Pirate ship to its sixth pennant, even though Kiki Cuyler was benched for half the season for refusing to bat second in the order. But Paul Waner's younger brother Lloyd arrived to join Paul in the outfield, and the pair tore up the league, finishing one-two in hits (237 and 223) as Paul also took crowns in batting (.380; Lloyd was third at .355), RBIs and total bases, while Lloyd led in runs scored. In and out of first place throughout the season, the Pirates moved into the lead a final time at the start of September and held on to edge the St. Louis Cardinals by 1½ games. In the World Series, though (played with Cuyler on the bench), the Pirates were swept by a Yankee team widely acclaimed as the greatest of all time.

Barney Dreyfuss died in February 1932. Ownership of the Pirates passed to his widow, who named their son-in-law Bill Benswanger president. The team finished a competitive second in 1932 and 1933, but then fell back until 1938, when—with Pie Traynor now manager—they moved out in front in midseason and held their lead comfortably until late September, when ten straight Chicago victories (including three against Pittsburgh) dropped the Pirates to second place, where they finished, 2 games back.

The Pirates showcased some great players in their lean years, like shortstop Arky Vaughan in the 1930s and early '40s, and slugger Ralph Kiner, who won or shared the

league home run title all seven of his seasons with Pittsburgh in the 1940s and '50s. But after 1938 the club finished no closer than eight games from the top for twenty-one years. They finished as high as second only twice (in 1944 and 1958), and in the eight years 1950–1957 wound up each season either last or next-to-last, reaching their nadir in 1952 with 112 losses and a last-place finish 54½ games out of first.

The Pirates had been purchased in 1946 by a four-man syndicate that included singer Bing Crosby and real estate tycoon John W. Galbreath. Galbreath later bought a majority interest in the club and, as president, hired Branch Rickey to rebuild the Pirates into contenders. Barney Dreyfuss had resisted the development of minor league farm systems (a Rickey innovation at St. Louis and Brooklyn), preferring to scour unaffiliated minor league teams himself for young talent. Rickey's ministrations helped build a foundation for the Pirate resurgence of 1958–1960.

No one threatened the 1958 Milwaukee Braves' preeminence in the NL after July, but Pittsburgh came closer than anyone, finishing second, eight games back. Six of the eight regulars who would lead the Pirates to their next championship in 1960 were already in the lineup, including Dick Groat, Bill Mazeroski, and Roberto Clemente; and the leading pitchers of 1958—Bob Friend, Vern Law, and reliever Roy Face—topped the 1960 staff, too.

In 1959 the Pirates fell back to fourth place, barely above .500, but the next year they began strong and, shaking off their last challenger in late July, built up a 7-game margin of victory by season's end. League batting champion Groat paced a balanced offense that led the league in hitting, and pitcher Law, with 20 wins, enjoyed the finest season of his career. Facing the Yankees in the World Series, the Pirates were overwhelmed in the three games they lost, but they won the world title with four close wins, capped by Mazeroski's famous home run in the bottom of the ninth inning of the final game.

Pittsburgh again led the league in batting in 1961, with Clemente (whose .351 batting average led the league) and first baseman Dick Stuart (35 home runs, 117 RBIs) enjoying especially fine seasons. But the Pirate pitching fell apart (Vern Law lost most of the season to arm trouble), and the club dropped to sixth place.

When the Pirates next made a serious run for the pennant, in 1966, Harry Walker managed the team and center fielder Matty Alou (newly acquired from San Francisco) won the batting crown. (His brother Felipe of Atlanta was runner-up—the only one-two brother finish ever.) In a season-long three-way race, the Pirates took a lead in August but lost it early in September and finished third, 3 games out. They dropped to sixth again the next season and remained out of the pennant race for three years.

In 1970 the majors experienced their second season of divisional play, John Galbreath's son Daniel was named Pirates' president, and Danny Murtaugh returned a third time to pilot the Pirates. (His second stint was for half a season in 1967.) The team began slowly and entered June with a record under .500. But they were already on their way up, and by mid-July, when they moved out of aging Forbes Field into the brand-new Three Rivers Stadium, they were at the top of the NL East. They slipped into a

three-way tangle in mid-September, but shot ahead later in the month to take the division title by 5 games. Most of the team was new since 1960—the power was now supplied by first baseman Bob Robertson and outfielder Willie Stargell. But Roberto Clemente was still in top form, and Bill Mazeroski was still at second base, though nearing the end of his career.

In the 1970 League Championship Series, the Pirates were swept by Cincinnati. But they came back the next season to overwhelm the East in a race that was no race after June, then defeated San Francisco for their eighth pennant, three games to one. Their slugging—paced by Stargell's league-leading 48 home runs—led the league, and reliever Dave Giusti saved a league-leading 30 games in support of a balanced pitching staff. Clemente hit .414 in the World Series (with half his hits going for extra bases) as the Pirates overcame a 0–2 deficit to edge Baltimore in seven games for their fourth world title.

In 1972, after a slow start, Pittsburgh (now managed by their former center fielder Bill Virdon) rocketed to their third straight division championship—by 11 games over Chicago. The club lost, narrowly, to Cincinnati in the LCS, then suffered an even greater loss when Clemente was killed that winter in a plane crash. They played poorly the next season, yet even with a losing record finished third, only 2½ games behind the champion New York Mets in a five-way divisional race. Danny Murtaugh returned as manager a fourth (and final) time late in the season and piloted the club to two more NL East titles the next two years.

The 1974 championship drive featured a comeback from last place in early July to first by late August, followed by a nip-and-tuck race in September with St. Louis that was settled by a tenth-inning Pirate victory over Chicago in the season's final game. Stargell's bat was joined by those of Al Oliver and Richie Zisk as the Pirates outhit the rest of the league. In the LCS, though, the Los Angeles Dodgers overcame Pittsburgh handily, three games to one.

The Pirates won the 1975 race more easily, holding the lead from early June as right fielder Dave Parker, in his first full big league season, led the club in home runs and RBIs, and the league in slugging. But once again, for the fourth time in five tries, Pittsburgh lost the pennant in the LCS—swept this time by the awesome Cincinnati Reds, winners of 108 regular season games.

A distant second-place finish in 1976 was followed that December by manager Murtaugh's untimely death. His successor, Chuck Tanner, kept the Pirates competitive in his first two seasons, steering them to within 5 games of the champion Phillies in 1977, then—with an amazing August-September spurt from way below .500—to within 1½ games of the Phillies in 1978.

In 1979 the Pirates again started slowly but began to move up in May and pushed to the front, ahead of Montreal, in late July. By mid-September, though, the Expos had caught up, and it was not until the final day that an Expo loss and Pirate win gave Pittsburgh its sixth NL East title. Parker and the aging Stargell (now called "Pops") were still the club's big bats, but submariner Kent Tekulve had emerged as the bullpen ace, and one of six Pirate pitchers to win 10 games or more.

In the LCS the Pirates repaid Cincinnati for their 1975

humiliation, sweeping to the pennant in three games. In the World Series they seemed to have met their match in Baltimore, falling behind three games to one. But Pops rallied his "family" to victory in the final three must-win contests, and Pittsburgh for a fifth time reigned at the top of the baseball world.

For seven years the Pirates drifted downhill. The club's family spirit disintegrated, fans deserted the team, and it seemed for a time that the Pirates would leave Pittsburgh. But in 1985 a group of local corporations and individuals purchased the club from the Galbreaths, determined (with the assistance of a loan from the city of Pittsburgh) to keep the Pirates in town. Syd Thrift, a trader of consummate skill, was named general manager, and Chicago White Sox coach Jim Leyland was hired to his first job as a big league pilot. Under the new regime the club improved gradually, until in 1988 it once again proved itself a serious contender for the NL championship of the East. Thrift had built a team second only to New York's mighty Mets. But Thrift's unwillingness to share with his superiors the top-level decision making bulked larger, in the eyes of the Pirate directors, than his achievement and he was fired at the season's end.

Plagued all season by injuries, Pittsburgh plunged to fifth in 1989. But in 1990, as Doug Drabek put together a career season on the mound and the bats of Barry Bonds and Bobby Bonilla burst into full bloom, the Pirates arrived at the All-Star break in first place by half a game over New York. With Drabek and Zane Smith (newly acquired from Montreal) all but unbeatable down the stretch, the Pirates, after exchanging the lead with New York several times, swept a Met series in early September to extend a narrow lead and clinched the NL East title at the end of the month with eight straight wins.

The Pirates repeated as division champions in 1991 and 1992. Bonds and Bonilla again led the offense in 1991 and pitcher John Smiley won 20 games. In 1992, even the departure of Bonilla (who signed with the Mets as a free agent) and Smiley (dealt to Minnesota) didn't hamper the Pirates. Center fielder Andy Van Slyke took up the offensive slack with one of his best seasons, and pitcher Tim Wakefield rose from the minors at the end of July to compile an 8-1 record as the Pirate ship breezed to the title by 9 games. But the three-time division champions could not win a pennant. In the 1990 LCS they fell to Cincinnati in six games. The next year they built a 3-1 lead over Atlanta, but lost the final two games. And in 1992, down three games to two, they fought back to within one out of victory in Game Seven before an Atlanta pinch hit cut them down once again.

St. Louis Cardinals

The club that is now the Cardinals first fielded a team in 1881, and the next season became a charter member of the American Association, a new major league formed in part to offer fans the beer and Sunday baseball forbidden by the older National League. Chris Von der Ahe, one of the club's founders and its first president, at first saw in baseball simply a source of customers for his St. Louis saloon and beer garden, but he developed a love for the game itself as his Brown Stockings—or Browns—developed into one of the era's greatest teams.

After a losing season in 1882, Von der Ahe hired Ted Sullivan, a noted judge of baseball talent, to manage the Browns. Sullivan brought in third baseman Arlie Latham and pitcher Tony Mullane to strengthen a team that already boasted a fine pitcher in Jumbo McGinnis (25–18 in 1882) and one of the game's premier first baseman in Charlie Comiskey. Although Sullivan quit before the end of his first season because of the continued interference of the volatile Von der Ahe, the Browns finished second in the AA, just a game behind champion Philadelphia.

When Mullane bolted the Browns in 1884, the club slipped to fourth. But help was on the way. In July Von der Ahe purchased the Bay City, Michigan, club to acquire its heavy-hitting pitcher Dave Foutz, and in September added another hitting pitcher, "Parisian Bob" Caruthers, to the roster. In 1885—with Comiskey now the manager, left fielder Tip O'Neill blossoming into one of baseball's best hitters, and Caruthers and Foutz winning 40 and 33 games—the Browns rose to the top, 16 games ahead of second-place Cincinnati. They finished on top four years in a row, tying Chicago's White Stockings (3–3–1) in the 1885 World Series and defeating them four games to two the next year for the AA's only Series triumph over their NL rivals.

Pitcher Silver King joined the club in 1887, and outfielder Tommy McCarthy arrived the following year. They helped keep the Browns at the top of the AA through 1888 (although the team lost the World Series both years). But Von der Ahe's sale of Foutz and Caruthers to Brooklyn following the 1887 season boosted Brooklyn to second place in 1888. The next year Brooklyn edged the Browns for the pennant, and the club's first era of greatness was over.

When the AA folded after the 1891 season, the Browns were taken into the NL, but fared poorly there, finishing ninth and eleventh of the twelve clubs in the divided season of 1892. They rose no higher than ninth in the remaining years of Von der Ahe's ownership, dropping into the cellar (63½ games out) in 1897 and returning to the bottom with a club-worst 111 losses the next season.

New owners Frank and Stanley Robison (who also controlled the Cleveland club) transferred the best Cleveland players and their manager to St. Louis in 1899. Dubbed the Perfectos, the revitalized St. Louis club fell short of perfection, but did rise to a first-division fifth place that year and (now known as the Cardinals) rose to fourth in 1901 before sinking back into the second division for a dozen years.

After Stanley Robison died in 1911 (his brother Frank had died in 1905), the club passed into the possession of Frank's daughter Helene Britton, who ran it behind the scenes until, in 1916, she sold it to a syndicate headed by her attorney James C. Jones. Jones hired Branch Rickey away from the AL Browns to run the club.

Rickey took over a team with two chief assets: manager Miller Huggins and a promising young infielder, Rogers Hornsby. Huggins had managed the Cards to third place in 1914, before Hornsby arrived, and after a pair of losing seasons brought them up to third again in 1917. Huggins was lost to the New York Yankees the next year, and Rickey left the club temporarily for military service in the Great War. When Rickey returned in 1919, he took over

as manager himself, and in 1921 and 1922 saw the team finish third, closer to the leaders than the club had finished since joining the NL in 1891. Led by Hornsby's .397 and .401 batting, the team hit over .300 both seasons.

Sam Breadon, one of the Jones group of owners, increased his investment in the Cardinals until by 1920 he was majority stockholder and club president, with Rickey as vice president and general manager. Breadon moved the Cards out of the inadequate wooden Cardinal Park during the 1920 season into the more modern Sportsman's Park, owned by the Browns (and built on the site of Von der Ahe's original grounds).

Early in the 1925 season, with the Cards in last place, Breadon replaced Rickey as field manager with second baseman Hornsby. The switch worked. In 1925 the Cards rebounded to fourth, and in 1926 they captured their first pennant since the glory days of the old Browns four decades earlier—edging Cincinnati in the final week of the season after an August spurt had shot them into pennant contention. The season was made perfect by victory in the World Series over Miller Huggins's Yankees.

But Breadon and his irascible player-manager had a falling out, and Hornsby found himself traded that winter to the New York Giants for second baseman Frank Frisch and pitcher Jimmy Ring. The trade enraged Cardinal fans, but the team finished a close second in 1927, and returned to the top (under new manager Bill McKechnie) in a tight race the following season.

McKechnie, fired after the Yankees swept the Cards in the 1928 World Series and rehired in the midst of a Cardinal slump the next season, left to manage the Boston Braves in 1930. Former catcher Gabby Street, who replaced him, led the Cards back to the top again for successive pennants in 1930 and 1931, and in 1931 to a World Series victory over the Philadelphia Athletics. The 1930 race saw the club shoot from below .500 in mid-June to 30 games above .500 by season's end, overtaking three other teams to clinch the flag just three games from the finish. The 1931 team ran away with the pennant, leading all the way and finishing 13 games in front. Outfielder Chick Hafey and first baseman Jim Bottomley finished first and third in NL batting, and pitcher Bill Hallahan led the league in strikeouts (for the second year in a row) and tied for the lead in wins, with 19. Four of the league's top five base stealers—led by Frank Frisch and including outfielder Pepper Martin in his first full season—were Cardinals.

When the Cards dropped to sixth place in 1932 and showed little improvement the following year, Breadon replaced manager Street with Frisch. As when he had named Hornsby to manage, Breadon's move paid immediate dividends. Though the club finished fifth that season, their record improved after Frisch took over, and the next year, in a season-long uphill struggle, the Cards won thirteen of their final fifteen games to pass the front-running New York Giants in the final week.

Writers labeled the 1934 Cardinals the "Gashouse Gang" for their rowdy and daring play. In addition to team veterans Frisch and Martin (who had been shifted from the outfield to third base), the gang included shortstop Leo Durocher, left fielder Joe "Ducky" Medwick, and the team's leading hitter and slugger, first baseman Rip Collins, who in a career-best season led the league in

slugging average and tied for first in home runs.

Cardinal pitching was headed by the league-leading Jerome "Dizzy" Dean (30–7) and his rookie brother Paul (19–11). Of the team's final nine wins, Diz and Paul accounted for seven. Each won another pair in the Cards' World Series triumph over Detroit.

The next two seasons the Cardinals moved into the lead late in the season only to wind up second. After the team slipped into the second division in 1938, Breadon replaced Frisch as manager with Ray Blades, who led a late-season run for the flag in 1939 but finished second. When the Cards failed to contend in 1940, Breadon brought up Rochester manager Billy Southworth for a second time. Southworth had failed as McKechnie's replacement in 1929, but this time he stuck, becoming one of the club's greatest helmsmen.

Through all these years Branch Rickey was revolutionizing baseball as he built the game's first and most extensive "farm system" of minor league clubs. The Cardinals' farm teams would—until the other major league clubs caught on and caught up—provide St. Louis with a competitive advantage in the recruitment and development of young players.

In the closing days of the 1941 season, perhaps the Cardinal system's greatest product arrived at the big club: Stan Musial. Southworth brought the club in a close second that year after a season-long back-and-forth struggle with Brooklyn. The next year—Musial's first full season—the Cardinals enjoyed their winningest season ever: 106 victories. They needed them all, too, for Brooklyn won 104 games, leading the race until mid-September, when the Cardinals passed them and held on to a narrow lead by winning twelve of their final thirteen games. St. Louis pitchers Mort Cooper and Johnny Beazley finished one-two in National League wins and ERA, while Enos Slaughter and Musial paced the Cardinal offense. The club maintained its momentum in the World Series, taking the Yankees in five games.

St. Louis retained its preeminence for two more years as baseball gradually lost players to military service in World War Two. Slaughter and Beazley were gone by 1943. But Cooper remained to compile two more 20-plus winning seasons, and Musial was not called until after the 1944 season. With 105 wins in both 1943 and 1944, the Cards ran away with two more pennants, losing to the Yankees in the 1943 World Series, but taking their sixth world title the next year from their St. Louis landlords, the AL champion Browns.

Owner Breadon had fired Branch Rickey in 1942 (objecting to the personal profit Rickey made from selling the club's unneeded farm players), and Southworth left to manage the Boston Braves after the 1945 season (in which the Cards failed to catch the leading Chicago Cubs, finishing second). Rickey went to head the Brooklyn Dodgers, building for them a farm system and tapping the large reservoir of black players. In 1946, the last year of all-white major league ball, the Cards (managed now by Eddie Dyer) and the Dodgers waged a two-team pennant race, ending the season in the first major league tie for first place. St. Louis won the first two games in a best-of-three playoff and went on to surprise the favored Boston Red Sox in the World Series. With the war over, the team was back at full strength. Slaughter led the league in

RBIs, and Musial led it in most other offensive categories; pitcher Howie Pollett led the league in ERA (as he had in 1943 before leaving for the war) and in wins, with 21.

But St. Louis was slow to integrate its club and lost ground to teams like Brooklyn, whose black players brought an immediate upswing in the club's success. The Cards began poorly in 1947, but recovered to finish second to Brooklyn, though never offering a serious challenge for the flag. After the season Breadon sold the club to Fred Saigh and Robert Hannegan (the U.S. Postmaster General). Musial enjoyed his finest season in 1948, but the club finished second again in a lackluster race. The next year, though, the Cards and Dodgers tangled in a season-long struggle for first place that was not resolved until the season's last day—with Brooklyn on top.

The Cardinals threatened to move to Milwaukee, but beer magnate August Busch, Jr., purchased the club early in 1953 and the same year bought Sportsman's Park from the Browns (who were moving to Baltimore). With Busch's infusion of money and enthusiasm, the club slowly revived. They made runs for the pennant in 1957, 1960, and 1963, but each time tailed off sharply in the final week of the season.

The Cards were playing below .500, in seventh place, in mid-June 1964 when the arrival (via a trade with the Cubs) of speedy young Lou Brock sparked a revival of both the team and player. Brock, who had been hitting .251 in Chicago, with 10 stolen bases, hit .348 the rest of the season and stole 33 more bases as the Cards hurtled into the midst of a four-way race for the pennant that was settled only when they took the flag with an 11–5 win on the final day. After surprising the Yankees in the World Series, the Cardinals were themselves surprised when manager Johnny Keane left to take the Yankee helm. The club slipped into the second division for a couple of years under the management of their great former second baseman Red Schoendienst.

But owner Busch built them a striking new stadium in 1966, and the next season the team rebounded to the top again, running away from the field in the last half of the season behind the heavy hitting of Orlando Cepeda, the bat and speed of Lou Brock, and a pitching staff of remarkable breadth and balance. Bob Gibson's three World Series wins over Boston edged the Cards to a ninth world title and set the stage for Gibson's astonishing season the following year.

With his 22 wins leading the Cards to another pennant in 1968, Gibson hurled 13 shutouts and compiled an ERA of just 1.12—both feats the best in more than half a century, both ranking among the top five big league performances ever. After winning two World Series games, Gibson lost Game Seven as Detroit took the crown.

Red Schoendienst continued as Cardinal manager through 1976—a club record twelve years—but led the team to no more championships. When divisional play was inaugurated in 1969, geography was ignored as the Cards were installed in the East to add strength to what seemed the weaker division. But it was fourteen years before they won their first divisional championship. Four times they finished second, losing twice by only 1½ games, in the back-to-back tight races of 1973 and 1974.

Dorrell "Whitey" Herzog was in his first full season as Cardinal manager before the club again finished that near the top. In the strike-shortened divided season of 1981, the Cards compiled the best overall record in the NL East, but because they had finished the two halves of the season second to Philadelphia and Montreal they were ineligible for postseason play.

With the defensive wizard shortstop Ozzie Smith (acquired from San Diego) and rookie speedster Willie McGee bolstering an already strong team, the Cardinals of 1982, after prevailing against the Phillies in the race for the East, swept West champion Atlanta for the pennant and captured their tenth World Series crown in a seven-game struggle with Milwaukee.

After two seasons out of the running, the Cards in 1985 gained the power of veteran Jack Clark (acquired from San Francisco) and the speed of rookie Vince Coleman. With career-best seasons from Willie McGee and newly acquired pitcher John Tudor, the team edged the New York Mets for the division title and defeated Los Angeles for the pennant—but lost the World Series in seven games to Kansas City.

Jack Clark missed two-thirds of the 1986 season to injury, and the Cards finished below .500, but they rebounded to edge the Mets again for the championship of the East in 1987 as Clark and Vince Coleman enjoyed their finest seasons at the bat. But the reinjured Clark made only a token appearance as the Cards edged San Francisco for the league championship, and he missed the World Series entirely as St. Louis bowed to Minnesota in seven games. That winter Clark signed as a free agent with the Yankees and in 1988 the Cardinals dropped to fifth place, 25 games out.

With solid pitching and hitting, and the league's best fielding, the 1989 Cardinals drew within half a game of the division lead on September 8, then fell out of the race with six straight losses, finishing third. As the season drew to its close, long-time owner August Busch, Jr., died at age ninety. The next July, with the club uncharacteristically mired at the bottom of the NL East, manager Whitey Herzog resigned. Under new manager Joe Torre the Cards revived briefly, but then dropped their final seven games to insure their first basement finish in seventy-two years.

Reliever Lee Smith provided the key to St. Louis's 1991 rebound to second place: his 47 saves—a new NL record—preserved more than half the wins of a team that won 37 of its games by a single run. Smith saved another 43 games in 1992, but this time the Cards finished third.

San Diego Padres

In their first fifteen years the Padres put together only one winning season. In their sixteenth, they won the National League pennant. Founded in the 1969 expansion that saw the two major leagues divide into East and West divisions, the Padres finished last in the six-team NL West their first six seasons, ending each year from 28½ to 42 games behind the division champion.

Their first season was their worst. With 110 losses, the Padres finished not only 41 games out of first but 29 games out of *fifth*. First baseman Nate Colbert, with 24 home runs, provided San Diego's brightest ray of hope. He proved to be one of the Padres' standout performers

through their last-place years, and in 1972 became the first Padre to drive in more than 100 runs.

Big league baseball was not an instant hit in San Diego. Home attendance barely topped half a million in the Padres' first year, and though it rose a little over the next few seasons, the increase was not enough to make the club viable. Owner C. Arnholt Smith decided early in 1974 to sell the franchise to a buyer who planned to move the team to Washington, D.C. New uniforms had been manufactured and the club's files were packed for the move, when the builder of the McDonald's fast-food empire, longtime baseball fan Ray Kroc, stepped in with an offer to buy the Padres for cash and keep them in San Diego. His bid was accepted.

Though Kroc's 1974 Padres finished last with the same 60–102 record they had posted the year before, his sense of showmanship drew spectators. Home attendance shot up 76 percent, rising above a million for the first time. The Padres then began to draw fans on their own merits as they finally pulled themselves out of the cellar. Pitcher Randy Jones, who in 1974 had led the league with 22 losses, turned his record around and for two years shone as one of the game's finest pitchers. He halved his 1974 ERA to a league-leading 2.24, winning 20 games as the Padres rose to fourth place in 1975 and posted a winning percentage over .400 for the first time. The next year Jones won a league-high 22 games and earned the Cy Young Award—the first major award to come to a San Diego player.

Although 1976 proved to be Jones's last winning season, the Padres were by then attracting other top-quality players. Outfielder Dave Winfield came up as a rookie in 1973, and the following year became the team RBI leader, a position he held in six of his seven full seasons with the Padres. Reliever Rollie Fingers signed as a free agent. In each of his four seasons in San Diego (1977–1980) he led the team in saves, twice also leading the league. In 1978 the Padres acquired veteran pitcher Gaylord Perry from Texas and installed rookie Ozzie Smith at shortstop. Perry's sparkling 21–6 season gave San Diego its second Cy Young winner, and together with Smith's play in the field, Winfield's bat (.308, 97 RBIs) and Fingers's 37 saves, brought the Padres their first winning season.

All these stars had gone—and owner Kroc had recently died—by the time the Padres recorded a second winning season six years later, and won the division title and NL pennant with a new blend of experience and youth. Sparked by recently acquired veterans Steve Garvey at first, Graig Nettles at third, and Goose Gossage in the bullpen, and by a bevy of younger stars like batting champ Tony Gwynn and hard-hitting outfielder Kevin McReynolds, the Padres moved into first place to stay in early June. From August 3 to the end of the season, they played only .500 ball but still won the championship of the weak Western Division by 12 games. Underdogs in the League Championship Series, the Padres lost the first two games in Chicago, but pulled themselves together to take the pennant with three come-from-behind wins at home.

Their decline began with their World Series loss to Detroit. The end of 1985 saw them tied for third, and in 1986 they slipped below .500 and into fourth place. In 1987 Gwynn won his second batting title, and rookie catcher Benito Santiago capped the season with a 34-

game hitting streak to cop Rookie of the Year honors. But with most of the 1984 standouts faded or traded, the Padres' decline was complete: the club for the ninth time in its nineteen years finished last.

In late May 1988, with the team at 16–30, Padre general manager Jack McKeon took over as field manager from Larry Bowa. Under McKeon the Padres went 67–48, with nine wins in their final ten games, shot from sixth place to third in the NL West.

In 1989 a trio of veteran pitchers—starters Bruce Hurst (lured from Boston as a free agent) and Ed Whitson, and closer Mark Davis—attained new peaks of performance. Slugger Jack Clark (newly acquired from the Yankees) turned on the power after a slow start to complement Tony Gwynn's fourth season as NL batting leader. The Padres stumbled through the first half, arriving at the All-Star break four games below .500, but climbed steadily through the final two months to a second-place finish with their second-best winning percentage ever.

With the loss of free agent Davis in 1990, plus injuries to Clark and catcher Santiago, even the new power of Joe Carter (traded from Cleveland) could not lift the club above a tie for fourth. New owners, headed by TV producer Tom Werner, took control of the Padres from Ray Kroc's widow Joan in mid-June. Jack McKeon resigned his managerial position, which went to coach Greg Riddoch a month later, and was fired as general manager in September.

Slugger Fred McGriff arrived for 1991 (in a trade that sent Carter to Toronto) and helped power the Padres into third place. In 1992 he was joined by Gary Sheffield, who revived after an injury-ridden season at Milwaukee to lead the NL in batting and rank with McGriff among the league leaders in home runs and RBIs. The Padres again finished third.

San Francisco Giants

The expulsion of Troy and Worcester from the National League after the 1882 season cleared the way for the league to reestablish clubs in the major markets of Philadelphia and New York. Manufacturer John B. Day was awarded the New York franchise. Purchasing the defunct Troy club, he divided their players between the new NL Gothams and his other club, the Metropolitans of the American Association, and set them up on adjoining grounds north of Central Park, on a field once used for polo.

The Mets fared better than the Gothams, finishing fourth in 1883 to the Gothams' sixth, and winning the AA pennant the next year while the Gothams rose only to fifth in the NL. Since the NL, with greater prestige and higher ticket prices, offered potentially greater profit, Day switched some of his Mets to the Gothams in 1885, including ace hurler Tim Keefe and manager Jim Mutrie. The results were immediate: the Mets sank to seventh place while the Gothams (dubbed "my Giants" by an enthusiastic Mutrie) rose to the thick of a pennant race with Chicago. At the finish Chicago was on top by two games, but the Giants had won more than three games out of four for a .759 winning percentage that is not only the club's best ever, but one of the highest in major-league

history. Pitchers Keefe and Mickey Welch together won 76 of the team's 85 victories, and first-baseman Roger Connor led the league in batting.

The Giants won their first pennant in 1888 by nine games over Chicago, and their second the next year in a one-game squeaker over Boston. Keefe and Welch, still going strong, combined for 61 wins in '88 and 55 in '89. Continuing their winning ways in the World Series, the Giants triumphed easily over St. Louis in 1888, and overcame a 1-3 deficit to vanquish Brooklyn the next year.

In 1890, ravaged by the loss of players to the rival Players League, the Giants finished sixth, but they recovered several players when the PL folded at the end of the season. (They also moved into the PL ballpark, named it after their original Polo Grounds, and played there 67 years). They rose to third in 1891, but Day could no longer afford to maintain the team and sold out to financier Edward Talcott. Talcott brought back former Giant star J. M. Ward to manage the club, and in 1894 saw the team rise to a close second-place finish behind Baltimore. Pitchers Amos Rusie and Jouett Meekin tied for the league lead with 36 wins apiece. In postseason Temple Cup play, the Giants swept Baltimore in four games for their third world championship.

That winter Talcott sold control of the club to Tammany Hall politician Andrew Freedman. Giant fortunes sank under Freedman's abrasive and heavy-handed rule. As he ran through a succession of managers, the Giants fell to ninth (of twelve clubs) in 1895 and—apart from a third-place finish in 1897—rose no higher than seventh while he controlled the franchise. In 1902, his final year of ownership, the Giants suffered their lowest winning percentage—.353—and most distant finish ever—53½ games behind champion Pittsburgh.

In the midst of the 1902 season, though, a skirmish in the war between the NL and the upstart American League led to a Giant turnaround. John T. Brush, owner of the NL Cincinnati Reds, bought the AL Baltimore Orioles, then released Oriole manager John McGraw and several key players to sign with NL clubs. Five joined the Giants, including McGraw, catcher Roger Bresnahan, and pitcher Joe "Iron Man" McGinnity. That winter, Brush sold the Reds and Orioles and bought the Giants.

In 1903, with Bresnahan hitting .350 and McGinnity winning a league-high 31 games (closely followed by third-year Giant Christy Mathewson's 30 wins), manager McGraw saw his Giants win thirty-six more games than they had in 1902 and finish a solid second in the standings. In McGraw's twenty-nine full seasons at the helm, the team would win ten pennants and finish second eleven times.

Just two years after their worst season ever, McGraw in 1904 led the Giants to one of their best. Their 106 wins and 13-game winning margin remain Giant highs to this day. The club led the NL in pitching, hitting, fielding, and base stealing. McGinnity led league pitchers in several categories with a career-best 35–8, 1.61 ERA season. Mathewson, right behind with 33 wins, led the league in strikeouts.

The only Giant disappointment of 1904 was McGraw's refusal to face Boston in a World Series. His rejection of the AL champions as worthy opponents was the last shot fired in the war between the two leagues. By the time the Giants had repeated as NL pennant winners a year later, the World Series was an official and permanent feature of the baseball landscape. Mathewson led NL pitchers in 1905 with 31 wins and an ERA of 1.27, and outfielder "Turkey Mike" Donlin, acquired from Cincinnati the previous July, erupted with the best season of his career, batting a team-high .356 and scoring a league-high 124 runs. The Giants won only one game less than the year before and held a comfortable lead throughout the season. Matty's three shutouts against the Philadelphia Athletics in the World Series secured the club's fourth world crown.

It was 1911 before the Giants won their next pennant. Despite 96 wins in 1906 they finished a distant second to Chicago's mighty Cubs, who won a record 116 games. In 1908 the Giants came within a disputed play of the pennant. On September 23, playing Chicago (with whom they were tied at the top of a three-way race), Giant baserunner Fred Merkle failed to run to second on a single by Al Bridwell that would have driven in the winning run from third. Merkle was forced at second after the ball (or a second ball—the argument still rages) was recovered amid the horde of fans who overran the field. The force out at second negated the run, and the game was ruled a tie. At season's end, when the two clubs found themselves again tied at the top, the "Merkle boner" game was replayed. The Cubs won the game and flag, leaving the Giants in a second-place tie with Pittsburgh.

In 1911 the Giants pulled away from the Cubs in September for the first of three straight pennants. (Early in the season most of the Polo Grounds was rebuilt in concrete after fire destroyed the wooden stands.) The following year the Giants took the lead in May and held it comfortably the rest of the way. In 1913 they didn't move into first until late June, but then quickly put the flag out of reach and finished 12½ games ahead of the faltering Phillies. Mathewson led the team in victories over the three years, with 74, followed closely by Rube Marquard (who with 73 wins enjoyed the three best seasons of his career). Matty led the NL in ERA in 1911 and 1913; Giant rookie Jeff Tesreau took the honors in 1912 (winning 17 games that season and 22 the next). Giant pitching led the league all three seasons, as did their hitting, which featured a balanced offense paced by infielders Larry Doyle and Art Fletcher and catcher John "Chief" Meyers.

In the World Series, though, the Giants three times fell short of the title. Philadelphia's Athletics defeated them handily in 1911 and 1913, but the Giants carried the 1912 Series against the Boston Red Sox to the tenth inning of the final game before a pair of Giant fielding lapses enabled Boston to rally for the win.

Boston's "miracle" Braves, in their 1914 surge from last place to the pennant, passed the front-running Giants for good in early September. The next year, five of the eight NL clubs found themselves bunched within 3½ games of one another at the lower end of the standings as the season ended—with the Giants at the very bottom. And in a 1916 Giant season characterized by dips and surges, even a 26-game winning streak in September couldn't raise the team higher than fourth. But in 1917 a balanced pitching staff—paced by Ferdie Schupp's one big season (21–7, 1.95 ERA)—hurled the Giants to the front early in June and kept them there to the finish. Once more, though, the

World Series proved a disappointment, with a loss to the Chicago White Sox in six games.

Three years of second-place finishes followed, in the midst of which the Giants changed owners. Brush had died in 1912 and was succeeded as president by his son-in-law Harry Hempstead. But in January 1919 Brush's heirs sold the club to financier and racehorse fancier Charles A. Stoneham, with manager McGraw a minority stockholder.

In 1921 McGraw brought home the first of four straight winners for Stoneham. Seven regulars hit over .300 (led by third baseman Frank Frisch's .341); first baseman George Kelly's 23 home runs topped the NL. The club hung close to Pittsburgh through August, then broke into a lead which the fading Pirates could not challenge. In postseason play the Giants lost the first two games to the Yankees, but charged back to win their fifth world title. The next year outfielder Emil "Irish" Meusel celebrated his first full season in New York with a team-high 132 RBIs, as the Giants fended off a midseason challenge from St. Louis to pull away to a comfortable margin at the end. The World Series was especially sweet: a four-game sweep of the Yankees.

Cincinnati and Pittsburgh hung just behind the Giants through much of 1923, but never quite caught up. The Giants' league-leading offense was led by individual NL highs in RBIs (Meusel), runs scored (outfielder Ross Youngs), and hits and total bases (Frisch). But the Yankees finally caught the Giants in the World Series, 4–2.

George Kelly took the NL RBI title in 1924. The club's hitting remained the league's best, and by early August the Giants had taken a ten-game lead. But they then leveled off while Brooklyn and Pittsburgh surged. Brooklyn, in fact, took over the lead for a day in early September, but the Giants emerged triumphant at the end by 1½ games. The World Series, though, was as heartbreaking as the pennant race had been heartstopping: the Giants lost to Washington in the last of the twelfth inning of the seventh game when a Senator grounder bounced over the head of rookie third baseman Fred Lindstrom to drive in the Series-ending run.

Close finishes—2 games out—in 1927 and 1928 were the nearest McGraw's Giants came to another pennant. Player relations with the demanding manager had seldom been harmonious, and they had reached a low point when, ill and tired, he quit early in the 1932 season with the team in last place, naming first baseman Bill Terry to replace him. Under Terry the Giants rose only to sixth that season, but McGraw had built a squad fit for a new era of greatness. He had persuaded Terry to leave a career with Standard Oil for one with the Giants; he had saved Mel Ott's unique but effective batting stance from revision by well-meaning minor league managers by keeping Ott out of the minors; and he had rescued pitcher Carl Hubbell from mediocrity by encouraging the screwball pitch other managers had tried to suppress.

Hubbell and Ott formed the heart of the club that would win a trio of pennants under Terry's management. In 1933 the Giants moved to the front in June and, despite a late-September slump, finished well ahead of runner-up Pittsburgh. Ott, with what was for him an off-year, powered the Giant offense with 23 homers and 103 RBIs,

while Hubbell led the league in wins, shutouts, and ERA. Hubbell also hurled two wins against Washington in the World Series, and Ott won it all for New York with a tenth-inning home run in Game Five. McGraw, still the club's vice president, threw a party for "his" Giants after the Series. The following February he died, at age sixty.

As they had the previous season, the Giants of 1934 emerged from the crowd to take and hold first place into late September. They rose higher than they had in 1933 and didn't slump as far at the end. But their five end-of-season losses were enough to drop them 2 games behind the surging Cardinals at the finish. Again in 1935 they led the league much of the season. But they had begun to level off in mid-July and finished the season well back in third. Charles Stoneham died in January 1936, and his son Horace—who at age thirty-three had already run the club for a year—assumed the club presidency.

In 1936, and again in 1937, the Giants came from behind to take the flag. Hubbell sparked their second-half resurgence in 1936, winning his final 16 decisions of the season as the Giants rose from fourth to first. In the World Series, though, Hubbell, after one win, was stopped by the Yankees in his try for a second. The Yankees took the Series in six games.

Again the next year the Giants hid behind the leaders most of the season until a surge in late August coincided with a Chicago decline and shot the Giants to the front. The Cubs recovered, but New York continued its winning ways and finished ahead by 3 games. But again the Yankees dominated the World Series, winning 4–1.

Hubbell's years of greatness were now over, and while the Giants led the NL through the first half of 1938, they finished third, 5 games out. It would be twelve years before they again finished that close to the top. Mel Ott replaced Terry as manager in 1942, but the Giants sank to the cellar in 1943 with their second-worst season ever, and finished last again three years later. One bright spot: in 1947 they rose to fourth with a barrage of 221 home runs (led by Johnny Mize's 51) that remained the major league record (though tied by Cincinnati in 1956) until the 1961 Yankees topped it with 240.

Halfway through the 1948 season the baseball world was startled to learn that Leo Durocher, the fiery manager of the Brooklyn Dodgers, had switched his allegiance to their arch foes, the Giants. Durocher discarded the three top Giant home run hitters of 1947 (but presciently retained the fourth, Bobby Thomson), and added agile infielders Alvin Dark and Eddie Stanky to the roster. By 1950, with the blossoming of Sal Maglie into a first-rank pitcher and the timely midseason purchase of hurler Jim Hearn, the Giants were once more a challenger, spurting in the second half from below .500 to within 5 games of the top.

After losing their first eleven games the next year, the Giants began a long climb. A sixteen-game August winning streak and a seven-game streak at season's end tied them with Brooklyn and forced a three-game playoff. After a win and a loss, the Giants entered the last of the ninth inning of Game Three trailing 1–4. Two singles and a double cut the deficit by a run and brought on Dodger Ralph Branca to face Bobby Thomson, whose two-run homer had provided the Giants' margin of victory in Game One. Thomson homered again, and the Giants won

the pennant. Their defeat by the Yankees in the World Series dimmed the miracle a bit, but couldn't detract from the career bests of pitchers Maglie and Larry Jansen, who tied for the NL lead with 23 wins apiece, and of former Negro League great Monte Irvin, who hit .312 and led the league in RBIs.

The next year Irvin was lost until August with a broken ankle, Jansen (with a back problem) fell off to 11–11, and Willie Mays—a promising rookie in 1951—left early in the season for a hitch in the Army. Still, the Giants hung close to Brooklyn for much of the summer and finished second. In 1953, though, they fell apart in midseason and wound up in fifth, 35 games out.

Mays returned in 1954 to enjoy one of his strongest seasons at the bat, and pitchers Johnny Antonelli (newly acquired from Milwaukee), sophomore Ruben Gomez, and reliever Marv Grissom all burst forth with the best seasons of their careers. The Giants pulled away from Brooklyn in July and held on with a late-season rush to finish 5 games up. Underdogs to powerful Cleveland in the World Series, they stunned the Indians (and the rest of the baseball world) with a four-game sweep. It was their eighth world title—and, so far, their last.

Manager Durocher retired after a distant third-place finish in 1955, and Bill Rigney, who replaced him (the first of seven straight rookie managers to be hired by the Giants over the next twenty years), presided over a pair of sixth-place seasons in the club's final years in New York. Persuaded by the Dodgers' Walter O'Malley that California was the land of baseball opportunity, Giant owner Stoneham announced in August 1957 his decision to move the club to San Francisco before the next season.

The move succeeded. Home attendance doubled, even though the team had to play in a former minor league park that seated fewer than 23,000 fans. When new Candlestick Park opened in 1960 attendance climbed to nearly 1.8 million, a new club high. Better still, rookie sensations like Orlando Cepeda in 1958 and Willie McCovey in 1959, plus the continuing mastery of Willie Mays, made the Giants competitive once again. In their first fourteen San Francisco seasons, they compiled winning records—a longer string than they had ever known in New York.

Candlestick Park, though, proved a cold and windy place to watch baseball, and after its inaugural season fans began to drift away. Attendance picked up some in 1962, however, as the Giants battled for first all summer with the Los Angeles Dodgers. Mays, Cepeda, and Felipe Alou headlined the league's best offense, and a pair of veteran pitchers—Jack Sanford and Billy O'Dell—garnered the most wins of their careers (24 and 19) as part of a balanced staff that also got 16 wins from veteran Billy Pierce and 18 from the emerging great Juan Marichal. Still, the Giants trailed the Dodgers most of the season until a Dodger loss and Giant win on the final day threw the teams into a tie and another playoff. As in 1951, the Giants won the first game and lost the second, and overcame a ninth-inning deficit in the finale to win the pennant. Also as in 1951, they lost the World Series to the Yankees, although this time they held on until the final out of Game Seven before losing their grip on the crown.

The 1963 Giants offered little challenge to the leaders after June, but the next three years found them locked to the end in tight struggles for the flag. Although they finished fourth in 1964, they were still in contention with just two games to play, in one of the closest four-way races ever. The next year they took the lead from the Dodgers early in September, only to lose it in the final week. And in 1966, in a season-long three-way race with the Dodgers and Pirates, the Giants weren't eliminated until the final day.

The turbulence of these races was reflected in the team itself. Cepeda (until traded to St. Louis in 1966) continually railed against his managers and his low pay. Alvin Dark, after four winning seasons as manager, was fired in 1964 when some of his racist comments ended up in print. And Marichal was fined and suspended for nine days in 1965 for hitting Dodger catcher John Roseboro over the head with his bat.

After a pair of distant second-place finishes, the Giants in 1969 (with the fine work of Marichal and McCovey augmented by the speed and power of young outfielder Bobby Bonds) found themselves in the thick of a five-way race for the championship of the newly created NL West. The race wasn't settled until the final week, when Atlanta's ten-game winning streak knocked the Giants out of first. Two years later, with Bonds the chief source of offensive power and fine pitching from starters Marichal and Gaylord Perry and reliever Jerry Johnson, the Giants moved out in front at the start of the season and held their lead all the way. A September slump coinciding with a Dodger surge narrowed the lead to one game in midmonth, but the Giants held on for the division crown. In their first experiences with a League Championship Series, though, they succumbed to Pittsburgh with three losses after an opening-game win.

The LCS loss signaled the end of an era. McCovey was past his prime and Marichal had enjoyed his last big year. Mays, after twenty Giant seasons, was sold to the Mets in 1972 so he could close out his career in New York, where it began. That year the Giants suffered their first losing season in San Francisco, and attendance for the first time dropped below what it had been in their final New York season.

Attendance had reached such a low point by the mid-1970s that Stoneham negotiated the club's sale to a Canadian brewery which planned to move it to Toronto. But San Francisco's mayor George Moscone delayed the sale until a buyer could be found who would keep the Giants in the city. San Francisco realtor Robert Lurie stepped forth with half the purchase price, and Arizona cattleman Arthur "Bud" Herseth provided the rest. (Toronto settled for an expansion club, the Blue Jays.)

After six years out of the running, the Giants in 1978 played at the top of the NL East through much of the summer before dropping to third (and home attendance jumped more than a million above the previous year). But they fell below .500 the next two years—making seven losing seasons in the nine that followed their division title of 1971.

In 1982 the Giants—paced by the slugging of Jack Clark and Greg Minton's sparkling relief pitching—made one of the most impressive comebacks since divisional play was instituted in 1969, driving from ten games below .500 in late June to just 2 games from champion Atlanta at season's end. But they dropped to fifth the following

year, and to a last-place sixth in 1984 and 1985.

When Roger Craig was called on to manage the final weeks of the 1985 season, there was no stopping the Giants' slide to a club-record 100 losses. But the next year, inspiring a "can do" spirit among the players, Craig turned the club around. Veteran hurler Mike Krukow won a career-high 20 games, eight players contributed more than 40 RBIs each, and the team captured 26 of their 83 wins in their final at-bat. In first place at midseason, the Giants slipped (in part because of injuries) to third by season's end, but the fans were back—over 700,000 more than a year earlier.

The club set a new home attendance record of more than 1.9 million in 1987 as it returned to the top of the NL West for the first time in sixteen years. Sophomore first baseman Will Clark led a balanced offense, and several shrewd in-season acquisitions by the front office spurred a second-half drive from five games back to a 6-game lead at the finish. But after taking a 3–2 advantage over St. Louis in the LCS, the Giants failed to score in the final two games and the Cardinals captured the flag.

Injuries contributed to the Giants' decline to fourth place the next year, but in 1989 Will Clark enjoyed his strongest season yet, and left fielder Kevin Mitchell erupted with league-high power (47 HRs, 125 RBIs, .635 slugging) to lead another successful Giant assault on the division title. For the first time, the Giants passed the 2 million mark in home attendance. After holding first place from mid-June to the finish, they pushed past the stubborn Cubs in the LCS to their first pennant in twenty-seven years, their nineteenth over all. But the earthquake that delayed Game 3 of the World Series only postponed a sweep by mighty Oakland.

The Giants' downward slide over the next three years— to third place in 1990, fourth in 1991, and fifth in 1992— coincided with futile efforts to persuade Bay area voters to approve public funding for a new stadium to replace unpopular Candlestick Park. In August 1992, Giant owner Bob Lurie arranged to sell the club to a group of investors who planned to move it to St. Petersburg, Florida. In November, though, the sale and move were blocked by the other major league owners.

Seattle Mariners

The Mariners began play in 1977, returning major league baseball to the Pacific Northwest eight years after the Seattle Pilots had moved to Milwaukee after only one season. With a 64–98 inaugural season, the Mariners avoided last place in the American League West only because the Oakland A's had plummeted faster and farther. The hitting of first baseman Dan Meyer, outfielder Leroy Stanton, and rookie center fielder Ruppert Jones— who combined for 73 home runs—and the relief pitching of rookie Enrique (Romo) Romero, who contributed 16 saves and 8 wins, provided most of the high points of that first season.

There was less to cheer about the next year as the production of the first-season heroes fell off and the Mariners took possession of the cellar from mid-May on, losing a club-record 104 games. They finished 12 games out of sixth place, 35 out of first. Much of the offense that

was generated came from outfielder Leon Roberts. Acquired from Houston over the winter, Roberts put together his best season and became the Mariners' first .300 hitter.

The club moved up a notch in 1979, to sixth place. Meyer and Jones regained much of their 1977 power, first baseman Bruce Bochte hit .316 and drove in 100 runs, and DH Willie Horton, near the end of a long career, enjoyed one of his finest seasons, driving in 106 runs and leading the club with 29 homers.

As the Mariners, with the league's weakest hitting, dropped back into the cellar the next season, attendance fell to a new low, and some of the original owners decided to sell out. In January 1981 California real-estate magnate George Argyros purchased control of the club, and later bought out the remaining partners to take sole ownership.

In strike-divided 1981 the Mariners finished sixth and fifth in the two halves of the season. Second baseman Julio Cruz continued among the league's top base stealers, and right fielder Tom Paciorek's second-place .326 BA put a Seattle hitter high among the league's best for the first time. Paciorek was traded away that winter, but his replacement, veteran Al Cowens, came through with one of his best seasons in 1982. And Mariner pitching improved dramatically—from the bottom of the league in ERA in 1981 to fourth best in '82. Newcomers Bill Caudill and rookie Ed Vande Berg, working in relief, combined for 21 wins and 31 saves. Starter Floyd Bannister led the league in strikeouts while winning 12 games (tying Caudill for the team lead), and veteran Gaylord Perry added 10 victories, including his 300th career win in May. The team finished above .450 for the first time, fourth in the AL West, a new high.

Caudill's 26 saves in 1983 couldn't prevent a slide back into last place. But the club's farm system was beginning to produce quality talent, and 1984 saw the arrival of two standouts: first baseman Alvin Davis, whose 27 homers and 116 RBIs earned him AL Rookie of the Year honors, and pitcher Mark Langston, a 17-game winner in 1984 and AL strikeout leader in three of his first four seasons. Rookie third baseman Jim Presley hit 10 home runs in 70 games and proceeded to blossom into one of the Seattle club's leading power hitters the next year.

After sixth-place finishes in 1984 and '85, the Mariners fell off to last again in 1986. Langston's 19 wins led the team's 1987 rebound to fourth, with Lee Guetterman's 11–4 pitching and the power of Davis and Presley providing valuable assists. Infielder Harold Reynolds stole his sixtieth base in the final game to preserve his lead in that department and to give the Mariners their first league leader in an offensive category.

After dropping back into the cellar in 1988 and rising a notch to sixth in 1989, the Mariners revived under new ownership in 1990 to challenge the .500 barrier. Center fielder Ken Griffey, Jr., began to fulfill the promise he had shown as a nineteen-year-old rookie the previous summer. Sophomore hurler Erik Hanson—with 18 wins and an ERA among the league's best—replaced the traded Mark Langston as ace of a young pitching staff that compiled the league's third lowest ERA. The Mariners entered August third in the strong AL West, with a winning record which they maintained through mid-month before

stumbling to fifth place with their fourteenth straight losing season.

At last, in 1991, Seattle produced its first winning season, rising from an even .500 with six wins in the final eight games. Griffey Jr. overcame a lackluster first half to reach new Mariner heights in batting (.327) and slugging (.527), but the club still finished fifth, and manager Jim Lefebvre was fired. It also continued to lose money, so in June 1992, as the Mariners sailed for the sixth time toward the bottom of the AL West, the club was sold. The new ownership group included (for the first time) substantial local representation, but as major financing came from Hiroshi Yamauchi, the Japanese president of computer game giant Nintendo, and his son-in-law, a Washington State resident but Japanese national, the sale was delayed until jingoistic opposition to it subsided. The deal was restructured to insure American control of the club. On the field Griffey enjoyed another strong season, and third baseman Edgar Martinez hit .343 to give Seattle its first league batting champion.

Texas Rangers

As part of the first American League expansion, a new Washington club was added to the league in November 1960, to replace the old Senators, who were moving to Minnesota to become the Twins. The old Senators had languished in the second division their final 14 years in Washington, and the new Senators scarcely improved on that record. In each of their first four seasons they lost 100 games or more, tying for last place in 1961 and holding down the bottom all by themselves for two years before rising to ninth in 1964.

Although as an expansion team the new Senators had to make do at first with expendable players from the established clubs, they were not devoid of talent. In their first season, pitcher Dick Donovan led the league with a 2.40 earned run average, though injuries and the lack of offensive support held his won-lost record to 10–10. Perhaps their most promising player, he was traded with two teammates to Cleveland for outfielder Jimmy Piersall. Piersall proved a major disappointment in Washington, batting only .244 while Donovan was winning 20 games for his new club.

Not all the Senators' trades proved disastrous. In late 1964 they sent another promising pitcher—Claude Osteen—to the Dodgers in a deal that brought them five players, including third baseman Ken McMullen and outfielder Frank Howard. Osteen blossomed into a consistent winner in Los Angeles, but at the same time, McMullen brought strength to the Washington infield and Howard became one of the league's offensive stars.

The Senators' blend of youth and experience jelled in 1969 under rookie manager Ted Williams, as several key players—including McMullen and Howard—enjoyed career-best seasons. The club finished above .500 for the first time, driving with a late-season spurt to within a game of third-place Boston in the league's Eastern Division.

But 1969 was a one-year phenomenon. After losing seasons in 1970 and '71 (and the loss of much of their fan support), owner Bob Short pulled up stakes and moved the club to Arlington, Texas (midway between Fort Worth and Dallas), where, as the Texas Rangers, they have been ever since. Their first summer in Texas resembled their first in Washington: they lost 100 games (despite a strike-shortened season) and finished last. Williams was replaced by a new rookie manager—Whitey Herzog—but the club did no better in 1973.

Before the season's end Herzog gave way to Billy Martin. Martin came too late to save the Rangers from another lost season, but the next year he spurred the team to the kind of turnaround Williams had managed five years earlier. Behind the 25–12 pitching of Ferguson Jenkins (acquired in the offseason from the Cubs) and the hitting of league MVP Jeff Burroughs and rookie first baseman Mike Hargrove, the Rangers spurted in the second half of 1974 from a sub-.500 record to second place in the American League West, only 5 games behind Oakland.

Since 1974 the Rangers' fortunes have been up and down. After two losing seasons they rebounded in 1977 to their finest season yet (94–68, .580) and second place, behind strong pitching and the blooming of Jim Sundberg as a hitter to go along with his league-leading catching. Fergie Jenkins's return to the club (after two years in Boston), the sparkling 11–5 season of rookie Steve Comer, and a September surge kept the club competitive in 1978. Jim Kern's brilliant relief work the next season helped club recover from a nosedive in July and August to edge Minnesota for a strong third-place finish.

After a losing season in 1980, the Rangers bounced back in 1981 to record their second-best winning percentage ever (.543)—and finishes of second and third in the two halves of the strike-divided season. Then they slipped below .500 again for four more years. Pitcher Charlie Hough's knuckleball, and strong seasons at the bat from Pete O'Brien, Larry Parrish, and rookies Scott Fletcher and Pete Incaviglia helped new manager Bobby Valentine turn the Rangers around once again in 1986, lifting them to the club's fifth second-place finish after last-place seasons in 1984 and '85.

Once more, though, the turnaround was brief: in 1987 losses in their final games of the season dropped the Rangers into a tie at the bottom of the division, and in 1988 they finished only two games out of the cellar, in sixth place.

A group of investors headed by George W. Bush—the President's son—purchased control of the Rangers in March 1989, and strikeout king Nolan Ryan returned to the American League as a Ranger after nine years in Houston. The strong arms of starter Ryan (who recorded his 5,000th career strikeout during the season) and reliever Jeff Russell, the potent bats of outfielder Ruben Sierra and second baseman Julio Franco (newly acquired from Cleveland), and a 10–1 start that put the club in first place for a month highlighted a Ranger return to the winning side of the ledger. In 1990 Ryan hurled his 300th win and sixth no-hitter, first baseman Rafael Palmeiro peaked at the plate, and pitcher Bobby Witt enjoyed his finest season, with 17 wins. After a slow first half, the Rangers rose from sixth place to third, compiling an 83–79 record identical to that of the year before.

A fourteen-game win streak in May 1991 boosted the Rangers into first place for several days, although they again finished third. Jose Guzman joined Ryan (who

threw a sixth no-hitter) among the league's top pitchers, and young slugger Juan Gonzalez formed with Franco, Palmeiro, and Sierra a powerful quartet that made the Rangers the top scoring team in the majors. In 1992 pitcher Kevin Brown joined the Rangers from Milwaukee and won 21 games, and Gonzalez topped the majors in home runs. But an overall decline in offense, coupled with disastrous fielding and relief pitching, dropped the team below .500 after a competitive first half. In the year's biggest in-season trade, the club acquired Jose Canseco from Oakland for Sierra, Witt, and Russell.

Toronto Blue Jays

For a while, in February 1977, it looked as if the National League's San Francisco Giants would move to Toronto, where there were buyers eager for the club. But when the Giants were sold in March to new owners determined to keep them in San Francisco, the American League jumped in to establish Toronto as an American League city, setting up an expansion club, the Blue Jays.

It took seven years for the Jays to lift themselves out of last place in the seven-team American League East. For five years they had the cellar all to themselves, never finishing closer than 11 games behind the *sixth*-place club.

In their first season, the Jays' 107 losses left them 45½ games out of first, as the team performed at the bottom of the division in hitting, fielding, and pitching. In 1978 their fielding improved dramatically, but the Jays still lost over 100 games, and there was little doubt after April who would finish last.

The next year was the team's worst ever. While every other Eastern Division club was compiling a winning record, Toronto plunged relentlessly downward and, despite a brief rally in September, finished 28½ games out of sixth place (50½ out of first), with 109 losses.

The club's turnaround began in 1980. It was late June before the Jays began their drop away from the rest of the division, and for the first time they finished with fewer than 100 losses. Pitchers Jim Clancy and Dave Stieb lowered their ERAs below 4.00 for the first time, and newly acquired second baseman Damaso Garcia combined with shortstop Alfredo Griffin to form the league's best double-play combination. There were still two more seasons in the cellar, but in strike-divided 1981 the Jays played a creditable second half for the first time, and in 1982 they spurted in September to tie the Indians for sixth at season's end. Garcia in 1982 became a .300 hitter and a leading base stealer, Clancy put together his first winning season and Stieb his second, and Stieb's five shutouts led the league.

In 1983, with seven of the Blue Jays' eight principal pitchers enjoying winning seasons, and the Jays' hitters leading the league in team batting and slugging, Toronto recorded its first winning season—in fourth place, only 9 games out of first. Their balanced pitching and offense carried them to a repeat 89–73 record in 1984—this time for second place (though they finished a distant 15 games behind Detroit).

In 1985 the Blue Jays topped their division with 99 victories, edging the Yankees by 2 games. Their pitching

was better than ever. Doyle Alexander won 17 games, Jimmy Key and Dave Stieb contributed 14 each, and reliever Dennis Lamp compiled an impressive 11–0 record. Stieb led the league in ERA, with Key fourth. Tony Fernandez, in his first full big league season, sparkled as expected at short, but also proved unexpectedly solid at the bat. Eight Jays drove in more than 50 runs, with outfielders George Bell (95), Jesse Barfield (84), and Lloyd Moseby (71) pacing the club's balanced attack.

In the LCS the Jays won three of their first four games against Kansas City, but lost the next three—and the pennant. Equally discouraging was their drop to fourth place in 1986. Barfield, Bell, and Fernandez all improved at the plate, but the league-leading pitchers of 1985 dropped back to the middle of the pack in '86 (though rookie Mark Eichorn sparkled in long relief).

Toronto sprang back stronger than ever in 1987. Jim Clancy (15–11, 3.54 ERA) enjoyed his best season yet, as did Jimmy Key (17–8), whose 2.76 ERA led the league. Once again, as in 1985, the team ERA was the league's lowest. And the offense remained strong. (George Bell, league RBI leader with 134, was named the American League MVP at season's end.) The Jays led their division going into the season's final series against second-place Detroit, though four straight losses had reduced the lead to just one game. Needing to win two of the three games to take the AL East title, or one to tie the Tigers and force a playoff, the Jays' slumping bats remained quiet, and Toronto lost the first two games. In the season finale, Jimmy Key hurled a three-hitter, striking out eight. But one of the hits was a home run—the only run of the game, as it turned out. Toronto's seven-game losing streak had cost them what would have been their second title in three years.

In 1988, a rocky season made worse by George Bell's feud with manager Jimy Williams (who wanted the unwilling outfielder to serve as designated hitter), the Jays surged at the end—with six straight wins—into a tie for third place, only two games out of first. The season was highlighted by the emergence of Fred McGriff as one of the game's most powerful batsmen, and by ace Dave Stieb's two successive one-hitters in late September—both of which were no-hitters through 8⅔ innings.

When Toronto's front office replaced manager Williams with batting coach Cito Gaston in mid-May 1989, the Jays were drowning near the bottom of the AL East with a record of 12–24. By mid-August they had bobbed above .500 to stay, and on September 1 replaced Baltimore in first place. With a pair of one-run victories over the Orioles at the end of September, the Jays preserved their narrow lead and clinched the division title. But Oakland outplayed them in the LCS, taking the pennant in five games.

From mid-June 1990 to the final day of the season, the Blue Jays battled Boston for the division lead before settling for second. Dave Stieb (after two more one-hitters in 1989) at last hurled a no-hitter, and third baseman Kelly Gruber confirmed a place with Bell and McGriff among Toronto's power elite. But the brightest Toronto star of 1989–90 was the new SkyDome, with its 11,000-ton retractable roof and its restaurants and hotel rooms above the outfield wall. After the Jays moved into the Dome on June 5, 1989, attendance zoomed, and by season's end the

club set a new American League home attendance record of nearly 3.4 million. In 1990, with a full season in the Dome, the Jays attracted over a half million more fans than the year before, for a new major league record of 3,885,284.

SkyDome attendance continued to set new records in 1991 and 1992 as it rose above 4 million. McGriff and Bell had departed by 1991, but an improved Devon White, plus newly acquired slugger Joe Carter and second baseman Roberto Alomar, led an offense that—together with the league's stingiest pitching staff—brought the Jays to their fourth divisional title. For the fourth time, though, they crashed in the LCS, this time trampled by Minnesota in five games. With the addition of a pair of free-agent veterans—pitcher Jack Morris (who went 21–6) and DH–outfielder Dave Winfield (108 RBIs)—Toronto in 1992 finally completed the puzzle. The Jays sported a balanced offense (six players drove in 60 runs or more) and outstanding pitching from starter Juan Guzman (16–5; 2.64 ERA) and relievers Tom Henke and Duane Ward. Thus armed, they fended off Baltimore's challenge for the lead through much of the summer and resisted Milwaukee's late-season surge to repeat as AL East titlists. They then felled Oakland in six games to bring Canada its first major league baseball pennant, and stopped stubborn Atlanta in six games to carry home the championship of the world.

Defunct Clubs

In addition to the many Negro League teams, some 108 ballclubs have played in the major leagues since the first professional association was formed in 1871. The twenty-six that still do are described above; here are the other eighty-two, listed according to the league and year in which they first played major league ball. Official club names precede the name of the city; nicknames follow.

National Association, 1871–1875

Two of the twenty-three clubs that played at one time or another in baseball's first professional league still play in the majors: the Atlanta Braves (then the Boston Red Stockings) and the Chicago Cubs (then the White Stockings). The other twenty-one:

Athletic of Philadelphia: NA 1871–1875, NL 1876. Organized in 1860 as an amateur club, the Athletics became one of the dominant teams of the decade. As professionals they won the first NA pennant in 1871. After one year in the NL, they were expelled for failing to make the final western trip of the season.

Forest City of Cleveland, NA 1871–1872. In the midst of a second losing season, the club disbanded in August 1872.

Forest City of Rockford, Ill., NA 1871. As an amateur club, Forest City (with its sixteen-year-old pitcher Al Spalding) was the only team to defeat the famous Washington Nationals on their pioneering midwestern tour of 1867. As professionals, Forest City finished seventh of the nine NA teams in 1871.

Kekionga of Fort Wayne, NA 1871. The Kekiongas won the first NA game ever played, but dropped out of the association before the end of the season.

Mutual of New York, NA 1871–1875, NL 1876. Organized as an amateur club in 1857, the Mutuals were said to be backed financially by New York's notorious William M. "Boss" Tweed. Frequently accused of corrupt practices, the club was one of the leading eastern teams of the late 1860s. They were declared national champions of 1868, and proclaimed themselves national champions of 1870. On the demise of the NA the Mutuals entered the NL, but were expelled after one season (along with the Athletics) for failing to play their final games in the West.

Olympic of Washington, D.C., NA 1871–1872. Unsuccessful in 1872 after playing well the year before, the Olympics disbanded about midseason.

Union of Troy, N.Y., NA 1871–1872. The Haymakers, as they were popularly known, dropped out of the NA halfway through the 1872 season.

Atlantic of Brooklyn, NA 1872–1875. One of the greatest of the amateur clubs, the Atlantics (organized in 1855) went undefeated in 1864 and 1865, and won three successive national championships, 1864–1866. But in four NA seasons their combined won-lost record was only 49–139, including a dismal 2–42 in 1875.

Eckford of Brooklyn, NA 1872. Another great early amateur club—like the Atlantics, organized in 1855—they won the national championship in 1862, and again (with an undefeated season of ten games) the next year. The Eckfords actually joined the NA in August 1871, replacing Kekionga, but their 1871 games were later erased from the record because they had failed to enter the association at the start of the season.

Lord Baltimore of Baltimore, NA 1872–1874. After twice finishing third, the Lord Baltimores (or "Canaries," for their yellow silk jerseys) disbanded two games before the end of the 1874 season, while in last place.

Mansfield of Middletown, Ct., NA 1872. Disbanded in late August.

National of Washington, D.C., NA 1872–1873, 1875. Organized as amateurs in 1859, the Nationals were the first eastern club to tour as far west as Chicago and St. Louis. After skipping the 1874 race, the Nationals reentered the NA in 1875, but dropped out in July.

Maryland of Baltimore, NA 1873. Dropped out after only six games.

Philadelphia, NA 1873–1875. Known successively as the "White Stockings," "Pearls," and "Phillies," the team finished a strong second to Boston in their first season, but slipped to fourth and fifth the next two years.

Resolute of Elizabeth, N.J., NA 1873. Disbanded in August with a 2–21 record.

Hartford Dark Blues, NA 1874–1875, NL 1876–1877. After a weak first year, Hartford finished third in its next three seasons, as standings are reckoned today. But by the 1876 guidelines (which used the number of games won rather than winning percentage), Hartford that year placed second. In 1877 the club played its home games in Brooklyn, N.Y.

Centennial of Philadelphia, NA 1875. Dropped out in late May.

New Haven Elm Citys, NA 1875. Failed to play out their schedule.

St. Louis Brown Stockings, NA 1875, NL 1876–1877. George Bradley pitched all but 5 of the Browns' 39 wins

in 1875, when they finished fourth, and all 45 victories in 1876, when they finished a strong third (in number of victories; they were second in winning percentage). With Bradley lost to Chicago the next year, St. Louis dropped below .500—and out of the league.

St. Louis Red Stockings, NA 1875. A successful amateur club that decided to take a fling at pro ball, the Red Stockings played only a few games in the NA.

Western of Keokuk, Iowa, NA 1875. Disbanded in mid-June.

National League, 1876–

When the NL was founded to replace the ill-organized NA, it included six of the stronger NA clubs plus independent clubs in Cincinnati and Louisville. The league's composition was in continual flux to the end of the century as clubs were dropped and added, shrinking the league to as few as six teams and expanding it to as many as twelve. Two clubs that first played major league ball in the NL still do: the Philadelphia Phillies and the San Francisco (originally New York) Giants, both organized in 1883. (The Boston and Chicago franchises—that continue to this day as the Atlanta Braves and Chicago Cubs—had their starts in the National Association.) Those that have not survived:

Cincinnati Red Stockings, NL 1876–1880. From last place in 1876 (and 1877, when their games were not counted because of the club's reorganization and failure to pay its dues), the Reds—with seven new regulars—rose to second in 1878, only to fall back to fifth in 1879, and last again in 1880. That fall, when they refused to accept a new rule abolishing liquor sales and Sunday baseball on club grounds, they were dropped from league membership.

Louisville Grays, NL 1876–1877. The strong Louisville team led the league in mid-August, but seven suspicious losses to chief rivals Boston and Hartford dropped the Grays out of first place. After Boston clinched the pennant, Louisville revived to secure second place, but four players—including pitching ace Jim Devlin—were expelled from baseball for throwing games. Their expulsion showed the NL's determination to wipe out corruption, but it also caused the St. Louis Browns, who had planned to sign three of the four Louisville players for 1878, to resign from the league. Louisville, too, dropped out of the league before the next season, unable to find adequate replacements for the four.

Indianapolis Browns, NL 1878. Finished fifth of six teams.

Milwaukee Grays (or Cream Citys), NL 1878. Finished a last-place sixth.

Providence Grays, NL 1878–1885. One of the great teams in the NL's early years, Providence won pennants in 1879 and 1884, finishing no lower than third in seven of their eight seasons. In 1884, pitcher Charlie "Old Hoss" Radbourn won a record 59 games, then pitched the Grays to victory in baseball's first World Series with a three-game sweep of the American Association champion New York Mets. But as they dropped to fourth place the next year, finishing for the first time below .500, their fans deserted them. Late that autumn the club was dissolved.

Buffalo Bisons, NL 1879–1885. Buffalo moved up to the majors after winning the International Association pennant in 1878. Jim "Pud" Galvin pitched nearly 70 percent of Buffalo's victories as he led them to four first-division finishes in seven big league seasons. First baseman Dan Brouthers, in his five years with Buffalo, twice won the batting title and led NL sluggers five times.

Cleveland Blues, NL 1879–1884. Cleveland's fortunes rested in large measure with pitcher Jim McCormick (who also managed the club their first two seasons). In 1880, their best season, McCormick won a career-high 45 games to bring the Blues in third. In 1883 Cleveland was in first place when McCormick's injured arm put him out for the season after he had won twenty-three games. The Blues dropped to fourth. The club folded after a seventh-place finish in 1884, a season that saw McCormick and two other Blues jump to the UA.

Star of Syracuse, NL 1879. After finishing a close second to Buffalo in the International League in 1878, the Stars moved up with the Bisons to the NL, but disbanded after a single unsuccessful season.

Troy, N.Y., Trojans, NL 1879–1882. After four losing seasons the franchise was expelled to make room for a club in New York City.

Worcester, Mass., Brown Stockings, NL 1880–1882. After a pair of losing minor league seasons, Worcester was admitted to the NL to replace the defunct Stars of Syracuse. After finishing a respectable fifth in 1880, Worcester dropped into the cellar for two seasons before being ousted in 1883 for a new Philadelphia club.

Detroit Wolverines, NL 1881–1888. Buffalo's sale of its "big four" (Dan Brouthers, Hardy Richardson, Jack Rowe, and Deacon White) to Detroit late in 1885 transformed a perennial also-ran into a contender. The club finished second in 1886 and won the pennant in 1887. In a World Series played in ten different cities, the Wolverines trounced St. Louis ten games to five. In 1888, after finishing fifth, they expired.

Kansas City Cowboys, NL 1886. They finished seventh, 58½ games out.

Washington Senators, NL 1886–1889. In their four seasons, the Senators finished out of the cellar only once: next to last in 1887.

Indianapolis Hoosiers, NL 1887–1889. After dropping below Washington into the cellar in 1887, the Hoosiers and Senators traded places for their final two years.

American Association, 1882–1891

Three of the six clubs that formed the AA in 1882 still represent their cities in the majors today: Allegheny (Pittsburgh), Cincinnati, and St. Louis. Brooklyn, which entered the AA two years later, today represents Los Angeles. The others:

Athletic of Philadelphia, AA 1882–1890. After finishing a distant second in the AA's first season, the Athletics in 1883 took the pennant from St. Louis by a single game. First baseman Harry Stovey, who led AA batters in most offensive categories that year, was even more productive in 1884. But the A's dropped to seventh and never again challenged for the crown. Expelled from the AA after the 1890 season for financial reasons, they were replaced by the Philadelphia club from the defunct Players League.

Baltimore Orioles, AA 1882–1889, 1890–1891, NL

1892–1899. After eight seasons out of pennant contention (including four in last place), the Orioles dropped out of the AA to play minor league ball in 1890. But toward the end of the season, when Brooklyn's new franchise went under, the Orioles returned to complete Brooklyn's season (finishing a combined last). After rising to third in 1891, the AA's final year, the Orioles were invited into the expanding NL, where they dropped to a twelfth-place last (54½ games out) in 1892.

Ned Hanlon, hired to manage Baltimore early in the 1892 season, set about building a championship club. By 1894, with a lineup that included six future Hall of Famers, Hanlon led his club to a narrow pennant victory over New York, though the Giants swept the Orioles in the first Temple Cup World Series, 4–0.

For five years Hanlon's brand of scrappy, hustling play made the Orioles the terror of the NL. Led by shortstop Hughie Jennings and outfielders Willie Keeler and Joe Kelley, the club repeated as NL champions in 1895 and 1896, and finished second to Boston the next two years. They lost the Temple Cup to Cleveland (1–4) in 1895, but swept the Spiders the next year 4–0, and took the cup again in 1897, defeating Boston 4–1 in what turned out to be the Series swan song.

Baltimore owners Hanlon and Harry Von der Horst purchased a half-interest in the Brooklyn club in 1899 (retaining a half-interest in Baltimore), and switched Jennings, Kelley, and Keeler to Brooklyn. Hanlon also went over as manager, leaving third baseman John McGraw in charge of the Orioles. McGraw hit .391 and rookie pitcher Joe McGinnity won 28 games to bring the team in fourth. But Hanlon's Superbas won the pennant, and when the NL cut back to eight teams after the season, Baltimore got the ax.

Eclipse of Louisville/Louisville Colonels (or Cyclones), AA 1882–1891, NL 1892–1899. The club, which changed its official name from Eclipse to Louisville after the 1883 season, was one of only two teams to play all ten seasons of the major league AA. (St. Louis—the present Cardinals—was the other.) Louisville finished above .500 in five of its first six years, but only once in that time closed within ten games of the top—in 1884, when Guy Hecker's 52 wins brought the team in third. Slugger Pete Browning paced the Colonel offense in their early years, winning batting titles in 1882 (his rookie season), 1885 and 1886, and hammering a second-best .402 in 1887. (A bat made for him by woodworker John Hillerich inspired the creation of the Louisville Slugger.)

By 1889, though, the club had sunk to last place, finishing 66½ games out of first, with 111 losses. The next year, although Hecker and Browning defected to the outlaw PL, the club was less affected by deserters than other AA teams. The Colonels (paced by the league's best hitter, William "Chicken" Wolf, and its best pitcher, Scott Stratton) made one of the greatest turnarounds in big league history, winning the pennant by 10 games over second-place Columbus. In the World Series against Brooklyn, poor weather and small crowds ended play after the teams had tied once and won three apiece.

Even though the Colonels finished next to last in 1891, they were one of four clubs taken into the NL after the AA folded. They never finished higher than ninth in the NL, and for three straight years (1894–1896) they occu-

pied the cellar. When the league cut back from twelve teams to eight after the 1899 season, Louisville merged with the Pittsburgh Pirates.

Columbus Colts (or Senators), AA 1883–1884. From sixth place in 1883, Columbus climbed to second in 1884 behind the 34–13 pitching of rookie Ed Morris. But when the AA dropped back from twelve clubs to eight in 1885, Columbus was out.

Metropolitan of New York, AA 1883–1887. After success in minor league and independent play since 1880, the Mets entered the AA in 1883 as the association expanded from six clubs to eight. With 41 victories from pitcher Tim Keefe (who was picked up from disbanded Troy), the Mets finished fourth. The next season, with first baseman Dave Orr hitting .354 in his first full major league season and pitcher Jack Lynch matching Keefe with 37 wins apiece, the Mets won the AA pennant handily. But they lost baseball's first World Series to the Providence Grays. When manager Jim Mutrie, third baseman Dude Esterbrook, and pitcher Keefe were transferred in 1885 to the New York Giants (the two clubs had the same owner), the Mets sank to seventh place, where they finished in their final three seasons.

Indianapolis Blues, AA 1884. Finished eleventh of twelve clubs, 46 games behind.

Toledo Blue Stockings, AA 1884. Catcher Fleet Walker (who played in 42 games) and his brother Welday (5 games) were the major leagues' first black players—and the only blacks until Jackie Robinson broke the color bar for good in 1947.

Washington, D.C., AA 1884. The popularity of the city's UA Nationals proved too much for this inept AA club, which went under in early August.

Virginia of Richmond, AA 1884. When Washington disbanded in August, the Wilmington club of the Eastern League was invited to join the AA as its replacement. Wilmington declined (and later jumped to the UA), but Virginia—also a member of the EL—accepted the invitation and took over Washington's remaining games. Washington-Virginia finished a combined 24–81, in last place.

Cleveland Spiders, AA 1887–1888, NL 1889–1899. After two losing seasons in the AA, the Spiders moved to the NL, where they continued below .500 for three more years. But in 1892 Cy Young's league-leading pitching brought them the second-half championship of the league's experimental split season. Cleveland lost the World Series to first-half winner Boston, losing five after tying the first game.

Second-place finishes in 1895 and 1896 qualified the Spiders for the Temple Cup series against champion Baltimore. In 1895 they beat the Orioles for the world title four games to one, but were swept the next year 0–4.

In 1899, when owner Frank Robison transferred all the team's best players to St. Louis (which he also owned), Cleveland suffered the worst season in major league history, winning only 20 games while losing a record 134. They finished 35 games behind eleventh-place Washington and 84 games out of first. After the season the Spiders died, as the NL cut back from twelve teams to eight.

Kansas City Blues, AA 1888–1889. Finished last in 1888, next to last in 1889.

Columbus Colts (or Solons), AA 1889–1891. In 1890, with the AA weakened by the replacement of half its

franchises with new clubs and by defections to the outlaw PL, Columbus (which retained several of its regulars) rose from its 1889 sixth-place finish to second behind Louisville. When the PL folded and the defectors returned in 1891, Columbus dropped back to sixth.

Brooklyn Gladiators, AA 1890. Formed as a replacement for the Brooklyn club that forsook the AA for the NL in 1890, the Gladiators floundered and were replaced by Baltimore late in the season.

Rochesters, AA 1890. Played .500 ball, finishing fifth.

Syracuse Stars, AA 1890. Finished sixth.

Toledo Maumees, AA 1890. Finished fourth.

Cincinnati Porkers, AA 1891. Also known as "Kelly's Killers" for their manager Mike "King" Kelly, the club went bankrupt in August and was replaced by Milwaukee.

Milwaukee Brewers, AA 1891. This Western League club moved up to the AA in August. Taking five players and the 43–57 record from the defunct Cincinnati club, Milwaukee went 21–15 the rest of the way to lift the Cincinnati-Milwaukee combination from seventh to fifth by season's end.

Washington Senators, AA 1891, NL 1892–1899. Despite a cellar finish in the AA's final year, the Senators were taken into the expanding NL. Of its nine losing seasons, the best was a tie for sixth in the twelve-team NL of 1897.

Union Association, 1884

Formed in opposition to the reserve rule that governed players in the NL and AA, the UA struggled through one season. The first eight clubs listed here began the season. The other five are listed according to the month they entered the UA as replacement teams. All thirteen—like the UA itself—are long extinct:

Altoona, Pa., Unions, UA 1884. The first of several UA clubs to drop out of competition during the season, Altoona disbanded on May 31, but reorganized as an independent club two days later with many of the same players.

Baltimore Unions, UA 1884. Bill Sweeney's league-leading 40 wins accounted for 70 percent of third-place Baltimore's victories.

Boston Unions, UA 1884. Outfielder Tom McCarthy, the UA's only Hall of Famer, hit .215 in this, his rookie big league season. Boston finished fourth.

Chicago Browns/Pittsburgh Stogies, UA 1884. Financial woes caused the Chicago Browns to relocate in Pittsburgh in late August, but the club quit altogether less than a month later.

Cincinnati Outlaw Reds, UA 1884. With three 20-game winners—including Jim McCormick, who won 21 after defecting from the NL in midseason—Cincinnati compiled a strong 69–36 record, but still finished 21 games behind champion St. Louis.

Keystone of Philadelphia, UA 1884. In early August Keystone dropped out of the league and reorganized as an independent semipro club.

National of Washington, D.C., UA 1884. Finished sixth, 46½ games back.

St. Louis Maroons, UA 1884, NL 1885–1886. Batting 47 points above the league average, the Maroons scored

184 runs more than the next-best club to run away with the pennant. They were the only UA club to survive 1884 as a major league team, but in the NL—where they were dubbed "the black diamonds" because of their cast of previously expelled players—they were unable to fashion a winning season or finish higher than sixth.

Kansas City Unions, UA 1884. Formed to replace Altoona, Kansas City went 16–63 in its partial season.

Wilmington, Del., UA 1884. After Wilmington had gone 51–12 to sew up the Eastern League championship, they jumped to the UA in August to replace Philadelphia's Keystones. But as several players failed to make the jump with them, the move was a disaster on the field (2–16) and financially. They failed in mid-September.

Milwaukee Grays, UA 1884. One of only two teams left in the deteriorating Northwestern League, Milwaukee moved up to the UA in September to complete the schedule of dropout Wilmington.

St. Paul White Caps, UA 1884. With the disbanding of the Northwestern League in September, St. Paul joined the UA to take over Pittsburgh's remaining games.

Players League, 1890

Formed in rebellion against the Brush classification plan, a scheme to limit players' pay, the PL drew many of the finest players from the NL and AA, and proved the most popular league with the fans. But when only one club turned a profit, the clubs' financial backers deserted and the league died. Two clubs were admitted to the AA, and many of the rest merged with their National League counterparts:

Boston Red Stockings, PL 1890, AA 1891. Boston won the PL pennant with such stars as Dan Brouthers, Old Hoss Radbourne, Hardy Richardson, and manager King Kelly. The only PL club to make money, Boston joined the AA the next year and won another pennant. But when the popular Kelly defected to Boston's NL Beaneaters (who also won a pennant for the city in 1891), the fans defected too, and the Red Stockings died along with the AA at the end of the season.

Brooklyn Wonders, PL 1890. At the end of a season in which they edged New York for second place, the Wonders merged with Brooklyn's NL pennant-winners.

Buffalo Bisons, PL 1890. After a last-place finish 20 games back of their nearest competitor, the Bisons simply went out of business.

Chicago Pirates, PL 1890. Mark Baldwin, with a league-high 34 wins, and Charles "Silver" King, with 30, pitched Chicago into fourth place. Both went to Pittsburgh the next year, although the franchise was absorbed by Chicago's NL Colts.

Cleveland Infants, PL 1890. Like Cleveland's NL Spiders of 1890, the Infants finished next to last. But one of their three managers, infielder Oliver Wendell "Patsy" Tebeau, would go on to lead the Spiders to their finest seasons.

Philadelphia Quakers, PL 1890, *Athletic* AA 1891. Although they finished sixth in their PL season, the Quakers compiled a winning record. When the Athletics of the AA were expelled following the 1890 season, the Quakers were admitted in their place and awarded the name "Athletic." The team finished fourth in 1891, but

was not among the four clubs taken into the NL when the AA folded, because Philadelphia already had an NL team (the Phillies).

New York Giants, PL 1890. Paced by the hitting of first baseman Roger Connor and outfielder Jim O'Rourke, New York's PL Giants finished third. In November the club merged with the city's NL Giants.

Pittsburgh Burghers, PL 1890. After a sixth-place finish, the Pittsburgh PL club and the NL Allegheny Club combined to form the new Pittsburgh Athletic club, which still represents Pittsburgh in the NL.

American League, 1901–

When Western League president Ban Johnson renamed the circuit in 1900 and proclaimed it a major league the next year, he little knew how stable it would be. For over half a century (1903–1953) the same eight clubs represented the same eight cities. Even today, although the league has expanded and several clubs have moved to new cities, not one franchise has perished.

Federal League, 1914–1915

After an inaugural season as a six-team minor league in 1913, the FL expanded to eight teams and declared war on the NL and AL for their players. After two big league seasons, and despite two of the game's most exciting pennant races ever, the league died for lack of patronage, and with it went its eight franchises:

Baltimore Terrapins, FL 1914–1915. Jack Quinn and George Suggs, with 26 and 25 wins, pitched Baltimore to third place in 1914. But when Quinn and Suggs lost their stuff the next year, the club sank out of sight, 24 games behind seventh-place Brooklyn.

Brooklyn Tip-Tops (or Brookfeds), FL 1914–1915. Not even the acquisition of batting and base-stealing champ Benny Kauff could stop Brooklyn from slipping from fifth in 1914 to seventh the next year.

Buffalo Buffeds, FL 1914–1915. Finished fourth in 1914, sixth the next year.

Chicago Chifeds (or Whales), FL 1914–1915. After leading the league through July and much of August in 1914, only to lose out after a late-season struggle with Indianapolis, the Whales came back in 1915 to triumph in an even tighter race that saw the three top teams separated at the finish by only half a game. Owner Charles Weeghman was permitted to buy the NL Cubs in 1916, and many Whales joined the Cubs in play at what was then Weeghman Park and now is known as Wrigley Field.

Indianapolis Federals (or Hoosiers), FL 1914; *Newark Peps,* FL 1915. Five regulars hit over .300 (paced by Benny Kauff's league-leading .370) in 1914, and the team as a whole hit twenty-two points above the league average. From fourth place in August the Hoosiers fought back to capture the flag from Chicago by 1½ games, with seven consecutive wins at the end. The only major league pennant-winner to move to a new city the next year, the Hoosiers became the Peps in 1915. Though they remained competitive into September, an eight-game losing streak dropped them out of the race and they finished fifth.

Kansas City Packers, FL 1914–1915. After a sixth-place finish in 1914, the Packers competed in a five-way race through much of 1915. But from first place on August 21 they dropped to fifth a week later and finished fourth.

Pittsburgh Rebels, FL 1914–1915. After avoiding last place in 1914 only by St. Louis's late-season nosedive, Pittsburgh turned itself around the next year, luring first baseman Ed Konetchy from their NL rival Pirates, and pitcher Frank Allen from the NL Brooklyn Robins. Both enjoyed the best season of their careers to lead the Rebels into first place in late August, where they remained until they were dropped to third by losing three out of four at the end to the champion Whales.

St. Louis Terriers, FL 1914–1915. After finishing last in 1914, St. Louis added veteran pitcher Eddie Plank to its roster. From a club with two 20-game losers, the Terriers became in 1915 a team with three 20-game winners (including Plank), pulling up from fifth late in August to catch the leaders with a nine-game winning streak. At the finish, though, they ranked second—by less than one percentage point, the narrowest big league pennant margin ever. For 1916, Terriers' owner Phil Ball took over the AL St. Louis Browns.

## CHAPTER 4

Ballparks

Philip J. Lowry

What follows are the vital statistics of each of the current twenty-eight major league baseball stadiums and a selection of the storied parks of the past. My book, *Green Cathedrals,* from which much of this section is taken, encompassed the whole of major league history, from 1871 to the present, including the extraordinary variety of early playing sites, from cricket grounds and polo fields to agricultural fairgrounds and cow pastures. That book also covered Negro League ballparks in a depth beyond the scope possible here, including the vast array of barnstorming sites, even for official league games, that was characteristic of impoverished ballclubs looking to maximize their gate receipts in any way possible. All the same, despite the space constraints imposed upon this entry, the primary Negro League parks will be covered, as well as classic shrines such as Ebbets Field, Griffith Stadium, Forbes Field, and others.

The focus here is on ballpark geometry and the oddities in play that resulted from the unique configuration of the park. Dimensional changes are catalogued and dated, particularly in outfield fence distances and heights. This subject is crucial to an understanding of the statistical history of baseball, whether or not one is a devotee of the park-adjusted figures on display in this volume.

The following leagues are covered by this study. The accompanying abbreviations may be employed for the twentieth century's principal leagues:

NL	National League, 1876–
AL	American League, 1901–
FL	Federal League, 1914–1915
NNL	Negro National League, 1920–1931, 1933–1948
ECL	Eastern Colored League, 1923–1928
NAL	Negro American League, 1929, 1937–1950
NSL	Negro Southern League, 1932
NEWL	Negro East-West League, 1932

Before 1900, most parks were small wooden grandstands hastily constructed around recreation fields that often were not even enclosed by outfield fences. Beginning with the erection of Shibe park and Forbes Field in 1909, however, concrete-and-steel ballparks became the rule. These palaces signaled the growing prominence of baseball and constituted to my mind the best in ballpark design; the term I have applied to this type of park is "Major League Classic." In the 1950s a transitional type of park—one that retained the beauty of the older parks while affording some of the conveniences of the new—became the home of the Braves, transplanted from Boston to Milwaukee, and the Orioles, who flew into Baltimore from St. Louis, where they had been the Browns.

Diagrams are by Kevin Spleid.

Using the Outlines

"Style" defines the structural design of the park.

"A.K.A." (Also Known As) lists alternate names and nicknames used for the ballpark.

"Occupant" lists teams using the park in chronological order. Inclusive dates of play within the league follow.

"Event" contains postseason and All-Star Games.

"Location" lists the surrounding streets. When possible, fields and bases are associated with the streets. Geographical directions, (N) for North, (S) for South, (E) for East, and (W) for West, are provided when available.

Because all older stadiums had grass "surfaces," information concerning carpet or grass is included only for modern ballparks.

Under "Dimensions" the distance is given in feet from home plate to the fences, and to the backstop. Dates, in parentheses, denote the *first* month and/or year when the boundaries stood at the stated distance.

"Fences" lists the heights of the outfield fences in feet. Dates denote the *first* time the fences stood at the stated height.

"Former Use" describes how the site was utilized before stadium construction. Similarly, "Current Use" chronicles the development of the site after a ballpark was demolished or abandoned.

"Phenomena" is a more general category for historical data. Included here will be special features of the park's physical plant, important changes over the years, and events of note throughout the years of operation.

ANAHEIM, CALIFORNIA

ANAHEIM STADIUM
STYLE Superstructure with natural surface
A.K.A. Big A 1966, Bigger A 1980
OCCUPANT AL Angels April 19, 1966 to date
EVENT All Star Game 1967, 1989
LOCATION *Left Field (N)* Katella Avenue; *3rd Base (W)* 2000 State College Boulevard and Interstate 5; *1st Base (S)* Orangewood Freeway, then Santa Ana River; *Center Field (NE)* Amtrak Railroad Station
SURFACE Bluegrass
DIMENSIONS *Foul Lines:* 333; *Bullpens:* 362; *Power*

Alleys: 375 (1966), 369 (1973), 374 (1974), 370 (1989); *Deep Alleys:* 386; *Center Field:* 406 (1966), 402 (1973), 404 (1974); *Backstop:* 55 (1966), 60.5 (1973)
FENCES *Majority of the Fence:* 10 (wire 1966), 7.86 (wire 1973), 7.86 (padded 1981); *Corners Between Foul Poles and Bullpens:* 4.75 (steel 1966); *Left-center Between 386 and 404 Marks:* 7.5 (padded 1981); *Padded Posts at the Left Sides of Both Left and Right Field; Bullpen Gates:* 9 (padded 1981); *Bullpen Gates:* 9.95 (wire 1966)
FORMER USE Four farms—Camille Allec's 39 acres of orange and eucalyptus trees, Roland Reynolds' 70 acres of alfalfa, John Knutgen's 20 acres of corn, Bill Ross and George Lenney's 19 acres of corn

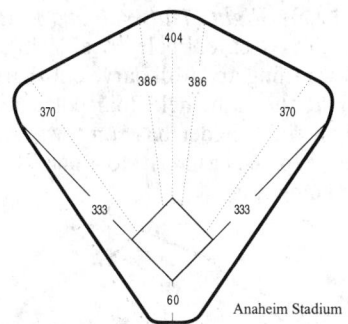

Anaheim Stadium

PHENOMENA
• Power hitter's park, the ball carries well.
• Huge 230-foot-high letter "A" stood behind the fence in left as a scoreboard support until 1980, then it was moved to the parking lot. The letter has a gold halo at its top.
• Sections 69 and 70 in center covered by green-canvas batters' background.
• Two thin black TV cables run in fair territory on the warning track from the left field corner bullpen gate to the foul pole, and then along the wall in foul territory about 50 feet toward third base, then into the stands.
• Outfield enclosed and tripledecked in 1980.
• 6 doors on ivy-covered wall in deep left-center behind outfield fence labeled: "warning track," "skin material," "screen clay mounds," "raw clay," "sand," "equipment."

ATLANTA, GEORGIA

ATLANTA-FULTON COUNTY STADIUM
STYLE Superstructure with natural surface
A.K.A. Atlanta Stadium 1965-74, Launching Pad
OCCUPANT NL Braves April 12, 1966 to date
EVENT All Star Game 1972
LOCATION *Left Field (NE)* Pullman Street and Interstate 20; *3rd Base (NW)* Washington Street and Interstate 75/85 and Georgia Avenue; *1st Base (SW)* 521 Capitol Avenue; *Right Field (SE)* Fulton Street
SURFACE Prescription Artificial Turf
DIMENSIONS *Foul Lines:* 325 (1966), 330 (1967); *Power Alleys:* 385 (1966), 375 (1969), 385 (1974); *Center Field:* 402 (1966), 400 (1969), 402 (1973); Back Stop: 59.92 (1973); *Foul Territory:* Large (1966), Medium (1977)
FENCES 6 (wire 1966), 10 (4 plexiglass above 6 wire 1983), 10 (plexiglass 1985)

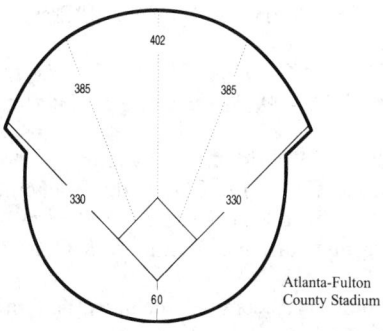

Atlanta-Fulton
County Stadium

PHENOMENA
• Three statues outside the stadium honor Ty Cobb, Hank Aaron, and Phil Niekro.
• Used by 1965 Triple A IL Crackers.
• Big Victor, a large totem-pole-styled figure, stood in the stadium in 1966. The huge head tilted and the eyes rolled whenever a Brave hit a home run.
• With an altitude of more than 1,000 feet above sea level, it was—until Denver entered the major leagues—the highest park in the majors, which results in many homers and the nickname "the Launching Pad."
• Chief Noc-A-Homa's Wigwam replaced Big Victor in 1967. From 1967 to 1971 the teepee stood on a 20-foot-square platform behind the left field fence. In 1972 the teepee was moved to right field. From 1973 to 1977 it returned to left field. From 1978 to August 1982 the teepee was moved to left-center, occupying 235 seats between aisles 128 and 130, rows 18-30. From August to early September, 1982, it was removed in anticipation of additional revenue in the playoffs, "causing" a disastrous tailspin for the first-place Braves. Its replacement coincided with the Braves' comeback to win the division crown in 1982. The teepee's removal on August 11, 1983, saw another losing streak which could not be overcome by its return on September 16. It stands today, a permanent outfield installation.
• 22-foot outfield wall never in play.
• 80-year-old calliope organ installed 1971.

BALTIMORE, MARYLAND

ORIOLE PARK AT CAMDEN YARDS
STYLE Superstructure with natural surface
A.K.A. Camden Yards
OCCUPANT AL Orioles April 6, 1992 to date
LOCATION *(N)* Camden Street; *(W)* Russell Street; *(E)* Howard Street; *(S)* Martin Luther King Boulevard

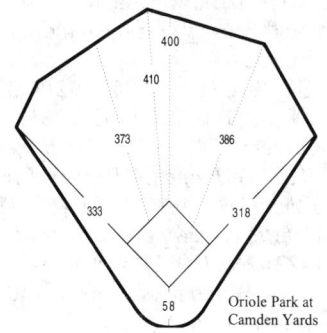

Oriole Park at
Camden Yards

SURFACE Maryland Bluegrass ("Prescription Athletic Turf")

DIMENSIONS *Left Field:* 333; *Left Center:* 410; *Center Field:* 400; *Right Center:* 373; *Right Field:* 318; *Backstop:* 58

FENCES 25 in right, 7 elsewhere

FORMER USE Le Comte de Rochambeau, French general, camped his troops here on the way to Yorktown in 1781; former station of Baltimore & Ohio Railroad

PHENOMENA

• Camden Yards complex includes the Baltimore & Ohio Warehouse, longest building on the East Coast (1,016 feet long but only 51 feet wide). Houses Orioles offices as well as a cafeteria, sports bar, and the exclusive Camden Club. Banks of lights are mounted on roof.

• Each aisle seat in the park features an 1890s Orioles logo.

• Unique doubledecked bullpens in left-center field.

• Hearing-impaired persons may hook into "hearing assistance channels" at their seats.

• Playing field is 16 feet below street level.

• Located only two blocks from Babe Ruth's birthplace; Babe's father operated Ruth's Cafe at 406 Conway Street, the site of which is now located in center field.

• Designed by HOK Sports Facility Group.

• Capacity: 48,041.

• Site of unique three league triple header on June 6, 1992. Fans could take in a morning game at Hagerstown, Md., an afternoon contest at Frederick, Md., and end up under the lights at Camden Yards.

• Built by Maryland Stadium Authority at an approximate cost of $105 million.

• Faced with brick to present a traditional appearance.

• Football stadium will be built adjacent to Camden Yards if an NFL team can be secured.

BOSTON, MASSACHUSETTS

FENWAY PARK

STYLE Major League Classic

OCCUPANT AL Red Sox April 20, 1912 to date

EVENT NL Braves vs. New York April 19, May 30, 1913; August 1 and 8, September 7 to 29, 1914; 1914 World Series; April 14 to July 26, 1915; All Star Game 1946, 1961

LOCATION *Left Field (N)* Lansdowne Street, Boston & Albany Railroad tracks, and Mass. Turnpike/Interstate 90; *3rd Base (W)* Brookline Avenue and 24 Jersey Street, renamed 24 Yawkey Way in 1976, also bowling alley building attached to park; *1st Base (S)* Van Ness Street (built after park was done); *Right Field (E)* Ipswich Street and Fenway Garage building

SURFACE Bluegrass

DIMENSIONS *Left Field:* 324 (1921), 320.5 (1926), 320 (1930), 318 (1931), 320 (1933), 312 (1934), 315 (1936); *Left-Center:* 379 (1934); *Deep Left-Center at Flagpole:* 388 (1934); *Flagpole Removed from Field of Play in 1970; Centerfield:* 488 (1922), 468 (1930), 388.67 (1934), 389.67 (1954); *Deepest Corner, Just Right of Center:* 550 (1922), 593 (1931), 420 (1934) [Note: 593 is cited in 1931-33 Bluebooks; this could be a mis-print.] *Right-Center, Just Right of Deepest Corner Where the Bullpen Begins:* 380 (1938), 383 (1955); *Right of Right Center:* 405 (1939), 382 (1940), 381 (1942), 380 (1943); *Right Field:* 313.5 (1921), 358.5 (1926), 358 (1930), 325 (1931) 358 (1933), 334 (1934), 332 (1936), 322 (1938), 332 (1939), 304 (1940), 302 (1942); *Backstop:* 68 (1912), 60 (1934); *Foul Territory:* Very small, smallest in the majors

FENCES *Left Field:* 25 (wood 1912), 37.17 (tin over wood over concrete lower section 1934), 37.17 (hard plastic 1976); *Left Field Wall to Center Bleacher Wall Behind Flagpole:* 18 sloping to 17 (concrete 1934), (padding 1976) crash pad added from 18 inches to 6 feet on left and center field walls (1976); *Center Field to Bullpen Fence:* 8.75 (wood 1940); *Right-Center Bullpen Fence:* 5.25 (wood 1940); *Right Field Wall and Railing:* Bullpen 3.42 sloping to 5.37 at foul pole (steel 1940); *Right Field Belly:* the low railing and wall curve out sharply from the 302 marker at the right field foul pole into deep right field—many a right fielder has run toward the foul line and watched helplessly as a 310-foot pop fly falls over the railing for a home run.

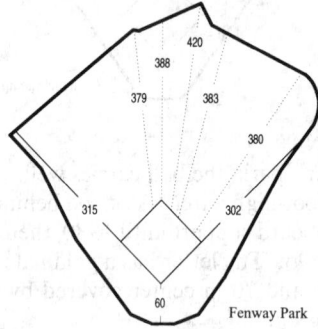

Fenway Park

PHENOMENA

• Seats made of oak.

• 1976 electronic scoreboard significantly altered the wind currents.

• 43 private 28-seat rooftop boxes added 1984.

• Duffy's Cliff was a 10-foot-high mound which formed an incline in front of the left field wall from 1912 to 1933, extending from the left field foul pole to the flag pole in center—named after Red Sox left fielder Duffy Lewis, who was the acknowledged master of defensive play on the cliff. It was greatly reduced but not completely eliminated in 1934.

• The Green Monster Wall in left completely dominates the field of play—now all green, it used to be covered with advertisements.

• Ladder starts near upper-left corner of scoreboard, 13 feet above ground, and rises to top of the Green Monster to allow groundskeeper to remove batting practice home run balls from the netting above the Wall.

• Scoreboard numbers—runs and hits: 16 inches by 16 inches, 3 pounds; errors, innings, pitcher's numbers: 12 inches by 16 inches, 2 pounds.

• Bleachers in foul territory down the left field line burned down in 1926. The charred remains were removed, increasing the size of foul territory there.

• No ball has ever been hit over the right field roof.

• Balls that hit uprights above the Wall, and should have been homers, were declared in play by the umpires.

• Wooden bleachers stood down the left field line in foul territory in the 1910s and 1920s, but burned down on May 8, 1926, and were not replaced. Wooden bleachers were completed in center and right-center by the 1912 World Series.

• Infield grass was transplanted from Huntington Avenue Baseball Grounds to Fenway in 1912.

• During the winter of 1933-34, all the wooden grandstands were replaced with concrete and steel. A big fire on January 5, 1934, destroyed much of what had already been built, but all was finished for the 1934 season opener on April 17.

• In 1935, a 23.33-foot net was placed atop the wall in left to protect windows on Landsdowne Street.

• Wind usually helps the batters. New pressbox built in late 1980s above home plate causes wind swirl which pushes foul balls back into fair territory. This is the park with the tiniest foul territory in the majors.

• When tin covered the two-by-fours on the Wall, balls hitting the tin over two-by-fours had a live bounce, but balls hitting between the two-by-fours were dead and just dropped straight down.

• In 1940, in an effort to help Ted Williams hit home runs, the Red Sox added the right field bullpens, called Williamsburg, which reduced the distance to the fence by 23 feet.

• In 1947 all advertisements were removed from the left field wall, which was painted green.

• Tom A. Yawkey's and his wife Jean R. Yawkey's initials, TAY and JRY, appear in Morse code in two vertical stripes on the scoreboard in left. The 1946 roof boxes were replaced in 1982.

• The screen behind home plate, designed to protect fans and allow foul balls to roll back down onto the field of play, was the first of its kind in the majors.

• Left field scoreboard installed on the Wall in 1934, moved 20 feet to the right in 1976.

• The low concrete base of the left and center field walls was padded after the 1975 World Series, during which Fred Lynn crashed into the concrete wall in center.

• The left field foul line was measured by Art Keefe and George Sullivan, authors of *The Picture History of the Boston Red Sox,* in October 1975 as 309 feet 5 inches. On October 19, 1975, the Boston *Globe* used aerial photography and measured it at 304.779 feet. Osborn Engineering Co. blueprints document the distance at 308 feet.

• Fenway—"where you can sit for hours and feel a security that does not exist anywhere else in the world."

CHICAGO, ILLINOIS

NEW COMISKEY PARK
STYLE   Superstructure with natural surface
A.K.A.   Comiskey II
OCCUPANT   AL White Sox April 18, 1991 to date
LOCATION   333 West 35th Street (South); Dan Ryan Expressway (East); Shields Ave. (West)
SURFACE   Natural Grass (Bluegrass)
DIMENSIONS   *Left field:* 347; *Left Center:* 383; *Center Field:* 400; *Right Center:* 383; *Right Field:* 347; *Backstop:* 60
FENCES   8

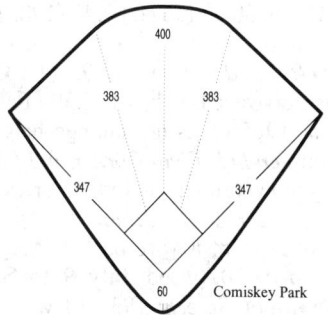

FORMER USE   Approximately 80 privately owned residential buildings
PHENOMENA
• Capacity: 44,702.

• Designed by HOK Sports Facility Group.

• Contains eighty-four luxury skyboxes on two levels, renting for $55,000 to $90,000 annually.

• Unlike the Picnic Area at old Comiskey Park, entry to the new Picnic Area's buffet costs $20 over the ticket price.

• Echoing the nickname of Charles Comiskey, food court contains a shop called Old Roman Pizza.

• Management boasts "Ratio of washroom fixtures to fan capacity, one of the best in baseball" but fans complain of long washroom lines.

• During construction was visible from former Comiskey Park, to which it was adjacent.

• Large scoreboard in center field replicates one designed by Bill Veeck at former Comiskey Park.

• Infield dirt transported here from old park.

• Built at a cost of $134.9 million; paid for in large part by a new hotel tax.

• Park's exterior is of precast colored concrete and features arched windows reminiscent of former park.

• Seats in front row of the upper deck are farther from home plate than those in last row at old Comiskey.

WRIGLEY FIELD
STYLE   Major League Classic
A.K.A.   North Side Ball Park, 1914; Weeghman Park, 1914-15; Cubs' Park, 1916-26; Whales Park, 1915; Eddie Dorr's House
OCCUPANT   FL Whales April 23, 1914 to October 3, 1915; NL Cubs April 20, 1916 to date
EVENT   All Star Game 1947, 1962, 1990
LOCATION   *Left Field (N)* West Waveland Avenue; *3rd Base (W)* Seminary Avenue; *Home Plate (SW)* North Clark Street; *1st Base (S)* 1060 West Addison Street; *Right Field (E)* North Sheffield Avenue
SURFACE   Grass, mixture of Merion Bluegrass and clover
DIMENSIONS   *Left Field:* 345 (April 1914), 310 (May 1914), 327 (June 1914), 343 (1921), 325 (1923), 348 (1926), 364 (1928), 355 (1938); *Left-Center Deepest:* 357 (1938); *Power Alleys:* 364 (1914), 368 (1938); *Center Field:* 440 (1914), 447 (1923), 436 (1928), 400 (1938); *Right-Center Deepest:* 363 (1938); *Right Field:* 356 (April 1914), 345 (June 1914), 321 (1915), 298 (1921), 399 (1922), 318 (1923), 321 (1928), 353 (1938); *Back-*

stop: 62.42 (1930), 60.5 (1957), 62.42 (1982); *Foul Territory:* Very small

FENCES *Left Field Corner:* 15.92 (11.33 brick with Boston and Bittersweet Ivy, below 4.59 plywood), 3 wire basket in front 1985 (does not change height of fence); *Transition Between Left Field Corner and Bleachers:* 12.5 (screen and yellow railing on top of brick wall); *Left-Center to Right-Center:* 8 (screen 1914), 11.33 (brick with ivy 1938); in front is wire basket (May 1970); *Left Field Scoreboard:* 40 (wood July 9 to September 3, 1937); *Center Field Screen:* 1933 (8 wire above 11.33 brick June 18, 1963 to October 1964); *Right Center Triangle:* 17.5 in front of catwalk steps sloping down to 15.5 (screen 1928, plywood 1979, removed 1985); *Right Field Corner:* 15.5 (11.33 brick with ivy, below 4.17 plywood), wire basket in front (1985)

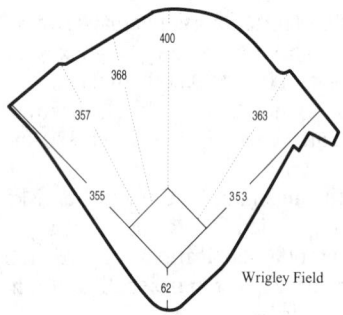

Wrigley Field

PHENOMENA

• IBM Home Run Distance calculation appears on center field scoreboard after a home run.

• The only remaining Federal League ballpark.

• Beautiful ivy vines on the outfield wall.

• After the game, a blue flag with a white W flying from the center field flag pole signifies a Cub win, a white flag with a blue L a Cub loss.

• Sea breeze off the lake favors pitchers.

• 452 seats added July 1985 to catwalks near foul pole, in fair territory.

• The center field 400 sign is slightly right of straight-away center.

• The only park where it's more difficult to hit a homer down the foul line than to hit one 50 or so feet out in fair territory because the bleachers protrude into the outfield.

• In 1923, the foul lines were shifted slightly amidst park renovations.

• During the 1930s Bobby Dorr, the groundskeeper, lived in a 6 room apartment at the ballpark, adjacent to the left field corner gate; the apartment is still there.

• Eight-foot-high batter's background wire fence, 64 feet wide, stood on top of the center field wall from June 18, 1963 through the end of the 1964 season. Called the Whitlow fence because Cub Athletic Director Robert Whitlow put it up. The screen prevented 10 homers, 4 by Cubs and 6 by visitors, 1 each by 500+ homer hitters Ernie Banks and Willie McCovey.

• Current green Astroturf cover on center field seats used for batters' background and debuted on May 18, 1967.

• In the winter of 1926-27, the left field bleachers were removed, the grandstand was doubledecked, and the playing area was lowered several feet.

• For World Series in 1929, 1932, and 1935, extra bleachers were built on the street on Waveland and Sheffield.

• The park was located so it would be easy for fans to get there on the Milwaukee Road train.

• The 27-foot-high, 75-foot-wide scoreboard was built in 1937 by Bill Veeck. Its top is 85 feet above the field. The 10 foot diameter clock was added in 1941.

• In 1937, the bleacher stairstep was created to allow potted plants and eight huge Chinese elm trees to grow, complementing the ivy. The trees eventually died.

• Ivy planted on the outfield walls in 1937 by Bill Veeck. Originally 350 Japanese bittersweet plants and 200 Boston ivy plants.

• During the 1937 season, new outfield bleachers were built, and the six gates in the brick wall were emplaced. They were red, repainted blue in 1981.

• The bleachers were expanded to their present state in the 1940s; famous Bleacher Bums formed here in 1966 by 10 bleacher fans.

• Lights were inside the park in the early 1940s ready to be installed, but Mr. Wrigley donated them to the war effort instead on December 8, 1941, thus allowing Wrigley Field to remain dark at night until 1988.

• The right field wall was remodeled in 1950-51.

• On April 14, 1976, Met Dave "King Kong" Kingman hit a homer 550 feet over Waveland and against a frame house 3 doors down on the east side of Kenmore Avenue. If the ball had carried 3 feet higher, it would have crashed through a window and smashed a TV screen on which Ms. Naomi Martinez was watching Mr. Kingman round the bases.

• Park is affected by wind conditions more than any other major league park, with the possible exception of Candlestick.

• More home runs than normal are caused by high altitude of over 600 feet above sea level, and by the heat involved in playing so many daylight games.

• Water fountain moved to the Cub Hall of Fame under the first base stands, near the Friendly Confines cafe.

• Arched dormers on the roof.

• Outfield wall distances before 1981 were marked on plywood markers screwed into the brick. Since then they have been painted directly on the brick.

• Foul pole screens have distances marked on plywood vertically "355" and "353."

• The most distant current outfield measurement sign is at Wrigley Field. On the roof of a house across Sheffield Avenue in right-center, the sign says "495."

• Winds blowing toward the lake take homers with them.

CINCINNATI, OHIO

RIVERFRONT STADIUM

STYLE   Superstructure with artificial surface
OCCUPANT   NL Reds June 30, 1970 to date
EVENT   All Star Game 1970
LOCATION   *Left Field (E)* Riverfront Coliseum, Central Bridge and Broadway; *3rd Base (N)* 201 East Second Street, renamed Pete Rose Way on September 10, 1985; *1st Base (W)* Interstate 71 Suspension Bridge Approach Ramp; *Right Field (S)* Mehring Way, railroad tracks, and Ohio River

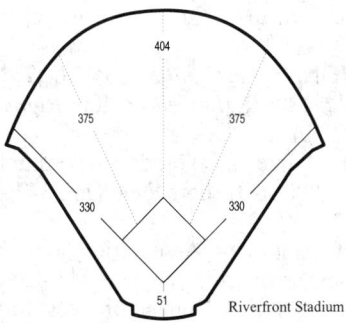

Riverfront Stadium

SURFACE Astroturf—hard, balls bounce high off it
DIMENSIONS *Foul Lines:* 330; *Power Alleys:* 375;
Center Field: 404; *Backstop:* 51; *Foul Territory:* Small
FENCES 12 (wood, 1970); 8 (wood, 1984)
PHENOMENA
• First to paint metric distances on outfield walls: 100.58
down the lines, 114.30 to the alleys, 123.13 to center.
• Uses Crosley Field's home plate.
• Parking garage beneath stadium.
• 4,192 circle in left center commemorates Pete Rose's
4,192nd hit here on 9/10/85 vs. the Padres.
• Reds and Pirates played slowest game ever here 8/30/
78—80.6 minutes per inning, called off after 3½ innings
and 3½ hours of rain delays at 12:47 A.M.
• Winds help righthanded hitters.

CLEVELAND, OHIO

CLEVELAND STADIUM
STYLE Summer Olympics Stadium
A.K.A. Lakefront Stadium 1930s, Cleveland Public
Municipal Stadium 1930s, Municipal Stadium 1940s and
1950s

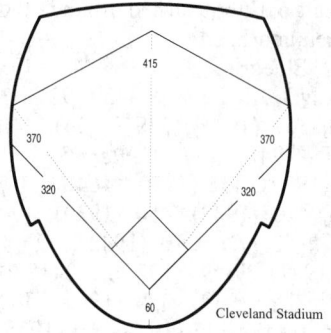

Cleveland Stadium

OCCUPANT AL Indians July 31, 1932 to September
24, 1933; August 2, 1936 vs. New York; AL Indians May
30 to September 6, 1937 Sundays and holidays only between Memorial Day and Labor Day; April 1938 to June
1939 Sundays, holidays and selected important games
only; AL Indians June 27, 1939 to September 1947
nights, Sundays, holidays, and selected important games
(this was a majority of home games in 1940, 1942-46); AL
Indians April 15, 1947 to date all games
EVENT All Star Game 1935, 1954, 1963, 1981

LOCATION *Center Field (NE)* East Ninth Street; *3rd
Base (NW)* Erieside Avenue and Donald Gray Lakefront
Gardens Port Authority Dock 28 and Lake Erie; *Home
Plate (SW)* West Third Street; *1st Base (SE)* Cleveland
Memorial Shoreway, Amtrak/Conrail railroad tracks;
Boudreau Boulevard encircles the park
SURFACE Bluegrass
DIMENSIONS *Foul Lines:* 322 (1932), 320 (1933),
321 (1948), 320 (1953); *Corners Where Inner Fence
Meets Stadium Walls:* 362 (1947), 370 (1980); *Power
Alleys:* 435 (1932), 365 (1947), 362 (1948), 385 (1949),
380 (1954), 400 (1965), 390 (1967), 395 (1968), 385
(1970), 395 (1991); *Left Center:* 377 (1980); *Right-
Center:* 385 (1980); *Deep Left-Center:* 387 (1980); *Deep
Right Center:* 395 (1980); *Bleacher Corners:* 463 (1932);
Grandstand Corners: 435 (1932); *Center Field:* 470
(1932), 467 (1938), 450 (1939), 410 (April 27, 1947), 408
(1966), 407 (1967), 410 (1968), 400 (1970); *Backstop:*
60; *Foul Territory:* Large
FENCES *Left and Right Field:* 5.25 (concrete 1932),
5.5 (wire April 27, 1947), 5.25 (concrete June 6, 1947), 6
(1955), 9 (1976), 8 (1977), 8 (canvas 1984)
PHENOMENA
• Architectural style has been called "stripped classi-
cism," and has been compared to later Memorial and
County Stadiums in Baltimore and Milwaukee.
• Groundskeepers' tools kept in foul territory in 1930s
and 1940s.
• Before the inner fences were installed on April 27 after
the first two weeks of the 1947 season, there was an incline
in front of the center field bleacher wall; strange shape in
power alleys caused by the end of the doubledecked
grandstand, where the fence jumped abruptly deeper to
the bleacher wall in center. The April 27 inner fence
curved all the way to the foul poles. On June 6, 1947, it
was changed so the inner fence just stretched across
center field, hitting the permanent wall at 362 mark.
• Teepees erected in 1946 in center.
• Foul poles are 32 feet 8 inches high, 27 inches wide, and
the screen on them is 22 inches wide.
• No one has ever hit a ball into the center field bleachers.
• Music bandstand in center field between fence and
bleachers set up in 1953.
• Wind usually blows out toward the lake.
• Center field standing-room area was a garden in 1957.
• Field was lowered 2 feet in 1976.
• Cleveland Stadium/League Park ratio of home games
from 1936 to 1946—1/77, 15/63, 18/58, 30/47, 49/33,
32/45, 46/34, 48/29, 44/34, 46/31, 41/36.
• Featured in 2 movies—*The Kid from Cleveland* in
1949, *Fortune Cookie* in mid-1960s.
• Opened formally on July 1, 1931—13 months before
the Indians' first home game on July 31, 1932.

DALLAS, TEXAS

ARLINGTON STADIUM
STYLE Expanded Minor League
A.K.A. Turnpike Stadium, 1965 to 1971
OCCUPANT AL Rangers April 21, 1972 to date
LOCATION Arlington, Texas—between Dallas and
Fort Worth; *Left Field (E)* Stadium Drive East and Six

Flags Over Texas Amusement Park; *3rd Base (N)* 1500 South Copeland Road; *1st Base (W)* Stadium Drive West; *Right Field (S)* Randol Mill Road
SURFACE   419 Bermuda grass
DIMENSIONS   *Foul Lines:* 330; *Power Alleys:* 380 (1972), 370 (1974), 383 (1981), 380 (1982); *Center Field:* 400; *Backstop:* 60; *Foul Territory:* Small
FENCES   11 (1972), 12 (1981), 11 (1986)
FORMER USE   Minor league ballpark from 1965 to 1971 called Turnpike Stadium

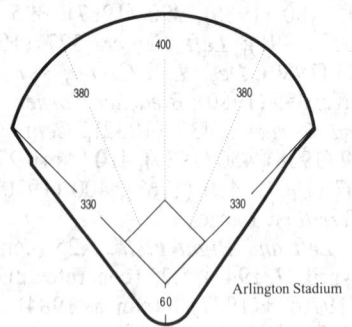

Arlington Stadium

PHENOMENA
• Built in 1965 as Turnpike Stadium.
• Like Dodger Stadium, the field is below the surrounding parking lots. Before 1978, when the upper deck was added, fans would walk in at the top of the stadium.
• Wind blows in directly from the outfield.
• Hottest park in the majors, which increases the number of home runs hit here since the warm humid air is not as dense as cooler drier air elsewhere and therefore does not offer as much resistance to the ball in flight.
• More advertising signs than any other major league park.
• The Lone Ranger on Diamond Vision scoreboard roots for the Rangers.

DENVER, COLORADO

MILE HIGH STADIUM
STYLE   Superstructure with natural surface
A.K.A.   Bears Stadium (Original Name)
OCCUPANT   Colorado Rockies, April 1993 to present

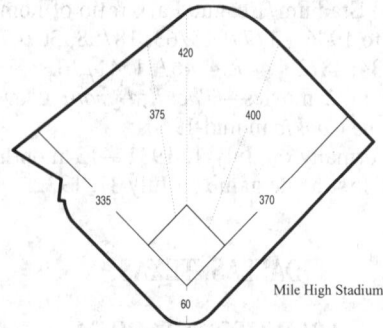

Mile High Stadium

LOCATION   Interstate 25, Routes 88 and 287, and Routes 70, 287 and 40; *Left Field* Clay Street; *3rd Base* West 20th Street; *1st Base* Elliot Street

SURFACE   Natural Grass ("Prescription Athletic Turf")
DIMENSIONS   *Left field:* 335; *Left Center:* 375; *Center Field:* 420; *Right Center:* 400; *Right Field:* 370
PHENOMENA
• Temporary home of Colorado Rockies until 1995 completion of 43,800-seat Coors Field (*LF:* 347; *LC:* 390; *CF:* 424; *RC:* 375; *RF:* 350).
• Home of American Association and Pacific Coast League's Denver Bears/Zephyrs, 1948–1992.
• Also home of NFL's Denver Broncos; former home of United States Football League's Denver Gold.
• Ownership assumed by City and County of Denver in 1968.
• Near McNichols Sports Arena, home of NBA Nuggets.
• Capacity: 19,000 (1960), 43,103 (1985), 75,123 (1985).
• Features 130 luxury suites.
• Entire east stands (built in 1977; capacity 21,000) are movable to accommodate both football and baseball; conversion time to football is ten hours; back to baseball, twelve hours.
• Playing field is heated electrically to prevent surface freezing and to allow year-round growth.
• First "fully distributed sound system" in any major US stadium—delivers "near stereo quality sound."

DETROIT, MICHIGAN

TIGER STADIUM
STYLE   Major League Classic
A.K.A.   Navin Field 1912 to 1937, Briggs Stadium 1938 to 1960
OCCUPANT   AL Tigers April 20, 1912 to date
EVENT   All Star Game 1941, 1951, 1971
LOCATION   *Left Field (NW)* Cherry Street, later Kaline Drive, and Interstate 75; *3rd Base (SW)* National Avenue, later Cochrane Avenue; *1st Base (SE)* Michigan Avenue; *Right Field (NE)* 2121 Trumbull Avenue, same site as Bennett park but turned around 90 degrees, in the Corktown neighborhood
SURFACE   Bluegrass
DIMENSIONS   *Left Field:* 345 (1921), 340.58 (1926), 339 (1930), 367 (1931), 339 (1934), 340 (1938), 342 (1939), 340 (1942); *Left Center:* 365 (1942); *Center Field:* 467 (1927), 455 (1930), 464 (1931), 459 (1936), 450 (1937), 440 (1938), 450 (1939), 420 (1942), 440 (1944); *Right Center:* 370 (1942), 375 (1982); *Right Field:* 370 (1921), 370.91 (1926), 372 (1930), 367 (1931), 325 (1936), 315 (1939), 325 (1942), 302 (1954), 325 (1955); *Backstop:* 54.35 (1954), 66 (1955); *Foul Territory:* Small
FENCES   *All Fences:* 5 concrete topped by screen; *Left Field:* 20 (1935), 30 (1937), 10 (1938), 12 (1940), 15 (1946), 12 (1953), 14 (1954), 12 (1955), 11 (1958), 9 (1962); *Center Field:* 9 (1940), 15 (1946), 11 (1950), 9 (1953), 14 (1954), 9 (1955); *Right of Flag Pole:* 7 (1946); *Right Field:* 8 (1940), 30 (1944), 10 (1945), 20 (1950), 8 (1953), 9 (1958), 30 (1961), 9 (1962); *Flag Pole:* 125 in play (5 feet in front of fence in center field, just left of dead center)

PHENOMENA

- First named for Frank Navin, a Tiger president.
- Right field second deck overhangs the lower deck by 10 feet. Screen in right in 1944 and in 1961 required balls to be hit into the second deck to be home runs.
- Only doubledecked bleachers in the majors—upper deck from left-center to center, lower deck from center to right-center.
- 125-foot-high flag pole in play in deep center, just to the left of the 440 mark—highest outfield obstacle ever in play in baseball history. The scoreboard now on the left field fence was orignally placed at the 440 mark in dead center in 1961 but was moved when Norm Cash, Al Kaline, and Charlie Maxwell complained that it hindered the batters' view of the pitch.
- There is a string of spotlights mounted under the overhang to illuminate the right field warning track which is shadowed from the normal light standards.
- Cobb's Lake—area in front of plate which was always soaked with water by the groundskeepers to slow down Ty Cobb's bunts.
- When slugging teams came to visit, manager Ty Cobb had the groundskeepers put in temporary bleachers in the outfield, so that long drives would be just ground-rule doubles.
- Sign above entrance to visitors' clubhouse: "Visitors' Clubhouse—No Visitors Allowed."
- Doubledecked in winter of 1923-24 from first to third base.
- Capacity increased in winter of 1935-36 by doubledecking the right field stands, and in the winter of 1937-38 by doubledecking both the left field stands and the center field bleachers.
- In the 1930s and 1940s, there was a 315 marker on the second deck in right field.
- In 1942 and 1943, the center field distance was only 420. The notches just left and right of dead center were closer than 420, at 405.
- Next-to-last classic old ballyard to put in lights, in 1948.

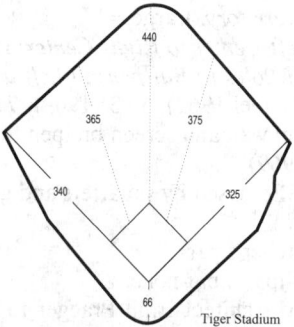

Tiger Stadium

- Saved in 1974 when owner John Fetzer told the Pontiac Silverdome committee, "This franchise belongs to the inner city of Detroit; I'm just the caretaker." Now that mantle of caretaker has been forfeited by owner Tom Monaghan to the Tiger Stadium Fan Club and the Cochrane Plan, an architectural plan to preserve the ballpark.
- First homer at Navin Field, on May 5, 1912, came on a fluke bounce which hopped through the side door of the left-center scoreboard.
- Home plate and batters' boxes oriented towards right-center rather than straight out to the mound. This tends to give righthanded pitchers more outside corner strike calls and can disorient visiting batters.

HOUSTON, TEXAS

ASTRODOME

STYLE Dome
A.K.A. Harris County Domed Stadium 1965, Eighth Wonder of the World 1960s
OCCUPANT NL Astros April 12, 1965 to date
EVENT All Star Game 1968, 1986
LOCATION *Center Field (E)* Fannin Street; *3rd Base (N)* Old Spanish Trail; *Home Plate (W)* Kirby Drive; *1st Base (S)* South Loop Freeway/Interstate 610; *Above:* Domed roof of 4796 Lucite panels and steel girders

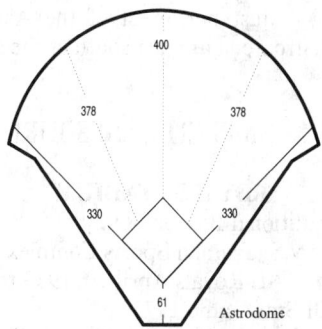

Astrodome

SURFACE *Infield:* Grass (1965) Tifway 419 Bermuda grass specially selected for indoor play—died; Astroturf, fast (April 1966 to date); *Outfield:* Grass (April 12, 1965 to July 19, 1966)—died too; Astroturf, fast (July 19, 1966 to date)
DIMENSIONS *Foul Lines:* 340 (1965), 330 (1972), 340 (1977), 330 (1985), 325 (1992); *Power Alleys:* 375 (1965), 390 (1966), 378 (1972), 390 (1977), 378 (1985), 375 (1992); *Center Field:* 406 (1965), 400 (1972), 406 (1977), 400 (1985); *Apex of Dome:* 208; *Backstop:* 60.5
FENCES *Left and Right Field:* 16 (9 concrete below 3 wire, 2 concrete, and 2 wire plus railing, 1965), 12 (concrete, 1969), 10 (concrete, 1977); *Center Field:* 12 (concrete, 1965), 10 (concrete, 1977)

PHENOMENA

- The second major league covered stadium, the first being the field under the Queensboro 59th Street Bridge in New York City used by the New York Cubans.
- Maximum height of the dome is 208 feet, just beyond second base.
- The roof had 4,796 clear panes of glass originally, but they caused a glare which prevented fielders from seeing the ball, thus two of the eight roof sections were painted white. This killed the grass and unfortunately introduced the world to Astroturf.
- Excepting Yankee Stadium's Death Valley, the most distant power alleys in the majors at 390 feet, until changed in 1985.
- Too much yellow, orange, and red.
- Hard to see through the screen from behind the plate.
- Site of 1992 Republican convention.
- In its inaugural season of 1965, the Astrodome was the

scene of a unique groundskeeping argument. The New York Mets claimed that the groundskeepers were roof-keeping as well by manipulating the air conditioning system so that the air currents helped Astro long balls and hindered visitors' long balls.

• The first game on a carpet was versus the Dodgers on April 8, 1966.

• Shoeshine stands behind home plate in lower deck.

• On April 28, 1965, Met announcer Lindsey Nelson broadcast a game from a gondola suspended from the apex of the dome.

• On June 10, 1974, Phillie Mike Schmidt hit the public address speaker 117 feet up and 329 feet from home—what would have been a 500-plus-foot homer ended up as a single as the ball dropped in center field.

• On June 15, 1976, a game was rained out because of flooding in the streets.

• The old location of Colt Stadium (now rebuilt in Toncon, Mexico) is just northwest of the Astrodome; Astrohall and Astroarena are just south of the Astrodome.

KANSAS CITY, MISSOURI

ROYALS STADIUM

STYLE Traditional Baseball Only
A.K.A. Harry S. Truman Sports Complex
OCCUPANT AL Royals April 10, 1973 to date
EVENT All Star Game 1973
LOCATION *Center Field (N)* Spectacular Drive, then Interstate 70; *3rd Base (W)* Lancer Lane, then Dutton Brookfield Drive; *Home Plate (S)* Royal Way, then Chiefs Way, Arrowhead Stadium, Raytown Road, and CRI&P Railroad tracks; *1st Base (E)* Red Coat Drive, then Blue Ridge Cut-Off; Stadium Drive encircles the park
SURFACE Astroturf—very fast
DIMENSIONS *Foul Lines:* 330; *Power Alleys:* 385; *Center Field:* 410; *Backstop:* 60; *Foul Territory:* Small

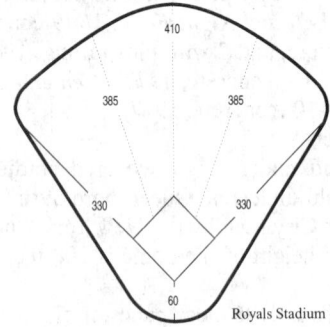
Royals Stadium

FENCES 12 (canvas)
PHENOMENA

• Waterfalls and fountains run for 322 feet on the embankment overlooking right-center.

• Best visibility for hitters in the majors.

• Homers few here because alleys are deep and the fence cuts away sharply from the 330 foul poles.

• Kenny Pippin, in his frogman suit, cleans the pond periodically in right-center.

• Royals 1985 World Series cup and other trophies are on display through the sixth inning of each game at Section 107.

• Upper deck fans near foul poles are in relative darkness.

• Best groundskeeper in baseball has the ironic job of maintaining an ugly plastic carpet. He keeps busy maintaining the Runway and the Boja, the grassy running area and the 125-tree forest beyond the left-center fence.

LOS ANGELES, CALIFORNIA

DODGER STADIUM

STYLE Traditional Baseball Only
A.K.A. Chavez Ravine during AL use 1962 to 1965 by Angels, Taj O'Malley, O'Malley's Golden Gulch

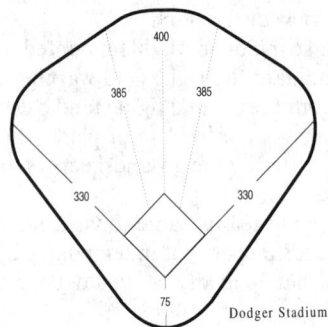
Dodger Stadium

OCCUPANT NL Dodgers April 10, 1962 to date; AL Angels April 17, 1962 to September 22, 1965
EVENT All Star Game 1980
LOCATION *Left Field (NW)* Glendale Boulevard; *3rd Base (SW)* Sunset Boulevard; *Home Plate (S)* 1000 Elysian Park Avenue; *1st Base (SE)* Pasadena Freeway; *Right Field (NE)* Los Angeles Police Academy, Elysian Park, and Golden State Freeway/Interstate; Stadium Way encircles the park; in Chavez Ravine, on a hill overlooking downtown Los Angeles
SURFACE Santa Ana Bermuda grass
DIMENSIONS *Foul Lines:* 330; *Power Alleys:* 380 (1962), 370 (1969), 385 (1983); *Center Field:* 410 (1962), 400 (1969); *Back Stop:* 65 (1962), 68.19 (1963), 75 (1969); *Foul Territory:* Large
FENCES *Left-Center to Right-Center:* 10 (wood 1962), 8 (1973); *Foul Poles to Bullpens in Left and Right Field Corners:* 3.75 (steel 1962), 3.83 (1969); *The Dip:* (where low corner steel wall and screen bullpen fence meet) 3.42 (1962), 3.5 (1969)
FORMER USE Used by squatters and goats.
PHENOMENA

• A classic pitcher's park.

• Cleanest ballpark, bar none.

• Designed by architect Emil Praeger to be expandable to 85,000 seats.

• Along with the modernized Yankee Stadium, Dodger Stadium is a modern stadium that has retained the classical character of the old ballparks and avoided the "concrete ashtray" appearance of most modern-era stadia.

• Infield dirt and outfield warning track made of 70 percent crushed red building brick and 30 percent mountain clay and calcium chlorate. Palm trees beyond the fence down the foul lines.

• See-through windows in bullpen fence installed in 1974.

• Although the center field 400 sign came down in 1980, the distance is still 400 to center; the two 395 signs are left and right of dead center.

• No drinking-water fountains when first built. Original design had a huge fountain in center field, like that in right-center at Royals Stadium.

• When foul poles were installed in 1962, discovered that they were positioned completely foul. Special dispensation was received from National League so they were recognized as fair, but the next year plate was moved so that poles are now actually fair.

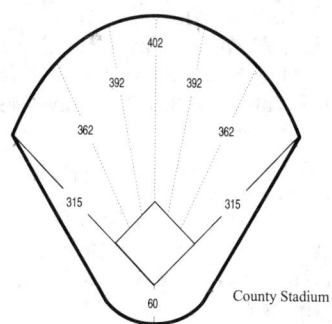

County Stadium

MIAMI, FLORIDA

JOE ROBBIE STADIUM
STYLE   Superstructure with Natural Surface
A.K.A.   JRS
OCCUPANT   Florida Marlins April 1993 to present
LOCATION   2269 N.W. 199th Street
SURFACE   Natural Grass ("Bermuda 419")
DIMENSIONS   *Left Field:* 335; *Left Center:* 380; *Center Field:* 410; *Right Center:* 380; *Right Field:* 345
FENCES   3 to 13 in extreme left, 3 to 16.2 in extreme right, 8 otherwise

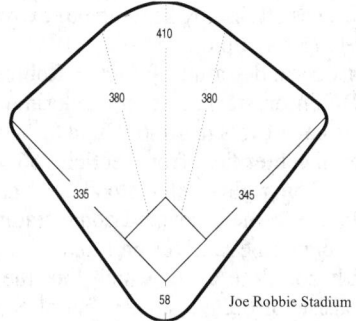

Joe Robbie Stadium

PHENOMENA
• Opening Day for football: August 16, 1987 (Bears vs. Dolphins).
• First baseball game: Los Angeles Dodgers vs. Baltimore Orioles on March 11, 1988.
• Architect: HOK Sports Facility Group.
• Capacity: 48,000.
• Parking for 14,970 cars and 254 buses plus a helipad.
• Retrofitted for baseball at a cost of $10 million.

MILWAUKEE, WISCONSIN

COUNTY STADIUM
STYLE   1950s transitional
OCCUPANT   NL Braves April 14, 1953 to September 22, 1965; AL White Sox for nine 1968 games and and eleven in 1969; games from May 15, 1968 to September 26, 1969; AL Brewers April 7, 1970 to date
EVENT   All Star Game 1955, 1975
LOCATION   *Left Field (E)* Menominee River and South 44th Street, later US-41 Stadium Freeway; *3rd Base (N)* Story Parkway and Interstate 94; *1st Base (W)* General Mitchell Boulevard; *Right Field (S)* West National Avenue and the National Soldiers Home
SURFACE   Bluegrass
DIMENSIONS   *Left Field:* 320 (1953), 315 (1975); *Power Alleys:* 355 (1953), 362 (1962); *Deep Alleys:* 397 (1953), 392 (1955); *Center Field:* 404 (1953), 410 (1954),

402 (1955); *Right Field:* 320 (1953), 315.37 (1954); *Backstop:* 60
FENCES   *Left Field:* 4 (1953), 8 (1955), 8.33 (1959), 10 (1985); *Center Field:* 4 (1953), 8 (1955), 8.33 (1959), 10 (1985); *Right Field:* 4 (1953), 10 (1955)
FORMER USE   Story Quarry
PHENOMENA
• Surveyor's mark on right field foul pole: "315.37."
• Before the park was expanded from 1953 to 1973, hospital patients at the National Soldiers Home V.A. Hospital sat outside their rooms on Mockingbird Hill overlooking right field and watched the game for free.
• Perini's Woods, spruce and fir trees behind center field fence, planted in 1954, replaced by bleachers in 1961.
• Braves Reservation, a picnic area down the left field line, was inaugurated in 1961.
• Bernie Brewer slides into a huge beer stein in right-center whenever a Brewer hits a homer.
• Only homer ever hit over left field roof was hit by Jose Canseco.
• Scene of Midwest League minor league game on August 27, 1966 between Fox Cities and Wisconsin Rapids.
• Braves hosted both the Reds and the Cards on September 24, 1954. The first game was the finish of a game two days earlier whose conclusion on a disputed double play was successfully protested by the Reds. The Reds tied the game after the protested game's resumption, but the Braves won 4-3 in the bottom of the ninth, and then beat the Cards 4-2.

MINNEAPOLIS, MINNESOTA

HUBERT H. HUMPHREY METRODOME
STYLE   Dome
A.K.A.   Minnedome, Bounce Dome, Hump Dome, Homer Dome, Hubie Dome, Sweat Box (before June 28, 1983, when air conditioning arrived), Domed Stadium, Thunderdome
OCCUPANT   AL Twins April 6, 1982 to date
EVENT   All Star Game 1985
LOCATION   *Left Field (SW)* Fourth Street South; *3rd Base (NW)* 501 Chicago Avenue South; *1st Base (NE)* Sixth Street South; *Right Field (SE)* Tenth Avenue South; *Above:* Domed roof
SURFACE   SporTurf (1982 to 1986—liveliest bounce ever), Astroturf (1987 to date)
DIMENSIONS   *Apex of Dome:* 186; *Left Field:* 344 (1982), 343 (1983); *Left-Center:* 385; *Center Field:* 407 (1982), 408 (1983); *Right Center:* 367; *Right Field:* 327;

Backstop: 60; *Foul Territory:* Small
FENCES   *Left Field:* 7 (canvas 1982), 13 (6 plexiglass above 7 canvas 1983); *Center Field:* 7 (canvas 1982); *Right Field:* 7 (canvas 1982), 13 (canvas 1983), 23 (canvas 1985)

PHENOMENA

• A power hitter's park.
• Right field wall called Hefty Bag.
• Almost an exact duplicate of the domed stadiums in Seattle, Pontiac, and Vancouver. All four were built by the same engineering firm.
• Game on April 27, 1986 delayed as violent rainstorm knocked out the lights and had the scoreboard and roof swaying.
• The white air-supported fabric Teflon roof makes it difficult to see the ball when hit high in the air.
• Playoffs and World Series of 1987 set new decibel records for sound in the Thunderdome.
• Sections 107 to 113 are football seats which in baseball season are tilted up and back to create a 40-foot wall behind the right field fence.
• The roof collapsed in the fall of 1982 but was repaired quickly.
• Twin batter Randy Bush hit a ball off the roof in 1983. The ball was caught foul for an out by Blue Jays catcher Buck Martinez.
• On May 4, 1984, in the top of the fourth inning, A's batter Dave Kingman hit a ball through the roof. It should have been a homer, but Kingman got only a double.

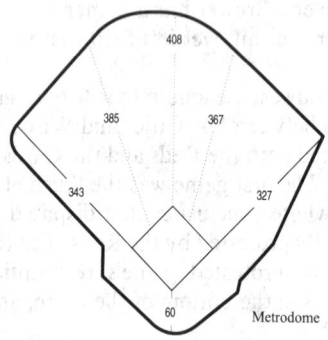

Metrodome

• Balls bounced very high off the carpet used from 1982 to 1986.
• More home runs tend to be hit when the air conditioning is turned off.
• Curvature of wall behind plate causes wild pitches and passed balls to bounce directly toward first base.

MONTREAL, QUEBEC

STADE OLYMPIQUE

STYLE   Summer Olympics Stadium/Dome
A.K.A.   Olympic Stadium, Big O, Big Owe
OCCUPANT   NL Expos April 15, 1977 to date
EVENT   All Star Game 1982
LOCATION   *Left Field (NW)* rue Sherbrooke; *3rd Base (SW)* boulevard Pie-IX; *1st Base (SE)* 4549, avenue Pierre-de-Coubertin; *Right Field (NE)* boulevard Viau
SURFACE   Astroturf

DIMENSIONS   *Foul Lines:* 325 (1977), 330 (1981), 325 (1983); *Power Alleys:* 375; *Center Field:* 404 (1977), 405 (1979), 404 (1980), 400 (1981), 404 (1983); *Apex of Dome:* 171; *Backstop:* 62 (1977), 65 (1983), 53 (1989); *Foul Territory:* Large
FENCES   12 (wood 1977), 12 (foam 1989)

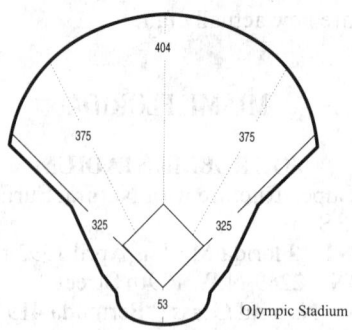

Olympic Stadium

PHENOMENA

• Labatt's Noise-Meter high above right field is baseball's answer to the NBA Sacramento Kings' Arco Arena Noise-Meter.
• Roof improves offense by keeping out extreme cold.
• Built for 1976 Olympics.
• Plaque inside and statue of Jackie Robinson at main entrance. Robinson starred at the Delorimer Downs for the IL Montreal Royals in 1946. Huge 623-foot-high umbrella tower in center field from section 766 in left-center to section 767 in right-center stood half finished from 1976 to 1987. Became a covered-dome stadium in 1989. The retractable dome is silver on top, and orange on the bottom, with 26 white cones which link the roof to the tower. It consists of 60,696 square feet of Kevlar, weighing 50 tons. Retractable roof not actually retractable until 1988 due to generator problems.

NEW YORK, NEW YORK

YANKEE STADIUM

STYLE   Major League Classic
A.K.A.   House That Ruth Built
OCCUPANT   AL Yankees April 18, 1923 to September 30, 1973; NEWL Black Yankees 1932; NNL Black Yankees 1946 to 1948; Negro League World Series 3rd game, 1942; 1st game 1947; AL Yankees April 15, 1976 to date
EVENT   All Star Game 1939, 1960, 1977
LOCATION   *Left Field (NE)* East 161st Street; *3rd Base (NW)* Doughty Street, later Ruppert Place; *Home Plate (W)* Major Degan Expressway/Interstate 87 and Harlem River; *1st Base (SW)* East 157th Street; *Right Field (SE)* River Avenue and IRT elevated tracks; In the southwest Bronx
SURFACE   Grass—Merion Bluegrass
DIMENSIONS   *Left Field:* 280.58 (1923), 301 (1928), 312 (1976), 318 (1988); *Left Side of Bullpen Gate in Short Left-Center:* 395 (1923), 402 (1928), 387 (1976), 379 (1985); *Right Side of Bullpen Gate:* 415 (1937); *Deepest Left-Center:* 500 (1923), 490 (1924), 457 (1937), 430 (1976), 411 (1985), 399 (1988); *Left Side of Center Field Screen:* 466 (1937); *Center Field:* 487 (1923), 461 (1937), 463 (1967), 417 (1976), 410 (1985), 408 (1988);

Deepest Right Center: 429 (1923), 407 (1937), 385 (1976); *Left Side of Bullpen Gate in Short Right Center:* 350 (1923), 367 (1937), 353 (1976); *Right Side of Bullpen Gate:* 344 (1937); *Right Field:* 294.75 (1923), 295 (1930), 296 (1939), 310 (1976), 314 (1988); *Backstop:* 82 (1942), 80 (1953), 84 (1976); *Foul Territory:* Large for the catcher behind home plate, but small for fielders down the foul lines

FENCES *Left Field–Foul Line:* 3.92 (3 wire above .92 concrete 1923), 8 (canvas 1976); *Left Center–Left of Visitors' Bullpen:* 3.58 (3 wire above .58 concrete); *Right of Visitors' Bullpen:* 7.83 (3 wire above 4.83 concrete), 7 (canvas 1976); *Center Field-Left Screen When Up for Hitters' Background:* 20 (1953), 22.25 (1959), 22.42 (1954); *Screen When Down:* 13.83,7 (canvas 1976); *Right Center-Right of Screen:* 14.5 (3 wire above 11.5 concrete 1923); *Left of Home Bullpen:* 7.83 (3 wire above 4.83 concrete 1923); *Right of Home Bullpen:* 3.58 (3 wire above .58 concrete 1923), 8 (canvas 1976), 9 (canvas 1979); *Right Field-Foul Line:* 3.75 (3 wire above .75 concrete 1923), 10 (canvas 1976)

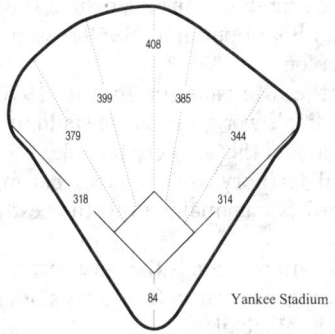

Yankee Stadium

PHENOMENA

• Left-center field monuments and plaques: Yankee Stadium (I) Monuments in fair territory, Lou Gehrig on the left, Miller Huggins in the middle, Babe Ruth on the right; Yankee Stadium (II) Monuments beyond the fence; same as Yankee Stadium I. Plaques beyond the fence, Ed Barrow, Jacob Ruppert, Joe DiMaggio, Mickey Mantle, Casey Stengel, Joe McCarthy, Pope Paul VI, Thurman Munson, Pope John Paul II, Billy Martin.

• A ball hitting the foul pole in the 1930s was in play, not a homer.

• "Death Valley" in left-center.

• Green curtain in center sometimes raised and lowered like a window shade to force visiting batters to face a background of white-shirted bleacher fans but allow Yankee hitters to face a dark green background. Removed in World Series to sell more seats.

• Bleachers in right-center often called Ruthville and Gehrigville.

• Warning track red cinders; later on, red brick dust.

• Extra grass kept near monuments in center, in play.

• Underneath second base in Yankee Stadium (I), there was a 15-foot-deep brick-lined vault with electrical, telephone, and telegraphic connections for boxing events.

• As originally constructed, from May 5, 1922, to April 18, 1923, three concrete decks extended from behind home plate to each corner, with a single deck in left-center, and wooden bleachers around the rest of the outfield.

• In the winter of 1927-28, second and third decks were added to left-center, and several rows of box seats were removed in left, extending the foul pole from 281 to 301.

• During the 1936 season, the winter of 1936-37, and continuing through the 1937 season, the wooden bleachers were replaced with concrete ones. During the 1937 season, second and third decks were added in right-center. The bleacher changes shortened straightaway center from 490 to 461 and reduced seating capacity from the 80,000s to the 70,000s.

• As the outfield bench seats were gradually replaced with chair seats, in the 1930s and 1940s, the seating capacity gradually dropped from over 70,000 to about 67,000.

• Bloody Angle—between bleachers and RF foul line in 1923 season was very asymmetric and caused crazy bounces. Eliminating this in 1924 caused the plate to be moved 13 feet, and the deepest left center corner to change from 500 to 490.

• Auxiliary scoreboards were built in the late 1940s, which covered up the 367 right-center sign and the 415 left-center sign.

• Minor modifications were made in the winter of 1966-67. During this work, a new 463 sign and a 433 sign appeared in the power alleys, and the exterior was painted blue and white.

• During 1974-75 renovation, iron third deck distinctive facade was removed, and a portion was placed in the bleachers.

SHEA STADIUM

STYLE Superstructure with natural surface
A.K.A. William A. Shea Municipal Stadium
OCCUPANT NL Mets April 17, 1964 to date; AL Yankees, April 6, 1974 to September 28, 1975
EVENT All Star Game 1964
LOCATION *Centerfield (E)* 126th Street; *3rd Base (N)* Whitestone Expressway/Interstate 678, and Flushing Bay; *Home Plate (W)* Grand Central Parkway; *1st Base (S)* Roosevelt Avenue; In Queens, near Flushing Meadow Park, site of 1939 and 1964 World's Fairs, just southeast of La Guardia Airport
SURFACE Bluegrass

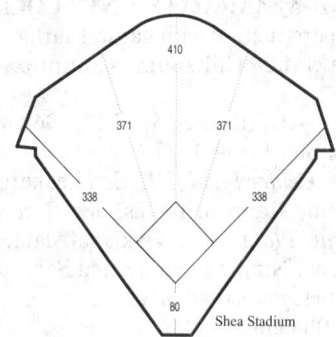

Shea Stadium

DIMENSIONS *Foul Line:* 330 (marked 1964), 341 (actual 1964), 341 (1965), 338 (1979); *Power Alleys:* 371; *Center Field:* 410; *Backstop:* 80 (1964); *Foul Territory:* Very large
FENCES *Foul Lines:* 16.33 (4 wire and railing above 12.33 brick 1964), 12.33 (brick 1965), 8 (wood 1979); *Power Alleys:* 8 (wood); *Center Field:* Small section 8.75 (wood), most 8 (wood)

PHENOMENA

- Designed to be expandable to 90,000 seats.
- Noisiest outdoor ballpark; frequent La Guardia Airport air traffic noise overhead.
- Named for attorney William Shea, who obtained the Mets franchise for New York by organizing the Continental League.
- Right-center scoreboard is largest in majors, 86 feet high with Bulova clock on top, about 25 feet behind the outfield fence, and 175 feet long.
- Practice facilities under the right field stands.
- Behind fence in center, just to the right of the 410 mark, is a Mets Magic Top Hat. When a Met hits a homer, a red Big Apple rises out of the black top hat, which actually looks more like a big kettle.
- Foul lines from 1965 to 1978 had an orange home run line painted at the top of the 12-foot, 4-inch brick wall. Above this was a 4-foot wire screen and railing. A ball was a homer if it hit above the line. Like a similar ground rule at Crosley Field in center field, this caused many controversies, so in 1979 an inner 8-foot wooden fence was installed.
- Worst visibility for hitters in the majors.
- Churchlike spire beyond center field fence with "Serval Zippers" sign.
- Outfield fences also marked as 358 and 396. From 1973 to 1979, there were also distance markers, outside the field of play, on the rear bullpen walls at 428, base of left-center light tower at 442, bottom edge of right-center scoreboard at 405 on right field end and 420 on center field end.
- 1964 Mets Banner Day—"Mongolia Loves The Mets" (in Mongolian) banner carried by the author; other banners included "E=mc2" (or Errors = Mets times customers squared),"Eamus Metropoli" (Let's go Mets in Latin).
- Christened April 16, 1964 with Dodger Holy Water from the Gowanus Canal in Brooklyn and Giant Holy Water from the Harlem River at the exact location where it passed the old Polo Grounds.

OAKLAND, CALIFORNIA

OAKLAND-ALAMEDA COUNTY COLISEUM

STYLE Superstructure with natural surface
A.K.A. Oakland Coliseum Complex, Oakland Mausoleum
OCCUPANT AL Athletics April 17, 1968 to date
EVENT All Star Game 1987
LOCATION *Center Field (NE)* San Leandro Street and Southern Pacific Railroad tracks; *3rd Base (NW)* 66th Avenue; *Home Plate (SW)* Oakland-Alameda County Coliseum Arena, Nimitz Freeway, and San Leandro Bay; *1st Base (SE)* Hegenberger Drive
SURFACE Bluegrass
DIMENSIONS *Foul Lines:* 330; *Power Alleys:* 378 (1968), 375 (1969), 372 (1981); *Center Field:* 410 (1968), 400 (1969), 396 (1981), 397 (1982), 400 (1990); *Backstop:* 90 (1968), 60 (1969); *Foul Territory:* Huge, largest in the majors
FENCES 8 (plywood 1968), 10 (canvas over plywood and plexiglass 1981), 8 (1986)

PHENOMENA

- Surrounded by beautiful green ivy slope.
- Backstop is a notch cut in stands.
- Possible to watch game for free from concourse behind the field seats by peering between wooden slats on cyclone fence.
- Steel shell of pitcher's mound was exposed on Opening Day April 17, 1968 and had to keep being covered between innings.

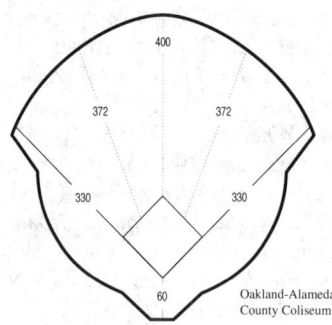

Oakland-Alameda
County Coliseum

- Right field scoreboard installed June 1968.
- Finley Fun Board put in for 1969 season—24 feet high and 126 feet long.
- Named the Mausoleum in the 1970s when the scoreboard didn't work, the entire stadium was gray concrete in color, and the A's were terrible.
- Huge foul territory area reduces batting average by roughly 5 to 7 points, making this the best pitcher's park in the AL.
- Fun picnic atmosphere is the very best in the majors of all new concrete circular ugly ashtray stadia.
- Best food in baseball.
- Winds favor lefthanded batters.
- Next door to Jewel Box, home of the NBA Golden State Warriors.
- Scoreboard shows upcoming home stands, with A's annihilating the opposition.
- Fans sitting at the foul poles can catch home run fair balls by reaching in front of the foul pole screens.
- Hand-operated scoreboard showing major league line scores installed in 1986.

PHILADELPHIA, PENNSYLVANIA

VETERANS STADIUM

STYLE Superstructure with artificial surface
A.K.A. Vet

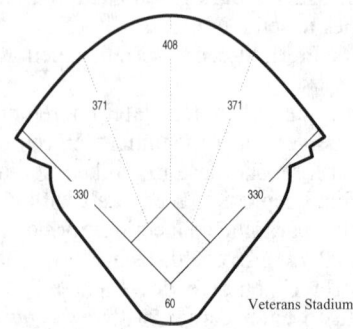

Veterans Stadium

OCCUPANT   April 10, 1971 to date
EVENT   All Star Game 1976
LOCATION   *Left Field (NE)* Packer Street and Interstate 76; *3rd Base (NW)* Broad Street and Philadelphia Naval Hospital; *1st Base (SW)* Pattison Avenue, Spectrum, and JFK Stadium; *Right Field (SE)* Tenth Street
SURFACE   Astroturf—fast, but slower since 1977
DIMENSIONS   *Foul Lines:* 330; *Power Alleys:* 371; *Center Field:* 408; *Backstop:* 60; *Foul Territory:* Large
FENCES   6 (wood April 1972); 8 (wood June 1971); 12 (6 plexiglass above 6 wood 1972)
PHENOMENA
• The park's rounded rectangular shape is called an octorad by the architects.
• Connie Mack Stadium's home plate was transplanted here.
• Plastic tarp covered unfinished right field wall in April 1971.
• "Liberty Bell" used to hang from center field roof in fourth level—hit only by Greg Luzinski on May 16, 1972.
• First ball dropped from a helicopter on April 10, 1971.
• Smallest hot dogs and loudest boos in baseball.
• Statues of Connie Mack and a sliding runner outside the park.

PITTSBURGH, PENNSYLVANIA

THREE RIVERS STADIUM
STYLE   Superstructure with artificial surface
A.K.A.   House That Clemente Built
OCCUPANT   NL Pirates July 16, 1970 to date
EVENT   All Star Game 1974

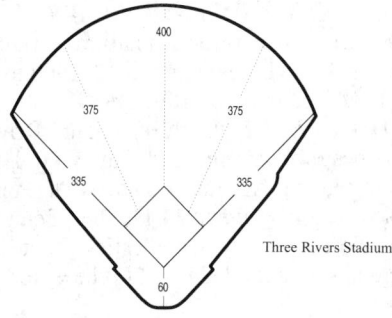

Three Rivers Stadium

LOCATION   *Left Field (E)* Interstate 279 Fort Duquesne Bridge approach ramp; *3rd Base (N)* Reedsdale Street; *1st Base (W)* Allegheny Avenue, Ohio River, and the original point where the Monongahela River joins the Allegheny River to form the Ohio River; *Right Field (S)* North Shore Avenue, Roberto Clemente Memorial Park, Allegheny River; Stadium Circle encircles the park
SURFACE   Carpet—Tartanturf 1970 to 1982; Astroturf 1983 to date
DIMENSIONS   *Foul Lines:* 340 (1970), 335 (1975); *Power Alleys:* 385 (1970), 375 (1975); *Center Field:* 410 (1970), 400 (1975); *Backstop:* 60; *Foul Territory:* Large
FENCES   10 (wood)
PHENOMENA
• On a site that was an island during the French and Indian Wars. It had been an Indian burial ground, a fact discovered when the Big Flood of 1763 uncovered many graves. Named Kilbuck Island after a friendly Delaware Indian chief. Back channels filled with silt, and it was no longer an island in 1852.
• Numbers painted on seats in right field upper deck where Willie Stargell's homers landed.
• Without the inner fence, the outfield would be 342 down the lines and 434 to center.
• The Honus Wagner statue, which used to stand outside of Forbes Field, now stands outside of Three Rivers Stadium.
• An 8- by 12-foot area of the 406 marker section of the Forbes Field brick wall, 12 Romanesque window frames, and the Babe Ruth plaque showing where his 714th home run landed are in the Allegheny Club at Three Rivers.
• Original design by Erik Sirko was for a "Stadium Over the Monongahela," with stadium above two parking lot levels, all sitting above the Monongahela River with plenty of room for boats to pass beneath on the river.

ST. LOUIS, MISSOURI

BUSCH STADIUM (II)
STYLE   Superstructure with artificial surface
A.K.A.   Civic Center Stadium 1966, Busch Memorial Stadium 1966 to 1983

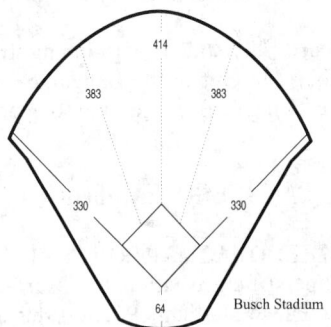

Busch Stadium

OCCUPANT   NL Cardinals May 12, 1966 to date
EVENT   All Star Game 1966
LOCATION   *Left Field (E)* Broadway, Interstate 70, Gateway Arch and Mississippi River; *3rd Base (N)* Walnut Street; *1st Base (W)* Seventh Street and 300 Stadium Plaza; *Right Field (S)* Spruce Street; Stadium Plaza surrounds the park
SURFACE   Grass 1966 to 1969. Carpet—very fast—1970 to date. From 1970 to 1976, the entire field was carpeted except for the part of the infield that is normally dirt on a grass field. In 1977, this was carpeted except for the sliding pits. This is one of only two instances where there was a full dirt infield, with an otherwise fully carpeted field, the other being Candlestick in 1971.
DIMENSIONS   *Foul Lines:* 330; *Power Alleys:* 386 (1966), 376 (1973), 386 (1977), 383 (July 1983), 375 (1992); *Center Field:* 414 (1966), 410 (1971), 414 (1972), 404 (1973), 414 (1977), 402 (1992); *Backstop:* 64 (Vin Scully's unofficial measurement during 1985 World Series showed this to be 50 rather than 64); *Foul Territory:* Large
FENCES   *Left and Right Fields:* 10.5 (padded concrete), 8 (padded canvas 1992); *Center Field:* 10.5 (padded concrete 1966), 8 (wood 1973), 10.5 (padded concrete 1977), 8 (padded canvas 1992)

PHENOMENA

- A line drive park because of the deep alleys and deep center field and the quick turf.
- Open arches surround the field just below the roof.
- From 1966 to 1982 right field scoreboard lights showed a cardinal in flight when a Cardinal hit a home run; same show was put on each time Lou Brock set a new base-stealing record.
- Home plate transplanted from old Busch Stadium at opener on May 12, 1966.
- Next to the Gateway Arch and the Mississippi River; you can see the Arch from the top deck in right field.
- Statue of "Stan the Man" Musial outside the stadium was unveiled in 1968.
- Small sections of bleachers in the outfield.
- Chicken wire basket (à la Wrigley Field in Chicago), installed in front of left-center and right-center bleacher sections in July 1983, is 2 feet high and reduces distance to fence by 3 feet (386 to 383 in power alleys). It does not raise the height of the 10½ foot wall. No basket in center field bleacher section since it is used only for football.
- At league direction, the site designated for any Cubs playoffs or World Series home games from 1986 until 1988, when Wrigley Field got lights.
- Most fans at the stadium seem to be wearing Cardinal red.
- Seventh inning brings the Clydesdale horses to the scoreboard.
- Only ballpark where the seventh-inning stretch does not bring on "Take Me Out to the Ballgame." Instead, here they play the "King of Beers" theme song on the organ.

FENCES *Left and Right Fields:* 17.5 (concrete 1969), 9 (line painted on concrete 1973), 18 (concrete 1974), 8.5 (canvas 1982); *Center Field:* 17.5 (concrete 1969), 10 (wood 1973), 18 (concrete 1978), 8.5 (canvas 1982), one section in right center 9 (canvas 1982)

FORMER USE San Diego River ran through the area, which was then a marshy swampland.

PHENOMENA

- Named for sports editor who campaigned to bring major league baseball to San Diego.
- Noticeable lack of Spanish-speaking fans and Spanish language advertisements in the only major league ballpark on the Mexican border.
- The stadium is circular but open in right.
- Foul poles sit two feet behind the fence, and one foot in front of the wall.
- The right-center scoreboard sits directly behind the right center seats, and is so hot that fans there feel the heat on their backs.
- Only park where bullpen dirt area touches the foul lines.
- Only park where a foul ball can be caught out of sight of all umpires and most players. Location is in either bullpen near the foul poles.
- After 1981 season, the plate was moved 5 feet back toward the backstop.
- Expanded during 1983 football season by adding seats in right and right-center.
- Ivy put on center field fence in 1980.
- 20-foot-wide black batter's eye section on both center field wall and fence July-October 1982.

SAN DIEGO, CALIFORNIA

SAN DIEGO JACK MURPHY STADIUM

STYLE Superstructure with natural surface
A.K.A. San Diego Stadium 1969 to 1980, Jack Murphy Stadium thereafter

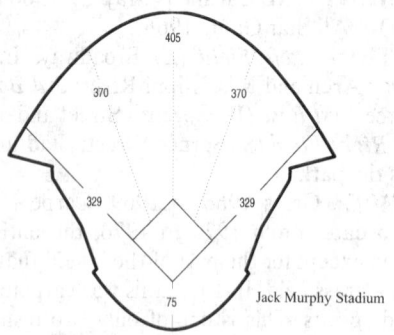

Jack Murphy Stadium

OCCUPANT NL Padres April 8, 1969 to date
EVENT All Star Games 1978, 1992
LOCATION *Left Field (N)* 9449 Friars Road; *3rd Base (W)* Stadium Way and a quarry; *1st Base (S)* San Diego River, Camino del Rio North, and Interstate 8; *Right Field (E)* Interstate 15
SURFACE Santa Ana Bermuda grass
DIMENSIONS *Foul Lines:* 330 (1969), fence 327 (1982), foul poles 329 (1982); *Power Alleys:* 375 (1969), 370 (1982); *Center Field:* 420 (1969), 410 (1973), 420 (1978), 405 (1982); *Backstop:* 80 (1969), 75 (1982)

SAN FRANCISCO, CALIFORNIA

CANDLESTICK PARK

STYLE Superstructure with natural surface
OCCUPANT NL Giants April 12, 1960 to date
EVENT All Star Game 1961, 1984
LOCATION *Left Field (NW)* Giants Drive; *3rd Base (SW)* Jamestown Avenue and Bay View Hill; *1st Base (SE)* Jamestown Avenue, Candlestick Point and San Francisco; *Right Field (NE)* Hunters Point Expressway and San Francisco Bay; Candlestick Point, with its rock outcroppings, was leveled to fill in the water for the parking lots.
SURFACE Grass (1960), Carpet (1971), Bluegrass (1979)

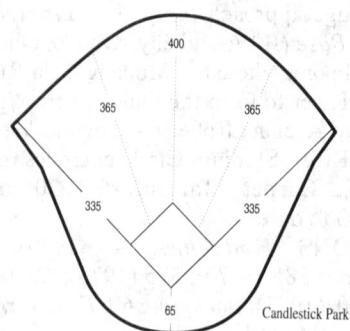

Candlestick Park

DIMENSIONS *Left Field:* 330 (1960), 335 (1968); *Left-Center:* 397 (1960), 365 (1961); *Center Field:* 420

(1960), 410 (1961), 400 (1982); *Right-Center:* 397 (1960), 330 (1970), 335 (1981); *Backstop:* 73 (1960), 70 (1961), 55 (1975), 65 (1982), 66 (1985); *Foul Territory:* Very large

FENCES   10 (wire 1960); 8 (wire 1972); 12 (6 canvas below 6 plexiglass 1975); 9 (6 canvas below 3 plexiglass 1982); 9 (wire 1984), 9.5 (fence posts 1984)

PHENOMENA

• Named for jagged rocks and trees which rise from the tidelands like giant candlesticks.

• Bay View Hill overlooks the park from behind 3rd base.

• Many fans arrived by boat in 1960s.

• Only hot-water-heated open-air stadium in the majors.

• Before the bleachers were enclosed, so many fans would stream out of the bleachers in right-center when Mays and McCovey batted and crowd up against the flimsy cyclone fence, that a white line was painted on the asphalt 20 feet behind the fence. Fans had to stand behind this line.

• Fifty-nine posts every 20 feet or so on the outfield fence can cause strange bounces—their tips extend 6 inches above the 9 foot wire fence.

• Wind, wind, and more wind! Before the stadium was enclosed, wind blew in from left-center and out toward right-center. Now that it is enclosed, the wind is a swirling monster, just as strong as before.

• Six Giants retired numbers on white baseballs on the right field fence.

• Maury's Lake—the basepath between first and second was drenched before the game to make it more difficult for Dodger Maury Wills to steal second.

• Umps protested location of foul poles completely in fair territory in third inning of opening game on April 12, 1960.

• Stu Miller was blown off the mound by the wind in the 1961 All-Star Game.

• The stadium was enlarged and fully enclosed in the winter of 1971-72 to house the 49ers.

• Architect John Bolles' boomerang-shaped concrete shell baffle behind the upper tier's last row of seats was intended to protect the park from wind; it didn't work.

• In the winter of 1978-79, the Giants ripped up their carpet and replaced it with grass.

• Coldest park in the majors, resulting in less home runs.

• Croix de Candlestick pin awarded to fans at conclusion of night extra-inning games.

SEATTLE, WASHINGTON

KINGDOME

STYLE   Dome

A.K.A.   King County Stadium, Tomb (1980s), Puget Puke (1980s)

OCCUPANT   AL Mariners April 6, 1977 to date

EVENT   All Star Game 1979

LOCATION   *Left Field (N)* 201 South King Street; *3rd Base (W)* 589 Occidental Avenue South; *1st Base (S)* South Royal Brougham Way; *Right Field (E)* Fourth Avenue South and Burlington Northern Railroad tracks; *Above:* Domed roof

DIMENSIONS   *Left Field:* 315 (1977), 316 (marked 1978), 314 (actual 1978), 324 (1990), 331 (1991); *Left Center:* 375 (1977), 365 (1978), 357 (1981), 362 (1990),

376 (1991); *Deep Left-Center:* 385 (1990); *Center Field:* 405 (1977), 410 (1978), 405 (1981), 410 (1986), 405 (1991); *Deep Right Center:* 375 (1990); *Right Center:* 375 (1977), 365 (1978), 357 (1981), 352 (1990); *Right Field:* 315 (1977), 316 (1978), 314 (1990); *Speakers in Left (3), Left Center, and Center:* 110 (1977), 133.5 (1981); 11 other speakers 130; *Backstop:* 63; *Apex of Dome:* 250; *Foul Territory:* Large

FENCES   *Left Field:* 11.5 (wood 1977), 17.5 (6 plexiglass over wood); *Center Field:* 11.5 (wood 1977); *Right Field:* 11.5 (wood 1977), 23.25 (wood 1982), 11.5 (wood 1988)

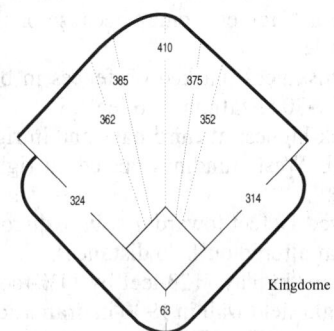

PHENOMENA

• Large American flag flies above the concrete dome.

• 23-foot Mini-Green Monster in right and right-center is called the Walla Walla.

• Carpet is rolled out by the Rhinoceros machine, and smoothed by the Grasshopper machine after it has been zipped together.

• Baby-changing areas in aisles 111, 113, 201, 203.

• Domed roof looks from below like it's made of thousands of bricks.

• Sick's Stadium home plate on display in Royal Brougham trophy case.

• In the winter of 1980-81, the three speakers above left, left-center, and center were raised from 102 to 133.5 feet to reduce the chance of their being hit again.

• Two foul balls have gone up but never come down: August 4, 1979—Ruppert Jones of Mariners hit a foul ball that stuck in the speaker above the first base dugout, thus disproving the old adage of physics that what goes up must come down. On May 20, 1983, Brewer Ricky Nelson did the same. By some arcane logic, both fly balls were ruled strikes.

• Four foul balls have bounced off speakers and been caught for outs: August 3, 1979, caught by A's pitcher Matt Keough; September 3, 1979, caught by Mariners' first baseman; May 19, 1980, caught by Mariners' first baseman; April 25, 1985, caught by Mariners' pitcher Mark Langston.

• Other foul balls have bounced off the Seattle Supersonics basketball speakers above first base and the basketball scoreboard above and behind home plate, without being caught.

• One fair ball bounced off a roof support wire and remained in play on April 11, 1985—a ball hit by Dave Kingman of A's was caught for an out in deep left: it would have been a home run. One fair ball has struck the right field speaker—Ken Phelps of the Mariners hit a tape-measure homer on August 13, 1987—the ball landed foul.

- Seven fair balls have bounced off speakers and remained in play.
- Called the Tomb by visiting sportswriters because it's sickeningly gray concrete and quiet.
- Roof's hanging red, white, and blue streamers can tangle up an infield fly and deflect it from the pitcher's mound to behind second base.
- U.S.S. *Mariner*—a huge yellow sailing ship behind the center-field fence which fires a cannon after every Mariner homer.
- 42 air-conditioning units, 16 in fair territory, 26 in foul territory, 8 ducts in each unit. These blow air in toward the field which means fewer home runs in what would normally be a "Homer Dome" because of the short 357 foot power alleys.
- Outfield distances marked on fences in both feet and fathoms 1977-80 (1 fathom = 6 feet).
- Third deck highest at third base and in right field. AL East and AL West standings posted on right field third deck facade.
- Plate moved 10 feet toward first base dugout in 1990 in a change that altered outfield distances.
- New classic "in-play" 123-feet by 11½-foot scoreboard placed on right field wall in 1990 in dramatic facelift.
- Scene of Funny Nose-Eye Glasses night.

- SkyDome Fitness Club boasts the world's largest indoor running track (2.2 lap per mile circuit) at the top of the stadium.
- Only park to draw over 4 million fans in a season.
- SkyDome's retractable four-panel, 11,000-ton roof takes twenty minutes to open or close; uses $500 in electricity in doing so.
- When roof is opened 91 percent of all seats are exposed to sky.
- Overruns ballooned costs from an estimated $202 million to $495 miilion.
- Facilities include a Hard Rock Cafe and the 650-seat Windows on SkyDome restaurant.
- Site of first World Series games played outside United States.
- Also home to the Toronto Argonauts of the Canadian Football League.
- Contains 161 private skyboxes on the 300 and 400 level, ranging in price from $150,000 to $225,000 yearly.

Storied Parks of the Past

BALTIMORE, MARYLAND

MEMORIAL STADIUM

STYLE 1950s Transitional
OCCUPANT AL Orioles April 15, 1954 to September 30, 1991
EVENT All Star Game 1958
LOCATION *Center Field (N)* East 36th Street; *3rd Base (W)* Ellerslie Avenue; *Home Plate (S)* 1000 East 33rd Street, section of 33rd Street near ballpark is known as Babe Ruth Plaza; *1st Base (E)* Ednor Road
SURFACE Bluegrass
DIMENSIONS *Foul Lines:* 309; where the 7-foot fence meets the 14-foot wall, 360; *Power Alleys:* 446 (1954), 447 (1955), 405 (1956), 380 (1958), 370 (1962), 385 (1970), 375 (1976), 378 (1977), 376 (1980), 378 (1990); *Center Field:* 445 (1954), 450 (1955), 425 (1956), 410 (1958), 400 (1976), 405 (1977), 410 (1978), 405 (1980); *Backstop:* 78 (1954), 58 (1961), 54 (1980), 75 (1987); *Foul Territory:* Large

TORONTO, ONTARIO

SKYDOME

STYLE Dome
OCCUPANT AL Blue Jays June 5, 1989 to date
EVENT All Star Game 1991; World Series 1992

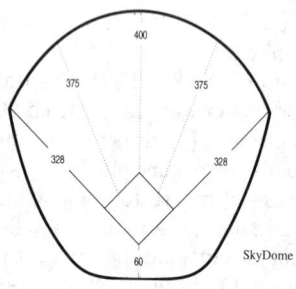

SkyDome

LOCATION *Center Field (N)* Front Street West; *3rd Base (W)* Spadina Avenue; *Home Plate (S)* Gardiner Expressway; *1st Base (E)* John Street and CN Tower, the world's largest free-standing structure
SURFACE Astroturf
DIMENSIONS *Left Field:* 328; *Left Center:* 375; *Center Field:* 400; *Right Center:* 375; *Right Field:* 328
FENCES 10
FORMER USE Water Supply pumping station where second base is now
PHENOMENA
- Capacity: 50,516.
- 31 stories high (Astrodome is just 18).
- SkyDome's $17 million Jumbotron scoreboard is the world's biggest video display board (115 by 33 feet).
- Hotel inside SkyDome has 348 rooms, 70 with a view of (and by) the stadium.

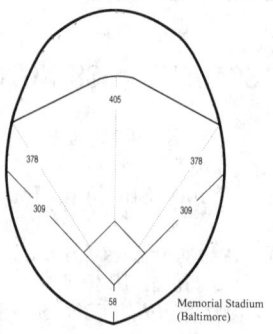

Memorial Stadium
(Baltimore)

FENCES *Foul Line Corners:* 11.33 (concrete 1954), 14 (11 concrete below 3 plywood 1959); these walls bounce balls toward center, reducing triples; *Left-Center to Right-Center:* 10 (hedges April and May, 1954), 8 (wire June 1954), 7 (wire 1955), 6 (wire 1958), 14 (wire 1961), 6 (wire 1963), 7 (canvas 1977)

FORMER USE Venable Stadium
PHENOMENA
• Beautiful trees on an embankment beyond the fence in center.
• Oriole Landing was a picnic area in the upper deck in the 1960s.
• At the beginning of the 1954 season, hedges served as the center field fence. In June 1954 a wire fence was erected which stood right in front of a row of high hedges. The top 6 feet of the fence were covered with canvas padding in 1958 after Harvey Kuenn cut his face trying to catch a home run ball by climbing the fence. The walls in the left and right field corners were also padded after Curt Blefary injured his hip chasing a Max Alvis fly.
• Fans yelled "O" (for Orioles) in unison when "The Star-Spangled Banner" reaches "O say does that star-spangled banner yet wave . . ."
• Wind usually helps lefthanded hitters.
• Venable Stadium, a football stadium also used for baseball after the July 4, 1944 fire destroyed Oriole Park (V), was torn down to make way for Memorial Stadium. Home plate was moved from where it had been in the north to its current location in the south.
• Home of the best crabcakes in baseball; crab races in the bottom of the sixth on the scoreboard between Wee Willie in orange, Paco in blue, and Mugsy in yellow.
• Inscribed into the concrete facade: "Dedicated as a memorial to all who so valiantly fought in the world wars with eternal gratitude to those who made the supreme sacrifice to preserve equality and freedom throughout the world—time will not dim the glory of their deeds."

BROOKLYN, NEW YORK

EBBETS FIELD
STYLE Major League Classic
OCCUPANT NL Dodgers April 9, 1913 to September 24, 1957, NNL Eagles 1935
EVENT All Star Game 1949
LOCATION *Left Field (NE)* Montgomery Street; *3rd Base (NW)* Franklin Avenue, later Cedar Place, later McKeever Place; *1st Base (SW)* 55 Sullivan Place; *Right Field (SE)* Bedford Avenue; in the Pigtown/Crown Heights district of Flatbush, near the Gowanus Canal.
DIMENSIONS *Left Field:* 419 (1913), 410 (1914), 418.75 (1921), 383.67 (1926), 382.83 (1930), 384 (1931), 353 (1932), 356.33 (1934), 365 (1938), 357 (1939), 365 (1940), 356 (1942), 357 (1947), 343 (1948), 348 (1953), 343 (1955), 348 (1957). There is some confusion about distances because the left field foul line and grandstand wall were the same near the corner between the 343 and 357 markers. *Left-Center:* 365 (1932), 351 (1948); *Deep Left-Center at Bend in Wall:* 407 (1932), 393 (1948), 395 (1954); *Center Field:* 450 (1914), 466 (1930), 460.79 (early 1931), 447 (late 1931), 399.42 (1932), 399 (1936), 402 (1938), 400 (1939), 399 (1947), 384 (1948), 393 (1955); *Right Side of Center Field Grandstand:* 390 (1932), 376 (1948); *Right-Center's Deepest Corner:* 500 (1913), 476.75 (1926), 415 (1932), 403 (1948), 405 (1950), 403 (1955); *Right Side of Right-Center Field Exit Gate:* 399 (1932); *Right-Center:* 352; *Scoreboard:* left side 344, right side 318; *Right Field:* 301 (1913), 300 (1914), 296.17 (1921), 292 (1922), 301 (1926), 296.08 (1930), 295.92 (1931), 296.5 (1934), 297 (1938); *Backstop:* 64 (1942), 70.5 (1954), 72 (1957)
FENCES *Left Field to Left-Center:* 20 (1913), 3 (wood 1920), 9.87 (concrete 1931); *Center Field:* 20 (1913), 393 marker: 9.87 (concrete 1931) sloping upward; 376 marker: 15 (concrete 1931); *Right-Center:* 9 (concrete 1913), from 376 point to screen: 15 sloping upward to 19, then down to 13; *Right-Center to Right Field:* 38 (top 19 screen, bottom 19 concave concrete wall, bent at 9.5 mid-point, vertical top half, concave angled bottom half); *Screen in Center Field:* 20 (screen above sloping concrete 1920s); *Right Field Before the Screen:* 9 (concrete 1913)
FORMER USE The Pigtown garbage dump

Ebbets Field

CURRENT USE Scoreboard clock now sits on top of right field scoreboard at McCormick Field, Asheville, North Carolina. Ebbets Field Apartments housing development built in 1963 and the I.S. 320 Intermediate School is across the road. Apartments renamed Jackie Robinson Apartments at Ebbets Field in 1972; renamed Ebbets Field Apartments in mid-1970s. Jackie Robinson School, previously known as Crown Heights, houses the Brooklyn Dodger Hall of Fame.
PHENOMENA
• Rotunda was 80-foot circle enclosed in Italian marble with floor tiled with stitches of a baseball, a chandelier with 12 baseball-bat arms holding 12 globes shaped like baseballs. There were 12 turnstiles and 12 gilded ticket windows. The domed ceiling was 27 feet high at its center.
• Little kids watched the game through a gap under the metal gate in right-center.
• Cobblestoned Bedford Avenue was a hill, climbing from a low point in right field to higher ground in center field.
• Right field wall and scoreboard had approximately 289 different angles—the scoreboard jutted out 5 feet from the wall at a 45-degree angle. Overhang of the center field second deck hung out over the field. Scoreboard built after 1930.
• Schaefer Beer sign on the top of the right-center scoreboard notified fans of official scorer's decision—the "H" in Schaefer lit up for a hit, an "E" for an error—the sign was erected after World War II.
• Abe Stark sign offered a free suit at 1514 Pitkin Avenue to any batter hitting the 3-foot-by-30-foot sign.
• Opened on April 5, 1913 for an exhibition game vs. the Yankees; it was discovered that the flag, a press box, and the keys to the bleachers had been forgotten. A press box was finally added in 1929.
• In the winter of 1931-32, the double deck was extended

from 3rd base to the left field corner and across to center field.

• According to Roger Kahn, the park was "a narrow cockpit of iron and concrete along a steep cobblestone slope."

• In the winter of 1937-38, box seats were added in center field.

• In the winter of 1947-48, more seats were added to left and center.

• Demolition began on February 23, 1960. Same wrecking ball used 4 years later to demolish Polo Grounds. Eight light towers were moved to Downing Stadium on Randall's Island.

• George Cutshaw of Dodgers hit groundball home run in 1916 which bounced crazily up the concave wall in right and over the fence, to the amazement of Phillies rightfielder Gavvy Cravath.

LOS ANGELES, CALIFORNIA

LOS ANGELES MEMORIAL COLISEUM
STYLE   Summer Olympics Stadium
A.K.A.   O'Malley's Chinese Theatre, O'Malley's Alley
OCCUPANT   NL Dodgers April 18, 1958 to September 20, 1961
EVENT   All Star Game 1959
LOCATION   *Left Field (N)* Exposition Boulevard and museums; *3rd Base (W)* Merlo Avenue and Los Angeles Olympic Swimming Stadium; *1st Base (S)* Santa Barbara Avenue, now Martin Luther King, Jr. Drive; *Right Field (E)* 3911 South Figueroa Street and Los Angeles Memorial Sports Arena

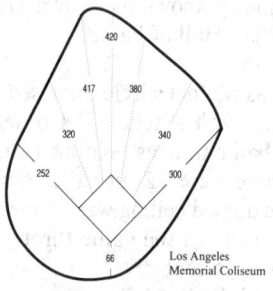

Los Angeles
Memorial Coliseum

DIMENSIONS   *Left Field:* 250 (1958), 251.6 (1959); *Left-Center:* 320 at end of screen rectangle; *Left-Center Where Fence Met Wall:* 425 (1958), 417 (1959); *Center Field:* 425 (1958), 420 (1959); *Right-Center:* 440 (1958), 375 (1959), 394 (1960), 380 (1961); *Right Field Where Fence Met Wall:* 390 (1958), 333 (1959), 340 (1960); *Right Field:* 301 (1958), 300 (1959); *Back-stop:* 60 (1958), 66 (1959); *Foul Territory:* Large; tremendous area on 3rd base line, but almost none on 1st base line
FENCES   *Left Field:* 40 (screen 1958), 42 (screen 1959); 60 (2 support towers for screen 1958); *Left Center:* 40 (fence (1958); from foul pole 140 feet into left center, 42 sloping to ground at 30 degree angle from 320 mark to 348 mark for a distance of 24 feet (1959 to 1960); 4 steps down from 42 to 8: 1st step left corner 42 sloping to 41, 2nd step 31, 3rd step 20, 4th step 12 (1961); *Right of Screen in Left-Center:* 8 (wire); *Center Field to Right Field Corner:* 6 (wire); *Right Field Corner:* 4 (concrete)

FORMER USE   Agriculture Park in 1890s—fairs, livestock shows, amusement park booths, horse-racing track and barns, saloons. Exposition Park—armory, museum, gardens from 1908 to 1921 along with gravel pit
PHENOMENA
• Wall in left-center jutted out twice, going from chest to thigh level, jutting out to ankle level, jutting out to thigh level, then back again to chest level.

• Concrete wall in the right field corner was the wall surrounding the football field. It sloped sharply away, creating a Fenway-like belly, and allowing a situation where a long drive near the right field foul line would be an out but a short fly down the line would be a home run.

• Huge tunnel behind home plate.

• First used for baseball by USC Trojans, who worked out here before the Dodgers opened the 1958 season.

• O'Malley considered using the Rose Bowl in Pasadena for the first years after the move from Brooklyn and before the Dodgers' Stadium opened. It would have been laid out differently from the Coliseum. Ten rows would have been removed in right and left to deepen the foul lines to 300 feet, and center field would have been 460. The field would have been symmetrical, because home plate would have been in one endzone and center field in the other endzone. Box seats were to have been added behind the plate and between 1st and 3rd.

• The 42-foot screen in left placed to prevent 251 foot popups from becoming homers.

• Commissioner Ford Frick attempted to order the Dodgers to construct a second screen in left, in the seats at 333 feet. A ball clearing both screens would be a home run, but a ball clearing just the shorter screen would be a double. The California Earthquake Law made construction of such a screen illegal.

• 79 rows of seats.

• 700 feet to furthest seats under peristylum.

• Two stones are on exhibit under the peristylum atop the bleachers in right-center at one end of the oval—the one on the left from Altis, Olympia, Greece, and the one on the right from the Colosseum, Rome, Italy.

• Rim of stadium 110 feet above ground level, field 33 feet below ground level.

• Cable and towers and wires above screen in play.

• Small green light pole in field of play in right field.

• 74,000 seats built from 1921 to 1923, expanded to 105,000 seats for the 1932 Olympic games.

• The right-center fence was shortened in 1959 after 182 homers were hit to left but only 3 to center and 8 to right. In 1959, there were 132 homers to left, 1 to center, 39 to right. In 1960, 155 to left, 3 to center, 28 to right. In 1961, 147 to left, 7 to center, 38 to right.

CHICAGO, ILLINOIS

COMISKEY PARK
STYLE   Major League Classic
A.K.A.   White Sox Park (II) 1910 to 1912, Charles A. Comiskey's Baseball Palace 1910, White Sox Park(III) May 1962 to 1975
OCCUPANT   AL White Sox July 1, 1910 through September 30, 1990; NL Cubs 1918 World Series; NAL American Giants 1941 to 1950

EVENT All Negro League East-West All Star games, 1933 to 1950; Negro League World Series, eighth through tenth games, 1926; third game, 1943; fifth game, 1946; fourth game, 1947

LOCATION *Left Field (N)* West 34th; *3rd Base (W)* Portland Avenue, later called South Shield's Avenue; *1st Base (S)* 324 West 35th Street; *Right Field (E)* South Wentworth Avenue, later Dan Ryan Expressway/I-94

SURFACE *Outfield:* Grass; *Infield:* Grass (1910), Carpet (1969), Grass (1976)

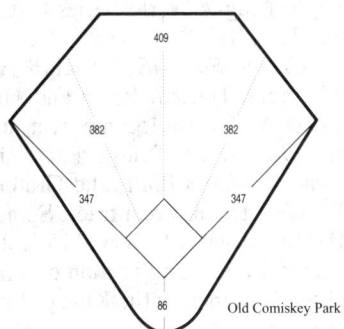

Old Comiskey Park

DIMENSIONS *Foul Lines:* 363 (1910), 362 (1911), 365 (1927), 362 (1930), 342 (1934), 353 (1935), 340 (1936), 352 (1937), 332 (April 22, 1949), 352 (May 5, 1949), 335 (1969), 352 (marked 1971), 349 (actual 1971), 341 (1983), 347 (1986); *Power Alleys:* 382 (1910), 375 (1927), 370 (1934), 382 (1942), 362 (April 22, 1949), 375 (May 5, 1949), 382 (1954), 365 (1955), 375 (1956), 365 (1959), 375 (1968), 370 (1969), 375 (marked 1971), 382 (actual 1971), 374 (1983), 382 (1986); *Center Field:* 420 (1910), 450 (1926), 455 (1927), 450 (1930), 436 (1934), 422 (1936), 440 (1937), 420 (April 22, 1949), 415 (May 5, 1949), 410 (1951), 415 (1952), 400 (1969), 440 (1976), 445 (1977), 402 (marked 1981), 409 (actual 1981), 401 (1983), 409 (1986); *Backstop:* 98 (1910), 71 (1933), 85 (1934), 86 (1955); *Foul Territory:* Large

FENCES *Foul Lines and Power Alleys:* 12 (concrete 1955), 9.83 (concrete 1959), 5 (wire 1969), 9.83 (concrete 1971); *Center Field:* 15 (1927), 30 (1948), 17 (1976), 18 (1980); *Left-Center to Right-Center Inner Fences:* 5 (canvas 1949), 6.5 (24-foot section in front of bullpens 1969), 9 (1974), 7 (canvas 1981), 7.5 (1982), 11 (1984), 7.5 (1986)

FORMER USE A truck garden owned by Signor Scavado, and/or a city dump. South Side Park (II) was almost on the same site, across Wentworth Avenue.

PHENOMENA
• Foul lines were old water hoses, painted white and squished flat.
• In 1910, there were bleachers in left and right, but not in center.
• In the winter of 1926-27, wooden bleachers were replaced with concrete and steel, and the pavilions from left around home plate to right were doubledecked. The scoreboard was moved from right center to two locations on the left field and right field walls.
• Center field bleachers were eliminated in 1947 to improve batter's visibility.
• Section of grandstand collapsed May 17, 1913.
• Special elevator for Lou Comiskey, in use from 1931 to 1982, had an inlaid tile floor.

• In 1950 the bullpens were moved from foul territory down the lines to behind the center field fence.
• In 1960 Bill Veeck installed the first exploding scoreboard in the majors, high above the bleachers in center. In 1982, when the Diamond Vision Board replaced the original, the pinwheels were retained.
• Green cornerstone laid on St. Patrick's Day in 1910 stayed green until 1960 when the exterior was painted all white by Bill Veeck.
• Scene of many masterful groundskeeping tricks by Roger, Gene, and Emil Bossard: (a) Camp Swampy in 1967 referred to the area in front of the plate, dug up and soaked with water when White Sox sinkerball pitchers were on the mound, but mixed with clay and gasoline and burned to provide hard soil if a sinkerballer was pitching for the visiting team. (b) Opposing team bullpen mounds were lowered or raised from the standard 10-inch height to upset visiting pitchers' rhythm. (c) Under Eddie Stanky's managerial tenure, the grass in front of shortstop was cut long because the Sox shortstop had limited range, but at second the grass was cut short because the Sox second sacker had very good range. (d) When the Sox had a lousy defensive outfield, the grass was cut long to turn triples into doubles. (e) When the Sox had speedy line drive hitters, the outfield grass was cut long to turn singles into doubles. (f) When the Sox had good bunters, more paint was added to the foul line in order to tilt the ball back fair.
• Nine speaker horns on the center field bleacher wall.
• Clock on wall in center to left of flag pole.
• Picnic areas, including Bullring in left and Bullpens I and II in right and right-center, Bavarian and Mexican restaurants and beer halls under the stands behind the plate.
• Showers in the bleachers in center.
• Foul poles bend back slightly to join the top of the roof.
• 540 center field listing in 1931-33 *Baseball Guides* is a misprint.
• Organist Nancy Faust played "Na-na-na-na, hey-hey, Good bye."
• Open arches between first and second decks.

CINCINNATI, OHIO

CROSLEY FIELD

STYLE Major League Classic
A.K.A. Redland Field 1912 to 1933

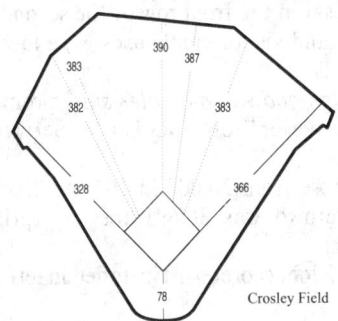

Crosley Field

OCCUPANT NL Cincinnati Reds April 11, 1912 to June 24, 1970; NAL Tigers 1937; NAL Clowns 1942 to 1945

EVENT All Star Games 1938, 1953

LOCATION *Left Field* (N) York Street; *3rd Base* (W) McLean Avenue; *1st Base* (S) Findlay Street; *Center Field* (NE) Western Avenue

DIMENSIONS *Left field:* 360 (1912), 320 (321), 352 (1926), 339 (1927), 328 (1938); *Scoreboard in Left Center* 380383 feet left to right; *Center Field:* 420 (1912), 417 (1926), 395 (1927), 393 (1930), 407 (1931), 393 (1933), 407 (1936), 387 (1938), 380 (1939), 387 (1940), 390 (1944), 387 (1955); *Right Center Field:* 383 (1955); *Deepest Corner:* 387 (1944); *Right Field:* 360 (1912), 384 (1921), 400 (1926), 383 (early 1927), 377 (late 1927), 366 (1938), 366 (1938), 342 (1942), 366 (June 30, 1950), 342 (1953), 366 (1958); *Backstop* 38 (1912), 58 (1927), 66 (1943), 78 (1953)

FENCES *Center Field* Canvas shield above fence to protect against street light glare (1935 to June 7, 1940); *Left Field* 18 (1938), 12 (1957), 14 (1962), 18 (1963); *Clock on top of the Scoreboard* 58 (1957), 45 (1967); *Left Center to Right Center* 18 (1954), 14 (1962), 13.5 (1963), 23 (9.5 plywood over 13.5 concrete 1965); *Right Field 7.5 (4.5 wire above 3 concrete 1938), 7.5 (4.5 wire above 3 wood 1942), 10 (7 wire above 3 wood 1949), 12 (9 wire above 3 concrete (June 30, 1950), 10 (7 wire above 3 wood 1953), 10 (7 wire above 3 concrete 1958), 9 (6 wire above 3 concrete 1959); Flagpole in left center 82, in play*

FORMER USE Brickyard, League Park (1884-1901), Palace of the Fans (1902-1911)

CURRENT USE Reconstructed on farm near Union, Kentucky (a replica has also been constructed at Blue Ash, Ohio). Site used for an industrial park.

PHENOMENA

• Designed by Harry Hake; built at cost of $225,000.

• In the 1920s rented out for movies and dancing, leading to complaints of "immoral dancing" and "vulgar conduct between boys and girls in unlighted portions of the grandstand."

• Steep incline in front of the fence all around the outfield; a pratfall on it by Babe Ruth on May 28, 1935 helped speed his retirement.

• Renamed for Reds owner Powel Crosley, manufacturer of radios, refrigerators and autos.

• Scene of first major league night game (vs. Phillies) on May 24, 1935.

• In January 1937 the Mill Creek flooded, covering the playing field with twenty-one feet of water. Pitcher Lee Grissom and Reds traveling secretary John McDonald rowed a boat over the center field fence.

• Pressbox was not erected until 1938. Prior to that sportswriters sat in the front row of the second deck.

• Both home and visitor clubhouses were located behind left field stands.

• *"Hit this sign and win a Siebler suit"* prominently displayed on Superior Towel & Linen Service Building across street.

• Capacity rose from 20,000 in 1912 to 29,488 in 1970 (yet largest crowd was 36,691 for an April 27, 1947 doubleheader).

• A 65 × 50.2 foot scoreboard installed in left center field in 1957.

NEW YORK, NEW YORK

POLO GROUNDS (IV)

STYLE Major League Classic

A.K.A. Brush Stadium 1911 to 1919, Coogan's Bluff, Coogan's Hollow, Matty Schwab's House, Harlem Meadow

OCCUPANT NL Giants June 28, 1911 to September 29, 1957; AL Yankees May 30, 1912 (morning game); April 17, 1913 to October 8, 1922; NL Mets April 13, 1962 to September 18, 1962

EVENT Negro League World Series first game, 1946; All Star Game 1934, 1942

LOCATION *Center Field (SE)* Eighth Avenue, then IRT elevated tracks, Harlem River and Harlem River Drive; *3rd Base (NE)* West 159th Street and IRT Rail Yards; *Home Plate (NW)* Bridge Park, then Harlem River Speedway, Coogan's Bluff, and Croton Aqueduct; *1st Base (SW)* West 157th Street trace; Same site as Polo Grounds (III); In Coogan's Hollow, 115 feet below Coogan's Bluff, the last remaining portion of a farm granted to Mr. John Lion Gardiner by the King of England in the seventeenth century

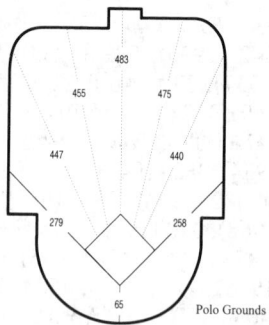

Polo Grounds

DIMENSIONS *Left Field:* 277 (1911), 286.67 (1921), 279.67 (1923), 279 (1930), 280 (1943), 279 (1955); *Left Field, Second Deck:* 250; *Left Center, Left of Bullpen:* 447; *Left-Center, Right of Bullpen:* 455; *Front Clubhouse Steps:* 460; *Center Field:* 433 (1911), 483 (1923), 484.75 (1927), 505 (1930), 430 (1931), 480 (1934), 430 (1938), 505 (1940), 490 (1943), 505 (1944), 480 (1945), 490 (1946), 484 (1947), 505 (1949), 483 (1952), 480 (1953), 483 (1954), 480 (1955), 475 (1962), 483 (1963); *Bleacher Corners:* 475; *Right-Center, Left of Bullpen:* 449; *Right-Center, Right of Bullpen:* 440; *Right Field:* 256.25 (1921), 257.67 (1923), 257.5 (1931), 257.67 (1942), 259 (1943), 257.67 (1944); *Right Field Photographers Perch:* 249; *Backstop:* 65 (1942), 70 (1943), 65 (1944), 70 (1946), 74 (1949), 65 (1954), 74 (1955), 65 (1962); *Foul Territory:* Very large. There's a lot of confusion here. During the Giants' stay it was 483 to the front of the clubhouse, and probably 505 to the rear clubhouse wall above the overhang. Why the 483 marker sometimes was changed to 480 or 475, is not known but it could have been due to remeasurements or a slight shift of home plate's location. Or it could have been a measurement to the base of the Eddie Grant Memorial. In the Giants' time, reading from left to right, the markers read 315, 360, 414, 447, 455, 483, 455, 449, 395, 338, 294. In the Mets' time, they read 306, 405, 475, 405, 281. The foul lines were never marked. One possibility is that it was 433

feet to the front of the bleachers, 475 to the beginning of the clubhouse overhang, 483 to the rear wall under the overhang, and 505 to the front of the high wall. The 21-foot overhang of the second deck in left reduced the distance to the second deck from 279 to 250, not 258, because of the angle involved.

FENCES—1911-22 *Left to Center:* 10 (concrete); *Center:* 20 (tarp); *Right-Center:* 10 (concrete); *Right Field:* 12 sloping to 11 at pole (concrete)

FENCES—1923-63 *Left Field:* 16.81 (concrete); *Left-Center:* 18 (concrete); *Where Left-Center Wall Ended at Bleachers:* 12 (concrete); *Center Field Bleachers Wall:* 8.5 (4.25 wire on top of 4.25 concrete) on both sides of clubhouse runway; *Center Field Hitters' Background:* 16.5 on both sides of clubhouse runway; *Center Field Clubhouse:* 60 high and 60 wide—50 high in 1963; *Center Field Top of Longines Clock:* 80; *Center Field Top of Right Side of Scoreboard:* 71; *Center Field Top of Left Side of Scoreboard:* 68; *Center Field Top of Middle of Scoreboard:* 64; *Center Field Top of 5 Right Scoreboard Windows:* 57; *Center Field Top of 4 Left Scoreboard Windows:* 55; *Center Field Bottom of 5 Right Scoreboard Windows:* 53; *Center Field Bottom of 4 Left Scoreboard Windows:* 48; *Center Field Bottom of Clubhouse Scoreboard:* 31; *Center Field Top of Rear Clubhouse Wall:* 28; *Center Field Top of Front Clubhouse Wall:* 19; *Center Field Top of 14 Lower Clubhouse Windows:* 16; *Center Field Bottom of 14 Lower Clubhouse Windows:* 11; *Center Field Clubhouse floor Overhang:* 8; *Center Field Top of Eddie Grant Memorial:* 5; *Center Field Width of Little Office on Top of Lower Clubhouse:* 10; *Right Center:* 12 (concrete); *Right Field:* 10.64 (concrete)

FORMER USE Underneath the Harlem River until filled in with dirt in the late 1870s.

CURRENT USE Polo Grounds Towers—four 30-story apartment buildings. Willie Mays Field—an asphalt playground with 6 basketball backboards where center field used to be, a brass historical marker in place.

PHENOMENA

• Originally named for owner John T. Brush.

• Second deck in right had 9-foot photographer's perch overhang 60 feet from foul pole out into right-center.

• Bullpens in fair territory in left-center and right-center.

• There was no line on the 60-foot-high center field clubhouse above which a ball would be a home run.

• The outfield was slightly sunken. A manager, standing in his dugout, could see only the top half of his outfielders. At the wall, the field was 8 feet below the infield.

• The left field second deck overhang meant that a homer to left was easier than a homer to right, even though the wall in left was 279 and the wall in right was 258. The overhang was 21 feet, but it effectively shortened the distance required for a pop-fly homer to the second deck in left to 250 feet because of the angle involved.

• The overhangs here and at Tiger Stadium and Shibe Park have more significance than one might suspect, according to research published by the professional society for physicists, the American Physical Society. The batted ball's trajectory consists of two component vectors, horizontal and vertical. The vertical deceleration is constant over time due to gravity, but the horizontal deceleration increases over time due to wind resistance and atmospheric drag. Near the end of its flight, the ball is coming down sharply, rather than arcing down as it arched up, as would occur in a vacuum. So many outfielders have watched helplessly as a ball they could catch dropped into the 2nd deck.

• Hitter's background extended beyond the end of the bleacher wall, several feet into the clubhouse gap.

• The field sloped in a "turtle back" just beyond the infield dirt. It sloped down 1.5 feet to drains about 20 feet into the outfield, then back up again.

• Right-center wall sloped gradually from 11 feet at pole to 12 feet at the bleachers.

• Left-center wall sloped from 16 feet 9.75 inches at the pole to 18 feet in left center, then abruptly fell to 16 feet and then to 14 feet and sloped gradually to 12 feet at the bleachers. When ad signs were removed in the 1940s, the abrupt changes in height in left-center disappeared.

• After the all-wooden Polo Grounds (III) burned down April 14, 1911, Polo Grounds (IV) was built with temporary stands for 1911. The infield stands were rebuilt with concrete for 1912, and the outfield concrete double deck was finished in 1922. The bleachers in left-center and center were wood remaining from before the fire.

• In 1914, there were 2 bends in the wall in right-center.

• In 1917, the fans exited from the field through gates under the center field bleachers.

• Morris James Mansion sat up on Coogan's Bluff, overlooking the ballpark.

• Brush Stairway led down from Coogan's Bluff to the Speedway and the ticket booths behind home plate.

• Coats of arms of all the teams in the National League on the top of the grandstand. Removed in the 1920s.

• Dedicated on May 30, 1921, to a former Giant killed in World War I, the Eddie Grant Memorial stood in center at the base of the clubhouse wall. It was 5 feet high. The Memorial reads:

In Memory of
Capt. Edward Leslie Grant
307th Infantry - 77th Division
A.E.F.
Soldier - Scholar - Athlete
Killed in action
Argonne Forest
October 5, 1918
Philadelphia Nationals
1907-1908-1909-1910
Cincinnati Reds
1911-1912-1913
New York Giants
1913-1914-1915
Erected by friends in Baseball,
Journalism, and the Service.

• In the winter of 1922-23, the concrete double decks were extended all the way to either side of the new concrete bleachers in center, housing the clubhouse. Unfortunately, the Roman Colosseum facade frescoes were removed during that winter also.

• Bleachers in center remodeled in 1923.

• In 1929, the first attempt was made to wire the umpires for sound and reconnect them into the PA system. It didn't work too well.

• Speaker placed above Grant Memorial in 1931.

• Field raised 4½ feet in 1949 to help with drainage. In

1609 and 1874 maps, the location is shown to be underneath the Harlem River. The water table was only 2-6 feet below the playing surface, and drainage was complicated by rainwater cascading off the 115-foot-high Coogan's Bluff down onto the site.

• During the 1950s, groundskeeper Matty Schwab and his family lived in an apartment under Section 3 of the left field stands built for him by Horace Stoneham. The apartment was the main bait in Mr. Stoneham's successful offer to grab Mr. Schwab away from the hated Dodgers in 1950.

• A two-foot-square section of sod from center field was removed and taken to San Francisco in the fall of 1957.

• Home plate was moved out toward center several feet by the Mets in the winter of 1961-62.

• During the Mets' stay in 1962 and 1963, Johnny McCarthy and his crew of groundskeepers painted Schwab's four rooms pink, installed a shower and plywood on the floor and lockers, and called it their Pink Room.

• In 1962 and 1963, the Howard Clothes sign on the outfield wall promised a boat to any player hitting it.

• Demolition started on April 10, 1964, with same wrecking ball that demolished Ebbets Field.

PHILADELPHIA, PENNSYLVANIA

BAKER BOWL

STYLE   Major League Classic
A.K.A.   Huntingdon Street Baseball Grounds 1895 to July 1913, National League Park (III) 1895 to 1938, Hump, Cigar Box, Band Box, Philadelphia Park

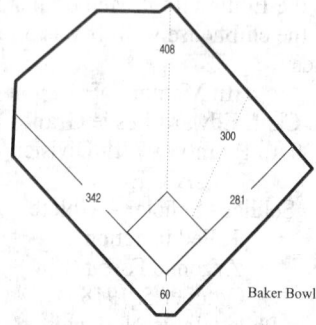

Baker Bowl

OCCUPANT   NL Phillies April 14, 1904 to May 14, 1927; NL Phillies June 24, 1927 to June 20, 1938; also neutral use by NL Cleveland versus Baltimore July 29, July 30, and August 11, 1898; and versus Washington August 5, 6, and 8, 1898
EVENT   Negro League World Series first and second games 1924, fifth and sixth games 1925, fourth and fifth games 1926
LOCATION   *Left Field (N)* West Lehigh Avenue; *3rd Base (W)* North 15th Street; *1st Base (S)* West Huntingdon Street; *Right Field (E)* North Broad Street; *Beneath* Philadelphia and Reading Railroad tracks in a tunnel
DIMENSIONS   *Left Field:* 335 (1921), 341.5 (1926), 341 (1930), 341.5 (1931); *Center Field:* 408; *Right-Center:* 300; *Right Field:* 272 (1921), 279.5 (1924), 280.5 (1925); *Backstop:* 60
FENCES   *Left Field:* 4 (1895), 12 July (1929); *Left-Center Field Clubhouse to Right-Center:* 35 (1895), 47

(with 12 screen on top 1915); *Right Field:* 40 (tin over brick 1895), 60 (40 tin over brick, topped by 20 screen 1915)
CURRENT USE   Parking lot and car wash in right-center, gas station in center, bus garage from home down right field foul line
PHENOMENA
• Named after Phillie owner William F. Baker.
• Named the Hump because it was on an elevated piece of ground that had a railroad tunnel underneath the outfield.
• Swimming pool in the basement of the center field clubhouse prior to World War I.
• Coke and "Health Soap Stops B.O." Lifebuoy signs on the high right field wall.
• Extra seats added in front of the fence in center for the 1915 World Series led directly to the Phillies losing the Series' last game.
• During Prohibition, the outfield wall liquor ads were boarded over with dirty grimy blank boards.
• Home plate moved back a foot in 1925, making the right field foul pole 280.5 rather than 279.5.
• Torn down in 1950.

SHIBE PARK

STYLE   Major League Classic
A.K.A.   Connie Mack Stadium 1953 to 1970
OCCUPANT   AL Athletics April 12, 1909 to September 19, 1954; NL Phillies May 16 to May 28, 1927; NL Phillies July 4, 1938 to October 1, 1970
EVENT   Negro League World Series fifth game 1942; fourth game 1945; third game 1947; All Star Game 1943, 1952
LOCATION   *Left Field (N)* West Somerset Street; *3rd Base (W)* North 21st Street; *1st Base (S)* West Lehigh Avenue; *Right Field (E)* North 20th Street
DIMENSIONS   *Left Field:* 360 (1909), 378 (late 1909), 380 (1921), 334 (1922), 312 (1926), 334 (1930); *Center:* 515 (1909), 502 (late 1909), 468 (1922), 448 (1950), 440 (1951), 460 (1953), 468 (1954), 447 (1956), 410 (1969); *Right Center:* 393 (1909), 390 (1969); *Right Center, Left of Scoreboard:* 400 (1942); *Right Field:* 360 (1909), 340 (late 1909), 380 (1921), 307 (1926), 331 (1931), 331 (to lower 1934), 329 (to upper iron fence 1934); *Backstop:* 90 (1942), 86 (1943), 78 (1956), 64 (1960)

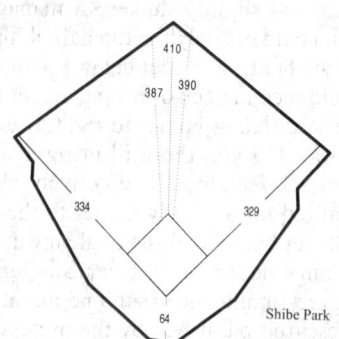

Shibe Park

FENCES   *Left Field to Left Center:* 12 (4 screen above 8 concrete 1949); *Center Field, Small Section:* 20 (1955), 8 (wood 1956), 3 (canvas 1969); *Right-Center Scoreboard:* 50 (top of black scoreboard 1956), 60 (top of

Ballantine Beer sign 1956); *Right Field:* 12 (concrete 1909), 34 (22 corrugated iron above 12 concrete 1935), 30 (1943), 50 (1949), 40 (1953), 30 (1954), 40 (1955), 32 (1956)

FORMER USE   City dog pound, also a brickyard in the Swampoodle neighborhood nearby

CURRENT USE   Vacant site. Several hundred of the seats are being used now in Duncan Park, home of the Sally League Phillies in Spartanburg, South Carolina, and in War Memorial Stadium, Greensboro, North Carolina

PHENOMENA

• The first concrete and steel stadium in the majors.

• Named for Ben Shibe, an A's stockholder and baseball manufacturer.

• French Renaissance churchlike dome on exterior roof behind the plate which housed Connie Mack's office.

• Sod transplanted here from Columbia Park.

• Highest pitcher's mound—20 inches high.

• Batting cage sat behind short fence in center when the measurement was only 447.

• Corrugated iron fence in right—balls bounced at crazy angles off it—top 22 feet of 34-foot fence—2-foot-deep frame—was 329 to front of frame, 231 to rear of frame where iron sheets were.

• Conduit on right field wall was in play.

• Slopes in front of the outfield fences in early years.

• Ladder in front of left field scoreboard, 1909—went all the way to the top.

• Doubledecked in 1925; also in that year left field stands added.

• Mezzanine added in 1929.

• Right field wall reinforcement in 1934 reduced distance to front of the frame from 331 to 329, but sign wasn't changed until 1956.

• Before 1935, 20th Street residents could sit in their front bedroom or on their roof and see the game free over the 12-foot right-field fence. Fans could see the lines of laundry on the roof of 20th Street houses. Connie Mack lost a suit to prevent this, so he built the high right-field fence.

• 1948 plans to add 18,000 seats in right field and reduce foul line to 315 feet never materialized.

• In 1956, the old Yankee Stadium scoreboard was installed in front of the right-center wall; later a clock was added—balls hitting the clock were homers—top of clock was 75 feet high; top of Ballantine Beer sign, 60 feet high.

• In 1956 the normal screen was replaced by see-through plexiglass—protected the fans behind the plate from foul balls.

• Home plate moved to Veterans Stadium in 1971.

• Fire damaged it on August 20, 1971.

• Last game on October 1, 1970.

• Torn down in June 1976.

PITTSBURGH, PENNSYLVANIA

FORBES FIELD

STYLE   Major League Classic

A.K.A.   Oakland Orchard, Dreyfuss' Folly

OCCUPANT   NL Pirates June 30, 1909 to June 28, 1970; NNL Grays 1939 to 1948

EVENT   Negro League World Series second game 1942; fourth and fifth games 1944; second game in 1945; All Star Game 1944, 1959

LOCATION   *Left Field (NE)* Schenley Park, then Bigelow Boulevard; *3rd Base (NW)* Sennott (also spelled "Sonnett" at times) Street, then Cathedral of Learning; *1st Base (SW)* Boquet (also spelled "Bouquet" at times) Street; *Right Field (SE)* Joncaire Street, Pierre Ravine, Junction Hollow, Junction Railroad tracks

DIMENSIONS   *Left Field:* 360 (1909), 356.5 (1921), 356 (1922), 360 (1926), 365 (1930), 335 (1947), 365 (1954); *Deepest Corner, Left of Straightaway Center, at the Flag Pole:* 462 (1909), 457 (1930); *Center Field:* 442 (1926), 435 (1930); *Right-Center, Right Side of Exit Gate:* 416 (1955); *Right-Center:* 375 (1942); *Bend at Left End of Screen:* 375; *Right Field:* 376 (1909), 376.5 (1921), 376 (1922), 300 (1925); *Backstop:* 110 (1909), 84 (1938), 80 (1947), 84 (1953), 75 (1959)

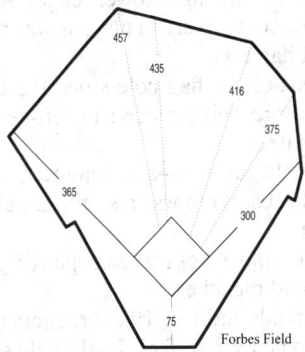

Forbes Field

FENCES   *Left Field Front Fence:* 8 (5 screen above 3 wood 1947), 12 (9 screen on top of 3 wood 1949), 14 (screen 1950); *Left Field Wall:* 12 (1909), 12 (brick and ivy 1946); *Left Field Scoreboard:* 25.42 (steel left and right sides), 27 (middle); *Wooden Marine Sergeant at Parade Rest to Right of Scoreboard:* 32 (June 26, 1943 to end of season); *Side Wall Angling Back to Meet Brick Wall in Left-Center:* 12 (wood, when front fence was up); *Cages Around Light Tower Just Right of Scoreboard and in Power Alleys:* 16.5; *Center Field:* 12 (wood 1909), 12 (brick and ivy 1946); *Right-Center:* 9.5 (concrete 1925); *Screen—Left Side at 375 Mark:* 24 (14.5 wire above 9.5 concrete 1932); *Screen—Right Side at Flag Pole:* 27.67 (18.17 wire above 9.5 concrete 1932)

FORMER USE   Part of Schenley Farms, a hothouse and livery stable. Land for grazing cows. Ravine where right field would be. Football site for University of Pennsylvania vs. Carnegie Tech October 31, 1908, game. Penn won on the rocky field.

CURRENT USE   Mervis Hall, out in right field, and the University of Pittsburgh's Forbes Quadrangle in the infield. The center field and right-center brick walls still stand, along with the base of the flag pole. Mazeroski Field, a Little League diamond beyond the left field brick wall, still remains. Roberto Clemente Drive now bisects the site, and runs about 10 feet under what used to be the playing surface of the infield.

PHENOMENA

• 1st base by a misspelled street: Boquet Street was named for General Henry Bouquet, a Swiss soldier who fought for the British in the French and Indian War's decisive battle at Fort Duquesne.

• Named for General John Forbes, a British general in the French and Indian War who captured Fort Duquesne and renamed it Fort Pitt in 1758.

• Ivy-covered brick wall in left and left-center.

• The 14-foot Longines clock with speaker horns on top of the left field scoreboard were out of play—a drive hitting it was a home run.

• Fans in the upper left corner of the left field bleachers could not see the plate because of the third base grandstand, which stood between them and the plate. Right field roof was 86 feet high.

• During World War II, the right field screen could not be replaced due to the priority given to the war effort. It deteriorated badly.

• No no-hitter was ever pitched here.

• Home plate remains in almost its exact original location, only now it is encased in glass on the first-floor walkway of the University of Pittsburgh's Forbes Quadrangle.

• The bottoms of the light-tower cages in left-center, center, and right-center were in play, as was the bottom of the center field flag pole.

• Just to the left of the flag pole stood the batting cage, also in play. Before being placed in left-center, it stood behind home plate.

• Very hard infield surface—ask Tony Kubek!

• Back in the 1910s, there was a small scoreboard on the center field wall.

• In 1920s, cars and trucks were repaired and sold beneath the left field bleachers.

• Right field stands built in 1925, reducing distance to right field foul pole by 76.5 feet. Right field screen added in 1932. It was taken down for a short period once, then put back up.

• Barney Dreyfuss Monument was just to the left of the exit gate in right-center where fans exited the ballpark into Schenley Park after a game. It was installed on June 30, 1934, on the park's 25th anniversary, and was made of granite with a bronze tablet.

• Greenberg Gardens, also called Kiner's Korner: the area between the scoreboard and a chicken coop wire short fence in left put there to increase home run production from 1947 to 1953—called Greenberg Gardens 1947, Kiner's Korner 1948 to 1953.

• When Greenberg Gardens were in place, a Western Union clock stood on top of the scoreboard, to the right of the familiar Gruen Clock. Torn down in 1972 and 1973.

• In 1938, with the Buccos apparently on their way to the World Series, they built a third deck of seats behind the plate called the Crow's Nest, which had the major leagues' first elevator. Bucs finally made the Series 22 years later.

• During World War II, from June 26 through the end of the 1943 season, a huge U.S. Marine made of wood stood against the left field wall, just to the right of the scoreboard. Standing at parade rest, the Marine sergeant was 32 feet high, 15 feet wide across his feet, and in play.

• Honus Wagner statue in Schenley Park erected 1955—18 feet high, 1,800 pounds—moved to Three Rivers with Bucs in 1970.

• A plaque today marks the spot where Bill Mazeroski's World Series-winning homer left the park in 1960 and flew into the trees above Yogi Berra's head.

• Green foam rubber crash pads placed on concrete wall in right and right-center, first in majors. Wooden walls

installed in left and center in 1909, replaced with brick and ivy in 1946.

• Street deadending into Sennott Street by 3rd base was called at various times Pennant Place and Forbes Field Avenue.

• Fires damaged park December 24, 1970, and July 17, 1971. Destruction began July 28, 1971.

• Site now occupied by Deliverance Evangelistic Church.

ST. LOUIS, MISSOURI

SPORTSMAN'S PARK (IV)

STYLE Major League Classic

A.K.A. Busch Stadium (I) 1953 to 1966, Bill Veeck's House

OCCUPANT AL Browns April 14, 1909 to September 27, 1953; NL Cardinals July 1, 1920 to May 8, 1966; NAL New Orleans–St. Louis Stars one game 1941

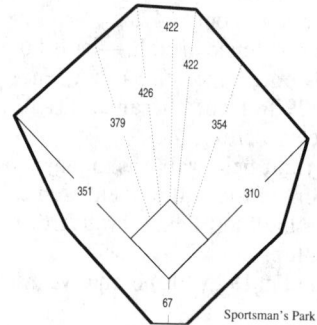

Sportsman's Park

EVENT All Star Game 1940, 1948, 1957

LOCATION *Left Field (NE)* Sullivan Avenue; *3rd Base (NW)* North Spring Avenue; *1st Base (SW)* 3623 Dodier Street; *Right Field (SE)* 2911 North Grand Avenue, later North Grand Boulevard. Same as earlier Sportsman's Parks, but turned around so that home plate was in the west-southwest corner

DIMENSIONS *Left Field:* 368 (1909), 340 (1921), 356 (1923), 355 (1926), 360 (1930), 351.1 (1931); *Left Center:* 379; *Center Field:* 430 (1926), 450 (1930), 445 (1931), 420 (1938), 422 (1939); *Deepest Corner Just Left of Dead Center:* 426 (1938); *Deepest Corner Just Right of Dead Center:* 422 (1938); *Right Center:* 354 (1942); *Right Field:* 335 (1909), 315 (1921), 320 (1926), 310 (1931), 332 (1938), 309.5 (1939); *Backstop:* 75 (1942), 67 (1953)

FENCES *Left to Center*: 11.5 (concrete); *354 Mark in Right-Center to Right*: 11.5 (1909), 33 (11.5 concrete below 21.5 wire July 5, 1929), 11.5 (1955), 36.67 (11.5 concrete below 25.17 wire 1956)

CURRENT USE Herbert Hoover Boys' Club, with a baseball diamond where the major league one used to be

PHENOMENA

• The local newspaper, the *Globe-Democrat*, had an ad on the right-center wall which showed the star of the previous game. Just to the right of this ad, the league standings for both leagues were listed.

• The Busch eagle would flap its wings after a Cardinal home run. It sat on top of the left-center scoreboard. During World War II, there was a War Chest sign there.

• Cards office was at 3623 Dodier, Browns office was at 2911 North Grand.

- Pavilion seats in the power alley in right center.
- Second deck from first to third added in 1909.
- Second deck expanded to foul poles in 1925.
- Bleachers were added to parts of outfield in 1926.
- Beginning in the 1940s, the outfield signs were 351, 358, 379, 400, 426, 425, 422, 422, 405, 354, 322, and 310. In the mid 1950s, the 426 and the right 422 signs that marked the corners just left and right of straightaway center were removed.
- Flag pole in fair territory until removed in the 1950s.
- Bill Veeck's family lived in an apartment under the stands in the 1950s.
- When he bought the stadium from the Browns in 1953, Card owner Gussie Busch almost named it Budweiser Stadium, but was prevented by league pressure.
- The wire screen in front of the right field pavilion was removed for the entire 1955 season. It had been installed on July 5, 1929.
- A helicopter carried home plate to Busch Memorial Stadium after the last game on May 8, 1966.
- The old 1902–8 grandstand behind home plate became the left field pavilion in this park from 1909 to 1925 when it was replaced.

SAN FRANCISCO, CALIFORNIA

SEALS STADIUM
STYLE Minor League
A.K.A. Home Plate Mine
OCCUPANT NL Giants April 15, 1958 to September 20, 1959

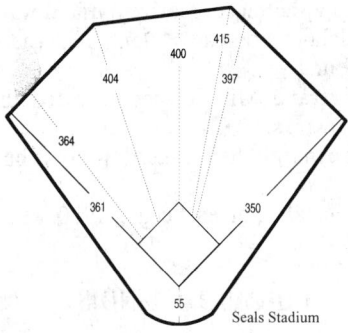
Seals Stadium

LOCATION *Left Field (E)* Potrero Avenue; *3rd Base (N)* Alameda Street; *1st Base (W)* Bryant Street; *Right Field (S)* 16th Street and Franklin Square Park
DIMENSIONS *Left Field:* 365 (1958), 361 (1959); *Left Center:* 375 (1958), 364 (1959); *Just Left of Straightaway Center in the Corner:* 404; *Center Field:* 410 (1958), 400 (1959); *Just Right of Straightaway Center in the Corner:* 415; *Just Right of the 415 Mark Where the Seats Jutted Out:* 397; *Right Field:* 355 (1958), 350 (1959); *Back Stop:* 55.42
FENCES *Left Field:* 15 (5 concrete below 10 wire); *Center Field Scoreboard:* 30.5; *Right Field:* 16 (5 concrete below 11 wire)
CURRENT USE San Francisco Auto Center
PHENOMENA
- Opened April 7, 1931.
- The original deed for the land under the park was listed as "Home Plate Mine."

- No warning track.
- Wind blew from right to left.
- Nearby Hamms Brewery still standing.

WASHINGTON, D.C.

GRIFFITH STADIUM
STYLE Major League Classic
A.K.A. National Park (III) 1911 to 1921, Clark Griffith Park 1922

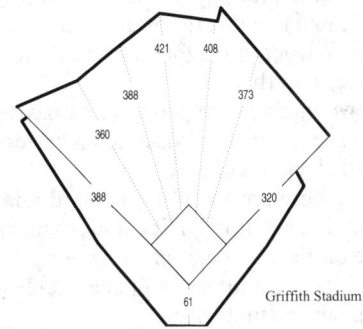
Griffith Stadium

OCCUPANT AL Senators (I) April 12, 1911 to October 2, 1960; ECL Potomacs 1924; NEWL Pilots 1932; NNL Elite Giants 1936 to 1937; NNL Washington-Homestead Grays half of their home games 1937 to 1948; NNL Black Senators 1938; AL Senators (II) April 10 to September 21, 1961; Negro League World Series first game 1942, first and second games 1943; third game 1945
EVENT All Star Game 1937, 1956
LOCATION *Left Field (E)* Larch Street, later Fifth Street NW; *3rd Base (N)* Howard University, then W Street NW; *1st Base (W)* J. Frank Kelley Lumber and Mill Works, then Georgia Avenue NW, also called Seventh Street NW; *Right Field (S)* Spruce Street, later U Street NW
DIMENSIONS *Left Field:* 407 (1911), 424 (1921), 358 (1926), 407 (1931), 402 (1936), 405 (1942), 375 (Opening Day 1947), 405 (remainder 1947), 402 (1948), 386 (1950), 408 (1951), 405 (1952), 388 (1954), 386 (1956), 350 (1957), 388 (1961); *Left of Left-Center at Corner:* 383 (1931), 366 (1954), 360 (1956); *Right of Left-Center at Bend in Bleachers: 409 (1942), 398 (1954), 383 (1955), 380 (1956); Left- Center:* 391 (1911), 380 (1950); *Center Field:* 421; *Center Field Corner to Left of Building Protection Wall:* 423 (1926), 441 (1930), 422 (1931), 426 (1936), 420 (1942), 426 (1948), 420 (1950), 394 (1951), 420 (1952) 421 (1953), 426 (1954), 421 (1955), 426 (1961); *Inner Tip of Building Protection Wall:* 409 (1943), 408 (1953); *Deepest Corner—Right End of Building Protection Wall; Right Center:* 378 (1954), 372 (1955), 373 (1956); *Right Field:* 328 (1909), 326 (1921), 328 (marked 1926), 320 (actual 1926), 320 (1956); *Back-stop:* 61
FENCES *Left Field:* 11.25 (foul pole to 408 mark concrete 1953), 12 (from 410 corner near left field foul pole to 408 mark just right of dead center 1954), 8 to 10 (wood in the corner in front of the bullpen at the foul pole 1955), 6.5 (wire and plywood in front of bullpen 1956); *Center Field:* 30 (concrete 408 mark to 457 mark 1953), 31 (concrete 408 mark to 457 mark 1954), 6 (wire and plywood 1956); *Right-Center:* to the left of the scoreboard in

front of the bullpen: 4 (wood from 457 mark to 435 mark 1953), 10 (wood 1955), 4 (wood 1959); *Right Center Scoreboard:* 41 (1946); *National Bohemian Beer Bottle:* 56 (1946); *Right Field:* 30 (concrete 1953), 31 (concrete 1954)

CURRENT USE Howard University Medical Center and Howard University College of Dentistry, 909 seats now in use at Tinker Field in Orlando, Florida

PHENOMENA

• Loudspeaker horn high on the wall in center.

• The center field wall detoured around 5 houses and a huge tree in center, jutting into the field of play.

• Right field foul line was the grandstand wall for the last 15 or so feet in front of the foul pole, so there was no way to catch a foul ball there.

• It was downhill from the plate to first base, supposedly to help save a step for slow Washington batters.

• Right field clock out of play.

• Ball rolling between top of scoreboard and bottom of the clock was in play: if it didn't come out, it was a homer; if it did, the outfielder could throw it back into play.

• U.S. presidents traditionally opened each season here by throwing out the first ball.

• Memorials honoring Walter Johnson and Clark Griffith stood outside the main entrance to the first base grandstand. The former now stands at Walter Johnson High School in Bethesda, Maryland; the latter at RFK Stadium.

• Height of National Bohemian Beer Bottle, above right-center scoreboard, approximately 50 feet.

• Park rebuilt after March 17, 1911 fire; completed on July 24, 1911.

• Doubledecked in 1920 from the bases down to the foul poles with a roof higher than the original second deck roof behind the plate.

• Temporary seats placed in front of left field bleachers for the 1924 World Series.

• In 1954, the visitor's bullpen was enclosed behind a screen fence in the left field corner in fair territory.

• Clark Calvin Griffith Memorial, dedicated by Vice President Nixon on August 8, 1956, was later moved to R.F.K. Stadium.

• In 1956, all the distances to the outfield fences were remeasured, and it was discovered that right field had lost 8 feet over the years!

• Also in 1956, 10 rows of temporary seats were added in front of the left field bleacher section.

• Park demolished from January 26 to August 14, 1965.

Negro League and Auxilliary Major League Baseball Sites

ATLANTA, GEORGIA

PONCE DE LEON PARK

STYLE Minor League
A.K.A. Spiller Park 1924 to 1932, Poncey
OCCUPANT NSL Black Crackers 1932; NAL Black Crackers 1938
LOCATION *Left Field (N)* Parking lot; *3rd Base (W)* North Boulevard; *1st Base (S)* 650 Ponce de Leon Boulevard; *Right Field (E) Southern Railroad tracks*

DIMENSIONS *Left Field:* 365 (1932), 330 (1949); *Left-Center, Left Side of Scoreboard:* 525; *Center Field:* 462 (1932), 448 (1938), 410 (1949); *Right Field:* 321 (1932), 324 (1938)
FENCES *Left Field:*2 (hedge, April 1949), 4 (cyclone fence, May 1949); *Left-Center:* 25 (scoreboard); *Center Field:* 6; *Right-Center:* Magnolia Tree halfway up very steep embankment, no fence; *Right Field:* 15
CURRENT USE Parking lot opposite Sears department store since being torn down in 1967
PHENOMENA

• First Ponce de Leon Park, built in 1907, burned down September 9, 1923.

• A 2-foot-high hedge formed the outfield fence from the left field line to the right side of the left-center scoreboard in 1949. It reduced the foul line from 365 to 330 and caused numerous arguments because a left fielder had to stay within the hedge. If he fell over it, the hit was a homer.

BROOKLYN, NEW YORK

DEXTER PARK

STYLE Negro League
A.K.A. Sterling Oval
OCCUPANT ECL Royal Giants 1923 to 1927
LOCATION Woodhaven, Long Island *Left (N)* Simpson Street, now called Park Lane South; *3rd Base (NW)* Cypress Hills Cemetery; *1st Base (W)* Elderta Lane and 75th Street; *Center Field (E)* Lott Avenue, now called 76th Street
PHENOMENA

• Had probably the most creative outfield wall billboard ever. An optician's ad read: "Don't Kill the Umpire— Maybe It's Your Eyes."

• Owners Max and Milt Rosner operated the semipro Brooklyn Bushwicks.

• Huge incline in right field caused by horse buried under the grass.

• First lights installed on east coast, 1930.

CHICAGO, ILLINOIS

SOUTH SIDE PARK (III)

STYLE Cricket Ground
A.K.A. 39th Street Grounds (II), White Stocking Park (III) 1901 to 1903, Chicago Cricket Club, White Sox Park (I) 1904 to 1910, American Giants Field 1911 to 1940, Schorling's Park 1920 to 1940
OCCUPANT AL White Sox April 24, 1901 to June 27, 1910; NNL Giants 1920; NNL American Giants 1920 to 1931, 1933 to 1935; NSL American Giants 1932; NAL American Giants 1937 to 1940; Neutral site use by NNL Cleveland Tigers 1928, by NNL Kansas City Monarchs in 1920s, by NNL Cuban Stars West in 1920s
LOCATION *Left Field (N) West 38th Street; 3rd Base (W)* South Princeton Avenue; *1st Base (S)* West 39th Street, now West Pershing Road; *Right Field (E)* Wentworth Avenue
DIMENSIONS *Left Field:* 355; *Left Center:* 400; *Center Field:* 450

FORMER USE Home of Wanderers cricket team

CURRENT USE Housing project three blocks from Comiskey Park

PHENOMENA
- Opened in 1900.
- Overhanging roof added in 1902.
- Fence cut back sharply around J. F. Kidwell Greenhouse buildings in right center, making right-center relatively short compared to center and right.
- Used as a dog racing track during the summer of 1933, forcing the NNL American Giants to move all their home games from May 28 through the end of the 1933 season to Indianapolis.
- Burned down Christmas Day 1940.

EAST ORANGE, NEW JERSEY

GROVE STREET OVAL

STYLE Negro League

A.K.A. Grove Street Senior Ball Diamond, Monte Irvin Field, East Orange Oval

OCCUPANT NNL Cubans 1940 to 1948; NAL Cubans 1949 to 1950; also neutral site used by NNL Newark Bears 1936 to 1948

LOCATION East Orange, New Jersey *Left Field (E)* Greenwood Avenue; *3rd Base (N)* Grove Place; *1st Base (W)* Grove Street North; *Right Field (S)* Eaton Place;

DIMENSIONS *Left Field:* 240; *Center Field:* 360 to the water fountain; *Right Field:* 280

FENCES *Left Field:* 25 (garage walls); *Center Field:* 4 (water fountain); *Right Field:* None

CURRENT USE Still used as a community ball diamond

PHENOMENA
- No fence in center field where there were some hedges.
- Water fountain in play in deepest center field.
- Trees in right, as well as tennis courts beyond.
- Scoreboard in left, as well as poplar trees.
- Clubhouse down right field line in foul territory.
- "Bujum" Jud Wilson hit longest ball ever hit over water fountain in center.
- Property purchased by city in October 1907 and park dedicated Labor Day 1908 in a game between the New Jersey State Senate and the New Jersey State General Assembly.
- Fire destroyed the first grandstand at 4 AM, May 3, 1925; new grandstand dedicated May 1, 1926.
- Renamed Monte Irvin Field at June 6, 1986 ceremony in culmination of 4 years effort initiated by this author and the SABR Negro Leagues Committee, who designed the plaque marking the site.

JERSEY CITY, NEW JERSEY

ROOSEVELT STADIUM

STYLE Minor League

OCCUPANT NL Dodgers for seven 1956 games and eight 1957 games from April 19, 1956 to September 3, 1957; some NNL New York Black Yankees games in 1940s

LOCATION *Left Field (NE)* Hackensack River; *3rd Base (NW)* Newark Bay; *1st Base (SW)* Danforth Avenue; *Right Field (SE)* State Highway 440; at Droyers Point

DIMENSIONS *Foul lines:* 330; *Power Alleys:* 397; *Center Field:* 411; *Backstop:* 60

FENCES *Foul Line Corners:* 11; *Left Field to Center Field:* 4; *Right-Center to Right Field:* 7

FORMER USE A landfill for dirt excavated from Holland Tunnel

PHENOMENA
- Built as a WPA project in 1937 and named for FDR.
- Newark Bay mist brought mosquitoes and mist into the outfield.
- Thanksgiving morning football games between St. Peter's and Dickinson were always sold out in the 1940s.
- Torn down in 1984.

NASHVILLE, TENNESSEE

SULPHUR DELL (II)

STYLE Minor League

A.K.A. Sulphur Springs Bottom, Sulphur Dell Park, Athletic Park, Dump, Suffer Hell

OCCUPANT NNL Elite Giants 1933 to 1934

LOCATION *Left Field (N)* Jackson Street; *3rd Base (W)* Summer Street, later 900 Fifth Avenue North; *1st Base (S)* Tennessee Central Railroad tracks; *Right Field (E)* Cherry Street, later Fourth Avenue North

DIMENSIONS *Left Field:* 334; *Center Field:* 421; *Right Field:* 262 (235 when fans sat behind ropes on the bank)

FENCES *All Around:* 16 (wood 1927); *Left and Center:* 16 (wood 1931); *Right Field:* 38.5 to 46 (16 wood below 22.5 to 30 screen to a point 186 feet from the right field foul line)

PHENOMENA
- Only one-quarter mile from the Cumberland River, the park was often flooded.
- Nicknamed "the Dump" in honor of the exceptional fragrance that drifted over from the nearby smoldering city dump and lent a unique character to Sulphur Dell hot dogs!
- Sulphur Dell had the craziest right field in history. Right fielders were called mountain goats because they had to go up and down the irregular hills in right-center and right. The incline in right rose 25 feet, beginning gradually behind first, then rising sharply at a 45-degree angle, then leveling off at a 10-foot-wide shelf one-third of the way up the incline, and then continuing at a 45-degree angle to the fence.
- Fielders used to play on the shelf, 235 feet from the plate. When overflow crowds were attracted to a game, a rope was extended in front of the shelf, and fans sat on the upper two thirds of the incline, reducing right field to 235 rather than 262.
- The stands were very close to the pancake-shaped diamond. First base was 42 feet from the seats; third base was 26 feet from the seats.
- Embankments began in left at 301 and in right at 224.
- Casey Stengel once joked that he hit a bunt home run down the 1st base line.

NEW YORK, NEW YORK

DYCKMAN OVAL

STYLE Negro League
OCCUPANT NNL Cuban Stars 1922; ECL Cuban Stars East 1923 to 1928; ECL Bachrach Giants many games 1923 to 1928; NAL Cuban Stars East 1929; NNL Cuban House of David 1931; NEWL Cuban Stars 1932
LOCATION *Left Field (NE)* West 204th Street; *3rd Base (NW)* Nagle Avenue; *1st Base (SW)* Academy Street; *Right Field (SE)* Tenth Avenue. In Upper Manhattan, 8 blocks east of the Henry Hudson Parkway, 5 blocks east of Inwood Hill Park, south of the Harlem Ship Canal, 4 blocks north of Dyckman Street, in Dyckman section
PHENOMENA
• The first major league park in New York to have lights for evening games. They were installed in 1930 by Cuban Stars owner Alex Pompez.

CAPITAL TEXTURE

STYLE Negro League
OCCUPANT ECL Lincoln Giants 1928; NAL Lincoln Giants 1929
LOCATION *(N)* East 138th Street; *(W)* Fifth Avenue; *(S)* East 135th Street; *(E)* Madison Avenue
CURRENT USE Riverton Apartments

CATHOLIC PROTECTORY OVAL

STYLE Amateur
OCCUPANT ECL Lincoln Giants 1923 to 1926; NNL Cubans 1935 to 1936
LOCATION *Left Field (E)* Hoguet Avenue; *3rd Base (N)* East Tremont Avenue; *1st Base (W)* White Plains Road; *Right Field (S)* McGraw Avenue. Bronx, 5 miles northeast of Yankee Stadium
CURRENT USE Parkchester Apartments, built by the Metropolitan Life Insurance Company—Unionport Road now crosses the site from home plate to center field; Metropolitan Avenue now runs from right field in to second base and then curves out to left field.
PHENOMENA
• The Protectory was a Catholic home and school for impoverished boys whose 50-piece marching band was much in demand. One of the students, Hank Greenberg, is now in the Hall of Fame.
• No grass in the infield.
• Leveled in 1939 so that Parkchester Apartments could be built.

TRIBOROUGH STADIUM

STYLE Football Stadium
A.K.A. Randall's Island Stadium, J. J. Downing Memorial Stadium
OCCUPANT NNL Black Yankees 1938
LOCATION *(N)* Bronx Kills and Harlem River, Eastern Parkway and Triborough Bridge; *(W)* House of Refuge, Vesta Avenue; *(S)* Little Hell Gate, East River, and Ward's Island, Sutter Avenue; *(E)* Sunken Meadow, Powell Street, Triborough Bridge
CURRENT USE Still standing, was used for WFL Stars football games in 1974 and NASL Cosmos soccer games in 1975

PHENOMENA
• A U-shaped stadium, open at the southwest end.
• Eight Ebbets Field light towers were moved here in 1939 when Ebbets had new lights installed.

PATERSON, NEW JERSEY

HINCHCLIFFE STADIUM

STYLE Football Stadium
OCCUPANT NNL Black Yankees 1936 to 1937, 1939 to 1945
LOCATION Paterson, New Jersey *Center Field (SE)* Passaic River; *3rd Base (NE)* Redwood Avenue; *Home Plate (NW)* Liberty Street; *1st Base (SW)* Maple Street
CURRENT USE Community baseball, still standing, opened 1932

PHILADELPHIA, PENNSYLVANIA

HILLDALE PARK

STYLE High School
A.K.A. Darby Catholic School Stadium
OCCUPANT ECL Hilldales 1923 to 1927; NAL Hilldales 1929; NEWL Hilldales 1932
LOCATION Yeadon, Pennsylvania *Left Field (N)* Bunting Lane, later MacDade Boulevard; *3rd Base (W)* Greenhouses and Cedar Avenue; *1st Base (S)* Chester Avenue; *Right Field (E)* Yeadon School In the suburbs of Philadelphia at a Catholic school on the Darby-Yeadon borderline
DIMENSIONS *Left Field:* 315; *Right Center:* 400; *Right Field:* 370
CURRENT USE Acme Super Saver supermarket and drive-in bank
PHENOMENA
• A huge tree sat beyond the fence in right-center; branches hung over the fence and were in play.

PITTSBURGH, PENNSYLVANIA

GUS GREENLEE FIELD

STYLE Negro League
OCCUPANT NEWL Grays 1932; NEWL Crawfords 1932; NNL Grays 1933, 1935 to 1938; NNL Crawfords 1933 to 1938
LOCATION In the Hill District *Left Field (N)* Ridgeway Street; *3rd Base (W)* Junilla Street; *1st Base (S)* 2500 Bedford Avenue; *Right Field (E)* Municipal Hospital and Francis Street
FORMER USE Entress Brick Company factory
CURRENT USE Pittsburgh Housing Authority projects
PHENOMENA
• Opened on April 29, 1932.
• Tin fence in outfield.
• Left field foul line was longer than at Forbes Field, where it was 365.
• The structure was torn down on December 10, 1938.

## CHAPTER 5

Major League Attendance

Robert L. Tiemann and Pete Palmer

If you have the patience to sift through them, the figures on the following pages, dating from 1890 through 1992, tell a remarkable story. Season attendance has exceeded 4 million in Toronto in 1991 and 1992, and it has been as little as 6,088 in Cleveland in 1899, when the awful Spiders went 20–134. The first club to pass the million mark was the New York Yankees of 1920, featuring a newcomer named Ruth and a ballpark borrowed from the Giants (who did not reach the mark themselves until 1945). In the depths of the Depression, the St. Louis Browns posted annual attendance figures (80,922 in 1935; 88,113 in 1933) below what a weekend set produces in many major-league venues.

Why did attendance stagnate in the 1890s? How much did the entry of the American League into National League strongholds New York, Chicago, Philadelphia, and St. Louis hurt the senior franchises? Were the Dodgers justified in leaving Brooklyn? How did baseball survive in Washington as long as it did, surpassing the million mark only once from 1892 to 1971? Has anyone noticed that Atlanta's attendance of 1990 doubled, and then tripled, over the next two years?

You get the picture. There's stuff here that permits you to chart trends in baseball that you already know about, and if you are eagle-eyed you may pick up an anomalous figure that prompts you to rethink what you thought you knew.

A researcher's goldmine, the tables that follow tell an interesting story for the average fan as well. Does winning a pennant correlate with higher attendance? Are first-division teams more profitable than those in the second division? What is the impact on attendance of a new stadium?

By the time the next edition rolls around we may be able to gather figures going back to the dawn of professional baseball. Here are some scattered tidbits:

• In their first year of existence, 1871, the Boston Red Stockings counted 32,600 fans in 18 home games.
• In 1882, the last year of its existence as an NL franchise, the Troy Haymakers drew a whopping 26,000 attendees for its 42 home games, with one late season date posting a recorded crowd of 12 (that's not a typo).
• The 1891 American Association, in its final year of operation, counted 1,296,000 fans, or an average of 162,000 per team, a figure very comparable to the 166,600 of the National League. In 1892, with the AA gone and the NL a twelve-team circuit, the average team attendance was less than 152,000. Is there a lesson to be drawn from this?

Yes, and the lesson is plain for magnates no less than for fans and students of the game.

	1890	1891	1892	1893	1894	1895	1896	1897	1898	1899
NATIONAL LEAGUE										
BAL			93,589	143,000	328,000	293,000	249,448	273,046	123,416	121,935
BOS	147,539	184,472	146,421	193,300	152,800	242,000	240,000	334,800	229,275	200,384
BRO	121,412	181,477	183,727	235,000	214,000	230,000	201,000	220,831	122,514	269,641
CHI	102,536	181,431	109,067	223,500	239,000	382,300	317,500	327,160	424,352	352,130
CIN	131,980	97,500	196,473	194,250	158,000	281,000	373,000	336,800	336,378	259,536
CLE	47,478	132,000	139,928	130,000	82,000	143,000	152,000	115,250	70,496	6,088
LOU			131,159	53,683	75,000	92,000	133,000	145,210	128,980	109,319
NY	60,667	210,568	130,566	290,000	387,000	240,000	274,000	390,340	265,414	121,384
PHI	148,366	217,282	193,731	293,019	352,773	474,971	357,025	290,027	265,414	388,933
PIT	16,064	128,000	177,205	184,000	159,000	188,000	197,000	165,950	150,900	251,834
STL			192,442	195,000	155,000	170,000	184,000	136,400	151,700	373,909
WAS			128,279	90,000	125,000	153,000	223,000	151,028	103,250	86,392
TOT	776,042	1,332,730	1,822,587	2,224,752	2,427,573	2,889,271	2,900,973	2,886,842	2,372,089	2,541,485
ML	776,042	1,332,730	1,822,587	2,224,752	2,427,573	2,889,271	2,900,973	2,886,842	2,372,089	2,541,485

	1900	1901	1902	1903	1904	1905	1906	1907	1908	1909
AMERICAN LEAGUE										
BAL		141,952	174,606							
BOS		289,448	348,567	379,338	623,295	468,828	410,209	436,777	473,048	668,965
CHI		354,350	337,898	286,183	557,123	687,419	585,202	666,307	636,096	478,400
CLE		131,380	275,395	311,280	264,749	316,306	325,733	382,046	422,262	354,627
DET		259,430	189,469	224,523	177,796	193,384	174,043	297,079	436,199	490,490
MIL		139,034								
NY				211,808	438,919	309,100	434,700	350,020	305,500	501,000
PHI		206,329	420,078	422,473	512,294	554,576	489,129	625,581	455,062	674,915
STL			272,283	380,405	318,108	339,112	389,157	419,025	618,947	366,274
WAS		161,661	188,158	128,878	131,744	252,027	129,903	221,929	264,252	205,199
TOT	0	1,683,584	2,206,454	2,344,888	3,024,028	3,120,752	2,938,076	3,398,764	3,611,366	3,739,870
NATIONAL LEAGUE										
BOS	202,000	146,502	116,960	143,155	140,694	150,003	143,280	203,221	253,750	195,188
BRO	183,000	198,200	199,868	224,670	214,600	227,924	277,400	312,500	275,600	321,300
CHI	248,577	205,071	263,700	386,205	439,100	509,900	654,300	422,550	665,325	633,480
CIN	170,000	205,728	217,300	351,680	391,915	313,927	330,056	317,500	399,200	424,643
NY	190,000	297,650	302,875	579,530	609,826	552,700	402,850	538,350	910,000	783,700
PHI	301,913	234,937	112,066	151,729	140,771	317,932	294,680	341,216	420,660	303,177
PIT	264,000	251,955	243,826	326,855	340,615	369,124	394,877	319,506	382,444	534,950
STL	270,000	379,988	226,417	226,538	386,750	292,800	283,770	185,377	205,129	299,982
TOT	1,829,490	1,920,031	1,683,012	2,390,362	2,664,271	2,734,310	2,781,213	2,640,220	3,512,108	3,496,420
ML	1,829,490	3,603,615	3,889,466	4,735,250	5,688,299	5,855,062	5,719,289	6,038,984	7,123,474	7,236,290

	1910	1911	1912	1913	1914	1915	1916	1917	1918	1919
AMERICAN LEAGUE										
BOS	584,619	503,961	597,096	437,194	481,359	539,885	496,397	387,856	249,513	417,291
CHI	552,084	583,208	602,241	644,501	469,290	539,461	679,923	684,521	195,081	627,186
CLE	293,456	406,296	336,844	541,000	185,997	159,285	492,106	477,298	295,515	538,135
DET	391,288	484,988	402,870	398,502	416,225	476,105	616,772	457,289	203,719	643,805
NY	355,857	302,444	242,194	357,551	359,477	256,035	469,211	330,294	282,047	619,164
PHI	588,905	605,749	517,653	571,896	346,641	146,223	184,471	221,432	177,926	225,209
STL	249,889	207,984	214,070	250,330	244,714	150,358	335,740	210,486	122,076	349,350
WAS	254,591	244,884	350,663	325,831	243,888	167,332	177,265	89,682	182,122	234,096
TOT	3,270,689	3,339,514	3,263,631	3,526,805	2,747,591	2,434,684	3,451,885	2,858,858	1,707,999	3,654,236
NATIONAL LEAGUE										
BOS	149,027	116,000	121,000	208,000	382,913	376,283	313,495	174,253	84,938	167,401
BRO	279,321	269,000	243,000	347,000	122,671	297,766	447,747	221,619	83,831	360,721
CHI	526,152	576,000	514,000	419,000	202,516	217,058	453,685	360,218	337,256	424,430
CIN	380,622	300,000	344,000	258,000	100,791	218,878	255,846	269,056	163,009	532,501
NY	511,785	675,000	638,000	630,000	364,313	391,850	552,056	500,264	256,618	708,857
PHI	296,597	416,000	250,000	470,000	138,474	449,898	515,365	354,428	122,266	240,424
PIT	436,586	432,000	384,000	296,000	139,620	225,743	289,132	192,807	213,610	276,810
STL	355,668	447,768	241,759	203,531	256,099	252,666	224,308	288,491	110,599	167,059
TOT	2,935,758	3,231,768	2,735,759	2,831,531	1,707,397	2,430,142	3,051,634	2,361,136	1,372,127	2,878,203
ML	6,206,447	6,571,282	5,999,390	6,358,336	4,454,988	4,864,826	6,503,519	5,219,994	3,080,126	6,532,439

	1920	1921	1922	1923	1924	1925	1926	1927	1928	1929
AMERICAN LEAGUE										
BOS	402,445	279,273	259,184	229,688	448,556	267,782	285,155	305,275	396,920	394,620
CHI	833,492	543,650	602,860	573,778	606,658	832,231	710,339	614,423	494,152	426,795
CLE	912,832	748,705	528,145	558,856	481,905	419,005	627,426	373,138	375,907	536,210
DET	579,650	661,527	861,206	911,377	1,015,136	820,766	711,914	773,716	474,323	869,318
NY	1,289,422	1,230,696	1,026,134	1,007,066	1,053,533	697,267	1,027,675	1,164,015	1,072,132	960,148
PHI	287,888	344,430	425,356	534,122	531,992	869,703	714,508	605,529	689,756	839,176
STL	419,311	355,978	712,918	430,296	533,349	462,898	283,986	247,879	339,497	280,697
WAS	359,260	456,069	458,552	357,406	584,310	817,199	551,580	528,976	378,501	355,506
TOT	5,084,300	4,620,328	4,874,355	4,602,589	5,255,439	5,186,851	4,912,583	4,612,951	4,221,188	4,662,470

	1920	1921	1922	1923	1924	1925	1926	1927	1928	1929
NATIONAL LEAGUE										
BOS	162,483	318,627	167,965	227,802	177,478	313,528	303,598	288,685	227,001	372,351
BRO	808,722	613,245	498,865	564,666	818,883	659,435	650,819	637,230	664,863	731,886
CHI	480,783	410,107	542,283	703,705	716,922	622,610	885,063	1,159,168	1,143,740	1,485,166
CIN	568,107	311,227	493,754	575,063	473,707	464,920	672,987	442,164	490,490	295,040
NY	929,609	973,477	945,809	820,780	844,068	778,993	700,362	858,190	916,191	868,806
PHI	330,998	273,961	232,471	228,168	299,818	304,905	240,600	305,420	182,168	281,200
PIT	429,037	701,567	523,675	611,082	736,883	804,354	798,542	869,720	495,070	491,377
STL	326,836	384,773	536,998	338,551	272,885	404,959	668,428	749,340	761,574	399,887
TOT	4,036,575	3,986,984	3,941,820	4,069,817	4,340,644	4,353,704	4,920,399	5,309,917	4,881,097	4,925,713
ML	9,120,875	8,607,312	8,816,175	8,672,406	9,596,083	9,540,555	9,832,982	9,922,868	9,102,285	9,588,183

	1930	1931	1932	1933	1934	1935	1936	1937	1938	1939
AMERICAN LEAGUE										
BOS	444,045	350,975	182,150	268,715	610,640	558,568	626,895	559,659	646,459	573,070
CHI	406,123	403,550	233,198	397,789	236,559	470,281	440,810	589,245	338,278	594,104
CLE	528,657	483,027	468,953	387,936	391,338	397,615	500,391	564,849	652,006	563,926
DET	649,450	434,056	397,157	320,972	919,161	1,034,929	875,948	1,072,276	799,557	836,279
NY	1,169,230	912,437	962,320	728,014	854,682	657,508	976,913	998,148	970,916	859,785
PHI	721,663	627,464	405,500	297,138	305,847	233,173	285,173	430,738	385,357	395,022
STL	152,088	179,126	112,558	88,113	115,305	80,922	93,267	123,121	130,417	109,159
WAS	614,474	492,657	371,396	437,533	330,074	255,011	379,525	397,799	522,694	339,257
TOT	4,685,730	3,883,292	3,133,232	2,926,210	3,763,606	3,688,007	4,178,922	4,735,835	4,445,684	4,270,602
NATIONAL LEAGUE										
BOS	464,835	515,005	507,606	517,803	303,205	232,754	340,585	385,339	341,149	285,994
BRO	1,097,329	753,133	681,827	526,815	434,188	470,517	489,618	482,481	663,087	955,668
CHI	1,463,624	1,086,422	974,688	594,112	707,525	692,604	699,370	895,020	951,640	726,663
CIN	386,727	263,316	356,950	218,281	206,773	448,247	466,345	411,221	706,756	981,443
NY	868,714	812,163	484,868	604,471	730,851	748,748	837,952	926,887	799,633	702,457
PHI	299,007	284,849	268,914	156,421	169,885	205,470	249,219	212,790	166,111	277,973
PIT	357,795	260,392	287,262	288,747	322,622	352,885	372,524	459,679	641,033	376,734
STL	508,501	608,535	279,219	256,171	325,056	506,084	448,078	430,811	291,418	400,245
TOT	5,446,532	4,583,815	3,841,334	3,162,821	3,200,105	3,657,309	3,903,691	4,204,228	4,560,827	4,707,177
ML	10,132,262	8,467,107	6,974,566	6,089,031	6,963,711	7,345,316	8,082,613	8,940,063	9,006,511	8,977,779

	1940	1941	1942	1943	1944	1945	1946	1947	1948	1949
AMERICAN LEAGUE										
BOS	716,234	718,497	730,340	358,275	506,975	603,794	1,416,944	1,427,315	1,558,798	1,596,650
CHI	660,336	677,077	425,734	508,962	563,539	657,981	983,403	876,948	777,844	937,151
CLE	902,576	745,948	459,447	438,894	475,272	558,182	1,057,289	1,521,978	2,620,627	2,233,771
DET	1,112,693	684,915	580,087	606,287	923,176	1,280,341	1,722,590	1,398,093	1,743,035	1,821,204
NY	988,975	964,722	922,011	618,330	789,995	881,845	2,265,512	2,178,937	2,373,901	2,283,676
PHI	432,145	528,894	423,487	376,735	505,322	462,631	621,793	911,566	945,076	816,514
STL	239,591	176,240	255,617	214,392	508,644	482,986	526,435	320,474	335,564	270,936
WAS	381,241	415,663	403,493	574,694	525,235	652,660	1,027,216	850,758	795,254	770,745
TOT	5,433,791	4,911,956	4,200,216	3,696,569	4,798,158	5,580,420	9,621,182	9,486,069	11,150,099	10,730,647
NATIONAL LEAGUE										
BOS	241,616	263,680	285,332	271,289	208,691	374,178	969,673	1,277,361	1,455,439	1,081,795
BRO	975,978	1,214,910	1,037,765	661,739	605,905	1,059,220	1,796,824	1,807,526	1,398,967	1,633,747
CHI	534,878	545,159	590,972	508,247	640,110	1,036,386	1,342,970	1,364,039	1,237,792	1,143,139
CIN	850,180	643,513	427,031	379,122	409,567	290,070	715,751	899,975	823,386	707,782
NY	747,852	763,098	779,621	466,095	674,483	1,016,468	1,219,873	1,600,793	1,459,269	1,218,446
PHI	207,177	231,401	230,183	466,975	369,586	285,057	1,045,247	907,332	767,429	819,698
PIT	507,934	482,241	448,897	498,740	604,278	604,694	749,962	1,283,531	1,517,021	1,449,435
STL	324,078	633,645	553,552	517,135	461,968	594,630	1,061,807	1,247,913	1,111,440	1,430,676
TOT	4,389,693	4,777,647	4,353,353	3,769,342	3,974,588	5,260,703	8,902,107	10,388,470	9,770,743	9,484,718
ML	9,823,484	9,689,603	8,553,569	7,465,911	8,772,746	10,841,123	18,523,289	19,874,539	20,920,842	20,215,365

	1950	1951	1952	1953	1954	1955	1956	1957	1958	1959
AMERICAN LEAGUE										
BAL					1,060,910	852,039	901,201	1,029,581	829,991	891,926
BOS	1,344,080	1,312,282	1,115,750	1,026,133	931,127	1,203,200	1,137,158	1,181,087	1,077,047	984,102
CHI	781,330	1,328,234	1,231,675	1,191,353	1,231,629	1,175,684	1,000,090	1,135,668	797,451	1,423,144
CLE	1,727,464	1,704,984	1,444,607	1,069,176	1,335,472	1,221,780	865,467	722,256	663,805	1,497,976
DET	1,951,474	1,132,641	1,026,846	884,658	1,079,847	1,181,838	1,051,182	1,272,346	1,098,924	1,221,221
KC						1,393,054	1,015,154	901,067	925,090	963,683
NY	2,081,380	1,950,107	1,629,665	1,537,811	1,475,171	1,490,138	1,491,784	1,497,134	1,428,438	1,552,030
PHI	309,805	465,469	627,100	362,113	304,666					
STL	247,131	293,790	518,796	297,238						
WAS	699,697	695,167	699,457	595,594	503,542	425,238	431,647	457,079	475,288	615,372
TOT	9,142,361	8,882,674	8,293,896	6,964,076	7,922,364	8,942,971	7,893,683	8,196,218	7,296,034	9,149,454
NATIONAL LEAGUE										
BOS	944,391	487,475	281,278							
BRO	1,185,896	1,282,628	1,088,704	1,163,419	1,020,531	1,033,589	1,213,562	1,028,258		
CHI	1,165,944	894,415	1,024,826	763,658	748,183	875,800	720,118	670,629	979,904	858,255

	1950	1951	1952	1953	1954	1955	1956	1957	1958	1959
CIN	538,794	588,268	604,197	548,086	704,167	693,662	1,125,928	1,070,850	788,582	801,298
LA									1,845,556	2,071,045
MIL				1,826,397	2,131,388	2,005,836	2,046,331	2,215,404	1,971,101	1,749,112
NY	1,008,878	1,059,539	984,940	811,518	1,155,067	824,112	629,179	653,923		
PHI	1,217,035	937,658	755,417	853,644	738,991	922,886	934,798	1,146,230	931,110	802,815
PIT	1,166,267	980,590	686,673	572,757	475,494	469,397	949,878	850,732	1,311,988	1,359,917
STL	1,093,411	1,013,429	913,113	880,242	1,039,698	849,130	1,029,773	1,183,575	1,063,730	929,953
SF									1,272,625	1,422,130
TOT	8,320,616	7,244,002	6,339,148	7,419,721	8,013,519	7,674,412	8,649,567	8,819,601	10,164,596	9,994,525
ML	17,462,977	16,126,676	14,633,044	14,383,797	15,935,883	16,617,383	16,543,250	17,015,819	17,460,630	19,143,979

	1960	1961	1962	1963	1964	1965	1966	1967	1968	1969
AMERICAN LEAGUE										
BAL	1,187,849	951,089	790,254	774,343	1,116,215	781,649	1,203,366	955,053	943,977	1,062,069
BOS	1,129,866	850,589	733,080	942,642	883,276	652,201	811,172	1,727,832	1,940,788	1,833,246
CAL						566,727	1,400,321	1,317,713	1,025,956	758,388
CHI	1,644,460	1,146,019	1,131,562	1,158,848	1,250,053	1,130,519	990,016	985,634	803,775	589,546
CLE	950,985	725,547	716,076	562,507	653,293	934,786	903,359	662,980	857,994	619,970
DET	1,167,669	1,600,710	1,207,881	821,952	816,139	1,029,645	1,124,293	1,447,143	2,031,847	1,577,481
KC	774,944	683,817	635,675	762,364	642,478	528,344	773,929	726,639		
LA		603,510	1,144,063	821,015	760,439					
MIN		1,256,723	1,433,116	1,406,652	1,207,514	1,463,258	1,259,374	1,483,547	1,143,257	1,349,328
NY	1,627,349	1,747,725	1,493,574	1,308,920	1,305,638	1,213,552	1,124,648	1,259,514	1,185,666	1,067,996
OAK									837,466	778,232
SEA										677,944
WAS	743,404	597,287	729,775	535,604	600,106	560,083	576,260	770,868	546,661	918,106
TOT	9,226,526	10,163,016	10,015,056	9,094,847	9,235,151	8,860,764	10,166,738	11,336,923	11,317,387	12,134,720
NATIONAL LEAGUE										
ATL							1,539,801	1,389,222	1,126,540	1,458,320
CHI	809,770	673,057	609,802	979,551	751,647	641,361	635,891	977,226	1,043,409	1,674,993
CIN	663,486	1,117,603	982,095	858,805	862,466	1,047,824	742,958	958,300	733,354	987,991
HOU			924,456	719,502	725,773	2,151,470	1,872,108	1,348,303	1,312,887	1,442,995
LA	2,253,887	1,804,250	2,755,184	2,538,602	2,228,751	2,553,577	2,617,029	1,664,362	1,581,093	1,784,527
MIL	1,497,799	1,101,441	766,921	773,018	910,911	555,584				
MON										1,212,608
NY			922,530	1,080,108	1,732,597	1,768,389	1,932,693	1,565,492	1,781,657	2,175,373
PHI	862,205	590,039	762,034	907,141	1,425,891	1,166,376	1,108,201	828,888	664,546	519,414
PIT	1,705,828	1,199,128	1,090,648	783,648	759,496	909,279	1,196,618	907,012	693,485	769,369
STL	1,096,632	855,305	953,895	1,170,546	1,143,294	1,241,201	1,712,980	2,090,145	2,011,167	1,682,783
SD										512,970
SF	1,795,356	1,390,679	1,592,594	1,571,306	1,504,364	1,546,075	1,657,192	1,242,480	837,220	873,603
TOT	10,684,963	8,731,502	11,360,159	11,382,227	12,045,190	13,581,136	15,015,471	12,971,430	11,785,358	15,094,946
ML	19,911,489	18,894,518	21,375,215	20,477,074	21,280,341	22,441,900	25,182,209	24,308,353	23,102,745	27,229,666

	1970	1971	1972	1973	1974	1975	1976	1977	1978	1979
AMERICAN LEAGUE										
BAL	1,057,069	1,023,037	899,950	958,667	962,572	1,002,157	1,058,609	1,195,769	1,051,724	1,681,009
BOS	1,595,278	1,678,732	1,441,718	1,481,002	1,556,411	1,748,587	1,895,846	2,074,549	2,320,643	2,353,114
CAL	1,077,741	926,373	744,190	1,058,206	917,269	1,058,163	1,006,774	1,432,633	1,755,386	2,523,575
CHI	495,355	833,891	1,177,318	1,302,527	1,149,596	750,802	914,945	1,657,135	1,491,100	1,280,702
CLE	729,752	591,361	626,354	615,107	1,114,262	977,039	948,776	900,365	800,584	1,011,644
DET	1,501,293	1,591,073	1,892,386	1,724,146	1,243,080	1,058,836	1,467,020	1,359,856	1,714,893	1,630,929
KC	693,047	910,784	707,656	1,345,341	1,173,292	1,151,836	1,680,265	1,852,603	2,255,493	2,261,845
MIL	933,690	731,531	600,440	1,092,158	955,741	1,213,357	1,012,164	1,114,938	1,601,406	1,918,343
MIN	1,261,887	940,858	797,901	907,499	662,401	737,156	715,394	1,162,727	787,878	1,070,521
NY	1,136,879	1,070,771	966,328	1,262,103	1,273,075	1,288,048	2,012,434	2,103,092	2,335,871	2,537,765
OAK	778,355	914,993	921,323	1,000,763	845,693	1,075,518	780,593	495,599	526,999	306,763
SEA								1,338,511	877,440	844,447
TEX			662,974	686,085	1,193,902	1,127,924	1,164,982	1,250,722	1,447,963	1,519,671
TOR								1,701,052	1,562,585	1,431,651
WAS	824,789	655,156								
TOT	12,085,135	11,868,560	11,438,538	13,433,604	13,047,294	13,189,423	14,657,802	19,639,551	20,529,965	22,371,979
NATIONAL LEAGUE										
ATL	1,078,848	1,006,320	752,973	800,655	981,085	534,672	818,179	872,464	904,494	769,465
CHI	1,642,705	1,653,007	1,299,163	1,351,705	1,015,378	1,034,819	1,026,217	1,439,834	1,525,311	1,648,587
CIN	1,803,568	1,501,122	1,611,459	2,017,601	2,164,307	2,315,603	2,629,708	2,519,670	2,532,497	2,356,933
HOU	1,253,444	1,261,589	1,469,247	1,394,004	1,090,728	858,002	886,146	1,109,560	1,126,145	1,900,312
LA	1,697,142	2,064,594	1,860,858	2,136,192	2,632,474	2,539,349	2,386,301	2,955,087	3,347,845	2,860,954
MON	1,424,683	1,290,963	1,142,145	1,246,863	1,019,134	908,292	646,704	1,433,757	1,427,007	2,102,173
NY	2,697,479	2,266,680	2,134,185	1,912,390	1,722,209	1,730,566	1,468,754	1,066,825	1,007,328	788,905
PHI	708,247	1,511,223	1,343,329	1,475,934	1,808,648	1,909,233	2,480,150	2,700,070	2,583,389	2,775,011
PIT	1,341,947	1,501,132	1,427,460	1,319,913	1,110,552	1,270,018	1,025,945	1,237,349	964,106	1,435,454
STL	1,629,736	1,604,671	1,196,894	1,574,046	1,838,413	1,695,270	1,207,079	1,659,287	1,278,215	1,627,256
SD	643,679	557,513	644,273	611,826	1,075,399	1,281,747	1,458,478	1,376,269	1,670,107	1,456,967
SF	740,720	1,106,043	647,744	834,193	519,987	522,919	626,868	700,056	1,740,477	1,456,402
TOT	16,662,198	17,324,857	15,529,730	16,675,322	16,978,314	16,600,490	16,660,529	19,070,228	20,106,921	21,178,419
ML	28,747,333	29,193,417	26,968,268	30,108,926	30,025,608	29,789,913	31,318,331	38,709,779	40,636,886	43,550,398

	1980	1981	1982	1983	1984	1985	1986	1987	1988	1989
AMERICAN LEAGUE										
BAL	1,797,438	1,024,247	1,613,031	2,042,071	2,045,784	2,132,387	1,973,176	1,835,692	1,660,738	2,535,208
BOS	1,956,092	1,060,379	1,950,124	1,782,285	1,661,618	1,786,633	2,147,641	2,231,551	2,464,851	2,510,012
CAL	2,297,327	1,441,545	2,807,360	2,555,016	2,402,997	2,567,427	2,655,872	2,696,299	2,340,925	2,647,291
CHI	1,200,365	946,651	1,567,787	2,132,821	2,136,988	1,669,888	1,424,313	1,208,060	1,115,749	1,045,651
CLE	1,033,827	661,395	1,044,021	768,941	734,079	655,181	1,471,805	1,077,898	1,411,610	1,285,542
DET	1,785,293	1,149,144	1,636,058	1,829,636	2,704,794	2,286,609	1,899,437	2,061,830	2,081,162	1,543,656
KC	2,288,714	1,279,403	2,284,464	1,963,875	1,810,018	2,162,717	2,320,794	2,392,471	2,350,181	2,477,700
MIL	1,857,408	874,292	1,978,896	2,397,131	1,608,509	1,360,265	1,265,041	1,909,244	1,923,238	1,970,735
MIN	769,206	469,090	921,186	858,939	1,598,692	1,651,814	1,255,453	2,081,976	3,030,672	2,277,438
NY	2,627,417	1,614,353	2,041,219	2,257,976	1,821,815	2,214,587	2,268,030	2,427,672	2,633,701	2,170,485
OAK	842,259	1,304,052	1,735,489	1,294,941	1,353,281	1,334,599	1,314,646	1,678,921	2,287,335	2,667,225
SEA	836,204	636,276	1,070,404	813,537	870,372	1,128,696	1,029,045	1,134,255	1,022,398	1,298,443
TEX	1,198,175	850,076	1,154,432	1,363,469	1,102,471	1,112,497	1,692,002	1,763,053	1,581,901	2,043,993
TOR	1,400,327	755,083	1,275,978	1,930,415	2,110,009	2,468,925	2,455,477	2,778,429	2,595,175	3,375,883
TOT	21,890,052	14,065,986	23,080,449	23,991,053	23,961,427	24,532,225	25,172,732	27,277,351	28,499,636	29,849,262
NATIONAL LEAGUE										
ATL	1,048,411	535,418	1,801,985	2,119,935	1,724,892	1,350,137	1,387,181	1,217,402	848,089	984,930
CHI	1,206,776	565,637	1,249,278	1,479,717	2,107,655	2,161,534	1,859,102	2,035,130	2,089,034	2,491,942
CIN	2,022,450	1,093,730	1,326,528	1,190,419	1,275,887	1,834,619	1,692,432	2,185,205	2,072,528	1,979,320
HOU	2,278,217	1,321,282	1,558,555	1,351,962	1,229,862	1,184,314	1,734,276	1,909,902	1,933,505	1,834,908
LA	3,249,287	2,381,292	3,608,881	3,510,313	3,134,824	3,264,593	3,023,208	2,797,409	2,980,262	2,944,653
MON	2,208,175	1,534,564	2,318,292	2,320,651	1,606,531	1,502,494	1,128,981	1,850,324	1,478,659	1,783,533
NY	1,192,073	704,244	1,323,036	1,112,774	1,842,695	2,761,601	2,767,601	3,034,129	3,055,445	2,918,710
PHI	2,651,650	1,638,752	2,376,394	2,128,339	2,062,693	1,830,350	1,933,335	2,100,110	1,990,041	1,861,985
PIT	1,646,757	541,789	1,024,106	1,225,916	773,500	735,900	1,000,917	1,161,193	1,866,713	1,374,141
STL	1,385,147	1,010,247	2,111,906	2,317,914	2,037,448	2,637,563	2,471,974	3,072,122	2,892,799	3,080,980
SD	1,139,026	519,161	1,607,516	1,539,815	1,983,904	2,210,352	1,805,716	1,454,061	1,506,896	2,009,031
SF	1,096,115	632,274	1,200,948	1,251,530	1,001,545	818,697	1,528,748	1,917,168	1,785,297	2,059,701
TOT	21,124,084	12,478,390	21,507,425	21,549,285	20,781,436	22,292,154	22,333,471	24,734,155	24,499,268	25,323,834
ML	43,014,136	26,544,376	44,587,874	45,540,338	44,742,863	46,824,379	47,506,203	52,011,506	52,998,904	55,173,096

	1990	1991	1992
AMERICAN LEAGUE			
BAL	2,415,189	2,552,753	3,567,819
BOS	2,528,986	2,562,435	2,468,574
CAL	2,555,688	2,416,236	2,065,444
CHI	2,002,357	2,934,154	2,681,156
CLE	1,225,240	1,051,863	1,224,094
DET	1,495,785	1,641,661	1,423,963
KC	2,244,956	2,161,537	1,867,689
MIL	1,752,900	1,478,729	1,857,351
MIN	1,751,584	2,293,842	2,482,428
NY	2,006,436	1,863,733	1,748,737
OAK	2,900,217	2,713,493	2,494,160
SEA	1,509,727	2,147,905	1,651,367
TEX	2,057,911	2,297,720	2,198,231
TOR	3,885,284	4,001,527	4,028,318
TOT	30,332,260	32,117,588	31,759,331
NATIONAL LEAGUE			
ATL	980,129	2,140,217	3,077,400
CHI	2,243,791	2,314,250	2,126,720
CIN	2,400,892	2,372,377	2,315,946
HOU	1,310,927	1,196,152	1,211,412
LA	3,002,396	3,348,170	2,473,266
MON	1,373,087	934,742	1,669,127
NY	2,732,745	2,284,484	1,779,534
PHI	1,992,484	2,050,012	1,927,448
PIT	2,049,908	2,065,302	1,829,395
STL	2,573,225	2,448,699	2,418,483
SD	1,856,396	1,804,289	1,721,406
SF	1,975,528	1,737,478	1,560,998
TOT	24,491,508	24,696,172	24,111,135
ML	54,823,768	56,813,760	55,870,466

## CHAPTER 6

Jackie Robinson's Signing: The Real, Untold Story

John Thorn and Jules Tygiel

October 1945. As the Detroit Tigers and Chicago Cubs faced off in the World Series, photographer Maurice Terrell arrived at an almost deserted minor league park in San Diego, California, to carry out a top-secret assignment: to surreptitiously photograph three black baseball players.

Terrell shot hundreds of motion-picture frames of Jackie Robinson and the two other players. A few photos appeared in print but the existence of the additional images remained unknown for four decades. In April 1987, as major league baseball prepared a lavish commemoration of the fortieth anniversary of Robinson's debut, John Thorn unearthed a body of contact sheets and unprocessed film from a previously unopened carton donated in 1954 by *Look* magazine to the Baseball Hall of Fame in Cooperstown, New York. This discovery triggered an investigation which led to startling revelations regarding Branch Rickey, the president of the Brooklyn Dodgers, and his signing of Jackie Robinson to shatter baseball's longstanding color line; the relationship between these two historic figures; and the still controversial issue of black managers in baseball.

The popular "frontier" image of Jackie Robinson as a lone gunman facing down a hostile mob has always dominated the story of the integration of baseball. But new information related to the Terrell photos reveals that while Robinson was the linchpin in Branch Rickey's strategy, in October 1945 Rickey intended to announce the signing of not just Jackie Robinson, but of several other Negro League stars. Political pressure, however, forced Rickey's hand, thrusting Robinson alone into the spotlight. And in 1950, after only three years in the major leagues, Robinson pressed Rickey to consider him for a position as field manager or front office executive, raising an issue with which the baseball establishment still grapples.

The story of these revelations began with the discovery of the Terrell photographs. The photos show a youthful, muscular Robinson in a battered cap and baggy uniform fielding from his position at shortstop, batting with a black catcher crouched behind him, trapping a third black player in a rundown between third and home, and sprinting along the basepaths more like a former track star than a baseball player. All three players wore uniforms emblazoned with the name "Royals." A woman with her back to the action is the only figure visible amid the vacant stands. The contact sheets are dated October 7, 1945.

The photos were perplexing. The momentous announcement of Jackie Robinson's signing with the Montreal Royals took place on October 23, 1945. Before that date his recruitment had been a tightly guarded secret. Why, then, had a *Look* photographer taken such an interest in Robinson two weeks earlier? Where had the pictures been taken? And why was Robinson already wearing a Royals uniform?

Thorn called Jules Tygiel, the author of *Baseball's Great Experiment: Jackie Robinson and His Legacy,* to see if he could shed some light on the photos. Tygiel knew nothing about them, but he did have in his files a 1945 manuscript by newsman Arthur Mann, who frequently wrote for *Look.* The article, drafted with Rickey's cooperation, had been intended to announce the Robinson signing but had never been published. The pictures, they concluded, were to have accompanied Mann's article; they decided to find out the story behind the photo session.

The clandestine nature of the photo session did not surprise the researchers. From the moment he had arrived in Brooklyn in 1942, determined to end baseball's Jim Crow traditions, Rickey had feared that premature disclosure of his intentions might doom his bold design. No blacks had appeared in the major leagues since 1884 when two brothers, Welday and Moses Fleetwood Walker, had played for Toledo in the American Association. Not since the 1890s had black players appeared on a minor league team. During the ensuing half century all-black teams and leagues featuring legendary figures like pitcher Satchel Paige and catcher Josh Gibson had performed on the periphery of Organized Baseball. Baseball executives, led by Commissioner Kenesaw Mountain Landis, had strictly policed the color line, barring blacks from both major and minor leagues. In 1943 when young Bill Veeck attempted to buy the Philadelphia Phillies and stock the team with Negro League stars, Landis had quietly but decisively blocked the move. Rickey therefore moved slowly and secretly to explore the issue and cover up his attempts to scout black players during his first three years in Brooklyn. He informed the Dodger owners of his plans but took few others into his confidence.

In the spring of 1945, as Rickey prepared to accelerate his scouting efforts, advocates of integration, emboldened by the impending end of World War II and the recent death of Commissioner Landis, escalated their campaign

to desegregate baseball. On April 6, 1945, black sportswriter Joe Bostic appeared at the Dodgers' Bear Mountain training camp with Negro League stars Terris McDuffie and Dave "Showboat" Thomas and forced Rickey to hold tryouts for the two players. Ten days later black journalist Wendell Smith, white sportswriter Dave Egan and Boston city councilman Isadore Muchnick engineered an unsuccessful audition with the Red Sox for Robinson and two other black athletes. In response to these events the major leagues announced the formation of a Committee on Baseball Integration. (Reflecting Organized Baseball's true intentions on the matter, the group never met.)

In the face of this heightened activity, Rickey created an elaborate smokescreen to obscure his scouting of black players. In May 1945 he announced the formation of a new franchise, the Brooklyn Brown Dodgers, and a new Negro League, the United States League. Rickey then dispatched his best talent hunters to observe black ballplayers, ostensibly for the Brown Dodgers, but in reality for the Brooklyn National League club.

A handwritten memorandum in the Rickey Papers offers a rare glimpse of Rickey's emphasis on secrecy in his instructions to Dodger scouts. The document, signed by Chas. D. Clark and accompanied by a Negro National League schedule for April-May 1945, is headlined "Job Analysis," and defines the following "Duties: under supervision of management of club":

1. To establish contact (silent) with all clubs (local or general).
2. To gain knowledge and abilities of all players.
3. To report all possible material (players).
4. Prepare weekly reports of activities.
5. Keep composite report of outstanding players . . . To travel and cover player whenever management so desire.

Clark's "Approch" [sic] was to "Visit game and loose [sic] self in stands; Keep statistical report (speed, power, agility, ability, fielding, batting, etc.) by score card"; and "Leave immediately after game."

Clark's directions, however, contain one major breach in Rickey's elaborate security precautions. According to his later accounts, Rickey had told most Dodger scouts that they were evaluating talent for a new "Brown Dodger" franchise. But Clark's first "Objective" was "To Cover Negro teams for possible major league talent." Had Rickey confided in Clark, a figure so obscure as to escape prior mention in the voluminous Robinson literature? Dodger superscout and Rickey confidante Clyde Sukeforth has no recollection of Clark, raising the possibility that Clark was not part of the Dodger family, but perhaps someone connected with black baseball. Had Clark himself interpreted his instructions in this manner?

Whatever the answer, Rickey successfully diverted attention from his true motives. Nonetheless, mounting interest in the integration issue threatened Rickey's careful planning. In the summer of 1945 Rickey constructed yet another facade. The Dodger President took Dan Dodson, a New York University sociologist who chaired Mayor Fiorello LaGuardia's Committee on Unity, into his confidence and requested that Dodson form a Committee on Baseball ostensibly to study the possibility of integration.

In reality, the committee would provide the illusion of action while Rickey quietly completed his own preparations. "This was one of the toughest decisions I ever had to make while in office," Dodson later confessed. "The major purpose I could see for the committee was that it was a stall for time. . . . Yet had Mr. Rickey not delivered . . . I would have been totally discredited."

Thus by late August, even as Rickey's extensive scouting reports had led him to focus on Jackie Robinson as his standard bearer, few people in or out of the Dodger organization suspected that a breakthrough was imminent. On August 28 Rickey and Robinson held their historic meeting at the Dodgers' Montague Street offices in downtown Brooklyn. Robinson signed an agreement to accept a contract with the Montreal Royals, the top Dodger affiliate, by November 1. Rickey, still concerned with secrecy, impressed upon Robinson the need to maintain silence. Robinson could tell the momentous news to his family and fiancee, but no one else.

For the conspiratorial Rickey, keeping the news sheltered while continuing arrangements required further subterfuge. Rumors about Robinson's visit had already spread through the world of black baseball. To stifle speculation Rickey "leaked" an adulterated version of the incident to black sportswriter Wendell Smith. Smith, who had recommended Robinson to Rickey and advised Rickey on the integration project, doubtless knew the true story behind the meeting. On September 8, however, he reported in the Pittsburgh *Courier* that the "sensational shortstop" and "colorful major league dynamo" had met behind "closed doors. . . . "The nature of the conference has not been revealed," Smith continued. Rickey claimed that he and Robinson had assessed "the organization of Negro baseball," but Smith noted that "it does not seem logical [Rickey] should call in a rookie player to discuss the future organization of Negro baseball." He closed with the tantalizing thought that "it appears that the Brooklyn boss has a plan on his mind that extends further than just the future of Negro baseball as an organization." The subterfuge succeeded. Neither black nor white reporters pursued the issue.

Rickey, always sensitive to criticism by New York sports reporters and understanding the historic significance of his actions, also wanted to be sure that his version of the integration breakthrough and his role in it be accurately portrayed. To guarantee this he persuaded Arthur Mann, his close friend and later a Dodger employee, to write a 3,000 word manuscript to be published simultaneously with the announcement of the signing.

Although it was impossible to confirm this in 1987 (it has since ben confirmed by Maurice Terrell himself, who was eventually located) it seemed highly likely that Terrell's photos, commissioned by *Look*, were destined to accompany Mann's article. Clearer prints of the negatives revealed that Terrell had taken the pictures in San Diego's Lane Stadium. This fit in with Robinson's autumn itinerary. After his meeting with Rickey, Robinson had returned briefly to the Kansas City Monarchs. With the Dodger offer securing his future and the relentless bus trips of the Negro League schedule wearing him down, he had left the Monarchs before season's end and returned home to Pasadena, California. In late September he hooked up with Chet Brewer's Kansas City Royals, a

postseason barnstorming team which toured the Pacific Coast, competing against other Negro League teams and major and minor league all-star squads. Thus the word "Royals" on Robinson's uniform, which had so piqued the interest of Thorn and Tygiel, ironically turned out not to relate to Robinson's future team in Montreal, but rather to his interim employment in California.

For further information Tygiel contacted Chet Brewer, who at age eighty still lived in Los Angeles. Brewer, one of the great pitchers of the Jim Crow era, had known Robinson well. He had followed Robinson's spectacular athletic career at UCLA and in 1945 they became teammates on the Monarchs. "Jackie was major league all the way," recalled Brewer. "He had the fastest reflexes I ever saw in a player."

Robinson particularly relished facing major league all-star squads. Against Bob Feller, Robinson once slashed two doubles. "Jack was running crazy on the bases," a Royal teammate remembered. In one game he upended Gerry Priddy, Washington Senator infielder. Priddy angrily complained about the hard slide in an exhibition game. "Any time I put on a uniform," retorted Robinson, "I play to win."

Brewer recalled that Robinson and two other Royals journeyed from Los Angeles to San Diego on a day when the team was not scheduled to play. He identified the catcher in the photos as Buster Haywood and the other player as Royals third baseman Herb Souell. Souell was no longer living, but Haywood, who, like Brewer lived in Los Angeles, vaguely recalled the event, which he incorrectly remembered as occurring in Pasadena. Robinson recruited the catcher and Souell, his former Monarch teammate, to "work out" with him. All three wore their Royal uniforms. Haywood found neither Robinson's request nor the circumstances unusual. Although he was unaware that they were being photographed, Haywood described the session accurately. "We didn't know what was going on," he stated. "We'd hit and throw and run from third base to home plate."

The San Diego pictures provide a rare glimpse of the pre-Montreal Robinson. The article which they were to accompany and related correspondence in the Library of Congress offer even rarer insights into Rickey's thinking. The unpublished Mann manuscript was entitled "The Negro and Baseball: "The National Game Faces a Racial Challenge Long Ignored." As Mann doubtless based his account on conversations with Rickey and since Rickey's handwritten comments appear in the margin, it stands as the earliest "official" account of the Rickey-Robinson story and reveals many of the concerns confronting Rickey in September 1945.

One of the most striking features of the article is the language used to refer to Robinson. Mann, reflecting the racism typical of postwar America, portrays Robinson as the "first Negro chattel in the so-called National pastime." At another point he writes, "Rickey felt the boy's sincerity," appropriate language perhaps for an 18-year-old prospect, but not for a 26-year-old former army officer.

"The Negro and Baseball" consists largely of the now familiar Rickey–Robinson story. Mann recreated Rickey's haunting 1904 experience as collegiate coach when one of his black baseball players, Charlie Thomas, was denied access to a hotel. Thomas cried and rubbed his hands, chanting, "Black skin! Black skin! If I could only make 'em white." Mann described Rickey's search for the "right" man, the formation of the United States League as a cover for scouting operations, the reasons for selecting Robinson, and the fateful Rickey–Robinson confrontation. Other sections, however, graphically illustrate additional issues Rickey deemed significant. Mann repeatedly cites the costs the Dodgers incurred: $5,000 to scout Cuba, $6,000 to scout Mexico, $5,000 to establish the "Brooklyn Brown Dodgers." The final total reaches $25,000, a modest sum considering the ultimate returns, but one which Rickey felt would counter his skinflint image.

Rickey's desire to show that he was not motivated by political pressures also emerges clearly. Mann had suggested that upon arriving in Brooklyn in 1942, Rickey "was beseiged by telephone calls, telegrams and letters of petition in behalf of black ball players," and that this "staggering pile of missives [was] so inspired to convince him that he and the Dodgers had been selected as a kind of guinea pig." In his marginal comments, Rickey vehemently wrote "No!" in a strong dark script. "I began all this as soon as I went to Brooklyn." Explaining why he had never attacked the subject during his two decades as general manager of the St. Louis Cardinals, Rickey referred to the segregation in that city. "St. Louis never permitted Negro patrons in the grandstand," he wrote, describing a policy he apparently had felt powerless to change.

Mann also devoted two of his twelve pages to a spirited attack on the Negro Leagues, repeating Rickey's charges that "they are the poorest excuse for the word league" and documented the prevalence of barnstorming, the uneven scheduling, absence of contracts, and dominance of booking agents. Mann revealingly traces Rickey's distaste for the Negro Leagues to the "outrageous" guarantees demanded by New York booking agent William Leuschner to place black teams in Ebbets Field while the Dodgers were on the road.

Rickey's misplaced obsession with the internal disorganization of the Negro Leagues had substantial factual basis. But Rickey had an ulterior motive. In his September 8 article, Wendell Smith addressed the issue of "player tampering," asking, "Would [Rickey] not first approach the owners of these Negro teams who have these stars under contract?" Rickey, argued Smith in what might have been an unsuccessful preemptive strike, "is obligated to do so and his record as a businessman indicated that he would." As Smith may have known, Rickey maintained that Negro League players did not sign valid contracts and so became free agents at the end of each season. Thus the Mahatma had no intention of compensating Negro League teams for the players he signed. His repeated attacks on black baseball, including the Mann article, served to justify this questionable position.

The one respect in which "The Negro and Baseball" departs radically from common picture of the Robinson legend is in its report of Robinson as one of a group of blacks about to be signed by the Dodgers. Mann's manuscript and subsequent correspondence from Rickey reveal that Rickey did not intend for Robinson to withstand the pressures alone. "Determined not to be charged with merely nibbling at the problem," wrote Mann, "Rickey

went all out and brought in two more Negro players," and "consigned them, with Robinson, to the Dodgers' top farm club, the Montreal Royals." Mann named pitcher Don Newcombe and, surprisingly, outfielder Sam Jethroe as Robinson's future teammates. Whether the recruitment of additional blacks had always been Rickey's intention or whether he had reached his decision after meeting with Robinson in August is unclear. But by late September, when he provided information to Mann for his article, Rickey had clearly decided to bring in other Negro League stars.

During the first weekend in October, Dodger Coach Chuck Dressen fielded a major league all-star team in a series of exhibition games against Negro League standouts at Ebbets Field. Rickey took the opportunity to interview at least three black pitching prospects, Newcombe, Roy Partlow and John Wright. The following week he met with catcher Roy Campanella. Campanella and Newcombe, at least, believed they had been approached to play for the "Brown Dodgers."

At the same time Rickey decided to postpone publication of Mann's manuscript. In a remarkable letter sent from the World Series in Chicago on October 7, Rickey informed Mann:

We just can't go now with the article. The thing isn't dead,-not at all. It is more alive than ever and that is the reason we can't go with any publicity at this time. There is more involved in the situation than I had contemplated. Other players are in it and it may be that I can't clear these players until after the December meetings, possibly not until after the first of the year. You must simply sit in the boat. . . .

There is a November 1 deadline on Robinson,-you know that. I am undertaking to extend that date until January 1st so as to give me time to sign plenty of players and make one break on the complete story. Also, quite obviously it might not be good to sign Robinson with other and possibly better players unsigned.

The revelations and tone of this letter surprised Robinson's widow, Rachel, forty years after the event. Rickey "was such a deliberate man," she recalled, "and this letter is so urgent. He must have been very nervous as he neared his goal. Maybe he was nervous that the owners would turn him down and having five people at the door instead of just one would have been more powerful."

Events in the weeks after October 7 justified Rickey's nervousness and forced him to deviate from the course stated in the Mann letter. Candidates in New York City's upcoming November elections, most notably black Communist City Councilman Ben Davis, made baseball integration a major issue in the campaign. Mayor LaGuardia's Democratic party also sought to exploit the issue. The Committee on Baseball had prepared a report outlining a modest, long-range strategy for bringing blacks into the game and describing the New York teams, because of the favorable political and racial climate in the city, as in a "choice position to undertake this pattern of integration." LaGuardia wanted Rickey's permission to make a pre-election announcement that "baseball would shortly begin signing Negro players," as a result of the committee's work.

Rickey, a committee member, had long ago subverted the panel to his own purposes. By mid-October, however, the committee had become "an election football." Again unwilling to risk the appearance of succumbing to political pressure and thereby surrendering what he viewed as his rightful role in history, Rickey asked LaGuardia to delay his comments. Rickey hurriedly contacted Robinson, who had joined a barnstorming team in New York en route to play winter ball in Venezuela, and dispatched him to Montreal. On October 23, 1945, with Rickey's carefully laid plans scuttled, the Montreal Royals announced the signing of Robinson, and Robinson alone.

Mann's article never appeared. *Look,* having lost its exclusive, published two strips of the Terrell pictures in its November 27, 1945 issue accompanying a brief summary of the Robinson story, by then old news. The unprocessed film and contact sheets were loaded into a box and nine years later shipped to the National Baseball Hall of Fame, where they remained, along with a picture of Jethroe, unpacked until April 1987.

Newcombe, Campanella, Wright and Partlow all joined the Dodger organization the following spring. Jethroe became a victim of the "deliberate speed" of baseball integration. Rickey did not interview Jethroe in 1945. Since few teams followed the Dodger lead, the fleet, powerful outfielder remained in the Negro Leagues until 1948, when Rickey finally bought his contract from the Cleveland Buckeyes for $5,000. Jethroe had two spectacular seasons at Montreal before Rickey, fearing a "surfeit of colored boys on the Brooklyn club," profitably sold him to the Boston Braves for $100,000. Jethroe won the Rookie of the Year Award in 1950, but his delayed entry into Organized Baseball foreshortened what should have been a stellar career. Until informed by the authors of this essay, Jethroe remained unaware of how close he came to joining Robinson, Newcombe and Campanella in the pantheon of integration pioneers.

For Robinson, who had always occupied center stage in Rickey's thinking, the early announcement intensified the pressures and enhanced the legend. The success or failure of integration rested disproportionately on his capable shoulders. He became the lightning rod for supporter and opponent alike, attracting the responsibility, the opprobrium, and ultimately the acclaim for his historic achievement.

Beyond these revelations about the Robinson signing, the Library of Congress documents add surprisingly little to the familiar story of the integration of baseball. The Rickey Papers copiously detail his post-Dodger career as general manager of the Pittsburgh Pirates, but are strangely silent about the criticial 1944–1948 period. Records for these years probably remained with the Dodger organization, which claims to have no knowledge of their whereabouts. National League documents for these years remain closed to the public.

In light of the controversy engendered by former Dodger General Manager Al Campanis's remarks about blacks in management, however, one exchange between Rickey and Robinson becomes particularly relevant. In 1950, after his fourth season with the Dodgers, Robinson appears to have written Rickey about the possibility of employment in baseball when his playing days ended. Robinson's original letter cannot be found in either the

Rickey papers or the Robinson family archives. However, Rickey's reply, dated December 31, 1950, survives. Rickey, who had recently left the Dodgers after an unsuccessful struggle to wrest control of the team from Walter O'Malley, responded to Robinson's inquiry with a long and equivocal answer.

"It is not at all because of lack of appreciation that I have not acknowledged your good letter of some time ago," began Rickey. "Neither your writing, nor sending the letter, nor its contents gave me very much surprise." On the subject of managing, Rickey replied optimistically, "I hope that the day will soon come when it will be entirely possible, as it is entirely right, that you can be considered for administrative work in baseball, particularly in the direction of field management." Rickey claimed to have told several writers that "I do not know of any player in the game today who could, in my judgement, manage a major league team better than yourself," but that the news media had inexplicably ignored these comments.

Yet Rickey tempered his encouragement with remarks that to a reader today seem gratuitous. "As I have often expressed to you," he wrote, "I think you carry a great responsibility for your people . . . and I cannot close this letter without admonishing you to prepare yourself to do a widely useful work, and, at the same time, dignifed and effective in the field of public relations. A part of this preparation, and I know you are smiling, for you have already guessed my oft repeated suggestion—to finish your college course meritoriously and get your degree." This advice, according to Rachel Robinson, was a "matter of routine" between the two men ever since their first meeting. Nonetheless, to the thirty-one-year-old Robinson, whose nonathletic academic career had been marked by indifferent success and whose endorsements and business acumen had already established the promise of a secure future, Rickey's response may have seemed to beg the question.

Rickey concluded with the promise, which seems to hinge on the completion of a college degree, that "It would be a great pleasure for me to be your agent in placing you in a big job after your playing days are finished. Believe me always." Shortly after writing this letter Rickey became the general manager of the Pittsburgh Pirates. Had Robinson ended his playing career before Rickey left the Pirates, perhaps the Mahatma would have made good on his pledge. But Rickey resigned from the Pirates at the end of the 1955 season, one year before Robinson's retirement, and never again had the power to hire a manager.

Robinson's 1950 letter to Rickey marked only the beginning of his quest to see a black manager in the major leagues. In 1952 he hoped to gain experience by managing in the Puerto Rican winter league, but, according to the New York Post, Commissioner Happy Chandler withheld his approval, forcing Robinson to cancel his plans. On November 30, 1952, the Dodger star raised the prospect of a black manager in a televised interview on "Youth Wants to Know," stating that both he and Campanella had been "approached" on the subject. In 1954, after the Dodgers had fired manager Chuck Dressen, speculation arose that either Robinson or Pee Wee Reese might be named to the post. But the team bypassed both men and

selected veteran minor league manager Walter Alston, who held the job for more than two decades.

Upon his retirement in 1956, Robinson, who had begun to manifest signs of the diabetes that would plague the rest of his life, had lost much of his enthusiasm for the prospect of managing, but nonetheless would probably have accepted another pioneering role. "He had wearied of the travel," states Rachel, "and no longer wanted to manage. He just wanted to be asked as a recognition of his accomplishments, his abilities as a strategist and to show that white men could be led by a black."

Ironically, in the early years of integration Organized Baseball had bypassed a large pool of qualified and experienced black managers: former Negro League players and managers like Chet Brewer, Ray Dandridge, and Quincy Trouppe. In the early 1950s Brewer and several other Negro League veterans managed all-black minor league teams, but no interracial club at any level offered a managerial position to a black until 1961, when former Negro League and major league infielder Gene Baker assumed the reins of a low-level Pittsburgh Pirate farm team, one of only three blacks to manage a major league affiliate before 1975.

This lack of opportunity loomed as a major frustration for those who had broken the color line. "We bring dollars into club treasuries while we play," protested Larry Doby, the first black American Leaguer, in 1964, "but when we stop playing, our dollars stop. When I retired in '59 I wanted to stay in the game, to be a coach or in some other capacity, or to manage in the minors until I'd qualify for a big league job. Baseball owners are missing the boat by not considering Negroes for such jobs." Monte Irvin, who had integrated the New York Giants in 1949 and clearly possessed managerial capabilities, concurred. "Among retired and active players [there] are Negroes with backgrounds suited to these jobs," wrote Irvin. "Owning a package liquor store, bowling alley or selling insurance is hardly the vocation for an athlete who has accumulated a lifetime knowledge of the game."

Had Robinson, Doby, Irvin or another black been offered a managerial position in the 1950s or early 1960s, and particularly if the first black manager had experienced success, it is possible that this would have opened the doors for other black candidates. As with Robinson's ascension to the major leagues, this example might ultimately have made the hiring and firing of a black manager more or less routine. Robinson dismissed the notion that a black manager might experience extraordinary difficulties. "Many people believe that white athletes will not play for a Negro manager," he argued in 1964. "A professional athlete will play with or for anyone who helps him make more money. He will respect ability, first, last and all the time. This is something that baseball's executives must learn—that any experienced player with leadership qualities can pilot a ball club to victory, no matter what the color of his skin."

On the other hand, the persistent biases of major league owners and their subsequent history of discriminatory hiring indicate that the solitary example of a Jackie Robinson regime would probably not have been enough to shake the complacency of the baseball establishment. Few baseball executives considered hiring blacks as managers even in the 1960s and 1970s. In 1960 Chicago

White Sox owner Bill Veeck, who had hired Doby in 1947 and represented the most enlightened thinking in the game, raised the issue, but even Veeck defined special qualifications needed for a black to manage. "A man will have to have more stability to be a Negro coach or manager and be slower to anger than if he were white," stated Veeck. "The first major league manager will have to be a fellow who has been playing extremely well for a dozen years or so so that he becomes a byword for excellence." The following year Veeck sold the White Sox; other owners ignored the issue entirely.

Robinson himself never flagged in his determination to see a black manager. In 1972 baseball commemorated the 25th anniversary of Robinson's major league debut at the World Series at Riverfront Stadium in Cincinnati. A graying, almost blind, but still defiant Robinson told a nationwide television audience, "I'd like to live to see a black manager." Nine days later he was dead.

"I would have eagerly welcomed the challenge of a managerial job before I left the game," Robinson revealed in his 1972 autobiography, *I Never Had It Made*. "I know I could have been a good manager." But despite his obvious qualifications, no one offered him a job. Thus, Jackie Robinson once again had been the first—the first of many worthy black baseball players denied the chance to manage in the major leagues.

The Players

## CHAPTER 7

The 100 Greatest Players

Michael Gershman

Picking baseball's hundred greatest players looks easy, which is why it's been tried more often than a Cub fan's patience. But in fact it requires the hand of a sculptor, the eye of an eagle, the nose of a sommelier, and the sensitivity of a redistricted Congressman up for reelection. Lacking these attributes, brass will suffice.

Part of the problem revolves around packing a hundred great players into just nine positions. It is easy to be blinded by power and pick just fireballing pitchers or slugging left fielders. Balance requires a different approach, with proper attention paid to fielding, baserunning, longevity, and other factors unrelated solely to batting or pitching statistics.

Accordingly, after poring over the contents of this volume, I have selected the players I considered the best:

- eight at each corner position (first and third base, left and right field);
- ten at each interior position (catcher, second base, shortstop, and center field);
- four who logged quality time in both infield and outfield (like Pete Rose);
- twenty-four pitchers (with representation for relievers).

One of the problems with this approach is that the eleventh best shortstop may very well be a better all-around ballplayer than the eighth best left fielder. Nevertheless, drawing the line—and thus obtaining focus—is what this exercise is all about. The great ones are easy to identify; the problem comes in separating the near great from the very good. Some of the players who didn't make the list were very good indeed—Johnny Mize, Pee Wee Reese, Early Wynn, and more.

It was tempting to pick a hundred Hall of Famers and let it go at that. But such a procedure would necessarily exclude players of today who are sure bets to make the Hall—such as Carlton Fisk, Nolan Ryan, and Ryne Sandberg. A second problem with an all-Hall top hundred is that I have the advantage of the records in this book, which are seemingly unfamiliar to those on the Hall of Fame Veterans Committee who place a Pop Haines in Cooperstown while keeping a Bid McPhee out, or those writers who persist in their snubs of Bill Mazeroski and Ron Santo.

Some members of the Baseball Hall of Fame are merely famous for being famous—like Candy Cummings, who may have invented the curveball—or famous for being pulled into the Hall by their more illustrious teammates, like the infield of the New York Giants of the 1920s. Such Hall of Famers are easy enough to exclude from any list of the top 100 baseball figures. But if fame alone is not enough to make the cut, how about great stats? While statistics are the lifeblood of *Total Baseball*, numbers can never adequately reflect the accomplishments of the game's pioneers, white or black. Dan Brouthers was the greatest offensive force in the game before 1900. His numbers would probably be very different if he were beamed down to play today, but then again he would not be playing the game of yesterday, and it could be said that he would not even be Dan Brouthers anymore. It is safe to assume, I believe, that while an average player of a century ago probably could not play in the 1990s, a star of an earlier period would be a star today. And as for Negro League baseball, statistics—even the scattered and fragmentary numbers unearthed by the Society for American Baseball Research—can only hint at the greatness of an Oscar Charleston or a Pop Lloyd. Such men were excluded during their active careers; they cannot be excluded here.

Having delivered the requisite caveats, it is now time to deliver the goods. I have tried to go beyond the stats and convey in each of these profiles a sense of the man, the era in which he performed, and why he deserves to be included in a list more elite than the roll call of the Baseball Hall of Fame.

Humorist Robert Benchley once said of baseball that "one of the chief duties of the fan is to engage in arguments with the man behind him. This department of the game has been allowed to run down fearfully." I hope this top hundred list stimulates a whole new bunch of arguments.

First Base (8)	*Second Base* (10)	Morgan, Joe	Maranville, Rabbit
Anson, Cap	Collins, Eddie	Sandberg, Ryne	Ripken, Cal
Brouthers, Dan	Evers, Johnny		Smith, Ozzie
Foxx, Jimmie	Frisch, Frankie	*Shortstop* (10)	Vaughan, Arky
Gehrig, Lou	Gehringer, Charlie	Aparicio, Luis	Wagner, Honus
Greenberg, Hank	Hornsby, Rogers	Appling, Luke	
Killebrew, Harmon	Lajoie, Nap	Banks, Ernie	*Third Base* (8)
McCovey, Willie	Mazeroski, Bill	Cronin, Joe	Baker, Home Run
Sisler, George	McPhee, Bid	Lloyd, John Henry	Boggs, Wade

Brett, George
Mathews, Eddie
Robinson, Brooks
Santo, Ron
Schmidt, Mike
Traynor, Pie

DiMaggio, Joe
Hamilton, Billy
Mantle, Mickey
Mays, Willie
Murphy, Dale
Snider, Duke
Speaker, Tris

Rose, Pete
Yount, Robin

Catchers (10)
Bench, Johnny
Berra, Yogi
Campanella, Roy
Carter, Gary
Cochrane, Mickey
Dickey, Bill
Ewing, Buck
Fisk, Carlton
Gibson, Josh
Hartnett, Gabby

Fingers, Rollie
Ford, Whitey
Gibson, Bob
Grove, Lefty
Hubbell, Carl
Keefe, Tim
Johnson, Walter
Koufax, Sandy
Mathewson, Christy
Nichols, Kid
Paige, Satchel
Palmer, Jim
Rusie, Amos
Ryan, Nolan
Seaver, Tom
Spahn, Warren
Walsh, Ed
Wilhelm, Hoyt
Young, Cy

Left Field (8)
Brock, Lou
Henderson, Rickey
Jackson, Joe
Kiner, Ralph
Musial, Stan
Simmons, Al
Stargell, Willie
Williams, Ted

Right Field (8)
Aaron, Hank
Clemente, Roberto
Jackson, Reggie
Kaline, Al
Robinson, Frank
Ruth, Babe
Thompson, Sam
Winfield, Dave

Center Field (10)
Ashburn, Richie
Charleston, Oscar
Cobb, Ty

Utility (4)
Bell, Cool Papa
Robinson, Jackie

Pitchers (24)
Alexander, Grover
Brown, Mordecai
Carlton, Steve
Clemens, Roger
Feller, Bob

HANK AARON
Right Field. Born Feb. 5, 1934 Mobile, Ala. Holds major league record for most lifetime home runs (755). NL MVP 1957.

Even though he led the NL in hits and batting average in 1956, Henry Louis Aaron, Jr., was pictured backward—batting lefthanded—on his 1957 baseball card.

That was fitting symbolism for the man who did everything quietly, except break Babe Ruth's record for career home runs. Hank Aaron integrated the Sally League, set records for career RBIs (2,297) and total bases (6,856), won two batting titles and four RBI crowns, and hit .300 or better in fourteen seasons—all very quietly.

No one exclaimed over his fielding, either, although Aaron played errorless defense in fourteen World Series games, won three Gold Gloves, led the league's outfielders three times in double plays, and twice in fielding runs. According to the Total Baseball Ranking, he was baseball's leading player from 1961 to 1990 and fifth overall, behind only Babe Ruth, Napoleon Lajoie, Ty Cobb, and Ted Williams.

Aaron hit crosshanded in Mobile, Alabama, and with the Indianapolis Clowns of the Negro AL. After the Braves bought his contract, he hit .326 in the Northern League and .362 to lead the Sally League. When Bobby Thomson broke his ankle in spring training in 1954, Aaron became a major league regular at age twenty.

Three years later, with characteristically little fanfare, he was named the NL's MVP as the Braves won the pennant, and he hit .393 in the World Series, including 3 home runs to lead all batters. Always rising to the occasion, Aaron hit home runs in two of the twenty-four All-Star Games in which he played, homered in all three playoff games in 1969, and amassed a lifetime World Series average of .364.

Number 44 attracted attention only with his home runs, hitting 44 in four different seasons; he won three National League home run crowns and tied for a fourth. In 1973 he hit 40 home runs in just 392 at bats. He broke Ruth's record the following year with a rocket off Al Downing in Atlanta, and finished his career with a record 755.

Although many fans discovered Aaron after most of his career was over, his colleagues knew how special he was. Stan Musial jumped onto the field to congratulate him when he joined the 3,000 hit club, and Mickey Mantle said of him, "Aaron was to my time what Joe DiMaggio was to the era when he played."

He was elected to the Hall of Fame in 1982.

GROVER CLEVELAND ALEXANDER
Pitcher. Born Feb. 26, 1887 St. Paul, Neb. Died Nov. 4, 1950 St. Paul,. Neb. Holds NL records for lifetime shutouts (90) and lifetime complete games (436).

Grover Cleveland Alexander got his big break when he was traded for a vote.

Charles Carr, owner of the American Association's Indianapolis team, had invested in a company that manufactured baseballs. Anxious to have his ball used in the New York State League, he told the owner of the Syracuse team, "If you'll vote for my ball, I'll give you a good pitcher for nothing."

The pitcher, Alexander, suffered from double vision at the time but recovered enough to win 29 games for Syracuse—13 of them shutouts. Drafted by the Phillies, he no-hit the Athletics in a five-inning exhibition game and won 28 games in 1911 to set the rookie record. He won 19, 22, and 27 his next three years to set the stage for the most successful three-year run enjoyed by any pitcher.

In 1915 he won 31 games (12 shutouts and a record 4 one-hitters) and outdid himself a year later by winning 33 games, 16 of them shutouts. In 1917 he won 30, two of them complete games in a Labor Day doubleheader against the Dodgers. If there were a "Triple Crown" for pitchers, as many have suggested, Alexander would have won it twice, leading the league in most wins, strikeouts, and lowest ERA for 1916 and 1920. The second time occurred after he returned from military duty deaf in one ear and suffering from epilepsy.

Occasional neurological fits and an eventually crippling

fondness for liquor didn't ruin his pitching. He led the league in ERA twice after his trade to the Chicago Cubs, for whom he won 27 games in 1920. Waived to the Cardinals six years later, he pitched the 15–1 underdogs to complete game victories in the second and sixth games and recorded the most dramatic "save" in Series history, striking out Tony Lazzeri with the bases loaded in the seventh inning of the seventh game.

Alex averaged 19.6 wins for nineteen years, pitched 90 lifetime shutouts (second only to Walter Johnson's 110), and won 373 games to tie Christy Mathewson as the NL lifetime leader. Even more impressive, he recorded the bulk of them at hitter-friendly parks—Philadelphia's Baker Bowl with its 290-foot right field fence and Wrigley Field. He joined the other immortals in Cooperstown in 1938.

ADRIAN "CAP" ANSON

First Baseman. Born Apr. 11, 1852 Marshalltown, Ia. Died Apr. 14, 1922 Chicago. Holds NL record for most seasons batting .300 or more (18). Most seasons of big-league play, 27 (5 NA, 22, NL).

Adrian Constantine "Cap" Anson was the first man to reach 3,000 hits, the first manager to rotate pitchers, and the first player to draw the color line against blacks in baseball.

A hard-driving disciplinarian, Anson was perhaps the most influential player in the nineteenth century. He played in the first professional league, the National Association, from its inception in 1871 and hit .331 in the NL twenty-five years later. Using a split grip, he hit .300 or better in twenty-five seasons, won two batting titles and eight RBI crowns, averaging an RBI every five at-bats over the course of his career.

Anson spent a year at Notre Dame, turned pro with the NA Rockford Forest Citys, played third base for the Philadelphia Athletics for four years, and joined Chicago when White Stockings owner William Hulbert formed the NL. Anson became the White Sox captain in 1878 and switched to first base exclusively when he took over as manager in 1879.

He managed Chicago to pennants from 1880 to 1882, 1884, and 1885, rotating his pitchers and using signals to his hitters and fielders. He has a claim to originating platooning and initiated preseason training. He also was fined regularly by umpires and league officials, earning the nickname "Baby" (for crybaby) before cleaning up his act to earn the nickname "Cap" (for captain). He used bed checks to keep tabs on his charges but also got them first-class hotel rooms and personally marched them onto the field single file before every game.

In 1883, Anson refused to play in an exhibition game at Toledo because the home team had a black catcher, Moses Fleetwood Walker. Although Anson backed down when threatened with forfeiture of the gate, he used his position and popularity to ban black pitcher George Stovey in 1887 when John Montgomery Ward tried to sign him to the Giants; no one tried to upset this "gentleman's agreement" until 1947.

Despite this black mark on his character, Anson later mellowed and eventually became known as "Pop" Anson. When he was fired in 1897, Chicago briefly became known as the Orphans, because they'd lost their Pop.

Anson managed the Giants for just twenty-five days, turned down $50,000 donated by Chicago fans, opened a billiard saloon, tried to organize a rival major league—the abortive American Association of 1899, entered vaudeville (doing skits written by Ring Lardner), and served a term as city clerk in Chicago. He was voted into the Hall of Fame in 1939.

LUIS APARICIO

Shortstop. Born Apr. 29, 1934 Maracaibo, Venezuela. Holds major league records for most games at shortstop (2,581), assists (8,016), and double plays (1,553).

Hank Greenberg had a choice of Venezuelan shortstops in the 1950s and guessed wrong. The Indians' general manager didn't think Luis Aparicio was worth a $10,000 bonus and traded instead for his countryman, Alfonso "Chico" Carrasquel. Carrasquel's career ended in 1959, the same year Aparicio led the "Go-Go Sox" to a pennant, the first for Chicago since the scandal year of 1919.

While Maury Wills is generally given credit with reinventing the stolen base in 1962, Aparicio had made pilferage pay six years earlier. In his rookie year, Aparicio led the league in stolen bases with 21, handled more chances than any AL shortstop, and was named Rookie of the Year. Aparicio led the league in stolen bases his first nine years in the AL (1956–1964), once stole 26 consecutive bases, and was successful on 79 percent of his base stealing attempts.

In truth, Aparicio was not a prototypical leadoff man, sporting an on base average of only .313. Part of his success was due to the bat-handling ability of second baseman and second-place hitter Nelson Fox. Looie hollered like Fox, spat tobacco juice like Fox, and named his son for Fox. When Fox won the MVP award in 1959, the year the Sox won the pennant, Aparicio was right behind him in second place.

Fox and Aparicio won more fielding titles together than any other double play combination, and no shortstop ever led his league in the major defensive categories as often as Looie. He won nine Gold Gloves, was selected to the *Sporting News* All-Star team five times, and the All-Star fielding team ten times. Aparicio attributed his success to using a heavier glove in infield practice to make his own feel lighter during the game.

In January 1963, the White Sox broke up the double play combination, trading Looie to the Orioles. Aparicio provided some of the leadership that enabled the Orioles to win the 1966 pennant and sweep the World Series. He began a second hitch with the White Sox in 1968, hit better than .300 for the only time in his career in 1970 (.313), and finished up playing three years for the Red Sox, giving him eighteen consecutive seasons in which he played 100 or more games. Aparicio was voted into the Hall of Fame in 1984.

LUKE APPLING

Shortstop. Born Apr. 2, 1907 High Point, N.C. Died Jan. 3, 1991 Cumming, Ga. Won two batting titles, including a record for shortstops of .388 in 1936.

They called him Old Aches and Pains, Fumblefoot, and Old Tanglehoof. But by the time he had retired, Luke Appling had hit .300 or better nine straight years and sixteen times in all; had set a major league record by

leading the AL in assists seven seasons in a row, and had played more games at shortstop than any ALr.

The hypochondriacal Appling would complain to White Sox manager Jimmy Dykes, saying "Honest, Jimmy, I'm dying." In actuality, over his long career Appling only broke a finger in 1930 and a leg in 1938. "Old Aches and Pains" was hung on him when he roomed with Chicago's trainer. The roomies would get to Comiskey Park early, and Appling would catch forty winks on the rubbing table; inquiring mates were told he was getting "special treatment for a muscle pull."

Lucius Benjamin Appling was healthy enough to consider pro football after playing fullback at Oglethorpe College, but joined the Atlanta Crackers instead. After hitting .326 in 104 games, he was told that the Cubs had bought his contract; however, Bill Veeck, Sr., had second thoughts, and Appling wound up with the Chicago White Sox instead.

Veeck must have felt relieved when the rookie started 1931 0-for-28 and averaged an error every other day; manager Lew Fonseca tried to trade him to no avail. He told Appling, "You're going to play 154 games if you hit .154 and field .154." By 1933, Luke was leading the AL in errors for the first of a record five times, but he also tied Billy Rogell for the lead in total chances and hit .322.

In 1936 he went 4-for-4 the final day of the season to become the first AL shortstop to win a batting title. He won his second in 1943 (.328) before going into the service. By 1949 he had become, at 42, the oldest regular shortstop in baseball history. He eclipsed Rabbit Maranville's record of 2,154 games at short, and retired with a career batting average of .310.

Appling won pennants managing Memphis (Southern Association) and Indianapolis (American Association) and managed the Kansas City A's in 1967. Elected to the Hall of Fame in 1964, he made an appearance in the Cracker Jack All-Star Game in 1984, homering at age 75 against Warren Spahn.

RICHIE ASHBURN
Center Field. Born Mar. 19, 1927 Tilden, Neb. Holds major league records for most years with 400 or more putouts (9) and 500 or more putouts (4).
When Richie Ashburn reported to spring training in 1948, all he had to do to win the center field job for the Phillies was beat out the man who had won the previous year's batting championship by 46 points—Harry "The Hat" Walker.

But Walker fouled a pitch off his foot one morning and was out of the lineup through May. By then, Ashburn was hitting .346 and had unseated him as the Phils' center fielder. The only rookie voted to the 1948 All-Star team, Ashburn had a pair of singles and a stolen base. Even though he broke a finger in August, no injury could spoil a year in which he had a 23-game hitting streak, led the league with 32 stolen bases, hit .333, and was named Rookie of the Year.

Some skeptics pointed out that, "He's not hitting .333; he's hitting .133 and running .200." But in a fifteen-year career, Ashburn hit .300 or better nine times, won two batting titles, got on base about 40 percent of the time, and posted a .308 career average, topping Pete Rose, Willie Mays, and Hank Aaron, among others. As an out-

fielder he set records by recording 500 or more putouts in four different seasons and 400 or more putouts in nine different seasons. He tied Max Carey's major league records by leading the league in that department nine times; he accepted the most chances nine times; he ranks fifth behind Carey, Willie Mays, Tris Speaker, and Ty Cobb in both career putouts and total chances.

"Whitey" Ashburn won batting titles in 1955 (.338) and 1958 (.350), but his greatest moment as a Phillie came in the field. On the last day of the 1950 season, the Dodgers, trailing Philadelphia by a game, played them at Ebbets Field. With the score tied, 1–1, in the bottom of the ninth inning, Brooklyn's Cal Abrams tried to score from second on Duke Snider's single; Ashburn cut him down by twenty feet, setting the stage for Dick Sisler's tenth-inning homer and clinching the Phils' first flag in thirty-five years.

Traded to the Cubs in 1961, Ashburn became one of the original Mets in 1962 and the expansion team's first All-Star, the fifth time he'd been named to an All-Star squad. Since retiring as a player, Ashburn has become the Phillies' longest-running broadcaster.

FRANK "HOME RUN" BAKER
Third Baseman. Born Mar. 13, 1886 Trappe, Md., Died Jun. 28, 1963 Trappe, Md.
By the end of the 1910 season, Frank Baker had hit just six home runs in 1,133 at bats. Up to that point, he was more noted as a base stealer than a power hitter, having stolen 20 or more bases every year and having led the league in triples in 1909 with 19.

Then Baker hit 11 homers in 1911 to lead the league for the first of four straight years and helped Connie Mack's Athletics to their second straight pennant. In the World Series, the Giants' Christy Mathewson won the opener, 2–1. Game Two was tied 1–1 in the sixth; New York's Rube Marquard had retired thirteen batters in a row; but, after Eddie Collins doubled, Baker pulled an inside pitch over the short right field wall at the Polo Grounds to give the A's a 3–1 win. The next day, Mathewson's ghost writer, John Wheeler, second-guessed Marquard and advised that "Baker should be pitched *outside*." Later that day, in Game Three, Mathewson retired Baker on two harmless grounders and a fly ball. When Baker came to bat for the fourth time, with the Giants ahead 1–0 with one out in the ninth, Mathewson got two strikes, but then Baker pulled an outside pitch into the right field seats; the A's won, 3–1 in 11 innings, and Frank Baker suddenly became "Home Run" Baker.

Baker batted cleanup, behind Eddie Collins, and sportswriters suggested that Collins's antics on the basepaths made Baker a better hitter. Collins laughed. "When it came to hitting," he said, "Baker needed help like Carnegie needed money." A .300 hitter in six different seasons, he led the league in RBIs twice and might have done even more damage if he hadn't missed two whole seasons.

When the A's were swept in the 1914 Series, Mack decided to punish his players with stiff pay cuts; Baker sat out the season instead and was sold to the Yankees. He also didn't play in 1920, the year his wife died, but helped New York win pennants in 1921 and 1922 as a spot player.

In 1961 sportswriter Joe Williams asked Baker how

many homers he would hit today. He replied, "I'd say 50 anyway. The year I hit 12, I also hit the right field fence at Shibe Park 38 times; all of those would have been home runs with the lively ball."

ERNIE "MR.CUB" BANKS
Shortstop/First Baseman. Born Jan. 31, 1931 Dallas, Tex. NL MVP 1958, 1959. Holds major league shortstop record for home runs in a season (47).

To the victors go the spoils—and most of the MVP Awards. Yet, once in baseball history, the shortstop of a club tied for fifth was named MVP two straight years. In 1958 Ernie Banks led the league in home runs (47), RBIs (129), and slugging percentage (.614), and played in every game. A year later, Banks led the league again with 143 ribbies. He hit 20 or more homers in thirteen seasons, hit .300 or better three times, and drove in 100 or more runs eight times. He led the league's shortstops in fielding three times and, after moving to first base in 1962, led all first basemen in putouts five times.

Banks never played minor league ball, jumping directly from the Kansas City Monarchs of the Negro AL to the Chicago Cubs. He hit .314 in ten games in 1953, took over as the Cubs' starting shortstop the following year, and had his first great season in 1955, knocking in 117 runs and hitting 44 homers, a record for shortstops; five of them came with the bases loaded, then a record (since broken by Don Mattingly).

By 1957 he was one of the most feared power hitters in the league. The late umpire Tom Gorman once recalled that, "in 1957 Banks was knocked down four times by four different pitchers—Don Drysdale, Bob Purkey, Bob Friend, and Jack Sanford. And each time he was knocked down, Banks hit their next pitch out of the park."

He led the league in RBIs in 1959 and homers again in 1960 (41). Only Eddie Mathews's 46th homer in a 1959 playoff game kept Banks, who had 45, from a share of three consecutive home run titles. He hit more home runs than any shortstop in the history of the game (293) and wound up with 512 for his career. Prior to his retirement in 1971, he was voted the Greatest Cub Player of All Time.

After becoming a minor league instructor for the Cubs, Banks belied his goody-two-shoes image by saying things like, "I like my players to be married and in debt. That's the way you motivate them." But Cub fans will always remember him as the ballplayer who said, "What a great day for baseball. Let's play two!"

JAMES "COOL PAPA" BELL
Infielder/Outfielder. Negro Leagues 1922–46; St. Louis Stars, Pittsburgh Crawfords, Detroit Wolves, Kansas City Monarchs, Chicago American Giants, Memphis Red Sox, Homestead Grays. Born May 17, 1903 Starkville, Miss. Died March 7, 1991 St. Louis, Mo.

Cool Papa Bell may have been the headiest and fastest baserunner of his time, and, maybe, all time.

He is credited with stealing 175 bases in 1933 and is said to have once rounded the bases in 12 seconds. (The official record is 13.3 seconds, set by Evar Swanson of the Reds in 1931.) Bell scored from first on a sacrifice in a 1940s exhibition against major leaguers. Satchel Paige bunted him over to second, then seeing third uncovered,

Bell took off; catcher Roy Partee gave chase, but Bell eluded him and slid home safely; he was forty-five at the time.

Originally a righthanded batter, Bell taught himself to switch hit and is credited with hitting .437 for Torreon of the Mexican League in 1940. Over an 89-game season, he led the league in runs (119), hits (167), triples (15), home runs (12) and RBIs (79). According to incomplete records, he hit .407 in 1944 and .402 in 1946.

Bill Veeck said, "Defensively, he was the equal of Tris Speaker, Joe DiMaggio or Willie Mays." Pro basketball pioneer and baseball scout Eddie Gottlieb said, "If he had played in the major leagues, he would have reminded the fans of Willie Keeler as a hitter and Ty Cobb as a baserunner—and he might have exceeded both."

Born in Starkville, Mississippi, James Bell played semi-pro ball with four of his brothers on the Compton Hill Cubs in St. Louis, breaking in as a lefthanded pitcher. After a particularly strong game in 1922, the St. Louis Stars signed him for $90 a month and switched him to the outfield to take advantage of his speed every day.

Named Cool Papa for his unflappability, he performed up to par in his few appearances against major league opposition. In 1929 he and other black stars barnstormed against a team headed by Hall of Famers Charlie Gehringer, Al Simmons, and Heinie Manush and won six games out of eight.

When his playing days were over, Bell had a hand in the development of Ernie Banks and others. Banks credits Bell with taking him from the Texas sandlots to Kansas City, and both Lou Brock and Maury Wills give Bell credit for helping them steal bases. He was elected to the Hall of Fame in 1974.

JOHNNY BENCH
Catcher. Born Dec. 7, 1947 Oklahoma City, Okla. NL MVP 1970, 1972.

Ted Williams has signed many autographs but none as prescient as one penned in spring training in 1965: "To Johnny Bench, a sure Hall of Famer."

Bench was named to the NL All-Star team fourteen times, played in every game from 1968 to 1975, and hit .409 with 3 home runs. He set a major league record for home runs by a catcher (327 plus 62 playing elsewhere), won two home run crowns, led the league in RBIs three times, and was chosen MVP twice.

While Bench is remembered most for his offense, he may have had his greatest impact behind the bat. He was the first receiver to use a protective helmet in the field, popularized catching onehanded, kept his throwing hand behind his back to protect it from foul tips, and said his father "taught me to throw 254 feet—twice the distance to second base—from a crouch."

Not known for keeping his counsel, Bench once said flatly, "I can throw out any runner alive," and brashly predicted that he would be the first catcher to be named Rookie of the Year. He did just that in 1968, caught 154 games, a rookie record, and won the first of ten straight Gold Gloves. Bench hit 45 homers and was chosen MVP for the first time in 1970, the year Bob Hunter, a Los Angeles sportswriter, first called Cincinnati "the Big Red Machine."

That year, the Reds ran into Brooks Robinson and, the

second time Bench was named MVP, in 1972, the Big Red Machine was derailed by the Oakland A's Mustache Gang. When the Reds squared off against the New York Yankees in 1976, the press played up the confrontation between Bench and the Yankees' catcher and captain, Thurman Munson.

Bench caught Mickey Rivers stealing in Game One, New York's only attempted theft in the Series, got two hits in each of the first three games, and hit two home runs in Game Four to lead the Reds to their first World Series sweep. Munson hit .529 with 2 RBIs; Bench hit .533 and knocked in 6 runs. Munson gave Bench his due, "The man deserves all the credit in the world."

Bench made Williams's prediction come true in 1989, the first year he was eligible. He is currently a broadcaster with CBS radio nationally and WLWT in Cincinnati.

LAWRENCE "YOGI" BERRA
Catcher. Born May 12, 1925 St. Louis, Mo. AL MVP, 1951, 1954, 1955.
Branch Rickey didn't make many mistakes, but blowing Yogi Berra for all of $250 was a real beaut.

In 1942 Rickey was the Cardinals' general manager and offered Berra $250 to sign, refusing to pay him the same $500 offered to his friend, Joe Garagiola. Berra turned down the $250 and, a year later, the Yankees signed him for the very same $500; not very long thereafter, they turned down a $50,000 offer from Giant manager Mel Ott, who had seen Berra play for the International League Newark Bears.

Berra eventually became a fifteen-time All-Star, a three-time MVP, and a Hall of Famer. He also holds numerous World Series records including games by a catcher (63), hits (71), and times on the winning team (10). Though lightly regarded as a manager, he was the first big league skipper to win pennants in both leagues in nearly forty years.

Born in "the Hill" section of St. Louis, Berra got his nickname when childhood friends watching a movie noted Berra's resemblance to a Hindu practicing yoga. Following stints in the navy and the minors, Yogi became a Yankee and shared catching duties with Aaron Robinson and Sherman Lollar until the Dodgers ran him ragged in the 1947 World Series. After being tutored by Bill Dickey, however, he became a standout catcher and accepted 950 errorless chances from July 28, 1957 to May 10, 1959.

Berra led AL catchers in putouts eight times, assists and fielding three times each, and handled the Yankee pitching staff masterfully. Although he never led the league in home runs or RBIs, Berra, a notorious bad-ball hitter, was a constant threat offensively, particularly with men on base; he was named Most Valuable Player in 1951, repeated in 1954 and 1955, and retired with a .285 lifetime average.

Named to manage the Yankees in 1964, he won the pennant but lost both a seven-game Series and his job, both to Johnny Keane. He joined the Mets as a coach and became the manager in 1973, taking them from fifth place to the pennant, ultimately losing the Series again in seven games, to the A's. He returned to the Yankees as coach and manager, was elected to the Hall of Fame in 1972 and ended his career as a coach with the Astros.

WADE BOGGS
Third Baseman. Born June 15, 1958 Omaha, Neb. Won four straight AL batting titles, 1985–1988, five straight on base percentage titles, 1985–1989.
Despite hitting a paltry .259 in 1992, Wade Boggs's lifetime average is still a robust .338, which ties him with Nap Lajoie and Jesse Burkett for eighteenth place.

Boggs scored 100 or more runs seven straight times, led the AL in batting five times, and notched 200 or more hits in seven straight seasons, a modern record. Named to the All-Star team in 1985, he has been a starter every year from 1986 to 1992.

The son of a retired Marine, Boggs grew up an all-state kicker in Tampa, Florida, signed with the Red Sox in 1976, and was playing for Elmira of the Eastern League shortly after graduating from high school. In 1980 he lost the International League batting title on the last day of the season but won it the next year on the last day of the season. Boggs became a regular in 1982 when Carney Lansford was injured. He booted the first two ground balls hit to him in the majors but hit .349, splitting his time between first base and third.

In 1983 he made 27 errors but led the majors in hitting (.361) and on-base percentage (.449). A year later, he topped all AL third basemen in errors but also had the most chances, double plays, assists, putouts, and fielding runs. In 1985 he hit .368 to win the first of four straight batting titles, reached base safely 340 times, and had 240 hits, the most since Babe Herman's 241 in 1930. He batted .357 to help the Red Sox win the pennant in 1986 and has hit .311 in three playoffs and World Series.

The "Chicken Man," so named by Jim Rice for his love of fowl, lives a disciplined life, getting up at the same time, going to the ballpark at the same time, eating chicken daily, and doing the same things the same way as often as possible. He fields exactly 150 grounders in practice, steps into the batting cage at 5:17 and, after private time in the clubhouse bouncing a baseball off a wall, hits the field at precisely 7:17 for wind sprints.

Boggs says his eyesight is his greatest asset. He told *Newsweek*, "I can observe the spin on a breaking ball. If it happens to be a fastball, I can still hit it to left. And if the pitch happens to be off-speed enough, believe it or not, I'll pull it."

GEORGE BRETT
Third Baseman. May 15, 1953 Glen Dale, W. Va. In 1980 had highest batting average since Ted Williams' .406 of 1941.
George Brett joined the exclusive 3,000-hit club on September 30, 1992. He was already the only player to win batting titles in three different decades, a thirteen-time All-Star, and the last modern player to make a serious run at hitting .400.

The younger brother of pitcher Ken Brett, he led the league in hits and triples in 1975, repeated in both categories in 1976, and added his first batting title that year, hitting .333 to edge Rod Carew and teammate Hal McRae, later his manager. From 1976 to 1978 the Royals lost three straight playoffs to the Yankees despite Brett's three-run homer in 1976 and his three consecutive homers off Catfish Hunter in 1978.

Just before the All-Star break in 1980 Brett was hitting

.337 when he strained ankle ligaments trying to steal a base; however, he got hot in July and even hotter in August, going 4-for-4 on the 17th to reach the magic figure of .400. With two weeks left, he slumped but finished strong (10-for-19), ending the season at .390; he also led the league in slugging (.664) and, to absolutely no one's surprise, was named MVP.

That year, the Royals broke the playoff jinx against the Yankees as Brett homered in Game One and hit an upper deck home run off Goose Gossage to win Game Three. Although the Phils beat KC in a six-game Series, Brett homered and went 9-for-24 in the Series. The Royals finally won a championship in 1985 as Brett starred offensively and defensively; he went 4-for-5 in Game Seven, robbed the Cardinals of five potential hits and went 10-for-27, scoring five runs.

On July 24, 1983, Brett made history in a different way. With New York leading Kansas City 4-3 in the ninth inning at Yankee Stadium, he homered with two out and a man on to put the Royals in front, 5-4. Yankee manager Billy Martin contended that Brett should be declared out and the runs shouldn't count, because his bat had pine tar more than 18 inches from the knob to the barrel; the umpires agreed, awarding the win to the Yankees. The Royals protested, however, and AL president Lee Mac-Phail ended the Great Pine Tar Incident by overruling his own umpires and declaring a resumption of play at a later date.

Brett won his third batting title in 1990.

LOU BROCK
Left Field. Born Jun. 18, 1939 ElDorado, Ark. Holds major league record for most consecutive years 50 or more stolen bases (12).
In 1978 the NL announced that its annual stolen base leader would receive the Lou Brock Award, making Brock the first active player to have an award named after him. The greatest base stealer baseball had produced to that time, Lou went on to break Ty Cobb's "modern" career record of 891 with 938 (Billy Hamilton had 912 in 1888–1901) although the record was eventually eclipsed, in turn, by Rickey Henderson.

Brock ensured that he'd get numerous chances to run by joining the exclusive 3,000-hit club (3,023) and finishing a nineteen-year career with seven .300 seasons and a lifetime batting average of .293. In 1968 he led the league in doubles, triples, and steals, the first NL player to accomplish that feat since Honus Wagner did it in 1908.

Lou could run, hit, and even hit with power occasionally; in 1967 he led the Cardinals in extra-base hits and knocked in 76 runs as a leadoff man. As a youngster with the Chicago Cubs, Brock even blasted a home run into the center field stands at the Polo Grounds, a startling feat that had been accomplished only once before, by certified slugger Joe Adcock.

After being traded from the Cubs to the Cardinals for Ernie Broglio in June 1964, he hit .348 and scored 81 runs in 103 games; during the stretch run, when the Phillies folded, he hit .461 to help the Cardinals win their first pennant in eighteen years. Although he hit .300, 1964 would prove to be his poorest offensive Series. In 1967 he batted .414 with 12 hits, stole a record 7 bases, and went 4-for-4 in Game One. A year later, he stole 7 bases again

and improved to .464 with 13 hits, tying Bobby Richardson's record; his 14 steals is a World Series career record, tying Eddie Collins.

In 1966 he broke Maury Wills's stranglehold on the stolen base championship with 74 thefts. That was the first of four straight base-stealing crowns, and, after Bobby Tolan interrupted his string in 1970, Lou won four more in a row. In 1974 he smashed Maury Wills's season mark of 104 stolen bases, ending with 118, and was named Man of the Year by the Sporting News. He was elected to the Hall of Fame in 1985.

DENNIS "BIG DAN" BROUTHERS
First Baseman. Born May 8, 1858 Sylvan Lake, N.Y. Died Aug. 3, 1932 East Orange, N.J. Highest slugging average of any player to perform before 900; led NL in slugging six years in a row (1881–1886).
Big Dan Brouthers holds the highest lifetime average of any first baseman (.342), batting .300 or better for fourteen straight years. He played on champions in three leagues, won five batting titles, and topped the NL in slugging six straight times.

Although he hit just 106 homers, the lefthanded Brouthers (rhymes with "soothers") was "the Babe Ruth of his era." John McGraw, his Oriole teammate, said, "When I first went with Baltimore there were little flags stuck on the fences of the different parks to show where Brouthers had driven balls out."

Brouthers got his baseball baptism with the semipro Wappingers Falls Actives. The Troy Haymakers brought him to the big leagues but, after he made 34 errors in 39 games in 1879, returned him to the minors. In 1881 Big Dan shuffled off to Buffalo, where he led the NL in homers (8) and topped all batsmen in 1882 (.368) and 1883 (.374).

Brouthers, James "Deacon" White, Hardy "Old True Blue" Richardson, and Jack Rowe constituted Buffalo's "Big Four." Although they failed to bring Buffalo a pennant, the quartet—sold as a unit to the Wolverines after the 1885 season—brought Detroit its first flag in 1887. Brouthers led the league in runs, doubles, and on-base percentage.

When the Wolverines disbanded a year later, Brouthers was awarded to the Boston Beaneaters, with whom he won his third batting title (.373) in 1889. The next year, he jumped to the Boston Reds, a Players League team; when it, too, disbanded, he joined a team of the same name that captured the American Association pennant and won the batting title again in 1891 (.350). Big Dan "revolved" (changed teams) and became a Brooklyn Superba, copped his fifth batting crown in 1892 (.335), and was traded to the Orioles with Willie Keeler. Brouthers had his last great year in 1894, hitting .347 and providing 128 RBIs to lead Baltimore to its first pennant.

After brief stops in Louisville and Philadelphia he continued his slugging exploits in the minors, winning the batting title of the Class C Hudson River League in 1904 at the age of 46, capping that incredible year with a two-game return to the big leagues for McGraw's Giants. He served as a press box attendant at the Polo Grounds until he died in 1932. He was elected to the Hall of Fame in 1945.

MORDECAI "THREE FINGER" BROWN

Pitcher. Born Oct. 19, 1876 Nyesville, Ind. Died Feb. 14, 1948 Terre Haute, Ind. ERA of 1.06 in 1906 stands as NL best since 1880.

Mordecai Brown's colorful nickname often obscures what a great pitcher he was.

He ranks third behind Ed Walsh and Addie Joss in lifetime ERA (2.06) and trails only Walsh, Joss, and Christy Mathewson in allowing the fewest runners per nine innings (9.80). Ty Cobb said of Brown's breaking ball, "It was the most devastating pitch I ever faced. Christy Mathewson's fadeaway was good, but it was nothing like that curve Three-Fingered Brown threw at you."

Brown was seven when he put the index finger of his right hand into his uncle's corn shredder; it was amputated just above the knuckle. A few weeks later he broke his third and fourth fingers while chasing a hog; they healed into a gnarled, unnatural shape. Despite his handicap, Brown became a semipro infielder. One day, the team's star pitcher broke his arm and Brown took over; in five innings, he struck out fourteen, using a curve ball that broke unusually because of the shape of his hand.

"Miner" Brown (so named because he was a coal miner before he became a ballplayer) joined the Cardinals, going 9–13 in his rookie season. Cubs' manager Frank Chance saw great potential and traded for the man he called "the greatest fielding pitcher the game ever had." Brown won 15 games in 1904, 18 in 1905, and 26 in 1906, posting a 1.04 ERA.

In 1908 Brown won 29 games against 9 losses, threw four consecutive shutouts, and helped Chicago catch the slumping Giants by winning both ends of a September doubleheader. The next day, Fred Merkle's baserunning boner turned a Giant victory in a tie, ultimately necessitating a playoff game. When the first three Giants hit safely and the next two walked, Brown took over from Jack Pfiester without warming up. He shut the Giants out the rest of the way and the Cubs won the game, 4–2, and the pennant.

In 1909 he led the league in wins (27), complete games (32), and saves (7) but wrenched a ligament in his right leg. He remained effective in 1910, but the glory years were behind him. Traded to the Reds in 1913, he won only 5 games. Following a stretch managing the St. Louis Federals, he rejoined the Cubs, and he and Mathewson pitched their finales against each other, Mathewson winning the atypically inept contest 10–7.

The great pitchers thus concluded their personal rivalry with Mathewson winning thirteen times against Brown's eleven. Matty was an original inductee into the Hall of Fame in 1936; Brown had to wait an additional thirteen years.

ROY CAMPANELLA

Catcher. Born Nov. 19, 1921 Philadelphia, Pa. NL MVP 1951, 1953, 1955.

Baseball's all-time record crowd wasn't attracted by a red-hot playoff or a World Series game. Instead, 93,103 fans filled the Los Angeles Coliseum on May 7, 1959, to honor Roy Campanella, whose baseball career had ended the previous year when the car he was driving skidded into a telephone pole, leaving him paralyzed.

A decade after that unique tribute, Campanella received baseball's ultimate honor and was inducted into the Hall of Fame despite a major league career that had lasted a mere ten years. Then again, Campy was named MVP in three of the nine full seasons in which he played; 1951, 1953, and 1955 to rank with Stan Musial and Mike Schmidt as the only three-time MVPs in the National League.

An outstanding handler of pitchers, Campanella caught three no-hitters, led the league in putouts six times, caught 100 or more games a year his last nine years in the majors, and nailed two of every three runners that tried to steal on him. Although his batting average oscillated wildly (.312 to .207 to .318 to .219 between 1953 and 1956), he was more consistent at the power game, averaging 27 homers between 1949 and 1956.

He joined the Negro NL's Baltimore Elite Giants right out of high school and eventually made $3,000 a month as a full-fledged star, being named to All-Star teams in 1941, 1944, and 1945. After that season he became Brooklyn's second black signee, taking $185 a month to play with Nashua in the New England League; by 1949 he was the Dodgers' regular catcher.

In 1951 he hit .325 with 33 homers and 108 RBIs but pulled a leg muscle in the final regular season game, missing the last two games of the playoff. Monte Irvin says, "If Campanella hadn't injured himself in Philadelphia, he might have settled Ralph Branca down after one high strike to Bobby Thomson."

After a modest 1952 season, Campy hit 41 homers in 1953 (40 as a catcher to set the major league record), batted .312, and led the league with 142 RBIs. In 1955 he hit .318 with 32 homers and 107 RBIs and was named to the *Sporting News* All-Star Team for the fourth time. He hit two home runs as Brooklyn won its only World Series.

STEVE CARLTON

Pitcher. Born Dec. 22, 1944 Miami, Fla. NL Cy Young Award 1972, 1977, 1980, 1982.

Steve Carlton never won the hearts and minds of baseball writers, but he led the NL in innings pitched and strikeouts five times each, won 329 games, and captured four Cy Young Awards.

He trained by using isometrics, kung fu, and twisting his hands in three-foot deep buckets of rice. The powerful lefty made 30 or more starts in 16 seasons. "I've never paced myself," he said, "I've always thrown everything as hard as I can for as long as I can."

Offered $4,000 by the Pirates as a junior college freshman, Carlton was signed by Cards' scout Howie Pollet for $5,000. On a Cards trip to Japan in 1968, he began developing the slider that became his "out" pitch. He fanned 19 Mets in a September 1969 game to set an NL record, finished the season 17–11, and won 20 games in 1971.

Instead of the big raise he expected, Carlton got traded to the Phillies and responded with a historic season. Lefty won 27 games for the last place Phils, notching an all-time record 45 percent of the team's wins. A Triple Crown pitcher, he also led in ERA (1.97) and strikeouts (310), won his first Cy Young Award, and negotiated a salary of $167,000, then a record for pitchers.

The bounces didn't go his way the next year and he became a 20-game loser. He bounced back to win 59

games as the Phils won division titles in 1976, 1977, and 1978. In 1980, Carlton was 24–9 in the regular season, captured his third Cy Young Award, and beat the Royals twice in the World Series to give the Phillies their only world championship.

Three years after his last Cy Young Award (1982), Carlton went on the DL for the first time and was released by the Phils a year later. He pitched briefly for the Giants, White Sox, Indians, and Twins before retiring in 1988 as the NL leader in career strikeouts (4,000) and the leading lefty in the majors (4,136).

GARY CARTER

Catcher. Born Apr. 8, 1954 Culver City, Cal. All-Star Game MVP 1981, 1984.

In an earlier edition of *Total Baseball*, Bob Carroll wrote of Gary Carter, "The guy is friendly, open, cooperative, thoughtful, enthusiastic and has never been involved in a scandal. What's he hiding?"

Carter's gee-whiz personality has led observers to discount his achievements; however, he has clearly been the National League's leading catcher since Johnny Bench. A three-time Gold Glover, Carter led the league five times in assists and six straight years in games and putouts. Offensively, he drove in more than a hundred runs four times and hit 20 or more homers nine times.

Carter passed on more than a hundred football scholarship offers to sign with the Expos and was shocked to discover that they saw him not as a shortstop but as a catcher. In the beginning, Carter says, "I was the worst catcher you ever saw—a real joke." (One of his minor league managers charged him a quarter for every ball he dropped and often collected three or four dollars a game.)

He caught and played first and the outfield until the Expos traded Barry Foote in 1977. In 1978 he set a major league record by allowing just a single passed ball in 157 games. By 1981, "Kid" was the All-Star starter and homered off Ken Forsch and Ron Davis to be named MVP, joining Al Rosen, Arky Vaughan, Willie McCovey, and Ted Williams as the only men to homer twice in an All-Star Game. That fall, Carter hit .421 against the Phils in the divisional playoff and .438 against the Dodgers in the NLCS.

In the 1984 All-Star Game Carter homered off Dave Stieb to break a 1–1 tie and win his second All-Star MVP award. That season, despite knee problems which required postseason surgery, he tied Mike Schmidt for the RBI crown (106) and hit 27 homers. Traded to the Mets, he hit 24 homers to help the Mets win the pennant in 1986, drove in 3 runs in both Games Three and Four of the World Series, and singled to ignite the come-from-behind rally that won Game Six. After being released by the Mets in 1989, he played a year each with the Giants, Dodgers, and Expos.

OSCAR CHARLESTON

Center Fielder. Born Oct. 14, 1896 Indianapolis, Ind. Died Oct. 5, 1954 Philadelphia, Pa. Batted .434 in the Negro National League of 1921.

Oscar Charleston is generally regarded as the greatest of all Negro League players.

It diminishes Negro Leaguers to equate them with white players as the "black" this or that; however,

Charleston's preeminence is such that he is known equally as "the black Tris Speaker" for his fielding, "the black Ty Cobb" for his baserunning, and "the black Babe Ruth" for his hitting. John McGraw said that he was simply the best, adding, "If only I could calcimine him."

He started out as batboy for the Indianapolis ABCs in his home town, joined the army at age fifteen, and was stationed in the Philippines with the all-black 24th Infantry. Even at that age, he was skilled enough to play in the otherwise all-white Manila League. He also ran track and was timed at the 220-yard dash in 23 seconds flat, giving rise to his nickname, "the Hoosier Comet."

He started professional play with the Indianapolis ABC's in 1915 and later moved on to the Chicago American Giants and St. Louis Giants. In a five-game series between Charleston's St. Louis Giants and the white St. Louis Cardinals, he is reported to have hit four home runs in one game, two of them off Hall of Famer Jesse "Pop" Haines.

Charleston became player-manager of the Eastern Colored League Harrisburg Giants from 1922 to 1925 and moved to Philadelphia, where he became friends with catcher Biz Mackey and third baseman Judy Johnson. After stints with the Hilldales and the Homestead Grays, Johnson and Charleston moved to Pittsburgh when Gus Greenlee persuaded Charleston to manage and play for the Crawfords. Charleston hit .363, second only to Josh Gibson, and led the team to a 99–36 record, with the help of fellow Hall of Famers Gibson, Johnson, and Satchel Paige.

When the Crawfords moved to Toledo and Indianapolis, Charleston stayed with them through 1940, moving on to the Philadelphia Stars in 1941. After the war, Charleston was signed to Branch Rickey's Brooklyn Brown Dodgers, where he had a hand in corralling both Jackie Robinson and Roy Campanella. He joined them in the Hall of Fame in 1976.

ROGER CLEMENS

Pitcher. Born Aug. 4, 1962 Dayton, Oh. AL Cy Young Award 1986, 1987, 1991.

In 1987 Roger Clemens became the third pitcher, along with Sandy Koufax and Jim Palmer, to win back-to-back Cy Young Awards outright (Denny McLain won the award in 1968 and tied for it in 1969). He picked up his third Cy Young in 1991. Nicknamed "Rocket," or "Rocket Man," after an Elton John song, Clemens burst on the scene the night of April 29, 1986, when he struck out 20 Mariners. That broke the nine-inning record previously held by Tom Seaver, Steve Carlton, and Clemens's idol, Nolan Ryan.

Clemens was destined for stardom. Offered $1,500 by the Twins, Clemens instead entered San Jacinto Junior College, then turned down a $20,000 bonus offered by the Mets and transferred to the University of Texas. (There he joined Bruce Ruffin, Calvin Schiraldi, and Greg Swindell.) After beating Alabama, 4–3, in the finals in 1983, Rocket became the Red Sox first pick in the June draft, signing for $121,000.

Called up the following May, Clemens was 9–4 in August when he strained a tendon in his right forearm and missed the rest of the season. He suffered a second arm injury in 1985 and required arthroscopic surgery in the

rotator cuff of his right shoulder; yet eight months later he was striking out 20 Mariners on his way to winning his first 14 decisions. Starting for the American League in the All-Star Game, he retired nine straight batters to be named MVP. Clemens finished the 1986 season 24–4 to lead Boston to a division title and was the unanimous winner of the Cy Young Award. Pitching with the flu on three days' rest, Clemens beat the Angels, 8–1, to clinch the pennant. He left two World Series games ahead, 6–3 (after 4⅓ innings in Game Two) and 3–2 after 7 innings of the ill-fated Game Six.

In 1990 Clemens put together a 21–6 season but missed most of September because of a shoulder injury. The Sox won their division and Clemens left Game One of the playoffs after six shutout innings and got no decision. He gave up three runs in Game Four and was ejected after arguing with plate umpire Terry Cooney. In 1991 and 1992 Clemens won 18 games and remained the game's best active pitcher.

ROBERTO CLEMENTE
Right Field. Born Aug. 18, 1934 Carolina, P.R. Died Dec. 31, 1972 San Juan, P.R. NL MVP, 1966.
When Roberto Clemente graduated from high school in Puerto Rico, he received not only the best wishes of his friends and family but also blessings in person from scouts for ten different big league teams.

He had played for Santurce in the Puerto Rican Winter League while still a student and had quickly attracted bird dogs with his hitting, fielding, and throwing ability. Although the Milwaukee Braves offered him a $30,000 signing bonus, he kept an earlier commitment to the Dodgers and signed for $10,000.

However, he never played for Brooklyn or Los Angeles. A rule then in effect required that any player signing for more than $4,000 be put on the big league roster after a year in the minors; otherwise, he could be signed by any other club for $4,000. Although the Dodgers tried to hide Clemente on their Montreal roster by not playing him, he was claimed by the Pirates on November 22, 1954, for $4,000.

It was the Bucs' best investment since Honus Wagner. Clemente batted over .300 in thirteen seasons, won four NL batting crowns, finished with an even 3,000 hits, and ended an eighteen-year career with a lifetime average of .317. The NL MVP in 1966, he was also selected for the All-Star game twelve times.

A textbook right fielder, Clemente won twelve straight Gold Gloves. In 1958 he threw out 22 runners to win the first of a NL record five assists titles. A World Series star, he led the Bucs to championships in 1960 and 1971 and hit safely in every World Series game in which he played. In 1971 he homered in the sixth and seventh games, hit .414 with 12 hits, fielded flawlessly, and was chosen the Series MVP.

Throughout his career Clemente was plagued by back injuries, the result of an arthritic spine caused by an automobile accident. He died in an airplane crash on New Year's Eve, 1972, carrying food and medical supplies to earthquake-stricken Nicaragua.

The customary five-year waiting period was waived, and in 1973 he became the first Hispanic member of the Hall of Fame. Later he became the second baseball player, after Jackie Robinson, to be pictured on a U.S. postage stamp.

TY COBB
Center Field. Born Dec. 18, 1886 Narrows, Ga. Died July 17, 1961 Atlanta. Holds major league record for lifetime batting average (.366), most years leading league in batting (12) and hits (8).
When Ty Cobb was 18, his mother shot his father fatally at her bedroom window; some say she mistook him for a burglar, others that he suspected her of infidelity.

Either way, the tragedy probably spurred Cobb to become the fiercest competitor in baseball as well as the game's greatest hitter. Since 1947, only Stan Musial, Ted Williams, Rod Carew, George Brett, Tony Gwynn, and Wade Boggs have, in single seasons, outhit Cobb's career average of .366. Virtually overlooked is his feat of leading the league in RBIs four out of five years and bettering 100 seven times, mostly in the dead-ball era.

One of the original five players elected to the Hall of Fame (he got seven more votes than Babe Ruth), Cobb is the only ALr to hit .400 or better in three different seasons. The Georgia Peach hit .300 or better every year from 1906 to 1928 and won the AL batting championship every year from 1907 to 1915 and from 1917 to 1919. (He slumped to .371 in 1916, when Tris Speaker hit .386.) Revisionist historians have deprived him of the batting titles in 1910 and 1914, but Cobb went to his grave with twelve batting championships.

While serving as player-manager of the Tigers in the mid-1920s Cobb benched himself when he was hitting .392. At the time, the Tigers had an all-.400 hitting outfield—Heinie Manush (.402), Fats Fothergill (.406), and Harry Heilmann (.410)—and Cobb didn't want to tamper with such statistics.

Although Pete Rose eclipsed Cobb's record for career hits, and Maury Wills, Lou Brock, and Rickey Henderson have broken most of his baserunning records, Cobb remains the career leader in steals of home (35); he also stole second, third, and home in the same inning three different times. While it cannot be documented statistically, his aggressive style produced balks, throwing errors, and lapses of concentration that counted as runs.

Cobb was shrewd as well as belligerent. He started the practice of swinging several bats in the on-deck circle so that one would feel light when it came time to hit. Similarly, he hunted in lead-weighted boots in the winter, practiced in them all spring, and switched to paper-thin shoes once the season started. (That same shrewdness led him to buy Coca-Cola at $1.18 a share and build a considerable fortune.)

Although Detroit won three straight pennants from 1907 to 1909, Cobb was never part of a world championship team and, as a manager, he never brought the Bengals home higher than second.

GORDON "MICKEY" COCHRANE
Catcher. Born Apr. 6, 1903 Bridgewater, Mass. Died Jun. 28, 1962 Lake Forest, Ill. AL MVP 1928, 1934.
Mickey Cochrane was a franchise player—literally. In 1924, Cochrane had hit .333 for Portland in the Pacific Coast League and carried a stiff $50,000 price tag. When Connie Mack found the whole club could be had for

$200,000, he bought the franchise, sold the other players at a profit, and got Cochrane at a bargain price.

"Black Mike" hit .331, .357 and .349 from 1929 to 1931 to lead the A's to three pennants. A lifetime .320 hitter, he hit .300 or better nine times in his career. After he was sold to the Tigers in 1934 as a player-manager, he led them to a pennant in 1934 and a world championship in 1935.

Cochrane hit .400 in the 1929 Series, but Commissioner Landis threatened to suspend him for his brutal bench jockeying. Chastened, Cochrane greeted the Cubs with , "Hello, sweethearts! We're gonna serve tea this afternoon." After the A's won Game Five to secure the championship, Landis congratulated every Athletic except Cochrane. Just before he left, the Judge said to Mickey, "Hello, sweetheart. I came in after my tea. Will you pour?"

Mack sold Cochrane to the Tigers after the 1933 season. Just as he had sparked the A's, Black Mike led a fifth place team to the pennant his first year. As the season wore on, the exhausted Cochrane played but spent the night in a nearby hospital. The Gashouse Gang won the 1934 classic in seven games. Next year it was Cochrane's turn. He scored the run that clinched the World Series and later said, "It was my greatest day in baseball."

There would not be too many others. In a game against the Yankees in May 1937, Cochrane homered off Bump Hadley. On his next trip to the plate he took a fastball to his right temple and collapsed in a heap. He was unconscious for ten days but finally pulled through; he never played again. Elected to the Hall of Fame in 1947, he went on to serve as general manager of the A's under Mack and became a Tiger VP in 1961.

EDDIE "COCKY" COLLINS

Second Baseman. Born May 2, 1887 Millerton, N.Y. Died Mar. 25, 1951 Boston, Mass. Holds major league record for most years leading league in fielding (9). AL MVP 1914.

Eddie Collins may have been "Cocky," but as a member of four world championship teams he'd earned the right to be confident about his abilities. He hit an even .333 lifetime and batted .300 or better every year from 1909 to 1916 and the period 1919–1928.

Had Ty Cobb not been so dominant while Collins was playing, he might have enjoyed even greater recognition. As it was, Cocky hit .369, .365, and .360 without ever winning a batting title. He did lead the league in stolen bases four times, winding up with 744 career steals, behind only Cobb and Billy Hamilton during his lifetime.

Defensively he played more games (2,650) and had more putouts (6,526), assists (7,630) and total chances (14,591) than any other second baseman. Collins won nine fielding titles and, with the exception of 1918 when he missed 57 games because of injuries, he led the league in one or another fielding category every year from 1909 to 1922.

In 1906, he made his debut under the name Sullivan until it was revealed that Sullivan was, in reality, Columbia University's junior quarterback and star infielder Eddie Collins. He was allowed to continue at Columbia as nonplaying captain and joined the A's after graduation.

Collins quickly became the keystone of the A's infield.

When shortstop Jack Barry, third baseman Frank "Home Run" Baker and first baseman John "Stuffy" McInnis joined the A's, the quartet became known as the "$100,000 infield" because Mack "wouldn't take that sum for all of them." The A's proceeded to roll to pennants in 1910, 1911, 1913, and 1914.

Sold to the White Sox in 1915 after winning the Chalmers Award as MVP in 1914, he hit .409 in the 1917 Series and scored the deciding run by slipping out of a rundown between third and home to beat the Giants' third baseman to the unprotected plate. Dispirited by some of his teammates' play in the Black Sox World Series of 1919, Collins batted only .226 but still stole a base to give him 14 career World Series thefts.

Inevitably, he became a manager, piloting the White Sox in 1925 and 1926 before returning to the Athletics as a pinch hitter—and leading the league in that department with a .353 average. He served as a highly placed Red Sox executive from 1932 until his death in 1951. Collins was elected to the Hall of Fame in 1939.

JOE CRONIN

Shortstop. Born Oct. 12, 1906 San Francisco, Cal. Died Sept. 7, 1984. AL MVP 1930.

Joe Cronin had 11 .300-plus seasons, hit .301 lifetime, won the Washington Senators' last pennant as a player-manager and, as a nonplaying manager, led the Red Sox to their only pennant in the 1940s.

Cronin grew up in San Francisco and signed with the Pirates but cooled his heels in the minors because the Bucs already had the league's leading shortstop in Glenn Wright. After Cronin signed with the Kansas City Blues, Joe Engel bought his contract for the Senators.

He finished 1928 in the big leagues, bettered .300 and 100 RBIs from 1930 to 1933, and also led the league in triples in 1932 (18) and in doubles in 1933 (45). Moreover, Cronin was the league's best shortstop in that time span, three times leading in putouts, assists, and double plays. Senators' owner Clark Griffith made him the manager at age twenty-six to replace Walter Johnson. Hailed as the Boy Manager, Cronin won the pennant in his first season, though the Senators lost the Series in five games to the Giants.

The Nats nosedived to seventh in 1934, and the high point of Cronin's season was marrying Griffith's adopted daughter, Mildred Robinson. While the two honeymooned, Red Sox boss Tom Yawkey angled to buy Cronin. When he offered a record $225,000 and shortstop Lyn Lary, the Boy Manager gave the go-ahead; in one move, Griffith had gotten rid of his shortstop, his manager and his son-in-law.

In 1938 Cronin hit a career high .325 and also led the league in doubles; however, the Sox finished second in four out of the five years between 1938 and 1942. Cronin stepped aside as shortstop in favor of Johnny Pesky, and prospered as a part-time player and pinch hitter, leading the league in 1943 with 18 hits in 42 at-bats, a .426 average. On one occasion he pinch hit home runs in both halves of a doubleheader. Ironically, the year he removed himself from the roster, 1946, the Red Sox won their first pennant since 1918, only to lose a seven-game Series to the Cardinals.

Cronin moved to the front office in 1948 and served as

Boston's general manager until 1959 when he became AL president. He was named to the Hall of Fame in 1956.

BILL DICKEY

Catcher. Born Jun. 6, 1907 Bastrop, Ga. Hit .362 in 1936, highest average for a catcher in this century.

Bill Dickey was the only Yankee quiet enough to play in the shadow of his roommate, the painfully shy Lou Gehrig, who had himself played in Babe Ruth's shadow.

Yet, with the passage of the years, it becomes clear that while Ruth started the Yankee mystique with his power and personality, the pinstriped legacy was passed along by quiet men—Gehrig, Dickey, Joe DiMaggio. An admiring Dan Daniel once wrote, "Dickey isn't just a catcher. He's a ball club. He isn't just a player. He's an influence."

With the Yanks and Reds scoreless in the ninth inning of the 1939 World Series opener, Charlie Keller tripled and Reds pitcher Paul Derringer walked Joe DiMaggio intentionally. Tommy Henrich says, "When I saw that—and this is the absolute gospel truth—I turned around and picked up my glove, because I knew the game was going to be over right now. And it was." (Dickey singled.)

One of the few nonpitchers in the Hall of Fame who never led the league in a single offensive category, he hit .300 or better eleven times—in 1936 a lofty .362, the highest mark for a backstop in this century—and compiled a lifetime average of .313. In the course of 6,300 at bats, he struck out only 289 times. As a bonus, Dickey caught 100 games in thirteen straight seasons, a record later tied by Johnny Bench.

At his best in October, Dickey hit .438 in the 1932 Classic, went 4-for-4 to open the 1938 edition, knocked in at least one run in every game in 1939, and finished off the Cardinals in Game Five of the 1943 Series with a two-run homer in the ninth.

Signed by Yankee scout Lena Blackburne on the back of an Elks Club card, Dickey tried to impress manager Miller Huggins with his home run swing. Huggins told him, "Stop unbuttoning your shirt on every pitch." With Ruth, Gehrig, and Lazzeri, the Yankees didn't need power from Dickey. What they wanted was steadiness. Dickey provided it, leading AL catchers three times each in assists and fielding and five times in putouts.

Given the job of turning Yogi Berra into a catcher, he looked up one day to find Joe Garagiola and Roy Campanella listening. In Yogi's phrase, Dickey "learned them all his experiences," too.

JOE DiMAGGIO

Center Field. Born Nov. 25, 1914 Martinez, Cal. Holds major league record for hitting in most consecutive games (56).

Babe Ruth played on seven pennant winners and four championship teams in his fifteen years as a Yankee; Joe DiMaggio played on ten pennant winners and nine championship teams in thirteen years.

At nineteen, he hit in 61 straight games for the San Francisco Seals, a Pacific Coast League record that still stands. Bought by the Yankees in 1936, he hit .323 as a rookie, led the league in home runs and runs scored the following year, and in 1939 led the league in batting and was named MVP for the first time.

He won the batting crown again in 1940 and the RBI

title in 1941, the year he hit in 56 straight games, winning the MVP award despite Ted Williams' mark of .406. A disc jockey wrote a hit song called "Joltin' Joe DiMaggio." A Cincinnati high school class was asked to name the greatest American of all time; George Washington finished second to DiMaggio.

After his return from military service, DiMaggio had a sub-par 1946, hitting only .290. The next spring, he was almost traded for Williams. DiMaggio responded by winning his third MVP award in 1947 and blasting two home runs in the World Series.

On February 7, 1949, DiMaggio became the first $100,000 ballplayer and, despite serious injuries, helped the Yanks win the pennant. In 1951 he retired with a .325 career batting average, having played on All-Star teams in every year of major league service. He was named to the Hall of Fame in 1955.

Despite serving on the boards of the A's and Orioles, a turbulent marriage to Marilyn Monroe, commercials for banks and coffeemakers, and an involvement in signing memorabilia for profit, DiMaggio retains his aura of heroism. In 1989 former All-Star outfielder Andy Pafko said, "Even today I look up to him. And he's never disappointed me."

JOHNNY EVERS

Second Baseman. Born July 21, 1881 Troy, N.Y. Died Mar. 28, 1947 Albany, N.Y. NL MVP 1914.

When Johnny Evers joined the Cubs in 1902 he played both ends of a Labor Day doubleheader; yet his mates thought so little of him that they refused to let him on the team bus; he had to ride on top instead.

As things turned out, Evers was a Hall of Fame second baseman and a winner in every sinew of his 125-pound body. An early incarnation of Eddie Stanky or Billy Martin, Evers single-mindedly drove himself and his mates to victory and his opponents to distraction. He was on five pennant winners, and all four times he played his team won the Series. (A broken leg kept him out of the 1910 Series, which the Cubs lost.)

Born in Troy, he was "the Trojan," but that nickname soon gave way to "the Crab." Like many other bantam-sized battlers, Evers had a chip on his shoulder and never ran from a fight. He and shortstop Joe Tinker had a falling out on September 14, 1905, when Evers took a cab to the park without waiting for Tinker; although they didn't speak for thirty-three years, they won three championships together.

The third championship came in 1908 when Evers batted 1.000 in the rules department. On September 4, with one out in the bottom of the tenth of a scoreless tie, the Pirates loaded the bases; John "Chief" Wilson singled, Fred Clarke scored the winning run, and Warren Gill, the runner on first, started for the clubhouse. Evers called for the ball, touched second, and told umpire Hank O'Day the side had been retired because Gill had been "forced." O'Day disallowed that protest but, when the same situation arose on September 23, Evers's alertness caused the controversial "Merkle boner" game to end in a tie and, eventually, give Chicago its third straight pennant.

In February 1914, Evers was sold to the Braves. He and Rabbit Maranville led the Miracle Braves from last place to the pennant, and Evers was named MVP and shone in

the World Series, hitting .438 to lead the Braves to a sweep. He ended his career in Philadelphia, although he played one game each for the Braves and White Sox while coaching with them. He, Tinker, and Frank Chance were reunited in the Hall of Fame in 1946.

WILLIAM "BUCK" EWING

Catcher. Born Oct. 17, 1859 Hoaglands, Oh. Died Oct. 20, 1906, Cincinnati, Oh.

In the 1919 *Reach Guide*, sportswriter Francis Richter picked the three greatest players of all time—Ty Cobb, Honus Wagner, and Buck Ewing—and said that, in his prime (1884–1890), Ewing was "the greatest player of the game." In the 1930 *Spalding Guide*, editor John Foster said Ewing "was the greatest all-around player ever connected with the game."

For one thing, Ewing did play all around literally, all nine positions. In addition to catching 636 games and leading all catchers in assists three times and double plays twice, he played 253 at first, 212 at the other infield slots, and 112 in the outfield. Finally, with the Giants involved in the pennant race in 1889 and short of pitchers, Ewing even pitched and won two games.

A lifetime .303 hitter, Ewing was fast enough to lead the league in triples in 1884 (20), and strong enough to outhomer it in 1883 (10). One of the few catchers to bat leadoff and be considered a real threat to run, Ewing stole 40 or more bases four times in his career. In one famous instance, he stole second, stole third, announced, "Now I'm stealing home," and made it. The moment was later immortalized in a famous lithograph.

But Ewing's greatest fame came as a defensive catcher and strategist. Mickey Welch, a Hall of Fame pitcher, said Ewing was "the thinking man's player" and credited him with inventing the pregame clubhouse meeting. It is said that Ewing also originated the practice of throwing from a crouch, saving precious fractions of a second to catch larcenous runners.

In 1888 John Montgomery Ward resigned as team captain, a position closer to today's manager, and Ewing took over and led the Giants to their first pennant. For the 1889 season, Ewing was paid $5,000, a princely sum, and hit .327 as the Giants repeated. When the Players League was founded, Ewing jumped to be player-manager of the New York team, rejoined the Giants when the league folded, and later played at Cleveland and Cincinnati, where he succeeded Charles Comiskey as the Reds' manager.

Ewing died a wealthy man from real estate investments. In 1936 he tied Cap Anson for the most "old-timer" votes in the intial selection of men for the Hall of Fame, and three years later, when the new museum opened, he and his old rival were immortalized with plaques.

BOB FELLER

Pitcher. Born Nov. 3, 1918 Van Meter, Ia. Threw three no-hitters and twelve one-hitters.

Bob Feller struck out 17 Athletics in a major league game in 1936, tying Dizzy Dean's record; then he went back to Van Meter, Iowa, to finish high school.

Feller generated statewide publicity at sixteen, and the Indians signed him to a contract before he completed high school, a violation of baseball rules. When he attracted attention pitching in Des Moines, the Tigers also offered him a bonus, and the truth was revealed. Commissioner Landis fined the Indians $7,500 and ruled that Feller was free to sign with any team. The bidding might have reached $100,000, an astronomical sum in those days, but Feller respected his contract and signed with the Indians.

Without any minor league experience, he faced the Cardinals in an exhibition game on July 6, 1936, and fanned eight members of the Gashouse Gang in three innings. "Rapid Robert" won his first big league start, 4–1, striking out 15 St. Louis Browns.

On the last day of the 1938 season, 30,000 people came to see Hank Greenberg try to break Babe Ruth's record of 60 home runs in a season. Instead, they saw Feller strike out 18 Tigers to set the major league record (since broken) and win the AL strikeout title, beating out Bobo Newsom. (He also led in bases on balls.)

By the time he was twenty-three Feller had won 107 games. He enlisted in the Navy the day after Pearl Harbor and was sworn in by former heavyweight champ Gene Tunney. Pitching anti-aircraft shells from the deck of the battleship *Alabama*, Feller missed nearly four full seasons but earned six battle citations as a gun crew chief.

Returning to baseball at the end of 1945, he had his best season ever in 1946, winning 26 games, striking out a record 348 batters in 371 innings, and recording 10 shutouts with an ERA of 2.18. In 1948, he two-hit the Braves in his only World Series game but lost. In 1951, he still had enough stuff to throw his third no-hitter and lead the league with a record of 22–8.

By the time he retired, Feller had pitched twelve one-hitters, won 20 or more games six times and rolled up 2,581 career strikeouts. Satchel Paige summed up his career this way: "If anybody threw that ball any harder than Rapid Robert, then the human eye couldn't follow it." He was elected to the Hall of Fame in 1962.

ROLLIE FINGERS

Pitcher. Born Aug. 25, 1946 Steubenville, Oh. AL Cy Young Award and MVP, 1981. Established major league record for saves, 341 (since surpassed).

If he hadn't been such a worrywart, Rollie Fingers might have been an average starter; instead, he fretted himself right into the bullpen and became a Hall of Fame fireman.

"I would plan my pitches days in advance of my start and get so wound up I couldn't sleep the night before my turn," he recalled. After finishing only four of thirty-five starts, he took immediately to the relief role in 1971 and finished with 17 saves. In 1972, he led the league with 11 relief wins and 21 saves to help Oakland win the division.

Fingers pitched in six of the seven games in the 1972 World Series, earning saves in Games Two and Seven and a win in Game Four. One year later, he pitched 3⅓ hitless innings in the Series opener against the Mets, saved Game Three for Paul Lindblad and Game Six for Catfish Hunter, and yielded only one unearned run in 3⅓ innings of relief in the finale.

In 1974, he led the A's to a third straight world championship. He got the win in Game One; for a change, Catfish Hunter got the save. The roles were reversed in Game Three when Fingers saved Hunter. Rollie got a second save the next day, and was named Series MVP.

When Fingers and the A's reached a contract impasse, owner Charlie Finley sold him to Boston, but Commissioner Bowie Kuhn voided the sale. With San Diego in 1977, Fingers appeared in 78 games and saved 35 (league-leading figures), and earned National League Fireman of the Year honors.

Four days after being traded to St. Louis in 1980, he moved again, to Milwaukee. During the strike-shortened 1981 season, he notched a league-leading 28 saves and posted a brilliant 1.04 ERA. Fingers won his fourth Fireman of the Year award, won the Cy Young Award, and was also named MVP.

After posting 29 saves in 1982, Fingers missed the World Series and the entire 1983 season because of tendinitis. He came back to notch 23 saves by July, 1984, when a herniated disk ended his season and career. He ranks first in wins plus saves (430) and was inducted into the Hall of Fame in 1992.

CARLTON FISK

Catcher. Born Dec. 26, 1947 Bellows Falls, Vt. Holds major league record for lifetime home runs by a catcher (350).

During a Yankees–White Sox game in May 1990, Carlton Fisk blasted Deion Sanders for not running out a pop fly, starting a brawl but enhancing Fisk's role as Defender of the Game. Moreover, it came at a time when Fisk, a ten-time All-Star, was trying to push an unknown pitching staff to a division title.

That year Fisk, already the oldest regular catcher in baseball history, hit 18 homers to pass Johnny Bench as baseball's leading home run-hitting catcher, extended his AL record of games caught, and added to his total as modern baseball's best base-stealing catcher. Fisk, Bench, and Yogi Berra are the only three receivers to hit 300 homers and both score and drive in 1,000 runs.

Carlton Ernest Fisk grew up in Charlestown, New Hampshire on the heavy side (5'4", 155) and was dubbed "Pudge" by a female relative. A three-sport MVP in high school, he earned a basketball scholarship to the University of New Hampshire but signed instead with the Red Sox in 1967.

Brought up late in 1971 for a look-see, he was the All-Star catcher by the summer of '72. That fall he became the first AL Rookie of the Year to be chosen unanimously. In 1975 injuries limited him to only 79 games during the regular season, but he created one of baseball's enduring moments in the World Series with a twelfth-inning, body English home run off the Reds' Pat Darcy to end the now fabled Game Six.

After the 1980 season, free agent Fisk signed with the White Sox. He had worn number 27 in Boston but sported number 72 in Chicago, because "it represents a turnaround in my career." Following a workmanlike 1982 season, Fisk slumped in early 1983 and was hitting only .136. Replaced in both halves of a June 12 doubleheader in Oakland, Fisk jawed with manager Tony LaRussa. LaRussa said, "He came out fighting, the way a winner reacts to a challenge." In the next 71 games, Fisk hit 16 homers, drove in 49 runs, raised his average more than 100 points, and helped Chicago clinch the division.

An Opening Day abdominal muscle hampered him in 1984. The next year, however, at age thirty-seven, Fisk

had his greatest campaign, knocking in 107 runs and hitting 37 homers. As of 1993, Fisk was within 21 games of equaling Bob Boone's major league record for most games caught.

ED "WHITEY" FORD

Pitcher. Born Oct. 21, 1928 New York, N.Y. Holds record for World Series wins (10); AL Cy Young Award, 1961.

Whitey Ford won 236 games and lost only 106 to register a lifetime .690 won-lost percentage, the lowest recorded by any pitcher since 1900. He also broke Babe Ruth's forty-five-year-old record of 29⅔ scoreless innings in World Series competition, ending up with 32. Ford also holds the records for most Series wins (10), strikeouts (94), and innings pitched (146).

Ford's Series stats are so impressive that his regular season numbers tend to get buried. He won 20 games only twice in sixteen seasons; however, from 1953 to 1960, he averaged nearly 16 wins against 7 losses. Casey Stengel, who manipulated the rotation so Ford faced the toughies (though he kept him out of Boston's Fenway Park), said, "If you had one game to win and your life depended on it, you'd want him to pitch it."

Even though he led the league in wins, innings pitched, and won-lost percentage and won the Cy Young Award in 1961, Ford's 25–4 record was almost overshadowed by Roger Maris's quest for home run number 61. He got more recognition by going 24–7 in 1963 and repeating in all three categories.

Ford was inducted into the Hall of Fame on August 12, 1974, along with Mickey Mantle, his partner in the long-running "Mick and Slick" Show. When writers recalled the spitter Ford used to strike out Willie Mays in the 1964 All-Star Game, Ford said, "Look, they didn't call me Slick for nothing."

JIMMIE FOXX

First Baseman. Born Oct. 22, 1907 Sudlersville, Md. Died July 21, 1967 Miami, Fla. Holds major league record for most consecutive years with 30 or more home runs (12). AL MVP 1932, 1933, 1938.

Jimmie Foxx hit some of baseball's most awesome home runs. He homered over the two-tiered left field stands in Shibe Park, drove a ball out of Comiskey Park some 600 feet from home plate, broke a seat in the upper deck of left field at Yankee Stadium, and hit what he considered his longest shot over the left-center field fence in Sportsman's Park to win Game Five of the 1930 Series. Ted Williams, not known for admiring other hitters, said of Foxx, "I never saw anyone hit a baseball harder."

Nicknamed "The Beast" and "Double X," Foxx won three MVP awards (1932, 1933, 1938), knocked in 100 or more runs in thirteen straight seasons, won five slugging titles, hit .300 or better thirteen times, and ended his career with a lifetime batting average of .325, 534 homers, and 1,922 RBIs. He also set a record by hitting 30 or more home runs in 12 consecutive seasons.

Appropriately enough this great home run hitter was discovered at age sixteen by none other than Home Run Baker. He entered Organized Baseball as a catcher. After several .300-plus seasons as a utility player, Foxx was installed at first base in 1929 and hit .354 with 33 homers. In 1932 he mounted the first serious challenge to Babe

Ruth's season record of 60 home runs with 58. (According to writer Fred Lieb, Foxx hit five doubles against the right field screen in Sportsman's Park, which hadn't been there in 1927 when Ruth hit 60 homers.) Foxx failed to win the Triple Crown when Dale Alexander was named batting champ, even though he didn't have 400 at bats. Nevertheless, the Beast led the league in homers (58), runs scored (151), RBIs (169), total bases (438) and slugging (.749) and finished second in batting average (.364) and hits (213) to win his first MVP award.

In 1933 he repeated as MVP, topped the league with a slugging percentage of .703, and captured the Triple Crown, hitting 48 homers, driving in 163 runs, and hitting .356. After tying Hank Greenberg for the home run crown in 1935, he was sold to the Red Sox. Foxx responded with another MVP year in 1938, leading the league with 175 RBIs and hitting 50 homers, second only to Greenberg's 58.

Foxx entered the pantheon at Cooperstown in 1951.

FRANKIE FRISCH

Second Baseman. Born Sept. 9, 1898 New York, N.Y. Died Mar. 12, 1973 Wilmington, Del. Holds major league records for most assists (641) and chances accepted (1,037) in a season, 1927; NL MVP 1931.

Frank Frisch, "The Fordham Flash," had something to prove in 1927.

Giants manager John McGraw, the man who had taken Frisch from Fordham to stardom, had traded him to the Cardinals after the 1926 season for Rogers Hornsby. McGraw had taught Frisch how to switch hit and play the hitters, and had been a father figure for Frisch, giving the trade a personal twist.

Frisch spent the winter toughening up and came out charging. He hit .337, led the league in steals, handled a record 1,059 chances (including a record 641 assists), made the most double plays, and just missed being named MVP, finishing second to Paul Waner. Cardinal catcher Bob O'Farrell, the MVP a year before, said, "The greatest player I ever saw in any one season was Frankie Frisch in 1927."

He'd served as captain of the baseball, football and basketball teams at Fordham and been a second-team All-America halfback when he joined the Giants in 1919. Frisch led the league in stolen bases in 1921 and hits in 1923, and the Giants won pennants every year from 1921–1924. He went 4-for-4 in the 1921 Series opener and averaged .363 in his first four Series.

The Flash also brought the Cardinals to three World Series as a player and one as a player-manager. The Yanks swept St. Louis in 1928 and the A's took them in six games in 1930, so 1931 was doubly sweet. Frisch sparked the Cardinals to a seventh-game win over the A's and was also named MVP. In the first All-Star Game, in 1933, Frisch singled and hit the first NL homer.

Shortly thereafter, he took over as player-manager of the Gashouse Gang, riding herd over Pepper Martin, Dizzy Dean, and company. In 1934 he hit .305 (one of thirteen times he hit .300 or better) and led the Redbirds to a pennant. In Game Seven of the Series, the Tigers intentionally walked Jack Rothrock to load the bases; Frisch unloaded them with a double and the Cardinals went on to a rout, 11–0.

After retiring as a player to devote himself to managing full time, Frisch never won another pennant with the Cardinals, Pirates, or Cubs; however, in 1947 he began a third successful career as a Giants broadcaster. In that same year he was reunited with McGraw in the Hall of Fame.

LOU GEHRIG

First Base. Born Jun. 19, 1903 New York, N.Y. Died June 2, 1941 Riverdale, N.Y. Holds major league records for consecutive games played (2,130) and grand salms (23); AL MVP 1927, 1936.

Playing in Babe Ruth's shadow may have robbed Lou Gehrig of the spotlight, but, as he himself said, "It's a pretty big shadow. It gives me lots of room to spread myself." The year Ruth retired (1935), Gehrig began a three-year streak of leading the league in walks, a good measure of the respect pitchers still had for him when he was in his mid-thirties.

Gehrig had 200 or more hits in eight seasons, never hit below .300 from 1926 to 1937, and had a career average of .340. He tied Ruth for the RBI lead in 1928 and led the league outright four times; his 184 ribbies in 1931 is still the league record. The "Iron Horse" led in homers in 1934 and 1936 and tied Ruth for the lead in 1931 with 46, when Lyn Lary's baserunning mistake—passing a runner on the bases—robbed him of his 47th. He also holds the record for career grand slams (23). On June 3, 1932, he was the first modern slugger to hit four home runs in a game, an achievement that was somewhat eclipsed because it happened on the same day as John McGraw's death.

Although Gehrig originally went to Columbia on a football scholarship, Giant manager John McGraw persuaded him to play pro baseball under an assumed name (Lewis) in 1921, making him ineligible for college ball; however, Gehrig's coach, Andy Coakley, persuaded the faculty to give Lou another chance. The contract was dissolved, and Gehrig resumed collegiate play.

In 1934, Ruth's last year as a Yankee, Gehrig won the Triple Crown, leading the AL in homers (49), RBIs (165), and batting average (.363). He batted .361 in World Series play, averaging an RBI a game for 34 games with 43 hits, 10 of them homers.

Suffering from the effects of amyotrophic lateral sclerosis, Gehrig took himself out of the lineup on May 2, 1939, after playing in 2,130 consecutive games. He entered the Hall of Fame later that year when the Baseball Writers Association waived the existing rule which required a player to be retired one year before he could be elected.

On Lou Gehrig Day at Yankee Stadium, the stoical slugger told a packed house, "I may have been given a bad break, but with all this I have a lot to live for. I consider myself the luckiest man on the face of the earth."

CHARLIE GEHRINGER

Second Baseman. Born May 11, 1903 Fowlerville, Mich. American League MVP 1937.

Describing Charlie Gehringer, Mickey Cochrane said of his teammate, "He says hello on opening day and goodbye on closing day, and in between he hits .350."

Gehringer was so quiet that when he was given a

"Day," the lefthander was given a set of righthanded golf clubs and learned to play the game righthanded. He celebrated the Day by homering on the first pitch thrown to him, getting three other hits, and stealing home to win the game.

"The Mechanical Man" had 200 or more hits seven times, bettered .300 fourteen times, and knocked in 100 or more runs seven times. In the field, he led the AL in fielding six times, putouts three times, and assists a record seven times. A measure of Gehringer's all-around excellence is the 1929 season, when he led the league in stolen bases, doubles, triples, hits, runs, games, putouts, and fielding while hitting .339. As for consistency, he hit .320 lifetime and .320 in twenty World Series games.

Like Bob Feller, Gehringer played his first baseball on a field carved out of a family farm. A third baseman at the University of Michigan, Gehringer was discovered by Tiger great Bobby Veach and, despite his quiet nature, became a favorite of manager Ty Cobb. Cobb resisted all efforts to change Gehringer's swing and said that, aside from Eddie Collins, Gehringer was "the best second baseman I ever saw."

After brief callups in 1924 and 1925, Gehringer became the Tigers' regular second baseman in 1926. In 1933 he started a string of six straight starts for the AL in the All-Star Game. He is the midsummer classic's lifetime batting leader with an even .500 average (10 for 20).

This splendid ballplaying machine was equally sparkling in World Series play, hitting .379, leading all Tiger hitters in a losing effort in 1934. In 1935, however, Detroit's "G-Men"—Hank Greenberg, Gehringer, and Goose Goslin—became champions, beating the Cubs as Gehringer hit .375 and handled 39 chances flawlessly.

In 1937 Gehringer reached the high-water mark of his career, hitting .371 and being named MVP. After three more .300-plus seasons, he played out the string during World War II. Elected to the Hall of Fame in 1949, he served as the Tigers' general manager from 1951 to 1953 and a vice president until 1959.

BOB GIBSON

Pitcher. Born Nov. 9, 1935 Omaha, Neb. Holds major league season record for lowest ERA in 300 or more innings (1.12), 1968. NL MVP 1968, Cy Young Award 1968, 1970.

Bob Gibson was a winner whether he was using his arm, his bat, or his glove.

In a fifteen-year career, he won 251 games, posted 56 shutouts, became the first major leaguer to strike out 200 or more in nine seasons, and posted a lifetime ERA of 2.91. He also hit 24 regular season home runs and earned a Gold Glove every year from 1965 to 1973.

Gibson suffered from rickets and asthma while growing up in Omaha and because of a heart murmur needed a doctor's permission to play ball. Nevertheless, he starred as the switch-hitting catcher-shortstop of a YMCA team, won a basketball scholarship to Creighton University, played with the Harlem Globetrotters for a year, joined the Cards for good in 1961, and had his first big year in 1963, going 18–9.

In 1964 his 19–12 record helped the Cards win the pennant, and he began an unprecedented streak of seven straight World Series wins by taking Game Five and, on two days' rest, Game Seven. On his way to another big year in 1967 (13 wins), Gibson was out when Roberto Clemente's smash fractured his left leg. Incredibly, after being sidelined for eight weeks, he came back to win three World Series games against the Red Sox, allowing just three earned runs and pitching three complete games.

In 1968 he was even better, posting a record of 22–9 with an ERA of 1.12, breaking Walter Johnson's 1913 record for the lowest ERA with 300 or more innings pitched. That year Gibson pitched 13 shutouts, and surrendered just 2 runs during one 95-inning stretch during the regular season to win both the MVP and Cy Young Awards. Awesome in the 1968 Series, he struck out 17 Tigers, a World Series record, while winning the opener.

In 1970 he was 23–7 and took his second Cy Young Award. On July 17, 1974, he became only the second pitcher (Walter Johnson was the first) to notch 3,000 strikeouts. Shortly before Gibson retired, 55,000 people at Busch Stadium gave him a ten-minute standing ovation. He was named to the Hall of Fame in 1981.

JOSH GIBSON

Catcher. Born Dec. 21, 1911 Buena Vista, Ga. Died Jan. 20, 1947 Pittsburgh, Pa.

Josh Gibson may have been the greatest catcher of all time. Walter Johnson said of him, "He hits the ball a mile. Throws like a rifle. Bill Dickey isn't as good a catcher." Roy Campanella, who saw Gibson at his peak, said, "When I broke in with the Baltimore Elite Giants in 1937 there were already a thousand legends about him; once you saw him play you knew they were all true."

According to a 1967 article in *The Sporting News*, Gibson hit a ball two feet from the top of the stadium wall circling the bleachers at Yankee Stadium, some 580 feet from home plate. His Hall of Fame plaque credits him with "almost 800 home runs," and various authorities say he hit 69, 75, 84, and 89 home runs in a season, albeit sometimes against semipro pitching. Gibson could also hit for average, compiling a .412 mark in 34 at bats against big league pitching. And, while he wasn't a great handler of pitchers or catcher of popups, few baserunners tried to steal on him because of his great arm.

He was born in Buena Vista, Georgia, and moved to Pittsburgh when he was twelve. As a youngster he won numerous swimming medals. At maturity, he stood 6' 2" and weighed 210.

Unable to break into the lineup of Pittsburgh's Homestead Grays, Gibson organized the semipro Crawford Colored Giants; He was in the stands when the Grays' regular catcher, Buck Ewing, split a finger in June 1930; he changed into a uniform and never left the lineup again.

In 1931 Gus Greenlee founded the Pittsburgh Crawfords, signed Gibson and Satchel Paige, and wrote ads that promised, "Josh Gibson will hit a home run and Satchel Paige will strike out the side on nine pitches." They nearly always delivered. Gibson also played winter ball extensively and said his greatest thrill was being chosen MVP of the Puerto Rican League in 1941.

Pirate owner Bill Benswanger reportedly signed him to a contract in 1943, but Commissioner Landis vetoed the signing. On January 20, 1947, three months before Jackie Robinson's major league debut, Gibson died of a stroke. He was elected to the Hall of Fame in 1972.

HANK GREENBERG

First Baseman. Born Jan. 1, 1911 New York, N.Y. Died Sept. 4, 1986 Beverly Hills, Cal. AL MVP 1935, 1940.

In 1934, the big question in Detroit was, "Should Hank Greenberg play on Rosh Hashanah and Yom Kippur?"

With the Tigers involved in a hot pennant race with the Yankees, the Jewish slugger sought spiritual guidance. After due deliberation, Rabbi Leo Franklin ruled that Greenberg should play on Rosh Hashanah, the Jewish New Year, a happy occasion; he did and hit a tenth-inning homer to win the game. However, Rabbi Franklin said the slugger should pray, not play, on Yom Kippur, the Day of Atonement. Greenberg acquiesced. Poet Edgar Guest commented:

We shall miss him in the infield and shall miss him at the bat
But he's true to his religion—and I honor him for that.

The Tigers won the pennant, and Greenberg homered in the World Series, as he would in all four Series in which he played. A year later, his 36 homers and 170 RBIs earned him the MVP award, but he missed the last four games of the Series with a broken wrist. Greenberg had a null year in 1936—67 at bats; however, in 1937, he drove in a mind-boggling 183 runs and, in 1938 fell just short of Babe Ruth's season home run record, with 58.

After hitting 33 homers and knocking in 112 runs in 1939, he was forced to take a $10,000 pay cut—if he stayed at first base. Instead he moved to the outfield, making way for good-hit, no-field Rudy York, and got a $10,000 raise. He was named MVP again in 1940, when the Tigers lost the Series in seven games to Cincinnati.

In May 1941 Greenberg was drafted into the Army and returned in July 1945, winning the pennant for the Tigers on the last day of the season with a grand slam in the bottom of the ninth inning. In 1947 he had a last fling with the Pirates, hitting 25 homers and knocking in 74 runs in his only NL season. When he retired that fall, he had led the league in RBIs four times, won home run honors outright four times and tied for the lead once, and hit 331 career home runs, even though he had lost four and a half seasons to the war and injury. He was elected to the Hall of Fame in 1956.

ROBERT "LEFTY" GROVE

Pitcher. Born Mar. 6, 1900 Lonaconing, Md. Died May 22, 1975 Norwalk, Oh. AL MVP 1931.

In 1931 Lefty Grove was en route to his seventeenth straight victory, which would have broken the AL record then shared by Walter Johnson and Smoky Joe Wood. Al Simmons had taken the day off, and the rookie outfielder subbing for him misjudged a fly ball, leading to an unearned run; Grove lost, 1–0. He said, "After that game I went in and tore the clubhouse up. Wrecked the place. Tore those stall lockers off the wall, giving Al Simmons hell all the while."

Grove recovered his composure, won another eight straight, was named MVP, and ended the season 31–4, possibly the single greatest season enjoyed by any hurler. The dominant pitcher of his era, he was the AL's strikeout leader his first seven years, led in ERA a record nine times, and went on to compile a won-lost record of 300–141, a winning percentage of .680. Normalized for league average and adjusted for home park, his 3.06 ERA is, quite simply, the best in baseball history.

He started in Organized Ball with Martinsburg, West Virginia, of the Blue Ridge League and joined the International League Orioles when Baltimore bartered for him, paying cash for Martinsburg's new center field fence. Owner Jack Dunn knew what he had in Grove and delayed his entry to the big leagues until the southpaw was twenty-five; he sold Grove to Connie Mack's A's for $100,600—$600 more than the Red Sox had paid for Babe Ruth in 1914.

Like Sandy Koufax after him, Grove had his troubles initially, winning 10 and losing 12 in 1925, his rookie year; however, the following year his ERA improved from 4.75 to 2.51, good enough to lead the league for the first time. By 1927, he was ready for his first 20-win season and tied George Pipgras for the league lead in wins (24) while losing only 8.

From 1929 to 1931 Grove was an awesome 79–15, and the A's won pennants every year as well as the Series the first two. By the time he was sold to the Red Sox for $125,000 in 1933, he had won 20, 24, 20, 28, 31, 25, and 24 games in seven consecutive seasons. Yet success didn't mellow him; in batting practice a Boston teammate once hit a ball back through the box; on the next pitch the batter hit the dust. Grove was elected to the Hall of Fame in 1947.

"SLIDING BILLY" HAMILTON

Center Fielder. Born Feb. 16, 1866 Newark, N.J. Died Dec. 16, 1940 Worcester, Mass. Holds major league record for runs scored in a season (196), 1894; stole 912 bases, a mark that stood for nine decades.

Although he was nicknamed for his daring, head-first slides, looking at the records, it's clear that Billy Hamilton should properly have been nicknamed "Scoring Billy."

Hamilton notched a record 1,690 runs in 1,591 games, making him the most effective leadoff man of all time. (For comparison, Rickey Henderson had, at the end of the 1992 season, 1,472 in 1,869 games.) What's more, Billy could hit as well as run. He missed hitting .300 only in his first and last seasons, led the league in hitting twice, and retired with a lifetime average of .344.

He was also a part of history's only all-.400 outfield, the Phillies' 1894 edition; Hamilton's puny .404 was dwarfed by the lusty .407 achieved by both his oversized garden mates, "Big Sam" Thompson and "Big Ed" Delahanty. (Incredibly, spare outfielder Tuck Turner, in over 300 at bats, hit for .416.)

Equally oversized is Hamilton's stolen base total. The record credits him with 912 steals—100-plus each in the years from 1889 to 1891. At the time, however, if a runner tagged up on a fly ball, went from first to third on a single, or moved up on a ground ball to the right side, he was credited with a stolen base. Beginning in 1892, steals were awarded to a runner only if there were "a possible chance and a palpable attempt made to retire him." Sliding Billy slid to only 57 and 43 steals the next two years but rebounded with 98 and 97 in 1894 and 1895 to lead the league. He also topped all NLrs in bases on balls, runs scored (a record 192 in 1894), and on-base percentage. In fact, his on-base percentage of .455 over nearly 1600

games is probably a greater achievement than all the stolen bases; he trails only Ted Williams, Babe Ruth, and John McGraw in this department.

Hamilton moved over to the Boston Beaneaters in 1896. He missed 59 games in 1899 because of injuries and played his last major league season in 1901. Far from ready to retire, he played ten more years in the Tri-State and New England Leagues. After becoming a Red Sox scout, he bought part of the Worcester team. Sliding Billy was named to the Hall of Fame in 1961.

CHARLES "GABBY" HARTNETT
Catcher. Born Dec. 20, 1900 Woonsocket, R.I. Died Dec. 20, 1972 Park Ridge, Ill. NL MVP 1935.
Gabby Hartnett had an active role in three of baseball's greatest moments. He caught Charlie Root when Babe Ruth "called his shot" in the 1932 World Series; flashed the signs when Carl Hubbell fanned Ruth and four other Hall of Fame sluggers in order in the 1934 All-Star Game; and, hit the "Homer in the Gloamin'" that put the Cubs ahead to stay in the 1938 pennant race.

The NL Bill Dickey, Hartnett was resilient, reliable, clever at picking pitches, and blessed with a shotgun for an arm. He caught 100 or more games twelve times, had a career average of .297, and set the standard for NL catchers defensively, leading four times in putouts, six times in assists, and six times in fielding percentage.

Hartnett was born in Woonsocket, Rhode Island to an unusual family; his mother had seven boys in a row and then seven girls in a row. Signed by the Cubs in high school, he was silent on his first train trip west to Catalina in 1922, and a reporter promptly dubbed him Gabby. His father had played semipro ball with Grover Cleveland Alexander, the Cubs' reigning star. Alexander insisted that Hartnett catch him on Opening Day, and Hartnett called the pitches for most of his starts thereafter.

By 1924 Gabby was doing the bulk of the catching, and Bob O'Farrell was traded to the Cardinals. Joe McCarthy became the Cubs' manager in 1926 and brought them a pennant winner in 1929 without Hartnett, who due to a dead arm caught in only one game. Hartnett's mother thought the pain in his arm was related to his wife's pregnancy; when the baby was born in December, the pain went away.

Hartnett came out charging in 1930. He led all the fielding categories, hit .339, and knocked in a career-high 122 runs; in 1935, he hit .344 and was named MVP. With the Cubs 5½ games behind Pittsburgh in July 1938, he became player-manager. On September 28, with darkness falling at Wrigley Field, Hartnett's homer to left in the bottom of the ninth off Pittsburgh's Mace Brown gave them a half-game lead they never relinquished. The famous blow was the highlight of a 21 game winning streak, the greatest stretch drive in the history of baseball.

The Cubs faltered the next two years, and Hartnett was released, eventually catching on as a player-coach with Bill Terry's Giants. He later managed in the minors and was elected to the Hall of Fame in 1955.

RICKEY HENDERSON
Left Field. Born Dec. 25, 1958 Chicago, Ill. Holds major league records for stolen bases season (130), 1982, and lifetime (1,042). AL MVP, 1990.

The most powerful leadoff man in history, Rickey Henderson broke Bobby Bonds's career record for leadoff homers in 1989 and had 55 at the end of the 1992 season. He was named the American League MVP in 1990, broke Lou Brock's record for career steals on May 1, 1991, and, a year later to the day, became the first man to steal 1,000 bases.

None of this surprised long-time Henderson watchers, who became convinced of his gifts when he played for Modesto of the California League. In 1977 Henderson stole a a record 95 bases, led league outfielders in total chances (313), hit .345 to be named MVP, and became only the fourth man in professional baseball to steal seven bases in a single game.

Brought up to Oakland in 1979, the "Man of Steal" absconded with 33 bases in 89 games and, a year later, became the first ALr to steal 100 bases in a season, was second in the AL in walks, third in on-base percentage, and fourth in runs scored. A year later, during the strike-shortened 1981 season, he led the league in hits (135), runs (89), and steals (56); he also led the league's outfielders in putouts and total chances and won a Gold Glove, the first of many.

In 1982 Henderson broke Lou Brock's record of 118 steals in a season, set in 1974, winding up with 130. After the 1984 season he became a Yankee in exchange for Tim Birtsas, Eric Plunk, Stan Javier, Jay Howell, and Jose Rijo. Although he missed the first 10 games of the 1985 season with a sprained left ankle, he hit 24 homers, knocked in 72 runs, batted .314, and led the league in runs scored (146) for the second time, the highest total since Ted Williams scored 150 in 1949.

Henderson led the league in steals every year from 1980 to 1990 except in 1987, when he missed 57 games due to injuries. Traded back to Oakland in June 1989, Henderson helped the A's win the division and starred in the playoffs, tying Jim Rice's record of 8 runs scored in a single series, stealing a record 8 bases, and being named MVP. He was chosen World Series MVP as well and was named regular season MVP in 1990 when he hit .325 and hit 28 homers. He has the highest Total Player Rating among active players and, with many years of optimum performance ahead, is already the fifteenth greatest player of all time.

ROGERS HORNSBY
Second Baseman. Born Apr. 27, 1896 Winters, Tex. Died Jan. 5, 1963 Chicago, Ill. Holds modern major league record for highest batting average in a season (.424), 1924, and NL record for highest batting average, lifetime (.359).
Rogers Hornsby was suspicious, short-tempered, and the greatest righthanded hitter that ever lived.

The Rajah hit .300 or better in fourteen full seasons, won the NL batting title six straight years (1920–1925), is the only righthanded hitter to bat .400 or better three times and ended his career with a lifetime average of .358, second only to Ty Cobb. Like Cobb, he was thorny and idiosyncratic, reserving the right to bet on horses and refusing to read books or see movies for fear it would hurt his eyesight.

His career didn't begin auspiciously; Hornsby made 58

errors at shortstop in the Texas League and was unimpressive in 18 games with the Cardinals in 1915. Manager Miller Huggins told him to put on weight and, 25 pounds heavier, the Rajah hit .313 to lead the Cardinals in 1916.

By the mid-1920s he was the dominant player in the NL, winning the Triple Crown in both 1922 and 1925, when he became the Cardinals player-manager and was also named MVP for the first time. For the five-year period 1921–1925 his batting average exceeded .400! In 1926 he slumped to .317 but he gave the Cardinals their first pennant and helped upset the Yanks in a seven-game Series.

Two months after his great triumph, on December 20, 1926, he was traded to the Giants for Frankie Frisch and Jimmy Ring. Before the trade could go through, Hornsby had to sell 1,000 shares of St. Louis stock lest a Giants player own stock in the Cardinals; he nearly tripled his money, finally settling for $120,000.

He was traded again to the Braves and then the Cubs. With Chicago in 1929, he hit .380 with 39 homers and 149 RBIs, to win his second MVP award in his last full year as a player. Hornsby managed the Cubs from the end of 1930 until August 2, 1932, when he was replaced by Charlie Grimm; the Cubs went on to win the pennant and demonstrated their affection for Hornsby by cutting him out of the World Series pool.

The Rajah finished up with the Browns and managed in the minor leagues for fifteen years before coming back to lead the Browns in 1952 and the Reds in 1953. He ended his career as a Mets scout and coach. Hornsby was elected to the Hall of Fame in 1942.

CARL HUBBELL
Pitcher. Born Jun. 22, 1903 Carthage, Mo. Died Nov. 21, 1988 Scottsdale, Ariz. NL MVP 1933, 1936.
Ty Cobb was convinced that Carl Hubbell's screwball, which Cobb called the "butterfly pitch," would ruin his arm and forbade Hubbell to throw it—even though the Tigers had paid Oklahoma City $20,000 for his services. The man who would later be known as the Giants' "Meal Ticket" languished without his favorite pitch and was eventually given his outright release.

Hubbell picked up the scroogie again with Beaumont of the Texas League and was signed by Dick Kinsella, a part-time Giant scout and bored Illinois delegate to the 1928 Democratic Convention in Houston. Hubbell won 10 of his 16 decisions that first season, no-hit the Pirates, 11–0, in his sophomore year, and really hit his stride in 1933. That year King Carl six-hit the Cardinals, 1–0, over eighteen innings, led the league in innings pitched (309), wins (23), shutouts (10), and ERA (1.66), and was named MVP.

In the World Series he beat Joe Cronin's Senators twice, 4–2 and 2–1, and pitched twenty innings without allowing an earned run as the Giants won in five games. On July 10, 1934, Hubbell started the second All-Star Game by giving up a single to Charlie Gehringer and walking Heinie Manush. He then struck out Babe Ruth, Lou Gehrig, and Jimmie Foxx consecutively to end the first inning and got Al Simmons and Joe Cronin to start the second, one of baseball's greatest feats.

Equally commanding during the regular season that year, Hubbell led the league with a 2.30 ERA and a 21–12 record, the second of five straight 20-game seasons. In 1936, he went 26–6 and was named MVP again. That July 17, he started a string of 24 straight victories over two seasons, eventually snapped by the Dodgers on May 27, 1937; he also won games in both the 1936 and 1937 World Series to post a 1.97 ERA in October.

In 1938, Hubbell experienced arm trouble and won only 13 games; in four more years he would never win more than 11, and he finally ended his pitching career at age 40 with 253 wins and 36 shutouts. Named to the Hall of Fame in 1947, he ran the Giants' farm system, directing player development from 1943 to 1977 and scouting from 1978 to 1985, eventually seeing fellow Hall of Famers like Willie Mays, Willie McCovey, and Juan Marichal take his place as the Giants' meal tickets.

"SHOELESS JOE" JACKSON
Outfielder. Born July 16, 1888 Brandon Mills, S.C. Died Dec. 5, 1951 Greenville, S.C. In ten years as a regular, 1911–1920, never hit below .300.
Babe Ruth once said, "I decided to pick out the greatest hitter to watch and study and Jackson was good enough for me."

Joseph Jefferson Jackson never learned to read or write, but he could hit, field, and run. He hit .356 lifetime (third highest behind Cobb and Rogers Hornsby), and his glove was named "the place triples go to die." Yet he remains under a cloud for his part in the Black Sox series of 1919.

Signed by the A's but assailed by homesickness, Shoeless Joe blossomed in Cleveland, making the biggest rookie splash in history by hitting .408 in 1911 and finishing second only to Ty Cobb in batting, slugging, hits, doubles, and total bases. Although his stats were nearly as good in 1912 (.395) and 1913 (.373), Cleveland was a last place club; sold to Chicago in the middle of 1915, Jackson helped the Sox win the pennant in 1917 and the World Series.

When Sox first baseman Chick Gandil approached Jackson about throwing the 1919 Series, Jackson called owner Charles Comiskey and asked to be benched, but Comiskey refused to hear him out. While Jackson was the leading hitter (.375), set a Series record for hits (12), and knocked in 6 runs, pitcher Lefty Williams gave Jackson $5,000 for his part in the fix, and, to his eternal discredit, Jackson took it.

In 1920 Jackson hit .382 but, that September, a Chicago grand jury investigated the fix; Jackson confessed, denied doing anything to throw the Series, but admitted taking the money. Although acquitted after their confessions "disappeared," Jackson and the other Black Sox were barred from baseball for life by Commissioner Landis. Shoeless Joe sued Comiskey for back pay and won a judgment for $16,711.04, but it was overturned; the sitting judge ordered him to jail for perjury and, after a brief stay, he accepted a small settlement from Comiskey,

Jackson ran several successful businesses in his home town of Brandon Mills, South Carolina but never learned to write his name. When the Cleveland Hall of Fame was started, in 1951, Jackson became the fourth highest vote-getter even though his name wasn't on the ballot. TV host Ed Sullivan heard the story and asked Jackson to be on the show; the day before he was scheduled to appear, Jackson died of a heart attack.

REGGIE JACKSON

Right Field. Born May 18, 1946 Wyncote, Pa. AL MVP 1973.

The only player to be named MVP in two World Series, Reggie Jackson earned the nickname "Mr. October" by setting a World Series record for slugging percentage (.755).

He's also baseball's all-time strikeout king, fanning 2,597 times, once every four at-bats. In addition to being all-or-nothing on offense, Jackson was next-to-nothing on defense. He is tied with Burt Shotton for leading the AL in errors the most times (five). Yet, from 1971 to 1982, Jackson helped three different clubs win ten division titles, six pennants, and five championships.

In 1968 he hit 29 homers, led the league in assists (14) and errors (12), and struck out 171 times in 553 at bats. In July 1969 he was two weeks ahead of Roger Maris's pace with 40, then hit only 7 more for the rest of the season and finished second to Harmon Killebrew. In 1973 he won the first of four home run crowns.

Jackson made his 1973 World Series debut memorable with four hits in Game Two, doubled twice to knock in both runs of Game Six, and hit a home run and made two spectacular catches to help Oakland win Game Seven; Jackson was voted MVP of the Series to go along with the MVP award he had won in the regular season.

He also homered in the opener of the 1974 Series, doubled in Game Two, and threw out a key base runner in Game Five. In the fall of 1977, Jackson fulfilled his destiny and truly became Mr. October. He homered in Games Four and Five and homered on three consecutive pitches in Game Six. Since he'd hit a homer on his last swing of Game Five and walked his first time up in Game Six, Jackson had hit four straight homers in four official at bats off four different pitchers. He set other Series records for homers in a Series (5), runs scored (10), and total bases (25).

After getting his name on a candy bar, Jackson won a third home run crown in 1980 with the Yankees, a fourth in 1982 with the Angels, and ended his career with the A's in 1987, retiring with 563 career homers to place sixth on the all-time list.

WALTER JOHNSON

Pitcher. Born Nov. 6, 1887 Humboldt, Kan. Died Dec. 10, 1946 Washington, D.C. Holds major league record for lifetime shutouts (110). AL MVP 1913, 1924.

Walter Johnson and the Senators were baseball's odd couple. From 1907 to 1927, Johnson compiled a record of 417–279 while the Senators won just two pennants. He lost 27 games by the score of 1–0; in all, he lost 65 games in which his team failed to score.

Not that he needed much support. On thirty-eight occasions when the Senators managed only a single run, Johnson held the opposition scoreless. He pitched seven Opening Day shutouts and wound up with more career whitewashes (110) than most big league pitchers have career wins.

Twelve of those shutouts came in 1913, when he was at his peak, finishing 36–7 to win his first MVP award. His 1.14 ERA was a record for fifty-five years, and he struck out 243 batters in 346 innings. "Barney" (after race driver Barney Oldfield) led the league in wins, ERA, and strike-outs again in 1918 and 1924, won 20 games or more in ten straight seasons, and had the lowest lifetime ERA (2.17) among AL pitchers with more than 2,000 innings. Considering all pitchers in all eras, Johnson ranks first in Total Pitcher Index.

A high school sensation, Johnson was ready to sign with the Pirates but was refused a $9 signing bonus; instead, he agreed to sign with the Senators on the condition that they pay his way home to Humboldt, Kansas, if he didn't make it in the big leagues. He made his debut on August 2, 1907, losing a five-hitter to the Tigers, 3–2. The following year, the "Big Train" arrived, shutting out the New York Highlanders (Yankees) three times in a four-day weekend series on four, three, and two hits.

Seventeen years later, when he should have been washed up, Johnson went 23–7 to win his second MVP award, and the hapless Senators finally reached the World Series. After losing twice to the Giants, Johnson won his first Series game by pitching four scoreless innings of relief in Game 7 as Washington beat the Giants, 4–3, in twelve innings. In the 1925 Series, Johnson won two games against the Pirates but lost the finale, 9–7, as his mates allowed four unearned runs.

When the first election was held for the Hall of Fame, Johnson joined Cobb, Babe Ruth, Honus Wagner, and Christy Mathewson as charter members, the "Five Immortals."

AL KALINE

Right Field. Born Dec. 19, 1934 Baltimore, Md. Won batting championship at age 20.

He was never named MVP, never led the league in home runs or RBIs, and managed to win only one batting title in twenty-two major league seasons. Yet, in 1980, Al Kaline became only the tenth player named to the Hall of Fame in his first year of eligibility.

Kaline had 100 or more hits eighteen times, hit 20 or more home runs nine times, hit .300 or better eight times. The first player to win Gold Gloves at two positions, he won ten in all. In 1971 at age thirty-six, Kaline played the entire season errorless as part of a 242-game streak without a miscue.

One week after signing with the Tigers on his high school graduation day, Kaline got into the lineup when Steve Souchock broke his wrist. Soon after, in a game against the White Sox, Kaline threw runners out at second, third, and home in successive innings. the next year he became the youngest player to win the batting title (.340) and was named AL Player of the Year by *The Sporting News*.

He started in the All-Star Game for the first of ten times in 1955 and played in sixteen summer classics without committing an error, hit .324, and homered in the 1959 Game and the second Game in 1960. He also won the slugging championship in 1959 (.530) and was named *Sporting News* Player of the Year a second time in 1963.

A's pitcher Lew Krausse hit him with a pitch in 1968, breaking his arm; six weeks later, Kaline returned as a first baseman and played the outfield during the Series. Down three games to one, the Tigers came back in Game Five when Kaline singled in the tying and go-ahead runs. In Game Six he singled twice in the ten-run third inning as the Tigers romped, 13–1. He wound up leading the

eventual World Champions with a .379 average and 8 RBIs.

In 1974 Kaline needed 139 hits to reach 3,000 and became a full-time DH. He got his 3,000th, doubling off Dave McNally, and retired with 3,007. While no Tiger uniform had been retired in deference to Ty Cobb, who didn't wear numerals, Kaline's number 6 was taken out of circulation in August 1980, after his election to the Hall of Fame.

TIM KEEFE

Pitcher. Born Jan. 1, 1857 Cambridge, Mass. Died Apr. 23, 1933 Cambridge, Mass. Posted all-time-low ERA of 0.80 in 1880.

The Mets' first great pitcher wasn't Tom Seaver. It was Tim Keefe, who won 41 games his first year and 37 in his second for the New York Metropolitans of the American Association.

Keefe notched 342 victories in just fourteen years, with a career ERA of 2.62, and established a major league record (since tied) by winning 19 straight games. In the 600 games Keefe pitched, he held the opposition to six or fewer hits on 235 occasions, more than a third of the time. In his streak season (1888), he managed this feat twenty-eight times in fifty-one starts, more than half the time.

His success depended partly on the changeup, of which he was the acknowledged pioneer, and partly on keeping meticulous records of opposing hitters in his own system of notation. (When fellow Giant John Montgomery Ward organized the Players League in 1890, Keefe was named secretary because he could take shorthand.)

Born in Cambridge, Massachusetts, he played with a string of semipro and minor-league New England teams before joining the Troy Haymakers in 1880. He first attracted national attention by going 41–27 with the Mets in 1883—including both ends of a doubleheader, a one-hitter and a two-hitter. He enjoyed even greater success with Jim Mutrie's New York Giants (42–20 in 1886) and became known as "Sir Timothy" for his pitching and manner.

Sir Tim's streak started on June 23, 1888, when he beat the Quakers (Phillies), 7–6, at the Baker Bowl. He went forty-five days before losing again, to the White Stockings (Cubs), 4–2, at the Polo Grounds. To cap off a dream season, Keefe was 4–0 in the World Series, yielding the American Association St. Louis Browns just 18 hits and 2 earned runs in 35 innings.

After jumping to the Players League, Keefe ended his playing days with the Phillies. He umpired in the NL before becoming a real estate mogul. He was elected to the Hall of Fame in 1964 and was proclaimed Cambridge's All-Time Greatest Athlete in a 1976 poll conducted by the Cambridge *Chronicle*.

HARMON KILLEBREW

First Baseman. Born Jun. 29, 1936 Payette, Ida. Holds AL record for most lifetime home runs, righthanded batter (573). AL MVP 1969.

Harmon Killebrew averaged a homer every 14.22 at-bats, more frequently than anyone but Babe Ruth and Ralph Kiner.

The fact is that Killebrew was better at hitting home runs than Ruth and Kiner—half the time—and worse

than Rabbit Maranville and Nellie Fox the other half. Baseball has had many streak hitters for average, but Killebrew was a bonafide streak hitter for power.

In 1962 the Killer beat Norm Cash for the home run title, 48 to 39; after a horrendous summer slump, he hit 11 homers in the last eleven games to beat Cash. In 1963 he pulled the same stunt, missing twenty games with a twisted knee, then hit seven homers in the last six games to outhomer Dick Stuart, 45 to 42. In all, he hit 573 homers to place fifth on the all-time list. He led the league in homers five times.

Killebrew is also the only Washington Senator to be discovered by an Idaho senator. The Honorable Herman Welker tipped Clark Griffith about Killebrew in 1954, comparing him to Mickey Mantle. The last time Welker had boasted about an Idaho boy, it had been Vernon Law, and Griffith hadn't listened. This time he sent Ossie Bluege to investigate, and Bluege signed Killebrew the day he first saw him.

In 1959 the Senators gave Killebrew the third base job; he responded with five two-homer games from May 1 through May 17 and ended the year with 42 to tie Rocky Colavito for the league lead. The Senators moved him to first base for two years, then to the outfield the year after moving to Minnesota. From 1962 through 1964, he led the league with 48, 45, and 49 homers.

When the Twins won their first pennant in 1965, he missed 48 games with a dislocated elbow but still hit 25 homers and won a fifth home run crown in 1967 (44). After missing nearly half the 1968 season with injuries, he had a banner year in 1969, leading the league in homers (49) and RBIs (140) and helped bring the Twins a Western Division title.

He hit 41 homers in 1970, his eighth 40-plus year, homered in his third All-Star Game in 1971 and ended his career in a Kansas City uniform; he was elected to the Hall of Fame in 1974.

RALPH KINER

Left Field. Born Oct. 27, 1922 Santa Rita, N.M. Hit home runs at a clip (home run percentage) faster than anyone except Babe Ruth.

Ralph Kiner set a home run record that even Babe Ruth and Hank Aaron couldn't top by leading or tying for the league lead in home runs the first seven years of his career. He is also the only player who hit home runs in three consecutive All-Star Games (1949–1951), averaged 35 homers a year in his ten-year major league career, and tied Rogers Hornsby for the then National League record in career grand slams with 12.

Never noted for his finesse with either arm or glove, Kiner ushered in the era of the pure slugger. Kiner had led the NL in 1946 with 23 home runs, the first rookie to do so since Harry Lumley in 1906; however, he really blossomed after slugger Hank Greenberg joined the Pirates in 1947. "Hank put me in a better position in the batter's box, which enabled me to pull outside pitches, and changed my stance and my whole approach to hitting, getting me not to swing at bad pitches," Kiner recalls. He hit 51 homers in 1947, 48 of them after June 1.

The good-looking Kiner also attracted a new kind of woman fan to baseball and became linked with movie stars like Elizabeth Taylor. He began doing personal ap-

pearances and became one of the first ballplayers to host his own local TV show.

Kiner reached his peak as a long ball hitter in 1949, hitting 54 homers, four of them grand slams. His mighty blasts attracted fans despite the Pirates' second-division finishes, and, by 1951, Kiner topped Stan Musial as the league's highest salaried player, at $90,000. Two years later the romance was over, and Kiner was traded to the Cubs. He ended his playing career with Cleveland, retiring at thirty-three when a back sprain held him to just 18 homers in 113 games.

Adept at putting people in the seats, he learned the business side of baseball as general manager of the San Diego Padres of the Pacific Coast League from 1955 to 1960. After a year as the radio voice of the White Sox, Kiner became part of the expansion Mets' announcing troika, with Lindsey Nelson and Bob Murphy. Named to the Hall of Fame in 1975, Kiner recently celebrated his thirtieth anniversary as a Mets announcer.

SANFORD "SANDY" KOUFAX
Pitcher. Born Dec. 30, 1935 Brooklyn, N.Y. Holds major league record for most consecutive years leading league in ERA (five). NL MVP 1963 and Cy Young Award 1963, 1965, 1966.
Sandy Koufax was the best pitcher in baseball for five seasons. From 1962 to 1966, he was 111–34 with 100 complete games, 33 of them shutouts. He led the NL in ERA all five years, in wins and strikeouts in 1963, 1965, and 1966, and won the Cy Young Award all three years.

Born Sanford Braun, he took the name of his stepfather, attorney Irving Koufax. He went to the University of Cincinnati on a basketball scholarship, but chose baseball after striking out 51 batters in 32 innings. In 1955 the nineteen-year old lefty joined the Dodgers and mopped up for three seasons. The first sign that he might be special came on August 31, 1959, when Koufax struck out 18 Cubs to tie Bob Feller's record; yet, frustrated with his progress, he nearly quit in 1960 after going 8–13.

One day, scout Kenny Meyers and catcher Norm Sherry asked him to throw at a spot and noticed that Koufax's motion obstructed his vision. Meyers said, "How can you hit that spot when you can't even see it?" Sherry persuaded Koufax to throw more deliberately, and controlling the speed of his delivery made all the difference between getting behind the hitters and throwing strikes.

In 1961, Koufax was 18–13, leading the league with 269 strikeouts. He blossomed fully in 1963, winning 25 of 30 regular season decisions and taking the first and last games of the World Series sweep of the Yankees. He also won the Cy Young Award and was named MVP.

Adhesions in his pitching arm broke loose in 1964, leading to the traumatic arthritis which would end his career. After throwing his third no-hitter in late August, Koufax was forced to stop pitching with a record of 19–5 and an ERA of 1.74. On medical orders, he didn't throw between starts in 1965 and went 26–8, crowning the regular season by pitching a perfect game against the Cubs on September 9; he shut out Minnesota twice in the World Series as the Dodgers won in seven games.

Koufax's final season was 1966, when he won 27 and lost 9 and led the league in ERA for the fifth year in a row (1.73). In 1972 he became the youngest player ever elected to the Hall of Fame and was also named Player of the Decade in the 1960s.

NAPOLEON "LARRY" LAJOIE
Second Baseman. Born Sept. 5, 1875 Woonsocket, R.I. Died Feb. 7, 1959 Daytona Beach, Fla. Holds AL record for highest season batting average, (.426), 1901.
Napoleon Lajoie was the complete package. No other second baseman has ever shone so brilliantly in so many ways for so long (twenty-one years).

In addition to leading ALrs in every fielding category in two different seasons, Lajoie won a Triple Crown and four batting titles, compiled 3,242 career hits and a lifetime batting average of .338. At one time or another, he led both leagues in RBIs, slugging average, and fielding percentage, and was so well-loved that his team adopted his nickname as its own.

Originally signed by the Phillies, Lajoie hit .361 in 1897 and won the slugging championship (.569). By 1900 he had gathered five straight .300 plus seasons but was earning only $2,400, the NL maximum. When Connie Mack offered him $4,000, he jumped to the new AL and won the Triple Crown in 1901, hitting .426 (still an AL record) with 14 home runs and 125 RBIs; it is a measure of his versatility that he also led in runs scored (145), hits (232), doubles (48) and slugging percentage (.643), putouts (395) and fielding percentage (.960).

The Phils sued Mack, and eventually the Pennsylvania Supreme Court enjoined Lajoie from playing with the Athletics. AL president Ban Johnson ordered that Lajoie be transferred to Cleveland where he could avoid Pennsylvania's jurisdiction but could still play in the AL; for the first few years, Lajoie always remained behind when the Bronchos (Indians) traveled to Philadelphia.

He won batting titles in 1903 (.344) and 1904 (.376) and was named Cleveland's player-manager in 1905; the team was renamed the Naps in his honor. Although the Naps improved, they never won a pennant under Lajoie, who resigned during the 1909 season to concentrate on playing.

Nap won a fourth, albeit tainted batting championship when he got seven bunt singles on the last day of the 1910 season, all because of the opposing manager's hatred for Ty Cobb, who was four points ahead. In retaliation, sportswriter Hugh Fullerton changed his ruling on a Cobb smash that he had ruled an error earlier in the season, helping to give Cobb a single extra hit and the championship. Seven decades later the controversy erupted anew as it was discovered that Cobb had been the beneficiary of a double entry of a game in which he had gone 2-for-3; Larry had the higher batting average in 1910, after all.

Lajoie was elected to the Hall of Fame in 1937.

JOHN HENRY "POP" LLOYD
Shortstop. Born Apr. 25, 1884 Palatka, Fla. Died Mar. 19, 1965 Atlantic City, N.J. At age forty-four, hit .564 and led the Negro NL in home runs.
Pop Lloyd was frequently called "the Black Honus Wagner." There is no record that Wagner was ever called "the white Pop Lloyd," but to have done so would have been high compliment indeed.

Wagner once commented about Lloyd, "After I saw him play, I felt honored that they should name such a

great ballplayer after me." Connie Mack added, "You could put Wagner and Lloyd in a bag together and whichever one you pulled out, you couldn't go wrong."

Lloyd may have been the single greatest black player of all time. A lefthanded line drive hitter, he was a gifted base runner and base stealer in both the United States and Cuba, where he played for twelve years and was an idol to fans and youngsters. They called him "El Cuchara"—"the Shovel," and writers talk of him scooping ground balls with dirt, twigs, and anything else that populated the primitive infields.

Born in Florida, he played semipro ball in Georgia with the Macon Acmes and moved on to the Cuban-X Giants. In Cuba he played against Ty Cobb in an exhibition game, tagging him out three times on attempted steals with catcher Bruce Petway delivering the ball. Lloyd also outhit Cobb, .500 to .369, and Cobb was so embarrassed that he vowed never to play against blacks again.

Perhaps the highlight of Lloyd's playing career came from 1914 to 1917 when he played for Rube Foster's Chicago American Giants and batted cleanup on a team that included Oscar Charleston, Bingo DeMoss, Smokey Joe Williams, and Cannonball Dick Redding.

As Lloyd's legs began to go, he switched to first base and signed on with the Brooklyn Royal Giants as player-manager for three seasons. From 1921 to 1928, he played with the Columbus Buckeyes, Hilldale, the Bacharach Giants, and the New York Lincoln Giants. At age forty-four he hit .564 and led the league in home runs.

When announced Graham McNamee asked Babe Ruth to name the greatest player of all time, Ruth said, "You mean major leaguers?" "No," replied McNamee, "the greatest player anywhere." "In that case," said Ruth, "I'd pick John Henry Lloyd." Lloyd was elected to the Hall of Fame in 1977.

MICKEY MANTLE

Center Field. Born Oct. 20, 1931 Spavinaw, Okla. AL MVP 1956, 1957, 1962.

Despite a chronic bone infection in his legs and operations on both knees, Mickey Mantle became baseball's most powerful switch hitter, hitting 536 home runs in the regular season and setting a World Series record with 18 more.

Named for Mickey Cochrane, his father's favorite player, Mantle learned to switch hit at age five and starred in high school baseball and football, developing osteomyelitis after bruising a leg in a football game. After a short (and error-filled) career as a minor league shortstop, he became the Yankees' regular right fielder before his twentieth birthday. He suffered his first serious injury during the 1951 Series when he tripped on a drain at Yankee Stadium and required surgery for torn knee cartilage.

Joe DiMaggio retired that fall, and Mantle moved to center field, hitting .311 in 142 games. He led the league in home runs (37) in 1955 and, a year later, won the Triple Crown, hitting 52 homers, knocking in 130 runs, and batting .353. The only player besides Jimmie Foxx to hit 50 homers and win a batting title, Mantle won the MVP award and shone in the World Series, hitting three homers as the Yanks beat Brooklyn in seven games.

In 1957 he was chosen MVP again as he hit .365. He won home run crowns again in 1958 (42) and 1960 (40), finishing second to Roger Maris's 61 homers in 1961 with

54. Mantle was named MVP a third time in 1962 when he hit .321. On June 5, 1963, he broke his left foot in Baltimore, ending a season in which he had 15 home runs in 172 at-bats, although he returned in time to hit a home run in the World Series.

His personal choice for most memorable homer was his ninth-inning shot off Cardinal Barney Schultz in 1964, which broke Babe Ruth's record for lifetime Series home runs and won Game Three. Mickey went on to hit two more in that Series, his last, and wound up his tenth Series with 18 homers, 42 runs scored, 123 total bases, and 40 RBIs—all records.

Despite his injuries, Mantle holds the Yankee record for games played—2,401. He retired during spring training in 1969, and, on June 8, received a ten-minute standing ovation at Yankee Stadium. He was named to the Hall of Fame in 1974.

WALTER "RABBIT" MARANVILLE

Shortstop. Born Nov. 11, 1891 Springfield, Mass. Died Jan. 5, 1954 New York, N.Y. Holds major league shortstop record for most years leading league in putouts (6) and lifetime putouts (5,133).

If you thought Jimmy Blake was, in the words of *Casey at the Bat,* "much-despised," consider Walter James Vincent "Rabbit" Maranville.

Every time suggestions are made to "prune" the Hall of Fame of its many undeserving members, Maranville's name is invariably suggested, mostly due to his limitations with the bat. The possessor of just 28 career home runs in more than 10,000 at bats, "Rabbit" bettered .300 just once in seventeen seasons as a regular, and never led the league in an offensive category.

Yet, in 1914 and again in 1919, Maranville led the league in both Fielding Runs and Total Player Rating. He saved 50 runs more than an average shortstop in 1914 and personally accounted for more wins than any player in the league. Casey Stengel, who later managed Maranville, said of him, "Shortstops who stay around more than twenty years are not clowns."

Maranville finished a close second to fellow Miracle Brave Johnny Evers in the voting for the Chalmers (MVP) Award. There was no MVP voting for the NL in 1919, but Maranville was third in 1913 and finished in the top twenty in MVP voting no less than seven times.

The colorful Maranville invented the "basket catch," but many of his antics were inspired by alcohol. He jumped into a water fountain fully clothed; dangled a teammate out of a twelfth-story hotel window; and, named manager of the Cubs in 1925, celebrated by pouring ice water on all his sleeping teammates. Waived to the Brooklyn Robins, Maranville was demoted to Rochester of the International League.

That's when he resolved to quit drinking. Asked to comment on the effects of Prohibition, he said, "There is much less drinking now than there was before 1927, because I quit drinking on May 24, 1927."

He joined the Cardinals later that year, started for the pennant-winning 1928 team, and hit .308 in the World Series. Back with the Braves in 1929, he started playing more second base; in 1932, at the age of forty-one, he led the league at that position in putouts and fielding. He still holds the major league record for career putouts by a

shortstop and was elected to the Hall of Fame shortly after his death in 1954.

EDDIE MATHEWS

Third Baseman. Born Oct. 13, 1931 Texarkana, Tex. Holds NL record, most consecutive years with 30 or more home runs (nine).

Eddie Mathews played a game-within-the-game. He said, "I'd take on the other third baseman ... I wanted to beat him in every department—fielding, hitting, running the bases. I played that game all my life, and it kept me on my toes."

It did indeed. Mathews was a seven-time All-Star. He hit 30 or more homers for nine straight seasons and 512 lifetime, led the NL's third basemen three times in assists, and teamed with Henry Aaron to form the greatest one-two home run punch in baseball history; as Braves teammates, they accounted for 863 homers.

The only Brave to play in Boston, Milwaukee and Atlanta, Mathews could have had his choice of teams. He was scouted by nine, but because Boston had the oldest third baseman (Bob Elliott), Mathews became a Brave at 12:01 a.m. the day following his high school graduation in 1949 and was sent to Atlanta, where Dixie Walker was the manager. Walker helped Mathews deal with lefthanded pitchers and Billy Jurges polished his fielding. By the fall of 1951, Ty Cobb said, "I've seen three or four perfect swings in my time. This lad has one of them."

In April 1952 Elliott was traded to the Giants, and Steady Eddie got his job. He became the first rookie to homer three times in a game, hit 25 homers, and proved there was no sophomore jinx by winning the home run title the following year with 47 round-trippers, finishing second only to Roy Campanella in the MVP voting.

Mathews starred in the 1957 World Series although the Yankees walked him eight times. He won Game Four with a tenth-inning homer, scored the only run in Game Five, and doubled in the first two runs of Game Seven; with the bases loaded and two out in the bottom of the ninth, he made a lunging stop on Bill Skowron's shot down the line and stepped on third to give the Milwaukee Braves their only championship.

In 1959 Mathews won his second home run crown. He was traded to the Astros on New Year's Eve, 1967, moved on to the Tigers, and played in his final World Series in 1968. He managed the Braves from 1972 to 1974 and entered the Hall of Fame in 1978.

CHRISTY MATHEWSON

Pitcher. Born Aug. 12, 1880 Factoryville, Pa. Died Oct. 7, 1925 Saranac Lake, N.Y. Holds NL record for most years winning 20 or more games (12).

If Mattel had made Barbie dolls in 1903, Christy Mathewson might have been the model for Ken.

Handsome, clean-cut, intelligent, clean-living, and heroic, Mathewson was one of the first players to attract women and children to the ballpark. An All-America college football player for Bucknell, he was nationally known as a checkers expert, too. Oh yes. He won 373 games in his major league career even though he didn't normally pitch on Sundays. (His mother had wanted him to become a minister.)

One of the "Five Immortals" elected when the Hall of Fame was established in 1936, Mathewson was called "Big Six" because his fastball reminded reporters of a famous New York fire engine. Nevertheless, it was his fadeaway (screwball) that drove National Leaguers crazy. He won 30 or more games four times, finished 434 of the 551 games he started, and completed 10 of 11 World Series games while posting an ERA of 1.15. A control whiz, he pitched 68 consecutive innings in 1913 without walking a batter.

Born to well-to-do parents in Factoryville, Pennsylvania, Mathewson studied forestry at Bucknell, headed two literary societies, was elected class president, and was the kicker on Walter Camp's 1900 All-America team. He became a Giant that fall, won 20 games in 1901, and became baseball's dominant pitcher starting in 1903, the first of three straight years with 30 or more wins.

In the 1905 World Series, Mathewson became a household name; in a Series decided entirely by shutouts, Matty contributed three—in five days. He four-hit Connie Mack's A's in the opener and, two days after Chief Bender blanked the Giants, four-hit the Mackmen again. Two days later Matty wound up the Series, giving up six hits this time, but nevertheless pitching his third shutout in six days. In 27 innings, Mathewson walked one man and stuck out 18.

Over the next ten years, Mathewson won at least 20 games a season. When the fadeaway began to fade, Mathewson's manager and best friend, John McGraw, arranged a trade to Cincinnati so he could take the helm of the Reds. Joining a chemical warfare unit in France during World War I, he was accidentally exposed to poison gas that weakened his lungs; he later contracted tuberculosis, which ultimately proved fatal. He had served as general manager of the Braves despite his poor health but died on the opening day of the 1925 World Series.

WILLIE MAYS

Center Field. Born May 6, 1931 Westfield, Ala. NL Rookie of the Year 1951, MVP 1954, 1965.

In 1951 Willie Mays chased a 457-foot shot to dead center in Forbes Field, hit the warning track, saw the ball hook right, and, with no time to reach across his body, made the catch bare-handed. Pirates general manager Branch Rickey, in his forty-eighth year of baseball, sent Mays a note: "That was the finest catch I have ever seen and the finest catch I ever hope to see."

Mays started with the Birmingham Black Barons of the Negro AL and, after hitting .477 in the opening months of the 1951 season with the Minneapolis Millers, was promoted to the Giants. When Mays had trouble hitting big league pitching, manager Leo Durocher assured him that center field was his—whether he hit or not. Mays responded by leading the Giants to the pennant and was named Rookie of the Year.

He spent most of 1952 and all of 1953 in the service, returning in 1954 to win his only batting title (.345) and to belt 41 homers. The Giants won another pennant and Mays collected his first MVP award. In Game One of the World Series, Mays made one of baseball's most famous catches, snaring Vic Wertz's drive to deep center over his shoulder to keep the game tied, 3–3; the Giants swept the Indians, and Mays won the Hickok Belt as Pro Athlete of the Year.

The "Say Hey Kid" only got better, winning the first of four home run titles in 1955 and becoming the complete player in 1957—winning a Gold Glove, stealing a league-leading 38 bases, and hitting 26 doubles, 20 triples, and 35 homers. He hit four home runs in a game on April 30, 1961, and hit 49 homers in 1962 to lead the league and drive the Giants to another pennant.

Voted the All-Star MVP in 1963 and 1968, he holds the All-Star Game record for career hits (23) and stolen bases (6) and says the best catch he ever made was one that robbed Ted Williams of a home run in the 1955 game at Milwaukee's County Stadium.

Willie earned eleven Gold Gloves, set records for career putouts and total chances, was the first man to hit 300 home runs and steal 300 bases, had 660 lifetime homers, and sported a lifetime batting average of .302. He has considerable support as the best ever to play the game. He was elected to the Hall of Fame in 1979, his first year of eligibility.

BILL MAZEROSKI
Second Baseman. Born Sept. 5, 1936 Wheeling, West Va. Holds major league record for lifetime double plays by a second baseman (1,706).
Bill Mazeroski, remembered best for his Series-winning home run in 1960, may have been baseball's best fielder. In *Baseball Ratings*, Charles Faber awards points for percentage, assists, chances, and range factor to all players with ten years' experience; Mazeroski leads every player from every era, regardless of position.

He set records for second basemen by leading his league the most years in assists (9) and double plays (8) and holds the record for career double plays by a second baseman (1706). Only three *first basemen* took part in more double plays; Lou Gehrig, for instance, played in one game more and figured in 136 fewer double plays.

Mazeroski won the first of eight Gold Gloves in 1956 and became an All-Star for the first of seven times in 1958. After hitting 19 home runs that year, he tried to pull everything and wound up with just seven homers and thirty-four-point drop in his batting average. When the slump continued into 1960, George Sisler made him stand deeper in the box to hit curveballs after they broke. Hitting .237 on August 3, Mazeroski ended the regular season at .273 as the Pirates won their first pennant in thirty-three years.

He started a double play in the first inning of Game One, hit a two-run homer in the fourth inning (the margin of victory in a 6–4 Pirate win), and turned his third double play in the ninth inning to end the game. With the Yanks and Pirates even in the Series, in the seventh game the Pirates went ahead, 9–7, in the eighth inning. The Yankees tied it in the top of the ninth, but, leading off in the bottom, Mazeroski hit Ralph Terry's second pitch over the left field wall to win the Series.

Maz set an NL record for double plays by a second baseman (144) in 1961 and smashed Gerry Priddy's AL record of 150 double plays in 1966; that year, he (161) and Gene Alley (128) recorded the most double plays for a shortstop and a second baseman in a season. A utility man in 1971, he retired in 1972. He later became an infield instructor for the Expos, and the Pirates retired his number 9 in 1987.

WILLIE "STRETCH" McCOVEY
First Baseman. Born Jan. 10, 1938 Mobile, Ala. Holds National League record for most lifetime home runs by a lefthanded batter (521). NL Rookie of the Year 1959, MVP 1969.
The man who left his heart in San Francisco wasn't Tony Bennett but Willie McCovey. After three seasons in San Diego and 11 games in Oakland, McCovey returned on Opening Day in 1977 and received a standing ovation that moved him to tears. He responded to the fans by hitting 28 homers at age thirty-nine and was named Comeback Player of the Year.

The love affair began on July 30, 1959, when McCovey made a spectacular debut. Called up from Phoenix, where he'd been tutored by Ted Williams, McCovey went 4-for-4 against Robin Roberts with two singles and two triples. But there was a problem. The Giants already had a first baseman, Orlando Cepeda, who had been named Rookie of the Year the year before. McCovey won the same honor in 1959, hitting .354, and the two see-sawed back and forth between first and the outfield; Cepeda got the first base job until he was injured in 1965, then was traded to the Cardinals.

By then McCovey was a star, having led the league with 44 homers in 1963. When he returned to first base full time, Willie led the league in 1968 with 36 homers, 105 RBIs, and a .545 slugging average. For an encore, he headed the same categories in 1969 with even better numbers—45 homers, 126 RBIs and a .656 slugging average.

NL pitchers, rather than pitch to McCovey in 1970, decided to walk him instead—a league-leading 137 times, including a record 45 intentional walks. "Stretch" (for his ability to keep one foot on the bag and reach off-the-mark throws) still hit 39 homers and led the league in slugging for the third straight year.

A series of injuries plagued him in the 1970s, and when he did play, pitchers continued to pitch around him. The Giants traded him and he played for three teams without leaving California. When he hung up his spikes in 1980, McCovey had played in four decades and hit 521 homers to tie Ted Williams, his idol and former mentor, for ninth on the all-time list. He also set the NL career record for grand slams (18), second only to Lou Gehrig's 23. He was elected to the Hall of Fame in 1985.

JOHN "BID" McPHEE
Second Baseman. Born Nov. 1, 1859 Messina, N.Y. Died Jan. 3, 1943 San Diego, Cal. Holds major league record for putouts by a second baseman (6,545).
John Alexander "Bid" McPhee made more putouts than any other major league second baseman, ranks fifth in Fielding Wins, ahead of star glove men like Tris Speaker and Ozzie Smith, stole more bases than Davey Lopes or Luis Aparicio. and, in Total Player Rating, beats out Hall of Fame second basemen Frankie Frisch, Bobby Doerr, and Billy Herman.

So how come you never heard of this guy?

Sometimes greatness can be boring, and that's certainly the case with "King Bid," as he was known. As historian Bob Carroll has noted, "In all of his eighteen years he was never fined. He was never even thrown out of a game!... McPhee showed up every day in shape, stayed sober, did his job, and went home to a good night's sleep."

About the only thing that made him colorful was the fact that he was the best defensive second baseman in the nineteenth century and for fourteen (of his eighteen) seasons he did it barehanded.

McPhee, who stood 5'8" and weighed 152 on a good day, was "biddy"—small. He joined the brand-new Cincinnati Reds of the brand-new American Association in 1882, leading the league in putouts, double plays, and fielding average, a habit he never quite broke. He was the double play champ eleven times and led in fielding nine times.

As you might expect, McPhee was a pesky hitter (.271 lifetime), speedy enough to steal 95 bases in 1887 and 568 lifetime. What might surprise is that Bid once "cranked out" 8 homers to lead the league in 1886. (Yes, they were all inside the park.) The other surprise is that McPhee's on-base percentage is .354, relatively low for a guy who walked 981 times.

When his contemporaries began using mitts, McPhee refused to go along. Although he toughened his hands every spring, he was no longer leading the league; however, he began 1896 with a sore finger and finally gave in. The results were instructive; at age 37, McPhee's fielding average was .978, a full 10 points above the recognized mark. The record stood until 1925 when Sparky Adams broke it.

He retired after the 1899 season, briefly managed the Reds, and scouted for them in Los Angeles, where he settled.

JOE MORGAN
Second Baseman. Born Sept. 19, 1943 Bonham, Tex. Holds major league record for seasons by a second baseman (22). NL MVP 1975, 1976.
When the Big Red Machine was operating in the 1970s, Joe Morgan was its generator. He got on base 41 percent of the time and, on a team with Johnny Bench and Pete Rose, was named MVP in both 1975 and 1976.

From 1972 through 1977, he averaged 60 stolen bases, scored more than 100 runs each year, and averaged 21 homers and 84 RBIs with a .301 batting average. Moreover, Little Joe won Gold Gloves in 1973–1977. Over twenty-two years, he helped his teammates win six divisional titles, four pennants and two world championships.

Born in Bonham, Texas, Morgan signed with the Astros and was named NL Rookie of the Year in 1965 by *The Sporting News*. Traded to Cincinnati before the 1972 season, he topped NL second basemen in putouts and fielding and led in walks (115) and runs scored (122).

In 1975 he hit .327, led all second basemen in fielding percentage, and stole 67 bases to be named MVP (he added six steals in the postseason). Morgan won Game Three of the World Series with a single in the bottom of the tenth and Game Seven with a single in the top of the ninth to give the Reds their first championship in thirty-five years.

The Reds repeated in 1976 and Morgan became the first back-to-back MVP since Ernie Banks. Little Joe won the slugging title (.576) and was runner-up in RBIs (111), runs scored (113), and steals (60). Morgan set a record for second basemen in 1977, making just five errors, but tailed off offensively in 1978 and 1979. He helped the Astros win their division in 1980 and went on to two solid

years with the San Francisco Giants. Reunited with Pete Rose and Tony Perez in Philadelphia for 1983, he hit 16 homers to help the Phillies win the pennant and homered twice in the World Series.

He made his 1984 farewell with Oakland memorable by replacing Rogers Hornsby as the most prolific home-run hitting second baseman of all time (268). A first-year selection to the Hall of Fame in 1990, Morgan has also been successful as a broadcaster for ESPN.

DALE MURPHY
Center Field. Born Mar. 12, 1956 Portland, Ore. NL MVP 1982, 1983.
Dale Murphy has hit 20 or more homers in twelve seasons, played in at least 154 games from 1982 to 1990, and became in 1983 the youngest player to be chosen MVP in two consecutive seasons.

He was the Braves' first-round draft choice two months after Hank Aaron set the record for career home runs. A catcher at the time, Murphy had impressed Atlanta management with his home run swing and rifle arm and was touted as "the next Johnny Bench." For a while, he wasn't even the next Biff Pocoroba. Shortly after being brought up to Atlanta, he developed a mysterious mental block about throwing to second base, and even tossing back to the pitcher.

Rather than let him languish behind Pocoroba and Bruce Benedict, manager Bobby Cox moved Murphy to first base, and he hit 23 homers in 1978. Moved again, to center field in 1980, Murphy became a superstar, hitting 33 homers and, two years later, leading the Braves to the Western Division championship. Murph finished second that year in homers (36 to Dave Kingman's 37), tied Al Oliver for the RBI lead with 109, won his first of five Gold Gloves, and was named MVP. Nolan Ryan said, "I can't imagine Joe DiMaggio was a better all-around player than Dale Murphy."

Five weeks later, he was working on his hitting; new manager Joe Torre was convinced that Murphy could become an even better hitter with two strikes. In 1983 he hit 36 home runs again, added 21 points to his batting average, and struck out 24 fewer times. He also stole 30 bases to become only the sixth 30–30 man in major league history. He was named MVP again at age twenty-seven—joining Ernie Banks, Joe Morgan, and Mike Schmidt as the only NLrs to be named MVP in back-to-back seasons.

In 1984 Murphy hit 36 home runs yet again to tie Mike Schmidt for the league lead; a year later, he led the league in walks (90), runs scored (118), and home runs (37). After perhaps his best all-around season in 1987, when he hit 44 homers and achieved personal bests in slugging (.580) and on base percentage (.420), Murphy had calamitous declines in 1988–1990. In August 1990 he was traded to Philadelphia.

Sidelined by injuries in 1992, Murphy had only 62 at bats, finishing the year at 398 lifetime homers to rank him twenty-fourth on the all-time list.

STAN "THE MAN" MUSIAL
Left Field. Born Nov. 21, 1920 Donora, Pa. Holds modern NL record for most years (seventeen) and consecutive years (sixteen) hitting .300 or better. NL MVP 1943, 1946, 1948.

In the bottom of the twelfth inning of the 1955 All-Star Game, Yogi Berra complained, "My feet are killing me." Stan Musial said, "Relax, I'll have you home in a minute." He hit a home run on the next pitch to win the game.

Musial's magic lit up twenty-four All-Star Games, and he holds the record for most All-Star homers (6), extra-base hits (8), and total bases (40). During the regular season he hit .300 or better in 17 of his 21 full years, won seven batting titles, and had a lifetime average of .331, with 475 homers and 1,951 RBIs.

His bat and glove helped the Cardinals reign over the NL in the 1940s as St. Louis won the pennant in 1943 and the World Series in 1942, 1944, and 1946. Musial was named MVP in 1942, 1946, and 1948 and won three straight batting titles from 1950 to 1952, around the time a Dodger fan nicknamed him by saying, "Uh, oh. Here comes that man again."

Musial's splendid hitting redeemed a promising pitching career that was ended by a shoulder injury. In 1940, Musial was 18–5 in the Florida State League when he fell on his arm and it went numb. Branch Rickey converted him to the outfield, and Musial's hitting got him to the big leagues in time to hit .426 in 12 games in 1941.

In twenty-two seasons as a Cardinal, he led the National League in runs scored five times, sharing the record with Rogers Hornsby and George Burns, and led the major leagues in total bases six times. At his retirement, he held major league records for most extra-base hits and total bases and the NL records for runs, hits, doubles, and RBIs.

Musial said his hitting secret was memory. "I consciously memorized the speed at which every pitcher in the league threw his fastball, curve, and slider; then, I'd pick up the speed of the ball in the first thirty feet of its flight and knew how it would move once it had crossed the plate."

When he retired, he became a Cardinal VP. The club honored him with a statue outside Busch Memorial Stadium in 1968, and he entered the Hall of Fame in 1969. Fully ten years later, when consumers were asked whose endorsement they would trust, Stan the Man still ranked first among athletes.

CHARLES "KID" NICHOLS

Pitcher. Born Sep. 14, 1869 Madison, Wis. Died Apr. 11, 1953 Kansas City, Mo. Won 30 games or more in seven of eight straight years (1891–1898)

Little recalled today, Kid Nichols won 361 games, completed 531 (as many as Walter Johnson), and finished behind only Johnson and Cy Young in Adjusted Pitching Runs, a measurement of how many runs a pitcher saved his team, beyond what an average pitcher would have done in his stead.

No pitcher has had more 30-win seasons than Nichols (seven), who pitched with no wind-up and, scorning the curveball, changed speeds with surpassing skill. The righthander led the Boston Beaneaters to five pre-1900 pennants and became the youngest pitcher to win 300 games, marking the anniversary before his thirty-first birthday.

He made his debut with Kansas City in 1887, when that city was in the Western League, and made his mark two years later with Omaha of the Western Association,

winning 36 games. When his manager, Frank Selee, went to Boston to manage the Beaneaters, Nichols went along and was an immediate sensation, winning 27 games his rookie year.

Called "Kid" for his slight build and baby face, Nichols soon became the workhorse of his era. He pitched more than 400 innings in each of his first five years, 300 or more in his first ten, and holds the record for most seasons with 300 innings pitched (twelve). He was relieved in only 24 of the 501 starts he made for Boston. Late in 1892, a year in which he finished at 35–16 in 453 innings, he pitched complete game wins three days in a row.

Named "Nervy Nick" for beating the Orioles twice in three days to win the 1897 pennant, Nichols held out for more than $2,400, the maximum allowable at the time, and was given a $285 bonus for winning the 1898 pennant. Nevertheless, he left the majors to buy a piece of the Kansas City team and returned after a two-year hiatus as player-manager of the Cardinals. Fading from the big leagues after the 1906 campaign, he returned to Kansas City and coached amateur clubs, one of which had a player named Charles Dillon "Casey" Stengel.

A vigorous man, he won the Kansas City bowling championship at age sixty-four and bowled competitively into his seventies. Elected to the Hall of Fame in 1949, he died in Kansas City four years later at the age of eighty-three.

LEROY "SATCHEL" PAIGE

Pitcher. Born July 7, 1905 Mobile, Ala. Died June 8, 1982 Kansas City, Mo. Pitched professionally from 1924 to 1959.

When the Cleveland Indians signed Satchel Paige to a contract in 1948, J.G. Taylor Spink, publisher of *The Sporting News,* wrote, "To bring in a pitching rookie of Paige's age is to demean the standards of baseball." Two days later, Paige demeaned the White Sox, holding them scoreless in two innings of relief. He pitched a shutout in his second start and finished his first big league season 6–1; since the Indians wound up in a tie with the Red Sox, they literally could not have won the pennant without him.

Satchel Paige had made it to the majors, but not when he was the best pitcher in baseball. In 1930 he struck out 22 big leaguers, including Hack Wilson and Babe Herman, in an exhibition game. A year later he joined the Pittsburgh Crawfords, who advertised—truthfully—that "Josh Gibson will hit two home runs and Satchel Paige will strike out the first nine batters."

As a member of the Crawfords in 1933 he was 31–4, winning 21 games in a row and once racking up 62 straight scoreless innings. In 1938 a sore arm threatened to put him out of baseball, but he learned to throw curves, and gradually his arm came back. He pitched the Kansas City Monarchs to five pennants, and, when one of his teammates, Jackie Robinson, made it to the majors, Paige figured rightly that his time had come.

After his sensational start with the Indians, Paige had a subpar season in 1949 and, following owner Bill Veeck's departure, was released. He rejoined Veeck as a member of the lowly Browns and, incredibly, became the AL's leading reliever in 1952 at age 46, winning 12 games and saving 10.

When the team moved to Baltimore, Satch pitched in the minors for seven more years. He came back at 59 to pitch three scoreless innings for the Kansas City A's in 1965. He was signed as a pitching coach in 1968 by the Braves to qualify for his pension. Fittingly, he was the first man elected to the Hall of Fame by the Committee on Negro Leagues formed in 1971.

JIM PALMER
Pitcher. Born Oct. 15, 1945 New York, N.Y. AL Cy Young Award 1973, 1975, 1976.

The best pitchers win the big ones. Jim Palmer clinched the first four pennants in Baltimore's post-1900 history and had a record of 8–3 and an ERA of 2.61 in postseason play. In 1983 he became the only pitcher to win a World Series game in three different decades.

Over eighteen years, Palmer won the Cy Young Award three times (1973, 1975, and 1976) and set Oriole records for career wins (268), shutouts (53), and complete games (211). He is, along with Walter Johnson and Lefty Grove, the only AL pitcher to win 20 games in eight or more seasons, and his ERA (2.86) ranks fifth among pitchers with 3,000 innings or more.

Palmer averaged 288 innings for nine straight years and led the league in that department four times. Despite this durability, he was frequently injured and acquired a reputation as a hypochondriac. When Oriole pitcher Steve Stone saw Palmer reading *Doctor Zhivago,* he quipped, "It must be about an elbow specialist."

Palmer led the Orioles in wins with 15 in 1966 and, before his twenty-first birthday, beat the Dodgers and Sandy Koufax in the southpaw's last game, 6–0, to become the youngest pitcher to throw a World Series shutout. The game was an apt symbol to divide the old and new orders of pitchers, but Palmer suffered a sore arm and was out of the majors for nearly two years.

He won 20 games eight out of nine years, from 1970 to 1973 and from 1975 to 1978. Numerous arm injuries slowed him down, and, when he sported an ERA of 7.44 in May 1982, it looked as though that might be his last year; however, Palmer recovered and won 11 in a row, nearly leading the Orioles to another pennant. When the O's won in 1983, Palmer pitched only once, winning Game Three as a relief pitcher.

After starting the 1984 season 0–3, Palmer pitched his last game on May 12. Although his plan to make a comeback in 1991—one year after he was inducted into the Hall of Fame!—never materialized, he remains in the public eye as a TV talk show host and corporate spokesman.

BROOKS "HOOVER" ROBINSON
Third Baseman. Born May 18, 1937 Little Rock, Ark. Holds major league third baseman records for highest fielding average (.971), putouts (2,697), assists (6,205), and double plays (618). AL MVP 1964.

Brooks Calbert Robinson, Jr. wasn't nicknamed "Hoover" for his resemblance to Herbert or J. Edgar but rather for his ability to suck up everything hit towards third base.

He won Gold Gloves every year from 1960 to 1975, led AL third basemen eleven times in fielding and eight times each in putouts and assists, and made more putouts, assists, chances, and double plays than any third baseman in

history. He also spent a record twenty-three years with one team, the Orioles. Sportswriter Gordon Beard said, "He never asked anyone to name a candy bar after him. In Baltimore people name their children after him."

Robinson made his debut as an Oriole in 1955 and collected 2,848 hits in the regular season; however, no amount of work could make up for his basic lack of speed; he grounded into more double plays than any other ALr (297) and stole only 28 bases in his entire career.

He won the MVP award in 1964, hitting .317 with 28 homers and shone in postseason play. In 39 playoff and World Series games, he hit 5 homers and went 44-for-145, a .303 average. He hit an even .500 in the 1969 playoffs and .583 in 1970 as the O's crushed the Twins.

The 1970 World Series was the Brooks Robinson Show. In the opener he backhanded Lee May's bullet to keep the go-ahead run off base in the sixth inning and, with the score tied 3–3 in the seventh, homered over the left field fence to give the Birds a 4–3 win; In Game Two he knocked in the game-winner in a 6–5 squeaker.

All that was prologue to Game Three when Robinson did for fielding what Esther Williams did for swimsuits. He made sparkling plays on Tony Perez's shot down the line in the first, Tommy Helms's slow roller in the second, Johnny Bench's line drive in the sixth. He went 4-for-4 in Game Four and was named MVP when the Orioles won Game Five and the Series. The ultimate accolade came from Johnny Bench: "I will become a lefthanded hitter to keep the ball away from that guy."

When he retired in 1977, the Orioles gave credit where it was due by holding Thanks Brooks Day on September 18. The occasion drew the largest regular season crowd in Memorial Stadium's history. He entered the Hall of Fame in 1983.

FRANK ROBINSON
Right Field. Born Aug. 31, 1935 Beaumont, Tex. NL Rookie of the Year 1956, MVP 1961. Won AL MVP and Triple Crown 1966.

Frank Robinson was in a class by himself as a two-league player.

He's the only man to be chosen MVP in both leagues, to hit All-Star Game homers for both, to hit 200 or more home runs in both, and to become the first black manager in both, piloting Cleveland from 1975 to 1977 and San Francisco from 1981 to 1984. In 1989, while managing Baltimore, he matched the Manager of the Year award he'd won in 1982 with the Giants.

Robinson also holds the record for hitting home runs in the most ballparks and, while his 586 homers place him fourth on the all-time list, Robinson also ranks in the top ten in career runs, RBIs, and total bases. The complete player, he stole 20 bases or more three times, and even led the majors in intentional walks in four straight years (1961–1964).

Like all professionals, he produced under pressure. Robby made a dramatic debut as a player-manager, homering in his first at bat for the Indians. Similarly, he won the hearts of Baltimore fans shortly after joining the Orioles by hitting the first home run—a 540-foot shot—out of Memorial Stadium.

Robinson broke in with Cincinnati in 1956, tied Wally Berger's rookie record by hitting 38 homers, and was

named Rookie of the Year. The first MVP award came in l96l, when he hit .323 with 37 homers, and stole 22 bases. In l966 he hit 49 homers, knocked in l22 runs, and hit .316 to win the Triple Crown; that year he led Baltimore to a pennant and earned his second MVP award. Robby's home run off Don Drysdale in the World Series provided the only run in Game Four of an Oriole sweep, and he was named MVP of the Series as well.

He played in six All-Star Games for the NL and five for the AL. Yet, he will probably always be remembered as an Oriole. When he was traded to the Dodgers, number 20 became the first Baltimore uniform to be retired, and it's the one he wears in his 1982 Hall of Fame portrait.

JACKIE ROBINSON
Infielder/Outfielder. Born Jan. 31, 1919 Cairo, Ga. Died Oct. 24, 1972 Stamford, Conn. First black player in twentieth-century major leagues. NL Rookie of the Year 1947, MVP 1949.
If all Jackie Robinson did was to integrate baseball, that alone would have ensured his place in the game's history. For the story of his valiant effort and his role not only in baseball's history but that of our nation as well, see the two pieces by Jules Tygiel (one of them with John Thorn) in this volume.

But Jackie Robinson did so much more than make baseball truly the national pastime. It is easy to overlook what a fabulous baseball player he was. He led the Brooklyn Dodgers to six pennants in ten years (plus their only world championship) and was named Rookie of the Year in 1947 and MVP in 1949.

While the Dodgers also had Hall of Famers Duke Snider, Pee Wee Reese, and Roy Campanella, Robinson forced them, by his example, to elevate their game, as he did all his other teammates. Cardinal second baseman Red Schoendienst once said, "If it wasn't for him, the Dodgers would be in the second division."

Driven by history and temperament, Robinson rattled pitchers by dancing off first base and had enough speed to steal home 19 times, 5 times in one season. He bettered .300 for six straight seasons, and retired with a .311 average. He was a regular at first, second, and third base and left field and led the league's second basemen in double plays four straight years (1949–1952).

UCLA's first four-letter man (baseball, basketball, football, and track), he went on to join the Army's Officer Candidate School. There he was court martialed, then acquitted, for refusing to sit in the back of a bus. After stints with the Kansas City Monarchs and the Dodgers' Montreal Royals farm club, he made his major league debut with the Dodgers in 1947 at the advanced age of twenty-eight; Robby hit .297, scored 125 runs, and led them to a pennant. That fall he finished second in a poll only to Bing Crosby as the most popular man in America.

Robinson, in just his second year, became the Dodgers' team leader. He started on the All-Star team for the first of five times (four as a second baseman) in 1949, led the league in hitting, was named MVP, and led the Dodgers to another pennant.

On the last day of the 1951 season, with Brooklyn needing to win to force a playoff with the Giants, Robinson made a spectacular, game-saving grab of Eddie Waitkus's liner to send the game into extra innings, then won it

with a homer in the fourteenth. The Dodgers fell short of the pennant that year thanks to Bobby Thomson, but recaptured the flag in four of Robinson's final five seasons.

Fifteen years after he'd integrated baseball, Robinson integrated the Baseball Hall of Fame.

PETE ROSE
Infielder/Outfielder. Born Apr. 14, 1941 Cincinnati, Oh. NL Rookie of the Year 1963, MVP 1973. Holds major league records for games played (3,562); most seasons, 200 or more hits (10); most lifetime hits (4,256).
In 1989 Commissioner Bart Giamatti suspended Pete Rose from baseball for life for gambling. In 1990 Rose served five months in prison for tax evasion. It all seemed a long way since spring training in 1963, when Rose ran out a walk and Whitey Ford dubbed him "Charlie Hustle."

Sadly, Rose is ineligible to be voted into the Hall of Fame, an honor he deserves for his accomplishments on the field. Rose was named Player of the Decade (1970–1979) by *The Sporting News,* played in sixteen All-Star Games, and holds the record for starting at most different positions (five)—first, second, and third bases, and left and right fields. He also played on three championship teams in six years—the 1975 and 1976 Reds and the 1980 Phillies. Rose holds playoff records for most hits (45) and batted .381 in 118 playoff at bats.

He grew up in Cincinnati and credited his father Harry, a former semipro football player, with influencing him to become an athlete. "He wanted me to share his love of sports and I did. One time Mom sent him to the store to buy a pair of shoes for my sister. Instead, he came back with a pair of boxing gloves for me."

In 1963 Rose hustled his way onto the Reds and turned out to be the sparkplug of the developing Big Red Machine. In 1970 Rose led the league in hits (205) for the third time. He repeated in 1972 and, in 1975 and 1976, he led the league in doubles and runs scored both times. In each of those years the Reds won the pennant.

In December 1978, the man who once said, "I'd go through hell in a gasoline suit to keep playing baseball," signed a four-year 3.2 million contract with the Phils to become the highest-paid player in team sports. Six years later, after playing briefly with the Expos, he returned to Cincinnati where he became a player-manager, breaking Ty Cobb's record for career hits. He retired as a player after the 1986 season and in six years as manager brought the Reds home second three times without winning a division title.

AMOS RUSIE
Pitcher. Born May 31, 1871 Indianapolis, Ind. Died Dec. 6, 1942 Seattle, Wash.
When Walter Johnson came along in 1907, writers seeking to compliment the young fireballer called him "another Rusie."

Baseball paid Rusie the ultimate compliment in 1893 when it changed the rules because of him. The mound was moved back from 50 feet to 60 feet, 6 inches, and several authorities claim the change was intended to make Rusie's heat less intimidating. (Rusie's first catcher, Dick Buckley, padded his glove with a thin sheet of lead to help absorb the impact of Rusie's hummer.) The Indianan led

the league in strikeouts five years out of six and won 30 games or more four years in a row.

The stocky righthander (6'1", 200) beat Boston and Washington in exhibition games before joining Indianapolis of the NL in 1889; when the franchise folded, Rusie and seven other players became Giants for $60,000. He arrived as a star in 1890, striking out 341 batters to lead the league. The media hero of his day, "the Hoosier Thunderbolt" was mentioned in a Mr. Dooley story as well as a Weber and Fields vaudeville skit; Lillian Russell, the sex symbol of that era, begged for an introduction to Rusie and got it.

At the end of the 1892 season the Giants, hoping to save half a month's pay, released him under a "gentlemen's agreement" that no club would sign him ... but the White Stockings did, for $6,250 plus a $2,000 bonus. The Giants eventually bought the contract back, then tried to count the bonus as part of Rusie's salary.

Rusie prevailed but in crossing swords with Giant boss Andrew Freedman he had bought a heap of trouble. Rusie later was fined for missing curfew and for thumbing his nose at Freedman in public, who withheld $200 from his last paycheck of 1895. Rusie pioneered the holdout, missing the entire 1896 season. He sued for damages and, just before the 1897 season, the NL owners pooled $5,000 to settle the suit.

Rusie picked up where he'd left off and went 28–10. He won 20 in 1898; however, he hurt his arm making a pick-off throw, and 1898 was his last full season. He stayed home in Washington State to tend to ailing wife and was disciplined by the Giants yet again. After sitting out a two-year suspension, he was traded to the Reds for Christy Mathewson. Matty at this point had no major league wins behind him but 373 ahead; Rusie had 245 in his pocket but, alas, none ahead. He started just two games, was blasted as he had never been in his prime, and retired. He was elected to the Hall of Fame in 1977.

GEORGE HERMAN "BABE" RUTH
Right Field. Born Feb. 6, 1895 Baltimore, Md. Died Aug. 16, 1948 New York, N.Y. Holds major league records for highest slugging percentage, season (.847, 1920) and lifetime (.690), most home runs by lefthanded batter (714), most years leading league in home runs (twelve)
Babe Ruth was one of baseball's best pitchers, its greatest player, greatest public figure, and the greatest hero in American sports.

When he was seven, George Herman Ruth was committed to Baltimore's St. Mary's Industrial School for repeated theft. Father Gilbert of St. Mary's later released him to pitch for the International League Baltimore Orioles and persuaded Orioles' owner-manager, Jack Dunn, to become Ruth's guardian, making Ruth his "Babe."

In 1914 Ruth was bought by the Red Sox, farmed out to Providence, and brought back to Boston after winning 22 games. He won 18 games for the big club in 1915, followed up with 23 wins in 1916, and pitched the longest complete game victory in World Series history that fall, a fourteen-inning 2–1 win over the Dodgers. The Babe became primarily an outfielder in 1918 (though he still pitched enough to go 13–7 in 1918 and 9–5 the following year). He left the mound in 1919 (not counting five cameo appearances over the next fourteen years, each of which

he won) as the only man to have pitched more than 1,000 innings and have a lifetime batting average over .300 (.304).

In 1918 Ruth led the league in home runs (with 11) for the first of a record twelve times. Harry Frazee, Red Sox owner and a theatrical producer deep in debt, was forced to sell him to the Yankees that December. Now playing his home games in the friendly Polo Grounds, which the Yanks shared with the Giants, Ruth changed the game by hitting 54 homers; the rest of the American League had only 315. His slugging average of .847 has never been approached, except by the Babe himself the following year, when he produced a mark of .846.

Fans rushed to see him in his first year in New York, producing the first million-plus attendance in baseball history and spurring the Yankees to erect a superstadium in 1923, "The House That Ruth Built." That year he hit .393 to lead the Yankees to their third straight pennant and first World Series their first of twenty-two World Series titles. He dominated the 1923 Series, hitting three home runs and batting .368.

From 1926 to 1930, he led the league in home runs every year and tied Lou Gehrig for the lead in 1931. Three years later, Ruth asked to manage the Yankees and was chagrined when owner Jacob Ruppert offered him New York's top farm club instead. He signed with the Braves and had a final moment of glory on May 25, 1935, hitting 3 home runs in a game, one of them a prodigious over the right-field roof at Pittsburgh's Forbes Field. The Babe retired a few weeks later with 714 home runs, a lifetime average of .342, and the highest slugging percentage in history (.690). In the inaugural ballot for the Hall of Fame the following year, he became one of the Founding Five members.

NOLAN RYAN
Pitcher. Born Jan. 31, 1947 Refugio, Tex. Holds major league record for no-hitters (7) and lifetime strikeouts (5,668).
Add up the lifetime strikeouts of Vida Blue (2,175), Hal Newhouser (1,796), and Carl Hubbell (1,677), and you still have 20 fewer than Nolan Ryan had all by himself as of 1992 (5,668).

The career of baseball's strikeout king parallels that of Sandy Koufax—the great fastball and overpowering curve, the control problems, early failure, final success—with Ryan's longevity being the obvious difference. Koufax retired at thirty-two, an age at which Ryan was leading the league in strikeouts for the sixth of twelve times.

Lynn Nolan Ryan was selected by the Mets on the eighth round of the free-agent draft in June 1965, when Tom Seaver was graduating from USC. In 1969 Seaver was the toast of the baseball world after winning 25 games in the regular season; Ryan was, by contrast, 6–3 as a relief pitcher although he saved Game Three of the World Series.

Traded to the Angels for Jim Fregosi, Ryan blossomed all at once, just as Koufax had a decade earlier. From 1972 to 1974, Ryan had a record of 62–48, with 1,079 strikeouts in 943 innings. In an eight-day period in 1972 he fanned 15 Rangers, 16 Red Sox, and 16 A's, on his way to winning 19 games, 9 of them shutouts. In 1973 he was

even better, no-hitting the Royals and the Tigers. Despite a torn calf muscle, he fanned Rich Reese for his 383rd and final K of the season, breaking Koufax's record for strikeouts in a season.

On August 12, 1974, he struck out 19 Red Sox to tie the record held by former teammate Tom Seaver and Steve Carlton. One month later he notched his third no-hitter, against the Twins. He tied Koufax with number four on June 1, 1975, beating the Orioles, 1-0. In 1979 Ryan signed with the Astros as a free agent.

Back in the NL, he eclipsed Koufax's record for no-hitters by beating the Dodgers, 5–0, at the Astrodome on September 26, 1981 and he led NL pitchers in that strike-shortened year with a 1.69 ERA. In 1983 he broke Walter Johnson's record for career strikeouts. Signing with the Texas Rangers after the 1988 season for what was antici-pated to be his fading farewell tour, Ryan instead turned up the heat. He added a sixth no-hitter in 1990 on the road against the A's and a seventh at home against the Blue Jays.

RYNE SANDBERG

Second Baseman. Born Sept. 18, 1959 Spokane, Wash. NL MVP 1984.
The Cubs weren't looked upon as a contender in 1984, but Ryne Sandberg changed that in a nationally televised game against the Cardinals. In both the ninth and tenth innings, Sandberg homered against Bruce Sutter to tie the game and went 5-for-6 with seven RBIs in a game the Cubs won, 12–11. Cards manager Whitey Herzog said, "One day I thought he was one of the best players in the NL. The next day I think he's one of the best players I've ever seen."

Sandberg attracted a lot of attention for his defense in 1990, by which time he'd gone nearly a year without making an error. The streak started on June 21, 1989, and ended on May 17, 1990; by that time, Sandberg had played in 123 consecutive games and accepted 582 chances without making an error, both records for all infielders except first basemen. Even more incredible, Sandberg has put together streaks of 30 or more errorless games fifteen times.

He grew up in Spokane, where he was the quarterback on *Parade* magazine's high school All-America team. Drafted by the Phillies, he played at Wichita, Spartan-burg, and Reading and spent winter ball learning all the infield positions, because the Phillies saw him as a utility man. Dealt to Chicago as a throw-in in a swap of short-stops Larry Bowa and Ivan DeJesus, Sandberg made the team as a third baseman, moving to second in 1983 when the Cubs signed Ron Cey.

Second baseman Sandberg became the first player to change positions and win a Gold Glove; he has since won eight more. In 1984 Jim Frey signed on as the manager and convinced Sandberg that he could become a power hitter by turning on 2–0 or 3–1 pitches. "Coaches and managers had always told me to hit the ball on the ground. He told me to swing for power and gave me confidence." Not coincidentally, the Cubs caught fire as a team, took the Eastern Division, and narrowly missed winning the pennant; Sandberg was named MVP.

After the 1991 season, Sandberg signed a contract which paid him $7.1 million a year. In 1992, he hit .304,

his fourth .300-plus season, hit 26 homers for the second straight year, and remained the all-time leader in fielding average among major league second basemen (.990).

RON SANTO

Third Baseman. Born Feb. 25, 1940 Seattle, Wash. Holds major league record for most times leading the league in total chances (nine), third baseman .
Ron Santo was the NL's best third baseman in the 1960s, the senior circuit's version of Brooks Robinson.

Although he won fewer Gold Gloves than Robinson, he set a major league record by leading third basemen in total chances the most times (nine) and shares NL records for leading the most times in putouts and assists (7) and double plays (6).

With 342 career homers, he was also a disciplined bat-ter who led the league in walks four times and twice in on-base percentage.

The durable Santo missed just 23 games in a ten-year period and played from 1961 to 1971 without injury. Bill James has plumped for Santo as a Hall of Famer, as have the editors of *Total Baseball*; James ranks him as the seventy-first best player of all time, ahead of contempo-raries Roberto Clemente and Billy Williams.

When Santo started out at San Antonio, he had such a wild arm, according to pitcher Jim Brosnan, that the GM "was going to sell first base box seats at a premium since fans who sat there were pretty sure to get a ball." Santo benefited from the coaching of Grady Hatton and was a polished third sacker by the time he reached Chicago. in his Cub debut he also knocked in five runs in a doubleheader.

If Billy Williams played in the shadow of Ernie Banks, Santo was even more invisible. Using the Total Player Rating, Santo was the best player in the NL in both 1966 and 1967 by a wide margin, yet finished thirteenth and fourth respectively in MVP voting. When the Cubbies came close to winning the division, in 1969, Santo led the league in runs produced (191) and drove in a career-high 123 runs.

Santo was also a success in business. He owned a print-ing company, started a baseball school, and got the rights to sell Pro's Pizza at Wrigley Field. (Every cover had a round baseball card of a Cub hero.) When the Cubs had a Day for him, he revealed that he had been diabetic since age eighteen; Santo buttons were sold, and all proceeds went to the Diabetes Association.

On December 11, 1973, he became the first ten-year veteran to veto a trade to another team, the Angels. (Given the timing, wits called this contract provision the "Santo clause.") Santo instead moved to the South Side and played second base with the White Sox, retiring after an unsatisfying 1974 season. He joined the Cub broadcast team in 1990.

MIKE SCHMIDT

Third Baseman. Born Sept. 27, 1949 Dayton, Oh. Holds major league record for most home runs by a third base-man (509 of his total 548).
Philadelphia's famous boobirds even booed baseball's greatest third baseman in 1978. They held Mike Schmidt's light hitting accountable for playoff losses to the Reds in 1976 and the Dodgers in 1977 and 1978.

When the Phillies beat Houston to face Kansas City in the 1980 World Series, Schmidt turned the boos to cheers. He:

- scored two runs in Game One;
- doubled in the winning run in Game Two;
- homered in a losing cause in Game Three;
- hit a two-run homer and singled to start a rally in the ninth inning of Game Five;
- singled in the first two runs in Game Six to win the championship.

Schmidt hit .381 and was named MVP of the Series to match the MVP award he'd won in the regular season, the first of three he earned. Over eighteen seasons, Schmidt homered more often than any other third baseman (509), hit 30 or more homers thirteen times, started seven All-Star Games, and won ten Gold Gloves, nine of them consecutively.

The shortstop on *The Sporting News* College All-America team for 1971 and the Pacific Coast League's All-Star second baseman the next year, he became the Phils' regular third baseman in 1973. He had a disastrous year, striking out 136 times in 367 at bats and hitting .196, the lowest average compiled that season by any major league regular.

One year later he led the NL in homers (36) for the first of three consecutive seasons and batted in 116 runs. He told *Sport* that winter ball in Puerto Rico had made the difference. "I found a swing that made things happen ... I was standing at the plate nice and relaxed and that sucker went off my bat a mile."

On April 17, 1976, he became the tenth major leaguer to hit four home runs in a game, as the Phillies beat the Cubs, 18–16. That same year he set a record for assists in a 162-game season (404) and topped the NL six more times to tie Ron Santo's record, as well as tying him in leading the league in double plays with six.

In the strike-shortened 1981 season, he led the majors in homers (31), RBIs (91), slugging (.644), and total bases (228) to earn his second consecutive MVP award. Fans named him the greatest Phillies player ever in 1983. Three years later, he led the league in homers (37) and RBIs (119) and became the only three-time NL MVP besides Stan Musial and Roy Campanella. He retired in 1989.

AL SIMMONS
Left Field. Born May 22, 1902 Milwaukee, Wis. Died May 26, 1956 Milwaukee, Wis. AL MVP 1929.
Striding toward third base, leaving the impression that he hit with his "foot in the bucket" (a venerable baseball term for a frightened batter, going back to the days when a water bucket sat at the end of the players' bench) didn't bother Al Simmons. He bettered .300 for eleven straight years, won back-to-back batting titles, hit .329 in nineteen World Series games, and .334 lifetime. Though unheralded for his defense, Simmons led the league in fielding twice. Joe Cronin said, "There never was a better left fielder in hustling to the foul line to turn a double into a single."

Born Aloysius Szymanski in Milwaukee in 1902, he turned pro with the Milwaukee Brewers in 1922, taking the name Simmons from a newspaper ad. Sold to the A's, Simmons worried that Connie Mack would change his stance, but Mack told him, "You can hold the bat in your teeth, provided you hit safely and often." Simmons hit .387 as a sophomore and led the league in hits (253), still a record for righthanded batsmen.

In 1929, he helped the A's to a pennant with 34 homers and a league-leading 157 RBIs and was named MVP. He drove in four runs in Game Two of the Series with a single and a homer, homered to start the famous ten-run rally in Game Four, and singled and doubled in Game Seven, scoring the Series-winning run on Bing Miller's double. If anything, Simmons improved in 1930, leading the league in runs (152) and hitting (.381), and homering in Games One and Six as the A's won their second straight championship.

Simmons held out in 1931, and, on Opening Day, Mack announced he would not play for the A's. Taking a cab to Shibe Park, Mack reached into his pocket to pay; the driver declined, saying, "If you can't afford Simmons, you can't afford me either." Hours later, Simmons signed a three-year contract and homered on the first pitch thrown to him.

In 1931, the Duke of Milwaukee hit .390 to lead the league for the second straight year and homered twice in the World Series, but he never again reached such heights. He said later, "When I finally decided I had it made, I was never again the ballplayer I was when I was hungry." Simmons went on to play with six other teams before finishing his career in a third tour of duty with the A's. He was named to the Hall of Fame in 1953.

GEORGE SISLER
First Baseman. Born Mar. 24, 1893 Manchester, Oh. Died Mar. 26, 1973 St. Louis, Mo. Holds major league record for hits in a season (257); AL MVP 1922.
George Sisler had the defensive ability, foot speed, and batting prowess to equal any first baseman. Originally a pitcher, Sisler was clearly more valuable as an everyday player. He led the league's first basemen in assists a record seven times, stole home nineteen times, and compiled a .340 career average.

In 1920 he played every inning of every game, had 140 assists, started 13 first-to-short-to-first double plays, stole 42 bases, batted .407, banged out 19 homers, and established what may be an unbeatable major league record with 257 hits. Two years later he led the league in hits, runs, doubles, and average, batting .420. Although Sisler earned the first League Award (MVP), the Yanks won the pennant by a single game, a sad end to a great season; Sisler never came close to another chance to play in a World Series.

Born in Manchester, Ohio, Sisler was an all-around athlete and signed with Akron of the Ohio-Penn League, although he received no money and never played for Akron. (He reported but was told the team didn't have a uniform small enough.) Instead, he starred for Branch Rickey at the University of Michigan. Rickey became a Browns scout in 1912, moved up to manager a year later, and signed Sisler when he graduated in 1915 with a degree in mechanical engineering.

The Pirates, who had purchased the Akron contract from Columbus, also claimed Sisler, and the case was

brought before the three-man National Commission, a predecessor of the commissioner's office. The NL and AL presidents voted along party lines, but Reds president Garry Herrmann broke ranks, and Sisler became a Brown.

As great as he was, Sisler might have been even better had he not contracted poisonous sinusitis and missed the entire 1923 season. Although he had three more 200-plus-hit seasons thereafter, he said, "I didn't consider that real good hitting." He once told *Baseball* magazine that his ambition was to "hang up a higher average than Ty Cobb's," and, indeed, Sisler's .41979 average in 1922 did edge the .41962 Cobb had in 1911. In fact, Cobb called him "the nearest thing to a perfect ballplayer."

Sisler was elected to the Hall of Fame in 1939, and in the 1940s and 1950s tutored two other Hall of Famers—Duke Snider and Roberto Clemente.

OZZIE SMITH

Shortstop. Born Dec. 26, 1954 Mobile, Ala. Holds NL record for most Gold Gloves (13).

Thomas Boswell of the *Washington Post* once wrote of Ozzie Smith, "Instead of '1' his number should be '8,' but turned sideways because the possibilities he brings to his position are almost infinite."

Already the NL's career leader in Gold Gloves and arguably baseball's best-fielding shortstop of all time, Smith has also made himself into an above-average hitter and high-average base-stealer. But what makes him a lock for the Hall of Fame when he hangs up his glove is ... his glove. Through the 1992 season, he had saved his teams 219 runs beyond what an average shortstop would have done, a mark unequaled at the position in this century.

"The Wizard of Oz" attended Locke High School in Los Angeles with Eddie Murray, and the Padres picked him in the fourth round of the 1977 free agent draft. After winning two Gold Gloves for San Diego and setting a record for assists in 1980 (621), Smith was traded to the Cardinals. Two years later, the Cardinals won their first championship in fifteen years as Smith led the league's shortstops in fielding for the first of a record seven times. (He also whacked two home runs, doubling his four-year output in San Diego.)

Learning to fit his talents to Busch Stadium, the switch-hitting Smith improved his batting average to .276 by 1985, when the Cardinals won their division again. Smith blossomed in the playoffs against the Dodgers, batting .435. With the score tied, 2–2, in Game Five, he homered in the bottom of the ninth to give the Cardinals a 3–2 edge in games. (To date, it is his only lefthanded major league home run.)

In 1987, for the fifth time in Smith's six years in St. Louis, the Cardinals led the league in team fielding. They won another pennant but lost a seven-game Series to the Royals. That year, the Wizard of Ahs finally reached the .300 mark (.303), won the accustomed Gold Glove, and finished second to Andre Dawson in voting for the Most Valuable Player.

In 1991 he set a record for NL shortstops, committing just 8 errors in 150 games, and won his thirteenth consecutive Gold Glove in 1992 to break a tie with Willie Mays and Roberto Clemente. By the end of the 1992 season he had also amassed 542 stolen bases.

EDWIN "DUKE" SNIDER

Center Field. Born Sept. 19, 1926 Los Angeles, Cal. Hit 40 or more home runs in five consecutive seasons (1952-56).

When New York had Willie (Mays), Mickey (Mantle), and the Duke (Snider), Snider always got third billing. Yet he hit more home runs in the 1950s than Mays, Mantle, or any other major leaguer (326) and tied Ralph Kiner's NL record of hitting 40 or more homers in five straight seasons. Kiner said of his fielding, "I'd say Duke covers more ground, wastes less motion, and is more consistent than anyone since DiMaggio."

Snider chose the Dodgers because of his admiration for Pete Reiser and Pee Wee Reese. General manager Branch Rickey put him in the batting cage three hours every day with Hall of Famer George Sisler—but not to hit. Snider recalls, "I was just supposed to call every pitch, ball or strike. It was amazing how wrong I was at the beginning. But I learned."

The Duke became a regular in 1949, hitting .292 with 23 homers, and clinched the pennant on the last day of the season by driving in the winning run. His World Series debut was a disaster (a .143 average and 8 strikeouts), but he redeemed himself in the 1952 World Series with ten hits, four of them home runs to tie the mark then shared by Babe Ruth and Lou Gehrig.

In 1955 Snider led the league in RBIs (136), led for a third time in runs scored (126), hit .309, and had 42 homers. He hit four more homers in the 1955 Series as Brooklyn won its only World Series and became the only man to hit four dingers in a Series twice. After the season, he was named Player of the Year by *The Sporting News*.

He led the league in home runs (43) in 1956, the only time he did so. The Dodgers moved to Los Angeles for the 1958 season, depriving the Duke of the cozy dimensions of Ebbets Field. He still had enough muscle to send out 23 homers and propel Los Angeles to the world championship, in which he homered again. That was Snider's last Series; he still holds the NL record for career World Series homers (11) and RBIs (26).

After two seasons as a Met and, even more incongruously, as a Giant, he retired with a lifetime batting average of .295 and 407 homers. He managed several Dodger farm teams, scouted for the Dodgers and Padres, and broadcast games for those two teams as well as the Expos. He was elected to the Hall of Fame in 1980.

WARREN SPAHN

Pitcher. Born Apr. 23, 1921 Buffalo, N.Y. Holds major league record for most games won by lefthanded pitcher (363).

Stan Musial once said, "I don't think Spahn will ever get into the Hall of Fame. He'll never stop pitching."

Musial's point was well taken. Warren Spahn pitched long enough to be a Brave under Casey Stengel in 1942 and a Met under Stengel again in 1965. In between, he became the winningest lefthander in major league history, emerging victorious in 363 games. He put 15,741 batters out of their misery, won 20 games or more in thirteen seasons, and had a lifetime ERA of 3.09.

Not regarded as a strikeout artist, he nonetheless recorded 2,583 whiffs in his career and led the NL four straight years, from 1949 to 1952. He led the league in

wins five times outright, had the most shutouts four times, and compiled the lowest ERA three times. He also started more double plays than any other major league pitcher (82) and also leads all NL pitchers in hitting home runs (35).

Brought up to the Boston Braves in 1942, he was sent back down when Stengel ordered him to throw at Pee Wee Reese and he refused. He enlisted in the Army, suffered shrapnel wounds in a battle along the Rhine, and was awarded the Purple Heart. He made his mark in 1947 by posting a 21–10 record, leading the league in ERA (2.33) and innings pitched (289⅔).

In 1948 the Braves won the pennant, fueled by the hopes for "Spahn and Sain and two days of rain." The franchise moved to Milwaukee in 1953. That year Spahn pitched in his third of seven All-Star Games and got the win. When the Braves won pennants in 1957 and 1958, he led the league in wins both years. He was given the Cy Young Award in 1957 (when there was only one award for both leagues) and won two games in the 1958 Series, shutting out the Yanks in Game 4.

When the 1960 season started, Spahn had won 267 major league games without pitching a no-hitter. He remedied this oversight on September 15, striking out 15 Phillies to win his 20th game of the season. Five days after his fortieth birthday, in 1961, Spahn pitched his second no-hitter.

After a losing season in 1964 (his first) and brief stays with the Mets and Giants in 1965, he coached in Mexico City and Japan. In line with Musial's prediction, Spahn interrupted his retirement to pitch in the Mexican League, thus delaying the onset of the mandatory five-year inactive period before induction into the Hall of Fame. Finally, however, Spahn left the mound for good and was elected to the Hall of Fame in 1973.

TRIS SPEAKER
Center Fielder. Born Apr. 4, 1888 Hubbard City, Tex. Died Dec. 8, 1958 Lake Whitney, Tex. Holds major league records for assists (450) and double plays (135) by an outfielder.

Like a wide receiver anticipating the throw of the quarterback, Tris Speaker revolutionized center fielding by moving before the pitch.

He acquired the knack as a Red Sox rookie, fielding fungos hit by Cy Young and trying to figure out which way the ball would go. He says, "In a few days I knew just by the way he swung whether the ball would go to my right or left. Then I began to study the batter during a game; when he started his swing, I knew if he would hit to my left or right and I was on my way."

Getting a head start allowed him to play shallow. The "Gray Eagle" participated in a record four unassisted double plays and set a record for outfielders with 448 career assists. He led AL outfielders seven times in put-outs, five times in double plays (some of them 4–8–3 or 6–8–3), three times in assists, and twice in fielding. Just as much a threat offensively, Speaker hit .345 during a twenty-two-year career, had eighteen .300-plus seasons, and compiled 3,514 hits.

Two of baseball's shrewdest operators didn't sign him: Pirate boss Barney Dreyfuss because "he smoked cigarettes"; and Giant manager John McGraw because "I had all the outfielders I needed." Speaker paid his way to the Red Sox training camp in Little Rock, Arkansas. Boston optioned Speaker and bartered him to Little Rock in lieu of their $400 rental fee. Several months later, he was burning up the league and became the Red Sox starting center fielder in 1909.

A star by 1912, Speaker tied Home Run Baker for most home runs (10) that year, led the league in doubles (53), hit .383, and won the Chalmers Award (a forerunner of the MVP award), and hit .340 as the Red Sox beat the Giants in the World Series. In 1916 Speaker, newly arrived in Cleveland, won the batting title (.386) from Ty Cobb, interrupting what would have been an uninterrupted string of 13 titles, and also led the league in doubles (41), hits (211), and slugging percentage (.503).

He took over as manager of the Indians during the 1919 season; a year later he steered them to a pennant and a World Series win over the Dodgers. Speaker was elected to the Hall of Fame in 1937 and returned to the Tribe as a coach during the Bill Veeck era.

WILVER "WILLIE" STARGELL
Left Field. Born Mar. 6, 1941. Earlsboro, Okla. NL co-MVP 1979.

Wilver Stargell was the Pittsburgh Pirates' Gold Star Father in 1979.

When a teammate distinguished himself with a clutch hit, heads-up move on the basepaths, or fielding gem, "Pops" Stargell marked the occasion with a gold star ceremony. Soon ballplayers earning $300,000 a year were putting out a little bit extra to get a gold "Stargell Star" and by the end of the season, the Pirates had the whole country singing "We Are Family," earning enough gold stars to become World Champions.

At thirty-nine, two years after his career had apparently ended, Stargell set a record for most MVP awards in a season. He was named MVP of both the playoffs and the World Series, divided regular season MVP honors with Keith Hernandez, and shared *Sports Illustrated's* Sportsman of the Year award with Steeler Terry Bradshaw.

Many of his 475 career home runs were titanic. Only eighteen balls were hit out of Forbes Field in sixty-one years (beginning with Babe Ruth's epic blast on May 25, 1935); Stargell hit seven of them. Only one player hit a ball completely out of Dodger Stadium—Stargell, who did it twice.

Stargell's 1977 season was plagued with injuries, but Pops hit 28 homers and drove in 97 runs in 1978 to earn Comeback Player of the Year. After the gold stars came out during spring training in 1979, Stargell hit 32 homers and the Pirates won the division, finishing two games ahead of Montreal.

In the playoffs against Cincinnati, he broke an 11-inning 2–2 tie with a three-run homer and homered again in Game Three as Pittsburgh swept the Big Red Machine. In the World Series against Baltimore, Stargell homered as the Orioles won the opener and went 3-for-5 with a homer in Game Four; however, Baltimore came up with six runs in the eighth inning to win, 9–6, and open up a 3–1 lead in games.

With the Pirates trailing, 1–0, in the bottom of the sixth inning of Game 5, Stargell hit a sacrifice fly to even the score and later singled to start a three-run inning. The

Pirates won, 7–1. After John Candelaria and Kent Tekulve shut Baltimore out in Game Six to bring the Buccos even, Stargell put on a batting show in the finale, going 4-for-5 with a two-run homer. Overall, he set a Series record with seven extra-base hits. He became a Hall of Famer in 1988.

SAM THOMPSON

Right Field. Born Mar. 5, 1860 Danville, Ind. Died Nov. 7, 1922 Detroit, Mich.

Sam Thompson was the power hitter par excellence of the nineteenth century and set a record for lifetime home runs that wasn't broken until Babe Ruth came along. Also possessed of a legendary throwing arm, "Big Sam" Thompson was still so highly regarded that he played eight games alongside rookie Ty Cobb in the Tiger outfield in 1906—at age 46.

The fifth of eleven children, Thompson started his big league career late. He played on the Danville team and worked in his father's carpentry business. When a scout offered to pay him the magnificent sum of $2.50 per game, Thompson joined Evansville of the Northwest League and hit .391 before the league folded. He signed with Indianapolis and, at age twenty-five, joined the NL Detroit Wolverines. When Gene Moriarty crashed into an outfield wall, Thompson took over and got 11 hits in his first 26 at bats. Moriarty never played another game for Detroit.

Thompson was an innovator in the outfield, too. Possessed of a rifle arm, he is said to have originated the one-hop throw to the plate, trying to catch a runner from third. He was so successful at this technique that in 1886 he led the league's outfielders in double plays (11) for the first of two times. In 1887, "Big Sam" (6'2", 207) had an awesome season at the bat, leading the league in hits (203), triples (23), batting (.372), and slugging (.571). He drove in an astounding 1.31 runs per game. This was a record that only he would ever surpass, with 1.42 in 1894 and 1.39 in 1895; for comparison, Hack Wilson, when he drove in 190 in 1930, had a mark of 1.23.

A sore arm sidelined him for most of 1888, and he was unceremoniously sold to the Philadelphia Quakers (Phillies). In 1889 Thompson rebounded with 20 home runs to lead the league, picked up another hit crown in 1890 (172), and in 1891 managed to accumulate 32 assists. In 1894 he led the league in fielding (.977) and hit .407 as part of an all-.400-hitting outfield, along with Ed Delahanty, Billy Hamilton, and Tuck Turner. His last great offensive year was 1895, when Big Sam led the league in homers (18), RBIs (165), and slugging (.654).

He still holds the major league record for ratio of RBIs to games played (.923, nipping Lou Gehrig) and was named to the Hall of Fame in 1974.

HAROLD "PIE" TRAYNOR

Third Baseman. Born Nov. 11, 1899 Framingham, Mass. Died Mar. 16, 1972 Pittsburgh, Pa. Holds NL record for lifetime putouts by third baseman (2,288).

Pie Traynor was the first third baseman whom the baseball writers voted into the Hall of Fame. (The Veterans' Committee previously selected Jimmy Collins.)

Traynor was also named the major leagues' outstanding third baseman by *The Sporting News* seven times and finished in the top ten in MVP voting six times between 1925 and 1933. While some analysts downplay his offensive accomplishments today, Hall of Famers of his era—Mickey Cochrane, Bill Dickey, Charlie Gehringer, Rogers Hornsby, and Carl Hubbell—named him to their All-Time All-Star teams.

Traynor hit .320 lifetime with ten seasons above .300, knocked in 100 or more runs seven times, and never struck out more than 28 times in seventeen seasons. In the field, he led in assists three times, double plays four straight years, led in putouts seven times (a record tied by Puddin' Head Jones and Ron Santo), and set the NL record for career putouts (2,289).

As a child Traynor yearned to play for the Somerville, Massachusetts, parish team coached by Father Nangle; instead, he chased balls. Taken to the grocery store as a reward, he would invariably say, "I'll take pie, Father," the source of his nickname. He was originally a shortstop, but after Traynor made 12 errors in his 17-game trial in 1920, the Pirates acquired Rabbit Maranville. Traynor's fielding improved when he moved to third base, and he began to hit with more power when Rogers Hornsby switched him to a forty-two-ounce bat.

The Pirates won the pennant in 1925. Traynor singled and homered against Walter Johnson in his first two World Series at bats and hit .346 as the Pirates won in seven. The Pie Man's bases-loaded single on the last day of the 1927 season gave the Pirates another pennant, but the Bucs were swept by the Yankees of Ruth and Gehrig.

Traynor hit .356 in 1929 and had his best batting average, .366, in 1930, but his career was essentially ended in 1934 when catcher Jimmy Wilson fell across his right arm and broke it. Pie took over as player-manager and just missed leading Pittsburgh to a pennant in 1938, when the Cubs' Gabby Hartnett hit his "Homer in the Gloamin'."

In retirement, Traynor ran a sporting goods store with Honus Wagner, coached at Duquesne, and was active as a sportscaster in Pittsburgh for thirty-three years. He was elected to the Hall of Fame in 1948.

ARKY VAUGHAN

Shortstop. Born Mar. 9, 1912 Clifty, Ark. Died Aug. 30, 1952 Eagleville, Cal. His .385 average of 1935 is not only the NL record for shortstops in this century but also a mark unequaled in the league since.

Arky Vaughan was, according to his Total Player Rating, the NL's leading player four times in seven years, from 1934 to 1940.

Using a unique flat-footed stance, Vaughan hit well over .300 ten straight years, twelve times in all, and set an all-time record for the league's shortstops by hitting .385 in 1935. Although it has become chic to deride Vaughan's fielding, he led the league three times each in putouts and assists (and, yes, errors) when such slick-fielding shortstops as Billy Jurges, Dick Bartell, and Eddie Miller were in their prime.

Born in Clifty, Arkansas (hence his nickname), Joseph Floyd Vaughan grew up in California and was a football star at Fullerton High School. (Fellow student Richard M. Nixon picked Vaughan for his All-Time All-Stars.) Signed by the Pirates, he led the league in errors his first two years but improved with help from his roommate, coach Honus Wagner, and from Pie Traynor.

Vaughan was named to the All-Star team for the first of seven times in 1934 and became the first man to homer twice in the midsummer classic, in 1941. His lifetime All-Star Game average was .364.

Traded to the Dodgers after the 1941 season, Vaughan became embroiled in a dispute between pitcher Bobo Newsom and catcher Bobby Bragan in 1943. Manager Leo Durocher suspended Newsom, and Vaughan led a successful "strike," after which Durocher backed down. Despite leading the league in runs scored for the third time, Vaughan was fed up and retired.

When Durocher was suspended in 1947, Vaughan came back and hit .325 to help the Dodgers win a pennant. Jackie Robinson said, "He went out of his way to be nice to me when I was a rookie. I needed it." After a sub-par 1948, he played briefly for the San Francisco Seals and retired.

On August 30, 1952, while fishing in Lost Lake, his companion tipped the boat over; Vaughan tried to rescue him but both went under and drowned. He was elected to the Hall of Fame in 1985. Among Hall of Fame shortstops, only Honus Wagner (.329) has a higher lifetime batting average than Vaughan (.318).

JOHN PETER "HONUS" WAGNER
Shortstop. Born Feb. 24, 1874 Carnegie, Pa. Died Dec. 6, 1955 Carnegie, Pa. Holds NL records for most years leading league in batting (eight) and most consecutive years hitting .300 or better (seventeen).

Honus Wagner and Babe Ruth finished in a tie behind Ty Cobb when the first players were voted into the Hall of Fame in 1936. The fan of today may look at the stats of these men and wonder why Wagner stands alongside the other two. Yet Bill Deane, in his "Awards and Honors" piece in this volume, credits Wagner with six "hypothetical" MVP awards during his career—for the years 1901–1903, 1907, and 1909, years in which no award was given. Only Ruth dominated a league for so long a time.

John Peter Wagner became "Johannes" and, later, "Honus" or "Hans," just as Wagner's nationality, German (a "Deutschman") became "Dutchman," hence Wagner's nickname, "the Flying Dutchman." Bowlegged, he "looked like a hoop rolling down the baselines" but reached the majors with Louisville. When the city was dropped from the league, owner Barney Dreyfuss bought Pittsburgh and took Wagner with him.

In 1900 Wagner won his first of eight batting titles, an NL record. He was stationed all over the diamond until Frederick "Bones" Ely, the regular shortstop, begged off. Wagner made three errors in an inning, then got lucky. With men on first and second, he gave the signal for a pickoff play and dashed toward second; the pitcher delivered to the plate instead, resulting in a one-hopper that Wagner turned into a double play. Wagner called it "the best play I ever made."

The Dutchman led the Pirates to pennants in 1901, 1902, 1903, and 1909, when he outplayed Cobb, and his batting average didn't fall below .300 until 1914. Wagner led the league five times in RBIs and stolen bases, six times in slugging, and seven times in doubles. When he retired as a player in 1917, he led the NL in hits, runs, singles, doubles, and triples.

After coaching at Carnegie Tech and owning a sporting goods store with Pie Traynor, Wagner fell on hard times. Early in 1933, Fred Lieb wrote a column about Wagner's plight, and new Pirate owner Bill Benswanger made him a coach. Honus boosted attendance and was given "Days," even in opposing cities.

In Larry Ritter's *The Glory of Their Times*, Paul Waner remembered, "He must have been sixty.... [He'd] get out there every once in a while [and hit] ... a hush would come over the whole ballpark, and every player on both teams would stand there, like a bunch of little kids ... I'll never forget it."

ED WALSH
Pitcher. Born May 14, 1881 Plains, Pa. Died May 26, 1959 Pompano Beach, Fla. Holds major league record for lowest lifetime ERA (1.82).

Ty Cobb said of Ed Walsh, "When this big moose had his stuff, he was just unbeatable, that's all."

The big spitballer (6'1", 193) won 40 games one year, led the league in saves five times, and is baseball's all-time leader in career ERA (1.82). He also set several fielding records for pitchers and was the first AL pitcher to steal home twice. Walsh, who also helped design Comiskey Park, pleased the crowds by fungoing balls into the stands and was not entirely unaware of his talents. Sportswriter Charlie Dryden said of him, "He's the only man I ever saw who could strut standing still." He is thought by many students of the game and literature to have been Ring Lardner's model for Jack Keefe, the cocksure narrator of *You Know Me, Al.*

Walsh joined the White Sox soon after Elmer Stricklett taught him how to throw the spitball in 1904. Exhibiting the endurance which marked his career, he pitched two complete game wins against the Red Sox on September 6, 1905, and led the league in 1906 with 10 shutouts in the regular season. He also won two World Series games, striking out 12 Cubs in Game Three, a record which stood until 1929, and taking Game Five even though the "Hitless Wonders" made five errors behind him.

In 1907 lack of offense hurt Walsh, who was shut out eight times but still posted a 24–18 record and set major league season records for assists and chances by a pitcher.

He had a nearly perfect year in 1908, leading the league in wins (40), shutouts (11), starts, complete games, strikeouts, and saves and set a post-1900 record for innings pitched (464) which still stands.

Chicago, Detroit, St. Louis, and Cleveland were neck-and-neck all season long, and Walsh pitched seven times in the last nine games. He won a doubleheader against Boston September 29 but lost his best-pitched game of the season on October 2; Walsh struck out 15 in eight innings only to lose 1–0 to Addie Joss's perfect game.

Bedeviled by a lack of offense again in 1910, Walsh became the only pitcher to lead the league in ERA (1.27) and lose 20 games. His team hit 7 homers all season long, batted .211, and made 314 errors.

After winning 27 games in both 1911 and 1912, he suffered arm trouble and retired in 1917. Walsh was named to the Hall of Fame in 1946.

HOYT WILHELM
Pitcher. Born Jul. 26, 1923 Huntersville, N.C. Holds major league record for games pitched (1,070) and most games won as a relief pitcher (124).

Hoyt Wilhelm, the first relief pitcher elected to the Hall of Fame, threw 36,000 knuckleballs to get there.

Pitching in twenty-one seasons, Wilhelm delivered those dipsy-doodles as an NL reliever, AL starter, and AL reliever. All told, he pitched in more games than any player in history (1,070), won the most in relief, (123) and finished the most (651).

After languishing in the minors, Wilhelm stuck with the Giants as a twenty-nine-year-old rookie and made a sensational debut in 1952, going 15–3 with 11 saves. He led the league in won-lost percentage (.833) and ERA (2.43) to become the first rookie ever to top his league in those two categories and the only rookie ever to win an ERA crown.

In 1955, Wilhelm was 4–1 but hadn't posted a single save in 59 appearances. He was traded to St. Louis, sold to Cleveland, and was picked up on waivers by Baltimore, mostly because Oriole manager Paul Richards had caught knuckleballer Dutch Leonard; after he lost three starts, Knuckles knew his days as an Oriole were numbered.

With his career hanging by a thread, Wilhelm got one last chance on September 20, 1958, against the Yankees. He pitched a no-hitter, winning 1–0 on Gus Triandos's homer. In 1959 he won his first nine starts and went on to lead the league in ERA (2.19), thus becoming the only pitcher to turn the trick in both circuits.

Traded to the White Sox, Wilhelm began his third career, posting a 2.64 ERA and a career-high 21 saves in 1963 and outdoing himself in 1964 with 27 saves, 12 wins and an ultra-stingy 1.99 ERA; his ERA didn't rise above 2.00 for four more seasons as he compiled 98 saves and 41 wins with the White Sox.

In the expansion draft of 1969 he was picked by the new Kansas City Royals, traded to the Angels, and passed along to the Braves, helping them take their division by winning 2 games and saving 4 in 8 appearances. After stints with the Cubs and Dodgers, he was released five days short of his 49th birthday. He was elected to the Hall of Fame in 1985.

TED WILLIAMS

Left Field. Born Aug. 30, 1918 San Diego, Cal. AL MVP 1946, 1949. Highest on base percentage of all time (.483), second only to Babe Ruth in slugging percentage and production.

He'll never be remembered for his fielding, throwing, running, or leadership, but by any measure Ted Williams is the greatest hitter of his era and perhaps of all time.

Despite missing five seasons to military service, the "Splendid Splinter" holds the records for most consecutive years leading the league in runs scored (five) and walks (six) and for career on-base percentage (.483) He also won four home run crowns, six batting titles, led the AL in slugging nine times, and finished with a career batting average of .344 and 521 home runs. At the close of the 1950s *The Sporting News* named him Player of the Decade.

Williams broke in with the San Diego Padres of the Pacific Coast League in 1936. In 1938 he won the Triple Crown at Minneapolis and became the Red Sox regular right fielder in 1939, moving to left later on. He set the rookie record for RBIs (145) to lead the AL. In 1941 his two-out, three-run homer off Claude Passeau won the All-Star Game and he concluded the year with a .406 batting average. He could have safeguarded his .400 average on the final day by sitting out, but instead he chose to play both ends of a doubleheader, going 6-for-8. He became the last player to top the magic number of .400, and the only one since 1930.

After winning the Triple Crown in 1942, the "Thumper" played for Uncle Sam from 1943 to 1945. He returned to star in the 1946 All-Star Game, hitting 2 homers and 2 singles, led the league in runs scored and slugging percentage, helped the Red Sox win the pennant, and was named MVP. He won his second Triple Crown in 1947. In 1949 he led the league in homers (43) and RBIs (159), hit .343, and was named MVP for a second time.

At thirty-four, he flew thirty-nine combat missions for the Marines in Korea and returned late in 1953 to hit .407 with 13 homers in 37 games. He had one of his greatest seasons at age thirty-nine in 1957, hitting .388 to become the oldest player ever to lead the league in hitting. To prove it was no fluke, he led the league again in hitting in 1958 at age 40, hitting .328, and ended his career at 42, hitting .316 with 29 home runs, including one in his last at-bat. He entered the Hall of Fame in 1966.

WINFIELD, DAVE

Right Field. Born Oct. 3, 1951 St. Paul, Minn. Oldest player to drive in 100 or more runs, 1992.

Dave Winfield was given a second chance and made the most of it.

Bedeviled by the memory a 1-for-22 batting slump in the 1981 World Series with the Yankees (and George Steinbrenner's subsequent characterization of him as "Mr. May," for his inability to produce in October), Winfield came to bat in the eleventh inning of Game Six in the 1992 Fall Classic as a member of the Toronto Blue Jays. With the score tied, 2–2, and two out, Winfield doubled down the left field line to give the Jays a 4–2 lead, and they hung on to win their first world championship.

It was sweet vindication for a man who had won seven Gold Gloves (two with the Padres, five with the Yankees), was an All-Star every year from 1977 to 1988, started All-Star Games in 1979, 1981, and every year from 1983 to 1988, and batted .361 in the twelve games.

Known as "Daddy Longlegs," the six-foot six-inch Winfield was a pitcher at the University of Minnesota, finished his senior year 13–1 and hit .400, and was the MVP of the College World Series. Drafted by the NBA's Atlanta Hawks, the ABA's Utah Stars, and the NFL's Minnesota Vikings—even though he had not played college football—Winfield was also selected by the Padres on June 5, 1973. Like Sandy Koufax and Al Kaline, Winfield had no minor league experience, and made his major league debut two weeks later.

In 1980, after leading the NL in RBIs (118), he signed a ten-year free agent contract with the Yankees; however, misinterpreting a cost-of-living clause led Steinbrenner to owe Winfield an extra $7 million and started a simmering feud which resulted in the Yankee owner paying a convicted felon, Howard Spira, for allegedly damaging information about Winfield. The damage instead was done to Steinbrenner, who was banished from baseball by Commissioner Fay Vincent.

Despite his problems with Steinbrenner, Winfield knocked in 100 runs or more from 1982 to 1986, the first Yankee to turn the trick in five consecutive seasons since Joe DiMaggio. In 1984, Winfield consciously shortened his stroke in an attempt to win a batting title and came close, hitting .340 to finish three points behind Don Mattingly. He underwent back surgery and missed the 1989 season; he joined the Angels for 1990. With the Angels, he drove in 72 runs in 112 games and won the Comeback Player of the Year Award. At the end of the 1992 season, Winfield had 432 career home runs to lead all active players and rank twenty-first behind Billy Williams on the all-time list.

DENTON TRUE "CY" YOUNG

Pitcher. Born Mar. 29, 1867 Gilmore, Oh. Died Nov. 4, 1955 Newcomerstown, Oh. Holds major league records for wins (511), starts (815), and complete games (749).

Had the honor been presented during his career, baseball's winningest pitcher might have had a shot at winning half a dozen Cy Young Awards.

He won at least 30 games in five seasons and, although he won a mere 26 in 1904, Young put together a string of 44 consecutive scoreless innings—23 of them hitless as well. He started with two hitless innings on April 25 against the A's, six on April 30 against Washington, and nine in the first post-1900 perfect game ever pitched, on May 5 against the A's. The streak ended on May 11 after he'd pitched six more hitless innings against the Tigers. (He did shut them out for fifteen innings.)

Pitching at a time when complete games were the rule, Young finished what he'd started 749 times. He'd take twelve warmup tosses and be ready to go. He pitched more than 400 innings in a season five times, more than 300 eleven other times, and said, "I never had a sore arm, and I pitched every third day. Once I pitched every other day for eighteen days."

Denton True Young was an instant sensation at Canton of the Tri-State League and got the name Cyclone (later shortened to Cy) after his pregame pitches splintered the fence that served as an outfield barrier.

Young threw a three-hitter in his big-league debut in 1890 and pitched both ends of a doubleheader that October, winning 5–1 and 7–3. In 1891, his first full season, he won 27 for the Cleveland Spiders, the first of nine straight seasons in which he won 20 games or more.

In 1903 Cy pitched the first of his three no-hitters and also won two games for the Boston Pilgrims (Red Sox) in the first World Series between the American and National leagues. He rebounded from losing seasons in 1905

and 1906 to win 21 games in 1907 and, at age forty-one, pitched his third no-hitter in 1908.

He retired with the most career victories (511), losses (316), innings pitched (7,354), and complete games (749) in history. In 1937 he was voted into the Hall of Fame.

ROBIN YOUNT

Infielder/Outfielder. Born Sept. 16, 1955 Danville, Ill. AL MVP 1982, 1989; joined 3,000-hit club in 1992.

Unlike the slowing veteran who moves from the outfield to first base, Robin Yount made a different move with different results. Seven years after being chosen MVP at one demanding defensive position, shortstop, Yount was selected as MVP again at another demanding position—center field.

Since 1974 Yount has been consistency itself, hitting in the high .280s (and over .300 six times) and playing 150 or more games eight times. He has won fielding titles at both positions, led the league in doubles, triples, and runs created twice each, and reached the 3,000 hit mark in 1992.

A high school All-America in Woodland Hills, California, Yount was the Brewers' number one pick in 1973 and the third player picked overall, behind David Clyde and John Stearns (and just ahead of Dave Winfield). He hit .285 at Newark, New York, in the New York–Penn League and went to spring training with the Brewers in 1974. When Brewers manager Del Crandall saw Yount play, he won the starting job; by the age of twenty-two, Yount had already qualified for his big league pension by playing for four years. During spring training in 1978, he left the Brewers briefly to become a pro golfer, returned a few months later, and has been with the Brewers ever since. In 1981, he led the league in fielding (.985) and fielding runs (28) and batted .316 in the divisional playoff series.

In 1982 Yount was the starting shortstop in the All-Star Game and had a career year; he became the first shortstop to lead the league in slugging and total bases and also topped his colleagues in hits, doubles, production, and Total Player Rating. He batted .414 with 6 RBIs in the World Series, although the Brewers lost to the Cardinals, and was named MVP in the off-season.

An All-Star starter again in 1983, Yount suffered back problems so severe that he was briefly shifted to DH. He moved to the outfield in 1985 and led the league's outfielders in fielding (.997), making just one error. On September 9, 1992, he joined baseball's exclusive 3,000-hit club by singling against Cleveland's Jose Mesa in Milwaukee and finished the season with 3,025 hits.

## CHAPTER 8

Baseball Families

Larry Amman

Just as the Wright brothers were first in flight, so were Wright brothers first in baseball. In the National Association's inaugural season of 1871, the Boston team featured Harry Wright as manager and reserve outfielder, and George at shortstop. Brother Sam joined them on the bench for the 1876 season, after an apprenticeship in New Haven the year before.

Since then there have been 336 brother combinations in the majors. The only season in which there was not at least one such pair was 1899. There were four new ones in 1991 and two more in 1992.

The first thing that strikes the eye as one reads the list is the large number who were teammates, however briefly—more than 25 percent.

Another observation one must make is how one-sided the big league performance was between so many of the combinations. For example, there are twenty-five members of the Hall of Fame who had brothers in the majors. Yet how many baseball fans have ever heard of the brothers of Bill Dickey, Christy Mathewson, or Honus Wagner? As another example, how many people remember the brothers of Steve Sax, Eddie Murray, and Robin Yount? All three of these current big names have brothers who played in the majors briefly.

Of course, being the brother of a major leaguer never guarantees success, nor even a shot at the big leagues. The five Delahantys, the three Boyers, and the two Ferrells all had other brothers who played minor league ball only.

Because the combinations in which more than one brother excelled are so rare, we can focus on the more outstanding ones.

In terms of balanced, outstanding achievement no group of three or more brothers can match the DiMaggios. The enduring folk hero status of Joe DiMaggio unfortunately has not done anything to keep alive the memory of his brothers, Vince and Dom. All three were gifted outfielders, good hitters, and fine all-around athletes. Vince, the oldest of these sons of a San Francisco fisherman, played for five different National League teams. In 1941 he had 21 homers and 100 RBIs for Pittsburgh. Four years later he hit four grand slams for the Phillies.

Dom DiMaggio was the youngest and smallest of the three brothers. Although lacking any of the power of the other two, he was the fastest on the bases and yielded nothing to his two brothers in the grace and skill he exhibited in the outfield. His lifetime batting average was just under .300.

In the 1941 All-Star Game, Dom went to right field as a late-inning substitute to play alongside Joe in center. This was a first in the mid-summer classic. In the eighth inning, Joe doubled and Dom singled him home. In the 1949 All-Star Game, Joe drove in Dom with what proved to be the margin of victory for the junior circuit.

Dominic, or the "Little Professor" as he was called, started four different All-Star games, including the 1946 contest. That year he was voted to start in center field ahead of his brother. On the season, Dom outhit Joe by 26 points (.316 to .290).

In the 1943 All-Star Game, Vince went 3 for 3, including a ninth-inning home run. While Joe and Dom were away in the military, Vince was ". . . maintaining the family tradition of excellence in All-Star Games."

The first time two brothers played against each other in an All-Star Game was in 1969. Carlos May of the White Sox came to bat as a pinch-hitter with brother Lee of the Reds playing first base. In the 1990 mid-summer classic, television cameras showed Sandy Alomar, Jr., at bat while Roberto Alomar set himself at second base, ready to field anything his brother might have hit his way. Both men were teammates for the junior circuit in the 1991 and 1992 games.

For the title of the best brother pitching combination, the competition is very close between the Niekros of Ohio and the Perrys of Williamston, North Carolina. In 1987 the ancient knuckleballing duo of Phil and Joe Niekro passed Jim and Gaylord Perry in wins. The two families remain very close in most statistical categories.

The Perry brothers had one full season as teammates—1974 with Cleveland, when the two combined for 39 victories, almost half of the team total. A year earlier, when Jim was with Detroit, the two made their only start against each other. Gaylord took the loss for Cleveland. Jim got a no-decision. In the 1970 All-Star Game, the National League pitcher in the sixth and seventh innings was Gaylord Perry of the Giants. On the mound for the American League in the seventh and eighth innings was Jim Perry of the Twins. This is the only time two brothers were rival pitchers in the mid-summer classic. Both have also won the Cy Young Award.

For Joe and Phil Niekro, pitching against each other was not that uncommon. It happened nine different times. The most noteworthy occasion came on September 26, 1978, in Atlanta. Before this, his last start of the season, Phil was 19–17 for the Braves; Joe was 12–14 for the Astros. Houston won 2–0, much to the dismay of victor Joe. He loathed the idea of pitching against his brother in these circumstances.

Harry and Stan Coveleski of the coal-mining country in

Pennsylvania were brother hurlers who refused to start games against each other. Stan, the younger, was in his first full season in the majors in 1916 at Cleveland while Harry was winning 20 for the third consecutive year at Detroit. Harry developed arm trouble and did not pitch another full season, but Stan went on to five 20-win seasons and a niche in the Hall of Fame.

Virtually every baseball fan has heard of the game on September 15, 1963, in which Felipe, Matty, and Jesus Alou formed the San Francisco outfield for one inning. A better story about this Dominican family, however, is the race for the 1966 National League batting title.

Going into the season, Felipe, with the Atlanta Braves, had established himself as a hitter of high average and respectable power. Younger brother Matty's career so far had been disappointing. With no power, his lifetime batting average was .260. In the off-season the Giants had traded him to Pittsburgh.

With the Bucs, Matty came under the special tutelage of manager Harry Walker. "Harry the Hat" taught his pupil to chop down on the ball and to hit to left field instead of trying to pull. This, plus over 20 bunt and 30 infield singles, propelled Matty to the top of the league batting race. Second or third to him almost all year was Atlanta leadoff man and first baseman Felipe Alou. Matty won the crown with a .342 average, while Felipe finished second at .327. The elder brother, however, led the circuit in runs, hits, and total bases.

It was only fitting that Harry Walker was the cause of the enormous jump in Matty's batting average. In 1947 Harry Walker the outfielder was traded from the Cardinals to the Phillies early in the season. There he won the batting title with an average 100 points higher than the year before. This was the second batting title in the family. In 1944 older brother Dixie had led the senior circuit with a .357 mark at Brooklyn.

Brother rivalries and brother teammates come into very sharp focus under the media glare of the World Series. The fall classics from 1921 to 1932 featured Bob Meusel of the Yankees versus older brother Emil or "Irish" of the Giants. These two outfielders were very similar in physical appearance and in capabilities.

Before the 1921 Series one writer summed up the pair:

Bob hits harder than Emil though he is not as consistent in garnering his hits. Bob also excels Emil as a thrower, but Emil is the more finished fielder. Bob is a left field hitter, and Emil often hits to right, so the play of "Meusel flied to Meusel" may be repeated frequently during the Series.

Indeed, it was so in all three series. In Game Three of the 1923 fall classic, each brother robbed the other of an extra-base hit. Over all, Irish emerged superior to Bob in every category—even in extra-base hits. Bob, however, had the last laugh, driving in the go-ahead run in Game Six of 1923 to give the Yankees their first world title.

For their entire careers, the Meusels startle the observer with the closeness of all their statistics. Irish averaged .310 to Bob's .309, both for 11 seasons. Bob leads in all other categories, but not by much. If Irish's totals were increased by prorating them based on his 100 fewer games, the two would look like clones. Each man led his league in RBIs one time.

Two brothers whose lifetime batting averages are identical are Bob and Roy Johnson. Both of these Oklahoma Indians hit .296 as American League outfielders in the 1930s. Bob amassed 2,000 hits and almost 300 home runs, playing mostly for Connie Mack. Elder brother Roy was a speedy singles and doubles hitter. He exceeded his brother only in stolen bases in his considerably shorter career.

The 1927 World Series featured Lloyd Waner leading off and playing center field for Pittsburgh while older brother Paul hit third and patrolled right field. In just his second season, Paul had won the batting title. Rookie Lloyd finished second in hits and third in batting average. The two combined for 460 hits during the season and were 11 for 30 in the World Series as the Yankees swept the Pirates in four games.

The Waners played parts of 16 seasons together, much longer than any other pair. Paul hit 17 points higher in batting and almost 70 points higher in slugging. However, "Big Poison" was actually shorter than Lloyd. Paul's moniker came from all the doubles and triples he delivered.

In 1934 Dizzy and Paul Dean had the greatest year any pitching brothers have ever enjoyed. "Me 'n' Paul" together won 49 games during the regular season and all four of the games the Cardinals won from the Tigers in the World Series. In 1935 their combined victory total was only two less. These two 19-win seasons were Paul's only full years in the majors.

An even more memorable year in St. Louis Cardinal history was 1942. In the last week of August, the Red Birds were five games behind the defending champion Brooklyn Dodgers. Five weeks later the Cardinals clinched first place with a record September rush. Winning five games in the last month for a total of 22 on the season was Mort Cooper. Catching him was younger brother Walker, in his first season as a regular. Mort won his September games with great flair. He was called the "fashion plate" for wearing the number on his back which equaled the victory he was seeking that day. The Cardinals beat the Yankees in a five-game World Series to shock all of baseball. Walker Cooper contributed several timely hits to the Series upset.

Mort also won 20 for the 1943 and 1944 pennant winners and had a victory in each of the World Series. Both brothers were named to *The Sporting News* All-Star team in 1944. Walker hit an even .300 for three Fall Classics.

The Coopers may have been the best of the 15 brother battery combinations, but Wes and Rick Ferrell have to be a close second. Rick caught his younger brother for five straight seasons. Wes won 20 the first two years together.

The next great brother act in the World Series was in 1964, when Ken and Clete Boyer were the opposing third basemen. Elder brother Ken was the National League's Most Valuable Player with a league-leading 119 RBIs for St. Louis. Clete had hit an anemic .219 for the Yankees. Still, this was his chance to show the baseball world he was Ken's equal in the field.

Although neither hit for a high average in the seven games, both did well with the glove. Ken gave his team all its runs in Game Four with a grand-slam homer. St. Louis won that contest 4–3. In the seventh game, Ken scored the first run and later homered. Brother Clete helped make the finish exciting as he hit one of the two solo home

runs off Bob Gibson in the ninth inning. Like the Coopers, the Boyers were born and raised in the "Show Me" state. Both parents were in the stands maintaining their strict neutrality and feeling great pride.

The integrity of play when brothers square off against each other has been taken for granted for many years. This wasn't always the case. In 1933 Joe Sewell, playing third base for the Yankees, and Luke Sewell, catching for Washington, found themselves on opposite sides of a hot pennant race. They had been teammates at Cleveland for a number of years.

Reporting on a crucial game in the 1933 AL race, Shirley Povich of the *Washington Post* wrote:

It was brother versus brother in the seventh when Joe Sewell made a whale of a stop and throw to cut down Luke. It's things like that help prove the honesty of baseball.

The shadow of the Black Sox Scandal still hung over the game.

Now for a trivia windup: There have been five brother shortstop–second base combinations in big league history: Granny and Garvin Hamner of the 1945 Phillies, Lou and Dino Chiozza of the 1935 Phillies, Milt and Frank Bolling

of the 1958 Tigers, Eddie and Johnny O'Brien of the Pirates in the mid-1950s, and Cal and Bill Ripken of the 1987 Orioles. The O'Briens were one of seven sets of twins in the majors.

Josh Clarke with Louisville in the National League in 1898 and George "White Wings" Tebeau of Cleveland in 1894–1895 must have felt some sense of constraint in criticizing their managers. In both cases it was a brother: Fred Clarke and Patsy Tebeau. Both pilots were regular players those seasons as well. Ed Hengle, who never played in the majors, managed his brother Moxie in the Union Association for the entry that began the season in Chicago. By the end of the campaign, both Mengels were gone, and the club had moved to Pittsburgh.

Wes and Rick Ferrell have something in common with Jesse and Lee Tannehill. In each case the pitching brother—Wes and Jesse—had a higher career batting average and more home runs than the brother who played every day.

No, Henry and Tommie Aaron were not the first "soul-brother" brother combination in major-league baseball. The game's first black siblings were Fleet and Welday Walker, who both played for Toledo of the American Association in 1884. That circuit was then considered a major league.

Brothers' Combined Totals (*Still active)

Seasons		Games		Hits		Doubles		Triples	
Alou	47	Alou	5,129	Waner	5,611	DiMaggio	906	Waner	308
Niekro	46	Waner	4,541	Alou	5,094	Waner	884	Delahanty	280
Delahanty	41	DiMaggio	4,245	DiMaggio	4,853	Delahanty	769	Wagner	256
Perry	39	Boyer	3,872	Delahanty	4,211	Alou	765	Clarke	233
Waner	38	Aaron	3,735	Aaron	3,987	Sewell	709	Connor	225
Boyer	36	Delahanty	3,595	Sewell	3,619	Johnson	671	DiMaggio	212
Sewell	35	Sewell	3,532	Boyer	3,559	Aaron	666	Meusel	187
DiMaggio	34	May	3,236	Wagner	3,489	Wagner	658	Johnson	178
Ferrell	33	Cruz	3,077	Johnson	3,343	Meusel	618	Ewing	178
Forsch	32	Johnson	3,016	Meusel	3,214	*Brett	612	Wheat	177
*Brett	34			*Brett	3,096				

Home Runs		Runs		RBI's		Batting Average (10 seasons)		Steals	
Aaron	768	DiMaggio	2,927	DiMaggio	2,739	Manush	.329	Wagner	726
DiMaggio	573	Waner	2,827	Aaron	2,391	Wagner	.326	Delahanty	685
Boyer	444	Delahanty	2,309	Delahanty	2,153	*Gwynn	.321	Clarke	557
May	444	Aaron	2,276	Waner	1,907	Waner	.325	Milan	501
Nettles	406	Alou	2,213	Meusel	1,887	Connor	.314	*Sax	437
Allen	358	Johnson	1,956	Johnson	1,839	Delahanty	.311	Cruz	322
*Murray	418	Sewell	1,794	Boyer	1,803	*Brett	.305	Alou	294
Johnson	346	Wagner	1,762	May	1,780	Meusel	.309	Meusel	253
*Brett	308	Boyer	1,761	Wagner	1,750	Wheat	.309	Moriarty	250
*Ripken	286	Clarke	1,744	Sewell	1,747	Clarke	.308	Aaron	249
Bando	269					O'Rourke	.308	*Yount	262

Brother Pitching Totals

Games		Innings		Wins		Losses		Strikeouts		Shutouts		Complete Games	
Niekro	1,566	Niekro	8,690	Niekro	538	Niekro	478	Perry	5,110	Perry	85	Clarkson	571
Perry	1,407	Perry	8,637	Perry	529	Perry	439	Niekro	5,089	Niekro	74	Weyhing	455
Forsch	1,019	Clarkson	5,616	Clarkson	383	Forsch	249	Mathewson	2,504	Coveleski	51	Mathewson	436
McDaniel	1,006	Forsch	4,921	Coveleski	296	Weyhing	239	Clarkson	2,326	Clarkson	43	Perry	412
Reuschel	755	Mathewson	4,793	Forsch	282	Clarkson	232	Forsch	2,180	Forsch	37	Niekro	352
		Reuschel	3,865									Coveleski	308

Fathers and Sons

Shortly after breaking into the majors, Dale Berra was asked about similarities between himself and his famous father, Yogi. The younger Berra replied, "Our similarities are different."

Like the many malapropisms of Yogi Berra, this one by his son may appear foolish on the surface, but it contains quite a bit of underlying wisdom. In fact, it can serve as a metaphor for father-son combinations in major league baseball.

Of the 128 combinations, only forty feature both

generations at the same position. There are nineteen father-son pitcher combinations, five cases where both father and son caught, one where both played first, two where both played shortstop, and thirteen where both father and son were outfielders. Very few fathers and sons at any position have career totals that are at all close.

Another important generalization is the great increase in father-son combinations since World War Two, especially in the last twenty years. The first son of a former big leaguer to break into the majors was Jack Doscher in 1903 as a pitcher for the Chicago Cubs—one of the three teams with whom his father, Herm, had toiled as a utility player twenty years earlier. By 1945 the number of father-son combinations was 36. In 1965 the total was 66. That means almost 40 percent of today's number has been added in the last two decades.

Is the son of a big league ballplayer more apt to develop into a major leaguer than the average boy? Some people think not. In the 1950s, Hall of Famer George Sisler was asked this very question. The two-time .400 hitter shook his head over how two of his offspring had made the majors. He pointed out that baseball players are absentee fathers. They don't have much opportunity to teach their boys the fundamentals of the game or to practice with them.

If not their fathers, perhaps other well-qualified professionals have instructed the second generation. A worthwhile study could be conducted to determine how many second-generation players who have broken in during the last two decades attended baseball camps as boys. If the number is significant, this could explain the big increase during this period.

Certainly, the Sisler family deserves special attention. Father George broke into the majors just before World War One as a pitcher for the St. Louis Browns. After being switched to first base, he spent fifteen years as one of the greatest performers ever at that position. Accordingly, it is only fitting that he should have one son, Dick, who was a good hitter and another son, Dave, who pitched in the majors briefly. Dick's home run on the last day of the 1950 season, which gave the Philadelphia Whiz Kids the pennant, has given him an identity independent of his father. Also, these two men both managed in the majors for a short time. Currently they are the only father-son combination in this category.

Baseball families fall into one of three categories: famous fathers only, famous sons only, and equals.

Let us consider the famous son category first. Another way of describing these men would be to call them "fathers of . . . " Two families stand out in this category. They are the Muellers and the Walkers.

Walter Mueller was a reserve outfielder for the Pirates for four seasons in the 1920s. His son, Don, hit .296 in twelve seasons as a National League outfielder. In 1954 Mueller and teammate Willie Mays battled all season for the batting title on the pennant-winning Giants. Mays finished first in hitting by three points, but Mueller led the league in hits with 212.

Dixie Walker was a pitcher for the Washington team from 1909 through 1912. His lifetime record was 24–30. Both his sons, Fred (or "Dixie") and Harry, won batting titles.

These two are the only clear cases of a son of All-Star

quality who had a father whose career in the majors was forgettable. Other families with "fathers of . . . " are Coleman, Grimsley, and Smalley.

In contrast, the list of "sons of . . . " is a long one. There are eight baseball fathers in the Hall of Fame. Averill, Berra, Collins, Lindstrom, Mack, O'Rourke and Walsh had offspring who fit this category. Four more families—Bagby, Camilli, Trosky, and Wood—had fathers of All-Star quality and sons who are footnotes to their careers. Hegan, Wills, and Trout are families where the sons had respectable careers and characteristics similar to those of the fathers, but the older generation was clearly superior.

We must consider first whether some of the "sons of . . ." got to the majors, or second, stayed longer than they merited, because of the family name. I would cite Collins, Walsh, and Wood to prove the former proposition, and Dale Berra and Marc Sullivan as support for the latter.

The younger Berra and Sullivan not only had the temerity to go into their father's business, but, like Bill and Cal Ripken, Jr., of Baltimore, they had dad for their boss. The Ripkens (in 1988) and Dale Berra (in 1985) saw their fathers dismissed as managers early in the season. Cal Ripken, Sr., was not only the first father to manage two sons at once, but the first without major league playing experience to manage his sons.

Sullivan, whose father owned part of the Red Sox, traded his son to the Houston Astros organization before the 1988 season, where he could commiserate with the Berras on the difficulties of combining a baseball career with family obligations.

By far the most interesting category is that of the fathers and sons whose careers parallel or equal each other.

The two Billy Sullivans caught for both the White Sox and the Tigers. Both played other positions as well as caught in one World Series. Sullivan Senior caught the older Ed Walsh; Junior caught the younger Ed Walsh—both at Chicago. Junior hit for what appears a much higher average, but we must remember that Senior played in the Dead-Ball Era, and Junior in the high-hitting 1930s.

Jim and Mike Hegan were a father-son combination well known for defensive ability. Father Jim was a great handler of pitchers for Cleveland. Mike played first base and the outfield for several American League teams. Both appeared in two World Series. Mike broke into the majors just four seasons after his father's finale.

The father-son pitching combinations have few parallels. Both Thornton and Don Lee gave up home runs to Ted Williams. Only two families have had both father and son pitch in a World Series. Jim Bagby, Sr. pitched for Cleveland in the 1920 Series and his son for the Red Sox in 1946. Mel Stottlemyre went 1–1 for the Yankees in the 1964 Series. Todd Stottlemyre pitched for Toronto in the 1992 fall classic.

Joe Schultz, Junior, received some unwanted publicity in Jim Bouton's book *Ball Four*, for being Bouton's manager. Schultz and his father, Joe Senior, each spent almost a decade in the majors as reserve players. Senior was 46 for 170 as a pinch-hitter. Junior went 43 for 160 in that same role.

It is only fitting that Buddy Bell spent a portion of his fine career with the Cincinnati Reds, the team on which his father Gus spent his best years. The two ended their

careers with nearly identical batting averages and home run totals.

Five father-son combinations have played in All-Star Games. Prior to 1990 only the Bell and Boone families could have made that boast. Then Barry Bonds, Ken Griffey, Jr., and both Alomar sons made their debuts in the mid-summer classic. The Bells and Boones have similar statistics. Gus was 2 for 6, hitting a home run his first time up; Buddy was 1 for 7, hitting a triple in his first plate appearance. Ray Boone went 1 for 5 in All-Star games with a homer; Bob is 2 for 5 in three games. Both Griffeys have been the Most Valuable Player in an All Star Game: Senior in 1980 and Junior in 1992. Currently the Seattle center fielder is 5 for 8 in the mid-summer classic. His father was 5 for 7 in three games. Each has a home run to his credit.

In Game One of the 1984 World Series, a two-run double by San Diego catcher Terry Kennedy was noted by the television announcers as something significant. This was the first time in the history of the fall classic that both a father and son had a World Series RBI. Terry's father, Bob, knocked in a run for Cleveland as an outfielder in the 1948 Series. There have been seven families in which the father and son both played in a World Series. Five have been mentioned already; there is also Ernie and Don Johnson. The father was a substitute infielder for the Yankees in the 1923 Series. Don was the regular second baseman for the Cubs in the 1945 fall classic. Stan Javier in 1988 and 1989 with Oakland makes seven; his father, Julian, played in four World Series.

An interesting father-son parallel to watch for in the future is that between Bobby and Barry Bonds. The son, an outfielder for Pittsburgh, has his father's penchant for home runs, stolen bases, and strikeouts.

The Bondses are not the first black father-son combination. That honor goes to the Hairstons. Father Sam caught two games for the White Sox in 1951. Son Jerry was a respected pinch-hitter for that team for over a decade.

Since the first edition of this book two significant events have taken place. In September 1990 Ken Griffey, Senior took a place in the Seattle Mariner outfield next to his son. Late in the 1992 season, Bret Boone made his major league debut as the Seattle second baseman. Baseball now has a three-generation family. Bret's father was Bob Boone and his grandfather was Ray Boone. It is hard to imagine what could top these two events in fan interest, but we are sure to see many more family combinations in the years to come.

Father-Son Hitters

	Years	Games	Runs	Hits	Homers	RBIs	BA	Steals
ALOMAR								
Sandy, Sr.	15	1,481	588	1,168	13	282	.245	227
Robby	5	761	439	862	39	302	.291	192
Sandy, Jr.	5	280	93	248	12	105	.261	7
AVERILL								
Earl, Sr.	13	1,669	1,224	2,020	238	1,165	.318	69
Earl, Jr.	9	449	137	249	44	159	.242	3
BELL								
Gus	15	1,741	865	1,823	206	942	.281	30
Buddy	18	2,405	1,150	2,514	201	1,106	.279	55
BERRA								
Yogi	19	2,120	1,175	2,150	358	1,430	.285	30
Dale	11	853	236	603	49	278	.236	32
BONDS								
Bobby	14	1,849	1,258	1,886	332	1,024	.268	461
Barry	7	1,010	672	984	176	556	.274	251
BOONE								
Ray	13	1,373	645	1,260	151	737	.275	21
Bob	19	2,264	679	1,838	105	826	.254	38
CAMILLI								
Dolf	12	1,490	936	1,482	239	950	.277	60
Doug	9	313	56	153	18	80	.199	0
GRIFFEY								
Ken, Sr.	19	2,090	1,129	2,143	152	859	.296	200
Ken, Jr.	4	578	311	652	87	344	.301	60

	Years	Games	Runs	Hits	Homers	RBIs	BA	Steals
HEGAN								
Jim	17	1,666	550	1,087	92	525	.228	15
Mike	12	965	281	504	53	229	.242	28
KENNEDY								
Bob	16	1,483	514	1,176	63	514	.254	45
Terry	14	1,491	474	1,313	113	628	.264	6
SCHOFIELD								
Ducky	19	1,321	394	699	21	211	.227	12
Dick	10	1,202	452	874	52	314	.229	109
SISLER								
George	15	2,055	1,283	2,812	99	1,175	.340	375
Dick	8	799	302	720	55	360	.276	6
SMALLEY								
Roy, Jr.	11	872	277	601	61	305	.227	4
Roy, III	13	1,653	745	1,454	163	694	.257	27
SULLIVAN								
Billy, Sr.	16	1,146	363	777	20	378	.212	98
Billy, Jr.	12	962	347	820	29	388	.289	30
TRESH								
Mike	12	1,027	326	788	2	297	.249	19
Tom	9	1,192	595	1,041	153	530	.245	45
WILLS								
Maury	14	1,942	1,067	2,134	20	458	.281	586
Bump	6	831	472	807	36	302	.266	196

Father-Son Pitchers

	Years	Games	W-L	SO	CG	ERA
BAGBY						
Jim, Sr.	9	316	127–89	450	132	3.10
Jim, Jr.	10	303	97–96	431	84	3.96
COLEMAN						
Joe, Sr.	10	223	52–76	444	60	4.38
Joe, Jr.	15	484	142–135	1728	94	3.69

	Years	Games	W-L	SO	CG	ERA
KRAUSSE						
Lew, Sr.	2	23	5–1	17	3	4.48
Lew, Jr.	12	321	68–91	721	21	4.00
LEE						
Thornton	16	374	117–124	937	155	3.56
Don	9	244	40–44	467	13	3.61

PILLETTE						
Herman	4	107	34–32	148	33	3.45
Duane	8	188	38–66	305	34	4.40
QUEEN						
Mel, Sr.	8	146	27–40	328	15	5.09
Mel, Jr.	9	140	20–17	302	6	3.14
SISLER						
George	7	24	5–6	63	9	2.35
Dave	7	247	38–44	355	12	4.33
TROUT						
Paul	15	521	170–161	1,256	158	3.23
Steve	12	301	88–92	656	32	4.18
WALSH						
Ed, Sr.	14	430	195–126	2,346	250	1.82
Ed, Jr.	4	79	11–24	107	15	5.57

Baseball Families

KEY

tm teammates
F-S father-son

BROTHERS

AARON   Henry & Tommie tm
ACOSTA   Jose & Merito
ADAMS   Bobby & Dick F-S also
ALLEN   Dick, Hank & Ron tm
ALLISON   Art & Doug tm
ALOMAR   Roberto & Sandy Jr.
ALOU   Felipe, Matty & Jesus tm
ANDERSON   Kent & Mike
ANDREWS   Rob & Mike
ASPROMONTE   Bob & Ken

BAILEY   Ed & Jim tm
BAKER   Dave & Doug
BANDO   Chris & Sal
BANNON   Jimmy & Tom
BARNES   Jesse & Virgil
BARRETT   Marty & Tom
BAXES   Jim & Mike
BELL   Charlie & Frank
BELL   George & Juan
BENNETT   Dave & Dennis tm
BERGEN   Bill & Marty
BIGBEE   Carson & Lyle tm
BLANKENSHIP   Homer & Ted tm
BLUEGE   Ossie & Otto
BOLLING   Frank & Milt tm
BOONE   Danny & Ike
BOYER   Clete, Ken & Cloyd tm
BOYLE   Buzz & Jim
BOYLE   Eddie & Jack
BRADY   Steve & Tom
BRASHEAR   Kitty & Roy
BREEDEN   Danny & Hal tm
BRETT   George & Ken
BREWER   Mike & Tony
BRINKMAN   Chuck & Ed
BROWN   Dick & Larry
BROWN   Jackie & Paul
BROWN   Oscar & Ollie
BROWN   Curtis & Leon

CAMNITZ   Harry & Howie tm
CAMP   Kid & Llewellan tm
CAMPBELL   Hugh & Mat tm
CANSECO   Jose & Ozzie
CANTWELL   Mike & Tom
CARLYLE   Cleo & Roy
CASEY   Dan & Dennis tm
CHIOZZA   Dino & Lou tm
CHRISTOPHER   Lloyd & Russ
CLAPP   Aaron & John
CLARK   Jerald & Phil
CLARKE   Fred & Josh tm
CLARKE   Sumpter & Rufe
CLARKSON   Dad, John & Walter tm
CLIBURN   Stan & Stew
COFFMAN   Dick & Slick
COHEN   Andy & Syd
CONIGLIARO   Billy & Tony
CONNELL   Gene & Joe
CONNOR   Joe & Roger
CONWAY   Jim & Pete
CONWAY   Bill & Dick tm
COONEY   Jimmy & Johnny tm F-S also
COOPER   Mort & Walker tm
CORCORAN   Larry & Mike tm
COSCARART   Joe & Pete
COVELESKI   Harry & Stan
COVINGTON   Sam & Tex
CROSS   Amos, Frank & Lave tm

CRUZ   Hector, Jose & Tommy tm
CUCCINELLO   Al & Tony

DAILY   Con & Ed
DALY   Joe & Tom
DANNING   Harry & Ike
DARINGER   Cliff & Rolla
DAVALILLO   Vic & Yo-Yo
DAVENPORT   Claude & Dave
DAVIS   Mark & Mike
DEAN   Dizzy & Paul tm
DEASLEY   Jim & Pat
DELAHANTY   Ed, Frank, Jim, Joe & Tom tm
DEMONTREVILLE   Gene & Lee
DICKEY   Bill & George
DILLON   Packy & Joe tm
DIMAGGIO   Vince, Joe & Dom
DONAHUE   Jiggs & Pat
DONNELLY   Pete & John
DONOVAN   Jerry & Tom
DORGAN   Jerry & Mike
DOWNS   Kelly & Dave
DOYLE   Brian & Doyle
DRAKE   Sammy & Solly
DUGAN   Bill & Ed tm

EDWARDS   Dave, Marshall & Mike (twins)
ENS   Jewel & Mutz
ERAUTT   Eddie & Joe
EVERS   Joe & Johnny
EWING   Buck & John tm

FALK   Bibb & Chet
FERRELL   Rick & Wes tm
FERRY   Cy & Jack
FINNEY   Hal & Lou
FISHER   Bob & Newt
FISHER   Chauncey & Tom
FOGARTY   Jim & Joe
FORD   Gene & Russ
FOREMAN   Brownie & Frank tm
FORSCH   Bob & Ken
FOUTZ   Dave & Frank
FOWLER   Art & Jesse
FREESE   Gene & George
FRIEL   Bill & Pat
FULLER   Harry & Shorty
FULMER   Chick & Washington

GAGLIANO   Phil & Ralph
GANZEL   Charlie & John F-S also
GARBARK   Bob & Mike
GARDELLA   Al & Danny tm
GARRETT   Adrian & Wayne
GASTON   Alex & Milt tm
GEISS   Bill & Emil
GENTRY   Harvey & Rufe
GILBERT   Harry & John tm
GILBERT   Charlie & Tookie F-S also
GLEASON   Bill & Jack tm
GLEASON   Harry & Kid
GRABOWSKI   Al & Reggie
GRAVES   Joe & Sid
GREGG   Dave & Vean
GRIMES   Ray & Roy (twins) F-S also
GRISSOM   Lee & Marv
GROH   Heine & Lew
GUMBERT   Ad & Billy
GWYNN   Chris & Tony

HACKETT   Mert & Walter tm
HAFEY   Bud & Tom
HAIRSTON   Jerry & John F-S also

HAMNER   Garvin & Granny tm
HANDLEY   Gene & Lee
HARGRAVE   Bubbles & Pinky
HATFIELD   Gil & John
HAYWORTH   Ray & Red
HEMPHILL   Charlie & Frank
HENGLE   Emery (Moxie) & Ed tm
HEVING   Joe & Johnnie
HIGH   Andy, Charlie & Hugh
HILL   Hugh & Still Bill
HINCHMAN   Bill & Harry tm
HITCHCOCK   Billy & Jim
HOGAN   George & Happy
HOVLIK   Hick & Joe
HOWARD   Del & Ivon
HUGHES   Jim & Mickey
HUGHES   Ed & Tom
HUNTER   Bill & George

IGNASIAK   Gary & Mike
IORG   Dane & Garth
IRWIN   Arthur & John

JEFFCOAT   George & Hal
JIMENEZ   Elvio & Manny
JONES   Darryl & Lynn
JONES   Gary & Steve
JOHNSON   Bob & Roy
JOHNSON   Chet & Earl
JOHNSTON   Doc & Jimmy
JONNARD   Bubber & Claude (twins)
JORGENS   Arndt & Orville

KAPPEL   Heinie & Joe
KELL   George & Skeeter
KELLER   Charlie & Hal
KELLNER   Alex & Walt tm
KELLY   George & Ren
KENNEDY   Jim & Junior
KEOUGH   Marty & Joe F-S also
KILLEFER   Bill & Red
KILROY   Matt & Mike tm
KLAUS   Billy & Bobby
KLING   Bill & Johnny
KNODE   Mike & Ray
KNOTHE   Fritz & George
KOPF   Larry & Wally
KRSNICH   Mike & Rocky

LACHEMANN   Marcel & Rene
LANNING   Johnny & Tom
LANSFORD   Carney & Joe
LARY   Al & Frank
LEITER   Al & Mark
LELIVELT   Bill & Jack
LILLARD   Bill & Gene tm
LOBERT   Frank & Hans
LOOK   Bruce & Dean
LOWDERMILK   Grover & Lou tm
LUSH   Billy & Ernie

MACHA   Ken & Mike
MADDUX   Greg & Mike
MAHLER   Mickey & Rick tm
MAISEL   Fritz & George
MANCUSO   Frank & Gus
MANGUAL   Angel & Pepe
MANSELL   John, Mike & Tom tm
MANUSH   Frank & Heine
MANZANILLO   Josias & Ravelo
MARION   Marty & Red
MARTINEZ   Pedro & Ramon tm
MASKREY   Harry & Leech tm
MATHEWSON   Christy & Henry tm
MATTOX   Cloy & Jim
MAY   Carlos & Lee

MAYER   Erskine & Sam
MCDANIEL   Lindy & Von tm
MCFARLAN   Alex & Dan
MCFARLAND   Lamont & Charles
MCGEEHAN   Connie & Dan
MCLAUGHLIN   Barney & Frank tm
MEUSEL   Bob & Irish
MILAN   Clyde & Horace tm
MILLER   Jake & Russ
MILLER   Bing & Ralph tm
MITCHELL   John & Charlie
MOFFETT   Joe & Sam
MORIARTY   Bill & George
MORRISON   Johnny & Phil tm
MORRISSEY   John & Tom
MOTA   Andy & Jose F-S also
MUELLER   Clarence & Walter F-S also
MURRAY   Eddie & Rich
MYERS   Billy & Lynn

NETTLES   Graig & Jim
NEWKIRK   Floyd & Joel
NIEKRO   Joe & Phil tm
NIXON   Otis & Donnell
NYMAN   Chris & Nyls

O'BRIEN   Eddie & Johnny (twins) tm
OGDEN   Curley & Jack
OLIVO   Chi Chi & Diomedes
O'NEILL   Jack, Jim, Mike & Steve tm
ONSLOW   Eddie & Jack
O'ROURKE   Jim & John F-S also
ORTIZ   Baby & Roberto tm
O'TOOLE   Denny & Jim
OWEN   Dave & Spike

PACIOREK   John, Tom & Jim
PARKER   Jay & Doc
PARROTT   Jiggs & Tom tm
PASCUAL   Camilo & Carlos
PATTERSON   Ham & Pat
PEITZ   Heine & Joe tm
PENA   Ramon & Tony
PEPLOSKI   Henry & Pepper
PERRY   Gaylord & Jim tm
PEREZ   Pascual & Melido
PFEFFER   Big Jeff & Jeff
PIERSON   Dave & Dick
PIKE   Jay & Lip
PIPGRAS   Ed & George
POTTER   Dykes & Squire

RAJSICH   Dave & Gary
REACH   Al & Bob
RECCIUS   John & Phil (twins) tm
REUSCHEL   Paul & Rick tm
REYNOLDS   Hal & Don
RICKETTS   Dick & Dave
RIDDLE   Elmer & Johnny tm
RIPKEN   Cal & Billy   tm F-S also
ROBINSON   Bruce & Dave
ROBINSON   Fred & Wilbert
ROENICKE   Gary & Ron
ROETTGER   Oscar & Wally
ROMO   Vicente & Romero Enrique
ROOF   Gene & Phil
ROSENBERG   Harry & Lou
ROTH   Braggo & Frank
ROWE   Dave & Jack
ROY   Charlie & Luther
RUSSELL   Allan & Lefty

SADOWSKI   Bob, Eddie & Ted
SAUER   Ed & Hank

SAX   Dave & Steve *tm*
SAY   Jimmie & Lou *tm*
SCANLAN   Doc & Frank
SCHANG   Bobby & Wally
SCHAREIN   Art & George
SCHMIDT   Boss & Walt
SCHULTE   Herman & Leonard
SEWELL   Luke, Joe & Tommie *tm*
SHAFFER   Orator & Taylor *tm*
SHANNON   Joe & Red *tm*
SHANTZ   Billy & Bobby *tm*
SHERLOCK   Monk & Vince
SHERRY   Larry & Norm *tm*
SISLER   Dave & Dick *F-S also*
SMITH   Charlie & Fred
SOWDERS   Bill, John & Len
STAFFORD   John & Jim
STANICEK   Steve & Pete
STANLEY   Buck & Joe
STOTTLEMYRE   Mel, Jr. & Todd
STOVALL   George & Jessie
SURHOFF   Bill & Rich
SUTHERLAND   Darrell & Gary

TANNEHILL   Jesse & Lee
TEBEAU   Patsy & White Wings *tm*
THIELMAN   Henry & Jake
THOMAS   Bill & Roy *tm*
THOMPSON   Homer & Tommy *tm*
THRONEBERRY   Faye & Marv
TOBIN   Jim & Johnny
TORRE   Frank & Joe *tm*
TRAFFLEY   Bill & John
TREACEY   Fred & Pete *tm*
TREVINO   Alex & Bobby
TWOMBLY   Babe & George
TYLER   Fred & Lefty *tm*
TYRONE   Jim & Wayne

UNDERWOOD   Pat & Tom
UPTON   Bill & Tom

VAN CUYK   Chris & Johnny

WADE   Ben & Jake
WAGNER   Butts & Honus
WALKER   Dixie Sr. & Ernie *F-S also*
WALKER   Dixie Jr. & Harry
WALKER   Gee & Hub *tm*
WALKER   Fleet & Welday *tm*
WANER   Lloyd & Paul *tm*
WATT   Al & Frank
WEILAND   Bob & Ed
WESTLAKE   Jim & Wally
WEYHING   Gus & John
WHEAT   Mack & Zack
WHITE   Deacon & Will *tm*
WHITNEY   Art & Frank

WILLIAMS   Gus & Harry
WILTSE   Hooks & Snake
WINGO   Al & Ivy
WOOD   Fred & Pete *tm*
WRIGHT   George, Harry & Sam *tm*
YOCHIM   Len & Ray
YOUNT   Larry & Robin

FATHERS-SONS

ADAMS   Bobby-Mike
ALOMAR   Sandy-Roberto & Sandy Jr.
ALOU   Felipe-Moises
AMARO   Ruben Sr. & Jr.
ARAGON   Angel-Jack
AVERILL   Earl-Earl

BAGBY   Jim Sr. & Jr.
BARNHART   Clyde-Vic
BEAMON   Charlie-Charlie
BELL   Gus-Buddy
BERRA   Yogi-Dale
BERRY   Charlie-Charlie
BERRY   Joe-Joe
BONDS   Bobby-Barry
BOONE   Ray-Bob
BOONE   Bob-Bret
BORBON   Pedro-Pedro
BRICKELL   Fred-Fritzie
BRUCKER   Earle Sr. & Jr.
BRUMLEY   Mike-Tony

CAMILLI   Dolf-Doug
CAMPANIS   Alex-Jim
CARREON   Camilo-Mark
COLEMAN   Joe-Joe
COLLINS   Ed Sr. & Jr.
CONNOLLY   Ed Sr. & Jr.
COONEY   Jimmy-Jimmy & John
CORRIDEN   Red-John
CROUCH   Bill-Wilmer

DOSCHER   Herm-Jack

ELLSWORTH   Dick-Steve
ESCHEN   Jim-Larry

FRANCONA   Tito-Terry

GABRIELSON   Len-Len
GANZEL   Charlie-Babe
GILBERT   Larry-Charlie & Tookie
GRAHAM   Peaches-Jack
GREEN   Fred-Gary
GRIFFEY   Ken Sr. & Jr. *tm*
GRIMES   Ray-Oscar
GRIMSLEY   Ross-Ross

HAIRSTON   Sam-Jerry & John
HANEY   Larry-Chris
HEGAN   Jim-Mike
HEINTZELMAN   Ken-Tom
HOOD   Wally Sr. & Jr.
HOWARD   Bruce-David
HUNDLEY   Randy-Todd

JAVIER   Julian-Stan
JETER   Johnny-Shawn
JOHNSON   Adam-Adam
JOHNSON   Ernie-Don

KENNEDY   Bob-Terry
KEOUGH   Marty-Matty
KRAUSE   Lew Sr. & Jr.
KUNKEL   Bill-Jeff

LANDRUM   Joe-Bill
LANIER   Max-Hal
LAW   Vern-Vance
LEE   Thornton-Don
LERCHEN   Dutch-George
LIEBHARDT   Glenn-Glenn
LINDSTROM   Fred-Charlie
LIVELY   Jack-Bud

MACK   Connie-Earle
MAGGERT   Harl-Harl
MALAY   Charlie-Joe
MARTIN   Barney-Jerry
MATTICK   Wally-Bobby
MAY   Dave-Derrick
MAY   Pinky-Milt
MCKNIGHT   Jim-Jeff
MCRAE   Hal-Brian
MEINKE   Frank-Bob
MILLS   Willie-Art
MONTEAGUDO   Rene-Aurelio
MOORE   Eugene Sr. & Jr.
MORTON   Guy Sr. & Jr.
MOTA   Manny-Andy & Jose
MUELLER   Walter-Don

NARLESKI   Bill-Ray
NAVARRO   Julio-Jaime
NICHOLS   Chet Sr. & Jr.
NORTHEY   Ron-Scott

OKRIE   Frank-Len
OLIVARES   Ed-Omar
OLIVO   Diomedes-Gilbert Rondon
O'ROURKE   Patsy-Joe
O'ROURKE   Jim-Queenie
OSBORNE   Tiny-Bobo

PARTENHEIMER   Steve-Stan
PILLETTE   Herman-Duane

QUEEN   Mel-Mel

RIPLEY   Walt-Allen

SAVIDGE   Ralph-Don
SCHOFIELD   Ducky-Dick
SCHULTZ   Joe Sr. & Jr.
SEGUI   Diego-David
SHEELY   Earl-Bub
SIEBERT   Dick-Paul
SISLER   George-Dick & Dave
SKINNER   Bob-Joel
SMALLEY   Roy Jr.-Roy III
SPRAGUE   Ed Sr. & Jr.
ST. CLAIRE   Ebba-Randy
STENHOUSE   Dave-Mike
STEPHENSON   Joe-Jerry
STILLWELL   Ron-Kurt
STOTTLEMYRE   Mel-Todd & Mel Jr.
SULLIVAN   Billy Sr.-Jr.
SULLIVAN   Haywood-Marc
SUSCE   George-George

TANNER   Chuck-Bruce
TARTABULL   Jose-Danny
TORRES   Ricardo-Gil
TRESH   Mike-Tom
TROSKY   Hal Sr. & Jr.
TROUT   Paul-Steve

UNSER   Al-Del

VIRGIL   Ozzie Sr. & Jr.

WAKEFIELD   Howard-Dick
WALKER   Dixie-Dixie & Harry
WALSH   Ed-Ed
WHITE   JoJo-Mike
WILLS   Maury-Bump
WINE   Bobby-Robbie
WOOD   Joe-Joe

YOUNG   Del-Del

GREAT GRANDFATHER-GREAT GRANDSON

Jim Bluejacket & Bill Wilkinson

GRANDFATHER-GRANDSON

George Rooks-Lou Possehl
Shano Collins-Bob Gallagher
Bill Brubaker-Dennis Rasmussen
Marty & Ed Herrmann
Lloyd & Jim Spencer
Lennie & Matt Merullo
Ray & Bret Boone

## CHAPTER 9

Scandals and Controversies

Stephen S. Hall

Scandal is in the eye of the beholder. The biggest scandal of baseball's 1876 season was the failure of the New York Mutuals and Philadelphia Athletics to fulfill their obligatory season-ending western road trip, resulting in their expulsion from the National League. Yet when black players were virtually excluded from the first eight decades of organized ball, few saw it as a long-running institutional scandal. When the likable but wayward Babe Ruth cut a broad swath through most notions of civilized behavior, the Sultan of Swat's charmed, forgiving public responded with winks and nods. But when Walter O'Malley, in a business decision calculated to maximize profits (surely one of baseball's most enduring and honored traditions), moved his Dodgers to Los Angeles after the 1957 season, he traumatized an entire generation of Brooklyn fans. When several New York Met players faced allegations of rape (ultimately not prosecuted) in 1992, the story blazed from the back pages of tabloids for weeks. But when baseball owners secretly conspired between 1985 and 1988 to subvert the economic spirit of free agency, cheating their employees out of tens of millions of dollars in potential salaries, the crime of collusion merited only a few grey paragraphs on the sport pages.

From its earliest days, baseball has indulged gamblers, fixers, drunkards, brawlers, disreputable moguls, bad actors, felons, homicidal maniacs, crooked umpires, vindictive owners, pyromaniacal fans, and at least one ax murderer. Just as a Dickens novel reflects all the voices and vices of Victorian London, baseball hears from all precincts of the American experience, including the seedy. And just as in Dickens, baseball's seediness is not confined to gambling parlors and bars, but extends to the executive suite. A harbinger of the economic controversies and financial hardball to come can be read in the ouster of baseball commissioner Francis (Fay) Vincent in September of 1992 by a majority of owners, in what more than one writer described as baseball's "civil war."

A Commissioner "Resigns"

Although Vincent's three-year tenure was not without its own controversial moments (his handling of the Steinbrenner expulsion, for one, and his peremptory manner in dealing with critics), the orchestrated movement that drove him from office reiterated a baseball truism overlooked in times of economic and sportive harmony: the commissioner serves, and always has served, at the pleasure of the owners. Circa 1992, the pleasure of the owners seems to be to force a confrontation with the players union on the issue of contracts, free agency, and spiraling salaries. Vincent threatened to act as a dangerously moderating force in that looming power struggle, for his track record suggests he would have been likely to invoke his favorite clause—the commissioner's power to act "in the best interests of baseball"—to squelch a possible 1993 spring training lockout of the players by ownership.

The whispering campaign to unseat Vincent bore a strong Chicago accent. The ringleaders of this insurrection, according to numerous press accounts, were Chicago White Sox owner Jerry Reinsdorf and Stanton Cook of the Tribune Company, owners not only of the Cubs but of television stations that broadcast games of seven teams (the Cubs, White Sox, Yankees, Angels, Phillies, Dodgers, and Rockies—all of whom, incidentally, opposed Vincent's continued service). Chief among the allies of the Chicago crowd were Dodger owner Peter O'Malley and Milwaukee owner Bud Selig. Their campaign to depose Vincent provides a map of the economic controversies that may well convulse major league baseball in the coming years.

Vincent took over as interim commissioner on September 2, 1989, one day after the death of A. Bartlett Giamatti, and one of his earliest official acts may have sealed the enmity with which many owners viewed his leadership. In the spring of 1990 Vincent intervened in a labor dispute, helping both to end a month-long spring training lockout and to negotiate a four-year collective bargaining agreement with the Major League Baseball Players Association. Many owners viewed the agreement as too accommodating to the union, and Vincent's unpopularity only grew over his handling of the ban of Yankee owner George Steinbrenner, his position on television contracts, and divisional realignment.

To all appearances, discontent boiled to a head in early July, when Vincent, invoking "the best interests of baseball," announced his decision to realign the National League. According to the plan (and common-sense geography), Atlanta and Cincinnati would join the eastern division while Chicago and St. Louis would shift to the west. The Tribune Company, arguing hardship for Cub fans (a novel strategy, given the club's history), promptly sued the commissioner.

But in fact the anti-Vincent sniping had begun as early as the winter of 1990–1991, when the commissioner acknowledged the discontent and stated publicly, "I'm not going to resign. Unless somebody has a technique that I'm not aware of, the decision whether I stay or go is mine." Fueled not so much by a technique as by a technology, disgruntled owners began to whip up anti-Vincent senti-

ment by fax, and this country club coup d'etat was well underway in the summer of 1992. Ominously, the labor issue resurfaced that June, when Reinsdorf, Brewers owner Selig, and Richard Ravitch—the owners' chief labor representative—tried to persuade Vincent to relinquish his authority in labor relations; he would not. The labor issue was the handwriting on Vincent's crumbling wall of support.

The owners convened in Chicago on September 3 to hold a vote of confidence on Vincent's stewardship. By an 18–9 vote, they requested his resignation (the teams voting for Vincent's ouster were the White Sox, Cubs, Dodgers, Yankees, Brewers, Angels, Twins, Phillies, Pirates, Indians, Blue Jays, Cardinals, Giants, Mariners, Padres, Tigers, Braves, and Rockies; Cincinnati abstained, and the rest voted for Vincent). For one tense weekend (ironically, the Labor Day holiday weekend), Vincent refused to cave in, vowing to fight the issue all the way to the Supreme Court and hiring Brendan V. Sullivan, Jr., the lawyer who so ably defended Oliver North during the Iran-Contra hearings, to give sinew to the threat. Still reeling from the Pete Rose debacle, Major League Baseball seemed headed for yet another major showdown in court.

But upon reflection Vincent thought better of going the court route, and in a capitulatory statement issued with his resignation on September 8, Vincent explained his decision, perhaps with intended irony, by invoking the very governing clause that most annoyed his detractors: "Simply put, I've concluded that resignation—not litigation—should be my final act as Commissioner, 'in the best interests' of baseball." The following day, September 9, baseball's executive council met in St. Louis to assume control of the game and unanimously elected Bud Selig to be chairman of the council, acting in effect as a caretaker commissioner.

Baseball's palace coup comes at a time when the owners, having fueled the fires of free agency for 15 years, now claim to have been burned by it. The game's economic woes are indeed pressing: numerous teams are pleading dwindling profits (if not poverty); the league's billion-dollar national television contract with CBS expires at the end of the 1993 season (with little chance of a similarly stratospheric bid being offered next time around); ESPN announced that it would not renew its option to televise games beyond the 1993 season because of flagging viewership; and the resistance to revenue sharing between teams in large and small markets threatens to carve the leagues' talent pool into haves and have-nots.

But the controversial dumping of Vincent stirred up even deeper problems, arousing the concern of several U.S. senators, including Howard Metzenbaum of Ohio and Alan Simpson of Wyoming. The former's antitrust subcommittee of the Senate Judiciary Committee scheduled a one-day hearing in December of 1992 to examine baseball's antitrust exemption. "If decisions about the direction and the future of Major League Baseball are going to be dictated by the financial interests of team owners," said Metzenbaum, "then maybe baseball should be required to operate under the same business rules as any other sport." At the same time, that exemption came under renewed inspection in light of the proposed sale of the San Francisco Giants to a group of investors in St.

Petersburg, Florida, for an estimated $115 million—a sale blocked by National League owners in favor of a lower bid from a San Francisco based group. The vote renewed scrutiny from potential outside regulators. "If they don't accept the offer," said Florida senator Connie Mack, grandson of the legendary Athletics manager, prior to the decision, "there is serious question about the exemption baseball enjoys from antitrust laws."

All this comes at a time when the the owners were already a bit thin in both integrity and the wallet following a series of legal setbacks in the landmark collusion judgments. On September 17, 1990, baseball arbitrator George Nicolau ruled that the owners had secretly coordinated efforts to prevent the free agent market from working in the 1987 and 1988 seasons, and ordered the owners to pay $102.5 million in compensation. Coupled with previous rulings and factoring in salary losses from 1986 to 1990, the owners reached an agreement to pay the players union the staggering total of $280 million. In financial terms alone, the owners' collusion to violate baseball's basic labor agreement—in effect, a secret plan that not only cheated the players but arguably cheated fans from seeing the best possible home team on the field—surely ranks as the greatest scandal of baseball's modern era. The willingness of owners to undermine the basic agreement, despite the enormous financial and public relations cost of such high-risk sabotage, suggests the degree to which they are willing to take a hard line in labor negotiations with the players in the future. And the absence of a nominally independent commissioner to mediate those deep divisions virtually ensures economic controversy for years to come.

Gambling, Bribery, and Game-Fixing

Baseball's greatest scandal is unquestionably the fixing of the 1919 World Series, but the Black Sox scandal merely climaxed more than five decades of dubious collusion between players and gamblers. Half a century before the World Series fix, in 1872, the New York Times harumphed editorially that the aim of baseball was "to employ professional players to perspire in public for the benefit of gamblers . . ." Many small scandals lit the way to the disgrace of 1919.

Baseball began as a gentlemanly avocation, but any disputatious athletic event quickly caught the attention of gamblers. As early as 1857, crowds at Elysian Fields in Hoboken, New Jersey, one of amateur baseball's most hallowed venues, came to bet on games. It was but a short step from gambling to influencing the outcome of games. Soon word drifted eastward that gamblers on the West Coast were not averse to firing their guns into the air at crucial moments to disrupt the concentration of fielders— and, of course, to protect their investments.

A slang term, "hippodroming," soon emerged to indicate a game played with the illusion of spontaneity when, in fact, the outcome had already been fixed. Gamblers reportedly harassed members of the Brooklyn Excelsiors in an 1860 game with the Brooklyn Atlantics—after which the Excelsiors refused to play the Atlantics again. Another team, the Haymakers of Troy, New York, was suspected of hippodroming, largely because its owners included renowned New York gamblers like John Morris-

sey. Rumors of fixed games so dogged baseball in its early years that a Buffalo writer once suggested, "Any professional base ball club will 'throw' a game if there is money in it. A horse race is a pretty safe thing to speculate on, in comparison with an average ball match."

Gamblers freely circulated in baseball parks, occasioning such warnings as the BETTING POSITIVELY PROHIBITED sign that graced the wall of the Washington Nationals' ballpark in 1867. A forerunner of bookmaking, called pool selling, sprung up in conjunction with baseball, and by the 1870s as much as $70,000 might be riding on a single game. With all the betting, it was inevitable that gamblers would approach players with bribes—even during the "amateur" era. Players of that era—ill educated, often immigrants—were particularly susceptible; the under-the-table payments they received as amateurs did little to instill moral probity. Indeed, patronage jobs were often offered in lieu of outright salaries by such well-connected owners as Boss Tweed, part owner of the New York Mutuals. A lot of baseball players found well-paying jobs in such unlikely spots as the U.S. Treasury Department in Washington and the coroner's office in New York.

Indeed, a scant six years after the formation of the amateur National Association, organized baseball confronted its first gambling scandal. On September 28, 1865, the heavily favored New York Mutuals lost to the Brooklyn Eckfords, 28–11. It later developed that two Mutuals players, Ed Duffy and William Wansley, offered money to Mutuals shortstop Thomas Devyr to throw the game. For their role in the conspiracy, which was investigated by the Judicial Committee of the National Association, Duffy and Wansley were banned from match play; the Mutuals, in desperate need of a shortstop, helped to have charges against Devyr dismissed. By 1870, all three players had won reinstatement—a prophetic indication that organized baseball was not yet prepared to take a firm stand against gambling.

A little-known footnote to the amazing 60–0 season of the 1869 Cincinnati Red Stockings, baseball's first avowedly professional team, is that the lone blemish in their record came as the result of a tie with the hippodroming Haymakers of Troy, who walked off the field in the sixth inning of a 17–17 game on some reportedly dubious pretext to save their gambling bosses from a probable loss. Five years into the professional era, the legendary baseball writer Henry Chadwick felt compelled to charge in print that players were in cahoots with gamblers and had staged "rather questionable" games during the 1874 campaign. The charges remained just that—accusations—until the Louisville Grays scandal of 1877. It was, according to historian J. E. Findling, "the first documented case of player crookedness after the founding of the National League."

The senior circuit was barely a year old when Chadwick's worst fears came true. The National League had been organized in February of 1876, at least in part as a response to growing public disenchantment with baseball's wayward ways—the influence of gamblers, the appearance of fixed games, the drunken, salacious antics of players. In August of 1877 the league-leading Louisville Grays embarked on a long eastern road trip. After a disastrous stretch of seven losses and a tie, in part facilitated by suspiciously inept play, the team returned home.

Sportswriters openly hinted that Louisville had dumped its games and deliberately blown the pennant.

Since a Louisville newspaper magnate served as club president, the *Courier-Journal* ran speculative articles intended to smoke out the suspected fixers. The ploy worked when one of the players confessed. On October 30, 1877, the Louisville directors expelled four players—Jim "Terror" Devlin, George "Gentleman George" Hall, Bill "Butcher" Craver, and Al "Slippery Elm" Nichols—for life. Nichols, a utility player, had befriended a "pool seller" named James McCloud, who paid Devlin and Hall $100 to throw a game. An examination of Western Union telegrams conclusively established links between the gambler and the players. Craver refused to sign a loyalty oath, thus earning his expulsion, but Devlin, Hall, and Nichols were accused of selling games and "tampering with players." In their defense, they claimed that the Louisville management had failed to pay their salaries as promised—not an unlikely charge, given the parlous finances of the nineteenth-century clubs. All four were banned for life, and the Louisville Grays were disbanded before the start of the 1878 season. The *Louisville Courier-Journal* attributed the dissolution to "the rascality of last year's players and the general conviction that dishonest players on other clubs were more the rule than the exception . . ."

Umpires were not immune to the emoluments of gamblers either. As a player for the Chicago White Stockings, Richard Higham's desultory attitude and outright ineptitude had aroused suspicion. As umpire, Higham handled many games involving the Detroit Wolverines at the outset of the 1882 season, and a number of observers—including Wolverine owner William Thompson—believed that many of the close calls went against Detroit. Thompson, who also happened to be mayor of Detroit, assigned a private detective to investigate Higham. The detective ultimately uncovered the scam: Higham placed bets by telegram with a well-known gambler on the very games he was scheduled to umpire, then made calls favoring the team he'd bet on. Baseball officials confronted Higham with the evidence and banished him from the game. It represented no midlife crisis for Higham, however—he promptly became a bookie based in Chicago. This expulsion marks the only documented case of dishonesty by an umpire in the history of major league baseball.

The influence—or at least suspicion—of gambling did not subside after the Louisville Grays and Higham scandals. Contemporary commentators speak of "a little odor" hovering over the pennant races of 1891 and 1892, but no details ever emerged. Then, at the turn of the century, baseball took a two-decade running start toward the scandal that would forever blacken its name.

The lassitude with which baseball viewed the gambling establishment by 1900 affected every part of the game. Players openly associated with gamblers; and, indeed, in some cases that was a politic thing to do, for those gamblers happened to be team owners. The original bankrollers of the New York Highlanders, Frank Farrell and William "Big Bill" Devery, typified the unhealthy cross-pollination of sports and gaming. Devery went unbowed by his reputation as New York's most corrupt police commissioner, and Farrell's notorious gambling habits placed him many chits above the middling pool seller. One of

their favorite pals was the player known as "Prince Hal": Hal Chase, probably the most corrupt ballplayer ever.

Chase began his career with the Highlanders in 1905 and was an extraordinarily gifted fielder at first base. He was also a well-known gambler who thought nothing of betting on his own team, and sometimes even against it. Many of his managers—including George Stallings of the Highlanders, Frank Chance of the Yankees (as the Highlanders came to be called), and Christy Mathewson in Cincinnati—suggested at one time or another that he threw games. It is typical of the *laissez-faire* days before the Black Sox scandal that when Stallings publicly complained about Chase, American League President Ban Johnson did not investigate the alleged game fixing, but rather dressed down Chase's manager for smearing the reputation of a big gate attraction. By 1918, when he was suspended by the Reds for gambling and attempting to bribe an opposing pitcher, Chase's appearance on the field was sometimes greeted with cynical cries of "What are the odds?"

At least once, and probably on many occasions, Chase offered bribes to teammates and opposing players to give substandard performances. He concluded his malodorous career with the 1919 New York Giants; true to form, he was blacklisted from the game in February 1920. It later emerged that Chase and third baseman Heinie Zimmerman, who was indefinitely suspended by the Giants in September 1919, offered an $800 bribe to Giant pitcher Rube Benton to throw a game; bribes were also offered to Benny Kauff, Lee Magee, Fred Toney, and Jean Dubuc. Despite no public explanation, Giants manager John McGraw later suggested that Chase and Zimmerman's questionable play against Cincinnati helped the Reds win the pennant—lending, if true, a rarely noted but fitting symmetry to that year's corrupt World Series. Prince Hal's crowning achievement in this record of deceit was to bring gamblers and fixers together to throw the 1919 World Series.

Hal Chase's machinations were merely the most obvious symptoms of pervasive corruption in the period 1900–1920, according to baseball historian David Quentin Voight. There was a reported attempt to bribe players in the first two World Series, in 1903 and 1905; in the former year, Boston catcher Lou Criger was offered a bribe to "lay down," while in the latter year, Philadelphia pitcher Rube Waddell did not play due to an injury, when he had allegedly received a $17,000 offer not to play. It was widely believed that gamblers tried to fix the 1908 season. In 1916, the New York Giants were rumored to have helped the Dodgers beat out the Phillies in the pennant race, and the 1918 World Series may have been tampered with as well. There was even the bizarre attempt, on the last day of the 1910 season, to bribe an official scorer, so that Cleveland's popular Nap Lajoie could beat out the detested Ty Cobb for the batting crown. The unsuccessful attempt—to change an error into a hit for Lajoie—resulted in dismissal for St. Louis Browns coach Harry Howell; St. Louis manager Jack O'Connor, too, got fired for ordering his third baseman to play so deep that Lajoie got seven bunt singles in the season-ending doubleheader. Yet these transgressions were more of degree than nature. Since at least the 1890s, it was commonplace for teams to reward opposition players with clothes, cigars, even money for a good performance against rivals; it no doubt took but a short step to rewarding bad performances as well.

All the corruption came home to roost in 1919. Even before the very first pitch had been thrown in what became Cincinnati's "improbable" World Series victory over the Chicago White Sox, rumors swirled that the fix was on. It took a year for the rumors to come true. The initial reaction was to dismiss the allegations, including reports that gamblers had offered Cincinnati pitcher Hod Eller a $5,000 bribe which he turned down.

But the 1920 season was a cauldron of renewed rumors of bribery and game fixing. No less than seven clubs—the Giants, Cubs, Yankees, Braves, Red Sox, Indians, and White Sox—were suspected of throwing games that season. Cub players Lee Magee and Claude Hendrix were blacklisted, Hendrix toward the end of the 1920 season for trying to fix a game with the Phillies. Finally, in September 1920, a Chicago grand jury convened to investigate charges about the 1919 World Series. Meanwhile, an article appeared on September 27, 1920, in the *Philadelphia North American* in which local gambler Bill Maharg went beyond innuendo and blew open the scandal. Maharg described how White Sox pitcher Eddie Cicotte volunteered to fix the Series; how Maharg and his partner, former major leaguer Billy Burns, promised to pay $100,000 to eight White Sox players; how the gamblers double-crossed the players by paying them only $10,000 at first; how the players double-crossed the gamblers by winning a game they were supposed to lose; and how Burns and Maharg got double-crossed by a rival fixer, New York gambler (and former boxing champion) Abe Attell, who *also* was bribing the players. The following day, Cicotte agreed to testify to the grand jury and named the names ever after branded the "Black Sox": pitchers Cicotte and Claude Williams, batting star Joe Jackson, infielders Buck Weaver (who had "guilty knowledge" of the fix but refused to take part in it), Swede Risberg, and Chick Gandil, outfielder Oscar "Happy" Felsch, and even a utility man, Fred McMullin. Not only did they throw the 1919 World Series to the Reds, but, in a disreputable postscript to their season of infamy, they dumped the 1920 pennant race to the Indians, too.

In grand jury testimony, Gandil emerged as the ringleader, pocketing $35,000. Cicotte received $10,000; Jackson got $5,000 (he was earning about $6,000 a year from the tight-fisted White Sox owner Charles Comiskey). Arnold Rothstein, the notorious gangster, reputedly masterminded the fix, although his role was never legally proven and he was never charged with a crime. The scandal left no one untainted. Joe Jackson wrote a letter to Comiskey shortly after the calamitous Series, stating that the Series outcome was questionable and volunteering to meet with the owner to provide details, but Comiskey—said to be concerned about the effect of such revelations on attendance and profits, not to mention his equity in the franchise—never followed up on Jackson's offer.

Following the mysterious disappearance of their confessions and other legal skullduggery, the "eight" Black Sox won acquittal during their June 1921 conspiracy trial; none of the big-fish gamblers and fixers went to trial. But the newly appointed baseball commissioner, Kenesaw Mountain Landis, in an extraordinarily usurptive move

aimed at restoring public confidence in the game, suspended all eight players for life. The sentence was particularly brutal for Weaver, who had not participated in the scam, and Jackson. "Shoeless Joe," in throwing the series, batted .375, and it was his apparently accurate throw to the plate in the tense fourth game, inexplicably cut off by pitcher Cicotte, which convinced cognoscenti in the stands beyond a doubt that the White Sox were deliberately tossing the games. In the roundelay of accusations that later emerged, Rube Benton charged that Hal Chase made $40,000 betting on the Reds; others charged that Benton knew of the fix and had made $3,200; and St. Louis infielder Joe Gedeon won $600 following a tip from Swede Risberg.

Bill James, in his *Historical Baseball Abstract,* estimates that a total of thirty-eight major league ballplayers were implicated in scandals during the period 1917–1927, and that nineteen were formally banned or effectively blacklisted (James's list includes several players, however, who were suspended not for corruption, but for such offenses as contract jumping). In addition to the Chase and Black Sox scandals, James cites the allegations of Jimmy O'Connell, who claimed to have offered $500 to Philadelphia player Heinie Sand to fix a game in 1924; O'Connell and Giants coach Cozy Dolan were banned for life, but Frankie Frisch denied he'd known about the fix.

Under Landis's stern tutelage, baseball took a far less tolerant view of gamblers, though tales of the corrupt teens continued to trickle out. In 1926, player-managers Ty Cobb of the Tigers and Tris Speaker of the Indians both resigned under a cloud; the public later learned that ex-pitcher Dutch Leonard alleged that they had conspired to fix the last game of the 1919 season so that Detroit could win third-place money and that Smoky Joe Wood allegedly placed bets for Cobb and Speaker. And in 1927, "Black Sox" Swede Risberg publicly charged that some fifty players had known of a four-game series in 1917 that the Tigers threw to the White Sox.

Compared to the tormented twenties, the Depression and war years seemed peaceably upright. But never entirely so. In 1943, for example, Phillies owner William D. Cox received a swift and permanent suspension from Landis for betting on Philadelphia games. It would be perhaps naive to think that Landis's crowd-pleasing gestures totally eliminated gambling from the game, but they certainly sent a message to players and administrators alike that, if caught, the price would be steep. The antigambling fervor carried over into the commissionership of A. B. "Happy" Chandler, who in the spring of 1947 suspended Brooklyn manager Leo Durocher for one year for "conduct detrimental to baseball." Personality clashes and baseball politics apparently influenced Chandler's decision, but he had previously warned Durocher against associating with gamblers and other "unsavory" characters, including actor George Raft. Durocher, not heeding the warning, had actually been living in Raft's home the previous fall.

Commissioner Bowie Kuhn prided himself on an aggressive Landis-style stance against even the *appearance* of association with gamblers, and so in 1969 presented an ultimatum to four prominent baseball people, including Oakland owner Charles O. Finley and Atlanta Brave directors Bill Bartholomay, John Louis, and Del Coleman.

All four had interests in the Parvin-Dohrmann Co., which owned and operated the Fremont, Stardust, and Aladdin casinos in Las Vegas. Faced with choosing baseball or gaming, Finley sold his stock, and all but Coleman resigned their directorships. Somewhat more controversial (and problematic) was Kuhn's insistence that players or coaches employed by baseball teams could not accept public relations work at casinos. Thus Mets batting instructor Willie Mays (in 1979) and Yankee spring training instructor Mickey Mantle (in 1983) were forced to give up their baseball jobs in order to serve as greeters at Atlantic City casinos. Shortly after Kuhn left office, incoming Commissioner Peter Ueberroth revoked the orders.

Baseball's next great gambling scandal unwittingly reaffirmed the old Graig Nettles adage about going from Cy Young to Sayonara. Detroit pitcher Denny McLain made the trip in four years, winning the prestigious award outright in 1968 with a 31–6 record and sharing it again in 1969, only to bounce out of the majors by 1972. Around the beginning of 1970, word circulated that a Detroit grand jury had begun investigating McLain. Against a backdrop of personal financial difficulties, McLain's rumored involvement with gamblers prompted a meeting with Bowie Kuhn, at which the pitcher admitted investing $5,700 in a bookmaking operation at a bar he frequented in Flint, Michigan. The confession preceded by several days a *Sports Illustrated* article on February 17, 1970, which described McLain's involvement in the bookmaking operation. The article went on to suggest that when McLain failed to pay out $46,600 on a winning bet in 1967, organized crime enforcer Tony Giacalone allegedly stomped on the pitcher's foot, dislocating several toes and causing him to miss at least two September starts during Detroit's heated pennant race with Boston. The article further alleged that Detroit mobster Billy Giacalone, brother of Tony, bet heavily on Boston to win the pennant, and also against Detroit in their final game of the season, which McLain started and the Tigers lost; in all, McLain lost his last three decisions of the 1967 season. The bookie connection and the allegations earned an indefinite suspension from Kuhn, although the commissioner later stated there was no proof of McLain's having bet on baseball games.

Unindicted but never clear of the clouds over his head, McLain returned to the Tigers in July. He received two more suspensions that season amid increasingly bizarre behavior: threatening a parking lot attendant, dumping a bucket of ice water on two sportswriters, and violating federal law by carrying a gun on a commercial airliner. McLain was traded to the Senators, and tried comebacks with Oakland and Atlanta before bouncing entirely out of baseball in 1972. In 1985, he was found guilty in a Florida trial and sentenced to twenty-three years in jail on charges of racketeering, loan sharking, extortion, and possession of cocaine with intent to distribute. After serving nearly thirty months, McLain won his appeal and regained freedom. (Late in 1988, however, he pled guilty to several of the charges and once again faced a jail term.) In allegedly dabbling both in gambling and drugs, McLain bridged the gap between baseball's more traditional vices and the modern fascination with controlled substances.

Even McLain's peccadilloes pale compared to those of

Pete Rose. It is difficult to choose one aspect of the Rose scandal that is richer with outrage or pathos than another: that the greatest hitter the game has seen would be forced to peddle, reportedly because of gambling debts, the bat with which he broke Ty Cobb's seemingly unassailable hit record; that "Charlie Hustle," the quintessential gamer, was banned for life from the game; that the rough-hewn moptop who played with such boyish abandon would end up in jail with the most hardened of men. But all the career hits (4,256), all the career games (3,562), all twelve major league records provided no immunity when Peter Edward Rose was permanently banned from baseball on August 24, 1989. It represented baseball's darkest moment since the Black Sox scandal of 1919.

No one knows when Rose's gambling problems got out of control; his legal problems with baseball began to surface in February 1989, when then-commissioner Peter Ueberroth called him to a meeting in New York—a meeting, it was soon reported, to discuss allegations of gambling. Press reports began to appear soon thereafter describing Rose's predilection for dog races and horse tracks, and then the commissioner's office confirmed that a special investigation was underway. In selecting John Dowd to head the probe, baseball entrusted its inquiry to a man who had successfully investigated a sitting FBI director (Clarence Kelley, ultimately dismissed for improprieties) and a sitting congressman (Rep. Daniel Flood, ultimately convicted of illegal campaign contributions). Dowd would not submit the results of his investigation until May 9, but in the course of its preparation, he interviewed and deposed more than half a dozen figures who professed knowledge of Rose's gambling activities.

On March 21, *Sports Illustrated* published a well-documented investigative article reporting that Rose bet on baseball games—a violation of baseball rule 21(d), which states that any player who bets on a game "shall be declared ineligible for one year" and any player who bets on his own team "shall be declared permanently ineligible." These public allegations of improprieties mirrored the charges privately being assembled by Dowd. But on April 18, 1989, the new commissioner, A. Bartlett Giamatti, committed a legal blunder that provided Rose's lawyers with the maneuvering room that allowed them to keep the issue churning in court, and on the front pages, all summer. In a letter to a federal judge in charge of sentencing one of Dowd's sources, an Ohio bookmaker named Ron Peters, Giamatti wrote that Peters had been "candid, forthright and truthful . . ." That last word, "truthful," with its implication that Giamatti accepted the veracity of Peters' allegation before hearing Rose's side of the story, allowed Rose and his lawyers to claim that Giamatti had prejudged the case. Indeed, when Giamatti requested Rose to appear at a May 25 hearing, Rose's lawyers asked for a thirty-day postponement and laid the grounds for an epic lawsuit that would challenge the very authority of the commissioner's office to rule on his—and, by implication, any player's—fate. The battle thus joined, it overshadowed the season for the next four months.

It was a classic battle pitting two considerable antagonists. Giamatti was erudite but tough, well spoken, as blue blood as the son of an immigrant could get, a Renaissance scholar conversant with the sense as well as the syntax of Macchiavelli, a man with an almost poetic love of the

game; Rose was the diehard, in-your-face burr-headed hustler, blue-collar and rough-edged, not terribly conversant with the kings's English, but willing to do anything to win. For all that, Rose's lawyers sought an early settlement in April, but discussions broke down and they filed suit against baseball on June 19, 1989, challenging Giamatti's ability to be fair and requesting a temporary restraining order barring the commissioner from holding his scheduled June 26 hearing with Rose. In granting the request on June 26, Hamilton County Common Pleas Court Judge Norbert A. Nadel ruled that Giamatti had prejudged the case. The stunning decision, widely criticized at the time, nonetheless raised the stakes considerably. Rose's suit, in effect, challenged the right of the baseball commissioner to adjudicate internal matters—threatened, in short, to chisel away at the bedrock on which the authority of baseball rests, and of which the sport, understandably, is most loathe to entertain the slightest erosion.

The Nadel ruling triggered a furious round of legal thrusts and parries by both sides that lasted nearly two months. As is often the case, broad issues took a back seat to nuts-and-bolts skirmishes over jurisdiction. Organized baseball methodically won these skirmishes. Baseball's lawyers got Rose's suit against Giamatti assigned to a federal court, and U.S. District Court Judge John Holschuh scheduled a hearing for August 28 on Rose's request. Once the case moved to federal court, historically sympathetic to baseball's arguments of self-administration, Rose faced a difficult legal battle, at enormous cost, to pursue the issue, and it is believed that this contributed to his decision to reach a settlement.

With the distraction of court arguments and rulings and reassignments, it was easy to forget that the Rose case was ultimately about gambling, not the authority of the commissioner. One day after his June 26 ruling, Judge Nadel was compelled to make public—against both his and baseball's wishes—the report compiled by John Dowd. This 225-page report, and seven supporting volumes of evidence, provided a comprehensive and devastating portrait of Rose the Gambler in the years 1985–87.

The Dowd report revealed that Rose routinely bet not only on baseball games (typically $2,000 per game), but that he bet on Cincinnati games—a violation of baseball rules that would automatically draw a permanent expulsion from the game. In the first three months of the 1987 season alone, for example, gambling records indicated that Rose bet on the Reds to win fifty-two times, winning twenty-nine times (there was no evidence that Rose bet against his own team). He typically used intermediaries named Thomas Gioiosa or Paul Janszen, both convicted felons and both destined to join the names Abe Attell and Bill Maharg in the tainted pantheon of baseball low-lifes; these gambling gofers would then place Rose's bets either with Ohio bookie Ron Peters or an unnamed bookmaker in Staten Island, N.Y. Baseball investigators obtained dated betting slips in Rose's handwriting—and, according to an FBI analysis cited in the *New York Times*, with Rose's fingerprints—to document his gambling activities.

Rose's gambling habits were certainly out of control by 1985. Gambling debts in fall 1985 forced Rose to borrow $47,000 from Michael Fry, who authorities allege was

involved in a cocaine ring operating between Florida and southwest Ohio; Rose reportedly came under investigation for involvement in the drug ring, though no charges were ever filed. Among the nine individuals making allegations against Rose, however, his principal accusers—Gioiosa, Peters, Janszen, and Fry—all faced legal difficulties and had reason to seek the leniency of the courts. Their testimony was never challenged by Rose's representatives in a hearing.

Through it all, Rose—firm of jaw, defiant as ever—steadfastly denied he had ever bet on baseball. But behind the scenes, with damaging evidence and legal costs mounting, Rose's lawyers once again approached the commissioner's office in mid-July with a proposed settlement. The sticking point was Rose's refusal to admit he bet on baseball games. Only after Rose's lawsuit was headed for federal court did a settlement get ironed out. On August 24, 1989, a grim and infamous Thursday in baseball history, A. Barlett Giamatti announced "the sad end of a sorry episode" by declaring Pete Rose "permanently ineligible" for employment in baseball—the most prolific hitter in the game, banned for life.

As part of the settlement, the language of the agreement did not explicitly accuse Rose of betting on baseball games, only of "conduct not to be in the best interests of Baseball." In exchange for that legalistic blurring of culpability, Rose agreed to drop all litigation against Giamatti, acknowledged that the commissioner had acted in good faith and had sole and exclusive authority to decide the issue. Rose neither denied nor admitted he bet on baseball (not since Spiro Agnew had nolo contendere boasted such a celebrated practitioner). Then Giamatti went and undid all the legal tiptoeing, in reply to a question at the ensuing press conference, by saying yes, his personal opinion was that Rose bet on baseball, Reds games included. Rose, stung, felt he'd been betrayed. Under the rules of baseball, Rose was eligible to apply for reinstatement after one year. "The burden to show a redirected, reconfigured, or rehabilitated life," Giamatti told reporters, "is entirely Pete Rose's." Three months later, Rose publicly admitted he had a gambling problem.

The settlement was widely viewed as a complete capitulation by Rose. But not everyone viewed Rose's lawsuit as frivolous. In the view of *Los Angeles Times* columnist Jim Murray, for example, "Baseball commissioner Giamatti just wanted to get the matter out of the courts. Baseball fears the courts the way safecrackers do." Was a deal struck? Giamatti emphatically denied it at the time. At least three newspapers—the *Los Angeles Times*, *Chicago Tribune*, and *Dayton Daily News*—quoted sources on the eve of the August 24 announcement saying that Rose agreed to a settlement only when the commissioner agreed that the expulsion would not be permanent. In the unlikely event that a deal was struck, Giamatti may well have taken the secret with him to the grave, for he died of a heart attack little more than a week after the decision was rendered.

Will Pete Rose make it back into baseball's graces? Precedent suggests not. Of the fourteen people previously booted out of the game, none has ever won reinstatement. Circumstances suggest not. One of the negotiators who represented baseball and worked on the Rose settlement reportedly took the position that Rose shouldn't even be allowed to *apply* for reinstatement for seven years; that negotiator was Francis (Fay) Vincent, who succeeded Giamatti as commissioner. And Rose's subsequent problems suggest not. In April 1990 Rose pled guilty in federal court to two counts of filing false income tax returns, dating back to 1985 and 1987, and in July he received a sentence of five months in the federal minimum security Correctional Institution Camp in Marion, Illinois. In July he received a sentence of five months in jail and fines of $50,000.

On August 8, 1990, shortly after noon, Rose began serving his five month sentence for tax evasion in the minimum-security federally run Southern Illinois Prison Camp in Marion, Illinois, where he wore jersey number 01832061 and worked as a welder in the prison machine shop. Following his release on January 7, 1991, Rose returned to Cincinnati and served an additional three months in the Talbert House halfway house, performing 1,000 hours of community service as part of his sentence. He continued to appear at autograph and card shows, although he needed to obtain permission from his parole officer to leave Cincinnati. He was eligible to apply for reinstatement one year after Giamatti's expulsion, but through the end of 1992 had declined to do so.

While still serving his sentence, Rose's hopes of eventually making his way into the Hall of Fame suffered a serious setback. The board of directors of the Hall of Fame, in an attempt to preempt the baseball writers from even considering Rose's induction, voted 12–0 in February 1991 to amend the institution's by-laws so that anyone deemed ineligible to work in baseball would be similarly ineligible for the Hall of Fame. According to some press reports, then-commissioner Vincent was behind the recommended rule change, although Vincent rejected that suggestion. Museum officials insisted that the rule change was unrelated to Rose's situation, although the Hall had existed peaceably for fifty-five seasons without the clarification. "I don't remember his name being specifically mentioned," Hall of Fame president Edward Stack told the press. Stack also clarified the policy of continuing to display Rose memorabilia in the National Baseball Museum. "Rose's bats are all right," he said, "but Rose isn't."

Rose has consistently referred to baseball's judgment as a "suspension," and he remarked at the time of the August 24 settlement that "to think that I'll be out of baseball for a very short time hurts." This seeming belief in the ban's temporary nature may simply reflect the same fierce denial that fueled Rose in his battle against the game. Whatever the decision, the hurt it causes Pete Rose can be inferred from a remark Charlie Hustle made earlier in his career. "I'd go through hell in a gasoline suit," he said, "to play baseball."

Nor can it be said that Rose's penalty served as a deterrent to would-be gamblers. In 1991 Philadelphia outfielder Lenny Dykstra, embarking on a troubled season that would include a near-fatal car wreck, received a year's probation from the commissioner for gambling activities. Dykstra's losing touch came to public attention in March of 1991, when he testified at the federal trial of Herbert Kelso, a man accused of running a betting parlor in Indianola, Mississippi. Dykstra revealed that he had dropped at least $78,000 in gambling losses to Kelso between 1988 and 1990.

In August of 1991, the New York *Times* reported that one National League umpire and one American League umpire had been placed on one-year probation, dating from December 1990, for gambling. The paper quoted sources saying the two umpires, whose identities have never been revealed, placed "relatively small bets" on non-baseball sporting events; their telephone numbers turned up when federal investigators tapped a bookie's phone.

Alcohol and Controlled Substances

John Barleycorn's name has never been entered into a major league scorecard, but alcohol has undoubtedly affected the outcome of games and certainly determined the length of careers. Two anecdotes a century apart suggest just how endemic drink—and drunks—have been to the game. When the Philadelphia Athletics won the pennant in 1871 (and in those days, it was a *real* pennant), the flag flew not from a stadium flagpole, nor did someone hoist it up in the clubhouse. No, it was promptly hung in a Philadelphia saloon. In 1974, after both Whitey Ford and Mickey Mantle won election to the Hall of Fame, restauranteur Toots Shor remarked, "It shows what you can accomplish if you stay up all night drinking whiskey all the time." In the 1970s and 1980s, drug use by the players became pervasive, leading to baseball's worst scandal since the days of the Black Sox.

Nineteenth-century ballplayers were inordinately fond of what they called "German tea," and "lushers" were common on every team. In 1880, in a dispute as political as it was moral, the Cincinnati ball club was expelled from the National League for selling liquor at the stadium (as well as for playing on Sunday). Shortly before his death in 1882, National League president William A. Hulbert issued lifetime suspensions to the "ten chronic lushers" in the league. "Drinking, late hours, and wenching were more common in the early decades of professionalism than they are now," historian Harold Seymour wrote in 1963, "or at least more regularly publicized in the newspapers."

Drinking by ballplayers had become so bad that it had attracted the notice and interest of temperance groups, as well as self-ordained protectors of the game's image. Thus in the 1880s, *The Sporting News* attacked such popular gate attractions as Mike "King" Kelly, Jim McCormick, Pete Browning, and Curt Welch for their notorious drinking. The most flagrant violator was probably Welch. An outfielder for St. Louis, Welch could be seen out in the field sneaking sips of beer, which he hid behind the billboards of Sportsman's Park. This may in part explain why he was known for his circus catches.

In 1886, Chicago White Stockings owner A. G. Spalding went on the warpath against his boozing players. He dangled $350 bonuses in front of two of his stars, Kelly and McCormick, if they would curtail their heavy drinking. They did not. Prior to their departure for spring training that year, the White Stockings even gathered en masse in Spalding's sporting goods store in Chicago to take public vows of temperence, with Chicago manager Adrian "Cap" Anson administering the oaths. Spalding then packed them off to the thermal waters of Hot Springs, Arkansas; the express purpose, according to one

writer, was "to boil out the alcoholic microbes." Lushing being a league-wide problem, many teams added Hot Springs to their February itineraries.

Many outstanding players have achieved notoriety with their drinking escapades. Chicago manager Anson got into a drunken fistfight in a saloon and was arrested on one occasion; Rube Waddell, the turn-of-the-century left-hander, often disappeared after long benders. The most tragic victim of drinking may well have been Ed Delahanty. Suspended by the Washington Senators for disciplinary problems in Detroit in July of 1903, Big Ed headed back east by train, got drunk and abusive on board, and had to be put off in Canada, just north of the Niagara River. He started to walk across the railroad bridge that led to the U.S., got into a tussle with the night watchman, and tumbled into the Niagara River; eight days later, his body washed up below Niagara Falls, some eleven miles downstream from the bridge.

In the era of prohibition, Babe Ruth was a walking advertisement for the ease with which alcohol could be obtained. That fine Yankee tradition was upheld by Mantle and Ford, aided and abetted by their drinking partner Billy Martin. But alcoholism unquestionably shortened the career of Cub outfielder Hack Wilson, and drinking problems came to be associated with such players as Paul Waner, Jimmie Foxx, Don Newcombe, Ryne Duren, and Dennis Martinez, to mention but a few. For many decades, during which sportswriting shared more with hagiography than journalism, incidents of alcohol abuse never reached the public. It could be argued that only upon the publication of *Ball Four* by Jim Bouton in 1970 did the hangover earn its rightful spot in the locker room.

While baseball clubs naturally condemned alcohol and drug use, teams continued to sell beer in the stands, of course. This hypocritical policy reached a sodden apotheosis on June 4, 1974, in Cleveland's Municipal Stadium, when the Indians sponsored a 10¢ beer night. Increasingly rowdy as the game progressed, drunken Cleveland fans spilled out onto the field and pelted the visiting Texas Rangers with firecrackers. By the bottom of the ninth inning of a 5–5 game, dozens of fans streamed onto the field, threatened Texas players, and ignited a riot requiring police action to quell. Cleveland lost the game on a forfeit.

Alcohol abuse continued to be a problem into the 1980s. In 1980, Dodger pitcher Bob Welch publicly acknowledged a drinking problem that occasioned a five-week stay in The Meadows, which would become a popular substance-abuse treatment center. That same year, Kansas City catcher Darrell Porter checked in for drug and alcohol counseling. Among major leaguers who recently faced charges of driving under the influence of alcohol were Braves players Brian Hunter and Keith Mitchell and Angels relief pitcher Bryan Harvey; in addition, Indians outfielder Albert Belle spent ten weeks in an alcohol rehabilitation program during the summer of 1990.

Without a doubt, however, Philadelphia outfielder Lenny "Nails" Dykstra gave the loudest seminar on the risks of driving while intoxicated. Early in the morning of May 6, 1991, while he and teammate Darren Daulton were returning from a bachelor party for Phillies player John Kruk, Dykstra lost control of his brand new Merce-

des sports car. The car slammed sideways into two trees, and Dykstra suffered fractures of the right collarbone, right cheekbone, and three ribs, also puncturing a lung; Daulton broke a bone below his left eye. Police charged Dykstra with driving under the influence, reckless driving, and driving at an unsafe speed. "Nails" served as a negative role model on two counts: his blood-alcohol level, according to police, measured eight beers an hour for a man his size, and he neglected (as did Daulton) to wear a seat belt. Phillies team physician Phillip Marone said, "If they don't go to church, they better start because they're very lucky."

Baseball players reflected general social trends with their increasing experimentation with drugs during the 1960s and 1970s, although a lot of disposable income and free time contributed to crash courses in recreational pharmacology. Access to drugs was easy. Many players routinely used "greenies," amphetamine-barbiturate combos, that allegedly gave them a lift before games. In some cases, the pills were distributed by club physicians, and the problem had become sufficiently widespread that in 1971 Commissioner Bowie Kuhn instituted baseball's first Drug Education and Prevention Program. Its effectiveness was questionable: in 1980, the team physician for the Phillies' Reading farm team was arrested for illegally writing prescriptions for amphetamines. The charges were later dismissed, but the doctor, Patrick A. Mazza, testified that he prescribed the pep pills at the request of seven Philadelphia players.

Baseball formally entered the era of mind-altering drugs on August 25, 1980, when Texas pitcher Ferguson Jenkins was arrested at the Toronto airport for possession of two ounces of marijuana, two grams of hashish, and four grams of cocaine; he was later found guilty of cocaine possession. Unofficially, baseball had tipped its hand during the previous decade. Pitcher Bill Lee, then of Montreal, had openly admitted use of marijuana. More startlingly, Pittsburg pitcher Dock Ellis, reportedly suffering a hangover on a day he didn't expect to pitch, flung a no-hitter (with eight walks) against the San Diego Padres on June 12, 1970. Ellis later denied that he was working on a hangover; he was working, rather, on a tab of LSD.

By the 1980s, the list of baseball's drug abusers began to read like a crime wave in a "good neighborhood." July 1982—San Diego infielder Alan Wiggins was arrested for cocaine possession. November 1982—Dodger relief pitcher Steve Howe began the first of three treatment regimens for drug abuse, which culminated with his suspension for the entire 1984 season. October 1983—four Kansas City Royal players (Willie Aikens, Vida Blue, Jerry Martin, and Willie Wilson) pled guilty to charges of attempting to possess cocaine and later served time in prison. January 1984—Atlanta pitcher Pascual Perez was arrested in the Dominican Republic with half of a gram of cocaine; found guilty, he paid about $400 in fines. May 1984—Anthony J. Peters, a former ice cream salesman in Milwaukee, received twenty-two years in jail for selling cocaine; at least ten players on the Milwaukee Brewers, Chicago White Sox, and Cleveland Indians were customers, and players Dick Davis, Paul Molitor, and Claudell Washington all reportedly admitted cocaine use during interviews with federal agents. In 1985 San Francisco outfielder Chili Davis publicly admitted using cocaine in 1983, but stopped when the Federal Bureau of Investigation reportedly questioned him about it.

These incidents were symptomatic of the widespread drug use that became a matter of record in the celebrated drug trials of 1985. In the spring of that year, a federal grand jury in Pittsburg heard testimony from eleven active major league players, resulting in a May 31, 1985, indictment of seven drug dealers who associated with players from December 1979 to January 1985. The dealers had access to the clubhouse and team flights of the Pittsburgh Pirates, and in one of the more bizarre twists on baseball's already bizarre modern-day marketing, FBI agents wired the Pittsburgh mascot, the Pirate Parrot, to obtain evidence used in the indictments.

During the trials in September, seven active or former players testified under grants of immunity: Dale Berra (Yankees), Enos Cabell (L.A. Dodgers), Keith Hernandez (Mets), Jeff Leonard (S.F. Giants), John Milner (ex-Pirate), Dave Parker (Reds), and Lonnie Smith (Cardinals). All confessed to extensive drug use, and several implicated peers during their testimony. Milner, for example, indicated that former Pittsburgh teammates Parker, Berra, Lee Lacy, and Rod Scurry used cocaine during the 1981 and 1982 seasons. Parker and Berra testified that Pirate stars Bill Madlock and Willie Stargell distributed amphetamines to team players (a charge denied by the two, who were never prosecuted); Parker also said he had arranged sales of cocaine to Dusty Baker, Steve Howe, and Derrell Thomas of the Dodgers as well as Cabell and J. R. Richard of the Astros. Smith and Hernandez implicated their former Cardinal teammate Joaquin Andujar. In gripping testimony, Hernandez described cocaine as "the devil on this earth" and shocked observers by estimating that by 1980 40 percent of all major league baseball players used cocaine.

Not a single player went on trial, however. Pittsburgh juries separately convicted part-time caterer Curtis Strong of Philadelphia and Robert McCue of drug-trafficking charges. Free-lance photographer Dale Shiffman of Pittsburgh and Philadelphia salesman Shelby Greer pled guilty and received sentences of twelve years, and three other Pittsburgh men entered guilty pleas. (In a tragic footnote to the Pittsburgh drug trials, the former Pirate Scurry died November 5, 1992 in Reno, Nevada at age thirty-six, a week after falling into a coma while scuffling with police officers. The police had responded to calls from neighbors and found Scurry outside his home, reportedly complaining that snakes were crawling through the house and biting him.)

In a 1985 interview with the *New York Times,* Montreal President John McHale flatly stated that cocaine use by eight of his players cost the Expos the National League Eastern Division race in 1982. Drug use was so widespread and casual, according to Lonnie Smith, that opposing players sometimes exchanged information on drug availability when they met at midfield during pregame warmup sprints. The extent of the involvement became pathetically clear when Montreal outfielder Tim Raines, the National League's leading base stealer, admitted that he often slid headfirst into second base during a steal so as to protect the gram bottle of cocaine he kept in his back pocket.

And still the roll call continued. Two former Cy Young winners, LaMarr Hoyt of San Diego and Dwight Gooden of the New York Mets, became involved in drug use. Gooden underwent treatment for cocaine and missed the first six weeks of the 1987 season. Hoyt served time for drug trafficking following his release by the Padres in 1987. Dale Berra, Yogi's son and one of the "Pittsburgh Seven," faced renewed difficulties when he was arrested at his New Jersey home for possession of cocaine with intent to sell in April 1990.

Drug use interrupted the careers of several prominent players in the early 1990s, but in a tragic intrusion of real life into the game of boys, drug abuse was apparently linked to baseball's first victim of acquired immune deficiency syndrome, or AIDS. Former San Diego infielder Alan Wiggins, a star on the Padres team that went to the World Series in 1984, died on January 6, 1991 of an AIDS-related pneumonia, according to the Los Angeles *Times* and other press reports. In addition to his arrest for cocaine possession in 1982, Wiggins suffered a drug-related relapse in 1985 and reportedly failed a drug test while with the Orioles, leading to his indefinite suspension from baseball on August 31, 1987. Only thirty-two years old, the fleet and gifted athlete had wasted away to only seventy-five pounds at the time of death.

Two notable drug casualties were Atlanta's Otis Nixon, enjoying his best season in the majors at the time of his suspension, and Yankee relief pitcher Steve Howe. Nixon, who had pled guilty to a reduced charge related to drug possession in 1987 while in Cleveland's minor league system, was leading the majors in stolen bases when he reportedly tested positive for cocaine on September 7, 1991. Following a second positive test, commissioner Vincent suspended Nixon for sixty days. Nixon, who had passed more than 250 drug tests since the 1987 incident, later told the Atlanta *Journal-Constitution* that a pharmacist friend had suggested imbibing a concoction of herbal tea and vinegar to mask his drug use.

After enjoying a remarkable comeback season in 1991 and having signed a contract that could pay him up to $2.5 million for the 1992 season, Howe, the southpaw stopper, simply couldn't slam the door on his own addiction. He was arrested on December 19, 1991 in Kalispell, Montana, near his off-season home, when he attempted to buy a gram of cocaine from an underground drug agent for $100. Howe pled innocent to two federal charges, one of attempt to buy and the other of possession of two grams of cocaine, but after considerable legal maneuverings he pled guilty to one misdemeanor count of possession in June 1992. Vincent promptly banned the six-time offender for life, but at this writing an arbitrator has given Howe yet another reprieve. Speaking of Otis Nixon's problems with a reporter, Howe once remarked, "It's an addiction, it's something you can't control. Your rationality is gone. You don't think of anything else. If you haven't done it, you can't understand. You just can't."

The ever-vigilant New Jersey authorities also busted White Sox outfielder Dan Pasqua in October 1991, for receiving a shipment of marijuana in the mail at his Dumont, New Jersey home. Several other players tested positive for drug use, including Montreal catcher Gilberto Reyes (his sixty-day suspension in 1992 was overturned by an arbitrator following a grievance proceeding), Yan-

kee pitcher Pasqual Perez (who received a one-year suspension in March of 1992), and Giant outfielder Rick Leach (suspended for sixty days in August 1991 and then released by the team the following spring).

Brawlers, Perverts, Felons and Fellow Travelers

From the origins of baseball until well into the 1890s, baseball players were regarded mainly as roughnecks, quick to anger, quicker to fight. Fans were rowdy, and brawls between players and the public were not unusual (a doozy occurred in Louisville in 1896, when the bellicose Cleveland Spiders, protesting the umpire's decision to call the game, sparked a riot that required police intervention—and landed all the Spiders in jail). In 1904, during a spring training exhibition game in Mobile, Alabama, the New York Giants became so enraged by the calls of a hometown umpire that they finally attacked the man and beat him unconscious. John McGraw hustled his team out of town, even as warrants were being sworn for the players' arrest.

Sometimes the violence has been more serious. In 1883, former National League pitcher Terry Larkin shot his wife Catherine after she complained about his drinking. In the game's goriest story, Marty Bergen, became baseball's first and only ax murderer in January of 1900, when he killed his wife and two children in North Brookfield, Massachusetts, before committing suicide. In 1917, in a crime with racial overtones, Milwaukee (of the American Association) manager Danny Shay shot and killed a black waiter in an Indianapolis hotel during an argument over the amount of sugar in a sugar bowl; Shay was later acquitted.

Debt, the impending end of his career, and an unfortunate pitch that he couldn't take back apparently pushed former Angels relief pitcher Donnie Moore, thirty-five, over the brink in July 1989. Moore shot his wife of sixteen years, Tonya, three times with a pistol during an argument at their suburban Anaheim home, then shot himself in the head in front of his three children and died instantly (his wife survived). Beset with financial difficulties and marital problems, Moore never recovered from surrendering a two-out, two-strike home run to Dave Henderson in the 1986 American League Championship Series, which allowed Boston to tie a game they later won in extra innings. Moore blamed himself too harshly, though, because the Red Sox had to win two more games (which they did) to go on to the World Series. "I think insanity set in," David Pinter, Moore's agent, later told the press. "He could not live with himself after Henderson hit the home run. He kept blaming himself."

In perhaps the most celebrated shooting in baseball history, a "disturbed" nineteen-year-old woman, said to be a "fan," shot Phillie first baseman Eddie Waitkus in a Chicago hotel on June 15, 1949. Waitkus missed the rest of the 1949 season and had to undergo four operations, but he returned to play six more seasons—and to serve as a model for a similar incident in Bernard Malamud's baseball novel, *The Natural*. Cesar Cedeno of the Houston Astros was implicated in a more lethal incident. On December 11, 1973, the twenty-two-year-old outfielder was charged with voluntary manslaughter in the Dominican Republic when the body of a nineteen-year-old

woman, shot to death, was found in his motel room. The charges were later changed—without much explanation—to involuntary manslaughter; Cedeno paid a small fine (about $100) and court costs. There have been no shootings between teammates, but not for lack of paranoia: Ty Cobb got along so poorly with his Detroit teammates during his early years that he retired to his railroad berth at night with a loaded pistol. Possibly the closest thing to an on-the-field homicide occurred in 1965, when San Francisco Giant pitcher Juan Marichal assaulted Los Angeles Dodger catcher John Roseboro with a bat.

The Mets' Darryl Strawberry enlivened the 1990 off-season when, in January, blood tests proved definitively he was the father in a paternity suit brought by a St. Louis woman. Two days later he was arrested by police in Encino, California, for threatening his wife Lisa with a loaded semiautomatic pistol. According to police, Strawberry slapped his wife during an argument (he had previously broken her nose in a tiff during the 1986 World Series); when she responded by striking him several times with a fire poker, he reached into a closet and produced the gun. Strawberry originally faced charges of assault with a deadly weapon, but the charges were later dropped. Within a week of the incident, the Mets slugger checked into New York's Smithers Clinic for alcohol rehabilitation.

Milwaukee relief pitcher Julio Machado faced more serious charges—"unintentional" murder—in his native Venezuela following a December 1991 shooting incident in which a woman died. Following an altercation over a late-night car accident, Machado told authorities he felt he was in physical danger, according to press reports, and fired his 9 mm. pistol into a car, killing the woman seated in the car's passenger seat.

The use of the baseball itself as an assault weapon, meanwhile, enjoyed a brief vogue during the 1992 campaign. Cincinnati pitcher Rob Dibble received a four-game suspension for hurling a ball into the stands at Riverfront Stadium on April 28, 1991; the ball struck a female spectator in the arm. The gifted and troubled Albert Belle of Cleveland, in May 1991, fired a high hard one at a heckler in the stands from a distance of fifteen feet, causing a chest bruise and incurring a week-long suspension (later shortened to six days).

In the old days, it was not uncommon for players to duke it out with their managers. One of the most savage beatings was administered in 1929 by White Sox player Art "Whattaman" Shires, a notorious drunkard and self-styled boxer. Shires cornered Chicago manager Lena Blackburne and the team's traveling secretary in a hotel room and thrashed both; it took four men, including two hotel detectives, to drag Shires off. He beat up his manager three times in one year. More recently, in 1977, Texas infielder Lenny Randle landed several punches on the face of manager Frank Lucchesi, shattering his cheekbone and requiring plastic surgery. The Rangers suspended Randle, fined him $10,000 and then released him; in court, Randle plea-bargained a felony charge down to simple battery and paid a $1,000 fine, along with medical expenses.

Umpires have not escaped controversy. In September 1988, National League umpire Dave Pallone—one of the original "scab" umpires hired during the 1979 season—

took a leave of absence after news reports incorrectly linked him to an investigation of sex crimes against teenage boys in Saratoga Springs, New York. Pallone, who later admitted he was homosexual, was never charged with any crime, but headlines like "Ump Tied to Sex Ring" (New York *Daily News*) helped turn the leave into a permanent resignation. National League ump Bob Engel, meanwhile, resigned from baseball in July 1990 after pleading no contest to a shoplifting charge. The previous April he had been arrested for stealing less than $200 worth of merchandise from a convenience store in Bakersfield, California. The merchandise? Baseball cards.

Although still only a minor leaguer as a menace to society, outfielder Jose Canseco continued to show signs of graduating to major league mayhem. In February 1991 Canseco was flagged by the Florida Highway Patrol for doing 104 miles per hour in a 55 mph zone of Miami (this in addition to four previous moving violations in 1988–1989, as well as an arrest in San Francisco for carrying a concealed weapon). In a dramatic duel of nouveau riche vehicles early on the morning of February 13, 1992, Canseco chased after his estranged wife, Esther, in his Porsche, sideswiped her BMW twice, and ran her off the road. Alarmed motorists notified police and Canseco was charged with aggravated assault; the charge was later dropped when he agreed to undergo psychological counseling.

In the twentieth century, three figures stand out for their combativeness as well as their ability to arouse controversy over the long haul: Ty Cobb, Babe Ruth, and Billy Martin.

Ty Cobb is generally considered the meanest player ever to don spikes. Cobb had to leave his first major league spring training camp, in 1906, to attend the trial of his mother, Amanda Cobb, who was acquitted of voluntary manslaughter charges in the death of Ty's father; she had shot him in 1905, believing him to be a prowler. Cobb seemed to carry a chip on his shoulder throughout his career. Thin-skinned, bigoted, a nasty street fighter, Cobb forever blemished his reputation in 1912 when he dove into the stands in New York to silence a heckler, kicking and spiking the man. The spectator turned out to be a man with no hands. Cobb's response was "I don't care if he has no feet"; American League president Ban Johnson's response was to suspend Cobb for ten days. (His Tiger teammates, in sympathy with Cobb, launched a strike that lasted one game.) During his career, Cobb engaged in drawn-out, knock-down fights with umpires, teammates, opposing players, fans, even a hotel watchman (the latter resulted in an indictment in Cleveland in 1909 for felonious assault). A racist with a broad palette, Cobb tarred all races with his brush: he liked to refer to Honus Wagner as "Kraut-head" and once refused to room with Babe Ruth, believing Ruth's dark complexion suggested black ancestry.

Ruth, on the other hand, enjoyed the reputation of a good-hearted, if adolescently rambunctious, personality; although he often indulged in scandalous behavior, he never amounted to a scandal. A man of immense and uncontrollable appetites, Ruth set new standards for eating, drinking, and whoring off the field just as he set longball standards on it. Particularly in the early days of his career, Ruth had little control of his temper. In 1917, as a

Boston pitcher, he attacked umpire Brick Owens, and once went into the stands with a bat to chase a heckler; in the 1922 season alone, he was suspended five times, usually for swearing at umpires. He drank whiskey and ginger ale for breakfast, spent countless hours and dollars at the racetrack, partied past curfews in any time zone, frequented illegal breweries, and never wanted for liquor during Prohibition. A legendary philanderer, Ruth once bragged that he had slept with every girl in a St. Louis whorehouse, and even when his first wife Helen accompanied him on road trips, teammates facilitated Ruth's infidelities by making their rooms available for the Babe's liaisons. For all his energetic rutting, Ruth apparently contracted venereal disease more than once. A $50,000 paternity suit filed against Ruth by a Long Island woman accelerated the demise of his marriage, which was also undermined by Ruth's open affair with Claire Merritt Hodgson (she later became his second wife). Ruth's behavior struck many as reckless and often infantile, but it was rarely malicious and often perversely innocent, which is why he never lost the admiration and love of the public. That strange brew of raging hormones and American innocence is perfectly summed up by an incident during a barnstorming trip to the Orient in the 1930s: brought to a geisha house, Ruth mistook it for a bordello and promptly started to undress.

Innocence seems lamentably absent from the adventures of infielder Billy Martin, who gave new, darker meaning to the word "scrappy." He was involved in at least five major fights on the field. He beat up one of his own pitchers, Dave Boswell, while managing the Twins in 1969 (Boswell required twenty stitches in the face); had punched out reporters (*Nevada State Journal* writer Ray Hagar in 1978) and marshmallow sales man (Joseph Cooper in 1979); got into a vicious fight with another member of his pitching staff while managing the Yankees (Ed Whitson in 1985); and brawled in a Texas strip joint (1988). He earned his reputation as "King of the Sucker Punch" in 1960 when, playing for the Reds, he sucker-punched Cub pitcher Jim Brewer after an inside pitch, shattering Brewer's cheekbone and landing him in the hospital for two weeks. No crass gesture has been too small or juvenile to be excluded from the Martin oeuvre: for his 1972 baseball card, as manager of the Detroit Tigers, Martin reverted to the classic junior high school prank of extending his middle finger in an unmistakably vulgar gesture while leaning on a bat.

The Billy Martin story came, inevitably, to a tragic end on an ice-slick country road near his home outside Binghamton, New York. On Christmas Day 1989, Martin's pickup truck skidded off the road and tumbled down an embankment; Martin died of massive internal injuries. William Reedy, a Detroit saloon owner and long-time Martin drinking companion, was charged with driving while intoxicated. Press reports indicated that the two men had been drinking for several hours, and Martin, too, was apparently drunk at the time of his death. Martin's widow Jill filed a lawsuit in July 1990, charging that Reedy's reckless driving caused Martin's death. In September of that year a jury in upstate New York found William Reedy guilty of driving the car with a blood-alcohol content above the legal limit. Reedy was cleared of the lesser charge of driving with impaired ability be-

cause, according to an Associated Press account, the jury "thought that Reedy was not impaired because of his high tolerance level for alcohol. . . ."

Although often suspected of prevarication, Martin spoke the absolute truth when he once referred to his boss as a "convicted felon." Indeed, Yankee principal owner George Steinbrenner had the dubious distinction of dragging baseball down into the Watergate scandal. In 1974, a federal grand jury in Cleveland indicted Steinbrenner on fourteen felony counts for illegal corporate contributions (by his American Shipbuilding Company) to the reelection campaign of Richard Nixon as well as for obstruction of justice. Represented by famed criminal attorney Edward Bennet Williams, Steinbrenner struck a deal with Watergate special prosecutor Leon Jaworski and pled guilty to a single felony charge.

Some observers considered Steinbrenner's light sentence (a $15,000 fine; no jail term) puzzling, since the Yankee owner admitted in court to such grave offenses as causing his employees to lie to the FBI and give false testimony to a federal grand jury. Williams literally saved Steinbrenner's baseball career; Commissioner Kuhn later admitted he would have expelled Steinbrenner for life had he received a jail sentence. Instead, Kuhn suspended Steinbrenner for two years, later reduced to one season. To the bewilderment of lawyers who prosecuted the case, Ronald Regan pardoned Steinbrenner in 1989. Steinbrenner, incidentally, was not the first owner to commit a felonious offense. In 1953, St. Louis owner Fred Saigh was forced to divest his control of the Cardinals when he began a fifteen-month sentence for tax evasion; that paved the way for Saigh's sale of the team to Anheuser-Busch.

Steinbrenner ran permanently afoul of the baseball establishment in 1990, when commissioner Fay Vincent ordered him to resign as general partner of the Yankees and, in effect, banned him from any active management of the club's baseball affairs. The decision culminated Steinbrenner's most tumultuous year in baseball. There was the usual nonfelonious bullying and double-talk; the usual revolving-door style of management (at final count, nineteen managerial changes in eighteen seasons); the usual odor of suspicious hijinx, as in the probe of former team official Syd Thrift for "scouting improprieties" (an investigation, it turns out, triggered by Steinbrenner himself and which yielded naught); and the usual good sportsmanship historically associated with the Yankees, as in allegations that Steinbrenner's famous "baseball people" spent part of their evenings sneaking into the visitors' locker room at Yankee Stadium, at the boss's orders, to search for corked bats (*et tu,* George Brett?). In July baseball fined Steinbrenner $25,000 and ordered him to pay the Angels $200,000 for tampering with Dave Winfield following his trade to California. His shipbuilding company faced mounting losses. And to add insult to the usual injury, a poll conducted in summer 1990 by the *New York Times* revealed that Met fans outnumbered Yankee fans in New York by three to one, and that only one in ten Yankee fans gave Steinbrenner a "favorable" rating.

A cloud of considerably darker and more ominous nature dogged Steinbrenner beginning in spring 1990. On March 18, 1990, the New York *Daily News* reported that Steinbrenner had paid $40,000 to an admitted small-time gambler named Howard Spira, allegedly in exchange for

damaging information about Dave Winfield. Claiming Steinbrenner had reneged on the promise of a job, Spira demanded an additional $110,000, at which point Steinbrenner filed a complaint of extortion; Spira was later indicted by a federal grand jury in Tampa. Just another day at the office in the Bronx.

According to press accounts, Spira first contacted Steinbrenner on December 17, 1986, with an offer to provide negative information about Winfield, with whom Steinbrenner had feuded for nearly a decade. Winfield, it will be recalled, locked horns with the Yankee owner over the latter's contributions to the outfielder's nonprofit Winfield Foundation, and relations further deteriorated when Winfield vetoed several trades. The prevailing theory was that Steinbrenner sought negative information about Winfield as a bargaining chip to get the player to accept a trade.

Whatever the merit of the charges and countercharges, they got a full airing in the national press. The *New York Times* published excerpts from taped telephone conversations in which Steinbrenner told Spira, "I'm anxious to hear what you want to tell me, what you have to say . . ." Spira reportedly dished the following dirt: He claimed that Winfield and his agent, the late Al Frohman, concocted phony death threats against Winfield during the 1981 World Series to distract attention from the player's poor on-field performance, that Winfield Foundation funds were misused and misappropriated, and that Winfield had once held a gun to Spira's head and threatened to kill him if he didn't pay back a loan of $15,000. Whatever the substance of these allegations (denied by Winfield), there was nothing casual about the contacts between Spira and Yankee representatives. Spira conversed primarily with Philip McNiff, a former FBI agent who served as a vice president at Steinbrenner's American Shipbuilding Company in Tampa. Records show that Spira called McNiff at least 426 times between December 1986 and December 1989. According to the *New York Times*, McNiff sent Spira a card on his thirtieth birthday with the inscription, "Howie, may all your dreams come true."

Spira, to the contrary, became Steinbrenner's worst nightmare. The Yankee owner acknowledged paying Spira $40,000 as the first press reports came out, but said he did it "out of the goodness of my heart." Even George conceded the inherent implausibility of that explanation, for he soon changed his story and said the payoff was to prevent Spira from disclosing embarrassing information about former Yankee employees. Steinbrenner changed his story once again while pleading his case in a private meeting with commissioner Fay Vincent—the transcript of which was leaked almost immediately and appeared first in *The National*. This time Steinbrenner claimed he paid Spira because he feared for the safety of his family and himself; dragging more names into the widening scandal, Steinbrenner also said Spira threatened to go public with information about Lou Piniella's gambling habits (an understandably touchy topic in Cincinnati, where Piniella replaced an admitted gambler as manager) and misappropriation of funds by two other Yankee employees. Vincent attached no merit to either charge.

Vincent had already enlisted John Dowd, head of the Rose investigation, to check out the Spira affair. Stein-

brenner hired two high-powered criminal lawyers to represent his side of the story, and for the second time in two summers, it appeared that baseball was headed for a confrontation in court. But after an eleven-hour meeting with Steinbrenner on July 30, 1990, Vincent met with the press to announce his severe decision. Citing Steinbrenner's bad judgment, questioning his "candor and contrition," and expressing puzzlement over "a pattern of behavior that borders on the bizarre," Vincent said Steinbrenner's actions had not been in the best interests of baseball and ordered him to reduce his ownership in the Yankees to less than 50 percent by August 20, 1991. In booting Steinbrenner out of baseball, Vincent faulted Steinbrenner for paying a gambler money in "a furtive fashion" and for initiating an investigation of a player with the help of Spira without notifying the commissioner, he dismissed Steinbrenner's claims of extortion as "not credible," and he charged Steinbrenner with an attempt to cover up the Spira payment. As to the accusation that he had been unfair, Vincent wrote in the ruling, "In my view, Mr. Steinbrenner's dilemma is not with the procedures I have utilized, but with his inability to rewrite history." Ronald Reagan acceded to this revisionism; Vincent did not.

According to the guidelines established by Vincent, Steinbrenner could no longer participate in baseball decisions involving the Yankees and would even have to obtain permission in writing from the commissioner in order to attend games. Vincent did not rule out the possibility that Steinbrenner's son Hank might assume day-to-day management of the team; however, the commissioner's assertion that severe restrictions would apply seemed, short of wiretaps and full-time surveillance, virtually impossible to enforce. Within twenty-four hours, Steinbrenner—who pronounced himself "very happy" with Vincent's ruling—tabbed his son to take over the club as general partner. As if Vincent's decision was not enough of a bombshell, the commissioner later revealed that he had planned only to suspend Steinbrenner for two years; it was Steinbrenner who pushed for a second decision that amounted to a permanent ban. "From where I sit," Vincent later said, "the second proposal [penalty] was stronger. I don't understand why he took it." When word of Vincent's decision reached Yankee Stadium on the night of July 30, fans cheered the news with a ninety-second standing ovation. "Christmas in July" is how one fan characterized the end of Steinbrenner's reign of terror in New York baseball.

Steinbrenner earned a measure of satisfaction the following spring. On May 8, 1991, following a four-week trial in Manhattan during which Steinbrenner fought back tears while testifying and Spira stuck out his tongue at photographers, a federal jury found the thirty-two-year-old Bronx gambler guilty of eight charges, including five attempts to extort money from the Yankee owner. The charges involved the additional $110,000 Spira sought; they did not address the $40,000 payment that led to Steinbrenner's ouster from baseball. In December, Spira was sentenced to two-and-a-half years in prison, to be followed by three years of probation and 200 hours of community service. Among Spira's last words before being led off to jail: "I sure hope George Steinbrenner never gets the team back."

George did, but not without the usual slam-dance of

litigation that could have been choreographed by the Marx Brothers. Steinbrenner's agreement with Vincent explicitly prevented the Boss from suing the commissioner. But it didn't say anything about Steinbrenner's partners, and so, with the marionette's strings clearly showing, two minority owners of the Yankees, Daniel Mc-Carthy and Harold Bowman, filed suit against the commissioner in August, arguing that Steinbrenner's exile could harm the franchise and thus the partners' financial stake. The following month, minority partner Leonard Kleinman filed a $22 million suit against Vincent, claiming the commissioner blocked his ascent to managing partner because of his involvement in the Spira affair. In this case, the strings were particularly visible; Kleinman's suit, it turned out, was financed by Steinbrenner.

When Vincent made it adamantly clear that there would be no discussion of reinstatement for Steinbrenner until the lawsuits were dropped, George called off his attack dogs. Problem was, one of the dogs refused to heel. To Steinbrenner's reported displeasure, and to the amusement of just about all other observers, Kleinman doggedly refused to drop his suit. The Yankees partners even fired Kleinman, the team's chief operating officer, in February 1992, when he continued to refuse to drop his suit. Finally, following long and contentious negotiations, Vincent agreed in July 1992 to reinstate Steinbrenner, whose repatriation to the Bronx was scheduled for March 1, 1993.

One of Steinbrenner's old nemeses made news during this period as well. Former commissioner Bowie Kuhn, that balding paragon of probity, received a bad haircut in the press in early 1990 when, as a *New York Times* headline had it, "Bowie Kuhn Is Said to Be in Hiding." Bowie's bad luck began the previous year, when his law firm Myerson & Kuhn overbilled a client and was ordered to pay back $1 million. By December 1989, the law firm had filed for bankruptcy protection, but one of the creditors, Marine Midland Bank, sued Kuhn to recover $3.1 million in loans. In court papers, the bank charged that Kuhn had sold his New Jersey home and fled to Florida, where state laws exempt residences from being seized in bankruptcy proceedings. Kuhn told the *Florida Times-Union* that he and his wife Luisa had simply moved to Florida for a change of pace.

No Sex, Please; We're Heroes

As baseball became popular, so too did public interest in its practitioners extend beyond the field to the home, and sometimes right on through the bedroom door. Within the bounds of Victorian society, one of baseball's earliest sex "scandals" involved the hard-fighting Walter "Arlie" Latham, third baseman of the St. Louis Browns. Around 1885, his second wife filed for divorce on the grounds of assault, desertion, infidelity, and perversion.

Sports pages in the 1880s also carried accounts of Sam Crane, infielder for the Metropolitans and later a prominent sportswriter, who was arrested for running off with $1,500 belonging to a Scranton fruit dealer named Travenfelter—*and* with his wife Hattie. Edwin "Ned" Bligh was among the earliest of players named in a paternity suit; Bligh just missed more serious charges, since his accuser was seventeen-year-old Zella Coleman. By the end of the century, domestic problems—such as the di-

vorces of popular players like John Montgomery Ward, Amos Rusie, and Tony Mullane—became fodder for reporters.

Probably the most tragic scandal involved minor league pitcher Edgar McNabb, who made it to the majors for one season with Baltimore in 1893. McNabb had been carrying on an affair with actress Louise Kellogg, wife of Seattle businessman R. E. Rockwell. The idyll came to an end on February 28, 1894, in a room at the Hotel Eiffel in Pittsburgh. For reasons that remain a mystery to this day, McNabb shot Kellogg twice (paralyzing her but not killing her), then turned the gun on himself and showed better control. In another romance-related suicide, Red Sox manager Chick Stahl took his life in 1907 after facing pressure from a woman who'd become pregnant by him.

On the whole, though, twentieth century sex scandals in baseball have been more elliptical than explicit. Apart from Ruth's legendary wenching, there was little to arouse prurient interest, except perhaps the vicarious experience of Joe DiMaggio's marriage to Marilyn Monroe or perhaps Bo Belinsky's dalliance with Mamie Van Doren. In 1988, Dave Winfield's bout with Ruth Roper, mother-in-law of Mike Tyson, brought VD into the courts. But in terms of vague but suggestive explanations, nothing beats the adventure of Brooklyn pitcher Van Lingle Mungo during spring training in 1941 in Havana. Authors Gene Karst and Martin J. Jones, Jr., note that the Dodger player had to be hustled hastily back to the mainland after he "became involved with a former bullfighter and his girlfriend." No further explanations offered.

Amidst the usual paternity suits (Darryl Strawberry, Pascual Perez), wife beatings, and even the rare case of mother beating (Jim Presley of Atlanta), Margo Adams provided an unusually juicy sex scandal in June 1988 when she filed a $6 million palimony suit against Boston third baseman Wade Boggs. The perennial AL All-Star and batting champ admitted he'd had a four-year affair with the California woman. When Adams's lawyer sought to depose nine other players, tensions rose on the Red Sox, including reports of an ugly confrontation between Boggs and teammate Dwight Evans. Boggs won the suit, Adams landed a pictorial in *Penthouse,* and none of the pictures Boggs allegedly took showing Red Sox teammates in compromising positions—so they wouldn't talk about his affair with Adams, it was said—ever saw the light of day. Everything you need to know about the baseball ethic in this arena of activity, however, can be inferred from a remark Boggs made at the end of the controversy: *One-night stands are acceptable,* he said, *but two-year affairs are not.*

Boggs's mantle passed the following season to former Dodger and Padre first baseman Steve Garvey. Baseball's former "Mr. Clean" managed to impregnate two women while pursuing and marrying a third, occasioning the appearance of two young children in the world and bumper stickers in Southern California that read: "Steve Garvey is not *my* Padre." Garvey's woes were complicated by a nasty child-custody suit with ex-wife Cyndi and his postbaseball career suffered a further setback in 1990, when he was fired by a San Diego radio station because of poor ratings for his talk show.

Back in the junior circuit, so to speak, Yankee outfielder Luis Polonia spent October 1989 in a Milwaukee

jail, serving a sixty-day sentence (later reduced to thirty days) for having had sexual intercourse with a minor when the Yankees visited the Brewers in August. Polonia claimed he was set up by the fifteen-year-old girl; the judge remained unconvinced, imposing fines and contributions totaling $11,500. The incident may have encouraged the Yankees to trade Polonia in 1990, but probably didn't influence Polonia's bizarre assessment of the transaction. "They only had one thing on their mind," Polonia charged, "and I don't know what it is."

The combustible mix of sex-related criminal allegations and the easily inflamed New York tabloid press created high-octane fireworks in the spring of 1992. No players were charged with any crime, but the police investigation, ultimately made public, exposed to public scrutiny the laissez-faire sexual adventures of modern-day lockerroom Romeos. Against the background of the Clarence Thomas–Anita Hill controversy in the fall of 1991, baseball too witnessed a "he said, she said" drama with racial overtones, in which the alleged transgression involved not sexual harassment but the far more serious charge of rape.

The case came to light in March 1992, when three unidentified New York Mets were reported to be under investigation for sexual assault in St. Lucie, Florida, where the Mets hold their spring training camp. Over the ensuing weeks, it emerged that an unidentified thirty-one-year-old New York woman, trained as an architect, had filed a complaint alleging that the three players—pitcher Dwight Gooden and outfielders Daryl Boston and Vince Coleman—had sexually assaulted her on the evening of March 30, 1991. Details of the woman's allegations became public when police released the 456-page file of the investigation. Among many lurid and startling details, the file revealed that the woman had been, at the time of the alleged incident, a companion of Met pitcher David Cone.

Hounded by reporters throughout spring training, Met players responded to the scandal by refusing to talk to members of the press. After police declined to pursue charges, several team members insisted that the name of the woman complainant be revealed. Said shortstop Kevin Elster: "I can't think of a reason why not."

But hardly a sex scandal in any field quite measures up to a wife-swapping scheme that became public in March 1973. New York Yankee pitchers Fritz Peterson and Mike Kekich pulled off one of the most daring trades in baseball history: they exchanged wives and children. In a straight-up deal, Peterson received Susanne Kekich, her two young daughters, and the Kekich family dog, in exchange for Marilyn "Chip" Peterson, her two young sons, and the Peterson family pet. If, as is often said, you cannot judge the value of a trade until five years have passed, it must be stated that neither side came out ahead on this one. Marilyn Peterson left Kekich and both pitchers were out of baseball by 1980.

## CHAPTER 10

Tragedies and Shortened Careers

Joseph M. Overfield

If, of all words of tongue and pen,
The saddest are, "It might have been,"
More sad are these we daily see:
"It is, but hadn't ought to be."
— Bret Harte

In the eleventh century in the reign of William the Conqueror, detailed information about the landowners of England and their assets was gathered and then recorded in what were called *Domesday Books.* Much of what is known of the demographics of early England is derived from these books.

Baseball also has its *Domesday Books,* but they are called *Encyclopedias.* They list the name, vital statistics, and records of every player who ever appeared in a major league game, beginning with the formation of the National Association in 1871. So assiduously have baseball's *Domesday Books* been corrected, refined, and updated, it is safe to say that detailed information is more readily available about ballplayers, even the most obscure, than it is for statesmen, authors, artists, poets, or captains of industry.

Informative as they are, the *Encyclopedias* still leave much unsaid. For example, why did Bert Shepard play but a single game, while Jim McGuire played for twenty-six seasons? Short careers, like Shepard's, usually mean a lack of ability or, perhaps, the failure to receive a fair opportunity; but often they are short for other reasons— death, illness, injury, accident, suicide, or even murder. It is with such tragically shortened careers that this chapter will deal. Although the subject was carefully researched, no assertion of 100 percent completeness is proffered.

Since baseball's *Domesday Books* are limited to major league players and managers, no listing will be found there for minor leaguers like Bill Thomas of the 1906 Buffalo Bisons or Ralph Worrell of the 1918 Baltimore Orioles or Jeff Hoffman of the 1992 Albany Colonie Yankees.

James Creighton was the star pitcher of the Excelsior Club, a famous Brooklyn amateur nine of the 1850s and 1860s. Before Creighton's day, it was customary for pitchers to toss the ball gently to the plate. Creighton changed all this by developing a snap throw that gave speed and spin to the ball. In addition, he was one of the most powerful hitters of his day. It is said that he completed one entire season without being put out. On October 14, 1862, the Excelsiors were playing the Union Club of Morrisania in their final match of the season. Creighton, at bat for the Excelsiors, swung mightily and sent the ball beyond the reach of the outfielders. As he crossed first base,

he collapsed, obviously in great pain. Legend has it that he staggered around the bases for a home run. He was immediately taken home by his teammates. Four days later, the twenty-one-year-old pitcher was dead. According to an account in the *Brooklyn Eagle,* headlined "Obsequies of a Celebrated Ballplayer," Creighton had ruptured his bladder with the force of his final swing and died from internal bleeding.

A. G. Spalding, in his book *Baseball, America's National Game,* devoted two pages to Creighton, with his picture and a view of the towering granite monument his teammates erected in his memory on Tulip Hill in Brooklyn's Greenwood Cemetery. The monument is embossed with crossed bats, a cap, a base, and a scorebook.

The circumstances of the death of Bill Thomas, a twenty-five-year-old Buffalo pitcher, in April 1906, are still a mystery. Thomas had been a big winner in the Pacific Coast League, and manager George Stallings of Buffalo had brought him east to test his mettle in the stronger Eastern League. He was successful in his first start at Baltimore. The Bisons then finished a series at Providence and took a train to New Bedford, Massachusetts, from which point they boarded the night boat *Richard Peck,* en route to New York City. Thomas had left word with the porter and with his roommate, pitcher Joe Galaski, that he wanted an early call so he could see the New York skyline at sunrise. In the morning, when the porter came into the stateroom, the Thomas bunk, which had been slept in, was empty. Thomas was never seen again.

In 1918 Ralph Worrell, only nineteen, won 25 games for Jack Dunn's Baltimore Orioles, but he never pitched again. Instead of becoming another Lefty Grove (also a Jack Dunn discovery), Worrell failed to survive the winter, dying in the terrible World War One flu epidemic.

Just as tragic was the death of twenty-nine-year-old Yankee farmhand Jeff Hoffman of the Albany Colonie–Yankees, August 29, 1992. The young righthanded pitcher collapsed in his Binghamton (N.Y.) hotel room and died later that day in a local hospital. There was no evidence of foul play or drug alcohol use. After several days it was determined he had died from a heart deficiency, previously undetected. He left his wife Teresa, who was expecting their first child.

The deaths of young, vigorous, and supposedly healthy athletes like Creighton, Thomas, Worrell, and Hoffman are sad and decidedly against the odds, but in the muster rolls of major league players in baseball's *Domesday Books,* such cases are far from rare.

Fatal Illnesses of Players and Managers

Elmer White was long thought to be a brother of James "Deacon" White and Will White. The early encyclopedias listed him as playing 15 games for the Forest Cities of Cleveland in 1872, but nothing more. A trip by the writer to the village of Caton in New York's southern tier and to the cemetery behind the Methodist Church there resulted in the finding of Elmer White's grave. The inscription on the tombstone, which showed he was Jim's and Will's cousin, not a brother, told with great economy of words the story of a short life and a short baseball career: "Born December 7, 1850. Died March 17, 1873."

Of all the deaths of active major leaguers to be recounted here, significantly, only one—that of Ray Chapman, who was killed by a Carl Mays pitch—resulted directly from activity on the diamond. Many of the deaths, especially those in the first fifty years, were from illnesses routinely controlled today. Typhoid fever, for example, killed first baseman Alex McKinnon of Pittsburgh (NL) on July 24, 1887. He played in the July 4 game, complained of not feeling well, and was taken home. He died twenty days later at the age of thirty. Less than a year later, on April 29, 1888, Charlie Ferguson, an outstanding young pitcher who had won 21, 26, 30, and 22 games for Philadelphia (NL) from 1884 through 1887 and was a strong hitter as well (.288 in four seasons), died from the same disease, twelve days after his twenty-fifth birthday.

Edward "Sy" Sutcliffe, a catcher for most of his career, had shifted to first base for Baltimore (NL) in 1892 and had done quite well, batting .279 in 66 games. In the off-season, the twenty-nine-year-old native of Wheaton, Illinois, developed Bright's disease. He died February 13, 1893.

Joe Cassidy, an infielder for the Washington Senators in 1904 and 1905, was a third victim of the deadly typhoid. He was only twenty-three when he died at his home in Chester, Pennsylvania, March 25, 1906. Just a year and four days later, March 29, 1907, Patrick Henry "Cozy" Dolan, a nine-year outfielder in the majors, most recently with Boston (NL), also died of typhoid. He took ill during Boston's spring training trip, and died in a Louisville hospital, at age thirty-four. News of his death was overshadowed in the Boston papers by the extensive coverage given to the sensational suicide of manager Chick Stahl of the other Boston club, the day before in West Baden, Indiana.

Mike Powers, who caught in the majors from 1898 to 1909, mainly with the Philadelphia Athletics, was an anomaly in those hard-bitten days of the game's history, in that he held a degree from Holy Cross College and had also attended Notre Dame Medical School. Powers, incidentally, recruited the legendary Louis "Chief" Sockalexis for both of his alma maters, as shall be seen later. Powers was not a strong hitter (.216 lifetime), but he was considered a fine defensive catcher. He was behind the plate in an early season game in 1909, when he complained of nausea and asked to be taken to a hospital. He underwent three stomach operations, and then gangrene set in. He died April 26, 1909, at the age of thirty-eight.

Alan Storke was an infielder for Pittsburgh and St. Louis (NL) from 1906 through 1909. He never made it to spring training in 1910. He was a mere twenty-five when he died in Newton, Massachusetts, March 18, 1910, following a lung operation. Less than two years later, February 1, 1912, another National League infielder, thirty-year-old Jimmy Doyle, who had batted .282 for the Cubs in 1911, died in Syracuse, New York, after an appendicitis operation.

Addie Joss pitched in the majors only eight seasons and part of a ninth, but his record was so extraordinary that he was elected to the Hall of Fame (in 1978), despite his short tenure. With Cleveland from 1902 to 1910, he won 160 games, lost 97, and compiled an ERA of 1.88 (second on the all-time list). He pitched a perfect game on October 2, 1908, defeating Big Ed Walsh, 1–0, with first place on the line. Joss had another no-hitter on April 20, 1910, also against the White Sox, just before his health began to fail.

Joss made only 13 appearances in 1910, and still felt weak when he went south in 1911. He collapsed on the bench during an exhibition game at Chattanooga, Tennessee, then became ill again when the team reached Cincinnati. Doctors said it was pleurisy and sent him home to Toledo. On April 14, 1911, two days after his team had opened the season in St. Louis, he died at the age of thirty-one. The cause of his death was given as tubercular meningitis. Famed ballplayer-preacher Billy Sunday presided at his funeral, said to have been the biggest ever seen in Toledo.

Leonard "King" Cole, a righthanded pitcher who had won 20 games for the Cubs in 1910 and 18 the following season, was, like Charlie Ferguson, to have a brilliant career nipped in the bud by a fatal illness. During the 1915 season, when Cole was with the Yankees, it was discovered that he had been suffering from tuberculosis. He returned to his home in Bay City, Michigan, where he died on January 6, 1916, at twenty-nine. He left a splendid 56–27 (.675) won–lost record.

Joe Leonard, a twenty-five-year-old infielder who began with Pittsburgh in 1914 and played for Washington in 1916, 1917, and 1919, appeared in only one game for the Senators in 1920, became ill, and was taken to George Washington Hospital. He died there on May 1, following an appendicitis operation.

In 1922, the St. Louis Cardinals lost two young ballplayers within nine months. First to go was William "Pickles" Dillhoefer, who had caught in the majors since 1917, usually in a backup role. He was twenty-seven when he died in a St. Louis hospital, February 22, 1922, of that old bugaboo, typhoid fever. Outfielder Austin McHenry had started with the Cardinals in 1918, but had not really blossomed until 1921, when he batted .350 and hit 37 doubles, 8 triples, and 17 home runs. The following year he began to have difficulties in judging fly balls. Manager Branch Rickey sent him to a doctor, who diagnosed his problem as a brain tumor. An operation proved unsuccessful, and he died at Jefferson Township, Ohio, November 27, 1922. He was twenty-seven, the same age as Dillhoefer.

The 1924 season saw the deaths of two veterans of the Cincinnati Reds within eight months. Pat Moran was a catcher in the majors from 1901 to 1914 and then a highly successful manager, first with the Phillies and then with the Reds. In nine managerial seasons, he compiled a record of 748–586 and won a pennant with each team. His

1915 Phillies lost the World Series to Boston, in five games, while his 1919 Reds won the tainted 1919 Series from the White Sox, 5–3. Moran was forty-eight when he died of Bright's disease at Orlando, Florida, March 7, 1924, while at spring training with the Reds. The second Red to die that year was Jake Daubert, a fancy-fielding first baseman who could hit (.303 in fifteen years with the Dodgers and the Reds). Although forty years old, he played 102 games for the Reds in 1924, batted .281 and fielded .990. He became ill in October and was taken to Good Samaritan Hospital in Cincinnati, where he died on October 9 following an appendicitis operation, just as Jimmy Doyle and Joe Leonard had before him.

Legendary New York Giants outfielder and future Hall of Famer Ross Youngs was at the height of his career when he was struck down by Bright's disease, diagnosed during spring training in 1926. Despite his illness, he played 95 games and batted .306. All through the season, he was accompanied by a male nurse hired by manager John McGraw. Youngs was bedridden for the entire 1927 season and died on October 22 at the age of thirty. Despite his relatively short career, nine seasons and part of another, his record was impressive enough to earn him election to the Hall of Fame in 1972. McGraw said he was the greatest outfielder he had ever seen.

Urban Shocker was an outstanding pitcher for the great Yankee teams of the 1925–1927 period. His record was 18–6 for the 1927 Yankees, but illness kept him out of the World Series. His thirteen-year record with the St. Louis Browns and the Yankees is in Hall of Fame country—187–117 (.615)—and he never had a losing season. His health continued to fail in 1928, and he appeared in only one game before being released. On September 9, 1928, in Denver, he died of heart disease and pneumonia. He was thirty-eight.

Shocker's manager, Miller Huggins, was to survive him little more than a year. On September 20, 1929, Huggins, who had managed the Yankees since 1918 and had won six pennants and three world's championships, asked coach Art Fletcher to take over for him, so that he could check into a hospital. Five days later, he was dead of erysipelas, a streptococcal skin infection. Huggins, who was of Munchkin size at 5'6" and 140 pounds, had been in the majors since 1904, batting a career .265, and winning 1,413 games and losing 1,134 as a manager. His showdowns with his rambunctious slugger, Babe Ruth, are part of baseball lore. Huggins was elected to the Hall of Fame in 1964.

On May 28, 1930, Hal Carlson, thirty-eight-year-old righthanded pitcher of the Chicago Cubs, and a fourteen-year veteran of the National League, called several of his teammates to his apartment in a Chicago hotel, saying that he was in severe pain. Shortly after the team physician arrived, Carlson was dead from what was described as "an internal hemorrhage." He left a three-year-old son and his wife, who was expecting another child.

Twenty-nine-year-old infielder Mickey Finn, who had played for the Dodgers from 1930 to 1932 and then for the Phillies, became ill midway through the 1933 season. Owner Gerry Nugent of the Phillies summoned his brother-in-law, Dr. H. P. Boyle, who diagnosed Finn's trouble as a duodenal ulcer. Surgery was performed in an Allentown, Pennsylvania, hospital. He seemed on the road to recovery, but unforeseen medical problems arose, leading to his death on July 7, 1933.

On August 28, 1949, Ernie Bonham, who had pitched seven seasons for the Yankees and appeared in three World Series, but who was now with the Pirates, pitched his team to an 8–2 win over the Phillies. He had complained of some discomfort during the game, and as a precaution was taken to a Pittsburgh hospital, where appendicitis was diagnosed. The normally routine operation extended for three hours when complications developed. He was very weak when manager Billy Meyer visited him a few days later. "Billy, they are hitting me all over the field, and I can't get anybody out," he mumbled. On September 15, minutes before Meyer and coach Goldie Holt arrived for another visit, he passed away. Bonham, who was thirty-six, left an impressive 103–72 record.

Perhaps the closest parallel to the death of James Creighton in the preprofessional era was the shocking and tragic passing of first baseman Harry Agganis of the Boston Red Sox, on June 27, 1955 at the age of twenty-five. Like Creighton, Agganis was young and talented, with a glorious career seemingly assured.

At 6'2", 200 pounds, and lefthanded, Agganis was a drawing-board first baseman. "The Golden Greek," as he was called, was the most publicized athlete to come out of Boston University since Mickey Cochrane in 1923. Such were Agganis's skills as a quarterback that he was a first-round draft pick of the Cleveland Browns, who offered him $25,000 to sign. When the Boston Red Sox upped this figure by $10,000, he chose baseball. After the 1953 season at Louisville (American Association), where he batted .281, had 23 home runs, 108 RBIs, and played in 155 games, he took over at first base for the parent club in 1954. He batted only .251 his first season. In the early going in 1955, he was over .300 when he developed pneumonia and was hospitalized for ten days. He returned to the lineup, but became ill again in Kansas City. He flew back to Boston and checked into Santa Maria Hospital in nearby Cambridge. He was thought to be recovering nicely, when suddenly on June 27, he died. The cause of his death was given as a massive pulmonary embolism.

Agganis's body lay in state at St. George's Greek Orthodox Church in his home town of Lynn, Massachusetts. On the day before the funeral, ten thousand mourners passed the bier.

Righthanded pitcher Jim Umbricht of Houston underwent a cancer operation on March 8, 1963. By May 9 he was back in uniform, and he finished the year with a 4–3 record and an ERA of 2.61 in 35 appearances. He did not make it into the next season. The malignancy spread, and he died on April 8, 1964, at age thirty-three.

According to present information, two active major leaguers succumbed to leukemia. Both were twenty-nine when they died and both at one time played with Minnesota. The first was giant 6'7" Walter Bond, who started with Cleveland in 1960, moved to Houston in 1964 and then to Minnesota in 1967, when illness forced him to quit. He died in Houston, September 14, 1967.

The second, infielder Danny Thompson, who broke in with Minnesota in 1970, had played for three years in the majors when he learned he had leukemia. He continued to play, however, and on June 1, 1976, he was involved in one of the big trades of the year, when he was bundled with

pitcher Bert Blyleven and shipped to Texas for Roy Smalley, Bill Singer, Mike Cubbage, Jim Gideon, and $250,000. Thompson finished the season with Texas, but it was to be his last. Baseball's Most Courageous Performer (he was so voted in 1974) was only twenty-nine when he died December 10, 1976, at Rochester, Minnesota.

In a single year, 1966, the Detroit Tigers lost two managers to illness and subsequent death, a tragic sequence not duplicated in major league history. On May 16 Charley Dressen, who had managed in the majors for sixteen seasons, suffered a heart attack and was succeeded by coach Bob Swift. Dressen died three months later at the age of sixty-seven. Swift himself became ill in July and was hospitalized, with another coach, Frank Skaff, taking over. It was found that Swift had an advanced case of lung cancer. He died October 16 at the age of fifty-one.

Quiet, efficient, and soft-spoken Dick Howser was an American League infielder from 1961 to 1968 with Kansas City, Cleveland, and New York. He became manager of the Yankees in 1980 and led them to 103 wins and a division title. After the Yankees lost the league championship series to Kansas City, 0–3, owner George Steinbrenner made things so uncomfortable for Howser that he resigned. He moved to Kansas City in 1981, winning a division title in 1984, then a pennant and a world's championship in 1985.

Early in the 1986 season, Howser began to suffer from headaches and to experience visual and memory problems. On July 18, he learned he had a malignant brain tumor. Operations followed, and he recovered sufficiently to return to uniform in 1987. But his health continued to deteriorate and he was forced to give up his managerial duties. He was fifty years old when he died, June 17, 1987.

Suicides and Other Violent Deaths

According to present information, five active major leaguers and one league president ended their lives by their own hands. Four others killed themselves in the year after they had been sent to the minors. Another Johnny Mostil, attempted suicide but recovered. There is also some intimation that the violent deaths of Len Koenecke and Ed Delahanty might have been "death wish" situations.

On February 28, 1894, Edgar McNabb, a pitcher who had won eight games for the Baltimore Orioles in 1893, checked in at the Eiffel Hotel on Smithfield Street in Pittsburgh. He told the clerk that his wife had gone to Braddock to visit her ailing parents and that he should give her the room key when she returned. Earlier that day, the McNabbs had run into a friend, one Louis Gillen, and the three had agreed to attend the theater that evening.

When the agreed time for the meeting passed, Gillen became concerned and went to the McNabbs' room. As he stood outside the door, he heard a woman's screams. He called for help, and when the room clerk opened the door, the two were shocked and sickened by the bloody and grisly scene before them. Mrs. McNabb lay on the floor, bleeding horribly from bullet holes in her neck and head, but still breathing. Lying beside her, dead, with bullet holes in the head, was Edgar McNabb. A pistol was still in his hand.

As the story unfolded, it became more than a tragic domestic confrontation. The dying woman was not Mrs. McNabb at all. She was Mrs. E. E. Rockwell, wife of a prominent Seattle businessman who had once been president of the Pacific Northwest Baseball League. She was an actress by profession and used the stage name of Louise Kellogg.

It appeared that Miss Kellogg, who had just finished a theatrical engagement in New York, had asked McNabb to meet her in Pittsburgh. According to a newspaper account, she was planning to break off her relationship with the ballplayer. Letters found in the room indicated that she had been sending him money to tide him over the winter, and further that there had been recent disagreements between them. In the judgment of the police who investigated, an argument had developed, culminating in McNabb's shooting of Miss Kellogg and then turning the gun on himself.

Among McNabb's possessions on the scene was a copy of a message which read: IN GREAT TROUBLE, TELEGRAPH $100 IMMEDIATELY. SEE YOU IN TWO WEEKS. It was probably this message that led Edgar McNabb and Louise Kellogg to their fateful rendezvous at the Eiffel Hotel. Miss Kellogg miraculously survived her wounds but was paralyzed.

Even more shocking than the McNabb affair was the sad denouement of Marty Bergen, first-string catcher for Frank Selee's Boston (NL) club from 1896 to 1899.

On the morning of January 19, 1900, Marty's father, Michael Bergen, who was staying at the house of a neighbor, walked to his son's property, which was called "Snowball Farm," to get some milk. Seeing no activity around the house, he left. He returned at noon and still saw no signs of life. He walked through the unlocked kitchen door, only to be confronted by a scene of unspeakable horror. On the kitchen floor, lay the body of his six-year-old granddaughter Florence. In the adjoining room, he found the body of his daughter-in-law Harriet Bergen and next to her that of her three-year-old son Joseph. Mrs. Bergen's hands were raised as though in supplication or as though trying to ward off a blow. A bloody ax, the apparent murder weapon, was found on the scene. Bergen himself had committed suicide with a straight razor, almost severing his head from his body.

Dr. W. E. Norwood, the medical examiner, made an almost on-the-spot judgment, ruling that the crime had been committed "in a fit of insanity," and that no autopsies would be necessary. According to the account in The Sporting Life, the funeral service at St. Joseph's Church in North Brookfield was somber and brief, and "only a few words suitable to the occasion were spoken." The only prominent baseball people present were Connie Mack of the Milwaukee club and Billy Hamilton, a Bergen teammate.

What triggered the carnage at Snowball Farm will never be known. Bergen's manager, Frank Selee, said that he seemed, at times, to act irrationally and to be pursued by hallucinations. It was also revealed that he had sought help from his pastor and his doctor, and that on one occasion he had accused the latter of trying to kill him. Bergen was not a drinker and apparently had no pressing money problems. He was buying the farm on the installment plan and had $2,000 in cash.

On January 12, 1903, not quite three years after the Bergen murder-suicide, the baseball world was stunned by the self-inflicted death of another prominent player. George Barclay "Win" Mercer was a versatile performer who had played every position but catcher in nine years in the majors, winning 131 games as a pitcher and batting .285. He was manager-designate for Detroit, where he had played in 1902.

Mercer was on the West Coast for a series of exhibition games between teams from the American and National leagues. A small man with striking good looks, he had a weakness for fast women and slow horses, a deadly combination that apparently was to do him in. On the fatal day, he did not appear when expected in the dining room of the San Francisco hotel where the players were staying. When the door of his room was opened, Mercer's body was found. A rubber hose was connected to a gas jet. He had died of self-inflicted asphyxiation.

Mercer left a suicide note in which he warned of the evils of women and gambling. He also left a note for his mother and one for his fiancée in East Liverpool, Ohio. Another letter was addressed to Tip O'Neill, manager of the ballplayer troupe, for which Mercer was in charge of finances. Even though Mercer had recently incurred heavy gambling losses, it was reported that his baseball accounts were in order.

Charles "Chick" Stahl had batted .307 in ten major league seasons and was considered one of the game's premier defensive outfielders. Stahl, a Marty Bergen teammate at Boston (NL) from 1897 to 1899, had been named manager of the Boston Puritans (AL) late in the 1906 season, succeeding his friend and roommate Jimmy Collins. Stahl was handsome, popular, well paid for his era, and recently married. Despite his oft-expressed distaste for managing and a recent attempt to resign, it seemed he had almost every reason to be on top of the world; but on March 28, 1907, in his room at the West Baden Hotel in West Baden, Indiana, he ingested a lethal dose of carbolic acid. As he staggered toward his bed, roommate Collins went to his assistance, just in time to hear him gasp: "Boys, I couldn't help it; it drove me to it."

For years, baseball historians pondered Stahl's cryptic words, then usually concluded it was the pressure of managing that forced him to swallow the poison. Dissenting was Harold Seymour, who, in his *Baseball, The Early Years,* strongly hints at the real reason: *cherchez la femme.* In the May 1986 issue of *Boston Magazine,* author Glenn Stout dug out the rest of the Stahl story and wrote it.

Stahl, according to Stout, although in love with a young lady named Julia Harmon of Roxbury, Massachusetts, was also attracted to other young ladies, the groupies of his day. Furthermore, according to Stout, one of his admirers, a Lulu Ortman, demanded that Stahl marry her. When he spurned her, she twice tried to shoot him but missed. Meanwhile, on November 14, 1906, Stahl had married Miss Harmon at St. Francis de Sales Church in Roxbury. It seems that he had also been involved, late in the 1906 season, with another woman, who now claimed to be pregnant by him. She pressured Stahl to marry her on pain of exposure. He told her that marriage was impossible, since he was already married. She persisted that spring, and it was this pressure, concludes Stout, not the pressure of managing, that led to his suicide.

A sad postscript to the Stahl suicide was the fate of his wife, Julia. Shortly after his death, she attempted suicide herself, but survived. On November 15, 1908, she was found dead in the doorway of a house in South Boston, after a night on the town. An autopsy showed that she had died of edema of the brain.

Little more than two years after the Stahl tragedy, another suicide rocked the game, but it had none of the nasty characteristics of the McNabb, Bergen, or Stahl cases.

Richard Cory, in Edwin Arlington Robinson's poem of the same name, was young, elegant, and well thought of, but one summer night he "went home and put a bullet through his head." Harry Clay Pulliam, president of the National League, was baseball's Richard Cory. On June 28, 1909, Pulliam went to his room in the New York Athletic Club and fired a shot through his head. He died the next morning. The forty-year-old bachelor left no suicide note. Presumably it was a combination of poor health (he had been on leave of absence for health reasons) and the burdens of his job that caused him to do it.

On December 13, 1910, Dennis "Dan" McGann, former captain of the New York Giants and a premier first baseman for thirteen seasons, but most recently a member of the Milwaukee club of the American Association, was found dead in a Louisville hotel room, a bullet hole in his heart and a revolver in his hand. He had been seen around the hotel during the day and had appeared to be in good spirits. One explanation was that he was depressed over the suicide of a brother the past summer.

On March 28, 1927, at the Youree Hotel in Shreveport, Louisiana, spring training headquarters of the Chicago White Sox, Johnny Mostil, the team's star center fielder, slashed both wrists and wounded himself in the chest, throat, and legs with a razor blade and a knife. Early reports, giving him little chance to survive, were wrong. He did recover, played later that same season, and two more seasons thereafter, followed by a long career in the game as a scout. The only explanation for his act seems to have been his hypochondriacal nature. He constantly worried and brooded over his health, although a physical examination that spring had revealed no serious problems.

In eight major league seasons, Cincinnati righthander Benny Frey had struggled to a 57–82 record. At the end of the 1936 season, the best of his career (he was 10–8), he was sent to Nashville to work an ailing arm back into shape. Apparently despondent over the failure of his arm to recover, Frey, on November 1, 1937, at Jackson, Michigan, sat in his car with the motor running and a rubber hose attached to the exhaust pipe. When police found the thirty-one-year-old pitcher, he was dead from carbon monoxide poisoning.

It was August 3, 1940, and the Cincinnati Reds were in Boston. Pleading illness, catcher Willard Hershberger told his roommate, Bill Baker (some accounts say it was Lew Riggs), that he would not be able to come to the ballpark until later. When he did not appear and his telephone was not answered, manager Bill McKechnie

sent Dan Cohen, Hershberger's close friend, to the hotel to get him. When the room was entered, Hershberger's body was found in the bathroom, his jugular vein severed by a razor.

Hershberger was young (just thirty), successful, and single, and there seemed no apparent reason for his act. As in the McGann case, there had been a previous suicide in the family. Hershberger's father had shot himself to death in 1928. It has been theorized that the catcher was depressed over his recent failures on the diamond. He had gone hitless in a crucial game, and on another occasion had supposedly called a wrong pitch to Harry Danning of the Giants, who then had hit a home run to beat the Reds in the ninth inning. On the other hand, it was no secret that he had been contemplating suicide. He had told manager McKechnie as much in recent weeks. Also, he had recently purchased a $500 bond, placed it in the hotel safe, and asked that it be given to his mother "if anything happens to me."

With all the obvious planning, it is curious that no suicide note was found. Suicidal tendencies notwithstanding, a hitless game and the call of a wrong pitch hardly seem sufficient to have provoked the deed. It took almost eighty years for the truth to be revealed about the Stahl suicide. Someday, perhaps, more light will be shed on the Hershberger story.

In seven seasons with the Chicago White Sox, Mexican-born righthander Hector Barrios compiled a 38–38 record. After the 1981 season, during which he had entered a Chicago hospital for drug and alcohol treatment, he was released. On April 4, 1982, he died at his parents' home in Hermosillo, Mexico, of heart failure brought on by an overdose of heroin.

Donnie Ray Moore had a combined 52 saves in 1985 and 1986 for the California Angels, only to become the goat of the 1986 championship series loss to Boston when he gave up a two-out, two-run home run to Dave Henderson that cost the Angels the title. He spent most of the next season on the disabled list, was released by the Angels in 1988 and then signed with Omaha of the American Association. He was released by the Royals on June 12 after seven appearances and a 1–2 record. On July 18 he shot his estranged wife (she recovered) and then killed himself with a bullet to the brain as his ten-year-old son watched in horror. Moore's agent attributed all of Moore's troubles to his brooding over the Henderson home run.

Over the years, ballplayers have died violently, other than by suicide. The bizarre death of Hall of Famer Ed Delahanty is a case in point. In 1903 he was with Washington of the American League, but wanted to be with the Giants in New York, where he felt he could earn more money. He dealt with his unhappiness by consuming generous doses of alcohol, starting with a drinking spree in Cleveland. Later, in Detroit, where he took out an accident policy in favor of his daughter, he was heard to threaten to take his own life.

On July 2, 1903, Delahanty boarded a Michigan Central train at Detroit with a ticket to Buffalo, from where, it is believed, he planned to catch another train to Washington to meet his wife. The conductor said Delahanty was "under the weather" when he got on at Detroit and that he had downed at least five shots of whiskey along

the way. Not only was he boisterous, but he also threatened some passengers with a razor. At Bridgeburg, Ontario, just across the Niagara River from Buffalo, the conductor ejected him from the train. Delahanty, in the darkness, began to walk across the International Bridge, a railroad bridge connecting Bridgeburg and Buffalo. Bridge watchman Sam Kingston had just escorted a freight across the bridge and, lantern in hand, was walking back to the Canadian side when he confronted Delahanty. Words were exchanged and a scuffle ensued. It is not clear (Kingston told conflicting stories) if Delahanty fell, jumped, or was pushed into the river. Eight days later, his body was found at Niagara Falls, below the Horseshoe Falls.

Subsequently, Delahanty's widow filed suit in the Ontario courts against the Michigan Central Railroad, seeking $20,000 damages for the wrongful death of her husband. She was awarded $3,000, and her daughter received $2,000.

When Walter "Big Ed" Morris won 19 games for the last-place Boston Red Sox in 1928 and then came back with 14 wins for another cellar Boston club in 1929, he became one of the most sought-after pitchers in the league. One story had the Red Sox turning down a $100,000 offer. A sore arm slowed Morris in 1930 and 1931, and his record retrogressed to 4–9 and 5–7. Confident that his arm had regained its strength, he prepared to go to spring training in 1932. As a going-away present, some of his buddies arranged a party for him at a tavern in Century, Florida, just across the state line from Morris's hometown of Flomaton, Alabama. Unfortunately, the party began to get out of hand, and soon the guest of honor was involved in a fight with Joe White, a gas station attendant from Brewton, Alabama. When Morris slipped to the floor, White pulled a knife and stabbed him twice, fatally. Morris was thirty-one and left a widow and two children.

Len Koenecke was an impressive-looking athlete—broad of shoulder, slim of waist, and ruggedly handsome. He was said to have been the last player personally scouted by John McGraw, who arranged for his purchase from Indianapolis (American Association) in 1931 for players valued at $75,000. The young outfielder failed to live up to his minor league billings and was farmed to Jersey City in 1932 and to Buffalo in 1933. An outstanding season for the Bisons in 1933 led to his sale to Brooklyn, where in 1934 he batted .320 and fielded a league-leading .994. But he slumped in 1935, and late that year manager Casey Stengel sent Koenecke and two other players home from St. Louis so that he could try out some young prospects.

On the flight from St. Louis to Detroit, Koenecke, who had been drinking, created a disturbance, and when the airport was reached he was ordered off the plane. Although it was late in the evening, he decided to charter a private plane and fly to Buffalo, where he had friends. The plane he chartered had an interesting past. It had once been owned by Smith Reynolds of the tobacco family and his wife, torch singer Libby Holman, who were principals in one of the most sensational murder cases of the 1930s. When Reynolds was shot to death at the family estate in Winston-Salem, N.C., his wife was charged with the crime but was later cleared.

While the plane was still over Canada, Koenecke tried to take over the controls from pilot William Mulqueeny. Irwin Davis, the copilot, attempted to restrain the husky ballplayer but was pushed to the floor. Mulqueeny, while trying to guide the plane with one hand, picked up a fire extinguisher with the other and bludgeoned Koenecke until he was dead. Mulqueeny had no idea where he was until he spotted the lights of Toronto. Seeing a racetrack on the outskirts of the city, he decided to use the backstretch as an airport and brought the plane safely down. Then, to cap their night of terror, the two men were attacked by watch dogs as they left the plane. The dogs eventually backed off, and they were able to summon help.

After two hearings in Canadian courts, Mulqueeny and Davis were absolved of all blame in Koenecke's death. Blood tests had shown that the dead ballplayer was drunk. At one of the hearings, Edward J. Murphy, attorney for the pilots, alleged that Koenecke was trying to commit suicide and to do it "in a grand and glorious manner."

In the early hours of January 5, 1975, Don Wilson, star righthanded pitcher of the Houston Astros, who had won 104 games in nine major league seasons and pitched two no-hitters, drove his luxury car into the garage of his suburban Houston home and left the motor running. At one P.M. his lifeless body was found slumped in the passenger seat. The ignition was on, the battery was dead, the gas tank was empty, and there were exhaust-fume stains on the garage floor. In the room above the garage, his five-year-old son Alexander was dead from the fumes. His wife, Bernice, and his daughter, Denise, were taken to the hospital in serious condition. Bernice Wilson also had a badly bruised jaw, which was never explained, but which could have been caused by a fall.

Mrs. Wilson and her daughter both recovered. Tests on the twenty-nine-year-old Don Wilson revealed a blood-alcohol content of .167. On February 5, 1975, the medical examiner ruled the deaths of father and son were accidental.

Mickey Fuentes, a righthanded pitcher who was 1–3 for Seattle in 1969, never made it to spring training in 1970. He was shot to death in a tavern brawl in his native Loiza Aldea, Puerto Rico, January 29, 1970. He was only twenty years old.

With Lyman Bostock, who had starred for Minnesota (in 1975–1977) and then had signed a lucrative free-agent contract with California, it was a case of being in the wrong place at the wrong time. On September 23, 1978, in Gary, Indiana, he was in a car being driven by his uncle when he was shot by a man named Leonard Smith, whose apparent target was Smith's estranged wife, seated next to Bostock in the back seat. Three hours after the assault, the twenty-seven-year-old Bostock was dead. There was whispering that something was going on between Bostock and Mrs. Smith. Actually they had met only twenty minutes before and were heading for different destinations.

Leonard Smith was twice tried for murder. The first trial, in which insanity was pleaded, ended in a hung jury. In the second trial, he was found not guilty by reason of insanity, spent six months in a mental hospital, and then was a free man. Outrage over the outcome of the two trials resulted in a change in the Indiana law, whereby an accused can now be judged both insane and guilty of a crime.

Planes, Cars, Trucks, and a Dune Buggy

When superstars Roberto Clemente and Thurman Munson lost their lives in air crashes, it was front-page news all over the country. In Clemente's case, the coverage was international in scope because of the mercy mission in which he was involved.

Clemente and Munson were not the first active major leaguers to perish in airplane accidents. There were at least six prior air fatalities—seven if Koenecke is included. Marvin Goodwin, a righthanded spitball pitcher who saw action with the Senators, Cardinals, and Reds from 1916 through 1925, was the first. In 1925, nearing the end of his career, he was pitcher-manager of Houston of the Texas League, on assignment from the Cardinals. He did so well at Houston (21–9) that Cincinnati purchased him conditionally late in the season, with the understanding that final payment on the deal would be made only if he lasted thirty days into the 1926 season. He made four September appearances for the Reds with no wins and no losses.

Goodwin had been a flying instructor in World War One and was still a lieutenant in the reserve. On October 18, 1925, he took off on a practice flight from Ellington Field, near Houston, with a mechanic on board. The engine failed at 200 feet, and the plane crashed. The mechanic miraculously survived, but Goodwin, who suffered two broken legs and internal injuries, died four days later. The fatality had a ghoulish aftermath. The following year, the Cardinals demanded full payment for Goodwin's contract. The Reds refused on the grounds that he was not on their roster thirty days into the 1926 season. The case was referred to the commissioner's office. Judge Landis, citing the terms of the contract, ruled in favor of the Reds.

Elmer Joseph Gedeon played in the outfield for the Washington Senators in 1939. He had been a track star at the University of Michigan and had given up a chance to run in the Olympic Games to go into baseball. But then World War Two came along, and Gedeon gave up baseball to become an early volunteer in the Air Corps. He died April 15, 1944, when his plane was shot down over France. (Two others who played in the majors in 1939 also died in battle. Bob Neighbors, a shortstop for seven games with the St. Louis Browns, died in North Korea in 1952, and Harry O'Neill, who caught one game for the Philadelphia Athletics, perished in the assault on Iwo Jima in 1945.)

After his graduation from Boston University in 1955, catcher Tom Gastall pocketed a $40,000 bonus from the Baltimore Orioles. He was used sparingly, playing 20 games in 1955 and 32 in 1956. On September 20, 1956, he took off in a light plane from Harbor Field, near Baltimore. He landed at Easton, from where he later took off for the return flight over the Chesapeake Bay. Five days later, his body and the wreckage of the plane were found in the water off Riviera Beach. Gastall was just twenty-four.

A little over two months later, on November 27, 1956, outfielder Charlie Peete, who had played 23 games for the St. Louis Cardinals that summer, died in a plane crash in the mountains of Venezuela, near Caracas, while en route to play winter ball. His wife and three children also perished in the crash.

Another victim of a Venezuelan air disaster was twenty-one-year-old Nestor Chavez, a San Francisco Giant farmhand who played in two games for the Giants in 1967. On March 16, 1969, the young pitcher was on his way to join the Giants' Phoenix farm club when his plane crashed, killing 155 passengers. It was one of the worst accidents in aviation history.

Ken Hubbs, playing 160 games for the Chicago Cubs in 1962, handled 148 consecutive chances without an error and was Rookie of the Year. He tailed off in 1963 but was still rated one of the game's rising young stars. At the end of the 1963 season, he began to take flying lessons. In early February 1964, shortly after he had received his license, Hubbs, who lived in Colton, California, flew to Provo, Utah, with a friend, Dennis Doyle, to visit Doyle's in-laws. On February 15, Hubbs and Doyle took off in a snowstorm for their return trip to California. Only five miles from Provo, the plane crashed into Utah Lake, killing Hubbs and Doyle.

After investigation, the Civil Aeronautics Board reported the probable cause as "Hubbs's attempt to continue visual flight into an area of adverse weather." The twenty-two-year-old Hubbs, who was not licensed for instrument flying, left a log book which showed he had flown just 71 hours, 16 minutes.

On September 30, 1972, Roberto Clemente, who had batted .317 in eighteen seasons with Pittsburgh, touched Jon Matlack of the Mets for a base hit. It was Clemente's 3,000th and last hit. On December 31, 1972, Clemente and four others were killed when a plane carrying food, clothing, and medical supplies to earthquake-stricken Nicaragua crashed moments after takeoff from San Juan, Puerto Rico.

Clemente's career had all the elements of a Horatio Alger tale. Born August 18, 1934, in Carolina, Puerto Rico, the son of a sugar plantation foreman, he was signed by Al Campanis of the Dodgers as a teenager. The Dodgers tried to cover him up on the Montreal (International League) roster, but Pittsburgh general manager Branch Rickey, who knew all about him from his days with the Dodgers, drafted him for a piddling $4,000. It was one of the greatest bargains in baseball history. Clemente immediately became a regular and won all manner of plaudits for his hitting, fielding, and magnificent throwing arm. He was Most Valuable Player in 1966, batted .310 and .414 in two World Series (1960, 1971), and was *Sporting News*'s Gold Glove outfielder twelve times. Twice he hit three home runs in one game, and five times he led National League outfielders in assists.

Clemente was voted into the Baseball Hall of Fame in 1973 in a special election, with the usual five-year waiting period waived by a change of the voting rules.

Thurman Munson was the only New York Yankee to win both Rookie of the Year (1970) and Most Valuable Player (1976) awards. He was the regular Yankee catcher from 1970, averaging more than 140 games a year, despite aching knees, a beaning, and a foul ball in the throat.

He was one of the league's top clutch hitters, with 701 RBIs and a .292 average over eleven seasons. His clashes with Reggie Jackson over which of them was the straw that stirred the Yankee drink drew national attention.

On August 2, 1979, an off-day, Munson flew his new Cessna Citation jet from New York to Canton, Ohio, to visit his family. Late in the afternoon, he was practicing takeoffs and landings at the Akron-Canton Airport when the plane crashed a thousand feet short of the runway. Munson's flying companions, David Hall and Jerry Anderson, survived and at great danger to themselves, attempted to pull Munson from the flaming wreckage. But there was no chance. Munson, who was thirty-two, left his wife, Diane, and three children, not to mention millions of mourning baseball fans. On August 6 of that year, 51,000 fans at Yankee Stadium participated in an impressive nine-minute salute to the Yankee captain, who, with a few more years under his belt, could well have been a good bet for the Hall of Fame.

As far as is known, the first active major leaguer to die in a vehicular accident was Norman Boeckel, a .298 hitter for the 1923 Boston Braves. The thirty-one-year-old third baseman died February 16, 1924, in a San Diego hospital, from pelvic injuries sustained the day before in a collision between his car and a truck. Earlier, Boeckel had played a fringe role in another piece of baseball history. He had submitted an affidavit to National League President John Heydler, attesting that he had heard pitcher Rube Benton boast of winning $3,200 on the 1919 World Series on a tip from Hal Chase. Benton was thrown out of baseball, but was later reinstated by Judge Landis.

The year 1929 saw the deaths of two major leaguers in vehicular accidents. Denny Williams, a twenty-nine-year-old outfielder, who had played with the Reds in 1921 and the Red Sox in 1924, 1925 and 1928, was killed in Los Angeles, March 21. Seven months later, on October 22, Walter "Peck" Lerian, regular catcher for the Phillies in 1928 and 1929, died in a Baltimore hospital, after being hit by a truck that vaulted over a curb and pinned him against the wall of a building.

Catcher Al Montgomery was only twenty years old when he appeared in 42 games for the Boston Braves in 1941. While returning from spring training on April 26, 1942, having been assigned to Hartford of the Eastern League, he was involved in a car accident near Waverly, Virginia, and killed.

While Paul Edmondson, a twenty-seven-year-old pitcher who had been 1–6 with the 1969 White Sox, was en route to spring training, he was involved in a fatal auto accident February 13, 1970, near Santa Barbara, California. Another victim of a California crash was Chico Ruiz, who had been in the majors for eight years, first with Cincinnati and most recently with California. He was killed in San Diego February 9, 1972.

The pitching career of Bob Moose was a series of highs and lows. In ten years with the Pirates, he won 76 games and lost 71. One of his wins was a no-hitter against the New York Mets on September 20, 1969. On the other side of the coin is the wild pitch he uncorked in the final game of the 1972 league championship series that permitted Cincinnati to defeat Pittsburgh. He also made three appearances in the 1971 World Series, but had no decisions. On October 9, 1976, at Martin's Ferry, Ohio, he suffered

fatal injuries in an automobile accident. It was his twenty-ninth birthday.

Righthanded pitcher Danny Frisella, who in ten years in the majors saw action with the Mets, Braves, Padres, Cardinals, and Brewers (34–40), took a dune buggy out in the desert near Phoenix on New Year's Day, 1977. When the buggy overturned, he was killed instantly.

Just six days later, on January 6, Mike Miley, a twenty-three-year-old shortstop with California in 1975 and 1976, was killed in a car crash at Baton Rouge.

On Friday night, December 19, 1986, Honolulu native Joe DeSa hit four doubles to help his Ponce Lions defeat the Mayaguez Indians, 11–8, in a Puerto Rico winter league game. At four A.M. on December 20, DeSa was killed in a head-on crash on the Las Americas Expressway. DeSa, who had played for Buffalo (American Association) in 1985 and 1986 and was the team's most valuable player in the latter year, had signed with Kansas City and was due to report in the spring for his third hitch in the majors.

The two known deaths of active players by drowning are separated by almost one hundred years. The first was England-born Al Thake, second baseman for the Brooklyn Atlantics. He drowned off Fort Hamilton, New York, while fishing, September 1, 1872. Almost a century later, on December 14, 1970, Herman Hill, twenty-five-year-old outfielder with Minnesota in 1969 and 1970, was in Venezuela for winter ball when he drowned off Valencia.

Bean Balls

Every time a batter steps to the plate, it is an act of courage. With pitches hurtling toward him at 90 miles per hour, he has but a fraction of a second to decide if he should swing, take, or bail out. Modern helmets with ear flaps have removed much of the peril, but not all. Prior to the 1950s, batters had no head protection at all; and before 1893 the risk was even greater, since the pitching distance was only 50 feet.

Considering the danger involved, it is somewhat of a miracle that only one batter has been killed by a pitched ball in the long history of major league baseball. No definitive statistics are available, but it is known that many have been killed at the amateur level and at least six in minor league play.

Major league baseball's only bean ball fatality, and its only diamond fatality for any reason, occurred on August 16, 1920, at the Polo Grounds, New York, in a game between the New York Yankees and the Cleveland Indians. It was the first half of the fifth inning, and shortstop Ray Chapman of the Indians was at bat, faced by Yankee submarine-baller Carl Mays. Chapman liked to crowd the plate and crouch over it. Mays, who had a mean streak, was not averse to throwing at any batter who encroached on his territory. Mays's first pitch was a strike, his second a ball, as Chapman seemed to edge even closer to the plate. Predictably the third pitch was high and inside. There was an ominous crack that was heard all over the Polo Grounds. Mays, thinking his pitch had hit Chapman's bat, fielded the ball and started to throw to Wally Pipp at first base, but then he saw Chapman slumped in the arms of catcher Muddy Ruel and he knew the batter

had been hit. A doctor was summoned from the stands and Chapman was temporarily revived. Assisted by two of his teammates, he began the long walk to the clubhouse in center field, but he soon collapsed and was carried the rest of the way.

When a preliminary examination in the clubhouse showed the injury was extremely serious, he was taken to nearby St. Lawrence Hospital, where an operation was performed. He was still under ether when he died at five A.M. the following day, August 17.

The repercussions were immediate and furious. Mays, a surly sort and never popular among his peers, was strongly criticized. Detroit and Boston players demanded that he be barred for life, while those on the Washington and St. Louis clubs threatened to strike if Mays was allowed to pitch again. But Mays did have his defenders. Cleveland pitcher Ray Caldwell, a former Yankee, said it seemed to him that Chapman had turned his head right into the ball. Connie Mack, venerable skipper of the Philadelphia Athletics, while deploring the fatal accident, pleaded for sympathy for Mays. Catcher Muddy Ruel, who caught Chapman when he fell, said in later years that the pitch could have been a strike.

Mays appeared before the district attorney and, after a deposition, was cleared of any criminal charges. He said he was not trying to hit Chapman, only to pitch him tight. That spring, Mays pointed out, he had seen Yankee infielder Chick Fewster nearly killed by a pitch delivered by Jeff Pfeffer of the Dodgers, and from that time on he had been reluctant even to throw inside pitches, let alone throw at batters. He then suggested the fatality might have been averted had plate umpire Tom Connolly not refused to remove from play the scuffed ball that hit Chapman. This drew a sharp rejoinder from American League umpires Billy Evans and Bill Dinneen, who charged that Mays was one of the league's most notorious scuffers. They said further that club owners had complained to Ban Johnson, league president, that too many balls were being thrown out, and that Johnson had responded by sending out a directive, instructing umpires to keep balls in play, "except those which are dangerous."

In the *New York Times* of August 19, there was an impassioned plea for the development and use of batting helmets, but it was to be more than thirty years before this advice would be heeded.

At least six minor leaguers have been killed by pitched balls. On August 9, 1906, Joe Yaeger of Fall River of the New England League hit Tom Burke of Lynn in the head with a pitch. Two days later, Burke was dead. Two days after attending Burke's funeral, Yaeger took his turn on the mound, only to be arrested by Lynn police on a manslaughter charge. Shortly thereafter, the charges were dropped. Jaeger, who had pitched for six years in the majors with Brooklyn and Detroit, completed the season with a 15–19 record.

In the second game of a Central League doubleheader, played in gathering darkness at Dayton, September 14, 1909, Charles "Cupid" Pinkney, twenty-year-old Dayton second baseman, was beaned by Casey Hageman of Grand Rapids. At first, it was thought he would recover, but his condition deteriorated, and he

died following an operation. Pinkney's father, who had traveled from Cleveland to watch his son play, was at his side when he died.

On June 18, 1916, Johnny Dodge, infielder for Mobile of the Southern Association, was hit on the head by Tom "Shotgun" Rogers of Nashville and died the next day of a fractured skull. It is believed that Dodge was thrown at in retaliation for the beaning of a Nashville player the previous day. By the strangest of coincidences, Rogers and Carl Mays were to be teammates briefly on the 1921 Yankees.

On July 4, 1933, at Omaha, Jesse Batterson, nineteen-year-old third baseman for Springfield of the Western League, suffered a fractured skull when hit by a pitch thrown by Omaha's Floyd "Swede" Carlson. He was able to get to his feet and walk to the clubhouse, but then collapsed and was taken to a hospital. He died there following an operation, with pitcher Carlson at his bedside.

Twenty-year-old James (Stormy) Davis was off to a great start for Ballinger (Texas) of the Longhorn League. In 48 games he had hit 19 home runs and had 59 RBIs. On July 3, 1947 he was beaned by Stan (Midnight) Wilson of Sweetwater. The young outfielder died a week later.

A sixth fatality occurred in the Alabama-Florida League on June 2, 1951. Lefty Jack Clifton of Headland hit Ottis Johnson of the Dothan Browns on the head and killed him. In his next start, Clifton, who had already hit twelve batters that season, pitched a no-hit, no-run game against Panama City. According to Ken Brooks in his book *The Last Rebel Yell,* every Panama City batter had one foot in the dugout.

In major league history there have been countless beanings. In most cases, the batters came back, but often were not the same hitters as before. Lowell Reidenbaugh, in his *Cooperstown,* writes that Hughie Jennings survived three skull fractures. His most serious injury was from a pitch delivered by Amos Rusie of New York, said to have been the swiftest pitcher of his day. The blow left Jennings near death and unconscious for four days. Some historians say it was Rusie's speed and the fear that he might kill someone that brought about the lengthening of the pitching distance in 1893 to the present 60 feet, 6 inches.

At Ebbets Field on September 3, 1932, Giants shortstop Ed Marshall was beaned by a Van Lingle Mungo fastball. He survived despite lapsing into "unsafe condition." The incident ended his major league career although Marshall did play thereafter in the minors.

On May 25, 1937, future Hall of Famer Mickey Cochrane, player-manager of the Detroit Tigers, lost sight of a pitch by Bump Hadley of the Yankees. It hit him in the right temple and fractured his skull. He lay unconscious for ten days but eventually recovered, although he never played again. He did, however, resume his managerial duties and also served with distinction in the Navy in World War Two.

Tony Conigliaro of the Boston Red Sox, who hit 166 home runs in six full seasons and parts of two others (all with the Red Sox, except for 74 games and 4 home runs for California in 1971), surely would have racked up more impressive numbers had he not been hit in the face

and nearly killed by a Jack Hamilton (of California) pitch on August 18, 1967. He was out of the game for a year and a half, but then came back to hit 20 home runs in 1969 and 36 in 1970. On October 11, 1970, in a most controversial deal, he was traded to California, where he was to see only limited duty. He returned to Boston for 21 games in 1975 and then was out of baseball. He died February 24, 1990.

Dickie Thon was the All-Star National League shortstop for Houston in 1983 and also led the league in game-winning hits. In the fifth game of the 1984 season, he was hit in the eye by a Mike Torrez (Mets) fastball. Despite permament damage to his eye, he was able to return to action, and through the 1992 season was playing more or less regularly for the Texas Rangers.

Don Zimmer, 1988 manager of the Chicago Cubs, suffered two serious beanings and still carries a metal plate in his head from the injuries. Paul Blair, center field magician of the Baltimore Orioles, Minnie Minoso of the White Sox, and Wayne Terwilliger, utility player for several clubs, were others whose careers were interrupted or affected by bean balls.

Sore Arms, Illnesses, Injuries, and Accidents

Up to this point, the subject has been (with a few exceptions) deaths off or on the diamond. But fatalities are only part of the story. Many a baseball career has aborted for reasons not resulting in death, at least, not at once.

In the old days, sore arms were usually rested. If there was any treatment at all, it was by the likes of John D. "Bonesetter" Reese, a self-trained muscle manipulator of Youngstown, Ohio. Nobody ever heard of the rotator cuff or even dreamed of such sophisticated operations as those which prolonged the careers of Tommy John, Ken Dayley, and others.

Charles "Lady" Baldwin was one old-timer who could have used a Tommy John bionic arm. In 1886 he won 42 games for Detroit (NL) and pitched 487 innings. He then developed arm trouble and dropped to 13 wins in 1887 and to 3 each in 1888 and 1890, after which he retired for good to his Michigan farm. Hall of Famer Christy Mathewson's arm went dead in 1916, but by then he was thirty-eight, had won 373 games, and had achieved immortality. Smoky Joe Wood was another sore arm victim, but he did beat the rap in a way. After winning 23 games for the Red Sox in 1911 and then 34 in 1912, including 16 in a row, he developed a sore arm the following spring. His days as an intimidating fireballer were over, although he did win 35 games for the Sox over the next three seasons. Realizing he could no longer pitch, he decided to become a sore-armed outfielder, and played that position with fair success for Cleveland through the 1922 season. Altogether he played in fourteen major league seasons and left a 116–57 pitching record and a career batting mark of .283.

Undocumented are the names of countless other pitchers of the game's early years who dropped out prematurely because of so-called dead arms. More is known of modern pitchers, like Dave Ferris and Karl Spooner. Ferris joined the Boston Red Sox in 1945, having been mustered out of the Army because of asthma. He raised plenty of eyebrows with a 21–10 record in the last year of wartime baseball, but then made believers out of every-

one by winning 25 and losing just 6 in 1946. But in a night game in Cleveland in June of 1947, he suffered a shoulder injury, from which he never fully recovered although he did hang on until 1950. His career log shows 65–30 for a phenomenal .684 percentage. No pitcher ever made a more dazzling entrance or faded as fast as Karl Spooner.

The twenty-three-year-old lefthander was called up by Brooklyn from Fort Worth (Texas), late in the 1954 season. He pitched shutouts against New York and Pittsburgh in his first two starts, allowing just 7 hits and striking out 27. Hampered by a sore arm, he struggled to an 8–6 record in 1955, made two appearances in the World Series (0–1), then never pitched again.

In 1966 another Dodger lefthander, Hall of Famer Sandy Koufax was 27–9, with 5 shutouts and an ERA of 1.73 in 323 innings of work. Talk about going out on top! No pitcher in major league history ever matched that in a final season. He pitched against Baltimore in the 1966 World Series (0–1), but at the age of thirty his career was over. Traumatic arthritis in the left elbow, triggered by a fall on his left arm when attempting a pickoff during the 1964 season, made it impossible for him to continue. Had Koufax been able to pitch as long as, say Warren Spahn, there is no telling what his record might have been. As it was, he left an imposing mark of 165–87 (.655) and an ERA of 2.76.

Mark Fidrych, the colorful Detroit pitcher known as "the Bird," was 19–9 in 1976 and was the starting pitcher in the All-Star game. But plagued by arm trouble, he faded to a combined 10–11 record over the next four seasons. He was only twenty-six when he pitched his final big league game in 1980. Twice he tried comebacks in the minors, but failed.

Lefty Don Gullett, the only man to pitch the opening game in successive World Series for two different teams (Cincinnati Reds, 1976; and New York Yankees, 1977), was just twenty-seven when his career ended with a bad arm after the 1978 season. He had been one of the first free agents signed by the Yankees, and was certainly one of their most expensive, costing them $2 million for his 18 wins in two seasons.

Righthander Wayne Garland of the Indians was operated on for a rotator cuff tear on May 5, 1978. He had won 33 games the two previous seasons. After the operation, he came back, hanging on until 1981, but he was never the same pitcher. And like Gullett, he was working on a lucrative long-term contract.

The previous pages have told of the surprising number of active major leaguers who succumbed to illness. Many others became ill and were forced to give up the game or see their baseball livelihoods interrupted. An early example was Jimmy Wood, who played for Chicago, Brooklyn, and Philadelphia in the National Association from 1871 to 1873. In 1873 he developed a leg abscess which he attempted to lance with a penknife. A severe infection developed, resulting in the loss of his leg. His playing days, of course, were over, but he did return as a manager in 1874 and 1875.

In 1890 first baseman Dave Orr of Brooklyn (in the Players' League) batted .373, hit 32 doubles, 13 triples, and 6 home runs, while striking out only 11 times. For a nonpitcher, this was the ultimate in final seasons. In the off-season, the thirty-one-year-old Orr suffered a stroke

and never played again. He died in Brooklyn on June 3, 1915. He had been caretaker of Ebbets Field for many years.

Hall of Famer Amos Rusie won 243 games in nine seasons and part of a tenth, but saw his career shrouded by misfortune, some of his own making. The so-called "Hoosier Thunderbolt," who almost killed Hughie Jennings with a bean ball, himself took a line drive to the head which permanently damaged his hearing. He threw out his arm in 1898 and was out of the game for two years. He compounded his other problems with heavy drinking. Although he tried to come back in 1901, he failed. At the age of thirty he was through.

The aforementioned Jennings, another Hall of Famer, had a baseball life replete with illness and adversity. In addition to the almost fatal beaning by Rusie, he suffered a nervous breakdown in 1925, after taking over as manager of the New York Giants when John McGraw became ill. Jennings died of spinal meningitis in 1928 at the age of fifty-eight.

Often documented is the tragic accident that terminated the career of catcher Charley Bennett, who played in the majors from 1878 to 1893 (except for 1879). In January of 1894, while on a hunting trip, he tried to catch and board a moving train at Wellsville, Kansas, but lost his grip and fell under the wheels, losing both legs.

Shortstop Charlie Hollocher, who played for the Cubs from 1918 to 1924, was constantly bedeviled by illness, real and imaginary, blunting what some observers feel could have been a Hall of Fame–level career. His tormented life came to an end on August 14, 1940, when he parked his car on a quiet Clayton, Missouri, street, then tore his throat apart with a blast from a sixteen-gauge shotgun.

Jackie Hayes, outstanding second baseman and shortstop for the Senators and the White Sox (1927–1940), was 3 for 3 in a 1940 Sox spring game; then in the shower room he noticed a cloudiness in one eye. He played 18 games that year, but by August he had lost his sight in the clouded eye. In a matter of three years, he had lost his sight in the other. Similarly, George "Specs" Toporcer, a former major league infielder, had lost his sight while managing Buffalo (International League) in 1951. Both men learned to live with their blindness and went on to lead productive lives, Hayes as the tax collector of Chilton County, Alabama, and Toporcer as a writer and lecturer.

Righthanded pitcher Monty Stratton (15–5 and 15–9 for the Chicago White Sox in 1937 and 1938) was hunting rabbits near his mother's home in Greenville, Texas, after the 1938 season, when he accidentally discharged a .22-caliber pistol. The slug lodged in his right knee, severing the main artery and necessitating amputation of the leg. Stratton did not pitch again in the majors, but he was a White Sox coach for three seasons. In 1946 he pitched for Sherman in the Class C East Texas League, where, remarkably, he won 18 games. Hollywood thought it saw a story in the courageous way he had faced his tragedy and made a much-acclaimed movie of his life, *The Stratton Story*, starring Jimmy Stewart.

A third victim of a leg injury was Joe Cronin, Hall of Fame shortstop who played twenty years for Washington and Boston, and probably would have played a few more had he not fractured his leg three games into the 1945

season. He never played again, but continued in the game for many years as a manager, front office executive, and as American League president.

He looked so indestructible that they called him "The Iron Horse." Henry Louis Gehrig, in seventeen years at first base for the New York Yankees, averaged .340, hit 535 doubles, 162 triples, and 493 home runs. He scored 1,888 runs, had 1,990 RBIs, and posted a slugging percentage of .632. His incredible record of playing in 2,130 consecutive games at one time seemed unassailable, but is now being challenged by Cal Ripken of the Baltimore Orioles, who played in 1,735 consecutive games through the end of the 1992 season. On May 2, 1939, Gehrig approached manager Joe McCarthy, told him he was not feeling well. Gehrig thought he was hurting the team, and he asked to be taken from the lineup. McCarthy, of course, complied, and so for the first time since pinch-hitting for Pee-Wee Wanninger on May 31, 1925, Gehrig missed a Yankee game.

A few months later the bad news came from the Mayo Clinic. The indestructible one, "The Iron Horse," had been stricken with amyotrophic lateral sclerosis, a disease of the central nervous system for which no cure was known. On July 4, 1939, 61,000 gathered at Yankee Stadium for a gigantic Gehrig tribute. There he spoke his memorable words: "I consider myself the luckiest man on the face of the earth."

In the short time left to him, Gehrig devoted himself to public service. On June 2, 1941, exactly sixteen years from the day he replaced Pipp at first base, he died. He was thirty-seven years old. The malady that killed him is now generally referred to as Lou Gehrig's disease. Unfortunately it is almost as much a medical mystery today as it was fifty years ago when it struck him.

Catcher Bill DeLancey was a product of the St. Louis Cardinal farm system. After playing eight games for the parent club in 1932 and then spending a year at Columbus (American Association), he became a regular member of the "Gas House Gang" in 1934. In 1935 he found that he had tuberculosis and faced a long recovery period. It was not until 1940 that he made it back, and then it was just for 15 games. By then, he knew it was no use. His career was over. He died November 28, 1946, on his forty-fifth birthday.

When Don Black went to the mound for the Cleveland Indians against the St. Louis Browns on September 13, 1948, he could have looked back on an undistinguished six-year record with the Athletics and Indians (34–55). But there were two victories—one off the diamond—that he could recall with pride. The first was against the bottle; the second was a no-hit, no-run game against the Philadelphia Athletics on July 10, 1947.

In the late-season game against the Browns, upon retiring the Browns in the first two innings, Black came to bat against Bill Kennedy. After swinging mightily at the first pitch and fouling it back, he began to stagger and finally sank to his knees. Umpire Bill Summers bent over to assist Black and heard him whisper, "That last pitch to [Ed] Pellagrini did it." (He had struck out the Browns' shortstop with a curve ball to end the top of the second.) Apparently, that pitch plus the force of his swing had caused an aneurism to rupture, sending blood to his brain and spinal cord. (Shades of James Creighton, who had

injured himself fatally while batting on August 14, 1862.) An eminent neurosurgeon was summoned. He ruled out surgery as too risky, but said Black had just a 50-50 chance of surviving. But Black did survive and on September 22 he was recipient of a large purse from a benefit game against the Red Sox that attracted a crowd of 76,772.

The Indians went on to win the pennant and then defeated the Boston Braves in the World Series, but without Black, who never pitched again. He died April 21, 1959 at the age of 42.

Baseball's *Domesday Books* credit lefthanded pitcher Bert Shepard with one major league appearance. What the books do not say is that this game was pitched by a one-legged man. When Shepard's call to World War Two service came, he was a promising young pitcher. The fortunes of war took him to the European front, where he was downed over Germany on his thirty-fifth mission and taken prisoner. Doctors removed his shattered right leg, after which a fellow prisoner of war fashioned him a wooden leg. After his recapture and return to the States, he was signed by the Washington Senators as a batting practice pitcher. In his one appearance in a regular game, he allowed one run in 5⅓ innings for an ERA of 1.69.

Lou Brissie, like Bert Shepard, was a victim of World War Two combat. Brissie, who joined the Army in 1942 as a teenager, was badly wounded on the Italian front and forced to undergo twenty-three operations. Despite the handicap of a steel leg brace and a leather guard, he never gave up his dream of becoming a major league pitcher. In 1947, for Savannah of the Sally League, he won 23 games and earned a late-season call-up from the Philadelphia Athletics. From 1947 to 1953, he won 44 games for the A's and the Indians, to whom he was traded in 1951. His best year was 1949, when he won 16 games and pitched in the All-Star Game. He was only twenty-nine when his career came to a close. He then became national director of the American Legion baseball program.

Herb Score was a third American League lefty to see his career abbreviated by injury. In 1955, Score won 16 games for Cleveland and struck out 245; then in 1956 he improved to 20 wins and 263 strikeouts. Along the banks of Lake Erie, he was hailed as a lefthanded Bob Feller. But it was not to be. On May 7, 1957, at Municipal Stadium in Cleveland, he was hit in the eye by a torrid line drive off the bat of Gil McDougald of the New York Yankees and seriously injured.

His recovery was slow, and he did not return to the Indians until 1958 and then only for 12 games. On April 18, 1960, he was traded to the White Sox for Barry Latman. After three seasons of limited duty for the Sox, he called it a day. He remains in baseball as the play-by-play announcer for the Indians.

Brooklyn catcher Roy Campanella was thirty-six and in the twilight of a remarkable career that had seen him win three Most Valuable Player awards, when disaster struck on a January night in 1958. He was driving to his Long Island home in the early hours of the morning when his borrowed car skidded on a slippery spot in the road and slammed into a utility pole. The two broken vertebrae he suffered doomed him to a long and excruciatingly painful period of recovery and rehabilitation, not to mention life-long confinement to a wheelchair.

On May 7, 1959, before a crowd of 93,103 fans at the Los Angeles Coliseum, the Dodgers and the Yankees met in a mammoth benefit for the paralyzed Campanella. It was an emotional affair, rivaling similar tributes to Yankee greats Gehrig and Ruth at Yankee Stadium.

The courage Campanella displayed in his rehabilitation was an inspiration to many others who suffered severe spinal injuries. He received baseball's highest honor in 1969—election to the Hall of Fame.

Mike Pazik, a lefthander from Lynn, Mass., who appeared briefly for Minnesota in 1975, 1976, and 1977, saw his pitching career terminated when he suffered multiple fractures of both legs in a 1977 automobile accident. He returned to the game in 1980 as a coach for the White Sox. Later, he served four years as a roving pitching instructor for the Milwaukee Brewers, and then in late 1987 he was named pitching coach for Charlotte of the Double-A Southern League.

Houston righthander J. R. Richard, at 6'8" and 222 pounds, was an intimidating figure on the mound. From 1976 through 1979, his strikeout log showed 214, 214, 303, and 313, respectively, while his victories totaled 74. In 1980, even though slowed by arm and shoulder injuries, he was chosen to start for the National League in the All-Star Game at Los Angeles. But, as fate would have it, he was to pitch just two more innings for the Astros before being laid low by a stroke. The rehabilitation was painfully slow, but there always seemed to be hope that his career could be salvaged, but such hopes proved to be futile. Twice (in 1982 and 1983) he tried to pitch in the lower minors, but the illness had taken too great a toll.

In 1988, while with the San Francisco Giants, lefty Dave Dravecky developed a cancerous growth on his pitching arm. An operation and a long recuperation followed. He tried to come back in 1989, but in a late-season game against Montreal his pitching arm broke as he was delivering a ptich. Subsequently his arm was amputated, bringing to an end a once promising career. His major league record was 64–57 with an ERA of 3.13.

First baseman Nick Esasky enjoyed a career year with the Boston Red Sox in 1989, with 30 home runs and 108 RBIs. He then signed a lucrative free agent contract with the Atlanta Braves. During spring training he began to suffer from vertigo. He played only nine regular season games in 1990 before being disabled. His failure to recover baffled a horde of medical experts. He did not play at all in 1991, tried to come back in '92, but was eventually released by the Braves. Going into the 1993 season, his baseball future remains a question mark.

Bo Jackson of the Kansas City Royals was one of the most exciting players to hit the majors in years. He could run, throw, field, and hit with power. He was also a superstar in football and that proved to be his downfall. An innocent-looking sideline tackle while he was playing for the Los Angeles Raiders in 1990 resulted in a serious hip injury. Released by the Royals, he was given another chance by the White Sox in 1991. He played in only 23 late-season games, batting .225 with three home runs. His hip continued to deteriorate and eventually had to be surgically replaced. He did not play at all in 1992, but is still carried on the White Sox disabled list. It is unlikely he will ever play again.

Careers cut short for psychological reasons are not common, but there have been a few. Steve Blass, hero of the 1971 Pittsburgh World Series victory over Baltimore and winner of 19 games in 1972, suddenly could not throw strikes. So severe was the mental block that his baseball life ended in 1972 when he was only thirty-two. Kevin Saucier, a lefthanded relief pitcher for Detroit, had 13 saves and 4 wins in 1981; then, inexplicably, he developed the Steve Blass syndrome and could not throw strikes. In his case it was a fear of hitting and injuring a batter. He could not overcome the problem, and at twenty-six he was out of baseball. Joe Cowley, who pitched for the Braves, Yankees, White Sox, and Phillies, and who has a no-hit game to his credit, simply could not throw strikes and was sent to the minors by the Phillies in 1987. He could not throw strikes there either and finally was sent home.

At least one career came to a premature end because of a fear of flying. Jackie Jensen, who hit 199 home runs in eleven seasons with the Yankees, Senators, and Red Sox, retired first in 1959, tried again in 1961, but then quit for good at the age of thirty-four.

Alcohol and Drugs

It is impossible to put a number on the baseball careers shortened or adversely affected by the excessive use of alcohol. In at least four cases (Delahanty, Koenecke, Morris, and Wilson), dealt with elsewhere in this chapter, fatalities resulted. Countless players of the game's early years were lushes. Liquor was readily available to them, often on the house, and there was plenty of time for carousing, especially when on the road. Some of the worst offenders were quietly blacklisted and faded from the game. Others who were heavy drinkers continued in uniform, because they were star players and the owners winked at their alcoholic escapades. Future Hall of Famer Michael "King" Kelly, for example, drank as hard as he played; yet in 1887 Boston paid an unheard of $10,000 to Chicago for his contract. Toward the end of his career, he opened a saloon in New York, which was like putting the fox in charge of the chicken coop. His performance level deteriorated rapidly, and by 1894 he was in the minors. That fall he developed pneumonia, and on November 8 he died at the age of thirty-six.

Terry Larkin, who won 29 games for Hartford in 1877, and 29 and 31, respectively, for Chicago in 1878 and 1879, was another nineteenth-century player whose career self-destructed from the ravages of strong drink. In 1883, while drunk, he shot his wife (she recovered) and then tried to commit suicide in jail. In 1886, while employed as a bartender in Brooklyn, he showed up for work with two pistols and challenged his employer to a duel. Police ware called and he was thrown into jail until he sobered up. He died in Brooklyn in 1894.

Equally melancholy is the story of James (The Troy Terrier) Egan, who pitched, caught and played the outfield for Troy (NL) in 1882 and then was blacklisted for drunkenness. Supposedly rehabilitated, he was given a chance with Brooklyn (AA) in 1884, but before he played a game he was arrested for theft and jailed. He died of what was described as "brain fever" in a New Haven, Connecticut, jail, September 26, 1884.

Few players have come to the majors with more raw talent than Louis Sockalexis, a Penobscot Indian from

Old Towne, Maine. He played college baseball at both Holy Cross and Notre Dame. While at the latter school in 1897, he and a companion broke up an establishment run by a certain "Popcorn Jennie" and threw the furniture out the windows. When the good fathers who ran Notre Dame read about this caper in the *South Bend Tribune,* they promptly threw him out. Future major league catcher Mike Powers, who had been instrumental in getting Sockalexis into both Holy Cross and Notre Dame, wired the Cleveland Club, with whom the Indian had signed a contract to take effect at the end of the school year, and suggested it send someone to South Bend to bail him out. Manager Patsy Tebeau caught the next train west, and in a few days Sockalexis was in a Cleveland uniform. He impressed with his strength, speed, and magnificent arm. In later years, both John McGraw and Hughie Jennings said he was the greatest natural talent they had ever seen. Even allowing for the hyperbole that often accompanies such reminiscence, it is apparent that he was a player of exceptional ability. But just as exceptional was his appetite for strong drink. Frequently interrupted by binges and injuries (once he jumped from a second-floor window and severely injured an ankle), his major league career was limited to 94 games in three seasons.

Sockalexis died in Burlington, Maine, on December 24, 1913, at the age of forty-two. His baseball monument is not his .313 batting average but the Cleveland Indians baseball club, which was nicknamed after him.

Hall of Famer Rube Waddell gained almost as much notoriety for his drinking as he did recognition for his pitching. Lowell Reidenbaugh, in his *Cooperstown,* tells how Waddell would come into a bar, penniless, and whisper to the bartender, "Give me a drink, and I will give you the ball I used to defeat Cy Young in twenty innings." According to Reidenbaugh, hundreds of bartenders "displayed what they considered to be the historic souvenir."

Despite the abuse he gave his body, the Rube lasted for thirteen major league seasons and won 191 games. But his indiscretions led to tuberculosis and he died in San Antonio, Texas, on April Fool's Day, 1914, at the age of thirty-seven.

Waddell contemporary Arthur (Bugs) Raymond was not the pitcher the Rube was, but he was his equal in the drinking department. The efforts of Giant manager John McGraw to rein him in are a part of the lore and legend of baseball. Raymond finally became so uncontrollable that the Giants let him go in the spring of 1912. Later that year Raymond, while drunk, was watching a sandlot game in Chicago when a spectator picked up a broken piece of pottery and threw it, hitting Raymond in the face. A fight ensued in which Raymond was badly beaten up. He went back to his hotel room, where six days later he died of a cerebral hemorrhage, caused by a skull facture. He was only thirty years old. One former teammate said of him, "Bugs paid too much too soon for too many drinks."

The problem of alcoholism continues in the modern game, but added to it is an affliction even more virulent— the use of illegal drugs. Careers are being shortened or interrupted by excessive drinking or the ingestion of drugs, or by a combination of both. In the old days, when a player drank too much, he was either shunted aside or his problem was swept under the rug. Now, the usual pattern is a confession of the problem, or exposure, fol-

lowed by treatment, rehabilitation, sometimes suspension, but then a return to the game.

In 1983 the baseball world was rocked by the news that four players on the Kansas City Royals—Willie Wilson, Willie Aikens, Jerry Martin, and Vida Blue (no longer with the team)—had been involved with illegal drugs. All were suspended for one year by Commissioner Bowie Kuhn, although later an arbitrator reduced the suspensions, except for Blue's. Meanwhile, indictments were handed down and all were convicted and sentenced to one year in jail, with the last nine months suspended. Eventually Wilson returned to the Royals. Aikens was traded to Toronto but then went to the minors. Martin and Blue are out of baseball.

Pitcher Steve Howe of the Los Angeles Dodgers was suspended for the 1984 season for alleged drug use and did not challenge it. After at least two relapses, he was signed by the Texas Rangers and appeared for them late in the 1987 season. He was out of baseball in '88 and '89, but made a comeback in 1991 and eventually worked himself up to a prominent place in the New York Yankee bullpen. After his conviction in 1992 in Kalispell, Montana, for drug possession, he was barred from baseball "for life" by Commissioner Fay Vincent, but was given yet another chance to play in 1993. Atlanta pitcher Pascual Perez spent three months in a Dominican Republic jail on drug charges during the 1983–1984 off-season and was also suspended by Commissioner Kuhn. Arbitrator Richard I. Bloch, who had also ruled in the Willie Wilson et al. cases, subsequently threw out the Perez suspension because of lack of evidence.

Also in 1983, pitcher Dickie Noles of the Cubs spent time in jail after a drunken brawl in Cincinnati. Outfielder Ron LeFlore was arrested on drug and weapons charges in 1982 while with the Chicago White Sox. Although found not guilty, he was released by the Sox in April 1983.

Bob Welch, talented righthanded pitcher of the Dodgers, best remembered for his classic confrontation with Reggie Jackson of the Yankees in the 1978 World Series, revealed that he had been an alcoholic for many years. After rehabilitation and relegation to the minors, he returned to the Dodgers in 1986 and Oakland two years later. He has written a book about his experiences, *Five O'Clock Comes Early.*

A much-publicized drug trial that began in Pittsburgh on September 5, 1985, exposed the drug involvement of numerous players, including Keith Hernandez of the Mets (formerly with the Cardinals) and Dave Parker of the Reds (formerly with the Pirates). After the trial, Commissioner Peter Ueberroth meted out penalties to twenty-one players, ranging from heavy fines to be paid to drug prevention programs, orders to participate in random drug testing, and the performance of drug-related community service.

The shocking disclosures of widespread drug use that came out of the 1985 trial and the severe penalties that followed seemed to have a favorable impact on the drug problem, but did not eliminate it entirely. In 1986 San Diego pitcher LaMarr Hoyt, a Cy Young Award winner in 1983 when he was with the White Sox, was arrested three times on drug-related charges, and after the third was sentenced to forty-five days in federal prison. Hoyt's sus-

pension from baseball was later overturned, and he was ordered reinstated with back pay, much to the dismay of the baseball hierarchy.

Hoyt then signed with his old club, the Chicago White Sox, but his troubles were far from over. He tested positive for cocaine three times in October 1987, and then on December 4 he was arrested in his Columbia, S.C., apartment and charged with intent to distribute cocaine and marijuana. He was convicted the following year and sentenced to one year in prison. How widespread has been the use of illegal drugs by major league players? In a recent book, *Baseball Babylon*, author Dan Gutman lists 83 players who have been so involved.

The list of tragedies and shortened careers has been a long one and sad. It has included paragons and playboys, teetotalers and tosspots, the great, the near-great, and the never-were; some who self-destructed and many more who were simply the victims of the cruelest of bad luck. However classified, for each player the hypothetical question remains: Had his tragedy not occurred, what might have been?

Careers Shortened by Blacklisting or Expulsion

Listed below, but not discussed in this chapter, are players blacklisted or expelled from baseball for gambling, dishonest play (or knowledge of same), criminal activity, or, in one case—that of Ray Fisher—violation of a contract. The players involved in the 1877 Louisville and 1919 Chicago White Sox scandals, all of whom were barred for life, are grouped; the others are listed alphabetically:

1877 Louisville players   Bill Craver, Jim Devlin, George Hall, Al Nichols.

1919 Chicago White Sox players   Eddie Cicotte, Oscar Felsch, Chick Gandil, Joe Jackson, Fred McMullin, Swede Risberg, Buck Weaver, Claude Williams.

Others   George Bechtel, Rube Benton (who was later reinstated and returned to the majors), Hal Chase, Cozy Dolan, Phil Douglas, Jean Dubuc (who returned as a coach with Detroit in 1931), Ray Fisher, Joe Gedeon, Claude Hendrix, Richard Higham (umpire), Benny Kauff, Hubert Leonard, Lee Magee, Jimmy O'Connell, Eugene Paulette, Pete Rose, Heinie Zimmerman. [Former major leaguers banned from baseball for their activities in the minor leagues include Babe Borton, Gene Dale, Jess Levan, Harl Maggert, Tom Seaton and Joe Tipton.]

## CHAPTER 11

The Pinch Hitters

L. Robert Davids

It was approximately 100 years ago, in 1891, when baseball rules were amended to allow substitute batters for other than emergency conditions. There apparently were a few occasions earlier when a batter was substituted because of an injury to a regular player. In fact, historian Al Kermisch has documented such an occurrence as early as 1876, the first year of the National League, but the batter did not make a hit. There might have been others who did hit safely, but the narrative reporting of the time was usually quite limited, and it was fairly typical for substitutes to be omitted from the box score.

For many years it was believed that the first successful pinch hit occurred June 7, 1892, when Jack Doyle of Cleveland batted for pitcher George Davies and delivered a ninth-inning single against Brooklyn. However, there were two earlier pinch hits achieved that season. On April 29, 1892, Philadelphia was playing in Chicago and losing in the ninth, 4–2. Manager Harry Wright called on Charles Reilly, a switch hitter, to bat in place of pitcher Kid Carsey. He singled sharply to center off Wild Bill Hutchison, but the game ended two outs later.

A more dramatic pinch hit was achieved about two weeks later with Brooklyn playing at Boston. The Boston *Journal* described the May 14 circumstance as follows:

Boston could do nothing in the ninth. Ward [Brooklyn manager John M. Ward] meant business in his turn at bat and instead of sending Collins [the left fielder] to bat he substituted Tom Daly. Hardly had the spectators recognized the newcomer when he lifted one of Clarkson's slow balls over the left field fence and the game was tied.

That description is quoted to confirm that Hub Collins, who was not feeling well, was replaced at bat in the ninth rather than in the field one-half inning earlier. There was a tragic footnote to this first pinch home run as it was soon learned that Collins had typhoid fever. He never returned to the lineup and died a week later.

In spite of three successful pinch hits in the first six weeks of the 1892 season, there was very limited use of substitute batsmen in that period. In fact, in the middle of the 1892 season, roster sizes would be reduced from 15 to 13. With a roster that small, most of the extra players had to be pitchers. Consequently, those pitchers who could also fill in as outfielders were the most available and most used in the early years. The first player to collect two pinch hits in a season was Kid Gleason in 1894. He was then a hurler with St. Louis and Baltimore. Jack Stivetts of Boston was the second player to hit a pinch homer, on June 28, 1894, and probably was the first to hit a pinch triple on August 15, 1895. We will include a separate section later in this chapter on the contributions of pitchers as pinch hitters.

Catchers also made an early contribution to pinch hitting. They were very vulnerable to injury in those days and it was always necessary to have available a second backstop. One or the other then could be used as a substitute batter. Jack Clements, best known as the lefthanded catcher of the Phillies, hit baseball's third pinch home run on May 5, 1896. However, he did poorly off the bench after that, collecting only 1 hit in 12 at bats in 1898. Duke Farrell of New York and Washington had much better success, going 10–4, 14–8, and 10–5 in 1896–97–98, and winding up with a 59–23 (.389) career mark in 1904.

In spite of Farrell's good record, there were still some low spots in pinch hitting after 1900. In 1904, for example, which was the first year of the 154-game schedule in this century, the AL leader in pinch hits had only two for the season. There were seven tied with that number, and you had to give the nod to catcher Jim McGuire, who was 2 for 2. The Deacon didn't do particularly well as a substitute batter until he became forty years old. From 1904 through 1908 he was 9–6. While managing Boston in 1907, he inserted himself as a pinch hitter against Detroit on July 27. He made quite a hit with Boston fans by slamming a home run in the ninth to tie the game at 2–2. It was only the second pinch homer hit in the American League. More significantly, McGuire, at age 43 years and 8 months, was the oldest ever to hit a pinch homer.

There was a significant change in the level of pinch hitter activity in 1908, when the St. Louis Browns acquired a big pitcher-first baseman named Dode Criss. He did not pitch very well and his fielding was of the same caliber, but he did bat .341 that first year as a substitute. He set new records for pinch-hit at bats with 41 and hits with 12, and he led the AL in both categories for the next three years as well. Since he pinch-hit in about 70 percent of his major league games, he logically could be described as the first professional pinch hitter.

The regular use of Criss as a substitute batter opened the doors for several other "have bat, will travel" types. They included Moose McCormick, Ted Easterly, Ham Hyatt, Doc Miller, and Bill Rumler. McCormick of the Giants wasn't really the pioneer pinch hitter of this era as later described by New York writers. Most of the stories on this subject stated that John McGraw popularized pinch hitting by his use of McCormick. McCormick did not make much impression until 1912, when he collected 11 hits in 30 at bats. Criss, who played on a second-

division team, had left the majors by that time. McCormick played on pennant winners and gained additional publicity when he pinch-hit in the 1912 and 1913 World Series. In seven appearances, he hit two singles and a sacrifice fly, and knocked in one run. More about World Series pinch hitters later.

Ted Easterly was a catcher who came up with Cleveland in 1909. In 1912 he set a new mark for hits when he collected 13 in 30 at bats (.433). He also established career records with 152 at bats and 45 hits by 1915. That was good for a pinch-hit average of .296, outstanding for the Dead Ball Era.

Doc Miller, a Canadian-born outfielder, did practically no pinch hitting in his first two years with the Boston Braves in 1910–11, but when he was traded to the Phillies in 1912, he was called on frequently. In fact, in 1913 he set new marks for at bats with 56 and hits with 20 (.357). In 1917, catcher Bill Rumler of the Browns, one of the few righthanded pinch-hit specialists in this era, upped the at bats to 71 and slapped out 16 hits along the way. The seventh-place Browns, still trying to get their act together, used a record 14 different pinch batters and averaged at least one appearance per game for the 154-game schedule.

Ham Hyatt, a well-built outfielder-first baseman and a recognized hitter in the minors, made his mark in the majors as a power hitter in the pinch. He broke in with the Pirates in 1909 and his 9 pinch hits that year included 3 triples. This was a season record, since tied, and he also shares the career mark with 5. In 1913 he became the first to hit three pinch homers in a season and he was the first to hit four in a career. He also was the first to reach the 50 level in hits. He closed out his major league career with the Yankees in 1918 with 57 hits in 240 at bats.

Hyatt's successor as career pinch-hit leader was even more sturdy in appearance. In fact, at 5-10 and 230 pounds, he was *fat*. Bob (Fatty) Fothergill also had fun poked at him by Catholic teammates because of his last name. There was no kidding around, however, when the Detroit outfielder was at bat as he compiled a career batting average (1923–33) of .326. In the pinch he was at an even .300, based on 76 hits in 253 at bats.

In 1933, while Fothergill was still an active player, he suffered the embarrassment of being passed on the pinch-hit list by a National Leaguer, and a pitcher at that. It was Charles "Red" Lucas, a dumpy-looking righthander who pitched for the second-division Cincinnati Reds. But on the mound he was a master craftsman with offspeed pitches and pinpoint control, and at the plate he swung with confidence from the left side. In the five years from 1929 to 1933, he averaged 13 pinch hits a season. Traded to Pittsburgh, he was used less as a pinch batter but went on to push the pinch-hit record seemingly out of reach by 1937, at which time he had 114 career pinch hits.

Lucas's hit record lasted almost thirty years; in fact, no one came close in the next quarter century. Sam Leslie, Bill Terry's backup first baseman with the Giants, had a big season in 1932, when he banged out 22 hits in 72 trips. Both were new season marks, but Leslie wound up in 1938 with only 59 career hits. The colorful and unpredictable Frenchy Bordagaray had one of the great pinch-hit seasons with the Cardinals in 1938, when he produced 20 hits in 43 at bats for a lofty .452 mark. However, when he

finished his career with the Dodgers in 1945 he had accumulated only 54 pinch hits.

Pinch hitting expanded in general after World War II, a process enhanced in part by Casey Stengel's success at platooning players. Peanuts Lowrey of the Cardinals had two of the best back-to-back seasons when he had 14 hits in 28 at bats (.500) in 1952, and 21 hits in 59 at bats the next season. This righthanded batter closed out in 1955 with 62 career hits. Switch hitters also began to be used more in the pinch. Dave Philley of the Phillies was a primary example. In 1958 he had 18 hits in 44 at bats (.409), and this included eight in a row at the end of the season. In 1961 with the Orioles, he established a new pinch-hit record with 24 in 72 at bats. When he retired the next year, he had 93 career pinch-hits, the closest to Lucas's 114. Red Schoendienst was another good switch hitter of this period. In 1962, he almost duplicated Philley's great 1961 season with 22 hits in 72 at bats.

Another leading pinch hitter of the post–World War II period was Elmer Valo, a native of Czechoslovakia. Actually he was the leading "pinch walker." He summed up his role in terms of "There are times when all a pinch hitter has to do is to get a pass. In that sort of situation, the trick is to walk and forget your temptation to go for a long hit." In 1960 with the Senators and Yankees, he was on base 33 times with 18 walks, 14 hits, and 1 hit-by-pitch. Over his career, he received a record 91 walks while collecting 90 pinch hits. Research on this anomaly reveals that Harry McCurdy of the 1933 Phillies had 16 walks to go with 15 hits, and Dom Dallessandro of the 1946 Cubs had 15 walks and only 6 pinch hits. Dom's diminutive stature (5 feet, 6 inches) might have been a contributing factor. More recently, Merv Rettenmund of the 1977 Padres had 16 walks and 21 hits in 86 appearances. No pinch hitter has been on base more often.

The major assault on Lucas's long-standing pinch-hit record of 114 came in the mid-1960s. Catcher Smoky Burgess and outfielder Jerry Lynch both reached the century level in 1965, and Smoky had enough momentum from a 20-hit season to pass Lucas with his last hit of the year. Lynch finished his career in 1966 with 116 hits—only two beyond Lucas. Since all of his career was spent in the NL, he at least held that record. Burgess, on the other hand, didn't look back. Essentially a full-time pinch hitter with the White Sox, he had 21 hits in 1966 and 8 in 1967, and wound up his career with 145.

Just as Lucas's pinch-hit total seemed secure at 114—and it was for 28 years—so did Smoky's grand total of 145. However, the man to break his record was already hitting well for the Pirates. It was Manny Mota of the Dominican Republic, one of the growing number of Latin Americans entering the major leagues. Unlike most other players, who did their pinch hitting in their later years, Mota was a substitute batter some 20–30 times a season in the first part of his long career, slacked off somewhat in the middle, and pushed for a record in the later years. He pinch-hit in every one of his 20 seasons, passing Burgess's mark in 1979 and winding up with a round 150 in 1980. It looked like Greg Gross might challenge his career mark, but the latter was released after the 1989 season with 143 hits in a record 588 at bats. Ironically, not one of Gross's 143 hits went for a home run. On the other hand, not one of Burgess's 145 hits went for a triple.

Pinch Home Runs

Home runs, the most dramatic and productive of pinch hits, have played an important role ever since the first pinch home run was hit by Tom Daly on May 14, 1892. National League pinch hitters had slammed ten homers by the time the AL entered the majors in 1901, and had hit six more by the time Germany Schaefer of Detroit hit the Junior Circuit's first on June 25, 1906, in Chicago. Doc White, who had hit a pinch homer for the Phillies in 1902, was on the mound for the White Sox and leading 2–1 in the ninth. With a Tiger on base, Schaefer hit a long drive which skipped around in the outfield long enough for both to circle the bases for a 3–2 win.

In 1910, Beals Becker of the Giants was the first to hit 2 pinch homers in a season, one coming with the bases loaded. Ham Hyatt was the first to hit 3 with Pittsburgh in 1913. Cliff Cravath of Philadelphia hit 2 that season, the second off Christy Mathewson on July 4. The NL exploded for 11 pinch four-baggers in all. Cravath again showed up the Giants on April 20, 1920, when, as manager of the Phillies, he inserted himself as a pinch batter in a scoreless game and hit a 3-run game-winner. It was his last in the majors and his sixth in the pinch, a record that lasted until an old Phillies teammate, Cy Williams, connected for his seventh on April 16, 1928. That round-tripper also came against the Giants, when a young and not-so-fat Freddie Fitzsimmons served up a knuckleball with two on base. Williams hit 3 pinch home runs that season and 2 in 1929, to close out his career with 11. That mark was expected to last for years and did.

Johnny Frederick of Brooklyn had a good crack at it, but his six-year career was too short. He concentrated most of his pinch-hit prowess in the 1932 season, when he collected 9 pinch hits in 29 at bats. However, a spectacular 6 of those hits went the distance. When Ford Sawyer, an early authority on pinch hitting, had this story published in *The Sporting News* in October 1932, the bold headline read: FREDERICK'S SIX PINCH-HIT HOME RUNS EPOCHAL ACHIEVEMENT OF MAJOR HISTORY. That might have sounded a bit exaggerated, but the standing record after forty years of pinch hitting was only 3 pinch homers. And even now, almost sixty years later, no one else has hit more than five. Frederick, who went "downtown" off such notable hurlers as Burleigh Grimes, Carl Hubbell, Lon Warneke, and Pat Malone, also hit 2 pinch doubles, giving him 29 total bases in 29 pinch at bats for a 1.000 slugging mark. His short career ended with 8 pinch-hit homers.

Red Sox manager Joe Cronin had an exceptionally productive year in 1943, when he batted .429 (43–18), hit 4 doubles and 5 homers, and batted in a record 25 runs, since tied. Six of the RBIs came in a June 17 twinbill, when he blasted a 3-run homer in each game. Ironically those 5 pinch homers became his career total as well. Hal Breeden of Montreal was the only other to duplicate this doubleheader feat. He apparently was not affected by superstition because his twin blasts came on Friday the thirteenth of July, 1973, and resulted in a split with Atlanta.

Cy Williams's record of 11 career pinch homers remained on the books for 31 years until George Crowe swept it away with a four-homer flourish in 1960 that raised his total to 14. Jerry Lynch then took over, not with four in a season, but one each season for 1963–64–65–66. His total of 18 was passed by Cliff Johnson, who was primarily a designated hitter, in 1985. Johnson's record of 20 pinch homers in 277 at bats gives him a frequency factor of 1 per 13.9 at bats. Among players with ten or more pinch homers, only Joe Adcock's 12.8 (153–12) and Cy Williams's 12.9 (142–11) rank ahead of him.

What about that ultimate dream hit, the pinch grand slam? It happens anywhere from two to seven times a year now but was very rare in the early days. More than 200 pinch slams have been hit, all in this century. Ironically, the first was hit by a pitcher, Mike O'Neill of the Cardinals, in a victory over the Boston NL team on June 3, 1902. Mike's brother Jack, one of four O'Neills who played in the majors, caught this game and also rode home on Mike's blast, which was inside the park in Boston. The second pinch slam occurred just two months later, hit by catcher Pat Moral of Boston, but then it was eight years before Beals Becker connected for the Giants. The first AL pinch slam did not take place until September 24, 1916, when Marty Kavanagh, a utility infielder for Cleveland, hit a hard liner off Hub Leonard of the Red Sox. The ball rolled through a hole in the fence and everyone scored.

Two playing managers looked good by inserting themselves in the box and belting the ball. Rogers Hornsby hit a pinch slam for his Cubs in the eleventh inning against the Braves on September 13, 1931. Phil Cavarretta also hit one for the Cubs shortly after taking over the helm on July 29, 1951. His came off Robin Roberts when the latter was a leading hurler. Pitcher Early Wynn hit one for Washington on September 15, 1946. He was the only player to experience both the ecstasy and the agony as he also served one up to Bob Cerv on May 28, 1961.

Jimmie Foxx was the first player to experience the emotional impact of hitting two pinch grand slams. The first was for the Athletics on September 21, 1931. His memory had faded by the time he hit the next one, which was for the Phillies on May 18, 1945, his last season. Ron Northey was the first to hit the jackpot three times—for the Cardinals in 1947 and 1948, and with the Cubs in 1950. Later Rich Reese did it three times for the Twins and Willie McCovey connected twice for the San Francisco Giants and once for the Padres. Chuck Klein is believed to have been the only player to hit two pinch-hit triples with the bases loaded. He delivered for the Phillies on May 8, 1939, and September 14, 1940.

Pitchers as Pinch Hitters

Pitcher Don Robinson's pinch home run for the Giants on June 19, 1990, the first hit by a hurler in nineteen years, serves as a reminder that special mention should be made of their contribution as substitute batters. They were among the first used in 1891, when pinch hitters were officially allowed. Bob Caruthers and Jack Stivetts made their initial efforts that season. On June 28, 1894, when Stivetts was with Boston, he went to the plate for Kid Nichols in the ninth with Boston trailing St. Louis 10–7. The Boston Strong Boy belted a home run with two on to tie the game. He then went in to pitch, and the Beantowners won in the tenth, 11–10. He hit two more before closing out his career in 1899.

Pitchers used most frequently as pinch hitters at the turn of the century were Jim Callahan, Win Mercer, Mike O'Neill, Jesse Tannehill, Al Orth, Frank Kitson, and George Mullin. There was one game on July 17, 1901, when Vic Willis was hurling for the Boston NL team, where two other Beantown hurlers were called off the bench to pinch hit in the ninth. Kid Nichols hit a triple and Bill Dinneen scored him with a single.

A memorable highlight for pinch-hitting pitchers came on June 10–11, 1915, when Ray Caldwell of the Yankees hit pinch homers in consecutive games against the White Sox. The second was a three-run shot against Red Faber. This was the first time this feat was achieved by any pinch batter and was not duplicated for twenty-eight years.

Over the years, several hurlers led all substitute batsmen in season pinch-hit average. Examples included Frank Lange in 1911, who had 8 hits in 19 trips; Clarence Mitchell, 6 for 18 in 1920; Jack Bentley, 10 for 20 in 1923; George Uhle, 11 for 26 in 1924; Ervin Brame, 10 for 21 in 1930; Red Ruffing, 8 for 18 in 1935; and Chubby Dean, 10 for 26 in 1939.

The major pinch-hitting role of Red Lucas has already been discussed. However, there was another red-headed hurler over in the AL who made his contribution. Red Ruffing was not as active as Red Lucas, but he had a longer career. He banged out 58 hits as a substitute swinger. Teammates he batted for included Joe Sewell, Bill Dickey, and Tommy Henrich. Red faced Lefty Grove 15 times and hit him safely 5 times. He got his last pinch hit on August 8, 1947, when he was 43 years old. It was an RBI single off Hal Newhouser, then at the top of his form. Ruffing was proud of his pinch-hitting prowess; in fact, he wanted to be paid a little extra for that work and held out for a while in the spring of 1937.

Ranking after Lucas and Ruffing in pitcher pinch hits were George Uhle with 44, Ray Caldwell 36, Dutch Ruether 34, Wes Ferrell 31, and Chubby Dean and Bob Lemon with 30. Gary Peters was the hurler hitting the most pinch home runs with 4, followed by Lynn Nelson with 3. Peters had only 16 career pinch hits to his credit, but he made them count. His first homer, on July 19, 1964, came in the thirteenth inning and gave the White Sox a 3–2 win over Kansas City. His fourth pinch homer came on September 4, 1971, and was the last one until Don Robinson's recent clout.

Effects of the Designated-Hitter Rule

The introduction of the designated hitter in the AL in 1973 not only sharply reduced hitting by pitchers, but disrupted a fairly balanced pinch-hitter competition between the two leagues since 1901. Over that period, the level of activity was about the same in each circuit, as were the pinch-hit batting averages. The NL did show surprising superiority in pinch homers, even in the AL power era of 1920–40. Apparently those sluggers like Ruth, Gehrig, Foxx, and Greenberg were hitting all those home runs as regular players. For whatever the reason, NL pinch batters hit 1,123 home runs from 1901 through 1972, and their AL counterparts hit 991.

A review of pinch-hit stats in the two leagues in the four years (1969–72) prior to the DH, and the four years after its introductory season (1974–77), show that AL pinch-hitter activity was cut almost in half. The reason, of course, is that the clubs' best substitute batters were already in the batting order. In prior years, most pinch batters entered the game to bat for the pitcher, but that role was usurped by the DH. It is true that sometimes when opposing pitchers are changed, a new DH may be inserted, and the first time he bats he is a pinch hitter. But that hasn't changed the sharply reduced use of pinch batters in the AL. This disparity continued through 1991. In the latter year, for example, the fourteen-team AL had 1954 pinch hit at bats and 474 hits (.243), while the twelve-team NL had 2901 at bats and 627 hits (.216). The AL is making up the difference with more home runs per pinch hit, belting 44 to 50 for the NL. In 1985 the AL actually surpassed the NL in homers 47 to 41.

One Season Pinch-Hit Analysis

The ultimate success of a pinch batter is measured by his ability to knock in the winning run in a close game. This should make him a hero in the eyes of his manager, at least until the next game. The late John Tattersall, who was an authority on pinch hitting as well as home runs, analyzed the 1962 season to determine how many games were won by pinch hitters who came through in the clutch. He found there were 33 such dramatic victories during the year, 17 in the AL and 16 in the NL. All but 5 would be one-run victories, but 12 would be come-from-behind triumphs. Ten of the 33 would be wins in extra innings. Pinch singles won 17 games, doubles 2, and homers 12. A sacrifice fly and a bases-loaded walk won 2 other contests. A brief discussion of some of these games might flavor the analysis.

Jim Lemon of the Minnesota Twins was the first to wear the halo on April 25, 1962, when he was sent in to hit in the ninth against Baltimore with the score tied 1–1. He homered with a man on for a 3–1 victory.

At the Polo Grounds on May 5, Cal Koonce of the Cubs walked Mets pinch batter Hobie Landrith in the thirteenth with the bases full. Landrith got the 6–5 game-winning RBI.

Three games were won by 1–0 scores. On June 6, a sacrifice fly by Tom Burgess of the Angels with the bases full in the ninth drove in the only run against the White Sox. At Baltimore on June 26, Charlie Lau, who would later teach players how to hit, demonstrated with a pinch single off Johnny Buzhardt of the White Sox in the ninth to give the Orioles the 1–0 win. At Cleveland on Independence Day, Gene Green burned Hank Aguirre of the Tigers with a single in the tenth to give Jim Perry a 1–0 squeaker.

Canada's Pete Ward had an auspicious debut with Baltimore on September 21. With the Orioles trailing the Twins 2–1 in the seventh, he drove in two Birds with a sharp single off Camilo Pascual to win the game 3–2.

On August 11, Don Drysdale of the Dodgers had the Giants beaten 4–2 in the sixth when Willie McCovey belted a 3-run homer for a 5–4 win. McCovey would hit 12 of his career homers off Drysdale. The bases were loaded with Cardinals on September 9 when Carl Sawatski swatted a homer in the ninth for a 5–3 come-from-behind triumph over the Reds.

The New York Mets won only 40 games and lost 120 in

1962, but Marv Throneberry won the nickname of "Marvelous Marv" with his energetic exploits. He delivered a 2-run homer on July 7, and a 3-run homer on August 21, each time in the ninth inning, to win come-from-behind games from the Cardinals and Pirates. In the AL, Vic Wertz of the Tigers also won 2 games with pinch blows. On May 1, he hit a tenth-inning single which drove in 2 runs to beat the Athletics 3–2. His July 6 contribution was a ninth-inning homer off Hoyt Wilhelm to beat Baltimore 5–4.

Pinch Hitters in the World Series

There have been some outstanding game or single Series exploits by pinch hitters, but nothing very significant has been compiled by substitute batsmen on a "career" basis. In fact, in the long history of World Series play, no player has collected more than 3 pinch hits. Four players did that, two from the Yankees. Bobby Brown had 7 pinch hit appearances in four World Series but concentrated almost all his production in the 1947 classic. He had a single, 2 doubles, a walk, and 3 RBIs. Johnny Blanchard had 10 at bats in 5 World Series between 1960 and 1964 and collected 3 singles. Nothing outstanding there. Ken O'Dea, backup catcher for the Cubs and Cardinals in 5 World Series between 1935 and 1944, never had more than one pinch hit in a Series but knocked in 4 runs.

Although Chuck Essegian hit 2 pinch homers for the Los Angeles Dodgers in the 1959 World Series, both were solo shots and neither won a game. Bernie Carbo of the Red Sox also hit two round-trippers for the Red Sox in the 1975 Series, one being a solo circling of the bases and the other a 3-run homer which temporarily tied the game with the Reds.

No pinch hitter dominated a World Series more than Dusty Rhodes with the New York Giants in 1954. In the Fall Classic with Cleveland, which had won a record 111 games during the season, he led the New Yorkers to a dramatic 5–2 opening-game victory on September 29 with a 3-run home run in the tenth. In the second game he singled in the tying run (and then homered after going into the lineup). Ironically, Rhodes, a .253 lifetime hitter, batted for future Hall of Famer Monte Irvin in his first two appearances. In the third game he knocked in 2 runs with a single. He didn't even have to get off the bench as the Giants swept the fourth game and the Series. He had knocked in 6 runs with his 3 pinch hits, not only a record for one Series but for all Series.

For individual one-game dramatics, Kirk Gibson of the 1988 Dodgers probably takes the cake. In the first game of the 1988 Series against the powerful Oakland A's on October 15, the Dodgers were down 4–3 with two down in the last of the ninth. With Mike Davis on base with a walk, Gibson, unable to play in the regular lineup because of a leg injury, was called in to bat for pitcher Alejandro Pena. On a 3-2 pitch from relief ace Dennis Eckersley, he drove the ball into the right field bleachers for a 5–4 Los Angeles victory. It was his only appearance in the Series, which was won by the Dodgers in 5 games.

More recently, 1992 postseason play saw pinch hitters heroically succeed in two crucial games. In the ninth inning of the final NLCS game on October 15, the Braves' Francisco Cabrera hit a two-out, two-run single to give Atlanta a 3–2 come-from-behind win over Pittsburgh. Then on October 18 in the second game of the World Series between the Braves and the Blue Jays, Toronto's Ed Sprague smashed a ninth-inning, two-run homer off Atlanta's Jeff Reardon to provide the Blue Jays with a 5–4 victory. Both Cabrera and Sprague were players of undistinguished reputation prior to entering the pantheon of pinch-hit heroes.

Season Pinch Hitting Records

At Bats	Rusty Staub, Mets, 1983	81	
Hits	Jose Morales, Expos, 1976	25	
Doubles	Vic Davalillo, Cards, 1970	8	
Triples	Ham Hyatt, Pirates, 1909	3	
	Gene Robertson, Browns, 1926	3	
	Vic Davalillo, Cards, 1970	3	
Homers	John Frederick, Dodgers, 1932	6	
Walks	Elmer Valo, Yanks-Senators, 1960	18	
RBIs	Joe Cronin, Red Sox, 1943	25	
	Jerry Lynch, Reds, 1961	25	
	Rusty Staub, Mets, 1983	25	
High BA	Bruce Boisclair, Mets, 1976	.571	(21–12)
	Peanuts Lowrey, Cards, 1952	.500	(28–14)
	Ed Kranepool, Mets, 1974	.486	(35–17)
	Frenchy Bordagaray, Cards, 1938	.465	(43–20)

Career Pinch Hitting Records

At Bats	Greg Gross (1973–89)	588	
Hits	Manny Mota (1962–82)	150	
Doubles	Smoky Burgess (1949–67)	27	
Triples	Ham Hyatt (1909–18)	5	
	Gates Brown (1963–75)	5	
Homers	Cliff Johnson (1972–86)	20	
Walks	Elmer Valo (1940–61)	91	
RBIs	Smoky Burgess (1949–67)	142	
High BA	Gordon Coleman (1959–67)	.333	(120–40)
	Tommy Davis (1959–76)	.320	(197–63)
	Bob Fothergill (1922–33)	.300	(253–76)
	Dave Philley (1941–62)	.299	(311–95)
	Manny Mota (1962–82)	.297	(505–150)

First Players to Collect 50 (or More) Pinch Hits

50		**60**		**70**		**80**		**90**	
1915	Ham Hyatt	1932	Bob Fothergill	1933	Red Lucas	1933	Red Lucas	1935	Red Lucas
1930	Bob Fothergill	1932	Red Lucas	1933	Bob Fothergill	1961	Elmer Valo	1962	Dave Philley
1931	Red Lucas	1947	Ernie Lombardi	1958	Enos Slaughter	1961	Dave Philley	1962	Elmer Valo
1934	Harvey Hendrick	1954	Peanuts Lowrey	1959	George Crowe	1961	Smoky Burgess	1963	Jerry Lynch
1937	Sam Leslie	1958	Enos Slaughter	1960	Elmer Valo	1962	Jerry Lynch	1964	Smoky Burgess
1941	Red Ruffing	1958	Smoky Burgess	1960	Smoky Burgess	1970	Tito Francona	1974	Gates Brown
1941	Billy Sullivan	1959	Elmer Valo	1961	Dave Philley	1971	Gates Brown	1975	Manny Mota
1945	Frenchy	1959	George Crowe	1961	Jerry Lynch	1972	Dalton Jones	1979	Vic Davalillo
	Bordagaray	1960	Dave Philley	1970	Tito Francona	1974	Manny Mota	1979	Ed Kranepool
1945	Debs Garms	1961	Julio Becquer	1970	Gates Brown	1978	Vic Davalillo	1980	Mike Lum
1945	Ernie Lombardi								

100		**110**		**120**		**130**		**140**	
1936	Red Lucas	1937	Red Lucas	1966	Smoky Burgess	1966	Smoky Burgess	1967	Smoky Burgess
1965	Smoky Burgess	1965	Smoky Burgess	1977	Manny Mota	1978	Manny Mota	1979	Manny Mota
1965	Jerry Lynch	1966	Jerry Lynch	1983	Jose Morales	1988	Greg Gross	1989	Greg Gross
1974	Gates Brown	1977	Manny Mota	1987	Greg Gross				
1976	Manny Mota	1983	Jose Morales					**150**	
1981	Mike Lum	1985	Steve Braun					1980	Manny Mota
1982	Jose Morales	1987	Greg Gross						
1982	Terry Crowley								
1984	Steve Braun								
1985	Rusty Staub								

Evolution of Pinch Home Runs

Seven		**Eight**		**Nine**		**Ten**		**Eleven**	
Cy Williams	1928	Cy Williams	1928	Cy Williams	1929	Cy Williams	1929	Cy Williams	1929
Johnny Frederick	1932	Johnny Frederick	1934	Bobby Hofman	1955	Smoky Burgess	1959	George Crowe	1960
Ernie Lombardi	1946	Ernie Lombardi	1947	Ron Northey	1957	Gus Zernial	1959	Smoky Burgess	1960
Bill Nicholson	1952	Bobby Hofman	1955	Gus Zernial	1958	George Crowe	1959	Bob Cerv	1961
Johnny Mize	1953	Ron Northey	1956	Smoky Burgess	1959	Jerry Lynch	1961	Jerry Lynch	1962
Bobby Hofman	1955	Gus Zernial	1958	George Crowe	1959	Bob Cerv	1961	Joe Adcock	1966
Ron Northey	1956	Smoky Burgess	1958	Jerry Lynch	1961	Wally Post	1962	Fred Whitfield	1967
Ted Williams	1957	George Crowe	1959	Bob Cerv	1960	Joe Adcock	1966	Gates Brown	1971
Gus Zernial	1958	Bob Cerv	1960	Yogi Berra	1962	Fred Whitfield	1967	Willie McCovey	1975
Smoky Burgess	1958	Jerry Lynch	1961	Wally Post	1962	Gates Brown	1971	Cliff Johnson	1978

Twelve		**Thirteen**		**Fourteen**		**Fifteen**		**Sixteen**	
George Crowe	1960	George Crowe	1960	George Crowe	1960	Jerry Lynch	1963	Jerry Lynch	1964
Bob Cerv	1961	Jerry Lynch	1963	Jerry Lynch	1963	Smoky Burgess	1967	Smoky Burgess	1967
Jerry Lynch	1963	Smoky Burgess	1965	Smoky Burgess	1965	Gates Brown	1974	Gates Brown	1975
Smoky Burgess	1964	Gates Brown	1974	Gates Brown	1974	Willie McCovey	1979	Willie McCovey	1979
Joe Adcock	1966	Will McCovey	1977	Willie McCovey	1978	Cliff Johnson	1980	Cliff Johnson	1981
Gates Brown	1972	Cliff Johnson	1980	Cliff Johnson	1980				
Willie McCovey	1976								
Cliff Johnson	1979								
Jose Morales	1983								
Graig Nettles	1988								

Seventeen		**Eighteen**		**Nineteen**		**Twenty**	
Jerry Lynch	1965	Jerry Lynch	1966	Cliff Johnson	1985	Cliff Johnson	1986
Cliff Johnson	1983	Cliff Johnson	1984				

Multiple Pinch Grand Slams			**Career Pinch Home Run Leader**		
Jimmie Foxx	1931, 1945		Jack Stivetts	3	1898
Ron Northey	1947, 1948, 1950		Ham Hyatt	4	1914
Bill Skowron	1954, 1957		Cliff Cravath	5	1919
Vic Wertz	1958, 1960		Cliff Cravath	6	1920
Ed Bailey	1962, 1963		Cy Williams	7	1928
Willie McCovey	1960, 1965, 1975		Cy Williams	8	1928
Rick Reese	1969, 1970, 1972		Cy Williams	9	1929
Reggie Jackson	1970, 1976		Cy Williams	10	1929
Dave Johnson	1978, 1978		Cy Williams	11	1929
Mike Ivie	1978, 1978		George Crowe	12	1960
			George Crowe	13	1960
			George Crowe	14	1960
			Jerry Lynch	15	1963
			Jerry Lynch	16	1964
			Jerry Lynch	17	1965
			Jerry Lynch	18	1966
			Cliff Johnson	19	1985
			Cliff Johnson	20	1986

## CHAPTER 12

Two-Sport Stars

Stan Grosshandler

There was a time when the first pitch of Opening Day was in early April and the last out of the World Series occurred during the first week of October. The NFL kicked off the second week of September and finished their Championship Game shortly after Thanksgiving. Basketball was just something to occupy the time until Opening Day came again.

It was relatively easy for a gifted athlete to exchange his steel baseball spikes for the long, hard rubber cleats used in football; therefore early in this century the two-sport star was not unusual, and most of these are found in the first four decades of this century.

Professional baseball has always been well defined, dating back to the National Association of 1871; however, prior to the formation of the American Professional Football League in 1920, it is difficult to determine what football teams were truly professional.

It is the opinion of knowledgeable sports historians that several teams that played in western Pennsylvania and central Ohio at the turn of the century were indeed professional teams. These clubs recruited the best athletes available, therefore the majority of two-sport players played for cities like Latrobe and Greensburg, Pennsylvania, and the Ohio cities of Canton and Massillon.

Ed "Batty" Abbattichio was the first and one of the most successful of the two-sport players. The husky 5'11", 170-pound native of Latrobe was a slick-fielding second sacker for Philadelphia, Boston, and Pittsburgh of the National League from 1897 through 1910 and a hard-running and -punting fullback for Latrobe from 1895 to the turn of the century.

The most famous of all early two-sport athletes was Christy Mathewson, the legendary Giants pitcher who between 1900 and 1916 won 373 games. He was a member of the first group of players voted into the Coopers-town Hall of Fame. Christy had played football at Bucknell, where he was a star fullback and punter. He played the 1900 season with the Pittsburgh Stars, winning several games with his punting.

In 1900 a team with the unusual name of the Homestead Library and Athletic Club did a fine job of recruiting, signing two great Brown halfbacks, Fred Crolius and John Gammons, plus David Fultz of Dartmouth. All three proved to be among the top football players of the day; but they also played major league baseball.

All three were outfielders: Fred Crolius played a total of 58 games in 1901 for the Boston Braves and for the 1902 Pittsburgh Pirates. John Gammons was a teammate of Crolius on the 1901 Braves, getting into only 28 games.

David Fultz, who spent one season as a player-coach with the Athletic Club, enjoyed success between 1898 and 1905 with Philadelphia and Baltimore of the NL and with Philadelphia and New York of the AL. His career average was .271. He also earned a law degree at N.Y.U. and was to become an early-day advocate for the rights of players.

In 1912 he organized the Players Fraternity, challenging the treatment of players and the reserve clause. Prior to the 1916 season he threatened a strike which never materialized. Baseball was not quite ready for a union, and David eventually became president of the International League.

In 1902 Philadelphia Athletic manager Connie Mack and owner Ben Shibe were convinced to organize a football team to take advantage of the many rivalries within the state. Connie put together a team and included Rube Waddell, allegedly to keep track of the eccentric southpaw pitcher during the off-season. Though Rube was supposed to have gotten into a few games briefly as a lineman, there is no real documentation that he ever played pro football.

Charles Moran, who had two cups of coffee with the Cardinals, one in 1903 as a pitcher and a second in 1908 as a catcher, played halfback for the powerful 1905 Massillon Tigers.

"Uncle Charley," as he came to be known, gained considerable fame as a football coach. His Centre College team was nationally known as the "Praying Colonels," as a result of Charley's asking them to have a prayer session prior to each game. Moran then went on to a second career, umpiring in the National League from 1917 through 1939.

The lives of Jim Thorpe and Earle "Greasy" Neale seem to intertwine on both the diamond and gridiron.

After his great triumph in the 1912 Olympic Games, Jim Thorpe joined the New York Giants as an outfielder. His great power and speed made him very attractive as a baseball player; however, pitchers soon found out that "the world's greatest athlete" could not hit a curve. Jim's lackadaisical approach to the game did not go well with the tough Giant manager John McGraw; yet Jim played for the Giants intermittently from 1913 through 1919.

In April 1917 Jim was sold to the Cincinnati Reds. On May 2, 1917, he was playing right field when Fred Toney of the Reds opposed Jim "Hippo" Vaughn of the Cubs. Each pitched hitless ball until the top of the tenth, when with runners on second and third and two out Thorpe, who had struck out twice, hit the ball on the handle, resulting in a high hopper to Vaughn. The pitcher realized he could not throw the fleet Thorpe out at first, so he threw home

late and the only run of the game scored. Jim was given credit for a single and the RBI that broke up the only double no-hitter ever played.

In August he was sold back to the Giants and played in one game of the World Series. In his final season with both the Giants and Braves, Jim hit .327 over 62 games.

Jim Thorpe was a member of the Canton Bulldogs from 1915 until they became part of the new professional league in 1920. Thorpe was actually elected president of the league, an obvious figurehead position. He went on to play for several NFL clubs, retiring in 1929 at age forty-two.

Hitting ahead of Thorpe and playing center field the day of the double no-hitter was Earle "Greasy" Neale. A sharp lefthanded hitter, Greasy was a Red from 1916 through '24, had a career .259 average, with his best season in 1917 when he batted .294. Neale's zenith on the diamond came in the 1919 World Series. His .357 was the best on the club as the Reds won the Series.

Greasy Neale was coaching at West Virginia Wesleyan when he played end for the 1917 Canton Bulldogs under the name of Foster. Thorpe was running the team, and he asked Greasy to play several backfield positions during the year due to many injuries. In 1917 he played backfield and coached the Dayton Triangles.

It is as a coach that Greasy Neale gained his highest accolades. He took an underdog Washington and Jefferson team to the Rose Bowl in 1921 and tied a powerful California team. After several successful college coaching jobs, he took over the Philadelphia Eagles in 1941, and before he retired after the 1950 season, he had built the club into an NFL power, winning three divisional and two league titles. He is in both the college and pro Halls of Fame for his coaching ability.

The star of the 1919 Rose Bowl, George Halas joined the New York Yankees that spring. A switch-hitting outfielder, Halas injured his hip sliding into third at Cleveland. After 12 games and an .091 average, his diamond career was over.

George then turned his attention to pro football, organizing the Decatur Staleys, who were to become the Chicago Bears. Halas played end, coached, and owned this franchise, developing it into one of the all-time greatest sports franchises.

On the 1920 Decatur Staleys were a 5'6", 145-pound quarterback and a 5'8", 155-pound halfback. The quarterback, Chuck Dressen, played third base seven years for the Reds and one for the Giants, compiling a career .272 mark. He then spent sixteen years as a manager, leading the Cincinnati Reds, Brooklyn Dodgers, Washington Senators, Milwaukee Braves, and Detroit Tigers. His Dodger teams were defeated in the 1952 and '53 World Series.

The halfback, Paddy Driscoll, played in only 13 games for the 1917 Chicago Cubs. He was to have a Hall of Fame career as an NFL player and coach.

On April 22, 1922, Ty Cobb injured his ankle and rookie Johnny Mohardt took his place on the bases. Mohardt had played football at Notre Dame in the same backfield as George Gipp and was now trying to win a spot in the Tiger outfield.

Mohardt only played in 5 games, batted just once (he got a hit, so his career average was 1.000), and then left baseball. Mohardt played for five seasons in the NFL, financing his medical training. He eventually became a distinguished surgeon and the Assistant Medical Director of the Veterans Administration.

Hinkey Haines appeared in 14 regular and 2 World Series games for the 1923 World Champion Yankees, his only season of major league baseball. He was also a member of the 1927 New York Giants, the NFL champs, making Hinkey the only man to be a member of two major league championship teams in different sports.

Hinkey had played college football at Penn State, where his coach was Hugo Bezdek.

"He was a tough guy," recalled Hinkey, "but we all felt he was very fair. He had emigrated from Czechoslovakia and learned his football with Stagg at Chicago. [Bezdek] is the only man to take three different schools to the Rose Bowl, manage a big league baseball team (the Pittsburgh Pirates), and coach an NFL team (the Cleveland Rams)."

Charlie Berry, a Walter Camp All-American end at Lafayette College in 1924, joined the 1925 Philadelphia Athletics as a catcher. On the A's he found outfielder Walter French, who had starred at West Point, and Mickey Cochrane, a former Boston College football player. Unfortunately for Charlie, Cochrane was one of the greatest catchers the game has ever seen, so Berry only played in 10 games that year.

In the fall he and French played for the Pottstown Maroons, an NFL power at the time. Exhibiting great pass-catching and field goal-kicking ability, Berry was the top scorer in the league with 72 points, while French averaged 5.4 yards per carry.

Both Berry and French soon gave up the gridiron. Berry caught for eleven years with the Red Sox, White Sox, and A's, while French was a gifted pinch hitter and a career .303 batter for six seasons as an A.

When Berry graduated from Lafayette, his place at end was taken by Frank Grube, who caught for seven seasons in the AL, was a teammate of Berry's on the Chisox, and also played in the NFL.

After finishing his active career, Berry remained with Connie Mack as a coach until 1940. He officiated in the NFL from 1941 to 1961 and was also an American League ump from 1942 to 1962. In 1958 Charlie Berry had the unique experience of officiating the World Series and the NFL Championship Game, the sudden-death game, one of sports' all-time great events.

Whether it was Connie Mack's brief football experience back in 1902 or the fact that he liked college-educated men on his teams, he seemed to have a proclivity for hiring football stars. Besides Cochrane and French, he signed All-Americans Berry, Ace Parker, Sam Chapman, and Eric Tipton (though the latter two never played pro football).

Ace Parker was a highly acclaimed Duke athlete when he joined the A's in 1937. On April 30 of that year, he made his initial appearance at bat as a pinch hitter and hit a home run. This was the first time an American League rookie had ever hit a homer in his first at bat as a pinch hitter.

That fall Parker wanted to join the Brooklyn Dodgers of the NFL, but Connie Mack would not grant permission; however, by November the old gentleman relented and Ace entered the NFL, where he became a Hall of

Famer. His baseball career ended after his second season.

Other dual-sport players on the A's were Lyle Bigbee, Jim Castiglia, Bruno Haas, Bert Kuczynski, and Ernie Orwell.

Perhaps because they were always desperate for talent, the St. Louis Browns usually had a two-sport man on the team. By far the most notable was Ernie Nevers, a terrific all-round athlete from Stanford.

"When I finished in college in 1926, I was offered a $25,000 bonus by the Browns and another $25,000 bonus by the Duluth Eskimos of the NFL," Ernie recalled several years before his death. "I took both."

"My greatest thrill in baseball was just pitching to those famous players like Ruth [he gave up Babe's eighth and forty-first homers in 1927], Foxx, and others. My fondest recollection was one of the first times I faced Walter Johnson. I never saw his first two pitches. Johnson then called time and motioned the catcher out. When he got back, he told me Walter was going to groove it. When I uttered my disbelief, he replied that Walter always means what he says.

"Well, I started swinging as he wound up and hit the ball to the wall for a double. When I got to second, he was smiling for he had let a raw rookie look good."

In three years for the Browns, Nevers posted only a 6–12 record due to a sore arm. He then devoted his time to the gridiron. His biggest day in football was Thanksgiving Day of 1929. Playing for the Chicago Cardinals against the Bears, he scored 6 touchdowns and kicked 4 extra points, a total of 40 points, a record that has never been surpassed.

Though he had a brief NFL career as both a player and coach, his impact was such that he is a member of the Pro Football Hall of Fame.

Other Brownies who performed on the gridiron were outfielder Red Badgro, now in the Pro Football Hall of Fame; outfielder-third baseman Larry Bettencourt, now in the College Football Hall of Fame; catcher Russ Young; shortstop Jim Levey; and outfielder Pete Layden.

The most prominent dual-sport stars of the 1950s were Vic Janowicz, who won the 1950 Heisman Award as a junior at Ohio State, and Carroll Hardy from Colorado.

Janowicz caught for the 1953 Pirates with little success and switched to third the next season, again without success. That fall he joined the Washington Redskins and gave up the diamond sport. A terrific runner, passer, and kicker, he was the number-two scorer in the NFL the next season; however, a postseason accident finished his great sports career.

Carroll Hardy had been a defensive back and punter at Colorado when he joined the '49ers in 1955.

"I was picked as a defensive back and punter," Carroll recalls. "However, they had an unusual amount of injuries and I ended up playing in the offensive backfield with Y. A. Tittle, Hugh McElhenny, Joe Perry, and John Henry Johnson—all of whom made the Pro Football Hall of Fame."

"I had a pretty good season, caught 12 passes for 4 TDs, one of which was a 79-yarder from Tittle. Hank Greenberg, G.M. of the Indians, convinced me to concentrate on baseball."

Hardy then joined the Cleveland Indians for the 1958 season and later played until 1968 with the Boston Red Sox, Houston Astros, and Minnesota Twins.

"I am probably the only man to pinch-hit for Ted Williams, Roger Maris, and Carl Yastrzemski. On September 30, 1960, Ted was hitting against Hector Brown of the Orioles in the first inning when he fouled a ball off his leg and just walked off the field. Manager Pinky Higgins yelled at me to get up there and I promptly lined into a double play. I later found out I was the only man who had ever pinch-hit for Ted Williams.

"I hit for Roger while we were with the Indians as Billy Pierce, a lefty, was pitching. There were two men on in the eleventh, and I hit a ball I was positive was foul, but the ump called it fair and we won."

One of the last to try both sports until the present day was Tom Brown, a lefthanded, switch-hitting first sacker. Tom opened the 1963 season with the Senators but was soon back in the minors. He then opted for football, joined the Green Bay Packers in time to enjoy their most successful period, and is the only man to play in the Super Bowl and major league baseball. It would be twenty-four years until another athlete attempted both baseball and football.

Bo Jackson won the Heisman Award in 1985 and joined the Kansas City Royals. In 1987 he became a running back for the L.A. Raiders; however, a football injury at the end of the 1990 season finished both careers. Bo hit more homers (112) and scored more touchdowns (18) than any other two sport player.

Deion Sanders and Brian Jordan were both defensive backs for the Atlanta Falcons (1989–91). In 1992 Sanders continued to play both sports while Jordan concentrated on baseball with the Cardinals.

By playing for the Atlanta Braves in the 1992 World Series Deion Sanders joins both Jim Thorpe and Greasy Neale as the only men to play in a World Series and pro football the same fall.

D. J. Dozier played running back for the Minnesota Vikings 1987–91. In 1992 he played in the outfield for the New York Mets.

Umpires have also been two-sport stars. Cal Hubbard, an American League arbitrator for twenty-five years, was such a fine football player that he has been elected to both the College and Professional Halls of Fame.

Hank Soar is a three-sport man. An AL man in blue for twenty-four years, he was also a star halfback for the Giants and briefly coached Providence in the BAA.

"My greatest baseball thrill," Hank stated, "was the day I was at first and Don Larsen pitched his perfect game. My only close call was on Jackie Robinson in the second and nobody complained. One of my best football days was the 1938 Championship Game, when I caught the winning TD pass. The basketball job was a fluke. I worked for the team and was the only one they could get to coach it that season."

With Soar on the 1943 and '44 Giants was guard Frank Umont, who called balls and strikes in the AL for nineteen years.

Bill Stewart is best remembered in sports as the ump who missed the Feller-Masi pickoff play in the 1948 Series, but Bill deserves better. An NL umpire for twenty-two years, he was the first American-born referee in the NHL, where he officiated for fourteen years. In 1937–38 he became coach of the Chicago Black Hawks. The team

won but 14 games; however, they captured the Stanley Cup. The next season Bill was fired halfway into the schedule.

Because of the length of a baseball season and the physical demands of football, it takes a very talented man with exceptional endurance to play both in the same year. One of the most unusual groups to participate in both sports are the six who hit a home run and scored a touchdown the same year. This elite club includes Pid Purdy, Red Badgro, Ace Parker, Steve Filipowicz, Bo Jackson, and Deion Sanders.

Professional basketball has a history very similar to pro football. At the turn of the century several professional teams appeared, mostly on the East Coast. Eventually leagues appeared that were considered major leagues by some historians and minor leagues by others. The first professional basketball league to be considered a major league by most historians is the ABL, which existed from 1925 to 1931.

As the schedules of major league baseball and basketball were somewhat compatible, it is not surprising to find diamond stars playing the court sport for extra money and to stay in condition.

Perhaps the most successful of all the dual athletes was Gene Conley, who starred in both major league baseball and the NBA.

The 6'8" Conley joined the 1952 Boston Braves as a pitcher and the Celtics the same year as a C-F. For the next several years Gene concentrated on baseball with the Milwaukee Braves, pitching in one World Series and three All-Star Games. In 1959 he returned to the Celtics and proved a perfect backup man for the super stars of that team as they won three straight titles.

"There is no doubt my greatest thrill in sports came in the 1955 All-Star Game. I was the losing pitcher the previous year, and as this game was in Milwaukee, I really wanted to pitch. I finally got to in the twelfth inning and struck out Al Kaline, Mickey Vernon, and Al Rosen. We won on a Stan Musial home run in the bottom of the inning.

"One day I was sitting in front of my locker," Gene continued, "when coach Red Auerbach walked up and asked me if I realized I was the only man to have a World Series and NBA Championship ring. Until Red mentioned it, I was unaware of the fact."

The only member of the Baseball Hall of Fame who played major league basketball is shortstop Lou Boudreau.

Lou joined Cleveland in late 1938 and then played guard for the Hammond Ciesar All-Americans, where his fellow guard was John Wooden, who became one of the game's greatest coaches. The next season Boudreau was briefly a nonplaying coach.

A career .295 hitter, Lou hit over .300 four times in his career, leading the league in hitting in 1944 and batting a tremendous .355 in 1948, when he captured the MVP Award.

The Indians realized that twenty-four-year-old Boudreau was a natural leader and appointed him as manager in 1942. He won the World Series in 1948 and managed through 1950. He then spent six seasons managing the Red Sox and one with the Cubs.

Dick Groat led the nation's college basketball players in scoring as a junior at Duke. In 1952 he went directly from the campus to the Pittsburgh Pirates, becoming one of thirty-nine men to go directly to the big leagues and never play minor league ball.

"The Pirates were not going anywhere," Dick said, "so they had nothing to lose by putting me at short. That fall I played with Fort Wayne. I had returned to Duke to finish my studies, and the owner of the team sent his private plane to take me to games. I then was called into the service, and when I got out, Branch Rickey of the Pirates convinced me the hard gym floor would ruin my legs for baseball, so I never returned to basketball, though it was my favorite game."

A fourteen-year player in the National League, Dick was captain of the World Champion 1960 Pirates, leading the league in hitting and winning the MVP Award. Dick played in a second Series with the Cards in 1964. A career .286 hitter, he surpassed the .300 mark four times.

Frank Baumholtz played the outfield for ten years in the senior circuit. In 1952 he finished second to Stan Musial in the batting race and posted a lifetime .290 mark. Frankie, a star at Ohio U., played for Youngstown of the NBL in 1946–47 and Cleveland of the BBA in 1947–48; he was a top scorer both years.

Dave DeBusschere and Ron Reed were forwards on the 1965–66 Detroit Pistons, where Dave was the player-coach. Both were aspiring major league pitchers whose careers took different turns. Dave's fame was made on the basketball court, while Ron made it on the diamonds of the National League.

DeBusschere's baseball career consisted of two undistinguished years on the mound for the White Sox; however, he had twelve brilliant seasons in the NBA. After six seasons with the Pistons, two as a player-coach, he joined the great Knicks of the early 1970s and enjoyed their championship seasons. He later served briefly as Commissioner of the ABA. His career scoring average was 16.1 per game.

Reed spent nineteen years playing for several NL teams. As a starter for Atlanta, his best season was an 18–10 mark in 1969. When he joined the Phillies, he became a relief artist and in 1979 led the league in relief wins. Ron appeared in five World Series games for the Phillies and posted a career record of 146–140, with 103 saves and an ERA of 3.46.

Steve Hamilton played for the 1958–59 Minneapolis Lakers, but, like Reed, he found his talents were more successful in baseball. A southpaw, he pitched for twelve years in both leagues and, upon joining the New York Yankees, became an outstanding bullpen man, appearing in three games of the 1963 and '64 World Series, recording one save. Steve's career ERA was a very respectable 3.05.

Several major league players who had brief pro basketball careers were George Crowe, a top National League pinch hitter for ten years; Irv Noren, who played the outfield in both leagues for twelve seasons; and Del Rice, a longtime catcher.

Howie Schultz, of whom great slugging feats were expected when he joined the Dodgers in 1943, found greater success as a scorer in the NBL and NBA. In 1950 he was a player-coach for Anderson of the NBL. Another NBL coach was Red Rolfe, the great third baseman of the

Bronx Bombers of the 1930s, who led Toronto of the NBL for a single season.

The only dual-sport player to pitch a no-hitter was Bill McCahan, who joined the Philadelphia Athletics after his military duty. In 1947 he threw a no-hit game against the Washington Senators.

Chuck Connors, who had brief careers in both professional baseball and basketball, found his real calling in T.V. series and the movies, gaining genuine stardom in those fields.

The latest man to try both sports was Danny Ainge, who after three seasons with the Toronto Blue Jays joined the Boston Celtics, where his great athletic ability became more apparent.

Key

The following are keys for abbreviations used in Two-Sport Stars.

The name of the player will be followed by his position and then the college he attended, if any. CHF after the player's name indicates that he has been inducted into the College Football Hall of Fame. PHF indicates induction into the Professional Football Hall of Fame and BHF indicates induction into the Baseball Hall of Fame.

There have been several professional football leagues since 1920. Prior to that professional teams did not play in any organized leagues. The leagues are:

AAFC	All-American Football Conference	1946–49
AFL	American Football League	1926
		1936–37
		1940–41
		1960–69
APFL	American Professional Football League	1920–21
CFL	Canadian Football League	1958–present
NFL	National Football League	1922–present
WFL	World Football League	1974–75

Major league basketball has had a multitude of professional leagues since the 1890s. Many of these leagues were in existence for only a few years before folding. New leagues later appeared and often adopted the name of a former league. The leagues and their life spans are:

ABA	American Basketball Association	1967–76
ABL	American Basketball League	1903–04
		1925–31
		1933–46
		1961–63
BAA	Basketball Association of America	1947–49
CBL	Central Basketball League	1906–12

CSL	Connecticut State League	1917–18
		1920–21
EBL	Eastern Basketball League	1909–18
		1919–23
		1931–33
EL	Eastern League	1909–18
		1919–23
		1931–33
IL	Interstate League (New York Area)	1915–17
		1919–20
MBC	Midwest Basketball Conference	1935–37
MBL	Metropolitan Basketball League	1921–28
		1931–33
NBA	National Basketball Association	1949–present
NBL	National Basketball League	1898–1904
		1926–27
		1929–30
		1932–33
		1937–49
		1950–51
NYSL	New York State League	1911–15
		1916–17
		1919–23
PBLA	Professional Basketball League of America	1947–48
PSL	Pennsylvania State League	1914–18
		1919–21
WBT	World Basketball Tournament	1938–48
WMBL	Western Massachusetts Basketball League	1903–04

The only professional hockey major league mentioned in this table is the National Hockey League (NHL), which has been in existence since 1917.

BASEBALL—FOOTBALL

Ed Abbaticchio
Fullback, Mt. St. Mary's
1895–1900, Latrobe.

Cliff Aberson
Halfback
1946, Green Bay, NFL.

Red Badgro (PFH)
End, Southern California
1927–28, New York Yankees, NFL; 1930–35, New York Giants, NFL; 1936, Brooklyn, NFL.

George Barclay
Halfback, Bucknell, Lafayette
189698, Greensburg.

Norman Bass
Defensive Halfback, University of the Pacific
1964, Denver, AFL.

Jim Bedford
End, Southern Methodist University
1925, Rochester, NFL; 1926, Hammond, NFL.

Dutch Bergman
Head Coach, Notre Dame
1943, Washington, NFL.

Charles Berry (CHF)
End/Linesman, Lafayette
1925–26, Pottsville, NFL; 1940–60, NFL head linesman.

Joe Berry
Halfback, Pennsylvania, Muhlenberg
1921, Rochester, NFL.

Larry Bettencourt (CHF)
Center, St. Mary's
1933, Green Bay, NFL.

Hugo Bezdek (CHF)
Coach, Chicago
1937–38, Cleveland, NFL.

Lyle Bigbee
End, Oregon
1922, Milwaukee.

Tom Brown
Defensive Halfback, Maryland
1964–68, Green Bay, NFL; 1969, Washington, NFL.

Garyland Buckeye
Guard
1920, Chicago Tigers, NFL; 1921–24, Chicago Cardinals; 1926, Chicago, AFL.

Bruce Caldwell
Halfback, Brown, Yale
1928, New York Giants.

Ralph Capron
Halfback, Minnesota
1920, Chicago Tigers, NFL.

Jim Castiglia
Halfback, Georgetown
1941, 1945–46, Philadelphia; 1947, Baltimore, AAFC; 1947–48, Washington.

Chuck Corgan
Halfback, Arkansas
1924–26, Kansas City, NFL; 1926, Hartford; 1927, New York Giants.

Fred Crolius
Halfback, Brown
1900–01, Homestead; 1902, Pittsburgh.

D. J. Dozier
Halfback, Penn State
1987–90, Minnesota.

Paul Desjardien (CHF)
Guard, Chicago University
1920, Chicago Tigers, NFL; 1922, Minneapolis.

Charles Dressen
Quarterback
1920, Decatur; 1922–23, Racine.

Paddy Driscoll (PHF, CHF)
Quarterback, Northwestern
1919, Hammond; 1920, Decatur, APFL; 1920–25, Chicago Cardinals; 1926–29, Chicago Bears; 1942–45, 1956–57, Chicago Bears, head coach.

Oscar Eckhardt
Halfback, Texas
1928, New York Giants.

Steve Filipowicz
Quarterback, Fordham
1945–46, New York Giants.

Paul Florence
End, Loyola
1920, Chicago Cardinals.

Walter French
Halfback, Army
1922, Rochester; 1925, Pottsville.

David Fultz
Halfback, Brown
1900–01, Homestead.

John Gammons
Halfback, Brown
1898–99, Duquesne; 1900–01, Homestead; 1902, Pittsburgh.

Walter Gilbert
Halfback, Valparaiso
1923–26, Duluth.

Norman Glockson
Guard
1922, Racine.

Frank Grube
End, Lafayette
1928, New York Yankees.

Bruno Haas
Halfback, Worcester
1921, Cleveland; 1921, Akron; 1922, Dayton.

Hinky Haines
Halfback, Penn State
1925–28, New York Giants; 1929, 1931, Staten
Island.

George Halas (PHF)
End, Coach, Owner, Illinois
1919, Hammond; 1920, Decatur, APFL; 1921,
Chicago, APFL; 1922–83, Chicago, NFL.

Carroll Hardy
Halfback, Colorado
1955, SF, NFL.

Cal Hubbard (BHF, PHF, CHF)
Tackle, Centenary, Geneva
1927–28, 1936, New York Giants; 1929–33,
Green Bay; 1936, Pittsburgh.

Bo Jackson
Halfback, Auburn
1987–90, Los Angeles Raiders.

Vic Janowicz (CHF)
Halfback, Ohio State
1954–55, Washington.

Rex Johnston
Halfback, Southern California
1960, Pittsburgh.

Brian Jordan
Defensive Back, Richmond
1989–91, Atlanta.

Matt Kinzer
Punter, Purdue
1987, Detroit.

Bert Kuczynski
End, Pennsylvania
1943, Detroit; 1946, Philadelphia.

Pete Layden
Halfback, Texas
1948–49, New York, AAFC; 1950, New York
Yankees.

Jim Levey
Halfback
1934–36, Pittsburgh.

Dean Look
Quarterback, Michigan State
1962, New York, AFL.

Wally MacPhee
Halfback, Princeton
1926, Providence.

Howard Maple
Halfback, Oregon State
1930, Chicago Cardinals.

Walter Masters
Halfback, Pennsylvania
1936, Philadelphia; 1943, Cardinals; 1944,
Cardinals–Pittsburgh.

Christy Mathewson (BHF)
Fullback, Bucknell
1902, Pittsburgh Stars.

Jim McKean
Quarterback,
1964–65, Montreal, CFL.

John Mohardt
Halfback, Notre Dame
1922–23, Chicago Cardinals; 1924, Racine; 1925,
Chicago Bears; 1926, Chicago, AFL.

Charles Moran
Halfback, Tennessee
1905–06, Massillon.

Earle Neale (PHF, CHF)
Halfback, West Virginia Wesleyan
1916–17, Canton; 1918, Dayton; 1941–50, Philadelphia, coach.

Ernie Nevers (PHF, CHF)
Fullback, Stanford
1926–27, Duluth; 1929–31, Chicago Cardinals;
1939, Cardinals, head coach.

Ossie Orwoll
Halfback, Luther
1926, Milwaukee.

Ace Parker (PHF, CHF)
Halfback, Duke
1937–41, Brooklyn, NFL; 1945, Boston; 1946,
New York, AAFC.

John Perrin
Halfback, Michigan
1926, Hartford.

Al Pierotti
C/G/T, Washington & Lee
1920, Akron, NFL; 1920, Cleveland; 1921, New
York; 1923–24, Milwaukee; 1923, Racine; 1926,
Boston, AFL; 1927, Providence; 1929, Boston.

Pid Purdy
Halfback, Beloit
1926–27, Green Bay.

Dick Reichle
End, Illinois
1923, Milwaukee.

Deion Sanders
Defensive Back, Florida State
1989–   , Atlanta.

John Scalzi
Halfback, Georgetown
1931, Brooklyn.

John Singleton
Halfback
1929, Dayton.

Red Smith
Halfback, Notre Dame
1927, 1929, Green Bay; 1928, 1931, New York
Giants; 1928, New York Yankees; 1930, Newark.

Hank Soar
Halfback, Providence
1936, Boston, AFL; 1937–44, 1946, New York
Giants.

Evar Swanson
End, Lombard
1924, Milwaukee; 1925, Rock Isle; 1925–27,
Chicago Cardinals.

Jim Thorpe (PHF, CHF)
Halfback, Carlisle
1915–19, Canton; 1920, Canton, APFA; 1921,
Cleveland, NFL; 1922–23, Oorang; 1924, Rock
Isle; 1925, New York Giants; 1926, Canton; 1928,
Chicago Cardinals.

Andy Tomasic
Halfback, Temple
1942, 1946, Pittsburgh.

Frank Umont
Guard
1943–45, New York Giants.

Louis Urban
End, Boston College
1921–23, Buffalo.

Joe Vance
Halfback, Southwest Texas
1931, Brooklyn.

Ernie Vick (CHF)
Center, Michigan
1925, 1928, Detroit; 1927–28, Chicago Bears.

Tom Whalen
End/Center, Georgetown, Notre Dame
1920, Canton; 1921, Cleveland.

Mike Wilson
End, Lehigh
1923–24, Rock Isle.

Hoge Workman
Halfback, Ohio State
1924, 1931, Cleveland; 1932, New York Giants.

Ab Wright
Halfback, Oklahoma A&M
1930, Frank.

Tom Yewcic
Quarterback, Michigan State
1961–66, Boston, AFL.

Russ Young
Halfback
1925, Dayton.

BASEBALL—BASKETBALL

Danny Ainge
Guard, Brigham Young
1981–89, Boston; 1989–   , Sacramento.

Ernie Andres
Guard/Forward, Indiana
1939–40, 1945–48, Indianapolis, NBL.

Babe Barna
Forward, West Virginia
1939–40, Clarksburg, WBT.

Rex Barney
Guard
1947–48, Omaha, PBLA.

Bill Barrett
Guard/Forward
1921–22, Worcester, IL.

Frank Baumholtz
Guard, Ohio University
1945–46, Youngstown, NBL; 1946–47, Cleveland,
BAA.

Bozie Berger
Forward, Maryland
1938–39, Washington, ABL.

Hank Biasetti
Guard, Assumption (Canada)
1946–47, Toronto, NBL.

Lou Boudreau (BHF)
Guard/Forward, Illinois
1938–39, Hammond, NBL; 1939–40, Hammond,
coach, NBL.

Art Bramhall
Guard/Forward
1929–31, Chicago, ABL.

Frank Bruggy
Forward
1909–10, Elizabeth, EL; 1913–14, Gloversville,
NYSL; 1914–15, South Philadelphia, EL, Gloversville, NYSL; 1915–16, Kingston, Elizabeth, North
Hudson, IL; 1916–17, Paterson, IL; 1917–18, Ansonia, CSL, Providence–Scranton, PSL;
1919–20, Germantown, EL, Scranton, PSL
(coach), Jersey City, IL; 1920–21, Scranton, PSL
(coach), Germantown, EL, Easthamp-
ton–Springfield, IL; 1921–22, Brooklyn, MBL,
Scranton-Wilkes-Barre, EL; 1922–23, Elizabeth,
MBL (coach), Atlantic City, EL; 1924–25, Paterson, MBL.

Frank Carswell
Guard, Rice
1947–48, Houston, PBLA, Flint, NBL.

Gene Conley
Forward, Washington State
1952–53, 1958–61, Boston; 1962–64, New York,
NBA.

Chuck Connors
Center/Forward, Seton Hall
1945–46, Rochester, NBL; 1946–48, Boston,
BAA.

Jerry Conway
Guard/Forward, St. Anselm
1919–20, Turners Falls, IL; 1920–21, Holyoke, IL;
1921–22, Holyoke, IL, Glens Falls; 1922–23, Holyoke, IL, Albany, NYSL; 1925–26, Washington,
ABL; 1927–28, Albany, MBL.

Bill Crouch
Forward/Guard, Michigan, Eastern Michigan
1935–26, Windsor, MBC.

George Crowe
Forward/Center, Indiana Central
1946–48, New York, WBT; 1948–49, Dayton,
NBL.

Snake Deal
Center/Forward
1898–99, Germantown, Philadelphia, NBL;
1899–1900, Chester, Camden, NBL; 1900–01,
Philadelphia, NBL; 1901–03, Camden, NBL;
1903–04, Pittsfield–Chicopee–Springfield,
WMBL; 1905–06, East Falls, PBL; 1906–08, East
Liverpool, CBL; 1908–10, Johnstown, CBL;
1914–15, Tamaqua, PSL.

Dave DeBusschere
Forward, Detroit University
1962–69, Detroit; 1968–74, New York; 1975–76,
commissioner, ABA.

Brooks Dowd
Forward, Lehigh, Springfield
1916–17, Mohawk, NYSL; 1919–20, Springfield,
IL, Mohawk, NYSL; 1920–21, Springfield (coach),
IL, Mohawk, NYSL; 1921–22, Mohawk, NYSL,
Springfield, IL; 1922–23, Springfield, IL; 1925–26,
Boston, ABL; 1926–27, Baltimore, ABL.

Grant Dunlap
Forward
College of the Pacific, Occidental
1947–48, Birmingham, PBLA; 1950–51, Anderson, NBL.

Joe Evers
Forward
1913–14, Troy, NYSL; 1915–16, Carbondale,
PSL; 1916–17, Hudson, NYSL, Nanticoke, PSL;
1919–20, Troy, NYSL; 1920–21, Cohoes, NYSL;
1921–22, Gloversville–Troy, NYSL; 1922–23,
Troy–Schenectady, NYSL; 1927–28, Troy (coach),
MBL.

Frankie Frisch (BHF)
Guard/Forward, Fordham
1919–20, New York, IL.

Les Fuchs
Referee, John Marshall
1938–46, ABL.

Johnny Gee
Center/Forward, Michigan
1946–47, Syracuse, NBL.

Tom Gorman
Forward
1944–45, New York, ABL; 1945–46, Trenton,
ABL.

Don Grate
Forward/Guard, Ohio State
1947–48, Indiana, NBL; 1949–50, Sheboygan.

Hank Greenberg (BHF)
Center/Forward, New York University
1931–32, Brooklyn Jewish Center, MBL;
1932–33, Brooklyn Jewels, MBL.

Dick Groat
Guard, Duke
1952–53, Fort Wayne, NBA.

Steve Hamilton
Forward/Center, Morehead State
1959–60, Minnesota, NBA.

Walter Hammond
Forward, Colgate
1919–20, Amsterdam, NYSL; 1920–21, Westfield,
IL; 1920–21, 1922–23, Amsterdam, NYSL.

Bucky Harris (BHF)
Guard
1915–18, Pittston, PSL; 1917–18, Bridgeport,
Jersey City, CSL; 1919–20, Pittston, PSL;
1919–20, Paterson, Brooklyn, IL; 1920–21,
Pittston, PSL; 1923–24, Glens Falls, NYSL.

Doug Harvey
Referee, San Diego State
1967–69, ABA.

Buddy Hassett
Guard, Manhattan
1933–34, Union City, ABL; 1934–35, Jersey, ABL.

Rick Herrscher
Guard, Southern Methodist University
1961–62, Hawaii, ABL.

Orel Hildebrand
Forward, Butler
1935–36, Indianapolis, MBC.

Waite Hoyt (BHF)
Forward, Middlebury
1925–26, Brooklyn, ABL.

Carl Husta
Forward/Guard
1925–30, Cleveland; 1930–31, Cleveland, Fort
Wayne, ABL.

Ted Kearns
Guard/Forward
1925–26, Washington; 1926–27, Baltimore–Washington; 1927–28, Philadelphia;
1928–29, Trenton; 1929–30, Syracuse, ABL.

Al Kellett
Center, Penn State
1926–28, Philadelphia; 1928–29, Trenton–Chicago; 1929–30, Chicago; 1930–31,
Brooklyn, ABL.

Fritz Knothe
Forward, Pennsylvania
1925–26, Passaic, MBL; 1926–27, Baltimore,
ABL, Kingston, MBL; 1927–28, Rochester, ABL,
Kingston, MBL; 1928–29, Paterson, ABL.

Pip Koehler
Guard, Penn State
1927–28, Fort Wayne; 1929–31, Toledo, ABL.

Stan Landes
Referee
1953–54, NBA.

Bert Lewis
Forward
1925–26, Buffalo, ABL.

Jerry Loeber
Referee, Rhode Island
1969–76, NBA.

Bill McCahan
Forward/Guard, Duke
1928–49, Syracuse, NBL; 1943–44, 1948–49,
Wilmington, ABL.

Mel McGaha
Guard, Arkansas
1948–49, New York, NBL.

Ralph Miller
Guard
1925–30, Fort Wayne; 1930–31, Fort Wayne,
Chicago, ABL.

Cotton Nash
Forward/Center, Kentucky
1964–65, Los Angeles, San Francisco; 1967–68,
Kentucky, ABA.

Irv Noren
Forward, Pasadena College
1946–47, Chicago, NBL.

Ron Reed
Forward, Notre Dame
1966–67, Detroit, NBA.

Del Rice
Forward
1943–44, Rochester, WBT; 1945–46, Rochester,
NBL.

Dick Ricketts
Forward, Duquesne
1955–56, St. Louis; 1955–57, Rochester;
1957–58, Cincinnati, NBA.

Harry Riconda
Forward
1926–27, Philadelphia; 1928–29, Paterson;
1929–30, New York, ABL.

Red Rolfe
Coach, Dartmouth
1946–47, Toronto, NBL.

Rusty Saunders
Forward
1925–26, Brooklyn, Washington; 1926–27, Washington; 1927–28, Brooklyn, Fort Wayne; 1928–31,
Fort Wayne, ABL; 1940–41, Detroit; 1945–46, Indianapolis, NBL.

John Scalzi
Referee, Georgetown
1948–49, BAA; 1949–51, NBA.

Howie Schultz
Center/Forward, Hamline
1947–49, Anderson, NBL; 1949–50, PC;
1949–50, Fort Wayne, NBA; 1952–53, Minnesota.

Danny Silva
Forward
1921–22, Worcester, IL.

John Simmons
Guard, New York University
1946–47, Boston, BAA.

Hank Soar
Head Coach, Providence
1947–48, Providence, BAA.

Keith Thomas
Guard/Referee, Kansas State
1947–48, Kansas City, PBLA; 1961–62, referee,
ABL.

Bucky Walters
Center
1931–32, Philadelphia Moose, EBL; 1932–33,
Philadelphia Broadcasters, EBL.

Ed Wineapple
Forward Providence
1929–30, Syracuse, ABL.

BASEBALL—HOCKEY

Bill Stewart
Referee/Coach
1928–37, 1940–44, NHL referee; 1937–38, Chicago, NHL, coach.

## CHAPTER 13

Casey at the Bat:
A Ballad of the Republic

Donald Hall

A century ago, on June 3, 1888, a twenty-five-year-old Harvard graduate, one-poem poet Ernest Lawrence Thayer, published "Casey at the Bat" in the pages of the San Francisco *Examiner*. I suppose it's the most popular poem in our country's history, if not exactly in its literature. Martin Gardner collected twenty-five sequels and parodies to print in his prodigy of scholarship, *The Annotated Casey at the Bat* (1967; rev. 1984). Will the next Casey bat clean-up in a St. Petersburg Over-Ninety Softball League? Perhaps, instead, we will hear of a transparent Casey on an Elysian diamond, shade swinging the shadow of a bat while wraith pitcher uncoils phantom ball—or spheroid, I should say.

The author of this people's poem was raised in Worcester, Massachusetts: gentleman and scholar, son of a mill owner. At Harvard he combined scholastic and social eminence, not always feasible on the banks of the Charles. A bright student of William James in philosophy, he graduated magna cum laude and delivered the Ivy Oration at graduation. On the other hand, he was editor of the *Lampoon*, for which traditional requirements are more social than literary; he belonged to Fly, a club of decent majesty. It is perhaps not coincidence, considering Victorian Boston's social prejudices, that Thayer's vainglorious mock hero carries an Irish name.

After his lofty graduation, Thayer drifted about in Europe. One of his Harvard acquaintances had been young William Randolph Hearst, business manager of the *Lampoon*, expelled from Harvard for various pranks while Thayer was pulling a magna. The disgraced young Hearst was rewarded by his father with editorship of the San Francisco *Examiner*, where he offered Thayer work as humorous columnist. By the time "Casey" appeared, Thayer had left California to return to Worcester, where he later managed a mill for his father and studied philosophy in his spare time.

He received five dollars for "Casey" and never claimed reward for its hundreds of further printings. By all accounts, "Casey's" author found his notoriety problematic. As with all famous nineteenth-century recitation pieces— "The Night Before Christmas," "Backward Turn Backward O Time in Thy Flight"—other poets claimed authorship, which annoyed Thayer first because he *did* write it, and second because he wasn't especially proud of it. There was the additional annoyance that old ballplayers continually asserted themselves the *original* Casey of the ballad: Thayer insisted that he made the poem up. The author of "Casey at the Bat" died in Santa Barbara in 1940 without ever doing another notable thing.

The poem's biography is richer than the poet's: At first "Casey" blushed unseen, wasting its sweetness on the desert air, until an accident blossomed it into eminence. In New York, DeWolf Hopper, a young star of comic opera, was acting in *Prince Methusalem*. On August 15, 1888, management invited players from the New York Giants and the Chicago White Stockings to attend a performance, and Hopper gave thought to finding a special bit that he might perform in the ballplayers' honor. His friend the novelist Archibald Clavering Gunter, recently returned from San Francisco, showed him a clipping from the San Francisco *Examiner*.

In Hopper's autobiography, he noted that when "[I] dropped my voice to B-flat, below low C, at the 'multitude was awed,' I remember seeing Buck Ewing's gallant mustachios give a single nervous twitch." Apparently Hopper's recitation left everyone in the house twitching with joy, and not only the Giants' hirsute catcher. For the rest of his life, Hopper repeated his performance by demand, no matter what part he sang or played, doomed to recite the poem (five minutes and forty seconds) an estimated ten thousand times before his death in 1935. As word spread from Broadway, the poem was reprinted in newspapers across the country, clipped out, memorized, and performed for the millions who would never hear De Wolf Hopper. Eventually the ballad was set to music, made into silent movies, and animated into cartoons; radio broadcast it, there were recordings by Hopper and others, and William Schuman wrote an opera called *The Mighty Casey* [premiere 1953].

When he first recited the poem, Hopper had no notion who had written it. Thayer had signed it "Phin.," abbreviating his college nickname of Phinny. Editors reprinted the poem anonymously or made up a name that sounded reasonable. When Hopper played Worcester early in the 1890s, he met the retiring Thayer—and poet recited poem for actor, as Hopper later reported, without a trace of elocutionary ability.

There are things in any society that *we always knew*. We do not remember when we first heard about Ground Hog Day or Thirty Days Hath September. Who remem-

bers first hearing "Casey at the Bat"? Although I cannot remember my original exposure, I remember many splendid renditions from early in my life by the great ham actor of my childhood. My New Hampshire grandfather, Wesley Wells, was locally renowned for his powers of recitation—for speaking pieces, as we called it. He farmed bad soil in central New Hampshire: eight Holsteins, fifty sheep, a hundred chickens. In the tie-up for milking, morning and night, he leaned his bald head into warm Holstein ribs and recited poems with me for audience; he kept time as his hands pulled blue milk from long teats. When he got to the best part, he let go the nozzles, leaned back in his milking chair, spread his arms wide and opened his mouth in a great O, the taught gestures of elocution. He spellbound me as he set the line out on the warm cowy air: "But there is no joy in Mudville—mighty Casey has struck out!" The old barn (with its whitewash over rough boards, with its spider webs and straw, with its patched harness and homemade ladders and pitchforks shiny from decades of hand labor) paused in its shadowy hugeness and applauded again the ringing failure of the hero.

If he had not recited it for me lately, I reminded him. He recited a hundred other poems also, a few from Whittier and Longfellow, but mostly from newspapers by poets without names. I don't suppose he knew "Ernest Lawrence Thayer" or the history of the poem, but "Casey" itself was as solid as the rocks of his fields. The word that left Broadway and traveled was: *This poem is good to say out loud.* Earlier, the same news traveled about Edgar Allan Poe's "The Raven" and Bret Harte's "The Heathen Chinee." Public schooling once consisted largely of group memorization and recitation. The New England Primer taught theology and the alphabet together: "In Adam's fall / We sinnèd all" through "Zacchaeus he / Did climb a tree / His Lord to see." Less obviously the Primer instilled pleasures of rhyme and oral performance. When we decided fifty and sixty years ago that rote memorization was bad teaching, we threw out not only the multiplication table but also "Barbara Frietchie." Recitation of verse was turned over to experts.

Earlier, for two hundred years at least, recitation and performance took center stage in the one-room schools; but it did not end there. At schools, recitation as performance—not merely to retain information—climbed toward competitive speaking, elimination and reward on Prize Speaking Day, when the athletes of elocution recited in contest before judges. The same athletes did not stop when school stopped, and recitation exfoliated into the adult world as a major form of entertainment. Hamlets and cities alike formed clubs meeting weekly for mutual entertainment that variously included singing, playing the violin and the piano, recitation, and political debate. In the country towns and villages, which couldn't afford to hire Mr. Hopper to entertain them (nor earlier Mr. Emerson to instruct and inspire them), citizens made their own Lyceums and Chautauquas. In my grandfather's South Danbury, New Hampshire, young people founded the South Danbury Debating and Oratorical Society. Twice a month they met for programs that began with musical offerings and recitations, paused for coffee and doughnuts, and concluded with a political debate. "Resolved:

That the United States should Cease from Territorial Expansion."

While recitation thrived, the recitable poem became a way of entertaining ideas and each other, of exposing or exercising public concerns. Poetry in the United States was briefly a public art. But after the Great War came cars, radios, and John Dewey; recitation departed, and poets have been blamed ever since for losing their audience. The blame is unfair, because the connection between poetry and a mass audience was brief, nor did it work for all poetry. John Donne never had a great audience; neither did George Herbert nor Andrew Marvell, nor in America Walt Whitman or Emily Dickinson. These poets made poems with a fineness of language that required sophisticated reading.

All the same, *some* nineteenth-century poets wrote poems both popular and fine—without being as popular as baseball or as fine as Gerard Manley Hopkins. This moment was the fragile age of elocution. Many poets turned in one direction to talk to the people, and in another to talk to the ages. Longfellow's best work—the *Divine Comedy* sonnets, "The Jewish Cemetery at Newport"—is dense, sophisticated, adult poetry of the second order. But in his nationalistic fervor he also wrote epics of the Republic's prehistory like *Evangeline*, or lyrics of the common life like "The Village Blacksmith." Making these poems, he made recitation pieces; without intending to, he wrote poems for children and for entertainment. When Whittier made "Barbara Frietchie" in his abolitionist passion, he made willy-nilly a patriotic poem for schoolkids to recite. Meantime Walt Whitman—who had notions about poetry for the people—went relatively unread as he went unrecited. Mind you, he showed he could turn his hand to the recitation piece: "O Captain My Captain" is poetically inferior to "Casey."

The twin phenomena of recitation and the popular poem thrived in England at the same time, and Macaulay's *The Lays of Ancient Rome* turned up in American school readers and on prize-speaking days. The public Tennyson, laureate not melancholic, wrote verses often memorized for performance; lyrical Wordsworth and bouncy Browning served as well. There were many English sources, even for "Casey at the Bat": Thayer remembered reading W.S. Gilbert's *Bab Ballads* before composing "Casey."

At my school in the 1930s we memorized American poets: Whitman for "O Captain My Captain," Joaquin Miller's "Columbus," something by James Whitcomb Riley. The trajectory of the recitation piece, of which "Casey" is a late honorable example, began its descent early. James Whitcomb Riley scored hits with "Little Orphant Annie" and others, but Riley was mostly hokum. Then there was Eugene Field, whose "Little Boy Blue" is gross sentimentality accomplished with skill; then there is Ella Wheeler Wilcox; then there is Edgar Lee Guest. [The Canadian Robert Service is a late recitable anomaly.] Vachel Lindsay and Carl Sandburg were themselves performers who did not give rise to performance in others; they led from recitation toward the poetry reading. There are poets today as sentimental and popular as Edgar Guest, but they write free verse and no one recites them.

The tradition of recitation survives only in backwaters, like Danbury, New Hampshire. If you come on Prize

Speaking Day and sit in the school cafeteria-gymnasium-assembly, a miniature elocutionist may break your heart reciting "Little Boy Blue," or you may watch a rawboned young outfielder, straight out of central casting, begin: "The outlook wasn't brilliant for the Mudville nine that day. . ."

Among the thousands of pieces memorized and recited, few survive. Why "Casey at the Bat"? For a hundred years this mock heroic ballad has lurked alive at the edges of American consciousness. It has endured past the culture that spawned it. When an artifact like this old clownish poem persists for a century, surviving not only its moment but its natural elocutionary habitat, there must be reasons. There must be public reasons for public endurance.

We might as well ask: Why has baseball survived? Neither the Black Sox scandal nor the Crash nor two World Wars nor the National Football League have ended the game of baseball. Every year more people buy tickets to sit in wooden seats over a diamond of grass—or in plastic seats over plastic grass, as may be. We need to ask: *Has* baseball survived? Casey's game pitted town against town with five thousand neighbors watching. Maybe the descendant of Casey's game is industrial league softball played under the lights by teams wearing rainbow acrylics. These days when we speak of baseball we mostly mean the Major Leagues, millionaire's hardball, where our box seats place us half a mile from the symmetrical petro-chemical field. Do we watch the game that Mudville watched?

Yes.

As "Casey at the Bat" survives the culture of recitation, the game's shape and import survive its intimate origins. Not without *change*: If the five thousand ghosts of the Mudville crowd, drinking a Mississippi of blood to turn solid, reconstituted themselves on a Friday night at Three Rivers Stadium to witness combat between Cincinnati's team and Pittsburgh's, they would gape in spiritual astonishment at the zircon light of a distant diamond under the velvet darkness, at the pool-table green of imitation grass, at amenities of Lite, at the wave, at the skin color of many players, at tight uniforms, and at a scoreboard that shows moving pictures of what just happened.

But in their ectoplasmic witness they would also observe the template of an unaltered game. They would watch a third baseman move to his right, a second baseman flip underhand to a shortstop pivoting toward first for the double play, and an outfielder charge a line drive while setting himself to throw. Above all, they would see a pitcher facing a batter late in the game with men on base. They would see a cleanup man approaching the batter's box with defiance curling his lip. "Casey at the Bat" survives—to begin with—because it crystallizes baseball's moment, the medallion carved at the center of the game, where pitcher and batter confront each other.

There are other reasons, literary and historical. When a poem is so popular, one needs to quote Mallarmé again, and observe that poems are made of words. "Casey's" language is a small, consistent, comic triumph of irony. The diction is mock heroic, big words for small occasions: When a few fans go home in the ninth inning, they depart not in discouragement but "in deep despair." The remain-

ing five thousand illustrate a learned illusion: In his *Essay on Man*, Alexander Pope wrote that, "Hope springs eternal in the human breast. . ." and Thayer of course knew the source of his saw; but Pope, like Shakespeare, is largely composed of book titles and proverbs: Thayer uses Pope not as literary allusion but as appeal to common knowledge by way of common elevated sentiment.

Elevation is fundamental: Despite the flicker of hope, the crowd is a "grim multitude"—a language appropriate to Milton's hell—and if the hero is mocked, hero worshippers are twice mocked. Thayer's poetic similes are Homeric—as if Achilles faced Hector instead of Casey the pitcher; or if Casey is not quite Achilles, at least he is Ajax. Imagery of noise, loud in Homer and his echo Virgil, rouses Thayer to exalted moments: A yell "rumbled through the valley, it rattled in the dell; / It knocked upon the mountain and recoiled upon the flat. . ." This yell is cousin to the "roar / Like the beating of the stormwaves on a stern and distant shore." It is noise again when Thayer's crowd reacts to a called strike: "'Fraud!' cried the maddened thousands, and echo answered fraud. . ." These days at Fenway Park the bleacherites divide themselves for a rhythmic double chant, but they do not say "Fraud." When they feel polite they cry "less filling" and echo answers "tastes great."

Possibly crowds were not chanting "Fraud" in the late 1880s either. It was a major form of Victorian humor to elevate diction over circumstance. Mr. Micawber soared with paraphrastic euphemism to admit that he was in debt; W. C. Fields was an orotund low-comedy grandson. For a hundred years it was witty or amusing to call kissing osculation, and to refer to a house as a domicile. If somebody missed our tone, we sounded pompous, but usually people understood us: When we enjoyed something common or vulgar (like baseball) we could show a humorous affection for it, yet retain our superiority by calling the ball a spheroid.

This habit of language has not entirely disappeared, but more and more it looks like an anglophile or academic *tic*. The late poet and renowned advocate of baseball, Marianne Moore, always talked this way, never more than when she spoke of the game. When she identified the Giants' pitcher, "Mr. Mathewson," she noted: "I've read his instructive book on the art of pitching, and it's a pleasure to note how unerringly his execution supports his theories." Another St. Louis poet was T. S. Eliot, born the same year as "Casey," and, like Moore, expert in the humor of a polysyllabic synonym. Eliot is the most eminent poet influenced by "Casey at the Bat." *Old Possum's Book of Practical Cats* includes "Growltiger's Last Stand," conflation of Custer and Casey, written in metrical homage and in allusion: "Oh there was joy in Wapping when the news flew through the land. . ." Growltiger is a vicious fellow, racist or at least nationalist ("But most to Cats of foreign race his hatred has been vowed"), and loathed by felines of an Asian provenance. Absorbed in romantic adventure he is surrounded by a "fierce Mongolian horde," captured, and made to walk the plank.

The author of *Four Quartets* and "The Love Song of J. Alfred Prufrock" grew up in the age of recitation; we could be certain that he knew "Casey" even if "Growltiger" were not written in homage. Like many poets he could write high or low, wide or narrow; unlike some

poets, when he wrote for children he recognized that he was doing it.

Mockery is "Casey's" point, with humor to soften it. After the crowd (which is us), the great Casey himself takes the brunt of our laughter. His name is the poem's mantra, repeated twenty-two times, often twice in a line: As he puffs with vainglory, "Defiance gleamed in Casey's eye, a sneer curled Casey's lip." The hero's role is written in the script of gesture. After five stanzas of requisite exposition, we catch sight of the rumored Casey in the sixth stanza: "There was ease in Casey's manner. . ." By this phrase we are captured and the double-naming locks us in: "There was pride in Casey's bearing and a smile on Casey's face." We know the smile's message, and we know how Casey doffs his cap. Casey is Godlike: "With a smile of Christian charity. . ." he "stilled the rising tumult"; if we remember that this metaphoric storm occurs at sea ("the beating of the stormwaves"), we may understand that Casey's charity earns its adjective.

And every time we hear "Casey at the Bat," the hero strikes out. We require this failure.

Not all of us. My grandfather, who was sanguine, always regretted that Casey struck out. He memorized the sequels and tried them all, especially "The Volunteer." In Clarence P. MacDonald's poem, printed in the San Francisco *Examiner* in 1908, the home team plays with no bench; behind in the game, it loses its catcher to an injury, and the captain calls for a substitute from the stands: A gray-headed volunteer finishes the game as catcher and his home run wins the game in the ninth. Besieged by teammates and fans to reveal his identity, the weeping stranger proclaims: "I'm mighty Casey who struck out just twenty years ago."

Wonderful.

But it won't do. None of the triumphant sequels will do. None show the flair of Thayer's ballad, its vigorous bumpety septameter and mostly well-earned rhymes, or its consistently overplayed language. Most important, none celebrate failure: Casey must strike out: Casey's failure makes the poem.

When Thayer first published "Casey at the Bat" in 1888, it bore a subtitle seldom reprinted: "A Ballad of the Republic." Once we lived in heroic times: once—and then again. When we suffer wars and undertake explorations we require heroes, and Jeb Stuart must gallop behind Union lines, Lindbergh fly the Atlantic, Davey Crockett enter the wilderness alone, Washington endure Valley Forge, the *Merrimack* attack the *Monitor*, Neil Armstrong step on the moon, and U.S. stand for Ulysses S., Unconditional Surrender, *and* the United States.

The Civil War, which ripped the country apart, began the work of stitching it together again. (One small agent of integrity was baseball, as blue and gray troops played the game at rest and even in prison camps, even North against South, as legend tells us.) For five years North and South lived through the triumphs and disasters of heroes. Although nameless boys charged stone walls blazing with rifle fire, we concentrated our attention on heroic leaders, from dandified cavalrymen to dignified generals. Sons born to veterans, late in the sixties and early in the seventies, were christened Forrest, Jackson, Sherman, Grant, Lee, Bedford, Beauregard. . .

But hero worship is dangerous and needs correction, especially in a democracy if we will remain democratic. To survive hero worship we mock our heroes; if we don't, we become their victims. Odysseus came home to slay the suitors; Ulysses S. allowed them to fatten on our larder: Heroic governance became disaster as the triumphant General Grant turned into the ruinous President. Many other heroes struck out. When the romantic vainglorious George Custer, with his shoulder-length hair, made combat with Crazy Horse and Sitting Bull in 1876, Growltiger walked the plank. Affluence and corruption, defeat and corruption bred irony. Violence of reconstruction and violence of anti-reconstruction eventually encouraged detachment from crowd passion.

Whatever young Thayer had in mind as he wrote his "Ballad of the Republic," 1888 was of course a Presidential year. We elected the mighty Benjamin Harrison President, a former officer of the Union Army, who took the job in a deal and installed as Secretary of State the notorious James G. Blaine. De Tocqueville stands behind this poem as much as Homer does. Democracies choose figures to vote in and out of office—to argue over, to ridicule: We do not want gods or kings—that's why we crossed the ocean west—but human beings, fallible like us.

We pretend to forgive failure; really we celebrate it. Bonehead Merkle lives forever and Bill Mazeroski's home run fades in memory. We fail, we all fail, we fail all our lives. The best hitters fail, two out of three at bats. If from time to time we succeed, our success is only prelude to further failure—and success's light makes failure darker still. Triumph's pleasures are intense but brief; failure remains with us forever, a featherbed, a mothering nurturing common humanity. With Casey we all strike out. Although Bill Buckner won a thousand games with his line drives and brilliant fielding, he will endure in our memories in the ninth inning of the sixth game of a World Series, one out to go, as the ball inexplicably, ineluctably, and eternally rolls between his legs.

And now, the immortal Casey
and his most worthy successors:

Casey at the Bat

A Ballad of the Republic, Sung in the Year 1888

The outlook wasn't brilliant for the Mudville nine that day;
The score stood four to two with but one inning more to play.
And then when Cooney died at first, and Barrows did the same,
A sickly silence fell upon the patrons of the game.

A straggling few got up to go in deep despair. The rest
Clung to that hope which springs eternal in the human breast;
They thought if only Casey could but get a whack at that—
We'd put up even money now with Casey at the bat.

But Flynn preceded Casey, as did also Jimmy Blake,
And the former was a lulu and the latter was a cake;
So upon that stricken multitude grim melancholy sat,
For there seemed but little chance of Casey's getting to
  the bat.

But Flynn let drive a single, to the wonderment of all,
And Blake, the much despis-ed, tore the cover off the ball;
And when the dust had lifted, and the men saw what had
  occurred,
There was Johnnie safe at second and Flynn a-hugging
  third.

Then from 5,000 throats and more there rose a lusty yell;
It rumbled through the valley, it rattled in the dell;
It knocked upon the mountain and recoiled upon the flat,
For Casey, mighty Casey, was advancing to the bat.

There was ease in Casey's manner as he stepped into his
  place;
There was pride in Casey's bearing and a smile on Casey's
  face.
And when, responding to the cheers, he lightly doffed his
  hat,
No stranger in the crowd could doubt 'twas Casey at the
  bat.

Ten thousand eyes were on him as he rubbed his hands
  with dirt;
Five thousand tongues applauded when he wiped them on
  his shirt.
Then while the writhing pitcher ground the ball into his
  hip,
Defiance gleamed in Casey's eye, a sneer curled Casey's
  lip.

And now the leather-covered sphere came hurtling
  through the air,
And Casey stood a-watching it in haughty grandeur there.
Close by the sturdy batsman the ball unheeded sped—
"That ain't my style," said Casey. "Strike one," the um-
  pire said.

From the benches, black with people, there went up a
  muffled roar,
Like the beating of the storm-waves on a stern and distant
  shore.
"Kill him! Kill the umpire!" shouted some one on the
  stand;
And it's likely they'd have killed him had not Casey raised
  his hand.

With a smile of Christian charity great Casey's visage
  shone;
He stilled the rising tumult; he bade the game go on;
He signaled to the pitcher, and once more the spheroid
  flew;
But Casey still ignored it, and the umpire said, "Strike
  two."

"Fraud!" cried the maddened thousands, and echo answered fraud;
But one scornful look from Casey and the audience was
  awed.
They saw his face grow stern and cold, they saw his
  muscles strain,
And they knew that Casey wouldn't let that ball go by
  again.

The sneer is gone from Casey's lip, his teeth are clenched
  in hate;
He pounds with cruel violence his bat upon the plate.
And now the pitcher holds the ball, and now he lets it go,
And now the air is shattered by the force of Casey's blow.

Oh, somewhere in this favored land the sun is shining
  bright;
The band is playing somewhere, and somewhere hearts
  are light,
And somewhere men are laughing, and somewhere children shout;
But there is no joy in Mudville—mighty Casey has struck
  out.

                                Ernest Lawrence Thayer

Casey's Revenge

There were saddened hearts in Mudville for a week or
  even more;
There were muttered oaths and curses—every fan in town
  was sore.
"Just think," said one, "how soft it looked with Casey at
  the bat,
And then to think he'd go and spring a bush league trick
  like that!"

All his past fame was forgotten—he was now a hopeless
  "shine."
They called him "Strike-Out Casey," from the mayor
  down the line;
And as he came to bat each day his bosom heaved a sigh,
While a look of hopeless fury shone in mighty Casey's eye.

He pondered in the days gone by that he had been their
  king,
That when he strolled up to the plate they made the
  welkin ring;
But now his nerve had vanished, for when he heard them
  hoot
He "fanned" or "popped out" daily, like some minor
  league recruit.

He soon began to sulk and loaf, his batting eye went lame;
No home runs on the score card now were chalked against
  his name;
The fans without exception gave the manager no peace,
For one and all kept clamoring for Casey's quick release.

The Mudville squad began to slump, the team was in the air;
Their playing went from bad to worse—nobody seemed to care.
"Back to the woods with Casey!" was the cry from Rooters' Row.
"Get some one who can hit the ball, and let that big dub go!"

The lane is long, some one has said, that never turns again,
And Fate, though fickle, often gives another chance to men;
And Casey smiled; his rugged face no longer wore a frown—
The pitcher who had started all the trouble came to town.

All Mudville had assembled—ten thousand fans had come
To see the twirler who had put big Casey on the bum;
And when he stepped into the box, the multitude went wild;
He doffed his cap in proud disdain, but Casey only smiled.

"Play ball!" the umpire's voice rang out, and then the game began.
But in that throng of thousands there was not a single fan
Who thought that Mudville had a chance, and with the setting sun
Their hopes sank low—the rival team was leading "four to one."

The last half of the ninth came round, with no change in the score;
But when the first man up hit safe, the crowd began to roar;
The din increased, the echo of ten thousand shouts was heard
When the pitcher hit the second and gave "four balls" to the third.

Three men on base—nobody out—three runs to tie the game!
A triple meant the highest niche in Mudville's hall of fame;
But here the rally ended and the gloom was deep as night,
When the fourth one "fouled to catcher" and the fifth "flew out to right."

A dismal groan in chorus came; a scowl was on each face
When Casey walked up, bat in hand, and slowly took his place;
His bloodshot eyes in fury gleamed, his teeth were clenched in hate;
He gave his cap a vicious hook and pounded on the plate.

But fame is fleeting as the wind and glory fades away;
There were no wild and wooly cheers, no glad acclaim this day;
They hissed and groaned and hooted as they clamored: "Strike him out!"
But Casey gave no outward sign that he had heard this shout.

The pitcher smiled and cut one loose—across the plate it sped;
Another hiss, another groan. "Strike one!" the umpire said.
Zip! Like a shot the second curve broke just below the knee.
"Strike two! the umpire roared aloud; but Casey made no plea.

No roasting for the umpire now—his was an easy lot;
But here the pitcher whirled again—was that a rifle shot?
A whack, a crack, and out through the space the leather pellet flew,
A blot against the distant sky, a speck against the blue.

Above the fence in center field in rapid whirling flight
The sphere sailed on—the blot grew dim and then was lost to sight.
Ten thousand hats were thrown in air, ten thousand threw a fit,
But no one ever found the ball that might Casey hit.

O, somewhere in this favored land dark clouds may hide the sun,
And somewhere bands no longer play and children have no fun!
And somewhere over blighted lives there hangs a heavy pall,
But Mudville hearts are happy now, *for Casey hit the ball*.

Grantland Rice

Casey—Twenty Years Later

The Mudville team was desperate in that big championship game;
The chances were they'd bite the dust and kiss goodbye to fame;
Three men were hurt and two were benched; the score stood six to four.
They had to make three hard-earned runs in just two innings more.

"It can't be done," the captain said, a pallor on his face;
"I've got two pitchers in the field, a mutt on second base;
And should another man get spiked or crippled in some way,
The team would sure be down and out, with only eight to play.

"We're up against it anyhow as far as I can see;
My boys ain't hitting like they should and that's what worries me;
The luck is with the other side, no pennant will we win;
It's mighty tough! There's nought to do but take it on the chin."

The eighth round opened; one, two, three—the enemy went down;
The Mudville boys went out the same, the captain wore a frown;

The first half of the ninth came round, two men had been
called out,
When Mudville's catcher broke a thumb and could not go
the route.

A deathly silence settled o'er the crowd assembled there.
Defeat, defeat was what all sensed! Defeat hung in the air!
With only eight men in the field 'twould be a gruesome
fray;
Small wonder that the captain cursed the day he learned
to play.

"Lend me a man to finish with," he begged the other
team;
"Lend you a man?" the foe replied; "My boy, you're in a
dream!
We want that dear old pennant, pal." And then, a final
jeer—
"There's only one thing you can do—*call for a volunteer.*"

The captain stood and pondered in a listless sort of way;
He never was a quitter and wouldn't quit today!
"Is there within the grandstand here"—his voice rang
loud and clear—
"A man who has the sporting blood to be a volunteer?"

A sense of death now settled o'er that sickly multitude;
Was there a man among them with such recklessness
imbued?
The captain stood with cap in hand, and hopeless was his
glance,
And then a big old man cried out, "Say, Cap, I'll take a
chance."

Into the field he bounded with a step both firm and light;
"Give me the mask and mitt," he said; "let's finish up the
fight.
The game is not beyond recall; a winner you have found;
Although I'm ancient, I'm a brute and muscular and
sound."

His hair was sprinkled here and there with little streaks of
gray;
Around his eyes and on his brow a bunch of wrinkles lay.
The captain smiled despairingly and slowly turned away.
"Why, he's all right," one rooter yelled. "C'mon, Cap, let
him play!"

"All right, go on," the captain sighed; the stranger turned
around,
Took off his coat and collar, too, and threw them on the
ground.
The humor of the situation seemed to hit them one and
all,
And as the stranger donned his mask, the umpire yelled,
"Play ball!"

Three balls the pitcher at him hurled, three balls of lightning speed;
The oldster caught them all with ease and did not seem to
heed.
Each ball had been pronounced a strike, the side had been
put out,
And as he walked in towards the bench, he heard the
rooters shout.

One Mudville boy went out on strikes, and one was killed
at first;
The captain saw his hopes all dashed, and gnashed his
teeth and cursed.
But the next man smashed a double and the fourth man
swatted clear;
Then, in a thunder of applause, up came the volunteer.

His feet were planted in the earth, he swung a warlike
club;
The captain saw his awkward pose and softly whispered,
"Dub!"
The pitcher looked at him and grinned, then heaved a
mighty ball;
The echo of that fearful swat still lingers with us all.

High, fast and far that spheroid flew; it sailed and sailed
away;
It ne'er was found, so it's supposed it still floats on today.
Three runs came in, the pennant would be Mudville's for a
year;
The fans and players gathered round to cheer the
volunteer.

"What is your name?" the captain asked. "Tell us your
name," cried all,
And down the unknown's cheeks great tears and rivulets
did fall.
For one brief moment he was still, then murmured soft
and low:
"I'm mighty Casey who struck out—just twenty years
ago!"

Clarence Patrick McDonald

The Highlights of the Game

## CHAPTER 14

Streaks and Feats

Jack Kavanagh

The past of baseball is accented by feats of accomplishment. The heroics of individual players or collective efforts of teams are listed in record books as bare statistics. It is the purpose of this section to clothe these with accounts of how such records were made.

These are the achievements of mortals whom we have made into heroes by giving great value to things they have done. Deeds of baseball players are valued more highly than scholarship, skills in creative crafts, or sustaining a precarious balance of world peace. We can name more Cy Young Award winners than we can list those given the Nobel Peace Prize; we can rattle off batting champions but not name holders of the Pulitzer Prize.

It is axiomatic that all records are made to be broken, yet it is wasteful to throw away old records which have been cherished by generations of fans and only replace them with a newly minted line of agate type. Those who have been on the top of the list, or came close to the peak, have been recognized by relying on lists which sustain enough depth to single out the most noteworthy performances in the many categories which are represented.

As the former mayor of New York City, the dapper, perceptive Jimmy Walker, once admonished Babe Ruth when he had fallen from grace in the eyes of fans, "The cheers of yesterday have a short echo."

The Streaks

Most records are, eventually, displaced by new ones. Some survive because the conditions under which they were made have been altered by changing circumstances in baseball. Some, such as the accumulation of sheer totals, are pushed higher. This is not so much a matter of accomplishment as it is of perseverance and lengthened seasons.

Longest Hitting Streaks

Joe DiMaggio's feat of hitting safely in 56 consecutive games is the type of record which is in jeopardy of being broken when each new baseball season begins. It is in jeopardy because every player has the same chance as DiMaggio to hit safely in every game he plays. Stringing enough of these games together to reach the level DiMaggio did in 1941 tests both a player's skill and his nerve.

The way baseball is played has not altered significantly since 1941. That year DiMaggio batted .357. In 1987 Wade Boggs was a threat to topple DiMaggio's record, batting .363. He even temporarily moved into DiMaggio's

class as a home run hitter, with 24. In 1941 DiMaggio had hit 30. Boggs was also dropped from batting first or second to hitting third. Players with power have a different approach to collecting base hits than did Willie Keeler, whose nineteenth-century record of 44 consecutive games in which he hit safely was broken by Joe DiMaggio. Those with extra-base power are expected to sacrifice the string-extending single for a game-winning home run when the occasion rises. In setting his record, DiMaggio never once bunted for a base hit.

DiMaggio's streak is mind-boggling in its length, yet temptingly attainable by batters capable of hitting for high averages. And any player might get on a hot streak and sustain it long enough to challenge DiMaggio's total. However, those who have set extended streaks did it while accomplishing a high season's average. The trick is to string those games with base hits together. The more games in which a batter has hit safely, the greater the possibility these will come in succession for long stretches.

Until the New York press, wire services, and broadcast industry made Joe DiMaggio's consecutive-game hitting streak a matter of national awareness and interest, this kind of feat was not noted with a daily fanaticism. Streaks drew comment, but this was mostly reserved to be relished during the winter's Hot Stove League sessions among sport-starved fans.

Although Willie Keeler's consecutive-game string became the target for future attempts to exceed it, it might have been only one of the records made under special circumstances. Keeler's 44 consecutive games might only be unusual in retrospect because the string began on Opening Day, 1897. Had Bad Bill Dahlen not had a most peculiar bad day on August 7, 1894, even Joe DiMaggio's 56-game streak would only be a "modern record" set after 1900. As it is, Bill Dahlen appears high on the list with the 42 games in which he hit safely.

DiMaggio was stopped by stellar infield play. Bill Dahlen was stopped by his own inability to fatten his record in a game in which almost everyone else did. Dahlen's team, the Chicago Colts, had 17 hits, winning a ten-inning game from Cincinnati 13–11. Dahlen's blanking was more evident because it was sandwiched between the feats that day of his teammates, Jimmy Ryan and Walter Wilmot. Ryan, the leadoff batter, had five hits, three of them doubles, and Walter Wilmot, who followed Dahlen in the batting order, also had five hits, two of them triples.

Dahlen was at bat a half dozen times, but the Reds' pitchers, Chauncey Fisher and Tom Parrott, found him, uniquely that day, an easy out. Dahlen's feat was obscured. When Willie Keeler, a star of greater national

awareness, hit safely in 44 games three years later, the eclipsed record was simply noted but not recounted in the detail which was later paid to the strings which exceeded it. Although appearing in 121 games and batting .362, Dahlen was not a regular shortstop at that time, dividing his games between short and third.

It was Keeler's feat which caught the public fancy, particularly as it began on Opening Day, April 22, 1897, and continued for 44 games into the season. He was eventually stopped on June 18. Until then, it seemed he had found an unending series of opportunities to "hit 'em where they ain't"—his simplistic explanation for his base-hit totals. Keeler's record not only stood the test of time until Joe DiMaggio broke it in 1941, it still stands as the National League record, tied only by Pete Rose in 1978.

It wasn't until 1922 that the feat of hitting successfully in successive games became a real target for seekers of new records. Keeler's streak had been regarded more as evidence of his great ability to rap out base hits than as a model of daily consistency. He was a widely admired player, the leadoff batter for the Baltimore Orioles, three times pennant winners prior to the 1897 season.

When Ty Cobb came along, the fact that he nearly equaled Keeler's mark in 1911, when he set an American League record with 40 successive games in which he got at least one hit, was also taken as a sign of his superiority, not necessarily observed as a model event.

But in 1922 the public and press were ready for new records, and they had popular heroes to set them. In 1922 both George Sisler and Rogers Hornsby created new marks in hitting safely in consecutive games. Sisler broke Cobb's American League record and Hornsby notched 33 games in a row in which he had a base hit. This was hailed as a new record for righthanded batters, at least since 1900. Dahlen's 42 had been made before the turn of the century. While such a demarcation might be a dubious distinction, it serves to create new records. (Eventually those who are insatiable for "new records" will draw a line across some point in the twentieth century and begin proclaiming new records by ignoring those which, like DiMaggio's 56-game streak, seem unbreakable.)

Consider, too, that Ty Cobb, the American League record holder, whose 1911 mark was Sisler's target, was still quite capable of breaking his own record in 1922. Although the hit which raised his final average that year to .401 was argued about, he was still a high-average batter and needed only to string enough games together to set a new mark. Hitting safely in consecutive games was a trademark for Cobb. He hit in 20 or more games in a row seven times during his career.

George Sisler was a very popular player. A college product when the campus was not a direct line to the major leagues, with superlative skills and a gentlemanly manner, he was widely admired. In addition, his team, the St. Louis Browns, was engaged in a hot pennant battle with the New York Yankees.

Sisler began his string on July 27 and continued through August and past Labor Day, getting his base hit in game after game. Then, with his targets in sight—Cobb's American League record and Keeler's major league record, set in the National League—Sisler injured his right shoulder. It was thought at first that not only might he not be able to keep his consecutive string going,

but he might not be able to finish the season.

Ironically Sisler found himself at the threshhold of Cobb's record while playing against the Detroit Tigers, managed by Cobb, who patrolled center field. Sisler notched games 37 and 38 when the Tigers came to Sportsman's Park in St. Louis. On September 11, struggling to keep his streak alive, Sisler tried for game 39, one short of Cobb's record.

Sisler had been granted a streak-extending single by a generous scorer on a fly ball which Bobby Veach had reached but couldn't hold, but in 1922 there were no message boards or public address systems to inform fans of scorer's decisions. So Cobb, playing center field, was too far away from the press box to see the scorer hold up one finger, the traditional sign of a safe hit. He didn't know Veach's muff had been ruled a hit. As far as he knew, Sisler, coming to bat in the bottom of the ninth, with two out, a runner on first, and the score 4–3 in favor of Detroit, was hitless.

Manager Cobb had a choice. He could order Sisler, the Browns' most dangerous hitter, walked. This would move the tying run into scoring position and put the winning run on base. It would have been bad baseball and worse sportsmanship to order an intentional walk. Cobb might have been tempted to deny his rival what he thought was a last chance, but he didn't. He did take the precaution of removing Bob "Fatty" Fothergill, a slow-footed fielder, and replacing him in right with a better defensive player, Ira Flagstead. Then he signaled Howard Ehmke to pitch. He did, and Sisler lined a triple between Cobb and Flagstead. He scored the game-winning run a moment later on a Marty McManus single. Cobb had lost a game he might have won by passing Sisler, and George had moved to within one game of tying Ty's record.

At this point Sisler's shoulder ached so much he couldn't play the next four games, a series against the last-place Boston Red Sox. It was one of those "might have been" situations. He might have set a new American League record then against the Red Sox. However, it was much more dramatically attained when the Yankees, a half game ahead of the Browns in a torrid pennant race's final stages, came to St. Louis for a crucial three-game series.

Sisler played. His shoulder and right arm were bandaged, and he could only swing his bat with one hand. But, he played and, in a 2–1 loss, he managed a lone hit off Bob Shawkey to tie Cobb's record. The next day, September 17, the Browns evened the series as Babe Ruth's nemesis, Hub Pruett, stopped the Yankees. Ruth did get a home run, but more importantly Sisler managed another one-handed base hit to break Cobb's record.

The final game of the series was won by the Yankees as Joe Bush gained his twenty-fifth victory and Sisler went hitless in four plate appearances, never making solid contact. The Yankees left town with an increased lead they nursed to a pennant by a one-game margin. With his team still in contention, Sisler was unable to play. He pinch-hit unsuccessfully the next day, as Walter Johnson defeated the Browns, then sat out games until he returned to action with a hit against the Athletics on September 23. He hit safely the next day, and then, in a peculiarity of the 1922 season, the whole league was idle for four days.

When the league resumed for the final Friday, Satur-

day, and Sunday, the Browns were unable to catch the Yankees, although George Sisler hit safely in the three final games. Leave out the pinch-hit effort against Walter Johnson, a desperate attempt by a player who, if he had been swinging with two hands, would have played the full game. Without an injured shoulder, Sisler arguably might have kept his string alive against Joe Bush. He might not have missed those four games against the pitching-poor Red Sox or the two final games against the Senators. He might have hit safely in all of those games as well as the three he added at the season's end. If he had, he would have finished the season, with no more games to play to extend his streak, with 52 games in which he hit consecutively. Think what a target that would have been for Joe DiMaggio in 1941.

The DiMaggio Streak

Joe DiMaggio was playing poorly when his epochal feat began. He wasn't thinking about hitting in 56 straight games; he was worrying about getting a hit in the game of May 15. In spring training DiMaggio hit safely in every exhibition game, a forecast of the record-setting year ahead. His momentum carried through the first eight games of the 1941 season. Then he was thrown into a slump by a junk-ball pitcher, Lester McCrabbe of the Philadelphia Athletics.

By mid-May DiMaggio was still floundering, hitting below .300 and without his usual authority. On May 15 he managed a scratch single. It was an unimpressive handle hit off Cotton Ed Smith of the Chicago White Sox. However, it began a streak that wouldn't end until another pitcher named Smith, Al Smith, paired with Jim Bagby, Jr., held Joe hitless in a game against the Cleveland Indians.

The well-known DiMaggio batting eye that had produced batting championships the two preceding seasons, grew sharper, although in most games he made only a single hit. There were to be 34 games in which the string was kept alive with a lone hit. Not only was this a precarious way to sustain a batting streak, it did not, in its opening stages, draw attention to the feat that was under way. Fans followed Joe's rising batting average but not his successive daily contributions to it. He was thought to be in a contest with Ted Williams, not with the ghosts of record holders whose feats had been both unchallenged and unnoticed since the 1920s. He never caught Williams, who was enjoying the last season a champion would bat over .400.

As DiMaggio's string lengthened, the days of another Yankee immortal, Lou Gehrig, grew fewer. The Iron Horse, who had set another sort of consecutive streak by appearing in 2,130 games, died on June 2, as DiMaggio's skein reached 19.

As the string stretched into the twenties, reporters began digging into record books. The last time this arcane event excited interest had been in 1922, when George Sisler broke Ty Cobb's American League record but was stopped short of Willie Keeler's total. In 1938 another St. Louis Browns first baseman, George McQuinn, had run off a string of 34 games in which he had hit safely. Since McQuinn was playing in the anonymity of the second division, little attention was paid to his challenge.

Because there are two major leagues, record setters have two targets. DiMaggio was required first to set a league mark at 42 and then proceed to reach 45 and set an all-time mark by breaking Keeler's total set in the past century.

By regarding DiMaggio first as a righthanded batter, he could challenge the closer record of Rogers Hornsby, who had hit in 33 straight games in 1922. No mention was made of Bill Dahlen's record of 1894. Perhaps the reporters assumed it had been made under different playing conditions and shouldn't count. They were wrong; the pitching distance had been established at sixty feet, six inches in 1893, and bunts fouled off counted as strikes from 1894. In any case, Dahlen's 42 games was less than Keeler's total, which became the ultimate target.

When DiMaggio passed Rogers Hornsby's total, the public's attention was heightened. Sisler's American League record was only a week's play away. The hype went into full swing. Les Brown's orchestra hurried a phonograph record onto the market, "Jolting Joe DiMaggio." As banal a tune as ever came from Tin Pan Alley, the song became a pep rally number as the band chanted, "Joe, Joe, DiMaggio, we want you on our side."

Bill "Bojangles" Robinson, who had tap-danced in movies with little Shirley Temple, did routines atop the Yankees dugout while he sprinkled what he called "goofer dust" to enhance DiMaggio's luck.

Despite the distractions of people pressing their attention on the reserved, unemotional DiMaggio, he continued his consistent, game-after-game pursuit of the next milestone, Sisler's league record. At the same time, he was carrying the Yankees toward a pennant. They had lost the title in 1940 after four successive world championships under manager Joe McCarthy. They were out to recapture their league's title.

Interest in Joe DiMaggio's quest went beyond the readers of the sports pages. The wire services carried stories assuring newspaper readers that Joe had extended his string before they gave the account of the game in which he did it. Radio newscasts began with bulletins about Joe's progress.

Cynics and debunkers, who concentrated their suspicions on anything coming out of New York, particularly if it gave credit to the Yankees, watched closely for scoring decisions which would give DiMaggio a favored ruling.

Rival managers juggled pitching rotations to bring their best to the mound when DiMaggio and the Yankees came to town.

Dan Daniel, a prolific and conscientious sportswriter and editor, was the official scorer for games at Yankee Stadium in 1941, and he covered the team on the road for his paper. He has written extensively about DiMaggio's 56-game hitting streak. He saw every game.

The scorer's circumstances at Yankee Stadium, as described by Daniel, placed him in view of rabid Yankee supporters who gathered behind him to demand a base hit no matter how glaring the error which allowed DiMaggio to reach base.

Daniel wrote afterward that he had to have his home phone number changed. He also insisted both he and the other scorers around the league became hyperattentive every time DiMaggio came to bat once his string had become established as a potential record breaker.

Daniel also explained that players on the opposing teams were keyed up when DiMaggio batted, none wanting to contribute to extending the string by loafing on a ball and turning it into a hit. DiMaggio's streak lifted the quality of play, umpiring, and press coverage. Everyone, including DiMaggio, wanted him to earn a new record.

Years afterward, DiMaggio looked back on the 56 games and could only find one where he wished the play had not been as judgmental as it was. It came in the thirtieth game, when he was still short of Hornsby's record. The White Sox came to the Stadium, and Johnny Rigney was the pitcher. He had twice been DiMaggio's victim in earlier games in the streak but on this day had stopped the Yankee Clipper until the seventh inning.

Then DiMaggio hit a routine grounder to Luke Appling. The future Hall of Fame shortstop moved for the ball, but it took a bad bounce, hitting him in the shoulder. In his rush to recover, Appling grabbed at the ball, dropped it, then threw too late. A bad-hop single? Butter-fingered retrieval? The official scorer, Dan Daniel, ruled it a hit. Lucky for Joe and fortunate for legend, too, because on his last time up, in the ninth, Taft Wright made a leaping catch to snatch a home run out of the right field stands. Joe would have been blanked.

The next day DiMaggio got another streak-extending break, almost the same way. This time the ball was hard hit and Appling could only knock it down. He couldn't make a throw. Too hard to handle? Scorer Daniel ruled so and the fans relaxed. A few days later Hornsby's record for righthanded batters would be broken and DiMaggio would be headed for Sisler's mark. However, it took another break for DiMaggio to get there.

Eldon Auker, a St. Louis submarine-ball pitcher, held Joe hitless until the eighth inning at Yankee Stadium. Unless one of the first three batters kept the inning alive, Joe, due up fourth, would not bat again. The Yankees were ahead by two runs, and it did not appear as though there would be a bottom of the ninth.

Johnny Sturm popped up, but Red Rolfe drew a walk. Tommy Henrich, the next batter, had a dilemma. He could still deprive Joe of a chance to bat if he hit into a double play. With manager McCarthy's consent, Henrich bunted and moved Rolfe to second base. Now, with first base open, it was Auker who had a dilemma. He could walk DiMaggio, hit him with a pitch (a strategy as underhanded as his delivery), or pitch to him.

DiMaggio stood at the plate, unruffled. Coolly he smashed the first pitch into left field for a double. It was a close call, but now Sisler's record was in reach.

In a Sunday doubleheader with Washington at Griffith Stadium, on June 29, DiMaggio tied Sisler's record in the first game and broke it in the nightcap. The record-tying hit came off knuckleballer Dutch Leonard and was broken with a last-chance single off the unknown Arnold Anderson. DiMaggio was one game short of tying Willie Keeler's 1897 record.

The only mark left for DiMaggio to eclipse was tied in the second game of a July 1 doubleheader with the Boston Red Sox and broken the next day.

The day DiMaggio claimed the American League record was marked by two extremes of luck. It was fortunate his record-tying hit came early in the game because a downpour deluged Yankee Stadium and the game was called after five innings. It was unfortunate that during the rain delay no one kept an eye on the bat rack. A souvenir hunter reached over the dugout and pulled out a bat. He grabbed DiMaggio's favorite club.

Although he was upset, the man who rarely showed emotion quietly borrowed a bat from teammate Tommy Henrich the next day. It was an identical thirty-six-inch, thirty-six-ounce bat, and Joe used it to break Keeler's record. His record-smashing hit was a prodigeous home run off Dick Newsome, a 19-game winner for the Red Sox. It carried high over the head of his rival, Ted Williams, into the left field stands.

Joe DiMaggio did not rest on his laurels. Actually, with the pressure to produce at least one base hit each game lifted, he began pounding out hits in clusters. He passed the 50-game mark and his luck still held. In the fifty-fourth game, he again came up against Johnny Rigney of the White Sox. This time he would have been stopped except for a topped roller. A typical lusty swing sent a dribbler slowly toward third base where Bob Kennedy was playing fearfully deep, a precaution normally taken by rival third baseman against DiMaggio. It worked to Joe's advantage that day as he beat out the slowly hit ball for his only hit. However, it would work to his disadvantage a few days later in Cleveland.

Although Joe DiMaggio said after his streak had ended, "I wish it could have gone on forever," like all good things it had to come to an end. Joe had reached 56 games when the kind of luck which occasionally had sustained him, such as the topped roller against Chicago, turned around. The Yankees came into Cleveland and crowds came, divided between fans' wishes to witness the streak extended and hometeam rooters' hopes that their team could bring the mighty DiMaggio to a halt.

What could only be a matter of time happened. As a minor league star in his native San Francisco, a nineteen-year-old Joe DiMaggio had been stopped after hitting in 61 consecutive games. After the 1941 streak ended, the *San Francisco Chronicle,* which had made daily reports of DiMaggio's record-breaking games, observed that the Pacific Coast League string had been ended by the son of a former major league pitching star, Bob Walsh, whose father, Big Ed Walsh, would be elected to the Hall of Fame. It was pointed out that DiMaggio's major league string was ended, in part, by Jim Bagby, Jr., another son of a successful major leaguer, a 31-game winner for the 1920 world champion Cleveland Indians.

It wasn't so much the pitching of starter Al Smith or reliever Bagby that halted DiMaggio as the glove work on the right side of the Indians' infield. Twice Ken Keltner, playing a very deep third base, took drives down the baseline and turned them into outs. And Joe's last chance found him deserted by luck on a bad bounce. A ball headed up the middle took an erratic hop, and shortstop Lou Boudreau grabbed it and flipped to second to start a double play that closed off DiMaggio's chance to keep safely intact the stretch of games in which he had hit.

Although the DiMaggio streak had been stopped, he was still a hot hitter, and even his favorite bat was back. An embarrassed fan from Newark admitted the theft and returned the bat, and Joe used it to continue his torrid hitting. He kept pounding out hits on a daily basis until he had hit safely in 16 more consecutive games. This meant

Joe DiMaggio's 1941 Hitting Streak

Game No.	Date	Club and Pitcher	AB	R	H
1	5-15	White Sox, Smith	4	0	1
2	5-16	White Sox, Lee	4	2	2
3	5-17	White Sox, Rigney	3	1	1
4	5-18	Browns, Harris, Niggeling	3	3	3
5	5-19	Browns, Galehouse	3	0	1
6	5-20	Browns, Auker	5	1	1
7	5-21	Tigers, Rowe, Benton	5	0	2
8	5-22	Tigers, McKain	4	0	1
9	5-23	Red Sox, Newsome	5	0	1
10	5-24	Red Sox, Johnson	4	2	1
11	5-25	Red Sox, Grove	4	0	1
12	5-27	Senators, Chase, Anderson, Carrasquel	5	3	4
13	5-28	Senators, Hudson	4	1	1
14	5-29	Senators, Sundra	3	1	1
15	5-30	Red Sox, Johnson	2	1	1
16	5-30	Red Sox, Harris	3	0	1
17	6-1	Indians, Milnar	4	1	1
18	6-1	Indians, Harder	4	0	1
19	6-2	Indians, Feller	4	2	2
20	6-3	Tigers, Trout	4	1	1
21	6-5	Tigers, Newhouser	5	1	1
22	6-7	Browns, Muncrief, Allen, Caster	5	2	3
23	6-8	Browns, Auker	4	3	2
24	6-8	Browns, Caster, Kramer	4	1	2
25	6-10	White Sox, Rigney	5	1	1
26	6-12	White Sox, Lee	4	1	2
27	6-14	Indians, Feller	2	0	1
28	6-15	Indians, Bagby	3	1	1
29	6-16	Indians, Milnar	5	0	1
30	6-17	White Sox, Rigney	4	1	1
31	6-18	White Sox, Lee	3	0	1
32	6-19	White Sox, Smith, Ross	3	2	3
33	6-20	Tigers, Newsom, McKain	5	3	4
34	6-21	Tigers, Trout	4	0	1
35	6-22	Tigers, Newhouser, Newsom	5	1	2
36	6-24	Browns, Muncrief	4	1	1
37	6-25	Browns, Galehouse	4	1	1
38	6-26	Browns, Auker	4	0	1
39	6-27	Athletics, Dean	3	1	2
40	6-28	Athletics, Babich, Harris	5	1	2
41	6-29	Senators, Leonard	4	1	1
42	6-29	Senators, Anderson	5	1	1
43	7-1	Red Sox, Harris, Ryba	4	0	2
44	7-1	Red Sox, Wilson	3	1	1
45	7-2	Red Sox, Newsome	5	1	1
46	7-5	Athletics, Marchildon	4	2	1
47	7-6	Athletics, Babich, Hadley	5	2	4
48	7-6	Athletics, Knott	4	0	2
49	7-10	Browns, Niggling	2	0	1
50	7-11	Browns, Harris, Kramer	5	1	4
51	7-12	Browns, Auker, Muncrief	5	1	2
52	7-13	White Sox, Lyons, Hallett	4	2	3
53	7-13	White Sox, Lee	4	0	1
54	7-14	White Sox, Rigney	3	0	1
55	7-15	White Sox, Smith	4	1	2
56	7-16	Indians, Milnar, Krakauskas	4	3	3
Totals			223	55	91

he would have reached an incredible 73 games had not Keltner and Boudreau pulled off outstanding defensive plays after game 56.

As it is, hitting safely in 72 of 73 games is almost unimaginable. Historians had to go back to the overlooked Bad Bill Dahlen to find a comparable feat for DiMaggio to eclipse almost half a century later. Back in 1894, after he had run up a string of 42 games, Dahlen ran off another stretch of 28 games in which he hit safely. He had left a neglected legacy of hitting in 70 of 71 games for DiMaggio to top with 72 in 73.

During his 56-game streak, Joe DiMaggio batted .408. Although he finished the 1941 season with a .357 average, he was second to Ted Williams's league-leading .406. However, DiMaggio had led his team to a championship and this, with the incredible feat of hitting in 56 straight

games, earned him the Most Valuable Player Award by a close margin.

Those whose interest in statistics match, if not exceed, a curiosity about the drama of making them, will want to know that, in hitting .408 during the 56 games, DiMaggio scored 56 runs and batted in 55. He hit 15 home runs, half his season's total, and had 35 extra-base hits among the 91 hits he collected in 223 at-bats. He walked 21 times, was hit by a pitch twice, and struck out only 7 times.

The Yankees went on to defeat the Brooklyn Dodgers in the World Series and, as the Japanese went on to bomb Pearl Harbor and involve the United States in World War Two, Joe was asked to take a $2,500 cut in salary for 1942. He managed to get a $5,000 raise and play the 1942 season before entering military service in possession of a unique feat which still attracts its new challengers.

The Pete Rose Challenge

The year 1978 was a tremendous one for Pete Rose, whose career with the Cincinnati Reds qualified him as a potential challenger for Joe DiMaggio's record of hitting safely in 56 consecutive games. Although he did not hit for the high averages of the other streakers who had held records—Keeler, Sisler, Hornsby, and DiMaggio—Rose batted leadoff and had amassed 10 seasons with 200 or more hits. Even more, he was the kind of player who would rise to any occasion. He loved a challenge.

Longest Hitting Streaks, NL

Player	Team	Year	G
Willie Keeler	BAL	1897	44
Pete Rose	CIN	1978	44
Bill Dahlen	CHI	1894	42
Tommy Holmes	BOS	1945	37
Billy Hamilton	PHI	1894	36
Fred Clarke	LOU	1895	35
Benito Santiago	SD	1987	34
George Davis	NY	1893	33
Rogers Hornsby	STL	1922	32
Ed Delahanty	PHI	1899	31
Willie Davis	LA	1969	31
Rico Carty	ATL	1970	31
Elmer Smith	CIN	1898	30
Stan Musial	STL	1950	30
Jerome Walton	CHI	1989	30

Longest Hitting Streaks, AL

Player	Team	Year	G
Joe DiMaggio	NY	1941	56
George Sisler	STL	1922	41
Ty Cobb	DET	1911	40
Paul Molitor	MIL	1987	39
Ty Cobb	DET	1917	35
George Sisler	STL	1925	34
John Stone	DET	1930	34
George McQuinn	STL	1938	34
Dom DiMaggio	BOS	1949	34
Heinie Manush	WAS	1933	33
Sam Rice	WAS	1924	31
Ken Landreaux	MIN	1980	31
Tris Speaker	BOS	1912	30
Bing Miller	PHI	1929	30
Goose Goslin	DET	1934	30
Ron LeFlore	DET	1976	30
George Brett	KC	1980	30

Pete Rose's 1978 Hitting Streak

Game No.	Date	Club and Pitcher	AB	R	H
1	6-14	Cubs, Roberts	4	1	2
2	6-16	Cardinals, Denny	4	1	2
3	6-17	Cardinals, Yuckovich, Schultz	4	2	2
4	6-18	Cardinals, Martinez	4	1	1
5	6-20	Giants, Montefusco	5	2	2
6	6-21	Giants, Halicki	4	0	1
7	6-22	Giants, Knepper	4	0	1
8	6-23	Dodgers, Hooton	4	0	1
9	6-24	Dodgers, Welch	5	1	4
10	6-25	Dodgers, John	3	1	2
11	6-26	Astros, Lemongello	5	1	1
12	6-27	Astros, Niekro	4	1	1
13	6-28	Astros, Dixon	4	0	1
14	6-29	Astros, Bannister	3	0	1
15	6-30	Dodgers, Rautzhan	4	1	1
16	6-30	Dodgers, Welch, Forster, Hough	5	1	3
17	7-1	Dodgers, Rhoden	5	0	1
18	7-2	Dodgers, Rau	4	1	1
19	7-3	Astros, Bannister, McLaughlin	5	1	3
20	7-4	Astros, Richard	4	1	1
21	7-5	Astros, Niekro	4	0	1
22	7-6	Giants, Blue, Curtis	5	1	3
23	7-7	Giants, Barr	4	0	1
24	7-8	Giants, Montefusco	4	1	1
25	7-9	Giants, Halicki, Knepper	4	1	3
26	7-13	Mets, Koosman, Lockwood	5	0	2
27	7-14	Mets, Zachry	5	0	2
28	7-15	Mets, Swan	2	2	1
29	7-16	Mets, Siebert	5	1	1
30	7-17	Expos, Bahnsen	4	0	1
31	7-18	Expos, Dues	4	0	2
32	7-19	Phillies, Reed	4	1	1
33	7-20	Phillies, Kaat	5	1	1
34	7-21	Expos, Grimsley	3	1	1
35	7-22	Expos, Schatzeder	3	0	1
36	7-23	Expos, Rogers, Knowles	6	0	2
37	7-24	Mets, Zachry, Lockwood	5	2	2
38	7-25	Mets, Swan	4	1	3
39	7-26	Mets, Espinosa	3	0	1
40	7-28	Phillies, Lerch	2	1	1
41	7-28	Phillies, Carlton	4	0	1
42	7-29	Phillies, Lonborg, Kaat	4	1	3
43	7-30	Phillies, Christenson	5	0	2
44	7-31	Braves, Niekro	4	0	1
Totals			182	30	70

Willie Keeler's 1897 Hitting Streak

Game No.	Date	AB	R	H
1	April 22	5	2	2
2	April 23	4	1	2
3	April 24	4	1	2
4	April 26	4	0	1
5	April 27	5	2	2
6	April 28	5	1	3
7	April 29	4	1	2
8	April 20	4	3	3
9	May 3	4	0	1
10	May 4	4	0	2
11	May 5	4	0	1
12	May 6	5	0	3
13	May 7	6	2	1
14	May 8	3	1	1
15	May 10	4	0	1
16	May 11	5	1	2
17	May 12	5	0	3
18	May 14	6	2	2
19	May 15	6	2	2
20	May 16	6	3	3
21	May 17	4	1	2
22	May 18	6	1	1
23	May 19	4	1	1
24	May 20	4	1	3
25	May 21	3	1	2
26	May 22	4	2	2
27	May 25	5	0	1
28	May 26	5	1	2
29	May 27	5	1	3
30	May 29	6	2	2
31	May 30	4	0	1
32	May 31	4	1	1
33	May 31	5	2	1
34	June 2	5	1	4
35	June 5	5	1	1
36	June 7	4	1	1
37	June 9	5	2	2
38	June 10	4	0	2
39	June 11	4	0	2
40	June 12	5	2	2
41	June 14	5	1	2
42	June 15	3	0	1
43	June 16	5	2	1
44	June 18	4	3	3
Totals		201	49	82

Before he got around to taking a swing at DiMaggio's record, Rose had, as his first order of business, the matter of making his 3,000th career base hit. He opened the 1978 season needing 34 hits to reach a plateau only twelve others had gained. On May 5 Rose reached 3,000 with a single off Montreal pitcher Steve Rogers, before a hometown crowd at Riverfront Stadium.

"Charlie Hustle" was having an epoch-making season and, with one landmark reached, he soon found himself en route to another. Consecutive-game hitting streaks begin without signaling their advent. It is only as they grow that they attract attention.

Pete Rose was only batting .267 when he got a pair of hits against the Cubs on June 14. He kept adding hits in the games he played and, eventually, it was decided he had enough in a row to start looking for a record to be broken.

DiMaggio's 56-game streak in 1941 loomed far beyond expectation. However, the record keepers had gerrymandered Willie Keeler, holder of the National League record at 44, out of the books. There was a modern mark of 37, set during the wartime year of 1945, by Tommy Holmes of the Boston Braves.

Pete Rose hustled onward and, as luck would have it, came into Shea Stadium for a series with the Mets on the verge of knocking Holmes out of the record book. The patron saint of hype was on the ball, and a now sixty-one-year-old Tommy Holmes was on hand to root for Rose. He was there in a dual capacity. Tommy Holmes was also the Mets' community relations director.

There was another reward in having Pete Rose break Holmes's record in front of the Mets' fans. In 1973 Pete had been *persona non grata* when he had wrestled on the ground with skinny shortstop Bud Harrelson in a League Championship Game after a takeout slide by Rose at second base. The Mets fans remembered Rose calling them "animals" as they threatened to avenge the honor of the team by challenging the wives and children of the Reds' players in field boxes behind the Cincinnati dugout. However, hype places a statute of limitations on vengeance in New York. Whipped to a frenzy of impartiality by the Mets' announcers and a record-hungry press, people filled Shea Stadium ready to cheer Rose on while trusting he'd not be so unappreciative as to make his record-extending safety a game-winning hit.

On July 24 Pete Rose equaled the record of Tommy Holmes and to chants of "Go, Pete, Go!" broke it the next night against Craig Swan. An appreciative Holmes, pleased to have been a short-term celebrity, came onto the field to shake the hand of the man who had erased him from the record books. Pete now held the "modern" National League record for hitting safely in consecutive

games. In fairness, he would now try to reach Willie Keeler's mark of 44, a feat turned before the century began. Pete continued his quest. He had the skill, the competitive instincts, and the attitude to do it. He was unruffled by press attention, accustomed to it as the consequence of being the game's most colorful player of his time. Would he break DiMaggio's seemingly unreachable mark? If anyone could, Pete Rose could do it. But first he had to lay the ghost of Willie Keeler and his 81-year-old record.

It was a struggle, as the whole streak had been, but Rose reached Keeler's mark on July 31 in Atlanta. His record-equaling hit came off the knuckleball pitching of Phil Niekro, a man whose own feats as a middle-aged ballplayer also merited recognition.

Keeler had been caught. Would he be passed? No. The next night a rookie lefthander, Larry McWilliams, held Pete Rose hitless through most of the game, and reliever Gene Garber provided the final denial. He struck Rose out.

Pete Rose is joined with Willie Keeler, linked now, regardless of the era when the feat was accomplished, as coholders of the National League record for hitting safely in consecutive games.

Consecutive Games Played

On May 31, 1925, no one thought the young substitute pinch-hitting for the New York Yankees was launching the most extraordinary streak of durability the game would ever see. The next day Lou Gehrig took the place of the team's star first baseman, Wally Pipp, and continued his uncertain start toward a goal so distant it was unimaginable.

Gehrig had played for Hartford in the Eastern League after the Yankees signed him off the campus of Columbia University. It was thought he would make the major league grade, but he had not been handed a starting job. Only when Pipp complained of a headache and was given the day off by manager Miller Huggins did Gehrig get a chance to start a game. So uncertain of the rookie's skills was management that two days later Aaron Ward pinch-hit for Gehrig and Pipp finished the game in the field.

Before June ended, Gehrig had been taken out of games three times for pinch hitters, although he continued to start games. On July 5 he wasn't even the starting first baseman. Fred Merkle, who in 1908, as a rookie himself, had failed to run to second on what appeared to be a game-winning single, started the game. Merkle, whose gaffe eventually cost the New York Giants a pennant to the Chicago Cubs, had been forever more labeled Bonehead by unforgiving fans. Gehrig was destined for adulation. This day he made a ninth-inning appearance, an unsuspected extension of a fledgling feat.

Of course at the time there was no suspicion that young Lou Gehrig had launched a string of consecutive-game appearances which wouldn't end until fourteen years later. He began it as a young giant in the prime of his life and ended it a dying man, forced out of the lineup with a rare disease. From start to finish it became a matter of drama as the survival of the string became a compelling goal which Gehrig sustained despite injury, sickness, accident, and managed to avoid ending inadvertently.

Gehrig is remembered, or known to people who never saw him play, as the gentle giant who was portrayed by actor Gary Cooper in the movie *The Pride of the Yankees*. In reality, particularly in his early years, Gehrig was a hard-nosed, competitive player who would readily leap into argument with umpires and enemy players. He was ejected from a major league game a half dozen times without drawing a suspension which would have ended his string of games.

Durable, yes. Gehrig was well dubbed "the Iron Horse" for his rawboned toughness. However, he never spared himself. A statistic which astonishes fans is that he stole home 15 times, risking crashing into a plate-blocking catcher. He ran the bases with surprising speed and fearless abandon. Babe Ruth and Lou Gehrig are remembered for the home runs they hit; yet they were also daring base runners.

Once Gehrig's penchant for never missing a game was established, just being in the boxscore was the goal. He could have simultaneously set records for consecutive games played at first base, while extending his string of boxscore appearances. However, while in the sixth year of his developing string, in a late-season game, the Yankees promoted a game in which Babe Ruth would pitch while Lou Gehrig took his place in the outfield. Harry Rice, an outfielder who sometimes spelled Gehrig late in one-sided games, played first base.

Gehrig's 2,130-game skein, stretched over fourteen seasons, was not simply a matter of having him go out to first base day after day. For one thing, there were times when he could hardly play. When the Iron Horse was no longer a frisky colt, he developed lumbago, and it hobbled him from time to time. In midseason of 1934, Lou was seized by an attack and, immobilized, had to be helped off the field.

There was a conscious awareness on the part of the Yankees of the consecutive games Gehrig played, and this was kept alive by the sportswriters who covered the team. Everett Scott had astonished baseball with his consecutive-game appearances at shortstop, ending a string of 1,307 in 1925, the season Gehrig, his rookie roommate, began his string. Scott had started his run of games with the Boston Red Sox, and when he was bought by the Yankees in 1923, he carried on the string without interruption. He slowed down drastically early in 1925 and was first benched, then sold to the Senators. Unlike Scott, Lou Gehrig, the Iron Horse, would never be put out to pasture. However, Scott had left a legend behind, and it served to lead Gehrig toward new standards of durability.

The day after Gehrig had been helped off the field, with his string at 1,426, and Scott's record broken, he made a contrived appearance in the lineup. Hardly able to stand, he was in the lineup of the visiting Yankees in Detroit as the leadoff batter, penciled in to play shortstop. Despite his pain, he lined out a single and, with his appearance established in the boxscore, gave way to pinch runner Red Rolfe, who finished the game at short while Gehrig took his aching back to the hotel. Jack Saltzgaver, a utility infielder who, over the years, replaced Gehrig at first base more often than any other player, filled in at first that day.

Gehrig was back in the regular lineup the next day, collecting four hits, three of them doubles. He was on his

way to the only batting title he ever won and the Triple Crown for 1934. But it wasn't a pain-free future ahead for Lou. Lumbago continued to be a problem. He left games early because he was feeling ill, and he had a thumb injury in 1938 which he ignored to keep his string going.

It was during 1938 that the perpetual machine began to show signs of wearing out. For the first time he batted below .300; his stats—a .295 average, 29 home runs, and 107 runs batted in—would have pleased most players. But they were substandard for Lou, and so was his general play. Just age catching up, it was thought, just the way it had slowed Everett Scott in 1925 when Gehrig was starting out.

In spring training the next season, it was evident that something was amiss, but manager Joe McCarthy left it to Gehrig to decide when to call it quits. It was on May 2, 1939, after eight feebly played games had brought his string to 2,130, that Gehrig advised McCarthy to replace him.

The longest streak of its kind, seemingly impossible to ever exceed despite the longer seasons, ended. For fourteen years Gehrig had played despite a broken thumb, a broken toe, back spasms, frequent colds, and recurring attacks of lumbago. He had been forced from the lineup by something no one could foresee and almost no one had ever heard about. When the tests at Mayo Clinic proved that he had amyotrophic lateral sclerosis, it was so singular an affliction that it was renamed Lou Gehrig's Disease. It was incurable then and still is. Gehrig was a doomed man. He knew it, as did his wife, Eleanor. They bravely pretended to each other that Lou would regain his strength.

He continued to carry the lineup card to home plate during the 1939 pennant-winning season, as the team captain, but soon he had to surrender even that role. On July 4, 1939, a Lou Gehrig Day was arranged at Yankee Stadium. The scene was repeated in the Gary Cooper movie and is seen often in filmed highlights of baseball history.

Babe Ruth, who had broken relationships with Gehrig during a 1934 postseason tour to the Pacific and Japan, embraced his former teammate, and the occasion came to a climax as Gehrig, a man who knew his life was nearly over, stood at a microphone, surrounded by the Yankees who had been his fellow players. He told a choked-up audience, "Today, I consider myself the luckiest man on the face of the earth." He died on June 2, 1941.

Far in the Distance—But Closing In

Lou Gehrig's legacy of stamina and determination reached such a length that once historians could only measure the sturdiest of subsequent players to see who might become a runner-up. However, at the end of the 1992 season the durable Cal Ripken, Jr. of the Baltimore Orioles loomed as a legitimate, if still distant, challenger. In 1991 he moved into second place ahead of Everett Scott. Barring an accident or illness which would sideline him, he will overtake Lou Gehrig late in the 1996 season.

Scott, whose record Gehrig had eclipsed, now is third on the list, just ahead of Steve Garvey's 1,207 games. For many years, Joe Sewell ranked third behind Scott. Sewell is best remembered for his avoidance of strikeouts. Twice he fanned only 4 times in a whole season. Once he went 115 games without striking out in 437 times at bat. He set his consecutive-game string with Cleveland, later moving to the Yankees where he played for three years as Lou Gehrig's teammate. He was elected to the Hall of Fame in 1977.

During the 1930s, Gus Suhr, a fine-fielding first baseman for the Pittsburgh Pirates, reached 822 consecutive games played. It was dwarfed, even as he made it, by Gehrig's still intact string, but he far exceeded earlier National League marks.

Gus Suhr's National League record was broken by Stan Musial, who played in 895 straight games, ending in 1957 at age thirty-six. This provided a target for Billy Williams when his career with the Cubs got under way in 1963 and daily appearances were part of his routine. He sailed past Musial to claim the National League record at 1,117. He stopped in 1970, and the occasional rest did him good. He led the National League in batting in 1972 and his career ended with Oakland in 1975. He has been elected to the Hall of Fame.

Williams's new National League record provided an attainable goal for Steve Garvey, who exuded the stamina and will power required to catch Gehrig. He just didn't get started soon enough. Gehrig was twenty-two when his streak began; Garvey was twenty-six.

Also, Garvey did not become an everyday regular with the Los Angeles Dodgers until 1975, his sixth season with the team. He had been regarded as erratic at third base but, once moved across the diamond in 1974, he delivered with consistency in the field, at the bat, with power, and refused to budge from the lineup.

He left the Dodgers with his string intact after the 1982 season and took his Iron Man act to San Diego. A hand injury took him out of the lineup on July 29, 1983. He had broken Billy Williams's record the previous season, and all told he played in 1,207 consecutive games.

A special recognition is due to Pete Rose. Had he not paused to catch his breath during the 1978 season, when he was thirty-seven years old, he would hold the National League record. In 1978 Rose had more realistic aims than Gehrig's too distant goal. During that season he reached the 3,000-hit mark and set aim on Ty Cobb's all-time total. He also captured the headlines with his assault on Joe DiMaggio's 56-game hitting streak.

The year 1978 was also Rose's last season with the Cincinnati Reds and, in a celebrated case of free agency, he moved to Philadelphia. There he not only resumed his climb toward Cobb's hit totals, but played again on a daily basis. When he sat down for two games in 1978 with the Reds, he snapped a somewhat modest run of 678 games. When he finally left the daily lineup in Philadelphia, in 1983, he had run off an even longer string of 745 games. Add them together and Rose's total is 1,423 games, longer than anyone's stretch except Gehrig's and now Ripken's.

Most Consecutive Games Played

2,130	Lou Gehrig
1,735	Cal Ripken (through 1992)
1,307	Everett Scott
1,207	Steve Garvey
1,117	Billy Williams
1,103	Joe Sewell
895	Stan Musial
829	Eddie Yost
822	Gus Suhr
798	Nellie Fox

Successive Pitching Victories

The 1912 baseball season produced a bumper crop of pitchers winning successive victories. Rube Marquard of the New York Giants topped everyone by running up a total of 19. This tied the record set by Tim Keefe, also of New York. Keefe had won his games in 1888, when the pitching distance was only fifty feet between pitcher and batter, but he had won them in a row and that is the measurement of this feat. The present distance of sixty feet, six inches (actually, this is only about 55 feet from the pitcher's point of release) was set in 1893, Keefe's last season.

Marquard's mark remains unmatched within the confines of a single season. The record for consecutive wins beginning in the midst of one season and extending into the next season is held by Carl Hubbell, whose 24 consecutive victories, starting in 1936 and continuing into 1937, tops the list.

However, 1912 produced more than just Marquard's record. It also produced a new American League record and an immediate challenger to it. Even while Rube Marquard was engaged in his run in the National League, Walter Johnson, almost concurrently, was setting the American League record at 16. And by the time he was stopped, another streak was under way, this one by Smokey Joe Wood of the Boston Red Sox.

No one could ask for a better matchup in 1912 than the one which brought Walter Johnson, the record holder, to the mound at Fenway Park to face Joe Wood the challenger. Johnson was the premier pitcher in the American League and its strikeout king. Wood had dazzled the baseball world while en route to a 34–5 season, with 10 shutouts. He won three more games in the 1912 World Series. Then he injured his arm and never returned to his single-season pinnacle.

Walter Johnson, himself a 32-game winner in 1912, had broken the former American League record of 14 straight, set by Jack Chesbro in 1904. By winning his sixteenth straight game on August 23, he had set a new league mark and had his sights on the brand-new record of Rube Marquard. The New York lefthander had won his 19 by July 3. Johnson never caught Marquard.

Johnson was a victim of both bad luck and a scoring rule which today would not have cost him a loss. He lost a game in relief, taking over in the seventh inning of a tie game. There were two runners on base, and before Johnson could get the side out, one of them scored the winning run. Today the loss would be charged to the starting pitcher, Tom Hughes, who had allowed the runner to get on base. At that time the loss went against whoever was pitching when the winning run scored.

Even so, in 1912 the scorer's decision was denounced by the press and sympathetic fans. However, Ban Johnson, not only president of the American League but its iron-fisted founder, decreed the loss be placed against Walter Johnson's record, and there it remains forever. He had been stopped at 16.

When the 1912 penchant for pitchers winning consecutive victories identified the next challenger as Smokey Joe Wood of the pennant-bound Boston Red Sox, Johnson was called upon to stop him personally. The schedule brought the Washington Senators to Fenway Park to play the Red Sox, and the management was well aware they had a great gate attraction. Johnson was asked to pitch a day sooner so he would face Wood. He was glad to do it.

Whatever the capacity of Fenway Park in 1912, it was far exceeded when, on a weekday, over 30,000 baseball fans crowded the park. The crowd overflowed the stands. In fact, the players could not sit in their dugouts. Instead, they sat on chairs arranged in front of the throngs that stood just outside the baselines. Thousands more people stood in the outfield, behind ropes, reducing the area for the great Red Sox outfield to cover. Tris Speaker, Duffy Lewis, and Harry Hooper would not be able to roam back to catch deep fly balls. These would be automatic doubles if they reached the crowd herded behind the ropes.

Walter Johnson held the American League record, a string of 16 straight victories. Joe Wood had drawn nearer to Johnson's mark in his last start, beating New York on September 2 for his thirteenth win without a loss during the streak. Today he was after his fourteenth straight, Chesbro's old mark, and Walter Johnson didn't want him to get it. Unless Johnson himself stopped Wood, his own record, and possibly Marquard's, were in danger.

The game lived up to expectations. It was a pitcher's battle. Great defensive plays snuffed out rallies, and both pitchers stopped scoring threats with clutch strikeouts. A scoreless tie was broken in the sixth inning, when Tris Speaker hit a fly ball that reached the roped-back crowd for a ground-rule double and Duffy Lewis hit an opposite-field double down the right field foul line. It just eluded the grab of Danny Moeller and Speaker scored. And that was it. The game ended 1–0 as Walter Johnson lost another game in which his team failed to get him any runs. He lost 65 games during his career when his team was shut out.

When Wood pitched next, in Chicago, he was not in top form but held a 5–3 lead going into the bottom of the ninth. When the first two White Sox batters reached base with hits, manager Jake Stahl replaced Wood with reliever Charles "Sea Lion" Hall. A sacrifice fly made the final score 5–4, but Hall retired the White Sox without further damage and Joe Wood was within one game of tying Walter Johnson.

The Red Sox rode on to St. Louis in Pullman cars for a game on September 15, and Joe Wood pitched another strong game, a 2–1 victory in eight innings to tie Johnson's record. Darkness caused the game to be called after Wood himself had scored the go-ahead run in the top of the eighth inning.

It all came to an end on September 20 in Detroit. Wood failed to break Walter Johnson's mark. He went the distance but mostly on the sufferance of manager Jake Stahl. Although two of the Tigers' runs were unearned, the 6–4 final score indicated Joe Wood's fastball lacked its usual smoke that day.

The Marquard Inheritance

When Rube Marquard wrote his way into the record books in 1912, with 19 consecutive victories, he established a benchmark which has been approached but never equaled, or excelled, since that time. Although Walter Johnson's American League mark, itself never beaten, took on extra importance because of the affection and awe he inspired in baseball fans, Marquard set the standard for all others to challenge.

The Johnson-Wood confrontation excited the imagination, and other challenges have created their own temporary focus, but always there stands the record of Marquard. It is the pinnacle toward which others climb and never reach, on a single-season, starting pitcher basis. It has only been exceeded by joining the end of one season to the start of the next.

Perhaps even more than the way Walter Johnson was revered in the American League, Rube Marquard's teammate, Christy Mathewson, overshadowed everyone. Marquard's record was the sort of achievement Matty should have had. Until 1912 all the heroics on the Giants' staff had been his. Rube's emergence took everyone by surprise; he was still living down the onerous nickname "the $11,000 Lemon."

Just a kid pitcher, only eighteen, when the Giants bought him from Indianapolis where he had won 28 games in 1908, Marquard had been a disappointment until the 1912 season. Then he began his streak with his first start of the season and, as he added to it, he began to attract favorable attention for the first time. When he won his sixth game, he exceeded any previous high; when he won the tenth game, he had won more than he had in his first two seasons combined.

Rube Marquard had been dubbed "the $11,000 Lemon" because John McGraw, with an eye to publicity value, had paid that much so it would top the $10,000 paid for Mike "King" Kelly when he was sold by Chicago to Boston in the previous century. In 1912, "the Lemon" turned it all around. He started right in on April 11 and didn't lose a game until July 8.

Actually, under the present scoring rules, Marquard's record would total 20 consecutive victories. In a game at the Polo Grounds, McGraw inserted Rube in the eighth inning of a game against the Brooklyn Dodgers which was tied at 3–3. Marquard inherited a bases-loaded situation but stopped Zach Wheat and Jake Daubert, both to become batting champions, and retired George Cutshaw, without a run being scored. The Giants won the game in the bottom of the ninth, but the rules then gave the victory to the starting pitcher.

The Giants, in 1912, were winning the middle of three successive pennants, and Marquard joined with Christy Mathewson to lead the Giants' staff. He was called "Rube," a nickname often given to lefthanders with a superior fastball. This was a tribute to Rube Waddell and

had no bucolic significance: Marquard was no innocent country boy turned loose on Broadway.

Marquard married a vaudeville headliner, Blossom Seeley, who was even more popular than he was. Her life story was later made into a motion picture which ignored Marquard in favor of Blossom's subsequent husband, song-and-dance man Benny Fields.

However, Rube had held up his end of the vaudeville act, serving as a straight man for the comedienne and added female impersonations, in which he sang and danced as well. This too is a performance unlikely to be duplicated by a modern player.

Streakers Blurred by Time

Although it is convenient to separate the "modern era" of baseball from its ancient past at 1900, the better dividing line would be 1893. That year the pitcher was moved back from fifty feet to the still-prevailing sixty feet, six inches. He had been allowed to throw overhand since 1884.

Until the 1890s, teams rarely used more than two principal pitchers. More open dates existed in the schedules, and two strong-armed men could carry the bulk of the work. A third pitcher, or a general substitute, could help out in doubleheaders. However, the regular duo met most occasions and had many more opportunities to reel off long strings of victories.

When Tim Keefe set the mark at 19 straight, he required only seven weeks to do it. Between June 23 and August 10, 1888, he won all his starts, 17 of them complete games. He alternated on the mound with Mickey Welch, himself the owner of an impressive winning streak. In 1885 Smiling Mickey had run off 17 in a row. That had been one less than the record Hoss Radbourn set in 1884. Pitchers in those years were capable of putting together long winning streaks.

Another contemporary, Jim McCormick of Chicago, won 14 in a row in 1885 and 16 straight the next year. When Keefe set his mark in 1888, the public was impressed but not stunned by its magnitude. After all, it only topped the recent mark of Radbourn's by one.

The New York Giants of 1888 were the toast of the town. They were led by Jim Mutrie, who had dubbed them "my Giants," marveling at the magnitude of the star players. Such stalwarts as Roger Connor, Montgomery Ward, and Buck Ewing—all future Hall of Fame members—were in the lineup. Keefe and Welch, pitching in tandem, were also destined for Cooperstown and immortality. The Giants were easy pennant winners over Cap Anson's Chicago team.

Tim Keefe began his 19-game winning streak on June 23. He had lost his previous start to yet another star pitcher, John Clarkson. Also elected to the Hall of Fame, even before Keefe and Welch, Clarkson had won 13 straight in 1885.

Keefe's first win was a squeaker, 7–6, over Philadelphia. Then he marched along, and when he won his twelfth in a row, his opponent was Clarkson. During the streak Tim Keefe pitched 17 complete games. The two he failed to finish included one in which he was hit on the arm by a line drive while leading 8–3 in the sixth inning. A replacement with a name more domineering than the

record he left behind, Cannonball Eddie Crane, held on for a 9–6 victory credited to Keefe.

The other incomplete game would not have been added to his string by today's scoring rules. On July 16, while leading Chicago 9–0, Keefe was excused for the day after two innings. The practices of the time gave him the win.

Tim Keefe's string came to an end on August 14, when his defense betrayed him and two unearned runs were the difference in a 4–2 loss. Gus Krock, of the Chicago White Stockings, was a lefthanded rookie who soon disappeared from the major leagues, but he had the satisfaction of stopping Keefe at 19.

Considering the winning streaks his contemporaries had run off, it was probably thought that Keefe's record was temporary. Had it not been for the victory gained in that two-inning start, it would have been. He would have been tied with Hoss Radbourn at 18 and eclipsed when Rube Marquard reached 19 in 1912. As it is, more than a century after his feat, Tim Keefe stands beside Marquard with a total no one has surpassed.

American League Record Tied

It wasn't until 1931 that the lesser American League record of 16 consecutive pitching victories was challenged. Lefty Grove came very close to setting a new record in the American League and narrowly missed being the pitcher to break Marquard's mark of 19. Grove had a 31–4 season, figures which could have accommodated both record-breaking streaks.

However, the luck even the best must have to sustain a long streak deserted Grove at the critical point. He was luckless in the game which would have moved him past Walter Johnson and Smokey Joe Wood, coholders of the American League mark.

The 1931 Philadelphia Athletics were awesome. Connie Mack's last championship team won its third pennant in a row. Responding to Depression-related financial pressures, Mack would break up the team, selling off its stars, including Grove, who went to the Red Sox. Future Hall of Famers Jimmie Foxx, Mickey Cochrane, Al Simmons, and Grove himself were at the peak of their careers. The members of the supporting cast—Max Bishop, Jimmie Dykes, Mule Haas, Bing Miller, and others—were all excellent role players. This was a team which did not beat itself.

As the season advanced into August, the Athletics were virtually coasting to a pennant. They would win 107 games and distance the runner-up New York Yankees by 13 games. Grove, pitching every fourth game and appearing in relief when needed, was on his personal roll. For the first time in many years, it appeared the American League record for consecutive victories could be broken by a pitcher. It was possible to project that Grove might go on and catch Marquard's record. There was enough time left.

Lefty Grove tied the American League record on August 19 and was expected to break it four days later with his seventeenth straight win. The day the record coheld by Walter Johnson and Joe Wood since 1912 was to fall was Sunday, August 23.

The St. Louis Browns, a second-division team and perennial victim, would provide only token opposition, and the unheralded Dick Coffman would be the sacrificial pitching opponent. Grove pitched with close to his usual brilliance, limiting the Browns to six hits, allowing only one run, and striking out six.

However, Dick Coffman, on that particular day, outpitched Grove and shut out the Athletics with only three hits. Grove's streak came to an end at 16 straight victories. He had only joined Johnson and Wood at the top of the American League's list.

Lefty Grove had never been a gracious, philosophical loser. He refused to accept defeat gracefully. He blamed the loss on the absence of Al Simmons from the lineup. True, Simmons was at home, in Milwaukee, seeing a doctor, and his replacement, Jim Moore, was far from being a sure-handed defensive player. When Moore misjudged a fly ball, which became the game-winning hit, Grove fumed that Simmons would have caught the ball. Further, he complained, Simmons, the league-leading batter, would surely have knocked in a few runs as well as preventing the Browns from scoring a tainted one.

Grove complained every time he was asked about the end of his streak, and the image of Simmons idling away the afternoon, thumbing through *National Geographics* in a doctor's waiting room, persisted. Actually, Simmons had an infected ankle and had already been out of the lineup for a week.

What made the defeat more bitter in retrospect was that Grove went on to win his next five starts. These victories would have put the record at 21, eclipsing not only the American League record but topping Marquard's all-time total of 19. (Grove won his next two starts, incidentally, with Simmons still missing from the lineup.) He did not lose until the final game of the season, on September 27.

Schoolboy Rowe's Row

It was only a few years later, in 1934, when the next assault was made on the American League record, now held by Lefty Grove as well as by Walter Johnson and Joe Wood. This time it was the colorful Schoolboy Rowe, blessed with a rural candor that the press found refreshing and the public fascinating, who made the run.

Mickey Cochrane, Grove's former battery mate, was a first-term manager, having been sold by the Athletics to Detroit. Still a great player and catcher, Cochrane had his team headed for the pennant and Schoolboy Rowe led the way. Rowe had been a pitcher of promise and Cochrane had brought about its fulfillment. Rowe had made a slow start, splitting his first eight decisions. His inauspicious beginning offered no portent that when, on June 15, he won his fifth victory, it was the start of a record-equaling skein. During the summer months Rowe shared the spotlight with Dizzy Dean of the National League. However, while Dean was garnering the victories which would eventually reach 30 for the season, he did not string them together the way Rowe did.

Rowe won his sixteenth straight game on August 26 but then ran into the barrier which had blocked other American League pitchers at that point. He joined Grove, Johnson, and Wood at the top of the list but also joined them among the frustrated who could not go past that point.

Rowe stumbled from the path toward a new record on

August 29, when the Tigers met the now lowly Philadelphia Athletics in a doubleheader. Gone from Connie Mack's A's were Lefty Grove, Mickey Cochrane, Al Simmons, George Earnshaw, and Rube Walberg. Only Jimmie Foxx remained from the recent championship teams.

It was the second game of an August 29 doubleheader, and Rowe was far off form. He was knocked out in the sixth inning. Unlike the contentious Lefty Grove, Rowe blamed no one but himself, saying without rancor that he'd just had an off-day. He refused the alibi offered by his manager, Mickey Cochrane, who contended that the demands of the press and public on the young pitcher had produced more turmoil than Schoolboy could handle. Rowe scoffed at the idea and went on to finish the season with 24 wins. He didn't face Dizzy Dean in the 1934 World Series, but he split two decisions, as the Cardinals won a seven-game series from Detroit. Another pennant year followed for Detroit, with Rowe winning 19 games. After that a chronic arm problem hindered his career, although he lasted a long while in the major leagues, winning 158 games, with a .610 winning average, over fifteen years.

Carl Hubbell's Fabulous Streak

When one adds the start of one season to the end of the preceding one, one finds a 17-game streak for Cleveland's Johnny Allen in 1936–1937 and another for Baltimore's Dave McNally in 1969–1970. But in this area Carl Hubbell claims all the records.

In the quirky way that records for consecutive victories by pitchers seem to come almost simultaneously, the same two seasons which provided Johnny Allen's 17 straight wins, also produced one of the most fabulous feats of all time. As had been the case with 1912, there was a magic about 1936–1937.

Carl Hubbell, between July 17, 1936, and May 27, 1937, won 24 games in a row. He won his last 16 decisions in 1936 and added 8 more victories before losing a game in 1937.

Carl Hubbell, and the team which would support him in his quest for a record, the New York Giants, were at their best in 1936 and 1937. They were the best in the National League at a time when their crosstown rivals, the Yankees, were dominant in the American League and also in the World Series. They beat the Giants both years despite Hubbell's presence. The Giants won only three World Series games in the two years and Hubbell won two of them.

Carl Hubbell was the ace of the Giants staff and the National League's most valuable player in 1936. He led the league in 1936 with 26 victories, an .813 winning percentage, and a 2.31 ERA. In 1937 he again topped the league in wins with 22 and percentage with .733 and added the strikeout crown with 159, his career high.

It was this kind of consistency that earned Carl Hubbell the nickname "the Meal Ticket." His manager, Bill Terry, knew Hubbell would pitch in rotation and stop any losing streak before it gained momentum.

The Giants were off to a bad start in 1936, although Hubbell was winning two of every three decisions. The day Hubbell's winning streak began, July 17, the Giants were in fifth place, barely over .500 at 42–41 and 10

games behind the defending champion Chicago Cubs. Hubbell had lost his last start, a tough two-hit 1–0 game, to the Cubs' Big Bill Lee. Chicago's run was unearned.

Appropriately Hubbell got the Giants back on a winning track by shutting out Pittsburgh, 6–0. The game contained a streak of another kind. In the first inning Joe Moore, Mel Ott, and Hank Leiber hit successive triples. Before the inning ended, Eddie Mayo, a utility infielder, added another triple. Not only was Hubbell off on a personal winning streak that wouldn't end until the next year, the Giants had found their own victory pace.

Oddly, considering the magnitude of Hubbell's record, the streak-starting shutout was the last one he pitched in 1936. He had a season-opening shutout the next year. However, low-run games predominated, and he produced an ERA of 1.95 for the run of 24 games.

Carl Hubbell's great rival was Dizzy Dean, and duels between the two were matchups between two titans. Hubbell's lefthanded screwball was matched against the fastball of the colorful screwball of the Cardinals. These confrontations were arranged as often as possible for their gate appeal, and Dean tried to head off Hubbell's march toward glory three times during the string.

Twice he failed gloriously and once ingloriously. During the 1936 portion of the skein, Dean lost 2–1 in an extrainning game and lost another 2–1 game in the regulation nine innings. These were typical Hubbell-Dean matchups, with both pitchers rising to the occasion. Hubbell, over the years, rose higher more often.

Probably in frustration, when the streak reached 22 on May 19, 1937, Dean lost both the game and his temper when umpire George Barr called a balk against Dizzy for the third time. It gave a reprieve to the batter, Dick Bartell, who had flied out. He then hit a line drive which Pepper Martin dropped, and a flurry of runs followed.

Dean's retaliation was to throw beanballs at every Giant batter who dared step to the plate. In this pre-helmet time such tactics were not viewed kindly, and outfielder Jimmy Ripple offered to take Dean on in a one-to-one fistfight. Dean, who spent a career vainly trying to find someone he could lick, accepted the challenge. He was engulfed by Giant bodies, topped by players in Cardinal uniforms, in what turned into one of the best displays of belligerence ever seen on a ballfield. Individual fights ranged all around the diamond. There were no peacemakers among the players. Among the few who chose to be spectators was Carl Hubbell. He had better use for his arm than swinging it at someone. When order was restored, Hubbell finished pitching a one-run, seven-hit game.

Dean protested his subsequent fine and threatened to boycott the upcoming All Star Game. As usual his threat was unfulfilled. It would have been far better for him if he had stayed away. It was in the 1937 All Star Game that Dean was hit on the foot by an Earl Averill line drive. He tried to pitch while favoring a broken toe and ruined a great right arm.

The end of Hubbell's streak came on May 31 at the hands of the team which considered any victory over the Giants as compensation for an otherwise dismal season. The Brooklyn Dodgers invaded the Polo Grounds for a doubleheader which drew the second-largest crowd that had ever crammed into the Giants home field.

The Dodgers had always been a tough team for

Pitchers with 12 or More Straight Victories in Season

National League (36)

Year	Pitcher	Won
1888	Timothy Keefe, N.Y.	19
1912	Richard Marquard, N.Y.	19
1884	Charles Radbourn, Provi.	18
1885	Michael Welch, N.Y.	17
1890	John Luby, Chi.	17
1959	El Roy Face, Pitts.	17
1886	James McCormick, Chi.	16
1936	Carl Hubbell, N.Y.	16
1947	Ewell Blackwell, Cinn.	16
1962	John Sanford, S.F.	16
1924	Arthur Vance, Brook.	15
1968	Robert Gibson, St. L.	15
1972	Steven Carlton, Phila.	15
1885	James McCormick, Chi.	14
1886	John Flynn, Chi.	14
1904	Joseph McGinnity, N.Y.	14
1909	Edward Reulbach, Chi.	14
1984	Richard Sutcliffe, Chi.	14
1985	Dwight Gooden, N.Y.	14
1880	Lawrence Corcoran, Chi.	13
1884	Charles Buffinton, Bos.	13
1892	Denton Young, Cleve.	13
1893	Frank Killen, Pitts.	13
1896	Frank Dwyer, Cin.	13
1897	Fred Klobedanz, Bos.	13
1898	Ted Lewis, Bos.	13
1909	Chris. Mathewson, N.Y.	13
1910	Charles Phillippe, Pitts.	13
1927	Burleigh Grimes, N.Y.	13
1956	Brooks Lawrence, Cin.	13
1966	Philip Regan, L.A.	13
1971	Dock Ellis, Pitts.	13
1992	Tom Glasine, Atl.	13
1885	John Clarkson, Chi.	13
1886	Charles Ferguson, Phila.	12
1902	John Chesbro, Pitts.	12
1904	George Wiltse, N.Y.	12
1906	Edward Reulbach, Chi.	12
1975	Burt Hooton, L.A.	12

American League (37)

Year	Pitcher	Won
1912	Walter Johnson, Wash.	16
1912	Joseph Wood, Bos.	16
1931	Robert Grove, Phila.	16
1934	Lynwood Rowe, Det.	16
1932	Alvin Crowder, Wash.	15
1937	John Allen, Cleve.	15
1969	David McNally, Balt.	15
1974	Gaylord Perry, Cleve.	15
1904	John Chesbro, N.Y.	14
1913	Walter Johnson, Wash.	14
1914	Charles Bender, Phila.	14
1928	Robert Grove, Phila.	14
1961	Edward Ford, N.Y.	14
1980	Steven Stone, Balt.	14
1986	W. Roger Clemens, Bos.	14
1924	Walter Johnson, Wash.	13
1925	Stanley Coveleski, Wash.	13
1930	Wesley Ferrell, Cleve.	13
1940	Louis Newsom, Det.	13
1949	Ellis Kinder, Bos.	13
1971	David McNally, Balt.	13
1973	James Hunter, Oak.	13
1978	Ronald Guidry, N.Y.	13
1983	D. LaMarr Hoyt, Chi.	13
1990	Bobby Witt, Tex.	13
1991	Scott Erickson, Minn.	13
1901	Denton Young, Bos.	12
1910	Russell Ford, N.Y.	12
1914	Hubert Leonard, Bos.	12
1929	Jonathan Zachary, N.Y.	12
1931	George Earnshaw, Phila.	12
1938	John Allen, Cleve.	12
1939	Atley Donald, N.Y.	12
1946	David Ferriss, Bos.	12
1961	Luis Arroyo, N.Y.	12
1963	Edward Ford, N.Y.	12
1968	David McNally, Balt.	12
1971	Patrick Dobson, Balt.	12
1985	Ronald Guidry, N.Y.	12

Hubbell. He had beaten them five times during his 24-game streak, twice in relief, but in the opening game of the doubleheader Brooklyn closed the door on Hubbell's feat.

Carl Hubbell took the long walk from the mound to the clubhouse in center field during the third inning. Five runs had scored. There had been seven hits and three walks. In came Dick Coffman, who had been Lefty Grove's nemesis. It would have been fitting if he had stopped the Dodgers in their tracks and the Giants had rallied to save Hubbell's streak so he could extend it the next time. Neither happened; Brooklyn scored five more runs, the Giants only tallied three runs for the whole game.

Lost in the Crowd

By winning 24 games in a row over two seasons, Carl Hubbell obscured the feat of Roy Face in 1958 and 1959 when the forkballer won 22 consecutive games, all in relief. That stands as the best achievement for a reliever. Also in 1959, Face equaled Johnny Allen's mark of 17 consecutive wins, doing it all in one season.

Roy Face, only five-eight and weighing just 160 pounds, didn't lose his first decision in 1959 until September 11. He had entered the game in relief and gave up the winning run in the ninth inning of a game at Los Angeles when Charlie Neal hit a single. Until then, it appeared that Roy Face was destined to never lose a game. Even when his forkball wasn't working its usual magic, he won.

A modest man, Face would point to six or seven games when the Pirates' hitters bailed him out. The most extreme of these times came in a June 11 game, when the San Francisco Giants played Pittsburgh. Face came in to protect a 7–5 lead in the eighth inning. The Giants had two men on base and Willie Mays came up as a pinch hitter. He homered and the Giants led, 8–7. In the bottom of the inning, the Pirates erupted with five runs and Face had a win instead of a loss.

During his string, Face won eleven of his games in extra innings.

Consecutive Base Hits

The feat of making a dozen consecutive base hits has been accomplished only twice in all the years major league baseball has been played. The record has rested there for thirty-five years and might never see the time when a batter delivers a baker's dozen to provide a new record. The hitter who reaches 13 will cap a slow, gradual climb toward a peak shared by Pinky Higgins and Walt Dropo, both American Leaguers. The National League's record is 10.

The history of consecutive base hits goes back to 1897, when Ed Delahanty, whom you would expect to set such standards, and Jake Gettman, whom you wouldn't, each got ten hits in a row during the season. Delahanty, one of five major-league-playing brothers, batted .377 for Philadelphia in 129 games. Gettman, who only played one season as a regular, got his ten straight while appearing in only 36 games for Washington. He hit .315 overall. The National League record is still 10 consecutive hits, and six others have joined the original pair.

Tris Speaker was the first to top 10, getting 11 straight hits in 1920. Speaker had eclipsed Doc Johnson's Ameri-

can League total of 9, hit in 1919, the same season Brooklyn's Ed Konetchy had joined Delahanty and Gettman with 10.

The next year, when Speaker moved the major league record up a notch, his feat came amid such epoch record-setting as Babe Ruth's 54 home runs. This had broken Ruth's own mark of 29 set the season before. It dwarfed Speaker's rattling off 11 straight hits. In fact, Speaker's own accomplishment, leading the Cleveland Indians to a World Series victory despite the loss of shortstop Ray

Most Consecutive Hits

American League

Player	Team	Year	H
Pinky Higgins	Bos.	1938	12
Walt Dropo	Det.	1952	12
Tris Speaker	Cleve.	1920	11
Johnny Pesky	Bos.	1946	11
George Sisler	St.L.	1921	10
Harry Heilmann	Det.	1922	10
Harry McCurdy	Chi.	1926	10
Ken Singleton	Balt.	1981	10
Kirby Puckett	Minn.	1987	10
Doc Johnston	Cleve.	1919	9
Ty Cobb	Det.	1925	9
Sam Rice	Wash.	1925	9
Hal Trosky	Cleve.	1936	9
Ted Williams	Bos.	1939	9
Tony Oliva	Minn.	1967	9
Nap Lajoie	Cleve.	1910	8
George Sisler	St.L.	1922	8
	St.L.	1927	8
Buddy Myer	Wash.	1929	8
Oscar Melillo	St.L.	1931	8
Sammy West	St.L.	1933	8
Hank Bauer	N.Y.	1952	8
Johnny Groth	Det.	1950	8
Don Baylor	Cal.	1978	8
Dan Ford	Cal.	1979	8
Jorge Orta	Cleve.	1980	8

National League

Player	Team	Year	H
Ed Delahanty	Phila.	1897	10
Jake Gettman	Wash.	1897	10
Ed Konetchy	Brook.	1919	10
Kiki Cuyler	Pitts.	1925	10
Chick Hafey	St.L.	1929	10
Joe Medwick	St.L.	1936	10
Buddy Hassett	Bos.	1940	10
Woody Williams	Cin.	1943	10
Bip Roberts	Cin.	1992	10
Joe Kelley	Balt.	1894	9
Rogers Hornsby	St.L.	1924	9
Taylor Douthit	St.L.	1926	9
Babe Herman	Brook.	1926	9
Bill Jurges	N.Y.	1941	9
Terry Moore	St.L.	1947	9
Dave Philley	Phila.	1958	9
	Phila.	1959	9
Felipe Alou	S.F.	1962	9
Willie Stargell	Pitts.	1966	9
Rennie Stennett	Pitts.	1975	9
Ron Cey	L.A.	1977	9
Roger Connor	St.L.	1895	8
Sammy Strang	Chi.	1900	8
Jack Fournier	Brook.	1923	8
Jimmy Johnston	Brook.	1923	8
Glenn Wright	Pitts.	1924	8
Chick Hafey	St.L.	1928	8
Lefty O'Doul	N.Y.	1933	8
Kiki Cuyler	Cin.	1936	8
Augie Galan	Brook.	1944	8
Wayne Terwilliger	Chi.	1949	8
Dick Sisler	Phila.	1950	8
Eddie Waitkus	Phila.	1950	8
Sid Gordon	Bos.	1952	8
Lee Walls	Chi.	1958	8
Curt Flood	St.L.	1964	8
Jerry Grote	N.Y.	1970	8
Billy Williams	Chi.	1972	8
Dave Winfield	S.D.	1979	8

Chapman to a fatal beaning during the pennant chase, overshadowed his own batting feats. This included a runner-up .388 to George Sisler's league-leading batting average of .407.

However, Speaker's 11 straight stood the test of time. During the 1920s others made a run at the record but couldn't get beyond 10 straight hits. They included Sisler in 1921 and Harry Heilmann in 1922. Kiki Cuyler in 1925 and Chick Hafey in 1929, all future Hall of Famers, got up to 10 straight in the National League. In 1936 another Hall of Famer to be, Joe Medwick, hit in 10 straight times at bat.

One outsider who edged onto the list with those headed for baseball's Hall of Fame was a reserve catcher, Harry McCurdy. A rookie with the White Sox in 1926, he only played in 33 games, but cracked out 10 straight hits while batting .326. He might have played in more games, but he had a month's vacation in August. He was claimed by the Yankees on waivers, but when New York discovered this included an obligation for the rookie's bonus of $30,000, they refused to complete the deal. The White Sox insisted they were honor-bound. As is usual in baseball, honor lost and McCurdy remained a substitute catcher with Chicago.

Speaker's record finally tumbled in 1938, when Mike "Pinky" Higgins, the Boston Red Sox third baseman, began by going 4 for 4 against the White Sox in Chicago. The next day the team was in Detroit to play a doubleheader with the Tigers. When Higgins went 4 for 4, with a walk, against Roxie Lawson in the first game, and singled his first time up in the second game, Cal Hubbard, umpiring on the bases, observed, "That makes you 5 for 5 for the day."

Higgins told Hubbard he was 9 for 9, counting the previous day in Chicago. It wasn't enough that Higgins put pressure on himself, but after he got his tenth straight hit, the field announcer at Briggs Field, Ty Tyson, made a public-address announcement that Higgins could tie Speaker's record if he got another hit the next time up.

Higgins shook off the hex and got the hit and, with everyone knowing a new record was on the line, ripped a single off Tommy Bridges, the best curveballer in the league, the next time up. It was an unlucky 13, however, as Higgins fanned his last time at bat. The catcher in both games of the doubleheader was Rudy York. It was the year the Tigers tried to find a place for him to play.

Even though he was to be described by Tom Meany as "part Indian, part first baseman," when Hank Greenberg moved to the outfield so York could play where he'd do the least damage, the one season as a catcher had been a disaster. Higgins later confided he had little trouble guessing a fastball was coming as York had become known to avoid complications by refusing to call for curveballs.

In 1952 the slugging first baseman of the Red Sox, Walt Dropo, tied Higgins's record. He had debuted in 1950 with a sensational season, hitting .322, but he never hit above .300 again. Dropo had begun the season with Boston, but in a multiplayer deal in June, he had been traded to Detroit. Going along with Dropo was Johnny Pesky, longtime shortstop for the Red Sox and, in the way of coincidences in record setting, had reached 11 straight hits, one behind Higgins's record, in 1946. Pesky was at shortstop in the games when Dropo tied him first for

runner-up, a spot he now shared with Speaker. He watched as Dropo got his twelfth straight.

Like Higgins, Walt Dropo made his run in a doubleheader. He had gone 5 for 5 against the Yankees in a single game on July 14, and the next day, in Griffith Stadium, he had four straight in the first game. All the hits had been singles, but starting off in the first inning of the nightcap, the powerful Dropo hit a triple with the bases loaded.

In the third inning he had his eleventh straight hit, another single, and Mickey Vernon, the Washington first baseman, told him he could tie the record with a hit the next time at bat. He did with a double. And he had another time at bat coming, in the seventh inning. Despite Dropo's hitting, the Tigers trailed, 7–6. He swung from the heels but only lifted a foul fly which catcher Mickey Grasso caught at the edge of the field boxes. The streak was over. Dropo added a single in the ninth inning but had to settle for a shared record which has stood against more recent assaults.

Ken Singleton of Baltimore got 10 in 1981, and Kirby Puckett of Minnesota reached 10 in 1987. Bip Roberts of Cincinnati managed the feat in 1992.

Team Winning Streaks

The two longest winning streaks by teams had different outcomes. Twice National League clubs won 21 in a row and the pennant. When the Chicago White Stockings did it, under Cap Anson, in 1880, they were simply running away from the pack. They won the pennant by 15 games.

However, when their descendants, the Chicago Cubs, won 21 in a row in 1935, the drive capped a sensational stretch battle that caught and passed their rivals, the St. Louis Cardinals, within a few days of the season's end.

These two 21-game streaks are not the longest on record. The record of 26 games won in a row by the 1916 New York Giants stands as the most perverse record of achievement in baseball. No other team has won so many games so convincingly to such little purpose. The Giants came in fourth, despite having had another win streak the same season of 17 straight. Even more peculiarly, the 26 games in a row were all played at home. Maybe the Giants could only win at the Polo Grounds? No. The 17 straight were all won on the road.

John McGraw did a remarkable thing in 1916. He rebuilt the team well into the season, after they had won 17 in a row. The season had started dismally, and before they hit their stride, they had lost thirteen of the first fifteen games played. When they ran off a streak of wins, it only made up for previously lost ground. Then they flattened out again. McGraw acted.

He had a flawed infield. Shortstop Art Fletcher was a gem, but the other positions were played by former stars, Fred Merkle at first and Larry Doyle at second. Bill McKechnie, the third baseman, would someday be a Hall of Famer, but as a manager.

John McGraw had a love-hate relationship with Buck Herzog. He loved him as a player, but hated him as an individual. Herzog had been a rookie with the Giants and was traded away to the Braves, then swapped back again

to star on three successive pennant winners, in 1911 through 1913. Then he was exiled again.

McGraw coveted Herzog, an unrepentant infielder who could hit and play any place with superb skill. They met privately, agreed that the money and opportunity involved was more important than any blood feud, and McGraw swapped the immortal Christy Mathewson, whose fade-away pitch had failed, to Cincinnati, where he would become manager. He sent McKechnie along and a young outfielder of promise but little playing time, Edd Roush. The next year and two years later Roush won the batting championships. McGraw never regretted his move. He had laid the groundwork for the 1917 pennant.

Even though the season was well along, McGraw shipped his former captain, Larry Doyle, to Chicago for Heinie Zimmerman. Doyle, who had shouted in boyish enthusiasm, "It's great to be young and a Giant," was no longer young and no longer a Giant.

Fred Merkle, forgiven the blunder of 1908, when he failed to touch second as an apparent winning run scored and cost the Giants a pennant, had also grown old in McGraw's service and was shipped out so a rookie, Walter Holke, could finish the season at first base. When Zimmerman arrived, Herzog was shifted to second, and double plays began to be turned, base hits became infield outs, and the pitchers relished their new-found support. The Giants' drive began as late as September 7, when they were in fourth place, ten games out of third. Ferdie Schupp emerged as a star pitcher and won six games in the string. Pol Perritt won the first game of a doubleheader on September 9 and enjoyed it so much he came back and pitched a shutout in the second game. Regulars won, and rookies debuted and won. The Giants won, but they didn't move up.

The Giants ripped off 12 in a row and then paused for a rain-stopped tie game, 1–1, as Burleigh Grimes, who lost 13 in a row that season, managed a tie game for Pittsburgh. The streak resumed the next day and went on and on, although the Giants had been eliminated from catching Brooklyn in first place. It was the Phillies who were breathing on the necks of the Dodgers, with a chance to tie on the last day.

The Giants' streak was stopped in their last home game of the season, when they lost to the Boston Braves. They crossed the bridge to Brooklyn to close out the season on October 2, and McGraw set off wide speculation in the press by leaving the bench during the game and intimating afterward that the Giants had deliberately lost the game to ensure a Dodger pennant. Brooklyn was managed by Wilbert Robinson, once McGraw's closest crony, his coach and developer of pitchers. Some argument, some twist to the volatile McGraw temper had made them enemies. McGraw, who hated to lose, loathed losing to Brooklyn and Uncle Robbie. Maybe that's all there was to it, just another symptom of McGraw being a sore loser. Yet just ahead was the Black Sox scandal, and playing for the Giants were two non-Chicago players who were to be swept out of baseball when Judge Landis purged its suspect characters—Heinie Zimmerman and Bennie Kauff. McGraw's 1916 Giants finished in fourth place—right where they were when they began their 26-game streak!—and 7 games out of first place.

The 1935 Chicago Cubs, whose 21 straight wins car-

ried them to a pennant, were a streaky team that year and the next year, too. In 1935 they faced a task made tougher by the schedule. The St. Louis Cardinals, the Gas House Gang world champions from 1934, not only led by 2 games, but the indomitable Deans, Dizzy and Paul, headed the staff. Even more comforting for the Cards, the schedule called for the Cubs to play the last five games of the season at Sportsman's Park in St. Louis.

In 1935 the Cubs picked up momentum, and it took them past the Cards in the middle of the streak. They took the lead on September 14 as they won their eleventh game and were three games ahead of the crumbling Cards when they reached St. Louis for the final five games. Lon Warneke beat Paul Dean 1–0 in the opener, and Bill Lee won his twentieth game of the season, beating Dizzy Dean 6–3 to clinch the pennant. It was the first game of a doubleheader, and the Cubs reached 21 straight by taking the nightcap.

They lost the next game, a meaningless one in the pennant race, in extra innings on Joe Medwick's second home run of the game. The Cards won the season's finale, 2–1, but it was the Cubs who went on to the World Series.

The next year was also a season of streaks. Again the Cubs got in gear with an impressive run of victories, taking 15 straight before midseason was reached. It did not lead to a pennant. Another 15-game winning streak, by the New York Giants, brought the championship to the Polo Grounds.

It was a streak that started late in the season and ran, in part, concurrently with Carl Hubbell's own string of 16 wins. While the Giants were racking up 15 straight, Hubbell appeared in ten consecutive games. He never ran out of steam, only games to win. The season ended with Hubbell experiencing a 16-game streak. He extended it by winning his first 8 decisions the next year to reach 24 straight wins over two seasons.

Other very long winning streaks in the National League that added late-season zest to pennant races were those of the 1924 Dodgers and, of course, the 1951 Giants. It was Dazzy Vance against the world in 1924 when he dominated the league and was the MVP. The Dodgers came up short, unable to catch the leading Giants, who added a fourth straight pennant in 1924, when Brooklyn's 15 straight were not enough.

In 1951 the same traditional rivals reversed roles, but not results. It was the Dodgers who were far in front when the Giants, managed by former Dodger skipper Leo Durocher, began a late-season drive. The Giants had started with the wrong kind of a streak. They lost their first 11 games and spent the season trying to catch the fast-flying Dodgers. They were 13 games behind when they won the first of 16 straight decisions on August 12 and began to close the gap the Dodgers had opened.

The Giants slowly edged closer and into a tie with a game to play. When both teams won their final games, the Dodgers on Jackie Robinson's extra-inning heroics in Philadelphia, the stage was set for a playoff series. It was won by Bobby Thomson's dramatic home run in the last of the ninth of the third, and decisive, game.

The American League's consecutive winning streaks have been turned in mostly by powerhouse teams headed for easy pennant triumphs. However, the 1906 American League season produced long strings of wins by two teams

locked in a hotly contested pennant race. The Chicago White Sox set a record, since tied by the 1947 Yankees and the 1988 Boston Red Sox, of 19 straight wins.

Dubbed "the Hitless Wonders" because of a .230 team batting average, the White Sox engaged in a dramatic scenario with the New York team, then called the Highlanders.

In early August the White Sox were in fourth place. Ahead of them were Philadelphia, New York, and Cleveland. Day after day the White Sox chipped away at the lead held by the teams ahead of them. They eventually passed Philadelphia and Cleveland.

The Highlanders proved the hardest to catch. They had benefited from a winning streak of their own, 15 in a row. However, in the final surge of the pennant race, it was the White Sox who came home in first place. New York became the only team to win 15 in a row and not win a pennant in the American League. In the National League since 1900, three teams have won at least 15 in a row and not won the pennant. The most glaring example, of course, was the 1916 Giants, winners of 26 and 17 straight. The 1936 Cubs won 15 in a row and finished second to the Giants, also winners of 15 straight. The 1907 Giants had the poorest finish. Despite 17 straight wins, they finished fourth, 25 games out of first place.

In the main, however, if a team wants to ensure winning a pennant, a good way to do it is rack up 15 or more consecutive victories along the way, preferably in the stretch run.

The Feats

What follows is a celebration of three of baseball's most rare and heroic feats: the triple crowns of batting and pitching, and the triple putout by one player, better known as the unassisted triple play. These feats do not rank with the central records of the game: Henry Aaron's 755 homers, Cy Young's 511 wins, Pete Rose's 4,256 hits, Ty Cobb's lifetime batting average of .366. They are not as distant in memory as a .400 hitter or a 40-game winner. But they are remarkable achievements and—unlike those mentioned above—are not evident from a perusal of the leaders tables found later in this book.

Triple Crown Winners—Batting

Baseball's first Triple Crown winner, Paul Hines, waited ninety years to be enthroned. The crown consists of three jewels: the batting, home run, and runs-batted-in titles must be won in a single season. The RBI count was a late starter among baseball stats and had to be reconstructed for earlier seasons. However, it was not for lack of the RBI distinction that Hines, of the Providence Grays, waited for belated recognition. His feat went unacknowledged until researchers turned up information which made him the true 1878 batting champion.

A special Baseball Records Committee met in 1968 and put a stamp of approval on statistics which had been

in dispute or unverified from baseball's past. The new information appeared the next year when Macmillan published the first edition of *The Baseball Encyclopedia*.

Abner Dalrymple had gone to his grave in 1939, the year the Baseball Hall of Fame Museum opened in Cooperstown, New York, with one baseball honor to his name. He had won the National League batting championship in 1878. Paul Hines, who died in 1935, was remembered only as the winner of the 1879 title. New data—coming from the two tie games he played and the one for Dalrymple—have revealed that Hines was a repeat batting champion who won both the 1878 and 1879 championships, and Abner Dalrymple has been demoted into relative obscurity.

Paul Hines, who had previously been credited with making an unassisted triple play, then lost that distinction as historians and researchers perused boxscores, gained two others—and eventually will regain his unassisted triple play, but more on that soon.

With his newly acknowledged batting title, the RBI leadership which resulted from reconstructed stats and the small but clearly superior total of 4 home runs, Paul Hines had attained the first Triple Crown. In addition, when he won the batting title again in 1879, again through later research efforts, he became the first to repeat as hitting leader.

Another nineteenth-century player, Hugh Duffy, had—since 1969, when his RBI data first was published—been considered the first to wear the Triple Crown. In 1894 he had won the three necessary titles but had almost obscured his own feat by batting .438, later corrected upward to .440. This remains the highest batting average of all time and has always interested interviewers more than the Triple Crown. Duffy's 18 home runs and 145 runs batted in led the league in these departments in 1894, but the idea of linking them as a diadem had not yet been formed. No one knew Paul Hines had done it and few cared that Hugh Duffy had. Although the RBI was known as a baseball stat as early as 1879, it was not commonly used until the 1910s, and not an official measure until 1920.

Hugh Duffy, a twinkle-eyed New Englander, told about his batting record for the fifty subsequent years that he spent in major league baseball, the last several decades as a coach for the Boston Red Sox. When a rookie named Ted Williams arrived in the big leagues in 1939, Hugh Duffy became his first mentor. Duffy proclaimed Williams as the greatest hitter he ever saw and watched while Williams won two Triple Crowns and missed a third by the closest margin possible.

The player who placed the stamp of the superstar most firmly on the concept of the Triple Crown was Nap Lajoie, who was the dominant player in the game when the American League was formed and ushered in twentieth-century baseball. The great Napoleon Lajoie had become the star of the Philadelphia Phillies as the nineteenth century closed. He was the prize recruit for the new league, remaining in Philadelphia where Connie Mack was establishing a new franchise. Lajoie put the team and the American League on the baseball map in 1901, when he provided the league-leading totals in the three prize categories. He batted .426, hit 14 home runs in the dead-ball era of the time, as later research showed, and, batted in

145 runs. It was the greatest season the immortal would ever have. He would win two more batting titles and again lead the league in RBIs. However, home runs were not his specialty.

Still, his Triple Crown brought instant respect to the new league and, together with other stars who had switched leagues, forced acceptance that the American League was a full-fledged major league and would be part of the basis of baseball's structure from then on.

Lajoie was succeeded as the American League's superstar by Ty Cobb, who also laid claim to the Triple Crown in 1909. As with Lajoie, hitting home runs was not Cobb's dominant ability, and despite ten batting championships and four RBI titles, he wore the Triple Crown but once. He came close two other times, in 1907 and 1911, finishing second in home runs each of those years.

Cobb's great rival was the National League's Honus Wagner, who never wore the Triple Crown, although he too missed it by a close margin. In 1908 he was second in home runs, the most difficult final jewel for the superstars of the dead-ball era to achieve. Wagner's eight batting titles and four RBI championships were never accompanied by a home run leadership.

While the list of those who have won the Triple Crown is short, it is a quality list. All but one Triple Crown holder in this century—the suspect Heinie Zimmerman—are in the Hall of Fame.

In 1912 Heinie Zimmerman, one of the best major league third basemen, put together the greatest season he would ever have. Honus Wagner failed to repeat as batting champion, and his 102 RBI total was one less than Zimmerman's, according to the tabulations of Ernie Lanigan. The 14 home runs Zimmerman hit edged teammate Wildfire Schulte, who had led the league in four-baggers the two previous seasons, by one. Only in batting average, where Zimmerman's .372 far distanced the field, did he have a clear superiority, but a Triple Crown by any measure is a rare treasure and it was Heinie's without dispute, that is until the researchers of Information Concepts, Inc., the group that compiled *The Baseball Encyclopedia*, downgraded his RBI total to 99. Later, an editor of *The Baseball Encyclopedia* fudged Zim's RBI count back up to 103 to restore his Triple Crown, but we cannot subscribe to such nonsense.

It was 1922 before the Triple Crown would again rest on a player's head, but when it did, it landed on the brow of the royally nicknamed "Rajah" Hornsby and just eluded Babe Ruth, "the Sultan of Swat."

Hornsby strung together six successive batting titles, from 1920 through 1925, and added another in 1928. Although he had home run power to go with his high averages, the title escaped him in 1921, when George Kelly outhomered him by two. It would have been the first Triple Crown for the Rajah and would have given him an eventual three, a total no one has ever achieved.

Babe Ruth, who got two legs up on the Triple Crown seven times without ever winning one, had many home run titles and frequently topped the league in RBIs. However, the competition for batting championships in the 1920s, when Cobb, Sisler, and Heilmann topped .400 and Heilmann alone accounted for four batting titles, was tough. Ruth managed one hitting title but lost the RBI leg that year, 1924, to Goose Goslin. The Babe won many

honors, but the Triple Crown was not among them.

In the 1930s a quartet of superstars and future Hall of Fame members competed for the Triple Crown during most of the decade, and each took a single turn wearing it.

The American League had two great first baseman, Jimmie Foxx and Lou Gehrig. Each was a threat to claim the Crown every year, but when Foxx narrowly failed on two occasions, it was not Gehrig who stymied him. In 1932 Jimmie came frustratingly close. He was edged out of the batting title by the clumsy-fielding Dale Alexander in 1932. Called "Moose," Alexander split the season between Detroit and Boston, the first player to win a batting title while appearing with two teams. Alexander barely qualified for the championship, but his .367 topped the .364 by Foxx. The following year, 1933, Foxx won his lone Triple Crown.

Alexander was long gone back to the minor leagues before Jimmie Foxx had his second near-miss of the Triple Crown in 1938. This time it was the home run lead that eluded him. Although Foxx hit 50 home runs in 1938, while winning the batting and RBI honors, Hank Greenberg hit 58 homers to almost equal Babe Ruth's record of 60.

While Gehrig and Foxx were trying on the Triple Crown for size in the American League, two sluggers in the National League were sharing domination of their league. Chuck Klein was the league's outstanding batter during the early 1930s and Joe Medwick took over for the final half of the decade. Both wore the Triple Crown, Klein getting his in 1933 when Jimmie Foxx was doing likewise. It was the only year that each league produced a Triple Crown winner. Medwick won his in 1937.

The next to claim the Triple Crown was Ted Williams. A brash rookie when he reported to the Boston Red Sox in 1939, he had little to learn from the old guy hitting fungos in practice. Hugh Duffy took one look at Williams's swing and knew the only part he could serve was as a role model. Williams had his eye on hitting .400. When he did it, in 1941, his .406 was far short of Duffy's .440, the all-time record.

Williams was also one leg short of the Triple Crown in 1941. He added the home run title to his batting championship, but his main rival, Joe DiMaggio, had topped the RBI column. DiMaggio had piled up his runs-batted-in totals largely during his 56-game hitting streak that season.

Ted Williams won all three titles for the Triple Crown the next season, 1942, and then went off to serve in World War Two. Several wartime players won two legs of the Triple Crown: Rudy York, with the Detroit Tigers in 1943, and Bill Nicholson, a Chicago Cubs outfielder in 1943 and 1944. Both hit home runs and batted in runs at league-leading levels, but they were far outdistanced for the batting-average honors.

Ted Williams returned from the war in 1946 and finished second in each of the Triple Crown categories. Mickey Vernon beat him out for the batting title, and Hank Greenberg, who had blocked Jimmie Foxx in 1938, had his last hurrah with the Tigers, topping Williams in both home runs and runs batted in.

The next year, with Greenberg gone to the National League, Ted Williams claimed his second Triple Crown. No one was close to him in any of the three prize categories, and despite three prime seasons lost to wartime service, the Red Sox star seemed most likely to be the first to wear the Triple Crown three times. He had won in 1942 and 1947.

In 1948 his old nemesis, Joe DiMaggio, who was never to win a Triple Crown, picked off two of the crown jewels, leading the American League in home runs with 39 and in runs batted in with 155. Ted Williams was far ahead of the pack as batting champion with a .369 average.

It was 1949 that proved the greatest disappointment to Williams. DiMaggio was injured much of the season and did not compete for individual honors. However, the pennant race was tightly contested between the Yankees and Red Sox, and more interest was focused on that than on the seemingly assured third Triple Crown to be worn by Ted Williams.

As the season reached the final weekend, Boston came to New York for two games between the Red Sox and Yankees. Boston was a game ahead and needed to win only one to gain the pennant. They lost on Saturday, and the teams were tied when Sunday's game began.

The biggest threat to Ted Williams' third Triple Crown came from teammate Vern Stephens, a slugging shortstop who was tied with Ted for RBIs. Williams held a small but probably secure batting lead over George Kell of the Detroit Tigers.

However, Williams and the Red Sox were in a slump, and it cost both the team and the individual their honors. The final game of the season between the Yankees and Red Sox was one of the most exciting of all time, if you were a Yankee fan. If you were among the generations of faithful Red Sox followers who have seen their team fail in the final situation, one frustrating season after another, it was a bitter end. The Yankees staved off a three-run Red Sox rally to win 5–3.

Williams had gone hitless and ended up not only missing a World Series appearance but his third Triple Crown. While Williams had sputtered in the final games, George Kell, who had missed two stretches of games with injuries, got back in the lineup for Detroit's final three games. With only a batting title at stake, Kell had two hits in his final game. When the final statistics were known, George Kell had batted .3429 and Ted Williams .3427. It was the closest any player ever came to a Triple Crown without actually winning it and the closest anyone has come to earning the honor three times.

The year before, in the National League, Stan Musial had narrowly missed his bid for a Triple Crown, when he was one behind Johnny Mize and Ralph Kiner, who tied for the home run title with 40.

In 1953 Al Rosen had a near-miss almost as tight as Ted Williams had had in 1949. Rosen won the home run and RBI titles but was edged out, .337 to .336, for the batting championship by Mickey Vernon, who had blocked Williams's bid in that category in 1946.

Mickey Mantle hit his peak in 1956 when he put the necessary ingredients together to win a Triple Crown. He hit .353 for the only batting title he would win, had top totals in home runs with 52, and piled up 130 runs batted in.

Ten years later, in 1966, Frank Robinson reacted to being traded out of the National League by winning the Triple Crown in the American League. His .316 batting

average was one of only two above .300 that year in the American League. He had switched leagues just in time. A .316 average wouldn't have made the top five in the National League in 1966. He won the home run and RBI titles comfortably.

In 1967, the year of the Red Sox "Impossible Dream," the team was driven to a surprise championship by the captain, Carl Yastrzemski, who had an astounding year. Yaz won the only home run title of his career and also the lone RBI championship he would record. He joined these with one of his three batting crowns and ended the season with what was to become an elusive honor, the Triple Crown.

He is the last player to wear the title, although a number of players have gained two legs, including Yaz's teammate, Jim Rice, who did this twice. In the American League the inability of power hitters to achieve a high batting average has resulted in a parade of sluggers leading in home runs and runs batted in but falling short in base-hit percentage.

Harmon Killebrew, who tied with Yaz for home runs in Yastrzemski's crown-winning season, Frank Howard, Dick Allen, Reggie Jackson, George Scott, Eddie Murray, Tony Armas, and Jose Canseco have won two legs but failed the batting title.

Since Yaz won the last Triple Crown, two National Leaguers have won batting titles and the RBI championship, but failed in home runs. Joe Torre in 1971 and Al Oliver in 1982 earned two legs one way, and Johnny Bench, Willie Stargell, George Foster, Andre Dawson, and Mike Schmidt have done it with the home run and RBI crowns. Foster did it twice and Schmidt four times.

Combining a high batting average with power is a rare characteristic in contemporary baseball. Players such as Rod Carew and Wade Boggs, who won frequent batting championships without expectation of adding the other elements of the Triple Crown, served to reduce the likelihood that a pure power hitter would also annex a batting title, especially in the course of the same season.

Carl Yastrzemski might not have been just part of a vanishing breed. He might have been the last example of a breed that has already vanished.

Triple Crown Winners—Pitching

Tommy Bond, the only nineteenth-century pitcher on the list of Triple Crown Winners who is not in the Hall of Fame, has, at least, the honor of turning the feat first. When the National League was formed in 1876, Bond was an established star in the National Association. The others who eventually won the pitchers' Triple Crown, for the most wins and strikeouts and the lowest ERA in a single season, began their careers in the National League.

Although he was only twenty-one when he won the Triple Crown in 1877, Bond had been pitching for prominent teams since he had been sixteen and joined the Athletics of Brooklyn. He entered the National League with Hartford but moved to Boston for his best seasons. He was Boston's only pitcher during 1877 and 1878 and pitched the great majority of games in 1879. He won 123

Triple Crown Hitters

American League

Player	Team	Year	HR	RBI	BA
Nap Lajoie	Phila.	1901	14	125	.422
Ty Cobb	Det.	1909	9	115	.377
Jimmie Foxx	Phila.	1933	48	163	.356
Lou Gehrig	N.Y.	1934	49	165	.363
Ted Williams	Bos.	1942	36	137	.356
	Bos.	1947	32	114	.343
Mickey Mantle	N.Y.	1956	52	130	.353
Frank Robinson	Bal.	1966	49	122	.316
Carl Yastrzemski	Bos.	1967	44	121	.326

National League

Player	Team	Year	HR	RBI	BA
Paul Hines	Prov.	1878	4	50	.358
Hugh Duffy	Bos.	1894	18	145	.438
Heinie Zimmerman*	Chi.	1912	14	103	.372
Rogers Hornsby	St.L.	1922	42	152	.401
	St.L.	1925	39	143	.403
Chuck Klein	Phila.	1933	28	120	.368
Joe Medwick	St.L.	1937	31	154	.374

*Zimmerman ranked first in RBIs as calculated by Ernie Lanigan, but only third as calculated by ICI research in 1969.

of the 204 games Boston played in those early years of short schedules.

Bond, who later coached baseball at Harvard, was celebrated for his victories and strikeouts. The measurement of earned runs was done retroactively.

As Bond's career lapsed, the next to claim the Triple Crown of pitching emerged. Old Hoss Radbourn reached the peak year that gave him his nickname for durability in 1884. He pitched the Providence Grays to the National League pennant, almost singlehandedly, after Charlie Sweeney's departure had left only Radbourn as the team's pitcher.

His 60 victories is the most ever won by a pitcher in a season. It shines brightest among all such jewels in the Triple Crowns worn by those who came after him. Radbourn won 308 games in his big league career, but the 60 he totaled in his 1884 season—including a streak of 26 wins in 27 decisions—gave him a celebrity which was recognized when he was named to the Hall of Fame in its opening year, 1939.

A Triple Crown is an exacting measurement of a pitcher's superiority at any time. However, because of the circumstance that he started so many games for the league's best team, Radbourn's win totals and strikeout numbers can largely be attributed to sheer volume. However, it is his 1.38 ERA at a time when the league mark was 2.98 that stamps Old Hoss as truly remarkable for his time.

Tim Keefe, the next pitcher to annex a Triple Crown, wore his for a season that has kept his name in the active files of modern baseball writers. Whenever a pitcher runs off a string of victories, this prompts a review of the record book, and Keefe's 19 in a row is remembered as the highest total, shared with Rube Marquard's 1912 season total of 19 straight. In all, Tim Keefe won 35 games for the New York Giants in 1888, just edging out the man who would take the Triple Crown the next year.

John Clarkson pitched Boston to a pennant in 1889, winning the Triple Crown as the workhorse of a staff which included the worn Old Hoss Radbourn. Clarkson won 49 games and Radbourn 20.

Clarkson's career was overlapped by that of Amos

Rusie, the most awesome pitcher of the 1890s. A burly farm boy, "the Hoosier Thunderbolt" was the principal reason the distance of the pitcher's box was pushed back in 1893. Rusie responded the following year by continuing to dominate the league in strikeouts, while topping all pitchers with 36 wins and an ERA of 2.78.

Probably because of the increased pitching distance, the league ERA ballooned to 5.32 and batters averaged .309 in 1894. This was the year Hugh Duffy won the batter's Triple Crown and set a still-unexcelled .440 batting record.

Rusie's career peaked in 1894. The next season one of the most oppressive men to own a big league team, Andrew Freedman, bought the Giants and began a blood feud with Rusie. Rusie sat out the 1896 season, but returned as a reluctant star for two more 20-game-winning seasons. Then he tore his arm muscles and retired. A token appearance in 1901 was the tenth season which qualified him for election to the Hall of Fame.

Just as Nap Lajoie marked the American League's inaugural in 1901 by winning a Triple Crown for batters, another established star, Cy Young, did the same for the pitchers' version. Young, in midcareer as a big league pitcher, won 33 games, a total almost dwarfed among the 511 he won in his career. This latter is a mark certain to stand permanently.

With two major leagues now offering the potential of a Triple Crown winner each year, it took only until 1905 to have both the American and National Leagues produce such winners. Christy Mathewson won the first of the two Triple Crowns he would win for the New York Giants, and the eccentric Rube Waddell had his last great year with the Philadelphia Athletics.

Matty won 31 games, struck out 206, and had an ERA of 1.43. The Rube produced 26 wins, 287 strikeouts, and an ERA of 1.48. The World Series, inaugurated in 1903 but boycotted by the Giants in 1904, was resumed in 1905. It would have provided marvelous theater for the two Triple Crown winners. The confrontation would have been the only one of its kind. Never since have two pennant winners also had pitching's Triple Crown winners. Alas, the colorful Rube Waddell injured his arm while wrestling a teammate just before the Series began.

Without Waddell to oppose him, Christy Mathewson won three games, all shutouts, and the Giants took the Series in five. Matty won the Triple Crown again in 1908 but lost his last start when the Chicago Cubs won the playoff game of a season which had ended in a tie. It was the failure of Fred Merkle to reach second as the winning run scored, resulting in his becoming an inning-ending force out, that deprived Matty of a second opportunity to wear his Triple Crown into a World Series.

Walter Johnson, the next to sport a Triple Crown, won three at widely spaced intervals in his long career. The first came in 1913, the next in 1918, and the last in 1924 when, in his eighteenth season, Johnson once more topped the American League in the three prize categories. This time it also brought a pennant to the Senators, the first in their history. The World Series came close to being a disappointing anticlimax for Johnson. He lost the opener to the New York Giants in extra innings, then lost again, but salvaged glory by winning the deciding seventh game in relief.

Earlier, during Walter Johnson's widely spaced crown jewels, Grover Alexander produced the most impressive reign ever enjoyed by a Triple Crown winner. Pitching for the Philadelphia Phillies, he had three successive seasons with 30 or more victories, starting with the pennant-winning 1915 season; each time he led the NL in ERA and K's as well. What stopped Alexander's run of mastery was World War One. Old Pete swapped his baseball uniform for the khaki of the Army and his Triple Crown honors for a sergeant's stripes.

While Pete was in the Army, another pitcher claimed the Triple Crown. Hippo Vaughn in 1917 had achieved immortality by engaging in a double no-hit game, losing in the tenth inning. In 1918, with Alexander away, Vaughn won the Triple Crown pitching for the Cubs.

Ironically Grover Alexander had served his Army hitch as a new member of the Cubs. With his battery mate, Reindeer Bill Killefer, he had been sold to Chicago after winning his third Triple Crown, in 1917. He pitched only three games in 1918 while Vaughn was in the star's role, and in 1919 the two teammates competed for the Triple Crown. Alexander led the league in ERA and Vaughn in strikeouts. Between them they won 37 games, but neither came close to topping the league.

However, in 1920 Grover Alexander again emerged as the Triple Crown winner. It was his fourth, the most ever won by a pitcher. He continued to star, despite personal and physical problems, during the 1920s without again leading in any of the categories which make up the diadem of the Triple Crown.

Next to wear the Triple Crown of pitchers was Dazzy Vance. Like Rusie, Waddell, and Johnson, Vance began with expectation of finishing each season with a league-leading total in strikeouts. In 1924 he won the Most Valuable Player Award, even though the Brooklyn Dodgers as a team could not win the pennant. To his strikeout superiority, the Dazzler added leadership in wins with 24 and an ERA of 2.16. His domination of the league can best be measured by comparing his ERA to a league total of 3.87 as the lively ball bounded off hitters' bats.

Lefty Grove of the Philadelphia Athletics won back to back Triple Crowns in 1930 and 1931, having missed one of the three legs in 1929. The A's won pennants all three of those years, and Grove was their leading pitcher. In 1929 teammate George Earnshaw topped him in wins, 24 to 20, as Grove missed getting decisions in an unusual number of games.

Another southpaw ace, Lefty Gomez, succeeded Lefty Grove as a Triple Crown winner. Like Grove, he wore the title twice, but not consecutively. He won his first Triple Crown, oddly, in a season when his team, the New York Yankees, didn't win a pennant, 1934. His next came in 1937 as the Yankees were in the midst of a run of four straight pennants.

Gomez was only a spot starter in 1939, when the Yankees met the Reds in the World Series, but Cincinnati had a converted third baseman, Bucky Walters heading their staff, the first National Leaguer to win the Triple Crown in fifteen years.

During World War Two, Hal Newhouser emerged as a superlative pitcher who might have been equally impressive against peacetime competition. He missed the Triple Crown in 1944, winning two legs but coming in second to

Detroit Tiger teammate Dizzy Trout for ERA honors. In 1945, the final wartime year, Newhouser topped the American League in the three prize categories, and winning the Triple Crown went into a long hiatus when the 1946 season resumed with the star pitchers back from service.

Despite leading the league in victories six times and in strikeouts seven, Bob Feller never won an official ERA title to match up with the other components of the Triple Crown. Although Feller's ERA in 1940 is today regarded as the lowest for that year, at that time Ernie Bonham won the title despite pitching only 99 innings.

Warren Spahn topped the National League in victories eight times, led in strikeouts four times, and even took ERA honors three times, but he could never link them up in a single season.

Robin Roberts, like Feller, never won an ERA title, so despite leading in victories four times and strikeouts twice, the singular honor of the Triple Crown eluded him, as it did all other pitchers once baseball had returned to the normalcy of peacetime play.

Triple Crown Pitchers

American League

Player	Team	Year	W	L	SO	ERA
Cy Young	Bos.	1901	33	10	158	1.62
Rube Waddell	Phila.	1905	26	11	287	1.48
Walter Johnson	Wash.	1913	36	7	303	1.09
	Wash.	1918	23	13	162	1.27
	Wash.	1924	23	7	158	2.72
Lefty Grove	Phila.	1930	28	5	209	2.54
	Phila.	1931	31	4	175	2.06
Lefty Gomez	N.Y.	1934	26	5	158	2.33
	N.Y.	1937	21	11	194	2.33
Hal Newhouser	Det.	1945	25	9	212	1.81

National League

Player	Team	Year	W	L	SO	ERA
Tommy Bond	Bos.	1877	40	17	170	2.11
Old Hoss Radbourn	Prov.	1884	60	12	441	1.38
Tim Keefe	N.Y.	1888	35	12	333	1.74
John Clarkson	Bos.	1889	49	19	284	2.73
Amos Rusie	N.Y.	1894	36	13	195	2.78
Christy Mathewson	N.Y.	1905	31	8	206	1.27
	N.Y.	1908	37	11	259	1.43
Grover Alexander	Phila.	1915	31	10	241	1.22
	Phila.	1916	33	12	167	1.55
	Phila.	1917	30	13	201	1.86
Hippo Vaughn	Chi.	1918	22	10	148	1.74
Grover Alexander	Chi.	1920	27	14	173	1.91
Dazzy Vance	Brook.	1924	28	6	262	2.16
Bucky Walters	Cin.	1939	27	11	137	2.29
Sandy Koufax	L.A.	1963	25	5	306	1.88
	L.A.	1965	26	8	382	2.04
	L.A.	1966	27	9	317	1.73
Steve Carlton	Phila.	1972	27	10	310	1.97
Dwight Gooden	N.Y.	1985	24	4	268	1.53

It wasn't until Sandy Koufax reached stardom when the Dodgers were transplanted to Los Angeles and notched three Triple Crown titles that the distinction was again achieved. Koufax topped the three needed categories in 1963, 1965, and 1966. Unlike any other winner of the Triple Crown, Koufax retired with the honor. An aching arthritic arm caused his early retirement, leaving a final season of 27 victories, 317 strikeouts, and an ERA of 1.73.

A Triple Crown-winning pitcher has not always meant a pennant for his team, although the two have gone together more often than not. However, in 1972 Steve Carlton took the honor despite pitching for a last-place team. There has never been such a contrast in the success of a team's best

pitcher and the rest of its staff. The Phillies won 59 games, and Carlton was responsible for 27 of them. He also led, for the only time, in ERA, with 1.97, and struck out 310.

Again a drought followed, despite the presence of such star pitchers as Tom Seaver, Fergie Jenkins, Juan Marichal, Jim Palmer, Gaylord Perry, and others who led in some of the prize-earning stats. Then in 1985 Dwight Gooden took up the challenge and claimed the Triple Crown with a remarkable record: 24-4, 1.53, and 268 strikeouts. Gooden faltered the next year, but Roger Clemens came forward to just miss the honor by finishing second in strikeouts while winning the other two legs.

The Unassisted Triple Play

On May 30, 1987, family and friends of ninety-three-year-old Jimmy Cooney gathered at his home to celebrate the sixtieth anniversary of his unassisted triple play. Rare? It was the last one made in the National League. Only three have been made since that long ago Memorial Day—one, oddly, the day after Cooney's.

Letters from National League president A. Bartlett Giamatti and Dallas Green, the general manager of the Chicago Cubs, congratulated Jimmy Cooney. He had worn a Chicago Cubs uniform the day fate had decreed he be in the right place at the right time. A much-traveled infielder, he had worn six major league uniforms in seven seasons. It was a happy coincidence that he was Chicago's shortstop when he made his unassisted triple play. His father, the first Jimmy Cooney, had been Chicago's shortstop in 1890, '91, and part of '92.

Jimmy's younger brother John had logged twenty years in the big leagues as a pitcher, and after his arm went lame, he had become an outfielder and first baseman.

Jimmy Cooney was no stranger to unassisted triple plays. Two seasons earlier, when he was shortstop for the St. Louis Cardinals, he was doubled off second by the Pirate shortstop Glenn Wright, who next tagged out Rogers Hornsby coming from first base. Wright had snared a line drive off the bat of Jim Bottomley to start his triple play. He watched from the Pirates' bench the day Cooney emulated his feat in much the same manner.

Paul Waner provided the line drive to make the first out, with Cooney snaring it as he ran toward second base. Clyde Barnhart had broken for second on the pitch, and Lloyd Waner, the runner on second, had dashed for third as his brother, Paul, swung. Lloyd was doubled off second, and Cooney simply tagged the startled Barnhart, who thought the ball had gone into center field for a base hit.

There are certain similarities among nine of the ten unassisted triple plays which have been recorded. These have occurred with runners on first and second, have been made by infielders, and have required the complicity of base runners either attempting a double steal or racing away on a hit-and-run play. The tenth—which is soon to be revealed—was by an outfielder, with runners on second and third.

Even the most celebrated unassisted-triple-play feat had an explanation that almost absolved the victims, the Brooklyn Dodgers, of bonehead base running. This was the only such event to happen in a World Series, and it was turned in by Bill Wambsganss, the Cleveland Indian

second baseman in 1920. Those who have examined the boxscore have questioned the tactics of Uncle Wilbert Robinson, the Brooklyn manager whose strategies often were charitably called "unusual." It was the fifth inning, and Brooklyn, behind 7–0, had the first two runners on base. Play it safe? Not Uncle Robbie.

Despite being scoreless, the Dodgers had been hitting the Cleveland pitcher, Jim Bagby, hard. It was a game in which they made thirteen hits and scored a lone run. Bill Wambsganss, who told the story hundreds of times, explained that he chose to play very deep when Clarence Mitchell, a very good-hitting pitcher came to bat in the fifth inning. He didn't think a seven-run lead was too secure the way the Dodgers had been hitting.

When Mitchell cracked the ball on a line, the batters took off, not thinking that Wamby was where the ball was going. He was and ran over and doubled Kilduff off second and turned and found a dumbfounded Otto Miller standing in the baseline. He tagged him out and, as has been the case after every unassisted triple play, trotted off the field in silence. It always takes the crowd a minute or more to realize what has happened.

In the early years of baseball, outfielder Paul Hines of the Providence Grays, had been credited with making an unassisted triple play. Later-day research indicated Hines had made an unassisted double play but had thrown to a base for the third out. But according to the rules of 1878, Hines did indeed register an unassisted triple play.

In 1928, Providence sportswriter W. D. "Bill" Perrin—who at that time had covered the Providence Grays for nearly half a century—described Hines' actions in the game played on May 8, 1878, in Providence. "The circumstances of this play have afforded more arguments than any other known play. That the play was made is not disputed, but whether Hines made the play unassisted or whether [second baseman Charles] Sweasy completed it by retiring the third man. . . . Here is what happened: [Jim] O'Rourke drew a base on balls and scored when Sweasy threw [Jack] Manning's drive over [Providence first baseman Tim] Murnane's head, Manning going to third on the error. Murnane muffed [Ezra] Sutton's fly, Manning holding third [as Sutton took second]. [Jack] Burdock was next up and dropped the ball just over [shortstop Tom] Carey's head for what looked like a safe hit. . . .

"The story in the *Providence Journal* of the next day thus describes the play: 'Manning and Sutton proceeded to the home plate,' meaning that both rounded third. 'Hines ran in and caught the ball, and kept going to tag third.' The rule then as now requires that when a base runner is forced to retrace his steps he must retouch the bases passed in reverse order. As Hines touched third with the ball in his hand, after making the catch, before either Manning or Sutton could get back, both were out automatically. It is true that Hines then on a signal from Sweasy threw the ball to second, but this was unnecessary as both runners were out at third."

To confirm Perrin's view, let's look at the playing rules for 1878, the year in which Hines made his celebrated play. Rule V, Section 1 reads: "Players running the bases must touch each base in regular order, viz., first, second, third, and home bases; and when obliged to return to bases they have occupied they must retouch them in re-

verse order. . . ." And Rule V, Section 15 reads: "Any base-runner failing to touch the base he runs for shall be declared out if the ball be held by a fielder, while touching said base, before the base-runner returns and touches it." Henry Chadwick's gloss on the latter rule stated: ". . . it is only necessary for a fielder to hold the ball on the base, which should have been touched, in order to put the runner out."

Eureka! The controversy of over a century is thus resolved, and in favor of Paul Hines and his unassisted triple play. Rewrite the record books!

Johnny Neun had read in the morning paper of May 31, 1927, about Jimmy Cooney's unassisted triple play in the National League. As first baseman for the Detroit Tigers, known for his fielding and base stealing, Neun was alert to all possibilities when Homer Summa's line drive landed in his glove. Charlie Jamieson was a dead duck, caught off first and easily tagged for the second out. Shortstop Jackie Tavener was jumping up and down at second base calling for the ball. Slow-footed Glen Myatt was lumbering back from third base.

Neun waved his shortstop out of the way and raced toward second base, implausibly shouting, "I'm running into the Hall of Fame."

In a nice touch of journalistic enterprise, *Sports Illustrated,* in 1987, noted that both Jimmy Cooney and Johnny Neun were still alive and arranged for them to talk on the telephone about their unique plays made sixty years earlier. They had been contemporaries but had played in different leagues and had never met.

When each had gone back to the minor leagues, they played against each other in the International League but simply passed each other without fraternal comment, despite having shared such an extremely rare experience. They had a very nice talk, and months later, when Jimmy reached his anniversary a day ahead of Johnny, it was Neun who called to extend congratulations.

On July 30, 1968, Ron Hansen, playing shortstop for the Washington Senators, made an unassisted triple play, following the process all other shortstops have used. He grabbed a line drive off the bat of Joe Azcue, stepped on second to retire Dave Nelson, and tagged Russ Snyder coming from first. It was the first time the feat had been pulled since 1927, forty-one years earlier.

It was the most memorable event of Hansen's week, which was an unusual one in other ways as well. Following his play, he struck out six consecutive times, perhaps still stunned by the event. Then he regained his batting eye to hit a grand-slam home run. His unassisted triple play had been made on a road trip. He could expect applause when he came to bat the first time before hometown Washington fans when the team returned home. But he didn't get this. Instead, he was traded to the White Sox.

The first unassisted triple play of the twentieth century was made on July 19, 1909, by a Cleveland shortstop, Neal Ball. Overall Cleveland has been involved in five of the ten unassisted triple plays in the major leagues. Three times the event has taken place there, twice executed by Cleveland players, and in all a Cleveland player has been involved somewhere five times. It all began with Neal Ball, who snagged a liner hit by Boston's Amby McConnell and retired Charley Wagner and Jake Stahl on the basepaths.

George Burns, playing for the Boston Red Sox between stints as a member of the Indians, turned the tables for Boston and made Cleveland the victim in 1923. He caught Frank Brower's liner, tagged Rube Lutzke off first, and ran to second to get Riggs Stephenson before he could return.

Burns made his play on September 14, and on October 6 another unassisted triple play occurred, making the feat which had been so rare appear almost commonplace, for a while. This time Ernie Padgett, a redheaded shortstop for the Boston Braves, turned the trick. Again the play was made in typical fashion—a line drive, a runner doubled off second base, and a surprised baserunner from first being tagged out.

The rare unassisted triple play occurred again late in the 1992 season. Rookie second baseman Mickey Morandini of the Philadelphia Phillies made a diving catch of a line drive off the bat of Pittsburgh's Jeff King. Morandini scrambled to second base to double off Andy Van Slyke. Then Barry Bonds, running from first base, bumbled into the surprised second baseman, who pushed him away with a climaxing third-out tag. Unaware of the rarity of his sudden feat, the rookie infielder rolled the ball toward the mound. The ball that was used to make the first play of its kind in the big leagues in 24 seasons was put into play the next inning and probably disappeared as a foul ball into the stands.

Unassisted Triple Plays

Player/Team	Date	Pos.	Opp.	Opp. Batter
Paul Hines, Prov.	May 8, 1878	OF	Bos.	Jack Burdock
Neal Ball, Cleve.	July 19, 1909	SS	Bos.	Amby McConnell
Bill Wambsganss, Cleve.	October 10, 1920	2B	Brook.	Clarence Mitchell
George Burns, Bos.	September 14, 1923	1B	Cleve.	Frank Brower
Ernie Padgett, Bos.	October 6, 1923	SS	Phila.	Walter Holke
Glenn Wright, Pitts.	May 7, 1925	SS	St.L.	Jim Bottomley
Jimmy Cooney, Chi.	May 30, 1927	SS	Pitts.	Paul Waner
Johnny Neun, Det.	May 31, 1927	1B	Cleve.	Homer Summa
Ron Hansen, Wash.	July 29, 1968	SS	Cleve.	Joe Azcue
Mickey Morandini, Phi.	September 23, 1992	2B	Pitt.	Jeff King

The No-Hitters

What follows is the traditional honor roll of the 200-plus pitchers who have attained the no-hit heights. Also provided is a list of those handful of ugly-duckling no-hitters that didn't go nine innings, and those 32 games in which a pitcher retired 27 or more batters in succession. Concerning the last-named group, only 13 are officially recognized as perfect games—the rest were deprived of perfection by their fielding support, their stars, or like Dick Bosman, simply themselves.

No-hit games, nine or more innings.

(Number to left is career total if greater than one)
   (Home team is that of pitcher, unless team is in italics)

Joe Borden, Phi vs. Chi NA, 4-0; July 28, 1875.
George Bradley, StL vs. Har NL, 2-0' July 15, 1876.
Lee Richmond, Wor vs. Cle NL, 1-0; June 12, 1880 (perfect game).
Monte Ward, Pro vs. Buf NL, 5-0; June 17, 1880.
Larry Corcoran, Chi vs. Bos NL, 6-0; August 19, 1880.
Jim Galvin, Buf vs. Wor NL, 1-0; August 20, 1880.

Tony Mullane, Lou vs. Cin AA, 2-0; September 19, 1882.
Guy Hecker, Lou vs. Pit AA, 3-1; September 19, 1882
2 Larry Corcoran, Chi vs. Wor NL, 5-0; September 20, 1882.
Hoss Radbourn, Pro vs. Cle NL, 8-0; July 25, 1883
Hugh (One Arm). Daily, Cle vs. Phi NL, 1-0; September 13, 1883.
Al Atkisson, Phi vs. Pit AA, 10-1; May 24, 1884.
Ed Morris, Col vs. Pit AA, 5-0; May 29, 1884.
Frank Mountain, Col vs. Was AA, 12-0; June 5, 1884.
3 Larry Corcoran, Chi vs. Pro NL, 6-0; June 27, 1884.
2 Jim Galvin, Buf vs. Det NL, 18-0; August 4, 1884.
Dick Burns, Cin vs. KC UA, 3-1; August 26, 1884.
Ed Cushman, Mil vs. Was UA, 5-0; September 28, 1884.
Sam Kimber, Bro vs. Tol AA, 0-0; October 4, 1884 (10 innings, tie).
John Clarkson, Chi vs. Pro NL, 4-0; July 27, 1885.
Charlie Ferguson, Phi vs. Pro NL, 1-0; August 29, 1885.
2 Al Atkisson, Phi vs. NY AA, 3-2; May 1, 1886.
Adonis Terry, Bro vs. StL AA, 1-0; July 24, 1886.
Matt Kilroy, Bal vs. Pit AA, 6-0; October 6, 1886.
2 Adonis Terry, Bro vs. Lou AA, 4-0; May 27, 1888.
Henry Porter, KC vs. Bal AA, 4-0; June 6, 1888.
Ed Seward, Phi vs. Cin AA, 12-2; July 26, 1888.
Gus Weyhing, Phi vs. KC AA, 4-0; July 31, 1888.
Cannonball Titcomb, Roch vs. Syr AA, 7-0; September 15, 1890.
Tom Lovett, Bro vs. NY NL, 4-0; June 22, 1891.
Amos Rusie, NY vs. Bro NL, 6-0; July 31, 1891.
Ted Breitenstein, StL vs. Lou AA, 8-0; October 4, 1891 (1st game). (first start in the major leagues).
Jack Stivetts, Bos vs. Bro NL, 11-0; August 6, 1892.
Ben Sanders, Lou vs. Bal NL, 6-2; August 22, 1892.
Bumpus Jones, Cin vs. Pit NL, 7-1; October 15, 1892. (first game in the major leagues).
Bill Hawke, Bal vs. Was NL, 5-0; August 16, 1893.
Cy Young, Cle vs. Cin NL, 6-0; September 18, 1897 (1st game).
2 Ted Breitenstein, Cin vs. Pit NL, 11-0; April 22, 1898.
Jim Hughes, Bal vs. Bos NL, 8-0; April 22, 1898.
Red Donahue, Phi vs. Bos NL, 5-0; July 8, 1898.
Walter Thornton, Chi vs. Bro NL, 2-0; August 21, 1898 (2nd game).
Deacon Phillippe, Lou vs. NY NL, 7-0; May 25, 1899.
Vic Willis, Bos vs. Was NL, 7-1; August 7, 1899.
Noodles Hahn, Cin vs. Phi NL, 4-0; July 12, 1900.
Earl Moore, Cle vs. Chi AL, 2-4; May 9, 1901 (lost on two hits in 10th).
Christy Mathewson, NY vs. StL NL, 5-0; July 15, 1901.
Jim Callahan, Chi vs. Det AL, 3-0; September 20, 1902 (1st game).
Chick Fraser, Phi vs. Chi NL, 10-0; September 18, 1903 (2nd game).
2 Cy Young, Bos vs. Phi AL, 3-0; May 5, 1904 (perfect game).
Bob Wicker, Chi vs. NY NL, 1-0; June 11, 1904. (won in 12 innings after allowing one hit in the 10th).
Jesse Tannehill, Bos vs. Chi AL, 6-0; August 17, 1904.
2 Christy Mathewson, NY vs. Chi NL, 1-0; June 13, 1905.
Weldon Henley, Phi vs. StL AL, 6-0; July 22, 1905 (1st game).
Frank Smith, Chi vs. Det AL, 15-0; September 6, 1905 (2nd game).
Bill Dinneen, Bos vs. Chi AL, 2-0; September 27, 1905 (1st game).
Johnny Lush, Phi vs. Bro NL, 6-0; May 1, 1906.
Mal Eason, Bro vs. StL NL, 2-0; July 20, 1906.
Harry McIntyre, Bro vs. Pit NL, 0-1; August 1, 1906. (lost on four hits in 13 innings after allowing first hit in 11th).
Frank (Jeff). Pfeffer, Bos vs. Cin NL, 6-0; May 8, 1907.
Nick Maddox, Pit vs. Bro NL, 2-1; September 20, 1907.
3 Cy Young, Bos vs. NY AL, 8-0; June 30, 1908.
Hooks Wiltse, NY vs. Phi NL, 1-0; July 4, 1908 (first game, ten innings).
Nap Rucker, Bro vs. Bos NL, 6-0; September 5, 1908 (2nd game).
Dusty Rhoades, Cle vs. Bos AL, 2-1; September 18, 1908.
2 Frank Smith, Chi vs. Phi AL, 1-0; September 20, 1908.
Addie Joss, Cle vs. Chi AL, 1-0; October 2, 1908 (perfect game).
Red Ames, NY vs. Bro NL, 0-3; April 15, 1909. (lost on seven hits in 13 innings after allowing first hit in 10th).
2 Addie Joss, Cle vs. Chi AL, 1-0; April 20, 1910.
Chief Bender, Phi vs. Cle AL, 4-0; May 12, 1910.
Tom L. Hughes, NY vs. Cle AL, 0-5; August 30, 1910 (2nd game). (lost on seven hits in 11 innings after allowing first hit in 10th).
Joe Wood, Bos vs. StL AL, 5-0; July 29, 1911 (1st game).
Ed Walsh, Chi vs. Bos AL, 5-0; August 27, 1911.
George Mullin, Det vs. StL AL, 7-0; July 4, 1912 (2nd game).
Earl Hamilton, StL vs. Det AL, 5-1; August 30, 1912.
Jeff Tesreau, NY vs. Phi NL, 3-0; September 6, 1912 (1st game).
Jim Scott, Chi vs. Was AL, 0-1; May 14, 1914 (lost on 2 two hits in 10th).
Joe Benz, Chi vs. Cle AL, 6-1; May 31, 1914.
George Davis, Bos vs. Phi NL, 7-0; September 9, 1914 (2nd game).
Ed Lafitte, Bro vs. KC FL, 6-2; September 19, 1914.
Rube Marquard, NY vs. Bro NL, 2-0; April 15, 1915.
Frank Allen, Pit vs. StL FL, 2-0; April 24, 1915.
Claude Hendrix, Chi vs. Pit FL, 10-0; May 15, 1915.
Alex Main, KC vs Buf FL, 5-0; August 16, 1915.
Jimmy Lavender, Chi vs. NY NL, 2-0; August 31, 1915 (1st game).
Dave Davenport, StL vs. Chi FL, 3-0; September 7, 1915.
2 Tom L. Hughes, Bos vs. Pit NL, 2-0; June 16, 1916.
Rube Foster, Bos vs. NY AL, 2-0; June 16, 1916.
Joe Bush, Phi vs. Cle AL, 5-0; August 26, 1916.
Hubert (Dutch) Leonard, Bos vs. StL AL, 4-0; August 30, 1916
Eddie Cicotte, Chi vs. StL AL, 11-0; April 14, 1917.
George Mogridge, NY vs. Bos AL, 2-1; April 24, 1917.
Fred Toney, Cin vs. Chi NL, 1-0; May 2, 1917 (10 innings).

Hippo Vaughn, Chi vs. Cin NL, 0-1; May 2, 1917. (lost on two hits in 10th; Toney pitched a no-hitter in this game).

Ernie Koob, StL vs. Chi AL, 1-0; May 5, 1917.

Bob Groom, StL vs. Chi AL, May 6, 1917 (2nd game).

Ernie Shore, Bos vs. Was AL, 3-0; June 23, 1917 (1st game). (perfect game). (Shore relieved Babe Ruth in the first inning after Ruth had been thrown out of the game for protesting a walk to the first batter. The runner was caught stealing and Shore retired the remaining 26 batters in order).

2 Hubert (Dutch). Leonard, Bos vs. Det AL, 5-0; June 3, 1918.

Hod Eller, Cin vs. StL NL, 6-0; May 11, 1919.

Ray Caldwell, Cle vs. NY AL, 3-0; September 10, 1919 (1st game).

Walter Johnson, Was vs. Bos AL, 1-0; July 1, 1920.

Charlie Robertson, Chi vs. Det AL, 2-0; April 30, 1922 (perfect game).

Jesse Barnes, NY vs. Phi NL, 6-0; May 7, 1922.

Sam Jones, NY vs. Phi AL, 2-0; September 4, 1923.

Howard Ehmke, Bos vs. Phi AL, 4-0; September 7, 1923.

Jesse Haines, StL vs Bos NL, 5-0; July 17, 1924.

Dazzy Vance, Bro vs. Phi NL, 10-1; September 13, 1925 (1st game).

Ted Lyons, Chi vs. Bos AL, 6-0; August 21, 1926.

Carl Hubbell, NY vs. Pit NL, 11-0; May 8, 1929.

Wes Ferrell, Cle vs. StL AL, 9-0; April 29, 1931.

Bobby Burke, Was vs. Bos AL, 5-0; August 8, 1931.

Bobo Newsom, StL vs Bos AL, 1-2; September 18, 1934 (lost on one hit in 10th).

Paul Dean, StL vs. Bro NL, 3-0; September 21, 1934 (2nd game).

Vern Kennedy, Chi vs. Cle AL, 5-0; August 31, 1935.

Bill Dietrich, Chi vs. StL AL, 8-0; June 1, 1937.

Johnny Vander Meer, Cin vs. Bos NL, 3-0; June 11, 1938.

2 Johnny Vander Meer, Cin vs. Bro NL, 6-0; June 15, 1938 (next start after June 11).

Monte Pearson, NY vs. Cle AL, 13-0; August 27, 1938 (2nd game).

Bob Feller, Cle vs. Chi AL, 1-0; April 16, 1940 (opening day).

Tex Carleton, Bro vs. Cin NL, 3-0; April 30, 1940.

Lon Warneke, StL vs. Cin NL, 2-0; August 30, 1941.

Jim Tobin, Bos vs. Bro NL, 2-0; April 27, 1944.

Clyde Shoun, Cin vs. Bos NL, 1-0; May 15, 1944.

Dick Fowler, Phi vs. StL AL, 1-0; September 9, 1945 (2nd game).

Ed Head, Bro vs. Bos NL, 5-0; April 23, 1946.

2 Bob Feller, Cle vs. NY AL, 1-0; April 30, 1946.

Ewell Blackwell, Cin vs. Bos NL, 6-0; June 18, 1947.

Don Black, Cle vs. Phi AL, 3-0; July 10, 1947 (1st game).

Bill McCahan, Phi vs. Was AL, 3-0; September 3, 1947.

Bob Lemon, Cle vs. Det AL, 2-0; June 30, 1948.

Rex Barney, Bro vs. NY NL, 2-0; September 9, 1948.

Vern Bickford, Bos vs. Bro NL, 7-0; August 11, 1950.

Cliff Chambers, Pit vs. Bos NL, 3-0; May 6, 1951 (2nd game).

3 Bob Feller, Cle vs. Det AL, 2-1; July 1, 1951 (1st game).

Allie Reynolds, NY vs. Cle AL, 1-0; July 12, 1951.

2 Allie Reynolds, NY vs. Bos AL, 8-0; September 28, 1951 (1st game).

Virgil Trucks, Det vs. Was AL, 1-0; May 15, 1952.

Carl Erskine, Bro vs. Chi NL, 5-0; June 19, 1952.

2 Virgil Trucks, Det vs. NY AL, 1-0; August 25, 1952.

Bobo Holloman, StL vs. Phi AL, 6-0; May 6, 1953 (first start in the major leagues).

Jim Wilson, Mil vs. Phi NL, 2-0; June 12, 1954.

Sam Jones, Chi vs Pit NL, 4-0; May 12, 1955.

2 Carl Erskine, Bro vs. NY NL, 3-0; May 12, 1956.

Johnny Klippstein (7 innings), Hershell Freeman (1 inning) and Joe Black (3 innings)., Cin vs. Mil NL, 1-2; May 26, 1956. (lost on three hits in 11 innings after allowing first hit in 10th).

Mel Parnell, Bos vs. Chi AL, 4-0; July 14, 1956.

Sal Maglie, Bro vs. Phi NL, 5-0; September 25, 1956.

Don Larsen, NY AL vs. Bro NL, 2-0; October 8, 1956. (World Series). (perfect game).

Bob Keegan, Chi vs. Was AL, 6-0; August 20, 1957 (2nd game).

Jim Bunning, Det vs. Bos AL, 3-0; July 20, 1958 (1st game).

Hoyt Wilhelm, Bal vs. NY AL, 1-0; September 20, 1958.

Harvey Haddix, Pit vs. Mil NL, 0-1; May 26, 1959 (lost on one hit in 13 innings after pitching 12 perfect innings).

Don Cardwell, Chi vs. StL NL, 4-0; May 15, 1960 (2nd game).

Lew Burdette, Mil vs. Phi NL, 1-0; August 18, 1960.

Warren Spahn, Mil vs. Phi NL, 4-0; September 16, 1960.

2 Warren Spahn, Mil vs. SF NL, 1-0; April 28, 1961.

Bo Belinsky, LA vs. Bal AL, 2-0; May 5, 1962.

Earl Wilson, Bos vs. LA AL, 2-0; June 26, 1962.

Sandy Koufax, LA vs. NY NL, 5-0; June 30, 1962.

Bill Monbouquette, Bos vs. Chi AL, 1-0; August 1, 1962.

Jack Kralick, Min vs. KC AL, 1-0; August 26, 1962.

2 Sandy Koufax, LA vs. SF NL, 8-0; May 11, 1963.

Don Nottebart, Hou vs. Phi NL, 4-1; May 17, 1963.

Juan Marichal, SF vs. Hou NL, 1-0; June 15, 1963.

Ken T. Johnson, Hou vs. Cin NL, 0-1; April 23, 1964 (lost game).

3 Sandy Koufax, LA vs. Phi NL, 3-0; June 4, 1964.

2 Jim Bunning, Phi vs. NY NL, 6-0; June 21, 1964 (1st game; perfect game).

Jim Maloney, Cin vs. NY NL, 0-1; June 14, 1965 (lsot on two hits in 11 innings after pitching 10 hitless innings).

Jim Maloney, Cin vs. Chi NL, 1-0; August 19, 1965 (1st game; 10 innings).

4 Sandy Koufax, LA vs. Chi NL, 1-0; September 9, 1965 (perfect game).

Dave Morehead, Bos vs. Cle AL, 2-0; September 16, 1965.

Sonny Siebert, Cle vs. Was AL, 2-0; June 10, 1966.

Steve D. Barber (8⅔ innings). and Stu Miller (⅓ inning) Bal vs. Det AL, 1-2; April 30, 1967 (1st game; lost game).

Don Wilson, Hou vs. Atl NL, 2-0; June 18, 1967.

Dean Chance, Min vs. Cle AL, 2-1; August 25, 1967 (2nd game).

Joe Horlen, Chi vs. Det AL, 6-0; September 10, 1967 (1st game).

Tom Phoebus, Bal vs. Bos AL, 6-0; April 27, 1968.

Catfish Hunter, Oak vs. Min AL, 4-0; May 8, 1968 (perfect game).

George Culver, Cin vs. Phi NL, 6-1; July 29, 1968 (2nd game).

Gaylord Perry, SF vs. StL NL, 1-0; Sept. 17, 1968.

Ray Washburn, StL vs. SF NL, 2-0; September 18, 1968.

Bill Stoneman, Mon vs. Phi NL, 7-0; April 17, 1969.

3 Jim Maloney, Cin vs. Hou NL, 10-0; April 30, 1969.

2 Don Wilson, Hou vs. Cin NL, 4-0; May 1, 1969.

Jim Palmer, Bal vs. Oak AL, 8-0; August 13, 1969.

Ken Holtzman, Chi vs. Atl NL, 3-0; August 19, 1969.

Bob Moose, Pit vs. NY NL, 4-0; September 20, 1969.

Dock Ellis, Pit vs. SD NL, 2-0; June 12, 1970 (1st game).

Clyde Wright, Cal vs. Oak AL, 4-0; July 3, 1970.

Bill Singer, LA vs. Phi NL, 5-0; July 20, 1970.

Vida Blue, Oak vs. Min AL, 6-0; September 21, 1970.

2 Ken Holtzman, Chi vs. Cin NL, 1-0; June 3, 1971.

Rick Wise, Phi vs. Cin NL, 4-0; June 23, 1971.

Bob Gibson, StL vs. Pit NL, 11-0; August 14, 1971.

Burt Hooton, Chi vs. Phi NL, 4-0; April 16, 1972.

Milt Pappas, Chi vs. SD NL, 8-0; September 2, 1972.

2 Bill Stoneman, Mon vs. NY NL, 7-0; October 2, 1972 (1st game).

Steve Busby, KC vs. Det AL, 3-0; April 27, 1973.

Nolan Ryan, Cal vs. KC AL, 3-0; May 15, 1973.

2 Nolan Ryan, Cal vs. Det AL, 6-0; July 15, 1973.

Jim Bibby, Tex vs. Oak AL, 6-0; July 20, 1973.

Phil Niekro, Atl vs. SD NL, 9-0; August 5, 1973.

2 Steve Busby, KC vs. Mil AL, 2-0; June 19, 1974.

Dick Bosman, Cle vs. Oak AL, 4-0; July 19, 1974.

3 Nolan Ryan, Cal vs. Min AL, 4-0; September 28, 1974

4 Nolan Ryan, Cal vs. Bal AL, 1-0; June 1, 1975.

Ed Halicki, SF vs. NY NL, 6-0; August 24, 1975 (2nd game).

Vida Blue (5 innings), Glenn Abbott (1 inning), Paul Lindblad (1 inning), and Rollie Fingers (2 innings), Oak vs. Cal AL, 5-0; September 28, 1975.

Larry Dierker, Hou vs. Mon NL, 5-0; July 9, 1976.

Blue Moon Odom (5 innings) and Francisco Barrios (4 innings), Chi vs. Oak AL, 6-0; July 28, 1976.

John Candelaria, Pit vs. LA NL, 2-0; August 9, 1976.

John Montefusco, SF vs. Atl NL, 9-0; September 29, 1976.

Jim Colborn, KC vs. Tex AL, 6-0; May 14, 1977.

Dennis Eckersley, Cle vs. Cal AL, 1-0; May 30, 1977.

Bert Blyleven, Tex vs. Cal AL, 6-0; September 22, 1977.

Bob Forsch, StL vs. Phi NL, 5-0; April 16, 1978.

Tom Seaver, Cin vs. StL NL, 4-0; June 16, 1978.

Ken Forsch, Hou vs. Atl NL, 6-0; April 7, 1979.

Jerry Reuss, LA vs. SF NL, 8-0; June 27, 1980.

Charlie Lea, Mon vs. SF NL, 4-0; May 10, 1981 (2nd game).

Len Barker, Cle vs. Tor AL, 3-0; May 15, 1981 (perfect game).

5 Nolan Ryan, Hou vs. LA NL, 5-0; September 26, 1981.

Dave Righetti, NY vs. Bos AL, 4-0; July 4, 1983.

2 Bob Forsch, StL vs. Mon NL, 3-0; September 26, 1983.

Mike Warren, Oak vs. Chi AL, 3-0; September 29, 1983.

Jack Morris, Det vs. Chi AL, 4-0; April 7, 1984.

Mike Witt, Cal vs. Tex AL, 1-0; September 30, 1984 (perfect game).

Joe Cowley, Chi vs. Cal AL, 7-1; September 19, 1986.

Mike Scott, Hou vs. SF NL, 2-0; September 25, 1986.

Juan Nieves, Mil vs. Bal AL, 7-0; April 15, 1987.

Tom Browning, Cin vs. LA NL, 1-0; September 16, 1988 (perfect game).

Mark Langston (7 innings) and Mike Witt (2 innings), Cal vs Sea AL, 1-0; April 11, 1990.

Randy Johnson, Sea vs Det AL, 2-0; June 2, 1990.

6 Nolan Ryan, Tex vs Oak AL, 5-0; June 11, 1990.

Dave Stewart, Oak vs Tor AL, 5-0; June 29, 1990.

Fernando Valenzuela, LA vs Stl NL, 6-0; June 29, 1990.

Andy Hawkins, NY vs Chi AL, 0-4; July 1, 1990 (8 innings, lost the game).

Terry Mulholland, Phi vs SF NL, 6-0; August 15, 1990.

Dave Stieb, Tor vs Det AL, 3-0; September 2, 1990.

7 Nolan Ryan, Tex vs Tor AL, 3-0; May 1, 1991.

Tommy Greene, Phi vs Mont NL, 2-0; May 23, 1991.

Bob Milacki (6 innings), Mike Flanagan (1 inning), Mark Williamson (1 inning), Gregg Olson (1 inning) vs Oak AL, 2-0; July 13, 1991.

Mark Gardner, Mont vs LA NL, 0-1; July 26, 1991 (9 innings, lost game in 10th).

Dennis Martinez, Mont vs LA NL, 2-0; July 28, 1991 (perfect game).

Wilson Alvarez, Chi vs Balt AL, 7-0; August 11, 1991.

Bret Saberhagen, KC vs Chi AL, 7-0; August 26, 1991.

Kent Mercker (6 innings), Mark Wohlers (2 innings), Alejandro Pena (1 inning), Atl vs SD NL, 1-0; September 11, 1991.

Matt Young, Bos vs Cle AL, 1-2; April 12, 1992 (8 innings, lost game).

Kevin Gross, LA vs SF NL, 2-0; August 17, 1992.

No-hit games, fewer than nine innings

(Home team is that of pitcher, unless team is in italics)

Larry McKeon, six innings, Ind vs. Cin AA, 0-0; May 6, 1884.

Charlie Gagus, eight innings, Was vs. Wil UA, 12-1; August 21, 1884.

Charlie Getzien, six innings, Det vs. Phi NL, 1-0; October 1, 1884.

Charlie Sweeney (3 innings) and Henry Boyle (2 innings), five innings, StL vs. StP U.A., 0-1; October 5, 1884.

Dupee Shaw, five innings, Pro vs. *Buf* NL, 4-0; October 7, 1885 (1st game).
George Van Haltren, six innings, Chi vs. Pit NL, 1-0; June 21, 1888.
Cannonball Crane, seven innings, NY vs. Was NL, 3-0; September 27, 1888.
Matt Kilroy, seven innings, Bal vs. StL AA, 0-0; July 29, 1889 (2nd game).
Silver King, eight innings, Chi vs. Bro PL, 0-1; June 21, 1890.
George Nicol, seven innings, StL vs. Phi AA, 21-2; September 23, 1890.
Hank Gastright, eight innings, Col vs. Tol AA, 6-0; October 12, 1890.
Jack Stivetts, five innings, Bos vs. *Was* NL, 6-0; October 15, 1892 (2nd game).
Icebox Chamberlain, seven innings, Cin vs. Bos NL, 6-0; September 23, 1893 (2nd game).
Ed Stein, six innings, Bro vs. Chi NL, 6-0; June 2, 1894.
Red Ames, five innings, NY vs. *StL* NL, 5-0; September 14, 1903 (2nd game).
Rube Waddell, five innings, Phi vs. StL AL, 2-0; August 15, 1905.
Jake Weimer, seven innings, Cin vs. Bro NL, 1-0; August 24, 1906 (2nd game).
Jimmy Dygert (3 innings) and Rube Waddell (2 innings), five innings, Phi vs. Chi AL, 4-3; September 24, 1906.
Stoney McGlynn, seven innings, StL vs. Bro NL, 1-1; September 24, 1906 (2nd game).
Lefty Leifield, six innings, Pit vs. Phi NL, 8-0; September 26, 1906, (2nd game).
Ed Walsh, five innings, Chi vs. NY AL, 8-1; May 26, 1907.

Ed Karger, seven perfect innings, StL vs. Bos NL, 4-0; August 11, 1907 (2nd game).
Howie Camnitz, five innings, Pit vs. *NY* NL, 1-0; August 23, 1907 (2nd game).
Rube Vickers, five perfect innings, Phi vs. *Was* AL, 4-0; October 5, 1907 (2nd game).
Johnny Lush, six innings, StL vs. *Bro* NL, 2-0; August 6, 1908.
King Cole, seven innings, Chi vs. *StL* NL, 4-0; July 31, 1910 (2nd game).
Jay Cashion, six innings, Was vs. Cle AL, 2-0; August 20, 1910 (2nd game).
Walter Johnson, seven innings, Was vs. StL Al, 2-0; August 25, 1910.
Fred Frankhouse, seven and two-thirds innings, Bro vs. Cin NL, 5-0; August 27, 1937.
John Whitehead, six innings, StL vs. Det AL, 4-0; August 5, 1940 (2nd game).
Jim Tobin, five innings, Bos vs. Phi NL, 7-0; June 22, 1944 (2nd game).
Mike McCormick, five innings, SF vs. Phi NL, 3-0; June 12, 1959.
Sam Jones, seven innings, SF vs. *StL* NL, 4-0; September 26, 1959.
Dean Chance, five perfect innings, Min vs. Bos AL, 2-0; August 6, 1967.
Dave Palmer, five perfect innings, Mon vs. *StL* NL, 4-0; April 21, 1984 (2nd game).
Pascual Perez, five innings, Mon vs. *Phi* NL, 1-0; September 24, 1988.
Melido Perez, five innings, rain, Chi at NY AL, 8-0; July 12, 1990.

Perfection Plus

Year	Pitcher	Batters	Opponent	Notes
1959	Harvey Haddix	36	Milwaukee	(12 innings)
1919	Waite Hoyt	34	Yanks	(2nd-13th inning)
1880	Pud Galvin	33	Worcester	(6 errors)
1884	Charlie Buffinton	32	Providence	(5 errors)
1971	Rick Wise	32	Chicago	(2nd-12th inning)
1908	Nap Rucker	30	Braves	(3 errors)
1885	John Clarkson	29	Providence	(3 errors, 1 DP)
1970	Bill Singer	29	Philadelphia	(2 errors, both his own)
1883	Hoss Radbourn	28	Cleveland	(1 error)
1884	Pud Galvin	28	Detroit	(1 error)
1905	Christy Mathewson	28	Cubs	(2 errors, one DP)
1910	Tom Hughes	28	Cleveland	(1 error)
1920	Walter Johnson	28	Red Sox	(1 error)
1947	Bill McCahan	28	Washington	(1 error)
1967	Joel Horlen	28	Detroit	(1 error)
1974	Dick Bosman	28	Oakland	(1 error, his own)
1980	Jerry Reuss	28	San Francisco	(1 error)
1880	J. L. Richmond	27	Cleveland	
1880	J. M. Ward	27	Buffalo	
1904	Cy Young	27	Philadelphia	

Year	Pitcher	Batters	Opponent	Notes
1906	Lefty Leifield	27	Cubs	(8 innings, 3 errors)
1908	Addie Joss	27	White Sox	
1922	Charlie Robertson	27	Detroit	
1956	Don Larsen	27	Brooklyn	
1964	Jim Bunning	27	Mets	
1965	Sandy Koufax	27	Cubs	
1968	Catfish Hunter	27	Minnesota	
1981	Len Barker	27	Toronto	
1984	Mike Witt	27	Texas	
1988	Tom Browning	27	Los Angeles	
1991	Dennis Martinez	27	Los Angeles	
1954	Robin Roberts	27*	Cincinnati	
1981	Jim Bibby	27*	Atlanta	
1917	Ernie Shore	26	Washington	

*Retired last twenty-seven batters in a row after giving up a hit to leadoff man.
†Starter Babe Ruth walked the first man and promptly slugged the umpire in the jaw and was banished. Ernie Shore rushed in from the bull pen, got the runner on a steal attempt, and retired the next twenty-six.
Note: Hooks Wiltse in 1908 and Lew Burdette in 1960 missed perfection because each hit a batter, with Wiltse hitting the *last* batter—the opposing pitcher—with an 0-2 count.

## CHAPTER 15

Awards and Honors

Bill Deane

This chapter presents the history and voting results of baseball's most prestigious awards and honors, including the complete balloting and current constituency of the Baseball Hall of Fame. This material will be of interest to the fan who wonders how a player of the past was viewed by his contemporaries. I have ventured an additional section of "what if" awards: what if the Cy Young Award had been instituted long before its actual inception in 1956, or the Rookie of the Year before its real debut in 1947, and so on. What follows is divided into six sections:

MVP Award: history and balloting.
Rookie of the Year Award: history and balloting.
Cy Young Award: history and balloting.
Hypothetical Awards: explanation and selections.
Gold Glove Award: history, discussion, and list of winners.
Hall of Fame: history of elections and balloting.

Balloting tables and lists of winners include each player's first initial, last name, and club city abbreviation (and point total, if applicable).

Most Valuable Player Award: History

The concept of most valuable player awards dates back more than a century. The first documented MVP-type honor in pro ball was bestowed upon James "Deacon" White of the 1875 Boston Red Stockings in the National Association. Catcher White sparked Boston to a remarkable 71–8 record that year, scoring 77 runs in 80 games and batting .355. An ardent Red Stockings' admirer presented Deacon with a silver tray, water pitcher, and loving cup inscribed with the words: WON BY JIM WHITE AS MOST VALUABLE PLAYER TO BOSTON TEAM, 1875.

The first official MVP honor was initiated some thirty-five years later. Prior to the 1910 season, baseball fan Hugh Chalmers, president and general manager of the Chalmers Motor Company, announced that he would present one of his company's automobiles—a Chalmers "30"—to the major league player who compiled the highest batting average. What appeared to be a harmless promotional gimmick was to soon turn into a public relations disaster.

The rules specified that players must accumulate a specific minimum number of times at bat, depending on position, to qualify for the award. For infielders and outfielders, it was a minimum of 350 at-bats; for catchers, 250 at-bats; and for pitchers, 100 at-bats. Interest in the award was tremendous from the outset. Ty Cobb, who already owned a Chalmers "30" roadster, wrote: "I am glad that something besides medals and trophies is offered for the championship in batting. I think the offer of a Chalmers "30" is simply great and I hope to be lucky enough to own a new Chalmers next fall."

It developed into a two-man race, with Detroit's Cobb and Cleveland's Napoleon Lajoie, both American Leaguers, the only serious challengers for the coveted prize. Throughout the season there were charges and counter-charges of favoritism by scorers in various cities. Furthermore, the general consensus of the press was that Cobb's selfish pursuit of this individual honor had cost his team the pennant. The controversy was capped by scandalous circumstances on the final day of the season.

Through games of September 16, Cobb held a solid lead over Lajoie, .368 to .357 (although, because of the era's sloppy record keeping, few actually knew the official figures at the time). From then through October 8, Cobb batted a torrid .532 (25 for 47) to seemingly lock up the crown with a .383 average. But Lajoie refused to surrender, going 30 for 54 (.556) in that same span to enter the final day, October 9, with a .376 mark. Cobb chose to sit out his final game, while Lajoie played the infamous doubleheader with the St. Louis Browns in which he went 8 for 8, including *seven bunt hits*—remarkable for a slow-footed slugger—to apparently edge out Cobb in the batting race. Browns' manager Jack O'Connor had instructed his rookie third baseman, Red Corriden, to play deep on Lajoie, advice with which Corriden complied. Lajoie took advantage of the strange defensive arrangement with the repeated safe bunts. Although neither Lajoie nor Corriden were implicated, there were charges of a Browns' frame-up to give the coveted batting title (and car) to the respected Lajoie over the disliked Cobb.

O'Connor lost his job due to his role in the alleged fix. Subsequently, AL President Ban Johnson announced that a "discrepancy" had been found in the official records, and that Cobb had actually won the batting crown after all (although this point is challenged by many current researchers, who have evidence that Cobb was credited wrongly for a 2 for 4 game). Meanwhile, Hugh Chalmers, attempting to divorce himself from the controversy, presented autos to both Cobb and Lajoie. It was generally acknowledged that this fiasco doomed the future of individual awards of any kind.

Hoping to salvage some goodwill out of the whole idea, Chalmers came up with a new proposal for the 1911 season. This time he would award an auto to one player in each league who "should prove himself as the most impor-

tant and useful player to his club and to the league at large in point of deportment and value of services rendered." The decision for this honor was to be made by a committee of baseball writers, one writer from each club city in each league. Each writer was to make eight selections, with a first-place ballot scoring eight points, on down to an eighth-place vote counting one point. Thus was born the short-lived Chalmers Award, with Ty Cobb and Frank Schulte earning recognition in 1911. Both Cobb and Schulte voluntarily withdrew from the competition in 1912, although the former received seventeen points anyway.

Interest in the award diminished within a few years. By 1914 the public was distracted by baseball's battles with the new Federal League and the escalation of the World War in Europe. The timing was right for the Chalmers Award to quietly disappear; it was noted that Mr. Chalmers had agreed to present vehicles for five years and that the 1914 awards marked the fifth presentations.

On July 15, 1922, the newly formed American League Trophy Committee adopted a set of rules governing the selection of an annual award-winner. The rules specified that "the purpose of the American League Trophy is to honor the baseball player who is of greatest all-round service to his club and credit to the sport during each season; to recognize and reward uncommon skill and ability when exercised by a player for the best interests of his team, and to perpetuate his memory." The rules further instructed voters to seek out the "winning ball player," reminding them that "combined offensive and defensive ability is not always indicated by any system of records."

Eight baseball writers, one from each AL city, were enfranchised, with each required to select exactly one player from each team, for a total of eight selections. Player-managers and previous winners were to be excluded from consideration. Points were distributed the same as in the Chalmers Award: eight for first place, down to one for eighth.

The intention of AL President Ban Johnson was to have a monument to baseball erected in East Potomac Park, Washington, D.C., engraved with the names of winners of the AL Award. This proposal was introduced as a congressional resolution in 1924, and passed in the House of Representatives before dying on the Senate Floor.

The AL voting rules led to growing criticism for several reasons, one of which was the limitation on the number of vote-getters from each team. For example, when the Browns' George Sisler won the first AL Award in 1922, he was named on all eight ballots—thus disqualifying his teammates from receiving any votes. As a result, fellow Brownie Ken Williams, who led the league in home runs (39), RBIs (155), and total bases (367) and became the first player ever to have 30 homers and 30 stolen bases in the same season, was shut out in the League Award voting.

Secondly, the rule prohibiting player-managers from eligibility drew fire. In 1925, when this rule eliminated five solid candidates from consideration, *The New York Times* wrote, "to say that it is impossible or impractical to divorce a man's managerial skill from his talents purely as a player is to reflect on the intelligence of the committee that awards the prize."

The *Times* further editorialized on the fallacy of as-

suming that no player can be the "most valuable" more than one year: "the purpose, of course, is to pass the honor around, but the effect is to pass an empty honor around." This rule became increasingly ridiculous when it eliminated Babe Ruth (and his 60 home runs) from consideration in 1927; by the following year, both Ruth and teammate Lou Gehrig, who were in the process of finishing one-two in the AL home run derby in five consecutive seasons, were ineligible for the League Award.

In 1924 the National League instituted its own award, with radical differences in the selection method: each writer voted for ten players rather than eight (ten points for first place, and so on); he was not bound to vote for a certain number of players from each team; he was free to select a player-manager; and, later, he was allowed to consider previous winners of the award. Additionally, the NL offered a cash "present" of $1,000 to the award-winner.

At various times between 1925–51, writers were permitted to name "honorable mention" candidates, whose vote totals were listed but not counted in the balloting. Another feature of early voting reports was the listing of "cumulative vote leaders"—a forerunner to Bill James's "award shares"—over a period of years.

A number of factors led to the demise of the AL Award, including the award's loss of credibility due to the previously mentioned shortsighted voting rules. Secondly, Ban Johnson, having failed to secure the erection of his proposed monument, felt the award had fallen short of its aim. Finally, management was concerned with the efforts of award-winners to parlay their honors into substantial pay raises. The AL Award was officially voted out at a special league meeting on May 6, 1929.

The National League followed suit with the AL's decision, but agreed to continue its award through the 1929 season.

In October 1929, the Baseball Writers' Association of America (BBWAA) announced the results of an "unofficial" AL most valuable player poll, whose winner was Lew Fonseca of Cleveland. Two months later, *The Sporting News* (TSN) conducted a poll of the eight writers who had previously voted on the League Award, thereby reporting Al Simmons as the "unofficial" AL Award-winner. Combining the results of these two unofficial polls gives Fonseca 77 points, followed by Heinie Manush (57), Simmons (56), Tony Lazzeri (55) and Charlie Gehringer (44).

The Sporting News announced that, thereafter, they would take it upon themselves to conduct an annual poll to substitute for the defunct league awards. However, they retained the stipulation that each voter must select just one player on each team. In 1930, TSN chose Joe Cronin in the AL and Bill Terry in the NL. Earlier, the Associated Press also had a special committee of writers make an unofficial AL selection for 1930, while the BBWAA did the same for the NL (adding a check for $1,000 for the winner). The respective selections here were Cronin in the AL and Hack Wilson in the NL. Again combining the two sets of polls, the AL leaders were Cronin (100), Al Simmons (85), Lou Gehrig (68), Charlie Gehringer (67), and Ted Lyons (56). The NL pace-setters were Hack Wilson (111), Frankie Frisch (107), Bill Terry (105), Chuck Klein (57), and Floyd "Babe" Herman (52).

In an effort to standardize MVP voting, the BBWAA, in its annual winter meeting in New York on December 11, 1930, decided to appoint two committees (one in each league) to elect most valuable players, with the association to "award suitable emblems to the players selected." Thus was born what is considered the modern MVP Award, with most of the flaws of its forerunners eliminated.

TSN, however, continued to make its own selections in bitter competition with the BBWAA. Finally, beginning in 1938, TSN agreed to unify the award by abiding with BBWAA balloting, and presenting The Sporting News Trophy to the winner. Among the various prizes awarded to the winners were wristwatches and shotguns.

At a meeting during the 1944 World Series, the BBWAA decided to begin issuing its own trophy, the Kenesaw Mountain Landis Award, in honor of the ailing commissioner. Landis died a month later and the official MVP Award has born his name ever since. A plaque engraved with the names of the winners hangs in the National Baseball Library in Cooperstown, New York.

The Sporting News went back to naming its own MVPs in 1944 and '45. Then, at the request of the new commissioner, Happy Chandler, TSN "withdrew from the field to cooperate in making the Landis Awards, provided by the major leagues, the official designations of the year." In 1948, however, TSN went back to its own awards, selecting a Player of the Year and Pitcher of the Year in each league, as they have done ever since. For some reason, TSN awards have never received the public recognition that the BBWAA honors have.

Two major changes in the MVP voting began in 1938. The BBWAA began polling three writers in each major league city, rather than just one, which remained in effect until it was reduced to two writers per city, starting in 1961. Also in 1938, the process was initiated to award fourteen points for each first-place vote, rather than ten.

"Split votes," which have since infiltrated all the major awards, first appeared in MVP Awards in 1959. The American League MVP race that year, by consensus, was between second baseman Nellie Fox and shortstop Luis Aparicio of the champion Chicago White Sox. Late in the season, the suggestion often arose that the two ought to share the award. When the votes were in, Fox had received fourteen first-place votes, Aparicio had gotten six, and four writers had split their votes between the two. Tickled with the idea of a split vote, one NL writer also resorted to this option, dividing his first-place nomination between Ernie Banks and Ed Mathews. The cop-out vote, having been allowed in '59, has since surfaced in sixteen more MVP Awards, ten Rookie of the Year, and six Cy Young Award elections. The ultimate folly of this practice was best exemplified in 1979. One NL writer split his fourth-place vote between pitching brothers Phil and Joe

Niekro, evidently convinced that the two were identical twins. But the writer was still permitted to make six more selections. That meant that his fifth-, sixth-, and seventh-place selections received more points (six, five and four, respectively) than his fourth-place co-selections, who were credited with just three and a half points apiece!

There has long been debate about the consideration of pitchers for the MVP Award, the theory (by some) that a man who plays every fourth game cannot be as valuable as a man who plays every day. The debate escalated after the inception of the Cy Young Award in 1956, giving pitchers their own exclusive honor, and the increasing practice of five-man rotations in the 1970s, giving starting pitchers even less of a chance to contribute. As far as Jack Lang, executive secretary of the BBWAA, is concerned, there is no room for controversy. "The rules that are sent out to the voters on the [MVP] committee state: 'Keep in mind that all players are eligible. That includes pitchers, starters and relievers,' " says Lang. "Anybody on the committee that feels they cannot vote for a pitcher, we replace them. In my twenty-four years running the elections, only two writers have said that to me." Since 1931, pitchers have won the award ten times in the AL and nine times in the NL.

There have been twelve occasions in which one player received all of the available first-place MVP votes in his league. The AL players so honored are Ty Cobb (1911), Babe Ruth (1923), Hank Greenberg (1935), Al Rosen (1953), Mickey Mantle (1956), Frank Robinson (1966), Denny McLain (1968), Reggie Jackson (1973), and Jose Canseco (1988). The three unanimous NL selections are Carl Hubbell (1936), Orlando Cepeda (1967), and Mike Schmidt (1980). Hubbell's distinction is disputable, as two of the eight writers did not submit ballots that year and were not replaced on the selection committee.

Following are the maximum possible point totals that could have been earned by an individual receiving the first-place nomination of every writer polled:

National League		American League	
1911–14	64	1911–14	64
1924–29	80	1922–28	64
1931–37	80	1931–37	80
1938–60	336	1938–60	336
1961	224	1961–68	280
1962–68	280	1969–76	336
1969–present	336	1977–present	392

There have been numerous cases in which the MVP vote point totals did not add up to the correct figure. Reasons for this include inaccuracies in tabulation, inaccuracies in reporting, and writers who failed to vote or to complete their ballots. However, the total impact of all these errors is a small fraction of 1 percent of the total voting over the years.

Following is a complete tabulation of all the recognized MVP elections since 1911:

MVP Award
Chalmers Award, 1911–14

1911 NATIONAL						
F. Schulte, CHI 29	F. Merkle, NY 19	M. Doolan, PHI 6	B. Sweeney, BOS . . .3	J. Kling, BOS 1	E. Collins, PHI 32
C. Mathewson, NY . .25	R. Marquard, NY . . .19	B. Harmon, SL 6	O. Knabe, PHI 2	B. Adams, PIT 1	J. Jackson, CLE . .28
L. Doyle, NY 23	J. Daubert, BKN . . .16	J. Archer, CHI 5	E. Konetchy, SL 2	N. Rucker, BKN 1	W. Johnson, WAS . .19
H. Wagner, PIT 23	J. Tinker, CHI 11	H. Lobert, PHI 4	D. Hoblitzell, CIN . . .2		B. Cree, NY 16
G. Alexander, PHI . .23	C. Meyers, NY 11	G. Gibson, PIT 4	J. Walsh, PHI 2	1911 AMERICAN	T. Speaker, BOS . . .16
M. Huggins, SL 21	J. Sheckard, CHI . . .9	M. Brown, CHI 4	J. Devore, NY 2	T. Cobb, DET 64	I. Thomas, PHI 12
	M. Mitchell, CIN 9	B. Bescher, CIN 4	F. Luderus, PHI 1	E. Walsh, CHI 35	C. Milan, WAS 10

(continued)

- V. Gregg, CLE ... 9
- F. Baker, PHI ... 8
- J. Coombs, PHI ... 6
- N. Lajoie, CLE ... 4
- J. Knight, NY ... 4
- S. Crawford, DET ... 4
- B. Lord, PHI ... 4
- D. Bush, DET ... 4
- R. Ford, NY ... 3
- J. Barry, PHI ... 3
- J. Austin, SL ... 2
- F. LaPorte, SL ... 2
- S. McInnis, PHI ... 1
- G. McBride, WAS ... 1

1912 NATIONAL

- L. Doyle, NY ... 48
- H. Wagner, PIT ... 43
- C. Meyers, NY ... 25
- J. Tinker, CHI ... 22
- B. Bescher, CIN ... 17
- B. Sweeney, BOS ... 16
- H. Zimmerman, CHI ... 16
- R. Marquard, NY ... 13
- O. Wilson, PIT ... 13
- J. Daubert, BKN ... 13
- O. Knabe, PHI ... 10
- E. Konetchy, SL ... 8
- C. Mathewson, NY ... 8
- D. Paskert, PHI ... 6
- J. Tesreau, NY ... 6
- R. Murray, NY ... 5
- M. Huggins, SL ... 5
- A. Marsans, CIN ... 4
- F. Merkle, NY ... 4
- J. Evers, CHI ... 2
- C. Hendrix, PIT ... 2
- J. Archer, CHI ... 1
- G. Alexander, PHI ... 1

1912 AMERICAN

- T. Speaker, BOS ... 59
- E. Walsh, CHI ... 30
- W. Johnson, WAS ... 28
- C. Milan, WAS ... 23
- J. Wood, BOS ... 22
- E. Collins, PHI ... 18
- F. Baker, PHI ... 17
- T. Cobb, DET ... 17
- J. Jackson, CLE ... 16
- H. Wagner, BOS ... 12
- C. Gandil, WAS ... 7
- B. Shotton, SL ... 6
- D. Pratt, SL ... 5
- E. Foster, WAS ... 4
- L. Gardner, BOS ... 4
- S. Crawford, DET ... 4
- J. Barry, PHI ... 4
- B. Carrigan, BOS ... 3
- G. Moriarty, DET ... 3
- J. Birmingham, CLE ... 2
- D. Moeller, WAS ... 1
- G. McBride, WAS ... 1
- S. McInnis, PHI ... 1
- B. Daniels, NY ... 1

1913 NATIONAL

- J. Daubert, BKN ... 50
- G. Cravath, PHI ... 40
- R. Maranville, BOS ... 23
- C. Mathewson, NY ... 21
- C. Meyers, NY ... 20
- V. Saier, CHI ... 15
- L. Cheney, CHI ... 12
- D. Miller, PIT ... 11
- H. Wagner, PIT ... 11
- J. Evers, CHI ... 10
- T. Seaton, PHI ... 9
- A. Fletcher, NY ... 7
- J. Archer, CHI ... 6
- M. Doolan, PHI ... 6
- B. Sweeney, BOS ... 6
- J. Viox, PIT ... 6
- J. Doyle, NY ... 5
- T. Shafer, NY ... 5
- R. Murray, NY ... 5
- H. Zimmerman, CHI ... 4
- O. Knabe, PHI ... 4
- B. Adams, PIT ... 3
- G. Cutshaw, BKN ... 3
- G. Burns, NY ... 2
- A. Marsans, CIN ... 2
- B. Humphries, CHI ... 2
- M. Brown, CIN ... 1

1913 AMERICAN

- W. Johnson, WAS ... 54
- J. Jackson, CLE ... 43
- E. Collins, PHI ... 30
- T. Speaker, BOS ... 26
- F. Baker, PHI ... 21
- C. Gandil, WAS ... 14
- S. McInnis, PHI ... 12
- W. Schang, PHI ... 11
- C. Milan, WAS ... 8
- J. Barry, PHI ... 8
- N. Lajoie, CLE ... 7
- D. Bush, DET ... 6
- H. Wagner, BOS ... 6
- R. Russell, CHI ... 5
- B. Shotton, SL ... 5
- G. McBride, WAS ... 5
- J. Scott, CHI ... 5
- G. Stovall, SL ... 5
- S. Crawford, DET ... 5
- T. Cobb, DET ... 3
- R. Schalk, CHI ... 3
- C. Bender, PHI ... 2
- T. Turner, CLE ... 2
- S. O'Neill, CLE ... 1
- H. Hooper, BOS ... 1

1914 NATIONAL

- J. Evers, BOS ... 50
- R. Maranville, BOS ... 44
- B. James, BOS ... 33
- G. Burns, NY ... 31
- J. Miller, SL ... 18
- J. Tesreau, NY ... 15
- D. Rudolph, BOS ... 14
- S. Magee, PHI ... 14
- Z. Wheat, BKN ... 10
- G. Alexander, PHI ... 9
- R. Bresnahan, CHI ... 6
- L. Magee, SL ... 6
- B. Doak, SL ... 5
- J. Viox, PIT ... 5
- A. Fletcher, NY ... 4
- C. Mathewson, NY ... 4
- V. Saier, CHI ... 4
- B. Schmidt, BOS ... 4
- J. Daubert, BKN ... 4
- L. McCarty, BKN ... 3
- H. Groh, CIN ... 2
- T. Clark, CIN ... 2
- G. Cravath, PHI ... 1

1914 AMERICAN

- E. Collins, PHI ... 63
- S. Crawford, DET ... 35
- D. Bush, DET ... 17
- F. Baker, PHI ... 17
- J. Jackson, CLE ... 15
- R. Schalk, CHI ... 13
- E. Foster, WAS ... 11
- B. Weaver, CHI ... 11
- S. McInnis, PHI ... 11
- D. Pratt, SL ... 10
- W. Schang, PHI ... 10
- T. Speaker, BOS ... 9
- T. Walker, SL ... 9
- T. Cobb, DET ... 7
- E. Scott, BOS ... 7
- J. Barry, PHI ... 6
- D. Leonard, BOS ... 6
- E. Plank, PHI ... 5
- G. McBride, WAS ... 5
- D. Lewis, BOS ... 4
- H. Hooper, BOS ... 4
- F. Maisel, NY ... 3
- R. Peckinpaugh, NY ... 2
- C. Milan, WAS ... 2
- S. Agnew, SL ... 2
- H. Hartzell, NY ... 2
- E. Cicotte, CHI ... 1
- G. Moriarty, DET ... 1

(No official awards, 1915–21)

MVP Award
League Awards, 1922–29

1922 AMERICAN

- G. Sisler, SL ... 59
- E. Rommel, PHI ... 31
- R. Schalk, CHI ... 26
- L. Bush, NY ... 19
- E. Collins, CHI ... 18
- J. Bassler, DET ... 13
- S. O'Neill, CLE ... 13
- J. Judge, WAS ... 12
- W. Pipp, NY ... 12
- L. Blue, DET ... 11
- C. Galloway, PHI ... 10
- H. Heilmann, DET ... 8
- D. Pratt, BOS ... 7
- W. Schang, NY ... 7
- B. Meusel, NY ... 6
- E. Scott, NY ... 6
- W. Johnson, WAS ... 5
- U. Shocker, SL ... 5
- C. Jamieson, CLE ... 4
- J. Sewell, CLE ... 4
- G. Burns, BOS ... 4
- J. Dykes, PHI ... 2
- B. Harris, WAS ... 2
- R. Peckinpaugh, WAS ... 2
- B. Wambsganss, CLE ... 2
- G. Cutshaw, DET ... 1
- C. Perkins, PHI ... 1

1923 AMERICAN

- B. Ruth, NY ... 64
- E. Collins, CHI ... 37
- H. Heilmann, DET ... 31
- W. Gerber, SL ... 20
- J. Sewell, CLE ... 20
- C. Jamieson, CLE ... 19
- J. Bassler, DET ... 17
- C. Galloway, PHI ... 13
- G. Uhle, CLE ... 13
- G. Burns, BOS ... 8
- H. Ehmke, BOS ... 7
- M. Ruel, WAS ... 7
- R. Peckinpaugh, WAS ... 6
- U. Shocker, SL ... 5
- J. Judge, WAS ... 4
- M. McManus, SL ... 4
- K. Williams, SL ... 4
- J. Harris, BOS ... 3
- B. Harris, WAS ... 3
- J. Hauser, PHI ... 1
- W. Johnson, WAS ... 1
- C. Perkins, PHI ... 1

(No National League awards, 1922–23)

1924 NATIONAL

- D. Vance, BKN ... 74
- R. Hornsby, SL ... 62
- F. Frisch, NY ... 40
- Z. Wheat, BKN ... 40
- R. Youngs, NY ... 35
- G. Kelly, NY ... 34
- R. Maranville, PIT ... 33
- K. Cuyler, PIT ... 25
- J. Fournier, BKN ... 21
- E. Roush, CIN ... 12
- G. Wright, PIT ... 10
- A. High, BKN ... 9
- B. Pinelli, CIN ... 7
- R. Bressler, CIN ... 6
- G. Hartnett, CHI ... 5
- B. Grimes, BKN ... 5
- J. Bottomley, SL ... 4
- J. Johnston, BKN ... 3
- M. Carey, PIT ... 3
- T. Jackson, NY ... 3
- E. Yde, PIT ... 2
- C. Williams, PHI ... 1
- E. Rixey, CIN ... 1
- G. Alexander, CHI ... 1
- H. DeBerry, BKN ... 1

1924 AMERICAN

- W. Johnson, WAS ... 55
- E. Collins, CHI ... 49
- C. Jamieson, CLE ... 25
- H. Pennock, NY ... 24
- J. Bassler, DET ... 22
- L. Severeid, SL ... 17
- J. Hauser, PHI ... 13
- W. Jacobson, SL ... 11
- H. Heilmann, DET ... 9
- J. Sewell, CLE ... 9
- M. Ruel, WAS ... 7
- W. Schang, NY ... 7
- A. Simmons, PHI ... 7
- W. Pipp, NY ... 6
- H. Ehmke, BOS ... 5
- I. Flagstead, BOS ... 5
- W. Gerber, SL ... 4
- E. Whitehill, DET ... 4
- L. Blue, DET ... 3
- I. Boone, BOS ... 2
- J. Harris, BOS ... 2
- C. Galloway, PHI ... 1
- K. Williams, SL ... 1

1925 NATIONAL

- R. Hornsby, SL ... 73
- K. Cuyler, PIT ... 61
- G. Kelly, NY ... 52
- G. Wright, PIT ... 43
- D. Vance, BKN ... 42
- D. Bancroft, BOS ... 41
- J. Bottomley, SL ... 28
- P. Traynor, PIT ... 27
- F. Frisch, NY ... 13
- E. Roush, CIN ... 12
- M. Carey, PIT ... 11
- I. Meusel, NY ... 6
- D. Luque, CIN ... 5
- C. Grimm, CHI ... 5
- Z. Wheat, BKN ... 4
- P. Donohue, CIN ... 4
- B. Hargrave, CIN ... 4
- G. Harper, PHI ... 3
- J. Sand, PHI ... 3
- W. Gautreau, BOS ... 2
- V. Aldridge, PIT ... 1

1925 AMERICAN

- R. Peckinpaugh, WAS ... 45
- A. Simmons, PHI ... 41
- J. Sewell, CLE ... 21
- H. Heilmann, DET ... 20
- H. Rice, SL ... 18
- E. Sheely, CHI ... 17
- I. Flagstead, BOS ... 10
- W. Jacobson, SL ... 10
- J. Mostil, CHI ... 10
- O. Bluege, WAS ... 8
- M. Cochrane, PHI ... 8
- L. Blue, DET ... 7
- S. Coveleski, WAS ... 7
- W. Kamm, CHI ... 7
- E. Rommel, PHI ... 7
- R. Schalk, CHI ... 7
- A. Wingo, DET ... 7
- E. Combs, NY ... 6
- B. Meusel, NY ... 6
- T. Lyons, CHI ... 5
- G. Burns, CLE ... 4
- M. McManus, SL ... 4
- H. Pennock, NY ... 4
- B. Bengough, NY ... 2
- H. Ehmke, BOS ... 2
- L. Gehrig, NY ... 2
- I. Boone, BOS ... 1
- J. Dugan, NY ... 1
- P. Todt, BOS ... 1

1926 NATIONAL

- B. O'Farrell, SL ... 79
- H. Critz, CIN ... 60
- R. Kremer, PIT ... 32
- T. Thevenow, SL ... 30
- H. Wilson, CHI ... 25
- L. Bell, SL ... 24
- B. Hargrave, CIN ... 24
- F. Rhem, SL ... 20
- F. Lindstrom, NY ... 17
- D. Bancroft, BOS ... 17
- H. Carlson, PHI ... 16
- P. Waner, PIT ... 15
- P. Traynor, PIT ... 14
- W. Pipp, CIN ... 12
- E. Brown, BOS ... 10
- F. Herman, BKN ... 8
- C. Root, CHI ... 8
- R. Hornsby, SL ... 7
- J. Butler, BKN ... 5
- B. Southworth, SL ... 5
- G. Alexander, SL ... 5
- C. Mays, CIN ... 4
- G. Kelly, NY ... 2
- C. Walker, CIN ... 1

1926 AMERICAN

- G. Burns, CLE ... 63
- J. Mostil, CHI ... 33
- H. Pennock, NY ... 32
- S. Rice, WAS ... 18
- H. Heilmann, DET ... 16
- H. Manush, DET ... 16
- A. Simmons, PHI ... 16
- L. Grove, PHI ... 12
- G. Goslin, WAS ... 9
- L. Gehrig, NY ... 7
- T. Lazzeri, NY ... 7
- B. Falk, CHI ... 6
- F. Fothergill, DET ... 6
- H. Rice, SL ... 6
- O. Bluege, WAS ... 5
- P. Todt, BOS ... 5
- M. Cochrane, PHI ... 4
- M. McManus, SL ... 4
- B. Meusel, NY ... 3
- E. Rigney, BOS ... 3
- I. Flagstead, BOS ... 2
- W. Gerber, SL ... 2
- T. Zachary, SL ... 2
- W. Jacobson, BOS ... 1

1927 NATIONAL

- P. Waner, PIT ... 72
- F. Frisch, SL ... 66
- R. Hornsby, NY ... 54
- C. Root, CHI ... 46
- T. Jackson, NY ... 42
- L. Waner, PIT ... 25
- P. Traynor, PIT ... 18
- J. Haines, SL ... 16
- R. Kremer, PIT ... 14
- G. Hartnett, CHI ... 12
- R. Lucas, CIN ... 10
- H. Wilson, CHI ... 9
- B. Terry, NY ... 6
- J. Bottomley, SL ... 6
- J. Hargrave, CIN ... 6
- C. Williams, PHI ... 6
- E. Farrell, BOS ... 4
- B. Grimes, NY ... 4
- M. Carey, BKN ... 3
- R. Stephenson, CHI ... 3
- G. Alexander, SL ... 3
- C. Hill, PIT ... 2
- J. Petty, BKN ... 2
- F. Ulrich, PHI ... 2
- C. Hafey, SL ... 1

1927 AMERICAN

- L. Gehrig, NY ... 56
- H. Heilmann, DET ... 35
- T. Lyons, CHI ... 34
- M. Cochrane, PHI ... 18
- A. Simmons, PHI ... 18
- G. Goslin, WAS ... 15
- M. Ruel, WAS ... 15
- J. Dykes, PHI ... 14
- J. Sewell, CLE ... 13
- J. Sewell, CLE ... 9
- T. Lazzeri, NY ... 8
- R. Reeves, WAS ... 6
- F. O'Rourke, SL ... 6
- J. Tavener, DET ... 6
- E. Miller, SL ... 5
- A. Metzler, CHI ... 4
- I. Flagstead, BOS ... 3
- C. Jamieson, CLE ... 3
- W. Schang, SL ... 3
- F. Schulte, SL ... 3
- W. Hudlin, CLE ... 2
- W. Regan, BOS ... 2
- J. Rothrock, BOS ... 2
- B. Harriss, BOS ... 1
- P. Todt, BOS ... 1

1928 NATIONAL

- J. Bottomley, SL ... 76
- F. Lindstrom, NY ... 70
- B. Grimes, PIT ... 53
- L. Benton, NY ... 37
- H. Critz, CIN ... 37
- P. Traynor, PIT ... 28
- H. Wilson, CHI ... 21
- S. Hogan, NY ... 17
- T. Jackson, NY ... 16
- R. Maranville, SL ... 14
- D. Vance, BKN ... 13
- C. Hafey, SL ... 11
- R. Hornsby, BOS ... 10
- G. Hartnett, CHI ... 6
- P. Waner, PIT ... 5
- R. Richbourg, BOS ... 5
- T. Douthit, SL ... 5
- D. Bissonette, BKN ... 3
- D. Flowers, BKN ... 3
- J. Wilson, SL ... 3
- A. Whitney, PHI ... 3
- H. Ford, CIN ... 2
- L. Thompson, PHI ... 1

1928 AMERICAN

- M. Cochrane, PHI ... 53
- H. Manush, SL ... 51
- J. Judge, WAS ... 27
- T. Lazzeri, NY ... 27
- W. Kamm, CHI ... 15
- G. Goslin, WAS ... 13
- E. Combs, NY ... 13
- C. Gehringer, DET ... 12
- C. Myer, BOS ... 11
- W. Hoyt, NY ... 8
- J. Foxx, PHI ... 7
- J. Sewell, CLE ... 6
- L. Sewell, CLE ... 6
- I. Flagstead, BOS ... 5
- E. Morris, BOS ... 4

H. Heilmann, DET ... 4
C. Lind, CLE ... 4
W. Cissell, CHI ... 4
A. Thomas, CHI ... 4
O. Carroll, DET ... 3
H. Rice, DET ... 3
L. Fonseca, CLE ... 2
T. Lyons, CHI ... 2
J. Hodapp, CLE ... 2
A. Metzler, CHI ... 1
W. Regan, BOS ... 1

1929 NATIONAL
R. Hornsby, CHI ... 60
L. O'Doul, PHI ... 54
B. Terry, NY ... 48
B. Grimes, PIT ... 35
L. Waner, PIT ... 30
R. Lucas, CIN ... 29
P. Traynor, PIT ... 27
H. Wilson, CHI ... 24
F. Herman, BKN ... 24
G. Bush, CHI ... 16
C. Klein, PHI ... 15
M. Ott, NY ... 15
T. Douthit, SL ... 14
C. Grimm, CHI ... 13
T. Jackson, NY ... 8
R. Maranville, BOS ... 8
H. Critz, CIN ... 5
B. Friberg, PHI ... 4
P. Malone, CHI ... 3
F. Frisch, SL ... 2
P. Whitney, PHI ... 2
J. Frederick, BKN ... 2
R. Stephenson, CHI 1
Z. Taylor, BOS-CHI ... 1

(There were no official selections for the American League in 1929 or for either league in 1930.)

MVP Award
Baseball Writers' Association of America Awards, 1931-Present

1931 NATIONAL
F. Frisch, SL ... 65
C. Klein, PHI ... 55
B. Terry, NY ... 53
W. English, CHI ... 30
C. Hafey, SL ... 29
J. Wilson, SL ... 28
T. Jackson, NY ... 24
C. Grimm, CHI ... 21
E. Adams, SL ... 18
E. Brandt, BOS ... 15
R. Maranville, BOS ... 15
K. Cuyler, CHI ... 14
P. Traynor, PIT ... 12
R. Lucas, CIN ... 10
L. Waner, PIT ... 8
J. Bottomley, SL ... 8
J. Elliott, PHI ... 6
J. Quinn, BKN ... 6
N. Finn, BKN ... 5
W. Clark, BKN ... 3
P. Derringer, SL ... 3
C. Root, CHI ... 3
D. Bartell, PHI ... 2
J. Vergez, NY ... 2
F. Fitzsimmons, NY ... 1
L. O'Doul, BKN ... 1
G. Wright, BKN ... 1
T. Cuccinello, CIN ... 1
C. Gelbert, SL ... 1

1931 AMERICAN
L. Grove, PHI ... 78
L. Gehrig, NY ... 59
A. Simmons, PHI ... 51
E. Averill, CLE ... 43
B. Ruth, NY ... 40
E. Webb, BOS ... 22
J. Cronin, WAS ... 18
O. Melillo, SL ... 17
S. West, WAS ... 16
M. Cochrane, PHI ... 16
G. Earnshaw, PHI ... 12
W. Ferrell, CLE ... 12
F. Marberry, WAS ... 11
H. Rhyne, BOS ... 10
B. Chapman, NY ... 7
J. Stone, DET ... 6
C. Gehringer, DET ... 4
L. Blue, DET ... 4
R. Kress, SL ... 3
C. Reynolds, CHI ... 2
W. Stewart, SL ... 2
G. Goslin, SL ... 2
D. MacFayden, BOS ... 2
T. Oliver, BOS ... 2
J. Foxx, PHI ... 1

1932 NATIONAL
C. Klein, PHI ... 78
L. Warneke, CHI ... 68
L. O'Doul, BKN ... 58
P. Waner, PIT ... 37
R. Stephenson, CHI 32
B. Terry, NY ... 25
D. Hurst, PHI ... 24
P. Traynor, PIT ... 17
B. Herman, CHI ... 16
M. Ott, NY ... 15
R. Brown, BOS ... 10
F. Herman, CIN ... 8
L. Waner, PIT ... 6
W. Berger, BOS ... 6
H. Wilson, BKN ... 6
E. Orsatti, SL ... 6
R. Maranville, BOS ... 5
J. Wilson, SL ... 5
T. Cuccinello, BKN ... 4
J. Dean, SL ... 4
F. Frisch, SL ... 3
R. Collins, SL ... 3
A. Vaughan, PIT ... 1
G. Bush, CHI ... 1

1932 AMERICAN
J. Foxx, PHI ... 75
L. Gehrig, NY ... 55
H. Manush, WAS ... 41
E. Averill, CLE ... 37
L. Gomez, NY ... 27
J. Cronin, WAS ... 26
B. Ruth, NY ... 26
T. Lazzeri, NY ... 21
A. Simmons, PHI ... 13
C. Gehringer, DET ... 13
D. Alexander, DET-BOS ... 10
W. Cissell, CLE ... 10
R. Ferrell, SL ... 9
L. Grove, PHI ... 8
J. Allen, NY ... 8
B. Dickey, NY ... 8
G. Goslin, SL ... 7
M. Weaver, WAS ... 6
H. Davis, DET ... 5
D. Harris, WAS ... 5
W. Ferrell, CLE ... 5
J. Levey, SL ... 5
T. Lyons, CHI ... 5
B. Sullivan, CHI ... 3
E. McNair, PHI ... 3
S. Jolley, BOS ... 3
G. Crowder, WAS ... 2
M. McManus, BOS ... 2
G. Walker, DET ... 1
J. Sewell, NY ... 1

1933 NATIONAL
C. Hubbell, NY ... 77
C. Klein, PHI ... 48
W. Berger, BOS ... 44
B. Terry, NY ... 35
P. Martin, SL ... 31
G. Mancuso, NY ... 24
J. Dean, SL ... 23
P. Traynor, PIT ... 20
B. Ryan, NY ... 19
A. Lopez, BKN ... 18
B. Cantwell, BOS ... 18
H. Schumacher, NY ... 11
R. Maranville, BOS ... 11
G. Bush, CHI ... 11
L. French, PIT ... 10
F. Frisch, SL ... 7
J. Bottomley, CIN ... 6
J. Medwick, SL ... 5
G. Hartnett, CHI ... 5
L. Warneke, CHI ... 4
R. Lucas, CIN ... 3
D. Bartell, PHI ... 3
A. Vaughan, PIT ... 2
R. Moore, BOS ... 2
V. Davis, PHI ... 1
C. Hafey, CIN ... 1
D. Luque, NY ... 1

1933 AMERICAN
J. Foxx, PHI ... 74
J. Cronin, WAS ... 62
H. Manush, WAS ... 54
L. Gehrig, NY ... 39
L. Grove, PHI ... 35
C. Gehringer, DET ... 32
G. Crowder, WAS ... 28
A. Simmons, CHI ... 19
E. Whitehill, WAS ... 18
O. Melillo, SL ... 12
S. West, SL ... 11
R. Ferrell, BOS ... 9
B. Dickey, NY ... 9
T. Lazzeri, NY ... 6
J. Kuhel, WAS ... 5
E. Averill, CLE ... 5
C. Myer, WAS ... 5
M. Cochrane, PHI ... 5
B. Johnson, PHI ... 5
B. Chapman, NY ... 4
M. Bishop, PHI ... 1
L. Appling, CHI ... 1
W. Kamm, CLE ... 1

1934 NATIONAL
J. Dean, SL ... 78
P. Waner, PIT ... 50
J. Moore, NY ... 42
T. Jackson, NY ... 39
M. Ott, NY ... 37
J. Collins, SL ... 32
B. Terry, NY ... 30
C. Davis, PHI ... 18
P. Dean, SL ... 16
H. Schumacher, NY ... 16
C. Hubbell, NY ... 16
W. Berger, BOS ... 13
L. Warneke, CHI ... 10
G. Hartnett, CHI ... 9
G. Slade, CIN ... 5
K. Cuyler, CHI ... 4
B. Frey, CIN ... 4
F. Frankhouse, BOS ... 4
R. Boyle, BKN ... 4
B. Herman, CHI ... 4
F. Frisch, SL ... 4
W. Hoyt, PIT ... 2
A. Lopez, BKN ... 1
V. Mungo, BKN ... 1
A. Vaughan, PIT ... 1

1934 AMERICAN
M. Cochrane, DET ... 67
C. Gehringer, DET ... 65
L. Gomez, NY ... 60
S. Rowe, DET ... 59
L. Gehrig, NY ... 54
H. Greenberg, DET ... 29
H. Trosky, CLE ... 18
W. Ferrell, BOS ... 16
M. Owen, DET ... 13
J. Foxx, PHI ... 11
A. Simmons, CHI ... 9
W. Werber, BOS ... 8
R. Johnson, BOS ... 8
G. Goslin, DET ... 6
S. West, SL ... 5
M. Harder, CLE ... 4
F. Higgins, PHI ... 3
E. Averill, CLE ... 3
B. Knickerbocker, CLE ... 2

1935 NATIONAL
G. Hartnett, CHI ... 75
J. Dean, SL ... 66
A. Vaughan, PIT ... 45
B. Herman, CHI ... 38
J. Medwick, SL ... 37
C. Hubbell, NY ... 20
W. Berger, BOS ... 20
B. Terry, NY ... 20
A. Galan, CHI ... 18
P. Martin, SL ... 16
H. Leiber, NY ... 11
L. Warneke, CHI ... 9
E. Lombardi, CIN ... 8
F. Frisch, SL ... 7
C. Blanton, PIT ... 5
J. Moore, PHI ... 5
E. Allen, PHI ... 4
G. Mancuso, NY ... 4
P. Derringer, CIN ... 4
M. Ott, NY ... 3
P. Dean, SL ... 2
R. Collins, SL ... 2
C. Davis, PHI ... 2
P. Waner, PIT ... 1
B. Lee, CHI ... 1
T. Jackson, NY ... 1
D. Camilli, PHI ... 1

1935 AMERICAN
H. Greenberg, DET ... 80
W. Ferrell, BOS ... 62
J. Vosmik, CLE ... 39
C. Myer, WAS ... 36
L. Gehrig, NY ... 29
C. Gehringer, DET ... 26
M. Cochrane, DET ... 24
R. Cramer, PHI ... 18
J. Solters, SL ... 16
R. Hemsley, SL ... 16
J. Foxx, PHI ... 11
T. Bridges, DET ... 11
T. Lyons, CHI ... 10
L. Grove, BOS ... 8
Z. Bonura, CHI ... 7
L. Appling, CHI ... 7
L. Sewell, CHI ... 7
J. Allen, NY ... 5
J. Whitehead, CHI ... 4
F. Higgins, PHI ... 3
J. Marcum, PHI ... 3
E. Auker, DET ... 2
M. Harder, CLE ... 2
L. Lary, SL ... 1

1936 NATIONAL
C. Hubbell, NY ... 60
J. Dean, SL ... 53
B. Herman, CHI ... 37
J. Medwick, SL ... 30
P. Waner, PIT ... 29
M. Ott, NY ... 28
F. Demaree, CHI ... 17
G. Mancuso, NY ... 13
D. MacFayden, BOS ... 12
L. Durocher, SL ... 8
P. Derringer, CIN ... 6
G. Hartnett, CHI ... 6
B. Whitehead, NY ... 6
A. Lopez, BOS ... 5
V. Mungo, BKN ... 5
W. Berger, BOS ... 4
D. Camilli, PHI ... 4
G. Phelps, BKN ... 3
D. Bartell, NY ... 2
E. Lombardi, CIN ... 1
T. Moore, SL ... 1

1936 AMERICAN
L. Gehrig, NY ... 73
L. Appling, CHI ... 65
E. Averill, CLE ... 48
C. Gehringer, DET ... 39
B. Dickey, NY ... 29
V. Kennedy, CHI ... 27
J. Kuhel, WAS ... 27
J. DiMaggio, NY ... 26
T. Bridges, DET ... 25
H. Trosky, CLE ... 19
J. Foxx, BOS ... 16
G. Walker, DET ... 14
B. Bell, SL ... 10
W. Moses, PHI ... 7
L. Grove, BOS ... 5
J. Dykes, CHI ... 3
R. Radcliff, CHI ... 3
S. West, SL ... 2
Z. Bonura, CHI ... 1
E. McNair, BOS ... 1

1937 NATIONAL
J. Medwick, SL ... 70
G. Hartnett, CHI ... 68
C. Hubbell, NY ... 52
J. Turner, BOS ... 30
L. Fette, BOS ... 29
D. Bartell, NY ... 26
M. Ott, NY ... 24
P. Waner, PIT ... 21
B. Herman, CHI ... 19
J. Mize, SL ... 18
C. Melton, NY ... 17
C. Root, CHI ... 15
P. Whitney, PHI ... 13
H. Danning, NY ... 10
F. Demaree, CHI ... 9
L. Warneke, SL ... 6
B. Jurges, CHI ... 4
J. Cooney, BKN ... 4
B. Myers, CIN ... 2
L. Grissom, CIN ... 2
H. Manush, BKN ... 1

1937 AMERICAN
C. Gehringer, DET ... 78
J. DiMaggio, NY ... 74
H. Greenberg, DET ... 48
L. Gehrig, NY ... 42
L. Sewell, CHI ... 22
B. Dickey, NY ... 22
J. Cronin, BOS ... 19
R. Ruffing, NY ... 18
L. Gomez, NY ... 14
M. Kreevich, CHI ... 13
C. Travis, WAS ... 12
W. Moses, PHI ... 12
J. Allen, CLE ... 11
H. Clift, SL ... 11
R. Radcliff, CHI ... 10
B. Lewis, WAS ... 7
L. Appling, CHI ... 5
B. Bell, SL ... 5
E. Averill, CLE ... 4
L. Lary, CLE ... 4
R. Lawson, DET ... 4
G. Walker, DET ... 3
R. York, DET ... 1
P. Fox, DET ... 1

1938 NATIONAL
E. Lombardi, CIN ... 229
B. Lee, CHI ... 166
A. Vaughan, PIT ... 163
M. Ott, NY ... 132
F. McCormick, CIN ... 130
J. Rizzo, PIT ... 96
S. Hack, CHI ... 87
P. Derringer, CIN ... 70
M. Brown, PIT ... 62
G. Hartnett, CHI ... 61
J. Medwick, SL ... 55
J. Mize, SL ... 28
T. Cuccinello, BOS ... 23
P. Young, PIT ... 19
C. Bryant, CHI ... 16
H. Danning, NY ... 13
I. Goodman, CIN ... 11
J. VanderMeer, CIN ... 6
L. Durocher, BKN ... 6
D. Coffman, NY ... 6
A. Lopez, BOS ... 5
L. Waner, PIT ... 5
D. Garms, BOS ... 5
D. Camilli, BKN ... 5
C. Root, CHI ... 3
J. Moore, NY ... 3
J. Hudson, BKN ... 3
H. Mulcahy, PHI ... 3
L. Handley, PIT ... 2
L. Warneke, SL ... 1
F. Fitzsimmons, BKN ... 1
H. Martin, PHI ... 1

1938 AMERICAN
J. Foxx, BOS ... 305
B. Dickey, NY ... 196
H. Greenberg, DET ... 162
R. Ruffing, NY ... 146
B. Newsom, SL ... 111
J. DiMaggio, NY ... 106
J. Cronin, BOS ... 92
E. Averill, CLE ... 34
C. Travis, WAS ... 33
C. Gehringer, DET ... 27
J. Heath, CLE ... 24
J. Gordon, NY ... 23
H. Trosky, CLE ... 22
K. Keltner, CLE ... 16
M. Stratton, CHI ... 15
M. Harder, CLE ... 14
B. Johnson, PHI ... 13
H. Clift, SL ... 11
L. Gehrig, NY ... 10
P. Fox, DET ... 9
J. Vosmik, BOS ... 7
G. McQuinn, SL ... 7
L. Grove, BOS ... 7
B. Lewis, WAS ... 5
R. Rolfe, NY ... 5
C. Myer, WAS ... 5
E. Brucker, PHI ... 5
J. Allen, CLE ... 3
F. Crosetti, NY ... 2
L. Gomez, NY ... 1
D. Cramer, BOS ... 1

1939 NATIONAL
B. Walters, CIN ... 303
J. Mize, SL ... 178
P. Derringer, CIN ... 174
F. McCormick, CIN ... 159
C. Davis, SL ... 106
J. Brown, SL ... 99
J. Medwick, SL ... 81
L. Durocher, BKN ... 52
H. Danning, NY ... 33
L. Hamlin, BKN ... 32
M. Ott, NY ... 21
B. Jurges, NY ... 20
D. Camilli, BKN ... 20
W. Myers, CIN ... 18
S. Hack, CHI ... 17
A. Galan, CHI ... 15
T. Moore, SL ... 15
M. Arnovich, PHI ... 10
L. Frey, CIN ... 8
B. Lee, CHI ... 8
E. Slaughter, SL ... 8
W. Werber, CIN ... 6
M. West, BOS ... 5
G. Hartnett, CHI ... 5
I. Goodman, CIN ... 4
B. Hassett, BOS ... 4
P. Coscarart, BKN ... 4
E. Fletcher, BOS-PIT ... 4
C. Lavagetto, BKN ... 3

P. Lowrey, CHI 2
E. Miller, CIN 2
A. Pafko, CHI 1

1947 AMERICAN
J. DiMaggio, NY . . 202
T. Williams, BOS . . 201
L. Boudreau, CLE . 168
J. Page, NY 167
G. Kell, DET 132
G. McQuinn, NY . . . 77
J. Gordon, CLE 59
B. Feller, CLE 58
P. Marchildon, PHI . . 47
L. Appling, CHI 43
E. Joost, PHI 35
B. McCosky, PHI . . . 35
T. Henrich, NY 33
F. Shea, NY 23
Y. Berra, NY 18
A. Reynolds, NY . . . 18
B. Dillinger, SL 13
J. Pesky, BOS 11
F. Fain, PHI 9
W. Johnson, NY 9
S. Spence, WAS 9
F. Hutchison, DET . . . 8
E. Wynn, WAS 7
B. Doerr, BOS 6
B. Rosar, PHI 6
M. Christman, WAS . . 4
B. McCahan, PHI 4
D. Mitchell, CLE 4
R. Cullenbine, DET . . 3
J. Dobson, BOS 3
J. Heath, SL 1
E. Lopat, CHI 1
V. Stephens, SL 1
T. Wright, CHI 1

1948 NATIONAL
S. Musial, SL 303
J. Sain, BOS 223
A. Dark, BOS 174
S. Gordon, NY 72
H. Brecheen, SL . . . 61
P. Reese, BKN 60
R. Kiner, PIT 55
E. Slaughter, SL 55
D. Murtaugh, PIT . . . 52
S. Rojek, PIT 51
R. Ashburn, PHI . . . 48
J. Schmitz, CHI 37
R. Elliott, BOS 33
W. Spahn, BOS 31
J. Robinson, BKN . . 30
A. Pafko, CHI 25
J. Mize, NY 22
R. Barney, BKN 15
J. VanderMeer, CIN . 13
J. Wyrostek, CIN 9
R. Branca, BKN 8
R. Campanella, BKN . 8
B. Chesnes, PIT 8
P. Cavaretta, CHI 6
E. Miller, PHI 4
D. Ennis, PHI 3
G. Hatton, CIN 3
L. Jansen, NY 2
D. Walker, PIT 2
G. Hodges, BKN 1
W. Lockman, NY 1
H. Sauer, CIN 1

1948 AMERICAN
L. Boudreau, CLE . 324
J. DiMaggio, NY . . 213
T. Williams, BOS . . 171
V. Stephens, BOS . . 121
B. Lemon, CLE . . . 101
J. Gordon, CLE 63
T. Henrich, NY 63
G. Bearden, CLE . . . 52
H. Newhouser, DET . 48
E. Joost, PHI 39
H. Majeski, PHI 23
B. Tebbetts, BOS . . . 23
V. Raschi, NY 23
K. Keltner, CLE 18
G. Priddy, SL 16
G. Kell, DET 14
W. Evers, DET 13
A. Zarilla, SL 11
B. Doerr, BOS 10
B. Dillinger, SL 10
J. Hegan, CLE 10
L. Appling, CHI 8
B. Feller, CLE 6
L. Brissie, PHI 5
F. Fain, PHI 5
J. Dobson, BOS 5
B. Goodman, BOS . . 4
B. McCosky, PHI 4
Y. Berra, NY 3
D. DiMaggio, BOS . . . 3
L. Doby, CLE 3
C. Fannin, SL 2
P. Mullin, DET 1
P. Rizzuto, NY 1

1949 NATIONAL
J. Robinson, BKN . 264
S. Musial, SL 226
E. Slaughter, SL . . . 181
R. Kiner, PIT 133
P. Reese, BKN 118
C. Furillo, BKN 68
W. Spahn, BOS 60
D. Newcombe, BKN 55
K. Heintzelman, PHI 48
R. Schoendienst, SL 30
G. Hodges, BKN . . . 29
H. Pollet, SL 29
D. Ennis, PHI 28
B. Thomson, NY . . . 25
R. Campanella, BKN 22
P. Roe, BKN 21
G. Hamner, PHI 9
W. Lockman, NY 9
R. Meyer, PHI 8
K. Raffensberger, CIN 8
H. Sauer, CHI 8
T. Wilks, SL 8
R. Ashburn, PHI 6
J. Schmitz, CHI 6
A. Dark, BOS 3
M. Marion, SL 3
W. Jones, PHI 2
W. Marshall, NY 2
E. Torgeson, BOS . . . 2
S. Gordon, NY 1
D. Sisler, PHI 1

1949 AMERICAN
T. Williams, BOS . . 272
P. Rizzuto, NY 175
J. Page, NY 166
M. Parnell, BOS . . . 151
E. Kinder, BOS . . . 122
T. Henrich, NY 121
V. Stephens, BOS . 100
G. Kell, DET 80
B. Lemon, CLE 57
V. Wertz, DET 51
V. Raschi, NY 19
J. DiMaggio, NY . . . 18
E. Joost, PHI 11
L. Boudreau, CLE . . 10
Y. Berra, NY 9
D. DiMaggio, BOS . . . 7
B. Doerr, BOS 7
A. Kellner, PHI 6
E. Robinson, WAS . . . 6
R. Sievers, SL 6
B. Tebbetts, BOS 6
L. Appling, CHI 3
A. Houtteman, DET . . 3
J. Priddy, SL 3
V. Trucks, DET 3
D. Mitchell, CLE 2
A. Reynolds, NY 2

1950 NATIONAL
J. Konstanty, PHI . . 286
S. Musial, SL 158
E. Stanky, NY 144
D. Ennis, PHI 104
R. Kiner, PIT 91
G. Hamner, PHI 79
R. Roberts, PHI 68
G. Hodges, BKN . . . 55
D. Snider, BKN 53
S. Maglie, NY 51
E. Blackwell, CIN . . . 41
A. Pafko, CHI 38
R. Campanella, BKN 29
A. Seminick, PHI . . . 25
J. Robinson, BKN . . 23
C. Simmons, PHI . . . 22
P. Roe, BKN 15
T. Kluszewski, CIN . . 14
W. Spahn, BOS 14
D. Newcombe, BKN 14
J. Sain, BOS 12
S. Gordon, BOS . . . 11
J. Hearn, NY 10
P. Reese, BKN 8
E. Waitkus, PHI 8
R. Elliott, BOS 8
E. Torgeson, BOS . . . 6
S. Jethroe, BOS 6
H. Sauer, CHI 5
V. Bickford, BOS 4
C. Furillo, BKN 4
W. Westrum, NY 3
D. Sisler, PHI 2
H. Thompson, NY . . . 2
L. Jansen, NY 2
W. Jones, PHI 1

1950 AMERICAN
P. Rizzuto, NY 284
B. Goodman, BOS 180
Y. Berra, NY 146
G. Kell, DET 127
B. Lemon, CLE . . . 102
W. Dropo, BOS 75
V. Raschi, NY 63
L. Doby, CLE 57
J. DiMaggio, NY . . . 54
V. Wertz, DET 50
W. Evers, DET 38
C. Carrasquel, CHI . 21
D. Trout, DET 21
D. DiMaggio, BOS . . 17
I. Noren, WAS 16
B. Doerr, BOS 15
J. Mize, NY 11
J. Priddy, DET 11
A. Rosen, CLE 11
E. Yost, WAS 8
M. Parnell, BOS 7
W. Ford, NY 7
T. Williams, BOS 7
N. Garver, SL 6
V. Stephens, BOS . . . 6
A. Houtteman, DET . . 6
S. Lollar, SL 4
E. Lopat, NY 3
K. Wood, SL 2
S. Dente, WAS 1
D. Philley, CHI 1

1951 NATIONAL
R. Campanella, BKN 243
S. Musial, SL 191
M. Irvin, NY 166
S. Maglie, NY 153
P. Roe, BKN 138
J. Robinson, BKN . . 92
R. Ashburn, PHI . . . 69
B. Thomson, NY . . . 62
M. Dickson, PIT 59
R. Kiner, PIT 49
W. Spahn, BOS 45
A. Dark, NY 30
R. Roberts, PHI 27
L. Jansen, NY 26
P. Reese, BKN 15
G. Hodges, BKN . . . 10
S. Gordon, BOS . . . 10
K. Raffensberger, CIN 8
J. Wyrostek, CIN 6
E. Blackwell, CIN 6
C. Furillo, BKN 6
D. Newcombe, BKN . 3
P. Cavaretta, CHI 1
H. Sauer, CHI 1

1951 AMERICAN
Y. Berra, NY 184
N. Garver, SL 157
A. Reynolds, NY . . . 125
M. Minoso, CHI . . . 120
B. Feller, CLE 118
F. Fain, PHI 103
E. Kinder, BOS 66
V. Raschi, NY 64
G. McDougald, NY . 63
B. Avila, CLE 49
P. Rizzuto, NY 47
E. Lopat, NY 44
T. Williams, BOS . . . 35
E. Joost, PHI 32
G. Kell, DET 30
E. Wynn, CLE 29
N. Fox, CHI 25
B. Goodman, BOS . 21
D. DiMaggio, BOS . . 16
G. Zernial, CHI-PHI . 15
B. Shantz, PHI 14
M. Garcia, CLE 11
G. Coan, WAS 8
M. Parnell, BOS 7
E. Robinson, CHI 7
G. Woodling, NY 5
J. Pesky, BOS 5
I. Noren, WAS 4
D. Mitchell, CLE 4
V. Trucks, DET 2
E. Yost, WAS 2
J. Busby, CHI 2
J. Mize, NY 2

1952 NATIONAL
H. Sauer, CHI 226
R. Roberts, PHI . . . 211
J. Black, BKN 208
H. Wilhelm, NY . . . 133
S. Musial, SL 127
E. Slaughter, SL 92
J. Robinson, BKN . . 31
P. Reese, BKN 29
D. Snider, BKN 29
R. Campanella, BKN 25
R. Schoendienst, SL 25
A. Dark, NY 24
M. Dickson, PIT 22
D. Ennis, PHI 18
W. Lockman, NY . . . 18
B. Thomson, NY . . . 17
F. Baumholtz, CHI . . 16
T. Kluszewski, CIN . . 16
G. Hodges, BKN . . . 15
R. McMillan, CIN . . . 15
E. Mathews, BOS . . . 13
B. Adams, CIN 9
B. Cox, BKN 8
W. Hacker, CHI 8
R. Kiner, PIT 8
S. Maglie, NY 8
K. Raffensberger, CIN 8
W. Spahn, BOS 8
P. Roe, BKN 7
S. Gordon, BOS 6
G. Hamner, PHI 5
S. Hemus, SL 5
M. Irvin, NY 5
G. Shuba, BKN 5
E. Yuhas, SL 5
A. Brazle, SL 3
J. Logan, BOS 3
T. Atwell, CHI 2
C. Metkovich, PIT . . . 2
W. Cooper, BOS 1

1952 AMERICAN
B. Shantz, PHI 280
A. Reynolds, NY . . 183
M. Mantle, NY 143
Y. Berra, NY 104
E. Wynn, CLE 99
F. Fain, PHI 66
N. Fox, CHI 59
B. Lemon, CLE 58
M. Garcia, CLE 52
A. Rosen, CLE 51
E. Robinson, CHI . . . 47
L. Doby, CLE 46
L. Easter, CLE 40
P. Rizzuto, NY 33
E. Joost, PHI 20
B. Goodman, BOS . 18
J. Jensen, NY-WAS . 12
S. Paige, SL 12
V. Raschi, NY 12
D. Mitchell, CLE 11
H. Bauer, NY 10
G. Woodling, NY . . . 10
P. Runnels, WAS 8
C. Courtney, SL 7
D. Gernert, BOS 6
W. Dropo, DET 5
S. Rogovin, CHI 4
S. White, BOS 4
B. Avila, CLE 3
B. Pierce, CHI 3
J. Sain, NY 3
B. Young, SL 3
J. Collins, NY 2
C. Marrero, WAS 1
B. Porterfield, WAS . . 1

1953 NATIONAL
R. Campanella, BKN 297
E. Mathews, MIL . . 216
D. Snider, BKN . . . 157
R. Schoendienst, SL 155
W. Spahn, MIL 120
R. Roberts, PHI . . . 106
T. Kluszewski, CIN . . 69
S. Musial, SL 62
C. Erskine, BKN . . . 54
C. Furillo, BKN 54
P. Reese, BKN 27
J. Robinson, BKN . . 19
D. Ennis, PHI 14
G. Hodges, BKN . . . 13
M. Irvin, NY 11
D. O'Connell, PIT . . . 10
H. Haddix, SL 9
F. Thomas, PIT 6
R. Ashburn, PHI 5
G. Bell, CIN 3
J. Logan, MIL 3
R. Gomez, NY 2
G. Hamner, PHI 2
D. Crandall, MIL 1
H. Thompson, NY . . . 1

1953 AMERICAN
A. Rosen, CLE 336
Y. Berra, NY 167
M. Vernon, WAS . . 162
M. Minoso, CHI . . . 100
V. Trucks, CHI 81
P. Rizzuto, NY 76
B. Porterfield, WAS . 64
R. Boone, CLE-DET 59
J. Piersall, BOS 56
B. Pierce, CHI 55
E. Kinder, BOS 41
H. Bauer, NY 37
A. Reynolds, NY . . . 37
M. Parnell, BOS 27
H. Kuenn, DET 23
B. Lemon, CLE 22
E. Lopat, NY 18
G. Zernial, PHI 16
D. Philley, PHI 11
W. Ford, NY 8
B. Goodman, BOS . . 5
M. Mantle, NY 4
G. Woodling, NY 3
E. Yost, WAS 3
B. Martin, NY 2
C. Carrasquel, CHI . . 1
G. Kell, BOS 1
T. Williams, BOS 1

1954 NATIONAL
W. Mays, NY 283
T. Kluszewski, CIN 217
J. Antonelli, NY . . . 154
D. Snider, BKN . . . 135
A. Dark, NY 110
S. Musial, SL 97
R. Roberts, PHI 70
J. Adcock, MIL 60
P. Reese, BKN 53
G. Hodges, BKN 40
W. Spahn, MIL 38
D. Mueller, NY 30
R. Schoendienst, SL 24
F. Thomas, PIT 24
H. Wilhelm, NY 17
E. Banks, CHI 14
D. Crandall, MIL . . . 13
J. Logan, MIL 9
E. Mathews, MIL 5
G. Hamner, PHI 5
R. Ashburn, PHI 5
S. Maglie, NY 4
G. Conley, MIL 3
M. Grissom, NY 2
R. McMillan, CIN 2
D. Rhodes, NY 1
H. Sauer, CHI 1

1954 AMERICAN
Y. Berra, NY 230
L. Doby, CLE 210
B. Avila, CLE 203
M. Minoso, CHI . . . 186
B. Lemon, CLE . . . 179
E. Wynn, CLE 72
T. Williams, BOS . . . 65
H. Kuenn, DET 37
M. Vernon, WAS . . . 30
N. Fox, CHI 30
B. Grim, NY 25
J. Finigan, PHI 19
V. Trucks, CHI 19
J. Jensen, BOS 17
M. Mantle, NY 16
I. Noren, NY 16
A. Rosen, CLE 16
J. Busby, WAS 7
J. Coleman, BAL 6
B. Goodman, BOS . . 6
M. Garcia, CLE 6
J. Hegan, CLE 5
H. Bauer, NY 4
A. Kaline, DET 4
B. Turley, BAL 4
S. Gromek, DET 1
C. Abrams, BAL 1
R. Boone, DET 1
R. Sievers, WAS 1

1955 NATIONAL
R. Campanella, BKN 226
D. Snider, BKN . . . 221
E. Banks, CHI . . . 195
W. Mays, NY 165
R. Roberts, PHI . . . 159
T. Kluszewski, CIN 111
D. Newcombe, BKN 89
S. Musial, SL 46
H. Aaron, MIL 36
P. Reese, BKN 36
J. Logan, MIL 24
W. Post, CIN 23
D. Ennis, PHI 21
R. Ashburn, PHI 17
C. Labine, BKN 11
B. Friend, PIT 10
D. Crandall, MIL 8
E. Mathews, MIL 6
D. Long, PIT 3
J. Meyer, PHI 3
G. Baker, CHI 2
C. Furillo, BKN 2
V. Law, PIT 1
F. Thomas, PIT 1

1955 AMERICAN
Y. Berra, NY 218
A. Kaline, DET 201
A. Smith, CLE 200
T. Williams, BOS . . 143
M. Mantle, NY 113
R. Narleski, CLE . . . 90
N. Fox, CHI 84
H. Bauer, NY 64
V. Power, KC 53
J. Jensen, BOS 39

S. Lollar, CHI . . . 37
G. McDougald, NY . 34
B. Klaus, BOS . . . 27
T. Byrne, NY . . . 24
W. Ford, NY . . . 21
R. Boone, DET . . . 16
R. Sievers, WAS . . . 9
H. Kuenn, DET . . . 8
B. Pierce, CHI . . . 8
D. Philley, CLE-BAL . . 6
E. Wynn, CLE . . . 6
E. Valo, KC . . . 5
M. Vernon, WAS . . . 4
B. Hoeft, DET . . . 1
D. Mossi, CLE . . . 1
F. Sullivan, BOS . . . 1
G. Triandos, BAL . . . 1
J. Valdivielso, WAS . . 1
S. White, BOS . . . 1

1956 NATIONAL
D. Newcombe, BKN . . . 223
S. Maglie, BKN . . . 183
H. Aaron, MIL . . . 146
W. Spahn, MIL . . . 126
J. Gilliam, BKN . . . 103
R. McMillan, CIN . . . 96
F. Robinson, CIN . . . 79
P. Reese, BKN . . . 71
S. Musial, SL . . . 62
D. Snider, BKN . . . 55
J. Adcock, MIL . . . 54
B. Friend, PIT . . . 38
H. Freeman, CIN . . . 25
J. Antonelli, NY . . . 18
T. Kluszewski, CIN . . 18
J. Robinson, BKN . . 17
W. Mays, NY . . . 14
E. Bailey, CIN . . . 13
B. Virdon, SL-PIT . . . 13
S. Lopata, PHI . . . 11
C. Furillo, BKN . . . 9
L. Burdette, MIL . . . 8
B. Buhl, MIL . . . 7
R. Roberts, PHI . . . 7
B. Lawrence, CIN . . . 6
D. Long, PIT . . . 4
W. Moon, SL . . . 3
E. Banks, CHI . . . 2
K. Boyer, SL . . . 2
C. Labine, BKN . . . 1
J. Logan, MIL . . . 1
R. Ashburn, PHI . . . 1

1956 AMERICAN
M. Mantle, NY . . . 336
Y. Berra, NY . . . 186
A. Kaline, DET . . . 142
H. Kuenn, DET . . . 80
B. Pierce, CHI . . . 75
T. Williams, BOS . . . 70
B. Nieman, CHI-BAL . . . 55
G. McDougald, NY . 55
V. Wertz, CLE . . . 45
B. Lemon, CLE . . . 40
H. Simpson, KC . . . 37
W. Ford, NY . . . 33
E. Wynn, CLE . . . 32
J. Piersall, BOS . . . 28
N. Fox, CHI . . . 28
S. Lollar, CHI . . . 27
F. Lary, DET . . . 24
P. Runnels, WAS . . . 24
H. Score, CLE . . . 18
J. Jensen, BOS . . . 15
M. Vernon, BOS . . . 14
T. Brewer, BOS . . . 11
H. Bauer, NY . . . 8
C. Maxwell, DET . . . 8
L. Aparicio, CHI . . . 7
G. Triandos, BAL . . . 6
F. Bolling, DET . . . 3
M. Minoso, CHI . . . 3
V. Power, KC . . . 3
J. Kucks, NY . . . 2
R. Sievers, WAS . . . 1

1957 NATIONAL
H. Aaron, MIL . . . 239
S. Musial, SL . . . 230
R. Schoendienst, NY-MIL . . . 221
W. Mays, NY . . . 174
W. Spahn, MIL . . . 131
E. Banks, CHI . . . 60
G. Hodges, BKN . . . 54
E. Mathews, MIL . . . 45
F. Robinson, CIN . . . 42
J. Sanford, PHI . . . 39
D. Hoak, CIN . . . 31
D. Blasingame, SL . . 26
E. Bouchee, PHI . . . 26
B. Buhl, MIL . . . 15
D. Ennis, SL . . . 13
D. Groat, PIT . . . 13
A. Dark, SL . . . 12
D. Snider, BKN . . . 10
F. Thomas, PIT . . . 8
D. Drysdale, BKN . . . 8
R. McMillan, CIN . . . 6
D. Drott, CHI . . . 6
G. Hamner, PHI . . . 3
L. Burdette, MIL . . . 2
J. Logan, MIL . . . 1
H. Anderson, PHI . . . 1

1957 AMERICAN
M. Mantle, NY . . . 233
T. Williams, BOS . . 209
R. Sievers, WAS . . 205
N. Fox, CHI . . . 193
G. McDougald, NY . . . 165
V. Wertz, CLE . . . 61
F. Malzone, BOS . . . 58
M. Minoso, CHI . . . 55
J. Bunning, DET . . . 46
A. Kaline, DET . . . 40
B. Pierce, CHI . . . 35
B. Gardner, BAL . . . 22
D. Donovan, CHI . . . 19
Y. Berra, NY . . . 18
G. Woodling, CLE . . 13
B. Grim, NY . . . 9
B. Boyd, BAL . . . 9
C. Maxwell, DET . . . 5
W. Held, KC . . . 4
W. Ford, NY . . . 4
V. Power, KC . . . 3
J. Piersall, BOS . . . 2
B. Skowron, NY . . . 2
H. Kuenn, DET . . . 2
S. Lollar, CHI . . . 2
T. Kubek, NY . . . 1
B. Shantz, NY . . . 1

1958 NATIONAL
E. Banks, CHI . . . 283
W. Mays, SF . . . 185
H. Aaron, MIL . . . 166
F. Thomas, PIT . . . 143
W. Spahn, MIL . . . 108
B. Friend, PIT . . . 98
R. Ashburn, PHI . . . 62
B. Mazeroski, PIT . . 61
O. Cepeda, SF . . . 57
D. Crandall, MIL . . . 48
L. Burdette, MIL . . . 47
S. Musial, SL . . . 39
K. Boyer, SL . . . 31
J. Temple, CIN . . . 26
B. Skinner, PIT . . . 18
W. Covington, MIL . . 16
E. Face, PIT . . . 8
H. Anderson, PHI . . . 5
J. Gilliam, LA . . . 4
B. Purkey, CIN . . . 4
F. Robinson, CIN . . . 4
J. Adcock, MIL . . . 2
C. Furillo, LA . . . 1

1958 AMERICAN
J. Jensen, BOS . . . 233
B. Turley, NY . . . 191
R. Colavito, CLE . . 181
B. Cerv, KC . . . 164
M. Mantle, NY . . . 127
R. Sievers, WAS . . . 95
T. Williams, BOS . . . 89
N. Fox, CHI . . . 88
S. Lollar, CHI . . . 57
P. Runnels, BOS . . . 29
G. Triandos, BAL . . . 27
D. Hyde, WAS . . . 26
H. Kuenn, DET . . . 24
C. McLish, CLE . . . 18
V. Power, KC-CLE . . 15
F. Bolling, DET . . . 10
E. Howard, NY . . . 9
Y. Berra, NY . . . 6
M. Minoso, CLE . . . 6
A. Kaline, DET . . . 5
G. McDougald, NY . . 5
R. Duren, NY . . . 4
F. Lary, DET . . . 3
J. Harshman, BAL . . . 2
D. Donovan, CHI . . . 1
F. Malzone, BOS . . . 1

1959 NATIONAL
E. Banks, CHI . . 232½
E. Mathews, MIL . . . 189½
H. Aaron, MIL . . . 174
W. Moon, LA . . . 161
S. Jones, SF . . . 130
W. Mays, SF . . . 85
E. Face, PIT . . . 67
C. Neal, LA . . . 64
F. Robinson, CIN . . . 52
K. Boyer, SL . . . 37
D. Crandall, MIL . . . 27
L. Burdette, MIL . . . 14
R. Craig, LA . . . 12
J. Cunningham, SL . 12
V. Pinson, CIN . . . 11
J. Temple, CIN . . . 8
D. Hoak, PIT . . . 6
G. Hodges, LA . . . 4
O. Cepeda, SF . . . 3
V. Law, PIT . . . 3
W. Spahn, MIL . . . 3
G. Conley, PHI . . . 1
W. McCovey, SF . . . 1
D. Snider, LA . . . 1

1959 AMERICAN
N. Fox, CHI . . . 295
L. Aparicio, CHI . . . 255
E. Wynn, CHI . . . 123
R. Colavito, CLE . . . 117
T. Francona, CLE . . 102
A. Kaline, DET . . . 84
J. Landis, CHI . . . 66
H. Kuenn, DET . . . 64
S. Lollar, CHI . . . 44
J. Jensen, BOS . . . 40
C. McLish, CLE . . . 35
Y. Berra, NY . . . 26
M. Minoso, CLE . . . 26
F. Malzone, BOS . . . 24
H. Killebrew, WAS . . 21
G. Woodling, BAL . . 18
M. Mantle, NY . . . 13
B. Richardson, NY . . 11
C. Pascual, WAS . . . 9
B. Shaw, CHI . . . 8
G. Triandos, BAL . . . 8
B. Daley, KC . . . 7
V. Power, CLE . . . 5
B. Tuttle, KC . . . 5
J. Lemon, WAS . . . 4
P. Runnels, BOS . . . 2
T. Williams, BOS . . . 2
B. Allison, WAS . . . 1
G. Staley, CHI . . . 1

1960 NATIONAL
D. Groat, PIT . . . 276
D. Hoak, PIT . . . 162
W. Mays, SF . . . 155
E. Banks, CHI . . . 100
L. McDaniel, SL . . . 95
K. Boyer, SL . . . 80
V. Law, PIT . . . 80
R. Clemente, PIT . . . 62
E. Broglio, SL . . . 58
E. Mathews, MIL . . . 52
H. Aaron, MIL . . . 49
E. Face, PIT . . . 47
D. Crandall, MIL . . . 31
W. Spahn, MIL . . . 27
N. Larker, LA . . . 21
S. Musial, SL . . . 18
M. Wills, LA . . . 7
V. Pinson, CIN . . . 6
J. Adcock, MIL . . . 5
S. Burgess, PIT . . . 2
F. Robinson, CIN . . . 2
L. Sherry, LA . . . 2
P. Herrera, PHI . . . 1

1960 AMERICAN
R. Maris, NY . . . 225
M. Mantle, NY . . . 222
B. Robinson, BAL . 211
M. Minoso, CHI . . . 141
R. Hansen, BAL . . . 110
A. Smith, CHI . . . 73
R. Sievers, CHI . . . 58
E. Battey, WAS . . . 57
B. Skowron, NY . . . 56
J. Lemon, WAS . . . 36
T. Kubek, NY . . . 29
C. Estrada, BAL . . . 28
T. Williams, BOS . . . 25
V. Wertz, BOS . . . 22
Y. Berra, NY . . . 21
J. Gentile, BAL . . . 21
P. Runnels, BOS . . . 18
N. Fox, CHI . . . 11
V. Power, CLE . . . 11
S. Barber, BAL . . . 7
L. Aparicio, CHI . . . 6
J. Perry, CLE . . . 6
G. Staley, CHI . . . 4
J. Bunning, DET . . . 3
G. Woodling, BAL . . . 3
H. Kuenn, CLE . . . 3
B. Daley, KC . . . 3
M. Fornieles, BOS . . . 2
C. Maxwell, DET . . . 2
J. Piersall, CLE . . . 2

1961 NATIONAL
F. Robinson, CIN . . 219
O. Cepeda, SF . . . 117
V. Pinson, CIN . . . 104
R. Clemente, PIT . . . 81
J. Jay, CIN . . . 74
W. Mays, SF . . . 70
K. Boyer, SL . . . 43
H. Aaron, MIL . . . 39
M. Wills, LA . . . 36
J. O'Toole, CIN . . . 31
W. Spahn, MIL . . . 31
S. Miller, SF . . . 26
W. Moon, LA . . . 22
G. Altman, CHI . . . 9
J. Podres, LA . . . 9
R. McMillan, MIL . . . 8
E. Mathews, MIL . . . 7
S. Koufax, LA . . . 5
J. Roseboro, LA . . . 4
J. Brosnan, CIN . . . 3
J. Torre, MIL . . . 2
L. Jackson, SL . . . 1
J. Lynch, CIN . . . 1
B. Malkmus, PHI . . . 1
D. Stuart, PIT . . . 1

1961 AMERICAN
R. Maris, NY . . . 202
M. Mantle, NY . . . 198
J. Gentile, BAL . . . 157
N. Cash, DET . . . 151
W. Ford, NY . . . 102
L. Arroyo, NY . . . 95
F. Lary, DET . . . 53
R. Colavito, DET . . . 51
A. Kaline, DET . . . 35
E. Howard, NY . . . 30
H. Killebrew, MIN . . . 29
L. Aparicio, CHI . . . 16
J. Piersall, CLE . . . 10
S. Barber, BAL . . . 7
D. Schwall, BOS . . . 7
N. Siebern, KC . . . 7
D. Donovan, WAS . . . 5
B. Phillips, CLE . . . 5
B. Robinson, BAL . . . 4
C. Schilling, BOS . . . 4
T. Morgan, LA . . . 3
A. Smith, CHI . . . 3
Y. Berra, NY . . . 2
B. Richardson, NY . . . 1
J. Romano, CLE . . . 1
L. Thomas, LA . . . 1
H. Wilhelm, BAL . . . 1

1962 NATIONAL
M. Wills, LA . . . 209
W. Mays, SF . . . 202
T. Davis, LA . . . 175
F. Robinson, CIN . . 164
D. Drysdale, LA . . . 85
H. Aaron, MIL . . . 72
J. Sanford, SF . . . 62
B. Purkey, CIN . . . 33
F. Howard, LA . . . 32
S. Musial, SL . . . 19
J. Pagan, SF . . . 13
D. Demeter, PHI . . . 12
F. Alou, SF . . . 10
B. White, SL . . . 10
O. Cepeda, SF . . . 9
D. Groat, PIT . . . 7
R. Clemente, PIT . . . 6
E. Banks, CHI . . . 5
K. Boyer, SL . . . 5
J. Callison, PHI . . . 5
H. Kuenn, SF . . . 5
J. Marichal, SF . . . 4
B. Skinner, PIT . . . 4
J. Davenport, SF . . . 3
S. Koufax, LA . . . 3
D. Crandall, MIL . . . 2
A. Mahaffey, PHI . . . 2
E. Roebuck, LA . . . 2
E. Kasko, CIN . . . 1
E. Mathews, MIL . . . 1

1962 AMERICAN
M. Mantle, NY . . . 234
B. Richardson, NY . . . 152
H. Killebrew, MIN . . . 99
L. Wagner, LA . . . 85
D. Donovan, CLE . . . 64
A. Kaline, DET . . . 58
N. Siebern, KC . . . 53
R. Rollins, MIN . . . 47
B. Robinson, BAL . . 41
F. Robinson, CHI . . . 33
L. Thomas, LA . . . 32
T. Tresh, NY . . . 30
B. Moran, LA . . . 28
R. Terry, NY . . . 19
C. Pascual, MIN . . . 14
R. Colavito, DET . . . 13
H. Aguirre, DET . . . 10
J. Cunningham, CHI . 9
P. Runnels, BOS . . . 9
C. Yastrzemski, BOS . . . 9
V. Power, MIN . . . 8
D. Radatz, BOS . . . 8
J. Bunning, DET . . . 8
Z. Versalles, MIN . . . 8
J. Lumpe, KC . . . 7
E. Bressoud, BOS . . . 6
B. Rodgers, LA . . . 6
W. Ford, NY . . . 6
R. Herbert, CHI . . . 5
C. Hinton, WAS . . . 5
F. Malzone, BOS . . . 3
N. Cash, DET . . . 3
A. Smith, CHI . . . 1

1963 NATIONAL
S. Koufax, LA . . . 237
D. Groat, SL . . . 190
H. Aaron, MIL . . . 135
R. Perranoski, LA . 130
W. Mays, SF . . . 102
J. Gilliam, LA . . . 62
B. White, SL . . . 56
T. Davis, LA . . . 41
R. Santo, CHI . . . 41
V. Pinson, CIN . . . 32
J. Marichal, SF . . . 31
W. Spahn, MIL . . . 30
K. Boyer, SL . . . 19
R. Clemente, PIT . . . 12
J. Callison, PHI . . . 11
T. Taylor, PHI . . . 10
W. McCovey, SF . . . 9
M. Wills, LA . . . 9
D. Ellsworth, CHI . . . 7
J. Maloney, CIN . . . 7
D. Demeter, PHI . . . 3
D. Drysdale, LA . . . 3
T. Gonzalez, PHI . . . 2
C. Flood, SL . . . 1

1963 AMERICAN
E. Howard, NY . . . 248
A. Kaline, DET . . . 148
W. Ford, NY . . . 125
H. Killebrew, MIN . . . 85
D. Radatz, BOS . . . 84
C. Yastrzemski, BOS . . . 81
E. Battey, MIN . . . 57
G. Peters, CHI . . . 55
P. Ward, CHI . . . 52
B. Richardson, NY . . 43
T. Tresh, NY . . . 38
C. Pascual, MIN . . . 29
D. Stuart, BOS . . . 25
A. Pearson, LA . . . 22
B. Allison, MIN . . . 15
J. Bouton, NY . . . 11
M. Alvis, CLE . . . 10
J. Pepitone, NY . . . 10
L. Wagner, LA . . . 9
S. Miller, BAL . . . 9
W. Causey, KC . . . 5
R. Rollins, MIN . . . 5
L. Aparicio, BAL . . . 3
B. Dailey, MIN . . . 3
J. Fregosi, LA . . . 3
N. Fox, CHI . . . 2
T. Kubek, NY . . . 1
F. Robinson, CHI . . . 1
N. Siebern, KC . . . 1

1964 NATIONAL
K. Boyer, SL . . . 243
J. Callison, PHI . . . 187
B. White, SL . . . 106½
F. Robinson, CIN . . . 98
J. Torre, MIL . . . 85
W. Mays, SF . . . 66
R. Allen, PHI . . . 63
R. Santo, CHI . . . 59
R. Clemente, PIT . . . 56
L. Brock, CHI-SL . . . 40
C. Flood, SL . . . 38
L. Jackson, CHI . . . 26
J. Bunning, PHI . . . 23
H. Aaron, MIL . . . 22
J. Marichal, SF . . . 14
S. Ellis, CIN . . . 13
S. Koufax, LA . . . 7½
V. Pinson, CIN . . . 6
J. Hart, SF . . . 6
B. Williams, CHI . . . 6
R. Amaro, PHI . . . 5
T. Davis, LA . . . 4
B. Gibson, SL . . . 2
C. Short, PHI . . . 2
R. Hunt, NY . . . 1
B. Schultz, SL . . . 1

1964 AMERICAN
B. Robinson, BAL . 269
M. Mantle, NY . . . 171
E. Howard, NY . . . 124
T. Oliva, MIN . . . 99
D. Chance, LA . . . 97
P. Ward, CHI . . . 67½
B. Freehan, DET . . . 44
G. Peters, CHI . . . 44
D. Radatz, BOS . . . 37
H. Killebrew, MIN . . . 31
B. Powell, BAL . . . 28
W. Bunker, BAL . . . 23
J. Fregosi, LA . . . 21
A. Kaline, DET . . . 17
F. Robinson, CHI . . . 14
R. Hansen, CHI . . . 10
B. Richardson, NY . . . 9
L. Wagner, CLE . . . 9
J. Pizarro, CHI . . . 8
H. Wilhelm, CHI . . . 8
J. Horlen, CHI . . . 7
W. Ford, NY . . . 7
B. Allison, MIN . . . 5
R. Colavito, KC . . . 5
M. Stottlemyre, NY . . 4
R. Maris, NY . . . 4
W. Causey, KC . . . 4
L. Aparicio, BAL . . 3½
D. Stuart, BOS . . . 3
E. Bressoud, BOS . . . 2

C. Osteen, WAS.....2
D. Wickersham, DET............2
D. Lock, WAS......1

1965 NATIONAL
W. Mays, SF....224
S. Koufax, LA.....177
M. Wills, LA.....164
D. Johnson, CIN...108
D. Drysdale, LA...77
P. Rose, CIN.....67
H. Aaron, MIL....58
R. Clemente, PIT..56
J. Marichal, SF...26
W. McCovey, SF...25
J. Torre, MIL....23
B. Williams, CHI...21
F. Linzy, SF.....16
W. Stargell, PIT....15
C. Flood, SL....13
J. Hart, SF.....13
V. Law, PIT......12
F. Robinson, CIN...11
R. Santo, CHI....11
E. Mathews, MIL....8
L. Cardenas, CIN....7
J. Maloney, CIN....7
L. Lefebvre, LA....7
J. Callison, PHI....6
L. Johnson, LA.....5
C. Rojas, PHI......5
J. Roseboro, LA....5
R. Allen, PHI......4
T. Cloninger, MIL....4
J. Gilliam, LA.....3
J. Morgan, HOU....1

1965 AMERICAN
Z. Versalles, MIN..275
T. Oliva, MIN.....174
B. Robinson, BAL..150
E. Fisher, CHI....122
R. Colavito, CLE...89
J. Grant, MIN....74
S. Miller, BAL....45
W. Horton, DET....24
T. Tresh, NY.....23
E. Battey, MIN....22
D. Wert, DET.....22
C. Yastrzemski, BOS............22
J. Hall, MIN.....19
M. Stottlemyre, NY..17
H. Killebrew, MIN...15
A. Kaline, DET......9
J. Adair, BAL......7
R. Hansen, CHI.....7
S. McDowell, CLE...7
B. Richardson, NY...6
V. Davalillo, CLE...5
J. Fregosi, CAL....5
F. Whitfield, CLE...5
B. Knoop, CAL.....4
D. Buford, CHI.....3
M. Mantle, NY.....3
P. Richert, WAS....3
F. Robinson, CHI...3
B. Campaneris, KC...2
F. Howard, WAS....2
R. Kline, WAS.....2
F. Mantilla, BOS....2
N. Cash, DET.....1
T. Conigliaro, BOS...1

1966 NATIONAL
R. Clemente, PIT..218
S. Koufax, LA....208
W. Mays, SF.....111
R. Allen, PHI....107
F. Alou, ATL.....83
J. Marichal, SF....74
P. Regan, LA.....66
H. Aaron, ATL....57
M. Alou, PIT.....36
P. Rose, CIN.....31
G. Alley, PIT.....24
R. Santo, CHI....23
J. Roseboro, LA...22
O. Cepeda, SF-SL..22
W. Stargell, PIT...19
J. Torre, ATL....18
W. McCovey, SF...12

J. Lefebvre, LA....8
G. Perry, SF......8
C. Flood, SL......7
M. Wills, LA......5
R. Staub, HOU....4
B. Mazeroski, PIT...3
G. Beckert, CHI....3
J. Maloney, CIN....3
B. White, PHI.....3
L. Brock, SL......2
B. Shaw, SF-NY....1
C. Short, PHI.....1
W. Davis, LA......1

1966 AMERICAN
F. Robinson, BAL..280
B. Robinson, BAL..153
B. Powell, BAL....122
H. Killebrew, MIN...96
J. Kaat, MIN.....84
T. Oliva, MIN.....71
A. Kaline, DET....66
T. Agee, CHI.....63
L. Aparicio, BAL...51
B. Campaneris, KC..36
S. Miller, BAL....27
N. Cash, DET.....23
J. Aker, KC......22
E. Wilson, BOS-DET......13
D. McLain, DET....12
B. Freehan, DET....9
A. Etchebarren, BAL..7
B. Knoop, CAL.....6
M. Mantle, NY.....5
T. Tresh, NY......5
J. Sanford, CAL....4
R. Reichardt, CAL...4
F. Valentine, WAS...4
W. Horton, DET....4
L. Wagner, CLE....4
P. Richert, WAS....3
J. Pepitone, NY....2
T. Conigliaro, BOS...1
S. Siebert, CLE....1
C. Yastrzemski, BOS............1
J. Fregosi, CAL....1

1967 NATIONAL
O. Cepeda, SL....280
T. McCarver, SL....136
R. Clemente, PIT..129
R. Santo, CHI....103
H. Aaron, ATL....79
M. McCormick, SF..73
L. Brock, SL.....49
T. Perez, CIN.....43
J. Javier, SL.....41
P. Rose, CIN.....40
J. Wynn, HOU.....29
F. Jenkins, CHI....26
C. Flood, SL.....24
E. Banks, CHI....22
N. Briles, SL.....20
R. Staub, HOU....12
D. Hughes, SL.....10
J. Hart, SF......10
R. Allen, PHI......9
T. Abernathy, CIN...8
T. Boyer, ATL.....6
B. Gibson, SL.....5
R. Hundley, CHI....5
J. Bunning, PHI....5
T. Seaver, NY.....5
T. Davis, NY......3
G. Alley, PIT.....3
T. Gonzalez, PHI...3
W. McCovey, SF....2

1967 AMERICAN
C. Yastrzemski, BOS............275
H. Killebrew, MIN..161
B. Freehan, DET...137
J. Horlen, CHI....91
A. Kaline, DET....88
J. Lonborg, BOS...82
C. Tovar, MIN.....70
J. Fregosi, CAL....70
G. Peters, CHI....37
G. Scott, BOS.....33
F. Robinson, BAL...31

E. Wilson, DET....20
D. Chance, MIN....19
R. Hansen, CHI....13
J. Adair, CHI-BOS..11
P. Blair, BAL......9
R. Petrocelli, BOS...7
E. Howard, NY-BOS..7
T. Oliva, MIN......6
J. Kaat, MIN......4
P. Casanova, WAS...3
D. Mincher, CAL....3
M. Lolich, DET.....2
M. Rojas, CAL.....1

1968 NATIONAL
B. Gibson, SL....242
P. Rose, CIN.....205
W. McCovey, SF...135
C. Flood, SL.....116
J. Marichal, SF....93
L. Brock, SL......73
M. Shannon, SL....55
B. Williams, CHI...48
G. Beckert, CHI....40
F. Alou, ATL.....33
M. Alou, PIT......32
H. Aaron, ATL....19
W. Mays, SF......14
E. Banks, CHI.....14
J. Koosman, NY....14
J. Bench, CIN.....11
P. Regan, LA-CHI...7
F. Jenkins, CHI.....6
T. Perez, CIN.....5
N. Briles, SL......4
D. Maxvill, SL.....4
S. Blass, PIT......3
T. Haller, LA......3
R. Santo, CHI......2
C. Carroll, ATL-CIN..1
T. Helms, CIN.....1

1968 AMERICAN
D. McLain, DET...280
B. Freehan, DET...161
K. Harrelson, BOS..........103
W. Horton, DET...102
D. McNally, BAL....78
L. Tiant, CLE.....78
D. McAuliffe, DET...71
F. Howard, WAS....63
C. Yastrzemski, BOS............50
M. Stottlemyre, NY..43
B. Campaneris, OAK..........39
R. White, NY......17
J. Northrup, DET...15
L. Aparicio, CHI...13
J. Fregosi, CAL....11
D. Buford, BAL....11
B. Robinson, BAL...8
R. Jackson, OAK....8
T. Oliva, MIN.....5
D. Cater, OAK.....5
M. Andrews, BOS...4
B. Powell, BAL.....4
N. Cash, DET......3
C. Tovar, MIN.....3
M. Stanley, DET....2
W. Wood, CHI.....2
T. Uhlaender, MIN...1

1969 NATIONAL
W. McCovey, SF...265
T. Seaver, NY....243
H. Aaron, ATL....188
P. Rose, CIN.....127
R. Santo, CHI....124
T. Agee, NY......89
C. Jones, NY......82
R. Clemente, PIT...51
P. Niekro, ATL....47
T. Perez, CIN.....28
M. Wills, MON-LA...17
E. Banks, CHI.....15
R. Carty, ATL.....12
J. Bench, CIN.....12
D. Kessinger, CHI...8
T. Gonzalez, SD-ATL..........8
R. Hunt, SF.......8

D. Menke, HOU.....8
W. Granger, CIN....8
J. Wynn, HOU.....8
W. Davis, LA......8
W. Stargell, PIT....7
J. Marichal, SF.....6
B. Williams, CHI....6
J. Koosman, NY....6
J. Torre, SL......6
M. Alou, PIT......6
L. Dierker, HOU....6
T. Haller, LA......3
B. Gibson, SL.....2
B. Bonds, SF......2
R. Hundley, CHI....2
L. May, CIN......2
T. Sizemore, LA....2
W. Parker, LA.....2
J. Edwards, HOU...1
R. Staub, MON....1
O. Cepeda, ATL....1

1969 AMERICAN
H. Killebrew, MIN..294
B. Powell, BAL....227
F. Robinson, BAL..162
F. Howard, WAS...115
R. Jackson, OAK...110
D. McLain, DET....85
R. Petrocelli, BOS...71
M. Cuellar, BAL....55
J. Perry, MIN.....40
R. Carew, MIN....30
P. Blair, BAL.....28
L. Cardenas, MIN...27
R. Perranoski, MIN..25
D. McNally, BAL....25
T. Oliva, MIN.....21
S. Bando, OAK....18
C. Tovar, MIN......9
M. Stottlemyre, NY...8
C. Yastrzemski, BOS............8
E. Brinkman, WAS...7
J. Fregosi, CAL....7
R. Smith, BOS.....5
D. Unser, WAS.....5
B. Robinson, BAL...5
M. Epstein, WAS....4
M. Andrews, BOS...3
D. Bosman, WAS....3
B. Freehan, DET....3
T. Harper, SEA.....3
A. Messersmith, CAL..........2
R. Reese, MIN.....2
K. Tatum, CAL.....2
R. White, NY......2
M. Belanger, BAL...2
D. Green, OAK.....1
J. Northrup, DET...1
L. Piniella, KC.....1

1970 NATIONAL
J. Bench, CIN....326
B. Williams, CHI...218
T. Perez, CIN.....149
B. Gibson, SL....110
W. Parker, LA.....91
D. Giusti, PIT.....72
P. Rose, CIN.....54
J. Hickman, CHI...52
W. McCovey, SF....47
R. Carty, ATL.....43
M. Sanguillen, PIT..36
R. Clemente, PIT...33
D. Clendenon, NY...26
G. Perry, SF......24
W. Stargell, PIT....20
B. Tolan, CIN......17
H. Aaron, ATL....16
J. Torre, SL......15
T. Agee, NY......13
B. Harrelson, NY...10
F. Jenkins, CHI.....8
J. Merritt, CIN.....8
D. Kessinger, CHI...5
C. Gaston, SD.....5
D. Johnson, PHI....4
L. Walker, PIT.....4
C. Morton, MON....3
B. Robertson, PIT...3
T. Seaver, NY.....2

W. Granger, CIN....1

1970 AMERICAN
B. Powell, BAL....234
T. Oliva, MIN.....157
H. Killebrew, MIN..152
C. Yastrzemski, BOS............136
F. Howard, WAS...91
T. Harper, MIL.....78
B. Robinson, BAL...75
A. Johnson, CAL....70
J. Perry, MIN.....63
F. Robinson, BAL...60
M. Cuellar, BAL....45
R. Perranoski, MIN..35
J. Fregosi, CAL....35
L. Aparicio, CHI...35
R. White, NY......25
D. McNally, BAL....22
S. McDowell, CLE...22
C. Tovar, MIN.....16
T. Munson, NY.....15
D. Buford, BAL....12
C. Wright, CAL.....8
L. McDaniel, NY....8
R. Fosse, CLE......7
B. Campaneris, OAK............5
J. Palmer, BAL.....4
R. Smith, BOS.....3
S. Bando, OAK.....3
T. Horton, CLE.....1
B. Oliver, KC......1

1971 NATIONAL
J. Torre, SL.....318
W. Stargell, PIT...222
H. Aaron, ATL....180
B. Bonds, SF.....139
R. Clemente, PIT...87
M. Wills, LA......74
F. Jenkins, CHI....71
M. Sanguillen, PIT..49
T. Seaver, NY.....46
A. Downing, LA....36
G. Beckert, CHI....35
L. May, CIN......28
L. Brock, SL......20
D. Giusti, PIT.....16
W. McCovey, SF....15
T. Simmons, SL....13
W. Davis, LA......13
J. Johnson, SF....12
W. Mays, SF......11
R. Staub, MON....11
B. Williams, CHI...10
B. Harrelson, NY....4
B. Gibson, SL.....3
R. Garr, ATL......3
D. Roberts, SD.....1
P. Rose, CIN......1

1971 AMERICAN
V. Blue, OAK....268
S. Bando, OAK....182
F. Robinson, BAL..170
B. Robinson, BAL..163
M. Lolich, DET....155
F. Patek, KC......77
B. Murcer, NY.....72
A. Otis, KC......67
W. Wood, CHI.....54
T. Oliva, MIN.....36
D. McNally, BAL....26
N. Cash, DET.....21
B. Melton, CHI....18
R. Jackson, OAK...15
C. Rojas, KC......15
K. Sanders, MIL....13
P. Dobson, BAL.....9
R. Smith, BOS.....9
D. Johnson, BAL....8
M. Rettenmund, BAL............8
H. Killebrew, MIN...5
J. Palmer, BAL.....5
L. Cardenas, MIN...5
M. Cuellar, BAL....5
C. Tovar, MIN.....4
G. Scott, BOS.....3
D. Buford, BAL.....2
J. Hunter, OAK.....1

G. Nettles, MIN.....1

1972 NATIONAL
J. Bench, CIN....263
B. Williams, CHI...211
W. Stargell, PIT...201
J. Morgan, CIN...197
S. Carlton, PHI...124
C. Cedeno, HOU...112
A. Oliver, PIT.....52
N. Colbert, SD....45
L. May, HOU......30
T. Simmons, SL....22
M. Marshall, MON..22
P. Rose, CIN......19
R. Clemente, PIT...16
C. Carroll, CIN....16
L. Brock, SL......13
H. Aaron, ATL....12
M. Sanguillen, PIT..12
S. Blass, PIT......9
R. Garr, ATL......9
G. Clines, PIT.....6
B. Tolan, CIN......6
D. Baker, ATL.....5
M. Mota, LA......4
D. Kingman, SF....3
T. McGraw, NY.....2
R. Staub, NY......2
T. Seaver, NY.....2
J. Cardenal, CHI....1
F. Jenkins, CHI....1
C. Speier, SF.....1

1972 AMERICAN
R. Allen, CHI....321
J. Rudi, OAK.....164
S. Lyle, NY......158
C. Fisk, BOS......96
B. Murcer, NY.....89
G. Perry, CLE.....88
W. Wood, CHI.....78
L. Tiant, BOS....70½
E. Brinkman, DET..62
M. Lolich, DET....60
J. Hunter, OAK....57
J. Mayberry, KC....27
J. Palmer, BAL....21
B. Grich, BAL.....16
R. Carew, MIN....16
B. Campaneris, OAK............11
M. Epstein, OAK....11
L. Aparicio, BOS....9½
R. Petrocelli, BOS...9
R. Jackson, OAK....9
C. May, CHI......6
G. Scott, MIL......6
D. Thompson, MIN...5
T. Harper, BOS.....4
A. Kaline, DET.....4
B. Freehan, DET....3
K. McMullen, CAL...3
B. Robinson, BAL...3
R. Smith, BOS.....3
S. Bando, OAK.....2
N. Ryan, CAL.....2
A. Otis, KC......1
L. Piniella, KC.....1

1973 NATIONAL
P. Rose, CIN....274
W. Stargell, PIT...250
B. Bonds, SF.....174
J. Morgan, CIN...102
M. Marshall, MON...93
L. Brock, SL......65
T. Perez, CIN.....59
T. Seaver, NY.....57
K. Singleton, MON..52
J. Bench, CIN.....41
C. Cedeno, HOU...39
H. Aaron, ATL....35
D. Johnson, ATL...34
T. Simmons, SL....20
T. McGraw, NY.....17
F. Millan, NY......12
W. Davis, LA......12
D. Evans, ATL.....11
L. May, HOU......8
T. Fuentes, SF.....8
B. Watson, HOU....7
J. Ferguson LA.....7

J. Cardenal, CHI ... 6
J. Billingham, CIN ... 6
A. Oliver, PIT 6
R. Hunt, MON 5
R. Bryant, SF 5
G. Maddox, SF 3
B. Harrelson, NY ... 2
B. Williams, CHI 2
G. Luzinski, PHI 2
B. Russell, LA 1

1973 AMERICAN
R. Jackson, OAK .. 336
J. Palmer, BAL ... 172
A. Otis, KC 112
R. Carew, MIN 83
J. Hiller, DET 83
S. Bando, OAK 83
J. Mayberry, KC ... 76
D. May, MIL 65
B. Murcer, NY 53
T. Davis, BAL 47
J. Hunter, OAK 47
T. Munson, NY 43
T. Harper, BOS 33
G. Scott, MIL 25
O. Cepeda, BOS ... 21
F. Robinson, CAL .. 21
N. Ryan, CAL 20
C. Fisk, BOS 16
B. Grich, BAL 9
C. Yastrzemski,
  BOS 9
M. Belanger, BAL .. 8
D. Johnson, OAK ... 8
J. Briggs, MIL 6
J. Coleman, DET ... 6
C. Rojas, KC 5
B. Blyleven, MIN ... 4
G. Perry, CLE 4
B. Campaneris,
  OAK 4
V. Blue, OAK 3
C. May, CHI 3
W. Horton, DET 3
B. North, OAK 3
P. Blair, BAL 2
D. Nelson, TEX 2
R. Allen, CHI 1

1974 NATIONAL
S. Garvey, LA 270
L. Brock, SL 233
M. Marshall, LA ... 146
J. Bench, CIN 141
J. Wynn, LA 137
M. Schmidt, PHI .. 136
A. Oliver, PIT 87
J. Morgan, CIN 72
R. Zisk, PIT 54
W. Stargell, PIT ... 43
R. Smith, SL 39
R. Garr, ATL 11
T. Simmons, SL 7
D. Cash, PHI 6
D. Concepcion, CIN . 5
J. Billingham, CIN .. 4
C. Cedeno, HOU ... 4
A. Hrabosky, SL ... 4
A. Messersmith, LA . 4
B. Capra, ATL 3
L. McGlothen, SL ... 2
B. McBride, SL 2
R. Hebner, PIT 2
R. Stennett, PIT ... 2
B. Buckner, LA 1
R. Cey, LA 1

1974 AMERICAN
J. Burroughs, TEX . 248
J. Rudi, OAK ... 161½
S. Bando, OAK .. 143½
R. Jackson, OAK .. 119
F. Jenkins, TEX ... 118
J. Hunter, OAK ... 107
R. Carew, MIN 70
E. Maddox, NY 59
B. Grich, BAL 49
M. Cuellar, BAL ... 42
L. Tiant, BOS 41
B. Robinson, BAL .. 30
P. Blair, BAL 27
N. Ryan, CAL 24

B. Campaneris,
  OAK 23
R. Fingers, OAK ... 21
G. Perry, CLE 18
C. Yastrzemski,
  BOS 14
K. Henderson, CHI . 12
J. Hiller, DET 11
L. Randle, TEX 10
B. Murcer, NY 10
L. Piniella, NY 8
R. Allen, CHI 8
S. Lyle, NY 7
T. Munson, NY 6
T. Davis, BAL 6
M. Belanger, BAL .. 6
D. Money, MIL 5
T. Murphy, MIL 3
H. McRae, KC 3
S. Busby, KC 3
G. Scott, MIL 2
P. Dobson, NY 1

1975 NATIONAL
J. Morgan, CIN .. 321½
G. Luzinski, PHI .. 154
D. Parker, PIT 120
J. Bench, CIN 117
P. Rose, CIN 114
T. Simmons, SL ... 103
W. Stargell, PIT ... 69
A. Hrabosky, SL ... 66
T. Seaver, NY 65
R. Jones, SD 54
S. Garvey, LA 50
B. Madlock, CHI ... 45
D. Cash, PHI 26
R. Staub, NY 20
T. Perez, CIN 18
M. Schmidt, PHI ... 16
M. Sanguillen, PIT . 16
R. Cey, LA 11½
D. Kingman, NY 9
B. Watson, HOU ... 8
L. Brock, SL 6
L. Bowa, PHI 5
J. Reuss, PIT 2
A. Messersmith, LA . 1
W. Montanez,
  PHI-SF 1

1975 AMERICAN
F. Lynn, BOS 326
J. Mayberry, KC .. 157
J. Rice, BOS 154
R. Fingers, OAK .. 129
R. Jackson, OAK .. 118
J. Palmer, BAL 82
T. Munson, NY 69
G. Scott, MIL 64½
R. Carew, MIN .. 54½
K. Singleton, BAL .. 44
G. Brett, KC 37½
J. Hunter, NY 31
R. Burleson, BOS .. 28
C. Washington,
  OAK 22
T. Harrah, TEX 16
M. Torrez, BAL 12
R. Gossage, CHI ... 11
P. Lindblad, OAK ... 7
G. Tenace, OAK 7
B. Powell, CLE ... 6½
D. Baylor, BAL 6
B. Campaneris,
  OAK 6
B. Lee, BOS 5
J. Todd, OAK 5
D. Doyle, BOS 5
R. Wise, BOS 4
J. Rudi, OAK 3
J. Kaat, CHI 2
L. May, BAL 2
B. Bonds, NY 1
C. Yastrzemski,
  BOS 1

1976 NATIONAL
J. Morgan, CIN ... 311
G. Foster, CIN ... 221
M. Schmidt, PHI .. 179
P. Rose, CIN 131
G. Maddox, PHI ... 98

B. Madlock, CHI ... 51
S. Garvey, LA 51
G. Luzinski, PHI ... 49
K. Griffey, CIN 49
R. Jones, SD 48
B. Watson, HOU ... 38
A. Oliver, PIT 30
R. Eastwick, CIN .. 26
J. Koosman, NY ... 20
S. Carlton, PHI 16
D. Cash, PHI 15
J. Richard, HOU ... 12
R. Monday, CHI 11
D. Kingman, NY 11
D. Parker, PIT 10
B. Robinson, PIT ... 9
D. Sutton, LA 7
R. Cey, LA 6
W. Montanez,
  SF-ATL 4
L. Brock, SL 3
C. Cedeno, HOU ... 3
C. Geronimo, CIN .. 3
R. Zisk, PIT 3
L. Bowa, PHI 1

1976 AMERICAN
T. Munson, NY ... 304
G. Brett, KC 217
M. Rivers, NY .. 179½
H. McRae, KC 99
C. Chambliss,
  NY 71½
R. Carew, MIN 71
A. Otis, KC 58
B. Campbell, MIN .. 56
L. May, BAL 51
J. Palmer, BAL 47
M. Fidrych, DET ... 41
J. Rudi, OAK 35
S. Bando, OAK 31
C. Yastrzemski,
  BOS 26
F. Tanana, CAL ... 19
R. Jackson, BAL ... 17
G. Nettles, NY 17
G. Tenace, OAK ... 13
R. Fingers, OAK ... 12
V. Blue, OAK 10
E. Figueroa, NY 9
S. Lyle, NY 8
R. LeFlore, DET 6
M. Littell, KC 5
R. Carty, CLE 5
W. White, NY 3
L. Tiant, BOS 3
J. Mayberry, KC 1
B. Wynegar, MIN ... 1

1977 NATIONAL
G. Foster, CIN ... 291
G. Luzinski, PHI .. 255
D. Parker, PIT ... 156
R. Smith, LA 112
S. Carlton, PHI .. 100
S. Garvey, LA 98
B. Sutter, CHI 68
R. Cey, LA 60
T. Simmons, SL ... 58
M. Schmidt, PHI ... 48
B. Robinson, PIT .. 34
J. John, LA 33
G. Templeton, SL .. 20
R. Fingers, SD 17
P. Rose, CIN 15
J. Burroughs, ATL .. 9
A. Oliver, PIT 9
J. Candelaria, PIT .. 8
R. Stennett, PIT ... 7
W. McCovey, SF ... 5
J. Bench, CIN 3
R. Reuschel, CHI ... 3
B. Valentine, MON .. 3
T. McGraw, PHI 2
L. Bowa, PHI 1
T. Seaver, NY-CIN .. 1

1977 AMERICAN
R. Carew, MIN ... 273
A. Cowens, KC ... 217
K. Singleton, BAL . 200
J. Rice, BOS 163
G. Nettles, NY ... 112

S. Lyle, NY 79
T. Munson, NY 70
R. Jackson, NY 67
C. Fisk, BOS 67
B. Campbell, BOS .. 65
M. Rivers, NY 59
L. Hisle, MIN 54
G. Brett, KC 51
R. Zisk, CHI 34
J. Sundberg, TEX .. 30
B. Bonds, CAL 28
C. Yastrzemski,
  BOS 25
R. Guidry, NY 11
J. Palmer, BAL 11
R. LeFlore, DET 7
J. Thompson, DET .. 6
R. Burleson, BOS ... 5
B. Hobson, BOS 4
N. Ryan, CAL 3
G. Scott, BOS 3
H. McRae, KC 3
L. Bostock, MIN ... 2
T. Johnson, MIN ... 2
C. Chambliss, NY .. 1
O. Gamble, CHI 1
D. Leonard, KC 1

1978 NATIONAL
D. Parker, PIT 320
S. Garvey, LA 194
L. Bowa, PHI 189
R. Smith, LA 164
J. Clark, SF 107
G. Foster, CIN 104
G. Luzinski, PHI ... 48
G. Perry, SD 45
W. Stargell, PIT ... 39
D. Winfield, SD 37
P. Rose, CIN 35
B. Blue, SF 33
K. Tekulve, PIT 23
R. Fingers, SD 16
B. Hooton, LA 15
D. Lopes, LA 12
P. Niekro, ATL 11
B. Buckner, CHI 8
J. Burroughs, ATL .. 7
B. Sutter, CHI 5
G. Maddox, PHI 4
E. Cabell, HOU 2
B. Boone, PHI 1

1978 AMERICAN
J. Rice, BOS 352
R. Guidry, NY ... 291
L. Hisle, MIL 201
A. Otis, KC 90
R. Staub, DET 88
G. Nettles, NY 86
D. Baylor, CAL 51
E. Murray, BAL 50
C. Fisk, BOS 48
D. Porter, KC 48
R. Carew, MIN 46
M. Caldwell, MIL ... 41
R. Gossage, NY 39
A. Oliver, TEX ... 26½
J. Sundberg, TEX .. 24
R. LeFlore, DET ... 21
R. Jackson, NY 18
C. Yastrzemski,
  BOS 17
G. Brett, KC 14
A. Thornton,
  CLE 12½
L. Piniella, NY 11
T. Munson, NY 9
L. Bostock, CAL 8
L. Gura, KC 8
F. Lynn, BOS 6
M. Rivers, NY 6
B. Stanley, BOS 6
D. LaRoche, CAL ... 6
D. Money, MIL 5
W. Randolph, NY ... 5
D. Eckersley, BOS .. 4
H. McRae, KC 4
L. Roberts, SEA 3
R. Gale, KC 2
K. Singleton, BAL ... 2
R. Burleson, BOS ... 1
F. Tanana, CAL 1

1979 NATIONAL
W. Stargell, PIT ... 216
K. Hernandez, SL . 216
D. Winfield, SD ... 155
L. Parrish, MON .. 128
R. Knight, CIN 82
J. Niekro, HOU .. 75½
B. Sutter, CHI 69
K. Tekulve, PIT 64
D. Concepcion,
  CIN 63
D. Parker, PIT 56
D. Kingman, CHI .. 53
G. Foster, CIN 34
M. Schmidt, PHI ... 32
S. Garvey, LA 30
O. Moreno, PIT 23
P. Rose, PHI 23
G. Carter, MON ... 15
B. Madlock,
  SF-PIT 14
J. Richard, HOU ... 12
P. Niekro, ATL ... 11½
J. Sambito, HOU ... 9
T. Seaver, CIN 9
J. Bench, CIN 7
A. Dawson, MON ... 6
G. Templeton, SL ... 5
G. Matthews, ATL ... 4
D. Collins, CIN 3
B. Horner, ATL 1

1979 AMERICAN
D. Baylor, CAL ... 347
K. Singleton, BAL . 241
G. Brett, KC 226
F. Lynn, BOS ... 160½
J. Rice, BOS 124
M. Flanagan, BAL . 100
G. Thomas, MIL .. 87
B. Grich, CAL 58
D. Porter, KC 52
B. Bell, TEX 48
E. Murray, BAL .. 25½
J. Kern, TEX 25
M. Marshall, MIN .. 25
B. Downing, CAL ... 24
S. Lezcano, MIL ... 18
R. Smalley, MIN ... 16
W. Wilson, KC 15
S. Kemp, DET 15
M. Clear, CAL 12
P. Molitor, MIL 8
R. Burleson, BOS ... 7
T. John, NY 5
C. Cooper, MIL 4
R. Jackson, NY 3
W. Horton, SEA 3
D. Ford, CAL 1
R. Guidry, NY 1
M. Hargrove, CLE ... 1

1980 NATIONAL
M. Schmidt, PHI .. 336
G. Carter, MON .. 193
J. Cruz, HOU 166
D. Baker, LA 138
S. Carlton, PHI ... 134
S. Garvey, LA 131
A. Dawson, MON .. 72
G. Hendrick, SL ... 50
B. Horner, ATL 42
B. McBride, PHI ... 32
K. Hernandez, SL .. 29
D. Murphy, ATL ... 23
C. Cedeno, HOU ... 14
B. Bibby, PIT 11
B. Buckner, CHI ... 11
T. McGraw, PHI ... 10
J. Bench, CIN 7
J. Clark, SF 6
J. Niekro, HOU 2
B. Easler, PIT 2
J. Reuss, LA 2
K. Griffey, CIN 1
R. LeFlore, MON ... 1
R. Richards, SD 1
R. Scott, MON 1

1980 AMERICAN
G. Brett, KC 335
R. Jackson, NY ... 234
R. Gossage, NY ... 218

W. Wilson, KC 169
C. Cooper, MIL ... 160
E. Murray, BAL ... 106
R. Cerone, NY 77
D. Quisenberry,
  KC 76½
S. Stone, BAL 53
R. Henderson,
  OAK 51
A. Oliver, TEX ... 31½
T. Armas, OAK 29
A. Bumbry, BAL ... 27
B. Oglivie, MIL 27
W. Randolph, NY ... 10
M. Norris, OAK 10
R. Yount, MIL 8
M. Rivers, TEX 7
B. Bell, TEX 7
A. Trammell, DET ... 6
K. Singleton, BAL ... 4
T. Perez, BOS 2
M. Dilone, CLE 2
F. Lynn, BOS 1
J. Wathan, KC 1

1981 NATIONAL
M. Schmidt, PHI .. 321
A. Dawson, MON .. 215
G. Foster, CIN 146
D. Concepcion,
  CIN 108
F. Valenzuela, LA .. 90
G. Carter, MON ... 77
D. Baker, LA 65
B. Sutter, SL 59
S. Carlton, PHI 41
T. Seaver, CIN 35
P. Rose, PHI 35
B. Buckner, CHI ... 35
G. Matthews, PHI .. 31
J. Cruz, HOU 25
G. Hendrick, SL ... 25
N. Ryan, HOU 23
B. Madlock, PIT ... 20
A. Howe, HOU 16
T. Raines, MON ... 15
R. Camp, ATL 9
K. Hernandez, SL ... 9
T. Herr, SL 7
G. Minton, SF 4
W. Cromartie, MON . 3
S. Garvey, LA 1
M. May, SF 1

1981 AMERICAN
R. Fingers, MIL .. 319
R. Henderson,
  OAK 308
D. Evans, BOS 140
T. Armas, OAK ... 139
E. Murray, BAL ... 137
C. Lansford, BOS . 109
D. Winfield, NY 98
C. Cooper, MIL 96
R. Gossage, NY 62
T. Paciorek, SEA ... 46
D. Murphy, OAK ... 45
K. Gibson, DET 40
S. McCatty, OAK ... 22
B. Grich, CAL 17
J. Morris, DET 17
A. Oliver, TEX 8
R. Yount, MIL 7
B. Bell, TEX 7
B. Almon, CHI 6
J. Mumphrey, NY ... 5
M. Hargrove, CLE ... 4
A. Trammell, DET ... 4
K. Singleton, BAL ... 3
S. Kemp, DET 3
D. Martinez, BAL ... 3
G. Luzinski, CHI ... 3
D. Stieb, TOR 1
G. Brett, KC 1

1982 NATIONAL
D. Murphy, ATL .. 283
L. Smith, SL 218
P. Guerrero, LA .. 175
A. Oliver, MON .. 175
B. Sutter, SL 134
M. Schmidt, PHI .. 54
J. Clark, SF 53

G. Minton, SF 44
S. Carlton, PHI 41
B. Buckner, CHI 38
B. Madlock, PIT 37
G. Carter, MON 35
O. Smith, SL 25
G. Hendrick, SL 20
T. Kennedy, SD 20
J. Morgan, SF 17
K. Hernandez, SL ..12
J. Thompson, PIT ..12
G. Garber, ATL 6
J. Andujar, SL 6
F. Valenzuela, LA ...3
A. Dawson, MON ...3
C. Chambliss, ATL ..2
G. Matthews, PHI ...2
R. Knight, HOU 1

1982 AMERICAN
R. Yount, MIL 385
E. Murray, BAL ...228
D. DeCinces, CAL .178
H. McRae, KC 175
C. Cooper, MIL 152
R. Jackson, CAL ...107
D. Evans, BOS 57
G. Thomas, MIL ...44½
D. Quisenberry, KC .39
R. Henderson, OAK ..38
D. Winfield, NY ...33
P. Molitor, MIL ...29½
L. Parrish, DET 26
B. Downing, CAL ...22
W. Wilson, KC 16
R. Fingers, MIL 12
B. Boone, CAL 12
P. Vuckovich, MIL ..11
J. Rice, BOS 10
T. Harrah, CLE 9
H. Baines, CHI 9
G. Brett, KC 9
D. Baylor, CAL 8
A. Thornton, CLE ...8
B. Stanley, BOS 6
J. Palmer, BAL 5
D. Garcia, TOR 5
R. Carew, CAL 5
B. Caudill, SEA 4
B. Bell, TEX 3
C. Ripken, BAL 3
C. Lansford, BOS ...1
R. Sutcliffe, CLE ...1
G. Ward, MIN 1

1983 NATIONAL
D. Murphy, ATL ...318
A. Dawson, MON .213
M. Schmidt, PHI ...191
P. Guerrero, LA ...182
T. Raines, MON 83
J. Cruz, HOU 76
D. Thon, HOU 67
B. Madlock, PIT 45
A. Holland, PHI 42
T. Kennedy, SD 37
G. Hendrick, SL 33
T. Pena, PIT 25
J. Denny, PHI 24
M. Soto, CIN 16
D. Evans, SF 16
R. Ramirez, ATL 15
J. Orosco, NY 14
L. Smith, CHI 8½
A. Oliver, MON 3
J. Leonard, SF 2
L. Smith, SL 1½
J. Davis, CHI 1
K. Hernandez, SL-NY 1
B. Horner, ATL 1
O. Smith, SL 1

1983 AMERICAN
C. Ripken, BAL ...322
E. Murray, BAL ...290
C. Fisk, CHI 209
J. Rice, BOS 150
C. Cooper, MIL ...123
D. Quisenberry, KC 107½
D. Winfield, NY 85

L. Whitaker, DET ..84
L. Parrish, DET 66
H. Baines, CHI 49
W. Upshaw, TOR .41½
W. Boggs, BOS 25
L. Hoyt, CHI 24½
L. Moseby, TOR 21
B. Stanley, BOS ..11½
A. Trammell, DET ...11
G. Luzinski, CHI 9
R. Yount, MIL 6
T. Simmons, MIL ...4
R. Dotson, CHI ...3½
R. Law, CHI 2
R. Guidry, NY 2
J. Morris, DET 2
J. Cruz, SEA-CHI ...1
R. Henderson, OAK ..1
G. Wright, TEX 1
T. Martinez, BAL ...½

1984 NATIONAL
R. Sandberg, CHI .326
K. Hernandez, NY ..195
T. Gwynn, SD 184
R. Sutcliffe, CHI ...151
G. Matthews, CHI ...70
B. Sutter, SL 67
M. Schmidt, PHI ..55½
J. Cruz, HOU 53
D. Murphy, ATL ..52½
J. Davis, CHI 49
T. Raines, MON 41
L. Durham, CHI 38
R. Gossage, SD 34
G. Carter, MON 32
D. Gooden, NY 28
A. Wiggins, SD 14
K. McReynolds, SD ..6
R. Cey, CHI 6
R. Dernier, CHI 6
S. Garvey, SD 5
B. Brenly, SF 1
J. Samuel, PHI 1
J. Leonard, SF 1

1984 AMERICAN
W. Hernandez, DET 306
K. Hrbek, MIN 247
D. Quisenberry, KC 235
E. Murray, BAL ...197
D. Mattingly, NY ..113
K. Gibson, DET 96
T. Armas, BOS ...87½
D. Winfield, NY 83
A. Trammell, DET 76½
W. Wilson, KC 61
D. Evans, BOS 39
A. Davis, SEA 26
J. Rice, BOS 10
H. Baines, CHI 10
D. Kingman, OAK ...10
L. Parrish, DET 8
W. Upshaw, TOR 8
B. Downing, CAL ...6
S. Balboni, KC 5
A. Thornton, CLE ...5
J. Bell, TOR 5
B. Bell, TEX 4
D. Stieb, TOR 4
L. Moseby, TOR 4
J. Beniquez, CAL ...2
M. Boddicker, BAL ..2
D. Alexander, TOR ..1
C. Ripken, BAL 1

1985 NATIONAL
W. McGee, SL 280
D. Parker, CIN ...220
P. Guerrero, LA ...208
D. Gooden, NY ...162
T. Herr, SL 119
G. Carter, NY 116
D. Murphy, ATL 63
K. Hernandez, NY ..61
J. Tudor, SL 61
J. Clark, SL 20
V. Coleman, SL 16
T. Raines, MON 15
R. Sandberg, CHI ..14

M. Marshall, LA 11
H. Brooks, MON ...11
O. Hershiser, LA 9
K. Moreland, CHI ...8
O. Smith, SL 5
M. Scioscia, LA 5
J. Reardon, MON ...4
J. Cruz, HOU 2
B. Doran, HOU 2
M. Duncan, LA 1
T. Gwynn, SD 1
F. Valenzuela, LA ...1
G. Wilson, PHI 1

1985 AMERICAN
D. Mattingly, NY ..367
G. Brett, KC 274
R. Henderson, NY .174
W. Boggs, BOS ...159
E. Murray, BAL ...130
D. Moore, CAL 96
J. Barfield, TOR 88
J. Bell, TOR 84
H. Baines, CHI 49
B. Saberhagen, KC .45
D. Quisenberry, KC .39
C. Fisk, CHI 29
D. Winfield, NY 35
Dr. Evans, DET 17
R. Guidry, NY 15
P. Bradley, SEA 12
C. Ripken, BAL 9
K. Gibson, DET 7
S. Balboni, KC 6
T. Henke, TOR 5
D. Lamp, TOR 3
K. Puckett, MIN 3
D. Alexander, TOR ..3
D. Garcia, TOR 2
R. Gedman, BOS ...1

1986 NATIONAL
M. Schmidt, PHI ..287
G. Davis, HOU ...231
G. Carter, NY 181
K. Hernandez, NY .179
D. Parker, CIN ...144
T. Raines, MON 99
K. Bass, HOU 73
V. Hayes, PHI 41
T. Gwynn, SD 34
M. Scott, HOU 33
B. Doran, HOU 32
E. Davis, CIN 21
S. Sax, LA 13
R. Knight, NY 9
M. Krukow, SF 8
T. Worrell, SL 7
R. McDowell, NY ...5
D. Smith, HOU 5
F. Valenzuela, LA ...4
L. Dykstra, NY 4
B. Ojeda, NY 2
D. Murphy, ATL 2
C. Maldonado, SF ..2

1986 AMERICAN
R. Clemens, BOS .339
D. Mattingly, NY ..258
J. Rice, BOS 241
J. Bell, TOR 125
J. Barfield, TOR ...107
K. Puckett, MIN ...105
W. Boggs, BOS 87
W. Joyner, CAL 74
J. Carter, CLE 72
D. Righetti, NY 71
D. DeCinces, CAL ..56
W. Witt, CAL 34
D. Baylor, BOS 32
T. Fernandez, TOR .17
T. Higuera, MIL 7
G. Gaetti, MIN 6
P. O'Brien, TEX 5
S. Fletcher, TEX 5
M. Barrett, BOS 5
J. Canseco, OAK ...3
J. Presley, SEA 2
D. Schofield, CAL ...1

1987 NATIONAL
A. Dawson, CHI ...269
O. Smith, SL 193

J. Clark, SL 186
T. Wallach, MON ..165
W. Clark, SF 128
D. Strawberry, NY ..95
T. Raines, MON 80
T. Gwynn, SD 75
E. Davis, CIN 73
H. Johnson, NY 42
D. Murphy, ATL 34
V. Coleman, SL 20
J. Samuel, PHI 19
M. Schmidt, PHI ...13
P. Guerrero, LA 12
S. Bedrosian, PHI ...6
M. Thompson, PHI ..4
B. Doran, HOU 1
T. Pendleton, SL ...1

1987 AMERICAN
J. Bell, TOR 332
A. Trammell, DET ..311
K. Puckett, MIN ...201
Dw. Evans, BOS ..127
P. Molitor, MIL ...125
M. McGwire, OAK .109
D. Mattingly, NY ...92
T. Fernandez, TOR .79
W. Boggs, BOS 64
G. Gaetti, MIN 47
J. Reardon, MIN ...37
Dr. Evans, DET 21
D. Alexander, DET ..17
T. Henke, TOR 17
W. Joyner, CAL 17
M. Hrbek, MIN 11
D. Tartabull, KC ...10
R. Yount, MIL 8
R. Clemens, BOS ...7
J. Morris, DET 5
K. Seitzer, KC 5
R. Sierra, TEX 5
J. Canseco, OAK ...4
M. Nokes, DET 1

1988 NATIONAL
K. Gibson, LA 272
D. Strawberry, NY .236
K. McReynolds, NY 162
A. Van Slyke, PIT .160
W. Clark, SF 135
O. Hershiser, LA ..111
A. Galarraga, MON 105
G. Davis, HOU 72
D. Jackson, CIN ...41
D. Cone, NY 37
T. Gwynn, SD 29
J. Franco, CIN 23
E. Davis, CIN 14
B. Bonilla, PIT 7
A. Dawson, CHI 6
B. Myers, NY 5
B. Butler, SF 2
S. Sax, LA 1

1988 AMERICAN
J. Canseco, OAK ..392
M. Greenwell, BOS 242
K. Puckett, MIN ...219
D. Winfield, NY ...164
D. Eckersley, OAK .156
W. Boggs, BOS ...107
A. Trammell, DET ..62
P. Molitor, MIL 79
Dw. Evans, BOS ...49
F. Viola, MIN 39
R. Yount, MIL 34
G. Brett, KC 29
D. Henderson, OAK .28
B. Hurst, BOS 15
D. Jones, CLE 11
J. Reardon, MIN ...11
F. McGriff, TOR 9
R. Henderson, NY ..8
M. McGwire, OAK ..8
J. Carter, CLE 5
L. Smith, BOS 4
G. Gaetti, MIN 3
D. Plesac, MIL 3
D. Stewart, OAK ...3
J. Franco, CLE 2

T. Fernandez, TOR ..1

1989 NATIONAL
K. Mitchell, SF ...314
W. Clark, SF 225
P. Guerrero. SL ...190
R. Sandberg, CHI .157
H. Johnson, NY ...153
M. Davis, SD 76
G. Davis, HOU 64
T. Gwynn, SD 57
E. Davis, CIN 44
M. Williams, CHI ...41
L. Smith, ATL 34
J. Clark, SD 16
J. Walton, CHI 14
M. Grace, CHI 9
M. Scott, HOU 6
B. Bonilla, PIT 5
B. Butler, SF 3
T. Raines, MON 3
M. Thompson, SL ...3
G. Garrelts, SF 2

1989 AMERICAN
R. Yount, MIL 256
R. Sierra, TEX 228
C. Ripken, BAL ...216
J. Bell, TOR 205
D. Eckersley, OAK .116
F. McGriff, TOR 96
K. Puckett, MIN 84
B. Saberhagen, KC .82
R. Henderson, NY-OAK 67
B. Jackson, KC 46
D. Parker, OAK 44
G. Olson, BAL 35
B. Blyleven, CAL ...32
D. Stewart, OAK ...30
D. Mattingly, NY ...25
J. Carter, CLE 23
C. Lansford, OAK ..20
N. Esasky, BOS 19
T. Fernandez, TOR ..9
M. Moore, OAK 6
W. Boggs, BOS 3
S. Sax, NY 3
A. Davis, SEA 2
N. Ryan, TEX 2
C. Davis, CAL 1
M. McGwire, OAK ...1
M. Wilson, TOR 1

1990 NATIONAL
B. Bonds, PIT 331
B. Bonilla, PIT 212
D. Strawberry, NY .167
R. Sandberg, CHI .151
E. Murray, LA 123
M. Williams, SF 95
B. Larkin, CIN 82
D. Drabek, PIT 59
L. Dykstra, PHI 41
T. Wallach, MON ...36
K. Mitchell, SF 20
E. Davis, CIN 12
C. Sabo, CIN 11
D. Gooden, NY 10
R. Martinez, LA 9
J. Carter, SD 7
R. Myers, CIN 7
P. O'Neill, CIN 6
J. Rijo, CIN 6
A. Dawson, CHI 6
D. Magadan, NY ...4
B. Santiago, SD 3
B. Butler, SF 2
D. Justice, ATL 2
P. Guerrero, SL 2
K. Daniels, LA 1
A. Van Slyke, PIT ...1

1990 AMERICAN
R. Henderson, OAK 317
C. Fielder, DET ...286
R. Clemens, BOS .212
K. Gruber, TOR ...175
B. Thigpen, CHI ...170
D. Eckersley, OAK .112
G. Brett, KC 60

D. Stewart, OAK ...56
B. Welch, OAK 54
F. McGriff, TOR 30
M. McGwire, OAK ..29
J. Canseco, OAK ...26
E. Burks, BOS 25
R. Palmeiro, TEX ...22
C. Fisk, CHI 16
D. Parker, MIL 11
O. Guillen, CHI 10
J. Reed, BOS 9
K. Griffey, Jr., SEA ..7
A. Trammell, DET ...7
T. Pena, BOS 6
W. Boggs, BOS 5
D. Jones, CLE 3
C. Ripken, BAL 2
N. Ryan, TEX 1
D. Stieb, Tor 1

1991 NATIONAL
T. Pendleton, ATL .274
B. Bonds, PIT 259
B. Bonilla, PIT 191
W. Clark, SF 118
H. Johnson, NY ...112
R. Gant, ATL 110
B. Butler, LA 103
L. Smith, SL 89
D. Strawberry, LA ..76
F. McGriff, SD 23
T. Glavine, ATL 16
D. Justice, ATL 11
J. Bell, PIT 11
A. Dawson, CHI 5
J. Smiley, PIT 5
T. Gwynn, SD 4
J. Kruk, PHI 2
R. Sandberg, CHI ..2
B. Larkin, CIN 2
D. Martinez, MON ..1
C. Sabo, CIN 1
O. Smith, SL 1

1991 AMERICAN
C. Ripken, BAL ...318
C. Fielder, DET ...286
F. Thomas, CHI ...181
J. Canseco, OAK ..145
J. Carter, TOR 136
R. Alomar, TOR ...128
K. Puckett, MIN 78
R. Sierra, TEX 63
K. Griffey, SEA 62
R. Clemens, BOS ...57
P. Molitor, MIL 51
D. Tartabull, KC ...32
J. Morris, MIN 29
C. Davis, MIN 21
J. Franco, TEX 17
D. White, TOR 15
S. Erickson, MIN ...12
R. Aguilera, MIN ...11
R. Palmeiro, TEX 6
R. Ventura, CHI 3
D. Henderson, OAK .1

1992 NATIONAL
B. Bonds, PIT 304
T. Pendleton, ATL .232
G. Sheffield, SD ...204
A. Van Slyke, PIT .145
L. Walker, MON ...111
D. Daulton, PHI ...100
F. McGriff, SD 100
B. Roberts, CIN 64
M. Grissom, MON ..54
T. Glavine, ATL 18
G. Maddux, CHI ...14
R. Sandberg, CHI ..12
B. Larkin, CIN 12
D. Jones, HOU 8
J. Kruk, PHI 8
M. Grace, PHI 6
D. DeShields, MON .6
R. Lankford, SL 5
J. Bagwell, HOU 4
D. Hollins, PHI 3
B. Butler, LA 2
O. Smith, SL 2
O. Nixon, ATL 1
J. Wetteland, MON ..1

1992 AMERICAN					
D. Eckersley, OAK .306	M. McGwire, OAK .155	F. Thomas, CHI ...108	E. Martinez, SEA ...29	J. Gonzalez, TEX ...15	J. Bell, CHI 3
K. Puckett, MIN ...209	D. Winfield, TOR ..141	C. Fielder, DET 83	J. Morris, TOR ...18	K. Griffey, SEA 13	M. Bordick, OAK 2
J. Carter, TOR 201	R. Alomar, TOR ...118	P. Molitor, MIL 63	R. Clemens, BOS ..16	P. Listach, MIL 8	M. Mussina, BAL 2
	M. Devereaux, BAL 109	C. Baerga, CLE 31	B. Anderson, BAL ..16	J. McDowell, CHI....5	A. Belle, CLE 1

Rookie of the Year Award: History

The Chicago chapter of the Baseball Writers' Association of America (BBWAA) established an award recognizing the major leagues' top rookie following the 1940 season, selecting Lou Boudreau for the honor. This procedure continued for six more years before going national. The subsequent winners of the Chicago chapter's award were Pete Reiser (1941), Johnny Beazley (1942), Bill Johnson (1943), Bill Voiselle (1944), Boo Ferriss (1945), and Eddie Waitkus (1946).

The Sporting News began naming its own Rookie of the Year in 1946, with the selection of Del Ennis. Their award has competed with that of the BBWAA ever since. In 1949 they began recognizing a winner from each league and in 1957 they started selecting both a rookie player and rookie pitcher of the year for each league.

In 1947 thirty-three baseball writers were asked to name five rookies in order of preference, with votes distributed on a 5–4–3–2–1 basis. Thus, Jackie Robinson became the first nationally recognized winner of the BBWAA Rookie of the Year Award, or the J. Louis Comiskey Memorial Award, as it was called. During the 1987 Hall of Fame induction ceremony, Commissioner Peter Ueberroth announced that, hereafter, the Rookie of the Year Award would be officially known as the Jackie Robinson Award.

In 1948 forty-eight writers took part in the award, this time naming only a single candidate on each ballot. In 1949 the BBWAA began the process of choosing a top rookie in each league. Three writers from each league city, the same men who decided on the MVP Awards, participated in the voting. Voters were free to use their individual judgments as to the eligibility of rookie candidates, which created some problems, especially in 1950 when Al Rosen, and his league-leading 37 homers, was ignored by Rookie of the Year voters. Apparently they felt that Rosen's 58 previous major league at-bats were tantamount to veteran status, while winner Walt Dropo's 41 previous at-bats were not.

In 1957 formal guidelines were finally established for determining rookie status. A player could not have accumulated more than 75 at-bats, 45 innings pitched, or have been on a major league roster between May 15 and September 1 of any previous season. Shortly after, the guidelines were changed to 90 at-bats, 45 innings pitched or 45 days on a major league roster before September 1. Finally, in 1971, the guidelines were set at 130 at-bats, 50 innings, or 45 days on a roster.

There were several instances, especially in the early days of the award, in which some Rookie of the Year voters didn't bother to exercise their franchise. In 1961, as with the MVP Award, the number of voters was reduced from three to two writers from each league city.

Following two tie votes in four years (1976 NL, 1979 AL), the writers adopted the system used in Cy Young Award balloting: naming three rookies on each ballot, in order of preference, with votes distributed on a 5–3–1 basis. This system began in 1980.

The maximum possible point total available to Rookie of the Year candidates was 165 in 1947, 48 in 1948, and 24 in each league in 1949–60. In the National League, it was 16 in 1961, 20 in 1962–68, 24 in 1969–79, and 120 from 1980 to the present. In the American League, it was 20 in 1961–68, 24 in 1969–76, 28 in 1977–79, and 140 from 1980 to the present.

There have been eight unanimous Rookie of the Year selections since 1947: Frank Robinson (NL, 1956), Orlando Cepeda (NL, 1958), Willie McCovey (NL, 1959), Carlton Fisk (AL, 1972), Vince Coleman (NL, 1985), Benito Santiago (NL, 1987), Mark McGwire (AL, 1987), and Sandy Alomar (AL, 1990).

Rookie of the Year Award

1947
J. Robinson, BKN (NL) 129
L. Jansen, NY (NL) 105
F. Shea, NY (AL)....67
F. Fain, PHI (AL) 43
F. Baumholtz, CIN (NL) 42
(Rest of voting unknown)

1948
A. Dark, BOS (NL) ..27
G. Bearden, CLE (AL) 8
R. Ashburn, PHI (NL) .7
L. Brissie, PHI (AL) ..3
B. Goodman, BOS (AL) 3

1949 NATIONAL
D. Newcombe, BKN 21
D. Crandall, BOS 3

1949 AMERICAN
R. Sievers, SL 10
A. Kellner, PHI 5

G. Coleman, NY 4
B. Kuzava, CHI 1
J. Groth, DET 1
M. Garcia, CLE 1

1950 NATIONAL
S. Jethroe, BOS ...11
B. Miller, PHI 5
D. O'Connell, PIT ...4
E. Church, PHI......2
B. Serena, CHI 1

1950 AMERICAN
W. Dropo, BOS 15
W. Ford, NY 6
C. Carrasquel, CHI ..2

1951 NATIONAL
W. Mays, NY 18
C. Nichols, BOS 5
C. Labine, BKN 2

1951 AMERICAN
G. McDougald, NY .13
M. Minoso, CHI ...11

1952 NATIONAL
J. Black, BKN 19
H. Wilhelm, NY ...3

D. Groat, PIT 1
E. Mathews, BOS ...1

1952 AMERICAN
H. Byrd, PHI 9
C. Courtney, SL 8
S. White, BOS 7

1953 NATIONAL
J. Gilliam, BKN 11
H. Haddix, SL 4
R. Jablonski, SL 3
R. Repulski, SL 2
B. Bruton, MIL......2
F. Baczewski, CIN ..1
J. Greengrass, CIN ..1

1953 AMERICAN
H. Kuenn, DET 23
T. Umphlett, BOS ...1

1954 NATIONAL
W. Moon, SL 17
E. Banks, CHI 4
G. Conley, MIL 2
H. Aaron, MIL 1

1954 AMERICAN
B. Grim, NY 15

J. Finigan, PHI 8
A. Kaline, DET 1

1955 NATIONAL
B. Virdon, SL 15
J. Meyer, PHI 7
D. Bessent, BKN ...2

1955 AMERICAN
H. Score, CLE 18
B. Klaus, BOS 5
N. Zauchin, BOS ...1

1956 NATIONAL
F. Robinson, CIN ...24

1956 AMERICAN
L. Aparicio, CHI 22
T. Francona, BAL....1
R. Colavito, CLE 1

1957 NATIONAL
J. Sanford, PHI 16
E. Bouchee, PHI ...4
D. Drott, CHI 3
B. Hazle, MIL.......1

1957 AMERICAN
T. Kubek, NY 23

F. Malzone, BOS 1

1958 NATIONAL
O. Cepeda, SF 21

1958 AMERICAN
A. Pearson, WAS ...14
R. Duren, NY 7
G. Bell, CLE........3

1959 NATIONAL
W. McCovey, SF ...24

1959 AMERICAN
B. Allison, WAS 18
J. Perry, CLE 5
R. Snyder, KC 1

1960 NATIONAL
F. Howard, LA 12
P. Herrera, PHI......4
A. Mahaffey, PHI ...3
R. Santo, CHI 2
T. Davis, LA 1

1960 AMERICAN
R. Hansen, BAL....22
C. Estrada, BAL 1
J. Gentile, BAL 1

1961 NATIONAL
B. Williams, CHI....10
J. Torre, MIL 5
J. Curtis, CHI.......1

1961 AMERICAN
D. Schwall, BOS ...7
D. Howser, KC 6
Fl. Robinson, CHI ...2
C. Schilling, BOS ...2
L. Thomas, LA 2
J. Wood, DET 1

1962 NATIONAL
K. Hubbs, CHI 19
D. Clendenon, PIT ...1

1962 AMERICAN
T. Tresh, NY 13
B. Rodgers, LA 4
B. Allen, MIN 1
D. Chance, LA 1
D. Radatz, BOS 1

1963 NATIONAL
P. Rose, CIN 17
R. Hunt, NY 2
R. Culp, PHI 1

1963 AMERICAN
G. Peters, CHI 10
P. Ward, CHI 6
J. Hall, MIN 4

1964 NATIONAL
R. Allen, PHI 18
R. Carty, MIL 1
J. Hart, SF 1

1964 AMERICAN
T. Oliva, MIN 19
W. Bunker, BAL 1

1965 NATIONAL
J. Lefebvre, LA 13
J. Morgan, HOU 4
F. Linzy, SF 3

1965 AMERICAN
C. Blefary, BAL 12
M. Lopez, CAL 8

1966 NATIONAL
T. Helms, CIN 12
S. Jackson, HOU 3
T. Fuentes, SF 2
R. Hundley, CHI 1
C. Jones, NY 1
L. Jaster, SL 1

1966 AMERICAN
T. Agee, CHI 16
J. Nash, KC 2
D. Johnson, BAL 1
G. Scott, BOS 1

1967 NATIONAL
T. Seaver, NY 11
D. Hughes, SL 6
G. Nolan, CIN 3

1967 AMERICAN
R. Carew, MIN 19
R. Smith, BOS 1

1968 NATIONAL
J. Bench, CIN 10½
J. Koosman, NY .. 9½

1968 AMERICAN
S. Bahnsen, NY 17
D. Unser, WAS 3

1969 NATIONAL
T. Sizemore, LA 14
C. Laboy, MON 3
A. Oliver, PIT 3
B. Didier, ATL 2
L. Hisle, PHI 2

1969 AMERICAN
L. Piniella, KC 9
M. Nagy, BOS 6
C. May, CHI 5
K. Tatum, CAL 4

1970 NATIONAL
C. Morton, MON ... 11
B. Carbo, CIN 8
L. Bowa, PHI 3
W. Simpson, CIN ... 1
C. Cedeno, HOU 1

1970 AMERICAN
T. Munson, NY 23

R. Foster, CLE 1

1971 NATIONAL
E. Williams, ATL ... 18
W. Montanez, PHI ... 6

1971 AMERICAN
C. Chambliss, CLE .11
B. Parsons, MIL 5
A. Mangual, OAK 4
D. Griffin, BOS 3
P. Splittorff, KC 1

1972 NATIONAL
J. Matlack, NY 19
Dv. Rader, SF 4
J. Milner, NY 1

1972 AMERICAN
C. Fisk, BOS 24

1973 NATIONAL
G. Matthews, SF ... 11
S. Rogers, MON ... 3½
B. Boone, PHI 2
E. Sosa, SF 2
D. Driessen, CIN ... 2
R. Cey, LA 1
D. Lopes, LA 1
J. Grubb, SD 1
R. Zisk, PIT .... ½

1973 AMERICAN
A. Bumbry, BAL .. 13½
P. Garcia, MIL 3
D. Porter, MIL 2
S. Busby, KC 2
D. Medich, NY 2
R. Coggins, BAL .. 1½

1974 NATIONAL
B. McBride, SL 16
G. Gross, HOU 7
B. Madlock CHI 1

1974 AMERICAN
M. Hargrove,
  TEX 16½
B. Dent, CHI 3
G. Brett, KC 2
R. Burleson, BOS . 1½
J. Sundberg, TEX ... 1

1975 NATIONAL
J. Montefusco, SF . 12
G. Carter, MON 9
Lr. Parrish, MON 1
R. Eastwick, CIN 1
M. Trillo, CHI 1

1975 AMERICAN
F. Lynn, BOS 23½
J. Rice, BOS .... ½

1976 NATIONAL
B. Metzger, SD 11
P. Zachry, CIN 11
H. Cruz, SL 2

1976 AMERICAN
M. Fidrych, DET ... 22
B. Wynegar, MIN ... 2

1977 NATIONAL
A. Dawson, MON .. 10

S. Henderson, NY ... 9
G. Richards, SD 4
F. Bannister, HOU ... 1

1977 AMERICAN
E. Murray, BAL .. 12½
M. Page, OAK 9½
B. Wills, TEX 4
D. Rozema, DET ... 2

1978 NATIONAL
B. Horner, ATL ... 12½
O. Smith, SD 8½
D. Robinson, PIT ... 3

1978 AMERICAN
L. Whitaker, DET ... 21
P. Molitor, MIL 3
C. Lansford, CAL ... 2
R. Gale, KC 1
A. Trammell, DET ... 1

1979 NATIONAL
R. Sutcliffe, LA 20
J. Leonard, HOU 3
S. Thompson, CHI ... 1

1979 AMERICAN
J. Castino, MIN 7
A. Griffin, TOR 7
M. Clear, CAL 5
R. Davis, NY 3
R. Baumgarten, CHI .3
P. Putnam, TEX 3

1980 NATIONAL
S. Howe, LA 80
B. Gullickson,
  MON 53
L. Smith, PHI 49
R. Oester, CIN 16
D. Smith, HOU 13
J. Reardon, NY 2
A. Holland, SF 1
L. Durham, SL 1
B. Walk, PHI 1

1980 AMERICAN
J. Charboneau,
  CLE 102
D. Stapleton, BOS .. 40
D. Corbett, MIN 38
D. Garcia, TOR 35
B. Burns, CHI 33
R. Peters, DET 3
R. Dotson, CHI 1

1981 NATIONAL
F. Valenzuela, LA . 107
T. Raines, MON 85
H. Brooks, NY 8½
B. Berenyi, CIN 5
J. Bonilla, SD 5
T. Pena, PIT 4
M. Wilson, NY ... 1½

1981 AMERICAN
D. Righetti, NY ... 127
R. Gedman, BOS ... 64
B. Ojeda, BOS 36
M. Jones, KC 8
D. Engle, MIN 4½
M. Witt, CAL 4
S. Babitt, OAK 4
J. Bell, TOR 2

G. Ward, MIN 1½
B. Havens, MIN 1

1982 NATIONAL
S. Sax, LA 63
J. Ray, PIT 57
W. McGee, SL 39
C. Davis, SF 32
L. DeLeon, SD 10
R. Sandberg, CHI ... 9
S. Bedrosian, ATL .. 4
D. LaPoint, SL 1
E. Show, SD 1

1982 AMERICAN
C. Ripken, BAL ... 132
K. Hrbek, MIN 90
W. Boggs, BOS .. 10½
E. Vande Berg, SEA ..9
G. Gaetti, MIN 4
D. Hostetler, TEX ... 3
V. Hayes, CLE 2
J. Barfield, TOR ... 1½

1983 NATIONAL
D. Strawberry, NY . 106
M. McMurtry, ATL .. 49
M. Hall, CHI 32
G. Redus, CIN 8
B. Doran, HOU 7
F. DiPino, HOU 6
G. Brock, LA 3
J. DeLeon, PIT 3
M. Thurmond, SD .. 1
L. Tunnell, PIT 1

1983 AMERICAN
R. Kittle, CHI 104
J. Franco, CLE 78
M. Boddicker, BAL . 70

1984 NATIONAL
D. Gooden, NY ... 118
J. Samuel, PHI 67
O. Hershiser, LA ... 15
M. Gladden, SF 9
R. Darling, NY 3
C. Martinez, SD 2
J. Stone, PHI 1
T. Pendleton, SL ... 1

1984 AMERICAN
A. Davis, SEA 134
M. Langston, SEA .. 82
K. Puckett, MIN 23
T. Teufel, MIN 5
M. Young, BAL 3
R. Clemens, BOS ... 2
M. Gubicza, KC 1
A. Nipper, BOS 1
R. Romanick, CAL .. 1

1985 NATIONAL
V. Coleman, SL ... 120
T. Browning, CIN .. 72
M. Duncan, LA 9
C. Brown, SF 7
G. Davis, HOU 3
R. McDowell, NY ... 2
J. Orsulak, PIT 2
J. Hesketh, MON 1

1985 AMERICAN
O. Guillen, CHI.... 101

T. Higuera, MIL ... 67
E. Riles, MIL 29
O. McDowell, TEX .. 25
S. Cliburn, CAL 16
B. Fisher, NY 7
T. Henke, TOR 5
M. Salas, MIN 2

1986 NATIONAL
T. Worrell, SL 118
R. Thompson, SF .. 46
K. Mitchell, NY 22
K. Kerfeld, HOU ... 17
W. Clark, SF 5
Br. Bonds, PIT 4
J. Deshaies, HOU .. 1
B. Larkin, CIN 1
B. Ruffin, PHI 1
J. Kruk, SD 1

1986 AMERICAN
J. Canseco, OAK .. 110
W. Joyner, CAL ... 98
M. Eichhorn, TOR .. 23
C. Snyder, CLE 16
D. Tartabull, SEA ... 4
R. Sierra, TEX 2

1987 NATIONAL
B. Santiago, SD .. 120
M. Dunne, PIT 66
J. Magrane, SL ... 10
C. Candaele, MON ..9
G. Young, HOU 7
C. James, PHI 1
L. Lancaster, CHI ... 1
G. Mathews, SL 1
R. Myers, NY 1

1987 AMERICAN
M. McGwire, OAK . 140
K. Seitzer, KC 64
M. Nokes, DET 32
M. Greenwell, BOS ..9
D. White, CAL 5
M. Henneman, DET .1
N. Liriano, TOR 1

1988 NATIONAL
C. Sabo, CIN 79
M. Grace, CHI 61
T. Belcher, LA 35
R. Gant, ATL 22
R. Alomar, SD 11
D. Berryhill, CHI ... 3
G. Jefferies, NY 3
R. Jordan, PHI 2

1988 AMERICAN
W. Weiss, OAK ... 103
B. Harvey, CAL 49
J. Reed, BOS 48
D. August, MIL 22
D. Gallagher, CHI .. 18
M. Perez, CHI 9
M. Schooler, SEA ... 2
C. Espy, TEX 1

1989 NATIONAL
J. Walton, CHI 116
D. Smith, CHI 68
G. Jefferies, NY 18
D. Lilliquist, ATL 6
A. Benes, SD 3

C. Hayes, PHI 3
G. Harris, SD 2

1989 AMERICAN
G. Olson, BAL 136
T. Gordon, KC 67
K. Griffey, SEA 21
C. Worthington, Bal .16
J. Abbott, Cal..... 10
K. Brown, TEX..... 2

1990 NATIONAL
D. Justice, ATL ... 118
D. DeShields, MON . 60
H. Morris, CIN 13
J. Burkett, SF 12
M. Harkey, CHI 7
T. Zeile, SL 4
M. Grissom, MON ... 1
L. Walker, MON 1

1990 AMERICAN
S. Alomar, CLE ... 140
K. Maas, NY 47
K. Appier, KC 31
J. Olerud, TOR 13
K. Tapani, MIN 5
T. Fryman, DET 5
R. Ventura, CHI 3
B. McDonald, BAL...2
A. Cole, CLE 1
S. Radinsky, CHI ... 1

1991 NATIONAL
J. Bagwell, HOU .. 118
O. Merced, PIT 53
R. Lankford, SL ... 28
B. Hunter, ATL 7
B. Barberie, MON ... 3
W. Chamberlain, PHI .3
C. McElroy, CHI 3
M. Stanton, ATL 1

1991 AMERICAN
C. Knoblauch, MIN 136
J. Guzman, TOR ... 68
M. Cuyler, DET 22
I. Rodriguez, TEX .. 10
B. DeLucia, SEA 7
M. Timlin, TOR 2
M. Whitten, CLE 2
L. Gomez, BAL 1
D. Henry, MIL 1
B. Mayne, KC 1
C. Nagy, CLE 1
P. Plantier, BOS 1

1992 NATIONAL
E. Karros, LA 116
M. Alou, MON 30
T. Wakefield, PIT .. 29
R. Sanders, CIN ... 23
D. Osborne, SL 12
M. Perez, SL 2
B. Rivera, PHI 1
F. Seminara, SD 1
B. Williams, HOU ... 1
M. Wohlers, ATL 1

1992 AMERICAN
P. Listach, MIL 122
K. Lofton, CLE 85
C. Fleming, SEA ... 23
C. Eldred, MIL 22

Cy Young Award: History

Commissioner Ford Frick, troubled by pitchers' lack of representation in MVP voting, spearheaded the 1956 effort to initiate a "most valuable pitcher" award. Cy Young, baseball's winningest pitcher, who had died the previous November, was the logical choice to name the honor after. At a special meeting on July 9, 1956, the Baseball Writers' Association of America approved, by the slim margin of 14-12, the establishment of the Cy Young Memorial Award, designed to honor the major leagues' outstanding pitcher each year beginning in '56. Ironically, the first winner, Brooklyn's Don Newcombe, also won his league's MVP Award.

One writer from each major league city participated in the balloting. In case of a tie vote, a second balloting was to be taken between the deadlocked pitchers. Hurlers were not to be eligible to win the award more than once, a rule which was evidently scrapped within two years.

Frick was adamantly opposed to the commonly voiced

idea to recognize a Cy Young winner in each league but, not long after his December 1965 retirement, the idea became a reality. On March 1, 1967, Frick's successor William Eckert approved the plan for dual awards, with two writers from each league city to select.

The system of having each writer make only one selection prevailed until 1969, when Detroit's Denny McLain and Baltimore's Mike Cuellar tied for the AL Cy Young Award. Thereafter, writers were instructed to name three pitchers in each league, with 5 points allotted for each first-place vote, 3 for second, and 1 for third.

The maximum number of points available for one pitcher was 16 from 1956–60, 18 in 1961, 20 in 1962–68, 24 in 1969, 120 in 1970–76 (AL) and 1970–present (NL), and 140 in 1977–present (AL). As with every other major award, there have been a few instances in Cy Young voting where at least one writer failed to return a ballot.

Unanimous winners of the Cy Young Award are Sandy Koufax (NL, 1963, '65, and '66), Bob Gibson (NL, 1968), Denny McLain (AL, 1968), Steve Carlton (NL, 1972), Ron Guidry (AL, 1978), Rick Sutcliffe (NL, 1984), Dwight Gooden (NL, 1985), Roger Clemens (AL, 1986), and Orel Hershiser (NL, 1988).

Relief pitchers, once overlooked in Cy Young balloting, have become strong candidates in recent years. Until 1970 only one reliever — Lindy McDaniel in 1960 — had received even a single vote. The new voting system helped open opportunities for bullpen aces and in 1974 the Dodgers' Mike Marshall became the first reliever to win the Cy Young Award. He has been followed in that distinction by Sparky Lyle (AL, 1977), Bruce Sutter (NL, 1979), Rollie Fingers (AL, 1981), Willie Hernández (AL, 1984), Steve Bedrosian (NL, 1987), Mark Davis (NL, 1989), and Dennis Eckersley (AL, 1992).

Cy Young Award

1956
D. Newcombe, BKN (NL) 10
S. Maglie, BKN (NL) . 4
W. Spahn, MIL (NL) . . 1
W. Ford, NY (AL) 1

1957
W. Spahn, MIL (NL) . . 15
D. Donovan, CHI (AL) 1

1958
B. Turley, NY (AL) 5
W. Spahn, MIL (NL) . . 4
B. Friend, PIT (NL) . . . 3
L. Burdette, MIL (NL) 3

1959
E. Wynn, CHI (AL) . . 13
S. Jones, SF (NL) . . . 2
B. Shaw, CHI (AL) . . . 1

1960
V. Law, PIT (NL) 8
W. Spahn, MIL (NL) . . 4
E. Broglio, SL (NL) . . . 1
L. McDaniel, SL (NL) . 1

1961
W. Ford, NY (AL) 9
W. Spahn, MIL (NL) . . 6
F. Lary, DET (AL) 2

1962
D. Drysdale, LA (NL) 14
J. Sanford, SF (NL) . . 4
B. Purkey, CIN (NL) . . 1
B. Pierce, SF (NL) . . . 1

1963
S. Koufax, LA (NL) . . 20

1964
D. Chance, LA (AL) . . 17
L. Jackson, CHI (NL) . 2
S. Koufax, LA (NL) . . . 1

1965
S. Koufax, LA (NL) . . 20

1966
S. Koufax, LA (NL) . . 20

1967 NATIONAL
M. Mc Cormick, SF . 18
F. Jenkins, CHI 1
J. Bunning, PHI 1

1967 AMERICAN
J. Lonborg, BOS . . . 18
J. Horlen, CHI 2

1968 NATIONAL
B. Gibson, SL 20

1968 AMERICAN
D. McLain, DET . . . 20

1969 NATIONAL
T. Seaver, NY 23
P. Niekro, ATL 1

1969 AMERICAN
M. Cuellar, BAL . . . 10
D. McLain, DET . . . 10
J. Perry, MIN 3
D. McNally, BAL . . . 1

1970 NATIONAL
B. Gibson, SL 118
G. Perry, SF 51
F. Jenkins CHI . . . 16
D. Giusti, PIT 8
J. Merritt, CIN 8
G. Nolan, CIN 5
T. Seaver, NY 4
W. Granger, CIN . . . 3
C. Morton, MON . . 2
L. Walker, PIT 1

1970 AMERICAN
J. Perry, MIN 55
D. McNally, BAL . . 47
S. McDowell, CLE . 45
M. Cuellar, BAL . . 44
J. Palmer, BAL . . . 11
C. Wright, CAL 9
R. Perranoski, MIN . 5

1971 NATIONAL
F. Jenkins, CHI . . . 97
T. Seaver, NY 61
A. Downing, LA . . . 40
D. Ellis, PIT 9
B. Gibson, SL 3
J. Johnson, SF . . . 2
D. Roberts, SD . . . 2
J. Marichal, SF 1
B. Stoneman, MON . 1

1971 AMERICAN
V. Blue, OAK 98
M. Lolich, DET . . . 85
W. Wood, CHI . . . 23
D. McNally, BAL . . 8
D. Drago, KC 1
A. Messersmith, CAL 1

1972 NATIONAL
S. Carlton, PHI . . 120
S. Blass, PIT 35
F. Jenkins, CHI . . . 23
M. Marshall, MON . 8
G. Nolan, CIN 6
T. Seaver, NY 6

C. Carroll, CIN 6
D. Sutton, LA 6
B. Gibson, SL 3
M. Pappas, CHI 3

1972 AMERICAN
G. Perry, CLE 64
W. Wood, CHI . . . 58
M. Lolich, DET . . . 27
J. Hunter, OAK . . . 26
J. Palmer, BAL . . . 20
L. Tiant, BOS 16
S. Lyle, NY 3
N. Ryan, CAL 2

1973 NATIONAL
T. Seaver, NY 71
M. Marshall, MON . 54
R. Bryant, SF 50
J. Billingham, CIN . 30
D. Sutton, LA 7
F. Norman, SD-CIN . 3
D. Giusti, PIT 1

1973 AMERICAN
J. Palmer, BAL . . . 88
N. Ryan, CAL 62
J. Hunter, OAK . . . 52
J. Hiller, DET 6
W. Wood, CHI . . . 3
J. Colborn, MIL . . . 2
V. Blue, OAK 1
B. Blyleven, MIN . . 1
G. Perry, CLE 1

1974 NATIONAL
M. Marshall, LA . . . 96
A. Messersmith, LA 66
P. Niekro, ATL . . . 15
D. Sutton, LA 12
A. Hrabosky, SL . . 9
J. Billingham, CIN . 8
D. Gullett, CIN . . . 5
C. Carroll, CIN . . . 2
D. Giusti, PIT 1
D. Capra, ATL 1
L. McGlothen, SL . . 1

1974 AMERICAN
J. Hunter, OAK . . . 90
F. Jenkins, TEX . . . 75
N. Ryan, CAL 28
G. Perry, CLE 8
L. Tiant, BOS 8
M. Cuellar, BAL . . . 6
J. Hiller, DET 1

1975 NATIONAL
T. Seaver, NY 98
R. Jones, SD 80
A. Hrabosky, SL . . 33
J. Montefusco, SF . 2
D. Gullett, CIN . . . 1

A. Messersmith, LA . . 1
D. Sutton, LA 1

1975 AMERICAN
J. Palmer, BAL 98
J. Hunter, NY 74
R. Fingers, OAK . . . 25
F. Tanana, CAL 7
J. Kaat, CHI 7
V. Blue, OAK 2
R. Gossage, CHI . . . 2
R. Wise, BOS 1

1976 NATIONAL
R. Jones, SD 96
J. Koosman, NY . 69½
D. Sutton, LA . . . 25½
S. Carlton, PHI . . . 11
R. Eastwick, CIN . . 6
J. Matlack, NY . . . 5
J. Richard, HOU . . 2
T. Seaver, NY 1

1976 AMERICAN
J. Palmer, BAL . . . 108
M. Fidrych, DET . . 51
F. Tanana, CAL . . . 18
E. Figueroa, NY . . 12
L. Tiant, BOS 10
V. Blue, OAK 8
B. Campbell, MIN . 7
R. Fingers, OAK . . 1
W. Garland, BAL . . 1

1977 NATIONAL
S. Carlton, PHI . . 104
T. John, LA 54
T. Seaver, NY-CIN . 18
R. Reuschel, CHI . . 18
J. Candelaria, PIT . 17
B. Sutter, CHI 5

1977 AMERICAN
S. Lyle, NY 56½
J. Palmer, BAL . . . 48
N. Ryan, CAL 46
D. Leonard, KC . . 45
B. Campbell, BOS 25½
D. Goltz, MIN 19
R. Guidry, NY 5
D. Rozema, DET . . 4
F. Tanana, CAL . . . 3

1978 NATIONAL
G. Perry, SD 116
B. Hooton, LA . . . 38
V. Blue, SF 17
J. Richard, HOU . . 13
K. Tekulve, PIT . . . 12
P. Niekro, ATL . . . 10
R. Grimsley, MON . 7
R. Fingers, SD . . . 1
T. John, LA 1

D. Robinson, PIT 1
D. Sutton, LA 1

1978 AMERICAN
R. Guidry, NY 140
M. Caldwell, MIL . . 76
J. Palmer, BAL . . . 14
D. Eckersley, BOS . 10
R. Gossage, NY . . . 4
F. Jenkins, TEX . . . 2
E. Figueroa, NY . . . 1
L. Gura, KC 1
D. Leonard, KC . . . 1
M. Marshall, MIN . . 1
P. Splittorff, KC . . . 1
B. Stanley, BOS . . . 1

1979 NATIONAL
B. Sutter, CHI 72
J. Niekro, HOU . . . 66
J. Richard, HOU . . 41
T. Seaver, CIN . . . 20
K. Tekulve, PIT . . . 14
P. Niekro, ATL . . . 3

1979 AMERICAN
M. Flanagan, BAL . 136
T. John, NY 51
R. Guidry, NY 26
J. Kern, TEX 25
M. Marshall, MIN . . 7
J. Koosman, MIN . . 5
D. Eckersley, BOS . 1
A. Lopez, DET 1

1980 NATIONAL
S. Carlton, PHI . . . 118
J. Reuss, LA 55
J. Bibby, PIT 28
J. Niekro, HOU . . . 11
T. McGraw, PHI . . . 1
S. Rogers, MON . . 1
J. Sambito, HOU . . 1
M. Soto, CIN 1

1980 AMERICAN
S. Stone, BAL 100
M. Norris, OAK . . . 91
R. Gossage, NY . . 37½
T. John, NY 14
D. Quisenberry, KC 7½
L. Gura, KC 1
S. McGregor, BAL . 1

1981 NATIONAL
F. Valenzuela, LA . . 70
T. Seaver, CIN . . . 67
S. Carlton, PHI . . . 50
N. Ryan, HOU 28
B. Sutter, SL 1

1981 AMERICAN
R. Fingers, MIL . . . 126
S. McCatty, OAK . 84½

J. Morris, DET 21
P. Vuckovich, MIL . 8½
D. Martinez, BAL . . 3½
R. Gossage, NY . . . 3
R. Guidry, NY 2½
B. Burns, CHI 2
L. Gura, KC 1

1982 NATIONAL
S. Carlton, PHI . . . 112
S. Rogers, MON . . 29
F. Valenzuela, LA . 25½
B. Sutter, SL 25
P. Niekro, ATL . . . 18
G. Minton, SF 4
J. Andujar, SL 1
G. Garber, ATL . . . 1
M. Soto, CIN . . . . ½

1982 AMERICAN
P. Vuckovich, MIL . 87
J. Palmer, BAL . . . 59
D. Quisenberry, KC . 40
D. Stieb, TOR 36
R. Sutcliffe, CLE . . 14
G. Zahn, CAL 7
B. Stanley, BOS . . 4
B. Caudill, SEA . . . 4
D. Petry, DET 1

1983 NATIONAL
J. Denny, PHI 103
M. Soto, CIN 61
J. Orosco, NY 19
S. Rogers, MON . . 15
L. McWilliams, PIT . 7
A. Holland, PHI . . . 4
C. McMurtry, ATL . 3
B. Welch, LA 2
N. Ryan, HOU 1
L. Smith, CHI 1

1983 AMERICAN
L. Hoyt, CHI 116
D. Quisenberry, KC . 81
J. Morris, DET 38
R. Dotson, CHI . . . 9
R. Guidry, NY 5
S. McGregor, BAL . 3

1984 NATIONAL
R. Sutcliffe, CHI . . 120
D. Gooden, NY . . . 45
B. Sutter, SL 33½
J. Andujar, SL . . . 12½
R. Gossage, SD . . 3
M. Soto, CIN 2

1984 AMERICAN
W. Hernandez, DET 88
D. Quisenberry, KC . 71
B. Blyleven, CLE . . 45
M. Boddicker, BAL . 41

D. Petry, DET 3	**1986 NATIONAL**	**1987 AMERICAN**	O. Hershiser, LA 7	**1990 AMERICAN**	J. McDowell, CHI ...3
F. Viola, MIN 2	M. Scott, HOU 98	R. Clemens, BOS .124	J. Magrane, SL 7	B. Welch, OAK 107	D. Ward, TOR 3
J. Morris, DET 1	F. Valenzuela, LA ...88	J. Key, TOR 64	T. Belcher, LA 4	R. Clemens, BOS ...77	
D. Stieb, TOR 1	M. Krukow, SF 15	D. Stewart, OAK ...32	S. Garrelts, SF 4	D. Stewart, OAK ...43	**1992 NATIONAL**
	B. Ojeda, NY 9	D. Alexander, DET ...8	R. Reuschel, SF 3	B. Thigpen, CHI 20	G. Maddux, CHI ...112
1985 NATIONAL	R. Darling, NY 2	M. Langston, SEA ...7	M. Bielecki, CHI.....1	D. Eckersley, OAK ...2	T. Glavine, ATL.....78
D. Gooden, NY ...120	R. Rhoden, PIT 2	T. Higuera, MIL 5	M. Williams, CHI 1	D. Stieb, TOR 2	B. Tewksbury, SL ...22
J. Tudor, SL 65	D. Gooden, NY 1	F. Viola, MIN 5		C. Finley, CAL 1	L. Smith, SL........3
O. Hershiser, LA ...17	S. Fernandez, NY ...1	J. Reardon, MIN 4	**1989 AMERICAN**		D. Drabek, PIT......1
J. Andujar, SL 6		J. Morris, DET 3	B. Saberhagen, KC ...	**1991 NATIONAL**	
F. Valenzuela, LA 4	**1986 AMERICAN**		138	T. Glavine, ATL ...110	**1992 AMERICAN**
T. Browning, CIN ...3	R. Clemens, BOS ...140	**1988 NATIONAL**	D. Stewart, OAK ...80	L. Smith, SL 60	D. Eckersley, OAK .107
J. Reardon, MON ...1	T. Higuera, MIL 42	O. Hershisher, LA .120	M. Moore, OAK 10	J. Smiley, PIT 26	J. McDowell, CHI ...51
	M. Witt, CAL 35	D. Jackson, CIN ...54	B. Blyleven, CAL 9	J. Rijo, CIN 13	R. Clemens, BOS ..48
1985 AMERICAN	D. Righetti, NY.....20	D. Cone, NY 42	N. Ryan, TEX 5	D. Martinez, MON ...4	M. Mussina, BAL...26
B. Saberhagen,	J. Morris, DET 13		J. Ballard, BAL 3	S. Avery, ATL 1	J. Morris, TOR 10
KC 127	M. Eichhorn, TOR ...2	**1988 AMERICAN**	D. Eckersley, OAK ...3	A. Benes, SD 1	K. Brown, TEX 9
R. Guidry, NY 88		F. Viola, MIN 138	G. Olson, BAL 3	M. Williams, PHI ...1	C. Nagy, CLE.......1
B. Blyleven, MIN 9	**1987 NATIONAL**	D. Eckersley, OAK ..52	J. Russell, TEX 1		
D. Quisenberry, KC ..9	S. Bedrosian, PHI ..57	M. Gubicza, KC 26		**1991 AMERICAN**	
C. Leibrandt, KC ...7	R. Sutcliffe, CHI 55	D. Stewart, OAK ...16	**1990 NATIONAL**	R. Clemens, BOS .119	
D. Alexander, TOR ...5	R. Reuschel, SF 54	B. Hurst, BOS 12	D. Drabek, PIT 118	S. Erickson, MIN ...56	
B. Burns, CHI 2	O. Hershiser, LA ...14	R. Clemens, BOS ...8	R. Marinez, LA 70	J. Abbott, CAL.....26	
D. Moore, CAL 2	D. Gooden, NY 12		F. Viola, NY 19	J. Morris, MIN 17	
D. Stieb, TOR 2	N. Ryan, HOU 12	**1989 NATIONAL**	D. Gooden, NY 8	B. Harvey, CAL 10	
M. Moore, SEA 1	M. Scott, HOU 9	M. Davis, SD 107	R. Myers, CIN 1	M. Langston, CAL ...7	
	B. Welch, LA 3	M. Scott, HOU 65		K. Tapani, MIN 6	
		G. Maddux, CHI 17		B. Gullickson, DET ..5	

Hypothetical Awards

As the "expert" in baseball award-voting, I have been asked to make a set of hypothetical award selections for the years no official honors were given; i.e., pre-1956 Cy Young, pre-1947 Rookie of the Year, and pre-1911 MVP Awards, along with awards for any other "missing" years.

While this assignment gave me unusual freedom, I felt a certain responsibility to make my selections consistent with the perceptions and voting trends of a particular era. For example, although there were better NL players than Cincinnati's Edd Roush in 1919, he did two things which, combined, would have virtually guaranteed him the MVP Award: he won the batting crown, which was *the* individual title in the dead-ball era; and he played on a pennant-winner, which has always been a key factor in MVP voting. Thus, I felt obliged to make Roush my hypothetical selection.

Besides my own opinions and intuitions, several sources were instrumental in my selection process, including:

1. SABR retroactive award surveys, which have been done for pre-1949 Rookie of the Year and pre-1967 Cy Young Awards. SABR (the Society for American Baseball Research) is comprised of more than six thousand hard-core fans, hundreds of whom chose to participate in these surveys. The ballots were tremendously helpful in screening candidates and the voting results were carefully compared to my own choices.

2. Linear Weights, an overall player rating system devised by Pete Palmer, first used in *The Hidden Game of Baseball* (Doubleday, 1984, 1985), and continued in *Total Baseball*.

3. MVP voting results, for comparing Cy Young and Rookie candidates. If rookie "A" receives 75 points in the MVP election, while comparable rookie "B" receives just 10, I am forced to conclude that the on-the-spot observers discerned some important difference that we can't see in the statistics and that "A" is probably the better choice.

(Incidentally, the criteria used to determine rookies was a maximum of 90 at-bats or 45 innings pitched in any previous seasons.)

4. Unofficial awards, including 1940–46 Rookie and 1929–30 MVP selections.

5. Cy Young (1956–66) and Rookie of the Year (1947–48) balloting, for years in which one league had no official winner.

The resulting selections are not necessarily ones the average reader will agree with, nor even that the *writer* agrees with; rather, they are the ones which can be *best justified with the available evidence.* I am prepared to defend any of my choices.

In comparison with the Palmer system, my selections concurred 54 percent with top player selections and 59 percent with top pitcher nominations. In comparison with the SABR surveys, my selections agreed 84 percent in the Rookie of the Year Award and 79 percent in the Cy Young Award.

The big winner in the hypothetical awards is Christy Mathewson, who picks up a Rookie of the Year, two MVPs, and eight Cy Young Awards. Other pitchers capturing at least three Cy Youngs are Walter Johnson (7); Lefty Grove (6, consecutively); Warren Spahn (4, to add to the one he actually did win); Grover Alexander (4); Burleigh Grimes, Carl Hubbell, Bob Feller, Bucky Walters, Bob Lemon, and appropriately, Cy Young himself (3 each).

Notable Rookies of the Year include Grover Alexander, Babe Ruth, Rogers Hornsby, Dizzy Dean, Joe DiMaggio, and Ted Williams.

Honus Wagner cops six MVP Awards, including four in succession. Three-time MVPs are Nap Lajoie, Alexander, Ruth, and Hornsby. Ruth (once) and Hornsby (twice) also won official MVP Awards.

The following pages contain my hypothetical Cy Young (124), Rookie of the Year (97), and MVP (42) selections for this century.

Hypothetical Cy Young Award

American League Pitcher/Club	Year	American League Pitcher/Club	Year	American League Pitcher/Club	Year	National League Pitcher/Club	Year	National League Pitcher/Club	Year	National League Pitcher/Club	Year
C. Young, BOS	1901	G. Uhle, CLE	1923	D. Trout, DET	1944	J. McGinnity, BKN	1900	J. Vaughn, CHI	1918	B. Walters, CIN	1939
C. Young, BOS	1902	W. Johnson, WAS	1924	H. Newhouser, DET	1945	N. Hahn, CIN	1901	J. Vaughn, CHI	1919	B. Walters, CIN	1940
C. Young, BOS	1903	S. Coveleski, WAS	1925	H. Newhouser, DET	1946	J. Taylor, CHI	1902	G. Alexander, CHI	1920	W. Wyatt, BKN	1941
J. Chesbro, NY	1904	G. Uhle, CLE	1926	J. Page, NY	1947	C. Mathewson, NY	1903	B. Grimes, BKN	1921	M. Cooper, SL	1942
R. Waddell, PHI	1905	W. Moore, NY	1927	B. Lemon, CLE	1948	J. McGinnity, NY	1904	W. Cooper, PIT	1922	M. Cooper, SL	1943
O. Hess, CLE	1906	L. Grove, PHI	1928	M. Parnell, BOS	1949	Mathewson, NY	1905	D. Luque, CIN	1923	B. Walters, CIN	1944
E. Walsh, CHI	1907	L. Grove, PHI	1929	B. Lemon, CLE	1950	M. Brown, CHI	1906	D. Vance, BKN	1924	H. Wyse, CHI	1945
E. Walsh, CHI	1908	L. Grove, PHI	1930	N. Garver, SL	1951	Mathewson, NY	1907	D. Vance, BKN	1925	H. Pollet, SL	1946
F. Smith, CHI	1909	L. Grove, PHI	1931	B. Shantz, PHI	1952	Mathewson, NY	1908	R. Kremer, PIT	1926	E. Blackwell, CIN	1947
J. Coombs, PHI	1910	L. Grove, PHI	1932	B. Pierce, CHI	1953	Mathewson, NY	1909	C. Root, CHI	1927	J. Sain, BOS	1948
W. Johnson, WAS	1911	L. Grove, PHI	1933	B. Lemon, CLE	1954	Mathewson, NY	1910	B. Grimes, PIT	1928	W. Spahn, BOS	1949
J. Wood, BOS	1912	L. Gomez, NY	1934	R. Narleski, CLE	1955	Mathewson, NY	1911	B. Grimes, PIT	1929	J. Konstanty, PHI	1950
W. Johnson, WAS	1913	W. Ferrell, BOS	1935	B. Pierce, CHI	1956	R. Marquard, NY	1912	P. Malone, CHI	1930	S. Maglie, NY	1951
W. Johnson, WAS	1914	T. Bridges, DET	1936	J. Bunning, DET	1957	Mathewson, NY	1913	E. Brandt, BOS	1931	R. Roberts, PHI	1952
W. Johnson, WAS	1915	L. Gomez, NY	1937	C. Estrada, BAL	1960	B. James, BOS	1914	L. Warneke, CHI	1932	W. Spahn, MIL	1953
B. Ruth, BOS	1916	R. Ruffing, NY	1938	D. Donovan, CLE	1962	G. Alexander, PHI	1915	C. Hubbell, NY	1933	J. Antonelli, NY	1954
E. Cicotte, CHI	1917	B. Feller, CLE	1939	W. Ford, NY	1963	G. Alexander, PHI	1916	D. Dean, SL	1934	R. Roberts, PHI	1955
W. Johnson, WAS	1918	B. Feller, CLE	1940	E. Fisher, CHI	1965	G. Alexander, PHI	1917	D. Dean, SL	1935	W. Spahn, MIL	1958
W. Johnson, WAS	1919	B. Feller, CLE	1941	J. Kaat, MIN	1966			C. Hubbell, NY	1936	S. Jones, SF	1959
J. Bagby, CLE	1920	T. Hughson, BOS	1942					C. Hubbell, NY	1937	W. Spahn, MIL	1961
R. Faber, CHI	1921	S. Chandler, NY	1943					B. Lee, CHI	1938	L. Jackson, CHI	1964
E. Rommel, PHI	1922										

Hypothetical Federal League Awards

	1914	1915
Most Valuable Player	B. Kauff, IND	D. Zwilling, CHI
Cy Young	C. Hendrix, CHI	G. McConnell, CHI
Rookie of the Year	B. Kauff, IND	E. Johnson, SL

Hypothetical Rookie of the Year Award

American League Player/Club	Year	American League Player/Club	Year	American League Player/Club	Year	National League Player/Club	Year	National League Player/Club	Year	National League Player/Club	Year
S. Seybold, PHI	1901	J. Bagby, CLE	1916	J. Allen, NY	1932	E. Scott, CIN	1900	T. Long, SL	1915	W. Berger, BOS	1930
A. Joss, CLE	1902	A. Sothoron, SL	1917	B. Johnson, PHI	1933	C. Mathewson, NY	1901	R. Hornsby, SL	1916	P. Derringer, SL	1931
C. Bender, PHI	1903	S. Perry, PHI	1918	H. Trosky, CLE	1934	H. Smoot, SL	1902	L. Cadore, BKN	1917	D. Dean, SL	1932
F. Glade, SL	1904	D. Kerr, CHI	1919	J. Powell, WAS	1935	J. Weimer, CHI	1903	C. Hollocher, CHI	1918	F. Demaree, CHI	1933
G. Stone, SL	1905	B. Meusel, NY	1920	J. DiMaggio, NY	1936	H. Lumley, BKN	1904	O. Tuero, SL	1919	C. Davis, PHI	1934
C. Rossman, CLE	1906	J. Sewell, CLE	1921	R. York, DET	1937	J. Reulbach, CHI	1905	J. Haines, SL	1920	C. Blanton, PIT	1935
S. Nicholls, PHI	1907	H. Pillette, DET	1922	K. Keltner, DET	1938	J. Pfiester, CHI	1906	R. Grimes, CHI	1921	J. Mize, SL	1936
E. Summers, DET	1908	H. Summa, CLE	1923	T. Williams, BOS	1939	N. Rucker, BKN	1907	H. Miller, CHI	1922	J. Turner, BOS	1937
F. Baker, PHI	1909	A. Simmons, PHI	1924	W. Judnich, SL	1940	G. McQuillan, PHI	1908	G. Grantham, CHI	1923	J. Rizzo, PIT	1938
R. Ford, NY	1910	E. Combs, NY	1925	P. Rizzuto, NY	1941	D. Miller, PIT	1909	K. Cuyler, PIT	1924	H. Casey, BKN	1939
V. Gregg, CLE	1911	T. Lazzeri, NY	1926	J. Pesky, BOS	1942	K. Cole, CHI	1910	J. Welsh, BOS	1925	B. Young, NY	1940
D. Pratt, SL	1912	W. Moore, NY	1927	B. Johnson, NY	1943	G. Alexander, PHI	1911	P. Waner, PIT	1926	E. Riddle, CIN	1941
R. Russell, CHI	1913	E. Morris, BOS	1928	J. Berry, PHI	1944	L. Cheney, CHI	1912	L. Waner, PIT	1927	J. Beazley, SL	1942
R. Bressler, PHI	1914	D. Alexander, DET	1929	B. Ferriss, BOS	1945	J. Viox, PIT	1913	D. Bissonette, BKN	1928	L. Klein, SL	1943
B. Ruth, BOS	1915	S. Jolley, CHI	1930	B. Lemon, CLE	1946	J. Pfeffer, BKN	1914	J. Frederick, BKN	1929	B. Voiselle, NY	1944
		J. Vosmik, CLE	1931	F. Shea, NY	1947					K. Burkhart, SL	1945
				G. Bearden, CLE	1948					D. Ennis, PHI	1946

Hypothetical Most Valuable Player Award

American League Player/Club	Year	American League Player/Club	Year	American League Player/Club	Year	National League Player/Club	Year	National League Player/Club	Year	National League Player/Club	Year
N. Lajoie, PHI	1901	T. Cobb, DET	1907	B. Ruth, BOS	1918	H. Wagner, PIT	1900	H. Wagner, PIT	1907	J. Vaughn, CHI	1918
C. Young, BOS	1902	E. Walsh, CHI	1908	J. Jackson, CHI	1919	H. Wagner, PIT	1901	C. Mathewson, NY	1908	E. Roush, CIN	1919
N. Lajoie, CLE	1903	T. Cobb, DET	1909	B. Ruth, NY	1920	H. Wagner, PIT	1902	H. Wagner, PIT	1909	R. Hornsby, SL	1920
J. Chesbro, NY	1904	J. Coombs, PHI	1910	B. Ruth, NY	1921	H. Wagner, PIT	1903	S. Magee, PHI	1910	R. Hornsby, SL	1921
R. Waddell, PHI	1905	E. Collins, CHI	1915	L. Fonseca, CLE	1929	J. McGinnity, NY	1904	G. Alexander, PHI	1915	R. Hornsby, SL	1922
N. Lajoie, CLE	1906	T. Speaker, CLE	1916	J. Cronin, WAS	1930	C. Mathewson, NY	1905	G. Alexander, PHI	1916	D. Luque, CIN	1923
		E. Cicotte, CHI	1917			F. Chance, CHI	1906	G. Alexander, PHI	1917	H. Wilson, CHI	1930

Gold Glove Award: History

In a 1956 spring training survey, Elmer A. Blasco—employed by Rawlings Sporting Goods as advertising, public relations and sales manager—found that 83 percent of the active regular major league players wore Rawlings gloves or mitts. Noting that Hillerich & Bradsby (the major leagues' leading baseball bat supplier) awarded Silver Bats to the leagues' top hitters, Blasco reasoned that Rawlings ought to sponsor some sort of fielding award.

After his idea was accepted by Rawlings' management, Blasco contacted the Brown Shoe Company of St. Louis and obtained from them a hide of gold lamé-tanned leather used to make ladies' formal slippers. A glove was crafted from this hide, laced and stamped as a regular fielders glove, and attached to a metal fixture on a walnut base with an appropriate engraved plate.

Thus was born the Gold Glove Award.

The October 2, 1957, edition of *The Sporting News* featured a full-page advertisement/announcement: "Rec-

ognizing the importance of superior individual fielding performance to the advancement of baseball as America's national game, Rawlings (Sporting Goods Company) has established Annual Gold Glove Awards beginning with the 1957 season.

"Each of the nine Major League players chosen for *The Sporting News* All-Star Fielding Team will be honored with a Rawlings Gold Glove Award. Selections will be made by a Committee named by *The Sporting News*.

"Awards will be Rawlings custom-built gloves or mitts hand-crafted of special metallic gold-finished leather, each mounted on a suitable hardwood stand bearing an engraved plate."

TSN publisher J. G. Taylor Spink appointed nineteen noted sportswriters for the selection task. They included Shirley Povich, Edgar Munzel, Hy Hurwitz, Earl Lawson, Bob Broeg, Allen Lewis, and Hal Lebowitz. A contest to predict the winners, open to baseball-playing boys, was sponsored by Rawlings.

The first Gold Glove winners were announced with great pomp and circumstance in the December 18, 1957, issue of TSN. "Too long neglected, the magicians of the defense have had no real recognition," the article explained, adding that the selections were made "solely on the basis of their defensive ability."

Rawlings and TSN also joined forces that year in the establishment of the Silver Glove Award, given to the top minor league fielder at each position—based entirely on fielding averages.

In 1958 the Gold Glove selection privilege was turned over to the major league players and an All-Star Fielding Team was selected for each league (as it still is).

In 1961 the method for selecting outfielders was changed. Rather than choosing a left-, center-, and right fielder for each league, each voter was instructed to name three outfielders regardless of position (still the practice today).

In 1965 the managers and coaches of each team took over the voting responsibility, which they have retained ever since. Voters are not permitted to select players on their own teams. In 1987, 139 different managers and coaches took part in the balloting.

Perhaps because of its originality, the Gold Glove is the one *Sporting News* award that has gained universal acceptance and prestige in the baseball world. However, as with any award, the selections often draw criticism.

One complaint is that too much importance is given to fielding average. Most of us realize that FA is not always a reliable indicator of defensive ability, but how much does it influence the Gold Glove voters?

Of the 366 FA leaders at the various positions between 1957–87 (discounting pitchers and counting only one outfielder per league each year), 118 (32 percent) also won their respective Gold Glove Awards (see Table 1). We can say, then, that if a player leads his league in FA, he has about a one-in-three chance of winning the Gold Glove—not an overwhelming correlation, but about four times better than random chance.

This raises some interesting questions. Since official fielding statistics are not published until months *after* Gold Gloves are voted on, any voter relying on fielding stats would probably have to consult (or remember) the *previous* year's data. Therefore, if FA itself really does

impress voters, we should expect to see many players winning a Gold Glove the year *after* they lead in FA. Do they? Well, no (see Table 2). The percentage here is 25 percent or one-in-four—again, considerably better than chance, but less of a factor than leading in FA in the current year.

And what about the influence of Gold Gloves on fielding averages? Is an official scorer less likely to charge an error against a player simply because he won a Gold Glove the previous year? Apparently not (see Table 3). The percentage of Gold Glove recipients leading in FA the following year is 23 percent.

"It is my belief that a lot more is considered than fielding percentage," says *TSN* editor Tom Barnidge, citing "range, throwing arm, the headiness of the ballplayer." Cincinnati's Pete Rose, a two-time Gold Glove winner concurred: "There are a lot of intangibles involved in voting for the Gold Glove. Take an outfielder. The coaches and managers watch these guys all the time. How they play the hitters, how strong their arms are, how often they hit the cutoff man, and all that is taken into consideration—things that do not show up in the statistics."

Another criticism of the Gold Glove is that batting performance plays a role in the selections, contrary to the award's philosophy. As *USA Today* baseball editor Hal Bodley puts it, "A player who is outstanding on defense and respectable on offense has a much better chance of getting a Gold Glove than a counterpart whose forte is fielding alone."

Other factors can be distractions to the voters: flashiness, reputations, and the selection process itself. For insight on some of these and their effects, I consulted an expert on the Gold Glove: Wes Parker, a six-time winner of the award at first base.

Parker, it should be noted, would seem to have no reason to gripe about the award. He grasped the honor from a seven-time winner; he won it even when he batted as low as .239; and he became one of only two nonpitchers (Roberto Clemente is the other) to win the award in his final major league season.

"I would say many, if not most, coaches and managers fail to take their voting responsibility seriously," says Parker. "They don't treat it as a vital act. They are usually much more concerned with their team and the pennant race and, as a result, tend to zip through the ballots (distributed in September). So they wind up voting for the most recognizable names."

Parker brings out another rarely discussed procedural problem: "Since players [when they were voting] and coaches are forbidden to vote for anyone on their own team, they often won't vote for the guy who is contending with their team's leading candidate for the same award. That increases their teammate's chances."

On the subject of reputation, Parker asserts that it "has a lot to do with it, absolutely. In 1966, Bill White won the award (for the seventh consecutive time), although even White admitted that I probably deserved it. It takes a couple of years for your reputation to catch up with you, but that can work to your advantage at the end of your career.

"Flashiness is a factor too," continues Parker. "It puts the player's name in the forefront of the voter's minds." Wes also concurs with the theory that a player's bat can

be the difference in winning this 'fielding' award.

"[Four-time Gold Glove winner Steve] Garvey is a good example of someone who won it with his bat and notoriety, a perfect example, in fact," opines Parker. "Garvey was vastly overrated defensively . . . he had no range, no arm, and no aggressiveness. He would hold the ball and allow opposing runners to take extra bases to avoid throwing errors. That's how he compiled his high

[fielding] averages at first base. Remember, he was a terrible third baseman, worst I ever saw." (In 1972, Garvey's last season as a third-sacker, he led the NL with 28 errors in just 85 games, posting a woeful .902 percentage.)

"Amazingly, despite these prejudices," Parker concludes, "I think the Gold Glove choices have been excellent. At first base I think they have been perfect, with the exception of Garvey."

TABLE 1 Fielding Average Leaders Winning Gold Glove, 1957-87 (Maximum 61 Each Position).

POS.	NL	AL	TOT.	PCT.
C	7	7	14	23
1B	13	13	26	43
2B	14	5	19	31
3B	4	15	19	31
SS	14	12	26	43
OF	6	8	14	23
TOT.	58	60	118	32

TABLE 2 Fielding Average Leaders Winning Gold Glove in Following Season, 1956-86 (Maximum 61 Each Position).

POS.	NL	AL	TOT.	PCT.
C	7	7	14	23
1B	8	11	19	31
2B	9	6	15	25
3B	3	13	16	26
SS	11	9	20	33
OF	2	5	7	11
TOT.	40	51	91	25

TABLE 3 Fielding Average Leaders Who Won Gold Glove in Previous Season, 1958-87 (Maximum 59 Each Position).

POS.	NL	AL	TOT.	PCT.
C	3	7	10	17
1B	11	8	19	32
2B	8	2	10	17
3B	2	12	14	24
SS	10	9	19	32
OF	6	5	11	19
TOT.	40	43	83	23

While the Gold Glove Award has adequately filled the need for a subjective fielding award, there is still something to be said about fielding statistics. It is fashionable to say that fielding stats are meaningless, but, as analyst Bill James says, "If a baseball statistic is meaningless to you, that is simply because you don't know what it means."

With the understanding of which fielding statistics *are* meaningful for each position, it is possible to make a pretty reliable judgment of a player's defensive skills based on stats alone. In recent years, several analysts have attempted to measure individual fielding performance on the basis of numbers.

One newer method is Linear Weights, Pete Palmer's translation of individual batting, pitching, and fielding statistics into runs gained and thus games won. The fielding portion of the system, Fielding or Defensive Wins, incorporates data (variously weighted according to position) on putouts, assists, errors, and double plays, comparing a player's totals against the league averages.

The formula first determines how many runs a player saves (or costs) his team as compared to an "average" player at the same position. Runs are then translated into wins, based on the league average of runs per win. For example, second baseman Glenn Hubbard was computed to have won about three and a half games for the Braves with his glove in 1986, the top Defensive Wins total in the majors.

Of the sixty players identified by the Palmer system as the best fielders in their leagues between 1957–86, twenty-eight also won their respective Gold Glove Awards.

Palmer has drawn criticism for comparing players with average, rather than replacement-level, players; for over-emphasizing the double play; and for the use of arbitrary weighting schemes. It is particularly—and admittedly—inadequate in evaluating catchers.

Bill James has also presented a fielding measurement system, Defensive Won/Lost Percentage (DW/L%), although he hasn't used it since 1984. The formula varies

from position to position, using four arbitrarily weighted components at each. These components range from readily available statistics (fielding average, assists per game, and so on) to abstruse estimations and calculations, using some data unavailable to the average researcher. The formula is not designed for cross-era comparisons.

The results of these calculations produce the DW/L%, which in turn is translated into defensive wins and losses, based on still more arbitrary assignments of defensive games at each position (ranging from 3 at first base to 11 at shortstop).

Of the thirty-two players identified by DW/L% as the best at their positions and leagues for the 1983–84 seasons, twelve (38 percent) also won their respective Gold Gloves.

The use of a series of arbitrary values is the glaring flaw of DW/L%. Criticism is also due for the complexity and lack of adaptability of the system(s).

The Elias Sports Bureau has demonstrated a simple and generally effective system for evaluating fielders: comparing the number of runs scored per nine innings while a player is on the field to the number scored when he isn't. For example, Elias calculated that the 1982–86 Cardinals averaged allowing 3.85 runs per nine innings with Ozzie Smith at shortstop, as compared to 4.04 per game with other shortstops.

There is nothing new or brilliant about this concept; the difference is that Elias has the data available to make this type of measurement, right down to thirds of an inning, at least since 1975. Since they generally choose not to share this data with the public, however, it is of no value at present.

So, when all is said and done about modern statistical fielding measurements, a subjective measurement—the Gold Glove—is probably still the best tool we have available to rate fielders.

The following pages list the winners of the Gold Glove at each position since 1957. Complete balloting for Gold Glove elections is, unfortunately, neither available nor researchable.

Gold Glove Award

Pitchers

Year	National League	American League
1957	(No selection)	B. Shantz, NY
1958	H. Haddix, CIN	B. Shantz, NY
1959	H. Haddix, PIT	B. Shantz, NY
1960	H. Haddix, PIT	B. Shantz, NY
1961	B. Shantz, PIT	F. Lary, DET
1962	B. Shantz, SL	J. Kaat, MIN
1963	B. Shantz, SL	J. Kaat, MIN
1964	B. Shantz, PHI	J. Kaat, MIN
1965	B. Gibson, SL	J. Kaat, MIN
1966	B. Gibson, SL	J. Kaat, MIN
1967	B. Gibson, SL	J. Kaat, MIN
1968	B. Gibson, SL	J. Kaat, MIN
1969	B. Gibson, SL	J. Kaat, MIN
1970	B. Gibson, SL	J. Kaat, MIN
1971	B. Gibson, SL	J. Kaat, MIN
1972	B. Gibson, SL	J. Kaat, MIN
1973	B. Gibson, SL	J. Kaat, MIN
1974	A. Messersmith, LA	J. Kaat, CHI
1975	A. Messersmith, LA	J. Kaat, CHI
1976	J. Kaat, PHI	J. Palmer, BAL
1977	J. Kaat, PHI	J. Palmer, BAL
1978	P. Niekro, ATL	J. Palmer, BAL
1979	P. Niekro, ATL	J. Palmer, BAL
1980	P. Niekro, ATL	M. Norris, OAK
1981	S. Carlton, PHI	M. Norris, OAK
1982	P. Niekro, ATL	R. Guidry, NY
1983	P. Niekro, ATL	R. Guidry, NY
1984	J. Andujar, SL	R. Guidry, NY
1985	R. Reuschel, PIT	R. Guidry, NY
1986	F. Valenzuela, LA	R. Guidry, NY
1987	R. Reuschel, SF	M. Langston, SEA
1988	O. Hershiser, LA	M. Langston, SEA
1989	R. Darling, NY	B. Saberhagen, KC
1990	G. Maddux, CHI	M. Boddicker, BOS
1991	G. Maddux, CHI	M. Langston, CAL
1992	G. Maddux, CHI	M. Langston, CAL

Catchers

Year	National League	American League
1957	(No selection)	S. Lollar, CHI
1958	D. Crandall, MIL	S. Lollar, CHI
1959	D. Crandall, MIL	S. Lollar, CHI
1960	D. Crandall, MIL	E. Battey, WAS
1961	J. Roseboro, LA	E. Battey, MIN
1962	D. Crandall, MIL	E. Battey, MIN
1963	J. Edwards, CIN	E. Howard, NY
1964	J. Edwards, CIN	E. Howard, NY
1965	J. Torre, MIL	B. Freehan, DET
1966	J. Roseboro, LA	B. Freehan, DET
1967	R. Hundley, CHI	B. Freehan, DET
1968	J. Bench, CIN	B. Freehan, DET
1969	J. Bench, CIN	B. Freehan, DET
1970	J. Bench, CIN	R. Fosse, CLE
1971	J. Bench, CIN	R. Fosse, CLE
1972	J. Bench, CIN	C. Fisk, BOS
1973	J. Bench, CIN	T. Munson, NY
1974	J. Bench, CIN	T. Munson, NY
1975	J. Bench, CIN	T. Munson, NY
1976	J. Bench, CIN	J. Sundberg, TEX
1977	J. Bench, CIN	J. Sundberg, TEX
1978	B. Boone, PHI	J. Sundberg, TEX
1979	B. Boone, PHI	J. Sundberg, TEX
1980	G. Carter, MON	J. Sundberg, TEX
1981	G. Carter, MON	J. Sundberg, TEX
1982	G. Carter, MON	B. Boone, CAL
1983	T. Pena, PIT	Lc. Parrish, DET
1984	T. Pena, PIT	Lc. Parrish, DET
1985	T. Pena, PIT	Lc. Parrish, DET
1986	J. Davis, CHI	B. Boone, CAL
1987	M. LaValliere, PIT	B. Boone, CAL
1988	B. Santiago, SD	B. Boone, CAL
1989	B. Santiago, SD	B. Boone, CAL
1990	B. Santiago, SD	S. Alomar, CLE
1991	T. Pagnozzi, SL	T. Pena, BOS
1992	T. Pagnozzi, SL	I. Rodriguez, TEX

First Baseman

Year	National League	American League
1957	G. Hodges, BKN	(No selection)
1958	G. Hodges, LA	V. Power, CLE
1959	G. Hodges, LA	V. Power, CLE
1960	B. White, SL	V. Power, CLE
1961	B. White, SL	V. Power, CLE
1962	B. White, SL	V. Power, MIN
1963	B. White, SL	V. Power, MIN
1964	B. White, SL	V. Power, LA
1965	B. White, SL	J. Pepitone, NY
1966	B. White, PHI	J. Pepitone, NY
1967	W. Parker, LA	G. Scott, BOS
1968	W. Parker, LA	G. Scott, BOS
1969	W. Parker, LA	J. Pepitone, NY
1970	W. Parker, LA	J. Spencer, CAL
1971	W. Parker, LA	G. Scott, BOS
1972	W. Parker, LA	G. Scott, MIL
1973	M. Jorgenson, MON	G. Scott, MIL
1974	S. Garvey, LA	G. Scott, MIL
1975	S. Garvey, LA	G. Scott, MIL
1976	S. Garvey, LA	G. Scott, MIL
1977	S. Garvey, LA	J. Spencer, CHI
1978	K. Hernandez, SL	C. Chambliss, NY
1979	K. Hernandez, SL	C. Cooper, MIL
1980	K. Hernandez, SL	C. Cooper, MIL
1981	K. Hernandez, SL	M. Squires, CHI
1982	K. Hernandez, SL	E. Murray, BAL
1983	K. Hernandez, SL-NY	E. Murray, BAL
1984	K. Hernandez, NY	E. Murray, BAL
1985	K. Hernandez, NY	D. Mattingly, NY
1986	K. Hernandez, NY	D. Mattingly, NY
1987	K. Hernandez, NY	D. Mattingly, NY
1988	K. Hernandez, NY	D. Mattingly, NY
1989	A. Galarraga, MON	D. Mattingly, NY
1990	A. Galarraga, MON	M. McGwire, OAK
1991	W. Clark, SF	D. Mattingly, NY
1992	M. Grace, CHI	D. Mattingly, NY

Second Basemen

Year	National League	American League
1957	(No selection)	N. Fox, CHI
1958	B. Mazeroski, PIT	F. Bolling, DET
1959	C. Neal, LA	N. Fox, CHI
1960	B. Mazeroski, PIT	N. Fox, CHI
1961	B. Mazeroski, PIT	B. Richardson, NY
1962	K. Hubbs, CHI	B. Richardson, NY
1963	B. Mazeroski, PIT	B. Richardson, NY
1964	B. Mazeroski, PIT	B. Richardson, NY
1965	B. Mazeroski, PIT	B. Richardson, NY
1966	B. Mazeroski, PIT	B. Knoop, CAL
1967	B. Mazeroski, PIT	B. Knoop, CAL
1968	G. Beckert, CHI	B. Knoop, CAL
1969	F. Millan, ATL	D. Johnson, BAL
1970	T. Helms, CIN	D. Johnson, BAL
1971	T. Helms, CIN	D. Johnson, BAL
1972	F. Millan, ATL	D. Griffin, BOS
1973	J. Morgan, CIN	B. Grich, BAL
1974	J. Morgan, CIN	B. Grich, BAL
1975	J. Morgan, CIN	B. Grich, BAL
1976	J. Morgan, CIN	B. Grich, BAL
1977	J. Morgan, CIN	F. White, KC
1978	D. Lopes, LA	F. White, KC
1979	M. Trillo, PHI	F. White, KC
1980	D. Flynn, NY	F. White, KC
1981	M. Trillo, PHI	F. White, KC
1982	M. Trillo, PHI	F. White, KC
1983	R. Sandberg, CHI	L. Whitaker, DET
1984	R. Sandberg, CHI	L. Whitaker, DET
1985	R. Sandberg, CHI	L. Whitaker, DET
1986	R. Sandberg, CHI	F. White, KC
1987	R. Sandberg, CHI	F. White, KC
1988	R. Sandberg, CHI	H. Reynolds, SEA
1989	R. Sandberg, CHI	H. Reynolds, SEA
1990	R. Sandberg, CHI	H. Reynolds, SEA
1991	R. Sandberg, CHI	R. Alomar, TOR
1992	J. Lind, PIT	R. Alomar, TOR

Third Basemen

Year	National League	American League
1957	(No selection)	F. Malzone, BOS
1958	K. Boyer, SL	F. Malzone, BOS
1959	K. Boyer, SL	F. Malzone, BOS
1960	K. Boyer, SL	B. Robinson, BAL
1961	K. Boyer, SL	B. Robinson, BAL
1962	J. Davenport, SF	B. Robinson, BAL
1963	K. Boyer, SL	B. Robinson, BAL
1964	R. Santo, CHI	B. Robinson, BAL
1965	R. Santo, CHI	B. Robinson, BAL
1966	R. Santo, CHI	B. Robinson, BAL
1967	R. Santo, CHI	B. Robinson, BAL
1968	R. Santo, CHI	B. Robinson, BAL
1969	C. Boyer, ATL	B. Robinson, BAL
1970	D. Rader, HOU	B. Robinson, BAL
1971	D. Rader, HOU	B. Robinson, BAL
1972	D. Rader, HOU	B. Robinson, BAL
1973	D. Rader, HOU	B. Robinson, BAL
1974	D. Rader, HOU	B. Robinson, BAL
1975	K. Reitz, SL	B. Robinson, BAL
1976	M. Schmidt, PHI	A. Rodriguez, DET
1977	M. Schmidt, PHI	G. Nettles, NY
1978	M. Schmidt, PHI	G. Nettles, NY
1979	M. Schmidt, PHI	B. Bell, TEX
1980	M. Schmidt, PHI	B. Bell, TEX
1981	M. Schmidt, PHI	B. Bell, TEX
1982	M. Schmidt, PHI	B. Bell, TEX
1983	M. Schmidt, PHI	B. Bell, TEX
1984	M. Schmidt, PHI	B. Bell, TEX
1985	T. Wallach, MON	G. Brett, KC
1986	M. Schmidt, PHI	G. Gaetti, MIN
1987	T. Pendleton, SL	G. Gaetti, MIN
1988	T. Wallach, MON	G. Gaetti, MIN
1989	T. Pendleton, SL	G. Gaetti, MIN
1990	T. Wallach, MON	K. Gruber, TOR
1991	M. Williams, SF	R. Ventura, CHI
1992	T. Pendleton, ATL	R. Ventura, CHI

Shortstops

Year	National League	American League
1957	R. McMillan, CIN	(No selection)
1958	R. McMillan, CIN	L. Aparicio, CHI
1959	R. McMillan, CIN	L. Aparicio, CHI
1960	E. Banks, CHI	L. Aparicio, CHI
1961	M. Wills, LA	L. Aparicio, CHI
1962	M. Wills, LA	L. Aparicio, CHI
1963	B. Wine, PHI	Z. Versalles, MIN
1964	R. Amaro, PHI	L. Aparicio, BAL
1965	L. Cardenas, CIN	Z. Versalles, MIN
1966	G. Alley, PIT	L. Aparicio, BAL
1967	G. Alley, PIT	J. Fregosi, CAL
1968	D. Maxvill, SL	L. Aparicio, CHI
1969	D. Kessinger, CHI	M. Belanger, BAL
1970	D. Kessinger, CHI	L. Aparicio, CHI
1971	B. Harrelson, NY	M. Belanger, BAL
1972	L. Bowa, PHI	E. Brinkman, DET
1973	R. Metzger, HOU	M. Belanger, BAL
1974	D. Concepcion, CIN	M. Belanger, BAL
1975	D. Concepcion, CIN	M. Belanger, BAL
1976	D. Concepcion, CIN	M. Belanger, BAL
1977	D. Concepcion, CIN	M. Belanger, BAL
1978	L. Bowa, PHI	M. Belanger, BAL
1979	D. Concepcion, CIN	R. Burleson, BOS
1980	O. Smith, SD	A. Trammell, DET
1981	O. Smith, SD	A. Trammell, DET
1982	O. Smith, SL	R. Yount, MIL
1983	O. Smith, SL	A. Trammell, DET
1984	O. Smith, SL	A. Trammell, DET
1985	O. Smith, SL	A. Griffin, OAK
1986	O. Smith, SL	T. Fernandez, TOR
1987	O. Smith, SL	T. Fernandez, TOR
1988	O. Smith, SL	T. Fernandez, TOR
1989	O. Smith, SL	T. Fernandez, TOR
1990	O. Smith, SL	O. Guillen, CHI
1991	O. Smith, SL	C. Ripken, BAL
1992	O. Smith, SL	C. Ripken, BAL

National League Outfielders

YEAR	PLAYERS		
1957	W. Mays, NY (CF)	(No other selections)	
1958	F. Robinson, CIN (LF)	W. Mays, SF (CF)	H. Aaron, MIL (RF)
1959	J. Brandt, SF (LF)	W. Mays, SF (CF)	H. Aaron, MIL (RF)
1960	W. Moon, LA (LF)	W. Mays, SF (CF)	H. Aaron, MIL (RF)
1961	W. Mays, SF	R. Clemente, PIT	V. Pinson, CIN
1962	W. Mays, SF	R. Clemente, PIT	B. Virdon, PIT
1963	W. Mays, SF	R. Clemente, PIT	C. Flood, SL
1964	W. Mays, SF	R. Clemente, PIT	C. Flood, SL
1965	W. Mays, SF	R. Clemente, PIT	C. Flood, SL
1966	W. Mays, SF	C. Flood, SL	R. Clemente, PIT
1967	R. Clemente, PIT	C. Flood, SL	W. Mays, SF
1968	W. Mays, SF	R. Clemente, PIT	C. Flood, SL
1969	R. Clemente, PIT	C. Flood, SL	P. Rose, CIN
1970	R. Clemente, PIT	T. Agee, NY	P. Rose, CIN
1971	R. Clemente, PIT	B. Bonds, SF	W. Davis, LA
1972	R. Clemente, PIT	C. Cedeno, HOU	W. Davis, LA
1973	B. Bonds, SF	C. Cedeno, HOU	W. Davis, LA
1974	C. Cedeno, HOU	C. Geronimo, CIN	B. Bonds, SF
1975	C. Cedeno, HOU	C. Geronimo, CIN	G. Maddox, PHI
1976	C. Cedeno, HOU	C. Geronimo, CIN	G. Maddox, PHI
1977	C. Geronimo, CIN	G. Maddox, PHI	D. Parker, PIT
1978	G. Maddox, PHI	D. Parker, PIT	E. Valentine, MON
1979	G. Maddox, PHI	D. Parker, PIT	D. Winfield, SD
1980	A. Dawson, MON	G. Maddox, PHI	D. Winfield, SD
1981	A. Dawson, MON	G. Maddox, PHI	D. Baker, LA
1982	A. Dawson, MON	D. Murphy, ATL	G. Maddox, PHI
1983	A. Dawson, MON	D. Murphy, ATL	W. McGee, SL
1984	D. Murphy, ATL	B. Dernier, CHI	A. Dawson, MON
1985	W. McGee, SL	D. Murphy, ATL	A. Dawson, MON
1986	T. Gwynn, SD	D. Murphy, ATL	W. McGee, SL
1987	E. Davis, CIN	T. Gwynn, SD	A. Dawson, CHI
1988	A. Van Slyke, PIT	E. Davis, CIN	A. Dawson, CHI
1989	A. Van Slyke, PIT	E. Davis, CIN	T. Gwynn, SD
1990	A. Van Slyke, PIT	T. Gwynn, SD	B. Bonds, PIT
1991	A. Van Slyke, PIT	T. Gwynn, SD	B. Bonds, PIT
1992	A. Van Slyke, PIT	L. Walker, MON	B. Bonds, PIT

American League Outfielders

YEAR	PLAYERS		
1957	M. Minoso, CHI (LF)	A. Kaline, DET (RF)	(No other selection)
1958	N. Siebern, NY (LF)	J. Piersall, BOS (CF)	A. Kaline, DET (RF)
1959	M. Minoso, CLE (LF)	A. Kaline, DET (CF)	J. Jensen, BOS (RF)
1960	M. Minoso, CHI (LF)	J. Landis, CHI (CF)	R. Maris, NY (RF)
1961	A. Kaline, DET	J. Piersall, CLE	J. Landis, CHI
1962	J. Landis, CHI	M. Mantle, NY	A. Kaline, DET
1963	A. Kaline, DET	C. Yastrzemski, BOS	J. Landis, CHI
1964	A. Kaline, DET	J. Landis, CHI	V. Davalillo, CLE
1965	A. Kaline, DET	T. Tresh, NY	C. Yastrzemski, BOS
1966	A. Kaline, DET	T. Agee, CHI	T. Oliva, MIN
1967	C. Yastrzemski, BOS	P. Blair, BAL	A. Kaline, DET
1968	M. Stanley, DET	C. Yastrzemski, BOS	R. Smith, BOS
1969	P. Blair, BAL	M. Stanley, DET	C. Yastrzemski, BOS
1970	M. Stanley, DET	P. Blair, BAL	K. Berry, CHI
1971	P. Blair, BAL	A. Otis, KC	C. Yastrzemski, BOS
1972	P. Blair, BAL	B. Murcer, NY	K. Berry, CAL
1973	P. Blair, BAL	A. Otis, KC	M. Stanley, DET
1974	P. Blair, BAL	A. Otis, KC	J. Rudi, OAK
1975	P. Blair, BAL	J. Rudi, OAK	F. Lynn, BOS
1976	J. Rudi, OAK	Dw. Evans, BOS	R. Manning, CLE
1977	J. Beniquez, TEX	C. Yastrzemski, BOS	A. Cowens, KC
1978	F. Lynn, BOS	Dw. Evans, BOS	R. Miller, CAL
1979	Dw. Evans, BOS	S. Lezcano, MIL	F. Lynn, BOS
1980	F. Lynn, BOS	D. Murphy, OAK	W. Wilson, KC
1981	D. Murphy, OAK	Dw. Evans, BOS	R. Henderson, OAK
1982	Dw. Evans, BOS	D. Winfield, NY	D. Murphy, OAK
1983	Dw. Evans, BOS	D. Winfield, NY	D. Murphy, OAK
1984	Dw. Evans, BOS	D. Winfield, NY	D. Murphy, OAK
1985	G. Pettis, CAL	D. Winfield, NY	Dw. Evans, BOS & D. Murphy, OAK
1986	G. Pettis, CAL	J. Barfield, TOR	K. Puckett, MIN
1987	J. Barfield, TOR	K. Puckett, MIN	D. Winfield, NY
1988	K. Puckett, MIN	D. White, CAL	G. Pettis, DET
1989	D. White, CAL	G. Pettis, DET	K. Puckett, MIN
1990	G. Pettis, TEX	K. Griffey, Jr., SEA	E. Burks, BOS
1991	K. Puckett, MIN	K. Griffey, Jr., SEA	D. White, TOR
1992	K. Puckett, MIN	K. Griffey, Jr., SEA	D. White, TOR

Hall of Fame Elections: History

In the 1930s plans were being made to celebrate baseball's 100th anniversary, based on the findings of the Mills Commission three decades earlier: "The first scheme for playing baseball, according to the best evidence obtainable to date, was devised by Abner Doubleday at Cooperstown, New York, in 1839." A small-scale baseball museum was established in Cooperstown, and a Centennial Committee composed of six baseball bigwigs ordered the first Hall of Fame election. On January 29, 1936, the results of this election were announced, with five immortals qualifying for enshrinement (although actual induction was delayed until formal opening of the Hall on June 12, 1939).

Actually, there were two elections in 1936: one a poll of 226 members of the Baseball Writers' Association of America (BBWAA), and the other held by a special veterans' committee of 78 designed to choose from among "old-timers." No specific guidelines were set as to who was eligible for consideration (several active players received strong support), nor to which committee would consider whom (resulting in Cy Young's split vote: 49 percent in the writers' election, 41 percent in the veterans'). A 75 percent majority was necessary for election by either committee, a voting feature which has survived a half century of Hall of Fame elections.

Elections were held by both the BBWAA and an old-timers' committee for each of the next three years, resulting in a total of 26 inductees in 1939. After that, BBWAA elections were scheduled at three-year intervals, with only one player elected in 1942 and none in 1945. A decision was made to hold annual elections beginning in 1946. This continued through 1956, when it was decided to hold elections only every other year. Annual elections were resumed a decade later and continue to this day.

A nominating system was installed after the 1945 election, providing for the top twenty vote-getters in a preliminary balloting to be listed alphabetically on a second and final ballot. The preliminary election's vote totals were not to be divulged until after the final balloting (so as not to influence voters), nor would they assure anyone of automatic election. However, this system proved an utter failure in 1946 and was amended in December of that year. Thereafter, anyone receiving 75 percent of the votes on the nominating ballot would be automatically elected, eliminating the runoff election.

No runoff was required until 1949, when Charlie Gehringer was elected on the second ballot. The nominating system was discontinued after that year but revived from 1960 to 1968 (providing for reconsideration of the top thirty vote-getters), being put into practice in 1964 and 1967.

Currently, an eligible candidate must have played at least ten seasons in the majors and been active at some point during a period beginning twenty years and ending five years before a given election. The five-year wait rule was first implemented in 1954 (excepting candidates who had already received 100 or more votes in a previous election); a one-year wait had been in effect from 1946–53, and no wait was specified before then (due to World War II, it was sometimes unclear who was still "active"). At the other end of the span, the twenty-year

rule has been in effect since 1962; the cutoff was thirty years from 1956–62, and twenty-five years from 1946–56.

Following Roberto Clemente's tragic death, a rule was passed in 1973 providing for the immediate consideration of an eligible candidate who dies while still active, or before the five-year waiting period has elapsed. Clemente was inducted overwhelmingly (393 of 424 votes) in a special election held that March. A few months later, the new rule was amended to allow consideration at least six months after a player's death (or five years after his retirement, whichever is less). The infamous "Pete Rose Rule" was added to the books in February 1991: "Any player on Baseball's ineligible list shall not be an eligible candidate."

Ten-year active and honorary members of the BBWAA are eligible to vote in the annual election (the 10-year restriction was installed in 1947). About 400 writers submit ballots each year, voting for up to ten eligible candidates apiece. At various times over the past three decades, it has been suggested that the enfranchisement be limited to a few dozen of the top baseball writers.

A candidate Screening Committee was first employed in 1968, limiting the ballot to forty candidates. Standards were relaxed somewhat after former pitcher Milt Pappas vociferously objected to his elimination by this committee (Pappas was allowed on the ballot in 1979, receiving 5 of 432 votes). Nomination by two of the six members of the Screening Committee now ensures a candidate at least one try on the BBWAA ballot; however, if he receives less than 5 percent of the vote, he is eliminated from future consideration. (Fortunately for many, this rule has not always been existent; more than seventy current Hall of Famers received less than 5 percent of the vote in their first tries!)

The Baseball Hall of Fame Committee on Baseball Veterans was established in July 1953. Previously, special old-timers' committees had elected new members in 1936–39, 1944–46, and 1949.

The new committee was composed of eleven members. This number was increased to twelve in 1960, eighteen in 1979, and twenty in 1987. Elections were held every other year at first, but have been held annually since 1961.

In most years the committee has been limited to naming no more than two new inductees per election. Exceptions occurred in the elections of 1953 (six), 1963 (four), 1964 (six), 1970 (three), 1971 (seven), and 1972–77 (three each). Voting details are not released to the public.

Individuals considered by the Veterans' Committee include managers, umpires, executives, and players no longer eligible through the BBWAA (except members of the committee). For eligibility under the former three groups, a person must have been retired five years, or six months if he has reached the age of sixty-five (a rule tailor-made for Casey Stengel's election in 1966). For players, the minimum wait is twenty-three years; previously, it was twenty-five years (1953–56, 1974–84), thirty years (1957–62), or twenty years (1963–73).

On June 10, 1971, a nine-member Baseball Hall of Fame Committee on Negro Baseball Leagues was established. Candidates were to have totaled at least ten years of service in the pre-1946 Negro Leagues and/or the major leagues, without being eligible for BBWAA election. A rule specified that the "Committee shall serve

until it shall dissolve itself of its own motion or until further notice from the Board of Directors" of the Hall.

At least one new member was inducted by this committee in each year between 1971 and 1977. By 1975 the committee had only 6 remaining members, and by 1979 it had been dissolved and absorbed into the Veterans' Committee. Only two Negro League representatives have been enshrined since 1977.

As far back as 1944, it was suggested that a special "Roll of Honor," distinct from actual Hall of Fame induction, be established for distinguished baseball writers and similar contributors to the baseball world. In 1962 the J. G. Taylor Spink Award was initiated to honor individuals "for meritorious contributions to baseball writing." In 1978 the Ford C. Frick Award was established to dignify broadcasters "for major contributions to the game of Baseball." The awards are presented annually during the Hall of Fame induction ceremonies and the winners' names are engraved on a plaque hanging in the National Baseball Library (explaining references to a writers' or broadcasters' "wing" at the Hall of Fame). Through 1992 there had been forty-three winners of the Spink Award, and fourteen recipients of the Frick trophy.

There have been a total of 215 men inducted into the National Baseball Hall of Fame and Museum through 1992, including 166 major league players, twenty-one 'classified as pioneers or executives, eleven Negro Leaguers, ten managers and seven umpires (many of the latter four groups also played in the majors or minors); eighty-three individuals have been elected by the BBWAA, 123 by the various veterans' committees, and nine by the Negro Leagues' Committee.

What follows is, first, a roster of the 215 members of the Hall of Fame named between 1936 and 1992; second, an index of every man who ever received so much as a single vote for the Hall of Fame, detailing each man's total for each year he received support; and third, the top ten finishers in the voting for each year of balloting since 1936. Men named to the Hall of Fame by special committee action, such as Alexander Cartwright or Josh Gibson, may not have received votes in an election, but they are included in this index as well. (There have been four such committee groupings: the Centennial Commission of 1937–1938, the Old Timers' Committee of 1939–1949, the Veterans Committee of 1953–present, and the Negro Leagues Committee of 1971–1977.)

Of special interest are some prominent players who were not elected or named to the Hall: Gil Hodges, who received the most votes for the Hall of Fame but remains outside it; Herman Long, who finished among the top ten vote-getters in the Veterans Ballot of 1936, which during later years produced twenty-nine future Hall of Famers; Hank Gowdy, who in the 1950s experienced a fate similar to Long's; and Marty Marion, and Allie Reynolds, other long-term vote-getters who were not able to bunch their support in a given year. And don't get White Sox fans talking about Nellie Fox and the election of 1985, when, in his final year of eligibility for the Baseball Writers Election, Fox fell only two votes short of the 297 that would have granted him enshrinement—the closest any man has ever come without making it.

The Hall of Fame balloting results were researched and compiled by Pete Palmer.

Hall of Fame Roster

FIRST BASEMEN
Anson, Cap
Beckley, Jake
Bottomley, Jim
Brouthers, Dan
Chance, Frank
Connor, Roger
Foxx, Jimmie
Gehrig, Lou
Greenberg, Hank
Kelly, George
Killebrew, Harmon
McCovey, Willie
Mize, Johnny
Sisler, George
Stargell, Willie
Terry, Bill

SECOND BASEMEN
Carew, Rod
Collins, Eddie
Doerr, Bobby
Evers, Johnny
Frisch, Frankie
Gehringer, Charlie
Herman, Billy
Hornsby, Rogers
Lajoie, Nap
Lazzeri, Tony
Morgan, Joe
Robinson, Jackie
Schoendienst, Red

SHORTSTOPS
Aparicio, Luis
Appling, Luke
Bancroft, Dave
Banks, Ernie
Boudreau, Lou
Cronin, Joe
Jackson, Travis

Jennings, Hugh
Maranville, Rabbit
Reese, Pee Wee
Sewell, Joe
Tinker, Joe
Vaughan, Arky
Wagner, Honus
Wallace, Bobby
Ward, Monte

THIRD BASEMEN
Baker, Frank
Collins, Jimmy
Kell, George
Lindstrom, Fred
Mathews, Eddie
Robinson, Brooks
Traynor, Pie

LEFT FIELDERS
Brock, Lou
Burkett, Jesse
Clarke, Fred
Delahanty, Ed
Goslin, Goose
Hafey, Chick
Kelley, Joe
Kiner, Ralph
Manush, Heinie
Medwick, Joe
Musial, Stan
O'Rourke, Jim
Simmons, Al
Wheat, Zack
Williams, Billy
Williams, Ted
Yastrzemski, Carl

CENTER FIELDERS
Averill, Earl
Carey, Max

Cobb, Ty
Combs, Earle
DiMaggio, Joe
Duffy, Hugh
Hamilton, Billy
Mantle, Mickey
Mays, Willie
Roush, Edd
Snider, Duke
Speaker, Tris
Waner, Lloyd
Wilson, Hack

RIGHT FIELDERS
Aaron, Hank
Clemente, Roberto
Crawford, Sam
Cuyler, Kiki
Flick, Elmer
Heilmann, Harry
Hooper, Harry
Kaline, Al
Keeler, Willie
Kelly, King
Klein, Chuck
McCarthy, Tommy
Ott, Mel
Rice, Sam
Robinson, Frank
Ruth, Babe
Slaughter, Enos
Stargell, Willie
Thompson, Sam
Waner, Paul
Youngs, Ross

CATCHERS
Bench, Johnny
Berra, Yogi
Bresnahan, Roger
Campanella, Roy

Cochrane, Mickey
Dickey, Bill
Ewing, Buck
Ferrell, Rick
Hartnett, Gabby
Lombardi, Ernie
Schalk, Ray

PITCHERS
Alexander, Grover
Bender, Chief
Brown, Mordecai
Chesbro, Jack
Clarkson, John
Coveleski, Stan
Dean, Dizzy
Drysdale, Don
Faber, Red
Feller, Bob
Fingers, Rollie
Ford, Whitey
Galvin, Pud
Gibson, Bob
Gomez, Lefty
Grimes, Burleigh
Grove, Lefty
Haines, Jess
Hoyt, Waite
Hubbell, Carl
Hunter, Catfish
Jenkins, Fergie
Johnson, Walter
Joss, Addie
Keefe, Tim
Koufax, Sandy
Lemon, Bob
Lyons, Ted
Marichal, Juan
Marquard, Rube
Mathewson, Christy

McGinnity, Joe
Newhouser, Hal
Nichols, Kid
Palmer, Jim
Pennock, Herb
Perry, Gaylord
Plank, Eddie
Radbourn, Charles
Rixey, Eppa
Roberts, Robin
Ruffing, Red
Rusie, Amos
Seaver, Tom
Spahn, Warren
Vance, Dazzy
Waddell, Rube
Walsh, Ed
Welch, Mickey
Wilhelm, Hoyt
Wynn, Early
Young, Cy

FROM NEGRO LEAGUES
Bell, Cool Papa
Charleston, Oscar
Dandridge, Ray
Dihigo, Martin
Foster, Rube
Gibson, Josh
Irvin, Monte
Johnson, Judy
Leonard, Buck
Lloyd, John
Paige, Satchel

MANAGERS
Alston, Walter
Harris, Bucky
Huggins, Miller

Lopez, Al
Mack, Connie
McCarthy, Joe
McGraw, John
McKechnie, Bill
Robinson, Wilbert
Stengel, Casey

UMPIRES
Barlick, Al
Conlan, Jocko
Connolly, Tom
Evans, Billy
Hubbard, Cal
Klem, Bill
McGowan, Bill

PIONEERS AND EXECUTIVES
Barrow, Ed
Bulkeley, Morgan
Cartwright, Alexander
Chadwick, Henry
Chandler, Albert
Comiskey, Charles
Cummings, Candy
Frick, Ford
Giles, Warren
Griffith, Clark
Harridge, Will
Johnson, Ban
Landis, Kenesaw
MacPhail, Larry
Rickey, Branch
Spalding, Al
Veeck, Bill
Weiss, George
Wright, George
Wright, Harry
Yawkey, Tom

Hall of Fame Balloting: Vote Totals of All Candidates

Hank Aaron
Inducted in 1982
1982 406

Babe Adams
1937 8
1938 11
1939 11
1942 11
1945 7
1946 NOM 6
1947 22
1948 4
1949 5
1950 6
1951 12
1952 9
1953 17
1954 13
1955 24

Sparky Adams
1958 1
1960 1

Bobby Adams
1966 1

Pete Alexander
Inducted in 1938
1936 55
1937 125
1938 212

Dick Allen
1983 14
1985 28
1986 41
1987 55
1988 52
1989 35
1990 58
1991 59
1992 69

Johnny Allen
1955 1

Doug Allison
1936 V 1

Felipe Alou
1980 3

Jay Alou
1985 1

Matty Alou
1980 5

Walt Alston
Inducted in 1983
Manager
1983 ...... Vet. Com.

Nick Altrock
1937 3
1938 7
1939 6
1953 1
1954 2
1958 20
1960 18

Cap Anson
Inducted in 1939
1936 V 40
1939 ...... O/T Com.

Luis Aparicio
Inducted in 1984
1979 120
1980 124

1981 48
1982 174
1983 252
1984 341

Luke Appling
Inducted in 1964
1953 2
1955 3
1956 14
1958 77
1960 72
1962 48
1964 142
1964 RO 189

Jimmy Archer
1937 6
1938 7
1939 3

Richie Ashburn
1968 6
1969 10
1970 11
1971 10
1972 11
1973 25
1974 56
1975 76
1976 85
1977 139
1978 158
1979 130
1980 134
1981 142
1982 126

Jimmy Austin
1958 1

Earl Averill
Inducted in 1975
1949 1
1952 2
1955 2
1956 3
1958 14
1960 11
1962 3
1975 ...... Vet. Com.

Bob Bailey
1984 1

Dusty Baker
1992 4

Frank Baker
Inducted in 1955
1936 1
1937 13
1938 32
1939 30
1942 39
1945 26
1946 NOM 39
1946 36
1947 49
1948 4
1950 4
1951 8
1955 ...... Vet. Com.

Dave Bancroft
Inducted in 1971
1937 3
1938 2
1939 1
1946 NOM 1
1948 4
1949 5
1950 9
1951 9
1952 11
1953 10

1954 10
1955 19
1956 15
1958 43
1960 30
1971 ...... Vet. Com.

Sal Bando
1987 3

Ernie Banks
Inducted in 1977
1977 321

Al Barlick
Inducted in 1989
Umpire
1989 ...... Vet. Com.

Ross Barnes
1936 V 3

Ed Barrow
Inducted in 1953
Executive
1953 ...... Vet. Com.

Jack Barry
1938 3
1939 1

Dick Bartell
1948 1
1951 1
1958 1
1960 1

Joe Battin
1936 V 1

Hank Bauer
1967 23
1967 RO 9

Ginger Beaumont
1938 1
1942 1
1945 1
1946 NOM 1

Glenn Beckert
1981 1

Jake Beckley
Inducted in 1971
1936 V 1
1942 1
1971 ...... Vet. Com.

Mark Belanger
1988 16

Cool Papa Bell
Inducted in 1974
1974 ...... Neg. Com.

Johnny Bench
Inducted in 1989
1989 431

Chief Bender
Inducted in 1953
1936 2
1937 17
1938 33
1939 40
1942 55
1945 40
1946 NOM 39
1946 35
1947 72
1948 5

1949 2
1950 6
1951 35
1952 70
1953 104
1953 ...... Vet. Com.

Charlie Bennett
1936 V 3

Larry Benton
1958 1

Moe Berg
1958 3
1960 5

Marty Bergen
1937 2
1938 1
1939 1

Wally Berger
1956 1
1958 2

Yogi Berra
Inducted in 1972
1971 242
1972 339

Charlie Berry
1955 1
1958 3

Jim Bibby
1990 1

Carson Bigbee
1948 1

Jack Billingham
1986 1

Max Bishop
1955 1
1956 1
1958 4
1960 5

Ewell Blackwell
1968 5
1969 11
1970 14

Ray Blades
1958 1
1960 1

Paul Blair
1986 8

Steve Blass
1980 2

Lu Blue
1954 1

Vida Blue
1992 23

Ossie Bluege
1948 2
1949 1
1954 1
1956 2
1958 2
1960 3

Ping Bodie
1937 2

1949 1

Joe Boley
1942 1

Tommy Bond
1936 V 1

Bobby Bonds
1987 24
1988 27
1989 29
1990 30
1991 39
1992 40

Jim Bottomley
Inducted in 1974
1948 4
1949 8
1950 8
1951 6
1952 7
1953 10
1954 16
1955 26
1956 42
1958 57
1960 89
1962 20
1974 ...... Vet. Com.

Lou Boudreau
Inducted in 1970
1956 2
1958 64
1960 35
1962 12
1964 68
1964 RO 43
1966 115
1967 143
1967 RO 68
1968 146
1969 218
1970 232

Jim Bouton
1984 3

Larry Bowa
1991 11

Clete Boyer
1978 1
1979 3

Ken Boyer
1975 9
1976 15
1977 14
1978 18
1979 20
1985 68
1986 95
1987 96
1988 109
1989 62
1990 78
1991 58
1992 71

Bill Bradley
1936 1
1937 5
1938 2
1939 1
1942 1
1946 NOM 1

Harry Brecheen
1960 7
1968 3
1969 2
1970 3

1971 7
1972 5
1973 3

Ted Breitenstein
1937 1

Roger Bresnahan
Inducted in 1945
1936 47
1937 43
1938 67
1939 67
1942 57
1945 133
1945 ...... O/T Com.

Jim Brewer
1982 2

Tommy Bridges
1956 3
1958 11
1960 4
1962 1
1964 15
1964 RO 1
1966 16

Lou Brock
Inducted in 1985
1985 315

Dan Brouthers
Inducted in 1945
1936 V 2
1945 ...... O/T Com.

Gates Brown
1981 1

Mordecai Brown
Inducted in 1949
1936 6
1937 31
1938 54
1939 54
1942 63
1945 46
1946 NOM 56
1946 48
1949 ...... O/T Com.

Bill Bruton
1971 1

Morgan Bulkeley
Inducted in 1937
Executive
1937 ...... Cen. Com.

Jim Bunning
1977 146
1978 181
1979 147
1980 177
1981 164
1982 138
1983 138
1984 201
1985 214
1986 279
1987 289
1988 317
1989 283
1990 257
1991 282

Lew Burdette
1973 12
1974 14
1975 11
1976 21
1977 85

1978	76
1979	53
1980	66
1981	48
1982	43
1983	43
1984	97
1985	82
1986	96
1987	96

Smoky Burgess

1973	1
1974	2

Jesse Burkett
Inducted in 1946

1936 V	1
1937	1
1938	2
1942	4
1945	2
1946 NOM	2
1946	O/T Com.

George J. Burns

1937	3
1938	3
1939	1
1949	1
1950	2

Jeff Burroughs

1991	1

Guy Bush

1956	2

Joe Bush

1958	5

Donie Bush

1937	1
1939	2
1942	2
1945	1
1946 NOM	2
1953	1

Leon Cadore

1948	1

Johnny Callison

1979	1

Dolf Camilli

1948	1
1956	1
1958	4
1960	3

Howie Camnitz

1945	1

Roy Campanella
Inducted in 1969

1964	115
1964 RO	138
1966	197
1967	204
1967 RO	170
1968	205
1969	270

Bert Campaneris

1989	14

Jose Cardenal

1986	1

Leo Cardenas

1981	1
1982	1

Rod Carew
Inducted in 1991

1991	401

Max Carey
Inducted in 1961

1937	6
1938	6
1939	7
1945	1
1948	9
1949	12
1950	14
1951	27
1952	36
1953	55
1954	55
1955	119
1956	65
1958	136
1961	Vet. Com.

Chico Carrasquel

1966	1

Bill Carrigan

1937	5
1938	4
1939	2
1945	3

Clay Carroll

1984	1

Rico Carty

1985	1

Alex Cartwright
Inducted in 1938
Pioneer

1938	Cen. Com.

George Case

1958	1
1960	1
1962	1
1964	2

Dave Cash

1986	2

Norm Cash

1980	6

Phil Cavaretta

1962	2
1964	22
1964 RO	9
1966	9
1967	15
1967 RO	4
1968	23
1969	37
1970	51
1971	83
1972	61
1973	73
1974	61
1975	129

Cesar Cedeno

1992	2

Orlando Cepeda

1980	48
1981	77
1982	42
1983	59
1984	124
1985	114
1986	152
1987	179
1988	199
1989	176
1990	211
1991	192
1992	246

Henry Chadwick
Inducted in 1938
Pioneer

1938	Cen. Com.

Frank Chance
Inducted in 1946

1936	5
1937	49
1938	133
1939	158
1942	136
1945	179
1946 NOM	144
1946	150
1946	O/T Com.

Happy Chandler
Inducted in 1982
Executive

1982	Vet. Com.

Spud Chandler

1950	2
1951	1
1956	1
1962	2
1964	6

Ben Chapman

1949	1
1952	1

Ray Chapman

1938	1

Sam Chapman

1958	1

Oscar Charleston
Inducted in 1976

1976	Neg. Com.

Hal Chase

1936	11
1937	18

Jack Chesbro
Inducted in 1946

1937	1
1938	2
1939	6
1946 NOM	1
1946	O/T Com.

Bill Cissell

1937	1

Watty Clark

1958	1

Fred Clarke
Inducted in 1945

1936 V	9
1936	1
1937	22
1938	63
1939	59
1942	58
1945	53
1945	O/T Com.

John Clarkson
Inducted in 1963

1936 V	5
1946 NOM	1
1963	Vet. Com.

Roberto Clemente
Inducted in 1973

1973	Spec. El.

Andy Coakley

1938	1

Ty Cobb
Inducted in 1936

1936	222

Mickey Cochrane
Inducted in 1947

1936	80
1939	28
1942	88
1945	125
1946 NOM	80
1946	65
1947	128

Rocky Colavito

1974	2
1975	1

Eddie Collins
Inducted in 1939

1936	60
1937	115
1938	175
1939	213

Jimmy Collins
Inducted in 1945

1936 V	8
1936	58
1937	66
1938	79
1939	72
1942	68
1945	121
1945	O/T Com.

Shano Collins

1937	1

Earle Combs
Inducted in 1970

1937	4
1938	7
1939	3
1945	1
1948	6
1949	6
1950	3
1952	1
1953	3
1955	1
1956	14
1958	34
1960	43
1962	6
1970	Vet. Com.

Charlie Comiskey
Inducted in 1939
Executive

1936 V	6
1939	O/T Com.

Jocko Conlan
Inducted in 1974
Umpire

1974	Vet. Com.

Tommy Connolly
Inducted in 1953
Umpire

1953	Vet. Com.

Roger Connor
Inducted in 1976

1976	Vet. Com.

Wid Conroy

1945	1

Jack Coombs

1937	2
1938	2
1946 NOM	2
1948	2
1951	1

Mort Cooper

1956	2
1958	3
1960	1
1969	3

Walker Cooper

1968	8
1969	5
1970	9
1971	7
1972	8
1973	8
1974	9
1975	13
1976	56
1977	45

Wilbur Cooper

1938	1
1939	1
1948	2
1949	4
1951	1
1952	2
1953	9
1954	7
1955	11

Clint Courtney

1967	1

Stan Coveleski
Inducted in 1969

1938	1
1948	2
1949	3
1950	1
1958	34
1969	Vet. Com.

Billy Cox

1962	1

Doc Cramer

1956	4
1958	2
1960	1
1962	1
1964	12

Del Crandall

1976	15
1977	8
1978	6
1979	9

Doc Crandall

1938	1

Gavvy Cravath

1937	2
1938	2
1939	2
1946 NOM	1
1947	2

Sam Crawford
Inducted in 1957

1936	1
1937	5
1938	11
1939	6
1942	2
1945	4
1946 NOM	9
1957	Vet. Com.

Lou Criger

1936 V	1
1936	7
1937	16
1938	11
1939	2
1946 NOM	6

Hughie Critz

1956	2

Joe Cronin
Inducted in 1956

1947	6
1948	25
1949	33
1949 RO	16
1950	33
1951	44
1952	48
1953	69
1954	85
1955	135
1956	152

Frank Crosetti

1950	1
1952	1
1956	1
1958	5
1960	8
1968	15

Lave Cross

1939	1
1942	1

Al Crowder

1958	1
1960	1

Walt Cruise

1938	1

Tony Cuccinello

1956	1
1958	3

Candy Cummings
Inducted in 1939
Pioneer

1939	O/T Com.

Kiki Cuyler
Inducted in 1968

1948	3
1949	4
1950	11
1951	8
1952	10
1953	18
1954	20
1955	35
1956	55
1958	90
1960	72
1962	31
1968	Vet. Com.

Bill Dahlen

1936 V	1
1938	1

Ray Dandridge
Inducted in 1987

1987	Vet. Com.

Harry Danning

1958	1
1960	1

Alvin Dark

1966	17
1967	38
1967 RO	7
1968	36
1969	48
1970	55
1971	54
1972	55
1973	53
1974	54
1975	48
1976	62
1977	66

1978	60
1979	80
1980	43

Jake Daubert

1936 V	1
1937	2
1938	1
1939	1
1951	1
1955	1

Curt Davis

1958	1

Harry Davis

1945	1
1946 NOM	2

Tommy Davis

1982	5

Spud Davis

1948	1
1949	1

Dizzy Dean
Inducted in 1953

1945	17
1946 NOM	40
1946	45
1947	88
1948	40
1949	88
1949 RO	81
1950	85
1951	145
1952	152
1953	209

Ed Delahanty
Inducted in 1945

1936 V	22
1936	17
1937	70
1938	132
1939	145
1942	104
1945	111
1945	O/T Com.

Jerry Denny

1936 V	6

Bucky Dent

1990	3

Paul Derringer

1948	1
1950	1
1951	1
1955	1
1956	12
1958	15
1960	8

Bill Dickey
Inducted in 1954

1945	17
1946 NOM	40
1946	32
1948	39
1949	65
1949 RO	39
1950	78
1951	118
1952	139
1953	179
1954	202

Martin Dihigo
Inducted in 1977

1977	Neg. Com.

Dom DiMaggio

1960	4
1962	2

1964	12
1968	8
1969	13
1970	15
1971	15
1972	36
1973	43

Joe DiMaggio
Inducted in 1955

1945	1
1953	117
1954	175
1955	223

Bill Dinneen

1938	4
1939	7
1942	1
1945	1
1946 NOM	1

Bill Doak

1958	3

Larry Doby

1966	7
1967	10
1967 RO	1

Bobby Doerr
Inducted in 1986

1953	2
1956	5
1958	25
1960	15
1962	10
1964	24
1964 RO	5
1966	30
1967	35
1967 RO	15
1968	48
1969	62
1970	75
1971	78
1986	Vet. Com.

Mike Donlin

1937	6
1938	5
1939	5
1945	1

Bill Donovan

1937	3
1938	1
1939	2
1945	3
1946 NOM	4

Red Dooin

1937	1
1938	1

Jack Doyle

1936 V	1

Larry Doyle

1937	2
1938	4
1939	1

Walt Dropo

1967	1

Don Drysdale
Inducted in 1984

1975	76
1976	114
1977	197
1978	219
1979	233
1980	238
1981	243
1982	233
1983	242

1984	316

Hugh Duffy
Inducted in 1945

1936 V	4
1937	7
1938	24
1939	34
1942	77
1945	64
1945	O/T Com.

Joe Dugan

1937	1
1938	1
1948	3
1949	2
1956	1
1958	5
1960	8

Fred Dunlap

1936 V	2

Jack Dunn

1942	1
1945	1
1946 NOM	1

Leo Durocher

1948	1
1949	1
1952	1
1956	1
1958	28
1960	10
1962	1
1964	15
1964 RO	2

Eddie Dyer

1947	1

Jimmy Dykes

1948	5
1949	7
1950	2
1951	3
1952	5
1953	5
1955	1
1956	1
1958	26
1960	27
1962	6

George Earnshaw

1948	3
1949	2
1950	2
1955	2
1956	3

Hank Edwards

1960	2

Howard Ehmke

1938	1
1949	1
1951	1
1952	1
1953	3
1954	4
1955	8
1956	8
1958	7
1960	12

Kid Elberfeld

1936	1
1937	1
1938	2
1942	1
1945	2

Jumbo Elliott

1958	1

Bob Elliott

1960	2
1962	1
1964	4

Dock Ellis

1985	1

Del Ennis

1966	3
1967	2

Jewel Ens

1950	1

Carl Erskine

1966	6
1968	9
1969	4
1970	2
1971	3
1972	4
1973	4
1974	11

Billy Evans
Inducted in 1973
Umpire

1973	Vet. Com.

Johnny Evers
Inducted in 1946

1936	6
1937	44
1938	91
1939	107
1942	91
1945	134
1946 NOM	130
1946	110
1946	O/T Com.

Buck Ewing
Inducted in 1939

1936 V	40
1939	2
1939	O/T Com.

Red Faber
Inducted in 1964

1937	3
1938	1
1939	3
1942	1
1948	3
1949	6
1950	9
1951	8
1952	9
1953	9
1954	12
1955	27
1956	34
1958	68
1960	83
1962	30
1964	Vet. Com.

Elroy Face

1976	23
1977	33
1978	27
1979	35
1980	21
1981	23
1982	22
1983	32
1984	65
1985	62
1986	74
1987	78
1988	79
1989	47
1990	50

Ron Fairly

1985	3

Cy Falkenberg

1937	1

Bob Feller
Inducted in 1962

1962	150

Rick Ferrell
Inducted in 1984

1956	1
1958	1
1960	1
1984	Vet. Com.

Wes Ferrell

1948	1
1949	1
1956	7
1960	8
1962	1

Rollie Fingers
Inducted in 1992

1991	291
1992	349

Fred Fitzsimmons

1948	2
1949	2
1950	1
1956	3
1958	16
1960	13
1962	1

Art Fletcher

1937	2
1938	3
1939	1
1947	3
1948	3
1949	1
1950	1
1951	4

Elmer Flick
Inducted in 1963

1938	1
1963	Vet. Com.

Curt Flood

1977	16
1978	8
1979	14
1985	28
1986	45
1987	50
1988	48
1989	27
1990	35
1991	23
1992	42

Lew Fonseca

1948	1
1950	2
1956	2
1958	3
1960	3

Whitey Ford
Inducted in 1974

1973	255
1974	284

Eddie Foster

1938	2

George Foster

1992	24

Rube Foster
Inducted in 1981
Manager

1981	Vet. Com.

Nellie Fox

1971	39
1972	64
1973	73
1974	79
1975	76
1976	174
1977	152
1978	149
1979	174
1980	161
1981	168
1982	127
1983	173
1984	246
1985	295

Jimmie Foxx
Inducted in 1951

1936	21
1946 NOM	26
1947	10
1948	50
1949	85
1949 RO	89
1950	103
1951	179

Curt Fraser

1939	1

Bill Freehan

1982	2

Jim Fregosi

1984	4

Ford Frick
Inducted in 1970
Executive

1970	Vet. Com.

Frankie Frisch
Inducted in 1947

1936	14
1939	26
1942	84
1945	101
1946 NOM	104
1946	67
1947	136

Carl Furillo

1966	2
1967	2
1970	2
1971	5
1972	2

Augie Galan

1968	2
1970	3

Jim Galvin
Inducted in 1965

1965	Vet. Com.

Ned Garver

1967	1

Lou Gehrig
Inducted in 1939

1936	51
1939	Spec. El.

Charlie Gehringer
Inducted in 1949

1945	10
1946 NOM	43
1946	23
1947	105
1948	52
1949	102
1949 RO	159

Charlie Gelbert

1947	1
1949	2
1950	1
1951	1

Josh Gibson
Inducted in 1972

1972	Neg. Com.

Bob Gibson
Inducted in 1981

1981	337

Warren Giles
Inducted in 1979
Executive

1979	Vet. Com.

Dave Giusti

1983	1

Jack Glasscock

1936 V	2

Kid Gleason

1937	1
1938	1
1939	1
1945	1

Lefty Gomez
Inducted in 1972

1945	7
1946 NOM	4
1947	1
1948	16
1949	17
1950	18
1951	23
1952	29
1953	35
1954	38
1955	71
1956	89
1958	76
1960	51
1962	20
1972	Vet. Com.

Mike Gonzales

1950	1
1952	1
1953	1
1958	3
1960	2

Joe Gordon

1945	1
1955	1
1956	4
1958	11
1960	11
1962	4
1964	30
1964 RO	1
1966	31
1967	66
1967 RO	13
1968	77
1969	97
1970	79

Goose Goslin
Inducted in 1968

1948	1
1949	4
1950	2
1954	1
1955	7
1956	26
1958	26
1960	30
1962	14
1968	Vet. Com.

Hank Gowdy

1937	2
1938	8
1939	4
1942	8
1945	3
1947	1
1948	3
1949	10
1950	6
1951	26
1952	34
1953	58
1954	51
1955	90
1956	49
1958	45
1960	38

Eddie Grant

1938	1
1939	2
1942	3
1945	2
1946 NOM	1

George Grantham

1958	1

Hank Greenberg
Inducted in 1956

1945	3
1949	67
1949 RO	44
1950	64
1951	67
1952	75
1953	80
1954	97
1955	157
1956	164

Bobby Grich

1992	11

Clark Griffith
Inducted in 1946
Executive

1937	4
1938	10
1939	20
1942	71
1945	108
1946 NOM	73
1946	82
1946	O/T Com.

Burleigh Grimes
Inducted in 1964

1937	1
1938	1
1939	1
1948	7
1949	8
1950	6
1951	5
1952	9
1953	9
1955	3
1956	25
1958	71
1960	92
1962	43
1964	Vet. Com.

Charlie Grimm

1939	1
1945	1
1946 NOM	1
1948	6
1949	10
1950	13
1951	9
1952	6
1953	9
1958	26
1960	13
1962	2

Marv Grissom

1966	2

Dick Groat

1973	7
1974	4
1975	4
1976	7
1977	4
1978	3

Heinie Groh

1937	1
1938	3
1945	1
1948	1
1950	2
1954	1
1955	5
1960	1

Steve Gromek

1964	1

Orval Grove

1958	5
1960	7

Lefty Grove
Inducted in 1947

1936	12
1945	28
1946 NOM	71
1946	61
1947	123

Frank Gustine

1958	3

Mule Haas

1955	1
1956	1
1958	1
1960	1

Stan Hack

1948	2
1949	4
1950	8
1951	3
1956	1
1958	6
1960	6

Harvey Haddix

1971	10
1972	9
1973	1
1974	8
1975	8
1976	8
1977	7
1978	7
1979	8
1985	15

Chick Hafey
Inducted in 1971

1948	1
1949	2
1950	4
1951	1
1952	1
1953	2
1954	2
1955	4
1956	16
1958	12
1960	29
1962	7
1971	Vet. Com.

Noodles Hahn

1939	1

Jesse Haines
Inducted in 1970

1939	1
1947	1
1948	2
1949	2
1950	11
1953	4
1954	6
1955	10
1956	14
1958	22
1960	20
1962	3
1970	Vet. Com.

Bill Hallahan

1948	1
1956	1
1958	1
1960	2

Billy Hamilton
Inducted in 1961

1936 V	2
1942	1
1961	Vet. Com.

Mel Harder

1949	4
1950	2
1951	1
1952	10
1953	8
1958	6
1960	12
1962	7
1964	51
1964 RO	14
1966	34
1967	52
1967 RO	14

Bubbles Hargrave

1947	1
1958	1
1960	1

Mike Hargrove

1991	1

Toby Harrah

1992	1

Bud Harrelson

1986	1

Will Harridge
Inducted in 1972
Executive

1972	Vet. Com.

Bucky Harris
Inducted in 1975
Manager

1938	1
1939	1
1948	3
1949	11
1950	4
1951	9
1952	12
1953	21
1958	45
1960	31
1975	Vet. Com.

Gabby Hartnett
Inducted in 1955

1945	2
1946 NOM	2
1947	2
1948	33
1949	35
1949 RO	7
1950	54
1951	57
1952	77

Grady Hatton

1966	4
1967	1

Jim Hearn

1966	1
1967	1

Richie Hebner

1991	1

Jim Hegan

1966	5
1967	2

Harry Heilmann
Inducted in 1952

1937	10
1938	14
1939	8
1942	4
1945	5
1946 NOM	23
1947	65
1948	40
1949	59
1949 RO	52
1950	87
1951	153
1952	203

Tommy Helms

1983	1

Solly Hemus

1966	1

Tommy Henrich

1952	4
1953	10
1956	2
1958	11
1960	10
1962	3
1964	13
1968	22
1969	50
1970	62

Babe Herman

1942	1
1948	2
1949	5
1950	2
1951	1
1952	3
1953	2
1954	1
1955	5
1956	11
1958	13
1960	7

Billy Herman
Inducted in 1975

1948	1
1956	2
1958	7
1962	1
1964	26
1964 RO	9
1966	28
1967	59
1967 RO	14
1975	Vet. Com.

Buck Herzog

1938	1

Jim Hickman

1980	1

Mike Higgins

1950	2
1951	1
1958	6
1960	3

John Hiller

1986	11

Bill Hinchman

1937	1

Gil Hodges

1969	82
1970	145
1971	180
1972	161
1973	218
1974	198
1975	188
1976	233
1977	224
1978	226
1979	242
1980	230
1981	241
1982	205
1983	237

Tommy Holmes

1958	2
1960	2

Ken Holtzman

1985	4
1986	5

Harry Hooper
Inducted in 1971

1937	6
1938	4
1939	5
1948	2
1950	2
1951	3
1971	Vet. Com.

Burt Hooton

1991	1

Rogers Hornsby
Inducted in 1942

1936	105
1937	53
1938	46
1939	176
1942	182

Willie Horton

1986	4

Art Houtteman

1964	2

Elston Howard

1974	19
1975	23
1976	55
1977	43
1978	41
1979	30
1980	29
1981	83
1982	40
1983	32
1984	45
1985	54
1986	51
1987	44
1988	53

Frank Howard

1979	6

Waite Hoyt
Inducted in 1969

1939	1
1942	1
1946 NOM	1
1948	7
1949	7
1950	11
1951	13
1952	12
1953	14
1954	14
1955	33
1956	37
1958	37
1960	29
1962	18
1969	Vet. Com.

Al Hrabosky

1988	1

Cal Hubbard
Inducted in 1976
Umpire

1976	Vet. Com.

Carl Hubbell
Inducted in 1947

1945	24
1946 NOM	101
1946	75
1947	140

Miller Huggins
Inducted in 1964
Manager

1937	5
1938	48
1939	97
1942	111
1945	133
1946 NOM	129
1946	106
1948	4
1950	2
1964	Vet. Com.

Catfish Hunter
Inducted in 1987

1985	212
1986	289
1987	315

Fred Hutchinson

1962	1
1964	10

Monte Irvin
Inducted in 1973

1973	Neg. Com.

Charlie Irwin

1938	1
1939	1

Joe Jackson

1936	2
1946 NOM	2

Sonny Jackson

1980	1

Travis Jackson
Inducted in 1982

1948	5
1949	6
1950	6
1951	4
1952	1
1953	2
1954	1
1955	5
1956	14
1958	11
1960	11
1962	1

1982 ..... Vet. Com.

Fergie Jenkins
Inducted in 1991

1989	234
1990	296
1991	334

Hughie Jennings
Inducted in 1945

1936 V	11
1937	4
1938	23
1939	33
1942	64
1945	92
1945	O/T Com.

Jackie Jensen

1967	3
1968	3
1969	1
1970	1
1971	2
1972	1

Ban Johnson
Inducted in 1937
Executive

1937	Cen. Com.

Dave Johnson

1984	3

Judy Johnson
Inducted in 1975

1975	Neg. Com.

Bob Johnson

1948	1
1956	1

Walter Johnson
Inducted in 1936

1936	189

Fielder Jones

1946 NOM	1

Sam P. Jones

1939	1
1955	1
1956	1

Tim Jordan

1951	1

Mike Jorgensen

1991	1

Addie Joss
Inducted in 1978

1937	11
1938	18
1939	28
1942	33
1945	23
1946 NOM	14
1960	1
1978	Vet. Com.

Joe Judge

1937	1
1938	2
1949	1
1955	2
1956	2
1958	9
1960	15

Billy Jurges

1949	2
1958	1

Jim Kaat

1989	87
1990	79
1991	62
1992	114

Al Kaline
Inducted in 1980

1980	340

Willie Kamm

1958	3
1960	1

Tim Keefe
Inducted in 1964

1936 V	1
1964	Vet. Com.

Willie Keeler
Inducted in 1939

1936 V	33
1936	40
1937	115
1938	177
1939	207

George Kell
Inducted in 1983

1964	33
1964 RO	8
1966	29
1967	40
1967 RO	11
1968	47
1969	60
1970	90
1971	105
1972	115
1973	114
1974	94
1975	114
1976	129
1977	141
1983	Vet. Com.

Charlie Keller

1953	1
1956	2
1958	9
1960	7
1962	1
1964	12
1968	11
1969	14
1970	7
1971	14
1972	24

Joe Kelley
Inducted in 1971

1939	1
1942	1
1971	Vet. Com.

George Kelly
Inducted in 1973

1947	1
1948	2
1949	1
1956	2
1958	2
1960	5
1962	1
1973	Vet. Com.

Mike Kelly
Inducted in 1945

1936 V	15
1945	O/T Com.

Ken Keltner

1958	1
1960	1

Dickie Kerr

1937	1

1938 3
1939 5
1942 1
1945 1
1949 1
1951 3
1952 9
1953 13
1954 13
1955 25

Don Kessinger

1985	2

Harmon Killebrew
Inducted in 1984

1981	239
1982	246
1983	269
1984	335

Bill Killefer

1946 NOM	1

Matt Kilroy

1936 V	1

Ellis Kinder

1964	3

Ralph Kiner
Inducted in 1975

1962	5
1964	31
1964 RO	3
1966	74
1967	124
1967 RO	41
1968	118
1969	137
1970	167
1971	212
1972	235
1973	235
1974	215
1975	273

Dave Kingman

1992	3

Chuck Klein
Inducted in 1980

1948	3
1949	9
1950	14
1951	15
1952	19
1954	11
1955	25
1956	44
1958	36
1960	37
1962	18
1964	56
1964 RO	18
1980	Vet. Com.

Bill Klem
Inducted in 1953
Umpire

1953	Vet. Com.

Johnny Kling

1936	8
1937	20
1938	26
1939	14
1942	15
1945	12
1946 NOM	20
1948	2
1953	1

Ted Kluszewski

1967	9
1968	14
1969	11
1970	8

1971 9
1972 10
1973 14
1974 28
1975 33
1976 50
1977 55
1978 51
1979 58
1980 50
1981 56

Otto Knabe

1939	1
1946 NOM	1

Jerry Koosman

1991	4

Sandy Koufax
Inducted in 1972

1972	344

Ray Kremer

1948	1
1958	2

Red Kress

1958	1
1960	3

Harvey Kuenn

1977	57
1978	58
1979	63
1980	83
1981	93
1982	62
1983	77
1984	106
1985	125
1986	144
1987	144
1988	168
1989	115
1990	107
1991	100

Joe Kuhel

1956	1

Bob Kuzava

1964	1

Nap Lajoie
Inducted in 1937

1936 V	2
1936	146
1937	168

Judge Landis
Inducted in 1944
Executive

1944	O/T Com.

Bill Lange

1936 V	6
1953	1

Hal Lanier

1979	1

Don Larsen

1974	29
1975	23
1976	47
1977	39
1978	32
1979	53
1980	31
1981	33
1982	32
1983	22
1984	25
1985	32
1986	33
1987	30

1988 31

Arlie Latham

1936 V	1
1938	1
1942	1

Cookie Lavagetto

1958	4
1960	2

Vern Law

1973	9
1974	5
1975	6
1976	9
1977	5
1978	6
1979	9

Tony Lazzeri
Inducted in 1991

1945	1
1947	1
1948	21
1949	20
1949 RO	6
1950	21
1951	27
1952	29
1953	28
1954	30
1955	66
1956	64
1958	80
1960	59
1962	8
1991	Vet. Com.

Fred Leach

1958	2
1960	1

Tommy Leach

1937	1
1939	1

Bill Lee

1988	3

Sam Leever

1937	1

Bob Lemon
Inducted in 1976

1964	24
1964 RO	3
1966	21
1967	35
1967 RO	7
1968	47
1969	56
1970	70
1971	90
1972	117
1973	177
1974	190
1975	233
1976	305

Buck Leonard
Inducted in 1972

1972	Neg. Com.

Dennis Leonard

1992	1

Emil Leonard

1960	2
1968	5
1969	4
1970	5
1971	3
1972	5
1973	6

Duffy Lewis
1937 ... 3
1938 ... 5
1939 ... 6
1945 ... 1
1951 ... 2
1952 ... 11
1953 ... 20
1954 ... 20
1955 ... 34

Fred Lindstrom
Inducted in 1976
1949 ... 1
1956 ... 3
1958 ... 5
1960 ... 6
1962 ... 7
1976 ... Vet. Com.

John Henry Lloyd
Inducted in 1977
1977 ... Neg. Com.

Hans Lobert
1937 ... 2
1938 ... 1
1939 ... 2
1960 ... 1

Whitey Lockman
1966 ... 4

Mickey Lolich
1985 ... 78
1986 ... 86
1987 ... 84
1988 ... 109
1989 ... 47
1990 ... 27
1991 ... 33
1992 ... 45

Ernie Lombardi
Inducted in 1986
1950 ... 3
1951 ... 3
1956 ... 8
1958 ... 4
1960 ... 6
1962 ... 5
1964 ... 33
1964 RO ... 9
1966 ... 34
1967 ... 43
1967 RO ... 25
1986 ... Vet. Com.

Jim Lonborg
1985 ... 3
1986 ... 3

Herman Long
1936 V ... 16
1937 ... 1
1938 ... 1
1939 ... 1
1945 ... 1
1946 NOM ... 1

Ed Lopat
1968 ... 2
1969 ... 2
1970 ... 2
1971 ... 4
1972 ... 2

Al Lopez
Inducted in 1977
Manager
1949 ... 1
1952 ... 2
1953 ... 2
1956 ... 1
1958 ... 34
1960 ... 26
1962 ... 11
1964 ... 57

1964 RO ... 34
1966 ... 109
1967 ... 114
1967 RO ... 50
1977 ... Vet. Com.

Bobby Lowe
1936 V ... 2
1942 ... 1
1945 ... 2

John Lowenstein
1991 ... 1

Red Lucas
1949 ... 2
1950 ... 1
1958 ... 1

Dolph Luque
1937 ... 1
1938 ... 1
1939 ... 1
1950 ... 1
1952 ... 1
1953 ... 1
1956 ... 1
1958 ... 15
1960 ... 4

Greg Luzinski
1990 ... 1

Sparky Lyle
1988 ... 56
1989 ... 25
1990 ... 25
1991 ... 15

Ted Lyons
Inducted in 1955
1945 ... 4
1946 NOM ... 3
1948 ... 15
1949 ... 29
1949 RO ... 14
1950 ... 42
1951 ... 71
1952 ... 101
1953 ... 139
1954 ... 170
1955 ... 217

Connie Mack
Inducted in 1937
Manager
1936 ... 1
1937 ... Cen. Com.

Larry MacPhail
Inducted in 1978
Executive
1978 ... Vet. Com.

Sherry Magee
1937 ... 2
1938 ... 2
1939 ... 1
1942 ... 1
1945 ... 1
1946 NOM ... 1
1950 ... 1
1951 ... 2

Sal Maglie
1964 ... 13
1968 ... 11

Jim Maloney
1978 ... 2
1979 ... 2

Gus Mancuso
1958 ... 1

Mickey Mantle
Inducted in 1974
1974 ... 322

Heinie Manush
Inducted in 1964
1948 ... 1
1949 ... 1
1956 ... 13
1958 ... 22
1960 ... 20
1962 ... 15
1964 ... Vet. Com.

Rabbit Maranville
Inducted in 1954
1937 ... 25
1938 ... 73
1939 ... 82
1942 ... 66
1945 ... 51
1946 NOM ... 50
1946 ... 29
1947 ... 91
1948 ... 38
1949 ... 58
1949 RO ... 39
1950 ... 66
1951 ... 110
1952 ... 133
1953 ... 164
1954 ... 209

Firpo Marberry
1938 ... 1
1950 ... 1
1958 ... 5
1960 ... 2
1962 ... 2

Juan Marichal
Inducted in 1983
1981 ... 233
1982 ... 305
1983 ... 313

Marty Marion
1956 ... 1
1960 ... 37
1962 ... 16
1964 ... 50
1964 RO ... 17
1966 ... 86
1967 ... 90
1967 RO ... 22
1968 ... 89
1969 ... 112
1970 ... 120
1971 ... 123
1972 ... 120
1973 ... 127

Roger Maris
1974 ... 78
1975 ... 70
1976 ... 87
1977 ... 72
1978 ... 83
1979 ... 127
1980 ... 111
1981 ... 94
1982 ... 69
1983 ... 69
1984 ... 107
1985 ... 128
1986 ... 177
1987 ... 176
1988 ... 184

Rube Marquard
Inducted in 1971
1936 ... 1
1937 ... 13
1938 ... 10
1939 ... 4
1946 NOM ... 6
1947 ... 18
1948 ... 6
1949 ... 4

1951 ... 3
1952 ... 9
1953 ... 19
1954 ... 15
1955 ... 35
1971 ... Vet. Com.

Mike Marshall
1987 ... 6

Billy Martin
1967 ... 1

Pepper Martin
1942 ... 2
1945 ... 1
1946 NOM ... 1
1948 ... 7
1949 ... 16
1950 ... 7
1951 ... 19
1952 ... 31
1953 ... 43
1956 ... 46
1958 ... 46
1960 ... 29
1962 ... 6
1964 ... 19
1964 RO ... 5

Morrie Martin
1966 ... 2

Eddie Mathews
Inducted in 1978
1974 ... 118
1975 ... 148
1976 ... 189
1977 ... 239
1978 ... 301

Christy Mathewson
Inducted in 1936
1936 ... 205

Lee May
1988 ... 2

Carl Mays
1958 ... 6

Willie Mays
Inducted in 1979
1979 ... 409

Bill Mazeroski
1978 ... 23
1979 ... 36
1980 ... 33
1981 ... 38
1982 ... 28
1983 ... 48
1984 ... 74
1985 ... 87
1986 ... 100
1987 ... 125
1988 ... 143
1989 ... 134
1990 ... 131
1991 ... 142
1992 ... 182

Jim McAleer
1936 V ... 1

Joe McCarthy
Inducted in 1957
Manager
1939 ... 3
1947 ... 2
1951 ... 1
1953 ... 1
1958 ... 2
1957 ... Vet. Com.

Tommy McCarthy
Inducted in 1946
1936 V ... 1
1946 ... O/T Com.

Tim McCarver
1986 ... 16

Frank McCormick
1956 ... 3
1962 ... 1
1964 ... 6
1968 ... 3

Willie McCovey
Inducted in 1986
1986 ... 346

Lindy McDaniel
1981 ... 1
1982 ... 3

Gil McDougald
1966 ... 5
1967 ... 4
1968 ... 4
1969 ... 3
1970 ... 1
1971 ... 4
1972 ... 4
1973 ... 2
1974 ... 3

Joe McGinnity
Inducted in 1946
1937 ... 12
1938 ... 36
1939 ... 32
1942 ... 59
1945 ... 44
1946 NOM ... 53
1946 ... 47
1946 ... O/T Com.

Bill McGowan
Inducted in 1992
Umpire
1992 ... Vet. Com.

John McGraw
Inducted in 1937
Manager
1936 V ... 17
1936 ... 4
1937 ... 35
1937 ... Cen. Com.

Tug McGraw
1990 ... 6

Stuffy McInnis
1937 ... 1
1938 ... 4
1939 ... 4
1948 ... 5
1949 ... 8
1950 ... 1
1951 ... 3

Bill McKechnie
Inducted in 1962
Manager
1945 ... 2
1946 NOM ... 2
1950 ... 1
1951 ... 8
1962 ... Vet. Com.

Denny McLain
1978 ... 1
1979 ... 3
1985 ... 2

Larry McLean
1937 ... 1

Don McMahon
1980 ... 1

Marty McManus
1958 ... 2
1960 ... 2

Roy McMillan
1972 ... 9
1973 ... 5
1974 ... 4

Dave McNally
1981 ... 5
1982 ... 5
1985 ... 7
1986 ... 12

Cal McVey
1936 V ... 1

Lee Meadows
1958 ... 2

Ducky Medwick
Inducted in 1968
1948 ... 1
1956 ... 31
1958 ... 50
1960 ... 38
1962 ... 34
1964 ... 108
1964 RO ... 130
1966 ... 187
1967 ... 212
1967 RO ... 248
1968 ... 240

Andy Messersmith
1985 ... 3
1986 ... 3

Bob Meusel
1937 ... 1
1938 ... 1
1945 ... 1
1948 ... 6
1949 ... 3
1950 ... 2
1952 ... 1
1955 ... 2
1956 ... 1
1958 ... 5
1960 ... 10

Eddie Miksis
1964 ... 1

Clyde Milan
1938 ... 1
1950 ... 1
1951 ... 1
1952 ... 1
1953 ... 1
1954 ... 3
1955 ... 6

Felix Millan
1983 ... 1

Bing Miller
1958 ... 1
1960 ... 6

Dots Miller
1948 ... 1

Hack Miller
1937 ... 1

Minnie Minoso
1969 ... 6
1986 ... 89
1987 ... 82
1988 ... 90

1989 59
1990 51
1991 38
1992 69

Johnny Mize
Inducted in 1981
1960 45
1962 14
1964 54
1964 RO 12
1966 81
1967 89
1967 RO 14
1968 103
1969 116
1970 126
1971 157
1972 157
1973 157
1981 ...... Vet. Com.

Rick Monday
1990 2

Don Money
1989 1

Wally Moon
1971 2

Jo-Jo Moore
1950 1

Terry Moore
1950 1
1953 1
1958 12
1960 7
1962 1
1964 14
1967 3
1968 33

Pat Moran
1937 1
1938 1
1939 1
1945 1

Joe Morgan
Inducted in 1990
1990 363

Wally Moses
1958 1
1960 1
1968 4
1969 4
1970 5
1971 7

Johnny Mostil
1956 1
1958 1

Manny Mota
1988 18
1989 9

Hugh Mulcahy
1948 1

Van Mungo
1945 1
1948 1
1958 2
1960 2

Thurman Munson
1981 62
1982 26
1983 18
1984 29
1985 32
1986 35
1987 28
1988 32
1989 31
1990 33
1991 28
1992 32

Bobby Murcer
1989 3

Danny Murphy
1937 1
1945 1

Red Murray
1937 1
1938 1

Stan Musial
Inducted in 1969
1969 317

Buddy Myer
1949 1

Art Nehf
1937 3
1938 5
1939 1
1949 1
1950 2
1951 4
1952 3
1953 4
1954 7
1955 7
1958 13

Don Newcombe
1966 7
1967 18
1967 RO 2
1968 9
1969 3
1970 5
1971 8
1972 7
1973 11
1974 7
1975 11
1976 21
1977 43
1978 48
1979 52
1980 59

Hal Newhouser
Inducted in 1992
1962 4
1964 26
1964 RO 3
1966 32
1967 62
1967 RO 13
1968 67
1969 82
1970 80
1971 94
1972 92
1973 79
1974 73
1975 155
1992 ...... Vet. Com.

Bobo Newsom
1960 6
1962 3
1964 17
1964 RO 1
1966 25
1967 19
1967 RO 6
1968 22
1969 32
1970 12
1971 17
1972 31
1973 33

Kid Nichols
Inducted in 1949
1936 V 3
1938 3
1939 7
1942 5
1945 5
1946 NOM 1
1949 ...... O/T Com.

Bill Nicholson
1960 1

Ron Northey
1964 1

Jim Northrup
1981 1

Lefty O'Doul
1948 4
1949 4
1950 9
1951 13
1952 19
1953 11
1956 5
1958 27
1960 45
1962 13

Joe Oeschger
1948 1

Bob O'Farrell
1950 4
1958 3
1960 3

Charlie O'Leary
1953 1
1958 1
1960 1

Tony Oliva
1982 63
1983 75
1984 124
1985 114
1986 154
1987 160
1988 202
1989 135
1990 142
1991 160
1992 175

Al Oliver
1991 19

Steve O'Neill
1948 2
1949 6
1950 1
1951 3
1952 10
1953 13
1958 10

Jim O'Rourke
Inducted in 1945
1945 ...... O/T Com.

Claude Osteen
1981 2

Mel Ott
Inducted in 1951
1949 94
1949 RO 128
1950 115
1951 197

Charlie Pabor
1936 V 1

Andy Pafko
1966 2
1967 1

Satchel Paige
Inducted in 1971
1951 1
1971 ...... Neg. Com.

Jim Palmer
Inducted in 1990
1990 411

Milt Pappas
1979 5

Camilo Pascual
1977 3
1978 1

Dode Paskert
1937 1

Monte Pearson
1958 1

Roger Peckinpaugh
1937 3
1938 2
1939 1
1942 2
1949 1
1952 2
1953 2
1954 1
1955 1

Herb Pennock
Inducted in 1948
1937 15
1938 37
1939 40
1942 72
1945 45
1946 NOM 41
1946 16
1947 86
1948 94

Hub Perdue
1938 1
1939 1

Tony Perez
1992 215

Cy Perkins
1958 2

Ron Perranoski
1979 6

Gaylord Perry
Inducted in 1991
1989 304
1990 320
1991 342

Jim Perry
1981 6
1983 7

Johnny Pesky
1960 1

Rico Petrocelli
1982 3

Deacon Phillippe
1939 1
1942 1
1945 2
1946 NOM 1

Billy Pierce
1970 5
1971 7
1972 4
1973 4
1974 4

Lip Pike
1936 V 1

Lou Piniella
1990 2

Vada Pinson
1981 18
1982 6
1983 12
1985 19
1986 43
1987 48
1988 67
1989 33
1990 36
1991 30
1992 36

Wally Pipp
1958 1

Eddie Plank
Inducted in 1946
1937 23
1938 38
1939 28
1942 63
1945 33
1946 NOM 34
1946 ...... O/T Com.

Johnny Podres
1975 3
1976 2
1977 3

Bob Porterfield
1966 1

Boog Powell
1983 5

Vic Power
1971 2
1972 3

Herb Pruett
1949 1
1950 1
1951 1
1952 1
1953 1

Jack Quinn
1948 2
1958 9
1960 2

Charlie Radbourn
Inducted in 1939
1936 V 16
1939 ...... O/T Com.

Vic Raschi
1962 1
1964 8
1968 1
1969 3
1971 2
1972 4
1973 7
1974 3
1975 37

Bugs Raymond
1937 1

Pee Wee Reese
Inducted in 1984
1964 73
1964 RO 47
1966 95
1967 89
1967 RO 16
1968 81
1969 89
1970 97
1971 127
1972 129
1973 126
1974 141
1975 154
1976 186
1977 163
1978 169
1984 ...... Vet. Com.

Pete Reiser
1958 6
1960 8

Jack Remsen
1936 V 1

Jerry Remy
1990 1

Allie Reynolds
1956 1
1960 24
1962 15
1964 35
1964 RO 6
1966 60
1967 77
1967 RO 19
1968 95
1969 98
1970 89
1971 110
1972 105
1973 93
1974 101

Del Rice
1966 2

Sam Rice
Inducted in 1963
1938 1
1948 1
1949 3
1950 1
1951 1
1952 1
1953 3
1954 9
1955 28
1956 45
1958 90
1960 143
1962 81
1963 ...... Vet. Com.

J. R. Richard
1986 7

Hardy Richardson
1936 V 1

Bobby Richardson
1972 8
1973 2
1974 5

Branch Rickey
Inducted in 1967
Executive
1942 3
1945 2
1967 ...... Vet. Com.

Jimmy Ring

1949 1

Claude Ritchey

1945 1

Mickey Rivers

1990 2

Eppa Rixey
Inducted in 1963

1937 1
1938 2
1945 1
1947 2
1948 5
1949 4
1950 6
1951 5
1952 3
1953 3
1954 5
1955 8
1956 27
1958 32
1960 142
1962 49
1963 ..... Vet. Com.

Phil Rizzuto

1956 1
1962 44
1964 45
1964 RO 11
1966 54
1967 71
1967 RO 14
1968 74
1969 78
1970 79
1971 92
1972 103
1973 111
1974 111
1975 117
1976 149

Robin Roberts
Inducted in 1976

1973 213
1974 224
1975 263
1976 337

Dave Robertson

1953 1

Brooks Robinson
Inducted in 1983

1983 344

Frank Robinson
Inducted in 1982

1982 370

Jackie Robinson
Inducted in 1962

1962 124

Wilbert Robinson
Inducted in 1945
Manager

1936 V 6
1937 5
1938 17
1939 46
1942 89
1945 81
1945 ..... O/T Com.

Preacher Roe

1960 1
1962 1
1968 2
1970 1
1971 3
1972 2

Red Rolfe

1950 7
1951 6
1952 4
1953 5
1956 3
1958 13
1960 10
1962 1

Eddie Rommel

1948 3
1949 2
1950 1
1951 1
1952 2
1953 1
1958 7
1960 12

Charlie Root

1945 1
1948 3
1949 1
1950 1
1958 6
1960 2

Pete Rose

1992 41

Edd Roush
Inducted in 1962

1936 2
1937 10
1938 9
1939 8
1942 1
1945 5
1946 NOM 11
1947 25
1948 17
1949 14
1950 16
1951 21
1952 24
1953 32
1954 52
1955 97
1956 91
1958 112
1960 146
1962 ..... Vet. Com.

Schoolboy Rowe

1958 12
1960 3
1968 6
1969 17

Nap Rucker

1936 1
1937 11
1938 12
1939 13
1942 15
1945 10
1946 NOM 13

Dick Rudolph

1937 1
1951 1

Muddy Ruel

1946 NOM 1
1950 4
1951 1
1952 1
1953 8
1954 5
1955 11
1956 16
1958 10
1960 9

Red Ruffing
Inducted in 1967

1948 4
1949 22
1949 RO 4
1950 12
1951 9
1952 10
1953 24
1954 29
1955 60
1956 97
1958 99
1960 86
1962 72
1964 141
1964 RO 184
1966 208
1967 212
1967 RO 266

Amos Rusie
Inducted in 1977

1936 V 12
1937 1
1938 8
1939 6
1942 1
1945 1
1977 ..... Vet. Com.

Bill Russell

1992 3

Babe Ruth
Inducted in 1936

1936 215

Ray Sadecki

1983 2

Johnny Sain

1962 1
1964 3
1968 7
1969 8
1970 9
1971 11
1972 21
1973 47
1974 51
1975 123

Manny Sanguillen

1986 2

Ron Santo

1980 15
1985 53
1986 64
1987 78
1988 108
1989 75
1990 96
1991 116
1992 136

Hank Sauer

1966 4

Al Schacht

1939 1
1948 2
1951 4
1956 1

Germany Schaefer

1942 1
1953 1

Ray Schalk
Inducted in 1955

1936 4
1937 24
1938 45
1939 35
1942 53
1945 33
1946 NOM 36
1947 50
1948 22
1949 24
1949 RO 17
1950 16
1951 37
1952 44
1953 52
1954 54
1955 113
1955 ..... Vet. Com.

Wally Schang

1948 1
1950 1
1956 1
1958 8
1960 11

Red Schoendienst
Inducted in 1989

1969 65
1970 97
1971 123
1972 104
1973 96
1974 110
1975 94
1976 129
1977 105
1978 130
1979 159
1980 164
1981 166
1982 135
1983 146
1989 ..... Vet. Com.

Ossie Schreck

1937 2
1938 2
1939 2

Frank Schulte

1937 1

Hal Schumacher

1948 1
1955 1
1956 2
1958 1
1960 11
1962 1
1964 10

Everett Scott

1937 2
1938 2
1939 1
1942 1
1947 1
1948 3
1949 3
1950 3
1951 2
1952 4
1953 5
1954 4
1955 8
1956 1

George Scott

1986 1

Jack Scott

1958 1

Tom Seaver
Inducted in 1992

1992 425

George Selkirk

1948 1
1949 1
1950 1
1951 2
1952 1
1953 1

Hank Severeid

1948 1

Joe Sewell
Inducted in 1977

1937 1
1948 1
1954 1
1955 1
1956 3
1958 1
1960 23
1977 ..... Vet. Com.

Luke Sewell

1948 1
1958 3
1960 3
1962 1

Rip Sewell

1958 1
1962 1
1964 1

Cy Seymour

1945 1

Bobby Shantz

1970 7
1971 5
1972 9
1973 5
1974 3

Jim Sheckard

1938 1
1945 1
1946 NOM 1

Bill Sherdel

1948 1
1949 1
1950 1
1951 1
1953 1
1955 1
1956 1
1958 2
1960 2

Urban Shocker

1938 1
1939 1
1948 1
1949 2
1958 4

Chris Short

1979 1

Sonny Siebert

1981 1

Roy Sievers

1971 4
1972 3

Al Simmons
Inducted in 1953

1936 4
1946 NOM 1
1947 6
1948 60
1949 89
1949 RO 76
1950 90
1951 116
1952 141
1953 199

Curt Simmons

1973 5
1974 3

George Sisler
Inducted in 1939

1936 77
1937 106
1938 179
1939 235

Sibby Sisti

1960 1

Enos Slaughter
Inducted in 1985

1966 100
1967 123
1967 RO 48
1968 129
1969 128
1970 133
1971 165
1972 149
1973 145
1974 145
1975 177
1976 197
1977 222
1978 261
1979 297
1985 ..... Vet. Com.

Roy Smalley

1964 1

Earl Smith

1948 1
1956 1

Reggie Smith

1988 3

Sherry Smith

1948 1

Duke Snider
Inducted in 1980

1970 51
1971 89
1972 84
1973 101
1974 111
1975 129
1976 159
1977 212
1978 254
1979 308
1980 333

Billy Southworth

1945 1
1946 NOM 1
1949 7
1950 1
1951 4
1952 1
1953 2
1958 18

Warren Spahn
Inducted in 1973

1973 316

Al Spalding
Inducted in 1939
Pioneer

1936 V 4
1939 ..... O/T Com.

Tully Sparks

1946 NOM 1

Tris Speaker
Inducted in 1937

1936 133
1937 165

Jake Stahl

1938 1

1939 1

Eddie Stanky

1960 3

Mickey Stanley

1984 2

Willie Stargell
Inducted in 1988

1988 352

Rusty Staub

1991 28
1992 26

Harry Steinfeldt

1937 1
1939 1
1942 1

Casey Stengel
Inducted in 1966
Manager

1938 2
1939 6
1945 2
1948 1
1949 3
1950 3
1951 8
1952 27
1953 61
1966 . . . . . Vet. Com.

Riggs Stephenson

1956 2
1958 1
1960 4
1962 1

Mel Stottlemyre

1980 3

Harry Stovey

1936 V 6

Gabby Street

1937 1
1938 1
1953 1

Gus Suhr

1956 1
1958 1
1960 1

Clyde Sukeforth

1958 1

Billy Sullivan

1937 1
1946 NOM 1

Bill Sweeney

1945 1

Jess Tannehill

1946 NOM 1

Birdie Tebbetts

1958 8
1960 1

Gene Tenace

1989 1

Fred Tenney

1936 V 1
1937 5
1938 8
1939 3
1942 1
1946 NOM 1

Bill Terry
Inducted in 1954

1936 9
1938 7
1939 16
1942 36
1945 32
1946 NOM 31
1947 46
1948 52
1949 81
1949 RO 48
1950 105
1951 148
1952 155
1953 191
1954 195

Tommy Thevenow

1950 2

Ira Thomas

1938 1

Sam Thompson
Inducted in 1974

1974 . . . . . Vet. Com.

Bobby Thomson

1966 12
1967 10
1967 RO 1
1968 13
1969 6
1970 4
1971 4
1972 10
1973 3
1974 6
1975 10
1976 9
1977 10
1978 5
1979 11

Luis Tiant

1988 132
1989 47
1990 42
1991 32
1992 50

Joe Tinker
Inducted in 1946

1937 15
1938 16
1939 12
1942 36
1945 49
1946 NOM 55
1946 45
1946 . . . . . . O/T Com.

Jim Tobin

1956 2

Fred Toney

1949 1

Earl Torgeson

1967 2

Joe Torre

1983 20
1984 45
1985 44
1986 60
1987 47
1988 60
1989 40
1990 55
1991 41
1992 62

Mike Torrez

1990 1

Pie Traynor
Inducted in 1948

1936 16
1938 3
1939 10
1942 45
1945 81
1946 NOM 65
1946 53
1947 119
1948 93

Dizzy Trout

1964 1

Virgil Trucks

1964 4

Jim Turner

1956 1

Terry Turner

1947 2

George Uhle

1956 1
1958 4
1960 4

Ellis Valentine

1991 1

Elmer Valo

1967 2

Dazzy Vance
Inducted in 1955

1936 1
1937 10
1938 10
1939 15
1942 37
1945 18
1946 NOM 31
1947 50
1948 23
1949 33
1949 RO 15
1950 52
1951 70
1952 105
1953 150
1954 158
1955 205

Johnny Vander Meer

1945 1
1956 3
1958 35
1960 31
1962 5
1964 51
1964 RO 20
1966 72
1967 87
1967 RO 35
1968 79
1969 95
1970 88
1971 98

George Van Haltren

1936 V 1

Arky Vaughan
Inducted in 1985

1953 1
1954 2
1955 4
1956 9
1958 6
1960 10
1962 6
1964 17
1964 RO 6
1966 36
1967 46

1967 RO 19
1968 82
1985 . . . . . Vet. Com.

Bobby Veach

1937 1

Bill Veeck
Inducted in 1991
Executive

1991 . . . . . Vet. Com.

Mickey Vernon

1966 20
1967 14
1967 RO 2
1968 22
1969 21
1970 10
1971 12
1972 12
1973 23
1974 27
1975 22
1976 52
1977 52
1978 66
1979 88
1980 96

Bill Virdon

1974 3
1975 1

Rube Waddell
Inducted in 1946

1936 33
1937 67
1938 148
1939 179
1942 126
1945 154
1946 NOM 122
1946 87
1946 . . . . . . O/T Com.

Honus Wagner
Inducted in 1936

1936 V 5
1936 215

Rube Walberg

1958 1
1960 1

Dixie Walker

1962 1
1964 6
1968 6
1969 9

Harry Walker

1958 1

Bobby Wallace
Inducted in 1953

1936 V 1
1937 1
1938 7
1939 5
1942 2
1945 3
1953 . . . . . Vet. Com.

Ed Walsh
Inducted in 1946

1936 20
1937 56
1938 110
1939 132
1942 113
1945 137
1946 NOM 115
1946 106
1946 . . . . . . O/T Com.

Bucky Walters

1950 4
1952 3
1953 10
1956 5
1958 33
1960 19
1962 5
1964 35
1964 RO 8
1966 56
1967 65
1967 RO 24
1968 67
1969 20
1970 29

Bill Wambsganss

1942 1
1950 1
1953 1
1954 4
1955 5
1956 1

Lloyd Waner
Inducted in 1967

1949 3
1950 1
1951 1
1952 1
1956 18
1958 39
1960 22
1962 5
1964 47
1964 RO 12
1967 . . . . . Vet. Com.

Paul Waner
Inducted in 1952

1946 NOM 4
1948 51
1949 73
1949 RO 63
1950 95
1951 162
1952 195

Monte Ward
Inducted in 1964

1936 V 3
1964 . . . . . Vet. Com.

Lon Warneke

1949 2
1958 2
1960 4
1962 2
1964 13

Bob Watson

1990 3

George Weiss
Inducted in 1971
Executive

1971 . . . . . Vet. Com.

Mickey Welch
Inducted in 1973

1973 . . . . . Vet. Com.

Billy Werber

1949 1
1950 1
1952 1
1958 3

Vic Wertz

1970 2
1971 2
1972 4
1973 2
1974 2
1975 5
1976 5
1977 4

1978 4

Sam West

1948 1

Wes Westrum

1964 2

Zach Wheat
Inducted in 1959

1937 5
1938 7
1939 4
1942 3
1945 2
1946 NOM 6
1947 37
1948 15
1949 15
1950 17
1951 19
1952 30
1953 32
1954 33
1955 51
1956 26
1959 . . . . . Vet. Com.

Deacon White

1936 V 1

Will White

1975 7
1976 7
1977 4

Burgess Whitehead

1956 1

Earl Whitehill

1956 1
1958 2
1960 3

Hoyt Wilhelm
Inducted in 1985

1978 158
1979 168
1980 209
1981 238
1982 236
1983 243
1984 290
1985 331

Billy Williams
Inducted in 1987

1982 97
1983 153
1984 202
1985 252
1986 315
1987 354

Fred Williams

1938 1
1945 1
1948 1
1949 2
1950 9
1951 7
1952 4
1953 4
1954 4
1955 3
1956 11
1958 6
1960 11

Ken Williams

1956 1
1958 1

Ted Williams
Inducted in 1966

1966 282

Ned Williamson

1936 V	2

Maury Wills

1978	115
1979	166
1980	146
1981	163
1982	91
1983	77
1984	104
1985	93
1986	124
1987	113
1988	127
1989	95
1990	95
1991	61
1992	110

Jimmie Wilson

1948	8
1949	6
1950	4
1951	2
1952	7
1953	10
1954	8
1955	13
1956	17
1958	3
1960	6
1962	4

Jim Wilson

1964	2

Hack Wilson
Inducted in 1979

1937	1
1939	1
1942	1
1948	2
1949	24
1949 RO	12
1950	16
1951	21
1952	21
1953	43
1954	48
1955	81
1956	74
1958	94
1960	72
1962	39
1979	Vet. Com.

Whitey Witt

1949	1

Joe Wood

1937	13
1938	6
1939	2
1942	1
1946 NOM	5
1947	29
1948	5
1950	1
1951	5

Wilbur Wood

1984	14
1985	16
1986	23
1987	26
1988	30
1989	14

Glenn Wright

1948	2
1949	1
1950	2
1951	1
1952	1
1953	3
1954	1
1955	4
1956	3

1958	8
1960	18
1962	1

George Wright
Inducted in 1937
Pioneer

1936 V	6
1937	Cen. Com.

Harry Wright
Inducted in 1953
Pioneer

1953	Vet. Com.

Whit Wyatt

1958	1

Early Wynn
Inducted in 1972

1969	95
1970	140
1971	240
1972	301

Tom Yawkey
Inducted in 1980
Executive

1980	Vet. Com.

Carl Yastrzemski
Inducted in 1989

1989	423

Steve Yeager

1992	2

Steve Yerkes

1945	1

Rudy York

1962	1
1964	10

Cy Young
Inducted in 1937

1936 V	32
1936	111
1937	153

Pep Young

1958	1

Ross Youngs
Inducted in 1972

1936	10
1937	16
1938	40
1939	34
1942	44
1945	22
1946 NOM	25
1947	36
1948	19
1949	20
1949 RO	11
1950	17
1951	34
1952	34
1953	31
1954	34
1955	48
1956	19
1972	Vet. Com.

Tom Zachary

1958	1
1960	1

Chief Zimmer

1938	1

1936 Veterans
Needed to Elect: 59

Cap Anson	40
Buck Ewing	40

Willie Keeler	33
Cy Young	32
Ed Delahanty	22
John McGraw	17
Herman Long	16
Charlie Radbourn	16
Mike Kelly	15
Amos Rusie	12

1936
Needed to Elect: 170

Ty Cobb	222
Babe Ruth	215
Honus Wagner	215
Christy Mathewson	205
Walter Johnson	189
Nap Lajoie	146
Tris Speaker	133
Cy Young	111
Rogers Hornsby	105
Mickey Cochrane	80

1937
Needed to Elect: 151

Nap Lajoie	168
Tris Speaker	165
Cy Young	153
Pete Alexander	125
Eddie Collins	115
Willie Keeler	115
George Sisler	106
Ed Delahanty	70
Rube Waddell	67
Jimmy Collins	66

1938
Needed to Elect: 197

Pete Alexander	212
George Sisler	179
Willie Keeler	177
Eddie Collins	175
Rube Waddell	148
Frank Chance	133
Ed Delahanty	132
Ed Walsh	110
Johnny Evers	91
Jimmy Collins	79

1939
Needed to Elect: 206

George Sisler	235
Eddie Collins	213
Willie Keeler	207
Rube Waddell	179
Rogers Hornsby	176
Frank Chance	158
Ed Delahanty	145
Ed Walsh	132
Johnny Evers	107
Miller Huggins	97

1942
Needed to Elect: 175

Rogers Hornsby	182
Frank Chance	136
Rube Waddell	126
Ed Walsh	113
Miller Huggins	111
Ed Delahanty	104
Johnny Evers	91
Wilbert Robinson	89
Mickey Cochrane	88
Frankie Frisch	84

1945
Needed to Elect: 185

Frank Chance	179
Rube Waddell	154
Ed Walsh	137
Johnny Evers	134
Roger Bresnahan	133
Miller Huggins	133
Mickey Cochrane	125
Jimmy Collins	121
Ed Delahanty	111
Clark Griffith	108

1946 Nominating Total Voting: 202

Frank Chance	144
Johnny Evers	130
Miller Huggins	129
Rube Waddell	122
Ed Walsh	115
Frankie Frisch	104
Carl Hubbell	101
Mickey Cochrane	80
Clark Griffith	73
Lefty Grove	71

1946
Needed to Elect: 197

Frank Chance	150
Johnny Evers	110
Miller Huggins	106
Ed Walsh	106
Rube Waddell	87
Clark Griffith	82
Carl Hubbell	75
Frankie Frisch	67
Mickey Cochrane	65
Lefty Grove	61

1947
Needed to Elect: 121

Carl Hubbell	140
Frankie Frisch	136
Mickey Cochrane	128
Lefty Grove	123
Pie Traynor	119
Charlie Gehringer	105
Rabbit Maranville	91
Dizzy Dean	88
Herb Pennock	86
Chief Bender	72

1948
Needed to Elect: 91

Herb Pennock	94
Pie Traynor	93
Al Simmons	60
Charlie Gehringer	52
Bill Terry	52
Paul Waner	51
Jimmie Foxx	50
Dizzy Dean	40
Harry Heilmann	40
Bill Dickey	39

1949
Needed to Elect: 115

Charlie Gehringer	102
Mel Ott	94
Al Simmons	89
Dizzy Dean	88
Jimmie Foxx	85
Bill Terry	81
Paul Waner	73
Hank Greenberg	67
Bill Dickey	65
Harry Heilmann	59

1949 Run Off
Needed to Elect: 140
One Player Maximum

Charlie Gehringer	159
Mel Ott	128
Jimmie Foxx	89
Dizzy Dean	81
Al Simmons	76
Paul Waner	63
Harry Heilmann	52
Bill Terry	48
Hank Greenberg	44
Bill Dickey	39
Rabbit Maranville	39

1950
Needed to Elect: 125

Mel Ott	115
Bill Terry	105
Jimmie Foxx	103
Paul Waner	95
Al Simmons	90
Harry Heilmann	87
Dizzy Dean	85
Bill Dickey	78

Rabbit Maranville	66
Hank Greenberg	64

1951
Needed to Elect: 170

Mel Ott	197
Jimmie Foxx	179
Paul Waner	162
Harry Heilmann	153
Bill Terry	148
Dizzy Dean	145
Bill Dickey	118
Al Simmons	116
Rabbit Maranville	110
Ted Lyons	71

1952
Needed to Elect: 176

Harry Heilmann	203
Paul Waner	195
Bill Terry	155
Dizzy Dean	152
Al Simmons	141
Bill Dickey	139
Rabbit Maranville	133
Dazzy Vance	105
Ted Lyons	101
Gabby Hartnett	77

1953
Needed to Elect: 198

Dizzy Dean	209
Al Simmons	199
Bill Terry	191
Bill Dickey	179
Rabbit Maranville	164
Dazzy Vance	150
Ted Lyons	139
Joe DiMaggio	117
Chief Bender	104
Gabby Hartnett	104

1954
Needed to Elect: 189

Rabbit Maranville	209
Bill Dickey	202
Bill Terry	195
Joe DiMaggio	175
Ted Lyons	170
Dazzy Vance	158
Gabby Hartnett	151
Hank Greenberg	97
Joe Cronin	85
Max Carey	55

1955
Needed to Elect: 188

Joe DiMaggio	223
Ted Lyons	217
Dazzy Vance	205
Gabby Hartnett	195
Hank Greenberg	157
Joe Cronin	135
Max Carey	119
Ray Schalk	113
Edd Roush	97
Hank Gowdy	90

1956
Needed to Elect: 145

Hank Greenberg	164
Joe Cronin	152
Red Ruffing	97
Edd Roush	91
Lefty Gomez	89
Hack Wilson	74
Max Carey	65
Tony Lazzeri	64
Kiki Cuyler	55
Hank Gowdy	49

1958
Needed to Elect: 200

Max Carey	136
Edd Roush	112
Red Ruffing	99
Hack Wilson	94
Kiki Cuyler	90
Sam Rice	90
Tony Lazzeri	80

Luke Appling	77
Lefty Gomez	76
Burleigh Grimes	71

1960
Needed to Elect: 202

Edd Roush	146
Sam Rice	143
Eppa Rixey	142
Burleigh Grimes	92
Jim Bottomley	89
Red Ruffing	86
Red Faber	83
Luke Appling	72
Kiki Cuyler	72
Hack Wilson	72

1962
Needed to Elect: 120

Bob Feller	150
Jackie Robinson	124
Sam Rice	81
Red Ruffing	72
Eppa Rixey	49
Luke Appling	48
Phil Rizzuto	44
Burleigh Grimes	43
Hack Wilson	39
Ducky Medwick	34

1964
Needed to Elect: 151

Luke Appling	142
Red Ruffing	141
Roy Campanella	115
Ducky Medwick	108
Pee Wee Reese	73
Lou Boudreau	68
Al Lopez	57
Chuck Klein	56
Johnny Mize	54
Mel Harder	51
Johnny Vander Meer	51

1964 Run Off
Needed to Elect: 170
One Player Maximum

Luke Appling	189
Red Ruffing	184
Roy Campanella	138
Ducky Medwick	130
Pee Wee Reese	47
Lou Boudreau	43
Al Lopez	34
Johnny Vander Meer	20
Chuck Klein	18
Marty Marion	17

1966
Needed to Elect: 227

Ted Williams	282
Red Ruffing	208
Roy Campanella	197
Ducky Medwick	187
Lou Boudreau	115
Al Lopez	109
Enos Slaughter	100
Pee Wee Reese	95
Marty Marion	86
Johnny Mize	81

1967
Needed to Elect: 219

Ducky Medwick	212
Red Ruffing	212
Roy Campanella	204
Lou Boudreau	143
Ralph Kiner	124
Enos Slaughter	123
Al Lopez	114
Marty Marion	90
Johnny Mize	89
Pee Wee Reese	89

1967 Run Off
Needed to Elect: 230
One Player Maximum

Red Ruffing	266

Ducky Medwick . . . 248
Roy Campanella . . 170
Lou Boudreau 68
Al Lopez 50
Enos Slaughter 48
Ralph Kiner 41
Johnny Vander Meer . .
. 35
Ernie Lombardi 25
Bucky Walters 24

1968
Needed to Elect: 212

Ducky Medwick . . . 240
Roy Campanella . . . 205
Lou Boudreau 146
Enos Slaughter . . . 129
Ralph Kiner 118
Johnny Mize 103
Allie Reynolds 95
Marty Marion 89
Arky Vaughan 82
Pee Wee Reese . . . 81

1969
Needed to Elect: 255

Stan Musial 317
Roy Campanella . .270
Lou Boudreau 218
Ralph Kiner 137
Enos Slaughter . . .128
Johnny Mize 116
Marty Marion 112
Allie Reynolds 98
Joe Gordon 97
Johnny Vander Meer . .
. 95
Early Wynn 95

1970
Needed to Elect: 225

Lou Boudreau 232
Ralph Kiner 167
Gil Hodges 145
Early Wynn 140
Enos Slaughter . . .133
Johnny Mize 126
Marty Marion 120
Pee Wee Reese . . .97
Red Schoendienst . .97
George Kell 90

1971
Needed to Elect: 270

Yogi Berra 242
Early Wynn 240
Ralph Kiner 212
Gil Hodges 180
Enos Slaughter . . .165

Johnny Mize 157
Pee Wee Reese . . .127
Marty Marion 123
Red Schoendienst .123
Allie Reynolds 110

1972
Needed to Elect: 297

Sandy Koufax 344
Yogi Berra 339
Early Wynn 301
Ralph Kiner 235
Gil Hodges 161
Johnny Mize 157
Enos Slaughter . . .149
Pee Wee Reese . . .129
Marty Marion 120
Bob Lemon 117

1973
Needed to Elect: 285

Warren Spahn 316
Whitey Ford 255
Ralph Kiner 235
Gil Hodges 218
Robin Roberts 213
Bob Lemon 177
Johnny Mize 157
Enos Slaughter . . .145
Marty Marion 127
Pee Wee Reese . . .126

1974
Needed to Elect: 274

Mickey Mantle 322
Whitey Ford 284
Robin Roberts 224
Ralph Kiner 215
Gil Hodges 198
Bob Lemon 190
Enos Slaughter . . .145
Pee Wee Reese . . .141
Eddie Mathews . . .118
Phil Rizzuto 111
Duke Snider 111

1975
Needed to Elect: 272

Ralph Kiner 273
Robin Roberts 263
Bob Lemon 233
Gil Hodges 188
Enos Slaughter . . .177
Hal Newhouser . . .155
Pee Wee Reese . . .154
Eddie Mathews . . .148
Phil Cavaretta 129
Duke Snider 129

1976
Needed to Elect: 291

Robin Roberts 337
Bob Lemon 305
Gil Hodges 233
Enos Slaughter . . .197
Eddie Mathews . . .189
Pee Wee Reese . . .186
Nellie Fox 174
Duke Snider 159
Phil Rizzuto 149
George Kell 129
Red Schoendienst .129

1977
Needed to Elect: 287

Ernie Banks 321
Eddie Mathews . . .239
Gil Hodges 224
Enos Slaughter . . .222
Duke Snider 212
Don Drysdale 197
Pee Wee Reese . . .163
Nellie Fox 152
Jim Bunning 146
George Kell 141

1978
Needed to Elect: 284

Eddie Mathews . . .301
Enos Slaughter . . .261
Duke Snider 254
Gil Hodges 226
Don Drysdale 219
Jim Bunning 181
Pee Wee Reese . . .169
Richie Ashburn . . .158
Hoyt Wilhelm 158
Nellie Fox 149

1979
Needed to Elect: 324

Willie Mays 409
Duke Snider 308
Enos Slaughter . . .297
Gil Hodges 242
Don Drysdale 233
Nellie Fox 174
Hoyt Wilhelm 168
Maury Wills 166
Red Schoendienst .159
Jim Bunning 147

1980
Needed to Elect: 289

Al Kaline 340

Duke Snider 333
Don Drysdale 238
Gil Hodges 230
Hoyt Wilhelm 209
Jim Bunning 177
Red Schoendienst .164
Nellie Fox 161
Maury Wills 146
Richie Ashburn . . .134

1981
Needed to Elect: 301

Bob Gibson 337
Don Drysdale 243
Gil Hodges 241
Harmon Killebrew .239
Hoyt Wilhelm 238
Juan Marichal 233
Nellie Fox 168
Jim Bunning 164
Maury Wills 163

1982
Needed to Elect: 311

Hank Aaron 406
Frank Robinson . .370
Juan Marichal 305
Harmon Killebrew .246
Hoyt Wilhelm 236
Don Drysdale 233
Gil Hodges 205
Luis Aparicio 174
Jim Bunning 138
Red Schoendienst .135

1983
Needed to Elect: 281

Brooks Robinson .344
Juan Marichal 313
Harmon Killebrew .269
Luis Aparicio 252
Hoyt Wilhelm 243
Don Drysdale 242
Gil Hodges 237
Nellie Fox 173
Billy Williams 153
Red Schoendienst .146

1984
Needed to Elect: 302

Luis Aparicio 341
Harmon Killebrew .335
Don Drysdale 316
Hoyt Wilhelm 290
Nellie Fox 246

Billy Williams 202
Jim Bunning 201
Orlando Cepeda . .124
Tony Oliva 124
Roger Maris 107

1985
Needed to Elect: 296

Hoyt Wilhelm 331
Lou Brock 315
Nellie Fox 295
Billy Williams 252
Jim Bunning 214
Catfish Hunter 212
Roger Maris 128
Harvey Kuenn 125
Orlando Cepeda . .114
Tony Oliva 114

1986
Needed to Elect: 319

Willie McCovey . . .346
Billy Williams 315
Catfish Hunter 289
Jim Bunning 279
Roger Maris 177
Tony Oliva 154
Orlando Cepeda . .152
Harvey Kuenn 144
Maury Wills 124
Bill Mazeroski 100

1987
Needed to Elect: 310

Billy Williams 354
Catfish Hunter 315
Jim Bunning 289
Orlando Cepeda . .179
Roger Maris 176
Tony Oliva 160
Harvey Kuenn 144
Bill Mazeroski 125
Maury Wills 113
Ken Boyer 96
Lew Burdette 96

1988
Needed to Elect: 320

Willie Stargell 352
Jim Bunning 317
Tony Oliva 202
Orlando Cepeda . .199
Roger Maris 184
Harvey Kuenn 168
Bill Mazeroski 143
Luis Tiant 132

Maury Wills 127
Ken Boyer 109
Mickey Lolich 109

1989
Needed to Elect: 335

Johnny Bench 431
Carl Yastrzemski . .423
Gaylord Perry 304
Jim Bunning 283
Fergie Jenkins 234
Orlando Cepeda . .176
Tony Oliva 135
Bill Mazeroski 134
Harvey Kuenn 115
Maury Wills 95

1990
Needed to Elect: 333

Jim Palmer 411
Joe Morgan 363
Gaylord Perry 320
Fergie Jenkins 296
Jim Bunning 257
Orlando Cepeda . .211
Tony Oliva 142
Bill Mazeroski 131
Harvey Kuenn 107
Ron Santo 96

1991
Needed to Elect: 333

Rod Carew 401
Gaylord Perry 342
Ferguson Jenkins .334
Rollie Fingers 291
Jim Bunning 282
Orlando Cepeda . .192
Tony Oliva 160
Bill Mazeroski 142
Ron Santo 116
Harvey Kuenn 100

1992
Needed to Elect: 323

Tom Seaver 425
Rollie Fingers 349
Orlando Cepeda . .246
Tony Perez 215
Bill Mazeroski 182
Tony Oliva 175
Ron Santo 136
Jim Kaat 114
Maury Wills 110
Ken Boyer 71

## CHAPTER 16

The All-Star Game

Frederick Ivor-Campbell

Although the tradition of All-Star Games in baseball dates back to an 1858 series between teams of stars from Brooklyn and New York (they were called "picked nines" in those days), the current All-Star series began when Arch Ward, sports editor of the *Chicago Tribune*, persuaded hesitant league owners to go along with his proposal for a game between stars from the American and National leagues, to be played in Chicago during that city's Century of Progress Exposition in 1933.

All-Star managers (who, except for the first game, have been the pilots of the previous year's pennant winners) shared with fans the selection of players for the first two games. From 1935 through 1946 the manager selected his whole squad. Since 1947, he has chosen his pitchers and all other players except the eight members of the starting lineup. The fans chose the starters in 1947–1957; after an incident of ballot-box stuffing by Cincinnati partisans in 1957, the major league players, coaches, and managers made the choice in 1958–1969; in 1970 the selection of starting lineups was returned to the fans.

The American League dominated the early years of the series, winning the first three games, and extending their winning margin to eight games (12–4) by 1949. The National League cut the lead in half with four straight wins, and by 1964 had drawn even in the series (17–17–1). From 1965 through 1985 the National Leaguers continued their drive, winning 19 All-Star Games while losing only two, to build a commanding 36–19 lead in the series. In recent years, though, the American Leaguers have begun to come back, winning in 1992 their sixth game in seven years, and their fifth in a row. But even if they were to continue winning every year, it would take them until 2004 to catch up.

GAME 1
Comiskey Park, Chicago
July 6, 1933
AL, 4–2

```
NL   000 002 000    2  8  0
AL   012 001 00X    4  9  1
```

Pitchers: HALLAHAN, Warneke (3), Hubbell (7) vs GOMEZ, Crowder (4), Grove (7)
Home Runs: Ruth-A, Frisch-N
Attendance: 49,200

Baseball's two grand old managers—Connie Mack and John McGraw—were chosen to lead the American and National League squads in the first All-Star Game, and American starting pitcher Lefty Gomez of the Yankees took home honors both as the first All-Star winning pitcher and as the first player to drive in an All-Star run (singling in Jimmie Dykes in the second inning). But it was another "grand old man"—Babe Ruth—who made the game's headlines. At thirty-eight, in his next-to-last season as a Yankee, he lined a two-run homer in the third to make the score 3–0, and as right fielder in the eighth he robbed Chick Hafey of a hit with a remarkable running catch of Hafey's line drive.

Frank Frisch homered for the Nationals, following up Pepper Martin's RBI with a solo shot in the National League's two-run sixth. But the American stars countered with an insurance run in the bottom of the sixth, as Earl Averill singled in Joe Cronin to end the scoring. Carl Hubbell for the Nationals and Lefty Grove for the Americans blanked the opposition through the final innings.

GAME 2
Polo Grounds, New York
July 10, 1934
AL, 9–7

```
AL   000 261 000    9  14  1
NL   103 030 000    7  8   1
```

Pitchers: Gomez, Ruffing (4), HARDER (5) vs Hubbell, Warneke (4), MUNGO (5), J.Dean (6), Frankhouse (9)
Home Runs: Frisch-N, Medwick-N
Attendance: 48,363

This was the game in which Carl Hubbell struck out Babe Ruth, Lou Gehrig, Jimmie Foxx, Al Simmons, and Joe Cronin in order in the first two innings. Hubbell also walked two and gave up two hits in his three innings of work, but allowed no run to score as his Nationals took a 4–0 lead on homers by Frank Frisch in the first and Joe Medwick (for three runs) in the third off American starter (and first-game winner) Lefty Gomez.

But with Hubbell gone, the Americans pounced on Lon Warneke and Van Lingle Mungo for four runs each in the fourth and fifth innings. The Nationals battled back for three off Red Ruffing in their half of the fifth, to come within a run of tying the game. But Mel Harder relieved Ruffing with none out and put out the fire, one-hitting the National stars over the final five innings. The Americans picked up an insurance run in the sixth off Dizzy Dean before Dean and Fred Frankhouse shut them down, too, through the final three frames.

GAME 3
Municipal Stadium, Cleveland
July 8, 1935
AL, 4–1

```
NL   000 100 000    1  4  1
AL   210 010 00X    4  8  0
```

Pitchers: WALKER, Schumacher (3), Derringer (7), J.Dean (8) vs GOMEZ, Harder (7)
Home Runs: Foxx-A
Attendance: 69,812

Lefty Gomez started his third All-Star Game, and pitched a record six innings to pick up his second All-Star win. For three innings he shut out the Nationals as the Americans built a lead behind him on Jimmie Foxx's two-run homer in the first, and Rollie Hemsley's triple and Joe Cronin's run-scoring fly in the second.

The National Leaguers tried to catch up in the fourth, when they put together two of their three hits off Gomez—a double by Arky Vaughan and a single by Bill Terry—and scored a run. But an inning later Foxx nullified the National run, singling Joe Vosmik home for his third RBI.

Gomez blanked the National stars through two more innings before yielding to Mel Harder, who came in to close his second All-Star Game. Harder had created an All-Star record the previous year with his five consecutive scoreless innings pitched, and extended the record to eight, with three more shutout innings to end the game.

GAME 4
Braves Field, Boston
July 7, 1936
NL, 4–3

```
AL   000 000 300    3  7  1
NL   020 020 00X    4  9  0
```

Pitchers: GROVE, Rowe (4), Harder (7) vs J.DEAN, Hubbell (4), C.Davis (7), Warneke (7)
Home Runs: Galan-N, Gehrig-A
Attendance: 25,534

The National League, which had not yet won an All-Star Game, scored first in the second when Gabby Hartnett tripled in a run off Lefty Grove—rookie Joe DiMaggio missing his try for a shoe-top catch of Hartnett's drive to right field. Pinky Whitney then singled in Hartnett. Augie Galan homered off Schoolboy Rowe (and the right field foul pole) in the fifth, and DiMaggio's bobble of Billy Herman's single a batter later put Herman in position to score an unearned fourth run, on Joe Medwick's single, that proved to be the margin of victory.

The Americans, shut out through six by Dizzy Dean and Carl Hubbell, nearly tied the game in the seventh off Curt Davis as Lou Gehrig homered and Luke Appling singled in two more. But Lon Warneke took over and, after loading the bases with a walk, escaped disaster as shortstop Leo Durocher snared DiMaggio's vicious line drive to his right for the third out. Warneke shut the Americans out over the final two innings to preserve the one-run lead and the National League's first All-Star win.

GAME 5
Griffith Stadium, Washington
July 7, 1937
AL, 8-3

| NL | 000 | 111 | 000 | 3 | 13 | 0 |
| AL | 002 | 312 | 00X | 8 | 13 | 2 |

Pitchers: J.DEAN, Hubbell (4), Blanton (4), Grissom (5), Mungo (6), Walters (8) vs GOMEZ, Bridges (4), Harder (7)
Home Runs: Gehrig-A
Attendance: 31,391

President Franklin Roosevelt attended the game. Lou Gehrig homered and doubled to drive in half the American League's eight runs in an easy American win. Lefty Gomez started his fourth All-Star Game in five years, winning his third. And American reliever Mel Harder pitched the final innings for the fourth All-Star Game in a row, pushing his record for consecutive All-Star shutout innings to 13. But the game is remembered not for any of these things, but for Earl Averill's line drive in the third inning which fractured Dizzy Dean's toe and led to the premature end of his spectacular career. (Dean recovered from the broken toe, but tried to resume his pitching too soon. In favoring the toe, he changed his delivery and irreparably injured his pitching arm.)

The Americans began their scoring when Gehrig, who preceded Averill in the batting order, homered off Dean in the third, with one aboard. They added to their score in each of the next three innings, so that although the Nationals countered with single runs in the three middle innings, they only fell farther behind.

GAME 6
Crosley Field, Cincinnati
July 6, 1938
NL, 4-1

| AL | 000 | 000 | 001 | 1 | 7 | 4 |
| NL | 100 | 100 | 20X | 4 | 8 | 0 |

Pitchers: GOMEZ, Allen (4), Grove (7) vs VANDER MEER, Lee (4), Brown (7)
Attendance: 27,607

For the fifth (and final) time, Lefty Gomez started for the American League, and although he gave up only two hits and no earned runs in his three innings, he was saddled with the loss when an error by shortstop Joe Cronin paved the way for a National League run in the first.

The Nationals scored their only earned run in the fourth when Mel Ott tripled and Ernie Lombardi singled him home. But in the seventh they recorded two more unearned runs when Leo Durocher bunted to move Frank McCormick to second. Both McCormick and Durocher scored as third baseman Jimmie Foxx threw wildly to first and right fielder Joe DiMaggio (who chased the ball down) missed home plate with his throw.

In the ninth DiMaggio singled and Cronin doubled him home in partial atonement for their errors. But as Johnny Vander Meer and Big Bill Lee had each blanked the American stars on one hit in their three-inning stints, and some fine outfield catches had kept them from scoring more than this one run off Mace Brown, the Americans' errors cost them the game.

GAME 7
Yankee Stadium, New York
July 11, 1939
AL, 3-1

| NL | 001 | 000 | 000 | 1 | 7 | 1 |
| AL | 000 | 210 | 00X | 3 | 6 | 1 |

Pitchers: Derringer, LEE (4), Fette (7) vs Ruffing, BRIDGES (4), Feller (6)
Home Runs: J.DiMaggio-A
Attendance: 62,892

Six Yankees started for the American League, and one of them—Joe DiMaggio—hit the game's only home run. But it was a young Cleveland pitcher—twenty-year-old Bob Feller, playing in his first All-Star Game—who turned in the most memorable performance.

The Nationals scored first, with a run in the third on three hits off the American League starter, Red Ruffing. But the Americans came back with two runs in the fourth on a walk, two singles, and a bobbled grounder by shortstop Arky Vaughan. DiMaggio hit his insurance homer an inning later.

In the top of the sixth, after two singles and an error had loaded the bases with National stars, with only one out, Feller replaced Tommy Bridges to face Vaughan (who had earlier singled and scored his team's only run). One pitch got Feller out of the inning as Vaughan grounded into a 4-6-3 double play. Feller shut out the National stars over the final three innings, striking out Johnny Mize and Stan Hack in the ninth to end the game and give the Americans their fifth All-Star victory.

GAME 8
Sportsman's Park, St. Louis
July 9, 1940
NL, 4-0

| AL | 000 | 000 | 000 | 0 | 3 | 1 |
| NL | 300 | 000 | 01X | 4 | 7 | 0 |

Pitchers: RUFFING, Newsom (4), Feller (7) vs DERRINGER, Walters (3), Wyatt (5), French (7), Hubbell (9)
Home Runs: West-N
Attendance: 32,373

The National Leaguers made short work of the Americans, scoring three times in the first inning and holding the opposing stars to three hits for the All-Star Game's first shutout. Before American League starter Red Ruffing retired a single National batter in the bottom of the first inning, three of the game's four runs had been scored, on singles by Arky Vaughan and Billy Herman and Max West's home run to right center.

Ruffing then settled down, and he and Buck Newsom held the Nationals to just three additional hits through the seventh. Bob Feller gave up the Nationals' fourth run in the eighth, on a walk, a sacrifice, and Harry Danning's single.

Five National League pitchers combined for the shutout, permitting only five batters to reach base while striking out seven. Starter Paul Derringer, who struck out three men in his two innings, was awarded the win.

GAME 9
Briggs Stadium, Detroit
July 8, 1941
AL, 7–5

NL	000	001	220	5	10	2
AL	000	101	014	7	11	3

Pitchers: Wyatt, Derringer (3), Walters (5), PASSEAU (7) vs Feller, Lee (4), Hudson (7), SMITH (8)
Home Runs: Vaughn-N (2), Williams-A
Attendance: 54,674

The National Leaguers entered the last of the ninth with a 5–3 lead and hopes of nailing down their first back-to-back All-Star victories. The American stars had scored their first run in the fourth. The Nationals tied the score in the top of the sixth, but the Americans countered with a run later in the inning. The Nationals' Arky Vaughan then made a bid to be the game's hero, homering in the seventh off Sid Hudson with a man aboard to restore the National lead, and homering again an inning later off Edgar Smith for two more runs.

A double and single by the DiMaggio brothers Joe and Dom brought the Americans a run closer in the eighth, but they still needed two to tie as they faced Claude Passeau in the bottom of the ninth. Two one-out singles and a walk loaded the bases, and a force play at second (that just missed being a game-ending double play) scored Ken Keltner from third. With two men now out and the Americans still down a run, Ted Williams homered on a letter-high fastball against the upper parapet in right for three more runs and another American League victory.

GAME 10
Polo Grounds, New York
July 6, 1942
AL, 3–1

AL	300	000	000	3	7	0
NL	000	000	010	1	6	1

Pitchers: CHANDLER, Benton (5) vs M.COOPER, Vander Meer (4), Passeau (7), Walters (9)
Home Runs: Boudreau-A, York-A, Owen-N
Attendance: 33,694

Home runs accounted for all the scoring as the American League, in something of a reverse of the 1940 game, scored three times in the top of the first to defeat the Nationals. Lou Boudreau, leading off, hit the game winner off Mort Cooper's second pitch, into the upper deck in left field. A double and two outs later, Rudy York put one over the fence near the short right field foul line for two more runs.

The Americans hit safely only four more times, and scored no more runs, but they already had more than enough, as Spud Chandler and Al Benton combined to shut out the National League stars for seven innings, until Mickey Owen, pinch-hitting for pitcher Claude Passeau in the eighth, hit his only home run of the summer.

This was the second All-Star Game played in the Polo Grounds. It had been Brooklyn's turn to host the game at Ebbets Field, but because the proceeds were destined for the war effort, the site was shifted to the larger stadium. The game might as well have been held in Brooklyn, though, as a pregame rain held attendance to well below the Polo Grounds' capacity.

GAME 11
Shibe Park, Philadelphia
July 13, 1943
AL, 5–3

NL	100	000	101	3	10	3
AL	031	010	00X	5	8	1

Pitchers: M.COOPER, Vander Meer (3), SeweLL (6), Javery (7) vs LEONARD, Newhouser (4), Hughson (7)
Home Runs: Doerr-A, V.DiMaggio-N
Attendance: 31,938

For the first time, the All-Star Game was played at night. And for the only time in All-Star history, no Yankee played—although six had been named to the American League squad. But Yankee Joe McCarthy (serving for the sixth time as American manager) was piqued by criticism that he favored his own players, and retaliated by keeping them all on the bench.

The only DiMaggio in this wartime game was Pittsburgh's Vince, and he provided most of the National League power—batting 3 for 3, with eight total bases and two of his team's three runs. But after the Nationals had jumped to a one-run lead in the first, Bobby Doerr of the Americans homered off Mort Cooper with two aboard in the second to put the American stars ahead. They added to their lead with a run in the third and another in the fifth. DiMaggio scored in the seventh after tripling off Tex Hughson and added a homer against Hughson in the ninth, but his heroics were not enough to overcome the American League's march to its third win in a row, and its eighth in eleven tries.

GAME 12
Forbes Field, Pittsburgh
July 11, 1944
NL, 7–1

AL	010	000	000	1	6	3
NL	000	040	21X	7	12	1

Pitchers: Borowy, HUGHSON (4), Muncrief (5), Newhouser (7), Newsom (8) vs Walters, RAFFENSBERGER (4), Sewell (6), Tobin (9)
Attendance: 29,589

For the second time the game was played at night, and for the seventh time Joe McCarthy managed the American League team. But this time—unlike Game 11—he let his Yankees play. He started Yankee pitcher Hank Borowy, who not only shut out the Nationals in his three innings but drove in a run in the second to give his team the lead.

But that was all the American stars got. For the first four innings it was enough, but in the fifth a double, four singles, a walk, an error, and a stolen base brought in four National League runs. In the seventh, Whitey Kurowski doubled in two more National runs, and in the eighth a missed third strike, two walks, and a fly ball produced a seventh and final tally.

No home runs were hit in the game, only the second time that had happened in All-Star play. But Phil Cavarretta of the Nationals tripled—and reached base four additional times on a single and three walks for a new All-Star on-base record.

GAME 13
Fenway Park, Boston
July 9, 1946
AL, 12–0

```
NL   000 000 000     0  3  0
AL   200 130 24X    12 14  1
```

Pitchers: PASSEAU, Higbe (4),
Blackwell (5), Sewell (8) vs FELLER,
Newhouser (4), Kramer (7)
Home Runs: Keller-A, Williams-A (2)
Attendance: 34,906

No All-Star Game was played in
1945 because of restrictions on
wartime travel, but when the
classic resumed in 1946 the
American stars avenged their
1944 loss with the most decisive
All-Star victory to date: 12–0.
American pitchers Bob Feller,
Hal Newhouser, and Jack
Kramer combined to hold the
National stars to three singles
and a walk, as their teammates
pounded National pitching for 14
hits, including two doubles and
three home runs.

But the game belonged to Ted
Williams. Back after three years
at war, and playing before his
hometown fans, he equaled Phil
Cavarretta's 1944 on-base record
in spectacular fashion, with one
walk, two singles, and two home
runs: one a drive into the center
field bleachers and the other the
first homer ever hit off Rip Sewell's looping "eephus" pitch. He
scored the game's first run in the
first inning as Charlie Keller followed his walk with a homer, and
went on to break an All-Star record by scoring three more times,
while driving in a record five
runs.

GAME 14
Wrigley Field, Chicago
July 8, 1947
AL, 2–1

```
AL   000 001 100     2  8  0
NL   000 100 000     1  5  1
```

Pitchers: Newhouser, SHEA (4),
Masterson (7), Page (8) vs
Blackwell, Brecheen (4), SAIN (7),
Spahn (8)
Home Runs: Mize-N
Attendance: 41,123

Johnny Mize homered for the
National League off rookie Spec
Shea in the fourth inning for the
game's first run, after three
one-hit innings by the two lanky
starters, Ewell Blackwell of the
Nationals and Hal Newhouser of
the Americans. Mize's run remained the only score until the
sixth inning, when the American
Leaguers tied the game on two
singles and a double-play
grounder.

Sharp baserunning by Bobby
Doerr—plus a little luck—led to
the Americans' second run an inning later. Doerr singled, then
stole second. He took third when
pitcher Johnny Sain's pickoff
throw bounced off Doerr's back
into the outfield. Pinch hitter
Stan Spence then singled Doerr
home with what proved to be the
game's final—and winning—run.
The Nationals put men on first
and third in the eighth, but shortstop Lou Boudreau's spectacular
stop of a hot grounder and sharp
throw to first retired the side and
ended the threat.

GAME 15
Sportsman's Park, St. Louis
July 13, 1948
AL, 5–2

```
NL   200 000 000     2  8  0
AL   011 300 00X     5  6  0
```

Pitchers: Branca, SCHMITZ (4),
Sain (4), Blackwell (6) vs
Masterson, RASCHI (4),
Coleman (7)
Home Runs: Musial-N, Evers-A
Attendance: 34,009

Vic Raschi pitched three shutout
innings for the American stars
and drove in two go-ahead runs
with a fourth-inning single as the
American League—for the third
time since the All-Star Game
originated in 1933—won its third
classic in a row. The Nationals
scored first on Stan Musial's
two-run homer in the top of the
first. But that was all they got, as
starter Walt Masterson settled
down and shut out the Nationals
through the second and third innings. Raschi then came on for
his shutout stint, and Joe Coleman stopped the Nationals without even a hit over the final three
innings.

Meanwhile, the Americans
scored a run in the second on
Hoot Evers's homer, and tied the
game with another run in the
third on two walks, a double steal,
and an outfield fly. Then in the
fourth, when two walks and a single had loaded the bases, pitcher
Raschi singled in the third and
fourth American runs. Joe
DiMaggio's pinch-hit fly scored a
fifth run. Johnny Sain and Ewell
Blackwell shut out the Americans
the rest of the way, but the damage had been done.

GAME 16
Ebbets Field, Brooklyn
July 12, 1949
AL, 11–7

```
AL   400 202 300    11 13  1
NL   212 002 000     7 12  5
```

Pitchers: Parnell, TRUCKS (2),
Brissie (4), Raschi (7) vs Spahn,
NEWCOMBE (2), Munger (5),
Bickford (6), Pollet (7), Blackwell (8),
Roe (9)
Home Runs: Musial-N, Kiner-N
Attendance: 32,577

Each team scored seven earned
runs in this game which saw a
total of 25 hits, including seven
doubles and two home runs. But
two first-inning National League
errors let in four unearned American runs to provide the margin
for the American League's fourth
consecutive All-Star win. Stan
Musial and Ralph Kiner each
drove in two National runs with
homers, but Eddie Joost singled
in two runs for the Americans and
Joe DiMaggio singled and doubled in three more to lead the
American attack. For the second
year in a row, Vic Raschi shut out
the National stars for three innings, this time holding the
American lead over the final
third of the game.

The game was notable as the
first to include black players:
three Dodgers (Jackie Robinson,
Roy Campanella, and Don Newcombe) for the National League,
and Larry Doby for the American. With the Americans now
ahead 12–4, it also marked the
farthest extent of American
League domination of the mid-
summer classic.

GAME 17
Comiskey Park, Chicago
July 11, 1950
NL, 4–3

NL	020 000 001 000 01	4	10	0
AL	001 020 000 000 00	3	8	1

Pitchers: Roberts, Newcombe (4),
    Konstanty (6), Jansen (7),
    BLACKWELL (12) vs Raschi,
    Lemon (4), Houtteman (7),
    Reynolds (10), GRAY (13), Feller (14)
Home Runs: Kiner-N,
    Schoendienst-N
Attendance: 46,127

For the first time, the All-Star
Game went into extra innings,
and for the first time the National
League won a game as the visiting team. Three pitchers each
hurled three innings of shutout
ball: Bob Lemon and Allie Reynolds for the American League
and Ewell Blackwell (who finished the game and got the win)
for the Nationals. But top pitching honors were earned by National Leaguer Larry Jansen, who
struck out six and gave up only
one hit over *five* shutout innings
(7–11).

The National stars scored first
with two runs in the second. The
Americans came back with one in
the third, and tied and took the
lead in the fifth on George Kell's
run-scoring fly and an RBI single
by Ted Williams (who, it was
later learned, had broken his left
elbow making an off-the-wall
catch in the first inning). But in
the top of the ninth, Ralph Kiner
of the Nationals hit a game-tying
homer, and 4½ scoreless innings
later Red Schoendienst—on the
first pitch of the fourteenth inning—homered off American
Ted Gray with what proved to be
the game winner.

GAME 18
Briggs Stadium, Detroit
July 10, 1951
NL, 8–3

NL	100 302 110	8	12	1
AL	010 110 000	3	10	2

Pitchers: Roberts, MAGLIE (3),
    Newcombe (6), Blackwell (9) vs
    Garver, LOPAT (4), Hutchinson (5),
    Parnell (8), Lemon (9)
Home Runs: Musial-N, Elliott-N,
    Wertz-A, Kell-A, Hodges-N, Kiner-N
Attendance: 52,075

In a game moved from Philadelphia to help Detroit celebrate its
250th birthday, hometowners Vic
Wertz and George Kell of the
Tigers hit solo homers in the
fourth and fifth innings to bring
the American stars within a run
of the Nationals. But they came
no closer, as the National Leaguers pulled away for a convincing 8–3 victory.

The Nationals, aided by six innings of shutout pitching (including three by Don Newcombe),
produced four home runs of their
own to drive in six of their eight
runs. With the score tied 1–1 going into the fourth inning, Stan
Musial greeted Ed Lopat's first
pitch with a shot to the right field
upper deck, and Bob Elliott
added two more runs later in the
inning with a homer to left. Gil
Hodges increased the National
League lead to 6–3 with a
two-run homer in the sixth, and
Ralph Kiner concluded the Nationals' scoring with a solo up-
per-deck shot to left center in the
eighth. For the first time in
All-Star play, the National
League had won two games in a
row.

GAME 19
Shibe Park, Philadelphia
July 8, 1952
NL, 3–2

AL	000 20	2	5	0
NL	100 20	3	3	0

Pitchers: Raschi, LEMON (3),
    Shantz (5) vs Simmons, RUSH (4)
Home Runs: J.Robinson-N, Sauer-N
Attendance: 32,785

No sun shone for this rain-short-
ened game, but two hometown
pitchers did. Curt Simmons of
the Phillies held the American
stars to one hit as he shut them
out over the first three innings.
And the Athletics' Bobby
Shantz—in the midst of an MVP
season—struck out the side in the
fifth for the Americans.

But home runs and rain determined the final outcome. Jackie
Robinson opened the scoring with
a homer off Vic Raschi in the bottom of the first to give the Nationals a 1–0 lead. In the fourth the
Americans came back to take the
lead briefly with two runs on a
double, a walk, and two singles
off eventual winner Bob Rush.
But in the bottom of the inning,
Hank Sauer's home run off Bob
Lemon with one aboard returned
the lead to the National League.
And there it stayed through a
scoreless fifth, when the rain,
which had fallen throughout the
game, at last brought the soggy
festivities to the All-Star series'
first premature conclusion.

GAME 20
Crosley Field, Cincinnati
July 14, 1953
NL, 5–1

AL	000 000 001	1	5	0
NL	000 020 12X	5	10	0

Pitchers: Pierce, REYNOLDS (4),
    Garcia (6) Paige (8) vs Roberts,
    SPAHN (4), Simmons (6),
    Dickson (8)
Attendance: 30,846

For the first 4½ innings, pitchers
for both sides held the opposition
scoreless, with one hit each. Then
the National Leaguers got to Allie Reynolds for two runs in the
bottom of the fifth on a hit batsman, a walk, and two singles.

This proved margin enough for
the National League's fourth consecutive victory, as four National
pitchers held the Americans to
just two hits through eight innings before three singles in the
ninth gave the American Leaguers their only run. For good
measure, though, the National
stars added a run in the seventh,
and two more in the eighth (with
three singles and a walk off
Satchel Paige in his only All-Star
appearance).

Enos Slaughter of the Nationals provided much of the game's
excitement. With two singles, a
walk, and a stolen base, he drove
in one run and scored two others,
and defensively made a spectacular diving catch in right field. Pee
Wee Reese's double in the seventh (scoring Slaughter) was the
game's only extra-base hit.

GAME 21
Municipal Stadium, Cleveland
July 13, 1954
AL, 11–9

```
NL   000 520 020    9 14 0
AL   004 121 03X   11 17 1
```

Pitchers: Roberts, Antonelli (4), Spahn (6), Grissom (6), CONLEY (8), Erskine (8) vs Ford, Consuegra (4), Lemon (4), Porterfield (5), Keegan (8), STONE (8), Trucks (9)
Home Runs: Rosen-A (2), Boone-A, Kluszewski-N, Bell-N, Doby-A
Attendance: 68,751

American starter Whitey Ford gave up only one hit in three shutout innings, and National starter Robin Roberts shut out the American stars through two. But in the bottom of the third Al Rosen tagged Roberts for a three-run homer, and Ray Boone followed with a solo shot. By the end of the game new All-Star records had been set for hits (31), runs (20), and pitchers used (13), and the record of 6 home runs had been equaled.

The Nationals topped the American four-run lead with five straight hits off Sandy Consuegra in the fourth, for five runs. The Americans tied the game with a run in their half of the fourth, but Ted Kluszewski homered in the fifth for two more National League runs. In the bottom of the fifth, Rosen homered again, for two, to bring the Americans even again.

A run in the sixth put the Americans ahead, but Gus Bell's two-run blast in the eighth returned the Nationals to the top by one. They were threatening to lengthen that lead when Dean Stone entered the contest in relief of Bob Keegan with two out and Red Schoendienst on third. Before Stone's first delivery, Schoendienst broke for home and was tagged out, setting the stage for Stone to become the winning pitcher without making a pitch. American Larry Doby tied it up again later in the eighth with a home run, and Nellie Fox drove in the game's final two runs a few batters later with a bases-loaded single.

In the ninth, the Nationals' Stan Musial blasted two over the fence—both foul—with a man aboard. But Virgil Trucks retired him and Gil Hodges, who followed, to preserve the American League's first victory in five games.

GAME 22
County Stadium, Milwaukee
July 12, 1955
NL, 6–5

```
AL   400 001 000 000   5 10 2
NL   000 000 230 001   6 13 1
```

Pitchers: Pierce, Wynn (4), Ford (7), SULLIVAN (8) vs Roberts, Haddix (4), Newcombe (7), Jones (8), Nuxhall (8), CONLEY (12)
Home Runs: Mantle-A, Musial-N
Attendance: 45,314

Down 0–5 in the seventh inning, the National Leaguers came back to tie the game and send it into extra innings. The Americans attacked early, scoring four runs off Robin Roberts (three of them on Mickey Mantle's home run to center) before the game's first out had been recorded. They added a fifth run in the sixth inning. Meanwhile, pitchers Billy Pierce and Early Wynn were shutting the Nationals down on four hits.

In the seventh, though, two singles, a walk, and an American error gave the Nationals two runs, and in the eighth, four two-out singles and another error tied the game. Joe Nuxhall for the Nationals and the Americans' Frank Sullivan prevented further scoring through the eleventh. In the top of the twelfth, Gene Conley replaced Nuxhall and struck out the side: Al Kaline, Mickey Vernon, and Al Rosen. Sullivan returned for the Americans to face Stan Musial in the bottom of the twelfth. Musial hit the first pitch—a fastball—over the screen in right and the game was over.

GAME 23
Griffith Stadium, Washington
July 10, 1956
NL, 7–3

```
NL   001 211 200   7 11 0
AL   000 003 000   3 11 0
```

Pitchers: FRIEND, Spahn (4), Antonelli (6) vs PIERCE, Ford (4), Wilson (5), Brewer (6), Score (8), Wynn (9)
Home Runs: Mays-N, Williams-A, Mantle-A, Musial-N
Attendance: 28,843

Four of the game's greatest sluggers—Willie Mays, Stan Musial, Ted Williams, and Mickey Mantle—hit home runs, three of them off two of the game's greatest pitchers—Whitey Ford and Warren Spahn. But the star of the game was National League third baseman Ken Boyer, who went 3 for 5, scoring one run and driving in another, while making three spectacular diving and leaping plays in the field.

The National stars scored five times—including twice in the fourth on Mays's homer off Ford—before the Americans put a run on the board. But in the bottom of the sixth, Williams homered for two runs off Spahn, and Mantle followed him with another homer to bring the Americans within two. But that was the end of their scoring, as Johnny Antonelli relieved Spahn to stop the American stars the rest of the way. The Nationals scored twice more in the seventh—one of the runs coming on Musial's homer—ensuring them a comfortable 7–3 victory.

GAME 24
Busch Stadium, St. Louis
July 9, 1957
AL, 6–5

```
AL   020 001 003   6 10 0
NL   000 000 203   5  9 1
```

Pitchers: BUNNING, Loes (4), Wynn (7), Pierce (7), Mossi (9), Grim (9) vs SIMMONS, Sanford (6), Jackson (7), Labine (9)
Attendance: 30,693

Cincinnati fans stuffed the ballot boxes and elected Reds to start everywhere but first base. Commissioner Ford Frick removed two elected starters, but left five Reds in the lineup. They could not bring the National League the victory, though.

The Americans scored twice in the second on singles and walks to take a lead they held to the finish. Although reliever Lew Burdette—after walking in the second run—stopped the American stars through the fifth, Jim Bunning and Billy Loes were combining to keep the Nationals from scoring through the first six innings. The Americans, meanwhile, added a third run in the top of the sixth on a double, a wild pitch, and a single.

The Nationals scored their first two in the seventh, on two singles and a double, to draw within a run of a tie. But in the top of the ninth the Americans combined two singles, an error, a sacrifice bunt, and Minnie Minoso's pinch double for three more runs. They needed them all, for the Nationals responded in their half of the ninth with three runs of their own on a blend of walks, hits (including Willie Mays's triple), and a wild pitch. With two out and a runner at second, Gil Hodges lined one deep to left center. But Minoso, now in left field, snared the drive on the run to end the game.

GAME 25
Memorial Stadium, Baltimore
July 8, 1958
AL, 4–3

NL	210 000 000	3	4	2
AL	110 011 00X	4	9	2

Pitchers: Spahn, FRIEND (4), Jackson (6), Farrell (7) vs Turley, Narleski (2), WYNN (6), O'Dell (7)
Attendance: 48,829

Although American League pitchers held the National Leaguers to only four hits (all singles), the Nationals took a quick lead, and held it for half the game before they were overtaken. Willie Mays and Stan Musial singled in the top of the first, both scoring as American starter Bob Turley proceeded to give up a sacrifice fly, hit a batter, walk a man, and unload a wild pitch.

The Americans came back with one run in their half of the first, but the Nationals drove Turley out with their third run as Mays (who had reached on a fielder's choice) worked his way around the bases on a steal, an error, and Bob Skinner's single. Once again the Americans answered with a run, but they didn't tie the game until Mickey Vernon scored on a bases-loaded ground out in the fifth. An inning later they took the lead when pinch hitter Gil McDougald singled home Frank Malzone.

Billy O'Dell set down the Nationals in order over the final three innings to preserve the lead and give the American Leaguers their second consecutive victory.

GAME 26
Forbes Field, Pittsburgh
July 7, 1959
NL, 5–4

AL	000 100 030	4	8	0
NL	100 000 22X	5	9	1

Pitchers: Wynn, Duren (4), Bunning (7), FORD (8), Daley (8) vs Drysdale, Burdette (4), Face (7), ANTONELLI (8), Elston (9)
Home Runs: Mathews-N, Kaline-A
Attendance: 35,277

For the third year in a row, the game was decided by one run, with the National League celebrating the city of Pittsburgh's bicentennial by breaking the American League's win streak at two.

Eddie Mathews homered for the Nationals in the bottom of the first for the only run in the first three innings, as Don Drysdale stopped the Americans without a hit or walk, fanning four. Al Kaline tied the game in the top of the fourth with an American home run for the only score of the middle three innings, as Ryne Duren one-hit the Nationals, like Drysdale striking out four.

In the last of the seventh, though, a double and two singles off Jim Bunning put the Nationals ahead by two runs. The NL lead lasted only briefly, however, as the Americans moved back into the lead with three runs in the eighth off Roy Face, with two singles, a walk, and a double after Face had retired the first two men. But in their half of the eighth the Nationals hit on Whitey Ford, tying the game with a single-sacrifice-single, and scoring the game winner on Willie Mays's triple to center.

GAME 27
Memorial Coliseum, Los Angeles
August 3, 1959
AL, 5–3

AL	012 000 110	5	6	0
NL	100 010 100	3	6	3

Pitchers: WALKER, Wynn (4), Wilhelm, (6), O'Dell (7), McLish (8) vs DRYSDALE, Conley (4), Jones (6), Face (8)
Home Runs: Malzone-A, Berra-A, F. Robinson-N, Gilliam-N, Colavito-A
Attendance: 55,105

To raise extra money for the players' pension fund and other causes, a second All-Star Game was scheduled for 1959, the first ever to be played in August, and the first on the West Coast. The American stars avenged their earlier defeat with a 5–3 win, out-homering the Nationals three to two.

The National Leaguers scored first on a first-inning double and sacrifice fly, but Frank Malzone tied the score with the game's first home run. Yogi Berra homered an inning later with one on for a 3–1 American lead, but Frank Robinson brought the Nationals back to within one with his homer in the fifth. The Americans replaced that run in the top of the seventh on a walk, two errors, and a single, but Junior Gilliam countered with a home run in the last of the inning. Rocky Colavito scored the game's final run for the Americans in the eighth with the game's final homer.

Don Drysdale, the pitching standout of the July game, struck out five this time, but also walked three and gave up three runs on homers to take the loss.

GAME 28
Municipal Stadium, Kansas City
July 11, 1960
NL, 5–3

NL	311 000 000	5	12	4
AL	000 001 020	3	6	1

Pitchers: FRIEND, McCormick (4), Face (6), Buhl (8), Law (9) vs MONBOUQUETTE, Estrada (3), Coates (4), Bell (6), Lary (8), Daley (9)
Home Runs: Banks-N, Crandall-N, Kaline-A
Attendance: 30,619

The day was hot—the temperature broke 100—and so were the National League bats. Willie Mays went 3 for 4, including a leadoff triple and a double; Ernie Banks homered and doubled; Del Crandall homered and singled; and Joe Adcock doubled and singled for three-fourths of the Nationals' 12 hits as the National League scored five unanswered runs in the first three innings to take an unbeatable lead. Starter Bob Friend, meanwhile, blanked the Americans on one hit through three innings and Mike McCormick held them scoreless for two more before yielding the first American run in the sixth on Nellie Fox's bases-loaded single. Roy Face then came on to douse the fire, getting Luis Aparicio to ground into a double play.

Four American League pitchers stopped the National stars after the third inning, and Al Kaline homered for two more American runs in the eighth. In the ninth the Americans put men on first and second with one away. But their comeback fell short, as Vern Law came on to retire Brooks Robinson and Harvey Kuenn and preserve the National victory.

GAME 29
Yankee Stadium, New York
July 13, 1960
NL, 6-0

```
NL   021 000 102    6 10 0
AL   000 000 000    0  8 0
```

Pitchers: LAW, Podres (3), S.Williams (5), Jackson (7), Henry (8), McDaniel (9) vs FORD, Wynn (4), Staley (6), Lary (8), Bell (9)
Home Runs: Mathews-N, Mays-N, Musial-N, Boyer-N
Attendance: 38,362

Only two days after the first All-Star Game, the squads met a second time before fewer than 39,000 fans in capacious Yankee Stadium. It was no contest. Vern Law, who had completed and saved the first game, started and won this one. His two shutout innings set the pace for the five National pitchers who followed him to fashion the first National League shutout in twenty years. The American stars got only two fewer hits than the Nationals (8 to 10), but only one was for extra bases, whereas four of the National League hits were home runs.

Eddie Mathews began the scoring with a two-run homer in the second, and Willie Mays (on his way to a second straight 3-for-4 game) homered for the third National run an inning later. No one scored through the three middle innings, but in the seventh Stan Musial broke his own record with his sixth All-Star homer—a mighty shot three tiers up in right—and in the ninth Ken Boyer completed the rout with a two-run shot to left.

GAME 30
Candlestick Park, San Francisco
July 11, 1961
NL, 5-4

```
AL   000 001 002 1   4  4 2
NL   010 100 010 2   5 11 5
```

Pitchers: Ford, Lary (4), Donovan (4), Bunning (6), Fornieles (8), WILHELM (8) vs Spahn, Purkey (4), McCormick (6), Face (9), Koufax (9), MILLER (9)
Home Runs: Killebrew-A, Altman-N
Attendance: 44,115

National League pitchers began the game where they had left off the year before. For five innings Warren Spahn and Bob Purkey shut out the American stars without a hit or base on balls. In the sixth, Harmon Killebrew homered off Mike McCormick to end the American drought, but it was the only hit McCormick yielded through the eighth.

Meanwhile, the Nationals had taken a 3–1 lead with runs in the second and fourth innings and George Altman's homer in the eighth. But in the top of the ninth, Candlestick's notorious winds helped put the Americans back in the game. Their second and third hits of the game brought in one run, and their fourth (and last) hit put another man on base. The tying run came in when the wind first of all blew pitcher Stu Miller off the mound for a balk to advance the runners, and then twisted a grounder out of third baseman Ken Boyer's grasp for a run-scoring error. In the tenth, the wind may have contributed to the Americans' go-ahead run as Boyer's throw to first sailed into the outfield, allowing Nellie Fox (who had walked) to score from first.

But in the last of the tenth the wind finally came to the aid of the Nationals, rendering useless the famous knuckleball of American reliever Hoyt Wilhelm, who gave up the tying run on hits by Hank Aaron and Willie Mays and lost the game when Roberto Clemente singled in Mays from second.

GAME 31
Fenway Park, Boston
July 31, 1961
Tie, 1-1

```
NL   000 001 000    1 5 1
AL   100 000 000    1 4 0
```

Pitchers: Purkey, Mahaffey (3), Koufax (5), Miller (7) vs Bunning, Schwall (4), Pascual (7)
Home Runs: Colavito-A
Attendance: 31,851

In the second All-Star Game of 1961, the weather again played a crucial role, as heavy rain at the end of the ninth inning forced the first (and, so far, only) All-Star tie.

Rocky Colavito's home run for the Americans in the first inning turned out to be his squad's only run, as four National League pitchers combined to shut out the American stars on only three singles the rest of the way. The American League pitching was just as effective, with starter Jim Bunning and finisher Camilo Pascual each pitching three no-hit innings. Don Schwall, who pitched the middle three innings, gave up all five National League hits and the Nationals' one run. But even that might have been prevented.

In the sixth, with two on and two out, American shortstop Luis Aparicio waited for a slow grounder, failing to get the ball in time to throw the batter out and end the inning. The Nationals scored on the next play, Bill White's hot ground single up the middle, which Aparicio stopped brilliantly to prevent more than one run from scoring, but which did drive in the game's tying—and final—run.

GAME 32
D.C. Stadium, Washington
July 10, 1962
NL, 3-1

```
NL   000 002 010    3 8 0
AL   000 001 000    1 4 0
```

Pitchers: Drysdale, MARICHAL (4), Purkey (6), Shaw (8) vs Bunning, PASCUAL (4), Donovan (7), Pappas (9)
Attendance: 45,480

The stadium was new, President Kennedy threw out the first ball, and starters Don Drysdale of the Nationals and Jim Bunning of the Americans both pitched three innings of one-hit shutout ball. But Maury Wills stole the show. Entering the game in the sixth inning to run for forty-one-year-old Stan Musial, who had singled, Wills stole second, then scored on Dick Groat's single up the middle for the game's first run. Another single, a long fly out, and a ground out scored Groat with the second (and, as it turned out, winning) run.

Two singles and a fly out by Roger Maris brought in an American run in the bottom of the sixth off Bob Purkey. But that was all they got, as Purkey and Bob Shaw one-hit the American stars through the final three innings.

In the eighth inning Wills manufactured an insurance run for the Nationals. On first with a leadoff single, he somehow reached third on Jim Davenport's single to short left, racing from second to third as left fielder Rocky Colavito threw in to second. He scored after tagging on a foul out to right.

GAME 33
Wrigley Field, Chicago
July 30, 1962
AL, 9–4

AL	001	201	302	9	10	0
NL	010	000	111	4	10	4

Pitchers: Stenhouse, HERBERT (3), Aguirre (6), Pappas (9) vs Podres, MAHAFFEY (3), Gibson (5), Farrell (7), Marichal (8)
Home Runs: Runnels-A, Wagner-A. Colavito-A, Roseboro-N
Attendance: 38,359

With this second game of 1962, the leagues ended their four-year experiment of playing two All-Star games a year. The Americans out-homered the Nationals to spoil the National League's attempt to even the series at 16 wins apiece. But no matter—the American stars would win only once again in the next twenty years.

The National stars scored first on a double and single in the second, but Pete Runnels evened the score in the third with a solo homer, and Leon Wagner put the Americans ahead with a two-run shot an inning later. After Tom Tresh doubled home a fourth American run in the sixth, Rocky Colavito put the game out of reach with a three-run blast in the seventh.

The Nationals tried to come back with runs in the seventh and eighth, but the Americans neutralized them with two more of their own in the ninth (on two errors, two Juan Marichal wild pitches, a double, and a long fly out). With the score now 9–3, John Roseboro's solo homer in the last of the ninth put the Nationals in the home-run column, but that was all.

GAME 34
Municipal Stadium, Cleveland
July 9, 1963
NL, 5–3

NL	012	010	010	5	6	0
AL	012	000	000	3	11	1

Pitchers: O'Toole, JACKSON (3), Culp (5), Woodeshick (6), Drysdale (8) vs McBride, BUNNING (4), Bouton (6), Pizarro (7), Radatz (8)
Attendance: 44,160

Willie Mays sparked the National League to victory with his baserunning and timely hitting. Although he had only one hit—a single—he scored two runs and drove in two others in the Nationals' 5–3 win.

The National stars scored first when Mays walked in the second inning, stole second, and came in on a single by Dick Groat. The Americans tied the game in the last of the second, but in the top of the third Mays singled in one run, stole second again, and scored his second run on Ed Bailey's single.

Once again the Americans came back in the bottom of the third to tie the game on Albie Pearson's double, followed by two singles sandwiched around an infield out. But these were their last runs, as four National pitchers shut them out on four singles the rest of the way. Meanwhile, Mays drove in what proved to be the winning run with a ground out in the fifth. In the eighth the Nationals scored a final run when Ron Santo singled home Bill White, who had singled and stolen second.

GAME 35
Shea Stadium, New York
July 7, 1964
NL, 7–4

AL	100	002	100	4	9	1
NL	000	210	004	7	8	0

Pitchers: Chance, Wyatt (4), Pascual (5), RADATZ (7) vs Drysdale, Bunning (4), Short (6), Farrell (7), MARICHAL (9)
Home Runs: B.Williams-N, Boyer-N, Callison-N
Attendance: 50,850

A new stadium in the midst of a World's Fair was the venue for this game in which the National League at last drew even with the American at 17 wins apiece.

The American stars jumped into the lead with an unearned run in the first, but the Nationals (after Dean Chance had shut them out through three innings) overtook the Americans in the fourth, on home runs by Billy Williams and Ken Boyer, and Dick Groat doubled in a third run in the fifth. In the top of the sixth the Americans tied the score when Brooks Robinson tripled in a pair, and took the lead again an inning later on a sacrifice fly that barely scored Elston Howard ahead of Willie Mays's throw from center.

The Americans held their slim lead into the bottom of the ninth. But Mays walked (after fouling off five third strikes), stole second, and scored the tying run on a single to short right and an errant throw home. One intentional walk and two outs later, Johnny Callison hit Dick Radatz's 1–2 fastball over the fence in right to win the game.

GAME 36
Metropolitan Stadium, Bloomington, Minnesota
July 13, 1965
NL, 6–5

NL	320	000	100	6	11	0
AL	000	140	000	5	8	0

Pitchers: Marichal, Maloney (4), Drysdale (5), KOUFAX (6), Farrell (7), Gibson (8) vs Pappas, Grant (2), Richert (4), McDOWELL (6), Fisher (8)
Home Runs: Mays-N, Torre-N, Stargell-N, McAuliffe-A, Killebrew-A
Attendance: 46,706

For a while it looked as though the Nationals would run away with the game. Willie Mays led off with a home run in the first, and Joe Torre added two runs with a homer later in the inning. In the second Willie Stargell homered for two more runs to make the score 5–0. National starter Juan Marichal stopped the Americans on one hit through three innings.

But the American stars battled back. A single, a walk, and another single off Marichal's replacement, Jim Maloney, brought in one run in the fourth. Maloney retired the first two men in the fifth, but then he gave up a walk followed by a home run to Dick McAuliffe, and a scratch single followed by a Harmon Killebrew homer—and the score was tied at 5–5.

Only one more run was scored. In the seventh, Willie Mays, who had walked and gone to third on Hank Aaron's single, scored on Ron Santo's infield hit to short. The Nationals held off American threats in the eighth and ninth to take the All-Star series lead for the first time.

GAME 37
Busch Memorial Stadium, St. Louis
July 12, 1966
NL, 2-1

```
AL  010 000 000 0   1 6 0
NL  000 100 000 1   2 6 0
```

Pitchers: McLain, Kaat (4), Stottlemyre (6), Siebert (8), RICHERT (10) vs Koufax, Bunning (4), Marichal (6), G.PERRY (9)
Attendance: 49,936

The celebration of another new stadium and the city's bicentennial—and a temperature of 106°F—greeted participants in the 1966 classic. Pitching dominated: seven pitchers hurled two innings or more each of shutout ball. American starter Denny McLain threw three perfect innings, but the National League's Sandy Koufax gave the Americans a run in the second when he let loose a wild pitch after Brooks Robinson had tripled.

The Nationals tied the score in the fourth with three singles off Jim Kaat, but that ended the scoring for both sides through the regulation nine innings. In the top of the tenth, Gaylord Perry stopped the American stars. But in the last half of the inning, National Leaguer Tim McCarver singled off Pete Richert, was sacrificed to second, and came across with the winning run on Maury Wills's single to right.

GAME 38
Anaheim Stadium, Anaheim, California
July 11, 1967
NL, 2-1

```
NL  010 000 000 000 001   2 9 0
AL  000 001 000 000 000   1 8 0
```

Pitchers: Marichal, Jenkins (4), Gibson (7), Short (9), Cuellar (11), DRYSDALE (13), Seaver (15) vs Chance, McGlothlin (4), Peters (6), Downing (9), HUNTER (11)
Home Runs: Allen-N, B.Robinson-A, Perez-N
Attendance: 46,309

This was a game of strikeouts, home runs, and extra innings. Every one of the twelve pitchers used in the game struck out at least one batter. American Leaguers Gary Peters (who pitched three perfect middle innings) and Catfish Hunter struck out four apiece, while Ferguson Jenkins of the Nationals tied the All-Star record with six. The game total of 30 strikeouts shattered the previous record of 20 set in 1955.

Apart from the splendid pitching, three home runs provided the only excitement—and the only scoring—in this longest All-Star Game. Richie Allen of the Nationals scored first, homering to center off Dean Chance in the second inning. The Americans' Brooks Robinson tied the score in the sixth with a shot off Jenkins. And 8½ innings later, in the top of the fifteenth, National Leaguer Tony Perez homered off Hunter for the game's third and final run. Tom Seaver set down the Americans in the bottom of the fifteenth, and the game—after a record 3 hours and 41 minutes—was history.

GAME 39
Astrodome, Houston
July 9, 1968
NL, 1-0

```
AL  000 000 000   0 3 1
NL  100 000 00X   1 5 0
```

Pitchers: TIANT, Odom (3), McLain (5), McDowell (7), Stottlemyre (8), John (8) vs DRYSDALE, Marichal (4), Carlton (6), Seaver (7), Reed (9), Koosman (9)
Attendance: 48,321

This game could be described by what was missing: fresh air and real grass (it was the first All-Star Game held indoors), hitting (the eight hits were a new low for a nine-inning All-Star Game), and earned runs (the game's only run came with the help of an error). In fact, if it weren't for thirty-seven-year-old Willie Mays, the game might not have had any runs at all. Starting only because of an injury to Pete Rose, National Leaguer Mays led off the bottom of the first with a single, and took second when first baseman Harmon Killebrew mishandled pitcher Luis Tiant's pickoff throw for an error. Mays took third as the rattled Tiant threw a wild pitch to walk Curt Flood, and scored when Willie McCovey grounded into a double play.

The pitching on both sides was superb, but the National Leaguers shone especially bright. Tom Seaver gave up two of the Americans' three hits (all of which were doubles), but struck out five in his two innings. Juan Marichal hurled two perfect innings, fanning three. And none of the six National pitchers walked a man. One American, Killebrew, couldn't walk. Stretching for a throw at first, the slugger tore a hamstring and missed the next two months, the most serious All-Star Game casualty since Ted Williams's broken elbow 18 years earlier.

GAME 40
R.F.K. Memorial Stadium, Washington, D.C.
July 23, 1969
NL, 9-3

```
NL  125 100 000   9 11 0
AL  011 100 000   3  6 2
```

Pitchers: CARLTON, Gibson (4), Singer (5), Koosman (7), Dierker (8), P.Niekro (9) vs STOTTLEMYRE, Odom (3), Knowles (3), McLain (4), McNally (5), McDowell (7), Culp (9)
Home Runs: Bench-N, Howard-A, McCovey-N (2), Freehan-A
Attendance: 45,259

After four one-run victories in a row, the National Leaguers finally broke loose, massing 10 of their 11 hits in the first four innings for nine runs and a crushing win. Scoring an unearned run in the first on a dropped outfield fly, and two in the second on Johnny Bench's home run, the Nationals erupted in the third for five runs off Blue Moon Odom before two outs had been recorded. Willie McCovey's two-run homer began the third-inning scoring, and an error, single, and two doubles added three more runs before Odom was mercifully relieved. McCovey homered again in the fourth for the Nationals' final tally.

The American bats were not wholly silent, but the solo homers by Frank Howard and Bill Freehan in the second and third, and a third run in the fourth, couldn't counter the Nationals' attack.

The final five innings of the game were as quiet as the opening four had been noisy. No runs scored, and the two teams together managed only three hits.

GAME 41
Riverfront Stadium, Cincinnati
July 14, 1970
NL, 5–4

```
AL  000 001 120 000   4 12  0
NL  000 000 103 001   5 10  0
```
Pitchers: Palmer, McDowell (4), J.Perry (7), Hunter (9), Peterson (9), Stottlemyre (9), WRIGHT (11) vs Seaver, Merritt (4), G.Perry (6), Gibson (8), OSTEEN (10)
Home Runs: Dietz-N
Attendance: 51,838

In a new stadium, opened only two weeks earlier, no one scored for the first five innings, as Jim Palmer and Sam McDowell of the Americans and Tom Seaver and Jim Merritt of the Nationals held the opposition to two hits per team. The Americans finally scored a run in the sixth, and another in the seventh. The Nationals got one back in the last of the seventh, but the Americans increased their lead to 4–1 in the eighth when Brooks Robinson tripled home two baserunners.

Fans had already begun to leave the park when the Nationals' Dick Dietz homered off Catfish Hunter to lead off the last of the ninth. Two pitchers, three singles, and a sacrifice fly later, the game was tied and headed for extra innings. Claude Osteen held the Americans scoreless from the tenth through the twelfth, and the Nationals also failed to score in the tenth and eleventh. But in the last of the twelfth, with two out, Pete Rose, Billy Grabarkewitz, and Jim Hickman singled. Hometowner Rose, racing home from second on Hickman's hit, crashed into catcher Ray Fosse with a force that injured both players and still provokes controversy—but which also gave the National League its eighth straight victory.

GAME 42
Tiger Stadium, Detroit
July 13, 1971
AL, 6–4

```
NL  021 000 010   4 5  0
AL  004 002 00X   6 7  0
```
Pitchers: ELLIS, Marichal (4), Jenkins (6), Wilson (7) vs BLUE, Palmer (4), Cuellar (6), Lolich (8)
Home Runs: Bench-N, Aaron-N, Jackson-A, F.Robinson-A, Killebrew-A, Clemente-N
Attendance: 53,559

With an assist from a favorable wind, six all-time greats homered to account for all the scoring as the American League broke its eight-game All-Star drought with a 6–4 victory. Johnny Bench put the Nationals in front with a two-run homer in the second inning off Vida Blue, and Hank Aaron—with his first All-Star home run—added a third run off Blue an inning later. But the Americans, shut out by Dock Ellis through the first two innings, rocked him in the bottom of the third as Reggie Jackson and Frank Robinson wrested the lead from the Nationals with a pair of two-run homers. (Robinson's made him the first player to hit an All-Star home run for both leagues.)

Ferguson Jenkins yielded the game's fifth homer, Harmon Killebrew's two-run shot for the Americans in the sixth. Roberto Clemente brought the Nationals a run closer with his solo homer off Mickey Lolich in the eighth, but that ended the team's scoring, and (for a year, anyway) the National League's All-Star stranglehold.

GAME 43
Atlanta Stadium, Atlanta
July 25, 1972
NL, 4–3

```
AL  001 000 020 0   3 6  0
NL  000 002 001 1   4 8  0
```
Pitchers: Palmer, Lolich (4), G.Perry (6), Wood (8), McNALLY (10) vs Gibson, Blass (3), Sutton (4), Carlton (6), Stoneman (7), McGRAW (9)
Home Runs: Aaron-N, Rojas-A
Attendance: 53,107

The American Leaguers tried to extend their All-Star win streak to two games, and for a time it looked as though they might do it. In the third, they scored the only run of the first half of the game as Jim Palmer and Mickey Lolich held the Nationals to two hits through the first five innings. In the sixth Hank Aaron thrilled the hometown crowd with a two-run homer deep to left to shift the lead to the National League. But Cookie Rojas restored the American lead with his own two-run shot in the eighth.

The Americans held their lead into the bottom of the ninth, but after two singles and a force out, the score was tied. Tug McGraw set down the American stars in order in the tenth, but American reliever Dave McNally was not so fortunate. He walked leadoff batter Nate Colbert, who was sacrificed to second. Joe Morgan then sent the American Leaguers back into the ranks of losers with a sharp RBI single to right center. His single also gave the Nationals their seventh win in seven extra-inning games.

GAME 44
Royals Stadium, Kansas City
July 24, 1973
NL, 7–1

```
NL  002 122 000   7 10  0
AL  010 000 000   1 5  0
```
Pitchers: WISE, Osteen (3), Sutton (5), Twitchell (6), Giusti (7), Seaver (8), Brewer (9) vs Hunter, Holtzman (2), BLYLEVEN (3), Singer (4), Ryan (6), Lyle (8), Fingers (9)
Home Runs: Bench-N, Bonds-N, W.Davis-N
Attendance: 40,849

Once again a new stadium was chosen to host the All-Star Game, and once again the National League emerged victorious. The Americans scored first, with a run in the second when Reggie Jackson scored from second on a single after doubling off the center field wall. But that was the beginning and end of their offense, as six National pitchers shut them out on three hits the rest of the way.

Meanwhile the National League hitters came to life, producing seven runs in four innings. Two walks and two singles in the third brought in two runs, and Johnny Bench's homer in the fourth made the score 3–1. In the fifth, Bobby Bonds—in the midst of his finest season—homered for two more National runs. And in the sixth, Willie Davis's home run completed the game's scoring, bringing in the Nationals' sixth and seventh runs.

The final third of the game was anticlimactic, as only two hits were made after the sixth inning. But Bonds brought the crowd to life briefly in the seventh, stretching one of those hits into a double with some audacious baserunning (ensuring his selection as the game's MVP).

GAME 45
Three Rivers Stadium,
Pittsburgh
July 23, 1974
NL, 7-2

AL	002 000 000	2	4	1
NL	010 210 12X	7	10	1

Pitchers: G.Perry, TIANT (4),
Hunter (6), Fingers (8) vs
Messersmith, BRETT (4),
Matlack (6), McGlothen (7),
Marshall (8)
Home Runs: R.Smith-N
Attendance: 50,706

Steve Garvey, who was elected to the National League starting lineup on write-in votes (his name was omitted from the fans' All-Star ballot), sparked the Nationals to yet another convincing win over the hapless American stars. After singling in the second inning, he scored the game's first run on Ron Cey's double.

The Americans took the lead with two runs in the top of the third, capitalizing on two walks and an error sandwiched between Thurman Munson's leadoff double and Dick Allen's single. They might have scored more had not Garvey snared Bobby Murcer's hot grounder for an assist on the third out.

Garvey doubled in the tying run in the fourth, and Cey's RBI ground out restored the Nationals' lead. Lou Brock added a run in the fifth with a single and some inspired baserunning, and Reggie Smith homered for another in the seventh. Don Kessinger's triple and a wild pitch by Rollie Fingers in the eighth contributed to two final National League runs.

GAME 46
County Stadium, Milwaukee
July 15, 1975
NL, 6-3

NL	021 000 003	6	13	1
AL	000 003 000	3	10	1

Pitchers: Reuss, Sutton (4),
Seaver (6), MATLACK (7),
R.Jones (9) vs Blue, Busby (3),
Kaat (5), HUNTER (7), Gossage (9)
Home Runs: Garvey-N, Wynn-N,
Yastrzemski-A
Attendance: 51,480

When National stars Steve Garvey and Jim Wynn led off the second with back-to-back homers and their teammates added another run in the third, it looked as if the National League might be on its way to another easy win. But the American pitchers shut down the National League offense for the next five innings, and Carl Yastrzemski made a contest of it with a three-run homer in the sixth off Tom Seaver to tie the score.

In the top of the ninth, though, the Americans all but gave the game away. Left fielder Claudell Washington dropped a fly on the run (it was scored a hit) and misplayed a line drive that went for a double. Goose Gossage came in to relieve Catfish Hunter on the mound and hit the next batter to load the bases. Bill Madlock then drove in two of the baserunners with a single through the drawn-in infield, and Pete Rose knocked in the third run of the inning with a sacrifice fly.

Randy Jones set the Americans down in order in the bottom of the ninth, and—voilà!—the National League had won again.

GAME 47
Veterans Stadium,
Philadelphia
July 13, 1976
NL, 7-1

AL	000 100 000	1	5	0
NL	202 000 03X	7	10	0

Pitchers: FIDRYCH, Hunter (3),
Tiant (5), Tanana (7) vs R.JONES,
Seaver (4), Montefusco (6),
Rhoden (8), K.Forsch (9)
Home Runs: Foster-N, Lynn-A,
Cedeno-N
Attendance: 63,974

Tom Seaver gave up a home run to Fred Lynn in the fourth inning, but that was the Americans' only score as the Nationals held the American stars to five hits while celebrating the nation's bicentennial with ten hits and seven runs.

Rookie standout Mark Fidrych was chosen to start for the Americans and was promptly rapped for two runs. Pete Rose led off with a single and was tripled home by Steve Garvey, who scored himself on a ground out. The Nationals doubled their score in the third inning as George Foster tagged Catfish Hunter for two runs with a mighty home run to left center, and capped their assault with three more in the eighth off Frank Tanana, including a two-run homer by Cesar Cedeno.

The fans had elected five members of Cincinnati's "big red machine" to the National League starting lineup, and Sparky Anderson, the Reds' and National squad's manager, added two more. They provided the bulk of the Nationals' offense, with seven hits, four RBIs, and four runs scored.

GAME 48
Yankee Stadium, New York
July 19, 1977
NL, 7-5

NL	401 000 020	7	9	1
AL	000 002 102	5	8	0

Pitchers: SUTTON, Lavelle (4),
Seaver (6), R.Reuschel (8),
Gossage (9) vs PALMER, Kern (3),
Eckersley (4), LaRoche (6),
Campbell (7), Lyle (8)
Home Runs: Morgan-N, Luzinski-N,
Garvey-N, Scott-A
Attendance: 56,683

The Nationals' Joe Morgan homered off Jim Palmer to open the game, and before Palmer escaped the first inning three more National Leaguers had crossed the plate on a single, double, and Greg Luzinski's homer. Palmer got through the second inning without further damage, but before he was relieved in the third Steve Garvey had homered to give the Nationals a 5-0 lead.

The Americans fought back against Tom Seaver in the sixth and seventh. Seaver retired two in the sixth, but then gave up two singles, and two runs as Richie Zisk doubled the runners home. Two more singles in the seventh produced a third American run.

But the Nationals—assisted by pitcher Sparky Lyle's wild pitch and hit batsman—put a sixth and seventh run on the board in the eighth with a double and single. The Americans added two final runs of their own in the bottom of the ninth on George Scott's homer off Goose Gossage, but fell short of victory once again.

GAME 49
San Dieg Stadium,
July 11, 1978
NL, 7–3

AL	201	000	000	3	8	1
NL	003	000	04X	7	10	0

Pitchers: Palmer, Keough (3), Sorensen (4), Kern (7), Guidry (7), GOSSAGE (8) vs Blue, Rogers (4), Fingers (6), SUTTER (8), P.Niekro (9)
Attendance: 51,549

Rod Carew led off both the first and third innings with triples—an All-Star record— scoring both times as the Americans took a 3–0 lead into the bottom of the third. But then Jim Palmer, who had shut the Nationals out on one hit through the first two innings, lost his touch. After yielding a leadoff single, he retired two batters, but then issued three walks to force in a run, and when Steve Garvey singled past the shortstop two more runs scored to tie the game.

No one scored through the next 4½ innings, with Larry Sorensen turning in the game's top pitching performance as he shut the Nationals out on one hit through the three middle innings. But in the last of the eighth, Gosse Gossage (the National League closer the previous year) took the mound this year for the Americans. Garvey greeted him with a leadoff triple and scored what proved to be the winning run on a wild pitch. A walk and three singles added three insurance runs before the inning ended. Bruce Sutter and Phil Niekro blanked the Americans in the ninth, and the Nationals has extended their current win streak to seven.

GAME 50
Kingdome, Seattle
July 17, 1979
NL, 7–6

NL	211	001	011	7	10	0
AL	302	001	000	6	10	0

Pitchers: Carlton, Andujar (2), Rogers (4), G.Perry (6), Sambito (6), LaCoss (6), SUTTER (8) vs Ryan, Stanley (3), Clear (5), KERN (7), Guidry (9)
Home Runs: Lynn-A, Mazzilli-N
Attendance: 58,905

Mike Schmidt tripled and George Foster doubled to drive in the game's first runs as the Nationals began their scoring in the top of the first. The Americans fought back to take the lead later in the inning as Don Baylor doubled home one run and Fred Lynn homered for two more. The Nationals tied the score with a run in the second and went ahead again in the third when Schmidt scored after doubling. But the Americans recaptured the lead in the bottom of the third, scoring twice on a single, wild pitch, ground out, hit batsman, single, and error.

Three innings later the Nationals again tied the game, but the Americans went ahead for the third time with a run in their half of the sixth. Outstanding throws by right fielder Dave Parker, who notched two assists, helped to keep the Americans from pulling away. In the eighth the Nationals' Lee Mazzilli homered for yet another tie, and an inning later Ron Guidry walked Mazzilli with the bases loaded to force in the Nationals' go-ahead seventh run. When Bruce Sutter kept the Americans from scoring in the bottom of the ninth, the National Leaguers had for the second time defeated the Americans eight years in a row.

GAME 51
Dodger Stadium,
Los Angeles
July 8, 1980
NL, 4–2

AL	000	020	000	2	7	1
NL	000	012	10X	4	7	0

Pitchers: Stone, JOHN (4), Farmer (6), Stieb (7), Gossage (8) vs Richard, Welch (3), REUSS (6), Bibby (7), Sutter (8)
Home Runs: Lynn-A, Griffey-N
Attendance: 56,088

For 4⅔ innings J.R. Richard and Bob Welch held the American stars scoreless. But then Rod Carew singled and Fred Lynn drove in the game's first runs with his third All-Star homer.

The Americans' Steve Stone and Tommy John pitched even better, setting the Nationals down in order through four innings. John continued the perfect streak through the first two outs of the fifth, but then Ken Griffey homered, and the Americans' spell on the National Leaguers was broken.

While three National pitchers limited the Americans to a single and a walk over the final four innings, three singles and an error sent the Nationals into the lead in the sixth. A passed ball surrounded by two wild pitches moved Dave Concepcion around the bases in the seventh (he had reached on a fielder's choice) for the Nationals' fourth run. They didn't really need it, though, as Bruce Sutter—the winning pitcher in the two previous All-Star games—saved this one with two final innings of no-hit ball for the Nationals' ninth successive win.

GAME 52
Municipal Stadium,
Cleveland
August 9, 1981
NL, 5–4

NL	000	011	120	5	9	1
AL	010	003	000	4	11	1

Pitchers: Valenzuela, Seaver (2), Knepper (3), Hooton (5), Ruthven (6), BLUE (7), Ryan (8), Sutter (9) vs Morris, Barker (3), K.Forsch (5), Norris (6), Davis (7), FINGERS (8), Stieb (8)
Home Runs: Singleton-A, Carter-N (2), Parker-N, Schmidt-N
Attendance: 72,086

The game, delayed until August by the midseason players' strike, drew an All-Star record crowd of more than 72,000 fans, and the managers set a new record by using 56 players. But the game itself followed a familiar pattern.

The Americans scored first in the second inning on Ken Singleton's home run off Tom Seaver, and held their slim lead into the fifth on Len Barker's two innings of perfect pitching. But Ken Forsch replaced Barker in the fifth and Gary Carter homered off his first pitch to tie the score. Dave Parker's homer off Mike Norris an inning later put the Nationals ahead for the first time, but the Americans came right back in the bottom of the inning, putting together four singles and a sacrifice fly for three runs and a two-run advantage.

Gary Carter's second home run of the game—this time off Ron Davis's first pitch—brought the Nationals within one in the seventh, and Mike Schmidt's two-run blast off Rollie Fingers in the eighth restored their lead. Three National pitchers shut out the Americans without a hit over the final three innings as closer Bruce Sutter picked up his second consecutive All-Star save and the National Leaguers their tenth consecutive victory.

GAME 53
Olympic Stadium, Montreal
July 13, 1982
NL, 4–1

```
AL   100 000 000    1  8  2
NL   021 001 00X    4  8  1
```

Pitchers: ECKERSLEY, Clancy (4), Bannister (5), Quisenberry (6), Fingers (8) vs ROGERS, Carlton (4), Soto (6), Valenzuela (8), Minton (8), Howe (9), Hume (9)
Home Runs: Concepcion-N
Attendance: 59,057

In the first All-Star Game held outside the United States, the American League for the third year in a row put the first run on the board, but for the eleventh year in a row the final score showed the National League the winner. Two singles, a wild pitch, and a sacrifice fly gave the Americans a run in the top of the first. But starter Steve Rogers of the host Expos held the Americans scoreless for the remainder of his three innings while the Nationals struck back for two runs in the second on Dave Concepcion's home run, and added another in the third when Ruppert Jones—who had tripled to open the inning—scored on a sacrifice fly.

Six National League pitchers (and shortstop Ozzie Smith's spectacular stop and throw to first with two on in the eighth) joined Rogers in holding the American stars scoreless after the first inning. Two hometowners put together the Nationals' final run in the sixth. Al Oliver, leading off, doubled down the line in left and took third as the ball got by left fielder Rickey Henderson. Two outs later Gary Carter lined a pitch to center, scoring Oliver as Willie Wilson's dive for the ball came up short.

GAME 54
Comiskey Park, Chicago
July 6, 1983
AL, 13–3

```
NL   100 110 000     3  8  3
AL   117 000 22X    13 15  2
```

Pitchers: SOTO, Hammaker (3), Dawley (3), Dravecky (5), Perez (7), Orosco (7), L.Smith (8) vs STIEB, Honeycutt (4), Stanley (6), Young (8), Quisenberry (9)
Home Runs: Rice-A, Lynn-A
Attendance: 43,801

The game returned to the park where it had originated fifty years earlier, and the American League, after eleven years of All-Star losses, unleashed its pent-up fury to produce the greatest margin of victory in thirty-seven years. The game began, though, as an embarrassment of errors. American starter Dave Stieb struck out the side in the first, but along the way two errors (one of them Stieb's) let in a run. An unearned run in the bottom of the first tied the score and another in the second put the American League ahead for good (making a loser out of the unfortunate National starter Mario Soto).

The hitting began in earnest in the last of the third as the Americans scored seven times for a new one-inning record. Among their six hits (also a record for an All-Star inning) were a homer by Jim Rice, a triple by George Brett, and a bases-loaded blast by Fred Lynn—his fourth All-Star home run and the first grand slam in All-Star history. With the score now 9–1, the National League's single runs in the fourth and fifth were exercises in futility, and the Americans' two each in the seventh and eighth served chiefly to boost the winning total to 13—another All-Star high.

GAME 55
Candlestick Park,
San Francisco
July 10, 1984
NL, 3–1

```
AL   010 000 000    1  7  2
NL   110 000 01X    3  8  0
```

Pitchers: STIEB, Morris (3), Dotson (5), Caudill (7), Hernandez (8) vs LEA, Valenzuela (3), Gooden (5), Soto (7), Gossage (9)
Home Runs: Brett-A, Carter-N, Murphy-N
Attendance: 57,756

Only four times in the previous fifty-four All-Star Games had a pitcher struck out the side in order. In this game, three more pitchers did it. And, on this fiftieth anniversary of Carl Hubbell's five consecutive strikeouts, two of those pitchers combined to break Hubbell's record with six back-to-back whiffs. Hubbell, who threw out the first ball, also saw an All-Star nine-inning record set with 21 total Ks (11 by National League pitchers, 10 by American).

In the fourth inning, National star Fernando Valenzuela mowed down three of the game's premier sluggers: Dave Winfield, Reggie Jackson, and George Brett. If the three men Dwight Gooden retired on strikes an inning later (Lance Parrish, Chet Lemon, and rookie Alvin Davis) were slightly less formidable, still, it was an impressive performance for a nineteen-year-old rookie (the youngest player in All-Star history). The three that American Leaguer Bill Caudill struck out in the seventh were no slouches either: Tim Raines, Ryne Sandberg (in the midst of an MVP season), and Keith Hernandez.

Three of the four runs scored in the game were homers. The National League's run in the first was unearned, but the Americans' George Brett homered to center to tie the game in the second, and the Nationals' go-ahead run later in the inning came on Gary Carter's blast to left. In the eighth, National Leaguer Dale Murphy also put one over the left field fence to end the scoring.

GAME 56
H. Humphrey Metrodome,
Minneapolis
July 16, 1985
NL, 6–1

```
NL   011 020 002    6  9  1
AL   100 000 000    1  5  0
```

Pitchers: HOYT, Ryan (4), Valenzuela (7), Reardon (8), Gossage (9) vs MORRIS, Key (3), Blyleven (4), Stieb (6), Moore (7), Petry (9), Hernandez (9)
Attendance: 54,960

The American Leaguers scored first, as Rickey Henderson led off the bottom of the first with a single and circled the bases on a steal, error, and sacrifice fly. But the five National pitchers blanked the Americans the rest of the way on only four more singles.

Meanwhile, the National stars methodically dismantled the Americans for their thirty-sixth All-Star victory. In the top of the second, after Darryl Strawberry singled and stole second, Terry Kennedy, whose error had led to the American League run, redeemed himself by singling Strawberry home. An inning later, with two out, Tom Herr doubled and scored the go-ahead (and winning) run on Steve Garvey's single.

In the fifth the Nationals scored two more runs on a hit batsman, Tim Wallach's ground-rule double, and Ozzie Virgil's single, and finished their scoring in the ninth with another pair on three walks and Willie McGee's double—another ground-rule bounce out of play off the lively Metrodome surface. Goose Gossage struck out the final two American batters in the bottom of the ninth, and the Nationals had increased their winning margin in the series to a new high of seventeen games.

GAME 57
Astrodome, Houston
July 15, 1986
AL, 3–2

AL	020 000 100	3	5	0
NL	000 000 020	2	5	1

Pitchers: CLEMENS, Higuera (4), Hough (7), Righetti (8), Aase (9) vs GOODEN, Valenzuela (4), Scott (7), Fernandez (8), Krukow (9)
Home Runs: Whitaker-A, White-A
Attendance: 45,774

National League pitchers struck out 12 Americans, led by Fernando Valenzuela's five in a row, which matched the mark set by Carl Hubbell in 1934. (Two years earlier Valenzuela had helped set a multipitcher All-Star record of six consecutive strikeouts.) In the eighth inning Sid Fernandez, after walking two, struck out the next three.

Though the American Leaguers struck out fewer men, their pitching was more effective over all. Starter Roger Clemens hurled three perfect innings (3 balls and 21 strikes), and Teddy Higuera one-hit the Nationals over the next three. Charlie Hough struck out three in the eighth after yielding the Nationals' only extra-base hit (a double) to Chris Brown. But catcher Rich Gedman couldn't handle Hough's knuckleball, and Brown advanced to third on the first strikeout (ruled a wild pitch) and scored on the second, a passed ball which also enabled batter Hubie Brooks to reach first safely. Brooks moved up on a balk and scored the Nationals' second run on Steve Sax's single.

But home runs had already undone the Nationals. With two gone in the second, Dave Winfield doubled off starter Dwight Gooden, and Lou Whitaker clubbed an 0–2 pitch over the fence in right. And in the seventh, Frank White (hitting for Whitaker) knocked Mike Scott's 0–2 pitch over the fence in left center for what proved the margin of American League victory.

GAME 58
Oakland-Alameda County
Stadium, Oakland
July 14, 1987
NL, 2–0

NL	000 000 000 000 2	2	8	2
AL	000 000 000 000 0	0	6	1

Pitchers: Scott, Sutcliffe (3), Hershiser (5), R.Reuschel (7), Franco (8), Bedrosian (9), L.SMITH (10), S. Fernandez (13) vs Saberhagen, Morris (4), Langston (6), Plesac (8), Righetti (9), Henke (9), J.HOWELL (12)
Attendance: 49,671

None of the previous fifty-seven All-Star Games had gone more than five innings without at least one run crossing the plate. But this game went more than twice that before National Leaguer Tim Raines tripled in two runs in the top of the thirteenth for the game's only scoring. It was the National League's eighth win in eight extra-inning All-Star games.

Both teams missed scoring opportunities in the ninth inning. Raines singled for the Nationals with only one out, and became the game's first runner to reach third when a throw from first on his attempted steal went into center field. But a fly to short right and a foul out left him stranded. In the bottom of the ninth, the Americans came close to winning the game as Dave Winfield headed for home from second on a missed 4–6–1 double play. But National pitcher Steve Bedrosian, covering first, snared the off-center throw from short and fired it home to catch Winfield for the third out.

The Americans again reached third in the eleventh as Larry Parrish singled and moved around on a sacrifice and ground out. But pitcher Lee Smith (whose three shutout innings earned him the win) struck out Tony Fernandez to end the threat.

GAME 59
Riverfront Stadium,
Cincinnati
July 12, 1988
AL, 2–1

AL	001 100 000	2	6	2
NL	000 100 000	1	5	0

Pitchers: VIOLA, Clemens (3), Gubicza (4), Stieb (6), Russell (7), Jones (8), Plesac (8), Eckersley (9) vs GOODEN, Knepper (4), Cone (5), Gross (6), Davis (7), Walk (7), Hershiser (8), Worrell (9)
Home Run: Steinbach-A
Attendance: 55,837

Oakland's Terry Steinbach was not among the ten top American League catchers in batting; because of time lost to injuries, he was not even his club's leading catcher in games played. But the fans voted him to start in the All-Star Game, and he won it for the American Leaguers with a home run in his first trip to the plate and a sacrifice fly his next time up. Steinbach's homer—a drive off Dwight Gooden that led off the third inning—caromed off the glove of a leaping Darryl Strawberry over the wall in right for the game's first score. His sacrifice fly—high and deep to left in the fourth inning—scored Dave Winfield (aboard with his record seventh All-Star double) to put the Americans ahead 2–0.

Steinbach also contributed negatively to the National League run later in the fourth. His throwing error on Vince Coleman's steal of second enabled Coleman to advance to third, whence he scored on a wild pitch by Mark Gubicza.

American starter Frank Viola, the midseason league leader in wins, was awarded the victory for his two perfect innings pitched. Dennis Eckersley, the majors' top reliever, preserved the win for the Americans with a perfect ninth inning.

GAME 60
Anaheim Stadium,
Anaheim, California
July 11, 1989
AL, 5–3

NL	200 000 010	3	9	1
AL	212 000 00X	5	12	0

Pitchers: Reuschel, SMOLTZ (2), Sutcliffe (3), Burke (4), M. Davis (6), Howell (7), Williams (8) vs Stewart, RYAN (2), Gubicza (4), Moore (5), Swindell (6), Russell (7), Plesac (8), Jones (8)
Home Runs: Jackson-A, Boggs-A
Attendance: 64,036

The National stars struck early with a pair of two-out runs in the top of the first inning, and a double steal put two more runners in scoring position. But left fielder Bo Jackson stifled the assault with a fine running catch, then opened the American half of the first with a massive home run to center field off Rick Reuschel. Wade Boggs, the next man up, added insult to the forty-year-old Reuschel's first All-Star start, tying the game with another homer.

In the second inning Jackson drove in the American League's go-ahead run with a slow grounder off young John Smoltz, and an inning later four American singles produced two more runs. A quartet of National League pitchers held the Americans scoreless on just three hits over the final six innings, and their teammates rallied for a third National run in the eighth. But Doug Jones (the majors' top reliever in 1989) came on to get the final out of the eighth, and in the ninth preserved the American lead to give the American Leaguers their first repeat All-Star victory in thirty-one years.

National League hurler Smoltz, at age twenty-two the youngest player in the lineup, took the loss. Nolan Ryan, back in the American League after nine National League seasons, earned the win with two shutout innings. Not only was he the oldest player on either side, at forty-two he was the oldest All-Star winning pitcher ever.

GAME 61
Wrigley Field, Chicago
July 10, 1990
AL, 2-0

AL	000 000 200	2 7 0
NL	000 000 000	0 2 1

Pitchers: Welch, Stieb (3), SABERHAGEN (5), Thigpen (7), Finley (8), Eckersley (9) vs Armstrong, R. Martinez (3), D. Martinez (4), Viola (5), D. Smith (6), BRANTLEY (6), Dibble (7), Myers (8), Franco (9)
Attendance: 39,071

Back-to-back American League singles off Jeff Brantley had put men on third and first and brought Julio Franco to the plate in the seventh inning, when heavy rain halted the game for more than an hour. During the delay Brantley's side stiffened, so when Franco finally got his turn at bat he faced a new National pitcher, Rob Dibble. Franco lined Dibble's third pitch into the gap in right center for a double—the only extra-base hit of the game— driving in what proved to be the game's only runs.

Damp air and a stiff breeze in from left field helped tame the offense. American League batters managed to accumulate seven hits, but the Nationals were held to two—an All-Star all-time low. No runner advanced as far as third base. No National Leaguer reached that far, and if it weren't for Barry Larkin's third-inning steal, no National runner would even have stood on second base.

American hurler Bret Saberhagen's two perfect middle innings earned him the win, and Dennis Eckersley, after yielding a leadoff hit in the ninth, retired the final three batters to record his second All-Star save in three years. The victory was the third in a row for the American Leaguers, the first time they had put together such a string of triumphs in forty-one years.

GAME 62
SkyDome, Toronto
July 9, 1991
AL, 4-2

NL	100 100 000	2 10 1
AL	003 000 10X	4 8 0

PITCHERS: Glavine, MARTINEZ (3), Viola (5), Harnisch (6), Smiley (7), Dibble (7), Morgan (8) vs Morris, KEY (3), Clemens (4), McDowell (5), Reardon (7), Aguilera (7), Eckersley (9)
HOME RUNS: Ripken-A, Dawson-N
ATTENDANCE: 52,383

The National League took an early 1-0 lead on singles by Tony Gwynn, Will Clark, and Bobby Bonilla in the top of the first, and held it for two innings on Tom Glavine's strong pitching, which included three strikeouts. But Dennis Martinez yielded successive singles to Rickey Henderson and Wade Boggs in the third inning, and the next batter, Cal Ripken, Jr., homered to center to give the Americans all the runs they would need for victory.

National Leaguer Andre Dawson led off the fourth inning with a massive home run to center off Roger Clemens. This brought the Nationals within a run of tying the game, but they scored no more, as a succession of American pitchers shut them down on a walk and four singles the rest of the way. In the seventh inning the Americans added an insurance run when Joe Carter singled and moved around the bases on a call of catcher interference (the first in All-Star history), a sacrifice bunt, and Harold Baines's sacrifice liner to right.

Jimmy Key, the pitcher of record when Ripken's three-run homer put the American League ahead, was awarded the win. Dennis Eckersley, who pitched a perfect ninth, earned a record third All-Star save.

It was only the second time in All-Star history that the American League had won four games in a row.

GAME 63
San Diego/Jack Murphy
Stadium
San Diego
July 14, 1992
AL, 13-6

AL	411 004 030	13 19 1
NL	000 001 032	6 12 1

PITCHERS: BROWN, McDowell (2), Guzman (3), Clemens (4), Mussina (5), Langston (6), Nagy (7), Montgomery (8), Aguilera (8), Eckersley (9) vs GLAVINE, Maddux (2), Cone (4), Tewksbury (5), Smoltz (6), Martinez (7), Jones (8), Charlton (9)
HOME RUNS: Sierra-A, Griffey-A, Clark-N
ATTENDANCE: 59,372

By the time the National Leaguers pushed across their first run in the sixth inning, the Americans had already scored ten times, and although National bats caught fire for five more runs in the eighth and ninth, they were powerless to prevent the American League from stretching its All-Star win streak to five games. National starting pitcher Tom Glavine could not repeat his strong 1991 start: before his relief after 1⅔ innings he was tagged for nine singles and five runs. In the third inning, Ken Griffey, Jr., who had driven in one of the first-inning runs, added the sixth American score with a homer off Greg Maddux. When he came up again to lead off the sixth inning, Griffey doubled to initiate a new American scoring spree, which included two-out doubles by Carlos Baerga and Robin Ventura, capped by Ruben Sierra's home run—all off Bob Tewksbury, who had set down the Americans 1-2-3 an inning earlier. Travis Fryman's RBI single and Roberto Kelly's two-run double in the eighth closed out the American League scoring.

Will Clark's two-out blast off Rick Aguilera in the last of the eighth was the National League's first three-run homer since 1964, but it was too little to make more than a dent in the American lead. With two men out in the ninth, a pair of singles off Dennis Eckersley loaded the bases, and Bip Roberts' single drove in two of the baserunners to bring the NL run total to six (enough to have defeated the AL in the seven previous All-Star Games).

Starter Kevin Brown was awarded the win; Glavine took the loss.

## CHAPTER 17

Postseason Play

Frederick Ivor-Campbell

As we all know, major-league baseball doesn't end with the end of the season. There follows the *post-season*—the League Championship Series and the World Series—when even the most casual fan is stirred to follow the games which determine, eventually, the world's best team.

Once there was much more baseball played in the postseason. In the 1880s, for example, nearly every major-league club played a couple of weeks of postseason games, generally exhibitions against clubs they didn't face during the regular season—like teams from the other major league, or a minor league.

Before there was a World Series there were city and regional series. In 1882 Cleveland defeated Cincinnati for the championship of Ohio, and the next year teams in Philadelphia and New York played for the championships of those cities. These were informal series, arranged by the clubs themselves without official league sanction, and varied in the number of games scheduled according to the desires of the clubs involved.

The same held true for the early World Series, which had their beginnings in 1884. Two years earlier, the champions of the National League and the brand-new American Association played a pair of postseason contests (in which each team recorded a shutout against the other). Some would like to call these games the first World Series, but no one in 1882 saw them as more than exhibition games. In fact, because the NL didn't yet recognize the legitimacy of the AA and forbade its clubs to play those of the new league, the NL champion Chicago White Stockings had to release their players from their season contracts so they could face AA champion Cincinnati as technically independent players.

That winter the two major leagues made their peace, and although a proposed series between the 1883 NL and AA titlists was called off, the 1884 champion Providence Grays (NL) and the Metropolitan Club of New York (AA) played three games "for the championship of the United States." The winning Grays were acclaimed in the press as "champions of the world," and the World Series was born.

The brief 1884 Series set the stage for more elaborate World Series to follow. From 1885 through 1890 the NL and AA pennant-winners met in Series that ranged in length from six games to 15.

The demise of the AA after the 1891 season caused a one-year gap in World Series play. When the National League expanded from eight clubs to twelve the next year (by absorbing four teams from the defunct AA), it divided the regular season into two halves, with the first-half winner playing the winner of the second half for the world title. Boston defeated Cleveland in the first official World Series, but the unpopular divided season was not repeated (that is, until the strike year of 1981).

Two years later a new World Series scheme was devised when one William C. Temple offered a prize cup to the winner of a postseason series between the first- and second-place finishers in the NL. For four years these best-of-seven Temple Cup games served as the officially recognized world championship. But by the end of four lopsided Series (only one of which was won by the pennant-winning club), fan interest—never robust—had declined so much that the trophy was returned to its donor and the series abandoned.

In 1900, partisans of second-place Pittsburgh felt that their Pirates were the equal of pennant-winning Brooklyn, and a Pittsburgh newspaper, the *Chronicle-Telegraph*, offered a silver trophy cup to the winner of a best-of-five series between the clubs, to be played entirely in Pittsburgh. Described in the press as the "world's championship series," the games confirmed the superiority of Brooklyn's Superbas, who needed only four games to subdue the hometown Pirates.

The upgrading of the American League from minor- to major-league status in 1901 made a return to interleague World Series play theoretically possible, but it was not until after the NL and AL had made peace in 1903 that the first modern Series was contested. The owners of NL champion Pittsburgh and AL champion Boston arranged a best-of-nine postseason Series in 1903, which proved both popular and financially successful—a firm foundation for future Series. When the NL pennant-winning Giants refused to meet repeating AL titlist Boston in 1904, press and fan disappointment led baseball's National Commission to establish the World Series officially and permanently in 1905.

The end of the 1903 season saw not only the first modern World Series, but also a revival of city and regional series (which had lapsed when the AA folded) in Chicago, Philadelphia, St. Louis, and Ohio. In 1905 the National Commission offered to oversee these series, too, and give them the stability of official sanction. Until the manpower needs of the World War halted the 1918 season a month early (discouraging postseason play apart from the World Series), most of the city and regional series—and occasional series between other clubs, like Cleveland and Pittsburgh, and the Boston Red Sox and New York Giants—were played under National Commission auspices.

After the war's end, only Chicago's Cubs and White Sox resumed a city series; they played 16 series between 1921 and 1942, when World War II intervened. For 26 years thereafter the World Series alone remained of the once multifaceted major-league postseason—until the AL and NL split into two divisions each in 1969 and ushered in a new layer of playoffs: the League Championship Series. (In 1981, to recoup some of

the money and fan interest lost during a midseason players' strike that split the season in half, a one-time third layer of postseason playoffs was added, pitting the first-half and second-half winners in each division against each other for the division titles—an aberration that made even more of a mockery of the divisional races than the strike itself had done.) From 1969 through 1984 the LCS were played as best-of-five series, but in 1985 they were expanded to match the best-of-seven World Series.

Key to the Statistics

The statistics in this section of *Total Baseball* are standard—there is little point in applying newer analytical measures to performances that run to seven games or fewer. We do offer, however, stats that were not standard at the time, such as earned run averages for years before 1912 and runs batted in before 1920 (which were determined from box scores and play-by-plays) and saves before 1969. Beyond our powers of reconstruction were the following: runs batted in for the World Series of 1884 and 1885; stolen bases for 1884 and 1885; and batter strikeouts for 1885.

Ignoring the odd 1887 custom of counting walks as base hits, we present the cumulative box score for that year's World Series in accordance with modern practice. Other curiosities of early postseason play include the use of neutral sites for some games in 1885 and 1888 and for the majority of games in 1887, and the use of players who did not appear in so much as an inning for that team during the regular season (Tom Forster, New York Mets, 1884; Bug Holliday, Chicago, 1885; Sy Sutcliffe, Detroit, 1887; Jumbo Davis, Brooklyn 1889).

The length of the World Series varied from three games in 1884 all the way up to fifteen in 1887 and ten the following year. The best-of-seven format came in with the Temple Cup Series of 1894 and has been the norm for World Series ever since (excepting 1900, 1903, and 1919–1921). In recent years this format has become the norm for League Championship Series as well.

If a player appeared at more than one position during the Series, the number of games he played at each is noted (for example, a man who divided seven games at shortstop and third base would carry the notation *ss-4, 3b-3*). Other abbreviations are as follows:

POS	Position	SB	Stolen Bases
AVG	Batting average	W	Wins
G	Games	L	Losses
AB	At bats	ERA	Earned run average
R	Runs	GS	Games started
H	Hits	CG	Complete games
2B	Doubles	SHO	Shutouts
3B	Triples	SV	Saves
HR	Home runs	IP	Innings pitched
RB	Runs batted in	ER	Earned runs
BB	Bases on Balls	SO	Strikeouts

After a flurry of boasts and challenges, Met manager Jim Mutrie and the Grays' Frank Bancroft arranged a three-game series in New York to determine which team was the nation's best. These were not the first games between NL and AA pennant winners. In 1882, the AA's first season, champion Cincinnati met NL titlist Chicago twice as part of its postseason schedule, in games viewed simply as exhibition contests. (Each team won one). The next year a postseason series was proposed between champions Boston (NL) and the Athletics of Philadelphia (AA), but the Athletics fared so poorly in exhibitions against lesser NL teams that they refused to face Boston.

The 1884 Series was touted as "for the championship of the United States," but the influential weekly *Sporting Life* established precedent for future Series hype by naming victorious Providence "Champions of the World." The weather turned cold and windy as the Series got under way. A hardy opening game crowd of 2,500 saw the Grays' great Charlie "Old Hoss" Radbourn blank the Mets on two singles. Met pitcher Tim Keefe, wild at the start, paved the way for two first-inning Providence runs by hitting the first two men to face him and assisted them around the bases with a pair of wild pitches. Paul Hines singled in the third frr the Grays' first hit and scored as a passed ball and two more wild pitches brought him home. Keefe yielded only four other hits, but they came back to back in the seventh to produce the Grays' final three runs.

The 1,000 spectators at Game Two witnessed the Series' closest contest. Keefe and Radbourn overwhelmed their opposition for four innings, but in the top of the fifth the Grays bunched three of their five hits for three two-out runs as Jerry Denny homered over the center field fence. The Mets responded with a run in the last of the fifth, but scored no more before darkness ended the game after seven innings.

The Grays had clinched the championship with their second win, and when they saw only a few hundred diehards in the stands for Game Three, they wanted to go home. The Mets must have regretted their insistence on playing the game. Although darkness halted it after only six innings, rookie Met pitcher Buck Becannon (replacing Keefe, who umpired) and awful Mets fielding gave Providence eleven or twelve runs (scorers lost count), while Radbourn held the New Yorkers to a pair of unearned tallies.

Providence Grays (NL), 3; New York Mets (AA), 0

PRO (N)

PLAYER/POS	AVG	G	AB	R	H	2B	3B	HR	RB	BB	SO	SB
Cliff Carroll, of	.100	3	10	2	1	0	0	0		1	1	
Jerry Denny, 3b	.444	3	9	3	4	0	1	1		0	3	
Jack Farrell, 2b	.444	3	9	3	4	2	0	0		0	0	
Barney Gilligan, c	.444	3	9	3	4	2	0	0		0	1	
Paul Hines, of	.250	3	8	5	2	0	0	0		3	0	
Arthur Irwin, ss	.222	3	9	2	2	0	1	0		0	2	
Charlie Radbourn, p	.100	3	10	1	1	0	0	0		3	3	
Paul Radford, of	.000	3	7	1	0	0	0	0		0	1	
Joe Start, 1b	.100	3	10	0	1	0	0	0		0	2	
TOTAL	.235		81	20	19	4	2	1		5	13	

PITCHER	W	L	ERA	G	GS	CG	SV	SHO	IP	H	ER	BB	SO
Charlie Radbourn	3	0	0.00	3	3	3	0	1	22.0	11	0	0	16
TOTAL	3	0	0.00	3	3	3	0	1	22.0	11	0	0	16

NY (A)

PLAYER/POS	AVG	G	AB	R	H	2B	3B	HR	RB	BB	SO	SB
Buck Becannon, p	.500	1	2	0	1	0	0	0		0	0	
Steve Brady, of	.000	3	10	1	0	0	0	0		0	1	
Dude Esterbrook, 3b	.300	3	10	0	3	1	0	0		0	3	
Tom Forster, 2b	.000	1	3	0	0	0	0	0		0	1	
Bill Holbert, c	.000	1	2	0	0	0	0	0		0	1	
Tim Keefe, p	.200	2	5	0	1	0	0	0		0	4	
Ed Kennedy, of	.000	3	7	0	0	0	0	0		0	2	
Candy Nelson, ss	.100	3	10	0	1	0	0	0		0	1	
Dave Orr, 1b	.111	3	9	0	1	0	0	0		0	0	
Charlie Reipschlager, c	.000	2	5	1	0	0	0	0		0	1	
Chief Roseman, of	.333	3	9	1	3	0	0	0		0	1	
Dasher Troy, 2b	.200	2	5	0	1	0	0	0		0	1	
TOTAL	.143		77	3	11	1	0	0		0	16	

PITCHER	W	L	ERA	G	GS	CG	SV	SHO	IP	H	ER	BB	SO
Buck Becannon	0	1	3.00	1	1	1	0	0	6.0	9	2	2	1
Tim Keefe	0	2	3.60	2	2	2	0	0	15.0	10	6	3	12
TOTAL	0	3	3.43	3	3	3	0	0	21.0	19	8	5	13

GAME 1 AT NY OCT 23

NY	000	000	000	0	2	0
PRO	201	000	30X	6	5	2

Pitchers: KEEFE vs RADBOURN
Attendance: 2,500

GAME 2 AT NY OCT 24

PRO	000	030	0	3	5	4
NY	000	010	0	1	3	1

Pitchers: RADBOURN vs KEEFE
Home Runs: Denny-PRO
Attendance: 1,000
(Game called at end of seventh, darkness)

GAME 3 AT NY OCT 25

PRO	120	044	11	9	3
NY	000	011	2	6	9

Pitchers: RADBOURN vs BECANNON
Attendance: 300
(Game called at end of sixth, darkness)

Before the start of the final game, the two clubs agreed to throw out Game Two, which had been forfeited to Chicago, leaving the Series tied at two wins apiece, plus the one tie. But after the Browns won the seventh game for their third victory, Chicago manager Cap Anson decided his club should retain its forfeit win after all, and a select committee agreed, leaving the Series in a tie instead of a White Stocking defeat.

Game One, in Chicago, was called for darkness after eight innings, with the score tied 5–5. The Browns scored first with a run in the second and added four more in the top of the fourth. But Chicago came back with a run in the last of the fourth, and in the bottom of the eighth scored four more on a walk, two singles, and Fred Pfeffer's game-tying three-run homer.

The Series moved to St. Louis for the next three games. Chicago was leading 5–4 in the sixth inning of Game Two when Browns manager Charlie Comiskey pulled his team off the field, objecting to the umpiring of David Sullivan. Umpire Sullivan later forfeited the game to the White Stockings; he worked no more in the Series. The Browns won Game Three, scoring five unearned runs with two out in the top of the first, and holding on for a 7–4 win. Chicago lost again the next day in a much closer game. The Browns scored first with a run in the third inning, but Abner Dalrymple's two-run homer in the fifth gave the White Stockings a 2–1 lead. In the bottom of the eighth, however, St. Louis scored twice and held on for the 3–2 win.

The Series took to the road for its final three games. In Pittsburgh for Game Five, Chicago overwhelmed the Browns 9–2, scoring four runs in the first inning, and their final three just before darkness ended the game after seven innings.

Game Six and Seven were played in Cincinnati. The White Stockings won the sixth game by the same 9–2 score as Game Five. The Browns' two runs were unearned, as Chicago's Jim McCormick stopped St. Louis on just two hits, both singles. The Brown's victory in the finale was a runaway 13–4, called in the eighth for darkness. St. Louis' six-run fourth inning typified the game's sloppy play, the runs scoring on five hits, four errors, and two passed balls.

Chicago White Stockings (NL), 3; St. Louis Browns (AA), 3; tie, 1

CHI (N)

PLAYER/POS	AVG	G	AB	R	H	2B	3B	HR	RB	BB	SO	SB
Cap Anson, 1b	.423	7	26	8	11	1	1	0		2		
Tom Burns, ss-4,3b-3	.080	7	25	3	2	0	1	0		0		
John Clarkson, p-2,of-2	.154	4	13	1	2	1	0	0		0		
Abner Dalrymple, of	.269	7	26	4	7	2	0	1		2		
Silver Flint, c	.143	4	14	0	2	0	0	0		0		
George Gore, of	.000	1	3	1	0	0	0	0		1		
Bug Holliday, of	.000	1	4	0	0	0	0	0		0		
King Kelly, of-4,c-3	.346	7	26	9	9	3	1	0		2		
Jim McCormick, p	.176	5	17	1	3	0	0	0		0		
Fred Pfeffer, 2b	.407	7	27	5	11	2	0	1		0		
Billy Sunday, of	.273	6	22	5	6	2	0	0		2		
N. Williamson, 3b-4,ss-3	.087	7	23	1	2	0	0	0		4		
TOTAL	.243		226	38	55	11	3	2		13		

PITCHER	W	L	ERA	G	GS	CG	SV	SHO	IP	H	ER	BB	SO
John Clarkson	0	1	1.13	2	2	2	0	0	16.0	15	2	1	15
Jim McCormick	3	2	2.00	5	5	5	0	0	36.0	27	8	6	19
TOTAL	3	3	1.73	7	7	7	0	0	52.0	42	10	7	34

STL (A)

PLAYER/POS	AVG	G	AB	R	H	2B	3B	HR	RB	BB	SO	SB
Sam Barkley, 2b	.087	7	23	3	2	0	0	0		2		
Doc Bushong, c	.154	4	13	1	2	0	0	0		0		
Bob Caruthers, p-3,of-2	.200	5	15	1	3	0	1	0		1		
Charlie Comiskey, 1b	.292	7	24	6	7	0	0	0		0		
Dave Foutz, p	.167	4	12	1	2	0	0	0		0		
Bill Gleason, ss	.231	7	26	5	6	2	0	0		1		
Arlie Latham, 3b	.318	7	22	5	7	3	0	0		2		
Hugh Nicol, of	.000	1	2	0	0	0	0	0		0		
Tip O'Neill, of	.208	7	24	4	5	0	0	0		0		
Yank Robinson, of-4,c-3	.174	7	23	5	4	0	1	0		1		
Curt Welch, of	.148	7	27	5	4	1	1	0		0		
TOTAL	.199		211	36	42	6	3	0		7		

PITCHER	W	L	ERA	G	GS	CG	SV	SHO	IP	H	ER	BB	SO
Bob Caruthers	1	1	2.42	3	3	3	0	0	26.0	25	7	4	16
Dave Foutz	2	2	0.61	4	4	4	0	0	29.1	30	2	9	14
TOTAL	3	3	1.46	7	7	7	0	0	55.1	55	9	13	30

GAME 1 AT CHI OCT 14

STL	010 400 00	5	7	2
CHI	000 100 04	5	5	10

Pitchers: CARUTHERS vs CLARKSON
Home Runs: Pfeffer-CHI
Attendance: 2,000
(Game called at end of eighth, darkness)

GAME 2 AT STL OCT 15

CHI	110 003	5	6	5
STL	300 10X	4	2	4

Pitchers: McCORMICK vs FOUTZ
Attendance: 2,000
(Game forfeited to Chicago in bottom of sixth)

GAME 3 AT STL OCT 16

CHI	111 000 001	4	8	7
STL	500 002 00X	7	8	4

Pitchers: CLARKSON vs CARUTHERS
Attendance: 3,000

GAME 4 AT STL OCT 17

CHI	000 020 000	2	8	3
STL	001 000 02X	3	6	7

Pitchers: McCORMICK vs FOUTZ
Home Runs: Dalrymple-CHI
Attendance: 3,000

GAME 5 AT PITA OCT 22

CHI	400 110 3	9	7	1
STL	010 000 1	2	4	7

Pitchers: CLARKSON vs FOUTZ
Attendance: 500
(Game called at end of seventh, darkness)

GAME 6 AT CINA OCT 23

CHI	200 111 040	9	11	7
STL	002 000 000	2	2	7

Pitchers: McCORMICK vs CARUTHERS
Attendance: 1,500

GAME 7 AT CINA OCT 24

CHI	200 020 00	4	9	9
STL	004 621 0X	13	13	5

Pitchers: McCORMICK vs FOUTZ
Attendance: 1,200
(Game called in eighth, darkness)

It was a winner-take-all Series, with the club that won four games pocketing the entire proceeds. Attendance, very good for those days, averaged over 7,000 per game and brought the victorious Browns about $14,000.

The first three games were played in Chicago. The White Stockings won the opener on a sparkling five-hit shutout by their ace John Clarkson. But St. Louis's Bob Caruthers improved on Clarkson's performance the next day, blanking Chicago on just two singles as his Browns turned thirteen hits and thirteen Chicago errors into twelve runs (in a game shortened by darkness to eight innings). The White Stockings improved their fielding in the next game (which was also called after eight innings), and this time their bats came alive. With eleven hits (including home runs by Mike "King" Kelly and George Gore) combining with seven St. Louis errors, they regained the Series advantage with an easy 11–4 win.

When the venue shifted to St. Louis, though, the Browns battled back. In a back-and-forth battle in Game Four, Chicago tied the game at 5–5 with a pair of runs in the sixth, but St. Louis scored three final runs a half inning later, winning when darkness ended play in the middle of the seventh.

Game Five repeated Game Two's innovation: two umpires (instead of the usual one), plus a "referee" who stood between the pitcher and second base. The umpiring satisfied everyone, but Chicago, handicapped by their scheduled pitcher's sore arm, lost when they sent shortstop Ned Williamson and right fielder Jimmy Ryan into the box. In the 6½ innings before dark, St. Louis got to Williamson and Ryan for eleven hits and ten runs as their Nat Hudson held Chicago batters to three hits and three unearned runs.

The finale proved to be the Series' best-played and closest game. Chicago's Clarkson shut out the Browns through seven innings as his mates built a three-run lead—one of them scored on Fred's Pfeffer's homer in the fourth. Rain (and a rowdy crowd which poured onto the field) halted play for a while in the fifth. But the game resumed and the rain subsided. In the last of the eighth, Charlie Comiskey scored the Browns' first run on a single, errant throw and run-scoring fly out, and Arlie Latham tripled home two more runners later in the inning to tie the game. The score remained 3–3 into the last of the tenth, when the Browns' Curt Welch singled (for

only the fourth St. Louis hit), went to second on an infield hit, and took third on a sacrifice. Welch then attempted to steal home but catcher Kelly had smelled out the play and called for a pitch out. Clarkson's delivery was poor and bobbled by Kelly, allowing Welch to steal home with a "$15,000 slide" for the Browns' triumph.

St. Louis Browns (AA), 4; Chicago White Stockings (NL), 2

STL (A)

PLAYER/POS	AVG	G	AB	R	H	2B	3B	HR	RB	BB	SO	SB
Doc Bushong, c	.188	6	16	4	3	1	0	0	2	4	5	0
Bob Caruthers, p-3,of-3	.250	6	24	6	6	1	2	0	5	1	4	1
Charlie Comiskey, 1b	.292	6	24	2	7	1	0	0	2	0	4	0
Dave Foutz, p-2,of-2	.200	4	15	2	3	1	1	0	3	0	3	0
Bill Gleason, ss	.208	6	24	3	5	0	0	0	5	1	3	0
Nat Hudson, p-1,of-1	.167	2	6	1	1	0	1	0	0	1	3	0
Arlie Latham, 3b-6,c-1	.174	6	23	4	4	0	1	0	3	3	4	2
Tip O'Neill, of	.400	6	20	4	8	0	2	2	5	4	5	2
Yank Robinson, 2b	.316	6	19	5	6	1	1	0	3	2	3	2
Curt Welch, of	.350	6	20	7	7	2	0	0	1	3	4	2
TOTAL	.262		191	38	50	7	8	2	29	19	38	9

PITCHER	W	L	ERA	G	GS	CG	SV	SHO	IP	H	ER	BB	SO
Bob Caruthers	2	1	2.42	3	3	3	0	1	26.0	18	7	6	12
Dave Foutz	1	1	3.60	2	2	2	0	0	15.0	16	6	6	7
Nat Hudson	1	0	2.57	1	1	1	0	0	7.0	3	2	3	3
TOTAL	4	2	2.81	6	6	6	0	1	48.0	37	15	15	22

CHI (N)

PLAYER/POS	AVG	G	AB	R	H	2B	3B	HR	RB	BB	SO	SB
Cap Anson, 1b-6,c-2	.238	6	21	3	5	1	0	0	1	4	0	1
Tom Burns, 3b-6,of-1	.286	6	21	2	6	2	1	0	1	0	2	0
John Clarkson, p-4,of-1	.067	4	15	0	1	0	0	0	1	0	2	1
Abner Dalrymple, of	.190	6	21	2	4	1	1	0	2	0	5	1
Silver Flint, c	.000	1	3	0	0	0	0	0	0	1	0	0
George Gore, of	.174	6	23	4	4	0	0	1	2	3	3	0
King Kelly, c-5,ss-2,1b-1,3b-1	.208	6	24	4	5	0	0	1	1	2	2	1
Jim McCormick, p	.000	1	3	0	0	0	0	0	0	0	0	0
Fred Pfeffer, 2b	.286	6	21	7	6	0	0	1	4	2	1	2
Jimmy Ryan, of-6,p-1,ss-1	.250	6	20	4	5	1	0	0	2	0	1	1
Ned Williamson, ss-6,p-2,c-1,of-1	.056	6	18	2	1	0	1	0	3	4	5	1
TOTAL	.195		190	28	37	5	3	3	18	15	22	8

PITCHER	W	L	ERA	G	GS	CG	SV	SHO	IP	H	ER	BB	SO
John Clarkson	2	2	2.01	4	4	3	0	1	31.1	25	7	12	28
Jim McCormick	0	1	6.75	1	1	1	0	0	8.0	13	6	2	4
Jimmy Ryan	0	0	9.00	1	0	0	0	0	5.0	8	5	4	4
Ned Williamson	0	1	4.50	2	1	0	0	0	2.0	4	1	1	2
TOTAL	2	4	3.69	8	6	4	0	1	46.1	50	19	19	38

GAME 1 AT CHI OCT 18

STL	000	000	000	0	5	3
CHI	200	001	03X	6	10	4

Pitchers: FOUTZ vs CLARKSON
Attendance: 6,000

GAME 2 AT CHI OCT 19

STL	200	230	50	12	13	2
CHI	000	000	00	0	2	10

Pitchers: CARUTHERS vs McCORMICK
Home Runs: O'Neill-STL (2)
Attendance: 8,000
(Game called at end of eighth, darkness)

GAME 3 AT CHI OCT 20

CHI	200	112	32	11	11	2
STL	010	002	01	4	9	7

Pitchers: CLARKSON, Williamson (8) vs CARUTHERS
Home Runs: Kelly-CHI, Gore-CHI
Attendance: 6,000
(Game called at end of eighth, darkness)

GAME 4 AT STL OCT 21

CHI	300	002	0	5	6	4
STL	011	033	X	8	7	4

Pitchers: CLARKSON vs FOUTZ
Attendance: 8,000
(Game called in seventh, darkness)

GAME 5 AT STL OCT 22

CHI	011	100	00	3	3	3
STL	214	003	0X	10	11	3

Pitchers: WILLIAMSON, Ryan (2) vs HUDSON
Attendance: 10,000
(Game called in eighth, darkness)

GAME 6 AT STL OCT 23

CHI	010	101	000	0	3	6	2
STL	000	000	030	1	4	5	3

Pitchers: CLARKSON vs CARUTHERS
Home Runs: Pfeffer-CHI
Attendance: 8,000

Even though their star slugger Dan Brouthers was sidelined for all but one game by a sprained ankle, the Wolverines—in baseball's longest World Series, played in ten different cities—followed up their only pennant with an easy triumph over repeating AA champion St. Louis. The Browns won the opener at home, though, 6–1. They played errorless ball (rare in that era) as pitcher Bob Caruthers held Detroit scoreless until the ninth inning, and drove in the Browns' second run himself with a first-inning single.

The Wolverines came back to win the next three games. They took an early lead in Game Two and held on for a 5–3 win in St. Louis to even the Series. Then, in the Series' tightest game (played in Detroit) the Wolverines defeated Caruthers 2–1 in the last of the thirteenth when their pitcher Charlie Getzien led off with a single, advanced to second and third on ground outs, and scored on an infield error. In Game Four (in Pittsburgh) Detroit's Charles "Lady" Baldwin stopped the Browns on two hits for an easy 8–0 win.

Caruthers hurled a seven-hitter in Brooklyn for St. Louis's second win, but Detroit took the next four. Getzien contributed a two-hit shutout in New York, and Baldwin overcame Caruthers 3–1 in Philadelphia the next day. Getzien yielded eight hits the day after that in Boston, but Caruthers gave up thirteen, including two home runs to Sam Thompson, and Detroit took the game 9–2. Back in Philadelphia for Game Nine, St. Louis broke a 1–1 tie with a run in the top of the sixth. But the Wolverines scored two in the seventh and a final run in the eighth. The win gave Detroit a 7–2 Series advantage.

Game Ten, scheduled for the next day in Washington, was postponed because of rain until the following morning. Detroit's Hardy Richardson opened the game with a home run, but the Wolverines lost an opportunity to clinch the Series as the Browns overwhelmed Getzien with sixteen hits for an 11–4 victory featuring a triple play. But that afternoon, in Baltimore, Detroit took the deciding game as decisively as they had lost in the morning, knocking the Browns' Dave Foutz for fourteen hits (including four by Richardson and three—including a home run—by Larry Twitchell) as Baldwin held St. Louis to two hits in a 13–3 win.

The Browns and Wolverines split the final four meaningless games, played in Brooklyn,

Detroit Wolverines (NL), 10; St. Louis Browns (AA), 5

DET (N)

PLAYER/POS	AVG	G	AB	R	H	2B	3B	HR	RB	BB	SO	SB
Lady Baldwin, p	.235	5	17	4	1	0	0	1	2	2	1
Charlie Bennett, c-10,1b-3	.262	11	42	6	11	2	1	0	9	3	5	5
Dan Brouthers, 1b	.667	1	3	0	2	0	0	0	0	0	0	0
Pete Conway, p	.000	4	12	0	0	0	0	0	0	0	2	0
Fred Dunlap, 2b	.150	11	40	5	6	0	1	0	1	0	4	4
Charlie Ganzel, 1b-10,c-7	.224	14	58	5	13	1	0	0	2	1	2	3
Charlie Getzien, p	.300	6	20	5	6	2	0	0	3	6	1
Ned Hanlon, of	.220	15	50	5	11	1	1	0	4	5	1	7
Hardy Richardson, of-10,2b-5,3b-1	.197	15	66	12	13	5	2	1	4	1	9	7
Jack Rowe, ss	.333	15	63	12	21	1	1	0	7	2	1	5
Cy Sutcliffe, 1b-3,c-1	.091	4	11	1	1	0	0	0	0	1	1	1
Sam Thompson, of	.362	15	58	8	21	2	0	2	7	3	3	5
Larry Twitchell, of	.250	6	20	5	5	1	0	1	3	0	1	1
Deacon White, 3b-14,1b-1	.207	15	58	8	12	1	1	0	3	2	0	2
TOTAL	.243		518	73	126	17	7	4	43	23	37	42

PITCHER	W	L	ERA	G	GS	CG	SV	SHO	IP	H	ER	BB	SO
Lady Baldwin	4	1	1.50	5	5	5	0	1	42.0	28	7	10	4
Pete Conway	2	2	3.00	4	4	4	0	0	33.0	31	11	6	10
Charlie Getzien	4	2	2.48	6	6	6	0	1	58.0	61	16	15	17
TOTAL	10	5	2.30	15	15	15	0	2	133.0	120	34	31	31

STL (A)

PLAYER/POS	AVG	G	AB	R	H	2B	3B	HR	RB	BB	SO	SB
Jack Boyle, c	.208	6	24	1	5	0	0	0	1	0	4	0
Doc Bushong, c	.241	9	29	3	7	0	0	0	1	4	1	0
Bob Caruthers, p-8,of-3	.239	10	46	2	11	0	0	0	3	1	1	3
Charlie Comiskey, 1b-14,of-1	.306	15	62	8	19	2	0	0	2	1	1	4
Dave Foutz, of-11,p-3,1b-1	.169	15	59	4	10	2	1	0	1	2	3	0
Bill Gleason, ss	.163	13	49	3	8	0	0	1	1	3	2	1
Silver King, p	.071	4	14	0	1	0	0	0	0	0	3	0
Arlie Latham, 3b	.293	15	58	12	17	1	0	1	1	9	2	15
Harry Lyons, ss	.286	2	7	3	2	0	0	0	1	0	0	0
Tip O'Neill, of	.200	15	65	7	13	2	1	1	5	0	2	0
Yank Robinson, 2b	.326	15	46	5	15	5	1	0	4	10	6	4
Curt Welch, of	.207	15	58	6	12	3	1	1	6	0	2	1
TOTAL	.232		517	54	120	15	4	2	25	31	27	28

PITCHER	W	L	ERA	G	GS	CG	SV	SHO	IP	H	ER	BB	SO
Bob Caruthers	4	4	2.13	8	8	8	0	0	71.2	64	17	12	19
Dave Foutz	0	3	3.46	3	3	3	0	0	26.0	36	10	9	6
Silver King	1	3	2.03	4	4	4	0	0	31.0	26	7	2	21
TOTAL	5	10	2.38	15	15	15	0	0	128.2	126	34	23	46

Detroit, Chicago, and St. Louis. For the first time in a World Series, two umpires officiated at all the games.

GAME 1 AT STL OCT 10

STL	200 040 000	6	12	0
DET	000 000 001	1	4	5

Pitchers: CARUTHERS vs GETZIEN
Attendance: 4,208

GAME 2 AT STL OCT 11

DET	022 000 100	5	10	2
STL	000 000 120	3	8	7

Pitchers: CONWAY vs FOUTZ
Attendance: 6,408

GAME 3 AT DET OCT 12

STL	010 000 000 000 0	1	13	7
DET	000 000 010 000 1	2	6	1

Pitchers: CARUTHERS vs GETZIEN
Attendance: 4,509

GAME 4 AT PIT OCT 13

DET	410 012 000	8	11	1
STL	000 000 000	0	2	6

Pitchers: BALDWIN vs KING
Attendance: 2,447

GAME 5 AT BRO OCT 14

STL	200 002 100	5	5	4
DET	000 020 000	2	7	5

Pitchers: CARUTHERS vs CONWAY
Attendance: 6,796

GAME 6 AT NY OCT 15

DET	330 000 003	9	12	1
STL	000 000 000	0	2	8

Pitchers: GETZIEN vs FOUTZ
Attendance: 5,797

GAME 7 AT PHI OCT 17

STL	000 000 001	1	8	1
DET	030 000 00X	3	6	1

Pitchers: CARUTHERS vs BALDWIN
Home Runs: O'Neill-STL
Attendance: 6,478

GAME 8 AT BOS OCT 18

DET	031 003 200	9	13	2
STL	100 000 010	2	8	5

Pitchers: GETZIEN vs CARUTHERS
Home Runs: Thompson-DET (2)
Attendance: 2,891

GAME 9 AT PHI OCT 19

STL	000 101 000	2	9	2
DET	000 100 21X	4	6	3

Pitchers: KING vs CONWAY
Attendance: 2,389

GAME 10 AT WAS OCT 21 (AM)

DET	200 010 001	4	8	3
STL	200 031 41X	11	16	5

Pitchers: GETZIEN vs CARUTHERS
Home Runs: Latham-STL, Welch-STL, Richardson-DET
Attendance: 1,261

GAME 11 AT BAL OCT 21 (PM)

STL	110 010 000	3	2	7
DET	100 344 10X	13	14	7

Pitchers: FOUTZ vs BALDWIN
Home Runs: Twitchell-DET
Attendance: 2,707
(Detroit wins best of 15 series 8 to 3)

GAME 12 AT BRO OCT 22

DET	000 100 0	1	5	3
STL	410 000 X	5	10	2

Pitchers: CONWAY vs KING
Attendance: 1,138
(Game called in seventh, darkness)

GAME 13 AT DET OCT 24

DET	020 100 120	6	12	3
STL	100 010 001	3	4	5

Pitchers: BALDWIN vs CARUTHERS
Attendance: 3,389

GAME 14 AT CHI OCT 25

STL	000 002 100	3	10	5
DET	300 010 00X	4	4	4

Pitchers: KING vs GETZIEN
Attendance: 378

GAME 15 AT STL OCT 26

STL	340 110	9	11	5
DET	011 000	2	8	7

Pitchers: CARUTHERS vs BALDWIN
Attendance: 659
(Game called after sixth, cold)

St. Louis, AA champions for the fourth straight year, battled the Giants closely through several games, but blowout losses in Games Six and Eight undid them. The first three games were played in New York. In a splendidly pitched opener, Brown ace Charles "Silver" King held New York to two hits and a walk while Giant ace Tim Keefe limited the Browns to three hits and a walk, striking out nine on his way to a narrow 2–1 win. St. Louis evened the Series in Game Two behind the shutout pitching of Elton "Icebox" Chamberlain. Tommy McCarthy scored the Browns' first run in the second inning when, after singling, he moved around to third on two passed balls by Giant catcher Buck Ewing and came home on Ewing's failed attempt to throw out a runner stealing second. Two more runs in the ninth gave St. Louis more than enough insurance for the win.

The Giants scored twice in the first inning of Game Three, and increased their lead to 4–0 before allowing St. Louis a pair of harmless runs in the final innings. They also scored first and led all the way in Game Four (played in Brooklyn) as another St. Louis rally fell short. The Browns took a 4–1 lead into the bottom of the eighth in Game Five (in New York), but a five-run Giant rally reversed the lead—and the outcome—as the game was called for darkness with St. Louis at bat in the ninth.

Giant Mickey Welch hurled a three-hitter (in Philadelphia) the next day, but St. Louis, capitalizing on walks and a questionable "safe" call at home, carried a 4–1 lead into the sixth inning. New York exploded in the late innings for 11 runs, however, and when darkness ended the game after eight the Giants were just one win away from the title.

The final four games were played in St. Louis. The Browns spoiled New York's hope of quick victory in Game Seven, coming from behind to tie the score with three runs in the fourth, and—after New York had scored twice in the sixth—recovering with a four-run eighth for a 7–5 lead before darkness again halted play after eight innings. But the Browns' win only delayed the inevitable. The Giants hammered Icebox Chamberlain for twelve hits in Game Eight (including home runs by Buck Ewing and Mike Tiernan) to clinch their first world championship with an 11–3 win.

New York Giants (NL), 6;
St. Louis Browns (AA), 4

NY (N)

PLAYER/POS	AVG	G	AB	R	H	2B	3B	HR	RB	BB	SO	SB
Willard Brown, c	.375	2	8	1	3	1	0	0	0	0	0	0
Roger Connor, 1b	.304	7	23	7	7	1	2	0	3	4	0	4
Ed Crane, p	.143	2	7	1	1	0	0	0	2	0	1	0
Buck Ewing, c-6,1b-1	.346	7	26	5	9	0	2	1	6	1	3	5
Bill George, p-1,1b-1	.333	2	9	2	3	1	0	1	4	0	2	0
George Gore, of-2,3b-1	.455	3	11	5	5	1	0	0	0	2	2	2
Gil Hatfield, p-1,2b-1,ss-1	.250	2	8	2	2	0	0	0	1	1	2	1
Tim Keefe, p	.091	4	11	2	1	0	0	0	0	2	2	1
Pat Murphy, c	.100	3	10	1	1	0	0	0	1	0	0	0
Jim O'Rourke, of-7,1b-2,ss-1	.222	10	36	4	8	0	0	0	1	4	2	3
Danny Richardson, 2b	.167	9	36	6	6	2	0	0	6	3	5	3
Mike Slattery, of-10,2b-1	.205	10	39	6	8	2	0	0	5	0	5	6
Mike Tiernan, of	.342	10	38	8	13	0	0	1	6	8	2	5
Ledell Titcomb, p-1,of-1	.500	1	4	1	2	1	0	0	1	0	0	0
Monte Ward, ss	.379	8	29	4	11	1	0	0	6	1	0	6
Mickey Welch, p	.286	2	7	2	2	0	0	0	1	0	0	0
Art Whitney, 3b-9,of-1	.324	10	37	7	12	0	1	0	12	1	4	2
TOTAL	.277		339	64	94	10	5	3	55	27	30	38

PITCHER	W	L	ERA	G	GS	CG	SV	SHO	IP	H	ER	BB	SO
Ed Crane	1	1	2.12	2	2	2	0	0	17.0	15	4	6	12
Bill George	0	1	7.20	1	1	1	0	0	10.0	15	8	3	4
Gil Hatfield	0	0	12.60	1	0	0	0	0	5.0	12	7	3	2
Tim Keefe	4	0	0.51	4	4	4	0	0	35.0	18	2	9	30
Ledell Titcomb	0	1	6.75	1	1	0	0	0	4.0	5	3	2	2
Mickey Welch	1	1	2.65	2	2	2	0	0	17.0	10	5	9	2
TOTAL	6	4	2.97	11	10	9	0	0	88.0	75	29	32	52

STL (A)

PLAYER/POS	AVG	G	AB	R	H	2B	3B	HR	RB	BB	SO	SB
Jack Boyle, c-4,of-1	.438	4	16	4	7	0	1	0	4	2	2	3
Icebox Chamberlain, p	.000	5	13	3	0	0	0	0	0	4	3	1
Charlie Comiskey, 1b-10,of-1	.268	10	41	6	11	1	1	0	3	1	1	4
Jim Devlin, p	.000	1	3	0	0	0	0	0	0	0	0	0
Ed Herr, of	.091	3	11	2	1	0	0	0	0	0	5	1
Silver King, p	.067	5	15	1	1	0	0	0	0	1	6	0
Arlie Latham, 3b	.250	10	40	10	10	0	0	0	3	5	6	11
Harry Lyons, of	.118	5	17	0	2	0	0	0	1	1	5	0
Tommy McCarthy, of	.244	10	41	10	10	1	0	1	9	0	0	6
Jocko Milligan, c-8,1b-1	.400	8	25	5	10	2	1	0	4	3	3	0
Tip O'Neill, of	.243	10	37	8	9	1	0	2	11	6	3	0
Yank Robinson, 2b	.250	10	36	7	9	2	1	0	7	6	12	2
Bill White, ss	.143	10	35	4	5	1	0	0	4	3	6	1
TOTAL	.227		330	60	75	8	4	3	46	32	52	29

PITCHER	W	L	ERA	G	GS	CG	SV	SHO	IP	H	ER	BB	SO
Icebox Chamberlain	2	3	5.32	5	5	5	0	1	44.0	52	26	16	13
Jim Devlin	1	0	2.57	1	0	0	0	0	7.0	5	2	2	5
Silver King	1	3	2.31	5	5	4	0	0	35.0	37	9	9	12
TOTAL	4	6	3.87	11	10	9	0	1	86.0	94	37	27	30

The final two games meant nothing to the outcome, and both clubs used reserve pitchers in Game Nine. But St. Louis rewarded the small crowd with a two-run rally in the ninth to tie the game at 11-all and scored three more runs in the tenth to win it. The finale the next day again featured heavy hitting on both sides, including a trio of home runs (one of them Tip O'Neill's second in two days) and an 18–7 St. Louis romp.

GAME 1 AT NY OCT 16

STL	001	000	000	1	3	5
NY	011	000	00X	2	2	4

Pitchers: KING vs KEEFE
Attendance: 4,876

GAME 2 AT NY OCT 17

STL	010	000	002	3	7	4
NY	000	000	000	0	6	1

Pitchers: CHAMBERLAIN vs WELCH
Attendance: 5,575

GAME 3 AT NY OCT 18

STL	000	000	011	2	5	5
NY	200	100	10X	4	5	2

Pitchers: KING vs KEEFE
Attendance: 5,780

GAME 4 AT BRO OCT 19

NY	104	010	000	6	8	2
STL	001	000	020	3	7	4

Pitchers: CRANE vs CHAMBERLAIN
Attendance: 3,062

GAME 5 AT NY OCT 20

STL	100	000	05	6	9	2
NY	003	001	00	4	5	5

Pitchers: KING vs KEEFE
Attendance: 9,124
(Game called at end of eighth, darkness)

GAME 6 AT PHI OCT 22

NY	000	103	35	12	13	5
STL	301	000	01	5	3	7

Pitchers: WELCH vs CHAMBERLAIN
Attendance: 3,281
(Game called at end of eighth, darkness)

GAME 7 AT STL OCT 24

NY	030	002	00	5	11	3
STL	000	300	04	7	8	3

Pitchers: CRANE vs KING
Attendance: 4,624
(Game called at end of eighth, darkness)

GAME 8 AT STL OCT 25

NY	103	100	006	11	12	2
STL	000	100	110	3	5	6

Pitchers: KEEFE vs CHAMBERLAIN
Home Runs: Ewing-NY, Tiernan-NY
Attendance: 4,865
(New York wins best of 10 series, 6 to 2)

GAME 9 AT STL OCT 26

STL	140	020	202	3	14	15	4
NY	035	000	120	0	11	14	5

Pitchers: King, DEVLIN (4) vs GEORGE
Home Runs: O'Neill-STL
Attendance: 711

GAME 10 AT STL OCT 27

STL	010	505	421	18	17	3
NY	310	000	021	7	13	8

Pitchers: CHAMBERLAIN vs TITCOMB, Hatfield (5)
Home Runs: George-NY, O'Neill-STL, McCarthy-STL
Attendance: 412

Six wins was the magic number this year, and it was agreed that—unlike most previous Series—play would not continue beyond the deciding game. At first it seemed Brooklyn might prevail, with an assistant from the dark of night. The Giants wanted the opening game called for darkness after the seventh inning, when they led 10–8. But the umpires held off until Brooklyn, in the deepening gloom, had scored four runs in the last of the eighth to go ahead 12–10.

The next day, in Brooklyn before more than 16,000 spectators (by far the largest World Series crowd to that time), Giant Ed "Cannonball" Crane held the Grooms to four hits as New York evened the Series. But Brooklyn won the next two for a 3–1 Series advantage. In Game Three, ahead 8–7 in the sixth inning, the Grooms began stalling, waiting for darkness to fall. The score was still 8–7 when the game was finally halted in the top of the ninth with one out and three Giants on base.

Darkness for a third time gave Brooklyn the victory in Game Four. New York overcame a 7–2 Bridegroom lead to tie the score with five runs in the top of the sixth, but in the bottom of the inning Brooklyn's Tom "Oyster" Burns homered in the dark for three runs. The umpires then halted the game.

The five remaining contests went the distance, and the Giants won them all. Cannonball Crane in Game Five gave up eight hits, but homered in his own behalf, driving in two runs in his Giants' 11–3 rout. Game Six was a pitching duel between New York's Hank O'Day and Brooklyn's William "Adonis" Terry. The Grooms scored a run in the second inning, but New York tied the game with two outs in the last of the ninth (when Monte Ward singled, stole second and third, and scored on Roger Connor's single), and won it with two away in the eleventh as Ward drove in a speedy Mike Slattery from second with an infield hit.

Back-to-back homers by Giants Dan Richardson and Jim O'Rourke highlighted an eight-run second inning in Game Seven. The Giants' eventual 11–7 win gave them their first Series advantage. In Game Eight, two of Brooklyn's five hits were home runs. But the Giants outscored the Grooms 12–2 over the first four innings and beat them 16–7.

With their backs to the wall, the Bridegrooms scored first in

New York Giants (NL), 6;
Brooklyn Bridegrooms (AA), 3

NY (N)

PLAYER/POS	AVG	G	AB	R	H	2B	3B	HR	RB	BB	SO	SB
Willard Brown, c	.600	1	5	3	3	0	0	1	2	0	0	0
Roger Connor, 1b	.343	9	35	9	12	2	2	0	12	3	2	8
Ed Crane, p	.278	5	18	3	5	1	1	1	5	1	2	0
Buck Ewing, c	.250	8	36	5	9	4	0	0	7	2	5	1
George Gore, of	.333	5	21	5	7	1	1	0	1	3	0	2
Tim Keefe, p	.500	2	4	1	2	1	0	0	0	1	1	0
Hank O'Day, p	.167	3	6	0	1	0	0	0	0	2	2	0
Jim O'Rourke, of	.389	9	36	7	14	2	2	2	7	2	2	3
Danny Richardson, 2b	.314	9	35	8	11	1	1	3	8	3	5	3
Mike Slattery, of	.188	4	16	6	3	0	0	0	1	3	1	1
Mike Tiernan, of	.289	9	38	12	11	1	1	1	5	5	3	3
Monte Ward, ss	.417	9	36	10	15	0	1	0	7	5	2	10
Mickey Welch, p	.333	1	3	0	1	1	0	0	0	0	0	0
Art Whitney, 3b	.229	9	35	4	8	2	1	0	3	1	0	0
TOTAL	.315		324	73	102	16	10	8	58	31	26	31

PITCHER	W	L	ERA	G	GS	CG	SV	SHO	IP	H	ER	BB	SO
Ed Crane	4	1	3.72	5	5	4	0	0	38.2	29	16	32	19
Tim Keefe	0	1	8.18	2	1	1	0	0	11.0	17	10	2	4
Hank O'Day	2	0	1.17	3	2	2	0	0	23.0	10	3	14	12
Mickey Welch	0	1	9.00	1	1	0	0	0	5.0	11	5	3	1
TOTAL	6	3	3.94	11	9	7	1	0	77.2	67	34	51	36

BRO (A)

PLAYER/POS	AVG	G	AB	R	H	2B	3B	HR	RB	BB	SO	SB
Oyster Burns, of	.229	9	35	8	8	3	0	2	11	5	6	0
Doc Bushong, c	.000	3	8	0	0	0	0	0	0	1	0	0
Bob Caruthers, p	.250	4	8	1	2	0	0	0	1	3	3	0
Bob Clark, c	.417	4	12	3	5	2	0	0	3	2	2	0
Hub Collins, 2b	.371	9	35	13	13	3	0	1	2	7	5	6
Pop Corkhill, of	.208	9	24	4	5	1	0	1	5	6	2	1
Jumbo Davis, ss	.000	1	4	0	0	0	0	0	0	0	0	0
Dave Foutz, 1b-9,p-1	.286	9	35	7	10	2	0	1	9	4	2	3
Mickey Hughes, p	.333	1	3	1	1	1	0	0	0	1	2	0
Tom Lovett, p	.000	1	1	0	0	0	0	0	0	0	0	0
Darby O'Brien, of	.161	9	31	8	5	0	1	0	4	12	6	6
George Pinckney, 3b	.258	9	31	2	8	2	0	0	3	4	2	2
Germany Smith, ss	.172	8	29	2	5	2	1	0	2	3	2	2
Adonis Terry, p-5,1b-1	.167	5	18	1	3	0	0	0	1	1	1	1
Joe Visner, c-3,of-2	.125	5	16	2	2	1	0	0	0	2	3	0
TOTAL	.231		290	52	67	17	2	5	41	51	36	21

PITCHER	W	L	ERA	G	GS	CG	SV	SHO	IP	H	ER	BB	SO
Bob Caruthers	0	2	3.75	4	2	2	1	0	24.0	28	10	6	6
Dave Foutz	0	0	7.20	1	0	0	0	0	5.0	5	4	2	2
Mickey Hughes	1	0	7.71	1	1	0	0	0	7.0	14	6	3	3
Tom Lovett	0	1	24.00	1	1	0	0	0	3.0	8	8	2	1
Adonis Terry	2	3	5.97	5	5	4	0	0	37.2	47	25	18	14
TOTAL	3	6	6.22	12	9	6	1	0	76.2	102	53	31	26

Game Nine and held a 2–1 lead after five innings. But New York tied the score in the sixth and went ahead 3–2 on a passed ball in the seventh. Meanwhile Giant pitcher

Hank O'Day (although he walked five batters) blanked the Grooms on just two hits after the first inning to bring New York its second straight world championship.

The Bridegrooms, AA pennant winners in 1889, switched to the NL and returned to World Series play as champions of their new league. Louisville, meanwhile, rose from a last-place finish in 1889 to replace Brooklyn at the top of the AA. The Series, though, seemed meaningless to many who believed that pennant-winning Boston of the outlaw Players League (which had drawn off many of the best NL and AA players) could beat both Louisville and Brooklyn if given the opportunity.

The first four games of the Series were played in Louisville before an ever decreasing number of spectators. The largest crowd—5,600—saw the Cyclones humiliated in the opener 9–0 as Brooklyn's Adonis Terry stopped them on two singles. The Grooms won the second game, too, breaking a 2–2 tie with a pair of runs in the fourth and holding on for a 5–3 win.

Louisville played catch-up throughout Game Three and entered the last of the eighth still behind 7–4. But a walk, three hits, a sacrifice fly, and a passed ball brought to score to 7-all—where it remained when darkness ended the game. Only 1,050 spectators attended the final contest in Louisville, but they saw the first Louisville win. The Cyclones scored three runs in the first inning, but Brooklyn countered with three an inning later, and both teams scored single runs in the third. Louisville's Red Ehret blanked the Grooms the rest of the way, but Brooklyn's Tom Lovett yielded the Cyclones a winning run in the seventh when Tim Shinnick tripled and was sacrificed home.

Rain postponed the first game in Brooklyn for two days, but when it was played—on a cold, muddy day before a small crowd of 1,000—the Grooms took the lead on Oyster Burns's two-run homer in the first inning and held it all the way for their third win. As the weather grew colder, the crowds declined for the final two games. Louisville captured its second win by a 9–8 margin when a three-run Brooklyn rally in the eighth inning of Game Six stalled one run short of a tie. Only abut 300 diehards saw the Cyclones even the Series in the finale, 6–2 behind Red Ehret's four-hitter. A tie-breaking eighth game seemed called for, but there was not enough interest in playing any further in the bitter cold.

Brooklyn Bridegrooms (NL), 3; Louisville Cyclones (AA), 3; tie, 1

BRO (N)

PLAYER/POS	AVG	G	AB	R	H	2B	3B	HR	RB	BB	SO	SB
Oyster Burns, of-4,3b-3	.222	7	27	6	6	2	0	1	5	3	4	0
Doc Bushong, c	.000	2	6	0	0	0	0	0	0	0	1	0
Bob Caruthers, of	.000	2	6	0	0	0	0	0	0	2	0	0
Bob Clark, c	.667	1	3	2	2	0	1	0	1	0	0	0
Hub Collins, 2b	.310	7	29	7	9	0	1	0	1	3	0	2
Tom Daly, c-6,1b-1	.182	6	22	1	4	2	0	0	3	0	4	2
Patsy Donovan, of	.471	5	17	5	8	1	0	0	3	2	1	3
Dave Foutz, 1b-7,of-1	.300	7	30	6	9	2	1	0	4	0	1	1
Tom Lovett, p-4,of-1	.067	5	15	0	1	0	0	0	0	0	4	0
Darby O'Brien, of	.125	6	24	3	3	0	1	0	3	1	5	3
George Pinckney, 3b	.357	4	14	4	5	0	2	0	3	2	1	1
Germany Smith, ss	.276	7	29	3	8	0	2	0	7	0	3	1
Adonis Terry, p-3,of-3	.050	6	20	5	1	1	0	0	0	6	3	1
TOTAL	.231		242	42	56	8	8	1	30	19	27	14

PITCHER	W	L	ERA	G	GS	CG	SV	SHO	IP	H	ER	BB	SO
Tom Lovett	2	2	2.83	4	4	4	0	0	35.0	29	11	6	14
Adonis Terry	1	1	3.60	3	3	3	0	1	25.0	25	10	10	8
TOTAL	3	3	3.15	7	7	7	0	1	60.0	54	21	16	22

LOU (A)

PLAYER/POS	AVG	G	AB	R	H	2B	3B	HR	RB	BB	SO	SB
Ned Bligh, c	.000	2	3	0	0	0	0	0	0	0	1	0
Ed Daily, of-4,p-2	.136	6	22	1	3	1	1	0	3	1	2	2
Red Ehret, p	.429	3	7	1	3	0	1	0	0	0	0	0
Charlie Hamburg, of	.269	7	26	3	7	1	0	0	2	0	3	0
George Meakim, p	.500	1	2	0	1	0	0	0	0	0	0	0
Harry Raymond, ss-5,ss-3	.148	7	27	5	4	1	1	0	1	2	5	1
John Ryan, c	.053	6	19	0	1	0	0	0	2	0	1	1
Tim Shinnick, 2b	.292	7	24	3	7	1	1	0	3	2	2	2
Scott Stratton, p-3,of-1	.222	4	9	4	2	1	0	0	0	2	1	3
Harry Taylor, 1b	.300	7	30	6	9	1	0	0	2	2	3	3
Phil Tomney, ss	.200	3	5	1	1	0	0	0	0	3	1	0
Farmer Weaver, of	.259	7	27	4	7	1	0	0	4	1	2	5
Pete Weckbecker, c	.000	1	4	0	0	0	0	0	0	0	1	0
Chicken Wolf, 3b-5,of-3	.360	7	25	4	9	3	1	0	8	3	0	2
TOTAL	.235		230	32	54	10	5	0	25	16	22	19

PITCHER	W	L	ERA	G	GS	CG	SV	SHO	IP	H	ER	BB	SO
Ed Daily	0	2	2.65	2	2	2	0	0	17.0	12	5	8	5
Red Ehret	2	0	1.35	3	2	2	1	0	20.0	12	3	6	13
George Meakim	0	0	0.00	1	0	0	0	0	4.0	6	0	1	1
Scott Stratton	1	1	2.37	3	3	1	0	0	19.0	26	5	4	8
TOTAL	3	3	1.95	9	7	5	1	0	60.0	56	13	19	27

GAME 1 AT LOU OCT 17

BRO	300 030 30	9 11 1
LOU	000 000 00	0 2 6

Pitchers: TERRY vs STRATTON
Attendance: 5,600

GAME 2 AT LOU OCT 18

BRO	020 201 000	5 5 3
LOU	101 000 001	3 6 5

Pitchers: LOVETT vs DAILY
Attendance: 2,860

GAME 3 AT LOU OCT 20

BRO	020 130 10	7 10 2
LOU	001 012 03	7 11 3

Pitchers: Terry vs Stratton, Meakim (4)
Attendance: 2,500

GAME 4 AT LOU OCT 21

BRO	031 000 000	4 7 2
LOU	301 000 10X	5 9 2

Pitchers: LOVETT vs EHRET
Attendance: 1,050

GAME 5 AT BRO OCT 25

LOU	010 010 000	2 5 6
BRO	210 200 20X	7 7 0

Pitchers: DAILY vs LOVETT
Home Runs: Burns-BRO
Attendance: 1,000

GAME 6 AT BRO OCT 27

LOU	012 101 220	9 13 3
BRO	100 004 030	8 12 3

Pitchers: STRATTON, Ehret (7) vs TERRY
Attendance: 600

GAME 7 AT BRO OCT 28

LOU	103 000 020	6 8 3
BRO	200 000 000	2 4 1

Pitchers: EHRET vs LOVETT
Attendance: 300

Interleague squabbling prevented a World Series in 1891, and the AA folded before the next season. Four AA clubs were taken into the NL, expanding the NL to twelve teams. To create a postseason championship series, the regular season was divided in half, with first-half winner Boston meeting second-half victor Cleveland for both the league and world titles.

The first game, in Cleveland, was a pitching and fielding classic. Boston's Jack Stivetts and Cleveland's Cy Young blanked the opposition for eleven innings before darkness halted the game. Young yielded just six hits and Stivetts four—all singles. Just as remarkable in an era when errors were commonplace, Cleveland committed only one and Boston none; several outstanding plays were made in the field.

Boston center fielder Hugh Duffy was the offensive and defensive star of Game Two. He drove in three of the Beaneaters' four runs (with a fly out, a triple, and a double), and scored the fourth himself after tripling a second time. And in the bottom of the ninth he snared a leadoff liner with a great running catch. As it was, Cleveland scored once in the inning to pull within a run of a tie; Duffy's catch prevented a certain tie and a possible Cleveland win. Game Three was just as close. Pitchers Stivetts and Young each gave up two early runs, but then blanked their foes until the seventh inning, when Boston's Tommy McCarthy singled in Stivetts (who had doubled) with what proved the winning run.

The Series moved to Boston for the next three games. In Game Four, Boston ace Kid Nichols shut out the Spiders, scattering seven hits and fanning eight. Cleveland's Nig Cuppy yielded only six hits, but one was a home run ball to Hugh Duffy for two runs in the third inning, and another was a two-run single to Joe Quinn in the sixth. Cleveland pitcher John Clarkson helped his own cause the next day with a three-run homer in the Spider's six-run second inning. But Boston pitcher Jack Stivetts—with the score now 7–5 Cleveland in the sixth—tripled in a run and scored the tying run. In the seventh, Stivetts scored Boston's twelfth (and final) run after singling, while holding Cleveland scoreless through the final four innings.

Two days later the Beaneaters brought the Series to an end with their fifth straight win. The Spiders scored first, with a three-run third, but pitcher Kid Nichols

Boston Beaneaters, 5; Cleveland Spiders, 0; tie, 1

BOS (N)

PLAYER/POS	AVG	G	AB	R	H	2B	3B	HR	RB	BB	SO	SB
Charlie Bennett, c	.286	2	7	2	2	0	0	1	1	0	2	1
Hugh Duffy, of	.462	6	26	3	12	3	2	1	9	1	0	3
Charlie Ganzel, c	.500	2	8	1	4	0	0	0	2	1	0	0
King Kelly, c	.000	2	8	0	0	0	0	0	0	0	2	1
Herman Long, ss	.222	6	27	4	6	0	0	0	1	0	0	2
Bobby Lowe, of	.130	6	23	8	3	0	0	0	0	1	2	1
Tommy McCarthy, of	.381	6	21	2	8	2	0	0	2	6	1	3
Billy Nash, 3b	.167	6	24	3	4	0	0	0	4	2	3	2
Kid Nichols, p	.286	2	7	1	2	0	0	0	2	0	1	1
Joe Quinn, 2b	.286	6	21	2	6	1	1	0	4	1	2	0
Harry Staley, p	.000	1	4	0	0	0	0	0	0	0	3	0
Jack Stivetts, p	.250	3	12	3	3	1	1	0	1	0	2	0
Tommy Tucker, 1b	.261	6	23	2	6	0	0	1	2	0	1	0
TOTAL	.265		211	31	56	7	4	3	28	12	19	14

PITCHER	W	L	ERA	G	GS	CG	SV	SHO	IP	H	ER	BB	SO
Kid Nichols	2	0	1.00	2	2	2	0	1	18.0	17	2	4	13
Harry Staley	1	0	3.00	1	1	1	0	0	9.0	10	3	1	0
Jack Stivetts	2	0	0.93	3	3	3	0	1	29.0	21	3	7	17
TOTAL	5	0	1.29	6	6	6	0	2	56.0	48	8	12	30

CLE (N)

PLAYER/POS	AVG	G	AB	R	H	2B	3B	HR	RB	BB	SO	SB
Jesse Burkett, of	.320	6	25	3	8	1	0	0	1	0	2	4
Cupid Childs, 2b	.409	6	22	3	9	0	2	0	0	5	1	0
John Clarkson, p	.250	2	8	1	2	0	0	1	3	0	1	0
Nig Cuppy, p	.000	1	3	0	0	0	0	0	0	0	2	0
George Davis, 3b-2	.167	3	6	0	1	0	0	0	0	0	1	0
Jimmy McAleer, of	.182	6	22	0	4	0	0	0	1	2	2	1
Ed McKean, ss	.440	6	25	2	11	0	0	0	6	1	3	0
Jack O'Connor, of	.136	6	22	1	3	0	0	0	0	2	3	0
Patsy Tebeau, 3b	.000	5	18	1	0	0	0	0	0	0	2	1
Jake Virtue, 1b	.125	6	24	1	3	0	0	0	0	2	5	1
Cy Young, p	.091	3	11	1	1	0	0	0	0	0	5	0
Chief Zimmer, c	.261	6	23	2	6	1	1	0	2	0	3	0
TOTAL	.230		209	15	48	2	3	1	13	12	30	7

PITCHER	W	L	ERA	G	GS	CG	SV	SHO	IP	H	ER	BB	SO
John Clarkson	0	2	5.29	2	2	2	0	0	17.0	24	10	5	9
Nig Cuppy	0	1	1.13	1	1	1	0	0	8.0	6	1	4	1
Cy Young	0	2	3.00	3	3	3	0	1	27.0	26	9	3	9
TOTAL	0	5	3.46	6	6	6	0	1	52.0	56	20	12	19

held them scoreless after that and singled home Boston's tying and go-ahead runs himself as the Beaneaters tagged Cy Young for eight runs over the final six innings.

GAME 1 AT CLE OCT 17

CLE	000 000 000 00	0	4	1
BOS	000 000 000 00	0	6	0

Pitchers: YOUNG vs STIVETTS
Attendance: 6,000

GAME 2 AT CLE OCT 18

BOS	101 010 010	4	10	4
CLE	001 100 001	3	10	2

Pitchers: STALEY vs CLARKSON
Attendance: 6,700

GAME 3 AT CLE OCT 19

CLE	200 000 000	2	8	0
BOS	110 000 10X	3	9	2

Pitchers: YOUNG vs STIVETTS
Attendance: 5,000

GAME 4 AT BOS OCT 21

CLE	000 000 000	0	7	3
BOS	002 002 00X	4	6	0

Pitchers: CUPPY vs NICHOLS
Home Runs: Duffy-BOS
Attendance: 6,547

GAME 5 AT BOS OCT 22

CLE	060 010 000	7	9	4
BOS	000 324 30X	12	14	3

Pitchers: CLARKSON vs STIVETTS
Home Runs: Clarkson-CLE,
   Tucker-BOS
Attendance: 3,466

GAME 6 AT BOS OCT 24

CLE	003 000 000	3	10	5
BOS	002 211 11X	8	11	5

Pitchers: YOUNG vs NICHOLS
Home Runs: Bennett-BOS
Attendance: 2,300

As the divided season of 1892 was not repeated, no "world series" was held in 1893. But in 1894 Pittsburgh sportsman William C. Temple offered an elegant trophy to the winner of a series between the NL's first- and second-place finishers. For four years the Temple Cup games determined the world championship. In this first matchup, second-place New York swept the feisty pennant-winning Orioles.

Game One, in Baltimore, was a shutout through four innings as New York's Amos Rusie and Baltimore's Duke Esper held their opponents at bay. But Giant George Van Haltren tripled in the fifth inning and scored the game's first run on a fly to left. The Giants also scored single runs in the sixth, seventh, and eighth innings, while Rusie continued his shutout pitching through the eighth. In the ninth Oriole John McGraw singled, and he came around on a sacrifice, stolen base, and single to spoil the shutout. But the Oriole effort was too little to deprive Rusie of his win.

Some two hundred policemen patrolled the second game the next day to protect the umpires and New York's players and fans from the abusive Orioles and the crowd in the stands whom the Oriole players egged on. Baltimore scored first with two runs in the second and, after losing and regaining the lead, completed the eighth inning tied 5–5. But in the top of the ninth, the Giants put together their second four-run inning of the game. Once again the Orioles came up with a run in the last of the ninth, but once again came up short.

More than 22,000 spectators showed up for Game Three as the Series shifted to New York—a huge crowd for that era, even for a Saturday. As in Game One, the Giants' Amos Rusie hurled a 4–1 victory. New York broke a 1–1 tie with a run in the fifth on a throwing error and a ground out, and scored the game's final runs an inning later. Threatening weather held down attendance at Game Four to about 12,000. Baltimore jumped to a quick lead with two runs in the top of the first, but New York pitcher Jouett Meekin held the Orioles to just one run after that as the Giants piled up runs for a 16–3 advantage by the time darkness forced an end to play after eight innings. Meekin, in winning his second game of the Series, connected for three hits himself—half as many as he permitted the whole Oriole team.

New York Giants, 4;
Baltimore Orioles, 0

NY (N)

PLAYER/POS	AVG	G	AB	R	H	2B	3B	HR	RB	BB	SO	SB
Eddie Burke, of	.389	4	18	3	7	1	0	0	2	1	0	1
George Davis, 3b	.313	4	16	5	5	2	2	0	5	2	0	2
Jack Doyle, 1b	.588	4	17	4	10	1	1	0	6	1	1	6
Duke Farrell, c	.400	4	15	5	6	0	0	0	2	1	1	1
Shorty Fuller, ss	.286	4	14	4	4	0	0	0	2	2	0	1
Jouett Meekin, p	.556	2	9	2	5	0	0	0	3	0	1	0
Yale Murphy, of	.000	1	1	0	0	0	0	0	0	0	0	0
Amos Rusie, p	.429	2	7	1	3	1	0	0	1	0	1	0
Mike Tiernan, of	.294	4	17	5	5	0	1	0	3	2	2	0
George Van Haltren, of	.500	4	14	3	7	1	1	0	0	2	2	2
Monte Ward, 2b	.294	4	17	1	5	0	0	0	6	0	0	0
TOTAL	.393		145	33	57	6	5	0	30	11	8	13

PITCHER	W	L	ERA	G	GS	CG	SV	SHO	IP	H	ER	BB	SO
Jouett Meekin	2	0	1.59	2	2	2	0	0	17.0	13	3	8	6
Amos Rusie	2	0	0.50	2	2	2	0	0	18.0	14	1	3	9
TOTAL	4	0	1.03	4	4	4	0	0	35.0	27	4	11	15

BAL (N)

PLAYER/POS	AVG	G	AB	R	H	2B	3B	HR	RB	BB	SO	SB
Frank Bonner, ss-1,of-1	.000	2	5	0	0	0	0	0	0	0	2	0
Steve Brodie, of	.000	4	15	2	0	0	0	0	0	2	1	1
Dan Brouthers, 1b	.188	4	16	2	3	0	0	0	0	0	1	3
Duke Esper, p	.000	1	2	0	0	0	0	0	0	1	1	0
Kid Gleason, p	.200	2	5	0	1	0	1	0	1	0	1	0
Bill Hawke, p	.000	1	2	0	0	0	0	0	0	0	1	0
George Hemming, p	.000	1	3	0	0	0	0	0	0	1	1	0
Hughie Jennings, ss	.143	4	14	0	2	0	0	0	1	0	2	0
Willie Keeler, of	.250	3	12	1	3	0	0	0	1	1	0	0
Joe Kelley, of	.333	4	15	2	5	1	1	0	0	3	2	1
John McGraw, 3b	.250	4	16	2	4	0	0	0	2	0	0	1
Heinie Reitz, 2b	.333	4	15	1	5	0	0	0	4	1	3	1
Wilbert Robinson, c	.267	4	15	1	4	0	0	0	1	1	1	1
TOTAL	.200		135	11	27	1	2	0	10	11	15	8

PITCHER	W	L	ERA	G	GS	CG	SV	SHO	IP	H	ER	BB	SO
Duke Esper	0	1	4.00	1	1	1	0	0	9.0	13	4	1	3
Kid Gleason	0	1	9.69	2	1	1	0	0	13.0	25	14	6	3
Bill Hawke	0	1	9.00	1	1	0	0	0	4.0	9	4	1	0
George Hemming	0	1	1.13	1	1	1	0	0	8.0	10	1	3	2
TOTAL	0	4	6.09	5	4	3	0	0	34.0	57	23	11	8

GAME 1 AT BAL OCT 4

NY	000	011	110	4	13	2
BAL	000	000	001	1	7	1

Pitchers: RUSIE vs ESPER
Attendance: 9,000

GAME 2 AT BAL OCT 5

NY	004	000	014	9	14	3
BAL	022	000	101	6	7	2

Pitchers: MEEKIN vs GLEASON
Attendance: 11,000

GAME 3 AT NY OCT 6

BAL	000	100	000	1	7	4
NY	100	012	00X	4	10	4

Pitchers: HEMMING vs RUSIE
Attendance: 22,000

GAME 4 AT NY OCT 8

BAL	201	000	00	3	6	3
NY	101	351	50	16	20	4

Pitchers: HAWKE, Gleason (5) vs MEEKIN
Attendance: 12,000
(Game called at end of eighth, darkness)

Baltimore, repeating as NL pennant winner, returned to Temple Cup play against new runner-up Cleveland. The first 4½ innings of the opener—played in Cleveland—featured a scoreless duel between Baltimore veteran John "Sadie" McMahon and the Spiders' great Cy Young. After Cleveland scored the game's first run in the last of the fifth, the teams traded runs and the lead, completing the eighth inning tied 3–3. In the top of the ninth, doubles by Wilbert Robinson and John McGraw restored the edge to Baltimore. But in the bottom of the inning, four straight Spider hits pushed across the tying run and filled the bases. One runner was forced at home for the first out, but a grounder that just missed being a double-play ball drove in the winning Cleveland run.

The next three games were not so closely contested. A large and enthusiastic Cleveland crowd watched its Spiders jump on Baltimore for three runs in the bottom of the first inning of Game Two and coast to a 7–2 win behind the strong pitching of Nig Cuppy, who held the Orioles to five singles. Cleveland repeated itself in Game Three, again exploding for three runs in the bottom of the first on the way to a seven-run total. Cy Young was just as effective in the box as Cuppy had been, scattering four hits over seven shutout innings before Baltimore put together three singles in the eighth for their only run.

When the teams shifted to Baltimore for Game Four, the Orioles sprang to life. While their pitcher Duke Esper strangled the Spiders on just five singles—only two Cleveland runners advanced as far as second base—Oriole batters tagged Nig Cuppy for five runs and their first Temple Cup win in two years of trying.

It proved to be their only win of the Series. The next day, in the first close struggle since the opener, Cy Young and Baltimore's rookie ace Bill Hoffer dueled scorelessly through six innings. But in the top of the seventh, Young doubled to start what became a three-run rally, and an inning later the Spiders scored twice more. Baltimore scored a single run in the last of the seventh, and, with two out in the ninth, loaded the bases on two walks and a hit batsman. A Cleveland error brought in the Orioles' second run as the bases remained full for Steve Brodie. But despite the pleas of Baltimore partisans to hit a homer or triple, Brodie "failed miserably" and Cleveland copped the cup.

Cleveland Spiders, 4;
Baltimore Orioles, 1

CLE (N)

PLAYER/POS	AVG	G	AB	R	H	2B	3B	HR	RBI	BB	SO	SB
Harry Blake, of	.250	5	20	1	5	3	0	0	2	0	2	0
Jesse Burkett, of	.450	5	20	3	9	2	0	0	2	0	0	1
Cupid Childs, 2b	.190	5	21	4	4	1	0	0	2	1	0	1
Nig Cuppy, p	.167	2	6	1	1	1	0	0	1	0	0	0
Jimmy McAleer, of	.286	5	21	2	6	0	0	0	2	0	0	1
Chippy McGarr, 3b	.368	5	19	3	7	2	0	0	1	1	0	2
Ed McKean, ss	.300	5	20	2	6	1	1	0	4	3	0	1
Patsy Tebeau, 1b	.286	5	21	3	6	1	0	0	3	1	1	0
Cy Young, p	.250	3	12	3	3	1	0	0	1	0	1	0
Chief Zimmer, c	.333	4	18	2	6	2	0	0	3	3	4	0
TOTAL	.298		178	24	53	14	1	0	21	9	9*	6

PITCHER	W	L	ERA	G	GS	CG	SV	SHO	IP	H	ER	BB	SO
Nig Cuppy	1	1	3.18	2	2	2	0	0	17.0	14	6	4	6
Cy Young	3	0	2.33	3	3	3	0	0	27.0	28	7	4	2
TOTAL	4	1	2.66	5	5	5	0	0	44.0	42	13	8	8

BAL (N)

PLAYER/POS	AVG	G	AB	R	H	2B	3B	HR	RBI	BB	SO	SB
Steve Brodie, of	.200	5	20	1	4	0	0	0	2	0	0	0
Scoops Carey, 1b	.263	5	19	0	5	1	0	0	1	0	0	0
Boileryard Clarke, c	.286	2	7	1	2	0	0	0	0	0	0	2
Duke Esper, p	.000	1	3	0	0	0	0	0	0	1	2	0
Kid Gleason, 2b	.105	5	19	0	2	0	0	0	0	0	1	0
Bill Hoffer, p	.000	2	7	0	0	0	0	0	0	0	2	0
Hughie Jennings, ss	.368	5	19	3	7	2	0	0	2	1	0	1
Willie Keeler, of	.235	5	17	3	4	0	0	0	1	3	1	0
Joe Kelley, of	.368	5	19	1	7	0	0	0	5	1	1	1
John McGraw, 3b	.400	5	20	4	8	2	0	0	1	2	0	2
Sadie McMahon, p	.000	2	7	0	0	0	0	0	0	0	0	0
Wilbert Robinson, c	.250	3	12	1	3	1	0	0	0	0	1	0
TOTAL	.249		169	14	42	6	0	0	12	8	8	6

PITCHER	W	L	ERA	G	GS	CG	SV	SHO	IP	H	ER	BB	SO
Duke Esper	1	0	0.00	1	1	1	0	1	9.0	5	0	0	3
Bill Hoffer	0	2	4.24	2	2	2	0	0	17.0	21	8	6	4
Sadie McMahon	0	2	5.94	2	2	2	0	0	16.2	27	11	3	2
TOTAL	1	4	4.01	5	5	5	0	1	42.2	53	19	9	9

* While the total strikeouts for the team have been confirmed as 9, research has failed, to this point, to identify the missing batter strikeout.

Baltimore captured its third consecutive pennant and for the second year in a row faced runner-up Cleveland in the Temple Cup games. But this time the Orioles emerged triumphant—with a sweep in which their margin of victory was never less than four runs.

Aces Bill Hoffer of Baltimore and the Spiders' Cy Young faced each other in the opener, in Baltimore. Hoffer walked four men, but gave up only five hits while the Orioles bombarded Young for thirteen. When the game ended, Hoffer and Baltimore had a 7–1 win.

Bobby Wallace (who had not yet discovered his role at shortstop that would propel him into the Hall of Fame) pitched for Cleveland in Game Two. He lost the game in the first inning when two Spider errors, a hit batsman, three hits, and a steal of home put four Baltimore runs on the board. The Orioles added two runs in the third and another in the fifth, while their promising twenty-year-old pitcher Joe Corbett held the Spiders to two runs on seven hits.

The Orioles' Hoffer gave up ten hits to Cleveland in Game Three —two more than the Birds made off Spider Nig Cuppy. But all the hits off Hoffer were singles, and he walked only one. Half of Cleveland's hits went toward producing just two runs. Their second run tied the score in the fifth inning, but in the sixth Baltimore regained the lead as John McGraw singled, stole second, took third on an error, and came home on an outfield fly. In the eighth the Orioles bunched four of their eight hits for three insurance runs.

The Series moved to Cleveland for the fourth game. Young Joe Corbett was again sent into the box for Baltimore, this time to face Nig Cuppy. For six innings the game was a scoreless duel. Baltimore hit safely in every inning but the second, but failed to score until the seventh, when Joe Kelley's double and Jack Doyle's single scored the only run they would need. But the Orioles added a second run in that inning and three more in the eighth. Two of the four Cleveland hits against Corbett put men on base in the eighth inning, and Corbett walked two in the ninth to raise Cleveland's hopes. But no Spider scored, and with the 5–0 win the Orioles were world champions at last.

Baltimore Orioles, 4;
Cleveland Spiders, 0

BAL (N)

PLAYER/POS	AVG	G	AB	R	H	2B	3B	HR	RB	BB	SO	SB
Steve Brodie, of	.067	4	15	1	1	0	0	0	3	0	0	1
Joe Corbett, p	.500	2	6	1	3	1	0	0	0	1	1	0
Jack Doyle, 1b	.294	4	17	3	5	1	0	0	4	0	0	2
Bill Hoffer, p	.286	2	7	1	2	0	2	0	0	0	1	0
Hughie Jennings, ss	.333	4	15	5	5	2	0	0	3	1	2	1
Willie Keeler, of	.471	4	17	4	8	1	2	0	4	0	0	1
Joe Kelley, of	.471	4	17	3	8	1	0	0	4	0	1	2
John McGraw, 3b	.267	4	15	4	4	0	0	0	1	0	0	4
Joe Quinn, 3b	.000	1	3	1	0	0	0	0	0	0	0	0
Heinie Reitz, 2b	.133	4	15	1	2	0	0	0	2	1	0	0
Wilbert Robinson, c	.267	4	15	1	4	1	0	0	2	0	3	0
TOTAL	.296		142	25	42	7	4	0	23	3	8	11

PITCHER	W	L	ERA	G	GS	CG	SV	SHO	IP	H	ER	BB	SO
Joe Corbett	2	0	0.50	2	2	2	0	1	18.0	11	1	7	10
Bill Hoffer	2	0	1.50	2	2	2	0	0	18.0	15	3	5	10
TOTAL	4	0	1.00	4	4	4	0	1	36.0	26	4	12	20

CLE (N)

PLAYER/POS	AVG	G	AB	R	H	2B	3B	HR	RB	BB	SO	SB
Harry Blake, of	.071	4	14	1	1	0	0	0	0	1	1	1
Jesse Burkett, of	.333	4	15	1	5	0	0	0	0	2	3	0
Cupid Childs, 2b	.231	4	13	2	3	0	0	0	0	4	0	1
Nig Cuppy, p	.143	2	7	0	1	0	0	0	0	0	1	0
Jimmy McAleer, of	.133	4	15	0	2	0	0	0	1	1	2	1
Chippy McGarr, 3b	.063	4	16	0	1	0	0	0	0	0	3	2
Ed McKean, ss	.313	4	16	0	5	1	1	0	1	1	2	1
Jack O'Connor, 1b	.286	4	14	1	4	0	0	0	1	1	2	0
Patsy Tebeau, 1b	.000	1	1	0	0	0	0	0	0	0	0	0
Bobby Wallace, p-1	.200	3	5	0	1	0	0	0	0	0	0	0
Cy Young, p	.000	1	3	0	0	0	0	0	0	0	0	0
Chief Zimmer, c	.214	4	14	0	3	1	0	0	1	2	6	0
TOTAL	.195		133	5	26	2	1	0	4	12	20	6

PITCHER	W	L	ERA	G	GS	CG	SV	SHO	IP	H	ER	BB	SO
Nig Cuppy	0	2	4.76	2	2	2	0	0	17.0	19	9	0	4
Bobby Wallace	0	1	4.50	1	1	1	0	0	8.0	10	4	2	4
Cy Young	0	1	6.00	1	1	1	0	0	9.0	13	6	1	0
TOTAL	0	4	5.03	4	4	4	0	0	34.0	42	19	3	8

GAME 1 AT BAL OCT 2

BAL	002 001 310	7 13 1
CLE	000 000 001 000	1 5 4

Pitchers: HOFFER vs YOUNG
Attendance: 4,000

GAME 2 AT BAL OCT 3

BAL	402 010 00	7 10 3
CLE	001 001 00	2 7 3

Pitchers: CORBETT vs WALLACE
Attendance: 3,100
(Game called at end of eighth, darkness)

GAME 3 AT BAL OCT 5

BAL	011 001 030	6 8 2
CLE	001 010 000	2 10 2

Pitchers: HOFFER vs CUPPY
Attendance: 2,000

GAME 4 AT CLE OCT 8

CLE	000 000 000	0 4 2
BAL	000 000 23X	5 11 1

Pitchers: CUPPY vs CORBETT
Attendance: 1,500

Boston had edged Baltimore in a close race for the NL pennant, but the Orioles turned the tables on the Beaneaters in Temple Cup play. The Series was a high-scoring affair, the winner of each game averaging eleven runs, the loser eight.

The opener, in Boston, set the tone for the games. Baltimore sent four runners across the plate in the top of the first inning, and Boston followed in its half with three. The Beaneaters recorded only twelve hits in the game to the Orioles' twenty, but they also received seven walks from Baltimore hurler Jerry Nops, and five of those runners scored. The lead switched back and forth in the middle innings, but Boston scored two final runs in the eighth and hung on for a 13–12 win.

Baltimore's Joe Corbett gave up sixteen hits (one a home run) and four walks in Game Two as Boston scored eleven times. But Boston's two pitchers, Fred Klobedanz and Jack Stivetts, were even more generous, handing out seventeen hits (including three homers—one of them to opposing pitcher Corbett, who also hit a double and two singles) and five walks as the Orioles evened the Series with their thirteen-run attack.

Game Three was the Series' lowest in run production, with Baltimore scoring four in the second inning and another four in the third for an 8–3 win. But rain ended the game before Boston could complete its time at bat in the last of the eighth, which erased from the record four more Oriole runs scored earlier in the inning. Rather than waste the two free days before the Series resumed in Baltimore, the two clubs played a pair of exhibition games in Worcester and Springfield, Massachusetts. Baltimore won them both, 11–10 and 8–6.

The Orioles continued their roll in Series Game Four, with another close but high-scoring victory, 12–11. It looked at first like a blowout as Baltimore scored six runs in the first inning and five more in the second. But Ted Lewis relieved Boston starter Jack Stivetts and held Baltimore to just one further run as the Beaneaters fought back to within one run of a tie before faltering in the ninth.

Boston batters hit Oriole Bill Hoffer safely fifteen times in Game Five, but only three Beaneaters scored. Baltimore, with two fewer hits, garnered six more runs than Boston and, with their fourth win, the right to hold the cup for another year. But at-

tendance at the final game was so small the embarrassed Baltimore management refused to release the figures, and the league gave the cup back to Mr. Temple rather than sponsor another unprofitable Series. There was no postseason championship contest in 1898 or 1899.

Baltimore Orioles, 4; Boston Beaneaters, 1

BAL (N)

PLAYER/POS	AVG	G	AB	R	H	2B	3B	HR	RBI	BB	SO	SB
Frank Bowerman, c-1,1b-1	.500	2	8	2	4	0	1	0	4	0	0	0
Boileryard Clarke, c	.563	4	16	5	9	1	1	1	4	1	0	0
Joe Corbett, p	.667	2	6	2	4	1	0	1	2	0	1	0
Jack Doyle, 1b	.526	5	19	7	10	2	0	0	9	0	1	2
Bill Hoffer, p	.250	2	8	2	2	1	0	0	0	0	0	0
Hughie Jennings, ss	.318	5	22	5	7	2	0	0	3	4	0	0
Willie Keeler, of	.391	5	23	5	9	2	0	0	2	4	0	0
Joe Kelley, of	.313	4	16	7	5	3	0	0	5	5	0	0
John McGraw, 3b	.300	5	20	6	6	1	1	0	6	7	0	0
Jerry Nops, p	.286	2	7	0	2	0	0	0	1	1	5	0
Tom O'Brien, of	.400	1	5	2	2	1	0	0	0	0	0	0
Heinie Reitz, 2b	.250	5	20	4	5	1	0	1	4	2	0	0
Jake Stenzel, of	.381	5	21	7	8	1	1	0	3	2	0	2
TOTAL	.382		191	54	73	16	4	3	43	26	7	4

PITCHER	W	L	ERA	G	GS	CG	SV	SHO	IP	H	ER	BB	SO
Joe Corbett	1	0	9.00	2	1	1	0	0	12.0	21	12	8	5
Bill Hoffer	2	0	3.38	2	2	2	0	0	16.0	25	6	4	2
Jerry Nops	1	1	12.86	2	2	1	0	0	14.0	23	20	9	3
TOTAL	4	1	8.14	6	5	4	0	0	42.0	69	38	21	10

BOS (N)

PLAYER/POS	AVG	G	AB	R	H	2B	3B	HR	RBI	BB	SO	SB
Marty Bergen, c	.500	1	4	0	2	0	0	0	1	0	1	1
Jimmy Collins, 3b	.182	5	22	2	4	0	0	0	4	1	0	0
Hugh Duffy, of	.524	5	21	6	11	1	0	0	7	1	0	0
Billy Hamilton, of	.500	4	16	6	8	1	0	0	2	5	3	2
Charlie Hickman, p-1,of-1	.250	1	4	0	1	1	0	0	1	0	0	0
Fred Klobedanz, p	1.000	2	5	3	5	0	0	0	0	0	0	0
Fred Lake, c	.000	1	4	0	0	0	0	0	0	1	0	0
Ted Lewis, p	.500	3	6	1	3	1	0	0	1	1	0	0
Herman Long, ss	.286	5	21	4	6	1	1	1	5	2	2	1
Bobby Lowe, 2b	.391	5	23	6	9	2	0	0	6	1	0	1
Kid Nichols, p	.000	1	3	0	0	0	0	0	1	0	0	0
Chick Stahl, of	.400	5	20	6	8	1	0	0	6	3	2	2
Jack Stivetts, p-2,of-1	.000	3	7	1	0	0	0	0	0	1	0	1
Jim Sullivan, p	.000	1	1	0	0	0	0	0	0	0	0	0
Fred Tenney, 1b	.300	5	20	4	6	0	0	0	2	4	1	2
George Yeager, c	.500	3	12	2	6	1	1	0	2	2	0	0
TOTAL	.365		189	41	69	9	2	1	38	21	10	10

PITCHER	W	L	ERA	G	GS	CG	SV	SHO	IP	H	ER	BB	SO
Charlie Hickman	0	1	3.60	1	1	0	0	0	5.0	7	2	2	0
Fred Klobedanz	0	1	9.35	2	1	0	0	0	8.2	12	9	8	0
Ted Lewis	1	1	6.17	3	1	0	0	0	11.2	18	8	9	4
Kid Nichols	0	0	12.00	1	1	0	0	0	6.0	14	8	0	3
Jack Stivetts	0	1	17.55	2	1	0	0	0	6.2	16	13	7	0
Jim Sullivan	0	0	3.00	1	0	0	0	0	3.0	6	1	0	0
TOTAL	1	4	9.00	10	5	0	0	0	41.0	73	41	26	7

GAME 1 AT BOS OCT 4

BAL	401 023 200	12	20	4
BOS	300 125 02X	13	12	4

Pitchers: NOPS vs Nichols, LEWIS (7)
Attendance: 9,600

GAME 2 AT BOS OCT 5

BAL	130 160 110	13	17	2
BOS	002 620 100	11	16	3

Pitchers: CORBETT vs KLOBEDANZ, Stivetts (5)
Home Runs: Reitz-BAL, Clarke-BAL, Corbett-BAL, Long-BOS
Attendance: 6,500

GAME 3 AT BOS OCT 6

BAL	044 000 0	8	9	2
BOS	003 000 0	3	10	2

Pitchers: HOFFER vs LEWIS, Klobedanz (4)
Attendance: 5,000
(Game called in eighth, rain)

GAME 4 AT BAL OCT 9

BOS	000 024 320	11	16	3
BAL	650 001 00X	12	14	3

Pitchers: STIVETTS, Lewis (3) vs NOPS, Corbett (7)
Attendance: 2,500

GAME 5 AT BAL OCT 11

BOS	020 000 001	3	15	3
BAL	023 000 22X	9	13	2

Pitchers: HICKMAN, Sullivan (7) vs HOFFER
Attendance: 700

Pennant-winning Brooklyn led the NL in hitting, but runner-up Pittsburgh claimed the best pitching. Honus Wagner was the only Pirate regular to hit over .300, but he enjoyed what turned out to be his finest season offensively, leading the league with a .381 batting average. Pittsburghers believed their club superior to Brooklyn and a best-of-five "world championship" series was arranged, with all the games to be played in Pittsburgh for a silver cup donated by the *Pittsburgh Chronicle-Telegraph*. Brooklyn, however, proved that its pennant was no fluke.

Two of the game's best pitchers faced off in the opener: Pittsburgh's Rube Waddell, who had led the league in ERA, and Joe "Iron Man" McGinnity, whose 29 regular-season wins totaled nine more than those of the league's runners-up. McGinnity prevailed, shutting out the Pirates until two unearned runs came across in the top of the ninth. Pirate errors also gave Brooklyn a pair of unearned runs, but Waddell lost the game on hits—thirteen in all, including six in the Superbas' three-run third inning.

In Game Two, Brooklyn's Frank Kitson held Pittsburgh to four hits, and although his Superbas scored only one earned run, six Pirate errors gave them their second win, 4–2.

The Pirates staved off a Series sweep with sharp pitching and heavy hitting in Game Three. Deacon Phillippe shut out Brooklyn on six hits as the Pirates jumped on Harry Howell for thirteen. All the Pirate hits were singles, but combined with Brooklyn errors they were good for ten runs, seven of them unearned.

Three Brooklyn singles and a fumble by Pirate pitcher Sam Leever in the fourth inning of Game Four gave the Superbas three runs and a 4–0 lead the Pirates could not overcome. Brooklyn hurler McGinnity scattered nine Pirate hits and, supported by flawless fielding, held Pittsburgh to a single run to bring Brooklyn its first World Series triumph in three tries—and its last until 1955. The Brooklyn players voted to award their trophy to McGinnity for his fine pitching. The cup may be seen today—along with the Temple Cup and the current World Series trophy—at baseball's Hall of Fame in Cooperstown.

Brooklyn Superbas, 3; Pittsburgh Pirates, 1

BRO (N)

PLAYER/POS	AVG	G	AB	R	H	2B	3B	HR	RB	BB	SO	SB
Lave Cross, 3b	.278	4	18	2	5	0	1	0	1	0	0	1
Bill Dahlen, ss	.176	4	17	3	3	0	1	0	2	0	3	1
Tom Daly, 2b	.154	4	13	2	2	1	0	0	1	3	1	0
Duke Farrell, c	.375	2	8	0	3	0	0	0	1	0	0	1
Harry Howell, p	.000	1	3	0	0	0	0	0	0	0	2	0
Hughie Jennings, 1b	.167	4	18	1	3	1	0	0	2	1	1	0
Fielder Jones, of	.278	4	18	3	5	0	0	0	4	1	1	1
Willie Keeler, of	.353	4	17	0	6	0	0	0	0	1	0	0
Joe Kelley, of	.176	4	17	2	3	0	0	0	1	2	3	0
Frank Kitson, p	.000	1	3	0	0	0	0	0	0	1	2	0
Joe McGinnity, p	.143	2	7	1	1	0	0	0	1	0	2	0
Deacon McGuire, c	.375	2	8	1	3	1	0	0	0	0	1	0
TOTAL	.231		147	15	34	3	2	0	13	9	16	4

PITCHER	W	L	ERA	G	GS	CG	SV	SHO	IP	H	ER	BB	SO
Harry Howell	0	1	3.38	1	1	1	0	0	8.0	13	3	2	3
rrank Kitson	1	0	1.00	1	1	1	0	0	9.0	4	1	1	2
Joe McGinnity	2	0	0.00	2	2	2	0	0	18.0	14	0	3	5
TOTAL	3	1	1.03	4	4	4	0	0	35.0	31	4	6	10

PIT (N)

PLAYER/POS	AVG	G	AB	R	H	2B	3B	HR	RB	BB	SO	SB
Ginger Beaumont, of	.267	4	15	2	4	0	0	0	1	1	0	1
Fred Ely, ss	.286	4	14	1	4	1	0	0	0	1	1	2
Tommy Leach, of	.176	4	17	4	3	0	0	0	1	1	2	0
Sam Leever, p	.250	2	4	0	1	0	0	0	0	0	1	1
Tom O'Brien, 1b	.125	4	16	1	2	1	0	0	2	0	1	0
Jack O'Connor, c	.250	2	4	0	1	0	0	0	1	1	0	0
Deacon Phillippe, p	.000	1	4	1	0	0	0	0	0	0	1	0
Claude Ritchey, 2b	.333	4	15	3	5	1	0	0	1	1	0	0
Pop Schriver, ph	.000	1	1	0	0	0	0	0	0	0	0	0
Rube Waddell, p	.200	2	5	0	1	0	0	0	0	0	1	0
Honus Wagner, of	.400	4	15	2	6	1	0	0	3	0	1	2
Jimmy Williams, 3b	.214	4	14	0	3	0	0	0	0	1	0	0
Chief Zimmer, c	.111	3	9	1	1	0	0	0	1	0	2	1
TOTAL	.233		133	15	31	4	0	0	10	6	10	7

PITCHER	W	L	ERA	G	GS	CG	SV	SHO	IP	H	ER	BB	SO
Sam Leever	0	2	1.38	2	2	1	0	0	13.0	13	2	4	4
Deacon Phillippe	1	0	0.00	1	1	1	0	1	9.0	6	0	2	5
Rube Waddell	0	1	1.93	2	1	1	0	0	14.0	15	3	3	7
TOTAL	1	3	1.25	5	4	3	0	1	36.0	34	5	9	16

GAME 1 AT PIT OCT 15

BRO	003	101	000	5	13	1
PIT	000	000	002	2	5	4

Pitchers: McGINNITY vs WADDELL
Attendance: 4,000

GAME 2 AT PIT OCT 16

BRO	010	003	000	4	7	0
PIT	000	100	100	2	4	6

Pitchers: KITSON vs LEEVER
Attendance: 1,800

GAME 3 AT PIT OCT 17

BRO	000	000	000	0	6	3
PIT	310	020	13X	10	13	1

Pitchers: HOWELL vs PHILLIPPE
Attendance: 2,500

GAME 4 AT PIT OCT 18

BRO	100	311	000	6	8	0
PIT	000	001	000	1	9	3

Pitchers: McGINNITY vs LEEVER, Waddell (6)
Attendance: 2,335

When the Boston Pilgrims of the young American League accepted a challenge from owner Barney Dreyfuss of the National League Pirates, the modern World Series was born. (In 1901–02, the National and American Leagues were warring, and did not stage a postseason series.) Pittsburgh was favored to win but entered the Series weakened by injuries to pitching ace Sam Leever and shortstop Honus Wagner, and by the loss of pitcher Ed Doheny to mental illness.

Deacon Phillippe, the Pirates' one healthy starter, faced Cy Young in the opener, winning handily as Pirate batters, with two out in the top of the first, jumped on Young (and a porous defense) for four runs. Right fielder Jimmy Sebring starred offensively for the Pirates, with four RBIs and the Series's first home run. Boston came back in Game Two as Bill Dinneen shut out the Pirates on three hits. His teammates scored three runs off the sore-armed Leever and reliever Bucky Veil, two coming on homers by Patsy Dougherty. (They were the last World Series home runs for five years.)

Phillippe, with only a day's rest, started Game Three and again pitched Pittsburgh into the Series lead, holding Boston to four hits. After a Sunday travel day to Pittsburgh and a day of rain, Phillippe defeated Boston a third time, though he yielded three ninth-inning runs before emerging with a 5–4 win.

The tide began to turn against the Pirates the next day, as Boston knocked five ground-rule triples into the overflow crowd, scoring ten runs in the sixth and seventh innings to give Young an 11–2 victory. Dinneen bested Leever for a second time in Game Six, holding the Pirates scoreless in eight of their nine innings for a 6–3 win. And in Game Seven, Phillippe finally lost, Young winning his second game as Boston numbered 5 more triples among its 11 hits.

After another travel Sunday and another rainout, Phillippe for the fifth time faced the Pilgrims. He pitched well, giving up three runs (only two of them earned). But Bill Dinneen pitched better, holding the Pirates to four hits as he shut them out for the second time to give Boston the Series.

Boston Pilgrims (AL), 5;
Pittsburgh Pirates (NL), 3

BOS (A)

PLAYER/POS	AVG	G	AB	R	H	2B	3B	HR	RB	BB	SO	SB
Jimmy Collins, 3b	.250	8	36	5	9	1	2	0	1	1	1	3
Lou Criger, c	.231	8	26	1	6	0	0	0	4	2	3	0
Bill Dinneen, p	.250	4	12	1	3	0	0	0	0	2	2	0
Patsy Dougherty, of	.235	8	34	3	8	0	2	2	5	2	6	0
Duke Farrell, ph	.000	2	2	0	0	0	0	0	1	0	0	0
Hobe Ferris, 2b	.290	8	31	3	9	0	1	0	5	0	6	0
Buck Freeman, of	.281	8	32	6	9	0	3	0	4	2	2	0
Tom Hughes, p	.000	1	0	0	0	0	0	0	0	0	0	0
Candy La Chance, 1b	.222	8	27	5	6	2	1	0	4	3	2	0
Jack O'Brien, ph	.000	2	2	0	0	0	0	0	0	0	1	0
Freddy Parent, ss	.281	8	32	8	9	0	3	0	4	1	1	0
Chick Stahl, of	.303	8	33	6	10	1	3	0	3	1	2	2
Cy Young, p	.133	4	15	1	2	0	1	0	3	0	3	0
TOTAL	.252		282	39	71	4	16	2	34	14	29	5

PITCHER	W	L	ERA	G	GS	CG	SV	SHO	IP	H	ER	BB	SO
Bill Dinneen	3	1	2.06	4	4	4	0	2	35.0	29	8	8	28
Tom Hughes	0	1	9.00	1	1	0	0	0	2.0	4	2	2	0
Cy Young	2	1	1.85	4	3	3	0	0	34.0	31	7	4	17
TOTAL	5	3	2.15	9	8	7	0	2	71.0	64	17	14	45

PIT (N)

PLAYER/POS	AVG	G	AB	R	H	2B	3B	HR	RB	BB	SO	SB
Ginger Beaumont, of	.265	8	34	6	9	0	1	0	1	2	4	2
Kitty Bransfield, 1b	.207	8	29	3	6	0	2	0	1	1	6	1
Fred Clarke, of	.265	8	34	3	9	2	1	0	2	1	5	1
Brickyard Kennedy, p	.500	1	2	0	1	1	0	0	0	0	0	0
Tommy Leach, 3b	.273	8	33	3	9	0	4	0	7	1	4	1
Sam Leever, p	.000	2	4	0	0	0	0	0	0	0	0	0
Ed Phelps, c-7	.231	8	26	1	6	2	0	0	1	1	6	0
Deacon Phillippe, p	.222	5	18	1	4	0	0	0	1	0	3	0
Claude Ritchey, 2b	.111	8	27	2	3	1	0	0	2	4	7	1
Jimmy Sebring, of	.367	8	30	3	11	0	1	1	3	1	4	0
Harry Smith, c	.000	1	3	0	0	0	0	0	0	0	0	0
Gus Thompson, p	.000	1	1	0	0	0	0	0	0	0	0	0
Bucky Veil, p	.000	1	2	0	0	0	0	0	0	0	2	0
Honus Wagner, ss	.222	8	27	2	6	1	0	0	3	3	4	3
TOTAL	.237		270	24	64	7	9	1	21	14	45	9

PITCHER	W	L	ERA	G	GS	CG	SV	SHO	IP	H	ER	BB	SO
Brickyard Kennedy	0	1	5.14	1	1	0	0	0	7.0	11	4	3	3
Sam Leever	0	2	5.40	2	2	1	0	0	10.0	13	6	3	2
Deacon Phillippe	3	2	2.86	5	5	5	0	0	44.0	38	14	3	22
Gus Thompson	0	0	4.50	1	0	0	0	0	2.0	3	1	0	1
Bucky Veil	0	0	1.29	1	0	0	0	0	7.0	6	1	5	1
TOTAL	3	5	3.34	10	8	6	0	0	70.0	71	26	14	29

GAME 1 AT BOS OCT 1

PIT	401	100	100	7	12	2
BOS	000	000	000	3	6	4

Pitchers: PHILLIPPE vs YOUNG
Home Runs: Sebring-PIT
Attendance: 16,242

GAME 2 AT BOS OCT 2

PIT	000	000	000	0	3	2
BOS	200	001	00X	3	9	0

Pitchers: LEEVER, Vail (2) vs DINNEEN
Home Runs: Dougherty-BOS(2)
Attendance: 9,415

GAME 3 AT BOS OCT 3

PIT	012	000	010	4	7	0
BOS	000	100	010	2	4	2

Pitchers: PHILLIPPE vs HUGHES, Young (3)
Attendance: 18,801

GAME 4 AT PIT OCT 6

BOS	000	010	003	4	9	1
PIT	100	010	30X	5	12	1

Pitchers: DINNEEN vs PHILLIPPE
Attendance: 7,600

GAME 5 AT PIT OCT 7

BOS	000	006	410	11	14	2
PIT	000	000	020	2	6	4

Pitchers: YOUNG vs KENNEDY, Thompson (8)
Attendance: 12,322

GAME 6 AT PIT OCT 8

BOS	003	020	100	6	10	1
PIT	000	000	300	3	10	3

Pitchers: DINNEEN vs LEEVER
Attendance: 11,556

GAME 7 AT PIT OCT 10

BOS	200	202	010	7	11	4
PIT	000	101	001	3	10	3

Pitchers: YOUNG vs PHILLIPPE
Attendance: 17,038

GAME 8 AT BOS OCT 13

PIT	000	000	000	0	4	3
BOS	000	201	00X	3	8	0

Pitchers: PHILLIPPE vs DINNEEN
Attendance: 7,455

After a year's gap caused by the Giants' refusal to play the American League champion Boston Pilgrims, the World Series—now established on an official and permanent basis—resumed with a pitching classic. Even though the A's ERA league leader Rube Waddell had ostensibly injured his shoulder and could not pitch in the Series—rumor had it that gamblers had reached him—the Philadelphia staff recorded a Series ERA of only 1.47. But the Giants' staff—led by Christy Mathewson's three shutouts—registered a matchless ERA of 0.00, permitting only three unearned runs to score in their only Series loss. Every victory in the Series was a shutout.

Mathewson, a 31-game winner in the regular season, continued his winning ways in the Series opener. Though three of the four hits he yielded were doubles, he permitted no more than one hit in any inning, and stopped the only scoring threat, fielding a squeeze bunt to throw out the runner at the plate in the sixth inning.

The A's came back to tie the Series the next day. This time it was Chief Bender's turn to hurl a four-hit shutout. Joe McGinnity also pitched well for the Giants, but New York errors in the third and eighth innings let in three unearned runs—the only runs, as it turned out, to be scored against the Giants in the Series.

Mathewson, pitching with only two days' rest in Game Three, once again permitted only four hits (all singles this time), and Philadelphia's flawed fielding let in seven unearned runs to help give Matty an easy 9–0 win. In Game Four, McGinnity, the hard-luck loser of Game Two, tried again. This time the Giants supported him almost flawlessly, while he gave up only five singles on his way to victory in the Series' tightest game. An A's error led to a single Giant run, and a loss for Eddie Plank, who had pitched even better than McGinnity, giving up only four hits while fanning six.

Chief Bender, the A's winner in Game Two, pitched a five-hitter in Game Six, but he also yielded three walks, all of which contributed to the two Giant runs. Mathewson, though he gave up six hits, walked none, retiring the final ten batters to conclude his record third shutout—and the Series.

New York Giants (NL), 4; Philadelphia Athletics (AL), 1

NY (N)

PLAYER/POS	AVG	G	AB	R	H	2B	3B	HR	RB	BB	SO	SB
Red Ames, p	.000	1	0	0	0	0	0	0	0	0	0	0
Roger Bresnahan, c	.313	5	16	3	5	2	0	0	1	4	0	1
George Browne, of	.182	5	22	2	4	0	0	0	1	0	2	2
Bill Dahlen, ss	.000	5	15	1	0	0	0	0	1	3	2	3
Art Devlin, 3b	.250	5	16	0	4	1	0	0	1	1	3	3
Mike Donlin, of	.263	5	19	4	5	1	0	0	1	2	1	2
Billy Gilbert, 2b	.235	5	17	1	4	0	0	0	2	0	2	1
Christy Mathewson, p	.250	3	8	1	2	0	0	0	0	1	1	0
Dan Mc Gann, 1b	.235	5	17	1	4	2	0	0	4	2	7	0
Joe Mc Ginnity, p	.000	2	5	0	0	0	0	0	0	0	2	0
Sam Mertes, of	.176	5	17	2	3	1	0	0	2	2	5	0
Sammy Strang, ph	.000	1	1	0	0	0	0	0	0	0	1	0
TOTAL	.203		153	15	31	7	0	0	13	15	26	12

PITCHER	W	L	ERA	G	GS	CG	SV	SHO	IP	H	ER	BB	SO
Red Ames	0	0	0.00	1	0	0	0	0	1.0	1	0	1	1
Christy Mathewson	3	0	0.00	3	3	3	0	3	27.0	14	0	1	18
Joe Mc Ginnity	1	1	0.00	2	2	1	0	1	17.0	10	0	3	6
TOTAL	4	1	0.00	6	5	4	0	4	45.0	25	0	5	25

PHI (A)

PLAYER/POS	AVG	G	AB	R	H	2B	3B	HR	RB	BB	SO	SB
Chief Bender, p	.000	2	5	0	0	0	0	0	0	0	1	0
Andy Coakley, p	.000	1	2	0	0	0	0	0	0	0	0	0
Lave Cross, 3b	.105	5	19	0	2	0	0	0	0	1	1	0
Monte Cross, ss	.176	5	17	0	3	0	0	0	0	0	7	0
Harry Davis, 1b	.200	5	20	0	4	1	0	0	0	0	1	0
Topsy Hartsel, of	.294	5	17	1	5	1	0	0	0	2	1	2
Danny Hoffman, ph	.000	1	1	0	0	0	0	0	0	0	1	0
Bris Lord, of	.100	5	20	0	2	0	0	0	2	0	5	0
Danny Murphy, 2b	.188	5	16	0	3	1	0	0	0	0	2	0
Eddie Plank, p	.167	2	6	0	1	0	0	0	0	0	2	0
Mike Powers, c	.143	3	7	0	1	1	0	0	0	0	0	0
Ossee Schreckengost, c	.222	3	9	2	2	1	0	0	0	0	0	0
Socks Seybold, of	.125	5	16	0	2	0	0	0	0	2	3	0
TOTAL	.161		155	3	25	5	0	0	2	5	25	2

PITCHER	W	L	ERA	G	GS	CG	SV	SHO	IP	H	ER	BB	SO
Chief Bender	1	1	1.06	2	2	2	0	1	17.0	9	2	6	13
Andy Coakley	0	1	2.00	1	1	1	0	0	9.0	8	2	5	2
Eddie Plank	0	2	1.59	2	2	2	0	0	17.0	14	3	4	11
TOTAL	1	4	1.47	5	5	5	0	1	43.0	31	7	15	26

GAME 1 AT PHI OCT 9

NY	000 020 001	3	10	1
PHI	000 000 000	0	4	0

Pitchers: MATHEWSON vs PLANK
Attendance: 17,955

GAME 2 AT NY OCT 10

PHI	001 000 020	3	6	2
NY	000 000 000	0	4	2

Pitchers: BENDER vs McGINNITY, Ames (9)
Attendance: 24,992

GAME 3 AT PHI OCT 12

NY	200 050 002	9	9	1
PHI	000 000 000	0	4	5

Pitchers: MATHEWSON vs COAKLEY
Attendance: 10,991

GAME 4 AT NY OCT 13

PHI	000 000 000	0	5	2
NY	000 100 00X	1	4	1

Pitchers: PLANK vs McGINNITY
Attendance: 13,598

GAME 5 AT NY OCT 14

PHI	000 000 000	0	6	0
NY	000 010 01X	2	5	1

Pitchers: BENDER vs MATHEWSON
Attendance: 24,187

The Cubs and White Sox have played more postseason City Series than any other clubs, but this was their only all-Chicago World Series. The Cubs were the clear favorites: league leaders in batting, fielding, and pitching (with a team ERA of only 1.76). They were one of baseball's greatest teams ever, with a still-record 116 wins, finishing 20 games ahead of the second-place Giants. The White Sox, by contrast, although their pitching and fielding were good enough to rank second in the American League, were the junior circuit's weakest hitters, batting as a team only .230, 32 points below the Cubs. But in the Series the "hitless wonders" prevailed. Though they hit only .198 and yielded eight unearned runs to the Cubs' two, the Sox bunched their hits for 20 earned runs—double the Cubs' total. Meanwhile, Sox pitchers held the Cubs to a .196 BA, and produced a team ERA less than half that of Cub pitchers.

Game One was a pitcher's duel as the Cubs' Mordecai (Three Finger) Brown and the Sox' Nick Altrock traded four-hitters and one earned run apiece. But Brown lost the game when his error in the seventh led to the Sox' second run. The Cubs snapped back to take Game Two on Ed Reulbach's one-hit 7–1 win. Although Reulbach issued six walks, he didn't really need the five unearned runs handed his club by Sox errors.

In Game Three the Sox regained the Series lead as Ed Walsh two-hit the Cubs, fanning 12 for the Series' first shutout. The Cubs' Jack Pfiester also pitched shutout ball in eight of his nine innings, but George Rohe's bases-loaded triple in the sixth gave the Sox more than enough to defeat him. Brown brought the Cubs back the next day, evening the Series with a two-hit shutout of his own, winning when Altrock yielded his only run on pairs of singles and sacrifice bunts in the seventh.

The rest of the Series belonged to the hitless wonders, who rocked three Cub pitchers for 12 hits and eight runs to take Game Five, and buried Brown and Orval Overall under 14 hits and another eight runs in Game Six to capture their first world championship.

Chicago White Sox (AL), 4; Chicago Cubs (NL), 2

CHI (A)

PLAYER/POS	AVG	G	AB	R	H	2B	3B	HR	RB	BB	SO	SB
Nick Altrock, p	.250	2	4	0	1	0	0	0	0	1	1	0
George Davis, ss	.308	3	13	4	4	3	0	0	6	0	1	1
Jiggs Donahue, 1b	.333	6	18	0	6	2	1	0	4	3	3	0
Patsy Dougherty, of	.100	6	20	1	2	0	0	0	1	3	4	2
Eddie Hahn, of	.273	6	22	4	6	0	0	0	0	1	1	0
Frank Isbell, 2b	.308	6	26	4	8	4	0	0	4	0	6	1
Fielder Jones, of	.095	6	21	4	2	0	0	0	0	3	3	0
Ed Mc Farland, ph	.000	1	1	0	0	0	0	0	0	0	0	0
Bill O'Neill, of	.000	1	1	1	0	0	0	0	0	0	0	0
Frank Owen, p	.000	2	0	0	0	0	0	0	0	0	1	0
George Rohe, 3b	.333	6	21	2	7	1	2	0	4	3	1	2
Billy Sullivan, c	.000	6	21	0	0	0	0	0	0	0	9	0
Lee Tannehill, ss	.111	3	9	1	1	0	0	0	0	0	2	0
Babe Towne, ph	.000	1	1	0	0	0	0	0	0	0	0	0
Ed Walsh, p	.000	2	4	1	0	0	0	0	0	3	3	0
Doc White, p	.000	3	3	0	0	0	0	0	0	1	0	0
TOTAL	.198		187	22	37	10	3	0	19	18	35	6

PITCHER	W	L	ERA	G	GS	CG	SV	SHO	IP	H	ER	BB	SO
Nick Altrock	1	1	1.00	2	2	2	0	0	18.0	11	2	2	5
Frank Owen	0	0	3.00	1	0	0	0	0	6.0	6	2	3	2
Ed Walsh	2	0	1.20	2	2	1	0	1	15.0	7	2	6	17
Doc White	1	1	1.80	3	2	1	1	0	15.0	12	3	7	4
TOTAL	4	2	1.50	8	6	4	1	1	54.0	36	9	18	28

CHI (N)

PLAYER/POS	AVG	G	AB	R	H	2B	3B	HR	RB	BB	SO	SB
Mordecai Brown, p	.333	3	6	0	2	0	0	0	0	0	4	0
Frank Chance, 1b	.238	6	21	3	5	1	0	0	0	2	1	2
Johnny Evers, 2b	.150	6	20	2	3	1	0	0	1	1	3	2
Doc Gessler, ph	.000	2	1	0	0	0	0	0	0	1	0	0
Solly Hofman, of	.304	6	23	3	7	1	0	0	2	3	5	1
Johnny Kling, c	.176	6	17	2	3	1	0	0	0	4	3	0
Pat Moran, ph	.000	2	2	0	0	0	0	0	0	0	0	0
Orval Overall, p	.250	2	4	1	1	1	0	0	0	1	1	0
Jack Pfiester, p	.000	2	2	0	0	0	0	0	0	0	1	0
Ed Reulbach, p	.000	2	3	0	0	0	0	0	0	1	0	0
Frank Schulte, of	.269	6	26	1	7	3	0	0	3	1	3	0
Jimmy Sheckard, of	.000	6	21	0	0	0	0	0	1	2	4	1
Harry Steinfeldt, 3b	.250	6	20	2	5	1	0	0	2	1	0	0
Joe Tinker, ss	.167	6	18	4	3	0	0	0	1	2	2	3
TOTAL	.196		184	18	36	9	0	0	11	18	28	9

PITCHER	W	L	ERA	G	GS	CG	SV	SHO	IP	H	ER	BB	SO
Mordecai Brown	1	2	3.20	3	3	2	0	1	19.2	14	7	4	12
Orval Overall	0	0	2.25	2	0	0	0	0	12.0	10	3	3	8
Jack Pfiester	0	2	6.10	2	1	1	0	0	10.1	7	7	3	11
Ed Reulbach	1	0	2.45	2	2	1	0	0	11.0	6	3	8	4
TOTAL	2	4	3.40	9	6	4	0	1	53.0	37	20	18	35

GAME 1 AT CHI-N OCT 9

CHI-A	000	011	000	2	4 1
CHI-N	000	001	000	1	4 2

Pitchers: ALTROCK vs BROWN
Attendance: 12,693

GAME 2 AT CHI-A OCT 10

CHI-N	031	001	020	7	10 2
CHI-A	000	010	000	1	1 2

Pitchers: REULBACH vs WHITE, Owen (4)
Attendance: 12,595

GAME 3 AT CHI-N OCT 11

CHI-A	000	003	000	3	4 1
CHI-N	000	000	000	0	2 2

Pitchers: WALSH vs PFIESTER
Attendance: 13,667

GAME 4 AT CHI-A OCT 12

CHI-N	000	000	100	1	7 1
CHI-A	000	000	000	0	2 1

Pitchers: BROWN vs ALTROCK
Attendance: 18,385

GAME 5 AT CHI-N OCT 13

CHI-A	102	401	000	8	12 6
CHI-N	300	102	000	6	6 0

Pitchers: WALSH, White (7) vs Reulbach, PFIESTER (3), Overall (4)
Attendance: 23,257

GAME 6 AT CHI-A OCT 14

CHI-N	100	010	001	3	7 0
CHI-A	340	000	01X	8	14 3

Pitchers: BROWN, Overall (2) vs WHITE
Attendance: 19,249

The two-run lead that Detroit took into the bottom of the ninth inning of Game One proved to be its biggest of the Series. And it was short-lived, as Chicago—after Frank Chance's leadoff single—took advantage of a hit batsman, a fumble at third base, and a dropped third strike to even the score. Three scoreless extra innings later, darkness ended the game in a 3–3 tie.

The Tigers pitched well enough in the Series. Wild Bill Donovan and George Mullin, who provided more than 80 percent of Detroit's pitching, allowed only four earned runs each for a combined 1.89 ERA. But Cub pitchers gave up only four earned runs *as a team,* suffocating the Tigers with a team ERA of 0.75. And while Tiger fielders made one less error than the Cubs, their misplays proved more costly, permitting eight unearned runs to the Cubs' two.

Detroit's three-run eighth in the opener provided half of their Series scoring. Nine Tiger hits in Game Two produced only one run, while the Cubs bunched six of their nine hits into two innings for three runs and the Series' first win. In Games Three and Four, while the Tigers were twice again limited to a single run, the Cubs increased their run production to five and six, clustering 40 percent of their hits into two three-run innings, one in each game. Mordecai (Three Finger) Brown wrapped up the Series for Chicago with a shutout, as his Cubs blended a hit in each of the first two innings with three stolen bases and a Tiger error for the game's only two runs.

Detroit's twenty-year-old Ty Cobb, the American League batting, RBI, and stolen base leader in his first full big league season, hit an anemic .200 in the World Series, stealing no bases and driving in no Tiger runs. If there was an offensive hero, it was Cub centerfielder Jimmy Slagle. At age thirty-four, nearing the end of a ten-year major league career, he led both clubs with four RBIs (nearly quadruple his season's per-game output) and six stolen bases.

Chicago Cubs (NL), 4;
Detroit Tigers (AL), 0; tie, 1

CHI (N)

PLAYER/POS	AVG	G	AB	R	H	2B	3B	HR	RB	BB	SO	SB
Mordecai Brown, p	.000	1	3	0	0	0	0	0	0	1	0	0
Frank Chance, 1b	.214	4	14	3	3	1	0	0	0	3	2	3
Johnny Evers, 2b-5,ss-1	.350	5	20	2	7	2	0	0	1	0	1	3
Del Howard, 1b-1	.200	2	5	0	1	0	0	0	0	0	2	1
Johnny Kling, c	.211	5	19	2	4	0	0	0	1	1	4	0
Pat Moran, ph	.000	1	0	0	0	0	0	0	0	0	0	0
Orval Overall, p	.200	2	5	0	1	0	0	0	2	0	1	0
Jack Pfiester, p	.000	1	2	0	0	0	0	0	0	0	1	0
Ed Reulbach, p	.200	2	5	0	1	0	0	0	1	0	0	0
Frank Schulte, of	.250	5	20	3	5	0	0	0	2	1	2	0
Jimmy Sheckard, of	.238	5	21	0	5	2	0	0	2	0	4	1
Jimmy Slagle, of	.273	5	22	3	6	0	0	0	4	2	3	6
Harry Steinfeldt, 3b	.471	5	17	2	8	1	1	0	2	1	2	1
Joe Tinker, ss	.154	5	13	4	2	0	0	0	1	3	3	1
Heinie Zimmerman, 2b	.000	1	1	0	0	0	0	0	0	0	1	0
TOTAL	.257		167	19	43	6	1	0	16	12	26	16

PITCHER	W	L	ERA	G	GS	CG	SV	SHO	IP	H	ER	BB	SO
Mordecai Brown	1	0	0.00	1	1	1	0	1	9.0	7	0	1	4
Orval Overall	1	0	1.00	2	2	1	0	0	18.0	14	2	4	11
Jack Pfiester	1	0	1.00	1	1	1	0	0	9.0	9	1	1	3
Ed Reulbach	1	0	0.75	2	1	1	0	0	12.0	6	1	3	4
TOTAL	4	0	0.75	6	5	4	0	1	48.0	36	4	9	22

DET (A)

PLAYER/POS	AVG	G	AB	R	H	2B	3B	HR	RB	BB	SO	SB
Jimmy Archer, c	.000	1	3	0	0	0	0	0	0	0	1	0
Ty Cobb, of	.200	5	20	1	4	0	1	0	0	0	3	0
Bill Coughlin, 3b	.250	5	20	0	5	0	0	0	0	1	4	1
Sam Crawford, of	.238	5	21	1	5	1	0	0	3	0	3	0
Bill Donovan, p	.000	2	8	0	0	0	0	0	0	0	3	0
Davy Jones, of	.353	5	17	1	6	0	0	0	0	4	0	3
Ed Killian, p	.500	1	2	1	1	0	0	0	0	0	0	0
George Mullin, p	.000	2	6	0	0	0	0	0	0	0	1	0
Charley O'Leary, ss	.059	5	17	0	1	0	0	0	0	1	3	0
Fred Payne, c-1	.250	2	4	0	1	0	0	0	1	0	0	1
Claude Rossman, 1b	.400	5	20	1	8	0	1	0	2	1	0	1
Germany Schaefer, 2b	.143	5	21	1	3	0	0	0	0	0	3	0
Boss Schmidt, c-3	.167	4	12	0	2	0	0	0	0	2	1	0
Ed Siever, p	.000	1	1	0	0	0	0	0	0	0	0	0
TOTAL	.209		172	6	36	1	2	0	6	9	22	6

PITCHER	W	L	ERA	G	GS	CG	SV	SHO	IP	H	ER	BB	SO
Bill Donovan	0	1	1.71	2	2	2	0	0	21.0	17	4	5	16
Ed Killian	0	0	2.25	1	0	0	0	0	4.0	3	1	1	1
George Mullin	0	2	2.12	2	2	2	0	0	17.0	16	4	6	8
Ed Siever	0	1	4.50	1	1	0	0	0	4.0	7	2	0	1
TOTAL	0	4	2.15	6	5	4	0	0	46.0	43	11	12	26

GAME 1 AT CHI OCT 8

DET	000 000 030 000	3	9	3
CHI	000 100 002 000	3	10	5

Pitchers: Donovan vs Overall, Reulbach (10)
Attendance: 24,377

GAME 2 AT CHI OCT 9

DET	010 000 000	1	9	1
CHI	010 200 00X	3	9	1

Pitchers: MULLIN vs PFIESTER
Attendance: 21,901

GAME 3 AT CHI OCT 10

DET	000 001 000	1	6	1
CHI	010 310 00X	5	10	1

Pitchers: SIEVER, Killian (5) vs REULBACH
Attendance: 13,114

GAME 4 AT DET OCT 11

CHI	000 020 301	6	7	2
DET	000 100 000	1	5	2

Pitchers: OVERALL vs DONOVAN
Attendance: 11,306

GAME 5 AT DET OCT 12

CHI	110 000 000	2	7	1
DET	000 000 000	0	7	2

Pitchers: BROWN vs MULLIN
Attendance: 7,370

The Tigers won their final game of the season to take their second straight pennant, and the Cubs won their third pennant in a row by defeating the Giants in a replay of an earlier tie. Ty Cobb and Detroit improved on their 1907 Series performance, as Cobb led his club in batting, hits, and RBIs, and the Tigers won a game. But the Cubs as a team hit 90 percentage points higher than Detroit, and outscored them 24–15, to take the Series with relative ease.

In Game One, the Tigers took advantage of the Cubs' ragged fielding to score two runs in the eighth for a 6–5 lead. But in the top of the ninth, the Cubs erupted for five runs on six consecutive singles and a double steal, to win the game. The next day Chicago's Orval Overall held Detroit to four hits and one ninth-inning run. The Tigers' Wild Bill Donovan pitched even better for seven innings, holding Pittsburgh to a single in the sixth. But in the eighth, Joe Tinker's two-run homer—the first in a World Series since 1903—began an assault that ended only after six Cubs had crossed the plate.

Detroit finally manufactured a Series win, pummeling Jack Pfiester in Game Three for ten hits (six of them in the sixth inning) and an 8–3 victory. But that was their last burst. As the Series moved to Detroit for Games Four and Five, the Tiger offense collapsed. Three Finger Brown, the winner as a reliever in Game One, won Game Four as a starter, shutting out the Tigers on four hits. The Cubs needed only three of their ten hits, combining them with a couple of walks and stolen bases, and a muffed fly ball, to score twice in the third inning and once in the ninth.

Only 6,210 spectators—the smallest World Series crowd of the century—saw Overall strike out four Tigers in the first inning of Game Five (one reached first on a wild pitch) in what became a three-hit shutout. Meanwhile, his Cubs unloaded for ten hits, defeating Donovan a second time, scoring runs in the first and fifth innings. Overall—after yielding a leadoff walk to Cobb in the fifth—retired Cobb on a force play and set down the final 11 men to face him.

Chicago Cubs (NL), 4;
Detroit Tigers (AL), 1

CHI (N)

PLAYER/POS	AVG	G	AB	R	H	2B	3B	HR	RB	BB	SO	SB
Mordecai Brown, p	.000	2	4	0	0	0	0	0	0	0	2	0
Frank Chance, 1b	.421	5	19	4	8	0	0	0	2	3	1	5
Johnny Evers, 2b	.350	5	20	5	7	1	0	0	2	1	2	2
Solly Hofman, of	.316	5	19	2	6	0	1	0	4	1	4	2
Del Howard, ph	.000	1	1	0	0	0	0	0	0	0	0	0
Johnny Kling, c	.250	5	16	2	4	1	0	0	2	2	2	0
Orval Overall, p	.333	3	6	0	2	0	0	0	0	0	1	0
Jack Pfiester, p	.000	1	2	0	0	0	0	0	0	0	2	0
Ed Reulbach, p	.000	2	3	0	0	0	0	0	0	0	1	0
Frank Schulte, of	.389	5	18	4	7	0	1	0	2	2	1	2
Jimmy Sheckard, of	.238	5	21	2	5	2	0	0	1	2	3	1
Harry Steinfeldt, 3b	.250	5	16	3	4	0	0	0	3	2	5	1
Joe Tinker, ss	.263	5	19	2	5	0	0	1	4	0	2	2
TOTAL	.293		164	24	48	4	2	1	20	13	26	15

PITCHER	W	L	ERA	G	GS	CG	SV	SHO	IP	H	ER	BB	SO
Mordecai Brown	2	0	0.00	2	1	1	0	1	11.0	6	0	1	5
Orval Overall	2	0	0.98	3	2	2	0	1	18.1	7	2	7	15
Jack Pfiester	0	1	7.87	1	1	0	0	0	8.0	10	7	3	1
Ed Reulbach	0	0	4.70	2	1	0	0	0	7.2	9	4	1	5
TOTAL	4	1	2.60	8	5	3	0	2	45.0	32	13	12	26

DET (A)

PLAYER/POS	AVG	G	AB	R	H	2B	3B	HR	RB	BB	SO	SB
Ty Cobb, of	.368	5	19	3	7	1	0	0	4	1	2	2
Bill Coughlin, 3b	.125	3	8	0	1	0	0	0	1	0	1	0
Sam Crawford, of	.238	5	21	2	5	1	0	0	1	1	2	0
Bill Donovan, p	.000	2	4	0	0	0	0	0	0	1	1	1
Red Downs, 2b	.167	2	6	1	1	1	0	0	1	1	2	0
Davy Jones, ph	.000	3	2	1	0	0	0	0	0	1	1	0
Ed Killian, p	.000	1	0	0	0	0	0	0	0	0	0	0
Matty Mc Intyre, of	.222	5	18	2	4	1	0	0	0	3	2	1
George Mullin, p	.333	1	3	1	1	0	0	0	1	1	0	0
Charley O'Leary, ss	.158	5	19	2	3	0	0	0	0	0	3	0
Claude Rossman, 1b	.211	5	19	3	4	0	0	0	3	1	4	1
Germany Schaefer, 2b-3,3b-2	.125	5	16	0	2	0	0	0	0	1	4	1
Boss Schmidt, c	.071	4	14	0	1	0	0	0	1	0	2	0
Ed Summers, p	.200	2	5	0	1	0	0	0	1	0	2	0
Ira Thomas, c-1	.500	2	4	0	2	1	0	0	1	1	0	0
George Winter, p-1	.000	2	0	0	0	0	0	0	0	0	0	0
TOTAL	.203		158	15	32	5	0	0	14	12	26	6

PITCHER	W	L	ERA	G	GS	CG	SV	SHO	IP	H	ER	BB	SO
Bill Donovan	0	2	4.24	2	2	2	0	0	17.0	17	8	4	10
Ed Killian	0	0	11.57	1	1	0	0	0	2.1	5	3	3	1
George Mullin	1	0	0.00	1	1	1	0	0	9.0	7	0	1	8
Ed Summers	0	2	4.30	2	1	0	0	0	14.2	18	7	4	7
George Winter	0	0	0.00	1	0	0	0	0	1.0	1	0	1	0
TOTAL	1	4	3.68	7	5	3	0	0	44.0	48	18	13	26

GAME 1 AT DET OCT 10

CHI	004	000	105	10	14 2
DET	100	000	320	6	10 4

Pitchers: Reulbach, Overall (7), BROWN (8) vs Killian, SUMMERS (3)
Attendance: 10,812

GAME 2 AT CHI OCT 11

DET	000	000	001	1	4 1
CHI	000	000	06X	6	7 1

Pitchers: DONOVAN vs OVERALL
Home Runs: Tinker-CHI
Attendance: 17,760

GAME 3 AT CHI OCT 12

DET	100	005	020	8	11 4
CHI	000	300	000	3	7 2

Pitchers: MULLIN vs PFIESTER, Reulbach (9)
Attendance: 14,543

GAME 4 AT DET OCT 13

CHI	002	000	001	3	10 0
DET	000	000	000	0	4 1

Pitchers: BROWN vs SUMMERS, Winter (9)
Attendance: 12,907

GAME 5 AT DET OCT 14

CHI	100	010	000	2	10 0
DET	000	000	000	0	3 0

Pitchers: OVERALL vs DONOVAN
Attendance: 6,210

Babe Adams, a twenty-seven-year-old rookie pitcher, was only the fifth biggest winner on the Pittsburgh staff. But his fine 12–3 record was supported by a team-best 1.11 ERA, and manager Fred Clarke started him in the Series opener against Detroit's ace George Mullin (who had led the American League with a career-high 29 wins). Mullin pitched well, giving up only one earned run—manager/outfielder Clarke's homer in the fourth inning. But four Tiger errors led to three Pirate runs in the fifth and sixth. Meanwhile, Adams, after yielding a run in the first, pitched shutout ball the rest of the way for the win.

Detroit came back in Game Two with seven runs (including Ty Cobb's theft of home) as Wild Bill Donovan held the Pirates to two runs on five hits. In Game Three the Pirates took an early lead, which Detroit, despite rallies in the seventh and ninth innings, was unable to overcome. Errors determined most of the scoring, as only one of Detroit's six runs and two of Pittsburgh's eight were earned.

Mullin shut out the Pirates on five hits in Game Four, striking out ten men as Detroit scored five runs (all earned, despite Pittsburgh's six errors) to drive out starter Lefty Leifield after four innings. The seesaw Series continued in Game Five, with Babe Adams winning his second game behind his Pirates' ten-hit, eight-run attack. Adams gave up leadoff homers to Davy Jones in the first and Sam Crawford in the eighth. But Pittsburgh's Clarke more than countered these with his three-run shot in the seventh. (All three homers were hit into temporary seats in center field.)

Back in Detroit for Game Six, the Tigers evened the Series for the third time, Mullin winning his second game in a close contest that saw Pittsburgh pull within a run of tying the game in the ninth before a runner thrown out at home and a game-ending double play cut their rally dead.

In the finale it was Babe Adams once again, scattering six Tiger hits for an easy 8–0 win, his third of the Series. Detroit had done better than ever, but still lost their third World Series in three consecutive attempts. A quarter century would pass before they would have a chance to try again.

Pittsburgh Pirates (NL), 4; Detroit Tigers (AL), 3

PIT (N)

PLAYER/POS	AVG	G	AB	R	H	2B	3B	HR	RB	BB	SO	SB
Ed Abbaticchio, ph	.000	1	1	0	0	0	0	0	0	0	0	0
Bill Abstein, 1b	.231	7	26	3	6	2	0	0	2	3	10	1
Babe Adams, p	.000	3	9	0	0	0	0	0	0	0	1	0
Bobby Byrne, 3b	.250	7	24	5	6	1	0	0	0	1	4	1
Howie Camnitz, p	.000	2	1	0	0	0	0	0	0	0	0	0
Fred Clarke, of	.211	7	19	7	4	0	0	2	7	5	3	3
George Gibson, c	.240	7	25	2	6	2	0	0	2	1	1	2
Ham Hyatt, of-1	.000	2	4	1	0	0	0	0	1	1	0	0
Tommy Leach, of-7,3b-1	.360	7	25	8	9	4	0	0	2	2	1	1
Lefty Leifield, p	.000	1	1	0	0	0	0	0	0	0	1	0
Nick Maddox, p	.000	1	4	0	0	0	0	0	0	0	1	0
Dots Miller, 2b	.250	7	28	2	7	1	0	0	4	2	5	3
Paddy O'Connor, ph	.000	1	1	0	0	0	0	0	0	0	1	0
Deacon Phillippe, p	.000	2	1	0	0	0	0	0	0	0	1	0
Honus Wagner, ss	.333	7	24	4	8	2	1	0	6	4	2	6
Vic Willis, p	.000	2	4	0	0	0	0	0	0	0	1	0
Chief Wilson, of	.154	7	26	2	4	1	0	0	1	0	2	1
TOTAL	.224		223	34	50	13	1	2	25	20	34	18

PITCHER	W	L	ERA	G	GS	CG	SV	SHO	IP	H	ER	BB	SO
Babe Adams	3	0	1.33	3	3	3	0	1	27.0	18	4	6	11
Howie Camnitz	0	1	9.82	2	1	0	0	0	3.2	8	4	2	2
Lefty Leifield	0	1	11.25	1	1	0	0	0	4.0	7	5	1	0
Nick Maddox	1	0	1.00	1	1	1	0	0	9.0	10	1	2	4
Deacon Phillippe	0	0	0.00	2	0	0	0	0	6.0	2	0	1	2
Vic Willis	0	1	3.97	2	1	0	0	0	11.1	10	5	8	3
TOTAL	4	3	2.80	11	7	4	0	1	61.0	55	19	20	22

DET (A)

PLAYER/POS	AVG	G	AB	R	H	2B	3B	HR	RB	BB	SO	SB
Donie Bush, ss	.261	7	23	5	6	1	0	0	3	5	3	1
Ty Cobb, of	.231	7	26	3	6	3	0	0	5	2	2	2
Sam Crawford, of-7,1b-1	.250	7	28	4	7	3	0	1	4	1	1	1
Jim Delahanty, 2b	.346	7	26	2	9	4	0	0	4	2	5	0
Bill Donovan, p	.000	2	4	0	0	0	0	0	0	0	1	0
Davy Jones, of	.233	7	30	6	7	0	0	1	1	2	1	1
Tom Jones, 1b	.250	7	24	3	6	1	0	0	2	2	0	1
Matty McIntyre, of-1	.000	4	3	0	0	0	0	0	0	1	0	0
George Moriarty, 3b	.273	7	22	4	6	1	0	0	1	3	1	0
George Mullin, p-4	.188	6	16	1	3	1	0	0	0	1	3	0
Charley O'Leary, ss	.000	1	3	0	0	0	0	0	0	0	0	0
Boss Schmidt, c	.222	6	18	0	4	2	0	0	4	2	0	0
Oscar Stanage, c	.200	2	5	0	1	0	0	0	2	0	2	0
Ed Summers, p	.000	2	2	0	0	0	0	0	0	0	2	0
Ed Willett, p	.000	2	2	0	0	0	0	0	0	0	0	0
Ralph Works, p	.000	1	0	0	0	0	0	0	0	0	0	0
TOTAL	.236		233	28	55	16	0	2	26	20	22	6

PITCHER	W	L	ERA	G	GS	CG	SV	SHO	IP	H	ER	BB	SO
Bill Donovan	1	1	3.00	2	2	1	0	0	12.0	7	4	8	7
George Mullin	2	1	2.25	4	3	3	0	1	32.0	23	8	8	20
Ed Summers	0	2	8.59	2	2	0	0	0	7.1	13	7	4	4
Ed Willett	0	0	0.00	2	0	0	0	0	7.2	3	0	0	1
Ralph Works	0	0	9.00	1	0	0	0	0	2.0	4	2	0	2
TOTAL	3	4	3.10	11	7	4	0	1	61.0	50	21	20	34

GAME 1 AT PIT OCT 8

DET	100	000	000	1	6	4
PIT	000	121	00X	4	5	0

Pitchers: MULLIN vs ADAMS
Home Runs: Clarke-PIT
Attendance: 29,264

GAME 2 AT PIT OCT 9

DET	023	020	000	7	9	3
PIT	200	000	000	2	5	1

Pitchers: DONOVAN vs CAMNITZ, Willis (3)
Attendance: 30,915

GAME 3 AT DET OCT 11

PIT	510	000	002	8	10	3
DET	000	000	402	6	10	5

Pitchers: MADDOX vs SUMMERS, Willett (1), Works (8)
Attendance: 18,277

GAME 4 AT DET OCT 12

PIT	000	000	000	0	5	6
DET	020	300	00X	5	8	0

Pitchers: LEIFIELD, Phillippe (5) vs MULLIN
Attendance: 17,036

GAME 5 AT PIT OCT 13

DET	100	002	010	4	6	1
PIT	111	000	41X	8	10	2

Pitchers: SUMMERS, Willett (8) vs ADAMS
Home Runs: D.Jones-DET, Crawford-DET, Clarke-PIT
Attendance: 21,706

GAME 6 AT DET OCT 14

PIT	300	000	001	4	7	3
DET	100	211	00X	5	10	3

Pitchers: WILLIS, Camnitz (6), Phillippe (7) vs MULLIN
Attendance: 10,535

GAME 7 AT DET OCT 16

PIT	020	203	010	8	7	0
DET	000	000	000	0	6	3

Pitchers: ADAMS vs DONOVAN, Mullin (4)
Attendance: 17,562

Pitcher Jack Coombs burst into stardom in 1910, emerging as the ace of a Philadelphia pitching staff which dominated the American League with an ERA of only 1.79. Coombs himself led league pitchers with 31 wins and 13 shutouts, and finished second to Chicago's Ed Walsh with an ERA of 1.30—all career bests. He continued his domination into the World Series, pitching three complete-game victories in the Athletics' surpisingly easy triumph over the Cubs.

The Series' finest pitching performance, though, was turned in by the A's Chief Bender in the opener. Only two batters reached base over the first eight innings—on a single and walk—and both of them were cut down trying to steal second. In the ninth, two Cub singles and two Athletic errors produced an unearned run, but as the A's had scored four runs (Bender himself providing the margin of victory with the game's second RBI in the second inning), the Cubs' run did no damage.

Coombs started Game Two and gave up a Cub run in the top of the first inning. But Athletic bats were hot in the Series (their team .316 batting average stood as a Series record for fifty years), and their 14 hits in this game (including four doubles and six runs in the seventh) sank Three Finger Brown and gave Coombs an easy win. Connie Mack also started Coombs in Game Three, two days later, and again the result was a lopsided win. Coombs himself drove in three of his team's 12 runs, and right fielder Danny Murphy added three more with the Series' only home run.

Bender pitched Game Four and suffered the A's only loss, as the Cubs tied the game at 3–3 with a run in the bottom of the ninth, and won it for reliever Three Finger Brown with a two-out RBI single an inning later.

Coombs faced Brown a second time in Game Five. Both clubs made nine hits, but the A's put four of them together with a walk, a wild pitch, and two stolen bases for five runs in the eighth to sink Brown as they had in Game Two, breaking a tight game wide open for Coombs's third win and the Athletics' first world championship.

Philadelphia Athletics (AL), 4;
Chicago Cubs (NL), 1

PHI (A)

PLAYER/POS	AVG	G	AB	R	H	2B	3B	HR	RB	BB	SO	SB
Frank Baker, 3b	.409	5	22	6	9	3	0	0	4	2	1	0
Jack Barry, ss	.235	5	17	3	4	2	0	0	3	1	3	0
Chief Bender, p	.333	2	6	1	2	0	0	0	1	1	1	0
Eddie Collins, 2b	.429	5	21	5	9	4	0	0	3	2	0	4
Jack Coombs, p	.385	3	13	0	5	1	0	0	3	0	3	0
Harry Davis, 1b	.353	5	17	5	6	3	0	0	2	3	4	0
Topsy Hartsel, of	.200	1	5	2	1	0	0	0	0	0	1	2
Jack Lapp, c	.250	1	4	0	1	0	0	0	1	0	2	0
Bris Lord, of	.182	5	22	3	4	2	0	0	1	1	3	0
Danny Murphy, of	.350	5	20	6	7	3	0	1	9	1	0	1
Amos Strunk, of	.278	4	18	2	5	1	1	0	2	2	5	0
Ira Thomas, c	.250	4	12	2	3	0	0	0	1	4	1	0
TOTAL	.316		177	35	56	19	1	1	30	17	24	7

PITCHER	W	L	ERA	G	GS	CG	SV	SHO	IP	H	ER	BB	SO
Chief Bender	1	1	1.93	2	2	2	0	0	18.2	12	4	4	14
Jack Coombs	3	0	3.33	3	3	3	0	0	27.0	23	10	14	17
TOTAL	4	1	2.76	5	5	5	0	0	45.2	35	14	18	31

CHI (N)

PLAYER/POS	AVG	G	AB	R	H	2B	3B	HR	RB	BB	SO	SB
Jimmy Archer, c-2,1b-1	.182	3	11	1	2	1	0	0	0	0	3	0
Ginger Beaumont, ph	.000	3	2	1	0	0	0	0	0	1	1	0
Mordecai Brown, p	.000	3	7	0	0	0	0	0	0	0	1	0
Frank Chance, 1b	.353	5	17	1	6	1	1	0	4	0	3	0
King Cole, p	.000	1	2	0	0	0	0	0	0	0	2	0
Solly Hofman, of	.267	5	15	2	4	0	0	0	2	4	3	0
Johnny Kane, pr	.000	1	0	0	0	0	0	0	0	0	0	0
Johnny Kling, c-3	.077	5	13	0	1	0	0	0	1	1	2	0
Harry Mc Intire, p	.000	2	1	0	0	0	0	0	0	0	1	0
Tom Needham, ph	.000	1	1	0	0	0	0	0	0	0	0	0
Orval Overall, p	.000	1	1	0	0	0	0	0	0	0	0	0
Jack Pfiester, p	.000	1	2	0	0	0	0	0	0	0	1	0
Ed Reulbach, p	.000	1	0	0	0	0	0	0	0	0	0	0
Lew Richie, p	.000	1	0	0	0	0	0	0	0	0	0	0
Frank Schulte, of	.353	5	17	3	6	3	0	0	2	2	3	0
Jimmy Sheckard, of	.286	5	14	5	4	2	0	0	1	7	2	1
Harry Steinfeldt, 3b	.100	5	20	2	2	1	0	0	1	0	4	0
Joe Tinker, ss	.333	5	18	2	6	2	0	0	0	2	2	1
Heinie Zimmerman, 2b	.235	5	17	0	4	1	0	0	2	1	3	1
TOTAL	.222		158	15	35	11	1	0	13	18	31	3

PITCHER	W	L	ERA	G	GS	CG	SV	SHO	IP	H	ER	BB	SO
Mordecai Brown	1	2	5.50	3	2	1	0	0	18.0	23	11	7	14
King Cole	0	0	3.38	1	1	0	0	0	8.0	10	3	3	5
Harry Mc Intire	0	1	6.75	2	0	0	0	0	5.1	4	4	3	3
Orval Overall	0	1	9.00	1	1	0	0	0	3.0	6	3	1	1
Jack Pfiester	0	0	0.00	1	0	0	0	0	6.2	9	0	1	1
Ed Reulbach	0	0	9.00	1	1	0	0	0	2.0	3	2	2	0
Lew Richie	0	0	0.00	1	0	0	0	0	1.0	1	0	0	0
TOTAL	1	4	4.70	10	5	1	0	0	44.0	56	23	17	24

GAME 1 AT PHI OCT 17

CHI	000	000	001	1	3	1
PHI	021	000	01X	4	7	2

Pitchers: OVERALL, McIntire (4) vs BENDER
Attendance: 26,891

GAME 2 AT PHI OCT 18

CHI	100	000	101	3	8	3
PHI	002	010	60X	9	14	4

Pitchers: BROWN, Richie (8) vs COOMBS
Attendance: 24,597

GAME 3 AT CHI OCT 20

PHI	125	000	400	12	15	1
CHI	120	000	020	5	6	5

Pitchers: COOMBS vs Reulbach, McINTIRE (3), Pfiester (3)
Home Runs: Murphy-PHI
Attendance: 26,210

GAME 4 AT CHI OCT 22

PHI	001	200	000	0	3	11	3
CHI	100	100	001	1	4	9	1

Pitchers: BENDER vs Cole, BROWN (9)
Attendance: 19,150

GAME 5 AT CHI OCT 23

PHI	100	010	050	7	9	1
CHI	010	000	010	2	9	2

Pitchers: COOMBS vs BROWN
Attendance: 27,374

Connie Mack's pitching aces out-dueled Christy Mathewson, and Frank Baker hit two crucial home runs to become "Home Run" Baker forever more, as the A's avenged their 1905 Series loss to the Giants. Game One, though, belonged to Matty and New York. Philadelphia scored first, but the Giants tied the game with an unearned run in the fourth inning, and won it with two doubles in the seventh, setting at naught Chief Bender's otherwise splendid 11-strikeout performance.

The A's came back to take three in a row. In Game Two Eddie Plank held the Giants to one run and Baker hit the first of his homers, breaking a tie in the sixth with a two-run blast off Rube Marquard. The next day, the A's and Jack Coombs handed Mathewson his first World Series loss. Both pitchers went the distance in an 11-inning duel that saw Matty hold the A's scoreless through eight, only to give up a game-tying home run to Baker in the ninth, and two unearned runs in the eleventh. Coombs, meanwhile, pitched two-hit, one-run ball through ten innings. In the last of the eleventh, a third Giant hit and an A's error let in a second Giant run, but the rally died when Beals Becker was cut down for the final out trying to steal second.

After a week of rain, Mathewson and Bender squared off in Game Four. The Giants jumped on Bender for two runs in the first, and held the lead until the fourth. But in the last of the fourth, three successive A's doubles and a run-scoring fly put the A's in front to stay as Bender held New York scoreless over the final 8 innings.

In Game Five, a three-run homer by the A's Rube Oldring off Rube Marquard in the third provided the only scoring through 6½ innings. But the Giants crept back with one run in the seventh, and two more in the last of the ninth tied the score. Plank replaced Coombs for the A's in the tenth and took the loss as Larry Doyle led off with a double, took third on a missed force play, and scored on Fred Merkle's fly to deep right.

After five closely contested games, Game Six was a laugher. It, too, was close at first—tied 1–1 after 3½ innings. But the A's scored four runs in the fourth on singles and errors, once in the sixth, and seven times in the seventh on a barrage of hits, an error, and a two-run wild pitch. Chief Bender, who gave up only four hits and two unearned runs, was the beneficiary of this largesse, taking his second win of the Series and giving the A's their second consecutive world title.

Philadelphia Athletics (AL), 4; New York Giants (NL), 2

PHI (A)

PLAYER/POS	AVG	G	AB	R	H	2B	3B	HR	RB	BB	SO	SB
Frank Baker, 3b	.375	6	24	7	9	2	0	2	5	1	5	0
Jack Barry, ss	.368	6	19	2	7	4	0	0	2	0	2	2
Chief Bender, p	.091	3	11	0	1	0	0	0	0	0	1	0
Eddie Collins, 2b	.286	6	21	4	6	1	0	0	1	2	2	2
Jack Coombs, p	.250	2	8	1	2	0	0	0	0	0	0	0
Harry Davis, 1b	.208	6	24	3	5	1	0	0	5	0	3	0
Jack Lapp, c	.250	2	8	1	2	0	0	0	0	0	1	0
Bris Lord, of	.185	6	27	2	5	2	0	0	1	0	5	0
Stuffy Mc Innis, 1b	.000	1	0	0	0	0	0	0	0	0	0	0
Danny Murphy, of	.304	6	23	4	7	3	0	0	3	0	3	0
Rube Oldring, of	.200	6	25	2	5	2	0	1	3	0	5	0
Eddie Plank, p	.000	2	3	0	0	0	0	0	0	0	2	0
Amos Strunk, pr	.000	1	0	0	0	0	0	0	0	0	0	0
Ira Thomas, c	.083	4	12	1	1	0	0	0	0	1	1	0
TOTAL	.244		205	27	50	15	0	3	21	4	31	4

PITCHER	W	L	ERA	G	GS	CG	SV	SHO	IP	H	ER	BB	SO
Chief Bender	2	1	1.04	3	3	3	0	0	26.0	16	3	8	20
Jack Coombs	1	0	1.35	2	2	1	0	0	20.0	11	3	6	16
Eddie Plank	1	1	1.86	2	1	1	0	0	9.2	6	2	0	8
TOTAL	4	2	1.29	7	6	5	0	0	55.2	33	8	14	44

NY (N)

PLAYER/POS	AVG	G	AB	R	H	2B	3B	HR	RB	BB	SO	SB
Red Ames, p	.500	2	2	0	1	0	0	0	0	0	1	0
Beals Becker, ph	.000	3	3	0	0	0	0	0	0	0	0	0
Doc Crandall, p-2	.500	3	2	1	1	1	0	0	1	2	0	0
Josh Devore, of	.167	6	24	1	4	1	0	0	3	1	8	0
Larry Doyle, 2b	.304	6	23	3	7	3	1	0	1	2	1	2
Art Fletcher, ss	.130	6	23	1	3	1	0	0	1	0	4	0
Buck Herzog, 3b	.190	6	21	3	4	2	0	0	2	3	2	2
Rube Marquard, p	.000	3	2	0	0	0	0	0	0	0	2	0
Christy Mathewson, p	.286	3	7	0	2	0	0	0	0	1	3	0
Fred Merkle, 1b	.150	6	20	1	3	1	0	0	1	2	6	0
Chief Meyers, c	.300	6	20	2	6	2	0	0	2	0	3	0
Red Murray, of	.000	6	21	0	0	0	0	0	0	2	5	0
Fred Snodgrass, of	.105	6	19	1	2	0	0	0	1	2	7	0
Art Wilson, c	.000	1	1	0	0	0	0	0	0	0	0	0
Hooks Wiltse, p	.000	2	1	0	0	0	0	0	0	0	1	0
TOTAL	.175		189	13	33	11	1	0	10	14	44	4

PITCHER	W	L	ERA	G	GS	CG	SV	SHO	IP	H	ER	BB	SO
Red Ames	0	1	2.25	2	1	0	0	0	8.0	6	2	1	6
Doc Crandall	1	0	0.00	2	0	0	0	0	4.0	2	0	0	2
Rube Marquard	0	1	1.54	3	2	0	0	0	11.2	9	2	1	8
Christy Mathewson	1	2	2.00	3	3	2	0	0	27.0	25	6	2	13
Hooks Wiltse	0	0	18.90	2	0	0	0	0	3.1	8	7	0	2
TOTAL	2	4	2.83	12	6	2	0	0	54.0	50	17	4	31

GAME 1 AT NY OCT 14

PHI	010	000	000	1	6	2
NY	000	100	10X	2	5	0

Pitchers: BENDER vs MATHEWSON
Attendance: 38,281

GAME 2 AT PHI OCT 16

NY	010	000	000	1	5	3
PHI	100	002	00X	3	4	0

Pitchers: MARQUARD, Crandall (8) vs PLANK
Home Runs: Baker-PHI
Attendance: 26,286

GAME 3 AT NY OCT 17

PHI	000	000	001 02	3	9	2
NY	001	000	000 01	2	3	5

Pitchers: COOMBS vs MATHEWSON
Home Runs: Baker-PHI
Attendance: 37,216

GAME 4 AT PHI OCT 24

NY	200	000	000	2	7	3
PHI	000	310	00X	4	11	1

Pitchers: MATHEWSON, Wiltse (8) vs BENDER
Attendance: 24,355

GAME 5 AT NY OCT 25

PHI	003	000	000 0	3	7	1
NY	000	000	102 1	4	9	2

Pitchers: Coombs, PLANK (10) vs Marquard, Ames (4), CRANDALL (8)
Home Runs: Oldring-PHI
Attendance: 33,228

GAME 6 AT PHI OCT 26

NY	100	000	001	2	4	3
PHI	001	401	70X	13	13	5

Pitchers: AMES, Wiltse (5), Marquard (7) vs BENDER
Attendance: 20,485

The Giants outhit the Red Sox by 50 percentage points, and their pitchers let in one less earned run per game. But this was the Series in which Fred Snodgrass's famous muff of a routine fly to center in the tenth inning of the final game helped turn a slim Giant lead into a Red Sox world championship. In all fairness, it must be admitted that Snodgrass followed his muff with a brilliant catch off the next batter, and indecision by the catcher and first baseman permitted a pop foul to drop, keeping the Sox alive to score the tying and winning runs. For that matter, this final game might not have been needed at all if Snodgrass and Beals Becker hadn't both been cut down trying to steal second in the eleventh inning of Game Two, which ended in a tie because of darkness. If either had gone on to score, the Giants would have won the Series in seven games.

Boston's Smokey Joe Wood followed up his spectacular 34–5 regular season with Series wins in Games One and Four, before being rocked for six runs in the first inning of Game Seven for a loss. Relieving in the eighth inning of the finale, he stopped the Giants for two innings, but gave up what would have been the losing run in the tenth had not the Giants' fielding in the last of the inning turned the game around, giving Wood the win and the Sox the Series.

Although Wood won three games, the best pitching of the Series was turned in by the Giants' Rube Marquard and Boston's Hugh Bedient. Marquard (who in the regular season had tied a major league record with 19 consecutive wins) won two of his club's three victories (Games Three and Six), allowing three runs—only one of them earned. Bedient, in two starts and two relief appearances, matched Marquard's 0.50 earned run average, winning a duel with Christy Mathewson in Game Five, and hurling seven effective innings against Matty in the finale.

Mathewson was the Series' hard-luck pitcher: his one tie and two losses were all decided by unearned runs.

Boston Red Sox (AL), 4;
New York Giants (NL), 3; tie, 1

BOS (A)

PLAYER/POS	AVG	G	AB	R	H	2B	3B	HR	RB	BB	SO	SB
Neal Ball, ph	.000	1	1	0	0	0	0	0	0	0	1	0
Hugh Bedient, p	.000	4	6	0	0	0	0	0	0	0	0	0
Hick Cady, c	.136	7	22	1	3	0	0	0	1	0	3	0
Bill Carrigan, c	.000	2	7	0	0	0	0	0	0	0	0	0
Ray Collins, p	.000	2	5	0	0	0	0	0	0	0	2	0
Clyde Engle, ph	.333	3	3	1	1	1	0	0	2	0	0	0
Larry Gardner, 3b	.179	8	28	4	5	2	1	1	4	2	5	0
Charley Hall, p	.750	2	4	0	3	1	0	0	0	1	0	0
Olaf Henricksen, ph	1.000	2	1	0	1	1	0	0	1	0	0	0
Harry Hooper, of	.290	8	31	3	9	2	1	0	2	4	4	2
Duffy Lewis, of	.156	8	32	4	5	3	0	0	2	2	2	0
Buck O'Brien, p	.000	2	2	0	0	0	0	0	0	0	2	0
Tris Speaker, of	.300	8	30	4	9	1	2	0	2	4	2	1
Jake Stahl, 1b	.281	8	32	3	9	2	0	0	2	0	6	2
Heinie Wagner, ss	.167	8	30	1	5	1	0	0	3	6	1
Joe Wood, p	.286	4	7	1	2	0	0	0	1	1	0	0
Steve Yerkes, 2b	.250	8	32	3	8	0	2	0	4	2	3	0
TOTAL	.220		273	25	60	14	6	1	21	19	36	6

PITCHER	W	L	ERA	G	GS	CG	SV	SHO	IP	H	ER	BB	SO
Hugh Bedient	1	0	0.50	4	2	1	0	0	18.0	10	2	7	7
Ray Collins	0	0	1.88	2	1	0	0	0	14.1	14	3	0	6
Charley Hall	0	0	3.38	2	0	0	0	0	10.2	11	4	9	1
Buck O'Brien	0	2	5.00	2	2	0	0	0	9.0	12	5	3	4
Joe Wood	3	1	3.68	4	3	2	0	0	22.0	27	9	3	21
TOTAL	4	3	2.80	14	8	3	0	0	74.0	74	23	22	39

NY (N)

PLAYER/POS	AVG	G	AB	R	H	2B	3B	HR	RB	BB	SO	SB
Red Ames, p	.000	1	0	0	0	0	0	0	0	0	0	0
Beals Becker, of-1	.000	2	4	1	0	0	0	0	0	2	0	0
Doc Crandall, p	.000	1	1	0	0	0	0	0	0	0	1	0
Josh Devore, of	.250	7	24	4	6	0	0	0	0	7	5	4
Larry Doyle, 2b	.242	8	33	5	8	1	0	1	2	3	2	2
Art Fletcher, ss	.179	8	28	1	5	1	0	0	3	1	4	1
Buck Herzog, 3b	.400	8	30	6	12	4	1	0	4	1	3	2
Rube Marquard, p	.000	2	4	0	0	0	0	0	0	1	0	0
Christy Mathewson, p	.167	3	12	0	2	0	0	0	0	0	4	0
Moose Mc Cormick, ph	.250	5	4	0	1	0	0	0	1	0	0	0
Fred Merkle, 1b	.273	8	33	5	9	2	1	0	3	0	7	1
Chief Meyers, c	.357	8	28	2	10	0	1	0	3	2	3	1
Red Murray, of	.323	8	31	5	10	4	1	0	5	2	2	0
Tillie Shafer, ss	.000	3	0	0	0	0	0	0	0	0	0	0
Fred Snodgrass, of	.212	8	33	2	7	2	0	0	2	2	5	1
Jeff Tesreau, p	.375	3	8	0	3	0	0	0	2	1	3	0
Art Wilson, c	1.000	2	1	0	1	0	0	0	0	0	0	0
TOTAL	.270		274	31	74	14	4	1	25	22	39	12

PITCHER	W	L	ERA	G	GS	CG	SV	SHO	IP	H	ER	BB	SO
Red Ames	0	0	4.50	1	0	0	0	0	2.0	3	1	1	0
Doc Crandall	0	0	0.00	1	0	0	0	0	2.0	1	0	0	2
Rube Marquard	2	0	0.50	2	2	2	0	0	18.0	14	1	2	9
Christy Mathewson	0	2	1.26	3	3	3	0	0	28.2	23	4	5	10
Jeff Tesreau	1	2	3.13	3	3	1	0	0	23.0	19	8	11	15
TOTAL	3	4	1.71	10	8	6	0	0	73.2	60	14	19	36

GAME 1 AT NY OCT 8

BOS	000 001 300	4	6	1
NY	002 000 001	3	8	1

Pitchers: WOOD vs TESREAU, Crandall (8)
Attendance: 35,730

GAME 2 AT BOS OCT 9

NY	010 100 030 10	6	11	5
BOS	300 010 010 10	6	10	1

Pitchers: Mathewson vs Collins, Hall (8), Bedient (11)
Attendance: 30,148

GAME 3 AT BOS OCT 10

NY	010 010 000	2	7	1
BOS	000 000 001	1	7	0

Pitchers: MARQUARD vs O'BRIEN, Bedient (9)
Attendance: 34,624

GAME 4 AT NY OCT 11

BOS	010 100 001	3	8	1
NY	000 000 100	1	9	1

Pitchers: WOOD vs TESREAU, Ames (8)
Attendance: 36,502

GAME 5 AT BOS OCT 12

NY	000 000 100	1	3	1
BOS	002 000 00X	2	5	1

Pitchers: MATHEWSON vs BEDIENT
Attendance: 34,683

GAME 6 AT NY OCT 14

BOS	020 000 000	2	7	2
NY	500 000 00X	5	11	2

Pitchers: O'BRIEN, Collins (2) vs MARQUARD
Attendance: 30,622

GAME 7 AT BOS OCT 15

NY	610 002 101	11	16	4
BOS	010 000 210	4	9	3

Pitchers: TESREAU vs WOOD, Hall (2)
Home Runs: Doyle-NY, Gardner-BOS
Attendance: 32,694

GAME 8 AT BOS OCT 16

NY	001 000 000 1	2	9	2
BOS	000 000 100 2	3	8	5

Pitchers: MATHEWSON vs Bedient, WOOD (8)
Attendance: 17,034

Third baseman Frank Baker and catcher Wally Schang drove in more than 60 percent of the Athletics' runs, as Philadelphia dispatched the Giants in five games. Chief Bender led A's pitchers with two wins, and rookie Bullet Joe Bush hurled a nifty five-hitter in Game Three, but the Series highlights were two duels between the A's Eddie Plank and the Giant's Christy Mathewson. The A's heavy hitting made Bender's wins possible and Bush's win easy, but pitching dominated the Plank-Matty games.

Bender yielded 11 hits in the opener, as did the Giants' pitchers. But five of the game's six extra-base hits belonged to the A's—including Baker's two-run homer and triples by Schang and Eddie Collins—and Bender emerged victorious. In Game Two, Plank and Mathewson pitched shutout ball through nine innings, but in the top of the tenth Matty himself singled in the game's first run and scored the second. Taking a 3–0 lead into the bottom of the inning, he set the A's down in order for New York's only Series win.

In Game Three, Schang's solo homer and Collins's three hits (including his second Series triple) and three RBIs led a 12-hit A's attack which, with Bush's fine pitching, put Philadelphia back into the Series lead. Bender won again in Game Four, shutting out the Giants through six innings as his A's scored six runs. But in the seventh, New York's Fred Merkle homered for three runs, and a single, double, and triple in the eighth brought in two more Giant runs. With his lead cut to a single run, Bender bore down in the ninth and retired the side in order.

Plank avenged his earlier loss with a brilliant two-hitter in Game Five, facing the minimum three batters in eight of the nine innings. (His own error in the fifth—a dropped pop-up—led to the Giants' only run.) Mathewson pitched well, too, yielding only six singles. But four of them came in the first and third innings, combining with two sacrifice flies and an error for three runs. Only one Athletic batter reached base in the final six innings, but with Plank pitching as he was, the game and the title were in Philadelphia's pocket.

Philadelphia Athletics (AL), 4; New York Giants (NL), 1

PHI (A)

PLAYER/POS	AVG	G	AB	R	H	2B	3B	HR	RB	BB	SO	SB
Frank Baker, 3b	.450	5	20	2	9	0	0	1	7	0	2	1
Jack Barry, ss	.300	5	20	3	6	3	0	0	2	0	0	0
Chief Bender, p	.000	2	8	0	0	0	0	0	1	0	1	0
Joe Bush, p	.250	1	4	0	1	0	0	0	0	0	1	0
Eddie Collins, 2b	.421	5	19	5	8	0	2	0	3	1	2	3
Jack Lapp, c	.250	1	4	0	1	0	0	0	0	0	1	0
Stuffy Mc Innis, 1b	.118	5	17	1	2	1	0	0	2	0	2	0
Eddie Murphy, of	.227	5	22	2	5	0	0	0	0	2	0	0
Rube Oldring, of	.273	5	22	5	6	0	1	0	0	0	1	1
Eddie Plank, p	.143	2	7	0	1	0	0	0	0	0	0	0
Wally Schang, c	.357	4	14	2	5	0	1	1	6	2	4	0
Amos Strunk, of	.118	5	17	3	2	0	0	0	0	2	2	0
TOTAL	.264		174	23	46	4	4	2	21	7	16	5

PITCHER	W	L	ERA	G	GS	CG	SV	SHO	IP	H	ER	BB	SO
Chief Bender	2	0	4.00	2	2	2	0	0	18.0	19	8	1	9
Joe Bush	1	0	1.00	1	1	1	0	0	9.0	5	1	4	3
Eddie Plank	1	1	0.95	2	2	2	0	0	19.0	9	2	3	7
TOTAL	4	1	2.15	5	5	5	0	0	46.0	33	11	8	19

NY (N)

PLAYER/POS	AVG	G	AB	R	H	2B	3B	HR	RB	BB	SO	SB
George Burns, of	.158	5	19	2	3	2	0	0	1	1	5	1
Claude Cooper, pr	.000	2	0	0	0	0	0	0	0	0	0	1
Doc Crandall, p-2	.000	4	4	0	0	0	0	0	0	0	0	0
Al Demaree, p	.000	1	1	0	0	0	0	0	0	0	0	0
Larry Doyle, 2b	.150	5	20	1	3	0	0	0	2	0	1	0
Art Fletcher, ss	.278	5	18	1	5	0	0	0	4	1	1	1
Eddie Grant, ph	.000	2	1	1	0	0	0	0	0	0	0	0
Buck Herzog, 3b	.053	5	19	1	1	0	0	0	0	0	1	0
Rube Marquard, p	.000	2	1	0	0	0	0	0	0	0	0	0
Christy Mathewson, p	.600	2	5	1	3	0	0	0	1	1	0	0
Moose Mc Cormick, ph	.500	2	2	1	1	0	0	0	0	0	0	0
Larry Mc Lean, c-4	.500	5	12	0	6	0	0	0	2	0	0	0
Fred Merkle, 1b	.231	4	13	3	3	0	0	1	3	1	2	0
Chief Meyers, c	.000	1	4	0	0	0	0	0	0	0	0	0
Red Murray, of	.250	5	16	2	4	0	0	0	1	2	2	2
Tillie Shafer, of-5,3b-1	.158	5	19	2	3	1	1	0	1	2	3	0
Fred Snodgrass, 1b-1,of-1	.333	2	3	0	1	0	0	0	0	0	0	0
Jeff Tesreau, p	.000	2	2	0	0	0	0	0	0	0	1	0
Art Wilson, c	.000	3	3	0	0	0	0	0	0	0	2	0
Hooks Wiltse, 1b	.000	2	2	0	0	0	0	0	0	0	1	0
TOTAL	.201		164	15	33	3	1	1	15	8	19	5

PITCHER	W	L	ERA	G	GS	CG	SV	SHO	IP	H	ER	BB	SO
Doc Crandall	0	0	3.86	2	0	0	0	0	4.2	4	2	0	2
Al Demaree	0	1	4.50	1	1	0	0	0	4.0	7	2	1	0
Rube Marquard	0	1	7.00	2	1	0	0	0	9.0	10	7	3	3
Christy Mathewson	1	1	0.95	2	2	2	0	1	19.0	14	2	2	7
Jeff Tesreau	0	1	6.48	2	1	0	0	0	8.1	11	6	1	4
TOTAL	1	4	3.80	9	5	2	0	1	45.0	46	19	7	16

GAME 1 AT NY OCT 7

PHI	000 320 010	6 11 1
NY	001 030 000	4 11 0

Pitchers: BENDER vs MARQUARD, Crandall (6), Tesreau (8)
Home Runs: Baker-PHI
Attendance: 36,291

GAME 2 AT PHI OCT 8

NY	000 000 000 3	3 7 2
PHI	000 000 000 0	0 8 2

Pitchers: MATHEWSON vs PLANK
Attendance: 20,563

GAME 3 AT NY OCT 9

PHI	320 000 210	8 12 1
NY	000 010 100	2 5 1

Pitchers: BUSH vs TESREAU, Crandall (7)
Home Runs: Schang-PHI
Attendance: 36,896

GAME 4 AT PHI OCT 10

NY	000 000 320	5 8 2
PHI	010 320 00X	6 9 0

Pitchers: MARQUARD vs BENDER
Home Runs: Merkle-NY
Attendance: 20,568

GAME 5 AT NY OCT 11

PHI	102 000 000	3 6 1
NY	000 010 000	1 2 2

Pitchers: PLANK vs MATHEWSON
Attendance: 36,682

The Athletics, easy winners of their fourth pennant in five years, were clear favorites over Boston. But the "Miracle Braves"—who moved from last place to first between July 18 and August 25 and kept going to take the pennant by 10½ games—had the momentum and swept the Series.

Boston pitcher Dick Rudolph (who won 27 games during the season) limited the A's to five hits and an unearned run, to take the opener behind the Braves' heavy hitting, 7–1. But the rest of the games were not won so easily.

Philadelphia's Eddie Plank held the Braves scoreless through eight innings of Game Two, and gave up only one run in the ninth. But the Braves' Bill James (26–7 during the season) allowed only two hits and no runs at all.

Game Three was a seesaw affair not settled until the twelfth inning. Through ten innings, starters Lefty Tyler of Boston and Joe Bush of the A's traded runs. Philadelphia scored one in the top of the first, but Braves' catcher Hank Gowdy doubled in the tying run in the second. The teams traded runs again in the fourth, but no one else crossed the plate until the tenth, when Frank Baker's bases-loaded single drove in two. For the third time, the Braves came back to tie it up. Gowdy opened the last of the tenth with the Series' only home run, and after a walk and single, a sacrifice fly knotted the score. Bill James came on to pitch no-hit ball through the eleventh and twelfth. Bush remained in for the A's, retiring the side in the eleventh. But an inning later Gowdy opened with his third crucial hit of the game, a double. Les Mann replaced him as runner, and after a walk, bunt, and wild throw to third, Mann scampered home with the winning run.

Two of Connie Mack's most promising young pitchers, Bob Shawkey and Herb Pennock (who would later find stardom as New York Yankees), shared the A's pitching in Game Four, and gave up only six hits between them. But a walk and an error led to a Boston run in the fourth, and although Shawkey himself doubled in the tying run a half inning later, two more Braves scored in the last of the fifth on Johnny Evers's single. Pennock came on to pitch three innings of shutout relief, but Rudolph held the A's hitless over the final four innings to preserve his second win and the Braves' crown.

Boston Braves (NL), 4; Philadelphia Athletics (AL), 0

BOS (N)

PLAYER/POS	AVG	G	AB	R	H	2B	3B	HR	RB	BB	SO	SB
Ted Cather, of	.000	1	5	0	0	0	0	0	0	0	1	0
Joe Connolly, of	.111	3	9	1	1	0	0	0	1	1	1	0
Charlie Deal, 3b	.125	4	16	1	2	2	0	0	0	0	0	2
Josh Devore, ph	.000	1	1	0	0	0	0	0	0	0	1	0
Johnny Evers, 2b	.438	4	16	2	7	0	0	0	2	2	2	1
Larry Gilbert, ph	.000	1	0	0	0	0	0	0	0	1	0	0
Hank Gowdy, c	.545	4	11	3	6	3	1	1	3	5	1	1
Bill James, p	.000	2	4	0	0	0	0	0	0	0	4	0
Les Mann, of-2	.286	3	7	1	2	0	0	0	1	0	1	0
Rabbit Maranville, ss	.308	4	13	1	4	0	0	0	3	1	1	2
Herbie Moran, of	.077	3	13	2	1	1	0	0	0	1	1	1
Dick Rudolph, p	.333	2	6	1	2	0	0	0	0	1	1	0
Butch Schmidt, 1b	.294	4	17	2	5	0	0	0	2	0	2	1
Lefty Tyler, p	.000	1	3	0	0	0	0	0	0	0	1	0
Possum Whitted, of	.214	4	14	2	3	0	1	0	2	3	1	1
TOTAL	.244		135	16	33	6	2	1	14	15	18	9

PITCHER	W	L	ERA	G	GS	CG	SV	SHO	IP	H	ER	BB	SO
Bill James	2	0	0.00	2	1	1	0	1	11.0	2	0	6	9
Dick Rudolph	2	0	0.50	2	2	2	0	0	18.0	12	1	4	15
Lefty Tyler	0	0	3.60	1	1	0	0	0	10.0	8	4	3	4
TOTAL	4	0	1.15	5	4	3	0	1	39.0	22	5	13	28

PHI (A)

PLAYER/POS	AVG	G	AB	R	H	2B	3B	HR	RB	BB	SO	SB
Frank Baker, 3b	.250	4	16	0	4	2	0	0	2	1	3	0
Jack Barry, ss	.071	4	14	1	1	0	0	0	0	1	3	1
Chief Bender, p	.000	1	2	0	0	0	0	0	0	0	0	0
Joe Bush, p	.000	1	5	0	0	0	0	0	0	0	2	0
Eddie Collins, 2b	.214	4	14	0	3	0	0	0	1	2	1	1
Jack Lapp, c	.000	1	1	0	0	0	0	0	0	0	0	0
Stuffy Mc Innis, 1b	.143	4	14	2	2	1	0	0	0	3	3	0
Eddie Murphy, of	.188	4	16	2	3	2	0	0	0	2	2	0
Rube Oldring, of	.067	4	15	0	1	0	0	0	0	0	5	0
Herb Pennock, p	.000	1	1	0	0	0	0	0	0	0	0	0
Eddie Plank, p	.000	1	2	0	0	0	0	0	0	0	1	0
Wally Schang, c	.167	4	12	1	2	1	0	0	0	1	4	0
Bob Shawkey, p	.500	1	2	0	1	1	0	0	1	0	1	0
Amos Strunk, of	.286	2	7	0	2	0	0	0	0	0	2	0
Jimmy Walsh, of-2	.333	3	6	0	2	1	0	0	1	3	1	0
Weldon Wyckoff, p	1.000	1	1	0	1	1	0	0	0	0	0	0
TOTAL	.172		128	6	22	9	0	0	5	13	28	2

PITCHER	W	L	ERA	G	GS	CG	SV	SHO	IP	H	ER	BB	SO
Chief Bender	0	1	10.13	1	1	0	0	0	5.1	8	6	2	3
Joe Bush	0	1	3.27	1	1	1	0	0	11.0	9	4	4	4
Herb Pennock	0	0	0.00	1	0	0	0	0	3.0	2	0	2	3
Eddie Plank	0	1	1.00	1	1	1	0	0	9.0	7	1	4	6
Bob Shawkey	0	1	3.60	1	1	0	0	0	5.0	4	2	2	0
Weldon Wyckoff	0	0	2.45	1	0	0	0	0	3.2	3	1	1	2
TOTAL	0	4	3.41	6	4	2	0	0	37.0	33	14	15	18

GAME 1 AT PHI OCT 9

BOS	020 013 010	7 11 2
PHI	010 000 000	1 5 0

Pitchers: RUDOLPH vs BENDER, Wyckoff (6)
Attendance: 20,562

GAME 2 AT PHI OCT 10

BOS	000 000 001	1 7 1
PHI	000 000 000	0 2 1

Pitchers: JAMES vs PLANK
Attendance: 20,562

GAME 3 AT BOS OCT 12

PHI	100 100 000 200	4 8 2
BOS	010 100 000 201	5 9 1

Pitchers: BUSH vs Tyler, JAMES (11)
Home Runs: Gowdy-BOS
Attendance: 35,520

GAME 4 AT BOS OCT 13

PHI	000 010 000	1 7 0
BOS	000 120 00X	3 6 0

Pitchers: SHAWKEY, Pennock (6) vs RUDOLPH
Attendance: 34,365

Boston's five runs in Game Five were the most scored by either team in a Series characterized by outstanding pitching. It was also one of the most closely contested Series: the deciding run was not scored until the ninth inning in three of the games, and only in Game One was the margin of victory as much as two runs.

Grover Cleveland Alexander pitched the opener for the Phillies, and while the Red Sox tagged him for eight hits, they were all singles, and not until the eighth inning did one manage to drive a runner home. Boston's Ernie Shore pitched just as well, giving up only five singles and four walks. But two Phillie hits produced a run in the fourth, and an alternating pair of walks and infield hits in the eighth broke the tie with two runs for the Phillies' only win.

The next three games were 2–1 Boston victories. Rube Foster held the Phillies to three hits in Game Two, and led his team at the bat, going 3 for 4, including a double in the fifth. But it was his single in the ninth with a man on second that produced what proved to be the winning run as he retired the side in the bottom of the ninth to preserve his win. Dutch Leonard duplicated Foster's three-hit pitching two days later as the Series moved to Boston's spacious new Braves Field for Game Three. Before a new Series record crowd of 42,300, Leonard defeated the great Alexander, as the Sox' Duffy Lewis—with his third hit of the game—singled over second base to score Harry Hooper from third with two out in the bottom of the ninth.

Ernie Shore returned to the mound for Boston in Game Four, and although he gave up more hits (seven) than he had in Game One, his Sox had scored their two runs before the Phillies put across their one in the eighth.

Rube Foster was not as effective in Game Five as he had been in Game Two, twice giving the Phillies a two-run lead as Phillie first baseman Fred Luderus drove in three runs with a double and a home run. But from the fifth inning on, Foster held Philadelphia scoreless on two hits, while Duffy Lewis evened the score with a two-run homer in the eighth, and Harry Hooper (who had tied the score earlier with a home run in the third) won the game and the Series with a second homer in the top of the ninth.

Boston Red Sox (AL), 4;
Philadelphia Phillies (NL), 1

BOS (A)

PLAYER/POS	AVG	G	AB	R	H	2B	3B	HR	RB	BB	SO	SB
Jack Barry, 2b	.176	5	17	1	3	0	0	0	1	1	2	0
Hick Cady, c	.333	4	6	0	2	0	0	0	0	1	2	0
Bill Carrigan, c	.000	1	2	0	0	0	0	0	0	1	1	0
Rube Foster, p	.500	2	8	0	4	1	0	0	1	0	2	0
Del Gainer, 1b	.333	1	3	1	1	0	0	0	0	0	0	0
Larry Gardner, 3b	.235	5	17	2	4	0	1	0	4	1	0	0
Olaf Henricksen, ph	.000	2	2	0	0	0	0	0	0	0	0	0
Dick Hoblitzel, 1b	.313	5	16	1	5	0	0	0	1	0	1	1
Harry Hooper, of	.350	5	20	4	7	0	0	2	3	2	4	0
Hal Janvrin, ss	.000	1	1	0	0	0	0	0	0	0	0	0
Dutch Leonard, p	.000	1	3	0	0	0	0	0	0	0	2	0
Duffy Lewis, of	.444	5	18	1	8	1	0	1	5	1	4	0
Babe Ruth, ph	.000	1	1	0	0	0	0	0	0	0	0	0
Everett Scott, ss	.056	5	18	0	1	0	0	0	0	0	3	0
Ernie Shore, p	.200	2	5	0	1	0	0	0	0	0	3	0
Tris Speaker, of	.294	5	17	2	5	0	1	0	0	4	1	0
Pinch Thomas, c	.200	2	5	0	1	0	0	0	0	0	0	0
TOTAL	.264		159	12	42	2	2	3	11	11	25	1

PITCHER	W	L	ERA	G	GS	CG	SV	SHO	IP	H	ER	BB	SO
Rube Foster	2	0	2.00	2	2	2	0	0	18.0	12	4	2	13
Dutch Leonard	1	0	1.00	1	1	1	0	0	9.0	3	1	0	6
Ernie Shore	1	1	2.12	2	2	2	0	0	17.0	12	4	8	6
TOTAL	4	1	1.84	5	5	5	0	0	44.0	27	9	10	25

PHI (N)

PLAYER/POS	AVG	G	AB	R	H	2B	3B	HR	RB	BB	SO	SB
Pete Alexander, p	.200	2	5	0	1	0	0	0	0	0	1	0
Dave Bancroft, ss	.294	5	17	2	5	0	0	0	1	2	2	0
Beals Becker, of	.000	2	0	0	0	0	0	0	0	0	0	0
Ed Burns, c	.188	5	16	1	3	0	0	0	0	1	2	0
Bobby Byrne, ph	.000	1	1	0	0	0	0	0	0	0	0	0
George Chalmers, p	.333	1	3	0	1	0	0	0	0	0	1	0
Gavvy Cravath, of	.125	5	16	2	2	1	1	0	1	2	6	0
Oscar Dugey, pr	.000	2	0	0	0	0	0	0	0	0	0	1
Bill Killefer, ph	.000	1	1	0	0	0	0	0	0	0	0	0
Fred Luderus, 1b	.438	5	16	1	7	2	0	1	6	1	4	0
Erskine Mayer, p	.000	2	4	0	0	0	0	0	0	0	2	0
Bert Niehoff, 2b	.063	5	16	1	1	0	0	0	0	1	5	0
Dode Paskert, of	.158	5	19	2	3	0	0	0	0	1	2	0
Eppa Rixey, p	.500	1	2	0	1	0	0	0	0	0	0	0
Milt Stock, 3b	.118	5	17	1	2	1	0	0	0	1	0	0
Possum Whitted, of-5,1b-1	.067	5	15	0	1	0	0	0	1	1	0	1
TOTAL	.182		148	10	27	4	1	1	9	10	25	2

PITCHER	W	L	ERA	G	GS	CG	SV	SHO	IP	H	ER	BB	SO
Pete Alexander	1	1	1.53	2	2	2	0	0	17.2	14	3	4	10
George Chalmers	0	1	2.25	1	1	1	0	0	8.0	8	2	3	6
Erskine Mayer	0	1	2.38	2	2	1	0	0	11.1	16	3	2	7
Eppa Rixey	0	1	4.05	1	0	0	0	0	6.2	4	3	2	2
TOTAL	1	4	2.27	6	5	4	0	0	43.2	42	11	11	25

GAME 1 AT PHI OCT 8

BOS	000	000	010	1	8	1
PHI	000	100	02X	3	5	1

Pitchers: SHORE vs ALEXANDER
Attendance: 19,343

GAME 2 AT PHI OCT 9

BOS	100	000	001	2	10	0
PHI	000	010	000	1	3	1

Pitchers: FOSTER vs MAYER
Attendance: 20,306

GAME 3 AT BOS OCT 11

PHI	001	000	000	1	3	0
BOS	000	100	001	2	6	1

Pitchers: ALEXANDER vs LEONARD
Attendance: 42,300

GAME 4 AT BOS OCT 12

PHI	000	000	010	1	7	0
BOS	001	001	00X	2	8	1

Pitchers: CHALMERS vs SHORE
Attendance: 41,096

GAME 5 AT PHI OCT 13

BOS	011	000	021	5	10	1
PHI	200	200	000	4	9	1

Pitchers: FOSTER vs Mayer, RIXEY (3)
Home Runs: Hooper-BOS (2),
Lewis-BOS, Luderus-PHI
Attendance: 20,306

In close pennant races, the Red Sox repeated as league champions and Brooklyn won its first pennant since 1900. The first three games of the Series were tightly contested, and the outcomes were determined by only one run apiece. For 6½ innings in the opener, Brooklyn's Rube Marquard dueled Boston's Ernie Shore about equally. But in the last of the seventh the Sox capitalized on a double, some sloppy Brooklyn fielding, and a couple of sacrifice hits for three runs, adding another off reliever Jeff Pfeffer in the eighth for a 6–1 lead. The Robins fought back in the ninth, driving out Shore and drawing within one run of a tie before reliever Carl Mays retired the final man with the bases loaded.

Game Two was even tighter. Boston starter Babe Ruth gave up a first-inning inside-the-park homer to Hy Myers, but in the third he drove in Everett Scott (who had tripled) to tie the game at 1–1. Then for the next ten innings he and Robin pitcher Sherry Smith shut off all scoring. Ruth continued to blank Brooklyn in the fourteenth, and in the last of the inning a walk, sacrifice, and single over the head of the third baseman gave Boston and Ruth the victory.

Brooklyn veteran Jack Coombs took a 4–0 lead into the sixth inning of Game Three before weakening. But after giving up a third Boston run on Larry Gardner's one-out homer, he was relieved by Jeff Pfeffer, who set the Sox down in order the rest of the way. In saving what proved to be Coombs's last World Series appearance (as well as the Robins' only Series win), Pfeffer preserved Coombs's perfect Series won-lost record at 5–0.

Games Four and Five proved anticlimactic. In Game Four, Gardner's second homer of the Series—inside the park for three runs—overcame the Robins' two runs in the first. The Sox added a run here and there to increase their lead, while Sox starter Dutch Leonard shut Brooklyn out through the final eight innings for a comfortable 6–2 win. And in what became the Series finale, Ernie Shore held the Robins to three singles and one unearned run as his Sox took advantage of a bad-hop triple in the second and two third-inning errors by Robin shortstop Ivy Olson to take the lead—and their fourth world championship.

Boston Red Sox (AL), 4; Brooklyn Robins (NL), 1

BOS (A)

PLAYER/POS	AVG	G	AB	R	H	2B	3B	HR	RB	BB	SO	SB
Hick Cady, c	.250	2	4	1	1	0	0	0	0	3	0	0
Bill Carrigan, c	.667	1	3	0	2	0	0	0	1	0	1	0
Rube Foster, p	.000	1	1	0	0	0	0	0	0	0	1	0
Del Gainer, ph	1.000	1	1	0	1	0	0	0	1	0	0	0
Larry Gardner, 3b	.176	5	17	2	3	0	0	2	6	0	2	0
Olaf Henricksen, ph	.000	1	0	1	0	0	0	0	0	1	0	0
Dick Hoblitzel, 1b	.235	5	17	3	4	1	1	0	2	6	0	0
Harry Hooper, of	.333	5	21	6	7	1	1	0	1	3	1	1
Hal Janvrin, 2b	.217	5	23	2	5	3	0	0	1	0	6	0
Dutch Leonard, p	.000	1	3	0	0	0	0	0	0	1	3	0
Duffy Lewis, of	.353	5	17	3	6	2	1	0	1	2	1	0
Carl Mays, p	.000	2	1	0	0	0	0	0	0	0	1	0
Mike Mc Nally, pr	.000	1	0	1	0	0	0	0	0	0	0	0
Babe Ruth, p	.000	1	5	0	0	0	0	0	0	1	0	2	0
Everett Scott, ss	.125	5	16	1	2	0	1	0	1	1	1	0
Ernie Shore, p	.000	2	7	0	0	0	0	0	0	0	2	0
Chick Shorten, of	.571	2	7	0	4	0	0	0	2	0	1	0
Pinch Thomas, c	.143	3	7	0	1	0	1	0	0	0	1	0
Tilly Walker, of	.273	3	11	1	3	0	1	0	1	1	2	0
Jimmy Walsh, of	.000	1	3	0	0	0	0	0	0	0	0	0
TOTAL	.238		164	21	39	7	6	2	18	18	25	1

PITCHER	W	L	ERA	G	GS	CG	SV	SHO	IP	H	ER	BB	SO
Rube Foster	0	0	0.00	1	0	0	0	0	3.0	3	0	0	1
Dutch Leonard	1	0	1.00	1	1	1	0	0	9.0	5	1	4	3
Carl Mays	0	1	5.06	2	1	0	1	0	5.1	8	3	3	2
Babe Ruth	1	0	0.64	1	1	1	0	0	14.0	6	1	3	4
Ernie Shore	2	0	1.53	2	2	1	0	0	17.2	12	3	4	9
TOTAL	4	1	1.47	7	5	3	1	0	49.0	34	8	14	19

BRO (N)

PLAYER/POS	AVG	G	AB	R	H	2B	3B	HR	RB	BB	SO	SB
Larry Cheney, p	.000	1	0	0	0	0	0	0	0	0	0	0
Jack Coombs, p	.333	1	3	0	1	0	0	0	1	0	0	0
George Cutshaw, 2b	.105	5	19	2	2	1	0	0	2	1	1	0
Jake Daubert, 1b	.176	4	17	1	3	0	1	0	0	2	3	0
Wheezer Dell, p	.000	1	0	0	0	0	0	0	0	0	0	0
Gus Getz, ph	.000	1	1	0	0	0	0	0	0	0	0	0
Jimmy Johnston, of-2	.300	3	10	1	3	0	1	0	0	1	0	0
Rube Marquard, p	.000	2	3	0	0	0	0	0	0	0	1	0
Fred Merkle, 1b-1	.250	3	4	0	1	0	0	0	0	1	2	0
Chief Meyers, c	.200	3	10	0	2	0	1	0	0	0	1	0
Otto Miller, c	.125	2	8	0	1	0	0	0	0	0	1	0
Harry Mowery, 3b	.176	5	17	2	3	0	0	0	1	3	2	0
Hy Myers, of	.182	5	22	2	4	0	1	1	3	0	3	0
Ivy Olson, ss	.250	5	16	1	4	0	1	0	2	2	2	0
Ollie O'Mara, ph	.000	1	1	0	0	0	0	0	0	0	1	0
Jeff Pfeffer, p-3	.250	4	4	0	1	0	0	0	0	0	2	0
Nap Rucker, p	.000	1	0	0	0	0	0	0	0	0	0	0
Sherry Smith, p	.200	1	5	0	1	0	1	0	0	0	0	0
Casey Stengel, of-3	.364	4	11	2	4	0	0	0	0	0	1	0
Zack Wheat, of	.211	5	19	2	4	0	1	0	1	2	2	1
TOTAL	.200		170	13	34	2	5	1	11	14	19	1

PITCHER	W	L	ERA	G	GS	CG	SV	SHO	IP	H	ER	BB	SO
Larry Cheney	0	0	3.00	1	0	0	0	0	3.0	4	1	1	5
Jack Coombs	1	0	4.26	1	1	0	0	0	6.1	7	3	1	1
Wheezer Dell	0	0	0.00	1	0	0	0	0	1.0	1	0	0	0
Rube Marquard	0	2	6.55	2	2	0	0	0	11.0	12	8	6	9
Jeff Pfeffer	0	1	1.69	3	1	0	1	0	10.2	7	2	4	5
Nap Rucker	0	0	0.00	1	0	0	0	0	2.0	1	0	0	3
Sherry Smith	0	1	1.35	1	1	1	0	0	13.1	7	2	6	2
TOTAL	1	4	3.04	10	5	1	1	0	47.1	39	16	18	25

GAME 1 AT BOS OCT 7

BRO	000 100 004	5 10 4
BOS	001 010 31X	6 8 1

Pitchers: MARQUARD, Pfeffer (8) vs SHORE, Mays (9)
Attendance: 36,117

GAME 2 AT BOS OCT 9

BRO	100 000 000 000 00	1 6 2
BOS	001 000 000 000 01	2 7 1

Pitchers: SMITH vs RUTH
Home Runs: H.Myers-BRO
Attendance: 41,373

GAME 3 AT BRO OCT 10

BOS	000 002 100	3 7 1
BRO	001 120 00X	4 10 0

Pitchers: MAYS, Foster (6) vs COOMBS, Pfeffer (7)
Home Runs: Gardner-BOS
Attendance: 21,087

GAME 4 AT BRO OCT 11

BOS	030 110 100	6 10 1
BRO	200 000 000	2 5 4

Pitchers: LEONARD vs MARQUARD, Cheney (5), Rucker (8)
Home Runs: Gardner-BOS
Attendance: 21,662

GAME 5 AT BOS OCT 12

BRO	010 000 000	1 3 3
BOS	012 010 00X	4 7 2

Pitchers: PFEFFER, Dell (8) vs SHORE
Attendance: 42,620

Easy winners in their pennant races, the White Sox and Giants traded pairs of victories in the Series before the Sox came up with a second pair to take the title in six games. In the opener, Happy Felsch's solo homer in the fourth inning gave Sox starter Eddie Cicotte the margin he needed to defeat Giant Slim Sallee 2–1, and in Game Two Red Faber went all the way, as his Sox broke a 2–2 tie in the fourth inning with five runs on six singles for Chicago's second win.

The clubs traveled to New York for Games Three and Four, and Giant pitchers rewarded their fans with a pair of shutouts to even the Series. In Game Three, a triple, double, and single against the Sox' Cicotte in the fourth inning produced the only scoring, as Giant Rube Benton blanked the Sox on five hits, walking none. Giant ace Ferdie Schupp (a 21-game winner during the season) did the honors in Game Four, scattering seven hits, as teammate Benny Kauff, with his first Series hit in the fourth inning, homered inside the park to deep center against Red Faber for the deciding run. Two later runs against Faber and two more in the eighth (on Kauff's second homer) against reliever Dave Danforth made Schupp's win easy.

But Faber, the loser in Game Four, came in to pitch two innings of perfect relief two days later in Chicago for his second win, as the Sox rebounded from a 2–5 deficit with three runs in the bottom of the seventh to tie the game and three more an inning later to win it.

After a day of rest and a return to New York, Faber was given his third start. He pitched well enough, but his third win and the Series clincher was really the gift of some infamous Giant fielding. In the fourth inning, the first two Sox batters—Eddie Collins and Joe Jackson—reached on a high throw to first and a dropped fly. Happy Felsch, the third man up, reached on a fielder's choice as Giant third baseman Heinie Zimmerman chased Collins across the plate in a botched rundown. Jackson and Felsch scored the second and third unearned runs as Chick Gandil singled off the hapless Rube Benton. The Giants recovered to score two runs an inning later, but Faber shut them out the rest of the way to give his Sox the Series.

Chicago White Sox (AL), 4;
New York Giants (NL), 2

CHI (A)

PLAYER/POS	AVG	G	AB	R	H	2B	3B	HR	RB	BB	SO	SB
Eddie Cicotte, p	.143	3	7	0	1	0	0	0	0	1	2	0
Eddie Collins, 2b	.409	6	22	4	9	1	0	0	2	2	3	3
Shano Collins, of	.286	6	21	2	6	1	0	0	0	0	2	0
Dave Danforth, p	.000	1	0	0	0	0	0	0	0	0	0	0
Red Faber, p	.143	4	7	0	1	0	0	0	0	0	3	0
Happy Felsch, of	.273	6	22	4	6	1	0	1	3	1	5	0
Chick Gandil, 1b	.261	6	23	1	6	1	0	0	5	0	2	1
Joe Jackson, of	.304	6	23	4	7	0	0	0	2	1	0	1
Nemo Leibold, of	.400	2	5	1	2	0	0	0	2	1	1	0
Byrd Lynn, ph	.000	1	1	0	0	0	0	0	0	0	1	0
Fred Mc Mullin, 3b	.125	6	24	1	3	1	0	0	2	1	6	0
Swede Risberg, ph	.500	2	2	0	1	0	0	0	1	0	0	0
Reb Russell, p	.000	1	0	0	0	0	0	0	0	0	0	0
Ray Schalk, c	.263	6	19	1	5	0	0	0	0	2	1	1
Buck Weaver, ss	.333	6	21	3	7	1	0	0	1	0	2	0
Lefty Williams, p	.000	1	0	0	0	0	0	0	0	0	0	0
TOTAL	.274		197	21	54	6	0	1	18	11	28	6

PITCHER	W	L	ERA	G	GS	CG	SV	SHO	IP	H	ER	BB	SO
Eddie Cicotte	1	1	1.96	3	2	2	0	0	23.0	23	5	2	13
Dave Danforth	0	0	18.00	1	0	0	0	0	1.0	3	2	0	2
Red Faber	3	1	2.33	4	3	2	0	0	27.0	21	7	3	9
Reb Russell	0	0	INF	1	1	0	0	0	0.0	2	1	1	0
Lefty Williams	0	0	9.00	1	0	0	0	0	1.0	2	1	0	3
TOTAL	4	2	2.77	10	6	4	0	0	52.0	51	16	6	27

NY (N)

PLAYER/POS	AVG	G	AB	R	H	2B	3B	HR	RB	BB	SO	SB
Fred Anderson, p	.000	1	0	0	0	0	0	0	0	0	0	0
Rube Benton, p	.000	2	4	0	0	0	0	0	0	0	3	0
George Burns, of	.227	6	22	3	5	0	0	0	2	2	6	1
Art Fletcher, ss	.200	6	25	2	5	1	0	0	0	0	2	0
Buck Herzog, 2b	.250	6	24	1	6	0	1	0	2	1	4	0
Walter Holke, 1b	.286	6	21	2	6	2	0	0	1	0	6	0
Benny Kauff, of	.160	6	25	2	4	1	0	2	5	0	2	1
Lew Mc Carty, c-2	.400	3	5	1	2	0	1	0	1	0	0	0
Pol Perritt, p	1.000	3	2	0	2	0	0	0	0	0	0	0
Bill Rariden, c	.385	5	13	2	5	0	0	0	2	2	1	0
Dave Robertson, of	.500	6	22	3	11	1	1	0	1	0	0	2
Slim Sallee, p	.167	2	6	0	1	0	0	0	1	0	2	0
Ferdie Schupp, p	.250	2	4	0	1	0	0	0	1	0	1	0
Jeff Tesreau, p	.000	1	0	0	0	0	0	0	0	0	0	0
Jim Thorpe, of	.000	1	0	0	0	0	0	0	0	0	0	0
Joe Wilhoit, ph	.000	2	1	0	0	0	0	0	0	1	0	0
Heinie Zimmerman, 3b	.120	6	25	1	3	0	1	0	0	0	0	0
TOTAL	.256		199	17	51	5	4	2	16	6	27	4

PITCHER	W	L	ERA	G	GS	CG	SV	SHO	IP	H	ER	BB	SO
Fred Anderson	0	1	18.00	1	0	0	0	0	2.0	5	4	0	3
Rube Benton	1	1	0.00	2	2	1	0	1	14.0	9	0	1	8
Pol Perritt	0	0	2.16	3	0	0	0	0	8.1	9	2	3	3
Slim Sallee	0	2	5.28	2	2	1	0	0	15.1	20	9	4	4
Ferdie Schupp	1	0	1.74	2	2	1	0	1	10.1	11	2	2	9
Jeff Tesreau	0	0	0.00	1	0	0	0	0	1.0	0	0	1	1
TOTAL	2	4	3.00	11	6	3	0	2	51.0	54	17	11	28

GAME 1 AT CHI OCT 6

NY	000	010	000	1	7	1
CHI	001	100	00X	2	7	1

Pitchers: SALLEE vs CICOTTE
Home Runs: Felsch-CHI
Attendance: 32,000

GAME 2 AT CHI OCT 7

NY	020	000	000	2	8	1
CHI	020	500	00X	7	14	1

Pitchers: Schupp, ANDERSON (2), Perritt (4), Tesreau (8) vs FABER
Attendance: 32,000

GAME 3 AT NY OCT 10

CHI	000	000	000	0	5	3
NY	000	200	00X	2	8	2

Pitchers: CICOTTE vs BENTON
Attendance: 33,616

GAME 4 AT NY OCT 11

CHI	000	000	000	0	7	0
NY	000	110	12X	5	10	1

Pitchers: FABER, Danforth (8) vs SCHUPP
Home Runs: Kauff-NY (2)
Attendance: 27,746

GAME 5 AT CHI OCT 13

NY	200	200	100	5	12	3
CHI	001	001	33X	8	14	6

Pitchers: SALLEE, Perritt (8) VS Russell, Cicotte (1), Williams (7), FABER (8)
Attendance: 27,323

GAME 6 AT NY OCT 15

CHI	000	300	001	4	7	1
NY	000	020	000	2	6	3

Pitchers: FABER vs BENTON, Perritt (6)
Attendance: 33,969

Although both clubs had lost key players to military service, so had other major league teams, and after a season shortened by a month because of the war, the Red Sox and Cubs found themselves opponents in an early-September World Series.

In the opener, Babe Ruth pushed his string of consecutive scoreless World Series innings to 22, holding the Cubs to six singles as he went the distance. The Cubs' Hippo Vaughn pitched just as well, but two of the five singles he yielded followed a leadoff walk in the fourth and produced the game's only run. Chicago evened the Series in Game Two, bunching four of their seven hits after a walk in the second inning to take a 3–0 lead. Successive triples in Boston's ninth spoiled Lefty Tyler's shutout but not his victory.

Hippo Vaughn lost another close one in Game Three when he gave up two runs in the fourth inning on a hit batsman and a succession of singles. The Cubs got him one run back in the fifth, but the Sox' Carl Mays held Chicago to that one run as he hurled Boston back into the Series lead. Ruth pushed the Sox farther ahead the next day in another squeaker. As he continued his mastery over Cub hitters, he drove Boston into the lead with a two-run triple in the fourth inning (his only Series hit). But in the eighth a run-scoring ground out ended his record setting string of scoreless innings at 29⅔, and a single drove in another run to tie the game. The Sox, though, scored a third run on a Chicago error in the last of the eighth, and reliever Bullet Joe Bush shut down a threat in the ninth to save Ruth's win.

Vaughn, in his third start, finally found what was needed for victory—a shutout, on five hits, as the Cubs added hits to walks from Boston's Sad Sam Jones in the third and eighth to push across their three runs. But in Game Six the Sox scored two unearned runs on a dropped line drive to right in the third inning. It was their only scoring off Lefty Tyler, but Boston's Carl Mays was on his way to a one-run three-hitter that brought the Red Sox their fifth world championship in five tries. To date, although they have tried four more times, they have not won a sixth.

Boston Red Sox (AL), 4; Chicago Cubs (NL), 2

BOS (A)

PLAYER/POS	AVG	G	AB	R	H	2B	3B	HR	RB	BB	SO	SB
Sam Agnew, c	.000	4	9	0	0	0	0	0	0	0	0	0
Joe Bush, p	.000	2	2	0	0	0	0	0	0	1	0	0
Jean Dubuc, ph	.000	1	1	0	0	0	0	0	0	0	1	0
Harry Hooper, of	.200	6	20	0	4	0	0	0	0	2	2	0
Sam Jones, p	.000	1	1	0	0	0	0	0	0	1	0	0
Carl Mays, p	.200	2	5	1	1	0	0	0	0	1	0	0
Stuffy Mc Innis, 1b	.250	6	20	2	5	0	0	0	1	1	1	0
Hack Miller, ph	.000	1	1	0	0	0	0	0	0	0	0	0
Babe Ruth, p-2,of-2	.200	3	5	0	1	0	1	0	2	0	2	0
Wally Schang, c	.444	5	9	1	4	0	0	0	1	2	3	1
Everett Scott, ss	.095	6	21	0	2	0	0	0	1	1	1	0
Dave Shean, 2b	.211	6	19	2	4	1	0	0	0	4	3	1
Amos Strunk, of	.174	6	23	1	4	1	1	0	0	0	5	0
Fred Thomas, 3b	.125	6	16	0	2	0	0	0	0	1	2	0
George Whiteman, of	.250	6	20	2	5	0	1	0	1	2	1	1
TOTAL	.186		172	9	32	2	3	0	6	16	21	3

PITCHER	W	L	ERA	G	GS	CG	SV	SHO	IP	H	ER	BB	SO
Joe Bush	0	1	3.00	2	1	1	1	0	9.0	7	3	3	0
Sam Jones	0	1	3.00	1	1	1	0	0	9.0	7	3	5	5
Carl Mays	2	0	1.00	2	2	2	0	0	18.0	10	2	3	5
Babe Ruth	2	0	1.06	2	2	1	0	1	17.0	13	2	7	4
TOTAL	4	2	1.70	7	6	5	1	1	53.0	37	10	18	14

CHI (N)

PLAYER/POS	AVG	G	AB	R	H	2B	3B	HR	RB	BB	SO	SB
Turner Barber, ph	.000	3	2	0	0	0	0	0	0	0	0	0
Charlie Deal, 3b	.176	6	17	0	3	0	0	0	0	0	1	0
Phil Douglas, p	.000	1	0	0	0	0	0	0	0	0	0	0
Max Flack, of	.263	6	19	2	5	0	0	0	0	4	1	1
Claude Hendrix, p-1	1.000	2	1	0	1	0	0	0	0	0	0	0
Charlie Hollocher, ss	.190	6	21	2	4	0	1	0	1	1	1	1
Bill Killefer, c	.118	6	17	2	2	1	0	0	2	2	0	0
Les Mann, of	.227	6	22	0	5	2	0	0	2	0	0	0
Bill Mc Cabe, ph	.000	3	1	1	0	0	0	0	0	0	0	0
Fred Merkle, 1b	.278	6	18	1	5	0	0	0	1	4	3	0
Bob O'Farrell, c-1	.000	3	3	0	0	0	0	0	0	0	0	0
Dode Paskert, of	.190	6	21	0	4	1	0	0	2	2	2	0
Charlie Pick, 2b	.389	6	18	2	7	1	0	0	0	1	1	1
Lefty Tyler, p	.200	3	5	0	1	0	0	0	2	2	0	0
Hippo Vaughn, p	.000	3	10	0	0	0	0	0	0	0	5	0
Chuck Wortman, 2b	.000	1	1	0	0	0	0	0	0	0	0	0
Rollie Zeider, 3b	.000	2	0	0	0	0	0	0	0	2	0	0
TOTAL	.210		176	10	37	5	1	0	10	18	14	3

PITCHER	W	L	ERA	G	GS	CG	SV	SHO	IP	H	ER	BB	SO
Phil Douglas	0	1	0.00	1	0	0	0	0	1.0	1	0	0	0
Claude Hendrix	0	0	0.00	1	0	0	0	0	1.0	0	0	0	0
Lefty Tyler	1	1	1.17	3	3	1	0	0	23.0	14	3	11	4
Hippo Vaughn	1	2	1.00	3	3	3	0	1	27.0	17	3	5	17
TOTAL	2	4	1.04	8	6	4	0	1	52.0	32	6	16	21

In the bottom of the first inning of Game One, White Sox pitcher Eddie Cicotte hit the first batter to face him, a prearranged signal to gamblers that "the fix was on"—that the Sox would throw the Series. The eight Chicago conspirators—pitching aces Cicotte and Lefty Williams, outfielders Joe Jackson and Happy Felsch, and infielders Chick Gandil, Buck Weaver, Fred McMullin and Swede Risberg—received no more than a fraction of the $100,000 promised them but "honored" their end of the deal. Cicotte (winner of 29 regular-season games, with a 1.82 ERA) gave up seven hits and six runs in the opening innings of Game One en route to a 1–9 loss, and Williams, though he held the Reds to four hits in Game Two, uncharacteristically walked six and fanned only one, a performance bad enough for a 2–4 loss.

Dickie Kerr, Chicago's third-best pitcher and not in on the fix, won Game Three with a three-hit shutout. But although Cicotte pitched well in Game Four, Chicago lost a third time as the Reds' Jimmy Ring hurled a three-hit shutout of his own (all three hits coming, ironically, off the bats of conspirators Jackson, Felsch, and Gandil).

Cincinnati's Hod Eller beat Chicago in Game Five with the Series' third successive three-hit shutout. Loser Lefty Williams once again yielded only four hits, but three came in a four-run sixth inning which also saw a walk and a throwing error by Felsch. (The win, the Reds' fourth, did not decide the Series, which had been expanded to the best five of nine in the exuberance which followed the end of the Great War.)

Chicago exerted itself to win the next two games. In Game Six, Kerr's second win depended on crucial hits by Jackson and Gandil in the tenth inning; and in Game Seven Cicotte held the Reds to one run as Jackson and Felsch drove in all the Sox' four.

But in Game Eight, Williams gave up two singles and two doubles before being pulled with only one away in the first. Jackson homered in the third. And he doubled and Gandil tripled to drive in three Chicago runs in the eighth. But by then the Reds had scored ten runs on their way to an easy win and their tainted world title.

Cincinnati Reds (NL), 5; Chicago White Sox (AL), 3

CIN (N)

PLAYER/POS	AVG	G	AB	R	H	2B	3B	HR	RB	BB	SO	SB
Jake Daubert, 1b	.241	8	29	4	7	0	1	0	1	1	2	1
Pat Duncan, of	.269	8	26	3	7	2	0	0	8	2	2	0
Hod Eller, p	.286	2	7	2	2	1	0	0	0	0	2	0
Ray Fisher, p	.500	2	2	0	1	0	0	0	0	0	0	0
Heinie Groh, 3b	.172	8	29	6	5	2	0	0	2	6	4	0
Larry Kopf, ss	.222	8	27	3	6	0	2	0	3	3	2	0
Dolf Luque, p	.000	2	1	0	0	0	0	0	0	0	1	0
Sherry Magee, ph	.500	2	2	0	1	0	0	0	0	0	0	0
Greasy Neale, of	.357	8	28	3	10	1	1	0	4	2	5	1
Bill Rariden, c	.211	5	19	0	4	0	0	0	2	0	0	1
Morrie Rath, 2b	.226	8	31	5	7	1	0	0	2	4	1	2
Jimmy Ring, p	.000	2	5	0	0	0	0	0	0	0	2	0
Edd Roush, of	.214	8	28	6	6	2	1	0	7	3	0	2
Dutch Ruether, p-2	.667	3	6	2	4	1	2	0	4	1	0	0
Slim Sallee, p	.000	2	4	0	0	0	0	0	0	0	0	0
Jimmy Smith, pr	.000	1	0	0	0	0	0	0	0	0	0	0
Ivey Wingo, c	.571	3	7	1	4	0	0	0	1	3	1	0
TOTAL	.255		251	35	64	10	7	0	34	25	22	7

PITCHER	W	L	ERA	G	GS	CG	SV	SHO	IP	H	ER	BB	SO
Hod Eller	2	0	2.00	2	2	2	0	1	18.0	13	4	2	15
Ray Fisher	0	1	2.35	2	1	0	0	0	7.2	7	2	2	2
Dolf Luque	0	0	0.00	2	0	0	0	0	5.0	1	0	0	6
Jimmy Ring	1	1	0.64	2	1	1	0	1	14.0	7	1	6	4
Dutch Ruether	1	0	2.57	2	2	1	0	0	14.0	12	4	4	1
Slim Sallee	1	1	1.35	2	2	1	0	0	13.1	19	2	1	2
TOTAL	5	3	1.63	12	8	5	0	2	72.0	59	13	15	30

CHI (A)

PLAYER/POS	AVG	G	AB	R	H	2B	3B	HR	RB	BB	SO	SB
Eddie Cicotte, p	.000	3	8	0	0	0	0	0	0	0	3	0
Eddie Collins, 2b	.226	8	31	2	7	1	0	0	1	1	2	1
Shano Collins, of	.250	4	16	2	4	1	0	0	0	0	0	0
Happy Felsch, of	.192	8	26	2	5	1	0	0	3	1	4	0
Chick Gandil, 1b	.233	8	30	1	7	0	1	0	5	1	3	1
Joe Jackson, of	.375	8	32	5	12	3	0	1	6	1	2	0
Bill James, p	.000	1	2	0	0	0	0	0	0	0	1	0
Dickie Kerr, p	.167	2	6	0	1	0	0	0	0	0	0	0
Nemo Leibold, of	.056	5	18	0	1	0	0	0	0	2	3	1
Grover Lowdermilk, p	.000	1	0	0	0	0	0	0	0	0	0	0
Byrd Lynn, c	.000	1	1	0	0	0	0	0	0	0	0	0
Erskine Mayer, p	.000	1	0	0	0	0	0	0	0	0	0	0
Fred Mc Mullin, ph	.500	2	2	0	1	0	0	0	0	0	0	0
Eddie Murphy, ph	.000	3	2	0	0	0	0	0	0	0	1	0
Swede Risberg, ss	.080	8	25	3	2	0	1	0	0	5	3	1
Ray Schalk, c	.304	8	23	1	7	0	0	0	2	4	2	1
Buck Weaver, 3b	.324	8	34	4	11	4	1	0	0	0	2	0
Roy Wilkinson, p	.000	2	2	0	0	0	0	0	0	0	1	0
Lefty Williams, p	.200	3	5	0	1	0	0	0	0	0	3	0
TOTAL	.224		263	20	59	10	3	1	17	15	30	5

PITCHER	W	L	ERA	G	GS	CG	SV	SHO	IP	H	ER	BB	SO
Eddie Cicotte	1	2	2.91	3	3	2	0	0	21.2	19	7	5	7
Bill James	0	0	5.79	1	0	0	0	0	4.2	8	3	3	2
Dickie Kerr	2	0	1.42	2	2	2	0	1	19.0	14	3	3	6
Grover Lowdermilk	0	0	9.00	1	0	0	0	0	1.0	2	1	1	0
Erskine Mayer	0	0	0.00	1	0	0	0	0	1.0	0	0	0	0
Roy Wilkinson	0	0	1.23	2	0	0	0	0	7.1	9	1	4	3
Lefty Williams	0	3	6.61	3	3	1	0	0	16.1	12	12	8	4
TOTAL	3	5	3.42	13	8	5	0	1	71.0	64	27	25	22

GAME 1 AT CIN OCT 1

| CHI | 010 000 000 | 1 6 1 |
| CIN | 100 500 21X | 9 14 1 |

Pitchers: CICOTTE, Wilkinson (4), Lowdermilk (8) vs RUETHER
Attendance: 30,511

GAME 2 AT CIN OCT 2

| CHI | 000 000 200 | 2 10 1 |
| CIN | 000 301 00X | 4 4 2 |

Pitchers: WILLIAMS vs SALLEE
Attendance: 29,690

GAME 3 AT CHI OCT 3

| CIN | 000 000 000 | 0 3 1 |
| CHI | 020 100 00X | 3 7 0 |

Pitchers: FISHER, Luque (8) vs KERR
Attendance: 29,126

GAME 4 AT CHI OCT 4

| CIN | 000 020 000 | 2 5 2 |
| CHI | 000 000 000 | 0 3 2 |

Pitchers: RING vs CICOTTE
Attendance: 34,363

GAME 5 AT CHI OCT 6

| CIN | 000 004 001 | 5 4 0 |
| CHI | 000 000 000 | 0 3 3 |

Pitchers: ELLER vs WILLIAMS, Mayer (9)
Attendance: 34,379

GAME 6 AT CIN OCT 7

| CHI | 000 013 000 1 | 5 10 3 |
| CIN | 002 200 000 0 | 4 11 0 |

Pitchers: KERR vs Ruether, RING (6)
Attendance: 32,006

GAME 7 AT CIN OCT 8

| CHI | 101 020 000 | 4 10 1 |
| CIN | 000 001 000 | 1 7 4 |

Pitchers: CICOTTE vs SALLEE, Fisher (5), Luque (6)
Attendance: 13,923

GAME 8 AT CHI OCT 9

| CIN | 410 013 010 | 10 16 2 |
| CHI | 001 000 040 | 5 10 1 |

Pitchers: ELLER vs WILLIAMS, James (1), Wilkinson (6)
Home Runs: Jackson-CHI
Attendance: 32,930

The Indians outscored the Robins in the Series, 21 runs to 8. Yet after losing the opener in Brooklyn, the Robins fought back to take the next two, and held the Series lead as the teams traveled to Cleveland for the next four games.

Both clubs garnered five hits in Game One, but an error, walk, single, and double gave the Indians two runs in the second and a lead they never yielded, as Stan Coveleski outlasted Rube Marquard for the win. In Game Two, both clubs increased their hit totals to seven, but the Robins bunched six of theirs into three innings for three runs, while Burleigh Grimes, only once yielding two hits in an inning, shut the Indians out. The two runs Brooklyn scored in the first inning of Game Three were all Sherry Smith needed to give the Robins their second win behind his three-hit pitching. But Brooklyn scored only twice more in the Series as the Indians swept to the championship with four wins in Cleveland.

With the Indians scoring four runs in Game Four before Brooklyn put its one run on the board, Coveleski breezed to his second five-hit Series run. Jim Bagby had it even easier the next day. The Robins tagged him for 13 hits, but not until the ninth inning were they able to put them together for a run. Meanwhile Bagby and his teammates were registering a couple of Series firsts as they moved to an eight-run lead. Right fielder Elmer Smith opened the scoring in the first inning with the first World Series grand slam, and Bagby himself homered for three more in the fourth—the first pitcher to hit a Series home run.

But the 1920 Series is best remembered for second baseman Bill Wambsganss's unassisted triple play in the fifth inning. With runners on first and second going on pitcher Clarence Mitchell's liner, Wambsganss snared the ball for the first out, stepped on second to force one runner, and tagged the runner coming in from first to retire the side.

In Game Six Duster Mails, a late-season addition to the team, shut out Brooklyn on three hits in a 1–0 squeaker over Sherry Smith. Coveleski won the clincher the next day, also via the shutout, with his third five-hitter of the Series and his third Series win.

Cleveland Indians (AL), 5; Brooklyn Robins (NL), 2

CLE (A)

PLAYER/POS	AVG	G	AB	R	H	2B	3B	HR	RB	BB	SO	SB
Jim Bagby, p	.333	2	6	1	2	0	0	1	3	0	0	0
George Burns, 1b-4	.300	5	10	1	3	1	0	0	2	3	3	0
Ray Caldwell, p	.000	1	0	0	0	0	0	0	0	0	0	0
Stan Coveleski, p	.100	3	10	2	1	0	0	0	0	0	4	0
Joe Evans, of	.308	4	13	0	4	0	0	0	0	1	0	0
Larry Gardner, 3b	.208	7	24	1	5	1	0	0	2	1	1	0
Jack Graney, of-2	.000	3	3	0	0	0	0	0	0	0	2	0
Charlie Jamieson, of-5	.333	6	15	2	5	1	0	0	1	1	0	1
Doc Johnston, 1b	.273	5	11	1	3	0	0	0	0	2	1	1
Harry Lunte, 2b	.000	1	0	0	0	0	0	0	0	0	0	0
Duster Mails, p	.000	2	5	0	0	0	0	0	0	0	1	0
Les Nunamaker, c-1	.500	2	2	0	1	0	0	0	0	0	0	0
Steve O'Neill, c	.333	7	21	1	7	3	0	0	2	4	3	0
Joe Sewell, ss	.174	7	23	4	0	0	0	0	0	2	1	0
Elmer Smith, of	.308	5	13	1	4	0	1	1	5	1	1	0
Tris Speaker, of	.320	7	25	6	8	2	1	0	1	3	1	0
Pinch Thomas, c	.000	1	0	0	0	0	0	0	0	0	0	0
George Uhle, p	.000	2	0	0	0	0	0	0	0	0	0	0
Bill Wambsganss, 2b	.154	7	26	3	4	0	0	0	1	2	1	0
Joe Wood, of	.200	4	10	2	2	1	0	0	0	1	2	0
TOTAL	.244		217	21	53	9	2	2	17	21	21	2

PITCHER	W	L	ERA	G	GS	CG	SV	SHO	IP	H	ER	BB	SO
Jim Bagby	1	1	1.80	2	2	1	0	0	15.0	20	3	1	3
Ray Caldwell	0	1	27.00	1	1	0	0	0	0.1	2	1	1	0
Stan Coveleski	3	0	0.67	3	3	3	0	1	27.0	15	2	2	8
Duster Mails	1	0	0.00	2	1	1	0	1	15.2	6	0	6	6
George Uhle	0	0	0.00	2	0	0	0	0	3.0	1	0	0	3
TOTAL	5	2	0.89	10	7	5	0	2	61.0	44	6	10	20

BRO (N)

PLAYER/POS	AVG	G	AB	R	H	2B	3B	HR	RB	BB	SO	SB
Leon Cadore, p	.000	2	0	0	0	0	0	0	0	0	0	0
Tommy Griffith, of	.190	7	21	1	4	2	0	0	3	0	2	0
Burleigh Grimes, p	.333	3	6	1	2	0	0	0	0	0	0	0
Jimmy Johnston, 3b	.214	4	14	2	3	0	0	0	0	0	2	1
Pete Kilduff, 2b	.095	7	21	0	2	0	0	0	0	1	4	0
Ed Konetchy, 1b	.174	7	23	0	4	0	1	0	2	3	2	0
Ernie Krueger, c-3	.167	4	6	0	1	0	0	0	0	1	0	0
Bill Lamar, ph	.000	3	3	0	0	0	0	0	0	0	0	0
Al Mamaux, p	.000	3	1	0	0	0	0	0	0	0	1	0
Rube Marquard, p	.000	2	1	0	0	0	0	0	0	0	0	0
Bill Mc Cabe, pr	.000	1	0	0	0	0	0	0	0	0	0	0
Otto Miller, c	.143	6	14	0	2	0	0	0	0	1	2	0
Clarence Mitchell, p-1	.333	2	3	0	1	0	0	0	0	0	0	0
Hy Myers, of	.231	7	26	0	6	0	0	0	1	0	1	0
Bernie Neis, of-2	.000	4	5	0	0	0	0	0	0	1	0	0
Ivy Olson, ss	.320	7	25	2	8	1	0	0	0	3	1	0
Jeff Pfeffer, p	.000	1	1	0	0	0	0	0	0	0	0	0
Ray Schmandt, ph	.000	1	1	0	0	0	0	0	0	0	0	0
Jack Sheehan, 3b	.182	3	11	0	2	0	0	0	0	0	1	0
Sherry Smith, p	.000	2	6	0	0	0	0	0	0	0	2	0
Zack Wheat, of	.333	7	27	2	9	2	0	0	2	1	2	0
TOTAL	.205		215	8	44	5	1	0	8	10	20	1

PITCHER	W	L	ERA	G	GS	CG	SV	SHO	IP	H	ER	BB	SO
Leon Cadore	0	1	9.00	2	1	0	0	0	2.0	4	2	1	1
Burleigh Grimes	1	2	4.19	3	3	1	0	1	19.1	23	9	9	4
Al Mamaux	0	0	4.50	3	0	0	0	0	4.0	2	2	0	5
Rube Marquard	0	1	1.00	2	1	0	0	0	9.0	7	1	3	6
Clarence Mitchell	0	0	0.00	1	0	0	0	0	4.2	3	0	3	1
Jeff Pfeffer	0	0	3.00	1	0	0	0	0	3.0	4	1	2	1
Sherry Smith	1	1	0.53	2	2	2	0	1	17.0	10	1	3	3
TOTAL	2	5	2.44	14	7	3	0	1	59.0	53	16	21	21

GAME 1 AT BRO OCT 5

CLE	020	100	000	3	5 0
BRO	000	000	100	1	5 1

Pitchers: COVELESKI vs MARQUARD, Mamaux (7), Cadore (9)
Attendance: 23,753

GAME 2 AT BRO OCT 6

CLE	000	000	000	0	7 1
BRO	101	010	00X	3	7 0

Pitchers: BAGBY, Uhle (7) vs GRIMES
Attendance: 22,559

GAME 3 AT BRO OCT 7

CLE	000	100	000	1	3 1
BRO	200	000	00X	2	6 1

Pitchers: CALDWELL, Mails (1), Uhle (8) VS SMITH
Attendance: 25,088

GAME 4 AT CLE OCT 9

BRO	000	100	000	1	5 1
CLE	202	001	00X	5	12 2

Pitchers: CADORE, Mamaux (2), Marquard (3), Pfeffer (6) vs COVELESKI
Attendance: 25,734

GAME 5 AT CLE OCT 10

BRO	000	000	001	1	13 1
CLE	400	310	00X	8	12 2

Pitchers: GRIMES, Mitchell (4) vs BAGBY
Home Runs: E.Smith-CLE, Bagby-CLE
Attendance: 26,884

GAME 6 AT CLE OCT 11

BRO	000	000	000	0	3 0
CLE	000	001	00X	1	7 3

Pitchers: SMITH vs MAILS
Attendance: 27,194

GAME 7 AT CLE OCT 12

BRO	000	000	000	0	5 2
CLE	000	110	10X	3	7 3

Pitchers: GRIMES, Mamaux (8) vs COVELESKI
Attendance: 27,525

Since both the Giants and Yankees called the Polo Grounds home, all eight games were played there, with the two clubs alternating from game to game as the hometeam. Pitching dominated the first two games—especially Yankee pitching. In Game One, Giant third baseman Frank Firsch went 4 for 4 against Carl Mays. But Mays gave up only one other hit and walked no one, to fashion a shutout. The next day Art Nehf of the Giants allowed the Yankees only three singles. But the Yankees capitalized on two of them, together with one of Nehf's seven walks, a couple of Giant errors, and Bob Meusel's steal of home to score three times, as pitcher Waite Hoyt shut out the Giants on two singles to put the Yanks two up in the Series.

In Game Three the hitters finally came alive. With the score tied 4–4 in the last of the seventh, the Giants unloaded for eight hits which, with two walks and a sacrifice fly, produced eight runs and the first Giant win. They evened the Series the next day, scoring three runs in the eighth to take a 3–1 lead, adding another in the ninth. Babe Ruth's first World Series home run, a solo shot in the bottom of the ninth, thrilled the fans but had no effect on the game's outcome.

The Yankees regained the Series lead in Game Five. Waite Hoyt was not as sharp as he had been in the opener, yielding ten hits. But the only run scored against him came as the result of a first-inning error, a deficit his Yankee teammates overcame for a 3–1 win. In Game Six the Yankees took a quick 3–0 lead in the first. The Giants tied it in the top of the second on home runs by Irish Meusel and Frank Snyder, but Chick Fewster hit a two-run shot a half inning later to restore the Yankee lead. In the fourth inning, though, the Giants parlayed four singles and an error into four runs and a lead that held up for a Series-tying win.

The Yankees scored only one run the rest of the way as the Giants took the final two games on unearned runs. In Game Seven, Mays and the Giants' Phil Douglas dueled into the seventh tied 1–1. But in the last of the seventh, Giant Frank Snyder's double drove in Johnny Rawlings, who had reached on an error, for the game's deciding run. In Game Eight, Hoyt held the Giants to four hits and completed his third game without giving up an earned run. But a Giant runner had scored in the first inning when a grounder shot through the legs of shortstop Roger Peckinpaugh. It turned out to be the game's only run, as Art Nehf and his Giants'

New York Giants (NL), 5; New York Yankees (AL), 3

NY (N)

PLAYER/POS	AVG	G	AB	R	H	2B	3B	HR	RB	BB	SO	SB
Dave Bancroft, ss	.152	8	33	3	5	1	0	0	3	1	5	0
Jesse Barnes, p	.444	3	9	3	4	0	0	0	0	0	0	0
George Burns, of	.333	8	33	2	11	4	1	0	2	3	5	1
Phil Douglas, p	.000	3	7	0	0	0	0	0	0	0	2	0
Frankie Frisch, 3b	.300	8	30	5	9	0	1	0	1	4	3	3
George Kelly, 1b	.233	8	30	3	7	1	0	0	4	3	10	0
Irish Meusel, of	.345	8	29	4	10	2	1	1	7	2	3	1
Art Nehf, p	.000	3	9	0	0	0	0	0	0	1	3	0
Johnny Rawlings, 2b	.333	8	30	2	10	3	0	0	4	0	3	0
Earl Smith, c-2	.000	3	7	0	0	0	0	0	0	1	0	0
Frank Snyder, c-6	.364	7	22	4	8	1	0	1	3	0	2	0
Fred Toney, p	.000	2	0	0	0	0	0	0	0	0	0	0
Ross Youngs, of	.280	8	25	3	7	1	1	0	4	7	2	2
TOTAL	.269		264	29	71	13	4	2	28	22	38	7

PITCHER	W	L	ERA	G	GS	CG	SV	SHO	IP	H	ER	BB	SO
Jesse Barnes	2	0	1.65	3	0	0	0	0	16.1	10	3	6	18
Phil Douglas	2	1	2.08	3	3	2	0	0	26.0	20	6	5	17
Art Nehf	1	2	1.38	3	3	3	0	1	26.0	13	4	13	8
Fred Toney	0	0	23.63	2	2	0	0	0	2.2	7	7	3	1
TOTAL	5	3	2.54	11	8	5	0	1	71.0	50	20	27	44

NY (A)

PLAYER/POS	AVG	G	AB	R	H	2B	3B	HR	RB	BB	SO	SB
Frank Baker, 3b-2	.250	4	8	0	2	0	0	0	0	1	0	0
Rip Collins, p	.000	1	0	0	0	0	0	0	0	0	0	0
Al De Vormer, c-1	.000	2	1	0	0	0	0	0	0	0	0	0
Chick Fewster, of	.200	4	10	3	2	0	0	1	2	3	3	0
Harry Harper, p	.000	1	0	0	0	0	0	0	0	0	0	0
Waite Hoyt, p	.222	3	9	0	2	0	0	0	1	0	1	0
Carl Mays, p	.111	3	9	0	1	0	0	0	0	0	1	0
Mike Mc Nally, 3b	.200	7	20	3	4	1	0	0	1	1	3	2
Bob Meusel, of	.200	8	30	6	6	2	0	0	3	2	5	1
Elmer Miller, of	.161	8	31	3	5	1	0	0	2	5	5	0
Roger Peckinpaugh, ss	.179	8	28	2	5	1	0	0	0	4	3	0
Bill Piercy, p	.000	1	0	0	0	0	0	0	0	0	0	0
Wally Pipp, 1b	.154	8	26	1	4	1	0	0	2	2	3	1
Jack Quinn, p	.000	1	2	0	0	0	0	0	0	0	1	0
Tom Rogers, p	.000	1	0	0	0	0	0	0	0	0	0	0
Babe Ruth, of	.313	6	16	3	5	0	0	1	4	5	8	2
Wally Schang, c	.286	8	21	1	6	1	1	0	1	5	4	0
Bob Shawkey, p	.500	2	4	2	2	0	0	0	0	0	1	0
Aaron Ward, 2b	.231	8	26	1	6	0	0	0	4	2	6	0
TOTAL	.207		241	22	50	7	1	2	20	27	44	6

PITCHER	W	L	ERA	G	GS	CG	SV	SHO	IP	H	ER	BB	SO
Rip Collins	0	0	54.00	1	0	0	0	0	0.2	4	4	1	0
Harry Harper	0	0	20.25	1	1	0	0	0	1.1	3	3	2	1
Waite Hoyt	2	1	0.00	3	3	3	0	1	27.0	18	0	11	18
Carl Mays	1	2	1.73	3	3	3	0	1	26.0	20	5	0	9
Bill Piercy	0	0	0.00	1	0	0	0	0	1.0	2	0	0	2
Jack Quinn	0	1	9.82	1	0	0	0	0	3.2	8	4	2	2
Tom Rogers	0	0	6.75	1	0	0	0	0	1.1	3	1	0	1
Bob Shawkey	0	1	7.00	2	1	0	0	0	9.0	13	7	6	5
TOTAL	3	5	3.09	13	8	6	0	2	70.0	71	24	22	38

flawless fielding blanked the Yankees to give manager John McGraw his first world championship since 1905.

GAME 1 AT NY -N OCT 5

```
NY-A  100 011 000   3 7 0
NY-N  000 000 000   0 5 0
```
Pitchers: MAYS vs DOUGLAS, Barnes (9)
Attendance: 30,202

GAME 2 AT NY -A OCT 6

```
NY-N  000 000 000   0 2 3
NY-A  000 100 02X   3 3 0
```
Pitchers: NEHF vs HOYT
Attendance: 34,939

GAME 3 AT NY -N OCT 7

```
NY-A  004 000 010    5  8 0
NY-N  004 000 81X   13 20 0
```
Pitchers: Shawkey, QUINN (3), Collins (7), Rogers (8) vs Toney, BARNES (3)
Attendance: 36,509

GAME 4 AT NY -A OCT 9

```
NY-N  000 000 031   4 9 1
NY-A  000 010 001   2 7 1
```
Pitchers: DOUGLAS vs MAYS
Home Runs: Ruth-NY(A)
Attendance: 36,372

GAME 5 AT NY -N OCT 10

```
NY-A  001 200 000   3  6 1
NY-N  100 000 000   1 10 1
```
Pitchers: HOYT vs NEHF
Attendance: 35,758

GAME 6 AT NY -A OCT 11

```
NY-N  030 401 000   8 13 0
NY-A  320 000 000   5  7 2
```
Pitchers: Toney, BARNES (1) vs Harper, SHAWKEY (2), Piercy (9)
Home Runs: E.Meusel-NY(N), Snyder-NY(N), Fewster-NY(A)
Attendance: 34,283

GAME 7 AT NY -N OCT 12

```
NY-A  010 000 000   1 8 0
NY-N  000 100 10X   2 6 0
```
Pitchers: MAYS vs DOUGLAS
Attendance: 36,503

GAME 8 AT NY -A OCT 13

```
NY-N  100 000 000   1 6 0
NY-A  000 000 000   0 4 1
```
Pitchers: NEHF vs HOYT
Attendance: 25,410

The Giants didn't quite sweep the Series—a tie in Game Two interrupted their string of victories—but they shut down the Yankee offense, holding Yankee scoring to three runs or less per game, and Babe Ruth to two hits and a .118 BA. This Series restored the best-of-seven-games format after three years of best-of-nine.

The Giants had to come from behind to take Game One. Yankee Bullet Joe Bush and Giant Art Nehf hurled shutout ball through five innings before the Yankees scored single runs in the sixth and seventh innings (Ruth driving in the Series' first run for the second year in a row with his single in the sixth). But in the eighth, Bush gave up four straight singles and two runs before Waite Hoyt relieved him with the score tied and men on first and third. Hoyt set down all three men he faced, but the first out—Ross Youngs's fly to center—drove in what proved to be the Giants' winning run.

The Giants led off Game Two with three first-inning runs on Irish Meusel's home run, but scored no more as Bob Shawkey stopped them for nine innings while his Yankees picked up runs in the first, fourth (on Aaron Ward's homer), and eighth to tie it all up. At the end of the tenth, with forty-five minutes left before sundown, the umpires called the game for darkness and provoked a storm of seat cushions and bottles from the stands.

The Giants resumed their winning ways in Game Three behind Jack Scott's shutout. Scott—picked up by the Giants in midseason—gave up only four Yankee hits, walking one, in the Series' top pitching performance. In Game Four the Yankees scored twice in the first inning, but in the fifth the Giants pounced on Carl Mays for four hits and two runs before the first out was recorded. Before the inning ended, a ground out and another hit had brought two more Giants across the plate, enough to survive Aaron Ward's second Series home run for a 4–3 win.

Game Five, the clincher, showed Nehf the winner by two runs at game's end, but the game went back and forth before the outcome was decided. Nehf gave up only five hits—all singles—but all of them contributed toward scoring Yankee runs in the first, fifth, and seventh innings. The Giants took the lead in the second with a pair of runs, but again fell behind until four hits and a walk in the eighth undid Yankee pitcher Joe Bush's fine effort, giving the Giants three additional runs and John McGraw his third world title.

New York Giants (NL), 4; New York Yankees (AL), 0; tie, 1

NY (N)

PLAYER/POS	AVG	G	AB	R	H	2B	3B	HR	RB	BB	SO	SB
Dave Bancroft, ss	.211	5	19	4	4	0	0	0	2	2	1	0
Jesse Barnes, p	.000	1	4	0	0	0	0	0	0	0	0	0
Bill Cunningham, of	.200	4	10	0	2	0	0	0	2	2	1	0
Frankie Frisch, 2b	.471	5	17	3	8	1	0	0	2	1	0	1
Heinie Groh, 3b	.474	5	19	4	9	0	1	0	0	2	1	0
George Kelly, 1b	.278	5	18	0	5	0	0	0	2	0	3	0
Lee King, of	1.000	2	1	0	1	0	0	0	1	0	0	0
Hugh Mc Quillan, p	.250	1	4	1	1	0	0	0	0	0	1	0
Irish Meusel, of	.250	5	20	3	5	0	0	1	7	0	1	0
Art Nehf, p	.000	2	3	0	0	0	0	0	0	2	0	0
Rosy Ryan, p	.000	1	0	0	0	0	0	0	0	0	0	0
Jack Scott, p	.250	1	4	0	1	0	0	0	0	0	1	0
Earl Smith, c-1	.143	4	7	0	1	0	0	0	0	0	2	0
Frank Snyder, c	.333	4	15	1	5	0	0	0	0	0	1	0
Casey Stengel, of	.400	2	5	0	2	0	0	0	0	0	1	0
Ross Youngs, of	.375	5	16	2	6	0	0	0	2	3	1	0
TOTAL	.309		162	18	50	2	1	1	18	12	15	1

PITCHER	W	L	ERA	G	GS	CG	SV	SHO	IP	H	ER	BB	SO
Jesse Barnes	0	0	1.80	1	1	1	0	0	10.0	8	2	2	6
Hugh Mc Quillan	1	0	3.00	1	1	1	0	0	9.0	8	3	2	4
Art Nehf	1	0	2.25	2	2	1	0	0	16.0	11	4	3	6
Rosy Ryan	1	0	0.00	1	0	0	0	0	2.0	1	0	0	2
Jack Scott	1	0	0.00	1	1	1	0	1	9.0	4	0	1	2
TOTAL	4	0	1.76	6	5	4	0	1	46.0	32	9	8	20

NY (A)

PLAYER/POS	AVG	G	AB	R	H	2B	3B	HR	RB	BB	SO	SB
Frank Baker, ph	.000	1	1	0	0	0	0	0	0	0	0	0
Joe Bush, p	.167	2	6	0	1	0	0	0	1	0	0	0
Joe Dugan, 3b	.250	5	20	4	5	1	0	0	0	0	1	0
Waite Hoyt, p	.500	2	2	0	1	0	0	0	0	0	0	0
Sam Jones, p	.000	2	0	0	0	0	0	0	0	0	0	0
Carl Mays, p	.000	1	2	0	0	0	0	0	0	0	0	0
Norm Mc Millan, of	.000	1	2	0	0	0	0	0	0	0	0	0
Mike Mc Nally, 2b	.000	1	0	0	0	0	0	0	0	0	0	0
Bob Meusel, of	.300	5	20	2	6	1	0	0	2	1	3	1
Wally Pipp, 1b	.286	5	21	0	6	1	0	0	3	0	2	1
Babe Ruth, of	.118	5	17	1	2	1	0	0	1	2	3	0
Wally Schang, c	.188	5	16	0	3	1	0	0	0	0	3	0
Everett Scott, ss	.143	5	14	0	2	0	0	0	1	1	0	0
Bob Shawkey, p	.000	1	4	0	0	0	0	0	0	0	1	0
Elmer Smith, ph	.000	2	2	0	0	0	0	0	0	0	2	0
Aaron Ward, 2b	.154	5	13	3	2	0	0	2	3	3	3	0
Whitey Witt, of	.222	5	18	1	4	1	1	0	0	1	2	0
TOTAL	.203		158	11	32	6	1	2	11	8	20	2

PITCHER	W	L	ERA	G	GS	CG	SV	SHO	IP	H	ER	BB	SO
Joe Bush	0	2	4.80	2	2	1	0	0	15.0	21	8	5	6
Waite Hoyt	0	1	1.13	2	0	0	0	0	8.0	11	1	2	4
Sam Jones	0	0	0.00	2	0	0	0	0	2.0	1	0	1	0
Carl Mays	0	1	4.50	1	1	0	0	0	8.0	9	4	2	1
Bob Shawkey	0	0	2.70	1	1	1	0	0	10.0	8	3	2	4
TOTAL	0	4	3.35	8	5	2	0	0	43.0	50	16	12	15

GAME 1 AT NY -N OCT 4

NY-A	000	001	100	2	7	0
NY-N	000	000	03X	3	11	3

Pitchers: BUSH, Hoyt (8) vs Nehf, RYAN (8)
Attendance: 36,514

GAME 2 AT NY -A OCT 5

NY-N	300	000	000	0	3	8	1
NY-A	100	100	010	0	3	8	0

Pitchers: Barnes vs Shawkey
Home Runs: E.Meusel-NY(N), Ward-NY(A)
Attendance: 37,020

GAME 3 AT NY -N OCT 6

NY-A	000	000	000	0	4	1
NY-N	002	000	10X	3	12	1

Pitchers: HOYT, Jones (8) vs J.SCOTT
Attendance: 37,620

GAME 4 AT NY -A OCT 7

NY-N	000	040	000	4	9	1
NY-A	200	000	100	3	8	0

Pitchers: McQUILLAN vs MAYS, Jones (9)
Home Runs: Ward-NY(A)
Attendance: 36,242

GAME 5 AT NY -N OCT 8

NY-A	100	010	100	3	5	0
NY-N	020	000	03X	5	10	0

Pitchers: BUSH vs NEHF
Attendance: 38,551

After two Series played entirely in the Polo Grounds, the Giants and Yankees in 1923 had Yankee Stadium across the river to play alternate games in. Celebrating the opener in the new "house that Ruth built," the Yankees took an early three-run lead. In the third inning, though, the Giants drove out starter Waite Hoyt, emerging with four runs. Yankee reliever Joe Bush prevented further Giant scoring for several innings as the Yankees picked up a tying run in the seventh. But with the game still knotted in the top of the ninth, Giant Casey Stengel legged out an inside-the-park homer to win it.

Babe Ruth gave Herb Pennock his first World Series win with a pair of homers in Game Two. The first, a solo blast over the roof in right, broke a 1–1 tie in the fourth, and the second, an inning later, concluded Yankee scoring in their 4–2 win that evened the Series. Stengel sent the Giants ahead in the seventh inning of Game Three, lifting a home run over the fence this time for the game's only score. The run gave Art Nehf the win in his duel with Sad Sam Jones, and again gave the Giants the Series lead.

Giant Ross Youngs's fourth hit of Game Four, an inside-the-park homer into the Polo Grounds' deep outfield, gave the Giants a fourth run to lead off the bottom of the ninth, but as a rally it fell short; the Yankees, who had already scored eight, took the game to even the Series. In Game Five Joe Bush gave up only three Giant hits—a single, double, and triple to Irish Meusel. Irish scored the only Giant run, but his Yankee brother Bob drove in three runs with his three hits—sharing RBI honors with Joe Dugan, whose four hits included the Series' third inside-the-park home run, a three-run shot in the second inning. Final score: 8–1.

In Game Six, Herb Pennock yielded four Giant runs in his seven innings on the mound and seemed on the edge of defeat. But in the top of the eighth, Art Nehf (who had pitched one-hit ball since Ruth homered for a Yankee run in the first) lost his stuff. With one out, two singles followed by two walks (on eight pitches) forced in a run. Rosy Ryan replaced Nehf and walked in another run. Ruth struck out, but Bob Meusel's single and a wild throw from center cleared the bases to put the Yankees ahead 6–4, where they remained to game's end for the first of their twenty-two world championships.

New York Yankees (AL), 4; New York Giants (NL), 2

NY (A)

PLAYER/POS	AVG	G	AB	R	H	2B	3B	HR	RB	BB	SO	SB
Joe Bush, p-3	.429	4	7	2	3	1	0	0	1	1	1	0
Joe Dugan, 3b	.280	6	25	5	7	2	1	1	5	3	0	0
Hinky Haines, of	.000	2	1	1	0	0	0	0	0	0	0	0
Harvey Hendrick, ph	.000	1	1	0	0	0	0	0	0	0	0	0
Fred Hoffmann, ph	.000	2	1	0	0	0	0	0	0	1	0	0
Waite Hoyt, p	.000	1	1	0	0	0	0	0	0	0	0	0
Ernie Johnson, ss-1	.000	2	0	1	0	0	0	0	0	0	0	0
Sam Jones, p	.000	2	2	0	0	0	0	0	0	0	1	0
Bob Meusel, of	.269	6	26	1	7	1	2	0	8	0	3	0
Herb Pennock, p	.000	3	6	0	0	0	0	0	0	0	2	0
Wally Pipp, 1b	.250	6	20	2	5	0	0	0	2	4	1	0
Babe Ruth, of-6,1b-1	.368	6	19	8	7	1	1	3	3	8	6	0
Wally Schang, c	.318	6	22	3	7	1	0	0	0	1	2	0
Everett Scott, ss	.318	6	22	2	7	0	0	0	3	0	1	0
Bob Shawkey, p	.333	1	3	0	1	0	0	0	1	0	0	0
Aaron Ward, 2b	.417	6	24	4	10	0	0	1	2	1	3	1
Whitey Witt, of	.240	6	25	1	6	2	0	0	4	1	1	0
TOTAL	.293		205	30	60	8	4	5	29	20	22	1

PITCHER	W	L	ERA	G	GS	CG	SV	SHO	IP	H	ER	BB	SO
Joe Bush	1	1	1.08	3	1	1	0	0	16.2	7	2	4	5
Waite Hoyt	0	0	15.43	1	1	0	0	0	2.1	4	4	1	0
Sam Jones	0	1	0.90	2	1	0	1	0	10.0	5	1	2	3
Herb Pennock	2	0	3.63	3	2	1	1	0	17.1	19	7	1	8
Bob Shawkey	1	0	3.52	1	1	0	0	0	7.2	12	3	4	2
TOTAL	4	2	2.83	10	6	2	2	0	54.0	47	17	12	18

NY (N)

PLAYER/POS	AVG	G	AB	R	H	2B	3B	HR	RB	BB	SO	SB
Dave Bancroft, ss	.083	6	24	1	2	0	0	0	1	1	2	1
Virgil Barnes, p	.000	2	1	0	0	0	0	0	0	0	1	0
Jack Bentley, p-2	.600	5	5	0	3	1	0	0	0	0	0	0
Bill Cunningham, of-3	.143	4	7	0	1	0	0	0	0	1	1	0
Frankie Frisch, 2b	.400	6	25	2	10	0	1	0	1	0	0	0
Dinty Gearin, pr	.000	1	0	0	0	0	0	0	0	0	0	0
Hank Gowdy, c-2	.000	3	4	0	0	0	0	0	0	1	0	0
Heinie Groh, 3b	.182	6	22	3	4	0	1	0	2	3	1	0
Travis Jackson, ph	.000	1	1	0	0	0	0	0	0	0	0	0
Claude Jonnard, p	.000	2	0	0	0	0	0	0	0	0	0	0
George Kelly, 1b	.182	6	22	1	4	0	0	0	1	1	2	0
Freddie Maguire, pr	.000	2	0	1	0	0	0	0	0	0	0	0
Hugh Mc Quillan, p	.000	2	3	0	0	0	0	0	0	0	1	0
Irish Meusel, of	.280	6	25	3	7	1	1	1	2	0	2	0
Art Nehf, p	.167	2	6	0	1	0	0	0	0	0	4	0
Jimmy O'Connell, ph	.000	2	1	0	0	0	0	0	0	0	1	0
Rosy Ryan, p	.000	3	2	0	0	0	0	0	0	0	1	0
Jack Scott, p	.000	2	1	0	0	0	0	0	0	0	0	0
Frank Snyder, c	.118	5	17	1	2	0	0	1	2	0	2	0
Casey Stengel, of	.417	6	12	3	5	0	0	2	4	4	0	0
Mule Watson, p	.000	1	0	0	0	0	0	0	0	0	0	0
Ross Youngs, of	.348	6	23	2	8	0	0	1	3	2	0	1
TOTAL	.234		201	17	47	2	3	5	17	12	18	1

PITCHER	W	L	ERA	G	GS	CG	SV	SHO	IP	H	ER	BB	SO
Virgil Barnes	0	0	0.00	2	0	0	0	0	4.2	4	0	0	4
Jack Bentley	0	1	9.45	2	1	0	0	0	6.2	10	7	4	1
Claude Jonnard	0	0	0.00	2	0	0	0	0	2.0	1	0	1	1
Hugh Mc Quillan	0	1	5.00	2	1	0	0	0	9.0	11	5	4	3
Art Nehf	1	1	2.76	2	2	1	0	1	16.1	10	5	6	7
Rosy Ryan	1	0	0.96	3	0	0	0	0	9.1	11	1	3	3
Jack Scott	0	1	12.00	2	1	0	0	0	3.0	9	4	1	2
Mule Watson	0	0	13.50	1	1	0	0	0	2.0	4	3	1	1
TOTAL	2	4	4.25	16	6	1	0	1	53.0	60	25	20	22

GAME 1 AT NY -A OCT 10

NY-N	004	000	001	5	8	0
NY-A	120	000	100	4	12	1

Pitchers: Watson, RYAN (3) vs Hoyt, BUSH (3)
Home Runs: Stengel-NY(N)
Attendance: 55,307

GAME 2 AT NY -N OCT 11

NY-A	010	210	000	4	10	0
NY-N	010	001	000	2	9	2

Pitchers: PENNOCK vs McQUILLAN, Bentley (4)
Home Runs: Ward-NY(A), E.Meusel-NY(N), Ruth-NY(A) (2)
Attendance: 40,402

GAME 3 AT NY -A OCT 12

NY-N	000	000	100	1	4	0
NY-A	000	000	000	0	6	1

Pitchers: NEHF vs JONES, Bush (8)
Home Runs: Stengel-NY(N)
Attendance: 62,430

GAME 4 AT NY -N OCT 13

NY-A	061	100	000	8	13	1
NY-N	000	000	031	4	13	1

Pitchers: SHAWKEY, Pennock (8) vs J.SCOTT, Ryan (2), McQuillan (3), Jonnard (8), Barnes (9)
Home Runs: Youngs-NY(N)
Attendance: 46,302

GAME 5 AT NY -A OCT 14

NY-N	010	000	000	1	3	2
NY-A	340	100	00X	8	14	0

Pitchers: BENTLEY, J.Scott (4), Barnes (4), Jonnard (8) vs BUSH
Home Runs: Dugan-NY(A)
Attendance: 62,817

GAME 6 AT NY -N OCT 15

NY-A	100	000	050	6	5	0
NY-N	100	111	000	4	10	1

Pitchers: PENNOCK, Jones (8) vs NEHF, Ryan (8)
Home Runs: Ruth-NY(A), Snyder-NY(N)
Attendance: 34,172

Four of the seven games in this exciting Series were decided by one run—two of them after twelve innings. Pitcher Walter Johnson, in his first World Series after eighteen big-league seasons and 376 victories, opened for Washington against the Giants' Art Nehf. Although fourteen Giants reached base on hits or walks in the first nine innings, only two scored—George Kelly and Bill Terry, both of whom homered. In the bottom of the ninth, the Senators scored their second run to send the game into extra innings. Johnson shut out the Giants for two more frames, but in the top of the twelfth, two walks and three singles put New York ahead by two. Washington came back with a run and had a man on third. But Kelly at second base stopped Goose Goslin's grounder with his bare hand, and Nehf had the Giants' first win.

Goslin and manager/second baseman Bucky Harris homered in Game Two to give the Senators a 3–0 lead through six innings. The Giants scored once in the seventh and drove out starter Tom Zachary with two more in the ninth to tie the game, but in the last of the ninth Senator Roger Peckinpaugh doubled in the tie breaker to even the Series.

The Giants took an early lead in Game Three and held it to retake the Series lead, but Washington (led by Goslin's three-run homer in the third) unleashed a 13-hit, seven-run attack the next day to even the Series once more. In Game Five, though, New York pulled ahead again, defeating Johnson a second time as winning pitcher Jack Bentley put the Giants into the lead for good with a two-run homer in the fifth. In Game Six, Washington's two runs in the fifth inning overcame a first-inning Giant run and gave Tom Zachary all he needed for the Senators' third win, which set the stage for one of the most memorable games in Series history.

Washington scored first in Game Seven on manager Harris's homer in the fourth inning, but the Giants scored three runs in the sixth (two of them on Senator errors) to go ahead 3–1. In the last of the eighth, though, Harris's grounder to third bounced over the head of rookie Freddie Lindstrom for two more Senator runs and a 3–3 tie. Walter Johnson came in to face the Giants in the ninth, and shut them out through the twelfth, fanning five. Then in the bottom of the twelfth, with one out, Muddy Ruel (given a second chance after Giant catcher Hank Gowdy caught his foot in his mask and missed Ruel's pop foul) doubled to left. Pitcher Johnson then reached first when

shortstop Travis Jackson bobbled what ought to have been a third-out grounder. With men on second and first, Earl McNeely bounced to Lindstrom at third. But again the ball bounced over Lindstrom's head, and Ruel raced home with Johnson's first Series win and Washington's first world championship.

Washington Senators (AL), 4; New York Giants (NL), 3

WAS (A)

PLAYER/POS	AVG	G	AB	R	H	2B	3B	HR	RB	BB	SO	SB
Ossie Bluege, ss-5,3b-4	.192	7	26	2	5	0	0	0	2	3	4	1
Goose Goslin, of	.344	7	32	4	11	1	0	3	7	0	7	0
Bucky Harris, 2b	.333	7	33	5	11	0	0	2	7	1	4	0
Walter Johnson, p	.111	3	9	0	1	0	0	0	0	0	0	0
Joe Judge, 1b	.385	7	26	4	10	1	0	0	0	5	2	0
Nemo Leibold, of-1	.167	3	6	1	1	1	0	0	0	1	0	0
Firpo Marberry, p	.000	4	2	0	0	0	0	0	0	0	0	0
Joe Martina, p	.000	1	0	0	0	0	0	0	0	0	0	0
Earl Mc Neely, of	.222	7	27	4	6	3	0	0	1	4	4	1
Ralph Miller, 3b	.182	4	11	0	2	0	0	0	2	1	0	0
George Mogridge, p	.000	2	5	0	0	0	0	0	0	0	5	0
Curly Ogden, p	.000	1	0	0	0	0	0	0	0	0	0	0
Roger Peckinpaugh, ss	.417	4	12	1	5	2	0	0	2	1	0	1
Sam Rice, of	.207	7	29	2	6	0	0	0	1	3	2	2
Muddy Ruel, c	.095	7	21	2	2	1	0	0	0	6	1	0
Allan Russell, p	.000	1	0	0	0	0	0	0	0	0	0	0
Mule Shirley, ph	.500	3	2	1	1	0	0	0	1	0	0	0
By Speece, p	.000	1	0	0	0	0	0	0	0	0	0	0
Bennie Tate, ph	.000	3	0	0	0	0	0	0	1	3	0	0
Tommy Taylor, 3b	.000	3	2	0	0	0	0	0	0	0	2	0
Tom Zachary, p	.000	2	5	0	0	0	0	0	0	0	1	0
TOTAL	.246		248	26	61	9	0	5	24	29	34	5

PITCHER	W	L	ERA	G	GS	CG	SV	SHO	IP	H	ER	BB	SO
Walter Johnson	1	2	2.25	3	2	2	0	0	24.0	30	6	11	20
Firpo Marberry	0	1	1.13	4	1	0	2	0	8.0	9	1	4	10
Joe Martina	0	0	0.00	1	0	0	0	0	1.0	0	0	0	0
George Mogridge	1	0	2.25	2	1	0	0	0	12.0	7	3	6	5
Curly Ogden	0	0	0.00	1	1	0	0	0	0.1	0	0	1	1
Allan Russell	0	0	3.00	1	0	0	0	0	3.0	4	1	0	0
By Speece	0	0	9.00	1	0	0	0	0	1.0	3	1	0	0
Tom Zachary	2	0	2.04	2	2	1	0	0	17.2	13	4	3	3
TOTAL	4	3	2.15	15	7	3	2	0	67.0	66	16	25	40

NY (N)

PLAYER/POS	AVG	G	AB	R	H	2B	3B	HR	RB	BB	SO	SB
Harry Baldwin, p	.000	1	0	0	0	0	0	0	0	0	0	0
Virgil Barnes, p	.000	2	4	0	0	0	0	0	0	1	2	0
Jack Bentley, p-3	.286	5	7	1	2	0	0	1	2	1	1	0
Wayland Dean, p	.000	1	0	0	0	0	0	0	0	0	0	0
Frankie Frisch, 2b-7,3b-1	.333	7	30	1	10	4	1	0	0	4	1	1
Hank Gowdy, c	.259	7	27	4	7	0	0	0	1	2	2	0
Heinie Groh, ph	1.000	1	1	0	1	0	0	0	0	0	0	0
Travis Jackson, ss	.074	7	27	3	2	0	0	0	1	1	4	1
Claude Jonnard, p	.000	1	0	0	0	0	0	0	0	0	0	0
George Kelly, 1b-4,of-4,2b-1	.290	7	31	7	9	1	0	1	4	1	8	0
Fred Lindstrom, 3b	.333	7	30	1	10	2	0	0	4	3	6	0
Hugh Mc Quillan, p	1.000	3	1	0	1	0	0	0	1	1	0	0
Irish Meusel, of	.154	4	13	0	2	0	0	0	1	2	0	0
Art Nehf, p	.429	3	7	1	3	0	0	0	0	0	0	0
Rosy Ryan, p	.500	2	2	1	1	0	0	1	2	0	0	0
Frank Snyder, ph	.000	1	1	0	0	0	0	0	0	0	0	0
Billy Southworth, of-2	.000	5	1	1	0	0	0	0	0	0	0	0
Bill Terry, 1b-4	.429	5	14	3	6	0	1	1	1	3	1	0
Mule Watson, p	.000	1	0	0	0	0	0	0	0	0	0	0
Hack Wilson, of	.233	7	30	1	7	1	0	0	3	1	9	0
Ross Youngs, of	.185	7	27	3	5	1	0	0	2	5	6	1
TOTAL	.261		253	27	66	9	2	4	22	25	40	3

PITCHER	W	L	ERA	G	GS	CG	SV	SHO	IP	H	ER	BB	SO
Harry Baldwin	0	0	0.00	1	0	0	0	0	2.0	1	0	0	1
Virgil Barnes	0	1	5.68	2	2	0	0	0	12.2	15	8	1	9
Jack Bentley	1	2	3.71	3	2	1	0	0	17.0	18	7	8	10
Wayland Dean	0	0	4.50	1	0	0	0	0	2.0	3	1	0	2
Claude Jonnard	0	0	INF	1	0	0	0	0	0.0	0	0	1	0
Hugh Mc Quillan	0	0	2.57	3	1	0	1	0	7.0	2	2	6	2
Art Nehf	1	1	1.83	3	2	1	0	0	19.2	15	4	9	7
Rosy Ryan	1	0	3.18	2	0	0	0	0	5.2	7	2	4	3
Mule Watson	0	0	0.00	1	0	0	1	0	0.2	0	0	0	0
TOTAL	3	4	3.24	17	7	2	2	0	66.2	61	24	29	34

GAME 1 AT WAS OCT 4

```
NY    010 100 000 002   4 14 1
WAS   000 001 001 001   3 10 1
```

Pitchers: NEHF vs JOHNSON
Home Runs: Kelly-NY, Terry-NY
Attendance: 35,760

GAME 2 AT WAS OCT 5

```
NY    000 000 102   3 6 0
WAS   200 010 001   4 6 1
```

Pitchers: BENTLEY vs ZACHARY, Marberry (9)
Home Runs: Goslin-WAS, Harris-WAS
Attendance: 35,922

GAME 3 AT NY OCT 6

```
WAS   000 200 011   4 9 2
NY    021 101 01X   6 12 0
```

Pitchers: MARBERRY, Russell (4), Martina (7), Speece (8) vs McQuillan, RYAN (4), Jonnard (9), Watson (9)
Home Runs: Ryan-NY
Attendance: 47,608

GAME 4 AT NY OCT 7

```
WAS   003 020 020   7 13 3
NY    100 001 011   4 6 1
```

Pitchers: MOGRIDGE, Marberry (8) vs BARNES, Baldwin (6), Dean (8)
Home Runs: Goslin-WAS
Attendance: 49,243

GAME 5 AT NY OCT 8

```
WAS   000 100 010   2 9 1
NY    001 020 03X   6 13 0
```

Pitchers: JOHNSON vs BENTLEY, McQuillan (8)
Home Runs: Bentley-NY, Goslin-WAS
Attendance: 49,211

GAME 6 AT WAS OCT 9

```
NY    100 000 000   1 7 1
WAS   000 020 00X   2 4 0
```

Pitchers: NEHF, Ryan (8) vs ZACHARY
Attendance: 34,254

GAME 7 AT WAS OCT 10

```
NY    000 003 000 000   3 8 3
WAS   000 100 020 001   4 10 4
```

Pitchers: Barnes, McQuillan (8), Nehf (10), BENTLEY (11) vs Ogden, Mogridge (1), Marberry (6), JOHNSON (9)
Home Runs: Harris-WAS
Attendance: 31,667

Repeating as pennant winners, the Senators found themselves again locked in a tight Series, this time with the Pirates, who hadn't won a pennant since 1909. Again Walter Johnson pitched the Series opener, winning this time with a strong five-hit, ten-strikeout performance, giving up only one run on Pie Traynor's homer in the fifth. Home runs by Pirates Kiki Cuyler and Glenn Wright and Senator Joe Judge accounted for four of the five runs scored in Game Two, in which Pirate Vic Aldridge dueled Senator Stan Coveleski to a narrow 3–2 win, evening the Series.

Washington took Games Three and Four, though, for a 3–1 Series advantage, Goose Goslin's solo homer in the sixth inning providing the margin of victory in Game Three, and homers by Goslin (for three runs) and Joe Harris the next day providing all the scoring as Johnson shut the Pirates out.

Harris hit his third Series homer in Game Five, but Pirate bats overwhelmed Coveleski as he lost to Aldridge for a second time. And although Goslin's third homer gave the Senators an early lead in Game Six, Pittsburgh's Ray Kremer shut Washington out from the third inning on as his teammates pulled even with two runs in the bottom of the third, and Eddie Moore's homer in the fifth gave him the run he needed for a win that sent the Series into a seventh game.

Both clubs went with their best in the finale as Johnson, winner of Games One and Four, faced Aldridge, victor in Games Two and Five. But Aldridge was wild, issuing three walks and two wild pitches in addition to two hits before being yanked with only one out in the top of the first. Johnson was hardly more effective: although he lasted the whole game, he gave up 15 hits and five earned runs. But if there was a Series goat, it would have to be Senator shortstop Roger Peckinpaugh, the American League MVP. Though he drove in a run in the first and homered for another in the eighth, his dropped pop fly in the seventh and wild throw in the eighth (his seventh and eighth errors of the Series) opened the way to four unearned runs and Pittsburgh's 9–7 triumph.

Pittsburgh Pirates (NL), 4;
Washington Senators (AL), 3

PIT (N)

PLAYER/POS	AVG	G	AB	R	H	2B	3B	HR	RB	BB	SO	SB
Babe Adams, p	.000	1	0	0	0	0	0	0	0	0	0	0
Vic Aldridge, p	.000	3	7	0	0	0	0	0	0	0	0	0
Clyde Barnhart, of	.250	7	28	1	7	1	0	0	5	3	5	1
Carson Bigbee, of-1	.333	4	3	1	1	1	0	0	1	0	0	1
Max Carey, of	.458	7	24	6	11	4	0	0	2	2	3	3
Kiki Cuyler, of	.269	7	26	3	7	3	0	1	6	1	4	0
Johnny Gooch, c	.000	3	3	0	0	0	0	0	0	0	0	0
George Grantham, 1b-4	.133	5	15	0	2	0	0	0	0	0	3	1
Ray Kremer, p	.143	3	7	0	1	0	0	0	0	1	5	0
Stuffy Mc Innis, 1b-3	.286	4	14	0	4	0	0	0	1	0	2	0
Lee Meadows, p	.000	1	1	0	0	0	0	0	0	1	1	0
Eddie Moore, 2b	.231	7	26	7	6	1	0	1	2	5	2	0
Johnny Morrison, p	.500	3	2	1	1	0	0	0	0	0	0	0
Red Oldham, p	.000	1	0	0	0	0	0	0	0	0	0	0
Earl Smith, c	.350	6	20	0	7	1	0	0	0	1	2	0
Pie Traynor, 3b	.346	7	26	2	9	0	2	1	4	3	1	1
Glenn Wright, ss	.185	7	27	3	5	1	0	1	3	1	4	0
Emil Yde, p-1	.000	2	1	1	0	0	0	0	0	0	0	0
TOTAL	.265		230	25	61	12	2	4	25	17	32	7

PITCHER	W	L	ERA	G	GS	CG	SV	SHO	IP	H	ER	BB	SO
Babe Adams	0	0	0.00	1	0	0	0	0	1.0	2	0	0	0
Vic Aldridge	2	0	4.42	3	3	2	0	0	18.1	18	9	9	9
Ray Kremer	2	1	3.00	3	2	2	0	0	21.0	17	7	4	9
Lee Meadows	0	1	3.38	1	1	0	0	0	8.0	6	3	0	4
Johnny Morrison	0	0	2.89	3	0	0	0	0	9.1	11	3	1	7
Red Oldham	0	0	0.00	1	0	0	1	0	1.0	0	0	0	2
Emil Yde	0	1	11.57	1	1	0	0	0	2.1	5	3	3	1
TOTAL	4	1	3.69	13	7	4	1	0	61.0	59	25	17	32

WAS (A)

PLAYER/POS	AVG	G	AB	R	H	2B	3B	HR	RB	BB	SO	SB
Spencer Adams, 2b-1	.000	2	1	0	0	0	0	0	0	0	0	0
Win Ballou, p	.000	2	0	0	0	0	0	0	0	0	0	0
Ossie Bluege, 3b	.278	5	18	2	5	1	0	0	2	1	4	0
Stan Coveleski, p	.000	2	3	0	0	0	0	0	0	0	2	0
Alex Ferguson, p	.000	2	4	0	0	0	0	0	0	0	3	0
Goose Goslin, of	.308	7	26	6	8	1	0	3	6	3	3	0
Joe Harris, of	.440	7	25	5	11	2	0	3	6	3	4	0
Bucky Harris, 2b	.087	7	23	2	2	0	0	0	0	1	3	0
Walter Johnson, p	.091	3	11	0	1	0	0	0	0	0	3	0
Joe Judge, 1b	.174	7	23	2	4	1	0	1	3	3	2	0
Nemo Leibold, ph	.500	3	2	1	1	1	0	0	0	1	0	0
Firpo Marberry, p	.000	2	0	0	0	0	0	0	0	0	0	0
Earl Mc Neely, of-2	.000	4	0	2	0	0	0	0	0	0	0	1
Buddy Myer, 3b	.250	3	8	0	2	0	0	0	0	1	2	0
Roger Peckinpaugh, ss	.250	7	24	1	6	1	0	1	3	1	2	1
Sam Rice, of	.364	7	33	5	12	0	0	0	3	0	1	0
Muddy Ruel, c	.316	7	19	0	6	1	0	0	1	3	2	0
Dutch Ruether, ph	.000	1	1	0	0	0	0	0	0	0	1	0
Hank Severeid, c	.333	1	3	0	1	0	0	0	0	0	0	0
Bobby Veach, ph	.000	2	1	0	0	0	0	0	1	0	0	0
Tom Zachary, p	.000	1	0	0	0	0	0	0	0	0	0	0
TOTAL	.262		225	26	59	8	0	8	25	17	32	2

PITCHER	W	L	ERA	G	GS	CG	SV	SHO	IP	H	ER	BB	SO
Win Ballou	0	0	0.00	2	0	0	0	0	1.2	0	0	1	1
Stan Coveleski	0	2	3.77	2	2	1	0	0	14.1	16	6	5	3
Alex Ferguson	1	1	3.21	2	2	1	0	0	14.0	13	5	6	11
Walter Johnson	2	1	2.08	3	3	3	0	1	26.0	26	6	4	15
Firpo Marberry	0	0	0.00	2	0	0	1	0	2.1	3	0	0	2
Tom Zachary	0	0	10.80	1	0	0	0	0	1.2	3	2	1	0
TOTAL	3	4	2.85	12	7	5	1	1	60.0	61	19	17	32

GAME 1 AT PIT OCT 7

WAS	010	020	001	4	8	1
PIT	000	010	000	1	5	0

Pitchers: JOHNSON vs MEADOWS, Morrison (9)
Home Runs: J.Harris-WAS, Traynor-PIT
Attendance: 41,723

GAME 2 AT PIT OCT 8

WAS	010	000	001	2	8	2
PIT	000	100	02X	3	7	0

Pitchers: COVELESKI vs ALDRIDGE
Home Runs: Judge-WAS, Wright-PIT, Cuyler-PIT
Attendance: 43,364

GAME 3 AT WAS OCT 10

PIT	010	101	000	3	8	3
WAS	001	001	20X	4	10	1

Pitchers: KREMER vs FERGUSON, Marberry (8)
Home Runs: Goslin-WAS
Attendance: 36,495

GAME 4 AT WAS OCT 11

PIT	000	000	000	0	6	1
WAS	004	000	00X	4	12	0

Pitchers: YDE, Morrison (3), Adams (8) vs JOHNSON
Home Runs: Goslin-WAS, J.Harris-WAS
Attendance: 38,701

GAME 5 AT WAS OCT 12

PIT	002	000	211	6	13	0
WAS	100	100	100	3	8	1

Pitchers: ALDRIDGE vs COVELESKI, Ballou (7), Zachary (8), Marberry (9)
Home Runs: J.Harris-WAS
Attendance: 35,899

GAME 6 AT PIT OCT 13

WAS	110	000	000	2	6	2
PIT	002	010	00X	3	7	1

Pitchers: FERGUSON, Ballou (8) vs KREMER
Home Runs: Goslin-WAS, Moore-PIT
Attendance: 43,810

GAME 7 AT PIT OCT 15

WAS	400	200	010	7	7	2
PIT	003	010	23X	9	15	2

Pitchers: JOHNSON vs Aldridge, Morrison (1), KREMER (5), Oldham (9)
Home Runs: Peckinpaugh-WAS
Attendance: 42,856

The Yankees, returning to the World Series after a two-year absence, faced the Cardinals, who had won their first pennant since joining the National League in 1892. Both clubs led their league in slugging and runs scored; this power erupted occasionally in the Series, but over all, pitching dominated as each staff bettered its regular-season earned run average by nearly a run per game.

Herb Pennock of the Yankees pitched a splendid three-hitter in the opener. After yielding two hits and a run in the first inning, he shut out the Cards the rest of the way, holding them hitless until the ninth. Cardinal starter Bill Sherdel also pitched effectively, but three walks in the first and a hit-sacrifice-hit sandwich in the sixth brought in enough runs to beat him.

In Game Two, the veteran Grover Cleveland Alexander evened the Series, striking out ten and holding the Yankees to four singles (three of them in the two-run second) as Billy Southworth and Tommy Thevenow homered for four of St. Louis's six runs. Two days later Jesse Haines put the Cards into the lead, winning the game both ways with a five-hit shutout and a two-run homer.

New York's big bats finally awoke in Game Four. Five Yankees doubled, and Babe Ruth hit three home runs (a World Series record) in a 14-hit, 10-run assault on half the Cardinal pitching staff. Yankee pitcher Waite Hoyt also gave up 14 hits, but 12 were singles and only five runs scored. In contrast, Game Five was a pitchers' duel. Pennock and Sherdel again faced each other and held the opposition to two runs apiece through nine innings. But in the tenth, rookie Tony Lazzeri's sacrifice fly gave New York a 3–2 lead, which Pennock held in the last of the tenth for his second win.

With St. Louis down three games to two, the Series moved to hostile New York for the final games. This didn't seem to trouble the Cardinals, who erupted in Game Six for their own ten-run game, four of them driven in by Les Bell's first-inning single and seventh-inning home run. Alexander pitched a complete game for his second Series win, and came back the next day to relieve Haines in the seventh with a 3–2 lead and the bases full. He struck out Lazzeri to end the inning and kept the Yankees off the bases until he issued Babe Ruth his eleventh Series walk with two away in the ninth. But Ruth, trying to steal second, was caught, and the Cards were world champions.

St. Louis Cardinals (NL), 4; New York Yankees (AL), 3

STL (N)

PLAYER/POS	AVG	G	AB	R	H	2B	3B	HR	RB	BB	SO	SB
Pete Alexander, p	.000	3	7	1	0	0	0	0	0	0	2	0
Hi Bell, p	.000	1	0	0	0	0	0	0	0	0	0	0
Les Bell, 3b	.259	7	27	4	7	1	0	1	6	2	5	0
Jim Bottomley, 1b	.345	7	29	4	10	3	0	0	5	1	2	0
Taylor Douthit, of	.267	4	15	3	4	2	0	0	1	3	2	0
Jake Flowers, ph	.000	3	3	0	0	0	0	0	0	0	1	0
Chick Hafey, of	.185	7	27	2	5	2	0	0	0	0	7	0
Jesse Haines, p	.600	3	5	1	3	0	0	1	2	0	1	0
Bill Hallahan, p	.000	1	0	0	0	0	0	0	0	0	0	0
Wattie Holm, of-4	.125	5	16	1	2	0	0	0	1	1	2	0
Rogers Hornsby, 2b	.250	7	28	2	7	1	0	0	4	2	2	1
Vic Keen, p	.000	1	0	0	0	0	0	0	0	0	0	0
Bob O'Farrell, c	.304	7	23	2	7	1	0	0	2	2	2	0
Art Reinhart, p	.000	1	0	0	0	0	0	0	0	0	0	0
Flint Rhem, p	.000	1	1	0	0	0	0	0	0	0	1	0
Bill Sherdel, p	.000	2	5	0	0	0	0	0	0	0	2	0
Billy Southworth, of	.345	7	29	6	10	1	1	1	4	0	0	1
Tommy Thevenow, ss	.417	7	24	5	10	1	0	1	4	0	1	0
Specs Toporcer, ph	.000	1	0	0	0	0	0	0	0	1	0	0
TOTAL	.272		239	31	65	12	1	4	30	11	30	2

PITCHER	W	L	ERA	G	GS	CG	SV	SHO	IP	H	ER	BB	SO
Pete Alexander	2	0	1.33	3	2	2	1	0	20.1	12	3	4	17
Hi Bell	0	0	9.00	1	0	0	0	0	2.0	4	2	1	1
Jesse Haines	2	0	1.08	3	2	1	0	1	16.2	13	2	9	5
Bill Hallahan	0	0	4.50	1	0	0	0	0	2.0	2	1	3	1
Vic Keen	0	0	0.00	1	0	0	0	0	1.0	0	0	0	0
Art Reinhart	0	1	INF	1	0	0	0	0	0.0	1	4	4	0
Flint Rhem	0	0	6.75	1	1	0	0	0	4.0	7	3	2	4
Bill Sherdel	0	2	2.12	2	2	1	0	0	17.0	15	4	8	3
TOTAL	4	3	2.71	13	7	4	1	1	63.0	54	19	31	31

NY (A)

PLAYER/POS	AVG	G	AB	R	H	2B	3B	HR	RB	BB	SO	SB
Spencer Adams, ph	.000	2	0	0	0	0	0	0	0	0	0	0
Pat Collins, c	.000	3	2	0	0	0	0	0	0	0	1	0
Earle Combs, of	.357	7	28	3	10	2	0	0	2	5	2	0
Joe Dugan, 3b	.333	7	24	2	8	1	0	0	2	1	1	0
Mike Gazella, 3b	.000	1	0	0	0	0	0	0	0	0	0	0
Lou Gehrig, 1b	.348	7	23	1	8	2	0	0	4	5	4	0
Waite Hoyt, p	.000	2	6	0	0	0	0	0	0	0	1	0
Sam Jones, p	.000	1	0	0	0	0	0	0	0	0	0	0
Mark Koenig, ss	.125	7	32	2	4	1	0	0	2	0	6	0
Tony Lazzeri, 2b	.192	7	26	2	5	1	0	0	3	1	6	0
Bob Meusel, of	.238	7	21	3	5	1	1	0	0	6	1	0
Ben Paschal, ph	.250	5	4	0	1	0	0	0	1	1	2	0
Herb Pennock, p	.143	3	7	1	1	1	0	0	0	0	0	0
Dutch Ruether, p-1	.000	3	4	0	0	0	0	0	0	0	0	0
Babe Ruth, of	.300	7	20	6	6	0	0	4	5	11	2	1
Hank Severeid, c	.273	7	22	1	6	1	0	0	1	1	2	0
Bob Shawkey, p	.000	3	2	0	0	0	0	0	0	0	1	0
Urban Shocker, p	.000	2	0	0	0	0	0	0	0	0	2	0
Myles Thomas, p	.000	2	0	0	0	0	0	0	0	0	0	0
TOTAL	.242		223	21	54	10	1	4	20	31	31	1

PITCHER	W	L	ERA	G	GS	CG	SV	SHO	IP	H	ER	BB	SO
Waite Hoyt	1	1	1.20	2	2	1	0	0	15.0	19	2	1	10
Sam Jones	0	0	9.00	1	0	0	0	0	1.0	2	1	2	1
Herb Pennock	2	0	1.23	3	2	2	0	0	22.0	13	3	4	8
Dutch Ruether	0	1	4.15	1	1	0	0	0	4.1	7	2	2	1
Bob Shawkey	0	1	5.40	3	1	0	0	0	10.0	8	6	2	7
Urban Shocker	0	1	5.87	2	1	0	0	0	7.2	13	5	0	3
Myles Thomas	0	0	3.00	2	0	0	0	0	3.0	3	1	0	0
TOTAL	3	4	2.86	14	7	3	0	0	63.0	65	20	11	30

GAME 1 AT NY OCT 2

STL	100 000 000	1 3 1
NY	100 001 00X	2 6 0

Pitchers: SHERDEL, Haines (8) vs PENNOCK
Attendance: 61,658

GAME 2 AT NY OCT 3

STL	002 000 301	6 12 1
NY	020 000 000	2 4 0

Pitchers: ALEXANDER vs SHOCKER, Shawkey (8), Jones (9)
Home Runs: Southworth-STL, Thevenow-STL
Attendance: 63,600

GAME 3 AT STL OCT 5

NY	000 000 000	0 5 1
STL	000 310 00X	4 8 0

Pitchers: RUETHER, Shawkey (5), Thomas (8) vs HAINES
Home Runs: Haines-STL
Attendance: 37,708

GAME 4 AT STL OCT 6

NY	101 142 100	10 14 1
STL	100 300 001	5 14 0

Pitchers: HOYT vs Rhem, REINHART (5), H.Bell (5), Hallahan (7), Keen (9)
Home Runs: Ruth-NY (3)
Attendance: 38,825

GAME 5 AT STL OCT 7

NY	000 001 001 1	3 9 1
STL	000 100 100 0	2 7 1

Pitchers: PENNOCK vs SHERDEL
Attendance: 39,552

GAME 6 AT NY OCT 9

STL	300 010 501	10 13 2
NY	000 100 100	2 8 1

Pitchers: ALEXANDER vs SHAWKEY, Shocker (7), Thomas (8)
Home Runs: L.Bell-STL
Attendance: 48,615

GAME 7 AT NY OCT 10

STL	000 300 000	3 8 0
NY	001 001 000	2 8 3

Pitchers: HAINES, Alexander (7) vs HOYT, Pennock (7)
Home Runs: Ruth-NY
Attendance: 38,093

The Pirates, who struggled to a narrow pennant win in a four-team race, were no slouches at the bat. Their team BA of .305 led the National League, and in the Waner brothers—Paul and Lloyd—and Pie Traynor they had three of the league's five top hitters. But in the World Series they came up against a Yankee team that is still widely regarded as the game's greatest ever. With 110 season victories and a 19-game margin over second-place Philadelphia, the Yankees led the American League in nearly every offensive category. Three Yankees—Earle Combs, Lou Gehrig, and Babe Ruth—hit over .350, and divided among them league crowns in runs, hits, doubles, triples, home runs (Ruth's 60), RBIs, and slugging average. The Yankees not only hit: their pitching staff boasted the league's lowest earned run average.

In the Series, though, it was Pittsburgh's erratic play that brought about the first American League sweep. The Pirates scored four times off Yankee starter Waite Hoyt in Game One, and might have won the game. But Paul Waner misplayed a Gehrig fly for a run-scoring triple in the first, and in the third, two Pirate errors led to three more Yankee runs. A final run in the fifth was all New York needed to win, 5–4.

The Yankees won the next two games more convincingly, with strong pitching and timely hitting. George Pipgras held Pittsburgh to two runs in Game Two as his Yankees bunched seven of their 11 hits into the third and eighth innings (also taking advantage of two walks and a hit batsman in the eighth) for their six runs. And in Game Three—as Herb Pennock pitched perfectly into the eighth inning before yielding two hits and a run—Yankee batters again bunched most of their hits into two innings, scoring two runs on Gehrig's first-inning triple and six more in the seventh, climaxed by Ruth's three-run homer.

Pittsburgh took advantage of two Yankee errors in the seventh inning of Game Four to score two runs and tie the game at three-all. But in the last of the ninth, after the Pirates' Johnny Miljus had struck out Gehrig and Bob Meusel with the bases loaded, his second wild pitch of the inning undid him—Combs scored from third with the Series' winning run.

New York Yankees (AL), 4; Pittsburgh Pirates (NL), 0

NY (A)

PLAYER/POS	AVG	G	AB	R	H	2B	3B	HR	RB	BB	SO	SB
Benny Bengough, c	.000	2	4	1	0	0	0	0	0	0	1	0
Pat Collins, c	.600	2	5	0	3	1	0	0	0	3	0	0
Earle Combs, of	.313	4	16	6	5	0	0	0	2	1	2	0
Joe Dugan, 3b	.200	4	15	2	3	0	0	0	0	0	0	0
Cedric Durst, ph	.000	1	1	0	0	0	0	0	0	0	0	0
Lou Gehrig, 1b	.308	4	13	2	4	2	2	0	4	3	3	0
Johnny Grabowski, c	.000	1	2	0	0	0	0	0	0	0	0	0
Waite Hoyt, p	.000	1	3	0	0	0	0	0	0	0	0	0
Mark Koenig, ss	.500	4	18	5	9	2	0	0	2	0	2	0
Tony Lazzeri, 2b	.267	4	15	1	4	1	0	0	2	1	4	0
Bob Meusel, of	.118	4	17	1	2	0	0	0	1	1	7	1
Wilcy Moore, p	.200	2	5	0	1	0	0	0	0	0	3	0
Herb Pennock, p	.000	1	4	1	0	0	0	0	0	1	0	0
George Pipgras, p	.333	1	3	0	1	0	0	0	0	0	1	0
Babe Ruth, of	.400	4	15	4	6	0	0	2	7	2	2	1
TOTAL	.279		136	23	38	6	2	2	19	13	25	2

PITCHER	W	L	ERA	G	GS	CG	SV	SHO	IP	H	ER	BB	SO
Waite Hoyt	1	0	4.91	1	1	0	0	0	7.1	8	4	1	2
Wilcy Moore	1	0	0.84	2	1	1	1	0	10.2	11	1	2	2
Herb Pennock	1	0	1.00	1	1	1	0	0	9.0	3	1	0	1
George Pipgras	1	0	2.00	1	1	1	0	0	9.0	7	2	1	2
TOTAL	4	0	2.00	5	4	3	1	0	36.0	29	8	4	7

PIT (N)

PLAYER/POS	AVG	G	AB	R	H	2B	3B	HR	RB	BB	SO	SB
Vic Aldridge, p	.000	1	2	0	0	0	0	0	0	0	0	0
Clyde Barnhart, of	.313	4	16	0	5	1	0	0	4	0	0	0
Fred Brickell, ph	.000	2	2	1	0	0	0	0	0	0	0	0
Mike Cvengros, p	.000	2	0	0	0	0	0	0	0	0	0	0
Joe Dawson, p	.000	1	0	0	0	0	0	0	0	0	0	0
Johnny Gooch, c	.000	3	5	0	0	0	0	0	0	1	1	0
George Grantham, 2b	.364	3	11	0	4	1	0	0	0	1	1	0
Heinie Groh, ph	.000	1	1	0	0	0	0	0	0	0	0	0
Joe Harris, 1b	.200	4	15	0	3	0	0	0	1	0	0	0
Carmen Hill, p	.000	1	1	0	0	0	0	0	0	1	0	0
Ray Kremer, p	.500	1	2	1	1	1	0	0	0	0	1	0
Lee Meadows, p	.000	1	2	0	0	0	0	0	0	0	0	0
Johnny Miljus, p	.000	2	2	0	0	0	0	0	0	0	2	0
Hal Rhyne, 2b	.000	1	4	0	0	0	0	0	0	0	0	0
Earl Smith, c-2	.000	3	8	0	0	0	0	0	0	0	0	0
Roy Spencer, c	.000	1	1	0	0	0	0	0	0	0	0	0
Pie Traynor, 3b	.200	4	15	1	3	1	0	0	0	0	1	0
Lloyd Waner, of	.400	4	15	5	6	1	1	0	0	1	0	0
Paul Waner, of	.333	4	15	0	5	1	0	0	3	0	1	0
Glenn Wright, ss	.154	4	13	1	2	0	0	0	2	0	0	0
Emil Yde, pr	.000	1	1	0	0	0	0	0	0	0	0	0
TOTAL	.223		130	10	29	6	1	0	10	4	7	0

PITCHER	W	L	ERA	G	GS	CG	SV	SHO	IP	H	ER	BB	SO
Vic Aldridge	0	1	7.36	1	1	0	0	0	7.1	10	6	4	4
Mike Cvengros	0	0	3.86	2	0	0	0	0	2.1	3	1	0	2
Joe Dawson	0	0	0.00	1	0	0	0	0	1.0	0	0	0	0
Carmen Hill	0	0	4.50	1	1	0	0	0	6.0	9	3	1	6
Ray Kremer	0	1	3.60	1	1	0	0	0	5.0	5	2	3	1
Lee Meadows	0	1	9.95	1	1	0	0	0	6.1	7	7	1	6
Johnny Miljus	0	1	1.35	2	0	0	0	0	6.2	4	1	4	6
TOTAL	0	4	5.19	9	4	0	0	0	34.2	38	20	13	25

GAME 1 AT PIT OCT 5

```
NY   103 010 000   5 6 1
PIT  101 010 010   4 9 2
```
Pitchers: HOYT, Moore (8) vs KREMER, Miljus (6)
Attendance: 41,467

GAME 2 AT PIT OCT 6

```
NY   003 000 030   6 11 0
PIT  100 000 010   2 7 2
```
Pitchers: PIPGRAS vs ALDRIDGE, Cvengros (8), Dawson (9)
Attendance: 41,634

GAME 3 AT NY OCT 7

```
PIT  000 000 010   1 3 1
NY   200 000 60X   8 9 0
```
Pitchers: MEADOWS, Cvengros (7) vs PENNOCK
Home Runs: Ruth-NY
Attendance: 60,695

GAME 4 AT NY OCT 8

```
PIT  100 000 200   3 10 1
NY   100 010 001   4 12 2
```
Pitchers: Hill, MILJUS (7) vs MOORE
Home Runs: Ruth-NY
Attendance: 57,909

After squandering a 13½-game lead and falling briefly behind the Athletics in early September, the Yankees recovered to meet the Cardinals—winners of another tight National League race—in the Series. With Herb Pennock lost to arm trouble, the Yankees made do with just three pitchers in extending their Series win streak to eight games.

The four games offered little suspense, but for Yankee fans there were thrills aplenty. The Bronx Bombers' nine home runs (including four by Lou Gehrig and three by Babe Ruth) nearly equalled St. Louis's total scoring (ten runs), and Gehrig himself drove in as many runs (nine) as the entire Cardinal offense. Ruth and Gehrig started things off with successive doubles and a run in the first inning of the opener, and when Bob Meusel followed Ruth's second double with a home run in the fourth, the Yanks had more than they would need to support Waite Hoyt's three-hitter. The Cardinals' Jim Bottomley homered off Hoyt in the seventh, but successive singles by Mark Koenig, Ruth, and Gehrig produced a fourth Yankee run and concluded the scoring.

Gehrig homered in the first inning of Game Two to get New York off to a 3–0 lead against forty-one-year-old Grover Cleveland Alexander. The Cards snapped back to tie the game, but the Yankees retook the lead with a run in the last of the second and put together four hits, two walks, and a hit batsman for four more in the third. A final Yankee run in the seventh capped a 9–3 four-hit win for pitcher George Pipgras.

Jim Bottomley gave St. Louis its first lead of the Series with a two-run triple in the first inning of Game Three. But Yankee Tom Zachary gave up only one more run, taking the third Yankee win as Gehrig drove in three runs with homers in the second and fourth, and his teammates scored three more in the sixth (thanks in large part to two Cardinal errors and Meusel's steal of home) and a final (unearned) run an inning later.

New York completed its second straight Series sweep with another 7–3 win two days later. Waite Hoyt gained his second victory, mostly on the strength of five solo Yankee homers, including three by Babe Ruth.

New York Yankees (AL), 4; St. Louis Cardinals (NL), 0

NY (A)

PLAYER/POS	AVG	G	AB	R	H	2B	3B	HR	RB	BB	SO	SB
Benny Bengough, c	.231	4	13	1	3	0	0	0	1	1	1	0
Pat Collins, c	1.000	1	1	0	1	1	0	0	0	0	0	0
Earle Combs, ph	.000	1	0	0	0	0	0	0	1	0	0	0
Joe Dugan, 3b	.167	3	6	0	1	0	0	0	1	0	0	0
Leo Durocher, 2b	.000	4	2	0	0	0	0	0	0	0	1	0
Cedric Durst, of	.375	4	8	3	3	0	0	1	2	0	1	0
Lou Gehrig, 1b	.545	4	11	5	6	1	0	4	9	6	0	0
Waite Hoyt, p	.143	2	7	0	1	0	0	0	0	0	0	0
Mark Koenig, ss	.158	4	19	1	3	0	0	0	0	0	1	0
Tony Lazzeri, 2b	.250	4	12	2	3	1	0	0	0	1	0	2
Bob Meusel, of	.200	4	15	5	3	1	0	1	3	2	5	2
Ben Paschal, of	.200	3	10	0	2	0	0	0	1	1	0	0
George Pipgras, p	.000	1	2	0	0	0	0	0	0	1	0	0
Gene Robertson, 3b	.125	3	8	1	1	0	0	0	2	1	0	0
Babe Ruth, of	.625	4	16	9	10	3	0	3	4	1	2	0
Tom Zachary, p	.000	4	4	0	0	0	0	0	0	0	1	0
TOTAL	.276		134	27	37	7	0	9	25	13	12	4

PITCHER	W	L	ERA	G	GS	CG	SV	SHO	IP	H	ER	BB	SO
Waite Hoyt	2	0	1.50	2	2	2	0	0	18.0	14	3	6	14
George Pipgras	1	0	2.00	1	1	1	0	0	9.0	4	2	4	8
Tom Zachary	1	0	3.00	1	1	1	0	0	9.0	9	3	1	7
TOTAL	4	0	2.00	4	4	4	0	0	36.0	27	8	11	29

STL (N)

PLAYER/POS	AVG	G	AB	R	H	2B	3B	HR	RB	BB	SO	SB
Pete Alexander, p	.000	2	1	0	0	0	0	0	0	1	0	0
Ray Blades, ph	.000	1	1	0	0	0	0	0	0	0	0	0
Jim Bottomley, 1b	.214	4	14	1	3	0	1	1	3	2	6	0
Taylor Douthit, of	.091	3	11	1	1	0	0	0	1	1	1	0
Frankie Frisch, 2b	.231	4	13	1	3	0	0	0	1	2	2	2
Chick Hafey, of	.200	4	15	0	3	0	0	0	0	1	4	0
Jesse Haines, p	.000	1	2	0	0	0	0	0	0	0	0	0
George Harper, of	.111	3	9	1	1	0	0	0	0	2	2	0
Andy High, 3b	.294	4	17	1	5	2	0	0	1	1	3	0
Wattie Holm, of-1	.167	3	6	0	1	0	0	0	0	1	0	1
Syl Johnson, p	.000	2	0	0	0	0	0	0	0	0	0	0
Rabbit Maranville, ss	.308	4	13	2	4	1	0	0	0	1	1	1
Pepper Martin, pr	.000	1	0	1	0	0	0	0	0	0	0	0
Clarence Mitchell, p	.000	1	2	0	0	0	0	0	0	0	0	0
Ernie Orsatti, of-1	.286	4	7	1	2	1	0	0	0	1	3	0
Flint Rhem, p	.000	1	0	0	0	0	0	0	0	0	0	0
Bill Sherdel, p	.000	2	5	0	0	0	0	0	0	0	2	0
Earl Smith, c	.750	1	4	0	3	0	0	0	0	0	0	0
Tommy Thevenow, ss	.000	1	0	0	0	0	0	0	0	0	0	0
Jimmie Wilson, c	.091	3	11	1	1	1	0	0	1	0	3	0
TOTAL	.206		131	10	27	5	1	1	9	11	29	3

PITCHER	W	L	ERA	G	GS	CG	SV	SHO	IP	H	ER	BB	SO
Pete Alexander	0	1	19.80	2	1	0	0	0	5.0	10	11	4	2
Jesse Haines	0	1	4.50	1	1	0	0	0	6.0	6	3	3	3
Syl Johnson	0	0	4.50	2	0	0	0	0	2.0	4	1	1	1
Clarence Mitchell	0	0	1.59	1	0	0	0	0	5.2	2	1	2	2
Flint Rhem	0	0	0.00	1	0	0	0	0	2.0	0	0	0	1
Bill Sherdel	0	2	4.72	2	2	0	0	0	13.1	15	7	3	3
TOTAL	0	4	6.09	9	4	0	0	0	34.0	37	23	13	12

GAME 1 AT NY OCT 4

STL	000	000	100	1	3	1
NY	100	200	01X	4	7	0

Pitchers: SHERDEL, Johnson (8) vs HOYT
Home Runs: Meusel-NY, Bottomley-STL
Attendance: 61,425

GAME 2 AT NY OCT 5

STL	030	000	000	3	4	1
NY	314	000	10X	9	8	2

Pitchers: ALEXANDER, Mitchell (3) vs PIPGRAS
Home Runs: Gehrig-NY
Attendance: 60,714

GAME 3 AT STL OCT 7

NY	010	203	100	7	7	2
STL	200	010	000	3	9	3

Pitchers: ZACHARY vs HAINES, Johnson (7), Rhem (8)
Home Runs: Gehrig-NY (2)
Attendance: 39,602

GAME 4 AT STL OCT 9

NY	000	100	420	7	15	2
STL	001	100	001	3	11	0

Pitchers: HOYT vs SHERDEL, Alexander (7)
Home Runs: Ruth-NY (3), Durst-NY, Gehrig-NY
Attendance: 37,331

The surprising success of a surprise starter and the ultimate in big innings highlighted the return of the Athletics to World Series play after a gap of fifteen years. In the opener, A's manager Connie Mack passed over the aces of his pitching staff in favor of Howard Ehmke, an aging journeyman who that season had started only eight times and pitched under 55 innings. But Ehmke, who (per Mack's instructions) had studied the Cubs' hitters in a series of late-season games, held the Cubs scoreless through the first eight innings of Game One (yielding an unearned run in the last of the ninth) while fanning 13 batters for a new Series record. Chicago's Charlie Root also pitched effectively until Jimmie Foxx's solo homer in the seventh gave the A's the game's first score. A pair of errors by Cub shortstop Woody English in the ninth set up two unearned runs against reliever Guy Bush and gave Ehmke and the A's all the lead they needed.

Home runs by Foxx and Al Simmons drove in five of the A's nine runs in Game Two as Philadelphia took a 2–0 Series lead. But Guy Bush held Mack's sluggers to nine singles and one run in Game Three as his Cubs scored three runs in the sixth to take their first win.

The Cubs seemed well on their way to tying the Series in Game Four as they entered the last of the seventh with an 8–0 lead. But Simmons led off with a homer to erase Charlie Root's shutout, and five of the next six batters singled. Art Nehf relieved Root, but the first batter to face him—Mule Haas—lofted a fly to center which Hack Wilson lost in the sun for a three-run inside-the-park homer, and the score was 8–7. After walking Mickey Cochrane, Nehf was replaced by Sheriff Blake, who gave up two singles and saw the tying run come home before Pat Malone took the mound with two men still on base and only one away. Malone struck out two in a row to end the inning—but not until he first hit a batter and gave up a double by Jimmy Dykes for the two runs that gave the A's a 10–8 win and a 3–1 Series advantage.

Game Five, although inevitably anticlimactic, was not decided until the final at-bat. Chicago scored twice off Ehmke in the fourth as Malone shut out the A's with only two hits through eight. But in the last of the ninth a single and Haas's home run tied the score, and—with two men out—Simmons doubled, Foxx was walked intentionally, Bing Miller doubled, and the Series was history.

Philadelphia Athletics (AL), 4; Chicago Cubs (NL), 1

PHI (A)

PLAYER/POS	AVG	G	AB	R	H	2B	3B	HR	RB	BB	SO	SB
Max Bishop, 2b	.190	5	21	2	4	0	0	0	0	1	2	3	0
Joe Boley, ss	.235	5	17	1	4	0	0	0	1	0	3	0
George Burns, ph	.000	1	2	0	0	0	0	0	0	0	1	0
Mickey Cochrane, c	.400	5	15	5	6	1	0	0	0	7	0	0
Jimmy Dykes, 3b	.421	5	19	2	8	1	0	0	4	1	1	0
George Earnshaw, p	.000	2	5	1	0	0	0	0	0	0	4	0
Howard Ehmke, p	.200	2	5	0	1	0	0	0	0	0	0	0
Jimmie Foxx, 1b	.350	5	20	5	7	1	0	2	5	5	1	0
Walter French, ph	.000	1	1	0	0	0	0	0	0	0	1	0
Lefty Grove, p	.000	2	2	0	0	0	0	0	0	0	1	0
Mule Haas, of	.238	5	21	3	5	0	0	2	6	1	3	0
Bing Miller, of	.368	5	19	1	7	1	0	0	4	0	2	0
Jack Quinn, p	.000	1	2	0	0	0	0	0	0	0	2	0
Eddie Rommel, p	.000	1	0	0	0	0	0	0	0	0	0	0
Al Simmons, of	.300	5	20	6	6	1	0	2	5	1	4	0
Homer Summa, ph	.000	1	1	0	0	0	0	0	0	0	1	0
Rube Walberg, p	.000	2	0	0	0	0	0	0	0	0	0	0
TOTAL	.281		171	26	48	5	0	6	26	13	27	0

PITCHER	W	L	ERA	G	GS	CG	SV	SHO	IP	H	ER	BB	SO
George Earnshaw	1	1	2.63	2	2	1	0	0	13.2	14	4	6	17
Howard Ehmke	1	0	1.42	2	2	1	0	0	12.2	14	2	3	13
Lefty Grove	0	0	0.00	2	0	0	2	0	6.1	3	0	1	10
Jack Quinn	0	0	9.00	1	1	0	0	0	5.0	7	5	2	2
Eddie Rommel	1	0	9.00	1	0	0	0	0	1.0	2	1	1	0
Rube Walberg	1	0	0.00	2	0	0	0	0	6.1	3	0	0	8
TOTAL	4	1	2.40	10	5	2	2	0	45.0	43	12	13	50

CHI (N)

PLAYER/POS	AVG	G	AB	R	H	2B	3B	HR	RB	BB	SO	SB
Footsie Blair, ph	.000	1	1	0	0	0	0	0	0	0	0	0
Sheriff Blake, p	1.000	2	1	0	1	0	0	0	0	0	0	0
Guy Bush, p	.000	2	3	1	0	0	0	0	0	1	3	0
Hal Carlson, p	.000	2	0	0	0	0	0	0	0	0	0	0
Kiki Cuyler, of	.300	5	20	4	6	1	0	0	4	1	7	0
Woody English, ss	.190	5	21	1	4	2	0	0	0	1	6	0
Mike Gonzalez, c-1	.000	2	1	0	0	0	0	0	0	0	1	0
Charlie Grimm, 1b	.389	5	18	2	7	0	0	1	4	1	2	0
Gabby Hartnett, ph	.000	3	3	0	0	0	0	0	0	0	3	0
Cliff Heathcote, ph	.000	2	1	0	0	0	0	0	0	0	0	0
Rogers Hornsby, 2b	.238	5	21	4	5	1	1	0	1	1	8	0
Pat Malone, p	.250	3	4	0	1	1	0	0	0	0	2	0
Norm Mc Millan, 3b	.100	5	20	0	2	0	0	0	0	2	6	1
Art Nehf, p	.000	2	0	0	0	0	0	0	0	0	0	0
Charlie Root, p	.000	2	5	0	0	0	0	0	0	0	3	0
Riggs Stephenson, of	.316	5	19	3	6	1	0	0	3	2	2	0
Zack Taylor, c	.176	5	17	0	3	0	0	0	3	0	3	0
Chick Tolson, ph	.000	1	1	0	0	0	0	0	0	0	1	0
Hack Wilson, of	.471	5	17	2	8	0	1	0	4	3	0	0
TOTAL	.249		173	17	43	6	2	1	15	13	50	1

PITCHER	W	L	ERA	G	GS	CG	SV	SHO	IP	H	ER	BB	SO
Sheriff Blake	0	1	13.50	2	0	0	0	0	1.1	4	2	0	1
Guy Bush	1	0	0.82	2	1	1	0	0	11.0	12	1	2	4
Hal Carlson	0	0	6.75	2	0	0	0	0	4.0	7	3	1	3
Pat Malone	0	2	4.15	3	2	1	0	0	13.0	12	6	7	11
Art Nehf	0	0	18.00	2	0	0	0	0	1.0	1	2	1	0
Charlie Root	0	1	4.72	2	2	0	0	0	13.1	12	7	2	8
TOTAL	1	4	4.33	13	5	2	0	0	43.2	48	21	13	27

GAME 1 AT CHI OCT 8

PHI	000 000 102	3	6	1
CHI	000 000 001	1	8	2

Pitchers: EHMKE vs ROOT, Bush (8)
Home Runs: Foxx-PHI
Attendance: 50,740

GAME 2 AT CHI OCT 9

PHI	003 300 120	9	12	0
CHI	000 030 000	3	11	1

Pitchers: EARNSHAW, Grove (5) vs MALONE, Blake (4), Carlson (6), Nehf (9)
Home Runs: Simmons-PHI, Foxx-PHI
Attendance: 49,987

GAME 3 AT PHI OCT 11

CHI	000 003 000	3	6	1
PHI	000 010 000	1	9	1

Pitchers: BUSH vs EARNSHAW
Attendance: 29,921

GAME 4 AT PHI OCT 12

CHI	000 205 100	8	10	2
PHI	000 000 100X	10	15	2

Pitchers: Root, Nehf (7), BLAKE (7), Malone (7), Carlson (8) vs Quinn, Walberg (6), ROMMEL (7), Grove (8)
Home Runs: Grimm-CHI, Haas-PHI, Simmons-PHI
Attendance: 29,921

GAME 5 AT PHI OCT 14

CHI	002 000 000	2	8	1
PHI	000 000 003	3	6	0

Pitchers: MALONE vs Ehmke, WALBERG (4)
Home Runs: Haas-PHI
Attendance: 29,921

Pitching 85 percent of the Series with a combined ERA of 1.02, Philadelphia aces George Earnshaw and Lefty Grove chilled the hot Cardinals, who had hit .314 and averaged 6½ runs per game during the season. The A's hit only .197 themselves in the Series, but more than half their hits went for extra bases as they outscored St. Louis 21–12 and took their second consecutive world championship in six games.

Grove faced Cardinal spitballer Burleigh Grimes in the opener, giving up nine hits, including four singles in the Cards' two-run third. The Athletics, for their part, touched Grimes for only five hits, all in separate innings. But every hit—a double, two triples, and home runs by Al Simmons and Mike Cochrane—resulted in a run, and Grove and the A's emerged 5–2 victors. In the first inning of Game Two, Cochrane again homered, sending Earnshaw on his way to Philadelphia's second win, 6–1.

When the Series moved to St. Louis, though, the Cards came alive. Wild Bill Hallahan (their leading winner during the season, with 15) spaced seven hits for a shutout. Taylor Douthit's fourth-inning home run off Rube Walberg was the first Cardinal hit, but the Cards knocked out nine more for four more runs before they were finished. A pair of unearned runs evened the Series the next day when A's third baseman Jimmy Dykes's wild throw to first in the fourth inning let in a tie-breaking second Cardinal run and led to a third against the ultimate loser Lefty Grove. Meanwhile, Cardinal veteran Jesse Haines, after yielding three Philadelphia hits and a run in the first inning, shut out the A's on one hit the rest of the way.

Earnshaw and Grove combined to restore the Series lead to the Athletics in Game Five with a three-hit shutout. Grove, who took over when Earnshaw left for a pinch hitter in the eighth, garnered his second Series win as Jimmie Foxx homered off Grimes in the top of the ninth for the game's only runs. After a travel day to Philadelphia, Earnshaw pitched again for the A's in Game Six, and pushed the Cardinals' scoreless streak to 21 innings before allowing them a token run in the ninth. But by then seven A's had crossed the plate and the Series was theirs.

Philadelphia Athletics (AL), 4;
St. Louis Cardinals (NL), 2

PHI (A)

PLAYER/POS	AVG	G	AB	R	H	2B	3B	HR	RB	BB	SO	SB
Max Bishop, 2b	.222	6	18	5	4	0	0	0	0	7	3	0
Joe Boley, ss	.095	6	21	1	2	0	0	0	1	0	1	0
Mickey Cochrane, c	.222	6	18	5	4	1	0	2	4	5	2	0
Jimmy Dykes, 3b	.222	6	18	2	4	3	0	1	5	5	3	0
George Earnshaw, p	.000	3	9	0	0	0	0	0	0	0	5	0
Jimmie Foxx, 1b	.333	6	21	3	7	2	1	1	3	2	4	0
Lefty Grove, p	.000	3	6	0	0	0	0	0	0	0	3	0
Mule Haas, of	.111	6	18	1	2	0	1	0	1	1	3	0
Eric Mc Nair, ph	.000	1	1	0	0	0	0	0	0	0	0	0
Bing Miller, of	.143	6	21	0	3	2	0	0	3	0	4	0
Jim Moore, of-1	.333	3	3	0	1	0	0	0	0	1	1	0
Jack Quinn, p	.000	1	0	0	0	0	0	0	0	0	0	0
Bill Shores, p	.000	1	0	0	0	0	0	0	0	1	0	0
Al Simmons, of	.364	6	22	4	8	2	0	2	4	2	2	0
Rube Walberg, p	.000	1	2	0	0	0	0	0	0	0	1	0
TOTAL	.197		178	21	35	10	2	6	21	24	32	0

PITCHER	W	L	ERA	G	GS	CG	SV	SHO	IP	H	ER	BB	SO
George Earnshaw	2	0	0.72	3	3	2	0	0	25.0	13	2	7	19
Lefty Grove	2	1	1.42	3	2	2	0	0	19.0	15	3	3	10
Jack Quinn	0	0	4.50	1	0	0	0	0	2.0	3	1	0	1
Bill Shores	0	0	13.50	1	0	0	0	0	1.1	3	2	0	0
Rube Walberg	0	1	3.86	1	1	0	0	0	4.2	4	2	1	3
TOTAL	4	2	1.73	9	6	4	0	0	52.0	38	10	11	33

STL (N)

PLAYER/POS	AVG	G	AB	R	H	2B	3B	HR	RB	BB	SO	SB
Sparky Adams, 3b	.143	6	21	0	3	0	0	0	1	0	4	0
Hi Bell, p	.000	1	0	0	0	0	0	0	0	0	0	0
Ray Blades, of-3	.111	5	9	2	1	0	0	0	0	2	2	0
Jim Bottomley, 1b	.045	6	22	1	1	1	0	0	0	2	9	0
Taylor Douthit, of	.083	6	24	1	2	0	0	1	2	0	2	0
George Fisher, ph	.500	2	2	0	1	0	0	0	0	0	1	0
Frankie Frisch, 2b	.208	6	24	1	5	2	0	0	0	0	0	1
Charlie Gelbert, ss	.353	6	17	2	6	0	1	0	2	3	3	0
Burleigh Grimes, p	.400	2	5	0	2	0	0	0	0	0	1	0
Chick Hafey, of	.273	6	22	2	6	5	0	0	2	1	3	0
Jesse Haines, p	.500	1	2	0	1	0	0	0	1	0	0	0
Bill Hallahan, p	.000	2	2	0	0	0	0	0	0	1	1	0
Andy High, 3b	.500	1	2	1	1	0	0	0	0	0	0	0
Syl Johnson, p	.000	2	0	0	0	0	0	0	0	0	0	0
Jim Lindsey, p	1.000	2	1	0	1	0	0	0	0	0	0	0
Gus Mancuso, c	.286	2	7	1	2	0	0	0	0	1	2	0
Ernie Orsatti, ph	.000	1	1	0	0	0	0	0	0	0	0	0
George Puccinelli, ph	.000	1	1	0	0	0	0	0	0	0	0	0
Flint Rhem, p	.000	1	1	0	0	0	0	0	0	0	1	0
George Watkins, of	.167	4	12	2	2	0	0	1	1	1	3	0
Jimmie Wilson, c	.267	4	15	0	4	1	0	0	2	0	1	0
TOTAL	.200		190	12	38	10	1	2	11	11	33	1

PITCHER	W	L	ERA	G	GS	CG	SV	SHO	IP	H	ER	BB	SO
Hi Bell	0	0	0.00	1	0	0	0	0	1.0	0	0	0	0
Burleigh Grimes	0	2	3.71	2	2	2	0	0	17.0	10	7	6	13
Jesse Haines	1	0	1.00	1	1	1	0	0	9.0	4	1	4	2
Bill Hallahan	1	1	1.64	2	2	1	0	1	11.0	9	2	8	8
Syl Johnson	0	0	7.20	2	0	0	0	0	5.0	4	4	3	4
Jim Lindsey	0	0	1.93	2	0	0	0	0	4.2	1	1	1	2
Flint Rhem	0	1	10.80	1	1	0	0	0	3.1	7	4	2	3
TOTAL	2	4	3.35	11	6	4	0	1	51.0	35	19	24	32

GAME 1 AT PHI OCT 1

STL	002	000	000	2	9	0
PHI	010	101	11X	5	5	0

Pitchers: GRIMES vs GROVE
Home Runs: Cochrane-PHI, Simmons-PHI
Attendance: 32,295

GAME 2 AT PHI OCT 2

STL	010	000	000	1	6	2
PHI	202	200	00X	6	7	2

Pitchers: RHEM, Lindsey (4), Johnson (7) vs EARNSHAW
Home Runs: Cochrane-PHI, Watkins-STL
Attendance: 32,295

GAME 3 AT STL OCT 4

PHI	000	000	000	0	7	0
STL	000	110	21X	5	10	0

Pitchers: WALBERG, Shores (5), Quinn (7) vs HALLAHAN
Home Runs: Douthit-STL
Attendance: 36,944

GAME 4 AT STL OCT 5

PHI	100	000	000	1	4	1
STL	001	200	00X	3	5	1

Pitchers: GROVE vs HAINES
Attendance: 39,946

GAME 5 AT STL OCT 6

PHI	000	000	002	2	5	0
STL	000	000	000	0	3	1

Pitchers: Earnshaw, GROVE (8) vs GRIMES
Home Runs: Foxx-PHI
Attendance: 38,844

GAME 6 AT PHI OCT 8

STL	000	000	001	1	5	1
PHI	201	211	00X	7	7	0

Pitchers: HALLAHAN, Johnson (3), Lindsey (6), Bell (8) vs EARNSHAW
Home Runs: Dykes-PHI, Simmons-PHI
Attendance: 32,295

For the second year in a row, the A's met the Cardinals in the Series, and once again pitchers Lefty Grove and George Earnshaw provided more than 80 percent of the Athletics' pitching, performing splendidly and winning three games between them. But this time Cardinal pitchers Wild Bill Hallahan and Burleigh Grimes outshone them, winning two games apiece to bring St. Louis the world championship.

Grove gave up four hits and two runs in the first inning of the opener, but shut out the Cards the rest of the way as the A's scored six off Paul Derringer to take the Series lead. Earnshaw also held St. Louis to two runs the next day—both manufactured by Pepper Martin's daring baserunning. But they were more than enough for Hallahan, who shut out the A's on three singles.

The Cardinals took their first Series lead in Game Three, scoring five times off Grove and reliever Roy Mahaffey while Grimes held the A's hitless through seven innings and scoreless through eight before giving up a harmless two-run homer to Al Simmons in the bottom of the ninth. But the A's came back to even the Series the next day on Earnshaw's two-hit shutout.

Pepper Martin, the Cardinal hero of Game Two, homered for two runs in Game Five, and drove in two more of St. Louis's five runs with a sacrifice fly and a single. Meanwhile pitcher Hallahan held Philadelphia to a lone run, returning the Series lead to the Cardinals with his second win.

Game Six pitted Grove and Derringer against each other again as in the opener, and again Grove emerged the victor, holding the Cardinals to one run and five hits. The Athletics scored four unearned runs in the fifth off the unfortunate Derringer who, after an error put a runner on base to open the inning, gave up two singles and walked four, including two with the bases full, before leaving the game. Four more Philadelphia runs in the seventh (two of them scoring on a dropped fly ball) gave the A's the Series' only lopsided win.

In the finale, Grimes once again held the A's scoreless through eight before giving up two runs in the ninth. And once again the runs proved harmless against an early Cardinal lead, as Hallahan came on to retire Max Bishop for the final out.

St. Louis Cardinals (NL), 4; Philadelphia Athletics (AL), 3

STL (N)

PLAYER/POS	AVG	G	AB	R	H	2B	3B	HR	RB	BB	SO	SB
Sparky Adams, 3b	.250	2	4	0	1	0	0	0	0	0	1	0
Ray Blades, ph	.000	2	2	0	0	0	0	0	0	0	2	0
Jim Bottomley, 1b	.160	7	25	2	4	1	0	0	2	2	5	0
Ripper Collins, ph	.000	2	2	0	0	0	0	0	0	0	1	0
Paul Derringer, p	.000	3	2	0	0	0	0	0	0	0	1	0
Jake Flowers, 3b-4	.091	5	11	1	1	1	0	0	0	1	0	0
Frankie Frisch, 2b	.259	7	27	2	7	2	0	0	1	1	2	1
Charlie Gelbert, ss	.261	7	23	0	6	1	0	0	3	0	4	0
Burleigh Grimes, p	.286	2	7	0	2	0	0	0	2	0	2	0
Chick Hafey, of	.167	6	24	1	4	0	0	0	0	0	5	1
Bill Hallahan, p	.000	3	6	0	0	0	0	0	0	0	3	0
Andy High, 3b	.267	4	15	3	4	0	0	0	0	0	2	0
Syl Johnson, p	.000	3	2	0	0	0	0	0	0	0	2	0
Jim Lindsey, p	.000	2	0	0	0	0	0	0	0	0	0	0
Gus Mancuso, c-1	.000	2	1	0	0	0	0	0	0	0	0	0
Pepper Martin, of	.500	7	24	5	12	4	0	1	5	2	3	5
Ernie Orsatti, of	.000	1	3	0	0	0	0	0	0	0	3	0
Flint Rhem, p	.000	1	0	0	0	0	0	0	0	0	0	0
Wally Roettger, of	.286	3	14	1	4	1	0	0	0	0	3	0
George Watkins, of	.286	5	14	4	4	1	0	1	2	2	1	1
Jimmie Wilson, c	.217	7	23	0	5	0	0	0	2	1	1	0
TOTAL	.236		229	19	54	11	0	2	17	9	41	8

PITCHER	W	L	ERA	G	GS	CG	SV	SHO	IP	H	ER	BB	SO
Paul Derringer	0	2	4.26	3	2	0	0	0	12.2	14	6	7	14
Burleigh Grimes	2	0	2.04	2	2	1	0	0	17.2	9	4	9	11
Bill Hallahan	2	0	0.49	3	2	2	1	1	18.1	12	1	8	12
Syl Johnson	0	1	3.00	3	1	0	0	0	9.0	10	3	1	6
Jim Lindsey	0	0	5.40	2	0	0	0	0	3.1	4	2	3	2
Flint Rhem	0	0	0.00	1	0	0	0	0	1.0	1	0	0	1
TOTAL	4	3	2.32	14	7	3	1	1	62.0	50	16	28	46

PHI (A)

PLAYER/POS	AVG	G	AB	R	H	2B	3B	HR	RB	BB	SO	SB
Max Bishop, 2b	.148	7	27	4	4	0	0	0	0	3	5	0
Joe Boley, ph	.000	1	1	0	0	0	0	0	0	0	1	0
Mickey Cochrane, c	.160	7	25	2	4	0	0	1	5	2	0	0
Doc Cramer, ph	.500	2	2	0	1	0	0	0	2	0	0	0
Jimmy Dykes, 3b	.227	7	22	2	5	0	0	0	2	5	1	0
George Earnshaw, p	.000	3	8	0	0	0	0	0	0	0	2	0
Jimmie Foxx, 1b	.348	7	23	3	8	0	0	1	3	6	5	0
Lefty Grove, p	.000	3	10	0	0	0	0	0	0	0	7	0
Mule Haas, of	.130	7	23	1	3	1	0	0	2	3	5	0
Johnnie Heving, ph	.000	1	1	0	0	0	0	0	0	0	0	0
Waite Hoyt, p	.000	1	2	0	0	0	0	0	0	0	0	0
Roy Mahaffey, p	.000	1	0	0	0	0	0	0	0	0	0	0
Eric Mc Nair, 2b-1	.000	2	2	1	0	0	0	0	0	0	1	0
Bing Miller, of	.269	7	26	3	7	1	0	0	1	0	4	0
Jim Moore, of-1	.333	2	3	0	1	0	0	0	0	0	1	0
Eddie Rommel, p	.000	1	0	0	0	0	0	0	0	0	0	0
Al Simmons, of	.333	7	27	4	9	2	0	2	8	3	3	0
Phil Todt, ph	.000	1	0	0	0	0	0	0	0	1	0	0
Rube Walberg, p	.000	2	0	0	0	0	0	0	0	0	0	0
Dib Williams, ss	.320	7	25	2	8	1	0	0	1	2	9	0
TOTAL	.220		227	22	50	5	0	3	20	28	46	0

PITCHER	W	L	ERA	G	GS	CG	SV	SHO	IP	H	ER	BB	SO
George Earnshaw	1	2	1.88	3	3	2	0	1	24.0	12	5	4	20
Lefty Grove	2	1	2.42	3	3	2	0	0	26.0	28	7	2	16
Waite Hoyt	0	1	4.50	1	1	0	0	0	6.0	7	3	0	1
Roy Mahaffey	0	0	9.00	1	0	0	0	0	1.0	1	1	1	0
Eddie Rommel	0	0	9.00	1	0	0	0	0	1.0	3	1	0	0
Rube Walberg	0	0	3.00	2	0	0	0	0	3.0	3	1	2	4
TOTAL	3	4	2.66	11	7	4	0	1	61.0	54	18	9	41

GAME 1 AT STL OCT 1

PHI	004 000 200	6	11	0
STL	200 000 000	2	12	0

Pitchers: GROVE vs DERRINGER, Johnson (8)
Home Runs: Simmons-PHI
Attendance: 38,529

GAME 2 AT STL OCT 2

PHI	000 000 000	0	3	0
STL	010 000 10X	2	6	1

Pitchers: EARNSHAW vs HALLAHAN
Attendance: 35,947

GAME 3 AT PHI OCT 5

STL	020 200 001	5	12	0
PHI	000 000 002	2	2	0

Pitchers: GRIMES vs GROVE, Mahaffey (9)
Home Runs: Simmons-PHI
Attendance: 32,295

GAME 4 AT PHI OCT 6

STL	000 000 000	0	2	1
PHI	100 002 00X	3	10	0

Pitchers: JOHNSON, Lindsey (6) vs EARNSHAW
Home Runs: Foxx-PHI
Attendance: 32,295

GAME 5 AT PHI OCT 7

STL	100 002 011	5	12	0
PHI	000 000 100	1	9	0

Pitchers: HALLAHAN vs HOYT, Walberg (7), Rommel (9)
Home Runs: Martin-STL, Watkins-STL
Attendance: 32,295

GAME 6 AT STL OCT 9

PHI	000 040 400	8	8	1
STL	000 001 000	1	5	2

Pitchers: GROVE vs DERRINGER, Johnson (5), Lindsey (7), Rhem (9)
Attendance: 39,401

GAME 7 AT STL OCT 10

PHI	000 000 002	2	7	1
STL	202 000 00X	4	5	0

Pitchers: EARNSHAW, Walberg (8) vs GRIMES, Hallahan (9)
Attendance: 20,805

Lou Gehrig, who hit .529 and scored nearly a quarter of New York's runs, led both clubs in batting, slugging, hits, runs, and RBIs as the Yankees crushed the Cubs in four games. But the Series is best remembered for Babe Ruth's "called" shot in Game Three, when he pointed his bat atp itcher Charlie Root in the fifth inning and broke the game's 4–4 tie a moment later with a massive home run into the center field bleachers. Debate has raged ever since about whether Ruth intended his gesture as a home run prediction. Whether intended or not, it erased from public memory Gehrig's home run that followed Ruth's (and the homers both men had hit earlier in the game), and made memorable an otherwise undistinguished Series.

Chicago scored in the first inning of each game, taking early leads in three of the four, but held no lead beyond the sixth inning. In Game One, the Cubs connected for ten hits to the Yankees' eight, but managed to score only half as many runs as the New Yorkers, who put what had been a close game out of reach with five runs in the sixth (on four walks, two singles, and a ground out) and three more in the seventh (a walk, two singles, a hit batsman, a sacrifice fly, and a wild pitch).

Chicago's Lon Warneke walked four batters in Game Two, and three of them went on to score as the Yankees countered single Cub runs in the first and third with pairs of their own on two walks and two singles in each frame. (A fifth Yankee run—on two singles without bases on balls—concluded the scoring for the game.)

Game Three featured not only the two homers each by Ruth and Gehrig, but home runs by the Cubs' Kiki Cuyler and Gabby Hartnett. Hartnett's solo shot in the last of the ninth brought Chicago to within two runs of New York for the Series' closest finish.

Four first-inning singles, Frank Demaree's three-run homer, and a Yankee error gave the Cubs a 4–1 advantage early in Game Four—their biggest lead of the Series. But by game's end, 19 Yankee hits (including two home runs by Tony Lazzeri and one by Earle Combs) had created 13 Yankee runs, and the world title was theirs.

New York Yankees (AL), 4; Chicago Cubs (NL), 0

NY (A)

PLAYER/POS	AVG	G	AB	R	H	2B	3B	HR	RB	BB	SO	SB
Johnny Allen, p	.000	1	0	0	0	0	0	0	0	0	0	0
Sammy Byrd, of	.000	1	0	0	0	0	0	0	0	0	0	0
Ben Chapman, of	.294	4	17	1	5	2	0	0	6	2	4	0
Earle Combs, of	.375	4	16	8	6	1	0	1	4	4	3	0
Frankie Crosetti, ss	.133	4	15	2	2	1	0	0	0	2	3	0
Bill Dickey, c	.438	4	16	2	7	0	0	0	4	2	1	0
Lou Gehrig, 1b	.529	4	17	9	9	1	0	3	8	2	1	0
Lefty Gomez, p	.000	1	3	0	0	0	0	0	0	0	2	0
Myril Hoag, pr	.000	1	0	1	0	0	0	0	0	0	0	0
Tony Lazzeri, 2b	.294	4	17	4	5	0	0	2	5	2	1	0
Wilcy Moore, p	.333	1	3	0	1	0	0	0	0	0	2	0
Herb Pennock, p	.000	2	1	0	0	0	0	0	0	0	0	0
George Pipgras, p	.000	1	5	0	0	0	0	0	0	0	5	0
Red Ruffing, p-1	.000	2	4	0	0	0	0	0	0	1	1	0
Babe Ruth, of	.333	4	15	6	5	0	0	2	6	4	3	0
Joe Sewell, 3b	.333	4	15	4	5	1	0	0	3	4	0	0
TOTAL	.313		144	37	45	6	0	8	36	23	26	0

PITCHER	W	L	ERA	G	GS	CG	SV	SHO	IP	H	ER	BB	SO
Johnny Allen	0	0	40.50	1	1	0	0	0	0.2	5	3	0	0
Lefty Gomez	1	0	1.00	1	1	1	0	0	9.0	9	1	1	8
Wilcy Moore	1	0	0.00	1	0	0	0	0	5.1	2	0	0	1
Herb Pennock	0	0	2.25	2	0	0	2	0	4.0	2	1	1	4
George Pipgras	1	0	4.50	1	1	0	0	0	8.0	9	4	3	1
Red Ruffing	1	0	4.00	1	1	1	0	0	9.0	10	4	6	10
TOTAL	4	0	3.25	7	4	2	2	0	36.0	37	13	11	24

CHI (N)

PLAYER/POS	AVG	G	AB	R	H	2B	3B	HR	RB	BB	SO	SB
Guy Bush, p	.000	2	1	0	0	0	0	0	0	1	0	0
Kiki Cuyler, of	.278	4	18	2	5	1	1	1	2	0	3	1
Frank Demaree, of	.286	2	7	1	2	0	0	1	4	1	0	0
Woody English, 3b	.176	4	17	2	3	0	0	0	1	2	2	0
Burleigh Grimes, p	.000	2	1	0	0	0	0	0	0	0	1	0
Charlie Grimm, 1b	.333	4	15	2	5	2	0	0	1	2	2	0
Marv Gudat, ph	.000	2	2	0	0	0	0	0	0	0	1	0
Stan Hack, ph	.000	1	0	0	0	0	0	0	0	0	0	0
Gabby Hartnett, c	.313	4	16	2	5	2	0	1	1	1	3	0
Rollie Hemsley, c-1	.000	3	3	0	0	0	0	0	0	0	3	0
Billy Herman, 2b	.222	4	18	5	4	1	0	0	1	1	3	0
Billy Jurges, ss	.364	3	11	1	4	1	0	0	1	0	1	2
Mark Koenig, ss-1	.250	2	4	1	1	0	1	0	1	1	0	0
Pat Malone, p	.000	1	0	0	0	0	0	0	0	0	0	0
Jakie May, p	.000	2	2	0	0	0	0	0	0	0	0	0
Johnny Moore, of	.000	2	7	1	0	0	0	0	0	2	1	0
Charlie Root, p	.000	2	0	0	0	0	0	0	0	0	1	0
Bob Smith, p	.000	1	0	0	0	0	0	0	0	0	0	0
Riggs Stephenson, of	.444	4	18	2	8	1	0	0	4	0	0	0
Bud Tinning, p	.000	2	0	0	0	0	0	0	0	0	0	0
Lon Warneke, p	.000	2	4	0	0	0	0	0	0	0	3	0
TOTAL	.253		146	19	37	8	2	3	16	11	24	3

PITCHER	W	L	ERA	G	GS	CG	SV	SHO	IP	H	ER	BB	SO
Guy Bush	0	1	14.29	2	2	0	0	0	5.2	5	9	6	2
Burleigh Grimes	0	0	23.63	2	0	0	0	0	2.2	7	7	2	0
Pat Malone	0	0	0.00	1	0	0	0	0	2.2	1	0	4	4
Jakie May	0	1	11.57	2	0	0	0	0	4.2	9	6	3	4
Charlie Root	0	1	10.38	1	1	0	0	0	4.1	6	5	3	4
Bob Smith	0	0	9.00	1	0	0	0	0	1.0	2	1	0	1
Bud Tinning	0	0	0.00	2	0	0	0	0	2.1	0	0	0	3
Lon Warneke	0	1	5.91	2	1	1	0	0	10.2	15	7	5	8
TOTAL	0	4	9.26	13	4	1	0	0	34.0	45	35	23	26

GAME 1 AT NY SEPT 28

CHI	200 000 220	6 10 1
NY	000 305 31X	12 8 2

Pitchers: BUSH, Grimes (6), Smith (8) vs RUFFING
Home Runs: Gehrig-NY
Attendance: 41,459

GAME 2 AT NY SEPT 29

CHI	101 000 000	2 9 0
NY	202 010 00X	5 10 1

Pitchers: WARNEKE vs GOMEZ
Attendance: 50,709

GAME 3 AT CHI OCT 1

NY	301 020 001	7 8 1
CHI	102 100 001	5 9 4

Pitchers: PIPGRAS, Pennock (9) vs ROOT, Malone (5), May (7), Tinning (9)
Home Runs: Ruth-NY (2), Gehrig-NY (2), Cuyler-CHI, Hartnett-CHI
Attendance: 49,986

GAME 4 AT CHI OCT 2

NY	102 002 404	13 19 4
CHI	400 001 001	6 9 1

Pitchers: Allen, MOORE (1), Pennock (7) vs Bush, Warneke (1), MAY (4), Tinning (7), Grimes (9)
Home Runs: Demaree-CHI, Lazzeri-NY (2), Combs-NY
Attendance: 49,844

Although John McGraw had retired from managing the Giants in 1932, he continued to regard them as "his" team. Led now by first baseman Bill Terry, the Giants faced a club also led by an active player, shortstop Joe Cronin in his rookie managerial season.

Giant ace Carl Hubbell dominated the first game, striking out ten while limiting the Senators to five singles and a pair of unearned runs. Mel Ott set the tone for New York with a two-out two-run homer in the first inning, and singled home a third Giant run in the third to build a lead Washington would not overcome. The next day the Senators scored first, on Goose Goslin's solo homer in the third. But that was the only run scored off Giant pitcher Hal Schumacher, and when the Giants drove out Senator starter Alvin Crowder with six runs in the sixth they had their second win well in hand.

The Senators revived when the Series moved to Washington for Game Three. Each of second baseman Buddy Myer's three hits scored or drove in a run, providing a growing cushion for pitcher Earl Whitehill, who recorded the Series' only shutout.

Games Four and Five went to New York, but not without a struggle. In the fourth game, manager Terry's home run broke the ice in the fourth inning, but Giant pitcher Hubbell muffed a bunt in the seventh which led to the tying run. Hubbell and Senator starter Monty Weaver dueled without further scoring until shortstop Blondy Ryan's single in the top of the eleventh put New York up by one. Hubbell let men reach second and third with one out in the last of the eleventh, but an intentional walk set up the hoped-for double play to end the game.

New York had built a three-run lead in Game Five when Senator Fred Schulte evened the score in the last of the sixth with a three-run homer. Relievers Jack Russell and Dolf Luque then dueled scorelessly into the tenth, when Giant Mel Ott (whose homer had begun the Series' scoring in the first inning of Game One) homered once again for what proved the Series' final run. Luque shut down the Senators in their half of the tenth, and "McGraw's Giants" were for the fourth time the world's finest. But before the advent of another spring, McGraw was dead.

New York Giants (NL), 4;
Washington Senators (AL), 1

NY (N)

PLAYER/POS	AVG	G	AB	R	H	2B	3B	HR	RB	BB	SO	SB
Hi Bell, p	.000	1	0	0	0	0	0	0	0	0	0	0
Hughie Critz, 2b	.136	5	22	2	3	0	0	0	0	1	0	0
Kiddo Davis, of	.368	5	19	1	7	1	0	0	0	0	3	0
Freddie Fitzsimmons, p	.500	1	2	0	1	0	0	0	0	0	0	0
Carl Hubbell, p	.286	2	7	0	2	0	0	0	0	0	0	0
Travis Jackson, 3b	.222	5	18	3	4	1	0	0	2	1	3	0
Dolf Luque, p	1.000	1	1	0	1	0	0	0	0	0	0	0
Gus Mancuso, c	.118	5	17	2	2	1	0	0	2	3	0	0
Jo-Jo Moore, of	.227	5	22	1	5	1	0	0	1	1	3	0
Lefty O'Doul, ph	1.000	1	1	0	1	0	0	0	0	2	0	0
Mel Ott, of	.389	5	18	3	7	0	0	2	4	4	4	0
Homer Peel, of-1	.500	2	2	0	1	0	0	0	0	0	0	0
Blondy Ryan, ss	.278	5	18	0	5	0	0	0	1	1	5	0
Hal Schumacher, p	.286	2	7	0	2	0	0	0	3	0	3	0
Bill Terry, 1b	.273	5	22	3	6	1	0	1	1	0	0	0
TOTAL	.267		176	16	47	5	0	3	16	11	21	0

PITCHER	W	L	ERA	G	GS	CG	SV	SHO	IP	H	ER	BB	SO
Hi Bell	0	0	0.00	1	0	0	0	0	1.0	0	0	0	0
Freddie Fitzsimmons	0	1	5.14	1	1	0	0	0	7.0	9	4	0	2
Carl Hubbell	2	0	0.00	2	2	2	0	0	20.0	13	0	6	15
Dolf Luque	1	0	0.00	1	0	0	0	0	4.1	2	0	2	5
Hal Schumacher	1	0	2.45	2	2	1	0	0	14.2	13	4	5	3
TOTAL	4	1	1.53	7	5	3	0	0	47.0	37	8	13	25

WAS (A)

PLAYER/POS	AVG	G	AB	R	H	2B	3B	HR	RB	BB	SO	SB
Ossie Bluege, 3b	.125	5	16	1	2	1	0	0	0	1	6	0
Cliff Bolton, ph	.000	2	2	0	0	0	0	0	0	0	0	0
Joe Cronin, ss	.318	5	22	1	7	0	0	0	2	0	2	0
General Crowder, p	.250	2	4	0	1	0	0	0	0	0	0	0
Goose Goslin, of	.250	5	20	2	5	1	0	1	1	1	3	0
Dave Harris, of-1	.000	3	2	0	0	0	0	0	0	0	0	0
John Kerr, pr	.000	1	0	0	0	0	0	0	0	0	0	0
Joe Kuhel, 1b	.150	5	20	1	3	0	0	0	1	1	4	0
Heinie Manush, of	.111	5	18	2	2	0	0	0	0	2	1	0
Alex Mc Coll, p	.000	1	0	0	0	0	0	0	0	0	0	0
Buddy Myer, 2b	.300	5	20	2	6	1	0	0	2	2	3	0
Sam Rice, ph	1.000	1	1	0	1	0	0	0	0	0	0	0
Jack Russell, p	.000	3	2	0	0	0	0	0	0	1	2	0
Fred Schulte, of	.333	5	21	1	7	1	0	1	4	1	1	0
Luke Sewell, c	.176	5	17	1	3	0	0	0	1	2	0	1
Lefty Stewart, p	.000	1	1	0	0	0	0	0	0	0	1	0
Tommy Thomas, p	.000	2	0	0	0	0	0	0	0	0	0	0
Monte Weaver, p	.000	1	4	0	0	0	0	0	0	0	2	0
Earl Whitehill, p	.000	1	3	0	0	0	0	0	0	0	0	0
TOTAL	.214		173	11	37	4	0	2	11	13	25	1

PITCHER	W	L	ERA	G	GS	CG	SV	SHO	IP	H	ER	BB	SO
General Crowder	0	1	7.36	2	2	0	0	0	11.0	16	9	5	7
Alex Mc Coll	0	0	0.00	1	0	0	0	0	2.0	0	0	0	0
Jack Russell	0	1	0.87	3	0	0	0	0	10.1	8	1	0	7
Lefty Stewart	0	1	9.00	1	1	0	0	0	2.0	6	2	0	0
Tommy Thomas	0	0	0.00	2	0	0	0	0	1.1	1	0	0	2
Monte Weaver	0	1	1.74	1	1	0	0	0	10.1	11	2	4	3
Earl Whitehill	1	0	0.00	1	1	1	0	1	9.0	5	0	2	2
TOTAL	1	4	2.74	11	5	1	0	1	46.0	47	14	11	21

GAME 1 AT NY OCT 3

WAS	000 100 001	2	5	3
NY	202 000 00X	4	10	2

Pitchers: STEWART, Russell (3), Thomas (8) vs HUBBELL
Home Runs: Ott-NY
Attendance: 46,672

GAME 2 AT NY OCT 4

WAS	001 000 000	1	5	0
NY	000 006 00X	6	10	0

Pitchers: CROWDER, Thomas (6), McColl (7) VS SCHUMACHER
Home Runs: Goslin-WAS
Attendance: 35,461

GAME 3 AT WAS OCT 5

NY	000 000 000	0	5	0
WAS	210 000 10X	4	9	1

Pitchers: FITZSIMMONS, Bell (8) vs WHITEHILL
Attendance: 25,727

GAME 4 AT WAS OCT 6

NY	000 100 000 01	2	11	1
WAS	000 000 100 00	1	8	0

Pitchers: HUBBELL vs WEAVER, Russell (11)
Home Runs: Terry-NY
Attendance: 26,762

GAME 5 AT WAS OCT 7

NY	020 001 000 1	4	11	1
WAS	000 003 000 0	3	10	0

Pitchers: Schumacher, LUQUE (6) vs Crowder, RUSSELL (6)
Home Runs: Schulte-WAS, Ott-NY
Attendance: 28,454

Pitching brothers Dizzy and Paul Dean won seven games in ten days to give the Cardinals the pennant on the final day of the season. In the Series they continued their winning ways, chalking up all four Cardinal victories. Dizzy pitched the opener in Detroit. Given a 3–0 lead, thanks to five Tiger errors in the first three innings, he breezed to an 8–3 win.

Detroit's Schoolboy Rowe brought the Tigers back with a pitching masterpiece in Game Two. After giving up single runs in the second and third innings, he allowed only one runner to reach base over the next nine as his Tigers tied the score in the ninth, and won it on two walks and a single in the twelfth.

Paul Dean nearly pitched a shutout in Game Three, yielding a harmless run with two out in the ninth after the Cards had built him a 4–0 lead. Brother Diz figured in a curious and painful play in Game Four. Pinch-running in the fourth inning, he was beaned by a would-be double-play throw as he ran to second. The tying run scored from third on the play, but Detroit's pitcher Eldon Auker shut out the Cards through the final five innings, and his teammates scored six more runs to bury St. Louis 10–4, evening the Series at two apiece. Diz was rushed to the hospital, but as no damage was found he started Game Five the next day. He pitched well enough, but Detroit's Tommy Bridges pitched better, giving the Cardinals only one run to the Tigers' three.

Paul Dean evened the Series again with a win against Rowe in a closely contested sixth game. A grounder through Dean's legs allowed the Tigers to tie the game in the sixth inning, but Paul redeemed his error in the seventh when he singled in the tie-breaking—and as it turned out, winning—run. Dizzy came back after only a day's rest to hurl a six-hit shutout in the finale. He also scored the game's first run and drove in the sixth with a double and single in his team's seven-run third. Three innings later, frustrated Tiger fans, angered by Cardinal Joe Medwick's rough slide into their third baseman, pelted Medwick with food and bottles, halting the game for twenty minutes until Commissioner Landis ordered Medwick from the game. The delay only forestalled Detroit's defeat, as the Cards took the title game 11–0.

St. Louis Cardinals (NL), 4; Detroit Tigers (AL), 3

STL (N)

PLAYER/POS	AVG	G	AB	R	H	2B	3B	HR	RB	BB	SO	SB
Tex Carleton, p	.000	2	1	0	0	0	0	0	0	0	0	0
Ripper Collins, 1b	.367	7	30	4	11	1	0	0	3	1	2	0
Pat Crawford, ph	.000	2	2	0	0	0	0	0	0	0	0	0
Spud Davis, ph	1.000	2	2	0	2	0	0	0	1	0	0	0
Dizzy Dean, p-3	.250	4	12	3	3	2	0	0	1	0	3	0
Paul Dean, p	.167	2	6	0	1	0	0	0	2	0	1	0
Bill De Lancey, c	.172	7	29	3	5	3	0	1	4	2	8	0
Leo Durocher, ss	.259	7	27	4	7	1	1	0	0	0	0	0
Frankie Frisch, 2b	.194	7	31	2	6	1	0	0	4	0	1	0
Chick Fullis, of	.400	3	5	0	2	0	0	0	0	0	0	0
Jesse Haines, p	.000	1	0	0	0	0	0	0	0	0	0	0
Bill Hallahan, p	.000	1	3	0	0	0	0	0	0	0	1	0
Pepper Martin, 3b	.355	7	31	8	11	3	1	0	4	3	3	2
Joe Medwick, of	.379	7	29	4	11	0	1	1	5	1	7	0
Jim Mooney, p	.000	1	0	0	0	0	0	0	0	0	0	0
Ernie Orsatti, of	.318	7	22	3	7	0	1	0	2	3	1	0
Jack Rothrock, of	.233	7	30	3	7	3	1	0	6	1	2	0
Dazzy Vance, p	.000	1	0	0	0	0	0	0	0	0	0	0
Bill Walker, p	.000	2	2	0	0	0	0	0	0	0	2	0
Burgess Whitehead, ss	.000	1	0	0	0	0	0	0	0	0	0	0
TOTAL	.279		262	34	73	14	5	2	32	11	31	2

PITCHER	W	L	ERA	G	GS	CG	SV	SHO	IP	H	ER	BB	SO
Tex Carleton	0	0	7.36	2	1	0	0	0	3.2	5	3	2	2
Dizzy Dean	2	1	1.73	3	3	2	0	1	26.0	20	5	5	17
Paul Dean	2	0	1.00	2	2	2	0	0	18.0	15	2	7	11
Jesse Haines	0	0	0.00	1	0	0	0	0	0.2	1	0	0	2
Bill Hallahan	0	0	2.16	1	1	0	0	0	8.1	6	2	4	6
Jim Mooney	0	0	0.00	1	0	0	0	0	1.0	1	0	0	0
Dazzy Vance	0	0	0.00	1	0	0	0	0	1.1	2	0	1	3
Bill Walker	0	2	7.11	2	0	0	0	0	6.1	6	5	6	2
TOTAL	4	3	2.34	13	7	4	0	1	65.1	56	17	25	43

DET (A)

PLAYER/POS	AVG	G	AB	R	H	2B	3B	HR	RB	BB	SO	SB
Eldon Auker, p	.000	2	4	0	0	0	0	0	0	0	2	0
Tommy Bridges, p	.143	3	7	0	1	0	0	0	0	1	4	0
Mickey Cochrane, c	.214	7	28	2	6	1	0	0	1	4	3	0
General Crowder, p	.000	2	1	0	0	0	0	0	0	0	0	0
Frank Doljack, of-1	.000	2	2	0	0	0	0	0	0	0	0	0
Pete Fox, of	.286	7	28	1	8	6	0	0	2	1	4	0
Charlie Gehringer, 2b	.379	7	29	5	11	1	0	1	2	3	0	1
Goose Goslin, of	.241	7	29	2	7	1	0	0	2	3	1	0
Hank Greenberg, 1b	.321	7	28	4	9	2	1	1	7	4	9	1
Ray Hayworth, c	.000	1	0	0	0	0	0	0	0	0	0	0
Chief Hogsett, p	.000	3	3	0	0	0	0	0	0	0	1	0
Firpo Marberry, p	.000	2	0	0	0	0	0	0	0	0	0	0
Marv Owen, 3b	.069	7	29	0	2	0	0	0	1	0	5	1
Billy Rogell, ss	.276	7	29	3	8	1	0	0	4	1	4	1
Schoolboy Rowe, p	.000	3	7	0	0	0	0	0	0	0	5	0
Gee Walker, ph	.333	3	3	0	1	0	0	0	1	0	1	0
Jo-Jo White, of	.130	7	23	6	3	0	0	0	0	8	4	1
TOTAL	.224		250	23	56	12	1	2	20	25	43	5

PITCHER	W	L	ERA	G	GS	CG	SV	SHO	IP	H	ER	BB	SO
Eldon Auker	1	1	5.56	2	2	1	0	0	11.1	16	7	5	2
Tommy Bridges	1	1	3.63	3	2	1	0	0	17.1	21	7	1	12
General Crowder	0	1	1.50	2	1	0	0	0	6.0	6	1	1	2
Chief Hogsett	0	0	1.23	3	0	0	0	0	7.1	6	1	3	3
Firpo Marberry	0	0	21.60	2	0	0	0	0	1.2	5	4	1	0
Schoolboy Rowe	1	1	2.95	3	2	2	0	0	21.1	19	7	0	12
TOTAL	3	4	3.74	15	7	4	0	0	65.0	73	27	11	31

GAME 1 AT DET OCT 3

STL	021	014	000	8	13	2
DET	001	001	010	3	8	5

Pitchers: J.DEAN vs CROWDER, Marberry (6), Hogsett (6)
Home Runs: Medwick-STL, Greenberg-DET
Attendance: 42,505

GAME 2 AT DET OCT 4

STL	011 000 000 000	2	7	3
DET	000 100 001 001	3	7	0

Pitchers: Hallahan, W.WALKER (9) vs ROWE
Attendance: 43,451

GAME 3 AT STL OCT 5

DET	000	000	001	1	8	2
STL	110	020	00X	4	9	1

Pitchers: BRIDGES, Hogsett (5) vs P.DEAN
Attendance: 34,073

GAME 4 AT STL OCT 6

DET	003	100	150	10	13	1
STL	011	200	000	4	10	5

Pitchers: AUKER vs Carleton, Vance (3), W.Walker (5), Haines (8), Mooney (9)
Attendance: 37,492

GAME 5 AT STL OCT 7

DET	010	002	000	3	7	0
STL	000	000	100	1	7	1

Pitchers: BRIDGES vs J.DEAN, Carleton (9)
Home Runs: Gehringer-DET, Delancey-STL
Attendance: 38,536

GAME 6 AT DET OCT 8

STL	100	020	100	4	10	2
DET	001	002	000	3	7	1

Pitchers: P.DEAN vs ROWE
Attendance: 44,551

GAME 7 AT DET OCT 9

STL	007	002	200	11	17	1
DET	000	000	000	0	6	3

Pitchers: J.DEAN vs AUKER, Rowe (3), Hogsett (3), Bridges (4), Marberry (8), Crowder (9)
Attendance: 40,902

With a 21-game September winning streak, the Cubs vaulted over the Giants and Cardinals to face Detroit in the Series, and for a moment it seemed as if their momentum might carry them past the Tigers as well. Chicago scored two runs off Schoolboy Rowe in the top of the first in the opener, and right fielder Frank Demaree homered to open the ninth as Lon Warneke blanked the Tigers on four hits. But Detroit retaliated quickly in Game Two, driving out starter Charlie Root in the first inning with four runs (including Hank Greenberg's two-run homer) before Root had had a chance to record even one out. Tiger pitcher Rocky Bridges gained an easy 8–3 win, but Greenberg broke a wrist and was finished for the Series.

In Game Three the Cubs scored three times before Detroit countered with their first run in the sixth. But a walk and four Tiger hits in the eighth put the Bengals ahead 4–3, and Billy Rogell's baserunning as he turned a foiled steal into a rundown permitted a fifth Tiger to cross the plate. Two Cub runs in the last of the ninth tied the score, but Detroit pulled out the victory in the eleventh as a pair of singles sandwiched Fred Lindstrom's error at third to give them an unearned run.

Detroit's Alvin "General" Crowder followed up the Tigers' advantage the next day with a neat five-hit 2–1 win. Once again the Cubs bobbled away the game, this time with two sixth-inning errors that enabled Detroit to score the winning run without a hit. Chuck Klein's two-run homer saved Chicago from elimination in Game Five as Lon Warneke and Bill Lee shut out the Tigers through eight before letting in a harmless run in the ninth.

Chicago's Larry French and Tiger Rocky Bridges yielded 12 hits apiece in Game Six. Cub second baseman Billy Herman singled in a run in the third to tie the score, and homered for two more runs in the fifth to put the Cubs ahead. But the Tigers tied it up an inning later, and took their first world title ever when Goose Goslin singled in Mickey Cochrane with two out in the bottom of the ninth.

Detroit Tigers (AL), 4; Chicago Cubs (NL), 2

DET (A)

PLAYER/POS	AVG	G	AB	R	H	2B	3B	HR	RB	BB	SO	SB
Eldon Auker, p	.000	1	2	0	0	0	0	0	0	0	1	0
Tommy Bridges, p	.125	2	8	1	1	0	0	0	1	0	3	0
Flea Clifton, 3b	.000	4	16	1	0	0	0	0	0	2	4	0
Mickey Cochrane, c	.292	6	24	3	7	1	0	0	1	4	1	0
General Crowder, p	.333	1	3	1	1	0	0	0	0	1	0	0
Pete Fox, of	.385	6	26	1	10	3	1	0	4	0	1	0
Charlie Gehringer, 2b	.375	6	24	4	9	3	0	0	4	2	1	1
Goose Goslin, of	.273	6	22	2	6	1	0	0	3	5	0	0
Hank Greenberg, 1b	.167	2	6	1	1	0	0	1	2	1	0	0
Chief Hogsett, p	.000	1	0	0	0	0	0	0	0	0	0	0
Marv Owen, 1b-4,3b-2	.050	6	20	2	1	0	0	0	1	2	3	0
Billy Rogell, ss	.292	6	24	1	7	2	0	0	1	2	5	0
Schoolboy Rowe, p	.250	3	8	0	2	1	0	0	0	0	1	0
Gee Walker, of-1	.250	3	4	1	1	0	0	0	0	1	0	0
Jo-Jo White, of	.263	5	19	3	5	0	0	0	1	5	7	0
TOTAL	.248		206	21	51	11	1	1	18	25	27	1

PITCHER	W	L	ERA	G	GS	CG	SV	SHO	IP	H	ER	BB	SO
Eldon Auker	0	0	3.00	1	1	0	0	0	6.0	6	2	2	1
Tommy Bridges	2	0	2.50	2	2	2	0	0	18.0	18	5	4	9
General Crowder	1	0	1.00	1	1	1	0	0	9.0	5	1	3	5
Chief Hogsett	0	0	0.00	1	0	0	0	0	1.0	0	0	1	0
Schoolboy Rowe	1	2	2.57	3	2	2	0	0	21.0	19	6	1	14
TOTAL	4	2	2.29	8	6	5	0	0	55.0	48	14	11	29

CHI (N)

PLAYER/POS	AVG	G	AB	R	H	2B	3B	HR	RB	BB	SO	SB
Tex Carleton, p	.000	1	1	0	0	0	0	0	0	1	1	0
Phil Cavaretta, 1b	.125	6	24	1	3	0	0	0	0	0	5	0
Frank Demaree, of	.250	6	24	2	6	1	0	2	2	1	4	0
Larry French, p	.250	2	4	1	1	0	0	0	0	0	2	0
Augie Galan, of	.160	6	25	2	4	1	0	0	2	2	2	0
Stan Hack, 3b-6,ss-1	.227	6	22	2	5	1	1	0	0	2	2	1
Gabby Hartnett, c	.292	6	24	1	7	0	0	1	2	0	3	0
Roy Henshaw, p	.000	1	1	0	0	0	0	0	0	0	0	0
Billy Herman, 2b	.333	6	24	3	8	2	1	1	6	0	2	0
Billy Jurges, ss	.250	6	16	3	4	0	0	0	1	4	4	0
Chuck Klein, of-3	.333	5	12	2	4	0	0	1	2	0	2	0
Fabian Kowalik, p	.500	1	2	1	1	0	0	0	0	0	0	0
Bill Lee, p	.000	2	1	0	0	0	0	0	1	0	0	0
Fred Lindstrom, of-4,3b-1	.200	4	15	0	3	1	0	0	0	1	1	0
Ken O'Dea, ph	1.000	1	1	0	1	0	0	0	1	0	0	0
Charlie Root, p	.000	2	0	0	0	0	0	0	0	0	0	0
Walter Stephenson, ph	.000	1	1	0	0	0	0	0	0	0	1	0
Lon Warneke, p	.200	3	5	0	1	0	0	0	0	0	0	0
TOTAL	.238		202	18	48	6	2	5	17	11	29	1

PITCHER	W	L	ERA	G	GS	CG	SV	SHO	IP	H	ER	BB	SO
Tex Carleton	0	1	1.29	1	1	0	0	0	7.0	6	1	7	4
Larry French	0	2	3.38	2	1	1	0	0	10.2	15	4	2	8
Roy Henshaw	0	0	7.36	1	0	0	0	0	3.2	2	3	5	2
Fabian Kowalik	0	0	2.08	1	0	0	0	0	4.1	3	1	1	1
Bill Lee	0	0	3.48	2	1	0	1	0	10.1	11	4	5	5
Charlie Root	0	1	18.00	2	1	0	0	0	2.0	5	4	1	2
Lon Warneke	2	0	0.54	3	2	1	0	1	16.2	9	1	4	5
TOTAL	2	4	2.96	12	6	2	1	1	54.2	51	18	25	27

GAME 1 AT DET OCT 2

CHI	200 000 001	3	7	0
DET	000 000 000	0	4	3

Pitchers: WARNEKE vs ROWE
Home Runs: Demaree-CHI
Attendance: 47,391

GAME 2 AT DET OCT 3

CHI	000 010 200	3	6	1
DET	400 310 00X	8	9	2

Pitchers: ROOT, Henshaw (1), Kowalik (4) vs BRIDGES
Home Runs: Greenberg-DET
Attendance: 46,742

GAME 3 AT CHI OCT 4

DET	000 001 040 01	6	12	2
CHI	020 010 002 00	5	10	3

Pitchers: Auker, Hogsett (7), ROWE (8) vs Lee, Warneke (8), FRENCH (10)
Home Runs: Demaree-CHI
Attendance: 45,532

GAME 4 AT CHI OCT 5

DET	001 001 000	2	7	0
CHI	010 000 000	1	5	2

Pitchers: CROWDER vs CARLETON, Root (8)
Home Runs: Hartnett-CHI
Attendance: 49,350

GAME 5 AT CHI OCT 6

DET	000 000 001	1	7	1
CHI	002 000 10X	3	8	0

Pitchers: ROWE vs WARNEKE, Lee (7)
Home Runs: Klein-CHI
Attendance: 49,237

GAME 6 AT DET OCT 7

CHI	001 020 000	3	12	0
DET	100 101 001	4	12	1

Pitchers: FRENCH vs BRIDGES
Home Runs: Herman-CHI
Attendance: 48,420

The Giants managed to win two games, but this first Series between the cross-river rivals in thirteen years was really no contest. Babe Ruth was gone, but Lou Gehrig was still there, and Joe DiMaggio had arrived. The Yankees outhit the Giants by 56 percentage points and outscored them by 20 runs.

Giant ace Carl Hubbell, who had won his final 16 decisions of the regular season, continued his streak in the Series opener. The Yankees scored first on George Selkirk's third-inning homer, but Giant shortstop Dick Bartell homered to even things in the fifth. Hubbell held the Yankees to that one run, but the Giants roughed up Red Ruffing for five more runs, to give the Polo Grounders a brief Series advantage.

Game Two was a Yankee blowout, as the Yankees hammered five Giant pitchers for 18 runs—four of them on Tony Lazzeri's grand slam in the third—to give Lefty Gomez an easy win. By contrast, Game Three was a pitchers' duel. Although the Giants touched Bump Hadley and Pat Malone for 11 hits, only Jimmy Ripple's fifth-inning homer produced a run. Giant Freddie Fitzsimmons was much more stingy with hits, yielding only four. But one was Gehrig's home run in the second inning, and another was Frank Crosetti's game-winning RBI single in the eighth.

Gehrig homered again in the third inning of Game Four to give the Yankees an insurmountable lead—and Hubbell his first loss in months. Down three games to one, the Giants struggled back in Game Five. They took a first-inning 3–0 lead, but the Yankees clawed their way back, and by the end of six the score was 4–4. There it stayed until the tenth, when a double, sacrifice, and fly to center put the Giants ahead by a run. Hal Schumacher, who had pitched the whole game, held the Yankees scoreless one more time for the win.

Fitzsimmons, who had pitched so well in his third-game loss, didn't last four innings in Game Six. Though the Giants scored first, Yankee Jake Powell (who led all Series hitters at .455) tied the game with a two-run homer in the top of the second. Two more runs in the fourth drove out Fitzsimmons, but the game stayed close until the top of the ninth, when five Yankees singles and three walks produced seven runs and a Series-ending 13–5 rout.

New York Yankees (AL), 4;
New York Giants (NL), 2

NY (A)

PLAYER/POS	AVG	G	AB	R	H	2B	3B	HR	RB	BB	SO	SB
Frankie Crosetti, ss	.269	6	26	5	7	2	0	0	3	3	5	0
Bill Dickey, c	.120	6	25	5	3	0	0	1	5	3	4	0
Joe DiMaggio, of	.346	6	26	3	9	3	0	0	3	1	3	0
Lou Gehrig, 1b	.292	6	24	5	7	1	0	2	7	3	2	0
Lefty Gomez, p	.250	2	8	1	2	0	0	0	3	0	3	0
Bump Hadley, p	.000	1	2	0	0	0	0	0	0	0	1	0
Roy Johnson, ph	.000	2	1	0	0	0	0	0	0	0	1	0
Tony Lazzeri, 2b	.250	6	20	4	5	0	0	1	7	4	4	0
Pat Malone, p	1.000	2	1	0	1	0	0	0	0	0	0	0
Johnny Murphy, p	.500	2	2	1	1	0	0	0	1	0	1	0
Monte Pearson, p	.500	1	4	0	2	1	0	0	0	0	0	0
Jake Powell, of	.455	6	22	8	10	1	0	1	5	4	4	1
Red Rolfe, 3b	.400	6	25	5	10	0	0	0	4	3	1	0
Red Ruffing, p-2	.000	3	5	0	0	0	0	0	0	1	2	0
Bob Seeds, pr	.000	1	0	0	0	0	0	0	0	0	0	0
George Selkirk, of	.333	6	24	6	8	0	1	2	3	4	4	0
TOTAL	.302		215	43	65	8	1	7	41	26	35	1

PITCHER	W	L	ERA	G	GS	CG	SV	SHO	IP	H	ER	BB	SO
Lefty Gomez	2	0	4.70	2	2	1	0	0	15.1	14	8	11	9
Bump Hadley	1	0	1.13	1	1	0	0	0	8.0	10	1	1	2
Pat Malone	0	1	1.80	2	0	0	1	0	5.0	2	1	1	2
Johnny Murphy	0	0	3.38	1	0	0	1	0	2.2	1	1	1	1
Monte Pearson	1	0	2.00	1	1	1	0	0	9.0	7	2	2	7
Red Ruffing	0	1	4.50	2	2	0	0	0	14.0	16	7	5	12
TOTAL	4	2	3.33	9	6	2	2	0	54.0	50	20	21	33

NY (N)

PLAYER/POS	AVG	G	AB	R	H	2B	3B	HR	RB	BB	SO	SB
Dick Bartell, ss	.381	6	21	5	8	3	0	1	3	4	4	0
Slick Castleman, p	.500	1	2	0	1	0	0	0	0	0	0	0
Dick Coffman, p	.000	2	0	0	0	0	0	0	0	0	0	0
Harry Danning, c-1	.000	2	2	0	0	0	0	0	0	0	1	0
Kiddo Davis, ph	.500	4	2	2	1	0	0	0	0	0	0	0
Freddie Fitzsimmons, p	.500	2	4	0	2	0	0	0	0	0	1	0
Frank Gabler, p	.000	2	0	0	0	0	0	0	0	1	0	0
Harry Gumbert, p	.000	2	0	0	0	0	0	0	0	0	0	0
Carl Hubbell, p	.333	2	6	0	2	0	0	0	1	0	0	0
Travis Jackson, 3b	.190	6	21	1	4	0	0	0	1	1	3	0
Mark Koenig, 2b-1	.333	3	3	0	1	0	0	0	0	0	1	0
Hank Leiber, of	.000	2	6	0	0	0	0	0	0	2	2	0
Sam Leslie, ph	.667	3	3	0	2	0	0	0	0	0	0	0
Gus Mancuso, c	.263	6	19	3	5	2	0	0	1	3	3	0
Eddie Mayo, 3b	.000	1	1	0	0	0	0	0	0	0	0	0
Jo-Jo Moore, of	.214	6	28	4	6	2	0	1	1	1	4	0
Mel Ott, of	.304	6	23	4	7	2	0	1	3	3	1	0
Jimmy Ripple, of	.333	5	12	2	4	0	0	1	3	3	3	0
Hal Schumacher, p	.000	2	4	0	0	0	0	0	0	1	3	0
Al Smith, p	.000	1	0	0	0	0	0	0	0	0	0	0
Bill Terry, 1b	.240	6	25	1	6	0	0	0	5	1	4	0
Burgess Whitehead, 2b	.048	6	21	1	1	0	0	0	2	1	3	0
TOTAL	.246		203	23	50	9	0	4	20	21	33	0

PITCHER	W	L	ERA	G	GS	CG	SV	SHO	IP	H	ER	BB	SO
Slick Castleman	0	0	2.08	1	0	0	0	0	4.1	3	1	2	5
Dick Coffman	0	0	32.40	2	0	0	0	0	1.2	5	6	1	1
Freddie Fitzsimmons	0	2	5.40	2	2	1	0	0	11.2	13	7	2	6
Frank Gabler	0	0	7.20	2	0	0	0	0	5.0	7	4	4	0
Harry Gumbert	0	0	36.00	2	0	0	0	0	2.0	7	8	4	2
Carl Hubbell	1	1	2.25	2	2	1	0	0	16.0	15	4	2	10
Hal Schumacher	1	1	5.25	2	2	1	0	0	12.0	13	7	10	11
Al Smith	0	0	81.00	1	0	0	0	0	0.1	2	3	1	0
TOTAL	2	4	6.79	14	6	3	0	0	53.0	65	40	26	35

GAME 1 AT NY -N SEPT 30

NY-A   001 000 000   1 7 2
NY-N   000 011 04X   6 9 1

Pitchers: RUFFING vs HUBBELL
Home Runs: Bartell-NY(N),
  Selkirk-NY(A)
Attendance: 39,419

GAME 2 AT NY -N OCT 2

NY-A   207 001 206   18 17 0
NY-N   010 300 000   4 6 1

Pitchers: GOMEZ vs SCHUMACHER,
  Smith (3), Coffman (3), Gabler (5),
  Gumbert (9)
Home Runs: Dickey-NY(A),
  Lazzeri-NY(A)
Attendance: 43,543

GAME 3 AT NY -A OCT 3

NY-N   000 010 000   1 11 0
NY-A   010 000 01X   2 4 0

Pitchers: FITZSIMMONS vs HADLEY,
  Malone (9)
Home Runs: Gehrig-NY(A),
  Ripple-NY(N)
Attendance: 64,842

GAME 4 AT NY -A OCT 4

NY-N   000 100 010   2 7 1
NY-A   013 000 01X   5 10 1

Pitchers: HUBBELL, Gabler (8) vs
  PEARSON
Home Runs: Gehrig-NY(A)
Attendance: 66,669

GAME 5 AT NY -A OCT 5

NY-N   300 001 000 1   5 8 3
NY-A   011 002 000 0   4 10 1

Pitchers: SCHUMACHER vs Ruffing,
  MALONE (7)
Home Runs: Selkirk-NY(A)
Attendance: 50,024

GAME 6 AT NY -N OCT 6

NY-A   021 200 017   13 17 2
NY-N   200 010 110   5 9 1

Pitchers: GOMEZ, Murphy (7) vs
  FITZSIMMONS, Castleman (4),
  Coffman (9), Gumbert (9)
Home Runs: Moore-NY(N), Ott-NY(N),
  Powell-NY(A)
Attendance: 38,427

For the second year in a row, the Yankees overwhelmed the Giants, this time in just five games. Giant ace Carl Hubbell, who took the opener in 1936, was unable to repeat this year. For five innings he held the Yankees to one hit. But in the sixth everything fell apart. Before Hubbell was taken out, two walks, five singles, and a Giant error had let in five runs. And the two runners Hubbell left on base scored later on a second Giant error and two walks by reliever Dick Coffman. The Yankees' Lefty Gomez also yielded six hits, but wider spacing and better field support held the Giants to one run in the fifth. Tony Lazzeri's homer in the eighth made the final score 8–1.

The Yankees spread their runs a bit more evenly in Game Two. For the second time the Giants gained a 1–0 lead. Rookie phenom Cliff Melton held the Yankees scoreless through four, but four straight hits for two runs at the start of the fifth drove him out. Reliever Ad Gumbert stopped the Yankees in the rest of the inning but gave up four more hits—and four more runs—in the sixth before Coffman stepped in to stop the assault. But Coffman gave up two final Yankee runs in the seventh, to complete a second straight 8–1 Yankee win, as Red Ruffing held the Giants scoreless through the final eight innings.

The Yankees had scored five times off Hal Schumacher in Game Three before the Giants got their one run in the seventh. But Yankee starter Monte Pearson made the game tighter as he yielded a single and two walks to load the bases in the ninth before Johnny Murphy came on to record the final out.

Giant bats finally came alive in the second inning of Game Four. Seven singles, plus a walk and a missed play at the plate gave the club a 6–1 lead, which starter Hubbell protected for the only Giant win of the Series.

Solo homers by Myril Hoag in the second and Joe DiMaggio in the third gave the Yankees a 2–0 lead early in Game Five, but Giant Mel Ott tied it up with a two-run shot off Lefty Gomez in the last of the third. But Gomez shut the Giants down the rest of the way, and singled in Lazzeri in the fifth with what proved the game winner (scoring himself on Lou Gehrig's double for the final run of the Series).

New York Yankees (AL), 4;
New York Giants (NL), 1

NY (A)

PLAYER/POS	AVG	G	AB	R	H	2B	3B	HR	RB	BB	SO	SB
Ivy Andrews, p	.000	1	2	0	0	0	0	0	0	0	1	0
Frankie Crosetti, ss	.048	5	21	2	1	0	0	0	0	3	2	0
Bill Dickey, c	.211	5	19	3	4	0	1	0	3	2	2	0
Joe DiMaggio, of	.273	5	22	2	6	0	0	1	4	0	3	0
Lou Gehrig, 1b	.294	5	17	4	5	1	1	1	3	5	4	0
Lefty Gomez, p	.167	2	6	2	1	0	0	0	1	2	1	0
Bump Hadley, p	.000	1	0	0	0	0	0	0	0	0	0	0
Myril Hoag, of	.300	5	20	4	6	1	0	1	2	0	1	0
Tony Lazzeri, 2b	.400	5	15	3	6	0	1	1	2	3	3	0
Johnny Murphy, p	.000	1	0	0	0	0	0	0	0	0	0	0
Monte Pearson, p	.000	1	3	0	0	0	0	0	0	1	1	0
Jake Powell, ph	.000	1	1	0	0	0	0	0	0	0	1	0
Red Rolfe, 3b	.300	5	20	3	6	2	1	0	1	3	2	0
Red Ruffing, p	.500	1	4	0	2	1	0	0	3	0	0	0
George Selkirk, of	.263	5	19	5	5	1	0	0	6	2	0	0
Kemp Wicker, p	.000	1	0	0	0	0	0	0	0	0	0	0
TOTAL	.249		169	28	42	6	4	4	25	21	21	0

PITCHER	W	L	ERA	G	GS	CG	SV	SHO	IP	H	ER	BB	SO
Ivy Andrews	0	0	3.18	1	0	0	0	0	5.2	6	2	4	1
Lefty Gomez	2	0	1.50	2	2	2	0	0	18.0	16	3	2	8
Bump Hadley	0	1	33.75	1	1	0	0	0	1.1	6	5	0	0
Johnny Murphy	0	0	0.00	1	0	0	1	0	0.1	0	0	0	0
Monte Pearson	1	0	1.04	1	1	0	0	0	8.2	5	1	2	4
Red Ruffing	1	0	1.00	1	1	1	0	0	9.0	7	1	3	8
Kemp Wicker	0	0	0.00	1	0	0	0	0	1.0	0	0	0	0
TOTAL	4	1	2.45	8	5	3	1	0	44.0	40	12	11	21

NY (N)

PLAYER/POS	AVG	G	AB	R	H	2B	3B	HR	RB	BB	SO	SB
Dick Bartell, ss	.238	5	21	3	5	1	0	0	1	0	3	0
Wally Berger, ph	.000	3	3	0	0	0	0	0	0	0	1	0
Don Brennan, p	.000	2	0	0	0	0	0	0	0	0	0	0
Lou Chiozza, of	.286	2	7	0	2	0	0	0	0	1	1	0
Dick Coffman, p	.000	2	1	0	0	0	0	0	0	0	1	0
Harry Danning, c	.250	3	12	0	3	1	0	0	2	0	2	0
Harry Gumbert, p	.000	2	0	0	0	0	0	0	0	0	0	0
Carl Hubbell, p	.000	2	6	1	0	0	0	0	1	0	0	0
Hank Leiber, of	.364	3	11	2	4	0	0	0	2	1	1	0
Sam Leslie, ph	.000	2	1	0	0	0	0	0	0	1	0	0
Gus Mancuso, c-2	.000	3	8	0	0	0	0	0	0	1	0	0
Johnny Mc Carthy, 1b	.211	5	19	1	4	1	0	0	1	1	2	0
Cliff Melton, p	.000	3	2	0	0	0	0	0	0	1	1	0
Jo-Jo Moore, of	.391	5	23	1	9	1	0	0	1	0	1	0
Mel Ott, 3b	.200	5	20	1	4	0	0	1	3	1	4	0
Jimmy Ripple, of	.294	5	17	2	5	0	0	0	0	3	1	0
Blondy Ryan, ph	.000	1	1	0	0	0	0	0	0	0	1	0
Hal Schumacher, p	.000	1	1	0	0	0	0	0	0	0	1	0
Al Smith, p	.000	2	0	0	0	0	0	0	0	0	0	0
Burgess Whitehead, 2b	.250	5	16	1	4	2	0	0	0	0	2	1
TOTAL	.237		169	12	40	6	0	1	12	11	21	1

PITCHER	W	L	ERA	G	GS	CG	SV	SHO	IP	H	ER	BB	SO
Don Brennan	0	0	0.00	2	0	0	0	0	3.0	1	0	1	1
Dick Coffman	0	0	4.15	2	0	0	0	0	4.1	2	2	5	1
Harry Gumbert	0	0	27.00	2	0	0	0	0	1.1	4	4	1	1
Carl Hubbell	1	1	3.77	2	2	1	0	0	14.1	12	6	4	7
Cliff Melton	0	2	4.91	3	2	0	0	0	11.0	12	6	6	7
Hal Schumacher	0	1	6.00	1	1	0	0	0	6.0	9	4	4	3
Al Smith	0	0	3.00	2	0	0	0	0	3.0	2	1	0	1
TOTAL	1	4	4.81	14	5	1	0	0	43.0	42	23	21	21

GAME 1 AT NY -A OCT 6

```
NY-N   000 010 000   1 6 2
NY-A   000 007 01X   8 7 0
```
Pitchers: HUBBELL, Gumbert (6), Coffman (6), Smith (8) vs GOMEZ
Home Runs: Lazzeri-NY(A)
Attendance: 60,573

GAME 2 AT NY -A OCT 7

```
NY-N   100 000 000   1 7 0
NY-A   000 024 20X   8 12 0
```
Pitchers: MELTON, Gumbert (5), Coffman (6) vs RUFFING
Attendance: 57,675

GAME 3 AT NY -N OCT 8

```
NY-A   012 110 000   5 9 0
NY-N   000 000 100   1 5 4
```
Pitchers: PEARSON, Murphy (9) vs SCHUMACHER, Melton (7), Brennan (9)
Attendance: 37,385

GAME 4 AT NY -N OCT 9

```
NY-A   101 000 001   3 6 0
NY-N   060 000 10X   7 12 3
```
Pitchers: HADLEY, Andrews (2), Wicker (8) vs HUBBELL
Home Runs: Gehrig-NY(A)
Attendance: 44,293

GAME 5 AT NY -N OCT 10

```
NY-A   011 020 000   4 8 0
NY-N   002 000 000   2 10 0
```
Pitchers: GOMEZ vs MELTON, Smith (6), Brennan (8)
Home Runs: DiMaggio-NY(A), Hoag-NY(A), Ott-NY(N)
Attendance: 38,216

As they had six years earlier, the Cubs faced the Yankees in the World Series, and as they had six years earlier, New York swept the Series in four games. Although Cub batters made nearly as many hits as the Yankees, they did much less damage, driving in 13 fewer runs. In Game One, Yankee ace Red Ruffing scattered nine Cub hits, holding Chicago to a single run. The Cubs' Bill Lee was nearly as effective in scattering hits, but a base on balls in the second (the game's only walk) followed by a pair of singles sandwiched around an error accounted for two runs—all the Yankees would need for the win (though they scored once more in the sixth).

In Game Two the Cubs outhit the Yankees 11 to 7, but scored only half as many runs as the New Yorkers. Chicago's Dizzy Dean, pitching on craft and guile with his fastball gone, managed to keep the game close until the final innings. With a 3–2 lead going into the eighth, though, he gave up a two-run homer to Frank Crosetti, and the same to Joe DiMaggio in the ninth before being relieved. Yankee fireman Johnny Murphy, meanwhile, held Chicago scoreless over the final two innings to preserve Lefty Gomez's win.

Utility outfielder Joe Marty drove in both Chicago runs in Game Three with a grounder to third in the fifth and a homer in the eighth. (His .500 BA was tops for both teams, and he drove in five of the Cubs' nine Series runs.) But again the Cubs fell short, as Yankee rookie second baseman Joe Gordon homered to tie the score in the bottom of the fifth with the first of what would be five Yankee runs by the time Bill Dickey's homer in the eighth ended the scoring for the day.

Cub second baseman Billy Herman's wild throw with two out in the second inning of Game Four led to three unearned runs, and a Yankee lead they would not relinquish. Though their lead was cut to one run (4–3) when Chicago scored twice in the top of the eighth, the Yankees took advantage of two wild pitches and two walks to turn their four hits into four runs that crushed Cub hopes and gave the New Yorkers a record third consecutive world championship.

New York Yankees (AL), 4;
Chicago Cubs (NL), 0

NY (A)

PLAYER/POS	AVG	G	AB	R	H	2B	3B	HR	RB	BB	SO	SB
Frankie Crosetti, ss	.250	4	16	1	4	2	1	1	6	2	4	0
Bill Dickey, c	.400	4	15	2	6	0	0	1	2	1	0	1
Joe DiMaggio, of	.267	4	15	4	4	0	0	1	2	1	1	0
Lou Gehrig, 1b	.286	4	14	4	4	0	0	0	0	2	3	0
Lefty Gomez, p	.000	1	2	0	0	0	0	0	0	0	0	0
Joe Gordon, 2b	.400	4	15	3	6	2	0	1	6	1	3	1
Tommy Henrich, of	.250	4	16	3	4	1	0	1	1	0	1	0
Myril Hoag, of-1	.400	2	5	3	2	1	0	0	1	0	0	0
Johnny Murphy, p	.000	1	0	0	0	0	0	0	0	0	0	0
Monte Pearson, p	.333	1	3	1	1	0	0	0	0	1	0	0
Jake Powell, of	.000	1	0	0	0	0	0	0	0	0	0	0
Red Rolfe, 3b	.167	4	18	0	3	0	0	0	1	0	3	1
Red Ruffing, p	.167	2	6	1	1	0	0	0	1	1	0	0
George Selkirk, of	.200	3	10	0	2	0	0	0	1	2	1	0
TOTAL	.274		135	22	37	6	1	5	21	11	16	3

PITCHER	W	L	ERA	G	GS	CG	SV	SHO	IP	H	ER	BB	SO
Lefty Gomez	1	0	3.86	1	1	0	0	0	7.0	9	3	1	5
Johnny Murphy	0	0	0.00	1	0	0	1	0	2.0	2	0	1	1
Monte Pearson	1	0	1.00	1	1	1	0	0	9.0	5	1	2	9
Red Ruffing	2	0	1.50	2	2	2	0	0	18.0	17	3	2	11
TOTAL	4	0	1.75	5	4	3	1	0	36.0	33	7	6	26

CHI (N)

PLAYER/POS	AVG	G	AB	R	H	2B	3B	HR	RB	BB	SO	SB
Clay Bryant, p	.000	1	2	0	0	0	0	0	0	0	1	0
Tex Carleton, p	.000	1	0	0	0	0	0	0	0	0	0	0
Phil Cavaretta, of-3	.462	4	13	1	6	1	0	0	0	0	1	0
Ripper Collins, 1b	.133	4	15	1	2	0	0	0	0	0	3	0
Dizzy Dean, p	.667	2	3	0	2	0	0	0	0	0	0	0
Frank Demaree, of	.100	3	10	1	1	0	0	0	0	1	2	0
Larry French, p	.000	3	0	0	0	0	0	0	0	0	0	0
Augie Galan, ph	.000	2	2	0	0	0	0	0	0	0	1	0
Stan Hack, 3b	.471	4	17	3	8	1	0	0	1	1	2	0
Gabby Hartnett, c	.091	3	11	0	1	0	1	0	0	0	2	0
Billy Herman, 2b	.188	4	16	1	3	0	0	0	0	1	4	0
Billy Jurges, ss	.231	4	13	0	3	1	0	0	0	1	3	0
Tony Lazzeri, ph	.000	2	2	0	0	0	0	0	0	0	1	0
Bill Lee, p	.000	2	3	0	0	0	0	0	0	0	1	0
Joe Marty, of	.500	3	12	1	6	1	0	1	5	0	2	0
Ken O'Dea, c-1	.200	3	5	1	1	0	0	1	2	1	0	0
Vance Page, p	.000	1	0	0	0	0	0	0	0	0	0	0
Carl Reynolds, of-3	.000	4	12	0	0	0	0	0	0	1	3	0
Charlie Root, p	.000	1	0	0	0	0	0	0	0	0	0	0
Jack Russell, p	.000	2	0	0	0	0	0	0	0	0	0	0
TOTAL	.243		136	9	33	4	1	2	8	6	26	0

PITCHER	W	L	ERA	G	GS	CG	SV	SHO	IP	H	ER	BB	SO
Clay Bryant	0	1	6.75	1	1	0	0	0	5.1	6	4	5	3
Tex Carleton	0	0	INF	1	0	0	0	0	0.0	1	2	2	0
Dizzy Dean	0	1	6.48	2	1	0	0	0	8.1	8	6	1	2
Larry French	0	0	2.70	3	0	0	0	0	3.1	1	1	1	2
Bill Lee	0	2	2.45	2	2	0	0	0	11.0	15	3	1	8
Vance Page	0	0	13.50	1	0	0	0	0	1.1	2	2	0	0
Charlie Root	0	0	3.00	1	0	0	0	0	3.0	3	1	0	1
Jack Russell	0	0	0.00	2	0	0	0	0	1.2	1	0	1	0
TOTAL	0	4	5.03	13	4	0	0	0	34.0	37	19	11	16

GAME 1 AT CHI OCT 5

NY	020 000 100	3	12	1
CHI	001 000 000	1	9	1

Pitchers: RUFFING vs LEE, Russell (9)
Attendance: 43,642

GAME 2 AT CHI OCT 6

NY	020 000 022	6	7	2
CHI	102 000 000	3	11	0

Pitchers: GOMEZ, Murphy (8) vs J.DEAN, French (9)
Home Runs: Crosetti-NY, DiMaggio-NY
Attendance: 42,108

GAME 3 AT NY OCT 8

CHI	000 010 010	2	5	1
NY	000 022 01X	5	7	2

Pitchers: BRYANT, Russell (6), French (7) vs PEARSON
Home Runs: Dickey-NY, Gordon-NY, Marty-CHI
Attendance: 55,236

GAME 4 AT NY OCT 9

CHI	000 100 020	3	8	1
NY	030 001 04X	8	11	1

Pitchers: LEE, Root (4), Page (7), French (8), Carleton (8), J.Dean (8) vs RUFFING
Home Runs: Henrich-NY, O'Dea-CHI
Attendance: 59,847

The Yankees won their fourth consecutive World Series with their second sweep in a row. This time the victim was Cincinnati, in the Series for the first time since their tainted triumph over the Black Sox two decades earlier. New York had lost the power of Lou Gehrig (whose illness forced his retirement early in the season), but in the Series rookie outfielder Charlie Keller took up the slack. He led both clubs in batting, slugging, home runs, RBIs, hits, and runs, and hit one of the Series' two triples. His eight runs scored equalled those of the whole Cincinnati team.

The Yankees' Red Ruffing and Cincinnati's Paul Derringer hurled matching four-hitters through eight innings of Game One. With the score tied 1–1, Ruffing set the Reds down in order in the ninth. But in the bottom of the ninth Keller tripled off Derringer with one away, and scored the deciding run on catcher Bill Dickey's single.

Babe Dahlgren, Gehrig's replacement at first base, doubled in the third and later scored the Yankees' first run in Game Two, and homered in the next inning for New York's fourth and final run of the game. Red starter Bucky Walters stopped the Yankees after that, but they had more than enough runs for the win, as Monte Pearson held the Reds hitless through seven and wound up with a two-hit shutout.

Keller provided the margin of victory with a pair of two-run homers in the first and fifth innings of Game Three. Joe DiMaggio's two-run homer in the third and Bill Dickey's solo shot that followed Keller's homer in the fifth accounted for the rest of New York's runs in their 7–3 win.

No one scored through six innings of Game Four. Keller and Dickey then homered in the top of the seventh, but Red Rolfe's error at third in the last of the inning opened the way for the Reds to go ahead with three unearned runs. They earned a fourth run an inning later, but the Yankees tied it up with two in the ninth (one unearned) and took the lead in the tenth with three more runs (two unearned) on a walk, a single, and three more Red errors. Reliever Johnny Murphy held off a Red threat in the last of the tenth and the Series was over.

New York Yankees (AL), 4; Cincinnati Reds (NL), 0

NY (A)

PLAYER/POS	AVG	G	AB	R	H	2B	3B	HR	RB	BB	SO	SB
Frankie Crosetti, ss	.063	4	16	2	1	0	0	0	1	2	2	0
Babe Dahlgren, 1b	.214	4	14	2	3	2	0	1	2	0	4	0
Bill Dickey, c	.267	4	15	2	4	0	0	2	5	1	2	0
Joe DiMaggio, of	.313	4	16	3	5	0	0	1	3	1	1	0
Lefty Gomez, p	.000	1	1	0	0	0	0	0	0	0	1	0
Joe Gordon, 2b	.143	4	14	1	2	0	0	0	1	0	2	0
Bump Hadley, p	.000	1	3	0	0	0	0	0	0	0	0	0
Oral Hildebrand, p	.000	1	1	0	0	0	0	0	0	0	1	0
Charlie Keller, of	.438	4	16	8	7	1	1	3	6	1	2	0
Johnny Murphy, p	.000	1	2	0	0	0	0	0	0	0	1	0
Monte Pearson, p	.000	1	2	0	0	0	0	0	0	0	1	0
Red Rolfe, 3b	.125	4	16	2	2	0	0	0	0	0	0	0
Red Ruffing, p	.333	1	3	0	1	0	0	0	0	0	1	0
George Selkirk, of	.167	4	12	0	2	1	0	0	0	3	2	0
Steve Sundra, p	.000	1	0	0	0	0	0	0	0	0	1	0
TOTAL	.206		131	20	27	4	1	7	18	9	20	0

PITCHER	W	L	ERA	G	GS	CG	SV	SHO	IP	H	ER	BB	SO
Lefty Gomez	0	0	9.00	1	1	0	0	0	1.0	3	1	0	1
Bump Hadley	1	0	2.25	1	0	0	0	0	8.0	7	2	3	2
Oral Hildebrand	0	0	0.00	1	1	0	0	0	4.0	2	0	0	3
Johnny Murphy	1	0	2.70	1	0	0	0	0	3.1	5	1	0	2
Monte Pearson	1	0	0.00	1	1	0	0	1	9.0	2	0	1	8
Red Ruffing	1	0	1.00	1	1	1	0	0	9.0	4	1	1	4
Steve Sundra	0	0	0.00	1	0	0	0	0	2.2	4	0	1	2
TOTAL	4	0	1.22	7	4	2	0	1	37.0	27	5	6	22

CIN (N)

PLAYER/POS	AVG	G	AB	R	H	2B	3B	HR	RB	BB	SO	SB
Wally Berger, of	.000	4	15	0	0	0	0	0	1	0	4	0
Nino Bongiovanni, ph	.000	1	1	0	0	0	0	0	0	0	0	0
Frenchy Bordagaray, pr	.000	2	0	0	0	0	0	0	0	0	0	0
Harry Craft, of	.091	4	11	0	1	0	0	0	0	0	6	0
Paul Derringer, p	.200	2	5	0	1	0	0	0	0	0	0	0
Lonny Frey, 2b	.000	4	17	0	0	0	0	0	0	1	4	0
Lee Gamble, ph	.000	1	1	0	0	0	0	0	0	0	1	0
Ival Goodman, of	.333	4	15	3	5	1	0	0	1	1	2	1
Lee Grissom, p	.000	1	0	0	0	0	0	0	0	0	0	0
Willard Hershberger, c-2	.500	3	2	0	1	0	0	0	1	0	0	0
Ernie Lombardi, c	.214	4	14	0	3	0	0	0	2	0	1	0
Frank Mc Cormick, 1b	.400	4	15	1	6	1	0	0	1	0	1	0
Whitey Moore, p	.000	1	1	0	0	0	0	0	0	0	0	0
Billy Myers, ss	.333	4	12	2	4	0	1	0	0	2	3	0
Al Simmons, of	.250	1	4	1	1	1	0	0	0	0	0	0
Junior Thompson, p	1.000	1	1	0	1	0	0	0	0	0	0	0
Bucky Walters, p	.000	2	3	0	0	0	0	0	0	0	0	0
Billy Werber, 3b	.250	4	16	1	4	0	0	0	2	2	0	0
TOTAL	.203		133	8	27	3	1	0	8	6	22	1

PITCHER	W	L	ERA	G	GS	CG	SV	SHO	IP	H	ER	BB	SO
Paul Derringer	0	1	2.35	2	2	1	0	0	15.1	9	4	3	9
Lee Grissom	0	0	0.00	1	0	0	0	0	1.1	0	0	1	0
Whitey Moore	0	0	0.00	1	0	0	0	0	3.0	0	0	0	2
Junior Thompson	0	1	13.50	1	1	0	0	0	4.2	5	7	4	3
Bucky Walters	0	2	4.91	2	1	1	0	0	11.0	13	6	1	6
TOTAL	0	4	4.33	7	4	2	0	0	35.1	27	17	9	20

GAME 1 AT NY OCT 4

CIN	000 100 000	1	4	0
NY	000 010 001	2	6	0

Pitchers: DERRINGER vs RUFFING
Attendance: 58,541

GAME 2 AT NY OCT 5

CIN	000 000 000	0	2	0
NY	003 100 00X	4	9	0

Pitchers: WALTERS vs PEARSON
Home Runs: Dalhgren-NY
Attendance: 59,791

GAME 3 AT CIN OCT 7

NY	202 030 000	7	5	1
CIN	120 000 000	3	10	0

Pitchers: Gomez, HADLEY (2) vs
THOMPSON, Grissom (5), Moore (7)
Home Runs: Keller-NY (2),
DiMaggio-NY, Dickey-NY
Attendance: 32,723

GAME 4 AT CIN OCT 8

NY	000 000 202 3	7	7	1
CIN	000 000 310 0	4	11	4

Pitchers: Hildebrand, Sundra (5),
MURPHY (7) vs Derringer,
WALTERS (8)
Home Runs: Keller-NY, Dickey-NY
Attendance: 32,794

The Tigers outpitched and out-slugged the Reds, and scored six more runs than the Reds did. What they failed to do was win the Series.

Tiger ace Bobo Newsom, who had enjoyed what would be his finest season in a long career, carried his mastery into the Series opener. Detroit gave him an early lead, driving out Red starter Paul Derringer with five runs in the second inning, and added a pair of runs in the fifth on Bruce Campbell's home run. Newsom, meanwhile, held the Reds to single runs in the fourth and eighth.

Cincinnati's Bucky Walters walked the first two Tigers he faced in Game Two, and both scored. But two Red runs in the second tied the game, Jimmy Ripple's two-run homer an inning later gave them the lead, and pitcher Walters scored an insurance run in the fourth after doubling. Another Tiger walk in the sixth led to their third run, but Walters retired the remaining Tigers in order.

The Series moved to Detroit and the lead to the Tigers in Game Three. Detroit's Rocky Bridges yielded ten hits and four runs, but his teammates responded with 13 hits and seven runs, including a pair of two-run homers by Rudy York and Pinky Higgins in the seventh. Cincinnati again evened the Series the next day, though, with five runs to support Derringer's five-hit, two-run pitching. Although Newsom's father had suffered a fatal heart attack the day after seeing his son win the opener, the son pitched Game Five, and improved on his previous performance with a three-hit shutout. Hank Greenberg's homer in the third inning accounted for the first three of the Tigers' eight runs in their lopsided win.

The Reds returned home needing to win the final two games. Like Newsom, Bucky Walters bettered his earlier win with a shutout in Game Six, and drove in two of the Reds' four runs, one with a solo homer in the eighth. In the Series finale, Newsom and Derringer found themselves evenly matched. The Tigers scored a run in the third, while Newsom held Cincinnati scoreless through six. But in the seventh, leadoff doubles by Frank McCormick and Jimmy Ripple, plus a successful bunt and a fly to deep center, gave the Reds two runs—all they needed as Derringer stopped the Tigers through the final six innings for the victory.

Cincinnati Reds (NL), 4;
Detroit Tigers (AL), 3

CIN (N)

PLAYER/POS	AVG	G	AB	R	H	2B	3B	HR	RB	BB	SO	SB
Morrie Arnovich, of	.000	1	1	0	0	0	0	0	0	0	0	0
Bill Baker, c	.250	3	4	1	1	0	0	0	0	0	1	0
Joe Beggs, p	.000	1	0	0	0	0	0	0	0	0	0	0
Harry Craft, ph	.000	1	1	0	0	0	0	0	0	0	0	0
Paul Derringer, p	.000	3	7	0	0	0	0	0	0	0	1	0
Lonny Frey, ph	.000	3	2	0	0	0	0	0	0	0	0	0
Ival Goodman, of	.276	7	29	5	8	2	0	0	5	0	3	0
Johnny Hutchings, p	.000	1	0	0	0	0	0	0	0	0	0	0
Eddie Joost, 2b	.200	7	25	0	5	0	0	0	2	1	2	0
Ernie Lombardi, c-1	.333	2	3	0	1	1	0	0	0	1	0	0
Frank Mc Cormick, 1b	.214	7	28	2	6	1	0	0	0	1	1	0
Mike Mc Cormick, of	.310	7	29	1	9	3	0	0	2	1	6	0
Whitey Moore, p	.000	3	2	0	0	0	0	0	0	0	1	0
Billy Myers, ss	.130	7	23	0	3	0	0	0	2	2	5	0
Elmer Riddle, p	.000	1	0	0	0	0	0	0	0	0	0	0
Lew Riggs, ph	.000	3	3	1	0	0	0	0	0	0	2	0
Jimmy Ripple, of	.333	7	21	3	7	2	0	1	6	4	2	0
Junior Thompson, p	.000	1	0	0	0	0	0	0	0	0	1	0
Jim Turner, p	.000	1	2	0	0	0	0	0	0	0	0	0
Johnny Vander Meer, p	.000	1	0	0	0	0	0	0	0	0	0	0
Bucky Walters, p	.286	2	7	2	2	1	0	1	2	0	1	0
Billy Werber, 3b	.370	7	27	5	10	4	0	0	2	4	2	0
Jimmie Wilson, c	.353	6	17	2	6	0	0	0	0	1	2	1
TOTAL	.250		232	22	58	14	0	2	21	15	30	1

PITCHER	W	L	ERA	G	GS	CG	SV	SHO	IP	H	ER	BB	SO
Joe Beggs	0	0	9.00	1	0	0	0	0	1.0	3	1	0	1
Paul Derringer	2	1	2.79	3	3	2	0	0	19.1	17	6	10	6
Johnny Hutchings	0	0	9.00	1	0	0	0	0	1.0	2	1	1	0
Whitey Moore	0	0	3.24	3	0	0	0	0	8.1	8	3	6	7
Elmer Riddle	0	0	0.00	1	0	0	0	0	1.0	0	0	0	2
Junior Thompson	0	1	16.20	1	1	0	0	0	3.1	8	6	4	2
Jim Turner	0	1	7.50	1	1	0	0	0	6.0	8	5	0	4
Johnny Vander Meer	0	0	0.00	1	0	0	0	0	3.0	2	0	3	2
Bucky Walters	2	0	1.50	2	2	2	0	1	18.0	8	3	6	6
TOTAL	4	3	3.69	14	7	4	0	1	61.0	56	25	30	30

DET (A)

PLAYER/POS	AVG	G	AB	R	H	2B	3B	HR	RB	BB	SO	SB
Earl Averill, ph	.000	3	3	0	0	0	0	0	0	0	0	0
Dick Bartell, ss	.269	7	26	2	7	2	0	0	3	3	3	0
Tommy Bridges, p	.000	1	3	0	0	0	0	0	0	0	1	0
Bruce Campbell, of	.360	7	25	4	9	1	0	1	5	4	4	0
Frank Croucher, ss	.000	1	0	0	0	0	0	0	0	0	0	0
Pete Fox, ph	.000	1	1	0	0	0	0	0	0	0	0	0
Charlie Gehringer, 2b	.214	7	28	3	6	0	0	0	1	2	0	0
Johnny Gorsica, p	.000	2	4	0	0	0	0	0	0	0	2	0
Hank Greenberg, of	.357	7	28	5	10	2	1	1	6	2	5	0
Pinky Higgins, 3b	.333	7	24	2	8	3	1	1	6	3	3	0
Fred Hutchinson, p	.000	1	0	0	0	0	0	0	0	0	0	0
Barney Mc Cosky, of	.304	7	23	5	7	1	0	0	1	7	0	0
Archie Mc Kain, p	.000	1	0	0	0	0	0	0	0	0	0	0
Bobo Newsom, p	.100	3	10	1	1	0	0	0	0	0	1	0
Schoolboy Rowe, p	.000	2	1	0	0	0	0	0	0	0	1	0
Clay Smith, p	.000	1	1	0	0	0	0	0	0	0	1	0
Billy Sullivan, c-4	.154	5	13	3	2	1	0	0	0	5	2	0
Birdie Tebbetts, c-3	.000	4	11	0	0	0	0	0	0	0	0	0
Dizzy Trout, p	.000	1	1	0	0	0	0	0	0	0	0	0
Rudy York, 1b	.231	7	26	3	6	0	1	1	2	4	7	0
TOTAL	.246		228	28	56	9	3	4	24	30	30	0

PITCHER	W	L	ERA	G	GS	CG	SV	SHO	IP	H	ER	BB	SO
Tommy Bridges	1	0	3.00	1	1	1	0	0	9.0	10	3	1	5
Johnny Gorsica	0	0	0.79	2	0	0	0	0	11.1	6	1	4	4
Fred Hutchinson	0	0	9.00	1	0	0	0	0	1.0	1	1	1	1
Archie Mc Kain	0	0	3.00	1	0	0	0	0	3.0	4	1	0	0
Bobo Newsom	2	1	1.38	3	3	3	0	1	26.0	18	4	4	17
Schoolboy Rowe	0	2	17.18	2	2	0	0	0	3.2	12	7	1	1
Clay Smith	0	0	2.25	1	0	0	0	0	4.0	1	1	3	1
Dizzy Trout	0	1	9.00	1	1	0	0	0	2.0	6	2	1	1
TOTAL	3	4	3.00	12	7	4	0	1	60.0	58	20	15	30

Dodger catcher Mickey Owen's dropped third strike in Game Four was the Series' memorable boner, but it was not the chief cause of Brooklyn's downfall. Yankee pitching was. Three Yankee starters hurled complete-game wins, with each giving the Dodgers only one earned run. And relief ace Johnny Murphy hurled two-hit shutout ball in six innings over two games, winning one.

Yankee Joe Gordon opened the Series scoring with a solo homer in the second inning of Game One, and the Yankees added runs in the fourth and sixth. Owen tripled in the Dodgers' first run in the fifth, and pinch hitter Lew Riggs singled in an unearned run in the seventh. But Yankee starter Red Ruffing held on to his slim lead through the final two innings for the win.

Dodger ace Whitlow Wyatt gave the Yankees single runs in the second and third innings of Game Two, but held them scoreless the rest of the way. Meanwhile, the Dodgers tied the game in the fifth, and scored an unearned run in the sixth to finish the scoring and give Brooklyn its only win of the Series.

Freddie Fitzsimmons, with the Dodgers' best pitching of the Series, dueled Yankee Marius Russo through seven scoreless innings in Game Three. But Fitzsimmons's final out of the seventh—a line drive by Russo that bounced off Fitzsimmons's leg into the glove of shortstop Pee Wee Reese—broke his kneecap. Hugh Casey, who replaced Fitzsimmons in the eighth, retired the first batter, but then gave up four straight singles for two runs before being removed. The Yankees scored no more, and Brooklyn came up with a run in the last of the eighth. But Russo stopped the Dodgers in order in the ninth to preserve his lead for the Yankees' second win.

In Game Four, for the first time in the Series, the margin of victory was more than one run, thanks to catcher Owen's famous boner. Brooklyn held the lead 4–3 with two out in the top of the ninth. Dodger reliever Casey, who had shut out the Yankees since coming on in the fifth inning, then struck out Tommy Henrich for what should have been the game-ending out. But Owen let the ball get by him, and before the third out was recorded Casey had given up a single, two doubles, and two walks—and four runs, for Brooklyn's third loss.

The Yankees scored twice off Wyatt in the second inning of Game Five, and once more in the fifth (on Henrich's home run), as Tiny Bonham held Brooklyn to four hits and a single run to clinch the ninth Yankee world title.

New York Yankees (AL), 4; Brooklyn Dodgers (NL), 1

NY (A)

PLAYER/POS	AVG	G	AB	R	H	2B	3B	HR	RB	BB	SO	SB
Tiny Bonham, p	.000	1	4	0	0	0	0	0	0	0	4	0
Frenchy Bordagaray, pr	.000	1	0	0	0	0	0	0	0	0	0	0
Marv Breuer, p	.000	1	1	0	0	0	0	0	0	0	0	0
Spud Chandler, p	.500	1	2	0	1	0	0	0	1	0	0	0
Bill Dickey, c	.167	5	18	3	3	1	0	0	1	3	1	0
Joe DiMaggio, of	.263	5	19	1	5	0	0	0	1	2	2	0
Atley Donald, p	.000	1	2	0	0	0	0	0	0	0	1	0
Joe Gordon, 2b	.500	5	14	2	7	1	1	1	5	7	0	0
Tommy Henrich, of	.167	5	18	4	3	1	0	1	1	3	3	0
Charlie Keller, of	.389	5	18	5	7	2	0	0	5	3	1	0
Johnny Murphy, p	.000	2	2	0	0	0	0	0	0	0	1	0
Phil Rizzuto, ss	.111	5	18	0	2	0	0	0	0	3	1	1
Red Rolfe, 3b	.300	5	20	2	6	0	0	0	0	2	1	0
Buddy Rosar, c	.000	1	0	0	0	0	0	0	0	0	0	0
Red Ruffing, p	.000	1	3	0	0	0	0	0	0	0	0	0
Marius Russo, p	.000	1	4	0	0	0	0	0	0	0	1	0
George Selkirk, ph	.500	2	2	0	1	0	0	0	0	0	0	0
Johnny Sturm, 1b	.286	5	21	0	6	0	0	0	2	0	2	1
TOTAL	.247		166	17	41	5	1	2	16	23	18	2

PITCHER	W	L	ERA	G	GS	CG	SV	SHO	IP	H	ER	BB	SO
Tiny Bonham	1	0	1.00	1	1	1	0	0	9.0	4	1	2	2
Marv Breuer	0	0	0.00	1	0	0	0	0	3.0	3	0	1	2
Spud Chandler	0	1	3.60	1	1	0	0	0	5.0	4	2	2	2
Atley Donald	0	0	9.00	1	1	0	0	0	4.0	6	4	3	2
Johnny Murphy	1	0	0.00	2	0	0	0	0	6.0	2	0	1	3
Red Ruffing	1	0	1.00	1	1	1	0	0	9.0	6	1	3	5
Marius Russo	1	0	1.00	1	1	1	0	0	9.0	4	1	2	5
TOTAL	4	1	1.80	8	5	3	0	0	45.0	29	9	14	21

BRO (N)

PLAYER/POS	AVG	G	AB	R	H	2B	3B	HR	RB	BB	SO	SB
Johnny Allen, p	.000	3	0	0	0	0	0	0	0	0	0	0
Dolph Camilli, 1b	.167	5	18	1	3	1	0	0	1	1	6	0
Hugh Casey, p	.500	3	2	0	1	0	0	0	0	0	1	0
Pete Coscarart, 2b	.000	3	7	1	0	0	0	0	0	1	2	0
Curt Davis, p	.000	1	2	0	0	0	0	0	0	0	0	0
Freddie Fitzsimmons, p	.000	1	2	0	0	0	0	0	0	0	0	0
Herman Franks, c	.000	1	1	0	0	0	0	0	0	0	0	0
Larry French, p	.000	2	0	0	0	0	0	0	0	0	0	0
Augie Galan, ph	.000	2	2	0	0	0	0	0	0	0	1	0
Billy Herman, 2b	.125	4	8	0	1	0	0	0	0	2	0	0
Kirby Higbe, p	1.000	1	1	0	1	0	0	0	0	0	0	0
Cookie Lavagetto, 3b	.100	3	10	1	1	0	0	0	0	2	0	0
Joe Medwick, of	.235	5	17	1	4	1	0	0	0	1	2	0
Mickey Owen, c	.167	5	12	1	2	0	1	0	2	3	0	0
Pee Wee Reese, ss	.200	5	20	1	4	0	0	0	2	0	0	0
Pete Reiser, of	.200	5	20	1	4	1	1	1	3	1	6	0
Lew Riggs, 3b-2	.250	3	8	0	2	0	0	0	1	1	1	0
Dixie Walker, of	.222	5	18	3	4	2	0	0	0	2	1	0
Jimmy Wasdell, of-1	.200	3	5	0	1	1	0	0	2	0	0	0
Whit Wyatt, p	.167	2	6	1	1	1	0	0	0	0	1	0
TOTAL	.182		159	11	29	7	2	1	11	14	21	0

PITCHER	W	L	ERA	G	GS	CG	SV	SHO	IP	H	ER	BB	SO
Johnny Allen	0	0	0.00	3	0	0	0	0	3.2	1	0	3	0
Hugh Casey	0	2	3.38	3	0	0	0	0	5.1	9	2	2	1
Curt Davis	0	1	5.06	1	1	0	0	0	5.1	6	3	3	1
Freddie Fitzsimmons	0	0	0.00	1	1	0	0	0	7.0	4	0	3	1
Larry French	0	0	0.00	2	0	0	0	0	1.0	0	0	0	0
Kirby Higbe	0	0	7.36	1	1	0	0	0	3.2	6	3	2	1
Whit Wyatt	1	1	2.50	2	2	2	0	0	18.0	15	5	10	14
TOTAL	1	4	2.66	13	5	2	0	0	44.0	41	13	23	18

GAME 1 AT NY OCT 1

BRO	000	010	100	2	6 0
NY	010	101	00X	3	6 1

Pitchers: DAVIS, Casey (6), Allen (7) vs RUFFING
Home Runs: Gordon-NY
Attendance: 68,540

GAME 2 AT NY OCT 2

BRO	000	021	000	3	6 2
NY	011	000	000	2	9 1

Pitchers: WYATT vs CHANDLER, Murphy (6)
Attendance: 66,248

GAME 3 AT BRO OCT 4

NY	000	000	020	2	8 0
BRO	000	000	010	1	4 0

Pitchers: RUSSO vs Fitzsimmons, CASEY (8), French (8), Allen (9)
Attendance: 33,100

GAME 4 AT BRO OCT 5

NY	100	200	004	7	12 0
BRO	000	220	000	4	9 1

Pitchers: Donald, Breuer (5), MURPHY (8) VS Higbe, French (4), Allen (5), CASEY (5)
Home Runs: Reiser-BRO
Attendance: 33,813

GAME 5 AT BRO OCT 6

NY	020	010	000	3	6 0
BRO	001	000	000	1	4 1

Pitchers: BONHAM vs WYATT
Home Runs: Henrich-NY
Attendance: 34,072

Cardinal rookies Stan Musial and Whitey Kurowski drove in game-winning runs for rookie-pitcher Johnny Beazley in Games Two and Five as the major leagues' youngest team upset the Yankees. New York won only the opener, building a seven-run lead for starter Red Ruffing, who shut out St. Louis on one hit through 8⅓ innings before giving up four hits and four harmless runs in the last of the ninth.

The Cardinals scored first in Game Two on catcher Walker Cooper's two-run double in the first inning. Kurowski tripled in a third Cardinal run in the seventh, but pitcher Beazley, after holding the Yankees scoreless through seven innings, gave up three runs in the eighth on two singles and Charlie Keller's two-run homer. St. Louis regained the lead a half inning later when Musial singled home Enos Slaughter (who had doubled), and stifled a threat in the ninth as Slaughter's great throw from right field nailed a Yankee runner at third.

Second-year Cardinal pitcher Ernie White turned in the Series' top mound performance with a six-single, no-walk shutout in Game Three (aided by outfielders Musial and Slaughter, who hauled in a pair of potential home run blasts in the seventh inning). The Cards managed only five singles themselves, but they combined one with a walk, sacrifice, and ground out for a run in the third, and sandwiched a Yankee error with two hits in the nineth for an unearned insurance run.

Game Four saw the Series' heaviest hitting. New York scored once in the first, but the Cards exploded in the fourth for six runs on six hits and two walks. The Yankees tied it up two innings later, with Keller's three-run homer the feature of the five-run inning. St. Louis took the lead for good with two runs in the seventh, and added a ninth run in the ninth.

Beazley and Ruffing tangled in Game Five. Phil Rizzuto's solo homer put New York ahead in the first inning. Slaughter's fourth-inning home run tied the score, but the Yankees regained the lead with a run later in the inning. The Cards retied the game in the sixth, and took the final lead when Kurowski homered for two runs in the top of the ninth. The Yankees threatened in the last of the ninth, putting their first two men on with a single and error. But catcher Cooper picked a runner off second, second baseman Jimmy Brown redeemed his earlier error with a sparkling catch, then fielded a routine grounder for the final out and the Cardinal triumph.

St. Louis Cardinals (NL), 4; New York Yankees (AL), 1

STL (N)

PLAYER/POS	AVG	G	AB	R	H	2B	3B	HR	RB	BB	SO	SB
Johnny Beazley, p	.143	2	7	0	1	0	0	0	0	0	5	0
Jimmy Brown, 2b	.300	5	20	2	6	0	0	0	1	3	0	0
Mort Cooper, p	.200	2	5	1	1	0	0	0	2	0	1	0
Walker Cooper, c	.286	5	21	3	6	1	0	0	4	0	1	0
Creepy Crespi, pr	.000	1	0	1	0	0	0	0	0	0	0	0
Harry Gumbert, p	.000	2	0	0	0	0	0	0	0	0	0	0
Johnny Hopp, 1b	.176	5	17	3	3	0	0	0	0	1	1	0
Whitey Kurowski, 3b	.267	5	15	3	4	0	1	1	5	2	3	0
Max Lanier, p	1.000	2	1	0	1	0	0	0	1	0	0	0
Marty Marion, ss	.111	5	18	2	2	0	1	0	3	1	2	0
Terry Moore, of	.294	5	17	2	5	1	0	0	2	2	3	0
Stan Musial, of	.222	5	18	2	4	1	0	0	2	4	0	0
Ken O'Dea, ph	1.000	1	1	0	1	0	0	0	1	0	0	0
Howie Pollet, p	.000	1	0	0	0	0	0	0	0	0	0	0
Ray Sanders, ph	.000	2	1	0	0	0	0	0	0	1	0	0
Enos Slaughter, of	.263	5	19	3	5	1	0	1	2	3	2	0
Harry Walker, ph	.000	1	1	0	0	0	0	0	0	0	1	0
Ernie White, p	.000	2	2	0	0	0	0	0	0	0	0	0
TOTAL	.239		163	23	39	4	2	2	23	17	19	0

PITCHER	W	L	ERA	G	GS	CG	SV	SHO	IP	H	ER	BB	SO
Johnny Beazley	2	0	2.50	2	2	2	0	0	18.0	17	5	3	6
Mort Cooper	0	1	5.54	2	2	0	0	0	13.0	17	8	4	9
Harry Gumbert	0	0	0.00	2	0	0	0	0	0.2	1	0	0	0
Max Lanier	1	0	0.00	2	0	0	0	0	4.0	3	0	1	1
Howie Pollet	0	0	0.00	1	0	0	0	0	0.1	0	0	0	0
Ernie White	1	0	0.00	1	1	1	0	1	9.0	6	0	0	6
TOTAL	4	1	2.60	10	5	3	0	1	45.0	44	13	8	22

NY (A)

PLAYER/POS	AVG	G	AB	R	H	2B	3B	HR	RB	BB	SO	SB
Tiny Bonham, p	.000	2	2	0	0	0	0	0	0	1	0	0
Hank Borowy, p	.000	1	1	0	0	0	0	0	0	0	1	0
Marv Breuer, p	.000	1	0	0	0	0	0	0	0	0	0	0
Spud Chandler, p	.000	2	2	0	0	0	0	0	0	0	1	0
Frankie Crosetti, 3b	.000	1	3	0	0	0	0	0	0	0	1	0
Roy Cullenbine, of	.263	5	19	3	5	1	0	0	2	1	2	1
Bill Dickey, c	.263	5	19	1	5	0	0	0	0	1	0	0
Joe DiMaggio, of	.333	5	21	3	7	0	0	0	3	0	1	0
Atley Donald, p	.000	1	2	0	0	0	0	0	0	0	0	0
Joe Gordon, 2b	.095	5	21	1	2	1	0	0	0	0	7	0
Buddy Hassett, 1b	.333	3	9	1	3	1	0	0	2	0	1	0
Charlie Keller, of	.200	5	20	2	4	0	0	2	5	1	3	0
Jerry Priddy, 1b-3,3b-1	.100	3	10	0	1	1	0	0	1	1	0	0
Phil Rizzuto, ss	.381	5	21	2	8	0	0	1	1	2	1	2
Red Rolfe, 3b	.353	4	17	5	6	2	0	0	0	1	2	0
Buddy Rosar, ph	1.000	1	1	0	1	0	0	0	0	0	0	0
Red Ruffing, p-2	.222	4	9	0	2	0	0	0	0	0	2	0
George Selkirk, ph	.000	1	1	0	0	0	0	0	0	0	0	0
Tuck Stainback, pr	.000	2	0	0	0	0	0	0	0	0	0	0
Jim Turner, p	.000	1	0	0	0	0	0	0	0	0	0	0
TOTAL	.247		178	18	44	6	0	3	14	8	22	3

PITCHER	W	L	ERA	G	GS	CG	SV	SHO	IP	H	ER	BB	SO
Tiny Bonham	0	1	4.09	2	1	1	0	0	11.0	9	5	3	3
Hank Borowy	0	0	18.00	1	1	0	0	0	3.0	6	6	3	1
Marv Breuer	0	0	INF	1	0	0	0	0	0.0	2	0	0	0
Spud Chandler	0	1	1.08	2	1	0	1	0	8.1	5	1	1	3
Atley Donald	0	1	6.00	1	0	0	0	0	3.0	3	2	2	1
Red Ruffing	1	1	4.08	2	2	1	0	0	17.2	14	8	7	11
Jim Turner	0	0	0.00	1	0	0	0	0	1.0	0	0	1	0
TOTAL	1	4	4.50	10	5	2	1	0	44.0	39	22	17	19

GAME 1 AT STL SEPT 30

NY	000 110 032	7	11	0
STL	000 000 004	4	7	4

Pitchers: RUFFING, Chandler (9) vs M.COOPER, Gumbert (8), Lanier (9)
Attendance: 34,769

GAME 2 AT STL OCT 1

NY	000 000 030	3	10	2
STL	200 000 110	4	6	0

Pitchers: BONHAM vs BEAZLEY
Home Runs: Keller-NY
Attendance: 34,255

GAME 3 AT NY OCT 2

STL	001 000 001	2	5	1
NY	000 000 000	0	6	1

Pitchers: WHITE vs CHANDLER, Breuer (9), Turner (9)
Attendance: 69,123

GAME 4 AT NY OCT 4

STL	000 600 201	9	12	1
NY	100 040 010	6	10	1

Pitchers: M.Cooper, Gumbert (6), Pollet (6), LANIER (7) vs Borowy, DONALD (4), Bonham (7)
Home Runs: Keller-NY
Attendance: 69,902

GAME 5 AT NY OCT 5

STL	000 101 002	4	9	4
NY	100 100 000	2	7	1

Pitchers: BEAZLEY vs RUFFING
Home Runs: Rizzuto-NY, Slaughter-STL, Kurowski-STL
Attendance: 69,052

Although both clubs had lost players to military service since the previous World Series, history seemed to be repeating itself. The Cardinals lost to the Yankees in the opener and won the second game, as they had the previous year. But this year it was the Yankees who took the next three games and the Series, as fine Cardinal pitching gave way to even finer Yankee mound work.

Yankee pitcher Spurgeon (Spud) Chandler, coming off his finest season (20–4, 1.64 ERA), continued to overwhelm the opposition in the Series. He held the Cards to two runs (only one earned) in Game One, and the Yankees took advantage of a wild pitch to score two runs of their own in the sixth inning, breaking a 2–2 tie for a 4–2 win. Cardinal shortstop Marty Marion homered in the third inning for the first Cardinal run the next day, and first baseman Ray Sanders homered for two more runs in a three-run fourth. Cardinal ace Mort Cooper held New York to one run on four hits through eight innings, but he weakened in the last of the ninth, giving up a double and triple to the first two batters. But only two runs scored as he retired the next three men for St. Louis's only victory.

The Cardinals carried a 2–1 lead into the last of the eighth inning of Game Three, when a pair of errors, two walks, and five Yankee hits (including Billy Johnson's three-run triple) undid them. Yankee fireman Johnny Murphy retired the Cards in order in the ninth to save Hank Borowy's win. Max Lanier and Harry Brecheen held New York to just two runs (and six hits) in Game Four, but Yankee pitcher Marius Russo gave up only one run—and that was scored only because of two Yankee errors in the seventh inning.

In the fifth and (as it turned out) final game, St. Louis couldn't score even an unearned run, although they knocked Spud Chandler for ten hits. But they were all singles and were spaced harmlessly over eight of the nine innings. Three St. Louis pitchers held the Yankees to just seven hits, six of them singles. But in the sixth inning Bill Dickey followed one of the Yankee singles with the game's only extra-base hit—a home run—to produce the game's only scoring, and bring the Yankees yet another world championship, their tenth.

New York Yankees (AL), 4;
St. Louis Cardinals (NL), 1

NY (A)

PLAYER/POS	AVG	G	AB	R	H	2B	3B	HR	RB	BB	SO	SB
Tiny Bonham, p	.000	1	2	0	0	0	0	0	0	0	0	0
Hank Borowy, p	.500	1	2	1	1	0	0	0	0	0	1	0
Spud Chandler, p	.167	2	6	0	1	0	0	0	0	0	2	0
Frankie Crosetti, ss	.278	5	18	4	5	0	0	0	1	2	3	1
Bill Dickey, c	.278	5	18	1	5	0	0	1	4	2	2	0
Nick Etten, 1b	.105	5	19	0	2	0	0	0	2	1	2	0
Joe Gordon, 2b	.235	5	17	2	4	1	0	1	2	3	3	0
Billy Johnson, 3b	.300	5	20	3	6	1	1	0	3	0	3	0
Charlie Keller, of	.222	5	18	3	4	0	1	0	2	2	5	1
Johnny Lindell, of	.111	4	9	1	1	0	0	0	0	1	4	0
Bud Metheny, of	.125	2	8	0	1	0	0	0	0	0	2	0
Johnny Murphy, p	.000	2	0	0	0	0	0	0	0	0	0	0
Marius Russo, p	.667	1	3	1	2	2	0	0	0	1	1	0
Tuck Stainback, of	.176	5	17	0	3	0	0	0	0	0	2	0
Snuffy Stirnweiss, ph	.000	1	1	1	0	0	0	0	0	0	0	0
Roy Weatherly, ph	.000	1	1	0	0	0	0	0	0	0	0	0
TOTAL	.220		159	17	35	5	2	2	14	12	30	2

PITCHER	W	L	ERA	G	GS	CG	SV	SHO	IP	H	ER	BB	SO
Tiny Bonham	0	1	4.50	1	1	0	0	0	8.0	6	4	3	9
Hank Borowy	1	0	2.25	1	1	0	0	0	8.0	6	2	3	4
Spud Chandler	2	0	0.50	2	2	2	0	1	18.0	17	1	3	10
Johnny Murphy	0	0	0.00	2	0	0	1	0	2.0	1	0	1	1
Marius Russo	1	0	0.00	1	1	1	0	0	9.0	7	0	1	2
TOTAL	4	1	1.40	7	5	3	1	1	45.0	37	7	11	26

STL (N)

PLAYER/POS	AVG	G	AB	R	H	2B	3B	HR	RB	BB	SO	SB
Al Brazle, p	.000	1	3	0	0	0	0	0	0	0	1	0
Harry Brecheen, p	.000	3	0	0	0	0	0	0	0	0	0	0
Mort Cooper, p	.000	2	5	0	0	0	0	0	0	0	3	0
Walker Cooper, c	.294	5	17	1	5	0	0	0	0	0	1	0
Frank Demaree, ph	.000	1	1	0	0	0	0	0	0	0	0	0
Murry Dickson, p	.000	1	0	0	0	0	0	0	0	0	0	0
Debs Garms, of-1	.000	2	5	0	0	0	0	0	0	0	2	0
Johnny Hopp, of	.000	1	4	0	0	0	0	0	0	0	0	0
Lou Klein, 2b	.136	5	22	0	3	0	0	0	0	1	2	0
Howie Krist, p	.000	1	0	0	0	0	0	0	0	0	0	0
Whitey Kurowski, 3b	.222	5	18	2	4	1	0	0	1	0	3	0
Max Lanier, p	.250	3	4	0	1	0	0	0	1	0	0	0
Danny Litwhiler, of-4	.267	5	15	0	4	1	0	0	2	2	4	0
Marty Marion, ss	.357	5	14	1	5	2	0	1	2	3	1	1
Stan Musial, of	.278	5	18	2	5	0	0	0	0	2	2	0
Sam Narron, ph	.000	1	1	0	0	0	0	0	0	0	0	0
Ken O'Dea, c-1	.667	2	3	0	2	0	0	0	0	0	0	0
Ray Sanders, 1b	.294	5	17	3	5	0	0	1	2	3	4	0
Harry Walker, of	.167	5	18	0	3	1	0	0	0	0	2	0
Ernie White, pr	.000	1	0	0	0	0	0	0	0	0	0	0
TOTAL	.224		165	9	37	5	0	2	8	11	26	1

PITCHER	W	L	ERA	G	GS	CG	SV	SHO	IP	H	ER	BB	SO
Al Brazle	0	1	3.68	1	1	0	0	0	7.1	5	3	2	4
Harry Brecheen	0	1	2.45	3	0	0	0	0	3.2	5	1	3	3
Mort Cooper	1	1	2.81	2	2	1	0	0	16.0	11	5	3	10
Murry Dickson	0	0	0.00	1	0	0	0	0	0.2	0	0	1	0
Howie Krist	0	0	INF	1	0	0	0	0	0.0	1	0	0	0
Max Lanier	0	1	1.76	3	2	0	0	0	15.1	13	3	3	13
TOTAL	1	4	2.51	11	5	1	0	0	43.0	35	12	12	30

GAME 1 AT NY OCT 5

STL	010	010	000	2	7 2
NY	000	202	00X	4	8 2

Pitchers: LANIER vs CHANDLER
Home Runs: Gordon-NY
Attendance: 68,676

GAME 2 AT NY OCT 6

STL	001	300	000	4	7 2
NY	000	100	002	3	6 0

Pitchers: M.COOPER vs BONHAM, Murphy (9)
Home Runs: Marion-STL, Sanders-STL
Attendance: 68,578

GAME 3 AT NY OCT 7

STL	000	200	000	2	6 4
NY	000	001	05X	6	8 0

Pitchers: BRAZLE, Krist (8), Brecheen (8) VS BOROWY, Murphy (9)
Attendance: 69,990

GAME 4 AT STL OCT 10

NY	000	100	010	2	6 2
STL	000	000	100	1	7 1

Pitchers: RUSSO vs Lanier, BRECHEEN (8)
Attendance: 36,196

GAME 5 AT STL OCT 11

NY	000	002	000	2	7 1
STL	000	000	000	0	10 1

Pitchers: CHANDLER vs M.COOPER, Lanier (8), Dickson (9)
Home Runs: Dickey-NY
Attendance: 33,872

The Cardinals—a much stronger team in the regular season—entered the World Series against their landlord Browns (who owned Sportsman's Park, where both teams played) as clear favorites. They won the Series in six games, but if the Browns' fielding had been as good as their pitching the outcome might have been different.

The Browns won the opener on Denny Galehouse's strong pitching. Galehouse gave up seven hits and four walks, but held the Cards scoreless for 8⅔ innings before yielding a run in the ninth. Cardinal ace Mort Cooper also pitched well in six of his seven innings. He allowed the Browns only two hits, but they came back to back in the fourth inning—a single followed by George McQuinn's home run—to give the Browns all the scoring they needed.

Brown pitcher Nelson Potter's two errors (a fumble and a wild throw) on a bunt in the third inning of Game Two led to an unearned run, and third baseman Mark Christman's fumble an inning later set up a second unearned run. The Browns tied the score with a pair of runs on three two-out hits in the seventh—enough to have won an error-free game—but lost when the Cardinals singled a run across in the last of the eleventh.

Two Brown errors led to a pair of unearned runs in Game Three, but Jack Kramer held the Cards scoreless apart from that, striking out ten. Meanwhile, Brown hitters tied together five singles with two out in the third inning for three runs, adding a fourth run on a wild pitch before the inning ended. In the seventh the Browns tacked on two more runs for a comfortable win and a 2–1 Series advantage.

The Cardinals came back to earn victory in Games Four and Five, knocking three Brown pitchers for 12 hits in Game Four (including Stan Musial's two-run homer in the first) and a 5–1 win for pitcher Harry Brecheen, then rapping Denny Galehouse for two solo homers in Game Five (by Danny Litwhiler and Ray Sanders) for the game's only scoring as Mort Cooper fanned 12 Browns while shutting them out.

Two of the Cardinals' three runs in the fourth inning of Game Six were made possible by Brown shortstop Vern Stephens's throwing error. They provided the margin of victory, as Cardinal pitchers Max Lanier and Ted Wilks held the Browns to three hits and a single run, and brought the Cards their second world title in three years.

St. Louis Cardinals (NL), 4; St. Louis Browns (AL), 2

STL (N)

PLAYER/POS	AVG	G	AB	R	H	2B	3B	HR	RB	BB	SO	SB
Augie Bergamo, of-2	.000	3	6	0	0	0	0	0	1	2	3	0
Harry Brecheen, p	.000	1	4	0	0	0	0	0	0	0	1	0
Bud Byerly, p	.000	1	0	0	0	0	0	0	0	0	0	0
Mort Cooper, p	.000	2	4	0	0	0	0	0	0	0	2	0
Walker Cooper, c	.318	6	22	1	7	2	1	0	2	3	2	0
Blix Donnelly, p	.000	2	1	0	0	0	0	0	0	0	1	0
George Fallon, 2b	.000	2	2	0	0	0	0	0	0	0	1	0
Debs Garms, ph	.000	2	2	0	0	0	0	0	0	0	0	0
Johnny Hopp, of	.185	6	27	2	5	0	0	0	0	0	8	0
Al Jurisich, p	.000	1	0	0	0	0	0	0	0	0	0	0
Whitey Kurowski, 3b	.217	6	23	2	5	1	0	0	1	1	4	0
Max Lanier, p	.500	2	4	0	2	0	0	0	1	0	0	0
Danny Litwhiler, of	.200	5	20	2	4	1	0	1	1	2	7	0
Marty Marion, ss	.227	6	22	1	5	3	0	0	2	2	3	0
Stan Musial, of	.304	6	23	2	7	2	0	1	2	2	0	0
Ken O'Dea, ph	.333	3	3	0	1	0	0	0	2	0	0	0
Ray Sanders, 1b	.286	6	21	5	6	0	0	1	1	5	8	0
Freddy Schmidt, p	.000	1	1	0	0	0	0	0	0	0	1	0
Emil Verban, 2b	.412	6	17	1	7	0	0	0	2	2	0	0
Ted Wilks, p	.000	2	2	0	0	0	0	0	0	0	2	0
TOTAL	.240		204	16	49	9	1	3	15	19	43	0

PITCHER	W	L	ERA	G	GS	CG	SV	SHO	IP	H	ER	BB	SO
Harry Brecheen	1	0	1.00	1	1	1	0	0	9.0	9	1	4	4
Bud Byerly	0	0	0.00	1	0	0	0	0	1.1	0	0	0	1
Mort Cooper	1	1	1.13	2	2	1	0	1	16.0	9	2	5	16
Blix Donnelly	1	0	0.00	2	0	0	0	0	6.0	2	0	1	9
Al Jurisich	0	0	27.00	1	0	0	0	0	0.2	2	2	1	0
Max Lanier	1	0	2.19	2	2	0	0	0	12.1	8	3	8	11
Freddy Schmidt	0	0	0.00	1	0	0	0	0	3.1	1	0	1	1
Ted Wilks	0	1	5.68	2	1	0	1	0	6.1	5	4	3	7
TOTAL	4	2	1.96	12	6	2	1	1	55.0	36	12	23	49

STL (A)

PLAYER/POS	AVG	G	AB	R	H	2B	3B	HR	RB	BB	SO	SB
Floyd Baker, 2b	.000	2	2	0	0	0	0	0	0	0	2	0
Milt Byrnes, ph	.000	3	2	0	0	0	0	0	0	1	2	0
Mike Chartak, ph	.000	2	2	0	0	0	0	0	0	0	0	0
Mark Christman, 3b	.091	6	22	0	2	0	0	0	1	0	6	0
Ellis Clary, ph	.000	1	1	0	0	0	0	0	0	0	0	0
Denny Galehouse, p	.200	2	5	0	1	0	0	0	0	1	1	0
Don Gutteridge, 2b	.143	6	21	1	3	1	0	0	0	3	5	0
Red Hayworth, c	.118	6	17	1	2	1	0	0	1	3	1	0
Al Hollingsworth, p	.000	1	1	0	0	0	0	0	0	0	0	0
Sig Jakucki, p	.000	1	0	0	0	0	0	0	0	0	0	0
Jack Kramer, p	.000	2	4	0	0	0	0	0	0	0	2	0
Mike Kreevich, of	.231	6	26	0	6	3	0	0	0	0	5	0
Chet Laabs, of-4	.200	5	15	1	3	1	1	0	0	2	6	0
Frank Mancuso, c-1	.667	2	3	0	2	0	0	0	0	1	0	0
George Mc Quinn, 1b	.438	6	16	2	7	2	0	1	5	7	2	0
Gene Moore, of	.182	6	22	4	4	0	0	0	0	3	6	0
Bob Muncrief, p	.000	2	1	0	0	0	0	0	0	0	1	0
Nelson Potter, p	.000	2	4	0	0	0	0	0	0	0	1	0
Tex Shirley, p	.000	2	0	0	0	0	0	0	0	0	0	0
Vern Stephens, ss	.227	6	22	2	5	1	0	0	0	3	3	0
Tom Turner, ph	.000	1	1	0	0	0	0	0	0	0	0	0
Al Zarilla, of-3	.100	4	10	1	1	0	0	0	1	0	4	0
TOTAL	.183		197	12	36	9	1	1	9	23	49	0

PITCHER	W	L	ERA	G	GS	CG	SV	SHO	IP	H	ER	BB	SO
Denny Galehouse	1	1	1.50	2	2	2	0	0	18.0	13	3	5	15
Al Hollingsworth	0	0	2.25	1	0	0	0	0	4.0	5	1	2	1
Sig Jakucki	0	1	9.00	1	1	0	0	0	3.0	5	3	0	4
Jack Kramer	1	0	0.00	2	1	1	0	0	11.0	9	0	4	12
Bob Muncrief	0	1	1.35	2	0	0	0	0	6.2	5	1	4	4
Nelson Potter	0	1	0.93	2	2	0	0	0	9.2	10	1	3	6
Tex Shirley	0	0	0.00	2	0	0	0	0	2.0	2	0	1	1
TOTAL	2	4	1.49	12	6	3	0	0	54.1	49	9	19	43

GAME 1 AT STL-N OCT 4

STL-A	000	200	000	2	2 0
STL-N	000	000	001	1	7 0

Pitchers: GALEHOUSE vs M.COOPER, Donnelly (8)
Home Runs: McQuinn-STL(A)
Attendance: 33,242

GAME 2 AT STL-N OCT 5

STL-A	000	002	000 0	2	7 4
STL-N	001	100	000 1	3	7 0

Pitchers: Potter, MUNCRIEF (7) vs Lanier, DONNELLY (8)
Attendance: 35,076

GAME 3 AT STL-A OCT 6

STL-N	100	000	100	2	7 0
STL-A	004	000	20X	6	8 2

Pitchers: WILKS, Schmidt (3), Jurisich (7), Byerly (7) vs KRAMER
Attendance: 34,737

GAME 4 AT STL-A OCT 7

STL-N	202	001	000	5	12 0
STL-A	000	000	010	1	9 1

Pitchers: BRECHEEN vs JAKUCKI, Hollingsworth (4), Shirley (8)
Home Runs: Musial-STL(N)
Attendance: 35,455

GAME 5 AT STL-A OCT 8

STL-N	000	001	010	2	6 1
STL-A	000	000	000	0	7 1

Pitchers: M.COOPER vs GALEHOUSE
Home Runs: Sanders-STL(N), Litwhiler-STL(N)
Attendance: 36,568

GAME 6 AT STL-N OCT 9

STL-A	010	000	000	1	3 2
STL-N	000	300	00X	3	10 0

Pitchers: POTTER, Muncrief (4), Kramer (7) vs LANIER, Wilks (6)
Attendance: 31,630

As World War Two ended during the summer, military major leaguers began returning to their clubs. Hank Greenberg's return in July provided the spark needed for Detroit's narrow pennant victory, and his three-run homer in Game Two of the World Series proved to be the decisive blow in the Tigers' successful struggle for the world title.

Chicago started strong as Cub ace Hank Borowy shut out the Tigers on six singles while his teammates drove out Tiger ace Hal Newhouser with seven runs in the first three innings, to win 9–0. Chicago continued its assault the next day with a run in the top of the fourth, but in the fifth inning Tiger Doc Cramer—with two out and two on—singled in the tying run, and Greenberg followed with his tie-breaking homer for three additional runs. Detroit pitcher Virgil Trucks (who had returned from the Navy in time to pitch in the regular-season finale) held the Cubs scoreless after the fourth inning for the Tiger win.

Chicago's Claude Passeau moved the Cubs back into the Series lead with a one-hit shutout in Game Three, but Tiger Dizzy Trout's five-hitter in Game Four again evened the Series. The Tigers bunched four of their seven hits in the fourth inning for all four of their runs.

Detroit took the Series lead for the first time with an 8–4 win in Game Five. Borowy and Newhouser faced each other as they had in the opener, but this time Borowy was hit hard. Driven out when four Tigers opened the sixth inning with safe hits, he took the loss as Newhouser went the distance for the win.

In Game Six, Chicago concluded the seventh inning of a heavy-hitting game leading 7–3. Detroit tied the score with four runs in the top of the eighth (capped by Greenberg's home run), but in the last of the twelfth the Cubs' Stan Hack doubled home the winning run to keep Chicago's hopes alive.

Two days later in the finale, Cub manager Charlie Grimm started Borowy, who had relieved for four shutout innings to win Game Six. But this third appearance in four days proved too much. Removed after the first three batters to face him singled, he took the loss, as the Tigers went on to score nine runs to the Cubs' three.

Detroit Tigers (AL), 4; Chicago Cubs (NL), 3

DET (A)

PLAYER/POS	AVG	G	AB	R	H	2B	3B	HR	RB	BB	SO	SB
Al Benton, p	.000	3	0	0	0	0	0	0	0	0	0	0
Red Borom, ph	.000	2	1	0	0	0	0	0	0	0	0	0
Tommy Bridges, p	.000	1	0	0	0	0	0	0	0	0	0	0
George Caster, p	.000	1	0	0	0	0	0	0	0	0	0	0
Doc Cramer, of	.379	7	29	7	11	0	0	0	4	1	0	1
Roy Cullenbine, of	.227	7	22	5	5	2	0	0	4	8	2	1
Zeb Eaton, ph	.000	1	1	0	0	0	0	0	0	0	1	0
Hank Greenberg, of	.304	7	23	7	7	3	0	2	7	6	5	0
Joe Hoover, ss	.333	1	3	1	1	0	0	0	1	0	0	0
Chuck Hostetler, ph	.000	3	3	0	0	0	0	0	0	0	0	0
Bob Maier, ph	1.000	1	1	0	1	0	0	0	0	0	0	0
Eddie Mayo, 2b	.250	7	28	4	7	1	0	0	2	2	2	0
John Mc Hale, ph	.000	3	3	0	0	0	0	0	0	0	1	0
Ed Mierkowicz, of	.000	1	0	0	0	0	0	0	0	0	0	0
Les Mueller, p	.000	1	0	0	0	0	0	0	0	0	0	0
Hal Newhouser, p	.000	3	8	0	0	0	0	0	0	1	1	0
Jimmy Outlaw, 3b	.179	7	28	1	5	0	0	0	3	2	1	1
Stubby Overmire, p	.000	1	1	0	0	0	0	0	0	0	0	0
Paul Richards, c	.211	7	19	0	4	2	0	0	6	4	3	0
Bob Swift, c	.250	3	4	1	1	0	0	0	0	2	0	0
Jim Tobin, p	.000	1	1	0	0	0	0	0	0	0	0	0
Dizzy Trout, p	.167	2	6	0	1	0	0	0	0	0	0	0
Virgil Trucks, p	.000	2	4	0	0	0	0	0	0	1	1	0
Hub Walker, ph	.500	2	2	1	1	1	0	0	0	0	0	0
Skeeter Webb, ss	.185	7	27	4	5	0	0	0	1	3	1	0
Rudy York, 1b	.179	7	28	1	5	1	0	0	3	3	4	0
TOTAL	.223		242	32	54	10	0	2	32	33	22	3

PITCHER	W	L	ERA	G	GS	CG	SV	SHO	IP	H	ER	BB	SO
Al Benton	0	0	1.93	3	0	0	0	0	4.2	6	1	0	5
Tommy Bridges	0	0	16.20	1	0	0	0	0	1.2	3	3	3	1
George Caster	0	0	0.00	1	0	0	0	0	0.2	0	0	0	1
Les Mueller	0	0	0.00	1	0	0	0	0	2.0	0	0	1	1
Hal Newhouser	2	1	6.10	3	3	2	0	0	20.2	25	14	4	22
Stubby Overmire	0	1	3.00	1	1	0	0	0	6.0	4	2	2	2
Jim Tobin	0	0	6.00	1	0	0	0	0	3.0	4	2	1	0
Dizzy Trout	1	1	0.66	2	2	1	0	0	13.2	9	1	3	9
Virgil Trucks	1	0	3.38	2	2	1	0	0	13.1	14	5	5	7
TOTAL	4	3	3.84	15	7	4	0		65.2	65	28	19	48

CHI (N)

PLAYER/POS	AVG	G	AB	R	H	2B	3B	HR	RB	BB	SO	SB
Heinz Becker, ph	.500	3	2	0	1	0	0	0	0	1	1	0
Cy Block, pr	.000	1	0	0	0	0	0	0	0	0	0	0
Hank Borowy, p	.167	4	6	1	1	1	0	0	0	0	3	0
Phil Cavaretta, 1b	.423	7	26	7	11	2	0	1	5	4	3	0
Bob Chipman, p	.000	1	0	0	0	0	0	0	0	0	0	0
Paul Derringer, p	.000	3	0	0	0	0	0	0	0	0	0	0
Paul Erickson, p	.000	4	0	0	0	0	0	0	0	0	0	0
Paul Gillespie, c-1	.000	3	6	0	0	0	0	0	0	0	0	0
Stan Hack, 3b	.367	7	30	1	11	3	0	0	4	4	2	0
Roy Hughes, ss	.294	6	17	1	5	1	0	0	3	4	5	0
Don Johnson, 2b	.172	7	29	4	5	2	1	0	0	0	8	1
Mickey Livingston, c	.364	6	22	3	8	3	0	0	4	1	1	0
Peanuts Lowrey, of	.310	7	29	4	9	1	0	0	0	1	2	0
Clyde Mc Cullough, ph	.000	1	1	0	0	0	0	0	0	0	1	0
Lennie Merullo, ss	.000	3	2	0	0	0	0	0	0	0	1	0
Bill Nicholson, of	.214	7	28	1	6	1	1	0	8	2	5	0
Andy Pafko, of	.214	7	28	5	6	2	1	0	2	2	5	1
Claude Passeau, p	.000	3	7	1	0	0	0	0	1	0	4	0
Ray Prim, p	.000	2	0	0	0	0	0	0	0	0	0	0
Ed Sauer, ph	.000	2	2	0	0	0	0	0	0	0	2	0
Bill Schuster, ss-1	.000	2	1	1	0	0	0	0	0	0	0	0
Frank Secory, ph	.200	5	5	0	1	0	0	0	0	0	2	0
Hy Vandenberg, p	.000	3	1	0	0	0	0	0	0	0	0	0
Dewey Williams, c-1	.000	2	2	0	0	0	0	0	0	0	1	0
Hank Wyse, p	.000	3	3	0	0	0	0	0	0	0	2	0
TOTAL	.259		247	29	64	16	3	1	27	19	48	2

PITCHER	W	L	ERA	G	GS	CG	SV	SHO	IP	H	ER	BB	SO
Hank Borowy	2	2	4.00	4	3	1	0	1	18.0	21	8	6	8
Bob Chipman	0	0	0.00	1	0	0	0	0	0.1	0	0	1	0
Paul Derringer	0	0	6.75	3	0	0	0	0	5.1	5	4	7	1
Paul Erickson	0	0	3.86	4	0	0	0	0	7.0	8	3	3	5
Claude Passeau	1	0	2.70	3	2	1	0	1	16.2	7	5	8	3
Ray Prim	0	1	9.00	2	1	0	0	0	4.0	4	4	1	1
Hy Vandenberg	0	0	0.00	3	0	0	0	0	6.0	1	0	3	3
Hank Wyse	0	1	7.04	3	1	0	0	0	7.2	8	6	4	1
TOTAL	3	4	4.15	23	7	2	0	2	65.0	54	30	33	22

GAME 1 AT DET OCT 3

CHI	403	000	200	9	13	0
DET	000	000	000	0	6	0

Pitchers: BOROWY vs NEWHOUSER, Benton (3), Tobin (5), Mueller (8)
Home Runs: Cavaretta-CHI
Attendance: 54,637

GAME 2 AT DET OCT 4

CHI	000	100	000	1	7	0
DET	000	040	00X	4	7	0

Pitchers: WYSE, Erickson (7) vs TRUCKS
Home Runs: Greenberg-DET
Attendance: 53,636

GAME 3 AT DET OCT 5

CHI	000	200	100	3	8	0
DET	000	000	000	0	1	2

Pitchers: PASSEAU vs OVERMIRE, Benton (7)
Attendance: 55,500

GAME 4 AT CHI OCT 6

DET	000	400	000	4	7	1
CHI	000	000	100	1	5	1

Pitchers: TROUT vs PRIM, Derringer (4), Vandenberg (6), Erickson (8)
Attendance: 42,923

GAME 5 AT CHI OCT 7

DET	001	004	102	8	11	0
CHI	001	000	201	4	7	2

Pitchers: NEWHOUSER vs BOROWY, Vandenberg (6), Chipman (6), Derringer (7), Erickson (9)
Attendance: 43,463

GAME 6 AT CHI OCT 8

DET	010	000	240	000	7	13	1
CHI	000	041	200	001	8	15	3

Pitchers: Trucks, Caster (5), Bridges (6), Benton (7), TROUT (8) vs Passeau, Wyse (7), Prim (8), BOROWY (9)
Home Runs: Greenberg-DET
Attendance: 41,708

GAME 7 AT CHI OCT 10

DET	510	000	120	9	9	1
CHI	100	100	010	3	10	0

Pitchers: NEWHOUSER vs BOROWY, Derringer (1), Vandenberg (2), Erickson (6), Passeau (8), Wyse (9)
Attendance: 41,590

With World War Two over, the majors were at full strength for the first time in five years. Boston's big bats were back, and the Sox ran away with the American League pennant. St. Louis had Stan Musial back, but they struggled to their pennant, finishing the regular schedule tied with Brooklyn, and defeating them in the first major league tie-breaker playoff, two games to none.

Favored Boston edged St. Louis in the opener, but it took a home run by Rudy York in the top of the tenth to spoil Cardinal ace Howie Pollet's strong showing. Harry Brecheen brought the Cards back the next day with the first of his three Series wins—a four-hit shutout.

Boston regained the lead in Game Three. Sox ace Dave Ferriss spaced six hits and a walk, one per inning, in shutting out the Cardinals, and Rudy York hit his second game-winning homer, this time a three-run shot in the first inning. The next day, though, St. Louis exploded for a record-tying 20 hits—four apiece by Enos Slaughter, Joe Garagiola and Whitey Kurowski—to give Cardinal pitcher George Munger (who had completed only two of his seven regular-season starts) an easy complete-game 12–3 victory.

For the third time the Red Sox took the Series lead, winning Game Five 6–3 behind Joe Dobson's four-hit pitching (the Cards' three runs were unearned), but St. Louis tied the Series for the third time with a win in Game Six. Brecheen, in his second start, again pitched splendidly, holding Boston to a single run in the seventh inning, long after the Cards had driven out Sox starter Mickey Harris with three runs in the third.

The final game, like the Series itself, was a seesaw battle. Boston scored the first run in the top of the first, but St. Louis tied the score an inning later. The Cards took a two-run lead on three hits in the fifth, but the Sox came back in the eighth to tie it up as Dom DiMaggio doubled off reliever Brecheen to drive in a pair of pinch hitters who had singled and doubled off starter Murry Dickson. The Series' final run came a half inning later. Slaughter opened with a single, but moved no farther as the next two batters were retired. Then Harry Walker hit a liner over short. Slaughter, off with the crack of the bat, never paused and beat the relay to the plate with what proved the winning run, as Brecheen held the Sox in the ninth for his third win of the Series and the Cardinals' seventh world title.

St. Louis Cardinals (NL), 4; Boston Red Sox (AL), 3

STL (N)

PLAYER/POS	AVG	G	AB	R	H	2B	3B	HR	RB	BB	SO	SB
Johnny Beazley, p	.000	1	0	0	0	0	0	0	0	0	0	0
Al Brazle, p	.000	1	2	0	0	0	0	0	0	0	0	0
Harry Brecheen, p	.125	3	8	2	1	0	0	0	1	0	1	0
Murry Dickson, p	.400	2	5	1	2	2	0	0	1	0	1	0
Erv Dusak, of	.250	4	4	0	1	1	0	0	0	2	2	0
Joe Garagiola, c	.316	5	19	2	6	2	0	0	4	0	3	0
Nippy Jones, ph	.000	1	1	0	0	0	0	0	0	0	1	0
Whitey Kurowski, 3b	.296	7	27	5	8	3	0	0	2	0	3	0
Marty Marion, ss	.250	7	24	1	6	2	0	0	4	1	1	0
Terry Moore, of	.148	7	27	1	4	0	0	0	2	2	6	0
Red Munger, p	.250	1	4	0	1	0	0	0	0	0	2	0
Stan Musial, 1b	.222	7	27	3	6	4	1	0	4	4	2	1
Howie Pollet, p	.000	2	0	0	0	0	0	0	0	0	1	0
Del Rice, c	.500	3	6	2	3	1	0	0	0	2	0	0
Red Schoendienst, 2b	.233	7	30	3	7	1	0	0	1	0	2	1
Dick Sisler, ph	.000	2	2	0	0	0	0	0	0	0	0	0
Enos Slaughter, of	.320	7	25	5	8	1	1	1	2	4	3	1
Harry Walker, of	.412	7	17	3	7	2	0	0	6	4	2	0
Ted Wilks, p	.000	1	0	0	0	0	0	0	0	0	0	0
TOTAL	.259		232	28	60	19	2	1	27	19	30	3

PITCHER	W	L	ERA	G	GS	CG	SV	SHO	IP	H	ER	BB	SO
Johnny Beazley	0	0	0.00	1	0	0	0	0	1.0	1	0	0	1
Al Brazle	0	1	5.40	1	0	0	0	0	6.2	7	4	6	4
Harry Brecheen	3	0	0.45	3	2	2	0	1	20.0	14	1	5	11
Murry Dickson	0	1	3.86	2	2	0	0	0	14.0	11	6	4	7
Red Munger	1	0	1.00	1	1	1	0	0	9.0	9	1	3	2
Howie Pollet	0	1	3.48	2	2	1	0	0	10.1	12	4	4	3
Ted Wilks	0	0	0.00	1	0	0	0	0	1.0	2	0	0	0
TOTAL	4	3	2.32	11	7	4	0	1	62.0	56	16	22	28

BOS (A)

PLAYER/POS	AVG	G	AB	R	H	2B	3B	HR	RB	BB	SO	SB
Jim Bagby, p	.000	1	1	0	0	0	0	0	0	0	0	0
Mace Brown, p	.000	1	0	0	0	0	0	0	0	0	0	0
Paul Campbell, pr	.000	1	0	0	0	0	0	0	0	0	0	0
Leon Culberson, of-3	.222	5	9	1	2	0	0	1	1	1	2	1
Dom DiMaggio, of	.259	7	27	2	7	3	0	0	3	2	2	0
Joe Dobson, p	.000	3	3	0	0	0	0	0	0	0	2	0
Bobby Doerr, 2b	.409	6	22	1	9	1	0	1	3	2	2	0
Clem Dreisewerd, p	.000	1	0	0	0	0	0	0	0	0	0	0
Dave Ferriss, p	.000	2	6	0	0	0	0	0	0	0	1	0
Don Gutteridge, 2b-2	.400	3	5	1	2	0	0	0	1	0	0	0
Mickey Harris, p	.333	2	3	0	1	0	0	0	0	0	1	0
Pinky Higgins, 3b	.208	7	24	1	5	1	0	0	2	2	0	0
Tex Hughson, p	.333	3	3	0	1	0	0	0	0	0	0	0
Earl Johnson, p	.000	3	1	0	0	0	0	0	0	0	0	0
Bob Klinger, p	.000	1	0	0	0	0	0	0	0	0	0	0
Tom Mc Bride, of-2	.167	5	6	0	2	0	0	0	1	0	1	0
Catfish Metkovich, ph	.500	2	2	1	1	1	0	0	0	0	0	0
Wally Moses, of	.417	4	12	1	5	0	0	0	0	1	2	0
Roy Partee, c	.100	5	10	1	1	0	0	0	1	1	2	0
Johnny Pesky, ss	.233	7	30	2	7	0	0	0	0	1	3	1
Rip Russell, 3b-1	1.000	2	2	1	2	0	0	0	0	0	0	0
Mike Ryba, p	.000	1	0	0	0	0	0	0	0	0	0	0
Hal Wagner, c	.000	5	13	0	0	0	0	0	0	0	1	0
Ted Williams, of	.200	7	25	2	5	0	0	0	1	5	5	0
Rudy York, 1b	.261	7	23	6	6	1	1	2	5	6	4	0
Bill Zuber, p	.000	1	0	0	0	0	0	0	0	0	0	0
TOTAL	.240		233	20	56	7	1	4	18	22	28	2

PITCHER	W	L	ERA	G	GS	CG	SV	SHO	IP	H	ER	BB	SO
Jim Bagby	0	0	3.00	1	0	0	0	0	3.0	6	1	1	1
Mace Brown	0	0	27.00	1	0	0	0	0	1.0	4	3	1	0
Joe Dobson	1	0	0.00	3	1	1	0	0	12.2	4	0	3	10
Clem Dreisewerd	0	0	0.00	1	0	0	0	0	0.1	0	0	0	0
Dave Ferriss	1	0	2.03	2	2	1	0	1	13.1	13	3	2	4
Mickey Harris	0	2	3.72	2	2	0	0	0	9.2	11	4	4	5
Tex Hughson	0	1	3.14	3	2	0	0	0	14.1	14	5	3	8
Earl Johnson	1	0	2.70	3	0	0	0	0	3.1	1	1	2	1
Bob Klinger	0	1	13.50	1	0	0	0	0	0.2	2	1	1	0
Mike Ryba	0	0	13.50	1	0	0	0	0	0.2	2	1	0	0
Bill Zuber	0	0	4.50	1	0	0	0	0	2.0	3	1	1	1
TOTAL	3	4	2.95	19	7	2	0	1	61.0	60	20	19	30

GAME 1 AT STL OCT 6

BOS	010 000 001 1	3 9 2
STL	000 001 010 0	2 7 0

Pitchers: Hughson, JOHNSON (9) vs POLLET
Home Runs: York-BOS
Attendance: 36,218

GAME 2 AT STL OCT 7

BOS	000 000 000	0 4 1
STL	001 020 00X	3 6 0

Pitchers: HARRIS, Dobson (8) vs BRECHEEN
Attendance: 35,815

GAME 3 AT BOS OCT 9

STL	000 000 000	0 6 1
BOS	300 000 01X	4 8 0

Pitchers: DICKSON, Wilks (8) vs FERRISS
Home Runs: York-BOS
Attendance: 34,500

GAME 4 AT BOS OCT 10

STL	033 010 104	12 20 1
BOS	000 100 020	3 9 4

Pitchers: MUNGER vs HUGHSON, Bagby (3), Zuber (6), Brown (8), Ryba (9), Dreisewerd (9)
Home Runs: Slaughter-STL, Doerr-BOS
Attendance: 35,645

GAME 5 AT BOS OCT 11

STL	010 000 002	3 4 1
BOS	110 001 30X	6 11 3

Pitchers: Pollet, BRAZLE (1), Beazley (8) vs DOBSON
Home Runs: Culberson-BOS
Attendance: 35,982

GAME 6 AT STL OCT 13

BOS	000 000 100	1 7 0
STL	003 000 01X	4 8 0

Pitchers: HARRIS, Hughson (3), Johnson (8) vs BRECHEEN
Attendance: 35,768

GAME 7 AT STL OCT 15

BOS	100 000 020	3 8 0
STL	010 020 01X	4 9 1

Pitchers: Ferriss, Dobson (5), KLINGER (8), Johnson (8) vs Dickson, BRECHEEN (8)
Attendance: 36,143

Two of the most memorable plays in World Series history brought Brooklyn victory in Games Four and Six, but when the Series had ended the Yankees were world champions for the eleventh time. Dodger ace Ralph Branca set New York down in order through the first four innings of Game One. But the first five batters to face him in the fifth inning reached base. Branca was lifted, but before the inning was over five Yankees had crossed the plate—more than enough for their first win.

The Yankees went two-up the next day, rocking four Brooklyn pitchers for 15 hits and an easy 10–3 win. Brooklyn finally made its presence felt in Game Three, another heavy-hitting affair, scoring six times in the second inning to establish a lead the Yankees could not overcome. Both teams recorded 13 hits, but Dodger fireman Hugh Casey extinguished the last Yankee flame in the seventh inning, and preserved a narrow 9–8 Dodger lead the rest of the way.

Shortstop Pee Wee Reese's error and a bases-loaded walk gave the Yankees an unearned run in the first inning of Game Four, and they earned a second run in the fourth. Meanwhile, Yankee pitcher Bill Bevens, although he averaged a walk an inning, had allowed no Dodger hits and only one run as the game entered the last of the ninth. Bevens retired two in the ninth, but walked his ninth and tenth batters (one intentionally), then lost both his no-hitter and the game as Dodger pinch hitter Cookie Lavagetto doubled home the two baserunners to even the Series at two-all.

Yankee Spec Shea (the winning pitcher in Game One) held Brooklyn to four hits and one run in Game Five. Joe DiMaggio homered in the fifth inning for New York's second run, enough to put the Yankees back in the Series lead. The Dodgers rebounded in Game Six to build an early 4–0 lead. But the Yankees tied the score in the last of the third and took a lead in the fourth. Brooklyn regained the lead in the sixth with four runs, but when DiMaggio hit a long fly to left with two on in the Yankee half of the inning, it looked as if the score would be tied. But substitute left fielder Al Gionfriddo (in what turned out to be his last big league game) raced to the bullpen fence 415 feet out to rob DiMag of the home run. New York scored a run in the ninth, but thanks to Gionfriddo's catch it was not enough to win the game.

Brooklyn scored first in the finale with a pair of second-inning runs, but Yankee relievers Bill

New York Yankees (AL), 4; Brooklyn Dodgers (NL), 3

NY (A)

PLAYER/POS	AVG	G	AB	R	H	2B	3B	HR	RB	BB	SO	SB
Yogi Berra, c-4,of-2	.158	6	19	2	3	0	0	1	2	1	2	0
Bill Bevens, p	.000	2	4	0	0	0	0	0	0	0	2	0
Bobby Brown, ph	1.000	4	3	2	3	2	0	0	3	1	0	0
Spud Chandler, p	.000	1	0	0	0	0	0	0	0	0	0	0
Allie Clark, of-1	.500	3	2	1	1	0	0	0	1	1	0	0
Joe DiMaggio, of	.231	7	26	4	6	0	0	2	5	6	2	0
Karl Drews, p	.000	2	2	0	0	0	0	0	0	0	2	0
Lonny Frey, ph	.000	1	1	0	0	0	0	0	1	0	0	0
Tommy Henrich, of	.323	7	31	2	10	2	0	1	5	2	3	0
Ralph Houk, ph	1.000	1	1	0	1	0	0	0	0	0	0	0
Billy Johnson, 3b	.269	7	26	8	7	0	3	0	2	3	4	0
Johnny Lindell, of	.500	6	18	3	9	3	1	0	7	5	2	0
Sherm Lollar, c	.750	2	4	3	3	2	0	0	1	0	0	0
George Mc Quinn, 1b	.130	7	23	3	3	0	0	0	1	5	8	0
Bobo Newsom, p	.000	2	0	0	0	0	0	0	0	0	0	0
Joe Page, p	.000	4	4	0	0	0	0	0	0	0	1	0
Jack Phillips, 1b-1	.000	2	0	0	0	0	0	0	0	0	0	0
Vic Raschi, p	.000	2	0	0	0	0	0	0	0	0	0	0
Allie Reynolds, p	.500	2	4	2	2	0	0	0	1	0	0	0
Phil Rizzuto, ss	.308	7	26	3	8	1	0	0	2	4	0	2
Aaron Robinson, c	.200	3	10	2	2	0	0	0	1	2	1	0
Spec Shea, p	.400	3	5	2	2	1	0	0	1	0	2	0
Snuffy Stirnweiss, 2b	.259	7	27	3	7	0	1	0	3	8	8	0
Butch Wensloff, p	.000	1	0	0	0	0	0	0	0	0	0	0
TOTAL	.282		238	38	67	11	5	4	36	38	37	2

PITCHER	W	L	ERA	G	GS	CG	SV	SHO	IP	H	ER	BB	SO
Bill Bevens	0	1	2.38	2	1	1	0	0	11.1	3	3	11	7
Spud Chandler	0	0	9.00	1	0	0	0	0	2.0	2	2	3	1
Karl Drews	0	0	3.00	2	0	0	0	0	3.0	2	1	1	0
Bobo Newsom	0	1	19.29	2	1	0	0	0	2.1	6	5	2	0
Joe Page	1	1	4.15	4	0	0	1	0	13.0	12	6	2	7
Vic Raschi	0	0	6.75	2	0	0	0	0	1.1	1	1	0	1
Allie Reynolds	1	0	4.76	2	2	1	0	0	11.1	15	6	3	6
Spec Shea	2	0	2.35	3	3	1	0	0	15.1	10	4	8	10
Butch Wensloff	0	0	0.00	1	0	0	0	0	2.0	0	0	0	0
TOTAL	4	3	4.09	19	7	3	1	0	61.2	52	28	30	32

BRO (N)

PLAYER/POS	AVG	G	AB	R	H	2B	3B	HR	RB	BB	SO	SB
Dan Bankhead, pr	.000	1	0	1	0	0	0	0	0	0	0	0
Rex Barney, p	.000	3	1	0	0	0	0	0	0	0	0	0
Hank Behrman, p	.000	5	0	0	0	0	0	0	0	0	0	0
Bobby Bragan, ph	1.000	1	1	0	1	1	0	0	1	0	0	0
Ralph Branca, p	.000	3	4	0	0	0	0	0	0	0	1	0
Hugh Casey, p	.000	6	1	0	0	0	0	0	0	0	1	0
Bruce Edwards, c	.222	7	27	3	6	1	0	0	2	2	7	0
Carl Furillo, of	.353	6	17	2	6	2	0	0	3	3	0	0
Al Gionfriddo, of-1	.000	4	3	2	0	0	0	0	0	1	0	1
Hal Gregg, p	.000	3	3	0	0	0	0	0	0	1	1	0
Joe Hatten, p	.333	4	3	1	1	0	0	0	0	0	0	0
Gene Hermanski, of	.158	7	19	4	3	0	1	0	1	3	3	0
Gil Hodges, ph	.000	1	1	0	0	0	0	0	0	0	1	0
Spider Jorgensen, 3b	.200	7	20	1	4	2	0	0	3	2	4	0
Cookie Lavagetto, 3b-3	.143	5	7	0	1	1	0	0	3	0	2	0
Vic Lombardi, p-2	.000	3	3	0	0	0	0	0	0	0	0	0
Eddie Miksis, 2b-1,of-1	.250	5	4	1	1	0	0	0	0	0	1	0
Pee Wee Reese, ss	.304	7	23	5	7	1	0	0	4	6	3	3
Pete Reiser, of-3	.250	5	8	1	2	0	0	0	3	1	0	0
Jackie Robinson, 1b	.259	7	27	3	7	2	0	0	3	2	4	2
Eddie Stanky, 2b	.240	7	25	4	6	1	0	0	2	3	2	0
Harry Taylor, p	.000	1	0	0	0	0	0	0	0	0	0	0
Arky Vaughan, ph	.500	3	2	0	1	1	0	0	0	1	0	0
Dixie Walker, of	.222	7	27	1	6	1	0	1	4	3	1	1
TOTAL	.230		226	29	52	13	1	1	26	30	32	7

PITCHER	W	L	ERA	G	GS	CG	SV	SHO	IP	H	ER	BB	SO
Rex Barney	0	1	2.70	3	1	0	0	0	6.2	4	2	10	3
Hank Behrman	0	0	7.11	5	0	0	0	0	6.1	9	5	5	3
Ralph Branca	1	1	8.64	3	1	0	0	0	8.1	12	8	5	8
Hugh Casey	2	0	0.87	6	0	0	1	0	10.1	5	1	1	3
Hal Gregg	0	1	3.55	3	1	0	0	0	12.2	9	5	8	10
Joe Hatten	0	0	7.00	4	0	0	0	0	9.0	12	7	7	4
Vic Lombardi	0	1	12.15	3	0	0	0	0	6.2	14	9	1	5
Harry Taylor	0	0	INF	1	1	0	0	0	0.0	2	0	1	0
TOTAL	3	4	5.55	27	7	0	1	0	60.0	67	37	38	37

Bevens and Joe Page shut them out through the final seven innings as their teammates gradually built a Series-clinching 5–2 victory.

GAME 1 AT NY SEPT 30

BRO	100 001 100	3	6 0
NY	000 050 00X	5	4 0

Pitchers: BRANCA, Behrman (5), Casey (7) vs SHEA, Page (6)
Attendance: 73,365

GAME 2 AT NY OCT 1

BRO	001 100 001	3	9 2
NY	101 121 40X	10	15 1

Pitchers: LOMBARDI, Gregg (5), Behrman (7), Barney (7) vs REYNOLDS
Home Runs: Walker-BRO, Henrich-NY
Attendance: 69,865

GAME 3 AT BRO OCT 2

NY	002 221 100	8	13 0
BRO	061 200 00X	9	13 1

Pitchers: NEWSOM, Raschi (2), Drews (3), Chandler (4), Page (6) vs Hatten, Branca (5), CASEY (7)
Home Runs: DiMaggio-NY, Berra-NY
Attendance: 33,098

GAME 4 AT BRO OCT 3

NY	100 100 000	2	8 1
BRO	000 010 002	3	1 3

Pitchers: BEVENS vs Taylor, Gregg (1), Behrman (8), CASEY (9)
Attendance: 33,443

GAME 5 AT BRO OCT 4

NY	000 110 000	2	5 0
BRO	000 001 000	1	4 1

Pitchers: SHEA vs BARNEY, Hatten (5), Behrman (7), Casey (8)
Home Runs: DiMaggio-NY
Attendance: 34,379

GAME 6 AT NY OCT 5

BRO	202 004 000	8	12 1
NY	004 100 001	6	15 2

Pitchers: Lombardi, BRANCA (3), Hatten (6), Casey (9) vs Reynolds, Drews (3), PAGE (5), Newsom (6), Raschi (7), Wensloff (8)
Attendance: 74,065

GAME 7 AT NY OCT 6

BRO	020 000 000	2	7 0
NY	010 201 10X	5	7 0

Pitchers: GREGG, Behrman (4), Hatten (6), Barney (6), Casey (7) vs Shea, Bevens (2), PAGE (5)
Attendance: 71,548

Boston outpitched and outhit Cleveland, and the clubs tied in runs scored. But the Braves scored most of their runs in one game, and the Indians, spreading theirs more evenly, took the Series. Boston ace Johnny Sain dueled Bob Feller in the opener. Feller gave up only two singles, but one of them followed a walk and a sacrifice (and a controversial pickoff play at second, in which the Boston runner was ruled safe although photos later showed him clearly out) and drove in the game's only run. Both teams registered eight hits in Game Two, but Cleveland's led to four runs, while Indian hurler Bob Lemon held Boston to just one—and that was unearned.

Cleveland's rookie sensation Gene Bearden shut out the Braves on five hits in Game Three as the Series moved to Cleveland's huge Municipal Stadium. Bearden himself, after doubling in the third, scored on a Boston error what proved to be the winning run. A record 81,897 fans saw Sain face Steve Gromek in Game Four. Only five Indians hit Sain safely, but a first-inning single and double put Cleveland on the board, and Larry Doby's home run two innings later made the score 2–0. Boston's Marv Rickert homered in the seventh to narrow Cleveland's lead, but that ended the scoring.

Another attendance record was set at Game Five as 86,288 fans gathered to watch Bob Feller sew up the title for Cleveland. They went home disappointed. In a game that featured five of the Series' eight home runs, Boston jumped ahead on Bob Elliott's three-run blast in the first. Dale Mitchell opened Cleveland's half of the inning with a home run, but Elliott neutralized it in the third with his second homer. The Indians drove out Boston starter Nelson Potter with four runs in the fourth inning (three coming on Jim Hegan's homer). But Warren Spahn (who had lost Game Two) hurled one-hit shutout relief over the final five frames as his Braves tied the game on Bill Salkeld's homer in the sixth, and blew out Feller and two relievers with six runs in the seventh. The fourth Indian pitcher, Satchel Paige (in his only World Series appearance), retired two batters to end the inning, but the damage had been done.

A day later though, back in Boston, Cleveland edged the Braves 4–3 for the title. Gene Bearden's relief pitching allowed two inherited baserunners to score in the eighth, but halted Boston's rally one run short of a tie.

Cleveland Indians (AL), 4;
Boston Braves (NL), 2

CLE (A)

PLAYER/POS	AVG	G	AB	R	H	2B	3B	HR	RB	BB	SO	SB
Gene Bearden, p	.500	2	4	1	2	1	0	0	0	0	1	0
Ray Boone, ph	.000	1	1	0	0	0	0	0	0	0	0	0
Lou Boudreau, ss	.273	6	22	1	6	4	0	0	3	1	1	0
Russ Christopher, p	.000	1	0	0	0	0	0	0	0	0	0	0
Allie Clark, of	.000	1	3	0	0	0	0	0	0	0	1	0
Larry Doby, of	.318	6	22	1	7	1	0	1	2	2	4	0
Bob Feller, p	.000	2	4	0	0	0	0	0	0	0	2	0
Joe Gordon, 2b	.182	6	22	3	4	0	0	1	2	1	2	1
Steve Gromek, p	.000	1	3	0	0	0	0	0	0	0	0	0
Jim Hegan, c	.211	6	19	2	4	0	0	1	5	1	4	1
Wally Judnich, of	.077	4	13	1	1	0	0	0	1	1	4	0
Ken Keltner, 3b	.095	6	21	3	2	0	0	0	0	2	3	0
Bob Kennedy, of	.500	3	2	0	1	0	0	0	1	0	1	0
Ed Klieman, p	.000	1	0	0	0	0	0	0	0	0	0	0
Bob Lemon, p	.000	2	7	0	0	0	0	0	0	0	0	0
Dale Mitchell, of	.174	6	23	4	4	1	0	1	1	2	0	0
Bob Muncrief, p	.000	1	0	0	0	0	0	0	0	0	0	0
Satchel Paige, p	.000	1	0	0	0	0	0	0	0	0	0	0
Hal Peck, of	.000	1	0	0	0	0	0	0	0	0	0	0
Eddie Robinson, 1b	.300	6	20	0	6	0	0	0	1	1	0	0
Al Rosen, ph	.000	1	1	0	0	0	0	0	0	0	0	0
Joe Tipton, ph	.000	1	1	0	0	0	0	0	0	0	1	0
Thurman Tucker, of	.333	1	3	1	1	0	0	0	0	1	0	0
TOTAL	.199		191	17	38	7	0	4	16	12	26	2

PITCHER	W	L	ERA	G	GS	CG	SV	SHO	IP	H	ER	BB	SO
Gene Bearden	1	0	0.00	2	1	1	1	1	10.2	6	0	4	4
Russ Christopher	0	0	INF	1	0	0	0	0	0.0	2	1	0	0
Bob Feller	0	2	5.02	2	2	1	0	0	14.1	10	8	5	7
Steve Gromek	1	0	1.00	1	1	1	0	0	9.0	7	1	1	2
Ed Klieman	0	0	INF	1	0	0	0	0	0.0	1	3	2	0
Bob Lemon	2	0	1.65	2	2	1	0	0	16.1	16	3	7	6
Bob Muncrief	0	0	0.00	1	0	0	0	0	2.0	1	0	0	0
Satchel Paige	0	0	0.00	1	0	0	0	0	0.2	0	0	0	0
TOTAL	4	2	2.72	11	6	4	1	1	53.0	43	16	16	19

BOS (N)

PLAYER/POS	AVG	G	AB	R	H	2B	3B	HR	RB	BB	SO	SB
Red Barrett, p	.000	2	0	0	0	0	0	0	0	0	0	0
Vern Bickford, p	.000	1	0	0	0	0	0	0	0	0	0	0
Clint Conatser, of	.000	2	4	0	0	0	0	0	1	0	0	0
Alvin Dark, ss	.167	6	24	2	4	1	0	0	0	0	2	0
Bob Elliott, 3b	.333	6	21	4	7	0	0	2	5	2	2	0
Tommy Holmes, of	.192	6	26	3	5	0	0	0	1	0	0	0
Phil Masi, c	.125	5	8	1	1	1	0	0	1	0	0	0
Frank McCormick, 1b-1	.200	3	5	0	1	0	0	0	0	0	2	0
Mike McCormick, of	.261	6	23	1	6	0	0	0	2	0	4	0
Nelson Potter, p	.500	2	2	0	1	0	0	0	0	0	1	0
Marv Rickert, of	.211	5	19	2	4	0	0	1	2	0	4	0
Connie Ryan, ph	.000	2	1	0	0	0	0	0	0	0	1	0
Johnny Sain, p	.200	2	5	0	1	0	0	0	0	0	0	0
Bill Salkeld, c	.222	5	9	2	2	0	0	1	1	5	1	0
Ray Sanders, ph	.000	1	1	0	0	0	0	0	0	0	0	0
Sibby Sisti, 2b	.000	2	1	0	0	0	0	0	0	0	0	0
Warren Spahn, p	.000	3	4	0	0	0	0	0	1	0	0	0
Eddie Stanky, 2b	.286	6	14	0	4	1	0	0	1	7	1	0
Earl Torgeson, 1b	.389	5	18	2	7	3	0	0	1	2	1	1
Bill Voiselle, p	.000	2	2	0	0	0	0	0	0	0	0	0
TOTAL	.230		187	17	43	6	0	4	16	16	19	1

PITCHER	W	L	ERA	G	GS	CG	SV	SHO	IP	H	ER	BB	SO
Red Barrett	0	0	0.00	2	0	0	0	0	3.2	1	0	0	1
Vern Bickford	0	1	2.70	1	1	0	0	0	3.1	4	1	5	1
Nelson Potter	0	0	8.44	2	1	0	0	0	5.1	6	5	2	1
Johnny Sain	1	1	1.06	2	2	2	0	1	17.0	9	2	0	9
Warren Spahn	1	1	3.00	3	1	0	0	0	12.0	10	4	3	12
Bill Voiselle	0	1	2.53	2	1	0	0	0	10.2	8	3	2	2
TOTAL	2	4	2.60	12	6	2	0	1	52.0	38	15	12	26

GAME 1 AT BOS OCT 6

CLE	000 000 000	0	4	0
BOS	000 000 01X	1	2	2

Pitchers: FELLER vs SAIN
Attendance: 40,135

GAME 2 AT BOS OCT 7

CLE	000 210 001	4	8	1
BOS	100 000 000	1	8	3

Pitchers: LEMON vs SPAHN, Barrett (5), Potter (8)
Attendance: 39,633

GAME 3 AT CLE OCT 8

BOS	000 000 000	0	5	1
CLE	001 100 00X	2	5	0

Pitchers: BICKFORD, Voiselle (4), Barrett (8) vs BEARDEN
Attendance: 70,306

GAME 4 AT CLE OCT 9

BOS	000 000 100	1	7	0
CLE	101 000 00X	2	5	0

Pitchers: SAIN vs GROMEK
Home Runs: Doby-CLE, Rickert-BOS
Attendance: 81,897

GAME 5 AT CLE OCT 10

BOS	301 001 600	11	12	0
CLE	100 400 000	5	6	2

Pitchers: Potter, SPAHN (4) vs FELLER, Klieman (7), Christopher (7), Paige (7), Muncrief (8)
Home Runs: Elliott-BOS (2), Mitchell-CLE, Hegan-CLE, Salkeld-BOS
Attendance: 86,288

GAME 6 AT BOS OCT 11

CLE	001 002 010	4	10	0
BOS	000 100 020	3	9	0

Pitchers: LEMON, Bearden (8) vs VOISELLE, Spahn (8)
Home Runs: Gordon-CLE
Attendance: 40,103

Casey Stengel, in the first of his twelve years as Yankee manager, edged his team past the Boston Red Sox for his first of ten American League pennants, then past the Dodgers for his first of seven world championships. New York and Brooklyn traded 1–0 wins to begin the Series. In Game One Yankee Allie Reynolds dueled Dodger rookie Don Newcombe scorelessly through 8½ innings—until Tommy Henrich led off the last of the ninth with a Yankee home run. Dodger Jackie Robinson scored after doubling off Vic Raschi in the second inning of Game Two for that game's only score, while Dodger ace Preacher Roe permitted the Yankees just six scattered hits—never more than one per inning.

The teams entered the ninth inning of Game Three tied 1–1. But in the top of the ninth, Dodger starter Ralph Branca, after loading the bases on two walks and a single, gave up another single to pinch hitter Johnny Mize for two runs. Jerry Coleman's single off reliever Jack Banta drove in another run before the third out was made. In the last of the ninth, Yankee fireman Joe Page (who had held Brooklyn scoreless since coming on with the bases loaded in the fourth) finally weakened. But after yielding solo homers to Luis Olmo and Roy Campanella, he struck out pinch hitter Bruce Edwards for New York's second win.

The Yankees' victory in Game Four came a little easier. They scored first, driving out starter Don Newcombe with three runs in the fourth, and rapping reliever Joe Hatten for three more runs an inning later. Brooklyn retaliated in the sixth, sending Yankee starter Ed Lopat to the showers with seven singles for four runs. But Allie Reynolds came on for 3⅓ innings of no-hit relief to preserve the Yankees lead—and his Series 0.00 earned run average.

After four closely contested games, the Yankees erupted in Game Five for ten runs in the first six innings as Brooklyn was held to just two. In the last of the seventh, the Dodgers came back, driving out starter Vic Raschi with a four-run rally, capped by Gil Hodges's three-run homer. But Joe Page came on to get the final out of the seventh, and held the Dodgers scoreless over the final two innings to bring the Yankees' world titles to an even dozen.

New York Yankees (AL), 4; Brooklyn Dodgers (NL), 1

NY (A)

PLAYER/POS	AVG	G	AB	R	H	2B	3B	HR	RB	BB	SO	SB
Hank Bauer, of	.167	3	6	0	1	0	0	0	0	0	0	0
Yogi Berra, c	.063	4	16	2	1	0	0	0	1	1	3	0
Bobby Brown, 3b-3	.500	4	12	4	6	1	2	0	5	2	2	0
Tommy Byrne, p	1.000	1	1	0	1	0	0	0	0	0	0	0
Gerry Coleman, 2b	.250	5	20	0	5	3	0	0	4	0	4	0
Joe DiMaggio, of	.111	5	18	2	2	0	0	1	2	3	5	0
Tommy Henrich, 1b	.263	5	19	4	5	0	0	1	1	3	0	0
Billy Johnson, 3b	.143	2	7	0	1	0	0	0	0	0	2	1
Johnny Lindell, of	.143	2	7	0	1	0	0	0	0	0	2	0
Ed Lopat, p	.333	1	3	0	1	1	0	0	1	0	0	0
Cliff Mapes, of	.100	4	10	3	1	1	0	0	2	2	4	0
Johnny Mize, ph	1.000	2	2	0	2	0	0	0	2	0	0	0
Gus Niarhos, c	.000	1	0	0	0	0	0	0	0	0	0	0
Joe Page, p	.000	3	4	0	0	0	0	0	0	0	2	0
Vic Raschi, p	.200	2	5	0	1	0	0	0	0	1	1	0
Allie Reynolds, p	.500	2	4	0	2	1	0	0	0	0	1	0
Phil Rizzuto, ss	.167	5	18	2	3	0	0	0	1	1	3	1
Charlie Silvera, c	.000	1	2	0	0	0	0	0	0	0	0	0
Snuffy Stirnweiss, ph	.000	1	0	0	0	0	0	0	0	0	0	0
Gene Woodling, of	.400	3	10	4	4	3	0	0	3	0	0
TOTAL	.226		164	21	37	10	2	2	20	18	27	2

PITCHER	W	L	ERA	G	GS	CG	SV	SHO	IP	H	ER	BB	SO
Tommy Byrne	0	0	2.70	1	1	0	0	0	3.1	2	1	2	1
Ed Lopat	1	0	6.35	1	1	0	0	0	5.2	9	4	1	4
Joe Page	1	0	2.00	3	0	0	1	0	9.0	6	2	3	8
Vic Raschi	1	1	4.30	2	2	0	0	0	14.2	15	7	5	11
Allie Reynolds	1	0	0.00	2	1	1	1	1	12.1	2	0	4	14
TOTAL	4	1	2.80	9	5	1	2	1	45.0	34	14	15	38

BRO (N)

PLAYER/POS	AVG	G	AB	R	H	2B	3B	HR	RB	BB	SO	SB
Jack Banta, p	.000	3	1	0	0	0	0	0	0	0	0	0
Rex Barney, p	.000	1	0	0	0	0	0	0	0	0	0	0
Ralph Branca, p	.000	1	3	0	0	0	0	0	0	0	3	0
Tommy Brown, ph	.000	2	2	0	0	0	0	0	0	0	1	0
Roy Campanella, c	.267	5	15	2	4	1	0	1	2	3	1	0
Billy Cox, 3b-1	.333	2	3	0	1	0	0	0	0	0	1	0
Bruce Edwards, ph	.500	2	2	0	1	0	0	0	0	0	1	0
Carl Erskine, p	.000	2	0	0	0	0	0	0	0	0	0	0
Carl Furillo, of-2	.125	3	8	0	1	0	0	0	0	1	0	0
Joe Hatten, p	.000	2	0	0	0	0	0	0	0	0	0	0
Gene Hermanski, of	.308	4	13	1	4	0	1	0	2	3	3	0
Gil Hodges, 1b	.235	5	17	2	4	0	0	1	4	1	4	0
Spider Jorgensen, 3b-3	.182	4	11	1	2	2	0	0	0	2	2	0
Mike Mc Cormick, of	.000	1	0	0	0	0	0	0	0	0	0	0
Eddie Miksis, 3b-2	.286	3	7	0	2	1	0	0	0	0	1	0
Paul Minner, p	.000	1	0	0	0	0	0	0	0	0	0	0
Don Newcombe, p	.000	2	4	0	0	0	0	0	0	0	3	0
Luis Olmo, of	.273	4	11	2	3	0	0	1	2	0	2	0
Erv Palica, p	.000	1	0	0	0	0	0	0	0	0	0	0
Marv Rackley, of	.000	2	5	0	0	0	0	0	0	0	2	0
Pee Wee Reese, ss	.316	5	19	2	6	1	0	1	2	1	0	1
Jackie Robinson, 2b	.188	5	16	2	3	1	0	0	2	4	2	0
Preacher Roe, p	.000	1	3	0	0	0	0	0	0	0	3	0
Duke Snider, of	.143	5	21	2	3	1	0	0	0	0	8	0
Dick Whitman, ph	.000	1	1	0	0	0	0	0	0	0	1	0
TOTAL	.210		162	14	34	7	1	4	14	15	38	1

PITCHER	W	L	ERA	G	GS	CG	SV	SHO	IP	H	ER	BB	SO
Jack Banta	0	0	3.18	3	0	0	0	0	5.2	5	2	1	4
Rex Barney	0	1	16.88	1	1	0	0	0	2.2	3	5	6	2
Ralph Branca	0	1	4.15	1	1	0	0	0	8.2	4	4	4	6
Carl Erskine	0	0	16.20	2	0	0	0	0	1.2	3	3	1	0
Joe Hatten	0	0	16.20	2	0	0	0	0	1.2	4	3	2	0
Paul Minner	0	0	0.00	1	0	0	0	0	1.0	1	0	0	0
Don Newcombe	0	2	3.09	2	2	1	0	0	11.2	10	4	3	11
Erv Palica	0	0	0.00	1	0	0	0	0	2.0	1	0	1	1
Preacher Roe	1	0	0.00	1	1	1	0	1	9.0	6	0	0	3
TOTAL	1	4	4.30	14	5	2	0	1	44.0	37	21	18	27

GAME 1 AT NY OCT 5

```
BRO   000 000 000   0 2 0
NY    000 000 001   1 5 1
```
Pitchers: NEWCOMBE vs REYNOLDS
Home Runs: Henrich-NY
Attendance: 66,224

GAME 2 AT NY OCT 6

```
BRO   010 000 000   1 7 2
NY    000 000 000   0 6 1
```
Pitchers: ROE vs RASCHI
Attendance: 70,053

GAME 3 AT BRO OCT 7

```
NY    001 000 003   4 5 0
BRO   000 100 002   3 5 0
```
Pitchers: Byrne, PAGE (4) vs BRANCA, Banta (9)
Home Runs: Reese-BRO, Olmo-BRO, Campanella-BRO
Attendance: 32,788

GAME 4 AT BRO OCT 8

```
NY    000 330 000   6 10 0
BRO   000 004 000   4 9 1
```
Pitchers: LOPAT, Reynolds (6) VS NEWCOMBE, Hatten (4), Erskine (6), Banta (7)
Attendance: 33,934

GAME 5 AT BRO OCT 9

```
NY    203 113 000   10 11 1
BRO   001 001 400    6 11 2
```
Pitchers: RASCHI, Page (7) vs BARNEY, Banta (3), Erskine (6), Hatten (6), Palica (7), Minner (9)
Home Runs: DiMaggio-NY, Hodges-BRO
Attendance: 33,711

Philadelphia's Whiz Kids, who had capped an exciting pennant race with the Phillies' first flag in thirty-five years, carried the excitement into the World Series but couldn't quite catch up with the Yankees. New York scored only one run in the opener; Philadelphia didn't score any. The Phillies did score a run in the second game, but the Yankees scored two. In Game Three the Phillies scored two runs, the Yankees three.

Jim Konstanty, the National League's ace reliever (and MVP), started his first major league game in four years to lead off the Series, and held the Yankees to just four hits in eight innings of work. But Bobby Brown's double in the fourth was followed by two long flies which moved Brown around to the plate—all the scoring New York needed as Vic Raschi held the Phillies to two singles and a walk.

Robin Roberts and Allie Reynolds dueled in Game Two. New York scored first with a run on a walk and two singles in the second inning, but two Phillie singles and a fly to left tied the game in the last of the fifth. There matters stood until the top of the tenth, when Joe DiMaggio led off with a home run to the upper deck in left. Reynolds held the Phillies in the bottom of the tenth for the second Yankee win.

The Phillies took a lead for the only time in the Series when they broke a 1–1 tie with a run in the seventh inning of Game Three. But New York scored on a Phillie error to tie the game again in the eighth, and in the last of the ninth—with two outs—Yankees Gene Woodling, Phil Rizzuto, and Jerry Coleman singled to produce the winning run.

Rookie sensation Whitey Ford started Game Four and held Philadelphia scoreless into the ninth inning as his Yankees scored twice in the first and three more times in the sixth. He was taken out with two away in the ninth after two singles, a hit batsman, and a Yankee error had permitted two Phillies to score. But reliever Allie Reynolds struck out the final batter to secure for the Yankees a Series sweep.

New York Yankees (AL), 4;
Philadelphia Phillies (NL), 0

NY (A)

PLAYER/POS	AVG	G	AB	R	H	2B	3B	HR	RB	BB	SO	SB
Hank Bauer, of	.133	4	15	0	2	0	0	0	0	1	0	0
Yogi Berra, c	.200	4	15	2	3	0	0	1	2	2	1	0
Bobby Brown, 3b	.333	4	12	2	4	1	1	0	1	0	0	0
Gerry Coleman, 2b	.286	4	14	2	4	1	0	0	3	2	0	0
Joe Collins, 1b	.000	1	0	0	0	0	0	0	0	0	0	0
Joe Di Maggio, of	.308	4	13	2	4	1	0	1	2	3	1	0
Tom Ferrick, p	.000	1	0	0	0	0	0	0	0	0	0	0
Whitey Ford, p	.000	1	3	0	0	0	0	0	0	0	2	0
Johnny Hopp, 1b	.000	3	2	0	0	0	0	0	0	0	0	0
Jackie Jensen, pr	.000	1	0	0	0	0	0	0	0	0	0	0
Billy Johnson, 3b	.000	4	6	0	0	0	0	0	0	0	3	0
Ed Lopat, p	.500	1	2	0	1	0	0	0	0	0	1	0
Cliff Mapes, of	.000	1	4	0	0	0	0	0	0	0	1	0
Johnny Mize, 1b	.133	4	15	0	2	0	0	0	0	0	1	0
Vic Raschi, p	.333	1	3	0	1	0	0	0	0	0	0	0
Allie Reynolds, p	.333	2	3	0	1	0	0	0	0	1	2	0
Phil Rizzuto, ss	.143	4	14	1	2	0	0	0	0	3	0	1
Gene Woodling, of	.429	4	14	2	6	0	0	0	1	2	0	0
TOTAL	.222		135	11	30	3	1	2	10	13	12	1

PITCHER	W	L	ERA	G	GS	CG	SV	SHO	IP	H	ER	BB	SO
Tom Ferrick	1	0	0.00	1	0	0	0	0	1.0	1	0	1	0
Whitey Ford	1	0	0.00	1	1	0	0	0	8.2	7	0	1	7
Ed Lopat	0	0	2.25	1	1	0	0	0	8.0	9	2	0	5
Vic Raschi	1	0	0.00	1	1	1	0	1	9.0	2	0	1	5
Allie Reynolds	1	0	0.87	2	1	1	1	0	10.1	7	1	4	7
TOTAL	4	0	0.73	6	4	2	1	1	37.0	26	3	7	24

PHI (N)

PLAYER/POS	AVG	G	AB	R	H	2B	3B	HR	RB	BB	SO	SB
Richie Ashburn, of	.176	4	17	0	3	1	0	0	1	0	4	0
Jimmy Bloodworth, 2b	.000	1	0	0	0	0	0	0	0	0	0	0
Putsy Caballero, ph	.000	3	1	0	0	0	0	0	0	0	1	0
Del Ennis, of	.143	4	14	1	2	1	0	0	0	0	1	0
Mike Goliat, 2b	.214	4	14	1	3	0	0	0	1	1	2	0
Granny Hamner, ss	.429	4	14	1	6	2	1	0	0	1	2	1
Ken Heintzelman, p	.000	1	2	0	0	0	0	0	0	0	0	0
Ken Johnson, pr	.000	1	0	1	0	0	0	0	0	0	0	0
Willie Jones, 3b	.286	4	14	1	4	1	0	0	0	0	3	0
Jim Konstanty, p	.250	3	4	0	1	0	0	0	0	0	1	0
Stan Lopata, c-1	.000	2	1	0	0	0	0	0	0	0	1	0
Jackie Mayo, of-1	.000	3	0	0	0	0	0	0	0	1	0	0
Russ Meyer, p	.000	2	0	0	0	0	0	0	0	0	0	0
Bob Miller, p	.000	1	0	0	0	0	0	0	0	0	0	0
Robin Roberts, p	.000	2	2	0	0	0	0	0	0	0	1	0
Andy Seminick, c	.182	4	11	0	2	0	0	0	0	1	3	0
Ken Silvestri, c	.000	1	0	0	0	0	0	0	0	0	0	0
Dick Sisler, of	.059	4	17	0	1	0	0	0	1	0	5	0
Eddie Waitkus, 1b	.267	4	15	0	4	1	0	0	0	2	0	0
Dick Whitman, ph	.000	3	2	0	0	0	0	0	0	1	0	0
TOTAL	.203		128	5	26	6	1	0	3	7	24	1

PITCHER	W	L	ERA	G	GS	CG	SV	SHO	IP	H	ER	BB	SO
Ken Heintzelman	0	0	1.17	1	1	0	0	0	7.2	4	1	6	3
Jim Konstanty	0	1	2.40	3	1	0	0	0	15.0	9	4	4	3
Russ Meyer	0	1	5.40	2	0	0	0	0	1.2	4	1	0	1
Bob Miller	0	1	27.00	1	1	0	0	0	0.1	2	1	0	0
Robin Roberts	0	1	1.64	2	1	1	0	0	11.0	11	2	3	5
TOTAL	0	4	2.27	9	4	1	0	0	35.2	30	9	13	12

GAME 1 AT PHI OCT 4

NY	000 100 000	1	5	0
PHI	000 000 000	0	2	1

Pitchers: RASCHI vs KONSTANTY, Meyer (9)
Attendance: 30,746

GAME 2 AT PHI OCT 5

NY	010 000 000 1	2	10	0
PHI	000 010 000 0	1	7	0

Pitchers: REYNOLDS vs ROBERTS
Home Runs: DiMaggio-NY
Attendance: 32,660

GAME 3 AT NY OCT 6

PHI	000 001 100	2	10	2
NY	000 000 001	3	7	0

Pitchers: Heintzelman, Konstanty (8), MEYER (9) vs Lopat, FERRICK (9)
Attendance: 64,505

GAME 4 AT NY OCT 7

PHI	000 000 002	2	7	1
NY	200 003 00X	5	8	2

Pitchers: MILLER, Konstanty (1), Roberts (8) vs FORD, Reynolds (9)
Home Runs: Berra-NY
Attendance: 68,098

The Giants—who caught Brooklyn with a tremendous late-season drive, then defeated them for the pennant on Bobby Thomson's ninth-inning home run in Game Three of the tie-breaker playoff series—carried their momentum through Game Three of the World Series before bowing to the Yankees. Dave Koslo (the only Giant starter not to see action in the playoff) pitched the Series opener and held the Yankees to one run. Monte Irvin's steal of home for the Giants' second run in the top of the first was enough for the win, but Al Dark made Koslo's lead more secure with a three-run homer in the sixth.

The Yankees evened the Series in Game Two, scoring two early runs (one of them Joe Collins's home run) off Larry Jansen, and holding on for the win behind Ed Lopat's five-hit pitching. But the Giants regained the lead in Game Three with five unearned runs (three of them on Whitey Lockman's homer) in a fifth inning prolonged by two Yankee errors, as pitchers Jim Hearn and Sheldon Jones combined to hold the Bronx Bombers to five hits and a pair of runs (though Hearn issued eight walks).

But that was the end of the Giants' drive. Although they scored first in games Four and Five with first-inning runs, they couldn't hold the lead either time. In Game Four Allie Reynolds held the Giants to two runs as his Yankees scored six—including a two-run homer by Joe DiMaggio in the fifth inning that proved to be the last home run of his career. DiMag drove in three more Yankee runs in Game Five, as did Phil Rizzuto, and rookie infielder Gil McDougald contributed a grand slam as the Bombers earned their nickname in obliterating Giant pitching with 13 runs. Ed Lopat, meanwhile, hurled his second five-hitter of the Series for his second win.

Yankee Hank Bauer tripled with the bases full in the sixth inning of Game Six to break a tie and give the Yankees a 4–1 lead. The Giants loaded the bases with three straight singles to open the top of the ninth, and scored two runners on successive flies to left, to come within one run of a tie. But pinch hitter Sal Yvars (in his only Series at-bat) lined out to right and the Yankees had their fourteenth world title.

New York Yankees (AL), 4; New York Giants (NL), 2

NY (A)

PLAYER/POS	AVG	G	AB	R	H	2B	3B	HR	RB	BB	SO	SB
Hank Bauer, of	.167	6	18	0	3	0	1	0	3	1	1	0
Yogi Berra, c	.261	6	23	4	6	1	0	0	0	2	1	0
Bobby Brown, 3b-4	.357	5	14	1	5	1	0	0	2	1	0	0
Gerry Coleman, 2b	.250	5	8	2	2	0	0	0	0	1	2	0
Joe Collins, 1b-6,of-1	.222	6	18	2	4	0	0	1	3	2	1	0
Joe Di Maggio, of	.261	6	23	3	6	2	0	1	5	2	4	0
Bobby Hogue, p	.000	2	0	0	0	0	0	0	0	0	0	0
Johnny Hopp, ph	.000	1	0	0	0	0	0	0	0	1	0	0
Bob Kuzava, p	.000	1	0	0	0	0	0	0	0	0	0	0
Ed Lopat, p	.125	2	8	0	1	0	0	0	1	0	2	0
Mickey Mantle, of	.200	2	5	1	1	0	0	0	0	2	1	0
Billy Martin, pr	.000	1	0	1	0	0	0	0	0	0	0	0
Gil Mc Dougald, 3b-5,2b-4	.261	6	23	2	6	1	0	1	7	2	2	0
Johnny Mize, 1b-2	.286	4	7	2	2	1	0	0	1	2	0	0
Tom Morgan, p	.000	1	0	0	0	0	0	0	0	0	0	0
Joe Ostrowski, p	.000	1	0	0	0	0	0	0	0	0	0	0
Vic Raschi, p	.000	2	2	0	0	0	0	0	0	0	2	0
Allie Reynolds, p	.333	2	6	0	2	0	0	0	0	1	0	0
Phil Rizzuto, ss	.320	6	25	5	8	0	0	1	3	2	3	0
Johnny Sain, p	.000	1	1	0	0	0	0	0	0	0	0	0
Gene Woodling, of-5	.167	6	18	6	3	1	1	1	1	5	3	0
TOTAL	.246		199	29	49	7	2	5	25	26	23	0

PITCHER	W	L	ERA	G	GS	CG	SV	SHO	IP	H	ER	BB	SO
Bobby Hogue	0	0	0.00	2	0	0	0	0	2.2	1	0	0	0
Bob Kuzava	0	0	0.00	1	0	0	1	0	1.0	0	0	0	0
Ed Lopat	2	0	0.50	2	2	2	0	0	18.0	10	1	3	4
Tom Morgan	0	0	0.00	1	0	0	0	0	2.0	2	0	1	3
Joe Ostrowski	0	0	0.00	1	0	0	0	0	2.0	1	0	0	1
Vic Raschi	1	1	0.87	2	2	0	0	0	10.1	12	1	8	4
Allie Reynolds	1	1	4.20	2	2	1	0	0	15.0	16	7	11	8
Johnny Sain	0	0	9.00	1	0	0	0	0	2.0	4	2	2	2
TOTAL	4	2	1.87	12	6	3	1	0	53.0	46	11	25	22

NY (N)

PLAYER/POS	AVG	G	AB	R	H	2B	3B	HR	RB	BB	SO	SB
Al Corwin, p	.000	1	0	0	0	0	0	0	0	0	0	0
Alvin Dark, ss	.417	6	24	5	10	3	0	1	4	2	3	0
Clint Hartung, of	.000	2	4	0	0	0	0	0	0	0	0	0
Jim Hearn, p	.000	2	3	0	0	0	0	0	0	0	1	0
Monte Irvin, of	.458	6	24	3	11	0	1	0	2	2	1	2
Larry Jansen, p	.000	3	2	0	0	0	0	0	0	0	0	0
Sheldon Jones, p	.000	2	0	0	0	0	0	0	0	0	0	0
Monte Kennedy, p	.000	2	0	0	0	0	0	0	0	0	0	0
Alex Konikowski, p	.000	1	0	0	0	0	0	0	0	0	0	0
Dave Koslo, p	.000	2	5	0	0	0	0	0	0	0	2	0
Whitey Lockman, 1b	.240	6	25	1	6	2	0	1	4	1	2	0
Jack Lohrke, ph	.000	2	2	0	0	0	0	0	0	0	1	0
Sal Maglie, p	.000	1	1	0	0	0	0	0	0	0	1	0
Willie Mays, of	.182	6	22	1	4	0	0	0	1	2	2	0
Ray Noble, c	.000	2	2	0	0	0	0	0	0	0	1	0
Bill Rigney, ph	.250	4	4	0	1	0	0	0	1	1	1	0
Hank Schenz, pr	.000	1	0	0	0	0	0	0	0	0	0	0
George Spencer, p	.000	2	0	0	0	0	0	0	0	0	0	0
Eddie Stanky, 2b	.136	6	22	3	3	0	0	0	1	3	2	0
Hank Thompson, of	.143	5	14	3	2	0	0	0	0	5	2	0
Bobby Thomson, 3b	.238	6	21	1	5	1	0	0	2	5	0	0
Wes Westrum, c	.235	6	17	1	4	1	0	0	0	5	3	0
Davey Williams, ph	.000	2	1	0	0	0	0	0	0	0	0	0
Sal Yvars, ph	.000	1	1	0	0	0	0	0	0	0	0	0
TOTAL	.237		194	18	46	7	1	2	15	25	22	2

PITCHER	W	L	ERA	G	GS	CG	SV	SHO	IP	H	ER	BB	SO
Al Corwin	0	0	0.00	1	0	0	0	0	1.2	1	0	0	1
Jim Hearn	1	0	1.04	2	1	0	0	0	8.2	5	1	8	1
Larry Jansen	0	2	6.30	3	2	0	0	0	10.0	8	7	4	6
Sheldon Jones	0	0	2.08	2	0	0	1	0	4.1	5	1	1	2
Monte Kennedy	0	0	6.00	2	0	0	0	0	3.0	3	2	1	4
Alex Konikowski	0	0	0.00	1	0	0	0	0	1.0	1	0	0	0
Dave Koslo	1	1	3.00	2	2	1	0	0	15.0	12	5	7	6
Sal Maglie	0	1	7.20	1	1	0	0	0	5.0	8	4	2	3
George Spencer	0	0	18.90	2	0	0	0	0	3.1	6	7	3	0
TOTAL	2	4	4.67	16	6	1	1	0	52.0	49	27	26	23

GAME 1 AT NY-A OCT 4

NY-N	200 003 000	5	10	1
NY-A	010 000 000	1	7	1

Pitchers: KOSLO vs REYNOLDS, Hogue (7), Morgan (8)
Home Runs: Dark-NY(N)
Attendance: 65,673

GAME 2 AT NY-A OCT 5

NY-N	000 000 100	1	5	1
NY-A	110 000 01X	3	6	0

Pitchers: JANSEN, Spencer (7) vs LOPAT
Home Runs: Collins-NY(A)
Attendance: 66,018

GAME 3 AT NY-N OCT 6

NY-A	000 000 011	2	5	2
NY-N	010 050 00X	6	7	2

Pitchers: RASCHI, Hogue (5), Ostrowski (7) vs HEARN, Jones (8)
Home Runs: Lockman-NY(N), Woodling-NY(A)
Attendance: 52,035

GAME 4 AT NY-N OCT 8

NY-A	010 120 200	6	12	0
NY-N	100 000 001	2	8	2

Pitchers: REYNOLDS vs MAGLIE, Jones (6), Kennedy (9)
Home Runs: DiMaggio-NY(A)
Attendance: 49,010

GAME 5 AT NY-N OCT 9

NY-A	005 202 400	13	12	1
NY-N	100 000 000	1	5	3

Pitchers: LOPAT vs JANSEN, Kennedy (4), Spencer (6), Corwin (7), Konikowski (9)
Home Runs: McDougald-NY(A), Rizzuto-NY(A)
Attendance: 47,530

GAME 6 AT NY-A OCT 10

NY-N	000 010 002	3	11	1
NY-A	100 003 00X	4	7	0

Pitchers: KOSLO, Hearn (7), Jansen (8) VS RASCHI, Sain (7), Kuzava (9)
Attendance: 61,711

In four of the seven games, home runs provided the margin of victory. Homers accounted for five of the six runs scored in the opener, with Duke Snider's two-run blast in the sixth putting Brooklyn ahead to stay. Star Dodger reliever Joe Black, in only his third start of the year, held New York to six hits and two runs in defeating Yankee ace Allie Reynolds.

Four home runs enlivened the next three games but did not govern the outcomes. Billy Martin's three-run shot was the centerpiece of the Yankee assault in Game Two, but New York would have won without it behind Vic Raschi's one-run three-hitter. Brooklyn needed no homers to regain the Series advantage in Game Three. In the top of the ninth, with the Dodgers leading by a run, Pee Wee Reese and Jackie Robinson singled (driving out starter Ed Lopat) and pulled a double steal. Both then scored on a passed ball. Yankee pinch hitter Johnny Mize homered in the last of the ninth, but Preacher Roe escaped without further scoring for a complete-game 5–3 win.

Black opposed Reynolds again in Game Four and bettered his earlier performance, holding New York to three hits and one run (a Mize homer) in seven innings. But Reynolds improved even more, fanning ten as he shut the Dodgers out.

Snider hit his second homer of the Series and Mize his third in the fifth inning of Game Five. Mize's shot put New York ahead, but Brooklyn tied the game in the seventh and took a 6–5 lead when Snider doubled home a run in the eleventh. Dodger right fielder Carl Furillo's leaping catch in the last of the eleventh robbed Mize of another home run, and starter Carl Erskine held on for the win, giving Brooklyn a 3–2 Series lead.

Snider's home run in the last of the sixth ended Vic Raschi's shutout in Game Six, but Yogi Berra, the first Yankee up in the seventh, tied the game and spoiled Billy Loes's shutout with his home run, and pitcher Raschi singled home the go-ahead run two outs later. Yankee sophomore Mickey Mantle's blast in the eighth (the first of his record 18 World Series home runs) made the score 3–1. Snider's fourth homer of the Series gave the Dodgers a second run in the eighth, but Allie Reynolds relieved Raschi and prevented further scoring, sending the Series to a seventh game.

Joe Black traded three shutout innings with Yankee Ed Lopat in the finale before both clubs scored single runs in the fourth and fifth innings. Mantle homered off Black in the sixth for a third Yankee run that proved the Series

New York Yankees (AL), 4; Brooklyn Dodgers (NL), 3

NY (A)

PLAYER/POS	AVG	G	AB	R	H	2B	3B	HR	RB	BB	SO	SB
Hank Bauer, of	.056	7	18	2	1	0	0	0	1	4	3	0
Yogi Berra, c	.214	7	28	2	6	1	0	2	3	2	4	0
Ewell Blackwell, p	.000	1	1	0	0	0	0	0	0	0	0	0
Joe Collins, 1b	.000	6	12	1	0	0	0	0	0	1	3	0
Tom Gorman, p	.000	1	0	0	0	0	0	0	0	0	0	0
Ralph Houk, ph	.000	1	1	0	0	0	0	0	0	0	0	0
Bob Kuzava, p	.000	1	1	0	0	0	0	0	0	0	0	0
Ed Lopat, p	.333	2	3	0	1	0	0	0	1	1	1	0
Mickey Mantle, of	.345	7	29	5	10	1	1	2	3	3	4	0
Billy Martin, 2b	.217	7	23	2	5	0	0	1	4	2	2	0
Gil Mc Dougald, 3b	.200	7	25	5	0	0	0	1	3	5	2	1
Johnny Mize, 1b-4	.400	5	15	3	6	1	0	3	6	3	1	0
Irv Noren, of-3	.300	4	10	0	3	0	0	0	1	1	3	0
Vic Raschi, p	.167	3	6	0	1	0	0	0	1	1	2	0
Allie Reynolds, p	.000	4	7	0	0	0	0	0	0	0	2	0
Phil Rizzuto, ss	.148	7	27	2	4	1	0	0	0	5	2	0
Johnny Sain, p-1	.000	2	3	0	0	0	0	0	0	0	0	0
Ray Scarborough, p	.000	1	0	0	0	0	0	0	0	0	0	0
Gene Woodling, of-6	.348	7	23	4	8	1	1	1	1	3	3	0
TOTAL	.216		232	26	50	5	2	10	24	31	32	1

PITCHER	W	L	ERA	G	GS	CG	SV	SHO	IP	H	ER	BB	SO
Ewell Blackwell	0	0	7.20	1	1	0	0	0	5.0	4	4	3	4
Tom Gorman	0	0	0.00	1	0	0	0	0	0.2	1	0	0	0
Bob Kuzava	0	0	0.00	1	0	0	1	0	2.2	0	0	0	2
Ed Lopat	0	1	4.76	2	2	0	0	0	11.1	14	6	4	3
Vic Raschi	2	0	1.59	3	2	1	0	0	17.0	12	3	8	18
Allie Reynolds	2	1	1.77	4	2	1	1	1	20.1	12	4	6	18
Johnny Sain	0	1	3.00	1	0	0	0	0	6.0	6	2	3	3
Ray Scarborough	0	0	9.00	1	0	0	0	0	1.0	1	1	0	1
TOTAL	4	3	2.81	14	7	2	2	1	64.0	50	20	24	49

BRO (N)

PLAYER/POS	AVG	G	AB	R	H	2B	3B	HR	RB	BB	SO	SB
Sandy Amoros, ph	.000	1	0	0	0	0	0	0	0	0	0	0
Joe Black, p	.000	3	6	0	0	0	0	0	0	1	6	0
Roy Campanella, c	.214	7	28	0	6	0	0	0	1	1	6	0
Billy Cox, 3b	.296	7	27	4	8	2	0	0	0	3	4	0
Carl Erskine, p	.000	3	6	1	0	0	0	0	0	0	1	0
Carl Furillo, of	.174	7	23	1	4	2	0	0	0	3	3	0
Gil Hodges, 1b	.000	7	21	1	0	0	0	0	1	5	6	0
Tommy Holmes, of	.000	3	1	0	0	0	0	0	0	0	0	0
Ken Lehman, p	.000	1	0	0	0	0	0	0	0	0	0	0
Billy Loes, p	.333	2	3	0	1	0	0	0	0	0	1	1
Bobby Morgan, 3b	.000	2	1	0	0	0	0	0	0	0	0	0
Rocky Nelson, ph	.000	4	3	0	0	0	0	0	0	1	2	0
Andy Pafko, of-5	.190	7	21	0	4	0	0	0	2	0	4	0
Pee Wee Reese, ss	.345	7	29	4	10	0	0	1	4	2	2	1
Jackie Robinson, 2b	.174	7	23	4	4	0	0	1	2	7	5	2
Preacher Roe, p	.000	3	2	0	0	0	0	0	0	0	0	0
Johnny Rutherford, p	.000	1	0	0	0	0	0	0	0	0	0	0
George Shuba, of-3	.300	4	10	0	3	1	0	0	0	0	4	0
Duke Snider, of	.345	7	29	5	10	2	0	4	8	1	5	1
TOTAL	.215		233	20	50	7	0	6	18	24	49	5

PITCHER	W	L	ERA	G	GS	CG	SV	SHO	IP	H	ER	BB	SO
Joe Black	1	2	2.53	3	3	1	0	0	21.1	15	6	8	9
Carl Erskine	1	1	4.50	3	2	1	0	0	18.0	12	9	10	10
Ken Lehman	0	0	0.00	1	0	0	0	0	2.0	2	0	1	0
Billy Loes	0	1	4.35	2	1	0	0	0	10.1	11	5	5	5
Preacher Roe	1	0	3.18	3	1	1	0	0	11.1	9	4	6	7
Johnny Rutherford	0	0	9.00	1	0	0	0	0	1.0	1	1	1	1
TOTAL	3	4	3.52	13	7	3	0	0	64.0	50	25	31	32

winner, as three Yankee relievers held Brooklyn scoreless through the final four frames.

GAME 1 AT BRO OCT 1

NY	010 000 010	2	6	2
BRO	010 002 01X	4	6	0

Pitchers: REYNOLDS, Scarborough (8) vs BLACK
Home Runs: Robinson-BRO, Snider-BRO, Reese-BRO, McDougald-NY
Attendance: 34,861

GAME 2 AT BRO OCT 2

NY	000 115 000	7	10	0
BRO	001 000 000	1	3	1

Pitchers: RASCHI vs ERSKINE, Loes (6), Lehman (8)
Home Runs: Martin-NY
Attendance: 33,792

GAME 3 AT NY OCT 3

BRO	001 010 012	5	11	0
NY	010 000 011	3	6	2

Pitchers: ROE vs LOPAT, Gorman (9)
Home Runs: Berra-NY, Mize-NY
Attendance: 66,698

GAME 4 AT NY OCT 4

BRO	000 000 000	0	4	1
NY	000 100 01X	2	4	1

Pitchers: BLACK, Rutherford (8) VS REYNOLDS
Home Runs: Mize-NY
Attendance: 71,787

GAME 5 AT NY OCT 5

BRO	010 030 100 01	6	10	0
NY	000 050 000 00	5	5	1

Pitchers: ERSKINE vs Blackwell, SAIN (6)
Home Runs: Snider-BRO, Mize-NY
Attendance: 70,536

GAME 6 AT BRO OCT 6

NY	000 000 210	3	9	0
BRO	000 001 010	2	8	1

Pitchers: RASCHI, Reynolds (8) vs LOES, Roe (9)
Home Runs: Snider-BRO (2), Berra-NY, Mantle-NY
Attendance: 30,037

GAME 7 AT BRO OCT 7

NY	000 111 100	4	10	4
BRO	000 110 000	2	8	1

Pitchers: Lopat, REYNOLDS (4), Raschi (7), Kuzava (7) vs BLACK, Roe (6), Erskine (8)
Home Runs: Woodling-NY, Mantle-NY
Attendance: 33,195

Although the Yankees easily won the American League pennant, the Dodgers seemed even more overwhelming, with a team batting average of .285 and a club-record 105 season wins. But when the Series was over, the Yankees had added a record fifth straight world championship to their record fifth straight pennant.

Dodger ace Carl Erskine lasted only one inning of the Series opener, giving up three walks and two triples for four Yankee runs. By the middle of the seventh inning, the Dodgers had tied the score at 5–5. But Yankee Joe Collins homered to break the tie in the last of the seventh, and reliever Johnny Sain ensured his own win with a two-run double an inning later. The Dodgers outhit New York in Game Two, and held a 2–1 lead entering the bottom of the seventh. But Billy Martin (who hit .500 and slugged .958 in the Series) tied the game with a leadoff homer in the seventh, and Mickey Mantle won it with a two-run blast in the eighth.

Down 0–2, Brooklyn evened the Series at home with victories in Games Three and Four. Erskine redeemed his poor start in Game One with a record-setting 14-strikeout performance in Game Three. But it was a narrow win, settled only when Roy Campanella homered in the last of the eighth to break a 2–2 tie. In Game Four, Duke Snider made Billy Loes's three-run pitching a winning performance, driving in four of the Dodgers' seven runs with two doubles and a homer.

But Brooklyn never even took the lead in the final two games. Four Yankee home runs (including a Mantle grand slam) rocked Dodger pitching in Game Five as the Bombers built a lead which Dodger home runs in the eighth and ninth were unable to overcome. In Game Six the Yankees built a 3–0 lead over Erskine in the first two innings. Brooklyn fought back with a run in the sixth, and tied the game on Carl Furillo's two-run homer in the top of the ninth. But with men on first and second in the last of the ninth, Yankee Billy Martin singled in the game-ending, Series-winning run. It was Martin's twelfth hit, a new record for a six-game Series.

New York Yankees (AL), 4; Brooklyn Dodgers (NL), 2

NY (A)

PLAYER/POS	AVG	G	AB	R	H	2B	3B	HR	RB	BB	SO	SB
Hank Bauer, of	.261	6	23	6	6	0	1	0	1	2	4	0
Yogi Berra, c	.429	6	21	3	9	1	0	1	4	3	3	0
Don Bollweg, 1b-1	.000	3	2	0	0	0	0	0	0	0	2	0
Joe Collins, 1b	.167	6	24	4	4	1	0	1	2	3	8	0
Whitey Ford, p	.333	2	3	0	1	0	0	0	0	0	0	0
Tom Gorman, p	.000	1	1	0	0	0	0	0	0	0	1	0
Bob Kuzava, p	.000	1	1	0	0	0	0	0	0	0	1	0
Ed Lopat, p	.000	1	3	0	0	0	0	0	0	0	2	0
Mickey Mantle, of	.208	6	24	3	5	0	0	2	7	3	8	0
Billy Martin, 2b	.500	6	24	5	12	1	2	2	8	1	2	1
Jim Mc Donald, p	.500	1	2	0	1	1	0	0	1	1	1	0
Gil Mc Dougald, 3b	.167	6	24	2	4	0	1	2	4	1	3	0
Johnny Mize, ph	.000	3	3	0	0	0	0	0	0	0	1	0
Irv Noren, ph	.000	2	1	0	0	0	0	0	0	1	0	0
Vic Raschi, p	.000	1	2	0	0	0	0	0	0	0	1	0
Allie Reynolds, p	.500	3	2	0	1	0	0	0	0	0	1	0
Phil Rizzuto, ss	.316	6	19	4	6	1	0	0	0	3	2	1
Johnny Sain, p	.500	2	2	1	1	1	0	0	2	0	1	0
Art Schallock, p	.000	1	0	0	0	0	0	0	0	0	0	0
Gene Woodling, of	.300	6	20	5	6	0	0	1	3	6	2	0
TOTAL	.279		201	33	56	6	4	9	32	25	43	2

PITCHER	W	L	ERA	G	GS	CG	SV	SHO	IP	H	ER	BB	SO
Whitey Ford	0	1	4.50	2	2	0	0	0	8.0	9	4	2	7
Tom Gorman	0	0	3.00	1	0	0	0	0	3.0	4	1	0	1
Bob Kuzava	0	0	13.50	1	0	0	0	0	0.2	2	1	0	1
Ed Lopat	1	0	2.00	1	1	1	0	0	9.0	9	2	4	3
Jim Mc Donald	1	0	5.87	1	1	0	0	0	7.2	12	5	0	3
Vic Raschi	0	1	3.38	1	1	1	0	0	8.0	9	3	3	4
Allie Reynolds	1	0	6.75	3	1	0	1	0	8.0	9	6	4	9
Johnny Sain	1	0	4.76	2	0	0	0	0	5.2	8	3	1	1
Art Schallock	0	0	4.50	1	0	0	0	0	2.0	2	1	1	1
TOTAL	4	2	4.50	13	6	2	1	0	52.0	64	26	15	30

BRO (N)

PLAYER/POS	AVG	G	AB	R	H	2B	3B	HR	RB	BB	SO	SB
Wayne Belardi, ph	.000	2	2	0	0	0	0	0	0	0	1	0
Joe Black, p	.000	1	0	0	0	0	0	0	0	0	0	0
Roy Campanella, c	.273	6	22	6	6	0	0	1	2	2	3	0
Billy Cox, 3b	.304	6	23	3	7	3	0	1	6	1	4	0
Carl Erskine, p	.250	3	4	0	1	0	0	0	0	0	1	0
Carl Furillo, of	.333	6	24	4	8	2	0	1	4	1	3	0
Jim Gilliam, 2b	.296	6	27	4	8	3	0	2	4	0	2	0
Gil Hodges, 1b	.364	6	22	3	8	0	0	1	1	3	3	1
Jim Hughes, p	.000	1	1	0	0	0	0	0	0	0	1	0
Clem Labine, p	.000	3	4	0	0	0	0	0	0	0	0	0
Billy Loes, p	.667	1	3	0	2	0	0	0	0	0	0	0
Russ Meyer, p	.000	1	1	0	0	0	0	0	0	0	1	0
Bob Milliken, p	.000	1	0	0	0	0	0	0	0	0	0	0
Bobby Morgan, ph	.000	1	1	0	0	0	0	0	0	0	1	0
Johnny Podres, p	1.000	1	1	0	1	0	0	0	0	0	0	0
Pee Wee Reese, ss	.208	6	24	0	5	0	1	0	0	4	1	0
Jackie Robinson, of	.320	6	25	3	8	2	0	0	2	1	0	1
Preacher Roe, p	.000	1	3	0	0	0	0	0	0	0	2	0
George Shuba, ph	1.000	2	1	1	1	0	0	1	2	0	0	0
Duke Snider, of	.320	6	25	3	8	3	0	1	5	2	6	0
Don Thompson, of	.000	2	0	0	0	0	0	0	0	0	0	0
Ben Wade, p	.000	2	0	0	0	0	0	0	0	0	0	0
Dick Williams, ph	.500	3	2	0	1	0	0	0	0	0	1	0
TOTAL	.300		213	27	64	13	1	8	26	15	30	2

PITCHER	W	L	ERA	G	GS	CG	SV	SHO	IP	H	ER	BB	SO
Joe Black	0	0	9.00	1	0	0	0	0	1.0	1	1	0	2
Carl Erskine	1	0	5.79	3	3	1	0	0	14.0	14	9	9	16
Jim Hughes	0	0	2.25	1	0	0	0	0	4.0	3	1	1	3
Clem Labine	0	2	3.60	3	0	0	1	0	5.0	10	2	1	3
Billy Loes	1	0	3.38	1	1	0	0	0	8.0	8	3	2	8
Russ Meyer	0	0	6.23	1	0	0	0	0	4.1	8	3	4	5
Bob Milliken	0	0	0.00	1	0	0	0	0	2.0	2	0	1	0
Johnny Podres	0	1	3.38	1	1	0	0	0	2.2	1	1	2	0
Preacher Roe	0	1	4.50	1	1	1	0	0	8.0	5	4	4	4
Ben Wade	0	0	15.43	2	0	0	0	0	2.1	4	4	1	2
TOTAL	2	4	4.91	15	6	2	1	0	51.1	56	28	25	43

GAME 1 AT NY SEPT 30

BRO	000	013	100	5	12 2
NY	400	010	13X	9	12 0

Pitchers: Erskine, Hughes (2), LABINE (6), Wade (8) vs Reynolds, SAIN (6)
Home Runs: Gilliam-BRO, Hodges-BRO, Shuba-BRO, Berra-NY, Collins-NY
Attendance: 69,374

GAME 2 AT NY OCT 1

BRO	000	200	000	2	9 1
NY	100	000	12X	4	5 0

Pitchers: ROE vs LOPAT
Home Runs: Martin-NY, Mantle-NY
Attendance: 66,786

GAME 3 AT BRO OCT 2

NY	000	010	010	2	6 0
BRO	000	011	01X	3	9 0

Pitchers: RASCHI vs ERSKINE
Home Runs: Campanella-BRO
Attendance: 35,270

GAME 4 AT BRO OCT 3

NY	000	020	001	3	9 0
BRO	300	102	10X	7	12 0

Pitchers: FORD, Gorman (2), Sain (5), Schallock (7) vs LOES, Labine (9)
Home Runs: McDougald-NY, Snider-BRO
Attendance: 36,775

GAME 5 AT BRO OCT 4

NY	105	000	311	11	11 1
BRO	010	010	041	7	14 1

Pitchers: McDONALD, Kuzava (8), Reynolds (9) vs PODRES, Meyer (3), Wade (8), Black (9)
Home Runs: Woodling-NY, Mantle-NY, Martin-NY, McDougald-NY, Cox-BRO, Gilliam-BRO
Attendance: 36,775

GAME 6 AT NY OCT 5

BRO	000	001	002	3	8 3
NY	210	000	001	4	13 0

Pitchers: Erskine, Milliken (5), LABINE (7) vs Ford, REYNOLDS (8)
Home Runs: Furillo-BRO
Attendance: 62,370

The Indians, who had won a league-record 111 games to break the American League domination of the New York Yankees, entered the World Series as strong favorites to humble the Giants. It was not to be.

Cleveland would have won the opener had it not been played in New York's Polo Grounds, with their short foul lines and deep center field. Most of the game was a pitchers' duel. Vic Wertz (the only Indian to hit safely in all four games) tripled off Sal Maglie to give Cleveland a two-run lead in the top of the first, but three Giant singles and a walk in the third off Bob Lemon tied the score. Lemon then settled down to hold New York scoreless through the ninth. Cleveland threatened in the eighth when the first two batters reached base, bringing Wertz to the plate. As he had already hit Maglie safely three times, Don Liddle was brought in to pitch to him. Wertz responded with a fly to deep center that would have been a home run in Cleveland, but in New York turned into the most famous catch in World Series history as Willie Mays raced out and tracked down the ball about 425 feet from the plate. Marv Grissom replaced Liddle on the mound and issued a walk to load the bases, but he retired the next two batters and (despite Wertz's double in the top of the tenth) held Cleveland scoreless the rest of the way. In the last of the tenth, Lemon retired the first batter, but Mays walked and stole second, and Hank Thompson was walked intentionally to set up the double play. Pinch hitter Dusty Rhodes then entered the hall of heroes with a short fly to right that—though it would have been an out in Cleveland—fell into the Polo Grounds stands for three runs and a Giant victory.

The rest of the Series was anticlimax. In the second game Rhodes, with half the Giants' four hits, drove in two runs on a single and another homer, providing the margin of victory for Giant ace Johnny Antonelli, who allowed only one of Cleveland's 14 baserunners to score. Game Three was no contest. New York had scored all six of its runs before the Indians managed to come up with single runs in both the seventh and eighth. Pinch hitter Hank Majeski's three-run homer put Cleveland on the board in the fifth inning of Game Four. But as New York had already scored seven times, even a fourth Cleveland run in the seventh proved too little to prevent a Giant sweep.

New York Giants (NL), 4; Cleveland Indians (AL), 0

NY (N)

PLAYER/POS	AVG	G	AB	R	H	2B	3B	HR	RBI	BB	SO	SB
Johnny Antonelli, p	.000	2	3	0	0	0	0	0	1	0	0	0
Alvin Dark, ss	.412	4	17	2	7	0	0	0	0	1	1	0
Ruben Gomez, p	.000	1	4	0	0	0	0	0	0	0	2	0
Marv Grissom, p	.000	1	1	0	0	0	0	0	0	0	1	0
Monte Irvin, of	.222	4	9	1	2	1	0	0	2	0	3	0
Don Liddle, p	.000	2	3	0	0	0	0	0	0	0	2	0
Whitey Lockman, 1b	.111	4	18	2	2	0	0	0	0	1	2	0
Sal Maglie, p	.000	1	3	0	0	0	0	0	0	0	2	0
Willie Mays, of	.286	4	14	4	4	1	0	0	3	4	1	1
Don Mueller, of	.389	4	18	4	7	0	0	0	1	0	1	0
Dusty Rhodes, of-2	.667	3	6	2	4	0	0	2	7	1	2	0
Hank Thompson, 3b	.364	4	11	6	4	1	0	0	2	7	1	0
Wes Westrum, c	.273	4	11	0	3	0	0	0	3	1	3	0
Hoyt Wilhelm, p	.000	2	1	0	0	0	0	0	0	0	1	0
Davey Williams, 2b	.000	4	11	0	0	0	0	0	1	2	2	0
TOTAL	.254		130	21	33	3	0	2	20	17	24	1

PITCHER	W	L	ERA	G	GS	CG	SV	SHO	IP	H	ER	BB	SO
Johnny Antonelli	1	0	0.84	2	1	1	1	0	10.2	8	1	7	12
Ruben Gomez	1	0	2.45	1	1	0	0	0	7.1	4	2	3	2
Marv Grissom	1	0	0.00	1	0	0	0	0	2.2	1	0	3	2
Don Liddle	1	0	1.29	2	1	0	0	0	7.0	5	1	1	2
Sal Maglie	0	0	2.57	1	1	0	0	0	7.0	7	2	2	2
Hoyt Wilhelm	0	0	0.00	2	0	0	0	1	2.1	1	0	0	3
TOTAL	4	0	1.46	9	4	1	2	0	37.0	26	6	16	23

CLE (A)

PLAYER/POS	AVG	G	AB	R	H	2B	3B	HR	RBI	BB	SO	SB
Bobby Avila, 2b	.133	4	15	1	2	0	0	0	0	2	1	0
Sam Dente, ss	.000	3	3	1	0	0	0	0	0	1	0	0
Larry Doby, of	.125	4	16	0	2	0	0	0	0	2	4	0
Mike Garcia, p	.000	2	0	0	0	0	0	0	0	0	0	0
Bill Glynn, 1b-1	.500	2	2	1	1	1	0	0	0	0	1	0
Mickey Grasso, c	.000	1	2	0	0	0	0	0	0	0	0	0
Jim Hegan, c	.154	4	13	1	2	1	0	0	0	1	1	0
Art Houtteman, p	.000	1	0	0	0	0	0	0	0	0	0	0
Bob Lemon, p-2	.000	3	6	0	0	0	0	0	0	1	1	0
Hank Majeski, 3b-1	.167	4	6	1	1	0	0	1	3	0	1	0
Dale Mitchell, ph	.000	3	2	0	0	0	0	0	0	1	0	0
Don Mossi, p	.000	3	0	0	0	0	0	0	0	0	0	0
Hal Naragon, c	.000	1	0	0	0	0	0	0	0	0	0	0
Ray Narleski, p	.000	2	0	0	0	0	0	0	0	0	0	0
Hal Newhouser, p	.000	1	0	0	0	0	0	0	0	0	0	0
Dave Philley, of-2	.125	4	8	0	1	0	0	0	0	1	3	0
Dave Pope, of-2	.000	3	3	0	0	0	0	0	0	1	1	0
Rudy Regalado, 3b-1	.333	4	3	0	1	0	0	0	1	0	0	0
Al Rosen, 3b	.250	3	12	0	3	0	0	0	0	1	0	0
Al Smith, of	.214	4	14	2	3	0	0	1	2	2	2	0
George Strickland, ss	.000	3	9	0	0	0	0	0	0	0	2	0
Vic Wertz, 1b	.500	4	16	2	8	2	1	1	3	2	2	0
Wally Westlake, of	.143	2	7	0	1	0	0	0	0	1	3	0
Early Wynn, p	.500	1	2	0	1	1	0	0	0	0	1	0
TOTAL	.190		137	9	26	5	1	3	9	16	23	0

PITCHER	W	L	ERA	G	GS	CG	SV	SHO	IP	H	ER	BB	SO
Mike Garcia	0	1	5.40	2	1	0	0	0	5.0	6	3	4	4
Art Houtteman	0	0	4.50	1	0	0	0	0	2.0	2	1	1	1
Bob Lemon	0	2	6.75	2	2	1	0	0	13.1	16	10	8	11
Don Mossi	0	0	0.00	3	0	0	0	0	4.0	3	0	1	0
Ray Narleski	0	0	2.25	2	0	0	0	0	4.0	1	1	1	2
Hal Newhouser	0	0	INF	1	0	0	0	0	0.0	1	1	1	0
Early Wynn	0	1	3.86	1	1	0	0	0	7.0	4	3	2	5
TOTAL	0	4	4.84	12	4	1	0	0	35.1	33	19	17	24

GAME 1 AT NY SEPT 29

CLE	200	000	000	0	2	8	0
NY	002	000	000	3	5	9	3

Pitchers: LEMON vs Maglie, Liddle (8), GRISSOM (8)
Home Runs: Rhodes-NY
Attendance: 52,751

GAME 2 AT NY SEPT 30

CLE	100	000	000	1	8	0
NY	000	020	10X	3	4	0

Pitchers: WYNN, Mossi (8) vs ANTONELLI
Home Runs: Smith-CLE, Rhodes-NY
Attendance: 49,099

GAME 3 AT CLE OCT 1

NY	103	011	000	6	10	1
CLE	000	000	110	2	4	2

Pitchers: GOMEZ, Wilhelm (7) vs GARCIA, Houtteman (4), Narleski (6), Mossi (9)
Home Runs: Wertz-CLE
Attendance: 71,555

GAME 4 AT CLE OCT 2

NY	021	040	000	7	10	3
CLE	000	030	100	4	6	2

Pitchers: LIDDLE, Wilhelm (7), Antonelli (8) vs LEMON, Newhouser (5), Narleski (5), Mossi (6), Garcia (8)
Home Runs: Majeski-CLE
Attendance: 78,102

The Dodgers and Yankees, after a year's absence, faced each other again in the World Series—their sixth Series confrontation in fifteen years. And after Brooklyn had lost the first two games it began to look as though 1955 might also mark the Yankees' sixth Series triumph over the Dodgers. But this was Brooklyn's year.

The opener was a hitters' game, but closely contested. Both teams scored twice in the second inning and once in the third, but Yankee first baseman Joe Collins's leadoff homer in the last of the fourth gave New York its first lead of the game, and his two-run blast in the sixth made the score 6–3. Brooklyn clawed back in the eighth for two runs—including Jackie Robinson's steal of home—to pull within one run of a tie, but they came no closer. In Game Two, Yankee pitcher Tommy Byrne held the Dodgers to five hits and two runs, and won his own game at the bat with a two-run single that capped the Yankees' four-run fourth.

The Series turned around as the Dodgers captured the next three games in Brooklyn. Roy Campanella's two-run homer in the first inning of Game Three gave Brooklyn a quick lead. New York tied the game with a pair of runs in the second (one of them a homer by Mickey Mantle, who appeared in only three Series games because of a leg injury). But two more Dodger runs in the last of the second drove out Yankee starter Bob Turley and put them ahead to stay as Dodger hurler Johnny Podres held the Yankees to three runs. Home runs by Campanella, Gil Hodges, and Duke Snider accounted for six of Brooklyn's eight runs in Game Four as the Dodgers evened the Series at two-all. Sandy Amoros's second-inning homer initiated the scoring in Game Five, and Snider's blasts in the third and fifth (which made him the first player to hit four home runs in two different Series) gave Brooklyn a 4–1 lead, which even late-inning Yankee homers by Bob Cerv and Yogi Berra could not overcome.

New York bounced back in Game Six, scoring all five of their runs in the first inning (including three on Bill Skowron's homer) to give Whitey Ford a comfortable lead, which he held with a one-run four-hitter. But in the finale, Gil Hodges drove in two Brooklyn runs with a single in the fourth and a sacrifice fly in the sixth. They were all Brooklyn got, but they proved more than enough to carry the Dodgers to their first world title in fifty-five years, as left fielder Sandy Amoros stifled New York's only real scoring threat with a spectacular running catch in the sixth that started a double play and preserved Johnny Podres's second Series win.

Brooklyn Dodgers (NL), 4; New York Yankees (AL), 3

BRO (N)

PLAYER/POS	AVG	G	AB	R	H	2B	3B	HR	RB	BB	SO	SB
Sandy Amoros, of	.333	5	12	3	4	0	0	1	3	4	4	0
Don Bessent, p	.000	3	1	0	0	0	0	0	0	0	1	0
Roy Campanella, c	.259	7	27	4	7	3	0	2	4	3	3	0
Roger Craig, p	.000	1	0	0	0	0	0	0	0	1	0	0
Carl Erskine, p	.000	1	1	0	0	0	0	0	0	0	0	0
Carl Furillo, of	.296	7	27	4	8	1	0	1	3	3	5	0
Jim Gilliam, 2b-5,of-4	.292	7	24	2	7	1	0	0	3	8	1	1
Don Hoak, 3b-1	.333	3	3	0	1	0	0	0	0	2	0	0
Gil Hodges, 1b	.292	7	24	2	7	0	0	1	5	3	2	0
Frank Kellert, ph	.333	3	3	0	1	0	0	0	0	0	0	0
Clem Labine, p	.000	4	4	0	0	0	0	0	0	0	3	0
Billy Loes, p	.000	1	1	0	0	0	0	0	0	0	0	0
Russ Meyer, p	.000	1	2	0	0	0	0	0	0	0	1	0
Don Newcombe, p	.000	1	3	0	0	0	0	0	0	0	0	0
Johnny Podres, p	.143	2	7	1	1	0	0	0	0	0	1	0
Pee Wee Reese, ss	.296	7	27	5	8	1	0	0	2	3	5	0
Jackie Robinson, 3b	.182	6	22	5	4	1	1	0	1	2	1	1
Ed Roebuck, p	.000	1	0	0	0	0	0	0	0	0	0	0
George Shuba, ph	.000	1	1	0	0	0	0	0	0	0	0	0
Duke Snider, of	.320	7	25	5	8	1	0	4	7	2	6	0
Karl Spooner, p	.000	2	0	0	0	0	0	0	0	0	0	0
Don Zimmer, 2b	.222	4	9	2	2	0	0	0	0	2	5	0
TOTAL	.260		223	31	58	8	1	9	30	33	38	2

PITCHER	W	L	ERA	G	GS	CG	SV	SHO	IP	H	ER	BB	SO
Don Bessent	0	0	0.00	3	0	0	0	0	3.1	3	0	1	1
Roger Craig	1	0	3.00	1	1	0	0	0	6.0	4	2	5	4
Carl Erskine	0	0	9.00	1	1	0	0	0	3.0	3	3	2	3
Clem Labine	1	0	2.89	4	0	0	1	0	9.1	6	3	2	2
Billy Loes	0	1	9.82	1	1	0	0	0	3.2	7	4	1	5
Russ Meyer	0	0	0.00	1	0	0	0	0	5.2	4	0	2	4
Don Newcombe	0	1	9.53	1	1	0	0	0	5.2	8	6	2	4
Johnny Podres	2	0	1.00	2	2	2	0	1	18.0	15	2	4	10
Ed Roebuck	0	0	0.00	1	0	0	0	0	2.0	1	0	0	0
Karl Spooner	0	1	13.50	2	1	0	0	0	3.1	4	5	3	6
TOTAL	4	3	3.75	17	7	2	1		60.0	55	25	22	39

NY (A)

PLAYER/POS	AVG	G	AB	R	H	2B	3B	HR	RB	BB	SO	SB
Hank Bauer, of-5	.429	6	14	1	6	0	0	0	1	0	1	0
Yogi Berra, c	.417	7	24	5	10	1	0	1	2	3	1	0
Tommy Byrne, p-2	.167	3	6	0	1	0	0	0	2	0	2	0
Andy Carey, ph	.500	2	2	0	1	0	1	0	1	0	0	0
Tom Carroll, pr	.000	2	0	0	0	0	0	0	0	0	0	0
Bob Cerv, of-4	.125	5	16	1	2	0	0	1	1	0	4	0
Gerry Coleman, ss	.000	3	3	0	0	0	0	0	0	0	1	0
Rip Coleman, p	.000	1	0	0	0	0	0	0	0	0	0	0
Joe Collins, 1b-5,of-1	.167	5	12	6	2	0	0	2	3	6	4	1
Whitey Ford, p	.000	2	6	1	0	0	0	0	0	1	1	0
Bob Grim, p	.000	3	2	0	0	0	0	0	0	0	0	0
Elston Howard, of	.192	7	26	3	5	0	0	1	3	1	8	0
Johnny Kucks, p	.000	4	0	0	0	0	0	0	0	0	0	0
Don Larsen, p	.000	1	2	0	0	0	0	0	0	0	0	0
Mickey Mantle, of-2	.200	3	10	1	2	0	0	1	1	0	2	0
Billy Martin, 2b	.320	7	25	2	8	1	1	0	4	1	5	0
Gil Mc Dougald, 3b	.259	7	27	2	7	0	0	1	1	2	6	0
Tom Morgan, p	.000	2	0	0	0	0	0	0	0	0	0	0
Irv Noren, of	.063	5	16	0	1	0	0	0	1	1	1	0
Phil Rizzuto, ss	.267	7	15	2	4	0	0	0	1	5	1	2
Eddie Robinson, 1b-1	.667	4	3	0	2	0	0	0	1	1	0	0
Bill Skowron, 1b-3	.333	5	12	4	4	2	0	1	3	0	1	0
Tom Sturdivant, p	.000	2	0	0	0	0	0	0	0	0	0	0
Bob Turley, p	.000	3	1	0	0	0	0	0	0	0	0	0
TOTAL	.248		222	26	55	4	2	8	25	22	39	3

PITCHER	W	L	ERA	G	GS	CG	SV	SHO	IP	H	ER	BB	SO
Tommy Byrne	1	1	1.88	2	2	1	0	0	14.1	8	3	8	8
Rip Coleman	0	0	9.00	1	0	0	0	0	1.0	5	1	0	1
Whitey Ford	2	0	2.12	2	2	1	0	0	17.0	13	4	8	10
Bob Grim	0	1	4.15	3	1	0	1	0	8.2	8	4	5	8
Johnny Kucks	0	0	6.00	4	0	0	0	0	3.0	4	2	1	1
Don Larsen	0	1	11.25	1	1	0	0	0	4.0	5	5	2	4
Tom Morgan	0	0	4.91	2	0	0	0	0	3.2	3	2	3	1
Tom Sturdivant	0	0	6.00	2	0	0	0	0	3.0	5	2	2	2
Bob Turley	0	1	8.44	3	1	0	0	0	5.1	7	5	4	7
TOTAL	3	4	4.20	18	7	2	1	0	60.0	58	28	33	38

GAME 1 AT NY SEPT 28

BRO	021	000	020	5	10	0
NY	021	102	00X	6	9	1

Pitchers: NEWCOMBE, Bessent (6), Labine (8) vs FORD, Grim (9)
Home Runs: Furillo-BRO, Snider-BRO, Howard-NY, Collins-NY (2)
Attendance: 63,869

GAME 2 AT NY SEPT 29

BRO	000	110	000	2	5	2
NY	000	400	00X	4	8	0

Pitchers: LOES, Bessent (4), Spooner (5), Labine (8) vs BYRNE
Attendance: 64,707

GAME 3 AT BRO SEPT 30

NY	020	000	100	3	7	0
BRO	220	200	20X	8	11	1

Pitchers: TURLEY, Morgan (2), Kucks (5), Sturdivant (7) vs PODRES
Home Runs: Campanella-BRO, Mantle-NY
Attendance: 34,209

GAME 4 AT BRO OCT 1

NY	110	102	000	5	9	0
BRO	001	330	10X	8	14	0

Pitchers: LARSEN, Kucks (5), R.Coleman (6), Morgan (7), Sturdivant (8) VS Erskine, Bessent (4), LABINE (5)
Home Runs: McDougald-NY, Campanella-BRO, Hodges-BRO, Snider-BRO
Attendance: 36,242

GAME 5 AT BRO OCT 2

NY	000	100	110	3	6	0
BRO	021	010	01X	5	9	2

Pitchers: GRIM, Turley (7) vs CRAIG, Labine (7)
Home Runs: Cerv-NY, Berra-NY, Amoros-BRO, Snider-BRO (2)
Attendance: 36,796

GAME 6 AT NY OCT 3

BRO	000	100	000	1	4	1
NY	500	000	00X	5	8	0

Pitchers: SPOONER, Meyer (1), Roebuck (7) vs FORD
Home Runs: Skowron-NY
Attendance: 64,022

GAME 7 AT NY OCT 4

BRO	000	101	000	2	5	0
NY	000	000	000	0	8	1

Pitchers: PODRES vs BYRNE, Grim (6), Turley (8)
Attendance: 62,465

The 1956 Series was a mirror image of 1955. With both teams repeaters as league champions, the Yankees this year followed Brooklyn's winning pattern of the previous Series: losing the first two games, winning the next three, then splitting the final pair.

Sal Maglie outlasted Yankee ace Whitey Ford in the opener. Maglie gave up nine hits and three runs (on homers by Mickey Mantle and Billy Martin), but struck out ten and took the win as Jackie Robinson and Gil Hodges contributed homers for four of Brooklyn's six runs. Dodger ace Don Newcombe was blown out by six Yankee runs (capped by Yogi Berra's grand slam) in the first two innings of Game Two. But Brooklyn came back with six unearned runs in their half of the second (three of them on Duke Snider's homer) and proceeded to run through seven Yankee pitchers for a 13–8 win and a two-game Series edge.

Whitey Ford tried again in Game Three, and this time held on for a complete-game 5–3 win, supported by Billy Martin's game-tying solo homer in the second and forty-year-old Enos Slaughter's go-ahead three-run shot in the sixth. Tom Sturdivant duplicated Ford's effectiveness and success the next day with a six-hit 6–2 win to even the Series.

Sal Maglie pitched Game Five for Brooklyn and improved on his winning performance of Game One, yielding only two runs and holding New York hitless until Mantle's two-out homer in the fourth inning. But no one was a match for Yankee pitcher Don Larsen that day. There was a close out on a deflected Dodger liner in the second inning, and center fielder Mantle made a fine running catch to prevent a hit in the fifth. But Larsen retired the rest routinely, and when Dale Mitchell fanned in the ninth Larsen had his perfect game—a feat still unique in World Series history.

Brooklyn reliever Clem Labine was started in Game Six against Yankee fastballer Bob Turley. No runner scored for either side until the last of the tenth inning when, with two out, Jackie Robinson lined a Turley pitch over the head of the left fielder, scoring Jim Gilliam from second and forcing New York into a seventh game.

The finale proved an anticlimactic disaster for Brooklyn. Once again Dodger starter Newcombe was driven out—this time by Yogi Berra's two two-run homers and Elston Howard's solo shot. By the time it was over, Bill Skowron had increased the Yankee run total to nine with a grand slam, and Yankee starter Johnny Kucks had shut Brooklyn out on three

singles. For New York it was world title number seventeen.

New York Yankees (AL), 4;
Brooklyn Dodgers (NL), 3

NY (A)

PLAYER/POS	AVG	G	AB	R	H	2B	3B	HR	RB	BB	SO	SB
Hank Bauer, of	.281	7	32	3	9	0	0	1	3	0	5	1
Yogi Berra, c	.360	7	25	5	9	2	0	3	10	4	1	0
Tommy Byrne, p-1	.000	2	1	0	0	0	0	0	0	0	0	0
Andy Carey, 3b	.158	7	19	2	3	0	0	0	0	1	6	0
Bob Cerv, ph	1.000	1	1	0	1	0	0	0	0	0	0	0
Gerry Coleman, 2b	.000	2	2	0	0	0	0	0	0	0	0	0
Joe Collins, 1b-5	.238	6	21	2	5	2	0	0	2	2	3	0
Whitey Ford, p	.000	2	4	0	0	0	0	0	0	0	3	0
Elston Howard, of	.400	5	5	1	2	1	0	1	1	0	0	0
Johnny Kucks, p	.000	3	3	0	0	0	0	0	0	0	1	0
Don Larsen, p	.333	2	3	1	1	0	0	0	1	0	1	0
Mickey Mantle, of	.250	7	24	6	6	1	0	3	4	6	5	1
Billy Martin, 2b-7,3b-1	.296	7	27	5	8	0	0	2	3	1	6	0
Maury Mc Dermott, p	1.000	1	1	0	1	0	0	0	0	0	0	0
Gil Mc Dougald, ss	.143	7	21	0	3	0	0	0	1	3	6	0
Tom Morgan, p	1.000	2	1	1	1	0	0	0	0	0	0	0
Norm Siebern, ph	.000	1	1	0	0	0	0	0	0	0	0	0
Bill Skowron, 1b-2	.100	3	10	1	1	0	0	1	4	0	3	0
Enos Slaughter, of	.350	6	20	6	7	0	0	1	4	4	0	0
Tom Sturdivant, p	.333	2	3	0	1	0	0	0	0	0	1	0
Bob Turley, p	.000	3	4	0	0	0	0	0	0	0	1	0
George Wilson, ph	.000	1	1	0	0	0	0	0	0	0	1	0
TOTAL	.253		229	33	58	6	0	12	33	21	43	2

PITCHER	W	L	ERA	G	GS	CG	SV	SHO	IP	H	ER	BB	SO
Tommy Byrne	0	0	0.00	1	0	0	0	0	0.1	0	0	0	1
Whitey Ford	1	1	5.25	2	2	1	0	0	12.0	14	7	2	8
Johnny Kucks	1	0	0.82	3	1	1	0	1	11.0	6	1	3	2
Don Larsen	1	0	0.00	2	2	1	0	1	10.2	1	0	4	7
Maury Mc Dermott	0	0	3.00	1	0	0	0	0	3.0	2	1	3	3
Tom Morgan	0	1	9.00	2	0	0	0	0	4.0	6	4	4	3
Tom Sturdivant	1	0	2.79	2	1	1	0	0	9.2	8	3	8	9
Bob Turley	0	1	0.82	3	1	1	0	0	11.0	4	1	8	14
TOTAL	4	3	2.48	16	7	5	0	2	61.2	42	17	32	47

BRO (N)

PLAYER/POS	AVG	G	AB	R	H	2B	3B	HR	RB	BB	SO	SB
Sandy Amoros, of	.053	6	19	1	1	0	0	0	1	2	4	0
Don Bessent, p	.500	2	2	0	1	0	0	0	1	1	1	0
Roy Campanella, c	.182	7	22	2	4	1	0	0	3	3	7	0
Gino Cimoli, of	.000	1	0	0	0	0	0	0	0	0	0	0
Roger Craig, p	.500	2	2	0	1	0	0	0	0	0	0	0
Don Drysdale, p	.000	1	0	0	0	0	0	0	0	0	0	0
Carl Erskine, p	.000	2	0	0	0	0	0	0	0	0	0	0
Carl Furillo, of	.240	7	25	2	6	2	0	0	1	2	3	0
Jim Gilliam, 2b-6,of-1	.083	7	24	2	2	0	0	0	2	7	3	1
Gil Hodges, 1b	.304	7	23	5	7	2	0	1	8	4	4	0
Ransom Jackson, ph	.000	3	3	0	0	0	0	0	0	0	2	0
Clem Labine, p	.250	2	4	0	1	1	0	0	0	0	2	0
Sal Maglie, p	.000	2	5	0	0	0	0	0	0	0	2	0
Dale Mitchell, ph	.000	4	4	0	0	0	0	0	0	0	1	0
Charlie Neal, 2b	.000	1	4	0	0	0	0	0	0	0	1	0
Don Newcombe, p	.000	2	1	0	0	0	0	0	0	0	0	0
Pee Wee Reese, ss	.222	7	27	3	6	0	1	0	2	2	6	0
Jackie Robinson, 3b	.250	7	24	5	6	1	0	1	2	5	2	0
Ed Roebuck, p	.000	3	0	0	0	0	0	0	0	0	0	0
Duke Snider, of	.304	7	23	5	7	1	0	1	4	6	8	0
Rube Walker, ph	.000	2	2	0	0	0	0	0	0	0	0	0
TOTAL	.195		215	25	42	8	1	3	24	32	47	1

PITCHER	W	L	ERA	G	GS	CG	SV	SHO	IP	H	ER	BB	SO
Don Bessent	1	0	1.80	2	0	0	0	0	10.0	8	2	3	5
Roger Craig	0	1	12.00	2	1	0	0	0	6.0	10	8	3	4
Don Drysdale	0	0	9.00	1	0	0	0	0	2.0	2	2	1	1
Carl Erskine	0	1	5.40	2	1	0	0	0	5.0	4	3	2	2
Clem Labine	1	0	0.00	2	1	1	0	1	12.0	8	0	3	7
Sal Maglie	1	1	2.65	2	2	2	0	0	17.0	14	5	6	15
Don Newcombe	0	1	21.21	2	2	0	0	0	4.2	11	11	3	4
Ed Roebuck	0	0	2.08	3	0	0	0	0	4.1	1	1	0	5
TOTAL	3	4	4.72	16	7	3	0	1	61.0	58	32	21	43

GAME 1 AT BRO OCT 3

NY	200	100	000	3	9	1
BRO	023	100	00X	6	9	0

Pitchers: FORD, Kucks (4), Morgan (6) vs MAGLIE
Home Runs: Mantle-NY, Robinson-BRO, Hodges-BRO, Martin-NY
Attendance: 34,479

GAME 2 AT BRO OCT 5

NY	150	100	001	8	12	2
BRO	061	220	02X	13	12	0

Pitchers: Larsen, Kucks (2), Byrne (2), Sturdivant (3), MORGAN (3), Turley (5), McDermott (6) vs Newcombe, Roebuck (2), BESSENT (3)
Home Runs: Berra-NY, Snider-BRO
Attendance: 36,217

GAME 3 AT NY OCT 6

BRO	010	001	100	3	8	1
NY	010	003	01X	5	8	1

Pitchers: CRAIG, Labine (7) vs FORD
Home Runs: Martin-NY, Slaughter-NY
Attendance: 73,977

GAME 4 AT NY OCT 7

BRO	000	100	001	2	6	0
NY	100	201	20X	6	7	2

Pitchers: ERSKINE, Roebuck (5), Drysdale (7) vs STURDIVANT
Home Runs: Mantle-NY, Bauer-NY
Attendance: 69,705

GAME 5 AT NY OCT 8

BRO	000	000	000	0	0	0
NY	000	101	00X	2	5	0

Pitchers: MAGLIE vs LARSEN
Home Runs: Mantle-NY
Attendance: 64,519

GAME 6 AT BRO OCT 9

NY	000	000	000	0	0	7	0
BRO	000	000	000	1	1	4	0

Pitchers: TURLEY vs LABINE
Attendance: 33,224

GAME 7 AT BRO OCT 10

NY	202	100	400	9	10	0
BRO	000	000	000	0	3	1

Pitchers: KUCKS vs NEWCOMBE, Bessent (4), Craig (7), Roebuck (7), Erskine (9)
Home Runs: Berra-NY (2), Howard-NY, Skowron-NY
Attendance: 33,782

Overall, the Yankees pitched better, hit oftener, and scored more runs than the Braves. But the Braves had Lew Burdette, and with him they won the Series.

The opener pitted the Braves' established great Warren Spahn against New York's emerging great Whitey Ford. Ford prevailed, with a five-hit 3–1 win as Spahn was chased in the sixth. Burdette, winner of 17 regular-season games, started Game Two against veteran Bobby Shantz, the American League ERA leader. After a scoreless first inning, both pitchers gave up a run in the second and another in the third. Two go-ahead runs in the top of the fourth ended the Braves' scoring, but they were enough, as Burdette blanked New York through the final six innings to even the Series. Before he was finished, Burdette would stretch his consecutive scoreless innings to 24.

The Yankees exploded in Game Three, in Milwaukee, running through six Brave pitchers for a 12–3 rout. Braves fans even ended up cheering Yankee second baseman Tony Kubek—a Milwaukee native—who opened the scoring with a solo homer in the first, scored again after singling in the fourth (on Mickey Mantle's home run), and concluded the Yankee scoring in the seventh with his second homer, with two aboard.

Warren Spahn carried a 4–1 Braves lead into the ninth inning of Game Four, but after retiring the first two batters in the ninth, he gave up singles to Yogi Berra and Gil McDougald, and a game-tying home run to Elston Howard. In the top of the tenth, Hank Bauer tripled in a go-ahead Yankee run, but Milwaukee's Johnny Logan doubled to tie it up in the last of the tenth, and Eddie Mathews homered to give Spahn a shaky victory.

Burdette faced Ford in Game Five. In the sixth inning the Braves put half their hits—three singles—back to back for a run. It was all they needed as Burdette spaced seven singles for the shutout. Back in New York the next day, all the scoring came on home runs. Each club hit a pair, but Berra's in the third was the only one with a man aboard. Brave blasts in the fifth (Frank Torre) and seventh (Hank Aaron) tied the score, but Bauer answered Aaron's homer in the last of the seventh with what proved the winning shot. Bob Turley, who yielded just four hits while fanning eight (the Series high) claimed the Yankee victory.

In the finale, Burdette, with only two days' rest, scattered four hits over the first eight innings as the Braves gave him a 5–0 lead. In

the bottom of the ninth, though, three Yankee singles loaded the bases with two out. But third baseman Eddie Mathews snared Bil Skowron's sharp grounder and stepped on the bag for a force out that preserved Burdette's second shutout and gave Milwaukee its first world championship.

Milwaukee Braves (NL), 4; New York Yankees (AL), 3

MIL (N)

PLAYER/POS	AVG	G	AB	R	H	2B	3B	HR	RB	BB	SO	SB
Hank Aaron, of	.393	7	28	5	11	0	1	3	7	1	6	0
Joe Adcock, 1b	.200	5	15	1	3	0	0	0	2	0	2	0
Bob Buhl, p	.000	2	1	0	0	0	0	0	0	0	1	0
Lew Burdette, p	.000	3	8	0	0	0	0	0	0	1	2	0
Gene Conley, p	.000	1	0	0	0	0	0	0	0	0	0	0
Wes Covington, of	.208	7	24	1	5	1	0	0	1	2	6	1
Del Crandall, c	.211	6	19	1	4	0	0	1	1	1	1	0
John De Merit, pr	.000	1	0	0	0	0	0	0	0	0	0	0
Bob Hazle, of	.154	4	13	2	2	0	0	0	0	1	2	0
Ernie Johnson, p	.000	3	1	0	0	0	0	0	0	0	1	0
Nippy Jones, ph	.000	3	2	0	0	0	0	0	0	0	0	0
Johnny Logan, ss	.185	7	27	5	5	1	0	1	2	3	6	0
Felix Mantilla, 2b-3	.000	4	10	1	0	0	0	0	0	1	1	0
Eddie Mathews, 3b	.227	7	22	4	5	3	0	1	4	8	5	0
Don Mc Mahon, p	.000	3	0	0	0	0	0	0	0	0	0	0
Andy Pafko, of-5	.214	6	14	1	3	0	0	0	0	0	1	0
Juan Pizarro, p	.000	2	1	0	0	0	0	0	0	0	0	0
Del Rice, c	.167	2	6	0	1	0	0	0	0	1	2	0
Carl Sawatski, ph	.000	2	2	0	0	0	0	0	0	0	2	0
Red Schoendienst, 2b	.278	5	18	0	5	1	0	0	2	0	1	0
Warren Spahn, p	.000	2	4	0	0	0	0	0	0	0	1	2	0
Frank Torre, 1b	.300	7	10	2	3	0	0	2	3	2	0	0
Bob Trowbridge, p	.000	1	0	0	0	0	0	0	0	0	0	0
TOTAL	.209		225	23	47	6	1	8	22	22	40	1

PITCHER	W	L	ERA	G	GS	CG	SV	SHO	IP	H	ER	BB	SO
Bob Buhl	0	1	10.80	2	2	0	0	0	3.1	6	4	6	4
Lew Burdette	3	0	0.67	3	3	3	0	2	27.0	21	2	4	13
Gene Conley	0	0	10.80	1	0	0	0	0	1.2	2	2	1	0
Ernie Johnson	0	1	1.29	3	0	0	0	0	7.0	2	1	1	8
Don Mc Mahon	0	0	0.00	3	0	0	0	0	5.0	3	0	3	5
Juan Pizarro	0	0	10.80	1	0	0	0	0	1.2	3	2	2	1
Warren Spahn	1	1	4.70	2	2	1	0	0	15.1	18	8	2	2
Bob Trowbridge	0	0	45.00	1	0	0	0	0	1.0	2	5	3	1
TOTAL	4	3	3.48	16	7	4	0	2	62.0	57	24	22	34

NY (A)

PLAYER/POS	AVG	G	AB	R	H	2B	3B	HR	RB	BB	SO	SB
Hank Bauer, of	.258	7	31	3	8	2	1	2	6	1	6	0
Yogi Berra, c	.320	7	25	5	8	1	0	1	2	4	0	0
Tommy Byrne, p	.500	2	2	0	1	0	0	0	0	0	1	0
Andy Carey, 3b	.286	2	7	0	2	1	0	0	1	1	0	0
Gerry Coleman, 2b	.364	7	22	2	8	2	0	0	2	3	1	0
Joe Collins, 1b-5	.000	6	5	0	0	0	0	0	0	0	3	0
Art Ditmar, p	.000	2	1	0	0	0	0	0	0	0	1	0
Whitey Ford, p	.000	2	5	0	0	0	0	0	0	0	1	0
Bob Grim, p	.000	2	0	0	0	0	0	0	0	0	0	0
Elston Howard, 1b-3	.273	6	11	2	3	0	0	1	3	1	3	0
Tony Kubek, of-5,3b-2	.286	7	28	4	8	0	0	2	4	0	4	0
Johnny Kucks, p	.000	1	0	0	0	0	0	0	0	0	0	0
Don Larsen, p	.000	2	2	1	0	0	0	0	0	0	2	0
Jerry Lumpe, 3b-3	.286	6	14	0	4	0	0	0	2	1	1	0
Mickey Mantle, of-5	.263	6	19	3	5	0	0	1	2	3	1	0
Gil Mc Dougald, ss	.250	7	24	3	6	0	0	0	2	3	3	1
Bobby Richardson, 2b-1	.000	2	0	0	0	0	0	0	0	0	0	0
Bobby Shantz, p	.000	3	1	0	0	0	0	0	0	0	0	0
Harry Simpson, 1b-4	.083	5	12	0	1	0	0	0	1	0	4	0
Bill Skowron, 1b	.000	5	4	0	0	0	0	0	0	0	0	0
Enos Slaughter, of	.250	5	12	2	3	1	0	0	3	2	0	0
Tom Sturdivant, p	.000	2	1	0	0	0	0	0	0	0	0	0
Bob Turley, p	.000	3	4	0	0	0	0	0	0	0	2	0
TOTAL	.248		230	25	57	7	1	7	25	22	34	4

PITCHER	W	L	ERA	G	GS	CG	SV	SHO	IP	H	ER	BB	SO
Tommy Byrne	0	0	5.40	2	0	0	0	0	3.1	1	2	2	1
Art Ditmar	0	0	0.00	2	0	0	0	0	6.0	2	0	0	2
Whitey Ford	1	1	1.13	2	2	1	0	0	16.0	11	2	5	7
Bob Grim	0	1	7.71	2	0	0	0	0	2.1	3	2	0	2
Johnny Kucks	0	0	0.00	1	0	0	0	0	0.2	1	0	1	1
Don Larsen	1	1	3.72	2	1	0	0	0	9.2	8	4	5	6
Bobby Shantz	0	1	4.05	3	1	0	0	0	6.2	8	3	2	7
Tom Sturdivant	0	0	6.00	2	1	0	0	0	6.0	6	4	1	2
Bob Turley	1	0	2.31	3	2	1	0	0	11.2	7	3	6	12
TOTAL	3	4	2.89	19	7	2	0	0	62.1	47	20	22	40

GAME 1 AT NY OCT 2

MIL	000	000	100		1	5	0
NY	000	012	00X		3	9	1

Pitchers: SPAHN, Johnson (6), McMahon (7) vs FORD
Attendance: 69,476

GAME 2 AT NY OCT 3

MIL	011	200	000		4	8	0
NY	011	000	000		2	7	2

Pitchers: BURDETTE vs SHANTZ, Ditmar (4), Grim (8)
Home Runs: Logan-MIL, Bauer-NY
Attendance: 65,202

GAME 3 AT MIL OCT 5

NY	302	200	500		12	9	0
MIL	010	020	000		3	8	1

Pitchers: Turley, LARSEN (2) vs BUHL, Pizarro (1), Conley (3), Johnson (5), Trowbridge (7), McMahon (8)
Home Runs: Kubek-NY (2), Mantle-NY, Aaron-MIL
Attendance: 45,804

GAME 4 AT MIL OCT 6

NY	100	000	003	1	5	11	0
MIL	000	400	000	3	7	7	0

Pitchers: Sturdivant, Shantz (5), Kucks (8), Byrne (8), GRIM (10) vs SPAHN
Home Runs: Aaron-MIL, Torre-MIL, Howard-NY, Mathews-MIL
Attendance: 45,804

GAME 5 AT MIL OCT 7

NY	000	000	000		0	7	0
MIL	000	001	00X		1	6	1

Pitchers: FORD, Turley (8) vs BURDETTE
Attendance: 45,811

GAME 6 AT NY OCT 9

MIL	000	010	100		2	4	0
NY	002	000	10X		3	7	0

Pitchers: Buhl, JOHNSON (3), McMahon (8) vs TURLEY
Home Runs: Berra-NY, Torre-MIL, Aaron-MIL, Bauer-NY
Attendance: 61,408

GAME 7 AT NY OCT 10

MIL	004	000	010		5	9	1
NY	000	000	000		0	7	3

Pitchers: BURDETTE vs LARSEN, Shantz (3), Ditmar (4), Sturdivant (6), Byrne (8)
Home Runs: Crandall-MIL
Attendance: 61,207

After four games, Milwaukee held a 3–1 Series advantage, but New York rebounded to take the final three games and avenge their loss to the Braves the year before. As in the previous series, Warren Spahn faced Whitey Ford in the opener. The durable Spahn emerged the victor when Bill Bruton singled home the Braves' winning run off reliever Ryne Duren in the last of the tenth. In Game Two, home runs by Bruton and pitcher Lew Burdette (for three runs) helped put the Braves ahead 7–1 in the first inning. Milwaukee scored off five Yankee hurlers in their eventual 13–5 win.

Don Larsen and Ryne Duren combined for a shutout in Game Three to give New York its first victory. Hank Bauer drove in all four Yankee runs with a two-run single in the fifth and his third home run in three games in the seventh. Warren Spahn held Bauer hitless in Game Four, blanking New York on two hits to defeat Whitey Ford and bring Milwaukee within a win of the championship.

Yankee Bob Turley came up with a shutout of his own the next day, though, fanning ten men along the way. Gil McDougald's solo homer in the third inning was all the offense Turley needed, but as insurance the Yankees bunched six of their ten hits into the sixth inning for six more runs.

Spahn and Ford, with only two days' rest, confronted each other a third time in Game Six. Ford lasted less than two innings, but Spahn (despite Hank Bauer's fourth Series home run in the first inning) endured into extra innings, when McDougald put New York ahead with a leadoff homer in the tenth. Two outs and two hits later, Spahn was removed, and Bill Skowron's single off reliever Don McMahon drove home another Yankee run. Milwaukee scored once in the last of the tenth and threatened further damage with men on first and third. But Bob Turley came on to retire the final batter and send the Series to a seventh game.

In the sixth inning of the finale, the Braves' Del Crandall homered against Turley (who had relieved Don Larsen in the third) to tie the game 2–2. But four Yankee runs off starter Lew Burdette in the top of the eighth (including Skowron's three-run homer) made the score 6–2, where it remained, as Turley held on to bring Casey Stengel his seventh (and last) Series triumph—and the Yankees their eighteenth.

New York Yankees (AL), 4; Milwaukee Braves (NL), 3

NY (A)

PLAYER/POS	AVG	G	AB	R	H	2B	3B	HR	RB	BB	SO	SB
Hank Bauer, of	.323	7	31	6	10	0	0	4	8	0	5	0
Yogi Berra, c	.222	7	27	3	6	3	0	0	2	1	0	0
Andy Carey, 3b	.083	5	12	1	1	0	0	0	0	0	3	0
Murry Dickson, p	.000	2	0	0	0	0	0	0	0	0	0	0
Art Ditmar, p	.000	1	1	0	0	0	0	0	0	0	0	0
Ryne Duren, p	.000	3	3	0	0	0	0	0	0	0	2	0
Whitey Ford, p	.000	3	4	1	0	0	0	0	0	0	2	0
Elston Howard, of	.222	6	18	4	4	0	0	0	2	1	4	1
Tony Kubek, ss	.048	7	21	0	1	0	0	0	1	1	7	0
Johnny Kucks, p	1.000	2	1	0	1	0	0	0	0	0	0	0
Don Larsen, p	.000	2	2	0	0	0	0	0	0	0	1	0
Jerry Lumpe, 3b-3,ss-2	.167	6	12	0	2	0	0	0	0	0	1	2
Duke Maas, p	.000	1	0	0	0	0	0	0	0	0	0	0
Mickey Mantle, of	.250	7	24	4	6	0	1	2	3	7	4	0
Gil Mc Dougald, 2b	.321	7	28	5	9	2	0	2	4	2	4	0
Zach Monroe, p	.000	1	0	0	0	0	0	0	0	0	0	0
Bobby Richardson, 3b	.000	4	5	0	0	0	0	0	0	0	0	0
Norm Siebern, of	.125	3	8	1	1	0	0	0	0	0	3	0
Bill Skowron, 1b	.259	7	27	3	7	0	0	2	7	1	4	0
Enos Slaughter, ph	.000	4	3	1	0	0	0	0	0	0	1	0
Marv Throneberry, ph	.000	1	1	0	0	0	0	0	0	0	1	0
Bob Turley, p	.200	4	5	0	1	0	0	0	0	2	0	0
TOTAL	.210		233	29	49	5	1	10	29	21	42	1

PITCHER	W	L	ERA	G	GS	CG	SV	SHO	IP	H	ER	BB	SO
Murry Dickson	0	0	4.50	2	0	0	0	0	4.0	4	2	0	1
Art Ditmar	0	0	0.00	1	0	0	0	0	3.2	2	0	0	2
Ryne Duren	1	1	1.93	3	0	0	1	0	9.1	7	2	6	14
Whitey Ford	0	1	4.11	3	3	0	0	0	15.1	19	7	5	16
Johnny Kucks	0	0	2.08	2	0	0	0	0	4.1	4	1	1	0
Don Larsen	1	0	0.96	2	2	0	0	0	9.1	9	1	6	9
Duke Maas	0	0	81.00	1	0	0	0	0	0.1	3	3	1	0
Zach Monroe	0	0	27.00	1	0	0	0	0	1.0	3	3	1	1
Bob Turley	2	1	2.76	4	2	1	1	1	16.1	10	5	7	13
TOTAL	4	3	3.39	19	7	1	2	1	63.2	60	24	27	56

MIL (N)

PLAYER/POS	AVG	G	AB	R	H	2B	3B	HR	RB	BB	SO	SB
Hank Aaron, of	.333	7	27	3	9	2	0	0	2	4	6	0
Joe Adcock, 1b	.308	4	13	1	4	0	0	0	0	1	3	0
Billy Bruton, of	.412	7	17	2	7	0	0	1	2	5	5	0
Lew Burdette, p	.111	3	9	1	1	0	0	1	3	0	3	0
Wes Covington, of	.269	7	26	2	7	0	0	0	4	2	4	0
Del Crandall, c	.240	7	25	4	6	0	0	1	3	3	10	0
Harry Hanebrink, ph	.000	2	2	0	0	0	0	0	0	0	0	0
Johnny Logan, ss	.120	7	25	3	3	2	0	0	2	2	4	0
Felix Mantilla, ss-1	.000	4	0	1	0	0	0	0	0	0	0	0
Eddie Mathews, 3b	.160	7	25	3	4	2	0	0	3	6	11	1
Don Mc Mahon, p	.000	3	0	0	0	0	0	0	0	0	0	0
Andy Pafko, of	.333	4	9	0	3	1	0	0	1	0	0	0
Juan Pizarro, p	.000	1	0	0	0	0	0	0	0	0	0	0
Bob Rush, p	.000	1	2	0	0	0	0	0	0	0	2	0
Red Schoendienst, 2b	.300	7	30	5	9	3	1	0	0	2	1	0
Warren Spahn, p	.333	7	12	0	4	0	0	0	3	0	6	0
Frank Torre, 1b	.176	7	17	0	3	0	0	0	1	2	0	0
Carl Willey, p	.000	1	0	0	0	0	0	0	0	0	0	0
Casey Wise, ph	.000	2	1	0	0	0	0	0	0	0	1	0
TOTAL	.250		240	25	60	10	1	3	24	27	56	1

PITCHER	W	L	ERA	G	GS	CG	SV	SHO	IP	H	ER	BB	SO
Lew Burdette	1	2	5.64	3	3	1	0	0	22.1	22	14	4	12
Don Mc Mahon	0	0	5.40	3	0	0	0	0	3.1	3	2	3	5
Juan Pizarro	0	0	5.40	1	0	0	0	0	1.2	2	1	1	3
Bob Rush	0	1	3.00	1	1	0	0	0	6.0	3	2	5	2
Warren Spahn	2	1	2.20	3	3	2	0	1	28.2	19	7	8	18
Carl Willey	0	0	0.00	1	0	0	0	0	1.0	0	0	0	2
TOTAL	3	4	3.71	12	7	3	0	1	63.0	49	26	21	42

GAME 1 AT MIL OCT 1

NY	000 120 000 0	3	8 1
MIL	000 200 010 1	4	10 0

Pitchers: Ford, DUREN (8) vs SPAHN
Home Runs: Skowron-NY, Bauer-NY
Attendance: 46,367

GAME 2 AT MIL OCT 2

NY	100 100 003	5	7 0
MIL	710 000 23X	13	15 1

Pitchers: TURLEY, Maas (1), Kucks (1), Dickson (5), Monroe (8) vs BURDETTE
Home Runs: Bruton-MIL, Burdette-MIL, Mantle-NY (2), Bauer-NY
Attendance: 46,367

GAME 3 AT NY OCT 4

MIL	000 000 000	0	6 0
NY	000 020 20X	4	4 0

Pitchers: RUSH, McMahon (7) vs LARSEN, Duren (8)
Home Runs: Bauer-NY
Attendance: 71,599

GAME 4 AT NY OCT 5

MIL	000 001 110	3	9 0
NY	000 000 000	0	2 1

Pitchers: SPAHN vs FORD, Kucks (8), Dickson (9)
Attendance: 71,563

GAME 5 AT NY OCT 6

MIL	000 000 000	0	5 0
NY	001 006 00X	7	10 0

Pitchers: BURDETTE, Pizarro (6), Willey (8) vs TURLEY
Home Runs: McDougald-NY
Attendance: 65,279

GAME 6 AT MIL OCT 8

NY	100 001 000 2	4	10 1
MIL	110 000 001	3	10 4

Pitchers: Ford, Ditmar (2), DUREN (6), Turley (10) vs SPAHN, McMahon (10)
Home Runs: Bauer-NY, McDougald-NY
Attendance: 46,367

GAME 7 AT MIL OCT 9

NY	020 000 040	6	8 0
MIL	100 001 000	2	5 2

Pitchers: Larsen, TURLEY (3) vs BURDETTE, McMahon (8)
Home Runs: Crandall-MIL, Skowron-NY
Attendance: 46,367

It took a nosedive from first to third by San Francisco and a Dodger playoff victory over Milwaukee (who had finished the season tied with the Dodgers), to bring Los Angeles the city's first major league pennant. But once they had made it to the Series, the Dodgers dispatched the White Sox in six games.

The opener, though, belonged to Chicago. In their first World Series in forty years, the White Sox overwhelmed Los Angeles with 11 runs in the first four innings as pitchers Early Wynn and Gerry Staley combined to blank the Dodgers. Chicago's big gun was veteran slugger Ted Kluszewski (acquired from Pittsburgh in late August), whose single and two homers drove in five runs. Chicago scored twice in the first inning the next day, but Dodger starter Johnny Podres settled down to blank the Sox over the next five innings as home runs by Charlie Neal in the fifth and pinch hitter Chuck Essegian and Neal (again) in the seventh put the Dodgers ahead by two. Rookie reliever Larry Sherry gave up a third Chicago run in the eighth on Al Smith's double, but a second runner was nailed at the plate, and Sherry set down the side in the ninth to save Podres's win.

When the Series moved to Los Angeles' cavernous Coliseum for the West Coast's first World Series games ever, fans turned out in record numbers, setting a new Series mark in each of the next three games. Dodger starter Don Drysdale yielded 11 hits and four walks in Game Three, but the only run scored against him came on a double-play after Larry Sherry had relieved him with two men on in the eighth. As Los Angeles had already scored twice, and added a third run in their half of the eighth, Drysdale emerged with the win and Sherry with his second save. In Game Four, the Sox's Sherm Lollar's three-run homer had tied the score by the time Sherry relieved Dodger starter Roger Craig in the eighth, so Gil Hodges's solo homer in the last of the eighth gave Sherry the win this time—and Los Angeles a 3–1 Series advantage.

Chicago's Bob Shaw dueled Dodger Sandy Koufax through seven innings of Game Five before 92,706 spectators (still a Series high). The Sox scored only once off Koufax, but one run was enough for their second win as a pair of Sox relievers continued Shaw's shutout through the final two innings.

Back in Chicago for Game Six, the Dodgers unloaded on Early Wynn and Dick Donovan for eight runs in the third and fourth innings. Ted Kluszewski's three-run

Los Angeles Dodgers (NL), 4; Chicago White Sox (AL), 2

LA (N)

PLAYER/POS	AVG	G	AB	R	H	2B	3B	HR	RB	BB	SO	SB
Chuck Churn, p	.000	1	0	0	0	0	0	0	0	0	0	0
Roger Craig, p	.000	2	3	0	0	0	0	0	0	0	2	0
Don Demeter, of	.250	6	12	2	3	0	0	0	0	1	3	0
Don Drysdale, p	.000	1	2	0	0	0	0	0	0	0	2	0
Chuck Essegian, ph	.667	4	3	2	2	0	0	2	2	1	1	0
Ron Fairly, of-4	.000	6	3	0	0	0	0	0	0	0	1	0
Carl Furillo, of-1	.250	4	4	0	1	0	0	0	0	2	1	0
Jim Gilliam, 3b	.240	6	25	2	6	0	0	0	0	2	2	2
Gil Hodges, 1b	.391	6	23	2	9	0	1	1	2	1	2	0
Johnny Klippstein, p	.000	1	0	0	0	0	0	0	0	0	0	0
Sandy Koufax, p	.000	2	2	0	0	0	0	0	0	0	1	0
Clem Labine, p	.000	1	0	0	0	0	0	0	0	0	0	0
Norm Larker, of	.188	6	16	2	3	0	0	0	0	2	3	0
Wally Moon, of	.261	6	23	3	6	0	0	1	2	2	2	1
Charlie Neal, 2b	.370	6	27	4	10	2	0	2	6	0	1	0
Joe Pignatano, c	.000	1	0	0	0	0	0	0	0	0	0	0
Johnny Podres, p-2	.500	3	4	1	2	1	0	0	1	0	0	0
Rip Repulski, of	.000	1	0	0	0	0	0	0	0	1	0	0
Johnny Roseboro, c	.095	6	21	0	2	0	0	0	1	0	2	0
Larry Sherry, p-4	.500	5	4	0	2	0	0	0	0	0	1	0
Duke Snider, of-3	.200	4	10	1	2	0	0	1	2	2	0	0
Stan Williams, p	.000	1	0	0	0	0	0	0	0	0	0	0
Maury Wills, ss	.250	6	20	2	5	0	0	0	0	1	3	1
Don Zimmer, ss	.000	1	1	0	0	0	0	0	0	0	0	0
TOTAL	.261		203	21	53	3	1	7	19	12	27	5

PITCHER	W	L	ERA	G	GS	CG	SV	SHO	IP	H	ER	BB	SO
Chuck Churn	0	0	27.00	1	0	0	0	0	0.2	5	2	0	0
Roger Craig	0	1	8.68	2	2	0	0	0	9.1	15	9	5	8
Don Drysdale	1	0	1.29	1	1	0	0	0	7.0	11	1	4	5
Johnny Klippstein	0	0	0.00	1	0	0	0	0	2.0	1	0	0	2
Sandy Koufax	0	1	1.00	2	1	0	0	0	9.0	5	1	1	7
Clem Labine	0	0	0.00	1	0	0	0	0	1.0	0	0	0	1
Johnny Podres	1	0	4.82	2	2	0	0	0	9.1	7	5	6	4
Larry Sherry	2	0	0.71	4	0	0	2	0	12.2	8	1	2	5
Stan Williams	0	0	0.00	1	0	0	0	0	2.0	0	0	2	1
TOTAL	4	2	3.23	15	6	0	2	0	53.0	52	19	20	33

CHI (A)

PLAYER/POS	AVG	G	AB	R	H	2B	3B	HR	RB	BB	SO	SB
Luis Aparicio, ss	.308	6	26	1	8	1	0	0	0	2	3	1
Norm Cash, ph	.000	4	4	0	0	0	0	0	0	0	2	0
Dick Donovan, p	.333	3	3	0	1	0	0	0	0	0	1	0
Sammy Esposito, 3b	.000	2	2	0	0	0	0	0	0	0	0	0
Nellie Fox, 2b	.375	6	24	4	9	3	0	0	4	4	1	0
Billy Goodman, 3b	.231	5	13	1	3	0	0	0	1	0	5	0
Ted Kluszewski, 1b	.391	6	23	5	9	1	0	3	10	2	0	0
Jim Landis, of	.292	6	24	6	7	0	0	0	1	1	7	1
Sherm Lollar, c	.227	6	22	3	5	0	0	1	5	1	3	0
Turk Lown, p	.000	3	0	0	0	0	0	0	0	0	0	0
Jim Mc Anany, of	.000	3	5	0	0	0	0	0	0	1	0	0
Ray Moore, p	.000	1	0	0	0	0	0	0	0	0	0	0
Bubba Phillips, 3b-3,of-1	.300	3	10	0	3	1	0	0	0	0	0	0
Billy Pierce, p	.000	3	0	0	0	0	0	0	0	0	0	0
Jim Rivera, of	.000	5	11	1	0	0	0	0	0	3	1	0
Johnny Romano, ph	.000	2	1	0	0	0	0	0	0	0	2	0
Bob Shaw, p	.250	2	4	0	1	0	0	0	0	0	2	0
Al Smith, of	.250	6	20	1	5	3	0	0	1	4	4	0
Gerry Staley, p	.000	4	1	0	0	0	0	0	0	1	1	0
Earl Torgeson, 1b-1	.000	3	1	1	0	0	0	0	0	1	0	0
Early Wynn, p	.200	3	5	0	1	0	0	0	1	0	2	0
TOTAL	.261		199	23	52	10	0	4	19	20	33	2

PITCHER	W	L	ERA	G	GS	CG	SV	SHO	IP	H	ER	BB	SO
Dick Donovan	0	1	5.40	3	1	0	1	0	8.1	4	5	3	5
Turk Lown	0	0	0.00	3	0	0	0	0	3.1	2	0	1	3
Ray Moore	0	0	9.00	1	0	0	0	0	1.0	1	1	0	1
Billy Pierce	0	0	0.00	3	0	0	0	0	4.0	2	0	2	3
Bob Shaw	1	1	2.57	2	2	0	0	0	14.0	17	4	2	2
Gerry Staley	0	1	2.16	4	0	0	1	0	8.1	8	2	0	3
Early Wynn	1	1	5.54	3	3	0	0	0	13.0	19	8	4	10
TOTAL	2	4	3.46	19	6	0	2	0	52.0	53	20	12	27

homer in the last of the fourth led to Larry Sherry's fourth relief appearance—and his second Series win, as he held the Sox scoreless the rest of the game to bring the world championship to the West Coast for the first time.

GAME 1 AT CHI OCT 1

| LA | 000 000 000 | 0 8 3 |
| CHI | 207 200 00X | 11 11 0 |

Pitchers: CRAIG, Churn (3), Labine (4), Koufax (5), Klippstein (7) vs WYNN, Staley (8)
Home Runs: Kluszewski-CHI (2)
Attendance: 48,013

GAME 2 AT CHI OCT 2

| LA | 000 010 300 | 4 9 1 |
| CHI | 200 000 010 | 3 8 0 |

Pitchers: PODRES, Sherry (7) vs SHAW, Lown (7)
Home Runs: Neal-LA (2), Essegian-LA
Attendance: 47,368

GAME 3 AT LA OCT 4

| CHI | 000 000 010 | 1 12 0 |
| LA | 000 000 21X | 3 5 0 |

Pitchers: DONOVAN, Staley (7) vs DRYSDALE, Sherry (8)
Attendance: 92,394

GAME 4 AT LA OCT 5

| CHI | 000 000 400 | 4 10 3 |
| LA | 004 000 01X | 5 9 0 |

Pitchers: Wynn, Lown (3), Pierce (4), STALEY (7) vs Craig, SHERRY (8)
Home Runs: Lollar-CHI, Hodges-LA
Attendance: 92,650

GAME 5 AT LA OCT 6

| CHI | 000 100 000 | 1 5 0 |
| LA | 000 000 000 | 0 9 0 |

Pitchers: SHAW, Pierce (7), Donovan (8) VS KOUFAX, Williams (8)
Attendance: 92,706

GAME 6 AT CHI OCT 8

| LA | 002 600 001 | 9 13 0 |
| CHI | 000 300 000 | 3 6 1 |

Pitchers: Podres, SHERRY (4) vs WYNN, Donovan (4), Staley (5), Pierce (8), Moore (9)
Home Runs: Snider-LA, Moon-LA, Kluszewski-CHI, Essegian-LA
Attendance: 47,653

Through six games and 8½ innings of the seventh, the Yankees had outscored the Pirates by 29 runs. But as Pirate second baseman Bill Mazeroski stepped to the plate to open the last of the ninth, the Series was even at three games apiece, and Game Seven was tied 9–9. The stage was set for Mazeroski to fulfill that ultimate baseball fantasy, and he did, on pitcher Ralph Terry's second pitch.

Yankee Roger Maris opened the Series scoring with a solo homer in the first inning of Game One, and Elston Howard added two more Yankee runs with a homer in the ninth. But between the home runs New York scored only one run to the Pirates' six (including a two-run homer by Mazeroski in the fourth).

The Yankees avenged their first-game loss with a blowout in Game Two—their first of three. Pittsburgh hit safely 13 times, but scored only three runs. New York, though, turned 19 hits (and a Pirate error) into 16 runs—five of them driven in by Mickey Mantle's two home runs. Continuing their assault in New York the next day, the Bronx Bombers scored six runs in the first inning and four in the fourth as Whitey Ford blanked the Pirates on four hits. Mantle homered again, and second baseman Bobby Richardson drove in a Series single-game record six runs with a grand slam and a single.

Pirate ace Vernon Law—the winner of Game One—started Game Four and, with relief help once again from Roy Face, held the Yankees to two runs to even the Series. Law's bat proved crucial, too, as he doubled in Pittsburgh's first run and scored the third in a three-run fifth that provided all the Pirate scoring. In Game Five, the Pirates' Mazeroski doubled in what proved the two decisive runs in a three-run second as Harvey Haddix and Roy Face (who recorded his third save of the Series) duplicated the previous day's achievement of limiting New York to two runs.

But once again the Yankees came back. Bobby Richardson drove in three of New York's 12 runs with two triples to establish a new Series record of 12 RBIs as the Yankees, behind Whitey Ford's second shutout, sent the Series into a seventh game.

Home runs dominated the finale. Rocky Nelson's two-run shot in the first opened the scoring, and Yankee homers by Bill Skowron in the fifth and Yogi Berra in the sixth contributed four of the five runs that put New York ahead 5–4. Pirate Hal Smith's three-run homer in the bottom of the eighth restored the lead to Pittsburgh,

9–7, and after the Yankees had tied the game in the top of the ninth (on three singles and a ground out), Mazeroski's immortal shot over the wall in left gave Pittsburgh its first world championship in thirty-five years.

Pittsburgh Pirates (NL), 4; New York Yankees (AL), 3

PIT (N)

PLAYER/POS	AVG	G	AB	R	H	2B	3B	HR	RB	BB	SO	SB
Gene Baker, ph	.000	3	3	0	0	0	0	0	0	0	1	0
Smoky Burgess, c	.333	5	18	2	6	1	0	0	0	2	1	0
Tom Cheney, p	.000	3	0	0	0	0	0	0	0	0	0	0
Joe Christopher, ph	.000	3	0	2	0	0	0	0	0	0	0	0
Gino Cimoli, of-6	.250	7	20	4	5	0	0	0	1	2	4	0
Roberto Clemente, of	.310	7	29	1	9	0	0	0	3	0	4	0
Roy Face, p	.000	4	3	0	0	0	0	0	0	0	0	0
Bob Friend, p	.000	3	1	0	0	0	0	0	0	0	0	0
Joe Gibbon, p	.000	2	0	0	0	0	0	0	0	0	0	0
Fred Green, p	.000	3	1	0	0	0	0	0	0	0	0	0
Dick Groat, ss	.214	7	28	3	6	2	0	0	2	0	1	0
Harvey Haddix, p	.333	2	3	0	1	0	0	0	0	0	1	0
Don Hoak, 3b	.217	7	23	3	5	2	0	0	3	4	1	0
Clem Labine, p	.000	5	0	0	0	0	0	0	0	0	0	0
Vern Law, p	.333	3	6	1	2	1	0	0	1	0	1	0
Bill Mazeroski, 2b	.320	7	25	4	8	2	0	2	5	0	3	0
Vinegar Bend Mizell, p	.000	2	0	0	0	0	0	0	0	0	0	0
Rocky Nelson, 1b-3	.333	4	9	2	3	0	0	1	2	1	1	0
Bob Oldis, c	.000	2	0	0	0	0	0	0	0	0	0	0
Dick Schofield, ss-2	.333	3	3	0	1	0	0	0	0	1	0	0
Bob Skinner, of	.200	2	5	2	1	0	0	0	1	1	0	1
Hal Smith, c	.375	3	8	1	3	0	0	1	3	0	0	0
Dick Stuart, 1b	.150	5	20	0	3	0	0	0	0	0	3	0
Bill Virdon, of	.241	7	29	2	7	3	0	0	5	1	3	1
George Witt, p	.000	3	0	0	0	0	0	0	0	0	0	0
TOTAL	.256		234	27	60	11	0	4	26	12	26	2

PITCHER	W	L	ERA	G	GS	CG	SV	SHO	IP	H	ER	BB	SO
Tom Cheney	0	0	4.50	3	0	0	0	0	4.0	4	2	1	6
Roy Face	0	0	5.23	4	0	0	3	0	10.1	9	6	2	4
Bob Friend	0	2	13.50	3	2	0	0	0	6.0	13	9	3	7
Joe Gibbon	0	0	9.00	2	0	0	0	0	3.0	4	3	1	2
Fred Green	0	0	22.50	3	0	0	0	0	4.0	11	10	1	3
Harvey Haddix	2	0	2.45	2	1	0	0	0	7.1	6	2	2	6
Clem Labine	0	0	13.50	4	0	0	0	0	4.0	13	6	1	2
Vern Law	2	0	3.44	3	3	0	0	0	18.1	22	7	3	8
Vinegar Bend Mizell	0	1	15.43	2	1	0	0	0	2.1	4	4	2	1
George Witt	0	0	0.00	3	0	0	0	0	2.2	5	0	2	1
TOTAL	4	3	7.11	28	7	0	3	0	62.0	91	49	18	40

NY (A)

PLAYER/POS	AVG	G	AB	R	H	2B	3B	HR	RB	BB	SO	SB
Luis Arroyo, p	.000	1	1	0	0	0	0	0	0	0	0	0
Yogi Berra, of-4,c-3	.318	7	22	6	7	0	0	1	8	2	0	0
Johnny Blanchard, c-2	.455	5	11	2	5	2	0	0	2	0	0	0
Clete Boyer, 3b-4,ss-1	.250	4	12	1	3	2	1	0	1	0	1	0
Bob Cerv, of-3	.357	4	14	1	5	0	0	0	1	0	3	0
Jim Coates, p	.000	3	1	0	0	0	0	0	0	0	1	0
Joe De Maestri, ss-3	.500	4	2	1	1	0	0	0	0	0	1	0
Art Ditmar, p	.000	2	0	0	0	0	0	0	0	0	0	0
Ryne Duren, p	.000	2	0	0	0	0	0	0	0	0	0	0
Whitey Ford, p	.250	2	8	1	2	0	0	0	2	0	2	0
Eli Grba, pr	.000	1	0	0	0	0	0	0	0	0	0	0
Elston Howard, c-4	.462	5	13	4	6	1	1	1	4	1	4	0
Tony Kubek, ss-7,of-2	.333	7	30	6	10	1	0	0	3	2	2	0
Dale Long, ph	.333	3	3	0	1	0	0	0	0	0	0	0
Hector Lopez, of-1	.429	3	7	0	3	0	0	0	0	0	0	0
Duke Maas, p	.000	1	0	0	0	0	0	0	0	0	0	0
Mickey Mantle, of	.400	7	25	8	10	1	0	3	11	8	9	0
Roger Maris, of	.267	7	30	6	8	1	0	2	2	2	4	0
Gil Mc Dougald, 3b	.278	6	18	4	5	1	0	0	2	2	3	0
Bobby Richardson, 2b	.367	7	30	8	11	2	2	1	12	1	1	0
Bobby Shantz, p	.333	3	3	0	1	0	0	0	0	0	0	0
Bill Skowron, 1b	.375	7	32	7	12	2	0	2	6	0	6	0
Bill Stafford, p	.000	2	1	0	0	0	0	0	0	0	1	0
Ralph Terry, p	.000	2	2	0	0	0	0	0	0	0	1	0
Bob Turley, p	.250	2	4	0	1	0	0	0	1	0	1	0
TOTAL	.338		269	55	91	13	4	10	54	18	40	0

PITCHER	W	L	ERA	G	GS	CG	SV	SHO	IP	H	ER	BB	SO
Luis Arroyo	0	0	13.50	1	0	0	0	0	0.2	2	1	0	1
Jim Coates	0	0	5.68	3	0	0	0	0	6.1	6	4	1	3
Art Ditmar	0	2	21.60	2	2	0	0	0	1.2	6	4	1	0
Ryne Duren	0	0	2.25	2	0	0	0	0	4.0	2	1	1	5
Whitey Ford	2	0	0.00	2	2	2	0	2	18.0	11	0	2	8
Duke Maas	0	0	4.50	1	0	0	0	0	2.0	2	1	0	1
Bobby Shantz	0	0	4.26	3	0	0	0	1	6.1	4	3	1	1
Bill Stafford	0	0	1.50	2	0	0	0	0	6.0	5	1	1	2
Ralph Terry	0	2	5.40	2	1	0	0	0	6.2	7	4	1	5
Bob Turley	1	0	4.82	2	2	0	0	0	9.1	15	5	4	0
TOTAL	3	4	3.54	20	7	2	1	2	61.0	60	24	12	26

Slugger Mickey Mantle sat out most of the Series with a thigh infection, but rookie manager Ralph Houk enjoyed an otherwise splendid finish to a splendid season as his Yankees mauled the Reds, 27 runs to 13. Yankee ace Whitey Ford, coming off one of his finest seasons (25–4), carried his mound mastery into the Series opener, holding Cincinnati to two singles and a walk as he hurled his third straight World Series shutout. New York recorded only six hits, but two of them were home runs by Elston Howard and Bill Skowron.

Gordy Coleman's two-run homer the next day in the top of the fourth inning broke Cincinnati's scoring drought and gave the Reds a 2–0 lead. Yogi Berra tied the score half an inning later with a two-run blast for New York, but that was all they would get. Red starter Joey Jay blanked the Yankees the rest of the way as his teammates put across four more runs to even the Series. Bob Purkey pitched for the Reds in Game Three and blanked New York on one hit through the first six innings, taking a 1–0 lead into the top of the seventh. A pair of Yankee singles sandwiched around a passed ball evened the score, but the Reds regained the lead with a run in the last of the seventh. But Yankee pinch hitter Johnny Blanchard homered to retie the game in the eighth and—while Yankee relief ace Luis Arroyo stopped the Reds through the final two innings—Roger Maris hit his sixty-second home run of the year to win the game and regain the Series lead for New York.

Cincinnati never again threatened. In Game Four, Whitey Ford held the Reds to four harmless singles until he was removed in the sixth because of an ankle injury. (In the third inning he passed Babe Ruth's World Series record of 29⅔ consecutive scoreless innings.) Reliever Jim Coates continued Ford's shutout as the Yankees scored seven runs for the decisive win. The fifth and final game also was no contest. Cincinnati did score five runs—three on Frank Robinson's third-inning home run and two on Wally Post's shot in the fifth. But the Yankees ran through eight Red pitchers, scoring 13 times. Seven of their 15 hits went for extra bases, including Johnny Blanchard's second home run of the Series, and a triple and homer by utility outfielder Hector Lopez.

New York Yankees (AL), 4; Cincinnati Reds (NL), 1

NY (A)

PLAYER/POS	AVG	G	AB	R	H	2B	3B	HR	RB	BB	SO	SB
Luis Arroyo, p	.000	2	0	0	0	0	0	0	0	0	0	0
Yogi Berra, of	.273	4	11	2	3	0	0	1	3	5	1	0
Johnny Blanchard, of-2	.400	4	10	4	4	1	0	2	3	2	0	0
Clete Boyer, 3b	.267	5	15	0	4	2	0	0	3	4	0	0
Jim Coates, p	.000	1	1	0	0	0	0	0	0	0	1	0
Buddy Daley, p	.000	2	1	0	0	0	0	0	0	1	0	0
Whitey Ford, p	.000	2	5	1	0	0	0	0	0	0	1	0
Billy Gardner, ph	.000	1	1	0	0	0	0	0	0	0	0	0
Elston Howard, c	.250	5	20	5	5	3	0	1	1	2	3	0
Tony Kubek, ss	.227	5	22	3	5	0	0	0	1	1	4	0
Hector Lopez, of-3	.333	4	9	3	3	0	1	1	7	2	3	0
Mickey Mantle, of	.167	2	6	0	1	0	0	0	0	0	2	0
Roger Maris, of	.105	5	19	4	2	1	0	1	2	4	6	0
Jack Reed, of	.000	3	0	0	0	0	0	0	0	0	0	0
Bobby Richardson, 2b	.391	5	23	2	9	1	0	0	0	0	0	1
Bill Skowron, 1b	.353	5	17	3	6	0	0	1	5	3	4	0
Bill Stafford, p	.000	1	2	0	0	0	0	0	0	0	0	0
Ralph Terry, p	.000	2	3	0	0	0	0	0	0	0	1	0
TOTAL	.255		165	27	42	8	1	7	26	24	25	1

PITCHER	W	L	ERA	G	GS	CG	SV	SHO	IP	H	ER	BB	SO
Luis Arroyo	1	0	2.25	2	0	0	0	0	4.0	4	1	2	3
Jim Coates	0	0	0.00	1	0	0	1	0	4.0	1	0	1	2
Buddy Daley	1	0	0.00	2	0	0	0	0	7.0	5	0	0	3
Whitey Ford	2	0	0.00	2	2	1	0	1	14.0	6	0	1	7
Bill Stafford	0	0	2.70	1	1	0	0	0	6.2	7	2	2	5
Ralph Terry	0	1	4.82	2	2	0	0	0	9.1	12	5	2	7
TOTAL	4	1	1.60	10	5	1	1	1	45.0	35	8	8	27

CIN (N)

PLAYER/POS	AVG	G	AB	R	H	2B	3B	HR	RB	BB	SO	SB
Gus Bell, ph	.000	3	3	0	0	0	0	0	0	0	0	0
Don Blasingame, 2b	.143	3	7	1	1	0	0	0	0	0	3	0
Jim Brosnan, p	.000	3	0	0	0	0	0	0	0	0	0	0
Leo Cardenas, ph	.333	3	3	0	1	1	0	0	0	0	1	0
Elio Chacon, 2b-3	.250	4	12	2	3	0	0	0	0	1	2	0
Gordie Coleman, 1b	.250	5	20	2	5	0	0	1	2	0	1	0
Johnny Edwards, c	.364	3	11	1	4	2	0	0	2	0	0	0
Gene Freese, 3b	.063	5	16	0	1	1	0	0	0	3	4	0
Dick Gernert, ph	.000	4	4	0	0	0	0	0	0	0	1	0
Bill Henry, p	.000	2	0	0	0	0	0	0	0	0	0	0
Ken Hunt, p	.000	1	0	0	0	0	0	0	0	0	0	0
Joey Jay, p	.000	2	4	0	0	0	0	0	0	0	2	0
Darrell Johnson, c	.500	2	4	0	2	0	0	0	0	0	0	0
Ken Johnson, p	.000	1	0	0	0	0	0	0	0	0	0	0
Sherman Jones, p	.000	1	0	0	0	0	0	0	0	0	0	0
Eddie Kasko, ss	.318	5	22	1	7	0	0	0	1	0	2	0
Jerry Lynch, ph	.000	4	3	0	0	0	0	0	0	1	1	0
Jim Maloney, p	.000	1	0	0	0	0	0	0	0	0	0	0
Jim O'Toole, p	.000	2	3	0	0	0	0	0	0	0	1	0
Vada Pinson, of	.091	5	22	0	2	1	0	0	0	0	1	0
Wally Post, of	.333	5	18	3	6	1	0	1	2	0	1	0
Bob Purkey, p	.000	2	3	0	0	0	0	0	0	0	3	0
Frank Robinson, of	.200	5	15	3	3	2	0	1	4	3	4	0
Jerry Zimmerman, c	.000	2	0	0	0	0	0	0	0	0	0	0
TOTAL	.206		170	13	35	8	0	3	11	8	27	0

PITCHER	W	L	ERA	G	GS	CG	SV	SHO	IP	H	ER	BB	SO
Jim Brosnan	0	0	7.50	3	0	0	0	0	6.0	9	5	4	5
Bill Henry	0	0	19.29	2	0	0	0	0	2.1	4	5	2	3
Ken Hunt	0	0	0.00	1	0	0	0	0	1.0	0	0	1	1
Joey Jay	1	1	5.59	2	2	1	0	0	9.2	8	6	6	6
Ken Johnson	0	0	0.00	1	0	0	0	0	0.2	0	0	0	0
Sherman Jones	0	0	0.00	1	0	0	0	0	0.2	0	0	0	0
Jim Maloney	0	0	27.00	1	0	0	0	0	0.2	4	2	1	1
Jim O'Toole	0	2	3.00	2	2	0	0	0	12.0	11	4	7	4
Bob Purkey	0	1	1.64	2	1	1	0	0	11.0	6	2	3	5
TOTAL	1	4	4.91	15	5	2	0	0	44.0	42	24	24	25

GAME 1 AT NY OCT 4

CIN	000	000	000	0	2	0
NY	000	101	00X	2	6	0

Pitchers: O'TOOLE, Brosnan (8) vs FORD
Home Runs: Howard-NY, Skowron-NY
Attendance: 62,397

GAME 2 AT NY OCT 5

CIN	000	211	020	6	9	0
NY	000	200	000	2	4	3

Pitchers: JAY vs TERRY, Arroyo (8)
Home Runs: Coleman-CIN, Berra-NY
Attendance: 63,083

GAME 3 AT CIN OCT 7

NY	000	000	111	3	6	1
CIN	001	000	100	2	8	0

Pitchers: Stafford, Daley (7), ARROYO (8) vs PURKEY
Home Runs: Blanchard-NY, Maris-NY
Attendance: 32,589

GAME 4 AT CIN OCT 8

NY	000	112	300	7	11	0
CIN	000	000	000	0	5	1

Pitchers: FORD, Coates (6) vs O'TOOLE, Brosnan (6), Henry (9)
Attendance: 32,589

GAME 5 AT CIN OCT 9

NY	510	502	000	13	15	1
CIN	003	020	000	5	11	3

Pitchers: Terry, DALEY (3) vs JAY, Maloney (1), K.Johnson (2), Henry (3), Jones (4), Purkey (5), Brosnan (7), Hunt (9)
Home Runs: Blanchard-NY, Robinson-CIN, Lopez-NY, Post-CIN
Attendance: 32,589

After edging Los Angeles for the pennant in a three-game playoff to break a regular-season tie, San Francisco battled to the final out of Game Seven before falling to New York in the World Series. The teams alternated wins throughout the Series. In the opener Roger Maris doubled two runs home for a quick Yankee lead. Whitey Ford gave up a run in the second (ending his record streak for consecutive scoreless World Series innings pitched at 33⅔) and a tying run an inning later. But he blanked the Giants after that, and won the game on Clete Boyer's homer in the seventh.

Giant Jack Sanford blanked the Yankees on three hits in Game Two, but in Game Three Yankee Bill Stafford restored the Series edge to New York with a four-hit 3–2 win (a shutout until Giant Ed Bailey's ninth-inning home run). Both clubs hit safely nine times in Game Four. But one of the Giants' hits was Chuck Hiller's tie-breaking grand slam in the seventh—more than enough for a Giant win and another Series tie. In Game Five Sanford brought a three-hit 2–2 tie into the last of the eighth. But after he had notched his tenth strikeout, two singles and Tom Tresh's home run drove him out and gave Yankee pitcher Ralph Terry all the margin he needed to avenge his second-game loss to Sanford, and put the Yankees ahead in the Series for the third time.

When play resumed in San Francisco after several days of rain, Billy Pierce held New York to just three hits. One was Roger Maris's solo homer in the fifth, but Pierce's Giants unloaded on Whitey Ford for five runs, driving Ford out and keeping Giant hopes alive.

The finale pitted Terry against Sanford for the third time. Both pitched effectively, but Terry carried a 1–0 lead into the last of the ninth. Pinch hitter Matty Alou led off with a bunt single, but Terry fanned the next two batters. Then Willie Mays doubled to right, but Roger Maris's slick fielding stopped Alou at third. As Terry faced Willie McCovey (who had homered off him in Game Two), he pondered the home run he had given up to Bill Mazeroski two years earlier to lose the 1960 World Series to Pittsburgh. McCovey lined Terry's third pitch toward right—but right at second baseman Bobby Richardson, who grabbed it for the Yankees' twentieth world title. It would be fifteen years before they saw another.

New York Yankees (AL), 4; San Francisco Giants (NL) 3

NY (A)

PLAYER/POS	AVG	G	AB	R	H	2B	3B	HR	RB	BB	SO	SB
Yogi Berra, c-1	.000	2	2	0	0	0	0	0	0	0	2	0
Johnny Blanchard, ph	.000	1	1	0	0	0	0	0	0	0	1	0
Clete Boyer, 3b	.318	7	22	2	7	1	0	1	4	1	3	0
Marshall Bridges, p	.000	2	0	0	0	0	0	0	0	0	0	0
Jim Coates, p	.000	2	0	0	0	0	0	0	0	0	0	0
Buddy Daley, p	.000	1	0	0	0	0	0	0	0	0	0	0
Whitey Ford, p	.000	3	7	0	0	0	0	0	0	1	3	0
Elston Howard, c	.143	6	21	1	3	1	0	0	1	1	4	0
Tony Kubek, ss	.276	7	29	2	8	1	0	0	1	1	3	0
Dale Long, 1b	.200	2	5	0	1	0	0	0	0	1	1	0
Hector Lopez, ph	.000	2	2	0	0	0	0	0	0	0	0	0
Mickey Mantle, of	.120	7	25	2	3	1	0	0	0	4	5	2
Roger Maris, of	.174	7	23	4	4	1	0	1	5	5	2	0
Bobby Richardson, 2b	.148	7	27	3	4	0	0	0	0	3	1	0
Bill Skowron, 1b	.222	6	18	1	4	0	1	0	1	1	5	0
Bill Stafford, p	.000	1	3	0	0	0	0	0	0	0	1	0
Ralph Terry, p	.125	3	8	0	1	0	0	0	0	1	6	0
Tom Tresh, of	.321	7	28	5	9	1	0	1	4	1	4	2
TOTAL	.199		221	20	44	6	1	3	17	21	39	4

PITCHER	W	L	ERA	G	GS	CG	SV	SHO	IP	H	ER	BB	SO
Marshall Bridges	0	0	4.91	2	0	0	0	0	3.2	4	2	2	3
Jim Coates	0	1	6.75	2	0	0	0	0	2.2	1	2	1	3
Buddy Daley	0	0	0.00	1	0	0	0	0	1.0	1	0	1	0
Whitey Ford	1	1	4.12	3	3	1	0	0	19.2	24	9	4	12
Bill Stafford	1	0	2.00	1	1	1	0	0	9.0	4	2	2	5
Ralph Terry	2	1	1.80	3	3	2	0	1	25.0	17	5	2	16
TOTAL	4	3	2.95	12	7	4	0	1	61.0	51	20	12	39

SF (N)

PLAYER/POS	AVG	G	AB	R	H	2B	3B	HR	RB	BB	SO	SB
Felipe Alou, of	.269	7	26	2	7	1	1	0	1	1	4	0
Matty Alou, of-4	.333	6	12	2	4	1	0	0	1	0	1	0
Ed Bailey, c-3	.071	6	14	1	1	0	0	1	2	0	3	0
Bobby Bolin, p	.000	2	0	0	0	0	0	0	0	0	0	0
Ernie Bowman, ss-1	.000	2	1	1	0	0	0	0	0	0	0	0
Orlando Cepeda, 1b	.158	5	19	1	3	1	0	0	2	0	4	0
Jim Davenport, 3b	.136	7	22	1	3	0	0	0	1	4	7	0
Tom Haller, c	.286	4	14	1	4	1	0	1	3	0	2	0
Chuck Hiller, 2b	.269	7	26	4	7	3	0	1	5	3	4	0
Harvey Kuenn, of	.083	4	12	1	1	0	0	0	0	1	1	0
Don Larsen, p	.000	3	0	0	0	0	0	0	0	0	0	0
Juan Marichal, p	.000	1	2	0	0	0	0	0	0	0	0	0
Willie Mays, of	.250	7	28	3	7	2	0	0	1	1	5	1
Willie Mc Covey, 1b-2,of-2	.200	4	15	2	3	0	1	1	1	1	3	0
Stu Miller, p	.000	2	0	0	0	0	0	0	0	0	0	0
Bob Nieman, ph	.000	1	0	0	0	0	0	0	0	1	0	0
Billy O'Dell, p	.333	3	3	0	1	0	0	0	0	0	0	0
John Orsino, c	.000	1	1	0	0	0	0	0	0	0	0	0
Jose Pagan, ss	.368	7	19	2	7	0	0	1	2	0	1	0
Billy Pierce, p	.000	2	5	0	0	0	0	0	0	0	1	0
Jack Sanford, p	.429	3	7	0	3	0	0	0	0	0	2	0
TOTAL	.226		226	21	51	10	2	5	19	12	39	1

PITCHER	W	L	ERA	G	GS	CG	SV	SHO	IP	H	ER	BB	SO
Bobby Bolin	0	0	6.75	2	0	0	0	0	2.2	4	2	2	2
Don Larsen	1	0	3.86	3	0	0	0	0	2.1	1	1	2	0
Juan Marichal	0	0	0.00	1	1	0	0	0	4.0	2	0	2	4
Stu Miller	0	0	0.00	2	0	0	0	0	1.1	1	0	2	0
Billy O'Dell	0	1	4.38	3	1	0	1	0	12.1	12	6	3	9
Billy Pierce	1	1	2.40	2	2	1	0	0	15.0	8	4	2	5
Jack Sanford	1	2	1.93	3	3	1	0	1	23.1	16	5	8	19
TOTAL	3	4	2.66	16	7	2	1	1	61.0	44	18	21	39

GAME 1 AT SF OCT 4

NY	200 000 121	6	11	0
SF	011 000 000	2	10	0

Pitchers: FORD vs O'DELL, Larsen (7), Miller (9)
Home Runs: Boyer-NY
Attendance: 43,852

GAME 2 AT SF OCT 5

NY	000 000 000	0	3	1
SF	100 000 10X	2	6	0

Pitchers: TERRY, Daley (8) vs SANFORD
Home Runs: McCovey-SF
Attendance: 43,910

GAME 3 AT NY OCT 7

SF	000 000 002	2	4	3
NY	000 000 30X	3	5	1

Pitchers: PIERCE, Larsen (7), Bolin (8) vs STAFFORD
Home Runs: Bailey-SF
Attendance: 71,434

GAME 4 AT NY OCT 8

SF	020 000 401	7	9	1
NY	000 002 001	3	9	1

Pitchers: Marichal, Bolin (5), LARSEN (6), O'Dell (7) vs Ford, COATES (7), Bridges (7)
Home Runs: Haller-SF, Hiller-SF
Attendance: 66,607

GAME 5 AT NY OCT 10

SF	001 010 001	3	8	2
NY	000 101 03X	5	6	0

Pitchers: SANFORD, Miller (8) vs TERRY
Home Runs: Pagan-SF, Tresh-NY
Attendance: 63,165

GAME 6 AT SF OCT 15

NY	000 010 010	2	3	2
SF	000 320 00X	5	10	1

Pitchers: FORD, Coates (5), Bridges (8) vs PIERCE
Home Runs: Maris-NY
Attendance: 43,948

GAME 7 AT SF OCT 16

NY	000 100 000	1	7	0
SF	000 000 000	0	4	1

Pitchers: TERRY vs SANFORD, O'Dell (8)
Attendance: 43,948

The Yankees won the American League pennant by 10½ games, but in the Series they were overwhelmed by Dodger pitching. The opener pitted two all-time greats against each other: Yankee Whitey Ford (24–7 that season) and Sandy Koufax (25–5). For an inning it was close. Ford fanned two of the first three batters to face him, and Koufax struck out the side. But in the top of the second the Dodgers' Frank Howard doubled with one out, and before Ford could record the second out, two singles and John Roseboro's home run had put four Dodger runs across. Koufax ran his consecutive Ks to five and had tied the Series single-game record of 14 by the time Tom Tresh tagged him for a two-run homer in the eighth. That was New York's only scoring, and Koufax ended the game with a new-record fifteenth strikeout an inning later.

Veteran Johnny Podres pitched shutout ball through 8⅓ innings of Game Two as his Dodgers built him a four-run lead (one of the runs a homer by ex-Yankee Bill Skowron). New York scored a run in the last of the ninth, but it was not enough to keep the Dodgers from returning to Los Angeles with a 2–0 Series advantage.

A first-inning walk, a wild pitch, and a single moved Dodger Jim Gilliam around the bases for the only scoring in Game Three as Yankee Jim Bouton hooked up in a duel with Don Drysdale. Bouton left after seven innings for Yankee relief ace Hal Reniff, who held Los Angeles hitless through the final frames. When Drysdale completed his shutout, only three singles had been hit against him, and he had struck out nine.

Ford and Koufax tangled again in the fourth game. Ford pitched much more impressively than he had in the opener, walking just one and yielding only two hits in seven innings. One of the Dodger hits was Frank Howard's solo homer in the fifth inning, but Mickey Mantle evened the score with a home run off Koufax in the seventh. But in the last of the seventh, Yankee first baseman Joe Pepitone lost sight of a throw from the third baseman for an error that sent batter Jim Gilliam all the way to third, and Willie Davis followed with a fly to center that scored Gilliam with the go-ahead run. No one else scored against Ford (or Reniff, who relieved him in the eighth), but no other Yankee scored against Koufax either, and the Dodgers, with just two hits, captured the game and the Series.

Los Angeles Dodgers (NL), 4; New York Yankees (AL), 0

LA (N)

PLAYER/POS	AVG	G	AB	R	H	2B	3B	HR	RB	BB	SO	SB
Tommy Davis, of	.400	4	15	0	6	0	2	0	2	0	2	1
Willie Davis, of	.167	4	12	2	2	2	0	0	3	0	6	0
Don Drysdale, p	.000	1	1	0	0	0	0	0	0	2	0	0
Ron Fairly, of	.000	4	1	0	0	0	0	0	0	3	0	0
Jim Gilliam, 3b	.154	4	13	3	2	0	0	0	0	3	1	0
Frank Howard, of	.300	3	10	2	3	1	0	1	1	0	2	0
Sandy Koufax, p	.000	2	6	0	0	0	0	0	0	0	2	0
Ron Perranoski, p	.000	1	0	0	0	0	0	0	0	0	0	0
Johnny Podres, p	.250	1	4	0	1	0	0	0	0	0	0	0
Johnny Roseboro, c	.143	4	14	1	2	0	0	1	3	0	4	0
Bill Skowron, 1b	.385	4	13	2	5	0	0	1	3	1	3	0
Dick Tracewski, 2b	.154	4	13	1	2	0	0	0	0	1	2	0
Maury Wills, ss	.133	4	15	1	2	0	0	0	0	1	3	1
TOTAL	.214		117	12	25	3	2	3	12	11	25	2

PITCHER	W	L	ERA	G	GS	CG	SV	SHO	IP	H	ER	BB	SO
Don Drysdale	1	0	0.00	1	1	1	0	1	9.0	3	0	1	9
Sandy Koufax	2	0	1.50	2	2	2	0	0	18.0	12	3	3	23
Ron Perranoski	0	0	0.00	1	0	0	1	0	0.2	1	0	0	1
Johnny Podres	1	0	1.08	1	1	0	0	0	8.1	6	1	1	4
TOTAL	4	0	1.00	5	4	3	1	1	36.0	22	4	5	37

NY (A)

PLAYER/POS	AVG	G	AB	R	H	2B	3B	HR	RB	BB	SO	SB
Yogi Berra, ph	.000	1	1	0	0	0	0	0	0	0	0	0
Johnny Blanchard, of-1	.000	1	3	0	0	0	0	0	0	0	0	0
Jim Bouton, p	.000	1	2	0	0	0	0	0	0	0	2	0
Clete Boyer, 3b	.077	4	13	0	1	0	0	0	0	1	6	0
Harry Bright, ph	.000	2	2	0	0	0	0	0	0	0	2	0
Al Downing, p	.000	1	1	0	0	0	0	0	0	0	1	0
Whitey Ford, p	.000	2	3	0	0	0	0	0	0	0	0	0
Steve Hamilton, p	.000	1	0	0	0	0	0	0	0	0	0	0
Elston Howard, c	.333	4	15	0	5	0	0	0	1	0	3	0
Tony Kubek, ss	.188	4	16	1	3	0	0	0	0	0	3	0
Phil Linz, ph	.333	3	3	0	1	0	0	0	0	0	1	0
Hector Lopez, of-2	.250	3	8	1	2	2	0	0	0	0	1	0
Mickey Mantle, of	.133	4	15	1	2	0	0	1	1	1	5	0
Roger Maris, of	.000	2	5	0	0	0	0	0	0	1	0	0
Joe Pepitone, 1b	.154	4	13	0	2	0	0	0	0	1	3	0
Hal Reniff, p	.000	3	0	0	0	0	0	0	0	0	0	0
Bobby Richardson, 2b	.214	4	14	0	3	1	0	0	0	1	3	0
Ralph Terry, p	.000	1	0	0	0	0	0	0	0	0	0	0
Tom Tresh, of	.200	4	15	1	3	0	0	1	2	1	6	0
Stan Williams, p	.000	1	0	0	0	0	0	0	0	0	0	0
TOTAL	.171		129	4	22	3	0	2	4	5	37	0

PITCHER	W	L	ERA	G	GS	CG	SV	SHO	IP	H	ER	BB	SO
Jim Bouton	0	1	1.29	1	1	0	0	0	7.0	4	1	5	4
Al Downing	0	1	5.40	1	1	0	0	0	5.0	7	3	1	6
Whitey Ford	0	2	4.50	2	2	0	0	0	12.0	10	6	3	8
Steve Hamilton	0	0	0.00	1	0	0	0	0	1.0	0	0	0	1
Hal Reniff	0	0	0.00	3	0	0	0	0	3.0	0	0	1	1
Ralph Terry	0	0	3.00	1	0	0	0	0	3.0	3	1	1	0
Stan Williams	0	0	0.00	1	0	0	0	0	3.0	1	0	0	5
TOTAL	0	4	2.91	10	4	0	0	0	34.0	25	11	11	25

GAME 1 AT NY OCT 2

LA	041	000	000	5	9	0
NY	000	000	020	2	6	0

Pitchers: KOUFAX vs FORD, Williams (6), Hamilton (9)
Home Runs: Roseboro-LA, Tresh-NY
Attendance: 69,000

GAME 2 AT NY OCT 3

LA	200	100	010	4	10	1
NY	000	000	001	1	7	0

Pitchers: PODRES, Perranoski (9) vs DOWNING, Terry (6), Reniff (9)
Home Runs: Skowron-LA
Attendance: 66,455

GAME 3 AT LA OCT 5

NY	000	000	000	0	3	0
LA	100	000	00X	1	4	1

Pitchers: BOUTON, Reniff (8) vs DRYSDALE
Attendance: 55,912

GAME 4 AT LA OCT 6

NY	000	000	100	1	6	1
LA	000	010	10X	2	2	1

Pitchers: FORD, Reniff (8) vs KOUFAX
Home Runs: F.Howard-LA, Mantle-NY
Attendance: 55,912

With late-season spurts the Cardinals edged the Reds and Phillies for their first pennant in eighteen years and the Yankees overtook the White Sox and Orioles for their fifteenth in eighteen years and their twenty-ninth over all. But when the Series was over, the long era of Yankee dominance had come to an end.

St. Louis won the opener, a 24-hit slugfest in which Curt Flood's RBI triple in the sixth proved the decisive blow. But New York came back to take the next two games. Rookie Mel Stottlemyre won Game Two, holding the Cards to three runs as his Yankees scored eight. (Loser Bob Gibson struck out nine Yankees, though, on his way to a new Series record of 31.) Game Three, by contrast, featured a pitchers' duel between Jim Bouton and Cardinal veteran Curt Simmons. Cardinal reliever Barney Schultz, who replaced Simmons for the last of the ninth with the score 1–1, lost the game on his first pitch when Mickey Mantle homered to deep right (his sixteenth World Series home run, which moved him ahead of Babe Ruth into the all-time Series lead).

Cardinal Ray Sadecki (the winner in Game One) left with one out in the first inning of Game Four after four Yankee batters hit safely, but relievers Roger Craig and Ron Taylor stopped New York on just two singles the rest of the way. The Cards were also held to six hits, but one was Ken Boyer's grand slam in the sixth, which erased a 3–0 Yankee lead and gave St. Louis runs enough to even the Series at two games apiece.

Gibson and Stottlemyre faced off a second time in Game Five. Gibson carried a 2–0 lead into the last of the ninth, when with two out Tom Tresh tagged him for a game-tying home run. In the top of the tenth, though, the Cards regained the lead on Tim McCarver's three-run homer and held on for the win as Gibson notched his thirteenth K of the game.

Bouton and Simmons tangled again in Game Five. Another 1–1 duel was shattered this time in the top of the sixth when Roger Maris and Mantle tagged Simmons for back-to-back home runs. New York put the game away in the eighth with five runs off Cardinal relievers—four of them on Joe Pepitone's grand slam.

With the series tied 3–3, Gibson and Stottlemyre were called upon to settle the title. Gibson pitched the whole game, striking out nine. Mantle touched him for a three-run homer in the sixth inning, and Clete Boyer and Phil Linz hit solo shots in the ninth.

St. Louis Cardinals (NL), 4; New York Yankees (AL), 3

STL (N)

PLAYER/POS	AVG	G	AB	R	H	2B	3B	HR	RB	BB	SO	SB
Ken Boyer, 3b	.222	7	27	5	6	1	0	2	6	1	5	0
Lou Brock, of	.300	7	30	2	9	2	0	1	5	0	3	0
Gerry Buchek, 2b	1.000	4	1	1	1	0	0	0	0	0	0	0
Roger Craig, p	.000	2	1	0	0	0	0	0	0	0	0	0
Curt Flood, of	.200	7	30	5	6	0	1	0	3	3	1	0
Bob Gibson, p	.222	3	9	1	2	0	0	0	0	0	3	0
Dick Groat, ss	.192	7	26	3	5	1	1	0	1	4	3	0
Bob Humphreys, p	.000	1	0	0	0	0	0	0	0	0	0	0
Charlie James, ph	.000	3	3	0	0	0	0	0	0	0	1	0
Julian Javier, 2b	.000	1	0	1	0	0	0	0	0	0	0	0
Dal Maxvill, 2b	.200	7	20	0	4	1	0	0	1	1	4	0
Tim McCarver, c	.478	7	23	4	11	1	1	1	5	5	1	1
Gordie Richardson, p	.000	2	0	0	0	0	0	0	0	0	0	0
Ray Sadecki, p	.500	2	2	0	1	0	0	0	1	0	1	0
Barney Schultz, p	.000	4	1	0	0	0	0	0	0	0	0	0
Mike Shannon, of	.214	7	28	6	6	0	0	1	2	0	9	1
Curt Simmons, p	.500	2	4	0	2	0	0	0	0	1	0	0
Bob Skinner, ph	.667	4	3	0	2	1	0	0	1	1	0	0
Ron Taylor, p	.000	2	1	0	0	0	0	0	0	0	1	0
Carl Warwick, ph	.750	5	4	2	3	0	0	0	1	1	0	0
Bill White, 1b	.111	7	27	2	3	1	0	0	2	2	6	1
TOTAL	.254		240	32	61	8	3	5	29	18	39	3

PITCHER	W	L	ERA	G	GS	CG	SV	SHO	IP	H	ER	BB	SO
Roger Craig	1	0	0.00	2	0	0	0	0	5.0	2	0	3	9
Bob Gibson	2	1	3.00	3	3	2	0	0	27.0	23	9	8	31
Bob Humphreys	0	0	0.00	1	0	0	0	0	1.0	0	0	0	1
Gordie Richardson	0	0	40.50	2	0	0	0	0	0.2	3	3	2	0
Ray Sadecki	1	0	8.53	2	2	0	0	0	6.1	12	6	5	2
Barney Schultz	0	1	18.00	4	0	0	1	0	4.0	9	8	3	1
Curt Simmons	0	1	2.51	2	2	0	0	0	14.1	11	4	3	8
Ron Taylor	0	0	0.00	2	0	0	1	0	4.2	0	0	1	2
TOTAL	4	3	4.29	18	7	2	2	0	63.0	60	30	25	54

NY (A)

PLAYER/POS	AVG	G	AB	R	H	2B	3B	HR	RB	BB	SO	SB
Johnny Blanchard, ph	.250	4	4	0	1	1	0	0	0	0	1	0
Jim Bouton, p	.143	2	7	0	1	0	0	0	1	0	2	0
Clete Boyer, 3b	.208	7	24	2	5	1	0	1	3	1	5	1
Al Downing, p	.000	3	2	0	0	0	0	0	0	0	2	0
Whitey Ford, p	1.000	1	1	0	1	0	0	0	1	2	0	0
Pedro Gonzalez, 3b	.000	1	1	0	0	0	0	0	0	0	0	0
Steve Hamilton, p	.000	2	0	0	0	0	0	0	0	0	0	0
Mike Hegan, ph	.000	3	1	1	0	0	0	0	0	1	1	0
Elston Howard, c	.292	7	24	5	7	1	0	0	2	4	6	0
Phil Linz, ss	.226	7	31	5	7	1	0	2	2	2	5	0
Hector Lopez, of-1	.000	3	2	0	0	0	0	0	0	0	2	0
Mickey Mantle, of	.333	7	24	8	8	2	0	3	8	6	8	0
Roger Maris, of	.200	7	30	4	6	0	0	1	1	1	4	0
Pete Mikkelsen, p	.000	4	0	0	0	0	0	0	0	0	0	0
Joe Pepitone, 1b	.154	7	26	1	4	1	0	1	5	2	3	0
Hal Reniff, p	.000	1	0	0	0	0	0	0	0	0	0	0
Bobby Richardson, 2b	.406	7	32	3	13	2	0	0	3	0	2	1
Rollie Sheldon, p	.000	2	0	0	0	0	0	0	0	0	0	0
Mel Stottlemyre, p	.125	3	8	0	1	0	0	0	0	0	6	0
Ralph Terry, p	.000	1	0	0	0	0	0	0	0	0	0	0
Tom Tresh, of	.273	7	22	4	6	2	0	2	7	6	7	0
TOTAL	.251		239	33	60	11	0	10	33	25	54	2

PITCHER	W	L	ERA	G	GS	CG	SV	SHO	IP	H	ER	BB	SO
Jim Bouton	2	0	1.56	2	2	1	0	0	17.1	15	3	5	7
Al Downing	0	1	8.22	3	1	0	0	0	7.2	9	7	2	5
Whitey Ford	0	1	8.44	1	1	0	0	0	5.1	8	5	1	4
Steve Hamilton	0	0	4.50	2	0	0	1	0	2.0	3	1	0	2
Pete Mikkelsen	0	1	5.79	4	0	0	0	0	4.2	4	3	2	4
Hal Reniff	0	0	0.00	1	0	0	0	0	0.1	2	0	0	0
Rollie Sheldon	0	0	0.00	2	0	0	0	0	2.2	0	0	2	2
Mel Stottlemyre	1	1	3.15	3	3	1	0	0	20.0	18	7	6	12
Ralph Terry	0	0	0.00	1	0	0	0	0	2.0	2	0	0	3
TOTAL	3	4	3.77	19	7	2	1	0	62.0	61	26	18	39

But as St. Louis had scored six times off Stottlemyre and his replacement Al Downing before the Yankees scored their first runs, the game ended with the Cards victors and world champions. Yogi Berra, New York's rookie manager, was fired the next day. The following season the Yankees finished sixth.

GAME 1 AT STL OCT 7

NY	030 010 010	5	12 2
STL	110 004 03X	9	12 0

Pitchers: FORD, Downing (6), Sheldon (8), Mikkelsen (9) vs SADECKI, Schultz (7)
Home Runs: Tresh-NY, Shannon-STL
Attendance: 30,805

GAME 2 AT STL OCT 8

NY	000 101 204	8	12 0
STL	001 000 011	3	7 0

Pitchers: STOTTLEMYRE vs GIBSON, Schultz (9), Craig (9)
Home Runs: Linz-NY
Attendance: 30,805

GAME 3 AT NY OCT 10

STL	000 010 000	1	6 0
NY	010 000 001	2	5 2

Pitchers: Simmons, SCHULTZ (9) vs BOUTON
Home Runs: Mantle-NY
Attendance: 67,101

GAME 4 AT NY OCT 11

STL	000 004 000	4	6 1
NY	300 000 000	3	6 1

Pitchers: Sadecki, CRAIG (1), Taylor (6) vs DOWNING, Mikkelsen (7), Terry (8)
Home Runs: K.Boyer-STL
Attendance: 66,312

GAME 5 AT NY OCT 12

STL	000 020 000 3	5	10 1
NY	000 000 002 0	2	6 2

Pitchers: GIBSON vs Stottlemyre, Reniff (8), MIKKELSEN (8)
Home Runs: Tresh-NY, McCarver-STL
Attendance: 65,633

GAME 6 AT STL OCT 14

NY	000 012 050	8	10 0
STL	100 000 011	3	10 1

Pitchers: BOUTON, Hamilton (9) VS SIMMONS, Taylor (7), Schultz (8), Richardson (9), Humphreys (9)
Home Runs: Maris-NY, Mantle-NY, Pepitone-NY
Attendance: 30,805

GAME 7 AT STL OCT 15

NY	000 003 002	5	9 2
STL	000 330 10X	7	10 1

Pitchers: STOTTLEMYRE, Downing (5), Sheldon (5), Hamilton (7), Mikkelsen (8) vs GIBSON
Home Runs: Brock-STL, Mantle-NY, K.Boyer-STL, C.Boyer-NY, Linz-NY
Attendance: 30,346

The Twins (bringing the World Series to Minnesota for the first time ever) featured heavy hitting, while Dodger hopes rested on great pitching and speed on the bases. For a while it looked as if batting power would triumph as the Twins took the first two games at home. They drove out Dodger starter Don Drysdale with seven runs in the first three innings of the opener—including home runs by Don Mincher and Zoilo Versalles—on the way to a convincing 8–2 win, and followed up with a 5–1 triumph the next day over Dodger ace Sandy Koufax (who had declined to pitch Game One on Yom Kippur, the holiest day of the Jewish year) and star reliever Ron Perranoski, who was tagged for three of the Twins' runs.

But when the Series moved to Los Angeles, Dodger pitching began to assert itself. Claude Osteen held Minnesota to five hits and no runs, while Los Angeles bunched seven of their ten hits in the middle three innings for four runs. Drysdale evened the Series in Game Four, avenging his first-game pounding with a second Dodger five-hitter. Twins Harmon Killebrew and Tony Oliva tagged him for a pair of solo homers, but that was Minnesota's only scoring—more than balanced by seven Dodger runs, including homers by Wes Parker and Lou Johnson. In Game Five the next day, Koufax avenged his earlier loss, carrying Los Angeles to its first Series lead with a shutout in which he allowed only four singles and a walk, while fanning ten Twins. Speedster Willie Davis stole three bases and Maury Wills stole another as the Dodgers parlayed fourteen hits into a 7–0 victory.

Back in Minnesota for Game Six, the Twins rallied, using the long ball to even the Series again with a 5–1 win. Bob Allison opened the scoring with a two-run shot off Dodger starter Claude Osteen in the fourth, and Minnesota pitcher Mudcat Grant insured his own win with a three-run blast two innings later.

In the finale, though, the visiting team won for the only time in the Series. Koufax again struck out ten men, stopping the Twins on three hits for his second shutout. Lou Johnson's second Series homer (a fourth-inning solo shot to left off Twin starter Jim Kaat that was barely fair) was all the Dodgers needed for their fifth world championship, but Ron Fairly followed Johnson with a double and Wes Parker singled home an insurance run that drove Kaat out and concluded the Series scoring.

Los Angeles Dodgers (NL), 4;
Minnesota Twins (AL) 3

LA (N)

PLAYER/POS	AVG	G	AB	R	H	2B	3B	HR	RB	BB	SO	SB
Jim Brewer, p	.000	1	0	0	0	0	0	0	0	0	0	0
Willie Crawford, ph	.500	2	2	0	1	0	0	0	0	0	1	0
Willie Davis, of	.231	7	26	3	6	0	0	0	0	0	2	3
Don Drysdale, p-2	.000	3	5	0	0	0	0	0	0	0	4	0
Ron Fairly, of	.379	7	29	7	11	3	0	2	6	0	1	0
Jim Gilliam, 3b	.214	7	28	2	6	1	0	0	2	1	0	0
Lou Johnson, of	.296	7	27	3	8	2	0	2	4	1	3	0
John Kennedy, 3b	.000	4	1	0	0	0	0	0	0	0	0	0
Sandy Koufax, p	.111	3	9	0	1	0	0	0	1	1	5	0
Jim Lefebvre, 2b	.400	3	10	2	4	0	0	0	0	0	0	0
Don Le John, ph	.000	1	1	0	0	0	0	0	0	0	1	0
Bob Miller, p	.000	2	0	0	0	0	0	0	0	0	0	0
Wally Moon, ph	.000	2	2	0	0	0	0	0	0	0	0	0
Claude Osteen, p	.333	2	3	0	1	0	0	0	0	0	0	0
Wes Parker, 1b	.304	7	23	3	7	0	1	1	2	3	3	2
Ron Perranoski, p	.000	2	0	0	0	0	0	0	0	0	0	0
Howie Reed, p	.000	2	0	0	0	0	0	0	0	0	0	0
Johnny Roseboro, c	.286	7	21	1	6	1	0	0	3	5	3	1
Dick Tracewski, 2b	.118	6	17	0	2	0	0	0	0	1	5	0
Maury Wills, ss	.367	7	30	3	11	3	0	0	3	1	3	3
TOTAL	.274		234	24	64	10	1	5	21	13	31	9

PITCHER	W	L	ERA	G	GS	CG	SV	SHO	IP	H	ER	BB	SO
Jim Brewer	0	0	4.50	1	0	0	0	0	2.0	3	1	0	1
Don Drysdale	1	1	3.86	2	2	1	0	0	11.2	12	5	3	15
Sandy Koufax	2	1	0.38	3	3	3	0	2	24.0	13	1	5	29
Bob Miller	0	0	0.00	2	0	0	0	0	1.1	0	0	0	0
Claude Osteen	1	1	0.64	2	2	1	0	1	14.0	9	1	5	4
Ron Perranoski	0	0	7.36	2	0	0	0	0	3.2	3	3	4	1
Howie Reed	0	0	8.10	2	0	0	0	0	3.1	2	3	2	4
TOTAL	4	3	2.10	14	7	4	0	3	60.0	42	14	19	54

MIN (A)

PLAYER/POS	AVG	G	AB	R	H	2B	3B	HR	RB	BB	SO	SB
Bob Allison, of	.125	5	16	3	2	1	0	1	2	2	9	1
Earl Battey, c	.120	7	25	1	3	0	1	0	2	0	5	0
Dave Boswell, p	.000	0	0	0	0	0	0	0	0	0	0	0
Mudcat Grant, p	.250	3	8	3	2	1	0	1	3	0	1	0
Jimmie Hall, of	.143	2	7	0	1	0	0	0	0	1	5	0
Jim Kaat, p	.167	3	6	0	1	0	0	0	2	0	5	0
Harmon Killebrew, 3b	.286	7	21	2	6	0	0	1	2	6	4	0
Johnny Klippstein, p	.000	2	0	0	0	0	0	0	0	0	0	0
Jim Merritt, p	.000	2	0	0	0	0	0	0	0	0	0	0
Don Mincher, 1b	.130	7	23	3	3	0	0	1	1	2	7	0
Joe Nossek, of-5	.200	6	20	4	4	0	0	0	0	0	1	0
Tony Oliva, of	.192	7	26	2	5	1	0	1	2	1	6	0
Camilo Pascual, p	.000	1	1	0	0	0	0	0	0	0	0	0
Jim Perry, p	.000	2	0	0	0	0	0	0	0	0	0	0
Bill Pleis, p	.000	1	0	0	0	0	0	0	0	0	0	0
Frank Quilici, 2b	.200	7	20	2	4	2	0	0	1	4	3	0
Rich Rollins, ph	.000	3	2	0	0	0	0	0	0	1	0	0
Sandy Valdespino, of-2	.273	5	11	1	3	1	0	0	0	0	1	0
Zoilo Versalles, ss	.286	7	28	3	8	1	1	1	4	2	7	1
Al Worthington, p	.000	2	0	0	0	0	0	0	0	0	0	0
Jerry Zimmerman, c	.000	2	1	0	0	0	0	0	0	0	0	0
TOTAL	.195		215	20	42	7	2	6	19	19	54	2

PITCHER	W	L	ERA	G	GS	CG	SV	SHO	IP	H	ER	BB	SO
Dave Boswell	0	0	3.38	1	0	0	0	0	2.2	3	1	2	3
Mudcat Grant	2	1	2.74	3	3	2	0	0	23.0	22	7	2	12
Jim Kaat	1	2	3.77	3	3	1	0	0	14.1	18	6	2	6
Johnny Klippstein	0	0	0.00	2	0	0	0	0	2.2	2	0	2	3
Jim Merritt	0	0	2.70	2	0	0	0	0	3.1	2	1	0	1
Camilo Pascual	0	1	5.40	1	1	0	0	0	5.0	8	3	1	0
Jim Perry	0	0	4.50	2	0	0	0	0	4.0	5	2	2	4
Bill Pleis	0	0	9.00	1	0	0	0	0	1.0	2	1	0	0
Al Worthington	0	0	0.00	2	0	0	0	0	4.0	2	0	2	2
TOTAL	3	4	3.15	17	7	3	0	0	60.0	64	21	13	31

GAME 1 AT MIN OCT 6

```
LA    010 000 001   2 10 1
MIN   016 001 00X   8 10 0
```
Pitchers: DRYSDALE, Reed (3), Brewer (5), Perranoski (7) vs GRANT
Home Runs: Fairly-LA, Mincher-MIN, Versalles-MIN
Attendance: 47,797

GAME 2 AT MIN OCT 7

```
LA    000 000 100   1 7 3
MIN   000 002 12X   5 9 0
```
Pitchers: KOUFAX, Perranoski (7), Miller (8) vs KAAT
Attendance: 48,700

GAME 3 AT LA OCT 9

```
MIN   000 000 000   0 5 0
LA    000 211 00X   4 10 1
```
Pitchers: PASCUAL, Merritt (6), Klippstein (8) vs OSTEEN
Attendance: 55,934

GAME 4 AT LA OCT 10

```
MIN   000 101 000   2 5 2
LA    110 103 01X   7 10 0
```
Pitchers: GRANT, Worthington (6), Pleis (8) vs DRYSDALE
Home Runs: Killebrew-MIN, Parker-LA, Oliva-MIN, Johnson-LA
Attendance: 55,920

GAME 5 AT LA OCT 11

```
MIN   000 000 000   0 4 1
LA    202 100 20X   7 14 0
```
Pitchers: KAAT, Boswell (3), Perry (6) vs KOUFAX
Attendance: 55,801

GAME 6 AT MIN OCT 13

```
LA    000 000 100   1 6 1
MIN   000 203 00X   5 6 1
```
Pitchers: OSTEEN, Reed (6), Miller (8) vs GRANT
Home Runs: Allison-MIN, Grant-MIN, Fairly-LA
Attendance: 49,578

GAME 7 AT MIN OCT 14

```
LA    000 200 000   2 7 0
MIN   000 000 000   0 3 1
```
Pitchers: KOUFAX vs KAAT, Worthington (4), Klippstein (6), Merritt (7), Perry (9)
Home Runs: Johnson-LA
Attendance: 50,596

The Orioles, with their first pennant since moving from St. Louis in 1954, won the franchise's first World Series ever, crushing Series repeater Los Angeles in four games. Back-to-back home runs by Frank and Brooks Robinson in the top of the first inning of the opener gave Baltimore a quick three-run lead, and the O's added a fourth run an inning later before the Dodgers attempted to come back with single runs in the second and third innings. But by then Oriole reliever Moe Drabowsky had come on to pitch, and he stopped the Dodgers on one hit the rest of the way, striking out eleven (including six in a row in the fourth and fifth innings). The Dodgers would not score again in the Series.

Sophomore Jim Palmer (a week shy of his twenty-first birthday) hurled a four-hit shutout at Los Angeles in Game Two, defeating the great—but critically sore-armed—Sandy Koufax, who, though only thirty years old himself, was pitching the final game of his career. Three errors by center fielder Willie Davis in the fifth (including a pair of flies lost in the sun) led to three unearned runs—the first scoring against Koufax. Frank Robinson's leadoff triple in the sixth and Boog Powell's single gave the Orioles an earned run before a double play ended the inning. Koufax was replaced after the inning by a succession of Dodger relievers as Baltimore went on to win 6–0.

Wally Bunker did the honors for the Orioles in Game Three, emerging the victor of a pitching duel with Dodger Claude Osteen on the strength of a fifth-inning home run by Paul Blair, a tremendous 430-foot shot to left. Osteen yielded only two other Orioles hits—both singles—in his seven innings, and Dodger reliever Phil Regan retired the side in the eighth. But one run was all Bunker needed for his shutout win.

Dave McNally, who had given up the Dodgers' only Series runs in Game One, mended his ways with a four-hit shutout in Game Four. He needed the shutout for the Oriole sweep, for Dodger Don Drysdale was also in top form. Drysdale, too, gave up only four hits. But one of them was Frank Robinson's second home run of the Series, a fourth-inning solo shot to left for the game's only scoring.

Baltimore Orioles (AL), 4;
Los Angeles Dodgers (NL) 0

BAL (A)

PLAYER/POS	AVG	G	AB	R	H	2B	3B	HR	RB	BB	SO	SB
Luis Aparicio, ss	.250	4	16	0	4	1	0	0	2	0	0	0
Paul Blair, of	.167	4	6	2	1	0	0	1	1	1	0	0
Curt Blefary, of	.077	4	13	0	1	0	0	0	0	2	3	0
Wally Bunker, p	.000	1	2	0	0	0	0	0	0	0	1	0
Moe Drabowsky, p	.000	1	2	0	0	0	0	0	0	1	1	0
Andy Etchebarren, c	.083	4	12	2	1	0	0	0	0	2	4	0
Davy Johnson, 2b	.286	4	14	1	4	1	0	0	1	0	1	0
Dave Mc Nally, p	.000	2	3	0	0	0	0	0	0	0	1	0
Jim Palmer, p	.000	1	4	0	0	0	0	0	0	0	2	0
Boog Powell, 1b	.357	4	14	1	5	1	0	0	1	0	1	0
Brooks Robinson, 3b	.214	4	14	2	3	0	0	1	1	1	0	0
Frank Robinson, of	.286	4	14	4	4	0	1	2	3	2	3	0
Russ Snyder, of	.167	3	6	1	1	0	0	0	1	2	0	0
TOTAL	.200		120	13	24	3	1	4	10	11	17	0

PITCHER	W	L	ERA	G	GS	CG	SV	SHO	IP	H	ER	BB	SO
Wally Bunker	1	0	0.00	1	1	1	0	1	9.0	6	0	1	6
Moe Drabowsky	1	0	0.00	1	0	0	0	0	6.2	1	0	2	11
Dave Mc Nally	1	0	1.59	2	2	1	0	1	11.1	6	2	7	5
Jim Palmer	1	0	0.00	1	1	1	0	1	9.0	4	0	3	6
TOTAL	4	0	0.50	5	4	3	0	3	36.0	17	2	13	28

LA (N)

PLAYER/POS	AVG	G	AB	R	H	2B	3B	HR	RB	BB	SO	SB
Jim Barbieri, ph	.000	1	1	0	0	0	0	0	0	0	1	0
Jim Brewer, p	.000	1	0	0	0	0	0	0	0	0	0	0
Wes Covington, ph	.000	1	1	0	0	0	0	0	0	0	1	0
Tommy Davis, of-3	.250	4	8	0	2	0	0	0	0	1	1	0
Willie Davis, of	.063	4	16	0	1	0	0	0	0	0	4	0
Don Drysdale, p	.000	2	2	0	0	0	0	0	0	0	1	0
Ron Fairly, of-2,1b-1	.143	3	7	0	1	0	0	0	0	2	4	0
Al Ferrara, ph	1.000	1	1	0	1	0	0	0	0	0	0	0
Jim Gilliam, 3b	.000	2	6	0	0	0	0	0	1	2	0	0
Lou Johnson, of	.267	4	15	1	4	1	0	0	0	1	1	0
John Kennedy, 3b	.200	2	5	0	1	0	0	0	0	0	0	0
Sandy Koufax, p	.000	1	2	0	0	0	0	0	0	0	0	0
Jim Lefebvre, 2b	.167	4	12	1	2	0	0	1	1	3	4	0
Bob Miller, p	.000	1	0	0	0	0	0	0	0	0	0	0
Joe Moeller, p	.000	1	0	0	0	0	0	0	0	0	0	0
Nate Oliver, pr	.000	1	0	0	0	0	0	0	0	0	0	0
Claude Osteen, p	.000	1	2	0	0	0	0	0	0	0	1	0
Wes Parker, 1b	.231	4	13	0	3	2	0	0	0	1	3	0
Ron Perranoski, p	.000	2	0	0	0	0	0	0	0	0	0	0
Phil Regan, p	.000	2	0	0	0	0	0	0	0	0	0	0
Johnny Roseboro, c	.071	4	14	0	1	0	0	0	0	0	3	0
Dick Stuart, ph	.000	2	2	0	0	0	0	0	0	0	1	0
Maury Wills, ss	.077	4	13	0	1	0	0	0	0	3	3	1
TOTAL	.142		120	2	17	3	0	1	2	13	28	1

PITCHER	W	L	ERA	G	GS	CG	SV	SHO	IP	H	ER	BB	SO
Jim Brewer	0	0	0.00	1	0	0	0	0	1.0	0	0	0	1
Don Drysdale	0	2	4.50	2	2	1	0	0	10.0	8	5	3	6
Sandy Koufax	0	1	1.50	1	1	0	0	0	6.0	6	1	2	2
Bob Miller	0	0	0.00	1	0	0	0	0	3.0	2	0	2	1
Joe Moeller	0	0	4.50	1	0	0	0	0	2.0	1	1	1	0
Claude Osteen	0	1	1.29	1	1	0	0	0	7.0	3	1	1	3
Ron Perranoski	0	0	5.40	2	0	0	0	0	3.1	4	2	1	2
Phil Regan	0	0	0.00	2	0	0	0	0	1.2	0	0	1	2
TOTAL	0	4	2.65	11	4	1	0	0	34.0	24	10	11	17

GAME 1 AT LA OCT 5

BAL	310 100 000	5	9	0
LA	011 000 000	2	3	0

Pitchers: McNALLY, DRABOWSKY (3) vs DRYSDALE, Moeller (3), Miller (5), Perranoski (8)
Home Runs: F.Robinson-BAL, B.Robinson-BAL, Lefebvre-LA
Attendance: 55,941

GAME 2 AT LA OCT 6

BAL	000 031 020	6	8	0
LA	000 000 000	0	4	6

Pitchers: PALMER vs KOUFAX, Perranoski (7), Regan (8), Brewer (9)
Attendance: 55,947

GAME 3 AT BAL OCT 8

LA	000 000 000	0	6	0
BAL	000 010 000	1	3	0

Pitchers: OSTEEN, Regan (8) vs BUNKER
Home Runs: Blair-BAL
Attendance: 54,445

GAME 4 AT BAL OCT 9

LA	000 000 000	0	4	0
BAL	000 100 000	1	4	0

Pitchers: DRYSDALE vs McNALLY
Home Runs: F.Robinson-BAL
Attendance: 54,458

The Cardinals cruised into the Series leading by 10½ games, whereas the Red Sox eked out their pennant over Minnesota and Detroit only by a dramatic win at season's end. The Sox continued to claw their way through six games of the Series before finally falling to superior pitching and hitting in the seventh game. Cardinal hurler Bob Gibson (who had missed a third of the season with a broken leg) edged Boston in the opener 2–1 with a six-hitter that included ten strikeouts. The only run against him came on a solo homer by opposing pitcher Jose Santiago in the third that tied the game. But Santiago was undone when Cardinal Lou Brock singled off him to open the seventh, then stole second, and moved around to score on a pair of ground outs.

Boston ace Jim Lonborg evened the Series the next day with a brilliant one-hit shutout. Sox Triple Crown winner Carl Yastrzemski accounted for four of Boston's five runs with homers in the fourth and seventh innings. Cardinal Nelson Briles outlasted a succession of Boston pitchers for a go-ahead 5–2 win in Game Three, and Gibson, with a five-hit shutout in Game Four, put St. Louis up three games to one.

But Boston's Lonborg kept Red Sox hopes alive with another pitching gem—a three-hitter in which the only extra-base hit was Roger Maris's harmless home run in the last of the ninth, after the Sox had already scored three runs (two of them unearned). Boston's bats came alive as the Series moved to Boston for Game Six, and the Sox evened the Series with an 8–4 win. The Cards used eight pitchers in a futile effort to hold off the Boston assault. Boston's score would have been greater had not all four Boston homers (including three in the fourth inning by Yastrzemski, Reggie Smith, and Rico Petrocelli—his second of the game) been solo shots.

With the Series tied at three-all, the Series' two-game winners, Gibson and Lonborg, faced off in the finale. It turned out to be no contest. Lonborg gave up ten hits and seven runs (including a homer by pitcher Gibson in the fifth and a three-run blast by Julian Javier an inning later) in six innings. Four Boston relievers held the Cards scoreless the rest of the game, but it was too late. Gibson's three-hitter included ten strikeouts and yielded only two Boston runs.

St. Louis Cardinals (NL), 4; Boston Red Sox (AL) 3

STL (N)

PLAYER/POS	AVG	G	AB	R	H	2B	3B	HR	RB	BB	SO	SB
Eddie Bressoud, ss	.000	2	0	0	0	0	0	0	0	0	0	0
Nelson Briles, p	.000	2	3	0	0	0	0	0	0	0	0	0
Lou Brock, of	.414	7	29	8	12	2	1	1	3	2	3	7
Steve Carlton, p	.000	1	1	0	0	0	0	0	0	0	0	0
Orlando Cepeda, 1b	.103	7	29	1	3	2	0	0	1	0	4	0
Curt Flood, of	.179	7	28	2	5	1	0	0	3	3	3	0
Phil Gagliano, ph	.000	1	1	0	0	0	0	0	0	0	0	0
Bob Gibson, p	.091	3	11	1	1	0	0	1	1	1	2	0
Joe Hoerner, p	.000	2	0	0	0	0	0	0	0	0	0	0
Dick Hughes, p	.000	2	3	0	0	0	0	0	0	0	3	0
Larry Jaster, p	.000	1	0	0	0	0	0	0	0	0	0	0
Julian Javier, 2b	.360	7	25	2	9	3	0	1	4	0	6	0
Jack Lamabe, p	.000	3	0	0	0	0	0	0	0	0	0	0
Roger Maris, of	.385	7	26	3	10	1	0	1	7	3	1	0
Dal Maxvill, ss	.158	7	19	1	3	0	1	0	1	4	1	0
Tim Mc Carver, c	.125	7	24	3	3	1	0	0	2	2	2	0
Dave Ricketts, ph	.000	3	3	0	0	0	0	0	0	0	0	0
Mike Shannon, 3b	.208	7	24	3	5	1	0	1	2	1	4	0
Ed Spiezio, ph	.000	1	1	0	0	0	0	0	0	0	0	0
Bobby Tolan, ph	.000	3	2	1	0	0	0	0	0	1	1	0
Ray Washburn, p	.000	2	0	0	0	0	0	0	0	0	0	0
Ron Willis, p	.000	3	0	0	0	0	0	0	0	0	0	0
Hal Woodeshick, p	.000	1	0	0	0	0	0	0	0	0	0	0
TOTAL	.223		229	25	51	11	2	5	24	17	30	7

PITCHER	W	L	ERA	G	GS	CG	SV	SHO	IP	H	ER	BB	SO
Nelson Briles	1	0	1.64	2	1	1	0	0	11.0	7	2	1	4
Steve Carlton	0	1	0.00	1	1	0	0	0	6.0	3	0	2	5
Bob Gibson	3	0	1.00	3	3	3	0	1	27.0	14	3	5	26
Joe Hoerner	0	0	40.50	2	0	0	0	0	0.2	4	3	1	0
Dick Hughes	0	1	5.00	2	2	0	0	0	9.0	9	5	3	7
Larry Jaster	0	0	0.00	1	0	0	0	0	0.1	2	0	0	0
Jack Lamabe	0	1	6.75	3	0	0	0	0	2.2	5	2	0	4
Ray Washburn	0	0	0.00	2	1	0	0	0	2.1	1	0	1	2
Ron Willis	0	0	27.00	3	0	0	0	0	1.0	2	3	4	1
Hal Woodeshick	0	0	0.00	1	0	0	0	0	1.0	1	0	0	0
TOTAL	4	3	2.66	20	7	4	0	1	61.0	48	18	17	49

BOS (A)

PLAYER/POS	AVG	G	AB	R	H	2B	3B	HR	RB	BB	SO	SB
Jerry Adair, 2b-4	.125	5	16	0	2	0	0	0	1	0	3	1
Mike Andrews, 2b-3	.308	5	13	2	4	0	0	0	0	1	1	0
Gary Bell, p	.000	3	0	0	0	0	0	0	0	0	0	0
Ken Brett, p	.000	2	0	0	0	0	0	0	0	0	0	0
Joe Foy, 3b-3	.133	6	15	2	2	1	0	0	1	5	5	0
Russ Gibson, c	.000	2	2	0	0	0	0	0	0	0	2	0
Ken Harrelson, of	.077	4	13	0	1	0	0	0	1	1	3	0
Elston Howard, c	.111	7	18	0	2	0	0	0	1	1	2	0
Dalton Jones, 3b-4	.389	6	18	2	7	0	0	0	1	1	3	0
Jim Lonborg, p	.000	3	9	0	0	0	0	0	0	0	7	0
Dave Morehead, p	.000	2	0	0	0	0	0	0	0	0	0	0
Dan Osinski, p	.000	2	0	0	0	0	0	0	0	0	0	0
Rico Petrocelli, ss	.200	7	20	3	4	1	0	2	3	3	8	0
Mike Ryan, c	.000	1	2	0	0	0	0	0	0	0	1	0
Jose Santiago, p	.500	3	2	1	1	0	0	1	1	0	1	0
George Scott, 1b	.231	7	26	3	6	1	0	0	3	6	0
Norm Siebern, of-1	.333	3	3	0	1	0	0	0	1	0	0	0
Reggie Smith, of	.250	7	24	3	6	1	0	2	3	2	2	0
Lee Stange, p	.000	1	0	0	0	0	0	0	0	0	0	0
Jerry Stephenson, p	.000	1	0	0	0	0	0	0	0	0	0	0
Jose Tartabull, of-6	.154	7	13	1	2	0	0	0	0	1	2	0
George Thomas, of-1	.000	2	2	0	0	0	0	0	0	0	1	0
Gary Waslewski, p	.000	2	1	0	0	0	0	0	0	0	1	0
John Wyatt, p	.000	2	0	0	0	0	0	0	0	0	0	0
Carl Yastrzemski, of	.400	7	25	4	10	2	0	3	5	4	1	0
TOTAL	.216		222	21	48	6	1	8	19	17	49	1

PITCHER	W	L	ERA	G	GS	CG	SV	SHO	IP	H	ER	BB	SO
Gary Bell	0	1	5.06	3	1	0	1	0	5.1	8	3	1	1
Ken Brett	0	0	0.00	2	0	0	0	0	1.1	0	0	1	1
Jim Lonborg	2	1	2.63	3	3	2	0	1	24.0	14	7	2	11
Dave Morehead	0	0	0.00	2	0	0	0	0	3.1	0	0	4	3
Dan Osinski	0	0	6.75	2	0	0	0	0	1.1	2	1	0	0
Jose Santiago	0	2	5.59	3	2	0	0	0	9.2	16	6	3	6
Lee Stange	0	0	0.00	1	0	0	0	0	2.0	3	0	0	0
Jerry Stephenson	0	0	9.00	1	0	0	0	0	2.0	3	2	1	0
Gary Waslewski	0	0	2.16	2	1	0	0	0	8.1	4	2	2	7
John Wyatt	1	0	4.91	2	0	0	0	0	3.2	1	2	3	1
TOTAL	3	4	3.39	21	7	2	1	1	61.0	51	23	17	30

In this "year of the pitcher," Tiger Denny McLain's 31 wins were the most for a major leaguer in thirty-seven years. Cardinal Bob Gibson's 1.12 ERA was the majors' best since Dutch Leonard's 1.01 in 1914, and his 13 season shutouts tied for third best of all time. In the Series, though, it was Detroit's second-best pitcher—Mickey Lolich—who emerged as the hero.

McLain came off second-best against Gibson in the opener. He yielded only three hits in his five innings, but two Cardinal singles in the fourth combined with a pair of walks and a Tiger error for three runs. Gibson, meanwhile, was in the process of striking out a Series-record 17 batters on the way to a five-hit shutout. But Lolich brought Detroit back in Game Two. He struck out nine, and his third-inning home run (the only one of his major league career) for the second Tiger run provided all the scoring needed for a Detroit victory, although the Tigers kept putting runs across for an eventual 8–1 win.

Home runs accounted for most of the scoring in Game Three. Veteran Al Kaline's two-run shot in the third opened the scoring, but Cardinal Tim McCarver's three-run blast in the fifth put St. Louis ahead. Tiger Dick McAuliffe's solo shot later in the inning brought Detroit within one run of a tie, but the Cardinals put the game away on Orlando Cepeda's three-run homer in the seventh.

McLain faced Gibson again in Game Four, and again came off second-best. Cardinal Lou Brock led off the game with a home run, and before the end of the third inning McLain was gone. Gibson gave up a solo homer to Tiger Jim Northrup in the fourth, but that was the only Detroit run he allowed. Gibson homered himself and struck out ten in an easy 10–1 win.

Down three games to one, the Tigers were saved from elimination by Lolich's arm. Although three Cardinal hits in the top of the first (including Orlando Cepeda's second homer of the Series) gave St. Louis a quick three runs, Lolich held the Cards scoreless the rest of the game as his Tigers fought back with two runs in the fourth and three more in the seventh (with a rally started by Lolich's single). McLain finally came through in Game Six, evening the Series with an easy 13–1 victory, in which Jim Northrup's grand slam provided the big blow of a ten-run third inning.

Lolich and Gibson—both 2–0 in the Series—faced off in the finale. Gibson broke his own World Series strikeout record in the third inning (finishing with 8 for the

game and 35 for the Series), and both pitchers hurled shutout ball through six innings. But four two-out Tiger hits in the top of the seventh—including a misplayed fly ball in center field—put three runs on the board, and another run in the ninth made the score 4–0. In the last of the ninth, Mike Shannon's solo homer spoiled Lolich's shutout, but not his third Series win—or the Tigers' comeback world title.

Detroit Tigers (AL), 4;
St. Louis Cardinals (NL) 3

DET (A)

PLAYER/POS	AVG	G	AB	R	H	2B	3B	HR	RB	BB	SO	SB
Gates Brown, ph	.000	1	1	0	0	0	0	0	0	0	0	0
Norm Cash, 1b	.385	7	26	5	10	0	0	1	5	3	5	0
Wayne Comer, ph	1.000	1	1	0	1	0	0	0	0	0	0	0
Pat Dobson, p	.000	3	0	0	0	0	0	0	0	0	0	0
Bill Freehan, c	.083	7	24	0	2	1	0	0	2	4	8	0
John Hiller, p	.000	2	0	0	0	0	0	0	0	0	0	0
Willie Horton, of	.304	7	23	6	7	1	1	1	3	5	6	0
Al Kaline, of	.379	7	29	6	11	2	0	2	8	0	7	0
Fred Lasher, p	.000	1	0	0	0	0	0	0	0	0	0	0
Mickey Lolich, p	.250	3	12	2	3	0	0	1	2	1	5	0
Tom Matchick, ph	.000	3	3	0	0	0	0	0	0	0	1	0
Eddie Mathews, 3b-1	.333	2	3	0	1	0	0	0	0	1	1	0
Dick Mc Auliffe, 2b	.222	7	27	5	6	0	0	1	3	4	6	0
Denny Mc Lain, p	.000	3	6	0	0	0	0	0	0	0	4	0
Don Mc Mahon, p	.000	2	0	0	0	0	0	0	0	0	0	0
Jim Northrup, of	.250	7	28	4	7	0	1	2	8	1	5	0
Ray Oyler, ss	.000	4	0	0	0	0	0	0	0	0	0	0
Daryl Patterson, p	.000	2	0	0	0	0	0	0	0	0	0	0
Jim Price, ph	.000	2	2	0	0	0	0	0	0	0	1	0
Joe Sparma, p	.000	1	0	0	0	0	0	0	0	0	0	0
Mickey Stanley, ss-7,of-4	.214	7	28	4	6	0	1	0	0	2	4	0
Dick Tracewski, 3b-1	.000	2	1	0	0	0	0	0	0	0	0	0
Don Wert, 3b	.118	6	17	1	2	0	0	0	2	6	5	0
Earl Wilson, p	.000	1	1	0	0	0	0	0	0	0	1	0
TOTAL	.242		231	34	56	4	3	8	33	27	59	0

PITCHER	W	L	ERA	G	GS	CG	SV	SHO	IP	H	ER	BB	SO
Pat Dobson	0	0	3.86	3	0	0	0	0	4.2	5	2	1	0
John Hiller	0	0	13.50	2	0	0	0	0	2.0	6	3	3	1
Fred Lasher	0	0	0.00	1	0	0	0	0	2.0	1	0	0	1
Mickey Lolich	3	0	1.67	3	3	3	0	0	27.0	20	5	6	21
Denny Mc Lain	1	2	3.24	3	3	1	0	0	16.2	18	6	4	13
Don Mc Mahon	0	0	13.50	2	0	0	0	0	2.0	4	3	0	1
Daryl Patterson	0	0	0.00	2	0	0	0	0	3.0	1	0	1	0
Joe Sparma	0	0	54.00	1	0	0	0	0	0.1	2	2	0	0
Earl Wilson	0	1	6.23	1	1	0	0	0	4.1	4	3	6	3
TOTAL	4	3	3.48	18	7	4	0		62.0	61	24	21	40

STL (N)

PLAYER/POS	AVG	G	AB	R	H	2B	3B	HR	RB	BB	SO	SB
Nelson Briles, p	.000	2	4	0	0	0	0	0	0	0	4	0
Lou Brock, of	.464	7	28	6	13	3	1	2	5	3	4	7
Steve Carlton, p	.000	2	0	0	0	0	0	0	0	0	0	0
Orlando Cepeda, 1b	.250	7	28	2	7	0	0	2	6	2	3	0
Ron Davis, of	.000	2	7	0	0	0	0	0	0	2	0	0
Johnny Edwards, ph	.000	1	1	0	0	0	0	0	0	0	1	0
Curt Flood, of	.286	7	28	4	8	1	0	0	2	2	2	3
Phil Gagliano, ph	.000	3	3	0	0	0	0	0	0	0	0	0
Bob Gibson, p	.125	3	8	2	1	0	0	1	2	1	2	0
Wayne Granger, p	.000	1	0	0	0	0	0	0	0	0	0	0
Joe Hoerner, p	.500	3	2	0	1	0	0	0	0	0	1	0
Dick Hughes, p	.000	1	0	0	0	0	0	0	0	0	0	0
Larry Jaster, p	.000	1	0	0	0	0	0	0	0	0	0	0
Julian Javier, 2b	.333	7	27	1	9	1	0	0	3	3	4	1
Roger Maris, of-5	.158	7	19	5	3	1	0	0	1	3	3	0
Dal Maxvill, ss	.000	7	22	1	0	0	0	0	0	3	5	0
Tim Mc Carver, c	.333	7	27	3	9	0	2	1	4	3	2	0
Mel Nelson, p	.000	1	0	0	0	0	0	0	0	0	0	0
Dave Ricketts, ph	1.000	1	1	0	1	0	0	0	0	0	0	0
Dick Schofield, ss-1	.000	2	0	0	0	0	0	0	0	0	0	0
Mike Shannon, 3b	.276	7	29	3	8	1	0	1	4	1	5	0
Ed Spiezio, ph	1.000	1	1	0	1	0	0	0	0	0	0	0
Bobby Tolan, ph	.000	1	1	0	0	0	0	0	0	0	1	0
Ray Washburn, p	.000	2	3	0	0	0	0	0	0	0	1	0
Ron Willis, p	.000	3	0	0	0	0	0	0	0	0	0	0
TOTAL	.255		239	27	61	7	3	7	27	21	40	11

PITCHER	W	L	ERA	G	GS	CG	SV	SHO	IP	H	ER	BB	SO
Nelson Briles	0	1	5.56	2	2	0	0	0	11.1	13	7	4	7
Steve Carlton	0	0	6.75	2	0	0	0	0	4.0	7	3	1	3
Bob Gibson	2	1	1.67	3	3	3	0	1	27.0	18	5	4	35
Wayne Granger	0	0	0.00	1	0	0	0	0	2.0	0	0	1	1
Joe Hoerner	0	1	3.86	3	0	0	1	0	4.2	5	2	5	3
Dick Hughes	0	0	0.00	1	0	0	0	0	0.1	2	0	0	0
Larry Jaster	0	0	INF	1	0	0	0	0	0.0	2	3	1	0
Mel Nelson	0	0	0.00	1	0	0	0	0	1.0	0	0	1	0
Ray Washburn	1	1	9.82	2	2	0	0	0	7.1	7	8	7	6
Ron Willis	0	0	8.31	3	0	0	0	0	4.1	2	4	4	3
TOTAL	3	4	4.65	19	7	3	1	1	62.0	56	32	27	59

GAME 1 AT STL OCT 2

| DET | 000 000 000 | 0 5 3 |
| STL | 000 300 10X | 4 6 0 |

Pitchers: McLAIN, Dobson (6), McMahon (8) vs GIBSON
Home Runs: Brock-STL
Attendance: 54,692

GAME 2 AT STL OCT 3

| DET | 011 003 102 | 8 13 1 |
| STL | 000 001 000 | 1 6 1 |

Pitchers: LOLICH vs BRILES, Carlton (6), Willis (7), Hoerner (9)
Home Runs: Horton-DET, Lolich-DET, Cash-DET
Attendance: 54,692

GAME 3 AT DET OCT 5

| STL | 000 040 300 | 7 13 0 |
| DET | 002 010 000 | 3 4 0 |

Pitchers: WASHBURN, Hoerner (6) vs WILSON, Dobson (5), McMahon (6), Patterson (7), Hiller (8)
Home Runs: Kaline-DET, McCarver-STL, McAuliffe-DET, Cepeda-STL
Attendance: 53,634

GAME 4 AT DET OCT 6

| STL | 202 200 040 | 10 13 0 |
| DET | 000 100 000 | 1 5 4 |

Pitchers: GIBSON vs McLAIN, Sparma (3), Patterson (4), Lasher (6), Hiller (8), Dobson (8)
Home Runs: Brock-STL, Gibson-STL, Northrup-DET
Attendance: 53,634

GAME 5 AT DET OCT 7

| STL | 300 000 000 | 3 9 0 |
| DET | 000 200 30X | 5 9 1 |

Pitchers: Briles, HOERNER (7), Willis (7) vs LOLICH
Home Runs: Cepeda-STL
Attendance: 53,634

GAME 6 AT STL OCT 9

| DET | 0 2 10 010 000 | 13 12 1 |
| STL | 00 0 000 001 | 1 9 1 |

Pitchers: McLAIN vs WASHBURN, Jaster (3), Willis (3), Hughes (3), Carlton (4), Granger (7), Nelson (9)
Home Runs: Northrup-DET, Kaline-DET
Attendance: 54,692

GAME 7 AT STL OCT 10

| DET | 000 000 301 | 4 8 1 |
| STL | 000 000 001 | 1 5 0 |

Pitchers: LOLICH vs GIBSON
Home Runs: Shannon-STL
Attendance: 54,692

Atlanta's Hank Aaron homered in each game and drove in a series-high seven runs. But the "Miracle Mets" as a team outhomered the Braves six to five, outhit them by seventy-two percentage points, and scored nearly twice as many runs.

Twice in the first game the Braves came from behind to lead by a run, but in the top of the eighth, five New York hits and poor Atlanta fielding buried starter Phil Niekro under five runs. In Game Two, home runs by Tommie Agee and Ken Boswell helped New York take an early 8–0 lead that even Aaron's three-run homer in the fifth couldn't damage.

In the third game the lead changed hands three times on home runs. Aaron began the barrage with a two-run shot in the first inning. Agee's homer in the third followed by Boswell's for two runs in the fourth put the Mets ahead—until Orlando Cepeda's two-run homer in the fifth gave Atlanta another lead. But in the bottom of the fifth, Met rookie Wayne Garrett's two-run blast reversed the lead one last time and, after four final shutout innings by twenty-two-year-old reliever Nolan Ryan, the Mets had swept to their first pennant.

New York Mets (East), 3; Atlanta Braves (West) 0

NY (E)

PLAYER/POS	AVG	G	AB	R	H	2B	3B	HR	RB	BB	SO	SB
Tommie Agee, of	.357	3	14	4	5	1	0	2	4	2	5	2
Ken Boswell, 2b	.333	3	12	4	4	0	0	2	5	1	2	0
Wayne Garrett, 3b	.385	3	13	3	5	2	0	1	3	2	2	1
Rod Gaspar, of	.000	3	0	0	0	0	0	0	0	0	0	0
Gary Gentry, p	.000	1	0	0	0	0	0	0	0	0	0	0
Jerry Grote, c	.167	3	12	3	2	1	0	0	1	1	4	0
Bud Harrelson, ss	.182	3	11	2	2	1	1	0	3	1	2	0
Cleon Jones, of	.429	3	14	4	6	2	0	1	4	1	2	2
Jerry Koosman, p	.000	1	2	1	0	0	0	0	0	1	2	0
Ed Kranepool, 1b	.250	3	12	2	3	1	0	0	1	1	2	0
J. C. Martin, ph	.500	2	2	0	1	0	0	0	2	0	0	0
Tug Mc Graw, p	.000	1	0	0	0	0	0	0	0	0	0	0
Nolan Ryan, p	.500	1	4	1	2	0	0	0	0	0	1	0
Tom Seaver, p	.000	1	3	0	0	0	0	0	0	0	0	0
Art Shamsky, of	.538	3	13	3	7	0	0	0	1	0	3	0
Ron Taylor, p	.000	2	0	0	0	0	0	0	0	0	0	0
Al Weis, 2b	.000	3	1	0	0	0	0	0	0	0	0	0
TOTAL	.327		113	27	37	8	1	6	24	10	25	5

PITCHER	W	L	ERA	G	GS	CG	SV	SHO	IP	H	ER	BB	SO
Gary Gentry	0	0	9.00	1	1	0	0	0	2.0	5	2	1	1
Jerry Koosman	0	0	11.57	1	1	0	0	0	4.2	7	6	4	5
Tug Mc Graw	0	0	0.00	1	0	0	1	0	3.0	1	0	1	1
Nolan Ryan	1	0	2.57	1	0	0	0	0	7.0	3	2	2	7
Tom Seaver	1	0	6.43	1	1	0	0	0	7.0	8	5	3	2
Ron Taylor	1	0	0.00	2	0	0	1	0	3.1	3	0	0	4
TOTAL	3	0	5.00	7	3	0	2	0	27.0	27	15	11	20

ATL (W)

PLAYER/POS	AVG	G	AB	R	H	2B	3B	HR	RB	BB	SO	SB
Hank Aaron, of	.357	3	14	3	5	2	0	3	7	0	1	0
Tommie Aaron, ph	.000	1	1	0	0	0	0	0	0	0	0	0
Felipe Alou, ph	.000	1	1	0	0	0	0	0	0	0	0	0
Bob Aspromonte, ph	.000	3	3	0	0	0	0	0	0	0	0	0
Clete Boyer, 3b	.111	3	9	0	1	0	0	0	3	2	3	0
Jim Britton, p	.000	1	0	0	0	0	0	0	0	0	0	0
Rico Carty, of	.300	3	10	4	3	2	0	0	0	3	1	0
Orlando Cepeda, 1b	.455	3	11	2	5	2	0	1	3	1	2	1
Bob Didier, c	.000	3	11	0	0	0	0	0	0	0	2	0
Paul Doyle, p	.000	1	0	0	0	0	0	0	0	0	0	0
Gil Garrido, ss	.200	3	10	0	2	0	0	0	0	1	1	0
Tony Gonzalez, of	.357	3	14	4	5	1	0	1	2	1	4	0
Sonny Jackson, ss	.000	1	0	0	0	0	0	0	0	0	0	0
Pat Jarvis, p	.000	1	2	0	0	0	0	0	0	0	2	0
Mike Lum, of-1	1.000	2	2	0	2	1	0	0	0	0	0	0
Felix Millan, 2b	.333	3	12	2	4	1	0	0	0	3	0	0
Gary Neibauer, p	.000	1	0	0	0	0	0	0	0	0	0	0
Phil Niekro, p	.000	1	3	0	0	0	0	0	0	0	1	0
Milt Pappas, p	.000	1	1	0	0	0	0	0	0	0	1	0
Ron Reed, p	.000	1	0	0	0	0	0	0	0	0	0	0
George Stone, p	.000	1	1	0	0	0	0	0	0	0	1	0
Bob Tillman, c	.000	1	0	0	0	0	0	0	0	0	0	0
Cecil Upshaw, p	.000	3	1	0	0	0	0	0	0	0	1	0
TOTAL	.255		106	15	27	9	0	5	15	11	20	1

PITCHER	W	L	ERA	G	GS	CG	SV	SHO	IP	H	ER	BB	SO
Jim Britton	0	0	0.00	1	0	0	0	0	0.1	0	0	1	0
Paul Doyle	0	0	0.00	1	0	0	0	0	1.0	2	0	1	3
Pat Jarvis	0	1	12.46	1	1	0	0	0	4.1	10	6	0	6
Gary Neibauer	0	0	0.00	1	0	0	0	0	1.0	0	0	0	1
Phil Niekro	0	1	4.50	1	1	0	0	0	8.0	9	4	4	4
Milt Pappas	0	0	11.57	1	0	0	0	0	2.1	4	3	0	4
Ron Reed	0	1	21.60	1	1	0	0	0	1.2	5	4	3	3
George Stone	0	0	9.00	1	0	0	0	0	1.0	2	1	0	0
Cecil Upshaw	0	0	2.84	3	0	0	0	0	6.1	5	2	1	4
TOTAL	0	3	6.92	11	3	0	0	0	26.0	37	20	10	25

GAME 1 AT ATL OCT 4

NY	020	200	050	9	10	1
ATL	012	010	100	5	10	2

Pitchers: SEAVER, Taylor (8) vs NIEKRO, Upshaw (9)
Home Runs: Gonzalez-ATL, H.Aaron-ATL
Attendance: 50,122

GAME 2 AT ATL OCT 5

NY	132	210	200	11	13	1
ATL	000	150	000	6	9	3

Pitchers: Koosman, TAYLOR (5), McGraw (7) VS REED, Doyle (2), Pappas (3), Britton (6), Upshaw (6), Neibauer (9)
Home Runs: Agee-NY, Boswell-NY, H.Aaron-ATL, Jones-NY
Attendance: 50,270

GAME 3 AT NY OCT 6

ATL	200	020	000	4	8	1
NY	001	231	00X	7	14	0

Pitchers: JARVIS, Stone (5), Upshaw (6) VS Gentry, RYAN (3)
Home Runs: H.Aaron-ATL, Agee-NY, Boswell-NY, Cepeda-ATL, Garrett-NY
Attendance: 53,195

Minnesota led the league in batting, Baltimore in pitching. In the LCS, pitching prevailed as the Twins were held to a series batting average 113 points below their season mark.

Still, Minnesota nearly won the first game with three runs on only four hits. But the Orioles tied the score on Boog Powell's homer in the bottom of the ninth and won the game three innings later on Paul Blair's suicide squeeze bunt with two away. In Game Two, Minnesota's Dave Boswell scattered seven Baltimore hits over 10⅔ scoreless innings before giving way to Ron Perranoski in the eleventh. But Oriole pitcher Dave McNally was more than a match for Boswell. He gave up only three Twin hits—none in the final 7⅔ innings of the 11 he pitched—and took the win when Baltimore pinch hitter Curt Motton lined a single off Perranoski to score Powell from second with the game's only run.

In the third game, the Twins fell apart as the Orioles battered seven Minnesota pitchers for eighteen hits. Baltimore's Jim Palmer gave up more than a hit an inning himself, but coasted to the pennant 11–2.

Baltimore Orioles (East), 3; Minnesota Twins (West) 0

BAL (E)

PLAYER/POS	AVG	G	AB	R	H	2B	3B	HR	RB	BB	SO	SB
Mark Belanger, ss	.267	3	15	4	4	0	1	1	1	1	0	0
Paul Blair, of	.400	3	15	1	6	2	0	1	6	2	2	0
Don Buford, of	.286	3	14	3	4	1	0	0	1	3	0	0
Mike Cuellar, p	.000	1	2	0	0	0	0	0	0	0	1	0
Andy Etchebarren, c	.000	2	4	0	0	0	0	0	0	0	0	0
Dick Hall, p	.000	1	0	0	0	0	0	0	0	0	0	0
Elrod Hendricks, c	.250	3	8	2	2	2	0	0	3	1	2	0
Davy Johnson, 2b	.231	3	13	2	3	0	0	0	0	2	1	0
Marcelino Lopez, p	.000	1	0	0	0	0	0	0	0	0	0	0
Dave May, ph	.000	1	1	0	0	0	0	0	0	0	0	0
Dave Nc Nally, p	.000	1	4	0	0	0	0	0	0	0	2	0
Curt Motton, ph	.500	2	2	0	1	0	0	0	1	0	0	0
Jim Palmer, p	.000	1	5	0	0	0	0	0	0	0	3	0
Boog Powell, 1b	.385	3	13	2	5	0	0	1	1	2	0	0
Merv Rettenmund, ph	.000	1	0	0	0	0	0	0	0	0	0	0
Pete Richert, p	.000	1	0	0	0	0	0	0	0	0	0	0
Brooks Robinson, 3b	.500	3	14	1	7	1	0	0	0	0	0	0
Frank Robinson, of	.333	3	12	1	4	2	0	1	2	3	3	0
Chico Salmon, ph	.000	1	1	0	0	0	0	0	0	0	0	0
Eddie Watt, p	.000	1	0	0	0	0	0	0	0	0	0	0
TOTAL	.293		123	16	36	8	1	4	15	13	14	0

PITCHER	W	L	ERA	G	GS	CG	SV	SHO	IP	H	ER	BB	SO
Mike Cuellar	0	0	2.25	1	1	0	0	0	8.0	3	2	1	7
Dick Hall	1	0	0.00	1	0	0	0	0	0.2	0	0	0	1
Marcelino Lopez	0	0	0.00	1	0	0	0	0	0.1	1	0	2	0
Dave Nc Nally	1	0	0.00	1	1	1	0	1	11.0	3	0	5	11
Jim Palmer	1	0	2.00	1	1	1	0	0	9.0	10	2	2	4
Pete Richert	0	0	0.00	1	0	0	0	0	1.0	0	0	2	2
Eddie Watt	0	0	0.00	1	0	0	0	0	2.0	0	0	0	2
TOTAL	3	0	1.13	7	3	2	0	1	32.0	17	4	12	27

MIN (W)

PLAYER/POS	AVG	G	AB	R	H	2B	3B	HR	RB	BB	SO	SB
Bob Allison, of	.000	2	8	0	0	0	0	0	1	0	0	0
Dave Boswell, p	.000	1	4	0	0	0	0	0	0	0	4	0
Leo Cardenas, ss	.154	3	13	0	2	0	1	0	0	0	7	0
Rod Carew, 2b	.071	3	14	0	1	0	0	0	0	1	4	0
Dean Chance, p	.000	1	0	0	0	0	0	0	0	0	0	0
Joe Grzenda, p	.000	1	0	0	0	0	0	0	0	0	0	0
Tom Hall, p	.000	1	0	0	0	0	0	0	0	0	0	0
Harmon Killebrew, 3b	.125	3	8	2	1	1	0	0	0	6	2	0
Chuck Manuel, ph	.000	1	0	0	0	0	0	0	0	1	0	0
Bob Miller, p	.000	1	0	0	0	0	0	0	0	0	0	0
George Mitterwald, c	.143	2	7	0	1	0	0	0	0	1	3	0
Graig Nettles, ph	1.000	1	1	0	1	0	0	0	0	0	0	0
Tony Oliva, of	.385	3	13	3	5	2	0	1	2	1	3	1
Ron Perranoski, p	.000	3	1	0	0	0	0	0	0	0	1	0
Jim Perry, p	.000	1	3	0	0	0	0	0	0	0	0	0
Rich Reese, 1b	.167	3	12	0	2	0	0	0	2	1	1	0
Rich Renick, ph	.000	1	1	0	0	0	0	0	0	0	0	0
John Roseboro, c	.200	2	5	0	1	0	0	0	0	0	0	0
Cesar Tovar, of	.077	3	13	0	1	0	0	0	0	1	2	1
Ted Uhlaender, of	.167	2	6	0	1	0	0	0	0	0	0	0
Dick Woodson, p	1.000	1	1	0	1	0	0	0	0	0	0	0
Al Worthington, p	.000	1	0	0	0	0	0	0	0	0	0	0
TOTAL	.155		110	5	17	3	1	1	5	12	27	2

PITCHER	W	L	ERA	G	GS	CG	SV	SHO	IP	H	ER	BB	SO
Dave Boswell	0	1	0.84	1	1	0	0	0	10.2	7	1	7	4
Dean Chance	0	0	13.50	1	0	0	0	0	2.0	4	3	0	2
Joe Grzenda	0	0	0.00	1	0	0	0	0	0.2	0	0	0	0
Tom Hall	0	0	0.00	1	0	0	0	0	0.2	0	0	0	0
Bob Miller	0	1	5.40	1	1	0	0	0	1.2	5	1	0	0
Ron Perranoski	0	1	5.79	3	0	0	0	0	4.2	8	3	0	2
Jim Perry	0	0	3.38	1	1	0	0	0	8.0	6	3	3	3
Dick Woodson	0	0	10.80	1	0	0	0	0	1.2	3	2	3	2
Al Worthington	0	0	6.75	1	0	0	0	0	1.1	3	1	0	1
TOTAL	0	3	4.02	11	3	0	0	0	31.1	36	14	13	14

GAME 1 AT BAL OCT 4

MIN	000 010 200 000	3	4	2
BAL	000 110 001 001	4	10	1

Pitchers: Perry, PERRANOSKI (9) VS Cuellar, Richert (9), Watt (10), Lopez (12), HALL (12)
Home Runs: F.Robinson-BAL, Belanger-BAL, Oliva-MIN, Powell-BAL
Attendance: 39,324

GAME 2 AT BAL OCT 5

MIN	000 000 000 00	0	3	1
BAL	000 000 000 01	1	8	0

Pitchers: BOSWELL, Perranoski (11) VS McNALLY
Attendance: 41,704

GAME 3 AT MIN OCT 6

BAL	030 201 023	11	18	0
MIN	100 010 000	2	10	2

Pitchers: PALMER vs MILLER, Woodson (2), Hall (4), Worthington (5), Grzenda (6), Chance (7), Perranoski (9)
Home Runs: Blair-BAL
Attendance: 32,735

The heavy-hitting, slick-fielding Orioles, who also boasted the majors' top pitching staff, entered the Series clear favorites against the upstart Mets. But the "Miracle Mets," after losing the opener, polished off Baltimore with four straight wins.

The clubs' big winners, Met Tom Seaver (25–7) and Mike Cuellar (23–11) faced each other in the opener. Baltimore's leadoff batter, Don Buford, greeted Seaver with a home run, and a three-run Oriole rally with two out in the fourth made the score 4–0 before the Mets scored their first Series run in the seventh. Cuellar held New York to that one run for the victory.

No one scored for three innings of Game Two off Oriole Dave McNally or even hit Met Jerry Koosman safely. But Met Donn Clendenon led off the fourth with a home run as Koosman continued to no-hit Baltimore for three more innings. In the seventh, though, Baltimore's Paul Blair spoiled Koosman's no-hitter with a leadoff single, and after stealing second, scored the tying run on Brooks Robinson's single. But those were the only hits the O's would get, and in the top of the ninth three successive two-out Met singles produced what proved to be the winning run.

Met pitchers Gary Gentry and Nolan Ryan (with the assist of two spectacular catches by center fielder Tommie Agee that saved a total of five runs) combined for a shutout in Game Three. Agee's leadoff homer against Jim Palmer in the first was all the scoring the Mets would need, but they added four more runs before the game ended. Game Four was the Series' tightest. Seaver went the distance for the win, holding a 1–0 lead until a sacrifice fly scored the tying Baltimore run in the top of the ninth. In the bottom of the tenth, the Mets finally won it as a bunt thrown to first hit the runner and bounded away, allowing pinch runner Rod Gaspar to score all the way from second.

Dave McNally and Jerry Koosman tangled a second time in Game Five, and again Koosman and the Mets emerged victorious. McNally's two-run homer in the third gave him a lead which Frank Robinson expanded with a solo shot. But in an eerie sixth inning reprise of Game Four of the 1957 World Series featuring Nippy Jones, the Mets' Cleon Jones was struck by a pitch on the foot and awarded first base after inspection by the home plate umpire revealed tell-tale shoe polish on the ball. Each Jones produced a key run, Cleon coming home on Donn Clendenon's home run which followed immediately. Al Weis

homered in the seventh for a 3–3 tie. With McNally now gone, two doubles off Eddie Watt in the eighth brought in the go-ahead Met run, and a pair of errors let in a run for insurance. Koosman held Baltimore scoreless in the ninth and the Met miracle was complete.

New York Mets (NL), 4; Baltimore Orioles (AL) 1

NY (N)

PLAYER/POS	AVG	G	AB	R	H	2B	3B	HR	RB	BB	SO	SB
Tommie Agee, of	.167	5	18	1	3	0	0	1	1	2	5	1
Ken Boswell, 2b	.333	1	3	1	1	0	0	0	0	0	0	0
Don Cardwell, p	.000	1	0	0	0	0	0	0	0	0	0	0
Ed Charles, 3b	.133	4	15	1	2	1	0	0	0	0	2	0
Donn Clendenon, 1b	.357	4	14	4	5	1	0	3	4	2	6	0
Duffy Dyer, ph	.000	1	1	0	0	0	0	0	0	0	0	0
Wayne Garrett, 3b	.000	2	1	0	0	0	0	0	0	2	1	0
Rod Gaspar, of-1	.000	3	2	1	0	0	0	0	0	0	0	0
Gary Gentry, p	.333	1	3	0	1	1	0	0	2	0	2	0
Jerry Grote, c	.211	5	19	1	4	2	0	0	1	1	3	0
Bud Harrelson, ss	.176	5	17	1	3	0	0	0	0	3	4	0
Cleon Jones, of	.158	5	19	2	3	1	0	0	0	0	1	0
Jerry Koosman, p	.143	2	7	0	1	1	0	0	0	0	4	0
Ed Kranepool, 1b	.250	1	4	1	1	0	0	1	1	0	0	0
J.C. Martin, ph	.000	1	0	0	0	0	0	0	0	0	0	0
Nolan Ryan, p	.000	1	0	0	0	0	0	0	0	0	0	0
Tom Seaver, p	.000	2	4	0	0	0	0	0	0	0	2	0
Art Shamsky, of-1	.000	3	6	0	0	0	0	0	0	0	0	0
Ron Swoboda, of	.400	4	15	1	6	1	0	0	1	1	3	0
Ron Taylor, p	.000	2	0	0	0	0	0	0	0	0	0	0
Al Weis, 2b	.455	5	11	1	5	0	0	1	3	4	2	0
TOTAL	.220		159	15	35	8	0	6	13	15	35	1

PITCHER	W	L	ERA	G	GS	CG	SV	SHO	IP	H	ER	BB	SO
Don Cardwell	0	0	0.00	1	0	0	0	0	1.0	0	0	0	0
Gary Gentry	1	0	0.00	1	1	0	0	0	6.2	3	0	5	4
Jerry Koosman	2	0	2.04	2	2	1	0	0	17.2	7	4	4	9
Nolan Ryan	0	0	0.00	1	0	0	1	0	2.1	1	0	2	3
Tom Seaver	1	1	3.00	2	2	1	0	0	15.0	12	5	3	9
Ron Taylor	0	0	0.00	2	0	0	1	0	2.1	0	0	1	3
TOTAL	4	1	1.80	9	5	2	2	0	45.0	23	9	15	28

BAL (A)

PLAYER/POS	AVG	G	AB	R	H	2B	3B	HR	RB	BB	SO	SB
Mark Belanger, ss	.200	5	15	2	3	0	0	0	1	2	1	0
Paul Blair, of	.100	5	20	1	2	0	0	0	0	2	5	1
Don Buford, of	.100	5	20	1	2	1	0	1	2	2	4	0
Mike Cuellar, p	.400	2	5	0	2	0	0	0	1	0	3	0
Clay Dalrymple, ph	1.000	2	2	0	2	0	0	0	0	0	0	0
Andy Etchebarren, c	.000	2	6	0	0	0	0	0	0	0	1	0
Dick Hall, p	.000	1	0	0	0	0	0	0	0	0	0	0
Elrod Hendricks, c	.100	3	10	1	1	0	0	0	0	1	0	0
Davy Johnson, 2b	.063	5	16	1	1	0	0	0	0	2	1	0
Dave Leonhard, p	.000	1	0	0	0	0	0	0	0	0	0	0
Dave May, of	.000	2	1	0	0	0	0	0	0	1	1	0
Dave Mc Nally, p	.200	2	5	1	1	0	0	1	2	0	2	0
Curt Motton, ph	.000	1	1	0	0	0	0	0	0	0	0	0
Jim Palmer, p	.000	1	2	0	0	0	0	0	0	0	0	0
Boog Powell, 1b	.263	5	19	0	5	0	0	0	1	1	4	0
Merv Rettenmund, pr	.000	1	0	0	0	0	0	0	0	0	0	0
Pete Richert, p	.000	1	0	0	0	0	0	0	0	0	0	0
Brooks Robinson, 3b	.053	5	19	0	1	0	0	0	2	0	3	0
Frank Robinson, of	.188	5	16	2	3	0	0	1	1	4	3	0
Chico Salmon, pr	.000	2	0	0	0	0	0	0	0	0	0	0
Eddie Watt, p	.000	2	0	0	0	0	0	0	0	0	0	0
TOTAL	.146		157	9	23	1	0	3	9	15	28	1

PITCHER	W	L	ERA	G	GS	CG	SV	SHO	IP	H	ER	BB	SO
Mike Cuellar	1	0	1.13	2	2	1	0	0	16.0	13	2	4	13
Dick Hall	0	1	INF	1	0	0	0	0	0.0	1	0	1	0
Dave Leonhard	0	0	4.50	1	0	0	0	0	2.0	1	1	1	1
Dave Mc Nally	0	1	2.81	2	2	1	0	0	16.0	11	5	5	13
Jim Palmer	0	1	6.00	1	1	0	0	0	6.0	5	4	4	5
Pete Richert	0	0	INF	1	0	0	0	0	0.0	0	0	0	0
Eddie Watt	0	1	3.00	2	0	0	0	0	3.0	4	1	0	3
TOTAL	1	4	2.72	10	5	2	0	0	43.0	35	13	15	35

GAME 1 AT BAL OCT 11

```
NY    000 000 100    1 6 1
BAL   100 300 00X    4 6 0
```

Pitchers: SEAVER, Cardwell (6), Taylor (7) vs CUELLAR
Home Runs: Buford-BAL
Attendance: 50,429

GAME 2 AT BAL OCT 12

```
NY    000 100 001    2 6 0
BAL   000 000 100    1 2 0
```

Pitchers: KOOSMAN, Taylor (9) vs McNALLY
Home Runs: Clendenon-NY
Attendance: 50,850

GAME 3 AT NY OCT 14

```
BAL   000 000 000    0 4 1
NY    120 001 01X    5 6 0
```

Pitchers: PALMER, Leonhard (7) VS GENTRY, Ryan (7)
Home Runs: Agee-NY, Kranepool-NY
Attendance: 56,335

GAME 4 AT NY OCT 15

```
BAL   000 000 001 0    1 6 1
NY    010 000 000 1    2 10 1
```

Pitchers: Cuellar, Watt (8), HALL (10), Richert (10) vs SEAVER
Home Runs: Clendenon-NY
Attendance: 57,367

GAME 5 AT NY OCT 16

```
BAL   003 000 000    3 5 2
NY    000 002 12X    5 7 0
```

Pitchers: McNally, WATT (8) vs KOOSMAN
Home Runs: McNally-BAL, F.Robinson-BAL, Clendenon-NY, Weis-NY
Attendance: 57,397

Pitching was the game and three the magic number, as Cincinnati swept Pittsburgh, scoring three runs in each game while holding the Pirates to just three runs for the whole series.

Pirate pitcher Dock Ellis matched the Reds' Gary Nolan for nine scoreless innings in Game One before a pinch-hit triple, a single, and a double undid him for three runs in the top of the tenth. In Game Two Pittsburgh scored its first series run, but Red center fielder Bobby Tolan scored three for Baltimore—including a home run—to give Cincinnati its second win.

The Pirates took a lead for the only time in the series with a run in the top of the first inning of Game Three. But Tony Perez and Johnny Bench homered in the bottom of the inning to put the Reds up 2–1. The Pirates tied the score in the fifth, but three Red relievers combined to shut them out over the final four innings, while Tolan sank the Pirate ship with his second game-winner in two days: a single in the eighth that drove in Cincinnati's third—and final—run.

Cincinnati Reds (West), 3;
Pittsburgh Pirates (East) 0

CIN (W)

PLAYER/POS	AVG	G	AB	R	H	2B	3B	HR	RB	BB	SO	SB
Johnny Bench, c	.222	3	9	2	2	0	0	1	1	3	1	0
Angel Bravo, ph	.000	1	1	0	0	0	0	0	0	0	0	0
Bernie Carbo, of	.000	2	6	0	0	0	0	0	0	0	3	0
Clay Carroll, p	.000	2	0	0	0	0	0	0	0	0	0	0
Ty Cline, of-1	1.000	2	1	2	1	0	1	0	0	1	0	0
Tony Cloninger, p	.000	1	0	0	0	0	0	0	0	1	0	0
Dave Concepcion, ss	.000	3	0	0	0	0	0	0	0	0	0	0
Wayne Granger, p	.000	1	0	0	0	0	0	0	0	0	0	0
Don Gullett, p	.000	2	1	0	0	0	0	0	0	0	0	0
Tommy Helms, 2b	.273	3	11	0	3	0	0	0	0	0	1	0
Lee May, 1b	.167	3	12	0	2	1	0	0	2	0	2	0
Hal Mc Rae, of-1	.000	2	4	0	0	0	0	0	0	0	1	0
Jim Merritt, p	.000	1	2	0	0	0	0	0	0	0	2	0
Gary Nolan, p	.333	1	3	0	1	0	0	0	0	0	0	0
Tony Perez, 3b-3,1b-1	.333	3	12	1	4	2	0	1	2	1	1	0
Pete Rose, of	.231	3	13	1	3	0	0	0	1	0	0	0
Jimmy Stewart, of	.000	1	2	0	0	0	0	0	0	0	0	0
Bobby Tolan, of	.417	3	12	3	5	0	0	1	2	1	1	1
Milt Wilcox, p	.000	1	0	0	0	0	0	0	0	0	0	0
Woody Woodward, ss-3,3b-3	.100	3	10	0	1	0	0	0	0	0	1	0
TOTAL	.220		100	9	22	3	1	3	8	8	12	1

PITCHER	W	L	ERA	G	GS	CG	SV	SHO	IP	H	ER	BB	SO
Clay Carroll	0	0	0.00	2	0	0	1	0	1.1	2	0	0	2
Tony Cloninger	0	0	5.40	1	1	0	0	0	5.0	7	3	4	1
Wayne Granger	0	0	0.00	1	0	0	0	0	0.2	1	0	0	0
Don Gullett	0	0	0.00	2	0	0	2	0	3.2	1	0	2	3
Jim Merritt	1	0	1.69	1	1	0	0	0	5.1	3	1	0	2
Gary Nolan	1	0	0.00	1	1	0	0	0	9.0	8	0	4	6
Milt Wilcox	1	0	0.00	1	0	0	0	0	3.0	1	0	2	5
TOTAL	3	0	1.29	9	3	0	3	0	28.0	23	4	12	19

PIT (E)

PLAYER/POS	AVG	G	AB	R	H	2B	3B	HR	RB	BB	SO	SB
PLAYER, POS	AVG	G	AB	R	H	2B	3B	HR	RB	BB	SO	SB
Gene Alley, ss	.000	2	7	0	0	0	0	0	0	1	2	0
Matty Alou, of	.250	3	12	1	3	1	0	0	0	2	1	0
Dave Cash, 2b	.125	2	8	1	1	1	0	0	0	1	1	0
Roberto Clemente, of	.214	3	14	1	3	0	0	0	1	0	4	0
Dock Ellis, p	.000	1	2	0	0	0	0	0	0	0	1	0
Joe Gibbon, p	.000	2	0	0	0	0	0	0	0	0	0	0
Dave Giusti, p	.000	2	0	0	0	0	0	0	0	0	0	0
Richie Hebner, 3b	.667	2	6	4	2	0	0	0	2	1	0
Johnny Jeter, of-1	.000	3	2	0	0	0	0	0	0	0	2	0
Bill Mazeroski, 2b	.000	1	2	0	0	0	0	0	0	2	0	0
Bob Moose, p	.000	1	4	0	0	0	0	0	0	0	1	0
Al Oliver, 1b	.250	2	8	0	2	0	0	0	1	1	0	0
Jose Pagan, 3b	.333	1	3	0	1	0	0	0	0	1	1	0
Freddie Patek, ss	.000	1	3	0	0	0	0	0	0	1	2	0
Bob Robertson, 1b-1	.200	2	5	0	1	1	0	0	0	0	0	0
Manny Sanguillen, c	.167	3	12	0	2	0	0	0	0	0	1	0
Willie Stargell, of	.500	3	12	0	6	1	0	0	1	1	1	0
Luke Walker, p	.000	1	2	0	0	0	0	0	0	0	1	0
TOTAL	.225		102	3	23	6	0	0	3	12	19	0

PITCHER	W	L	ERA	G	GS	CG	SV	SHO	IP	H	ER	BB	SO
Dock Ellis	0	1	2.79	1	1	0	0	0	9.2	9	3	4	1
Joe Gibbon	0	0	0.00	2	0	0	0	0	0.1	1	0	0	1
Dave Giusti	0	0	3.86	2	0	0	0	0	2.1	3	1	1	1
Bob Moose	0	1	3.52	1	1	0	0	0	7.2	4	3	2	4
Luke Walker	0	1	1.29	1	1	0	0	0	7.0	5	1	1	5
TOTAL	0	3	2.67	7	3	0	0	0	27.0	22	8	8	12

GAME 1 AT PIT OCT 3

CIN	000 000 000 3	3	9	0
PIT	000 000 000 0	0	8	0

Pitchers: NOLAN, Carroll (10) vs ELLIS, Gibbon (10)
Attendance: 33,088

GAME 2 AT PIT OCT 4

CIN	001 010 010	3	8	1
PIT	000 001 000	1	5	2

Pitchers: MERRITT, Carroll (6), Gullett (6) vs WALKER, Giusti (8)
Home Runs: Tolan-CIN
Attendance: 39,317

GAME 3 AT CIN OCT 5

PIT	100 010 000	2	10	0
CIN	200 000 01X	3	5	0

Pitchers: MOOSE, Gibbon (8), Giusti (8) VS Cloninger, WILCOX (6), Granger (9), Gullett (9)
Home Runs: Perez-CIN, Bench-CIN
Attendance: 40,538

For the second year in a row, Baltimore swept Minnesota in the LCS. In the first two games the Orioles' attack featured the big inning. The score was tied 2–2 in the first game as the Orioles came to bat in the top of the fourth. But by the time the Twins came to bat in the inning, they were seven runs behind—thanks in part to a grand slam by Baltimore pitcher Mike Cuellar. Harmon Killebrew's two-run homer in the fifth helped bring the Twins within three, but they came no closer.

Except for home runs to Killebrew and Tony Oliva in the fourth inning, Oriole pitcher Dave Mc-Nally stopped the Twins in Game Two, and Baltimore held a close 4–3 lead after eight. If they had been playing at home, they wouldn't have needed to bat at all in the ninth. But they did come to bat in the top of the ninth, and they once again buried Minnesota under a seven-run inning.

In the third game, for the second year in a row, Oriole pitcher Jim Palmer breezed through the series clincher. Baltimore scored five runs for him in the first three innings, and another in the eighth—four more than he needed to carry his club to another pennant.

Baltimore Orioles (East), 3; Minnesota Twins (West) 0

BAL (E)

PLAYER/POS	AVG	G	AB	R	H	2B	3B	HR	RB	BB	SO	SB
Mark Belanger, ss	.333	3	12	5	4	0	0	0	1	1	0	0
Paul Blair, of	.077	3	13	0	1	0	0	0	0	1	4	0
Don Buford, of	.429	2	7	2	3	1	0	1	3	2	0	0
Mike Cuellar, p	.500	1	2	1	1	0	0	1	4	0	1	0
Andy Etchebarren, c	.111	2	9	1	1	0	0	0	0	0	3	0
Dick Hall, p	.500	1	2	0	1	0	0	0	0	0	1	0
Elrod Hendricks, c	.400	1	5	2	2	0	0	0	0	0	1	0
Davy Johnson, 2b	.364	3	11	4	4	0	0	2	4	1	1	0
Dave Nc Nally, p	.400	1	5	1	2	1	0	0	1	0	1	0
Jim Palmer, p	.250	1	4	1	1	1	0	0	1	0	0	0
Boog Powell, 1b	.429	3	14	2	6	2	0	1	6	0	3	0
Merv Rettenmund, of	.333	1	3	1	1	0	0	0	1	2	1	1
Brooks Robinson, 3b	.583	3	12	4	7	2	0	0	1	0	1	0
Frank Robinson, of	.200	3	10	3	2	0	0	1	2	5	2	0
TOTAL	.330		109	27	36	7	0	6	24	12	19	1

PITCHER	W	L	ERA	G	GS	CG	SV	SHO	IP	H	ER	BB	SO
Mike Cuellar	0	0	12.46	1	1	0	0	0	4.1	10	6	1	2
Dick Hall	1	0	0.00	1	0	0	0	0	4.2	1	0	0	3
Dave Nc Nally	1	0	3.00	1	1	1	0	0	9.0	6	3	5	5
Jim Palmer	1	0	1.00	1	1	1	0	0	9.0	7	1	3	12
TOTAL	3	0	3.33	4	3	2	0	0	27.0	24	10	9	22

MIN (W)

PLAYER/POS	AVG	G	AB	R	H	2B	3B	HR	RB	BB	SO	SB
Bob Allison, ph	.000	3	2	0	0	0	0	0	0	1	1	0
Brant Alyea, of-2	.000	3	7	1	0	0	0	0	0	2	3	0
Bert Blyleven, p	.000	1	0	0	0	0	0	0	0	0	0	0
Leo Cardenas, ss	.182	3	11	1	2	0	0	0	1	1	1	0
Rod Carew, ph	.000	2	2	0	0	0	0	0	0	0	1	0
Tom Hall, p	.000	2	1	0	0	0	0	0	0	0	1	0
Jim Holt, of	.000	3	5	0	0	0	0	0	0	0	2	0
Jim Kaat, p	.000	1	1	0	0	0	0	0	0	0	0	0
Harmon Killebrew, 3b-2,1b-1	.273	3	11	2	3	0	0	2	4	2	4	0
Chuck Manuel, ph	.000	1	1	0	0	0	0	0	0	0	1	0
George Mitterwald, c	.500	2	8	2	4	1	0	0	2	0	2	0
Tony Oliva, of	.500	3	12	2	6	2	0	1	1	0	1	0
Ron Perranoski, p	.000	2	0	0	0	0	0	0	0	0	0	0
Jim Perry, p	.000	2	1	0	0	0	0	0	1	0	1	0
Frank Quilici, 2b-2	.000	3	2	0	0	0	0	0	0	0	1	0
Paul Ratliff, c	.250	1	4	0	1	0	0	0	0	0	1	0
Rich Reese, 1b	.143	2	7	0	1	0	0	0	0	1	1	0
Rich Renick, 3b-1	.200	2	5	0	1	0	0	0	0	0	1	0
Danny Thompson, 2b	.125	3	8	0	1	1	0	0	0	1	0	0
Luis Tiant, p	.000	1	0	0	0	0	0	0	0	0	0	0
Cesar Tovar, of-3,2b-1	.385	3	13	2	5	0	1	0	1	0	0	0
Stan Williams, p	.000	2	0	0	0	0	0	0	0	1	0	0
Dick Woodson, p	.000	1	0	0	0	0	0	0	0	0	0	0
Bill Zepp, p	.000	2	0	0	0	0	0	0	0	0	0	0
TOTAL	.238		101	10	24	4	1	3	10	9	22	0

PITCHER	W	L	ERA	G	GS	CG	SV	SHO	IP	H	ER	BB	SO
Bert Blyleven	0	0	0.00	1	0	0	0	0	2.0	2	0	0	2
Tom Hall	0	1	6.75	2	0	0	0	0	5.1	6	4	4	6
Jim Kaat	0	1	9.00	1	1	0	0	0	2.0	6	2	2	1
Ron Perranoski	0	0	19.29	2	0	0	0	0	2.1	5	5	1	3
Jim Perry	0	1	13.50	2	1	0	0	0	5.1	10	8	1	3
Luis Tiant	0	0	13.50	1	0	0	0	0	0.2	1	1	0	0
Stan Williams	0	0	0.00	2	0	0	0	0	6.0	2	0	1	2
Dick Woodson	0	0	9.00	1	0	0	0	0	1.0	2	1	1	0
Bill Zepp	0	0	6.75	2	0	0	0	0	1.1	2	1	2	2
TOTAL	0	3	7.62	14	3	0	0	0	26.0	36	22	12	19

GAME 1 AT MIN OCT 3

BAL	020	701	000	10 13 0
MIN	110	130	000	6 11 2

Pitchers: Cuellar, HALL (5) vs PERRY, Zepp (4), Woodson (5), Williams (6), Perranoski (9)
Home Runs: Cuellar-BAL, Buford-BAL, Powell-BAL, Killebrew-MIN
Attendance: 26,847

GAME 2 AT MIN OCT 4

BAL	102	100	007	11 13 0
MIN	000	300	000	3 6 2

Pitchers: McNALLY vs HALL, Zepp (4), Williams (5), Perranoski (8), Tiant (9)
Home Runs: F.Robinson-BAL, Killebrew-MIN, Oliva-MIN, Johnson-BAL
Attendance: 27,490

GAME 3 AT BAL OCT 5

MIN	000	010	000	1 7 2
BAL	113	000	10X	6 10 0

Pitchers: KAAT, Blyleven (3), Hall (5), Perry (7) vs PALMER
Home Runs: Johnson-BAL
Attendance: 27,608

With a near-sweep of Cincinnati, the Orioles helped Baltimore fans forget their 1969 Series humiliation by the New York Mets. Baltimore's first two wins, though, were closely contested. In the opener in Cincinnati (the first World Series game played on artificial grass), a Red run in the first inning and Lee May's third-inning two-run homer off Oriole starter Jim Palmer gave Cincinnati a 3–0 lead. But Orioles Boog Powell and Elrod Hendricks tagged Red starter Gary Nolan for home runs in the fourth and fifth that evened the score, and Brooks Robinson—whose otherworldly defense at third gave Reds righthanded hitters nightmares throughout the Series—homered in the seventh for a one-run Baltimore lead that held up as Palmer settled down to pitch one-hit ball from the fourth inning until he was relieved for the final out of the ninth.

Game Two was just as close. The Reds scored four runs in the first three innings, but Baltimore came back with six in the fourth and fifth. Johnny Bench's leadoff homer in the last of the sixth brought the Reds within one, but that was the end of the scoring for either side. In Game Three Oriole Dave McNally gave up nine hits and three runs. But he himself hit a grand slam in the sixth inning to cement what became a 9–3 victory.

On the verge of a Series sweep, the Orioles scored three runs in the last of the third inning of Game Four to take a 4–2 lead. But the Reds' Pete Rose homered in the fifth, and although Baltimore got the run back in the sixth, Lee May's three-run blast in the eighth overcame the Oriole lead and gave the Reds a narrow 6–5 win as Red reliever Clay Carroll permitted only one Oriole to hit safely over the final 3⅔ innings.

Mike Cuellar, driven out of Game Two in the third inning, hurled the complete game for Baltimore in Game Five, even though Cincinnati hammered him for four hits (three of them doubles) and three runs in the top of the first inning. But as Oriole home runs by Frank Robinson and Merv Rettenmund highlighted a Baltimore onslaught that produced fifteen hits and nine runs, Cuellar settled down, holding Cincinnati to a walk and a pair of harmless singles over the final eight innings to bring Baltimore its second world title in five years.

Baltimore Orioles (AL), 4;
Cincinnati Reds (NL) 1

BAL (A)

PLAYER/POS	AVG	G	AB	R	H	2B	3B	HR	RB	BB	SO	SB
Mark Belanger, ss	.105	5	19	0	2	0	0	0	0	1	1	2	0
Paul Blair, of	.474	5	19	5	9	1	0	0	3	2	4	0
Don Buford, of	.267	4	15	3	4	0	0	1	1	3	2	0
Terry Crowley, ph	.000	1	1	0	0	0	0	0	0	0	0	0
Mike Cuellar, p	.000	2	4	0	0	0	0	0	0	0	2	0
Moe Drabowsky, p	.000	2	1	0	0	0	0	0	0	0	1	0
Andy Etchebarren, c	.143	2	7	1	1	0	0	0	0	2	3	0
Dick Hall, p	.000	1	1	0	0	0	0	0	0	0	1	0
Elrod Hendricks, c	.364	3	11	1	4	1	0	1	4	1	2	0
Davy Johnson, 2b	.313	5	16	2	5	2	0	0	2	5	2	0
Marcelino Lopez, p	.000	1	0	0	0	0	0	0	0	0	0	0
Dave Mc Nally, p	.250	1	4	1	1	0	0	1	4	0	2	0
Jim Palmer, p	.143	2	7	1	1	0	0	0	0	0	3	0
Tom Phoebus, p	.000	1	0	0	0	0	0	0	0	0	0	0
Boog Powell, 1b	.294	5	17	6	5	1	0	2	5	5	2	0
Merv Rettenmund, of-1	.400	2	5	2	2	0	0	1	2	1	0	0
Pete Richert, p	.000	1	0	0	0	0	0	0	0	0	0	0
Brooks Robinson, 3b	.429	5	21	5	9	2	0	2	6	0	2	0
Frank Robinson, of	.273	5	22	5	6	0	0	2	4	0	5	0
Chico Salmon, ph	1.000	1	1	1	1	0	0	0	0	0	0	0
Eddie Watt, p	.000	1	0	0	0	0	0	0	0	0	0	0
TOTAL	.292		171	33	50	7	0	10	32	20	33	0

PITCHER	W	L	ERA	G	GS	CG	SV	SHO	IP	H	ER	BB	SO
Mike Cuellar	1	0	3.18	2	2	1	0	0	11.1	10	4	2	5
Moe Drabowsky	0	0	2.70	2	0	0	0	0	3.1	2	1	1	1
Dick Hall	0	0	0.00	1	0	0	1	0	2.1	0	0	0	0
Marcelino Lopez	0	0	0.00	1	0	0	0	0	0.1	0	0	0	0
Dave Mc Nally	1	0	3.00	1	1	1	0	0	9.0	9	3	2	5
Jim Palmer	1	0	4.60	2	2	0	0	0	15.2	11	8	9	9
Tom Phoebus	1	0	0.00	1	0	0	0	0	1.2	1	0	0	0
Pete Richert	0	0	0.00	1	0	0	1	0	0.1	0	0	0	0
Eddie Watt	0	1	9.00	1	0	0	0	0	1.0	2	1	1	3
TOTAL	4	1	3.40	12	5	2	2	0	45.0	35	17	15	23

CIN (N)

PLAYER/POS	AVG	G	AB	R	H	2B	3B	HR	RB	BB	SO	SB
Johnny Bench, c	.211	5	19	3	4	0	0	1	3	1	2	0
Angel Bravo, ph	.000	4	2	0	0	0	0	0	0	1	1	0
Bernie Carbo, of-2	.000	4	8	0	0	0	0	0	0	2	3	0
Clay Carroll, p	.000	4	1	0	0	0	0	0	0	0	1	0
Darrel Chaney, ss	.000	3	1	0	0	0	0	0	0	0	1	0
Ty Cline, ph	.333	3	3	0	1	0	0	0	0	0	0	0
Tony Cloninger, p	.000	2	2	0	0	0	0	0	0	0	1	0
Dave Concepcion, ss	.333	3	9	0	3	0	1	0	3	0	0	0
Pat Corrales, ph	.000	1	1	0	0	0	0	0	0	0	0	0
Wayne Granger, p	.000	2	0	0	0	0	0	0	0	0	0	0
Don Gullett, p	.000	3	1	0	0	0	0	0	0	0	1	0
Tommy Helms, 2b	.222	5	18	1	4	0	0	0	0	1	1	0
Lee May, 1b	.389	5	18	6	7	2	0	2	8	2	2	0
Jim Mc Glothlin, p	.000	1	2	0	0	0	0	0	0	0	1	0
Hal Mc Rae, of	.455	3	11	1	5	2	0	0	3	0	1	0
Jim Merritt, p	.000	1	1	0	0	0	0	0	0	0	1	0
Gary Nolan, p	.000	2	3	0	0	0	0	0	0	0	0	0
Tony Perez, 3b	.056	5	18	2	1	0	0	0	0	3	4	0
Pete Rose, of	.250	5	20	2	5	1	0	1	2	2	0	0
Jimmy Stewart, ph	.000	2	2	0	0	0	0	0	0	0	1	0
Bobby Tolan, of	.211	5	19	5	4	1	0	1	1	3	2	1
Ray Washburn, p	.000	1	0	0	0	0	0	0	0	0	0	0
Milt Wilcox, p	.000	2	0	0	0	0	0	0	0	0	0	0
Woody Woodward, ss-3	.200	4	5	0	1	0	0	0	0	0	0	0
TOTAL	.213		164	20	35	6	1	5	20	15	23	1

PITCHER	W	L	ERA	G	GS	CG	SV	SHO	IP	H	ER	BB	SO
Clay Carroll	1	0	0.00	4	0	0	0	0	9.0	5	0	2	11
Tony Cloninger	0	1	7.36	2	1	0	0	0	7.1	10	6	5	4
Wayne Granger	0	0	33.75	2	0	0	0	0	1.1	7	5	1	1
Don Gullett	0	0	1.35	3	0	0	0	0	6.2	5	1	4	4
Jim Mc Glothlin	0	0	8.31	1	1	0	0	0	4.1	6	4	2	2
Jim Merritt	0	1	21.60	1	1	0	0	0	1.2	3	4	1	0
Gary Nolan	0	1	7.71	2	2	0	0	0	9.1	9	8	3	9
Ray Washburn	0	0	13.50	1	0	0	0	0	1.1	2	2	0	0
Milt Wilcox	0	1	9.00	2	0	0	0	0	2.0	3	2	0	2
TOTAL	1	4	6.70	18	5	0	0	0	43.0	50	32	20	33

For the first time, an LCS went more than the minimum three games, as Pittsburgh rebounded from a loss in the opener to take the next three from San Francisco.

The Pirates scored first, with two runs in the third inning of Game One, but the Giants came back with a run in the bottom of the inning and put the game away in the fifth as Tito Fuentes and Willie McCovey both hit two-out two-run homers. Pirate first baseman Bob Robertson avenged his club's opening-game defeat the next day, battering four of the Giants' six pitchers for three home runs and a double—and five RBIs—in the Pirates' 9–5 win. Robertson continued his assault in Game Three, homering off Juan Marichal in the second. The Giants came back with a run in the sixth, but third baseman Richie Hebner put the game away with a second Pirate home run off Marichal in the eighth.

Both clubs scored five times in the first two innings of Game Four. But Pirate relievers Bruce Kison and Dave Giusti then pinned the Giants down for the final seven innings, while Roberto Clemente and Al Oliver combined for four RBIs in the sixth to capture the flag.

Pittsburgh Pirates (East), 3; San Francisco Giants (West), 1

PIT (E)

PLAYER/POS	AVG	G	AB	R	H	2B	3B	HR	RB	BB	SO	SB
Gene Alley, ss	.500	1	2	1	1	0	0	0	0	0	0	0
Steve Blass, p	.000	2	1	0	0	0	0	0	0	0	1	0
Dave Cash, 2b	.421	4	19	5	8	2	0	0	1	0	1	1
Roberto Clemente, of	.333	4	18	2	6	0	0	0	4	1	6	0
Gene Clines, of	.333	1	3	1	1	0	0	1	1	0	1	0
Vic Davalillo, ph	.000	2	2	0	0	0	0	0	0	0	1	0
Dock Ellis, p	.000	1	3	0	0	0	0	0	0	0	2	0
Dave Giusti, p	.000	4	0	0	0	0	0	0	0	0	0	0
Richie Hebner, 3b	.294	4	17	3	5	1	0	2	4	0	4	0
Jackie Hernandez, ss	.231	4	13	2	3	0	0	0	1	0	4	0
Bob Johnson, p	.000	1	2	0	0	0	0	0	0	0	1	0
Bruce Kison, p	.000	1	2	0	0	0	0	0	0	0	0	0
Milt May, ph	.000	1	1	0	0	0	0	0	0	0	0	0
Bill Mazeroski, ph	1.000	1	1	1	1	0	0	0	0	0	0	0
Bob Miller, p	.000	1	1	0	0	0	0	0	0	0	0	0
Bob Moose, p	.000	1	0	0	0	0	0	0	0	0	0	0
Al Oliver, of	.250	4	12	3	3	0	0	1	5	1	3	0
Jose Pagan, 3b	.000	1	1	0	0	0	0	0	0	0	0	0
Bob Robertson, 1b	.438	4	16	5	7	1	0	4	6	0	2	0
Manny Sanguillen, c	.267	4	15	1	4	0	0	0	1	1	1	1
Willie Stargell, of	.000	4	14	1	0	0	0	0	0	2	6	0
TOTAL	.271		144	24	39	4	0	8	23	5	33	2

PITCHER	W	L	ERA	G	GS	CG	SV	SHO	IP	H	ER	BB	SO
Steve Blass	0	1	11.57	2	2	0	0	0	7.0	14	9	2	11
Dock Ellis	1	0	3.60	1	1	0	0	0	5.0	6	2	4	1
Dave Giusti	0	0	0.00	4	0	0	3	0	5.1	1	0	2	3
Bob Johnson	1	0	0.00	1	1	0	0	0	8.0	5	0	3	7
Bruce Kison	1	0	0.00	1	0	0	0	0	4.2	2	0	2	3
Bob Miller	0	0	6.00	1	0	0	0	0	3.0	3	2	3	3
Bob Moose	0	0	0.00	1	0	0	0	0	2.0	0	0	0	0
TOTAL	3	1	3.34	11	4	0	3	0	35.0	31	13	16	28

SF (W)

PLAYER/POS	AVG	G	AB	R	H	2B	3B	HR	RB	BB	SO	SB
Jim Barr, p	.000	1	1	0	0	0	0	0	0	0	0	0
Bobby Bonds, of	.250	3	8	0	2	0	0	0	0	2	4	0
Ron Bryant, p	.000	1	0	0	0	0	0	0	0	0	0	0
Don Carrithers, p	.000	1	0	0	0	0	0	0	0	0	0	0
John Cumberland, p	.000	1	0	0	0	0	0	0	0	0	0	0
Dick Dietz, c	.067	4	15	0	1	0	0	0	0	2	5	0
Frank Duffy, ph	.000	1	1	0	0	0	0	0	0	0	1	0
Tito Fuentes, 2b	.313	4	16	4	5	1	0	1	2	1	3	0
Alan Gallagher, 3b	.100	4	10	0	1	0	0	0	0	0	2	0
Steve Hamilton, p	.000	1	0	0	0	0	0	0	0	0	0	0
Jim Ray Hart, 3b-1	.000	3	5	0	0	0	0	0	0	0	2	0
Ken Henderson, of	.313	4	16	3	5	1	0	0	2	2	1	1
Jerry Johnson, p	.000	1	0	0	0	0	0	0	0	0	0	0
Dave Kingman, of-2	.111	4	9	0	1	0	0	0	0	1	3	0
Hal Lanier, 3b	.000	1	1	0	0	0	0	0	0	0	0	0
Juan Marichal, p	.000	2	3	0	0	0	0	0	0	0	1	0
Willie Mays, of	.267	4	15	2	4	2	0	1	3	3	3	1
Willie Mc Covey, 1b	.429	4	14	2	6	0	0	2	6	4	2	0
Don Mc Mahon, p	.000	2	0	0	0	0	0	0	0	0	0	0
Gaylord Perry, p	.250	2	4	0	1	0	0	0	0	0	0	0
Jimmy Rosario, pr	.000	1	0	0	0	0	0	0	0	0	0	0
Chris Speier, ss	.357	4	14	4	5	1	0	1	1	1	1	0
TOTAL	.235		132	15	31	5	0	5	14	16	28	2

PITCHER	W	L	ERA	G	GS	CG	SV	SHO	IP	H	ER	BB	SO
Jim Barr	0	0	9.00	1	0	0	0	0	1.0	3	1	0	2
Ron Bryant	0	0	4.50	1	0	0	0	0	2.0	1	1	1	2
Don Carrithers	0	0	INF	1	0	0	0	0	0.0	3	3	0	0
John Cumberland	0	1	9.00	1	1	0	0	0	3.0	7	3	0	4
Steve Hamilton	0	0	9.00	1	0	0	0	0	1.0	1	1	0	3
Jerry Johnson	0	0	13.50	1	0	0	0	0	1.1	1	2	1	2
Juan Marichal	0	1	2.25	1	1	1	0	0	8.0	4	2	0	6
Don Mc Mahon	0	0	0.00	2	0	0	0	0	3.0	0	0	0	3
Gaylord Perry	1	1	6.14	2	2	1	0	0	14.2	19	10	3	11
TOTAL	1	3	6.09	11	4	2	0	0	34.0	39	23	5	33

GAME 1 AT SF OCT 2

PIT	002	000	200	4	9 0
SF	001	040	00X	5	7 2

Pitchers: BLASS, Moose (6), Giusti (8) VS PERRY
Home Runs: Fuentes-SF, McCovey-SF
Attendance: 40,977

GAME 2 AT SF OCT 3

PIT	010	210	401	9	15 0
SF	110	000	002	4	9 0

Pitchers: ELLIS, Miller (6), Giusti (9) VS CUMBERLAND, Barr (4), McMahon (5), Carrithers (7), Bryant (7), Hamilton (9)
Home Runs: Robertson-PIT (3), Clines-PIT, Mays-SF
Attendance: 42,562

GAME 3 AT PIT OCT 5

SF	000	001	000	1	5 2
PIT	010	000	01X	2	4 1

Pitchers: MARICHAL vs JOHNSON, Giusti (9)
Home Runs: Robertson-PIT, Hebner-PIT
Attendance: 38,322

GAME 4 AT PIT OCT 6

SF	140	000	000	5	10 0
PIT	230	004	00X	9	11 2

Pitchers: PERRY, Johnson (6), McMahon (8) VS Blass, KISON (3), Giusti (7)
Home Runs: Speier-SF, McCovey-SF, Hebner-PIT, Oliver-PIT
Attendance: 35,487

Baltimore, dividing its fifteen runs evenly among the three games, swept the ALCS for the third year in a row.

Oakland's Vida Blue took a 3–1 lead into the seventh inning of Game One, but with two away and men on first and third, an Oriole single and two doubles pushed across four runs to beat him 5–3, as Oriole starter Dave McNally and reliever Eddie Watt held the A's scoreless from the fifth inning on. In the second game Oakland managed only one run off Mike Cuellar, while the Orioles hammered Catfish Hunter for five runs on four homers—two of them by Boog Powell, including one in the eighth with a man aboard.

Reggie Jackson retaliated for the A's in Game Three with two home runs off Jim Palmer, and Sal Bando added a third. But Palmer permitted no other A's to score, and—supported by a Baltimore run in the first and two each in the fifth and seventh—preserved an Oriole lead throughout the game, for the third year in a row clinching the pennant for Baltimore with a complete-game victory.

Baltimore Orioles (East), 3;
Oakland A's (West) 0

BAL (E)

PLAYER/POS	AVG	G	AB	R	H	2B	3B	HR	RB	BB	SO	SB
Mark Belanger, ss	.250	3	8	1	2	0	0	0	1	3	2	0
Paul Blair, of	.333	3	9	1	3	1	0	0	2	0	3	0
Don Buford, of	.429	2	7	1	3	0	1	0	0	2	1	0
Mike Cuellar, p	.333	1	3	0	1	0	0	0	0	0	2	0
Andy Etchebarren, c	.000	2	5	0	0	0	0	0	0	0	0	0
Elrod Hendricks, c	.500	2	4	1	2	0	0	1	2	1	1	0
Davy Johnson, 2b	.300	3	10	2	3	2	0	0	0	3	1	0
Dave Nc Nally, p	.000	1	2	0	0	0	0	0	0	0	0	0
Curt Motton, ph	1.000	1	1	0	1	1	0	0	1	0	0	0
Jim Palmer, p-1	.200	2	5	1	1	0	0	0	0	0	1	0
Boog Powell, 1b	.300	3	10	4	3	0	0	2	3	3	3	0
Merv Rettenmund, of	.250	3	8	0	2	1	0	0	1	0	3	0
Brooks Robinson, 3b	.364	3	11	2	4	1	0	1	3	0	1	0
Frank Robinson, of	.083	3	12	2	1	1	0	0	1	1	4	0
Eddie Watt, p	.000	1	0	0	0	0	0	0	0	0	0	0
TOTAL	.274		95	15	26	7	1	4	14	13	22	0

PITCHER	W	L	ERA	G	GS	CG	SV	SHO	IP	H	ER	BB	SO
Mike Cuellar	1	0	1.00	1	1	1	0	0	9.0	6	1	1	2
Dave Nc Nally	1	0	3.86	1	1	0	0	0	7.0	7	3	1	5
Jim Palmer	1	0	3.00	1	1	1	0	0	9.0	7	3	3	8
Eddie Watt	0	0	0.00	1	0	0	1	0	2.0	2	0	0	1
TOTAL	3	0	2.33	4	3	2	1	0	27.0	22	7	5	16

OAK (W)

PLAYER/POS	AVG	G	AB	R	H	2B	3B	HR	RB	BB	SO	SB
Sal Bando, 3b	.364	3	11	3	4	2	0	1	1	1	0	0
Curt Blefary, ph	.000	1	1	0	0	0	0	0	0	0	1	0
Vida Blue, p	.000	1	3	0	0	0	0	0	0	0	3	0
Bert Campaneris, ss	.167	3	12	0	2	1	0	0	0	0	1	0
Tommy Davis, 1b-2	.375	3	8	1	3	1	0	0	0	0	0	0
Dave Duncan, c	.500	2	6	0	3	1	0	0	2	0	0	0
Mike Epstein, 1b-1	.200	2	5	0	1	0	0	0	0	0	3	0
Rollie Fingers, p	.000	2	0	0	0	0	0	0	0	0	0	0
Mudcat Grant, p	.000	1	0	0	0	0	0	0	0	0	0	0
Dick Green, 2b	.286	3	7	0	2	0	0	0	0	1	1	0
Mike Hegan, ph	.000	1	1	0	0	0	0	0	0	0	1	0
Catfish Hunter, p	.000	1	3	0	0	0	0	0	0	0	1	0
Reggie Jackson, of	.333	3	12	2	4	1	0	2	2	0	1	0
Darold Knowles, p	.000	1	0	0	0	0	0	0	0	0	0	0
Bob Locker, p	.000	1	0	0	0	0	0	0	0	0	0	0
Angel Mangual, of	.167	3	12	1	2	1	1	0	2	0	1	0
Rick Monday, of	.000	1	3	0	0	0	0	0	0	1	2	0
Joe Rudi, of	.143	2	7	0	1	1	0	0	0	1	0	0
Diego Segui, p	.000	1	2	0	0	0	0	0	0	0	0	0
Gene Tenace, c	.000	1	3	0	0	0	0	0	0	1	1	0
TOTAL	.229		96	7	22	8	1	3	7	5	16	0

PITCHER	W	L	ERA	G	GS	CG	SV	SHO	IP	H	ER	BB	SO
Vida Blue	0	1	6.43	1	1	0	0	0	7.0	7	5	2	8
Rollie Fingers	0	0	7.71	2	0	0	0	0	2.1	2	2	1	2
Mudcat Grant	0	0	0.00	1	0	0	0	0	2.0	3	0	0	2
Catfish Hunter	0	1	5.63	1	1	1	0	0	8.0	7	5	2	6
Darold Knowles	0	0	0.00	1	0	0	0	0	0.1	1	0	0	0
Bob Locker	0	0	0.00	1	0	0	0	0	0.2	0	0	2	0
Diego Segui	0	1	5.79	1	1	0	0	0	4.2	6	3	6	4
TOTAL	0	3	5.40	8	3	1	0	0	25.0	26	15	13	22

GAME 1 AT BAL OCT 3

OAK	020	100	000	3	9 0
BAL	000	100	40X	5	7 1

Pitchers: BLUE, Fingers (8) vs McNALLY, Watt (8)
Attendance: 42,621

GAME 2 AT BAL OCT 4

OAK	000	100	000	1	6 0
BAL	011	000	12X	5	7 0

Pitchers: HUNTER vs CUELLAR
Home Runs: B.Robinson-BAL, Powell-BAL (2), Hendricks-BAL
Attendance: 35,003

GAME 3 AT OAK OCT 5

BAL	100	020	200	5	12 0
OAK	001	001	010	3	7 0

Pitchers: PALMER vs SEGUI, Fingers (5), Knowles (7), Locker (7), Grant (8)
Home Runs: Jackson-OAK (2), Bando-OAK
Attendance: 33,176

In its third successive Series, Baltimore faced its third different opponent and beat the Pirates in the first two games. A walk, a wild pitch, two Baltimore errors, and a single in the second inning of the opener gave Pittsburgh an early 3–0 lead. But Oriole pitcher Dave McNally shut out the Pirates on two hits the rest of the game as Frank Robinson, Merv Rettenmund and Don Buford homered to give Baltimore a 5–3 victory. Jim Palmer took the win in Game Two as Baltimore hammered Pirate pitching for fourteen hits and eleven runs before Palmer issued Richie Hebner a three-run homer—Pittsburgh's only scoring—in the eighth.

The Pirates overtook the Orioles when the Series moved to Pittsburgh. Steve Blass pitched a three-hitter in Game Three, and while Frank Robinson's solo homer in the seventh ended Blass's shutout, a three-run shot by Pirate Bob Robertson in the last of the inning cemented a 5–1 Pittsburgh win. The next evening (in the first World Series night game ever), Baltimore scored three times in the top of the first inning, but two Pirate runs later in the inning and another run in the third tied the game. It remained tied until Pirate pinch hitter Milt May singled home the game winner with two away in the seventh.

With the Series now even at two wins apiece, Pittsburgh's Nelson Briles stopped the Orioles in Game Five on a pair of singles. Bob Robertson's leadoff homer in the second proved all the Pirates needed for the win, but Briles himself drove in an insurance run later in the inning and Pittsburgh went on to win 4–0.

The Pirates tried to win it all in Game Six, scoring single runs against the O's Jim Palmer in the second inning and the third (Roberto Clemente's home run). But Pirate starter Bob Moose was replaced after giving up a solo homer to Don Buford in the sixth, and a tying Baltimore run came home an inning later. A ninth-inning pinch hitter for Palmer produced nothing, but Baltimore won in the last of the tenth, when Frank Robinson scored on Brooks Robinson's sacrifice fly to shallow center.

Steve Blass, who had defeated Oriole Mike Cuellar in Game Three, faced him again in the finale and again emerged the victor of a pitching duel. Clemente's two-out homer in the fourth inning provided the game's only run until the eighth, when both teams scored single runs. Blass retired Baltimore in order in the ninth and the Pirates were world champions.

Pittsburgh Pirates (NL), 4;
Baltimore Orioles (AL) 3

PIT (N)

PLAYER/POS	AVG	G	AB	R	H	2B	3B	HR	RB	BB	SO	SB
Gene Alley, ss	.000	2	2	0	0	0	0	0	0	0	1	0
Steve Blass, p	.000	2	7	0	0	0	0	0	0	0	1	0
Nelson Briles, p	.500	1	2	0	1	0	0	0	1	0	1	0
Dave Cash, 2b	.133	7	30	2	4	1	0	0	1	3	1	1
Roberto Clemente, of	.414	7	29	3	12	2	1	2	4	2	2	0
Gene Clines, of	.091	3	11	2	1	0	1	0	0	1	1	1
Vic Davalillo, of-2	.333	3	3	1	1	0	0	0	0	0	0	0
Dock Ellis, p	.000	1	0	0	0	0	0	0	0	0	0	0
Dave Giusti, p	.000	3	0	0	0	0	0	0	0	0	0	0
Richie Hebner, 3b	.167	3	12	2	2	0	0	1	3	3	3	0
Jackie Hernandez, ss	.222	7	18	2	4	0	0	0	1	2	5	1
Bob Johnson, p	.000	2	3	0	0	0	0	0	0	0	2	0
Bruce Kison, p	.000	2	2	0	0	0	0	0	0	0	2	0
Milt May, ph	.500	2	2	0	1	0	0	0	1	0	0	0
Bill Mazeroski, ph	.000	1	1	0	0	0	0	0	0	0	0	0
Bob Miller, p	.000	3	0	0	0	0	0	0	0	0	0	0
Bob Moose, p	.000	3	2	0	0	0	0	0	0	0	1	0
Al Oliver, of-4	.211	5	19	1	4	2	0	0	2	2	5	0
Jose Pagan, 3b	.267	4	15	0	4	2	0	0	2	0	1	0
Bob Robertson, 1b	.240	7	25	4	6	0	0	2	5	4	8	0
Charlie Sands, ph	.000	1	1	0	0	0	0	0	0	0	1	0
Manny Sanguillen, c	.379	7	29	3	11	1	0	0	0	0	3	2
Willie Stargell, of	.208	7	24	3	5	1	0	0	1	7	9	0
Bob Veale, p	.000	1	0	0	0	0	0	0	0	0	0	0
Luke Walker, p	.000	1	0	0	0	0	0	0	0	0	0	0
TOTAL	.235		238	23	56	9	2	5	21	26	47	5

PITCHER	W	L	ERA	G	GS	CG	SV	SHO	IP	H	ER	BB	SO
Steve Blass	2	0	1.00	2	2	2	0	0	18.0	7	2	4	13
Nelson Briles	1	0	0.00	1	1	1	0	1	9.0	2	0	2	2
Dock Ellis	0	1	15.43	1	1	0	0	0	2.1	4	4	1	1
Dave Giusti	0	0	0.00	3	0	0	1	0	5.1	3	0	2	4
Bob Johnson	0	1	9.00	2	1	0	0	0	5.0	5	5	3	3
Bruce Kison	1	0	0.00	2	0	0	0	0	6.1	1	0	2	3
Bob Miller	0	1	3.86	3	0	0	0	0	4.2	7	2	1	2
Bob Moose	0	0	6.52	3	1	0	0	0	9.2	12	7	2	7
Bob Veale	0	0	13.50	1	0	0	0	0	0.2	1	1	2	0
Luke Walker	0	0	40.50	1	1	0	0	0	0.2	3	3	1	0
TOTAL	4	3	3.50	19	7	3	1	1	61.2	45	24	20	35

BAL (A)

PLAYER/POS	AVG	G	AB	R	H	2B	3B	HR	RB	BB	SO	SB
Mark Belanger, ss	.238	7	21	4	5	0	1	0	0	5	2	1
Paul Blair, of-3	.333	4	9	2	3	1	0	0	0	0	1	0
Don Buford, of	.261	6	23	3	6	1	0	2	4	3	3	0
Mike Cuellar, p	.000	2	3	0	0	0	0	0	0	1	2	0
Pat Dobson, p	.000	3	2	0	0	0	0	0	0	0	2	0
Tom Dukes, p	.000	2	0	0	0	0	0	0	0	0	0	0
Andy Etchebarren, c	.000	1	2	0	0	0	0	0	0	0	0	0
Dick Hall, p	.000	1	0	0	0	0	0	0	0	0	0	0
Elrod Hendricks, c	.263	6	19	3	5	1	0	0	1	3	3	0
Grant Jackson, p	.000	1	0	0	0	0	0	0	0	0	0	0
Davy Johnson, 2b	.148	7	27	1	4	0	0	0	3	0	1	0
Dave Leonhard, p	.000	1	0	0	0	0	0	0	0	0	0	0
Dave Mc Nally, p	.000	4	8	0	0	0	0	0	0	0	3	0
Jim Palmer, p	.000	2	4	0	0	0	0	0	2	2	2	0
Boog Powell, 1b	.111	7	27	1	3	0	0	0	1	1	3	0
Merv Rettenmund, of-6	.185	7	27	3	5	0	0	1	4	0	4	0
Pete Richert, p	.000	1	0	0	0	0	0	0	0	0	0	0
Brooks Robinson, 3b	.318	7	22	2	7	0	0	0	5	3	1	0
Frank Robinson, of	.280	7	25	5	7	0	0	2	2	2	8	0
Tom Shopay, ph	.000	5	4	0	0	0	0	0	0	0	0	0
Eddie Watt, p	.000	2	0	0	0	0	0	0	0	0	0	0
TOTAL	.205		219	24	45	3	1	5	22	20	35	1

PITCHER	W	L	ERA	G	GS	CG	SV	SHO	IP	H	ER	BB	SO
Mike Cuellar	0	2	3.86	2	2	0	0	0	14.0	11	6	6	10
Pat Dobson	0	0	4.05	3	1	0	0	0	6.2	13	3	4	6
Tom Dukes	0	0	0.00	2	0	0	0	0	4.0	2	0	0	1
Dick Hall	0	0	0.00	1	0	0	1	0	1.0	1	0	0	0
Grant Jackson	0	0	0.00	1	0	0	0	0	0.2	0	0	1	0
Dave Leonhard	0	0	0.00	1	0	0	0	0	1.0	0	0	1	0
Dave Mc Nally	2	1	1.98	4	2	1	0	0	13.2	10	3	5	12
Jim Palmer	1	0	2.65	2	2	0	0	0	17.0	15	5	9	15
Pete Richert	0	0	0.00	1	0	0	0	0	0.2	0	0	0	1
Eddie Watt	0	1	3.86	2	0	0	0	0	2.1	4	1	0	2
TOTAL	3	4	2.66	19	7	1	1	0	61.0	56	18	26	47

GAME 1 AT BAL OCT 9

				R	H	E
PIT	030	000	000	3	3	0
BAL	013	010	00X	5	10	3

Pitchers: ELLIS, Moose (3), Miller (7) VS McNALLY
Home Runs: F.Robinson-BAL, Rettenmund-BAL, Buford-BAL
Attendance: 53,229

GAME 2 AT BAL OCT 11

				R	H	E
PIT	000	000	030	3	8	1
BAL	010	361	00X	11	14	1

Pitchers: R.JOHNSON, Kison (4), Moose (4), Veale (5), Miller (6), Giusti (8) vs PALMER, Hall (9)
Home Runs: Hebner-PIT
Attendance: 53,239

GAME 3 AT PIT OCT 12

				R	H	E
BAL	000	000	100	1	3	3
PIT	100	001	30X	5	7	0

Pitchers: CUELLAR, Dukes (7), Watt (8) VS BLASS
Home Runs: F.Robinson-BAL, Robertson-PIT
Attendance: 50,403

GAME 4 AT PIT OCT 13

				R	H	E
BAL	300	000	000	3	4	1
PIT	201	000	10X	4	14	0

Pitchers: Dobson, Jackson (6), WATT (7), Richert (8) vs Walker, KISON (1), Giusti (8)
Attendance: 51,378

GAME 5 AT PIT OCT 14

				R	H	E
BAL	000	000	000	0	2	1
PIT	021	010	00X	4	9	0

Pitchers: McNALLY, Leonhard (5), Dukes (6) vs BRILES
Home Runs: Robertson-PIT
Attendance: 51,377

GAME 6 AT BAL OCT 16

					R	H	E
PIT	011	000	000	0	2	9	1
BAL	000	001	100	1	3	8	0

Pitchers: Moose, R.Johnson (6), Giusti (7), MILLER (10) vs Palmer, Dobson (10), McNALLY (10)
Home Runs: Clemente-PIT, Buford-BAL
Attendance: 44,174

GAME 7 AT BAL OCT 17

				R	H	E
PIT	000	100	010	2	6	1
BAL	000	000	010	1	4	0

Pitchers: BLASS vs CUELLAR, Dobson (9), McNally (9)
Home Runs: Clemente-PIT
Attendance: 47,291

Pittsburgh traded wins with Cincinnati through the first four games—winning the first and third—and took a lead into the ninth inning of the fifth game before a home run and a wild pitch undid them.

Cincinnati got eight hits in each of the first two games. In the first game, though, only Joe Morgan's first-inning homer produced a run, and the Reds lost 1–5. But the next day, five first-inning hits gave the Reds four runs and a lead the Pirates could not overcome.

Pirate catcher Manny Sanguillen brought Pittsburgh back in Game Three with a home run in the fifth and the game-winning RBI in the eighth. But Reds pitcher Ross Grimsley evened the series for Cincinnati the next day with a two-hitter, in the series' only complete-game performance.

Game Five was Pittsburgh's for 8½ innings. The Pirates scored first, and held the lead into the bottom of the ninth. But Johnny Bench opened the Reds' half of the ninth with a game-tying home run, and Tony Perez and Denis Menke followed him with singles. Bob Moose came in and retired the next two men, though George Foster (running for Perez) took third on a fly to right. Moose then threw away the pennant with a run-scoring, series-ending wild pitch.

Cincinnati Reds (West), 3;
Pittsburgh Pirates (East) 2

CIN (W)

PLAYER/POS	AVG	G	AB	R	H	2B	3B	HR	RB	BB	SO	SB
Johnny Bench, c	.333	5	18	3	6	1	1	1	2	1	3	2
Jack Billingham, p	.000	1	2	0	0	0	0	0	0	0	1	0
Pedro Borbon, p	.000	3	0	0	0	0	0	0	0	0	0	0
Clay Carroll, p	.000	2	0	0	0	0	0	0	0	0	0	0
Darrel Chaney, ss	.188	5	16	3	3	0	0	0	1	1	1	1
Dave Concepcion, ss-1	.000	3	2	0	0	0	0	0	0	0	0	0
George Foster, pr	.000	1	0	1	0	0	0	0	0	0	0	0
Cesar Geronimo, of	.100	5	20	2	2	0	0	1	1	0	2	0
Ross Grimsley, p	.500	1	4	0	2	1	0	0	1	0	1	0
Don Gullett, p	.500	2	2	0	1	0	0	0	0	0	0	0
Joe Hague, ph	.000	3	1	0	0	0	0	0	0	2	1	0
Tom Hall, p	.000	2	1	0	0	0	0	0	0	0	0	0
Jim Mc Glothlin, p	.000	1	0	0	0	0	0	0	0	0	0	0
Hal Mc Rae, ph	.000	1	0	0	0	0	0	0	0	0	0	0
Denis Menke, 3b	.250	5	16	1	4	1	0	0	4	3	0	0
Joe Morgan, 2b	.263	5	19	5	5	0	0	2	3	1	2	1
Gary Nolan, p	.000	1	2	0	0	0	0	0	0	0	1	0
Tony Perez, 1b	.200	5	20	4	4	1	0	0	2	0	7	0
Pete Rose, of	.450	5	20	1	9	4	0	0	2	1	2	0
Bobby Tolan, of	.238	5	21	3	5	1	1	0	4	0	4	0
Ted Uhlaender, ph	.500	2	2	0	1	0	0	0	0	0	0	0
TOTAL	.253		166	19	42	9	2	4	16	10	28	4

PITCHER	W	L	ERA	G	GS	CG	SV	SHO	IP	H	ER	BB	SO
Jack Billingham	0	0	3.86	1	1	0	0	0	4.2	5	2	2	4
Pedro Borbon	0	0	2.08	3	0	0	0	0	4.1	2	1	0	1
Clay Carroll	1	1	3.38	2	0	0	0	0	2.2	2	1	3	0
Ross Grimsley	1	0	1.00	1	1	1	0	0	9.0	2	1	0	5
Don Gullett	0	1	8.00	2	2	0	0	0	9.0	12	8	0	5
Tom Hall	1	0	1.23	2	0	0	0	0	7.1	3	1	3	8
Jim Mc Glothlin	0	0	0.00	1	0	0	0	0	1.0	0	0	0	0
Gary Nolan	0	0	1.50	1	1	0	0	0	6.0	4	1	1	4
TOTAL	3	2	3.07	13	5	1	0	0	44.0	30	15	9	27

PIT (E)

PLAYER/POS	AVG	G	AB	R	H	2B	3B	HR	RB	BB	SO	SB
Gene Alley, ss	.000	5	16	1	0	0	0	0	0	0	3	0
Steve Blass, p	.000	2	6	0	0	0	0	0	0	0	3	0
Nelson Briles, p	.000	1	2	0	0	0	0	0	0	0	1	0
Dave Cash, 2b	.211	5	19	0	4	0	0	0	3	0	0	0
Roberto Clemente, of	.235	5	17	1	4	1	0	1	2	3	5	0
Gene Clines, ph	.000	3	2	1	0	0	0	0	0	0	1	0
Vic Davalillo, ph	.000	1	0	0	0	0	0	0	0	1	0	0
Dock Ellis, p-1	.000	2	1	0	0	0	0	0	0	0	0	0
Dave Giusti, p	.000	3	1	0	0	0	0	0	0	0	0	0
Richie Hebner, 3b	.188	5	16	2	3	1	0	0	1	1	3	0
Ramon Hernandez, p	.000	3	0	0	0	0	0	0	0	0	0	0
Bob Johnson, p	.000	2	1	0	0	0	0	0	0	0	1	0
Bruce Kison, p	.000	2	0	0	0	0	0	0	0	0	0	0
Milt May, c	.500	1	2	0	1	0	0	0	1	0	0	0
Bill Mazeroski, ph	.500	2	2	0	1	0	0	0	0	0	1	0
Bob Miller, p	.000	1	0	0	0	0	0	0	0	0	0	0
Bob Moose, p	.000	2	0	0	0	0	0	0	0	0	0	0
Al Oliver, of	.250	5	20	3	5	2	1	1	3	0	4	0
Bob Robertson, 1b	.000	4	0	0	0	0	0	0	0	1	0	0
Manny Sanguillen, c	.313	5	16	4	5	1	0	1	2	0	0	0
Willie Stargell, 1b-5,of-1	.063	5	16	1	1	1	0	0	1	2	5	0
Rennie Stennett, of-5,2b-1	.286	5	21	2	6	0	0	0	1	1	0	0
Luke Walker, p	.000	1	0	0	0	0	0	0	0	0	0	0
TOTAL	.190		158	15	30	6	1	3	14	9	27	0

PITCHER	W	L	ERA	G	GS	CG	SV	SHO	IP	H	ER	BB	SO
Steve Blass	1	0	1.72	2	2	0	0	0	15.2	12	3	6	5
Nelson Briles	0	0	3.00	1	1	0	0	0	6.0	6	2	1	3
Dock Ellis	0	1	0.00	1	1	0	0	0	5.0	5	0	1	3
Dave Giusti	0	1	6.75	3	0	0	1	0	2.2	5	2	0	3
Ramon Hernandez	0	0	2.70	3	0	0	1	0	3.1	1	1	0	3
Bob Johnson	0	0	3.00	2	0	0	0	0	6.0	4	2	2	7
Bruce Kison	1	0	0.00	2	0	0	0	0	2.1	1	0	0	3
Bob Miller	0	0	0.00	1	0	0	0	0	1.0	1	0	0	1
Bob Moose	0	1	54.00	2	1	0	0	0	0.2	5	4	0	0
Luke Walker	0	0	18.00	1	0	0	0	0	1.0	3	2	0	0
TOTAL	2	3	3.30	18	5	0	2	0	43.2	42	16	10	28

GAME 1 AT PIT OCT 7

CIN	100	000	000	1	8	0
PIT	300	020	00X	5	6	0

Pitchers: GULLETT, Borbon (7) vs BLASS, R.Hernandez (9)
Home Runs: Morgan-CIN, Oliver-PIT
Attendance: 50,476

GAME 2 AT PIT OCT 8

CIN	400	000	010	5	8	1
PIT	000	111	000	3	7	1

Pitchers: Billingham, HALL (5) vs MOOSE, Johnson (1), Kison (6), R.Hernandez (7), Giusti (9)
Home Runs: Morgan-CIN
Attendance: 50,584

GAME 3 AT CIN OCT 9

PIT	000	010	110	3	7	0
CIN	002	000	000	2	8	1

Pitchers: Briles, KISON (7), Giusti (8) VS Nolan, Borbon (7), CARROLL (7), McGlothlin (9)
Home Runs: Sanguillen-PIT
Attendance: 52,420

GAME 4 AT CIN OCT 10

PIT	000	000	100	1	2	3
CIN	100	202	20X	7	11	1

Pitchers: ELLIS, Johnson (6), Walker (7), Miller (8) vs GRIMSLEY
Home Runs: Clemente-PIT
Attendance: 39,447

GAME 5 AT CIN OCT 11

PIT	020	100	000	3	8	0
CIN	001	010	002	4	7	1

Pitchers: Blass, R.Hernandez (8), GIUSTI (9), Moose (9) vs Gullett, Borbon (4), Hall (6), CARROLL (9)
Home Runs: Geronimo-CIN, Bench-CIN
Attendance: 41,887

Oakland turned back the Tigers in the first two games, but Detroit evened the series before succumbing in the fifth game.

In Game One, Tiger Al Kaline homered off Rollie Fingers in the eleventh to give starter Mickey Lolich a 2–1 lead. But in the last of the inning, pinch hitter Gonzalo Marquez singled off Tiger reliever Chuck Seelbach with two on to drive in the tying run, and Gene Tenace scored to win it on the same play as right fielder Kaline threw the ball away. Blue Moon Odom increased the A's series lead with a three-hit shutout in Game Two, but Detroit's Joe Coleman retaliated with 14 strikeouts and a shutout of his own to save the Tigers from elimination in Game Three.

In Game Four the A's pulled out of a 1–1 tie with two runs in the top of the tenth. But Detroit in its half of the inning went through three Oakland relievers for three runs and the win. In the finale, after Odom, the A's starter, had given Detroit a run and a brief lead in the first, he and Vida Blue divided eight shutout innings between them as the A's scored twice to capture their first pennant since Connie Mack won his last in Philadelphia forty-one years earlier.

Oakland A's (West), 3; Detroit Tigers (East) 2

OAK (W)

PLAYER/POS	AVG	G	AB	R	H	2B	3B	HR	RB	BB	SO	SB
Matty Alou, of	.381	5	21	2	8	4	0	0	2	0	2	1
Sal Bando, 3b	.200	5	20	0	4	0	0	0	0	0	3	0
Vida Blue, p	.000	4	1	0	0	0	0	0	0	0	0	0
Bert Campaneris, ss	.429	2	7	3	3	0	0	0	0	1	0	2
Tim Cullen, ss	.000	2	1	0	0	0	0	0	0	0	0	0
Dave Duncan, c	.000	2	2	0	0	0	0	0	0	1	1	0
Mike Epstein, 1b	.188	5	16	1	3	0	0	1	1	4	5	1
Rollie Fingers, p	.000	3	1	0	0	0	0	0	0	0	0	0
Dick Green, 2b	.125	5	8	0	1	1	0	0	0	0	0	0
Dave Hamilton, p	.000	1	0	0	0	0	0	0	0	0	0	0
Mike Hegan, 1b-1	.000	3	1	1	0	0	0	0	0	0	0	0
George Hendrick, of-1	.143	5	7	2	1	0	0	0	0	0	1	0
Ken Holtzman, p	.000	1	1	0	0	0	0	0	0	0	1	0
Joe Horlen, p	.000	1	0	0	0	0	0	0	0	0	0	0
Catfish Hunter, p	.167	2	6	0	1	0	0	0	0	0	2	0
Reggie Jackson, of	.278	5	18	1	5	1	0	0	2	1	6	2
Ted Kubiak, 2b-3,ss-1	.500	4	4	0	2	0	0	0	1	0	0	0
Bob Locker, p	.000	2	0	0	0	0	0	0	0	0	0	0
Angel Mangual, ph	.000	3	3	0	0	0	0	0	0	0	1	0
Gonzalo Marquez, ph	.667	3	3	1	2	0	0	0	1	0	0	0
Dal Maxvill, ss-4,2b-1	.125	5	8	0	1	0	0	0	0	1	2	1
Don Mincher, ph	.000	1	1	0	0	0	0	0	0	0	1	0
Blue Moon Odom, p-2	.250	3	4	0	1	1	0	0	0	0	1	0
Joe Rudi, of	.250	5	20	1	5	1	0	0	2	1	4	0
Gene Tenace, c-5,2b-2	.059	5	17	1	1	0	0	0	1	3	5	0
TOTAL	.224		170	13	38	8	0	1	10	12	35	7

PITCHER	W	L	ERA	G	GS	CG	SV	SHO	IP	H	ER	BB	SO
Vida Blue	0	0	0.00	4	0	0	1	0	5.1	4	0	1	5
Rollie Fingers	1	0	1.69	3	0	0	0	0	5.1	4	1	1	3
Dave Hamilton	0	0	INF	1	0	0	0	0	0.0	1	0	1	0
Ken Holtzman	0	1	4.50	1	1	0	0	0	4.0	4	2	2	2
Joe Horlen	0	1	INF	1	0	0	0	0	0.0	0	1	1	0
Catfish Hunter	0	0	1.17	2	2	0	0	0	15.1	10	2	5	9
Bob Locker	0	0	13.50	2	0	0	0	0	2.0	4	3	0	1
Blue Moon Odom	2	0	0.00	2	2	1	0	1	14.0	5	0	2	5
TOTAL	3	2	1.76	16	5	1	1	1	46.0	32	9	13	25

DET (E)

PLAYER/POS	AVG	G	AB	R	H	2B	3B	HR	RB	BB	SO	SB
Ed Brinkman, ss	.250	1	4	0	1	1	0	0	0	0	0	0
Ike Brown, 1b	.500	1	2	0	1	0	0	0	2	0	1	0
Gates Brown, ph	.000	3	2	1	0	0	0	0	0	1	0	0
Norm Cash, 1b	.267	5	15	1	4	0	0	1	2	2	3	0
Joe Coleman, p	.500	1	2	0	1	0	0	0	0	0	1	0
Bill Freehan, c	.250	3	12	2	3	1	0	1	3	0	1	0
Woody Fryman, p	.000	2	3	0	0	0	0	0	0	0	0	0
Tom Haller, ph	.000	1	1	0	0	0	0	0	0	0	0	0
John Hiller, p	.000	3	0	0	0	0	0	0	0	0	0	0
Willie Horton, of-3	.100	5	10	0	1	0	0	0	0	1	3	0
Al Kaline, of	.263	5	19	3	5	0	0	1	1	2	2	0
John Knox, pr	.000	1	0	0	0	0	0	0	0	0	0	0
Lerrin La Grow, p	.000	1	0	0	0	0	0	0	0	0	0	0
Mickey Lolich, p	.000	2	7	0	0	0	0	0	0	0	2	0
Dick Mc Auliffe, ss-4,2b-1	.200	5	20	3	4	0	0	1	1	1	4	0
Jim Northrup, of	.357	5	14	0	5	0	0	0	1	2	3	0
Aurelio Rodriguez, 3b	.000	5	16	0	0	0	0	0	0	2	2	0
Fred Scherman, p	.000	1	0	0	0	0	0	0	0	0	0	0
Chuck Seelbach, p	.000	2	0	0	0	0	0	0	0	0	0	0
Duke Sims, c-2,of-2	.214	4	14	0	3	2	1	0	0	1	2	0
Mickey Stanley, of-3	.333	4	6	0	2	0	0	0	0	0	0	0
Tony Taylor, 2b	.133	4	15	0	2	2	0	0	0	0	2	0
Chris Zachary, p	.000	1	0	0	0	0	0	0	0	0	0	0
TOTAL	.198		162	10	32	6	1	4	10	13	25	0

PITCHER	W	L	ERA	G	GS	CG	SV	SHO	IP	H	ER	BB	SO
Joe Coleman	1	0	0.00	1	1	1	0	1	9.0	7	0	3	14
Woody Fryman	0	2	3.65	2	2	0	0	0	12.1	11	5	2	8
John Hiller	1	0	0.00	3	0	0	0	0	3.1	1	0	1	1
Lerrin La Grow	0	0	0.00	1	0	0	0	0	1.0	0	0	0	1
Mickey Lolich	0	1	1.42	2	2	0	0	0	19.0	14	3	5	10
Fred Scherman	0	0	0.00	1	0	0	0	0	0.2	1	0	0	1
Chuck Seelbach	0	0	18.00	2	0	0	0	0	1.0	4	2	0	0
Chris Zachary	0	0	INF	1	0	0	0	0	0.0	0	1	1	0
TOTAL	2	3	2.14	13	5	1	0	1	46.1	38	11	12	35

GAME 1 AT OAK OCT 7

DET	010 000 000 01	2	6	2
OAK	001 000 000 02	3	10	1

Pitchers: LOLICH, Seelbach (11) VS Hunter, Blue (9), FINGERS (9)
Home Runs: Cash-DET, Kaline-DET
Attendance: 29,536

GAME 2 AT OAK OCT 8

DET	000 000 000	0	3	1
OAK	100 040 00X	5	8	0

Pitchers: FRYMAN, Zachary (5), Scherman (5), LaGrow (6), Hiller (7) VS ODOM
Attendance: 31,088

GAME 3 AT DET OCT 10

OAK	000 000 000	0	7	0
DET	000 200 01X	3	8	1

Pitchers: HOLTZMAN, Fingers (5), Blue (6), Locker (7) vs COLEMAN
Home Runs: Freehan-DET
Attendance: 41,156

GAME 4 AT DET OCT 11

OAK	000 000 100 2	3	9	2
DET	001 000 000 3	4	10	1

Pitchers: Hunter, Fingers (8), Blue (9), Locker (10), HORLEN (10), Hamilton (10) VS Lolich, Seelbach (10), HILLER (10)
Home Runs: McAuliffe-DET, Epstein-OAK
Attendance: 37,615

GAME 5 AT DET OCT 12

OAK	010 100 000	2	4	0
DET	100 000 000	1	5	2

Pitchers: ODOM, Blue (6) vs FRYMAN, Hiller (9)
Attendance: 50,276

Oakland slugger Reggie Jackson missed the Series with a pulled hamstring, but Gene Tenace (the A's backup catcher during the season) took up the slack, hitting four of the club's five homers and driving in nine of their sixteen runs.

Six of the seven games were decided by a single run. Oakland won the first two in Cincinnati, 3–2 and 2–1. Tenace made the difference in the opener, driving in all the A's runs with a two-run homer in the second inning and a solo shot in the fifth. In the second game, A's starting pitcher Catfish Hunter singled in a run in the second inning which proved the margin of his victory. His 8⅔-inning performance was the longest mound outing in a Series which saw the two clubs together use nearly seven pitchers per game.

Cincinnati took the first game in Oakland, 1–0. The A's' Blue Moon Odom dueled the Reds' Jack Billingham scorelessly on one hit through six innings before giving up the game's only run on a single-sacrifice-single in the seventh. Billingham, too, yielded only three hits in eight-plus innings before yielding to ace reliever Clay Carroll, who retired the side in the ninth.

Oakland won Game Four, 3–2. Tenace opened the scoring with a solo homer in the fifth. The Reds' Bobby Tolan doubled in a pair in the eighth to put Cincinnati ahead, but in the last of the ninth four successive A's singles scored two runs, with Tenace scoring the game winner on pinch hitter Angel Mangual's hit. Tenace homered again in Game Five for three runs, but it wasn't enough as the Reds tied the score in the eighth and won on Pete Rose's RBI single in the ninth.

The Reds produced the Series' only blowout with five runs in the seventh inning of Game Six to make the score 8–1, where it remained. The finale saw Tenace drive in a run in the top of the first for a narrow Oakland lead which held until the Reds tied the game in the fifth. In the sixth the A's scored twice—Tenace doubling in the go-ahead run. Cincinnati scored once more in the eighth as a runner inherited by A's reliever Rollie Fingers came home on a sacrifice fly. But Fingers permitted no other runs to score, and the A's took the crown with their fourth one-run victory.

Oakland Athletics (AL), 4; Cincinnati Reds (NL) 3

OAK (A)

PLAYER/POS	AVG	G	AB	R	H	2B	3B	HR	RB	BB	SO	SB
Matty Alou, of	.042	7	24	0	1	0	0	0	0	0	3	1
Sal Bando, 3b	.269	7	26	2	7	1	0	0	1	2	5	0
Vida Blue, p	.000	4	1	0	0	0	0	0	0	0	2	0
Bert Campaneris, ss	.179	7	28	1	5	0	0	0	0	1	4	0
Dave Duncan, c-1	.200	3	5	0	1	0	0	0	0	1	3	0
Mike Epstein, 1b	.000	6	16	1	0	0	0	0	0	5	3	0
Rollie Fingers, p	.000	6	1	0	0	0	0	0	0	0	0	0
Dick Green, 2b	.333	7	18	0	6	2	0	0	1	0	4	0
Dave Hamilton, p	.000	2	0	0	0	0	0	0	0	0	0	0
Mike Hegan, 1b-5	.200	6	5	0	1	0	0	0	0	0	2	0
George Hendrick, of	.133	5	15	3	2	0	0	0	0	1	2	0
Ken Holtzman, p	.000	3	5	0	0	0	0	0	0	0	0	0
Joe Horlen, p	.000	1	0	0	0	0	0	0	0	0	0	0
Catfish Hunter, p	.200	3	5	0	1	0	0	0	1	2	1	0
Ted Kubiak, 2b	.333	4	3	0	1	0	0	0	0	0	0	0
Allan Lewis, pr	.000	6	0	2	0	0	0	0	0	0	0	0
Bob Locker, p	.000	1	0	0	0	0	0	0	0	0	0	0
Angel Mangual, of-2	.300	4	10	1	3	0	0	0	1	0	4	0
Gonzalo Marquez, ph	.600	5	5	0	3	0	0	0	1	0	0	0
Don Mincher, ph	1.000	3	1	0	1	0	0	0	1	0	0	0
Blue Moon Odom, p-2	.000	4	4	0	0	0	0	0	0	0	3	0
Joe Rudi, of	.240	7	25	1	6	0	0	1	1	1	2	5	0
Gene Tenace, c-6,1b-1	.348	7	23	5	8	1	0	4	9	2	4	0
TOTAL	.209		220	16	46	4	0	5	16	21	37	1

PITCHER	W	L	ERA	G	GS	CG	SV	SHO	IP	H	ER	BB	SO
Vida Blue	0	1	4.15	4	1	0	1	0	8.2	8	4	5	5
Rollie Fingers	1	1	1.74	6	0	0	2	0	10.1	4	2	4	11
Dave Hamilton	0	0	6.75	2	0	0	0	0	1.1	2	1	2	1
Ken Holtzman	1	0	2.13	3	2	0	0	0	12.2	11	3	3	4
Joe Horlen	0	0	27.00	1	0	0	0	0	1.1	3	4	1	1
Catfish Hunter	2	0	2.81	3	2	0	0	0	16.0	12	5	6	11
Bob Locker	0	0	0.00	1	0	0	0	0	0.1	1	0	0	0
Blue Moon Odom	0	1	1.59	2	2	0	0	0	11.1	5	2	6	13
TOTAL	4	3	3.05	22	7	0	3	0	62.0	46	21	27	46

CIN (N)

PLAYER/POS	AVG	G	AB	R	H	2B	3B	HR	RB	BB	SO	SB
Johnny Bench, c	.261	7	23	4	6	1	0	1	1	5	5	2
Jack Billingham, p	.000	3	5	0	0	0	0	0	0	0	4	0
Pedro Borbon, p	.000	6	0	0	0	0	0	0	0	0	0	0
Clay Carroll, p	.000	5	0	0	0	0	0	0	0	0	0	0
Darrel Chaney, ss-3	.000	4	7	0	0	0	0	0	0	2	2	0
Dave Concepcion, ss-5	.308	6	13	2	4	0	1	0	2	2	2	1
George Foster, of-1	.000	2	0	0	0	0	0	0	0	0	0	0
Cesar Geronimo, of	.158	7	19	1	3	0	0	0	3	1	4	1
Ross Grimsley, p	.000	4	2	0	0	0	0	0	0	0	2	0
Don Gullett, p	.000	1	2	0	0	0	0	0	0	0	0	0
Joe Hague, of-1	.000	3	3	0	0	0	0	0	0	0	0	0
Tom Hall, p	.000	4	2	0	0	0	0	0	0	0	1	0
Julian Javier, ph	.000	4	2	0	0	0	0	0	0	0	0	0
Jim Mc Glothlin, p	.000	1	1	0	0	0	0	0	0	0	0	0
Hal Mc Rae, of-2	.444	5	9	1	4	1	0	0	2	0	1	0
Denis Menke, 3b	.083	7	24	1	2	0	0	1	2	2	6	0
Joe Morgan, 2b	.125	7	24	4	3	2	0	0	1	6	3	2
Gary Nolan, p	.000	2	3	0	0	0	0	0	0	0	0	0
Tony Perez, 1b	.435	7	23	3	10	2	0	0	2	4	4	0
Pete Rose, of	.214	7	28	3	6	0	0	1	2	4	4	1
Bobby Tolan, of	.269	7	26	2	7	1	0	0	6	1	4	5
Ted Uhlaender, ph	.250	4	4	0	1	1	0	0	0	0	1	0
TOTAL	.209		220	21	46	8	1	3	21	27	46	12

PITCHER	W	L	ERA	G	GS	CG	SV	SHO	IP	H	ER	BB	SO
Jack Billingham	1	0	0.00	3	2	0	1	0	13.2	6	0	4	11
Pedro Borbon	0	-1	3.86	7	0	0	0	0	7.0	7	3	2	4
Clay Carroll	0	1	1.59	5	0	0	1	0	5.2	6	1	4	3
Ross Grimsley	2	1	2.57	4	1	0	0	0	7.0	7	2	3	2
Don Gullett	0	0	1.29	1	1	0	0	0	7.0	5	1	2	4
Tom Hall	0	0	0.00	4	0	0	1	0	8.1	6	0	2	7
Jim Mc Glothlin	0	0	12.00	1	1	0	0	0	3.0	2	4	2	3
Gary Nolan	0	1	3.38	2	2	0	0	0	10.2	7	4	2	3
TOTAL	3	2	2.17	26	7	0	3	0	62.1	46	15	21	37

GAME 1 AT CIN OCT 14

OAK	020	010	000	3	4 0
CIN	010	100	000	2	7 0

Pitchers: HOLTZMAN, Fingers (6), Blue (7) VS NOLAN, Borbon (7), Carroll (8)
Home Runs: Tenace-OAK (2)
Attendance: 52,918

GAME 2 AT CIN OCT 15

OAK	011	000	000	2	9 2
CIN	000	000	001	1	6 0

Pitchers: HUNTER, Fingers (9) VS GRIMSLEY, Borbon (6), Hall (8)
Home Runs: Rudi-OAK
Attendance: 53,224

GAME 3 AT OAK OCT 18

CIN	000	000	100	1	4 2
OAK	000	000	000	0	3 2

Pitchers: BILLINGHAM, Carroll (9) VS ODOM, Blue (8), Fingers (8)
Attendance: 49,410

GAME 4 AT OAK OCT 19

CIN	000	000	020	2	7 1
OAK	000	010	002	3	10 1

Pitchers: Gullett, Borbon (8), CARROLL (9) vs Holtzman, Blue (8), FINGERS (9)
Home Runs: Tenace-OAK
Attendance: 49,410

GAME 5 AT OAK OCT 20

CIN	100	110	011	5	8 0
OAK	030	100	000	4	7 2

Pitchers: McGlothlin, Borbon (4), Hall (5), Carroll (7), GRIMSLEY (8), Billingham (9) vs Hunter, FINGERS (5), Hamilton (9)
Home Runs: Rose-CIN, Tenace-OAK, Menke-CIN
Attendance: 49,410

GAME 6 AT CIN OCT 21

OAK	000	010	000	1	7 1
CIN	000	111	50X	8	10 0

Pitchers: BLUE, Locker (6), Hamilton (7), Horlen (7) vs Nolan, GRIMSLEY (5), Borbon (6), Hall (7)
Home Runs: Bench-CIN
Attendance: 52,737

GAME 7 AT CIN OCT 22

OAK	100	002	000	3	6 1
CIN	000	010	010	2	4 2

Pitchers: Odom, HUNTER (5), Holtzman (8), Fingers (8) vs Billingham, BORBON (6), Carroll (6), Grimsley (7), Hall (8)
Attendance: 56,040

The Mets received strong pitching throughout the series, and their offense came through just often enough to defeat Cincinnati in five games.

Though three Reds pitchers held New York to three hits in Game One, the single Met run in the second seemed for a time enough for a win. But Tom Seaver gave up a home run to Pete Rose in the eighth and lost the game in the ninth when Johnny Bench homered. Not wanting another last-inning loss in Game Two, the Mets unloaded for four runs in the top of the ninth to add to their one in the fourth. But this time one would have been enough as Jon Matlack blanked the Reds on two hits.

The Mets made it easy for Jerry Koosman in Game Three in New York, scoring nine times in the first four innings. Things were more difficult for shortstop Bud Harrelson, who exchanged blows with Pete Rose following Rose's hard slide in the fifth inning. A bench-clearing melee ensued, and fans in the left field stands showered Rose with debris until a delegation of Tom Seaver, Willie Mays and Rusty Staub visited the area to calm nerves and eliminate the threat of a forfeit. In Game Four, though, Met bats were stifled once again as four Reds pitchers combined for a 12-inning three-hitter. The Reds won the game and tied the series on Rose's sweetly vengeful twelfth-inning homer.

In the finale the Mets took a quick two-run lead. Cincinnati tied the game in the top of the fifth, but New York retaliated with four more in the bottom of the inning. Seaver—and Tug Mc-Graw in the ninth—held the Reds scoreless the rest of the way.

New York Mets (East), 3;
Cincinnati Reds (West) 2

NY (E)

PLAYER/POS	AVG	G	AB	R	H	2B	3B	HR	RB	BB	SO	SB
Ken Boswell, ph	.000	1	1	0	0	0	0	0	0	0	0	0
Wayne Garrett, 3b	.087	5	23	1	2	1	0	0	1	0	5	0
Jerry Grote, c	.211	5	19	2	4	0	0	0	2	1	3	0
Don Hahn, of	.235	5	17	2	4	0	0	0	1	2	4	0
Bud Harrelson, ss	.167	5	18	1	3	0	0	0	2	1	1	0
Cleon Jones, of	.300	5	20	3	6	2	0	0	3	2	4	0
Jerry Koosman, p	.500	1	4	1	2	0	0	0	1	0	0	0
Ed Kranepool, of	.500	1	2	0	1	0	0	0	0	2	0	0
Jon Matlack, p	.000	1	2	0	0	0	0	0	0	1	2	0
Willie Mays, of	.333	1	3	1	1	0	0	0	1	0	0	0
Tug Mc Graw, p	.000	2	1	0	0	0	0	0	0	0	1	0
Felix Millan, 2b	.316	5	19	5	6	0	0	0	2	2	1	0
John Milner, 1b	.176	5	17	2	3	0	0	0	1	5	3	0
Harry Parker, p	.000	1	0	0	0	0	0	0	0	0	0	0
Tom Seaver, p	.333	2	6	1	2	2	0	0	1	1	1	0
Rusty Staub, of	.200	4	15	4	3	0	0	3	5	3	2	0
George Stone, p	.000	1	1	0	0	0	0	0	0	1	1	0
TOTAL	.220		168	23	37	5	0	3	22	19	28	0

PITCHER	W	L	ERA	G	GS	CG	SV	SHO	IP	H	ER	BB	SO
Jerry Koosman	1	0	2.00	1	1	1	0	0	9.0	8	2	0	9
Jon Matlack	1	0	0.00	1	1	1	0	1	9.0	2	0	3	9
Tug Mc Graw	0	0	0.00	2	0	0	1	0	5.0	4	0	3	3
Harry Parker	0	1	9.00	1	0	0	0	0	1.0	1	1	0	0
Tom Seaver	1	1	1.62	2	2	1	0	0	16.2	13	3	5	17
George Stone	0	0	1.35	1	1	0	0	0	6.2	3	1	2	4
TOTAL	3	2	1.33	8	5	3	1	1	47.1	31	7	13	42

CIN (W)

PLAYER/POS	AVG	G	AB	R	H	2B	3B	HR	RB	BB	SO	SB
Ed Armbrister, of-1	.167	3	6	0	1	0	0	0	0	0	5	0
Johnny Bench, c	.263	5	19	1	5	2	0	1	1	2	2	0
Jack Billingham, p	.000	2	3	0	0	0	0	0	0	0	1	0
Pedro Borbon, p	.000	4	0	0	0	0	0	0	0	0	0	0
Clay Carroll, p	.000	3	0	0	0	0	0	0	0	0	0	0
Darrel Chaney, ph	.000	5	9	0	0	0	0	0	0	3	4	0
Ed Crosby, ss	.500	2	2	0	1	0	0	0	0	0	1	0
Dan Driessen, 3b	.167	4	12	0	2	1	0	0	1	0	2	0
Phil Gagliano, ph	.000	3	3	0	0	0	0	0	0	2	0	0
Cesar Geronimo, of	.067	4	15	0	1	0	0	0	0	0	7	0
Ken Griffey, of-2	.143	3	7	0	1	1	0	0	0	0	0	0
Ross Grimsley, p	.000	2	0	0	0	0	0	0	0	0	0	0
Don Gullett, p	.000	3	1	0	0	0	0	0	0	0	0	0
Tom Hall, p	.000	3	0	0	0	0	0	0	0	0	0	0
Hal King, ph	.500	3	2	0	1	0	0	0	0	1	1	0
Andy Kosco, of	.300	3	10	0	3	0	0	0	0	2	3	0
Denis Menke, ss-2,3b-2	.222	3	9	1	2	0	0	1	1	1	2	0
Joe Morgan, 2b	.100	5	20	1	2	1	0	0	1	2	2	0
Roger Nelson, p	.000	1	1	0	0	0	0	0	0	0	1	0
Fred Norman, p	.000	1	1	0	0	0	0	0	0	0	1	0
Tony Perez, 1b	.091	5	22	1	2	0	0	1	2	0	4	0
Pete Rose, of	.381	5	21	3	8	1	0	2	2	2	2	0
Larry Stahl, ph	.500	4	4	1	2	0	0	0	0	0	1	0
Dave Tomlin, p	.000	1	0	0	0	0	0	0	0	0	0	0
TOTAL	.186		167	8	31	6	0	5	8	13	42	0

PITCHER	W	L	ERA	G	GS	CG	SV	SHO	IP	H	ER	BB	SO
Jack Billingham	0	1	4.50	2	2	0	0	0	12.0	9	6	4	9
Pedro Borbon	1	0	0.00	4	0	0	1	0	4.2	3	0	0	3
Clay Carroll	1	0	1.29	3	0	0	0	0	7.0	5	1	1	2
Ross Grimsley	0	1	12.27	2	1	0	0	0	3.2	7	5	2	3
Don Gullett	0	1	2.00	3	1	0	0	0	9.0	4	2	3	6
Tom Hall	0	0	67.50	3	0	0	0	0	0.2	3	5	4	1
Roger Nelson	0	0	0.00	1	0	0	0	0	2.1	0	0	1	0
Fred Norman	0	0	1.80	1	1	0	0	0	5.0	1	1	3	3
Dave Tomlin	0	0	16.20	1	0	0	0	0	1.2	5	3	1	1
TOTAL	2	3	4.50	20	5	0	1	0	46.0	37	23	19	28

GAME 1 AT CIN OCT 6

NY	010	000	000	1	3 0
CIN	000	000	011	2	6 0

Pitchers: SEAVER vs Billingham, Hall (9), BORBON (9)
Home Runs: Rose-CIN, Bench-CIN
Attendance: 53,431

GAME 2 AT CIN OCT 7

NY	000	100	004	5	7 0
CIN	000	000	000	0	2 0

Pitchers: MATLACK vs GULLETT, Carroll (6), Hall (9), Borbon (9)
Home Runs: Staub-NY
Attendance: 54,041

GAME 3 AT NY OCT 8

CIN	002	000	000	2	8 1
NY	151	200	00X	9	11 1

Pitchers: GRIMSLEY, Hall (2), Tomlin (3), Nelson (4), Borbon (7) vs KOOSMAN
Home Runs: Staub-NY (2), Menke-CIN
Attendance: 53,967

GAME 4 AT NY OCT 9

CIN	000 000 100 001	2	8 0
NY	001 000 000 000	1	3 2

Pitchers: Norman, Gullett (6), CARROLL (10), Borbon (12) vs Stone, McGraw, PARKER (12)
Home Runs: Perez-CIN, Rose-CIN
Attendance: 50,786

GAME 5 AT NY OCT 10

CIN	001	010	000	2	7 1
NY	200	041	00X	7	13 1

Pitchers: BILLINGHAM, Gullett (5), Carroll (5), Grimsley (7) vs SEAVER, McGraw (9)
Attendance: 50,323

The Orioles finally met their match in an LCS as Oakland took its second consecutive pennant. Baltimore started strong, chasing A's starter Vida Blue with four runs in the first inning as Jim Palmer—pitching the series opener for a change—blanked the A's on five hits. But Oakland snapped back in Game Two, with five of their six runs coming on homers by Sal Bando (two, for three runs), Joe Rudi, and Bert Campaneris.

Oriole Mike Cuellar and the A's Ken Holtzman cut down opposing batters for 10½ innings in Game Three before Oakland's Campaneris broke the 1–1 tie in the bottom of the eleventh with a leadoff home run. The next day Jim Palmer was driven out in the second inning by three Oakland runs, and the A's added to their lead with another run in the sixth. But Andy Etchebarren led a four-run Oriole comeback in the seventh with a three-run homer, and Bobby Grich's solo shot in the next inning gave the Orioles the margin they needed to win the game and tie the series.

The A's took it all in the finale, though, needing only one of their three runs as Catfish Hunter stopped Oakland cold on five scattered hits.

Oakland A's (West), 3;
Baltimore Orioles (East) 2

OAK (W)

PLAYER/POS	AVG	G	AB	R	H	2B	3B	HR	RB	BB	SO	SB
Jesus Alou, dh-1	.333	4	6	0	2	0	0	0	1	0	1	0
Mike Andrews, 1b-1,dh-1	.000	2	1	0	0	0	0	0	0	0	0	0
Sal Bando, 3b	.167	5	18	2	3	0	0	2	3	3	6	0
Vida Blue, p	.000	2	0	0	0	0	0	0	0	0	0	0
Pat Bourque, dh	.000	2	1	0	0	0	0	0	0	1	1	0
Bert Campaneris, ss	.333	5	21	3	7	1	0	2	3	2	2	3
Billy Conigliaro, of	.000	1	4	0	0	0	0	0	0	0	2	0
Vic Davalillo, 1b-2,of-2	.625	4	8	2	5	1	1	0	1	1	0	0
Rollie Fingers, p	.000	3	0	0	0	0	0	0	0	0	0	0
Ray Fosse, c	.091	5	11	2	1	1	0	0	3	2	2	0
Dick Green, 2b	.077	5	13	0	1	1	0	0	1	1	4	0
Ken Holtzman, p	.000	1	0	0	0	0	0	0	0	0	0	0
Catfish Hunter, p	.000	2	0	0	0	0	0	0	0	0	0	0
Reggie Jackson, of	.143	5	21	0	3	0	0	0	0	0	6	0
Deron Johnson, dh	.100	4	10	0	1	0	0	0	0	2	6	0
Ted Kubiak, 2b	.000	3	2	0	0	0	0	0	0	0	1	0
Allan Lewis, pr	.000	2	0	1	0	0	0	0	0	0	0	0
Angel Mangual, of	.111	3	9	1	1	0	0	0	0	0	3	0
Blue Moon Odom, p-2	.000	1	0	0	0	0	0	0	0	0	0	0
Horacio Pina, p	.000	1	0	0	0	0	0	0	0	0	0	0
Joe Rudi, of	.222	5	18	1	4	0	0	1	3	3	1	0
Gene Tenace, 1b-5,c-3	.235	5	17	3	4	1	0	0	0	2	4	0
TOTAL	.200		160	15	32	5	1	5	15	17	39	3

PITCHER	W	L	ERA	G	GS	CG	SV	SHO	IP	H	ER	BB	SO
Vida Blue	0	1	10.29	2	2	0	0	0	7.0	8	8	5	3
Rollie Fingers	0	1	1.93	3	0	0	1	0	4.2	4	1	2	4
Ken Holtzman	1	0	0.82	1	1	1	0	0	11.0	3	1	1	7
Catfish Hunter	2	0	1.65	2	2	1	0	0	16.1	12	3	5	6
Blue Moon Odom	0	0	1.80	2	0	0	0	0	5.0	6	1	2	4
Horacio Pina	0	0	0.00	1	0	0	0	0	2.0	3	0	1	1
TOTAL	3	2	2.74	11	5	2	1	0	46.0	36	14	16	25

BAL (E)

PLAYER/POS	AVG	G	AB	R	H	2B	3B	HR	RB	BB	SO	SB
Doyle Alexander, p	.000	1	0	0	0	0	0	0	0	0	0	0
Frank Baker, ss	.000	2	0	0	0	0	0	0	0	0	0	0
Don Baylor, of-3	.273	4	11	3	3	0	0	0	1	3	5	0
Mark Belanger, ss	.125	5	16	0	2	0	0	0	1	1	1	0
Paul Blair, of	.167	5	18	2	3	0	0	0	0	1	5	0
Larry Brown, 3b	.000	1	0	0	0	0	0	0	0	0	0	0
Al Bumbry, of	.000	2	7	1	0	0	0	0	0	2	2	1
Rich Coggins, of	.444	2	9	1	4	1	0	0	0	0	0	0
Terry Crowley, of-1	.000	2	5	0	0	0	0	0	0	0	0	0
Mike Cuellar, p	.000	1	0	0	0	0	0	0	0	0	0	0
Tommy Davis, dh	.286	5	21	1	6	1	0	0	2	1	0	0
Andy Etchebarren, c	.357	4	14	1	5	1	0	1	4	0	1	0
Bobby Grich, 2b	.100	5	20	1	2	0	0	1	1	2	5	0
Grant Jackson, p	.000	2	0	0	0	0	0	0	0	0	0	0
Dave Nc Nally, p	.000	1	0	0	0	0	0	0	0	0	0	0
Jim Palmer, p	.000	3	0	0	0	0	0	0	0	0	0	0
Boog Powell, 1b	.000	1	4	1	0	0	0	0	0	0	1	0
Merv Rettenmund, of	.091	3	11	1	1	0	0	0	0	3	2	0
Bob Reynolds, p	.000	2	0	0	0	0	0	0	0	0	0	0
Brooks Robinson, 3b	.250	5	20	1	5	2	0	0	2	1	1	0
Eddie Watt, p	.000	1	0	0	0	0	0	0	0	0	0	0
Earl Williams, 1b-4,c-1	.278	5	18	2	5	2	0	1	4	2	2	0
TOTAL	.211		171	15	36	7	0	3	15	16	25	1

PITCHER	W	L	ERA	G	GS	CG	SV	SHO	IP	H	ER	BB	SO
Doyle Alexander	0	1	4.91	1	1	0	0	0	3.2	5	2	0	1
Mike Cuellar	0	1	1.80	1	1	1	0	0	10.0	4	2	3	11
Grant Jackson	1	0	0.00	2	0	0	0	0	3.0	0	0	1	0
Dave Nc Nally	0	1	5.87	1	1	0	0	0	7.2	7	5	2	7
Jim Palmer	1	0	1.84	3	2	1	0	1	14.2	11	3	8	15
Bob Reynolds	0	0	3.18	2	0	0	0	0	5.2	5	2	3	5
Eddie Watt	0	0	0.00	1	0	0	0	0	0.1	0	0	0	0
TOTAL	2	3	2.80	11	5	2	0	1	45.0	32	14	17	39

GAME 1 AT BAL OCT 6

OAK	000	000	000	0	5 1
BAL	400	000	11X	6	12 0

Pitchers: BLUE, Pina (1), Odom (3), Fingers (8) vs PALMER
Attendance: 41,279

GAME 2 AT BAL OCT 7

OAK	100	002	021	6	9 0
BAL	001	000	010	3	8 0

Pitchers: HUNTER, Fingers (8) VS McNALLY, Reynolds (8), G.Jackson (9)
Home Runs: Campaneris-OAK, Rudi-OAK, Bando-OAK (2)
Attendance: 48,425

GAME 3 AT OAK OCT 9

BAL	010	000	000 00	1	3 0
OAK	000	000	010 01	2	4 3

Pitchers: CUELLAR vs HOLTZMAN
Home Runs: Williams-BAL, Campaneris-OAK
Attendance: 34,367

GAME 4 AT OAK OCT 10

BAL	000	000	410	5	8 0
OAK	030	001	000	4	7 0

Pitchers: Palmer, Reynolds (2), Watt (7), G.JACKSON (7) vs Blue, FINGERS (7)
Home Runs: Etchebarren-BAL, Grich-BAL
Attendance: 27,497

GAME 5 AT OAK OCT 11

BAL	000	000	000	0	5 2
OAK	001	200	00X	3	7 0

Pitchers: ALEXANDER, Palmer (4) vs HUNTER
Attendance: 24,265

For the second year in a row, the A's were outpitched and outscored by their Series opposition, and this time they were outhit as well. But again, when the dust of Game Seven had risen, they still wore the crown. A's starter Ken Holtzman, who because of the American League's new designated hitter rule had not batted all season, doubled for the A's first hit in the third inning of Game One and scored the first Oakland run on a Met error. The A's scored again in the inning, enough for the win as Holtzman and two relievers held New York to a single run.

The Mets evened things in a Game Two that lasted a record 4 hours 13 minutes, scoring four runs with two out in the top of the twelfth inning for a lead the A's were not able to overcome. (Three of the runs scored on a pair of errors by second-baseman Mike Andrews, prompting a flap that rocked the baseball world as A's owner Charlie Finley tried—unsuccessfully—to "fire" Andrews by declaring him injured.) Final score of the slugfest: 10–7.

In a somewhat more normal third game, the Mets grabbed an early lead on Wayne Garrett's leadoff homer in the bottom of the first and scored a second run on two singles and wild pitch for a 2–0 lead that held up until Oakland tied the game in the eighth. In the eleventh, the A's Ted Kubiak worked his way around the bases on a walk, passed ball, and single for a lead that reliever Rollie Fingers held in the bottom of the inning.

New York evened the Series on Rusty Staub's three-run homer in the first inning of Game Four (scoring three more times later for a 6–1 win). The Mets moved in front on a sparkling 2–0 three-hitter by Jerry Koosman and Tug McGraw in Game Five, but lost their edge as the Series returned to Oakland for Game Six, losing when Reggie Jackson's doubles in the first and third drove in two runs to give the A's a lead New York was unable to overtake.

Oakland made the finale look easy. Bert Campaneris and Jackson both hit two-run homers in the third inning, and Campaneris scored a fifth run two innings later before New York finally got on the board in the sixth. In the ninth inning the Mets scored a second run with two outs, but reliever Darold Knowles came on for a record seventh pitching appearance and retired the final batter for his second Series save.

Oakland Athletics (AL), 4;
New York Mets (NL) 3

OAK (A)

PLAYER/POS	AVG	G	AB	R	H	2B	3B	HR	RB	BB	SO	SB
Jesus Alou, of-6	.158	7	19	0	3	1	0	0	3	0	0	0
Mike Andrews, 2b-1	.000	2	3	0	0	0	0	0	0	1	1	0
Sal Bando, 3b	.231	7	26	5	6	1	1	0	1	4	7	0
Vida Blue, p	.000	2	4	0	0	0	0	0	0	0	4	0
Pat Bourque, 1b	.500	2	2	0	1	0	0	0	0	0	0	0
Bert Campaneris, ss	.290	7	31	6	9	0	1	1	3	1	7	3
Billy Conigliaro, ph	.000	3	3	0	0	0	0	0	0	0	1	0
Vic Davalillo, of-4,1b-1	.091	6	11	0	1	0	0	0	0	2	1	0
Rollie Fingers, p	.333	6	3	0	1	0	0	0	0	0	1	0
Ray Fosse, c	.158	7	19	0	3	1	0	0	0	1	4	0
Dick Green, 2b	.063	7	16	0	1	0	0	0	0	1	6	0
Ken Holtzman, p	.667	3	3	2	2	2	0	0	0	0	0	0
Catfish Hunter, p	.000	2	5	0	0	0	0	0	0	0	3	0
Reggie Jackson, of	.310	7	29	3	9	3	1	1	6	2	7	0
Deron Johnson, 1b-2	.300	6	10	0	3	1	0	0	1	0	4	0
Darold Knowles, p	.000	7	0	0	0	0	0	0	0	0	0	0
Ted Kubiak, 2b	.000	4	3	1	0	0	0	0	0	1	1	0
Allan Lewis, pr	.000	3	0	1	0	0	0	0	0	0	0	0
Paul Lindblad, p	.000	3	1	0	0	0	0	0	0	0	0	0
Angel Mangual, of-1	.000	5	6	0	0	0	0	0	0	0	3	0
Blue Moon Odom, p-2	.000	3	1	0	0	0	0	0	0	0	1	0
Horacio Pina, p	.000	2	0	0	0	0	0	0	0	0	0	0
Joe Rudi, of	.333	7	27	3	9	2	0	0	4	3	4	0
Gene Tenace, 1b-7,c-3	.158	7	19	0	3	1	0	0	3	11	7	0
TOTAL	.212		241	21	51	12	3	2	20	28	62	3

PITCHER	W	L	ERA	G	GS	CG	SV	SHO	IP	H	ER	BB	SO
Vida Blue	0	1	4.91	2	2	0	0	0	11.0	10	6	3	8
Rollie Fingers	0	1	0.66	6	0	0	2	0	13.2	13	1	4	8
Ken Holtzman	2	1	4.22	3	3	0	0	0	10.2	13	5	5	6
Catfish Hunter	1	0	2.03	2	2	0	0	0	13.1	11	3	4	6
Darold Knowles	0	0	0.00	7	0	0	2	0	6.1	4	0	5	5
Paul Lindblad	0	0	0.00	3	0	0	0	0	3.1	4	0	1	1
Blue Moon Odom	0	0	3.86	2	0	0	0	0	4.2	5	2	2	2
Horacio Pina	0	0	0.00	2	0	0	0	0	3.0	6	0	2	0
TOTAL	4	3	2.32	27	7	0	4	0	66.0	66	17	26	36

NY (N)

PLAYER/POS	AVG	G	AB	R	H	2B	3B	HR	RB	BB	SO	SB
Jim Beauchamp, ph	.000	4	4	0	0	0	0	0	0	0	1	0
Ken Boswell, ph	1.000	3	3	1	3	0	0	0	0	0	0	0
Wayne Garrett, 3b	.167	7	30	4	5	0	0	2	2	5	11	0
Jerry Grote, c	.267	7	30	2	8	0	0	0	0	0	1	0
Don Hahn, of	.241	7	29	2	7	1	1	0	2	1	6	0
Bud Harrelson, ss	.250	7	24	2	6	1	0	0	1	5	3	0
Ron Hodges, ph	.000	1	0	0	0	0	0	0	0	1	0	0
Cleon Jones, of	.286	7	28	5	8	2	0	1	1	4	2	0
Jerry Koosman, p	.000	2	4	0	0	0	0	0	0	0	3	0
Ed Kranepool, ph	.000	4	3	0	0	0	0	0	0	0	0	0
Ted Martinez, pr	.000	2	0	0	0	0	0	0	0	0	0	0
Jon Matlack, p	.250	3	4	0	1	0	0	0	0	2	1	0
Willie Mays, of-2	.286	3	7	1	2	0	0	0	1	0	1	0
Tug Mc Graw, p	.333	5	3	1	1	0	0	0	0	0	1	0
Felix Millan, 2b	.188	7	32	3	6	1	1	0	1	1	1	0
John Milner, 1b	.296	7	27	2	8	0	0	0	2	5	1	0
Harry Parker, p	.000	3	0	0	0	0	0	0	0	0	0	0
Ray Sadecki, p	.000	4	0	0	0	0	0	0	0	0	0	0
Tom Seaver, p	.000	2	5	0	0	0	0	0	0	0	2	0
Rusty Staub, of	.423	7	26	1	11	2	0	1	6	2	2	0
George Stone, p	.000	2	0	0	0	0	0	0	0	0	0	0
George Theodore, of-1	.000	2	2	0	0	0	0	0	0	0	0	0
TOTAL	.253		261	24	66	7	2	4	16	26	36	0

PITCHER	W	L	ERA	G	GS	CG	SV	SHO	IP	H	ER	BB	SO
Jerry Koosman	1	0	3.12	2	2	0	0	0	8.2	9	3	7	8
Jon Matlack	1	2	2.16	3	3	0	0	0	16.2	10	4	5	11
Tug Mc Graw	1	0	2.63	5	0	0	1	0	13.2	8	4	9	14
Harry Parker	0	1	0.00	3	0	0	0	0	3.1	2	0	2	2
Ray Sadecki	0	0	1.93	4	0	0	1	0	4.2	5	1	1	6
Tom Seaver	0	1	2.40	2	2	0	0	0	15.0	13	4	3	18
George Stone	0	0	0.00	2	0	0	1	0	3.0	4	0	1	3
TOTAL	3	4	2.22	21	7	0	3	0	65.0	51	16	28	62

GAME 1 AT OAK OCT 13

NY	000	100	000	1	7	2
OAK	002	000	00X	2	4	0

Pitchers: MATLACK, McGraw (7) VS HOLTZMAN, Fingers (6), Knowles (9)
Attendance: 46,021

GAME 2 AT OAK OCT 14

NY	011	004	000	004	10	15	1
OAK	210	000	102	001	7	13	5

Pitchers: Koosman, Sadecki (3), Parker (5), McGRAW (6), Stone (12) VS Blue, Pina (6), Knowles (6), Odom (8), FINGERS (10), Linblad (12)
Home Runs: Jones-NY, Garrett-NY
Attendance: 49,151

GAME 3 AT NY OCT 16

OAK	000	001	010	01	3	10	1
NY	200	000	000	00	2	10	2

Pitchers: Hunter, Knowles (7), LINDBLAD (9), Fingers (11) vs Seaver, Sadecki (9), McGraw (9), PARKER (11)
Home Runs: Garrett-NY
Attendance: 54,817

GAME 4 AT NY OCT 17

OAK	000	100	000	1	5	1
NY	300	300	00X	6	13	1

Pitchers: HOLTZMAN, Odom (1), Knowles (4), Pina (5), Linblad (8) VS MATLACK, Sadecki (9)
Home Runs: Staub-NY
Attendance: 54,817

GAME 5 AT NY OCT 18

OAK	000	000	000	0	3	1
NY	010	001	00X	2	7	1

Pitchers: BLUE, Knowles (6), Fingers (7) VS KOOSMAN, McGraw (7)
Attendance: 54,817

GAME 6 AT OAK OCT 20

NY	000	000	010	1	6	2
OAK	101	000	01X	3	7	0

Pitchers: SEAVER, McGraw (8) vs HUNTER, Knowles (8), Fingers (8)
Attendance: 49,333

GAME 7 AT OAK OCT 21

NY	000	001	001	2	8	1
OAK	004	010	00X	5	9	1

Pitchers: MATLACK, Parker (3), Sadecki (5), Stone (7) vs HOLTZMAN, Fingers (6), Knowles (9)
Home Runs: Campaneris-OAK, Jackson-OAK
Attendance: 49,333

Dodger pitcher Don Sutton—who had brought his won-lost record from 10–9 to 19–9 with a nine-game winning streak in the regular season—continued his winning ways in the LCS, surrendering only seven hits and one run in seventeen innings and taking both the opener and clincher of the four-game series. Los Angeles's Andy Messersmith followed up Sutton's opening-game shutout with six shutout innings of his own in Game Two before Pittsburgh scored its first two runs of the series in the seventh. They tied the score, but the Dodgers countered with three more in the top of the eighth to assure their second win.

The Pirates captured their only victory in Game Three, as Richie Hebner and Willie Stargell homered for five of the Bucs' seven runs, while Bruce Kison and Ramon Hernandez shut out the Dodgers on four hits.

Pittsburgh finally got to Sutton for a run when Stargell homered in the seventh inning of Game Four. But it was too little, and too late to stem a twelve-run Dodger attack led by Steve Garvey's four hits (two of them home runs) and four RBIs.

Los Angeles Dodgers (West), 3; Pittsburgh Pirates (East) 1

LA (W)

PLAYER/POS	AVG	G	AB	R	H	2B	3B	HR	RB	BB	SO	SB
Rick Auerbach, ph	1.000	1	1	0	1	1	0	0	0	0	0	0
Bill Buckner, of	.167	4	18	0	3	1	0	0	0	0	2	0
Ron Cey, 3b	.313	4	16	2	5	3	0	1	1	3	2	0
Willie Crawford, of	.250	2	4	1	1	0	0	0	1	1	1	0
Al Downing, p	.000	1	1	0	0	0	0	0	0	0	0	0
Joe Ferguson, of-3,c-2	.231	4	13	3	3	0	0	0	2	5	1	0
Steve Garvey, 1b	.389	4	18	4	7	1	0	2	5	1	1	0
Charley Hough, p	.000	1	0	0	0	0	0	0	0	0	0	0
Von Joshua, ph	.000	1	0	0	0	0	0	0	0	1	0	0
Lee Lacy, pr	.000	1	0	0	0	0	0	0	0	0	0	0
Davey Lopes, 2b	.267	4	15	4	4	0	1	0	3	5	1	3
Mike Marshall, p	.000	2	0	0	0	0	0	0	0	0	0	0
Ken Mc Mullen, ph	.000	1	1	0	0	0	0	0	0	0	1	0
Andy Messersmith, p	.000	1	3	0	0	0	0	0	0	0	1	0
Manny Mota, of-1	.333	3	3	0	1	0	0	0	1	0	0	0
Tom Paciorek, of	1.000	1	1	0	1	0	0	0	0	0	0	0
Doug Rau, p	.000	1	0	0	0	0	0	0	0	0	0	0
Bill Russell, ss	.389	4	18	1	7	0	0	0	3	1	0	0
Eddie Solomon, p	.000	1	0	0	0	0	0	0	0	0	0	0
Don Sutton, p	.286	2	7	0	2	0	0	0	1	1	2	0
Jimmy Wynn, of	.200	4	10	4	2	2	0	0	2	9	1	1
Steve Yeager, c	.000	3	9	1	0	0	0	0	0	3	3	1
TOTAL	.268		138	20	37	8	1	3	19	30	16	5

PITCHER	W	L	ERA	G	GS	CG	SV	SHO	IP	H	ER	BB	SO
Al Downing	0	0	0.00	1	0	0	0	0	4.0	1	0	1	0
Charley Hough	0	0	7.71	1	0	0	0	0	2.1	4	2	0	2
Mike Marshall	0	0	0.00	2	0	0	0	0	3.0	0	0	0	1
Andy Messersmith	1	0	2.57	1	1	0	0	0	7.0	8	2	3	0
Doug Rau	0	1	40.50	1	1	0	0	0	0.2	3	3	1	0
Eddie Solomon	0	0	0.00	1	0	0	0	0	2.0	2	0	1	1
Don Sutton	2	0	0.53	2	2	1	0	1	17.0	7	1	2	13
TOTAL	3	1	2.00	9	4	1	0	1	36.0	25	8	8	17

PIT (E)

PLAYER/POS	AVG	G	AB	R	H	2B	3B	HR	RB	BB	SO	SB
Ken Brett, p	.000	1	1	0	0	0	0	0	0	0	1	0
Gene Clines, of	.000	2	1	1	0	0	0	0	0	0	0	0
Larry Demery, p	.000	2	0	0	0	0	0	0	0	0	0	0
Dave Giusti, p	.000	3	0	0	0	0	0	0	0	0	0	0
Richie Hebner, 3b	.231	4	13	1	3	0	0	1	4	1	4	0
Ramon Hernandez, p	.000	2	1	0	0	0	0	0	0	0	1	0
Art Howe, ph	.000	1	1	0	0	0	0	0	0	0	0	0
Ed Kirkpatrick, 1b	.000	3	9	0	0	0	0	0	0	2	0	0
Bruce Kison, p	.000	1	3	0	0	0	0	0	0	0	2	0
Mario Mendoza, ss	.200	3	5	0	1	0	0	0	1	1	0	0
Al Oliver, of	.143	4	14	1	2	0	0	0	1	2	2	0
Dave Parker, of-2	.125	3	8	0	1	0	0	0	0	0	1	0
Juan Pizarro, p	.000	1	0	0	0	0	0	0	0	0	0	0
Paul Popovich, ss	.600	3	5	1	3	0	0	0	0	0	0	0
Jerry Reuss, p	.000	2	2	0	0	0	0	0	0	0	0	0
Bob Robertson, 1b	.000	1	5	1	0	0	0	0	0	0	0	0
Jim Rooker, p	.500	1	2	0	1	0	0	0	0	0	0	0
Manny Sanguillen, c	.250	4	16	0	4	1	0	0	0	0	0	0
Willie Stargell, of	.400	4	15	3	6	0	0	2	4	1	2	0
Rennie Stennett, 2b	.063	4	16	1	1	0	0	0	0	1	1	0
Frank Taveras, ss	.000	2	2	0	0	0	0	0	0	0	0	1
Richie Zisk, of-2	.300	3	10	1	3	0	0	0	0	0	3	0
TOTAL	.194		129	10	25	1	0	3	10	8	17	1

PITCHER	W	L	ERA	G	GS	CG	SV	SHO	IP	H	ER	BB	SO
Ken Brett	0	0	7.71	1	0	0	0	0	2.1	3	2	2	1
Larry Demery	0	0	27.00	2	0	0	0	0	1.0	3	3	2	0
Dave Giusti	0	1	21.60	3	0	0	0	0	3.1	13	8	5	1
Ramon Hernandez	0	0	0.00	2	0	0	0	0	4.1	3	0	1	2
Bruce Kison	1	0	0.00	1	1	0	0	0	6.2	2	0	6	5
Juan Pizarro	0	0	0.00	1	0	0	0	0	0.2	0	0	1	0
Jerry Reuss	0	2	3.72	2	2	0	0	0	9.2	7	4	8	3
Jim Rooker	0	0	2.57	1	1	0	0	0	7.0	6	2	5	4
TOTAL	1	3	4.89	13	4	0	0	0	35.0	37	19	30	16

GAME 1 AT PIT OCT 5

LA	010	000	002	3	9	2
PIT	000	000	000	0	4	0

Pitchers: SUTTON vs REUSS, Giusti (8)
Attendance: 40,638

GAME 2 AT PIT OCT 6

LA	100	100	030	5	12	0
PIT	000	000	200	2	8	3

Pitchers: MESSERSMITH, Marshall (8) VS Rooker, GIUSTI (8), Demery (8), Hernandez (8)
Home Runs: Cey-LA
Attendance: 49,247

GAME 3 AT LA OCT 8

PIT	502	000	000	7	10	0
LA	000	000	000	0	4	5

Pitchers: KISON, Hernandez (7) vs RAU, Hough (1), Downing (4), Solomon (8)
Home Runs: Stargell-PIT, Hebner-PIT
Attendance: 55,953

GAME 4 AT LA OCT 9

PIT	000	000	100	1	3	1
LA	102	022	23X	12	12	0

Pitchers: REUSS, Brett (3), Demery (6), Giusti (7), Pizarro (8) vs SUTTON, Marshall (9)
Home Runs: Garvey-LA (2), Stargell-PIT
Attendance: 54,424

After spotting Baltimore a win in the opener, Oakland took the next three games and their third consecutive pennant. Although the A's got nine hits in Game One—their series high—the Orioles hit harder, burying Oakland under home runs by Paul Blair, Brooks Robinson, and Bobby Grich. In Game Two, though, Ken Holtzman shut out Baltimore on five hits as Sal Bando and Ray Fosse homered. Bando homered again in the third game for the only Oakland run as Jim Palmer limited the A's to four hits. But one run was enough to defeat Baltimore, for Vida Blue shut them out on a masterly two-hitter.

Oriole starter Mike Cuellar walked nine men in 4⅔ innings of Game Four, including four in the fifth to force in Oakland's first run. Two innings later Reggie Jackson's double (the only Oakland hit of the game) off reliever Ross Grimsley drove in Oakland's second run, while starter Catfish Hunter was blanking the O's through seven-plus innings. After failing to score for thirty consecutive innings, the Orioles got to reliever Rollie Fingers for a run with two out in the bottom of the ninth. But Fingers then struck out Don Baylor, and the A's had their pennant.

Oakland A's (West), 3; Baltimore Orioles (East) 1

OAK (W)

PLAYER/POS	AVG	G	AB	R	H	2B	3B	HR	RB	BB	SO	SB
Jesus Alou, ph	1.000	1	1	0	1	0	0	0	0	0	0	0
Sal Bando, 3b	.231	4	13	4	3	0	0	2	2	4	0	0
Vida Blue, p	.000	1	0	0	0	0	0	0	0	0	0	0
Bert Campaneris, ss	.176	4	17	0	3	0	0	0	3	0	3	1
Rollie Fingers, p	.000	2	0	0	0	0	0	0	0	0	0	0
Ray Fosse, c	.333	4	12	1	4	1	0	1	3	1	2	0
Dick Green, 2b	.222	4	9	0	2	0	0	0	0	2	1	0
Jim Holt, 1b-1	.000	2	0	0	0	0	0	0	0	1	0	0
Ken Holtzman, p	.000	1	0	0	0	0	0	0	0	0	0	0
Catfish Hunter, p	.000	2	0	0	0	0	0	0	0	0	0	0
Reggie Jackson, dh-3,of-1	.167	4	12	0	2	1	0	0	1	5	2	0
Angel Mangual, dh	.250	1	4	0	1	0	0	0	0	0	0	0
Dal Maxvill, 2b	.000	1	1	0	0	0	0	0	0	0	1	0
Billy North, of	.063	4	16	3	1	1	0	0	0	2	1	1
Blue Moon Odom, p-1	.000	3	0	0	0	0	0	0	0	0	0	0
Joe Rudi, of	.154	4	13	0	2	0	1	0	3	2	0	0
Gene Tenace, 1b	.000	4	11	1	0	0	0	0	1	4	4	1
Manny Trillo, pr	.000	1	0	1	0	0	0	0	0	0	0	0
Claudell Washington, of-3	.273	4	11	1	3	1	0	0	0	0	0	0
Herb Washington, pr	.000	2	0	0	0	0	0	0	0	0	0	0
TOTAL	.183		120	11	22	4	1	3	11	22	16	3

PITCHER	W	L	ERA	G	GS	CG	SV	SHO	IP	H	ER	BB	SO
Vida Blue	1	0	0.00	1	1	1	0	1	9.0	2	0	0	7
Rollie Fingers	0	0	3.00	2	0	0	1	0	3.0	3	1	1	3
Ken Holtzman	1	0	0.00	1	1	1	0	1	9.0	5	0	2	3
Catfish Hunter	1	1	4.63	2	2	0	0	0	11.2	11	6	2	6
Blue Moon Odom	0	0	0.00	1	0	0	0	0	3.1	1	0	0	1
TOTAL	3	1	1.75	7	4	2	1	2	36.0	22	7	5	20

BAL (E)

PLAYER/POS	AVG	G	AB	R	H	2B	3B	HR	RB	BB	SO	SB
Frank Baker, ss	.000	2	0	0	0	0	0	0	0	0	0	0
Don Baylor, of	.267	4	15	0	4	0	0	0	0	0	2	0
Mark Belanger, ss	.000	4	9	0	0	0	0	0	0	1	3	0
Paul Blair, of	.286	4	14	3	4	0	0	1	2	2	2	0
Al Bumbry, ph	.000	2	1	0	0	0	0	0	0	0	1	0
Enos Cabell, of-1	.250	3	4	0	1	0	0	0	0	0	2	0
Rich Coggins, of	.000	3	11	0	0	0	0	0	0	0	3	0
Mike Cuellar, p	.000	2	0	0	0	0	0	0	0	0	0	0
Tommy Davis, dh	.267	4	15	0	4	0	0	0	1	0	1	0
Andy Etchebarren, c	.333	2	6	0	2	0	0	0	0	0	0	0
Wayne Garland, p	.000	1	0	0	0	0	0	0	0	0	0	0
Bobby Grich, 2b	.250	4	16	2	4	1	0	1	2	0	1	0
Ross Grimsley, p	.000	2	0	0	0	0	0	0	0	0	0	0
Elrod Hendricks, c	.167	3	6	1	1	0	0	0	0	1	3	0
Grant Jackson, p	.000	1	0	0	0	0	0	0	0	0	0	0
Dave Nc Nally, p	.000	1	0	0	0	0	0	0	0	0	0	0
Curt Motton, ph	.000	1	1	0	0	0	0	0	0	0	0	0
Jim Palmer, p-1	.000	2	0	0	0	0	0	0	0	0	0	0
Boog Powell, 1b	.125	2	8	0	1	0	0	0	1	0	0	0
Bob Reynolds, p	.000	1	0	0	0	0	0	0	0	0	0	0
Brooks Robinson, 3b	.083	4	12	1	1	0	0	1	1	1	0	0
Earl Williams, 1b	.000	2	6	0	0	0	0	0	0	0	2	0
TOTAL	.177		124	7	22	1	0	3	7	5	20	0

PITCHER	W	L	ERA	G	GS	CG	SV	SHO	IP	H	ER	BB	SO
Mike Cuellar	1	1	2.84	2	2	0	0	0	12.2	9	4	13	6
Wayne Garland	0	0	0.00	1	0	0	0	0	0.2	1	0	1	0
Ross Grimsley	0	0	1.69	2	0	0	0	0	5.1	1	1	2	2
Grant Jackson	0	0	0.00	1	0	0	0	0	0.1	1	0	0	1
Dave Nc Nally	0	1	1.59	1	1	0	0	0	5.2	6	1	2	2
Jim Palmer	0	1	1.00	1	1	1	0	0	9.0	4	1	1	4
Bob Reynolds	0	0	0.00	1	0	0	0	0	1.1	0	0	3	1
TOTAL	1	3	1.80	9	4	1	0	0	35.0	22	7	22	16

GAME 1 AT OAK OCT 5

BAL	100	140	000	6	10	0
OAK	001	010	001	3	9	0

Pitchers: CUELLAR, Grimsley (9) vs HUNTER, Odom (5), Fingers (9)
Home Runs: Blair-BAL, Robinson-BAL, Grich-BAL
Attendance: 41,609

GAME 2 AT OAK OCT 6

BAL	000	000	000	0	5	2
OAK	000	101	03X	5	8	0

Pitchers: McNALLY, Reynolds (7), G.Jackson (8) vs HOLTZMAN
Home Runs: Bando-OAK, Fosse-OAK
Attendance: 42,810

GAME 3 AT BAL OCT 8

OAK	000	100	000	1	4	2
BAL	000	000	000	0	2	1

Pitchers: BLUE vs PALMER
Home Runs: Bando-OAK
Attendance: 32,060

GAME 4 AT BAL OCT 9

OAK	000	010	100	2	1	0
BAL	000	000	001	1	5	1

Pitchers: HUNTER, Fingers (8) vs CUELLAR, Grimsley (5)
Attendance: 28,136

Although the A's were in a turmoil of dislike for owner Charlie Finley—and for each other—they played well enough together to take their third consecutive world championship in just five games. Still, victory didn't come easily, as three of Oakland's wins came by identical 3–2 scores (as did the Dodgers' one victory), and their biggest winning margin was three runs in Game Four. It was the first World Series held entirely on the West Coast.

The A's and Dodgers split the first two games in Los Angeles. Oakland won the opener on the strength of Reggie Jackson's home run in the second inning, pitcher Ken Holtzman's double in the fifth (he moved around on a wild pitch and squeeze bunt), and a Dodger throwing error in the eighth. The Dodgers evened the Series on Joe Ferguson's two-run homer in the sixth inning of the second game, which gave Los Angeles a 3–0 lead that an Oakland rally in the ninth failed to catch.

Los Angeles outhit Oakland in Game Three, but two of the A's runs were unearned, coming after Dodger catcher Ferguson bobbled what should have been a third-out play in the third inning.

Pitcher Ken Holtzman, who had now gone two regular seasons without a time at bat, produced in Game Four his second hit of the Series, this one a homer in the third inning for the game's first run. The Dodgers' Bill Russell tripled off him for two runs a half inning later, but in the last of the sixth inning Oakland regained the lead on three walks interspersed with a pair of singles and an RBI grounder to short. Four runs scored—more in this one inning than either team scored in any of the other four games.

Oakland took an early 2–0 lead in Game Five, with single runs in the first and second innings (the latter a Ray Fosse home run). The Dodgers put together a pinch-hit double, a walk, a pair of sacrifices (bunt and fly), and a single to tie the score in the sixth. But Joe Rudi hit the first pitch of Oakland's half of the seventh into the stands in left for the run that decided the game and the Series.

Oakland Athletics (AL), 4; Los Angeles Dodgers (NL) 1

OAK (A)

PLAYER/POS	AVG	G	AB	R	H	2B	3B	HR	RB	BB	SO	SB
Jesus Alou, ph	.000	1	1	0	0	0	0	0	0	0	1	0
Sal Bando, 3b	.063	5	16	3	1	0	0	0	2	2	5	0
Vida Blue, p	.000	2	4	0	0	0	0	0	0	0	4	0
Bert Campaneris, ss	.353	5	17	1	6	2	0	0	2	0	2	1
Rollie Fingers, p	.000	4	2	0	0	0	0	0	0	1	0	0
Ray Fosse, c	.143	5	14	1	2	0	0	1	1	1	5	0
Dick Green, 2b	.000	5	13	1	0	0	0	0	0	1	4	0
Larry Haney, c	.000	2	1	0	0	0	0	0	0	0	0	0
Jim Holt, 1b-1	.667	4	3	0	2	0	0	0	2	0	0	0
Ken Holtzman, p	.500	2	4	2	2	1	0	1	1	1	1	0
Catfish Hunter, p	.000	2	2	0	0	0	0	0	0	0	2	0
Reggie Jackson, of	.286	5	14	3	4	1	0	1	1	5	3	1
Angel Mangual, ph	.000	1	1	0	0	0	0	0	0	0	1	0
Dal Maxvill, 2b	.000	2	0	0	0	0	0	0	0	0	0	0
Billy North, of	.059	5	17	3	1	0	0	0	0	2	5	1
Blue Moon Odom, p	.000	2	0	0	0	0	0	0	0	0	0	0
Joe Rudi, of-5,1b-2	.333	5	18	1	6	0	0	1	4	0	3	0
Gene Tenace, 1b	.222	5	9	0	2	0	0	0	0	3	4	0
Claudell Washington, of	.571	5	7	1	4	0	0	0	0	1	1	0
Herb Washington, pr	.000	3	0	0	0	0	0	0	0	0	0	0
TOTAL	.211		142	16	30	4	0	4	14	16	42	3

PITCHER	W	L	ERA	G	GS	CG	SV	SHO	IP	H	ER	BB	SO
Vida Blue	0	1	3.29	2	2	0	0	0	13.2	10	5	7	9
Rollie Fingers	1	0	1.93	4	0	0	2	0	9.1	8	2	2	6
Ken Holtzman	1	0	1.50	2	2	0	0	0	12.0	13	2	4	10
Catfish Hunter	1	0	1.17	2	1	0	1	0	7.2	5	1	2	5
Blue Moon Odom	1	0	0.00	2	0	0	0	0	1.1	0	0	1	2
TOTAL	4	1	2.05	12	5	0	3	0	44.0	36	10	16	32

LA (N)

PLAYER/POS	AVG	G	AB	R	H	2B	3B	HR	RB	BB	SO	SB
Rick Auerbach, pr	.000	1	0	0	0	0	0	0	0	0	0	0
Jim Brewer, p	.000	1	0	0	0	0	0	0	0	0	0	0
Bill Buckner, of	.250	5	20	1	5	1	0	1	1	0	1	0
Ron Cey, 3b	.176	5	17	1	3	0	0	0	0	3	3	0
Willie Crawford, of-2	.333	3	6	1	2	0	0	0	1	1	0	0
Al Downing, p	.000	1	1	0	0	0	0	0	0	0	0	0
Joe Ferguson, of-4,c-2	.125	5	16	2	2	0	0	1	2	4	6	1
Steve Garvey, 1b	.381	5	21	2	8	0	0	0	1	0	3	0
Charley Hough, p	.000	1	0	0	0	0	0	0	0	0	0	0
Von Joshua, ph	.000	4	4	0	0	0	0	0	0	0	0	0
Lee Lacy, ph	.000	1	1	0	0	0	0	0	0	0	1	0
Davey Lopes, 2b	.111	5	18	2	2	0	0	0	0	3	4	2
Mike Marshall, p	.000	5	0	0	0	0	0	0	0	1	0	0
Andy Messersmith, p	.500	2	4	0	2	0	0	0	0	0	2	0
Tom Paciorek, ph	.500	3	2	1	1	1	0	0	0	0	0	0
Bill Russell, ss	.222	5	18	0	4	0	1	0	2	0	2	0
Don Sutton, p	.000	2	3	0	0	0	0	0	0	0	2	0
Jimmy Wynn, of	.188	5	16	1	3	1	0	1	2	4	4	0
Steve Yeager, c	.364	4	11	0	4	1	0	0	1	1	4	0
TOTAL	.228		158	11	36	4	1	4	10	16	32	3

PITCHER	W	L	ERA	G	GS	CG	SV	SHO	IP	H	ER	BB	SO
Jim Brewer	0	0	0.00	1	0	0	0	0	0.1	0	0	0	1
Al Downing	0	1	2.45	1	1	0	0	0	3.2	4	1	4	3
Charley Hough	0	0	0.00	1	0	0	0	0	2.0	0	0	1	4
Mike Marshall	0	1	1.00	5	0	0	0	1	9.0	6	1	1	10
Andy Messersmith	0	2	4.50	2	2	0	0	0	14.0	11	7	7	12
Don Sutton	1	0	2.77	2	2	0	0	0	13.0	9	4	3	12
TOTAL	1	4	2.79	12	5	0	1	0	42.0	30	13	16	42

GAME 1 AT LA OCT 12

OAK	010	010	010	3	6 2
LA	000	010	001	2	11 1

Pitchers: Holtzman, FINGERS (5), Hunter (9) vs MESSERSMITH, Marshall (9)
Home Runs: Jackson-OAK, Wynn-LA
Attendance: 55,974

GAME 2 AT LA OCT 13

OAK	000	000	002	2	6 0
LA	010	002	00X	3	6 1

Pitchers: BLUE, Odom (8) vs SUTTON, Marshall (9)
Home Runs: Ferguson-LA
Attendance: 55,989

GAME 3 AT OAK OCT 15

LA	000	000	011	2	7 2
OAK	002	100	00X	3	5 2

Pitchers: DOWNING, Brewer (4), Hough (5), Marshall (7) vs HUNTER, Fingers (8)
Home Runs: Buckner-LA, Crawford-LA
Attendance: 49,347

GAME 4 AT OAK OCT 16

LA	000	200	000	2	7 1
OAK	001	004	00X	5	7 0

Pitchers: MESSERSMITH, Marshall (7) VS HOLTZMAN, Fingers (8)
Home Runs: Holtzman-OAK
Attendance: 49,347

GAME 5 AT OAK OCT 17

LA	000	002	000	2	5 1
OAK	110	000	10X	3	6 1

Pitchers: Sutton, MARSHALL (6) vs Blue, ODOM (7), Fingers (8)
Home Runs: Fosse-OAK, Rudi-OAK
Attendance: 49,347

The Reds, who had steamrolled the National League during the season, continued their roll in the LCS. Red pitcher Don Gullett gave up three Pirate runs in the first game, but he drove in three himself with a home run and a single. Pitching the series' only complete game, he won easily behind his club's twelve-hit, eight-run attack. The Reds won just as handily in Game Two, with Fred Norman and reliever Rawley Eastwick holding the Pirates to one run as Tony Perez drove in half the Reds' six runs—two of them with a first-inning homer.

In Game Three the Pirates struggled gamely against elimination. Cincinnati scored first in the second, but in the sixth Al Oliver put Pittsburgh ahead with a two-run homer. In the eighth, though, Pete Rose restored the Reds' lead (and nullified rookie John Candelaria's fourteen-strikeout effort over 7⅔ innings) with his two-run shot. The Pirates were granted a brief reprieve when Red reliever Eastwick walked in the tying run in the bottom of the ninth. But in the tenth the Reds scored twice on three hits, and when Eastwick's replacement Pedro Borbon shut the Pirates down in the bottom of the tenth, Cincinnati had its series sweep.

Cincinnati Reds (West), 3; Pittsburgh Pirates (East) 0

CIN (W)

PLAYER/POS	AVG	G	AB	R	H	2B	3B	HR	RB	BB	SO	SB
Ed Armbrister, ph	.000	2	0	0	0	0	0	0	0	1	0	0
Johnny Bench, c	.077	3	13	1	1	0	0	0	0	1	6	1
Pedro Borbon, p	.000	1	0	0	0	0	0	0	0	0	0	0
Clay Carroll, p	.000	1	0	0	0	0	0	0	0	0	0	0
Dave Concepcion, ss	.455	3	11	2	5	0	0	1	1	1	2	2
Terry Crowley, ph	.000	1	0	0	0	0	0	0	0	0	0	0
Rawly Eastwick, p	.000	2	0	0	0	0	0	0	0	0	0	0
George Foster, of	.364	3	11	3	4	0	0	0	0	1	2	1
Cesar Geronimo, of	.000	3	10	0	0	0	0	0	0	1	7	0
Ken Griffey, of	.333	3	12	4	4	1	0	0	4	0	3	3
Don Gullett, p	.500	1	4	1	2	0	0	1	3	0	0	0
Will Mc Enaney, p	.000	1	0	0	0	0	0	0	0	0	0	0
Joe Morgan, 2b	.273	3	11	2	3	3	0	0	1	3	2	4
Gary Nolan, p	.000	1	2	0	0	0	0	0	0	0	2	0
Fred Norman, p	.000	1	1	0	0	0	0	0	1	0	0	0
Tony Perez, 1b	.417	3	12	3	5	0	0	1	4	1	2	0
Merv Rettenmund, ph	.000	2	1	0	0	0	0	0	0	1	0	0
Pete Rose, 3b	.357	3	14	3	5	0	0	1	2	0	2	0
TOTAL	.284		102	19	29	4	0	4	18	9	28	11

PITCHER	W	L	ERA	G	GS	CG	SV	SHO	IP	H	ER	BB	SO
Pedro Borbon	0	0	0.00	1	0	0	1	0	1.0	0	0	0	1
Clay Carroll	0	0	0.00	1	0	0	0	0	1.0	0	0	1	1
Rawly Eastwick	1	0	0.00	2	0	0	1	0	3.2	2	0	2	1
Don Gullett	1	0	3.00	1	1	1	0	0	9.0	8	3	2	5
Will Mc Enaney	0	0	6.75	1	0	0	0	0	1.1	1	1	0	1
Gary Nolan	0	0	3.00	1	1	0	0	0	6.0	5	2	0	5
Fred Norman	1	0	1.50	1	1	0	0	0	6.0	4	1	5	4
TOTAL	3	0	2.25	8	3	1	2	0	28.0	20	7	10	18

PIT (E)

PLAYER/POS	AVG	G	AB	R	H	2B	3B	HR	RB	BB	SO	SB
Ken Brett, p	.000	2	0	0	0	0	0	0	0	0	0	0
John Candelaria, p	.000	1	3	0	0	0	0	0	0	0	3	0
Larry Demery, p	.000	1	0	0	0	0	0	0	0	0	0	0
Duffy Dyer, ph	.000	1	0	0	0	0	0	0	1	1	0	0
Dock Ellis, p	.000	1	0	0	0	0	0	0	0	0	0	0
Dave Giusti, p	.000	1	0	0	0	0	0	0	0	0	0	0
Richie Hebner, 3b	.333	3	12	2	4	1	0	0	2	1	1	0
Ramon Hernandez, p	.000	1	0	0	0	0	0	0	0	0	0	0
Ed Kirkpatrick, ph	.000	2	2	0	0	0	0	0	0	0	0	0
Bruce Kison, p	.000	1	0	0	0	0	0	0	0	0	0	0
Al Oliver, of	.182	3	11	1	2	0	0	1	2	2	0	0
Dave Parker, of	.000	3	10	2	0	0	0	0	0	1	3	0
Willie Randolph, 2b-1	.000	2	2	1	0	0	0	0	0	0	1	0
Jerry Reuss, p	.000	1	1	0	0	0	0	0	0	0	0	0
Craig Reynolds, ss-1	.000	2	1	0	0	0	0	0	0	0	0	0
Bob Robertson, 1b-1	.500	3	2	0	1	0	0	0	1	1	0	0
Bill Robinson, ph	.000	2	2	0	0	0	0	0	0	0	1	0
Jim Rooker, p	.000	1	1	0	0	0	0	0	0	0	1	0
Manny Sanguillen, c	.167	3	12	0	2	0	0	0	0	0	0	0
Willie Stargell, 1b	.182	3	11	1	2	1	0	0	0	1	3	0
Rennie Stennett, 2b-3,ss-1	.214	3	14	0	3	0	0	0	0	0	1	0
Frank Taveras, ss	.143	3	7	0	1	0	0	0	1	1	2	0
Kent Tekulve, p	.000	2	0	0	0	0	0	0	0	0	0	0
Richie Zisk, of	.500	3	10	0	5	1	0	0	0	2	2	0
TOTAL	.198		101	7	20	3	0	1	7	10	18	0

PITCHER	W	L	ERA	G	GS	CG	SV	SHO	IP	H	ER	BB	SO
Ken Brett	0	0	0.00	2	0	0	0	0	2.1	1	0	0	1
John Candelaria	0	0	3.52	1	1	0	0	0	7.2	3	3	2	14
Larry Demery	0	0	18.00	1	0	0	0	0	2.0	4	4	1	1
Dock Ellis	0	0	0.00	1	0	0	0	0	2.0	2	0	0	2
Dave Giusti	0	0	0.00	1	0	0	0	0	1.1	0	0	0	1
Ramon Hernandez	0	1	27.00	1	0	0	0	0	0.2	3	2	0	0
Bruce Kison	0	0	4.50	1	0	0	0	0	2.0	2	1	1	0
Jerry Reuss	0	1	13.50	1	1	0	0	0	2.2	4	4	4	1
Jim Rooker	0	1	9.00	1	1	0	0	0	4.0	7	4	0	5
Kent Tekulve	0	0	6.75	2	0	0	0	0	1.1	3	1	1	2
TOTAL	0	3	6.58	12	3	0	0	0	26.0	29	19	9	28

The Oakland A's ran their domination of the American League West to five years, but an aroused Boston team stifled their try for a fourth straight pennant.

In the first game Luis Tiant held Oakland to three hits as his teammates—aided by four Oakland errors—scored seven times before giving the A's an unearned run in the eighth. Oakland scored first in Game Two on Reggie Jackson's two-run homer in the first inning and added a run in the fourth. But Carl Yastrzemski's two-run shot in the last of the fourth, followed by a Carlton Fisk double and a Fred Lynn single, drove out A's starter Vida Blue, and the tying run scored on a double play. Single Boston runs in the sixth, seventh, and eighth put the game away.

The A's started Ken Holtzman for the second time in Game Three, after only two days of rest. He held the Sox scoreless for three innings, but was driven from the game in the fifth. Boston scored four times before Oakland put a run on the board, and retained the lead to the game's conclusion.

Boston Red Sox (East), 3; Oakland A's (West) 0

BOS (E)

PLAYER/POS	AVG	G	AB	R	H	2B	3B	HR	RB	BB	SO	SB
Juan Beniquez, dh	.250	3	12	2	3	0	0	0	1	0	1	2
Rick Burleson, ss	.444	3	9	2	4	2	0	0	1	1	0	0
Reggie Cleveland, p	.000	1	0	0	0	0	0	0	0	0	0	0
Cecil Cooper, 1b	.400	3	10	0	4	2	0	0	1	0	2	0
Denny Doyle, 2b	.273	3	11	3	3	0	0	0	1	0	1	0
Dick Drago, p	.000	2	0	0	0	0	0	0	0	0	0	0
Dwight Evans, of	.100	3	10	1	1	1	0	0	1	1	2	0
Carlton Fisk, c	.417	3	12	4	5	1	0	0	2	0	2	1
Fred Lynn, of	.364	3	11	1	4	1	0	0	3	0	0	0
Roger Moret, p	.000	1	0	0	0	0	0	0	0	0	0	0
Rico Petrocelli, 3b	.167	3	12	1	2	0	0	1	2	0	3	0
Luis Tiant, p	.000	1	0	0	0	0	0	0	0	0	0	0
Rick Wise, p	.000	1	0	0	0	0	0	0	0	0	0	0
Carl Yastrzemski, of	.455	3	11	4	5	1	0	1	2	1	1	0
TOTAL	.316		98	18	31	8	0	2	14	3	12	3

PITCHER	W	L	ERA	G	GS	CG	SV	SHO	IP	H	ER	BB	SO
Reggie Cleveland	0	0	5.40	1	1	0	0	0	5.0	7	3	1	2
Dick Drago	0	0	0.00	2	0	0	2	0	4.2	2	0	1	2
Roger Moret	1	0	0.00	1	0	0	0	0	1.0	1	0	1	0
Luis Tiant	1	0	0.00	1	1	1	0	0	9.0	3	0	3	8
Rick Wise	1	0	2.45	1	1	0	0	0	7.1	6	2	3	2
TOTAL	3	0	1.67	6	3	1	2	0	27.0	19	5	9	14

OAK (W)

PLAYER/POS	AVG	G	AB	R	H	2B	3B	HR	RB	BB	SO	SB
Glenn Abbott, p	.000	1	0	0	0	0	0	0	0	0	0	0
Sal Bando, 3b	.500	3	12	1	6	2	0	0	2	0	3	0
Vida Blue, p	.000	1	0	0	0	0	0	0	0	0	0	0
Dick Bosman, p	.000	1	0	0	0	0	0	0	0	0	0	0
Bert Campaneris, ss	.000	3	11	1	0	0	0	0	0	1	1	0
Rollie Fingers, p	.000	1	0	0	0	0	0	0	0	0	0	0
Ray Fosse, c	.000	1	2	0	0	0	0	0	0	0	1	0
Phil Garner, 2b	.000	3	5	0	0	0	0	0	0	0	1	0
Tommy Harper, ph	.000	1	0	0	0	0	0	0	0	1	0	0
Jim Holt, 1b-1	.333	3	3	0	1	1	0	0	0	0	0	0
Ken Holtzman, p	.000	2	0	0	0	0	0	0	0	0	0	0
Don Hopkins, dh	.000	1	0	0	0	0	0	0	0	0	0	0
Reggie Jackson, of	.417	3	12	1	5	0	0	1	3	0	2	0
Paul Lindblad, p	.000	2	0	0	0	0	0	0	0	0	0	0
Ted Martinez, 2b	.000	3	0	0	0	0	0	0	0	0	0	0
Billy North, of	.000	3	10	0	0	0	0	0	1	2	0	0
Joe Rudi, 1b-2,of-1	.250	3	12	1	3	2	0	0	0	0	1	0
Gene Tenace, c-3,1b-1	.000	3	9	0	0	0	0	0	0	3	2	0
Jim Todd, p	.000	3	0	0	0	0	0	0	0	0	0	0
Cesar Tovar, 2b-1	.500	2	2	2	1	0	0	0	0	1	0	0
Claudell Washington, of-2,dh-1	.250	3	12	1	3	1	0	0	1	0	2	0
Billy Williams, dh-2	.000	3	8	0	0	0	0	0	0	1	1	0
TOTAL	.194		98	7	19	6	0	1	7	9	14	0

PITCHER	W	L	ERA	G	GS	CG	SV	SHO	IP	H	ER	BB	SO
Glenn Abbott	0	0	0.00	1	0	0	0	0	1.0	0	0	0	0
Vida Blue	0	0	9.00	1	1	0	0	0	3.0	6	3	0	2
Dick Bosman	0	0	0.00	1	0	0	0	0	0.1	0	0	0	0
Rollie Fingers	0	1	6.75	1	0	0	0	0	4.0	5	3	1	3
Ken Holtzman	0	2	4.09	2	2	0	0	0	11.0	12	5	1	7
Paul Lindblad	0	0	0.00	2	0	0	0	0	4.2	5	0	1	0
Jim Todd	0	0	9.00	3	0	0	0	0	1.0	3	1	0	0
TOTAL	0	3	4.32	11	3	0	0	0	25.0	31	12	3	12

The Red Sox entered the Series as underdogs to the mighty Reds, who had won 108 regular-season games. In the opening game, though, the Reds were surprised by veteran Sox starter Luis Tiant, who shut them out on five hits with the Series' first complete-game pitching effort in four years. Tiant also opened the Boston seventh with a single, starting a rally that ended only when he fouled out to end the inning after six runs had scored.

Boston took a 2–1 lead into the ninth inning of Game Two before Johnny Bench doubled to drive out starter Bill Lee, and Dave Concepcion and Ken Griffey drove in runs off reliever Dick Drago to turn the tide for Cincinnati. The Reds moved ahead in the Series with a tenth-inning victory in Game Three, a slugfest in which each club hit three home runs and used five pitchers. Boston tied the score on Dwight Evans's two-run homer in the ninth, but in the last of the tenth, the Reds' Joe Morgan drove one over the center fielder's head with the bases full to end the game.

Tiant pitched Game Four for Boston. Four of the nine hits against him went for extra bases, and each drove in a run. But the Sox bunched six of their eleven hits in the fourth inning for five runs—their only scoring, but enough for the win. Tiant himself scored the fifth run after singling. The Reds moved nearer the title in Game Five, though, as Tony Perez homered twice for four runs in a 6–2 win for a 3–2 Series advantage.

A day of travel to Boston and three days of rain between Games Five and Six brought Tiant back to the mound for a third time. Rookie standout Fred Lynn gave Tiant a three-run lead with a first-inning homer, but Ken Griffey's triple and Johnny Bench's long single drove in the tying Red runs in the fifth. Two more Red runs in the seventh and Cesar Geronimo's leadoff homer in the eighth drove out Tiant, but Boston pinch hitter Bernie Carbo homered to center in the last of the eighth for three runs that tied the score again. After a trio of Boston relievers had held Cincinnati in check through the top of the twelfth inning, the Sox leadoff hitter in the last of the twelfth, Carlton Fisk, ended the game dramatically with a home run to left on the first pitch that came within inches of being foul.

After the pyrotechnics of Game Six (ranked by some as the greatest World Series game ever), the seventh game, close as it was, came as an anticlimax. Boston scored three runs in the third inning, but the Reds began their

comeback with Tony Perez's two-run homer in the sixth, tied the game an inning later, and took a 4–3 lead on Joe Morgan's bloop RBI single in the ninth. Red reliever Will McEnaney came on to set the Sox down in order in the last of the ninth, and the Reds went home with their first world title in thirty-five years.

Cincinnati Reds (NL), 4; Boston Red Sox (AL) 3

CIN (N)

PLAYER/POS	AVG	G	AB	R	H	2B	3B	HR	RB	BB	SO	SB
Ed Armbrister, ph	.000	4	1	1	0	0	0	0	0	0	2	0
Johnny Bench, c	.207	7	29	5	6	2	0	1	4	2	4	0
Jack Billingham, p	.000	3	2	0	0	0	0	0	0	0	0	0
Pedro Borbon, p	.000	3	1	0	0	0	0	0	0	0	0	0
Clay Carroll, p	.000	5	0	0	0	0	0	0	0	0	0	0
Darrel Chaney, ph	.000	2	2	0	0	0	0	0	0	0	1	0
Dave Concepcion, ss	.179	7	28	3	5	1	0	1	4	0	1	3
Terry Crowley, ph	.500	2	2	0	1	0	0	0	0	0	0	0
Pat Darcy, p	.000	2	1	0	0	0	0	0	0	0	1	0
Dan Driessen, ph	.000	2	2	0	0	0	0	0	0	0	0	0
Rawly Eastwick, p	.000	5	1	0	0	0	0	0	0	0	0	0
George Foster, of	.276	7	29	1	8	1	0	0	2	1	1	1
Cesar Geronimo, of	.280	7	25	3	7	0	1	2	3	3	5	0
Ken Griffey, of	.269	7	26	4	7	3	1	0	4	4	2	2
Don Gullett, p	.286	3	7	1	2	0	0	0	0	0	2	0
Will Mc Enaney, p	1.000	5	1	0	1	0	0	0	0	0	0	0
Joe Morgan, 2b	.259	7	27	4	7	1	0	0	3	5	1	2
Gary Nolan, p	.000	2	1	0	0	0	0	0	0	0	0	0
Fred Norman, p	.000	2	1	0	0	0	0	0	0	0	0	0
Tony Perez, 1b	.179	7	28	4	5	0	0	3	7	3	9	1
Merv Rettenmund, ph	.000	3	3	0	0	0	0	0	0	0	1	0
Pete Rose, 3b	.370	7	27	3	10	1	1	0	2	5	1	0
TOTAL	.242		244	29	59	9	3	7	29	25	30	9

PITCHER	W	L	ERA	G	GS	CG	SV	SHO	IP	H	ER	BB	SO
Jack Billingham	0	0	1.00	3	1	0	0	0	9.0	8	1	5	7
Pedro Borbon	0	0	6.00	3	0	0	0	0	3.0	3	2	2	1
Clay Carroll	1	0	3.18	5	0	0	0	0	5.2	4	2	2	3
Pat Darcy	0	1	4.50	2	0	0	0	0	4.0	3	2	1	1
Rawly Eastwick	2	0	2.25	5	0	0	1	0	8.0	6	2	3	4
Don Gullett	1	1	4.34	3	3	0	0	0	18.2	19	9	10	15
Will Mc Enaney	0	0	2.70	5	0	0	1	0	6.2	3	2	2	5
Gary Nolan	0	0	6.00	2	2	0	0	0	6.0	6	4	1	2
Fred Norman	0	1	9.00	2	1	0	0	0	4.0	8	4	3	2
TOTAL	4	3	3.88	30	7	0	2	0	65.0	60	28	30	40

BOS (A)

PLAYER/POS	AVG	G	AB	R	H	2B	3B	HR	RB	BB	SO	SB
Juan Beniquez, of-2	.125	3	8	0	1	0	0	0	1	1	1	0
Rick Burleson, ss	.292	7	24	1	7	1	0	0	2	4	2	0
Jim Burton, p	.000	2	0	0	0	0	0	0	0	0	0	0
Bernie Carbo, of-2	.429	4	7	3	3	1	0	2	4	1	1	0
Reggie Cleveland, p	.000	3	2	0	0	0	0	0	0	0	2	0
Cecil Cooper, 1b	.053	5	19	0	1	1	0	0	1	0	3	0
Denny Doyle, 2b	.267	7	30	3	8	1	1	0	0	2	1	0
Dick Drago, p	.000	2	0	0	0	0	0	0	0	0	0	0
Dwight Evans, of	.292	7	24	3	7	1	1	1	5	3	4	0
Carlton Fisk, c	.240	7	25	5	6	0	0	2	4	7	7	0
Doug Griffin, ph	.000	1	1	0	0	0	0	0	0	0	0	0
Bill Lee, p	.167	2	6	0	1	0	0	0	0	0	3	0
Fred Lynn, of	.280	7	25	3	7	1	0	1	5	3	5	0
Rick Miller, of-2	.000	3	2	0	0	0	0	0	0	0	0	0
Bob Montgomery, ph	.000	1	1	0	0	0	0	0	0	0	0	0
Roger Moret, p	.000	3	0	0	0	0	0	0	0	0	0	0
Rico Petrocelli, 3b	.308	7	26	3	8	1	0	0	4	3	6	0
Dick Pole, p	.000	1	0	0	0	0	0	0	0	0	0	0
Diego Segui, p	.000	1	0	0	0	0	0	0	0	0	0	0
Luis Tiant, p	.250	3	8	2	2	0	0	0	0	0	2	0
Jim Willoughby, p	.000	3	0	0	0	0	0	0	0	0	0	0
Rick Wise, p	.000	2	2	0	0	0	0	0	0	0	0	0
Carl Yastrzemski, 1b-4,of-4	.310	7	29	7	9	0	0	0	4	4	1	0
TOTAL	.251		239	30	60	7	2	6	30	30	40	0

PITCHER	W	L	ERA	G	GS	CG	SV	SHO	IP	H	ER	BB	SO
Jim Burton	0	1	9.00	2	0	0	0	0	1.0	1	1	3	0
Reggie Cleveland	0	1	6.75	3	1	0	0	0	6.2	7	5	3	5
Dick Drago	0	1	2.25	2	0	0	0	0	4.0	3	1	1	1
Bill Lee	0	0	3.14	2	2	0	0	0	14.1	12	5	3	7
Roger Moret	0	0	0.00	3	0	0	0	0	1.2	2	0	3	1
Dick Pole	0	0	INF	1	0	0	0	0	0.0	0	1	2	0
Diego Segui	0	0	0.00	1	0	0	0	0	1.0	1	0	1	0
Luis Tiant	2	0	3.60	3	3	2	0	1	25.0	25	10	8	12
Jim Willoughby	0	1	0.00	3	0	0	0	0	6.1	3	0	0	2
Rick Wise	1	0	8.44	2	1	0	0	0	5.1	6	5	2	2
TOTAL	3	4	3.86	22	7	2	0	1	65.1	59	28	25	30

GAME 1 AT BOS OCT 11

CIN	000	000	000	0	5	0
BOS	000	000	60X	6	12	0

Pitchers: GULLETT, Carroll (7), McEnaney (7) vs TIANT
Attendance: 35,205

GAME 2 AT BOS OCT 12

CIN	000	100	002	3	7	1
BOS	100	001	000	2	7	0

Pitchers: Billingham, Borbon (6), McEnaney (7), EASTWICK (8) vs Lee, Drago (9)
Attendance: 35,205

GAME 3 AT CIN OCT 14

BOS	010	001	102 0	5	10	2
CIN	000	230	000 1	6	7	0

Pitchers: Wise, Burton (5), Cleveland (5), WILLOUGHBY (7), Moret (10) VS Nolan, Darcy (5), Carroll (7), McEnaney (7), EASTWICK (9)
Home Runs: Fisk-BOS, Bench-CIN, Concepcion-CIN, Geronimo-CIN, Carbo-BOS, Evans-BOS
Attendance: 55,392

GAME 4 AT CIN OCT 15

BOS	000	500	000	5	11	1
CIN	200	200	000	4	9	1

Pitchers: TIANT vs NORMAN, Borbon (4), Carroll (5), Eastwick (7)
Attendance: 55,667

GAME 5 AT CIN OCT 16

BOS	100	000	001	2	5	0
CIN	000	113	01X	6	8	0

Pitchers: CLEVELAND, Willoughby (6), Pole (8), Segui (8) vs GULLETT, Eastwick (9)
Home Runs: Perez-CIN (2)
Attendance: 56,393

GAME 6 AT BOS OCT 21

CIN	000	030	210	000	6	14	0
BOS	300	000	030	001	7	10	1

Pitchers: Nolan, Norman (3), Billingham (3), Carroll (5), Borbon (6), Eastwick (8), McEnaney (9), DARCY (10) VS Tiant, Moret (8), Drago (9), WISE (12)
Home Runs: Lynn-BOS, Geronimo-CIN, Carbo-BOS, Fisk-BOS
Attendance: 35,205

GAME 7 AT BOS OCT 22

CIN	000	002	101	4	9	0
BOS	003	000	000	3	5	2

Pitchers: Gullett, Billingham (5), CARROLL (7), McEnaney (9) vs Lee, Moret (7), Willoughby (7), BURTON (9), Cleveland (9)
Home Runs: Perez-CIN
Attendance: 35,205

Philadelphia outhit Cincinnati in two of the three games, but couldn't turn enough hits into runs, as the Reds for the second year in a row swept the LCS. The Phillies scored first in Game One with a run in the first inning. But pitcher Don Gullett held them scoreless for the next seven innings as his Reds caught up in the third, moved ahead in the sixth, and took a five-run lead into the last of the ninth. The Phillies scored twice in their half of the inning, but the rally fell short.

In the second game the Phillies outhit the Reds ten to six, scoring the game's first two runs while their starter Jim Lonborg threw a no-hitter for five innings. But in the sixth a walk and two singles drove Lonborg out and set the Reds off on a two-inning six-run spree for their second win.

Again in Game Three the Phillies outhit the Reds, this time going into the last of the ninth ahead by two runs. But George Foster and Johnny Bench hit back-to-back homers off Ron Reed to tie the score, and two relievers (and a single and two walks) later, the Reds brought home another pennant as Ken Griffey's high-bouncing chop glanced off first baseman Bobby Tolan's outstretched glove.

Cincinnati Reds (West), 3; Philadelphia Phillies (East) 0

CIN (W)

PLAYER/POS	AVG	G	AB	R	H	2B	3B	HR	RB	BB	SO	SB
Ed Armbrister, ph	.000	1	0	0	0	0	0	0	0	0	0	0
Johnny Bench, c	.333	3	12	3	4	1	0	1	1	1	2	1
Pedro Borbon, p	.000	2	2	1	0	0	0	0	0	0	2	0
Dave Concepcion, ss	.200	3	10	4	2	1	0	0	0	2	1	0
Dan Driessen, ph	.000	1	1	0	0	0	0	0	0	0	0	0
Rawly Eastwick, p	.000	2	0	0	0	0	0	0	0	0	0	0
Doug Flynn, 2b	.000	1	0	0	0	0	0	0	0	0	0	0
George Foster, of	.167	3	12	2	2	0	0	2	4	0	4	0
Cesar Geronimo, of	.182	3	11	0	2	0	1	0	2	1	3	0
Ken Griffey, of	.385	3	13	2	5	0	1	0	2	2	1	2
Don Gullett, p	.500	1	4	1	2	1	0	0	3	0	0	0
Mike Lum, ph	.000	1	1	0	0	0	0	0	0	0	0	0
Joe Morgan, 2b	.000	3	7	2	0	0	0	0	0	6	1	2
Gary Nolan, p	.000	1	0	0	0	0	0	0	0	1	0	0
Tony Perez, 1b	.200	3	10	1	2	0	0	0	3	1	2	0
Pete Rose, 3b	.429	3	14	3	6	2	1	0	2	1	0	0
Manny Sarmiento, p	.000	1	1	0	0	0	0	0	0	0	0	0
Pat Zachry, p	.000	1	1	0	0	0	0	0	0	0	0	0
TOTAL	.253		99	19	25	5	3	3	17	15	16	5

PITCHER	W	L	ERA	G	GS	CG	SV	SHO	IP	H	ER	BB	SO
Pedro Borbon	0	0	0.00	2	0	0	1	0	4.1	4	0	1	0
Rawly Eastwick	1	0	12.00	2	0	0	0	0	3.0	7	4	2	1
Don Gullett	1	0	1.13	1	1	0	0	0	8.0	2	1	3	4
Gary Nolan	0	0	1.59	1	1	0	0	0	5.2	6	1	2	1
Manny Sarmiento	0	0	18.00	1	0	0	0	0	1.0	2	2	1	0
Pat Zachry	1	0	3.60	1	1	0	0	0	5.0	6	2	3	3
TOTAL	3	0	3.33	8	3	0	1	0	27.0	27	10	12	9

PHI (E)

PLAYER/POS	AVG	G	AB	R	H	2B	3B	HR	RB	BB	SO	SB
Richie Allen, 1b	.222	3	9	1	2	0	0	0	0	3	2	0
Bob Boone, c	.286	3	7	0	2	0	0	0	1	1	0	0
Larry Bowa, ss	.125	3	8	1	1	1	0	0	1	3	0	0
Ollie Brown, of	.000	1	2	0	0	0	0	0	0	1	1	0
Steve Carlton, p	.000	1	2	0	0	0	0	0	0	0	0	0
Dave Cash, 2b	.308	3	13	1	4	1	0	0	1	0	0	0
Gene Garber, p	.000	2	0	0	0	0	0	0	0	0	0	0
Terry Harmon, pr	.000	1	0	1	0	0	0	0	0	0	0	0
Tom Hutton, ph	.000	1	1	0	0	0	0	0	0	0	0	0
Jay Johnstone, of-2	.778	3	9	1	7	1	1	0	2	1	0	0
Jim Kaat, p	.500	1	2	0	1	0	0	0	0	0	0	0
Jim Lonborg, p	.000	1	1	0	0	0	0	0	0	0	0	0
Greg Luzinski, of	.273	3	11	2	3	2	0	1	2	1	4	0
Garry Maddox, of	.231	3	13	2	3	1	0	0	2	2	0	0
Jerry Martin, of	.000	1	1	1	0	0	0	0	0	0	0	0
Tim Mc Carver, c-1	.000	2	4	0	0	0	0	0	0	0	1	0
Tug Mc Graw, p	.000	2	0	0	0	0	0	0	0	0	0	0
Johnny Oates, c	.000	1	1	0	0	0	0	0	0	0	0	0
Ron Reed, p	.000	2	1	0	0	0	0	0	0	0	0	0
Mike Schmidt, 3b	.308	3	13	1	4	2	0	0	2	0	1	0
Bobby Tolan, 1b-1,of-1	.000	3	2	0	0	0	0	0	0	0	0	0
Tom Underwood, p	.000	1	0	0	0	0	0	0	0	0	0	0
TOTAL	.270		100	11	27	8	1	1	11	12	9	0

PITCHER	W	L	ERA	G	GS	CG	SV	SHO	IP	H	ER	BB	SO
Steve Carlton	0	1	3.86	1	1	0	0	0	7.0	8	3	5	6
Gene Garber	0	1	40.50	2	0	0	0	0	0.2	2	3	1	0
Jim Kaat	0	0	3.00	1	1	0	0	0	6.0	2	2	2	1
Jim Lonborg	0	1	1.69	1	1	0	0	0	5.1	4	1	2	2
Tug Mc Graw	0	0	11.57	2	0	0	0	0	2.1	4	3	1	5
Ron Reed	0	0	7.71	2	0	0	0	0	4.2	6	4	2	2
Tom Underwood	0	0	0.00	1	0	0	0	0	0.1	1	0	2	0
TOTAL	0	3	5.47	10	3	0	0	0	26.1	25	16	15	16

Returning to postseason play after a dozen years' absence, the Yankees found themselves evenly matched with the first-time-champion Royals. They didn't really need their two ninth-inning runs in the first game: the two they scored in the first inning proved cushion enough for Catfish Hunter's one-run five-hitter. But Kansas City came back the next day, scoring first, losing the lead in the third, then regaining it for good in the sixth.

The Royals again took a first-inning lead in Game Three, but this time the Yankees, once they went ahead in the sixth, didn't let go. Kansas City held on to its early lead in Game Four, building on it throughout the game for a second win, despite Yankee Graig Nettles' two home runs.

But Game Five—like the series itself—was a seesaw affair. For the fourth time the Royals scored first, with a pair in the first on John Mayberry's home run. But the Yankees tied the game when they came to bat, and K.C. retook the lead in the second. New York went ahead again in the third and increased its lead to 6–3 in the sixth. But in the top of the eighth, George Brett's three-run homer tied the score once again, setting the stage for Chris Chambliss to win for the Yankees their thirtieth American League pennant with his first-pitch home run in the bottom of the ninth.

New York Yankees (East), 3; Kansas City Royals (West) 2

NY (E)

PLAYER/POS	AVG	G	AB	R	H	2B	3B	HR	RB	BB	SO	SB
Sandy Alomar, dh-1	.000	2	1	0	0	0	0	0	0	0	0	0
Chris Chambliss, 1b	.524	5	21	5	11	1	1	2	8	0	1	2
Dock Ellis, p	.000	1	0	0	0	0	0	0	0	0	0	0
Ed Figueroa, p	.000	2	0	0	0	0	0	0	0	0	0	0
Oscar Gamble, of	.250	3	8	1	2	1	0	0	1	1	1	0
Ron Guidry, pr	.000	1	0	0	0	0	0	0	0	0	0	0
Elrod Hendricks, ph	1.000	1	1	0	1	0	0	0	0	0	0	0
Catfish Hunter, p	.000	2	0	0	0	0	0	0	0	0	0	0
Grant Jackson, p	.000	2	0	0	0	0	0	0	0	0	0	0
Sparky Lyle, p	.000	1	0	0	0	0	0	0	0	0	0	0
Elliott Maddox, of	.222	3	9	0	2	1	0	0	1	0	1	0
Jim Mason, ss	.000	2	0	0	0	0	0	0	0	0	0	0
Carlos May, dh	.200	3	10	1	2	1	0	0	0	1	4	0
Thurman Munson, c	.435	5	23	3	10	2	0	0	3	0	1	0
Graig Nettles, 3b	.235	5	17	2	4	1	0	2	4	3	3	0
Lou Piniella, dh-3	.273	4	11	1	3	1	0	0	0	0	1	0
Willie Randolph, 2b	.118	5	17	0	2	0	0	0	1	3	1	1
Mickey Rivers, of	.348	5	23	5	8	0	1	0	0	1	1	0
Fred Stanley, ss	.333	5	15	1	5	2	0	0	2	0	0	0
Dick Tidrow, p	.000	3	0	0	0	0	0	0	0	0	0	0
Otto Velez, ph	.000	1	1	0	0	0	0	0	0	0	0	0
Roy White, of	.294	5	17	4	5	3	0	0	3	5	1	1
TOTAL	.316		174	23	55	13	2	4	21	16	15	4

PITCHER	W	L	ERA	G	GS	CG	SV	SHO	IP	H	ER	BB	SO
Dock Ellis	1	0	3.38	1	1	0	0	0	8.0	6	3	2	5
Ed Figueroa	0	1	5.84	2	2	0	0	0	12.1	14	8	2	5
Catfish Hunter	1	1	4.50	2	2	1	0	0	12.0	10	6	1	5
Grant Jackson	0	0	8.10	2	0	0	0	0	3.1	4	3	1	3
Sparky Lyle	0	0	0.00	1	0	0	1	0	1.0	0	0	1	0
Dick Tidrow	1	0	3.68	3	0	0	0	0	7.1	6	3	4	0
TOTAL	3	2	4.70	11	5	1	1	0	44.0	40	23	11	18

KC (W)

PLAYER/POS	AVG	G	AB	R	H	2B	3B	HR	RB	BB	SO	SB
Doug Bird, p	.000	1	0	0	0	0	0	0	0	0	0	0
George Brett, 3b	.444	5	18	4	8	1	1	1	5	2	1	0
Al Cowens, of	.190	5	21	3	4	0	1	0	0	1	1	2
Larry Gura, p	.000	2	0	0	0	0	0	0	0	0	0	0
Tom Hall, p	.000	1	0	0	0	0	0	0	0	0	0	0
Andy Hassler, p	.000	2	0	0	0	0	0	0	0	0	0	0
Dennis Leonard, p	.000	2	0	0	0	0	0	0	0	0	0	0
Mark Littell, p	.000	3	0	0	0	0	0	0	0	0	0	0
Buck Martinez, c	.333	5	15	0	5	0	0	0	4	1	3	0
John Mayberry, 1b	.222	5	18	4	4	0	0	1	3	1	0	0
Hal Mc Rae, dh-3,of-2	.118	5	17	2	2	1	1	0	1	1	4	0
Steve Mingori, p	.000	3	0	0	0	0	0	0	0	0	0	0
Dave Nelson, dh-1	.000	2	2	0	0	0	0	0	0	0	1	0
Amos Otis, of	.000	1	1	0	0	0	0	0	0	0	0	0
Freddie Patek, ss	.389	5	18	2	7	2	0	0	4	0	1	0
Marty Pattin, p	.000	2	0	0	0	0	0	0	0	0	0	0
Tom Poquette, of	.188	5	16	1	3	2	0	0	4	2	3	0
Jamie Quirk, dh-2	.143	4	7	1	1	0	1	0	2	0	2	0
Cookie Rojas, 2b	.333	4	9	2	3	0	0	0	1	0	0	1
Paul Splittorff, p	.000	2	0	0	0	0	0	0	0	0	0	0
Bob Stinson, c-1	.000	2	1	0	0	0	0	0	0	0	0	0
John Wathan, c	.000	1	0	0	0	0	0	0	0	0	0	0
Frank White, 2b	.125	4	8	2	1	0	0	0	0	0	1	0
Jim Wohlford, of	.182	5	11	3	2	0	0	0	0	3	1	2
TOTAL	.247		162	24	40	6	4	2	24	11	18	5

PITCHER	W	L	ERA	G	GS	CG	SV	SHO	IP	H	ER	BB	SO
Doug Bird	1	0	1.93	1	0	0	0	0	4.2	4	1	0	1
Larry Gura	0	1	4.22	2	2	0	0	0	10.2	18	5	1	4
Tom Hall	0	0	0.00	1	0	0	0	0	0.1	1	0	0	0
Andy Hassler	0	1	6.14	2	1	0	0	0	7.1	8	5	6	4
Dennis Leonard	0	0	19.29	2	2	0	0	0	2.1	9	5	2	0
Mark Littell	0	1	1.93	3	0	0	0	0	4.2	4	1	1	3
Steve Mingori	0	0	2.70	3	0	0	1	0	3.1	4	1	0	1
Marty Pattin	0	0	27.00	2	0	0	0	0	0.1	0	1	0	0
Paul Splittorff	1	0	1.93	2	0	0	0	0	9.1	7	2	5	2
TOTAL	2	3	4.40	18	5	0	1	0	43.0	55	21	16	15

The Reds led the National League in virtually every offensive category and in fielding as well. In the Series (which, incidentally, was the first to employ the designated hitter), the Big Red Machine continued its roll over the Yankees to become the first National League club in fifty-four years to repeat as world champions, as well as the first team to sweep both a League Championship and World Series. Red catcher Johnny Bench led the attack with eight hits, half of them for extra bases, for a batting average of .533 and a 1.133 average in slugging.

Joe Morgan's home run for Cincinnati in the first inning of Game One was the first hit of the Series, but New York pushed across a tying run half an inning later on a sacrifice fly. Red pitchers Don Gullett and Pedro Borbon held the Yankees scoreless after that as the Reds regained the lead with a run in the third and extended it in the sixth and seventh for a 5–1 win.

Game Two turned out to be the Reds' only narrow victory. They scored first, with three runs in the second inning. In the fourth the Yankees scored their first run, and they tied the score with two more runs in the seventh. But with two men out in the last of the ninth, a throwing error by Yankee shortstop Fred Stanley allowed the Reds' batter Ken Griffey to reach second, from where he scored the winning run on Tony Perez's line single to left.

In Game Three, four hits and a pair of stolen bases put Cincinnati ahead 3–0 in the second inning, and Dan Driessen homered in the fourth to make it 4–0 before the Yankees scored their first run. Another quartet of hits in the eighth gave the Reds two more runs and a 6–2 win.

New York took the lead for the only time in the Series when Chris Chambliss doubled in Thurman Munson in the first inning of Game Four. (Munson had singled with the third of what became six straight hits.) But the Reds' George Foster drove in a tying run in the fourth, and Johnny Bench followed him with a two-run homer. New York scored again an inning later to come close, but Bench's second home run, a three-run blast in the ninth, put the game out of reach, and a pair of ground-rule doubles touched by New York fans nailed the final run in the Yankee coffin.

Cincinnati Reds (NL), 4;
New York Yankees (AL) 0

CIN (N)

PLAYER/POS	AVG	G	AB	R	H	2B	3B	HR	RB	BB	SO	SB
Johnny Bench, c	.533	4	15	4	8	1	1	2	6	0	1	0
Jack Billingham, p	.000	1	0	0	0	0	0	0	0	0	0	0
Pedro Borbon, p	.000	1	0	0	0	0	0	0	0	0	0	0
Dave Concepcion, ss	.357	4	14	1	5	1	1	0	3	1	3	1
Dan Driessen, dh	.357	4	14	4	5	2	0	1	1	2	0	1
George Foster, of	.429	4	14	3	6	1	0	0	4	2	3	0
Cesar Geronimo, of	.308	4	13	3	4	2	0	0	1	2	2	2
Ken Griffey, of	.059	4	17	2	1	0	0	0	1	0	1	1
Don Gullett, p	.000	1	0	0	0	0	0	0	0	0	0	0
Will Mc Enaney, p	.000	2	0	0	0	0	0	0	0	0	0	0
Joe Morgan, 2b	.333	4	15	3	5	1	1	1	2	2	2	2
Gary Nolan, p	.000	1	0	0	0	0	0	0	0	0	0	0
Fred Norman, p	.000	1	0	0	0	0	0	0	0	0	0	0
Tony Perez, 1b	.313	4	16	1	5	1	0	0	2	1	2	0
Pete Rose, 3b	.188	4	16	1	3	1	0	0	1	2	2	0
Pat Zachry, p	.000	1	0	0	0	0	0	0	0	0	0	0
TOTAL	.313		134	22	42	10	3	4	21	12	16	7

PITCHER	W	L	ERA	G	GS	CG	SV	SHO	IP	H	ER	BB	SO
Jack Billingham	1	0	0.00	1	0	0	0	0	2.2	0	0	0	1
Pedro Borbon	0	0	0.00	1	0	0	0	0	1.2	0	0	0	0
Don Gullett	1	0	1.23	1	1	0	0	0	7.1	5	1	3	4
Will Mc Enaney	0	0	0.00	2	0	0	2	0	4.2	2	0	1	2
Gary Nolan	1	0	2.70	1	1	0	0	0	6.2	8	2	1	1
Fred Norman	0	0	4.26	1	1	0	0	0	6.1	9	3	2	2
Pat Zachry	1	0	2.70	1	1	0	0	0	6.2	6	2	5	6
TOTAL	4	0	2.00	8	4	0	2	0	36.0	30	8	12	16

NY (A)

PLAYER/POS	AVG	G	AB	R	H	2B	3B	HR	RB	BB	SO	SB
Doyle Alexander, p	.000	1	0	0	0	0	0	0	0	0	0	0
Chris Chambliss, 1b	.313	4	16	1	5	1	0	0	1	0	2	0
Dock Ellis, p	.000	1	0	0	0	0	0	0	0	0	0	0
Ed Figueroa, p	.000	1	0	0	0	0	0	0	0	0	0	0
Oscar Gamble, of-2	.125	3	8	0	1	0	0	0	1	0	0	0
Elrod Hendricks, ph	.000	2	2	0	0	0	0	0	0	0	0	0
Catfish Hunter, p	.000	1	0	0	0	0	0	0	0	0	0	0
Grant Jackson, p	.000	1	0	0	0	0	0	0	0	0	0	0
Sparky Lyle, p	.000	2	0	0	0	0	0	0	0	0	0	0
Elliott Maddox, of-1,dh-1	.200	2	5	0	1	0	1	0	0	1	2	0
Jim Mason, ss	1.000	3	1	1	1	0	0	1	1	0	0	0
Carlos May, dh	.000	4	9	0	0	0	0	0	0	0	1	0
Thurman Munson, c	.529	4	17	2	9	0	0	0	2	0	1	0
Graig Nettles, 3b	.250	4	12	0	3	0	0	0	2	3	1	0
Lou Piniella, of-2,dh-2	.333	4	9	1	3	1	0	0	0	0	0	0
Willie Randolph, 2b	.071	4	14	1	1	0	0	0	0	1	3	0
Mickey Rivers, of	.167	4	18	1	3	0	0	0	0	1	2	1
Fred Stanley, ss	.167	4	6	1	1	1	0	0	1	3	1	0
Dick Tidrow, p	.000	2	0	0	0	0	0	0	0	0	0	0
Otto Velez, ph	.000	3	3	0	0	0	0	0	0	0	3	0
Roy White, of	.133	4	15	0	2	0	0	0	0	3	0	0
TOTAL	.222		135	8	30	3	1	1	8	12	16	1

PITCHER	W	L	ERA	G	GS	CG	SV	SHO	IP	H	ER	BB	SO
Doyle Alexander	0	1	7.50	1	1	0	0	0	6.0	9	5	2	1
Dock Ellis	0	1	10.80	1	1	0	0	0	3.1	7	4	0	1
Ed Figueroa	0	1	5.63	1	1	0	0	0	8.0	6	5	5	2
Catfish Hunter	0	1	3.12	1	1	1	0	0	8.2	10	3	4	5
Grant Jackson	0	0	4.91	1	0	0	0	0	3.2	4	2	0	3
Sparky Lyle	0	0	0.00	2	0	0	0	0	2.2	1	0	0	3
Dick Tidrow	0	0	7.71	2	0	0	0	0	2.1	5	2	1	1
TOTAL	0	4	5.45	9	4	1	0	0	34.2	42	21	12	16

GAME 1 AT CIN OCT 16

				R	H	E
NY	010	000	000	1	5	1
CIN	101	001	20X	5	10	1

Pitchers: ALEXANDER, Lyle (7) vs GULLETT, Borbon (8)
Home Runs: Morgan-CIN
Attendance: 54,826

GAME 2 AT CIN OCT 17

				R	H	E
NY	000	100	200	3	9	1
CIN	030	000	001	4	10	0

Pitchers: HUNTER vs Norman, BILLINGHAM (7)
Attendance: 54,816

GAME 3 AT NY OCT 19

				R	H	E
CIN	030	100	020	6	13	2
NY	000	100	100	2	8	0

Pitchers: ZACHRY, McEnaney (7) vs ELLIS, Jackson (4), Tidrow (8)
Home Runs: Driessen-CIN, Mason-NY
Attendance: 56,667

GAME 4 AT NY OCT 21

				R	H	E
CIN	000	300	004	7	9	2
NY	100	010	000	2	8	0

Pitchers: NOLAN, McEnaney (7) vs FIGUEROA, Tidrow (9), Lyle (9)
Home Runs: Bench-CIN (2)
Attendance: 56,700

The Phillies took the first game, but the Dodgers proved better over all at turning hits into runs and swept the next three. Philadelphia jumped ahead in the first inning of Game One, and had built a 5–1 lead by the seventh, when Ron Cey tied the score with a Dodger grand slam. But the Phillies came back with two runs on three singles in the top of the ninth and held on for the win. As in Game One, both clubs again got nine hits apiece in Game Two, but this time Dodger pitcher Don Sutton scattered the Phillies' hits for a single run over nine innings, while Phillie starter Jim Lonborg—in the four innings he pitched—yielded five runs, including a grand slam to Dusty Baker.

In Game Three Los Angeles outhit the Phillies, but the Dodgers were nearly undone when starter Burt Hooton walked in three Philadelphia runs in the second inning. The Phillies took a two-run lead into the ninth, but after two men were out the Dodgers rebounded, thanks largely to a couple of old pros. Pinch hitter Vic Davalillo, age 38, beat out a drag bunt on a disputed call, and 39-year-old Manny Mota doubled to deep left. Two more Dodger singles scored three runs that proved enough for the win.

The Dodgers didn't even need all of their five hits to take the final game behind Tommy John's one-run seven-hitter, for one of those hits was another Dusty Baker home run with a man aboard.

Los Angeles Dodgers (West), 3; Philadelphia Phillies (East) 1

LA (W)

PLAYER/POS	AVG	G	AB	R	H	2B	3B	HR	RB	BB	SO	SB
Dusty Baker, of	.357	4	14	4	5	1	0	2	8	2	3	0
Glenn Burke, of	.000	4	7	0	0	0	0	0	0	0	3	0
Ron Cey, 3b	.308	4	13	4	4	1	0	1	4	2	4	1
Vic Davalillo, ph	1.000	1	1	1	1	0	0	0	0	0	0	0
Mike Garman, p	.000	2	0	0	0	0	0	0	0	0	0	0
Steve Garvey, 1b	.308	4	13	2	4	0	0	0	0	2	1	1
Ed Goodson, ph	.000	1	1	0	0	0	0	0	0	0	0	0
Jerry Grote, c-1	.000	2	0	0	0	0	0	0	0	1	0	0
Burt Hooton, p	1.000	1	1	0	1	1	0	0	0	0	0	0
Charley Hough, p	.000	1	0	0	0	0	0	0	0	0	0	0
Tommy John, p	.200	2	5	0	1	0	0	0	0	0	2	0
Lee Lacy, ph	1.000	1	1	1	1	0	0	0	0	0	0	0
Davey Lopes, 2b	.235	4	17	2	4	0	0	0	3	2	0	0
Rick Monday, of	.286	3	7	1	2	1	0	0	0	2	1	0
Manny Mota, ph	1.000	1	1	1	1	1	0	0	0	0	0	0
Doug Rau, p	.000	1	0	0	0	0	0	0	0	0	0	0
Lance Rautzhan, p	.000	1	0	0	0	0	0	0	0	0	0	0
Rick Rhoden, p	.000	1	1	0	0	0	0	0	0	0	0	0
Bill Russell, ss	.278	4	18	3	5	1	0	0	2	0	0	0
Reggie Smith, of	.188	4	16	2	3	0	1	0	1	2	5	1
Elias Sosa, p	.000	2	1	0	0	0	0	0	0	0	0	0
Don Sutton, p	.000	1	3	0	0	0	0	0	0	0	0	0
Steve Yeager, c	.231	4	13	1	3	0	0	0	2	1	3	0
TOTAL	.263		133	22	35	6	1	3	20	14	22	3

PITCHER	W	L	ERA	G	GS	CG	SV	SHO	IP	H	ER	BB	SO
Mike Garman	0	0	0.00	2	0	0	1	0	1.1	0	0	0	1
Burt Hooton	0	0	16.20	1	1	0	0	0	1.2	2	3	4	1
Charley Hough	0	0	4.50	1	0	0	0	0	2.0	2	1	0	3
Tommy John	1	0	0.66	2	2	1	0	0	13.2	11	1	5	11
Doug Rau	0	0	0.00	1	0	0	0	0	1.0	0	0	0	1
Lance Rautzhan	1	0	0.00	1	0	0	0	0	0.1	0	0	0	0
Rick Rhoden	0	0	0.00	1	0	0	0	0	4.1	2	0	2	0
Elias Sosa	0	1	10.13	2	0	0	0	0	2.2	5	3	0	0
Don Sutton	1	0	1.00	1	1	1	0	0	9.0	9	1	0	4
TOTAL	3	1	2.25	12	4	2	1	0	36.0	31	9	11	21

PHI (E)

PLAYER/POS	AVG	G	AB	R	H	2B	3B	HR	RB	BB	SO	SB
Bob Boone, c	.400	4	10	1	4	0	0	0	0	0	0	0
Larry Bowa, ss	.118	4	17	2	2	0	0	0	1	1	0	0
Ollie Brown, ph	.000	2	2	0	0	0	0	0	0	0	1	0
Warren Brusstar, p	.000	2	0	0	0	0	0	0	0	0	0	0
Steve Carlton, p	.500	2	4	0	2	0	0	0	1	0	2	0
Larry Christenson, p	.000	1	0	0	0	0	0	0	1	1	0	0
Gene Garber, p	.000	3	0	0	0	0	0	0	0	0	0	0
Richie Hebner, 1b-3	.357	4	14	2	5	2	0	0	0	0	1	0
Tom Hutton, 1b-1	.000	3	3	0	0	0	0	0	0	0	0	0
Davy Johnson, 1b	.250	1	4	0	1	0	0	0	2	0	1	0
Jay Johnstone, of	.200	2	5	0	1	0	0	0	0	0	1	0
Jim Lonborg, p	.000	1	1	0	0	0	0	0	0	0	0	0
Greg Luzinski, of	.286	4	14	2	4	1	0	1	2	3	3	1
Garry Maddox, of	.429	2	7	1	3	0	0	0	2	0	1	0
Jerry Martin, of-1	.000	3	4	0	0	0	0	0	0	0	2	0
Bake Mc Bride, of	.222	4	18	2	4	0	0	1	2	1	2	0
Tim Mc Carver, c-2	.167	3	6	1	1	0	0	0	0	1	3	0
Tug Mc Graw, p	.000	2	0	0	0	0	0	0	0	0	0	0
Ron Reed, p	.000	3	0	0	0	0	0	0	0	0	0	0
Mike Schmidt, 3b	.063	4	16	2	1	0	0	0	1	2	3	0
Ted Sizemore, 2b	.231	4	13	1	3	0	0	0	0	2	0	0
TOTAL	.225		138	14	31	3	0	2	12	11	21	1

PITCHER	W	L	ERA	G	GS	CG	SV	SHO	IP	H	ER	BB	SO
Warren Brusstar	0	0	3.38	2	0	0	0	0	2.2	2	1	1	2
Steve Carlton	0	1	6.94	2	2	0	0	0	11.2	13	9	8	6
Larry Christenson	0	0	8.10	1	1	0	0	0	3.1	7	3	0	2
Gene Garber	1	1	3.38	3	0	0	0	0	5.1	4	2	0	3
Jim Lonborg	0	1	11.25	1	1	0	0	0	4.0	5	5	1	1
Tug Mc Graw	0	0	0.00	2	0	0	1	0	3.0	1	0	2	3
Ron Reed	0	0	1.80	3	0	0	0	0	5.0	3	1	2	5
TOTAL	1	3	5.40	14	4	0	1	0	35.0	35	21	14	22

GAME 1 AT LA OCT 4

PHI	200 021 002	7	9	0
LA	000 010 400	5	9	2

Pitchers: Carlton, GARBER (7), McGraw (9) vs John, Garman (5), Hough (6), SOSA (8)
Home Runs: Luzinski-PHI, Cey-LA
Attendance: 55,968

GAME 2 AT LA OCT 5

PHI	001 000 000	1	9	1
LA	001 401 10X	7	9	1

Pitchers: LONBORG, Reed (5), Brusstar (7) vs SUTTON
Home Runs: McBride-PHI, Baker-LA
Attendance: 55,973

GAME 3 AT PHI OCT 7

LA	020 100 003	6	12	2
PHI	030 000 020	5	6	2

Pitchers: Hooton, Rhoden (2), Rau (7), Sosa (8), RAUTZHAN (8), Garman (9) vs Christenson, Brusstar (4), Reed (5), GARBER (7)
Attendance: 63,719

GAME 4 AT PHI OCT 8

LA	020 020 000	4	5	0
PHI	000 100 000	1	7	0

Pitchers: JOHN vs CARLTON, Reed (6), McGraw (7), Garber (9)
Home Runs: Baker-LA
Attendance: 64,924

As in 1976, the Royals met the Yankees in the LCS, and as in 1976 the series went five games, with the Royals outscoring New York by a single run. But this time Kansas City won the first game, and as the teams traded victories through the first four games and K.C. took a lead into the ninth inning of Game Five, it began to look as though this year the Royals might take the pennant.

Royal hitters began things with a bang, scoring six of their seven runs in Game One in the first three innings for an insurmountable lead. New York came back to take the second game 6–2 behind Ron Guidry's three-hitter, but the Royals reversed the score the next day as Dennis Leonard limited the Yankees to four hits. Yankee reliever Sparky Lyle shut K.C. down over the final five innings of Game Four after the Royals had drawn within a run of New York in the fourth inning, and the series was tied.

In the finale, Kansas City drew first blood with two runs in the bottom of the first and led by one run after eight. But with the pennant in sight, the Royals gave up three Yankee runs in the top of the ninth, scoring nothing themselves as reliever Lyle held them off to give the Yankees their thirty-first flag.

New York Yankees (East), 3; Kansas City Royals (West) 2

NY (E)

PLAYER/POS	AVG	G	AB	R	H	2B	3B	HR	RB	BB	SO	SB
Paul Blair, of	.400	3	5	1	2	0	0	0	0	0	0	0
Chris Chambliss, 1b	.059	5	17	0	1	0	0	0	0	3	4	0
Bucky Dent, ss	.214	5	14	1	3	1	0	0	2	1	0	0
Ed Figueroa, p	.000	1	0	0	0	0	0	0	0	0	0	0
Ron Guidry, p	.000	2	0	0	0	0	0	0	0	0	0	0
Don Gullett, p	.000	1	0	0	0	0	0	0	0	0	0	0
Reggie Jackson, of-4,dh-1	.125	5	16	1	2	0	0	0	1	2	2	1
Cliff Johnson, dh-4	.400	5	15	2	6	2	0	1	2	1	2	0
Sparky Lyle, p	.000	4	0	0	0	0	0	0	0	0	0	0
Thurman Munson, c	.286	5	21	3	6	1	0	1	5	0	2	0
Graig Nettles, 3b	.150	5	20	1	3	0	0	0	1	0	3	0
Lou Piniella, of-4,dh-1	.333	5	21	1	7	3	0	0	2	0	1	0
Willie Randolph, 2b	.278	5	18	4	5	1	0	0	2	1	0	0
Mickey Rivers, of	.391	5	23	5	9	2	0	0	2	0	2	1
Fred Stanley, ss	.000	2	0	0	0	0	0	0	0	0	0	0
Dick Tidrow, p	.000	2	0	0	0	0	0	0	0	0	0	0
Mike Torrez, p	.000	2	0	0	0	0	0	0	0	0	0	0
Roy White, of-1,dh-1	.400	4	5	2	2	2	0	0	0	1	0	0
TOTAL	.263		175	21	46	12	0	2	17	9	16	2

PITCHER	W	L	ERA	G	GS	CG	SV	SHO	IP	H	ER	BB	SO
Ed Figueroa	0	0	10.80	1	1	0	0	0	3.1	5	4	2	3
Ron Guidry	1	0	3.97	2	2	1	0	0	11.1	9	5	3	8
Don Gullett	0	1	18.00	1	1	0	0	0	2.0	4	4	2	0
Sparky Lyle	2	0	0.96	4	0	0	0	0	9.1	7	1	0	3
Dick Tidrow	0	0	3.86	2	0	0	0	0	7.0	6	3	3	3
Mike Torrez	0	1	4.09	2	1	0	0	0	11.0	11	5	5	5
TOTAL	3	2	4.50	12	5	1	0	0	44.0	42	22	15	22

KC (W)

PLAYER/POS	AVG	G	AB	R	H	2B	3B	HR	RB	BB	SO	SB
Doug Bird, p	.000	3	0	0	0	0	0	0	0	0	0	0
George Brett, 3b	.300	5	20	2	6	0	2	0	2	1	0	0
Al Cowens, of	.263	5	19	2	5	0	0	1	5	1	3	0
Larry Gura, p	.000	2	0	0	0	0	0	0	0	0	0	0
Andy Hassler, p	.000	1	0	0	0	0	0	0	0	0	0	0
Pete La Cock, 1b	.000	1	1	0	0	0	0	0	0	1	1	0
Joe Lahoud, dh	.000	1	1	2	0	0	0	0	0	2	0	0
Dennis Leonard, p	.000	2	0	0	0	0	0	0	0	0	0	0
Mark Littell, p	.000	2	0	0	0	0	0	0	0	0	0	0
John Mayberry, 1b	.167	4	12	1	2	1	0	1	3	1	2	0
Hal Mc Rae, dh-3,of-2	.444	5	18	6	8	3	0	1	2	3	1	0
Steve Mingori, p	.000	3	0	0	0	0	0	0	0	0	0	0
Amos Otis, of	.125	5	16	1	2	1	0	0	2	2	3	2
Freddie Patek, ss	.389	5	18	4	7	3	1	0	5	1	2	0
Marty Pattin, p	.000	1	0	0	0	0	0	0	0	0	0	0
Tom Poquette, of	.167	2	6	0	1	0	0	0	0	0	0	0
Darrell Porter, c	.333	5	15	3	5	0	0	0	0	3	0	0
Cookie Rojas, dh	.250	1	4	0	1	0	0	0	0	0	1	1
Paul Splittorff, p	.000	2	0	0	0	0	0	0	0	0	0	0
John Wathan, 1b-2,c-1,dh-1	.000	4	6	0	0	0	0	0	0	0	3	0
Frank White, 2b	.278	5	18	1	5	1	0	0	2	0	4	1
Joe Zdeb, of	.000	4	9	0	0	0	0	0	0	0	2	1
TOTAL	.258		163	22	42	9	3	3	21	15	22	5

PITCHER	W	L	ERA	G	GS	CG	SV	SHO	IP	H	ER	BB	SO
Doug Bird	0	0	0.00	3	0	0	0	0	2.0	4	0	0	1
Larry Gura	0	1	18.00	2	1	0	0	0	2.0	7	4	1	2
Andy Hassler	0	1	4.76	1	1	0	0	0	5.2	5	3	0	3
Dennis Leonard	1	1	3.00	2	1	1	0	0	9.0	5	3	2	4
Mark Littell	0	0	3.00	2	0	0	0	0	3.0	5	1	3	1
Steve Mingori	0	0	0.00	3	0	0	0	0	1.1	0	0	0	1
Marty Pattin	0	0	1.50	1	0	0	0	0	6.0	6	1	0	0
Paul Splittorff	1	0	2.40	2	2	0	0	0	15.0	14	4	3	4
TOTAL	2	3	3.27	16	5	1	0	0	44.0	46	16	9	16

This was the Series in which Yankee Reggie Jackson established his reputation as "Mr. October" with a record five home runs, including three in successive at-bats in the final game, and the Yankees showed that after a decade or so of decline they were once again the world's best. Los Angeles scored first in the opening game with a pair of first-inning runs. But New York gained back half the ground in the bottom of the first and tied the game on Willie Randolph's leadoff homer in the sixth. The clubs traded runs in the eighth and ninth to take the game into extra innings. The impasse was not breached until the last of the twelfth, when Randolph doubled and Paul Blair singled him home.

Game Two, by contrast, was a runaway Dodger victory. Home runs in the first three innings by Ron Cey, Steve Yeager, and Reggie Smith made the score 5–0 before New York scored its lone run in the fourth. Burt Hooton hurled the Dodger win, a five-hitter. And for good measure, Dodger Steve Garvey homered in the ninth inning. The Yankees returned to form two days later in Los Angeles, though, scoring three runs in the top of the first on pairs of doubles and singles (and a Dodger error). Dodger Dusty Baker's three-run homer tied the game in the third, but single Yankee runs in the next two innings provided pitcher Mike Torrez with runs enough for the win.

Two of the four hits yielded by emerging Yankee ace Ron Guidry in Game Four were pitcher Rick Rhoden's double followed by Davey Lopes's home run in the third inning. But the Yankees had already scored three times in the second, and Reggie Jackson homered in the sixth as Guidry held Los Angeles scoreless after the third for a 4–2 win. A Yankee assault against Dodger pitcher Don Sutton in Game Five included back-to-back home runs by Thurman Munson and Jackson in the eighth inning. But Los Angeles rocked Yankee pitching even harder, with homers by Steve Yeager and Reggie Smith producing five of the Dodgers' ten runs as the club evaded elimination with its second win.

The Dodgers scored first in the sixth game when Steve Garvey's first-inning triple drove in two runners. Yankee Chris Chambliss matched that an inning later with a two-run homer. Smith restored the lead to Los Angeles with a solo shot in the third inning, but Jackson put the Yankees back in front with the first of his three home runs, a two-run blast in the fourth. By the time he had homered again for two in the fifth and for the third time in the eighth, the

New York Yankees (AL), 4; Los Angeles Dodgers (NL) 2

NY (A)

PLAYER/POS	AVG	G	AB	R	H	2B	3B	HR	RB	BB	SO	SB
Paul Blair, of-3	.250	4	4	0	1	0	0	0	1	0	0	0
Chris Chambliss, 1b	.292	6	24	4	7	2	0	1	4	0	2	0
Ken Clay, p	.000	2	0	0	0	0	0	0	0	0	0	0
Bucky Dent, ss	.263	6	19	0	5	0	0	0	2	2	1	0
Ron Guidry, p	.000	1	2	0	0	0	0	0	0	0	1	0
Don Gullett, p	.000	2	2	0	0	0	0	0	0	0	2	0
Catfish Hunter, p	.000	2	0	0	0	0	0	0	0	0	0	0
Reggie Jackson, of	.450	6	20	10	9	1	0	5	8	3	4	0
Cliff Johnson, c-1	.000	2	1	0	0	0	0	0	0	0	0	0
Sparky Lyle, p	.000	2	2	0	0	0	0	0	0	0	2	0
Thurman Munson, c	.320	6	25	4	8	2	0	1	3	2	8	0
Graig Nettles, 3b	.190	6	21	1	4	1	0	0	2	2	3	0
Lou Piniella, of	.273	6	22	1	6	0	0	0	3	0	3	0
Willie Randolph, 2b	.160	6	25	5	4	2	0	1	1	2	2	0
Mickey Rivers, of	.222	6	27	1	6	2	0	0	1	0	2	1
Fred Stanley, ss	.000	1	0	0	0	0	0	0	0	0	0	0
Dick Tidrow, p	.000	2	1	0	0	0	0	0	0	0	0	0
Mike Torrez, p	.000	2	6	0	0	0	0	0	0	0	4	0
Roy White, ph	.000	2	2	0	0	0	0	0	0	0	0	0
George Zeber, ph	.000	2	2	0	0	0	0	0	0	0	2	0
TOTAL	.244		205	26	50	10	0	8	25	11	37	1

PITCHER	W	L	ERA	G	GS	CG	SV	SHO	IP	H	ER	BB	SO
Ken Clay	0	0	2.45	2	0	0	0	0	3.2	2	1	1	0
Ron Guidry	1	0	2.00	1	1	1	0	0	9.0	4	2	3	7
Don Gullett	0	1	6.39	2	2	0	0	0	12.2	13	9	7	10
Catfish Hunter	0	1	10.38	2	1	0	0	0	4.1	6	5	0	1
Sparky Lyle	1	0	1.93	2	0	0	0	0	4.2	2	1	0	2
Dick Tidrow	0	0	4.91	2	0	0	0	0	3.2	5	2	0	1
Mike Torrez	2	0	2.50	2	2	2	0	0	18.0	16	5	5	15
TOTAL	4	2	4.02	13	6	3	0	0	56.0	48	25	16	36

LA (N)

PLAYER/POS	AVG	G	AB	R	H	2B	3B	HR	RB	BB	SO	SB
Dusty Baker, of	.292	6	24	4	7	0	0	1	5	0	2	0
Glenn Burke, of	.200	3	5	0	1	0	0	0	0	0	1	0
Ron Cey, 3b	.190	6	21	2	4	1	0	1	3	3	5	0
Vic Davalillo, ph	.333	3	3	0	1	0	0	0	1	0	0	0
Mike Garman, p	.000	2	0	0	0	0	0	0	0	0	0	0
Steve Garvey, 1b	.375	6	24	5	9	1	1	1	3	1	4	0
Ed Goodson, ph	.000	1	1	0	0	0	0	0	0	1	0	0
Jerry Grote, c	.000	1	1	0	0	0	0	0	0	0	0	0
Burt Hooton, p	.000	2	5	0	0	0	0	0	0	0	2	0
Charley Hough, p	.000	2	0	0	0	0	0	0	0	0	0	0
Tommy John, p	.000	1	2	0	0	0	0	0	0	0	2	0
Lee Lacy, of-2	.429	4	7	1	3	0	0	0	2	1	1	0
Rafael Landestoy, pr	.000	1	0	0	0	0	0	0	0	0	0	0
Davey Lopes, 2b	.167	6	24	3	4	0	1	1	2	4	3	2
Rick Monday, of	.167	4	12	0	2	0	0	0	0	0	3	0
Manny Mota, ph	.000	3	3	0	0	0	0	0	0	0	1	0
Johnny Oates, c	.000	1	1	0	0	0	0	0	0	0	0	0
Doug Rau, p	.000	2	0	0	0	0	0	0	0	0	0	0
Lance Rautzhan, p	.000	1	0	0	0	0	0	0	0	0	0	0
Rick Rhoden, p	.500	2	2	1	1	1	0	0	0	0	0	0
Bill Russell, ss	.154	6	26	3	4	0	1	0	2	1	3	0
Reggie Smith, of	.273	6	22	7	6	1	0	3	5	4	3	0
Elias Sosa, p	.000	2	0	0	0	0	0	0	0	0	0	0
Don Sutton, p	.000	2	6	0	0	0	0	0	0	1	4	0
Steve Yeager, c	.316	6	19	2	6	1	0	2	5	1	1	0
TOTAL	.231		208	28	48	5	3	9	28	16	36	2

PITCHER	W	L	ERA	G	GS	CG	SV	SHO	IP	H	ER	BB	SO
Mike Garman	0	0	0.00	2	0	0	0	0	4.0	2	0	1	3
Burt Hooton	1	1	3.75	2	2	1	0	0	12.0	8	5	2	9
Charley Hough	0	0	1.80	2	0	0	0	0	5.0	3	1	0	5
Tommy John	0	1	6.00	1	1	0	0	0	6.0	9	4	3	7
Doug Rau	0	1	11.57	2	1	0	0	0	2.1	4	3	0	1
Lance Rautzhan	0	0	0.00	1	0	0	0	0	0.1	0	0	2	0
Rick Rhoden	0	1	2.57	2	0	0	0	0	7.0	4	2	1	5
Elias Sosa	0	0	11.57	2	0	0	0	0	2.1	3	3	1	1
Don Sutton	1	0	3.94	2	2	1	0	0	16.0	17	7	7	3
TOTAL	2	4	4.09	16	6	2	0	0	55.0	50	25	17	34

Yankees' twenty-first world title was well in hand.

GAME 1 AT NY OCT 11

LA	200 000 001 000	3	6	0
NY	100 001 010 001	4	11	0

Pitchers: Sutton, Rautzhan (8), Sosa (8), Garman (9), RHODEN (12) vs Gullett, LYLE (9)
Home Runs: Randolph-NY
Attendance: 56,668

GAME 2 AT NY OCT 12

LA	212 000 001	6	9	0
NY	000 100 000	1	5	0

Pitchers: HOOTON vs HUNTER, Tidrow (3), Clay (6), Lyle (9)
Home Runs: Cey-LA, Yeager-LA, Smith-LA, Garvey-LA
Attendance: 56,691

GAME 3 AT LA OCT 14

NY	300 110 000	5	10	0
LA	003 000 000	3	7	1

Pitchers: TORREZ vs JOHN, Hough (7)
Home Runs: Baker-LA
Attendance: 55,992

GAME 4 AT LA OCT 15

NY	030 001 000	4	7	0
LA	002 000 000	2	4	0

Pitchers: GUIDRY vs RAU, Rhoden (2), Garman (9)
Home Runs: Lopes-LA, Jackson-NY
Attendance: 55,995

GAME 5 AT LA OCT 16

NY	000 000 220	4	9	2
LA	100 432 00X	10	13	0

Pitchers: GULLETT, Clay (5), Tidrow (6), Hunter (7) vs SUTTON
Home Runs: Yeager-LA, Smith-LA, Munson-NY, Jackson-NY
Attendance: 55,955

GAME 6 AT NY OCT 18

LA	201 000 001	4	9	0
NY	020 320 01X	8	8	1

Pitchers: HOOTON, Sosa (4), Rau (5), Hough (7) vs TORREZ
Home Runs: Chambliss-NY, Smith-LA, Jackson-NY (3)
Attendance: 56,407

Steve Garvey hit half the Dodgers' eight home runs and Tommy John hurled the first LCS shutout in four years as Los Angeles, for the second year in a row, defeated the Phillies for the pennant in four games. Philadelphia's five runs in Game One would have been enough to win any of the other games, but not this one as the Dodgers outhomered the Phillies four to one (including two by Garvey) and scored nine times. Dodger Davey Lopes hit the game's only home run the next day (with a man aboard), but it was more than enough support for John's four-hit shutout.

The series' most decisive win went to the Phillies in Game Three. Steve Carlton allowed four Dodger runs to score, but he made up for it by driving in his own four runs on a homer and sacrifice fly. His teammates added five more, rendering futile Garvey's third series home run.

But Garvey's fourth homer, in Game Four, helped carry the Dodgers into the tenth inning, when Bill Russell—capitalizing on Gary Maddox's muff of Ron Cey's fly to center—singled home Cey with the Dodgers' unearned pennant winner.

Los Angeles Dodgers (West), 3;
Philadelphia Phillies (East), 1

LA (W)

PLAYER/POS	AVG	G	AB	R	H	2B	3B	HR	RB	BB	SO	SB
Dusty Baker, of	.467	4	15	1	7	2	0	0	1	3	0	0
Ron Cey, 3b	.313	4	16	4	5	1	0	1	3	2	4	0
Joe Ferguson, ph	.000	2	2	0	0	0	0	0	0	0	1	0
Terry Forster, p	.000	1	0	0	0	0	0	0	0	0	0	0
Steve Garvey, 1b	.389	4	18	6	7	1	1	4	7	0	1	0
Jerry Grote, c	.000	1	0	0	0	0	0	0	0	0	0	0
Burt Hooton, p	.000	1	2	0	0	0	0	0	0	0	1	0
Charley Hough, p	.000	1	0	0	0	0	0	0	0	0	0	0
Tommy John, p	.000	1	3	0	0	0	0	0	0	0	0	0
Lee Lacy, ph	.000	2	2	0	0	0	0	0	0	0	0	0
Davey Lopes, 2b	.389	4	18	3	7	1	1	2	5	0	1	1
Rick Monday, of	.200	3	10	2	2	0	1	0	0	1	5	0
Manny Mota, ph	1.000	2	1	0	1	1	0	0	0	0	0	0
Billy North, of	.000	4	8	0	0	0	0	0	0	0	1	0
Doug Rau, p	.000	1	0	0	0	0	0	0	0	0	0	0
Lance Rautzhan, p	.000	1	0	0	0	0	0	0	0	0	0	0
Rick Rhoden, p	.000	1	1	0	0	0	0	0	0	0	0	0
Bill Russell, ss	.412	4	17	1	7	1	0	0	2	1	1	0
Reggie Smith, of	.188	4	16	2	3	1	0	1	0	2	0	0
Don Sutton, p	.000	1	2	0	0	0	0	0	0	0	2	0
Bob Welch, p	.000	1	2	0	0	0	0	0	0	0	1	0
Steve Yeager, c	.231	4	13	2	3	0	0	1	2	2	2	1
TOTAL	.286		147	21	42	8	3	8	21	9	22	2

PITCHER	W	L	ERA	G	GS	CG	SV	SHO	IP	H	ER	BB	SO
Terry Forster	1	0	0.00	1	0	0	0	0	1.0	1	0	0	2
Burt Hooton	0	0	7.71	1	1	0	0	0	4.2	10	4	0	5
Charley Hough	0	0	4.50	1	0	0	0	0	2.0	1	1	0	1
Tommy John	1	0	0.00	1	1	1	0	1	9.0	4	0	2	4
Doug Rau	0	0	3.60	1	1	0	0	0	5.0	5	2	2	1
Lance Rautzhan	0	0	6.75	1	0	0	0	0	1.1	3	1	2	0
Rick Rhoden	0	0	2.25	1	0	0	0	0	4.0	2	1	1	3
Don Sutton	0	1	6.35	1	1	0	0	0	5.2	7	4	2	0
Bob Welch	1	0	2.08	1	0	0	0	0	4.1	2	1	0	5
TOTAL	3	1	3.41	9	4	1	0	1	37.0	35	14	9	21

PHI (E)

PLAYER/POS	AVG	G	AB	R	H	2B	3B	HR	RB	BB	SO	SB
Bob Boone, c	.182	3	11	0	2	0	0	0	0	0	1	0
Larry Bowa, ss	.333	4	18	2	6	0	0	0	0	1	2	0
Warren Brusstar, p	.000	3	0	0	0	0	0	0	0	0	0	0
Jose Cardenal, 1b	.167	2	6	0	1	0	0	0	0	1	1	0
Steve Carlton, p	.500	1	4	2	2	0	0	1	4	0	0	0
Larry Christenson, p	.000	1	1	0	0	0	0	0	0	0	1	0
Rawly Eastwick, p	.000	1	0	0	0	0	0	0	0	0	0	0
Barry Foote, ph	.000	1	1	0	0	0	0	0	0	0	1	0
Orlando Gonzalez, ph	.000	1	1	0	0	0	0	0	0	0	1	0
Richie Hebner, 1b-2	.111	3	9	0	1	0	0	0	1	0	0	0
Randy Lerch, p	.000	1	2	0	0	0	0	0	0	0	0	0
Greg Luzinski, of	.375	4	16	3	6	0	1	2	3	1	2	0
Garry Maddox, of	.263	4	19	1	5	0	0	0	2	0	3	0
Jerry Martin, of-3	.222	4	9	1	2	1	0	1	2	1	3	0
Bake Mc Bride, of-2	.222	3	9	2	2	0	0	1	1	0	2	0
Tim Mc Carver, c-1	.000	2	4	2	0	0	0	0	0	1	2	0
Tug Mc Graw, p	.000	3	0	0	0	0	0	0	0	0	0	0
Jim Morrison, ph	.000	1	1	0	0	0	0	0	0	0	1	0
Ron Reed, p	.000	2	0	0	0	0	0	0	0	0	0	0
Dick Ruthven, p	.000	1	1	0	0	0	0	0	0	0	1	0
Mike Schmidt, 3b	.200	4	15	1	3	2	0	0	1	2	2	0
Ted Sizemore, 2b	.385	4	13	3	5	0	1	0	1	1	0	0
TOTAL	.250		140	17	35	3	2	5	16	9	21	0

PITCHER	W	L	ERA	G	GS	CG	SV	SHO	IP	H	ER	BB	SO
Warren Brusstar	0	0	0.00	3	0	0	0	0	2.2	2	0	1	0
Steve Carlton	1	0	4.00	1	1	1	0	0	9.0	8	4	2	8
Larry Christenson	0	1	12.46	1	1	0	0	0	4.1	7	6	1	3
Rawly Eastwick	0	0	9.00	1	0	0	0	0	1.0	3	1	0	1
Randy Lerch	0	0	5.06	1	1	0	0	0	5.1	7	3	0	0
Tug Mc Graw	0	1	1.59	3	0	0	0	0	5.2	3	1	5	5
Ron Reed	0	0	2.25	2	0	0	0	0	4.0	6	1	0	2
Dick Ruthven	0	1	5.79	1	1	0	0	0	4.2	6	3	0	3
TOTAL	1	3	4.66	13	4	1	0	0	36.2	42	19	9	22

GAME 1 AT PHI OCT 4

LA	004 211 001	9 13 1
PHI	010 030 001	5 12 1

Pitchers: Hooton, WELCH (5) vs CHRISTENSEN, Brusstar (5), Eastwick (6), McGraw (7)
Home Runs: Garvey-LA (2), Lopes-LA, Yeager-LA, Martin-PHI
Attendance: 63,460

GAME 2 AT PHI OCT 5

LA	000 120 100	4 8 0
PHI	000 000 000	0 4 0

Pitchers: JOHN vs RUTHVEN, Brusstar (5), Reed (7), McGraw (9)
Home Runs: Lopes-LA
Attendance: 60,642

GAME 3 AT LA OCT 6

PHI	040 003 101	9 11 1
LA	012 000 010	4 8 2

Pitchers: CARLTON vs SUTTON, Rautzhan (6), Hough (8)
Home Runs: Carlton-PHI, Luzinski-PHI, Garvey-LA
Attendance: 55,043

GAME 4 AT LA OCT 7

PHI	002 000 100 0	3 8 2
LA	010 101 000 1	4 13 0

Pitchers: Lerch, Brusstar (6), Reed (7), McGRAW (9) vs Rau, Rhoden (6), FORSTER (10)
Home Runs: Luzinski-PHI, Cey-LA, Garvey-LA, McBride-PHI
Attendance: 55,124

It took Bucky Dent's pop-fly home run against Boston in an Eastern Division tiebreaker to carry the Yankees into the LCS. But once there they took the pennant, downing the Royals for the third year in a row. Reggie Jackson's three-run homer in the eighth inning of Game One capped a sixteen-hit, seven-run Yankee attack, as pitchers Jim Beattie and Ken Clay combined to limit Kansas City to two hits and a single run. The Royals, though, made it look just as easy the next day as their own sixteen hits and ten runs evened the series.

Twice in Game Three George Brett gave the Royals a lead with a home run, and he tied the game with a third homer in the fifth. But Jackson's two-run homer in the fourth brought the Yankees back, and Thurman Munson's two-run shot in the eighth gave New York a close win. Game Four was just as close, but more of a pitcher's duel. Dennis Leonard, who went the distance, gave up only four hits, but two of them were home runs to Graig Nettles and Roy White. Yankee starter Ron Guidry allowed a run in the first, but shut out the Royals for the next seven innings. Goose Gossage preserved Guidry's good work—and the pennant—in the ninth.

New York Yankees (East), 3; Kansas City Royals (West), 1

NY (E)

PLAYER/POS	AVG	G	AB	R	H	2B	3B	HR	RBI	BB	SO	SB
Jim Beattie, p	.000	1	0	0	0	0	0	0	0	0	0	0
Paul Blair, of-3,2b-1	.000	4	6	1	0	0	0	0	0	0	1	0
Chris Chambliss, 1b	.400	4	15	1	6	0	0	0	2	0	4	0
Ken Clay, p	.000	1	0	0	0	0	0	0	0	0	0	0
Bucky Dent, ss	.200	4	15	0	3	0	0	0	4	0	0	0
Brian Doyle, 2b	.286	3	7	0	2	0	0	0	1	1	1	0
Ed Figueroa, p	.000	1	0	0	0	0	0	0	0	0	0	0
Rich Gossage, p	.000	2	0	0	0	0	0	0	0	0	0	0
Ron Guidry, p	.000	1	0	0	0	0	0	0	0	0	0	0
Catfish Hunter, p	.000	1	0	0	0	0	0	0	0	0	0	0
Reggie Jackson, dh-3,of-1	.462	4	13	5	6	1	0	2	6	3	4	0
Cliff Johnson, ph	.000	1	1	0	0	0	0	0	0	0	0	0
Sparky Lyle, p	.000	1	0	0	0	0	0	0	0	0	0	0
Thurman Munson, c	.278	4	18	2	5	1	0	1	2	0	0	0
Graig Nettles, 3b	.333	4	15	3	5	0	1	1	2	0	1	0
Lou Piniella, of	.235	4	17	2	4	0	0	0	0	0	3	0
Mickey Rivers, of	.455	4	11	0	5	0	0	0	0	2	0	0
Fred Stanley, 2b	.200	2	5	0	1	0	0	0	0	0	2	0
Gary Thomasson, of	.000	3	1	0	0	0	0	0	0	0	0	0
Dick Tidrow, p	.000	1	0	0	0	0	0	0	0	0	0	0
Roy White, of-3,dh-1	.313	4	16	5	5	1	0	1	1	1	2	0
TOTAL	.300		140	19	42	3	1	5	18	7	18	0

PITCHER	W	L	ERA	G	GS	CG	SV	SHO	IP	H	ER	BB	SO
Jim Beattie	1	0	1.69	1	1	0	0	0	5.1	2	1	5	3
Ken Clay	0	0	0.00	1	0	0	1	0	3.2	0	0	3	2
Ed Figueroa	0	1	27.00	1	1	0	0	0	1.0	5	3	0	0
Rich Gossage	1	0	4.50	2	0	0	1	0	4.0	3	2	0	3
Ron Guidry	1	0	1.13	1	1	0	0	0	8.0	7	1	1	7
Catfish Hunter	0	0	4.50	1	1	0	0	0	6.0	7	3	3	5
Sparky Lyle	0	0	13.50	1	0	0	0	0	1.1	3	2	0	0
Dick Tidrow	0	0	4.76	1	0	0	0	0	5.2	8	3	2	1
TOTAL	3	1	3.86	9	4	0	2	0	35.0	35	15	14	21

KC (W)

PLAYER/POS	AVG	G	AB	R	H	2B	3B	HR	RBI	BB	SO	SB
Doug Bird, p	.000	2	0	0	0	0	0	0	0	0	0	0
Steve Braun, of-1	.000	2	5	0	0	0	0	0	0	1	1	0
George Brett, 3b	.389	4	18	7	7	1	1	3	3	0	1	0
Al Cowens, of	.133	4	15	2	2	0	0	0	1	0	2	0
Larry Gura, p	.000	1	0	0	0	0	0	0	0	0	0	0
Al Hrabosky, p	.000	3	0	0	0	0	0	0	0	0	0	0
Clint Hurdle, of-2	.375	4	8	1	3	0	1	0	1	2	3	0
Pete La Cock, 1b-3	.364	4	11	1	4	2	1	0	1	3	1	1
Dennis Leonard, p	.000	2	0	0	0	0	0	0	0	0	0	0
Hal Mc Rae, dh	.214	4	14	0	3	0	0	0	2	2	2	1
Steve Mingori, p	.000	1	0	0	0	0	0	0	0	0	0	0
Amos Otis, of	.429	4	14	2	6	2	0	0	1	3	5	4
Freddie Patek, ss	.077	4	13	2	1	0	0	1	2	1	4	0
Marty Pattin, p	.000	1	0	0	0	0	0	0	0	0	0	0
Tom Poquette, ph	.000	1	1	0	0	0	0	0	0	0	0	0
Darrell Porter, c	.357	4	14	1	5	1	0	0	3	2	0	0
Paul Splittorff, p	.000	1	0	0	0	0	0	0	0	0	0	0
John Wathan, 1b	.000	1	3	0	0	0	0	0	0	0	0	0
Frank White, 2b	.231	4	13	1	3	0	0	0	2	0	0	0
Willie Wilson, of	.250	3	4	0	1	0	0	0	0	0	2	0
TOTAL	.263		133	17	35	6	3	4	16	14	21	6

PITCHER	W	L	ERA	G	GS	CG	SV	SHO	IP	H	ER	BB	SO
Doug Bird	0	1	9.00	2	0	0	0	0	1.0	2	1	0	1
Larry Gura	1	0	2.84	1	1	0	0	0	6.1	8	2	2	2
Al Hrabosky	0	0	3.00	3	0	0	0	0	3.0	3	1	0	2
Dennis Leonard	0	2	3.75	2	2	1	0	0	12.0	13	5	2	11
Steve Mingori	0	0	7.36	1	0	0	0	0	3.2	5	3	3	0
Marty Pattin	0	0	27.00	1	0	0	0	0	0.2	2	2	0	0
Paul Splittorff	0	0	4.91	1	1	0	0	0	7.1	9	4	0	2
TOTAL	1	3	4.76	11	4	1	0	0	34.0	42	18	7	18

GAME 1 AT KC OCT 3

NY	011	020	030	7	16	0
KC	000	001	000	1	2	2

Pitchers: BEATTIE, Clay (6) vs LEONARD, Mingori (5), Hrabosky (8), Bird (9)
Home Runs: Jackson-NY
Attendance: 41,143

GAME 2 AT KC OCT 4

NY	000	000	220	4	12	1
KC	140	000	32X	10	16	1

Pitchers: FIGUEROA, Tidrow (2), Lyle (7) vs GURA, Pattin (7), Hrabosky (8)
Home Runs: Patek-KC
Attendance: 41,158

GAME 3 AT NY OCT 6

KC	101	010	020	5	10	1
NY	010	201	02X	6	10	0

Pitchers: Splittorff, BIRD (8), Hrabosky (8) vs Hunter, GOSSAGE (7)
Home Runs: Brett-KC (3), Jackson-NY, Munson-NY
Attendance: 55,535

GAME 4 AT NY OCT 7

KC	100	000	000	1	7	0
NY	010	001	00X	2	4	0

Pitchers: LEONARD vs GUIDRY, Gossage (9)
Home Runs: Nettles-NY, R.White-NY
Attendance: 56,356

The outcome was the same as in 1977: the Yankees over the Dodgers in six games. But this year New York overcame a two-game deficit by sweeping the next four, a feat never before achieved in a World Series.

Los Angeles overwhelmed New York in the opener. Home runs in the second and fourth innings by Dusty Baker and Davey Lopes (two, for five RBIs), and another run in the fifth, gave the Dodgers a 7–0 lead before Reggie Jackson's leadoff homer in the seventh gave New York its ifrst score. The Yankees scored four more times, but so did the Dodgers for an 11–5 win. Game Two was closer. The Yankees scored first and held a lead through the top of the sixth, but Ron Cey's three-run homer in the bottom of the inning gave Los Angeles the runs they needed to win 4–3.

Yankee Ron Guidry, coming off a spectacular 25–3 regular season, pitched Game Three as the Series moved to New York. He gave up eight hits and issued seven walks. But only one baserunner scored, thanks in large part to several memorable stops and throws by third baseman Graig Nettles. Meanwhile, Roy White's home run in the first inning began Yankee scoring in what would become a 5–1 win.

It took ten innings for New York to win Game Four. Starters Tommy John and Ed Figueroa hurled shutout ball until Dodger Reggie Smith tagged Figueroa for a three-run homer in the top of the fifth. The Yankees clawed back in the sixth. Reggie Jackson singled in one run, then—in a play that stirred great controversy—got in the way (the Dodgers claimed intentionally) of a throw from second on an attempted double play, deflecting the ball to the outfield and permitting a second run to score. In the eighth, Thurman Munson doubled home the tying Yankee run, and in the last of the tenth Lou Piniella's two-out drive to center scored baserunner Roy White with the game winner.

Game Five was a Yankee blowout. No one hit home runs, but the Yankees hit sixteen singles (a Series record) and two doubles for twelve runs (five of them driven in by Munson's three hits) to give Yankee pitcher Jim Beattie (nine hits, two runs) an easy win. Back in Los Angeles for the sixth game, the Yankees won the crown on the hitting of two men at the bottom of the batting order: Denny Doyle and Bucky Dent. With three hits each, they combined for five RBIs in the 7–2 win. For good measure, Reggie Jackson concluded the Series scoring with a mighty two-run homer in the seventh.

New York Yankees (AL), 4; Los Angeles Dodgers (NL), 2

NY (A)

PLAYER/POS	AVG	G	AB	R	H	2B	3B	HR	RB	BB	SO	SB
Jim Beattie, p	.000	1	0	0	0	0	0	0	0	0	0	0
Paul Blair, of	.375	6	8	2	3	1	0	0	0	1	4	0
Chris Chambliss, 1b	.182	3	11	1	2	0	0	0	0	1	1	0
Ken Clay, p	.000	1	0	0	0	0	0	0	0	0	0	0
Bucky Dent, ss	.417	6	24	3	10	1	0	0	7	1	2	0
Brian Doyle, 2b	.438	6	16	4	7	1	0	0	2	0	0	0
Ed Figueroa, p	.000	2	0	0	0	0	0	0	0	0	0	0
Rich Gossage, p	.000	3	0	0	0	0	0	0	0	0	0	0
Ron Guidry, p	.000	1	0	0	0	0	0	0	0	0	0	0
Mike Heath, c	.000	1	0	0	0	0	0	0	0	0	0	0
Catfish Hunter, p	.000	2	0	0	0	0	0	0	0	0	0	0
Reggie Jackson, dh	.391	6	23	2	9	1	0	2	8	3	7	0
Cliff Johnson, ph	.000	2	2	0	0	0	0	0	0	0	1	0
Jay Johnstone, of	.000	2	0	0	0	0	0	0	0	0	0	0
Paul Lindblad, p	.000	1	0	0	0	0	0	0	0	0	0	0
Thurman Munson, c	.320	6	25	5	8	3	0	0	7	3	7	1
Graig Nettles, 3b	.160	6	25	2	4	0	0	0	1	0	6	0
Lou Piniella, of	.280	6	25	3	7	0	0	0	4	0	0	1
Mickey Rivers, of-4	.333	5	18	2	6	0	0	0	1	0	2	1
Jim Spencer, 1b-3	.167	4	12	3	2	0	0	0	0	2	4	0
Fred Stanley, 2b	.200	3	5	0	1	1	0	0	0	1	0	0
Gary Thomasson, of	.250	3	4	0	1	0	0	0	0	0	1	0
Dick Tidrow, p	.000	2	0	0	0	0	0	0	0	0	0	0
Roy White, of	.333	6	24	9	8	0	0	1	4	4	5	2
TOTAL	.306		222	36	68	8	0	3	34	16	40	5

PITCHER	W	L	ERA	G	GS	CG	SV	SHO	IP	H	ER	BB	SO
Jim Beattie	1	0	2.00	1	1	1	0	0	9.0	9	2	4	8
Ken Clay	0	0	11.57	1	0	0	0	0	2.1	4	3	2	2
Ed Figueroa	0	1	8.10	2	2	0	0	0	6.2	9	6	5	2
Rich Gossage	1	0	0.00	3	0	0	0	0	6.0	1	0	1	4
Ron Guidry	1	0	1.00	1	1	1	0	0	9.0	8	1	7	4
Catfish Hunter	1	1	4.15	2	2	0	0	0	13.0	13	6	1	5
Paul Lindblad	0	0	11.57	1	0	0	0	0	2.1	4	3	0	1
Dick Tidrow	0	0	1.93	2	0	0	0	0	4.2	4	1	0	5
TOTAL	4	2	3.74	13	6	2	0	0	53.0	52	22	20	31

LA (N)

PLAYER/POS	AVG	G	AB	R	H	2B	3B	HR	RB	BB	SO	SB
Dusty Baker, of	.238	6	21	2	5	0	0	1	1	1	3	0
Ron Cey, 3b	.286	6	21	2	6	0	0	1	4	3	3	0
Vic Davalillo, dh-1	.333	2	3	0	1	0	0	0	0	0	0	0
Joe Ferguson, c	.500	2	4	1	2	2	0	0	0	0	1	0
Terry Forster, p	.000	3	0	0	0	0	0	0	0	0	0	0
Steve Garvey, 1b	.208	6	24	1	5	1	0	0	0	1	7	1
Jerry Grote, c	.000	2	0	0	0	0	0	0	0	0	0	0
Burt Hooton, p	.000	2	0	0	0	0	0	0	0	0	0	0
Charley Hough, p	.000	2	0	0	0	0	0	0	0	0	0	0
Tommy John, p	.000	2	0	0	0	0	0	0	0	0	0	0
Lee Lacy, dh	.143	4	14	0	2	0	0	0	1	1	3	0
Davey Lopes, 2b	.308	6	26	7	8	0	0	3	7	2	1	2
Rick Monday, of-4,dh-1	.154	5	13	2	2	1	0	0	0	4	3	0
Manny Mota, ph	.000	1	0	0	0	0	0	0	0	1	0	0
Billy North, of	.125	4	8	2	1	1	0	0	2	1	0	1
Johnny Oates, c	1.000	1	1	0	1	0	0	0	0	1	0	0
Doug Rau, p	.000	1	0	0	0	0	0	0	0	0	0	0
Lance Rautzhan, p	.000	2	0	0	0	0	0	0	0	0	0	0
Bill Russell, ss	.423	6	26	1	11	2	0	0	2	2	2	1
Reggie Smith, of	.200	6	25	3	5	0	0	1	5	2	6	0
Don Sutton, p	.000	2	0	0	0	0	0	0	0	0	0	0
Bob Welch, p	.000	3	0	0	0	0	0	0	0	0	0	0
Steve Yeager, c	.231	5	13	2	3	1	0	0	0	1	2	0
TOTAL	.261		199	23	52	8	0	6	22	20	31	5

PITCHER	W	L	ERA	G	GS	CG	SV	SHO	IP	H	ER	BB	SO
Terry Forster	0	0	0.00	3	0	0	0	0	4.0	5	0	1	6
Burt Hooton	1	1	6.48	2	2	0	0	0	8.1	13	6	3	6
Charley Hough	0	0	8.44	2	0	0	0	0	5.1	10	5	2	5
Tommy John	1	0	3.07	2	2	0	0	0	14.2	14	5	4	6
Doug Rau	0	0	0.00	1	0	0	0	0	2.0	1	0	0	3
Lance Rautzhan	0	0	13.50	2	0	0	0	0	2.0	4	3	0	0
Don Sutton	0	2	7.50	2	2	0	0	0	12.0	17	10	4	8
Bob Welch	0	1	6.23	3	0	0	0	1	4.1	4	3	2	6
TOTAL	2	4	5.47	17	6	0	1	0	52.2	68	32	16	40

GAME 1 AT LA OCT 10

NY	000 000 320	5	9	1
LA	030 310 31X	11	15	2

Pitchers: FIGUEROA, Clay (2), Lindblad (5), Tidrow (7) vs JOHN, Forster (8)
Home Runs: Baker-LA, Lopes-LA (2), Jackson-NY
Attendance: 55,997

GAME 2 AT LA OCT 11

NY	002 000 100	3	11	0
LA	000 103 00X	4	7	0

Pitchers: HUNTER, Gossage (7) vs HOOTON, Forster (7), Welch (9)
Home Runs: Cey-LA
Attendance: 55,982

GAME 3 AT NY OCT 13

LA	001 000 000	1	8	0
NY	110 000 30X	5	10	1

Pitchers: SUTTON, Rautzhan (7), Hough (8) vs GUIDRY
Home Runs: White-NY
Attendance: 56,447

GAME 4 AT NY OCT 14

LA	000 030 000 0	3	6	1
NY	000 002 010 1	4	9	0

Pitchers: John, Forster (8), WELCH (8) vs Figueroa, Tidrow (6), GOSSAGE (9)
Home Runs: Smith-LA
Attendance: 56,445

GAME 5 AT NY OCT 15

LA	101 000 000	2	9	3
NY	004 300 41X	12	18	0

Pitchers: HOOTON, Rautzhan (3), Hough (4) vs BEATTIE
Attendance: 56,448

GAME 6 AT LA OCT 17

NY	030 002 200	7	11	0
LA	000 000 020	2	7	1

Pitchers: HUNTER, Gossage (8) vs SUTTON, Welch (7), Rau (8)
Home Runs: Lopes-LA, Jackson-NY
Attendance: 55,985

The Pirates—with a better season's record than Cincinnati and stronger hitting and pitching—proved their superiority in the LCS as well, dominating the statistics and sweeping the series. Yet the games were closer than the stats alone would suggest. Pittsburgh won the first game by three runs—but they didn't come until Willie Stargell's homer in the eleventh inning broke a 2–2 tie.

In Game Two, Cincinnati scored first. The Pirates tied the game with a run in the fourth and took a narrow lead with another in the fifth. But the Reds came back on a game-tying pair of doubles in the ninth, and it wasn't until the tenth that Pittsburgh eked out its victory with a run on two singles and Don Robinson's shutout relief.

Only in the third game did the Pirates take a commanding lead, with six runs in the first four innings (two of them on home runs by Stargell and Bill Madlock). The Reds outhit Pittsburgh eight to seven, but only Johnny Bench's homer brought them a run, as Bert Blyleven overcame them in the series' only complete-game pitching performance.

Pittsburgh Pirates (East), 3; Cincinnati Reds (West), 0

PIT (E)

PLAYER/POS	AVG	G	AB	R	H	2B	3B	HR	RB	BB	SO	SB
Matt Alexander, pr	.000	1	0	1	0	0	0	0	0	0	0	0
Jim Bibby, p	.000	1	0	0	0	0	0	0	0	1	0	0
Bert Blyleven, p	.333	1	3	1	1	0	0	0	0	0	1	0
John Candelaria, p	.000	1	3	0	0	0	0	0	0	0	2	0
Mike Easler, ph	.000	1	1	0	0	0	0	0	0	0	0	0
Tim Foli, ss	.333	3	12	1	4	1	0	0	3	0	0	0
Phil Garner, 2b-3,ss-1	.417	3	12	4	5	0	1	1	1	1	0	0
Grant Jackson, p	.000	2	1	0	0	0	0	0	0	0	0	0
Bill Madlock, 3b	.250	3	12	1	3	0	0	1	2	2	0	2
John Milner, of	.000	3	9	0	0	0	0	0	0	2	0	0
Omar Moreno, of	.250	3	12	3	3	0	1	0	0	2	2	1
Ed Ott, c	.231	3	13	0	3	0	0	0	0	0	2	0
Dave Parker, of	.333	3	12	2	4	0	0	0	2	2	3	1
Dave Roberts, p	.000	1	0	0	0	0	0	0	0	0	0	0
Don Robinson, p	.000	2	0	0	0	0	0	0	0	0	0	0
Bill Robinson, of	.000	3	3	0	0	0	0	0	0	0	0	0
Enrique Romo, p	.000	2	0	0	0	0	0	0	0	0	0	0
Willie Stargell, 1b	.455	3	11	2	5	2	0	2	6	3	2	0
Rennie Stennett, 2b	.000	1	0	0	0	0	0	0	0	0	0	0
Kent Tekulve, p	.000	2	1	0	0	0	0	0	0	0	1	0
TOTAL	.267		105	15	28	3	2	4	14	13	13	4

PITCHER	W	L	ERA	G	GS	CG	SV	SHO	IP	H	ER	BB	SO
Jim Bibby	0	0	1.29	1	1	0	0	0	7.0	4	1	4	5
Bert Blyleven	1	0	1.00	1	1	1	0	0	9.0	8	1	0	9
John Candelaria	0	0	2.57	1	1	0	0	0	7.0	5	2	1	4
Grant Jackson	1	0	0.00	2	0	0	0	0	2.0	1	0	1	2
Dave Roberts	0	0	INF	1	0	0	0	0	0.0	0	0	1	0
Don Robinson	1	0	0.00	2	0	0	1	0	2.0	0	0	1	3
Enrique Romo	0	0	0.00	2	0	0	0	0	0.1	3	0	1	1
Kent Tekulve	0	0	3.00	2	0	0	0	0	3.0	2	1	2	2
TOTAL	3	0	1.48	12	3	1	1	0	30.1	23	5	11	26

CIN (W)

PLAYER/POS	AVG	G	AB	R	H	2B	3B	HR	RB	BB	SO	SB
Rick Auerbach, ph	.000	2	2	0	0	0	0	0	0	0	1	0
Doug Bair, p	.000	1	0	0	0	0	0	0	0	0	0	0
Johnny Bench, c	.250	3	12	1	3	0	1	1	1	2	2	0
Dave Collins, of	.357	3	14	0	5	1	0	0	1	0	2	2
Dave Concepcion, ss	.429	3	14	1	6	1	0	0	0	0	3	0
Hector Cruz, of-1	.200	2	5	1	1	1	0	0	0	0	1	0
Dan Driessen, 1b	.083	3	12	1	1	0	0	0	0	1	3	0
George Foster, of	.200	3	10	1	2	0	0	1	2	4	3	0
Cesar Geronimo, of	.143	2	7	0	1	0	0	0	0	0	5	0
Tom Hume, p	.000	3	1	0	0	0	0	0	0	0	1	0
Ray Knight, 3b	.286	3	14	0	4	1	0	0	0	0	2	1
Mike La Coss, p	.000	1	0	0	0	0	0	0	0	0	0	0
Charlie Leibrandt, p	.000	1	0	0	0	0	0	0	0	0	0	0
Joe Morgan, 2b	.000	3	11	0	0	0	0	0	0	3	1	1
Fred Norman, p	.000	1	1	0	0	0	0	0	0	0	1	0
Frank Pastore, p	.000	1	0	0	0	0	0	0	1	1	0	0
Tom Seaver, p	.000	1	2	0	0	0	0	0	0	0	1	0
Mario Soto, p	.000	1	0	0	0	0	0	0	0	0	0	0
Harry Spilman, ph	.000	2	2	0	0	0	0	0	0	0	0	0
Dave Tomlin, p	.000	3	0	0	0	0	0	0	0	0	0	0
TOTAL	.215		107	5	23	4	1	2	5	11	26	4

PITCHER	W	L	ERA	G	GS	CG	SV	SHO	IP	H	ER	BB	SO
Doug Bair	0	1	9.00	1	0	0	0	0	1.0	2	1	1	0
Tom Hume	0	1	6.75	3	0	0	0	0	4.0	6	3	0	2
Mike La Coss	0	1	10.80	1	1	0	0	0	1.2	1	2	4	0
Charlie Leibrandt	0	0	0.00	1	0	0	0	0	0.1	0	0	0	0
Fred Norman	0	0	18.00	1	0	0	0	0	2.0	4	4	1	1
Frank Pastore	0	0	2.57	1	1	0	0	0	7.0	7	2	3	1
Tom Seaver	0	0	2.25	1	1	0	0	0	8.0	5	2	2	5
Mario Soto	0	0	0.00	1	0	0	0	0	2.0	0	0	0	1
Dave Tomlin	0	0	0.00	3	0	0	0	0	3.0	3	0	2	3
TOTAL	0	3	4.34	13	3	0	0	0	29.0	28	14	13	13

GAME 1 AT CIN OCT 2

PIT	002 000 000 03	5 10 0
CIN	000 200 000 00	2 7 0

Pitchers: Candelaria, Romo (8), Tekulve (8), JACKSON (10), D.Robinson (11) vs Seaver, HUME (9), Tomlin (11)
Home Runs: Garner-PIT, Foster-CIN, Stargell-PIT
Attendance: 55,006

GAME 2 AT CIN OCT 3

PIT	000 110 000 1	3 11 0
CIN	010 000 001 0	2 8 0

Pitchers: Bibby, Jackson (8), Romo (8), Tekulve (8), Roberts (9), D.ROBINSON (9) vs Pastore, Tomlin (8), Hume (8), BAIR (10)
Attendance: 55,000

GAME 3 AT PIT OCT 5

CIN	000 001 000	1 8 1
PIT	112 200 01X	7 7 0

Pitchers: LaCOSS, Norman (2), Leibrandt (4), Soto (5), Tomlin (7), Hume (8) vs BLYLEVEN
Home Runs: Stargell-PIT, Madlock-PIT, Bench-CIN
Attendance: 42,240

Baltimore, returning to postseason play after a four-year absence, struggled with first-timer California through three games before blowing them away in the fourth. Game One went into the last of the tenth, tied 3–3, when Oriole pinch hitter John Lowenstein, up with two men on, ended it with a two-out, two-strike shot that just cleared the left field wall.

Game Two looked like a blow-out for Baltimore. Eddie Murray drove in four runs, and the rest of the team added five more to give the O's a 9–1 lead by the end of three. But California chipped away at the lead in the latter half of the game and drew within one in the ninth, before Brian Downing hit into a forceout with the bases full to end their scoring.

The Angels' late rally in Game Three was more successful. Down by a run in the bottom of the ninth, they scored twice, on a walk, a dropped outfield fly, and Larry Harlow's game-winning double. The final game, though, was all Baltimore's, as Scott Mc-Gregor—pitching the series' only complete game—blanked the Angels on six hits. The Orioles scored two in the third and another in the fourth, before Pat Kelly put Angel pennant hopes out of reach with a three-run homer in the O's five-run seventh.

Baltimore Orioles (East), 3;
California Angels (West), 1

BAL (E)

PLAYER/POS	AVG	G	AB	R	H	2B	3B	HR	RB	BB	SO	SB
Mark Belanger, ss	.200	3	5	0	1	0	0	0	1	0	2	0
Al Bumbry, of	.250	4	16	5	4	0	1	0	0	4	3	2
Terry Crowley, ph	.500	2	2	0	1	0	0	0	1	0	0	0
Rich Dauer, 2b	.182	4	11	0	2	0	0	0	0	0	1	0
Doug De Cinces, 3b	.308	4	13	4	4	1	0	0	3	1	1	0
Rick Dempsey, c	.400	3	10	3	4	2	0	0	2	1	0	1
Mike Flanagan, p	.000	1	0	0	0	0	0	0	0	0	0	0
Kiko Garcia, ss	.273	3	11	1	3	0	0	0	2	2	4	0
Pat Kelly, dh-2,of-1	.364	3	11	3	4	0	0	1	4	1	3	2
John Lowenstein, of-3	.167	4	6	2	1	0	0	1	3	2	2	0
Dennis Martinez, p	.000	1	0	0	0	0	0	0	0	0	0	0
Lee May, dh	.143	2	7	0	1	0	0	0	1	1	3	0
Scott Mc Gregor, p	.000	1	0	0	0	0	0	0	0	0	0	0
Eddie Murray, 1b	.417	4	12	3	5	0	0	1	5	5	2	0
Jim Palmer, p	.000	1	0	0	0	0	0	0	0	0	0	0
Gary Roenicke, of	.200	2	5	1	1	0	0	0	1	0	0	0
Ken Singleton, of	.375	4	16	4	6	2	0	0	2	1	2	0
Dave Skaggs, c	.000	1	4	0	0	0	0	0	0	0	0	0
Billy Smith, 2b	.000	1	4	0	0	0	0	0	0	0	1	0
Don Stanhouse, p	.000	3	0	0	0	0	0	0	0	0	0	0
TOTAL	.278		133	26	37	5	1	3	25	18	24	5

PITCHER	W	L	ERA	G	GS	CG	SV	SHO	IP	H	ER	BB	SO
Mike Flanagan	1	0	5.14	1	1	0	0	0	7.0	6	4	1	2
Dennis Martinez	0	0	3.24	1	1	0	0	0	8.1	8	3	0	4
Scott Mc Gregor	1	0	0.00	1	1	1	0	1	9.0	6	0	1	4
Jim Palmer	0	0	3.00	1	1	0	0	0	9.0	7	3	2	3
Don Stanhouse	1	1	6.00	3	0	0	0	0	3.0	5	2	3	0
TOTAL	3	1	2.97	7	4	1	0	1	36.1	32	12	7	13

CAL (W)

PLAYER/POS	AVG	G	AB	R	H	2B	3B	HR	RB	BB	SO	SB
Don Aase, p	.000	2	0	0	0	0	0	0	0	0	0	0
Jim Anderson, ss	.091	4	11	0	1	0	0	0	0	0	1	0
Mike Barlow, p	.000	1	0	0	0	0	0	0	0	0	0	0
Don Baylor, dh-3,of-1	.188	4	16	2	3	0	0	1	2	1	2	0
Bert Campaneris, ss	.000	1	0	0	0	0	0	0	0	0	0	0
Rod Carew, 1b	.412	4	17	4	7	3	0	0	1	0	0	1
Bobby Clark, of	.000	1	3	0	0	0	0	0	0	0	2	0
Mark Clear, p	.000	1	0	0	0	0	0	0	0	0	0	0
Willie Davis, ph	.500	2	2	1	1	1	0	0	0	0	0	0
Brian Downing, c	.200	4	15	1	3	0	0	0	1	1	1	0
Dan Ford, of	.294	4	17	2	5	1	0	2	4	0	0	0
Dave Frost, p	.000	2	0	0	0	0	0	0	0	0	0	0
Bobby Grich, 2b	.154	4	13	0	2	1	0	0	2	1	1	0
Larry Harlow, of-2	.125	3	8	0	1	1	0	0	1	1	2	0
Chris Knapp, p	.000	1	0	0	0	0	0	0	0	0	0	0
Carney Lansford, 3b	.294	4	17	2	5	0	0	0	3	1	2	1
Dave La Roche, p	.000	1	0	0	0	0	0	0	0	0	0	0
Rick Miller, of	.250	4	16	2	4	0	0	0	0	0	1	0
John Montague, p	.000	2	0	0	0	0	0	0	0	0	0	0
Merv Rettenmund, dh	.000	2	2	0	0	0	0	0	0	2	1	0
Nolan Ryan, p	.000	1	0	0	0	0	0	0	0	0	0	0
Frank Tanana, p	.000	1	0	0	0	0	0	0	0	0	0	0
Dickie Thon, ss	.000	1	0	1	0	0	0	0	0	0	0	0
TOTAL	.234		137	15	32	7	0	3	14	7	13	2

PITCHER	W	L	ERA	G	GS	CG	SV	SHO	IP	H	ER	BB	SO
Don Aase	1	0	1.80	2	0	0	0	0	5.0	4	1	2	6
Mike Barlow	0	0	0.00	1	0	0	0	0	1.0	0	0	0	0
Mark Clear	0	0	4.76	1	0	0	0	0	5.2	4	3	2	3
Dave Frost	0	1	18.69	2	1	0	0	0	4.1	8	9	5	1
Chris Knapp	0	1	7.71	1	1	0	0	0	2.1	5	2	1	0
Dave La Roche	0	0	6.75	1	0	0	0	0	1.1	2	1	1	1
John Montague	0	1	9.00	2	0	0	0	0	4.0	4	4	2	2
Nolan Ryan	0	0	1.29	1	1	0	0	0	7.0	4	1	3	8
Frank Tanana	0	0	3.60	1	1	0	0	0	5.0	6	2	2	3
TOTAL	1	3	5.80	12	4	0	0	0	35.2	37	23	18	24

GAME 1 AT BAL OCT 3

CAL	101	001	000	0	3	7	1
BAL	002	001	000	1	4	6	0

Pitchers: Ryan, MONTAGUE (8) vs Palmer, STANHOUSE (10)
Home Runs: Ford-CAL, Lowenstein-BAL
Attendance: 52,787

GAME 2 AT BAL OCT 4

CAL	100	001	132	8	10	1
BAL	441	000	00X	9	11	1

Pitchers: FROST, Clear (2), Aase (8) vs FLANAGAN, Stanhouse (8)
Home Runs: Ford-CAL, Murray-BAL
Attendance: 52,108

GAME 3 AT CAL OCT 5

BAL	000	101	100	3	8	3
CAL	100	100	002	4	9	0

Pitchers: D.Martinez, STANHOUSE (9) vs Tanana, AASE (6)
Home Runs: Baylor-CAL
Attendance: 43,199

GAME 4 AT CAL OCT 6

BAL	002	100	500	8	12	1
CAL	000	000	000	0	6	0

Pitchers: McGREGOR vs KNAPP, LaRoche (3), Frost (4), Montague (7), Barlow (9)
Home Runs: Kelly-BAL
Attendance: 43,199

Veteran Willie Stargell was "Pops," and in the Series he showed his Pirate "family" the way. Seven of his twelve hits went for extra bases, and he drove in a Series-high seven runs. What Stargell began, submarine reliever Kent Tekulve finished, appearing in five of the seven games and recording a record-tying three saves.

Stargell drove in a pair of runs in the opener—one of them with an eighth-inning homer—but Pittsburgh's four runs fell short of the five Baltimore had scored in the first inning. The only extra-base hits in Game Two came from the bat of Eddie Murray, who homered and doubled to drive in both Baltimore runs. But three singles and a sacrifice fly had already given Pittsburgh two runs in the second inning, and two more Pirate singles and a walk in the top of the ninth made the score 3–2. Tekulve came on in the last of the ninth to preserve the lead, fanning two as he retired the side in order.

Baltimore bounced back, though, to take the next two games in convincing fashion. The score favored the Orioles 8–4 when Tekulve came on to set the birds down in order over the final two innings. But Baltimore starter Scott McGregor had by then settled into his groove, retiring the final eleven Pirates with relative ease to preserve his lead and the Oriole win. It took four Orioles pitchers to hold the Pirates in Game Four. Stargell led the Bucs' seventeen-hit attack with a homer, double, and single, and the Pirates led 6–3 entering the eighth inning. But Baltimore loaded the bases in the top of the eighth, prompting Pirate manager Chuck Tanner to bring Tekulve in again. This one time the strategy failed, as Tekulve saw six runs score before he retired his first batter.

Down three games to one, the Pirates rebounded in Game Five, scoring seven times in the final three innings for a 7–1 victory. Baltimore starter Jim Palmer matched John Candelaria's shutout pitching through six innings of Game Six before the Pirates tagged him for pairs of runs in the seventh and eighth. Tekulve, meanwhile, continued Candelaria's shutout through the final three innings, retiring the last seven men in order, four by strikeout. Baltimore scored first in the finale on Rich Dauer's leadoff home run in the third inning, but Stargell put the Pirates ahead with a two-run homer in the sixth. Tekulve came in with two Orioles on base in the eighth to stifle the threat, and (after the Pirates had scored a pair of insurance runs in the top of the ninth) set Baltimore

Pittsburgh Pirates (NL), 4; Baltimore Orioles (AL), 3

PIT (N)

PLAYER/POS	AVG	G	AB	R	H	2B	3B	HR	RB	BB	SO	SB
Matt Alexander, of	.000	1	0	0	0	0	0	0	0	0	0	0
Jim Bibby, p	.000	2	4	0	0	0	0	0	0	0	1	0
Bert Blyleven, p	.000	2	3	0	0	0	0	0	0	0	0	0
John Candelaria, p	.333	2	3	0	1	0	0	0	0	0	2	0
Mike Easler, ph	.000	2	1	0	0	0	0	0	0	1	0	0
Tim Foli, ss	.333	7	30	6	10	1	1	0	3	2	0	0
Phil Garner, 2b	.500	7	24	4	12	4	0	0	5	3	1	0
Grant Jackson, p	.000	4	1	0	0	0	0	0	0	0	0	0
Bruce Kison, p	.000	1	0	0	0	0	0	0	0	0	0	0
Lee Lacy, ph	.250	4	4	0	1	0	0	0	0	0	1	0
Bill Madlock, 3b	.375	7	24	2	9	1	0	0	3	5	1	0
John Milner, of	.333	3	9	2	3	1	0	0	1	2	0	0
Omar Moreno, of	.333	7	33	4	11	2	0	0	3	1	7	0
Steve Nicosia, c	.063	4	16	1	1	0	0	0	0	0	0	0
Ed Ott, c	.333	3	12	2	4	1	0	0	3	3	0	0
Dave Parker, of	.345	7	29	2	10	3	0	0	4	2	7	0
Don Robinson, p	.000	4	0	0	0	0	0	0	0	0	0	0
Bill Robinson, of-6	.263	7	19	2	5	1	0	0	2	0	4	0
Enrique Romo, p	.000	2	1	0	0	0	0	0	0	0	0	0
Jim Rooker, p	.000	2	2	0	0	0	0	0	0	0	1	0
Manny Sanguillen, ph	.333	3	3	0	1	0	0	0	1	0	0	0
Willie Stargell, 1b	.400	7	30	7	12	4	0	3	7	0	6	0
Rennie Stennett, ph	1.000	1	1	0	1	0	0	0	0	0	0	0
Kent Tekulve, p	.000	5	2	0	0	0	0	0	0	0	0	0
TOTAL	.323		251	32	81	18	1	3	32	16	35	0

PITCHER	W	L	ERA	G	GS	CG	SV	SHO	IP	H	ER	BB	SO
Jim Bibby	0	0	2.61	2	2	0	0	0	10.1	10	3	2	10
Bert Blyleven	1	0	1.80	2	1	0	0	0	10.0	8	2	3	4
John Candelaria	1	1	5.00	2	2	0	0	0	9.0	14	5	2	4
Grant Jackson	1	0	0.00	4	0	0	0	0	4.2	1	0	2	2
Bruce Kison	0	1	108.00	1	1	0	0	0	0.1	3	4	2	0
Don Robinson	1	0	5.40	4	0	0	0	0	5.0	4	3	6	3
Enrique Romo	0	0	3.86	2	0	0	0	0	4.2	5	2	3	4
Jim Rooker	0	0	1.04	2	1	0	0	0	8.2	5	1	3	4
Kent Tekulve	0	1	2.89	5	0	0	3	0	9.1	4	3	3	10
TOTAL	4	3	3.34	24	7	0	3	0	62.0	54	23	26	41

BAL (A)

PLAYER/POS	AVG	G	AB	R	H	2B	3B	HR	RB	BB	SO	SB
Benny Ayala, of-3	.333	4	6	1	2	0	0	1	2	1	0	0
Mark Belanger, ss-4	.000	5	6	1	0	0	0	0	0	1	1	0
Al Bumbry, of	.143	7	21	3	3	0	0	0	1	2	1	0
Terry Crowley, ph	.250	5	4	0	1	1	0	0	2	1	0	0
Rich Dauer, 2b-5	.294	6	17	2	5	1	0	1	1	0	1	0
Doug De Cinces, 3b	.200	7	25	5	0	0	0	1	3	5	5	1
Rick Dempsey, c-6	.286	7	21	3	6	2	0	0	0	1	3	0
Mike Flanagan, p	.000	3	5	0	0	0	0	0	0	1	2	0
Kiko Garcia, ss	.400	6	20	4	8	2	1	0	6	1	3	0
Pat Kelly, ph	.250	5	4	0	1	0	0	0	0	1	1	0
John Lowenstein, of-3	.231	6	13	2	3	1	0	0	3	1	3	0
Tippy Martinez, p	.000	3	0	0	0	0	0	0	0	0	0	0
Dennis Martinez, p	.000	2	0	0	0	0	0	0	0	0	0	0
Lee May, ph	.000	2	1	0	0	0	0	0	0	1	1	0
Scott Mc Gregor, p	.000	2	4	1	0	0	0	0	0	2	1	0
Eddie Murray, 1b	.154	7	26	3	4	1	0	1	2	4	4	1
Jim Palmer, p	.000	2	4	0	0	0	0	0	0	0	3	0
Gary Roenicke, of-5	.125	6	16	1	2	1	0	0	0	0	6	0
Ken Singleton, of	.357	7	28	1	10	1	0	0	2	5	0	0
Dave Skaggs, c	.333	1	3	1	1	0	0	0	0	0	0	0
Billy Smith, 2b-2	.286	4	7	1	2	0	0	0	0	2	0	0
Don Stanhouse, p	.000	3	0	0	0	0	0	0	0	0	0	0
Sammy Stewart, p	.000	1	1	0	0	0	0	0	0	0	1	0
Tim Stoddard, p	1.000	4	1	0	1	0	0	0	0	1	0	0
Steve Stone, p	.000	1	0	0	0	0	0	0	0	0	0	0
TOTAL	.232		233	26	54	10	1	4	23	26	41	2

PITCHER	W	L	ERA	G	GS	CG	SV	SHO	IP	H	ER	BB	SO
Mike Flanagan	1	1	3.00	3	2	1	0	0	15.0	18	5	2	13
Tippy Martinez	0	0	6.75	3	0	0	0	0	1.1	3	1	0	1
Dennis Martinez	0	0	18.00	2	1	0	0	0	2.0	6	4	0	0
Scott Mc Gregor	1	1	3.18	2	2	1	0	0	17.0	16	6	2	8
Jim Palmer	0	1	3.60	2	2	0	0	0	15.0	18	6	5	8
Don Stanhouse	0	1	13.50	3	0	0	0	0	2.0	6	3	3	0
Sammy Stewart	0	0	0.00	1	0	0	0	0	2.2	4	0	1	0
Tim Stoddard	1	0	5.40	4	0	0	0	0	5.0	6	3	1	3
Steve Stone	0	0	9.00	1	0	0	0	0	2.0	4	2	2	2
TOTAL	3	4	4.35	21	7	2	0	0	62.0	81	30	16	35

down in order to complete the Pirate comeback.

In the tightest LCS yet, the Phillies took the opener 3–1 on the series' only home run—Greg Luzinski's two-run blast in the sixth inning. It was the only game not to go into extra innings.

The Astros evened the series in Game Two—demolishing a 3–3 tie with four runs in the tenth—and took the series lead in a Game Three pitchers' duel that saw Astro Joe Niekro hurl ten scoreless innings. Reliever Dave Smith continued the shutout and took the win as Joe Morgan's triple and Denny Walling's sacrifice fly off ace Phillie reliever Tug McGraw scored the game's only run in the bottom of the eleventh.

The Phillies rebounded, though, with their own set of extra-inning victories. In Game Four, a single and two doubles pushed across two go-ahead runs in the top of the tenth, and McGraw preserved the edge for his second series save. And in the finale—which saw the lead change hands three times—after Del Unser scored on Gary Maddox's tenth-inning double, Dick Ruthven held off Houston to bring the Phillies their first pennant in thirty years.

Philadelphia Phillies (East), 3; Houston Astros (West), 2

PHI (E)

PLAYER/POS	AVG	G	AB	R	H	2B	3B	HR	RB	BB	SO	SB
Ramon Aviles, pr	.000	1	0	1	0	0	0	0	0	0	0	0
Bob Boone, c	.222	5	18	1	4	0	0	0	2	1	2	0
Larry Bowa, ss	.316	5	19	2	6	0	0	0	0	3	3	1
Warren Brusstar, p	.000	2	1	0	0	0	0	0	0	0	1	0
Marty Bystrom, p	.000	1	2	0	0	0	0	0	0	0	0	0
Steve Carlton, p	.000	2	4	0	0	0	0	0	0	0	1	0
Larry Christenson, p	.000	1	2	0	0	0	0	0	0	0	1	0
Greg Gross, of-1	.750	4	4	2	3	0	0	0	1	0	0	0
Greg Luzinski, of	.294	5	17	3	5	2	0	1	4	0	6	0
Garry Maddox, of	.300	5	20	2	6	2	0	0	3	2	2	2
Bake Mc Bride, of	.238	5	21	0	5	0	0	0	0	1	5	2
Tug Mc Graw, p	.000	5	1	0	0	0	0	0	0	0	0	0
Keith Moreland, c-1	.000	2	1	0	0	0	0	0	1	0	0	0
Dickie Noles, p	.000	2	0	0	0	0	0	0	0	0	0	0
Ron Reed, p	.000	3	0	0	0	0	0	0	0	0	0	0
Pete Rose, 1b	.400	5	20	3	8	0	0	0	2	5	3	0
Dick Ruthven, p	.000	2	2	0	0	0	0	0	0	0	2	0
Kevin Saucier, p	.000	2	0	0	0	0	0	0	0	0	0	0
Mike Schmidt, 3b	.208	5	24	1	5	1	0	0	1	1	6	1
Lonnie Smith, of-2	.600	3	5	2	3	0	0	0	0	0	0	1
Manny Trillo, 2b	.381	5	21	1	8	2	1	0	4	0	2	0
Del Unser, of-2	.400	5	5	2	2	1	0	0	1	0	2	0
George Vukovich, of-1	.000	4	3	0	0	0	0	0	0	0	0	0
TOTAL	.289		190	20	55	8	1	1	19	13	37	7

PITCHER	W	L	ERA	G	GS	CG	SV	SHO	IP	H	ER	BB	SO
Warren Brusstar	1	0	3.38	2	0	0	0	0	2.2	1	1	1	0
Marty Bystrom	0	0	1.69	1	1	0	0	0	5.1	7	1	2	1
Steve Carlton	2	0	2.19	2	2	0	0	0	12.1	11	3	8	6
Larry Christenson	0	0	4.05	1	1	0	0	0	6.2	5	3	5	2
Tug Mc Graw	0	1	4.50	5	0	0	2	0	8.0	8	4	4	5
Dickie Noles	0	0	0.00	2	0	0	0	0	2.2	1	0	3	0
Ron Reed	0	1	18.00	3	0	0	0	0	2.0	3	4	1	1
Dick Ruthven	1	0	2.00	2	1	0	0	0	9.0	3	2	5	4
Kevin Saucier	0	0	0.00	2	0	0	0	0	0.2	1	0	2	0
TOTAL	3	2	3.28	20	5	0	2	0	49.1	40	18	31	19

HOU (W)

PLAYER/POS	AVG	G	AB	R	H	2B	3B	HR	RB	BB	SO	SB
Joaquin Andujar, p	.000	1	0	0	0	0	0	0	0	0	0	0
Alan Ashby, c	.125	2	8	0	1	0	0	0	1	0	0	0
Dave Bergman, 1b	.333	4	3	0	1	0	1	0	2	0	0	0
Bruce Bochy, c	.000	1	1	0	0	0	0	0	0	0	0	0
Enos Cabell, 3b	.238	5	21	1	5	1	0	0	0	1	3	0
Cesar Cedeno, of	.182	3	11	1	2	0	0	0	1	1	0	0
Jose Cruz, of	.400	5	15	3	6	1	1	0	4	8	1	0
Ken Forsch, p	1.000	2	2	0	2	0	0	0	0	0	0	0
Danny Heep, ph	.000	1	1	0	0	0	0	0	0	0	0	0
Art Howe, 1b-4	.200	5	15	0	3	1	1	0	2	2	2	0
Frank La Corte, p	.000	2	1	0	0	0	0	0	0	0	0	0
Rafael Landestoy, 2b-3,ss-1	.222	5	9	3	2	0	0	0	2	1	0	1
Jeffrey Leonard, of-1	.000	3	3	0	0	0	0	0	0	0	2	0
Joe Morgan, 2b	.154	4	13	1	2	1	1	0	0	6	1	0
Joe Niekro, p	.000	1	3	0	0	0	0	0	0	0	1	0
Terry Puhl, of-4	.526	5	19	4	10	2	0	0	3	3	2	2
Luis Pujols, c	.100	4	10	1	1	0	1	0	0	3	0	0
Craig Reynolds, ss	.154	4	13	2	2	1	0	0	0	3	1	0
Vern Ruhle, p	.000	1	3	0	0	0	0	0	0	0	1	0
Nolan Ryan, p	.000	2	4	1	0	0	0	0	0	1	2	0
Joe Sambito, p	.000	3	0	0	0	0	0	0	0	0	0	0
Dave Smith, p	.000	3	0	0	0	0	0	0	0	0	0	0
Denny Walling, of-2,1b-1	.111	3	9	2	1	0	0	0	2	1	0	0
Gary Woods, of-3	.250	4	8	0	2	0	0	0	1	1	3	1
TOTAL	.233		172	19	40	7	5	0	18	31	19	4

PITCHER	W	L	ERA	G	GS	CG	SV	SHO	IP	H	ER	BB	SO
Joaquin Andujar	0	0	0.00	1	0	0	1	0	1.0	0	0	1	0
Ken Forsch	0	1	4.15	2	1	1	0	0	8.2	10	4	1	6
Frank La Corte	1	1	3.00	2	0	0	0	0	3.0	7	1	2	2
Joe Niekro	0	0	0.00	1	1	0	0	0	10.0	6	0	1	2
Vern Ruhle	0	0	3.86	1	1	0	0	0	7.0	8	3	1	3
Nolan Ryan	0	0	5.40	2	2	0	0	0	13.1	16	8	3	14
Joe Sambito	0	1	4.91	3	0	0	0	0	3.2	4	2	2	6
Dave Smith	1	0	3.86	3	0	0	0	0	2.1	4	1	2	4
TOTAL	2	3	3.49	15	5	1	1	0	49.0	55	19	13	37

GAME 1 AT PHI OCT 7

HOU	001 000 000	1	7	0
PHI	000 002 10X	3	8	1

Pitchers: FORSCH vs CARLTON, McGraw (8)
Home Runs: Luzinski-PHI
Attendance: 65,277

GAME 2 AT PHI OCT 8

HOU	001 000 110 4	7	8	1
PHI	000 200 010 1	4	14	2

Pitchers: Ryan, Sambito (7), D.Smith (7), LaCORTE (9), AnduJar (10) vs Ruthven, McGraw (8), REED (9), Saucier (10)
Attendance: 65,476

GAME 3 AT HOU OCT 10

PHI	000 000 000 00	0	7	1
HOU	000 000 000 01	1	6	1

Pitchers: Christensen, Noles (7), McGRAW (8) vs Niekro, D.SMITH (11)
Attendance: 44,443

GAME 4 AT HOU OCT 11

PHI	000 000 030 2	5	13	0
HOU	000 110 001 0	3	5	1

Pitchers: Carlton, Noles (6), Saucier (7), Reed (7), BRUSSTAR (8), McGraw (10) vs Ruhle, D.Smith (8), SAMBITO (8)
Attendance: 44,952

GAME 5 AT HOU OCT 12

PHI	020 000 050 1	8	13	2
HOU	100 001 320 0	7	14	0

Pitchers: Bystrom, Brusstar (6), Christensen (7), Reed (7), McGraw (8), RUTHVEN (9) vs Ryan, Sambito (8), Forsch (8), LaCORTE (9)
Attendance: 44,802

Kansas City and New York met for the fourth time in the LCS, and this time the Royals swept to their first pennant. In the first game the Yankees scored first, with second-inning home runs by Rick Cerone and Lou Piniella, but the Royals' Frank White doubled in a pair later in the inning to tie it, and Willie Aikens's hit in the third gave K.C. the lead. They held it to the end as Larry Gura shut out New York the rest of the way.

The Royals scored three runs in the third inning of Game Two, on Willie Wilson's two-run triple and an RBI double by U. L. Washington. Yankee starter Rudy May stopped K.C. after that, but the Royals already had enough for the win as Dennis Leonard in eight innings held New York to two runs, and Dan Quisenberry kept the lid on in the ninth.

Game Three was decided by home runs. White scored first for the Royals with a solo shot in the fifth. New York took the lead briefly with a two-run sixth, but lost it—and the pennant—in the top of the seventh when Goose Gossage, relieving starter Tommy John with two out and a man on, gave up an infield single to Washington and a home run to George Brett.

Kansas City Royals (West), 3;
New York Yankees (East), 0

KC (W)

PLAYER/POS	AVG	G	AB	R	H	2B	3B	HR	RB	BB	SO	SB
Willie Aikens, 1b	.364	3	11	0	4	0	0	0	2	0	1	0
George Brett, 3b	.273	3	11	3	3	1	0	2	4	1	0	0
Larry Gura, p	.000	1	0	0	0	0	0	0	0	0	0	0
Clint Hurdle, of	.000	3	2	0	0	0	0	0	0	0	1	0
Pete La Cock, 1b	.000	1	0	0	0	0	0	0	0	0	0	0
Dennis Leonard, p	.000	1	0	0	0	0	0	0	0	0	0	0
Hal Mc Rae, dh	.200	3	10	0	2	0	0	0	0	1	3	0
Amos Otis, of	.333	3	12	4	4	1	0	0	0	0	3	2
Darrell Porter, c	.100	3	10	2	1	0	0	0	0	1	0	0
Dan Quisenberry, p	.000	2	0	0	0	0	0	0	0	0	0	0
Paul Splittorff, p	.000	1	0	0	0	0	0	0	0	0	0	0
U. L. Washington, ss	.364	3	11	1	4	1	0	0	1	2	3	0
John Wathan, of	.000	3	6	1	0	0	0	0	0	3	1	0
Frank White, 2b	.545	3	11	3	6	1	0	1	3	0	1	1
Willie Wilson, of	.308	3	13	2	4	2	1	0	4	1	2	0
TOTAL	.289		97	14	28	6	1	3	14	9	15	3

PITCHER	W	L	ERA	G	GS	CG	SV	SHO	IP	H	ER	BB	SO
Larry Gura	1	0	2.00	1	1	1	0	0	9.0	10	2	1	4
Dennis Leonard	1	0	2.25	1	1	0	0	0	8.0	7	2	1	8
Dan Quisenberry	1	0	0.00	2	0	0	1	0	4.2	4	0	2	1
Paul Splittorff	0	0	1.69	1	1	0	0	0	5.1	5	1	2	3
TOTAL	3	0	1.67	5	3	1	1	0	27.0	26	5	6	16

NY (E)

PLAYER/POS	AVG	G	AB	R	H	2B	3B	HR	RB	BB	SO	SB
Bobby Brown, of	.000	3	10	1	0	0	0	0	0	1	2	0
Rick Cerone, c	.333	3	12	1	4	0	0	1	2	0	1	0
Ron Davis, p	.000	1	0	0	0	0	0	0	0	0	0	0
Bucky Dent, ss	.182	3	11	0	2	0	0	0	0	0	1	0
Oscar Gamble, of-1,dh-1	.200	2	5	1	1	0	0	0	0	1	1	0
Rich Gossage, p	.000	1	0	0	0	0	0	0	0	0	0	0
Ron Guidry, p	.000	1	0	0	0	0	0	0	0	0	0	0
Reggie Jackson, of	.273	3	11	1	3	1	0	0	0	1	4	0
Tommy John, p	.000	1	0	0	0	0	0	0	0	0	0	0
Joe Lefebvre, of	.000	1	0	0	0	0	0	0	0	0	0	0
Rudy May, p	.000	1	0	0	0	0	0	0	0	0	0	0
Bobby Murcer, dh	.000	1	4	0	0	0	0	0	0	0	2	0
Graig Nettles, 3b	.167	2	6	1	1	0	0	1	1	0	1	0
Lou Piniella, of	.200	2	5	1	1	0	0	1	1	2	1	0
Willie Randolph, 2b	.385	3	13	0	5	2	0	0	1	1	3	0
Aurelio Rodriguez, 3b	.333	2	6	0	2	1	0	0	0	0	0	0
Eric Soderholm, dh	.167	2	6	0	1	0	0	0	0	0	0	0
Jim Spencer, ph	.000	1	1	0	0	0	0	0	0	0	0	0
Tom Underwood, p	.000	2	0	0	0	0	0	0	0	0	0	0
Bob Watson, 1b	.500	3	12	0	6	3	1	0	0	0	0	0
TOTAL	.255		102	6	26	7	1	3	5	6	16	0

PITCHER	W	L	ERA	G	GS	CG	SV	SHO	IP	H	ER	BB	SO
Ron Davis	0	0	2.25	1	0	0	0	0	4.0	3	1	1	3
Rich Gossage	0	1	54.00	1	0	0	0	0	0.1	3	2	0	0
Ron Guidry	0	1	12.00	1	1	0	0	0	3.0	5	4	4	2
Tommy John	0	0	2.70	1	1	0	0	0	6.2	8	2	1	3
Rudy May	0	1	3.38	1	1	1	0	0	8.0	6	3	3	4
Tom Underwood	0	0	0.00	2	0	0	0	0	3.0	3	0	0	3
TOTAL	0	3	4.32	7	3	1	0	0	25.0	28	12	9	15

GAME 1 AT KC OCT 8

NY	020	000	000	2	10	1
KC	022	000	12X	7	10	0

Pitchers: GUIDRY, Davis (4), Underwood (8) vs GURA
Home Runs: Cerone-NY, Piniella-NY, G.Brett-KC
Attendance: 42,598

GAME 2 AT KC OCT 9

NY	000	020	000	2	8	0
KC	003	000	00X	3	6	0

Pitchers: MAY vs LEONARD, Quisenberry (9)
Home Runs: Nettles-NY
Attendance: 42,633

GAME 3 AT NY OCT 10

KC	000	010	300	4	12	1
NY	000	002	000	2	8	0

Pitchers: Splittorff, QUISENBERRY (6) vs John, GOSSAGE (7), Underwood (8)
Home Runs: White-KC, G.Brett-KC
Attendance: 56,588

Both clubs had won divisional titles three years in a row—1976–1978—only to lose the League Championship Series. But both overcame the jinx in 1980 to face off in the World Series—the Phillies for the first time in thirty years, the Royals for the first time ever. Kansas City began with a rush in the opener, scoring two runs on Amos Otis's homer in the second inning and two more on Willie Aikens's blast an inning later. But the Phillies came back to take the lead in their half of the third with a five-run rally capped by Bake McBride's three-run homer. Single Phillie runs in each of the next two innings kept them out of reach of Aikens's second two-run shot in the eighth for a narrow 7–6 win. The Phillies extended their Series advantage with a 6–4 win in the second game, rebounding from a two-run deficit with four runs in the eighth inning.

The two clubs traded single runs throughout Game Three. Royal George Brett's first-inning homer began the scoring. The Phillies got the run back in the second inning, the Royals took the lead back in the fourth, Phillie Mike Schmidt homered to tie it again in the fifth, Amos Otis countered with a homer in the seventh, and Pete Rose singled in another tying Phillie run in the eighth. Phillie reliever Tug McGraw (who had a save in the opening game) came on to pitch the last of the tenth inning, but couldn't hold the tie, though two men were out before Willie Aikens singled in the Royals' winning run. The Royals evened the Series with their second victory the next day, scoring four times in the first inning and once in the second (with Willie Aikens for the second time in the Series hitting two home runs in a game), then holding on for a 5–3 win.

But the Phillies recovered to win the next two, and their first world crown. Mike Schmidt's fourth-inning two-run homer began the Phillies' scoring in Game Five. The Royals replied with one run in the fifth, and Amos Otis's home run an inning later tied the game. A second K.C. run in the inning put the Royals ahead until the top of the ninth, when pinch hitter Del Unser doubled home Schmidt to tie the game, and Manny Trillo drove home Unser with the go-ahead run. Tug McGraw, who had held K.C. scoreless through two innings of relief, loaded the bases in the last of the ninth with three walks, but at last fanned Jose Cardenal for the final out. In Game Six, with the Phillies ahead 4–0 in the eighth inning, McGraw relieved starter Steve Carlton with two men on,

and loaded the bases with a walk. One Royal scored on a sacrifice fly before McGraw got his third out. In the ninth, another McGraw walk and two singles again loaded the bases with only one away, but Frank White popped out foul, the ball bouncing off Bob Boone's catcher's mitt into Pete Rose's hand, and Willie Wilson struck out for the twelfth time to end the Series.

Philadelphia Phillies (NL), 4;
Kansas City Royals (AL), 2

PHI (N)

PLAYER/POS	AVG	G	AB	R	H	2B	3B	HR	RB	BB	SO	SB
Bob Boone, c	.412	6	17	3	7	2	0	0	4	4	0	0
Larry Bowa, ss	.375	6	24	3	9	1	0	0	2	0	0	3
Warren Brusstar, p	.000	1	0	0	0	0	0	0	0	0	0	0
Marty Bystrom, p	.000	1	0	0	0	0	0	0	0	0	0	0
Steve Carlton, p	.000	2	0	0	0	0	0	0	0	0	0	0
Larry Christenson, p	.000	1	0	0	0	0	0	0	0	0	0	0
Greg Gross, of-3	.000	4	2	0	0	0	0	0	0	0	0	0
Greg Luzinski, dh-2,of-1	.000	3	9	0	0	0	0	0	0	1	5	0
Garry Maddox, of	.227	6	22	1	5	2	0	0	1	1	3	0
Bake Mc Bride, of	.304	6	23	3	7	1	0	1	5	2	1	0
Tug Mc Graw, p	.000	4	0	0	0	0	0	0	0	0	0	0
Keith Moreland, dh	.333	3	12	1	4	0	0	0	1	0	1	0
Dickie Noles, p	.000	1	0	0	0	0	0	0	0	0	0	0
Ron Reed, p	.000	2	0	0	0	0	0	0	0	0	0	0
Pete Rose, 1b	.261	6	23	2	6	1	0	0	1	2	2	0
Dick Ruthven, p	.000	1	0	0	0	0	0	0	0	0	0	0
Kevin Saucier, p	.000	1	0	0	0	0	0	0	0	0	0	0
Mike Schmidt, 3b	.381	6	21	6	8	1	0	2	7	4	3	0
Lonnie Smith, of-5,dh-1	.263	6	19	2	5	1	0	0	1	1	1	0
Manny Trillo, 2b	.217	6	23	4	5	2	0	0	2	0	0	0
Del Unser, of	.500	3	6	2	3	2	0	0	2	0	1	0
Bob Walk, p	.000	1	0	0	0	0	0	0	0	0	0	0
TOTAL	.294		201	27	59	13	0	3	26	15	17	3

PITCHER	W	L	ERA	G	GS	CG	SV	SHO	IP	H	ER	BB	SO
Warren Brusstar	0	0	0.00	1	0	0	0	0	2.1	0	0	1	0
Marty Bystrom	0	0	5.40	1	1	0	0	0	5.0	10	3	1	4
Steve Carlton	2	0	2.40	2	2	0	0	0	15.0	14	4	9	17
Larry Christenson	0	1	108.00	1	1	0	0	0	0.1	5	4	1	0
Tug Mc Graw	1	1	1.17	4	0	0	2	0	7.2	7	1	8	10
Dickie Noles	0	0	1.93	1	0	0	0	0	4.2	5	1	2	6
Ron Reed	0	0	0.00	2	0	0	1	0	2.0	2	0	0	2
Dick Ruthven	0	0	3.00	1	1	0	0	0	9.0	9	3	0	7
Kevin Saucier	0	0	0.00	1	0	0	0	0	0.2	0	0	2	0
Bob Walk	1	0	7.71	1	1	0	0	0	7.0	8	6	3	3
TOTAL	4	2	3.69	15	6	0	3	0	53.2	60	22	27	49

KC (A)

PLAYER/POS	AVG	G	AB	R	H	2B	3B	HR	RB	BB	SO	SB
Willie Aikens, 1b	.400	6	20	5	8	0	1	4	8	6	8	0
George Brett, 3b	.375	6	24	3	9	2	1	1	3	2	4	1
Jose Cardenal, of	.200	4	10	0	2	0	0	0	0	0	3	0
Dave Chalk, 3b	.000	1	0	1	0	0	0	0	0	1	0	1
Onix Concepcion, pr	.000	3	0	0	0	0	0	0	0	0	0	0
Rich Gale, p	.000	2	0	0	0	0	0	0	0	0	0	0
Larry Gura, p	.000	2	0	0	0	0	0	0	0	0	0	0
Clint Hurdle, of	.417	4	12	1	5	1	0	0	0	2	1	1
Pete La Cock, 1b	.000	1	0	0	0	0	0	0	0	0	0	0
Dennis Leonard, p	.000	2	0	0	0	0	0	0	0	0	0	0
Renie Martin, p	.000	3	0	0	0	0	0	0	0	0	0	0
Hal Mc Rae, dh	.375	6	24	3	9	3	0	0	1	2	2	0
Amos Otis, of	.478	6	23	4	11	2	0	3	7	3	3	0
Marty Pattin, p	.000	1	0	0	0	0	0	0	0	0	0	0
Darrell Porter, c-4	.143	5	14	1	2	0	0	0	0	3	4	0
Dan Quisenberry, p	.000	6	0	0	0	0	0	0	0	0	0	0
Paul Splittorff, p	.000	1	0	0	0	0	0	0	0	0	0	0
U L Washington, ss	.273	6	22	1	6	0	0	0	2	0	6	0
John Wathan, c-2,of-1	.286	3	7	1	2	0	0	0	1	2	1	0
Frank White, 2b	.080	6	25	0	2	0	0	0	0	1	5	1
Willie Wilson, of	.154	6	26	3	4	1	0	0	0	4	12	2
TOTAL	.290		207	23	60	9	2	8	22	26	49	6

PITCHER	W	L	ERA	G	GS	CG	SV	SHO	IP	H	ER	BB	SO
Rich Gale	0	1	4.26	2	2	0	0	0	6.1	11	3	4	4
Larry Gura	0	0	2.19	2	2	0	0	0	12.1	8	3	3	4
Dennis Leonard	1	1	6.75	2	2	0	0	0	10.2	15	8	2	5
Renie Martin	0	0	2.79	3	0	0	0	0	9.2	11	3	3	2
Marty Pattin	0	0	0.00	1	0	0	0	0	1.0	0	0	0	2
Dan Quisenberry	1	2	5.23	6	0	0	1	0	10.1	10	6	3	0
Paul Splittorff	0	0	5.40	1	0	0	0	0	1.2	4	1	0	0
TOTAL	2	4	4.15	17	6	0	1	0	52.0	59	24	15	17

GAME 1 AT PHI OCT 14

KC	022 000 020	6	9	1
PHI	005 110 00X	7	11	0

Pitchers: LEONARD, Martin (4), Quisenberry (8) vs WALK, McGraw (8)
Home Runs: Otis-KC, Aikens-KC (2), McBride-PHI
Attendance: 65,791

GAME 2 AT PHI OCT 15

KC	000 001 300	4	11	0
PHI	000 020 04X	6	8	1

Pitchers: Gura, QUISENBERRY (7) vs CARLTON, Reed (9)
Attendance: 65,775

GAME 3 AT KC OCT 17

PHI	010 010 010 0	3	14	0
KC	100 100 100 1	4	11	0

Pitchers: Ruthven, McGRAW (10) vs Gale, Martin (5), QUISENBERRY (8)
Home Runs: Schmidt-PHI, G.Brett-KC, Otis-KC
Attendance: 42,380

GAME 4 AT KC OCT 18

PHI	010 000 110	3	10	1
KC	410 000 00X	5	10	2

Pitchers: CHRISTENSEN, Noles (1), Saucier (6), Brusstar (6) vs LEONARD, Quisenberry (8)
Home Runs: Aikens-KC (2)
Attendance: 42,363

GAME 5 AT KC OCT 19

PHI	000 200 002	4	7	0
KC	000 012 000	3	12	2

Pitchers: Bystrom, Reed (6), McGRAW (7) vs Gura, QUISENBERRY (7)
Home Runs: Schmidt-PHI, Otis-KC
Attendance: 42,369

GAME 6 AT PHI OCT 21

KC	000 000 010	1	7	2
PHI	002 011 00X	4	9	0

Pitchers: GALE, Martin (3), Splittorff (5), Pattin (7), Quisenberry (8) vs CARLTON, McGraw (8)
Attendance: 65,838

The Expos, who triumphed over the NL East in the second half of the season, won the first two play-off games at home by identical 3–1 scores over the first-half champion Phillies. The Phillies rapped Expo ace Steve Rogers for ten hits in Game One, but Keith Moreland's solo home run in the second was the only hit to produce a run. The homer tied the score briefly, but the Expos regained the lead in the last of the second inning on Chris Speier's double and increased it to 3–1, two innings later. The Expos scored their three runs early in Game Two on Speier's second-inning single and Gary Carter's two-run homer an inning later. Expo starter Bill Gullickson blanked the Phillies on three hits through 7⅔ innings, but three two-out hits in the eighth scored a Phillie run and brought on reliever Jeff Reardon, who ended the threat for his second save in as many days.

When the Series moved to Philadelphia, the Phillies recovered to even things with a pair of wins. After an easy 13-hit 6–2 victory in Game Three, they took a 4–0 lead into the fourth inning of Game Four. Montreal fought back to tie the game, fell behind again, then re-tied the score at 5–5 in the top of the seventh. The final innings featured a duel between relievers Tug McGraw and Jeff Reardon. McGraw stopped the Expos on one hit through three innings, and took the win when Reardon, after retiring eight Phillies in a row, gave up a leadoff homer to pinch hitter George Vukovich in the bottom of the tenth.

Steve Rogers won the division title for Montreal in the finale, hurling a six-hit shutout against the Phillies and driving in the first two of the Expos' three runs with a bases-loaded single through the box in the fifth inning.

Montreal Expos, 3; Philadelphia Phillies, 2

MON (E)

PLAYER/POS	AVG	G	AB	R	H	2B	3B	HR	RB	BB	SO	SB
Stan Bahnsen, p	.000	1	0	0	0	0	0	0	0	0	0	0
Ray Burris, p	.000	1	2	0	0	0	0	0	0	0	2	0
Gary Carter, c	.421	5	19	3	8	3	0	2	6	1	1	0
Warren Cromartie, 1b	.227	5	22	1	5	2	0	0	1	0	9	0
Andre Dawson, of	.300	5	20	1	6	0	1	0	0	1	6	2
Terry Francona, of	.333	5	12	0	4	0	0	0	0	2	2	0
Woody Fryman, p	.000	1	0	0	0	0	0	0	0	0	0	0
Bill Gullickson, p	.000	1	3	0	0	0	0	0	0	0	1	0
Wallace Johnson, ph	.500	2	2	0	1	0	0	0	0	1	0	0
Bill Lee, p	.000	1	0	0	0	0	0	0	0	0	0	0
Jerry Manuel, 2b	.071	5	14	0	1	0	0	0	0	2	5	0
Brad Mills, ph	.000	1	0	0	0	0	0	0	0	1	0	0
John Milner, ph	.500	2	2	0	1	0	0	0	0	1	0	0
Larry Parrish, 3b	.150	5	20	3	3	1	0	0	1	1	3	0
Mike Phillips, 2b	.000	1	1	0	0	0	0	0	0	0	0	0
Jeff Reardon, p	.000	3	1	0	0	0	0	0	0	0	1	0
Steve Rogers, p	.400	2	5	0	2	0	0	0	2	0	1	0
Scott Sanderson, p	.000	1	1	0	0	0	0	0	0	0	1	0
Elias Sosa, p	.000	2	0	0	0	0	0	0	0	0	0	0
Chris Speier, ss	.400	5	15	4	6	2	0	0	3	4	2	0
Tim Wallach, of-3	.250	4	4	1	1	1	0	0	0	4	0	0
Jerry White, of	.167	5	18	3	3	1	0	0	1	2	2	3
TOTAL	.255		161	16	41	10	1	2	16	18	36	7

PITCHER	W	L	ERA	G	GS	CG	SV	SHO	IP	H	ER	BB	SO
Stan Bahnsen	0	0	0.00	1	0	0	0	0	1.1	1	0	1	1
Ray Burris	0	1	5.06	1	1	0	0	0	5.1	7	3	4	4
Woody Fryman	0	0	6.75	1	0	0	0	0	1.1	3	1	1	0
Bill Gullickson	1	0	1.17	1	1	0	0	0	7.2	6	1	1	3
Bill Lee	0	0	0.00	1	0	0	0	0	0.2	2	0	0	1
Jeff Reardon	0	1	2.08	3	0	0	2	0	4.1	1	1	1	2
Steve Rogers	2	0	0.51	2	2	1	0	1	17.2	16	1	3	5
Scott Sanderson	0	0	6.75	1	1	0	0	0	2.2	4	2	2	2
Elias Sosa	0	0	3.00	2	0	0	0	0	3.0	4	1	0	1
TOTAL	3	2	2.05	13	5	1	2	1	44.0	44	10	13	19

PHI (E)

PLAYER/POS	AVG	G	AB	R	H	2B	3B	HR	RB	BB	SO	SB
Luis Aguayo, pr	.000	2	0	1	0	0	0	0	0	0	0	0
Ramon Aviles, ph	.000	1	0	0	0	0	0	0	0	1	0	0
Bob Boone, c	.000	3	5	0	0	0	0	0	0	0	0	0
Larry Bowa, ss	.176	5	17	0	3	1	0	0	1	0	0	0
Warren Brusstar, p	.000	2	0	0	0	0	0	0	0	0	0	0
Steve Carlton, p	.250	2	4	0	1	0	0	0	0	0	0	0
Larry Christensen, p	.000	1	2	0	0	0	0	0	0	0	1	0
Dick Davis, of	.000	1	2	0	0	0	0	0	0	0	1	0
Greg Gross, of-2	.000	4	4	0	0	0	0	0	0	0	0	0
Sparky Lyle, p	.000	3	0	0	0	0	0	0	0	0	0	0
Garry Maddox, of	.333	2	3	0	1	1	0	0	0	0	0	0
Gary Matthews, of	.400	5	20	3	8	0	1	1	1	0	2	0
Bake Mc Bride, of	.200	4	15	1	3	1	0	0	0	0	5	0
Tug Mc Graw, p	.000	2	0	0	0	0	0	0	0	0	0	0
Keith Moreland, c	.462	4	13	2	6	0	0	1	3	1	1	0
Dickie Noles, p	.000	1	0	0	0	0	0	0	0	1	0	0
Ron Reed, p	.000	4	0	0	0	0	0	0	0	0	0	0
Pete Rose, 1b	.300	5	20	1	6	1	0	0	2	2	0	0
Dick Ruthven, p	.000	1	1	0	0	0	0	0	0	0	0	0
Mike Schmidt, 3b	.250	5	16	3	4	1	0	1	2	4	2	0
Lonnie Smith, of	.263	5	19	1	5	1	0	0	0	0	4	0
Manny Trillo, 2b	.188	5	16	1	3	0	0	0	1	4	0	0
George Vukovich, of-3	.444	5	9	1	4	0	0	1	2	0	3	0
TOTAL	.265		166	14	44	6	1	4	12	13	19	0

PITCHER	W	L	ERA	G	GS	CG	SV	SHO	IP	H	ER	BB	SO
Warren Brusstar	0	0	4.91	2	0	0	0	0	3.2	5	2	1	3
Steve Carlton	0	2	3.86	2	2	0	0	0	14.0	14	6	8	13
Larry Christensen	1	0	1.50	1	1	0	0	0	6.0	4	1	1	8
Sparky Lyle	0	0	0.00	3	0	0	0	0	2.1	4	0	2	1
Tug Mc Graw	1	0	0.00	2	0	0	0	0	4.0	2	0	0	2
Dickie Noles	0	0	4.50	1	1	0	0	0	4.0	4	2	2	5
Ron Reed	0	0	3.00	4	0	0	0	0	6.0	5	2	3	4
Dick Ruthven	0	1	4.50	1	1	0	0	0	4.0	3	2	1	0
TOTAL	2	3	3.07	16	5	0	0	0	44.0	41	15	18	36

GAME 1 AT MON OCT 7

PHI	010 000 000	1	10	1
MON	110 100 00X	3	8	0

Pitchers: CARLTON, R.Reed (7) vs ROGERS, Reardon (9)
Home Runs: Moreland-PHI
Attendance: 34,327

GAME 2 AT MON OCT 8

PHI	000 000 010	1	6	2
MON	012 000 00X	3	7	0

Pitchers: RUTHVEN, Brusstar (5), Lyle (7), McGraw (8) vs GULLICKSON, Reardon (8)
Home Runs: Carter-MON
Attendance: 45,896

GAME 3 AT PHI OCT 9

MON	010 000 010	2	8	4
PHI	020 002 20X	6	13	0

Pitchers: BURRIS, Lee (6), Sosa (7) vs CHRISTENSON, Lyle (7), R.Reed (8)
Attendance: 36,835

GAME 4 AT PHI OCT 10

MON	000 112 100 0	5	10	1
PHI	202 001 000 1	6	9	0

Pitchers: Sanderson (3), Sosa (5), Fryman (6), REARDON (7) vs Noles, Brusstar (5), LyLE (6), R.Reed (7), McGRAW (8)
Home Runs: Carter-MON, Schmidt-PHI, Matthews-PHI, G.Vukovich-PHI
Attendance: 38,818

GAME 5 AT PHI OCT 11

MON	000 021 000	3	8	1
PHI	000 000 000	0	6	0

Pitchers: ROGERS vs CARLTON, R.Reed (9)
Attendance: 47,384

Cincinnati, with the league's best overall season record, failed to win either half season in the NL West, and watched from the sidelines as first-half winner Los Angeles, down 0–2, recovered to win the final three games—and the division title—from second-half victor Houston. In the opener, Astro Alan Ashby's two-run homer in the last of the ninth broke a 1–1 tie and gave Nolan Ryan a two-hit victory. The next day, Astro Denny Walling's two-out bases-loaded single in the last of the eleventh scored Phil Garner with the game's only run.

When the clubs shifted to Los Angeles for the remainder of the series, the Dodgers came alive. In Game Three, a first-inning double by Dusty Baker and home run by Steve Garvey drove in three Dodger runs. Pitcher Burt Hooton and two relievers held Houston to three hits in what became a 6–1 Dodger victory. The next day, Dodger Fernando Valenzuela and Astro Vern Ruhle hurled matching four-hitters. But Pedro Guerrero's home run in the fifth inning and a pair of Dodger singles sandwiched around a sacrifice and intentional walk in the seventh gave Los Angeles two runs, while Valenzuela held Houston to a single run in the ninth. In the finale, Jerry Reuss blanked the Astros on five hits while his Dodgers blended three of their seven hits with a walk and Astro error for three runs in the sixth. Two more hits produced a final run an inning later.

Los Angeles Dodgers, 3; Houston Astros, 2

LA (W)

PLAYER/POS	AVG	G	AB	R	H	2B	3B	HR	RB	BB	SO	SB
Dusty Baker, of	.167	5	18	2	3	1	0	0	1	2	0	0
Terry Forster, p	.000	1	0	0	0	0	0	0	0	0	0	0
Steve Garvey, 1b	.368	5	19	4	7	0	1	2	4	0	2	0
Pedro Guerrero, 3b	.176	5	17	1	3	1	0	1	1	2	4	1
Burt Hooton, p	.000	1	3	0	0	0	0	0	0	0	0	0
Steve Howe, p	.000	2	0	0	0	0	0	0	0	0	0	0
Jay Johnstone, ph	.000	1	1	0	0	0	0	0	0	0	0	0
Ken Landreaux, of	.200	5	20	1	4	1	0	0	1	0	1	0
Davey Lopes, 2b	.200	5	20	1	4	1	0	0	0	3	7	1
Mike Marshall, ph	.000	1	1	0	0	0	0	0	0	0	1	0
Rick Monday, of	.214	5	14	1	3	0	0	0	1	2	4	0
Tom Niedenfuer, p	.000	1	0	0	0	0	0	0	0	0	0	0
Jerry Reuss, p	.000	2	8	0	0	0	0	0	0	0	8	0
Bill Russell, ss	.250	5	16	1	4	1	0	0	2	3	1	0
Steve Sax, 2b	.000	1	0	0	0	0	0	0	0	0	0	0
Mike Scioscia, c	.154	4	13	0	2	0	0	0	1	1	2	0
Reggie Smith, ph	.000	2	1	0	0	0	0	0	1	0	1	0
Dave Stewart, p	.000	2	0	0	0	0	0	0	0	0	0	0
Derrel Thomas, of	.000	4	2	1	0	0	0	0	0	0	1	0
Fernando Valenzuela, p	.000	2	4	0	0	0	0	0	0	0	1	0
Bob Welch, p	.000	1	0	0	0	0	0	0	0	0	0	0
Steve Yeager, c	.400	2	5	1	2	1	0	0	0	0	1	0
TOTAL	.198		162	13	32	6	1	3	12	13	34	2

PITCHER	W	L	ERA	G	GS	CG	SV	SHO	IP	H	ER	BB	SO
Terry Forster	0	0	0.00	1	0	0	0	0	0.1	0	0	0	0
Burt Hooton	1	0	1.29	1	1	0	0	0	7.0	3	1	3	2
Steve Howe	0	0	0.00	2	0	0	0	0	2.0	1	0	0	2
Tom Niedenfuer	0	0	0.00	1	0	0	0	0	0.1	1	0	1	1
Jerry Reuss	1	0	0.00	2	2	1	0	1	18.0	10	0	5	7
Dave Stewart	0	2	40.50	2	0	0	0	0	0.2	4	3	0	1
Fernando Valenzuela	1	0	1.06	2	2	1	0	0	17.0	10	2	3	10
Bob Welch	0	0	0.00	1	0	0	0	0	1.0	0	0	1	1
TOTAL	3	2	1.17	12	5	2	0	1	46.1	29	6	13	24

HOU (W)

PLAYER/POS	AVG	G	AB	R	H	2B	3B	HR	RB	BB	SO	SB
Alan Ashby, c	.111	3	9	1	1	0	0	1	2	2	0	0
Cesar Cedeno, 1b	.231	4	13	0	3	1	0	0	0	2	2	2
Jose Cruz, of	.300	5	20	0	6	1	0	0	0	1	3	1
Kiko Garcia, ss-1	.000	2	4	0	0	0	0	0	0	0	1	0
Phil Garner, 2b	.111	5	18	1	2	0	0	0	0	3	3	0
Art Howe, 3b	.235	5	17	1	4	0	0	1	1	2	1	0
Bob Knepper, p	.000	1	1	0	0	0	0	0	0	0	0	0
Frank La Corte, p	.000	2	0	0	0	0	0	0	0	0	0	0
Joe Niekro, p	.000	1	2	0	0	0	0	0	0	0	0	0
Joe Pittman, ph	.000	2	2	0	0	0	0	0	0	0	0	0
Terry Puhl, of	.190	5	21	2	4	1	0	0	0	0	1	1
Luis Pujols, c	.000	2	6	0	0	0	0	0	0	0	1	0
Craig Reynolds, ss-1	.333	2	3	1	1	0	0	0	0	0	1	0
Dave Roberts, ph	.000	1	1	0	0	0	0	0	0	0	1	0
Vern Ruhle, p	.000	1	1	0	0	0	0	0	0	0	1	0
Nolan Ryan, p	.250	2	4	0	1	0	0	0	0	1	1	0
Joe Sambito, p	.000	2	0	0	0	0	0	0	0	0	0	0
Tony Scott, of	.150	5	20	0	3	0	0	0	2	1	6	0
Billy Smith, p	.000	1	0	0	0	0	0	0	0	0	0	0
Dave Smith, p	.000	2	0	0	0	0	0	0	0	0	0	0
Harry Spilman, ph	.000	1	1	0	0	0	0	0	0	0	0	0
Dickie Thon, ss	.182	4	11	0	2	0	0	0	0	1	0	0
Denny Walling, 1b-2	.333	3	6	0	2	0	0	0	1	0	1	0
Gary Woods, ph	.000	2	2	0	0	0	0	0	0	0	1	0
TOTAL	.179		162	6	29	3	0	2	6	13	24	4

PITCHER	W	L	ERA	G	GS	CG	SV	SHO	IP	H	ER	BB	SO
Bob Knepper	0	1	5.40	1	1	0	0	0	5.0	6	3	2	4
Frank La Corte	0	0	0.00	2	0	0	0	0	3.2	2	0	1	5
Joe Niekro	0	0	0.00	1	1	0	0	0	8.0	7	0	3	4
Vern Ruhle	0	1	2.25	1	1	1	0	0	8.0	4	2	2	1
Nolan Ryan	1	1	1.80	2	2	1	0	0	15.0	6	3	3	14
Joe Sambito	1	0	16.20	2	0	0	0	0	1.2	5	3	2	2
Billy Smith	0	0	0.00	1	0	0	0	0	0.1	0	0	0	0
Dave Smith	0	0	3.86	2	0	0	0	0	2.1	2	1	0	4
TOTAL	2	3	2.45	12	5	2	0	0	44.0	32	12	13	34

GAME 1 AT HOU OCT 6

LA	000	000	100		1	2	0
HOU	000	001	002		3	8	0

Pitchers: Valenzuela, STEWART (9) vs RYAN
Home Runs: Garvey-LA, Ashby-HOU
Attendance: 44,836

GAME 2 AT HOU OCT 7

LA	000	000	000	00	0	9	1
HOU	000	000	000	01	1	9	0

Pitchers: Reuss, S.Howe (1), STEWART (11), Forster (11), Niedenfuer (11) vs Niekro, D.Smith (9), SAMBITO (11)
Attendance: 42,398

GAME 3 AT LA OCT 9

HOU	001	000	000		1	3	2
LA	300	000	03X		6	10	0

Pitchers: KNEPPER, LaCorte (6), Sambito (8), B.Smith (8) vs HOOTON, S.Howe (8), Welch (9)
Home Runs: Garvey-LA, A.Howe-HOU
Attendance: 46,820

GAME 4 AT LA OCT 10

HOU	000	000	001		1	4	0
LA	000	010	10X		2	4	0

Pitchers: RUHLE vs VALENZUELA
Home Runs: Guerrero-LA
Attendance: 55,983

GAME 5 AT LA OCT 11

HOU	000	000	000		0	5	3
LA	000	003	10X		4	7	2

Pitchers: RYAN, D.Smith (7), LaCorte (7) vs REUSS
Attendance: 55,979

Fine pitching characterized the series, with the losing team held to one run in four of the five games. In the exception Expo Ray Burris hurled a shutout.

Montreal put men on base in each inning of the opener. But the pitching of Burt Hooton and Bob Welch—plus some fine Dodger fielding—kept the Expos from scoring until the ninth, when their one run was too little to overcome the Dodger lead. Burris's shutout evened the series in Game Two as the Expos scored three times against rookie sensation Fernando Valenzuela. The Expos took the series lead in Game Three, overcoming a 0–1 deficit with a two-out four-run burst in the sixth (capped by Jerry White's three-run homer).

In the end, though, the Dodgers prevailed. Through seven innings of Game Four, Hooton and the Expos' Bill Gullickson dueled at 1–1. But in the top of the eighth, Steve Garvey homered with a man aboard, and four more Dodger runs in the ninth put the game away. The finale—Burris vs. Valenzuela again—featured another 1–1 duel, this one reaching into the top of the ninth when, with two out, Dodger Rick Monday homered off reliever Steve Rogers. In the bottom of the ninth, Valenzuela walked two batters after retiring two, but Welch came on to save the game and the pennant.

Los Angeles Dodgers (West), 3;
Montreal Expos (East), 2

LA (W)

PLAYER/POS	AVG	G	AB	R	H	2B	3B	HR	RB	BB	SO	SB
Dusty Baker, of	.316	5	19	3	6	1	0	0	3	1	0	0
Bobby Castillo, p	.000	1	0	0	0	0	0	0	0	0	0	0
Ron Cey, 3b	.278	5	18	1	5	1	0	0	3	3	2	0
Terry Forster, p	.000	1	0	0	0	0	0	0	0	0	0	0
Steve Garvey, 1b	.286	5	21	2	6	0	0	1	2	0	4	0
Pedro Guerrero, of	.105	5	19	1	2	0	0	1	2	1	4	0
Burt Hooton, p	.000	2	5	0	0	0	0	0	0	0	2	0
Steve Howe, p	.000	2	0	0	0	0	0	0	0	0	0	0
Jay Johnstone, ph	.000	2	2	0	0	0	0	0	0	0	0	0
Ken Landreaux, of-3	.100	5	10	0	1	1	0	0	0	3	2	0
Davey Lopes, 2b	.278	5	18	0	5	0	0	0	0	1	3	5
Rick Monday, of-2	.333	3	9	2	3	0	0	1	1	0	4	0
Tom Niedenfuer, p	.000	1	0	0	0	0	0	0	0	0	0	0
Alejandro Pena, p	.000	2	0	0	0	0	0	0	0	0	0	0
Jerry Reuss, p	.000	1	2	0	0	0	0	0	0	0	0	0
Bill Russell, ss	.313	5	16	2	5	0	1	0	1	1	1	0
Steve Sax, 2b	.000	1	0	0	0	0	0	0	0	0	0	0
Mike Scioscia, c	.133	5	15	1	2	0	0	1	1	2	1	0
Reggie Smith, ph	1.000	1	1	0	1	0	0	0	1	0	0	0
Derrel Thomas, 3b-1,of-1	1.000	2	1	2	1	0	0	0	0	0	0	0
Fernando Valenzuela, p	.000	2	5	0	0	0	0	0	1	0	0	0
Bob Welch, p	.000	3	0	0	0	0	0	0	0	0	0	0
Steve Yeager, c	.500	1	2	1	1	0	0	0	0	0	0	0
TOTAL	.233		163	15	38	3	1	4	15	12	23	5

PITCHER	W	L	ERA	G	GS	CG	SV	SHO	IP	H	ER	BB	SO
Bobby Castillo	0	0	0.00	1	0	0	0	0	1.0	0	0	0	1
Terry Forster	0	0	0.00	1	0	0	0	0	0.1	0	0	0	1
Burt Hooton	2	0	0.00	2	2	0	0	0	14.2	11	0	6	7
Steve Howe	0	0	0.00	2	0	0	0	0	2.0	1	0	0	2
Tom Niedenfuer	0	0	0.00	1	0	0	0	0	0.1	2	0	0	0
Alejandro Pena	0	0	0.00	2	0	0	0	0	2.1	1	0	0	0
Jerry Reuss	0	1	5.14	1	1	0	0	0	7.0	7	4	1	2
Fernando Valenzuela	1	1	2.45	2	2	0	0	0	14.2	10	4	5	10
Bob Welch	0	0	5.40	3	0	0	1	0	1.2	2	1	0	2
TOTAL	3	2	1.84	15	5	0	1	0	44.0	34	9	12	25

MON (E)

PLAYER/POS	AVG	G	AB	R	H	2B	3B	HR	RB	BB	SO	SB
Ray Burris, p	.000	2	6	0	0	0	0	0	0	0	4	0
Gary Carter, c	.438	5	16	3	7	1	0	0	0	4	2	0
Warren Cromartie, 1b	.167	5	18	0	3	1	0	0	2	0	2	0
Andre Dawson, of	.150	5	20	2	3	0	0	0	0	0	4	0
Terry Francona, of-1	.000	2	1	0	0	0	0	0	0	0	1	0
Woody Fryman, p	.000	1	0	0	0	0	0	0	0	0	0	0
Bill Gullickson, p	.000	2	3	0	0	0	0	0	0	1	2	0
Bill Lee, p	.000	1	0	0	0	0	0	0	0	0	0	0
Jerry Manuel, pr	.000	1	0	0	0	0	0	0	0	0	0	0
John Milner, ph	.000	1	1	0	0	0	0	0	0	0	1	0
Larry Parrish, 3b	.263	5	19	2	5	2	0	0	2	1	1	0
Tim Raines, of	.238	5	21	1	5	2	0	0	1	0	3	0
Jeff Reardon, p	.000	1	0	0	0	0	0	0	0	0	0	0
Steve Rogers, p	.000	2	2	0	0	0	0	0	0	0	1	0
Rodney Scott, 2b	.167	5	18	0	3	0	0	0	0	1	3	1
Elias Sosa, p	.000	1	0	0	0	0	0	0	0	0	0	0
Chris Speier, ss	.188	5	16	0	3	0	0	0	0	2	0	0
Tim Wallach, ph	.000	1	1	0	0	0	0	0	0	0	0	0
Jerry White, of	.313	5	16	2	5	1	0	1	3	3	1	1
TOTAL	.215		158	10	34	7	0	1	8	12	25	2

PITCHER	W	L	ERA	G	GS	CG	SV	SHO	IP	H	ER	BB	SO
Ray Burris	1	0	0.53	2	2	1	0	1	17.0	10	1	3	4
Woody Fryman	0	0	36.00	1	0	0	0	0	1.0	3	4	1	1
Bill Gullickson	0	2	2.51	2	2	0	0	0	14.1	12	4	6	12
Bill Lee	0	0	0.00	1	0	0	0	0	0.1	1	0	0	0
Jeff Reardon	0	0	27.00	1	0	0	0	0	1.0	3	3	0	0
Steve Rogers	1	1	1.80	2	1	1	0	0	10.0	8	2	1	6
Elias Sosa	0	0	0.00	1	0	0	0	0	0.1	1	0	1	0
TOTAL	2	3	2.86	10	5	2	0	1	44.0	38	14	12	23

GAME 1 AT LA OCT 13

MON	000	000	001	1	9	0
LA	020	000	03X	5	8	0

Pitchers: GULLICKSON, Reardon (8) vs HOOTON, Welch (8), Howe (9)
Home Runs: Guerrero-LA, Scioscia-LA
Attendance: 51,273

GAME 2 AT LA OCT 14

MON	020	001	000	3	10	1
LA	000	000	000	0	5	1

Pitchers: BURRIS vs VALENZUELA, Niedenfuer (7), Forster (7), Pena (7), Castillo (9)
Attendance: 53,463

GAME 3 AT MON OCT 16

LA	000	100	000	1	7	0
MON	000	004	00X	4	7	1

Pitchers: REUSS, Pena (8) vs ROGERS
Home Runs: White-MON
Attendance: 54,372

GAME 4 AT MON OCT 17

LA	001	000	024	7	12	1
MON	000	100	000	1	5	1

Pitchers: HOOTON, Welch (8), Howe (9) vs GULLICKSON, Fryman (8), Sosa (9), Lee (9)
Home Runs: Garvey-LA
Attendance: 54,499

GAME 5 AT MON OCT 19

LA	000	010	001	2	6	0
MON	100	000	000	1	3	1

Pitchers: VALENZUELA, Welch (9) vs Burris, ROGERS (9)
Home Runs: Monday-LA
Attendance: 36,491

The home field didn't seem to offer any advantage. First-half winner New York captured both games played in Milwaukee, but when the Series moved to Yankee Stadium for the final three games, the second-half champion Brewers evened the series.

Milwaukee took a 2–0 lead early in the opener, but New York erupted for four runs in the fourth on Oscar Gamble's two-run homer and Rick Cerone's double, and held on to win 5–3. In Game Two, rookie starter Dave Righetti fanned ten Brewers in his six innings and Goose Gossage's brilliant relief earned him his second save in two days as the Yankees took a 3–0 win on homers by Lou Piniella and Reggie Jackson.

Milwaukee, struggling against elimination, took the lead in the seventh inning of Game Three on Ted Simmons' two-run homer. New York tied the score at 3–3 in their half of the inning, but Paul Molitor broke the tie in the eighth with a solo homer. Simmons doubled home an insurance run later in the inning for a 5–3 Brewer win. The Brewers tagged Yankee pitching for only four hits in Game Four, but three of them came in the fourth inning and combined with a sacrifice fly to produce the Brewers' two runs. New York scored once in the sixth, but baserunning errors an inning later ended their only other scoring threat.

In the finale Milwaukee scored two early runs, but the Yankees (as they had done in the opener) took the lead with a four-run fourth—this time on home runs by Reggie Jackson and Oscar Gamble, and Rick Cerone's single. Cerone later hit an insurance homer, as the home team finally won a game—and captured the division crown.

New York Yankees, 3;
Milwaukee Brewers, 2

NY (E)

PLAYER/POS	AVG	G	AB	R	H	2B	3B	HR	RB	BB	SO	SB
Bobby Brown, pr	.000	1	0	0	0	0	0	0	0	0	0	0
Rick Cerone, c	.333	5	18	1	6	2	0	1	5	0	2	0
Ron Davis, p	.000	3	0	0	0	0	0	0	0	0	0	0
Barry Foote, ph	.000	1	0	0	0	0	0	0	0	0	0	0
Oscar Gamble, dh	.556	4	9	2	5	1	0	2	3	1	2	0
Rich Gossage, p	.000	3	0	0	0	0	0	0	0	0	0	0
Ron Guidry, p	.000	2	0	0	0	0	0	0	0	0	0	0
Reggie Jackson, of	.300	5	20	4	6	0	0	2	4	1	5	0
Tommy John, p	.000	1	0	0	0	0	0	0	0	0	0	0
Rudy May, p	.000	1	0	0	0	0	0	0	0	0	0	0
Larry Milbourne, ss	.316	5	19	4	6	1	0	0	0	0	1	0
Jerry Mumphrey, of	.095	5	21	2	2	0	0	0	0	0	1	1
Bobby Murcer, ph	.000	2	1	0	0	0	0	0	0	1	0	0
Graig Nettles, 3b	.059	5	17	1	1	0	0	0	1	3	1	0
Lou Piniella, of	.200	4	10	1	2	1	0	1	3	0	0	0
Willie Randolph, 2b	.200	5	20	4	4	0	0	0	1	1	4	0
Rick Reuschel, p	.000	1	0	0	0	0	0	0	0	0	0	0
Dave Revering, 1b	.000	2	0	0	0	0	0	0	0	0	0	0
Dave Righetti, p	.000	2	0	0	0	0	0	0	0	0	0	0
Bob Watson, 1b	.438	5	16	2	7	0	0	0	1	1	1	0
Dave Winfield, of	.350	5	20	2	7	3	0	0	0	1	5	0
TOTAL	.269		171	19	46	8	0	6	18	9	22	1

PITCHER	W	L	ERA	G	GS	CG	SV	SHO	IP	H	ER	BB	SO
Ron Davis	1	0	0.00	3	0	0	0	0	6.0	1	0	2	6
Rich Gossage	0	0	0.00	3	0	0	3	0	6.2	3	0	2	8
Ron Guidry	0	0	5.40	2	2	0	0	0	8.1	11	5	3	8
Tommy John	0	1	6.43	1	1	0	0	0	7.0	8	5	2	0
Rudy May	0	0	0.00	1	0	0	0	0	2.0	1	0	0	1
Rick Reuschel	0	1	3.00	1	1	0	0	0	6.0	4	2	1	3
Dave Righetti	2	0	1.00	2	1	0	0	0	9.0	8	1	3	13
TOTAL	3	2	2.60	13	5	0	3	0	45.0	36	13	13	39

MIL (E)

PLAYER/POS	AVG	G	AB	R	H	2B	3B	HR	RB	BB	SO	SB
Sal Bando, 3b	.294	5	17	1	5	3	0	0	1	2	3	0
Dwight Bernard, p	.000	2	0	0	0	0	0	0	0	0	0	0
Thad Bosley, dh	.000	1	0	0	0	0	0	0	0	0	0	0
Mike Caldwell, p	.000	2	0	0	0	0	0	0	0	0	0	0
Cecil Cooper, 1b	.222	5	18	1	4	0	0	0	3	1	3	0
Jamie Easterly, p	.000	2	0	0	0	0	0	0	0	0	0	0
Marshall Edwards, of	.000	2	1	0	0	0	0	0	0	0	1	0
Rollie Fingers, p	.000	3	0	0	0	0	0	0	0	0	0	0
Jim Gantner, 2b	.143	4	14	1	2	1	0	0	0	0	2	0
Moose Haas, p	.000	2	0	0	0	0	0	0	0	0	0	0
Roy Howell, dh-3	.400	4	5	0	2	0	0	0	0	2	2	0
Randy Lerch, p	.000	1	0	0	0	0	0	0	0	0	0	0
Bob McClure, p	.000	3	0	0	0	0	0	0	0	0	0	0
Paul Molitor, of	.250	5	20	2	5	0	0	1	1	2	5	0
Don Money, 2b-1,dh-1	.000	2	3	0	0	0	0	0	0	0	0	0
Charlie Moore, of-2,dh-2	.222	4	9	0	2	0	0	0	1	1	2	0
Ben Oglivie, of	.167	5	18	0	3	1	0	0	1	0	7	0
Ed Romero, 2b	.500	2	2	1	1	0	0	0	0	0	1	0
Ted Simmons, c	.211	5	19	1	4	1	0	1	4	2	2	0
Jim Slaton, p	.000	4	0	0	0	0	0	0	0	0	0	0
Gorman Thomas, of-3,dh-2	.118	5	17	2	2	0	0	1	1	1	9	0
Pete Vuckovich, p	.000	2	0	0	0	0	0	0	0	0	0	0
Robin Yount, ss	.316	5	19	4	6	0	1	0	1	2	2	1
TOTAL	.222		162	13	36	6	1	3	13	13	39	1

PITCHER	W	L	ERA	G	GS	CG	SV	SHO	IP	H	ER	BB	SO
Dwight Bernard	0	0	0.00	2	0	0	0	0	2.1	0	0	0	0
Mike Caldwell	0	1	4.32	2	1	0	0	0	8.1	9	4	0	4
Jamie Easterly	0	0	6.75	2	0	0	0	0	1.1	2	1	0	1
Rollie Fingers	1	0	3.86	3	0	0	1	0	4.2	7	2	1	5
Moose Haas	0	2	9.45	2	2	0	0	0	6.2	13	7	1	1
Randy Lerch	0	0	1.50	1	1	0	0	0	6.0	3	1	4	3
Bob McClure	0	0	0.00	3	0	0	0	0	3.1	4	0	0	2
Jim Slaton	0	0	3.00	4	0	0	0	0	6.0	6	2	0	2
Pete Vuckovich	1	0	0.00	2	1	0	0	0	5.1	2	0	3	4
TOTAL	2	3	3.48	21	5	0	1	0	44.0	46	17	9	22

GAME 1 AT MIL OCT 7

NY	000 400 001	5 13 1
MIL	011 010 000	3 8 3

Pitchers: Guidry, DAVIS (5), Gossage (8) vs HAAS, Bernard (4), McClure (5), Slaton (6), Fingers (8)
Home Runs: Gamble-NY
Attendance: 35,064

GAME 2 AT MIL OCT 8

NY	000 100 002	3 7 0
MIL	000 000 000	0 7 0

Pitchers: RIGHETTI, Davis (7), Gossage (7) vs CALDWELL, Slaton (9)
Home Runs: Piniella-NY, Jackson-NY
Attendance: 26,395

GAME 3 AT NY OCT 9

MIL	000 000 320	5 9 0
NY	000 100 200	3 8 2

Pitchers: Lerch, FINGERS (7) vs JOHN, May (8)
Home Runs: Simmons-MIL, Molitor-MIL
Attendance: 56,411

GAME 4 AT NY OCT 10

MIL	000 200 000	2 4 2
NY	000 001 000	1 5 0

Pitchers: VUCKOVICH, Easterly (6), Slaton (7), McClure (8), Fingers (9) vs REUSCHEL, Davis (7)
Attendance: 52,077

GAME 5 AT NY OCT 11

MIL	011 000 100	3 8 0
NY	000 400 12X	7 13 0

Pitchers: HAAS, Caldwell (4), Bernard (4), McClure (6), Slaton (7), Easterly (8), Vuckovich (8) vs Guidry, RIGHETTI (5), Gossage (8)
Home Runs: Thomas-MIL, Jackson-NY, Gamble-NY, Cerone-NY
Attendance: 47,505

First-half winner Oakland, with the league's best win-loss record over the full season, swept the division title from second-half champ Kansas City (who, with a full-season record of 50–53, had become the only club in major-league history to qualify for postseason play with a losing record). Twice in the opener the Royals loaded the bases against Mike Norris with fewer than two outs, but both times failed to score. Meanwhile, after a Royal error had prolonged the A's fourth inning, Wayne Gross homered for three unearned Oakland runs. Dwayne Murphy's eighth-inning solo shot gave the A's a fourth run. The game ended with Norris possessor of a four-hit shutout.

Game Two was closer. Oakland's Tony Armas doubled in a run in the top of the first, and doubled home another in the eighth (his fourth hit of the game) to break a 1–1 tie and provide the margin needed for pitcher Steve McCatty's six-hit win. The A's Rick Langford yielded ten hits in Game Three (including Kansas City's only extra-base hit of the series, a double), but only one Royal scored, meanwhile the A's were sending four runs across the plate—three of them by Rickey Henderson, who reached base four times on pairs of hits and walks.

Oakland Athletics, 3;
Kansas City Royals, 0

KC (W)

PLAYER/POS	AVG	G	AB	R	H	2B	3B	HR	RB	BB	SO	SB
Willie Aikens, 1b	.333	3	9	0	3	0	0	0	0	3	2	0
George Brett, 3b	.167	3	12	0	2	0	0	0	0	0	0	0
Cesar Geronimo, pr	.000	1	0	0	0	0	0	0	0	0	0	0
Larry Gura, p	.000	1	0	0	0	0	0	0	0	0	0	0
Clint Hurdle, of	.273	3	11	0	3	0	0	0	0	1	1	0
Mike Jones, p	.000	1	0	0	0	0	0	0	0	0	0	0
Dennis Leonard, p	.000	1	0	0	0	0	0	0	0	0	0	0
Renie Martin, p	.000	2	0	0	0	0	0	0	0	0	0	0
Lee May, 1b	.000	1	0	0	0	0	0	0	0	0	0	0
Hal Mc Rae, dh	.091	3	11	0	1	1	0	0	0	1	1	0
Amos Otis, of	.000	3	12	0	0	0	0	0	1	0	4	0
Dan Quisenberry, p	.000	1	0	0	0	0	0	0	0	0	0	0
U. L. Washington, ss	.222	3	9	0	2	0	0	0	0	0	1	0
John Wathan, c	.300	3	10	1	3	0	0	0	0	1	1	0
Frank White, 2b	.182	3	11	1	2	0	0	0	0	1	1	0
Willie Wilson, of	.308	3	13	0	4	0	0	0	1	0	0	0
TOTAL	.204		98	2	20	1	0	0	2	7	11	0

PITCHER	W	L	ERA	G	GS	CG	SV	SHO	IP	H	ER	BB	SO
Larry Gura	0	1	7.36	1	1	0	0	0	3.2	7	3	3	3
Mike Jones	0	1	2.25	1	1	0	0	0	8.0	9	2	0	2
Dennis Leonard	0	1	1.13	1	1	0	0	0	8.0	7	1	1	3
Renie Martin	0	0	0.00	2	0	0	0	0	5.1	1	0	2	2
Dan Quisenberry	0	0	0.00	1	0	0	0	0	1.0	1	0	0	0
TOTAL	0	3	2.08	6	3	0	0	0	26.0	25	6	6	10

OAK (W)

PLAYER/POS	AVG	G	AB	R	H	2B	3B	HR	RB	BB	SO	SB
Tony Armas, of	.545	3	11	1	6	2	0	0	3	1	1	0
Dave Beard, p	.000	1	0	0	0	0	0	0	0	0	0	0
Rick Bosetti, of	.000	1	0	0	0	0	0	0	0	0	0	0
Keith Drumright, dh	.250	1	4	0	1	0	0	0	0	0	0	0
Wayne Gross, 3b-1	.400	2	5	1	2	0	0	1	3	0	0	0
Mike Heath, c	.000	2	8	0	0	0	0	0	0	0	1	0
Rickey Henderson, of	.182	3	11	3	2	0	0	0	0	2	0	2
Cliff Johnson, dh	.286	2	7	0	2	1	0	0	0	0	1	0
Mickey Klutts, 3b	.143	2	7	0	1	0	0	0	0	0	1	0
Rick Langford, p	.000	1	0	0	0	0	0	0	0	0	0	0
Steve Mc Catty, p	.000	1	0	0	0	0	0	0	0	0	0	0
Dave Mc Kay, 2b	.273	3	11	1	3	0	0	1	1	1	1	0
Kelvin Moore, 1b	.000	2	8	0	0	0	0	0	0	0	2	0
Dwayne Murphy, of	.545	3	11	4	6	1	0	1	2	1	1	0
Jeff Newman, c	.000	1	3	0	0	0	0	0	0	0	1	0
Mike Norris, p	.000	1	0	0	0	0	0	0	0	0	0	0
Rob Picciolo, ss	.333	1	3	0	1	0	0	0	0	0	0	0
Jim Spencer, 1b	.250	1	4	0	1	1	0	0	0	0	0	0
Fred Stanley, ss	.000	3	6	0	0	0	0	0	0	1	1	0
Tom Underwood, p	.000	1	0	0	0	0	0	0	0	0	0	0
TOTAL	.253		99	10	25	5	0	3	9	6	10	2

PITCHER	W	L	ERA	G	GS	CG	SV	SHO	IP	H	ER	BB	SO
Dave Beard	0	0	0.00	1	0	0	1	0	1.1	0	0	0	2
Rick Langford	1	0	1.23	1	1	0	0	0	7.1	10	1	0	3
Steve Mc Catty	1	0	1.00	1	1	1	0	0	9.0	6	1	4	3
Mike Norris	1	0	0.00	1	1	1	0	1	9.0	4	0	3	2
Tom Underwood	0	0	0.00	1	0	0	0	0	0.1	0	0	0	1
TOTAL	3	0	0.67	5	3	2	1	1	27.0	20	2	7	11

GAME 1 AT KC OCT 6

OAK	000 300 010	4	8	2
KC	000 000 000	0	4	1

Pitchers: NORRIS vs LEONARD, Martin (9)
Home Runs: Gross-OAK, Murphy-OAK
Attendance: 40,592

GAME 2 AT KC OCT 7

OAK	100 000 010	2	10	1
KC	000 010 000	1	6	0

Pitchers: McCATTY vs JONES, Quisenberry (9)
Attendance: 40,274

GAME 3 AT OAK OCT 9

KC	000 100 000	1	10	3
OAK	101 200 00X	4	7	0

Pitchers: GURA, Martin (4) vs LANGFORD, Underwood (8), Beard (8)
Home Runs: McKay-OAK
Attendance: 40,002

The A's scored only four runs to their opponents' twenty as the Yankees swept the series. And only two of the six Yankee pitchers permitted an Oakland runner to score, while not one of Oakland's eight pitchers held New York scoreless. Even so, two of the three games were closely contested.

Oakland's Mike Norris gave up a bases-loaded double to Graig Nettles in the first inning of Game One before settling down to pitch shutout ball. But the three runs Nettles drove in were more than enough, as Tommy John and two relievers held the A's to a single run.

Game Two was the series' only blowout, and even it remained close for three innings. But, led by a pair of three-run homers from Nettles and Lou Piniella, the Yankees parlayed nineteen hits into thirteen runs as Yankee reliever George Frazier held the A's scoreless over the final five frames.

Game Three remained tight until the ninth. Through eight innings the only run came on Yankee Willie Randolph's homer off Oakland starter Matt Keough. But in the top of the ninth, Graig Nettles tagged reliever Tom Underwood for his second bases-clearing double of the series. The three runs weren't really needed, as Dave Righetti, Ron Davis, and Goose Gossage combined to shut out the A's for the full nine.

New York Yankees (East), 3;
Oakland A's (West), 0

NY (E)

PLAYER/POS	AVG	G	AB	R	H	2B	3B	HR	RB	BB	SO	SB
Bobby Brown, of-2	1.000	3	1	2	1	0	0	0	0	0	0	0
Rick Cerone, c	.100	3	10	1	1	0	0	0	0	0	0	0
Ron Davis, p	.000	2	0	0	0	0	0	0	0	0	0	0
Barry Foote, c-1	1.000	2	1	0	1	0	0	0	0	0	0	0
George Frazier, p	.000	1	0	0	0	0	0	0	0	0	0	0
Oscar Gamble, dh-2,of-1	.167	3	6	2	1	0	0	0	1	5	3	0
Rich Gossage, p	.000	2	0	0	0	0	0	0	0	0	0	0
Reggie Jackson, of	.000	2	4	1	0	0	0	0	1	1	0	1
Tommy John, p	.000	1	0	0	0	0	0	0	0	0	0	0
Rudy May, p	.000	1	0	0	0	0	0	0	0	0	0	0
Larry Milbourne, ss	.462	3	13	4	6	0	0	0	1	0	0	0
Jerry Mumphrey, of	.500	3	12	2	6	1	0	0	0	3	2	0
Bobby Murcer, dh	.333	1	3	0	1	0	0	0	0	1	1	0
Graig Nettles, 3b	.500	3	12	2	6	2	0	1	9	1	0	0
Lou Piniella, dh-2,of-1	.600	3	5	2	3	0	0	1	3	0	0	0
Willie Randolph, 2b	.333	3	12	2	4	0	0	1	2	0	1	0
Dave Revering, 1b	.500	2	2	0	1	0	0	0	0	0	0	0
Dave Righetti, p	.000	1	0	0	0	0	0	0	0	0	0	0
Andre Robertson, ss	.000	1	1	0	0	0	0	0	0	0	0	0
Aurelio Rodriguez, 3b	.000	1	0	0	0	0	0	0	0	0	0	0
Bob Watson, 1b	.250	3	12	0	3	0	0	0	1	0	1	0
Dave Winfield, of	.154	3	13	2	2	1	0	0	2	2	2	1
TOTAL	.336		107	20	36	4	0	3	20	13	10	2

PITCHER	W	L	ERA	G	GS	CG	SV	SHO	IP	H	ER	BB	SO
Ron Davis	0	0	0.00	2	0	0	0	0	3.1	0	0	2	4
George Frazier	1	0	0.00	1	0	0	0	0	5.2	5	0	1	5
Rich Gossage	0	0	0.00	2	0	0	1	0	2.2	1	0	0	2
Tommy John	1	0	1.50	1	1	0	0	0	6.0	6	1	1	3
Rudy May	0	0	8.10	1	0	0	0	0	3.1	6	3	0	5
Dave Righetti	1	0	0.00	1	1	0	0	0	6.0	4	0	2	4
TOTAL	3	0	1.33	8	2	0	1	0	27.0	22	4	6	23

OAK (W)

PLAYER/POS	AVG	G	AB	R	H	2B	3B	HR	RB	BB	SO	SB
Tony Armas, of	.167	3	12	0	2	0	0	0	0	0	5	0
Dave Beard, p	.000	1	0	0	0	0	0	0	0	0	0	0
Rick Bosetti, of-1,dh-1	.250	2	4	1	1	1	0	0	0	0	1	0
Mike Davis, ph	1.000	1	1	0	1	0	0	0	0	0	0	0
Keith Drumright, dh-1	.000	3	4	0	0	0	0	0	0	1	0	0
Wayne Gross, 3b	.000	3	5	0	0	0	0	0	0	0	0	0
Mike Heath, c-2,of-1	.333	3	6	1	2	0	0	0	0	0	1	0
Rickey Henderson, of	.364	3	11	0	4	2	1	0	1	1	2	2
Cliff Johnson, dh	.000	2	6	0	0	0	0	0	0	2	2	0
Jeff Jones, p	.000	1	0	0	0	0	0	0	0	0	0	0
Matt Keough, p	.000	1	0	0	0	0	0	0	0	0	0	0
Brian Kingman, p	.000	1	0	0	0	0	0	0	0	0	0	0
Mickey Klutts, 3b	.429	3	7	1	3	0	0	0	0	0	1	0
Steve Mc Catty, p	.000	1	0	0	0	0	0	0	0	0	0	0
Dave Mc Kay, 2b	.273	3	11	0	3	0	0	0	1	0	2	0
Kelvin Moore, 1b	.222	3	9	0	2	0	0	0	0	0	1	0
Dwayne Murphy, of	.250	3	8	0	2	1	0	0	1	2	3	0
Jeff Newman, c	.000	2	5	0	0	0	0	0	0	0	2	0
Mike Norris, p	.000	1	0	0	0	0	0	0	0	0	0	0
Bob Owchinko, p	.000	1	0	0	0	0	0	0	0	0	0	0
Rob Picciolo, ss	.200	2	5	1	1	0	0	0	0	0	2	0
Jim Spencer, 1b	.000	2	0	0	0	0	0	0	0	0	0	0
Fred Stanley, ss	.333	2	3	0	1	0	0	0	0	1	0	1
Tom Underwood, p	.000	2	0	0	0	0	0	0	0	0	0	0
TOTAL	.222		99	4	22	4	1	0	4	6	23	2

PITCHER	W	L	ERA	G	GS	CG	SV	SHO	IP	H	ER	BB	SO
Dave Beard	0	0	40.50	1	0	0	0	0	0.2	5	3	0	0
Jeff Jones	0	0	4.50	1	0	0	0	0	2.0	2	1	1	0
Matt Keough	0	1	1.08	1	1	0	0	0	8.1	7	1	6	2
Brian Kingman	0	0	81.00	1	0	0	0	0	0.1	3	3	0	0
Steve Mc Catty	0	1	13.50	1	1	0	0	0	3.1	6	5	2	2
Mike Norris	0	1	3.68	1	1	0	0	0	7.1	6	3	2	4
Bob Owchinko	0	0	5.40	1	0	0	0	0	1.2	3	1	0	0
Tom Underwood	0	0	13.50	2	0	0	0	0	1.1	4	2	2	2
TOTAL	0	3	6.84	8	3	0	0	0	25.0	36	19	13	10

GAME 1 AT NY OCT 13

OAK	000	010	000	1	6	1
NY	300	000	00X	3	7	1

Pitchers: NORRIS, Underwood (8) vs JOHN, Davis (7), Gossage (8)
Attendance: 55,740

GAME 2 AT NY OCT 14

OAK	001	200	000	3	11	1
NY	100	701	40X	13	19	0

Pitchers: McCATTY, Beard (4), Jones (5), Kingman (7), Owchinko (7) vs May, FRAZIER (4)
Home Runs: Piniella-NY, Nettles-NY
Attendance: 48,497

GAME 3 AT OAK OCT 15

NY	000	001	003	4	10	0
OAK	000	000	000	0	5	2

Pitchers: RIGHETTI, Davis (7), Gossage (9) vs KEOUGH, Underwood (9)
Home Runs: Randolph-NY
Attendance: 47,302

What the Yankees had done to the Dodgers three years earlier, the Dodgers now did to the Yankees in this, their eleventh meeting in the Series: they took the crown with four straight wins after losing the first two games. In the opener Bob Watson's first-inning three-run homer gave New York an insurmountable lead. Yankee starter Ron Guidry pitched seven strong innings, yielding just one run on a Steve Yeager homer, but two eighth-inning Dodger runs charged to reliever Ron Davis madethings exciting until Yankee third baseman Graig Nettles dampened the rally with a splendid diving catch of Steve Garvey's line drive. In Game Two, Tommy John (now a Yankee) shut out his old teammates on three hits in seven innings. Reliever Goose Gossage completed the shutout, earning his second save in two days in the 3–0 Yankee victory.

But as the Series moved to Los Angeles, the Dodgers took the upper hand. Rookie ace Fernando Valenzuela experienced rocky going in the early innings of Game Three, yielding six hits (including home runs to Bob Watson and Rick Cerone) and four runs in the second and third innings. But Ron Cey's first-inning home run had given Los Angeles three early runs, and Dodger hitters added two more in the fifth as Valenzuela settled down to blank New York on three hits over the final six innings. The next day the Dodgers evened the Series with another close win. New York scored four times before the Dodgers got their first runs, but L.A. tied the game at 6–6 in the sixth and took an 8–6 lead an inning later. Reggie Jackson homered in the eighth to bring New York within one run of a tie, but they came no closer.

In Game Five, for the third day in a row, the Dodgers ovecame a Yankee lead to claim a one-run victory. Dodger pitcher Jerry Reuss gave the Yankees a run on two hits in the second inning, but shut them out on just three additional hits the rest of the way. Yankee starter Ron Guidry, meanwhile, stopped the Dodgers on two hits through the first six innings, but then gave up back-to-back homers to Pedro Guerrero and Steve Yeager in the seventh—runs enough for a 2–1 Dodger win. The final game was close for four innings, but in the fifth and sixth the Dodgers broke it open with seven runs and coasted in on Steve Howe's 3⅔ innings of shutout relief to a 9–2 win and, including 1900, their sixth world championship.

Los Angeles Dodgers (NL), 4; New York Yankees (AL), 2

LA (N)

PLAYER/POS	AVG	G	AB	R	H	2B	3B	HR	RB	BB	SO	SB
Dusty Baker, of	.167	6	24	3	4	0	0	0	1	1	6	0
Bobby Castillo, p	.000	1	0	0	0	0	0	0	0	0	0	0
Ron Cey, 3b	.350	6	20	3	7	0	0	1	6	3	3	0
Terry Forster, p	.000	2	0	0	0	0	0	0	0	0	0	0
Steve Garvey, 1b	.417	6	24	3	10	1	0	0	0	2	5	0
Dave Goltz, p	.000	2	0	0	0	0	0	0	0	0	0	0
Pedro Guerrero, of	.333	6	21	2	7	1	1	2	7	2	6	0
Burt Hooton, p	.000	2	4	1	0	0	0	0	0	1	3	0
Steve Howe, p	.000	3	2	0	0	0	0	0	0	0	2	0
Jay Johnstone, ph	.667	3	3	1	2	0	0	1	3	0	0	0
Ken Landreaux, of-3	.167	5	6	1	1	1	0	0	0	0	2	1
Davey Lopes, 2b	.227	6	22	6	5	1	0	0	2	4	3	4
Rick Monday, of-4	.231	5	13	1	3	1	0	0	0	3	6	0
Tom Niedenfuer, p	.000	2	0	0	0	0	0	0	0	0	0	0
Jerry Reuss, p	.000	2	3	0	0	0	0	0	0	0	1	2	0
Bill Russell, ss	.240	6	25	1	6	0	0	0	2	0	1	1
Steve Sax, 2b-1	.000	2	1	0	0	0	0	0	0	0	0	0
Mike Scioscia, c	.250	3	4	1	1	0	0	0	0	1	0	0
Reggie Smith, ph	.500	2	2	0	1	0	0	0	0	0	1	0
Dave Stewart, p	.000	2	0	0	0	0	0	0	0	0	0	0
Derrel Thomas, of-3,3b-2,ss-1	.000	5	7	2	0	0	0	0	1	1	2	0
Fernando Valenzuela, p	.000	1	3	0	0	0	0	0	0	0	1	0
Bob Welch, p	.000	1	0	0	0	0	0	0	0	0	0	0
Steve Yeager, c	.286	6	14	2	4	1	0	2	4	0	2	0
TOTAL	.258		198	27	51	6	1	6	26	20	44	6

PITCHER	W	L	ERA	G	GS	CG	SV	SHO	IP	H	ER	BB	SO
Bobby Castillo	0	0	9.00	1	0	0	0	0	1.0	0	1	5	0
Terry Forster	0	0	0.00	2	0	0	0	0	2.0	1	0	3	0
Dave Goltz	0	0	5.40	2	0	0	0	0	3.1	4	2	1	2
Burt Hooton	1	1	1.59	2	2	0	0	0	11.1	8	2	9	3
Steve Howe	1	0	3.86	3	0	0	1	0	7.0	7	3	1	4
Tom Niedenfuer	0	0	0.00	2	0	0	0	0	5.0	3	0	1	0
Jerry Reuss	1	1	3.86	2	2	1	0	0	11.2	10	5	3	8
Dave Stewart	0	0	0.00	2	0	0	0	0	1.2	1	0	2	1
Fernando Valenzuela	1	0	4.00	1	1	1	0	0	9.0	9	4	7	6
Bob Welch	0	0	INF	1	1	0	0	0	0.0	3	2	1	0
TOTAL	4	2	3.29	18	6	2	1	0	52.0	46	19	33	24

NY (A)

PLAYER/POS	AVG	G	AB	R	H	2B	3B	HR	RB	BB	SO	SB
Bobby Brown, of-2	.000	4	1	1	0	0	0	0	0	0	1	0
Rick Cerone, c	.190	6	21	2	4	1	0	1	3	4	2	0
Ron Davis, p	.000	4	0	0	0	0	0	0	0	0	0	0
Barry Foote, ph	.000	1	1	0	0	0	0	0	0	0	1	0
George Frazier, p	.000	3	2	0	0	0	0	0	0	0	1	0
Oscar Gamble, of-2	.333	3	6	1	2	0	0	0	1	1	0	0
Rich Gossage, p	.000	3	1	0	0	0	0	0	0	0	1	0
Ron Guidry, p	.000	2	5	0	0	0	0	0	0	0	3	0
Reggie Jackson, of	.333	3	12	3	4	1	0	1	1	2	3	0
Tommy John, p	.000	3	2	0	0	0	0	0	0	0	0	0
Dave La Roche, p	.000	1	0	0	0	0	0	0	0	0	0	0
Rudy May, p	.000	3	1	0	0	0	0	0	0	0	0	0
Larry Milbourne, ss	.250	6	20	2	5	2	0	0	0	3	4	0
Jerry Mumphrey, of	.200	5	15	2	3	0	0	0	0	3	2	1
Bobby Murcer, ph	.000	4	3	0	0	0	0	0	0	0	0	0
Graig Nettles, 3b	.400	3	10	1	4	1	0	0	0	1	1	0
Lou Piniella, of-3	.438	6	16	2	7	1	0	0	3	0	1	1
Willie Randolph, 2b	.222	6	18	5	4	1	1	2	3	9	0	1
Rick Reuschel, p	.000	2	2	0	0	0	0	0	0	0	1	0
Dave Righetti, p	.000	1	1	0	0	0	0	0	0	0	0	0
Andre Robertson, pr	.000	1	0	0	0	0	0	0	0	0	0	0
Aurelio Rodriguez, 3b-3	.417	4	12	1	5	0	0	0	0	1	2	0
Bob Watson, 1b	.318	6	22	2	7	1	0	2	7	3	0	0
Dave Winfield, of	.045	6	22	0	1	0	0	0	1	5	4	1
TOTAL	.238		193	22	46	8	1	6	22	33	24	4

PITCHER	W	L	ERA	G	GS	CG	SV	SHO	IP	H	ER	BB	SO
Ron Davis	0	0	23.14	4	0	0	0	0	2.1	4	6	5	4
George Frazier	0	3	17.18	3	0	0	0	0	3.2	9	7	3	2
Rich Gossage	0	0	0.00	3	0	0	2	0	5.0	2	0	2	5
Ron Guidry	1	1	1.93	2	2	0	0	0	14.0	8	3	4	15
Tommy John	1	0	0.69	3	2	0	0	0	13.0	11	1	0	8
Dave La Roche	0	0	0.00	1	0	0	0	0	1.0	0	0	0	2
Rudy May	0	0	2.84	3	0	0	0	0	6.1	5	2	1	5
Rick Reuschel	0	0	4.91	2	1	0	0	0	3.2	7	2	3	2
Dave Righetti	0	0	13.50	1	1	0	0	0	2.0	5	3	2	1
TOTAL	2	4	4.24	22	6	0	2	0	51.0	51	24	20	44

GAME 1 AT NY OCT 20

LA	000	010	020	3	5	0
NY	301	100	00X	5	6	0

Pitchers: REUSS, Castillo (3), Goltz (4), Niedenfuer (5), Stewart (8) vs GUIDRY, Davis (8), Gossage (8)
Home Runs: Watson-NY, Yeager-LA
Attendance: 56,470

GAME 2 AT NY OCT 21

LA	000	000	000	0	4	2
NY	000	010	02X	3	6	1

Pitchers: HOOTON, Forster (7), Howe (8), Stewart (8) vs JOHN, Gossage (8)
Attendance: 56,505

GAME 3 AT LA OCT 23

NY	022	000	000	4	9	0
LA	300	020	00X	5	11	1

Pitchers: Righetti, FRAZIER (3), May (5), Davis (7) vs VALENZUELA
Home Runs: Cey-LA, Watson-NY, Cerone-NY
Attendance: 56,236

GAME 4 AT LA OCT 24

NY	211	002	010	7	13	1
LA	002	013	20X	8	14	2

Pitchers: Reuschel, May (4), Davis (5), FRAZIER (5), John (7) vs Welch, Goltz (4), Forster (4), Niedenfuer (5), HOWE (7)
Home Runs: Johnstone-LA, Randolph-NY, Jackson-NY
Attendance: 56,242

GAME 5 AT LA OCT 25

NY	010	000	000	1	5	0
LA	000	000	20X	2	4	3

Pitchers: GUIDRY, Gossage (8) vs REUSS
Home Runs: Guerrero-LA, Yeager-LA
Attendance: 56,115

GAME 6 AT NY OCT 28

LA	000	134	010	9	13	1
NY	001	001	000	2	7	2

Pitchers: HOOTON, Howe (6) vs John, FRAZIER (5), Davis (6), Reuschel (6), May (7), LaRoche (9)
Home Runs: Guerrero-LA, Randolph-NY
Attendance: 56,513

The official records show Atlanta ahead and threatening only once in a three-game series swept by the Cardinals. But in the original Game One, Phil Niekro held a slim 1–0 Atlanta lead in the fifth inning when rain wiped out the game just before it could become official.

In the first official game, the Braves scored nothing at all as Bob Forsch held them to three hits. Atlanta's Pascual Perez gave up only one run through the first five innings, but the Cardinals exploded for five runs in the sixth to put the game away. Following another rainout, Niekro tried again in Game Two. He gave up a run in the first, but Atlanta came back with three before he yielded a second run in the sixth. Gene Garber, who relieved Niekro, gave up the tying run in the eighth and lost the game in the bottom of the ninth on Ken Oberkfell's RBI liner over the center fielder's head.

Joaquin Andujar shut out the Braves through six innings of Game Three before giving up two runs in the seventh. But by then St. Louis had scored five times. Bruce Sutter retired the last seven Braves in relief of Andujar, and the Cardinals had their pennant.

St. Louis Cardinals (East), 3; Atlanta Braves (West), 0

STL (E)

PLAYER/POS	AVG	G	AB	R	H	2B	3B	HR	RB	BB	SO	SB
Joaquin Andujar, p	.000	1	1	0	0	0	0	0	0	0	1	0
Doug Bair, p	.000	1	0	0	0	0	0	0	0	0	0	0
Steve Braun, ph	.000	1	1	0	0	0	0	0	0	0	0	0
Bob Forsch, p	.667	1	3	1	2	0	0	0	1	0	0	0
David Green, of	1.000	2	1	1	1	0	0	0	0	0	0	0
George Hendrick, of	.308	3	13	2	4	0	0	0	2	1	2	0
Keith Hernandez, 1b	.333	3	12	3	4	0	0	0	1	2	3	0
Tommy Herr, 2b	.231	3	13	1	3	1	0	0	0	1	2	0
Willie Mc Gee, of	.308	3	13	4	4	0	2	1	5	0	5	0
Ken Oberkfell, 3b	.200	3	15	1	3	0	0	0	2	0	0	0
Darrell Porter, c	.556	3	9	3	5	3	0	0	1	5	2	0
Lonnie Smith, of	.273	3	11	1	3	0	0	0	1	0	1	0
Ozzie Smith, ss	.556	3	9	0	5	0	0	0	3	3	0	1
John Stuper, p	.000	1	1	0	0	0	0	0	0	0	0	0
Bruce Sutter, p	.000	2	1	0	0	0	0	0	0	0	0	0
TOTAL	.330		103	17	34	4	2	1	16	12	16	1

PITCHER	W	L	ERA	G	GS	CG	SV	SHO	IP	H	ER	BB	SO
Joaquin Andujar	1	0	2.70	1	1	0	0	0	6.2	6	2	2	4
Doug Bair	0	0	0.00	1	0	0	0	0	1.0	2	0	3	0
Bob Forsch	1	0	0.00	1	1	1	0	1	9.0	3	0	0	6
John Stuper	0	0	3.00	1	1	0	0	0	6.0	4	2	1	4
Bruce Sutter	1	0	0.00	2	0	0	1	0	4.1	0	0	0	1
TOTAL	3	0	1.33	6	3	1	1	1	27.0	15	4	6	15

ATL (W)

PLAYER/POS	AVG	G	AB	R	H	2B	3B	HR	RB	BB	SO	SB
Steve Bedrosian, p	.000	2	0	0	0	0	0	0	0	0	0	0
Bruce Benedict, c	.250	3	8	1	2	1	0	0	0	2	1	0
Brett Butler, of-1	.000	2	1	0	0	0	0	0	0	0	0	0
Rick Camp, p	.000	1	0	0	0	0	0	0	0	0	0	0
Chris Chambliss, 1b	.000	3	10	0	0	0	0	0	0	1	0	0
Gene Garber, p	.000	2	1	0	0	0	0	0	0	0	0	0
Terry Harper, of	.000	1	1	1	0	0	0	0	0	0	0	0
Bob Horner, 3b	.091	3	11	0	1	0	0	0	0	0	2	0
Glenn Hubbard, 2b	.222	3	9	1	2	0	0	0	1	0	3	0
Rick Mahler, p	.000	1	0	0	0	0	0	0	0	0	0	0
Donnie Moore, p	.000	2	0	0	0	0	0	0	0	0	0	0
Dale Murphy, of	.273	3	11	1	3	0	0	0	0	0	2	1
Phil Niekro, p	.000	1	0	0	0	0	0	0	1	0	0	0
Pascual Perez, p	.000	2	3	0	0	0	0	0	0	0	1	0
Biff Pocoroba, ph	.000	1	1	0	0	0	0	0	0	0	0	0
Rafael Ramirez, ss	.182	3	11	1	2	0	0	0	1	1	1	0
Jerry Royster, of-3,3b-1	.182	3	11	0	2	0	0	0	0	0	2	0
Bob Walk, p	.000	1	0	0	0	0	0	0	0	0	0	0
Claudell Washington, of	.333	3	9	0	3	0	0	0	0	2	2	0
Larry Whisenton, ph	.000	2	2	0	0	0	0	0	0	0	1	0
TOTAL	.169		89	5	15	1	0	0	3	6	15	1

PITCHER	W	L	ERA	G	GS	CG	SV	SHO	IP	H	ER	BB	SO
Steve Bedrosian	0	0	18.00	2	0	0	0	0	1.0	3	2	1	2
Rick Camp	0	1	36.00	1	1	0	0	0	1.0	4	4	1	0
Gene Garber	0	1	8.10	2	0	0	0	0	3.1	4	3	1	3
Rick Mahler	0	0	0.00	1	0	0	0	0	1.2	3	0	2	0
Donnie Moore	0	0	0.00	2	0	0	0	0	2.2	2	0	0	1
Phil Niekro	0	0	3.00	1	1	0	0	0	6.0	6	2	4	5
Pascual Perez	0	1	5.19	2	1	0	0	0	8.2	10	5	2	4
Bob Walk	0	0	9.00	1	0	0	0	0	1.0	2	1	1	1
TOTAL	0	3	6.04	12	3	0	0	0	25.1	34	17	12	16

GAME 1 AT STL OCT 7

ATL	000	000	000		0	3	0
STL	001	005	01X		7	13	1

Pitchers: PEREZ, Bedrosian (6), Moore (6), Walk (8) vs FORSCH
Attendance: 53,008

GAME 2 AT STL OCT 9

ATL	002	010	000		3	6	0
STL	100	000	001		4	9	1

Pitchers: Niekro, GARBER (7) vs Stuper, Bair (7), SUTTER (8)
Attendance: 53,408

GAME 3 AT ATL OCT 10

STL	040	010	001		6	12	0
ATL	000	000	200		2	6	1

Pitchers: ANDUJAR, Sutter (7) vs CAMP, Perez (2), Moore (5), Mahler (7), Bedrosian (8), Garber (9)
Home Runs: McGee-STL
Attendance: 52,173

For the first time in LCS play, a club won the first two games but lost the series. The Angels overcame a 1–3 deficit to take Game One, with four runs in the third and three more later, while starter Tommy John settled down to stop the Brewers through the final six innings. In Game Two Bruce Kison prevailed, as the Angels built a 4–0 lead over Milwaukee and Pete Vuckovich before Kison gave up what proved to be a harmless two-run homer to Paul Molitor in the fifth.

With three chances to clinch the pennant, California three times fell short. In the third game, their three eighth-inning runs couldn't catch the Brewers, who already had five. In Game Four, Don Baylor's eighth-inning grand slam completed Angel scoring at five runs, but Milwaukee had already scored seven, and they added two more. In the finale, Kison held a 3–2 lead when he was relieved after five innings. But Cecil Cooper singled off Luis Sanchez in the seventh (with two out and the bases loaded) for two runs and a Brewer lead. Bob McClure and Pete Ladd held off the Angels through the final two innings, and the Brewers were on their way to their first World Series.

Milwaukee Brewers (East), 3; California Angels (West), 2

MIL (E)

PLAYER/POS	AVG	G	AB	R	H	2B	3B	HR	RB	BB	SO	SB
Dwight Bernard, p	.000	1	0	0	0	0	0	0	0	0	0	0
Mark Brouhard, of	.750	1	4	4	3	1	0	1	3	0	0	0
Mike Caldwell, p	.000	1	0	0	0	0	0	0	0	0	0	0
Cecil Cooper, 1b	.150	5	20	1	3	2	0	0	4	0	6	0
Marshall Edwards, dh-2,of-1	.000	3	1	2	0	0	0	0	0	0	0	1
Jim Gantner, 2b	.188	5	16	1	3	0	0	0	2	1	1	0
Moose Haas, p	.000	1	0	0	0	0	0	0	0	0	0	0
Roy Howell, dh	.000	1	3	0	0	0	0	0	0	0	1	0
Pete Ladd, p	.000	3	0	0	0	0	0	0	0	0	0	0
Bob Mc Clure, p	.000	1	0	0	0	0	0	0	0	0	0	0
Paul Molitor, 3b	.316	5	19	4	6	1	0	2	5	2	3	1
Don Money, dh	.182	4	11	2	2	0	0	0	1	3	1	0
Charlie Moore, of	.462	5	13	3	6	0	0	0	0	1	2	0
Ben Oglivie, of	.133	4	15	1	2	0	0	1	1	0	3	0
Ted Simmons, c	.167	5	18	3	3	0	0	0	1	1	4	0
Jim Slaton, p	.000	2	0	0	0	0	0	0	0	0	0	0
Don Sutton, p	.000	1	0	0	0	0	0	0	0	0	0	0
Gorman Thomas, of	.067	5	15	1	1	0	0	1	3	2	7	0
Pete Vuckovich, p	.000	2	0	0	0	0	0	0	0	0	0	0
Robin Yount, ss	.250	5	16	1	4	0	0	0	0	5	0	0
TOTAL	.219		151	23	33	4	0	5	20	15	28	2

PITCHER	W	L	ERA	G	GS	CG	SV	SHO	IP	H	ER	BB	SO
Dwight Bernard	0	0	0.00	1	0	0	0	0	1.0	0	0	0	0
Mike Caldwell	0	1	15.00	1	1	0	0	0	3.0	7	5	1	2
Moose Haas	1	0	4.91	1	1	0	0	0	7.1	5	4	5	7
Pete Ladd	0	0	0.00	3	0	0	2	0	3.1	0	0	0	5
Bob Mc Clure	1	0	0.00	1	0	0	0	0	1.2	2	0	0	0
Jim Slaton	0	0	1.93	2	0	0	1	0	4.2	3	1	1	3
Don Sutton	1	0	3.52	1	1	0	0	0	7.2	8	3	2	9
Pete Vuckovich	0	1	4.40	2	2	1	0	0	14.1	15	7	7	8
TOTAL	3	2	4.19	12	5	1	3	0	43.0	40	20	16	34

CAL (W)

PLAYER/POS	AVG	G	AB	R	H	2B	3B	HR	RB	BB	SO	SB
Don Baylor, dh	.294	5	17	2	5	1	1	1	10	2	0	0
Juan Beniquez, of	.000	2	0	0	0	0	0	0	0	0	0	0
Bob Boone, c	.250	5	16	3	4	0	0	1	4	0	2	0
Rod Carew, 1b	.176	5	17	2	3	1	0	0	0	4	4	1
Bobby Clark, of	.000	2	0	0	0	0	0	0	0	0	0	0
Doug De Cinces, 3b	.316	5	19	5	6	2	0	0	0	1	5	0
Brian Downing, of	.158	5	19	4	3	1	0	0	0	3	2	0
Tim Foli, ss	.125	5	16	0	2	0	0	0	1	0	3	0
Dave Goltz, p	.000	1	0	0	0	0	0	0	0	0	0	0
Bobby Grich, 2b	.200	5	15	1	3	1	0	0	1	2	7	0
Andy Hassler, p	.000	2	0	0	0	0	0	0	0	0	0	0
Reggie Jackson, of	.111	5	18	2	2	0	0	1	2	2	7	0
Ron Jackson, ph	1.000	1	1	0	1	0	0	0	0	0	0	0
Tommy John, p	.000	2	0	0	0	0	0	0	0	0	0	0
Bruce Kison, p	.000	2	0	0	0	0	0	0	0	0	0	0
Fred Lynn, of	.611	5	18	4	11	2	0	1	5	2	3	0
Luis Sanchez, p	.000	2	0	0	0	0	0	0	0	0	0	0
Rob Wilfong, ph	.000	2	1	0	0	0	0	0	0	0	1	0
Mike Witt, p	.000	1	0	0	0	0	0	0	0	0	0	0
Geoff Zahn, p	.000	1	0	0	0	0	0	0	0	0	0	0
TOTAL	.255		157	23	40	8	1	4	23	16	34	1

PITCHER	W	L	ERA	G	GS	CG	SV	SHO	IP	H	ER	BB	SO
Dave Goltz	0	0	7.36	1	0	0	0	0	3.2	4	3	2	2
Andy Hassler	0	0	0.00	2	0	0	0	0	2.2	0	0	0	2
Tommy John	1	1	5.11	2	2	1	0	0	12.1	11	7	6	6
Bruce Kison	1	0	1.93	2	2	1	0	0	14.0	8	3	3	12
Luis Sanchez	0	1	6.75	2	0	0	0	0	2.2	4	2	1	1
Mike Witt	0	0	6.00	1	0	0	0	0	3.0	2	2	2	3
Geoff Zahn	0	1	7.36	1	1	0	0	0	3.2	4	3	1	2
TOTAL	2	3	4.29	11	5	2	0	0	42.0	33	20	15	28

GAME 1 AT CAL OCT 5

MIL	021	000	000	3	7	2
CAL	104	210	00X	8	10	0

Pitchers: CALDWELL, Slaton (4), Ladd (7), Bernard (8) vs JOHN
Home Runs: Thomas-MIL, Lynn-CAL
Attendance: 64,406

GAME 2 AT CAL OCT 6

MIL	000	020	000	2	5	0
CAL	021	100	00X	4	6	0

Pitchers: VUCKOVICH vs KISON
Home Runs: Re.Jackson-CAL, Molitor-MIL
Attendance: 64,179

GAME 3 AT MIL OCT 8

CAL	000	000	030	3	8	0
MIL	000	300	20X	5	6	0

Pitchers: ZAHN, Witt (4), Hassler (7) vs SUTTON, Ladd (8)
Home Runs: Molitor-MIL, Boone-CAL
Attendance: 50,135

GAME 4 AT MIL OCT 9

CAL	000	001	040	5	5	3
MIL	030	300	02X	9	9	2

Pitchers: JOHN, Goltz (4), Sanchez (8) vs HAAS, Slaton (8)
Home Runs: Baylor-CAL, Brouhard-MIL
Attendance: 51,003

GAME 5 AT MIL OCT 10

CAL	101	100	000	3	11	1
MIL	100	100	20X	4	6	4

Pitchers: Kison, SANCHEZ (6), Hassler (7) vs Vuckovich, McCLURE (7), Ladd (9)
Home Runs: Oglivie-MIL
Attendance: 54,968

The Series was anticipated as a matchup of Cardinal speed and Brewer power. In the event, though, St. Louis outslugged the Brewers and wound up with their tenth world championship.

The Brewers, in their first World Series, looked unstoppable in the opening game. Hammering four Cardinal pitchers for seventeen hits (including a record five for Paul Molitor), they scored ten runs while pitcher Mike Caldwell was shutting out the Cards on three hits. In the second game Milwaukee continued the onslaught, building an early 3–0 lead. But St. Louis finally got on the scoreboard with two runs in the last of the third, and tied the game at 4–4 in the sixth on Darrell Porter's two-RBI double. And the Cards won the game on a bases-loaded walk in the eighth as relievers Doug Bair and Bruce Sutter held the Brewers scoreless over the final four innings.

St. Louis pushed into the Series lead in Game Three, thanks mostly to the 6⅓ shutout innings of starter Joaquin Andujar and the fielding and batting of center fielder Willie McGee. McGee drove in four of the six Cardinal runs with a pair of homers and prevented an extra-base hit and a two-run Brewer homer with leaping catches in the first and final innings. The Cards pressed their advantage in Game Four with four early runs. But in the last of the seventh (with the score now 5–1), an error by Cardinal pitcher Dave La Point opened the way for Milwaukee to win the game with six two-out runs on a barrage of hits (and the added assistance of a pair of walks and a wild pitch).

Brewer pitcher Mike Caldwell wasn't as effective in Game Five as he had been in the opener, yielding fourteen hits and four runs in 8⅓ innings of work. But he was never behind in the game as his teammates, with eleven hits of their own (four of them by Robin Yount, including a home run) and several fielding gems put Milwaukee ahead again in the Series with a 6–4 win.

The Cards had their backs to the wall as the Series moved to St. Louis for the final games. But in Game Six the Cards responded to their opening-game humiliation with a laugher of their own, 13–1, on John Stuper's four-hitter. And in the finale they rocked Brewer ace Pete Vuckovich and three relievers for fifteen hits and a 6–3 victory that gave starter Joaquin Andujar his second Series win and reliever Bruce Sutter his second save.

St. Louis Cardinals (NL), 4; Milwaukee Brewers (AL), 3

STL (N)

PLAYER/POS	AVG	G	AB	R	H	2B	3B	HR	RB	BB	SO	SB
Joaquin Andujar, p	.000	2	0	0	0	0	0	0	0	0	0	0
Doug Bair, p	.000	3	0	0	0	0	0	0	0	0	0	0
Steve Braun, dh	.500	2	2	0	1	0	0	0	2	1	0	0
Glenn Brummer, c	.000	1	0	0	0	0	0	0	0	0	0	0
Bob Forsch, p	.000	2	0	0	0	0	0	0	0	0	0	0
David Green, of-4,dh-3	.200	7	10	3	2	1	1	0	0	1	3	0
George Hendrick, of	.321	7	28	5	9	0	0	0	5	2	2	0
Keith Hernandez, 1b	.259	7	27	4	7	2	0	1	8	4	2	0
Tommy Herr, 2b	.160	7	25	2	4	2	0	0	5	3	3	0
Dane Iorg, dh	.529	5	17	4	9	4	1	0	1	0	0	0
Jim Kaat, p	.000	4	0	0	0	0	0	0	0	0	0	0
Jeff Lahti, p	.000	2	0	0	0	0	0	0	0	0	0	0
Dave La Point, p	.000	2	0	0	0	0	0	0	0	0	0	0
Willie Mc Gee, of	.240	6	25	6	6	0	0	2	5	1	3	2
Ken Oberkfell, 3b	.292	7	24	4	7	1	0	0	1	2	1	2
Darrell Porter, c	.286	7	28	1	8	2	0	1	5	1	4	0
Mike Ramsey, 3b-2	.000	3	1	1	0	0	0	0	0	0	1	0
Lonnie Smith, of-6,dh-1	.321	7	28	6	9	4	1	0	1	1	5	2
Ozzie Smith, ss	.208	7	24	3	5	0	0	0	1	3	0	1
John Stuper, p	.000	2	0	0	0	0	0	0	0	0	0	0
Bruce Sutter, p	.000	4	0	0	0	0	0	0	0	0	0	0
Gene Tenace, dh-1	.000	5	6	0	0	0	0	0	0	1	2	0
TOTAL	.273		245	39	67	16	3	4	34	20	26	7

PITCHER	W	L	ERA	G	GS	CG	SV	SHO	IP	H	ER	BB	SO
Joaquin Andujar	2	0	1.35	2	2	0	0	0	13.1	10	2	1	4
Doug Bair	0	1	9.00	3	0	0	0	0	2.0	2	2	2	3
Bob Forsch	0	2	4.97	2	2	0	0	0	12.2	18	7	3	4
Jim Kaat	0	0	3.86	4	0	0	0	0	2.1	4	1	2	2
Jeff Lahti	0	0	10.80	2	0	0	0	0	1.2	4	2	1	1
Dave La Point	0	0	3.24	2	1	0	0	0	8.1	10	3	2	3
John Stuper	1	0	3.46	2	2	1	0	0	13.0	10	5	5	6
Bruce Sutter	1	0	4.70	4	0	0	2	0	7.2	6	4	3	6
TOTAL	4	3	3.84	21	7	1	2	0	61.0	64	26	19	28

MIL (A)

PLAYER/POS	AVG	G	AB	R	H	2B	3B	HR	RB	BB	SO	SB
Dwight Bernard, p	.000	1	0	0	0	0	0	0	0	0	0	0
Mike Caldwell, p	.000	3	0	0	0	0	0	0	0	0	0	0
Cecil Cooper, 1b	.286	7	28	3	8	1	0	1	6	1	1	0
Marshall Edwards, of	.000	1	0	0	0	0	0	0	0	0	0	0
Jim Gantner, 2b	.333	7	24	5	8	4	1	0	4	1	1	0
Moose Haas, p	.000	2	0	0	0	0	0	0	0	0	0	0
Roy Howell, dh	.000	4	11	1	0	0	0	0	0	0	3	0
Pete Ladd, p	.000	1	0	0	0	0	0	0	0	0	0	0
Bob Mc Clure, p	.000	5	0	0	0	0	0	0	0	0	0	0
Doc Medich, p	.000	1	0	0	0	0	0	0	0	0	0	0
Paul Molitor, 3b	.355	7	31	5	11	0	0	0	3	2	4	1
Don Money, dh-4	.231	5	13	4	3	1	0	0	1	2	3	0
Charlie Moore, of	.346	7	26	3	9	3	0	0	2	1	0	0
Ben Oglivie, of	.222	7	27	4	6	0	1	1	2	4	0	0
Ted Simmons, c	.174	7	23	2	4	0	0	2	3	5	3	0
Jim Slaton, p	.000	2	0	0	0	0	0	0	0	0	0	0
Don Sutton, p	.000	2	0	0	0	0	0	0	0	0	0	0
Gorman Thomas, of	.115	7	26	0	3	0	0	0	3	2	7	0
Pete Vuckovich, p	.000	2	0	0	0	0	0	0	0	0	0	0
Ned Yost, c	.000	1	0	0	0	0	0	0	1	0	0	0
Robin Yount, ss	.414	7	29	6	12	3	0	1	6	2	2	0
TOTAL	.269		238	33	64	12	2	5	29	19	28	1

PITCHER	W	L	ERA	G	GS	CG	SV	SHO	IP	H	ER	BB	SO
Dwight Bernard	0	0	0.00	1	0	0	0	0	1.0	0	0	0	1
Mike Caldwell	2	0	2.04	3	2	1	0	1	17.2	19	4	3	6
Moose Haas	0	0	7.36	2	1	0	0	0	7.1	8	6	3	4
Pete Ladd	0	0	0.00	1	0	0	0	0	0.2	1	0	2	0
Bob Mc Clure	0	2	4.15	5	0	0	2	0	4.1	5	2	3	5
Doc Medich	0	0	18.00	1	0	0	0	0	2.0	5	4	1	0
Jim Slaton	1	0	4.05	2	0	0	0	0	2.2	1	0	2	1
Don Sutton	0	1	7.84	2	2	0	0	0	10.1	12	9	1	5
Pete Vuckovich	0	1	4.50	2	2	0	0	0	14.0	16	7	5	4
TOTAL	3	4	4.80	19	7	1	2	1	60.0	67	32	20	26

The Dodgers earned only four runs off Philadelphia pitching, and even though they doubled their run total to eight on unearned runs, the Phillies scored twice that number to take the pennant in four games.

Mike Schmidt homered off Jerry Reuss in the first inning of the opener for the game's only run. Phillie starter Steve Carlton loaded the bases in the eighth, but Al Holland came on to get the third out and preserve the shutout. The Phillies also scored only one run in the second game, on Gary Matthews's homer off Fernando Valenzuela in the second. But this time the run only tied the score, and in the fifth Pedro Guerrero tripled in two unearned runs to give Valenzuela the Dodgers' only win.

The Phillies' Charlie Hudson hurled the series' only complete game—a four-hitter—to win Game Three. Gary Matthews's four hits in Game Three and Four included his second and third series homers, and drove in half the Phillies' fourteen runs as they took the two games by identical 7–2 scores.

Philadelphia Phillies (East), 3; Los Angeles Dodgers (West), 1

PHI (E)

PLAYER/POS	AVG	G	AB	R	H	2B	3B	HR	RB	BB	SO	SB
Steve Carlton, p	.200	2	5	0	1	0	0	0	0	0	3	0
Ivan De Jesus, ss	.250	4	12	0	3	0	0	0	1	3	3	0
John Denny, p	.000	1	1	0	0	0	0	0	0	0	0	0
Bob Dernier, of	.000	1	0	0	0	0	0	0	0	0	0	0
Bo Diaz, c	.154	4	13	0	2	1	0	0	0	2	1	0
Greg Gross, of-3	.000	4	5	1	0	0	0	0	0	2	2	0
Von Hayes, of-1	.000	2	2	0	0	0	0	0	0	0	0	0
Al Holland, p	.000	2	0	0	0	0	0	0	0	0	0	0
Charles Hudson, p	.000	1	4	0	0	0	0	0	0	0	3	0
Joe Lefebvre, pr	.000	2	2	0	0	0	0	0	1	0	1	0
Sixto Lezcano, of	.308	4	13	2	4	0	0	1	2	1	1	0
Garry Maddox, of	.273	3	11	0	3	1	0	0	1	0	1	0
Gary Matthews, of	.429	4	14	4	6	0	0	3	8	2	1	1
Joe Morgan, 2b	.067	4	15	1	1	0	0	0	0	2	1	0
Tony Perez, ph	1.000	1	1	0	1	0	0	0	0	0	0	0
Ron Reed, p	.000	2	0	0	0	0	0	0	0	0	0	0
Pete Rose, 1b	.375	4	16	3	6	0	0	0	0	1	1	1
Juan Samuel, pr	.000	1	0	0	0	0	0	0	0	0	0	0
Mike Schmidt, 3b	.467	4	15	5	7	2	0	1	2	2	3	0
Ossie Virgil, ph	.000	1	1	0	0	0	0	0	0	0	1	0
TOTAL	.262		130	16	34	4	0	5	15	15	22	2

PITCHER	W	L	ERA	G	GS	CG	SV	SHO	IP	H	ER	BB	SO
Steve Carlton	2	0	0.66	2	2	0	0	0	13.2	13	1	5	13
John Denny	0	1	0.00	1	1	0	0	0	6.0	5	0	3	3
Al Holland	0	0	0.00	2	0	0	1	0	3.0	1	0	0	3
Charles Hudson	1	0	2.00	1	1	1	0	0	9.0	4	2	2	9
Ron Reed	0	0	2.70	2	0	0	0	0	3.1	4	1	1	3
TOTAL	3	1	1.03	8	4	1	1	0	35.0	27	4	11	31

LA (W)

PLAYER/POS	AVG	G	AB	R	H	2B	3B	HR	RB	BB	SO	SB
Dusty Baker, of	.357	4	14	4	5	1	0	1	1	2	0	0
Joe Beckwith, p	.000	2	0	0	0	0	0	0	0	0	0	0
Greg Brock, 1b	.000	3	9	1	0	0	0	0	0	0	3	0
Jack Fimple, c	.143	3	7	0	1	0	0	0	1	0	3	0
Pedro Guerrero, 3b	.250	4	12	1	3	1	1	0	2	3	3	0
Rick Honeycutt, p	.000	2	0	0	0	0	0	0	0	0	0	0
Rafael Landestoy, ph	.000	2	2	0	0	0	0	0	0	0	1	0
Ken Landreaux, of	.143	4	14	0	2	0	0	0	1	1	3	0
Candy Maldonado, ph	.000	2	2	0	0	0	0	0	0	0	1	0
Mike Marshall, 1b-3,of-2	.133	4	15	1	2	1	0	1	2	1	6	0
Rick Monday, ph	.000	1	0	0	0	0	0	0	0	0	0	0
Jose Morales, ph	.000	2	2	0	0	0	0	0	0	0	1	0
Tom Niedenfuer, p	.000	2	0	0	0	0	0	0	0	0	0	0
Alejandro Pena, p	1.000	1	1	0	1	0	0	0	0	0	0	0
Jerry Reuss, p	.000	2	3	0	0	0	0	0	0	0	3	0
Bill Russell, ss	.286	4	14	1	4	0	0	0	0	2	4	1
Steve Sax, 2b	.250	4	16	0	4	0	0	0	0	1	0	1
Derrel Thomas, of	.444	4	9	0	4	1	0	0	0	0	3	1
Fernando Valenzuela, p	.000	1	3	0	0	0	0	0	0	1	0	0
Bob Welch, p	.000	1	0	0	0	0	0	0	0	0	0	0
Steve Yeager, c	.167	2	6	0	1	1	0	0	0	0	0	0
Pat Zachry, p	.000	2	0	0	0	0	0	0	0	0	0	0
TOTAL	.209		129	8	27	5	1	2	7	11	31	3

PITCHER	W	L	ERA	G	GS	CG	SV	SHO	IP	H	ER	BB	SO
Joe Beckwith	0	0	0.00	2	0	0	0	0	2.1	1	0	2	3
Rick Honeycutt	0	0	21.60	2	0	0	0	0	1.2	4	4	0	2
Tom Niedenfuer	0	0	0.00	2	0	0	1	0	2.0	0	0	1	3
Alejandro Pena	0	0	6.75	1	0	0	0	0	2.2	4	2	1	3
Jerry Reuss	0	2	4.50	2	2	0	0	0	12.0	14	6	3	4
Fernando Valenzuela	1	0	1.13	1	1	0	0	0	8.0	7	1	4	5
Bob Welch	0	1	6.75	1	1	0	0	0	1.1	0	1	2	0
Pat Zachry	0	0	2.25	2	0	0	0	0	4.0	4	1	2	2
TOTAL	1	3	3.97	13	4	0	1	0	34.0	34	15	15	22

The White Sox and Orioles entered the LCS evenly matched, with similar season's records and stats. But in the LCS, Baltimore all but shut down Chicago's run production. Both teams had 28 hits, but the Sox, held to four for extra bases, found themselves outslugged by 116 percentage points and outscored by 16 runs.

Chicago won the first game, scoring two of their three series runs as LaMarr Hoyt shut Baltimore out for eight innings before letting in a run in the ninth. But the White Sox had concluded their effective scoring. In Game Two, Oriole rookie Mike Boddicker shut them out on five hits, striking out fourteen. In Game Three the Sox scored their final run. The Orioles got only two more hits than Chicago, but blended them with nine walks, a hit batsman, and a Sox error to score eleven runs. In the fourth game, Oriole pitchers Storm Davis and Tippy Martinez saw that ten Chicago hits scored no runs. Britt Burns held Baltimore scoreless, too, through nine innings. But Tito Landrum's solo homer in the top of the tenth drove Burns out, and two more Oriole runs provided more than enough scoring to win Baltimore the flag.

Baltimore Orioles (East), 3; Chicago White Sox (West), 1

BAL (E)

PLAYER/POS	AVG	G	AB	R	H	2B	3B	HR	RB	BB	SO	SB
Benny Ayala, dh	.000	1	0	0	0	0	0	0	0	1	0	0
Mike Boddicker, p	.000	1	0	0	0	0	0	0	0	0	0	0
Al Bumbry, of	.125	3	8	0	1	1	0	0	1	0	2	0
Todd Cruz, 3b	.133	4	15	0	2	0	0	0	1	0	5	0
Rich Dauer, 2b	.000	4	14	0	0	0	0	0	1	0	0	0
Storm Davis, p	.000	1	0	0	0	0	0	0	0	0	0	0
Rick Dempsey, c	.167	4	12	1	2	0	0	0	0	1	1	0
Jim Dwyer, of-1	.250	2	4	1	1	1	0	0	0	1	0	0
Mike Flanagan, p	.000	1	0	0	0	0	0	0	0	0	0	0
Dan Ford, of-1	.200	2	5	0	1	1	0	0	0	0	1	0
Tito Landrum, of-3	.200	4	10	2	2	0	0	1	1	0	2	0
John Lowenstein, of	.167	2	6	0	1	1	0	0	2	1	2	0
Tippy Martinez, p	.000	2	0	0	0	0	0	0	0	0	0	0
Scott Mc Gregor, p	.000	1	0	0	0	0	0	0	0	0	0	0
Eddie Murray, 1b	.267	4	15	5	4	0	0	1	3	3	3	1
Joe Nolan, ph	.000	1	0	0	0	0	0	0	1	0	0	0
Jim Palmer, pr	.000	1	0	0	0	0	0	0	0	0	0	0
Cal Ripken, ss	.400	4	15	5	6	2	0	0	1	2	3	0
Gary Roenicke, of	.750	3	4	4	3	1	0	1	4	5	0	0
John Shelby, of-2	.222	3	9	1	2	0	0	0	0	1	3	1
Ken Singleton, dh	.250	4	12	0	3	2	0	0	1	2	2	0
Sammy Stewart, p	.000	2	0	0	0	0	0	0	0	0	0	0
TOTAL	.217		129	19	28	9	0	3	17	16	24	2

PITCHER	W	L	ERA	G	GS	CG	SV	SHO	IP	H	ER	BB	SO
Mike Boddicker	1	0	0.00	1	1	1	0	1	9.0	5	0	3	14
Storm Davis	0	0	0.00	1	1	0	0	0	6.0	5	0	2	2
Mike Flanagan	1	0	1.80	1	1	0	0	0	5.0	5	1	0	1
Tippy Martinez	1	0	0.00	2	0	0	0	0	6.0	5	0	3	5
Scott Mc Gregor	0	1	1.35	1	1	0	0	0	6.2	6	1	3	2
Sammy Stewart	0	0	0.00	2	0	0	1	0	4.1	2	0	1	2
TOTAL	3	1	0.49	8	4	1	1	1	37.0	28	2	12	26

CHI (W)

PLAYER/POS	AVG	G	AB	R	H	2B	3B	HR	RB	BB	SO	SB
Juan Agosto, p	.000	1	0	0	0	0	0	0	0	0	0	0
Harold Baines, of	.125	4	16	0	2	0	0	0	0	1	3	0
Floyd Bannister, p	.000	1	0	0	0	0	0	0	0	0	0	0
Salome Barojas, p	.000	2	0	0	0	0	0	0	0	0	0	0
Britt Burns, p	.000	1	0	0	0	0	0	0	0	0	0	0
Julio Cruz, 2b	.333	4	12	0	4	0	0	0	0	3	4	2
Richard Dotson, p	.000	1	0	0	0	0	0	0	0	0	0	0
Jerry Dybzinski, ss	.250	2	4	0	1	0	0	0	0	0	0	0
Carlton Fisk, c	.176	4	17	0	3	1	0	0	0	1	3	0
Scott Fletcher, ss	.000	3	7	0	0	0	0	0	0	1	0	0
Jerry Hairston, of	.000	2	3	0	0	0	0	0	0	1	1	0
La Marr Hoyt, p	.000	1	0	0	0	0	0	0	0	0	0	0
Ron Kittle, of	.286	3	7	1	2	1	0	0	0	1	2	0
Jerry Koosman, p	.000	1	0	0	0	0	0	0	0	0	0	0
Dennis Lamp, p	.000	3	0	0	0	0	0	0	0	0	0	0
Rudy Law, of	.389	4	18	1	7	1	0	0	0	0	1	2
Vance Law, 3b	.182	4	11	0	2	0	0	0	1	1	3	0
Greg Luzinski, dh	.133	4	15	0	2	1	0	0	0	1	5	0
Tom Paciorek, 1b-3,of-2	.250	4	16	1	4	0	0	0	1	1	2	0
Aurelio Rodriguez, 3b	.000	2	0	0	0	0	0	0	0	0	0	0
Mike Squires, 1b-3	.000	4	4	0	0	0	0	0	0	0	0	0
Dick Tidrow, p	.000	1	0	0	0	0	0	0	0	0	0	0
Greg Walker, 1b-1	.333	2	3	0	1	0	0	0	0	1	2	0
TOTAL	.211		133	3	28	4	0	0	2	12	26	4

PITCHER	W	L	ERA	G	GS	CG	SV	SHO	IP	H	ER	BB	SO
Juan Agosto	0	0	0.00	1	0	0	0	0	0.1	0	0	0	0
Floyd Bannister	0	1	4.50	1	1	0	0	0	6.0	5	3	1	5
Salome Barojas	0	0	18.00	2	0	0	0	0	1.0	4	2	0	0
Britt Burns	0	1	0.96	1	1	0	0	0	9.1	6	1	5	8
Richard Dotson	0	1	10.80	1	1	0	0	0	5.0	6	6	3	3
La Marr Hoyt	1	0	1.00	1	1	1	0	0	9.0	5	1	0	4
Jerry Koosman	0	0	54.00	1	0	0	0	0	0.1	1	2	2	0
Dennis Lamp	0	0	0.00	3	0	0	0	0	2.0	0	0	2	1
Dick Tidrow	0	0	3.00	1	0	0	0	0	3.0	1	1	3	3
TOTAL	1	3	4.00	12	4	1	0	0	36.0	28	16	16	24

Near neighbors Baltimore and Philadelphia met in a World Series for the first time. Both clubs were led by new managers: Baltimore by Joe Altobelli, who inherited a team built under longtime Oriole manager Earl Weaver; and the Phillies by general manager Paul Owens, who replaced Pat Corrales with himself in mid-season. Both started their top game winners in the opener, and the result was a pitchers' duel, with all three runs scored on solo homers. Phillie John Denny gave up the first home run to Jim Dwyer in the first inning, but after that (with late-inning help from Al Holland) he blanked the Orioles, while Baltimore's Scott McGregor, after 5⅔ scoreless innings gave up home runs to Joe Morgan and (the game-loser two innings later) to Garry Maddox.

The Orioles swept the next four games. In Game Two, Mike Boddicker yielded just three singles (and no walks) to Phillie batters. Though one of the singles led to a run in the fourth inning, giving the Phillies a 1–0 lead, Oriole John Lowenstein tied the score with a home run in the fifth. Three more Oriole hits in the inning and a sacrifice fly made the score 3–1, and three two-out singles in the seventh inning brought in a fourth Baltimore run.

Philadelphia again scored first in Game Three, on leadoff home runs in the second and third innings by Gary Matthews and Joe Morgan. But the Orioles finally got to veteran starter Steve Carlton in the sixth for one run and drove him out after a second run scored an inning later. Carlton suffered the loss when the baserunner he left scored the tie-breaking run from second on an error by shortstop Ivan DeJesus.

The Phillies also lost Game Four by a single run. Baltimore scored first with two runs in the top of the fourth, but Philadelphia recovered with one run in the fourth and two an inning later. They would not lead again in the Series. Baltimore scored twice in the sixth to go ahead again, and once more in the seventh. The Phillies scored once more with two down in the ninth to draw within one run of a tie, but Joe Morgan lined out to second to end the game.

Home runs by Rick Dempsey and Eddie Murray (who hit two) accounted for four of Baltimore's five runs in the final game—more than enough to support Scott McGregor's five-hit shutout pitching.

Baltimore Orioles (AL), 4; Philadelphia Phillies (NL), 1

BAL (A)

PLAYER/POS	AVG	G	AB	R	H	2B	3B	HR	RB	BB	SO	SB
Benny Ayala, ph	1.000	1	1	1	1	0	0	0	1	1	0	0
Mike Boddicker, p	.000	1	3	0	0	0	0	0	0	0	1	0
Al Bumbry, of	.091	4	11	0	1	1	0	0	0	1	0	1
Todd Cruz, 3b	.125	6	16	1	2	0	0	0	0	1	3	0
Rich Dauer, 2b	.211	5	19	2	4	1	0	0	3	0	3	0
Storm Davis, p	.000	1	2	0	0	0	0	0	0	0	2	0
Rick Dempsey, c	.385	5	13	3	5	4	0	1	2	2	2	0
Jim Dwyer, of	.375	2	8	3	3	1	0	1	1	1	0	0
Mike Flanagan, p	.000	1	1	0	0	0	0	0	0	0	1	0
Dan Ford, of-4	.167	5	12	1	2	0	0	1	1	1	5	0
Tito Landrum, of	.000	3	3	0	0	0	0	0	0	0	0	1
John Lowenstein, of	.385	4	13	2	5	1	0	1	1	1	3	0
Tippy Martinez, p	.000	3	0	0	0	0	0	0	0	0	0	0
Scott Mc Gregor, p	.000	2	5	0	0	0	0	0	0	0	0	0
Eddie Murray, 1b	.250	5	20	2	5	0	0	2	3	1	4	0
Joe Nolan, c	.000	2	2	0	0	0	0	0	0	1	0	0
Jim Palmer, p	.000	1	0	0	0	0	0	0	0	0	0	0
Cal Ripken, ss	.167	5	18	2	3	0	0	0	1	3	4	0
Gary Roenicke, of-2	.000	3	7	0	0	0	0	0	0	0	2	0
Len Sakata, 2b	.000	1	1	0	0	0	0	0	0	0	0	0
John Shelby, of	.444	5	9	1	4	0	0	0	1	0	4	0
Ken Singleton, ph	.000	2	1	0	0	0	0	0	0	1	1	0
Sammy Stewart, p	.000	3	2	0	0	0	0	0	0	0	1	0
TOTAL	.213		164	18	35	8	0	6	17	10	37	1

PITCHER	W	L	ERA	G	GS	CG	SV	SHO	IP	H	ER	BB	SO
Mike Boddicker	1	0	0.00	1	1	1	0	0	9.0	3	0	0	6
Storm Davis	1	0	5.40	1	1	0	0	0	5.0	6	3	1	3
Mike Flanagan	0	0	4.50	1	1	0	0	0	4.0	6	2	1	1
Tippy Martinez	0	0	3.00	3	0	0	2	0	3.0	3	1	0	0
Scott Mc Gregor	1	1	1.06	2	2	1	0	1	17.0	9	2	2	12
Jim Palmer	1	0	0.00	1	0	0	0	0	2.0	2	0	1	0
Sammy Stewart	0	0	0.00	3	0	0	0	0	5.0	2	0	2	6
TOTAL	4	1	1.60	12	5	2	2	1	45.0	31	8	7	29

PHI (N)

PLAYER/POS	AVG	G	AB	R	H	2B	3B	HR	RB	BB	SO	SB
Larry Andersen, p	.000	2	0	0	0	0	0	0	0	0	0	0
Marty Bystrom, p	.000	1	0	0	0	0	0	0	0	0	0	0
Steve Carlton, p	.000	1	3	0	0	0	0	0	0	0	1	0
Ivan De Jesus, ss	.125	5	16	0	2	0	0	0	0	1	2	0
John Denny, p	.200	2	5	1	1	0	0	0	0	1	0	0
Bob Dernier, pr	.000	1	0	1	0	0	0	0	0	0	0	0
Bo Diaz, c	.333	5	15	1	5	1	0	0	0	1	2	0
Greg Gross, of	.000	2	6	0	0	0	0	0	0	0	0	0
Von Hayes, of-1	.000	4	3	0	0	0	0	0	0	0	1	0
Willie Hernandez, p	.000	3	0	0	0	0	0	0	0	0	0	0
Al Holland, p	.000	2	0	0	0	0	0	0	0	0	0	0
Charles Hudson, p	.000	2	2	0	0	0	0	0	0	0	0	0
Joe Lefebvre, of-2	.200	3	5	0	1	1	0	0	0	2	0	1
Sixto Lezcano, of-3	.125	4	8	0	1	0	0	0	0	0	2	0
Garry Maddox, of-3	.250	4	12	1	3	1	0	1	1	0	2	0
Gary Matthews, of	.250	5	16	1	4	0	0	1	1	2	2	0
Joe Morgan, 2b	.263	5	19	3	5	0	1	2	2	2	3	1
Tony Perez, 1b-2	.200	4	10	0	2	0	0	0	0	0	2	0
Ron Reed, p	.000	3	0	0	0	0	0	0	0	0	0	0
Pete Rose, 1b-3,of-1	.313	5	16	1	5	1	0	0	1	1	3	0
Juan Samuel, ph	.000	3	1	0	0	0	0	0	0	0	0	0
Mike Schmidt, 3b	.050	5	20	0	1	0	0	0	0	0	6	0
Ossie Virgil, c-1	.500	3	2	0	1	0	0	0	0	1	0	0
TOTAL	.195		159	9	31	4	1	4	9	7	29	1

PITCHER	W	L	ERA	G	GS	CG	SV	SHO	IP	H	ER	BB	SO
Larry Andersen	0	0	2.25	2	0	0	0	0	4.0	4	1	0	1
Marty Bystrom	0	0	0.00	1	0	0	0	0	1.0	0	0	0	1
Steve Carlton	0	1	2.70	1	1	0	0	0	6.2	5	2	3	7
John Denny	1	1	3.46	2	2	0	0	0	13.0	12	5	3	9
Willie Hernandez	0	0	0.00	3	0	0	0	0	4.0	0	0	1	4
Al Holland	0	0	0.00	2	0	0	1	0	3.2	1	0	0	5
Charles Hudson	0	2	8.64	2	2	0	0	0	8.1	9	8	1	6
Ron Reed	0	0	2.70	3	0	0	0	0	3.1	4	1	2	4
TOTAL	1	4	3.48	16	5	0	1	0	44.0	35	17	10	37

GAME 1 AT BAL OCT 11

PHI	000 001 010	2	5	0
BAL	100 000 000	1	5	1

Pitchers: DENNY, Holland (8) vs McGREGOR, Stewart (9), T.Martinez (9)
Home Runs: Morgan-PHI, Maddox-PHI, Dwyer-BAL
Attendance: 52,204

GAME 2 AT BAL OCT 12

PHI	000 100 000	1	3	0
BAL	000 030 10X	4	9	1

Pitchers: HUDSON, Hernandez (5), Andersen (6), Reed (8) vs BODDICKER
Home Runs: Lowenstein-BAL
Attendance: 52,132

GAME 3 AT PHI OCT 14

BAL	000 001 200	3	6	1
PHI	011 000 000	2	8	2

Pitchers: Flanagan, PALMER (5), Stewart (7), T.Martinez (9) vs CARLTON, Holland (7)
Home Runs: Matthews-PHI, Morgan-PHI, Ford-BAL
Attendance: 65,792

GAME 4 AT PHI OCT 15

BAL	000 202 100	5	10	1
PHI	000 120 001	4	10	0

Pitchers: DAVIS, Stewart (6), T.Martinez (8) vs DENNY, Hernandez (6), Reed (6), Andersen (8)
Attendance: 66,947

GAME 5 AT PHI OCT 16

BAL	011 210 000	5	5	0
PHI	000 000 000	0	5	1

Pitchers: McGREGOR vs HUDSON, Bystrom (5), Hernandez (6), Reed (9)
Home Runs: Murray-BAL (2), Dempsey-BAL
Attendance: 67,064

After two games in Chicago, the Cubs appeared headed for their first pennant in thirty-nine years. Rick Sutcliffe and Warren Brusstar shut out the Padres 13–0 in an opener enlivened by five Cub home runs. In a quieter second game, the Cubs built a 4–1 lead over the first four innings and held on for the win.

When the series moved to San Diego, though, the Padres came to life. In the fifth and sixth innings of Game Three, they obliterated a 1–0 Cub lead with seven runs, as Ed Whitson and Goose Gossage held the Cubs scoreless after the second inning for what turned into an easy Padres win.

Game Four was not so easy. San Diego scored first in the first inning, lost their lead in the fourth, tied in the fifth, went ahead in the seventh, and fell back into a 5–5 tie in the eighth. But in the bottom of the ninth, Padre Steve Garvey's two-run homer sent the series into a fifth game.

Leon Durham put the Cubs ahead with a two-run homer in the first inning of the finale, and Jody Davis added to the lead with a solo shot in the second. Rick Sutcliffe, meanwhile, was setting down Padres as he added five shutout innings to his seven from Game One. But he gave up two runs in the sixth, and after first baseman Durham saw a grounder go through his legs to let in the tying run in the seventh, the Cubs watched the pennant slip away as Tony Gwynn's double and Garvey's single drove in the game's three final runs.

San Diego Padres (West), 3; Chicago Cubs (East), 2

SD (W)

PLAYER/POS	AVG	G	AB	R	H	2B	3B	HR	RB	BB	SO	SB
Kurt Bevacqua, ph	.000	2	2	0	0	0	0	0	0	0	0	0
Greg Booker, p	.000	1	0	0	0	0	0	0	0	0	0	0
Bobby Brown, of	.000	3	4	1	0	0	0	0	0	1	2	1
Dave Dravecky, p	.000	3	0	0	0	0	0	0	0	0	0	0
Tim Flannery, ph	.500	3	2	2	1	0	0	0	0	0	0	0
Steve Garvey, 1b	.400	5	20	1	8	1	0	1	7	1	2	0
Rich Gossage, p	.000	3	0	0	0	0	0	0	0	0	0	0
Tony Gwynn, of	.368	5	19	6	7	3	0	0	3	1	2	0
Greg Harris, p	.000	1	0	0	0	0	0	0	0	0	0	0
Andy Hawkins, p	.000	3	0	0	0	0	0	0	0	0	0	0
Terry Kennedy, c	.222	5	18	2	4	0	0	0	1	1	3	0
Craig Lefferts, p	.000	3	0	0	0	0	0	0	0	0	0	0
Tim Lollar, p	.000	1	1	0	0	0	0	0	0	0	1	0
Carmelo Martinez, of	.176	5	17	1	3	0	0	0	0	2	4	0
Kevin Mc Reynolds, of	.300	4	10	2	3	0	0	1	4	3	1	0
Graig Nettles, 3b	.143	4	14	1	2	0	0	0	2	1	1	0
Mario Ramirez, ph	.000	2	2	0	0	0	0	0	0	0	0	0
Luis Salazar, of-2,3b-1	.200	3	5	0	1	0	1	0	0	0	1	0
Eric Show, p	.000	2	1	0	0	0	0	0	0	0	1	0
Champ Summers, ph	.000	2	2	0	0	0	0	0	0	0	1	0
Garry Templeton, ss	.333	5	15	2	5	1	0	0	2	2	0	1
Mark Thurmond, p	1.000	1	1	0	1	0	0	0	0	0	0	0
Ed Whitson, p	.000	1	3	0	0	0	0	0	0	0	1	0
Alan Wiggins, 2b	.316	5	19	4	6	0	0	0	1	2	2	0
TOTAL	.265		155	22	41	5	1	2	20	14	22	2

PITCHER	W	L	ERA	G	GS	CG	SV	SHO	IP	H	ER	BB	SO
Greg Booker	0	0	0.00	1	0	0	0	0	2.0	2	0	1	2
Dave Dravecky	0	0	0.00	3	0	0	0	0	6.0	2	0	0	5
Rich Gossage	0	0	4.50	3	0	0	1	0	4.0	5	2	1	5
Greg Harris	0	0	31.50	1	0	0	0	0	2.0	9	7	3	2
Andy Hawkins	0	0	0.00	3	0	0	0	0	3.2	0	0	2	1
Craig Lefferts	2	0	0.00	3	0	0	0	0	4.0	1	0	1	1
Tim Lollar	0	0	6.23	1	1	0	0	0	4.1	3	3	4	3
Eric Show	0	1	13.50	2	2	0	0	0	5.1	8	8	4	2
Mark Thurmond	0	1	9.82	1	1	0	0	0	3.2	7	4	2	1
Ed Whitson	1	0	1.13	1	1	0	0	0	8.0	5	1	2	6
TOTAL	3	2	5.23	19	5	0	1	0	43.0	42	25	20	28

CHI (E)

PLAYER/POS	AVG	G	AB	R	H	2B	3B	HR	RB	BB	SO	SB
Thad Bosley, ph	.000	2	2	0	0	0	0	0	0	0	2	0
Larry Bowa, ss	.200	5	15	1	3	1	0	0	1	1	0	0
Warren Brusstar, p	.000	3	1	0	0	0	0	0	0	0	0	0
Ron Cey, 3b	.158	5	19	3	3	1	0	1	3	3	3	0
Henry Cotto, of	1.000	3	1	1	1	0	0	0	0	0	0	0
Jody Davis, c	.389	5	18	3	7	0	0	2	6	0	3	0
Bob Dernier, of	.235	5	17	5	4	2	0	1	1	5	4	2
Leon Durham, 1b	.150	5	20	2	3	0	0	2	4	1	4	0
Dennis Eckersley, p	.000	1	2	0	0	0	0	0	0	0	1	0
George Frazier, p	.000	1	0	0	0	0	0	0	0	0	0	0
Richie Hebner, ph	.000	2	1	0	0	0	0	0	0	0	0	0
Steve Lake, c	1.000	1	1	0	1	1	0	0	0	0	0	0
Davey Lopes, of-1	.000	2	1	0	0	0	0	0	0	0	0	0
Gary Matthews, of	.200	5	15	4	3	0	0	2	5	6	4	1
Keith Moreland, of	.333	5	18	3	6	2	0	0	2	1	1	0
Ryne Sandberg, 2b	.368	5	19	3	7	2	0	0	2	3	2	3
Scott Sanderson, p	.000	1	2	0	0	0	0	0	0	0	1	0
Lee Smith, p	.000	2	0	0	0	0	0	0	0	0	0	0
Tim Stoddard, p	.000	2	0	0	0	0	0	0	0	0	0	0
Rick Sutcliffe, p	.500	2	6	1	3	0	0	1	1	0	2	0
Steve Trout, p	.500	2	2	0	1	0	0	0	0	0	0	0
Tom Veryzer, ss-2,3b-1	.000	3	1	0	0	0	0	0	0	0	0	0
Gary Woods, of	.000	1	1	0	0	0	0	0	0	0	1	0
TOTAL	.259		162	26	42	11	0	9	25	20	28	6

PITCHER	W	L	ERA	G	GS	CG	SV	SHO	IP	H	ER	BB	SO
Warren Brusstar	0	0	0.00	3	0	0	0	0	4.1	6	0	0	1
Dennis Eckersley	0	1	8.44	1	1	0	0	0	5.1	9	5	0	0
George Frazier	0	0	10.80	1	0	0	0	0	1.2	2	2	0	1
Scott Sanderson	0	0	5.79	1	1	0	0	0	4.2	6	3	1	2
Lee Smith	0	1	9.00	2	0	0	1	0	2.0	3	2	0	3
Tim Stoddard	0	0	4.50	2	0	0	0	0	2.0	1	1	2	2
Rick Sutcliffe	1	1	3.38	2	2	0	0	0	13.1	9	5	8	10
Steve Trout	1	0	2.00	2	1	0	0	0	9.0	5	2	3	3
TOTAL	2	3	4.25	14	5	0	1	0	42.1	41	20	14	22

GAME 1 AT CHI OCT 2

SD	000	000	000	0	6	1
CHI	203	062	00X	13	16	0

Pitchers: SHOW, Harris (5), Booker (7) vs SUTCLIFFE, Brusstar (8)
Home Runs: Dernier-CHI, Matthews-CHI (2), Sutcliffe-CHI, Cey-CHI
Attendance: 36,282

GAME 2 AT CHI OCT 3

SD	000	101	000	2	5	0
CHI	102	100	00X	4	8	1

Pitchers: THURMOND, Hawkins (4), Dravecky (6), Lefferts (8) vs TROUT, Smith (9)
Attendance: 36,282

GAME 3 AT SD OCT 4

CHI	010	000	000	1	5	0
SD	000	034	00X	7	11	0

Pitchers: ECKERSLEY, Frazier (6), Stoddard (8) vs WHITSON, Gossage (9)
Home Runs: McReynolds-SD
Attendance: 58,346

GAME 4 AT SD OCT 6

CHI	000	300	020	5	8	1
SD	002	010	202	7	11	0

Pitchers: Sanderson, Brusstar (5), Stoddard (7), SMITH (8) vs Lollar, Hawkins (5), Dravecky (6), Gossage (8), LEFFERTS (9)
Home Runs: Davis-CHI, Durham-CHI, Garvey-SD
Attendance: 58,354

GAME 5 AT SD OCT 7

CHI	210	000	000	3	5	1
SD	000	002	40X	6	8	0

Pitchers: SUTCLIFFE, Trout (7), Brusstar (8) vs Show, Hawkins (2), Dravecky (4), LEFFERTS (6), Gossage (8)
Home Runs: Durham-CHI, Davis-CHI
Attendance: 58,359

The heavily favored Tigers swept the series, but not without difficulty, despite a fourteen-hit, three-homer, 8–1 romp in the opener.

Games Two and Three were much tighter. In the second game, after Detroit had built a 3–0 lead over the first three innings, Royal rookie starter Bret Saberhagen settled down and blanked the Tigers for the next five innings as K.C. inched its way to a tie with runs in the fourth, seventh, and eighth. Through the ninth and tenth innings, Tiger reliever Aurelio Lopez and Royal Dan Quisenberry dueled scorelessly, but in the top of the eleventh Johnny Grubb doubled home two Tiger runs. Lopez struggled but held the Royals scoreless in the last of the eleventh for the win.

In Game Three, the Royals' Charlie Leibrandt and Tigers' Milt Wilcox and Willie Hernandez hurled matching three-hitters. But the Tigers secured the game—and the pennant—when Chet Lemon scored on a broken double play in the second inning for the game's only run.

Detroit Tigers (East), 3;
Kansas City Royals (West), 0

DET (E)

PLAYER/POS	AVG	G	AB	R	H	2B	3B	HR	RB	BB	SO	SB
Doug Baker, ss	.000	1	0	0	0	0	0	0	0	0	0	0
Dave Bergman, 1b-1	1.000	2	1	1	1	0	0	0	0	0	0	1
Tom Brookens, 2b-1,3b-1	.000	2	2	0	0	0	0	0	0	0	1	0
Marty Castillo, 3b	.250	3	8	0	2	0	0	0	2	0	3	1
Darrell Evans, 1b-3,3b-1	.300	3	10	1	3	1	0	0	1	1	0	1
Barbaro Garbey, dh-2	.333	3	9	1	3	0	0	0	0	0	1	0
Kirk Gibson, of	.417	3	12	2	5	1	0	1	2	2	1	1
Johnny Grubb, dh	.250	1	4	0	1	1	0	0	2	0	0	0
Willie Hernandez, p	.000	3	0	0	0	0	0	0	0	0	0	0
Larry Herndon, of	.200	2	5	1	1	0	0	1	1	1	2	0
Ruppert Jones, of	.000	2	5	1	0	0	0	0	0	1	1	0
Rusty Kuntz, of	.000	1	0	0	0	0	0	0	0	0	0	0
Chet Lemon, of	.000	3	13	1	0	0	0	0	0	0	1	0
Aurelio Lopez, p	.000	1	0	0	0	0	0	0	0	0	0	0
Jack Morris, p	.000	1	0	0	0	0	0	0	0	0	0	0
Lance Parrish, c	.250	3	12	1	3	1	0	1	3	0	3	0
Dan Petry, p	.000	1	0	0	0	0	0	0	0	0	0	0
Alan Trammell, ss	.364	3	11	2	4	0	1	1	3	3	1	0
Lou Whitaker, 2b	.143	3	14	3	2	0	0	0	0	0	3	0
Milt Wilcox, p	.000	1	0	0	0	0	0	0	0	0	0	0
TOTAL	.234		107	14	25	4	1	4	14	8	17	4

PITCHER	W	L	ERA	G	GS	CG	SV	SHO	IP	H	ER	BB	SO
Willie Hernandez	0	0	2.25	3	0	0	1	0	4.0	3	1	1	3
Aurelio Lopez	1	0	0.00	1	0	0	0	0	3.0	4	0	1	2
Jack Morris	1	0	1.29	1	1	0	0	0	7.0	5	1	4	4
Dan Petry	0	0	2.57	1	1	0	0	0	7.0	4	2	1	4
Milt Wilcox	1	0	0.00	1	1	0	0	0	8.0	2	0	2	8
TOTAL	3	0	1.24	7	3	0	1	0	29.0	18	4	6	21

KC (W)

PLAYER/POS	AVG	G	AB	R	H	2B	3B	HR	RB	BB	SO	SB
Steve Balboni, 1b	.100	3	10	0	1	0	0	0	0	0	4	0
Buddy Biancalana, ss	.000	2	1	0	0	0	0	0	0	0	1	0
Bud Black, p	.000	1	0	0	0	0	0	0	0	0	0	0
George Brett, 3b	.231	3	13	0	3	0	0	0	0	0	2	0
Onix Concepcion, ss	.000	3	7	0	0	0	0	0	0	0	0	0
Mark Huismann, p	.000	1	0	0	0	0	0	0	0	0	0	0
Dane Iorg, ph	.500	2	2	0	1	0	0	0	1	0	0	0
Lynn Jones, of-2	.200	3	5	1	1	0	0	0	0	0	0	0
Mike Jones, p	.000	1	0	0	0	0	0	0	0	0	0	0
Charlie Leibrandt, p	.000	1	0	0	0	0	0	0	0	0	0	0
Hal Mc Rae, ph	1.000	2	2	0	2	1	0	0	1	0	0	0
Darryl Motley, of	.167	3	12	0	2	0	0	0	1	1	3	0
Jorge Orta, dh	.100	3	10	1	1	0	1	0	1	0	2	0
Greg Pryor, 3b	.000	1	0	0	0	0	0	0	0	0	0	0
Dan Quisenberry, p	.000	1	0	0	0	0	0	0	0	0	0	0
Bret Saberhagen, p	.000	1	0	0	0	0	0	0	0	0	0	0
Pat Sheridan, of	.000	3	6	1	0	0	0	0	0	3	3	0
Don Slaught, c	.364	3	11	0	4	0	0	0	0	0	0	0
U. L. Washington, ph	.000	2	1	0	0	0	0	0	0	0	1	0
John Wathan, dh	.000	1	0	0	0	0	0	0	0	0	0	0
Frank White, 2b	.083	3	12	1	1	0	0	0	0	0	3	0
Willie Wilson, of	.154	3	13	0	2	0	0	0	0	1	2	0
TOTAL	.170		106	4	18	1	1	0	4	6	21	0

PITCHER	W	L	ERA	G	GS	CG	SV	SHO	IP	H	ER	BB	SO
Bud Black	0	1	5.40	1	1	0	0	0	5.0	7	3	1	3
Mark Huismann	0	0	10.13	1	0	0	0	0	2.2	6	3	1	2
Mike Jones	0	0	6.75	1	0	0	0	0	1.1	1	1	0	0
Charlie Leibrandt	0	1	1.13	1	1	1	0	0	8.0	3	1	4	6
Dan Quisenberry	0	1	3.00	1	0	0	0	0	3.0	2	1	1	1
Bret Saberhagen	0	0	2.25	1	1	0	0	0	8.0	6	2	1	5
TOTAL	0	3	3.54	6	3	1	0	0	28.0	25	11	8	17

GAME 1 AT KC OCT 2

DET	200	110	121	8	14	0
KC	000	000	100	1	5	1

Pitchers: MORRIS, Hernandez (8) vs BLACK, Huismann (6), M.Jones (8)
Home Runs: Herndon-DET, Trammell-DET, Parrish-DET
Attendance: 41,973

GAME 2 AT KC OCT 3

DET	201	000	000 02	5	8	1
KC	000	100	110 00	3	10	3

Pitchers: Petry, Hernandez (8), LOPEZ (9) vs Saberhagen, QUISENBERRY (9)
Home Runs: Gibson-DET
Attendance: 42,019

GAME 3 AT DET OCT 5

KC	000	000	000	0	3	3
DET	010	000	00X	1	3	0

Pitchers: LEIBRANDT vs WILCOX, Hernandez (9)
Attendance: 52,168

Few objective observers expected the Padres (playing in their first World Series) to best the mighty Tigers—and they didn't. Detroit's first two batters in Game One hit safely to produce the Series' first scoring before an out had been recorded. San Diego countered with three two-out hits in their half of the first to go ahead 2–1. But Detroit starter Jack Morris settled down to shut out the Padres over the final eight innings, and his Tigers scored the tying and winning runs in the fifth on Larry Herndon's two-run homer. The Tigers scored again in Game Two before the first out was recorded and drove out Padre starter Ed Whitson with three first-inning runs on five singles. But this time Detroit was shut out (by relievers Andy Hawkins and Craig Lefferts) over the final eight, while San Diego scored single runs in the first and fourth and the winning runs in the fifth on a three-run homer by the normally light-hitting Kurt Bevacqua.

The Tigers won Game Three on walks—a Series-record eleven—as the Series moved to Detroit. After scoring their first two runs in the inning on a single and Marty Castillo's home run, they continued on to put across two more in the inning on a pair of hits alternated with three walks (the last with the bases full). Three more walks an inning later, followed by a hit batsman, gave Detroit its final run in what became a 5–2 win.

Alan Trammell's two-run homer in the first inning of Game Four put the Tigers ahead to stay. Tiger pitcher Jack Morris gave up a solo home run to Terry Kennedy in the second, but Trammell swatted a second two-run shot an inning later for a 4–1 lead. Morris let a second Padre runner score on a wild pitch in the ninth, but then retired Kennedy for the third out and his second Series win. Kirk Gibson's two home runs framed Tiger scoring in the final game. His two-run shot in the first inning opened the game's scoring. San Diego tied it up with runs in the third and fourth, but Detroit took a 5–3 lead with runs in the fifth and seventh (the latter on Lance Parrish's homer). The unlikely Kurt Bevacqua brough the Padres within a run of tying the game with his second Series homer in the eighth (doubling his regular-season total), but Gibson ended the scoring—and Padre hopes—with a three-run blast half an inning later.

Detroit Tigers (AL), 4;
San Diego Padres (NL), 1

DET (A)

PLAYER/POS	AVG	G	AB	R	H	2B	3B	HR	RBI	BB	SO	SB
Doug Bair, p	.000	1	0	0	0	0	0	0	0	0	0	0
Dave Bergman, 1b	.000	5	5	0	0	0	0	0	0	1	0	0
Tom Brookens, 3b	.000	3	3	0	0	0	0	0	0	0	1	0
Marty Castillo, 3b	.333	3	9	2	3	0	0	1	2	2	1	0
Darrell Evans, 1b-4,3b-2	.067	5	15	1	1	0	0	0	1	4	4	0
Barbaro Garbey, dh-3	.000	4	12	0	0	0	0	0	0	0	2	0
Kirk Gibson, of	.333	5	18	4	6	0	0	2	7	4	4	3
Johnny Grubb, dh-2	.333	4	3	0	1	0	0	0	0	0	0	0
Willie Hernandez, p	.000	3	0	0	0	0	0	0	0	0	0	0
Larry Herndon, of	.333	5	15	1	5	0	0	1	3	3	2	0
Howard Johnson, ph	.000	1	1	0	0	0	0	0	0	0	0	0
Ruppert Jones, of	.000	2	3	0	0	0	0	0	0	0	1	0
Rusty Kuntz, ph	.000	2	1	0	0	0	0	0	1	1	1	0
Chet Lemon, of	.294	5	17	1	5	0	0	0	1	2	2	2
Aurelio Lopez, p	.000	2	0	0	0	0	0	0	0	0	0	0
Jack Morris, p	.000	2	0	0	0	0	0	0	0	0	0	0
Lance Parrish, c	.278	5	18	3	5	1	0	1	2	3	2	1
Dan Petry, p	.000	2	0	0	0	0	0	0	0	0	0	0
Bill Scherrer, p	.000	3	0	0	0	0	0	0	0	0	0	0
Alan Trammell, ss	.450	5	20	5	9	1	0	2	6	2	2	1
Lou Whitaker, 2b	.278	5	18	6	5	2	0	0	0	4	4	0
Milt Wilcox, p	.000	1	0	0	0	0	0	0	0	0	0	0
TOTAL	.253		158	23	40	4	0	7	23	24	27	7

PITCHER	W	L	ERA	G	GS	CG	SV	SHO	IP	H	ER	BB	SO
Doug Bair	0	0	0.00	1	0	0	0	0	0.2	0	0	0	1
Willie Hernandez	0	0	1.69	3	0	0	2	0	5.1	4	1	0	0
Aurelio Lopez	1	0	0.00	2	0	0	0	0	3.0	1	0	1	4
Jack Morris	2	0	2.00	2	2	2	0	0	18.0	13	4	3	13
Dan Petry	0	1	9.00	2	2	0	0	0	8.0	14	8	5	4
Bill Scherrer	0	0	3.00	3	0	0	0	0	3.0	5	1	0	0
Milt Wilcox	1	0	1.50	1	1	0	0	0	6.0	7	1	2	4
TOTAL	4	1	3.07	14	5	2	2	0	44.0	44	15	11	26

SD (N)

PLAYER/POS	AVG	G	AB	R	H	2B	3B	HR	RBI	BB	SO	SB
Kurt Bevacqua, dh	.412	5	17	4	7	2	0	2	4	1	2	0
Bruce Bochy, ph	1.000	1	1	0	1	0	0	0	0	0	0	0
Greg Booker, p	.000	1	0	0	0	0	0	0	0	0	0	0
Bobby Brown, of	.067	5	15	1	1	0	0	0	0	2	4	0
Dave Dravecky, p	.000	2	0	0	0	0	0	0	0	0	0	0
Tim Flannery, 2b	1.000	1	1	0	1	0	0	0	0	0	0	0
Steve Garvey, 1b	.200	5	20	2	4	2	0	0	2	0	2	0
Rich Gossage, p	.000	2	0	0	0	0	0	0	0	0	0	0
Tony Gwynn, of	.263	5	19	1	5	0	0	0	0	3	2	1
Greg Harris, p	.000	1	0	0	0	0	0	0	0	0	0	0
Andy Hawkins, p	.000	3	0	0	0	0	0	0	0	0	0	0
Terry Kennedy, c	.211	5	19	2	4	1	0	1	3	1	1	0
Craig Lefferts, p	.000	3	0	0	0	0	0	0	0	0	0	0
Tim Lollar, p	.000	1	0	0	0	0	0	0	0	0	0	0
Carmelo Martinez, of	.176	5	17	0	3	0	0	0	0	1	9	0
Graig Nettles, 3b	.250	5	12	2	3	0	0	0	2	5	0	0
Ron Roenicke, of-1	.000	2	0	0	0	0	0	0	0	0	0	0
Luis Salazar, of-2,3b-1	.333	4	3	0	1	0	0	0	0	0	0	0
Eric Show, p	.000	1	0	0	0	0	0	0	0	0	0	0
Champ Summers, ph	.000	1	1	0	0	0	0	0	0	0	1	0
Garry Templeton, ss	.316	5	19	1	6	1	0	0	0	0	3	0
Mark Thurmond, p	.000	2	0	0	0	0	0	0	0	0	0	0
Ed Whitson, p	.000	1	0	0	0	0	0	0	0	0	0	0
Alan Wiggins, 2b	.364	5	22	2	8	1	0	0	1	0	2	1
TOTAL	.265		166	15	44	7	0	3	14	11	26	2

PITCHER	W	L	ERA	G	GS	CG	SV	SHO	IP	H	ER	BB	SO
Greg Booker	0	0	9.00	1	0	0	0	0	1.0	0	1	4	0
Dave Dravecky	0	0	0.00	2	0	0	0	0	4.2	3	0	1	5
Rich Gossage	0	0	13.50	2	0	0	0	0	2.2	3	4	1	2
Greg Harris	0	0	0.00	1	0	0	0	0	5.1	0	0	3	5
Andy Hawkins	1	1	0.75	3	0	0	0	0	12.0	4	1	6	4
Craig Lefferts	0	0	0.00	3	0	0	1	0	6.0	2	0	1	7
Tim Lollar	0	1	21.60	1	1	0	0	0	1.2	4	4	4	0
Eric Show	0	1	10.13	1	1	0	0	0	2.2	4	3	1	2
Mark Thurmond	0	1	10.13	2	2	0	0	0	5.1	12	6	3	2
Ed Whitson	0	0	40.50	1	1	0	0	0	0.2	5	3	0	0
TOTAL	1	4	4.71	17	5	0	1	0	42.0	40	22	24	27

GAME 1 AT SD OCT 9

DET	100	020	000	3	8	0
SD	200	000	000	2	8	1

Pitchers: MORRIS vs THURMOND, Hawkins (6), Dravecky (8)
Home Runs: Herndon-DET
Attendance: 57,908

GAME 2 AT SD OCT 10

DET	300	000	000	3	7	3
SD	100	130	00X	5	11	0

Pitchers: PETRY, Lopez (5), Scherrer (6), Bair (7), Hernandez (8) vs Whitson, HAWKINS (1), Lefferts(7)
Home Runs: Bevacqua-SD
Attendance: 57,911

GAME 3 AT DET OCT 12

SD	001	000	100	2	5	0
DET	041	000	00X	5	7	0

Pitchers: LOLLAR, Booker (2), Harris (3) vs WILCOX, Scherrer (7), Hernandez (7)
Home Runs: Castillo-DET
Attendance: 51,970

GAME 4 AT DET OCT 13

SD	010	000	001	2	10	2
DET	202	000	00X	4	7	0

Pitchers: SHOW, Dravecky (3), Lefferts (7), Gossage (8) vs MORRIS
Home Runs: Trammell-DET (2), Kennedy-SD
Attendance: 52,130

GAME 5 AT DET OCT 14

SD	001	200	010	4	10	1
DET	300	010	13X	8	11	1

Pitchers: Thurmond, HAWKINS (1), Lefferts (5), Gossage (7) vs Petry, Scherrer (4), LOPEZ (5), Hernandez (8)
Home Runs: Gibson-DET (2), Parrish-DET, Bevacqua-SD
Attendance: 51,901

The Dodgers' league-leading pitchers held St. Louis to three runs over the first two games, even though the Cardinals recorded eight hits per game. But the Cards' league-leading hitters put their blows to better advantage in the next four games of the expanded LCS, scoring twenty-six times for four wins and the pennant.

Fernando Valenzuela captured Game One for the Dodgers, thanks in part to some ragged fielding by the usually sharp Cardinal infield. And as Orel Hershiser was holding St. Louis to two runs in Game Two, an errant Cardinal pickoff throw and heavy Dodger hitting gave him an increasingly comfortable lead.

When the series shifted to St. Louis for Game Three, the Cardinals revived, scoring twice in each of the first two innings for a quick lead, which they held for their first win. In Game Four they unloaded for nine runs in the second inning, and in Game Five—with the game and series tied in the bottom of the ninth—Ozzie Smith hit his first lefthanded home run ever to give St. Louis the series lead.

Back in Los Angeles, the Dodgers scored first in Game Six, and held a 4–1 lead after six innings. But three Cardinals scored on four hits in the seventh, and though Dodger Mike Marshall's eighth-inning home run restored the lead to Los Angeles, Cardinal Jack Clark settled things with a three-run homer in the ninth.

St. Louis Cardinals (East), 4;
Los Angeles Dodgers (West), 2

STL (E)

PLAYER/POS	AVG	G	AB	R	H	2B	3B	HR	RB	BB	SO	SB
Joaquin Andujar, p	.250	2	4	1	1	1	0	0	0	0	1	0
Steve Braun, ph	.000	2	2	0	0	0	0	0	0	0	0	0
Bill Campbell, p	.000	3	0	0	0	0	0	0	0	0	0	0
Cesar Cedeno, of-4	.167	5	12	2	2	1	0	0	0	2	3	0
Jack Clark, 1b	.381	6	21	4	8	0	0	1	4	5	5	0
Vince Coleman, of	.286	3	14	2	4	0	0	0	0	1	0	2
Danny Cox, p	.000	1	2	0	0	0	0	0	0	1	1	0
Ken Dayley, p	.500	5	2	0	1	0	0	0	0	0	0	0
Bob Forsch, p	.000	1	0	0	0	0	0	0	0	0	0	0
Brian Harper, ph	.000	1	1	0	0	0	0	0	0	0	0	0
Tommy Herr, 2b	.333	6	21	2	7	4	0	1	6	5	2	1
Rick Horton, p	.000	3	0	0	0	0	0	0	0	0	0	0
Mike Jorgensen, ph	.000	2	2	0	0	0	0	0	0	0	1	0
Jeff Lahti, p	.000	2	0	0	0	0	0	0	0	0	0	0
Tito Landrum, of-4	.429	5	14	2	6	0	0	0	4	1	1	0
Willie Mc Gee, of	.269	6	26	6	7	1	0	0	3	3	6	2
Tom Nieto, c	.000	1	3	1	0	0	0	0	0	1	2	0
Terry Pendleton, 3b	.208	6	24	2	5	1	0	0	4	1	3	0
Darrell Porter, c	.267	5	15	1	4	1	0	0	0	5	4	0
Ozzie Smith, ss	.435	6	23	4	10	1	1	1	3	3	1	1
John Tudor, p	.000	2	4	0	0	0	0	0	0	1	1	0
Andy Van Slyke, of	.091	5	11	1	1	0	0	0	0	1	2	0
Todd Worrell, p	.000	4	0	0	0	0	0	0	0	0	0	0
TOTAL	.279		201	29	56	10	1	3	26	30	34	6

PITCHER	W	L	ERA	G	GS	CG	SV	SHO	IP	H	ER	BB	SO
Joaquin Andujar	0	1	6.97	2	2	0	0	0	10.1	14	8	4	9
Bill Campbell	0	0	0.00	3	0	0	0	0	2.1	3	0	0	2
Danny Cox	1	0	3.00	1	1	0	0	0	6.0	4	2	5	4
Ken Dayley	0	0	0.00	5	0	0	2	0	6.0	2	0	1	3
Bob Forsch	0	0	5.40	1	1	0	0	0	3.1	3	2	2	0
Rick Horton	0	0	9.00	3	0	0	0	0	3.0	4	3	2	1
Jeff Lahti	1	0	0.00	2	0	0	0	0	2.0	2	0	0	1
John Tudor	1	1	2.84	2	2	0	0	0	12.2	10	4	3	8
Todd Worrell	1	0	1.42	4	0	0	0	0	6.1	4	1	2	3
TOTAL	4	2	3.46	23	6	0	2	0	52.0	46	20	19	31

LA (W)

PLAYER/POS	AVG	G	AB	R	H	2B	3B	HR	RB	BB	SO	SB
Dave Anderson, ss-3,3b-1	.000	4	5	1	0	0	0	0	0	3	1	0
Bob Bailor, 3b	.000	2	1	0	0	0	0	0	0	0	0	0
Greg Brock, 1b-4	.083	5	12	2	1	0	0	1	2	2	2	0
Enos Cabell, 1b-3	.077	5	13	1	1	0	0	0	0	0	3	0
Bobby Castillo, p	.000	1	2	0	0	0	0	0	0	0	1	0
Carlos Diaz, p	.000	2	0	0	0	0	0	0	0	0	0	0
Mariano Duncan, ss	.222	5	18	2	4	2	1	0	1	1	3	1
Pedro Guerrero, of	.250	6	20	2	5	1	0	0	4	5	2	2
Orel Hershiser, p	.286	2	7	1	2	0	0	0	1	0	2	0
Rick Honeycutt, p	.000	2	0	0	0	0	0	0	0	0	0	0
Ken Howell, p	.000	1	0	0	0	0	0	0	0	0	0	0
Jay Johnstone, ph	.000	1	1	0	0	0	0	0	0	0	0	0
Ken Landreaux, of	.389	6	18	4	7	3	0	0	2	1	1	0
Bill Madlock, 3b	.333	6	24	5	8	1	0	3	7	0	2	1
Candy Maldonado, of-3	.143	4	7	0	1	0	0	0	1	0	3	0
Mike Marshall, of	.217	6	23	1	5	2	0	1	3	1	3	0
Len Matuszek, 1b-1,of-1	1.000	3	1	1	1	0	0	0	0	0	0	0
Tom Niedenfuer, p	.000	3	1	0	0	0	0	0	0	0	1	0
Jerry Reuss, p	.000	1	0	0	0	0	0	0	0	0	0	0
Steve Sax, 2b	.300	6	20	1	6	3	0	0	1	1	5	0
Mike Scioscia, c	.250	6	16	2	4	0	0	0	1	4	0	0
Fernando Valenzuela, p	.200	2	5	0	1	0	0	0	0	0	0	0
Bob Welch, p	.000	1	1	0	0	0	0	0	0	0	1	0
Terry Whitfield, ph	.000	1	1	0	0	0	0	0	0	0	0	0
Steve Yeager, c	.000	1	2	0	0	0	0	0	0	1	1	0
TOTAL	.234		197	23	46	12	1	5	23	19	31	4

PITCHER	W	L	ERA	G	GS	CG	SV	SHO	IP	H	ER	BB	SO
Bobby Castillo	0	0	3.38	1	0	0	0	0	5.1	4	2	2	4
Carlos Diaz	0	0	3.00	2	0	0	0	0	3.0	5	1	1	2
Orel Hershiser	1	0	3.52	2	2	1	0	0	15.1	17	6	6	5
Rick Honeycutt	0	0	13.50	2	0	0	0	0	1.1	4	2	2	1
Ken Howell	0	0	0.00	1	0	0	0	0	2.0	0	0	0	2
Tom Niedenfuer	0	2	6.35	3	0	0	0	1	5.2	5	4	2	5
Jerry Reuss	0	1	10.80	1	1	0	0	0	1.2	5	2	1	0
F. Valenzuela	1	0	1.88	2	2	1	0	0	14.1	11	3	10	13
Bob Welch	0	1	6.75	1	1	0	0	0	2.2	5	2	6	2
TOTAL	2	4	3.86	15	6	1	1	0	51.1	56	22	30	34

GAME 1 AT LA OCT 9

STL	000	000	100	1	8	1
LA	000	103	00X	4	8	0

Pitchers: TUDOR, Dayley (6), Campbell (7), Worrell (8) vs VALENZUELA, Niedenfuer (7)
Attendance: 55,270

GAME 2 AT LA OCT 10

STL	001	000	001	2	8	1
LA	003	212	00X	8	13	1

Pitchers: ANDUJAR, Horton (5), Campbell (6), Dayley (7), Lahti (8) vs HERSHISER
Home Runs: Brock-LA
Attendance: 55,222

GAME 3 AT STL OCT 12

LA	000	100	100	2	7	2
STL	220	000	00X	4	8	0

Pitchers: WELCH, Honeycutt (3), Diaz (5), Howell (7) vs COX, Horton (7), Worrell (7), Dayley (9)
Home Runs: Herr-STL
Attendance: 53,708

GAME 4 AT STL OCT 13

LA	000	000	110	2	5	2
STL	090	110	01X	12	15	0

Pitchers: REUSS, Honeycutt (2), Castillo (2), Horton (8), Campbell (9) vs TUDOR
Home Runs: Madlock-LA
Attendance: 53,708

GAME 5 AT STL OCT 14

LA	000	200	000	2	5	1
STL	200	000	001	3	5	1

Pitchers: Valenzuela, NIEDENFUER (9) vs Forsch, Dayley (4), Worrell (7), LAHTI (9)
Home Runs: Madlock-LA, Smith-STL
Attendance: 53,708

GAME 6 AT LA OCT 16

STL	001	000	303	7	12	1
LA	110	020	010	5	8	0

Pitchers: Andujar, WORRELL (7), Dayley (9) vs Hershiser, NIEDENFUER (7)
Home Runs: Madlock-LA, Marshall-LA, Clark-STL
Attendance: 55,208

Were it not for the expansion of the LCS to a best-of-seven series, the Blue Jays would have won the pennant. But after winning three of the first four games, the Jays lost their steam and K.C. swept to their second pennant.

The pitching of Toronto ace Dave Stieb proved a key to the club's fortunes. Three times he started for the Jays. In the opener he threw eight shutout innings as the Jays won easily. In Game Four he continued to dominate batters, though three walks in the sixth helped the Royals score a go-ahead run before Toronto pulled it out (for reliever Tom Henke) with a three-run ninth. Had the series ended there, Stieb would have been a hero. But it didn't, and he was called upon again for Game Seven—perhaps with inadequate rest. This time he faltered. After giving up single runs in the second and fourth innings, he loaded the bases in the sixth with two walks and a hit batsman. Jim Sundberg unloaded them with a wind-blown triple, later scoring himself, and the Royals were on the road to victory.

George Brett keyed Kansas City's triumph. His four hits in Game Three (including two home runs) gave the club its first victory, and his RBI ground out in Game Five and go-ahead homer in Game Six proved game-winners in contests the Royals had to win.

Kansas City Royals (West), 4;
Toronto Blue Jays (East), 3

KC (W)

PLAYER/POS	AVG	G	AB	R	H	2B	3B	HR	RB	BB	SO	SB
Steve Balboni, 1b	.120	7	25	1	3	0	0	0	1	2	8	0
Buddy Biancalana, ss	.222	7	18	2	4	1	0	0	1	1	6	0
Bud Black, p	.000	3	0	0	0	0	0	0	0	0	0	0
George Brett, 3b	.348	7	23	6	8	2	0	3	5	7	5	0
Onix Concepcion, ss	.000	4	1	0	0	0	0	0	0	0	0	0
Steve Farr, p	.000	2	0	0	0	0	0	0	0	0	0	0
Mark Gubicza, p	.000	2	0	0	0	0	0	0	0	0	0	0
Dane Iorg, ph	.500	4	2	0	1	1	0	0	0	2	0	0
Danny Jackson, p	.000	2	0	0	0	0	0	0	0	0	0	0
Lynn Jones, of	.000	5	0	0	0	0	0	0	0	0	0	0
Charlie Leibrandt, p	.000	3	0	0	0	0	0	0	0	0	0	0
Hal Mc Rae, dh	.261	6	23	1	6	2	0	0	3	1	6	0
Darryl Motley, of	.333	2	3	1	1	0	0	0	1	1	2	0
Jorge Orta, dh-1	.000	2	5	0	0	0	0	0	0	0	1	0
Jamie Quirk, ph	.000	1	1	0	0	0	0	0	0	0	0	0
Dan Quisenberry, p	.000	4	0	0	0	0	0	0	0	0	0	0
Bret Saberhagen, p	.000	2	0	0	0	0	0	0	0	0	0	0
Pat Sheridan, of	.150	7	20	4	3	0	0	2	3	2	3	0
Lonnie Smith, of	.250	7	28	2	7	2	0	0	1	3	6	1
Jim Sundberg, c	.167	7	24	3	4	1	1	1	6	1	7	0
Frank White, 2b	.200	7	25	1	5	0	0	0	3	1	2	0
Willie Wilson, of	.310	7	29	5	9	0	0	1	2	1	5	1
TOTAL	.225		227	26	51	9	1	7	26	22	51	2

PITCHER	W	L	ERA	G	GS	CG	SV	SHO	IP	H	ER	BB	SO
Bud Black	0	0	1.69	3	1	0	0	0	10.2	11	2	4	8
Steve Farr	1	0	1.42	2	0	0	0	0	6.1	4	1	1	3
Mark Gubicza	1	0	3.24	2	1	0	0	0	8.1	4	3	4	4
Danny Jackson	1	0	0.00	2	1	1	0	1	10.0	10	0	1	7
Charlie Leibrandt	1	2	5.28	3	2	0	0	0	15.1	17	9	4	6
Dan Quisenberry	0	1	3.86	4	0	0	1	0	4.2	7	2	0	3
Bret Saberhagen	0	0	6.14	2	2	0	0	0	7.1	12	5	2	6
TOTAL	4	3	3.16	18	7	1	1	1	62.2	65	22	16	37

TOR (E)

PLAYER/POS	AVG	G	AB	R	H	2B	3B	HR	RB	BB	SO	SB
Jim Acker, p	.000	2	0	0	0	0	0	0	0	0	0	0
Doyle Alexander, p	.000	2	0	0	0	0	0	0	0	0	0	0
Jesse Barfield, of	.280	7	25	3	7	1	0	1	4	3	7	1
George Bell, of	.321	7	28	4	9	3	0	0	1	0	4	0
Jeff Burroughs, ph	.000	1	1	0	0	0	0	0	0	0	0	0
Jim Clancy, p	.000	1	0	0	0	0	0	0	0	0	0	0
Tony Fernandez, ss	.333	7	24	2	8	2	0	0	2	1	2	0
Cecil Fielder, ph	.333	3	3	0	1	1	0	0	0	0	1	0
Damaso Garcia, 2b	.233	7	30	4	7	4	0	0	1	3	3	0
Jeff Hearron, c	.000	2	0	0	0	0	0	0	0	0	0	0
Tom Henke, p	.000	3	0	0	0	0	0	0	0	0	0	0
Garth Iorg, 3b	.133	6	15	1	2	0	0	0	0	1	3	0
Cliff Johnson, dh	.368	7	19	1	7	2	0	0	2	1	4	0
Jimmy Key, p	.000	2	0	0	0	0	0	0	0	0	0	0
Dennis Lamp, p	.000	3	0	0	0	0	0	0	0	0	0	0
Gary Lavelle, p	.000	1	0	0	0	0	0	0	0	0	0	0
Manny Lee, 2b	.000	1	0	0	0	0	0	0	0	0	0	0
Lloyd Moseby, of	.226	7	31	5	7	1	0	0	4	2	3	1
Rance Mulliniks, 3b	.364	5	11	1	4	1	0	1	3	2	2	0
Al Oliver, dh	.375	5	8	0	3	1	0	0	3	0	0	0
Dave Stieb, p	.000	3	0	0	0	0	0	0	0	0	0	0
Lou Thornton, pr	.000	2	0	1	0	0	0	0	0	0	0	0
Willie Upshaw, 1b	.231	7	26	2	6	2	0	0	1	1	4	0
Ernie Whitt, c	.190	7	21	1	4	1	0	0	2	2	4	0
TOTAL	.269		242	25	65	19	0	2	23	16	37	2

PITCHER	W	L	ERA	G	GS	CG	SV	SHO	IP	H	ER	BB	SO
Jim Acker	0	0	0.00	2	0	0	0	0	6.0	2	0	0	5
Doyle Alexander	0	1	8.71	2	2	0	0	0	10.1	14	10	3	9
Jim Clancy	0	1	9.00	1	0	0	0	0	1.0	2	1	1	0
Tom Henke	2	0	4.26	3	0	0	0	0	6.1	5	3	4	4
Jimmy Key	0	1	5.19	2	2	0	0	0	8.2	15	5	2	5
Dennis Lamp	0	0	0.00	3	0	0	0	0	9.1	2	0	1	10
Gary Lavelle	0	0	INF	1	0	0	0	0	0.0	0	0	1	0
Dave Stieb	1	1	3.10	3	3	0	0	0	20.1	11	7	10	18
TOTAL	3	4	3.77	17	7	0	0	0	62.0	51	26	22	51

GAME 1 AT TOR OCT 8

KC	000 000 001	1	5	1
TOR	023 100 00X	6	11	0

Pitchers: LEIBRANDT, Farr (3), Gubicza (5), Jackson (8) vs STIEB, Henke (9)
Attendance: 39,115

GAME 2 AT TOR OCT 9

KC	002 100 001 1	5	10	3
TOR	000 102 010 2	6	10	0

Pitchers: Black, QUISENBERRY (8) vs Key, Lamp (4), Lavelle (8), HENKE (8)
Home Runs: Wilson-KC, Sheridan-KC
Attendance: 34,029

GAME 3 AT KC OCT 11

TOR	000 050 000	5	13	1
KC	100 112 01X	6	10	1

Pitchers: Alexander, Lamp (6), CLANCY (8) vs Saberhagen, Black (5), FARR (5)
Home Runs: Brett-KC (2), Barfield-TOR, Mulliniks-TOR, Sundberg-KC
Attendance: 40,224

GAME 4 AT KC OCT 12

TOR	000 000 003	3	7	0
KC	000 001 000	1	2	0

Pitchers: Stieb, HENKE (7) vs LEIBRANDT, Quisenberry (9)
Attendance: 41,112

GAME 5 AT KC OCT 13

TOR	000 000 000	0	8	0
KC	110 000 00X	2	8	0

Pitchers: KEY, Acker (6) vs JACKSON
Attendance: 40,046

GAME 6 AT TOR OCT 15

KC	101 012 000	5	8	1
TOR	101 001 000	3	8	2

Pitchers: GUBICZA, Black (6), Quisenberry (9) vs ALEXANDER, Lamp (6)
Home Runs: Brett-KC
Attendance: 37,557

GAME 7 AT TOR OCT 16

KC	010 104 000	6	8	0
TOR	000 010 001	2	8	1

Pitchers: Saberhagen, LEIBRANDT (4), Quisenberry (9) vs STIEB, Acker (6)
Home Runs: Sheridan-KC
Attendance: 32,084

The underdog Royals surprised St. Louis with superior hitting and pitching, and even outstole the speedy Cards six bases to two. Still, had an umpire not muffed a call at first base in Game Six, St. Louis might have emerged from the fray wearing the world crown.

The Cardinals broke a 1–1 tie in the fourth inning of the opener with back-to-back doubles off Royal starter Danny Jackson, and held on behind the strong pitching of John Tudor and reliever Todd Worrell for a 3–1 win. In Game Two, except for the fourth inning, when he yielded a single and two doubles (for two runs) before retiring his first batter, Cardinal starter Danny Cox held the Royals in check. Royal starter Charlie Leibrandt hurled even more effectively, holding St. Louis to two hits—until the ninth inning, when four Cardinal hits (three of them doubles) produced four runs and a second Card victory.

Kansas City finally demonstrated its punch in Game Three. Frank White hit a two-run homer in the fifth, and the Royals scored four more times to win behind the six-hit hurling of sophomore sensation Bret Saberhagen. The next day, though, Royal bats died again against John Tudor, who shut them out on five hits. Three Royal pitchers yielded only six hits to Cardinal batters, but two were home runs to Tito Landrum and Willie McGee, and one was a triple to Terry Pendleton, who scored on a sacrifice squeeze.

Down three games to one, the Royals hammered eleven hits in Game Five for six runs to win behind Danny Jackson's five-hitter. Seven Royal hits in the first eight innings of Game Six, though, scored no runs against Cardinal starter Danny Cox and reliever Ken Dayley. But in the last of the ninth, with the Cards ahead 1–0 and Todd Worrell now pitching, Royal pinch hitter Jorge Orta was ruled safe at first on what the cameras showed clearly as an out. This miscall, followed by a pop foul that first baseman Jack Clark should have caught but didn't, opened the door to Cardinal disintegration. A single and passed ball put Royals at second and third, and after an intentional walk to set up the double play, pinch hitter Dane Iorg singled home the tying and winning Royal runs.

The Cardinals threw seven pitchers at Kansas City in the finale in a vain attempt to halt the Royals' fourteen-hit, eleven-run attack, while Bret Saberhagen stopped the Cards cold on five hits to bring the Royals their first world title.

Kansas City Royals (AL), 4; St. Louis Cardinals (NL), 3

KC (A)

PLAYER/POS	AVG	G	AB	R	H	2B	3B	HR	RB	BB	SO	SB
Steve Balboni, 1b	.320	7	25	2	8	0	0	0	3	5	4	0
Joe Beckwith, p	.000	1	0	0	0	0	0	0	0	0	0	0
Buddy Biancalana, ss	.278	7	18	2	5	0	0	0	2	5	4	0
Bud Black, p	.000	2	1	0	0	0	0	0	0	0	1	0
George Brett, 3b	.370	7	27	5	10	1	0	0	1	4	7	1
Onix Concepcion, ss-2	.000	3	0	1	0	0	0	0	0	0	0	0
Dane Iorg, ph	.500	2	2	0	1	0	0	0	2	0	0	0
Danny Jackson, p	.000	2	6	0	0	0	0	0	0	0	5	0
Lynn Jones, of-4	.667	6	3	0	2	1	1	0	0	0	0	0
Charlie Leibrandt, p	.000	2	4	0	0	0	0	0	0	0	2	0
Hal Mc Rae, ph	.000	3	1	0	0	0	0	0	0	1	0	0
Darryl Motley, of-4	.364	5	11	1	4	0	0	1	3	0	1	0
Jorge Orta, ph	.333	3	3	0	1	0	0	0	0	0	0	0
Greg Pryor, 3b	.000	1	0	0	0	0	0	0	0	0	0	0
Dan Quisenberry, p	.000	4	0	0	0	0	0	0	0	0	0	0
Bret Saberhagen, p	.000	2	7	1	0	0	0	0	0	0	4	0
Pat Sheridan, of-4	.222	5	18	0	4	2	0	0	1	0	7	0
Lonnie Smith, of	.333	7	27	4	9	3	0	0	4	3	8	2
Jim Sundberg, c	.250	7	24	6	6	2	0	0	1	6	4	0
John Wathan, ph	.000	2	1	0	0	0	0	0	0	0	1	0
Frank White, 2b	.250	7	28	4	7	3	0	1	6	3	4	0
Willie Wilson, of	.367	7	30	2	11	0	1	0	3	1	4	3
TOTAL	.288		236	28	68	12	2	2	26	28	56	6

PITCHER	W	L	ERA	G	GS	CG	SV	SHO	IP	H	ER	BB	SO
Joe Beckwith	0	0	0.00	1	0	0	0	0	2.0	1	0	0	3
Bud Black	0	1	5.06	2	1	0	0	0	5.1	4	3	5	4
Danny Jackson	1	1	1.69	2	2	1	0	0	16.0	9	3	5	12
Charlie Leibrandt	0	1	2.76	2	2	0	0	0	16.1	10	5	4	10
Dan Quisenberry	1	0	2.08	4	0	0	0	0	4.1	5	1	3	3
Bret Saberhagen	2	0	0.50	2	2	2	0	1	18.0	11	1	1	10
TOTAL	4	3	1.89	13	7	3	0	1	62.0	40	13	18	42

STL (N)

PLAYER/POS	AVG	G	AB	R	H	2B	3B	HR	RB	BB	SO	SB
Joaquin Andujar, p	.000	2	1	0	0	0	0	0	0	0	1	0
Steve Braun, ph	.000	1	1	0	0	0	0	0	0	0	0	0
Bill Campbell, p	.000	3	0	0	0	0	0	0	0	0	0	0
Cesar Cedeno, of	.133	5	15	1	2	1	0	0	1	2	2	0
Jack Clark, 1b	.240	7	25	1	6	2	0	0	4	3	9	0
Danny Cox, p	.000	2	4	0	0	0	0	0	0	0	2	0
Ken Dayley, p	.000	4	0	0	0	0	0	0	0	0	0	0
Ivan De Jesus, ph	.000	1	1	0	0	0	0	0	0	0	0	0
Bob Forsch, p	.000	2	0	0	0	0	0	0	0	0	0	0
Brian Harper, ph	.250	4	4	0	1	0	0	0	1	0	1	0
Tommy Herr, 2b	.154	7	26	2	4	2	0	0	2	2	2	0
Rick Horton, p	.000	3	1	0	0	0	0	0	0	0	1	0
Mike Jorgensen, of-1	.000	2	3	0	0	0	0	0	0	0	0	0
Jeff Lahti, p	.000	3	0	0	0	0	0	0	0	0	0	0
Tito Landrum, of	.360	7	25	3	9	2	0	1	1	0	2	0
Tom Lawless, pr	.000	1	0	0	0	0	0	0	0	0	0	0
Willie Mc Gee, of	.259	7	27	2	7	2	0	1	2	1	3	1
Tom Nieto, c	.000	2	5	0	0	0	0	0	0	1	2	0
Terry Pendleton, 3b	.261	7	23	3	6	1	1	0	3	3	2	0
Darrell Porter, c	.133	5	15	0	2	0	0	0	0	2	5	0
Ozzie Smith, ss	.087	7	23	1	2	0	0	0	0	4	0	1
John Tudor, p	.000	3	5	0	0	0	0	0	0	0	4	0
Andy Van Slyke, of	.091	6	11	0	1	0	0	0	0	0	5	0
Todd Worrell, p	.000	3	1	0	0	0	0	0	0	0	1	0
TOTAL	.185		216	13	40	10	1	2	13	18	42	2

PITCHER	W	L	ERA	G	GS	CG	SV	SHO	IP	H	ER	BB	SO
Joaquin Andujar	0	1	9.00	2	1	0	0	0	4.0	10	4	4	3
Bill Campbell	0	0	2.25	3	0	0	0	0	4.0	4	1	2	5
Danny Cox	0	0	1.29	2	2	0	0	0	14.0	14	2	4	13
Ken Dayley	1	0	0.00	4	0	0	0	0	6.0	1	0	3	5
Bob Forsch	0	1	12.00	2	1	0	0	0	3.0	6	4	1	3
Rick Horton	0	0	6.75	3	0	0	0	0	4.0	4	3	5	5
Jeff Lahti	0	0	12.27	3	0	0	1	0	3.2	10	5	0	2
John Tudor	2	1	3.00	3	3	1	0	1	18.0	15	6	7	14
Todd Worrell	0	1	3.86	3	0	0	1	0	4.2	4	2	2	6
TOTAL	3	4	3.96	25	7	1	2	1	61.1	68	27	28	56

GAME 1 AT KC OCT 19

STL	001	100	001	3	7	1
KC	010	000	000	1	8	0

Pitchers: TUDOR, Worrell (7) vs JACKSON, Quisenberry (8), Black (9)
Attendance: 41,650

GAME 2 AT KC OCT 20

STL	000	000	004	4	6	0
KC	000	200	000	2	9	0

Pitchers: Cox, DAYLEY (8), Lahti (9) vs LEIBRANDT, Quisenberry (9)
Attendance: 41,656

GAME 3 AT STL OCT 22

KC	000	220	200	6	11	0
STL	000	001	000	1	6	0

Pitchers: SABERHAGEN vs ANDUJAR, Campbell (5), Horton (6), Dayley (8)
Home Runs: White-KC
Attendance: 53,634

GAME 4 AT STL OCT 23

KC	000	000	000	0	5	1
STL	011	010	00X	3	6	0

Pitchers: BLACK, Beckwith (6), Quisenberry (8) vs TUDOR
Home Runs: Landrum-STL, McGee-STL
Attendance: 53,634

GAME 5 AT STL OCT 24

KC	130	000	011	6	11	2
STL	100	000	000	1	5	1

Pitchers: JACKSON vs FORSCH, Horton (2), Campbell (4), Worrell (6), Lahti (8)
Attendance: 53,634

GAME 6 AT KC OCT 26

STL	000	000	010	1	5	0
KC	000	000	002	2	10	0

Pitchers: Cox, Dayley (8), WORRELL (9) vs Leibrandt, QUISENBERRY (8)
Attendance: 41,628

GAME 7 AT KC OCT 27

STL	000	000	000	0	5	0
KC	023	060	00X	11	14	0

Pitchers: TUDOR, Campbell (3), Lahti (5), Horton (5), Andujar (5), Forsch (5), Dayley (7) vs SABERHAGEN
Home Runs: Motley-KC
Attendance: 41,658

Houston pitcher Mike Scott overwhelmed the Mets in Games One and Four, and would have faced them a third time in Game Seven if the Astros had won Game Six. They tried, scoring three runs in the first as Bob Knepper shut out the Mets on two hits through eight innings. But in the top of the ninth New York tied the game and held on into extra innings. No one scored again until the Mets put a run across in the fourteenth. Astro Billy Hatcher tied it up again later in the fourteenth with a home run just inside the left field foul pole. Two innings later the Mets (aided by a pair of wild pitches) scored three runs. Again the Astros came back, scoring twice, but fell just short as Jesse Orosco struck out Kevin Bass with two men on base to win his third game of the series and give New York the pennant.

In the series opener Houston scored just one run off Dwight Gooden, but it was enough, as Mike Scott, fanning fourteen, shut out the Mets on five hits. New York came back with five runs in Game Two to win behind Bob Ojeda, who gave up ten hits but only one run. In Game Three the Astros held the lead into the last of the sixth, when New York tied the score with four runs. Houston retook the lead in the seventh with a run, but Met Len Dykstra won it for New York with a two-run homer in the bottom of the ninth.

The Astros' win in Game Four evened the series. Houston had scored three runs by the time Scott (on his way to a three-hitter) gave the Mets their only run in the eighth. Houston's Nolan Ryan gave up only two hits in the first nine innings of Game Five (one of them Darryl Strawberry's game-tying solo homer in the fifth), striking out twelve. But New York's Gooden also yielded only one run in ten innings of work. Astro Charlie Kerfeld shut out the Mets in the tenth and eleventh, and the Mets' Orosco stopped Houston in the eleventh and twelfth. But in the last of the twelfth, Met catcher Gary Carter singled home a run off Kerfeld to end the game (and his series-long batting slump)—setting the stage for the sixteen-inning marathon the next day.

New York Mets (East), 4;
Houston Astros (West), 2

NY (E)

PLAYER/POS	AVG	G	AB	R	H	2B	3B	HR	RB	BB	SO	SB
Rick Aguilera, p	.000	2	0	0	0	0	0	0	0	0	0	0
Wally Backman, 2b	.238	6	21	5	5	0	0	0	2	2	4	1
Gary Carter, c	.148	6	27	1	4	1	0	0	2	2	5	0
Ron Darling, p	.000	1	1	0	0	0	0	0	0	0	0	0
Lenny Dykstra, of	.304	6	23	3	7	1	1	1	3	2	4	1
Kevin Elster, ss	.000	4	3	0	0	0	0	0	0	0	1	0
Sid Fernandez, p	.000	1	1	0	0	0	0	0	0	0	0	0
Dwight Gooden, p	.000	2	5	0	0	0	0	0	0	0	2	0
Danny Heep, of-1	.250	5	4	0	1	0	0	0	1	0	2	0
Keith Hernandez, 1b	.269	6	26	3	7	1	1	0	3	3	6	0
Howard Johnson, ph	.000	2	2	0	0	0	0	0	0	0	0	0
Ray Knight, 3b	.167	6	24	1	4	0	0	0	2	1	5	0
Lee Mazzilli, ph	.200	5	5	0	1	0	0	0	0	0	3	0
Roger Mc Dowell, p	.000	2	1	0	0	0	0	0	0	0	0	0
Kevin Mitchell, of	.250	2	8	1	2	0	0	0	0	0	1	0
Bob Ojeda, p	.000	2	5	1	0	0	0	0	0	0	2	0
Jesse Orosco, p	.000	4	0	0	0	0	0	0	0	0	0	0
Rafael Santana, ss	.176	6	17	0	3	0	0	0	0	0	3	0
Doug Sisk, p	.000	1	0	0	0	0	0	0	0	0	0	0
Darryl Strawberry, of	.227	6	22	4	5	1	0	2	5	3	12	1
Tim Teufel, 2b	.167	2	6	0	1	0	0	0	0	0	0	0
Mookie Wilson, of	.115	6	26	2	3	0	0	0	1	1	7	1
TOTAL	.189		227	21	43	4	2	3	19	14	57	4

PITCHER	W	L	ERA	G	GS	CG	SV	SHO	IP	H	ER	BB	SO
Rick Aguilera	0	0	0.00	2	0	0	0	0	5.0	2	0	2	2
Ron Darling	0	0	7.20	1	1	0	0	0	5.0	6	4	2	5
Sid Fernandez	0	1	4.50	1	1	0	0	0	6.0	3	3	1	5
Dwight Gooden	0	1	1.06	2	2	0	0	0	17.0	16	2	5	9
Roger Mc Dowell	0	0	0.00	2	0	0	0	0	7.0	1	0	0	3
Bob Ojeda	1	0	2.57	2	2	1	0	0	14.0	15	4	4	6
Jesse Orosco	3	0	3.38	4	0	0	0	0	8.0	5	3	2	10
Doug Sisk	0	0	0.00	1	0	0	0	0	1.0	1	0	1	0
TOTAL	4	2	2.29	15	6	1	0	0	63.0	49	16	17	40

HOU (W)

PLAYER/POS	AVG	G	AB	R	H	2B	3B	HR	RB	BB	SO	SB
Larry Andersen, p	.000	2	0	0	0	0	0	0	0	0	0	0
Alan Ashby, c	.130	6	23	2	3	1	0	1	2	2	1	0
Kevin Bass, of	.292	6	24	0	7	2	0	0	0	4	4	2
Jeff Calhoun, p	.000	1	0	0	0	0	0	0	0	0	0	0
Jose Cruz, of	.192	6	26	0	5	0	0	0	2	1	8	0
Glenn Davis, 1b	.269	6	26	3	7	1	0	1	3	1	3	0
Bill Doran, 2b	.222	6	27	3	6	0	0	1	3	2	2	2
Phil Garner, 3b	.222	3	9	1	2	1	0	0	2	1	2	0
Billy Hatcher, of	.280	6	25	4	7	0	0	1	2	3	2	3
Charlie Kerfeld, p	.000	3	0	0	0	0	0	0	0	0	0	0
Bob Knepper, p	.000	2	5	0	0	0	0	0	0	1	2	0
Davey Lopes, ph	.000	2	1	0	0	0	0	0	0	1	0	0
Aurelio Lopez, p	.000	2	0	0	0	0	0	0	0	0	0	0
Jim Pankovits, ph	.000	2	2	0	0	0	0	0	0	0	1	0
Terry Puhl, ph	.667	3	3	0	2	0	0	0	0	0	0	1
Craig Reynolds, ss	.333	4	12	1	4	0	0	0	0	1	3	0
Nolan Ryan, p	.000	2	4	0	0	0	0	0	0	0	2	0
Mike Scott, p	.000	2	6	0	0	0	0	0	0	0	5	0
Dave Smith, p	.000	2	0	0	0	0	0	0	0	0	0	0
Dickie Thon, ss	.250	6	12	1	3	0	0	1	1	0	1	0
Denny Walling, 3b	.158	5	19	1	3	1	0	0	2	2	4	0
TOTAL	.218		225	17	49	6	0	5	17	17	40	8

PITCHER	W	L	ERA	G	GS	CG	SV	SHO	IP	H	ER	BB	SO
Larry Andersen	0	0	0.00	2	0	0	0	0	5.0	1	0	2	3
Jeff Calhoun	0	0	9.00	1	0	0	0	0	1.0	1	1	1	0
Charlie Kerfeld	0	1	2.25	3	0	0	0	0	4.0	2	1	1	4
Bob Knepper	0	0	3.52	2	2	0	0	0	15.1	13	6	1	9
Aurelio Lopez	0	1	8.10	2	0	0	0	0	3.1	7	3	4	3
Nolan Ryan	0	1	3.86	2	2	0	0	0	14.0	9	6	1	17
Mike Scott	2	0	0.50	2	2	2	0	1	18.0	8	1	1	19
Dave Smith	0	1	9.00	2	0	0	0	0	2.0	2	2	3	2
TOTAL	2	4	2.87	16	6	2	0	1	62.2	43	20	14	57

GAME 1 AT HOU OCT 8

NY	000 000 000	0 5 0
HOU	010 000 00X	1 7 1

Pitchers: GOODEN, Orosco (8) vs SCOTT
Home Runs: Davis-HOU
Attendance: 44,131

GAME 2 AT HOU OCT 9

NY	000 230 000	5 10 0
HOU	000 000 100	1 10 2

Pitchers: OJEDA vs RYAN, Andersen (6), Lopez (8), Kerfeld (9)
Attendance: 44,391

GAME 3 AT NY OCT 11

HOU	220 000 100	5 8 1
NY	000 004 002	6 10 1

Pitchers: Knepper, Kerfeld (8), SMITH (9) vs Darling, Aguilera (6), OROSCO (8)
Home Runs: Doran-HOU, Strawberry-NY, Dykstra-NY
Attendance: 55,052

GAME 4 AT NY OCT 12

HOU	020 010 000	3 4 1
NY	000 000 010	1 3 0

Pitchers: SCOTT vs FERNANDEZ, McDowell (7), Sisk (9)
Home Runs: Ashby-HOU, Thon-HOU
Attendance: 55,038

GAME 5 AT NY OCT 14

HOU	000 010 000 000	1 9 1
NY	000 010 000 001	2 4 0

Pitchers: Ryan, KERFELD (10) vs Gooden, OROSCO (11)
Home Runs: Strawberry-NY
Attendance: 54,986

GAME 6 AT HOU OCT 15

NY	000 000 003 000 010 3	7 11 0
HOU	300 000 000 000 010 2	6 11 1

Pitchers: Ojeda, Aguilera (6), McDowell (9), OROSCO (14) vs Knepper, Smith (9), Andersen (11), LOPEZ (14), Calhoun (16)
Home Runs: Hatcher-HOU
Attendance: 45,718

For the second time in the two years of the expanded LCS, a club that would have been eliminated in a five-game series came back to take the pennant in seven games. The first two games were one-sided. California scored five early runs off Roger Clemens and breezed to an easy 8–1 win in the opener. Boston retaliated in Game Two with nine runs, breaking the game open with six unanswered runs in the seventh and eighth innings.

Game Three was close until the Angels homered twice for three runs with two out in the seventh to break a 1–1 tie. In Game Four, the Angels were handed a tie in the last of the ninth when Boston reliever Calvin Schiraldi hit a batter with the bases loaded and won in the eleventh on Bobby Grich's RBI single.

The Red Sox, down three games to one, were on the brink of elimination in Game Five, with two out in the ninth, when Dave Henderson, after fouling off one third-strike pitch, hit the next for a two-run homer that gave Boston a one-run lead. The Angels tied the game in the last of the ninth, but Henderson's sacrifice fly in the eleventh put the Sox ahead for good.

Boston needed two more wins and got them with surprising ease, 10–4 and 8–1, as Oil Can Boyd and Clemens redeemed their earlier losses.

Boston Red Sox (East), 4; California Angels (West), 3

BOS (E)

PLAYER/POS	AVG	G	AB	R	H	2B	3B	HR	RB	BB	SO	SB
Tony Armas, of	.125	5	16	1	2	1	0	0	0	0	2	0
Marty Barrett, 2b	.367	7	30	4	11	2	0	0	5	2	2	0
Don Baylor, dh	.346	7	26	6	9	3	0	1	2	4	5	0
Wade Boggs, 3b	.233	7	30	3	7	1	1	0	2	4	1	0
Oil Can Boyd, p	.000	2	0	0	0	0	0	0	0	0	0	0
Bill Buckner, 1b	.214	7	28	3	6	1	0	0	3	0	2	0
Roger Clemens, p	.000	3	0	0	0	0	0	0	0	0	0	0
Steve Crawford, p	.000	1	0	0	0	0	0	0	0	0	0	0
Dwight Evans, of	.214	7	28	2	6	1	0	1	4	3	3	0
Rich Gedman, c	.357	7	28	4	10	1	0	1	6	0	4	0
Mike Greenwell, ph	.500	2	2	0	1	0	0	0	0	0	0	0
Dave Henderson, of	.111	5	9	3	1	0	0	1	4	2	2	0
Bruce Hurst, p	.000	2	0	0	0	0	0	0	0	0	0	0
Spike Owen, ss	.429	7	21	5	9	0	1	0	3	2	2	1
Jim Rice, of	.161	7	31	8	5	1	0	2	6	1	8	0
Ed Romero, ss	.000	1	2	0	0	0	0	0	0	0	0	0
Joe Sambito, p	.000	3	0	0	0	0	0	0	0	0	0	0
Calvin Schiraldi, p	.000	4	0	0	0	0	0	0	0	0	0	0
Bob Stanley, p	.000	3	0	0	0	0	0	0	0	0	0	0
Dave Stapleton, 1b	.667	4	3	2	2	0	0	0	0	1	0	0
TOTAL	.272		254	41	69	11	2	6	35	19	31	1

PITCHER	W	L	ERA	G	GS	CG	SV	SHO	IP	H	ER	BB	SO
Oil Can Boyd	1	1	4.61	2	2	0	0	0	13.2	17	7	3	8
Roger Clemens	1	1	4.37	3	3	0	0	0	22.2	22	11	7	17
Steve Crawford	1	0	0.00	1	0	0	0	0	1.2	1	0	2	1
Bruce Hurst	1	0	2.40	2	2	1	0	0	15.0	18	4	1	8
Joe Sambito	0	0	13.50	3	0	0	0	0	0.2	1	1	1	0
Calvin Schiraldi	0	1	1.50	4	0	0	1	0	6.0	5	1	3	9
Bob Stanley	0	0	3.18	3	0	0	0	0	5.2	7	2	3	1
TOTAL	4	3	3.58	18	7	1	1	0	65.1	71	26	20	44

CAL (W)

PLAYER/POS	AVG	G	AB	R	H	2B	3B	HR	RB	BB	SO	SB
Bob Boone, c	.455	7	22	4	10	0	0	1	2	1	3	0
Rick Burleson, 2b-2,dh-1	.273	4	11	0	3	0	0	0	0	0	0	0
John Candelaria, p	.000	2	0	0	0	0	0	0	0	0	0	0
Doug Corbett, p	.000	3	0	0	0	0	0	0	0	0	0	0
Doug De Cinces, 3b	.281	7	32	2	9	3	0	1	3	0	2	0
Brian Downing, of	.222	7	27	2	6	0	0	1	7	4	5	0
Chuck Finley, p	.000	3	0	0	0	0	0	0	0	0	0	0
Bobby Grich, 2b-3,1b-3	.208	6	24	1	5	0	0	1	3	0	8	0
George Hendrick, of-2,1b-1	.083	3	12	0	1	0	0	0	0	0	2	0
Jack Howell, ph	.000	2	1	0	0	0	0	0	0	1	1	0
Reggie Jackson, dh	.192	6	26	2	5	2	0	0	2	2	7	0
Ruppert Jones, of-5	.176	6	17	4	3	1	0	0	2	5	2	0
Wally Joyner, 1b	.455	3	11	3	5	2	0	1	2	2	0	0
Gary Lucas, p	.000	4	0	0	0	0	0	0	0	0	0	0
Kirk Mc Caskill, p	.000	2	0	0	0	0	0	0	0	0	0	0
Donnie Moore, p	.000	3	0	0	0	0	0	0	0	0	0	0
Jerry Narron, c-3	.500	4	2	1	1	0	0	0	0	1	1	0
Gary Pettis, of	.346	7	26	4	9	1	0	1	4	3	5	0
Vern Ruhle, p	.000	1	0	0	0	0	0	0	0	0	0	0
Dick Schofield, ss	.300	7	30	4	9	1	0	1	2	1	5	1
Don Sutton, p	.000	2	0	0	0	0	0	0	0	0	0	0
Devon White, of-3	.500	4	2	2	1	0	0	0	0	0	1	0
Rob Wilfong, 2b	.308	4	13	1	4	1	0	0	2	0	2	0
Mike Witt, p	.000	2	0	0	0	0	0	0	0	0	0	0
TOTAL	.277		256	30	71	11	0	7	29	20	44	1

PITCHER	W	L	ERA	G	GS	CG	SV	SHO	IP	H	ER	BB	SO
John Candelaria	1	1	0.84	2	2	0	0	0	10.2	11	1	6	7
Doug Corbett	1	0	5.40	3	0	0	0	0	6.2	9	4	2	2
Chuck Finley	0	0	0.00	3	0	0	0	0	2.0	1	0	0	1
Gary Lucas	0	0	11.57	4	0	0	0	0	2.1	3	3	1	2
Kirk Mc Caskill	0	2	7.71	2	2	0	0	0	9.1	16	8	5	7
Donnie Moore	0	1	7.20	3	0	0	1	0	5.0	8	4	2	0
Vern Ruhle	0	0	13.50	1	0	0	0	0	0.2	2	1	0	0
Don Sutton	0	0	1.86	2	1	0	0	0	9.2	6	2	1	4
Mike Witt	1	0	2.55	2	2	1	0	0	17.2	13	5	2	8
TOTAL	3	4	3.94	22	7	1	1	0	64.0	69	28	19	31

GAME 1 AT BOS OCT 7

CAL	041	000	030	8 11	0
BOS	000	001	000	1 5	1

Pitchers: WITT vs CLEMENS, Sambito (8), Stanley (8)
Attendance: 32,993

GAME 2 AT BOS OCT 8

CAL	000	110	000	2 11	3
BOS	110	010	33X	9 13	2

Pitchers: McCASKILL, Lucas (8), Corbett (8) vs HURST
Home Runs: Joyner-CAL, Rice-BOS
Attendance: 32,786

GAME 3 AT CAL OCT 10

BOS	010	000	020	3 9	1
CAL	000	001	31X	5 8	0

Pitchers: BOYD, Sambito (7), Schiraldi (8) vs CANDELARIA, Moore (8)
Home Runs: Schofield-CAL, Pettis-CAL
Attendance: 64,206

GAME 4 AT CAL OCT 11

BOS	000	001	020 00	3 6	1
CAL	000	000	003 01	4 11	2

Pitchers: Clemens, SCHIRALDI (9) vs Sutton, Lucas (7), Ruhle (7), Finley (8), FINLEY (8)
Home Runs: DeCinces-CAL
Attendance: 64,223

GAME 5 AT CAL OCT 12

BOS	020	000	004 01	7 12	0
CAL	001	002	201 00	6 13	0

Pitchers: Hurst, Stanley (7), Sambito (9), CRAWFORD (9), Schiraldi (11) vs Witt, Lucas (9), MOORE (9), Finley (11)
Home Runs: Gedman-BOS, Boone-CAL, Grich-CAL, Baylor-BOS, Henderson-BOS
Attendance: 64,223

GAME 6 AT BOS OCT 14

CAL	200	000	110	4 11	1
BOS	205	010	20X	10 16	1

Pitchers: McCASKILL, Lucas (3), Corbett (4), Finley (7) vs BOYD, Stanley (8)
Home Runs: Downing-CAL
Attendance: 32,998

GAME 7 AT BOS OCT 15

CAL	000	000	010	1 6	2
BOS	030	400	10X	8 8	1

Pitchers: CANDELARIA, Sutton (4), Moore (8) vs CLEMENS, Schiraldi (8)
Home Runs: Rice-BOS, Evans-BOS
Attendance: 33,001

In their three most recent Series appearances—1946, 1967, and 1975—the Red Sox had battled to a seventh game, only to lose. This time they came within one strike of winning the crown in the sixth game—but wound up losing again in Game Seven.

Boston surprised the favored Mets by taking the first two games in New York. Bruce Hurst (with relief from Calvin Schiradli in the ninth) pitched a four-hitter. New York's Ron Darling hurled just as well but lost when a seventh-inning walk, a wild pitch, and an error by second baseman Tim Teufel moved Jim Rice around the bases with the game's only run. Game Two, close for three innings, turned into a 9–3 Boston blowout as the Sox racked four of the five Met pitchers for eighteen hits, including home runs by Dave Henderson and Dwight Evans.

When the Series moved to Boston, though, the Mets revived to rap Sox starter Oil Can Boyd and two relievers for thirteen hits and seven runs (starting with Len Dykstra's leadoff home run in the first inning) as former Sox pitcher Bob Ojeda subdued his old teammates, giving up just one run on five hits in his seven innings of work. The next day Ron Darling redeemed his first-game loss with seven shutout innings as his teammates built him a 6–0 lead (five of the runs scoring on homers by Dykstra and a pair by Gary Carter). The game ended at 6–2, with the Series even at two wins apiece.

Boston recovered in its final home appearance, taking a 4–0 lead and holding it until Teufel spoiled Bruce Hurst's try for a second shutout by homering in the eighth inning. Hurst yielded a second run with two out in the ninth, but struck out Len Dykstra on three pitches to seal his second win.

The ninth inning of Game Six ended with the score tied 3–3. Boston's Dave Henderson led off the tenth with a home run and two more Sox hits made the score 5–3. Boston reliever Calvin Schiraldi retired the first two Mets in the last of the tenth on long flies, but then three Mets singled, driving in one run and driving out Schiraldi. Bob Stanley, his replacement, had two strikes on Mookie Wilson when a wild pitch let in the tying run, and then Wilson's grounder went through first baseman Bill Buckner's legs as the winning Met bounded across the plate.

The Red Sox nearly recovered in Game Seven. Second-inning home runs by Dwight Evans and Rich Gedman, a walk, sacrifice, and single gave Boston a 3–0 lead which they held into the sixth inning. But then starter Bruce Hurst

New York Mets (NL), 4; Boston Red Sox (AL), 3

NY (N)

PLAYER/POS	AVG	G	AB	R	H	2B	3B	HR	RB	BB	SO	SB
Rick Aguilera, p	.000	1	0	0	0	0	0	0	0	0	0	0
Wally Backman, 2b	.333	6	18	4	6	0	0	0	1	3	2	1
Gary Carter, c	.276	7	29	4	8	2	0	2	9	0	4	0
Ron Darling, p	.000	3	3	0	0	0	0	0	0	0	1	0
Lenny Dykstra, of	.296	7	27	4	8	0	0	2	3	2	7	0
Kevin Elster, ss	.000	1	1	0	0	0	0	0	0	0	0	0
Sid Fernandez, p	.000	3	0	0	0	0	0	0	0	0	0	0
Dwight Gooden, p	.500	2	2	1	1	0	0	0	0	0	0	0
Danny Heep, dh-2,of-1	.091	5	11	0	1	0	0	0	2	1	1	0
Keith Hernandez, 1b	.231	7	26	1	6	0	0	0	4	5	1	0
Howard Johnson, 3b-1,ss-1	.000	2	5	0	0	0	0	0	0	0	2	0
Ray Knight, 3b	.391	6	23	4	9	1	0	1	5	2	2	0
Lee Mazzilli, of-1	.400	4	5	2	2	0	0	0	0	0	0	0
Roger Mc Dowell, p	.000	5	0	0	0	0	0	0	0	0	0	0
Kevin Mitchell, of-2,dh-1	.250	5	8	1	2	0	0	0	0	0	3	0
Bob Ojeda, p	.000	2	2	0	0	0	0	0	0	0	1	0
Jesse Orosco, p	1.000	4	1	0	1	0	0	0	0	1	0	0
Rafael Santana, ss	.250	7	20	3	5	0	0	0	2	2	5	0
Doug Sisk, p	.000	1	0	0	0	0	0	0	0	0	0	0
Darryl Strawberry, of	.208	7	24	4	5	1	0	1	1	4	6	3
Tim Teufel, 2b	.444	3	9	1	4	1	0	1	1	1	2	0
Mookie Wilson, of	.269	7	26	3	7	1	0	0	0	1	6	3
TOTAL	.271		240	32	65	6	0	7	29	21	43	7

PITCHER	W	L	ERA	G	GS	CG	SV	SHO	IP	H	ER	BB	SO
Rick Aguilera	1	0	12.00	1	0	0	0	0	3.0	8	4	1	4
Ron Darling	1	1	1.53	3	3	0	0	0	17.2	13	3	10	12
Sid Fernandez	0	0	1.35	3	0	0	0	0	6.2	6	1	1	10
Dwight Gooden	0	2	8.00	2	2	0	0	0	9.0	17	8	4	9
Roger Mc Dowell	1	0	4.91	5	0	0	0	0	7.1	10	4	6	2
Bob Ojeda	1	0	2.08	2	2	0	0	0	13.0	13	3	5	9
Jesse Orosco	0	0	0.00	4	0	0	2	0	5.2	2	0	0	6
Doug Sisk	0	0	0.00	1	0	0	0	0	0.2	0	0	1	1
TOTAL	4	3	3.29	21	7	0	2	0	63.0	69	23	28	53

BOS (A)

PLAYER/POS	AVG	G	AB	R	H	2B	3B	HR	RB	BB	SO	SB
Tony Armas, ph	.000	1	1	0	0	0	0	0	0	0	1	0
Marty Barrett, 2b	.433	7	30	1	13	2	0	0	4	5	2	0
Don Baylor, dh-3	.182	4	11	1	2	1	0	0	1	1	3	0
Wade Boggs, 3b	.290	7	31	3	9	3	0	0	3	4	2	0
Oil Can Boyd, p	.000	1	0	0	0	0	0	0	0	0	0	0
Bill Buckner, 1b	.188	7	32	2	6	0	0	0	1	0	3	0
Roger Clemens, p	.000	2	4	0	0	0	0	0	0	0	1	0
Steve Crawford, p	.000	3	1	0	0	0	0	0	0	0	0	0
Dwight Evans, of	.308	7	26	4	8	2	0	2	9	4	3	0
Rich Gedman, c	.200	7	30	1	6	1	0	1	1	0	10	0
Mike Greenwell, ph	.000	4	3	0	0	0	0	0	0	1	2	0
Dave Henderson, of	.667	7	15	6	10	1	1	2	5	2	6	0
Bruce Hurst, p	.000	3	3	0	0	0	0	0	0	0	1	0
Al Nipper, p	.000	2	0	0	0	0	0	0	0	0	0	0
Spike Owen, ss	.300	7	20	2	6	0	0	0	2	5	6	0
Jim Rice, of	.333	7	27	6	9	1	1	0	0	6	9	0
Ed Romero, ss	.000	3	1	0	0	0	0	0	0	0	0	0
Joe Sambito, p	.000	2	0	0	0	0	0	0	0	0	0	0
Calvin Schiraldi, p	.000	3	1	0	0	0	0	0	0	0	1	0
Bob Stanley, p	.000	5	1	0	0	0	0	0	0	0	1	0
Dave Stapleton, 1b	.000	3	1	0	0	0	0	0	0	0	0	0
TOTAL	.290		238	27	69	11	2	5	26	28	53	0

PITCHER	W	L	ERA	G	GS	CG	SV	SHO	IP	H	ER	BB	SO
Oil Can Boyd	0	1	7.71	1	1	0	0	0	7.0	9	6	1	3
Roger Clemens	0	0	3.18	2	2	0	0	0	11.1	9	4	6	11
Steve Crawford	1	0	6.23	3	0	0	0	0	4.1	5	3	0	4
Bruce Hurst	2	0	1.96	3	3	1	0	0	23.0	18	5	6	17
Al Nipper	0	1	7.11	2	1	0	0	0	6.1	10	5	2	2
Joe Sambito	0	0	27.00	2	0	0	0	0	0.1	2	1	2	0
Calvin Schiraldi	0	2	13.50	3	0	0	1	0	4.0	7	6	3	2
Bob Stanley	0	0	0.00	5	0	0	1	0	6.1	5	0	1	4
TOTAL	3	4	4.31	21	7	1	2	0	62.2	65	30	21	43

lost his touch: four hits and a walk later the score was tied. A succession of five Sox relievers tried to hold the line, but the Mets scored five runs to Boston's two in the final innings for an 8–5 triumph.

GAME 1 AT NY OCT 18

BOS	000	000	100	1	5	0
NY	000	000	000	0	4	1

Pitchers: HURST, Schiradli (9) vs DARLING, McDowell (8)
Attendance: 55,076

GAME 2 AT NY OCT 19

BOS	003	120	201	9	18	0
NY	002	010	000	3	8	1

Pitchers: Clemens, CARWFORD (5), Stanley (7) vs GOODEN, Aguilera (6), Orosco (7), Fernandez (9), Sisk (9)
Home Runs: Henderson-BOS, Evans-BOS
Attendance: 55,063

GAME 3 AT BOS OCT 21

NY	400	000	210	7	13	0
BOS	001	000	000	1	5	0

Pitchers: OJEDA, McDowell (8) vs BOYD, Sambito (8), Stanley (8)
Home Runs: Dykstra-NY
Attendance: 33,595

GAME 4 AT BOS OCT 22

NY	000	300	210	6	12	0
BOS	000	000	020	2	7	1

Pitchers: DARLING, McDowell (7), Orosco (7) vs NIPPER, Crawford (7), Stanley (9)
Home Runs: Dykstra-NY, Carter-NY (2)
Attendance: 33,920

GAME 5 AT BOS OCT 23

NY	000	000	011	2	10	1
BOS	011	020	00X	4	12	0

Pitchers: GOODEN, Fernandez (5) vs HURST
Home Runs: Teufel-NY
Attendance: 34,010

GAME 6 AT NY OCT 25

BOS	110	000	100 2	5	13	3
NY	000	020	010 3	6	8	2

Pitchers: Clemens, SCHIRALDI (8), Stanley (10) vs Ojeda, McDowell (7), Orosco (8), AGUILERA (9)
Home Runs: Henderson-BOS
Attendance: 55,078

GAME 7 AT NY OCT 27

BOS	030	000	020	5	9	0
NY	000	003	32X	8	10	0

Pitchers: Hurst, SCHIRALDI (7), Sambito (7), Stanley (7), Nipper (8), Crawford (8) vs Darling, Fernandez (4), McDOWELL (8), Orosco (9)
Home Runs: Evans-BOS, Gedman-BOS, Knight-NY, Strawberry-NY
Attendance: 55,032

The Giants scored four times in the fourth inning of Game Five, winning the game and taking a 3–2 series advantage. But Cardinal pitchers shut them out the rest of the series (an NLCS record 22 innings) to capture the flag.

St. Louis won the opener 5–3, with pitcher Greg Mathews's two-run single in the sixth providing his margin of victory. The Giants came back in Game Two, supporting Dave Dravecky's two-hit shutout with home runs by Will Clark and Jeffrey Leonard. But the Cards retook the series lead in Game Three, overcoming a 0–4 deficit with two runs on Jim Lindeman's homer in the sixth and four more in the seventh (capped by Lindeman's sacrifice fly) for an eventual 6–5 win. The Giants snapped back with a pair of wins, scoring four runs on three homers in Game Four (including Leonard's fourth in successive games—an LCS record), and six runs in Game Five. But Dravecky and the Giants lost a heartbreaker in Game Six when right fielder Candy Maldonado lost Tony Pena's fly in the lights for a triple. Pena scored on a sacrifice fly for the game's only run, as John Tudor and two late-inning relievers blanked the Giants. Danny Cox pitched an easier shutout in the finale as his Cardinals hammered seven Giant pitchers for twelve hits and six runs.

St. Louis Cardinals (East), 4;
San Francisco Giants (West) 3

STL (E)

PLAYER/POS	AVG	G	AB	R	H	2B	3B	HR	RB	BB	SO	SB
Jack Clark, ph	.000	1	1	0	0	0	0	0	0	0	1	0
Vince Coleman, of	.269	7	26	3	7	1	0	0	4	4	6	1
Danny Cox, p	.333	2	6	0	2	0	0	0	1	0	2	0
Ken Dayley, p	.000	3	0	0	0	0	0	0	0	0	0	0
Dan Driessen, 1b-4	.250	5	12	1	3	2	0	0	1	1	1	0
Curt Ford, of	.333	4	9	2	3	0	0	0	0	1	1	0
Bob Forsch, p	.000	3	0	0	0	0	0	0	0	0	0	0
Tommy Herr, 2b	.222	7	27	0	6	0	0	0	3	0	1	1
Rick Horton, p	.000	1	0	0	0	0	0	0	0	0	0	0
Lance Johnson, pr	.000	1	0	1	0	0	0	0	0	0	0	1
Tom Lawless, 3b-2,of-1	.333	3	6	0	2	0	0	0	0	0	1	0
Jim Lindeman, 1b	.308	5	13	1	4	0	0	1	3	0	3	0
Joe Magrane, p	.000	1	1	0	0	0	0	0	0	0	0	0
Greg Mathews, p	1.000	2	2	0	2	0	0	0	2	0	0	0
Willie Mc Gee, of	.308	7	26	2	8	1	1	0	2	0	5	0
John Morris, of	.000	2	3	0	0	0	0	0	0	0	0	0
Jose Oquendo, of-5,3b-1	.167	5	12	3	2	0	0	1	4	3	2	0
Tom Pagnozzi, ph	.000	1	1	0	0	0	0	0	0	0	0	0
Tony Pena, c	.381	7	21	5	8	0	1	0	3	4	1	0
Terry Pendleton, 3b	.211	6	19	3	4	0	1	0	1	0	6	0
Ozzie Smith, ss	.200	7	25	2	5	0	1	0	1	3	4	0
John Tudor, p	.000	2	4	0	0	0	0	0	0	0	4	0
Todd Worrell, p-3,of-1	.000	3	1	0	0	0	0	0	0	0	1	0
TOTAL	.260		215	23	56	4	4	2	22	16	42	4

PITCHER	W	L	ERA	G	GS	CG	SV	SHO	IP	H	ER	BB	SO
Danny Cox	1	1	2.12	2	2	2	0	1	17.0	17	4	3	11
Ken Dayley	0	0	0.00	3	0	0	2	0	4.0	1	0	2	4
Bob Forsch	1	1	12.00	3	0	0	0	0	3.0	4	4	1	3
Rick Horton	0	0	0.00	1	0	0	0	0	3.0	2	0	0	2
Joe Magrane	0	0	9.00	1	1	0	0	0	4.0	4	4	2	3
Greg Mathews	1	0	3.48	2	2	0	0	0	10.1	6	4	3	10
John Tudor	1	1	1.76	2	2	0	0	0	15.1	16	3	5	12
Todd Worrell	0	0	2.08	3	0	0	1	0	4.1	4	1	1	6
TOTAL	4	3	2.95	17	7	2	3	1	61.0	54	20	17	51

SF (W)

PLAYER/POS	AVG	G	AB	R	H	2B	3B	HR	RB	BB	SO	SB
Mike Aldrete, of-3	.100	5	10	0	1	0	0	0	0	1	2	0
Bob Brenly, c	.235	6	17	3	4	1	0	1	2	3	7	0
Will Clark, 1b	.360	7	25	3	9	2	0	1	3	3	6	1
Chili Davis, of	.150	6	20	2	3	1	0	0	0	1	4	0
Kelly Downs, p	.000	1	0	0	0	0	0	0	0	0	0	0
Dave Dravecky, p	.167	2	6	0	1	0	0	0	0	0	1	0
Scott Garrelts, p	.000	2	0	0	0	0	0	0	0	0	0	0
Atlee Hammaker, p	.000	2	3	0	0	0	0	0	0	0	2	0
Mike Krukow, p	.000	1	2	0	0	0	0	0	0	1	0	0
Mike La Coss, p	.000	2	0	0	0	0	0	0	0	0	0	0
Craig Lefferts, p	.000	3	0	0	0	0	0	0	0	0	0	0
Jeffrey Leonard, of	.417	7	24	5	10	0	0	4	5	3	4	0
Candy Maldonado, of	.211	5	19	2	4	1	0	0	2	0	3	0
Bob Melvin, c-2	.429	3	7	0	3	0	0	0	0	1	1	0
Eddie Milner, of-4	.143	6	7	0	1	0	0	0	0	0	3	0
Kevin Mitchell, 3b	.267	7	30	2	8	1	0	1	2	0	3	1
Joe Price, p	.000	2	1	0	0	0	0	0	0	0	1	0
Rick Reuschel, p	.000	2	2	0	0	0	0	0	0	0	1	0
Don Robinson, p	.000	3	0	0	0	0	0	0	0	0	0	0
Chris Speier, 2b-1	.000	3	5	0	0	0	0	0	0	0	2	0
Harry Spilman, ph	.500	3	2	1	1	0	0	1	1	0	0	0
Rob Thompson, 2b-6	.100	7	20	4	2	0	1	1	2	5	7	2
Jose Uribe, ss	.269	7	26	1	7	1	0	0	2	0	4	1
TOTAL	.239		226	23	54	7	1	9	20	17	51	5

PITCHER	W	L	ERA	G	GS	CG	SV	SHO	IP	H	ER	BB	SO
Kelly Downs	0	0	0.00	1	0	0	0	0	1.1	1	0	0	0
Dave Dravecky	1	1	0.60	2	2	1	0	1	15.0	7	1	4	14
Scott Garrelts	0	0	6.75	2	0	0	0	0	2.2	2	2	4	4
Atlee Hammaker	0	1	7.87	2	2	0	0	0	8.0	12	7	0	7
Mike Krukow	1	0	2.00	1	1	1	0	0	9.0	9	2	1	3
Mike La Coss	0	0	0.00	2	0	0	0	0	3.1	1	0	3	2
Craig Lefferts	0	0	0.00	3	0	0	0	0	2.0	3	0	1	0
Joe Price	1	0	0.00	2	0	0	0	0	5.2	3	0	1	7
Rick Reuschel	0	1	6.30	2	2	0	0	0	10.0	15	7	2	2
Don Robinson	0	1	9.00	3	0	0	0	0	3.0	3	3	0	3
TOTAL	3	4	3.30	20	7	2	0	1	60.0	56	22	16	42

GAME 1 AT STL OCT 6

| SF | 100 100 010 | 3 | 7 | 1 |
| STL | 001 103 00X | 5 | 10 | 1 |

Pitchers: REUSCHEL, Lefferts (7), Garrelts (8) vs MATHEWS, Worrell (8), Dayley (8)
Home Runs: Leonard-SF
Attendance: 55,331

GAME 2 AT STL OCT 7

| SF | 020 100 020 | 5 | 10 | 0 |
| STL | 000 000 000 | 0 | 2 | 1 |

Pitchers: DRAVECKY vs TUDOR, Forsch (9)
Home Runs: Clark-SF, Leonard-SF
Attendance: 55,331

GAME 3 AT SF OCT 9

| STL | 000 002 400 | 6 | 11 | 1 |
| SF | 031 000 001 | 5 | 7 | 1 |

Pitchers: Magrane, FORSCH (5), Worrell (7) vs Hammaker, D.ROBINSON (7), Lefferts (7), LaCoss (8)
Home Runs: Lindeman-STL, Leonard-SF, Spilman-SF
Attendance: 57,913

GAME 4 AT SF OCT 10

| STL | 020 000 000 | 2 | 9 | 0 |
| SF | 000 120 01X | 4 | 9 | 2 |

Pitchers: COX vs KRUKOW
Home Runs: Thompson-SF, Leonard-SF, Brenly-SF
Attendance: 57,997

GAME 5 AT SF OCT 11

| STL | 101 100 000 | 3 | 7 | 0 |
| SF | 101 400 00X | 6 | 7 | 1 |

Pitchers: Mathews, FORSCH (4), Horton (4), Dayley (7), Price (5) vs Reuschel (5)
Home Runs: Mitchell-SF
Attendance: 59,363

GAME 6 AT STL OCT 13

| SF | 000 000 000 | 0 | 6 | 0 |
| STL | 010 000 00X | 1 | 5 | 0 |

Pitchers: DRAVECKY, D.Robinson (7) vs TUDOR, Worrell (8), Dayley (9)
Attendance: 55,331

GAME 7 AT STL OCT 14

| SF | 000 000 000 | 0 | 8 | 1 |
| STL | 040 002 00X | 6 | 12 | 0 |

Pitchers: HAMMAKER, Price (3), Downs (3), Garrelts (5), Lefferts (6), LaCoss (6), D.Robinson (8) vs COX
Home Runs: Oquendo-STL
Attendance: 55,331

The Tigers, with the best over-all won-lost record in the majors, were favored to defeat the ninth-ranked Twins, although Minnesota held the home field advantage and the major leagues' best record at home. Tiger pitcher Doyle Alexander—he had been 9–0 since joining Detroit in mid-August—took a 5–4 lead into the last of the eighth in Game One. But a single and double drove him out, and before the inning was over three more Twins had scored to sew up their first win. Detroit scored twice in the second inning the next day, but the Twins responded later in the inning with three runs, two on Tim Laudner's double off Tiger ace Jack Morris, and increased their lead in the fourth and fifth to seal Morris's first loss in Minnesota after eleven wins.

The Tigers won a game after the series moved to Detroit, when Pat Sheridan's two-run homer in the eighth inning of Game Three restored a lead they had squandered in the middle innings. But that was it for Detroit, as the Twins surprised everyone by subduing the Tigers in their den. In Game Four they took the lead for good on Greg Gagne's fourth-inning home run. And in Game Five, after initiating the scoring with four runs in the second, Minnesota pushed on to a 9–5 win and their first pennant in twenty-two years.

Minnesota Twins (West) 4;
Detroit Tigers (East), 1

MIN (W)

PLAYER/POS	AVG	G	AB	R	H	2B	3B	HR	RB	BB	SO	SB
Keith Atherton, p	.000	1	0	0	0	0	0	0	0	0	0	0
Don Baylor, dh	.400	2	5	0	2	0	0	0	1	0	0	0
Juan Berenguer, p	.000	4	0	0	0	0	0	0	0	0	0	0
Bert Blyleven, p	.000	2	0	0	0	0	0	0	0	0	0	0
Tom Brunansky, of	.412	5	17	5	7	4	0	2	9	4	3	0
Randy Bush, dh	.250	4	12	4	3	0	1	0	2	3	2	3
Sal Butera, c	.667	1	3	0	2	0	0	0	0	0	0	0
Mark Davidson, pr	.000	1	0	0	0	0	0	0	0	0	0	0
Gary Gaetti, 3b	.300	5	20	5	6	1	0	2	5	1	3	0
Greg Gagne, ss	.278	5	18	5	5	3	0	2	3	3	4	0
Dan Gladden, of	.350	5	20	5	7	2	0	0	5	2	1	0
Kent Hrbek, 1b	.150	5	20	4	3	0	0	1	1	3	0	0
Gene Larkin, ph	1.000	1	1	0	1	1	0	0	1	0	0	0
Tim Laudner, c	.071	5	14	1	1	1	0	0	2	2	5	0
Steve Lombardozzi, 2b	.267	5	15	2	4	0	0	0	1	2	2	0
Al Newman, 2b	.000	1	2	0	0	0	0	0	0	0	0	0
Kirby Puckett, of	.208	5	24	3	5	1	0	1	3	0	5	1
Jeff Reardon, p	.000	4	0	0	0	0	0	0	0	0	0	0
Dan Schatzeder, p	.000	2	0	0	0	0	0	0	0	0	0	0
Les Straker, p	.000	1	0	0	0	0	0	0	0	0	0	0
Frank Viola, p	.000	2	0	0	0	0	0	0	0	0	0	0
TOTAL	.269		171	34	46	13	1	8	33	20	25	4

PITCHER	W	L	ERA	G	GS	CG	SV	SHO	IP	H	ER	BB	SO
Keith Atherton	0	0	0.00	1	0	0	0	0	0.1	1	0	0	0
Juan Berenguer	0	0	1.50	4	0	0	1	0	6.0	1	1	3	6
Bert Blyleven	2	0	4.05	2	2	0	0	0	13.1	12	6	3	9
Jeff Reardon	1	1	5.06	4	0	0	2	0	5.1	7	3	3	5
Dan Schatzeder	0	0	0.00	2	0	0	0	0	4.1	2	0	0	5
Les Straker	0	0	16.88	1	1	0	0	0	2.2	3	5	4	1
Frank Viola	1	0	5.25	2	2	0	0	0	12.0	14	7	5	9
TOTAL	4	1	4.50	16	5	0	3	0	44.0	40	22	18	35

DET (E)

PLAYER/POS	AVG	G	AB	R	H	2B	3B	HR	RB	BB	SO	SB
Doyle Alexander, p	.000	2	0	0	0	0	0	0	0	0	0	0
Dave Bergman, 1b-1,dh-1	.250	4	4	0	1	0	0	0	0	2	0	1	0
Tom Brookens, 3b	.000	5	13	0	0	0	0	0	0	0	3	0
Darrell Evans, 1b-5,3b-1	.294	5	17	0	5	0	0	0	0	4	2	0
Kirk Gibson, of	.286	5	21	4	6	1	0	1	4	3	8	3
Johnny Grubb, dh-1	.571	4	7	0	4	0	0	0	0	0	1	0
Mike Heath, c	.286	3	7	1	2	0	0	1	2	0	0	0
Mike Henneman, p	.000	3	0	0	0	0	0	0	0	0	0	0
Willie Hernandez, p	.000	1	0	0	0	0	0	0	0	0	0	0
Larry Herndon, of-2,dh-1	.333	3	9	1	3	1	0	0	2	1	1	0
Eric King, p	.000	2	0	0	0	0	0	0	0	0	0	0
Chet Lemon, of	.278	5	18	4	5	0	0	2	4	1	4	0
Bill Madlock, dh	.000	1	5	0	0	0	0	0	0	0	3	0
Jack Morris, p-1,dh-1	.000	2	0	1	0	0	0	0	0	0	0	0
Jim Morrison, 3b-1,dh-1	.400	2	5	1	2	0	0	0	0	0	1	0
Matt Nokes, c-3,dh-2	.143	5	14	2	2	0	0	1	2	1	4	0
Dan Petry, p	.000	1	0	0	0	0	0	0	0	0	0	0
Jeff Robinson, p	.000	1	0	0	0	0	0	0	0	0	0	0
Pat Sheridan, of-4	.300	5	10	2	3	1	0	1	2	0	2	1
Frank Tanana, p	.000	1	0	0	0	0	0	0	0	0	0	0
Walt Terrell, p	.000	1	0	0	0	0	0	0	0	0	0	0
Mark Thurmond, p	.000	1	0	0	0	0	0	0	0	0	0	0
Alan Trammell, ss	.200	5	20	3	4	1	0	0	2	1	2	0
Lou Whitaker, 2b	.176	5	17	4	3	0	0	1	1	7	3	1
TOTAL	.240		167	23	40	4	0	7	21	18	35	5

PITCHER	W	L	ERA	G	GS	CG	SV	SHO	IP	H	ER	BB	SO
Doyle Alexander	0	2	10.00	2	2	0	0	0	9.0	14	10	1	5
Mike Henneman	1	0	10.80	3	0	0	0	0	5.0	6	6	6	3
Willie Hernandez	0	0	0.00	1	0	0	0	0	0.1	0	0	0	0
Eric King	0	0	1.69	2	0	0	0	0	5.1	3	1	2	4
Jack Morris	0	1	6.75	1	1	1	0	0	8.0	6	6	3	7
Dan Petry	0	0	0.00	1	0	0	0	0	3.1	1	0	0	1
Jeff Robinson	0	0	0.00	1	0	0	0	0	0.1	0	0	0	0
Frank Tanana	0	1	5.06	1	1	0	0	0	5.1	6	3	4	1
Walt Terrell	0	0	9.00	1	1	0	0	0	6.0	7	6	4	4
Mark Thurmond	0	0	0.00	1	0	0	0	0	0.1	0	0	0	0
TOTAL	1	4	6.70	14	5	1	0	0	43.0	46	32	20	25

GAME 1 AT MIN OCT 7

DET 001 001 120 5 10 0
MIN 010 030 04X 8 10 0

Pitchers: ALEXANDER, Henneman (8), Hernandez (8), King (8) vs Viola, REARDON (8)
Home Runs: Heath-DET, Gibson-DET, Gaetti-MIN (2)
Attendance: 53,269

GAME 2 AT MIN OCT 8

DET 020 000 010 3 7 1
MIN 030 210 00X 6 6 0

Pitchers: MORRIS vs BLYLEVEN, Berenguer (8)
Home Runs: Lemon-DET, Whitaker-DET, Hrbek-MIN
Attendance: 55,245

GAME 3 AT DET OCT 10

MIN 000 202 200 6 8 1
DET 005 000 02X 7 7 0

Pitchers: Straker, Schatzeder (3), Berenguer (7), REARDON (8) vs Terrell, HENNEMAN (7)
Home Runs: Gagne-MIN, Brunansky-MIN, Sheridan-DET
Attendance: 49,730

GAME 4 AT DET OCT 11

MIN 001 111 010 5 7 1
DET 100 011 000 3 7 3

Pitchers: VIOLA, Atherton (6), Berenguer (6), Reardon (9) vs TANANA, Petry (6), Thurmond (9)
Home Runs: Puckett-MIN, Gagne-MIN
Attendance: 51,939

GAME 5 AT DET OCT 12

MIN 040 000 113 9 15 1
DET 000 300 011 5 9 1

Pitchers: BLYLEVEN, Schatzeder (7), Berenguer (8), Reardon (8) vs ALEXANDER, King (2), Henneman (7), Robinson (9)
Home Runs: Brunansky-MIN, Nokes-DET, Lemon-DET
Attendance: 47,448

Although the Twins compiled a dismal record on the road during the season (29–52), their play at home (56–25) topped the majors. In postseason play they won all six games played in their Metrodome, including the four that won them the world championship. They overwhelmed St. Louis in the Series opener, the first World Series game ever played indoors. The Cardinals scored first, in the second inning, but Twin ace Frank Viola (with relief from Keith Atherton in the ninth) stopped them after that as his teammates unloaded for seven runs in the fourth inning (capped by Dan Gladden's grand slam) on their way to a 10–1 win. The Cardinals scored four runs in Game Two, but again the Twins enjoyed a big fourth inning—bunching six of their ten hits together for six runs—and scored two other runs on homers by Gary Gaetti and Tim Laudner.

When the Series moved to St. Louis, the Cardinals grabbed the home advantage to post their three wins. In Game Three, Cardinal pitchers John Tudor and Todd Worrell combined for a five-hitter as the Cards came from behind with a three-run seventh to win 3–1. The next day St. Louis broke a 1–1 tie with their own fourth-inning explosion, for six runs. The big blow was a three-run homer by utility infielder Tom Lawless—only the second home run of his big league career. Final score: 7–2. After five scoreless innings in Game Five, St. Louis moved out to a 4–0 lead in the sixth and seventh innings. Gaetti's eighth-inning triple put two Minnesota runs across, but the Cards held on for a 4–2 win.

Back in Minneapolis, St. Louis built up a 5–2 lead in Game Six before the Twins retaliated with four runs in the fifth inning (with Don Baylor's three-run homer providing the tying runs) and four more an inning later as Kent Hrbek's grand slam. A final Twins run in the eighth ended the scoring at 11–5.

The Cardinals scored first in Game Seven, with a pair of runs in the second inning, but the Twins edged their way to a tie with single runs in the second and fifth, and an inning later took the lead on three walks and an infield single. As Twin starter Frank Viola held St. Louis scoreless on two hits after the second inning, Minnesota made the score 4–2 with a final run in the eighth, and ace reliever Jeff Reardon retired the Cards in order in the ninth to bring Minnesota its first world championship.

Minnesota Twins (AL) 4; St. Louis Cardinals (NL), 3

MIN (A)

PLAYER/POS	AVG	G	AB	R	H	2B	3B	HR	RB	BB	SO	SB
Keith Atherton, p	.000	2	0	0	0	0	0	0	0	0	0	0
Don Baylor, dh-3	.385	5	13	3	5	0	0	1	3	1	1	0
Juan Berenguer, p	.000	3	0	0	0	0	0	0	0	0	0	0
Bert Blyleven, p	.000	2	1	0	0	0	0	0	0	0	1	0
Tom Brunansky, of	.200	7	25	5	5	0	0	0	2	4	4	1
Randy Bush, dh-2	.167	4	6	1	1	1	0	0	2	0	1	0
Sal Butera, c	.000	1	0	0	0	0	0	0	0	0	0	0
Mark Davidson, of-1	.000	2	1	0	0	0	0	0	0	0	0	0
George Frazier, p	.000	1	0	0	0	0	0	0	0	0	0	0
Gary Gaetti, 3b	.259	7	27	4	7	2	1	1	4	2	5	2
Greg Gagne, ss	.200	7	30	5	6	1	0	1	3	1	6	0
Dan Gladden, of	.290	7	31	3	9	2	1	1	7	3	4	2
Kent Hrbek, 1b	.208	7	24	4	5	0	0	1	6	5	3	0
Gene Larkin, 1b-1,dh-1	.000	5	3	1	0	0	0	0	0	0	1	0
Tim Laudner, c	.318	7	22	4	7	1	0	1	4	5	3	0
Steve Lombardozzi, 2b	.412	6	17	3	7	1	0	1	4	2	3	0
Al Newman, 2b-3	.200	4	5	0	1	0	0	0	0	1	1	0
Joe Niekro, p	.000	1	0	0	0	0	0	0	0	0	0	0
Kirby Puckett, of	.357	7	28	5	10	1	1	0	3	2	1	1
Jeff Reardon, p	.000	4	0	0	0	0	0	0	0	0	0	0
Dan Schatzeder, p	.000	3	0	0	0	0	0	0	0	0	0	0
Roy Smalley, ph	.500	4	2	0	1	1	0	0	0	2	0	0
Les Straker, p	.000	2	2	0	0	0	0	0	0	0	2	0
Frank Viola, p	.000	3	1	0	0	0	0	0	0	0	1	0
TOTAL	.269		238	38	64	10	3	7	38	29	36	6

PITCHER	W	L	ERA	G	GS	CG	SV	SHO	IP	H	ER	BB	SO
Keith Atherton	0	0	6.75	2	0	0	0	0	1.1	0	1	1	0
Juan Berenguer	0	1	10.38	3	0	0	0	0	4.1	10	5	0	1
Bert Blyleven	1	1	2.77	2	2	0	0	0	13.0	13	4	2	12
George Frazier	0	0	0.00	1	0	0	0	0	2.0	1	0	0	2
Joe Niekro	0	0	0.00	1	0	0	0	0	2.0	1	0	1	1
Jeff Reardon	0	0	0.00	4	0	0	1	0	4.2	5	0	0	3
Dan Schatzeder	1	0	6.23	3	0	0	0	0	4.1	4	3	3	3
Les Straker	0	0	4.00	2	2	0	0	0	9.0	9	4	3	6
Frank Viola	2	1	3.72	3	3	0	0	0	19.1	17	8	3	16
TOTAL	4	3	3.75	21	7	0	1	0	60.0	60	25	13	44

STL (N)

PLAYER/POS	AVG	G	AB	R	H	2B	3B	HR	RB	BB	SO	SB
Vince Coleman, of	.143	7	28	5	4	2	0	0	2	2	10	6
Danny Cox, p	.000	3	2	0	0	0	0	0	0	0	1	0
Ken Dayley, p	.000	4	1	0	0	0	0	0	0	0	1	0
Dan Driessen, 1b	.231	4	13	3	3	2	0	0	1	1	1	0
Curt Ford, of-4	.308	5	13	1	4	0	0	0	2	1	1	0
Bob Forsch, p	.000	3	2	0	0	0	0	0	0	0	0	0
Tommy Herr, 2b	.250	7	28	2	7	0	0	1	1	2	2	0
Rick Horton, p	.000	2	0	0	0	0	0	0	0	0	0	0
Lance Johnson, pr	.000	1	0	0	0	0	0	0	0	0	0	1
Steve Lake, c	.333	3	3	0	1	0	0	0	1	0	0	0
Tom Lawless, 3b	.100	3	10	1	1	0	0	1	3	0	4	0
Jim Lindeman, 1b-6,of-1	.333	6	15	3	5	1	0	0	2	0	3	0
Joe Magrane, p	.000	2	0	0	0	0	0	0	0	0	0	0
Greg Mathews, p	.000	1	1	0	0	0	0	0	0	0	0	0
Willie McGee, of	.370	7	27	2	10	2	0	0	4	0	9	0
John Morris, of	.000	2	2	0	0	0	0	0	0	0	1	0
Jose Oquendo, 3b-4,of-3	.250	7	24	2	6	0	0	0	2	1	4	0
Tom Pagnozzi, dh-1	.250	2	4	0	1	0	0	0	0	0	0	0
Tony Pena, c-6,dh-1	.409	7	22	2	9	1	0	0	4	3	2	1
Terry Pendleton, dh-2	.429	3	7	2	3	0	0	0	1	1	1	2
Ozzie Smith, ss	.214	7	28	3	6	0	0	0	2	2	3	2
John Tudor, p	.000	2	2	0	0	0	0	0	0	0	2	0
Lee Tunnell, p	.000	2	0	0	0	0	0	0	0	0	0	0
Todd Worrell, p	.000	4	0	0	0	0	0	0	0	0	0	0
TOTAL	.259		232	26	60	8	0	2	25	13	44	12

PITCHER	W	L	ERA	G	GS	CG	SV	SHO	IP	H	ER	BB	SO
Danny Cox	1	2	7.71	3	2	0	0	0	11.2	13	10	8	9
Ken Dayley	0	0	1.93	4	0	0	1	0	4.2	2	1	0	3
Bob Forsch	1	0	9.95	3	0	0	0	0	6.1	8	7	5	3
Rick Horton	0	0	6.00	2	0	0	0	0	3.0	5	2	0	1
Joe Magrane	0	1	8.59	2	2	0	0	0	7.1	9	7	5	5
Greg Mathews	0	0	2.45	1	1	0	0	0	3.2	2	1	2	3
John Tudor	1	1	5.73	2	2	0	0	0	11.0	15	7	3	8
Lee Tunnell	0	0	2.08	2	0	0	0	0	4.1	4	1	2	1
Todd Worrell	0	0	1.29	4	0	0	2	0	7.0	6	1	4	3
TOTAL	3	4	5.64	23	7	0	3	0	59.0	64	37	29	36

GAME 1 AT MIN OCT 17

```
STL   010 000 000   1  5 1
MIN   000 720 10X  10 11 0
```
Pitchers: MAGRANE, Forsch (4), Horton (7) vs VIOLA, Atherton (9)
Home Runs: Gladden-MIN, Lombardozzi-MIN
Attendance: 55,171

GAME 2 AT MIN OCT 18

```
STL   000 010 120   4  9 0
MIN   010 601 00X   8 10 0
```
Pitchers: COX, Tunnell (4), Dayley (7), Worrell (8) vs BLYLEVEN, Berenguer (8), Reardon (9)
Home Runs: Gaetti-MIN, Laudner-MIN
Attendance: 55,257

GAME 3 AT STL OCT 20

```
MIN   000 001 000   1  5 1
STL   000 000 30X   3  9 1
```
Pitchers: Straker, BERENGUER (7), Schatzeder (7) vs TUDOR, Worrell (8)
Attendance: 55,347

GAME 4 AT STL OCT 21

```
MIN   001 010 000   2  7 1
STL   001 600 00X   7 10 1
```
Pitchers: VIOLA, Schatzeder (4), Niekro (5), Frazier (7) vs Mathews, FORSCH (4), Dayley (7)
Home Runs: Gagne-MIN, Lawless-STL
Attendance: 55,347

GAME 5 AT STL OCT 22

```
MIN   000 000 020   2  6 1
STL   000 003 10X   4 10 0
```
Pitchers: BLYLEVEN, Atherton (7), Reardon (7) vs COX, Dayley (8), Worrell (8)
Attendance: 55,347

GAME 6 AT MIN OCT 24

```
STL   110 210 000   5 11 2
MIN   200 044 01X  11 15 0
```
Pitchers: TUDOR, Horton (5), Forsch (6), Dayley (6), Tunnell (7) vs Straker, SCHATZEDER (4), Berenguer (6), Reardon (9)
Home Runs: Herr-STL, Baylor-MIN, Hrbek-MIN
Attendance: 55,293

GAME 7 AT MIN OCT 25

```
STL   020 000 000   2  6 1
MIN   010 011 01X   4 10 0
```
Pitchers: Magrane, COX (5), Worrell (6) vs VIOLA, Reardon (9)
Attendance: 55,376

The Mets had defeated the Dodgers in 10 of 11 regular season games, but in the LCS the pitching of Dodger ace Orel Hershiser and rookie Tim Belcher, and the timely hitting of Mike Scioscia and Kirk Gibson, propelled L.A. to the pennant. The Dodgers scored a first-inning run in the opener and carried a 2–0 lead into the ninth. But three Met runs in the top of the ninth (the final two scoring with two outs on a fly to short center that bounced off the glove of a diving John Shelby) gave New York the victory.

Dodger pitcher Tim Belcher singled with two away in the second inning of Game Two to start a four-run rally—the margin of victory in Belcher's 6–3 win. In Game Three (played in a steady downpour after a rainout the night before), the Mets overcame a 3–4 deficit, rapping four Dodger pitchers for five runs in the last of the eighth to take the series lead.

Kirk Gibson's twelfth-inning solo homer the next night put the Dodgers ahead 5–4, after Mike Scioscia's ninth-inning home run had pulled them into a tie. In the last of the twelfth, Orel Hershiser (who had pitched seven innings to no decision in the previous game) took the mound with two out and the bases full, and saved the game as center fielder Shelby, on the run, snared Kevin McReynolds' looping fly.

Gibson homered again in Game Four—for three runs that provided the winning margin in a 7–4 Dodger victory. One game from the pennant, as the series moved back to Los Angeles, the Dodgers for the first time failed to score first and saw the series evened a third time as David Cone held them to five hits and one run while the Mets scored five. But in the finale, the Dodgers unloaded on Ron Darling for six runs in the first two innings and Hershiser blanked the Mets on five hits.

Los Angeles Dodgers (West), 4; New York Mets (East), 3

LA (W)

PLAYER/POS	AVG	G	AB	R	H	2B	3B	HR	RB	BB	SO	SB
Tim Belcher, p	.125	2	8	1	1	0	0	0	0	0	3	0
Mike Davis, ph	.000	4	2	0	0	0	0	0	0	1	0	0
Rick Dempsey, c-3	.400	4	5	1	2	2	0	0	2	1	0	0
Kirk Gibson, of	.154	7	26	2	4	0	0	2	6	3	6	2
Jose Gonzalez, of-3	.000	4	0	2	0	0	0	0	0	0	0	0
Alfredo Griffin, ss	.160	7	25	1	4	1	0	0	3	0	5	0
Jeff Hamilton, 3b	.217	7	23	2	5	0	0	0	1	3	4	0
Mickey Hatcher, 1b-6,of-1	.238	6	21	4	5	2	0	0	3	3	0	0
Danny Heep, ph	.000	3	1	0	0	0	0	0	0	1	1	0
Orel Hershiser, p	.000	4	9	1	0	0	0	0	1	1	2	0
Brian Holton, p	1.000	3	1	1	1	0	0	0	0	0	0	0
Rick Horton, p	.000	4	0	0	0	0	0	0	0	0	0	0
Jay Howell, p	.000	2	0	0	0	0	0	0	0	0	0	0
Tim Leary, p	.000	2	1	0	0	0	0	0	0	0	0	0
Mike Marshall, of	.233	7	30	3	7	1	1	0	5	2	9	0
Jesse Orosco, p	.000	4	0	0	0	0	0	0	0	0	0	0
Alejandro Pena, p	.000	3	0	0	0	0	0	0	0	0	0	0
Steve Sax, 2b	.267	7	30	7	8	0	0	0	3	3	3	5
Mike Scioscia, c	.364	7	22	3	8	1	0	1	2	1	2	0
Mike Sharperson, ss-1,3b-1	.000	2	1	0	0	0	0	0	1	1	0	0
John Shelby, of	.167	7	24	3	4	0	0	0	3	5	12	2
Franklin Stubbs, 1b-3	.250	4	8	0	2	0	0	0	0	0	4	0
John Tudor, p	.000	1	2	0	0	0	0	0	0	0	2	0
Tracy Woodson, 1b	.250	3	4	0	1	0	0	0	0	0	1	0
TOTAL	.214		243	31	52	7	1	3	30	25	54	9

PITCHER	W	L	ERA	G	GS	CG	SV	SHO	IP	H	ER	BB	SO
Tim Belcher	2	0	4.11	2	2	0	0	0	15.1	12	7	4	16
Orel Hershiser	1	0	1.09	4	3	1	1	1	24.2	18	3	7	15
Brian Holton	0	0	2.25	3	0	0	1	0	4.0	2	1	1	2
Rick Horton	0	0	0.00	4	0	0	0	0	4.1	4	0	2	3
Jay Howell	0	1	27.00	2	0	0	0	0	0.2	1	2	2	1
Tim Leary	0	1	6.23	2	1	0	0	0	4.1	8	3	3	3
Jesse Orosco	0	0	7.71	4	0	0	0	0	2.1	4	2	3	0
Alejandro Pena	1	1	4.15	3	0	0	1	0	4.1	1	2	5	1
John Tudor	0	0	7.20	1	1	0	0	0	5.0	8	4	1	1
TOTAL	4	3	3.32	25	7	1	3	1	65.0	58	24	28	42

NY (E)

PLAYER/POS	AVG	G	AB	R	H	2B	3B	HR	RB	BB	SO	SB
Rick Aguilera, p	.000	3	1	0	0	0	0	0	0	0	1	0
Wally Backman, 2b	.273	7	22	2	6	1	0	0	2	2	5	1
Gary Carter, c	.222	7	27	0	6	1	1	0	4	1	3	0
David Cone, p	.000	3	4	0	0	0	0	0	0	0	0	0
Ron Darling, p-2	.000	2	3	0	0	0	0	0	0	0	2	0
Lennie Dykstra, of	.429	7	14	6	6	3	0	1	3	4	0	0
Kevin Elster, ss	.250	5	8	1	2	1	0	0	1	3	0	0
Sid Fernandez, p	.000	1	1	0	0	0	0	0	0	0	0	0
Dwight Gooden, p	.200	3	5	0	1	0	0	0	0	0	2	0
Keith Hernandez, 1b	.269	7	26	2	7	0	0	1	5	6	7	1
Gregg Jefferies, 3b	.333	7	27	2	9	2	0	0	1	4	0	0
Howard Johnson, ss-5,3b-1	.056	6	18	3	1	0	0	0	0	1	6	1
Terry Leach, p	.000	3	0	0	0	0	0	0	0	0	0	0
Dave Magadan, ph	.000	3	3	0	0	0	0	0	0	0	2	0
Lee Mazzilli, ph	.500	4	2	0	1	0	0	0	0	0	0	1
Roger Mc Dowell, p	.000	4	0	0	0	0	0	0	0	0	0	0
Kevin Mc Reynolds, of	.250	7	28	4	7	2	0	2	4	3	5	2
Randy Myers, p	.000	3	0	0	0	0	0	0	0	0	0	0
Mackey Sasser, c-1	.200	4	5	0	1	0	0	0	0	0	1	0
Darryl Strawberry, of	.300	7	30	5	9	2	0	1	6	2	5	0
Tim Teufel, 2b	.000	1	3	0	0	0	0	0	0	0	1	0
Mookie Wilson, of-3	.154	4	13	2	2	0	0	0	1	2	2	0
TOTAL	.242		240	27	58	12	1	5	27	28	42	6

PITCHER	W	L	ERA	G	GS	CG	SV	SHO	IP	H	ER	BB	SO
Rick Aguilera	0	0	1.29	3	0	0	0	0	7.0	3	1	2	4
David Cone	1	1	4.50	3	2	1	0	0	12.0	10	6	5	9
Ron Darling	0	1	7.71	2	2	0	0	0	7.0	11	6	4	7
Sid Fernandez	0	1	13.50	1	1	0	0	0	4.0	7	6	1	5
Dwight Gooden	0	0	2.95	3	2	0	0	0	18.1	10	6	8	20
Terry Leach	0	0	0.00	3	0	0	0	0	5.0	4	0	1	4
Roger Mc Dowell	0	1	4.50	4	0	0	0	0	6.0	6	3	2	5
Randy Myers	2	0	0.00	3	0	0	0	0	4.2	1	0	2	0
TOTAL	3	4	3.94	22	7	1	0	0	64.0	52	28	25	54

GAME 1 AT LA OCT 4

NY	000 000 003	3	8	1
LA	100 000 100	2	4	0

Pitchers: Gooden, MYERS (8) vs Hershiser, J.HOWELL (9)
Attendance: 55,582

GAME 2 AT LA OCT 5

NY	000 200 001	3	6	0
LA	140 010 00X	6	7	0

Pitchers: CONE, Aguilera (3), Leach (6), McDowell (8) vs BELCHER, Orosco (9), Pena (9)
Home Runs: Hernandez-NY
Attendance: 55,780

GAME 3 AT NY OCT 8

LA	021 000 010	4	7	2
NY	001 002 05X	8	9	2

Pitchers: Hershiser, J.Howell (8), PENA (8), Orosco (8), Horton (8) vs Darling, McDowell (7), MYERS (8), Cone (9)
Attendance: 44,672

GAME 4 AT NY OCT 9

LA	200 000 002 001	5	7	1
NY	000 301 000 000	4	10	2

Pitchers: Tudor, Holton (6), Horton (7), PENA (9), Leary (12), Orosco (12), Hershiser (12) vs Gooden, Myers (9), McDOWELL (11)
Home Runs: Strawberry-NY, McReynolds-NY, Scioscia-LA, Gibson-LA
Attendance: 54,014

GAME 5 AT NY OCT 10

LA	000 330 001	7	12	0
NY	000 030 010	4	9	1

Pitchers: BELCHER, Horton (8), Holton (8) vs FERNANDEZ, Leach (5), Aguilera (6), McDowell (8)
Home Runs: Gibson-LA, Dykstra-NY
Attendance: 52,069

GAME 6 AT LA OCT 11

NY	101 021 000	5	11	0
LA	000 010 000	1	5	2

Pitchers: CONE vs LEARY, Holton (5), Horton (6), Orosco (8)
Home Runs: McReynolds-NY
Attendance: 55,885

GAME 7 AT LA OCT 12

NY	000 000 000	0	5	2
LA	150 000 00X	6	10	0

Pitchers: DARLING, Gooden (2), Leach (5), Aguilera (7) vs HERSHISER
Attendance: 55,693

Jose Canseco's three home runs and Dennis Eckersley's sparkling relief pitching highlighted Oakland's sweep to the pennant. In his six shutout innings, Eckersley gave up just one hit and a pair of walks while fanning five, to record an LCS record four saves.

Canseco's fourth-inning solo shot off the Sox's Bruce Hurst put the A's out in front in Game One. Boston tied it up in the seventh, but two former Boston players—Carney Lansford, who doubled, and Dave Henderson, who singled him home—put Oakland back in front in the eighth, and Eckersley (also an ex-Bostonian) held the Sox through the final two innings.

Oakland's Storm Davis and Boston's Roger Clemens dueled scorelessly through five innings of Game Two. The Sox took advantage of an Oakland error to score twice in the sixth, but four Oakland hits in the seventh (including a two-run homer by Canseco), a balk, and a wild pitch put the A's up 3–2. Rich Gedman's home run for Boston in the last of the seventh tied the score, but in the ninth Oakland's rookie shortstop Walt Weiss singled home what proved the game winner off Sox ace reliever Lee Smith.

Boston unloaded for five runs in the first two innings of Game Three. But Weiss's double and home runs by Mark McGwire and Carney Lansford in the last of the second brought the A's within one run of a tie, and Ron Hassey's two-run homer an inning later gave the A's a lead that they held to the end. Dave Henderson's two-run blast in the eighth capped the A's 10–6 victory.

Canseco's first-inning homer in Game Four put the A's ahead to stay, as starter Dave Stewart and relievers Rick Honeycutt and Eckersley combined for a four-hit, 4–1 pennant clincher.

Oakland Athletics (West), 4; Boston Red Sox (East), 0

OAK (W)

PLAYER/POS	AVG	G	AB	R	H	2B	3B	HR	RB	BB	SO	SB
Don Baylor, dh	.000	2	6	0	0	0	0	0	1	1	2	0
Greg Cadaret, p	.000	1	0	0	0	0	0	0	0	0	0	0
Jose Canseco, of	.313	4	16	4	5	1	0	3	4	1	2	1
Storm Davis, p	.000	1	0	0	0	0	0	0	0	0	0	0
Dennis Eckersley, p	.000	4	0	0	0	0	0	0	0	0	0	0
Mike Gallego, 2b	.083	4	12	1	1	0	0	0	0	0	3	0
Ron Hassey, c	.500	4	8	2	4	1	0	1	3	1	1	0
Dave Henderson, of	.375	4	16	2	6	1	0	1	4	1	7	0
Rick Honeycutt, p	.000	3	0	0	0	0	0	0	0	0	0	0
Stan Javier, of	.500	2	4	0	2	0	0	0	1	1	0	0
Carney Lansford, 3b	.294	4	17	4	5	1	0	1	2	0	2	0
Mark Mc Gwire, 1b	.333	4	15	4	5	0	0	1	3	1	5	0
Gene Nelson, p	.000	2	0	0	0	0	0	0	0	0	0	0
Dave Parker, dh-2,of-1	.250	4	12	1	3	1	0	0	0	0	0	0
Tony Phillips, of-2,2b-1	.286	2	7	0	2	1	0	0	0	1	4	0
Eric Plunk, p	.000	1	0	0	0	0	0	0	0	0	0	0
Luis Polonia, of-1	.400	3	5	0	2	0	0	0	0	1	1	0
Terry Steinbach, c	.250	2	4	0	1	0	0	0	0	0	2	0
Dave Stewart, p	.000	2	0	0	0	0	0	0	0	0	0	0
Walt Weiss, ss	.333	4	15	2	5	2	0	0	2	0	4	0
Bob Welch, p	.000	1	0	0	0	0	0	0	0	0	0	0
Curt Young, p	.000	1	0	0	0	0	0	0	0	0	0	0
TOTAL	.299		137	20	41	8	0	7	20	10	35	1

PITCHER	W	L	ERA	G	GS	CG	SV	SHO	IP	H	ER	BB	SO
Greg Cadaret	0	0	27.00	1	0	0	0	0	0.1	1	1	0	0
Storm Davis	0	0	0.00	1	1	0	0	0	6.1	2	0	5	4
Dennis Eckersley	0	0	0.00	4	0	0	4	0	6.0	1	0	2	5
Rick Honeycutt	1	0	0.00	3	0	0	0	0	2.0	0	0	2	0
Gene Nelson	2	0	0.00	2	0	0	0	0	4.2	5	0	1	0
Eric Plunk	0	0	0.00	1	0	0	0	0	0.1	0	0	0	0
Dave Stewart	1	0	1.35	2	2	0	0	0	13.1	9	2	6	11
Bob Welch	0	0	27.00	1	1	0	0	0	1.2	6	5	2	0
Curt Young	0	0	0.00	1	0	0	0	0	1.1	1	0	0	2
TOTAL	4	0	2.00	16	4	0	4	0	36.0	26	8	18	23

BOS (E)

PLAYER/POS	AVG	G	AB	R	H	2B	3B	HR	RB	BB	SO	SB
Marty Barrett, 2b	.067	4	15	2	1	0	0	0	0	1	0	0
Todd Benzinger, 1b-3	.091	4	11	0	1	0	0	0	0	1	3	0
Mike Boddicker, p	.000	1	0	0	0	0	0	0	0	0	0	0
Wade Boggs, 3b	.385	4	13	2	5	0	0	0	3	3	4	0
Ellis Burks, of	.235	4	17	2	4	1	0	0	1	0	3	0
Roger Clemens, p	.000	1	0	0	0	0	0	0	0	0	0	0
Dwight Evans, of	.167	4	12	1	2	1	0	0	1	3	5	0
Wes Gardner, p	.000	1	0	0	0	0	0	0	0	0	0	0
Rich Gedman, c	.357	4	14	1	5	0	0	1	1	2	1	0
Mike Greenwell, of	.214	4	14	2	3	1	0	1	3	3	0	0
Bruce Hurst, p	.000	2	0	0	0	0	0	0	0	0	0	0
Spike Owen, dh	.000	1	0	0	0	0	0	0	0	1	0	0
Larry Parrish, 1b-2	.000	4	6	0	0	0	0	0	0	0	2	0
Jody Reed, ss	.273	4	11	0	3	1	0	0	0	2	1	0
Jim Rice, dh	.154	4	13	0	2	0	0	0	1	2	4	0
Ed Romero, pr	.000	1	0	0	0	0	0	0	0	0	0	0
Kevin Romine, pr	.000	2	0	1	0	0	0	0	0	0	0	0
Lee Smith, p	.000	2	0	0	0	0	0	0	0	0	0	0
Mike Smithson, p	.000	1	0	0	0	0	0	0	0	0	0	0
Bob Stanley, p	.000	2	0	0	0	0	0	0	0	0	0	0
TOTAL	.206		126	11	26	4	0	2	10	18	23	0

PITCHER	W	L	ERA	G	GS	CG	SV	SHO	IP	H	ER	BB	SO
Mike Boddicker	0	1	20.25	1	1	0	0	0	2.2	8	6	1	2
Roger Clemens	0	0	3.86	1	1	0	0	0	7.0	6	3	0	8
Wes Gardner	0	0	5.79	1	0	0	0	0	4.2	6	3	2	8
Bruce Hurst	0	2	2.77	2	2	1	0	0	13.0	10	4	5	12
Lee Smith	0	1	8.10	2	0	0	0	0	3.1	6	3	1	4
Mike Smithson	0	0	0.00	1	0	0	0	0	2.1	3	0	0	1
Bob Stanley	0	0	9.00	2	0	0	0	0	1.0	2	1	1	0
TOTAL	0	4	5.29	10	4	1	0	0	34.0	41	20	10	35

GAME 1 AT BOS OCT 5

OAK	000 100 010	2	6	0
BOS	000 000 100	1	6	0

Pitchers: Stewart, HONEYCUTT (7), Eckersley (8) vs HURST
Home Runs: Canseco-OAK
Attendance: 34,104

GAME 2 AT BOS OCT 6

OAK	000 000 301	4	10	1
BOS	000 002 100	3	4	1

Pitchers: Davis, Cadaret (7), NELSON (7), Eckersley (9) vs Clemens, Stanley (8), SMITH (8)
Home Runs: Canseco-OAK, Gedman-BOS
Attendance: 34,605

GAME 3 AT OAK OCT 8

BOS	320 000 100	6	12	0
OAK	042 010 12X	10	15	1

Pitchers: BODDICKER, Gardner (3), Stanley (8) vs Welch, NELSON (2), Young (6), Plunk (7), Honeycutt (7), Eckersley (8)
Home Runs: Greenwell-BOS, McGwire-OAK, Lansford-OAK, Hassey-OAK, Henderson-OAK
Attendance: 49,261

GAME 4 AT OAK OCT 9

BOS	000 001 000	1	4	0
OAK	101 000 02X	4	10	1

Pitchers: HURST, Smithson (5), Smith (7), STEWART, Honeycutt (8), Eckersley (9)
Home Runs: Canseco-OAK
Attendance: 49,406

Mickey Hatcher's home run in the first inning of Game One set the tone for the Dodgers' surprising triumph over Oakland's mighty A's. Hatcher, who homered only once during the season, initiated the Series scoring with a two-run blast to left center. Half an inning later the A's Jose Canseco—baseball's leading slugger, with 42 season homers—erased the Dodger lead with his first career grand slam. But while Hatcher went on to hit safely six more times in the Series—including another home run—Canseco's first hit was also his last, as he went 0 for 19 the rest of the way. The Dodgers scored once in the sixth inning to draw within one run of a tie, but remained behind until the last of the ninth when, with two out and one on, Kirk Gibson pinch hit for pitcher Alejandro Peña. Gibson, the Dodgers' top source of power during the season, was so hobbled by leg injuries that he had, till that moment, sat out the game in the training room. But with two strikes on him he belted a home run off baseball's premier reliever, Dennis Eckersley, to win the game. It was Gibson's only Series appearance.

Dodger ace Orel Hershiser blanked the A's on three hits in Game Two and led the offense with three hits of his own. His single in the third inning began a five-run Dodger rally (capped by Mike Marshall's three-run homer), and his fourth-inning double drove in the Dodgers' sixth and final run.

When the Series moved to Oakland, the A's recovered for a dramatic win in Game Three, as Mark McGwire (who had homered 32 times during the season) broke a 1–1 tie with his only Series hit, a solo homer in the last of the ninth. In Game Four, Dodger reliever Jay Howell, who had yielded the losing home run the day before, got McGwire to pop up with the bases full to end the seventh inning, and blanked the A's the rest of the way to preserve a narrow 4–3 Dodger victory.

Hershiser returned to pitch Game Five. He allowed two runs in his four-hitter, but Mickey Hatcher had given the Dodgers the lead with a two-run homer in the first inning, and Mike Davis (who had homered just twice during the season) drove a 3–0 pitch into the stands for two more runs in the fourth. Veteran catcher Rick Dempsey (substituting for injured first-stringer Mike Scioscia) doubled home a fifth Los Angeles run in the sixth, and the Dodgers were on their way to a seventh world title.

Los Angeles Dodgers (NL), 4;
Oakland Athletics (AL), 1

LA (N)

PLAYER/POS	AVG	G	AB	R	H	2B	3B	HR	RBI	BB	SO	SB
Dave Anderson, dh	.000	1	1	0	0	0	0	0	0	0	1	0
Tim Belcher, p	.000	2	0	0	0	0	0	0	0	0	0	0
Mike Davis, dh-2,of-1	.143	4	7	3	1	0	0	2	2	4	0	2
Rick Dempsey, c	.200	2	5	0	1	1	0	0	1	1	2	0
Kirk Gibson, ph	1.000	1	1	1	1	0	0	1	2	0	0	0
Jose Gonzalez, of-3	.000	4	2	0	0	0	0	0	0	0	2	0
Alfredo Griffin, ss	.188	5	16	2	3	0	0	0	0	2	4	0
Jeff Hamilton, 3b	.105	5	19	1	2	0	0	0	0	1	4	0
Mickey Hatcher, of	.368	5	19	5	7	1	0	2	5	1	3	0
Danny Heep, of-1,dh-1	.250	3	8	0	2	1	0	0	0	0	2	0
Orel Hershiser, p	1.000	2	3	1	3	2	0	0	1	0	0	0
Brian Holton, p	.000	1	0	0	0	0	0	0	0	0	0	0
Jay Howell, p	.000	2	0	0	0	0	0	0	0	0	0	0
Tim Leary, p	.000	2	0	0	0	0	0	0	0	0	0	0
Mike Marshall, of	.231	5	13	2	3	0	1	1	3	0	5	0
Alejandro Pena, p	.000	2	0	0	0	0	0	0	0	0	0	0
Steve Sax, 2b	.300	5	20	3	6	0	0	0	0	1	1	1
Mike Scioscia, c	.214	4	14	0	3	0	0	0	1	0	2	0
John Shelby, of	.222	5	18	0	4	1	0	0	1	2	7	1
Franklin Stubbs, 1b	.294	5	17	3	5	2	0	0	2	1	3	0
John Tudor, p	.000	1	0	0	0	0	0	0	0	0	0	0
Tracy Woodson, 1b-3	.000	4	4	0	0	0	0	0	0	1	0	0
TOTAL	.246		167	21	41	8	1	6	19	13	36	4

PITCHER	W	L	ERA	G	GS	CG	SV	SHO	IP	H	ER	BB	SO
Tim Belcher	1	0	6.23	2	2	0	0	0	8.2	10	6	6	10
Orel Hershiser	2	0	1.00	2	2	2	0	1	18.0	7	2	6	17
Brian Holton	0	0	0.00	1	0	0	0	0	2.0	0	0	1	0
Jay Howell	0	1	3.38	2	0	0	1	0	2.2	3	1	1	2
Tim Leary	0	0	1.35	2	0	0	0	0	6.2	6	1	2	4
Alejandro Pena	1	0	0.00	2	0	0	0	0	5.0	2	0	1	7
John Tudor	0	0	0.00	1	1	0	0	0	1.1	0	0	0	1
TOTAL	4	1	2.03	12	5	2	1	1	44.1	28	10	17	41

OAK (A)

PLAYER/POS	AVG	G	AB	R	H	2B	3B	HR	RBI	BB	SO	SB
Don Baylor, ph	.000	1	1	0	0	0	0	0	0	0	1	0
Todd Burns, p	.000	1	0	0	0	0	0	0	0	0	0	0
Greg Cadaret, p	.000	3	0	0	0	0	0	0	0	0	0	0
Jose Canseco, of	.053	5	19	1	1	0	0	1	5	2	5	1
Storm Davis, p	.000	2	1	0	0	0	0	0	0	0	1	0
Dennis Eckersley, p	.000	2	0	0	0	0	0	0	0	0	0	0
Mike Gallego, 2b	.000	1	0	0	0	0	0	0	0	0	0	0
Ron Hassey, c-4	.250	5	8	2	2	0	0	0	1	3	3	0
Dave Henderson, of	.300	5	20	1	6	2	0	0	1	2	7	0
Rick Honeycutt, p	.000	3	0	0	0	0	0	0	0	0	0	0
Glenn Hubbard, 2b	.250	4	12	2	3	0	0	0	0	1	2	1
Stan Javier, of-2	.500	3	4	0	2	0	0	0	2	0	1	0
Carney Lansford, 3b	.167	5	18	2	3	0	0	0	1	2	2	0
Mark McGwire, 1b	.059	5	17	1	1	0	0	1	1	3	4	0
Gene Nelson, p	.000	3	0	0	0	0	0	0	0	0	0	0
Dave Parker, of-2,dh-2	.200	4	15	0	3	0	0	0	0	2	4	0
Tony Phillips, 2b-1,of-1	.250	2	4	1	1	0	0	0	0	1	2	0
Eric Plunk, p	.000	2	0	0	0	0	0	0	0	0	0	0
Luis Polonia, of-2	.111	3	9	1	1	0	0	0	0	0	2	0
Terry Steinbach, c-2,dh-1	.364	3	11	0	4	1	0	0	0	0	2	0
Dave Stewart, p	.000	2	3	1	0	0	0	0	0	1	3	0
Walt Weiss, ss	.063	5	16	1	1	0	0	0	0	0	2	0
Bob Welch, p	.000	1	0	0	0	0	0	0	0	0	0	0
Curt Young, p	.000	1	0	0	0	0	0	0	0	0	0	0
TOTAL	.177		158	11	28	3	0	2	11	17	41	3

PITCHER	W	L	ERA	G	GS	CG	SV	SHO	IP	H	ER	BB	SO
Todd Burns	0	0	0.00	1	0	0	0	0	0.1	0	0	0	0
Greg Cadaret	0	0	0.00	3	0	0	0	0	2.0	2	0	0	3
Storm Davis	0	2	11.25	2	2	0	0	0	8.0	14	10	1	7
Dennis Eckersley	0	1	10.80	2	0	0	0	0	1.2	2	2	1	2
Rick Honeycutt	1	0	0.00	3	0	0	0	0	3.1	0	0	0	5
Gene Nelson	0	0	1.42	3	0	0	0	0	6.1	4	1	3	3
Eric Plunk	0	0	0.00	2	0	0	0	0	1.2	0	0	3	3
Dave Stewart	0	1	3.14	2	2	0	0	0	14.1	12	5	5	5
Bob Welch	0	0	1.80	1	1	0	0	0	5.0	6	1	3	8
Curt Young	0	0	0.00	1	0	0	0	0	1.0	1	0	0	0
TOTAL	1	4	3.92	20	5	0	0	0	43.2	41	19	13	36

GAME 1 AT LA OCT 15

OAK	040	000	000	4	7	0
LA	200	001	002	5	7	0

Pitchers: Stewart, ECKERSLEY (9) vs Belcher, Leary (3), Holton (6), PENA (8) Home Runs: Hatcher-LA, Canseco-OAK, Gibson-LA
Attendance: 55,983

GAME 2 AT LA OCT 16

OAK	000	000	000	0	3	0
LA	005	100	00X	6	10	1

Pitchers: DAVIS, Nelson (4), Young (6), Plunk (7), Honeycutt (8) vs HERSHISER
Home Runs: Marshall-LA
Attendance: 56,051

GAME 3 AT OAK OCT 18

LA	000	010	000	1	8	1
OAK	001	000	001	2	5	0

Pitchers: Tudor, Leary (2), Pena (6), J.HOWELL (9) vs Welch, Cadaret (6), Nelson (6), HONEYCUTT (8)
Home Runs: McGwire-OAK
Attendance: 49,316

GAME 4 AT OAK OCT 19

LA	201	000	100	4	8	1
OAK	100	001	100	3	9	2

Pitchers: BELCHER, J.Howell (7) vs STEWART, Cadaret (7), Eckersley (9)
Attendance: 49,317

GAME 5 AT OAK OCT 20

LA	200	201	000	5	8	0
OAK	001	000	010	2	4	0

Pitchers: HERSHISER vs DAVIS, Cadaret (5), Nelson (5), Honeycutt (8), Plunk (9), Burns (9)
Home Runs: Hatcher-LA, Davis-LA
Attendance: 49,317

From the first inning of Game 1 when they drove in their teams' first runs, first basemen Will Clark of the Giants and Mark Grace of the Cubs dominated the offense, finishing with eight RBIs apiece and LCS record-shattering BAs of .650 and .647. Although Grace homered for two Chicago runs in the opener, the game belonged to Clark, whose four hits—two of them home runs, one a grand slam—drove in six of the eleven Giant runs. Grace led the Cubs' retaliation the next day with his second three-hit game, driving in four of Chicago's nine runs in the first and sixth innings. Kevin Mitchell, Matt Williams, and Rob Thompson—runners-up to Clark for Giant offensive honors in the series—all homered in the losing cause. Chicago scored first in the next three games but narrowly lost them all. Thompson's two-run homer in the last of the seventh put the Giants ahead for good in Game 3. The next day, Williams's two-run single in the third inning overcame Chicago's lead, and his two-run homer in the fifth broke a 4–4 tie to conclude the scoring.

Cub starter Mike Bielecki stopped San Francisco on a pair of singles through six innings of Game 5, and carried a 1–0 lead into the seventh, when Clark's triple and Mitchell's sacrifice fly tied the score. An inning later, after Bielecki loaded the bases with three two-out walks, relief ace Mitch Williams was called on to face Clark and got two strikes on him. But after fouling off a slider and fastball, Clark lined a single up the middle for two go-ahead Giant runs. San Francisco closer Steve Bedrosian yielded Chicago a second run in the ninth on a trio of two-out singles, but Ryne Sandberg (until then batting .421 in the series) grounded out, and the Giants owned their first pennant in twenty-seven years.

San Francisco Giants (West), 4; Chicago Cubs (East), 1

SF (W)

PLAYER/POS	AVG	G	AB	R	H	2B	3B	HR	RB	BB	SO	SB
Bill Bathe, ph	.000	2	1	0	0	0	0	0	0	0	1	0
Steve Bedrosian, p	.000	4	0	0	0	0	0	0	0	0	0	0
Jeff Brantley, p	.000	3	0	0	0	0	0	0	0	1	0	0
Brett Butler, of	.211	5	19	6	4	0	0	0	0	3	3	0
Will Clark, 1b	.650	5	20	8	13	3	1	2	8	2	2	0
Kelly Downs, p	.000	2	3	0	0	0	0	0	0	0	1	0
Scott Garrelts, p	.000	2	4	0	0	0	0	0	0	1	1	0
Atlee Hammaker, p	.000	1	0	0	0	0	0	0	0	0	0	0
Terry Kennedy, c	.188	5	16	0	3	1	0	0	0	1	4	0
Mike La Coss, p	.000	1	1	0	0	0	0	0	0	0	0	0
Craig Lefferts, p	.000	2	0	0	0	0	0	0	0	0	0	0
Greg Litton, 3b	1.000	1	1	0	1	0	0	0	0	0	0	0
Candy Maldonado, of	.000	3	3	1	0	0	0	0	1	2	0	0
Kirt Manwaring, c	.000	3	2	0	0	0	0	0	0	0	0	0
Kevin Mitchell, of	.353	5	17	5	6	0	0	2	7	3	3	0
Donell Nixon, of-2	.000	3	3	0	0	0	0	0	0	0	1	1
Ken Oberkfell, 3b-1	.000	3	4	0	0	0	0	0	0	0	0	0
Rick Reuschel, p	.000	2	2	0	0	0	0	0	0	0	0	0
Ernie Riles, ph	.000	1	1	0	0	0	0	0	0	0	0	0
Don Robinson, p	.000	1	0	0	0	0	0	0	0	0	0	0
Pat Sheridan, of	.154	5	13	1	2	0	1	0	0	0	4	0
Robby Thompson, 2b	.278	5	18	5	5	0	0	2	3	3	2	0
Jose Uribe, ss	.235	5	17	2	4	1	0	0	1	1	5	1
Matt Williams, 3b-5,ss-1	.300	5	20	2	6	1	0	2	9	0	2	0
TOTAL	.267		165	30	44	6	2	8	29	17	29	2

PITCHER	W	L	ERA	G	GS	CG	SV	SHO	IP	H	ER	BB	SO
Steve Bedrosian	0	0	2.70	4	0	0	3	0	3.1	4	1	2	2
Jeff Brantley	0	0	0.00	3	0	0	0	0	5.0	1	0	2	3
Kelly Downs	1	0	3.12	2	0	0	0	0	8.2	8	3	6	6
Scott Garrelts	1	0	5.40	2	2	0	0	0	11.2	16	7	2	8
Atlee Hammaker	0	0	0.00	1	0	0	0	0	1.0	1	0	0	0
Mike La Coss	0	0	9.00	1	1	0	0	0	3.0	7	3	0	2
Craig Lefferts	0	0	9.00	2	0	0	0	0	1.0	2	1	2	1
Rick Reuschel	1	1	5.19	2	2	9	0	0	8.2	12	5	2	5
Don Robinson	1	0	0.00	1	0	0	0	0	1.2	3	0	0	0
TOTAL	4	1	4.09	18	5	9	3	0	44.0	53	20	16	27

CHI (E)

PLAYER/POS	AVG	G	AB	R	H	2B	3B	HR	RB	BB	SO	SB
Paul Assenmacher, p	.000	2	0	0	0	0	0	0	0	0	0	0
Mike Bielecki, p	.200	2	5	0	1	0	0	0	2	0	2	0
Andre Dawson, of	.105	5	19	0	2	1	0	0	3	2	6	0
Shawon Dunston, ss	.316	5	19	2	6	0	0	0	0	1	1	1
Joe Girardi, c	.100	4	10	1	1	0	0	0	0	1	2	0
Mark Grace, 1b	.647	5	17	3	11	3	1	1	8	4	1	0
Paul Kilgus, p	.000	1	0	0	0	0	0	0	0	0	0	0
Lester Lancaster, p	.000	3	1	0	0	0	0	0	0	0	1	0
Vance Law, 3b-1	.000	2	3	0	0	0	0	0	0	0	3	0
Greg Maddux, p-2	.000	3	3	1	0	0	0	0	0	0	0	0
L. McClendon, c-2,of-1	.667	3	3	0	2	0	0	0	0	1	0	0
Domingo Ramos, ph	.000	1	1	0	0	0	0	0	0	0	0	0
Luis Salazar, 3b	.368	5	19	2	7	0	1	1	2	0	0	0
Ryne Sandberg, 2b	.400	5	20	6	8	3	1	1	4	3	4	0
Scott Sanderson, p	.000	1	0	0	0	0	0	0	0	0	0	0
Dwight Smith, of	.200	4	15	2	3	1	0	0	0	2	2	1
Rick Sutcliffe, p	.500	1	2	0	1	1	0	0	0	0	0	0
Jerome Walton, of	.364	5	22	4	8	0	0	0	2	2	2	0
Mitch Webster, of-2	.333	5	3	1	1	0	0	0	0	0	0	0
Curtis Wilkerson, 3b-1	.500	2	2	1	1	0	0	0	0	0	0	0
Mitch Williams, p	.000	2	0	0	0	0	0	0	0	0	0	0
Steve Wilson, p	.000	2	0	0	0	0	0	0	0	0	0	0
Rick Wrona, c	.000	2	5	0	0	0	0	0	0	0	3	0
Marvell Wynne, of-2	.167	4	6	0	1	0	0	0	0	0	0	0
TOTAL	.303		175	22	53	9	3	3	21	16	27	3

PITCHER	W	L	ERA	G	GS	CG	SV	SHO	IP	H	ER	BB	SO
P. Assenmacher	0	0	13.50	2	0	0	0	0	0.2	3	1	0	0
Mike Bielecki	0	1	3.65	2	2	0	0	0	12.1	7	5	6	11
Paul Kilgus	0	0	0.00	1	0	0	0	0	3.0	4	0	1	0
Lester Lancaster	1	1	6.00	3	0	0	0	0	6.0	6	4	1	3
Greg Maddux	0	1	13.50	2	2	0	0	0	7.1	13	11	4	5
Scott Sanderson	0	0	0.00	1	0	0	0	0	2.0	2	0	0	1
Rick Sutcliffe	0	1	4.50	1	1	0	0	0	6.0	5	3	4	2
Mitch Williams	0	0	0.00	2	0	0	0	0	1.0	1	0	0	2
Steve Wilson	0	0	4.91	2	0	0	0	0	3.2	3	2	1	4
TOTAL	1	4	5.57	16	5	0	0	0	42.0	44	26	17	29

GAME 1 AT CHI OCT 4

SF	301	400	030	11	13	0
CHI	201	000	000	3	10	1

Pitchers: GARRELTS, Brantley (8), Hammaker (9) vs MADDUX, Kilgus (5), Wilson (8)
Home Runs: Grace-CHI, Clark-SF (2), Sandberg-CHI, Mitchell-SF
Attendance: 39,195

GAME 2 AT CHI OCT 5

SF	000	200	021	5	10	0
CHI	600	003	00X	9	11	0

Pitchers: REUSCHEL, Downs (1), Lefferts (6), Brantley (7), Bedrosian (8) vs Bielecki, Assenmacher (5), LANCASTER (6)
Home Runs: Mitchell-SF, Williams-SF, Thompson-SF
Attendance: 39,195

GAME 3 AT SF OCT 7

CHI	200	100	100	4	10	0
SF	300	000	20X	5	8	3

Pitchers: Sutcliffe, Assenmacher (7), LANCASTER (7) vs LaCoss, Brantley (4), ROBINSON (7), Lefferts (8), Bedrosian (9)
Home Runs: Thompson-SF
Attendance: 62,065

GAME 4 AT SF OCT 8

CHI	110	020	000	4	12	1
SF	102	120	00X	6	9	1

Pitchers: Maddux, WILSON (4), Sanderson (6), Williams (8) vs Garrelts, DOWNS (5), Bedrosian (9)
Home Runs: Salazar-CHI, Williams-SF
Attendance: 62,078

GAME 5 AT SF OCT 9

CHI	001	000	001	2	10	1
SF	000	000	12X	3	4	1

Pitchers: BIELECKI, Williams (8), Lancaster (8) vs REUSCHEL, Bedrosian (9)
Attendance: 62,084

The awesome A's produced their share of heroes. Jose Canseco powered a truly heroic home run into the top deck of Toronto's SkyDome in Game 4; Dave Parker, in his seventh postseason series, at last hit his first post-season homer (and later his second); closer Dennis Eckersley added three saves to his four from 1988 to establish a new LCS record; and Carney Lansford was batting .455, with four RBIs, when a hamstring pull in Game 3 ended his series play. But the hero of heroes was leadoff batter Rickey Henderson. Oakland might have won the opener without Henderson, even though his hard slide into second in the sixth inning broke up a double play and forced a wide throw that gave the A's two runs and their first lead of the game. And the A's might also have won the next day even if Henderson had not rattled Toronto with four stolen bases. The A's suffered their loss in Game 3 despite an early 2–0 lead with Henderson scoring both runs—the first after walking, the second after a double and stolen base.

But in the final two games, Rickey Henderson's contribution made the difference between defeat and victory. A pair of two-run Henderson homers (together with Canseco's memorable blast and later RBI single) gave the A's their 6–5 win in Game 4. And in the first inning of Game 5, Henderson, after walking, stole his eighth base—a postseason series record—before Canseco singled him home with the A's first run. Two innings later Henderson tripled home the second Oakland run. The A's scored twice more in the seventh, but Toronto had narrowed Oakland's lead to one run when Eckersley fanned a final Blue Jay to secure the second straight Oakland pennant. Rickey Henderson was the unanimous choice for series MVP.

Oakland Athletics (West), 4; Toronto Blue Jays (East), 1

OAK (W)

PLAYER/POS	AVG	G	AB	R	H	2B	3B	HR	RB	BB	SO	SB
Lance Blankenship, 2b	.000	1	0	0	0	0	0	0	0	0	0	0
Jose Canseco, of	.294	5	17	1	5	0	0	1	3	3	7	0
Storm Davis, p	.000	1	0	0	0	0	0	0	0	0	0	0
Dennis Eckersley, p	.000	4	0	0	0	0	0	0	0	0	0	0
Mike Gallego, 2b-2,ss-2	.273	4	11	3	3	1	0	0	1	0	2	0
Ron Hassey, c	.167	2	6	0	1	0	0	0	1	1	2	0
Dave Henderson, of	.263	5	19	4	5	3	0	1	1	2	5	0
Rickey Henderson, of	.400	5	15	8	6	1	1	2	5	7	0	8
Rick Honeycutt, p	.000	3	0	0	0	0	0	0	0	0	0	0
Stan Javier, of	.000	1	2	0	0	0	0	0	0	0	1	0
Carney Lansford, 3b	.455	3	11	2	5	0	0	0	4	2	1	2
Mark McGwire, 1b	.389	5	18	3	7	1	0	1	3	1	4	0
Mike Moore, p	.000	1	0	0	0	0	0	0	0	0	0	0
Gene Nelson, p	.000	1	0	0	0	0	0	0	0	0	0	0
Dave Parker, dh	.188	4	16	2	3	0	0	2	3	0	0	0
Ken Phelps, ph	1.000	1	1	0	1	1	0	0	0	0	0	0
Tony Phillips, 2b-3,3b-3	.167	5	18	1	3	1	0	0	1	2	4	2
Terry Steinbach, c-3,dh-1	.200	4	15	0	3	0	0	0	1	1	5	0
Dave Stewart, p	.000	2	0	0	0	0	0	0	0	0	0	0
Walt Weiss, ss	.111	4	9	2	1	1	0	0	0	1	1	1
Bob Welch, p	.000	1	0	0	0	0	0	0	0	0	0	0
Matt Young, p	.000	1	0	0	0	0	0	0	0	0	0	0
TOTAL	.272		158	26	43	9	1	7	23	20	32	13

PITCHER	W	L	ERA	G	GS	CG	SV	SHO	IP	H	ER	BB	SO
Storm Davis	0	1	7.11	1	1	0	0	0	6.1	5	5	2	3
Dennis Eckersley	0	0	1.59	4	0	0	3	0	5.2	4	1	0	2
Rick Honeycutt	0	0	32.40	3	0	0	0	0	1.2	6	6	5	1
Mike Moore	1	0	0.00	1	1	0	0	0	7.0	3	0	2	3
Gene Nelson	0	0	0.00	1	0	0	0	0	1.1	1	0	0	2
Dave Stewart	2	0	2.81	2	2	0	0	0	16.0	13	5	3	9
Bob Welch	1	0	3.18	1	1	0	0	0	5.2	8	2	1	4
Matt Young	0	0	0.00	1	0	0	0	0	0.1	0	0	2	0
TOTAL	4	1	3.89	14	5	0	3	0	44.0	40	19	15	24

TOR (E)

PLAYER/POS	AVG	G	AB	R	H	2B	3B	HR	RB	BB	SO	SB
Jim Acker, p	.000	5	0	0	0	0	0	0	0	0	0	0
George Bell, dh-3,of-2	.200	5	20	2	4	0	0	1	2	0	3	0
Pat Borders, c	1.000	1	1	0	1	0	0	0	1	0	0	0
John Cerutti, p	.000	2	0	0	0	0	0	0	0	0	0	0
Junior Felix, of	.273	3	11	0	3	1	0	0	3	0	2	0
Tony Fernandez, ss	.350	5	20	6	7	3	0	0	1	1	2	5
Mike Flanagan, p	.000	1	0	0	0	0	0	0	0	0	0	0
Kelly Gruber, 3b	.294	5	17	2	5	1	0	0	1	3	2	1
Tom Henke, p	.000	3	0	0	0	0	0	0	0	0	0	0
Jimmy Key, p	.000	1	0	0	0	0	0	0	0	0	0	0
Manny Lee, 2b	.250	2	8	2	2	0	0	0	0	0	1	0
Nelson Liriano, 2b	.429	3	7	1	3	0	0	0	1	2	0	3
Lee Mazzilli, dh-2	.000	3	8	0	0	0	0	0	0	2	2	0
Fred McGriff, 1b	.143	5	21	1	3	0	0	0	3	0	4	0
Lloyd Moseby, of	.313	5	16	4	5	0	0	1	2	5	2	1
Rance Mulliniks, ph	.000	1	1	0	0	0	0	0	0	0	1	0
Dave Stieb, p	.000	2	0	0	0	0	0	0	0	0	0	0
Todd Stottlemyre, p	.000	1	0	0	0	0	0	0	0	0	0	0
Duane Ward, p	.000	2	0	0	0	0	0	0	0	0	0	0
David Wells, p	.000	1	0	0	0	0	0	0	0	0	0	0
Ernie Whitt, c	.125	5	16	1	2	0	0	1	3	2	3	0
Mookie Wilson, of	.263	5	19	2	5	0	0	0	2	2	2	1
TOTAL	.242		165	21	40	5	0	3	19	15	24	11

PITCHER	W	L	ERA	G	GS	CG	SV	SHO	IP	H	ER	BB	SO
Jim Acker	0	0	1.42	5	0	0	0	0	6.1	4	1	1	4
John Cerutti	0	0	0.00	2	0	0	0	0	2.2	0	0	3	1
Mike Flanagan	0	1	10.38	1	1	0	0	0	4.1	7	5	1	3
Tom Henke	0	0	0.00	3	0	0	0	0	2.2	0	0	0	3
Jimmy Key	1	0	4.50	1	1	0	0	0	6.0	7	3	2	2
Dave Stieb	0	2	6.35	2	2	0	0	0	11.1	12	8	6	10
Todd Stottlemyre	0	1	7.20	1	1	0	0	0	5.0	7	4	2	3
Duane Ward	0	0	7.36	2	0	0	0	0	3.2	6	3	3	5
David Wells	0	0	0.00	1	0	0	0	0	1.0	0	0	2	1
TOTAL	1	4	5.02	18	5	0	0	0	43.0	43	24	20	32

GAME 1 AT OAK OCT 3

TOR	020	100	000	3 5 1
OAK	010	013	02X	7 11 0

Pitchers: STIEB, Acker (6), Ward (8) vs STEWART, Eckersley (9)
Home Runs: D.Henderson-OAK, Whitt-TOR, McGwire-OAK
Attendance: 49,435

GAME 2 AT OAK OCT 4

TOR	001	000	020	3 5 1
OAK	000	203	10X	6 9 1

Pitchers: STOTTLEMYRE, Acker (6), Wells (6), Henke (7), Cerutti (8) vs MOORE, Honeycutt (8), Eckersley (9)
Home Runs: Parker-OAK
Attendance: 49,444

GAME 3 AT TOR OCT 6

OAK	101	100	000	3 8 1
TOR	000	400	30X	7 8 0

Pitchers: DAVIS, Honeycutt (7), Nelson (7), M.Young (8) vs KEY, Acker (7), Henke (9)
Home Runs: Parker-OAK
Attendance: 50,268

GAME 4 AT TOR OCT 7

OAK	003	020	100	6 11 1
TOR	000	101	120	5 13 0

Pitchers: WELCH, Honeycutt (6), Eckersley (8) vs FLANAGAN, Ward (5), Cerutti (8), Acker (9)
Home Runs: R.Henderson-OAK (2), Canseco-OAK
Attendance: 50,076

GAME 5 AT TOR OCT 8

OAK	101	000	200	4 4 0
TOR	000	000	012	3 9 0

Pitchers: STEWART, Eckersley (9) vs STIEB, Acker (7), Henke (9)
Home Runs: Moseby-TOR, Bell-TOR
Attendance: 50,024

Not even the devastating earthquake that blindsided baseball's first San Francisco Bay World Series could halt the Oakland juggernaut. The A's scored first in every game and, except for 1½ innings of Game 2 in which the score stood at 1–1, held their lead to the finish.   Athletic ace Dave Stewart shut out the Giants on five hits in the opener. Three second-inning Oakland runs initiated the Series scoring, and Dave Parker and Walt Weiss expanded Stewart's margin of comfort with solo homers in the third and fourth. In Game 2, doubles by Carney Lansford in the first inning and Parker in the fourth drove home the two runs the A's would need for victory; Terry Steinbach's three-run blast later in the fourth added frosting to Oakland's cake. A's starter Mike Moore yielded a pair of singles and the first Giant run of the Series in the third inning but held the Giants to just two more singles in his seven-plus innings of work. Relievers Rick Honeycutt and Dennis Eckersley hurled perfect ball in the eighth and ninth.   After a day off, the Series shifted eleven miles across the Bay to San Francisco for Game 3. But just as fans were settling into their seats, the earthquake struck, knocking out power to Candlestick Park and (as gradually became known) killing 67 people in scattered pockets of destruction throughout the Bay Area. The fans were sent home, but despite the pleas of a few Eastern reporters that the rest of the Series be cancelled, the overwhelming desire of Bay Area residents prevailed, and Game 3 came off at last, ten days late. Starter Dave Stewart gave up three Giant runs in seven innings, but by the time he was relieved, his A's had sent nine men across the plate. Four more runs in the eighth completed the Oakland scoring. The Giants put together their first big inning of the Series, scoring four runs in the last of the ninth. Although the Giants' effort fell far short of what was needed, pinch hitter Bill Bathe's home run—the game's seventh, including five by the A's—set a new World Series record.   Game 4 began as yet another Giant humiliation. Oakland's Rickey Henderson led off the game with a home run, and by the time Giant Kevin Mitchell homered in his team's first pair of runs in the sixth inning, the A's had scored eight times. The Giants struggled back, though, scoring four times in the seventh on a walk and a cycle of hits—home run, triple, double, and single—to draw within two runs of a tie. But they came no closer. Oakland scored a ninth run

Oakland Athletics (AL), 4; San Francisco Giants (NL), 0

OAK (A)

PLAYER/POS	AVG	G	AB	R	H	2B	3B	HR	RB	BB	SO	SB
Lance Blankenship, 2b	.500	1	2	1	1	0	0	0	0	0	0	0
Todd Burns, p	.000	2	0	0	0	0	0	0	0	0	0	0
Jose Canseco, of	.357	4	14	5	5	0	0	1	3	4	3	1
Dennis Eckersley, p	.000	2	0	0	0	0	0	0	0	0	0	0
Mike Gallego, 2b-1,3b-1	.000	2	1	0	0	0	0	0	0	0	0	0
Dave Henderson, of	.308	4	13	6	4	2	0	2	4	4	3	0
Rickey Henderson, of	.474	4	19	4	9	1	2	1	3	2	2	3
Rick Honeycutt, p	.000	3	0	0	0	0	0	0	0	0	0	0
Stan Javier, of	.000	1	0	0	0	0	0	0	0	0	0	0
Carney Lansford, 3b	.438	4	16	5	7	1	0	1	4	3	1	0
Mark McGwire, 1b	.294	4	17	0	5	1	0	0	1	1	3	0
Mike Moore, p	.333	2	3	1	1	1	0	0	2	0	1	0
Gene Nelson, p	.000	2	0	0	0	0	0	0	0	0	0	0
Dave Parker, dh-2	.222	3	9	2	2	1	0	1	2	0	2	0
Ken Phelps, ph	.000	1	1	0	0	0	0	0	0	0	0	0
	.235	4	17	2	4	1	0	1	3	0	3	0
Terry Steinbach, c	.250	4	16	3	4	0	1	1	7	2	1	0
Dave Stewart, p	.000	2	3	0	0	0	0	0	0	0	1	0
Walt Weiss, ss	.133	4	15	3	2	0	0	1	1	2	2	0
TOTAL	.301		146	32	44	8	3	9	30	18	22	4

PITCHER	W	L	ERA	G	GS	CG	SV	SHO	IP	H	ER	BB	SO
Todd Burns	0	0	0.00	2	0	0	0	0	1.2	1	0	1	0
Dennis Eckersley	0	0	0.00	2	0	0	1	0	1.2	0	0	0	0
Rick Honeycutt	0	0	6.75	3	0	0	0	0	2.2	4	2	0	2
Mike Moore	2	0	2.08	2	2	0	0	0	13.0	9	3	3	10
Gene Nelson	0	0	54.00	2	0	0	0	0	1.0	4	6	2	1
Dave Stewart	2	0	1.69	2	2	1	0	1	16.0	10	3	2	14
TOTAL	4	0	3.50	13	4	1	1	1	36.0	28	14	8	27

SF (N)

PLAYER/POS	AVG	G	AB	R	H	2B	3B	HR	RB	BB	SO	SB
Bill Bathe, ph	.500	2	2	1	1	0	0	1	3	0	0	0
Steve Bedrosian, p	.000	2	0	0	0	0	0	0	0	0	0	0
Jeff Brantley, p	.000	3	0	0	0	0	0	0	0	0	0	0
Brett Butler, of	.286	4	14	1	4	1	0	0	1	2	1	2
Will Clark, 1b	.250	4	16	2	4	1	0	0	0	1	3	0
Kelly Downs, p	.000	3	0	0	0	0	0	0	0	0	0	0
Scott Garrelts, p	.000	2	1	0	0	0	0	0	0	0	1	0
Atlee Hammaker, p	.000	2	0	0	0	0	0	0	0	0	0	0
Terry Kennedy, c	.167	4	12	1	2	0	0	0	2	1	3	0
Mike La Coss, p	.000	2	1	0	0	0	0	0	0	0	0	0
Craig Lefferts, p	.000	3	0	0	0	0	0	0	0	0	0	0
Greg Litton, 2b-2,3b-1	.500	2	6	1	3	1	0	1	3	0	0	0
Candy Maldonado, of-3	.091	4	11	1	1	0	1	0	0	0	4	0
Kirt Manwaring, c	1.000	1	1	1	1	1	0	0	0	0	0	0
Kevin Mitchell, of	.294	4	17	2	5	0	0	1	2	0	3	0
Donell Nixon, of	.200	2	5	1	1	0	0	0	0	1	1	0
Ken Oberkfell, 3b	.333	4	6	1	2	0	0	0	0	3	0	0
Rick Reuschel, p	.000	1	0	0	0	0	0	0	0	0	0	0
Ernie Riles, dh-2	.000	3	6	0	0	0	0	0	0	0	1	0
Don Robinson, p	.000	1	0	0	0	0	0	0	0	0	0	0
Pat Sheridan, of	.000	1	2	0	0	0	0	0	0	0	0	0
Robby Thompson, 2b	.091	4	11	0	1	0	0	0	0	2	4	0
Jose Uribe, ss	.200	3	5	1	1	0	0	0	0	0	0	0
Matt Williams, ss-4,ss-3	.125	4	16	1	2	0	0	1	1	0	6	0
TOTAL	.209		134	14	28	4	1	4	14	8	27	2

PITCHER	W	L	ERA	G	GS	CG	SV	SHO	IP	H	ER	BB	SO
Steve Bedrosian	0	0	0.00	2	0	0	0	0	2.2	0	0	2	2
Jeff Brantley	0	0	4.15	3	0	0	0	0	4.1	5	2	3	1
Kelly Downs	0	0	7.71	3	0	0	0	0	4.2	3	4	2	4
Scott Garrelts	0	2	9.82	2	2	0	0	0	7.1	13	8	1	8
Atlee Hammaker	0	0	15.43	2	0	0	0	0	2.1	8	4	0	2
Mike La Coss	0	0	6.23	2	0	0	0	0	4.1	4	3	3	2
Craig Lefferts	0	0	3.38	3	0	0	0	0	2.2	2	1	2	1
Rick Reuschel	0	1	11.25	1	1	0	0	0	4.0	5	5	4	2
Don Robinson	0	1	21.60	1	1	0	0	0	1.2	4	4	1	0
TOTAL	0	4	8.21	19	4	0	0	0	34.0	44	31	18	22

an inning later, and Todd Burns and Dennis Eckersley hurled the Series to its conclusion with 2⅓ innings of perfect relief.

GAME 1 AT OAK OCT 14

SF	000 000 000	0	5	1
OAK	031 100 00X	5	11	1

Pitchers: GARRELTS, Hammaker (5), Brantley (6), LaCoss (8) vs STEWART
Home Runs: Parker-OAK, Weiss-OAK
Attendance: 49,385

GAME 2 AT OAK OCT 15

SF	001 000 000	1	4	0
OAK	100 400 00X	5	7	0

Pitchers: REUSCHEL, Downs (5), Lefferts (7), Bedrosian (8) vs MOORE, Honeycutt (8), Eckersley (9)
Home Runs: Steinbach-OAK
Attendance: 49,388

GAME 3 AT SF OCT 27

OAK	200 241 040	13	14	0
SF	010 200 004	7	10	3

Pitchers: STEWART, Honeycutt (8), Nelson (9), Burns (9) vs GARRELTS, Downs (4), Brantley (5), Hammaker (8), Lefferts (9)
Home Runs: Williams-SF, D.Henderson-OAK (2), Phillips-OAK, Canseco-OAK, Lansford-OAK, Bathe-SF
Attendance: 62,038

GAME 4 AT SF OCT 28

OAK	130 031 010	9	12	0
SF	000 002 400	6	9	0

Pitchers: MOORE, Nelson (7), Honeycutt (7), Burns (7), Eckersley (9) vs ROBINSON, LaCoss (2), Brantley (6), Downs (6), Lefferts (8), Bedrosian (8)
Home Runs: R.Henderson-OAK, Mitchell-SF, Litton-SF
Attendance: 62,032

Fielding plays and misplays provided some of the most crucial moments of the series. After the Pirates had overcome a three-run deficit to tie the score in Game 1, for example, they won the game when Eric Davis misplayed Andy Van Slyke's fly to left field for a run-scoring double. Cincinnati right fielder Paul O'Neill evened the series in Game 2 by singling home the game's first run in the first inning, then (with the game tied 1–1 in the fifth) doubling in the go-ahead—and final—run on a fly Pirate left fielder Barry Bonds lost in the late afternoon sun. Finally, O'Neill gunned down Pittsburgh's potential tying run at third base when Van Slyke attempted to move up after Bonds's fly-out to right.   Two- and three-run homers by Reds Billy Hatcher and Mariano Duncan gave Cincinnati the series advantage in Game 3, and Chris Sabo's sacrifice fly and two-run blast proved the decisive blows a day later as the Reds pushed their series lead to 3–1. In that game left fielder Eric Davis, backing up Bobby Bonilla's double off the center field wall, prevented what would have become a game-tying run when, with a perfect throw to third, he nailed Bonilla trying for a triple.

The Pirates staved off elimination with a narrow 3–2 win in Game 5, a win preserved by a spectacular bases-loaded game-ending double play. But in Game 6, Pittsburgh's uncertain fielding in the first inning gave the Reds their first and, as it turned out, decisive run. In the ninth inning, with the Reds ahead 2–1, Reds right fielder Glen Braggs snared a deep fly with a leaping catch that prevented at least one, and perhaps two, Pirate runs from scoring. One strikeout later the Reds had snared the National League pennant.

Cincinnati Reds (West), 4; Pittsburgh Pirates (East), 2

CIN (W)

PLAYER/POS	AVG	G	AB	R	H	2B	3B	HR	RB	BB	SO	SB
Billy Bates, pr	.000	2	0	1	0	0	0	0	0	0	0	0
Todd Benzinger, 1b-2	.333	5	9	0	3	0	0	0	0	2	0	0
Glenn Braggs, of	.200	2	5	0	1	0	0	0	0	0	1	0
Tom Browning, p	.000	2	3	0	0	0	0	0	0	0	1	0
Norm Charlton, p	.000	4	0	0	0	0	0	0	0	0	0	0
Eric Davis, of	.174	6	23	2	4	1	0	0	2	1	9	0
Rob Dibble, p	.000	4	2	0	0	0	0	0	0	0	1	0
Mariano Duncan, 2b	.300	6	20	1	6	0	0	1	4	0	8	0
Billy Hatcher, of	.333	4	15	2	5	1	0	1	2	0	2	0
Danny Jackson, p	.000	2	3	0	0	0	0	0	0	0	2	0
Barry Larkin, ss	.261	6	23	5	6	2	0	0	1	3	1	3
Rick Mahler, p	.000	1	0	0	0	0	0	0	0	0	0	0
Hal Morris, 1b-4	.417	5	12	3	5	1	0	0	1	1	0	0
Randy Myers, p	.000	4	0	0	0	0	0	0	0	0	0	0
Ron Oester, 2b-2	.333	3	3	1	1	0	0	0	0	0	0	0
Joe Oliver, c	.143	5	14	1	2	0	0	0	0	0	2	0
Paul O'Neill, of	.471	5	17	1	8	3	0	1	4	1	1	1
Luis Quinones, ph	.500	3	2	1	1	0	0	0	2	0	0	1
Jeff Reed, c	.000	4	7	0	0	0	0	0	0	0	2	0
Jose Rijo, p	.000	2	5	0	0	0	0	0	0	0	1	0
Chris Sabo, 3b	.227	6	22	1	5	0	0	1	3	1	4	0
Scott Scudder, p	.000	1	0	0	0	0	0	0	0	0	0	0
Herm Winningham, of-2	.286	3	7	1	2	1	0	0	1	1	1	1
TOTAL	.255		192	20	49	9	0	4	20	10	37	6

PITCHER	W	L	ERA	G	GS	CG	SV	SHO	IP	H	ER	BB	SO
Tom Browning	1	1	3.27	2	2	0	0	0	11.0	9	4	6	5
Norm Charlton	1	1	1.80	4	0	0	0	0	5.0	4	1	3	3
Rob Dibble	0	0	0.00	4	0	0	1	0	5.0	0	0	1	10
Danny Jackson	1	0	2.38	2	2	0	0	0	11.1	8	3	7	8
Rick Mahler	0	0	0.00	1	0	0	0	0	1.2	2	0	0	0
Randy Myers	0	0	0.00	4	0	0	3	0	5.2	2	0	3	7
Jose Rijo	1	0	4.38	2	2	0	0	0	12.1	10	6	7	15
Scott Scudder	0	0	0.00	1	0	0	0	0	1.0	1	0	0	1
TOTAL	4	2	2.38	20	6	0	4	0	53.0	36	14	27	49

PIT (E)

PLAYER/POS	AVG	G	AB	R	H	2B	3B	HR	RB	BB	SO	SB
Wally Backman, 3b-2	.143	3	7	1	1	1	0	0	0	1	3	1
Stan Belinda, p	.000	3	0	0	0	0	0	0	0	0	0	0
Jay Bell, ss	.250	6	20	3	5	1	0	1	1	4	3	0
Barry Bonds, of	.167	6	18	4	3	0	0	0	1	6	6	2
Bobby Bonilla, of-5,3b-3	.190	6	21	0	4	1	0	0	1	3	1	0
Sid Bream, 1b	.500	4	8	1	4	1	0	1	3	2	3	0
Doug Drabeck, p	.167	2	6	0	1	0	0	0	0	0	2	0
Jeff King, 3b-4	.100	5	10	1	1	0	0	0	0	1	5	0
Bill Landrum, p	.000	2	0	0	0	0	0	0	0	0	0	0
Mike La Valliere, c	.000	3	6	1	0	0	0	0	0	3	1	0
Jose Lind, 2b	.238	6	21	1	5	1	1	1	2	1	4	0
Carmelo Martinez, 1b	.250	2	8	0	2	2	0	0	2	0	1	0
Bob Patterson, p	.000	2	0	0	0	0	0	0	0	0	0	0
Ted Power, p	.000	2	1	0	0	0	0	0	0	0	1	0
Gary Redus, 1b-2	.250	5	8	1	2	0	0	0	0	1	3	1
R. J. Reynolds, of-3	.200	6	10	0	2	0	0	0	0	2	2	1
Don Slaught, c	.091	4	11	0	1	1	0	0	1	2	3	0
John Smiley, p	.000	1	0	0	0	0	0	0	0	0	0	0
Zane Smith, p	.000	2	3	0	0	0	0	0	0	0	1	0
Andy Van Slyke, of	.208	6	24	3	5	1	1	0	3	1	6	1
Bob Walk, p	.000	2	4	0	0	0	0	0	0	0	4	0
TOTAL	.194		186	15	36	9	2	3	14	27	49	6

PITCHER	W	L	ERA	G	GS	CG	SV	SHO	IP	H	ER	BB	SO
Stan Belinda	0	0	2.45	3	0	0	0	0	3.2	3	1	0	4
Doug Drabeck	1	1	1.65	2	2	1	0	0	16.1	12	3	3	13
Bill Landrum	0	0	0.00	2	0	0	0	0	2.0	0	0	0	1
Bob Patterson	0	0	0.00	2	0	0	1	0	1.0	1	0	2	0
Ted Power	0	0	3.60	2	0	0	1	0	5.0	6	2	2	3
John Smiley	0	0	0.00	1	0	0	0	0	2.0	2	0	0	0
Zane Smith	0	2	6.00	2	1	0	0	0	9.0	14	6	1	8
Bob Walk	1	1	4.85	2	2	0	0	0	13.0	11	7	2	8
TOTAL	2	4	3.29	16	6	1	2	0	52.0	49	19	10	37

GAME 1 AT CIN OCT 4

PIT	001	200	100	4	7	1
CIN	300	000	000	3	5	0

Pitchers: WALK, Belinda (7), Patterson (9), Power (9) vs Rijo, CHARLTON (6), Dibble (9)
Home Runs: Bream-PIT
Attendance: 55,700

GAME 2 AT CIN OCT 5

PIT	000	010	000	1	6	0
CIN	100	010	00X	2	5	0

Pitchers: DRABEK vs BROWNING, Dibble (7), Myers (8)
Home Runs: Lind-PIT
Attendance: 54,456

GAME 3 AT PIT OCT 8

CIN	020	030	001	6	13	1
PIT	000	200	010	3	8	0

Pitchers: JACKSON, Dibble (6), Charlton (8), Myers (9) vs SMILEY, Landrum (6), Smiley (7), Belinda (9)
Home Runs: Duncan-CIN, Hatcher-CIN
Attendance: 45,611

GAME 4 AT PIT OCT 9

CIN	000	200	201	5	10	1
PIT	100	100	010	3	8	0

Pitchers: RIJO, Myers (8), Dibble (9) vs WALK, Power (9)
Home Runs: O'Neill-CIN, Sabo-CIN, Bell-PIT
Attendance: 50,461

GAME 5 AT PIT OCT 10

CIN	100	000	010	2	7	0
PIT	200	100	00X	3	6	1

Pitchers: BROWNING, Mahler (6), Charlton (7), Scudder (8) vs DRABEK, Patterson (9)
Attendance: 48,221

GAME 6 AT CIN OCT 12

PIT	000	010	000	1	1	3
CIN	100	000	10X	2	9	0

Pitchers: Power, SMITH (3), Belinda (7), Landrum (8) vs Jackson, CHARLTON (7), Myers (8)
Attendance: 56,079

The ejection of Boston ace Roger Clemens from Game 4 for mouthing off to an umpire provided a moment of raucous counterpoint to the surgical precision with which Oakland dismembered the Red Sox. While the A's pitchers anesthetized Boston's hitters, parceling out just one run per game, their batters sliced up the Sox with singles, steals, and sacrifices. In Game 1, Boston's Wade Boggs interrupted a pitchers' duel between Clemens and Oakland's Dave Stewart with the series' only home run. But in the top of the seventh—after a tiring Clemens had been relieved—the A's evened the score with a walk, single, and sacrifice fly, took the lead an inning later with a pair of singles sandwiched around a bunt and stolen base, then buried the Sox with seven runs in the ninth. DH Harold Baines provided Oakland's most productive offense in the second game, singling home the tying run in the fourth inning, driving in the tiebreaker with a groundout in the seventh, and doubling home a third run in the ninth. In Game 3, a double steal by Baines and Jose Canseco set up the A's tying and tiebreaking runs, which scored on a sacrifice fly and a single.   The A's scored first for the only time in the series in Game 4, on a pair of singles and a grounder to short in the second inning. Following the shouting match between the Sox and umpires that erupted when pitcher Clemens was thrown out for disputing a walk to the next batter, Mike Gallego doubled home two more Oakland runs. A trio of Boston relievers stopped the Athletics the rest of the way, and a pair of Red Sox hits in the ninth ended Dave Stewart's shutout bid. But Rick Honeycutt came on to preserve Stewart's second win of the series and sew up Oakland's third successive American League championship.

Oakland Athletics (West), 4; Boston Red Sox (East), 0

OAK (W)

PLAYER/POS	AVG	G	AB	R	H	2B	3B	HR	RB	BB	SO	SB
Harold Baines, dh	.357	4	14	2	5	1	0	0	3	2	1	1
Lance Blankenship, dh	.000	3	0	1	0	0	0	0	0	0	0	1
Jose Canseco, of	.182	4	11	3	2	0	0	0	1	5	5	2
Dennis Eckersley, p	.000	3	0	0	0	0	0	0	0	0	0	0
Mike Gallego, ss-3,2b-2	.400	4	10	1	4	1	0	0	2	1	1	0
Ron Hassey, c-1,dh-1	.333	2	3	0	1	0	0	0	0	2	0	0
Dave Henderson, of	.167	2	6	0	1	0	0	0	0	1	0	2
Rickey Henderson, of	.294	4	17	1	5	0	0	0	3	1	2	2
Rick Honeycutt, p	.000	3	0	0	0	0	0	0	0	0	0	0
Doug Jennings, of	.000	1	1	0	0	0	0	0	0	0	0	0
Carney Lansford, 3b	.438	4	16	2	7	1	0	0	2	0	1	0
Willie McGee, of-2,dh-1	.222	3	9	3	2	1	0	0	0	1	2	2
Mark McGwire, 1b	.154	4	13	2	2	0	0	0	2	3	3	0
Mike Moore, p	.000	1	0	0	0	0	0	0	0	0	0	0
Gene Nelson, p	.000	1	0	0	0	0	0	0	0	0	0	0
Jamie Quirk, ph	1.000	1	1	0	1	0	0	0	0	0	0	0
Willie Randolph, 2b	.375	4	8	1	3	0	0	0	3	1	0	0
Terry Steinbach, c	.455	3	11	2	5	0	0	0	1	1	2	0
Dave Stewart, p	.000	2	0	0	0	0	0	0	0	0	0	0
Walt Weiss, ss	.000	2	7	2	0	0	0	0	0	0	2	0
Bob Welch, p	.000	1	0	0	0	0	0	0	0	0	0	0
TOTAL	.299		127	20	38	4	0	0	18	19	21	9

PITCHER	W	L	ERA	G	GS	CG	SV	SHO	IP	H	ER	BB	SO
Dennis Eckersley	0	0	0.00	3	0	0	2	0	3.1	2	0	0	3
Rick Honeycutt	0	0	0.00	3	0	0	1	0	1.2	0	0	0	0
Mike Moore	1	0	1.50	1	1	0	0	0	6.0	4	1	1	5
Gene Nelson	0	0	0.00	1	0	0	0	0	1.2	3	0	0	0
Dave Stewart	2	0	1.13	2	2	0	0	0	16.0	8	2	2	4
Bob Welch	1	0	1.23	1	1	0	0	0	7.1	6	1	3	4
TOTAL	4	0	1.00	11	4	0	3	0	36.0	23	4	6	16

BOS (E)

PLAYER/POS	AVG	G	AB	R	H	2B	3B	HR	RB	BB	SO	SB
Larry Andersen, p	.000	3	0	0	0	0	0	0	0	0	0	0
Marty Barrett, 2b	.000	3	0	0	0	0	0	0	0	0	0	0
Mike Boddicker, p	.000	1	0	0	0	0	0	0	0	0	0	0
Wade Boggs, 3b	.438	4	16	1	7	1	0	1	1	0	3	0
Tom Bolton, p	.000	2	0	0	0	0	0	0	0	0	0	0
Tom Brunansky, of	.083	4	12	0	1	0	0	0	1	1	3	0
Ellis Burks, of	.267	4	15	1	4	2	0	0	0	1	1	1
Roger Clemens, p	.000	2	0	0	0	0	0	0	0	0	0	0
Dwight Evans, dh	.231	4	13	0	3	1	0	0	0	1	3	0
Jeff Gray, p	.000	2	0	0	0	0	0	0	0	0	0	0
Mike Greenwell, of	.000	4	14	1	0	0	0	0	0	2	2	0
Greg Harris, p	.000	1	0	0	0	0	0	0	0	0	0	0
Danny Heep, ph	.000	2	2	0	0	0	0	0	0	0	0	0
Dana Kiecker, p	.000	1	0	0	0	0	0	0	0	0	0	0
Randy Kutcher, pr	.000	2	0	0	0	0	0	0	0	0	0	0
Dennis Lamp, p	.000	1	0	0	0	0	0	0	0	0	0	0
Mike Marshall, ph	.333	3	3	0	1	0	0	0	0	0	0	0
Rob Murphy, p	.000	1	0	0	0	0	0	0	0	0	0	0
Tony Pena, c	.214	4	14	0	3	0	0	0	0	0	0	0
Carlos Quintana, 1b	.000	4	13	0	0	0	0	0	1	1	0	0
Jeff Reardon, p	.000	1	0	0	0	0	0	0	0	0	0	0
Jody Reed, 2b-4,ss-3	.133	4	15	0	2	0	0	0	1	0	2	0
Luis Rivera, ss	.222	4	9	1	2	1	0	0	0	0	2	0
TOTAL	.183		126	4	23	5	0	1	4	6	16	1

PITCHER	W	L	ERA	G	GS	CG	SV	SHO	IP	H	ER	BB	SO
Larry Andersen	0	1	6.00	3	0	0	0	0	3.0	3	2	3	3
Mike Boddicker	0	1	2.25	1	1	1	0	0	8.0	6	2	3	7
Tom Bolton	0	0	0.00	2	0	0	0	0	3.0	2	0	2	3
Roger Clemens	0	1	3.52	2	2	0	0	0	7.2	7	3	5	4
Jeff Gray	0	0	2.70	2	0	0	0	0	3.1	4	1	1	2
Greg Harris	0	1	27.00	1	0	0	0	0	0.1	3	1	0	0
Dana Kiecker	0	0	1.59	1	1	0	0	0	5.2	6	1	1	2
Dennis Lamp	0	0	108.00	1	0	0	0	0	0.1	2	4	2	0
Rob Murphy	0	0	13.50	1	0	0	0	0	0.2	2	1	1	0
Jeff Reardon	0	0	9.00	1	0	0	0	0	2.0	3	2	1	0
TOTAL	0	4	4.50	15	4	1	0	0	34.0	38	17	19	21

GAME 1 AT BOS OCT 6

OAK	000	000	117	9	13	0
BOS	000	100	000	1	5	1

Pitchers: STEWART, Eckersley (9) vs Clemens, ANDERSEN (7), Bolton (8), Gray (8), Lamp (9), Murphy (9)
Home Runs: Boggs-BOS
Attendance: 35,192

GAME 2 AT BOS OCT 7

OAK	000	100	102	4	13	1
BOS	001	000	000	1	6	0

Pitchers: WELCH, Honeycutt (8), Eckersley (8) vs Kiecker, HARRIS (6), Andersen (7), Reardon (8)
Attendance: 35,070

GAME 3 AT OAK OCT 9

BOS	010	000	000	1	8	3
OAK	000	202	00X	4	6	0

Pitchers: BODDICKER vs MOORE, Nelson (7), Honeycutt (8), Eckersley (9)
Attendance: 49,026

GAME 4 AT OAK OCT 10

BOS	000	000	001	1	4	1
OAK	030	000	00X	3	6	0

Pitchers: CLEMENS, Bolton (2), Gray (5), Andersen (8) vs STEWART, Honeycutt (9)
Attendance: 49,052

In the most stunning World Series sweep since 1954, Cincinnati's fired-up Reds roasted the team many were proclaiming baseball's newest dynasty. Reds left fielder Eric Davis, playing despite shoulder and knee injuries, provided the A's their first hint of what was to come when—on the first pitch thrown to him in the first inning—he homered over the center field wall for two runs. Billy Hatcher, on base with a walk, scored ahead of Davis, the first of his Series-high six runs. Hatcher would not be retired at the plate until Game 3. Final score: 7–0. For Oakland starter Dave Stewart, the loss ended a personal postseason six-game win streak. For the club, the loss ended a streak of ten postseason wins. The A's put up their best fight of the Series in Game 2, scoring first, then overcoming a 1–2 deficit in the third inning with three more runs for a 4–2 lead. Cincinnati narrowed the gap with a run in the fourth and tied the score in the eighth when Hatcher tripled—setting a World Series record with his seventh straight hit—and came home on a grounder to short. The A's held on until the tenth inning, when ace reliever Dennis Eckersley gave up three straight hits to lose the game.

Game 3 was another Cincinnati blowout, an 8–3 contest in which all eleven runs were scored in the second and third innings. Chris Sabo led the Reds assault with two home runs, and handled a Series-record ten chances at third base.

For seven innings of Game 4 the tide of battle seemed to be turning in Oakland's favor. Billy Hatcher—who was batting .750—left the game after a pitch hit his hand in the first inning. Later in the inning Eric Davis tore a kidney diving for a Willie McGee shot that went for a double. McGee went on to score, and Davis departed for the hospital. A renewed Dave Stewart, supported by sharp fielding, seemed capable of sustaining his 1–0 lead to the finish. But in the eighth the Reds, with just one solid hit, eked out the two runs they would need for victory. After loading the bases with a leadoff single, a third-strike bunt that went for a hit, and a sacrifice bunt that Stewart misplayed for an error, the Reds drove home the tying run with a grounder to short and took the lead on a sacrifice fly. Meanwhile Reds starter Jose Rijo held the A's hitless after the first inning, leveling twenty men in order from the second into the ninth, when ace closer Randy Myers relieved him for the final two outs of the splendid sweep.

Cincinnati Reds (NL), 4;
Oakland Athletics (AL), 0

CIN (N)

PLAYER/POS	AVG	G	AB	R	H	2B	3B	HR	RB	BB	SO	SB
Jack Armstrong, p	.000	1	0	0	0	0	0	0	0	0	0	0
Billy Bates, ph	1.000	1	1	1	1	0	0	0	0	0	0	0
Todd Benzinger, 1b-3	.182	4	11	1	2	0	0	0	0	0	0	0
Glenn Braggs, of-1	.000	2	4	0	0	0	0	0	2	1	0	0
Tom Browning, p	.000	1	0	0	0	0	0	0	0	0	0	0
Norm Charlton, p	.000	1	0	0	0	0	0	0	0	0	0	0
Eric Davis, of	.286	4	14	3	4	0	0	1	5	0	0	0
Rob Dibble, p	.000	3	0	0	0	0	0	0	0	0	0	0
Mariano Duncan, 2b	.143	4	14	1	2	0	0	0	1	2	2	1
Billy Hatcher, of	.750	4	12	6	9	4	1	0	2	2	0	0
Danny Jackson, p	.000	1	1	0	0	0	0	0	0	0	1	0
Barry Larkin, ss	.353	4	17	3	6	1	1	0	1	2	0	0
Hal Morris, 1b-2,dh-2	.071	4	14	0	1	0	0	0	2	1	1	0
Randy Myers, p	.000	3	0	0	0	0	0	0	0	0	0	0
Ron Oester, ph	1.000	1	1	0	1	0	0	0	0	1	0	0
Joe Oliver, c	.333	4	18	2	6	3	0	0	2	0	1	0
Paul O'Neill, of	.083	4	12	2	1	0	0	0	1	5	2	1
Jose Rijo, p	.333	2	3	0	1	0	0	0	0	0	0	0
Chris Sabo, 3b	.563	4	16	2	9	1	0	2	5	2	2	0
Scott Scudder, p	.000	1	0	0	0	0	0	0	0	0	0	0
Herm Winningham, of-1	.500	2	4	1	2	0	0	0	0	0	0	0
TOTAL	.317		142	22	45	9	2	3	22	15	9	2

PITCHER	W	L	ERA	G	GS	CG	SV	SHO	IP	H	ER	BB	SO
Jack Armstrong	0	0	0.00	1	0	0	0	0	3.0	1	0	0	3
Tom Browning	1	0	4.50	1	1	0	0	0	6.0	6	3	2	2
Norm Charlton	0	0	0.00	1	0	0	0	0	1.0	1	0	0	0
Rob Dibble	1	0	0.00	3	0	0	0	0	4.2	3	0	1	4
Danny Jackson	0	0	10.13	1	1	0	0	0	2.2	6	3	2	0
Randy Myers	0	0	0.00	3	0	0	1	0	3.0	2	0	0	3
Jose Rijo	2	0	0.59	2	2	0	0	0	15.1	9	1	5	14
Scott Scudder	0	0	0.00	1	0	0	0	0	1.1	0	0	2	2
TOTAL	4	0	1.70	13	4	0	1	0	37.0	28	7	12	28

OAK (A)

PLAYER/POS	AVG	G	AB	R	H	2B	3B	HR	RB	BB	SO	SB
Harold Baines, dh-2	.143	3	7	1	1	0	0	1	2	1	2	0
Lance Blankenship, ph	.000	1	1	0	0	0	0	0	0	0	1	0
Mike Bordick, ss	.000	3	0	0	0	0	0	0	0	0	0	0
Todd Burns, p	.000	2	0	0	0	0	0	0	0	0	0	0
Jose Canseco, of-3,dh-1	.083	4	12	1	1	0	0	1	2	2	3	0
Dennis Eckersley, p	.000	2	0	0	0	0	0	0	0	0	0	0
Mike Gallego, ss	.091	4	11	0	1	0	0	0	1	1	3	1
Ron Hassey, c-1	.333	3	6	0	2	0	0	0	1	0	0	0
Dave Henderson, of-3	.231	4	13	2	3	1	0	0	0	1	3	0
Rickey Henderson, of	.333	4	15	2	5	2	0	1	1	3	4	3
Rick Honeycutt, p	.000	1	0	0	0	0	0	0	0	0	0	0
Doug Jennings, ph	1.000	1	1	0	1	0	0	0	0	0	0	0
Joe Klink, p	.000	1	0	0	0	0	0	0	0	0	0	0
Carney Lansford, 3b	.267	4	15	0	4	0	0	0	1	1	0	1
Willie McGee, of-3	.200	4	10	1	2	1	0	0	0	0	2	1
Mark McGwire, 1b	.214	4	14	1	3	0	0	0	0	2	4	0
Mike Moore, p	.000	1	0	0	0	0	0	0	0	0	0	0
Gene Nelson, p	.000	2	0	0	0	0	0	0	0	0	0	0
Jamie Quirk, c	.000	1	3	0	0	0	0	0	0	0	2	0
Willie Randolph, 2b	.267	4	15	4	4	0	0	0	0	1	0	1
Scott Sanderson, p	.000	2	0	0	0	0	0	0	0	0	0	0
Terry Steinbach, c	.125	3	8	0	1	0	0	0	0	0	1	0
Dave Stewart, p	.000	2	1	0	0	0	0	0	0	0	1	0
Bob Welch, p	.000	1	3	0	0	0	0	0	0	0	2	0
Curt Young, p	.000	1	0	0	0	0	0	0	0	0	0	0
TOTAL	.207		135	8	28	4	0	3	8	12	28	7

PITCHER	W	L	ERA	G	GS	CG	SV	SHO	IP	H	ER	BB	SO
Todd Burns	0	0	16.20	2	0	0	0	0	1.2	5	3	2	0
Dennis Eckersley	0	1	6.75	2	0	0	0	0	1.1	3	1	0	1
Rick Honeycutt	0	0	0.00	1	0	0	0	0	1.2	2	0	1	0
Joe Klink	0	0	INF	1	0	0	0	0	0.0	0	0	1	0
Mike Moore	0	1	6.75	1	1	0	0	0	2.2	8	2	0	1
Gene Nelson	0	0	0.00	2	0	0	0	0	5.0	3	0	2	0
Scott Sanderson	0	0	10.80	2	0	0	0	0	1.2	4	2	1	0
Dave Stewart	0	2	3.46	2	2	1	0	0	13.0	10	5	6	5
Bob Welch	0	0	4.91	1	1	0	0	0	7.1	9	4	2	2
Curt Young	0	0	0.00	1	0	0	0	0	1.0	1	0	0	0
TOTAL	0	4	4.33	15	4	1	0	0	35.1	45	17	15	9

GAME 1 AT CIN OCT 16

OAK	000	000	000	0	9 1
CIN	202	030	00X	7	10 0

Pitchers: STEWART, Burns (5), Nelson (5), Sanderson (7), Eckersley (8) vs RIJO, Dibble (8), Myers (9)
Home Runs: Davis-CIN
Attendance: 55,830

GAME 2 AT CIN OCT 17

OAK	103	000	000 0		4 10
CIN	200	100	010 1		5 14

Pitchers: Welch, Honeycutt (8), ECKERSLEY (10) vs Jackson, Scudder (3), Armstrong (5), Charlton (8), DIBBLE (9)
Home Runs: Canseco-OAK
Attendance: 55,832

GAME 3 AT OAK OCT 19

CIN	017	000	000	8 14 1
OAK	021	000	000	3 7 1

Pitchers: BROWNING, Dibble (7), Myers (8) vs MOORE, Sanderson (3), Klink (4), Nelson (4), Burns (8), Young (9)
Home Runs: Sabo-CIN (2), Baines-OAK, R.Henderson-OAK
Attendance: 48,269

GAME 4 AT OAK OCT 20

CIN	000	000	020	2 7 1
OAK	100	000	000	1 2 1

Pitchers: RIJO, Myers (9) vs STEWART
Attendance: 48,613

Pitching dominated this back-and-forth series which featured four shutouts, including three 1–0 games. Three times Atlanta hurlers blanked Pittsburgh on the Pirates' home grounds, including a pair of must-win victories that brought the Braves back from the brink of defeat. Andy Van Slyke opened the series scoring with a first-inning Pirate home run. Pirate starter Doug Drabek held the Braves scoreless through six innings of the opener, before injuring himself on the basepath. By the time David Justice homered in the ninth for Atlanta's only score, the Pirates had the game well in hand.

Atlanta evened the series with its first of three shutouts in Game Two behind the pitching of young Steve Avery and (for the final ⅔ inning) Alejandro Pena, and the bat and glove of Mark Lemke. The Braves' second baseman doubled home that game's only run in the sixth inning and prevented a Pittsburgh run from scoring in the eighth with a diving stop of a grounder up the middle. In Atlanta for Game Three, the Braves took the series lead with a 10–3 route that featured home runs by Ron Gant, Greg Olson, and Sid Bream. (Orlando Merced and Derek Bell homered for Pittsburgh.)

Game Four was much closer; this time three Pirate runs brought them victory. The Braves took a quick lead with two first-inning runs, but Pittsburgh scored once in the second and tied the game in the fifth on a throwing error as Pirate pitching shut down Atlanta's offense. In the top of the tenth, Andy Van Slyke led off with a walk. With two away he stole second, and then scored what proved the winning run on Don Slaught's double. With the series even again, Atlanta lost a run in Game Five when David Justice was ruled out for missing third base as he dashed home from second. An inning later the Pirates parlayed a walk and a pair of singles into the only run they would need to carry the series advantage back to Pittsburgh.

In Game Six, though, the Braves returned the favor, tying the series once more with a gem of their own. Avery and Pena combined for their second 1–0 victory, holding Atlanta to just four singles. Drabek held the Braves scoreless into the ninth, when Olson doubled home the game's only run.

In the finale, Braves starter John Smoltz enjoyed a three-run lead when he took the mound in the bottom of the first inning. Rookie first baseman Brian Hunter (who had homered for two of the first-inning runs) doubled in an additional Atlanta run in the fifth. Meanwhile Smoltz stopped the Pirates on six hits to bring the Braves their first pennant since their move to Atlanta in 1966.

Atlanta Braves (West), 4;
Pittsburgh Pirates (East), 3

ATL (W)

PLAYER/POS	AVG	G	AB	R	H	2B	3B	HR	RB	BB	SO	SB
Steve Avery, p	.143	2	7	0	1	0	0	0	0	0	4	0
Rafael Belliard, ss	.211	7	19	0	4	0	0	0	1	3	3	0
Jeff Blauser, ss	.000	2	2	0	0	0	0	0	0	0	0	0
Sid Bream, 1b	.300	4	10	1	3	0	0	1	3	0	1	0
Jim Clancy, p	.000	1	0	0	0	0	0	0	0	0	0	0
Ron Gant, of	.259	7	27	4	7	1	0	1	3	2	4	7
Tom Glavine, p	.250	2	4	0	1	0	0	0	0	0	2	0
Tommy Gregg, ph	.250	4	4	0	1	0	0	0	0	0	2	0
Brian Hunter, 1b	.333	5	18	2	6	2	0	1	4	0	2	0
David Justice, of	.200	7	25	4	5	1	0	1	2	3	7	0
Charlie Leibrandt, p	.000	1	1	0	0	0	0	0	0	0	0	0
Mark Lemke, 2b	.200	7	20	1	4	1	0	0	1	4	0	0
Kent Mercker, p	.000	1	0	0	0	0	0	0	0	0	0	0
Keith Mitchell, of	.000	5	4	0	0	0	0	0	0	0	1	0
Greg Olson, c	.333	7	24	3	8	1	0	1	4	4	3	1
Alejandro Pena, p	.000	4	0	0	0	0	0	0	0	0	0	0
Terry Pendleton, 3b	.167	7	30	1	5	1	1	0	1	1	3	0
Lonnie Smith, of	.250	7	24	3	6	3	0	0	4	5	2	2
John Smoltz, p	.200	2	5	0	1	0	0	0	0	1	4	1
Mike Stanton, p	.000	3	0	0	0	0	0	0	0	0	0	0
Jeff Treadway, 2b	.333	1	3	0	1	0	0	0	0	0	0	0
Jerry Willard, ph	.000	2	2	0	0	0	0	0	0	0	1	0
Mark Wohlers, p	.000	3	0	0	0	0	0	0	0	0	0	0
TOTAL	.231		229	19	53	10	1	5	19	22	42	11

PITCHER	W	L	ERA	G	GS	CG	SV	SHO	IP	H	ER	BB	SO
Steve Avery	2	0	0.00	2	2	0	0	0	16.1	9	0	4	17
Jim Clancy	0	0	0.00	1	0	0	0	0	0.1	0	0	0	0
Tom Glavine	0	2	3.21	2	2	0	0	0	14.0	12	5	6	11
Charlie Leibrandt	0	0	1.35	1	1	0	0	0	6.2	8	1	3	6
Kent Mercker	0	1	13.50	1	0	0	0	0	0.2	0	1	2	0
Alejandro Pena	0	0	0.00	4	0	0	3	0	4.1	1	0	0	4
John Smoltz	2	0	1.76	2	2	1	0	1	15.1	14	3	3	15
Mike Stanton	0	0	2.45	3	0	0	0	0	3.2	4	1	3	3
Mark Wohlers	0	0	0.00	3	0	0	0	0	1.2	3	0	1	1
TOTAL	4	3	1.57	19	7	1	3	1	63.0	51	11	22	57

PIT (E)

PLAYER/POS	AVG	G	AB	R	H	2B	3B	HR	RB	BB	SO	SB
Stan Belinda, p	.000	3	0	0	0	0	0	0	0	0	0	0
Jay Bell, ss	.414	7	29	2	12	2	0	1	1	0	10	0
Barry Bonds, of	.148	7	27	1	4	1	0	0	0	2	4	3
Bobby Bonilla, of	.304	7	23	2	7	2	0	0	1	6	2	0
Steve Buechele, 3b	.304	7	23	2	7	2	0	0	4	6	0	0
Doug Drabek, p	.200	2	5	0	1	1	0	0	1	0	2	0
Cecil Espy, ph	.000	2	2	0	0	0	0	0	0	0	2	0
Bob Kipper, p	.000	1	0	0	0	0	0	0	0	0	0	0
Bill Landrum, p	.000	1	0	0	0	0	0	0	0	0	0	0
Mike La Valliere, c	.333	3	6	0	2	0	0	0	1	2	0	0
Jose Lind, 2b	.160	7	25	0	4	0	0	0	3	0	6	0
Roger Mason, p	.000	3	1	0	0	0	0	0	0	0	1	0
Lloyd Mc Clendon, 1b-1	.000	3	2	0	0	0	0	0	0	1	0	0
Orlando Merced, 1b-2	.222	3	9	1	2	0	0	1	1	0	1	0
Bob Patterson, p	.000	1	0	0	0	0	0	0	0	0	0	0
Gary Redus, 1b	.158	5	19	1	3	0	0	0	0	1	4	2
Rosario Rodriguez, p	.000	1	0	0	0	0	0	0	0	0	0	0
Don Slaught, c	.235	6	17	0	4	0	0	0	1	1	4	0
John Smiley, p	.000	2	0	0	0	0	0	0	0	0	0	0
Zane Smith, p	.000	2	5	0	0	0	0	0	0	0	4	0
Randy Tomlin, p	.000	1	2	0	0	0	0	0	0	0	0	0
Andy Van Slyke, of	.160	7	25	3	4	2	0	1	2	5	5	1
Gary Varsho, ph	.500	2	2	0	1	0	0	0	0	0	1	0
Bob Walk, p	.000	3	2	0	0	0	0	0	0	0	0	0
Curtis Wilkerson, ph	.000	4	4	0	0	0	0	0	0	0	3	0
TOTAL	.224		228	12	51	10	0	3	11	22	57	6

PITCHER	W	L	ERA	G	GS	CG	SV	SHO	IP	H	ER	BB	SO
Stan Belinda	1	0	0.00	3	0	0	0	0	5.0	0	0	3	4
Doug Drabek	1	1	0.60	2	2	1	0	0	15.0	10	1	5	10
Bob Kipper	0	0	4.50	1	0	0	0	0	2.0	2	1	0	1
Bill Landrum	0	0	9.00	1	0	0	0	0	1.0	2	1	2	2
Roger Mason	0	0	0.00	3	0	0	1	0	4.1	3	0	1	2
Bob Patterson	0	0	0.00	1	0	0	0	0	2.0	1	0	0	3
Rosario Rodriguez	0	0	27.00	1	0	0	0	0	1.0	1	3	2	1
John Smiley	0	2	23.63	2	2	0	0	0	2.2	8	7	1	3
Zane Smith	1	1	0.61	2	2	0	0	0	14.2	15	1	3	10
Randy Tomlin	0	0	3.00	1	1	0	0	0	6.0	6	2	2	1
Bob Walk	0	0	1.93	3	0	0	1	0	9.1	5	2	3	5
TOTAL	3	4	2.57	20	7	1	2	0	63.0	53	18	22	42

GAME 1 AT PIT OCT 9

ATL	000	000	001	1	5	1
PIT	102	001	01X	5	8	1

Pitchers: GLAVINE, Wohlers (7), Stanton (8) vs DRABEK, Walk (7)
Home Runs: Van Slyke-PIT, Justice-ATL
Attendance: 57,347

GAME 2 AT PIT OCT 10

ATL	000	001	000	1	8	0
PIT	000	000	000	0	6	0

Pitchers: AVERY, Pena (9) vs SMITH, Mason (8), Belinda (9)
Attendance: 57,533

GAME 3 AT ATL OCT 12

PIT	100	100	100	3	10	2
ATL	411	000	13X	10	11	0

Pitchers: SMILEY, Landrum (3), Patterson (4), Kipper (6), Rodriguez (8) vs SMOLTZ, Stanton (7), Wohlers (8), Pena (8)
Home Runs: Merced-PIT, Bell-PIT, Gant-ATL, Olson-ATL, Bream-ATL
Attendance: 50,905

GAME 4 AT ATL OCT 13

PIT	010	010	000	1	3	11	1
ATL	200	000	000	0	2	11	1

Pitchers: Tomlin, Walk (7), BELINDA (9) vs Leibrandt, Clancy (7), Stanton (8), MERCKER (10), Wohlers (10)
Attendance: 51,109

GAME 5 AT ATL OCT 14

PIT	000	010	000	1	6	2
ATL	000	000	000	0	9	1

Pitchers: SMITH, Mason (8) vs GLAVINE, Pena (9)
Attendance: 51,109

GAME 6 AT PIT OCT 16

ATL	000	000	001	1	7	0
PIT	000	000	000	0	4	0

Pitchers: AVERY, Pena (9) vs DRABEK
Attendance: 54,508

GAME 7 AT PIT OCT 17

ATL	300	010	000	4	6	1
PIT	000	000	000	0	6	0

Pitchers: SMOLTZ vs SMILEY, Walk (1), Mason (6), Belinda (8)
Home Runs: Hunter-ATL
Attendance: 46,932

Minnesota struggled to achieve a 2–1 advantage in the first three games, then blew the Jays out of their SkyDome in the next two. Game One looked as though it would be an easy win for the Twins, who drove out starter Tom Candiotti with five runs on eight hits in the first 2⅔ innings. But Toronto scored once in the fourth and chased Twin starter Jack Morris in the sixth with five straight singles and three more runs. Relievers Carl Willis and Rick Aguilera, though, held Toronto to just one more single to preserve the victory for Minnesota.

The Jays scored three times in Game Two before Minnesota put its first run across in the last of the third, and scored twice more in the seventh, taking their first—and, as it turned out, only—win behind the strong pitching of rookie Juan Guzman and relievers Tom Henke and Duane Ward. Toronto again scored early in Game Three, with a pair of two-out runs (one of them Joe Carter's homer) in the first inning. Jays starter Jimmy Key held the Twins scoreless until they got to him for a run in the fifth, and another in the sixth which evened the score. Meanwhile a string of Minnesota pitchers stifled the Blue Jay bats from the second inning on. In the tenth, pinch hitter Mike Pagliarulo won it for the Twins with a home run to right.

For the third game in a row, Toronto scored first, with a run in the second inning of Game Four. But Minnesota's Kirby Puckett homered in the fourth to tie the score, and by the time Toronto scored again two innings later, the Twins had upped its run total to six. Puckett's home run in the first inning of Game Five gave the Twins the first of two early runs, but the Jays came back with three runs in the third and two more in the fourth to drive out starter Kevin Tapani. They scored no more, however, as three Twin relievers held them to one single in the final five frames. In the sixth inning, meanwhile, Minnesota reawakened to tie the game with a trio of runs, and salted it—and the pennant—away in the eighth: with two out, Puckett doubled home the go-ahead run, and Kent Hrbek singled in two more for insurance.

Minnesota Twins (West), 4; Toronto Blue Jays (East), 1

MIN (W)

PLAYER/POS	AVG	G	AB	R	H	2B	3B	HR	RB	BB	SO	SB
Rick Aguilera, p	.000	3	0	0	0	0	0	0	0	0	0	0
Steve Bedrosian, p	.000	2	0	0	0	0	0	0	0	0	0	0
Jarvis Brown, dh	.000	1	0	1	0	0	0	0	0	0	0	0
Chili Davis, dh	.294	5	17	3	5	2	0	0	2	5	8	1
Scott Erickson, p	.000	1	0	0	0	0	0	0	0	0	0	0
Greg Gagne, ss	.235	5	17	2	4	0	0	0	1	1	5	0
Dan Gladden, of	.261	5	23	4	6	0	0	0	3	1	3	3
Mark Guthrie, p	.000	2	0	0	0	0	0	0	0	0	0	0
Brian Harper, c	.278	5	18	1	5	2	0	0	1	0	2	0
Kent Hrbek, 1b	.143	5	21	0	3	0	0	0	3	1	3	0
Chuck Knoblauch, 2b	.350	5	20	5	7	2	0	0	3	3	3	2
Gene Larkin, ph	.000	3	3	0	0	0	0	0	0	0	1	0
Scott Leius, 3b	.000	3	4	0	0	0	0	0	0	1	1	0
Shane Mack, of	.333	5	18	4	6	1	1	0	3	2	4	2
Jack Morris, p	.000	2	0	0	0	0	0	0	0	0	0	0
Al Newman, 2b-1,3b-1	.000	2	0	0	0	0	0	0	0	0	0	0
Junior Ortiz, c	.000	3	3	0	0	0	0	0	0	0	0	0
Mike Pagliarulo, 3b	.333	5	15	3	5	1	0	1	3	0	2	0
Kirby Puckett, of	.429	5	21	4	9	1	0	2	6	1	4	0
Paul Sorrento, ph	.000	1	1	0	0	0	0	0	0	0	1	0
Kevin Tapani, p	.000	2	0	0	0	0	0	0	0	0	0	0
David West, p	.000	2	0	0	0	0	0	0	0	0	0	0
Carl Willis, p	.000	3	0	0	0	0	0	0	0	0	0	0
TOTAL	.276		181	27	50	9	1	3	25	15	37	8

PITCHER	W	L	ERA	G	GS	CG	SV	SHO	IP	H	ER	BB	SO
Rick Aguilera	0	0	0.00	3	0	0	3	0	3.1	1	0	0	3
Steve Bedrosian	0	0	0.00	2	0	0	0	0	1.1	3	0	2	2
Scott Erickson	0	0	4.50	1	1	0	0	0	4.0	3	2	5	2
Mark Guthrie	1	0	0.00	2	0	0	0	0	2.2	0	0	0	0
Jack Morris	2	0	4.05	2	2	0	0	0	13.1	17	6	1	7
Kevin Tapani	0	1	7.84	2	2	0	0	0	10.1	16	9	3	9
David West	1	0	0.00	2	0	0	0	0	5.2	1	0	4	4
Carl Willis	0	0	0.00	3	0	0	0	0	5.1	2	0	0	3
TOTAL	4	1	3.33	17	5	0	3	0	46.0	43	17	15	30

TOR (E)

PLAYER/POS	AVG	G	AB	R	H	2B	3B	HR	RB	BB	SO	SB
Jim Acker, p	.000	1	0	0	0	0	0	0	0	0	0	0
Roberto Alomar, 2b	.474	5	19	3	9	0	0	0	4	2	3	2
Pat Borders, c	.263	5	19	0	5	1	0	0	2	0	0	0
Tom Candiotti, p	.000	2	0	0	0	0	0	0	0	0	0	0
Joe Carter, of-3,dh-2	.263	5	19	3	5	2	0	1	4	1	5	0
Rob Ducey, of	.000	1	1	0	0	0	0	0	0	0	0	0
Rene Gonzales, 1b-1,ss-1	.000	2	0	0	0	0	0	0	0	0	0	0
Kelly Gruber, 3b	.238	5	21	1	5	0	0	0	4	0	4	1
Juan Guzman, p	.000	1	0	0	0	0	0	0	0	0	0	0
Tom Henke, p	.000	2	0	0	0	0	0	0	0	0	0	0
Jimmy Key, p	.000	1	0	0	0	0	0	0	0	0	0	0
Manuel Lee, ss	.125	5	16	3	2	0	0	0	0	1	5	0
Rob Mac Donald, p	.000	1	0	0	0	0	0	0	0	0	0	0
Candy Maldonado, of	.100	5	20	1	2	1	0	0	1	1	6	0
Rance Mulliniks, dh-3	.125	5	8	1	1	0	0	0	0	3	0	0
John Olerud, 1b	.211	5	19	1	4	1	0	0	3	3	1	0
Todd Stottlemyre, p	.000	1	0	0	0	0	0	0	0	0	0	0
Pat Tabler, dh	.000	2	1	0	0	0	0	0	0	1	0	0
Mike Timlin, p	.000	4	0	0	0	0	0	0	0	0	0	0
Duane Ward, p	.000	2	0	0	0	0	0	0	0	0	0	0
David Wells, p	.000	4	0	0	0	0	0	0	0	0	0	0
Devon White, of	.364	5	22	5	8	1	0	0	0	2	3	3
Mookie Wilson, of-2	.250	3	8	1	2	0	0	0	0	1	3	1
TOTAL	.249		173	19	43	6	0	1	18	15	30	7

PITCHER	W	L	ERA	G	GS	CG	SV	SHO	IP	H	ER	BB	SO
Jim Acker	0	0	0.00	1	0	0	0	0	0.2	1	0	0	1
Tom Candiotti	0	1	8.22	2	2	0	0	0	7.2	17	7	2	5
Juan Guzman	1	0	3.18	1	1	0	0	0	5.2	4	2	4	2
Tom Henke	0	0	0.00	2	0	0	0	0	2.2	0	0	1	5
Jimmy Key	0	0	3.00	1	1	0	0	0	6.0	5	2	1	4
Rob Mac Donald	0	0	9.00	1	0	0	0	0	1.0	1	1	1	0
Todd Stottlemyre	0	1	9.82	1	1	0	0	0	3.2	7	4	1	3
Mike Timlin	0	1	3.18	4	0	0	1	0	5.2	5	2	2	5
Duane Ward	0	1	6.23	2	0	0	1	0	4.1	4	3	1	6
David Wells	0	0	2.35	4	0	0	0	0	7.2	6	2	2	9
TOTAL	1	4	4.60	19	5	0	1	0	45.0	50	23	15	37

By any measure, this World Series was one of the great ones. Five of the seven games were decided by a single run, three of them—including Games Six and Seven—in extra innings.

The opener in Minnesota gave no indication of the suspense to come, as the Twins opened up a 4–0 lead in the fifth inning en route to a 5–2 win. Game Two proved more difficult. Chili Davis put the Twins in front with a two-run homer in the first inning, but in the fifth Atlanta tied the score. Braves hurler Tom Glavine but lost the game when the Twins' Scott Leius lofted a homer to lead off the eighth.

Minnesota took a quick lead in Game Three, but Atlanta tied the game an inning later, and went ahead on solo homers by David Justice in the fourth inning and Lonnie Smith in the fifth. Home runs by Kirby Puckett and Chili Davis in the fifth and sixth re-tied the score, which remained at 4–4 into the last of the eleventh inning, when Justice scored from second on Mark Lemke's two-out single. Lemke's heroics also made the difference in Game Four. Mike Pagliarulo drove in a pair of runs for Minnesota with a single in the second and a home run in the seventh, but Braves Terry Pendleton and Lonnie Smith neutralized the runs with solo homers in the third and seventh. Lemke came to bat in the bottom of the ninth with one out and the score still 2–2. He tripled, and scored in a tight play to even the Series.

In Game Five the Braves assaulted five Minnesota pitchers for fourteen runs and the Series lead, but when play returned to Minnesota for Game Six the Twins revived with two first-inning runs. In the third inning Puckett prevented two Atlanta runs with a leaping catch above the wall, but in the fifth, Atlanta's Terry Pendleton evened the score with a two-run homer. Later in the inning the Twins regained the lead on Puckett's sacrifice fly. Atlanta knotted the score again in the seventh, at 2–2. In the last of the eleventh, leadoff batter Puckett lined the ball over the wall near where he had earlier made his game-saving catch.

No one scored through 9½ innings of Game Seven as Minnesota's Jack Morris dueled John Smoltz, Mike Stanton, and Alejandro Pena. If the Braves had scored in the eighth as they could have, they would have won the game and the crown. Lonnie Smith singled to lead off the inning and could have come around on Terry Pendleton's double to the wall in left center. But, decoyed by the Twins' middle infielders into thinking there was a play at

second, he paused just long enough after passing second to enable him to advance only to third. No one was out, but a grounder to first, an intentional walk to load the bases, and a smart 3–2–3 double play ended the Braves' threat.

Thus the game was still scoreless in the last of the tenth when Dan Gladden hustled his way into a broken-bat double and moved to third on Chuck Knoblauch's sacrifice bunt. Then, after the bases were loaded intentionally, pinch hitter Gene Larkin lobbed a hit over the head of the drawn-in left fielder. Gladden came home with the title for Minnesota.

Minnesota Twins (AL), 4; Atlanta Braves (NL), 3

MIN (A)

PLAYER/POS	AVG	G	AB	R	H	2B	3B	HR	RB	BB	SO	SB
Rick Aguilera, p	.000	4	1	0	0	0	0	0	0	0	0	0
Steve Bedrosian, p	.000	3	0	0	0	0	0	0	0	0	0	0
Jarvis Brown, of-2,dh-1	.000	3	2	0	0	0	0	0	0	0	0	0
Randy Bush, of-2	.250	3	4	0	1	0	0	0	0	0	1	0
Chili Davis, dh-4,of-1	.222	6	18	4	4	0	0	2	4	2	3	0
Scott Erickson, p	.000	2	1	0	0	0	0	0	0	0	1	0
Greg Gagne, ss	.167	7	24	1	4	1	0	1	3	0	7	0
Dan Gladden, of	.233	7	30	5	7	2	2	0	0	3	4	2
Mark Guthrie, p	.000	4	0	0	0	0	0	0	0	0	0	0
Brian Harper, c	.381	7	21	2	8	2	0	0	1	2	2	0
Kent Hrbek, 1b	.115	7	26	3	3	1	0	1	2	2	6	0
Chuck Knoblauch, 2b	.308	7	26	3	8	1	0	0	2	4	2	4
Gene Larkin, dh-1	.500	4	4	0	2	0	0	0	1	0	0	0
Terry Leach, p	.000	2	0	0	0	0	0	0	0	0	0	0
Scott Leius, 3b	.357	7	14	2	5	0	0	1	2	1	2	0
Shane Mack, of	.130	6	23	0	3	1	0	0	1	0	7	0
Jack Morris, p	.000	3	2	0	0	0	0	0	0	0	1	0
Al Newman, 3b-2,2b-1,ss-1	.500	4	2	0	1	0	1	0	1	0	0	0
Junior Ortiz, c	.200	3	5	0	1	0	0	0	1	0	1	0
Mike Pagliarulo, 3b	.273	6	11	1	3	0	0	1	2	1	2	0
Kirby Puckett, of	.250	7	24	4	6	0	1	2	4	5	7	1
Paul Sorrento, 1b-1	.000	3	2	0	0	0	0	0	0	1	2	0
Kevin Tapani, p	.000	2	1	0	0	0	0	0	0	0	0	0
David West, p	.000	2	0	0	0	0	0	0	0	0	0	0
Carl Willis, p	.000	4	0	0	0	0	0	0	0	0	0	0
TOTAL	.232		241	24	56	8	4	8	24	21	48	7

PITCHER	W	L	ERA	G	GS	CG	SV	SHO	IP	H	ER	BB	SO
Rick Aguilera	1	1	1.80	4	0	0	2	0	5.0	6	1	1	3
Steve Bedrosian	0	0	5.40	3	0	0	0	0	3.1	3	2	0	2
Scott Erickson	0	0	5.06	2	2	0	0	0	10.2	10	6	4	5
Mark Guthrie	0	1	2.25	4	0	0	0	0	4.0	3	1	4	3
Terry Leach	0	0	3.86	2	0	0	0	0	2.1	2	1	0	2
Jack Morris	2	0	1.17	3	3	1	0	1	23.0	18	3	9	15
Kevin Tapani	1	1	4.50	2	2	0	0	0	12.0	13	6	2	7
David West	0	0	INF	2	0	0	0	0	0.0	2	4	4	0
Carl Willis	0	0	5.14	4	0	0	0	0	7.0	6	4	2	2
TOTAL	4	3	3.74	26	7	1	2	1	67.1	63	28	26	39

ATL (N)

PLAYER/POS	AVG	G	AB	R	H	2B	3B	HR	RB	BB	SO	SB
Steve Avery, p	.000	2	3	0	0	0	0	0	0	0	2	0
Rafael Belliard, ss	.375	7	16	0	6	1	0	0	4	1	2	0
Jeff Blauser, ss	.167	5	6	0	1	0	0	0	0	1	1	0
Sid Bream, 1b	.125	7	24	0	3	2	0	0	0	3	4	0
Francisco Cabrera, c-1	.000	3	1	0	0	0	0	0	0	0	1	0
Jim Clancy, p	.000	3	1	0	0	0	0	0	0	0	1	0
Ron Gant, of	.267	7	30	3	8	0	1	0	4	2	3	1
Tom Glavine, p	.000	2	2	0	0	0	0	0	0	0	0	0
Tommy Gregg, ph	.000	4	3	0	0	0	0	0	0	0	2	0
Brian Hunter, 1b-4,of-4	.190	7	21	2	4	1	0	1	3	0	2	0
David Justice, of	.259	7	27	5	7	0	0	2	6	5	5	2
Charlie Leibrandt, p	.000	2	0	0	0	0	0	0	0	0	0	0
Mark Lemke, 2b	.417	6	24	4	10	1	3	0	4	2	4	0
Kent Mercker, p	.000	2	0	0	0	0	0	0	0	0	0	0
Keith Mitchell, of	.000	3	2	0	0	0	0	0	0	1	0	0
Greg Olson, c	.222	7	27	3	6	2	0	0	1	5	4	1
Alejandro Pena, p	.000	3	0	0	0	0	0	0	0	0	0	0
Terry Pendleton, 3b	.367	7	30	6	11	3	0	2	3	3	1	0
Randy St.Claire, p	.000	2	0	0	0	0	0	0	0	0	0	0
Lonnie Smith, dh-4,of-3	.231	7	26	5	6	0	0	3	3	3	4	1
John Smoltz, p	.000	2	2	0	0	0	0	0	0	0	1	0
Mike Stanton, p	.000	5	0	0	0	0	0	0	0	0	0	0
Jeff Treadway, 2b-1	.250	3	4	1	1	1	0	0	0	0	2	0
Jerry Willard, ph	.000	1	0	0	0	0	0	0	1	0	0	0
Mark Wohlers, p	.000	3	0	0	0	0	0	0	0	0	0	0
TOTAL	.253		249	29	63	10	4	8	29	26	39	5

PITCHER	W	L	ERA	G	GS	CG	SV	SHO	IP	H	ER	BB	SO
Steve Avery	0	0	3.46	2	2	0	0	0	13.0	10	5	1	8
Jim Clancy	1	0	4.15	3	0	0	0	0	4.1	3	2	4	2
Tom Glavine	1	1	2.70	2	2	1	0	0	13.1	8	4	7	8
Charlie Leibrandt	0	2	11.25	2	1	0	0	0	4.0	8	5	1	3
Kent Mercker	0	0	0.00	2	0	0	0	0	1.0	0	0	0	1
Alejandro Pena	0	1	3.38	3	0	0	0	0	5.1	6	2	3	7
Randy St.Claire	0	0	9.00	1	0	0	0	0	1.0	1	1	0	0
John Smoltz	0	0	1.26	2	2	0	0	0	14.1	13	2	1	11
Mike Stanton	1	0	0.00	5	0	0	0	0	7.1	5	0	2	7
Mark Wohlers	0	0	0.00	3	0	0	0	0	1.2	2	0	2	1
TOTAL	3	4	2.89	25	7	1	0	0	65.1	56	21	21	48

GAME 1 AT MIN OCT 19

ATL	000 001 010	2	6 1
MIN	001 031 00X	5	9 1

Pitchers: LEIBRANDT, Clancy (5), Wohlers (7), Stanton (8) vs MORRIS, Guthrie (8), Aguilera (8)
Home Runs: Gagne-MIN, Hrbek-MIN
Attendance: 55,108

GAME 2 AT MIN OCT 20

ATL	010 010 000	2	8 1
MIN	200 000 01X	3	4 1

Pitchers: GLAVINE vs TAPANI, Aguilera (9)
Home Runs: Davis-MIN, Leius-MIN
Attendance: 55,145

GAME 3 AT ATL OCT 22

MIN	100 000 120 000	4	10 1
ATL	010 120 000 001	5	8 2

Pitchers: Erickson, West (5), Leach (5), Bedrosian (6), Willis (8), Guthrie (10), AGUILERA (12) vs Avery, Pena (8), Stanton (10), Wohlers (12), Mercker (12), CLANCY (12)
Home Runs: Justice-ATL, Smith-ATL, Puckett-MIN, Davis-MIN
Attendance: 50,878

GAME 4 AT ATL OCT 23

MIN	010 000 100	2	7 0
ATL	001 000 101	3	8 0

Pitchers: Morris, Willis (7), GUTHRIE (8), Bedrosian (9) vs Smoltz, Wohlers (8), STANTON (8)
Home Runs: Pendleton-ATL, Pagliarulo-MIN, Smith-ATL
Attendance: 50,878

GAME 5 AT ATL OCT 24

MIN	000 003 011	5	7 1
ATL	000 410 63X	14	17 1

Pitchers: TAPANI, Leach (5), West (7), Bedrosian (7), Willis (8) vs GLAVINE, Mercker (6), Clancy (7), St.Claire (9)
Home Runs: Justice-ATL, Smith-ATL, Hunter-ATL
Attendance: 50,878

GAME 6 AT MIN OCT 26

ATL	000 020 100 00	3	9 1
MIN	200 010 000 01	4	9 0

Pitchers: Avery, Stanton (7), Pena (9), LEIBRANDT (11) vs Erickson, Guthrie (7), Willis (7), AGUILERA (10)
Home Runs: Pendleton-ATL, Puckett-MIN
Attendance: 55,155

GAME 7 AT MIN OCT 27

ATL	000 000 000 0	0	7 0
MIN	000 000 000 1	1	10 0

Pitchers: Smoltz, Stanton (8), PENA (9) vs MORRIS
Attendance: 55,118

Atlanta opened the series with a pair of one-sided wins but Pittsburgh pulled out a close victory in Game Three. After a third loss, the Piartes pummelled the Braves for two wins even more lopsided than their losses in the first two games. With the series now even, the stage was set for what turned out to be one of the most dramatic finishes in postseason history.

In Game One Pirate Jose Lind spoiled John Smoltz's shutout with his first home run of the season in the eighth inning. But by then the Braves had scored five times and held victory firmly in hand. Game Two was even easier. By the time the Pirates came up with four runs in the seventh inning (ending Steve Avery's LCS-record streak of scoreless innings at 22⅓), Atlanta had already compiled two four-run innings of their own (one of them on Ron Gant's grand slam). The Braves added five more runs in the last of the seventh to put the game out of reach.

At home for Game Three, the Pirates pulled themselves together behind the five-hit pitching of rookie knuckleballer Tim Wakefield. Sid Bream's solo homer in the fourth inning gave Atlanta a 1–0 lead, but Pirate Don Slaught homered to even the score an inning later and a pair of sixth-inning doubles put the Pirates ahead. Ron Gant's homer for Atlanta in the top of the seventh tied the score again, but a single, double, and sacrifice fly in the bottom of the inning put Pittsburgh on top to stay.

A 6–4 loss in Game Four brought the Pirates to the brink of elimination, but in Game Five they counterattacked, driving out Atlanta starter Steve Avery in the first inning with five hits (four of them doubles) and four runs, on their way to a 7–1 victory. With their feet still at the chasm's edge, the Pirates unloaded on Atlanta's Tom Glavine for eight runs in the second inning of Game Six before the first out was recorded, and pushed the assault to a 13–4 conclusion and a tied series.

While the Pirates scored single runs in the first and sixth innings of the final game, Pirate starter Doug Drabek (who had taken losses in Games One and Four) held Atlanta scoreless through eight innings. Then, in the last of the ninth, leadoff Brave Terry Pendleton doubled. He moved to third as David Justice reached on a grounder bobbled by the usually sure-handed second baseman Jose Lind. A walk to Sid Bream filled the bases. Stan Belinda replaced Drabek on the mound and retired Ron Gant on a fly to left, but Pen-

dleton scored Atlanta's first run after the catch. Damon Berryhill walked to reload the bases, and pinch hitter Brian Hunter popped out. Had there been no error, the game would have been over, with Pittsburgh waving the pennant. Instead, little-used pinch hitter Francisco Cabrera lined the ball safely to left, scoring Justice with the tying run and Bream with a repeat pennant for Atlanta.

Atlanta Braves (West), 4; Pittsburgh Pirates (East), 3

ATL (W)

PLAYER/POS	AVG	G	AB	R	H	2B	3B	HR	RB	BB	SO	SB
Steve Avery, p	.000	3	2	0	0	0	0	0	0	1	0	1	0
R. Belliard, ss-3,2b-1	.000	4	2	1	0	0	0	0	0	1	0	0
Damon Berryhill, c	.167	7	24	1	4	1	0	0	1	3	2	0
Jeff Blauser, ss	.208	7	24	3	5	0	1	1	4	3	2	0
Sid Bream, 1b	.273	7	22	5	6	3	0	1	2	3	0	0
Francisco Cabrera, ph	.500	2	2	0	1	0	0	0	2	0	0	0
Marvin Freeman, p	.000	3	0	0	0	0	0	0	0	0	0	0
Ron Gant, of	.182	7	22	5	4	0	0	2	6	4	4	1
Tom Glavine, p	.000	2	2	0	0	0	0	0	0	0	0	0
Brian Hunter, 1b-2	.200	3	5	1	1	0	0	0	0	0	1	0
David Justice, of	.280	7	25	5	7	1	0	2	6	6	2	0
Charlie Leibrandt, p	.000	2	1	0	0	0	0	0	0	0	1	0
Mark Lemke, 2b-7,3b-1	.333	7	21	2	7	1	0	0	2	5	3	0
Javier Lopez, c	.000	1	1	0	0	0	0	0	0	0	0	0
Kent Mercker, p	.000	2	0	0	0	0	0	0	0	0	0	0
Otis Nixon, of	.286	7	28	5	8	2	0	0	2	4	4	3
Terry Pendleton, 3b	.233	7	30	2	7	2	0	0	3	0	2	0
Jeff Reardon, p	.000	3	0	0	0	0	0	0	0	0	0	0
Deion Sanders, of-3	.000	4	5	0	0	0	0	0	0	0	3	0
Lonnie Smith, ph	.333	6	6	1	2	0	1	0	1	0	0	0
Pete Smith, p	.000	2	1	0	0	0	0	0	0	0	0	0
John Smoltz, p	.286	3	7	1	2	0	0	0	1	0	2	0
Mike Stanton, p	1.000	5	1	1	1	1	0	0	1	0	0	0
Jeff Treadway, 2b-1	.667	3	3	1	2	0	0	0	0	0	1	0
Mark Wohlers, p	.000	3	0	0	0	0	0	0	0	0	0	0
TOTAL	.244		234	34	57	11	2	6	32	29	28	5

PITCHER	W	L	ERA	G	GS	CG	SV	SHO	IP	H	ER	BB	SO
Steve Avery	1	1	9.00	3	2	0	0	0	8.0	13	8	2	3
Marvin Freeman	0	0	14.73	3	0	0	0	0	3.2	8	6	2	1
Tom Glavine	0	2	12.27	2	2	0	0	0	7.1	13	10	3	2
Charlie Leibrandt	0	0	1.93	2	0	0	0	0	4.2	4	1	3	3
Kent Mercker	0	0	0.00	2	0	0	0	0	3.0	1	0	1	1
Jeff Reardon	1	0	0.00	3	0	0	1	0	3.0	0	0	2	3
Pete Smith	0	0	2.45	2	0	0	0	0	3.2	2	1	3	3
John Smoltz	2	0	2.66	3	3	0	0	0	20.1	14	6	10	19
Mike Stanton	0	0	0.00	5	0	0	0	0	4.1	2	0	2	5
Mark Wohlers	0	0	0.00	3	0	0	0	0	3.0	2	0	1	2
TOTAL	4	3	4.72	28	7	0	1	0	61.0	59	32	29	42

PIT (E)

PLAYER/POS	AVG	G	AB	R	H	2B	3B	HR	RB	BB	SO	SB
Stan Belinda, p	.000	2	0	0	0	0	0	0	0	0	0	0
Jay Bell, ss	.172	7	29	3	5	2	0	1	4	3	4	0
Barry Bonds, of	.261	7	23	5	6	1	0	1	2	6	4	1
Alex Cole, of	.200	4	10	2	2	0	0	0	1	3	2	0
Danny Cox, p	.000	2	0	0	0	0	0	0	0	0	0	0
Doug Drabek, p	.000	3	6	0	0	0	0	0	0	1	4	0
Cecil Espy, of-2	.667	4	3	0	2	0	0	0	0	0	1	0
Carlos Garcia, 2b	.000	1	1	0	0	0	0	0	0	0	0	0
Danny Jackson, p	.000	1	0	0	0	0	0	0	0	0	0	0
Jeff King, 3b	.241	7	29	4	7	4	0	0	2	0	1	0
Mike La Valliere, c	.200	3	10	1	2	0	0	0	0	3	0	0
Jose Lind, 2b	.222	7	27	5	6	2	1	1	5	1	4	0
Roger Mason, p	.000	2	0	0	0	0	0	0	0	0	0	0
Lloyd Mc Clendon, of	.727	5	11	4	8	2	0	1	4	4	1	0
Orlando Merced, 1b	.100	4	10	0	1	1	0	0	2	2	4	0
Denny Neagle, p	.000	2	0	0	0	0	0	0	0	0	0	0
Bob Patterson, p	.000	2	0	0	0	0	0	0	0	0	0	0
Gary Redus, 1b	.438	5	16	4	7	4	1	0	3	2	3	0
Don Slaught, c	.333	5	12	5	4	1	0	1	5	6	3	0
Randy Tomlin, p	.000	2	0	0	0	0	0	0	0	0	0	0
Andy Van Slyke, of	.276	7	29	1	8	3	1	0	4	1	5	0
Gary Varsho, of-1	.500	5	2	0	1	0	0	0	0	0	0	0
Tim Wakefield, p	.000	2	6	1	0	0	0	0	0	0	0	0
Bob Walk, p	.000	2	5	0	0	0	0	0	0	0	1	0
John Wehner, ph	.000	2	2	0	0	0	0	0	0	0	2	0
TOTAL	.255		231	35	59	20	3	5	32	29	42	1

PITCHER	W	L	ERA	G	GS	CG	SV	SHO	IP	H	ER	BB	SO
Stan Belinda	0	0	0.00	2	0	0	0	0	1.2	0	0	0	2
Danny Cox	0	0	0.00	2	0	0	0	0	1.1	1	0	1	1
Doug Drabek	0	3	3.71	3	3	0	0	0	17.0	18	7	7	10
Danny Jackson	0	1	21.60	1	1	0	0	0	1.2	4	4	2	0
Roger Mason	0	0	0.00	2	0	0	0	0	3.1	0	0	2	1
Denny Neagle	0	0	27.00	2	0	0	0	0	1.2	4	5	3	0
Bob Patterson	0	0	5.40	2	0	0	0	0	1.2	3	1	1	1
Randy Tomlin	0	0	6.75	2	0	0	0	0	2.2	5	2	1	0
Tim Wakefield	2	0	3.00	2	2	2	0	0	18.0	14	6	5	7
Bob Walk	1	0	3.86	2	1	1	0	0	11.2	6	5	7	6
TOTAL	3	4	4.45	20	7	3	0	0	60.2	57	30	29	28

GAME 1 AT ATL OCT 6

PIT	000	000	010	1	5	1
ATL	010	210	10X	5	8	0

Pitchers: DRABEK, Patterson (5), Neagle (7), Cox (8) vs SMOLTZ, Stanton (9)
Home Runs: Lind-PIT, Blauser-ATL
Attendance: 51,971

GAME 2 AT ATL OCT 7

PIT	000	000	410	5	7	0
ATL	040	040	50X	13	14	0

Pitchers: JACKSON, Mason (2), Walk (3), Tomlin (5), Neagle (7), Patterson (7), Belinda (8) vs AVERY, Freeman (7), Stanton (7), Wohlers (8), Reardon (9)
Home Runs: Gant-ATL
Attendance: 51,975

GAME 3 AT PIT OCT 9

ATL	000	100	100	2	5	0
PIT	000	011	10X	3	8	1

Pitchers: GLAVINE, Stanton (7), Wohlers (8) vs WAKEFIELD
Home Runs: Bream-ATL, Gant-ATL, Slaught-PIT
Attendance: 56,610

GAME 4 AT PIT OCT 10

ATL	020	022	000	6	11	0
PIT	021	000	100	4	6	1

Pitchers: SMOLTZ, Stanton (7), Reardon (9) vs DRABEK, Tomlin (5), Cox (6), Mason (7)
Attendance: 57,164

GAME 5 AT PIT OCT 11

ATL	000	000	010	1	3	0
PIT	401	001	10X	7	13	0

Pitchers: AVERY, Smith (1), Leibrandt (5), Freeman (6), Mercker (8) vs WALK
Attendance: 52,929

GAME 6 AT ATL OCT 13

PIT	080	041	000	13	13	1
ATL	000	100	102	4	9	1

Pitchers: WAKEFIELD vs GLAVINE, Leibrandt (2), Freeman (5), Mercker (7), Wohlers (9)
Home Runs: Bell-PIT, Bonds-PIT, McClendon-PIT, Justice-ATL (2)
Attendance: 51,975

GAME 7 AT ATL OCT 14

PIT	100	001	000	2	7	1
ATL	000	000	003	3	7	0

Pitchers: DRABEK, Belinda (9) vs Smoltz, Stanton (7), Smith (7), Avery (7), REARDON (9)
Attendance: 51,975

Oakland had competed in three League Championship Series in the previous four years and won them all. Toronto in its first fifteen seasons of existence had competed three times in the LCS and never won. In the first game of the 1992 matchup, the Athletics scored first on Mark McGwire's two-run homer and the next batter, Terry Steinbach, pushed the score to 3–0 with another homer. Toronto's Pat Borders and Dave Winfield retaliated with solo homers in the fifth and sixth innings to narrow the gap, and the Blue Jays tied the score in the eighth when Winfield, who had doubled with two outs, came home on John Olerud's single. But in the top of the ninth, Harold Baines led off with the game's fifth home run to put Oakland back into the lead, and A's reliever Dennis Eckersley preserved it for his tenth LCS save.

After this encouraging beginning, though, the A's went into a three-game decline. In Game Two, fireballer David Cone held Oakland scoreless through eight innings while the Jays built a 3–0 lead on Kelly Gruber's two-run homer in the fifth inning and a third score two innings later. Oakland finally touched Cone for a run in the ninth, but reliever Tom Henke smothered the threat. The A's recovered from an early deficit in Game Three to tie the score in the fourth inning, but fell behind on Candy Maldonado's leadoff homer in the sixth and never regained the lead. In Game Four the A's rocked Toronto starter Jack Morris for five runs in the fifth, and added another in the sixth to take a 6–1 lead. But in the eighth, reliever Eckersley, who came on with one run in and two on, yielded singles on his first two pitches to let in two more runs, and in the ninth gave up a leadoff single and a game-tying home run to Roberto Alomar. Toronto finally took the lead in the eleventh as Derek Bell fouled off several pitches before drawing a walk, took third on Maldonado's single, and scored on Pat Borders' fly to left. Reliever Tom Henke held the lead.

Down three games to one, Oakland came out slugging in Game Five. Ruben Sierra homered for a pair of runs in the first inning and the A's added a third run two innings later. Dave Winfield homered in the Toronto fourth, but the A's took advantage of two Toronto errors to score three more runs an inning later, putting the game out of the Blue Jays' reach. But they couldn't sustain their comeback. Joe Carter's two-run homer in the first inning of Game Six, and Candy Maldonado's three-run blast two innings later, highlighted a 9–2 Toronto romp

that ended the team's string of failed opportunities and carried the American League pennant to Canada for the first time.

Toronto Blue Jays (East), 4
Oakland Athletics (West), 2

TOR (E)

PLAYER/POS	AVG	G	AB	R	H	2B	3B	HR	RB	BB	SO	SB
Roberto Alomar, 2b	.423	6	26	4	11	1	0	2	4	2	1	5
Derek Bell, of	.000	2	0	1	0	0	0	0	0	1	0	0
Pat Borders, c	.318	6	22	3	7	0	0	1	3	1	1	0
Joe Carter, of-6,1b-2	.192	6	26	2	5	0	0	1	3	2	4	2
David Cone, p	.000	2	0	0	0	0	0	0	0	0	0	0
Mark Eichhorn, p	.000	1	0	0	0	0	0	0	0	0	0	0
Alfredo Griffin, ss-1	.000	2	2	0	0	0	0	0	0	0	0	0
Kelly Gruber, 3b	.091	7	22	3	2	1	0	1	2	2	3	0
Juan Guzman, p	.000	2	0	0	0	0	0	0	0	0	0	0
Tom Henke, p	.000	4	0	0	0	0	0	0	0	0	0	0
Jimmy Key, p	.000	1	0	0	0	0	0	0	0	0	0	0
Manuel Lee, ss	.278	6	18	2	5	1	1	0	3	1	2	0
Candy Maldonado, of	.273	6	22	3	6	0	0	2	6	2	4	0
Jack Morris, p	.000	2	0	0	0	0	0	0	0	0	0	0
John Olerud, 1b	.348	6	23	4	8	2	0	1	4	2	5	0
Ed Sprague, ph	.500	2	2	0	1	0	0	0	0	0	1	0
Todd Stottlemyre, p	.000	1	0	0	0	0	0	0	0	0	0	0
Mike Timlin, p	.000	2	0	0	0	0	0	0	0	0	0	0
Duane Ward, p	.000	3	0	0	0	0	0	0	0	0	0	0
Devon White, of	.348	6	23	2	8	2	0	0	2	5	6	0
Dave Winfield, dh	.250	6	24	7	6	1	0	2	3	5	2	0
TOTAL	.281		210	31	59	8	1	10	30	23	29	7

PITCHER	W	L	ERA	G	GS	CG	SV	SHO	IP	H	ER	BB	SO
David Cone	1	1	3.00	2	2	0	0	0	12.0	11	4	5	9
Mark Eichhorn	0	0	0.00	1	0	0	0	0	1.0	0	0	0	0
Juan Guzman	2	0	2.08	2	2	0	0	0	13.0	12	3	5	11
Tom Henke	0	0	0.00	4	0	0	3	0	4.2	4	0	2	2
Jimmy Key	0	0	0.00	1	0	0	0	0	3.0	2	0	2	1
Jack Morris	0	1	6.57	2	2	1	0	0	12.1	11	9	9	6
Todd Stottlemyre	0	0	2.45	1	0	0	0	0	3.2	3	1	0	1
Mike Timlin	0	0	6.75	2	0	0	0	0	1.1	4	1	0	1
Duane Ward	1	0	6.75	3	0	0	0	0	4.0	5	3	1	2
TOTAL	4	2	3.44	18	6	1	3	0	55.0	52	21	24	33

OAK (W)

PLAYER/POS	AVG	G	AB	R	H	2B	3B	HR	RB	BB	SO	SB
Harold Baines, dh	.440	6	25	6	11	2	0	1	4	0	3	0
Lance Blankenship, 2b	.231	5	13	2	3	0	0	0	0	3	4	1
Mike Bordick, ss-4,2b-2	.053	6	19	1	1	0	0	0	0	1	2	1
Jerry Browne, 3b-2,of-1	.400	4	10	3	4	0	0	0	2	2	0	0
Jim Corsi, p	.000	3	0	0	0	0	0	0	0	0	0	0
Ron Darling, p	.000	1	0	0	0	0	0	0	0	0	0	0
Kelly Downs, p	.000	2	0	0	0	0	0	0	0	0	0	0
Dennis Eckersley, p	.000	3	0	0	0	0	0	0	0	0	0	0
Eric Fox, of-1,dh-1	.000	4	1	0	0	0	0	0	0	1	0	2
Rickey Henderson, of	.261	6	23	5	6	0	0	0	1	4	4	2
Rick Honeycutt, p	.000	2	0	0	0	0	0	0	0	0	0	0
Carney Lansford, 3b	.167	5	18	0	3	0	0	0	1	1	1	0
Mark Mc Gwire, 1b	.150	6	20	1	3	0	0	1	3	5	4	0
Mike Moore, p	.000	2	0	0	0	0	0	0	0	0	0	0
Jeff Parrett, p	.000	3	0	0	0	0	0	0	0	0	0	0
Jamie Quirk, ph	.000	1	1	0	0	0	0	0	0	0	0	0
Randy Ready, ph	.000	1	1	0	0	0	0	0	0	0	1	0
Jeff Russell, p	.000	3	0	0	0	0	0	0	0	0	0	0
Ruben Sierra, of	.333	6	24	4	8	2	1	1	7	2	1	1
Terry Steinbach, c	.292	6	24	1	7	0	0	1	5	2	7	0
Dave Stewart, p	.000	2	0	0	0	0	0	0	0	0	0	0
Walt Weiss, ss	.167	3	6	1	1	0	0	0	0	2	1	0
Bob Welch, p	.000	1	0	0	0	0	0	0	0	0	0	0
Willie Wilson, of	.227	6	22	0	5	1	0	0	0	1	5	7
Bobby Witt, p	.000	1	0	0	0	0	0	0	0	0	0	0
TOTAL	.251		207	24	52	5	1	4	23	24	33	16

PITCHER	W	L	ERA	G	GS	CG	SV	SHO	IP	H	ER	BB	SO
Jim Corsi	0	0	0.00	3	0	0	0	0	2.0	2	0	3	0
Ron Darling	0	1	3.00	1	1	0	0	0	6.0	4	2	2	3
Kelly Downs	0	1	3.86	2	0	0	0	0	2.1	3	1	1	0
Dennis Eckersley	0	0	6.00	3	0	0	1	0	3.0	8	2	0	2
Rick Honeycutt	0	0	0.00	2	0	0	0	0	2.0	0	0	0	1
Mike Moore	0	2	7.45	2	2	0	0	0	9.2	11	8	5	7
Jeff Parrett	0	0	11.57	3	0	0	0	0	2.1	6	3	0	1
Jeff Russell	1	0	9.00	3	0	0	0	0	2.0	2	2	4	0
Dave Stewart	1	0	2.70	2	2	1	0	0	16.2	14	5	6	7
Bob Welch	0	0	2.57	1	1	0	0	0	7.0	7	2	1	7
Bobby Witt	0	0	18.00	1	0	0	0	0	1.0	2	2	1	1
TOTAL	2	4	4.50	23	6	1	1	0	54.0	59	27	23	29

GAME 1 AT TOR OCT 7

OAK	030	000	001	4	6	1
TOR	000	011	010	3	9	0

Pitchers: Stewart, RUSSELL (8), Eckersley (9) vs MORRIS
Home Runs: Baines-OAK, McGwire-OAK, Steinbach-OAK, Winfield-TOR, Borders-TOR
Attendance: 51,039

GAME 2 AT TOR OCT 8

OAK	000	000	001	1	6	0
TOR	000	020	10X	3	4	0

Pitchers: MOORE, Corsi (8), Parrett (8) vs CONE, Henke (9)
Home Runs: Gruber-TOR
Attendance: 51,114

GAME 3 AT OAK OCT 10

TOR	010	110	211	7	9	1
OAK	000	200	210	5	13	3

Pitchers: GUZMAN, Ward (7), Timlin (8), Henke (8) vs DARLING, Downs (7), Corsi (8), Russell (8), Honeycutt (9), Eckersley (9)
Home Runs: Alomar-TOR, Maldonado-TOR
Attendance: 46,911

GAME 4 AT OAK OCT 11

TOR	010	000	032	01	7	17	4
OAK	005	001	000	00	6	12	2

Pitchers: Morris, Stottlemyre (8), Timlin (8), WARD (9), Henke (11) vs Welch, Parrett (8), Eckersley (8), Corsi (9), DOWNS (10)
Home Runs: Alomar-TOR, Olerud-TOR
Attendance: 47,732

GAME 5 AT OAK OCT 12

TOR	000	100	100	2	7	3
OAK	201	030	00X	6	8	0

Pitchers: CONE, Key (5), Eichhorn (8) vs STEWART
Home Runs: Winfield-TOR, Sierra-OAK
Attendance: 44,955

GAME 6 AT TOR OCT 14

OAK	000	001	010	2	7	1
TOR	204	010	02X	9	13	0

Pitchers: MOORE, Parrett (3), Honeycutt (5), Russell (7), Witt (8) vs GUZMAN, Ward (8), Henke (9)
Home Runs: Carter-TOR, Maldonado-TOR
Attendance: 51,335

Atlanta outscored Toronto in the Series 20 runs to 16, but the Blue Jays eked out four one-run victories to bring Canada its first world baseball championship. In the fourth inning of Game One, Atlanta's Tom Glavine gave up a leadoff homer to Joe Carter for the game's first run, but held the Jays to just one single the rest of the way. For five innings, meanwhile, Toronto starter Jack Morris shut out the Braves. But in the top of the sixth he gave up a deciding three-run homer to catcher Damon Berryhill. The next night, though, down 4–5 in the ninth inning, Toronto pinch hitter Derek Bell drew a walk from Braves closer Jeff Reardon, and pinch hitter Ed Sprague lined Reardon's first pitch over the left field wall.

Toronto moved ahead with another close victory in Game Three, the first World Series game ever played outside the United States. Atlanta threatened in the fourth inning when, with two on and none out, David Justice drove the ball to deep center. But in the defensive play of the Series, center fielder Devon White leaped high to snare the ball. Baserunner Terry Pendleton was ruled out for passing Deion Sanders on the basepath, and third baseman Kelly Gruber tagged Sanders, who was diving back into second base, to complete what seemed to be a triple play. The umpire didn't see the tag, however, and called Sanders safe. Still, no Brave scored, and Blue Jay Joe Carter homered for the game's first run in the last of the fourth. Atlanta tied the game in the sixth and took the lead in the top of the eighth. Gruber homered to re-tie it in the bottom of the inning, and after the Jays had filled the bases in the last of the ninth, Candy Maldonado tagged Reardon for a hit over the drawn-in outfield to bring home the winning run.

The Jays pushed their Series advantage to 3–1 in Game Four. Catcher Pat Borders opened the Toronto third with a home run, and Gruber scored from second on Devon White's seventh-inning single to push the Blue Jay lead to 2-0. The Braves got to Toronto starter Jimmy Key for a run in the eighth, but relievers Duane Ward and Tom Henke combined to stop them from scoring again.

In the fifth game the Blue Jays twice came from one run down to even the score. But in the fifth inning, after the Braves had once again built a one-run lead, Lonnie Smith extended it with a grand slam home run that sent the Series back to Atlanta.

Toronto Blue Jays (AL), 4; Atlanta Braves (NL), 2

TOR (A)

PLAYER/POS	AVG	G	AB	R	H	2B	3B	HR	RB	BB	SO	SB
Roberto Alomar, 2b	.208	6	24	3	5	1	0	0	0	3	3	2
Derek Bell, ph	.000	2	1	1	0	0	0	0	0	1	0	0
Pat Borders, c	.450	6	20	2	9	3	0	1	3	2	1	0
Joe Carter, of-4	.273	6	22	2	6	2	0	2	3	3	2	1
David Cone, p	.500	2	4	0	2	0	0	0	1	1	0	0
Mark Eichhorn, p	.000	1	0	0	0	0	0	0	0	0	0	0
Alfredo Griffin, ss	.000	2	0	0	0	0	0	0	0	0	0	0
Kelly Gruber, 3b	.105	6	19	2	2	0	0	1	1	2	5	1
Juan Guzman, p	.000	1	0	0	0	0	0	0	0	0	0	0
Tom Henke, p	.000	3	0	0	0	0	0	0	0	0	0	0
Jimmy Key, p	.000	2	1	0	0	0	0	0	0	0	0	0
Manuel Lee, ss	.105	6	19	1	2	0	0	0	0	1	2	0
Candy Maldonado, of-5	.158	6	19	1	3	0	0	1	2	2	5	0
Jack Morris, p	.000	2	2	0	0	0	0	0	0	0	2	0
John Olerud, 1b	.308	4	13	2	4	0	0	0	0	0	4	0
Ed Sprague, 1b-1	.500	3	2	1	1	0	0	1	2	1	0	0
Todd Stottlemyre, p	.000	4	0	0	0	0	0	0	0	0	0	0
Pat Tabler, ph	.000	2	2	0	0	0	0	0	0	0	0	0
Mike Timlin, p	.000	2	0	0	0	0	0	0	0	0	0	0
Duane Ward, p	.000	4	0	0	0	0	0	0	0	0	0	0
David Wells, p	.000	4	0	0	0	0	0	0	0	0	0	0
Devon White, of	.231	6	26	2	6	1	0	0	2	0	6	1
Dave Winfield, of-3,dh-3	.227	6	22	0	5	1	0	0	3	2	3	0
TOTAL	.230		196	17	45	8	0	6	17	18	33	5

PITCHER	W	L	ERA	G	GS	CG	SV	SHO	IP	H	ER	BB	SO
David Cone	0	0	3.48	2	2	0	0	0	10.1	9	4	8	8
Mark Eichhorn	0	0	0.00	1	0	0	0	0	1.0	0	0	0	1
Juan Guzman	0	0	1.13	1	1	0	0	0	8.0	8	1	1	7
Tom Henke	0	0	2.70	3	0	0	2	0	3.1	2	1	2	1
Jimmy Key	2	0	1.00	2	1	0	0	0	9.0	6	1	0	6
Jack Morris	0	2	8.71	2	2	0	0	0	10.1	13	10	6	12
Todd Stottlemyre	0	0	0.00	4	0	0	0	0	3.2	4	0	0	4
Mike Timlin	0	0	0.00	2	0	0	1	0	1.1	0	0	0	0
Duane Ward	2	0	0.00	4	0	0	0	0	3.1	1	0	1	6
David Wells	0	0	0.00	4	0	0	0	0	4.1	1	0	2	3
TOTAL	4	2	2.80	25	6	0	3	0	54.2	44	17	20	48

ATL (N)

PLAYER/POS	AVG	G	AB	R	H	2B	3B	HR	RB	BB	SO	SB
Steve Avery, p	.000	2	1	0	0	0	0	0	0	0	1	0
Rafael Belliard, ss-3,2b-1	.000	4	0	0	0	0	0	0	0	0	0	0
Damon Berryhill, c	.091	6	22	1	2	0	0	1	3	1	11	0
Jeff Blauser, ss	.250	6	24	2	6	0	0	0	0	1	9	2
Sid Bream, 1b	.200	5	15	1	3	0	0	0	0	4	0	0
Francisco Cabrera, ph	.000	1	1	0	0	0	0	0	0	0	0	0
Ron Gant, of-3	.125	4	8	2	1	1	0	0	0	1	2	2
Tom Glavine, p	.000	2	2	0	0	0	0	0	0	1	0	0
Brian Hunter, 1b-3	.200	4	5	0	1	0	0	0	2	0	1	0
David Justice, of	.158	6	19	4	3	0	0	1	3	6	5	1
Charlie Leibrandt, p	.000	1	0	0	0	0	0	0	0	0	0	0
Mark Lemke, 2b	.211	6	19	0	4	0	0	0	2	1	3	0
Otis Nixon, of	.296	6	27	3	8	1	0	0	1	1	3	5
Terry Pendleton, 3b	.240	6	25	2	6	2	0	0	2	1	5	0
Jeff Reardon, p	.000	2	0	0	0	0	0	0	0	0	0	0
Deion Sanders, of	.533	4	15	4	8	2	0	0	1	2	1	5
Lonnie Smith, dh-3	.167	5	12	1	2	0	0	1	5	1	4	0
Pete Smith, p	.000	1	1	0	0	0	0	0	0	0	1	0
John Smoltz, p-2	.000	3	3	0	0	0	0	0	0	0	2	0
Mike Stanton, p	.000	4	0	0	0	0	0	0	0	0	0	0
Jeff Treadway, ph	.000	1	1	0	0	0	0	0	0	0	0	0
Mark Wohlers, p	.000	2	0	0	0	0	0	0	0	0	0	0
TOTAL	.220		200	20	44	6	0	3	19	20	48	15

PITCHER	W	L	ERA	G	GS	CG	SV	SHO	IP	H	ER	BB	SO
Steve Avery	0	1	3.75	2	2	0	0	0	12.0	11	5	3	11
Tom Glavine	1	1	1.59	2	2	2	0	0	17.0	10	3	4	8
Charlie Leibrandt	0	1	9.00	1	0	0	0	0	2.0	3	2	0	0
Jeff Reardon	0	2	13.50	2	0	0	0	0	1.1	2	2	1	1
Pete Smith	0	0	0.00	1	0	0	0	0	3.0	3	0	0	0
John Smoltz	1	0	2.70	2	2	0	0	0	13.1	13	4	7	12
Mike Stanton	0	0	0.00	4	0	0	1	0	5.0	3	0	2	1
Mark Wohlers	0	0	0.00	2	0	0	0	0	0.2	0	0	1	0
TOTAL	2	4	2.65	16	6	2	1	0	54.1	45	16	18	33

Toronto scored a run in the first inning of Game Six. Atlanta tied the game in the third, but Candy Maldonado's leadoff homer in the fourth restored the advantage to Toronto. In the bottom of the ninth, the Braves scrabbled back to tie it up again. The score remained knotted at 2–2 until the top of the eleventh, when Toronto's Dave Winfield delivered runners from second and first with a two-out double into the left field corner. As it turned out, the Jays needed both runs, for Atlanta scored in the bottom of the eleventh. But with two out and the potential tying run on third, Otis Nixon, attempting a bunt single, just failed to reach safely, and the Series was over.

GAME 1 AT ATL OCT 17

TOR	000 100 000	1	4	0
ATL	000 003 00X	3	4	0

Pitchers: MORRIS, Stottlemyre (7), Wells (8) vs GLAVINE
Home Runs: Carter-TOR, Berryhill-ATL
Attendance: 51,763

GAME 2 AT ATL OCT 18

TOR	000 020 012	5	9	2
ATL	010 120 000	4	5	1

Pitchers: Cone, Wells (5), Stottlemyre (7), WARD (8), Henke (9) vs Smoltz, Stanton (8), REARDON (8)
Home Runs: Sprague-TOR
Attendance: 51,763

GAME 3 AT TOR OCT 20

ATL	000 001 010	2	9	0
TOR	000 100 011	3	6	1

Pitchers: AVERY, Wohlers (9), Stanton (9), Reardon (9) vs Guzman, WARD (9)
Home Runs: Carter-TOR, Gruber-TOR
Attendance: 51,813

GAME 4 AT TOR OCT 21

ATL	000 000 010	1	5	0
TOR	001 000 10X	2	6	0

Pitchers: GLAVINE vs KEY, Ward (8), Henke (9)
Home Runs: Borders-TOR
Attendance: 52,090

GAME 5 AT TOR OCT 22

ATL	100 150 000	7	13	0
TOR	010 100 000	2	6	0

Pitchers: SMOLTZ, Stanton (7) vs MORRIS, Wells (5), Timlin (7), Eichhorn (8), Stottlemyre (9)
Home Runs: Justice-ATL, L.Smith-ATL
Attendance: 52,268

GAME 6 AT ATL OCT 24

TOR	100 100 000 02	4	14	1
ATL	001 000 001 01	3	8	1

Pitchers: Cone, Stottlemyre, Wells (7), Ward (8), Henke (9), KEY (10), Timlin (11) vs Avery, P.Smith (5), Stanton (8), Wohlers (9), LEIBRANDT (10)
Home Runs: Maldonado-TOR
Attendance: 51,763

Other Leagues

CHAPTER 18

Rival Leagues

David Pietrusza

For nearly a century baseball has been dominated by two leagues, the National and American, and most fans think that this is the way it has always been and must forever be.

Yet it was not always thus. Throughout baseball history, rivals to the game's power structure have arisen. Sometimes they have been relatively solid structures, such as the American Association and the Federal League; other times single-season phenomena, such as the Players League or the Union Association, have emerged. And of a lesser magnitude, such hopeful enterprises as the Continental League or the United States League have quixotically tilted at Organized Baseball.

In 1876 the National League itself was such a challenge, but the circuit it confronted, the National Association, was so ephemeral that it evaporated as soon as the new league appeared. However, cities spurned by the National League soon coalesced into the loosely formed International Association. Generally not recognized as a major league, it nonetheless featured strong playing talent; but it was organizational incompetence that spelled its doom.

By 1882 the National League was a going concern, but it had excluded several of the nation's prime markets; after its inaugural season of 1876 it expelled New York and Philadelphia for not completing their final western road trips. Cincinnati was booted because it insisted on selling liquor in the stands. St. Louis and Louisville were two other large cities without big league teams. So in 1882 the upstart American Association moved into these vacant territories. Featuring Sunday baseball, 25-cent admissions, and strong drink, the "beer and whisky circuit" quickly established itself as the box-office equal of the NL.

Both leagues were making money, so other promoters tried to get in on the act. In 1884, twenty-six-year old St. Louis traction magnate (the contemporary term for a kingpin of trolleycars, wagons, carts, and carriages) Henry V. Lucas organized the Union Association. Featuring such lackluster franchises as Altoona and Wilmington, it lacked balance in both capital and playing talent (Lucas's St. Louis Maroons ran away and hid from the rest of the league). The weakest of all generally recognized big leagues, the Union Association collapsed at season's end when Lucas cut a deal allowing his Maroons into the National League.

The 1880s saw capital's control over labor intensify, culminating in a wholesale breakaway of top National League players in 1890 and the formation of the Players National League under the leadership of Giants shortstop John Montgomery Ward. Despite a glittering array of talent, the Players League collapsed at season's end when the investors bankrolling it caved in to National League bluff and bluster.

The rise and fall of the Players League resulted in further deterioration of the never very good feelings between the National League and American Association. Open conflict erupted in 1891, and in 1892 the AA dissolved and four of its franchises—Louisville, Washington, Baltimore, and St. Louis—were absorbed into a new twelve-team National League.

Abortive attempts to revive the American Association were made in 1894 and 1900. The American League, a souped-up version of the minor Western League, made the successful jump to major league status in 1901 after the National League abandoned its Washington, Cleveland, and Baltimore franchises in 1900.

Once again big profits attracted investors, and an unprecedented spate of half-baked challenges emerged: Alfred Lawson's Union League (1908), the "Burlesquers' League" (1910), "Daniel Fletcher's League" (1910), William Abbott Witman's United States League (1912–1913), and the Columbian League (1912). Most were utter fiascos that never took the field.

Not so absurd was the Federal League of 1914–1915. Led by "Fighting Jim" Gilmore and backed by such men of substance as the baking Ward Brothers in Brooklyn and restaurateur Charles Weeghman in Chicago (he built what later came to be called Wrigley Field for his Federal circuit Whales), the Feds threw a genuine scare into Organized Baseball. A 1915 lawsuit even threatened the very basis of O.B.—that it was a localized sport rather than a business conducted across state lines—but the action was stalled, mortally for the upstart league, by Federal Judge Kenesaw Mountain Landis. Seven years later the case wound up in United States Supreme Court, where Justice Holmes wrote the majority decision affirming Organized Baseball's immunity from antitrust legislation.

The Feds were the last serious stateside challenge to Major League hegemony. After that, challengers could no longer erect cheap wooden ballparks; all big league parks were expensive concrete-and-steel affairs. A pipe dream called the Continental League gathered a few headlines in 1921 as it promised unionization of players and an end to the reserve clause, but it never played an inning.

Following World War II, Mexico's wealthy Pascuel brothers made big cash offers to Ted Williams, Bob Feller and Stan Musial, and lured such talent as Junior Stephens, Mickey Owen, and Sal Maglie across the border before the league collapsed. No further confrontation occurred until Bill Shea and Branch Rickey's Continental League of 1959–1960, stimulated by the departure of the

two National League teams from New York City in 1957. Ultimately the Continental League forced major league expansion in 1961–1962, giving birth to the Los Angeles Angels, a new version of the Washington Senators, the New York Mets, and the Houston Colt .45's.

The laughable Global League actually took the field in Latin America in 1969 and claimed "franchises" in America and Japan. It left scores of players stranded in Venezuela.

In the late 1980s "The Baseball League," reputedly backed by Donald Trump, was rumored, but realistically the immediate possibility for any new rival big league is less than dim, as the financial resources necessary to build stadiums and develop talent are prohibitive.

## CHAPTER 19

Black Ball

Jules Tygiel

In 1987, Major League Baseball, amidst much fanfare and publicity, celebrated the 40th anniversary of the finest moment in the history of the national pastime—Jackie Robinson's heroic shattering of the color barrier. But baseball might also have commemorated the centennial of a related, but far less auspicious event—the banishment of blacks from the International League in 1887 which ushered in six disgraceful decades of Jim Crow baseball. During this era, some of America's greatest ballplayers plied their trade on all-black teams, in Negro Leagues, on the playing fields of Latin America, and along the barnstorming frontier of the cities and towns of the United States, but never within the major and minor league realm of "organized baseball." When slowly and grudgingly given their chance in the years after 1947, blacks conclusively proved their competitive abilities on the diamond, but discrimination persisted as baseball executives continued to deny them the opportunity to display their talents in managerial and front office positions.

Scattered evidence exists of blacks playing baseball in the antebellum period, but the first recorded black teams surfaced in Northern cities in the aftermath of the Civil War. In October 1867, the Uniques of Brooklyn hosted the Excelsiors of Philadelphia in a contest billed as the "championship of colored clubs." Before a large crowd of black and white spectators, the Excelsiors marched around the field behind a fife and drum corps before defeating the Uniques, 37–24. Two months later, a second Philadelphia squad, the Pythians, dispatched a representative to the inaugural meetings of the National Association of Base Ball Players, the first organized league. The nominating committee unanimously rejected the Pythian's application, barring "any club which may be composed of one or more colored persons." Using the impeccable logic of a racist society, the committee proclaimed, "If colored clubs were admitted there would be in all probability some division of feeling, whereas, by excluding them no injury could result to anyone." The Philadelphia Pythians, however, continued their quest for interracial competition. In 1869, they became the first black team to face an all-white squad, defeating the crosstown City Items, 27–17.

In 1876, athletic entrepreneurs in the nation's metropolitan centers established the National League which quickly came to represent the pinnacle of the sport. The new entity had no written policy regarding blacks, but precluded them nonetheless through a "gentleman's agreement" among the owners. In the smaller cities and towns of America, however, where under-funded teams and fragile minor league coalitions quickly appeared and faded, individual blacks found scattered opportunities to pursue baseball careers. During the next decade, at least two dozen black ballplayers sought to earn a living in this erratic professional baseball world.

Bud Fowler ranked among the best and most persistent of these trailblazers. Born John Jackson in upstate New York in 1858 and raised, ironically, in Cooperstown, Fowler first achieved recognition as a 20-year-old pitcher for a local team in Chelsea, Massachusetts. In April 1878, Fowler defeated the National League's Boston club, which included future Hall of Famers George Wright and Jim O' Rourke, 2–1, in an exhibition game, besting 40-game winner Tommy Bond. Later that season, Fowler hurled three games for the Lynn Live Oaks of the International Association, the nation's first minor league, and another for Worcester in the New England League. For the next six years, he toiled for a variety of independent and semi-professional teams in the United States and Canada. Despite a reputation as "one of the best pitchers on the continent," he failed to catch on with any major or minor league squads. In 1884, now appearing regularly as a second baseman, as well as a pitcher, Fowler joined Stillwater, Minnesota, in the Northwestern League. Over the next seven seasons, Fowler played for fourteen teams in nine leagues, seldom batting less than .300 for a season. In 1886, he led the Western League in triples. "He is one of the best general players in the country," reported *Sporting Life* in 1885, "and if he had a white face he would be playing with the best of them. . . Those who know, say there is no better second baseman in the country."

In 1886, however, a better second baseman did appear in the form of Frank Grant, perhaps the greatest black player of the nineteenth century. The light-skinned Grant, described as a "Spaniard" in the *Buffalo Express*, batted .325 for Meridien in the Eastern League. When that squad folded he joined Buffalo in the prestigious International Association and improved his average to .340, third best in the league.

Although not as talented as Fowler and Grant, bare-hand-catcher Moses Fleetwood Walker achieved the highest level of play of blacks of this era. The son of an Ohio physician, Fleet Walker had studied at Oberlin College, where in 1881 he and his younger brother Welday helped launch a varsity baseball team. For the next two years, the elder Walker played for the University of Michigan and in 1883 he appeared in 60 games for the pennant-winning Toledo squad in the Northwestern League. In 1884, Toledo entered the American Association, the

National League's primary rival, and Walker became the first black major leaguer. In an age when many catchers caught barehanded and lacked chest protectors, Walker suffered frequent injuries and played little after a foul tip broke his rib in mid-July. Nonetheless, he batted .263 and pitcher Tony Mullane later called him "the best catcher I ever worked with." In July, Toledo briefly signed Walker's brother, Welday, who appeared in six games batting .182. The following year, Toledo dropped from the league, ending the Walkers' major league careers.

These early black players found limited acceptance among teammates, fans, and opponents. In Ontario, in 1881, Fowler's teammates forced him off the club. Walker found that Mullane and other pitchers preferred not to pitch to him. Although he acknowledged Walker's skills, Mullane confessed, "I disliked a Negro and whenever I had to pitch to him I used anything I wanted without looking at his signals." At Louisville in 1884, insults from Kentucky fans so rattled Walker that he made five errors in a game. In Richmond, after Walker had actually left the team due to injuries, the Toledo manager received a letter from "75 determined men" threatening "to mob Walker" and cause "much bloodshed" if the black catcher appeared. On August 10, 1883, Chicago White Stockings star and manager Cap Anson had threatened to cancel an exhibition game with Toledo if Walker played. The injured catcher had not been slated to start, but Toledo manager Charlie Morton defied Anson and inserted Walker into the lineup. The game proceeded without incident.

In 1887, Walker, Fowler, Grant, Higgins, Stovey, and three other blacks converged on the International League, a newly reorganized circuit in Canada and upstate New York, one notch below the major league level. At the same time, a new six-team entity, the League of Colored Baseball Clubs, won recognition under baseball's National Agreement, a mutual pact to honor player contracts among team owners. Thus, an air of optimism pervaded the start of the season. But 1887 would prove a fateful year for the future of blacks in baseball.

On May 6, the Colored League made its debut in Pittsburgh with "a grand street parade and a brass band concert." Twelve hundred spectators watched the hometown Keystones lose to the Gorhams of New York, 11–8. Within days, however, the new league began to flounder. The Boston franchise disbanded in Louisville on May 8, stranding its players in the Southern city. Three weeks later, league-founder Walter Brown formally announced the demise of the infant circuit.

Meanwhile, in the International League, black players found their numbers growing, but their status increasingly uncertain. Six of the 10 teams fielded blacks, prompting Sporting Life to wonder, "How far will this mania for engaging colored players go?" In Newark, fans marveled at the "colored battery" of Fleet Walker, dubbed the "coon catcher" by one Canadian newspaper, and "headstrong" pitcher George Stovey. Stovey, one of the greatest black pitchers of the nineteenth century, won 35 games, still an International League record. Frank Grant, in his second season as the Buffalo second baseman, led the league in both batting average and home runs. Bud Fowler, one of two blacks on the Binghamton squad, compiled a .350 average through early July and stole 23 bases.

These athletes compiled their impressive statistics under the most adverse conditions. "I could not help pitying some of the poor black fellows that played in the International League," reported a white player. "Fowler used to play second base with the lower part of his legs encased in wooden guards. He knew that about every player that came down to second base on a steal had it in for him." Both Fowler and Grant, "would muff balls intentionally, so that [they] would not have to touch runners, fearing that they might injure [them]." In addition, "About half the pitchers try their best to hit these colored players when [they are] at bat." Grant, whose Buffalo teammates had refused to sit with him for a team portrait in 1886, reportedly saved himself from a "drubbing" at their hands in 1887, only by "the effective use of a club." In Toronto, fans chanted, "Kill the Nigger," at Grant, and a local newspaper headline declared, "THE COLORED PLAYERS DISTASTEFUL." In late June, Bud Fowler's Binghamton teammates refused to take the field unless the club removed him from the lineup. Soon after, on July 7, the Binghamton club submitted to these demands, releasing Fowler and a black teammate, a pitcher named Renfroe.

The most dramatic confrontations between black and white players occurred on the Syracuse squad, where a clique of refugees from the Southern League exacerbated racial tensions. In spring training, the club included a catcher named Dick Male, who, rumors had it, was a light-skinned black named Richard Johnson. Male charged "that the man calling him a Negro is himself a black liar," but when released after a poor preseason performance, he returned to his old club, Zanesville in the Ohio State League, and resumed his true identity as Richard Johnson. In May, Syracuse signed 19-year-old black pitcher Robert Higgins, angering the Southern clique. On May 25, Higgins appeared in his first International League game in Toronto. "THE SYRACUSE PLOTTERS," as a Sporting News headline called his teammates, undermined his debut. According to one account, they "seemed to want the Toronto team to knock Higgins out of the box, and time and again they fielded so badly that the home team were enabled to secure many hits after the side had been retired." "A disgusting exhibition," admonished The Toronto World. "They succeeded in running Male out of the club," reported a Newark paper, "and they will do the same with Higgins." One week later, two Syracuse players refused to pose for a team picture with Higgins. When manager "Ice Water" Joe Simmons suspended pitcher Doug Crothers for this incident, Crothers slugged the manager. Higgins miraculously recovered from his early travails and lack of support to post a 20–7 record.

On July 14, as the directors of the International League discussed the racial situation in Buffalo, the Newark Little Giants planned to send Stovey, their ace, to the mound in an exhibition game against the National League Chicago White Stockings. Once again manager Anson refused to field his squad if either Stovey or Walker appeared. Unlike 1883, Anson's will prevailed. On the same day, team owners, stating that "Many of the best players in the league are anxious to leave on account of the colored element," allowed current black players to remain, but voted by a six-to-four margin to reject all

future contracts with blacks. The teams with black players all voted against the measure, but Binghamton, which had just released Fowler and Renfroe, swung the vote in favor of exclusion.

Events in 1887 continued to conspire against black players. On September 11, the St. Louis Browns of the American Association refused to play a scheduled contest against the all-black Cuban Giants. "We are only doing what is right," they proclaimed. In November, the Buffalo and Syracuse teams unsuccessfully attempted to lift the International League ban on blacks. The Ohio State League, which had fielded three black players, also adopted a rule barring additional contracts with blacks, prompting Welday Walker, who had appeared in the league, to protest, "The law is a disgrace to the present age. . . There should be some broader cause—such as lack of ability, behavior and intelligence—for barring a player, rather than his color."

After 1887, only a handful of blacks appeared on integrated squads. Grant and Higgins returned to their original teams in 1888. Walker jumped from Newark to Syracuse. The following year, only Walker remained for one final season, the last black in the International League until 1946. Richard Johnson, the erstwhile Dick Male, reappeared in the Ohio State League in 1888 and in 1889 joined Springfield in the Central Interstate League, where he hit 14 triples, stole 45 bases, and scored 100 runs in 100 games. In 1890, Harrisburg in the Eastern Interstate League fielded two blacks, while Jamestown in the New York Penn League featured another. Bud Fowler and several other black players appeared in the Nebraska State League in 1892. Three years later, Adrian in the Michigan State League signed five blacks, including Fowler and pitcher George Wilson who posted a 29–4 record. Meanwhile Sol White, who later chronicled these events in his 1906 book, *The History of Colored Baseball*, played for Fort Wayne in the Western State League. In 1896, pitcher-outfielder Bert Jones joined Atchison in the Kansas State League where he played for three seasons before being forced out in 1898. Almost 50 years would pass before another black would appear on an interracial club in organized baseball.

While integrated teams grew rare, several leagues allowed entry to all black squads. In 1889, the Middle States League included the New York Gorhams and the Cuban Giants, the most famous black team of the age. The Giants posted a 55–17 record. In 1890, the alliance reorganized as the Eastern Interstate League and again included the Cuban Giants. Giants' star George Williams paced the circuit with a .391 batting average, while teammate Arthur Thomas slugged 26 doubles and 10 triples, both league-leading totals. The Eastern Interstate League folded in midseason, and in 1891 the Giants made one final minor league appearance in the Connecticut State League. When this circuit also disbanded, the brief entry of the Cuban Giants in organized baseball came to an end. In 1898, a team calling itself the Acme Colored Giants affiliated with Pennsylvania's Iron and Oil League, but won only eight of 49 games before dropping out, marking an ignoble conclusion to these early experiments in interracial play.

Overall, at least 70 blacks appeared in organized baseball in the late 19th century. About half played for all-black teams, the remainder for integrated clubs. Few lasted more than one season with the same team. By the 1890s, the pattern for black baseball that would prevail for the next half century had emerged. Blacks were relegated to "colored" teams playing most of their games on the barnstorming circuit, outside of any organized league structure. While exhibition contests allowed them to pit their skills against whites, they remained on the outskirts of baseball's mainstream, unheralded and unknown to most Americans.

As early as the 1880s and 1890s several all-black traveling squads had gained national reputations. The Cuban Giants, formed among the waiters of the Argyle Hotel to entertain guests in 1885, set the pattern and provided the recurrent nickname for these teams. Passing as Cubans, so as not to offend their white clientele, the Giants toured the East in a private railroad car playing amateur and professional opponents. In the 1890s, rivals like the Lincoln Giants from Nebraska, the Page Fence Giants from Michigan, and the Cuban X Giants in New York emerged. From the beginning these teams combined entertainment with their baseball to attract crowds. The Page Fence Giants, founded by Bud Fowler in 1895, would ride through the streets on bicycles to attract attention. In 1899, Fowler organized the All-American Black Tourists, who would arrive in full dress suits with opera hats and silk umbrellas. Their showmanship notwithstanding, the black teams of the 1890s included some of the best players in the nation. The Page Fence Giants won 118 of 154 games in 1895, with two of their losses coming against the major league Cincinnati Reds.

During the early years of the 20th century many blacks still harbored hopes of regaining access to organized baseball. Sol White wrote in 1906 that baseball, "should be taken seriously by the colored player. An honest effort of his great ability will open the avenue in the near future wherein he may walk hand-in-hand with the opposite race in the greatest of all American games—baseball." Rube Foster, the outstanding figure in black baseball from 1910-1926, stressed excellence because "we have to be ready when the time comes for integration."

But even clandestine efforts to bring in blacks met a harsh fate. In 1901, Baltimore Orioles Manager John McGraw attempted to pass second baseman Charlie Grant of the Columbia Giants off as an Indian named Chief Tokohama, until Chicago White Sox President Charles Comiskey exposed the ruse. In 1911, the Cincinnati Reds raised black hopes by signing two light-skinned Cubans, Armando Marsans and Rafael Almeida, prompting the *New York Age* to speculate, "Now that the first shock is over it would not be surprising to see a Cuban a few shades darker. . .breaking into the professional ranks. . .it would then be easier for colored players who are citizens of this country to get into fast company." But the Reds rushed to certify that Marsans and Almeida were "genuine Caucasians," and while light-skinned Cubans became a fixture in the majors, their darker brethren remained unwelcome. Over the years, tales circulated of United States blacks passing as Indians or Cubans, but no documented cases exist.

Although most blacks lived in the South, during the first two decades of the 20th century, the great black teams and players congregated in the metropolises and

industrial cities of the North. Chicago emerged as the primary center of black baseball with teams like the Leland Giants and the Chicago American Giants. In New York, the Lincoln Giants, which boasted pitching stars Smokey Joe Williams and Cannonball Dick Redding, shortstop John Henry Lloyd and catcher Louis Santop, reigned supreme. Other top clubs of the era included the Philadelphia Giants, the Hilldale Club (also of Philadelphia), the Indianapolis ABC's and the Bacharach Giants of Atlantic City. Player contracts were nonexistent or nonbinding and stars jumped frequently from team to team. "Wherever the money was," recalled John Henry Lloyd, "that's where I was."

Fans and writers often compared the great black players of this era to their white counterparts. Lloyd, one of the outstanding shortstops and hitters of that or any era, came to be known as "The Black Wagner," after his white contemporary Honus Wagner, who called it an "honor" and a "privilege" to be compared to the gangling black infielder. A St. Louis sportswriter once said when asked who was the best player in baseball history, "If you mean in organized baseball, the answer would be Babe Ruth; but if you mean in all baseball...the answer would have to be a colored man named John Henry Lloyd." Pitcher "Rube" Foster earned his nickname by outpitching future Hall of Famer Rube Waddell, and Cuban Jose Mendez was called "The Black Matty" after Christy Mathewson.

The talents of Foster and Mendez notwithstanding, the greatest black pitcher of the early twentieth century was 6'5" Smokey Joe Williams. Born in 1886, Williams spent a good part of his career pitching in his native Texas, unheralded until he joined the Leland Giants in 1909 at the age of 24. From 1912-1923 he won renown as a strikeout artist for Harlem's Lincoln Giants. Against major league competition Williams won six games, lost 4, and tied two, including a three-hit 1–0 victory over the National League champion Philadelphia Phillies in 1915. In 1925, he signed with the Homestead Grays and although approaching his fortieth birthday, starred for seven more seasons. A 1952 poll to name the outstanding black pitcher of the half-century, placed Williams in first place, ahead of the legendary Satchel Paige.

Oscar Charleston ranks as the greatest outfielder of the 1910s and 1920s. With tremendous speed and a strong, accurate arm, Charleston was the quintessential centerfielder. During his 15-year career starting in 1915, Charleston hit for both power and average and may have been the most popular player of the 1920s. After he retired he managed the Philadelphia Stars, Brooklyn Brown Dodgers, and other clubs.

Several major stars of this era labored outside the usual channels of black baseball. In 1914, white Kansas City promoter J. L. Wilkinson organized the All-Nations team, which included whites, blacks, Indians, Asians, and Latin Americans. Pitchers John Donaldson, Jose Mendez, and Bill Drake and outfielder Cristobel Torriente played for the All-Nations team, described by one observer as "strong enough to give any major league team a nip-and-tuck battle." A black Army team from the 25th Infantry Unit in Nogales, Arizona, featured pitcher Bullet Joe Rogan and shortstop Dobie Moore. In 1920, when Wilkinson formed the famed Kansas City Monarchs, the players from the All-Nations and 25th Infantry teams formed the

nucleus of his club. In 1921, the Monarchs challenged the minor league Kansas City Blues to a tournament for the city championship. The Blues won the series five games to three. In 1922, however, the Monarchs won five of six games to claim boasting honors in Kansas City. One week later, they swept a doubleheader from the touring Babe Ruth All-Stars.

In the years after 1910, Andrew "Rube" Foster emerged as the dominant figure in black baseball. Like many of his white contemporaries, Foster rose through the ranks of the national pastime from star player to field manager to club owner. Born in Texas in 1879, Foster accepted an invitation to pitch for Chicago's Union Giants in 1902. "If you play the best clubs in the land, white clubs as you say," he told owner Frank Leland, "it will be a case of Greek meeting Greek. I fear nobody." By 1903, he was hurling for the Cuban X Giants against the Philadelphia Giants in a series billed as the "Colored Championship of the World." His four victories in a best of nine series clinched the title. The following year, he had switched sides and registered two of three wins for the Philadelphia Giants in a similar matchup, striking out 18 batters in one game and tossing a two-hitter in another. In 1907, he rejoined the Leland Giants and, in 1910, pitched for and managed a reconstituted team of that name to a 123–6 record.

As a pitcher, Foster had ranked among the nation's best; as a manager, his skills achieved legendary proportions. A master strategist and motivator, Foster's teams specialized in the bunt, the steal, and the hit-and-run, which came to characterize black baseball. Fans came to watch him sit on the bench giving signs with a wave of his ever-present pipe. He became the friend and confidant of major league managers like John McGraw. Over the years, Foster trained a generation of black managers, like Dave Malarcher, Biz Mackey, and Oscar Charleston in the subtleties of the game.

In 1911, Foster entered the ownership ranks, uniting with white saloon keeper John Schorling (the son-in-law of White Sox owner Charles Comiskey) to form the Chicago American Giants. With Schorling's financial backing, Foster's managerial acumen, a regular home field in Chicago, and high salaries, the American Giants attracted the best black players in the nation. Throughout the decade, whether barnstorming or hosting opponents in Chicago, the American Giants came to represent the pinnacle of black baseball.

By World War One, Foster dominated black baseball in Chicago and parts of the Midwest. In most other areas, however, white booking agents controlled access to stadiums, and as one newspaperman charged in 1917, "used circus methods to drag a bunch of our best citizens out, only to undergo humiliation ... while [they sat] back and [grew] rich off a percentage of the proceeds." In the East, Nat Strong, the part owner of the Brooklyn Royal Giants, Philadelphia Giants, Cuban Stars, Cuban Giants, New York Black Yankees, and the renowned white semi-pro team, the Bushwicks, held a stranglehold on black competition. To break this monopoly and place the game more firmly under black control, Foster created the National Association of Professional Baseball Clubs, better known as the Negro National League, in 1920.

Foster's new organization marked the third attempt of

the century to meld black teams into a viable league. In 1906, the International League of Independent Baseball Clubs, which had four black and two white teams, struggled through one season characterized by shifting and collapsing franchises. Four years later, Beauregard Moseley, secretary of Chicago's Leland Giants attempted to form a National Negro Baseball League, but the association folded before a single game had been played.

The new Negro National League, which included the top teams from Chicago, St. Louis, Detroit, and other Midwestern cities, fared far better. At Foster's insistence, all clubs, with the exception of the Kansas City Monarchs, whom Foster reluctantly accepted, were controlled by blacks. J. L. Wilkinson, who owned the Monarchs, a major drawing card, had won the respect of his fellow owners and soon overcame Foster's reservations. He became the league secretary and Foster's trusted ally. Operating under the able guidance of Foster and Wilkinson, the league flourished during its early years. In 1923, it attracted 400,000 fans and accumulated $200,000 in gate receipts.

The success of the Negro National League inspired competitors. In 1923, booking agent Nat Strong formed an Eastern Colored League, with teams in New York, Brooklyn, Baltimore, New Jersey, and Philadelphia. With four of the six teams owned by whites, and Strong controlling an erratic schedule, the league had somewhat less legitimacy than Foster's circuit. Playing in larger population centers, however, the more affluent Eastern clubs successfully raided some of the top players of the Negro National League before the circuits negotiated an uneasy truce in 1924. Throughout the remainder of the decade, however, acrimony rather than harmony characterized interleague relations. A third association emerged in the South, where the stronger independent teams in major cities formed the Southern Negro League. While this group became a breeding ground for top players, the impoverished nature of its clientele, and the inability of clubs to bolster revenues with games against white squads, rendered them unable to prevent their best players from jumping to the higher paying Northern teams.

At their best the Negro Leagues of the 1920s were haphazard affairs. Since most clubs continued to rely on barnstorming for their primary livelihood, scheduling proved difficult. Teams played uneven numbers of games and especially in the Eastern circuit skipped official contests for more lucrative nonleague matchups. Several of the stronger independent teams, like the Homestead Grays, remained unaffiliated. Umpires were often incompetent and lacked authority to control conditions. Finally, players frequently jumped from one franchise to another, peddling their services to the highest bidder. In 1926, Foster grew ill, stripping the Negro National League of his vital leadership. Two years later, the Eastern Colored League disbanded and in 1931, less than a year after Foster's death, the Negro National League departed the scene, once again leaving black baseball with no organized structure.

With the collapse of Foster's Negro National League and the onset of the Great Depression, the always-borderline economics of operating a black baseball club grew more precarious. White booking agents, like Philadelphia's Eddie Gottlieb or Abe Saperstein of the Midwest, again reigned supreme. In the early 1930s, only the stronger independent clubs like the Homestead Grays or Kansas City Monarchs, novelty acts like the Cincinnati Clowns, or those teams backed by the "numbers kings" of the black ghettos could survive.

The Kansas City Monarchs emerged as the healthiest holdover from the old Negro National League. In 1929, owner Wilkinson had commissioned an Omaha, Nebraska, company to design a portable lighting system for night games. The equipment, consisting of a 250-horsepower motor and a 100-kilowatt generator, which illuminated lights atop telescoping poles 50 feet above the field, took about two hours to assemble. To pay for the innovation, Wilkinson mortgaged everything he owned and took in Kansas City businessman Tom Baird as a partner. But the gamble paid off. The novelty of night baseball allowed the Monarchs to play two and three games a day and made them the most popular touring club in the nation.

Meanwhile, in Pittsburgh, former basketball star Cumberland Posey, Jr. had forged the Homestead Grays into one of the best teams in America. Posey, the son of one of Pittsburgh's wealthiest black businessmen, had joined the Grays, then a sandlot team, as an outfielder in 1911. By the early 1920s he owned the club and began recruiting top national players to supplement local talent. In 1925, he signed 39-year-old Smokey Joe Williams, and the following year he lured Oscar Charleston, whom many consider the top black player of that era. Over the next several seasons Posey recruited Judy Johnson, Martin Dihigo, and Cool Papa Bell. In 1930, he added a catcher from the Pittsburgh sandlots named Josh Gibson, and in 1934 brought in first baseman Buck Leonard from North Carolina. Unwilling to subject himself to outside control, Posey preferred to remain free from league affiliations. Yet for two decades, the Homestead Grays reigned as one of the strongest teams in black baseball.

In the 1930s, Posey faced competition from crosstown rival Gus Greenlee, "Mr. Big" of Pittsburgh's North Side numbers rackets. Greenlee took over the Pittsburgh Crawfords, a local team, in 1930. Greenlee spent $100,000 to build a new stadium, and wooed established ballplayers with lavish salary offers. In 1931, he landed the colorful Satchel Paige, the hottest young pitcher in the land, and the following year raided the Grays, outbidding Posey for the services of Charleston, Johnson, and Gibson. In 1934, James "Cool Papa" Bell jumped the St. Louis Stars and brought his legendary speed to the Crawfords. With five future Hall of Famers, Greenlee had assembled one of the great squads of baseball history.

The emergence of Gus Greenlee marked a new era for black baseball, the reign of the numbers men. In an age of limited opportunities for blacks, many of the most talented northern black entrepreneurs turned to gambling and other illegal operations for their livelihood. Novelist Richard Wright explained, "They would have been steel tycoons, Wall Street brokers, auto moguls, had they been white." Like the political bosses of nineteenth century urban America, numbers operators provided an informal assistance network for needy patrons in the impoverished black communities and represented a major source of capital for black businesses. In city after city, the numbers barons, seeking an element of respectability or an outlet to shield gambling profits from the Internal Reve-

nue Service or merely the thrill of sports ownership, came to dominate black baseball. In Harlem, second-generation Cuban immigrant Alex Pompez, a powerful figure in the Dutch Schultz mob, ran the Cuban Stars, while Ed "Soldier Boy" Semler controlled the Black Yankees. Abe Manley of the Newark Eagles, Ed Bolden of the Philadelphia Stars, and Tom Wilson of the Baltimore Elite Giants all garnered their fortunes from the numbers game. Even Cum Posey, who had no connection with the rackets, had to bring in Homestead numbers banker Rufus "Sonnyman" Jackson as a partner and financier to stave off Greenlee's challenge.

In 1933, Greenlee unified the franchises owned by the numbers kings into a rejuvenated Negro National League. Under his leadership, writes Donn Rogosin, "The Negro National League meetings were enclaves of the most powerful black gangsters in the nation." This "unholy alliance" sustained black baseball in the Northeast through depression and war. Even the collapse of the Crawfords and demolition of Greenlee Stadium in 1939, failed to weaken the league which survived until the onset of integration. In 1937 a second circuit, the Negro American League was formed in the Midwest and South. Dominated by Wilkinson and the Kansas City Monarchs, the Negro American League relied less on numbers brokers, but more on white ownership for their financing.

The formation of the Negro American League encouraged the rejuvenation of an annual World Series, matching the champions of the two leagues. But the Negro League World Series never achieved the prominence of its white counterpart. The fact that league standings were often determined among teams playing uneven numbers of games, diluted the notion of a champion. Furthermore, impoverished urban blacks could not sustain attendance at a prolonged series. As a result, the Negro League World Series always took a back seat to the annual East-West All-Star Game played in Chicago. The East-West Game, originated by Greenlee in 1933, quickly emerged as the centerpiece of black baseball. Fans chose the players in polls conducted by black newspapers. By 1939, leading candidates received as many as 500,000 votes. Large crowds of blacks and whites watched the finest Negro League stars, and the revenues divided among the teams often spelled the difference between profit and loss at the season's end.

By the 1930s and 1940s, black baseball had become an integral part of Northern ghetto life. With hundreds of employees and millions of dollars in revenue, the Negro Leagues, as Donn Rogosin notes, "may rank among the highest achievements of black enterprise during segregation." In addition, baseball provided an economic ripple effect, boosting business in hotels, cafes, restaurants and bars. In Kansas City and other towns, games became social events, as black citizens, recalls manager Buck O'Neil, "wore their finery." The Monarch Booster Club was a leading civic organization and the "Miss Monarch Bathing Beauty" pageant a popular event.

Black baseball also represented a source of pride for the black community. "The Monarchs was Kansas City's team," boasted bartender Jesse Fisher. "They made Kansas City the talk of the town all over the world." In several cities, white politicians routinely appeared at Opening Day games to curry favor with their often neglected black constituents. When Greenlee Field launched its operations in Pittsburgh, the mayor, city council, and county commissioners lined the field boxes. Negro League owners also played a role in the fight against segregation. In Newark, Effa Manley, who ran the Eagles with her husband Abe, served as treasurer of the New Jersey NAACP and belonged to the Citizen's League for Fair Play which fought for black employment opportunities. Manley sponsored a "Stop Lynching" fundraiser at one Eagles home game.

The impact of the Negro Leagues, however, ranged beyond the communities whose names the teams bore. Throughout the age of Jim Crow baseball, even in those years when a substantial league structure existed, official league games accounted for a relatively small part of the black baseball experience. Black teams would typically play over 200 games a year, only a third of which counted in the league standings. The vast majority of contests occurred on the "barnstorming" circuit, pitting black athletes against a broad array of professional and semi-professional competition, white and black, throughout the nation. In the pre-television era, traveling teams brought a higher level of baseball to fans in the towns and cities of America and allowed local talent to test their skills against the professionals. While some all-white teams, like the "House of David" also trod the barnstorming trail, itinerancy was the key to survival for black squads. The capital needed to finance a Negro League team existed primarily in Northern cities, but the overwhelming majority of blacks lived in the South.

"The schedule was a rugged one," recalled Roy Campanella of the Baltimore Elite Giants. "Rarely were we in the same city two days in a row. Mostly we played by day and traveled by night." After the Monarchs introduced night baseball, teams played both day and night appearing in two and sometimes three different ballparks on the same day. Teams traveled in buses—"our home, dressing room, dining room, and hotel"—or sandwiched into touring cars. "We had little time to waste on the road," states Quincy Trouppe, "so it was a rare treat when the cars would stop at times to let us stretch out and exercise for a few minutes." Most major hotels barred black guests, so even when the schedule allowed overnight stays, the athletes found themselves in less than comfortable accommodations. Large cities usually had better black hotels where ballplayers, entertainers, and other members of the black bourgeoisie congregated. On the road, however, Negro Leaguers more frequently were relegated to Jim Crow roadhouses, "continually under attack by bedbugs."

The black baseball experience extended beyond the confines of the United States and into Central America and the Caribbean. Negro Leaguers appeared regularly in the Cuban, Puerto Rican, Venezuelan, and Dominican winter leagues where they competed against black and white Latin stars and major leaguers as well. Some blacks, like Willie Wells and Ray Dandridge, jumped permanently to the Mexican League, where several also became successful managers of interracial teams. As Wells explained, "I am not faced by the racial problem. . . I've found freedom and democracy here, something I never found in the United States. . . In Mexico, I am a man."

In the United States, however, blacks often found themselves in more distasteful roles. To attract crowds throughout the nation and to keep fans interested in the frequently one-sided contests against amateur competition, some black clubs injected elements of clowning and showmanship into their pre-game and competitive performances. As early as the 1880s, comedy had characterized many barnstorming teams. Black baseball, even in its most serious form, tended to be flashier and less formal than white play. Against inferior teams, players often showboated and flaunted their superior skills. Pitcher Satchel Paige would call in his outfielders or guarantee to strike out the first six or nine batters to face him against semi-professional squads. In the late 1930s, Olympic star Jesse Owens traveled with the Monarchs, racing against horses in pre-game exhibitions.

Black teams, like the Tennessee Rats and Zulu Cannibals, thrived on their minstrel show reputations. The most famous of these franchises were the "Ethiopian Clowns." Originating in Miami in the 1930s, the Clowns later operated out of Cincinnati and then Indianapolis. Their antics included a "pepperball and shadowball" performance (later emulated by basketball's Harlem Globetrotters), and mid-game vaudeville routines by comics Spec Bebop, a dwarf, and King Tut. Players like Pepper Bassett, "the Rocking Chair Catcher" and "Goose" Tatum, a talented first baseman and natural comedian, enlivened the festivities. By the 1940s, the Clowns, through the effort of booking agent Syd Pollack, dominated the baseball comedy market. In 1943, their popularity won the Clowns entrance into the Negro Leagues, although other owners demanded they drop the demeaning "Ethiopian" nickname. Although never one of the better black teams, the Clowns greatly bolstered Negro League attendance.

Their popularity notwithstanding, the comedy teams reflected one of the worst elements of black baseball. The Clowns and Zulus perpetuated stereotypes drawn from Stepin Fetchit and Tarzan movies. "Negroes must realize the danger in insisting that ballplayers paint their faces and go through minstrel show revues before each ball-game," protested sportswriter Wendell Smith. Many black players resented the image that all were clowns. "Didn't nobody clown in our league but the Indianapolis Clowns," objected Piper Davis. "We played baseball."

Even without the clowning, black baseball offered a more freewheeling and, in many respects, more exciting brand of baseball than the major leagues. Since the 1920s, when Babe Ruth had revolutionized the game, the majors had pursued power strategies, emphasizing the home run above all else. Although the great sluggers of the Negro Leagues rivaled those in the National and American Leagues, they comprised but one element in the speed-dominated universe of "tricky baseball." Black teams emphasized the bunt, the stolen base, and the hit-and-run. "We played by the 'coonsbury' rules," boasted second baseman Newt Allen. "That's just any way you think you can win, any kind of play you think you could get by on." In games between white and black all-star teams, this style of play often confounded the major leaguers. Centerfielder James "Cool Papa" Bell personified this approach. Bell was so fast, marveled rival third baseman Judy Johnson, "You couldn't play back in your regular position or you'd never throw him out." In one

game against a major league All-Star squad, Bell scored from first base on a sacrifice bunt! In center field, his great speed allowed him to lurk in the shallow reaches of the outfield, ranging great distances to make spectacular catches.

Negro League pitching also took on a peculiar caste. "Anything went in the Negro League," reported catcher Roy Campanella, "Spitballs, shineballs, emery balls; pitchers used any and all of them." Since league officials could not afford to replace the balls as frequently as in organized ball, scuffed and nicked baseballs remained in the game, giving pitchers great latitude for creative efforts. "I never knew what the ball would do once it left the pitcher's hand," recalled Campanella.

Since most rosters included only 14 to 18 men, Negro League players demonstrated a wide range of versatility. Each was required to fill in at a variety of positions. Star pitchers often found themselves in the outfield when not on the mound. Some won renown at more than one position. Ted "Double-Duty" Radcliffe often pitched in the first game of a doubleheader and caught in the second. Cuban Martin Dihigo, whom many rank as the greatest player of all time, excelled at every position. In 1938, in the Mexican League he led the league's pitchers with an 18–2 record and the league's hitters with a .387 average.

The manpower shortage offered opportunities for individuals to display their all-around talents, but it also limited the competitiveness of the black teams. While on a given day a Negro League franchise, featuring one of its top pitchers, might defeat a major league squad, most teams lacked the depth to compete on a regular basis. "The big leagues were strong in every position," remarks Radcliffe. "Most of the colored teams had a few stars but they weren't strong in every position."

While black teams may not have matched the top clubs in organized baseball, the individual stars of the 1930s and 1940s clearly ranked among the best of any age. Homestead Gray teammates Josh Gibson and Buck Leonard won renown as the Babe Ruth and Lou Gehrig of the Negro Leagues. The Grays discovered Gibson in 1929 as an 18-year-old catcher on the sandlots of Pittsburgh, where he had already earned a reputation for 500-foot home runs. For 17 years, he launched prodigious blasts off pitchers in the Negro Leagues, on the barnstorming tour, and in Latin America. As talented as any major league star, Gibson died in January 1947, at age 35, just three months before Jackie Robinson joined the Brooklyn Dodgers. Leonard, four-years older than Gibson, starred in both the Negro and Mexican Leagues as a sure-handed, power-hitting first baseman. The Newark Eagles in the early 1940s, boasted the "million dollar infield" of first baseman Mule Suttles, second baseman Dick Seay, shortstop Willie Wells, and third baseman Ray Dandridge. The acrobatic fielding skills of Seay, Wells and Dandridge led Roy Campanella to call this the greatest infield he ever saw.

Amidst the many talented Negro Leaguers of 1930s and 1940s, however, one long, lean figure came to personify black baseball to blacks and whites alike. Leroy "Satchel" Paige began his prolonged athletic odyssey in his hometown in 1924 as a 17-year-old pitcher with the semi-professional Mobile Tigers. He joined the Chattanooga Black Lookouts of the Negro Southern League in

1926. Two years later, the Lookouts sold his contract to the Birmingham Black Barons. By 1930, his explosive fastball, impeccable control, and eccentric mannerisms had made him a legend in the South. In 1932, Gus Greenlee brought Paige to the Pittsburgh Crawfords where the colorful pitcher embellished his reputation by winning 54 games in his first two years. Greenlee also began the practice of hiring out Paige to semi-professional clubs that needed a one-day box office boost.

For seven years Paige feuded with Greenlee, jumping the club when a better offer appeared, being banished "for life," and then returning. In the mid-1930s, in addition to his stints with the Crawfords, Paige won fame by boosting Bismarck, North Dakota, to the national semi-professional championships, hurling for the Dominican Republic at the behest of dictator Rafael Trujillo, in the Mexican League, and especially on the postseason barnstorming trail pitted against Dizzy Dean's Major League All-Stars. "That skinny old Satchel Paige with those long arms is my idea of the pitcher with the greatest stuff I ever saw," claimed the unusually immodest Dean.

Paige's appeal stemmed as much from his unusual persona as his pitching prowess. A born showman, Paige's lanky, lackadaisical presence evoked popular racial stereotypes of the age. "As undependable as a pair of second-hand suspenders," Paige often arrived late or failed to show. His names for his pitches (the "bee ball" which buzzed and all of a sudden, "be there"; the "jump ball"; and the "trouble ball") and his minstrel show one-liners enhanced the image. But on the mound, Paige invariably rose to the occasion against top competition or challenged inferior opponents by calling in the outfield or promising to strike out the side.

In 1938, a sore arm threatened to curtail Paige's career but the Kansas City Monarchs, hoping his reputation alone would draw fans, signed him for their traveling second team. On the road, Paige perfected a repertoire of curves and off-speed pitches, including his famous "hesitation" pitch. When his fastball returned in 1939, he became a better pitcher than ever. Promoted to the main Monarch club, Paige pitched the team to four consecutive Negro American League pennants. From 1941-1947, although officially still a Monarch, Paige spent far more time as an independent performer, hired out by Monarchs' owner J. L. Wilkinson to semi-pro and Negro League clubs. "He kept our league going," recalls Othello Renfroe. "Anytime a team got into trouble, it sent for Satchel to pitch." Paige also continued to hurl against major league All-Star teams. In the 1940s, the example of Satchel Paige, whose legend had spread into the white community, offered the most compelling argument for the desegregation of the National Pastime.

Paige's exploits against white players revealed a fundamental irony about baseball in the Jim Crow era. While organized baseball rigidly enforced its ban on black players within the major and minor leagues, opportunities abounded for black athletes to prove themselves against white competition along the unpoliced boundaries of the national pastime. During the 1930s, Western promoters sponsored tournaments for the best semi-professional teams in the nation. These squads often featured former and future major leaguers as well as top local talent. In 1934, the *Denver Post* tourney, "the little World Series of the West," invited the Kansas City Monarchs to compete for the $7,500 first prize. The Monarchs fought their way into the finals against the House of David team (also owned by J. L. Wilkinson) only to find themselves confronted on the mound by Paige, rented out to pitch this one game. Paige outdueled Monarchs ace, Chet Brewer, 2–1. Black teams became a fixture in the Post series, emerging victorious for several consecutive years.

In 1935, the National Baseball Congress began an annual tournament in Wichita, Kansas. The competition attracted community squads heartily bankrolled by local business leaders. Neil Churchill, an auto dealer from Bismarck, North Dakota, recruited a half-dozen black stars, including Paige and Brewer, to represent the town in the Wichita competition. Bismarck naturally swept the series, and thereafter teams that were either integrated or all black routinely appeared in the National Baseball Congress invitational each year.

In an age in which the major leagues were confined to the East and Midwest, and television had yet to bring baseball into people's homes, postseason tours by big league stars offered yet another opportunity for black players to prove their equality on the diamond. Games pitting blacks against whites were popular features of the barnstorming circuit. Until the late 1920s, when Commissioner Kenesaw Mountain Landis limited postseason play to all-star squads, black teams frequently met and defeated major league clubs in postseason competition. During the next decade, matchups between the Babe Ruth or Dizzy Dean "All-Stars" and black players became frequent. In the autumns of 1934 and 1935, Dean's team traveled the nation accompanied by the "Satchel Paige All-Stars." In one memorable 1934 game, called by baseball executive Bill Veeck, "the greatest pitching battle I have ever seen," Paige bested Dean 1–0. Surviving records of interracial contests during the 1930s reveal that blacks won two-thirds of the games. "That's when we played the hardest," asserted Judy Johnson, "to let them know, and to let the public know, that we had the same talent they did and probably a little better at times."

The rivalries proved particularly keen on the West Coast where Monarchs co-owner Tom Baird organized the California Winter League, which included black teams, white major and minor league stars, and some of Mexico's top players. In 1940, pitcher Chet Brewer formed the Kansas City Royals, which each year fielded one of the best clubs on the coast. One year the Royals defeated the Hollywood Stars, who had won the Pacific Coast League championship, six straight times. In 1945, Brewer's team, including Jackie Robinson and Satchel Paige, regularly defeated major league competition.

The most famous of the interracial barnstorming tours occurred in 1946, when Cleveland Indian pitcher Bob Feller organized a major league All-Star Team, rented two Flying Tiger aircraft and hopped the nation accompanied by the Satchel Paige All-Stars. With Feller and Paige each pitching a few innings a day, the tour proved extremely lucrative for promoters and players alike and gave widespread publicity to the skills of the black athletes.

The World War Two years marked the heyday of the Negro Leagues. With black and white workers flooding into Northern industrial centers, relatively full employ-

ment, and a scarcity of available consumer goods, attendance at all sorts of entertainment events increased dramatically. In 1942, three million fans saw Negro League teams play, while the East-West game in 1943 attracted over 51,000 fans. "Even the white folks was coming out big," recalled Satchel Paige.

But World War Two also generated forces which would challenge the foundations of Jim Crow baseball. In the armed forces, baseball teams like the Black Bluejackets of the Great Lakes Naval Station team posted outstanding records against teams featuring white major leaguers. In 1945, a well-publicized tournament of teams in the European theatre featured top black players like Leon Day, Joe Green, and Willard Brown in the championship round. More significantly, the hypocrisy of blacks fighting for their country but unable to participate in the national pastime grew steadily more apparent. As wartime manpower shortages forced major league teams to rely on a 15-year-old pitcher, over-the-hill veterans, and one-armed Pete Gray, their refusal to sign black players seemed increasingly irrational. "How do you think I felt when I saw a one-armed outfielder?" moaned Chet Brewer. Pitcher Nate Moreland protested, "I can play in Mexico, but I have to fight for America where I can't play." Pickets at Yankee Stadium carried placards asking, "If we are able to stop bullets, why not balls?"

Amidst this heightened awareness, organized baseball repeatedly walked to the precipice of integration, but always failed to take the final leap. In 1942, Moreland and All-American football star Jackie Robinson requested a tryout at a White Sox training camp in Pasadena, California. Robinson, in particular, impressed White Sox Jimmy Dykes but nothing came of the event. Brooklyn Dodger manager Leo Durocher publicly stated his willingness to sign blacks, only to receive a stinging rebuke from Commissioner Landis. Landis again short-circuited integration talk the following year. At the annual baseball meetings, black leaders led by actor Paul Robeson gained the opportunity to address major league owners on the issue, but Landis ruled all further discussion out of order.

In 1943, several minor and major league teams were rumored close to signing black players. In California, where winter league play had demonstrated the potential of black players, several clubs considered integration. The Los Angeles Angels of the Pacific Coast League announced tryouts for three black players, but pressure from other league owners doomed the plan. Oakland owner Vince DeVicenzi ordered Manager Johnny Vergez to consider pitcher Chet Brewer, the most popular black player on the West Coast, for the Oaks. Vergez refused and the issue died. Two years later, Bakersfield, a Cleveland Indian farm team in the California League, offered Brewer a position as player-coach, but the parent club vetoed the plan.

At the major league level, Washington Senators owner Clark Griffith called sluggers Josh Gibson and Buck Leonard into his office and asked if they would like to play in the major leagues. They answered affirmatively, but never heard from Griffith again. In Pittsburgh, *Daily Worker* sports editor Nat Low pressured Pirate owner William Benswanger to arrange a tryout for catcher Roy Campanella and pitcher Dave Barnhill. At the last minute, Benswanger canceled the audition, citing "unnamed

pressures." The most promising situation occurred in Philadelphia where young Bill Veeck had arranged to buy the Phillies. Veeck planned to stock the team with Negro League stars, whom he felt sure would guarantee Philadelphia the pennant. When Commissioner Landis learned of his plans, however, Veeck suddenly found his purchase blocked.

For more than two decades, the imperial Landis had reigned over baseball as an implacable foe of integration. While hypocritically denying the existence of any "rule, formal or informal, or any understanding—unwritten, subterranean, or sub-anything—against the signing of Negro players," Landis had stringently policed the color line. His death in 1944 removed a major barrier for integration advocates.

In April 1945, with World War Two entering its final months, the integration crusade gained momentum. On April 6, *People's Voice* sportswriter Joe Bostic appeared at the Brooklyn Dodger training camp at Bear Mountain, New York, with two Negro League players, Terris McDuffie and Dave "Showboat" Thomas, and demanded a tryout. An outraged, but outmaneuvered Dodger President Branch Rickey, allowed the pair to work out with the club. One week later, a more serious confrontation occurred in Boston. The Red Sox, under pressure from popular columnist Dave Egan and city councilman Isidore Muchnick, agreed to audition Sam Jethroe, the Negro League's leading hitter in 1944, second baseman Marvin Williams, and Kansas City Monarch shortstop Jackie Robinson, all top prospects in their mid-twenties. The Fenway Park tryout, however, proved little more than a formality and the players never again heard from the Red Sox.

The publicity surrounding these events, however, forced the major leagues to address the issue at its April meetings. At the urging of black sportswriter Sam Lacy, Leslie O'Connor, Landis's interim successor, established a Major League Committee on Baseball Integration in April 1945, to review the problem. In addition, the racial views of newly appointed Commissioner A. B. "Happy" Chandler came under close scrutiny. A former governor of the segregated state of Kentucky, Chandler nonetheless offered at least verbal support to the entry of blacks into organized ball. "If a black boy can make it on Okinawa and Guadalcanal, hell, he can make it in baseball," Chandler told black reporter Rick Roberts. Whether Chandler, however, unlike Landis, would reinforce his rhetoric with positive actions remained uncertain.

Unbeknownst to the integration advocates, baseball officials, and local politicians sand-dancing around the race issue, Branch Rickey, the president of the Brooklyn Dodgers, had already set in motion the events which would lead to the historic breakthrough.

Raised in rural Ohio in a strict Methodist family, Rickey, nicknamed by sportwriters "The Deacon" and "The Mahatma," had financed his way through college and law school playing and coaching baseball. His skills as a catcher merited two years in the major leagues. In 1913, he abandoned a fledgling law career to manage the St. Louis Browns, and in 1917 he began a 25-year relationship with the St. Louis Cardinals. Rickey served as the field manager of the Cardinals from 1919–1925, after which he became the club's vice-president and business

manager. In the 1920s and 1930s, Rickey perfected the farm system, whereby a major league team controlled young, undeveloped players through a chain of minor league franchises. This innovation allowed the Cardinals to compete equally with richer teams in larger cities, generating pennants for the "Gas House Gang" and allowing the team to profitably sell off surplus talent.

Although Rickey later claimed that his desire to integrate baseball dated from 1904, when an Indiana hotel had denied lodgings to a black player on his college squad, he gave no indication of any interest in the race issue during his years in St. Louis. Perhaps this stemmed from the fact that St. Louis was a Southern city with firmly entrenched segregationist traditions. Throughout Rickey's reign with the Cardinals, blacks sat in Jim Crow sections at Sportsman's Park, a policy which he never openly challenged.

Nonetheless, in 1942, when Rickey left the Cardinals and assumed control of the Brooklyn Dodgers, he informed the Dodger ownership of his intentions to recruit black players in the near future. Rickey never clearly explained the motivations for this dramatic turnaround. At times Rickey cited moral considerations, stating, "I couldn't face my God much longer knowing that His black creatures are held separate and distinct from His white creatures in the game that has given me all I own." On other occasions, he eschewed the role of "crusader," proclaiming, "My selfish objective is to win baseball games. . .The Negroes will make us winners for years to come." Some observers saw financial reasons behind Rickey's actions, citing the lure of the growing black population in Northern cities and the prospects of increased attendance. Certainly, Brooklyn offered a more congenial atmosphere for integration than St. Louis. In all probability, a combination of these factors—geographic, moral, competitive, and financial—coupled with Rickey's desire for a broader role in history, impelled him to seek black players.

From 1942–1945, Rickey, a conservative, cautious, and conspiratorial man, moved slowly, studying the philosophical and sociological ramifications of integration and taking few people into his confidence. During the spring and summer of 1945, under the guise of creating a new black baseball circuit, the United States League, Rickey's scouts combed the nation and the Caribbean for black players. Rickey sought one player who would spearhead the breakthrough and several other potential stars who would follow in his wake. By August 1945, scouting reports and Rickey's own investigations pointed to one man as the ideal candidate for the struggle ahead—Kansas City Monarch shortstop Jackie Robinson.

In Robinson, Rickey had found a rare combination of athletic ability, competitive fire, intelligence, maturity, and poise. Born in Georgia and raised in Pasadena, California, Robinson had won fame at UCLA as the nation's greatest all-around athlete, earning All-America honors in football, establishing broad-jump records, and leading his basketball conference in scoring, all in addition to his baseball exploits. In 1942, he enlisted in the army where he attended officer's candidate school and became a lieutenant. Two years later, while stationed in Texas, Robinson's refusal to move to the back of a bus resulted in a court martial and ultimate acquittal. This incident demonstrated his commitment to the cause of equal rights. After his discharge from the army, Robinson joined the Monarchs and earned a starting spot in the 1945 East-West All-Star Game. Robinson's college education, experience in interracial athletics, and army career complemented his playing talents. But his fiery pride and temper seemed a potential obstacle to his success.

On August 28, 1945, Robinson met with Rickey at the latter's Brooklyn offices. Rickey revealed his bold plan to integrate organized baseball and challenged Robinson to accept the primary role. The Mahatma flamboyantly playacted, assuming the role of racist players, fans and hotel clerks, impressing upon Robinson the need to "turn the other cheek" in the event of racial confrontations. By the end of the session, Robinson had signed a contract to play for the Montreal Royals in the International League, the top farm team in the Brooklyn system. Rickey promised that if Robinson's performance merited it, he would be promoted to the Dodgers.

Rickey intended to announce the Robinson signing along with that of several other black players, but political pressures stemming from the New York City fall elections forced him to abandon his original plans and, on October 23, 1945, to reveal the signing of Robinson alone. The announcement sent shock waves through the baseball establishment and placed Robinson into a spotlight that he would never relinquish. Numerous sports figures, from players to executives to reporters, predicted the ultimate failure of Rickey's "great experiment."

Robinson's first test came at spring training in Florida in 1946. Thrust into the deep South where Jim Crow reigned supreme, Robinson and black pitcher John Wright, whom Rickey had recruited to room with Robinson, found themselves unable to room with their teammates and barred from playing in Jacksonville and other Florida cities. In addition, a shoulder injury hindered Robinson's performance, raising doubts about his abilities.

On April 18, 1946, at Roosevelt Stadium in Jersey City, Robinson became the first black to appear in modern Organized Baseball (excepting Jimmy Claxton, who passed as white in 1916 for the Oakland Oaks of the Pacific Coast League). In the process he staged one of the most remarkable performances under pressure in the history of the game. In Robinson's second at-bat, he hit a three-run home run. He followed this with three singles and two stolen bases, scoring a total of four runs. As the New York Times reported, "This would have been a big day for any man, but under the circumstances, it was a tremendous feat."

In many respects, 1946 proved a nightmare season for Robinson. Fans jeered him in Baltimore, and opposing players tormented him with insults. Pitchers made him a frequent target of brushback pitches and baserunners attempted to spike and maim him at second base. As the season drew to a close, Robinson hovered on the brink of a nervous breakdown. Through it all, however, Robinson remained a dominant force on the field. His .349 batting average and 113 runs-scored led the league and paced the Royals to the International League pennant. His presence inspired new attendance records throughout the circuit. In the Little World Series, which pitted Montreal against the Louisville Colonels of the American Association,

Robinson braved the hostility of Kentucky fans and stroked game-winning hits in the final two games to give the Royals the championship.

Rickey's initiative and Robinson's dramatic success failed to inspire other team owners. In August, major league executives debated a controversial report discussing the "Race Question" which argued that integration would "lessen the value of several major league franchises." No other clubs moved to sign black players. Only four blacks, all in the Brooklyn system, joined Robinson in organized baseball in 1946. At Nashua, New Hampshire, in the New England League, the Dodger farm club fielded catcher Roy Campanella and pitcher Don Newcombe. The Nashua Dodgers won the league championship largely due to Campanella's hitting and Newcombe's hurling. In the small town of Trois Rivières in Quebec, pitchers John Wright and Roy Partlow, both of whom had appeared briefly with Robinson at Montreal, led a third Dodger farm team to the Canadian-American league crown. Nonetheless, at the start of the 1947 season, no additional black players appeared on major or minor league rosters.

Although Robinson's performance at Montreal merited promotion to the Dodgers, Robinson remained a Royal when he reported to spring training in 1947. Rickey hoped that the Brooklyn players themselves, when exposed to Robinson's talents, would request his addition to the team. He switched Robinson to first base, a weak spot on the Dodger squad, to make his case more compelling. Robinson compiled a .519 batting average against the major leaguers, but several Dodger players, instead of demanding his promotion, rebelled. Led by "Dixie" Walker, a group of mostly Southern Dodgers circulated a petition against Robinson. Rickey moved quickly to short-circuit the dissension, threatening to trade any athletes who opposed Robinson. In addition, the refusal of Pete Reiser, "Pee Wee" Reese and other Dodger stars to support the protestors, effectively squelched the petition drive. Finally, on April 10, just five days before the start of the 1947 season, Rickey officially announced that Robinson would join the Dodgers.

Throughout the early months of the 1947 campaign Robinson stoically endured crises and challenges. The Philadelphia Phillies, led by manager Ben Chapman, unleashed a barrage of verbal abuse against Robinson which horrified Dodger players and fans. The Benjamin Franklin Hotel in Philadelphia refused lodgings for Robinson and death threats appeared among his voluminous daily mail. In early May, rumors that the St. Louis Cardinals planned to strike rather than compete against Robinson prompted National League President Ford Frick to warn the players, "If you do this you will be suspended from the league." Opposing pitchers targeted Robinson's body at a record setting pace and an early season 0 for 20 batting drought led many to question his qualifications. "But for the fact that he is the first acknowledged Negro in major league history," observed a Cincinnati sportswriter, "he would have been benched a week ago."

Yet, as the season unfolded, Robinson converted doubters and enemies into admirers. By the end of June, a 21-game hitting streak had raised his batting average to .315 and propelled the Dodgers into first place. Robinson's daring baserunning, typical of Negro League play, evoked images of an "Ebony Ty Cobb." In city after city, record crowds flocked to experience Robinson's charismatic dynamism as five teams set new all-time season attendance marks. While periodic controversies erupted over baserunners who used their spikes "to make a pincushion out of Robinson" at first base, Robinson won the acceptance and respect of teammates and opponents alike. In September, as the Dodgers coasted to the pennant, the *Sporting News* named Robinson the major league Rookie of the Year. To cap his triumphant season, Robinson became the first black player to appear in the World Series.

Robinson's success on the field and at the box office stimulated some movement on the part of other clubs to hire black players. In Cleveland Bill Veeck recruited 23-year-old Larry Doby, who jumped straight from the Negro League Newark Eagles to the Indians in July. Used sparingly, Doby batted a meager .156, casting doubts upon his future. The St. Louis Browns, seeking to boost flagging attendance, signed Willard Brown and Hank Thompson of the Kansas City Monarchs. When the turnstiles failed to respond, the Browns released both Brown and Thompson, although the latter had established himself as a top prospect. In the National League, the Dodgers signed Dan Bankhead to bolster the club's pitching down the stretch. On August 25, Bankhead, the first black pitcher to appear in the major leagues, surrendered eight runs in three innings but also slammed a home run in his initial at bat.

In addition to the five athletes who appeared in the major leagues, a handful of blacks surfaced in the minors. Campanella succeeded Robinson at Montreal, earning accolades as "the best catcher in the business." Newcombe returned to Nashua where he won 19 games. The independent Stamford Bombers of the Colonial League fielded six black players, and two blacks, including future major leaguer Chuck Harmon, played in the Canadian-American League. Veteran Negro League hurler Nate Moreland won 20 games in California's Class C Sunset League. For the most part, however, organized baseball continued to ignore the treasure trove of black talent submerged in the Negro Leagues. A full year would pass before additional major league teams would add black players to their chains.

In 1948, the integration focus shifted from the Dodgers, where Robinson now reigned at second base, to the Cleveland Indians. In spring training, Larry Doby, who had performed so dismally in 1947, unexpectedly won a starting berth in the Cleveland outfield. After an erratic early season stretch in which Doby alternated errors and strikeouts with tape-measure home runs, he batted .301 and became a key performer for the American League champion Indians. In July, Cleveland owner Bill Veeck added the legendary Satchel Paige to the team. Amidst charges that his signing had been a publicity stunt, the 42-year-old Paige won six out of seven decisions, including back-to-back shutouts, and posted a 2.47 earned run average. Standing-room-only crowds greeted him in Washington, Chicago, Boston, and even in Cleveland's mammoth Municipal Stadium. The Indians, after defeating the Boston Red Sox in a pennant playoff, won the World Series in six games with Doby's .318 average leading the club.

In 1947, the Dodgers had integrated and reached the World Series; in 1948, the Indians had duplicated and

surpassed this achievement. Both teams had set all-time attendance records. Remarkably, as the 1948 season drew to a close, no other franchise had followed their lead. In the minor leagues, Roy Campanella became the first black in the American Association, stopping at St. Paul before permanently joining Robinson on the Dodgers. Newcombe and Bankhead each won more than 20 games for Brooklyn affiliates. The Dodgers also added fleet-footed Sam Jethroe to the Montreal roster, where he batted .322. The Indians also began to stockpile black talent, signing future major leaguers Al Smith, Dave Hoskins, and Orestes "Minnie" Minoso to minor league contracts. Several other blacks, including San Diego catcher John Ritchey, who broke the Pacific Coast League color line, played for independent teams.

In the interregnum between the 1948 and 1949 seasons four more teams—the Giants, Yankees, Braves, and Cubs—signed blacks to play in their farm systems, and 1949 would herald the beginning of widespread integration in the minor leagues. Blacks starred in all three Triple A leagues. In the Pacific Coast League, Luke Easter won acclaim as the "greatest natural hitter . . . since Ted Williams," amassing 25 home runs and 92 runs-batted-in in just 80 games before succumbing to a knee injury. Oakland's Artie Wilson led the league in hits, stolen bases, and batting average. In the International League, Jethroe scored 151 runs and stole 89 bases while Montreal teammate Dan Bankhead won 20 games for the second straight year. At Jersey City, Monte Irvin batted .373. The outstanding performer in the American Association was Ray Dandridge. Considered by many the greatest third baseman of all time, the acrobatic Dandridge, now in his late 30s, thrilled Minneapolis fans with his spectacular fielding, batting .364 in the process. Former Negro Leaguers turned in equally stellar performances at lower minor league levels as well.

In the major leagues, the spotlight again returned to Jackie Robinson. For three years, Robinson had honored his pledge to Branch Rickey "to turn the other cheek" and avoid confrontations. With his position in the majors firmly established, Robinson announced, "They better be prepared to be rough this year, because I'm going to be rough on them." The more combative Robinson produced his finest year, batting .342 and earning the Most Valuable Player Award. Complemented by teammates Newcombe and Campanella, Robinson led the Dodgers to another pennant.

By the end of the 1949 season, integration had achieved spectacular success at both the major and minor league level, but most teams moved "with all deliberate speed" in signing black players. The New York Giants joined the interracial ranks in 1949 when they promoted Monte Irvin and Hank Thompson. The following year, the Boston Braves purchased Jethroe from the Dodgers for $100,000 and installed him in the starting lineup. In 1951, the Chicago White Sox acquired Minnie Minoso in a trade with Cleveland, and Bill Veeck, who had acquired the hapless St. Louis Browns, brought back Satchel Paige for another major league stint. Yet, as late as August 1953, out of sixteen major league teams only these six fielded black players. Several teams displayed an interest in signing blacks but bypassed established Negro League stars who might have jumped directly to the majors, concen-

trating instead on younger prospects for the minor leagues. Still others like the Red Sox, Phillies, Cardinals, and Tigers continued to pursue a whites-only policy.

This failure to hire and promote blacks occurred amidst a continuing backdrop of outstanding performances by black players. The first generation of players from the Negro Leagues proved an extraordinary group. Jackie Robinson quickly established himself as one of the dominant stars in the national pastime, compiling a .311 batting average over his 10-year career while thrilling fans with his baserunning and clutch-hitting talents. Sportswriters called him, "the most dangerous man in baseball today." Campanella won accolades as the best catcher in the National League and won the Most Valuable Player Award in 1951, 1953, and 1955. Both Campanella and Robinson later won election to the Baseball Hall of Fame. Pitcher Don Newcombe averaged better than 20 wins a season during his first five full years with the Dodgers. In addition, from 1950-1953 Negro League graduates Sam Jethroe, Willie Mays, Joe Black, and Jim Gilliam each won the National League Rookie of the Year Award.

In the American League, where integration proceeded at a slower pace, several players compiled outstanding records. Larry Doby, while never achieving the superstar status many expected, nonetheless became a steady producer, twice leading the league in home runs and five times driving in more than 100 runs. His Cleveland teammate Luke Easter, who reached the majors in his mid-30s, slugged 86 home runs and drove in 300 runs in his brief three-season career. Satchel Paige, after a two-year stint with the Indians, joined the hapless St. Louis Browns from 1951-1953 and became one of the American League's best relief pitchers. On the Chicago White Sox, Minnie Minoso proved himself a consistent .300 hitter. Despite their relatively small numbers, teams with black players in both major leagues regularly finished high in the standings and only in 1950 did both pennant winners field all-white squads. In addition, the more aggressive stance of National League teams in recruiting black players gave that circuit a clear superiority in World Series and All-Star contests for more than two decades.

By the end of the 1953 season, the benefits of integration had grown apparent to all but the most recalcitrant of major league owners. In September, the Chicago Cubs purchased shortstop Ernie Banks from the Kansas City Monarchs and finally elevated longtime minor league standout Gene Baker. Connie Mack's Philadelphia Athletics ended their Jim Crow era by acquiring pitcher Bob Trice. At the start of the 1954 season, the Washington Senators, St. Louis Cardinals, Pittsburgh Pirates, and Cincinnati Reds all joined the interracial ranks. The sudden integration of six more clubs left only the Yankees, Tigers, Phillies, and Red Sox with all-white personnel. In addition, 1954 marked the debut of young Henry Aaron with the Braves and the return of Willie Mays, who had sparkled for the Giants in 1951, from military service.

The desegregation of organized baseball opened the way not only to blacks in the United States but to those in other parts of the Americas as well. Throughout the 20th century, baseball had imposed a curious double standard on Latin players, accepting those with light complexions but rejecting their darker countrymen. With the color barrier down, major league clubs found a wealth of talent

in the Carribbean. Minnie Minoso, the "Cuban Comet" who integrated the Chicago White Sox, became the first of the great Latin stars. Over a 15-year career, Minoso compiled a .298 batting average. In 1954, slick-fielding Puerto Rican Vic Power launched his career with the Athletics. The following year, Roberto Clemente, the greatest of the Latin stars, debuted with the Pittsburgh Pirates. The proud Puerto Rican won four batting championships and amassed 3,000 hits en route to a .317 lifetime batting average. In the late 1950s, the San Francisco Giants revealed the previously ignored treasure trove that existed in the Dominican Republic. In 1958, Felipe Alou became the first of three Alou brothers to play for the Giants, and in 1960 the Giants unveiled pitcher Juan Marichal, "the Dominican Dandy," who won 243 games en route to the Hall of Fame.

Among the early Latin players were two sons of stars of the Jim Crow age. Perucho Cepeda, who had won renown as "The Bull" in his native Puerto Rico, had refused to play in the segregated Negro leagues. His son Orlando, dubbed "The Baby Bull," went on to star for the Giants and Cardinals. Luis Tiant, Sr., a standout performer in both Cuba and the Negro Leagues, lived to see Luis, Jr. win over 200 major league games and excel in the 1975 World Series.

As the major leagues moved slowly toward complete desegregation, throughout the nation blacks invaded the minor leagues. In the Northern and Western states, these athletes, a combination of youthful prospects and Negro League veterans, were greeted by a storm of insults, beanballs, and discrimination. "I learned more names than I thought we had," states Piper Davis of his treatment by fans in the Pacific Coast League. At least a half-dozen blacks had to be carried off the field on stretchers after being hit by pitches between 1949 and 1951. In city after city, blacks found hotels and restaurants unwilling to serve them. "At the same time when they signed blacks and Latins," argues John Roseboro about his Dodger employers, "they should have made sure they would be welcome." But neither the Dodgers nor other clubs provided any special assistance for their black farmhands. Despite these conditions, blacks compiled remarkable records in league after league. In the early 1950s, blacks overcame adversity and dominated the lists of batting leaders at the Triple A level and in many of the lower circuits as well.

In 1952, blacks began to appear on minor league clubs in the Jim Crow South. The Dallas Eagles of the Texas League, hoping to boost sagging attendance, signed former Homestead Gray pitcher Dave Hoskins to become the "Jackie Robinson of the Texas League." Hoskins took the Lone Star State by storm, attracting record crowds en route to a 22–10 record. The black pitcher posted a 2.12 earned run average and also finished third in the league in batting with a .328 mark. By 1955, every Texas League club except Shreveport fielded black players.

Hoskins' performance inspired other teams throughout the South to scramble for black players. In 1953, 19-year-old Henry Aaron desegregated the South Atlantic League, which included clubs in Florida, Atlanta, and Georgia, while Bill White appeared in the Carolina League. Playing for Jacksonville (a city which seven years earlier had barred Jackie Robinson), Aaron "led the league in everything but hotel accommodations." By

1954, when the United States Supreme Court issued its historic *Brown* v. *Board of Education* decision ordering school desegregation, blacks had appeared in most Southern minor leagues.

The integration of the South, however, did not proceed without incidents. Black players recall these years as "an ordeal" or a "sentence" and described the South as "enemy country" or a "hellhole." In 1953, the Cotton States League barred brothers Jim and Leander Tugerson from competing. The following year, Nat Peeples broke the color line in the Southern Association, but lasted only two weeks. For the remainder of the decade, the league adhered to a whites-only policy, a strategy which contributed to the collapse of the Southern Association in 1961. As resistance to the civil rights movement mounted in the 1950s, black players found themselves in increasingly hostile territory. Even in the pioneering Texas League, teams visiting Shreveport, Louisiana, in 1956 had to leave their black players at home due to stricter segregation laws.

In the face of these obstacles, young black stars like Aaron, Curt Flood, Frank Robinson, Bill White, and Leon Wagner overcame their frustrations "by taking it out on the ball." "What had started as a chance to test my baseball ability in a professional setting," wrote Curt Flood, "had become an obligation to test myself as a man." Throughout the 1950s, blacks appeared regularly among the league leaders of the Texas, South Atlantic, Carolina, and other circuits, advancing both their own careers and the cause of integration.

As these events unfolded in the South, the major leagues completed their long overdue integration process. In 1955, the Yankees, after denying charges of racism for almost a decade, finally promoted Elston Howard to the parent club. Two more years passed before the Phillies integrated, and not until 1958 did a black player don a Tiger uniform. Thus, at the start of the 1959 season, only the Boston Red Sox, who had yet to hire either black scouts or representatives in the Caribbean, retained their Jim Crow heritage. A storm of protest arose when the Red Sox cut black infielder Elijah "Pumpsie" Green just before Opening Day, but on July 21, 1959, 12 years and 107 days after Jackie Robinson's Dodger debut, Green won promotion to the Boston club, completing the cycle of major league integration.

While integration became a reality in organized baseball, the Negro Leagues gradually faded into oblivion. As early as 1947, Negro League attendance, especially in cities close to National League parks, dropped precipitously. "People wanted to go Brooklynites," recalls Monarch pitcher Hilton Smith. "Even if we were playing here in Kansas City, people wanted to go over to St. Louis to see Jackie." Negro League owners hoped to offset declining attendance by selling players to organized baseball, but major league teams paid what Effa Manley called "bargain basement" prices for all-star talent. In 1948, the Manleys' Newark Eagles and New York Black Yankees disbanded. The Homestead Grays severed all league connections and returned to its roots as a barnstorming unit. Without these teams, the Negro National League collapsed. A reorganized 10-team Negro American League, most of whose franchises were located in minor league cities, vowed to go on, but the spread of integration quickly thinned its ranks. By 1951, the league had dwin-

dled to six teams. Two years later, only the Birmingham Black Barons, Memphis Red Sox, Kansas City Monarchs, and Indianapolis Clowns remained.

For several years in the early 1950s, the Negro Leagues remained a breeding ground for young black talent. The New York Giants plucked Willie Mays from the roster of the Birmingham Black Barons, while the Boston Braves discovered Hank Aaron on the Indianapolis Clowns. The Kansas City Monarchs produced more than two dozen major leaguers, including Robinson, Paige, Banks, and Howard. But for most black players, the demise of the Negro Leagues had disastrous effects. "The livelihoods, the careers, the families of 400 Negro ballplayers are in jeopardy," complained Effa Manley in 1948, "because four players were successful in getting into the major leagues." The slow pace of integration left most in a state of limbo set adrift by their former teams, but still unwelcomed in organized baseball. Some players like Buck Leonard and Cool Papa Bell were too old to be considered, while others like Ray Dandridge and Piper Davis found themselves relegated to the minor leagues, where outstanding records failed to win them promotion.

Throughout the 1950s the Negro American League struggled to survive, recruiting teenagers and second-rate talent for the modest four-team loop. In 1963, Kansas City hosted the 30th and last East-West All-Star Game and the following year the famed Monarchs ceased touring the nation. By 1965, the Indianapolis Clowns remained as a last vestige of Jim Crow baseball. Utilizing white as well as black players, the Clowns continued for another decade. "We are all show now," explained their owner. "We clown, clown, clown."

But the legacy of the Negro Leagues remained. Robinson and other early black players introduced new elements of speed and "tricky baseball" into the major leagues, transforming and improving the quality of play. Since 1947, blacks have led the National League in stolen bases in all but two seasons. In the American League, a black or Latin baserunner has topped the league every year since 1951 with only two exceptions. Nor did this injection of speed come at the expense of power. In the 1950s and 1960s, Hank Aaron, Willie Mays, and Frank Robinson reigned as the greatest power hitters in baseball. Thus, by the 1960s, the national pastime more closely resembled the well-balanced offensive structure of the Negro Leagues than the unidimensional power-oriented attack that had typified the all-white majors.

The demise of the Negro Leagues and the decline of segregation in the majors, however, did not end discrimination. Conditions on and off the field, in spring training and in the executive suites, repeatedly reminded the black athletes of their second-class status. In the early 1950s, all-white teams taunted their black opponents with racial insults. Blacks like Jackie and Frank Robinson, Minnie Minoso and Luke Easter repeatedly appeared among the league leaders in being hit by pitches. While black superstars like Willie Mays had little difficulty ascending to the major leagues, players of only slightly above average talent found themselves buried for years in the minors. Many observers charged that teams had imposed quotas on the number of blacks they would field at one time.

In cities like St. Louis, Washington, D. C., and, later, Baltimore, black ballplayers could not stay at hotels with their teammates. In 1954, they achieved a breakthrough of sorts when the luxury Chase Hotel in St. Louis informed Jackie Robinson and other Dodger players that they could room there, but had to refrain from using the dining room or swimming pool or loitering in the lobby. Ten years later, the hotel had removed these restrictions, but still relegated black players, according to Hank Aaron, to rooms "looking out over some old building or some green pastures or a blank wall, so nobody can see us through a window."

Blacks faced even greater discrimination each year in spring training in Florida. While all spring training sites now accepted blacks, segregation statutes and local traditions forced them to live in all-black boarding houses far from the luxury air-conditioned hotels which accommodated white players. "The whole set-up is wrong," protested Jackie Robinson. "There is no reason why we shouldn't be able to live with our teammates." When teams traveled from place to place, blacks could not join their fellow players in restaurants. Instead they had to wait on the bus until someone brought their food out to them. Some teams attempted to reduce the problems faced by blacks. Several clubs moved to Arizona, where conditions were only moderately improved. The Dodgers built a special spring training camp at Vero Beach where players could live together. Most organizations, however, did very little to assist their black employees.

By the time that Jackie Robinson retired in 1956, conditions had barely improved. "After 10 years of traveling in the South," he charged, " I don't think advances have been fast enough. It's my belief that baseball itself hasn't done all it can to remedy the problems faced by . . . players." Over the next decade, a new generation of black players militantly demanded change. Cardinal stars Bill White, Curt Flood, and Bob Gibson protested against conditions in St. Petersburg, while Aaron and other black Braves demanded changes in Bradenton. In many instances, however, significant changes awaited passage of the Civil Rights Act of 1965 barring segregation in public facilities.

By 1960, Robinson, Campanella, Doby, and the cadre of Negro League veterans who had formed the vanguard of baseball integration had retired. In their wake, a second generation of black players, most of whom had never appeared in the Negro Leagues, made most Americans forget that Jim Crow baseball had ever existed, as they shattered longstanding "unbreakable" records. In 1962, black shortstop Maury Wills stole 104 bases, eclipsing Ty Cobb's 47-year-old stolen base mark. Twelve years later, outfielder Lou Brock stole 118 bases en route to breaking Cobb's career stolen-base record as well. In 1966, Frank Robinson, who had won the National League Most Valuable Player Award in 1961, became the first player to win that honor in both leagues when he led the Baltimore Orioles to the American League pennant. By the end of his career, Robinson had slugged 586 home runs; only Babe Ruth among players of the Jim Crow era had hit more. Both Ernie Banks and Willie McCovey also amassed more than 500 home runs during this era. On the pitcher's mound, the indomitable Bob Gibson proved himself one of the greatest strikeout pitchers in the game's history. Upon retirement, Gibson had amassed more strikeouts than anyone except Walter Johnson.

Brock, Frank Robinson, Banks, McCovey, and Gibson all won election to the Hall of Fame in their first year of eligibility.

The greatness of these players notwithstanding, two other black players, Willie Mays and Hank Aaron, both of whom ironically had begun their careers in the Negro Leagues, reigned as the dominant stars of baseball in the 1950s and 1960s. Originally signed by the Birmingham Black Barons of the Negro American League, Mays had joined the New York Giants in midseason 1951, sparking their triumph in the most famous pennant race in history and winning the Rookie of the Year Award. After two years in the military, he returned in 1954 to bat a league-leading .345 and hit 41 home runs. The following year, he pounded 51 homers. A spectacular center fielder, Mays won widespread acclaim as the greatest all-around player in the history of the game. In 1969, he became only the second player in major league history to hit 600 home runs and took aim at Babe Ruth's legendary lifetime total of 714. Over the next four seasons, the aging Mays added 60 more homers before retiring, still well short of Ruth's record.

Unlike Mays, who had begun his career amidst the glare of the New York media, Hank Aaron had spent his career first in Milwaukee and later in Atlanta, far distant from the center of national publicity. Nonetheless, he steadily compiled record- threatening statistics in almost every offensive category. In 1972, at age 38, he surpassed Mays's home run total and set his sights on Ruth. Entering the 1973 season, he needed just 41 home runs to catch the Babe. Performing under tremendous pressure and fan-fare, Aaron stroked 40 homers, leaving him just one shy of the record. He tied Ruth's mark with his first swing of the 1974 season. Three days later, on April 8, 1974, a nation-wide television audience watched Aaron stroke home run number 715. Babe Ruth's "unreachable" record thus fell to a man whose career had started with the Indianapolis Clowns of the Negro Leagues. When Aaron retired in 1976, he boasted 755 home runs and held major league records for games played, at-bats, runs batted in and extra-base hits. He also ranked second to Ty Cobb in hits and runs scored.

By the 1970s, black players had become an accepted part of the baseball scene and regularly ranked among the most well-known symbols of the sport. Reggie Jackson, Willie Stargell, and Joe Morgan had succeeded Aaron, Mays, and the Robinsons as Hall of Fame caliber super-stars. Yet three decades after Jackie Robinson had broken the color barrier, racism and discrimination remained a persistent problem for baseball. Several studies demon-strated that baseball management channeled blacks into positions thought to require less thinking and fewer lead-ership qualities. In 1968, blacks accounted for more than half of the major league outfielders, but only 20 percent of other position players. Black catchers were rare and fewer than one in 10 pitchers were black. By 1986, the disparity had grown greater. American-born blacks comprised 70 percent of all outfield positions but only 7 percent of all pitcher, second basemen, and third basemen positions. There were no American-born black catchers in the major leagues at the start of the 1986 season.

While superior black players had open access to the major leagues, those of average or slightly above average skills often found their paths blocked. "The Negro player may have to be better qualified than a white player to win the same position," argued Aaron Rosenblatt in 1967. "The undistinguished Negro player is less likely to play in the major leagues than the equally undistinguished white player." Rosenblatt demonstrated that black major lea-guers on the whole batted 20 points higher than whites. As batting averages dropped, so did the proportion of blacks. This trend continued into the 1980s. A 1982 study revealed that 70 percent of all black non-pitchers were everyday starters, indicating a substantial bias against blacks who filled utility or pinch-hitting roles. Statistics compiled in 1986 showed a strikingly similar pattern.

The subtle nature of this on-the-field discrimination obscured it from public controversy. The failure of base-ball to provide jobs for blacks in managerial and front office positions, however, became an increasing embar-rassment. In the early years of integration, baseball exec-utives bypassed the substantial pool of experienced Negro Leaguers from consideration for managerial and coaching positions. A handful of blacks, including Sam Bankhead, Nate Moreland, Marvin Williams, and Chet Brewer man-aged independent, predominantly all-black teams in the minor leagues. The first generation of black major lea-guers fared no better. "We bring dollars into club treasur-ies when we play," exclaimed Larry Doby, "but when we stop playing, our dollars stop." No major league organiza-tion hired a black pilot at any level until 1961 when the Pittsburgh Pirates placed Gene Baker at the helm of their Batavia franchise. By the mid-1960s no blacks had man-aged in the majors and only two had held full-time major league coaching positions. The first black umpire did not appear in the majors until 1966, when Emmett Ashford appeared in the American League.

In the final years of his life, Jackie Robinson made repeated pleas for baseball to eliminate these lingering vestiges of Jim Crow. "I'd like to live to see a black manager," he stated before a national television audience at the 1972 World Series. Nine days later he died, his dream unfulfilled. In 1975, the Cleveland Indians hired Frank Robinson to be the first black major league man-ager. This precedent, however, opened few new doors. Robinson lasted two-and-a-half seasons with the Indians, later managed the San Francisco Giants for four years, and in 1988 was made manager of the Baltimore Orioles. Maury Wills and Larry Doby each had brief half-season stints as managers. After four decades of integration, only these three men had received major league managerial opportunities.

A similar situation existed in major league front offices. Only one black man, Bill Lucas of the Atlanta Braves, had served as a general manager. As late as 1982, a survey of 24 clubs (the Yankees and Red Sox refused to provide information) found that of 913 available white-collar baseball jobs, blacks held just 32 positions. Among 568 full-time major league scouts, only 15 were black. While many teams hired former players as announcers, few em-ployed blacks in these roles. Five years later, conditions had not improved. Of the top 879 administrative positions in baseball only 17 were filled by blacks and 15 by His-panics. Four teams in California—the Dodgers, Giants, Athletics, and Angels—accounted for almost two-thirds of the minority hiring. Ten out of 14 American League

teams, and five of 12 National League franchises had no blacks in management positions.

These shortcomings came to haunt baseball in 1987. Commissioner Peter Ueberroth had dedicated the season to the commemoration of the fortieth anniversary of Jackie Robinson's major league debut. As the celebration began, Los Angeles Dodger general manager Al Campanis, who had played with Robinson at Montreal, appeared on ABC-TV's *Nightline*. When asked about the dearth of black managers, Campanis explained that blacks "may not have some of the necessities to be, let's say, a field manager or general manager." Campanis's statement, which surely reflected the thinking of many baseball executives, evoked a storm of protest, and precipitated his resignation. An embarrassed Ueberroth pledged to take action to bring more blacks into leadership positions and hired University of California sociologist Harry Edwards to facilitate the process. Fifty blacks and Latins with past or present connections to baseball created their own Minority Baseball Network to apprise blacks of employment opportunities and to lobby clubs to recruit more minorities for front office jobs.

When the controversy of 1987 had subsided, few franchises had taken significant steps to increase minority hiring. Several clubs added blacks to administrative positions, but none offered field or general manager positions to nonwhite candidates (although Bill White was named National League president). In 1988 Frank Robinson received his third chance to manage in the major leagues,

this time with the Baltimore Orioles. At midseason 1989 Cito Gaston assumed the reins of the Toronto Blue Jays. When the squads managed by Robinson and Gaston had their initial confrontation, it marked, after 40 years of integration, the first time that two teams managed by black men had competed in a major league game. Fittingly, on the final weekend of the season, the Orioles and Blue Jays met face-to-face in a series to decide the championship of the American League Eastern Division. The spectacle offered a resounding rebuke to the shortsightedness and persistent discrimination that continues to plague the national pastime.

The 1992 season finally saw a black manager in a World Series as Toronto's Cito Gaston led his Jays to a world championship. Over in the National League Felipe Alou took over the Expos' reins and performed creditably by bringing his young team to a second place finish. Major League Baseball also took action to improve its image among minorities, announcing its embrace of John Young's RBI ("Reviving Baseball in the Inner Cities") program, an effort to entice black youth away from the hoop and back to the diamond. RBI was already backed by franchises in Cincinnati, Los Angeles, and New York.

Rumors even floated of Democratic Party National Chairman Ron Brown as a replacement for ousted Commissioner Fay Vincent. At season's end two more blacks joined the managerial ranks, Don Baylor as field pilot of the expansion Colorado Rockies and Tony Perez at Cincinnati.

## CHAPTER 20

The Minor Leagues

Bob Hoie

The International Association, founded in 1877, is frequently described as the first minor league. For two major reasons it shouldn't be so regarded. First, it was barely a league. Structurally it resembled the old National Association—there was virtually no central authority, no limitation on the number or location of member teams, no set schedule, and haphazard umpire selection. The league was so loosely assembled in fact that some member teams competed at the same time for the championships of other organizations like the New England Association and the League Alliance. Second, the International Association was originally established as a rival to the National League and never officially recognized itself as being subordinate. It was generally acknowledged that several of its teams were as good as or better than some in the National League. Various off-the-field problems, administrative weaknesses, and a lack of solidarity and resolve on the part of the member clubs assured its subordinate status.

A strong case could be made for the 1879 Northwestern League as the first minor league—it had a preset schedule and had no pretensions of rivaling the National League, but the absence of league-appointed umpires led to frequent forfeits due to charges of biased "hometown" umpiring, and the league folded after only two months.

The Eastern Association was founded in 1881, but this was another loose alliance with no set schedule.

The first recognized minor league was another Northwestern League, this one organized on October 27, 1882. At that time they requested of the National League cooperation and reciprocity in protecting player contracts. This was necessary because independent clubs frequently lost their best players during the course of the season to the National League and later to the American Association clubs. In response to this request, the National League, American Association, and Northwestern League signed a "Tripartite Agreement" in March 1883. This agreement bound the clubs to honor the contracts of players on reserve lists, assured mutual recognition of expulsions and suspensions, established territorial rights, and created an arbitration committee to settle disputes. Minimum salaries were established and pegged at a higher level in the National League and American Association than in the Northwestern League or "any other parties to the agreement," thus by implication assigning a "major" and "minor" status to the leagues.

The Interstate Association was established early in 1883 and was quickly accepted as an "alliance" league by the American Association, becoming a junior partner of the Tripartite Agreement. Both the Northwestern and the Interstate opened their seasons on May 1, 1883. Each had a formal league organization, a schedule that was preset before the season opening, and a complement of umpires appointed and paid for by the league. Both leagues recognized and accepted their status as subordinate to the two "majors." In 1884 the Interstate Association reorganized as the Eastern League and became a fourth member of what now became known as the National Agreement.

In October 1885 a new National Agreement was adopted which made the National League and American Association the principal parties and removed from minor league clubs the protection of the reserve clause. Two years later the reserve clause was reinstated for the minors, but the major-minor league distinction had been formalized. Following the collapse of the American Association in 1892, another National Agreement for the first time established minor league classifications and gave major league clubs the right to draft minor league players at fixed prices.

While these events were taking place, organized baseball expanded dramatically, going from two leagues in 1883 to seventeen by 1890. Baseball was played throughout the country, of course, but organized ball was confined to the northeast quadrant of the United States in 1884; it expanded to the South in 1885, to Colorado and the upper Midwest in 1886, California in 1887, Texas in 1888, and the Pacific Northwest in 1890. So in the year that the American frontier was officially declared closed, organized baseball had extended to all corners of the country.

In 1887 an organization called the Negro Baseball League, fearing player raids by the still moderately integrated minors, sought and received protection under the National Agreement. The league was to play in eight cities that also had major league teams, but it folded in less than two weeks. This was unfortunately characteristic of the era. Many teams and leagues were underfinanced and were ultrasensitive to changes in the national or local economy. In addition, being unable or unwilling to pay the required fees for reserving their players, they lost their better ones at the close of the season—and those teams that even managed to finish the season could usually consider themselves lucky. During the nineteenth century, more than one-third of the leagues that started a season failed to finish it. There was, however, a solid core of support for minor league baseball. Regardless of how many leagues started each season—usually about fifteen but sometimes up to nineteen—ten usually finished; the rest failed. The 1890s were not a period of expansion nor of stability as throughout the decade an average of 40 percent of the leagues that started a season failed to finish it. A depression in 1892–1893 and the Spanish-American War in 1898 were significant factors, but a proliferation of

"fly-by-night" operators played a role as well.

At the close of the 1900 season, the still minor American League withdrew from the National Agreement, announcing through that action its intention not to allow its players to be drafted and not to respect the reserve clause or territorial rights any longer.

In September 1901 the National League announced its intention to abrogate the National Agreement, contending that with the American League invading its cities and raiding its players the National League could not be expected to sit back and abide by restrictions which did not hinder its rival. Essentially this meant that the National, like the American, considered the players on minor league rosters "fair game."

In immediate reaction to this, the presidents of seven minor leagues met in Chicago on September 5, 1901, and in an act of self-protection they organized the National Association of Professional Baseball Leagues. On October 25 representatives of nine minor leagues met in New York and adopted a new "National Agreement." This new agreement established league classifications, roster and salary limits, and a draft system; it recognized reserve lists and created a Board of Arbitration which was given the power to suspend players, clubs, or officials for violations of the agreement. By the beginning of the 1902 season, the National Association included fifteen member leagues.

The American and National Leagues ratified a peace agreement early in 1903, and in late August the presidents of the two major leagues and the National Association drafted a National Agreement which was initially rejected by the minors. After some concessions were made by the majors, such as a prohibition on "farming," the plan was adopted in September. The agreement formalized relations between the majors and minors and established a National Commission to serve as a Board of Arbitration.

These agreements were necessary because the majors and minors were mutually dependent on each other. The majors needed the minors as a reliable source of talent, while the minors, many of whom relied on player sales to stay in business, needed assurances from the majors that they would recognize their property rights in players.

Despite this mutual dependence there was a basic buyer-seller conflict. The majors wanted to acquire players as cheaply as possible, while the minors wanted to sell them for as much as possible. This same conflict existed within the minors as well, with the highest-classification clubs wanting to buy cheaply from the lower minors and sell at high prices to the majors. Thus the National Agreement, the major-minor agreement, and the National Association itself were uneasy alliances of clubs and leagues with competing and often conflicting objectives, and the nearly annual revisions in draft rules and prices and limits on optional player assignments were required to maintain the equilibrium necessary to keep the alliance intact.

The majors favored an unlimited draft—i.e., any player on a minor league roster could be purchased for a fixed rate. As early as 1896, when Minneapolis of the Western League was decimated through what were in effect forced sales, it became clear that some limitations were necessary, so by 1905 only one player could be drafted from a club per year. The draft prices of top-classification minor

leaguers went from $750 to $1,000 in 1905 and then to $2,500 in 1911. While these prices were not particularly low for average prospects in that era, they were well below the value of the best prospects in the minors; thus the draft or the threat of it served as an incentive for minor league clubs at all levels to sell their better players to major or higher-classification minor league clubs at competitive market prices. From the players' standpoint, the draft had the positive effect of allowing them eventually to advance to whatever levels their ability would take them. The lower-classification minor league clubs received lower draft prices for their players but seemed relatively satisfied with the system—after all, this was an era when the contracts of Tris Speaker, Rogers Hornsby, and Ty Cobb were sold to major league clubs for $400, $500, and $700 respectively.

On the other hand, many of the higher-classification minor league clubs had never really been satisfied with the draft. As early as 1908, this dissatisfaction nearly caused the two top minor leagues at that time—the American Association and the Eastern League—to go independent. Several of the top minor league clubs drew more fans annually than some major league clubs and represented substantial investments; their owners were understandably not happy with a system that forced the sale of their top players for below-market prices to the majors; in addition to the challenge to club stability and autonomy caused by the draft, the gap between the market value of the top prospects and the draft price widened throughout the 1910s.

Despite the rumblings of discontent, the establishment of the National Association ushered in a period of minor league expansion to a fairly stable core of thirty leagues. While there were still leagues that failed to finish the season, the failure rate was down to 10–15 percent. For some reason, in 1910 the minors reached a level never to be topped until the post–World War Two boom era—fifty-two leagues started the season and forty-six finished it. For the next five years more leagues folded, but each season generally closed with forty leagues operating. Then, for reasons that ranged from the automobile, movies, the war in Europe, and the Federal League War, the bottom started to drop out. Forty-four leagues started in the 1914 season, and by the end of the 1918 season only one was operating (ten leagues had started that year—one folded and eight suspended operations due to the war).

After the 1918 season, with most of the lower minors driven out of business, the National Association, for the first time dominated by the higher minors, adopted a resolution demanding that the majors relinquish the right of the draft and end the practice of "farming out" players. When the majors as expected rejected these demands, the National Association withdrew from the National Agreement. Pending a new major agreement, the majors and minors reached general agreement on property rights in players and territorial rights, and the National Commission ruled that the major league draft would be suspended. In addition the minors would not accept major league players on option, meaning that any players owned or controlled by major league clubs in excess of the active player roster limit would have to be sold or released to minor league clubs.

A. R. Tierney, president of two minor leagues and a

leader in the fight to end the draft, said, "This means that the minor leagues will be able to build fences for themselves instead of for the major leagues." He predicted expansion of the minors and higher sale prices for the players. He was correct on both counts. With no players on option, the majors needed to buy more players from the minors, some of whom they had been forced to sell but now had to buy back at higher prices, and without the draft the minor league clubs could virtually name their own price. The minors expanded, as the leagues that had been driven out of business during the war now reentered the fold.

The reappearance of the low minors again shifted the balance of power within the minors. The higher minors had never been happy with the one-league, one-vote system in the National Association. Club owners were wary of having their investments affected by the vote of what they perceived as little more than "fly-by-night" operators, and on occasion they tried to change the arrangement. But just as the majors needed the minors, so the high minors needed the low minors. Thus the high minors always stopped short of enacting measures that might drive their underlings out of the Association.

As noted previously, many of the low minors needed the revenues they received from the draft to survive, and although the minor league draft still existed, it had ceased to be a dependable source of revenue as the combination of numerous prewar minor league failures and returning military veterans yielded more than enough talent to fill the higher minors' rosters. In addition, many of the low-minor clubs did not have the resources to scout for and sign enough players to remain competitive on the field and/or at the box office; thus they were dependent on receiving some players on option.

So while most of the higher minor leagues were prospering as never before under the new independence, by 1920 the low minors were ready to withdraw from the National Association if a new agreement with the majors restoring the draft was not adopted. In addition, some of the higher minor league clubs were upset that the "no-farming" rules were being circumvented by "gentleman's agreements" which enabled the major league clubs to "sell" a player to a minor league club and "buy" him back at the end of the season with little or no money actually changing hands.

On January 10, 1921, a new major-minor league agreement was signed which restored the major league draft with a top price of $5,000 but as a compromise gave individual minor leagues the right to be exempt from the draft; in addition major league clubs could option up to eight players for no more than two consecutive years, and a tax on player sales was instituted to help reduce the fake player transfers. Quickly the top three minors—the International League, Pacific Coast League, and the American Association—together with the Western and Three-I Leagues declared their exemption from the draft; this in turn prohibited them from drafting from the lower minors.

The prices the majors paid for top minor league players nearly doubled between 1919 and 1920, but they skyrocketed during the draft-exemption era. In 1921 the Giants paid $75,000 to San Francisco for Jimmy O'Connell; in 1922 the Giants paid $72,000 to Baltimore for Jack Bent-

ley and the White Sox paid $100,000 to San Francisco for Willie Kamm. The majors clearly were not happy with this situation, and in 1922 they offered to raise the draft price to $7,500, but this failed to lure back the draft-exempt leagues. In early 1923 the majors, after considering but eventually rejecting the idea of a maximum purchase price of $25,000 for any minor league player and/or a boycott of draft-exempt leagues, declared that all players sent to the minors either by sale or option would be subject to the draft and increased the number of players who could be optioned to fifteen. Western League clubs immediately began accepting players on option under these conditions.

The prices for ballplayers remained high in 1923. Baltimore of the International League was reportedly offered $100,000 by Brooklyn for Joe Boley and sold Max Bishop to the Philadelphia A's for $50,000. Salt Lake sold Paul Strand to the A's for a reported $70,000, Louisville sold Earle Combs to the Yankees for $50,000, Toronto sold Red Wingo to the Tigers for $50,000 and Rochester sold Maurice Archdeacon to the White Sox for $50,000, but these were isolated cases. Baltimore, aided by five years of draft exemption, had built a powerhouse, but many of the higher-classification minor league clubs had not been nearly as successful and found that they needed to receive players on option to fill holes and remain competitive. Therefore at the close of the 1923 season all exempt leagues but the International agreed to the modified draft which exempted only those players who had come up through the minors. In 1924, after Baltimore sold Lefty Grove for $100,000 to the A's, the International League also fell into line.

The modified draft did nothing to reduce the prices paid for top minor league stars: Louisville sold Wayland Dean to the Giants for $72,000 in 1924, San Francisco sold Paul Waner and Hal Rhyne to Pittsburgh for $100,000 in 1925, and Baltimore continued selling star players to the majors for big prices—Tommy Thomas to the White Sox in 1925, Joe Boley to the A's in 1926, John Ogden to the Browns and George Earnshaw to the A's in 1927. In 1927 Portland (of the PCL) sold Billy Cissel to the White Sox for a package of cash and players worth over $100,000 and Oakland sold Lyn Lary and Jimmy Reese to the Yankees for $100,000. With prices like these, clubs could afford to lose a Lefty O'Doul or Hack Wilson in the modified draft.

The major-minor agreement expired at the end of the 1927 season, with the National Association members deadlocked on the issue of the draft. The majors and minors were also at an impasse, so the modified draft continued and many of the higher minor league clubs continued to prosper, both through player sales and at the gate. The Los Angeles franchise and ballpark were valued at $2 million, and in 1928 the Oakland club was sold for $500,000. But in the lower minors all was not well through the 1920s. There were generally twenty-five or thirty leagues starting each year, and an average of three or four of these would fold during the season. Leagues were operating that never should have been admitted to the National Association—for example, one of the four leagues that not unexpectedly failed in 1924 was the West Arkansas, which included six towns within a 750-square-mile area with a combined population of 16,000.

In 1929 the rift between the high and low minors widened as the low minors, rebuffed in their efforts to nullify the modified draft agreement, now attempted to impose their own draft exemption—essentially exempting from the draft any player with fewer than two seasons of organized baseball.

Early in 1931 the majors and minors finally adopted a new National Agreement, including a provision which eliminated the modified draft and granted to major league clubs greater control of talent through revised option and draft rules. The higher minors had originally objected, but the majors told them to accept the universal draft or they would no longer have any relations with them—in other words, major league teams would not sell or option players to or buy players from the American Association, the International League, or the Pacific Coast League. While such threats had been taken relatively lightly by the minors in the early days of the draft-exempt leagues, they were now taken seriously enough that in less than a month the three recalcitrant leagues capitulated to the majors' terms. In exchange for all this and largely to secure the support of the low minors, the majors agreed to sign only collegian amateurs, leaving all high-schoolers and sandlotters to the minors. Of course, by this time farm systems had developed to the point that most major league clubs could still sign noncollegian amateurs through their farm clubs.

Milwaukee had sold Fred Schulte to the Browns for a reported $100,000 in 1928, but this was the end of an era. There would be no more $100,000 minor leaguers; in fact there would be few if any minor leaguers sold for as much as $50,000 again. It would be more than fifty years before minor league clubs ever sold for as much as $500,000, and at the 1928 National Association Convention, president Mike Sexton wondered when the majors would own enough clubs to control the National Association. The farm system, an old idea now in the process of being perfected by Branch Rickey, had clearly begun to alter the way the minors operated, and despite the efforts of some—most notably Judge Landis—the trend couldn't be reversed.

The Great Depression caused a contraction of the minors in the early 1930s, but even though a near-record low of fourteen leagues opened the 1933 season, none of them folded. The minors then entered an era of unprecedented growth and stability, reaching forty-four leagues in 1940, with only two leagues failing to finish the season between 1933 and 1941. This can be attributed in part to the substantial involvement of the major leagues through outright ownership or regular infusions of money through working agreements, but there were obviously other factors at work. Judge Bramham, on becoming president of the National Association, instituted a number of reforms, many of which were aimed at getting rid of "fly-by-night" or "shoestring" operators. Minor league baseball was better promoted—they had established a public relations department in 1934—and the advent of night baseball was of incalculable value in generating attendance, which reached 20 million in 1940. Interestingly, that year 54 percent of the minor league clubs were not affiliated with any major league clubs compared to just 37 percent that operated independently in 1936.

World War Two caused the minors to drop to just ten leagues in 1944, but in the first postwar year it was up to forty-three, increasing to an all-time high of fifty-nine in 1949, and during that time no leagues folded. (In 1946 the Mexican National League, set up by organized baseball to compete with the outlaw Mexican League, is listed by the National Association as having folded during the season, but actually it only withdrew from the Association and continued to operate independently.)

According to a general consensus, it was the coming of television that caused the minors to begin to disintegrate. Between 1949 and 1963 the number of minor leagues dropped from fifty-nine to eighteen. Attendance decreased even more sharply, going from 42 million to less than 10 million over the same time period.

By 1963, the minors had become nothing more than a training ground for the majors—90 percent of the clubs were major league affiliates, and most of those that weren't were in the largely autonomous Mexican League. While television was commonly cited as the cause of the minors' contraction, some contended it was a natural response to overexpansion. Gerry Hirn, in an April 1954 *Baseball Digest* article, contended that while the number of minor leagues had dropped from fifty-nine to thirty-six, that was still too many and the minors would be stronger and more efficient if only sixteen to twenty leagues operated. Interestingly, in 1954 three leagues failed to finish the season, the most failures in peacetime since 1932; they remain the last United States–based minor leagues that failed to finish a season (the Inter-American League, which had a team in Miami but was largely based in the Caribbean, failed to finish the 1979 season—the only year it operated).

For reasons that aren't entirely clear, minor league baseball exploded in popularity in the 1980s. Attendance, which had remained stuck at 10–11 million through the 1960s and most of the 1970s, took off in the late 1970s, topping 20 million in 1987 for the first time since 1953. Louisville, which dropped out of organized ball after drawing just 116,000 in 1972, topped a million in 1983. Nashville, which dropped out in 1963 after drawing just 54,000 for the season, drew over half a million in 1980. Buffalo, which drew only 78,000 in 1969 and saw its franchise shifted to Winnipeg the following year, came back to set an all-time minor league attendance record with 1.1 million in 1988. The Louisville franchise, which didn't exist in 1981 (what became the Louisville franchise was at that time in Springfield, Illinois, drawing 120,000), sold for more than $4 million in 1987. In 1990 the far less successful Vancouver franchise sold to Japanese interests for $5.5 million. Minor league franchises that could be picked up in the early 1970s by anyone who would pay the outstanding debts were selling for more than a million dollars.

The high prices being paid for franchises may have precipitated the major-minor-league crisis of 1990, reminiscent of the battles earlier in the century. The Professional Baseball Agreement which binds the majors and minors was set to expire at the end of 1990. The majors, who under that agreement provided substantial financial support for the minors, proposed a reduction in those subsidies. The majors believed that the now financially healthy minor league clubs should assume a greater share of operational expenses. In addition, the majors wanted

the Commissioner's office to have greater control over minor league affairs. The minors felt the majors were trying to usurp their autonomy and, to add injury to insult, charge them for the privilege. If there was no agreement, the majors threatened to place their entire farm systems in spring training complexes in Arizona and Florida. Some minor league operators threatened to go independent and even form a third major league.

In the end, however, the majority of minor league clubs capitulated, believing that they could not afford to operate without players supplied by the majors. The majors would still pick up most of the expenses, but the new agreement (a) eliminated the minors' share of big-league TV revenue, (b) required that the minors pay a share of their ticket revenues to the majors, and (c) established minimum standards that must be met by minor league facilities by 1994. It was generally believed that these changes, by reducing minor league clubs' profits, might stabilize or reduce the value of franchises. However, in 1992 the Las Vegas franchise sold for a record $7 million and some unsuccessful Class A franchises were sold for well over a million dollars each. And the fans kept coming—in 1992 minor league attendance topped 27 million for the first time since 1951, and Buffalo went over 1 million in attendance for the fifth consecutive year.

The positive trend of the past fifteen years is not unprecedented, but the minors have been riding a rollercoaster of success and failure over the past century—the Newark franchise which sold for a reported $600,000 during the depths of the Depression didn't even exist twenty years later. Even today the picture is not all positive: between 1987 and 1992 more than two dozen franchises were shifted, usually due to poor attendance; more than one quarter of the clubs still draw less than a thousand a game; and it is generally believed that many clubs substantially pad their attendance totals. So the current wave of success is somewhat deceptive and history tells us it won't last forever. However, regardless of fluctuations in popularity and economic viability, the minors have been and one can safely assume will continue to be the primary training ground for major league players.

The Players

Great players have passed through the minors, their careers frequently going in opposite directions and occasionally teaming up or crossing in unlikely locations such as Easton, Maryland, where in 1924 Jimmie Foxx broke into organized baseball as a catcher and the player-manager was Home Run Baker in his last season as an active player. There were many others: Rube Waddell and Red Faber with Minneapolis in 1911, young Waite Hoyt and ancient Jesse Burkett with Hartford in 1916, Dazzy Vance and Roger Bresnahan with Toledo in 1917, Chief Bender and Lefty Grove with Baltimore in 1923, and more recently Enos Slaughter and Billy Williams with Houston in 1960.

Former Negro Leaguers, their careers going in opposite directions, Ray Dandridge and Willie Mays were teammates at Minneapolis in 1951 where another teammate was a seven-year minor league veteran, Hoyt Wilhelm. Wilhelm, a twenty-eight-year-old knuckleballer with a background that included three years in Class D ball and

three more in the military service, at that time appeared to be a member of what in that era was a vast army of career minor leaguers, the best of whom held their own with the acknowledged major league greats passing through the minors, but who for a variety of reasons—some good, some not—would themselves spend the bulk of their careers in the minors.

For some of these players who were left behind, the DH rule came fifty years too late, because while they could hit both for average and power, they generally lacked speed or had defensive shortcomings. For others it is less clear what, if any, deficiencies kept them in the minors, but from these groups a few players emerged as true minor league greats whose impact on fans in minor league cities—Buzz Arlett in Oakland, Joe Hauser in Minneapolis, and Bunny Brief in Kansas City, to name a few—was as great as that of more renowned players in major league cities.

The greatest of the minor league players is generally acknowledged to be Buzz Arlett.

Arlett started his career as a right-handed spitball pitcher with the hometown Oakland Oaks in 1918 and went on to win 108 games, twice going over 25 wins in a season. The Detroit Tigers looked at him, but without the spitball, which he wouldn't be able to use in the majors, they did not consider him a prospect. After suffering arm trouble early in 1923, Buzz switched to the outfield. Although he had been nothing more than a fair-hitting pitcher, once becoming a regular he annually averaged nearly .360 with 30 homers and 140 RBIs through the rest of the 1920s, but early in his career as an outfielder a Cardinal scout labeled him "good hit, no field," and it stuck. Finally in 1931 he was purchased by the Phillies. The thirty-two-year-old switch-hitter batted .313 with 18 homers and 73 RBIs in a season when the National League introduced a "dead ball" in reaction to the hitting orgies of 1929–1930. However, at the end of the year Arlett was sent to Baltimore, where in 1932 he hit 4 homers in a game twice within a five-week period and led the league with 54 homers for the season, but he would never return to the majors. He spent another year with Baltimore, when he again won the home run title, a little over a month with Birmingham, and nearly three years with Minneapolis, where he had another home run championship. After a few games with Syracuse in 1937, Arlett's career was over.

In addition to his 108 wins, he hit 432 homers, a minor league record that held up until Hector Espino topped it in 1977. Arlett walked a lot, didn't strike out much, ran pretty well early in his career, had a .341 lifetime batting average—.350 after he became an outfielder—and was the only player to finish in the top five in home runs and slugging percentage in his only season in the majors. In addition, modern statistical analysis, including range factors, suggests he was nowhere near the defensive liability he was portrayed as being. He was big (6-4, 230) and gave the appearance of being lackadaisical, which apparently irritated some of his managers, but the evidence is strong that Arlett, despite nearly two decades spent in the minors, was a major-league-caliber player.

Ike Boone was another player whose hitting feats were not limited to the minors. Boone was a college teammate (at the University of Alabama) of Joe Sewell and Riggs

Stephenson; his lifetime major league batting average was .319, and in his only two full seasons in the majors—1924-1925 with the Boston Red Sox—he hit .333 and .330, but due to alleged defensive deficiencies most of his career was spent in the minors. In 1929 with the Missions of San Francisco, Boone probably had the finest season any player has had in the minors. On the all-time minor league list of single-season accomplishments, his 553 total bases that year are first, his 323 hits are second, his 195 runs scored are tied for third, and his 218 RBIs are fourth. On the all-time Pacific Coast League list, his .407 average is second, and his 55 home runs are tied for fourth.

Boone's greatness wasn't confined to a single season; in four of his first eight years in the minors he hit over .400 (he was on his way to perhaps his greatest season in 1930, batting .448 with 22 homers and 96 RBIs when he was sold to Brooklyn in late June). His .402 average with San Antonio in 1923 is the highest in twentieth-century Texas League history; his .389 with New Orleans in 1921 is the fifth highest in the Southern Association; he also led the International League in batting twice. His .370 lifetime average is the minor league record for players with ten or more seasons. He had an exceptional arm, but limited range in the outfield. Although he hit 77 home runs in a season and a half with the Missions, he was not generally regarded as a power hitter. He was, however, a great pure hitter; in eleven of his fourteen seasons in the minors, he hit over .350, and there is no evidence that he couldn't hit major league pitching.

Smead Jolley was an atrocious outfielder. Stories of his defensive lapses are legion, and the statistical evidence suggests those stories are more than isolated anecdotes. Like Boone, Jolley had a powerful arm but no speed; like Arlett, he was big and awkward; and like both, he could hit—majors or minors. In the equivalent of three full major league seasons with the White Sox and Red Sox, he hit .305 and averaged 15 homers and 105 RBIs. He won six minor league batting championships—leading the Pacific Coast League in hitting three times (winning the Triple Crown with San Francisco in 1928) and the International League once. Twice he had over 300 hits in a season, and twice he drove in more than 180 runs. In the thirteen minor league seasons in which he played over 100 games, he had this run: .370, .372, .346, .397, .404, .387, .360, .372, .373, .350, .309, .373, .345. Perhaps because he spent nearly six years in the low minors, the first four as a pitcher, and had a somewhat nomadic career (he was with thirteen minor league teams), he has not always been ranked in the top echelon of minor league greats, yet he may have been the finest hitter of them all.

Minor league stars generally fit two stereotypes: one-dimensional players who could hit but could do nothing else well enough to stay in the majors—justly or not, Arlett, Boone, and Jolley were consigned to this group. Then there are those who excelled in the minors but couldn't produce in the majors. Perhaps the classic example is Bunny Brief.

Brief, born Antonio Bordetski, may have been the most dominant power hitter in the minor leagues. In major league trials with the Browns, White Sox, and Pirates between 1912 and 1917, he was consistently unimpressive—in a combined 569 at-bats, he hit .223 with 5 homers, 59 RBIs, and nearly 100 strikeouts. In the minors,

however, it was a different story. Although he hit 40 or more homers only twice and never had more than 42, he had eight league home run championships. Before going up to the majors, he led the Michigan State League twice; later he led the Pacific Coast League once and the American Association five times. He also led the Association in RBIs five times (four in succession), including a league-record 191 in 1921. He had a six-year stretch (1921–1926) with Kansas City and Milwaukee, where he averaged 90 extra-base hits, 151 RBIs, and a .351 average per season. Brief also drew a lot of walks. Early in his career he had excellent speed, and although he played most of his career at first base, he was the best defensive outfielder of the big minor league sluggers, with good range and an excellent arm—yet for reasons that remain unclear, Brief never played in a major league game after his twenty-fifth birthday.

Nick Cullop was another minor league great who never produced in the majors. He, like many of the great minor league sluggers, began his career as a pitcher. In trials with the Yankees, Senators, Indians, Dodgers, and Reds between 1926 and 1931 he totaled 490 at-bats, hit 11 homers, drove in 67 runs, hit .249, and struck out 128 times. He was the first farm-system minor league star, playing 1,450 games in the Cardinal chain from 1932 to 1944. In the minors, he drove in 1,857 runs, the all-time career high, ten times exceeding 100 in a season. He hit 420 home runs, third on the all-time list.

Cullop had good speed early in his career and was a good enough outfielder to play center field into the late 1920s, but he slowed up considerably in the 1930s. While it is not clear why Brief never did well in the majors, Cullop struck out a lot even in the minors and didn't walk much—suggesting that he had holes which could be and were pitched to effectively in the majors.

Ox Eckhardt was a great football star at the University of Texas who after graduation signed with both Austin of the Texas Association and the Cleveland Indians. The resulting dispute delayed his real professional debut for three years until he was twenty-six years old. Ox quickly made up for lost time, hitting .376 with a league leading 27 triples for Wichita and Amarillo in the Western League in 1928. That fall he played for the New York Giants of the NFL. His baseball contract had been acquired by the Detroit Tigers and although he was on their spring roster in 1929, 1930, and 1931 he never got into a game with the big club. In 1929 he was sent to Seattle, where he hit .354 and again led the league in triples. In 1930 he went to Beaumont, where he led the Texas League with a .379 average. In 1931 he was sold to the Missions, for whom he led the PCL with a .369 average. In the spring of 1932 he was with the Boston Braves—he played 8 games at the start of the season as a pinch hitter and was then sent back to the Missions, where over the next four seasons he hit .371, .414, .378, and .399, winning the batting title three times. He went to the Dodgers in 1936, lasted 16 games batting just .182, and was sent to Indianapolis, where he hit .353 and .341 over the next two years. He hit .321 with Toledo and Beaumont in 1938, .361 with Memphis in 1939, and after hitting .293 with Dallas in 1940, he retired with a minor league career batting average of .367 and the highest career average in organized baseball—.365. (Ty Cobb's minor league re-

cord drops his overall average to .3630; Ike Boone's major league record drops his organized-baseball average to .3629.) Eckhardt has the highest single-season and career batting average in the PCL, and ten times he hit over .350.

Unlike many of the minor league stars, Eckhardt did not want for opportunities to play in the majors—counting a trial with the Indians in 1925, he had six shots, but they resulted in his playing in just 24 major league games. The reasons for his failure to make it in the majors are not obscure. Despite being an exceptional athlete with good speed early in his career, he was a poor fielder with a weak arm and no power. Although he was 6-1, 190, the left-handed-hitting Eckhardt sliced or punched almost every hit down the left field line. Reportedly managers tried to get him to pull the ball—an idea that should certainly have advanced his career in Detroit or Brooklyn—but it only served to foul up his swing, which he would rediscover after being returned to the minors.

A few minor league greats don't fit the stereotypes: Jigger Statz was the opposite of most—his strengths were speed and defense. Joe Hauser appeared to be on his way to a successful career in the majors, broke his leg, never regained his past form, and went to the minors, where he became the only player to have two 60-home-run seasons. Hector Espino spent virtually his entire career in Mexico, and while major league scouts believed he could hit in the majors, he apparently had no desire to leave his homeland.

Of the great minor league stars, Statz spent the most time in the majors—683 games—and the most time with one club: all of his eighteen minor league seasons were with Los Angeles. His 3,473 games in organized baseball were a record until broken by Pete Rose in 1983.

Statz was a great fielder; virtually all of his contemporaries considered him the best or one of the best they had seen. Playing very shallow, he reminded many of Tris Speaker. The statistics offer strong support for his claim to greatness. In four full seasons in the majors, he led the league in chances-per-game once and was second the other three years. Between 1922 and 1932 in the majors and minors he had a stretch of ten seasons in which he played in at least 100 games and never finished lower than second in chances-per-game. He had excellent speed, but during most of his career with the Angels they were a hard-hitting club that did not feature the running game, but that changed in the mid-1930s, and in the three seasons following his thirty-sixth birthday he stole 157 bases. His game was not just limited to speed and defense. A classic leadoff man of his era—a good contact hitter, small and fast—he hit .285 in the majors and .315 in the minors, collecting over 2,300 runs, 4,000 hits, 700 doubles, and 500 stolen bases in his organized-baseball career.

On April 7, 1925, the day of Babe Ruth's "big belly-ache," Joe Hauser a twenty-six-year-old first baseman beginning his fourth season with the Athletics, broke his leg in a non-contact play while fielding during a preseason game against the Phillies at Baker Bowl. He had a .304 average for his first three major league seasons and had hit 27 homers with 115 RBIs in 1924. The injury kept him out for the entire 1925 season. In 1926 he tried to come back but hit only .192. After an excellent season with Kansas City, he went back to the majors but didn't do much in stints with the Philadelphia A's and Indians. He went back to the minors and had 4½ remarkable seasons. In 1930 with Baltimore he set a professional record with 63 homers; then he dropped to 31 in 1931 but still led the league. In 1932 he went to Minneapolis, where he led the American Association in homers with 49. In 1933 he broke his own home run record with 69, and he was off to a great start in 1934—33 homers, 88 RBIs in 82 games—when he broke his kneecap, knocking him out for the season. He continued to play until 1942 but never came close to achieving the success he had in the early 1930s.

Hauser did not hit for a high average, and it has been suggested that he took enormous advantage of short right field fences in Baltimore and Minneapolis—no one would argue that point, since 50 of his 69 homers in 1933 came at home—but many greats played in Oriole and Nicollet Parks, and none came close to Hauser's two record-breaking seasons, which remain the two highest home run seasons in the high minors.

Hector Espino holds the minor league career home run record with 484, and all but 3 of those were hit in Mexico. At the end of the 1964 Mexican League season, the twenty-five-year-old first baseman, who had led the league with 46 homers and a .371 batting average, was sold by Monterrey to the St. Louis Cardinals' Jacksonville farm club. He hit .300 with those 3 homers in 100 at-bats and was invited to spring training by the Cards for 1965, but he never reported and was eventually returned to Monterrey. In the late 1960s, the California Angels coveted Espino, who had led the Mexican League in hitting in 1966–1968, but they were never able to consummate a deal. Espino was a legend in Mexico, but it has never been clear why he never tried the majors—he has given conflicting answers. Possibly he enjoyed being a big fish in a small pond—it wasn't the money, since he never made more than $18,000 a year in Mexico. He was notorious for marching to his own drummer, occasionally leaving clubs for a midseason vacation, and perhaps he was unwilling to sacrifice that independence.

Espino could hit for power and average—he led the Mexican League in batting five times and home runs four times—and scouts said he could have done the same in the majors, but like many players he played too long. His power started a sharp decline after his thirty-third birthday, and he was virtually helpless at the plate during his last two or three seasons. Nevertheless he ranks as perhaps the greatest minor league player who never played in the majors.

Great players do not have to be distributed evenly among all positions or across all eras, but the emphasis being on great hitters, the result is a number of outfielder-first baseman-designated hitter types, most of whom played in the high-scoring 1920s and 1930s.

Ray French was perhaps the best middle infielder in the minors. He spent twenty-eight years in the minors, most of it in the Pacific Coast League. He played 2,736 games at shortstop and was a brilliant fielder. In the fourteen seasons that he played more than 100 games at short, he led the league in chances-per-game seven times. He was not an outstanding hitter, but his fielding kept him around long enough for him to collect 3,254 hits—seventh on the all-time minor league list.

The two best nineteenth-century minor leaguers were first baseman Perry Werden and pitcher Willie Mains. Werden had good speed and power. He had several good years in the majors (twice leading the league in triples), won six minor league home run titles, including two seasons when he went over 40, and his .341 lifetime average was exceptionally high for that era.

Mains was the first minor league pitcher to win 300 games, reaching that figure early in 1905. A seven-time twenty-game winner, he was also an excellent hitter in an era when pitchers were frequently expected to take a shift in the outfield. Most of his career was in the New York State League, but in an interesting example of the mobility of players in the game's early years, in 1892–1893 Mains had back-to-back seasons in Portland, Oregon, and Portland, Maine.

A highly productive but not great player who deserves mention is Spencer Harris, a little lefthanded-hitting outfielder who holds the minor league career records for runs, hits, doubles, total bases, and walks. He reached those levels primarily because he kept playing until he was forty-eight years old. He did lead the American Association in homers in 1928 while at Minneapolis, but he was aided enormously by the friendly right field fence at Nicollet Park. (He averaged 17 homers a year in ten seasons with Minneapolis but only 6 a year in his sixteen other minor league seasons.) He was never thought of as the top player on his many minor league clubs—just as a good solid player of the type that formed the backbone of the minors for so many years.

There have been few minor league pitching stars of the magnitude of the great hitters. Perhaps this is because pitching is a one-dimensional skill—no pitchers were kept in the minors because they couldn't hit or field. Many of the outstanding minor league pitchers stayed there because they didn't have great stuff. Bill Thomas, who won 383 games, and Hal Turpin, who won 271 without ever getting shots at the majors, had the same statistical profile—they struck out few, walked even less, and allowed a lot of hits.

Two pitchers that didn't fit that profile, however, were Joe Martina and Dick Barrett. Martina was a power pitcher who spent most of his career with Beaumont and with his hometown New Orleans Pelicans. He held the minor league career strikeout record until ageless George Brunet broke it while toiling in the Mexican League in 1981. Martina was a workhorse, pitching over 250 innings thirteen times and was a seven-time twenty-game winner. He got his first and only big league opportunity at age thirty-five with the world champion Washington Senators in 1924.

Kewpie Dick Barrett didn't really find himself until he joined Seattle of the PCL in 1935, ten years into his professional career. A little lefthander with less than pinpoint control (he holds the minor league record for career bases on balls), he had good stuff and eight 20-win seasons.

Frank Shellenback is most frequently named as the greatest minor league pitcher. The Pacific Coast League career leader in wins with 295, Shellenback won 10 games with the White Sox as a nineteen-year-old rookie spitballer in 1918. After a poor start the following season, he was sent to Minneapolis. In February 1920 the baseball rules committee outlawed the spitball and other trick pitches. Each major league team was allowed to designate two spitball pitchers who would be able to continue using the pitch in the majors. Unfortunately for Shellenbeck, he was on the Vernon roster by this time and at age twenty-one would be consigned forever to pitching in the minors if he couldn't get by without the spitball. Throughout much of his career, articles would be written that usually declared that Shellenback would be a major league star if he was eligible to play there. He did have a great six-year stretch with Hollywood (1928–1933) when he went 142–59. He was a very popular player with the Stars as well as Vernon and a fine hitter with good power, but a review of his record suggests he was never as good as everyone thought he was—he led the PCL in wins twice but never led in another category. He had only five 20-win seasons.

Because of the spitball ban, Shellenback was viewed as a tragic figure, but he wasn't alone. Spitballer Paul Wachtel won 203 games in the Texas League after the ban, including five 20-win seasons. Rube Robinson won 148 games in the Southern Association, including two league-leading 26-win seasons. Wheeler Fuller, who never pitched in the majors, won 156 in the Eastern League after the ban.

Perhaps the greatest minor league pitcher was Tony Freitas, a little lefthander who spent all or part of fifteen seasons with Sacramento. He had great control, could get the strikeout, and had nine 20-win seasons (plus two 19-win seasons). If he hadn't lost three years to the military, he probably would have won 400 games in the minors. Freitas had an impressive major league debut, going 12–5 in less than a full season with the 1932 Philadelphia A's, but that was the last success he would have in the majors.

Four other pitchers worthy of mention are Sam Gibson, George Boehler, Bill Bailey, and George Brunet.

Gibson was an underappreciated pitcher who spent most of his career in the PCL—twelve years with San Francisco. He didn't make his organized-baseball debut until he was twenty-three years old. After two promising seasons with Detroit, he never had much success in the majors, but he was extremely effective in the minors. He had six 20-win seasons (plus three 19-win seasons) and, pitching in a high-scoring era, he had eight seasons where his ERA was below 3.00.

Boehler was a hard-throwing workhorse who spent most of his career in the Western League. Twice he pitched over 400 innings, six times over 300. Unfortunately he was terribly inconsistent: with Tulsa in 1921–1923 his seasonal win totals were 4–38–7. He was consistently ineffective in a number of major league trials.

Bailey had seven league-leading strikeout seasons in four different leagues (International, Texas, Southern, Western) but only three 20-win seasons. After a promising September debut with the Browns in 1907, he pitched over 200 games in the majors with five teams spread over fifteen years with no success.

Brunet pitched in organized ball for thirty-three years (1953-1985), and astonishingly he was a regular-rotation pitcher for all but the last year. When he was forty-eight years old, he had a 1.94 ERA pitching regularly in the Mexican League. He never won more than 17 games in a season, had only two 200-strikeout seasons (they were

twenty-one years apart), but he had a credible major league career and holds the minor league career strikeout record.

The Teams

There have been a number of debates about the greatest minor league teams. The 1937 Newark Bears, the 1934 Los Angeles Angels, the 1920-1925 Ft. Worth Panthers, and the 1919-1925 Baltimore Orioles usually draw the most support. All were dominant teams with good players.

The Bears included Charlie Keller, Joe Gordon, George McQuinn, Atley Donald, and five other players who would go to the majors the following year. They won the International League pennant by 25½ games with a 109–41 record. The Angels included Frank Demaree, Jigger Statz, Gene Lillard, and Fay Thomas, and they compiled an astounding 137–50 record. The Panthers (or Cats) won six straight pennants and five Dixie Series. They were led by the home run hitting of Big Boy Kraft and a fine pitching staff that included spitballer Paul Wachtel and Joe Pate.

It is doubtful that any of the three could have competed successfully in the majors. It is occasionally claimed that the 1937 Newark Bears were the Yankee B team and could have finished second in the American League, or at least in the first division. But that ignores the talent that was in the majors. The Red Sox finished fifth in 1937 with a club that included Jimmie Foxx, Joe Cronin, Lefty Grove, Pinky Higgins, Doc Cramer, Ben Chapman, Jack Wilson, and Bobo Newsom, all of whom, it is safe to say, would have started for the Bears. The same is true of the Angels, whose pitching staff chose 1934 to have career years, and of the Cats, who played well as a team but had few players that were even considered minor league standouts.

The Orioles were a different story. Thanks to the draft exemption, Jack Dunn was able to assemble a powerhouse comprised of players ready and capable of playing in the majors. The 1922 team was probably the best minor league club ever assembled. It had Jack Bentley, Max Bishop, Fritz Maisel, and Joe Boley in the infield, and Otis Lawry, Merwyn Jacobson, and Jimmy Walsh in the outfield. The catcher was Lena Styles, and the pitchers were Lefty Grove, John Ogden, Tommy Thomas, Rube Parnham, and Harry Frank with Bentley occasionally seeing action in that capacity.

Grove, Ogden, and Thomas combined for 60 wins and six years later would win a combined 56 games in the majors. Parnham, a free spirit who pitched when he wanted, was around long enough to win 16 (the following year he won 33). Frank won 22, but his career would soon be cut short by illness. Bentley hit .350 and won 13 games; he went to the Giants in 1923 as a pitcher but hit .427. Bishop and Boley, who hit .261 and .343 respectively, went on to become the double-play combo with the 1929-1930 world champion Philadelphia A's. Styles was just twenty-two years old and hit .315, but that was his peak. Maisel (.306), Walsh (.327), Jacobson (.304), and Lawry (.333) had all played briefly and/or ineffectively in the majors but would all go on to have great careers in the International League. A twenty-year-old rookie utility player on the team was Dick Porter, who hit .279 and

would have seven excellent seasons with the Orioles before going on to have several good years with the Indians.

As good as the Orioles were and as good as some of their players became, it is doubtful that even they could have finished in the first division of the American or National Leagues in 1922. Yet the strongest evidence of the attraction of minor league baseball and the hold it has long held on fans who were exposed to it is that those great Oriole, Bear, and Angel teams are far better known and more fondly remembered than hundreds of more talented second-division and higher major league clubs.

The Farm System

Farm teams are nearly as old as organized baseball. In 1884 the Boston Beaneaters of the National League owned a team called the Boston Reserves in the Massachusetts State Association. The Reserves, also called the Colts, were apparently intended to serve as a source of replacements for disabled members of the major league club. It has also been suggested that the farm team was a device to keep more players under contract and out of the hands of the Union Association that year. Whatever the origins of the idea, during the next decade a number of major league clubs operated such reserve teams, but they usually competed in local semipro leagues rather than in organized baseball and were viewed more as quick sources of replacements rather than as training grounds for players.

With John B. Day's joint ownership of the New York Gothams of the National League and the New York Metropolitans of the American Association as early as 1883 and with the proliferation of interlocking ownerships of major league clubs in the 1890s, it was only natural that some major and minor league clubs would come under joint ownership as well. The first instance of any significance, however, occurred when John T. Brush, owner of Cincinnati in the National League, entered the Indianapolis club in the newly formed Western League in 1894. While this was not the first case of joint major-minor league club ownership, Brush appears to have been the first to grasp the potential of such an arrangement. Indianapolis served as a place to develop talent that was not quite ready for the majors. The team gave Cincinnati an expanded roster as players were frequently shuffled to and from Indianapolis during the season; it also served as a source of profit because Indianapolis drew well at the gate, having become the dominant club in the Western League, with three pennants and two second-place finishes in five seasons (1895–1899). Indianapolis's success was aided in no small part by Brush's practice of drafting players from other Western League clubs and sending them to Indianapolis, thus simultaneously weakening the opposition and strenghtening the Hoosiers. Efforts were made by the other Western League club owners to control "farming" or to modify the draft rules to stop Brush, but none were successful.

Perhaps copying Brush's strategy, in 1896 several National League clubs obtained minor league affiliates: Pittsburgh had Toronto, Boston had Wilkes-Barre, and Cleveland had Ft. Wayne. Philadelphia had a Philadelphia farm club in the Pennsylvania State League, and

when that league folded, they shifted the junior club to the Atlantic Association. The New York Giants had the first farm "system," with the New York Mets in the Atlantic Association and Syracuse in the Eastern League.

When the National Agreement was adopted in 1903, it banned the "farming out" of players, but "farming" as defined in the agreement referred only to those efforts by major league clubs to exceed the limits on players who could be optioned through subterfuge—"fake transfers" such as loans or sell/buy-back arrangements with minor league clubs where title to a player was never actually surrendered.

The independent minor league operators saw farming as a curse for two reasons. First, it reduced their autonomy and potential revenue by placing more players under major league ownership, thus reducing the majors' need to buy or draft players from the minors. Second, clubs accepting players from the majors, either openly through options or secretly, might gain an unfair competitive advantage on the field. So while in 1905 the New York Giants' request to establish a working agreement with Bridgeport was validated by the National Commission, most of the legislation was focused on restricting farming, normally by limiting the number of players who could be optioned and the number of times each player could be optioned. For example, in 1904 a rule was adopted which required a player sent out on option to stay with the minor league club for the remainder of that season. In 1907 the rule was relaxed so that a major league club could option a player and recall him, but only once in a season. In 1911 a team could have no more than eight players out on option at one time.

Working agreements became quite common during this period. The major league club furnished the minor league club with its surplus players—youngsters in need of more experience or veterans past their prime who could still strengthen a minor league club—and/or cash. In return the major league club could obtain promising players from the minor league club. During this era the formal working agreement between major and minor league clubs was usually of short duration—a year or two at most—suggesting that major league clubs targeted certain minor league clubs that had two or three players they might be interested in and established a working agreement in order to get first claim on those that developed satisfactorily. There were also informal working agreements, generally based on friendships between major and minor league club operators, and it was usually through such arrangements that the "fake transfers" banned by the National Agreement took place. In the early 1900s, for example, there was substantial traffic in players between the White Sox and Milwaukee of the American Association and between the Dodgers and Baltimore in the Eastern League. (Brewer manager Joe Cantillon was a long-time friend of Charles Comiskey, and Brooklyn manager Ned Hanlon was also a minority owner of the Orioles.)

The most efficient and only legal method of circumventing the rules relating to major league control of players was through joint ownership of major and minor league clubs. By 1912 Charles W. Somers owned Cleveland and Toledo, and Charles Ebbets owned both Brooklyn and Newark. This enabled the Indians to hold title to

sixty players and the Dodgers to sixty-one. In 1913 a National Commission confidential bulletin directed major league clubs to divest their interest in minor league clubs by January 1, 1914, but neither Somers nor Ebbets complied until several years later (in fact, Somers secretly acquired New Orleans in 1913). In 1921 the joint ownership of major and minor league clubs was again permitted, and the New National Agreement, although retaining option limits, dropped the antifarming provisions that had been in it since 1903.

In 1921 the Cardinals, who had already acquired an interest in Ft. Smith of the Western Association and Houston of the Texas League, acquired a half interest in Syracuse of the International League. This was the beginning of Branch Rickey's farm system, but initially it attracted little attention as it didn't appear to represent anything particularly new. Major league clubs had long been signing young talent directly off the sandlots and developing it in the minors. In 1910, for example, Cleveland signed Roger Peckinpaugh out of the Cleveland City League, gave him a brief trial, and then optioned him to New Haven and Portland in successive seasons before recalling him when he was deemed ready for the majors. This practice had developed to the point that Mike Sexton, president of the National Association, in 1921 spoke out against the fact that the majors and higher minors had preempted the low minors' traditional role of discovering and signing young talent.

As we have seen, major league clubs had occasionally owned minor league clubs, primarily to expand the number of players under their control, but these were always higher-classification clubs, where talent was refined rather than developed. Rickey's approach was original because he was the first to assemble a system of teams at various levels or classifications. This enabled him to sign young talent and, through a hierarchy of minor league clubs, to develop and retain continuous title to a large number of players, his theory being that out of quantity comes quality. It didn't take long for the system to begin producing talent—the Cards, who had never finished higher than third in this century, won the World Series in 1926 with a team that included future Hall of Famers Jim Bottomley and Chick Hafey as well as regulars Taylor Douthit, Tommy Thevenow, Les Bell, Ray Blades, Flint Rhem, and Art Reinhardt plus reserves Watty Holm, Jake Flowers, Spec Toporcher, Ernie Vick, and Bill Hallahan—all of whom were products of a farm system that was less than seven years old. In addition, Billy Southworth was acquired from the Giants for Heinie Mueller, another product of the Cardinal farm system.

During those seven years when the Cardinals were discovering, signing, and developing unprecedented quantities of players at little expense, the other major league clubs were essentially operating as they always had, signing some players out of the amateur ranks, optioning them out for seasoning, and buying top prospects from minor league clubs, even though the new draft rules were driving the prices of such players to unprecedented levels. For example, the Yankee team the Cardinals defeated in the 1926 World Series had just one home-grown player—Lou Gehrig, who was signed out of Columbia University in 1923 and optioned to Hartford until ready. Although this had been an inexpensive acquisition, the Yankees subse-

quently had purchased, for $50,000 each, Earle Combs from Louisville, Mark Koenig from St. Paul (with whom the Yankees had a working agreement), and Tony Lazzeri from Salt Lake. In 1925, the year the Pirates won the World Series, they acquired Paul Waner and Hal Rhyne from the San Francisco Seals for $100,000 and also signed Joe Cronin off the San Francisco sandlots for little more than train fare to his first assignment—Johnstown, Pennsylvania.

But the escalating prices of players and the success of the Cardinals finally encouraged other clubs to begin acquiring minor league clubs. Shortly after the Cardinals acquired the half interest in Syracuse in 1921, William Wrigley, owner of the Cubs, acquired Los Angeles of the Pacific Coast League, but he treated them virtually as separate investments. By 1927, however, major league acquisition of minor league clubs was causing concern in the minors. The first formal notice came late that year, when the American Association adopted a new Constitution which effectively prohibited major league ownership of its clubs (excluding Columbus, which was already owned by Cincinnati). At the National Association meeting in December 1928, Mike Sexton wondered aloud when the majors would own enough clubs to control the National Association. Early in 1929 major league clubs owned or controlled twenty-seven minor league clubs. At that point Judge Landis, who until then had been remarkably quiet on the issue of farm systems, opened fire. He began granting free agency to minor leaguers "covered up" by various major league organizations. Later in 1929, Landis denounced the farm system, and announced his intention of destroying it. In response, Sam Breadon, owner of the Cardinals, cited letters from seven minor leagues saying the farm system was beneficial to them. Interestingly, in 1921 Landis had said, "The object of organized baseball is to facilitate the development of skill among ball players." No one could seriously argue that this wasn't the purpose of the farm system, but by 1929 Landis was accusing Rickey and Breadon of "raping the minors," robbing smalltown America of its precious heritage of independent minor league baseball.

Through the 1930s Landis tried to make good on his threat to destroy the farm system, but since it was not contrary to baseball law, he had to pick at the edges—by levying fines against teams having an interest in more than one team in a minor league or by granting free agency to players who were "covered up" through violations of the option rules or "secret agreements." Attracting much attention in Landis's crusade was his granting of free agency to seventy-four Cardinal farmhands in 1938, and to ninety-one Detroit minor leaguers in 1940, but these shots were fired after the war was lost.

More important than the fireworks that erupted between Landis and Breadon at the 1929 major league meeting was Yankees owner Jacob Ruppert's declaration at the same meetings that no ball club could afford the prices being paid for minor league players; Ruppert added that he was "going to be forced into owning minor league clubs, and so is every other major league owner in this room." At the time he spoke, the Yankees had already purchased the Chambersburg club of the Class D Blue Ridge League. In November 1931 Ruppert purchased Newark of the International League for a reported

$600,000 and soon thereafter hired Baltimore general manager George Weiss to develop a farm system. Thus the farm system, a concept that had been created largely out of necessity by Branch Rickey because the Cardinals didn't have the financial resources to compete with other clubs for top minor league prospects, had in less than a decade been embraced by the wealthiest club in baseball as being the most efficient method of acquiring talent. There would still be an occasional Joe DiMaggio or Ted Williams, signed by a minor league club and sold to the majors, but the major league club that didn't establish a farm system did so at its own peril—it cannot be coincidental that the eight teams which were the slowest to get on the bandwagon and had the thinnest farm systems in the 1930s—the Phillies, Athletics, Senators, White Sox, Giants, Cubs, Braves, and Pirates—were, aside from the Browns, the eight least successful teams in the 1940s. (The Browns and Reds established extensive farm systems in the 1930s, and overall they were the two most improved clubs of the 1940s.)

While several clubs caught on to what the Cardinals were doing, none could catch up as Rickey, taking advantage of the Depression, which had created a large pool of young men with few career options, signed players by the hundreds at tryout camps. Whereas during the 1920s the Cardinal system had only increased from three clubs to five, by 1936 it had expanded to twenty-eight teams—remarkable considering that there were only twenty-six minor leagues that year (the Cardinals had two teams each in the Nebraska State, Georgia-Florida, and Arkansas-Missouri Leagues). The Cardinal system finally topped out with thirty-three clubs in 1937—more than the two next-largest farm systems combined. Rickey's belief that out of quantity comes quality was proven on the field by the 1942 world champion Cardinals. Every player on the active roster, except for second-line pitchers Harry Gumbert and Whitey Moore, was a product of the Cardinal farm system, and Gumbert had been acquired in exchange for Cardinal farm graduate Bill McGee. In addition, the sale of players developed by the Cardinals kept the coffers full—in 1940–1941 alone, Johnny Mize, Joe Medwick, and Mickey Owen were exchanged to other clubs for $240,000 and nine players.

Thus from the perspective of the majors the farm system was a success, and the minors seemed to be flourishing—going from fourteen leagues in 1933 to forty-four by 1940. Sam Breadon, responding to another barrage of attacks by Landis in the late 1930s, claimed that the farm system had brought stability and strength to the minors, but there were other factors at work—the proliferation of night games, better promotion, and an influx of good young talent resulted in a per-club increase in attendance of 40 percent from 1937 to 1940. During that same period the portion of minor league clubs affiliated with the majors actually dropped from 61 to 46 percent. Rickey's theory that out of quantity comes quality might have had practical merit during a depression, or again immediately following World War Two when there was an influx of returning veterans. However, under normal circumstances huge farm systems were not cost-effective. While the minors were still expanding in the late 1930s, the Cardinals began pruning back their farm system of more than thirty teams; again while the minors were expanding

in the late 1940s, farm systems were contracting—in 1948 there were six farm systems of twenty or more teams; by 1951 there were none. The portion of minor league teams affiliated with major league teams dropped from 62 percent in 1946 to 47 percent in 1951 as major league farm systems collectively dropped from 280 to 175 clubs and outright major league ownership of minor league clubs dropped from 125 to 75.

In 1950 there were 232 minor league teams not affiliated with the majors. This was the highest number of independent teams in organized baseball since the early teens. Nine of the fifty-eight leagues had no teams with major league affiliations, and more than a dozen others had only one or two affiliates. These leagues operated virtually outside the player-development chain, existing much as a semipro team or league does—to provide entertainment and reflect civic pride. Their only source of revenue was through the turnstiles, and just as forty years earlier automobiles and the movies helped drive out the marginal teams and leagues, now TV did the same. This can be clearly seen as the heavily populated Northeast, the first region to be heavily penetrated by television, suffered the first wave of league failures.

Over the next few years, attendance declined sharply, most of the independent clubs folded, and farm systems continued to contract. In 1956 the majors established a "stabilization fund" of $500,000 to aid clubs and leagues in lower classifications, but the free-fall of leagues, clubs, and attendance continued. In 1959 the majors discontinued the stabilization fund and established a fund of $1 million to finance a player-development and promotional program for the minors. In 1962 the majors and minors adopted the Player Development Plan that, by requiring each major league club to have five farm teams, would guarantee the operation of at least one-hundred minor league teams, which the majors felt was adequate for their player-development purposes. The plan also included the Player Development Contract under the terms of which the parent major league club became responsible for all spring training costs and all or most of the salaries of players, managers, and coaches. After major league expansion in 1969, major league clubs were only required to support four farm clubs each, but their financial support of each was increased. By 1976 there were only 106

minor league teams with major league affiliations, the lowest peacetime total since 1935. American League expansion the following year created the need for additional minor league affiliates, and in subsequent years major league clubs expanded their farm systems—all of them back up to a minimum of five clubs by 1984. With the dramatic increase in minor league attendance and the resulting increase in the value of franchises in the 1980s, a new Professional Baseball Agreement was ratified by the majors and minors in 1990 that required the minors to assume a greater share of operational expenses but the majors continued to pay the salaries and meal money of all uniformed personnel (including umpires). And farm systems continued to grow—by 1992 each major league club had at least six farm clubs and the number of minor league teams with major league affiliations was up to 189 (including 18 in the Dominican Rookie League), the highest total since 1950. By the end of 1992 it appeared this trend might begin to change as several major league clubs announced cost-cutting measures that included a scaling down of their farm systems.

In 1928 Mike Sexton had asked how long it would be before the majors owned enough minor league clubs to control the National Association. Other than during World War Two, when the minors were severely constricted, major league clubs never have "owned" more than 28 percent of the minor league clubs; however, possibly as early as 1934, probably by 1935, and certainly by 1936, the majors through outright ownership, working agreements, or other interlocking devices "controlled" the National Association, and this situation was generally acknowledged throughout baseball by 1938.

Until about 1960 there was still some room for independent clubs and career minor league players, but since then the minors have existed almost exclusively to develop talent for the majors. While this has dismayed many minor league fans and traditionalists, it should be remembered that the principal role of the minors within organized baseball has always been to develop talent for the majors, and to receive money in exchange. The farm system, which owed its success in no small part to the greed of some minor league operators, was merely a different device by which talent moved to the majors and money moved to the minors.

Minor Leagues

Year	Leagues Started	Didn't Finish	Year	Leagues Started	Didn't Finish	Year	Leagues Started	Didn't Finish	Year	Leagues Started	Didn't Finish	Year	Leagues Started	Didn't Finish	Year	Leagues Started	Didn't Finish
1883	2		1901	14	3	1919	15	1	1937	37		1955	33		1973	18	
1884	7	4	1902	17	2	1920	22	1	1938	37		1956	28		1974	18	
1885	8	4	1903	20		1921	26		1939	41		1957	28		1975	18	
1886	10	1	1904	24	2	1922	30	2	1940	44	1	1958	24		1976	20	
1887	15	6	1905	32	5	1923	31	3	1941	41		1959	21		1977	19	
1888	17	7	1906	33	3	1924	29	4	1942	31	5	1960	22		1978	18	
1889	15	5	1907	37	4	1925	25	3	1943	10	1	1961	22		1979	18	1
1890	17	7	1908	40	11	1926	30	4	1944	10		1962	20		1980	17	
1891	14	3	1909	34	4	1927	24		1945	12		1963	18		1981	17	
1892	12	3	1910	51	6	1928	31	3	1946	43	1	1964	20		1982	17	
1893	7	5	1911	51	10	1929	26	2	1947	52		1965	19		1983	17	
1894	8	2	1912	47	11	1930	23	2	1948	58		1966	19		1984	17	
1895	18	8	1913	42	4	1931	19	3	1949	59		1967	19		1985	18	
1896	14	7	1914	43	6	1932	19	4	1950	58	1	1968	20		1986	17	
1897	17	7	1915	33	8	1933	14		1951	50	1	1969	21		1987	18	
1898	21	11	1916	27	6	1934	20	1	1952	43		1970	21		1988	19	
1899	14	4	1917	21	9	1935	21		1953	38		1971	20		1989	19	
1900	15	6	1918	10	9	1936	26		1954	36	3	1972	19		1990	19	
															1991	19	
															1992	19	

Major League Farm Systems
1936–1969

	36	37	38	39	40	41	42	43	44	45	46	47	48	49	50	51	52	53	54	55	56	57	58	59	60	61	62	63	64	65	66	67	68	69
Boston, AL	9	10	7	8	6	7	6	3	5	4	12	13	15	11	8	8	6	6	6	6	6	5	7	7	6	6	6	6	5	5	5	6	5	6
Chicago, AL	5	4	10	8	6	5	5	0	0	0	17	12	15	9	8	8	6	6	6	6	5	6	6	6	6	6	6	5	5	5	6	6	6	6
Cleveland, AL	5	7	13	16	8	9	8	3	3	3	11	18	20	20	16	12	10	8	8	9	9	8	8	8	7	5	6	5	4	4	4	4	5	5
Detroit, AL	11	8	12	7	5	11	8	2	3	2	7	11	16	14	9	8	7	7	8	10	9	8	10	7	8	8	6	6	5	5	5	5	6	6
New York, AL	11	15	15	15	14	12	9	5	5	5	15	22	24	22	15	14	10	11	9	10	11	10	10	8	8	7	7	6	5	7	7	6	6	6
Phila.-K.C.-Oakland, AL	5	3	3	3	4	5	3	2	2	4	7	15	10	11	15	9	8	8	6	7	7	9	8	8	8	8	8	6	5	5	6	6	6	6
St. Louis-Baltimore, AL	3	15	16	12	11	11	6	1	3	3	11	15	20	18	13	10	12	10	12	8	9	8	9	7	7	9	6	6	6	7	6	6	6	6
Wash.-Minnesota, AL	1	5	2	8	4	6	3	1	2	2	5	7	12	9	10	6	8	7	8	7	6	8	7	6	7	7	7	6	8	8	8	8	8	8
Milwaukee-Atlanta, NL	4	6	6	6	5	4	4	1	1	2	13	15	15	11	8	8	12	11	10	10	12	15	14	12	10	9	8	7	6	5	6	7	5	4
Brklyn.-Los Angeles, NL	5	14	14	11	18	14	10	4	7	9	21	25	26	26	22	19	17	15	15	16	14	13	12	12	12	11	9	7	8	6	6	6	6	6
Chicago, NL	5	6	5	2	2	9	11	4	6	7	18	23	19	16	15	14	10	9	9	8	8	10	8	6	6	6	5	5	5	5	6	6	5	5
Cincinnati, NL	16	10	10	10	8	8	5	2	1	3	4	8	11	10	7	4	6	7	9	9	9	11	11	8	8	6	5	5	5	4	5	5	5	5
N.Y.-San Francisco, NL	2	11	4	5	6	7	7	3	5	8	16	19	22	19	18	14	13	9	9	10	10	10	12	9	8	9	8	7	7	6	6	6	6	5
Philadelphia, NL	1	2	3	3	8	3	2	1	3	5	9	11	15	14	12	11	11	9	9	8	8	9	7	10	8	7	6	6	6	7	7	7	6	6
Pittsburgh, NL	4	5	7	7	9	8	7	4	4	4	13	14	19	13	13	11	15	11	10	13	13	10	11	9	7	7	7	6	6	6	6	6	6	6
St. Louis, NL	28	33	32	28	29	25	22	6	7	7	18	19	22	20	21	16	15	16	22	18	15	11	14	12	9	8	6	5	5	6	6	7	7	7
L.A.-California, AL																										2	4	6	6	6	5	5	5	5
Washington, AL																										2	4	4	4	4	4	4	5	5
Houston, NL																											2	4	5	5	5	6	6	6
New York, NL																										3	4	5	4	4	5	6	6	5
Kansas City, AL																																		7
Seattle, AL																																		4
Montreal, NL																																		3
San Diego, NL																																		4

Minor League Clubs/Major League Affiliations

Year	Minor League Clubs	Affiliated with Majors	Owned by Majors
1936	184	115	38
1937	251	154	39
1938	267	163	48
1939	292	149	47
1940	310	143	60
1941	304	143	61
1942	206	116	46
1943	66	42	23
1944	70	57	21
1945	85	68	33
1946	316	197	79
1947	406	247	103
1948	452	280	125
1949	461	243	116
1950	446	210	99
1951	373	172	75
1952	324	166	65
1953	292	152	50
1954	269	156	49
1955	243	155	40
1956	217	150	33
1957	209	153	32
1958	173	157	34
1959	150	132	30
1960	152	126	18
1961	147	129	21
1962	134	121	22
1963	127	114	22
1964	136	108	19
1965	136	110	28
1966	138	116	32
1967	141	118	36
1968	142	119	39
1969	155	128	46
1970	153	120	39
1971	155	127	45
1972	148	125	49
1973	147	117	38
1974	145	113	27
1975	137	109	26
1976	148	106	24
1977	150	113	23
1978	156	118	24
1979	155	119	
1980	155	125	
1981	152	133	
1982	160	136	
1983	162	139	
1984	164	140	
1985	168	140	
1986	162	143	
1987	172	149	
1988	188	168	
1989	197	179	
1990	202	183	
1991	207	184	
1992	209	189	

Annual Overall Minor League Pitching Percentage Leader (20 or more decisions)

Year	Player	Team (League)	W–L	Pct.	Overall W–L	Overall Pct.
1900	Willie Mains	Rome (N.Y. St.)	27–5	.844		
1901	Henry Allemang	Little Rock (So. Assn.)	20–4	.833		
1902	Louis Bruce	Toronto (Eastern)	18–2	.900		
1903	Ernest Nichols	Spokane (Pac. Nat.)	20–4	.833		
1904	Ed Craig	Springfield (Mo. Valley)	19–4	.826		
1905	Fred Steele	Oskaloosa (Iowa St.)	18–3	.857		
1906	Frank Dick	Marshalltown (Iowa St.)	18–3	.857		
1907	Harley Young	Wichita (West. Assn.)	29–4	.879		
1908	Harry Gaspar	Waterloo (Cent. Assn.)	32–4	.889		
1909	Ray Fisher	Hartford (Conn.)	24–5	.828		
1910	Cyrus Dahlgren	Superior (Minn.-Wis.)	22–3	.880		
1911	Howard Northrop	Reading (Inter.-St.)	27–4	.871		
1912	Larue Kirby	Traverse City (Mich. St.)	18–3	.857		
1913	Ralph Bell	Winona (Northern)	28–6	.824		
1914	Joe Chabek	Harrisburg (Tri-St.)	28–3	.903		
1915	Booth Hopper	Minneapolis (A.A.)	18–3	.857		
1916	Howard Ehmke	Syracuse (N.Y. St.)	31–7	.816		
1917	John Verbout	Wilkes-Barre (N.Y. St.)	26–7	.788		
1918	John Beckvermit	Binghamton (Int.)	17–4	.810		
1919	C. A. (Chief) Bender	Richmond (Va.)	29–2	.935		
1920	George Carmen	London (Mich.,-Ont.)	26–2	.926		
1921	Earl Keiser	Mitchell (Dakota)	20–2			
		Oakland (PCL)	3–0		23–2	.920
1922	Byrd Hodges	Joplin (West. Assn.)	26–3	.897		
1923	Emil Levsen	Cedar Rapids (Miss. Val.)	19–4	.826		
1924	Carl Dunagan	Dyersburg (Kitty)	19–2	.905		
1925	Lloyd Brown	Ardmore-Western Assn.	17–1	.944*		
1926	Frank Tubbs	Port Huron (Mich.-Ont.)	8–1			
		Port Huron (Mich. St.)	8–0			
		Oklahoma City (Western)	9–2		25–3	.893
1927	Ben Cantwell	Jacksonville (So'east.)	25–5	.833		
1928	Paul Fittery	Carrollton (Ga.-Ala.)	21–2	.913		
1929	Andrew Bednar	McCook (Neb. St.)	21–4	.840		

Year	Player	Team	W-L	Pct.	W-L	Pct.
1930	Jim Cameron	McCook (Neb. St.)	19-2	.905		
1931	Lyle (Bud) Tinning	Minneapolis (A.A.)	1-2			
		Des Moines (West. Assn.)	24-2		25-4	.862
1932	Marvin Duke	Erie (Central)	23-4	.852		
1933	Al Piechota	Davenport (Miss. Val.)	19-4	.826		
1934	Fay Thomas	Los Angeles (PCL)	28-4	.875		
1935	Lloyd Sterling	Winnipeg (Northern)	24-2	.923		
1936	Bill Yocke	Akron (Mid. Atl.)	1-2			
		Norfolk (Piedmont)	18-1		19-3	.864
1937	Joe Kohlman	Salisbury (E. Shore)	25-1	.962		
1938	Paige Dennis	Thomasville (N.C. St.)	28-2	.933		
1939	Charles Wensloff	Joplin (West. Assn.)	26-4	.867		
1940	Arthur Cyrolewski	Johnson City (App.)	20-3	.870		
	Mervin Hensley	La Crosse (Wis. St.)	20-3	.870		
1941	Frank Marino	Macon (Sally)	19-1	.950		
1942	Paul Minner	Elizabethton (App.)	18-2			
		Knoxville (So. Assn.)	1-0		19-2	.905
1943	Irvin Stein	Portsmouth (Piedmont)	24-6	.800		
1944	Pete Naktenis	Hartford (Eastern)	18-3	.857		
1945	Lewis Carpenter	Atlanta (So. Assn.)	22-2	.917		
1946	Bill Kennedy	Rocky Mount (C. Plain)	28-3	.903		
1947	Chris VanCuyk	Cambridge (E. Shore)	25-2	.926		
1948	Albert Tefft	Blackstone (Va.)	20-1	.952		
1949	Lynn Southworth	Thomasville (N.C. St.)	21-1	.955		
1950	Mike Hudak	Big Stone Gap (Mt. St.)	19-2	.905		
1951	Anderson Bush	Hagerstown (Int. St.)	22-3	.880		
1952	Russell Harris	Ozark (Ala-Fla.)	27-3	.900		
1953	Steve Kraly	Binghamton (Eastern)	19-2	.905		
1954	Bob Thorpe	Stockton (Calif.)	28-4	875		
1955	Jim Grant	Keokuk (I-I-I)	19-3	.864		
1956	Francisco Ramirez	Mexico City Reds (Mex.)	20-3	.870		
1957	Bob Riesner	Alexandria (Evang.)	20-0			
		New Orleans (So. Assn.)	0-2		20-2	.909
1958	Jerry Walker	Knoxville (Sally)	18-4	.818		
	Art Henriksen	St. Petersburg (Fla. St.)	17-3			
		New Orleans (So. Assn.)	0-1		18-4	.818
1959	Les Bass	Boise (Pioneer)	21-3	.875		
1960	Tom Haake	Grand Forks (Northern)	0-1			
		Dubuque (Midwest)	19-3		19-4	.826
1961	David Seeman	Selma (Ala.-Fla.)	17-3			
		Burlington (Carolina)	7-0		24-3	.889
1962	Bob Schmidt	Modesto (Calif.)	0-0			
		Jamestown (NYP)	17-3		17-3	.850
1963	Bob Lee	Batavia (NYP)	20-2			
		Asheville (Sally)	1-1		21-3	.875

Year	Player	Team	W-L	Pct.	W-L	Pct.
1964	Ed Watt	Aberdeen (Northern)	14-1			
		Elmira (Eastern)	3-1		17-2	.895**
1965	Billy MacLeod	Pittsfield (Eastern)	18-0	1.000†		
1966	Bob Snow	Winston-Salem (Carolina)	20-2	.909		
1967	John Parker	Spartanburg (W. Car.)	17-3	.850		
1968	Pablo Montes De Oca	Campeche (Mex. S.E.)	21-4	.840		
1969	Don Eddy	Appleton (Midwest)	18-3	.857		
1970	Jim Flynn	Albuquerque (Texas)	19-4	.826		
1971	Rich Gossage	Appleton (Midwest)	18-2	.900		
1972	Andres Ayon	Saltillo (Mexican)	22-3	.880		
1973	Silvano Quezada	Tampico (Mexican)	22-2	.917		
1974	Bob Knepper	Fresno (Calif.)	20-5	.800		
1975	Jerry Garvin	Reno (Calif.)	17-5	.773		
1976	Enrique Romo	Mexico City Reds (Mexican)	20-4	.833		
1977	Mike Chris	Lakeland (Fla. St.)	18-5	.783		
1978	Tomas Armas	Saltillo (Mexican)	22-4	.846		
1979	Miguel Solis	Saltillo (Mexican)	25-5	.833		
1980	Gene Nelson	Ft. Lauderdale (Fla. St.)	20-3	.870		
1981	Ted Power	Albuquerque (PCL)	18-3	.857		
1982	Mike Warren	Stockton-Modesto (Calif.)	19-4	.826		
1983	Alfonso Pulido	Mexico City Reds (Mexican)	17-3	.850		
1984	Mike Bielecki	Hawaii (PCL)	19-3	.864		
1985	Eleazar Beltran	Tampico (Mexican)	18-3	.857		
1986	George Ferran	Shreveport (Texas)	16-1	.941‡		
1987	Bob Faron	Springfield (Midwest)	19-2	.905		
1988	Jimmy Rodgers	Myrtle Beach (So. Atl.)	18-4	.818		
1989	Royal Clayton	Albany (Eastern)	16-4	.800		
1989	Mercedes Esquer	Yucatan (Mexican)	16-4	.800		
1989	Walt Trice	Osceola (Fla. St.)	16-4	.800		
1990	Randy Marshall	Fayetteville (So. Atl.)	13-0	1.000		
		Lakeland (Fla. St.)	7-2		20-2	.909
1991	Jose Martinez	Columbus (So. Atl.)	20-4	.833		
1992	John Fritz	Quad Cities (Midwest)	20-4	.833		

*Adding two losses to Brown's record giving him 20 decisions yields a .850 percent, better than John Schmutte, Johnstown Middie Atlantic, 19-4, .822
**Adding 1 loss to Watt's record, giving him 20 decisions, yields an .850 percentage, better than Dave Leonhard, Aberdeen (Northern), 16-4 .800
†Adding 2 losses to MacLeod's record, giving him 20 decisions, yields a .900 percentage, better than Dave Leonhard, Elmira (Eastern), 20-5 .800
‡Adding 3 losses to Ferran's record, giving him 20 decisions, yields an .800 percentage, better than Kevin Armstrong, Columbia (Sally), 17-5 .773

Annual Overall Minor League Batting Leader (400 or more at-bats)

Year	Player	Team (League)	G	AB	R	H	2B	3B	HR	RBI	SB	AVG.
1900	Kitty Bransfield	Worcester (Eastern)	122	501	115*	186*	30	8	17	—	40	.371*
1901	Frank Huelsman	Shreveport (So. Assn.)	121*	487	98	191*	31	10	9	—	15	.392*
1902	Emil Frisk	Denver (Western)	123	450	89	168	22	22	14*	—	20	.373*
1903	Frank Huelsman	Spokane (Pac. Int.)	98	418	89	160	35	11	6	—	14	.392*
1904	Billy Hamilton	Haverhill (New Eng.)	113	408	113*	168*	32	8	0	—	74*	.412*
1905	Charlie Hemphill	St. Paul (A. A.)	145	560	122	204*	38	12	5	—	40	.364*
1906	Mike Welday	Des Moines (Western)	129	549	93	197	—	—	—	—	31	.359
1907	Ed Householder	Aberdeen (Northwest)	127	499	64	173	30*	19	9	—	19	.347**
1908	Ward Miller	Wausau (Wis.-Ill.)	124	408	91*	156*	—	—	—	—	—	.382*
1909	Harry Welch	Omaha (Western)	151	527	81	196*	41	15	7	—	51	.372*
1910	Dave Callahan	Eau Claire (Minn.-Wis.)	126	460	92*	168*	25	17*	2	—	52	.365*
1911	Frank Huelsman	Great Falls (U.A.)	135	516	117	212	48	15	17*	125*	25	.411*
1912	Charlie Johnson	Trenton (Tri-State)	109	400	86	161	31	5	14	—	22	.403*
1913	Frank Huelsman	Salt Lake City (U.A.)	122	473	123*	200*	36*	20*	22*	126*	16	.423*
1914	Joe Harris	Bay City (So. Michigan)	139	510	135	197*	39	22*	10	—	42	.386*
1915	Big Bill Kay	Binghamton (N.Y. St.)	125	447	98*	169*	22	25*	7	—	35	.378*
1916	Hank Butcher	Denver (Western)	145	541	116	204	31	20*	15	—	32	.377*
1917	Nap Lajoie	Toronto (Int.)	151	581	83	221*	39*	4	5	—	4	.380*
1918	Polly McLarry	Shreveport (Texas)	29	84	12	24	3	1	1	—	6	.286
		Binghamton (Int.)	103	335	51	129	26	7	4	—	15	.385*
											overall	.365
1919	Joe Wilhoit	Seattle (PCL)	17	67	8	11	1	0	0	—	3	.164
		Wichita (Western)	128	526	126*	222*	41	10	7	—	13	.422*
											overall	.393
1920	Merwyn Jacobson	Baltimore (Int.)	154*	581	161*	235*	35	16*	7	—	18	.404*
1921	Jack Lelivelt	Omaha (Western)	166	659	149	274*	70*	9	14	—	24	.416*
1922	Jack Schaefer	London (Mich.-Ont.)	100	407	79	167	27	21	9	—	9	.410*
1923	Moses Solomon	Hutchinson (So'west.)	134	527	143*	222*	40*	15	49*	—	12	.421*
1924	T. P. Osborne	Mt. Pleasant (E. Tex.)	101	396	93	171*	48	3	23	—	46*	.432*¹
1925	Paul Waner	San Francisco (PCL)	174	599	167	280	75*	7	11	130	8	.401*
1926	Bill Diester	Salina (So'west.)	106	428	110*	190*	33*	4	27	—	10	.444*
		Tulsa (Western)	11	44	5	15	4	0	0	—	0	.341
											overall	.434
1927	Elton Langford	Des Moines (Western)	149	611	132	250	47	28*	8	—	31	.409*
1928	Danny Boone	High Point (Piedmont)	128	468	123	196*	40	11	38*	131*	11	.419*
1929	Ed Kallina	Midland(W. Tex.)	94	367	126	159	28	7	44*	—	16	.433*
		Sherman (Lone Star)	17	64	22	22	—	—	6	—	1	.344
											overall	.420
1930	Tony Antista	Bisbee (Arizona St.)	109*	444	127*	191*	36	16*	17	100	18	.430*
1931	Babe Phelps	Youngstown (Mid-Atl.)	115	436	71	178	29	9	15	88	9	.408*
1932	George Puccinelli	Rochester (Int.)	133	478	102	187	34	8	28	115	2	.391*
1933	Ox Eckhardt	Mission (PCL)	189*	760	145	315*	56	16	12	143	15	.414*

Year	Player	Team (League)	G	AB	R	H	2B	3B	HR	RBI	SB	AVG
1934	Frank Demaree	Los Angeles (PCL)	186	702	190*	269*	51*	4	45*	173*	41	.383*
1935	Ox Eckhardt	Mission (PCL)	172	710	149	283*	40	11	2	114	8	.399*
1936	Cal Lahman	Jamestown (Northern)	127	466	154*	182*	30	9	48*	162*	20	.391*
1937	Earl (Red) Martin	Beckley (Mt. St.)	91	360	80	144	39*	14*	8	96*	7	.400*
		Scranton (NYP)	11	41	7	10	1	0	0	4	1	.244
											overall	.384
1938	Murray Franklin	Beckley (Mt. St.)	94	385	91	169	31	13*	26*	110	13	.439*[2]
1939	Joe Schmidt	Duluth (Northern)	120	440	114*	194*	29	9	31*	133*	17	.441*
1940	Ed Schweda	Lubbock (W. Tex.-N.M.)	114	469	142	198	39	15	11	118	7	.422*
1941	Lew Flick	Elizabethton (App.)	117	502*	127*	210*	37*	13	5	116*	20	.418*
1942	Don Manno	Welch (Mt. St.)	117	457	136*	174*	32	14*	34*	122*	23	.381*
1943	George Kell	Lancaster (Inter-St.)	138	555	120*	220*	33	23*	5	79	14	.396*
1944	Roland Gladu	Hartford (Eastern)	119	417	92	155	28	14	7	102	8	.372
1945	Arden (Cotton) McCaskey	Bristol (App.)	106	437	72	164*	26*	14*	2	96	5	.375*
1946	Walt Forwood	Carbondale (N. Atl.)	111	419	98	170*	43*	7	3	101	22	.406*
1947	Jim Prince	Midland (Longhorn)	108	415	111	178	31	6	34	141	4	.429*
		Lubbock (W. Tex.-N.M.)	12	37	7	10	3	0	1	12	0	.270
											overall	.416
1948	Hershel Martin	Albuquerque (W. Tex.-N.M.)	132	447	133	190	61*	6	18	128	5	.425*
1949	Bob Montag	Pawtucket (New Eng.)	125	454	139*	192*	36	18*	21*	91	43*	.423*
1950	Oscar Sierra	Hornell (Pony)	93	358	99	151	28	2	21	114	12	.422*
		Newport News (Piedmont)	15	45	5	13	1	0	0	5	0	.289
											overall	.407
1951	D. C. (Pud) Miller	Hickory (N.C. St.)	119	426	115	181	32	1	40*	136*	2	.425*
1952	Don Stafford	Salisbury (N.C. St.)	105	392	99	160	31	3	18	90	1	.408*[3]
1953	Russ Snyder	McAlester (Sooner St.)	138	556	137	240*	32	16	2	84	74*	.432*
1954	Neal Cobb	Crestview (Ala.-Fla.)	115	435	108	188	27	8	5	124	3	.432*
1955	Tom Jordan	Artesia (Longhorn)	136	543	116	221*	69*	2	28	159*	4	.407*
1956	Len Tucker	Pampa (So'west)	140	565	181*	228	40	13	51	181	47*	.404*
1957	Fran Boniar	Reno (Calif.)	110	443	102	193	33	15	11	138*	4	.436*
		Pueblo (Western)	11	37	5	9	1	0	0	7	3	.243
											overall	.421
1958	Neb Wilson	Ft. Walton Beach-Pensacola (Ala.-Fla.)	119	409	102*	162	38*	3	24*	106*	3	.396*
1959	Tom Hamilton	St. Petersburg (Fla. St.)	125	401	109	155	20	3	20*	96	3	.387*
1960	Al Pinkston	Mexico City Reds (Mexican)	138	567	110	225*	41	11	26	144*	4	.397*
1961	Al Pinkston	Vera Cruz (Mexican)	109	406	79	152	26*	4	13	86	4	.374*
1962	Ramiro Caballero	Guanajuato (Mex. Center)	113	423	123	175*	25	0	59*	170	3	.414*
1963	Vinicio Garcia	Monterrey (Mexican)	122	475	107*	175	36*	5	21	88	3	.368*
1964	Ramiro Caballero	Leon (Mex. Center)	121	460	135*	175*	29	1	35*	145*	3	.380*
1965	Alfonso Peciado	Guanajuato (Mex. Center)	130	529	103	224*	48*	14*	11	147	11	.423*
1966	Heriberto Vargas	Vera Cruz (Mexican)	7	14	0	3	0	0	0	0	0	.214
		Guanajuato (Mex. Center)	127	481	168*	214	33	1	55*	174*	3	.445*
											overall	.438
1967	Hilario Pena	Campeche (Mex. S.E.)	102	404	60	159	61	3	1	49	9	.394*
1968	Jim Hicks	Tulsa (PCL)	117	407	100*	149	32	7	23	85	14	.366*
1969	Bernie Carbo	Indianapolis (A.A.)	111	404	83	145	37	2	21	76	7	.359*
1970	Miguel Suarez	Tampico (Mex. Center)	126	460	105	181*	37*	4	14	101	15	.393*
1971	Téolindo Acosta	Puebla (Mexican)	133	441	75	173	22	11	7	71	17	.392*
1972	Don Anderson	Jalisco (Mexican)	130	445	76	161	31	2	8	68	0	.362*
1973	Hector Espino	Tampico (Mexican)	116	422	82	159	20	2	22	107*	3	.377*
1974	Téolindo Acosta	Puebla (Mexican)	122	464	93*	170*	17	6	2	43	20	.366*
1975	Gene Richards	Reno (Calif.)	134	501*	148*	191*	29	10	12	58	85*	.381*
1976	Pat Putnam	Asheville (W. Car.)	138	538	100	194*	33*	3	24*	142*	8	.361*
1977	Rudy Law	Lodi (California)	122	451	124	174	22	5	9	88	37	.386*
1978	Champ Summers	Indianapolis (A.A.)	132	462	98	170*	25	5	34*	124*	11	.368
1979	Jimmie Collins	Chihuahua (Mexican)	124	470	95	206*	35	10	6	60	33	.438*
1980	Jimmie Collins	Chihuahua (Mex. #1)	91	346	62	131	19	13	4	52	19	.379
		Saltillo (Mex. #2)	39	137	25	52*	8	3*	2	31*	5	.380
											overall	.379
1981	Kent Hrbek	Visalia (Calif.)	121	462	119	175	25	5	27	111	12	.379*
1982	Randy Ready	El Paso (Texas)	132	475	122*	178*	33	5	20	99	13	.375*
1983	Chris Smith	Phoenix (PCL)	123	449	88	170	31	5	21	102	4	.379*
1984	Jimmie Collins	Mexico City Reds-Cordoba (Mexican)	109	403	81	166	35	4	6	59	12	.412*
1985	Oswaldo Olivares	Aguas.-Campeche (Mexican)	110	441	85	175*	22	14*	5	49	20	.397*
1986	Willie Aikens	Puebla (Mexican)	129	445	134	202*	38	3	46	154*	0	.454*
1987	Orlando Sanchez	Puebla (Mexican)	123	439	95	182	34	1	25	115	6	.415*
1988	Nelson Barrera	Mexico City Reds (Mexican)	129	460	90	171	26	0	31	124*	7	.372
1989	Willie Aikens	León (Mexican)	128	423	108*	167	40	1	37	131*	1	.395*
1990	Trench Davis	Saltillo (Mexican)	127	498	84	189*	33	4	5	50	20	.380
1991	Rich Renteria	Jalisco (Mexican)	104	382	90	169	30	6	24	106	17	.442*
		Indianapolis (A.A.)	20	72	6	17	5	0	1	5	0	.236
											overall	.410
1992	Raul Perez Tovar	Monclova (Mexican)	129	483	83	201	32	5	8	93	14	.416*

*Led league in category

[1]If charged with 400 at-bats, Osborne's average would be .428, higher than any player with 400 or more at-bats.
(George Rhinehardt, Greenville (Sally) G: 120, AB: 495, R: 110*, H: 200*, 2B: 45*, 3B: 18, HR: 8, RBI: 92, SB: 32*, AVG: .404*)

[2]If charged with 400 at-bats, Franklin's average would be .423, higher than any player with 400 or more at-bats.
(Butch Moran, Rogers (Ark.-Mo.) G: 105, AB: 406, R: 107, H: 159, 2B: 43*, 3B: 12, HR: 22*, RBI: 114, SB: 8, AVG: .392*)

[3]If charged with 400 at-bats, Stafford's average would be .400, higher than any player with 400 or more at-bats.
(Clint McCord, Clinton (Miss. Ohio Val.) G:119, AB: 482, R: 123, H: 189*, 2B: 40, 3B: 15, HR: 15, RBI: 109, SB: 20, AVG: .392*)

Minor League Career Records

Batters	Years	G	AB	R	H	2B	3B	HR	RBI	SB	AVG
Buzz Arlett	1918–37	2390	8001	1610	2726	598	107	432	1786	200	.341
Ike Boone	1920–37	1857	6807	1362	2521	477	128	215	1334	120	.370
Bunny Brief	1910–28	2426	8945	1776	2963	594	152	340	1776	247	.331
Nick Cullop	1920–44	2484	8571	1607	2670	523	147	420	1857	154	.312
Ox Eckhardt	1925–40	1926	7563	1275	2773	455	146	66	1037	140	.367
Hector Espino	1960–84	2500	8605	1597	2898	403	49	484	1678	54	.337
Ray French	1914–41	3278	12174	1769	3254	590	129	46	1029	363	.267
Spencer Harris	1921–48	3258	11377	2287	3617	743	150	258	1769	241	.318
Joe Hauser	1918–42	1854	6426	1430	1923	340	116	399	1353	109	.299
Smead Jolley	1922–41	2231	8298	1455	3037	633	78	336	1593	61	.366
Jigger Statz	1920–42	2790	10657	1996	3356	595	137	66	1044	466	.315
Perry Werden	1884–1908	1539	6233	1214	2124	392	87	169	—	350	.341

Pitchers	Years	G	IP	W	L	H	R	ER	BB	SO	ERA
Bill Bailey	1906–25	578	3730	242	219	3452	1572	612	1565	2375	2.87
Dick Barrett	1925–53	790	4961	325	257	4572	2170	1747	2096	2512	3.34
George Boehler	1911–30	562	3711	248	202	3421	1745	874	1464	2319	3.74
George Brunet	1953–85	668	4041	244	242	3761	1832	1466	1754	3175	3.27
Tony Freitas	1928–53	736	4905	342	238	5090	2073	1694	932	2324	3.11
Sam Gibson	1923–49	661	4469	307	200	4460	1860	1413	1073	2195	3.08
Willie Mains	1887–1906	545	4014	318	179	4399	2417	—	1280	1669	
Joe Martina	1910–31	833	5417	349	277	4950	2307	1355	1868	2770	3.22
Frank Shellenback	1917–38	638	4514	315	192	4922	2110	1775	1021	1742	3.55
Bill Thomas	1926–52	1016	5995	383	347	6721	3098	2211	1230	2204	3.71
Hal Turpin	1927–46	635	4084	271	203	4512	1917	1367	807	1254	3.28

## CHAPTER 21

Japanese Baseball

Yoichi Nagata and John B. Holway

Just when baseball arrived in Japan, and who introduced it, is not clear. Horace Wilson, a professor in Tokyo in the 1870s, is one of those credited with being the Abner Doubleday of Japan, teaching baseball to students who ran bases and flagged grounders in *geta,* or wooden clogs. They named it *yakyu* (yok-yoo')—field ball—or *beisu boru.* In 1908, the University of Washington team, the first American college team to visit Japan, won six games but lost four games to Japanese colleges.

In 1913 the Chicago White Sox and New York Giants stopped in Japan on a round-the-world tour, playing three games with Japanese college teams. In 1922 a big league All-Star team, including Casey Stengel, also sailed into Yokohama harbor. And in 1928 Ty Cobb himself went over to teach the Japanese his batting secrets.

By 1930 *yakyu* began to rival *sumo* as the Japanese national pastime. The two games still tug in opposite directions at the nation's sports psyche, the one traditional and native, the other newer and outward-looking, but baseball has far outdistanced *sumo* as the nation's most popular sport.

The game thrived in schools and colleges. In fact, scholastic baseball still has a grip on the fans, like college football in America, high school basketball in Indiana, or the Final Four of the NCAA basketball tourney. Japan's annual national high school tournaments in Osaka every March and August fill huge Koshien Stadium for two weeks and command dawn-to-dusk TV coverage.

Japan's first professional team, the Nihon Undo Kyokai (Japan Athletic Association), was formed in 1920, which was followed by a second club, somewhat like the U.S. Harlem Globetrotters. When the great earthquake of 1923 hit the Tokyo metropolitan area, the NUK was forced to disband. The next year the Hankyu Railway reorganized former NUK players into a third pro club, the Takarazuka Kyokai. However, those teams couldn't survive because of a lack of competition.

In the fall of 1931, Lou Gehrig, Lefty Grove, Frankie Frisch, and Lefty O'Doul arrived for a tour. Several black teams visited Japan in the 1920s and in 1932, with stars such as Bullet Joe Rogan and Biz Mackey, who later became Roy Campanella's mentor.

Japanese baseball reached a watershed in 1934 with the arrival of Babe Ruth, Gehrig, Jimmy Foxx, Al Simmons, Charlie Gehringer, and Lefty Gomez. Matsutaro Shoriki, owner of the Yomiuri newspapers, sponsored the tour and would become the great genius–father figure of professional baseball there. Ruth and the others, soon to receive plaques in Cooperstown, played sixteen games and easily won fifteen of them. Ruth hit thirteen home runs and clowned in right field, holding an umbrella, while Gehrig played first base in galoshes. But they weren't clowning when a high school boy, Eiji Sawamura, almost shut them out, whiffing Gehringer, Ruth, Gehrig, and Foxx in succession before losing 1–0. Sawamura became, and still is, a national hero, especially on his death, at twenty-six, in World War Two.

Shoriki signed a professional, Osamu Mihara (later famous as the "Magic Manager"), to his All-Japan team to oppose Ruth, although the Japanese looked down on professional sports as "unpure." At the end of the year he formed an all-pro team, Dai-Nippon (Greater Japan), with Sawamura, Mihara, the White Russian Vic Starffin, and others. They toured the United States the next year and would become the present-day Yomiuri (Tokyo) Giants (*Kyojin*), a nickname hung on them by O'Doul. Shoriki urged other businesses to form pro teams and by 1936 formed the country's first professional league, the Japan Pro-Baseball League.

World War Two interrupted baseball. American words, such as *out* and *safe*, became *hi-ké* (withdraw) and *yoshi* (good), etc., and Japanese soldiers shouted, "To hell with Beibu Rusu." The league succumbed completely in 1945, and the Giants' proud stadium became an ammo dump.

After the war General MacArthur ordered the stadium cleared and encouraged the rebirth of the game. O'Doul, a veteran of the 1931 and 1934 tours, brought his San Francisco Seals of the PCL in 1949 and won all seven games. He returned with Joe DiMaggio and other big leaguers in 1951.

The big league tours continued every other year or so, and, *mirabile dictu*, in 1953 the Americans even lost one game with two ties. In 1956 the champion Dodgers lost four games, and in 1966 they lost eight and won nine. Of course the players considered the tours as vacations for shopping and partying, but they were learning that unless they played their best, they could no longer waltz to easy victories.

In 1950 the JPBL split into two leagues, which now have six teams apiece. The Central League, dominated by the Giants, is by far the more popular, with the benefit of the nationwide publicity the Yomiuri empire gives its club. The Giants have drawn 3.5 million fans in a 65-game home schedule. That's nearly 53,000 per game, or 4.2 million for a U.S. schedule of 81 games. Even when they finished last in 1975, they drew 2.8 million. The Pacific League, struggling to break even, in 1973 instituted a split season (since abandoned) and the DH (still in effect). It now averages about 24,400 attendance per game, compared to 35,300 for the Central League. Average pay is $260,000, compared to over $1 million in the U.S. majors.

Three-time Triple Crown winner Hiromitsu Ochiai is the highest paid, at $2.5 million.

Of course every Japanese kid wants to grow up to play for the Giants, leaving the other eleven clubs talent-poor. A draft system, begun in 1966, has helped give the other teams a better chance to compete. Since 1974 the Pacific League has won twelve of the nineteen Japan Series.

Every night a Japanese *sarariman* (salaried man, or wage earner) who is *kichigai* (crazy) about *yakyu* can switch on nationwide TV to watch the Giants. Where America has one weekly sports paper, *The Sporting News* and the *USA Today Baseball Weekly*, Japan has seven sports *dailies*, which concentrate mostly on baseball.

Most teams are owned by large companies and operated as advertising write-offs. For years Hiroshima was the only club owned by a city, but it is now owned by the Mazda company. Nine of the twelve clubs play in the two metropolitan centers, Tokyo-Yokohama and Osaka-Kobe-Kyoto.

In the early 1950s, it was a shock for Tokyo fans when the American big leaguers arrived, standing a head taller than the Japanese. Today it is a shock for the same fan to visit a U.S. spring training camp and see visiting Japanese dressing at lockers next to the Americans: There isn't that much difference anymore. Sadaharu Oh and Hank Aaron could almost trade uniforms.

The Japanese began talking of a real World Series. Their victory over America in the 1984 Los Angeles Olympics stirred the fantasy even more.

In general, American observers say, Japanese outfielders and catchers don't have the arms of Americans and Latins. But their infielders are among the best in the world, many of their pitchers are outstanding, and their batters are beginning to hit with big league power.

Americans also say the draconian training methods leave the players burned out in the second half of the season. And especially the Japanese attitude that "the future is now" has led to sacrificing many a great young pitcher to brutal overwork until his arm is ruined forever. In 1961 Hiroshi Gondo won 35 games in 429 innings. The next year he won 30 in 362. The next year he was down to 10, then 6, then 1; then he was out. This, however, is changing, as the Japanese are beginning to adopt the American pitching rotation.

About half the teams play on artificial turf, and in 1988 Japan got its first dome, the Tokyo Dome, built on the site of historic Korakuen (Ko-ra′-kwen) Stadium, similar to Minnesota's Metrodome. Another fancy indoor stadium, Fukuoka Dome, will open for 1993 as the home of the Fukuoka Daiei Hawks.

Meanwhile Japanese baseball has produced some outstanding heroes and memorable moments.

A Gallery of Stars

Tetsuharu Kawakami "The God of Batting," he has also been called "Japan's Lou Gehrig." Wearing glasses and swinging his famous red bat, Kawakami hit cleanup on the great Tokyo Giant teams of 1938–1958 and hit a high of .377 in 1951. His lifetime .313 is fifth highest in Japanese annals. Against the Dodgers in 1956, he batted .364 with two home runs. His concentration was so intense, he said he could visually "stop" a pitch in midflight.

But Kawakami's hitting paled compared to his managing—11 pennants in fourteen years. He was the man at the helm as the Giants won nine straight Japan Series, a feat accomplished by no other professional team in any sport. The Negro League Homestead Grays won nine straight pennants 1937–1945, but they lost several Black World Series and one playoff.

The Grays had Josh Gibson and Buck Leonard. Kawakami had Sadaharu Oh and Shigeo Nagashima. And he did it without using a single foreign player, desiring to prove the superiority of a "pure" Japanese team with fighting spirit.

Hiroshi Oshita (O′-shta) A three-time batting champ and three-time home run leader, Oshita was the postwar hero who dueled with his blue bat against Kawakami's red bat and helped lift the nation's spirit after World War Two. He was popular with the fans and with visiting Americans, who nicknamed him "Oyster."

With a soft and graceful swing, he lofted balls that left lofty, graceful traces in the sky. His 20 homers in 1946 seem a modest total, but they were 10 percent of all the homers hit in the Japanese majors that year. He hit cleanup on the Lions' "H-Bomb Row" of the 1950s.

Futoshi Nakanishi A Japanese Hack Wilson, in Leo Durocher's phrase, Nakanishi hit the second-longest tape-measure home run in Japanese history—530 feet—as a sophomore in 1953. He led the league in homers five out of the six years 1953–1958 and, with Oshita and pitcher Kazuhisa Inao, helped the Nishitetsu Lions win three successive Japan championships, all over the hated Giants.

Nakanishi helped spark the Lions to an amazing comeback in 1958, beginning from eleven games behind the Hawks. In one September stretch, they won seventeen out of eighteen games, and Nakanishi's homer vanquished the Hawks in their final meeting.

Nakanishi's career was cut short by an injury to his left hand after 244 home runs and a .307 average.

He managed the Lions to the flag in another heroic comeback starting from fourteen games behind. An eight-game winning streak in October finally put them a half game ahead, and American Tony Roig's homer clinched it on the final day.

Katsuya Nomura (Kot′-su-ya) The slugging catcher Nomura was the first home run king Oh had to catch before he could go after Ruth and Aaron. Nomura played in Japan's smallest park, with 280-foot foul lines, but he was a legitimate star, with a high of 52 homers in 150 games in 1963, when he almost batted the Hawks to the pennant over the Lions. Nomura's lifetime homer total, 1954–1980, was 657. He led the Pacific League eight straight times—nine in all.

Nomura was the most enduring catcher of all time. His 2,921 games behind the plate are almost 1,000 more than the U.S. record, by Bob Boone. Six years Nomura played every game on the schedule. Once he caught every inning in 150 games, including 16 doubleheaders. Hard work only made him stronger. He hit a combined .235 in the first games of the doubleheaders, .339 in the second games.

Overshadowed by Oh and Nagashima of the Giants, who enjoyed a tremendous publicity advantage, Nomura called them "sunflowers" and himself "an evening primrose."

Slow afield and afoot (Americans called him "Moose"), Nomura admired Campanella, who taught him how to catch without blocking the ump's view of low pitches and how to give his pitchers more confidence. An intelligent catcher, Nomura played each game in his head, pitch by pitch, the night before. Batters swore he could read their minds.

Nomura made a reliever of strikeout king Enatsu and in 1959 caught Sugiura's magnificent 38–4 season, forming one of the finest batteries of all time.

In 1965 he won the Triple Crown, with a little help from the league's pitchers, who walked American Daryl Spencer to prevent him from winning the home run title.

Shigeo Nagashima (She-gay'-o) The most popular player ever to play in Japan, Nagashima came to the Yomiuri Giants in 1958 and led the league in homers and RBIs his rookie year. He went on to win another HR crown, four more RBI titles, six batting crowns, and five MVPs— pretty good for a man whose main rival for all these honors was Sadaharu Oh.

In fact, Oh joined the team the year after Nagashima, and the two of them gave the Giants the dreaded "O-N Cannons" that propelled them to nine straight Japan championships. With Nagashima hitting cleanup behind Oh, pitchers couldn't pitch around Sadaharu. In the first year of Nagashima's retirement, 1975, Oh lost his HR crown after thirteen straight years as king.

Nagashima was considered the greater clutch hitter. He was nicknamed "Mr. Giant" and "the burning man" for the intensity of his play. His years of greatness coincided with Japan's dramatic economic surge, a period of national pride that he seemed to symbolize.

In 1959 Nagashima won the most famous game ever played in Japan, before the Emperor and Empress, with a ninth-inning homer. Seven years later, in 1966, his majesty attended his second game, against the L.A. Dodgers. Nagashima homered off Alan Foster in the first, singled in the fourth after a brushback pitch, and singled again in the seventh, as the Japanese won 11–3. He was the first baseball player to receive an audience at the Imperial Palace.

At third base, Nagashima was compared to Ron Santo by Americans who saw him. Dodger G.M. Fresco Thompson said Los Angeles could have won two extra pennants with Nagashima on third.

Fans adored him. His every move on the bases, in the field, or at bat, delighted them. Even Oh admitted that Nagashima was the first Japanese to realize that the game belongs to the fans. Early on, Oh realized he would never be able to rival Nagashima in popularity and that he would have to concentrate on setting records instead.

Although the two Giants were not unfriendly, neither were they close friends. Never once, Oh says, did they meet socially off the field or even take a drink together.

Like Gehrig and Ruth, Oh was upstaged by Nagashima. In '64 Oh blasted 55 homers, a Japanese record. But that was the year Nagashima got married—

the number one sports story of the year.

When Oh won a then unprecedented second straight Triple Crown in 1974, he again had to take a back seat to Nagashima, whose retirement was the biggest story of the year. In true Ted Williams fashion, Nagashima hit his 444th, and last, home run on his final day, then tearfully toured the field, while his fans wept with him and implored him not to go.

The next year Nagashima succeeded Kawakami as manager. He was officially given the appointment before thousands in Korakuen Stadium in a ceremony which author Robert Whiting called "a coronation."

In his first year at the helm, the Giants came in last, a national shock. Nagashima led the team in a formal bow of apology to the fans on the final day. But they bounced back to first the next two years. In 1993, after a twelve-year absence, Nagashima will manage the Yomiuri Giants.

Sadaharu Oh The world home-run king, Oh smashed 868 to pass Ruth and Aaron by more than 100 and put the record out of sight for at least the rest of the twentieth century and probably for several generations into the twenty-first. Clete Boyer, who played and coached for many years in Japan, said Oh had the strength of Aaron and the eyes of Williams. Oh's homers were the result of his samurai dedication, his mastery of the martial arts of *aikido* and *kendo* (swordsmanship), and thousands of hours of work with his devoted coach, Hiroshi Arakawa.

Sadaharu hit .161 as a Yomiuri Giant rookie pitcher (!) in 1959. Then Oh and Arakawa began their search for The Way. Oh gave up late-night drinking bouts on the Ginza and studied with masters of martial arts to attain physical, mental, and spiritual mastery. From the legend of the swordsman Miyamoto Musashi, Oh learned that superior spirit conquers superior technique.

But a hitch in his swing still kept Oh back until Arakawa made him stand on one leg before the pitch. If he hitched, he'd topple over. Thus the famous dog-at-the-hydrant stance, which no one before or since has attempted. (Mel Ott's raised foot was entirely different.) The bat angle, with the barrel pointing toward the pitcher, was an integral part of the balance.

Aikido taught Oh patience at the plate. *Kendo* taught him hip action, a downward swing (the fastest path to the ball), and focusing *ki*, or energy, from the shoulders to the "sweet" part of the bat.

Oh put it together in 1962, and the home runs began to explode. For 14 of the next 15 years he hit 40–55 homers a year. True, Japanese fences are shorter, 300' down the line. But so is the Japanese season—130 games. And Oh saw a lot more junkball pitchers than American hitters do. In addition, they walked him as many as 166 times a year—he never came to bat 500 times in one year in his life. The result: home run totals that ranged up to 67 per 550 at-bats. The 67 came in 1974 with 49 homers in only 385 AB.

Some lifetime comparisons:

	AB	HR	HR/550AB
Aaron	12,364	755	34
Ruth	8,399	714	45
Oh	9,250	868	49

Some other stats on Oh:

- 15 HR titles (13 in a row)—Ruth had 12, Aaron four
- 13 RBI crowns
- 13 straight times leading in runs
- nine MVP's—Ruth and Aaron had one each
- five bat championships—Ruth won one, Aaron two
- two back-to-back Triple Crowns—no American has done it
- nine Gold Gloves (they call them Golden Gloves in Japan).

Early on, Arakawa instilled in Oh the goal of catching Ruth, then Aaron, then going for 800. Aaron and Oh met face to face in 1974 in a home run contest before 50,000 fans in Tokyo. Aaron was still shaking off jet lag when his tenth homer broke a 9–9 tie. Oh was sorry to see Aaron retire—the competition had given him a goal.

Besides becoming a great hitter, Oh also became an excellent pianist. He drinks a secret blend of ginseng tea, the traditional Korean brew for energy. His bats, like Pete Rose's bats and like the sword blades used by samurai warriors, were hand made for him. Oh insisted that his bats be fashioned from a rare tree found only in northern Japan—and only from the branches of female trees.

Isao Harimoto (E'-sow) The only member of Japan's 3,000-hit club, Harimoto set the then Japanese batting record with .383 in 1970, and many thought he could go on to become the country's first .400 hitter. He didn't, partly because he refused to bunt, but he did win two more titles, for a total of seven, slugged 504 home runs, and batted .319, fourth-highest lifetime average in Japan.

A Korean born in Hiroshima, he was being carried by his mother outside the city when the atom bomb went off. She shielded him, but a sister was killed. At the age of four, two fingers on his right hand were severely burned, making it difficult for him to swing a bat.

Harimoto used a "level-up" swing—the bat was level until it met the ball, then went sharply up on the follow-through. Like Willie Keeler, he hit to all fields, wherever "they ain't."

Harimoto was active in establishing pro ball in Korea.

Shinichi Eto (Shin-i'-chi Et-o) A husky first baseman, Eto hit 367 homers but had the misfortune to come up with the Chunichi Dragons the same year Oh joined the Giants, 1959, and in the same league. It cost Eto several home run crowns.

But he had the pleasure of costing Oh two Triple Crowns, beating him out of the batting titles in 1964 and 1965.

Koichi Tabuchi Big (six-three, 210 pounds), handsome Tabuchi is the man who ended Oh's home run reign in 1975 after thirteen straight titles. Tabuchi slugged 43 that year, in spite of playing in the country's largest park. He had done even better the year before with 45 to Oh's 49. The Japanese call him their Johnny Bench.

Japanese connoisseurs consider Tabuchi's homers even more beautiful than Oh's—long and high, with a lot of "hang time." He accumulated 474 in a career that stretched from 1969 to 1984.

Yutaka Fukumoto This fleet little (five-seven) Braves outfielder is the world's stolen base champ—with 1,065 as compared to Lou Brock's 938.

Thirteen straight times, in 1970–1982, Fukumoto led the league in steals. His high, 106 in 122 games in 1972, broke Maury Wills's then record of 104 in 148 games. Brock stole 118 in 1974, but he had many more opportunities:

Player	Year	1B	BB	OB*	SB	SB/OB
Wills	1962	150	59	209	104	.498
Brock	1974	159	61	220	118	.536
Cobb	1915	161	118	279	96	.344
Fukumoto	1972	97	65	163	106	.650

*Times reached first base

Fukumoto stole 95 more in 1973 and 94 in 1974.

In that thirteen-year span, the Braves won six pennants. No wonder they took out a half-million-dollar insurance policy on his legs.

Was he stealing on the weak arms of Japanese receivers? American Don Blasingame, who played for years in Japan, said Fukumoto could have stolen on Bench.

Fukumoto led the league in runs ten times, triples eight times, walks (+ HBP) six times, hits four times, and doubles three times, and won the MVP for his great performance in 1972.

Sachio Kinugasa (Sah'-chio Ke-nu-ga'-sa) Kinugasa passed Lou Gehrig's consecutive-game record in 1987 (2,215 games to Gehrig's 2,130) and topped him in lifetime homers as well, 504–493.

Breaking in with the doormat Hiroshima Carp in 1965, he teamed with college star Koji Yamamoto to lift the Carp to their first pennant in 1975. They won again in 1979 and 1980, the so-called "Red Helmet" era, like Cincinnati's "Big Red Machine"—both teams wore red helmets.

A "GI baby" (his father was black), Kinugasa played in Yamamoto's shadow, often taking practice swings in his hotel room until two A.M. It paid off in 1984, his twentieth season, when he hit .300 for the only time in his life, led in RBI, and won the MVP.

Kinugasa once confided that he would like to find his father someday. "Keep playing like that," a teammate answered, "and your father will find *you*."

Hiromitsu Ochiai (O'-che-aye) With Oh, Nomura, and the other hitters of the past retired, Ochiai ranks as the top Japanese slugger today. The winner of three Triple Crowns (in 1982, 1985, and 1986). At 300,000,000 Yen he is the highest paid player in Japan, although he has not produced a Triple Crown since his trade from the Lotte Orions to the Chunichi Dragons after the 1986 season.

Pitchers

Eiji Sawamura A true folk hero, in 1934 the eighteen-year-old Sawamura whiffed four of America's greatest Hall of Famers in a row—Gehringer (.356, 11 home runs), Ruth (.288, 22), Gehrig (.363, 49), and Foxx (.334, 44).

The Americans had been averaging four homers and eight runs per game until they met the schoolboy with the excellent fastball and drop. The kid considered the visi-

tors "gods" but gulped and took the mound against Earl Whitehill (14–11 for the seventh-place Senators).

With the score 0–0 going into the seventh, Ruth grounded out. (The sun got in his eyes, he said.) Next up was Gehrig, who led both majors in both batting and homers that year. Sawamura threw a strike past him. The next pitch was a high curve, which Lou slammed over the right field wall to win the game 1–0.

In the last of the seventh, the Japanese put a man on second with one out, and Shigeru Mizuhara pulled a low line drive down the right field foul line. A diving catch by Bing Miller saved one run and maybe more.

In all, the kid gave five hits, struck out nine, and walked one. Connie Mack was so impressed, he offered the boy a contract.

The next year Sawamura toured the States with Shoriki's Dai Nippon nine (later tagged the Tokyo Giants by Lefty O'Doul), playing PCL and semipro clubs. American fans crowded around for autographs, and one asked him to sign in English, not Japanese. Sawamura obliged, only to discover later that he had signed a contract! It took some fast talking, and perhaps some yen, to get Sawamura out of the scout's clutches.

Sawamura went on to lead the new pro league in 1936 with a 13–3 record. In the postseason playoff against the Osaka Tigers, he pitched all three games, holding them to a .116 batting average and an 0.19 ERA, as the Giants won, two games to one.

The next year he was 33–10.

In his brief five-year career, he pitched three no-hitters.

Sawamura was called away to military service in 1938–1939, and again in 1942 and 1944. In December 1944 his troop ship was torpedoed by a submarine off Formosa, and he went down with the ship.

Masaichi Kaneda (Masa-ichi Ka-nay'-da)   Only Cy Young and Walter Johnson have surpassed Kaneda's 400 victories. Akin to Johnson's experience, he won most of his with one of the weakest teams in Japan, the Kokutetsu Swallows, who finished in the first division only once in his fifteen years with them 1950–1964.

In 1958 the Swallows were last in homers and near last in batting. But Kaneda was 31–14 with a 1.30 ERA. The Swallows were 27–54 without him.

In all, he won 43 percent of the Swallows' victories. He won and lost more 1–0 games than anyone—21 victories, 23 defeats.

The lefthanded Kaneda was the first man to break Walter Johnson's lifetime strikeout record, as well as the first to break his scoreless innings streak. Nolan Ryan broke Kaneda's strikeout mark, 4,490, but no one has touched his mark of 64⅓ straight shutout innings.

Kaneda whiffed the great Nagashima four straight times in Nagashima's big league debut, the only pitcher ever to do that to the great batting star.

Kaneda finally joined the Giants for five years at the end of the line. His 16–5 in 1967 at the age of thirty-four got them off to the third of their nine straight championships.

Kaneda was also the Wes Ferrell of Japan. His 36 home runs are the Japanese record for pitchers.

A Japanese-born Korean (*kane* is the Japanese equivalent of the Korean name *Kim*), when he retired

with bone chips in his elbow, his glove was donated to the U.S. Hall of Fame in Cooperstown.

Takumi Otomo (Ta-ku'-me O'-to-mo)   The little submarine-baller beat the New York Giants and Hoyt Wilhelm 2–1 in 1953 in one of the ten greatest games in Japan's history. With Lefty O'Doul urging him to keep the ball high, Otomo stayed ahead in the count, then fed them bad balls until they popped up or rolled out.

He won the MVP that year with a 27–6 record, plus two wins in the Japan Series. His ERA, 1.85, was the highest he posted in a four-year period. The lowest: 1.63 in 1956. In 1955 he was 30–6.

Kazuhisa Inao (Ka-zu-hee'-sa E-now')   Until his arm finally weakened from overwork, Inao was one of the world's most amazing pitchers.

His record of pitching six Japan Series games in 1958 and winning the last four of them will probably never be done again by any pitcher in any country. He won 42 games in 1961, 35 in 1957, and 33 in 1958. He was voted best pitcher in the league five times.

A poor fisherman's son, he reported as an unknown rookie to the Nishitetsu Lions' camp, with muscles bulging from rowing his father's boat in rough seas. He threw up to 300 pitches a day, posted a 21–6 record with a 1.06 ERA, and lifted the Lions to the pennant. In 262 innings, he gave up two home runs. He won three more games in the Japan Series.

Nicknamed *"Tetsu Wan"*—Iron Arm—in 1957 Inao won a record 20 straight at the end of the year to lift the Lions from third to another pennant.

In 1961 he tied Vic Starffin's record of 42 wins and lost his bid for his forty-third, 1–0, in the first game of two on the final day. He considered coming back in Game Two and going for the record but at last decided to rest on his laurels.

Inao came back as a relief pitcher in 1966 and led the league in ERA once more, with 1.79.

His final totals: 276–137, 1.98, with 2,574 strikeouts.

Tadashi Sugiura (Su-ghee-u'-ra)   One year after Inao won four straight games in the Japan Series, the bespectacled Sugiura won four straight too. But he pitched all four games and won all four!

Nagashima's teammate in college, Sugiura had spurned the Yomiuri Giants after Nankai Hawk manager Tsuruoka bowed to him and said, "We need you to beat the Giants."

As a rookie Sugiura was 27–12, 2.05 with the second-place Hawks, though Inao (33–10) and the Lions won their third straight flag.

Then in 1959 it was Sugiura's turn. He pitched 371 innings, held enemy hitters to a 1.40 ERA, and posted a 38–4 record. He pitched 29 games in the last eight weeks, or virtually every other day. He was 17–1 after August 1 and won his last 13 in a row. The stretch included 54 straight shutout innings, an ERA of 0.10, 95 strikeouts, and only 4 walks! His final victory clinched the flag.

Then came the Japan Series against the Giants, who had just won their fifth straight flag. The Hawks had never beaten them.

In spite of a painful elbow, Sugiura went eight innings

in Game One, gave up nine hits, but won 10–7. The next day Sugiura pitched five innings of relief, gave three hits and one run, and got the victory 6-3.

After travel days Sugiura started Game Three in Tokyo. Midway through, a corn came off his pitching hand, and catcher Nomura suddenly found himself catching a bloody ball. In the samurai spirit, however, Sugiura refused to come out. He lost a 2–1 lead on a homer in the ninth, and the Giants put two more men on second and third with one out. "My God, I'm done for," he says he thought, desperately looking into the dugout for relief. Tsuruoka kept his eyes averted, however, sending a coach out with a good luck amulet instead. Sugiura buckled down and got the last two outs and won in the tenth 3–2. He gave up only one walk.

Rain gave Sugiura a day of rest. Would the Hawks give him another in Game Four? The finger still pained him. "Can you go?" Tsuruoka asked. "I can go," Sugiura answered. He went nine more innings and shut the Giants out on five hits.

Ecstatic Hawk fans rewarded their hero with a new car, license number 38–4.

In his first three years, he had won 96 games:

Year	Rank	G	IP	BB	SO	W–L	ERA	Series	Awards
1958	2	53	299	85	215	27–12	2.05		
1959	1	69	371	46	336	38–4	1.40*	4–0	MVP
1960	2	57	333	49	317	31–11	2.05		

But then the overwork finally told. After an operation on his arm, he fell to 20–9 in 1961. He dropped to 14–15, then 14–16, made a brief comeback in 1964 with 20–15, and then was sent to the bullpen. He was all pitched out.

His final totals: 187–106.

Tetsuya Yoneda (Tet'-su-ya Yo-nay-da) Like Kaneda or Phil Niekro, Yoneda slaved for a doormat team, the Braves. Yet he posted the second-highest winning total in Japan—350–285, second only to Kaneda's 400 wins.

In 1966 Yoneda led the league with 25–17, while his team finished next to last. His biggest year was 1968, when he went 29–13 as the Braves won the pennant. He was voted the MVP of the league.

Yoneda is second to Kaneda in hitting too, with 33 homers to Kaneda's 36. Yoneda might have passed his rival, but the coming of the DH rule stopped his bid.

He did pass Kaneda, and everyone, including Cy Young, in one department, total games—949.

Keishi Suzuki For six straight years, 1967–1972—eight years in all—the lefty Suzuki led the Pacific League in strikeouts. As a sophomore lefty in 1967, he was 21–13 for the last-place Kintetsu Buffaloes.

Like Robin Roberts, another fastballing control pitcher, Suzuki gave up a lot of homers—560.

He was a natural righthander, but his father had tied his right hand to force him to pitch as a lefty.

His final figures: 317–238, and 3,061 strikeouts.

Minoru Murayama In 1959 rookie fastballer Murayama faced Japan's best player, Nagashima, in the greatest game ever played in Japan, a contest before 50,000 fans, including the Emperor himself.

Murayama, as famous for his forkball as his fastball,

pitched for the Yomiuri Giants' biggest rivals, the Hanshin Tigers. An Osaka native and boyhood Tiger fan, he spurned a Giant bonus in order to stay home and pitch for the Tigers for half the amount the Giants offered.

The night before the big game, Murayama had come in in the ninth inning against the Giants and struck out the side, Nagashima included.

The next night, before their majesties, Koyama started for the Tigers and they took an early lead. Nagashima ripped a home run to tie the score. The Tigers went back into the lead, and in the seventh Nagashima struck out, but a rookie named Sadaharu Oh pumped a two-run home run to tie it again.

That brought in Murayama, who got the Giants out to end the seventh, then shut them out in the eighth, as the scoreboard clock inched toward nine-thirty, the time when the imperial couple would have to leave. They stayed in their seats, however, to see Nagashima and Murayama duel each other in the last of the ninth.

This was a classic Japanese showdown, or *shobu*. Under the unwritten rule, there could be no nibbling the corners or dirty tricks; it had to be a head-on challenge, strength against strength.

Murayama's first pitch was a forkball, for a ball. Next another forkball, for a strike. Then a fastball, which Nagashima fouled back.

Another fastball was outside, making the count 2–2. Then he uncorked still another fastball on the inside. Nagashima swung and parked it ten rows into the left field stands. To this day Murayama insists it was foul. But Nagashima circled the bases before the royal box, to be mobbed by his teammates waiting at the plate.

Nagashima went on to win the batting championship. Murayama went on to strike out 294 men in 295 innings; he won 18 and lost 10, with a 1.19 ERA, and won the Sawamura Award.

But nothing could erase the memory of that one fateful home run. Nagashima was invited to the palace for an audience. There was no imperial audience for Murayama, however. Ever after, he waited for his revenge.

When he neared the 1,500th strikeout of his career, he announced that he would get it against Nagashima; he did. Then he announced he was saving number 2,000 for Nagashima as well, and he delivered on that promise too.

In 1961 Murayama was 24–13; in 1962, 25–14 with a 1.20 ERA to lift the Tigers to the pennant. It was a partial revenge at least.

That fall Murayama took part of his anger out on the visiting Detroit Tigers. Murayama had been hit hard by the Americans earlier in the tour. But this day his fastball and forkball were snapping.

He struck out the first two hitters, Chico Fernandez (.249) and Bill Bruton (.278). Norm Cash (.243) walked, but Al Kaline (.304) was the third out.

For the next six innings not another Detroiter got on base. "I was keeping every ball down," Murayama said later. "My slider and forkball were working well. I was thinking no-hitter."

Former American League pitcher Tom Ferrick watched the game and repeated what he had said before: Murayama was the best pitcher in Japan; his fastballs were jamming the hitters, and he delivered both the fastball and the forkball with the same deceptive motion.

"No major leaguer could have hit Murayama today," Ferrick said.

For seven innings, no major leaguer did. In the eighth Dick McAuliffe (.263) led off with a walk, the first Detroit base runner since the first inning. Murayama retired Bubba Morton (.262) and Steve Boros (.228). Then Mike Roarke (.213) lined one into left field to break up the no-hitter. Lefthanded Bobo Osborne (.230) pinch-hit and popped to second.

Murayama got Fernandez out to open the ninth. Then Bruton dropped a bunt and beat it out for the second—and last—hit. Cash walked again. But Kaline lifted a foul to shortstop, McAuliffe hit a high fly to left, and the Tigers were finished. It was the first shutout a U.S. big league team had ever suffered in Japan.

The Detroiters probably didn't know what hit them, or why. As Murayama said, "I have become what I am because of Nagashima."

His final stats: 222–147, 2.09.

Yutaka Enatsu One of the most amazing athletes in Japanese baseball, in 1968 Enatsu struck out 401 men in 329 innings—that's eleven every nine innings. He was only twenty years old and just two years out of high school.

The lefty was one of the few pitchers who could get Nagashima and Oh out consistently. As a result his pennant-hungry managers worked him like a slave in every series against the Giants. Enatsu pitched the first and third games of a three-game series, and sometimes relieved in the middle game as well.

In 1970 he shut the Giants out twice in three days, then pitched the final game of the season with no rest and lost it 2–1 in ten innings. The Giants won by two games.

In 1971 Enatsu had elbow trouble and won only 15 games—but six of them were against the Giants, including 34 straight scoreless innings. And in the All-Star Game that summer he pitched three innings and struck out all nine men he faced. (In 1984 Suguru Egawa of the Giants almost matched him. He whiffed the first eight men on thirty-seven pitches, or about 4.5 per man, then got two fastball strikes on batter number nine. He shook off a sign for another fastball and instead threw a curve, which the batter hit on the ground for the final out.)

Enatsu was a free spirit who rebelled against the strict samurai-style workouts, saying he wanted to save himself for the season—the way they worked him, he was probably right. To dramatize his revolt one spring, he lay down in the outfield and went to sleep while the other pitchers ran. The Tigers finished last that year. They fired the manager and kept Enatsu.

Another time he was suspended for accepting a watch from a gambler.

In 1973 the Tigers were making a hard run at ending the Giants' pennant streak. On August 30, with one day of rest, Enatsu tossed an eleven-inning no-hitter, winning it himself 1–0 with a home run. In September he pitched a fourteen-inning one-hitter, retiring thirty-three straight batters in a row—the equal of eleven perfect innings—then lost 1–0.

When the Giants arrived for the climactic series, Enatsu faced them with two days rest and lost. As usual manager Murayama put him in to pitch the third game.

The exhausted pitcher was leading 3–1 in the seventh, when he loaded the bases on a walk, a single, and a bunt, with Oh at bat. Enatsu got two strikes on Oh, then walked him on four straight pitches. Nagashima followed with a single to win the game and, eventually, the pennant. Enatsu ended with 24–13. It was his last great year as a starter.

He became Japan's greatest relief ace and bounced to the Hawks, Carp, and Lions, fighting with most of his managers. Finally, at the age of thirty-eight, he came to America to try out with the Brewers. It was too late; his arm was gone. Fifteen years earlier, and who knows how he might have done? Red Schoendienst called him one of the greatest lefties he'd ever seen.

Enatsu's final record: 206–158, plus 193 saves. And 2,987 strikeouts.

"East is East, and west is West, and never the twain shall meet."—Rudyard Kipling

Gaijin—*Foreigners*

Next to trade policy, no area of U.S.-Japanese relations contains the seeds of more controversy than baseball. The two games may appear the same from the left field stands, but the two nations actually play two quite different games. The differences can sometimes lead to bitter misunderstanding.

According to U.S. observers, among the differences are:

Japanese managers . . .
- Conduct spring training like marine boot camp.
- Overwork their pitchers.
- Bench players in midgame for one error or one strikeout.
- Overemphasize home runs.
- Resent advice.
- Are too conservative.
- Won't let Americans excel.

Japanese players . . .
- Take half an hour batting practice every day.
- Don't miss signs.
- Don't dive for fly balls.
- Won't break up double plays.
- Don't block the plate.
- Don't backhand grounders.
- Don't chew tobacco.

Japanese pitchers . . .
- Throw sidearm and underhand more than in the States.
- Have good curves but mediocre fastballs.
- Throw brushback pitches to American hard hitters.
- Throw 300–500 pitches a day—just to stay in shape.
- Burn out early.

Japanese fans . . .
- Eat sushi instead of hotdogs at the game.
- Throw foul balls back.
- Never stop cheering with drums and trumpets throughout the game (big noise).

According to the Japanese, among the differences are:

American players . . .

- Are overpaid, stuck up, and out of shape.
- Won't work hard.
- Don't follow orders.
- Play dirty baseball.
- Bait the umpires.
- Are quick to punch opponents.
- Look down on the Japanese.
- Won't learn the language.
- Don't like Japanese food.

Still, like lovers having a quarrel, the two nations can't stay away from each other on the ballfield.

The Japanese have used 400 foreigners—in Japanese, *gaijin*, which means "outside people." There is an ambivalence toward these aliens. On the one hand, teams are tempted to use them to gain a competitive advantage (there's a cap of three per team). On the other hand, the Japanese yearn for the day that an all-Japanese team will win a *real* world series and reign as kings of the baseball world.

Although the Japanese regularly import players, they are paranoid about exporting any to the U.S. majors. America has a very favorable "balance-of-baseball" trade. And the currently devalued dollar means Japan can afford even more American shortstops—more Yanks for the yen.

In 1987 they gave Bob Horner of the Braves $1.4 million dollars. He rewarded them with six homers in his first four games and put an estimated quarter of a million more people in the park. But he spurned a $3 million offer to stay, preferring to go home to the Cards for $1 million rather than play "something like baseball."

The Japanese offered Dave Righetti a reported $8 million for two years and Reggie Jackson $2 million for one. They turned it down. But the Japanese teams landed Bill Madlock for $1 million, Bill Gullickson for $1.1 million, and Doug DeCinces for $1.5 million—this only four years after Japan's commissioner had announced a plan to ban all *gaijin*.

(Gullickson returned from Tokyo after signing his contract to report that he saw only two English words there—Sony and Mitsubishi.) However, 1989 was the most successful year for *gaijin* players, winning MVP and three batting titles of both leagues except the RBI title of the CL.

Here are some of the best—and the worst—foreigners to play in Japan.

Victor Starffin Now that baseball is an Olympic sport, the Russians have set themselves the goal of winning a gold medal some day. A preview of what the future may hold was big (six-four) Victor Starffin, the White Russian whose parents brought him to Japan fleeing the Bolshevik Revolution. He took to baseball like Khrushchev to vodka and became the greatest Russian baseball player of all time.

Joining the Dai-Nippon team, Starffin towered over the Japanese and opened a rivalry with teammate Sawamura. Vic was 28–11 in 1937, 33–5 in 1938, 42–15 in 1939 (two-thirds of the team's wins), and 38–12 (1.09) in 1940. Those 42 wins remained the record until Inao tied it in 1961.

On the U.S. tour in 1935, Americans assumed he spoke English. He didn't, once telling a waitress, "I am a chicken." (He later learned the language.)

Excused from military service as a stateless person, Starffin served as a Russian translator at the Tokyo war crimes trials. He spent his postwar years with some tailend teams but finished at 303–176, Japan's first 300-game winner.

He was killed soon afterward when he was driving his car home while drunk and hit a train. His plaque in Japan's Hall of Fame is inscribed in both Japanese and Russian.

Henry "Bozo" Wakabayashi (Wa-ka-bah-yah′-shee) The son of a Japanese immigrant to Hawaii, Wakabayashi first played in Japan in 1928, graduated from one of Tokyo's "Big Six" universities, and pitched for the Osaka Tigers from the beginning of pro ball in 1936. A finesse pitcher, Wakabayashi threw seven different pitches ("seven-color magic pitches"). In 1939 he was 30–7 with a 1.25 ERA. For six years in a row, 1939–1944, he had ERAs of under 1.81; his best was 1.06 in 1943.

Twice MVP, his most famous game came in the first Japan Series in 1950 at the age of forty-two, when he was the surprise starter in Game One against the Robins, who boasted a team batting average of .287. Bozo beat them 3-2.

Wakabayashi retired at 240–141 and 1.99 and remained a baseball ambassador for decades.

Bucky Harris Bucky Harris, another American (no, not the Senators' manager), was the Japanese home run king in the spring season of 1938 and the first foreigner to win the MVP. A veteran catcher from the American PCL, he had a good throwing arm and repeatedly won exhibitions throwing through a barrel at second base.

He studied hard to learn the language and, given a day of honor at his retirement, replied with a *sayonara* speech in Japanese.

Wally Yonamine (Yo-na′-mi-nay) The Jackie Robinson of Japan, Yonamine introduced a slashing, running game and blazed the way for American players there. This Hawaiian-born Nisei didn't know a word of Japanese when he left the San Francisco 49ers' backfield to join the Yomiuri Giants in 1951. (He'd played some baseball in the low U.S. minors; Brooklyn's Billy Loes, who pitched against him, said he was the toughest out he ever faced.)

Wally carried a double stigma. Not only was he an American, when the wounds of the war were still fresh, he was a Nisei (son of a Japanese who chooses another country), who was regarded by the Japanese in about the same way as Americans would regard a fellow countryman who had defected to Russia.

The Giants put him in center field and batted him leadoff, and he promptly hit .354. He also ran out sacrifice bunts, which surprised the Japanese, and threw rolling blocks into second basemen on the double play, which horrified them. And he played center like his stateside contemporary, Dom DiMaggio, who also wore glasses.

A Yonamine single, a hit-and-run, and a base hit by Kawakami was the usual Giant formula. They rose from third to first in Wally's first season and won the flag every year he was with them except one. Wally and Kawakami

were rivals for hitting honors, and a jealousy arose. Yonamine was much the better fielder and won three batting titles and one MVP, made seven All-Star teams, and ended with a .311 average, one of the highest in Japan. Against the Dodgers in 1956 Wally hit .347. The Japanese hailed him as the greatest leadoff man in their history, and he's probably still the biggest American star to play in Japan.

Another Nisei, Jun Hirota, caught for the Giants. When the New York Giants arrived in 1953, manager Leo Durocher, coaching at first, abandoned signals and merely told his runners to "go down on the next pitch." Hirota calmly threw them out. Leo didn't know Jun was a graduate of the University of Hawaii.

When Kawakami took over as Giant manager, he eased Wally off the team.

Yonamine got his revenge, however. As manager of the Dragons in 1974 he nipped Kawakami's Giants by one game, or .001 points, to end Kawakami's record of nine straight pennants.

Thereafter the U.S.-Japan baseball romance was a rocky one. Some Americans made a big hit. Others were big bombs.

Ugly Americans

Don Newcombe and Larry Doby   The first big-name American stars in Japan, Newcombe and Doby signed with the Chunichi Dragons in 1962. Both were in retirement, and Newk especially arrived overweight and out of shape. He pitched only 4 innings but batted .262 in 81 games in the field. Larry hit .225 with 10 home runs, although some of them were eye-popping 500-footers. The Dragons, who had finished second before they came, finished third with them. The pair were not invited back.

Marshall, Logan, Stuart, Johnson, Howard, Davis   Instead, in 1963 the optimistic Dragons signed Jim Marshall, a reserve first baseman for San Francisco with a .242 big league average, for $40,000, more than either Nagashima or Oh were making. Marshall stayed for three years, averaging .268 and 26 homers a year.

The thirty-seven-year-old Johnny Logan, a former star shortstop for the Milwaukee Braves, joined the Nankai Hawks in 1964. He hit .189 and set a Japanese record by going 38 straight at-bats without a hit.

Dick Stuart came well touted in 1967. He hit 33 homers his first year, but in his second fell to 17 homers and .217. They sent him home, where he signed with the California Angels, the first Japanese reject to return to play in the U.S. majors.

In 1973 Davey Johnson hit 43 homers for Atlanta, a record for big league second basemen. The next year the Tokyo Giants obtained him to replace the great Nagashima and integrate the Giants once again. It was a job no mortal man could fill, and Johnson didn't. He hit .197, as the Giants finished dead last. He did make a comeback the next year, and so did they, hitting .275 with 26 homers, as the Giants won the pennant. But Dave was happy to go home to the Phils, where he hit .321.

Big Frank Howard cost the Lions $80,000 in 1974. He hurt his knee, came to bat twice, and didn't get a hit. His salary came to $40,000 per at-bat.

In mid-season 1988, Dick Davis was arrested for co-

caine possession and immediately was dismissed from the Buffaloes.

Joe Pepitone   In 1973 the Yakult Atoms forked over $140,000 to Pepitone, a .258-hitting former Yankee. He arrived with shoulder-length hair, got a headache from bumping his head on low hotel room doors, complained about the food and high prices, played 14 games, hit .163, developed a "bad leg," and refused to play—but discoed into the morning. He finally flew home, leaving his roommate a $2,000 phone bill, and the Japanese with a new noun, *pepitone*, meaning "a goof-off."

The Japanese players' union protested against these high-priced foreigners who were taking jobs away from Japanese and getting paid more for doing less.

Some Handsome Americans

Blasingame, Boyer, Kirkland   Thank goodness Don Blasingame came to Japan in 1967 after hitting .258 for several teams in the States. He hit 20 points better for the Nankai Hawks, learned to speak good Japanese, was cheerful to his teammates, respectful to his manager, and popular with the fans.

When home run champ Katsuya Nomura took over as manager, he appointed "Blaser" as his head coach and *de facto* bench manager, while Nomura concentrated on his play in the field. They got along splendidly and won the pennant in 1973.

Clete Boyer, possibly the greatest fielding third baseman of all time, also won friends and influenced people as a gritty player for the Taiyo Whales in 1972–1975. He also enjoyed the people, spoke their language, ate their food, and showed them the same sensational play he had shown Yankee fans back home.

Willie Kirkland hit .240 with 20 homers a year for the San Francisco Giants and others before he joined the Hanshin Tigers in 1968. He gave them 37 homers his first year, stayed for six years, joked in Japanese with fans in the outfield, and thrilled them with long distance blasts— three in one game against the hated Giants. He hit .246, the same as he had in the States, and averaged 21 homers a year.

Leron and Leon Lee   Leron Lee, a vet of four big league teams (.250), owns the second highest lifetime batting average in Japan, .320, plus 283 homers in 11 seasons, 1977–1987. He almost won the Triple Crown in his rookie year, got an 800 percent raise, and brought his kid brother Leon over.

Leon, who never played in the majors, was almost as good, hitting .309 with 268 homers.

Both were considered "good *gaijin*," on and off the field. Leon learned Japanese well enough to act as Bob Horner's interpreter.

Xenophobia

The Japanese have not been blameless in their handling of the cross-cultural experiments. Sometimes their bias against *gaijin* is subtle, sometimes blatant.

Daryl Spencer   A 33-year-old infielder with fair power

and a .244 big league average, Spencer, at six-three, was a "monster" in Japanese eyes. In his first year, 1964, he hit 36 homers, second to Nomura's 41, and lifted the Hankyu Braves from last to second.

The next year Spencer was hitting .300 and leading Nomura by six homers in August, when, he said, his own coaches took him aside and told him to concentrate on the batting title and forget home runs, because Nomura usually finished strong. Spencer refused, so the Japanese pitchers sent their own message—they began walking him. At one stretch he got 16 straight balls. He even stepped into the box holding his bat upside down and still drew a walk. Of course, Nomura's Nankai Hawk pitchers were the most flagrant evaders of Spencer's strike zone. Nomura won the home run crown, 42–38, and took the batting crown too, .320 to .311. (He also won the RBI title for a Triple Crown.) The Braves fell to fourth.

A student of the game, Spencer analyzed every pitch and defensive alignment. One of his ideas: move the left field fence in ten feet to help him hit more homers. Spencer played for seven years. He told Whiting that his manager resented his advice. "I spoke my mind once too many times," Spencer told Whiting, "and I think I'm blackballed." Japanese observers, however, understood that manager Yukio Nishimoto had welcomed Spencer's help.

Other Americans felt a similar sense of discrimination. In 1968 Dave Roberts, a .239-hitting utility man with several big league clubs, hit 40 homers for the Sankei Atoms, to Oh's 49. The next year Roberts was leading for the Triple Crown, when a Giants pitcher ran into him at first base, breaking his shoulder. Dave was out for the rest of the year, and Oh and Nagashima took the three batting titles.

George Altman In 1968 the former National League outfielder (.269, fair power) started a new career in Japan at age thirty-five. He was an immediate success, hitting .320 with 34 homers and 100 RBI. In 1970 he helped pull the Lotte Orions into first place with .319 and 30 homers.

In 1969, George said, he got nothing but balls from the pitchers and nothing but strikes from the umps. He slumped to 21 homers and .269.

In 1971 Altman had his best year—39 homers and 103 RBI, and was in a race for the batting title with his teammate, Shinichi Eto. When Eto came up, he noticed, the infielders suddenly left a big hole between first and second, and Eto punched four hits through it in one game. "That," Altman told Whiting, "is when I figured my chances of winning the title were almost zero."

Randy Bass Big, bewhiskered Randy Bass played a little first base for the Padres and Rangers (batting .212) before joining the Japanese Hanshin Tigers in 1983. In 1985 he burst into stardom, winning the Triple Crown with .350, 134 RBIs, and 54 home runs.

He was just one home run short of tying Oh's Japanese record, with one game left—against the Giants, managed by Oh. The Giant pitchers walked him all four times he came to bat.

But Bass did lead the Tigers to the pennant over the hated Giants, and his home runs won two Japan Series games as the Tigers took the Japanese championship in seven games. He became a media star, his poster advertisements appearing all over Tokyo. He even agreed to shave his beard for a razor blade company.

Some Other Gaijin Stars

Some minor leaguers have done well in Japan.

Jack Bloomfield won batting titles in 1962–1963.

Pitcher Joe Stanka won an MVP, with 26–7 for the Nankai Hawks in 1964.

Gene Bacque (Bock'-ay) won a Sawamura (Cy Young) for pitching the Tigers to the 1964 pennant with a 29–9. However, his brushback pitches appalled the Japanese. When he tried one against the great Oh, the whole Giants team mobbed him. In the melee, Oh says, coach Hiroshi Arakawa, Oh's best friend and an *aikido* black belt, broke Gene's thumb and put him out for the rest of the season.

Clarence Jones won a home run crown in 1974.

Boomer Wells won the Triple Crown and MVP in 1984.

Richard Lancellotti was home run king in 1987 while batting .218.

New Trend: "Cup of Tea" Gaijin

Cecil Fielder's great success—.302 with 38 homers in 106 games in 1989—illustrates a new trend of U.S. players traveling to Japan for a "cup of coffee."

Far from being over the hill like most earlier U.S. arrivals, Fielder was only twenty-five when he arrived from the Blue Jays after a frustrating .230 season, when he was platooned against lefthanders only. He replaced long-time favorite Randy Bass of the Hanshin Tigers, even wearing Bass's uniform number, 44.

Japanese pitchers soon discovered Fielder's weakness, the high inside fastball, and his strikeouts earned him the nickname "The Big Fan." However, in June he came back with home run after home run, and his long shots excited the fans. He knocked two balls completely out of the park in one day. By September he was leading the league in homers (two more than Larry Parrish). Then Cecil, angry after a strikeout, tossed his bat, which bounced back, breaking his finger and ending his season. But with his new-found confidence, he returned to the States to blast 51 homers for the Tigers.

In 1989 pitcher Bill Gullickson, twenty-nine, came off a 4–2 season with the Yanks to sign with the Tokyo Giants for two years. He posted won-lost records of 14-9 and 7-5 before returning to Houston, where he was 10–14. In 1991 he won 20 games for Detroit.

Others who went from the U.S. majors to Japan and back to the majors were Vance Law, Warren Cromartie, Goose Gossage, and Tony Bernazard.

One investment fizzled badly. In 1992 the Japanese put out $1.5 million for the Dodgers' Mike Marshall, thirty-two, but he batted only .246 with 9 homers and was sent back home at the end of the season.

That year former Angel third baseman Jack Howell, thirty, had a great initial season in Japan. He won the Central League home run (38) and batting (.331) titles and was voted MVP. It earned him a 1993 contract for $1.5 million, tying Marshall's *gaijin* record but leaving him $500,000 short of former Yankee Mel Hall.

Japanese in America

Mashi Murakami Many Japanese have played in the U.S. minors and one in the majors.

The big leaguer was Masanori "Mashi" Murakami, who almost caused a complete rupture in U.S.-Japan diamond relations. Murakami was one of three members of the Nankai Hawks sent over to gain experience with the San Francisco Giants' farm teams in Fresno and Magic Valley in 1964. The twenty-year-old did so well (11–7) and was so well liked (bowing to teammates who made good plays behind him) that he was promoted to the Giants. He made his debut against the last-place Mets before 50,000 fans at Shea Stadium and pitched one inning of shutout relief. That year he won one and saved one with a 1.80 ERA. He struck out 15 men in 15 innings and walked only 1.

At this point the Giants invoked the fine print in their contract—the paragraph giving them the right to buy any of the three who made the parent club. The Japanese had never anticipated this development! They said Murakami had only been on loan. Besides, they said, he was homesick and didn't want to go back to the States. The boy dutifully agreed. The Hawks even charged that the contract was a forgery, thus enraging the Giants. Who did they think Murakami was, club president Chub Feeney demanded—Christy Mathewson?

U.S. Commissioner Ford Frick threatened to break relations with Japan if they didn't honor the contract. This could have cut off all further U.S. players going there to play.

At last a compromise broke the impasse. Murakami would play one more year in the States, then would be free to choose his own destiny.

Mashi flew back to San Francisco, won 4 games, lost 1, saved 8, and struck out 85 men in 74 innings. He was a darling of the San Francisco Nisei community.

In 1966 the Hawks enticed him home with a $40,000 contract, twice what the Giants had offered. The Hawks rubbed their hands in anticipation of seeing Murakami obliterate every pitching record in the book. Alas, he never lived up to his promise. He won a total of 9 games his first two years. He had only one good year, 1968, when he was 18–4. He was the first and last Japanese to play in the U.S. majors.

The Young Lions

In a second experiment, the Taiheiyo Lions bought a U.S. minor league team in Lodi, California, and stocked it with nine of their rookies plus a coach, along with U.S. players.

But the Japanese players, like some Americans in Japan, couldn't adjust to the food and the language. After two years the Lions sold their Lodi club and brought their players home.

Undaunted, in 1982 the Seibu Lions (bought by Seibu Railway Co. after the 1978 season) signed a working agreement with the Baltimore Orioles' Class A farm team at San Jose and each year have sent several rookies there for experience. The plan paid off big. The Lions won the pennant five of the next six years, and experts attributed it in part to their San Jose graduates. Most famous of the group was Koji Akiyama, the 1987 Japanese home run king.

In spring 1990, American baseball fans were irritated when a Japanese whiskey company, Suntory, bought the Birmingham Barons (AA) and in 1992 the Seattle Mariners were purchased by Japanese interests, the Nintendo company, as well.

The "Magic" Manager, Mihara

Two of the greatest managers in Japanese history were Osamu Mihara and Shigeru Mizuhara. Their duels are compared to the legendary duel of the greatest swordsmen of literature, Miyamoto Musashi and Sasaki Kojiro.

Mihara and Mizuhara attended rival high schools on Shikoku Island and went to rival colleges in the highly competitive Tokyo Big Six Conference. In 1931, before 65,000 fans, Mihara stole home against pitcher Mizuhara to lead his school to victory.

In 1934 both played on the All-Japan team against Babe Ruth's Stars. Then Mihara went into military service; Mizuhara toured the States with Dai-Nippon, sparked the Giants to several pennants (he was MVP in 1942), and then was drafted himself.

Mizuhara languished in a Soviet POW camp for four years after the war, while Mihara took over the Giants and rebuilt that once proud club into champs in 1949.

But Mihara's triumph was spoiled when Mizuhara was repatriated that same year. "I am Mizuhara," he announced. "I have returned." Mizuhara was given the manager's job and won eight pennants in ten years, 1950–1959. Mihara was kicked upstairs, where he spent his time playing *go*.

Then Mihara left to manage a new club, the Nishitetsu Lions, in faroff Kyushu. He lived in the dorm with his players, mostly recent high school kids like Nakanishi and slugging shortstop Yasumitsu Toyoda, and built them into champs in 1954. They won again in 1956 and beat Mizuhara's strutting Yomiuri Giants in the Japan Series. They did it again in 1957 and 1958. In the last year the Giants won the first three games, but the Lions, behind Inao, won the last four.

In 1960 Mihara moved back to the Central League with the Taiyo Whales, who had finished last for six straight years. Shades of the Mets! In Mihara's first year, he whipped the Giants for the pennant by 4½ games, then swept the Japan Series in four straight!

No wonder they called him "the Magician."

A Real World Series

Matsutaro Shoriki died in 1969 with one dream still unfulfilled—a real World Series between his Giants and the winner of the American World Series. It's a goal every Japanese fan keeps before his eyes.

In frequent series against U.S. big league teams, the Japanese have already established one thing: the Americans can still win, but they have to field strong teams and play hard to do it.

In 1966 the Giants played seven games against the NL champion Dodgers and won four of them. Overall, the Dodgers were 9–8–1 in Japan. Of course, Sandy Koufax and Don Drysdale didn't make the trip. But their number

three pitcher, Claude Osteen (17–14), did and was bombed out of the box five times.

In 1968 the NL champion Cards (Bob Gibson, Lou Brock, Orlando Cepeda, etc.) arrived fresh from the World Series. Beset by jet lag, they lost two of their first three games but came back to win 12 of their last 15 for a 13–5 record overall. The Japanese might have done better if Nagashima had not missed the series with an injury. Oh hit .356 with six homers.

In 1971, after a 9–6 spring training record against U.S. teams, Kawakami announced that "the Americans have nothing more to teach us." The nation looked confidently forward to the arrival that fall of the AL champ Orioles for what the Japanese were hailing as the long awaited "world series." Bowie Kuhn even threw out the first ball.

The Japanese knocked Jim Palmer (20–9) out three times, but Pat Dobson (20–8) pitched three shutouts, including a no-hitter. The O's held Oh to a .111 average. Nagashima hit .258, and the Orioles won 12 games to two, with four ties. But when the Americans sent subpar teams—the fifth-place Mets in 1974 and the fifth-place Orioles in 1984, the competition was closer.

The U.S.–Japan Series

Satellite TV brings U.S. major league games to fans in Japan, and as a result major league caps, jackets, and T-shirts sell well there.

In 1990 Japan stunned a visiting U.S. all star team, winning 4 games against 3 losses and a tie. The major leaguers included Barry Bonds, Cecil Fielder, Roberto Alomar, Kelly Cruber, Bobby Thigpen, Ramon Martinez, Dave Stewart, and others. Following Japan's 1984 Olympic gold medal, the results started speculation that the Japanese were approaching U.S. major league caliber.

However, in '92 Roger Clemens led another all star squad to Japan, and they won handily, 7 games to 1 with a tie. It seemed clear that Japan has not produced the formidable players it did in the 1960s, such as Oh, Nagashima, Nakanishi, Inao, Kaneda, etc.

Nonetheless, his league leading totals are prodigious:

RBI	1982, 1985, 1986, 1989, 1990
HR	1982, 1985, 1986, 1990, 1991
BA	1981, 1982, 1983, 1985, 1986

The 1992 season saw a decline in his batting: to a .292 average with 71 RBIs and just 22 homers.

There is still about a twenty-pound difference between the average U.S. and Japanese big leaguer, which means that today's Japanese player is about as big as a major leaguer of Babe Ruth's day.

Some Japanese doubt that Japan can ever catch up with the U.S. majors. They say the Olympics are a better arena for competition — Japan won the "demonstration" Olympic title in 1984, defeating the United States in the finale.

Will we ever see a *real* World Series? If so, when? In this generation? The next?

Japan's economic miracle, which surprised the world, suggests that one thing is certain—don't bet on anything.

Pennant Winners: Japan Pro-Baseball League

YEAR		TEAM	WON	LOST	PCT.	YEAR	TEAM	WON	LOST	PCT.
1936	FALL	TOKYO GIANTS	18	9	—	1942	TOKYO GIANTS	73	27	.730
1937	SPRING	TOKYO GIANTS	41	13	.759	1943	TOKYO GIANTS	54	27	.667
	FALL	OSAKA TIGERS	39	9	.813	1944	HANSHIN	27	6	.818
1938	SPRING	OSAKA TIGERS	29	6	.829	1945	PLAY SUSPENDED			
	FALL	TOKYO GIANTS	30	9	.769	1946	KINKI GREATRING	65	38	.631
1939		TOKYO GIANTS	66	26	.717	1947	OSAKA TIGERS	79	37	.681
1940		TOKYO GIANTS	76	28	.731	1948	NANKAI HAWKS	87	49	.640
1941		TOKYO GIANTS	62	22	.738	1949	YOMIURI GIANTS	85	48	.639

Pennant Winners: Central League

YEAR	TEAM	WON	LOST	PCT.	YEAR	TEAM	WON	LOST	PCT.
1950	SHOCHIKU ROBINS	98	35	.737	1972	YOMIURI GIANTS	74	52	.587
1951	YOMIURI GIANTS	79	29	.731	1973	YOMIURI GIANTS	66	60	.524
1952	YOMIURI GIANTS	83	37	.692	1974	CHUNICHI DRAGONS	70	49	.588
1953	YOMIURI GIANTS	87	37	.702	1975	HIROSHIMA CARP	72	47	.605
1954	CHUNICHI DRAGONS	86	40	.683	1976	YOMIURI GIANTS	76	45	.628
1955	YOMIURI GIANTS	92	37	.713	1977	YOMIURI GIANTS	80	46	.635
1956	YOMIURI GIANTS	82	44	.646	1978	YAKULT SWALLOWS	68	46	.596
1957	YOMIURI GIANTS	74	53	.581	1979	HIROSHIMA CARP	67	50	.573
1958	YOMIURI GIANTS	77	52	.596	1980	HIROSHIMA CARP	73	44	.624
1959	YOMIURI GIANTS	77	48	.612	1981	YOMIURI GIANTS	73	48	.603
1960	TAIYO WHALES	70	56	.554	1982	CHUNICHI DRAGONS	64	47	.577
1961	YOMIURI GIANTS	71	53	.569	1983	YOMIURI GIANTS	72	50	.590
1962	HANSHIN TIGERS	75	55	.577	1984	HIROSHIMA CARP	75	45	.625
1963	YOMIURI GIANTS	83	55	.601	1985	HANSHIN TIGERS	74	49	.602
1964	HANSHIN TIGERS	80	56	.588	1986	HIROSHIMA CARP	73	46	.613
1965	YOMIURI GIANTS	91	47	.659	1987	YOMIURI GIANTS	76	43	.639
1966	YOMIURI GIANTS	89	41	.685	1988	CHUNICHI DRAGONS	79	46	.632
1967	YOMIURI GIANTS	84	46	.646	1989	YOMIURI GIANTS	84	44	.656
1968	YOMIURI GIANTS	77	53	.592	1990	YOMIURI GIANTS	88	42	.677
1969	YOMIURI GIANTS	73	51	.589	1991	HIROSHIMA CARP	74	56	.569
1970	YOMIURI GIANTS	79	47	.627	1992	YAKULT SWALLOWS	69	61	.531
1971	YOMIURI GIANTS	70	52	.574					

Pennant Winners: Pacific League

YEAR		TEAM	WON	LOST	PCT.
1950		MAINICHI ORIONS	81	34	.704
1951		NANKAI HAWKS	72	24	.750
1952		NANKAI HAWKS	76	44	.633
1953		NANKAI HAWKS	71	48	.597
1954		NISHITETSU LIONS	90	47	.657
1955		NANKAI HAWKS	99	41	.707
1956		NISHITETSU LIONS	96	51	.646
1957		NISHITETSU LIONS	83	44	.648
1958		NISHITETSU LIONS	78	47	.619
1959		NANKAI HAWKS	88	42	.677
1960		DAIMAI ORIONS	82	48	.631
1961		NANKAI HAWKS	85	49	.629
1962		TOEI FLYERS	78	52	.600
1963		NISHITETSU LIONS	86	60	.589
1964		NANKAI HAWKS	84	63	.571
1965		NANKAI HAWKS	88	49	.642
1966		NANKAI HAWKS	79	51	.608
1967		HANKYU BRAVES	75	55	.577
1968		HANKYU BRAVES	80	50	.615
1969		HANKYU BRAVES	76	50	.603
1970		LOTTE ORIONS	80	47	.630
1971		HANKYU BRAVES	80	39	.672
1972		HANKYU BRAVES	80	48	.625
1973	1st HALF	*NANKAI HAWKS	38	26	.594
	2nd HALF	HANKYU BRAVES	43	19	.694
1974	1st HALF	HANKYU BRAVES	36	23	.610
	2nd HALF	*LOTTE ORIONS	38	23	.623

YEAR		TEAM	WON	LOST	PCT.
1975	1st HALF	*HANKYU BRAVES	38	25	.603
	2nd HALF	KINTETSU BUFFALOES	40	20	.667
1976	1st HALF	HANKYU BRAVES	42	21	.667
	2nd HALF	HANKYU BRAVES	37	24	.607
1977	1st HALF	*HANKYU BRAVES	35	25	.583
	2nd HALF	LOTTE ORIONS	33	24	.579
1978	1st HALF	HANKYU BRAVES	44	20	.688
	2nd HALF	HANKYU BRAVES	38	19	.667
1979	1st HALF	*KINTETSU BUFFALOES	39	19	.672
	2nd HALF	HANKYU BRAVES	36	23	.610
1980	1st HALF	LOTTE ORIONS	33	25	.569
	2nd HALF	*KINTETSU BUFFALOES	35	26	.574
1981	1st HALF	LOTTE ORIONS	35	26	.574
	2nd HALF	*NIPPON HAM FIGHTERS	37	23	.617
1982	1st HALF	*SEIBU LIONS	36	27	.571
	2nd HALF	NIPPON HAM FIGHTERS	35	23	.603
1983		SEIBU LIONS	86	40	.683
1984		HANKYU BRAVES	75	45	.625
1985		SEIBU LIONS	79	45	.637
1986		SEIBU LIONS	68	49	.581
1987		SEIBU LIONS	71	45	.612
1988		SEIBU LIONS	73	51	.589
1989		KINTETSU BUFFALOES	71	54	.568
1990		SEIBU LIONS	81	45	.643
1991		SEIBU LIONS	81	43	.653
1992		SEIBU LIONS	80	47	.630

*playoff winner

Japan Series

YEAR	TEAM/LEAGUE	WON	TEAM/LEAGUE	WON	
1950	MAINICHI ORIONS, PL	4	SHOCHIKU ROBINS, CL	2	
1951	YOMIURI GIANTS, CL	4	NANKAI HAWKS, PL	1	
1952	YOMIURI GIANTS, CL	4	NANKAI HAWKS, PL	2	
1953	YOMIURI GIANTS, CL	4	NANKAI HAWKS, PL	2	1 TIE
1954	CHUNICHI DRAGONS, CL	4	NISHITETSU LIONS, PL	3	
1955	YOMIURI GIANTS, CL	4	NANKAI HAWKS, PL	3	
1956	NISHITETSU LIONS, PL	4	YOMIURI GIANTS, CL	2	
1957	NISHITETSU LIONS, PL	4	YOMIURI GIANTS, CL	0	1 TIE
1958	NISHITETSU LIONS, PL	4	YOMIURI GIANTS, CL	3	
1959	NANKAI HAWKS, PL	4	YOMIURI GIANTS, CL	0	
1960	TAYIO WHALES, CL	4	DAIMAI ORIONS, PL	0	
1961	YOMIURI GIANTS, CL	4	NANKAI HAWKS, PL	2	
1962	TOEI FLYERS, PL	4	HANSHIN TIGERS, CL	2	1 TIE
1963	YOMIURI GIANTS, CL	4	NISHITETSU LIONS, PL	3	
1964	NANKAI HAWKS, PL	4	HANSHIN TIGERS	3	
1965	YOMIURI GIANTS, CL	4	NANKAI HAWKS, PL	1	
1966	YOMIURI GIANTS, CL	4	NANKAI HAWKS, PL	2	
1967	YOMIURI GIANTS, CL	4	HANKYU BRAVES, PL	2	
1968	YOMIURI GIANTS, CL	4	HANKYU BRAVES, PL	2	
1969	YOMIURI GIANTS, CL	4	HANKYU BRAVES, PL	2	
1970	YOMIURI GIANTS, CL	4	LOTTE ORIONS, PL	1	
1971	YOMIURI GIANTS, CL	4	HANKYU BRAVES, PL	1	
1972	YOMIURI GIANTS, CL	4	HANKYU BRAVES, PL	1	
1973	YOMIURI GIANTS, CL	4	NANKAI HAWKS, PL	1	
1974	LOTTE ORIONS, PL	4	CHUNICHI DRAGONS, CL	2	

YEAR	TEAM/LEAGUE	WON	TEAM/LEAGUE	WON	
1975	HANKYU BRAVES, PL	4	HIROSHIMA CARP, CL	0	2 TIES
1976	HANKYU BRAVES, PL	4	YOMIURI GIANTS, CL	3	
1977	HANKYU BRAVES, PL	4	YOMIURI GIANTS, CL	1	
1978	YAKULT SWALLOWS, CL	4	HANKYU BRAVES, PL	3	
1979	HIROSHIMA CARP, CL	4	KINTETSU BUFFALOES, PL	3	
1980	HIROSHIMA CARP, CL	4	KINTETSU BUFFALOES, PL	3	
1981	YOMIURI GIANTS, CL	4	NIPPON HAM FIGHTERS, PL	2	
1982	SEIBU LIONS, PL	4	CHUNICHI DRAGONS, CL	2	
1983	SEIBU LIONS, PL	4	YOMIURI GIANTS, CL	3	
1984	HIROSHIMA CARP, CL	4	HANYKU BRAVES, PL	3	
1985	HANSHIN TIGERS, CL	4	SEIBU LIONS, PL	2	
1986	SEIBU LIONS, PL	4	HIROSHIMA CARP, CL	3	1 TIE
1987	SEIBU LIONS, PL	4	YOMIURI GIANTS, CL	2	
1988	SEIBU LIONS, PL	4	CHUNICHI DRAGONS, CL	1	
1989	YOMIURI GIANTS, CL	4	KINTETSU BUFFALOES, PL	3	
1990	SEIBU LIONS, PL	4	YOMIURI GIANTS, CL	0	
1991	SEIBU LIONS, PL	4	HIROSHIMA CARP, CL	3	
1992	SEIBU LIONS, PL	4	YAKULT SWALLOWS, CL	3	

U.S. Major League Batters in Japan

Name	Yrs		G	HR	BA	Titles Won
Adair, Jerry	1	1971	90	7	.300	
Adduci, Jim	1	1987	82	13	.268	
Allen, Kim	2	1982-83	125	5	.265	
Allen, Rod	3	1989-91	245	45	.288	
Alou, Matty	3	1974-76	262	14	.283	
Altman, George	8	1968-75	935	205	.309	68 rbi, 71 ba
Andrews, Mike	1	1975-76	123	12	.231	
Arnold, Chris	3	1978-81	330	43	.274	
Aspromonte, Ken	3	1964-66	295	31	.273	
Ault, Doug	1	1981	102	18	.307	
Barbier, Jim	1	1970	93	9	.188	
Bass, Randy	6	1983-88	614	202	.337	85-86 hr-ba-rbi, 83-84 ba, 85 MVP
Bathe, Bill	2	1991-92	156	16	.236	
Batista, Rafael	1	1975	48	3	.204	
Baumer, Jim	5	1963-67	690	82	.251	
Bean, Billy	1	1992	7	0	.208	
Bernazard, Tony	3	1988-90	308	67	.289	
Bertoia, Reno	1	1964	20	1	.175	
Blasingame, Don	3	1967-69	366	15	.274	
Boisclair, Bruce	1	1980	80	1	.249	

Name	Yrs		G	HR	BA	Titles Won
Boles, Carl	6	1966-71	577	117	.265	
Boyer, Clete	4	1972-75	419	71	.257	
Bradford, Buddy	1	1977	56	4	.192	
Bradly, Phil	1	1991	121	21	.282	
Brant, Marshall	2	1984-85	118	25	.244	
Breedon, Hal	3	1976-78	260	79	.251	
Brewer, Tony	3	1986-89	389	82	.310	
Briggs, Dan	2	1982-83	176	18	.258	
Briggs, John	1	1976	47	7	.227	
Brouhard, Mark	2	1986-87	140	23	.265	
Brown, Marty	1	1992	109	19	.233	
Brown, Mike	1	1990	70	7	.282	
Bryant, Ralph	5	1988-92	493	172	.263	89 hr-MVP
Budaska, Mark	1	1982	86	3	.208	
Buford, Don	4	1973-76	490	65	.270	
Cage, Wayne	2	1981-82	252	62	.235	
Chance, Bob	2	1969-70	143	22	.271	
Christian, Bob	2	1971-72	232	27	.263	
Coggins, Frank	1	1973	13	2	.125	
Corey, Mark	1	1984	31	3	.215	
Cosey, Ray	1	1981	120	15	.251	

Name	Yrs		G	HR	BA	Titles Won
Cromartie, Warren	7	1984-90	779	171	.321	89 ba-MVP
Cruz, Hector	1	1983	58	4	.240	
Cruz, Tommy	6	1980-85	712	120	.310	
Dade, Paul	1	1981	37	1	.219	
Davis, Alvin	1	1992	40	5	.275	
Davis, Dick	5	1984-88	461	117	.331	
Davis, Willie	2	1977-78	199	43	.297	
Dayett, Brian	4	1988-91	145	121	.268	
DeCinces, Doug	1	1989	84	19	.244	
Destrade, Orestes	4	1989-92	471	154	.264	
Diaz, Mike	4	1989-92	350	114	.281	
Distefano, Benny	1	1990	56	39	.215	
Doby, Larry	1	1962	72	10	.225	
Dodson, Pat	1	1989	6	0	.313	
Doyle, Jeff	2	1984-85	243	29	.263	
Duncan, Taylor	1	1980	64	14	.235	
Dupree, Mike	1	1980	127	10	.266	
Easler, Mike	2	1988-89	142	26	.302	
Edwards, Mike	1	1983	53	1	.291	
Emery, Calvin	1	1970	94	8	.213	
Essegian, Chuck	1	1964	110	15	.263	
Ewing, Sam	1	1979	119	15	.286	
Fernandez, Chico	1	1965	52	1	.144	
Fielder, Cecil	1	1989	106	38	.302	
Gaines, Joe	1	1969	51	3	.205	
Gardner, Art	2	1981-82	218	30	.272	
Garrett, Adrian	3	1977-79	384	102	.260	
Garrett, Wayne	2	1979-80	192	28	.241	
Gentile, Jim	1	1969	65	8	.256	
Gonzales, Dan	1	1981	9	1	.174	
Gonzalez, Denny	2	1991-92	350	114	.281	
Gonzalez, Tony	1	1972	31	0	.297	
Goodwin, Danny	1	1986	83	8	.231	
Green, David	1	1986	67	10	.270	
Grunwald, Alfred	1	1962	70	3	.211	
Hadley, Kent	6	1962-67	781	131	.260	
Hammond, Steve	1	1987	115	9	.274	
Hampton, Ike	1	1981	72	15	.230	
Hansen, Jimmy	2	1977-78	232	31	.271	
Harlow, Larry	1	1982	42	4	.164	
Harper, Terry	1	1988	10	2	.143	
Harris, Vic	3	1981-83	280	35	.253	
Hengel, Dave	2	1990-91	21	4	.183	
Hicks, Jim	2	1973-74	183	33	.247	
Hilton, Dave	3	1978-80	251	38	.284	
Hinshaw, George	1	1989	53	8	.294	
Horner, Bob	1	1987	93	31	.327	
Hopkins, Gail	3	1975-77	360	69	.282	
Hostetler, Dave	2	1986-87	254	42	.270	
Howard, Frank	1	1974	1	0	.000	
Howell, Jack	1	1992	112	38	.332	
Ireland, Tom	2	1983-84	204	18	.275	
Jackson, Lou	3	1966-68	329	68	.257	
James, Skip	1	1980	111	21	.269	
Jestadt, Garry	2	1975-76	256	27	.239	
Johnson, Dave	2	1975-76	199	39	.241	
Johnson, Frank	1	1972	101	13	.232	
Johnson, Greg	1	1982	104	10	.256	
Johnson, Randy	2	1987-88	142	9	.306	
Johnson, Stan	1	1969	96	5	.242	
Jones, Bobby	2	1979-80	174	20	.284	
Jones, Clarence	8	1970-77	961	246	.239	74, 76 hr
Jones, Ruppert	1	1988	52	8	.254	
Keough, Marty	1	1968	134	17	.231	
Kirkland, Willie	6	1968-73	723	126	.246	
Kostro, Frank	1	1970	37	1	.200	
Klaus, Billy	1	1963	62	3	.257	
Krsnich, Mike	5	1963-67	506	90	.265	
Lacock, Pete	1	1981	90	10	.269	
Laga, Mike	1	1991	124	32	.236	
Larker, Norm	2	1965-66	224	14	.267	
Lancellotti, Rich	2	1987-88	200	55	.207	87 hr
Law, Vance	1	1990	122	29	.313	
Lee, Leron	11	1977-87	1315	283	.320	80 ba, 77 hr-rbi
Lefebvre, Jim	4	1973-76	330	60	.263	
Lezcano, Sixto	1	1987	20	3	.217	
Lind, Jack	1	1977	65	7	.237	
Lis, Joe	1	1978	95	6	.206	
Llenas, Winston	1	1976	101	6	.227	
Locklear, Gene	1	1978	108	8	.240	
Logan, Johnny	1	1964	96	7	.189	
Lolich, Ron	3	1974-76	272	56	.238	
Lopez, Arturo	6	1968-73	750	116	.290	
Loman, Doug	1	1986	126	14	.291	
Lum, Mike	1	1982	117	12	.269	
Lyttle, Jim	7	1977-83	876	166	.285	
Macha, Ken	4	1982-85	473	82	.304	
Madlock, Bill	1	1988	123	19	.263	
Manuel, Charlie	6	1976-81	621	189	.303	79-80 hr, 80 rbi, 79 MVP
Marshall, Jim	3	1963-65	408	78	.268	

Name	Yrs		G	HR	BA	Titles Won
Marshall, Mike	1	1992	67	9	.246	
Martin, Gene	6	1974-79	746	189	.272	
Martinez, Carmelo	1	1992	42	6	.227	
May, Carlos	4	1978-81	415	70	.309	
McFadden, Leon	1	1972	54	2	.283	
McGuire, Mickey	2	1973-74	207	11	.265	
McManus, Jim	2	1962-63	190	20	.236	
McNulty, Bill	1	1975	64	13	.190	
Mejias, Roman	1	1966	30	0	.288	
Meyer, Joey	1	1990	42	26	.275	
Millan, Felix	3	1978-80	325	12	.306	79 ba
Miller, John	3	1970-72	382	79	.245	
Mitchell, Bobby	4	1976-79	474	113	.250	78 hr
Money, Don	1	1984	29	8	.260	
Morton, Bubba	1	1970	48	3	.173	
Moseby, Lloyd	1	1992	96	25	.306	
Motley, Darryl	1	1992	25	5	.208	
Murphy, Dwayne	1	1990	34	5	.229	
Muser, Tony	1	1979	65	2	.196	
Nettles, Jim	1	1975	84	3	.234	
Newcombe, Don	1	1962	81	12	.262	
Nieman, Bob	1	1963	110	13	.301	
Nyman, Chris	2	1984-85	246	55	.276	
Oglivie, Ben	2	1987-88	224	46	.306	
O'Malley, Tom	2	1991-92	241	36	.315	
Ontiveros, Steve	6	1980-85	686	82	.312	
Ortenzio, Frank	2	1979-80	149	30	.250	
Paciorek, Jim	2	1988-89	248	29	.333	
Paciorek, Tom	5	1988-92	624	79	.322	
Paredes, Johnny	1	1992	53	3	.242	
Parker, Wes	1	1974	127	14	.301	
Parrish, Larry	1	1989-90	235	70	.260	89 hr
Palys, Stan	4	1964-67	446	66	.275	
Paredes, Johnny	1	1992	53	3	.242	
Parrish, Larry	1	1989-90	235	70	.260	
Pepitone, Joe	1	1973	14	1	.163	
Perlozzo, Sam	1	1980	118	5	.281	
Peterson, Carl	3	1961-63	357	58	.272	
Pierce, Jack	1	1977	95	13	.227	
Pointer, Aaron	3	1970-72	302	40	.230	
Ponce, Carlos	5	1986-90	533	119	.296	87 rbi, 88 hr-rbi
Powell, Alonzo	1	1992	88	13	.308	
Putnam, Pat	2	1986-87	243	37	.266	
Qualls, Jimmy	2	1972-73	162	15	.252	
Raines, Larry	3	1953-55	330	31	.302	54 ba, 53 sb
Rajsich, Gary	3	1986-88	317	76	.283	
Rawdon, Wade	2	1989-90	149	24	.289	
Ray, Johnny	2	1991-92	159	13	.269	
Reid, Jessie	2	1991-92	128	20	.250	
Reinback, Mike	5	1976-80	565	94	.296	
Repoz, Roger	5	1974-77	526	122	.262	
Reynolds, Robert	2	1991-92	231	34	.283	
Rivera, Bombo	2	1985-86	158	37	.240	
Rivera, German	1	1989	123	25	.260	
Roberts, Dave	7	1967-73	814	183	.275	
Robson, Tom	1	1976	37	3	.209	
Rodgers, Andre	1	1969	49	4	.210	
Roig, Tony	6	1963-78	779	126	.255	
Rosario, Jim	2	1975-76	131	5	.215	
Ryal, Mark	2	1991-92	124	24	.286	
Scheinblum, Rich	2	1975-76	239	33	.295	
Scott, John	3	1979-81	279	48	.262	
Sheets, Larry	1	1992	131	26	.308	
Shirley, Bart	2	1971-72	246	15	.183	
Sipin, John	9	1972-80	1036	218	.297	
Smith, Chris	2	1984-85	68	5	.202	
Smith, Reggie	2	1983-84	186	45	.271	
Smith, Willie	2	1972-73	170	29	.259	
Solaita, Tony	4	1980-83	510	155	.268	81 hr-rbi
Sorrell, Bill	2	1972-73	183	20	.278	
Spencer, Daryl	7	1964-70	731	152	.275	64, 65 ba
Spikes, Charlie	1	1981	26	1	.122	
Stanton, Leroy	1	1979	121	23	.225	
Stephens, Gene	1	1966	109	5	.224	
Stroughter, Steve	1	1983	28	5	.276	
Stuart, Dick	2	1967-68	208	49	.257	
Tatum, Jarvis	1	1971	31	1	.192	
Taylor, Robert	3	1973-75	358	30	.259	
Testa, Nick	1	1962	57	0	.136	
Thomas, Lee	1	1969	109	12	.263	
Thomasson, Gary	2	1981-82	167	20	.249	
Tolan, Bobby	1	1978	98	6	.267	
Torve, Kelvin	1	1992	96	11	.305	
Traber, Jim	2	1990-91	247	53	.287	
Tracy, Jim	2	1983-84	128	20	.301	
Tyrone, Jim	3	1979-82	435	74	.287	
Upshaw, Willie	2	1989-90	174	39	.245	
Valentine, Fred	1	1970	123	11	.246	
Venable, Max	1	1992	111	13	.268	
Versalles, Zoilo	1	1972	48	4	.189	

Name	Yrs		G	HR	BA	Titles Won
Vidal, Jose	1	1971	39	2	.221	
Vukovich, George	2	1986-87	222	32	.256	
Walls, Lee	1	1965	108	14	.239	
Walton, Danny	1	1978	75	9	.215	
Ward, Jay	1	1966	104	14	.238	
Wells, Greg	10	1983-92	1148	277	.317	84 hr-ba-rbi-MVP, 87 rbi, 89 ba-rbi
Werhas, Johnny	1	1971	100	8	.214	
White, Jerry	2	1984-85	218	37	.251	
White, Roy	3	1980-82	362	54	.283	
Whitfield, Terry	3	1981-83	374	85	.289	
Williams, Bernie	6	1975-80	718	96	.258	
Williams, Dallas	1	1988	100	10	.242	

Name	Yrs		G	HR	BA	Titles Won
Williams, Eddie	1	1991	49	5	.252	
Williams, Walt	2	1976-77	239	44	.277	
Wills, Bump	2	1983-84	203	16	.259	
Wilson, George	2	1963-64	225	27	.258	
Wilson, Jim	1	1990	6	1	.059	
Windhorn, Gordon	6	1964-69	641	86	.255	
Winters, Matt	3	1990-92	377	103	.281	
Wolfe, Larry	1	1982	88	14	.224	
Woods, Ron	2	1975-76	192	19	.263	
Wright, George	1	1988	89	11	.263	
Wynne, Marvell	1	1991	123	13	.230	
Young, Mike	1	1990	69	11	.234	
Zimmer, Don	1	1966	87	9	.182	

U.S. Major League Pitchers in Japan*

Name	Yrs		Won-Lost	ERA
Alexander, Bob	1	1959	2-5	4.67
Anderson, Scott	2	1991-92	18-21	4.00
Austin, Rich	1	1974	1-1	2.33
Bannister, Floyd	1	1990	3-2	4.04
Beene, Andy	1	1985	2-2	7.25
Birtsas, Tim	1	1991	3-5	5.61
Burnside, Pete	2	1964-65	10-22	3.10
Cary, Charles	1	1992	3-5	3.61
Castillo, Bobby	1	1987	1-1	7.84
Comstock, Keith	2	1985	8-10	4.47
Culver, George	1	1975	1-4	6.50
Davis, Ron	1	1989	4-5	3.97
Eichelberger, Juan	1	1989	0-3	7.04
Foytack, Paul	1	1965	2-3	3.16
Gail, Rich	2	1985-86	18-18	4.42
Gibson, Bob	1	1988	7-11	4.87
Gossage, Goose	1	1990	2-3	4.40
Grunwald, Alfred	1	1962	2-8	4.50
Gullickson, Bill	2	1988-89	21-14	3.29
Hoffman, Guy	3	1989-91	20-19	4.33
Kekich, Mike	1	1974	5-11	4.13
Keough, Matt	4	1987-90	45-44	3.73
Kiely, Leo	1	1953	6-0	1.80
Krueger, Rich	1	1979	2-1	4.66
Kuhaulua, Fred	1	1978	3-4	4.32

Name	Yrs		Won-Lost	ERA
Lesley, Brad	2	1986-87	7-5	3.00
Ley, Richard	2	1974-75	5-5	4.09
Mickens, Glenn	5	1959-63	45-51	2.50
Newcombe, Don	1	1962	0-0	4.50
Paine, Phil	1	1953	4-3	1.77
Palmquist, Ed	1	1963	0-1	3.00
Perez, Yorkis	1	1992	0-1	7.11
Rajsich, David	1	1984	0-1	3.18
Reynolds, Bob	1	1977	0-0	9.00
Rochford, Mike	1	1990	0-3	8.61
Sanchez, Luis	2	1986-87	4-4	2.54
Schulze, Don	3	1990-92	12-11	4.94
Shirley, Steve	2	1983-84	5-7	4.17
Smith, Willie	1	1972	0-1	81.00
Stanka, Joe	7	1960-66	100-72	3.03
Stone, Dean	1	1964	0-0	3.75
Tillotson, Thad	1	1971	3-4	6.40
Tunnell, Byron Lee	2	1991-92	8-11	4.94
Wright, Clyde	3	1976-78	22-18	3.97
Young, Raymond	2	1991-92	1-2	5.95
TOTALS			405-422	

* Lists compiled from Wayne Graczyk, *Americans in Japan 1950-1986,* and Isao Chiba, "Kiroku no Techo (Record Notes)," *Shukan Baseball,* March 28, 1988, and April 4, 1988.

## CHAPTER 22

Baseball in the Caribbean

Rob Ruck

Soon after the World Series marks the season's end in the United States, baseball springs back to life in and around the Caribbean. There, to the beat of *salsa* and *merengue* and against a backdrop of palm trees and seasonal labor, some of the best baseball in the world is played each winter. While most of South America follows football and the British West Indies follows cricket, the rest of the Caribbean basin plays baseball—and has for the better part of a century.

Since baseball fever first infected Cuba in the 1870s, the game has infiltrated the sporting psyches of Mexico, Nicaragua, the Dominican Republic, Venezuela, Puerto Rico, Panama, and Colombia. Although tied to major league baseball in four of these countries through a set of winter leagues and as a source of fresh talent, Caribbean baseball is not simply an appendage of the game that is played in the United States. Rather, baseball has acquired an autonomous persona as the peoples of the region have made the game into their own national pastimes.

More than simply recreation or a display of grace and competence, baseball has catalyzed national consciousness and cohesion in the Caribbean basin. A critical part of the fabric of everyday life, the sport has also influenced how these societies have come to define themselves, their relations with each other, and their ties to the United States. "It's more than a game," Dominican winter league general manager Winston Llenas once remarked. "It's our passion. It's almost our way of life."

Pedro Julio Santana stands at his office window in what was once the colonial zone of Santo Domingo. A sportsman at the center of Dominican baseball's evolution earlier this century, he searches for words to describe how the game penetrated his country and the rest of the basin. Glancing below to the hulking walls of the first Catholic cathedral in the western hemisphere, Santana finds his metaphor. "It is much the same as that which happened with Christianity. Jesus could be compared to the North Americans, but the apostles were the ones that spread the faith, and the apostles of baseball were Cubans. Even though the Dominican Republic and Puerto Rico were occupied by the North Americans, the Cubans first brought baseball here, and to Mexico and Venezuela, too."

Caribbean baseball's first epicenter was Cuba, which had fallen into orbit around the United States by the late nineteenth century. Baseball arrived there last century, brought by sailors, students, and businessmen from the United States as well as by Cubans who had traveled north. The U.S. military occupations that followed the

1898 conflict with Spain stimulated baseball's expansion there and across the basin. By the time the Good Neighbor Policy had supplanted the Big Stick in the 1930s, baseball was entrenched. Moreover, Cuban baseball had become the focal point of an international network that stretched from the Caribbean basin through the Negro Leagues.

What was likely the first ballgame in Cuba with local participation occurred in June 1866, when sailors of a U.S. ship taking on sugar invited Cuban longshoremen to play. *El Club Habana* (Havana) began two years later, crushing a team from Matanzas in the first organized contest of two Cuban teams.

Havana's victory over Matanzas featured two of Cuba's sporting pioneers, Esteban Bellan and Emilio Sabourín. Bellan became the first Latino in U.S. organized baseball, playing three seasons in the National Association (1871–1873). Sabourín, the A. G. Spalding of Cuban baseball, was the motivating force behind the *Liga de Beisbol Profesional Cubana,* whose inaugural tournament was won by Sabourín's reconstituted Havana club in 1878. Sabourín proselytized for his sport as well as for the cause of Cuban independence from Spain until his contribution of baseball revenues to the independence movement incurred the wrath of Spanish officials. They imprisoned Sabourín until his death and banned baseball in parts of their colony.

While initially a game of the more affluent and those with contact with the United States, baseball soon spread to all classes of Cuban society, both urban and rural. U.S. military occupations, support by companies and businessmen, and close ties to political elites would shape its subsequent development, much as these forces would elsewhere in the basin.

The game was organized on three overlapping levels in its early years. The first was an ad hoc player-organized, self-directed network of teams. The second involved clubs sponsored by businessmen, companies, and politicians who sought the promotional advantages of such patronage. The third level was that of professional (sometimes semiprofessional) baseball, which organized championships from 1878 until 1961, with a changing cast of teams and format. In some years, no tournaments were held, while in others both a summer and winter season took place. Havana, Almendares, Santa Clara, Cienfuegos, and Marianao were the league's mainstays.

Until the 1959 Cuban Revolution and the ensuing U.S. blockade, Cuba set the standard for Caribbean baseball. It sent the most players to the major and Negro leagues while its winter and summer tournaments featured the

highest caliber of Latin ball and attracted players from both the States and the basin. Cuban players, radio broadcasts, and emigrants, in turn, became baseball's emissaries to the rest of the region.

In the Dominican Republic, Cubans who had migrated to escape the turmoil of the Ten Years' War (1868–1878) were the first to form teams. Young Dominicans emulated them and joined with compatriots who had studied in the United States to establish a self-organized matrix of teams and tournaments well in place before the U.S. Marines arrived in 1916 for their eight-year occupation. Santo Domingo's *Licey,* the oldest of the six professional Dominican clubs, formed in 1907, while the forerunners of San Pedro de Macoris's *Estrellas Orientales,* Santiago's *Aguilas Cibaeñas,* and Santo Domingo's other club, *Escogido,* took to the field soon afterward.

While Dominicans refer to these early decades as the romantic epoch of baseball, commercial forces were already at work there and across the basin. Teams occasionally recruited players with the lure of financial reward and soon began importing Cubans and Puerto Ricans for championship tournaments. Moreover, local clubs often induced talented players with payment in cash or work. North American oil companies in Venezuela, rum distilleries and tobacco manufacturers in Cuba, and sugar cane companies in Nicaragua, Puerto Rico, Cuba, and the Dominican Republic sponsored or assisted workplace teams for recreation and community entertainment, but with an industrial agenda, too — winning their workers' hearts and minds.

During these "Yankee years," between 1898 and 1933, when the Marines hit the beaches thirty-four times in ten different basin countries, they found baseball already implanted in Cuba, Puerto Rico, Nicaragua, Mexico, and the Dominican Republic. They never made it to Venezuela, but would have found baseball there, too, as early as the organization of the Caracas club in 1895. The occupations, though, helped to push the sport along. While Nicaraguans had played on their Atlantic coast since 1888, the nation's longest-running pro team, *Boer,* was founded by the U.S. consul in Managua. In the Dominican Republic, U.S. marines and sailors played ball to bolster morale; they were frequently challenged by Dominican teams, for whom these contests were both a test of sporting abilities and national character. Far more baseball was in evidence by the end of the U.S. stay on the island.

While Cubans and some other basin natives had broken into baseball in the States during the first half of the century, the center of gravity for Caribbean baseball remained a regional one. A "Have Glove—Will Travel" mentality soon took hold of basin baseball and its ablest practitioners made the rounds of national tournaments. A core of the finest black players from the States—then barred from major league play by the color line, as were most Latinos—joined them in Cuba, the Dominican Republic, Puerto Rico, Venezuela, and Mexico.

Caribbean baseball's apogee was probably reached in the summer of 1937 in the Dominican Republic during a national championship dedicated to the re-election of the then state-of-the-art dictator Rafael Trujillo. Top Dominican players were joined by the best Cuban, Puerto Rican, and Negro league talent that the Dominican peso could buy to form a three-team league. Santiago boasted the services of Martín Dihigo, Luís Tiant Sr., and Horacio Martínez; San Pedro de Macoris countered with Tetelo Vargas, Ramón Bragaña, and Cocaína García, while the eventual victor, *Ciudad Trujillo* (a merger of *Licey* and *Escogido* that represented the city Trujillo had renamed in his own honor) relied on future Hall of Famers Josh Gibson, Cool Papa Bell, and Satchel Paige, as well as Silvío García, Perucho Cepeda, and Sam Bankhead. Baseball on the island was the equal of that played anywhere that summer. These players barnstormed year-round, and many of them later played together as *Santa Clara* in Cuba and as *La Concordia* in Venezuela.

The proprietary interest taken by caudillos such as Trujillo or Nicaragua's Anastasio Somoza ensured baseball of its most-favored sport status and contributed to the growth of strong regional rivalries. Caribbean participation in the *Mundiales,* the world amateur baseball championships that began in 1938, and later the Caribbean Series of pro circuits, which started in 1949, reinforced the game's hegemony.

Latin ball was an opportunity for North American players to supplement their income and hone their skills in encounters that sometimes surpassed the caliber of major league play. However, it was also a threat to organized baseball in the States. Major league teams had played in Cuba before the turn of the century, and afterward Negro league squads as well as individual black and white pros journeyed south. The 1937 raids on the Negro leagues by Dominican teams destroyed the Pittsburgh Crawfords, and other Negro league squads frequently lost their best players and gate attractions to basin teams. From 1939 until the demise of independent black baseball a decade later, Venezuelan and Mexican franchises vied for Negro leaguers during the summer months, enticing Josh Gibson, Ray Dandridge, and other stars to jump their Negro league teams. They offered better pay and a different atmosphere. "Not only do I get more money playing here, but I live like a king," Willie Wells wrote to *Pittsburgh Courier* sportswriter Wendell Smith in 1939 to explain his switch from the Newark Eagles to Vera Cruz. "I am not faced with the racial problem. . . . I've found freedom and democracy here, something I never found in the United States. . . . Here, in Mexico, I am a man."

The major leagues were less vulnerable to such competition, but even they blanched when Mexican liquor mogul Jorge Pasquel sought major leaguers in addition to Negro leaguers to bolster the six-team summer Mexican League in 1946. Railroad workers from the States taught the game to their Mexican colleagues as early as the 1880s and a strong semipro league formed in the 1920s. In Sonora and Mexico City, the game felt the pull of baseball across the northern border, which Mexican and black teams frequently crossed. In the Yucatan, baseball pointed more toward the Caribbean, especially Cuba. Pasquel, pumping new capital into the league, persuaded Mickey Owens, Sal Maglie, and Max Lanier to desert their major league teams, prompting the latter to ban them. Pasquel also pursued Stan Musial, reportedly placing $50,000 on the bed in his spring training hotel room at a time when the Cardinals' outfielder was making but $13,000 a season. Other basin leagues also lost top players in the Mexican effort to upgrade. Pasquel's challenge,

however, was blunted by organized baseball in the States, which tried to limit any competition for its players, and by the Mexican League's own logistical and financial difficulties. The challenge faded after the 1948 season. In the aftermath of the Mexican raids and with integration imminent, major league baseball began to sign accords with professional leagues throughout the basin, formalizing player movement and institutionalizing winter play.

That was especially important, for with the end of the color line in 1947 Latinos soon renewed their assault on major league ball. By the 1970s, the basin would constitute the freshest source of talent in the majors, especially important as the black community turned away from baseball as part of a general shift toward other sports in the United States. But Latin players—black and white—had played pro ball in the United States long before Jackie Robinson's historic debut.

Colombia's Luis Castro broke ground in baseball's modern era, after the creation of the National and American Leagues, but Cubans for the most part led the way. While Castro played only part of the 1902 season, Rafael Almeida and Armando Marsans spearheaded a Cuban invasion in 1911 that left its imprimatur on the game and numbered over thirty players before integration. Another ninety or so Cubans played major league ball after that divide.

The crucial factor controlling the entry of Cubans and other basin players into the major leagues was skin color. Barnstorming their way through black communities from the early century on, Cuban teams had become a mainstay of the Negro leagues that began in 1920. Popular draws, the Cuban Stars and the New York Cubans featured Latinos too dark to pass the color line into the majors. Playing most of their contests on the road, these Caribbean squads injected talent and a tropical allure to the game. Cubans Martín Dihigo, Alejandro Oms, Luís Tiant Sr., Orestes "Minnie" Miñoso, and Silvío García were joined by Dominicans Horacio Martínez and Tetelo Vargas, Puerto Rican Peruchin Cepeda, Panamanian Pat Scantlebury, and sometimes several black North Americans who passed for Cubans, on these pan-Caribbean aggregations. A few Cubans, such as Cristóbal Torriente, a powerful outfielder, and José de la Caridad Méndez, *"El Diamante Negro,"* who took a no-hitter into the ninth inning the first time he faced the barnstorming Cincinnati Reds, became mainstays of other Negro league franchises.

Lighter-skinned Cubans from that predominantly mixed island played on the other side of sport's racial boundary in the States, in the major leagues. Perhaps the greatest pre–Jackie Robinson Cuban major leaguer was Adolfo Luque, a pitcher whose twenty big league seasons were capped by a brilliant 27–8 record in 1923 and a winning relief stint of shutout ball in the seventh game of the 1933 World Series. Following that game, Clark Griffith, whose Washington Senators had lost the Series, decided to back a scouting exhibition to Cuba. He sent Joe Cambria.

"Papa Joe," as many still refer to Cambria, stocked the Senators with Cubans. Among his first signees was Roberto Estalella, from the sugarcane milltown that Hershey Chocolate operated in Cárdenas. The *Cincinnati Enquirer* had greeted the signings of Almeida and Mar-

sans in 1911 with relief, introducing them as "two of the purest bars of Castilian soap to ever wash upon our shores," but the darker-hued Estalella was more controversial. No one challenged this indirect breaching of the color line, although it prompted Red Smith to write his classic column in which he suspected that "there was a Senegambian somewhere in the Cuban batpile where Senatorial lumber was seasoned."

The player regarded in the Caribbean as the best Cuban ever, and arguably the finest ballplayer of all time, never played major league ball. Martín Dihigo displayed his talents in Cuba, the United States, Mexico, Venezuela, and the Dominican Republic, and is enshrined in the Hall of Fame of three of these nations. Dihigo excelled at the plate, on the mound, and as a manager, but integration came too late for him. His bust at Havana's *Estadio Latinoamericano* reads simply, *El Inmortal.*

The contradiction that some Cubans played in the majors and others in the Negro leagues was not lost upon blacks in the States or on Latin ballplayers. As early as Almeida's and Marsans' 1911 debut, the black press began to hope that black ballplayers would soon follow them into baseball's most exclusive league. And while Negro leaguers went south to adulation and greater pay, dark-skinned Latinos who came north encountered prejudice based on both skin color and nationality. As major leaguers such as Ty Cobb, Tris Speaker, and Carl Hubbell traveled south to play in winter ball, black North Americans and Latinos found that they could more than hold their own. These symbolic victories were appreciated both in the States and throughout the basin. North American blacks and the peoples of the region shared each other's athletes and appropriated each other's sporting heroes and symbols. If a proving ground was necessary to show that blacks could compete with whites, that the two could coexist on the same squad, or to dispel any other racial shibboleth, Caribbean baseball was just that.

Following integration, the more farsighted owners began scouring the islands for prospects. Soon a fresh wave of Latinos arrived in the majors, including three future Hall of Famers: Venezuela's Luís Aparicio, Puerto Rico's Roberto Clemente, and the Dominican Republic's Juan Marichal. They signaled, moreover, a shift away from Cuba as the primary spawning waters for Caribbean players.

With the 1959 Cuban Revolution and the subsequent deterioration of relations with the United States, Cuba fell out of organized baseball's system. The Havana Sugar Kings, an International League franchise affiliated with the Reds since 1954, were on their way to winning the Little World Series of the AAA minor leagues in 1959, just months after Fidel Castro came to power. The revolutionary government offered to underwrite the Sugar Kings' debts, and Castro sought to keep the franchise there, "even if I have to pitch," but the International League shipped the club to Jersey City during the 1960 season. Baseball in Cuba was cut off completely from baseball in the United States, and the movement of players and equipment halted. Cuba developed its own sporting goods industry and relied on the repatriated Dihigo, a political exile during the 1950s who had given money to Che Guevara and who now returned to help teach the game. Cuban baseball soon shed its commercial skin and

sought instead to advance the social and political aims of the revolution. Cuba has remained *the* powerhouse in world amateur baseball ever since, but the island stopped producing new major leaguers. After the Zoilo Versalles, Tony Oliva, Tony Pérez generations passed out of baseball, the next set of Cubans to reach the majors were those who, while born on the island, had grown up in the United States.

The fulcrum of baseball power, meanwhile, shifted one island to the east, where the Dominican Republic shared Hispaniola with French-speaking, soccer-playing Haiti. After the star-studded 1937 season, pro ball in the Dominican Republic entered a fourteen-year hiatus. While an occasional tournament celebrated an event such as the nation's centennial, Dominican pros Horacio Martínez and Tetelo Vargas plied their trade in Cuba, Venezuela, or the United States. But several forces revitalized Dominican baseball in the 1940s, and after the reappearance of a professional league in 1951, these dynamics propelled over a hundred players to the major leagues.

The first catalyst was the birth of the *Mundial,* an international championship tournament for amateur baseball. After its inauguration in England in 1938, the *Mundial* moved to the Caribbean. Held in the basin throughout the 1940s, with Cuba hosting five consecutive tournaments, the *Mundial* had a decidedly Latin flavor and became the most important sporting competition in which these nations competed on something approximating equal footing, both with each other and with the United States. Basin nations won every championship from 1940 through 1972, with Cuba winning eleven out of eighteen times.

National aspirations and international rivalries sometimes were injected into the *Mundial.* An irate Anastasio Somoza fired the Nicaraguan manager in the midst of one and took to the dugout to direct the team himself. Nicaraguan national honor was restored by a victory over Cuba in the final game of the 1972 series, an event still celebrated as one of the Central American nation's greatest sporting exploits. The Dominican victory in 1948, coming just months after virtually the entire national championship team perished in a plane crash by the Río Verde, captivated the Republic and lent impetus to pro ball's rebirth there.

A second factor in Dominican baseball's rejuvenation was the creation of the *Dirección General de Deportes.* Modeled in part after the comparable Cuban agency, this government body organized regional and then national tournaments for amateur baseball (often with semiprofessional overtones) that gave further purpose to local, company, and armed forces support. Many of the Dominicans that entered the majors from the late 1950s on, including Marichal, Manuel Mota, and the three Rojas Alou brothers, played on these squads.

The final catalysts to Dominican ascendancy were bananas and sugarcane, and the concentrations of baseball fervor and expertise which they fostered. While the sugarcane milltowns of the southeast produce the most prospects today, the banana region along the northwest border with Haiti was instrumental in cultivating the first contingent of pros in the late 1950s. There the Grenada Company, a United Fruit Company subsidiary, began two teams for its workers and their sons in the 1940s. The

squad won three national championships, and Juan Marichal and Guayubín Olivo passed through its ranks to the majors.

Dominican sugarcane milltowns, like those in Cuba, had long spawned ballclubs. The six-month long *tiempo muerto,* or dead season, when the cane required minimal attention and most workers were unemployed, contributed to an intense sporting environment, first for cricket and ultimately for baseball. In the 1920s and '30s, *Central La Romana's Papagayo* team was an amateur powerhouse, and in the 1940s the milltowns in and around San Pedro de Macoris made their play. There the descendants of cricket-playing migrants from the British West Indies brought to cut cane and work in the mills displayed an aptitude for playing baseball and an approach to organizing the game that made San Pedro baseball's Mecca. Since Rico Carty's breakthrough in the 1960s, San Pedro has contributed about one-third of the Dominicans to play in the big leagues. The town currently sends more of its native sons to the majors on a per-capita basis than any town ever has. There is probably no other place on earth where the game is played as well and as widely.

Since the end of the color line, ballplayers from Cuba, the Dominican Republic, Venezuela, Puerto Rico, Panama, Nicaragua, Mexico, Colombia, and even the Bahamas have played major league ball. Although the Dominican Republic leads this basin contingent, substantial numbers of Puerto Ricans and Venezuelans are present, too. Mexico, despite a population that dwarfs the rest of the region combined and its well-developed pro leagues, sends few players to the majors. Unlike the other basin leagues, Mexican teams retain first rights to sign any native amateur. A major league club, therefore, must buy the contract from a player's Mexican club, usually for more than it costs to sign a prospect elsewhere in the region. This relationship, the summer Mexican league, and perhaps cultural factors, too, persuade native ballplayers to remain in Mexico.

Cuba opted out of this network after its revolution, and Nicaragua, whose eleven-year fling with the pro winter leagues ended in 1967, followed suit after its 1979 revolution. Panama and Colombia have also tried winter ball, but financial pressures made play sporadic.

The flow of players continues to run both north and south. Minor and major leaguers from the United States still play in the winter leagues, which presently operate in Venezuela, Puerto Rico, the Dominican Republic, and Mexico. In their heyday during the 1950s and '60s, these winter leagues featured major leaguers like Tommy Lasorda, Whitey Ford, and Willie Stargell. But as major league salaries soared in the 1970s and unfavorable rates of exchanges weakened basin economies, the winter leagues restricted the number of North American imports. Minor leaguers and inexperienced major leaguers have replaced them. For them, these leagues provide the chance to play in the winter months, developing the potential that might allow them to crack a big league roster. They also earn higher pay than they do in the minors, encounter competition from top Latino players, and are treated as demigods by the impassioned *fanáticos* of the winter game.

The winners of the winter leagues have met in a *Serie del Caribe* since 1949. Between 1949 and 1960, the pen-

nant-winning squads of Cuba, Panama, Puerto Rico, and Venezuela played in early February to determine a champion of the Caribbean. Cuba won over half of these tournaments, but after the revolution, the series was discontinued. When it resumed in 1970, Mexico and the Dominican Republic replaced Cuba and Panama. The current round-robin format sends the teams that win their postseason tournaments to the *Serie del Caribe* along with a number of reinforcements, including North Americans, from their defeated opponents. Willie Mays, Monte Irvin, Camilo Pasqual, Rico Carty, and Vic Pellot Power are among those who have starred in these postseason celebrations.

Winter ball has descended from its zenith of the 1950s and '60s largely due to economic dynamics beyond the control of the Caribbean franchises. Rising player and fuel costs, devalued currencies, and underdevelopment pushed many into deficits, with government subsidies often vital to their continuation. Government support, long a feature of basin baseball, helps to keep current the Dominican saying that there will never be political trouble during the baseball season, only afterward. But by the middle of the 1980s, fewer of the established Latin major leaguers suited up for the October-through-January campaign. The demands of the regular season, the threat of injury, and the relatively inconsequential pay of winter ball suggest that this trend will continue. The pattern, however, has given younger Latin ballplayers the chance to play before knowledgeable fans and against competition that is often at a major league level.

While winter ball in the late 1980s was troubled and other sports were making inroads, baseball remains *el rey de deportes* (the king of sports) throughout the basin. From the rocky hillsides and arid plains of northern Mexico through the canefields of the islands to the basin's southernmost flank in the Andes, baseball commands a fascination approaching reverence.

Baseball's significance derives from the role that it has played in the coming together of these societies in the twentieth century. Knitting a common cultural fabric, serving as a vent to social and political tensions, and offering a vehicle not only for individual mobility but collective social affirmation, baseball indeed has been more than a game. It has offered the citizens of the basin a chance to enter a ritual kinship embracing all fans and players. And while reflecting the progressive penetration of the United States in the region, baseball has been more than a cultural transmission belt for North American values. Beating each other and excelling in the major leagues and international competitions at a time when the Caribbean basin has encountered difficulties in asserting either its political or economic autonomy have been tremendous sources of pride. And that symbolic recognition has become a catalyst to national cohesion and consciousness for the region in its troubled evolution this century.

The lights are going out in Santo Domingo, and like so many aspects of this nation's descent into economic chaos, it's affecting baseball. They still play the game, but this year the ballparks are eerily quiet, mute testimony to winter baseball's deepening crisis. And those close to the game are asking what it will take to ensure professional baseball's survival in the 1990s.

The streets outside *Estadio Quisqueya* in Santo Do-

mingo are dark; the players sprawl in clusters on the grass inside. A few take a form of batting practice, hitting balls tossed laterally from a few feet away, into a net. Soon, as darkness becomes nearly complete, they hit off a tee. Then, even that becomes impossible.

Gradually, the Big Dipper becomes visible, standing straight up to form a celestial question mark that might as well be asking if tonight's game will be played.

The question is answered when the generator kicks in with a fireworks-like flourish and bulbs pop on in the light stanchions. At first, nobody moves, then gradually bodies rise stiffly from the grass and walk out onto the field.

This barely averted blackout offers an exaggerated example of winter ball's woes. But the crisis, which has halved attendance here and in Puerto Rico, knocked one franchise out of action, and threatens others, has been brewing for over a decade.

"Dominicans haven't lost their love of the game," Winston Llenas, *Aguilas'* general manager attests. "But this society is in trouble, serious trouble. It's living dangerously now."

Over two years into an economic downturn in which inflation and the exchange rate for the *peso* with the U.S. dollar have soared and living standards have fallen, the Dominican Republic suffers from severe electrical shortages, a lack of potable water, and a transportation system in suspended motion. The ballparks, once a beacon of light in the evening sky, now often remain dark until shortly before game time.

The nation's collapse is part of a continental decline that has seen much of Latin America regress to an economic level last seen during the 1930s.

"Perhaps our biggest problem," Llenas adds, "is the lack of desire on the part of the established Dominican players to play." Indeed, as major league salaries have spiraled upward, the incentive for the better-known Latins to play winter ball has all but disappeared.

Llenas points to the benefits that have accrued to major league baseball from winter ball. "It's been a good partnership. Look at the résumés of players, managers, and even umpires in the United States. You have a saying there, 'What's good for General Motors is good for the USA.' Well, what's good for winter baseball is what's good for the major leagues. They should not let us die. Not when we need their help."

A few nights later in San Pedro de Macoris, La Romana's Jose Offerman goes deep in the hole, spins, and nabs the runner at first in a play that has even a few of San Pedro's players exchanging high fives. In La Romana's dugout, manager Victor Ramirez raises one hand in the air as if to give religious testimony and exclaims, "What a talent!"

Winter ball's lack of established major leaguers means that youths like Offerman are experiencing an accelerated development. By the end of the 1990 season, Offerman will be in the majors, and in coming years, he will attract Dominican fans back to the park. The cycle of regeneration is already at work.

But that process will take a few years—years that are not guaranteed. As the game concludes and a squadron of boys leaps from the top of the dugout onto the field, it seems improbable that such a vibrant institution as winter ball could end in the near future. But it could.

Luis Perez stands in the outfield grass, shaking his Hiroshima Carp cap in the air and chanting his Japanese team's slogan: "We will not tire. Our song is work." Then, the twenty-one-year-old second baseman from a nearby sugar milltown sprints to the dugout.

Besuboru has arrived in the tropic of baseball. In November 1990 the Hiroshima Carp inaugurated a state-of-the-art baseball academy amidst the canefields north of San Pedro de Macoris. "Its goal," says Cesar Geronimo, the former Cincinnati Red directing the camp, "is to make Dominican kids into Japanese major leaguers. We want to make a good ballplayer, but one who thinks like the Japanese."

A few months later, Luis Perez and four of his *compadres* were training in Japan, the third group of recruits to cross the Pacific. There they impressed their hosts, especially after Perez drilled a fastball into the stands off Carp ace Hiroshi Nagatomi in a showcase exhibition in Fukuyama, and two of them made the Hiroshima farm team for the 1992 season.

The Caribbean academy reflects a new Japanese approach to acquiring foreign talent, one that will reduce a onesided U.S. export. The Carp are recruiting and developing their own prospects, circumventing the U.S. major leagues and tapping the Dominican Republic, the best source of fresh talent in the game over the last twenty years. Since constructing the $4 million facility, the Carp have signed thirty-two Latin players, most of them seventeen- or eighteen-year olds. A dozen have left the team or been released; the remainder live at the academy or are with the Carp in Hiroshima.

"Japan is a different culture than the U.S. and baseball there is different, too," explained Takashi Tanaka, the academy's general manager, after the camp opened. "Your major leaguers have often been difficult for us and quite expensive. With what it would cost to sign two Americans, we can sign many Dominicans of high quality."

The Japanese recognize that foreigners inject new dimensions into their game, but cringe at the cultural fallout. U.S. major leaguers have offended their sensibilities by arguing with coaches and easing up on arduous pregame drills. Others deserted in midseason or placed family ahead of team, such as Randy Bass's much criticized absence from the Hanshin Tigers to be with his dying father.

Cultivating young Dominican talent is perceived as an alternative to United States players and as a way to infuse Japanese play with the verve of the Caribbean game without jeopardizing its overall stress on *wa*, or team harmony.

"Japan needs strong batters like Pedro Guerrero and George Bell," Tananka contended. "What we don't want is the temperament of a George Bell," said Tanaka of the San Pedro slugger who once told the city of Toronto that "They can kiss my Dominican ass." "With these boys, we

will teach the comportment, self-control, that they will need to play in Japan."

The camp, with two fields, a clubhouse, a weight room, a dining room and dorm, as well as indoor batting cages and pitching mounds, surpasses the dozen or so training complexes that major league teams operate on the island. It will be the hub of the Carp's Caribbean program, says Geronimo, who plans on scouting talent in Venezuela, Panama, and Nicaragua, too.

Living full-time in the enclave, the players are tightly supervised. They were not allowed to venture into nearby San Pedro for most of their first year here. The coaches, Dominicans who trained in Japan, have adapted the Carp approach to their regimen. That means less "play ball" than "work ball" under an unforgiving sun and the coaches' relentless scrutiny, where attitude is evaluated along with athleticism and grasp of the game.

A plume of smoke from the nearby Santa Fe sugar mill reminds any player who can't make it on the ballfield that the canefields await him. The monthly wage in one of San Pedro's five sugarmills is about 1000 *pesos*, about $80 U.S. Luis Perez, infielder, makes between 2500 and 3000 *pesos* playing for the Carp.

Perez and his teammates welcome anyone seeking to harvest the Dominican baseball crop, but U.S. clubs see the penetration of what had been their exclusive sporting preserve as a threat.

"It's a free enterprise system and they can do what they want in looking for talent," said Major League Baseball director of operations Bill Murray after the academy opened. "A number of clubs don't welcome the competition."

Hiroshima is the only one of the twelve Japanese pro teams to open a Caribbean academy. That could give them an advantage over other Japanese teams, which traditionally rely on a draft of Japanese amateurs supplemented by a few U.S. pros.

Since Japanese rules limit a club to three foreigners, the Carp cannot flood their roster with inexpensive Latin talent. They could sell these players to other Japanese teams, teams in Taiwan and Korea, or even U.S. clubs, Tanaka said.

These boys are hungry, Geronimo notes. The Carp seek to tap that hunger, which has made this nation of 6 million such a fecund source of talent. If they are successful, Japanese baseball will attain a new level of play, fueling speculation that the hidden motive is to take on the major leagues some day.

"I can't speculate on the Japanese agenda for global competition," answers Cleveland Indians GM John Hart, "but this inevitably spells head-to-head battle with American clubs. They're in the same business we are, which is to procure talent." But Hart evinces little concern over a larger Japanese challenge.

Geronimo offers a simpler explanation of the Carp's intentions. "The Japanese are losing games because they're holding back aggression on the field. I think our aggressive way of playing will help make Japanese baseball better."

First Major Leaguers from Caribbean Basin Countries

Country	Player	Year	Team
Belize	Chito Martinez	1991	Baltimore Orioles
Colombia	Luis "Jud" Castro	1902	Philadelphia Athletics
Cuba	Esteban Bellan	1871	Troy Haymakers
	Rafael Almeida	1911	Cincinnati Reds
	Armando Marsans	1911	Cincinnati Reds
Mexico	Baldomero "Mel" Almada	1933	Boston Red Sox
Venezuela	Alejandro Carrasquel	1939	Washington Senators
Puerto Rico	Hiram Bithorn	1942	Chicago Cubs
Panama	Héctor López	1955	Kansas City Athletics
	Humberto Robinson	1955	Milwaukee Braves
Dominican Republic	Osvaldo Virgil	1956	New York Giants
Virgin Islands	Joe Christopher	1959	Pittsburgh Pirates
Nicaragua	Dennis Martínez	1976	Baltimore Orioles
Honduras	Gerald Young	1987	Houston Astros
Curacao	Hensley Meulens	1990	New York Yankees

Serie del Caribe

Series	Year	Site	Winning Team/Country
I	1949	Cuba	Almendares/Cuba
II	1950	Puerto Rico	Carta Vieja/Panama
III	1951	Venezuela	Santurce/Puerto Rico
IV	1952	Panama	La Habana/Cuba
V	1953	Cuba	Santurce/Puerto Rico
VI	1954	Puerto Rico	Caguas/Puerto Rico
VII	1955	Venezuela	Santurce/Puerto Rico
VIII	1956	Panama	Cienfuegos/Cuba
IX	1957	Cuba	Marianao/Cuba
X	1958	Puerto Rico	Marianao/Cuba
XI	1959	Venezuela	Almendares/Cuba
XII	1960	Panama	Cienfuegos/Cuba
	1961–69	Not Held	
XIII	1970	Venezuela	Magallanes/Venezuela
XIV	1971	Puerto Rico	Licey/Dominican Republic
XV	1972	Dominican Republic	Ponce/Puerto Rico
XVI	1973	Venezuela	Licey/Dominican Republic
XVII	1974	Mexico	Caguas/Puerto Rico
XVIII	1975	Puerto Rico	Bayamón/Puerto Rico
XIX	1976	Dominican Republic	Hermosillo/Mexico
XX	1977	Venezuela	Licey/Dominican Republic
XXI	1978	Mexico	Mayagüez/Puerto Rico
XXII	1979	Puerto Rico	Magallanes/Venezuela
XXIII	1980	Dominican Republic	Licey/Dominican Republic
	1981	Not Held	
XXIV	1982	Mexico	Caracas/Venezuela
XXV	1983	Venezuela	Arecibo/Puerto Rico
XXVI	1984	Puerto Rico	Zulia/Venezuela
XXVII	1985	Mexico	Licey/Dominican Republic
XXVIII	1986	Venezuela	Mexicali/Mexico
XXIX	1987	Mexico	Caguas/Venezuela
XXX	1988	Dominican Republic	Escogido/Dominican Republic
XXXI	1989	Mazatlan	Zulia/Venezuela
XXXII	1990	Miami	Escogido/Dominican Republic
XXXIII	1991	Miami	Licey/Dominican Republic
XXXIV	1992	Mexico	Mayagüez/Puerto Rico

Dominican League Statistics

Year	Champion	BA Leader	HR Leader	Most Games Won
1951	Licey	Luis Villodas .346	Pedro Formental 13	Guayuabín Olivo 10
1952	Aguilas	Luis Olmo .344	Alonzo Perry 11	Terry McDuffie 14
1953	Licey	Tetelo Vargas .355	Alonzo Perry 11	Emilio Cueche 13
1954	Estrellas Orientales	Alonzo Perry .326	Bob Thurman 11	Carrao Bracho G. Olivo 8
1955–56	Escogido*	Bob Wilson .333	Willie Kirkland 9	Fred Waters 11
1956–57	Escogido	Osvaldo Virgil .312	Danny Kravitz 4	Pete Burnside 11
1957–58	Escogido	Alonzo Perry .332	Dick Stuart 14	Fred Kipp 11
1958–59	Licey	Felipe Alou .351	Jim McDaniels 12	Bennie Daniels 12
1959–60	Escogido	Felipe Alou .359	Frank Howard 9	Stan Williams 12
1960–61	Escogido	Manuel Mota .344	Manuel Jiménez 13 J.V. Nicolás Victor Ramirez Felipe Alou N. Saviñón Tied with 4	Danilo Riva 13
1961–62	Incomplete Season			
1962–63	Not Held			
1963–64	Licey	Manuel Mota .379	O. McFarlane 10	G. Olivo Steve Blass 9
1964–65	Aguilas	Manuel Mota .364	O. McFarlane 8	Dick LeMay 8
1965–66	Season not organized by league			
1966–67	Aguilas	Mateo Alou .363	Winston Llenas Bob Robertson 10	Dock Ellis 9
1967–68	Estrellas Orientales	Ricardo Carty .350	Bob Robertson 9	Silvano Quezada 11
1968–69	Escogido	Mateo Alou .390	Nate Colbert 8	Jay Ritchie 9
1969–70	Licey	Ralph Garr .387	Winston Llenas Byron Browne 9	G. Rounsaville 8
1970–71	Licey	Ralph Garr .457	César Cedeño 8	Rollie Fingers 9
1971–72	Aguilas	Ralph Garr .388	Charlie Sands 10	Gene Garber 9
1972–73	Licey	Von Joshua .358	Adrian Garrett 9	Pedro Borbón 9
1973–74	Licey	Dave Parker .345	Ricardo Carty 9	Rick Waits 8
1974–75	Aguilas	Bruce Bochte .352	Rafael Batista Bobby Darwin 8	James Richards 8
1975–76	Aguilas	Wilbur Howard .341	Wilbur Howard John Hale Gary Alexander 8 Larry Parrish G. Thomasson Bill Nahorodny Andre Thornton Tied with 4	Nino Espinosa Tom Dettore 8
1976–77	Licey	Mario Guerrero .365	Pedro Guerrero Ike Hampton 6	Angel Torres 10
1977–78	Aguilas	Omar Moreno .345	Dick Davis 8	Odell Jones Al Holland Mickey Mahler 7
1978–79	Aguilas	Ted Cox .319	Bob Beall Dick Davis 7	Bo McLaughlin Mike Proly 9
1979–80	Licey	Tony Peña .317	A. De Freitas Alberto Lois Leon Durham Samuel Mejía Pedro Guerrero Tied with 3	Jerry Hannahs 9
1980–81	Escogido	Ken Landreaux .394	Tony Peña 7	Mario Soto M. Mahler 7
1981–82	Escogido	Pedro Hernandez .408	Dave Hostetler 9	Pasqual Pérez 10
1982–83	Licey	César Geronimo .341	Howard Johnson 8	Pasqual Pérez 9
1983–84	Licey	Miguel Diloné .343	Reggie Whittemore 12	Orel Hershiser Frank Wills 8
1984–85	Licey	Junior Noboa .327	Ralph Bryant 9	Tom Filer 8
1985–86	Aguilas	Tony Fernández .364	Tony Peña 9	Mickey Mahler 8
1986–87	Aguilas	Stanley Javier .374	Ralph Bryant 13	Gibson Alba José Nuñez Eric Plunk Tied with 5
1987–88	Escogido	Stanley Javier .363	Mark Parent 10	José Bautista 8
1988–89	Licey	Julio Peguero .327	Domingo Michel 9	Melido Perez 8–3
1989–90	Escogido	Angel González .403	Denny González 5	Mel Rojas Jeff Shaw Kevin Wicklander Darren Holmes Tied with 6
1990–91	Licey	Hensley Meulens .338	Francisco Cabrera 8	Francesco De la Rosa 7
1991–92	Escogido	Luis Mercedes .333	Francisco Cabrera, Sammy Sosa, Geronimo Berroa, Kevin Koslofski, and Julian Yan tied with 4	José Nuñez 6

* First year held in winter

Cuban League Statistics

Year	Champion	BA Leader	HR Leader	Most Games Won
1878–79	Habana Undefeated			
1879–80	Habana			
1880–81	Not held			
1882	Disputed: Fe and Habana			
1882–83	Habana			
1885	Habana	Pablo Ronquilla .350		
1885–86	Habana Undefeated	Wenceslao Gálvez .345		Adolfo Luján 5–0
1887	Habana	R. Martínez .439		Adolfo Luján 5–0
1888	Fe	Antonio García .448		Francisco Hernández 10–2
1889	Habana	Francisco Salabarria .305		Adolfo Luján 10–3
1889–90	Habana	Antonio García .364		Miguel Prats 11–2

Year	Champion	BA Leader	HR Leader	Most Games Won
1890–91	Fe	Alfredo Crespo .375		Miguel Prats 9–4
1892	Habana	Antonio García .362		E. Hernández 4–1
1892–93	Matanzas	Antonio García .385		Francisco Hernández 4–1
1893–94	Almendares	Miguel Pratts .394		José Pastoriza 16–7
1894–95	Suspended due to War of Independence	Alfredo Arcaño .430		Enrique García 12–4
1897–98	Not finished			
1898	Habanista	Valentín González .394		José Romero 5–2
1900	San Francisco	Esteban Pratts .333		Luis Padrón 13–4
1901	Habana	Julián Castillo .454		Carlos Royer 12–3
1902	Habana Undefeated	Luis Padrón .463		Carlos Royer 17–0
1903	Habana	Julián Castillo .330		Cándido Fontanals 14–6
1904	Habana	Regino García .397		Carlos Royer 13–3
1905	Almendares	Regino García .305		Angel D'Meza 10–4
1905–6	Fe	Regino García .304		José Muñoz 8–1
1907	Almendares	Regino García .324		George Mack 4–2
1908	Almendares	Emilio Palomino .350		José Méndez 9–0
1908–9	Habana	Julián Castillo .315		L. Haggerman 15–6
1910	Almendares	Emilio Palomino .408		José Méndez 7–0
1910–11	Almendares	Preston Hill .365		José Méndez 11–2
1912	Habana	Emilio Palomino .440		José Junco 6–1
1913	Fe	Armando Marsans .400		Red Redding 7–2
1913–14	Almendares	Manuel Villa .351		José Méndez 10–0
1914–15	Habana	Cristóbal Torriente .387		José Acosta 5–1
1915–16	Almendares	Eustaquio Pedrosos .413		José Acosta 8–3
1917	Orientales	Adolfo Luque .355		José Acosta 2–1
1918–19	Habana	Manuel Cueto .344		José Acosta 16–10
1919–20	Almendares	Cristóbal Torriente .360		Emilio Palmero 5–1
1920–21	Habana	Pelayo Chacon .344	Cristóbal Torriente M. González B. Jiménez M. Guerra Tied with 1	José "Cheo" Hernández 4–1
1921*	Habana	Bienvenido Jiménez .619	Manuel Cueto 1	Julio Leblanc 2–0
1922–23	Marianao	Bernardo Baró .401	Cristóbal Torriente 4	Lucas Boada 10–4
1923–24	Santa Clara	Oliver Marcells .393	Bienvenido Jiménez 4	Bill Holland 10–2
1924–25	Almendares	Manuel Cueto .364	Esteban Mantalvo 5	José Acosta 4–1
1925–26	Almendares	Johnny Wilson .430	J. H. Lloyd Jud Wilson 3	César Alvarez 10–2
1926–27	Habana	Manuel Cueto .404	J. Hernández 4	Juan Olmo 3–0
1927–28	Habana	Johnny Wilson .424	Oscar Charleston 5	Oscar Levis 7–2
1928–29	Habana	Alejandro Oms .432	Cool Papa Bell 5	Adolfo Luque 9–2
1929–30	Cienfuegos	Alejandro Oms .380	Mule Suttles 7	Heliodoro "Yoyo" Diaz 13–3
1930–31*	Not finished	O. Charleston .373	Ernest Smith José Fernández 1	Martin Dihigo 2–0
1931–32	Almendares	Rámon Cueto .400	Alejandro Oms Ismael Morales 3	Juan Eckelson 5–1
1932–33	Tie: Habana Almendares	M. González .432	R. Estalella 3	Jésus Lorenzo 3–0
1933–34	No championship held			
1934–35	Almendares	Lázaro Salazar .407	Eleven tied with 1	Lázaro Salazar 6–1
1935–36	Santa Clara	Martín Dihigo .358	Willie Wells Jacinto Roque 5	Martín Dihigo 11–2
1936–37	Marianao	Harry Williams .349	H. Andrews R. Estalella 5	Raymond Brown 21–4
1937–38	Santa Clara	Sam Bankhead .366	Willie Wells R. Estalella Raymond Brown 4	Raymond Brown 12–5
1938–39	Santa Clara	Tony Castaños .371	Josh Gibson 11	Martín Dihigo 14–2
1939–40	Almendares	Tony Castaños .340	Mule Suttles 4	Rodolfo Fernández 7–4
1940–41	Habana	Lázaro Salazar .316	A. Crespo 3	Gilberto Torres 10–3
1941–42	Almendares	Silvío García .351		Macon Mayor Agapito Mayor 6–2
1942–43	Almendares	A. Crespo .337	Roberto Ortiz Saguita Hernández 2	Cocaina García 10–3
1943–44	Habana	Roberto Ortiz .337	Saguita Hernández 3	Martín Dihigo 8–1
1944–45	Almendares	Claro Duany .340	Claro Duany 3	Oliverio Ortiz 10–4
1945–46	Cienfuegos	L. Davenport .333	Dick Sisler 9	Adrián Zabala 9–3
1946–47	Almendares	Lou Klein .330	Roberto Ortiz 11	Cocaina García 10–3
1947–48	Habana	Harry Kimbro .346	Jesús Chanquilon Díaz 7	C. Marrero 12–2
1948–49	Almendares	A. Crespo .326	Monte Irvin 10	Octavio Rubert 8–1
1949–50	Almendares	P. Formental .336	Roberto Ortiz Don Lenhardt 15	Octavio Rubert 5–1
1950–51	Habana	Silvío García .347	P. Formental, Bert Hass Ed Mierkowitz Charles Grant Tied with 8	Vincente López]7–3
1951–52	Habana	Bert Hass .323	P. Formental James Basso 9	Joe Black 15–6
1952–53	Habana	Edmundo Amorós .373	Louis Klein 16	R. Alexander 10–3
1953–54	Almendares	Rocky Nelson .352	Earl Rapp Rafael Noble 10	Cliff Fanning 13–4
1954–55	Almendares	Angel Scull .370	Rocky Nelson 13	Joe Hatten 13–5
1955–56	Cienfuegos	Forrest Jacobs .321	Ultus Alvarez 10	Pedro Ramos 13–5
1956–57	Marianao	Orestes Miñoso .312	Archie Wilson 11	Camilo Pascual 15–5
1957–58	Marianao	Milton Smith .320	Daniel Morejon Norman Laker B. Robinson Frank Herrera 9	Billy O'Dell 7–2
1958–59	Almendares	Tony Taylor .303	Jim Baxes 9	Orlando Peña 13–5
1959–60	Cienfuegos	Octavio Rojas .322		
1960–61	Cienfuegos			

* Short season

## CHAPTER 23

Baseball in Canada

Bruce L. Prentice and Merritt Clifton

Baseball as we know it—with three bases and home, nine players to a side, and three outs to an inning—has been played in Canada at least since 1860, when the existing teams in London, Hamilton, St. Thomas, and Woodstock, Ontario, all accepted the rules of the New York Game popularized by Henry Chadwick. This was the game played on June 19, 1846 between the New York and Knickerbocker clubs on the Elysian Fields of Hoboken, New Jersey.

But a game differing from early baseball mainly in having five bases was played in Beechville, Ontario, as early as June 4, 1838, according to witness Adam Ford, who described it in a letter to *Sporting Life* published on May 5, 1886. The game included at least two "grey-headed men" who "used to play when they were boys."

Thus the Canadian baseball tradition certainly predates Abner Doubleday's apocryphal invention of the game at Cooperstown in 1839, and may go back as far as the U.S. tradition. Indeed, in both nations, ancestors of baseball including cricket and rounders had been played since the early 1700s, and determining exactly where their derivatives ended and baseball began may be well-nigh impossible.

Before the arrival of the New York Game, the southwestern Ontario teams played the Canadian Game, with five bases and eleven fielders. All eleven batters had to be retired to end an inning. Only after the New York rules were adopted did the game spread to the other provinces. By 1865 baseball had become so popular in Montreal that an ordinance was passed forbidding games in city parks as a menace to other users. The Montreal-based Crescents of St. John's claimed the Canadian championship in 1868. The Montreal game was apparently not up to U.S. standards, however, as in 1870 the New York Knickerbockers Lacrosse Club crushed the Montreal Baseball Club, 54–32.

Baseball reached Manitoba no later than 1874, supplanting a local ancestor game called "bat," which had been played around the Red River Settlement as early as the 1840s. A professional three-team Manitoba League failed in 1886, but the game had firmly caught on by 1902, when the Great Northern Railway sponsored a Winnipeg entry in the professional North Dakota League.

Saskatchewan had semiprofessional baseball by 1887, when future provincial prime minister Walter Scott led a Regina team to two successive regional championships. Amateur baseball emerged in Alberta at about the same time, with games recorded as early as 1886.

By 1903 baseball was even played in the Yukon, where games attracted heavy gambling. Professional baseball debuted the same year in British Columbia, as twenty-year-old Hal Chase—"Prince Hal," the slick-fielding first baseman—starred for a Victoria entry in an otherwise Washington-based league.

While major league baseball came late to Canada, Canadian entries in U.S.-based professional leagues won pennants as early as 1877, when the Tecumsehs of London, Ontario, led the International Association. The Tecumsehs reputedly declined a chance to join the two-year-old National League later that year, and disbanded from lack of fan support in early 1878. Ontario acquired another pennant winner in 1887, as Toronto began an only briefly interrupted eighty-year run as a mainstay of the International League, then called the Eastern League. Toronto either finished first during the regular season or won four-team playoffs fifteen times, with back-to-back winners in 1917–1918, 1956–1957, and 1965–1966.

Montreal's first Eastern League entry folded within weeks in 1890. While another Montreal club won the 1898 championship, the by then renamed International League didn't become lastingly situated there until 1928. Even then, Montreal's third entry struggled until it was acquired in 1935 by gas station magnate Charlie Trudeau, father of future Canadian prime minister Pierre Elliot Trudeau. Trudeau anchored the lineup with French-speaking Del Bissonnette and Quebec native Gus Dugas, who hit .327 with 191 homers in thirteen minor league seasons. Under manager Frank Shaughnessy, who became International League president in 1936 and originated the four-club playoff format many experts credit with saving minor league baseball, the Montreal Royals won the 1935 pennant.

Bought by the Brooklyn Dodgers in 1940, the Royals won either pennant or playoffs in ten of the next twenty years. Led by Quebecois Roland Gladu (12 homers, 105 RBIs, .338 batting average) and pitcher Jean Pierre Roy (25–11), the 1945 club was probably Montreal's favorite, but the 1946 Royals are best remembered: with them, second baseman Jackie Robinson (.349) broke the Organized Baseball color line that had prevailed for fifty-five years.

The color line had already been broken in Quebec by .392-hitting pitcher/outfielder Fred Wilson, who joined Granby of the then-outlaw Provincial League for the 1935 stretch run. The Provincial League had included a Montreal-based all-black entry, the Black Panthers, in 1936 and 1937; was all white again in 1940, during a one-year fling at Organized Baseball; and was reintegrated in 1946 by minor league hockey star Manny McIntyre, who signed with Sherbrooke only days after the Dodgers had

signed Robinson and optioned him to Montreal.

The Provincial League was the longest-running of numerous native Canadian circuits, many of which owed ancestry to the work of longtime Canadian Pacific Railway sports representative Joseph Page, who helped set up teams and leagues wherever the trains stopped. A former semi-pro teammate of Tip O'Neill, Page was involved with O'Neill in assembling Montreal's 1898 International League pennant winner. He later enlisted former major league pitcher Jean Dubuc to help him organize the Eastern Canada League, a.k.a. the Ontario-Quebec-Vermont League, of 1922–1924. This was an ancestor of three leagues of note, each of which sent over 100 players to the majors—the Provincial, which had already come together for single seasons in 1894 and 1900; the Canadian-American League, which could claim descent from the short lived, Ontario-based Canadian League of 1885; and the outlaw Northern League that flourished in New York and Vermont from 1935 to 1952.

Reorganized a fourth time, the Provincial League grew steadily from 1935 to 1940, was interrupted by World War II, resumed play in 1944, collapsed in 1956 after a disastrous six-year return to Organized Baseball, and struggled on as an outlaw circuit in 1958–1971. Stars were plentiful, from Quebec native Sam LaRoque (1900) to Felix Mantilla (1969), but the zenith came in 1948–1949, as the league attracted: black greats who were hoping to prove themselves against whites, displaced wartime major leaguers, and the so-called Mexican League Jumpers, who were barred from Organized Baseball in 1946–1950 after breaking their major league contracts in an ill-fated stand against the reserve clause. At least twenty-five major leaguers played in the Provincial League during those two years, among them Sal Maglie, Max Lanier, Vic Power, Gladu and Roy, and Negro League stars Dave Pope, Bus Clarkson, and Quincy Trouppe.

The less colorful Can-Am belonged to Organized Baseball from 1936 through 1951. Several of the Ontario teams continued as an outlaw league into the 1960s.

Page also helped promote the Western Canada League, which began play in 1907, continuing with frequent interruptions and occasional name changes into the late 1940s, when Edmonton and Calgary anchored the Big Four League. The Western Canada League's best year was probably 1921, when its stars included Babe Herman and Heinie Manush.

Canadian teams have also been part of the bygone Northern Copper Country League, which later became the Northern League; the Northwestern League and Western International League, which evolved into today's Northwest League; the Pacific Coast League; the American Association; the Eastern League; the New York–Pennsylvania League; and the Pioneer League.

As well as helping return blacks to Organized Baseball, Canada played a part in popularizing baseball in Japan, through the Asahis (Rising Suns), a team of Vancouver teenagers of Japanese descent (Niseis) formed in 1914. In 1921, twelve years after the first visit by a U.S. collegiate team and thirteen years before the first visit by U.S. major leaguers, the Asahis and a touring team from Seattle barnstormed Japan, playing both Japanese clubs and each other. The Asahis remained a power in Vancouver-

area amateur baseball and heroes to the substantial British Columbia Nisei population for over twenty years.

Despite the many major leaguers who have played for Canadian teams, relatively few Canadian natives have made the majors—a reflection of short summers and a paucity of places to play since television killed the old town teams and outlaw leagues in the 1950s. (Only one high school baseball team exists in Quebec; none in several other provinces.)

High school baseball programs have flourished in the Metro Toronto area since 1979, when four schools experimented with a short schedule. There are now close to seventy schools playing a spring schedule that culminates in a championship game played at the SkyDome, prior to a regular-season Blue Jays game. The winning team receives the "Blue Jays Cup."

College baseball was started in 1978, when Seneca College (near Toronto) joined the NJCAA, New York-Penn Conference, for five seasons and was the forerunner to the National Baseball Institute (NBI) located in British Columbia. This college program has produced Canadians now in the major leagues such as outfielder Kevin Reimer, lefthanded pitchers Steve Wilson and Dennis Boucher, and Expos outfielder Larry Walker.

The province of Quebec in 1989 began its own college program, and patterned after the successful NBI format will eventually prove to be a breeding ground for future big leaguers.

The Canadian Baseball Hall of Fame has identified a total of 163 Canadian major leaguers, 4 managers and 7 umpires. Among them are 86 Ontarians, 18 Quebecois and 22 Maritimers. Of the ten Canadian provinces, only Newfoundland hasn't produced a major leaguer.

Seven players from the late 1800s are listed by most record books as having been born in the U.S., but are believed to have altered their birth records for various reasons, including the 1894 Alien Exemption Act, which barred Canadian athletes from U.S. employment. In addition, several players who were born abroad actually grew up in Canada, e.g., Hank Biasatti and Reno Bertoia, natives of Italy but raised in Windsor, Ontario, and Jimmy Archer, born in Ireland, raised in Toronto, and signed into Organized Baseball from an independent team in Manitoba.

Many of the best Canadian players actually grew up in the U.S., among them infielder Pete Ward, son of former Montreal hockey great Jim Ward, who learned baseball in Oregon; pitcher Dick Lines, born in Montreal but raised in Florida; pitcher Kirk McCaskill, born in Kapuskasing, Ontario, but grew up in Burlington, Vermont; and infielder Sherry Robertson, born in Montreal but raised in Washington, D.C. (as the nephew of Senators and Twins club owner Calvin Griffith, who was also born in Montreal but was brought to Washington in 1921 by Senators owner Clark Griffith, who married Calvin's aunt).

Pitcher Sheldon Burnside reversed that pattern. Born in South Bend, Indiana, Burnside grew up in Toronto.

Not on the Canadian Baseball Hall of Fame list are a number of other special cases. Del Bissonnette and Napoleon Lajoie, for instance, were both born in the U.S., but were conceived in Quebec by Quebecois parents. Bissonnette actually spent more of his life in Quebec than anywhere else. After starring in the Cape Breton Colliery

League of New Brunswick, Bissonnette broke into Organized Baseball by hitting .395 for Cap Madeleine, Quebec, of the Eastern Canada League. Years later he ended his playing career with outlaw teams in Quebec City and Iberville. Bissonnette later managed the Toronto Maple Leafs of the International League. Subsequently, as scouts for the Braves, Bissonnette and his protégé Roland Gladu signed half a dozen other Canadian big leaguers. Mel Hall, born at Lyons, New York, has been a winter Montrealer since he married a Quebecois airline stewardess several years ago. Pitcher Lew LaClaire listed his birthplace as Milton, Vermont, but lived in Farnham, Quebec, where he and his family died in the influenza epidemic of 1918.

The first Canadian-born major leaguer was first baseman Bill Phillips, who played for Cleveland, Brooklyn, and Kansas City, from 1879 to 1888. Born in St. John, New Brunswick, Phillips actually grew up in Chicago.

Among the 150 to follow Phillips are active players Rob Ducey, Larry Walker, Kevin Reimer, and Matt Stairs, as well as pitchers Steve Wilson, Kirk McCaskill, Dennis Boucher, Mike Gardiner, Vince Horsman, Paul Quantrill, and Rheal Cormier. While the number of players by position is roughly proportional to the numbers on major league rosters, pitchers have won the most distinction, perhaps because pitching skills can be developed more readily in short amateur seasons. Bob Emslie of Guelph, Ontario, was the first Canadian pitcher of note, and won more games in a big league season than any other Canadian, posting a 32–17 mark for the 1884 Baltimore Orioles. A poor start in 1885 sent him back to the minors, with a career major league record of just 44–44. Emslie returned to the majors, however, as an umpire, serving thirty-five years before retiring in 1926.

Only George Washington Stovey won more games in a year in Organized Baseball than Emslie. Stovey, probably born in Ontario, was among the top black pitchers of the nineteenth century. A headstrong lefty fireballer, Stovey fanned 22 men in one game with Bridgeport of the Eastern League in 1886, but lost due to poor control. He set an all-time International League record with 35 wins for Newark the next year, 1887, then was ousted from Organized Baseball through the racist efforts of white players including Hall of Famer Cap Anson and slugger Tip O'Neill, whose refusal to play either with or against blacks drew the color line firm by 1890.

O'Neill, born at either Woodstock or Springfield, Ontario, in 1858, was the best Canadian hitter of his time or ever, batting .326 in a big-league career that ran from 1883 to 1892. Breaking into the majors with New York as a pitcher, O'Neill soon switched to the outfield. In 1886 he led the then-major league American Association in hits, doubles, triples, homers, runs scored, batting, and slugging. His batting average, at the time, was actually listed as .492, but 50 walks were counted as hits. Subtracting them, he still hit .435. Though O'Neill fell to .335 in 1887, he repeated as batting champion.

The best Canadian player of all was probably Hall of Famer Ferguson Jenkins, a 6'5" black righthander from Chatham, Ontario, who avenged the injustice done to Stovey with a 284–226 record over nineteen seasons from 1965 to 1983. At his peak, Jenkins won 20 games or more seven times in eight years. Noted for control, Jenkins

fanned over three times as many batters as he walked—and led the NL with 273 whiffs in 1969, retiring ninth on the all-time strikeout list. He earned the 1971 NL Cy Young Award by leading the league in wins (24), innings pitched, and, for the third time each, starts and complete games. He also hit 6 homers that year, one behind the NL record for home runs by a pitcher.

Other Canadian pitchers of note include Russ Ford, John Hiller, Reggie Cleveland, Phil Marchildon, Dick Fowler, Claude Raymond, and Ron Taylor. Ford, whose older brother also made the big leagues briefly, won 26 games for the New York Highlanders in 1910, his first full season. Hiller saved a then-record 38 games in 1973 and won an AL record 17 games in relief the next year, but is best known for his comeback from a 1971 heart attack. Marchildon and Fowler were half of the Athletics' rotation during the 1940s. On September 9, 1945, Fowler became the only Canadian to hurl a no-hitter, beating the Browns 1–0 for his only victory that year after coming back from military service. Marchildon peaked with 19 wins in 1947. Raymond is remembered as the first native Quebecois to play for the Expos, but was part of another bit of baseball trivia in 1959, as one of three Quebecois pitchers who helped Louisville to the American Association eastern division pennant. (The others were Georges Maranda and Ron Piche.) Taylor relieved for two World Champions, the 1964 Cardinals and the 1969 Mets, then became team physician for the Toronto Blue Jays.

Other top Canadian hitters were George Selkirk and Jeff Heath. Selkirk, who replaced Babe Ruth in the Yankees' lineup in 1934, hit .290 over nine seasons, topping .300 five times and twice driving in more than 100 runs. He played out the string in the early 1950s as a .300-hitting player-manager for Quebec City of the Provincial League and, following his retirement as a player, served as general manager of the Washington Senators for ten years. Heath, who reputedly never lived up to his potential, averaged .293 over fourteen years, beginning in 1936, with 194 homers. His best years were 1938 (21–112–.343) and 1941 (24–123–.340.) In between he led a player revolt against Indians manager Oscar Vitt. In his final full year, Heath hit .319 with twenty-four homers, pacing the Braves to the 1948 NL pennant, but broke his leg sliding during the last week of the season, missing his only chance at a World Series.

Canadian managers have included Art Irwin, Freddie Lake, Moon Gibson, and Bill Watkins, who led the Detroit Wolverines to the 1887 American Association pennant and had the only winning lifetime record among them.

Catcher Nig Clarke, from Amhurstburg, Ontario, won a spot in the minor league record books on June 15, 1902, hitting eight homers for Corsicana of the Texas League in a 51–3 rout of Texarkana. A Corsicana ordinance against Sunday baseball had forced the teams to play on a youth field at the nearby town of Ennis. Outfielder Jack Graney, of St. Thomas, Ontario, was reputedly the first major leaguer to wear a number, and was also both the first hitter to face Babe Ruth when the latter debuted as a pitcher, and the first ex-player to become a baseball broadcaster. Outfielder Glen Gorbous, of Drumheller, Alberta, made the *Guinness Book of Records* with the longest measured throw on record. Black pitcher Jimmy

Claxton, of New Westminster, British Columbia, briefly broke the color line by passing as an alleged Native American with Oakland of the Pacific Coast League in 1916.

Several Canadian women could also claim to have been major leaguers, having played in the All-American Girls' Pro Baseball League organized in 1943 by Branch Rickey and Phil Wrigley. The league, the only women's professional circuit to date, thrived in the Midwest until 1955. First batting champion was Toronto native Gladys Davis. Catcher-manager and off season fashion model Mary "Bonnie" Baker of Regina, Alberta, was the league's best-paid player in 1951 and 1952, earning $1,600 a month— more than many men in the National and American Leagues. Helen Callaghan St. Aubin, of Vancouver, stole 354 bases in 388 games, then became mother of former Expo infielder Casey Candaele. The three followed a tradition of Canadian women players begun by barnstorming star Nellie McClung in the 1880s.

National League baseball finally came to Canada with the expansion Montreal Expos in 1969. Hoping to get off to a good start, the Expos drafted mainly veterans, including Maury Wills, who became the only player to appear with Montreal in both the majors and the minors. Wills was soon traded for another veteran, Ron Fairly, who had led the University of Edmonton into the 1957 College World Series. A preseason swap of sluggers Donn Clendenon and Rusty Staub had to be rearranged when Clendenon quit rather than join the Astros. Clendenon eventually unretired and was swapped to the Mets. The affair was a milestone in the series of events that led to the overturn of the reserve clause in 1975. Although the Expos won both their first game and their home opener (on a home run by pitcher Dan McGinn), they finished last. No-hitters by Bill Stoneman in 1969 and 1972 were the club high points until 1973. Then, despite a 79–83 record, the Expos were in contention into the final week, paced by Ken Singleton, Ron Hunt, who set an all-time record by getting hit with pitches 50 times, rookie Steve Rogers, and reliever Mike Marshall, who saved 31 games and won 14 in 92 appearances.

Marshall was promptly traded to the Dodgers for Willie Davis, who staged a sit-down strike in center field before moving on. Singleton and pitcher Mike Torrez were sent to the Orioles a year later for former Cy Young Award winner Dave McNally and outfielder Rich Coggins. A thyroid ailment ended Coggins's career at age 25, while McNally played the 1975 season without a contract, then filed one of the two lawsuits that finally broke the reserve clause (Andy Messersmith of the Dodgers filed the other).

The Expos regrouped under new manager Dick Williams to win a club record 95 games in 1979. The arrival of young stars including Rogers, Andre Dawson, Gary Carter, Larry Parrish, Tim Raines, and Tim Wallach led management to bill the Expos as "The Team of the Eighties." The promise seemed real when the Expos won a playoff against the Phillies for the NL East title during the strike-shortened split season of 1981, and were leading the Dodgers 1–0 in the fifth inning of the final game of the NL Championship Series. But Rick Monday singled and scored the tying run, then won the game 2–1 with a two-out ninth inning homer off Rogers, who had come on in relief.

Toronto appeared ready to enter the National League in 1976 by purchasing the San Francisco Giants. When that deal fell through at the last minute, the American League admitted the Blue Jays as an expansion team in 1977. The Blue Jays drafted for the future, enduring six years in the cellar before winning 89 games to place fourth in 1983.

Good trades and a strong farm system loaded the lineup with sluggers George Bell, Jesse Barfield, Lloyd Moseby, and Willie Upshaw, plus hard-hitting infielders Tony Fernandez and Damaso Garcia, and produced a perennially strong pitching staff led by Dave Stieb and Jimmy Key. Ernie Whitt, an expansion draft selection, supplied power behind the plate through 1989. Winning 99 games and the AL East title in 1985, the Jays took a 3–1 lead in the Championship Series against Kansas City, but then dropped three games in a row to lose. Two years later, bolstered by emerging young longball hitters Fred McGriff and Kelly Gruber, the Blue Jays had a three-and-a-half-game lead over the Tigers with a week to play but, after injuries to Fernandez and Whitt, lost their last six games, including three one-run decisions to the Tigers on the final weekend.

The Jays partially redeemed a growing reputation for choking by besting the Orioles in a season-ending series to win the 1989 AL East, but were crushed by the Athletics, four games to one, in the Championship Series. The 1990 club started slowly. Closing fast, however, the Blue Jays overtook the slumping Red Sox with two weeks to play— and lost again, dropping two out of three games to the Bosox in a last-week direct confrontation.

By 1991 Canadian baseball really began taking hold. The Blue Jays broke the 4 million attendance figure for the second straight season. Meanwhile, the Expos were trying to solidify their precarious financial situation, as original owner Charles Bronfman put the club on the block. A group headed by club president Claude Brochu finally purchased the Expos, but had to face the prospect of losing his ballpark (built only in 1976) as a 50-ton block of concrete fell from the Olympic Stadium roof. The possibility that the stadium would be condemned left the Expos to consider relocating to another city, with Buffalo and St. Petersburg among the contenders. The Expos finished the final weeks of the season on the road, while all waited for stadium engineering reports—which proved positive. After extensive repairs were made, Le Stade Olympique was declared safe, and baseball stayed in Montreal.

Minor league teams were flourishing in Ontario as the New York-Penn League featured the Welland Pirates, St. Catherines Blue Jays, and Hamilton Redbirds and the Eastern League had the London Tigers. The Pacific Coast League included Vancouver, Edmonton, and Calgary, while the Rookie-Classification Pioneer League featured a Blue Jays farm club at Medicine Hat, Alberta. By 1993 the Hamilton club had moved to the States but the International League had awarded an expansion franchise to Ottawa.

As for grass-roots baseball, the Canadian National Under 21 Team won its first Gold Medal in the Pan-Am Games, defeating the USA in the final.

The 1991 Blue Jays again won their division, but after giving everyone a sense of "this is the year," collapsed in

the ALCS and lost to Minnesota. The mood in the Dominion, which by now had declared the Jays "Canada's Team," was one of despair. The rules of Williamsport's Little League World Series had recently been changed so that an American team would always be in the final game . . . maybe, just maybe, there was an unwritten rule about the Major League Baseball World Series, too, thought weary Canadians.

Pat Gillick, the mastermind of the Blue Jays, had been stuck by media and fans with the tag "Stand Pat," reflecting opinion that he was overly cautious. The 1991 winter meetings changed all that as Gillick pulled off one of the biggest trades ever made. He swapped the Blue Jays' leading hitter and RBI man, Fred McGriff, along with slick-fielding shortstop Tony Fernandez to the Padres for outfielder Joe Carter and future All-Star second baseman Robby Alomar. Now the gloves were off, and the owners' purse strings were loosened. Gillick proceeded to sign free agents Jack Morris (who had pitched brilliantly in leading the Twins to the World Championship in 1991) and Dave Winfield (who everyone thought was over the hill). With a 1992 payroll of $41 million, the Blue Jays were determined to crash the World Series.

Toronto held off the stubborn Baltimore Orioles, who faded in September, and the Milwaukee Brewers to capture the AL East. Led by Morris's 21 wins and a bullpen with baseball's best closer tandem, Duane Ward and Tom Henke, the Jays remained in first place for all but a few days in May. Forty-one-year-old Dave Winfield was the oldest player to knock in over 100 runs in a season. With 28 homers, he proved to be the spark that ignited the Jays. In the ALCS, Toronto defeated the Oakland A's in six games to capture the pennant.

In the World Series, after splitting the first two games in Atlanta, Canada was in a frenzy as the Blue Jays went up 3 games to 1. Jack Morris took the mound for the Jays in Game Five. How could they lose? But lose they did, as the Braves' Lonnie Smith hammered a grand slam off Morris in the fifth inning.

Hysteria set in. The press screamed, "Here we go again! Choke! The Blue Jays are choking!" Remember 1985 and the Royals, was the chant, when the Jays were up 3 games to 1 and lost. Blown out by the A's and Twins and Tigers when they were so close. All the seasons past were coming back to haunt the Blue Jays of 1992.

Game Six became one of the most exciting World Series contests ever. Leading 2–1 going into the bottom of the ninth, the Jays brought in top closer Tom Henke. The Toronto bullpen had been near perfect throughout the Series. But not this time. The Braves tied the score to force extra innings.

The top of the eleventh brought Dave Winfield to the plate with runners on first and second. The rest is history. The Blue Jays' 1992 slogans—"Three for Three" and "Win with Winfield"—all came together when Winfield doubled down the left field line, putting Toronto up by two runs. Reliever Mike Timlin held off an Atlanta rally that brought them to within one run of prolonging the game. The Blue Jays beat the Braves 4–3, and could now be called world champions.

Disgruntled Americans asked: How many Canadians were on the Blue Jays anyway? Yes, the players were either American, Dominican, Puerto Rican, or other non-Canadians. But just as the National Hockey League is made up of mostly Canadians and Europeans, it doesn't matter. The 1992 Blue Jays were Canada's team, as the World Series Trophy resided in their Toronto offices, to remain there until the 1993 world champions are crowned. Who knows, maybe it will be the Expos' turn? *Sacre bleu!*

[Thanks for research help to Eves Raja; Bill Humber; Donald Guay; and the Brome County Historical Society.]

Honored Members of The Canadian Baseball Hall of Fame

Inducted	Name/Career Facts
1990	Archer, Jimmy: Pit-N 1904, 1918; Det-A 1907; Chi-N 1909-17; Bro-N 1918; Cin-N 1918
1988	Bertoia, Reno Peter: Det-A 1953-58, 1961-62; Was-A 1959-60; Min-A 1961; KC-A 1961
1984	Bilesky, Andy: Little League coach
1988	Bowsfield, Ted: Bos-A 1958-60; Cle-A 1960; LA-A 1961-62; KC-A 1963-64
1984	Bronfman, Charles: executive
1989	Brown, Bob: minor league player, executive and club owner
1992	Burgess, Thomas (Tim): StL-N 1954; LA-A 1962, minor league manager 1964-1989
1985	Bush, Carmen: amateur player, coach, manager, umpire and administrator
1986	Cleveland, Reggie: StL-N 1969-73; Bos-A 1974-78; Tex-A 1978; Mil-A 1979-81
1985	Cooke, Jack Kent: minor league owner and executive
1983	Ducey, John: amateur player, minor league umpire and administrator
1986	Emslie, Bob: Bal-A 1883-85; NL umpire 1891-1924
1987	Ford, Russell William: NY-A 1909-13; Buf-F 1914-15
1985	Fowler, Dick: Phi-A 1941-42, 1945–52
1987	Gibson, George "Moonie": Pit-N 1905-16; NY-N 1917-18
1984	Graney, Jack: Cle-A 1908-22; broadcaster Cle-A 1932-53
1988	Heath, Jeff: Cle-A 1936-45; Was-A 1946; StL-A 1946-47; Bos-N 1948-49
1985	Hiller, John: Det-A 1965-70, 1972-80
1989	Irwin, Arthur: Wor-N 1880-82; Pro-N 1883-85; Phi-N 1886-89, 1894; Was-N 1889; Bos-P 1890; Bos-A 1891

Inducted	Name/Career Facts
1987	Jenkins, Ferguson: Phi-N 1965-66; Chi-N 1966-73, 1982-83; Tex-A 1974-75, 1978-81; Bos-A 1976-77
1985	Judd, Thomas "Lefty": Bos-A 1941-45; Phi-A 1945-48
1983	Marchildon, Phil: Phi-A 1940-42, 1945-49; Bos-A 1950
1987	Nelson, Glenn "Rocky": StL-N 1949-51, 1956; Tor-IL 1951, 1958, 1962; Pit-N 1951, 1959-61; Chi-A 1951; Bro-N 1952, 1956; Mon-IL 1952-56; Cle-A 1954
1983	O'Neill, James "Tip": NY-N 1883; StL-A 1884-1889; Chi-P 1890; Cin-N 1892
1983	Pearson, Lester B.: (Honorary Inductee) amateur player; former Prime Minister of Canada
1988	Phillips, Bill: Cle-N 1879-84; Bro-A 1885-87; KC-A 1888
1988	Piche, Ron: Mil-A 1960-63; Cal-A 1965; StL-N 1966
1986	Prentice, Bobby: minor league player and scout
1984	Raymond, Claude: Chi-A 1959; Mil-N 1961-63; Hou-N 1964-67; Atl-N 1967-69; Mon-N 1969-71
1991	Robinson, Jackie: Montreal Royals, International League, 1946; Bro-N 1947-56
1984	Rosen, Goody: Bro-N 1937-39, 1944-46; NY-N 1946
1983	Selkirk, George "Twinkletoes": NY-A 1934-42
1983	Shaughnessy, Sr., Frank "Shag": minor league administrator and executive
1985	Taylor, Ron: Cle-A 1962; StL-N 1963-65; Hou-N 1965-66; NY-N 1967-71; SD-N 1972
1991	Ward, Peter: Bal-A 1962; Chi-A 1963-69; NY-A 1970
1991	Williams, Jimmy: LA, Pacific Coast League, 1947-1964; minor league manager, 17 seasons; major league coach, Hou-N 1975; Bal-A 1981-1987

## CHAPTER 24

College Baseball

Cappy Gagnon

Intercollegiate baseball has come a long way since July 1, 1859, when the first match was played between Amherst and Williams Colleges, at Pittsfield, Massachusetts. Amherst won by a 73–32 score, on a playing field unrecognizable today. The pitcher was twenty-five feet closer to the batter, and the diamond was only sixty feet on a side. In keeping more with the academic orientation of the times, the two schools engaged in a chess match on the following day. The baseball game was played under the "Massachusetts rules," which eventually gave way to "New York rules," the forerunner of the game we know today. At the time of this game, Abraham Lincoln was not yet President. After the game there were rumors of some "ringers" being used by each team. This was a problem which haunted college sports for the next six decades.

Early college baseball thus preceded the National League by seventeen years. The colleges also provided one very significant equipment innovation. It was a Harvard man named Fred W. Thayer who invented the catcher's mask. Thayer gave his homemade creation to Harry Thatcher, the Crimson backstop (though several sources credit instead Harvard's star, James Tyng). After overcoming taunts about his "babyish and cowardly" act, Thatcher adjusted to wearing the mask. A short while later, Thayer saw the potential of this invention, and on February 12, 1878, he obtained a patent for it.

From the founding of the National Association in 1871 to the present there has been a collegiate influence on the national pastime. There is little evidence that this influence has raised the level of scholarship in the dugout, but unquestionably college baseball has provided an important feeder system for the majors. Initially, this role was important because major league teams of the pre-Rickey era did not have their own farm systems and competed vigorously with each other for raw playing talent. Colleges were an additional place for youngsters to develop.

The majors became more closely aligned with the campuses beginning in the 1890s, when veteran players began to serve as coaches of college teams. Until about 1910, college teams did not have full-time baseball field coaches. During February and March of each year, teams practiced in gymnasiums until weather permitted outside play. These practices were often supervised by a big leaguer, or other pro, limbering up for his own spring training to follow. He might have been a player from the neighboring area, as when Lou Criger of Elkhart, Indiana, or Harry Arndt of South Bend coached the Notre Dame teams. Or he might have been a recent graduate of the school, as when Jesse Burkett coached Holy Cross.

Such coaches usually retained an entrée with the college when his big league team was looking for prospects. Norwood Gibson and Red Morgan followed Criger to the Red Sox, Red Murray followed Arndt to the Cardinals, and Lou Sockalexis followed Burkett to the Cleveland Spiders.

Once the intercollegiate season began, there would be little or no involvement from university staff in the conduct of play. The team captain, a player, would function as the manager. Another student, a nonplayer, would function as the athletic director, scheduling games with other colleges and with independent and professional teams. George Huff, of Illinois, was probably the first paid full-time "coacher." His knowledge of the game helped make the Illini a "western" power, while at the same time developing future pros. Huff scouted for the Cubs and recruited players from his own teams and neighboring colleges for the Southsiders. In the former group were pitchers Carl Lundgren, Big Jeff Pfeffer, and Fred Beebe. Pitcher Ed Reulbach, of Notre Dame, was an example of the latter.

With a few exceptions in California (notably St. Mary's), college baseball until after World War Two was primarily a northeastern and midwestern sport. Because of travel difficulties and the location of all sixteen major league teams within a handful of eastern and midwestern states, college baseball became dominated by the eastern athletic powers (Harvard, Yale, Princeton, and Brown). "Western" upstarts like Illinois, Michigan, Chicago, and Notre Dame were lightly regarded by them. Because intersectional play did not occur until around 1910, however, there was no way to evaluate the competing claims of superiority. Catholic schools Boston College, Fordham, and Manhattan and the Ivy League were strong around the turn of the century, as were many small eastern colleges like Amherst. Harvard had such a strong team, they were able to defeat the defending and soon to repeat world champion Boston Red Sox, 1–0, on April 10, 1916.

Early collegians showed their cleverness in choosing pseudonyms. The two great Columbia players were known as "Sullivan" (Eddie Collins) and "Lewis" (Lou Gehrig). John Mohardt of Notre Dame had an interesting story as a result of his baseball alias: Mohardt became "Cavanaugh" when the entire Notre Dame team went to New Hampton, Iowa, for the summer of 1920. Mohardt picked up a girlfriend during that summer. He confided to her what the "ND" on the team caps stood for (his teammates claimed they were from North Dakota), but did not divulge his real name. Later that fall, when she sent a love note to "Johnny Cavanaugh, c/o Notre Dame," it was

delivered to the Reverend John Cavanaugh, C.S.C., president of the university, who was not amused.

Early "tramp athletes" went from school to school and played on semipro teams under various aliases. Some "collegiate" players were not even enrolled in the colleges they represented. Bert Daniels was one of a number of itinerant collegians. He played at Villanova, Notre Dame, and Bucknell—all under his own name, while playing minor league ball during the summers, using five different aliases. As "Ayres," at Altoona in 1910, he was called the "next Ty Cobb." Unfortunately, he was already twenty-seven years old and had already played ten years of college and semipro football. All this had taken its toll on his legs. Daniels did make good use of his schooling, however, becoming an engineer.

Big leaguers came from virtually every college, including small and lesser-known colleges. Mathewson of Bucknell, Coombs of Colby, Plank of Gettysburg, Thorpe of Carlisle, and Beaumont of Beloit were good examples of why the majors scouted even the small schools. Although college teams played fewer than thirty games at this time, due to cold weather and travel difficulties and perhaps an occasional class or two, the top collegiate players seemed to get in sufficient playing time to impress big league scouts. Semipro, Industrial League, and town-team leagues were three of the types of ball for which a skilled collegian could pick up a little money for tuition and supporting his family.

The rise of college programs in the South and Far West came much later. The first major leaguer from the University of Southern California was Fay Thomas in 1927. Rod Dedeaux of the 1935 Dodgers was the fourth. Notre Dame had at least forty men reach the big leagues by 1920. Brown had fourteen in the majors by 1900. Georgetown was another early producer of big leaguers.

Once there was full-time college baseball, the relationship between the majors and the colleges became even more pronounced. In 1909 Connie Mack installed Jack Barry, a Holy Cross collegian as the shortstop in his $100,000 infield. During his forty years as coach of the Crusaders (1921–1961), Barry sent at least twenty-three players to the majors, including Gene Desautels and Mike Hegan. Connie Mack sent his son Earle to Niagara and Notre Dame.

According to Ellery Clark in *Red Sox Forever,* the early Bosox team featured many collegians, including two stars from St. Mary's (Duffy Lewis and Harry Hooper) who formed two-thirds of the best outfield of its day and the two best players from Vermont's 1908 team (Ray Collins and Larry Gardner).

One factor which may have encouraged many players to matriculate instead of trying out with the majors was the number of them who were multiple-sports stars. Christy Mathewson played football and basketball; Robin Roberts played basketball at Michigan State; Alvin Dark was a football star at Louisiana State University; Ted Kluszewski and Moose Skowron were football players at Indiana and Purdue respectively; Joe Adcock was a scoring star in basketball at Louisiana State University; Lou Boudreau, Frank Baumholtz, and Dick Groat were All-Americans in basketball at Illinois, Ohio, and Duke; and Jackie Robinson starred in football and track at U.C.L.A.

Many players better known for football were major

leaguers too: George Halas, Ernie Nevers, Jim Thorpe, Sam Chapman, Red Badgro, Ace Parker, etc. Similarly, many collegiate baseball players achieved fame in other professional sports, like NFL quarterbacks Joe Theismann (ND) and John Elway (Stanford). The legendary George Gipp played a little baseball at Notre Dame. The Cubs allegedly offered him a contract after watching him play semipro baseball with Kiki Cuyler in Michigan.

College men were not always warmly received into the majors. Veteran players had a natural reluctance to accept anyone who was out to win a scarce job, in the days of sixteen teams and eighteen-man rosters. Secondly, the crude, often ill-educated pros were more than a little resentful of the more-cultured and better-educated collegians. Writing just before the turn of the century, sportswriter George E. Stackhouse quoted "a well-known professional catcher . . . [whose manager] . . . was beginning to get the college baseball fever." The player approached a collegian and asked him if he were thinking of becoming a professional. When the collegian said he had no idea of becoming a pro, the catcher replied, "with much warmth: 'Now that's square, old man. You know Greek, Latin, and something about the world. You can make a good living anywhere. Don't interfere with us fellows, because you don't have to.' "

Henry Edwards of the Major League Service Bureau estimated this percentage of collegians in the majors at almost one-third in 1932. This is a big jump from 1909, when only fifty-seven big leaguers—or approximately 14 percent—had college backgrounds.

Because of the harsh conditions they faced, many star baseballers took their schooling seriously and skipped the majors. Another factor is that player salaries, in an era long before Marvin Miller, were often not attractive enough to persuade a bright college man to give up a career in a profession.

According to the 1900 U.S. Census, fewer than 2 percent of twenty-three-year-old men were college graduates. The average annual earnings of a working man from 1900 through World War One ranged from a little more than $400 to a little less than $1,000. A college man stood a much better chance to earn more than his counterpart. Similarly, professional players did not earn much more than average, and their short careers and unpleasant travel conditions made it difficult to develop either a nest egg or a headstart on a post-playing career.

The Notre Dame baseball captain in 1900 was probably as good a player as Peaches O'Neill, Red Morgan, Bob Bescher, Henry Thielman, Norwood Gibson, Bert Keeley, Frank Shaughnessy, and several other of his teammates who went on to the majors. Instead, first baseman Angus MacDonald, a four-letter winner, took his business degree to New York City, where he went to work for the Southern Pacific Railroad, later becoming president of the railroad.

Despite the closer relationship, considerable hostility remained between organized ball and the colleges. An editorial in *The Sporting News* on March 14, 1946, defended major league baseball's plantation treatment of the colleges.

Referring to the case of Gale Bishop of Washington State, who was signed early and made ineligible for further collegiate play, "University authorities have com-

plained about this and similar practices, but few have shown any disposition to give the game an adequate place in their athletic programs, because of the emphasis placed on football and basketball." The fact that Bishop had no major league career to show for the disruption of his college athletics only exacerbated the problem.

On July 2, 1947, *The Sporting News* reported that a foundation was being laid for a truce between organized ball and the colleges. Earlier, Branch Rickey, himself a college man from Ohio Wesleyan and later George Sisler's baseball coach at Michigan when he was the country's top college pitcher, said that he felt the colleges had "dirty skirts" themselves and were in no position to lecture the majors. Rickey said he would continue to scout and sign collegians because he felt that some college teams had relationships with major league teams that were akin to their being farmclubs. And we know that Branch Rickey was not going to be "out-farmclubbed" by anyone.

One of the committee members representing organized baseball in its deliberations with the colleges was Frank "Shag" Shaughnessy, president of the International League. He said, "The player should not be compelled to wait to play professional ball if he needs the money to complete his education."

Shag was a star baseball and football player at Notre Dame who paid for his college education by playing semi-pro (as "Shannon") and professional ball.

Once the minor league teams were no longer able to sign and develop their own players, but were dependent upon "working agreements" with big league teams, long-term player development became a function of college baseball programs. Major league teams could avoid signing hundreds of players and maintaining ten or more minor league affiliates by simply letting the colleges do their work for them. College facilities and coaching were at least as good as the low minors. Players were "signed" to a scholarship and nurtured by the colleges. Big league scouts could watch their playing and learn something about their competitive abilities, injury history, and maturity. After two or three years, the best players would be drafted and sent to Rookie Ball or higher. Some think that a good college program might be the equivalent of Double-A baseball.

From the 1950s on, the major leagues changed their relationship with the minors dramatically, thereby thrusting the college game into an even more prominent role. Schools such as Arizona, Arizona State, and Texas began to produce big leaguers by the gross. When Dedeaux returned to his alma mater as coach, he increased their big league output dramatically while winning ten collegiate championships from 1958 to 1978.

From 1954 through 1980, there were only three years when U.S.C. did not send at least one player to the majors—forty-five players in twenty-seven years. Tom Seaver, Dave Kingman, Fred Lynn, Ron Fairly, and Don Buford were among this invasion. Commissioner Bowie Kuhn estimated in 1978 that more than two-thirds of major leaguers were college men.

There are also advantages for the collegians in this relationship. If an aspiring major leaguer's baseball apprenticeship does not work out, he can concentrate on his studies and find another vocation. He is in an environment where he has more opportunity for enrichment, for overall personal development, than would result from his being thrown into the minors at age seventeen or eighteen, as so often occurred during baseball's early days.

Great collegiate baseball teams can be evaluated in terms of two measures: the number of games won and the number of major league players produced. It is hard to argue with those who regard the University of Southern California as the greatest school on both counts. Since the inception of the Division I NCAA baseball championship in 1947, the U.S.C. Trojans have won eleven times and have finished as runner-up once. Next closest are Arizona State, with five firsts and three seconds; Texas with four firsts and one second; Arizona with three of each; and Minnesota with three titles. Oklahoma State, Cal State Fullerton, Florida State, Wichita State, and Miami are other schools with baseball programs that have been very strong during the past decade.

Pepperdine's 1992 championship kept the trophy in the Sun Belt for the twenty-fourth year in the past twenty-five. Only Wichita State's 1989 title interrupted the run which began after Ohio State's 1966 win.

Besides Barry and Dedeaux, former big leaguers coaching these NCAA championship teams have included Bibb Falk (at Texas), Ray Fisher and Don Lund (Michigan), Dick Siebert (Minnesota), and Jerry Kindall (Arizona).

The Trojans of USC, Texas Longhorns and Arizona Sun Devils are the three top schools in producing major leaguers. The next echelon, in order, includes Holy Cross, Michigan, Illinois and Notre Dame. The Michigan Wolverines are the only school to have produced a major leaguer in every decade since the founding of the National Association in 1871.

Texas has provided the majors with Roger Clemens, Greg Swindell, Burt Hooten, Calvin Schiraldi, and Keith Moreland among recent stars. Alabama claims Frank Lary, Riggs Stephenson, Joe Sewell, Del Pratt, and Butch Hobson. Michigan has sent an all-world infield combo which will be hard to top: George Sisler, Charlie Gehringer, Bill Freehan, Barry Larkin, and Chris Sabo. Brigham Young has been strong recently with Jack Morris, Wally Joyner, and Cory Snyder.

In 1973, the California Angels thought so much of the coaching of Bobby Winkles of the Arizona State Sun Devils that they hired him as their manager, the first time the majors had ever hired a college coach with no prior big league experience. Winkles managed two years each with the Angels and the A's. At Arizona State Winkles had coached Rick Monday, Reggie Jackson, and Sal Bando.

The NCAA has selected a championship Series Most Valuable Player since 1949. Winners of this award have included future big leaguers Tom Yewcic (C, Michigan State), Tom Borland (P, Oklahoma State), Cal Emery (P-1B, Penn State), Bob Garibaldi (P, Santa Clara), Sal Bando (3B, Arizona State), Steve Arlin (P, Ohio State), Jerry Tabb (1B, Tulsa), Dave Winfield (P-OF, Minnesota), Bob Horner (3B, Arizona State), Terry Francona (LF, Arizona), and Calvin Schiraldi (P, Texas).

CHAPTER 25

Women in Baseball

Debra A. Shattuck

Women have been associated with baseball, either as players or spectators, since the game's dawn in the early nineteenth century. Even before baseball emerged in its final form, girls and young women sometimes played precursors of the game like One Old Cat, Town Ball, and Stoolball in Colonial America. As time passed, and the boys' amusement became serious business for grown men, baseball's reputation as a masculine domain was established. In 1865, one year before Charles Peverelly observed that baseball "has now become beyond question the leading feature of the outdoor sports of the United States," *Harper's Weekly* proclaimed: "There is no nobler or manlier game than base-ball." During the latter half of the nineteenth century, women's presence as spectators at baseball games was tolerated and sometimes encouraged. Eventually promoters of the game hosted regular "Ladies Days" to attract women fans who would bring in added gate receipts and, hopefully, have a calming effect on the sometimes unruly crowds. Many women were content with their role as spectators and moral uplifters, but others yearned for the opportunity to try their hand at the national pastime. Those who lived out their fantasy often had to endure verbal and written derision from observers anxious to preserve the baseball status quo.

For the most part, the negative attitude toward women baseball players continues to this day. Many still share the opinion of an editorialist who noted in The St. Louis *Globe-Democrat* in 1885 that "The female has no place in base ball, except to the degradation of the game." The criticisms notwithstanding, uncounted women have pursued their own field of dreams, contributing their unique chapter to baseball's rich heritage.

Many of the first women baseball players were college students. The secluded atmosphere of all-girl's schools enabled women to play the game without attracting too much attention. Students at Vassar College organized two baseball clubs as early as 1866. In 1879, according to Vassar alumna Sophia Foster Richardson, the Vassar girls organized at least seven baseball clubs. The private grounds of college campuses did not always protect female players from public criticism, however. In a speech to an alumnae association in 1896, Richardson recalled, "The public, so far as it knew of our playing, was shocked, but in our retired grounds, and protected from observation even in these grounds by sheltering trees, we continued to play in spite of a censorious public." Within a few years, however, the "censorious public" and "disapproving mothers" had succeeded in stifling the game at Vassar.

But Vassar was not the only college where women tried their hand at baseball. In a letter to her former classmates at Smith College, Minnie Stephens (class of 1883) reminisced about the baseball clubs they had organized at the school in 1880. Stephens described the enthusiasm of the players and the keen competition at games. She also related how the Victorian-style clothing of the day, generally a hindrance to sporting endeavors, had actually benefited one of the players during a heated contest, "One vicious batter drove a ball directly into the belt line of her opponent, and had it not been for the rigid steel corset clasp worn in those days, she would have been knocked out completely." Like the women at Vassar, baseball players at Smith College faced opposition which eventually forced them to give up the game for a number of years.

Women baseball players were not limited to college campuses. In Springfield, Illinois, three men organized a women's baseball club in 1875. They were confident that the novelty of women playing baseball would attract large crowds and fatten their bankroll. On September 11, 1875, the club's teams, labeled the "Blondes" and "Brunettes," played their first match. Newspapers heralded the event as the "first game of baseball ever played in public for gate money between feminine ball-tossers." The concept evidently caught on, for numerous other male entrepreneurs copied the idea and organized women's baseball teams. One group started the "Young Ladies' Baseball Club" in Philadelphia in 1883. These owners billed their team's games as entertainment spectacles, not serious competition, and they continually stressed the femininity and moral respectability of their players. A newspaper account of one of the club's first games relayed the management's claim that players were "selected with tender solicitude from 200 applicants, variety actresses and ballet girls being positively barred." Furthermore the article noted, "Only three of the lot had ever been on the stage, and they were in the strictly legitimate business."

The Young Ladies Baseball Club played its first game on August 18, 1883, at Pastime Park in Philadelphia. Despite the supposed "200 applicants," only sixteen girls were mustered to form the two teams for the contest; two young men rounded out the rosters. The game was played on a regulation-size diamond, but, as one observer wrote, it was too large for the women. "A ball thrown from pitcher to second base almost invariably fell short and was stopped on the roll. The throw from first to third base was an utter impossibility." Five hundred spectators witnessed the club's debut and were caught up in "uncontrollable laughter" much of the time. From a financial standpoint, however, the venture was a success. More than 1,500 fans

turned out for the club's match at the Manhattan Athletic Club on September 23, 1883, where they "laughed themselves hungry and thirsty." Though one observer conceded that "four of the girls had become expert—for girls," it is obvious that "novelty" and not "ability" was the hallmark of women's baseball at the time.

Another novel group of women baseball players was the Bloomer Girls. Actually "Bloomer Girls" was a misnomer, since Bloomer Girls teams were composed of both men and women. Kansas City Bloomer Girls, New York Bloomer Girls, Texas Bloomer Girls, and Boston Bloomer Girls were just a few of the teams traveling from diamond to diamond in the late nineteenth and early twentieth centuries in search of fame and fortune. Despite the number of Bloomer Girl teams, they did not play each other and no formal league was set up. Instead, they journeyed from town to town, challenging men's amateur and semiprofessional teams. The Bloomer Girls teams relied on sideshow style appeal to draw fans and, not surprisingly, the bottom line was money. The manager of the Texas Bloomer Girls wrote to one prospective promoter in 1913, assuring him that the team's seven girls and four boys, "including the one-armed boy who plays center field," would draw enough fans to ensure the backer "three hundred dollars clear money" each week. A few of the male Bloomer Girls players like "Smoky Joe" Wood and Hall of Famer Rogers Hornsby went on to become successful big league ballplayers, but the future was not as bright for the female players who could not aspire to anything higher in the baseball world.

The Bloomer Girls teams were not the only option available to baseball-playing females around the turn of the century. Women's teams and mixed teams competed occasionally in "pickup" games. One such game took place in Kearsarge, New Hampshire, on August 7, 1903. An article in the *Boston Herald* the following day noted, "The teams were made up of young ladies gowned in white and young men decked out in girls' clothes, all New Englanders, guests at the hotel." On August 31, the newspaper announced an upcoming game at Forest Hills between the "Hickey and Clover clubs," each composed of five women and four men. One year later, in Flat Rock, Indiana, a group of women organized two baseball clubs, one consisting only of married players, the other only of single players.

While some women played on all-female or coed teams, others challenged social constraints of the day by playing on otherwise all-male teams. On June 12, 1903, the *Cincinnati Enquirer* printed an article about the efforts of a local woman, Miss M. E. Phelan, to get a job as center fielder with the all-male Flora Baseball Club of Indiana. Phelan wrote to the club's manager informing him, "I have played with a number of lady ball clubs and am considered the equal of the average country player." Whether the Flora club took Phelan up on her offer to play for them for "$60 per month and expenses" is unknown, but only four years later another Ohioan, Alta Weiss, became an overnight female baseball-playing sensation and, as one article put it, "perhaps the only girl in the United States to obtain [a] college education through skill as a baseball player."

Weiss, a native of Ragersville, Ohio, became a celebrity in the Cleveland area when she made her pitching debut with the all-male, semiprofessional Vermilion Independents on September 2, 1907. More than 1,200 fans attended the game in which Weiss pitched 5 innings, giving up only 4 hits and 1 run. By the time Weiss made her second appearance on September 8, she was already being heralded as the "Girl Wonder" in the press. According to the *Vermilion News,* so many fans wanted to see Weiss play that special trains had to be run to Vermilion from Cleveland and surrounding towns.

Weiss pitched 8 games for the Independents during their 1907 season. More than 13,000 fans saw the games, including a season high of 3,182, who witnessed her debut at Cleveland's League Park on October 2, 1907. At least a dozen newspapers covered her exploits. The following year her father bought a half-interest in a men's semiprofessional team which was known thereafter as the Weiss All-Stars. It was based in Cleveland and, with Alta as a drawing card, played for large crowds throughout Ohio and Kentucky.

Though Weiss was far and away the best-known woman baseball player in northern Ohio at this time, she was not the only one. On June 22, 1908, the *Cleveland Press* introduced fourteen-year-old Carita Masteller to the public. The paper reported that she had been playing baseball for eight or nine years and was as good as Weiss. That same month Weiss pitched against another female pitcher, Irma Gribble. The two dueled again in August. In another unique game, two sisters from Bellevue, Ohio, Irene and Ruth Basford, pitched for opposing men's teams.

Another well-known woman baseball player who played on men's teams was Rhode Islander Elizabeth Murphy. "Lizzie," as she liked to be called, played amateur and semiprofessional baseball from about 1915 to 1935 and was known as the "Queen of Baseball" throughout New England and eastern Canada. After playing for a number of amateur teams in Rhode Island, Murphy signed with the semiprofessional Providence Independents in 1918. A few years later she joined Ed Carr's All-Stars of Boston and earned quite a reputation for her skills as a first baseman.

In 1928, while Murphy was still impressing the fans in New England, fourteen-year-old Margaret Gisolo helped her Blanford, Indiana, American Legion boys' baseball team win county, district, sectional, and state championships. In seven tournament games she had 9 hits in 21 at-bats. She scored 10 putouts and 28 assists in the field, with no errors charged against her. A protest against her participation filed by opposing teams went all the way to the American Legion's National Americanism Commission, which referred it to the major league baseball commissioner, Judge Kenesaw Mountain Landis. Landis determined that American Legion rules did not specifically ban the participation of women and disallowed the protest.

Landis had to address a similar situation three years later when the "Barnum of Baseball," Chattanooga Lookouts manager Joe Engel, signed seventeen-year-old Jackie Mitchell to a contract with his Class AA minor league team, thus making her the first female professional baseball player. Mitchell had been taught to pitch by major leaguer Dazzy Vance and had once struck out nine men in a row in an amateur game. She became an overnight

celebrity on April 2, 1931, when she pitched in an exhibition game against the visiting New York Yankees—and struck out Babe Ruth and Lou Gehrig, back to back. Speculation continues as to whether Ruth and Gehrig were merely putting on a show or really trying to hit Mitchell's pitches. Mitchell contended that it was not a setup and that the only instructions to the Yankee players had been to try not to hit the ball straight through the pitcher's box. A number of Yankee players confirmed her story. Unfortunately Mitchell never had a chance to repeat her performance as a professional baseball player. A few days after her debut, Landis informed Engel that he had disallowed Mitchell's contract on the grounds that life in baseball was too strenuous for women. Organized baseball formalized the ban against women signing professional baseball contracts with men's teams on June 21, 1952; the ruling still stands.

The restriction on women playing professional baseball on men's teams did not prevent the formation of a women's professional baseball league, however. In 1943, with wartime manpower shortages threatening major league baseball, Chicago Cubs' owner Philip K. Wrigley decided to form a women's professional softball league which would play its games in the major league stadiums while the men were away at war. Within a year of its founding, the league modified its rules and the All-American Girls *Baseball* League (AAGBL) was born. The AAGBL made its debut in 1943, when four teams—the Rockford [Illinois] Peaches, the South Bend [Indiana] Blue Sox, the Racine [Wisconsin] Belles, and the Kenosha [Wisconsin] Comets—squared off during the League's 108-game schedule. Attendance that year was 176,000 fans, which, according to one contemporary, meant that the League was "drawing a higher percentage of the population [in league cities] than major league baseball ever did in its greatest attendance years." Attendance figures continued to rise year after year, reaching a peak in 1948, when the League's ten teams drew almost 1,000,000 fans. That same year, AAGBL teams drew more than 100,000 fans for a series of nine games in Puerto Rico.

Unlike women's teams of the past, the AAGBL relied on players' skills, not their gender, to draw fans to the ballpark. The 500 women who played in the AAGBL during its eleven-year existence were top-notch athletes. Many were veterans of championship school, community, or industrial softball teams, and a few had even played on boys' or men's baseball teams. In addition, many of the AAGBL managers were experienced professional baseball players—some, like Bill Wambsganss (the only player ever to achieve an unassisted triple play in a World Se-

ries), Max Carey, Jimmie Foxx, and Dave Bancroft, were legends.

The AAGBL represented one of the only times in history that women baseball players received widespread moral and financial support. Once World War II ended, however, social pressures for women to leave nontraditional jobs and return to household duties resumed. This fact, coupled with organizational problems and the rise of televised major league games, led to the demise of the AAGBL. Interest in the league all but disappeared until the 1980s, when a group of former players organized a players association and began lobbying to have the league honored in the National Baseball Hall of Fame. The popular media and serious scholars rediscovered the league and hundreds of articles about the AAGBL appeared in newspapers and magazines across the country. In October 1988, the Hall of Fame unveiled a permanent exhibit of AAGBL league memorabilia. In the summer of 1992, the AAGBL was further memorialized when it became the subject of the feature film, *A League of Their Own.*

Despite the newfound popularity of the AAGBL, modern-day women baseball players still face the same obstacles and criticisms endured by nineteenth century players. For the most part, organized teams and leagues remain closed to women. When Commissioner Ford Frick issued his ban against women players in 1952, his purpose was to prevent teams from using women players as publicity stunts. The end result of his edict was that even highly skilled women players (like those on the all-female team that tried, unsuccessfully, to gain admission to the men's Class A Florida State League in 1984) lost an important avenue for upward mobility and legitimacy in baseball. Women who challenge baseball's "men only" reputation rarely escape the experience unscathed. Julie Croteau, who gained notoriety in the late 1980s by playing first base for the St. Mary's (Maryland) College men's baseball team, earned school and conference honors yet still had to endure derisive comments from teammates. She left school in the middle of her junior year disillusioned with a system she believed treated women as inferior to men.

It is possible that baseball may one day lose its masculine cast and become equally accessible to women and men. Thanks to a series of court battles in the 1970s, generations of young girls have the opportunity to play baseball on Little League teams. As they mature and resist abandoning the game of their youth, perhaps more high schools and colleges will field girls' baseball, instead of softball, teams. If women baseball players become the rule instead of the exception, baseball will finally, truly become the national pastime.

The Game
Off the Field

## CHAPTER 26

The Business of Baseball

Steve Mann and David Pietrusza

Major league baseball, like every other professional sport, is an entertainment business. And the financial success of any top-level entertainment business rests on its ability to attract consistently large audiences. In order to meet that requirement, the business must do two things. It must assemble and maintain a group of the very best performers in their field, and it must provide pleasant accommodations for the spectators. Every other facet of the business is tied to these fundamental necessities.

In professional sports, the top performers are essentially world-class athletes. And, by definition, there is always a relatively scarce supply of such athletes. This scarcity demands constant vigilance on the part of club management in identifying and developing new talent. The task of maintaining an ample supply of highly skilled performers is difficult in any sport for the simple reason that the players have relatively short careers. But it is especially challenging in baseball because amateur players, no matter how gifted and experienced they are, almost invariably need intensive long-term training to compete at the major league level. To continue producing that level of talent, season after season, the clubs are obliged to invest heavily and continuously in scouting and player development.

Although the association between major league clubs and their towns runs deep, and one therefore tends to think that the clubs belong to their towns, major league baseball is actually a form of private enterprise. It is an industry made up of twenty-eight separate, semi-independent franchises, all of which are owned by private individuals, groups, or companies. Each franchise is contractually linked to a half dozen or more minor league clubs through which it develops its big league talent. The network of those two hundred or so clubs is organized under the Office of the Commissioner.

Like any other private industry, baseball has had to depend upon income and profits for its existence. In the game's earliest days, nearly all revenue came from tickets sales. As the sport grew in popularity, and as bigger and more comfortable stadiums were built, the sale of refreshments, scorecards, pennants and other team paraphernalia became significant new sources of club revenue. The advent of radio in the 1920s brought yet another form of income: advertising revenue. Sponsors paid radio stations handsomely for promoting their products during games. And the stations, in turn, paid the clubs for rights to carry the games. As listening audiences grew, the charges for broadcast rights increased. When television was introduced, a generation later, a flood of new advertising money washed over the major leagues. By the mid-1980s, total industry income from radio and television rights, in-stadium advertising and promotions, and club shares of ballpark concessions exceeded gate receipts.

Then, in 1987, commissioner Peter Ueberroth raised several million more dollars for the industry from an entirely new source, the national sponsor. Through this scheme, huge corporations pay large sums for the privilege of becoming the official "mega-sponsors" of baseball. Now, for example, International Business Machines and Chevrolet are the official computer and automobile manufacturers, respectively, of the major leagues.

While all of this new money was being raked in, baseball's resurgent popularity continued to soar. Attendance records were being broken year after year. In 1986, every club exceeded the 1 million mark in home attendance, a major league first. And in 1987, thanks largely to unprecedented parity on the field (fifteen of the twenty-six teams were still legitimate contenders on September 1), even more fans poured through the turnstiles. Teams such as the Dodgers, Mets, Twins, and Cardinals would exceed the 3 million mark. The Blue Jays crashed through the 4 million barrier.

The baseball business also generates revenue for publishers, sporting goods companies, T-shirt manufacturers, transportation companies, service stations, restaurants, bars, legal and illegal gambling operations, and a variety of other business interests. Consequently a major league franchise is not only a source of pride for its hometown fans but also an economic boon to the city that houses it.

Where all this money comes from, of course, is the fans. It is the fans who pay for the tickets, the fans who purchase the scorecards and yearbooks, the pennants and caps, the hotdogs and sodas that supplement the gate receipts. Furthermore it is the fans who ultimately pay for newspaper, radio, television, and in-stadium advertising, for it is they who absorb the built-in costs of advertising when they buy the sponsors' goods. And for the moment, at least, the fans seem quite willing to pay the increasing costs of their spectatorship.

Given the huge and still growing influx of income to the baseball owners' coffers, one would expect that the clubs are by now embarrassingly profitable. In truth, however, the baseball business is in trouble. The problem is that throughout the revenue bonanza of the 1980s, the rate of increase in the costs of running the clubs far exceeded the rate of increase in income. The startling rise in costs can be attributed almost entirely to a single category of club expenses—player salaries.

On the surface, the issue is simply money. Ownership claims that it still doesn't have enough of it, and the players seem to behave as though they can't get enough of it either. The sports news media tend to pay only sporadic attention to the dilemma, in part because cries of distress are hard to accept from either party, and in part because there is no base of popular support for either party. The fans are generally unsympathetic toward either camp. In fact, public sentiment on the subject is by and large measured in terms of resentment for one or both sides, with the players lately holding a distinct edge in unpopularity.

The financial situation is quite bleak—major league baseball actually is teetering on the brink of bankruptcy. The primary cause of baseball's paradoxical dilemma is the adversary relationship that has existed between the players and owners since 1879. It was then that the baseball owners first established a limited version of the infamous "reserve clause." This was a provision in certain players' contracts that made them captives, virtual slaves, of their owners. Within six years of its inception, the provision was extended to include all major and minor league players. The ballplayers did not obtain freedom from the reserve clause, and thus did not begin to receive a reasonable share of baseball's income, until the 1977 season.

For today's players, a century-old legacy of financial slavery and the personal animosity and political entrenchment that naturally flow from that condition are neither quickly nor easily erased. In light of the dubious practices of the clubs since the 1985 season, which include collusion in dealing with free agents, the players appear more than justified in maintaining their basic distrust of management.

For the owners, the eleven years since the players gained their freedom have been a horror show of fiscal ineptitude and mismanagement. They have watched their own club executives drive salaries to unthinkably high levels. In several instances they have themselves added significantly to the escalation. But while many of the baseball moguls privately blame their fellow owners and themselves for allowing the game's financial crisis to develop in the first place, their public anger is directed squarely at the players, their agents, and their union.

So contrary to popular opinion, the current standoff is not merely a case of two greedy opponents using hardball negotiating tactics to force concessions out of each other, all at the fans' expense. Rather it is a clash over rights and principles. And if greed is at all involved in baseball's internal conflict, then it is more as a manifestation of that conflict than a cause of it.

In fact, the history of the business of baseball is the history of the tension between individual rights on the one hand and the priorities and practices of businessmen on the other. Like the game itself, the story is uniquely American. In many respects it runs parallel to the history of labor-management relations in America. The story begins in 1846, with the first match game of the Knickerbocker Base Ball Club, and winds its way through the institution of the reserve clause and the many challenges to it over the years, the breaking of the color bar, transcontinental franchise shifts, rich television contracts, and league expansion. But as these events are detailed elsewhere in this volume, the present essay will focus on the turbulent years since 1968, when the Players Association and the owners signed the game's first bilateral agreement.

The Storm Before the Calm: 1968–1975

When Ford Frick retired as commissioner in 1965, the owners hired an unheralded Air Force general by the name of William D. Eckert. "Spike," as he was known, was openly pleased to be a ceremonial chief. But he asumed the job just at the time the Players Association was beginning to make bold moves.

To deal with the growing strength of the opposition, owners created a Player Relations Committee in 1967. The PRC, as it is commonly called, was headed by John J. Gaherin, former president of the New York City Newspaper Publishers Association. It included the two major league presidents and three owners from each league and was supported by a legal staff. As its name implied, the Player Relations Committee's sole function was to act as a link between the Players Association and the owners, delivering information to and from both bodies and assisting in the formulation of management policy.

The first big item on the PRC's agenda was a collective-bargaining agreement, something that the association had been angling to get for some time. The purpose of the agreement was to make some inroads into the standard contract. It was not yet time to launch a frontal attack on the reserve clause.

The document which emerged from the negotiations was officially entitled the Basic Agreement. Signed in February 1968, it was the first in a still unbroken series of such accords. It established a formal grievance procedure for the players and provided for subsequent study of the reserve clause by both parties. Probably the most important feature of the first Basic Agreement was that it would take official precedence over the old major league rules wherever they were found to be in conflict. This meant that players were involved in major league policymaking for the first time.

By now the players had racked up a series of important victories, and it was clear that William Eckert's administration was overmatched. During the short period in which Eckert held office, the players hired Marvin Miller, built their Park Avenue office, and successfully negotiated the first Basic Agreement. The war was on, but General Eckert was in the wrong army. The owners fired him in December 1968.

Within three months of Eckert's removal, and with the commissioner's job still vacant, the owners were confronted with a crisis. Management had offered the players a contract package that was a distinct improvement over the previous deal. The Players Association had rejected the offer because they felt they deserved additional increases in health care, life insurance, and pension benefits. Both sides were angry, and neither side would yield an inch of ground. So the players refused to sign contracts and threatened to strike. Spring training was scheduled to begin in a couple of weeks, and it appeared that the players were prepared to delay its start.

The PRC called on one of the National League lawyers, a big pleasant chap named Bowie Kent Kuhn, to see if he

could untie the knot. Kuhn, in a style which would become his trademark, devoted most of his time to calming
and soothing his irritated management colleagues. Having accomplished that not-so-easy feat, he gave the players everything they had asked for. Six months later, he
was rewarded for his efforts with an eight-year term as the
commissioner of baseball.

Within seven months after he assumed office, Kuhn
was confronted with the Curt Flood case. Flood had been
a very fine outfielder with the Cardinals for twelve years
when he was informed by a low-level club official after the
1969 season that he would be playing ball with the Phillies
in 1970. The Phillies had finished 24 games behind the
Cardinals, and Flood apparently didn't much like the
town of Philadelphia anyway. So he wrote a letter to the
commissioner requesting that he be permitted to "consider offers from other clubs before making any
decisions."

Kuhn could not grant the request without simultaneously and singlehandedly overturning the reserve clause.
He denied Flood's request. With the Players Association
behind him, Curt Flood decided to take the issue to court.
The case reached the United States Supreme Court, but,
as usual, yet another player went down in defeat.

Why did it always turn out that the lawmakers and
judges, many of whom were openly sympathetic to the
players' cause, were unwilling to rule in the players' favor?
Essentially it was because no less than the relationship
between government and private industry was at stake. If
Congress or the United States Supreme Court had chosen
to modify or overturn the reserve clause, it would have
immediately established a fundamentally different and
presumably more equal balance of power between the
players and the owners, but with unknown results. The
uncertainty was the hangup. Whatever the effects of altering the reserve clause might be, the publicity such an
action would receive would be enormous. Sports fans and
politics watchers, a sizable audience to say the least,
would be riveted to the issue. And if major league competition and franchise stability were indeed sacrificed
through the removal or modification of the reserve clause,
as the owners had been warning would happen since 1885,
then the government officials responsible for the decision,
either the Supreme Court justices or the members of
Congress, would be held accountable. If baseball could
not right itself in a reasonable amount of time or, worse, if
it were to collapse, this would be especially embarrassing
and possibly damaging to nothing less than a branch of
the United States government.

Except in the most extreme circumstances, neither
Congress nor the Supreme Court is inclined to take a
potentially profound step where the outcome of its decisions is so thoroughly unpredictable. Both bodies would
much prefer that basic struggles of this sort be brought to
a higher level of resolution before they will bring their
heavy conclusive weight to bear upon them. Not a single
meaningful aspect of the reserve system had been altered
yet. The real effects of altering or removing the controversial clause were still basically untested. So it is reasonable
to conclude that in the eyes of Washington politicos baseball's eternal adversaries had a long way to go before the
federal government would get seriously involved.

Despite the risks involved, the Supreme Court's deci-

sion to retain baseball's antitrust exemption in the case of
Flood v. *Kuhn* was a upheld by a narrow 5–3 margin.
Subsequent revelations concerning the justices who ruled
on the case suggest that the issue troubled a few of them
deeply and that the vote was even closer than the final
tally indicated. It could have gone either way. Furthermore public opinion at the time was overwhelmingly on
the side of Curt Flood.

These were definite signs that the owners were in a
lonelier position than they had ever been in before. Indeed, they were cornered. And Commissoner Kuhn's previous behavior as well as the personal risks his job entailed
should have been clear hints to the owners that he would
be more inclined to commiserate with them than fight for
them when the going got tough.

The Players Association, which had responsibly cautioned Flood against pursuing his case, was nonetheless
delighted that he had chosen to disregard their advice.
Flood's case would keep the reserve system in full public
view.

This was just the first loud shot in what would become
an unceasing legal siege on baseball management. Starting with the Flood case, the two sides have engaged in
major confrontations roughly once a year ever since. Just
during the time that the Flood case was being heard, the
association fought a battle over the second Basic Agreement in 1970, which it followed up with a players' strike in
1972, which was in turn followed by a third Basic Agreement in 1973 that gave the players the right to outside,
impartial salary arbitration.

Between these big surges, the union maintained a barrage of smaller assaults. And in what was effectively a
flanking operation, they directed a flurry of attacks on the
renewal clause of the uniform baseball contract. What the
renewal provision said, in brief, was that a player who did
not sign a new contract for the coming season at a salary
set by the club would still be the property of his current
club for one year—the renewal year. What it did not say
was what would happen after the renewal year. Would a
player be free to sell his services to any club at the conclusion of the renewal year? Thus a pivotal legal question
remained unanswered, a question that shared its legal
border with the reserve clause.

In 1969, pitcher Al Downing of the Yankees made a
serious inquiry into the matter. He wanted to play the
1970 season without signing so that he could become a
free agent the following year. After being cautioned by
Marvin Miller against testing the renewal clause, Downing was told by Yankees management that if he refused to
sign his 1970 contract, he might as well not bother to show
up at spring training. Downing signed. He was then
traded to Oakland before the 1970 season began.

In 1972 St. Louis catcher Ted Simmons came even
closer to testing the renewal clause. He played unsigned
for half a season before finally agreeing to a two-year
contract with the Cardinals. From 1973 to 1975, seventeen more players started seasons without contracts, all of
whom threatened to play out their options for a stab at
becoming free agents. Two of them, pitchers Dave Mc-
Nally and Andy Messersmith, carried out the threat—
they never did sign.

Meanwhile, association gains were piling up. The 1970
Basic Agreement had given the players the right to arbi-

trate grievances. The Flood case had led to the inclusion of the "five-and-ten" rule in the 1973 Basic Agreement, by which players with ten or more years of major league service who have played for at least the last five years with one club have the right to approve a trade to another club. Though the rule affected only a very small segment of the major league population, it marked the first time that any group of players had any control over where they would ply their trade. A breach of contract by Oakland A's owner Charles O. Finley had made pitcher Catfish Hunter a free agent in 1974. That decision had been of little direct value to other players, except to grant them protection against illegally drawn contracts. But it had demonstrated the determination and the growing strength of the union.

Next on the agenda was a full test of the renewal clause by Messersmith and McNally in the fall of 1975. Both pitchers had played the entire 1975 season without contracts. The bounds of the Basic Agreement had thus been exceeded, leaving the two pitchers in a legal no-man's-land. Would the parent clubs still own the contracts of the players after the renewal year, or would the players become free agents, thereby allowing them to sell their services to other teams? That was the multimillion-dollar question.

The case was to be heard by a three-man arbitration panel. The panel chairman was Peter Seitz, a man with twenty years of experience as an arbitrator. Marvin Miller and John Gaherin were the other panel members, so naturally their partisan votes on the case would cancel out. This meant that Seitz would, in effect, be making the most important decision in the history of baseball's labor-management relations all by himself.

Although the issue was ostensibly the renewal clause, it was really the reserve clause that was on trial. For if Seitz ruled that the two pitchers were free, then every other player in the major leagues could take the same circuitous route to freedom. It would be a cavernous loophole, but a perfectly legal one.

Seitz tried vigorously to get the two sides to work out the problem through bargaining. Like Congress and the Supreme Court, he felt that the matter was far too important to be adjudicated in any other way. He even went so far as to write a letter to management, explaining that the weight of the case was definitely on the side of the players and warning that he would not shrink from his duty to act, and act quickly, on the case. But the owners stonewalled it. They rejected Seitz's recommendation.

Two days before Christmas 1975, Mr. Seitz placed a nicely wrapped gift under the owners' tree—a sixty-one-page decision in favor of Andy Messersmith and Dave McNally.

The owners' first response was to fire Seitz. Then they sent their attorneys around to all of the courts that would listen, trying desperately to appeal the decision. The courts listened, but did not heed the call. Every appeal was rejected, the last one coming in March 1976. Spring training had not begun. The owners had locked the players out. Another delay in the start of a big league season was looming on the not-too-distant horizon.

Then, suddenly and very uncharacteristically, Bowie Kuhn defied the owners and opened the training camps. Recognizing the unpopularity of their position and having exhausted all of their legal options, the owners entered into negotiations with the Players Association for a new Basic Agreement. By this action, the owners had officially surrendered.

The specter of the Messersmith decision cast a pall over the management negotiators. They knew that they were going to have to yield expensive turf. The only question was how much. This was it, the big face-to-face showdown between baseball management and labor, and the culmination of an ancient quest by ballplayers for a proper share of major league revenue.

On the face of it, the Basic Agreement that emerged from the negotiations in July 1976 did not seem revolutionary. Indeed, to the astonishment of many, it retained nearly all of the elements of the original reserve clause. But there was one historic exception: a provision that any player with six or more years of major league service would now have the right to declare himself a free agent.

Was this what all of the commotion had been about—the freedom to sell one's services after six full major league seasons? The answer was a resounding "Yes!" The new provision gave the players all the freedom they would ever need. In fact, 1976 was a year of unsurpassable celebration for the union members. It marked the two-hundredth birthday of the United States of America, the one-hundredth birthday of major league baseball, and the erection of a fountain of wealth for the men who play the game.

Thus ended the first long chapter in the history of labor-management relations in major league baseball. Nearly a century of internal struggle had been devoted essentially to the revison of a single sentence in the standard player's contract, a single clause that meant the difference between economic slavery and economic freedom. Although the new 1976 version of the reserve clause still restricted that freedom, and although no one could predict what effects limited free agency would ultimately have, the players had finally built a tunnel to the outside from their financial prison. And golden rays of sunshine immediately began to pour into the cells of some of the veteran inmates.

The peculiarities of the baseball industry had produced a strange, even unique form of economic struggle. The last attempt to establish a third baseball league had been crushed sixty years before arbitrator Seitz's ruling. So the baseball players received none of the large and lasting financial boosts that the American Football League, the American Basketball Association, and the World Hockey League had generated for professional football, basketball, and hockey players. And with little more than expressions of positive sentiment on the part of the fans and the politicians, they had had to fight their salary battles in virtual isolation. The transiency of the major league labor force had made it extremely difficult for them to mount a sustained offensive. Furthermore, by paying many of the star players rather handsomely, ownership had bought most of them out of opposition. Given the ease with which the owners could remove ordinary players, who would not be terribly missed by the paying customers anyway, it was next to impossible for the players to get a grassroots movement started. Troublemakers and malcontents generally found themselves tied up in court, or quickly dispatched to the minor leagues, or dispensed with altogether. Be-

sides, it truly was a whole lot better to be turning double plays for a living than turning sod in a field or flapjacks on a grill.

Baseball players had always been a young, hungry, competitive lot, generally unschooled in and intimidated by corporate matters. So most of them were quite content to play ball for a living, regardless of the level of pay. And they tended to look back on their major league experience, their days in the sun, not with rancor, but with understandable pride and satisfaction. What resentment the players did harbor for the barons who owned them generally lasted no longer than their careers.

Under these circumstances, and given the socioeconomic climate of America during baseball's first seventy years, all that the baseball owners had had to do to protect their dictatorial monopoly was play hard-fisted defense. They and their cadre of lawyers and bureaucrats practiced the traditional corporate techniques of stonewalling, name-calling, delaying, and postponing. Furthermore they were an integral part of the business establishment. This had given them unfettered access to and clout with the sports media. Add to those advantages the reluctance of the Congress and the courts to intervene meaningfully on the players' behalf, plus the relative indifference of the fans to the whole matter, and management had been practically invulnerable. Being as ambitious, competitive, and self-interested as they were, management had never even attempted to accommodate the players, in any area, not even when Commissioners Kenesaw M. Landis and A. B. Chandler had advised them to do so.

The owners were The Club. And they had ruled with the club, primitively and uncompromisingly, for one hundred years. The only club the player had had was made of hickory or ash and called a bat. It was the only club he had had, that is, until the star players took up the cause.

The stars were the ones who had attracted the crowds in New York in the 1850s and 1860s and put baseball on the map. It was they who had received the game's first big paychecks and eventually prompted the restrictive methods adopted by the owners, including the oppressive reserve clause. It was the stars upon whom the hapless rival leagues had pinned their takeover attempts. And it was they to whom the established clubs had paid even higher salaries to keep them in the fold.

To the fans the stars were kings, to be envied. To the owners they were pawns, to be played against the other players and the rival leagues in the interest of minimizing salaries and maximizing profits. To the players the stars were the winners in an environment in which it was every man for himself.

Baseball's stars had let their teammates down for seventy-odd years. Ty Cobb's steely disregard for his fellow ballplayers at the Celler Committee hearings in 1952—when he spoke of the necessity for maintaining the reserve clause—was perhaps the most galling example. But in the early 1950s, the stars turned and the rest of the players gradually joined the effort. Perhaps the courage of Jackie Robinson in his fight for integration had inspired them to act. Perhaps Branch Rickey's treatment of Ralph Kiner—paying him far less than his performance warranted, simply because he played for an inferior team ("We could have finished last without you" were Rickey's immortal words)—was the pivotal event in their crusade.

Perhaps it was the continuing emergence of the Roosevelt-inspired middle class, or the conclusion of the war. Probably it was all of those things, and more. But whatever their personal reasons, the commitment of stars such as Bob Feller, Allie Reynolds, Ralph Kiner, and Robin Roberts to their fellow players, a commitment that led to the very formation of the Players Association in 1954 and would require their continued attention and devotion to the cause after their own careers were over, was the key to the success of the players' revolt. Others played very significant roles. Marvin Miller, Curt Flood, Andy Messersmith, and Dave McNally are among the most obvious. Dozens of lesser-known participants made important contributions, too. But when the stars finally took action, that is when the scenery really started to change. And by 1976 the stage was set for a new period in major league history—the free-agency era.

The baseball industry had undergone another dramatic change from the late 1950s to the mid-1970s. During that time the mantle of club ownership was being gradually handed over to a new genre of proprietor, the corporate magnate.

Prior to the 1950s, one did not need excessive wealth to become a club owner. Thanks to the reserve clause, operating costs had always been relatively low. And the monopoly status of the sport had served as protection against outside competition, especially after the Federal League incursion had been quashed in 1916. Clubs were generally owned by individuals or small groups of investors. Most franchises were family-run businesses that depended for their survival and success more upon baseball savvy and blood-and-guts determination than upon managerial sophistication or huge cash reserves. The ballclub, in most cases, was the livelihood of the owner. And his fortune normally rose and fell with the standing of his team or the general economic health of the major leagues.

Through the 1950s the motivation to own a ballclub came from the prestige that one automatically acquired, the profits that one stood a very good chance of making, and, perhaps above all, a deep devotion to the game. For without an abiding attachment to baseball, one would have succumbed to the unrelenting, undifferentiated demands of the job. The fact that the game was a cash business practically mandated that management personnel be family members or highly trusted friends. Someone, after all, always had to keep an eye on the till.

In those days, most owners assumed major responsibility for the day-to-day running of their clubs. In nearly all cases, it was they who dictated and negotiated player contracts. This gave the sport a head-to-head, man-to-man character. All were in it together—the owner, his cadre of management personnel, and the players. But the relative intimacy of ballclubs did not promote fair and equitable treatment for club employees. Most of the front-office people and their assistants fared no better than the players.

The fellowship that existed resembled the sort that is found in military organizations. There was a strict top-down chain of command, in which orders were obeyed, rights and privileges were decreed, and nonsense was not tolerated. But along with that stern order came a unity of purpose among all involved and a high level of camaraderie among the troops. Those qualities helped to keep the

teams and the sport intact throughout its embattled development.

The quasi-military nature of the sport helped to foster a public perception of team loyalty and stability. That perception grew after the Black Sox scandal and flourished during the Landis regime. In the meantime, the big league clubs had become embedded in their cities. For exactly fifty years, starting in 1903, not one of the sixteen American and National League franchises left its hometown. The music had stopped and the chairs were in place. The sport and each of its teams had become seemingly permanent features of the American cultural landscape.

Then, in 1953, all of that began to change. After having won the National League pennant in 1948 with a record of 91–62, the Boston Braves began to slide. By 1952, they had fallen to seventh place with a 64–89 record. The next year, the franchise moved to Milwaukee. This was the first in a rapid shakeout of two-team cities. Towns like Milwaukee had been aching to obtain major league clubs for years. Since there were as yet no firm plans to expand the major leagues, the obvious takeover targets for the disfranchised towns were the weaker clubs in two-team cities.

The next two teams to move out were both from the American League. The St. Louis Browns became the Baltimore Orioles in 1954, and the Philadelphia A's moved to Kansas City in 1955. Both clubs had been last-place finishers the year before they pulled up stakes. And both had been distinctly weaker, competitively and economically, than their National League counterparts for a long stretch of time. As a result, these first club relocations in a half-century were rather easily accepted by the hometown fans. And the general perception of franchise stability remained unshaken.

During this brief period, the Players Association was being formed, and television had begun to expand the reach and the income of the baseball business. A decade had passed since the end of World War Two, and the jet age was just beginning. It was a new world with new frontiers. And the big leagues could not buck the momentum of change.

After the 1957 season, the baseball industry was thoroughly introduced to the magnitude of that momentum, for it was then that the New York Giants and the Brooklyn Dodgers were moved to San Francisco and Los Angeles, respectively. Both franchises had maintained huge and loyal followings. Thus the decisions by Giants' owner Horace Stoneham and Dodgers' owner Walter O'Malley to go west sent shock waves through the baseball community. It was one thing to sell a wilting franchise to an enthusiastic new owner and a hungry new town. But it was quite a different matter for an owner simply to rip a solid club away from its faithful fans. The Brooklyn fans were particularly enraged. Their team had been one of the very best in baseball for the preceding decade. In their eyes, and in the eyes of many others, mainly from the East, baseball had broken a social contract by allowing the moves to take place.

From the perspective of Stoneham and O'Malley, the uprooting was strictly a sound business decision. Both viewed California as an untapped source of practically boundless opportunity. And despite the strong base of support in New York and Brooklyn, the industrial East was stagnating. Attendance at Giant and Dodger home games, though respectable, did not match the quality of the teams, especially in the case of the Dodgers. Walter O'Malley recognized that baseball was in the midst of a transition to a more demanding, higher profile, and more lucrative entertainment industry.

The Dodgers' first year in Los Angeles was a bust on the field. The club wound up the season in seventh place, 21 games behind the pennant-winning Braves. But the club set its all-time attendance record, reaching nearly 1,850,000. Only twice before had the Dodgers drawn in the 1.8 million range, in the immediate postwar years of 1946 and 1947. And this was only the beginning. After he built his own stadium in 1962 and assumed control of all ballpark concessions, O'Malley's new vision was complete. By putting a solid baseball organization in the booming Los Angeles area and securing ownership of all related property, O'Malley constructed the most successful baseball operation in the history of the sport. For the last twenty years, it has averaged close to 3 million. Until the Blue Jays moved into the SkyDome no other club has remotely approached that degree of success at the turnstiles.

Meanwhile, up the coast, the Giants were trying to win at the same game. The first several years, the years of Willie Mays, Juan Marichal, and Willie McCovey, were magical. Great talent continued to flow into the organization, enabling the club to be a serious contender for most of its first fourteen years in San Francisco, through the 1971 season. But attendance in the city by the bay never reached the dizzying heights attained by the Dodgers. From 1958 through 1967, average attendance held at around 1.5 million, which was well above the league average of roughly 1 million for the period.

Then, however, the A's moved from Kansas City to Oakland. The Giants' attendance plummeted overnight. By the time the club had lost its edge on the field, in 1972, annual attendance had settled in the 700,000 range, making it one of the weakest draws in the National League. Attendance languished at that level for five more years, during which time the A's were busy winning three World Series and attracting 900,000 fans per year. It was immediately evident that the San Francisco Bay area would have difficulty supporting and sustaining two major league clubs. And Candlestick Park, with its sixtyish temperatures and its erratic, blustery winds, was becoming progressively less acceptable, both to the fans and to the new principal owner of the club, Robert Lurie. Giant attendance bounced back, reaching an all-time high of 2,059,829 in 1989. But the club, at this writing scheduled to open the 1993 season in San Francisco, had a serious flirtation with St. Petersburg, Florida that may yet culminate in a long-lasting relationship.

By the mid-1960s, the financial stakes had become higher for the major league baseball business, and the new California teams highlighted some of the opportunities and risks involved.

The most important transformation in the character of big league club ownership started in the 1960s, when corporate interests began to replace family ownership groups. Overall baseball attendance had ebbed by then, due in part to a severe drop in run production caused by a

legislated increase in the size of the strike zone, and due in larger part to the ascendancy of the National Football League. The nation was in a countercultural frenzy at that time, with drugs, sex, rock-and-roll, and the Vietnam War sharing center stage. Under the circumstances, football was hot, baseball was not. There was a growing sense among the members of the major league establishment that the national pastime would have to kick into a higher gear to keep up with the faster pace and more indulgent interests of the society. The first big corporation to get into the act was the Columbia Broadcasting System. CBS purchased the New York Yankees in 1964.

One way to meet the demands of the time was to replace old, typically small, and in some cases dilapidated, baseball parks with large new all-purpose stadiums. Eighteen of the twenty-six stadiums in use in 1992 have been constructed since 1966. Yankee Stadium, one of the eight existing parks built before 1960, underwent massive reconstruction in 1974–1975. A few of the seven remaining older parks are soon to be replaced.

The new stadiums reflected the comparatively cold, artificial, plastic, hyped qualities of the new era they were ushering in. They were equipped with massive electronic scoreboards and message boards. Giant sound systems piped advertising jingles through the vast concrete terraces of plastic seats. Spectators were led in cheers, taunts, and songs by computer-graphic instructions flashed on the huge, usually garish message machines. In the Houston Astrodome, touted for its first several years of existence as the eighth manmade wonder of the world, fans were even prompted to applaud by the center field message board, where jerky animated figures of hands would suddenly appear, clapping to the synthesized beat of a high-technology organ.

By way of these innovations, several ballparks became enormous television studios, filled with all of the technical gadgetry and special accommodations needed to put on dazzling spectacles, both for the in-stadium and at-home spectators. Even the playing fields did not escape the reconstruction trend. Artificial grass was developed for the sun-starved floor of the Astrodome in 1966, and it soon spread through the big leagues, as though it was the real thing. Ten stadiums are now paved with plastic turf.

So by the mid-1970s the surface features of baseball had been altered markedly. For the clubs that joined in the reconstruction movement, the immediate and long-term financial costs were high. The new gimmickry, by itself, was very expensive. The cost of building a stadium had become so great by the mid-1960s that practically every one of the newer stadiums was funded by a local bond issue. And even with the local populaces paying for the ballparks, the annual rent charges to the clubs had become quite costly. Club organizations needed to become more diversified to keep up with the increasing complexities of the business. More importantly, to some of the old-style owners the game was turning into a promotion-ridden circus. The days of pure unadulterated baseball entertainment were numbered. As a result, the business was being invaded by public-relations-minded corporate magnates.

And the Messersmith-McNally decision was hanging over the industry, threatening to restructure its century-old financial foundations.

The Free-Agency Era: 1976–1989

The Messersmith-McNally arbitration decision put major league salary matters on hold for a full year while labor and management worked out the details for implementing free agency. Neither side could predict what effects the new arrangement would have, so both sides were inclined to proceed slowly and cautiously in laying it out. As a result, free-agent bidding did not begin until the fall of 1976. The two sides also agreed to suspend the salary arbitration process through the 1977 season.

What emerged from the 1976 bargaining talks was a salary system made up of four basic elements: a guaranteed minimum salary of $19,000, maximum salary cuts of 20 percent in one year and 30 percent over a two-year period, the right for players with at least two years but less than six years of major league service to have their salaries determined through arbitration, and the right for players with six or more years of service to declare free agency and sell their services to any club.

The first two components, the minimum salary and the maximum permissible cuts, were the players' defensive weapons. Both had been in place for many years. Arbitration, which was first adopted after the 1973 season, was designed to allow any player dissatisfied with a club salary offer to have his dispute heard and ruled upon by an impartial arbitrator. It was intended to give the player an opportunity to raise his income to a level commensurate with other players of similar ability and experience and thereby protect him against salary gouging. Free agency was strictly an offensive instrument. It enabled the player to determine his dollar value through free-market bidding by clubs.

In theory, an ordered salary structure would emerge from the new four-part system. There would now be three mutually exclusive "classes" of players.

At the bottom of the salary pyramid would be those players with less than two years of major league service, who would have no explicit rights beyond the major league minimum. Their salaries would be unilaterally determined by management. If such players felt they were underpaid, their only recourse would be to hold out, refusing to play unless and until they received higher pay. Holding out had been the players' only real source of negotiating leverage for one hundred years. Now, just those players with less than two years of service would be forced to rely on such an extreme negotiating measure, and only on rare occasions.

In the middle would be the arbitration eligibles. If they did not want to accept a club's offer, they would be free to take the matter to an arbitrator.

The salary arbitration procedure is essentially simple and straightforward. If, in the course of negotiations, a player has reason to believe that his club will not offer him as much money as he feels he is worth, then he officially files for arbitration by a specified date in early January. If he and the club are still unable to reach an accord as of a second deadline, at the end of January, then both sides are required to submit a salary figure. Within twenty-four hours of the submissions, the player, the club, the Players Association, and the Player Relations Committee are notified of the salary amounts that the two parties have submitted. An arbitration hearing is then scheduled for a

specific morning or afternoon between February 1 and February 20, the official arbitration period. If the two parties remain unable to reach a settlement before the appointed hearing, then the case is heard in a four- to six-hour session. The arbitrator then has twenty-four hours to select one of the two submissions. It is an either-or proposition; there is no middle ground. Thus if the player is seeking, say, $350,000 and the club is offering $250,000, the arbitrator must choose one or the other figure. He may not, for example, split the difference and award the player a $300,000 contract.

In its first two years of implementation, in 1974 and 1975, arbitration did not amount to much. Indeed, it could not amount to much because nearly all salaries were relatively low. The average salary was between $40,000 and $45,000; the median was between $30,000 and $35,000. In those years, arbitration battles were generally fought over differences in the $10,000 to $20,000 range.

The top salary class in the new structure would consist of the players eligible to be free agents. They would either receive enough income from their original clubs to stay with those clubs or they would declare themselves free and seek higher pay elsewhere. In either event, there would be pressure on the clubs to pay all players with six or more years of service well enough to secure their services, assuming, of course, that the clubs would uphold the letter and the spirit of the free agency rules by earnestly bidding for players.

The scheme, as a whole, follows the logic of military employment. Like the armed services, the owners would be giving the players training and instruction in the minor leagues in exchange for six years of active duty, at which point the soldiers of summer would be free to remain with their original employers or strike out on their own. Under the circumstances, this seems to have been a surprisingly fair and reasonable resolution of the players' ancient problem. Management had cornered itself, legally, in its dealings with the Players Association and with arbitrator Seitz. So they might well have been backed into a deeper hole by the players. But this final salary arrangement appeared to give the clubs plenty of financial breathing room.

When free agency was set into place in November 1976, it had immediate impact on veteran players. Their salaries took off. In that first year, the average major league salary increased by nearly 50 percent, jumping from $51,501 to $76,066. The median increased by a similar percentage, going from around $40,000 to around $58,000. But the extra $25,000 per player was not distributed evenly. The 1976 minimum salary of $19,000 was retained in 1977, which meant that the younger players had received no boost at the bottom end. So most of the significant raises were going to players with six or more years of major league service behind them. Those veterans represented approximately 40 percent of the player population. Thus what had happened was that the six-year veterans had realized an average increase of about $50,000, while the players with less than six years of service had, as a group, made only marginal gains. This dichotomy was to have been expected. For not only did the younger players not possess the valuable right of free agency, but they also had no access to arbitration. And even if they had been able to take salary disputes to

arbitration, the awards would have been limited by the fact that players of similar skill and experience were not making big salaries either.

Over the next three years, the same principles held. The result was a lopsided three-tiered salary structure, with the youngest players hovering around the minimum, the arbitration eligibles a full notch higher, and the veterans far, far ahead. And the costs of retaining the older players continued to climb steadily and dramatically, widening the gap even further.

The average salary for all players shot up to $113,500 by the end of the 1979 season. Management took on a siege mentality, with owners and executives privately and publicly predicting doom for the baseball business. But the new system created a good deal of interest in baseball's backstage politics. If anything, it contributed to a resurgence in the game's popularity—and in the owners' revenue. The American League's expansion in 1977, from twelve teams to fourteen, and increasing competitive balance on the field in both leagues provided additional boosts to club income. The dollar value of clubs began to skyrocket. More corporate owners bought into the business, and few family-owned and -operated clubs remained. With the stakes now so high, the small owner was simply unable to compete for the better players.

For the players, the last years of the 1970s were an exciting beginning. At long last some of them had started to share in the profits of the entertainment industry that they were the center of. But the huge gap between the arbitration eligibles and the free-agency eligibles kept growing. Even the star players with less than six years of major league service were unable to bridge that gap. What had happened was that the two groups had become segregated. Veterans were being compared with veterans, and younger players were being compared with younger players, due strictly to the difference in service. Consequently middling players with many years of service were generally earning quite a bit more than stars with less than six years of service.

This development kept the rate of salary inflation from getting completely out of control. It was the silver lining in the cloud that had formed over the owners. To the players and their union leaders, it was illogical and unfair that a number of over-the-hill veterans were making hundreds of thousands of dollars more per year than many outstanding young players, such as Eddie Murray, Keith Hernandez, Pete Vuckovich, and Dennis Eckersley. In their view, too much credit was being given for sheer longevity and not enough for quality of play. But under the new salary system, the only way the younger players could move toward the veteran salary range would be through arbitration. The owners certainly weren't going to elevate their salaries out of generosity.

Meanwhile, the arbitration arena was becoming an interesting sideshow feature of the big league circus. Once the combination of free agency and arbitration was permitted to function, after the 1977 season, arbitration began to take on the character of a high stakes pokerfest. The spreads between player demands and club offers were occasionally reaching six figures. Then, after the close of the 1979 season, a major showdown started to take shape. Relief pitcher Bruce Sutter of the Chicago Cubs had completed his fourth year of unsurpassed excellence on

the mound. Every big league club would have loved to have Sutter in its bullpen. At the winter meetings in Toronto, in December 1979, several club executives expressed the view that Sutter was among the three or four most valuable players in the game. Some felt that he was the topmost banana in the whole bunch. December trades and purchases of players had dried up considerably as a direct result of the new salary system. As a result, much of the attention of the press and the clubs was given to arbitration, especially to the Sutter matter. The rumors floating around the headquarters hotel suggested that Sutter would be seeking more than a half million dollars for the 1980 season, while the Cubs would not be willing to spend much more than a quarter of a million for his services.

In January the arbitration filing figures came out. The Cubs were offering their relief ace $350,000, a very high amount at that time for a player with barely four years of service, but not much higher than the income he had received the previous year. Sutter's demand was $700,000, a staggering figure that, if granted, would place him near the top of the salary pyramid despite his nonveteran status. In February the case was heard. And to the astonishment of management, Sutter was declared the winner.

This was the first big crack in the wall that separated the free agents from the younger players. The decision implied that a star is a star, regardless of his prior service time, and that he should be paid accordingly. That is to say, he should earn a salary consistent with, though perhaps not quite as high as, that of a veteran with a similar qualitative performance record.

Inside the baseball establishment there was a swirl of controversy surrounding the Cubs' handling of the case. Suggestions were made that Cubs' management committed one or two key tactical blunders. Whether those claims are valid or not, the Sutter case suggested that a few weak links among the clubs with respect to the negotiation and arbitration of salaries could have impact on all other cases and clubs. The case also helped to establish a new high-paid class of player, the relief ace.

The clubs were badly shaken by the Sutter decision. A few of the owners, particularly George Steinbrenner of the Yankees, Ray Kroc of the San Diego Padres, and Brad Corbett of the Texas Rangers, had already sent the salaries of free agents into the stratosphere. Now the clubs felt that they would have to give equal attention to the growing threat of salary arbitration. For even though the Sutter decision was the act of only a single arbitrator, the full impact of which would not be determined for at least a few years, it was a strong signal of danger.

How the clubs responded to their deteriorating position is mystifying. It is also of bottom-line importance to the history of the baseball business, because that response more than anything else is what led the clubs into the deep and dire financial straits in which they are currently mired. Management's convoluted strategy proceeded more or less along the following lines.

It was obvious to all of the clubs that free agency was costing them dearly. It was equally clear that the big bidders had not reached a plateau, so there was no telling when, where, or if the veterans' spiraling salaries would stop.

By 1980 the $1 million mark had been surpassed by several players. In the meantime, the overarching priority for nearly all of the clubs was still to put the best possible team on the field. That was their business. A handful of less well-off owners refused to enter the fray and simply turned their backs on free agents. But they were too few to buck the inflationary trend. They were on their way out of the industry anyway. For the rest, the problem was not only to decide if and to what extent they would get involved in bidding for free agents. They also had to figure out how they could keep their better young players on their teams once those players reached the sixth year of service and became free agents. Front-office people throughout both leagues dreaded the prospect of having to lose players whom they had selected, trained, and groomed for eight or more years just because some other club would be willing to pay more for them in free-agent bidding. The anxiety was particularly acute among the clubs in the smaller and less profitable media markets, such as Seattle, Pittsburgh, and Cincinnati. So a defensive contract strategy was needed.

A few clubs responded to the dilemma by entering into long-term contracts with their most prized young players. Such contracts had been virtually nonexistent prior to free agency. The reserve clause had made the player the permanent property of his club, so there had been no good reason for the clubs to guarantee anyone more than the coming year's salary. Now, however, there was a special incentive to sign players for several years at a time. The reasoning went as follows. If a club had an All-Star quality player with four years of service, then by signing that player for, say, five years the club would retain ownership of his contract through the player's ninth year of service. In other words, the club would in effect buy out three years' worth of the player's free agency rights. In practical terms, this meant that the clubs would be willing to risk wheelbarrows full of current dollars on players purely for the purpose of being able to hang on to them for an additional one, two, three years, or more.

The multiyear contract would typically be of great benefit to the player, for no matter what might happen during the term of the contract, most or all of the money would be fully guaranteed. Thus if the player's performance were to fall off, or if he were to become incapacitated through wear and tear or injury, his financial future would be secure.

There were only two risks to the player in agreeing to a multiyear deal. With salaries escalating at a wild rate, no one could know what the future dollar value of a player might be. Consequently a salary of $750,000 in year four of the contract might appear irresistible to the player upon signing, but he could actually be worth much more than that in the major league market by the time that fourth year rolled around. The other risk of entering into a long-term contract was that the player's performance might improve dramatically, again raising his relative dollar value. If both possibilities came to be, then the player might lose hundreds of thousands of dollars, or millions, by taking the multiyear offer. Though there weren't very many of them, future Hall of Famers Johnny Bench and Tom Seaver were among the principal victims of the multiyear contract. Each of them missed out on an income bonanza by agreeing to a long-term deal early in the free

agency era, before salaries went through the roof.

Having bitten the multiyear bullet, the question now facing the clubs was how exactly to design these long-term contracts. Since each player belonged to his club through year six, it seemed unnecessary to pay any player more than a fair wage for years three, four, or five. One would have expected, therefore, that the clubs would have granted modest raises prior to a player's sixth year of service, and that they would have built much larger raises into the contract for all subsequent years, raises that would make the player's pay consistent with free agents of similar ability. In fact, what the clubs started to do was to offer free-agent level salaries for each and every year of a multiyear contract.

A hypothetical example will help to illustrate this critical issue. Let's say a club had a better-than-average third baseman who had earned $100,000 in his third year of major league service in 1979. The club wanted to ensure that it would keep the player on the team for as long as reasonably possible. So it decided to offer the player a six-year deal covering the years 1980 through 1985. Comparable third basemen with less than six years of service were making between $150,000 and $250,000. Comparable free agent third basemen, however, were earning between $600,000 and $700,000 per year. With both the player and the club anticipating continued, rampant salary inflation, they might agree that the player would be worth more than $1 million by the beginning of the sixth year of the proposed contract. A fair contract, under these circumstances, might have been constructed as follows:

Calendar Yr.	Yrs. of Service	Contract Yr.	Salary
1979	3	—	$ 100,000
1980	4	1	200,000
1981	5	2	300,000
1982	6	3	700,000
1983	7	4	850,000
1984	8	5	1,000,000
1985	9	6	1,150,000
Tot. Cum. Salary			4,300,000

In the first two contract years, before the player would have reached free agent status, he would have been paid at a rate slightly higher than, but generally consistent with, the pay of other third basemen who had not accrued six years of service. Then his salary would have leaped up to the free-agent level in contract years three through six.

What the clubs in fact did in many such instances was draw up contracts that looked more like the following:

Calendar Yr.	Yrs. of Service	Contract Yr.	Salary
1979	3	—	$ 100,000
1980	4	1	500,000
1981	5	2	650,000
1982	6	3	800,000
1983	7	4	925,000
1984	8	5	1,050,000
1985	9	6	1,175,000
Tot. Cum. Salary			5,200,000

The first two years of this deal, while not quite at the free-agent level, are roughly double what a comparable player would have been worth in normal negotiations or arbitration. And the total value of the second contract is $900,000 greater than the first, more than a 20 percent boost.

Of course, by adopting this approach major league executives cost their clubs both immediate and long-term

cash. But, far more important than that, they set into motion a wave of big salary increases via the arbitration process. Why? Because the third baseman from the above example would be used as a basis of comparison by players of similar quality who had also not yet obtained free agency rights. In negotiations, a comparable young player would point to that contract and any others like it, claiming that if the other third baseman were worth $500,000 after just four years in the big leagues, then so, too, was he. And if the club didn't accept the claim, then the player would take the case to an arbitrator. More and more players did indeed take such cases to arbitration.

By the end of the 1983 season, this almost breathtaking act of fiscal self-destruction on the part of club management had become standard policy. Nearly every major league club had a few players with less than six years of service who were reaping very hefty incomes. As a result, the salaries of the arbitration eligibles, as a group, had increased by several hundred percent. Although they were still a clear notch or two behind the veterans in income, they had pulled away from the players with less than two years of service, who had no arbitration rights. Had the clubs not overplayed their new defensive strategy, which they clearly did not have to do, the arbitration eligibles might still have salaries within hailing distance of the major league minimum. It was by this time, of course, too late for the clubs to correct their grave strategic error. And the wall separating the younger players from the veterans had been reduced to an embattled trench.

To make matters worse for management, the Sutter precedent continued to exert its own upward pressure on the salaries of arbitration eligibles. That is, the players were still trying to establish the principle that a star is a star, regardless of his prior experience, and that he should be paid the full wages of a veteran star. The nub of their reasoning was that a young star has at least as much present value as an older star, and certainly greater future value to his club. The clubs continued to insist that service time is the bedrock of the salary structure, just as seniority is in other industries.

The first three years of the free agency era can be regarded as an experimental phase. No one on either side of the table knew precisely what was unfolding or how it would play itself out. As of 1980 it was evident to the clubs that free agency was producing an unchecked inflationary spiral and that arbitration would demand very serious attention.

Help for the clubs in the arbitration arena was already on the way. Talbot M. "Tal" Smith had been the president and general manager of the Houston Astros from 1975 through 1980. He was renowned in management circles as a tough but fair-minded chief executive with extraordinary skills in fiscal management. Smith had also brought the Astros from the depths of mediocrity to a division championship in his relatively brief tenure at Houston. But he and the new Astros owner, John McMullen, did not see eye to eye on a number of internal club matters, particularly the assignment of contracts. So despite his club's 1980 success on the field, Smith was fired almost immediately after the Astros lost the League Championship Series to the Eastern Division champion Phillies, three games to two.

Smith had gotten his feet wet in arbitration prior to his last season at the helm. Although he had lost both cases, his interest in the arbitration process had been piqued by the experience. He genuinely enjoyed the challenge of the specialized competition that arbitration is. So he decided to offer his personal services to a few of his front-office colleagues. The Oakland A's took him up on the offer. The club was headed toward contract battles with two of its best players, outfielder Tony Armas and pitcher Mike Norris. With Tal Smith representing them, the A's prevailed over both players in arbitration.

The victories prompted Smith to set up a business, Tal Smith Enterprises, to extend his salary services to other clubs. At the end of the 1981 season, six major league clubs retained Smith for support in salary negotiations and arbitration. Smith quickly assembled a small group of legal and statistical experts to round out his salary team. He had commented, privately, in his last months as the president of the Astros that backup catchers were now earning more than general managers. He felt strongly that the financial survival of major league baseball was in jeopardy and regarded his new role as a mission, a financial crusade, to save the game. His lament over fiscal conditions was sincere, and it was music to the ears of a lot of club executives.

Prior to the formation of Tal Smith Enterprises, the Player Relations Committee had been solely responsible for providing advice, counsel, and data support to the clubs. The PRC's executive director, Raymond Grebey, was a gruff and rather arrogant veteran of labor-management wars. He had headed the PRC since 1978, but had not scored many victories for the clubs. Instead of allying himself with Smith, Grebey seemed to view Smith as a competitor for Grebey's rightful role as management's protector. He even attempted in various ways to thwart Tal Smith's efforts. This bureaucratic pettiness exemplified management's internal divisions over policies and methods for combating the gains being racked up by the Players Association and its constituents.

Grebey notwithstanding, crusader Smith and his band of Young Turks put on a dazzling display in the 1982 arbitration campaign. Of the eight cases that went to hearings, the Smith team won seven. It was a previously unheard-of margin of victory, and it helped to quell Grebey's noisome opposition. More importantly, it sent a strong message to the players and their agents. They would have a better organized and much more formidable arbitration adversary than they had ever before encountered. A line had been drawn in the arbitration sand, giving the clubs a small but significant beachhead.

As the 1982 salary returns came in, it was plainly evident that the clubs were routinely granting enormous percentage increases to arbitration eligibles and free agents. There was a rising tide of salaries that was lifting nearly all boats. Furthermore, the clubs, inexplicably, were tendering virtually no salary cuts, even though they were empowered to do so. Equally difficult to explain was the fact that franchise sales were proceeding apace, with prices going up, way up. With the exception of the O'Malley family, the last of the family owners was gone, and corporate interests were evidently still anxious to gain membership in the baseball owners' club.

Tal Smith Enterprises' accomplishments the year before led six more clubs to sign up after the 1982 season. Smith had to expand his workforce and computerize his operation to keep up with the demand for his services. The client load increased to thirteen clubs the following year and remained at that level through 1986. Smith was, thus, representing half of the clubs in baseball.

Smith's presence no doubt tempered the submissions of a sizable percentage of players in arbitration, and it helped to slow the pace of inflation in normal negotiations carried out by his client clubs. But the Smith team compiled only a .500 record after its first splashy campaign. Inherent in the arbitration process is a tendency for the arbitrators to split their decisions, for if they come down too heavily on one side they are likely to be permanently removed from the pool of arbitrators by the opposing side. This worked against Smith, perhaps even unduly after his highly publicized rookie campaign. Moreover, even Smith's clients saw their payrolls rise at a bankrupting rate. The past practices of ill-prepared clubs had gone on too long and they were precedential. Those practices had helped to establish the micro-rules of the arbitration game, and there was little that Tal Smith or anyone else could do about it. Besides, of the more than 700 contracts that are signed each year, only 25 or so end up in hearings. And of that total, only about 60 percent, or roughly 15 cases, are handled by Smith. In other words, Smith brought too little, too late. The structural damage had already been done even before he had officially hung up his shingle. To make matters worse, by the end of the 1985 arbitration season many of the club executives and the player agents were complaining that arbitration had become a random process. Decisions were almost totally unpredictable. The term being bandied about was "crapshoot"—arbitration, many were saying, had turned into a crapshoot.

Throughout the first decade of the free agency era, labor-management relations worsened. The clubs' hiring of Smith had put an additional buffer between the players and the clubs, just as the cadre of player agents had done several years earlier. By adding such layers of representation, the ballplayers and their owners became a step more detached and alienated from each other. The more intimate love-hate relationship that had existed between the old family owners and their players, which was more akin to the relationship between troops and their generals, or between sons and their fathers, steadily gave way to an entrenched business relationship after World War Two. Meanwhile, salaries continued to rise. The labor-management war drums were beating, perhaps more loudly than ever before. But now the owners were the Indians.

More bad news greeted the besieged front offices after the 1985 season. Two years earlier, baseball had signed a six-year television contract with ABC and NBC that was worth approximately $8 million per year to each club. The $1.3 billion deal was triple the value of the prior network-TV contract. But now there was open talk that TV revenues had passed their peak. The networks were initiating an industry-wide reduction in personnel and a streamlining of their corporate structures. Accordingly, they were letting it be known that baseball could fully expect a decline in income—a fear that proved unfounded—when the next contract came up for negotiation in 1989. The clubs also began to see their cable television

income level off. And prices for tickets, parking, and concessions had all risen steadily as the players' salaries increased. Those prices were now barely, if at all, increasable. And radio and in-stadium advertising and promotions were rapidly reaching a saturation point.

To demonstrate the gravity of the situation, the owners made the unprecedented and startling decision to open the clubs' financial books in the fall of 1985. The central purposes of this action were to prove management's claims of insolvency and to obtain changes in the Basic Agreement that would reverse, or at least stem, the flow of red ink. By their accounting, the industry was losing roughly $58 million per year, or a bit more than $2 million per club. The Players Association had its own financial analysts review the data. They concluded that the clubs had actually netted $9 million in profits in 1985. According to one highly placed club executive, the financial data were so poorly organized, so incomplete, and so out of date that no one could draw reliable conclusions with respect to club costs or revenues.

Wherever the truth lay, it was clear that no more than two or three clubs were regularly showing profits. The Los Angeles Dodgers were, and still are, in their own special category at the top of the heap. The rest were fighting a losing battle. Nonetheless, between 1982 and 1985 the Detroit, Minnesota, and Cincinnati franchises were purchased—at astronomical prices. And there was talk, encouraged by the game's new commissioner, Peter V. Ueberroth, that the expansion of the major leagues to twenty-eight or thirty teams would take place in the relatively near future.

Given the extremely discouraging financial conditions of the baseball industry in the 1980s, one wonders why anyone, including the high rollers who had replaced their generally less wealthy predecessors, would want to get into the business. By 1985, every big league club was backed by at least one big corporate entity. In name, almost every club was owned by an individual or a group of individuals, but in reality the clubs belonged to large parent companies. The list included a variety of large media corporations, an international brewery, a blue-chip jeans manufacturer, a nationwide pizza franchise, a big-time law firm, a regional car dealership, and two major shipbuilding companies. What distinguished the new breed of owners from the earlier model was that the new baseball moguls were uninvolved in day-to-day club operations. Several owners meddled in important personnel and salary decisions, but club management was now essentially in the hands of front-office executives. This absentee style of ownership was a clear indication of the relative unimportance to the owners of the financial condition of their baseball franchises. It also suggested what the main motivation to own a ballclub had finally become—promotion. For whether or not a club made money, the individuals and the corporate interests that undergirded them would constantly be in the national limelight. Thus the clubs had turned into the promotional, public-relations playthings of their corporate overlords. How else can one explain the appreciation in club values in the midst of the game's financial plunge? Is the alternative view, that so many ultrawealthy parties are just slipshod businesspeople, really credible? After all, if the new owners are so terribly lacking in business acumen, how have they gotten to where they are?

Whatever their individual reasons for buying into the baseball business, the new hands-off owners relied on front-office personnel to oversee their organizations. Within the front offices there had always been a barrier between business and baseball. The baseball people—general managers, player personnel directors, farm system directors, assistants in those areas, scouts, and all the rest—had jealously protected their professional turf and the inside information upon which their jobs rested. They were also a relatively uneducated group, the bulk of whose professional experience was limited to the playing field. The finance people, stadium operations people, ticket office personnel, and so forth minded their own business. This kind of compartmentalization of responsibility and authority was another of the quasi-military aspects of the sport. The new owners in most cases empowered their one or two top baseball executives to hire and supervise the business personnel, thereby keeping the old order intact. As a result, salary matters generally fell to people ill-equipped to deal with salary techniques and strategies.

Salary determination is inherently a blend of performance evaluation and comparative salary analysis, and a rather exacting intellectual exercise. But with the owners basically uninvolved and with the traditional organizational barrier still standing, there were very few club personnel qualified to do a creditable job in the salary arena. The rapid and broad success of Tal Smith stood as proof that the clubs could not adequately manage their own salary matters. And if there was a single area on which the current and future financial health of each franchise depended, it was undeniably the area of salaries. It is for these reasons that free agency and arbitration led to rampant inflation. To put it another way, the Messersmith-McNally decision had freed only the veterans; it was the unsupervised and fiscally deficient baseball executives who had made the rest of the major league players wealthy. In effect, they had given away the store while the owners were fishing.

The first loud signal of ownership's recognition of its managerial shortcomings came when the owners' council selected the business entrepreneur Peter Ueberroth to replace the attorney Bowie Kuhn as baseball's commissioner. Ueberroth had demonstrated his take-charge, nononsense, profit-oriented approach to sports when he organized the 1984 Olympic Games held in Los Angeles. The owners' appointment of Ueberroth was nothing less than a reversion to the strong-commissioner strategy that had brought Judge Landis into baseball and saved the game in the aftermath of the Black Sox scandal. It showed that they were deeply concerned about the existing state of affairs. It was also a virtual admission that when the going gets tough, the ever-divided house of owners must seek outside help.

When Ueberroth took office as the commissioner at the beginning of 1985, baseball was awash in red ink and the tide was still rising. The clubs could not unilaterally rewrite the Basic Agreement. Nor could they control the behavior of arbitrators. They had opened their books, but the players remained unconvinced that they were in trouble. How, the players asked, could the clubs possibly be insolvent and at the same time have a string of anxious

buyers waiting in line to pay exorbitant and still escalating prices for those clubs? Management was becoming desperate.

The new commissioner was not the type of administrator who would simply sit back and allow a bad situation to deteriorate further. In late September of 1985, Ueberroth addressed the club owners and their representatives at a regularly scheduled quarterly meeting. After the season ended, he attended two more of management's private meetings. His broad message to the clubs at those gatherings was that they would have to exercise fiscal responsibility in order to keep their industry viable. His more specific advice to them came in the form of a negative statement that he made at the general managers' meeting at Tarpon Springs, Florida, in early November:

"It is not smart to sign long-term contracts."

Shortly after that meeting, sixty-two players filed for free agency. Though the list was long, it was perhaps the least impressive group, talentwise, since free agency was instituted. It was loaded with marginal and soon-to-retire players. One of the few exceptions, however, was All-Star outfielder Kirk Gibson. The twenty-eight-year-old Gibson had been with the Detroit Tigers for his entire professional career, and he was coming off his best season as a major leaguer. Many clubs would normally have had serious interest in obtaining a player of Gibson's caliber. But the deadline for bidding on free agents came and went, and not a single club made an offer to Gibson. In fact, practically all of the free agents had been completely ignored by the clubs. Of the group of sixty-two, only five changed clubs. And all five were players in whom their previous employers had officially indicated no interest by waiving their right to negotiate with them.

To the Players Association, it was obvious that the clubs had entered into a tacit agreement not to pursue any free agents that their most recent employers wished to retain. In their view, that amounted to a conspiracy to violate the terms of the Basic Agreement. The legal term for such behavior is collusion. So the association lodged a grievance against all twenty-six clubs, claiming that they had violated Article XVIII of the agreement, which states that "the Clubs shall not act in concert with the other Clubs" in signing free agents.

Veteran arbitrator Thomas Tuttle Roberts began hearing the case in the summer of 1986. In September the owners attempted to dismiss Roberts from the case. He had just ruled, in a separate case, that the clubs could not insert drug-testing provisions in players' contracts without the consent of the Players Association, and that had angered the owners, or so they claimed. The association felt that this was merely an excuse and that management was engaging, as it had done for more than a century, in delaying tactics. For the longer it would take to resolve the collusion case, the more opportunity the clubs would have to defy free agency and maybe even wreck it.

To the delight of management, the case dragged on through the winter of 1986–1987. This time, however, the free agent pool was one of the best on record. It included perennial All-Stars Tim Raines, Andre Dawson, Jack Morris, and Lance Parrish. But, true to form, the clubs continued the practice of the previous year. They made no bids for free agents whom their previous clubs wanted to

keep. And, not surprisingly, the Players Association filed another grievance.

Then the final 1985 salary tallies came in. What those results showed was that management's initial attack on free agency had had little if any effect on salaries. The major league payroll had continued to grow at a bankrupting pace. Management was sweating bullets, and they were looking more and more ready to fight back in other ways.

Some of the provisions of the Basic Agreement had been changed through prior negotiations between the players and the clubs. The changes went into effect after the 1986 season. The most important of them dealt with arbitration rights. Players now would have to complete three full years of major league service instead of just two to become eligible for arbitration. Using the new provision to full advantage, the clubs grossly underpaid some of the game's brightest young stars, including 1986 Cy Young Award winner Roger Clemens of the Boston Red Sox. It was, as it always had been, within the clubs' rights to unilaterally assign contracts to such players. But by recent standards, the salaries tendered to Clemens and a half dozen other outstanding young players were, in each instance, hundreds of thousands of dollars below the established scale. Several of the players threatened to hold out for the 1987 season. Clemens did hold out until shortly after the season began. In addition, the clubs took a firmer stand in arbitration than ever before. They submitted several offers that represented no raise over the previous year's salaries, and they even went so far as to try to cut a few salaries by way of arbitration. Given the almost total absence of holds and cuts in prior arbitration proceedings, these were highly risky actions.

The 1986–1987 arbitration results revealed the chaotic state into which the process had lapsed. At the bottom end of the salary scale, the clubs had cleaned up. Twenty-six players had taken their cases to arbitration and seven of them had returned without salary increases. Four of those had received cuts in pay. But at the high end, Yankee first baseman Don Mattingly received an award of $1,975,000, which was the largest arbitration award to date. Overall, the clubs won sixteen of the twenty-six cases. And the players realized the lowest percentage gain in income in the history of arbitration.

The most interesting case was that of Detroit pitcher Jack Morris. Morris had gone to arbitration four years earlier and had lost. After the 1986 season, he declared himself a free agent. But because the Tigers wanted to keep him, none of the other clubs would bid for his services. His agent, Richard Moss, decided to throw the Tigers a curveball. He advised his client to pursue a new option available to free agents, namely to withdraw his declaration of free agency and subject himself, once again, to arbitration. Detroit management was over a barrel. Morris was one of the best pitchers in the game, and he had plenty of statistical evidence to back up that assessment. So the club knew that if it were to accept the offer, it would stand a pretty good chance of getting clobbered in arbitration. On the other hand, if the club were to turn down the offer to arbitrate, it would not be permitted to negotiate with Morris until May 1, a full month into the 1987 season. The club consented to arbitrate. Jack Morris won this one, and it cost the club a whopping $1,850,000

to retain his services for the 1987 season.

When the final figures for 1987 came in at the end of November, it appeared that the array of extreme measures taken by management had at last reversed the salary inflation trend. In fact, the average major league salary had declined by a few thousand dollars. And Tal Smith Enterprises was still proudly leading the cost-reduction crusade on behalf of the ballclubs.

But it was not yet time for the owners to celebrate, because two months earlier arbitrator Tom Roberts ruled that the major league clubs had indeed operated "in concert" when they shunned the free agents after the 1985 season. In September 1989 that translated into awards of $10,528,086.71 to the 139 players he held had been victims of that first round of collusion. Seven players—including Kirk Gibson and Carlton Fisk—were given "new look" free agency.

In August 1988 arbitrator George Nicolau, after reviewing 8,346 pages of testimony, found owners guilty once more of collusion, this time against seventy-nine free agents following the 1986 season. In October—he had delayed his action to avoid disrupting the pennant races—he granted "new look" free agency to twelve more players, including Bob Boone, Jim Clancy, and Willie Randolph, all of whom signed with new teams.

A "Collusion III" case was filed by the union in January 1989 regarding those who had become free agents after the 1987 campaign. In July 1990 Nicolau again found for labor. Seventy-six players, including such stars as Jack Clark, Gary Gaetti, Jack Morris, Dave Righetti, Mike Witt, and Paul Molitor, were involved in the case, which revolved around management's creation of an "information bank" in the winter of 1986–87. This data bank reported all salary offers made to free agents. Nicolau wrote he found it a "quiet" form of cooperation between supposedly rival clubs endeavoring to keep tabs on what each competitor was offering on the supposedly free market. By the time damages would finally be determined, they would exceed the $100 million mark.

New Sources of Revenue

Reports of the demise of television's profitability proved grossly exaggerated. Toward the end of Ueberroth's tenure, a series of blockbuster broadcasting deals were negotiated. The biggest was a four-year deal with CBS in December 1988 for $1.06 billion. The network received rights to the All-Star Game, League Championship Series, World Series, and twelve regular-season weekend games. Criticism surrounded the cutback in regular-season broadcasts, but Ueberroth answered with an unprecedented deal with the cable industry. ESPN outbid such rivals as TNT and USA in January 1989 for a four-year, $400-million pact, featuring 175 regular-season games, including groundbreaking Sunday-night cablecasts. No one knew how successful the package would be, but even ESPN officials admitted they would lose money for at least the first two years. At the same time a $50-million, four-year agreement with CBS Radio for the Game of the Week, All-Star Game, and postseason contests was made final.

Not only was Organized Baseball as a whole cashing in; so were the individual clubs. George Steinbrenner obtained a $500-million, twelve-year agreement with Madison Square Garden cable. His colleagues worried that he would again attempt to corner the free-agent market. Big Apple fans, at least what Yankee fans remained, worried over the cost of their cable bills (as did fans nationwide following the ESPN negotiations), but the deal was done.

At the conclusion of Ueberroth's breathtaking round of broadcasting conquests, the commissioner noted baseball's newfound prosperity and respectfully requested owners to hold the line on ticket prices. He was ignored.

Another segment of the business of baseball—and an increasingly lucrative and ugly one—was memorabilia, autographs, and baseball cards. In 1989 it was estimated that these "extras" accounted for $1 billion in business. Its culmination came during a particularly dark day in baseball history. Hours after a disgraced Pete Rose was expelled from the game by Commissioner Giamatti, he appeared on a cable network and peddled $1.2 million in bats, plaques, and balls, taking home $100,000 in pocket money.

While that may have shocked many, it was not the only seaminess marring the trade. Ballplayers peddling autographs at card shows soured stomachs from Fenway to Anaheim. Forgeries and fakes surfaced with regularity. Jose Canseco was sued for his failure to appear at one card show. Two dealers were charged with ripping off an infirm "Cool Papa" Bell of his mementos. A seventy-five-year-old man was killed over memorabilia in the Midwest. By 1990 reports from the New York City area held that the boom was losing steam, that crowds were thinning out at shows, and that overpriced gimcracks were starting to gather dust. Perhaps.

Tying in to this facet of the game was the licensing of logos and related products. Initiated nearly three decades ago by the National Football League, licensed sports marketing now produces over a billion dollars in annual sales in baseball.

The Franchise Game

In 1988 Peter Ueberroth admitted that four years earlier twenty-one out of twenty-six big league clubs suffered financial losses. By 1987 the situation had seen a dramatic turnaround, and twenty-two out of twenty-six clubs either broke even or were profitable. There had always been an interest in ballclubs as rich men's toys, but when it appeared that once again money could be made at the national pastime, bidding went through the roof (dome?) for franchises.

Even the most moribund teams were selling for big bucks. Somewhat understandably the New York Mets changed hands for $100 million, and Baltimore sold for $70 million, but when the woeful Seattle Mariners were peddled for $77 million (George Argyros had paid $13.1 million for these latter-day St. Louis Browns in 1981), it was clear that the economic balance had been tilted.

Back in the early 1980s Commissioner Ueberroth had announced that the majors would feature two new AL and four new NL clubs by 2000, but calling progress snail-like would have exaggerated its speed. By the late 1980s the

game faced increased pressure from a number of sources for expansion. The Players Association wished to open up more jobs for its members. The U.S. Senate formed a fourteen-member panel on the subject. A new league, organized by agent Dick Moss and at one time backed by Donald Trump's ephemeral billions, was another threat in the summer of 1989. Baseball now announced a willingness to add two more NL franchises.

Nothing really happened until the summer of 1990. Slowing up matters, some said, were the recent TV contracts. Established owners were loath to share their newfound riches with any newcomers, and hence expansion would not occur until the current broadcasting contracts expired. Each of the twenty-six teams received $16 million yearly from the national package, but with more dollars going to such stars as Viola, Clark, and Canseco, the owners still felt they needed every last penny.

As a result, a 1993 target for expanding came into view. The National League would announce its two newest members in September 1991. The expansion franchises would draft entry-level minor-league players in late 1991 and actually operate farm systems in 1992. During that season, they would be able to draft college and high school players. Major league expansion drafts would occur in November 1992. An interesting—and definitely different—aspect of this draft is that the newest senior-circuit clubs may draft personnel (thirty-six for each club) from *both* major leagues, the logic being that if the two newcomers cut into the TV and radio revenues of all clubs, they should draft from all clubs. A corollary of this, of course, is that both the AL and the NL would divvy up the $95 million franchise fee each rookie owner would fork over.

While Organized Baseball is not exactly pooh-poohing those hefty initiation fees, they are not the only factors involved in the initiation process. Such considerations as "substantial financial resources" (obviously) and "long-term commitment" to their local communities were cited. Multipurpose stadiums were deemed passé. Local politicos were advised to be cognizant of "the necessity of the club receiving parking, concession, signage, pay TV, and luxury box revenue."

Frontrunners for the new franchises included Denver (where voters in 1990 approved a new 40,000-seat stadium), St. Petersburg (which nearly hijacked the White Sox in 1988), Miami (assisted by recently retired Mike Schmidt), Buffalo (where the Rich family runs a big-league operation at the AAA level), and Washington (a two-time loser, but a loser with political connections).

The huge franchise fees plus a projected $65 million in startup costs (a figure that ultimately reached $95 million) began to cause several prospective backers to think twice. Nonetheless, despite a downturn in the national economy, there was no shortage of takers.

Major league expansion would trigger minor league expansion, as the new clubs would require farm teams. With such franchises as Oklahoma City going for $4.5 million, the price tag at the AAA level would not be cheap. Most observers estimate it would be $5 million per club (consider that the Mets had cost $1.8 million in 1962 and the Kansas City Royals had cost just $5.55 million in 1969). Even applying for a minor league club required a $5,000 nonrefundable deposit (an unprecedented situa-

tion for the bushes), but in September 1990 eighteen groups sent in their checks.

As minor league franchises were being bought and sold for record prices, the major league clubs took notice. Claiming they no longer saw the wisdom of subsidizing such "profitable" ventures (in all too many cases the only profit comes from selling to the next party willing to take operating losses), the big leaguers started to place heavy-handed pressure on their farm clubs in 1990. On a single day in August 1990, sixty-three working agreements were dropped. That was followed by a threat to bring fifty-nine bush-league teams to Florida and Arizona in 1991 for summer versions of complex baseball. Hardball was the name of the game on all negotiating fronts.

The Lockout of 1990

Baseball's Basic Agreement expired on December 31, 1989, and despite the prosperity that both sides now enjoyed, open warfare was imminent. The Players Association was hardly blind to the marvelously round figures Ueberroth had pried out of the networks. Beyond that they were particularly irritated by the year of arbitration they had given away in the last settlement. Club owners, on the other hand, were tired of forking over millions through the arbitration process. The problem for management was not simply the cost of losing specific arbitration cases. Winning could also be costly. In the winter of 1989–90 the ten *losers* in the process received average raises of $477,050. Average salaries doubled for only the second time in the fifteen-year history of the process. First-year arbitration players saw paychecks skyrocket by 166 percent. While the vast majority of disputes were settled before they got to arbitration, they still involved huge increases, such as Teddy Higuera's $2,125,000 stipend and Tom Browning's pact for the same figure. Fred McGriff saw his income rise from $325,000 to $1,450,000 in a prearbitration settlement.

A showdown had to occur.

Negotiations dragged on during the winter of 1989–90, and it was widely believed that the players would collect their checks for a few months and then strike at midseason, when the owners were gearing up for large crowds and were most vulnerable. To thwart this plan, management struck first, engaging in yet another lockout of spring training camps.

The owners' strategy was to hold firm on the third-year threshold for arbitration. The PRC tendered a number of alternatives to the Players Association, including one granting 48 percent of club profits to players and another offering a cumbersome $4 million bonus-pool scheme to be shared by two-year players.

After thirty-two bitter days, Donald Fehr, the union's combative new representative, and Charles O'Connor, the new PRC negotiator, hammered out a compromise. Seventeen percent of the second-year players would now become eligible for arbitration. The minimum salary would rise from $68,000 to $100,000, the largest percentage increase ever. Management would contribute $55 million to the players' pension fund, up from $39 million. To the casual observer this seemed a victory for labor, but the players had wanted $80 million and the settlement was a

giant step back from the traditional one-third of national TV revenues that players had contended was their right. Additionally, it was written into the agreement that baseball would announce its long-stalled expansion plans within ninety days.

It was not a settlement that established any great principles, and most fans were no doubt just as puzzled as ever as to what all the shouting had been about, but it appeared that the process had cooled some tempers. Even the Players Association's Don Fehr, never one to look away from controversy, discerned a "measurably lower degree of hostility" at lockout's conclusion.

What is certain is that the ballplayers and the major league clubs remain deeply entrenched in financial warfare. The chairman of the board, president and chief executive officer of the Philadelphia Phillies, William Y. Giles, has been a baseball executive for more than thirty years. He was one of the principal negotiators in the lucrative six-year pact signed by the television networks. And he is widely regarded as one of the "nicest guys" in the business. When asked recently by a Philadelphia reporter how labor-management relations were faring, Giles said that the animosity between the parties is "at an all-time high."

Baseball Enters the Nineties

In the 1991 season, salaries, arbitration settlements, and attendance continued to climb in dizzying fashion. The average player salary soared an astonishing 42.5 percent to $851,383. The highest stipend was accorded to Los Angeles' Darryl Strawberry—$3,800,000—while the average Oakland paycheck was a handsome $1,394,119.

In January 1991, 159 players filed for arbitration. They secured average raises of $540,000—a 102 percent boost. Big winners were Wally Joyner ($2.1 million) and Doug Drabek ($3.35 million).

Overall, major league attendance hit an all-time high of 56,813,760, paced by Toronto's exceeding the 4 million mark, the first time a club had smashed that barrier.

Long-stalled National League expansion finally occurred in June 1991 with $95 million franchises being granted for the 1993 season to the Colorado Rockies, headed by wholesale beverage dealer John Antonucci, and the Florida Marlins, led by Blockbuster Video tycoon Wayne Huizenga. Huizenga's appointment of Pirates executive Carl Barger to be the Marlins' first president caused some controversy as Barger had played a key role in the expansion process. Also on board as Marlins GM was Dave Dombrowski, who had previously done much to fortify the Expos farm system. Commissioner Fay Vincent ruled that American League teams would receive $42 million of the franchise fees.

Issues such as disparities in local television revenue continued to fester. Local television, cable, and radio rights generated $200 million for Major League Baseball, but just four teams—the Yanks, Mets, Phils, and Dodgers—garnered more than 35 percent of the total. The Yankees' $41.5 million per year deal towered over the funding available to such small market franchises as Pittsburgh ($5.8 million), Kansas City ($5 million), and Seattle ($4 million). In September 1991 the American League voted to channel 20 percent of local broadcasting 'net revenues' into a pool which would be shared equally (the NL formula, on the other hand, now calls for sharing 25 percent). Controversy is expected over what revenue is to be considered "net."

As the 1991 season ended, another round of free agent signings ensued with the New York Mets snagging Pittsburgh's Bobby Bonilla with a five-year, $29 million pact. This largesse was soon eclipsed by the Cubs' signing of thirty-two-year-old Ryne Sandberg to a four-year $28.4 million agreement. At the lower end of the spectrum, the big league minimum wage inched up to $109,000—an almost meaningless figure with the average major league salary now at $1,043,156.

Big losers in the free agent–big salary game were the 1992 Mets, Dodgers, and Red Sox. These teams spent $130.5 million in finishing a collective 82 games out of first as their attendance plummeted by a total of 1.5 million paying customers.

Despite another 4-million-plus season in Toronto and the million-fan boost given by the opening of Baltimore's Camden Yards, major league attendance dropped by 1.6 percent in 1992. Major league profits plummeted from $143 million in 1990 to just $8.7 million in 1991 to virtually nothing in 1992. Nervousness increased over the coming end of the lucrative CBS television contract after the 1993 campaign. Given these alarming indicators of doom, it was anticipated that the unprecedently large number of free agents testing the market after the 1992 World Series—including such stars as Barry Bonds, David Cone, Kirby Puckett, and Greg Maddux—would find few takers.

As the World Series ended, a bombshell struck baseball's already shaky financial structure. ESPN announced it would not exercise its option for television coverage in 1994–1995. Claiming that so far it had lost more than half of its investment in the deal, the decision makers at ESPN chose a $13 million buyout rather than further payments of $250 million for the two seasons available to them. The cable network left the door open for negotiations, but obviously at a much lower starting point. Among other factors, baseball was losing its popularity with American youth: Neilsen ratings revealed a disconcerting 24 percent drop in viewership of regular season games by 12-to-17-year-olds from 1989 to 1992. In that time NFL ratings in that age group were up 16 percent; the NBA rose a startling 31 percent.

Meanwhile in the minors, 1992 provided the highest attendance total since 1950, with 27,180,170 fans passing through the turnstiles. Major league expansion had appeared to create a trickle-down growth for the minors. Yet the capital demands on minor league owners, a product of the hardball Professional Baseball Agreement that Major League Baseball had pushed on the National Association, were coming due in a recessionary atmosphere, and fewer municipalities were willing or able to foot the bill for new ballparks or for upgrades of existing facilities.

The saga of Bob Lurie and the San Francisco Giants went on and on. In June 1990 he received permission to shift the club thirty-five miles south to Santa Clara County, California. But that November voters in fifteen Santa Clara County cities turned thumbs down on a 1 percent utility tax to pay for a new stadium—the third

year in a row such a referendum had failed. In January 1992 Lurie announced plans to move to San Jose if a new $155 million, 48,000-seat stadium could be constructed. The plan foundered on the shoals of a projected 2 percent increase in the city's utility tax. On August 7, 1992, Lurie (who had paid $8 million for the franchise in 1976) announced the sale of his Giants for $115 million to a group headed by Vincent J. Naimoli bent on relocating the club to St. Petersburg, Florida. That triggered a $100 million counteroffer from local investors headed by Safeway magnate Peter Magowan and stockbroker Charles Schwab, who were intent on keeping the team in the Bay area. The National League, by a 9–4 vote on November 10, 1992, rejected the St. Petersburg offer, leaving the status of the Magowan offer up in the air. The maneuvering sparked new Congressional interest (particularly that of the Senate Judiciary Committee) in baseball's antitrust status.

Several other franchises changed hands in 1991–1992. On November 2, 1991, John Labatt Ltd. paid $67.5 million (Canadian) to acquire majority control (going from 45 percent to 90 percent ownership) of the Blue Jays. In a controversial move that sparked xenophobic and racial responses, Jeff Smulyan turned the woeful Seattle Mariners over to Japanese interests connected to the Nintendo corporation for $106 million. John McMullen unloaded the Astros to Texas business executive Drayton McLane, Jr., for $115 million. Finally, after draining an estimated $23 million from the Detroit Tigers' coffers, Domino's Pizza baron Tom Monaghan peddled the club to fellow pizza magnate Mike Ilitch (a former Tiger farmhand) for a relatively paltry $85 million. The Orioles were rumored to be on the block for $200 million.

The biggest casualty of the 1992 season was Commissioner Fay Vincent, who was ousted on September 7, 1992. (For more about his "resignation," see the articles by Stephen S. Hall and A. D. Suehsdorf.) Brewers owner Bud Selig stepped in as Commissioner Pro Tem. The first tangible result of Vincent's departure was recision of his controversial National League realignment plan, which would have placed the Cardinals and the Cubs in the NL West and the Reds and Braves in the NL East.

Some observers felt that Vincent's downfall was foreshadowed in December 1991 when owners hired Richard Ravitch, a one-time candidate for mayor of New York City, to the post of President of the Major League Player Relations Committee at a salary $100,000 greater than Vincent's. The owners did not want Vincent interfering in labor relations as he had when he intervened in the 1990 spring training lockout. Vincent's dismissal only fueled the rumors, already rampant, of an owner-generated lockout for 1993.

Sales of Major League Baseball licensed products continued to soar—from $200 million in 1987 to $1.5 billion in 1990 to $2 billion in 1992. Despite the fact that items with Mets and Yankees logos account for 20 percent of all sales, revenues are split equally among the twenty-eight franchises. To compete with the rival NBA and NFL in an increasingly global struggle for fan dollars, MLB started to promote overseas sales and by 1991 was doing $20 million a year in foreign sales.

In 1992 even the minors got into the act with a similar centralized licensing approach (under the control of Major League Baseball Properties, which can keep up to 30 percent of the royalties). National Association licensed sales in 1992 were an estimated $12 to $15 million. Hopeful plans are being drawn up to go "international" with bush league caps and gimcracks.

The Spoils of War

For the better part of a century, major league baseball players fought for a reasonable portion of the proceeds of their entertainment industry. However, with no viable competition from outside the baseball monopoly, the players were forced to accept whatever salaries and conditions their owners saw fit to give them. They eventually made progress, but only after they pulled together as a bargaining unit and slowly and painfully loosened the grip of the reserve clause. In the end, what they obtained was not a specified level of income but rather a system of salary determination. The system contained no financial guarantees beyond the major league minimum salary. How much money the players would ultimately receive through free agency and salary arbitration would rest entirely on the behavior of the clubs.

What the system did was create a form of free-market competition within the monopoly. In a sense, it turned a single business into twenty-eight separate businesses and unleashed a self-destructive frenzy of interclub competition. To the players' amazement and joy, they saw their salaries reach heights that they could not have imagined were possible.

To most of the fans and the press, the dizzying escalation in their incomes made the players appear baldly greedy. And when filthy-rich players began to complain that they were being underpaid compared to other individuals or groups of players, the public's growing distaste for them was understandable. But greed really was not the issue. What was at stake for the carping millionaire pitcher or outfielder was not the money but rather his standing as a ballplayer. Money had become the measure of his talent, and every player wanted and still wants his money to match his skills. So when he sees that a player whom he considers himself superior to is earning more than he is, he feels underrated, cheated. That is his value system.

Unfortunately, as long as the salary system remains a chaotic hodgepodge without fixed standards of evaluation, in which the negotiating skills of agents and club executives are often more of a factor in determining the players' worth than their actual on-the-field contributions to their teams are, a good number of players will always feel cheated. And the clubs will continue to be and to feel besieged.

The system is under attack now. Management has chosen to use unethical or illegal methods to achieve its ends, as it has since 1879 when the first version of the reserve clause was introduced. The latest ploy in the owners' bottomless bag of tricks is collusion. Consequently, trust and respect between management and labor are at a low. And whatever hope the clubs might have had of smoothing out their differences with the players and their union has been all but dashed.

The players will continue to earn astounding sums of

money and the club owners will continue to bask in the national limelight, thereby getting plenty of public-relations bang for their otherwise poorly managed bucks. And the fans will continue to be the ones who ultimately pay for the follies of both sides. Thus one of the key questions facing the major leagues is how long the fans will go on subsidizing the war of principle between the players and the clubs.

Whether or not the fee-per-game plan is implemented, the recent and steady shift from free over-the-air telecasts to paid-for cable-TV telecasts is continuing. This development is taking viewing opportunities away from those people who either do not have cable access or cannot afford to pay the monthly fee. The problem is already rather acute for New York Yankee fans, because there is no cable television in the Bronx at this time and the majority of Yankee games are broadcast exclusively on MSG, a cable-TV operation.

In the long run, the shift to cable may diminish the size of the baseball viewing audience, which would erode the major league fan population and thereby reduce the future income of the sport.

The shift also raises a fundamental question concerning baseball's exemption from antitrust laws. The matter has been addressed by Charles E. Schumer, a member of the House of Representatives from New York's Tenth Congressional district. In an article for the *New York Times* written in the summer of 1987, he posed the following challenge:

If baseball is simply a "business," then why should it have a special antitrust exemption? On the other hand, if baseball enjoys protection from the nation's laws because it is a national treasure, then Americans have a right to demand reasonable access to it.

Congressman Schumer has introduced legislation which would require that the Yankees and major league baseball choose between two alternatives. They must, in his words, "either act like a business and receive no governmental protection, or behave like a great national pastime by making sure that New Yorkers can see the game on cable or free TV."

There is an eerie quality to the maelstrom in which baseball now finds itself. For none of the central issues that have haunted the game since its inception has really been resolved. The business is still a monopoly. The reserve clause, though drastically altered, remains largely in force, and the owners are trying to resurrect the rest of

it by undermining free agency. Many individual players are still dissatisfied because they do not feel that their contracts reflect their relative value as on-the-field performers. Members of Congress are beginning to consider legislation aimed, as before, at removing baseball's antitrust exemption. And baseball's un-merry-go-round, the seamier side of the industry, keeps spinning on its own goofy axis. In the words of Yogi Berra, "It seems like déjà vu all over again."

Nevertheless, the game is bringing in more spectators and more money than ever before. And the irrepressible club owners, though they are now more a clique of promotion-minded high rollers than a league of dyed-in-the-wool baseball men, seem undaunted by the growing financial threats to their industry.

The Future of the Baseball Business

The industry faces two major threats to its well-being, one external and one internal.

The external threat comes from the fans, whose willingness to subsidize the excesses of the clubs and the players is being severely tested. Will the rising costs of attending games and viewing them on television reduce the fan base? Will spectatorship become a privilege available only to those who can afford it? Will spectatorship become a privilege available only to those who can afford it? With the national economy in the doldrums, at the close of the 1992 season several clubs took pains to proclaim a freeze in ticket and concession prices.

The internal threat concerns the salary system. By way of collusion, the clubs have discovered that they can beat free agency by simply abstaining from bidding for players. And even though that ploy has been officially ruled illegal, the fact remains that the clubs have learned how to use it. Does this mean that free agency is from this point forward unenforceable? If not, how then can the clubs be made to bid for players? And even if they could somehow be compelled to make bids, how could they be required to offer more money than they wish to offer? Does this mean that free agency is dead? Not if the players can figure out a way to sustain it. Does it mean that arbitration will replace free agency? Not if the owners can help it.

And the drums keep beating, and the music keeps playing, and both sides keep screaming baseball's most familiar war cry:

"Wait till next year!"

## CHAPTER 27

Baseball and the Law

Gary D. Hailey

Like many other members of our litigation-happy society, baseball players and team owners have spent their fair share of time in the courtroom. Judges have been asked to decide lawsuits involving everything from a team's liability for fan injuries from foul balls and thrown bats to the legality of the decision to resume the infamous Yankees-Royals "Pine Tar Game" nearly a month after George Brett's home run had been ruled a game-ending out.

But the most significant baseball-related court cases were a series of mostly unsuccessful challenges to organized baseball's attempts to limit competition—especially from rivals like the Players League and the Federal League—for players' services. That litigation has reached the United States Supreme Court three times, and all three times that Court has ruled that baseball is not governed by the antitrust laws. The reasoning behind this holding may have been perfectly logical when the first of those cases was decided in 1922, but it seemed bizarre and irrational when it was reiterated half a century later in *Flood* v. *Kuhn*.

From the game's earliest days, baseball owners have struggled to keep their expenses down and maintain control over the players, who often decide that the grass (and the money) is greener in someone else's ballpark. In 1870 the National Association of Base Ball Players tried to stop "revolving," or contract jumping, by adopting a rule requiring players to give 60 days' notice before leaving one club for another. Tougher controls were agreed to after word leaked that A. G. Spalding and three other Boston Red Stockings stars had signed contracts in the middle of the 1875 season to play for Chicago in 1876. In 1879 the National League secretly agreed to allow each team owner to "reserve" his five best players at the end of the season; other owners were prohibited from bidding for the services of the reserved players. The owners also agreed not to sign any player who refused to play for the team that reserved him.

The reserve rule and blacklist helped protect the National League owners from their fellows, but proved less useful against the newly formed American Association, which declared war on the NL in 1882. One of the biggest names to jump to the rival league was catcher Charles Bennett, who had played for the NL's Pittsburgh club in 1882. In August of that year, he accepted $100 in exchange for his written promise to sign a contract with Pittsburgh for the 1883 season. But before Bennett signed that contract, the Detroit AA team offered him more money. Pittsburgh got wind of what was happening and immediately filed suit in federal court, seeking an injunction ordering Bennett to sign the Pittsburgh contract.

Bennett's lawyers offered a number of legal defenses, some rather narrow and technical. The court ruled in Bennett's favor[1] but did not issue a written opinion, so it is unclear just which of his attorneys' arguments were persuasive. The dismissal may have resulted from the court concluding that the reserve system and blacklist illegally limited Bennett's freedom to earn a living. But the court may have refused to enjoin Bennett's jump to Detroit simply because of the timing of the lawsuit. The Pittsburgh club would have suffered no real harm from Bennett's refusal to sign an 1883 contract until it had to play a game without him in the lineup. Its October 1882 lawsuit was, in a sense, premature because Bennett might have changed his mind and returned to Pittsburgh before the opening day of the 1883 season.

Shortstop Sam Wise did Bennett one better. He signed a contract with the AA's Cincinnati club but then jumped back to Boston when they upped their original offer. Cincinnati got an Ohio court to order Boston not to play Wise, but they were unable to enforce the order in other states. Wise simply stayed at home when the Boston team came to Cleveland to play.

The National League and American Association made peace in 1883 and signed the "National Agreement," which contained a strengthened reserve rule. The promoters of the Union Association hoped to capitalize on the players' resentment of the one-sided terms of their contracts with organized baseball, but the established leagues fought back hard by adopting the "Day Resolution," an agreement to blacklist any reserved player who jumped to a Union club. Star pitcher Tony Mullane, who jumped from the St. Louis Browns to the St. Louis Maroons of the new league, tried to return to the Browns after hearing about the Day Resolution. The Browns refused to welcome their prodigal back because they knew the Maroons would haul them into court if they did. The Toledo AA club wanted Mullane, but the National Agreement did not provide for player trades or sales. The Browns simply released Mullane outright, and Toledo signed him. The Union Association failed to persuade an Ohio federal judge to order Mullane back to the Maroons.[2] After the demise of the upstart league at the end of the 1884 season, Toledo agreed to send Mullane back to the Browns, but the Cincinnati AA club—in flagrant violation of the National Agreement—signed the 35-game winner to a lucrative bonus contract. The Association's powers-that-be ultimately awarded Mullane to Cincinnati, but ordered him to sit out the 1885 season and give back part of his bonus.

Once the Union Association was dead and buried, organized baseball tightened the screws a bit more by trying to establish a maximum annual player salary of $2,000. In response the players formed the National Brotherhood of Professional Base Ball Players under the leadership of John Montgomery Ward, the New York Giants shortstop who attended Columbia University law school in the off-season. Ward claimed that the reserve clause, the blacklist, and other intimidating provisions of the standard player contract were legally unenforceable. When the owners refused to scrap the salary cap or to agree not to sell or trade players without their consent, the brotherhood went on to form the Players League, which fielded eight teams in 1890. Over 80 National League players and almost 30 from the American Association— including future Hall of Famers Dan Brouthers, John Clarkson, Hugh Duffy, "Buck" Ewing, "King" Kelly, Connie Mack, and "Old Hoss" Radbourne—signed up with the Players League.

Organized baseball used every weapon at its disposal to strike back at this new rival. The owners told fans that the players were aligned with radical unionists. Boston reportedly gave pitcher Clarkson $10,000—five times the average 1889 salary—to desert the brotherhood, while Spalding offered King Kelly a blank check to play for the White Stockings. When propaganda and bankrolls failed, the established league fielded a team of lawyers at courthouses around the country.

The reserve rule was originally adopted by the parties to the National Agreement as a sort of gentlemen's agreement not to compete for their fellow owners' players. When the National League tried to enforce the reserve clause against the Players League, it got nowhere. A federal court in New York City held that the Giants could not keep catcher Ewing from playing for their brotherhood rival because the reserve provisions in his 1889 contract were "merely a contract to make a contract" for 1890 "if the parties agree."[3] The reserve clause was valuable because it gave the Giants a "prior and exclusive" right to negotiate with Ewing that was enforceable against other clubs in organized baseball. But as a basis for an injunction preventing a player from taking the field for a Players League team, Ewing's contract was held "wholly nugatory" because it did not set forth in detail contract terms and conditions (including salary) for 1890. A party who seeks enforcement of a contract with vague or indefinite terms is really asking the court to fill in the blank spaces in that contract, which is something that courts are reluctant to do.

Other courts objected not only to the indefiniteness of player contracts but also to their one-sidedness, which they referred to as a "lack of mutuality." Owners could release players on ten days' notice, but the reserve clause purported to bind a player to one team for as long as the team wanted him. A New York state court judge expressed disgust at "the spectacle" of the Giants' attempt to enforce "a contract which binds [the player] for a series of years and [the team] for 10 days."[4] The National League spent $15,000 on lawyers' fees in New York alone fighting the Players League, but came away with nothing to show for it.

The Players League won the legal battles, but not the war—in fact, everyone lost money. Both sides agreed to Spalding's suggestion that some Players League teams be merged with existing NL and AA franchises and the rest be dissolved. After a bit of skirmishing over the rights to sign some of the returning Players League stars, the NL and AA merged their sixteen clubs into twelve after the 1891 season, and then signed a new National Agreement with the minor leagues. Players had little choice but to accept the terms offered by the "Baseball Trust," but a few rebelled. Amos Rusie won 22 games in 1895 and led the league in strikeouts, but Giants owner Andrew Freedman rewarded him by withholding $600 in fines from his paycheck. Rusie sat out 1896 and then sued the Giants when they invoked their reserve for 1897 as well. The case was settled before trial, with all the National League owners reportedly kicking in a portion of Rusie's $5,000 claim.

As usual the next baseball war set off a spate of contract jumping and legal skirmishes. Over half of the players who suited up for the American League's first season of play were ex-National Leaguers. The older league went to court to try to wrest back a number of their players, most notably Napoleon Lajoie. Lajoie signed a contract with the Phillies in 1900, but refused to be bound by the reserve clause and jumped to the Athletics before the 1901 season. The Pennsylvania Supreme Court held that the Phillies were entitled to an injunction barring the batting champ from playing for the A's.[5] But that decision turned in part on two unusual factors. First, the Phillies' contract reserved Lajoie for only three years and stated what salary would be paid in each of those three years, so it was not simply "a contract to make a contract." Second, Lajoie was a star of the very highest order. Courts are reluctant to order someone to perform a contract for personal services, although they are not at all reluctant to order the defendant to pay monetary damages equal to the harm caused by his nonperformance. Only when the harm cannot be measured in dollars or the contract involves something unique or irreplaceable are injunctions or other nonmonetary remedies granted by a court. The Phillies may have been able to find equally talented replacements for many of their players, but Lajoie—who led the AL in hits, doubles, home runs, runs, RBIs, batting average, and slugging average in 1901— was a unique talent.

The Phillies' legal victory proved hollow. The A's quickly dealt Lajoie to Cleveland. Whenever Cleveland was scheduled to play in Philadelphia, Lajoie stayed far away. His old team's attempts to obtain an injunction from an Ohio court were not successful.

Other National League efforts to hold on to players also failed. Citing a Supreme Court case holding that a contract that could be abandoned on one year's notice was not enforceable, a federal judge dismissed Brooklyn's suit against veteran catcher Deacon McGuire because the team could terminate his contract on only ten days' notice.[6] The judge also questioned whether McGuire's talents were so "unique and peculiar" that Brooklyn could not replace him. McGuire was a fine player, but he was no Nap Lajoie. A state judge in St. Louis went further in a case involving pitcher Jack Harper. Not only was the standard NL player contract lacking in mutuality, according to the court, but it also unreasonably restrained competition in violation of the Sherman Antitrust Act.[7]

After two years of rivalry, the National League agreed to recognize the American League as an equal. The two major leagues used blacklists and boycotts to bring "outlaw" minor leagues to their knees and keep control of players who had the audacity to hold out for higher salaries. When Ty Cobb refused to accept Detroit's 1913 salary offer, the Tigers suspended him. The impasse was broken only when two Georgia congressmen called for a federal investigation. The threat of government action got Ty Cobb a raise, but the players in general benefited much more from organized baseball's war with the Federal League, which no doubt had the National and American Leagues muttering "Two's company, three's a crowd" when the 1914 season opened.

The established leagues didn't even try to use the courts to stop reserve jumpers from playing for the Federal League, but they did seek injunctions against a number of players who jumped, even though they had signed contracts for the upcoming season. The irrepressible Hal Chase signed a 1914 contract with the White Sox, but then moved on to the new league. Teams could release players they didn't want on ten days' notice, so Chase gave Chicago ten days' warning and shuffled off to the Buffalo Federals. A New York state judge agreed with Chase's reasoning and turned down Chicago's request that he order Chase to return.[8] Not only did the contract lack mutuality, said the judge, but organized baseball placed so many limits on the freedom of players that they were left in a state of "*quasi* peonage" that was "contrary to the spirit of American institutions and . . . contrary to the spirit of the Constitution of the United States." The court's opinion did contain some good news for organized baseball: it ruled that baseball did not involve interstate commerce and, therefore, did not violate the Sherman Act.

The judges who heard cases involving contract jumpers occasionally showed real distaste for the whole nasty business. Phillies catcher Bill Killefer signed with the Chicago Federal League club for a substantial increase in salary, but re-signed with the Phillies only 12 days later when they topped Chicago's offer. When the Federals asked a Michigan federal judge to order Killefer not to play for Philadelphia, they were rudely received. Citing the opinions in the Ewing, Ward, and McGuire cases, Judge Sessions noted that the right of reservation in the Phillies' 1913 contract with Killefer did not bind him for the 1914 season because it was indefinite and lacked mutuality.[9] But he refused to enforce Chicago's contract because it came into court with "unclean hands." Killefer was under a moral, although not a legal obligation to play for Philadelphia in 1914, but Chicago persuaded him to repudiate that obligation. Both teams had "acted wrongfully and in bad faith," and the judge refused to lift a finger to help either one of them. He also let Killefer know what he thought of him, calling him "a person upon whose pledged word little or no reliance can be placed, and who, for gain to himself, neither scruples nor hesitates to disregard and violate his express engagements and agreements." Chicago appealed the decision but was unsuccessful. The Sixth Circuit Court of Appeals agreed with Judge Sessions that none of the parties to these underhanded dealings was deserving of any assistance from the courts.[10]

Knowing that they could not outlast their better-financed rivals, the Federal League owners filed an antitrust suit against organized baseball in Chicago on January 5, 1915. They asked federal Judge Kenesaw Mountain Landis, who had a reputation as a committed trustbuster, to declare the National Agreement's reserve and blacklisting provisions to be unreasonable and illegal restraints on competition. The trial was completed that month, but the Federal League's hopes for a quick verdict in their favor were in vain. The future baseball commissioner pondered the evidence all through the 1915 season, which resulted in another healthy dose of red ink for team owners. After waiting almost a year for Judge Landis to make up his mind, the rival leagues cut a deal. Organized baseball bought some of the Federal League's player contracts and stadiums—in reality, they were buying peace—and the Federals dropped the antitrust suit.

The final deal satisfied everyone except AL president Ban Johnson, who preferred to fight to the death rather than pay his enemies a nickel of tribute, and the Baltimore Federal League club, which wanted to buy an existing major league franchise and move it to Baltimore. Angered by Brooklyn owner Ebbets's scornful description of their city as "one of the worst minor league towns in this country," the Baltimore owners pledged $50,000 to finance a new antitrust suit against organized baseball and the Federal League owners who had sold the league out for a few pieces of silver. When the Department of Justice refused to investigate, Baltimore filed its complaint in federal district court in Washington, D.C., in 1917.

The testimony given at the trial, which didn't begin until March 1919, left little doubt that organized baseball's team owners had agreed to use the reserve clause and blacklisting to maintain tight control over the supply of players and paid the Federal League to go out of business in order to protect their monopoly over professional baseball. The judge's directions to the jury virtually directed a verdict for the plaintiffs. The Baltimore club won $254,000 in damages.

Organized baseball's lawyers immediately appealed the decision. They contended that baseball was not commerce because it involved "personal effort not related to [the] production" of material goods. If baseball did not involve interstate commerce, it was not subject to the Sherman Act or any other federal law. The court of appeals heard oral arguments on October 15, 1920, only three days after the final game of the World Series was played between the Cleveland Indians and the Brooklyn Dodgers. Only a few weeks later, it overturned the lower court's decision in favor of Baltimore.[11] The appellate court first noted that

The transportation in interstate commerce of the players and the paraphernalia used by them was but an incident to the main purpose of the appellants, namely the production of the game. It was for it they were in business— not for the purpose of transferring players, balls, and uniforms . . .

. . . So here, baseball is not commerce, though some of its incidents may be. Suppose a law firm in the city of Washington sends its members to points in different states to try lawsuits; they would travel, and probably carry briefs and records, in interstate commerce. Could it be correctly

said that the firm, in the trial of the lawsuits, was engaged in trade and commerce? Or, take the case of a lecture bureau, which employs persons to deliver lectures before Chautauqua gatherings at points in different states. It would be necessary for the lecturers to travel in interstate commerce, in order that they might fulfill their engagements; but would it not be an unreasonable stretch of the ordinary meaning of the words to say that the bureau was engaged in trade or commerce?

The court of appeals then cited with approval cases holding that those who produce theatrical exhibitions, practice medicine, or launder clothes are not engaged in commerce.

The Baltimore club tried to persuade the United States Supreme Court to reinstate the original verdict in its favor. But Justice Oliver Wendell Holmes, writing for a unanimous Court, upheld the decision of the court of appeals.[12]

[E]xhibitions of base ball . . . are purely state affairs. It is true that, in order to attain for the exhibitions the great popularity that they have achieved, competitions must be arranged between clubs from different cities and States. But the fact that in order to give the exhibitions the League must induce free persons to cross state lines and arrange and pay for their doing so is not enough to change the character of the business . . . [T]he transport is a mere incident, not the essential thing. That to which it is incident, the exhibition, although made for money would not be called trade or commerce in the commonly accepted use of those words. As it is put by the defendants, personal effort, not related to production, is not a subject of commerce. That which in its consummation is not commerce does not become commerce among the States because the transportation that we have mentioned takes place. To repeat the illustrations given by the Court below, a firm of lawyers sending out a member to argue a case, or the Chautauqua lecture bureau sending out lecturers, does not engage in such commerce because the lawyer or lecturer goes to another State.

Only a year later, the Court ruled that a company that presented vaudeville shows in cities around the country was, unlike major league baseball, engaged in interstate commerce.[13] Justice Holmes explained the different outcomes in the two cases by pointing to the difference in "the degree of interstate activity" in baseball games and vaudeville shows, but his reasoning is unconvincing.

The next challenge to organized baseball's hegemony came a quarter century later from Don Jorge Pasqual, the millionaire organizer of the Mexican League, who lured 18 major leaguers south of the border in 1946. In August of that year, the owners amended their Rule 15 to provide that any player who jumped to the new league would be ineligible to return to organized baseball for five years. The Cubs' general manager, who proposed the amendment, said that the prospect of being blacklisted for five years "will do a lot more to discourage Stan Musial from going to Mexico next winter than any suits we may file on the reserve clause."

The Rule 15 blacklist stemmed the southward flow of players. Commissioner A. B. "Happy" Chandler refused to reinstate the players who returned to the states in 1947. Catcher Mickey Owen was reduced to managing a semipro club in Winner, South Dakota, while several other Mexican League refugees signed with Cuban clubs.

When blacklisted outfielder Danny Gardella filed an antitrust complaint against organized baseball, a federal district judge in New York noted the "clear trend toward a broader conception of what constitutes interstate commerce" than had existed when *Federal Baseball Club of Baltimore* was decided over 25 years earlier, but felt bound to follow the Supreme Court's decision in that case.[14] But in February 1949 a federal court of appeals voted 2–1 to reverse the district court's dismissal of Gardella's complaint.[15] Judge Learned Hand distinguished *Federal Baseball* by emphasizing the importance to modern-day baseball of interstate radio and television broadcasts of major league games. Judge Frank's separate opinion strongly condemned the reserve system.

For the "reserve clause," as has been observed, results in something resembling peonage of the baseball player . . . Although many courts have refused to enforce the "reserve" clause, yet severe and practically efficacious extralegal penalties are imposed for violation. The most extreme of these penalties is the blacklisting of the player so that no club in organized baseball will hire him . . . The violator may perhaps become a . . . bartender or a street-sweeper, but his chances of ever playing baseball are exceedingly slim.

Gardella's victory was not a final one—it simply allowed him the opportunity to prove his allegations in a trial. Former Cardinals Fred Martin, Max Lanier, and Lou Klein filed a separate suit, and all four players asked the district court to order their immediate reinstatement pending the outcome of the trials, but the court declined to do so.[16] Faced with the prospect of spending the 1949 season in a courtroom rather than on a baseball field, the players were receptive to baseball's offer to settle the case. Commissioner Chandler later characterized his reinstatement of the four "good kids" who had "said they were sorry" for jumping their reserves as inspired by his desire to "temper justice with mercy." But the court of appeals decision—and Judge Frank's sentiments in particular— no doubt had an effect too. Gardella, who had been working as a hospital orderly after returning from Mexico, was reportedly given $60,000 to drop his case.

Subsequent litigation and congressional inquiries kept baseball's attorneys busy in the 1950s. Organized baseball was the defendant in eight pending antitrust suits when it sought relief from Congress in 1951. At its behest three separate bills that would have granted all professional sports leagues a complete exemption from the antitrust laws were introduced in the House of Representatives that year. After lengthy hearings, Congressman Emanuel Celler's Subcommittee on the Study of Monopoly Power recommended that the bills not be passed, and none of them were. The Celler Subcommittee did not favor blanket antitrust immunity, but did conclude that professional baseball could not operate successfully without some form of the reserve clause.[17]

After the Gardella decision, organized baseball's lawyers and the Subcommittee assumed that *Federal Base-*

ball was no longer good law. But the Supreme Court surprised them in 1953 in *Toolson* v. *New York Yankees.*[18] When Yankee farmhand George Toolson was placed on the ineligible list for refusing to accept a demotion to a lower-classification team, he sued the Yankees. A California federal judge dismissed the case before trial on the basis of *Federal Baseball.* "If [that] case is, as Judge Frank intimates [in his *Gardella* opinion], an 'impotent zombi,'" the judge wrote, "I feel that it is not my duty to so find but that the Supreme Court should so declare."[19] The Ninth Circuit Court of Appeals agreed,[20] and the Supreme Court reaffirmed *Federal Baseball* in a one-paragraph opinion.

In Federal Baseball . . . *this Court held that . . . professional baseball . . . was not within the scope of the federal antitrust laws. Congress has had the ruling under consideration but has not seen fit to bring such business under these laws by legislation having prospective effect. . . . The present cases ask us to overrule the prior decision, and, with retrospective effect, hold the [antitrust laws] applicable. We think that if there are evils in this field which now warrant application to it of the antitrust laws it should be by legislation. Without re-examination of the underlying issues, the judgments below are affirmed on the authority of* Federal Baseball . . .

The Court's conclusion that "Congress has had the ruling under consideration but has not seen fit to bring [baseball] under [the antitrust] laws by legislation" is questionable. The Celler Subcommittee report concluded that given the *Gardella* decision and cases subsequent to *Federal Baseball,* which took a broader view of what constituted interstate commerce, "it may be seriously doubted whether baseball should now be regarded as exempt from the antitrust laws." If Congress assumed that baseball was subject to the antitrust laws, its failure to act on bills granting an antitrust exemption was evidence that it did not intend baseball to be exempt—which was just the opposite of what the Court said in *Toolson.*

The next few years saw the Supreme Court hold that professional boxing and football did not share baseball's antitrust immunity. In *Radovich* v. *National Football League,*[21] the Court expressly limited the reach of the *Federal Baseball* precedent to baseball. Three justices dissented from this decision "to put baseball in a class by itself."

Another flurry of congressional activity followed. In 1957 the House Antitrust Subcommittee held fifteen days of hearings on seven different bills, some of which would have exempted all professional sports from antitrust liability. Congressman Celler introduced a bill exempting only those acts that were "reasonably necessary" to maintaining competitive balance and the integrity of sports, but the full House voted to give professional sports leagues a broader although not unlimited exemption. A Senate committee held more hearings in 1958—Casey Stengel, Mickey Mantle, Ted Williams, and Stan Musial testified the day after the All-Star Game was played in nearby Baltimore—but the full Senate never considered the bill. In a 1959 report to the membership, the Major League Baseball Players Association's lawyers said, "There does not seem any doubt that Congress will even-

tually pass a law concerning Baseball's right to continue its reserve clause," but Congress never came any closer to passing comprehensive sports antitrust legislation. Bills were introduced year after year—attempts to organize a third major league, franchise moves, and the CBS purchase of the Yankees inspired some of the legislative proposals—but none was enacted.

In 1972 the U.S. Supreme Court upheld *Federal Baseball* once more in *Flood* v. *Kuhn.*[22] When the Cardinals traded Curt Flood to the Phillies after the 1969 season, Flood refused to go. "I am [not] a piece of property to be bought and sold irrespective of my wishes," he wrote to Commissioner Bowie Kuhn. Kuhn refused to declare him a free agent, so Flood hired former Supreme Court Justice and Secretary of Labor Arthur Goldberg and filed suit. The lower court's dismissal of his case was eventually upheld by the Supreme Court. Justice Harry Blackmun's opinion noted that baseball's antitrust immunity was "an anomaly" and "an aberration," but he felt bound by history.

Remedial legislation has been introduced repeatedly in Congress but none has ever been enacted. The Court, accordingly, has concluded that Congress as yet has had no intention to subject baseball's reserve system to the reach of the antitrust statutes . . . If there is any inconsistency or illogic in all this, it is an inconsistency and illogic of long standing that is to be remedied by the Congress and not this Court.

The Court's opinion also noted that state antitrust laws could not apply to baseball. Flood's career had ended by the time the Supreme Court issued its decision. After sitting out the 1970 season, he was traded to the Senators in 1971, but retired after hitting only .200 in 13 games.

It seems unlikely that the Court would reach a different result if a similar antitrust case were presented to it today. But does baseball's antitrust exemption really matter today? The players' union has managed to win free agency, salary arbitration, and limits on trades without a player's consent through collective bargaining or arbitration. After two arbitrators' decisions that the owners violated the collective-bargaining agreement by failing to bid for free agents like Kirk Gibson and Tim Raines after the 1985 and 1986 seasons, the players seem to be in the catbird seat. But what if the baseball owners choose to hang as tough as the football owners did in the 1987 strike? The courts have held that neither labor nor management can be sued under the antitrust laws over provisions in a collective-bargaining agreement, even if those provisions are clearly anticompetitive. The football players are litigating whether the labor exemption applies after a union contract has expired. But even if they win, baseball's unique antitrust exemption might still serve as a shield for the baseball owners if the players ever file a similar suit.

Baseball's exemption might protect it from the players but not from other parties who have less connection to the on-the-field aspects of the business of baseball. For example, an anticompetitive owner conspiracy involving stadium concession or parking revenues might not be exempt.

But what if a maverick owner—say, Ted Turner—tried to move his team to another city without the approval of

his peers? Al Davis and Bob Irsay could move the Raiders and Colts to greener pastures because the antitrust laws prevent other NFL owners from agreeing to boycott them or take other punitive action. While there is some authority for the proposition that baseball's antitrust exemption is broad enough to cover that kind of situation, a court that was uncomfortable with the reasoning of *Federal Baseball* and its progeny could justify a different outcome in such a case much more easily than in a case involving free agency or other player-management disputes.

As noted above, the Supreme Court has referred to baseball's antitrust immunity as an "exception," an "anomaly," and an "aberration." According to another federal court, baseball's system of governance—under which the Commissioner has broad authority to prevent or remedy acts that are contrary, in his view, to the best interests of baseball—"is equally an exception, anomaly, and aberration."[23]

The 1921 Major League Agreement, which created the Office of the Commissioner, contained virtually no limits on the Commissioner's authority because Judge Landis refused to accept the job unless he was given carte blanche. The current version of that agreement provides that "[t]he functions of the Commissioner shall be . . . to investigate . . . any act, transaction, or practice . . . not in the best interests of the national game of Baseball" and "to determine . . . what preventive, remedial, or punitive action is appropriate . . . and to take such action."[24] The agreement also states that the club owners agree to be bound by the Commissioner's decisions, and "waive such right of recourse to the courts as would otherwise have existed in their favor."[25]

Perhaps former Oakland A's owner Charles O. Finley should have read that language more carefully before he signed the Major League Agreement. When Finley tried to sell Joe Rudi and Rollie Fingers to the Red Sox and Vida Blue to the Yankees just before the 1976 trading deadline, Commissioner Kuhn quickly nullified the transactions as "inconsistent with the best interests of baseball, the integrity of the game, and the maintenance of public confidence in it." Finley's lawyers tried to persuade a federal judge that Kuhn's action exceeded his authority, but the judge ruled that Kuhn's authority to void player transactions was not limited to cases involving rules violations or moral turpitude, as Finley argued. A federal appeals court later upheld that decision,[26] and also noted that the "waiver of recourse" provision quoted above kept Finley from going to court to challenge Kuhn's ruling unless he could show that the Major League Agreement was inconsistent with state or federal law or that the procedures followed by Kuhn "failed to follow the basic rudiments of due process of law."[27]

Pete Rose's 1989 lawsuit against A. Bartlett Giamatti relied on just that argument—that Rose was being denied the right to a fair hearing by an unbiased decisionmaker. When Rose asked a state court judge to issue an injunction stopping the Commissioner's pending disciplinary proceeding, Giamatti's lawyers filed a motion to remove the case to federal court. In most cases, state courts have jurisdiction if one or both of the parties to the lawsuit are citizens of that state; if the plaintiff and defendant are citizens of different states, federal courts usually have jurisdiction to hear the case. Because Rose was a citizen of Ohio and Giamatti was a citizen of New York, Giamatti was able to remove the case from the Ohio state court—which might favor Ohioans over New Yorkers—to a federal court.[28] After losing that legal skirmish, Rose withdrew his lawsuit and agreed to be suspended indefinitely from baseball, so the court never ruled on the merits of Rose's claim that the Commissioner was not treating him fairly.

[1]*Allegheny Base-ball Club* v. *Bennett*, 14 Fed. 257 (C.C.W.D. Pa., 1882).

[2]*St. Louis Athletic Ass'n* v. *Mullane*, No. 3642 (C.C.S.D. Ohio, May 13, 1884). Reprinted in *Sporting Life*, May 21, 1884, p.2, col.1.

[3]*Metropolitan Exhibition Co.* v. *Ewing*, 42 Fed. 198 (C.C.S.D. N.Y. 1890).

[4]*Metropolitan Exhibition Co.* v. *Ward*, 24 Abb.N.C. 414 (1890).

[5]*Philadelphia Base Ball Club* v. *Lajoie*, 51 Atl. 973 (Pa. S. Ct. 1902).

[6]*Brooklyn Baseball Club* v. *McGuire*, 116 Fed. 783 (C.C.E.D. Pa. 1902).

[7]*American Base Ball & Athletic Exhibition Co. of St. Louis* v. *Harper*, 54 Cent. L.J. 449 (St. Louis Cir. Ct. 1902).

[8]*American League Baseball Club of Chicago* v. *Chase*, 86 Misc. 441, 149 N.Y. Supp. 6 (Sup. Ct. 1914).

[9]*Weeghman* v. *Killefer*, 214 Fed. 168 (W.D. Mich. 1914).

[10]*Weeghman* v. *Killefer*, 215 Fed. 289 (6th Cir. 1914).

[11]*National League of Professional Baseball Clubs* v. *Federal Baseball Club of Baltimore*, 269 Fed. 681 (D.C. Cir. 1921).

[12]*Federal Baseball Club of Baltimore* v. *National League of Professional Baseball Clubs*, 259 U.S. 200 (1922).

[13]*Hart* v. *Keith Vaudeville Exchange*, 262 U.S. 271 (1923).

[14]*Gardella* v. *Chandler*, 79 F.Supp. 260 (S.D.N.Y. 1948).

[15]*Gardella* v. *Chandler*, 172 F.2d 402 (2d Cir. 1949).

[16]*Martin* v. *Chandler*, 174 F.2d 917 (2d. Cir. 1949); *Gardella* v. *Chandler*, 174 F.2d 919 (2d. Cir. 1949).

[17]H.R. Rep. 2002, 82d Cong., 2d Sess. 228–32 (1952).

[18]346 U.S. 356 (1953).

[19]*Toolson* v. *New York Yankees*, 101 F.Supp. 93 (S.D. Cal. 1951).

[20]200 F.2d 198 (9th Cir. 1952).

[21]358 U.S. 445 (1957).

[22]407 U.S. 258 (1972).

[23]*Charles O. Finley & Co., Inc.* v. *Kuhn*, 569 F.2d 527, 537 (1978).

[24]Major League Agreement, Art. I, Sec. 2.

[25]Id. at Art. VII, Sec. 2.

[26]*Finley* v. *Kuhn*, 569 F.2d 527 (1978).

[27]Id. at 544.

[28]*Rose* v. *Giamatti*, 721 F.Supp. 906 (1989).

## CHAPTER 28

Free Agency and Trades

Eliot Cohen

Before and after the advent of free agency, baseball team owners have viewed unimpeded movement for players as destabilizing. The reserve clause, written in the 1880s, bound players to teams for life, made them chattel, and promoted a tradition of player trading that fueled baseball interest and debate, in and out of season. Traditionalist doomsayers predicted that free agency, as prompted by the ruling arbitrator Peter Seitz in the 1975 cases of Andy Messersmith and Dave McNally, would ruin the fine art of baseball trading, not to mention the game itself, just as divisional play and the League Championship Series were supposed to kill the World Series.

Owners and fans had no reason to fear change. The post–Seitz free agent system has added new dimensions to baseball's trading game, as well as enhancing the game's competitive balance on the field and redistributing income. With players free to change teams after six years in the big leagues, teams had a new option for improving their rosters. The system also presented front offices with whole new reasons to trade players.

Let's look back at 1976. Free agency had barely come into being, and no baseball executive yet feared arbitration. Oakland A's owner Charles O. Finley was trying to sell his best players who could become free agents to the highest bidder. Finley, father of postseason night baseball, again displayed his near-infallible baseball instincts, pioneering what owners now do routinely.

Dire predictions of how the richest teams would get the best players and destroy the game's competitive balance under free agency conveniently ignored nearly a century of baseball history. Modern free agency didn't alter the flow of talent from the financially strapped teams to the better-off ones; it just altered the direction of the cash. The money went to the player in the form of salary instead of to his former team as the purchase price. From the dawn of the professional game, talent has moved from the strapped teams to the affluent ones. It was no coincidence that dynasties of the era before the amateur draft were built by the wealthy teams. The dirty little secret of the John J. McGraw New York Giants wasn't their connection to corrupt Tammany Hall politicians, but their wealth, which enabled them to search deeper for talent, sign more prospects, buy more talent from independent minor league operators, and pay the players they needed. Winning meant more revenue, which helped successful teams remain successful.

The next dynasty, the New York Yankees, shared that same big market—and for a time their home field—with the Giants. The Bronx dynasty began when Boston Red Sox owner Harry Frazee sold his stars, most notably Babe Ruth, to the Yanks to finance his theatrical ventures. Frazee's follies merely continued a Red Sox tradition; his predecessor, Joseph Lannin, sold Tris Speaker to Cleveland. Then, as now, salaries also mattered. Connie Mack twice broke up multiple–World Champion Philadelphia Athletics teams because they grew too costly. After all, the 1914 A's featured the $100,000 infield.

The St. Louis Cardinals under Branch Rickey developed the farm system as an antidote to wealthy teams' player purchases. His Cardinals joined the ranks of the rich by selling farm system excesses to other teams and became the dominant National League team between the wars.

Even though talent flowed to the richest teams in the past and today, teams have never been able to buy championships outright. After Tom Yawkey purchased the Red Sox in 1933, the team became renowned for its generosity to players and actively participated in the second breakup of the Athletics, acquiring stars such as Lefty Grove and Jimmy Foxx. Still, during six decades of Yawkey ownership, the Red Sox failed to duplicate their 1918 world championship. Similarly the Yankees of the 1980s had the best overall won-lost record of that decade, thanks in part to profligate free agent spending under owner George Steinbrenner, but failed to win a title except for the truncated 1981 season. The Mets and Dodgers, the teams with the National League's highest payrolls in 1992, inflated by free agent spending, were awful. Successful franchises have, almost to a rule, blended home-grown talent with players acquired from other teams, either through trades or free agent signings. Wise spending beats free spending every time.

The free agent rule change having the greatest impact on competition was the institution of the amateur draft in 1965. Prior to the draft, teams competed for prospects according to the golden rule—whoever has the gold rules. The pool of amateur players was baseball's first free market, with all teams competing equally to sign players and bind them to organizations for life through the reserve clause. Richer teams could outbid rivals for top prospects, even after bonus baby restrictions forced teams to keep high priced signees on the major league roster. Just as important as contract money, richer teams could outscout others, digging deeper to find talent and bird-dogging harder to build relationships with teenaged prospects and their families that were often as crucial to signings as money. The amateur draft, with the worst teams picking first, eliminated a prospect's right to choose his team, but it helped dismantle the dynasties by equalizing opportunities to acquire the best young talent. That foundation gave teams better players to keep and to trade.

The other boost to competitiveness came with major league free agency. The team with the best players could no longer hold on to them forever. After six full years of major league service, a player not under contract could offer his services in a free market, causing salaries to soar. Even collusion among owners following the 1985, 1986, and 1987 seasons failed to destroy the system and caused only a temporary pause in the dizzying pace of salary escalation. A record number of free agents after the 1992 season may have given owners a more useful lesson in controlling salaries. Scarcity has made multi-millionaires out of marginal players such as Danny Darwin, Matt Young, and Franklin Stubbs because they were the best available at their positions in that season's particular free agent class. When it became apparent that the reserve clause would fall, Finley, for one, proposed letting every player become a free agent every year. According to Finley, and most economists, in a free market, increased supply should lower prices.

Whether by design or happy accident, the system gave players their first taste of freedom at or near the peaks of their careers. Age, not sloth, suggests they'll likely earn less money for less output after signing lucrative free agent contracts. Even with salary arbitration pushing up their salaries after three years of major league service, young players generally deliver better value for salary dollars than veterans past their sixth big league season.

That fact of life may have contributed to team success cycles replacing the dynasties of old. As in the past, a team near the top will be most inclined to acquire current stars for a piece of their future, either by signing free agents or trading prospects. In most cases, their flow of minor league talent eventually dries up, their star players age, and their payroll is higher than their winning percentage, as happened to the Pittsburgh Pirates of the mid-1980s. Under General Manager Syd Thrift, after letting free agent Dave Parker walk, they traded away their aging stars and their salaries for unproven talent: John Candelaria, Al Holland and George Hendrick for Pat Clements, Bob Kipper and Mike Brown; Rick Rhoden, plus Clements and Cecilio Guante, for future Cy Young–winner Doug Drabek, Brian Fisher, and Logan Easley; Tony Pena for Andy Van Slyke, Mike LaValliere, and Mike Dunne. With smart drafts, including Barry Bonds (but Jeff King instead of Greg Swindell), and a terrific manager in Jim Leyland, they went—in the space of four seasons—from three straight last place finishes to the first of three straight division championships. Hit by free agency losses and economically inspired trades, the cycle appears to be spinning downward again as the mid-nineties approach. The Houston Astros, winner of the NL West in 1986, began their rebuilding process in earnest after the 1990 season, and after a last place finish in 1991, rebounded to .500 in 1992.

Even though major league free agency offers a method to acquire players without giving up one in return (under the current rules, signing a quality free agent costs a draft choice, so the bill comes due years later) trades remain the lifeblood of winning—and losing—teams, just as they have for over a century. There's rarely been a pennant winner without an important player from another organization, from Bob Carruthers and Dave Foutz of the 1889 Brooklyn Bridegrooms to David Cone of the 1992 Toronto Blue Jays. If not for trades, modern free agency may not have come into being. The 1969 trade of Curt Flood from St. Louis to Philadelphia (with Tim McCarver, Joe Hoerner, and Byron Browne for Dick Allen, Cookie Rojas, and Jerry Johnson; Philadelphia received Willie Montanez when Flood refused to report) began the players' march toward freedom, even though Flood lost his lawsuit against the reserve clause.

Free agency has actually lubricated the trade market. Impending free agency has created a new reason to trade a player. General managers can either risk letting a potential free agent walk at the end of the season, or trade him for something they want. When he owned the Chicago White Sox for the second time at the dawn of the free agent era, Bill Veeck pioneered the rent-a-player concept, acquiring players a year away from free agency, knowing he couldn't afford to sign them for long term deals. The Cone trade—in which the Toronto Blue Jays leased the Mets pitcher for forty days plus the postseason—illustrates the evolution of the art, and how much potential free agency devalues the player. For a twenty-nine-year-old pitcher en route to a third straight National League strikeout title with the best stuff in the game this side of Roger Clemens, the Mets received only unproven infielder Jeff Kent and marginal prospect Ryan Thompson.

The biggest blockbuster of 1992, in which the Oakland A's traded Jose Canseco for Ruben Sierra, plus pitchers Jeff Russell and Bobby Witt, was also inspired by free agency and its side effect, big salaries. The A's were obligated to pay Canseco nearly $15 million through the 1995 season. So, in addition to adding a couple of pitchers for the stretch drive, the A's lopped off a long term commitment, giving them time to assess whether salaries were indeed heading downward.

Some observers might cite these deals as proof of how the game has changed. Yet salaries inflated by the Federal League led to the breakup of the A's champions of the 1910s and the sale of Tris Speaker. Trades have always been a factor in the useful life of a player, which in the past meant solely age, rather than including today's contract considerations. The rules have changed and the possibilities have grown, but the sizzle of players changing teams—by their choice or that of their bosses—remains a baseball staple.

## CHAPTER 29

Baseball Commissioners

A. D. Suehsdorf

From the beginning, organized baseball has been controlled by the owners of the major league clubs. Acting in concert and accountable only to themselves, they have parceled out the franchises, built the grandstands, set the ticket prices, assembled the players, written the game's rules, defined league structure and operation, dominated the minor league dependencies, and, until recent times, bound their players absolutely through the reserve clause written into every contract. Virtually the only restraint on this monopoly power has been fear of alienating the fans from whom all profit flows by actions or circumstances threatening confidence in the honesty and integrity of the game. Even this, on occasion, has been put at risk.

Owner power has been matched by owner intractability. Whatever their virtues as individuals, baseball owners in the aggregate through much of their history have been quarrelsome, devious, inclined to factional fights, and to circumventing, if not subverting, the rules of their own National Agreement under which all baseball is expected to operate. In part this has resulted from their paradoxical position as cooperative competitors, in part from the entrepreneur's traditional resistance to authority.

During the quarter century of National League supremacy (1876-1900), it was of little consequence that the league presidents were figureheads and the owners' squabbles flagrant. But when Ban Johnson's American League established itself as an equal in 1901—the first and only competitor ever to do so—it became imperative to create an agency empowered to arbitrate matters between the still-touchy partners and to present a facade of unity to the outside world.

The result was the National Commission of 1903: the two league presidents, Ban Johnson of the American League and Harry Pulliam of the National, and August "Garry" Herrmann, president of the Cincinnati Reds, as unsalaried chairman. The National League's edge was more apparent than real. *Gemütlich* Garry was an old friend of Ban's and had won regard in both leagues for his efforts in mediating peace between them. Further, while Herrmann and Johnson served all seventeen years of the Commission's life, the National League had four presidents, breaks in continuity that diminished its role. And in any event the triumvirate was dominated by the dynamic Johnson, whose wit, energy, and administrative skill soon made him the acknowledged "Czar of Baseball."

Basically, the Commission's responsibility was interpretation and enforcement of the National Agreement, and punishment of violations by fines and suspensions. Neither the minor leagues nor the players were officially represented. The Commission assumed protection of their rights in grievances against individual clubs or the major leagues, although its

concern was paternalistic at best. Intra-league matters were left to the appropriate president and his board of directors.

Overall, historians give the Commission marks of fair to good for its efforts. The first twelve years of its existence were prosperous, relatively harmonious, and progressive insofar as they consolidated baseball as the national pastime. The final five were a time of anger, turmoil, and disruption.

Strain was inherent, for the concept of the National Commission was fundamentally flawed. League presidents, by their nature, could not view intra- and inter-league affairs equally. The club owners of each league expected the loyalty of their Commission representative and were infuriated when justice or equity required a decision that went against them. It also was impossible to select a neutral chairman from among the owners themselves, yet the money men were never pleased to do the bidding of commissioners who had no financial stake in the game.

In external affairs the Commission did reasonably well. Dealings with the Base Ball Players Fraternity (1912-17), while accompanied by bluster and stonewalling, were on the whole conducted fairly and brought about some improvements in player contracts. It contributed to settlement of the Federal League uprising and to keeping the game going during World War I.

Internally, it lacked the heart to confront long-range baseball problems, such as gambling, which was widespread in and around ballparks, and, in consequence, an undercurrent of crooked players, bribe offers, and thrown games. Investigations were tentative, conclusions irresolute: A coat of whitewash, or passing the buck to the league or teams concerned, while sighing with relief that no one outside baseball was the wiser.

As men of their time, the Commissioners shared proprietors' beliefs in the sanctity of property and the subservience of labor, and rigorously upheld the reserve and ten-day clauses, while assiduously avoiding any legal test of their validity. Yet despite this tilt toward their employers, they showed their best side in the justice of many difficult decisions affecting the commerce in players.

Under the National Agreement players had the right to advance as far and as fast as their talents permitted. Contrarily, they were not to be "farmed" or "covered up" or otherwise hindered from pursuing this goal. The Agreement was inspired less by a regard for players than by assurance of an open market for owners, so that by offering opportunity to baseball's best prospects the clubs would enjoy a competitive balance and hold fan interest. Yet for the owners a gentleman's agreement was always more compelling than the national one. They connived with each other to diddle the draft, waiver, and option processes, and, incidentally, to limit

salaries and rosters, hold up the pay of injured players, and burden released players with the travel costs of getting wherever they were being sent. Such sharp practice and cheeseparing economies were considered shrewd business, and the Commission, when it did not agree with them, was hard put to remedy any but the most egregious injustices.

Where it was most at risk was in settling conflicting claims to players—viz., Sisler to the Browns instead of the Pirates, Quinn to the Yankees, not the White Sox. These interclub fights were bitter and the losers nursed their grievances for years. Cumulatively, they were serious enough to topple the Commission. The last straw was President Johnson's suspension of Carl Mays in mid-1919. Having gone AWOL from the Red Sox, the pitcher was traded to New York in defiance of Ban's order that no deal be made until Mays had been disciplined. This enraged both clubs, as well as long-simmering malcontents in both leagues who had had enough of Ban, whether as president, commissioner, or czar. The Yankees got the suspension overturned in court. The American League drastically reduced Ban's authority by appointing a two-owner committee to review all but the most minor fines and suspensions. And the National League, long exasperated with Herrmann for being Johnson's docile creature, forced him to resign. Johnson, having lost his customary American League backing, was powerless to keep Garry in office, although he bullheadedly blocked the election of a new Commission chairman. As rancor led to impasse, the baseball establishment drifted.

To prod the owners out of their rut, Albert D. Lasker, a prominent Chicago advertising man and a substantial stockholder in the Cubs, proposed a new commission of three distinguished, disinterested public figures with "unreviewable authority" over owners, players, and franchises. Wearied as they were of bosses from within the ranks, the magnates did not welcome supervision by outsiders as an improvement. While they maundered, the Black Sox scandal broke.

Horrified, if not surprised, by this corruption of their enterprise, the owners took dramatic action to restore public confidence in the game. Although splintered by in-house controversy and intrigue, they mustered a majority vote to scrap the National Agreement and create a new three-man commission. Shortly after a Grand Jury heard evidence of the 1919 World Series fix, they named Kenesaw Mountain Landis as their principal Commissioner.

Then 53, Landis had been a Federal district court judge for fifteen years. He was meagerly educated, narrow in vision, and simplistic in his judicial decisions, many of which were overturned on appeal. Nonetheless, with his craggy face, dramatic shock of white hair, and flamboyant manner, not to mention an easily aroused sense of outrage, he had the public image of a fierce but twinkly eyed man of rectitude. The owners were certain he saw things their way. In 1915, he had delayed action on the Federal League's antitrust suit against the majors until a negotiated settlement could be reached and the need for a decision was past, thus avoiding once again a legal test of baseball's monopoly status. To the press and public, he had the common touch of a lifelong affection for the Cubs and, to all appearances, the backbone to clean up baseball's mess.

Commissioner Landis took office in January, 1921 (although not surrendering his seat on the Federal bench for another year). His mandate was to deal as he saw fit with anything deemed "detrimental" to baseball. His powers were written into a new National Agreement and incorporated in player contracts. His decisions and penalties were to be binding. There could be no recourse to the courts and no public criticism. Even the most tentative objections were met by threats of resignation before which the owners invariably quailed.

Landis relished the free hand he had demanded and got. The appointment of associate commissioners was forgotten, and even as advisers, the two league presidents—Johnson and John A. Heydler—generally were ignored.

The eight Black Sox were first to feel the Commissioner's wrath. Whatever the courts might determine, in Judge Landis's eyes their conduct had been atrociously detrimental to baseball and he banned them all, plus Joe Gedeon, who had "guilty knowledge," for life.

Player delinquency was a continuing embarrassment. Old villainies surfaced and new ones occurred. Over the next several years six more players were expelled and many others declared ineligible for varying periods. Landis's sweeping actions often were inconsistent, arbitrary, and unfair. Some rascals escaped scrutiny. Some great stars were acquitted on their own say-so. A few culprits were severely punished for trifles. Benny Kauff, indicted for, but acquitted of, auto theft, was ruled permanently ineligible because Landis decided he was probably guilty. Ray Fisher was blacklisted without explanation, hearing, or appeal, evidently for negotiating with an "outlaw" club. Petitions for reinstatement of such sinners as Buck Weaver were refused or went unanswered.

Landis opposed all forms of gambling—horse racing especially—and tried to keep gamblers out of the ballparks, but with indifferent success. He failed to act against the known gambling connections of Charles Stoneham of the Giants; the racing stables of Frank Navin of Detroit, or the betting proclivities of such dedicated horse players as John McGraw and Rogers Hornsby.

Still, by his vehemence and persistence he sent a clear message to baseball that crooks and cheats would not be tolerated, and he persuaded Americans that he was making their game honest again.

For all his harshness, he acted to protect the rights of players and professed sympathetic interest in them. He cracked down on cover-ups and other management maneuvering that impeded players' progress, although here, too, he was ever unpredictable. In two cover-up cases six months apart, he made the Indians turn Tommy Henrich loose, while allowing them to keep Bob Feller.

Similarly, he favored an unrestricted draft and fought a losing battle against the farm system, most prominently in skirmishes with Branch Rickey, farming's principal architect. In 1938, he made free agents of 91 Cardinal farmhands unfairly sequestered, and in 1940 another 91 young Tigers. Landis's resistance to the farm system began soon after he was installed as Commissioner and it remained a central issue of his many years in office. Whether farming killed minor league ball or kept it alive, it was an idea whose time had come, and Landis alienated many owners by his efforts to stamp it out.

The Judge loved to preside at the World Series each year. As an interleague affair, it always had been a National Commission responsibility, but Landis had his own czarist inclinations and went beyond scheduling, umpires, and distribution of receipts to make the event uniquely his own. He reduced the format from nine games to seven, negotiated the first

contracts for radio broadcasting, and, as he was always in attendance with his chin on the railing of a front-row box, he usurped the umpires' authority to call a game or oust a player—most notably the removal of Ducky Medwick in 1934.

It did not take the owners long to regret their hasty and comprehensive surrender of power. By the mid-1920s they were grumbling at Landis's interference in player transactions, and by 1932 voted limits on his jurisdiction in this area. The opprobrium once reserved for Ban Johnson was now applied to Landis, but stopped short of calling his bluff about quitting. Capricious, high-handed, and profane as he was, he was also an unassailable national institution. Among his last acts was the legitimate but Draconian expulsion of owner William D. Cox for betting on his Philadelphia Phillies. Frail and ill as his term reached 24 years, the Judge still was the only logical candidate for Commissioner on the owners' horizon. He died at 78 in 1944 and was elected to baseball's Hall of Fame.

Rid of the tyrant at last, the magnates threw off a few of their shackles. They restricted the detrimental-to-baseball authority by exempting from it all their major league rules and any action taken in compliance with them. They wiped out the gag that prohibited criticizing a Commissioner's ruling, or going to court to block it. And they changed the margin for approval of an interleague action from a simple majority to three quarters of the clubs of each league.

They then chose 47-year-old Senator Albert B. "Happy" Chandler of Kentucky as Landis's successor. It was a surprise appointment engineered by Larry MacPhail, then a Yankee owner, who brought his colleagues, divided and squabbling as usual, to a decision.

A greater contrast to Landis would have been hard to find. Happy was the prototypical politico: shrewd, ebullient, folksy, and smarter than he seemed. The owners obviously wanted a glad-handing good-will ambassador for baseball and a lightweight boss for themselves. They got the first, but not the second. Although rather too exuberant and good ol' boy for the New York press, which thought him foolish and began to ride him hard, Happy was his own man. He bluntly told his new employers that they did not own baseball, that it was America's game and would remain so as long as fans did not think it "a bloody business" run by profiteers. This did not sit well in baseball's councils; nor did his efforts to improve wages and working conditions for umpires and his support of benefits for players, such as a minimum wage ($5,000!), a 25 percent limit on salary cuts, and a pension plan to be funded by a percentage of the receipts from television and radio broadcasts of the World Series.

If the owners were displeased, they knew they were in a weak position from which to object. In 1946, the upstart Mexican League was an enticing alternative to players uncertain about the level and stability of their baseball earnings.

Chandler met the Mexican League threat by suspending 18 jumpers for five years (though granting amnesty in 1949, when the insurrection failed). Several of the disgruntled jumpers thereupon filed suits challenging the sacred reserve clause, which was a profound worry to the owners until the clubs involved persuaded the plaintiffs to withdraw. Still, Chandler was seen as having invited an unnecessary risk.

The most significant event of his regime was the integration of the major leagues by Brooklyn's introduction of Jackie Robinson; the most sensational was the one-year suspension of Brooklyn's manager, Leo Durocher, both in April 1947.

While not a prime mover in Robinson's arrival, Happy was openly and genuinely supportive of Branch Rickey's stunning assault on the game's long-standing color barrier. Unlike Landis, who addressed the matter only obliquely—in blocking Bill Veeck's attempt to buy the Phils and recruit Negro Leaguers for them—Chandler spoke forthrightly in favor of integration.

Durocher's suspension was brought on specifically by an unseemly confrontation between Leo and Larry MacPhail, but it appeared to stem from official exasperation with an accumulation of Durocher scrapes, altercations, dubious associations, on-field rows, and marital difficulties, all of which presumably added up to that convenient catchall, "conduct detrimental to baseball." It was the stiffest penalty ever levied against a manager.

Unfortunately, having pronounced judgment without citing the particulars on which it was based, Chandler enforced silence on all parties and refused to discuss it himself. In the confusion and controversy which followed, it was never made clear whether the suspension "year" was the duration of the baseball season or the calendar's twelve months, whether a suspended manager's contract was valid, and whether, at suspension's end, he could be rehired. Far from a salutary punishment, *l'affaire* Durocher made a martyr of Leo and lost face for Happy.

Throughout his term, the Commissioner was confronted by the ineradicable problems of owner manipulation of baseball rules and of inappropriate association with racing or gambling interests. In a remarkable burst of confidence, Alva Bradley of the Indians confessed blandly to generalized owner cheating, and Chandler encountered enough violations of the option process and premature signing of high school prospects to believe him.

As always, investigations of possible wrong-doing made no friends, and adverse decisions always made enemies. Hearing rumbles of dissatisfaction before the winter meetings of 1950, the penultimate year in which, by custom, reelection of the Commissioner would be considered, Happy asked for a vote of confidence. Nine were for, seven against—three short of the mandatory three quarters. Happy resigned, accepting one year's salary as severance. In 1982, he was elected to the Hall of Fame. He died June 15, 1991, age ninety-two.

Ford C. Frick, 56, a one-time "gee-whiz" sportswriter and, since 1934, president of the National League, was picked to replace Happy in 1951. He was a compromise candidate maneuvered into the job by Walter O'Malley of Brooklyn, an emerging power among the magnates.

Now fully recovered from the Landis era, the owners had acquired the complacent, pliable Commissioner most to their liking. In the span of Frick's two seven-year terms, baseball underwent revolutionary changes, not one of them bearing his imprint. He busied himself with administrative detail, pursuing the struggle against gambling, punishing management infractions of baseball rules, and occasionally freeing covered-up minor leaguers. He determined that Roger Maris's 61 homers should have separate mention in the record book because they took 162 games to achieve and, like Landis and Chandler before him, he refused an appeal to reinstate old Buck Weaver of the Black Sox. Beyond that, anything the owners wanted was all right with him.

He presided over an era when commonplace air travel, widening TV markets, and beckoning tax breaks prompted

the Braves, Browns, A's, Giants, and Dodgers to shift their franchises, when talk of a potential third big league was enough to hustle the majors into expanding to 10 clubs each, and when minor leagues were dying from all these invasions of their territories. The character of club ownership was changing from the rough-and-ready old-timers to big-money businessmen or corporations. Congress conducted hearings on baseball's curious exemption from the antitrust laws (though without taking action). Some prominent players were benefiting from exorbitant signing bonuses, while others were looking for greater security and considering unionization. Commissioner Frick saw these as league matters, outside his jurisdiction. In 1965, full of years, he resigned with an election to the Hall of Fame in prospect.

The choice of William D. "Spike" Eckert as Commissioner was a mistake and an embarrassment. A retired Air Force lieutenant general with a distinguished record in World War II, he had not sought the job, but was recommended by a brother officer, Curtis LeMay, bellicose boss of the Strategic Air Command, who refused to be a candidate himself. Spike, an amiable if diffident man, had become a business consultant with fair administrative skills and no knowledge of baseball. He immediately was dubbed "the Unknown Soldier." The owners supported him with four of their number to assist in his major areas of responsibility. Yet his ineptitude was obvious. He was deferential to his owners, limp with his league presidents, and had no awareness of baseball's problems or of the direction it should be headed. He aroused national indignation by failing to cancel games after the assassinations of Martin Luther King and Robert Kennedy.

In December 1968, with an organized players' strike in prospect, he was fired. As balm, he continued to receive his salary until his death in 1971. For this uncomfortable interlude, the owners had no one to blame but themselves.

When elected in 1969, Bowie Kuhn was baseball's youngest (42), tallest (six-five), and biggest (240 pounds) Commissioner ever. He had worked the Griffith Stadium scoreboard as a youth, graduated Princeton, and was well-acquainted with baseball through his New York law firm which had the National League as a client.

Kuhn's first act was to get negotiations between the Major League Players Association and the owner's Player Relations Committee, which had stalled over the terms of a pension package, moving again. He helped bring about a successful settlement which saved the 1969 season from the disruption of a player strike.

A positive man, though in his own words a bit stiff-necked and starchy, Kuhn believed that the still-extraordinary powers of the Commissioner had been granted in order to be used. Furthermore, the owners had decided that their governance needed "restructuring," and charged him with developing a plan for more efficient administration of their business. Kuhn and an ad hoc committee of baseball executives and management experts proposed a further concentration of power in the Commissioner's office. The plan was utterly rejected. Many owners felt that, with more lines on the organization chart leading to the Commissioner, they would be surrendering control of their franchises.

With many important areas of baseball business excluded from his purview, Kuhn resumed his role as persuader, counselor, and positive influence. He was never more than that in the fierce negotiations with the MLPA and its zealous executive director, Marvin Miller. For the owners, negotiations

were conducted by the PRC, a body of their peers. It was this group, with confirmation by the owners as a whole, which made the landmark concessions to union recognition, player agents, arbitration, free agency, the resulting destruction of the reserve clause, and skyrocketing salaries. During the 50-day player strike of 1981, cries were heard for Bowie's locking both sides in a room until they emerged with a settlement. In Landis's day, maybe, but things no longer worked that way. By 1978, the owners had made the PRC a separate corporation, distinctly separate from the Commissioner's office.

Where Kuhn acted boldly—more so than any of his predecessors—was in his dealings with owners and players. He cracked down on George Steinbrenner of the Yankees (two-year suspension), Ted Turner of the Braves (one-year suspension), and went head-to-head with Charlie Finley of the Oakland A's in what seemed unfair salary wrangles with Reggie Jackson, Vida Blue, and Catfish Hunter. In 1976, believing that Finley was liquidating, not rebuilding, his club, Kuhn negated sales of three A's for $3.5 million.

He met the emerging drug problem directly, despite opposition from owners who felt that acknowledging involvement made baseball "look bad," and from the MLPA, which resisted all disciplinary measures imposed by the Commissioner. He returned the All-Star Game voting to the fans, presided over a new and lucrative television contract, and brought the 1972 strike to a speedy conclusion.

Greater furors arose from making Willie Mays and Mickey Mantle sever their association with baseball while working for gambling casinos, and from acceding to television's demand for World Series games in prime-time hours at night.

Victims of his direct actions often became unforgiving enemies. What might be good for baseball was not necessarily good for an owner's corporate interests that underwrote his baseball venture. An insurrection that threatened his re-election in 1975 was headed off by a friendly majority. But by 1983, five National League owners were unalterably disaffected. Lingering unhappiness with the costly 1981 strike and its aftermath was a burden. A proposal for more equitable sharing of broadcasting revenues among rich and poor clubs was a new and divisive problem. And there were renewed calls for "restructuring." Magnates now said they wanted a chief executive officer—a real corporate CEO with the business skills to guide them through the complexities of baseball in the contemporary world. Views on the powers he would have were mixed.

In the voting, the National League dissidents held firm. (There were three inconsequential "no" votes in the American League.) With 18 out of 26 owners on his side—a 69 percent approval rating—Kuhn failed to get the necessary three-quarters majority in each league.

For all the complaints, Bowie Kuhn was probably the most capable Commissioner the owners ever had, and after more years in office than anyone but Landis, it was not easy to find an equally qualified replacement. Kuhn overstayed his term by a year until Peter V. Ueberroth, 47 years old and fresh from a triumph as head of the Los Angeles Olympic Organizing Committee, was unanimously elected to a five-year term in October 1984.

In this trim, composed, and self-confident executive, the owners finally acquired the leadership they knew was needed to deal with the complexities of contemporary life that were engulfing the baseball business.

Ueberroth became the game's CEO. All departments and

activities reported to him, as did the two league presidents, Dr. Bobby Brown of the American and A. Bartlett Giamatti of the National. The Commissioner's authority to discipline owners was greatly increased. He could transfer or deny any club's draft choices, and the limit on club fines was upped from $5,000 to $250,000. Reelection of the Commissioner reverted to a majority vote of the clubs, with a required minimum of five votes from each league. His salary was raised to a reported $450,000, nearly twice what Kuhn was paid.

Having concentrated power in his own hands, Ueberroth then demonstrated that his management style was to delegate responsibility. Although he took unilateral actions to tidy up baseball operations that he found "in disarray," he preferred to have problems solved by the people most closely involved. Cool and controlled in demeanor, yet insistent on high levels of performance and not afraid to make unpopular decisions—he once described himself as "shy and ruthless"—Ueberroth worked first to restore fiscal "sanity" to owners' operations. Many franchises—estimates ran as high as 21 of the 26—were losing money yet continuing to offer long-term player contracts at high wages, even to veterans headed for the inactive list. Exchanges of information to control this extravagance soon brought charges of collusion from the Players Association, which complained of a suspicious absence of bidding by clubs for free agents. Two arbitrators agreed that this was indeed the case during the 1986 and 1987 seasons. Ueberroth denied the allegation but did not dispute the judgment, insisting that baseball must find ways to improve financial stability before such looming problems as expansion could be faced. Tentatively, new franchises could be awarded by 1990 and new teams take the field by 1993.

Internally, baseball felt the impact of two pervasive social problems of the 1980s: drugs and job opportunities for minorities. Each club conducted its own rehabilitation program for drug users through its medical department. The Players Association objected to testing as an invasion of privacy and Ueberroth tended to agree, even though minor leaguers and front-office personnel were tested. The Commissioner also was empowered to suspend relapsed players for one year without pay.

The hiring of blacks and other minorities, particularly those individuals with distinguished baseball careers, for positions of responsibility on or off the field remained a sensitive issue. Ueberroth contended that all clubs had accepted the obligation, although at his departure few, if any, highly visible jobs (such as manager, which minority groups say will prove the point of good faith) had gone to blacks or Latinos.

In assaults on gambling, Ueberroth worked principally behind the scenes to eliminate club-owner investment in racing stables or tracks. In one of his first public gestures he won approval by lifting Kuhn's rather farfetched ban on Mantle and Mays.

At his urging the Cubs chose to install lights at Wrigley Field, rather than reimburse the leagues for lost night game revenues. While not involved in the owners' negotiations with players and umpires, he kept the parties bargaining until settlements were reached. He found a new source of income in persuading large corporations to pay for the privilege of having their products endorsed by Major League Baseball. He concluded enormous new TV contracts with CBS and ESPN. And he then announced his decision to resign as Commissioner, even if a second term were offered. Although the owners did not always welcome his assertiveness—an

outsider's voice in which they heard as much coercion as persuasion—they felt he had significantly improved baseball's finances, and they accepted his resignation with regret.

National League president A. Bartlett Giamatti was chosen unanimously as Ueberroth's successor in September 1988. The seventh Commissioner signed on for five years beginning April 1, 1989, six months before the traditional October date for transfers of power.

Bart Giamatti's background was intellectually glamorous. A magna cum laude graduate of Yale, he taught Renaissance literature there until elected the university's president in 1978. Eight years later, after the retirement of Charles "Chub" Feeney, he became president of the National League. His first move was to hire his good friend, Francis T. "Fay" Vincent, Jr., a lawyer with high-level business experience, as baseball's first-ever deputy commissioner.

Whether as league president or Commissioner, Giamatti was first of all a fan, with the New Englander's inevitable devotion to the Red Sox. He suspended players for corking bats and scuffing balls. During the 1988 season he held firm against protests of his thirty-day suspension of Reds' Manager Pete Rose for bumping an umpire and made an unpopular decision to enforce the balk rule strictly. He supported "social justice" as the only remedy for baseball's embarrassing and persistent refusal to hire minority managers, coaches, or executives at any level of the game. He also insisted that clubs improve the rowdy atmosphere of their parks. What charmed people most, however, was his unabashed love of baseball and the elegance with which he expressed his feelings—in speech or prose—for its place in American life. He was, in truth, a Commissioner not for owners, or players, or fans, but for the Game.

The major action of his 154-day term was banning Pete Rose from baseball for life. The basic question of whether Rose had engaged, as alleged, in sports gambling was never resolved, but a six-month investigation did establish his association with known gamblers and drug dealers. Rose agreed to a settlement charging him with violation of Major League Rule 21, which covers a miscellany of punishable misconduct. Rose, said Giamatti, had "engaged in a variety of acts which have stained the game, and he must now live with the consequences of those acts." Under another Major League Rule, Rose would be free to apply for reinstatement after one year.

It was generally agreed that Commissioner Giamatti had handled an awkward and difficult problem with distinction. Nine days later, after suffering a heart attack at his summer home on Martha's Vineyard, Massachusetts, he was dead at the age of fifty-one.

Within hours, baseball's executive council elevated Fay Vincent to Acting Commissioner, and the owners, by unanimous vote, made him their eighth Commissioner on September 13. If he lacked Giamatti's flair, he shared his friend's affection and respect for baseball. He preferred grass to turf and day games to night, liked wooden bats, disliked the designated hitter. He was a boyhood fan of the then-Philadelphia A's, but his own athletic career was cut short by a freak accident to his back while at Williams College. Damage to spinal nerves left him unable to stand comfortably for more than a few minutes at a time and forced him to walk with a cane. His qualifications for baseball's top job, however, were bona fide: Phi Beta Kappa at Williams, law degree from Yale, practicing attorney, prime mover (as president and CEO) in a turnaround of ailing Columbia Pictures, and, when the movie

company was sold to Coca-Cola, vice president of a new Coke entertainment division. He had rejoined a law firm when Giamatti lured him into baseball. As Giamatti's deputy he brought the record-setting television contract to a conclusion and supervised the complex Rose investigation.

As Commissioner he moved into the spotlight when the 1989 World Series between Oakland and San Francisco was halted by a severe northern California earthquake which struck minutes before Game Three at Candlestick Park. Fay acted quickly and surely. "We want to be very sensitive to the state of the community," he told a candlelit press conference. "Our modest little game is not a priority." When the Series was resumed ten days later he was widely praised for his calm and tactful demeanor.

As spring training for the 1990 season was about to begin, the owners' negotiations with the players for a new collective bargaining agreement broke down and led to a lockout. Vincent brought the two sides together, and a settlement was achieved by mid-March, an effort appreciated less by the owners than by the players.

In July Vincent banned George Steinbrenner, the obstreperous owner of the New York Yankees, from the "management or day-to-day operations" of his team. Steinbrenner acknowledged that he had acted contrary to the best interests of baseball, specifically by paying a known gambler $40,000 to provide damaging information about player Dave Winfield, who had a long-standing dispute with the owner about money allegedly owed to the outfielder's charitable foundation.

Like many baseball scandals, this one had ramifications aside from the unpleasantness of seeing an owner publicly chastised by a Commissioner. It had actually come to light during Peter Ueberroth's watch. Its clues led, like a pond's ripples, in many directions; some were pursued, others not. But Steinbrenner's admission of wrongdoing seemed to satisfy the Commissioner's office, which, as it had for Rose, pronounced Steinbrenner eligible for future reinstatement.

Subsequent decisions were criticized not only for the actions taken, but for how the Commissioner reached them. In June 1992, when the owners agreed to allow the National League to expand into Colorado and Florida, Vincent ruled that the American League would be tapped for 55 percent of the players drafted to stock the new teams but would receive only $45 million of the $190 million total the new entities were paying as franchise fees. It could be argued that the AL's fourteen teams were about 55 percent of the major leagues' twenty-six, or that the NL should receive the larger reward for letting newcomers into their club.

But Vincent took heat for two departures from precedent. In five previous league expansions franchise fees were awarded solely to the expanding league, and players were drafted only from the league in which they would be playing. Yet if the money division was unpopular, the owners had only themselves to blame. Failing to reach an agreement on their own, they had left Vincent to make the decision for them.

A few days later, when there were owner objections to sale of the Seattle Mariners to investors led by Nintendo, the Japanese video-games corporation, Vincent helped complete the deal ($125 million, the highest amount ever paid for a team) and was credited with preserving an ailing, small-market franchise.

Even so, his relations with the owners were deteriorating in an atmosphere of "disharmony and dissension." Fundamentally different views of the Commissioner's role were emerg-

ing. For Fay Vincent it meant preserving the integrity of the National Pastime for all constituencies—owners, players, fans, and for America itself. Many owners felt otherwise. They owned the game and Vincent was theirs to command. Hardliners on the owners' Labor Relations Committee made this all too clear. Fearful that the Commissioner might undermine their bargaining strategy—freely predicted as union-busting—in forthcoming negotiations with the Players Association, they asked Vincent to waive the power to intervene implicit under his catch-all authority to act in "the best interests of baseball." To their great displeasure, he flatly refused.

Unrest reached crisis proportions on July 6, when the Commissioner undertook a realignment of the National League. It was ridiculous, he argued, to have the Chicago Cubs and St. Louis Cardinals in the league's eastern division while the Atlanta Braves and Cincinnati Reds were in the west. For the sake of geograohic good sense, the teams should switch. Interestingly, his action was not taken unilaterally, but at the request of six NL owners who favored realignment.

Nonetheless, consternation and outrage greeted the announcement. The Tribune Company, owner of the Cubs, led the protest. It complained that traditional rivalries would be disrupted and that the Commissioner had acted arbitrarily and capriciously. It was also keenly aware that realignment would make a serious impact on its superstation operations.

Superstations have been a sore point in baseball for everybody who doesn't own one. Many teams argue that wide-ranging superstation broadcasts hurt local attendance and local television coverage. Who is going to watch the local tailender, either in the stands or on local TV, if a superstation's games involving top teams or a hot pennant race can be seen by anyone subscribing to cable? The Tribune Company, which pays handsomely to broadcast games of seven major league teams (Cubs, White Sox, Dodgers, Angels, Yankees, Phillies, Rockies) on one or another of its far-reaching TV stations, was not worrying about pennant races. Putting the Cubs on the West Coast would mean that games could not be seen in Chicago until 9 P.M., hardly prime time. Low rates for late-hour commercials could mean heavy losses of revenue. The Tribune Company went to court for an injunction to block the order.

Vincent was certain that as Commissioner he had jurisdiction in such matters as realignment. As chairman of Major League Baseball it was his sworn duty to protect the game from encroachment and to create the best possible conditions in which it could thrive. He did not see himself as the owners' errand boy, or as the guardian of their outside interests, particularly those interests in which baseball was reduced to a subordinate role. It seemed unlikely that Bart Giamatti would have acted otherwise.

Legally, several elements of baseball's governing documents were at issue. The National League consitution, as revised in 1981, clearly states that no club can be moved without its consent. The Cubs argued that this should take precedence over anything the Commissioner is empowered to do under the Major League Agreement.

Not so, said Vincent. He acted under Article I of the Agreement, which gives what courts have previously found to be "broad and unfettered" power to act in "the best interests of baseball."

But, said the Cubs, those powers cannot be used to interfere with "intimate business decisions." Furthermore, the Commissioner's power to settle disputes between clubs (Arti-

cle VII) applies only to those whose resolution is not "expressly provided" elsewhere—viz., the National League constitution. The District Court judge ruled that Article VII applied and could not be superseded by Article I's "best interest" power. A preliminary injunction was granted.

Dissident owners now pushed for a full-dress meeting of both leagues with their Commissioner to discuss his performance, perhaps to press for his resignation or, failing that, to fire him. Vincent saw no reason to oblige them. Article IX of the Agreement states that "no diminution of the compensation or powers of . . . the Commissioner shall be made during his term of office." Vincent's term ran to March 31, 1994, and, he said firmly, "I will not resign—ever."

Vincent had some support among the owners, but the movers and shakers were dead-set against him. On September 7, four days after an overwhelming vote of no confidence, he resigned. It would not serve baseball well to have its leadership endlessly involved in legal wrangling. "Owners have a duty," he said, "to take into consideration that they own a part of America's national pastime—in trust. This trust sometimes requires putting self-interest second."

Realignment pulled the trigger, but it was not the issue. It was a power struggle in which the owners have prevailed. More malleable Commissioners than Vincent survived this tug-of-war, but those who clung to the eroding power the owners, with fear and trembling, once gave Judge Landis to save their game were destined for defeat. With Vincent gone, the owners are where they have wanted to be: in absolute control of their industry, with no umpire to reconcile the competing claims of players or fans.

Until they decide otherwise, an executive council of the two league presidents plus eight owners will govern the game. They, or hired or appointed delegates, will deal with such outside relationships as those with the Players Association, the radio and TV broadcasters, and perhaps the Congress, as well as with such internal problems as finite sources of revenue in an era of sykyrocketing costs, the troublesome imbalance between large market teams (LA, NY) and small (Seattle, Pittsburgh), and, perhaps most painful, their historic inability to get along with each other.

## CHAPTER 30

How to Score a Game

Neil Cohen

If you're reading this page, chances are you've never kept score at a ballgame. Maybe you preferred to have your hands free for a hot dog and a beer. Or maybe you didn't realize what you were missing.

Keeping score focuses all your attention on the game and provides more insight than just watching casually. It slows the action so that you can watch each play and enables you to take the pulse of the game, appreciate its subtleties, and sometimes even predict its outcome. What's more, it can be as easy or as complex as you want it to be.

The scoring system fans and sportswriters use today was invented by Henry Chadwick in the 1850s, building upon the earlier scoring technique of New York sportswriter M. J. Kelly. Chadwick, one of the first to write about baseball in the newspapers, created a minutely detailed scorecard so he would have a point of reference and recollection when he wrote his articles about the game. He also invented the modern boxscore.

Chadwick assigned a letter or letters to each play that could take place on the field, usually the first or last letters of the word that described the play. Then, he assigned a number—from 1 to 9—to each of the players on the field, according to his defensive position. By combining letters and numbers, he could record what happened in a particular at bat and, if an out were made, which defensive players made the play.

Little has changed in scoring since Chadwick's day, except for the way some of the letters and numbers are assigned. Here's how we do it today.

- 1B—Single
- 2B—Double
- 3B—Triple
- HR—Home Run
- BB—Walk (Base on Balls); IBB—intentional walk
- FC—Fielder's Choice
- SB—Stolen Base
- CS—Caught Stealing
- WP—Wild Pitch
- PB—Passed Ball
- FO—Foul Out
- SAC—Sacrifice
- HBP—Hit by Pitch
- K—Strikeout; backwards K—Strikeout, looking

Why a K for a strikeout? Chadwick needed S for sacrifice, so he decided to go with K, the last letter in the word "struck," then a common term for striking out.

This is the way we number the defensive players:

- 1—Pitcher;
- 2—Catcher;
- 3—First Baseman;
- 4—Second Baseman;
- 5—Third Baseman;
- 6—Shortstop;
- 7—Left Fielder;
- 8—Center Fielder;
- 9—Right Fielder.

Shortstop is number 6, instead of number 5, because in the early days of the game, shortstop was still evolving as a position, and the player in that spot was considered more of a shallow outfielder than an infielder.

To save space, some plays are described simply with numbers. For a flyout, we just record the code number of the fielder who made the catch. For an unassisted groundout, we write the number of the infielder, followed by a period. For an assisted groundout, we would use the numbers of the two fielders handling the ball.

Now, imagine that each box on your scorecard is a miniature baseball diamond, with first base in the lower right corner, second base in the upper right corner, third base in the top left and home plate in the bottom left. If a batter reaches first, divide the box into quarters. This allows you to record the batter's progress in the square as he moves around the bases.

Here are two fictional innings to illustrate how this all comes together on a sample scorecard (below). Leading off for the All-Time All-Stars is left fielder Ty Cobb, who singles and steals second. The next batter, second baseman Rogers Hornsby, bounces a grounder to second and Cobb takes third. We mark a number 2 in the third base quadrant of Cobb's box to indicate that the No. 2 batter advanced him there. The next batter, Babe Ruth, hits a home run. We note that, plus a 3 in the home plate quadrant of Cobb's box to show how he scored. Batting fourth, Lou Gehrig flies out to center field.

Center fielder Tris Speaker walks and takes second on a passed ball. Honus Wagner doubles, but is thrown out by the leftfielder when he tries to stretch it into a triple. Speaker, however, advances to third and then scores before the third out is made. In the box below the inning boxes, we note the number of runs and hits made in that half-inning: two runs above the diagonal line, three hits below.

In the second inning, catcher Bill Dickey singles but is

erased when third baseman Pie Traynor grounds into a shortstop-to-second-to-first double play, shown by the 6–4 in Dickey's second-base quadrant. Pitcher Cy Young strikes out to end the inning. The totals: 0 runs, 1 hit.

It can be that simple. But it doesn't have to be. Scoring also has its creative side. Any scoring code is just a guideline; you can make up your own system to record whatever you're interested in tracking. For example, some scorers record base hits in shorthand: dashes or dots, one for each base. You can also embellish your scoring with other details of the game that you find interesting or would be fun to keep track of and think about later. The extra boxes at the end of the scoresheet (for at bats, runs, etc.) can come in handy if you need to branch out. You can, for example, record the count on each batter, or whether the pitcher was ahead or behind on a batter when the ball was put into play. That way you can tell how efficiently a pitcher is working in a game, and how he might fare in the later innings. If you have a good seat, or you're watching on television, you can also keep track of what pitch a pitcher uses to record outs and what pitches result in hits. You can record where fly balls are caught; if many batters are reaching the warning track, you know you have a lucky pitcher out there. Or, you can note where hits are made, to learn the patterns in which certain hitters perform.

Use your imagination. Keeping score enables you to study a game with as much concentration as a manager or coach in the dugout and to gain a feel for the underlying current of the game. And you can still have a hot dog and a beer. Like everything else in baseball, all you need is a sharp eye, a good pair of hands, and practice.

PLAYER	POS.	1	2	3	4	5	6	7	AB	R	H	BB	TB
									8	9	10	11	12
1. Cobb	⑦ LF	2 SB / 3 1B											
2. Hornsby	④ 2B	4-3											
3. Ruth	⑨ RF	HR											
4. Gehrig	③ 1B	8											
5. Speaker	⑧ CF	6 PB / 6 BB											
6. Wagner	⑥ SS	7-5 2B											
7. Dickey	② C		6-4 / 1B										
8. Traynor	⑤ 3B		6-4-3										
9. Young	① P		K										
R	2	0						
H	3	1						

PITCHER	IP	H	R	ER	BB	SO

TEAM _____

## CHAPTER 31

Baseball on the Air

Paul D. Adomites

The story of broadcast baseball actually begins almost seventy years before the first game was aired. Baseball owners have always been of two minds about any fan interest that wasn't satisfied at the game itself. The common sentiment was "They'll stay home instead of coming to the game." Yet these outside sources generated extra income, and owners are businessmen first of all. As early as the 1860s, it was already clear that baseball sold newspapers, and newspapers sold baseball. Yet some owners feared "giving the game away."

The owners' schizophrenic response also occurred with telegraphy. Even though telegraph operators paid for the privilege of relaying game reports to saloons and poolrooms, a "hot debate" over whether this "free" sport was keeping people away from the parks led some owners to try to ban telegraph machines from their operations.

In 1897, each team received $300 worth of free telegrams on a league-wide contract, and some owners complained that it was hurting attendance. Sixteen years later, Western Union offered each team $17,000 a year for five years for the telegraph rights. It was hard for the owners to say no.

Even the fledgling motion picture industry got into the act, paying baseball $500 in 1910 for the rights to film and show the World Series. American League President Ban Johnson, who saw movies as competition, suggested that baseball ask for ten times as much for rights to film the 1911 Series, figuring that it would frighten the moviemen away. It didn't. However, baseball had to settle for only seven times what it had received the year before.

The point is obvious—baseball was far from being overexposed. Even though he was talking about telegraphy, John R. Tunis in 1923 pointed out the real value of broadcasting baseball. He described the World Series thrilling people in New Orleans, San Francisco, Honolulu, and even "an excited group of Mongolians in Seoul, the capital of Korea." The point is, advanced communications create fans *everywhere*, even thousands of miles from the parks.

Radio Days

The first major league game was broadcast over radio on August 5, 1921, from Pittsburgh, home of the Westinghouse Corporation, over the new Westinghouse station, KDKA. Harold Arlin, a Westinghouse foreman, announced the Pirates-Phillies contest from Forbes Field. Westinghouse was eager to make a name for itself in the new industry. The next day, Arlin broadcast the U.S. Open tennis tournament, also near Pittsburgh. Two months later he did the first football broadcast.

That same year the first World Series broadcast was aired to a handful of fans on the East Coast. By 1922, the Series was heard "live by 5,000,000 people." Re-creations were heard by fans *on three continents*.

(Many of the early baseball broadcasts, and almost all away-game airings were re-created in a hometown radio studio, with announcers reading pitch-by-pitch information from ticker tapes, and using sound effects and canned crowd noises to simulate live action. In 1950, the Red Sox provided the first live coverage of all their away games. Within five years, major-league re-creations were antiques, as the teams were broadcasting all their games live. At the minor-league level, re-creation continued for away games into the 1960s.)

The first owner to see radio's promise to boost fan interest was the Cubs' boss Philip Wrigley. In 1925 he invited all the Chicago radio stations to carry all the Cubs' games. No charge. Sam Breadon, the Cardinals' owner, followed suit soon thereafter, in the first two attempts to develop regional followings.

In 1926 and 1927 the first great national radio networks began operation: NBC and CBS. This was the beginning of radio's golden era. Sales of radio equipment, a $60 million industry in 1922, were nearly a billion dollars in 1929.

Yet many owners were still wary. By the 1930s, the two-team cities of Boston, Philadelphia, St. Louis, and Chicago had an agreement not to broadcast away games. In other words, if the Braves were at home, you could hear *their* game on the radio, but not the Red Sox. The owners' wail ("they won't come to the park if you give the game away") seemed turned on its logical head under this arrangement, but home radio is where you ballyhoo home-game attendance, which was the concern, anyway.

The New York owners went one step further. In 1932 they agreed to ban all radio, even visitors' re-creations, from their parks.

Larry MacPhail took over the Reds in 1933 and sold a controlling interest in the club to Powel Crosley, owner of two Cincinnati radio stations. It was a match made in economic heaven: MacPhail knew that broadcasting games would promote the team (he hired southerner Red

Barber as his announcer), Crosley now could boost his radio ratings. The mutuality was akin to Chris von der Ahe, the St. Louis beer garden magnate, taking over the St. Louis club in the American Association in order to sell more beer.

Then, when MacPhail moved to Brooklyn in 1938, he brought Red Barber with him, and broke the New York ban. The next year was the first year that all the teams in the major leagues broadcast their games. Prophetically, it was also the year of the first *televised* baseball game.

In 1935, Judge Landis moved in to orchestrate the radio deal to cover the World Series. All three networks were involved, and baseball made $400,000. Landis, as ever, was imperious; he dismissed Ted Husing as announcer of the games, even though with five World Series under his belt, Ted was second only to the ubiquitous Graham MacNamee in Series-announcing experience.

The money for baseball broadcasting was growing. Gillette, the razor blade manufacturer, one of the first companies to realize the power of sports as an advertising vehicle, tried to flex their muscles by offering Red Barber a substantial amount to walk out on his Dodger contract to join Gillette on a new Yankees/Giants network. Barber refused. It's no wonder Gillette felt powerful; in 1946 they were rich enough to sign a ten-year deal for exclusive radio sponsorship of the World Series and All-Star Games, for $14 million.

But the World Series was the exception; otherwise, baseball remained locally dominated. However, in 1950, Gordon McLendon changed all that, when he founded a new radio network, one with daily baseball as its centerpiece: the Liberty Broadcasting System. His announcers re-created a game every day, plus extras on weekends. McLendon charged the stations $10 per game, and enrolled 300 of them. He paid his announcers $27.50 a week, netting himself a weekly profit of over $2,970.

But once again the moguls of baseball feared too much free publicity. A rule banned the Game of the Day from many areas because there were fears that it might conflict with local broadcasts within a 75-mile area.

The paradoxical result, according to Curt Smith, was "If you lived in Butte, Montana, or Amarillo, Texas, you got to hear every club in baseball," as many as ten games a week. But if you lived in a major league town (or near one), you could hear only the locals, and only when the club decided the broadcasts wouldn't "interfere" with attendance. McLendon's gold mine didn't last long: he lost a suit against baseball and folded. Yet the Mutual Broadcasting Network mimicked his strategy and succeeded.

In 1951 Liberty broadcast more than 200 games, almost 600 hours of baseball; Mutual did 145 games. That amount of time was more than quadruple the amount of total network time (via television and radio) that baseball would receive in *1984*. More importantly, the Liberty/Mutual style set a pattern for successful TV coverage years later.

TV or Not TV

Baseball on television began to take hold in the late 1950s. The Yankees were the first team to sell their TV rights (in 1946, for $75,000; in 1987 the Yankees earned 250 times as much for their TV rights). The first televised World Series was the memorable 1947 set. Harry Coyle, the NBC dean of baseball producers, was there. In Chicago, Jack Brickhouse was announcing White Sox telecasts in 1948.

By 1950 the World Series was televised as far west as Omaha; 38 million watched. The next year World Series baseball television reached the West Coast. (Radio still had strengths: the 1953 Brooklyn Dodgers Radio Network linked 117 stations, making the Bums the first "America's Team.")

The era of baseball broadcasting that began in 1953 should have opened the owners' eyes to the future, but it didn't. That year the first televised Game of the Week began (then on ABC). Naturally, it was banned from all major league cities. (Does this sound familiar?) Yet with the irrepressible Dizzy Dean at the microphone, it rolled up incredible ratings anyway: 11.4 percent of all households with sets, 51 percent of all sets in use. That translated to 75 percent of all sets in use not in big league cities.

And there was no doubt that the colorful Diz, with his demented grammar, malapropisms, and ambling yarn-weaving, *was* the program. In 1955, a slick advertising agency move landed the Game of the Week for CBS, and Curt Smith says, "the most transforming baseball series in television's show of shows ... was born." Two years later a group of Sunday games was added to the schedule. Baseball was on its way to becoming the *truly* national game; the owners just felt they could do it without the help of the fans in the cities where the teams played.

Television was becoming a national mania. By 1955 only three teams didn't televise (the Braves, Pirates, and A's). On the other hand, the Cubs, Dodgers, Yankees, and Giants broadcast every home game, the Indians and Cards every road game. The Reds televised all weekday afternoon home games; the Phillies showed 29 home and 27 road games; Baltimore showed 65 contests; even the Red Sox and Senators had TV on their schedule; six stations in Michigan showed 42 Tigers games; WGN televised every day game from Comiskey Park.

Then came football. The upstart NFL (and their very wise leader Pete Rozelle) realized that TV was the way to *build* fan interest. Baseball's less progressive owners still feared "giving it away," preferring local/regional efforts. As Harold Rosenthal explains, "Football fans were sold as National Football League fans—network television made them that way ... In Appleton, Wisconsin, a guy would turn on the tube and watch the Giants play the Browns ... Baseball fans were brought up to follow the Cardinals or Giants or Tigers ... the local coverage mattered, the local announcer."

When the NFL signed an immense contract with TV in the early 1960s, guaranteeing coverage, with all the NFL teams sharing the wealth, baseball wanted to copy the plan. They asked for millions, but they didn't get it.

What baseball got was the ABC Game of the Week: 28 telecasts a season; each of the clubs receiving $300,000. Curt Smith explains the upshot: "By 1966, instead of watching as many as 123 games on three networks, a majority of American viewers could behold only 28 tele-

casts on one network." The "common good" policy was a mistake, but baseball couldn't figure this out. They changed networks, to NBC, and we got a new announcer.

"Curt Gowdy emerged for an entire generation of listeners as the national signature of baseball broadcasting. From 1966 through 1975, he called play-by-play for every All-Star Game, every World Series game, and virtually every regular season network game" (Curt Smith). And that list doesn't even include Gowdy's work on seven Super Bowls, seven Olympic Games, twelve NCAA basketball championships, 13 Rose Bowls, the Pan Am Games, and twenty years of "The American Sportsman."

But Curt couldn't bring in the ratings; his highest regular season rating was still two full points below Dizzy Dean's first year (and remember, Dizzy wasn't allowed into any major league markets), and it dropped 15 percent by 1970; Curt's World Series ratings fell by nearly 20 percent, though it was certainly no fault of his own. Solid, professional, and competent, he was just never exciting. People never talked about him as they did about Dizzy or other announcers. And he was definitely overexposed.

Meanwhile football was coming on strong. In 1969 pro football televised three times as many games on network TV as baseball. (Three times!) By 1969 not even all the baseball postseason games were broadcast nationally. The NFL wasn't just growing; they were promoting. Their highlight films featured thrilling action, rich drama, and the golden voice of orator John Facenda.

Baseball, it was clear to everyone in the national press, was losing the battle. "Baseball is dead" was a cliché. A Lou Harris poll showed that football was now Americans' favorite sport. More importantly, another Harris poll showed how baseball's popularity paralleled the degree of its TV coverage. Where the big leagues were most heavily covered, baseball was most popular. Where fans received only network coverage, baseball ranked lowest.

But Commissioner Bowie Kuhn had something to say about the matter; he pushed for World Series night games (the first was in 1971) because they could attract a much larger audience. And while you could cynically dismiss this move as pure economics (bigger viewership means more advertising dollars), it worked.

In 1975 baseball announced a new kind of TV deal: Alternating coverage of the World Series, playoffs and All-Star Games between NBC and ABC. The networks saw the advantages: postseason baseball play was the perfect time to begin promoting the new fall TV season. The alternating feature built in an element of competition without economic overtones: quality of coverage.

Then came October 21, 1975. The Boston Red Sox, unable to win a World Series since 1918, were on their way to a loss in six games to Cincinnati's "Big Red Machine." But a three-run pinch-hit homer by Bernie Carbo tied the game in the eighth, and in the twelfth (by now it was 12:34 A.M.), Carlton Fisk hit a solo shot over the Green Monster to win the game. A total of 62 million people saw it, and television couldn't have planned it better, because as Fisk hit his homer, the camera in the left field scoreboard followed *him*, not the ball, and on replay the audience saw Fisk furiously trying to wave the ball fair: the first-ever home run reaction shot.

The next night, 75,890,000 people watched the seventh game, and baseball was definitely back. In 1976, baseball received revenue from radio and television near $51 million. Lou Harris said in 1977: "For the first time since 1968, more sports fans in the country follow baseball than football." Ten years later baseball received $350 million.

And 1977 is also the year that cable television broadcasts began to have their impact. The situation was analogous to the Liberty/Mutual networks' Game of the Day, or the Dizzy Dean/CBS Game of the Week. Now fans all over the country could see a lot of baseball, every day. By 1982, cable TV was in 35 percent of all American homes; in 1987 it passed the 50 percent mark.

Superstations like Ted Turner's Atlanta TBS, Chicago's WGN, and New York's WWOR and WPIX, along with the all-sports network, ESPN, were giving fans more baseball on a regular basis than they had ever had before. In 1986 Cubs' games were viewed by 20 million fans. For his definitive history, *Voices of the Game,* Curt Smith interviewed Cub fans in Kodiak, Alaska; Costa Rica; and Boise, Idaho—all because of Harry Caray's calls on the Chicago superstation. A Peter Ueberroth–inspired change in the rules to make superstations give the other teams a certain amount of money per viewer passed over Ted Turner's noisy objections. Sports-only premium cable networks have failed in several places, largely due to the availability of the "free" (part of the basic cable charge) coverage.

Even though the superstation teams do not benefit directly, in cash income, from sending their games around the country, (their parent corporations do, of course . . .), they do help to promote interest in baseball as a whole. (For example, every Atlanta Braves game can be seen in 48 percent of U.S. households, yet in 1987 the Braves' broadcast rights earned them the same as the Pittsburgh Pirates, whose five-station network reached as far as Johnstown.) As Harry Caray says, "We've made the Cubs part of their lives; they have to be interested."

By the late '80s, the advertising industry was announcing that the era of megabuck sports TV packages was over; advertisers just didn't have enough money to pay for them. What the ad pundits didn't realize was the value that network TV saw in televising the League Championship series and World Series—prime vehicles for introducing their new fall lineup. When time came to renegotiate a national TV package, NBC (which had carried the Saturday Game of the Week for years) and ABC (which had carried some Monday night games and alternated LCS and Series with NBC) were both outslugged at the bargaining table by third-rated CBS.

CBS's deal for a handful of Saturday games plus all postseason play was for $1.1 billion over four years. ESPN kicked in another $400 million for the same period of time, and each team became instantly richer to the tune of $14 million a year, plus change. The result was felt instantly on the field. Free-agency outrageousness reached new heights, as the $3 Million Man was created, then surpassed. When the owners tried to claim poverty at the 1990 labor negotiations, the players scoffed. And the average player increased his annual wealth by $70,000 overnight.

But before long CBS and ESPN were doubting the wisdom of their profligate ways. Viewership had not risen

enough to pay the bigger tab, and both claimed huge losses. Even though CBS admitted the postseason had helped their new lineup, they asked for (and were refused) rebates from baseball. The 1992 World Series was the second-lowest rated ever. During that Series ESPN announced it was willing to pay a $13 million penalty in order to forego its option to carry 1994–1995 games for $250 million. Owners, afraid that their glory days of net-

work TV billions were gone (and seeing another chance to poor-mouth), decided to reopen negotiations on the Basic Agreement a year early. Has the owners' century-old fear of "giving the game away" finally come true? Has the baseball fan finally seen all he or she can stand? No, and no. But flexibility and creativity—not hardline attitudes and bellicose posturing—are the needs of the moment.

## CHAPTER 32

Night Baseball

David Pietrusza

The story of night baseball is often boiled down to just two chapters: Cincinnati in 1935 and Wrigley Field in 1988. Yet this now familiar nocturnal habit struggled for acceptance throughout virtually all of baseball's history, before it finally propelled the game to new levels of popularity and prosperity. It has transformed the national pastime—but it was hardly achieved . . . overnight.

In fact, just eleven months after Edison perfected the incandescent bulb on September 2, 1880, the first night game was played at Nantasket Beach in Massachusetts, in an attempt by the Northern Electric Light Company to convince a skeptical world that electricity could rival gaslight for outdoor uses. Teams sponsored by two Boston department stores, Jordan White and R. H. White, battled to a nine-inning 16–16 tie. The Boston *Post* noted that "a clear, pure light was produced, very strong and yet pleasant to the sight," although the crude system produced only 30,000 candlepower, and visibility must have been tenuous at best. Nonetheless, experiments continued apace and would continue for decades.

In May 1883, a railway engineer named Charles S. Hull contrived a test of electric railroad headlights in Chambersburg, Pennsylvania, by mounting a dynamo on top of a flatcar, aiming its rays at teams representing "Captain Clay Heninger's Nine" and George Pensinger's Paint Shop. Allegedly, the contest "was played as easily as in daylight."

Just a few weeks later, on June 2, 1883, Charles Jenney of Fort Wayne's Jenney Electric Light Company staged a nighttime contest featuring the first professional squad to play under arcs—the Quincy squad of the Northwest League versus the local Methodist College nine. The professionals triumphed 19–11 in seven innings.

Other experiments followed, one after another, in varying degrees of seriousness. In 1887, the American Association's New York Mets toyed with the rather cockeyed idea of installing lights on the ground and shining them upwards. In Indianapolis in August 1888, owner John T. Brush installed flaming gaslights for possible National League play. "The crosspiece," noted *Sporting Life*, "has burners on the upper side, about six inches apart, and when the gas [is] turned on it makes a solid flame, say about four foot long."

Less solemn attempts occurred. In Seattle, in August 1891, an arclit contest featured the Northwest League's Spokane and Portland clubs in outlandish costumes. Kerosene lamps were used at Los Angeles' Athletic Park on July 2, 1893. Authorities also employed a searchlight (mounted on top of the grandstand) to assist fielders in tracking down fly balls.

In Wilmington, Delaware, on July 4, 1896, normally staid Ed Barrow brought his Paterson (N.J.) nine into town for a sunlit Atlantic League doubleheader and stayed for an after-dusk third contest that degenerated into a farce. Allegedly one pitch literally exploded in the face of Paterson's Honus Wagner. "The ball became lost so often and so many runs were made they were not counted," noted the Wilmington *Morning News*. Such horseplay did little to increase the respectability of night ball.

And in St. Louis Chris Von der Ahe may have used electric lights for an official game at Sportsman's Park sometime in the 1890s. It is known that the colorful Teuton installed lights there for night horseracing (one of many stunts). One story has it that as night was falling on a Browns contest, the switch was thrown and the game was finished under flickering arcs.

A series of highly publicized attempts to light night games occurred in 1909 and 1910. A trio of inventors—George, Thaddeus, and Arthur Cahill—interested major league owners in the possibility of a workable system. The Cahills brought their invention to the attention of Cincinnati Reds President Gerry Herrmann by *Sporting Life* editor Francis Richter ("If it should fall into the hands of speculative outsiders it would surely mean rival night-playing leagues. There are great commercial possibilities and probabilities in the invention, which should be kept within the present 'charmed circle.'") The Cahills staged a game at Cincinnati's park, the "Palace of the Fans," on June 18, 1909, that was played by two local Elks lodges. Despite some misjudged fly balls, Herrmann pronounced the effort a triumph, but Reds pilot Clark Griffith commented halfheartedly, "I don't believe night ball is destined to rival the daylight article, but I will say I was much surprised at the ease with which the game was played . . . tonight. Under improved lighting it will grow more popular."

The Cahills struck again at Grand Rapids, Michigan, on July 10, 1909, in a loosely played game between Grand Rapids and Zanesville of the Central League. A year later, lacrosse, soccer, and baseball (played by two strong local semipro squads) were showcased under Cahill arcs at newly christened Comiskey Park.

In 1915, the upstart Federal League saw evening competition as a way to salvage their faltering war with Organized Baseball. The Brooklyn Tip-Tops began installing lights in the final weeks of the 1915 season, projecting a few evening dates. Unfortunately, the games never materialized. If they had, the entire circuit was poised to schedule evening tilts on a regular basis for 1916—had the Feds survived, that is.

No further significant movement occurred until June 24, 1927, when Lynn and Salem of the New England League tangled under a General Electric–installed system at Lynn's home field. Looking on were members of the Red Sox and Senators. Surviving photos reveal a somewhat dim scene, but most observers were favorably impressed, including Goose Goslin, who found it "just as good ball as they play in daylight."

Nineteen-thirty witnessed the great breakthrough. A three-way race was on to convert night baseball from a gimmick into a paying proposition. The participants were Lee Keyser, owner of the Class A Western League's Des Moines Demons; M.L. Truby of the Class C Western Association's Independence Producers; and E.L. Wilkinson, proprietor of the Negro Leagues' legendary Kansas City Monarchs.

In the off-season, Keyser announced he would install the first modern, permanent lighting system on May 2, 1930, but Truby and Wilkinson both got the jump on him by successfully inaugurating systems of their own on April 17. That evening Independence hosted the barnstorming House of David, while at Enid, Oklahoma, the Monarchs engaged the Phillips University team using a highly innovative portable system. Then on Monday, April 28, Independence hosted the Muskogee Chiefs in the first Western Association night contest.

Nonetheless, it was still Keyser who caught the nation's attention. Eight thousand fans attended the Des Moines game, including many initially skeptical representatives of Organized Baseball and technicians for a worldwide radio hookup. All went away believers.

Throughout the minors the idea spread like wildfire. By season's end most bush league teams had lights—and every circuit save the Central had authorized night play. Significantly, it did return for the 1931 season.

Throughout the early 1930s, big league teams toyed with the idea of arclit play. The first two major league clubs to compete under mazdas were the White Sox and Giants, who tangled at Houston's Buff Stadium on March 22, 1931. The game was neither an artistic nor a financial success. Players groused about the damp of the evening, and management swooned at the attendance—possibly as low as 500 fans.

Cardinals owner "Singing Sam" Breadon made the most positive noises about night ball ("It makes every day a Sunday"), but since the rival Browns owned Sportsman's Park, where both teams played—and as they had no interest in the innovation—nothing happened in the big leagues until 1935, when Leland Stanford MacPhail was brought in to refurbish the threadbare Cincinnati franchise.

Just up from the minors, MacPhail was out to revive one of the majors' most moribund operations. Despite spirited opposition from Commissioner Landis and Giants owner Charles Stoneham, he secured National League permission to stage seven night contests per season.

But MacPhail was the only member of the Reds Board of Directors to vote *against* night ball—a little known fact. As part of his planning, the Roaring Redhead had scrupulously computed the payback on a new state-of-the-art system. Limited as he was to an annual quota of seven regular-season tilts, he calculated that he would have to stage exhibition games to turn a profit, but in January

1935 the National League had banned such displays in big league parks. Faced with a losing proposition and with the equipment still not ordered, MacPhail voted to scrap night ball. But because his "nay" was the only one cast, night baseball was approved.

Franklin Roosevelt threw the switch from the White House as 20,422 fans packed Crosley Field on the decidedly cold and damp evening of May 24, 1935. The Reds, behind Paul Derringer, stopped the hapless Phils 2–1 to decidedly mixed reactions. "There is no chance," Washington's Clark Griffith blustered, "of night baseball ever becoming popular in the bigger cities. People there are educated to see the best. High-class baseball cannot be played under artificial light."

Yet who could argue with results—a huge crowd paying to see the woeful Reds on an even more woeful night (the average Crosley Field afternoon contest would attract just 1,500), and the Reds continuing to draw whenever they played after dark. Still there was no further movement until the stormy MacPhail lost his job with the Reds and in 1938 signed with the equally pathetic Brooklyn Dodgers. The result was a page in baseball history—Brooklyn's debut under the lights on June 15 and Johnny Vander Meer's back end of his unprecedented "double no-hitter."

Night baseball quickly spread around the majors, as one by one other clubs followed: the A's (May 16, 1939), Phils (June 1, 1939), Indians (June 27, 1939), White Sox (August 14, 1939), Giants (May 24, 1940), Browns (May 24, 1940), Cardinals (June 4, 1940), Pirates (June 4, 1940) and Senators (May 28, 1941). Even mossbacks like Clark Griffith became believers, although not everyone was sold. Mrs. Liebrich, who lived across the street from the Philadelphia Athletics' park, "wanted to know what privacy she'd have in a bedroom, facing the park, illuminated by eight floodlights" when Connie Mack installed lights.

Even though President Roosevelt encouraged night play in his historic "green light" letter to Clark Griffith, which cleared baseball to continue operation during the war because it was a vital need of the American people, World War II interrupted the march of this innovation. Shortages of materials made new installations difficult, if not impossible. A drought in the Southeastern states threatened TVA-generated power and, consequently, night games. And on the east and west coasts, fear of enemy aircraft and submarines doused night baseball. The Pacific Coast League, Ebbets Field, and the Polo Grounds were notable casualties.

Despite blackout regulations, the last hour of the 1942 All Star Game at the Polo Grounds was played under lights, and the 1943 midsummer classic at Shibe Park was totally under the arcs. By war's end the government was actually encouraging new installations as a morale measure.

Following the war, the Braves (May 11, 1946), Yankees (May 28, 1946), Red Sox (June 13, 1947), and Tigers (June 15, 1948) fell into line. The Cubs, who like the Tigers had been on the verge of installing a system before Pearl Harbor, remained the last outpost of exclusively sunlit ball.

It was not until the threat of shifting Cubs League Championship and World Series games to distant St.

Louis that night play became a reality at Wrigley Field. Before 39,008 fans on August 8, 1988, the Cubbies took the field for their evening baptism. Baptism it was as rain washed out the historic event. The lights went on for keeps the next night as 36,399 saw the Cubs vanquish the Mets 6–4.

Some—and not just the terminally nostalgic—now say night ball is overdone. With games dragging on past the three-hour mark, it's tough to stay awake through nine full innings. Statistics prove that attendance can be higher at afternoon contests. Yet with television driving so many of baseball's decisions, a retreat from evening play seems unlikely.

## CHAPTER 33

Baseball Collecting

Barry Halper with Bill Madden

In the early 1970s baseball began to take on a new dimension—one that would transform the hobby of a dedicated few into a national phenomenon and, incidentally, a multimillion dollar industry.

The game's first century did not produce many collectors of baseball memorabilia. Oh, sure, there were a few baseball cards as early as the 1860s and extensive sets by the 1880s; even in the game's infancy there was always that legion of autograph-seekers waiting outside the players' gate at any given ballpark. But the cards were seldom saved (as evidenced by the scarcity today of early cards, even those produced in great quantities in the 1950s) and the autographs were a fancy of one's idol-worshiping days. There were no prices attached to such mementos of youthful infatuation, just as there was no business of collecting.

But then, in 1967, a man by the name of Jefferson Burdick published *The American Card Catalog*—a guide listing the origin, description, and estimated value of every card (baseball or otherwise) ever printed. It was a monumental volume, which took years of painstaking research. What his catalog did was to transform the informal and undocumented hobby of baseball card collecting into the more elevated and established rank of stamp and coin collecting. Prices and values, scarcity and condition—these commercial considerations, once they were applied to cards, quickly moved into just about anything associated with baseball: autographs, bats, balls, uniforms, photos, press pins, chinaware, publications, you name it.

Cards

In the beginning, though, there were the cards, and today they remain at the center of the baseball collecting hobby.

The most extensive early card set (it remains the largest ever issued, with 520 players in one to seventeen variants each!) was the Old Judge Cigarette Brand series of 1887–89, catalogued by Burdick as N172. These insert cards were really photographs mounted on board, in the same manner as the *cartes de visite* that were all the rage in the 1860s. In terms of interest today, however, the most popular early baseball card set was the 1909–11 tobacco issue that Burdick catalogued as the T206. These 523 cards, approximately 2¼ by 1½ inches, were inserted in packages of Sweet Caporal, Piedmont, Sovereign, Cycle, and assorted other cigarette brands of the American Tobacco Company.

Included in that T206 set are two of the most valuable cards in the history of collecting—the Honus Wagner and the Eddie Plank. Both cards are extremely rare for different reasons. According to legend Wagner, a nonsmoker, became incensed when he discovered that his picture on a card was being used to promote smoking. As a result, he ordered that his card be removed from the T206 set. (Evidently, though, he must have had a change of heart years later, as he is depicted in the 1948 Leaf Gum card set with at least two packs of chewing tobacco stuffed in his jaw.) Today, there are believed to be no more than twenty-five or so T206 Wagner cards in existence. The Plank card is believed to be equally as rare—a result of the printing plates for it having been accidentally destroyed back in 1909.

Burdick, acknowledging the scarcity of both cards, lists the Wagner card's value at $50 and the Plank card at $10. The rest of the T206s are listed at ten cents apiece. Today, the common T206 lists at $100 mint, a Plank at $25,000, and the Wagner at a peak of $451,000.

Besides the T206s, the most popular early lithographed tobacco cards then and today are the 1887–88 Allen & Ginters (N28, N29, and N43) and the 1911 T3 Turkey Reds. The Allen & Ginters maintain their value and popularity from their sheer beauty. The same size as the T206s, the N28 and N29 series were magnificent watercolor paintings of baseball players, printed on glossy stock. The N28 is generally considered the first of the tobacco card baseball sets and it includes ten players, among them Hall of Famers Cap Anson, John Clarkson, Charles Comiskey, King Kelly, John Montgomery Ward, and Tim Keefe. The N29, or second series, adds six players, among them Hall of Famer Buck Ewing. The Anson card is the most expensive today, listing at $2,000 mint. Burdick listed the average Allen & Ginter card at ten cents.

The T3s are classified as cabinet cards in that they measured a much larger 5¾ by 8 inches in size and were obtained by sending in coupons found in Turkey Red, Fez, and Old Mill brand cigarettes. They, too, are beautiful cards, depicting players in full-color portraits. All told, there are 100 baseball players in the Turkey Red set of 126 athletes, averaging $150 for commons and considerably more for Hall of Famers (Ty Cobb lists at $8,500). In 1967 Burdick listed the price of T3s at $1 apiece.

In the 1930s the tobacco companies gave way to the gum and confectionery companies as the prime dispensers of baseball cards. The most prominent of those companies was the Goudey Gum Company, which issued significant sets in 1933–41. These cards, like all the gum/confectionery cards of the 1930–50 era, measured 2½ by 3¼ inches.

The most popular of all the Goudey sets is still its initial 1933, effort which was comprised of 240 cards including one of the rarest of all, No. 106, Napoleon Lajoie. For some reason, the Lajoie card was inadvertently omitted from the original 1933 Goudey set, and when collectors inquired about the absence of card No. 106, the company offered it as a premium the following year. As a result, the few Lajoie cards that exist today contain the 1934 Goudey card design. Burdick listed the common R319 1933 Goudeys at twenty cents apiece and the Lajoie at a dollar. Today, the commons list at $150, the numerous Hall of Famers in the set at $250 and upwards, and the Lajoie at $30,000.

In 1939, Gum Inc. of Boston entered the baseball card field, issuing the first of its three Play Ball sets. The 1939 and '40 Play Balls were sepia toned, while the 1941 went to color. The 72-card 1941 Play Ball set is the most popular of the three, listing at $14,000 in mint condition. It also features the first color cards of Joe DiMaggio (mint today $2,500) and Ted Williams ($2,000).

World War II prompted a shutdown of the baseball card industry, and it did not renew production until 1948, when the Chicago-based Leaf Company issued its 168-card set of colorized photo cards with gum. That Leaf set, which contains a number of less-distributed cards, lists at $30,000 in mint condition today, the DiMaggio and Babe Ruth cards listing at $2,000 each, and the Satchel Paige, because of its alleged scarcity, also at $2,000.

In 1950 the Bowman Gum Company of Philadelphia displaced Leaf as the number one baseball card manufacturers. They remained atop the field until 1952, when the Topps Gum Company of Brooklyn began making big inroads into this burgeoning industry. Topps, which began modestly with two fifty-two-card sets in 1951, as well as a pair of now extremely valuable premium sets called Connie Mack and Current All Stars, broke historical ground in 1952 when it issued a 407-card set.

The 1952 Topps remains the Holy Grail of modern-day card sets for collectors, if only because of the difficulty in completing it. Cards number 311–407, it seems, were issued late in the year by Topps and reportedly only in the New York area and Canada. As a result, they are considerably harder to find. Burdick listed the 1952 Topps from 1 to 310 at ten cents apiece and 311 to 407 at thirty cents in 1967.

But making that final series even more valuable is the fact that Topps included many of the game's superstars of that year in it, including Mickey Mantle, Jackie Robinson, Pee Wee Reese, Bobby Thomson, Eddie Mathews, and Roy Campanella. All of them list today at over $1,000 mint, and the Mantle card, number 311, at $7,000–$10,000, is considered the *pièce de résistance* of all modern-day baseball cards. The 311–407 commons list at $150 apiece.

When Jefferson Burdick published his *American Card Catalog*, baseball card collecting was limited to just that—collecting. It was not until the mid-'70s, when card values began to be known nationwide, that baseball card shows and flea markets began to crop up across the country. Prior to that, there had been only a small network of what could be considered hard-core baseball card collectors: Frank Nagy of Detroit, Buck Barker of St. Louis, myself, and a few others would trade cards among our-

selves. There was never any selling of cards within that network, although on many occasions the trading would branch into other fields, such as trading an autograph for a suitable card or cards.

All in all, in 1972, there were about ten card dealers who would meet once a month in New York on Friday nights. No money ever changed hands. It was strictly trading.

A couple of years later, however, the hobby began to grow and groups of dealers began putting together once- or twice-a-year baseball card conventions in church basements around New York City and, soon, other large cities. These conventions served to arouse the public interest in baseball cards, rekindling the childhoods of many whose cards had long since been thrown away. As the demand for old cards increased and the prices of them quickly began to rise accordingly, the church basement card shows evolved into much larger productions held in hotels, convention centers, and even ballparks.

As an added attraction for these larger baseball card shows, promoters began bringing in old-time and current ballplayers to sign autographs at a modest price. From that was born the phenomenon that exists today: spectacular baseball card/autograph shows in which as many as ten or twelve Hall of Famers can be found signing autographs at upwards of $10 per item.

Autographs

For the longest time, baseball autographs were something to be personally treasured but not necessarily valued. No one, for instance, put a value on a Babe Ruth autograph even twenty years after the Babe's death. For one thing, a Ruth autograph was still one of the most common of all Hall of Famer autographs, simply because the Babe signed willingly for everyone he came in contact with. A Lou Gehrig, by contrast, was not nearly as common, although until the advent of the autograph-collecting boom—which occurred at the same time the baseball card boom hit in the mid 1970s—collectors paid little notice.

Today Ruth, simply because of who he was and what he is to baseball, remains one of the most sought-after and high-priced baseball autographs. Of the living players, Joe DiMaggio is still commanding top dollar on the autograph circuit, with Mickey Mantle and Willie Mays not far behind. But as autograph collectors will testify, it is the turn-of-the-century Hall of Famers such as Pud Galvin, Tommy McCarthy, King Kelly, John Clarkson, Roger Connor, Candy Cummings, and Cap Anson whose signatures rightfully command the highest prices. These are players who have been dead for well over sixty years and whose autographs are far more scarce than a Ruth, Gehrig, or Ty Cobb.

Perhaps the best way to sum up the modern-day baseball autograph craze is to recall an incident at the 1980 New York Yankees annual Old Timer's Day game. As usual, all the Yankee living legends, from Joe DiMaggio to Mickey Mantle, Yogi Berra, and Whitey Ford, were on hand for the occasion and, accordingly, were besieged throughout the day for autographs. Reggie Jackson, the Yankees' star right fielder at the time, was attempting—

at least for public consumption—to express dismay at all the autograph badgering around him. "I don't understand all this idolatry," Reggie told the assembled writers. The next day, however, in the New York *Daily News* coverage of the Old Timer's Day festivities, there was a picture of Reggie Jackson—getting an autograph on a baseball from Joe DiMaggio.

Press Pins

Press pins from the World Series, the All Star Game, and Hall of Fame induction ceremonies are about the only baseball collectibles that are totally separated from the players themselves. They have nothing to do with the actual games themselves, other than being displayed on the sports coats of attending sportswriters, and they can't be autographed. Nevertheless, in conjunction with the baseball collecting boom of the 1970s and '80s, press pins have become among the most sought after (and subsequently highly valued) memorabilia items.

The origin of the baseball press pin dates back to 1911. According to legend John McGraw, manager of the New York Giants, had invited many of his cronies to attend the hotly contested games of September 1908. However, because of the scarcity of tickets, McGraw assigned his friends seats in the press box, where they became rowdy, distracting the members of the working press.

It was because of this unwelcome intrusion into their working domain that the Baseball Writers Association of America was formed. And as a part of this new union, press pins were used to establish proper identity for the World Series, when every seat was spoken for. No one was permitted into the press boxes without a press pin.

As years went on, press accreditation for the World Series became far more sophisticated, but the press pins continued to be a tradition. Each World Series team designed its own press pin for the games in its ballpark and though most sportswriters kept their pins through the years, they didn't look at them as valuable collectibles. Again, it was not until the early 1970s, when collectors began to realize how genuinely scarce all those old press pins were (because of limited distribution and the fact that so many of them were thrown away through the years) that they suddenly became a valued baseball collectible.

The earliest press pins are now valued at upwards of $10,000 apiece. But even the press pins from the 1940s, '50s, and '60s have considerable value. Of these, the most valued of all the World Series pins is that of the 1956 Brooklyn Dodgers—primarily because it isn't a pin at all; it's a tie clasp. For some reason, that year the Dodgers chose to break tradition and issue to the working press tie clasps with a blue Brooklyn cap affixed to it. Probably because the tie clasps were actually worn by the writers long after the Series was over (instead of being stuffed away in a drawer with all the old press pins), a good many of the tie clasps vanished from the scene. As a result, today the Brooklyn Dodgers 1956 World Series tie clasp has commanded as much as $3,000 in collectors' markets as opposed to the $300 that the 1956 New York Yankees World Series press pin generally sells for.

In 1937 baseball extended its press pin tradition to the All Star Game and those pins, too, have risen greatly in value. (The reason no press pins were issued prior to 1937 is that the All Star Game's creator and founder, sportswriter Arch Ward, had envisioned his "gala" as being a one-time event. (Actually, even the 1937 pin, from Griffith Stadium in Washington, may, in fact, be a one-of-a-kind item since only the one in the Halper collection is known to exist.)

The prices of All Star press pins vary greatly, based primarily on the issuing city. One of the hardest-to-find All Star press pins—and consequently one of the most sought-after and most prized—is the 1948 pin issued by the host St. Louis Browns. It is a beautiful pin depicting the white Brownies cap with the brown bill and gold piping; it is dated 1948, and it lists for upwards of $3,500.

Finally, in 1982, the Hall of Fame got into the press pin field. Beginning that year the Hall of Fame issued commemorative press pins, listing the names of each year's inductees. Because there is a far more limited number of media personnel covering the Hall of Fame ceremonies, the distribution of the pins is believed to be about one-tenth that of the World Series pins. As a result, the Hall of Fame pins have quickly shot past their contemporary World Series and All Star pins in value. That first Hall of Fame pin in 1982, engraved with the names of inductees Hank Aaron, Happy Chandler, Frank Robinson, and Travis Jackson, was going for $650 in the collectors' market.

In the early years of press pins, the Dieges & Clust Company of John Street in New York was the primary manufacturer. In 1946 the Balfour Company of Attleboro, Massachusetts, assumed the contract from Major League Baseball to produce the pins. They remain the prime producers of pins and rings for the World Series and All Star Game, although some teams have, in the interest of cost-cutting, sought local companies to produce their pins (the workmanship of those pins, particularly the colors and the enamel, has suffered noticeably).

The advent of the playoff system also caused economic problems for the contending clubs that were compelled to commission press pins. It had long been the custom of clubs to date the pins for each year's World Series. In many cases, though, the club would not make it to the Series and those press pins produced for the event were rendered unusable for any future Series. As such, these so-called "phantom" pins, such as the 1951 Brooklyn Dodgers (who lost out in a playoff to the Giants on Bobby Thomson's historic home run), the 1938 Pittsburgh Pirates (victims of the Cubs' Gabby Hartnett's memorable "homer in the gloamin'"), or the 1949 Cardinals are harder to come by and just as valuable as the "official" Series press pins of those years.

As John Scarpellini, Balfour's longtime representative to baseball recalled: "The elimination of the dating of the pins came about when Dick O'Connell, general manager of the Red Sox, was asked by us about the kind of press pin he wanted designed for the 1975 World Series. Instead of committing himself, O'Connell opened up a closet door in his office and produced what had to be nearly 50,000 press pins. 'Look at these,' he said. 'They're all dated and therefore no good to us. I've got all these pins, which we've paid for, and we can't do anything with them.'

"After that, we came up with the idea of labeling the pins with the phrase 'Our Second World Series' or whatever number that particular World Series was for that particular team. That way, if the club was beaten out in the playoffs, but had already had to produce their pins, they could just put them away in a vault and use them whenever they made it."

Uniforms

In the entire spectrum of baseball collecting there is probably no item more personal or intimate than a uniform. Unfortunately, the collecting of uniforms from modern-day players has oftentimes become a risky venture because of the increase in counterfeits on the market. Because the modern-day doubleknits are so easy to manufacture, it is very difficult to tell a counterfeit from the real thing. That's why the source of such uniforms is so important.

More often than not, the source for legitimate modern-day uniforms is the clubhouse man for the major league ballclubs. This, of course, has created a serious problem for Major League Baseball. They are aware of how little clubhouse men are paid and, as such, how they can become easy prey for dealers in baseball memorabilia.

In some cases, the players themselves can be sources for uniforms. Pete Rose, for example, reportedly had a deal with the Cincinnati Reds that he be given twenty-five or more uniforms during the course of the season to do with as he wished. And in the game in which Rose tied Ty Cobb's all-time hits record, he wore a different uniform top for each at bat. Presumably, Rose sold all those uniform tops to different collectors.

Similarly, Gaylord Perry, in winning his 300th game against the New York Yankees, wore two different Seattle Mariner uniforms. The reason I know that is that Perry had promised his uniform from that game to me. But a couple of days before he pitched, I got a call from the visiting clubhouse man in Baltimore, who was also a dealer in memorabilia. The clubhouse man offered me Perry's Seattle uniform from his 300th-win game. It seems that Gaylord had decided that two uniforms were better than one when it came to maximizing his profit on 300 wins, and he decided to make a change after four innings. I wound up having to make separate deals with both Perry and the clubhouse man from Baltimore in order to have what was surely the uniform in which Perry won his 300th game.

The values of modern-day players' uniforms vary greatly. Naturally, the uniforms players wore performing historic feats such as Perry's 300th win or Rose's 4,192nd hit (both of which are in the Halper collection) are of considerably more value than just an everyday game-worn uniform. In the uniform-collecting hobby of the '90s, common players' uniforms were selling in the $200 range, star-quality players' from $750 to $1,200, and superstar/ Hall of Fame–caliber players' from $2,000 up.

Old-time uniforms are a far more challenging hobby, one that has been the most satisfying and exciting aspect of my collecting career. Why? Because I never believed so many of these old uniforms, particularly the ones from the pre-1900 Hall of Fame players, could still exist. And exist in such remarkable condition! Through the years, I have managed to amass some 964 uniforms, which I have stored on a dry cleaner conveyer belt that is computerized to stop at whichever uniform number I punch in. Included among those 964 are uniforms of every Hall of Famer who played or managed, and even some minor league uniforms of Hall of Fame executives (such as longtime Yankee business manager Ed Barrow) who never wore a major league uniform.

As one might expect, values for the oldest, turn-of-the-century uniforms far exceed those for any of the more recent Hall of Famers of the '30s on up. I have had values in excess of $100,000 each placed on uniforms of Babe Ruth, Lou Gehrig, and Ty Cobb—all autographed—in my collection. But I could not even begin to put a value on the uniforms of turn-of-the-century Hall of Famers such as Pud Galvin (Buffalo, 1879), John Clarkson (Saginaw, 1883), King Kelly (NY Giants, 1893), Charles Comiskey (Cincinnati, 1893), Hoss Radbourn (Boston, 1886), Roger Connor (NY Giants, 1893), Joe McGinnity (NY Giants, 1904), and Cy Young (Boston, 1903)—most of which are almost certain to be the only ones worn by those players that still survive.

The existence of these uniforms only adds to and rounds out the lore and history of baseball. How they were uncovered after all these years—the treasure hunt—is the most fulfilling aspect of collecting baseballiana.

It was during a conversation I once had with Pete Sheehy, the venerable New York Yankee clubhouse man from the days of Ruth in the '20s right up until the Don Mattingly–Dave Winfield Yankees of the '80s, that I got my most valuable tip in regard to uniform collecting. I asked Sheehy: "Pete, where are all the Pete Sheehys of yesterday? The clubhouse men who kept a vigil over all the old uniforms?"

Not surprisingly, in his days as Yankee clubhouse man, Sheehy did become friends with the clubhouse men from other clubs and they would correspond frequently. Most of his contemporaries had died when I talked to him about this, but he kept track of many of their relatives.

One person Sheehy put me in contact with was a man from Coxsackie, New York, who, Sheehy thought, was in possession of most of the old Yankee uniforms from 1927, the year of Murderers' Row. Sure enough, upon getting in touch with the man, I was able to acquire the 1927 Yankee uniforms of Ruth, Gehrig, Earle Combs, Waite Hoyt, Bob Meusel, Mark Koenig, Bob Shawkey, and about a half dozen others. Sheehy also put me in contact with the relatives of the equipment manager at Columbia University during the early '20s when Gehrig played there. It was through that contact that I was able to uncover Gehrig's Columbia uniform and the first uniform he ever wore as a professional, with Hartford. He had played there under the assumed name of Lewis in 1921 to protect his amateur standing at Columbia; that name is sewn into the bottom flap of the shirt.

All the uniforms from that pre-1920s period are identified by the players' names sewn somewhere on them since numbers did not come into existence until 1929. The Yankees that year introduced numbers on the backs of their uniforms in the order in which the players appeared in the batting order.

Another valuable source of old uniforms was Dick Bar-

tell, the pepperpot New York Giants and Detroit Tigers shortstop of the 1930s and '40s. Bartell put me in touch with Ollie O'Mara, an old ballplayer, then in his 80s, who lived in Reno, Nevada. O'Mara had had a brief major league career with the Brooklyn Dodgers from 1914 to 1919, a team that was managed by Hall of Famer Wilbert Robinson. Apparently O'Mara had maintained a close friendship with Robinson. That is the only explanation I can offer for the fact that he had in his possession the 1894 Baltimore Orioles uniforms of Robinson, Joe Kelley, Wee Willie Keeler, Dan Brouthers, and Hughie Jennings— Hall of Famers all. O'Mara never did tell me how he got the uniforms or why he had kept them all those years in near-perfect condition. In 1989 he went to his grave with that secret, but baseball historians can be forever grateful that he preserved so much of the game's valuable past.

Bats, Balls, Books

Until recent years vintage bats, balls, gloves, and other gear were a neglected area for collectors. One could find an antique glove or ball in a thrift store or flea market for just a few dollars; without an autograph or major-league player "association," the items were simply not viewed as desirable. The same could be said of baseball books and photos, though scorecards, guides (Spalding, Reach, Beadle, etc.), yearbooks, and programs—especially World Series programs— did attract collectors before the 1980s baseball-card boom.

A handful of early-baseball enthusiasts, myself included, picked up as many of these early items as we could, from club constitutions of the amateur era to thick-handled bats with "mushroom" knobs, from gold-painted trophy balls of the 1860s to sepia-toned photographs of unknown teams. These sorts of items increased in value over the years but not as spectacularly as, say, the cards of the 1950s. Where a 1952 Mickey Mantle card, of which may fine examples exist, might fetch $8,000, a genuinely rare 1868 book by Henry Chadwick might bring only $3,000. However, as card prices continued to soar sophisticated collectors and devoted fans who have been made nervous by the explosive speculation of the 1980s are beginning to see relative safety in the pursuit of older collectibles, where "the market" is driven by true scarcity more than widespread demand.

Despite dire predictions of a collapse in the market, I remain convinced that collecting baseball memorabilia is a hobby that is still in its infancy. Prices may go up or down with general economic conditions, but the lure of baseball and its collectibles is a constant.

The Registers, Leaders, and Rosters

Part II: Introduction

Part Two, the statistical section of *Total Baseball*, presents the record of major league contests played from 1871 through 1990—all 160,899 of them. It details the accomplishments of the game's 2,125 teams and 13,843 players more completely and more accurately than any other encyclopedic work; it applies to all of baseball's glorious past the "sabermetric" stats that fans first embraced in the 1980s; it introduces original measures of player performance. Yet for all its innovation, *Total Baseball* stands squarely in the tradition of baseball record keeping; it is—like each new spring of our national pastime—a link in a long, long chain. As the game of one hundred and fifty years ago lives on in the game of today, so is this volume enriched by the labors of statisticians from Henry Chadwick to Ernie Lanigan, from S. C. Thompson to David Neft to Bill James.

The Origins, 1845–1875

In fact, baseball and stats were a tandem from the outset of the game's history, as the editors of this volume first discussed in their earlier *Hidden Game of Baseball* (1984), from which portions of this introduction are adapted. The first box score appeared in the *New York Morning News* on October 22, 1845, just a month after Alexander Cartwright and his Knickerbocker teammates codified the first set of rules. Why did these early players and scribes measure individual performance rather than simply count the score? In part to imitate the custom of cricket; yet the larger explanation is that the numbers served to legitimize men's concern with a boys' pastime. The pioneers of baseball reporting—William Cauldwell of the *Sunday Mercury*, William Porter of *Spirit of the Times*, the unknown annalist at the *News*, and later Henry Chadwick—may indeed have reflected that if they did not cloak the game in the "importance" of statistics, it might not seem worthwhile for adults to read about, let alone play. Statistics elevated baseball from other boys' field games of the 1840s and '50s to make it somehow "serious," like business; its essential simplicity was adorned with intricate detail that suited it perfectly to quantification.

In the development of baseball statistics, no man is more important than Father Chadwick. Born in England in 1824, he came to these shores at age thirteen steeped in the tradition of cricket. In his teens he played the English game and in his twenties he reported on it for a variety of newspapers, including the *Long Island Star* and the *New York Times*. In the early 1840s, before the Knickerbocker rules eliminated the practice of retiring a base runner by throwing the ball at him rather than to the base, Chadwick occasionally played baseball too, but he was not favorably impressed, having received "some hard hits in the ribs." Not until 1856, by which time he had been a cricket reporter for a decade, were Chadwick's eyes opened to the possibilities in the American game, which had improved dramatically since his youth. In 1868 he recalled, "On returning from the early close of a cricket match on Fox Hill, I chanced to go through the Elysian Fields during the progress of a contest between the noted Eagle and Gotham clubs. The game was being sharply played on both sides, and I watched it with deeper interest than any previous ball game between clubs that I had seen. It was not long before I was struck with the idea that baseball was just the game for a national sport for Americans . . . as much so as cricket in England. At the time I refer to I had been reporting cricket for years, and, in my method of taking notes of contests, I had a plan peculiarly my own. It was not long, therefore, after I had become interested in baseball, before I began to invent a method of giving detailed reports of leading contests at baseball . . ."

Thus Chadwick's cricket background was largely the impetus to his method of scoring a baseball game, the format of his early box scores, and the copious if primitive statistics that appeared in his year-end summaries in the *New York Clipper*, Beadle's *Dime Base-Ball Player*, and other publications.

Actually, cricket had begun to shape baseball statistics even before Chadwick's conversion. The first box score reported on two categories, outs and runs: outs, or "hands out," counted both unsuccessful times at bat and outs run into on the basepaths; "runs" were runs scored, not those driven in. The reason for not recording hits in the early years, when coverage of baseball matches appeared alongside that of cricket matches, was that, unlike baseball, cricket had no such category as the successful hit which did not produce a run. To reach "base" in cricket is to run to the opposite wicket, which tallies a run; if you hit the ball and do not score a run, you have been put out.

Cricket box scores were virtual play-by-plays, a fact made possible by the lesser number of possible events. This play-by-play aspect was applied to a baseball box score as early as 1856; interestingly, despite the abundance of detail, hits were not accounted, nor did they appear in Chadwick's own box scores until 1867. The batting champion as declared by Chadwick, whose computations were immediately and universally accepted as "official," was the man with the highest average of runs per game. An inverse though imprecise measure of batting quality was outs per game. After 1863, when a fair

ball caught on one bounce was no longer an out, fielding leaders were those with the greatest total of fly catches, assists, and "foul bounds" (fouls caught on one bounce). Pitching effectiveness was based purely on control, with the leader recognized as the one whose delivery offered the most opportunities for outs at first base and led to the fewest passed balls.

In a sense, Chadwick's measuring of baseball as if it were cricket can be viewed as correct in that when you strip the game to its basic elements, those that determine victory or defeat, outs and runs are all that count in the end. No individual statistic is meaningful to the team unless it relates directly to the scoring of runs. Chadwick's blind spot in his early years of baseball reporting lay in not recognizing the linear character of the game, the sequential nature whereby a string of base hits or men reaching base on error (there were no walks then) was necessary in most cases to produce a run. In cricket each successful hit must produce at least one run, while in baseball, more of a team game on offense, a successful hit may produce none.

Early player stats were of the most primitive kind, the counting kind. They'd tell you *how many* runs, or outs, or fly catches had occurred—later, how many hits or total bases. Counting is the most basic of all statistical processes; the next step up is averaging, and Chadwick was the first to put this into practice.

As professionalism infiltrated the game, teams began to bid for star-caliber players. Stars were known not by their stats but by their style until 1865, when Chadwick began to record in the *Clipper* a form of batting average taken from the cricket pages—runs per game. Two years later, in his newly founded baseball weekly, *The Ball Players' Chronicle,* he began to record not only average runs and outs per game, but also home runs, total bases, total bases per game—and hits per game. The averages were expressed not with decimal places but in the standard cricket format of the "average and over." Thus a batter with 23 hits in 6 games would have an average expressed not as 3.83 but as "3-5"—an average of 3 with an overage, or remainder, of 5. Another innovation was to remove from the individual accounting all bases gained through errors. Runs scored by a team, beginning in 1867, were divided between those scored after a man reached base on a clean hit and those arising from a runner's having reached base on an error. This was, of course, a precursor of today's earned run average.

In 1868, despite Chadwick's derision, the *Clipper* continued to award the prize for the batting championship to the player with the greatest average of runs per game. Actually, the old yardstick had been less preposterous a measure of batsmanship than one might imagine today, because team defense was so much poorer and the pitcher, with severe restrictions on his method of delivery, was so much less important. If you reached first base, whether by a hit or by an error, your chances of scoring were excellent; indeed, teams of the mid-1860s registered more runs than hits! By 1876, the caliber of both pitching and defense had improved to the extent that the ratio of runs to hits was about 6.5 to 10; today the ratio stands at roughly 5 to 10.

By the end of the decade Chadwick was recording total bases and home runs, but he placed little stock in either, as conscious attempts at slugging violated his cricket-bred image of "form." Just as cricket aficionados watch the game for the many opportunities for fine fielding it affords, so was baseball from its inception perceived as a fielders' sport. The original Cartwright rules of 1845, in fact, specified that a ball hit out of the field—in fair territory or foul—was a foul ball! "Long hits are showy," Chadwick wrote in the *Clipper* in 1868, "but they do not pay in the long run. Sharp grounders insuring the first-base certain, and sometimes the second-base easily, are worth all the hits made for home-runs which players strive for."

Chadwick prevailed, and hits per game became the criterion for the *Clipper* batting championship and remained so until 1876, when the problem with using games as the denominator in the average at last became clear. If you were playing for a successful team, and thus were surrounded by good batters, or if your team played several weak rivals who committed many errors, the number of at-bats for each individual in that lineup would increase. The more at-bats one is granted in a game, the more hits one is likely to have. So, for example, if Player A had 10 at-bats in a game, which was not so unusual in the 1860s, he might have 4 base hits. In a more cleanly played game, Player B might bat only 6 times, and get 3 base hits. Yet Player A, with his 4-for-10, would achieve an average of 4.00; the average of Player B, who went 3-for-6, would be only 3.00. By modern standards, of course, Player A would be batting .400 while Player B would be batting .500.

In short, the batting average used in the 1860s is the same as that used today except in its denominator, with at-bats replacing games. Moreover, Chadwick created a measure in the 1860s that divided total bases by games played; change the denominator to at-bats and you have today's slugging average—which, incidentally, was not accepted by the National League as an official statistic until 1923 and by the American until 1946 (baseball was born and bred conservative).

Chadwick's "total bases average" represents the game's first attempt at a weighted average—an average in which the elements collected together in the numerator or the denominator are recognized numerically as being unequal. In this instance, a single is the unweighted unit, the double is weighted by a factor of two, the triple by three, and the home run by four. Statistically, this is a distinct leap forward from, first, counting, and next, averaging. The weighted average is in fact the cornerstone of today's statistical innovations, or "sabermetrics."

The 1870s gave rise to some new batting stats and to the first attempt to quantify thoroughly the other principal facets of the game, pitching and fielding. Although the *Clipper* recorded base hits and total bases as early as 1868, a significant wrinkle was added in 1870 when at-bats were listed as well. This was a critical introduction because it permitted the improvement of the batting average, first introduced in its current form by H. A. Dobson of Washington, D.C., in the *Dime Base-Ball Player* of 1872, and first computed officially—that is, for the National League—in 1876. Since then the batting average has not changed, except for 1876, when bases on balls were figured as outs, and 1887, when they were counted as hits. *Total Baseball* counts a walk as neither an at-bat nor an out for all years since 1871.

The objections to the batting average are well known, but to date have not dislodged it from its place as the most popular measure of hitting ability. First of all, the batting average makes no distinction between the single, the double, the triple, and the home run, treating all as the same unit. This objection had been addressed in 1868 by Chadwick's total bases average.

Second, it gives no indication of the effect of that base hit—that is, its value to the team. This was the reason Chadwick clung to runs per game as the best possible batting measure. Third, the batting average does not take into account those occasions when first base is reached via a walk, hit by pitch, or error. This last point was addressed at a surprisingly early date, too, as for 1879 the National League adopted as an official statistic a forerunner of the on-base percentage; it was called "reached first base," which included times reached by error as well as base on balls and base hits. (Being hit by a pitch did not give the batter first base until 1884 in the American Association, 1887 in the National League.)

The Flowering, 1876–1920

Ever since the Civil War, serial guides like Beadle and DeWitt and sporting columns like those in the *Clipper* had carried year-end tabulations of batting, fielding, and pitching exploits, varying from year to year with the brainstorms of Chadwick or other demon compilers like New York's M. J. Kelly or Philadelphia's Al Wright. But the year 1876 was special. It was significant not only for the founding of the National League and the official debut of the batting average in its current form, it was also the Centennial of the United States, which was marked by a giant exposition in Philadelphia celebrating the mechanical marvels of the day. American ingenuity reigned, and technology was seen as the new handmaiden of democracy. Baseball, that mirror of American life, reflected the fervor for things scientific with an explosion of statistics far more complex than those seen before, particularly in the previously neglected areas of pitching and fielding. The increasingly minute statistical examination of the game met a responsive audience, one primed to view complexity as a measure of worth.

The crossroads year of 1876 highlights how the game had changed to that point, as well as how it has changed since.

In that year, the number of offensive stats tabulated at season's end in any of the publications inspired by Chadwick or Spalding was six: games, at-bats, runs, hits, runs per game, and batting average. (And as with all the various guides until 1941, the stats of men who played in fewer than a specified minimum number of games were not noted.) Of these six, only runs and runs per game were common in the 1860s, while that decade's tabulation of total bases vanished. The number of offensive stats a hundred years later? Twenty. (Today the number is twenty-one, with the addition of on base percentage).

The number of pitching categories in 1876 was eleven, and there were some surprises, such as earned run average, hits allowed, hits per game, and opponents' batting average. Strikeouts were not recorded, for Chadwick saw them strictly as a sign of poor batting rather than good pitching (his view had such an impact that pitcher strike-

outs were not kept officially until 1889). The number of pitching stats today? Twenty-four.

The number of fielding categories in 1876 was six. One hundred years later it was still six (with the exception of the catcher, who gets a seventh: passed balls), dramatizing how the game, which originated as a showcase for fielders, had changed. The fielding stats of 1876 lumped "battery errors" with fielding errors, so that wild pitches and passed balls—in some years, even walks—diminished one's fielding percentage. This practice continued until 1887, but in *Total Baseball* battery errors are not included in fielding stats. Battery-mates' fielding stats were boosted by the awarding of an assist to the pitcher on strikeouts. This practice lasted until 1889, but is not reflected in *Total Baseball*.

The custom in 1876, as it is now, was to combine putouts, assists, and errors to form a "percentage of chances accepted," or what is today known as fielding average or fielding percentage. A "missing link" variant, devised by Al Wright in 1875, was to form averages by dividing the putouts by the number of games to yield a "putout average"; dividing the assists similarly to arrive at an "assist average"; and dividing putouts plus assists by games to get "fielding average." These averages took no account of errors. (Wright's "fielding average" was reborn a century later as Bill James's Range Factor.)

The public's appetite for new statistics was not sated by the outburst of 1876. New measures were introduced in dizzying profusion in the remaining years of the century. Some of these did not catch on and were soon dropped for all time, like the ridiculous "total bases run," while others fizzled only to reappear with new vigor in the twentieth century. These include (a) the above-mentioned "reached first base," which resurfaced in the early 1950s in an unofficial, improved form called on base percentage and became an official stat more than thirty years later, and (b) an 1860s stat, earned run average, which was periodically revived before dropping from sight in the 1880s, only to return triumphant to the NL in 1912 and the AL in 1913. In 1913 Ban Johnson not only proclaimed the ERA official but became so enamored with it that he also instructed American League scorers to compile *no* official won-lost records (this state of affairs lasted for seven years, 1913–1919).

Another stat that was "sent back to the minors" before its eventual adoption as an official stat in 1920 was the run batted in. Introduced by a Buffalo newspaper in 1879, the stat was picked up the following year by the *Chicago Tribune* and even became an official NL stat for the opening months of 1891. By season's end it had faded as most NL scorers declined to account for it in their summaries (The American Association, however, recorded it all year long.) Ernie Lanigan picked up the RBI baton with his reports to the *New York Press* in 1907, but only about a third of his data has been found, and he did not figure RBIs for men who played in fewer than ten games, or club totals for traded players. For *Total Baseball* we have placed much reliance upon the source material donated by Information Concepts, Inc. (ICI) to the National Baseball Library in Cooperstown following publication of its *Baseball Encyclopedia* for Macmillan in 1969. David Neft also kindly supplied us with his unpublished RBI data for the previously missing National League

seasons of 1880–1885. The John Tattersall collection of nineteenth century game accounts and box scores was valuable as well.

Other statistics introduced officially before the turn of the century were stolen bases (though not caught stealing); doubles, triples, and homers; and sacrifice bunts (though an at-bat was charged from 1889 through 1894). Pitcher strikeouts, bases on balls, and the hit-by-pitch also appeared before 1900, but hit-by-pitch stats were not kept for batters on a systematic basis until 1917 in the NL and 1920 in the AL. Through newspaper research, we have filled in HBP data from 1884 through 1916 in the National League, Players League, and American Association, from 1909 through 1919 in the American League, and the 1914–1915 Federal League; research continues for the 1903–1908 period in both the American and National leagues. We are indebted in this area to Alex Haas, John Schwartz, John Tattersall, and Bob Davids.

Hit into double play—including line outs as well as groundouts—was recorded erratically in the nineteenth century, but separate stats for groundouts into double plays have been kept by the leagues only since 1933 in the NL and 1939 in the AL. Batters' strikeouts were reported unofficially in 1891, but not as a league stat until 1910 in the NL and 1913 in the AL. Innings pitched were not kept until 1908 in the AL and 1910 in the NL.

Stolen bases were awarded not only for clean steals but also for extra bases taken through daring, from the first year in which totals were kept, 1886, until 1898 (the Macmillan *Baseball Encyclopedia* begins its record of stolen bases with 1887). Because the figures reported in the guides were grossly inflated (such as Harry Stovey's ostensible 156 steals in 1888), the figures in *Total Baseball* reflect game-by-game research and refiguring. Caught-stealing (CS) figures are available on a very sketchy basis in some of the later years of the century, as some newspapers carried the data in the box scores of hometown games. From 1912 on, Lanigan recorded CS in box scores of the *New York Press,* but the leagues did not keep the figure officially until 1920. The AL has tabulated CS from that year to the present, excepting 1927, which members of the Society for American Baseball Research reconstructed from newspaper box scores. National League caught-stealing data exists for 1920–1925, and for 1951 to the present.

The new century added little in the way of *new* official statistics—ERA, RBI, and slugging average are better regarded as revivals despite their respective adoption dates of 1912, 1920, and 1923. But back in 1908 there was a classic case of a statistic rushing in to fill a void, as Phillies' manager Billy Murray observed that his outfielder Sherry Magee had the happy facility of providing a long fly ball whenever presented with a situation of a man on third and fewer than two outs. Taking up the cudgels on his player's behalf, Murray protested to the National League office that it was unfair to charge Magee with an unsuccessful time at bat when he was in fact succeeding, doing precisely what the situation demanded. Murray won his point, but baseball flip-flopped a couple of times on this stat, in some years reverting to calling it a time at bat, in other years not even crediting an RBI. The sacrifice-fly rule was in effect from 1908 through 1930, with a sacrifice being given for advancing any runner, not just to home, for the final four years of this period. The rule was revived for one year in 1939. In none of these years was a distinction made between a sacrifice bunt or fly. When the rule came back into force in 1954, there was a breakdown of each.

More recent stats that have followed from this sort of perception—that something important was occurring on the field which had no verifiable reality because it was not yet being measured—are the save and the late, lamented game-winning RBI, which will be discussed later.

A signal event took place in 1912: the publication by *Baseball Magazine* editor John Lawres of *Who's Who in Baseball,* a small book that became the first to provide career statistics and personal facts for a group of players. Although thoroughly inadequate by today's standards— its only tabulations were games, batting average, and fielding average (even for pitchers, who were given no mound records!)—*Who's Who* was a groundbreaking work, giving rise to a much-expanded format in 1916 and inspiring two other significant encyclopedic works: in 1914, George Moreland's self-published opus called *Balldom* (grandiosely subtitled "The Britannica of Baseball," which it surely wasn't), and Ernest J. Lanigan's *Baseball Cyclopedia,* also sponsored by *Baseball Magazine,* which debuted in 1922 and was updated annually through 1933.

The Golden Age, 1920–1968

There have been other new statistical tabulations in this century, but generally of the counting sort: complete games (NL 1910, AL 1922), games started (AL 1926, NL 1938), games finished (NL 1920, AL 1926). And there were sacrifice bunts allowed (NL 1916, AL 1922), intentional bases on balls (only since 1955), and, in the next period, saves (1969) and game-winning RBIs (1980). The only new average since slugging average was adopted in 1923 has been the on base percentage, adopted in 1985. The ICI group computed saves for prior years. Another such stat that failed to survive, alas, was stolen bases off pitchers, which the American League recorded only in 1920–1924; it has been recorded on an unofficial basis in the 1980s by the Elias Sports Bureau and Project Scoresheet. The only new fielding measure was team double plays, added to the AL list in 1912 and the NL in 1919. Other new and more interesting stats appeared in the 1940s and '50s but have not yet gained the official stamp of approval, such as Ted Oliver's Weighted Rating System, Alfred P. Berry's Average Bases Allowed (opponents' slugging average), and Branch Rickey and Allan Roth's Isolated Power.

This period of baseball's history may have fielded its most dazzling array of stars, but strategically and statistically it was pretty dim. There was some excitement, however, in baseball record keeping. First came *Daguerreotypes,* issued by *The Sporting News* in 1934, featuring the playing records of many retired players both celebrated and obscure; most if not all of these statistical and biographical profiles originally appeared in the pages of *TSN.* Although its number of statistical categories was fewer than one might have wished, *Daguerreotypes* was very useful and, through its several editions ably edited by Paul MacFarlane, long-lived.

In 1940 came *The Sporting News's Baseball Register*, which supplied full records for active players, managers, coaches, and umpires, plus a grab bag of former stars. Since the expansion of the major leagues from sixteen teams to twenty-six, the *Register* has only accommodated contemporary players and managers, but it remains a valuable source. One year later, *TSN* issued a notable edition of its *Official Baseball Record Book,* giving for the first time full statistical lines for all men who played in a major league game the previous year.

In 1944 a little-known man named Ted Oliver published in obscurity a booklet called *Kings of the Mound*. It introduced a new stat called the Weighted Rating System for pitchers, a stat that we modified and continue to employ as Wins Above Team. Moved by the inadequacy of both the won-lost percentage and the ERA to reflect the value of a decent pitcher laboring for a lousy club, Oliver ingeniously subtracted the pitcher's decisions from his team's, then took the difference between the pitcher's won-lost percentage and his team's and multiplied that difference by the pitcher's number of decisions. Although his concept and his math were flawed, his principles—viewing a pitcher's record in relation to his team and weighting the result of his calculation by the number of decisions—were of unparalleled sophistication for the time. (Oliver's formula for his Weighted Rating System and its modification in *Total Baseball* are detailed in the Glossary, as are the calculations behind every statistic employed in this book.)

Then in 1951 came the first true encyclopedia of baseball, the claims of Moreland and Lanigan notwithstanding. Compiled by Hy Turkin and S. C. Thompson, *The Official Encyclopedia of Baseball* was published by the A. S. Barnes Company. Its 620 pages contained a wealth of features such as manager and umpire rosters, historical essays, playing tips, a bibliography, and much more. But the heart of the volume and the key to its subsequent success was a register of nearly nine thousand men who played one or more games at the major league level from 1871 through 1949 (the 1950 record of players appearing in ten games or more was tacked on to the end). In this register, Turkin/Thompson also offered birth and death data and what today seems fairly limited statistical information but by previous standards was a veritable cornucopia: year, club, league, position, games, and batting average or won-lost record. A landmark volume that did much to inspire this one, *The Official Encyclopedia of Baseball* lasted through ten revised editions, the last being published in 1979, ten years after the initial appearance of Macmillan's *Baseball Encyclopedia*.

The genesis of the Turkin/Thompson opus was one day in September 1944 when musician Thompson invited his neighbor, New York *Daily News* sportswriter Turkin, to "look over his baseball collection." What Turkin saw was a massive treasure chest of data, collected and collated over twenty years. "Tommy" Thompson was a baseball nut—a figure filbert, in the parlance of the time—who researched baseball just for the love of it. He was not alone in this pursuit, although very nearly so—other baseball archeologists of the time who contributed to this encyclopedia were Frank Marcellus, Tom Shea, Lee Allen, Ralph Lin Weber, Joe Overfield, Bob McConnell, and the aforementioned Ernie Lanigan.

The Official Encyclopedia of Baseball went a long way toward making the study of baseball history and records a respectable pursuit, just as a century earlier the statistical accounting of a boys' game had helped to make baseball a sport for grown men. The researchers' ranks expanded to include such men as Bob Davids, who in 1971, aided by other experts like Cliff Kachline, Bill Haber, Ray Nemec, John Pardon, and Joe Simenic, would create SABR, the Society for American Baseball Research (pronounced "saber"). Formerly the lonely pursuit of a handful of "nuts" like S. C. Thompson, baseball research and sabermetrics—a neologism coined in honor of SABR, signifying the statistical analysis of the game's records—would become the pastime of thousands.

An article in *Life* magazine by Branch Rickey on August 2, 1954, gave further impetus to the study of baseball statistics, but not just to set the historical record straight. Indeed, this article may be viewed as the opening shot of the sabermetric assault of the 1980s. In "Goodby to Some Old Baseball Ideas," Rickey, with the aid of some new mathematical tools supplied by Dodger statistician Allan Roth, sought to puncture some long-held conceptions about how the game was divided among its elements (batting, baserunning, pitching, fielding), who was best at playing it, and what caused one team to win and another to lose. This is a pretty fair statement of what sabermetrics is about.

Rickey attacked the batting average and proposed in its place the on base percentage; advocated the use of Isolated Power (extra bases beyond singles, divided by at-bats) as a better measure than slugging average; introduced a "clutch" measure of run-scoring efficiency for teams, and a similar concept for pitchers (earned runs divided by baserunners allowed); reaffirmed the basic validity of the ERA; saw the strikeout as the insubstantial thing it was—and more. But the most important thing Rickey did for baseball statistics was to pull it back from the wrong path it had taken with the introduction of the batting average in 1876: to strip the game and its stats to their essentials and start again, this time remembering that individual stats came into being as an attempt to apportion the players' contributions to achieving a team victory, for that is what the game is about.

Rickey and Roth devised a formula to measure a team's efficiency in turning its offensive and defensive statistics into runs, and thus wins. They realized, and had confirmed for them by mathematicians at the Massachusetts Institute of Technology, that just as the team which scores more runs in a game gets the win, so a team which over the course of a season scores more runs than it allows should win more games than it loses—and by an extent correlated to its run differential. From this startlingly simple (or rather, seemingly simple) observation in 1954 flowed: first, the trailblazing but little noted work of George Lindsey in the 1950s and early 1960s, when he developed a model for run-scoring probability from the twenty-four combinations of outs and bases occupied; the development of "percentage baseball" stats and strategies by Earnshaw Cook in the 1960s; the play-by-play analysis of complete seasons by the Mills brothers, Eldon and Harlan, in 1969–1970; and, over the next two decades, the statistical and historical works of several sabermetricians, most notably Bill James.

The Computer Age, 1969–

Despite the death of Turkin in 1957 and Thompson ten years later, their *Official Encyclopedia of Baseball* remained the dominant book of baseball statistics, although many fans were frustrated with the fragmentary records it presented. As Frank V. Phelps wrote in the 1987 edition of *The National Pastime,* "Gaps and obvious errors in official averages, the lack of many early records, difficulty in securing the records of players who appeared in only a few games, and frustrating discrepancies among existing guides and registers had long since created a desire for an ultimate, complete, correct set of major league records. But it wasn't until the mid-1960s that the development of sophisticated computers which could absorb, retain, order, and output huge amounts of data finally made a project feasible."

Beginning in 1967, a battalion of researchers commanded by David Neft foraged through the official records and newspaper box scores to provide freshly compiled figures for those who had no ERAs, RBIs, slugging averages, saves, and all manner of wonderful things. The material which finally appeared in the tome was entered into a data bank, and the book was the first typeset entirely by computer, now a common practice. Published in 1969, *The Baseball Encyclopedia* was a milestone in computer technology, but as indispensable as the computer were the old-fashioned scrapbooks and files of Lee Allen and John Tattersall. The result was a mammoth ledger book of the major leagues more thorough than any that had appeared before.

The Baseball Encyclopedia researchers not only found new data to correct old inaccuracies but also applied new yardsticks to men who had gone to their graves never having heard of an RBI or a save. They also raised the hackles of traditionalists with many of their findings, which prompted the formation of a Special Baseball Records Committee. Its members ruled upon such matters as whether, for the historical record, bases on balls should be counted as hits (as they were in 1887), outs (as they were in 1876), or neither (as has been the practice in all other years); or whether "sudden-death" home runs—thirty-seven game-winning blows with men on base that they identified as having occurred in the bottom half of the ninth or extra inning—would be credited as homers or, in the practice before 1920, would count for only as many bases as needed to push across the winning run. In the latter controversy, committee members first decided to count the disputed blows as homers, but then, when complaints arose that Babe Ruth's famous total of 714 would change to 715, they reversed themselves. They decided that the National Association of 1871–1875 was not a major league, while the Federal League, Union Association, and Players League were; and they ruled on several other issues, all of which were published in the Appendix to *The Baseball Encyclopedia.*

In *Total Baseball,* we have abided by most of the committee's decisions—not to preserve Ruth's total, but because there were many more such homers before 1920 than the thirty-seven the committee identified, and the disputes surrounding some of them are now beyond settling. We have, however, treated the National Association as a major league, as Turkin/Thompson and all previous

record books did, and in accordance with the views of most historians. And we have differed from the committee's ruling on awarding pitchers wins and losses in the years before 1920. Not finding any official scoring rule or practice for that time, they chose to apply 1950 guidelines to decisions awarded in 1876–1920. This well-intentioned decision produced substantial alterations in the records of such hurlers as Cy Young, Christy Mathewson, Grover Alexander, and others. In the ensuing years, the notable research of Frank Williams (reported in "All the Record Books Are Wrong," *The National Pastime,* 1982) revealed that there was indeed a pattern and a rationale for the way decisions were awarded in those days; the data in *Total Baseball* conforms with his findings.

ICI research created new stars, launching several previously underappreciated heroes of old into the Hall of Fame. Sam Thompson, Addie Joss, Roger Connor, Amos Rusie—their phenomenal level of play was hidden simply because statisticians back then were not recording the particular numbers which would show them off to best advantage. If sabermetrics consists of finding things in the existing data that were not seen before, or collecting that data which makes possible the application of new statistics to old performances, the first edition of *The Baseball Encyclopedia* was a monument in the course of sabermetrics.

However, its subsequent editions declined from that standard, dropping valuable data, jimmying figures for star players in a misguided homage to tradition, and making a shambles of individual/team balance in the totals. As Phelps wrote of the second edition, edited by Joseph L. Reichler for the Macmillan Company after the ICI group broke up and relinquished supervision:

"Players' batting statistics were changed without compensating for changes in the records of other players on the same teams or in the corresponding team and league totals. Later editions included even more unbalanced adjustments . . .

"Quite apart from the problem of record-balancing, the numerous changes in players' totals and averages has caused serious misapprehensions and confusions for fans, writers, and researchers. The records of Fred Clarke and Cy Young differ in all six editions [to 1987] even without counting Clarke's astronomical 1899 BA [in the third edition, Clarke was credited with a batting average of .986 that boosted his lifetime mark by 15 points]. The figures for Burkett, Chesbro, Duffy, Hornsby, Walter Johnson, Radbourn, Speaker, and Waddell differ in five of the six books. The same is so in four of six for at least twenty-three other Hall of Famers, and many more less gifted players." The seventh edition was issued in 1988 and, like the five that preceded it, was less accurate than the classic first issue. The eighth edition, published in 1990, corrected many of the errors in the seventh but—perhaps because of its marketing link with Major League Baseball—retained many once-contested errors that historians had long since expunged from the record. (David Neft of ICI, along with *Baseball Encyclopedia* staff alumni Dick Cohen and Jordan Deutsch, went on to form Sport Products, Inc. Since 1974 they have issued the excellent *Sports Encyclopedia: Baseball,* which has endured as the baseball reference of choice for thousands of sophisticated fans.)

We will have more to add about accuracy and balance in the "Errors and Controversies" section of this Introduction.

There were two other interesting developments in 1969. The first and less celebrated was a research project launched by Eldon and Harlan Mills that, like the ICI encyclopedia, could not have been contemplated without the computer. The Mills brothers tracked the entire major league seasons of 1969 and 1970 on a play-by-play basis. Then they applied to that record the probabilities of winning which derived from each possible outcome of a plate appearance, as determined by a computer simulation incorporating nearly eight thousand possibilities. What, for example, was the visiting team's chance of winning the game before the first pitch was thrown? Fifty percent, if we are pitting two theoretical teams of equal or unknown ability on a neutral site. If the first man fails to get on base, the chances of the visiting team winning are reduced to 49.8 percent; should he hit a double, the visiting team's chance of victory is raised to 55.9 percent, as determined by the probabilistic simulation. Every possible situation—combining half inning, score, men on base, and men out—was tested by the simulator to arrive at "Win Points."

The Millses' purpose was to determine the clutch value of, say, hitting a homer with two men on and one man out in the bottom of the ninth, with the team trailing by two runs, the situation Bobby Thomson faced in the climactic National League game of 1951—oddly, the rookie year of the first modern computer. (It gained for him 1,472 Win Points; had it come with no one on in the eighth inning of a game in which his team led 4–0, the homer would have been worth only 12 Win Points.) What the Mills brothers were attempting to do was to evaluate not only the *what* of a performance, which traditional statistics indicate, but the *when,* or clutch factor, which no statistic to that time could provide.

This project, detailed in a small book issued in 1970 called *Player Win Averages,* proceeded from the same impulse that led to other measures of clutch performance: the game winning RBI, introduced as an official major league stat in 1980 and scrapped in 1989; the measure of batting performance in late-inning pressure situations first published by Seymour Siwoff, Steve Hirdt, and Peter Hirdt of the Elias Sports Bureau in 1985; and the historically complete indexes of clutch hitting and clutch pitching developed for this book.

The other noteworthy baseball event of 1969 (besides the centennial of professional baseball and the miracle of the Mets) was the adoption by the major leagues of the save, the stat associated with the most significant strategic development since the advent of the gopher ball. Now shown in the papers on a daily basis, saves were not officially recorded at all until 1960; it was at the instigation of Jerry Holtzman of the *Chicago Sun-Times,* with the cooperation of *The Sporting News,* that this statistic was finally accepted. (Although Pat McDonough, a founding member of SABR, had developed a similar stat in 1924 which he called "games finished by relief hurlers"; its first appearance in print came in the *New York Telegram* three years later.) The need for the save arose because relievers operated at a disadvantage when it came to picking up wins. The bullpen specialists were a new breed, and as their role increased, the need arose to identify excellence, as it had long ago for batters, starting pitchers, and fielders. The save's prime statistical drawback is that there is no negative to counteract the positive, no stat for saves blown (except, all too often, a victory for the "fireman"); unofficial attempts to develop such a stat have accelerated in recent years, and now are part of the formula for the Fireman of the Year award.

August 10, 1971, marked another milestone, the founding in Cooperstown of SABR, the group in whose annual publications most of today's sabermetricians cut their analytical teeth. Its statistical analysis research committee, headed for more than a decade by Pete Palmer, has served as a sounding board for the inventive approaches of such men as Dallas Adams, Dick Cramer, Steve Mann, Craig Wright, and Bill James.

James published *The Baseball Abstract* from his home in Lawrence, Kansas, for five years to a minute if appreciative audience (its 1977 publication budget: $112.73). In 1982 Ballantine Books, recognizing the increasing sophistication of baseball fans in the computer age, assumed publication of the *Abstract,* and the audience for sabermetrics became sizable indeed, with James's annuals reaching the bestseller lists and his *Historical Baseball Abstract* becoming an essential book for anyone who viewed himself as a serious fan. James has popularized a different approach to the whole question of what baseball statistics are for—that they are not brass knuckles to beat a barroom adversary with, but a means of achieving a better understanding of the game and heightening one's pleasure in it.

Among the many valuable analytical tools he has developed are the Brock-2 System of projecting career totals, the Victory Important RBI, Offensive and Defensive Winning Percentages, Secondary Average, Range Factor, and Runs Created. The last-mentioned, perhaps because James developed it earlier in his career, is the most widely known, and we apply it in this book to all batters, in all fourteen variations of the formula, bringing in data for stolen bases, caught stealing, hit-by-pitch, and grounded into double play for those years in which it is available. (See the Glossary for the formulas.)

The 1980s also brought attention to another attempt to redefine the measure of individual performance. In 1978 Barry Codell of Chicago distributed a paper describing his new statistic, the Base-Out Percentage, to fellow statisticians and figures in the sports media. At about the same time, Tom Boswell, not a statistician by trade or inclination but rather a sportswriter for the *Washington Post,* developed a stat called Total Average. Like the Base-Out Percentage, Total Average is a gauge of offensive proficiency which takes into account not only batting but also base-running skills. (See the Glossary.)

Dallas Adams and Dick Cramer devoted themselves in the late 1970s to a discussion of average batting, pitching, and fielding skill, which more than a decade later remains a subject of intense interest and passionate disagreement. The question, roughly put, is: *How would Cy Young do against the batters of today? Or Wade Boggs against the pitchers of the 1890s? How many homers would Babe Ruth hit if he were active today? Or how many strikeouts would Nolan Ryan have registered in 1880, pitching from a fifty-foot distance?* In other words, how can we

adjust the statistics of players to reflect the certainty that the average batter, pitcher, and fielder have improved over time, thus narrowing the gap between each succeeding era's peak performance and its average one? (For more on this philosophically and mathematically complex subject, we refer you to *The Hidden Game of Baseball*.)

Adams and Cramer advanced a discussion that had begun in 1976 with the first article on cross-era comparison, in which David Shoebotham proposed a new statistic called the Relative Batting Average. Shoebotham recognized that a .320 batting average in 1893, when the National League batted .280, did not represent the same level of accomplishment as that average did in 1968 when, for a number of reasons, the National League batted a measly .243. His solution? To normalize the players' averages to their respective league averages simply by dividing the player's batting average by that of his league.

In this fashion he demonstrated, for example, that Pete Rose, who led the NL with a .335 BA in 1968, had a Relative BA of 1.38; while Ed Delahanty, who led the NL with a BA of .380 in 1893, had a Relative BA of only 1.36. Another way of stating this conclusion is that Rose's .335 was 38 percent above the average batting performance in the NL of 1968, while Delahanty exceeded his league's norm by 36 percent. The inferences that might be drawn from this approach are many: that batting skill has not declined since the days of Ruth, Gehrig, Foxx, et al., but that pitching skill might have increased; that no batting average of the years around 1930 ought to be taken without a carload of salt; that some of the most notable batting performances of all time, as measured by the batting average, have occurred right under our noses, unbeknownst to us.

Normalizing a statistic to its league average is a valuable analytical tool if employed logically. A Relative Batting Average, for example, tells a good deal more, and tells it more straightforwardly, than Relative Homers or Relative Strikeouts. The relativist approach works better with ratios such as batting average, on base percentage, or slugging average—or for that matter with Runs Created or Total Average—than it does for simple counter stats.

Another worthwhile adjustment to various averages is for home-park effects. The pioneering work in this area was done by Robert Kingsley, particularly in regard to why homers flew out of Atlanta's park despite its "normal" dimensions, but Pete Palmer was first to measure the effects of home parks on run totals and then to devise a park adjustment for the records of batters and pitchers. These were discussed in depth in *The Hidden Game of Baseball,* and the data base for park factor in this book has been upgraded to include runs scored *and* runs allowed at home parks instead of just the latter.

In 1984 the editors of this volume introduced, in *The Hidden Game,* the Linear Weights System of assessing players' contributions to their teams—at the bat, on the basepaths, in the field, or on the mound—in terms of runs, which are the currency of the game. Its back-to-basics foundation is the same as that underlying the Rickey formula of 1954 and most of the new statistics developed since then: that wins and losses are what the game is about; that wins and losses are proportional in some way to runs scored and runs allowed; and that runs in turn are proportional to the events which go into their making.

In the Linear Weights System, these events are expressed not in the familiar yet deceptive ratios—base hits to at-bats, wins to decisions, etc.—but in *runs themselves,* the runs contributed (by batting or base stealing) or saved (by pitching or fielding). Computer simulations of over 100,000 games produced the run values of, for example: a single (.47 runs), double (.78), triple (1.09), home run (1.40), walk (.33), steal (.30), caught stealing (−.60), out (−.25), and out made on base (−.50). Using a straightforward additive formula, one can calculate a batter or baserunner's contribution to his team in runs. These would be expressed in terms of runs contributed beyond what a league-average replacement player could contribute in his stead, and that average is defined as a baseline of zero. A team composed entirely of average performers would finish with a record of .500, as the league must—so each above-average player contributes positive runs toward a win, and each subpar player contributes negative runs.

Normalizing factors (to league average) are built into the formulas for all but base stealing, where league average is not a shaping force; these factors enable us to compute, for example, the number of runs (Batting Runs) that Cecil Fielder provided in 1990 beyond those an average hitter might have produced in an equivalent number of plate appearances. And by adjusting Fielder's Batting Runs for Detroit's homepark influences, the Linear Weights comparison may be extended to how many runs he accounted for beyond what an average player might have produced in the same number of at-bats *had he too played half his games in Tiger Stadium.*

Furthermore, having determined the number of runs above average required to transform a loss to a win in the final standings (generally around ten, historically in the range of nine to eleven; for more on the theory behind this, see the Glossary), we can convert a player's Linear Weights record—expressed as Batting Runs, Base Stealing Runs, Pitching Runs, or Fielding Runs—to the number of *wins above average* he alone contributed. What are individual statistics for if not to achieve some understanding of this? Last, by reviewing the win contributions of all a team's personnel, we may establish a solid assessment of that team's strength and weaknesses—either to predict a team's chances for success in the upcoming season or, in an encyclopedia like *Total Baseball*, to analyze how and even why it failed its reasonable statistical expectations or exceeded them.

Formulas for the Linear Weights measures for batting, baserunning, fielding, and pitching will be found in the Glossary.

Other developments of the decade include the previously mentioned adoption of the game-winning RBI (GWRBI) in 1980; it credited the batter who drove in a run to give his club a lead that it never relinquished. This stat was pilloried in the press from its introduction, with merit, until Major League Baseball finally gave up on it before the 1989 season. In 1984 on base percentage was made official, thirty years after its introduction to the general baseball public by Branch Rickey and Allan Roth. Subsequent years brought the Quality Start, which takes note of a pitcher who gives his club six innings or more while allowing three runs or less. Under this construction, an ERA of 4.50 in a mercifully shortened out-

ing is held to be commendable. The editors of this book do not regard the Quality Start as a quality stat.

More interesting are the situational stats which are the specialty of the Elias Sports Bureau and Project Scoresheet—performance in day games vs. night, grass vs. artificial turf, lefty vs. righty, day game following night, bases-loaded situations, and so on. When the data is drawn from a large enough sample, these stats can be provocative and meaningful; too often, however, television announcers desperate to maintain conversation flow will burden their listeners with something like, "Over the last two seasons, he's batted .375 against this guy" (not bothering to add that the figure represents three hits in eight times at bat). Situational stats are the wave of the future in baseball, but are not yet of much use for reviewing the past—Elias has kept them systematically only since 1975.

Total Baseball

The next major event in the history of baseball record keeping may be the book you now hold. Founded upon a unique historical database that Pete Palmer has cultivated for over twenty years—in the tradition of baseball archivists like S. C. Thompson, Bradshaw Swales, Leonard Gettelson, and John Tattersall—Total Baseball is the third-generation encyclopedia of the game. Just as the advent of the Macmillan/ICI encyclopedia supplanted Turkin/Thompson, the standard for two decades, Total Baseball has taken advantage of new technology and new research, notably by members of the Society for American Baseball Research, to present more accurate data than ever before, and more of it. There are, of course, the traditional stats one would expect in a baseball reference work; there are many of the new, more revealing stats discussed above; there are stats never published before and developed now for this book. And as you have seen in Part One, there is a recognition that baseball history and knowledge resides not only in its numbers.

But returning to the statistics and records which make up this second part of Total Baseball, here is a brief rundown of what's coming (full descriptions will be found in the separate introduction to each section):

- *The Annual Record:* Season-by-season standings and records for all teams since 1871, plus the top five league leaders in generally forty-eight categories per season.
- *The Rosters:* A completely revised manager roster, courtesy of some splendid research into the early years by SABR's Bob Tiemann and Richard Topp; and the application to all managers of the "actual vs. expected win" method introduced in the editors' *Baseball Annual 1990* (with Eliot Cohen); a definitive roster of the men in blue, compiled by expert Larry Gerlach; a roster of coaches, never before compiled; a roster of club owners and presidents; and a roster of all the black men who played professionally in the years of segregated ball.
- *The Player, Pitcher, and Relief Pitcher Registers:* The heart of this section of Total Baseball, presenting complete seasonal and lifetime records for every major leaguer, with twenty-three stats for players, twenty-five for pitchers, and ten for relievers.

- *All-Time Leaders:* The top one hundred lifetime and single-season performers in 219 categories, including important conventional stats not found in other encyclopedias and dozens of the sabermetric variety.

Now that the genealogy of the more significant records and record books has been described, it's time to say a few words about the measures you'll find in the main statistical sections of *Total Baseball:* the annual record and the player/pitcher registers. We will not attempt to define the basic counting stats such as games, at-bats, wins, losses, and so on; if these are puzzling to you, you have picked up the wrong book.

Batting

Let's start with the batting statistics, and the first of these to consider will be that venerable, uncannily durable fraud, the batting average. (It consists simply of hits divided by at-bats.) We know as well as anyone else that this monument just won't topple; the best that can be hoped is that in time fans and officials will recognize it as a bit of nostalgia, a throwback to the period of its invention when power counted for naught, bases on balls were scarce, and no one wanted to place a statistical accomplishment in historical context because there wasn't much history yet.

Time has given the batting average a powerful hold on the American baseball public; everyone knows that a man who hits .300 is a good hitter while one who hits .250 is not. Everyone knows that—no matter that it is not true. You want to trade Lenny Dykstra for Kevin Mitchell? Willie McGee for Will Clark? Batting average treats all hits in an egalitarian fashion. A two-out bunt single in the ninth with no one on base and your team trailing by six runs counts the same as Bobby Thomson's "shot heard 'round the world." And what about a walk? Say you foul off four 3–2 pitches, then watch a close one go by to take your base. Where's your credit for a neat bit of offensive work? Not in this stat. And a .250 batting average may have represented a distinct accomplishment in certain years, like 1968 when the American League mean was .230. That .250 hitter stood in the same relation to an average hitter of his season as a .282 hitter did in the American League in 1988—or a *329* hitter in the National League of 1930! If .329 and .282 and .250 all mean roughly the same thing, it raises questions about the value of the measure.

And yet, the batting champion each year is declared to be the one with the highest batting average, and this will not soon change. And the Hall of Fame is filled with .300 hitters who couldn't carry the pine tar of many who will stay forever on the outside looking in. Knowledgeable fans have long realized that the ability to reach base and to produce runs are not adequately measured by batting average, and they have looked to other measures—for example, the other two components of the Triple Crown, home runs and RBIs. Still more sophisticated fans have looked to the slugging average or on base percentage, and in the 1980s to various sabermetric measures.

The slugging average does acknowledge the role of the man whose talent is for the long ball and who may, with management's blessing, be sacrificing bat control and thus batting average in order to let'er rip. (Slugging aver-

age is the number of total bases divided by at-bats.) But the slugging average has its problems, too. It declares that a double is worth two singles, that a triple is worth one and a half doubles, and that a home run is worth four singles. All of these proportions are intuitively pleasing, for they relate to the number of bases touched on each hit, but in terms of the hits' value in generating runs, the proportions are wrong. One home run in four at-bats is not worth as much as four singles, for instance, in part because the total run potential for the team of four singles is greater, and in part because the man who hit the four singles did not also make three outs; yet the man who goes one for four at the plate, that one being a homer, has the same slugging percentage of 1.000 as a man who singles four times in four at-bats.

Moreover, it is possible to attain a high slugging average without being a slugger. In other words, if you have a high batting average, you must have a decent slugging average; it's difficult to hit .350 and have a slugging percentage of only .400. Even a bunt single boosts not only your batting average but also your slugging average. (The attempt to counteract this problem is a statistic called Isolated Power, which divides only extra bases by at-bats.) Other things the slugging average does not do are: indicate how many runs were produced by the hits; give any credit for other offensive categories, such as walks, hit-by-pitch, or steals; permit the comparison of sluggers from different eras (if Jimmie Foxx had a slugging percentage of .749 in 1932 and Mickey Mantle had one of .705 in 1957, was Fox 7 percent superior? The answer is no, and the reason is in the higher slugging average of the AL in 1932.

Well, how about on base percentage? (To calculate this stat, divide hits, walks, and hit-by-pitch by at-bats, walks, hit-by-pitch, and sacrifice flies.) On base percentage has the advantage of giving credit for walks and hit-by-pitch, but it is an unweighted average and thus makes no distinction between those two events and, say, a grand-slam homer. A fellow like Eddie Yost, who, in some years when he hit under .250, drew nearly a walk a game, gets his credit with this stat as does a Gene Tenace, one of those guys whose statistical line looks puny without his walks. Similarly, players like Mickey Rivers or Omar Moreno, leadoff hitters with a lot of speed, no power, and no patience, are exposed by the OBP as distinctly marginal major leaguers, even in years when their batting averages look respectable or excellent. In short, on base percentage does tell you more about a man's ability to get on than does the batting average, and thus is a better indicator of run generation, but it's not enough by itself to separate the "good" hitters from the "average" or "poor" ones.

Not by itself, no . . . but when you add it to slugging average, you come up with a very powerful indicator of batting ability. These two one-legged men, when joined together, make for a very sturdy tandem, the infirmity of the one being almost exactly compensated by the power of the other. The virtues of on base plus slugging, a combined stat called Production, are that it is easily computed from officially issued stats and that it is the most accurate of all the newer stats except those denominated directly in runs. Its weaknesses are that because it is stated as the sum of two averages, it is—like a batting average or earned run average or any other average—a measure of

the *rate* of success rather than the *amount,* and the fan needs considerable context to know what it means. Is a Production mark of .750 poor, average, or outstanding? (Answer: pretty good, because the league average figure in recent years has been in the low .700s—although in the NL of 1930 it exceeded .800.)

This second drawback may be eliminated in the same manner for all averages: by normalizing, or adjusting, each individual performance to the league average in that category for the year in which it took place. If a batter's Production was .700 in a year when the league average was .700, he performed at a rate of 100 (his Production divided by the league's, discarding the decimal point for ease of expression). If his Production was .800, his league-adjusted mark would be 114. The meaningfulness of that performance might be further refined by adjusting it once more, to take into account the run-producing characteristics of the man's home park: a batter whose home park was a hitters' haven like Wrigley Field might have his Production adjusted downward, while another playing half his games in the Astrodome might have his adjusted upward. In *Total Baseball,* figures adjusted for league average and park factor are denoted by "/A" following the raw figure, and the Park Factor (PF) is expressed with a baseline of 100—a hitter's park might have a factor of 110, a pitcher's park 90. In this third edition of *Total Baseball,* we state Production in the Player Register only in its normalized, park-adjusted form, here termed "Production+."

RBIs? Don't they indicate run production and clutch ability? Yes and no. The RBI does tell you something about run-producing ability, but not enough: it's a situation-dependent statistic, inextricably tied to factors which vary wildly for individuals on the same team or on others (including, importantly, the position of each player in the batting order). And the RBI makes no distinction between being hit by a pitch to drive in the twelfth run of a game that concludes 14–3 and, again for comparison, the Thomson blast. RBIs tell how many runs a batter pushed across the plate, all right, but they don't tell how many fewer he might have driven in had he batted eighth rather than fourth, or how many more he might have driven in on a team that put more men on base. They don't even tell how many more runs a batter might have driven in if he had delivered a higher proportion of his hits with men on base.

The American League kept RBI Opportunities—men on base presented to each batter—as an official stat for the first three weeks of 1918, then saw how much work was involved and ditched it. The problem remains: how to assess run productivity for batters. Pitchers are easier. Their accomplishments are directly measured in runs allowed. But batters, baserunners, and fielders make their contributions in the constituent parts of runs—outs, hits, and a variety of more or less successful other events. (Even a batter who hits a solo homer contributes more than one run to his team, because he permits another player to bat who otherwise would not have, and each batter has a potential for producing further runs.)

You hear a lot in the media about the value of Runs Produced, a stat we track in *Total Baseball* in the top five section of the Annual Record. Runs Produced is simply runs scored plus runs batted in, subtracting homers be-

cause a dinger gives a batter "double credit"—a run scored plus an RBI. The editors view Runs Produced as an odd linkage of one opportunity-dependent stat with another that depends upon largely the same factors, but we offer the stat for those who like that sort of thing.

And so we come to the recently formulated game-winning RBI (GWRBI)—a noble attempt at describing the value of a hit to the team, its "clutchness," but a measure which was misconceived in its presumption that a game could be won with a hit in the first inning. A man who drives in a run in the first inning is simply doing his job, not performing an extraordinary feat; if the pitcher makes that run hold up by throwing a shutout, bully for him, but why credit the hitter? Were he to drive in the lone run of the game in the seventh inning or later, that would be different. Nonetheless, the latest formulation of the stat gave the man who drove in that first-inning run a GWRBI even if his team eventually won 22–0, since it gave the team a lead that was never relinquished.

Worse, the GWRBI was situation-dependent to an even greater degree than the RBI. You can't play for a lousy team and lead the league in GWRBIs because there aren't enough games won to go around. And it's even harder to accumulate GWRBIs from the eighth place in the batting order than it is to accumulate RBIs. Last, if you put your team ahead with an RBI in the bottom of the eighth, why should you lose your GWRBI simply because the pitcher allows the lead to be lost? Wasn't your hit "clutch"? Say the pitcher allows the score to be tied, then a teammate might pick up the GWRBI that should have been safely tucked away for you. Nicely motivated, the GWRBI, but utterly without merit and thus we barred it from the first edition of Total Baseball, no matter that at the time we prepared that book the GWRBI was still an official Major League Baseball stat. It is no longer.

We do, however, present a measure called Clutch Hitting Index, which addresses the problem of run-producing opportunities on a historical basis. We offer this with several reservations, including the classic philosophical one about whether clutch ability exists at all. Is a man who hits .280 with men on base and .240 with the sacks clear a hero in the former situation or a bum in the latter? The Clutch Hitting Index measures actual RBIs over expected RBIs, which have been calculated on the basis of a man's extra-base hits and the opportunities he could have been expected to have, based on the average RBIs per league and where he batted in the lineup and who batted above him. This is, by admission, a rough measure indeed, but we think it's an interesting one. We included it in the Player Register in the first edition; since then we have confined the stat to the Annual Record and Leaders Sections. For teams, the measure of clutch hitting is more elegant: the ratio of its actual runs to its runs as calculated by the Linear Weights method.

Previously discussed were Runs Created, Total Average, and Batting Runs. Total Average numbers will tend to look like those of Production, which measures largely the same things only in a different manner; for this reason we have removed it from the Player Register while retaining it in the Annual Record and Leaders. The numerical expression of Runs Created exceeds that of Batting Runs, except that its baseline of zero defines the worst player in the league rather than the average one.

Base Stealing

Many fans understand, as a result of sabermetric findings of the 1980s, that a man with a lot of stolen bases is not necessarily the best baserunner, nor even an asset to his team; he might have been caught nearly as often as he stole and thus may have cost his team many runs on balance. The game's encyclopedic reference works have in years past contained stolen base totals, even if the tabulations for the early years were suspect because of unclear standards for what differentiated a steal from clever baserunning. What they have not offered is the flip side of the steal—the caught-stealing numbers that make sense of the steal itself.

As mentioned above, caught stealing was recorded officially in the AL beginning in 1920, then was dropped for 1927, was resumed in 1928, and has been continuously in use ever since. In the NL, it was computed for 1920–1925, then was dropped until 1951, when it resumed on a continuous basis. We have figures kept by Ernie Lanigan for the years 1914–1916 in the AL and for 1915–1916 in the NL, and in the second edition we added caught-stealing data for 1927 from newspaper accounts (about 90 percent complete). In Total Baseball we present, for those years in which the data exists, the raw CS data, Stolen Base Averages, and Stolen Base Runs. This last is expressed in runs, based on the computer-derived value of .30 runs for a stolen base and −.60 runs for a thwarted steal. To make a positive contribution to his team, a base thief must be successful in more than two-thirds of his attempts.

Fielding

When, back in 1954, Rickey and Roth came up with their "efficiency formula" for run scoring and run prevention, the defensive half of the equation was divided into five segments. The first was opponents' batting average; the second was opponents' reaching base through bases on balls or hit batsmen; the third was a measure of a pitcher's clutch ability; the fourth was his strikeout capability; and the fifth was fielding, to which they assigned a mathematical value of zero. "There is nothing on earth," Rickey declared, "anyone can do with fielding." Besides, he added, good fielding might account for the critical run in a ballgame only four or five times a year.

Was Rickey right? The central weakness of the fielding average has long been known: you can't make an error on a ball you don't touch. To counter this weakness in fielding average and to credit the plays made as well as the plays not made, total chances per game is a more useful statistic—and when errors are deducted from chances, you have a fielder's Range Factor. James pointed out how absurd it had become, in a time when the best-fielding second baseman might commit ten errors a season and the worst twenty, to focus on this difference of ten rather than on the 250–300 in total chances which might separate the most agile keystoner from the exemplar of Lot's wife.

Another difficulty with the fielding average is that to understand what figure represents mean performance (and thus be able to identify inferior and superior fielders), one must adjust for position: a shortstop who fields .980 has done quite well, but a first baseman, catcher, or

outfielder with that figure would have been below average. Thus the fan must bring to the fielding average a great deal of background knowledge—the mean for each fielding average for each position in each season. This is a demand that, on first reflection, is not created by the batting average (all men stepping to the plate occupy the same position—batter). On second thought, however, the knowledgeable fan recognizes that a batting line of .267, 10 HRs, 80 RBIs will mean different things when applied to a shortstop or to a left fielder. In other words, just as any evaluation of fielding performance carries an inherent positional bias, so does batting performance.

High double-play totals are believed to indicate excellence among middle infielders, but the more double plays a club turns, as a rule, the worse the pitching. Which teams had the most double plays in major league history? In the 154-game season, the Philadelphia A's of 1949 and the Los Angeles Dodgers of 1958; in the 162-game season, Toronto and Boston of 1980 and Pittsburgh of 1966. Of these, only the last-mentioned had a team ERA better than the league average. If the pitchers are putting a lot of men on base, the team can get a lot of double plays even without a great-fielding shortstop and second baseman.

So what to do? How do we assess fielding excellence? The idea of crediting stellar fielding plays individually has been proposed occasionally ever since 1868, when Chadwick wrote: "The best player in a nine is he who makes the most good plays in a match, not the one who commits the fewest errors, and it is in the record of his good plays that we are to look for the most correct data for an estimate of his skill in the position he occupies." Father Chadwick was correct to see that fielding percentage emphasized failure rather than success, but in truth the fielding percentage was a far better measure of ability in the 1860s, when one play in four produced an error, than now, when only two plays in a hundred are flubbed.

The choice in *Total Baseball* has been to concentrate on Total Chances but not to disregard the error, as Range Factor does; nor to include it in Total Chances, as David Neft would favor; nor to subtract it from Total Chances, as Barry Codell once advocated. The error may be infrequent today but it is not insignificant; instead, it is a peculiarly damaging event, turning an out (with its computer-derived run value of $-.25$) to, in effect, a hit (with its run value of $+.50$). This is a turnaround of .75 runs, or *the equivalent of three outs;* an outfield error costs even more, because it so often produces more than one base for batter and runners both. Thus the defensive stats we favor in this book and include in the Player Register and Pitcher Register, are Linear Weights formulas, expressed in runs and computed differently for the different positions (see the Glossary for the formulas, which have a significant refinement in this edition). However, in all cases the elements of the statistics are putouts, assists, double plays, and errors (and for catchers, passed balls).

Position players are gauged by Fielding Runs, a Linear Weights measure of the runs they saved (or allowed) through their play that an average man *at that position* would not have (second baseman are compared with other second baseman rather than, say, with left fielders—even the worst-fielding second sacker would cost his team fewer runs at the position than the best defensive left fielder). Pitcher Defense (like Pitcher Batting) is to be found in the Pitcher Register. Raw fielding statistics, of questionable value in and of themselves, have been excluded from this third edition of *Total Baseball*. An innovation this time around is the placement of the fielding average in the Player Register. It is computed for the position at which a man played the most games.

Pitching

On to the pitching statistics you will see in the Annual Record and Pitcher Register. First to be reviewed are wins and losses, and won-lost percentage. Wins are a team statistic, obviously, as are losses, but we credit a win entirely to one pitcher in each game. Why not to the shortstop? Or the left fielder? Or some combination of the three? In a 13–11 game, several players may have had more to do with the win than any pitcher. No matter. We're not going to change this custom, though Ban Johnson gave it a good try when he banished it from the American League records for seven years beginning in 1913.

To win many games a pitcher generally must play for a team that wins many games. Look at Red Ruffing's won-lost record with the miserable Red Sox of the 1930s, then at his mark with the Yankees. Or at Danny Jackson, first with Kansas City, then with Cincinnati. There is an endless list of good pitchers traded to stronger offensive clubs who "emerge" as stars.

The recognition of the weakness of this statistic came early. Originally it was not computed by such men as Chadwick because most teams leaned heavily, if not exclusively, on one starter, and relievers as we know them today did not exist. As the season schedules lengthened, the need for a pitching staff became evident, and separating out the team's record on the basis of who was in the box seemed a good idea. However, it was not then nor is it now a good measure of performance, for the simple reason that one may pitch poorly and win, or pitch well and lose.

The natural corrective to this deficiency of the won-lost percentage is the earned run average—which, strangely, preceded it, gave way to it in the 1880s, and then returned in 1912. Originally, the ERA was computed as earned runs per game because pitchers almost invariably went nine innings. In this century it has been calculated as earned runs times nine, divided by innings pitched.

The purpose of the earned run average is noble: to give a pitcher credit for doing what *he* can to prevent runs from scoring, aside from his own fielding lapses and those of the men around him. It succeeds to a remarkable extent in isolating the performance of the pitcher from his situation, but objections to the statistic remain. Say a pitcher retires the first two men in an inning, then has the shortstop kick a ground ball to allow the batter to reach first base. Six runs follow before the third out is secured. How many of these runs are earned? None.

The prime difficulty with the ERA in the early days, say 1913, when one of every four runs scored was unearned, was that a pitcher got a lot of credit in his ERA for playing with a bad defensive club. The errors would serve to cover up in the ERA a good many runs which probably should not have scored. Those runs would hurt the team, but not the pitcher's record. This situation has been aggravated further by the use of newly computed

ERAs for pitchers prior to 1913, the first year of its official status. Example: Bobby Mathews, sole pitcher for the New York Mutuals of 1876, allowed 7.19 runs per game, yet his ERA was only 2.86—almost a perfect illustration of the league's 40 percent proportion of earned runs.

It is not an accident that pitchers of the dead-ball era of this century (1900–1919) dominate the lifetime and seasonal leaders tables in ERA. Yes, there were circumstances away from the mound that depressed batting, but the pitchers of that period also benefited mightily in the ERA column from the high number of errors, as compared to today. How to compare the ERA of an Ed Walsh or Three Finger Brown with a Frank Viola or a Dwight Gooden? As with batting stats, normalize the ERA to league average and adjust for home park effects. A pitcher from 1908 whose Adjusted ERA was 150 can be compared to one from 1988 with the same Adjusted ERA—each stood in the same relation to his peers, that is, 50 percent better than average.

What gave rise to the ERA, and what we appreciate about it, is that like the batting average it is an attempt at an isolating stat, a measure of individual performance not dependent upon one's own team. Its principal shortcoming is that it indicates only a pitcher's *rate* of efficiency, not his actual benefit to the team. In a league with an ERA of 4.00, a starter who throws 300 innings with an ERA of 3.50 must be worth more to his team than a starter whose ERA is the same but who pitches in only half as many innings. Through the Linear Weights figures of Pitching Runs (broken out in the top-five section of the Annual Record as Starter Runs and Relief Runs), we can determine the number of runs a pitcher saved his team beyond what a pitcher performing at the league-average ERA would have allowed. A truly simple stat, it consists of nothing more than a pitcher's normalized, or league-adjusted, earned run average weighted by his innings pitched.

Because Pitching Runs has a built-in normalizing factor, when you see it in *Total Baseball* under a heading for "/A," that adjustment will be for park factor. Pitchers' park factor is calculated differently from batters' park factor, for a number of fairly complex reasons that technical-minded readers might best consult in the Glossary.

While the ERA is a far more accurate reflection of a pitcher's value than the BA is of a hitter's, it fails to a greater degree than the BA in offering an isolated measure. For a truly unalloyed individual pitching measure, we must look to the glamour statistic of strikeouts, the pitcher's mate to the home run (though home runs are highly dependent upon home park, strikeouts are to only a slight degree).

Is a strikeout artist a good pitcher? Maybe yes, maybe no; a good analogue would be to ask whether a home run slugger is a good hitter. The two stats run together: periods of high home run activity (as a percentage of all hits) invariably are accompanied by high strikeout totals. Strikeout totals, however, may soar even in the absence of overzealous swingers, say, as the result of a rules change such as the legalization of overhand pitching in 1884, the introduction of the foul strike (NL, 1901; AL, 1903), or the expanded strike zone in 1963.

Just as home run totals are a function of the era in

which one plays, so are strikeouts. The great nineteenth-century totals—Matches Kilroy's 513, Toad Ramsey's 499, One Arm Daily's 483—were achieved under different rules and fashions. No one in that era fanned batters at the rate of one per inning; indeed, among regular pitchers (those with 154 innings pitched or more), only Herb Score did until 1960. In the next five years the barrier was passed by Sandy Koufax, Jim Maloney, Bob Veale, Sam McDowell, and Sonny Siebert. Walter Johnson, Rube Waddell, and Bob Feller didn't run up numbers like that. Were they slower, or easier to hit, than Sonny Siebert?

Even in today's game, which lends itself to the accumulation of, by historic standards, high strikeout totals for a good many pitchers and batters, the strikeout is, as it always has been, just another way to make an out. Yes, it is a sure way to register an out without the risk of advancing baserunners and so is highly useful in a situation such as when there is a man on third with fewer than two outs; otherwise, it is a vastly overrated stat because it has nothing to do with victory or defeat—it is mere spectacle. A high strikeout total indicates raw talent and overpowering stuff, but the imperative of the pitcher is simply to retire the batter, not to crush him. What's not listed in your daily averages are strikeouts by batters—fans are not as interested in that because it's a negative measure—yet the strikeout may be a more significant stat for batters than it is for pitchers.

Bases on balls will drive a manager crazy and put lead in fielders' feet, but it is possible to survive, even to excel, without first-rate control—provided your stuff is good enough to hold down the number of hits. *Total Baseball* offers two stats that are, like strikeouts, highly interesting but ultimately of debatable value: Opponents' Batting Average and Opponents' On Base Percentage. (The same could be said of Fewest Hits Per Game and Fewest Walks Per Game, of course.) It is illuminating to compare one or the other with a pitcher's ERA or Pitching Runs, but both calculations are somewhat academic, for at the end of a game, season, or career, it doesn't matter how many men a pitcher puts on base. Theoretically he can put three men on every inning, leave the twenty-seven baserunners allowed, and pitch a shutout. A man who gives up one hit over nine innings can lose 1–0; it's even possible to allow no hits and lose. Who is the better pitcher? The man with the shutout and twenty-seven baserunners allowed, or the man who allows one hit? No matter how sophisticated your measurements for pitchers, the best ones are counted in runs.

The nature of baseball at all points is one man against nine. It's the pitcher against a series of batters. With that situation prevailing, we have tended to examine batting with intricate, ingenious stats, while viewing pitching through generally much weaker, though perhaps more copious, measurements. What if the game were to be turned around so that we had a "pitching order"— nine pitchers facing one batter? Think of that for a minute. The nature of the statistics would change, too, so that your batting stats would be vastly simplified. You wouldn't care about all the individual components of the batter's performance, all combining in some obscure fashion to reveal run production. You'd care only about *runs*. Yet what each of the nine pitchers did would bear intense scrutiny, and over the course of a year each pitcher's

Opponents' Batting Average, Opponents' On Base Percentage, Opponents' Slugging Average, and so forth, would be recorded and spun to come up with a sense of how many runs each pitcher had saved.

A pitching stat with an interesting history is complete games. This is your basic counter stat, but it's taken to mean more than most of those measurements by baseball people and knowledgeable fans. When everyone was completing 90–100 percent of his starts, the stat was without meaning and thus was not kept. As relief pitchers crept into the game after 1905, the percentage of completed games declined rapidly. By the 1920s it became a point of honor to complete three quarters of one's starts; today the man who completes half is quite likely to lead his league. So with these shifting standards, what do CGs tell you? About pitchers, not a lot anymore: about managers and bullpens, a great deal.

Can we say that a pitcher with 18 complete games out of 37 starts is better than one with 12 complete games in 35 starts? Not without a lot of supporting help, we can't, not without a store of knowledge about the individuals, the teams, and especially the eras involved. The more uses to which we attempt to put the stat, the weaker it becomes, the more attenuated its force. If we declare the hurler with 18 CGs "better," how are we to compare him with another pitcher from, say, fifty years earlier who completed 27 out of 30 starts? Or another pitcher of eighty years ago who completed all the games he started? (Jack W. Taylor completed every one of the 187 games he started *over five years*.) Or what about Will White, who in 1880 started 75 games and completed every blessed one of them? But the rules were different, you say, or the ball was less resilient, or they pitched from a different distance, with a different motion, or this, or that. The point is, there are limits to what a traditional, unadjusted baseball statistic can tell you about a player's performance in any given year, let alone compare his efforts to those of a player from a different era.

Of shutouts there is little to say that is not perfectly obvious, except that historical totals have been revised because (a) in 1920–1939 the American League did not count games of less than nine innings as shutouts, and (b) in those years and before, in both leagues, a pitcher was credited with a shutout even if he was pulled midway, if he had pitched enough innings of a combined whitewash. *Total Baseball* counts only complete-game shutouts.

Wins Above Team is, as discussed, a variation of Ted Oliver's stat made public in 1944, which he called the Weighted Rating System. Apart from modifying his math, we have taken Oliver's "points"—the thousands of points his formula gave to hurlers who performed well for poor teams—and by retaining the decimal that he would have discarded, we have come up with a stat that is expressed quite properly in wins. In this second edition, Wins Above Team is recorded only for the top hundred lifetime and season marks.

Newly developed for the first edition of this book was a Clutch Pitching Index that, like the measure for clutch hitting, could be applied to historical data. The CPI is figured by taking how many earned runs the pitcher should have allowed, based on the performance of the batters who faced him, and how many he actually allowed (see the Glossary for the formula). The Clutch Pitching

Index consists of expected runs over actual runs, so marks over 100 exceed league-average performance.

For relief pitchers, we have previously discussed saves, and Relief Runs (the Linear Weights category) are figured no differently than Starter Runs. Newly developed here is Relief Ranking, which adjusts Relief Runs for the greater situational importance of each run a bullpenner saves or yields. The other elements of the formula are wins, losses, and saves, in a proportion detailed in the Glossary. Games, innings, and ERA in relief are broken out in the new Relief Pitcher Register.

Bringing It All Together

Pitcher Batting and Pitcher Defense are recorded in the Pitcher Register as Linear Weights figures, expressed in runs. (Pitcher batting has been removed from league stats for such computations, so that the batting records of everyday players are compared only with those of their peers and pitchers' batting records are compared only with those of *their* peers.) For this edition we have added to Pitcher Batting Runs the seasonal totals for hits and the pitchers' batting averages. The totals for Pitcher Batting Runs and Fielding Runs are seldom of a great magnitude—and for AL pitchers since 1973, the batting figure is, of course, zero—but in earlier years a pitcher's ability to help himself and his team off the mound has occasionally counted for a great deal in a given season; spitballer Ed Walsh in 1907, the year before he won 40 games for the White Sox, accounted for an astounding 2.3 Fielding Wins. The hitting ability of a Wes Ferrell or Don Drysdale certainly counted for something in their teams' prospects for victory. In *Total Baseball* a pitcher's overall contribution is reflected in the Total Pitcher Index, converted from Runs above average to Wins, based on the Runs required to create an extra Win in that year.

For everyday position players, add Fielding Runs to Stolen Base Runs to Batting Runs, then convert those combined Runs to Wins, and you have the best measure of the complete ballplayer: the Total Player Rating. We believe, however, that a positional adjustment must be made to the above combination to reflect the greater skill required to play, for example, second base than left field; this adjustment is based on the average batting skill required at that position to hold a major league job. Historically, left fielders have presented the best record in Batting Runs and middle infielders the worst. In other words, a left fielder who accounted for 10 Fielding Runs should not be regarded as having the same value to a team as a shortstop who also contributed 10 Fielding Runs: Have the two men switch positions and you would soon see who made more of a defensive contribution. And because some positions—shortstop, catcher, second base, and third base—are harder to play than others, we see a relative scarcity of good hitters at these positions and an abundance at the others. Again, see the Glossary for more detail.

The ultimate stat brings together batters, pitchers, fielders, and baserunners in the Total Baseball Ranking. The equivalent of a Most Valuable Player Award and Cy Young Award wrapped into one, it reveals the best baseball player every season and the best ever. Relief pitchers and shortstops can compete on the same plane—wins

contributed to their team through all their accomplishments. In 1978 the MVP question in the American League was whether to vote for Jim Rice, who had 46 homers, 139 RBIs, and 400 total bases (the first time for an American Leaguer in forty-one years), or for Ron Guidry, 25–3 with an .893 won-lost percentage that was the all-time high for a starter with 20 or more wins, and whose ERA of 1.74 was less than half the league average. Why don't you flip to the page in the Annual Record for 1978 and see for yourself who deserved the MVP Award that year.

Total Baseball also sums things up on the team level. Fielding Runs are expressed as Wins in the team stats section of the Annual Record, as are Batting Runs, Stolen Base Runs, and Pitching Runs. This enables one to see the component parts of a team's predicted success or failure—that is, the wins or losses beyond the average (a .500 season) that the players' performance could have been expected to produce. The Differential figure (DIF) in this section of the Annual Record states the spread between the team's actual won-lost record and that predicted by the Linear Weights measures of batting, base stealing, fielding, and pitching. The miracle Mets of 1969 exceeded expectations by 13 Wins—in other words, instead of finishing 87–75 as their players' performance would have warranted, they finished 100–62. Did the Blue Jays also do it with mirrors in 1992? Check for yourself.

Errors and Controversies

The data ICI reported in the first edition of *The Baseball Encyclopedia* upset many people in baseball, for their numbers were different from those traditionally accepted; however, their changes were responsible ones, the product of new research that corrected errors of long standing, or in response to the rulings of the Special Baseball Records Committee. For example, much of the statistical information on Hall of Fame plaques was rendered obsolete. The result has been that through the ensuing editions, the offending data has been fudged to bring it into line with tradition—more on this in a moment.

Despite the uproar that greeted ICI's revised numbers, 1969 was hardly the first time corrections had been made to official data. In 1929 Grover Cleveland Alexander won his 373rd game, breaking Christy Mathewson's National League record, then thought to be 372. He never won another game. A number of years later, Joe Reichler found a game in which, by today's rules, Matty should have gotten the win, this game taking place on May 21, 1902. The record was changed and they were given a tie. The problem was that no one checked all of Mathewson's other games to see how many times he received a win under the old rules that wouldn't have been credited that way today. When ICI did their research in 1968, they found Matty had only 367 wins total by today's rules, while Alexander had 374. (Further research, notably by Frank Williams, has restored Alexander and Mathewson to a tie at 373 wins.) The Records Committee decided that all wins and losses should be awarded according to the present rules, so Macmillan printed the totals as such in the *Baseball Encyclopedia*. However, after the book came out, Commissioner Bowie Kuhn decided that it was better to show stats that agreed with previously published

recognized sources, so all records—not only those of Mathewson and Alexander—were supposed to be changed back in accordance with the scoring practices at the time. What happened in the next edition was that some records, especially those of the stars, were changed, while others were not; team totals and the records of other players on the same team were not; and the data base was corrupted.

Here's another celebrated example of record-book flip-flops. When the American League was formed in 1901, Nap Lajoie was credited with a .422 average, with 220 hits in 543 at-bats. After a number of years, someone noticed that if you take these at-bats and hits, the average comes out only to .405, so his average was changed. (Turkin/Thompson gave Nap a mark of .409 in its first edition.) Later in the 1950s, John Tattersall had his doubts and decided to go through his newspaper collection of box scores. He found 229 hits for Lajoie, not 220—the error had been in the figure for hits, not in the figure for batting average. Thus his average was restored to .422, which happened to be the highest in American League history. Then ICI research in this area came up with a .426 mark (232 for 544, based on newspaper accounts), which was published in the first edition, then trimmed back to .422 in subsequent editions. The .426 figure is the one this book uses.

Nap seemed to be involved in a number of controversies. ICI research found four more hits for him in 1902, raising his average from .369 to .378. Later editions have changed Lajoie's stats back to the old values; we have not.

In 1910 there was a very close batting race between Cobb and Lajoie. At the end of the season, most people thought Nap had won, based on his getting seven hits in a doubleheader on the final day of the season. There was talk that the opposing Browns had let him get a number of bunts by playing back, so that the hated Cobb would lose. However, the AL office went over their figures and gave Cobb the title, .385 to .384. Nearly eighty years later, Pete Palmer discovered a critical error: a game in which Cobb had two hits in three at-bats had been entered twice. This was found because Sam Crawford had 157 games on his official sheet yet the Tigers only played 156. It turned out that Detroit played a doubleheader on September 24, but the second game inadvertently was inserted in the official sheets as being played on September 25. Later, this second game of the twenty-fourth, which appeared to have been missing, was put in the scoresheets again. The League Office discovered this mistake soon after its official announcement that Cobb had won the batting title, because the double entry was corrected for all the other Detroit players. However, Ban Johnson had made a big deal out of how carefully his people had checked the figures in order to settle the controversy, so they kept quiet about the gaffe, leaving Cobb the winner.

Appeals to Commissioner Kuhn in 1981 to set the matter straight officially were to no avail, because that would not only have changed the outcome of the 1910 batting race, it would also have altered Cobb's lifetime hit total, then being pursued to massive media attention by Pete Rose. Kuhn's statement read, in part, "The passage of 70 years, in our judgment . . . constitutes a certain statute of limitation as to recognizing any changes in the records with confidence of the accuracy of such changes. . . .

Since a variety of questions have been raised through the years about the accuracy of the statistics of that period, the only way to make changes with confidence would be for a complete and thorough review of all team and individual statistics. That is not practical." It may not have not been practical, but we have done it, and are continuing to do it. A notable area of change reflected in this second edition of *Total Baseball* is the National Association period of 1871–1875, in which the research of Michael Stagno and a team of SABR researchers have not only supplied new, more accurate statistics but also a handful of new players, previously not included in any baseball encyclopedia.

In 1912, Heinie Zimmerman got credit for a Triple Crown victory, although it wasn't called that then. Ernie Lanigan's RBI figures gave him 98, compared to 94 for Honus Wagner. However, ICI research gave Wagner 102 and Zimmerman 99. Later editions of *The Baseball Encyclopedia* changed Zimmerman up to 103—giving him back his phony Triple Crown.

The National League batting data has been pretty accurate since 1910. That was the first year that the NL kept daily game records for teams as well as players and compared the team totals to the sum for the players for that team and tried to resolve any differences. Before then, the team totals simply *were* the sum for the players. The American League had team totals all the way back to 1905, but never compared them with the sum of the players and therefore had a great many errors. The AL, however, did introduce team pitching first in 1930, while the NL followed in 1941. The AL never published league totals, so the fact that the batter hits, strikeouts, walks, etc. did not agree with the corresponding pitcher totals was somewhat academic. However, the NL did publish league totals starting in 1926, and when they first presented team pitching, the totals did not agree. In order to make this look correct, they doctored the pitching totals to agree with the batting stats. After a few years, this was no longer necessary, as they took the time to resolve and correct differences. For the AL, most team totals did not agree with the sum of the players for that team until around 1935: the at-bats, runs, hits, and extra-base hits usually checked out, but walks and strikeouts did not add up until the 1960s. The AL converted to computer in 1973, while the NL did in 1981, improving accuracy.

On the whole there have been surprisingly few errors in the National League stats. Most of the bigger ones have involved innings pitched in the years before 1930. Because no one added up the innings and compared them to putouts to check for discrepancies, in 1926 Wayland Dean brought up the rear in ERA with a 6.10 mark. It turned out that his innings pitched had been added up incorrectly, and he should have had 204, not 164. This reduced his ERA to 4.90. For a game in 1920, Jimmy Ring had his faced batsman total of 35 put in the innings pitched column, giving him 26 extra innings pitched for the game. It would seem that someone adding up innings pitched would question a figure of 35 for one game, but it slipped through. Ring was also credited for nine extra innings in 1923. But the strangest mix-up in the NL was in 1909, the year before the team totals were kept. For some strange reason, 700 putouts were dropped from the team totals, all the result of adding mistakes for catchers. Pat Moran

and Red Dooin each lost 200, while Peaches Graham, Bill Bergen, and Doc Marshall lost 100 each.

The American League has had many errors of 100 or more putouts or assists over the years due to addition mistakes, as well as quite a few blunders in innings pitched. Ed Willett in 1910 lost 77 innings, showing only 147 instead of 224. The correction lowered his ERA from 3.60 to 2.36. However, this was still more than a run behind the leader, Ed Walsh. Frank Williams discovered a dozen or more errors in entering wins and losses for pitchers in the AL *every year* from 1905 through 1919. And John Tattersall, in his home run research, found over 100 official errors, about 80 percent in the AL and most before 1920. George Sisler picked up 3 new homers, These were on April 12, 1916, September 22, 1921, and June 29, 1929.

From 1912 to 1914, the AL statistician decided not to enter anything for a player who had all zeroes for his line in any given game. Most of these were relief pitchers, but they had entries on their pitching sheets and these games were restored by the ICI researchers. There were about 600 other cases where nonpitchers had games omitted. These are included in *Total Baseball*. This kind of record keeping over the early years kept some men out of the encyclopedias altogether, like pinch runners or defensive replacements. SABR research has added several of these one-time ciphers to *The Baseball Encyclopedia* over the years, as well as to *Total Baseball*.

For the American League records of 1913, the official sheets disagree with the data published in the baseball guides for almost every player. The only logical explanation is that the official figures weren't ready when it came time to publish the guide, so they must have used data from another source. *Total Baseball* uses the official figures, as they have daily sheets to support the data.

An interesting quirk in the way records are kept—and another reminder, as if one needed it, that baseball record keeping remains subject to error and controversy—occurred as recently as 1981. The league rule was to round off the innings pitched at the end of the season, although the weekly reports showed thirds of innings. Baltimore's Sammy Stewart had 29 earned runs in 112⅓ innings, while Oakland's Steve McCatty had 48 in 185⅔ innings. This gave Stewart the ERA title, 2.323 to 2.327. But when the innings were rounded off, McCatty won, 2.32 to 2.33. McCatty got the title, but the next year both leagues decided to count thirds of innings.

Sources

The computer has made possible the rapid analysis of mountains of raw baseball data based upon observed games or mathematically accurate, probabilistic computer simulations. Questions once thought to be unanswerable are mysteries no longer. What is the worth, in terms of its run-producing capacity, of a single, or a walk, or a homer? How valuable is a stolen base? Who were the best clutch hitters? But as invaluable as the computer has been in producing the statistical data for *Total Baseball,* the editors owe more to the people who have contributed their time, their expertise, their love of the game, and their passion for getting things right. These individuals are listed here, in the Acknowledgments, or in the table at

the end of the book of those readers of the first edition who helped us improve the accuracy of *Total Baseball* this time around. A collective debt is owed to the Society for American Baseball Research and the National Baseball Library.

The statistics were obtained primarily from the following sources:

- John Tattersall Collection of newspaper box scores and compilations for 1876–1890 NL.
- ICI computer printouts, National Baseball Library, 1891–1902 NL, 1882–1891 AA, 1884 UA, 1890 PL, 1901–1904 AL, 1914–1915 FL.
- Official league averages, 1903–date NL, 1905–date AL.
- Michael Stagno Collection of newspaper box scores and compilations for 1871–1875 NA, supplemented by research of SABR's nineteenth century research committee, headed by Bob Tiemann.

Supplemental sources were:

- For batters hit by pitch, 1884–1899 AA/NL/PL, 1909–1916 NL, 1909–1919 AL, research from newspapers by Alex Haas, Pete Palmer, John Schwartz, Bob Davids, John Tattersall, Lyle Spatz, and others. (Note: research continues for the 1897–1908 period, but the data is, at this writing, about 88 percent complete.)
- For home runs allowed by pitchers, 1876–1950 AL/ NL, the Tattersall Collection, reviewed and corrected by Bob McConnell.
- For runs batted in, 1903–1919 NL, 1905–1919 AL, ICI research.
- For runs batted in, 1880–1885 NL, David Neft.
- For pitcher saves (except 1901–1919 AL) 1876–1968 NL/AA/UA/PL/AL.
- For stolen bases, 1886 NL, *Spalding Baseball Guide.*
- For wins and losses for pitchers, 1876–1900 NL/ AA/PL, and for wins, losses, games started, complete games, shutouts, saves, 1900–1919 AL, and complete pitching data, 1892, research from newspa-

pers and official sheets by Frank Williams.
- For shutouts, 1876–1939, Joe Wayman.
- For biographical data, the biographical research committee of SABR, notably Richard Topp, Bill Carle.
- For caught-stealing data, 1914–1916 AL, 1915–1916 NL, Ernie Lanigan, courtesy of Bob Davids.
- For home/away data, 1876–1891 NL/AA/UA/PL, Bob McConnell.
- For game scores, 1876–1884 NL/AA/UA, Bob Tiemann.
- For game scores, 1885–1891 NL/AA/PL, Richard Topp.
- For runs and homers home/away, 1980s NL/AL, Bill Carr.

Missing data includes:

- Hit batters: 1897–1908, scattered data, especially for New York and Cincinnati.
- Caught stealing: 1886–1914, 1916 (players with more than 20 steals), 1917–1919, 1926–1950 NL; 1886–1891 AA; 1890 PL; 1901–1913, 1916 (players with more than 20 steals), 1917–1919, 1914–15 FL.
- Sacrifice hits: 1927–1930 (fly balls advancing runners to any base counted as sacrifice hits).
- Sacrifice flies: 1908–1930, 1939, 1940–1953.
- Runs batted in, 1882–1887, 1890 AA; 1884 UA.
- Strikeouts for batters: 1882–1888, 1890 AA; 1884 UA; 1897–1909 NL; 1901–1912 AL. (Team batting strikeouts are presented for 1897–1902 NL and 1901–1904 AL.)

Incomplete data for those years through 1902 NL and 1904 AL are available from the ICI computer printouts at the National Baseball Library. Additional research could turn up more data. If your research or sharp eye should detect errors or gaps in *Total Baseball,* please write us in care of the publisher and we'll be delighted to improve our data and credit your catch in the next edition.

Sabermetrics

John Thorn

Sabermetrics may be a new coinage for the statistical analysis of baseball but it is not a new phenomenon. Henry Chadwick, in the antebellum period, was as much a sabermetrician as Allan Roth or Bill James or Pete Palmer: he saw as clearly as they that because the object of the game is to win, runs are the best measure of player performance, just as they are of team performance at the end of a game.

After many decades in which this fundamental truth was lost (amid the general worship of false idols like batting average and pitcher won-lost percentage), today's sabermetricians have come around full circle to the game as it was originally understood. And what's remarkable about this is that in order to return to the primordial simplicity of the 1840s, '50s, and '60s, when runs and outs were all that went in to the box score, they have relied upon computer simulations and higher mathematics. In other words, with the new statistics, simplicity emerges from complexity; what baseball statistics have offered for the last hundred years or so has been, despite the appearance of simplicity, in fact extremely complex.

For the veteran fan as well as for Organized Baseball, new ideas, new statistics, and new discoveries that dispute long-held verities (Ty Cobb's hit total, Hoss Radbourn's number of victories in 1884, etc.) may represent a challenge to tradition and thus a threat to the very soul of baseball, its proud anachronism. Bernard Malamud wrote, "The whole history of baseball has the quality of mythology." The editors of *Total Baseball* relish the game's myths, from Abner Doubleday to the sacrifice bunt, and believe that in setting the record straight or turning conventional wisdom on its head, they are adding to the fan's enjoyment of the rich texture of the game. If you are one of the skeptics—like Earl Weaver, who once said, "There's no such thing as a new statistic"—please permit us to make the case for sabermetrics.

If you skipped over the preceding Introduction, which is largely taken up with an overview of baseball's traditional measures, we would encourage you to go back and read it before proceeding with this discussion of sabermetrics. As with the Introduction, much of the material in this section is adapted from the editors' earlier *The Hidden Game of Baseball.*

What's in a Number?

On April 27, 1983, the Montreal Expos came to bat in the bottom of the eighth inning trailing the Houston Astros 4–2. First up to face pitcher Nolan Ryan was Tim Blackwell, a lifetime .228 hitter who had struck out in his first time at bat. At this routine juncture of this commonplace game, Ryan stared down at Blackwell, but his invisible—yet, for all that, more substantial—opponent was a man who had died the month before Ryan was born, a man about whom Ryan knew nothing, he confessed, except his statistical line. For at this moment of his glorious big-league career, Ryan had accumulated a total of 3,507 strikeouts, only one short of the mark Walter Johnson set over twenty-one seasons, from 1907 to 1927. Long thought invulnerable, Johnson's record was in imminent danger of falling, in 1983, not only to Ryan but also to Steve Carlton and Gaylord Perry.

Ryan fanned Blackwell and then froze the next batter, pinch-hitter Brad Mills, with a 1-and-2 curveball. The pinnacle was his. Johnson had been baseball's all-time strikeout leader since 1921, when he surpassed Cy Young. Ryan would hold that title for just a few weeks, then would be overtaken by Carlton, only to display an incredible finishing kick and top the 5,000 mark in 1990. But at the time that Ryan topped Johnson, baseball savants scurried to assess the meaning of 3,509 for both the deposed King of K and the new.

In the aftermath of Ryan's feat, some writers pointed out that he only needed sixteen full seasons, plus fractions of two others, in which to record 3,509 strikeouts while Johnson needed twenty-one, or that Johnson pitched over 2,500 more innings than Ryan. Coming into the 1983 season, Ryan had fanned 9.44 men per nine innings, while Johnson was way down the list at 5.33. And Ryan allowed fewer hits per nine innings than Johnson, or, for that matter, anyone in the history of the game. So, it would seem 3,509 was not just one batter better than Johnson, but rather was mere confirmation for the masses of a superiority that was clear to the cognoscenti years before.

However, other writers introduced mitigating factors on Johnson's behalf, much as Ruth found supporters as the home run king even after Aaron hit number 715. These champions of the old order cited Johnson's won-lost record of 417–279 and earned run average of 2.17 while scoffing at Ryan's mark, entering 1983, of 205–186 with an ERA of 3.11. This tack led to further argument in print, bringing in the quality of the teams each man pitched for and against, the resiliency of the ball, the attitudes of the batters in each era toward the strikeout, the advent of night ball, integration, expansion, the designated hitter, the overall talent pool, competition from other professional sports . . . and on down into the black hole of subjectivism.

Why were so many things dragged into that discussion?

Because the underlying question about 3,509 was: Does this total make Ryan better than Johnson, or even a better *strikeout* pitcher than Johnson? At the least, does it make him a great pitcher? In our drive to identify excellence on the baseball field (or off it), we inevitably look to the numbers as a means of encapsulating and comprehending experience. This quantifying habit is at the heart of baseball's hidden game, the one ceaselessly played by Ryan and Johnson and Ruth and Aaron—and, thanks to baseball's voluminous records, more than 13,000 other players—in a stadium bounded only by the imagination.

What's in a number? The answer to "How Many?" and sometimes a great deal more. In this case, 3,509 men had come to the plate against Ryan and failed to put the ball in play, one more man than Johnson had returned to the dugout, cursing. So what's the big deal? That Ryan was .0002849 faster, scarier, tougher—better—than Johnson? An absolute number like 3,509, or 714 (the home-run record once thought invulnerable, too), or 4,191 (the erroneous hit total of Ty Cobb that Pete Rose finally surpassed) does not resound with meaning unless it is placed into some context that will give it life.

Baseball statistics are not the instruments of vivisection, taking the life out of the game in order to examine it; rather, statistics are themselves the vital part of baseball, the only tangible and imperishable remains of contests played yesterday or a hundred years ago. Baseball may be loved without statistics, but it cannot be understood without them. As the statistics reflect more accurately the reality of what happened on the field, greater understanding leads to a deeper love and appreciation of this great game—which is, essentially, the case for sabermetrics and the reason for *Total Baseball*.

The Linear Weights System

In 1982, Milwaukee's Robin Yount had the year of his life, batting .331 with 29 homers, 114 RBIs and 129 runs scored; he led the American League in hits, doubles, total bases, and slugging percentage, while finishing just one point behind the league leader in batting average. First of the two times in his career, he was voted the Most Valuable Player in the American League, being named first on all but one of the twenty-eight ballots cast by the baseball writers.

Over in the other league, Mike Schmidt of the Phillies was having an off year, batting only .280 with 35 homers and 87 RBIs; the previous year, when he was awarded the MVP, in only 102 games played he had totaled 31 homers and 91 RBIs. He did lead the league once again in 1982 in slugging percentage, and he did win the Gold Glove at third base for the seventh straight year, yet in the MVP balloting none of the ballots listed him higher than fourth; ten ballots were cast without listing him at all.

For Yount, 1982 was a crowning achievement; for Schmidt, a disappointment: That is the verdict reached by the baseball writers and conventional baseball statistics. Yet in terms of actual performance, as determined by the number of runs contributed, Schmidt's "off year" was scarcely different from Yount's. With the bat, Yount accounted for 50.3 runs beyond what an average batter might have contributed; Schmidt, 47.2. Through base

stealing, Yount added 2.4; Schmidt none. With the glove, Yount was 4 runs below league average at his position; Schmidt was 18.8 above average at *his* position. Total runs contributed: Yount 48.7, Schmidt 66.0. Total wins contributed beyond average by each: Yount 6.5, Schmidt 6.3. Both men had outstanding seasons, the best in their respective leagues, and both outstripped the second-best player by about the same margin.

Viewing player (and team) performance through this sort of prism frequently produces such illuminating results. Cecil Fielder had a wonderful year in 1990, with his 51 homers, 132 RBIs, and league-leading figures in slugging average and extra-base hits. But how did he convince any writer voting for MVP that he had a better year than Rickey Henderson? In *Total Baseball*, you could look it up: Fielder contributed 4.4 extra wins to his team (wins that an average player would not), which was the fourth-best figure in the American League that year; Henderson was responsible for a whopping 7.7, not only the top mark in 1990 but also the third-best mark in the AL since Ted Williams's epic season in 1941!

This is the kind of analysis of player performance possible with a variety of sabermetric measures, not just the Linear Weights System. The common ingredient of most of the new, as yet unofficial statistics is their creators' recognition of the relationship between runs and wins.

Runs and Wins

George Lindsey, in an article in *Operations Research* in 1963, was the first to assign run values to the various offensive events which lead to runs: Runs = (.41)1B + (.32)2B + (1.06)3B + (1.42)HR. He based these values on recorded play-by-play data and basic probability theory. Unlike Earnshaw Cook, who in the following year assigned run values on the basis of the sum of the individual scoring probabilities—that is, the *direct* run potential of the hit or walk plus those of the baserunners set in motion—Lindsey recognized that a substantial part of the run value of any non-out is that *it brings another man to the plate*. This additional batter has a one-in-three chance of reaching base and thus bringing another man to the plate with the same chance, as do the batters to follow. The *indirect* run potential of these batters cannot be ignored.

Steve Mann's Run Productivity Average (RPA) assigned these values based on observation of some 12,000 plate appearances: RPA = (.51)1B + (.82)2B + (1.38)3B + (2.63)HR + (.25)BB + (.15)SB − (.25)CS, all divided by plate appearances, then plus .016. His values were denominated in terms of the number of runs *and RBIs* each event produced. Bill James, at about the same time, came up with a similar formula, since shunned, with values based on runs plus RBIs *minus home runs*. The drawbacks to the approaches of Mann and James were the drawbacks of the RBI, which gives the entire credit for producing a run to the man who plates it, and of the run scored, which gives credit only to the man who touches home, no matter how he came to do so. For example, with no outs, a man reaches first on an error; the next batter hits a double, placing runners on second and third; the following batter taps a roller to short and is thrown out at

first, with the run scoring from third. The man who produced the out is given the credit for producing a run, while the man who started the sequence by reaching first on an error is likewise credited with a run. The man who hit the double, which was surely the key event in the sequence which produced the run, and the only one reflecting batting skill, receives no credit whatsoever. In this regard, any formula based on "Runs Produced" (whether R + RBI or R + RBI − HR) is philosophically inferior to the formula Lindsey proposed, despite his failure to account for walks, steals, and other events.

The run values in the Linear Weights formula for identifying batters' real contribution are derived from Pete Palmer's 1978 computer simulation of all major-league games played since 1901. All the data available concerning the frequencies of the various events was collected; following a test run, these were tabulated. Unmeasured quantities, such as the probability of a man going from first to third on a single vs. that of his advancing only one base, were assigned values based on play-by-play analysis of over 100 World Series contests. The goal was to get all the measured quantities very nearly equal to the league statistics; then the simulation would provide run values of each event in terms of net runs produced above average. Expressing the values in those terms would give a meaningful base line to individual performances, because if you are told that a player contributed 87 runs you don't know what that signifies unless you know the average level of run contribution in that year: 87 may sound like a lot, but if the norm was 80, then you know the player contributed only 7 runs beyond average.

The values obtained from the simulation are remarkably similar from one era to the next, confounding expectations that the home run would prove more valuable today than in the dead-ball era, or that the steal was once a primary offensive weapon. These values are expressed in beyond average runs.

Run Values of Various Events, by Periods

Event	Period			
	1901–20	1921–40	1941–60	1961–77
home run	1.36	1.40	1.42	1.42
triple	1.02	1.05	1.03	1.00
double	.82	.83	.30	.77
single	.46	.50	.47	.45
walk/HBP	.32	.35	.35	.33
stolen base	.20	.22	.19	.19
caught stealing	-.33	-.39	-.36	-.32
out*	-.24	-.30	-.27	-.25

*An out is considered to be a hitless at bat and its value is set so that the sum of all events times their frequency is zero, thus establishing zero as the base line, or norm, for performance.

In the years since this simulation was conducted, statistician Dave Smith ("Maury Wills and the Value of the Stolen Base," *Baseball Research Journal*, 1980) convinced Pete to adjust the values of the stolen base and caught stealing because of their situation-dependent, elective nature: Attempts are apt to occur more frequently in close games, where they would be worth more than if they were distributed randomly the way an event like a single or a home run would be. Pete revised the value for the steal upward to .30 runs, while for the caught stealing it becomes −.60 runs.

Just as these run values change marginally with changing conditions of play, they differ slightly up and down the batting order (a homer is not worth as much to the leadoff hitter as it is to the fifth-place batter; a walk is worth more for the man batting second than for the man batting eighth); however, these differences have been averaged out in the figures above. For evaluating runs contributed by any batter at any time, there is no better method than Batting Runs, the Linear Weights formula derived from the computer simulation which is the basis of the table above.

The Formula

Runs = (.47)1B + (.78)2B + (1.09)3B + (1.40)HR + (.33)(BB + HB) + (.30)SB − (.60)CS − (.25)(AB − H) − .50(OOB).

The events not included in the formula that you might have thought to see are sacrifices, sacrifice hits, grounded into double plays, and reached on error. The last is not known for most years and in the official statistics is indistinguishable from outs on base (OOB). The sacrifice has essentially canceling values, trading an out for an advanced base which, often as not, leaves the team in a situation with poorer run potential than it had before the sacrifice. The sacrifice fly has dubious run value because it is entirely dependent upon a situation not under the batter's control: While a single or a walk always has a potential run value, a long fly does not unless a man happens to be poised at third base (whether it is achieved by accident or design is open to question, as well, but that is beside the question—getting hit by a pitch is not a product of intent, either). Last, the grounded into double play is to a far greater extent a function of one's place in the batting order than it is of poor speed or failure in the clutch, and thus it does not find a home in a formula applicable to all batters. It is no accident that Henry Aaron, who ran well for most of his long career and wasn't too bad in the clutch, hit into more DP's than anyone else, nor that Roberto Clemente, Al Kaline, and Frank Robinson, who fit the same description, are also among the ten "worst" in this department. If Boston's Luis Rivera doesn't hit into many twin killings, it's not because of adept bat handling or blazing speed but because he bats ninth.

The Linear Weights formula for batters may be long, but it calls for only addition, subtraction, and multiplication and thus is as simple as the slugging average, whose incorrect weights (1, 2, 3, and 4) it revises and expands upon. Each event has a value and a frequency, just as in slugging average, yet as in no batting statistic you have ever seen, outs are treated as offensive events with a run value of their own (albeit a negative one), a truth so obvious it somehow escaped notice. Just as the run potential for a team in a given half inning is boosted by a man reaching base, it is diminished by a man being retired; not only has he failed to change the situation on the bases but he has deprived his team of the services of a man further down the order who might have come up in this half inning, either with men on base and/or with scores already in.

What Batting Runs does is to take every offensive event

and treat it in terms of its impact upon the team—an average team, so that a man does not benefit in his individual record for having the good fortune to bat cleanup with the Giants or suffer for batting seventh with the Astros. The relationship of individual performance to team play is stated poorly or not at all in conventional baseball statistics. In Batting Runs it is crystal clear: The linear progression, the sum of the various offensive events, when weighted by their accurately predicted run values, will total the runs contributed by that batter or that team beyond the league average.

Recognizing some dedicated readers of *Total Baseball* will wish to keep track of batting performance by computing Batting Runs themselves over the course of a season, and that they may be frustrated by the difficulty of calculating the "At Bats–Hits" factor for the league, which is necessary to determine the negative value of an out, we advise that using a fixed value of −.25 for outs will tend to work quite well if you wish to include pitcher batting performance, and a fixed value of −.27 will serve if you wish to delete it. Actually, any fixed value will suffice in midseason; it's only when all the numbers are in and you care to compare this year's results with last year's (or with those of the 1927 Yankees) that more precision is desirable. At that point the value of the out may be calculated by the ambitious among you, but ideally, your newspaper or the sporting press will provide accurate Batting Runs figures. Who, after all, calculates ERA for himself?

Batting Runs and Production

For those to whom calculation is anathema, or at the least no pleasure, Batting Runs has a "shadow stat" that tracks its accuracy to a remarkable degree and is a breeze to calculate: Production, which consists simply of On Base Percentage Plus Slugging Average. While it is not expressed in runs and thus lacks the philosophical appeal of Batting Runs, the standard deviation of its most complete version is 20.4 runs compared to the 19.8 of Batting Runs. In other words, the correlation between Batting Runs and Production over the course of an average team season is 99.7 percent.

However, as an average or ratio, Production measures the *rate* of batting success (efficiency), while Batting Runs measures the *amount* of success. For example, a batter who goes 2-for-5 with a walk in one game, those 2 hits being doubles, will have an On Base Percentage of .500 and a Slugging Average of .800; his Production will be 1.3, or as stated for convenience in *Total Baseball*, 130. Another batter, who in 162 games gets 200 hits and 100 walks in 500 at bats, with 400 total bases, will have an identical OBP, SLG, and PRO. Which player has contributed more to his team? Clearly, longevity, or *amount* of production, is no less important than *rate* of production.

To cite a specific instance in which Production and Batting Runs differ, take George Brett's remarkable 1980 season in which he batted .390, had 298 total bases, 75 bases through walks or HBP, and 118 RBIs—all in only 117 games played. In the table of all-time single-season leaders in production, the Kansas City third baseman ranks 44th when his PRO of 1.124 is normalized to the league average and adjusted for home-park effects. Yet in the table of park adjusted Batting Runs, Brett's season ranks out of the top 100 because he missed 45 games, in which his team derived no benefit from his performance. (Had Brett played 162 games and continued to perform at the same level, his Batting Runs would have been not 64.8 but 89.7, the 19th best mark in history.)

Because PRO is not expressed in runs, it is less versatile than Batting Runs. For just as runs are proportional to the events that form them, so are they proportional to wins and losses. This statement, a truism today, was a novelty in 1954 when Rickey and Roth first stated the correlation between run differentials and team standings. But they did not take the next step, to recognize that not only a team's standing *but even its won-lost record* could be predicted from the run totals.

"The initial published attempt on this subject," Pete wrote in the 1982 issue of the SABR annual *The National Pastime*, "was Earnshaw Cook's *Percentage Baseball*, in 1964. Examining major-league results from 1950 through 1960 he found winning percentage equal to .484 times runs scored divided by runs allowed. . . . Arnold Soolman, in an unpublished paper which received some media attention, looked at results from 1901 through 1970 and came up with winning percentage equal to .102 times runs scored per game minus .103 times runs allowed per game plus .505. . . . Bill James, in the *Baseball Abstract*, developed winning percentage equal to runs scored raised to the power x, divided by the sum of runs scored and runs allowed each raised to the power x. Originally, x was equal to two but then better results were obtained when a value of 1.83 was used. . . .

"My work showed that as a rough rule of thumb, each additional ten runs scored (or ten less runs allowed) produced one extra win, essentially the same as the Soolman study. However, breaking the teams into groups showed that high-scoring teams needed more runs to produce a win. This runs-per-win factor I determined to be ten times the square root of the average number of runs scored per inning by both teams. Thus in normal play, when 4.5 runs per game are scored by each club, each team scores .5 runs per inning—totaling one run, the square root of which is one, times ten."

Note that when Palmer refers to the need for approximately ten additional runs scored (or ten fewer allowed) to provide a team with an additional win, he does *not* mean that it takes ten runs to win any given game. Obviously, in a specific case, a one-run margin is all that is required; but statistics are designed for the long haul, not the short.

What does this have to do with Batting Runs? Remembering that Batting Runs are expressed not simply in runs but in beyond-average runs, the conversion from a batter's Linear Weights *runs* to his *wins* is a snap: simply divide Batting Runs by the number of runs it takes to gain an extra win in a given year. Taking the exploits of Babe Ruth in 1927, we see that through batting alone he contributed 100.7 runs, or 9.56 wins, since in the American League in 1927 it took 10.53 runs to produce an additional win. If every other player on the Yankees had performed at the league average, the New York record should have been 87–67; if each of the seven other batters had performed only half as well as Ruth and had added five extra wins (discounting reserves, pitchers, fielders,

and stealers, whom we shall presume for this discussion to have been average), the Yankees would have gained another 35 wins (7 × 5) to finish with a won-lost mark of 122–32.

Stolen Base Runs

The Linear Weights formula for batters contains a factor for base stealers, expressed in runs. How do you judge the effectiveness of a base stealer? Conventional baseball statistics will lead you to the conclusion that whoever has the most steals is the best thief; that is the sole criterion for *The Sporting News* annual "Golden Shoe Award" in each league. How often the man with the most steals may have been thrown out is of no concern.

An article in the 1981 *Baseball Research Journal* by Bob Davids offered something more sophisticated yet utterly simple: a stolen base percentage, which is simply stolen bases divided by attempts. The best stolen base average of all time, insofar as we know and based on a minimum of 30 attempts, is Max Carey's in 1922 when he stole 51 bases in 53 attempts. The most times caught stealing in the course of a season was Ty Cobb's 38 in 1915, until 1982 when Rickey Henderson was nabbed 42 times. But the best method yet devised, and the one that is pleasingly simple, is to apply the Linear Weights method to get Stolen Base Runs. One multiplies the steals by their run value of .30 and the failed attempts by −.60, and adds the two products. The implication for such men as Ty Cobb, Rickey Henderson, and Vince Coleman is clear: It takes a fabulous stealing performance to produce as much as one extra win for the team.

In 1915 Ty Cobb, when he established the modern stolen base record of 96, can be seen to have contributed to his team 28.8 runs, while his 38 foiled larcenies cost 22.8. Thus Cobb, for all his whirling-dervish activity, accounted for only 6 non-par runs—not even a single win. Whoa! You mean that not a single one of Cobb's steals produced a victory? That is not what is being said: the fact is that while the gain from the stolen base is entirely visible—an extra base which may be followed by a hit that would otherwise not have produced a run—the cost of the caught stealing is entirely invisible, or conjectural, except with the aid of statistics. How many big innings did Cobb run his team out of? How many batters reached base in ensuing innings who might, in an earlier inning, have had their contributions count for runs? What Stolen Base Runs indicate are that, *on balance*, not on a specific-case basis, the stolen base is at best a dubious method of increasing a team's run production.

Now let's take a look at what Henderson did. His record 130 stolen bases in 1982 produced 39 runs for his team. His 42 failed attempts took away 25.2 possible runs. Net effect: approximately 14 runs, or one and a half wins, a performance nearly *three times* as good as Cobb's. In 1983, stealing 22 fewer bases, he was even better, accounting for 21.0 runs. However, the all-time best stealing record is that of Maury Wills in 1962, when he stole 104 bases and was caught only 13 times. Wills's 104 stolen bases produced 31.2 runs; his 13 failed attempts cost only 7.8. So, his baserunning contribution was 23.4, or a little over two wins.

Fielding Runs

As mentioned earlier, in 1954 when Branch Rickey and Allan Roth came up with their "efficiency formula" for run scoring and run prevention, the defensive half of the equation was divided into five segments, the last of which was fielding, to which they assigned a mathematical value of zero. "There is nothing on earth," Rickey declared, "anyone can do with fielding."

Since then many have tried, with mixed results, to improve upon the mere toting up of raw data—putouts, assists, errors, double plays. In this second edition of *Total Baseball*, we have improved upon the Fielding Runs formula by calculating innings played at each position, plate appearances for all players on the team, and then rating each fielder based on his chances per inning. (Formerly we had rated each position on each team based on totals for all players on that team at that position; then we split up the total based on putouts. For more on the formula, see the Introduction to the new Fielding Register, and the Glossary.)

In the current edition we have also rated left fielders against left fielders, center fielders against center fielders, and right fielders against right fielders; where previously all outfield positions had been grouped together. We revised thoroughly the formula for catchers, which retains the highest degree of subjectivism because their primary defensive contribution comes not with the glove but through calling the pitches.

More on this complex subject at the head of the Fielding Register.

Pitching Runs

Determining the run contributions of pitchers is much easier than determining those of fielders or batters, though not quite so simple as that of base stealers. Actual runs allowed are known, as are innings pitched. Let's assume that a pitcher is responsible only for earned runs. Then why, we hear some of you asking, is the ERA not measure enough of his ability? Because it tells only the pitcher's rate of efficiency, not his actual benefit to the team. In a league with an ERA of 3.50, a starter who throws 300 innings with an ERA of 2.50 must be worth twice as much to his team as a starter with the same ERA who appears in only 150 innings. Through Pitching Runs, we seek to determine the number of beyond-average runs a pitcher saved—the number he prevented from scoring that an average pitcher would have allowed.

The formula for Earned Run Average is:

$$\text{ERA} = \frac{\text{Earned Runs} \times 9}{\text{Innings Pitched}}$$

The number of average, or par, runs for a pitcher, which is represented by a Pitching Runs figure of zero, is equal to:

$$\frac{\text{League ERA} \times \text{IP}}{9}$$

If the league ERA is 3.79 (as the National League's was in 1990) and a pitcher's ERA is also 3.79, he will by definition have held batters in check at the league average no matter how many innings he pitched. If, however, his ERA was 2.67 and he hurled 249 innings (as Frank Viola did for the Mets in '90), he will have saved a certain

number of runs that an average pitcher might have allowed in his place; to find that number we employ the Pitching Runs formula:

Pitcher's Runs =

$$\text{Innings Pitched} \times \left(\frac{\text{League ERA}}{9}\right) - \text{ER}$$

This represents the difference between the number of earned runs allowed at the league average for the innings pitched and the actual earned runs allowed. For the case of Viola, we get

$$\text{Runs} = 249 \times \frac{3.79}{9} - 74 = 31.2$$

Viola was 31.2 runs better than the average National League pitcher in 1990, and had he been transported to an average NL team—that mythical entity that scores as many runs as it allows while winning 81 and losing 81—he would have made that team's mark 84–78. An alternative way to calculate pitchers' Linear Weights, useful with oldtimers for whom you may have the ERA but not the number of earned runs allowed, is to use the pitcher's ERA, subtracted from the league's ERA, multiplying by the innings pitched, then dividing by nine. In Viola's case, this approach would look like:

$$(3.79 - 2.67) \times \frac{249}{9} = 31.0$$

The difference of two tenths of a point is accounted for because we are using the ERA of 2.69, which has been rounded off, rather than the absolute figure of the pitcher's earned runs allowed, 74.

The two parts of performance—efficiency and durability, or how well and how long—are incorporated into all Linear Weights measures. If you are performing at a better than average clip, the more regularly you do so, the more your team will benefit and thus the higher your Linear Weights measure. If you are stealing bases nine times out of ten, your team will benefit more from sixty attempts than from forty; if you are batting at an above average clip, it's better to play in 160 games than 110; if you're allowing one earned run per game less than the average pitcher, your LWTS will increase with innings pitched.

A problem emerges in this regard when trying to compare the Pitching Runs of a pitcher from 1978 like Ron Guidry, with that of Hoss Radbourn in 1884. In the "efficiency" component of the formula, which may be understood as the league ERA minus the individual's ERA, the two compare this way:

Guidry = 3.76 − 1.74 = 2.02
Radbourn = 2.98 − 1.38 = 1.60

Guidry's differential is "unfairly" boosted by the higher league ERA of 1978; in fact, if we had compared the two by their normalized ERAs, which is logically more sound, the results would have been:

$$\text{Guidry} = \frac{3.76}{1.74} = 2.16 \qquad \text{Radbourn} = \frac{2.98}{1.38} = 2.16$$

Yet because rules and playing conditions allowed Radbourn to extend his efficiency over 679 innings, while Guidry hurled "only" 274, their Pitching Runs look like this:

Guidry = 62.0   Radbourn = 120.6

There is a great deal more to say on the subject of pitching and sabermetric stats: see the Introduction to the Pitching Register and the Glossary.

Linear Weights in Practice

Having formulas for pitching, fielding, baserunning, and batting, we can assess the run-scoring contribution of every individual who has ever played the game, and thus the number of wins that he has contributed in a given season or over his career. The number of runs required to produce an additional win has varied over the years between 9 and 11 runs, with a very few league seasons outside those parameters.

Limited by conventional baseball statistics, one might, in 1990, have uttered something like, "Bobby Bonds hit .293 with 33 homers and 114 RBIs—the guy must have been worth 10 extra wins to Pittsburgh all by himself!" Or: "The White Sox are only one pitcher away from winning the division." Or: "The Yankees are only three players away from being a contender." Or, "Letting Darryl Strawberry get away was the worst thing the Mets ever did; they'll be a second-division club for a decade."

With Linear Weights, these statements, or rather the concerns they reflect, can be approached with some data and with some degree of objectivity. First: Bobby Bonds had a fine year in 1990, but to have contributed 10 wins by himself he would have had to account for nearly 100 Linear Weights runs, a mark that has been attained by only one man in major-league history. In fact, Bonds contributed 6.5 wins in '90, though he did post 9.0 wins in 1992.

As to the White Sox, they finished 94–68 in 1982, while their Linear Weights projected them to finish at 81–81. The Athletics, who won the AL West at 103–59, actually projected to finish 96–66. So, the Sox management might have asked, how to close ground on the Athletics? Could one pitcher—like Bob Welch, for whom they bid in the free-agent bazaar—make the difference? To do so, he would have to contribute about 150 Pitching Runs, a feat no pitcher has ever accomplished. In 1990, pitching for Oakland—and remember, the Linear Weights formula is divorced from considerations of batter support—Welch contributed 20.7 park-adjusted Pitching Runs. So presuming that he pitched as well for the White Sox as he did for the Athletics, or even slightly better, he would not be enough to "win" Chicago the flag on paper; Chicago would need help from other quarters.

Regarding the other statements, you get the picture: sabermetric analyses like the ones above will tend to puncture fantasies.

Park Factor

A central issue for sabermetricians is the network of illusion created by home-park dimensions, atmospheric conditions, and visibility for batters. How many home runs would Mark McGwire hit if he played half his games in Fenway Park? Will the Boston Red Sox and Chicago Cubs keep "failing" to put together solid pitching staffs—or has their pitching been adequate all along? Why have the American League leaders in triples so often worn a Royals uniform? One's home park has a powerful effect on a player or pitcher's record, elevating some good players to greatness and denying the spotlight to some outstanding performers.

It should be understood that the average player does better at home *regardless* of the park—familarity breeds success, it seems. Individuals bat and pitch at a rate 10 percent higher at home, on average. But parks don't create performance; they only affect it. For example, a left-handed hitter at Fenway can do very well indeed, as Wade Boggs has, by learning to take the outside pitch to left field. Likewise, a righthanded batter can make the friendly Green Monster into his nemesis by trying to pull every pitch.

For hard luck in home parks, it is tough to top the record of Dave Winfield, who has had the misfortune to call both San Diego and Yankee stadiums home before landing in the more or less neutral Big A in Anaheim. Through 1990, his lifetime Production, normalized to league average but not adjusted for park effects, was 117th best on the all time list of those playing in 1,000 games. Had he played his home games instead in Fenway Park, his PRO would have projected to the 45th best of all time. Had he even played in an average hitters' park—which is what PRO$^+$ measures—his record would show itself to be the 80th best ever.

If we desire to remove the silver spoon or the millstone that a home park can be, and measure individual ability alone, we must create a statistical balancer that diminishes the individual batting marks created in parks like Fenway and augments those created in San Diego. Pete Palmer developed an adjustment that enables us, for the first time, to measure a player's accomplishments apart from the influence of his home park.

Parks differ in so many ways that it may be hard to imagine how their differences can be quantified. The most obvious way in which they differ is in their dimensions, from home plate to the outfield walls, and from the base lines to the stands. The older arenas—Fenway Park, Wrigley Field, Tiger Stadium—tend to favor hitters in both regards, with reachable fences and little room to pursue a foul pop. The exception among the older parks was Chicago's Comiskey, which, in keeping with the theories of Charles Comiskey back in 1910 and the team's perceived strength, was built as a pitcher's park. Yet two parks can have nearly equal dimensions, like Pittsburgh's Three Rivers Stadium and Atlanta's Fulton County Stadium, yet have highly dissimilar impacts upon hitters because of climate (balls travel farther in hot weather), elevation (travel farther above sea level), and playing surface (travel faster and truer on artificial turf). Yet another factor is how well batters think they see the ball; Shea Stadium is notorious as a cause of complaints.

And perhaps more important than any of the objective park characteristics, suggested Robert Kingsley in a 1980 study of why so many homers were hit in Atlanta, is the attitude of the players, the way that the park changes their view of how the game must be played in order to win. Every team that comes into Atlanta in August knows that the ball is going to fly and, whether it is a team designed for power or not, it plays ball there as if it were the 1927 Yankees. In their own home park the Astros may peck and scratch for runs, but in Atlanta they will put the steal and hit-and-run in mothballs. Conversely, a team which comes into the Astrodome and plays for the big inning will generally get what it deserves—a loss. The successful team is one that can play its game at home—the game for which the team was constructed—yet is flexible enough to adapt when on the road. How to quantify attitude?

Rather than try to assign a numerical value to each of the six or more variables that might go into establishing an estimator of homepark impact, Pete looked to the single measure in which all these variables are reflected—runs. After all, why would we assign one value to dimensions, another to climate, and so on, except to identify their impact on scoring? If a stadium is a "hitters' park," it stands to reason that more runs would be scored there than in a park perceived as neutral, just as a "pitchers' park" could be expected to depress scoring.

The full and lengthy explanation for the computation of the Park Factor is left to the Glossary, where hardy readers might consider taking a peek right now. For most of us, though, it will be enough to understand that the Park Factor consists mainly of the team's home-road ratio of runs allowed, computed as it was above for the league, compared to the league's home-road ratio.

Just as Dave Winfield's stats suffered for the home parks he played in until he joined the California Angels, Dean Chance, star pitcher of the Angels in the mid-1960s, benefited from playing in Chavez Ravine when it was notoriously rough on hitters. This is not to say Chance had anything but a marvelous year in 1964: 20 wins, a 1.65 ERA, and 11 shutouts are hard to argue with. Still, in 81 home games in 1964, the Angels allowed 226 runs; in 81 games on the road, they allowed 325—44 percent more, where a 10 to 11 percent increase would have been normal. If one is to compare Chance and, say, Bert Blyleven in his years with Minnesota fairly, you must deny one the benefit of his home park and remove from the other the onus of his. This is what Park Factor does.

For decades, the all-time scoring squelcher was Chicago's South Side Park, which saw service at the dawn of the American League. From 1901 through 1909, its last full year of service to the White Sox, this cavernous stadium produced home run totals like the 2 in 1904, 3 in 1906, and 4 in 1909; in two years the Sox failed to hit *any* homers at home, thus earning the nickname "Hitless Wonders." In 1906, Chicago pitchers held opponents to 180 runs at South Side Park, an average of 2.28 runs per game, earned *and* unearned, in a decade when 4 of every 10 runs were unearned. This mark held until 1981, when the Astrodome intimidated opposing hitters to such a point that in the 51 home dates of that strike-shortened season, Astro hurlers were touched for only 106 runs—2.08 per game. The Pitcher Park Factor of .817 for the Astrodome was the lowest ever. Those who suspected that men like Joe Niekro, Don Sutton, Vern Ruhle, et al., were perhaps not world beaters after all were right: Look at the ERAs the Astro starters registered that year, and what these ERAs might have been in an average park like Shea that year (BPF: 1.00) or a moderately difficult pitchers' park like San Francisco (BPF: 1.06).

Houston Pitchers, 1982

	ERA	BPF: 1.00	BPF: 1.06
Nolan Ryan	1.69	2.07	2.19
Joe Niekro	2.82	3.43	3.64
Vern Ruhle	2.91	3.56	3.77
Bob Knepper	2.18	2.66	2.82
Don Sutton	2.60	3.17	3.36
HOUSTON (all)	2.66	3.24	3.44
SAN FRANCISCO (all)	3.28	3.09	3.28

Some observations prompted by this table: San Francisco with its team ERA of 3.28 had a better pitching staff than Houston with its 2.66; and Houston batters, regarded as a Punch-and-Judy crew by all observers, must have been a lot more effective than heretofore suspected. In fact, when Houston batters' totals (eighth in runs scored, eighth in LWTS) are adjusted for park, the Astros emerge on ability as the *best* hitting team in the National League of 1981! Even without the application of Park Factor, one might have come to a similar conclusion by examining the runs scored totals for all NL clubs on the road in 1981. Houston's total was exceeded only by those of the Dodgers and Reds.

Proceeding from a similar hunch, we may look at the batting record of the "Hitless Wonders" of 1906, who won the pennant (and the World Series, in four straight over a Cubs team which went 116–36 during the season). Baseball lore has it that a magnificent pitching staff (Ed Walsh, Doc White, Nick Altrock, and others) overcame a puny batting attack (BA of .230, 6 homers, slugging percentage of .286). In fact, the Sox scored more runs on the road than all but one AL team, and their Batting Linear Weights, when adjusted for park, was third in the league—the same rank achieved by their pitching. (How they won the pennant remains a mystery, though, for both Cleveland and New York had vastly superior teams on paper.)

Relativity

Sabermetric statistics can be marvelous tools for cross-era comparisons, enabling us to determine if baseball's history is truly a seamless web or if its seams are real enough, but are camouflaged by traditional statistics.

If Batter A presented himself to you for approval with these statistics—.330 batting average, 16 home runs, 107 RBIs—what would your reaction be? You'd like to have him on your team, right? And what to make of Batter B, who presents these numbers—.257 batting average, 14 home runs, 53 RBIs? Not bad for a middle infielder with a good glove, you say, but otherwise undistinguished? In fact, the "impressive" figures of Batter A represent the *average* performance of a National League outfielder in 1930, while the "blah" figures of Batter B are those of the average American League outfielder of 1968: The former has more than twice the RBIs of the latter, along with a batting average 73 points higher, yet the two performed at identical levels, and an argument could be made that Batter B was superior.

In a similar comparison involving those two years of extremes, Bill Terry led the National League in 1930 with a BA of .401, a mark surpassed by Ted Williams in 1941 but not equaled since; Carl Yastrzemski led the American League of 1968 with a performance that oldtimers held to be a disgrace, a lowly BA of .301, the worst ever to win a batting championship. Terry's mark was achieved at a time when most pitchers had only two pitches, a fastball and a curve, and not enough confidence in the latter to throw it when behind in the count at 2–0 or 3–1. The parks were smaller; there was no night ball; the game was segregated racially; and you played 22 games with each team, none farther west of the Mississippi than St. Louis. Moreover, 1930 was the year in which National League officials, attempting to match the popularity of the slugging American League, juiced the ball to such an extent that the entire *league* batted .312 (if you remove pitcher batting). In other words, the average nonpitcher in the NL of 1930 batted higher than the AL leader in 1968! When Yaz hit .301, pitchers dominated the game and the average American League nonpitcher hit .238. How to compare Terry and Yaz, who played under such different conditions thirty-eight years apart?

You could view Terry's .401 in relation to his league's BA of .312, concluding that Memphis Bill was a better hitter (by BA alone, which despite its previously cited deficiencies remains the most comfortable stat by which to introduce this technique) by 28.5 percent. You could compare Yaz's .301 to *his* league's BA of .238 and conclude that he was a better than average hitter by 26.5 percent. A mere 2 percentage points separate the men— had they both played in the National League of 1983, when the league average was .255, the Terry of 1930 might have hit .328, the Yaz of 1968, .323. (A further refinement of this method would be to delete Terry's at bats and hits from his league's, and those of Yastrzemski from his league's, so that the batters are not in effect compared with themselves. This, however, necessitates the use of at bats and hits rather than simply the averages and does not significantly alter the results.)

Why do we need relative measures? Basically, for the same reason we need statistics altogether, to compare, to interpret, and to comprehend, but in a more reasonable and accurate manner when the disparity of the data sources makes the use of absolute, unadjusted numbers illogical. If the analysis involves data produced under widely varying conditions, such as a sample including performances 20, 50, or 100 years apart, any comparison will be meaningless without dragging in a series of rather complex historical understandings to modify the analysis—and in a highly subjective, unreliable manner. To compare Terry's .401 with Yastrzemski's .301 with no recognition of the *context* in which these marks were achieved, that is, to infer that Terry was 100 points *better* than Yaz, is equivalent to comparing Babe Ruth's salary of $80,000 in 1930 with Pete Rose's $806,250 of fifty years later and concluding that Rose was $726,250 richer. To understand those figures we must place them within a context which includes such factors as I.R.S. regulations and inflation: We might think to re-express the two salaries in terms of their purchasing power, multiplying each by the Consumer Price Index of its time as expressed in 1967 dollars; doing this would be to compute a "relative salary" for Ruth and Rose, just as we computed a Relative Batting Average for Terry and Yaz. (And just as we discovered there was little difference between the BAs of the latter couple, we would discover there is little difference between the salaries of the former pair.)

Few are the fans who could cite the context of Ross Barnes's .429 batting average of 1876, let alone evaluate its ingredients (these include considerations of equipment, schedule, travel, physiology, racial exclusion, daytime games, rules variations, attitudes, and customs). A statistic removed from its historical context can be as deceptive as a quotation pulled out of context. How, then, to compare Barnes's .429 with, say, Bill Madlock's league-leading figure of .339 a century later? Should we discount Barnes's average 10 percent because in his day batters could demand a pitch above the waist or below? Or should we augment it 17 percent because a pitcher could throw eight "balls" before allowing a walk?

We are confronted with a similar problem in trying to quantify the various differences between home parks; our solution there was to look at the single measure which reflected all the variables—runs—and from that measure we proceeded to devise a formula for Park Factor. Similarly, the many variables that supply the context for Barnes in 1876 supplied an identical context for every other batter in *that year*—and the context in which Bill Madlock hit .339 prevailed for every other National League batter in 1976 (except for home park, of course). Accordingly, if we form a ratio of Barnes's .429 to his league's average (.265) and another of Madlock's to his league's average (.263) we obtain figures (1.62 for Barnes, 1.28 for Madlock—stated for convenience in *Total Baseball* as 162 and 128), which may reasonably be compared with each other: Barnes was 62 percent better than his league in BA, while Madlock was 28 percent better than his; these become the comparables, not the .429 and .339. The method will not become a time machine—putting Barnes on a modern club and Madlock on an old-time one—any more than Park Factor is a place machine, switching Joe DiMaggio to Beantown and Ted Williams to the Bronx. However, the relativist approach offers suggestive truths and does measure precisely the extent to which Barnes's and Madlock's BAs dominated those of their contemporaries.

Until the 1970s, when David Shoebotham ("Relative Batting Averages," *Baseball Research Journal*, 1976) and Merritt Clifton ("Relative Baseball," *Samisdat*, 1979) introduced the relativist approach, all baseball stats were absolute. And for cross-era comparison, that favorite Hot Stove League activity, absolute stats were absolutely useless, generating plenty of heat and precious little light. What the theory of relativity, baseball-style, does beautifully is to eliminate the need for bringing historical baggage to statistical analysis. The normalized or relative versions of *any* statistic—batting average, Production, ERA, slugging average, you name it; even homers or strikeouts, though there are problems with these—will be greater than 1.00 for all above-average performers (1.41, for example, means 41 percent better than average in the given category) while relative statistics less than 1.00 will indicate a below average level of play (0.88 means 12 percent below the norm).

It is as simple as can be. So Early Wynn had a 3.20 ERA in 1950? What does that *mean*? Well, the league ERA was 4.58, so Wynn did very well indeed. His normalized ERA thus was 143, a mark better than that earned by Tom Seaver in 1968, when he had an absolute ERA a full run lower at 2.20.

We cannot employ a Relative Won-Lost record, for the league average is every year the same: .500. (A logical corollary is that one cannot fruitfully use relative measures of any sort for a single season's analysis, as all like figures will be compared to the same league average. The numbers may be changed into normalized form, but the players' rankings will be unchanged: The top ten in batting average in 1990, for example, will retain their ranks in Relative Batting Average.)

Relativism in baseball echoes not only Einstein but also Shakespeare, whose words in *Hamlet* might be modified to read "There is nothing either good or bad, but context makes it so." No longer must we accept arbitrary assessments of performance or regard with awe such old-time figures as Hugh Duffy's BA of .438 in 1894 (not the accomplishment that Rod Carew's .388 was in 1977) or George Sisler's .407 in 1920 (not as good as Roberto Clemente's .357 in 1967). Conversely, a "mediocre" performance of recent years, such as Bobby Murcer's .292 of 1972, for instance, stacks up as the equal of Eddie Collins' .360 in 1923, while Charlie Grimm's seemingly solid .298 in 1929 compares unfavorably to Mike Cubbage's .260 in 1976.

Relativism redefines our understanding not only of particular accomplishments but also of baseball history itself. We see that the men who batted .400 with numbing regularity in the 1890s and 1920s were not supermen (would you swap Wade Boggs for Tuck Turner? George Brett for Harry Heilmann?) anymore than the sub-2.00 ERA pitchers of the late 1960s (Gary Peters, Bob Bolin, Dave McNally, et al.). Absolute figures lie. Are hitters today worse because none has hit .400 since 1941? Or are they superior because a Dave Kingman can average nearly 30 homers a year while Cap Anson only averaged 4? Are infielders better today because they make fewer errors than their counterparts of 50, 75, or 100 years ago? Do modern outfielders have limp-noodle arms because their assist totals pale before those registered in the early decades of the 1900s? Is baseball improving or declining, and has its rise or fall been steady? One can spit absolute stats on the hot stove all winter long and get no closer to the answer, but with relative statistics, the issues are clarified.

In the May 1983 issue of *The Coffin Corner*, the newsletter of the Professional Football Researchers Association, Bob Carroll offered a witty and perceptive dissection of the relative approach to football statistics. It was based upon a comparison of two great running backs, Tuffy Leemans of the New York Giants of the late 1930s and early '40s and George Rogers, then with the New Orleans Saints. "I've always liked the story," Carroll wrote, "of the little old lady who scornfully toured a Picasso exhibit and then sniffed, 'If Rembrandt were alive today, *he* wouldn't paint this way!' To which a bystander replied, 'Ah, but if Rembrandt were alive today, he wouldn't be Rembrandt.'"

There are things that relative baseball stats won't do, questions they won't answer. What would Ty Cobb bat if he were playing today? Lefty O'Doul was asked this question by a fan at an offseason baseball banquet in 1960. "Maybe .340," O'Doul answered. "Then why do you say Cobb was so great," the fan remarked, "if he could only hit .340 with the lively ball today?" "Well," O'Doul said,

"you have to take into consideration that the man is now 74 years old." Relative Batting Average cannot tell with certainty what Cobb would hit today, for as Carroll wrote of Tuffy Leemans, if Cobb were playing today he wouldn't be the same Cobb; he would be bigger, stronger, and faster, and he might choose to steal less and go for the long ball more.

Relief Pitching

Absent from the chapter to this point has been the relief pitcher, a modern specialist who because of his still-evolving role in baseball, presents a variety of sabermetric problems and opportunities. The nature of the job is such that his won-lost record is not meaningful (even less so today than ten or fifteen years ago, with the ace in most bullpens being called upon—in highly dubious wisdom—only when his team has a lead in the eighth or ninth inning). A reliever may pick up a win with as little as a third of an inning's work, if he is lucky, while a starter must go five innings; a reliever may also pick up a loss more easily, for if he allows a run there may be little or no opportunity for his teammates to get it back, as they can for a starter. Earned run average is meaningful for the reliever, but it must be .15 to .25 lower to equate with that of a starter of comparable ability: a reliever frequently begins his work with a man or two already out, and thus can put men on base and strand them without having to register three outs.

Ratios of hits to innings, strikeouts to innings, strikeouts to walks—all of these have their interest, but none is sufficient by itself to measure relief-pitcher effectiveness. Relievers may also have an edge in these ratios because they generally face each batter only once in a game, thus leading to fewer hits and more strikeouts per inning. Before discussing the modern alternatives of saves or Relief Points, and our own Relief Ranking, let's review briefly the rise of the relief pitcher from the role of a mere hanger-on to, some would say, the most indispensable part of a winning team.

Relief pitching before 1891 was limited, with rare exceptions, to the starting pitcher exchanging places with one of the fielders, who was known as the "change pitcher." Substitutions from the bench were not permitted except in case of injury until 1889, when a tenth man became entitled to designation as a substitute for all positions; free substitution came in two years later, but no relief specialists emerged until Claude Elliott, Cecil Ferguson, and Otis Crandall in the first decade of this century.

The next decade's best relievers were starters doing double duty—notably Ed Walsh, Chief Bender, and Three Finger Brown. The 1920s, and up to the end of World War II, brought the first firemen to be employed in the modern way, although they tended to work more innings and fewer games than today. These were men such as Firpo Marberry, Johnny Murphy, Ace Adams, and several other worthies.

When you think of a relief pitcher in the modern-day sense—that is, a man who can appear in 50 or more ballgames a year, all or nearly all in relief, and win/save 30 or more—you begin with Joe Page of the 1947–49 Yankees and Jim Konstanty of the 1950 Phils, though Marberry had one such season in 1926. None of the three, however, ever heard of a "save" in his playing days—this term wasn't introduced until 1960, the year after Larry Sherry's heroic World Series in which he finished all four Dodger victories, garnering two for himself and saving the others; 1959 was also the year fireman Roy Face went 18–1, not losing until September 11.

Before Jerry Holtzman of the Chicago *Sun Times* devised the save, baseball people were looking at really only one figure to measure a reliever's work, and that was the number of games in which he appeared; any other appreciation of his efforts was expressed impressionistically. A reliever did not work enough innings to qualify for an ERA title (Hoyt Wilhelm in 1952 being the exception), nor could he expect to win 20 games. The introduction of a specialized statistic for the fireman was acknowledgment of his specialized employment and conferred upon it a status it had never enjoyed, not even after the exploits of Konstanty, Page, Wilhelm, and Face. Only when the save came into being did the majority of relievers take pride in their work and stop regarding their time in the bullpen as an extended audition for a starting role.

When *The Sporting News*, spurred by Holtzman, began recording saves in its weekly record of the 1960 season, the save was defined in a way different from today. Then, upon entering the game, a reliever had to confront the tying or winning run on base or at the plate, and of course finish the game with the lead. This definition later became eased, so that simply finishing a game would get the reliever a save; a memorably absurd result of the new ruling was that the Mets' Ron Taylor gained a save in 1969 by pitching the final inning of a 20–6 win over Atlanta. This outraged sportswriters and fans alike, so in 1973 the definition was changed yet again: a reliever had to work three innings *or* come in with the tying or winning run on base or at bat. This definition was relaxed yet again in 1975 so that the tying run could be *on deck*, thus giving the relief pitcher license to allow a baserunner. It was a good thing for statisticians when Dan Quisenberry surpassed John Hiller's 1973 record of 38 saves by a decisive margin of 7. Today, of course, Bobby Thigpen's 1990 mark of 57 saves seems beyond challenge . . . but back in 1920 so did Babe Ruth's 29 homers.

There was a blip in the relievers' trend of rising importance when the American League introduced the designated hitter in 1973. The predicted outcome, based on the first few years' experience of the DH, was: increased offensive production, no more need to pinch-hit for the pitcher, and thus a greater number of complete games and fewer saves. All those things did happen in 1973–76, although not quite to the degree expected—and soon the American League's use of relief pitchers became as extensive as it had been in the early 1970s. In 1982, despite the DH, American League starters completed only 19.6 percent of their games, an all-time league low (though still substantially higher than the National League, where CGs dropped below 15 percent the last few years). In 1990 the AL and NL each logged complete games at about a 16 percent rate.

Relief Points *is* an improvement over saves, in all of its various incarnations including the one that provides a penalty for a blown save as well as for a defeat. Some folks still long for a measure of middle-relief

effectiveness, that statistical no-man's land. In April 1981 *Sports Illustrated* came up with an incredibly complicated series of tabulations to address these final injustices, and they were dazzling. However, the *SI* method dazzled in the same way that the Mills brothers' Player Win Average did—it was ingenious and well conceived, but involved too much work. Not only did it require play-by-play analysis, but it also reminded one (queasily) of the National Football League's quarterback-rating system. Quarterbacks are rated in four categories, variously weighted, to arrive at a number of "rating points." Not one fan in a thousand could tell you how the rating points are derived, and the same holds for the *SI* relievers' formulas.

The final relief statistic to be discussed is the one we think is the best—Relief Ranking, which is a weighted variant of park-adjusted Relief Runs (in the first edition of *Total Baseball*, we applied the measure to all pitchers who averaged less than three innings per appearance, and this resulted in some needless inclusions of pitchers who were primarily starters; this time around we have broken out all pitchers' relief innings). Relief Ranking tends to favor closers, while Relief Runs provides a good measure for middle-relief outings. See the Relief Pitcher Register,

a new feature in this third edition of *Total Baseball*.

The Future

The most exciting frontier for sabermetrics is in situational stats, the type employed by Elias and Project Scoresheet; as the years go by and their data bases grow, the sampling sizes of the data will enlarge and their figures for day vs. night, turf vs. grass, and so on, will be statistically meaningful as well as statistically correct. Cross-era comparison remains a subject of intense interest, and the debate over average-player skill rages on. Fielding and relieving, as discussed, also provide fertile ground for invention.

Fantasy baseball aficionados seem caught up in the competition and deal-making (as well as player evaluation), but some of the newsletters, such as John Benson's, provide sound analysis and trend-spotting tips. It would not be surprising if Rotisserie-type Leagues, rather than SABR, furnish the best sabermetricians of the 1990s. See also, in the Appendix, Gary Gillette's article, "Baseball, Computers, and New Statistics."

The Player Register

The Player Register consists of the central batting, baserunning, and fielding statistics of every man who has batted in major league play since 1871, excepting those men who were primarily pitchers. A pitcher's complete batting record, however, is included for those pitchers who also, over the course of their careers, played in 100 or more games at another position—including pinch hitter—or played in more than half of their total major league games at a position other than pitcher, or played more games at a position other than pitcher in at least one year. (Pitcher batting is also expressed in Batting Wins in the Pitcher Batting column of the Pitcher Register.)

The players are listed alphabetically by surname and, when more than one player bears the name, alphabetically by *given* name—not by "use name," by which we mean the name that may have been applied to him during his playing career. This is the standard method of alphabetizing used in other biographical reference works, and in the case of baseball it makes it easier to find a lesser-known player with a common surname like Smith or Johnson. This method also jibes with that employed in the Annual Record where, for example, Charles "Old Hoss" Radbourn is shown not as the puzzling O. Radbourn or H. Radbourn, as some reference books have it, but as C. Radbourn. On the whole, we have been conservative in ascribing nicknames, doing so only when the player was in fact known by that name during his playing days.

Each page of the Player Register is topped at the corner by a finding aid: in capital letters, the surname of, first, the player whose entry heads up the page and, second, the player whose entry concludes it. Another finding aid is the use of boldface numerals to indicate a league-leading total in those categories in which a player is truly attempting to excel (no boldface is given to the "leaders" in batter strikeouts, times caught stealing, at bats, or games played). An additional finding aid is an asterisk alongside the team for which a player appeared in post-season competition, thus making for easy cross-reference to the earlier section on postseason play. New to this edition are symbols denoting All Star Game selection and/or play; these appear to the right of the team/league column. Condensed type appears occasionally throughout this section; it has no special significance but is designed simply to accommodate unusually wide figures, such as the 4.000 slugging average of a man who, in his only at bat of the year, hit a home run.

The record for each man who played in more than one season is given in a line for each season, plus a career total line. If he played for more than one team in a given year, his totals for each team are stated on separate lines. And if the teams for which he played in his "traded year" are in the same league, then his full record is stated in both separate and combined fashion. (In the odd case of a man playing for three or more clubs in one year, with some of these clubs being in the same league, the combined total line will reflect only his play in that one league.) New in this edition, we include position data in the "Yr" line for traded players. A man who played in only one year will have no additional career total line, since it would be identical to his seasonal listing.

Batting records for the National Association are included in The Player Register because the editors, like most baseball historians, regard it as a major league, inasmuch as it was the only professional league of its day and supplied the National League of 1876 with most of its players. In this edition of *Total Baseball*, we benefit from the SABR research project referred to in the Introduction to the Annual Record—which to date has produced extra-base hits, corrected averages, walks, and some stolen bases, strikeouts, and other data heretofore unavailable; fielding data for the NA may be available for *Total Baseball 4*. Until Major League Baseball reverses the position it adopted in 1969 and restores the NA to offical major-league status, we will reluctantly continue the practice of carrying separate totals lines for the National Association years rather than integrating them into the career marks of those players whose major league tenures began before 1876 and concluded in that year or later.

Gaps remain elsewhere in the official record of baseball and in the ongoing process of sabermetric reconstruction. The reader will note occasional blank elements in biographical lines, or in single-season columns; these are not typographical lapses but signs that the information does not exist or has not yet been found. In the totals lines of many players, an underlined figure indicates that the total reflects partial data, such as caught stealing for a man whose career covers the National League of 1918–1930 (during which this data was available only for 1920–1925), or batter strikeouts for a man whose career spanned both sides of the year 1909.

For a discussion of which data is missing for particular years, see the general introduction to the statistical section. Here is a quick summation of the missing data:

Hit batters, 1897–1908 (12 percent missing);
Caught stealing, 1886–1914, 1916 for players with fewer than 20 stolen bases, 1917–1919, 1926–1950 NL; 1886–1891 AA; 1890 PL; 1901–1913, 1916 for players with fewer than 20 stolen bases, 1917–1919 AL (1927 data, missing from the first edition, is now 90 percent complete); 1914–15 FL;

Sacrifice hit, 1908–1930, 1939 (in these years fly balls scoring runners counted as sacrifice hits, and in 1927–1930 fly balls advancing runners to any base counted as sacrifices);

Sacrifice fly, 1908–1930, 1939 (counted but inseparable from sacrifice hits), 1940–1953 (not counted);

Runs batted in, 1882–1887, 1890 AA; 1884 UA;

Strikeouts for batters, 1882–1888, 1890 AA; 1884 UA; 1897–1909 NL; 1901-1912 AL.

For a key to the team and league abbreviations used in the Player Register, flip to the last page of this volume. For a guide to the other procedures and abbreviations employed in the Player Register, review the comments on the prodigiously extended playing record below.

Looking at the biographical line for any player, we see first his use name in full capitals, then his given name and nickname (and any other name he may have used or been born with, such as the matronymic of a Latin American

YEAR	TM/L	G	AB	R	H	2B	3B	HR	RBI	BB	SO	AVG	OBP	SLG	PRO+	BR	/A	RC	SB	CS	SBR	FA	FR	POS	TPR
■ **KID DE LEON**					Ponce de Leon, Juan "Castilian Kid" (also played in 1874 as Kid Madrid)																				
					b: 3/13/1460, Madrid, Spain d: 2/25/1963, St. Augustine, Fl. BR/TR, 5'11", 173 lbs. Deb: 5/21/1874 MUCH F																				
1874	Bos-n	52	277	73	94	7	4	1	14	2		.339	.342	.400	111	7	4	33						*2	0.2
1875	Wes-n	2	3	1	1	0	0	0		0		.333	.333	.333	95	0	0	0						/S	0.0
1883	Bal-a	28	121	12	33	2	1	1		8		.273	.318	.331	101	1	1	13				.901	0	CO/S	0.0
1884	Was-U	86	371	75	107	12	5	1		11		.288	.309	.356	127	4	5	42	0			.913	0	1OC	0.9
	KC-U	1	4	1	0	0	0	0		0		.000	.000	.000	-97	-0	-0	0	0			1.000	0	/1	0.0
	Yr	87	375	76	107	12	5	1		11		.287	.308	.355	126	-0	-0	42	0			.914	0	1OC	0.0
1890	Cin-P	1	1	1	1	0	0	1	1	0		1.000	1.000	4.000	700	1	1	2	0			.000	0	/2	0.0
1908	Pit-N	1	0	0	0	0	0	0	0	0	0	—	—	—	—	-0	0	0	0			.000	0	/3	0.0
	Phi-A	9	31	5	9	3	0	0	2	0		.290	.290	.387	113	1	0	3	0			.899	-1	/3	0.0
1909	Phi-A	148	541	73	165	27	**19**	4	85	26		.305	.343	.447	146	27	26	88	20			.920	-5	*3	3.0
1910	Phi-A	146	561	83	159	25	15	2	74	34		.283	.329	.392	123	14	13	77	21			.934	3	*3	2.4
1911	Phi-A	148	592	96	198	40	4	11	115	50		.334	.379	.505	157	33	38	121	38			.912	-8	*3	3.3
1912	Phi-A	149	577	116	200	40	21	10	130	50		**.347**	.404	.541	171	49	50	138	40			.930	9	*3	5.4
1913	Phi-A	149	564	116	190	34	9	12	117	63	31	.337	.413	.493	171	46	48	130	34			.927	7	*3	6.1
1914	Phi-A	150	570	84	182	23	10	9	89	53	37	.319	.380	.442	151	31	33	105	19	20	-6	.929	8	*3	4.1
1915	Nwk-F	2	8	5	4	2	1	1	4	0	2	.500	.500	1.38	304	3	3	3	0			.977	1	/3	0.1
1916	NY-A	100	360	46	97	23	2	10	52	36	30	.269	.344	.428	130	13	12	59	15			.931	3	3	2.1
1917	NY-A	146	553	57	156	24	2	6	71	48	27	.282	.345	.365	109	10	6	76	18			.940	11	*3	2.7
1918	NY-A	126	504	65	154	24	5	6	62	38	13	.306	.357	.409	138	17	20	79	8			.943	11	*3	3.4
1939	*NY-A	☆141	567	70	166	22	1	10	83	44	18	.293	.346	.388	100	4	-0	82	13			.944	-2	*3	0.9
1941	*NY-A	★ 94	330	46	97	16	2	9	71	26	12	.294	.353	.436	98	-0	-2	55	8	5	-1	.955	13	3	1.6
1942	*NY-A	† 69	234	30	65	12	3	7	36	15	14	.278	.327	.444	98	-1	-2	36	1	3	-2	.940	-8	3	-0.4
Total	2 n	54	280	74	95	7	4	1	14	2		.339	.348	.404	110	7	4	33						*2/S	0.2
Total	17	1694	6489	981	1983	329	100	100	992	502	184	.306	.354	.446	130	247	246	1109	235	28		.938	41	*3C/SO12	35.6

player). His date and place of birth follow "b" and his date and place of death follow "d." Years through 1900 are expressed fully, in four digits, and years after 1900 are expressed in their last two digits.

Then comes the player's manner of batting and throwing, abbreviated for a lefthanded batter who throws right as BL/TR (a switch-hitter would be shown as BB for "bats both" and a switch thrower as TB for "throws both").

Next, and for most players last, is the player's debut date in the major leagues, all of which are reported now.

Some players continue in major league baseball after their playing days are through, as managers, coaches, or even umpires. A player whose biographical line concludes with an M can be located in the Manager Roster; one whose line bears a C will be listed in the Coach Roster; and one with a U occupies a place in the Umpire Roster. (In the last case we have placed a U on the biographical line only for those players who umpired in at least six games in a year, for in the nineteenth century—and especially in the years of the National Association—literally hundreds of players were pressed into service as umpires for a game or two. It would be misleading to accord such players the same code we give to Bob Emslie or Babe Pinelli.) The select few who have been enshrined in the Baseball Hall of Fame at Cooperstown, NY, are noted with an H. They are also listed in the Hall of Fame Roster found toward the end of Bill Deane's "Awards and Honors" essay. New to this edition is an F in this line to denote family connection—father-son-grandson or brother.

The explanations for the statistical column heads follow; for more technical information about formulas and calculations, see the Glossary. The vertical rules in the column-header line separate the stats into seven logical groupings: year, team, league; fundamental counting stats for batters; hits and plate appearances broken out into their component counting stats; basic calculated averages; sabermetric figures of more complex calculation; baserunning stats; fielding stats and Total Player Rating.

Absent from the Player Register in this edition are some statistics present in the original: production as a raw, unadjusted figure (still available by simply adding OBP plus SLG, as well as in the Annual Record and Leaders sections); Park Factor for batters (still available from the Annual Record); Clutch Hitting Index, newly developed for *Total Baseball* but which we have judged to be of lesser interest and value than the more established sabermetric measures (like PRO, however, it is still present in the Annual Record and Leaders sections); and Total Average, a popular stat but one that is mirrored by Runs Created and Batting Runs, both of which are more accurate (TA is present in the Annual Record and Leaders sections). By deleting these statistics from the Register we have improved legibility, particularly by adding to the margin in the gutter of the book, and reduced some redundancy. Note that league leading totals appear in boldface.

YEAR   Year of play (when a space in the column is blank, this indicates that the man has played for two or more clubs in the last year stated in the column; if those clubs were in the same league, then the man will also have a combined total line, beginning with the abbreviation "Yr" placed in the TEAM/L column)

Yr   Year's totals for play with two or more clubs in

same league (see comments for YEAR)

*   Denotes postseason play, World Series or League Championship Series

TM/L   Team and League (see comments for YEAR)

★   Named to All Star Game, played

☆   Named to All Star Game, did not play

†   Named to All Star Game, replaced because of injury

G   Games

AB   At-bats

R   Runs

H   Hits (Bases on balls were counted as hits by scorers in 1887, but in *Total Baseball* they are not figured as times at bat, nor as hits.)

2B   Doubles

3B   Triples

HR   Home Runs

RBI   Runs Batted In

BB   Bases on Balls (Bases on balls were counted as outs by scorers in 1876, but in *Total Baseball* they are not figured as times at bat nor as outs.)

SO   Strikeouts

AVG   Batting Average (Figured as hits over at-bats; mathematically meaningless averages created through a division by zero are rendered as dashes; see Kid De Leon's entry for 1908 with Pit-N.)

OBP   On Base Percentage (See comments for AVG)

SLG   Slugging Average (See comments for AVG, and note the use of condensed type to express Kid De Leon's maximum SLG in 1890.)

PRO+   Production Plus, or Adjusted Production (On Base Percentage plus Slugging Average, normalized to league average and adjusted for home-park factor.) See comments for /A.

BR   Batting Runs (Linear Weights measure of runs contributed *beyond* what a league-average batter or team might have contributed, defined as zero. Occasionally the curious figure of −0 will appear in this column, or in the columns of other Linear Weights measures of batting, baseruning, fielding, and the TPR. This "negative zero" figure signifies a run contribution that falls below the league average, but to so small a degree that it cannot be said to have cost the team a run.)

/A   Adjusted (This signifies that the stat to the immediate left, in this instance Batting Runs, is here normalized to league average and adjusted for home-park factor. A mark of 100 is a league-average performance. Pitcher batting is removed from all league batting statistics before normalization, for a variety of reasons expanded upon in the Glossary. Three-year averages are used for batting park factors. If a team moved or the park changed dramatically, then two-year averages are employed; if the park was used for only one year, then of course only that run-scoring data is used.)

RC   Runs Created (Bill James's formulation for run contribution from a variety of batting and base-running events; calculated variably to make maximum use of the data available in a given year; see Glossary.)

SB   Stolen Bases (for 1886 to the present)

CS   Caught Stealing (Available 1915, 1916 for players with 20 or more stolen bases, 1920–1925, 1951–date NL; 1914–1915, 1916 for players with 20 or more stolen bases, 1920 to date AL with scattered data still missing from 1927.)

SBA   Stolen Base Average (Stolen bases divided by attempts; availability dependent upon CS as shown above.)

SBR   Stolen Base Runs (This is a Linear Weights measure of runs contributed *beyond* what a league-average base stealer might have gained, defined as zero and calculated on the basis of a 66.7 percent success rate, which computer simulations have shown to be the break-even point beyond which stolen bases have positive run value to the team; see the general introduction to Part Two and the Glossary. The presence of a figure in the SBR column in the Player Register is dependent upon the availability of CS as shown above. Lifetime Stolen Base Runs are not totaled where data is incomplete, but seasonal SBRs are reflected in the seasonal Total Player Ratings, which in turn are added to form the lifetime Total Player Rating.)

FA   Fielding Average, often called Fielding Percentage as well (putouts plus assists divided by putouts plus assists plus errors, here calculated only for the position at which a man played the most games in a season or career)

FR   Fielding Runs (The Linear Weights measure of runs saved *beyond* what a league-average player at that position might have saved, defined as zero; this stat is calculated to take account of the particular demands of the different positions; see Glossary for formulas, and note new method for the positional adjustment.)

POS   Positions played (This is a ranking from left to right by frequency of the positions played in the field or at designated hitter. An asterisk to the left of the position indicates, generally, that in a given year the man played about two-thirds of his team's scheduled games at that position; more precisely, it is figured at 20 games in 1871, 30 in 1872, 35 in 1873, 40 in 1874, and 50 in 1875; two-thirds of the scheduled games in 1876–1900, and 100 or more games since. When a slash separates positions, the man played those positions listed to the left of the slash in 10 or more games and the positions to the right of the slash in fewer than 10

games. If there is no slash, he played all positions listed in 10 or more games. For the POS [positions played] in the lifetime line, the asterisk signifies 1,000 games and the slash marks a dividing point of 100 games. The precise number of games played at each position, plus an array of fielding data, are available in the new Fielding Register. A player's POS column will list him as a pinch runner or pinch hitter in only those years in which he appeared at no other position. The positions and their abbreviations are)

1: First base	P: Pitcher
2: Second base	D: Designated hitter
S: Shortstop	R: Runner (pinch)
3: Third base	H: Hitter (pinch)
O: Outfield	M: Manager (playing)
C: Catcher	

TPR Total Player Rating (This is the sum of a player's Adjusted Batting Runs, Fielding Runs, and Base Stealing Runs, minus his positional adjustment, all divided by the Runs Per Win factor for that year—generally around 10, historically in the 9–11 range. For more information on the formula and the Runs Per Win concept, see the general introduction to the statistical section and the Glossary. In the lifetime line, the TPR is the sum of the seasonal TPRs. For men who were primarily pitchers but whose extent of play at other positions warrants a listing in the Player Register as well as the Pitcher Register, the TPR may be listed as 0.0; this signifies that their batting records are summed up in the Total Pitcher Index [TPI] column of the Pitcher Register.) Note that the TPR (and the TPI, Total Pitcher Index) in this third edition will differ from those in earlier volumes, for four reasons which are explained in greater detail in the Glossary. (1) A broader and more sophisticated computation of the positional adjustment to Batting Runs has improved the accuracy and reasonableness of the method, by which the TPR of those who play skill positions like shortstop and second base tend to be boosted and the TPR of the sluggers who customarily play first base and left field are generally diminished. (2) Because games in left, center, and right fields are now available for all outfielders, center fielders no longer need be compared to an aver-

age of the regular center fielders and now may be set against all the men who played center, thus tending to elevate their Fielding Runs. (3) Because Hit Batsmen data is now available for the 1903–1908 period, plus considerable data for the years 1897–1902, men like Frank Chance, who was hit over 100 times in his career, increase their Batter Ratings perceptibly. (4) And for players who were both batters and pitchers, the method of allocating Wins between TPR and TPI (Total Pitcher Index) was improved. Previously, if a pitcher pitched in over half his games, all his batting was included with his pitcher rating (TPI); if he pitched in less than half his games, his Batting Wins were thrown over to his batter rating (TPR), with his TPI including only his Pitching Wins and Pitcher Defense. The new method prorates batting proportionally with the number of games pitched. In addition, fielding ratings at nonpitching positions for players who pitched in over half their games, previously omitted, are now part of the Total Baseball Ranking. In any case, the TPR values of batter-pitchers should remain about the same. Thus in 1918, Babe Ruth now has a batter rating of 2.6 Wins and a pitcher rating of 2.8 (total 5.4). In previous editions his marks used to be 4.1 and 1.0, respectively, or 5.1 overall, with none of his batting counted in with his pitching record even though he pitched 20 of 95 games. The large jump in his pitcher rating is because now his pitcher batting is compared against average batting for pitchers.

Total For players whose careers include play in the National Association a well as other major leagues, two totals are given, as described above and as illustrated in Kid De Leon's record, where the record of his years in the National Association is shown alongside the notation "Total 2 n," where *2* stands for the number of years totaled and *n* stands for National Association. For players whose careers began in 1876 or later, the lifetime record is shown alongside the notation "Total x," where *x* stands for the number of post-1875 years totaled. Note the underlined entries in the record for Kid De Leon, reflecting the partial data for RBI, batter strikeouts, stolen bases, and times caught stealing.

■ HANK AARON

Aaron, Henry Louis "Hammerin' Hank" b: 2/5/34, Mobile, Ala. BR/TR, 6', 180 lbs. Deb: 4/13/54 FH

YEAR	TM/L	G	AB	R	H	2B	3B	HR	RBI	BB	SO	AVG	OBP	SLG	PRO+	BR	/A	RC	SB	CS	SBR	FA	FR	POS	TPR
1954	Mil-N	122	468	58	131	27	6	13	69	28	39	.280	.325	.447	105	-2	1	64	2	2	-1	.970	-2	*O	-0.6
1955	Mil-N★	153	602	105	189	**37**	9	27	106	49	61	.314	.369	.540	144	31	35	114	3	1	0	.967	6	*O2	3.6
1956	Mil-N★	153	609	106	**200**	**34**	14	26	92	37	54	**.328**	.369	.558	154	36	41	115	2	4	-2	.962	10	*O	4.1
1957	*Mil-N★	151	615	**118**	198	27	6	**44**	**132**	57	58	.322	.379	.600	170	48	54	136	1	1	-0	.983	2	*O	4.7
1958	*Mil-N★	153	601	109	196	34	4	30	95	59	49	.326	.387	.546	157	37	43	121	4	1	1	.984	2	*O	3.7
1959	Mil-N★	154	629	116	**223**	46	7	39	123	51	54	**.355**	.406	**.636**	**188**	**63**	**70**	**156**	8	0	2	.982	-2	*O/3	6.1
1960	Mil-N★	153	590	102	172	20	11	40	**126**	60	63	.292	.359	.566	160	37	43	119	16	7	1	.982	9	*O/2	4.5
1961	Mil-N★	155	603	115	197	**39**	10	34	120	56	64	.327	.386	.594	**165**	46	51	132	21	9	1	.982	-0	*O/3	4.2
1962	Mil-N★	156	592	127	191	28	6	45	128	66	73	.323	.393	.618	171	54	56	140	15	7	0	.980	-5	*O/1	4.1
1963	Mil-N★	161	631	**121**	201	29	4	**44**	**130**	78	94	.319	.394	**.586**	**180**	**63**	**64**	**149**	31	5	**6**	.979	-4	*O	**6.1**
1964	Mil-N★	145	570	103	187	30	2	24	95	62	46	.328	.394	.514	152	41	40	112	22	4	4	.983	9	*O2	4.9
1965	Mil-N★	150	570	109	181	**40**	1	32	89	60	81	.318	.384	.560	161	46	46	122	24	4	5	.987	9	*O	5.5
1966	Atl-N★	158	603	117	168	23	1	**44**	**127**	76	96	.279	.360	.539	144	37	36	118	21	3	5	.988	11	*O/2	4.5
1967	Atl-N★	155	600	**113**	184	37	3	**39**	109	63	97	.307	.373	**.573**	169	50	51	126	17	6	2	.979	12	*O/2	6.0
1968	Atl-N★	160	606	84	174	33	4	29	86	64	62	.287	.356	.498	154	39	39	104	28	5	5	.991	14	*O1	**5.5**
1969	*Atl-N★	147	547	100	164	30	3	44	97	87	47	.300	.398	.607	177	56	56	128	9	10	-3	.982	5	*O/1	5.0
1970	Atl-N★	150	516	103	154	26	1	38	118	74	63	.298	.389	.574	146	39	35	116	9	0	3	.977	3	*O1	3.2
1971	Atl-N★	139	495	95	162	22	3	47	118	71	58	.327	.414	**.669**	**190**	**65**	**62**	137	1	1	-0	.996	-9	1O	4.5
1972	Atl-N★	129	449	75	119	10	0	34	77	92	55	.265	.391	.514	142	35	30	91	4	0	1	.987	-0	*1O	2.1
1973	Atl-N★	120	392	84	118	12	1	40	96	68	51	.301	.406	.643	173	45	42	104	1	1	-0	.977	-2	*O	3.6
1974	Atl-N★	112	340	47	91	16	0	20	69	39	29	.268	.343	.491	126	13	11	58	1	0	0	.986	-10	O	-0.3
1975	Mil-A★	137	465	45	109	16	2	12	60	70	51	.234	.336	.355	95	-2	-2	56	0	1	-1	1.000	-1	*D/O	-0.4
1976	Mil-A	85	271	22	62	8	0	10	35	35	38	.229	.317	.369	102	0	1	31	0	1	-1	1.000	-0	D/O	0.0
Total	23	3298	12364	2174	3771	624	98	755	2297	1402	1383	.305	.377	.555	156	878	902	2550	240	73	28	.980	54	*O1D/23	84.6

■ TOMMIE AARON

Aaron, Tommie Lee b: 8/5/39, Mobile, Ala. d: 8/16/84, Atlanta, Ga. BR/TR, 6'1", 200 lbs. Deb: 4/10/62 FC

YEAR	TM/L	G	AB	R	H	2B	3B	HR	RBI	BB	SO	AVG	OBP	SLG	PRO+	BR	/A	RC	SB	CS	SBR	FA	FR	POS	TPR
1962	Mil-N	141	334	54	77	20	2	8	38	41	58	.231	.315	.374	86	-8	-6	40	6	0	2	.989	1	*1O/23	-0.9
1963	Mil-N	72	135	6	27	6	1	1	15	11	27	.200	.260	.281	57	-8	-7	8	0	3	-2	1.000	-4	1O/23	-1.5
1965	Mil-N	8	16	1	3	0	0	0	1	1	2	.188	.235	.188	21	-2	-2	1	0	0	0	.961	0	/1	-0.2
1968	Atl-N	98	283	21	69	10	3	1	25	21	37	.244	.296	.311	82	-6	-6	24	3	4	-2	.942	-4	O1/3	-1.8
1969	*Atl-N	49	60	13	15	2	0	1	5	6	6	.250	.318	.333	82	-1	-1	6	0	1	-1	1.000	1	1/O	-0.2
1970	Atl-N	44	63	3	13	2	0	2	7	3	10	.206	.242	.333	50	-4	-5	4	0	0	0	.955	-1	1O	-0.7
1971	Atl-N	25	53	4	12	2	0	0	3	3	5	.226	.268	.264	48	-3	-4	3	0	0	0	.974	2	1/3	-0.3
Total	7	437	944	102	216	42	6	13	94	86	145	.229	.293	.327	75	-32	-32	86	9	8	-2	.990	-5	1O/32	-5.6

■ JOHN ABADIE

Abadie, John b: 11/4/1854, Philadelphia, Pa. d: 5/17/05, Pemberton, N.J. BR/TR, 6', 192 lbs. Deb: 6/10/1875

YEAR	TM/L	G	AB	R	H	2B	3B	HR	RBI	BB	SO	AVG	OBP	SLG	PRO+	BR	/A	RC	SB	CS	SBR	FA	FR	POS	TPR
1875	Cen-n	11	45	3	10	0	0	0		0		.222	.222	.222	59	-2	-1	2						1	-0.1
	Atl-n	1	4	1	1	0	0	0		0		.250	.250	.250	84	-0	-0	0						/1	0.0
	Yr	12	49	4	11	0	0	0		0		.224	.224	.224	61	-2	-1	3						1	-0.1

■ ED ABBATICCHIO

Abbaticchio, Edward James "Batty" b: 4/15/1877, Latrobe, Pa. d: 1/6/57, Ft.Lauderdale, Fla. BR/TR, 5'11", 170 lbs. Deb: 9/04/1897

YEAR	TM/L	G	AB	R	H	2B	3B	HR	RBI	BB	SO	AVG	OBP	SLG	PRO+	BR	/A	RC	SB	CS	SBR	FA	FR	POS	TPR
1897	Phi-N	3	10	0	3	0	0	0	0	1		.300	.364	.300	78	-0	-0	1	0			.875	-2	/2	-0.2
1898	Phi-N	25	92	9	21	4	0	0	14	7		.228	.290	.272	64	-5	-4	9	4			.818	-13	3/2O	-1.6
1903	Bos-N	136	489	61	111	18	5	1	46	52		.227	.306	.290	74	-18	-15	54	23			.934	3	*2S	-0.6
1904	Bos-N	154	579	76	148	18	10	3	54	40		.256	.309	.337	104	-0	2	71	24			.915	2	*S	0.9
1905	Bos-N	153	610	70	170	25	12	3	41	35		.279	.324	.374	110	5	6	86	30			.919	-12	*S/O	-0.3
1907	Pit-N	147	496	63	130	14	7	2	82	65		.262	.357	.331	114	11	11	76	35			.951	-23	*2	-1.6
1908	Pit-N	146	500	43	125	16	7	1	61	58		.250	.336	.316	109	7	7	62	22			**.969**	-12	*2	-0.8
1909	*Pit-N	36	87	13	20	0	0	1	16	19		.230	.368	.264	89	1	-0	9	2			.966	2	S/2O	0.2
1910	Pit-N	3	3	0	0	0	0	0	0	0	0	.000	.000	.000	-95	-1	-1	0	0			.500	-0	/S	-0.1
	Bos-N	52	178	20	44	4	2	0	10	12	16	.247	.295	.292	68	-7	-8	16	2			.910	-3	S/2	-1.0
	Yr	55	181	20	44	4	2	0	10	12	16	.243	.290	.287	66	-7	-8	16	2			.907	-4	S/2	-1.1
Total	9	855	3044	355	772	99	43	11	324	289	16	.254	.325	.325	98	-7	-2	384	142			.949	-59	2S/3O	-5.1

■ CHARLIE ABBEY

Abbey, Charles S. b: 10/1868, Falls City, Neb. BL , 5'8.5", 169 lbs. Deb: 8/16/1893

YEAR	TM/L	G	AB	R	H	2B	3B	HR	RBI	BB	SO	AVG	OBP	SLG	PRO+	BR	/A	RC	SB	CS	SBR	FA	FR	POS	TPR
1893	Was-N	31	116	11	30	1	4	0	12	12	6	.259	.333	.336	82	-3	-3	16	9			.937	3	O	-0.1
1894	Was-N	129	523	95	164	26	18	7	101	58	38	.314	.389	.472	112	7	11	111	31			.909	14	*O	1.2
1895	Was-N	132	511	102	141	14	10	8	84	43	41	.276	.340	.389	91	-8	-7	80	28			.903	10	*O	-0.7
1896	Was-N	79	301	47	79	12	6	1	49	27	20	.262	.331	.352	82	-8	-8	43	16			.879	-6	O/P	-1.7
1897	Was-N	80	300	52	78	14	8	3	34	27		.260	.329	.390	90	-5	-5	43	9			.946	2	O	-0.8
Total	5	451	1751	307	492	67	46	19	280	167	105	.281	.351	.404	95	-17	-12	293	93			.910	21	O/P	-2.1

■ FRED ABBOTT

Abbott, Harry Frederick (b: Harry Frederick Winbigler)
b: 10/22/1874, Versailles, Ohio d: 6/11/35, Los Angeles, Cal. BR/TR, 5'10", 180 lbs. Deb: 4/25/03

YEAR	TM/L	G	AB	R	H	2B	3B	HR	RBI	BB	SO	AVG	OBP	SLG	PRO+	BR	/A	RC	SB	CS	SBR	FA	FR	POS	TPR
1903	Cle-A	77	255	25	60	11	3	1	25	7		.235	.270	.314	76	-8	-7	25	8			.958	9	C/1	0.9
1904	Cle-A	41	130	14	22	4	2	0	12	6		.169	.206	.231	38	-9	-9	7	2			.953	-4	C/1	-1.0
1905	Phi-N	42	128	9	25	6	1	0	12	6		.195	.248	.258	53	-8	-7	10	4			.954	-0	C/1	-0.5
Total	3	160	513	48	107	21	6	1	49	19		.209	.248	.279	61	-25	-24	43	14			.956	5	C/1	-0.6

■ ODY ABBOTT

Abbott, Ody Cleon b: 9/5/1888, New Eagle, Pa. d: 4/13/33, Washington, D.C. BR/TR, 6'2", 180 lbs. Deb: 9/10/10

YEAR	TM/L	G	AB	R	H	2B	3B	HR	RBI	BB	SO	AVG	OBP	SLG	PRO+	BR	/A	RC	SB	CS	SBR	FA	FR	POS	TPR
1910	StL-N	22	70	2	13	2	1	0	6	6	20	.186	.250	.243	46	-5	-5	5	3			.982	1	O	-0.5

■ DAVE ABERCROMBIE

Abercrombie, David b: 5/1840, Falkirk, Scotland d: 9/2/16, Baltimore, Md. Deb: 10/21/1871

YEAR	TM/L	G	AB	R	H	2B	3B	HR	RBI	BB	SO	AVG	OBP	SLG	PRO+	BR	/A	RC	SB	CS	SBR	FA	FR	POS	TPR
1871	Tro-n	1	4	0	0	0	0	0	0	0	0	.000	.000	.000	-99	-1	-1	0	0					/S	-0.1

■ CLIFF ABERSON

Aberson, Clifford Alexander "Kif" b: 8/28/21, Chicago, Ill. d: 6/23/73, Vallejo, Cal. BR/TR, 6', 200 lbs. Deb: 7/18/47

YEAR	TM/L	G	AB	R	H	2B	3B	HR	RBI	BB	SO	AVG	OBP	SLG	PRO+	BR	/A	RC	SB	CS	SBR	FA	FR	POS	TPR
1947	Chi-N	47	140	24	39	6	3	4	20	20	32	.279	.369	.450	121	3	4	23	0			.920	-1	O	0.1
1948	Chi-N	12	32	1	6	1	0	1	6	5	10	.188	.297	.313	68	-2	-1	3	0			.867	-1	/O	-0.2
1949	Chi-N	4	7	0	0	0	0	0	0	0	2	.000	.000	.000	-99	-2	-2	0	0			1.000	0	/O	-0.2
Total	3	63	179	25	45	7	3	5	26	25	44	.251	.343	.408	103	-0	1	26	0			.913	-2	/O	-0.3

■ SHAWN ABNER

Abner, Shawn Wesley b: 6/17/66, Hamilton, Ohio BR/TR, 6'1", 190 lbs. Deb: 9/08/87

YEAR	TM/L	G	AB	R	H	2B	3B	HR	RBI	BB	SO	AVG	OBP	SLG	PRO+	BR	/A	RC	SB	CS	SBR	FA	FR	POS	TPR
1987	SD-N	16	47	5	13	3	1	2	7	2	8	.277	.306	.511	116	1	1	8	1	0	0	.926	1	O	0.1
1988	SD-N	37	83	6	15	3	0	2	5	4	19	.181	.227	.289	48	-6	-6	5	0	1	-1	.982	-4	O	-1.2
1989	SD-N	57	102	13	18	4	0	2	14	5	20	.176	.215	.275	39	-8	-8	6	1	0	0	1.000	-9	O	-1.9
1990	SD-N	91	184	17	45	9	0	1	15	9	28	.245	.287	.310	64	-9	-9	16	2	3	-1	.991	-7	O	-1.9
1991	SD-N	53	115	15	19	4	1	1	5	7	25	.165	.220	.243	29	-11	-11	6	0	0	0	1.000	1	O	-1.2
	Cal-A	41	101	12	23	6	1	2	9	4	18	.228	.257	.366	71	-4	-4	8	1	2	-1	1.000	-1	O/D	-0.7
1992	Chi-A	97	208	21	58	10	1	1	16	12	35	.279	.327	.351	92	-3	-2	24	1	2	-1	1.000	-13	O/D	-1.8
Total	6	392	840	89	191	39	4	11	71	43	153	.227	.271	.323	65	-41	-40	72	6	8	-3	.993	-32	O/D	-8.6

■ CAL ABRAMS

Abrams, Calvin Ross b: 3/2/24, Philadelphia, Pa. BL/TL, 5'11", 195 lbs. Deb: 4/20/49

YEAR	TM/L	G	AB	R	H	2B	3B	HR	RBI	BB	SO	AVG	OBP	SLG	PRO+	BR	/A	RC	SB	CS	SBR	FA	FR	POS	TPR
1949	Bro-N	8	24	6	2	1	0	0	0	7	6	.083	.290	.125	15	-3	-3	1	1			.833	-1	/O	-0.4
1950	Bro-N	38	44	5	9	1	0	0	4	9	13	.205	.340	.227	51	-3	-3	4	0			1.000	-3	O	-0.6

YEAR	TM/L	G	AB	R	H	2B	3B	HR	RBI	BB	SO	AVG	OBP	SLG	PRO+	BR	/A	RC	SB	CS	SBR	FA	FR	POS	TPR
1951	Bro-N	67	150	27	42	8	0	3	19	36	26	.280	.419	.393	118	6	6	27	3	2	-0	.944	-1	O	0.3
1952	Bro-N	10	10	1	2	0	0	0	0	2	4	.200	.333	.200	51	-1	-1	1	0	0	0	.000	-0	/O	-0.1
	Cin-N	71	158	23	44	9	2	2	13	19	25	.278	.356	.399	109	2	2	25	1	0	0	1.000	-5	O	-0.4
	Yr	81	168	24	46	9	2	2	13	21	29	.274	.354	.387	106	2	2	25	1	0	0	1.000	-5	O	-0.5
1953	Pit-N	119	448	66	128	10	6	15	43	58	70	.286	.368	.435	109	6	7	77	4	4	-1	.973	5	*O	0.6
1954	Pit-N	17	42	6	6	1	1	0	2	10	9	.143	.308	.214	39	-4	-4	3	0	0	0	1.000	0	O	-0.4
	Bal-A	115	423	67	124	22	7	6	25	72	67	.293	.401	.421	135	17	21	76	1	4	-2	.977	4	*O	1.8
1955	Bal-A	118	309	56	75	12	3	6	32	89	69	.243	.416	.359	118	10	13	52	2	8	-4	.985	-13	O/1	-0.8
1956	Chi-A	4	3	0	1	0	0	0	0	2	1	.333	.600	.333	150	1	1	1	0	0	0	1.000	-0	/O	0.0
Total	8	567	1611	257	433	64	19	32	138	304	290	.269	.387	.392	113	33	40	268	12	18		.977	-14	O/1	-0.0
■ **JOE ABREU**	Abreu, Joseph Lawrence b: 5/24/16, Oakland, Cal. BR/TR, 5'8", 160 lbs. Deb: 4/23/42																								
1942	Cin-N	9	28	4	6	1	0	1	3	4	4	.214	.313	.357	96	-0	-0	3	0			.941	-1	/32	-0.1
■ **BILL ABSTEIN**	Abstein, William Henry "Big Bill" b: 2/2/1883, St.Louis, Mo. d: 4/8/40, St.Louis, Mo. BR/TR, 6', 185 lbs. Deb: 9/25/06																								
1906	Pit-N	8	20	2	4	0	0	0	3	0		.200	.200	.200	24	-2	-2	1	2			.769	-2	/2O	-0.4
1909	*Pit-N	137	512	51	133	20	10	1	70	27		.260	.302	.344	93	-2	-6	59	16			.982	-5	*1	-1.4
1910	StL-A	25	87	1	13	2	0	0	3	2		.149	.169	.172	7	-9	-9	3	3			.963	2	1	-0.8
Total	3	170	619	54	150	22	10	1	76	29		.242	.281	.315	80	-13	-17	63	21			.979	-5	1/2O	-2.6
■ **MERITO ACOSTA**	Acosta, Balmodero Pedro (Fernandez) b: 5/19/1896, Bauta, Cuba d: 11/17/63, Miami, Fla. BL/TL, 5'7", 140 lbs. Deb: 6/15/13 F																								
1913	Was-A	12	20	3	6	0	1	0	1	4	2	.300	.417	.400	136	1	1	4	2			.714	-3	/O	-0.2
1914	Was-A	39	74	10	19	2	2	0	4	11	18	.257	.353	.338	104	1	1	8	3	4	-2	.857	-2	O	-0.4
1915	Was-A	72	163	20	34	4	1	0	18	28	15	.209	.338	.245	73	-4	-4	17	8	4	0	.963	-4	O	-1.1
1916	Was-A	5	8	0	1	0	0	0	0	2	0	.125	.300	.125	28	-1	-1	0	0			1.000	1	/O	0.0
1918	Was-A	3	2	0	0	0	0	0	0	0	1	.000	.000	.000	-99	-0	-0	0	0			.000	0	H	-0.1
	Phi-A	49	169	23	51	3	3	0	14	18	10	.302	.369	.355	117	4	4	24	4			.944	-3	O	-0.2
	Yr	52	171	23	51	3	3	0	14	18	11	.298	.365	.351	115	4	3	24	4			.944	-3	O	-0.3
Total	5	180	436	56	111	9	7	0	37	63	46	.255	.354	.307	97	2	1	53	17	8		.933	-11	O	-2.0
■ **JIMMY ADAIR**	Adair, James Aubrey "Choppy" b: 1/25/07, Waxahachie, Tex. d: 12/9/82, Dallas, Tex. BR/TR, 5'10.5", 154 lbs. Deb: 8/24/31 C																								
1931	Chi-N	18	76	9	21	3	1	0	3	1	8	.276	.286	.342	67	-4	-4	7	1			.948	-1	S	-0.3
■ **JERRY ADAIR**	Adair, Kenneth Jerry b: 12/17/36, Sand Springs, Okla. d: 5/31/87, Tulsa, Okla. BR/TR, 6', 175 lbs. Deb: 9/02/58 C																								
1958	Bal-A	11	19	1	2	0	0	0	0	1	7	.105	.150	.105	-30	-3	-3	0	0	0	0	.967	2	S/2	-0.1
1959	Bal-A	12	35	3	11	0	1	0	2	1	5	.314	.333	.371	95	-0	-0	4	0	0	0	.932	-4	2/S	-0.3
1960	Bal-A	3	5	1	1	0	0	1	1	0	0	.200	.200	.800	159	0	0	1	0	0	0	1.000	0	/2	0.1
1961	Bal-A	133	386	41	102	21	1	9	37	35	51	.264	.329	.394	94	-5	-4	51	5	2	0	.987	-1	*2S/3	0.7
1962	Bal-A	139	538	67	153	29	4	11	48	27	77	.284	.321	.414	101	-4	-1	66	7	7	-2	.969	-10	*S2/3	0.0
1963	Bal-A	109	382	34	87	21	3	6	30	9	51	.228	.249	.346	66	-19	-18	27	3	3	-1	.985	-0	*2	-1.0
1964	Bal-A	155	569	56	141	20	3	9	47	28	72	.248	.284	.341	73	-21	-21	50	3	2	-0	**.994**	9	*2	0.0
1965	Bal-A	157	582	51	151	26	3	7	66	35	65	.259	.304	.351	84	-12	-13	55	6	4	-1	**.986**	12	*2	1.3
1966	Bal-A	17	52	3	15	1	0	0	3	4	8	.288	.339	.308	89	-1	-1	6	0	0	0	.969	-1	2	-0.1
	Chi-A	105	370	27	90	18	2	4	36	17	44	.243	.278	.335	81	-12	-9	31	3	2	-0	.975	-2	S2	-0.3
	Yr	122	422	30	105	19	2	4	39	21	52	.249	.286	.332	82	-13	-10	37	3	2	-0	.975	-3	S2	-0.4
1967	Chi-A	28	98	6	20	4	0	0	9	4	17	.204	.243	.245	46	-7	-6	5	0	1	-1	.985	-0	2	-0.6
	*Bos-A	89	316	41	92	13	1	3	26	13	35	.291	.323	.367	96	1	-2	34	1	4	-2	.952	-8	3S2	-1.0
	Yr	117	414	47	112	17	1	3	35	17	52	.271	.304	.338	85	-6	-8	38	1	5	-3	.976	-9	23S	-1.6
1968	Bos-A	74	208	18	45	1	0	2	12	9	28	.216	.252	.250	49	-12	-13	11	0	0	0	.976	-5	S2/31	-1.6
1969	KC-A	126	432	29	108	9	1	5	48	20	36	.250	.288	.310	67	-19	-20	32	1	3	-2	.984	-22	*2/S3	-3.6
1970	KC-A	7	27	0	4	0	0	0	1	5	3	.148	.281	.148	22	-3	-3	1	0	1	-1	1.000	2	/2	-0.1
Total	13	1165	4019	378	1022	163	19	57	366	208	499	.254	.294	.347	80	-117	-113	376	29	29	-9	.985	-30	2S/31	-6.6
■ **SPARKY ADAMS**	Adams, Earl John b: 8/26/1894, Zerbe, Pa. d: 2/24/89, Pottsville, Pa. BR/TR, 5'5.5", 151 lbs. Deb: 9/18/22																								
1922	Chi-N	11	44	5	11	0	1	0	3	4	3	.250	.313	.295	56	-3	-3	4	1	2	-1	.914	-4	2	-0.7
1923	Chi-N	95	311	40	90	12	0	4	35	26	10	.289	.346	.367	88	-5	-5	37	20	19	-5	.935	-6	S/O	-0.9
1924	Chi-N	117	418	66	117	11	5	1	27	40	20	.280	.344	.337	83	-9	-9	48	15	17	-6	.941	-8	S2	-1.3
1925	Chi-N	149	627	95	180	29	8	2	48	44	15	.287	.341	.368	80	-17	-19	80	26	12	1	**.983**	**28**	*2/S	1.2
1926	Chi-N	154	624	95	193	35	3	0	39	52	27	.309	.367	.375	99	2	1	86	27			.965	17	*23/S	2.2
1927	Chi-N	146	647	100	189	17	7	0	49	42	26	.292	.335	.340	81	-16	-17	73	26			.994	-1	23S	-0.8
1928	Pit-N	135	539	91	149	14	6	0	38	64	18	.276	.357	.325	76	-14	-17	65	8			.971	-11	*2S/O	-2.1
1929	Pit-N	74	196	37	51	8	1	0	11	15	5	.260	.316	.311	55	-13	-14	19	3			.901	-15	S23/O	-2.3
1930	*StL-N	137	570	98	179	36	9	0	55	45	27	.314	.365	.409	84	-11	-14	84	7			**.966**	-13	*32/S	-1.7
1931	*StL-N	143	608	97	178	**46**	5	1	40	42	24	.293	.340	.390	92	-4	-7	83	16			**.963**	-12	*3/S	-1.0
1932	StL-N	31	127	22	35	3	1	0	13	14	5	.276	.352	.315	79	-3	-3	15	0			.931	-4	3	-0.5
1933	StL-N	8	30	1	5	1	0	0	0	1	3	.167	.219	.200	19	-3	-3	1	0			.955	-2	/S3	-0.5
	Cin-N	137	538	59	141	21	1	1	22	44	30	.262	.320	.310	82	-12	-11	56	3			.963	-3	*3/S	-0.6
	Yr	145	568	60	146	22	1	1	22	45	33	.257	.315	.305	78	-15	-15	57	3			.959	-5	*3S	-1.1
1934	Cin-N	87	278	38	70	16	1	0	14	20	10	.252	.307	.317	69	-13	-12	29	2			.955	-3	32	-1.1
Total	13	1424	5557	844	1588	249	48	9	394	453	223	.286	.343	.353	82	-121	-133	679	154	50		.974	-37	23S/O	-10.1
■ **BUSTER ADAMS**	Adams, Elvin Clark b: 6/24/15, Trinidad, Col. d: 9/1/90, Rancho Mirage, Cal. BR/TR, 6', 180 lbs. Deb: 4/27/39																								
1939	StL-N	2	1	1	0	0	0	0	0	0	0	.000	.000	.000	-94	-0	-0	0	0			.000	0	H	0.0
1943	StL-N	8	11	1	1	1	0	0	1	4	4	.091	.333	.182	48	-1	-1	1	0			1.000	-1	/O	-0.2
	Phi-N	111	418	48	107	14	7	4	38	39	67	.256	.319	.352	98	-4	-2	48	2			.984	3	*O	-0.5
	Yr	119	429	49	108	15	7	4	39	43	71	.252	.320	.347	96	-4	-3	49	2			.984	2	*O	-0.7
1944	Phi-N	151	584	86	165	35	3	17	64	74	74	.283	.370	.440	132	22	24	99	2			.979	11	*O	2.8
1945	Phi-N	14	56	6	13	3	1	2	8	5	5	.232	.295	.429	103	-0	-0	7	0			1.000	-1	O	-0.2
	StL-N	140	578	98	169	26	0	20	101	57	75	.292	.359	.441	119	16	14	94	3			.978	1	*O	0.8
	Yr	154	634	104	182	29	1	22	109	62	80	.287	.353	.440	117	15	14	101	3			.979	0	*O	0.6
1946	StL-N	81	173	21	32	6	0	5	22	29	27	.185	.312	.306	73	-5	-6	19	3			.990	-9	O	-1.8
1947	Phi-N	69	182	21	45	11	1	2	15	26	29	.247	.341	.352	88	-4	-3	23	2			.954	-4	O	-0.9
Total	6	576	2003	282	532	96	12	50	249	234	281	.266	.346	.400	110	24	27	290	12			.979	0	O	-0.0
■ **GEORGE ADAMS**	Adams, George b: Grafton, Mass. 185 lbs. Deb: 6/14/1879																								
1879	Syr-N	4	13	0	3	0	0	0	0	1	1	.231	.286	.231	82	-0	-0	1				1.000	-1	/O1	-0.1
■ **GLENN ADAMS**	Adams, Glenn Charles b: 10/4/47, Northbridge, Mass. BL/TR, 6', 185 lbs. Deb: 5/04/75																								
1975	SF-N	61	90	10	27	2	1	4	15	11	25	.300	.382	.478	132	5	4	17	1	0	0	.941	-1	O	0.3
1976	SF-N	69	74	2	18	4	0	0	3	1	12	.243	.253	.297	54	-4	-5	5	1	0	0	1.000	-1	/O	-0.6
1977	Min-A	95	269	32	91	17	0	6	49	18	30	.338	.380	.468	132	11	11	46	0	2	-1	.969	-4	DO	0.5
1978	Min-A	116	310	27	80	18	1	7	35	17	32	.258	.297	.390	90	-4	-5	33	0	1	-1	1.000	-1	*D/O	-0.7
1979	Min-A	119	326	34	98	13	1	8	50	25	27	.301	.356	.420	104	4	2	50	2	2	-1	.958	-8	DO	-0.8
1980	Min-A	99	262	32	75	11	2	6	38	15	26	.286	.325	.412	94	-0	-3	31	2	4	-2	.947	-2	DO	-0.7
1981	Min-A	72	220	13	46	10	0	2	24	20	26	.209	.275	.282	57	-11	-13	15	0	1	-1	.000	0	D	-1.4

YEAR	TM/L	G	AB	R	H	2B	3B	HR	RBI	BB	SO	AVG	OBP	SLG	PRO+	BR	/A	RC	SB	CS	SBR	FA	FR	POS	TPR
1982	Tor-A	30	66	2	17	4	0	1	11	4	5	.258	.300	.364	74	-2	-3	7	0	0	0	.000	0	D	-0.3
Total	8	661	1617	152	452	79	5	34	225	111	183	.280	.327	.398	96	-2	-10	204	6	10	-4	.959	-16	DO	-3.7
■ DOUG ADAMS	Adams, Harold Douglas b: 1/27/43, Blue River, Wis. BL/TR, 6'3", 185 lbs. Deb: 9/08/69																								
1969	Chi-A	8	14	1	3	0	0	0	1	1	3	.214	.267	.214	34	-1	-1	1	0	0	0	1.000	-1	/C	-0.2
■ HERB ADAMS	Adams, Herbert Loren b: 4/14/28, Hollywood, Cal. BL/TL, 5'9", 160 lbs. Deb: 9/17/48																								
1948	Chi-A	5	11	1	3	1	0	0	0	1	1	.273	.333	.364	88	-0	-0	2	0	0	0	1.000	2	/O	0.1
1949	Chi-A	56	208	26	61	5	3	0	16	9	16	.293	.323	.346	79	-7	-7	23	1	2	-1	.975	-0	O	-1.0
1950	Chi-A	34	118	12	24	2	3	0	2	12	7	.203	.288	.271	45	-10	-10	10	3	0	1	.978	-1	O	-1.0
Total	3	95	337	39	88	8	6	0	18	22	24	.261	.310	.320	67	-18	-16	35	4	2	0	.978	0	/O	-1.9
■ JIM ADAMS	Adams, James J. b: 1868, E.St.Louis, Ill. TR , Deb: 4/21/1890																								
1890	StL-a	1	4	0	1	0	0	0		0		.250	.250	.250	43	-0	-0	0	0			1.000	-1	/C	-0.1
■ BERT ADAMS	Adams, John Bertram b: 6/21/1891, Wharton, Tex. d: 6/24/40, Los Angeles, Cal. BB/TR, 6'1", 185 lbs. Deb: 8/30/10																								
1910	Cle-A	5	13	1	3	0	0	0	0	0		.231	.231	.231	44	-1	-1	1	0			.964	3	/C	0.3
1911	Cle-A	2	5	0	1	0	0	0	0	1		.200	.333	.200	49	-0	-0	0	0			.900	-1	/C	-0.1
1912	Cle-A	20	54	5	11	2	1	0	6	4		.204	.259	.278	52	-3	-4	4	0			.942	2	C	0.0
1915	Phi-N	24	27	1	3	0	0	0	2	2	3	.111	.172	.111	-13	-4	-4	1	0			.974	-4	C/1	-0.8
1916	Phi-N	11	13	2	3	0	0	0	1	0	3	.231	.231	.231	40	-1	-1	1	0			.929	1	C	0.0
1917	Phi-N	43	107	4	22	4	1	1	7	0	20	.206	.206	.290	49	-7	-7	6	0			.994	1	C/1	-0.4
1918	Phi-N	84	227	10	40	4	0	0	12	10	26	.176	.214	.194	23	-20	-22	11	5			.976	-1	C	-2.0
1919	Phi-N	78	232	14	54	7	2	1	17	6	27	.233	.252	.293	59	-11	-12	17	4			.966	-2	C/1	-1.0
Total	8	267	678	37	137	17	4	2	45	23	79	.202	.229	.248	42	-46	-51	40	9			.970	-2	C/1	-4.0
■ DICK ADAMS	Adams, Richard Leroy b: 4/8/20, Tuolomne, Cal. BR/TL, 6', 185 lbs. Deb: 5/20/47 F																								
1947	Phi-A	37	89	9	18	2	3	2	11	2	18	.202	.220	.360	58	-6	-6	7	0	0	0	.995	0	1/O	-0.6
■ RICKY ADAMS	Adams, Ricky Lee b: 1/21/59, Upland, Cal. BR/TR, 6'2", 180 lbs. Deb: 9/15/82																								
1982	Cal-A	8	14	1	2	0	0	0	0	0	2	.143	.200	.143	-4	-2	-2	0	1	0	0	.947	-1	/S	-0.2
1983	Cal-A	58	112	22	28	2	0	2	6	5	12	.250	.300	.321	72	-4	-4	11	1	1	-0	.960	22	S3/2	1.9
1985	SF-N	54	121	12	23	3	1	2	10	5	23	.190	.228	.281	44	-10	-9	7	1	1	-0	.964	3	S3/2	-0.4
Total	3	120	247	35	53	5	1	4	16	10	37	.215	.260	.291	54	-16	-15	19	3	2	-0	.961	24	/S32	1.3
■ BOBBY ADAMS	Adams, Robert Henry b: 12/14/21, Tuolumne, Cal. BR/TR, 5'10", 170 lbs. Deb: 4/16/46 FC																								
1946	Cin-N	94	311	35	76	13	3	4	24	18	32	.244	.292	.344	83	-9	-8	31	16			.967	24	2/O3	2.2
1947	Cin-N	81	217	39	59	11	2	4	20	25	23	.272	.358	.396	101	0	1	33	9			.967	14	2	1.8
1948	Cin-N	87	262	33	78	20	3	1	21	25	23	.298	.361	.408	112	3	4	39	6			.965	-12	2/3	-0.4
1949	Cin-N	107	277	32	70	16	2	0	25	26	36	.253	.317	.325	72	-11	-11	29	4			.984	-9	23	-1.7
1950	Cin-N	115	348	57	98	21	8	3	25	43	29	.282	.361	.414	103	2	2	55	7			.981	-9	23	-0.6
1951	Cin-N	125	403	57	107	12	5	5	24	43	40	.266	.338	.357	86	-7	-7	49	4	10	-5	.956	-10	32/O	-2.1
1952	Cin-N	154	637	85	180	25	4	6	48	49	67	.283	.334	.363	93	-6	-6	77	11	9	-2	.962	9	*3	-0.2
1953	Cin-N	150	607	99	167	14	6	8	49	58	67	.275	.338	.357	81	-15	-16	78	3	2	-0	.951	8	*3	-1.1
1954	Cin-N	110	390	69	105	25	6	3	23	55	46	.269	.364	.387	93	-1	-3	58	2	5	-2	.951	1	3/2	-0.6
1955	Cin-N	64	150	23	41	11	2	2	20	20	21	.273	.370	.413	102	2	1	24	2	0	1	.969	3	3/2	0.5
	Chi-A	28	21	8	2	0	1	0	3	4	4	.095	.240	.190	16	-3	-3	1	0	0	0	.933	5	/32	0.2
1956	Bal-A	41	111	19	25	6	1	0	7	25	15	.225	.368	.297	84	-3	-1	15	1	1	-0	.984	-6	32	-0.6
1957	Chi-N	60	187	21	47	10	2	1	10	17	28	.251	.320	.342	79	-6	-5	21	0	3	-2	.949	-8	3/2	-1.4
1958	Chi-N	62	96	14	27	4	4	0	4	6	15	.281	.324	.406	93	-1	-1	13	2	0	1	.961	-2	1/32	-0.2
1959	Chi-N	3	2	0	0	0	0	0	0	0	1	.000	.000	.000	-99	-1	-1	0	0	0	0	.667	-0	/1	-0.1
Total	14	1281	4019	591	1082	188	49	37	303	414	447	.269	.340	.368	90	-54	-54	523	67	30		.955	10	32/1O	-4.3
■ BOB ADAMS	Adams, Robert Melvin b: 1/6/52, Pittsburgh, Pa. BR/TR, 6'2", 200 lbs. Deb: 7/10/77																								
1977	Det-A	15	24	2	6	1	0	2	2	0	5	.250	.250	.542	103	0	-0	3	0	0	0	1.000	-0	/1C	0.0
■ MIKE ADAMS	Adams, Robert Michael b: 7/24/48, Cincinnati, Ohio BR/TR, 5'9", 180 lbs. Deb: 9/10/72 F																								
1972	Min-A	3	6	0	2	0	0	0	0	0	1	.333	.333	.333	94	-0	-0	1	0	0	0	1.000	-0	/O	0.0
1973	Min-A	55	66	21	14	2	0	3	6	17	18	.212	.381	.379	110	2	2	11	2	1	0	.978	-1	O/D	0.0
1976	Chi-N	25	29	1	4	2	0	0	2	8	7	.138	.342	.207	54	-1	-2	3	0	0	0	1.000	-3	/O32	-0.5
1977	Chi-N	2	2	0	0	0	0	0	0	0	1	.000	.000	.000	-90	-1	-1	0	0	0	0	.000	0	/O	-0.1
1978	Oak-A	15	15	5	3	1	0	0	1	7	2	.200	.455	.267	113	1	1	3	0	0	0	1.000	-1	/23D	0.0
Total	5	100	118	27	23	5	0	3	9	32	29	.195	.375	.314	93	1	0	17	2	1	0	.980	-4	/O23D	-0.6
■ SPENCER ADAMS	Adams, Spencer Dewey b: 6/21/1898, Layton, Utah d: 11/24/70, Salt Lake City, Ut BL/TR, 5'9", 158 lbs. Deb: 5/08/23																								
1923	Pit-N	25	56	11	14	0	1	0	4	6	6	.250	.323	.286	60	-3	-3	5	2	1	0	.879	-6	2/S	-0.8
1925	*Was-A	39	55	11	15	4	1	0	4	5	4	.273	.333	.382	83	-2	-2	7	1	1	-0	.941	-2	2/S3	-0.3
1926	*NY-A	28	25	7	3	1	0	0	1	3	7	.120	.214	.160	-1	-4	-4	1	1	0	0	1.000	4	/23	0.1
1927	StL-A	88	259	32	69	11	3	0	29	24	33	.266	.333	.332	71	-10	-11	27	1	8	-5	.948	1	23	-1.2
Total	4	180	395	61	101	16	5	0	38	38	50	.256	.324	.322	66	-18	-20	40	5	10	-5	.944	-3	/23S	-2.2
■ JOE ADCOCK	Adcock, Joseph Wilbur b: 10/30/27, Coushatta, La. BR/TR, 6'4", 220 lbs. Deb: 4/23/50 M																								
1950	Cin-N	102	372	46	109	16	1	8	55	24	24	.293	.336	.406	94	-4	-4	48	2			.968	6	O1	-0.2
1951	Cin-N	113	395	40	96	16	4	10	47	24	29	.243	.288	.380	77	-13	-14	36	1	2	-1	.983	1	*O	-1.8
1952	Cin-N	117	378	43	105	22	4	13	52	23	38	.278	.321	.460	115	6	6	53	1	4	-2	.985	4	O1	0.4
1953	Mil-N	157	590	71	168	33	6	18	80	42	82	.285	.334	.453	110	1	6	85	3	2	-0	.991	-4	*1	-0.5
1954	Mil-N	133	500	73	154	27	5	23	87	44	58	.308	.367	.520	137	19	24	95	1	4	-2	.995	-11	*1	0.4
1955	Mil-N	84	288	40	76	14	0	15	45	31	44	.264	.340	.469	118	4	6	42	0	2	-1	.990	-5	1	-0.4
1956	Mil-N	137	454	76	132	23	1	38	103	32	86	.291	.339	.597	**154**	26	30	88	1	0	0	**.995**	-6	*1	1.7
1957	*Mil-N	65	209	31	60	13	2	12	38	20	51	.287	.352	.541	146	10	12	38	0	0	0	.996	-3	1	0.6
1958	*Mil-N	105	320	40	88	15	1	19	54	21	63	.275	.322	.506	125	5	9	47	0	0	0	.989	-1	1O	0.3
1959	Mil-N	115	404	53	118	19	2	25	76	32	77	.292	.344	.535	141	16	20	73	0	0	0	.998	10	1O	2.3
1960	Mil-N★	138	514	55	153	21	4	25	91	46	86	.298	.357	.500	142	21	26	89	2	2	-1	**.993**	3	*1	1.8
1961	Mil-N	152	562	77	160	20	0	35	108	59	94	.285	.355	.507	133	19	24	96	2	1	0	**.993**	-5	*1	0.7
1962	Mil-N	121	391	48	97	12	1	29	78	50	91	.248	.335	.506	126	11	12	62	2	0	1	**.997**	-4	*1	0.2
1963	Cle-A	97	283	28	71	7	1	13	49	30	53	.251	.323	.420	107	2	3	37	1	2	-1	.995	-4	1	-0.6
1964	LA-A	118	366	39	98	13	0	21	64	48	61	.268	.353	.475	142	14	18	59	0	2	-1	.993	-5	*1	0.8
1965	Cal-A	122	349	30	84	14	0	14	47	37	74	.241	.315	.401	104	1	2	43	2	2	-1	.996	-4	1	-0.9
1966	Cal-A	83	231	33	63	10	3	18	48	31	48	.273	.359	.576	168	19	19	43	2	2	-1	.997	-0	1	1.5
Total	17	1959	6606	823	1832	295	35	336	1122	594	1059	.277	.339	.485	125	158	198	1033	20	25		.994	-28	*1O	6.3
■ BOB ADDIS	Addis, Robert Gordon b: 11/6/25, Mineral, Ohio BL/TR, 6', 175 lbs. Deb: 9/01/50																								
1950	Bos-N	16	28	7	7	1	0	0	2	3	5	.250	.323	.286	66	-1	-1	3	1			1.000	-2	/O	-0.3
1951	Bos-N	85	199	23	55	7	0	1	24	9	10	.276	.308	.327	76	-8	-6	20	3	2	-0	.982	-0	O	-0.8
1952	Chi-N	93	292	38	86	13	2	1	20	23	30	.295	.346	.363	96	-1	-1	37	4	4	-1	.988	-2	O	-0.8
1953	Chi-N	10	12	2	2	1	0	0	1	2	0	.167	.286	.250	40	-1	-1	1	0	0	0	1.000	1	/O	0.0

YEAR	TM/L	G	AB	R	H	2B	3B	HR	RBI	BB	SO	AVG	OBP	SLG	PRO+	BR	/A	RC	SB	CS	SBR	FA	FR	POS	TPR
	Pit-N	4	3	0	0	0	0	0	0	0	2	.000	.000	.000	-99	-1	-1	0	0	0	0	.000	0	H	-0.1
	Yr	14	15	2	2	1	0	0	1	2	2	.133	.235	.200	15	-2	-2	1	0	0	0	1.000	1	/O	-0.1
Total	4	208	534	70	150	22	2	2	47	37	47	.281	.327	.341	84	-13	-11	61	8	6		.986	-3	O	-2.0
■ **JIM ADDUCI**	Adduci, James David b: 8/9/59, Chicago, Ill. BL/TR, 6′5″, 200 lbs. Deb: 9/12/83																								
1983	StL-N	10	20	0	1	0	0	0	0	1	6	.050	.095	.050	-59	-4	-4	0	0	0	0	1.000	0	/1O	-0.5
1986	Mil-A	3	11	2	1	1	0	0	0	1	2	.091	.167	.182	-5	-2	-2	0	0	0	0	1.000	0	/1	-0.2
1988	Mil-A	44	94	8	25	6	1	1	15	0	15	.266	.266	.383	79	-3	-3	9	0	1	-1	.969	-4	OD/1	-0.8
1989	Phi-N	13	19	1	7	1	0	0	0	0	4	.368	.368	.421	125	1	1	3	0	0	0	1.000	0	/1O	0.1
Total	4	70	144	11	34	8	1	1	15	2	27	.236	.247	.326	58	-8	-8	12	0	1	-1	.969	-3	/O1D	-1.4
■ **BOB ADDY**	Addy, Robert Edward "Magnet" b: 2/1845, Rochester, N.Y. d: 4/9/10, Pocatello, Idaho BL/TL, 5′8″, 160 lbs. Deb: 5/06/1871 M																								
1871	Rok-n	25	118	30	32	6	0	0	13	4	0	.271	.295	.322	81	-3	-2	14	8					*2/S	-0.2
1873	Phi-n	10	51	12	16	1	0	0	9	2	0	.314	.340	.333	95	0	-0	6						2	-0.1
	Bos-n	31	152	37	54	6	2	1	36	1	0	.355	.359	.441	124	6	4	24						*O	0.2
	Yr	41	203	49	70	7	2	1	45	3	0	.345	.354	.414	117	6	3	30						O2	0.1
1874	Har-n	50	211	25	50	9	2	0		2		.237	.244	.299	68	-6	-8	16						*2/3S	-0.8
1875	Phi-n	69	311	60	79	11	4	0		0		.254	.254	.315	92	-1	-3	26						*O/2M	-0.2
1876	Chi-N	32	142	36	40	4	1	0	16	5	0	.282	.306	.324	98	2	-1	14				.800	0	O	-0.1
1877	Cin-N	57	245	27	68	2	3	0	31	6	5	.278	.295	.310	102	-2	2	23				.805	5	*O/M	0.3
Total	4 n	185	843	164	231	33	8	1	58	9		.274	.282	.336	91	-5	-11	85						/O23S	-1.1
Total	2	89	387	63	108	6	4	0	47	11	5	.279	.299	.315	100	-1	1	37				.803	5	/O	0.2
■ **MORRIE ADERHOLT**	Aderholt, Morris Woodrow b: 9/13/15, Mt.Olive, N.C. d: 3/18/55, Sarasota, Fla. BL/TR, 6′1″, 188 lbs. Deb: 9/13/39																								
1939	Was-A	7	25	5	5	0	0	1	4	2	6	.200	.259	.320	51	-2	-2	2	0	1	-1	.872	0	/2	-0.2
1940	Was-A	1	2	0	0	0	0	0	0	0	0	.000	.000	.000	-99	-1	-1	0	0	0	0	1.000	0	/2	0.0
1941	Was-A	11	14	3	2	0	0	0	1	1	3	.143	.200	.143	-8	-2	-2	0	0	0	0	.818	0	/23	-0.2
1944	Bro-N	17	59	9	16	2	3	0	10	4	4	.271	.317	.407	105	0	0	8	0			.871	-1	O	-0.1
1945	Bro-N	39	60	4	13	1	0	0	6	3	10	.217	.254	.233	36	-5	-5	4	0			1.000	-2	/O	-0.8
	Bos-N	31	102	15	34	4	0	2	11	9	6	.333	.387	.431	127	4	4	18	3			.984	0	O/2	0.3
	Yr	70	162	19	47	5	0	2	17	12	16	.290	.339	.358	94	-1	-1	20	3			.985	-2	O/2	-0.5
Total	5	106	262	36	70	7	3	3	32	19	29	.267	.317	.351	85	-6	-6	32	3	1		.949	-2	/O23	-1.0
■ **DICK ADKINS**	Adkins, Richard Earl b: 3/3/20, Electra, Tex. d: 9/12/55, Electra, Tex. BR/TR, 5′10″, 165 lbs. Deb: 9/19/42																								
1942	Phi-A	3	7	2	1	0	0	0	0	2	2	.143	.333	.143	37	-0	-0	1	0	0	0	.875	-1	/S	-0.2
■ **HENRY ADKINSON**	Adkinson, Henry Magee b: 9/1/1874, Chicago, Ill. d: 5/1/23, Salt Lake City, Ut. Deb: 9/25/1895																								
1895	StL-N	1	5	1	2	0	0	0	0	0	2	.400	.400	.400	110	0	0	1	0			.667	-0	/O	0.0
■ **DAVE ADLESH**	Adlesh, David George b: 7/15/43, Long Beach, Cal. BR/TR, 6′, 187 lbs. Deb: 5/12/63																								
1963	Hou-N	6	8	0	0	0	0	0	0	0	4	.000	.000	.000	-99	-2	-2	0	0	0	0	.889	-2	/C	-0.4
1964	Hou-N	3	10	0	2	0	0	0	0	0	5	.200	.200	.200	14	-1	-1	0	0	0	0	1.000	-1	/C	-0.2
1965	Hou-N	15	34	2	5	1	0	0	3	2	12	.147	.216	.176	13	-4	-4	1	0	0	0	1.000	-1	C	-0.4
1966	Hou-N	3	6	0	0	0	0	0	0	0	4	.000	.000	.000	-99	-2	-2	0	0	0	0	1.000	1	/C	-0.1
1967	Hou-N	39	94	4	17	1	0	1	4	11	28	.181	.267	.223	43	-7	-7	5	0	0	0	.995	-3	C	-0.8
1968	Hou-N	40	104	3	19	1	1	0	4	5	27	.183	.227	.212	33	-8	-8	5	0	0	0	.990	-3	C	-1.0
Total	6	106	256	9	43	3	1	1	11	18	80	.168	.228	.199	26	-24	-23	12	0	0	0	.992	-8	/C	-2.9
■ **TROY AFENIR**	Afenir, Michael Troy b: 9/21/63, Escondido, Cal. BR/TR, 6′4″, 185 lbs. Deb: 9/14/87																								
1987	Hou-N	10	20	1	6	1	0	0	1	0	12	.300	.300	.350	74	-1	-1	2	0	0	0	.974	-1	C	-0.1
1990	Oak-A	14	14	0	2	0	0	0	2	0	6	.143	.143	.143	-21	-2	-2	0	0	0	0	1.000	-1	C/D	-0.3
1991	Oak-A	5	11	0	1	0	0	0	0	0	2	.091	.091	.091	-53	-2	-2	0	0	0	0	1.000	1	/CD	-0.1
1992	Cin-N	16	34	3	6	1	2	0	4	5	12	.176	.282	.324	68	-1	-1	4	0	0	0	1.000	-3	C	-0.4
Total	4	45	79	4	15	2	2	0	7	5	32	.190	.238	.266	39	-7	-7	6	0	0	0	.992	-4	/CD	-0.9
■ **TOMMIE AGEE**	Agee, Tommie Lee b: 8/9/42, Magnolia, Ala. BR/TR, 5′11″, 195 lbs. Deb: 9/14/62																								
1962	Cle-A	5	14	0	3	0	0	0	2	0	4	.214	.214	.214	16	-2	-2	1	0	0	0	1.000	-0	/O	-0.2
1963	Cle-A	13	27	3	4	1	0	1	3	2	9	.148	.207	.296	39	-2	-2	1	0	0	0	1.000	-1	O	-0.4
1964	Cle-A	13	12	0	2	0	0	0	0	0	3	.167	.167	.167	-7	-2	-2	0	0	0	0	1.000	-4	O	-0.6
1965	Chi-A	10	19	2	3	1	0	0	3	2	6	.158	.238	.211	30	-2	-2	1	0	1	-1	1.000	-2	/O	-0.5
1966	Chi-A★	160	629	98	172	27	8	22	86	41	127	.273	.328	.447	129	15	20	88	44	18	2	.982	11	*O	2.8
1967	Chi-A★	158	529	73	124	26	2	14	52	44	129	.234	.303	.371	102	-2	0	58	28	10	2	.969	2	*O	-0.3
1968	NY-N	132	368	30	80	12	3	5	17	15	103	.217	.256	.307	68	-15	-15	27	13	8	-1	.978	-12	*O	-3.9
1969	*NY-N	149	565	97	153	23	4	26	76	59	137	.271	.343	.464	121	17	15	91	12	9	-2	.986	2	*O	0.7
1970	NY-N	153	636	107	182	30	7	24	75	55	156	.286	.345	.469	115	12	12	101	31	15	0	.967	9	*O	1.3
1971	NY-N	113	425	58	121	19	0	14	50	50	84	.285	.363	.428	125	13	14	68	28	6	5	.978	7	*O	2.2
1972	NY-N	114	422	52	96	23	0	13	47	53	92	.227	.319	.374	99	-2	-0	46	8	9	-3	.962	3	*O	-0.6
1973	Hou-N	83	204	30	48	5	2	8	15	16	55	.235	.294	.397	90	-3	-3	22	2	5	-2	.983	2	O	-0.6
	StL-N	26	62	8	11	3	1	3	7	5	13	.177	.239	.403	75	-3	-2	3	1	0	0	.981	4	O	0.1
	Yr	109	266	38	59	8	3	11	22	21	68	.222	.281	.398	87	-6	-6	25	3	5	-2	.982	6	O	-0.5
Total	12	1129	3912	558	999	170	27	130	433	342	918	.255	.321	.412	108	26	34	507	167	81	2	.975	19	*O	-0.0
■ **HARRY AGGANIS**	Agganis, Harry "The Golden Greek" b: 4/30/30, Lynn, Mass. d: 6/27/55, Cambridge, Mass. BL/TL, 6′2″, 200 lbs. Deb: 4/13/54																								
1954	Bos-A	132	434	54	109	13	8	11	57	47	57	.251	.324	.394	86	-3	-9	57	6	3	0	.990	7	*1	-0.8
1955	Bos-A	25	83	11	26	10	1	0	10	10	10	.313	.387	.458	116	3	2	15	2	0	1	.987	0	1	0.2
Total	2	157	517	65	135	23	9	11	67	57	67	.261	.334	.404	91	-0	-7	72	8	3	1	.989	7	1	-0.6
■ **JOE AGLER**	Agler, Joseph Abram b: 6/12/1887, Coshocton, Ohio d: 4/26/71, Massillon, Ohio BL/TL, 5′11″, 165 lbs. Deb: 10/01/12																								
1912	Was-A	2	1	0	0	0	0	0	0	0		.000	.000	.000	-99	-0	-0	0	0			.000	0	/1	0.0
1914	Buf-F	135	463	82	126	17	6	0	20	77	78	.272	.376	.335	101	5	4	70	21			.985	5	1O	0.5
1915	Buf-F	25	73	11	13	1	2	0	2	20	14	.178	.355	.247	76	-1	-1	7	2			.973	-2	O/1	-0.4
	Bal-F	72	214	28	46	4	2	0	14	34	38	.215	.325	.252	68	-6	-7	24	15			.981	5	1/O2	-0.5
	Yr	97	287	39	59	5	4	0	16	54	52	.206	.333	.251	71	-7	-8	32	17			.981	3	1O/2	-0.9
Total	3	234	751	121	185	22	10	0	36	131	130	.246	.359	.302	89	-2	-5	101	38			.983	7	1/O2	-0.4
■ **SAM AGNEW**	Agnew, Samuel Lester "Slam" b: 4/12/1887, Farmington, Mo. d: 7/19/51, Sonoma, Cal. BR/TR, 5′11″, 185 lbs. Deb: 4/10/13																								
1913	StL-A	105	307	27	64	9	5	2	24	20	49	.208	.272	.290	66	-14	-13	26	11			.952	2	*C	-0.3
1914	StL-A	115	311	22	66	5	4	0	16	24	63	.212	.279	.254	63	-15	-14	23	10	8	-2	.961	3	*C	-0.4
1915	StL-A	104	295	18	60	4	2	0	19	12	36	.203	.247	.231	45	-21	-20	18	5	2	0	.934	6	*C	-0.7
1916	Bos-A	40	67	4	14	2	1	0	7	6	4	.209	.293	.269	69	-2	-3	6	0			.952	8	C	0.8
1917	Bos-A	85	260	17	54	6	2	0	16	19	30	.208	.267	.246	57	-14	-13	17	2			.965	-10	C	-1.9
1918	*Bos-A	72	199	11	33	8	0	0	6	11	26	.166	.221	.206	29	-17	-17	9	0			.965	11	C	-0.2
1919	Was-A	42	98	6	23	7	0	0	10	10	8	.235	.312	.306	74	-3	-3	10	1			.974	8	C	0.7
Total	7	563	1537	105	314	41	14	2	98	102	216	.204	.265	.253	56	-87	-83	111	29	10		.955	27	C	-2.0

YEAR	TM/L	G	AB	R	H	2B	3B	HR	RBI	BB	SO	AVG	OBP	SLG	PRO+	BR	/A	RC	SB	CS	SBR	FA	FR	POS	TPR
■ LUIS AGUAYO	Aguayo, Luis (Muriel) b: 3/13/59, Vega Baja, P.R. BR/TR, 5'9", 185 lbs. Deb: 4/19/80																								
1980	Phi-N	20	47	7	13	1	2	1	8	2	3	.277	.306	.447	102	0	-0	6	1	1	-0	.962	1	2/S	0.2
1981	*Phi-N	45	84	11	18	4	0	1	7	6	15	.214	.283	.298	62	-4	-4	8	1	0	0	.938	-4	2S/3	-0.7
1982	Phi-N	50	56	11	15	1	2	3	7	5	7	.268	.339	.518	133	2	2	9	1	1	-0	.966	3	2S/3	0.6
1983	Phi-N	2	4	1	1	0	0	0	0	1	2	.250	.400	.250	85	-0	-0	1	0	0	0	1.000	-2	/S	-0.2
1984	Phi-N	58	72	15	20	4	0	3	11	8	16	.278	.350	.458	123	2	2	12	0	0	0	.909	8	32S	1.1
1985	Phi-N	91	165	27	46	7	3	6	21	22	26	.279	.383	.467	133	9	8	29	1	0	0	.957	3	S2/3	1.6
1986	Phi-N	62	133	17	28	6	1	4	13	8	26	.211	.271	.361	70	-5	-6	13	1	1	-0	.967	-7	2S/3	-1.1
1987	Phi-N	94	209	25	43	9	1	12	21	15	56	.206	.275	.431	81	-6	-7	24	0	0	0	.971	-9	S/23	-1.1
1988	Phi-N	49	97	9	24	3	0	3	5	13	17	.247	.336	.371	101	1	0	13	2	0	1	.967	2	S3/2	0.5
	NY-A	50	140	12	35	4	0	3	8	7	33	.250	.291	.343	77	-5	-4	13	0	2	-1	.961	-2	32/S	-0.7
1989	Cle-A	47	97	7	17	4	1	1	8	7	19	.175	.245	.268	44	-7	-7	6	0	0	0	.950	5	3S2/D	-0.2
Total	10	568	1104	142	260	43	10	37	109	94	220	.236	.307	.393	91	-13	-16	133	7	5	-1	.960	-2	S2/3D	-0.0
■ CHARLIE AHEARN	Ahearn, Charles b: Troy, N.Y. Deb: 6/19/1880																								
1880	Tro-N	1	4	1	1	0	0	0	0	0	0	.250	.250	.250	67	-0	-0	0				.778	-0	/C	0.0
■ WILLIE AIKENS	Aikens, Willie Mays b: 10/14/54, Seneca, S.C. BL/TR, 6'3", 220 lbs. Deb: 5/17/77																								
1977	Cal-A	42	91	5	18	4	0	0	6	10	23	.198	.277	.242	45	-7	-7	6	1	2	-1	.971	0	1D	-0.8
1979	Cal-A	116	379	59	106	18	0	21	81	61	79	.280	.381	.493	138	19	21	71	1	3	-2	.996	-2	1D	1.4
1980	*KC-A	151	543	70	151	24	0	20	98	64	88	.278	.362	.433	116	13	13	82	1	0	0	.990	-9	*1D	-0.4
1981	*KC-A	101	349	45	93	16	0	17	53	62	47	.266	.382	.458	142	20	21	62	0	0	0	.992	-5	1	1.0
1982	KC-A	134	466	50	131	29	1	17	74	45	70	.281	.348	.457	119	12	12	69	0	1	-1	.994	-3	*1	0.1
1983	KC-A	125	410	49	124	26	1	23	72	45	75	.302	.374	.539	148	26	26	78	0	0	0	.989	-5	*1/D	1.5
1984	Tor-A	93	234	21	48	7	0	11	26	29	56	.205	.298	.376	82	-5	-6	26	0	0	0	1.000	0	D/1	-0.6
1985	Tor-A	12	20	2	4	1	0	1	5	3	6	.200	.304	.400	89	-0	-0	2	0	0	0	.000	0	D	0.0
Total	8	774	2492	301	675	125	2	110	415	319	444	.271	.358	.455	123	78	79	398	3	6	-3	.991	-24	1D	2.2
■ DANNY AINGE	Ainge, Daniel Ray b: 3/17/59, Eugene, Ore. BR/TR, 6'4", 175 lbs. Deb: 5/21/79																								
1979	Tor-A	87	308	26	73	7	1	2	19	12	58	.237	.270	.286	50	-22	-22	23	1	0	0	.977	-4	2	-1.9
1980	Tor-A	38	111	11	27	6	1	0	4	2	29	.243	.263	.315	55	-7	-7	9	3	0	1	.986	2	O/32D	-0.5
1981	Tor-A	86	246	20	46	6	2	0	14	23	41	.187	.259	.228	39	-18	-20	15	8	5	-1	.949	1	3/SO2D	-2.2
Total	3	211	665	57	146	19	4	2	37	37	128	.220	.265	.269	47	-46	-49	47	12	5	1	.977	-1	/23OSD	-4.6
■ EDDIE AINSMITH	Ainsmith, Edward Wilbur "Dorf" b: 2/4/1892, Cambridge, Mass. d: 9/6/81, Ft.Lauderdale, Fla BR/TR, 5'11", 180 lbs. Deb: 8/09/10																								
1910	Was-A	33	104	4	20	1	2	0	9	6		.192	.236	.240	52	-6	-6	6	0			.963	-4	C	-0.7
1911	Was-A	61	149	12	33	2	3	0	14	10		.221	.275	.275	55	-9	-9	12	5			.952	0	C	-0.4
1912	Was-A	61	186	22	42	7	2	0	22	14		.226	.280	.285	61	-10	-10	17	4			.958	15	C	1.1
1913	Was-A	84	229	26	49	4	4	2	20	12	41	.214	.262	.293	61	-12	-12	20	17			.967	6	C/P	0.0
1914	Was-A	62	151	11	34	7	0	0	13	9	28	.225	.273	.272	61	-7	-8	12	8	5	-1	.969	8	C	0.4
1915	Was-A	47	120	13	24	4	2	0	6	10	18	.200	.267	.267	59	-6	-6	9	7	4	-0	.988	6	C	0.2
1916	Was-A	51	100	11	17	4	0	0	8	8	14	.170	.231	.210	33	-8	-8	7	3			.959	13	C	0.7
1917	Was-A	125	350	38	67	17	4	0	42	40	48	.191	.280	.263	66	-14	-14	30	16			.971	15	*C	1.1
1918	Was-A	96	292	22	62	10	9	0	20	29	44	.212	.283	.308	80	-8	-8	27	6			.975	8	C	0.8
1919	Det-A	114	364	42	99	17	12	3	32	45	30	.272	.354	.409	117	7	8	54	9			.962	-11	*C	0.7
1920	Det-A	69	186	19	43	5	3	1	19	14	19	.231	.285	.306	58	-12	-11	17	4	3	-1	.955	-3	C/1	-1.1
1921	Det-A	35	98	6	27	5	2	0	12	13	7	.276	.360	.367	87	-2	-2	14	1	0	0	.947	-4	C	-0.3
	StL-N	27	62	5	18	0	1	0	5	3	4	.290	.323	.323	73	-2	-2	7	0	0	0	.956	1	C/1	0.0
1922	StL-N	119	379	46	111	14	4	13	59	28	43	.293	.343	.454	109	1	4	58	2	3	-1	.963	-2	*C	0.6
1923	StL-N	82	263	22	56	11	6	3	34	22	19	.213	.276	.335	62	-16	-15	26	4	0	1	.980	-8	C	-1.7
	Bro-N	2	10	0	2	0	0	0	2	0	0	.200	.200	.200	6	-1	-1	0	0	1	-1	1.000	1	/C	-0.1
	Yr	84	273	22	58	11	6	3	36	22	19	.212	.274	.330	60	-17	-16	26	4	1	1	.981	-7	C	-1.8
1924	NY-N	10	5	0	3	0	0	0	0	0	0	.600	.600	.600	229	1	1	2	0	0	0	1.000	-0	/C	0.1
Total	15	1078	3048	299	707	108	54	22	317	263	315	.232	.296	.324	76	-105	-99	317	86	16		.966	42	C/1P	1.4
■ GEORGE AITON	Aiton, George Wilson b: 12/29/1890, Kingman, Kan. d: 8/16/76, Van Nuys, Cal. BB/TR, 5'11.5", 175 lbs. Deb: 6/29/12																								
1912	StL-A	10	17	1	4	0	0	0	1	4		.235	.381	.235	80	-0	-0	1	0			.917	-0	/O	-0.1
■ JOHN AKE	Ake, John Leckie b: 8/29/1861, Altoona, Pa. d: 5/11/1887, LaCrosse, Wis. BR/TR, 6'1", 180 lbs. Deb: 5/12/1884																								
1884	Bal-a	13	52	1	10	0	1	0		0		.192	.208	.231	43	-3	-3	3				.677	-3	/3OS	-0.6
■ BILL AKERS	Akers, William G. "Bump" b: 12/25/04, Chattanooga, Tenn. d: 4/13/62, Chattanooga, Tenn. BR/TR, 5'11", 178 lbs. Deb: 9/08/29																								
1929	Det-A	24	83	15	22	4	1	1	9	10	9	.265	.351	.373	86	-2	-2	12	2	0	1	.935	-9	S	-0.6
1930	Det-A	85	233	36	65	8	5	9	40	36	34	.279	.375	.472	111	5	4	42	5	5	-2	.944	9	S3	1.6
1931	Det-A	29	66	5	13	2	2	0	3	7	6	.197	.274	.288	46	-5	-5	5	0	1	-1	.935	-2	S/2	-0.6
1932	Bos-N	36	93	8	24	3	1	1	17	10	15	.258	.330	.344	85	-2	-2	11	0			.927	-5	3/2S	-0.5
Total	4	174	475	64	124	17	9	11	69	63	64	.261	.349	.404	93	-4	-4	70	7	6		.936	-6	/S32	-0.1
■ GUS ALBERTS	Alberts, Augustus Peter b: 1861, Reading, Pa. d: 5/7/12, Idaho Springs, Colo BR/TR, 5'6.5", 180 lbs. Deb: 5/01/1884																								
1884	Pit-a	2	5	1	1	0	0	0		0		.200	.200	.200	32	-0	-0	0				.500	-1	/S	-0.2
	Was-U	4	16	4	4	0	0	0		4		.250	.400	.250	128	1	1	2				.870	2	/S	0.2
1888	Cle-a	102	364	51	75	10	6	1	48	41		.206	.299	.275	90	-3	-2	39	26			.862	4	S3	0.4
1891	Mil-a	12	41	6	4	0	0	0	2	7	5	.098	.260	.098	4	-5	-6	1	1			.814	-3	3	-0.8
Total	3	120	426	62	84	10	6	1	50	52	5	.197	.298	.256	79	-8	-8	42	27			.880	2	/3S	-0.4
■ BUTCH ALBERTS	Alberts, Francis Burt b: 5/4/50, Williamsport, Pa. BR/TR, 6'2", 205 lbs. Deb: 9/07/78																								
1978	Tor-A	6	18	1	5	1	0	0	0	0	2	.278	.278	.333	70	-1	-1	2	0	0	0	.000	0	/D	-0.1
■ JACK ALBRIGHT	Albright, Harold John b: 6/30/21, St.Petersburg, Fl BR/TR, 5'9", 175 lbs. Deb: 5/19/47																								
1947	Phi-N	41	99	9	23	4	0	2	5	10	11	.232	.303	.333	71	-5	-4	10	1			.943	3	S	0.0
■ LUIS ALCARAZ	Alcaraz, Angel Luis (Acosta) b: 6/20/41, Humacao, P.R. BR/TR, 5'9", 165 lbs. Deb: 9/13/67																								
1967	LA-N	17	60	1	14	1	0	0	3	1	13	.233	.246	.250	46	-4	-4	3	1	1	-0	.990	9	2	0.6
1968	LA-N	41	106	4	16	1	0	2	5	9	23	.151	.217	.217	33	-9	-8	5	1	1	-0	.979	3	23/S	-0.5
1969	KC-A	22	79	15	20	2	1	1	7	7	9	.253	.314	.342	83	-2	-2	8	0	0	0	.988	-5	2/3S	-0.5
1970	KC-A	35	120	10	20	5	1	1	14	4	13	.167	.194	.250	21	-13	-13	6	0	0	0	.993	-8	2	-2.0
Total	4	115	365	30	70	9	2	4	29	21	58	.192	.236	.260	43	-28	-27	22	2	2	-1	.988	-1	/23S	-2.4
■ SCOTTY ALCOCK	Alcock, John Forbes b: 11/29/1885, Wooster, Ohio d: 1/30/73, Wooster, Ohio BR/TR, 5'9.5", 160 lbs. Deb: 4/19/14																								
1914	Chi-A	54	156	12	27	4	2	0	7	7	14	.173	.213	.224	32	-13	-13	8	4	2	0	.905	4	3/2	-0.8
■ MIKE ALDRETE	Aldrete, Michael Peter b: 1/29/61, Carmel, Cal. BL/TL, 5'11", 185 lbs. Deb: 5/28/86																								
1986	SF-N	84	216	27	54	18	3	2	25	33	34	.250	.355	.389	110	2	4	31	1	3	-2	1.000	3	1O	0.2
1987	*SF-N	126	357	50	116	18	2	9	51	43	50	.325	.398	.462	133	15	17	68	6	0	2	.986	-2	O1	1.3
1988	SF-N	139	389	44	104	15	0	3	50	56	65	.267	.360	.329	103	2	4	47	6	5	-1	.982	-7	*O1	-0.9

YEAR	TM/L	G	AB	R	H	2B	3B	HR	RBI	BB	SO	AVG	OBP	SLG	PRO+	BR	/A	RC	SB	CS	SBR	FA	FR	POS	TPR
1989	Mon-N	76	136	12	30	8	1	1	12	19	30	.221	.321	.316	81	-3	-3	14	1	3	-2	.980	-3	O1	-0.9
1990	Mon-N	96	161	22	39	7	1	1	18	37	31	.242	.387	.317	100	1	2	22	1	2	-1	.982	-4	O1	-0.4
1991	SD-N	12	15	2	0	0	0	0	1	3	4	.000	.167	.000	-48	-3	-3	0	0	1	-1	1.000	0	/O	-0.4
	Cle-A	85	183	22	48	6	1	1	19	36	37	.262	.384	.322	97	1	1	26	1	2	-1	.994	-3	1O/D	-0.5
Total	6	618	1457	179	391	72	8	17	176	227	251	.268	.368	.364	107	15	21	208	16	16	-5	.984	-15	O1/D	-1.6
■ **CHUCK ALENO** Aleno, Charles b: 2/19/17, St.Louis, Mo. BR/TR, 6'1.5", 215 lbs. Deb: 5/15/41																									
1941	Cin-N	54	169	23	41	7	3	1	18	11	16	.243	.289	.337	76	-6	-6	16	3			.975	-4	3/1	-0.9
1942	Cin-N	7	14	1	2	1	0	0	0	3	3	.143	.294	.214	50	-1	-1	1	0			.727	1	/32	0.1
1943	Cin-N	7	10	0	3	0	0	0	1	2	1	.300	.417	.300	110	0	0	1	0			1.000	-1	/O	0.0
1944	Cin-N	50	127	10	21	3	0	1	15	15	15	.165	.259	.213	35	-11	-10	8	0			.952	-4	3/1S	-1.5
Total	4	118	320	34	67	11	3	2	34	31	35	.209	.281	.281	60	-17	-17	26	3			.954	-7	/31SO2	-2.3
■ **DALE ALEXANDER** Alexander, David Dale "Moose" b: 4/26/03, Greeneville, Tenn. d: 3/2/79, Greeneville, Tenn. BR/TR, 6'3", 210 lbs. Deb: 4/16/29																									
1929	Det-A	155	626	110	**215**	43	15	25	137	56	63	.343	.397	.580	148	43	42	140	5	9	-4	.988	-4	*1	1.8
1930	Det-A	154	602	86	196	33	8	20	135	42	56	.326	.372	.507	118	17	15	112	6	5	-1	.985	-7	*1	-0.7
1931	Det-A	135	517	75	168	47	3	3	87	64	35	.325	.401	.445	118	18	16	93	5	8	-3	.987	-8	*1/O	-0.7
1932	Det-A	23	16	0	4	0	0	0	4	6	2	.250	.455	.250	84	0	0	2	0	0	0	1.000	-0	/1	0.0
	Bos-A	101	376	58	140	27	3	8	56	55	19	.372	.454	.524	157	32	33	91	4	5	-2	.992	2	*1	2.3
	Yr	124	392	58	144	27	3	8	60	61	21	.367	.454	.513	152	32	33	93	4	5	-2	.992	2	*1	2.3
1933	Bos-A	94	313	40	88	14	1	5	40	25	22	.281	.336	.380	90	-5	-5	40	0	1	-1	.992	3	1	-0.9
Total	5	662	2450	369	811	164	30	61	459	248	197	.331	.394	.497	128	105	102	478	20	28	-11	.988	-14	1/O	1.8
■ **GARY ALEXANDER** Alexander, Gary Wayne b: 3/27/53, Los Angeles, Cal. BR/TR, 6'2", 200 lbs. Deb: 9/12/75																									
1975	SF-N	3	3	1	0	0	0	0	0	1	2	.000	.250	.000	-25	-0	-1	0	0	0	0	1.000	-1	/C	-0.1
1976	SF-N	23	73	12	13	1	1	2	7	10	16	.178	.277	.301	62	-3	-4	7	1	0	0	.964	-4	C	-0.7
1977	SF-N	51	119	17	36	4	2	5	20	20	33	.303	.411	.496	143	8	8	24	3	1	0	.968	-8	C/O	0.1
1978	Oak-A	58	174	18	36	6	1	10	22	22	66	.207	.299	.425	107	-0	1	19	0	3	-2	1.000	0	D/OC1	-0.1
	Cle-A	90	324	39	76	14	3	17	62	35	100	.235	.311	.454	114	4	5	47	0	2	-1	.983	-9	CD	-0.4
	Yr	148	498	57	112	20	4	27	84	57	166	.225	.307	.444	112	4	6	66	0	5	-3	.983	-9	DC/O1	-0.5
1979	Cle-A	110	358	54	82	9	2	15	54	46	100	.229	.319	.391	90	-5	-5	46	4	2	0	.961	-20	CD/O	-2.2
1980	Cle-A	76	178	22	40	7	1	5	31	17	52	.225	.292	.360	77	-6	-6	15	0	4	-2	.971	-2	DC/O	-1.0
1981	Pit-N	21	47	6	10	4	1	1	6	3	12	.213	.260	.404	84	-1	-1	5	0	0	0	.964	1	/1O	0.0
Total	7	432	1276	169	293	45	11	55	202	154	381	.230	.315	.411	99	-4	-3	163	8	12	-5	.969	-41	CD/O1	-4.4
■ **HUGH ALEXANDER** Alexander, Hugh b: 7/10/17, Buffalo, Mo. BR/TR, 6', 190 lbs. Deb: 8/15/37																									
1937	Cle-A	7	11	0	1	0	0	0	0	0	5	.091	.091	.091	-54	-3	-3	0	1	0	0	.667	-2	/O	-0.4
■ **MANNY ALEXANDER** Alexander, Manuel De Jesus b: 3/20/71, San Pedro De Macoris, D.R. BR/TR, 5'10", 150 lbs. Deb: 9/18/92																									
1992	Bal-A	4	5	1	1	0	0	0	0	0	3	.200	.200	.200	12	-1	-1	0	0	0	0	1.000	1	/S	0.0
■ **MATT ALEXANDER** Alexander, Matthew b: 1/30/47, Shreveport, La. BB/TR, 5'11", 169 lbs. Deb: 8/23/73																									
1973	Chi-N	12	5	4	1	0	0	0	1	1	1	.200	.333	.200	48	-0	-0	1	2	0	1	1.000	1	/O	0.1
1974	Chi-N	45	54	15	11	2	1	0	0	12	12	.204	.358	.278	76	-1	-1	6	8	4	0	.921	-1	3/O2	-0.2
1975	Oak-A	63	10	16	1	0	0	0	0	1	1	.100	.182	.100	-19	-2	-2	-7	17	10	-1	1.000	-2	DO/23	-0.5
1976	Oak-A	61	30	16	1	0	0	0	0	0	5	.033	.033	.033	-84	-7	-7	-2	20	7	2	1.000	-7	OD	-1.3
1977	Oak-A	90	42	24	10	1	0	0	2	4	6	.238	.304	.262	57	-2	-2	0	26	14	-1	1.000	-11	OS/23D	-1.4
1978	Pit-N	7	0	2	0	0	0	0	0	0	0	—	—	—	—	0	0	0	4	1	1	.000	0	R	0.1
1979	*Pit-N	44	13	16	7	0	1	0	1	0	0	.538	.538	.692	223	2	2	7	13	1	3	1.000	4	O/S	1.0
1980	Pit-N	37	3	13	1	1	0	0	0	0	0	.333	.333	.667	170	0	0	-5	10	3	1	1.000	4	/O2	0.6
1981	Pit-N	15	11	5	4	0	0	0	0	0	1	.364	.364	.364	104	0	0	1	3	2	-0	1.000	1	/O	0.1
Total	9	374	168	111	36	4	2	0	4	18	26	.214	.294	.262	56	-9	-9	1	103	42	6	1.000	-10	/OD3S2	-1.5
■ **WALT ALEXANDER** Alexander, Walter Ernest b: 3/5/1891, Atlanta, Ga. d: 12/29/78, Fort Worth, Tex. BR/TR, 5'10.5", 165 lbs. Deb: 6/21/12																									
1912	StL-A	37	97	5	17	4	0	0	5	8		.175	.245	.216	34	-9	-8	6	1			.969	-3	C	-0.8
1913	StL-A	43	110	5	15	2	1	0	7	4	36	.136	.174	.173	2	-14	-14	3	1			.947	4	C	-0.7
1915	StL-A	1	1	0	0	0	0	0	0	0	0	.000	.000	.000	-99	-0	-0	0	0			.000	0	/C	0.0
	NY-A	25	68	7	17	4	0	1	5	13	16	.250	.370	.353	117	2	2	10	2	1	0	.967	9	C	1.3
	Yr	26	69	7	17	4	0	1	5	13	16	.246	.366	.348	114	2	2	10	2	1	0	.967	9	C	1.3
1916	NY-A	36	78	8	20	6	1	0	3	13	20	.256	.376	.359	118	3	2	11	0			.960	2	C	0.6
1917	NY-A	20	51	1	7	2	1	0	4	4	11	.137	.200	.216	27	-5	-5	3	1			.951	0	C	-0.4
Total	5	162	405	26	76	18	3	1	24	42	83	.188	.271	.254	56	-23	-22	32	5	1		.959	11	C	-0.0
■ **NIN ALEXANDER** Alexander, William Henry b: 11/24/1858, Pana, Ill. d: 12/22/33, Pana, Ill. BR/TR, 5'4.5", 163 lbs. Deb: 6/07/1884																									
1884	KC-U	19	65	2	9	0	0	0		1		.138	.152	.138	-2	-7	-5	1				.907	-2	C/SO	-0.5
	StL-a	1	4	0	0	0	0	0		0		.000	.000	.000	-97	-1	-1	0				.667	-0	/CO	-0.1
Total	1	20	69	2	9	0	0	0		1		.130	.143	.130	-8	-7	-6	1				.895	-2	/COS	-0.6
■ **LUIS ALICEA** Alicea, Luis Rene (De Jesus) b: 7/29/65, Santurce, P.R. BB/TR, 5'9", 165 lbs. Deb: 4/23/88																									
1988	StL-N	93	297	20	63	10	4	1	24	25	32	.212	.278	.283	61	-15	-15	22	1	1	-0	.970	4	2	-0.9
1991	StL-N	56	68	5	13	3	0	0	0	8	19	.191	.276	.235	45	-5	-5	5	0	1	-1	1.000	-1	2/3S	-0.7
1992	StL-N	85	265	26	65	9	11	2	32	27	40	.245	.324	.385	102	0	1	32	2	5	-2	.989	2	2/S	0.2
Total	3	234	630	51	141	22	15	3	56	60	91	.224	.297	.321	76	-19	-19	59	3	7	-3	.979	4	2/S3	-1.4
■ **ANDY ALLANSON** Allanson, Andrew Neal b: 12/22/61, Richmond, Va. BR/TR, 6'5", 225 lbs. Deb: 4/07/86																									
1986	Cle-A	101	293	30	66	7	3	1	29	14	36	.225	.263	.280	49	-21	-20	22	10	1	2	.960	-7	C	-1.9
1987	Cle-A	50	154	17	41	6	0	3	16	9	30	.266	.307	.364	76	-5	-5	17	1	1	-0	.986	-7	C	-0.9
1988	Cle-A	133	434	44	114	11	0	5	50	25	63	.263	.307	.323	75	-13	-15	42	5	9	-4	.986	1	*C	-0.8
1989	Cle-A	111	323	30	75	9	1	3	17	23	47	.232	.291	.294	64	-15	-15	27	4	4	-1	.986	3	*C	-0.7
1991	Det-A	60	151	10	35	10	0	1	16	7	31	.232	.266	.318	60	-8	-9	12	0	1	-1	.979	6	C/1D	-0.1
1992	Mil-A	9	25	6	8	1	0	0	0	1	2	.320	.346	.360	100	-0	-0	3	3	1	0	.943	-2	/C	-0.1
Total	6	464	1380	137	339	44	4	13	128	79	209	.246	.290	.312	66	-63	-64	124	23	17	-3	.979	-5	C/1D	-4.5
■ **NICK ALLEN** Allen, Artemus Ward b: 9/14/1888, Norton, Kan. d: 10/16/39, Hines, Ill. BR/TR, 6', 180 lbs. Deb: 5/01/14																									
1914	Buf-F	32	63	3	15	1	0	0	4	3	12	.238	.273	.254	49	-4	-4	6	4			.969	2	C	-0.1
1915	Buf-F	84	215	14	44	7	1	0	17	18	34	.205	.269	.247	51	-13	-13	16	4			.956	7	C	-0.1
1916	Chi-N	5	16	1	1	0	0	0	1	0	3	.063	.063	.063	-56	-3	-3	0	0			.958	-1	/C	-0.4
1918	Cin-N	37	96	6	25	2	2	0	5	4	7	.260	.297	.323	91	-1	-1	9	0			.950	8	C	0.9
1919	Cin-N	15	25	7	8	0	1	0	5	2	6	.320	.393	.400	142	1	1	4	0			.958	3	C	0.5
1920	Cin-N	43	85	10	23	3	1	0	4	6	11	.271	.340	.329	94	-1	-0	10	0	0	0	.961	6	C	0.8
Total	6	216	500	41	116	13	5	0	36	33	73	.232	.288	.278	66	-21	-21	45	8	0		.958	25	C	1.6
■ **BERNIE ALLEN** Allen, Bernard Keith b: 4/16/39, E.Liverpool, O. BL/TR, 6', 185 lbs. Deb: 4/10/62																									
1962	Min-A	159	573	79	154	27	7	12	64	62	82	.269	.340	.403	96	-1	-3	80	0	1	-1	.983	-17	*2	-0.4
1963	Min-A	139	421	52	101	20	1	9	43	38	52	.240	.304	.356	83	-9	-10	46	0	0	0	.976	-24	*2	-2.5
1964	Min-A	74	243	28	52	8	1	6	20	33	30	.214	.310	.329	78	-7	-7	25	1	2	-1	.979	-11	2	-1.4

YEAR	TM/L	G	AB	R	H	2B	3B	HR	RBI	BB	SO	AVG	OBP	SLG	PRO+	BR	/A	RC	SB	CS	SBR	FA	FR	POS	TPR
1965	Min-A	19	39	2	9	2	0	0	6	6	8	.231	.333	.282	73	-1	-1	4	0	0	0	1.000	-2	2/3	-0.2
1966	Min-A	101	319	34	76	18	1	5	30	26	40	.238	.300	.348	80	-6	-8	31	2	3	-1	.974	-7	2/3	-1.1
1967	Was-A	87	254	13	49	5	1	3	18	18	43	.193	.246	.256	51	-16	-15	17	1	2	-1	.990	19	2	0.7
1968	Was-A	120	373	31	90	12	4	6	40	28	35	.241	.301	.343	98	-3	-1	38	2	0	1	**.991**	5	*2/3	1.1
1969	Was-A	122	365	33	90	17	4	9	45	50	35	.247	.337	.389	108	2	4	48	5	4	-1	.974	3	*2/3	1.4
1970	Was-A	104	261	31	61	7	1	8	29	43	21	.234	.342	.360	99	-1	0	34	0	2	-1	.969	-0	23	0.4
1971	Was-A	97	229	18	61	11	1	4	22	33	27	.266	.359	.376	115	3	5	33	2	1	0	.961	-11	23	-0.4
1972	NY-A	84	220	26	50	9	0	9	21	23	42	.227	.300	.391	108	1	2	26	0	1	-1	.940	-0	32	0.1
1973	NY-A	17	57	5	13	3	0	0	4	5	5	.228	.290	.281	64	-3	-3	5	0	0	0	.985	0	2/D	-0.2
	Mon-N	16	50	5	9	1	0	2	9	5	4	.180	.255	.320	56	-3	-3	4	0	0	0	.970	-1	/23	-0.4
Total	12	1139	3404	357	815	140	21	73	351	370	424	.239	.315	.357	91	-44	-42	391	13	16	-6	.980	-48	23/D	-2.9
■ JACK ALLEN	Allen, Cyrus Alban b: 10/2/1855, Woodstock, Ill. d: 4/21/15, Girard, Pa. 160 lbs. Deb: 5/01/1879																								
1879	Syr-N	11	48	7	9	2	1	0	3	1	5	.188	.204	.271	62	-2	-1	3				.655	-6	/3O	-0.7
	Cle-N	16	60	7	7	1	1	0	4	1	9	.117	.131	.167	-3	-6	-6	1				.845	3	3/O	-0.3
	Yr	27	108	14	16	3	2	0	7	2	14	.148	.164	.213	24	-9	-8	4				.790	-3	3/O	-1.0
■ ETHAN ALLEN	Allen, Ethan Nathan b: 1/1/04, Cincinnati, Ohio BR/TR, 6'1", 180 lbs. Deb: 6/21/26																								
1926	Cin-N	18	13	3	4	1	0	0	0	0	3	.308	.308	.385	88	-0	-0	1	0			1.000	-3	/O	-0.3
1927	Cin-N	111	359	54	106	26	4	2	20	14	23	.295	.325	.407	98	-3	-2	46	12			.988	-2	O	-1.0
1928	Cin-N	129	485	55	148	30	7	1	62	27	29	.305	.343	.402	96	-5	-4	65	6			.981	3	*O	-0.9
1929	Cin-N	143	538	69	157	27	11	6	64	20	21	.292	.317	.416	84	-18	-15	68	21			**.988**	-10	*O	-3.1
1930	Cin-N	21	46	10	10	1	0	3	7	5	2	.217	.294	.435	77	-2	-2	6	1			.969	-2	O	-0.4
	NY-N	76	238	48	73	9	2	7	31	12	23	.307	.340	.450	91	-5	-4	35	5			.985	-4	O	-1.1
	Yr	97	284	58	83	10	2	10	38	17	25	.292	.332	.447	89	-7	-6	41	6			.981	-6	O	-1.5
1931	NY-N	94	298	58	98	18	2	5	43	15	15	.329	.363	.453	121	7	8	49	6			.975	-7	O	-0.3
1932	NY-N	54	103	13	18	6	2	1	7	1	12	.175	.198	.301	33	-10	-10	6	0			.957	-4	O	-1.4
1933	StL-N	91	261	25	63	7	3	0	36	13	22	.241	.280	.291	60	-12	-14	22	3			.984	8	O	-1.0
1934	Phi-N	145	581	87	192	**42**	4	10	85	33	47	.330	.370	.468	108	18	8	99	6			.978	9	*O	1.0
1935	Phi-N	156	645	90	198	46	1	8	63	43	54	.307	.351	.419	96	5	-3	100	5			.980	17	*O	0.7
1936	Phi-N	30	125	21	37	3	1	1	9	4	8	.296	.318	.360	75	-3	-5	14	4			.954	-0	O	-0.6
	Chi-N	91	373	47	110	18	6	3	39	13	30	.295	.322	.399	91	-4	-5	47	12			.980	-2	O	-1.1
	Yr	121	498	68	147	21	7	4	48	17	38	.295	.321	.390	87	-8	-10	61	16			.972	-3	*O	-1.7
1937	StL-A	103	320	39	101	18	1	0	31	21	17	.316	.360	.378	86	-6	-7	43	3	4	-2	.980	-1	O	-1.1
1938	StL-A	19	33	4	10	3	1	0	4	2	4	.303	.343	.455	98	-0	-0	5	0	0	0	1.000	-1	/O	-0.2
Total	13	1281	4418	623	1325	255	45	47	501	223	310	.300	.336	.410	92	-40	-55	606	84	4		.981	-0	*O	-10.8
■ SLED ALLEN	Allen, Fletcher Manson b: 8/23/1886, West Plains, Mo. d: 10/16/59, Lubbock, Tex. BR/TR, 6'1", 180 lbs. Deb: 5/04/10																								
1910	StL-A	14	23	3	3	1	0	0	1	1		.130	.231	.174	29	-2	-2	1	0			.903	-6	C/1	-0.8
■ HANK ALLEN	Allen, Harold Andrew b: 7/23/40, Wampum, Pa. BR/TR, 6', 190 lbs. Deb: 9/09/66 F																								
1966	Was-A	9	31	2	12	0	0	1	6	3	6	.387	.441	.484	167	3	3	7	0	0	0	.917	0	/O	0.2
1967	Was-A	116	292	34	68	8	4	3	17	13	53	.233	.266	.318	75	-11	-10	22	3	4	-2	.980	-21	O	-4.0
1968	Was-A	68	128	16	28	2	2	1	9	7	16	.219	.265	.289	70	-5	-5	9	0	0	0	.895	-8	O32	-1.5
1969	Was-A	109	271	42	75	9	3	1	17	13	28	.277	.312	.343	88	-6	-5	26	12	3	2	.933	-15	O/32	-2.2
1970	Was-A	22	38	3	8	2	0	0	4	5	9	.211	.302	.263	60	-2	-2	3	0	0	0	1.000	-3	O	-0.6
	Mil-A	28	61	4	14	4	0	0	4	7	5	.230	.309	.295	67	-3	-3	5	0	1	-1	1.000	-1	O/21	-0.5
	Yr	50	99	7	22	6	0	0	8	12	14	.222	.306	.283	65	-5	-5	9	0	1	-1	1.000	-4	O/21	-1.1
1972	Chi-A	9	21	1	3	0	0	0	0	0	2	.143	.143	.143	-15	-3	-3	0	0	0	0	.905	3	/3	0.0
1973	Chi-A	28	39	2	4	2	0	0	0	1	9	.103	.125	.154	-21	-6	-6	0	0	1	-1	1.000	-0	/31OC2	-0.8
Total	7	389	881	104	212	27	9	6	57	49	128	.241	.282	.312	74	-34	-30	74	15	9	-1	.957	-46	O/321C	-9.4
■ HEZEKIAH ALLEN	Allen, Hezekiah "Ki" b: 2/25/1863, Westport, Conn. d: 9/21/16, Saugatuck, Conn. 5'11", 160 lbs. Deb: 5/16/1884																								
1884	Phi-N	1	3	0	2	0	0	0	0	0	0	.667	.667	.667	337	1	1	1				1.000	-1	/C	0.0
■ HAM ALLEN	Allen, Homer S. b: 8/1854, Hamden, Conn. d: 1/7/1892, Hamden, Conn. Deb: 4/27/1872																								
1872	Man-n	15	59	8	15	2	0	0	11	0	1	.254	.254	.288	71	-2	-2	4						O/S	-0.1
■ HORACE ALLEN	Allen, Horace Tanner "Pug" b: 6/11/1899, Deland, Fla. d: 7/5/81, Canton, N.C. BL/TR, 6', 187 lbs. Deb: 6/15/19																								
1919	Bro-N	4	7	0	0	0	0	0	0	0	2	.000	.000	.000	-98	-2	-2	0	0			1.000	0	/O	-0.2
■ JAMIE ALLEN	Allen, James Bradley b: 5/29/58, Yakima, Wash. BR/TR, 6', 205 lbs. Deb: 5/01/83																								
1983	Sea-A	86	273	23	61	10	0	4	21	33	52	.223	.309	.304	67	-11	-12	26	6	5	-1	.959	-6	3/D	-2.0
■ PETE ALLEN	Allen, Jesse Hall b: 5/1/1868, Columbiana, Ohio d: 4/16/46, Philadelphia, Pa. BR/TR, 5'8.5", 185 lbs. Deb: 8/04/1893																								
1893	Cle-N	1	4	0	0	0	0	0	0	0	0	.000	.000	.000	-94	-1	-1	0	0			1.000	-1	/C	-0.2
■ KIM ALLEN	Allen, Kim Bryant b: 4/5/53, Fontana, Cal. BR/TR, 5'11", 175 lbs. Deb: 9/02/80																								
1980	Sea-A	23	51	9	12	3	0	0	3	8	3	.235	.350	.294	78	-1	-1	6	10	3	1	.970	-2	2/OS	-0.2
1981	Sea-A	19	3	1	0	0	0	0	0	0	2	.000	.000	.000	-96	-1	-1	-0	2	1	0	.000	-1	/2OD	-0.2
Total	2	42	54	10	12	3	0	0	3	8	5	.222	.333	.278	69	-2	-2	6	12	4	1	.970	-4	/2ODS	-0.4
■ MYRON ALLEN	Allen, Myron Smith "Zeke" b: 3/22/1854, Kingston, N.Y. d: 3/8/24, Kingston, N.Y. BR/TR, 5'8", 150 lbs. Deb: 7/19/1883																								
1883	NY-N	1	4	0	0	0	0	0	1	0	2	.000	.000	.000	-99	-1	-1	0				1.000	-0	/P	0.0
1886	Bos-N	1	3	0	0	0	0	0	0	0	1	.000	.000	.000	-99	-1	-1	0	0			1.000	-0	/2	-0.1
1887	Cle-a	117	463	66	128	22	10	4		36		.276	.335	.393	108	3	5	71	26			.894	8	*O/3SP	0.9
1888	KC-a	37	136	23	29	6	4	0	10	9		.213	.267	.316	84	-2	-3	13	4			.931	7	O/P	0.2
Total	4	156	606	89	157	28	14	4	11	45	3	.259	.317	.371	100	-1	1	84	30			.903	15	O/P3S2	1.0
■ DICK ALLEN	Allen, Richard Anthony b: 3/8/42, Wampum, Pa. BR/TR, 5'11", 190 lbs. Deb: 9/03/63 F																								
1963	Phi-N	10	24	6	7	2	1	0	2	0	5	.292	.292	.458	114	0	0	2	0	0	0	.833	-1	/O3	-0.1
1964	Phi-N	162	632	**125**	201	38	**13**	29	91	67	138	.318	.383	.557	163	50	51	135	3	4	-2	.921	7	*3	5.7
1965	Phi-N★	161	619	93	187	31	14	20	85	74	150	.302	.378	.494	146	36	38	119	15	2	3	.943	-2	*3/S	3.7
1966	Phi-N★	141	524	112	166	25	10	40	110	68	136	.317	.398	**.632**	**181**	**57**	**57**	**131**	10	6	-1	.967	-10	3O	4.3
1967	Phi-N★	122	463	89	142	31	10	23	77	75	117	.307	**.404**	.566	**173**	46	46	109	20	5	3	.908	-6	*3/2S	4.4
1968	Phi-N	152	521	87	137	17	9	33	90	74	161	.263	.356	.520	160	38	38	97	7	7	-2	.973	-14	*O3	1.6
1969	Phi-N	118	438	79	126	23	3	32	89	64	144	.288	.378	.573	168	36	37	95	9	3	1	.985	-9	*1	2.0
1970	StL-N★	122	459	88	128	17	5	34	101	71	118	.279	.378	.560	145	30	29	97	5	4	-1	.993	-12	13/O	0.9
1971	LA-N	155	549	82	162	24	1	23	90	93	113	.295	.398	.468	154	35	39	102	8	1	2	.918	-11	3O1	2.5
1972	Chi-A★	148	506	90	156	28	5	**37**	**113**	**99**	126	.308	**.422**	**.603**	**199**	**66**	**65**	**131**	19	8	1	.995	-4	*1/3	**5.5**
1973	Chi-A†	72	250	39	79	20	3	16	41	33	51	.316	.398	.612	175	26	25	59	7	2	1	.994	0	1/2D	2.1
1974	Chi-A★	128	462	84	139	23	1	**32**	88	57	89	.301	.379	**.563**	164	39	38	96	7	1	2	.986	-11	*1/2D	2.1
1975	Phi-N	119	416	54	97	21	3	12	62	58	109	.233	.330	.385	94	-1	-3	52	11	2	2	.982	-1	*1	-1.0
1976	*Phi-N	85	298	52	80	16	1	15	49	37	63	.268	.349	.480	130	12	11	47	11	4	1	.989	-3	1	0.3
1977	Oak-A	54	171	19	41	4	0	5	31	24	36	.240	.337	.351	89	-2	-2	20	1	3	-2	.984	2	1/D	-0.5
Total	15	1749	6332	1099	1848	320	79	351	1119	894	1556	.292	.381	.534	156	470	469	1290	133	52	9	.989	-77	13O/2DS	33.5

YEAR	TM/L	G	AB	R	H	2B	3B	HR	RBI	BB	SO	AVG	OBP	SLG	PRO+	BR	/A	RC	SB	CS	SBR	FA	FR	POS	TPR

■ **BOB ALLEN** Allen, Robert (b: Alvah Charles Elliott) b: 10/13/1894, Muscoda, Wis. d: 12/18/75, Naperville, Ill. BR/TR, 5'10", 180 lbs. Deb: 8/20/19

| 1919 | Phi-A | 9 | 22 | 3 | 3 | 1 | 0 | 0 | 0 | 3 | 7 | .136 | .269 | .182 | 27 | -2 | -2 | 1 | 0 | | | .889 | -2 | /O | -0.5 |

■ **BOB ALLEN** Allen, Robert Gilman b: 7/10/1867, Marion, Ohio d: 5/14/43, Little Rock, Ark. BR/TR, 5'11", 175 lbs. Deb: 4/19/1890 M

1890	Phi-N	133	456	69	103	15	11	2	57	87	54	.226	.356	.320	97	3	1	58	13			.924	**39**	*S/M	4.2
1891	Phi-N	118	438	46	97	7	4	1	51	43	44	.221	.291	.263	62	-19	-21	38	12			.896	13	*S	-0.2
1892	Phi-N	152	563	77	128	20	14	2	64	61	60	.227	.304	.323	92	-6	-5	61	15			.919	18	*S	1.7
1893	Phi-N	124	471	86	126	19	12	8	90	71	40	.268	.369	.410	109	7	7	76	8			.919	18	*S	2.5
1894	Phi-N	40	149	26	38	10	3	0	19	17	11	.255	.335	.362	72	-7	-7	20	4			.915	-2	S	-0.5
1897	Bos-N	34	119	33	38	5	0	1	24	18		.319	.409	.387	104	3	1	20	1			.924	8	S/O2	0.8
1900	Cin-N	5	15	0	2	1	0	0	1	0		.133	.188	.200	7	-2	-2	1	0			.864	-1	/SM	-0.2
Total	7	606	2211	337	532	77	44	14	306	297	209	.241	.334	.334	90	-22	-25	274	53				93	S/2O	8.3

■ **ROD ALLEN** Allen, Roderick Bernet b: 10/5/59, Los Angeles, Cal. BR/TR, 6'1", 185 lbs. Deb: 4/07/83

1983	Sea-A	11	12	1	2	0	0	0	0	0	1	.167	.167	.167	-8	-2	-2	0	0	0	0	1.000	0	/OD	-0.2
1984	Det-A	15	27	6	8	1	0	0	3	2	8	.296	.367	.333	96	-0	-0	4	1	0	0	1.000	-0	D/O	0.0
1988	Cle-A	5	11	1	1	1	0	0	0	0	2	.091	.091	.182	-25	-2	-2	0	0	0	0	.000	0	/D	-0.2
Total	3	31	50	8	11	2	0	0	3	2	11	.220	.264	.260	45	-4	-4	4	1	0	0	1.000	-0	/DO	-0.4

■ **RON ALLEN** Allen, Ronald Frederick b: 12/23/43, Wampum, Pa. BB/TR, 6'3", 205 lbs. Deb: 8/11/72 F

| 1972 | StL-N | 7 | 11 | 2 | 1 | 0 | 0 | 1 | 1 | 3 | 5 | .091 | .286 | .364 | 84 | -0 | -0 | 1 | 0 | 0 | 0 | .968 | -0 | /1 | -0.1 |

■ **GARY ALLENSON** Allenson, Gary Martin b: 2/4/55, Culver City, Cal. BR/TR, 5'11", 185 lbs. Deb: 4/08/79 C

1979	Bos-A	108	241	27	49	10	2	3	22	20	42	.203	.267	.299	50	-16	-18	19	1	1	-0	.980	9	*C/3	-0.7
1980	Bos-A	36	70	9	25	6	0	0	10	13	11	.357	.458	.443	141	4	5	15	2	2	-1	.981	4	C/3D	0.9
1981	Bos-A	47	139	23	31	8	0	3	25	23	33	.223	.337	.388	92	2	1	18	0	0	0	.969	7	C	0.3
1982	Bos-A	92	264	25	54	11	0	6	33	38	39	.205	.307	.314	67	-10	-12	26	0	3	-2	.992	8	C	-0.3
1983	Bos-A	84	230	19	53	11	0	3	30	27	43	.230	.317	.317	70	-7	-10	23	0	1	-1	.984	4	C	-0.3
1984	Bos-A	35	83	9	19	2	0	2	8	9	14	.229	.304	.325	71	-3	-3	7	0	0	0	.987	0	C	-0.2
1985	Tor-A	14	34	2	4	1	0	0	3	0	10	.118	.118	.147	-27	-6	-6	0	0	0	0	1.000	-2	C	-0.7
Total	7	416	1061	114	235	49	2	19	131	130	192	.221	.309	.325	71	-35	-43	109	3	7	-3	.984	25	C/3D	-1.0

■ **GENE ALLEY** Alley, Leonard Eugene b: 7/10/40, Richmond, Va. BR/TR, 6', 165 lbs. Deb: 9/04/63

1963	Pit-N	17	51	3	11	1	0	0	2	12		.216	.245	.235	39	-4	-4	3	0	1	-1	.947	1	/32S	-0.3
1964	Pit-N	81	209	30	44	3	1	6	13	21	56	.211	.289	.321	72	-8	-8	20	0	1	-1	.966	24	S/32	2.0
1965	Pit-N	153	500	47	126	21	6	5	47	32	82	.252	.302	.348	82	-12	-12	52	7	2	1	.968	30	*S2/3	3.0
1966	Pit-N	147	579	88	173	28	10	7	43	27	83	.299	.336	.418	108	6	6	79	8	8	-2	.979	13	*S	3.1
1967	Pit-N★	152	550	59	158	25	7	6	55	36	70	.287	.339	.391	108	6	6	70	10	5	0	.967	8	*S	3.0
1968	Pit-N†	133	474	48	116	20	2	4	39	39	78	.245	.309	.321	91	-6	-5	45	13	5	1	.974	26	*S2	3.8
1969	Pit-N	82	285	28	70	3	2	8	32	19	48	.246	.295	.354	83	-8	-7	29	4	0	1	.977	7	2S/3	0.8
1970	*Pit-N	121	426	46	104	16	5	8	41	31	70	.244	.300	.362	78	-15	-14	46	7	3	0	.975	34	*S/23	3.3
1971	*Pit-N	114	348	38	79	8	7	6	28	35	43	.227	.298	.342	81	-9	-9	36	9	2	2	.958	-16	*S/3	-1.1
1972	*Pit-N	119	347	30	86	12	2	3	36	38	52	.248	.322	.320	85	-7	-6	36	3	4	-1	.970	-5	*S/3	0.3
1973	Pit-N	76	158	25	32	3	2	2	8	20	28	.203	.292	.285	62	-8	-8	12	1	0	0	.981	5	S/3	0.3
Total	11	1195	3927	442	999	140	44	55	342	300	622	.254	.312	.354	88	-65	-61	428	63	30	1	.970	125	S2/3	18.2

■ **GAIR ALLIE** Allie, Gair Roosevelt b: 10/28/31, Statesville, N.C. BR/TR, 6'1", 190 lbs. Deb: 4/13/54

| 1954 | Pit-N | 121 | 418 | 38 | 83 | 8 | 6 | 3 | 30 | 56 | 84 | .199 | .296 | .268 | 49 | -31 | -30 | 37 | 1 | 1 | -0 | .952 | -16 | S3 | -3.9 |

■ **BOB ALLIETTA** Allietta, Robert George b: 5/1/52, New Bedford, Mass. BR/TR, 6', 190 lbs. Deb: 5/06/75

| 1975 | Cal-A | 21 | 45 | 4 | 8 | 1 | 0 | 1 | 2 | 1 | 6 | .178 | .196 | .267 | 32 | -4 | -4 | 2 | 0 | 0 | 0 | 1.000 | 2 | C | -0.2 |

■ **ANDY ALLISON** Allison, Andrew K. b: 1848, New York, N.Y. 5'10", 150 lbs. Deb: 5/07/1872

| 1872 | Eck-n | 24 | 99 | 11 | 15 | 2 | 0 | 0 | 7 | 0 | 3 | .152 | .152 | .172 | -1 | -11 | -8 | 3 | | | | | | 1/O | -0.5 |

■ **ART ALLISON** Allison, Arthur Algernon b: 1/29/1849, Philadelphia, Pa. d: 2/25/16, Washington, D.C. 5'8", 150 lbs. Deb: 5/04/1871 F

1871	Cle-n	29	137	28	40	4	5	0	19	2	5	.292	.302	.394	104	-0	1	18	3					*O	0.2
1872	Cle-n	19	85	13	23	6	0	0	8	0	2	.271	.271	.341	92	-1	-0	8						O	0.0
1873	Res-n	23	99	12	32	5	0	0	11	0	1	.323	.323	.374	113	0	2	12						O/1C	0.2
1875	Was-n	26	110	18	24	3	1	0		1		.218	.225	.264	71	-3	-3	7						1/OC	-0.2
	Har-n	40	173	26	41	6	0	1		0		.237	.237	.289	77	-3	-5	12						O/2	-0.4
	Yr	66	283	44	65	9	1	1		1		.230	.232	.279	75	-7	-7	19						O1/C2	-0.6
1876	Lou-N	31	130	9	27	2	1	0	10	2	6	.208	.220	.238	45	-6	-10	7				.789	6	O/1	-0.4
Total	4 n	137	604	97	160	24	6	1	38	3	7	.265	.269	.329	90	-8	-4	57						O/1C2	-0.2

■ **DOUG ALLISON** Allison, Douglas L. b: 7/1845, Philadelphia, Pa. d: 12/19/16, Washington, D.C. BR/TR, 5'10.5", 160 lbs. Deb: 5/05/1871 F

1871	Oly-n	27	133	28	44	10	2	2	27	0	2	.331	.331	.481	137	5	6	22	1					*C	0.4
1872	Tro-n	23	118	23	34	5	2	0	20	1	3	.288	.294	.364	100	-0	0	13						C/S	-0.1
	Eck-n	18	79	18	27	2	1	0	6	1	2	.342	.350	.392	151	3	5	11						C	0.3
	Yr	41	197	41	61	7	3	0	26	2	5	.310	.317	.376	119	3	5	24						C/S	0.2
1873	Res-n	18	84	11	24	5	0	0	8	0	0	.286	.286	.345	92	-2	-0	8						C/O	0.0
	Mut-n	11	49	6	11	1	0	0	3	1	0	.224	.240	.245	43	-3	-3	3						C/O	-0.2
	Yr	29	133	17	35	6	0	0	11	1	0	.263	.269	.308	73	-5	-4	11						C/O	-0.2
1874	Mut-n	65	316	69	88	8	5	0		6		.278	.292	.335	96	-0	2	32						*OC	0.0
1875	Har-n	61	267	38	67	7	0	0		7		.251	.270	.277	85	-2	-5	20						*C/1	-0.2
1876	Har-N	44	163	19	43	4	0	0	15	3	9	.264	.277	.288	82	-2	-4	13				.881	11	C/O	0.7
1877	Har-N	29	115	14	17	2	0	0	6	3	7	.148	.169	.165	7	-12	-10	3				.896	2	C	-0.7
1878	Pro-N	19	76	9	22	2	0	0	7	1	8	.289	.299	.316	102	0	0	7				.911	-0	C/P	-0.1
1879	Pro-N	1	5	0	0	0	0	0	0	0	1	.000	.000	.000	-99	-1	-1	0				.833	0	/C	-0.1
1883	Bal-a	1	3	2	2	0	0	0		0		.667	.667	.667	321	1	1	1				.000	-1	/OC	0.2
Total	5 n	223	1046	193	295	38	10	2	64	16	7	.282	.293	.343	100	-0	1	110						C/O1S	0.2
Total	5	94	362	44	84	8	0	0	28	7	25	.232	.247	.254	63	-14	-14	25				.892	12	/COP	-0.1

■ **MILO ALLISON** Allison, Milo Henry b: 10/16/1890, Elk Rapids, Mich. d: 6/18/57, Kenosha, Wis. BL/TR, 6', 163 lbs. Deb: 9/26/13

1913	Chi-N	2	6	1	2	0	0	0	0	0	1	.333	.333	.333	90	-0	-0	1				1.000	0	/O	0.0
1914	Chi-N	1	1	0	1	0	0	0	0	0	0	1.000	1.000	1.000	497	0	0	1				.000	0	H	0.0
1916	Cle-A	14	18	10	5	0	0	0	0	6	1	.278	.458	.278	115	1	1	3	0			1.000	-0	O	0.0
1917	Cle-A	32	35	4	5	0	0	0	0	9	7	.143	.318	.143	38	-2	-2	3	3			1.000	-3	O	-0.6
Total	4	49	60	15	13	0	0	0	0	15	9	.217	.373	.217	74	-0	-1	7	4			1.000	-4	/O	-0.6

■ **BILL ALLISON** Allison, William Andrew b: 9/18/1848, Philadelphia, Pa. d: 6/12/23, Deb: 5/21/1872

| 1872 | Eck-n | 3 | 10 | 3 | 2 | 0 | 0 | 0 | 1 | 0 | 1 | .200 | .200 | .200 | 28 | -1 | -1 | 0 | | | | | | /O2 | 0.0 |

■ **BOB ALLISON** Allison, William Robert b: 7/11/34, Raytown, Mo. BR/TR, 6'4", 220 lbs. Deb: 9/16/58

| 1958 | Was-A | 11 | 35 | 1 | 7 | 1 | 0 | 0 | 0 | 2 | 5 | .200 | .243 | .229 | 31 | -3 | -3 | 1 | 0 | 2 | -1 | 1.000 | -0 | O | -0.5 |

YEAR	TM/L	G	AB	R	H	2B	3B	HR	RBI	BB	SO	AVG	OBP	SLG	PRO+	BR	/A	RC	SB	CS	SBR	FA	FR	POS	TPR
1959	Was-A☆	150	570	83	149	18	**9**	30	85	60	92	.261	.334	.482	122	15	15	85	13	8	-1	.974	-2	*O	0.5
1960	Was-A	144	501	79	126	30	3	15	69	92	94	.251	.370	.413	113	10	11	79	11	9	-2	.965	9	*O/1	1.1
1961	Min-A	159	556	83	136	21	3	29	105	103	100	.245	.367	.450	111	15	11	93	2	7	-4	.975	7	*O1	0.5
1962	Min-A	149	519	102	138	24	8	29	102	84	115	.266	.372	.511	130	26	23	102	8	5	-1	.977	7	*O	2.2
1963	Min-A★	148	527	**99**	143	25	4	35	91	90	109	.271	.381	.533	**150**	39	37	113	6	1	1	.971	11	*O	4.3
1964	Min-A★	149	492	90	141	27	4	32	86	92	99	.287	.406	.553	163	45	44	119	10	1	2	.986	-4	1O	3.8
1965	*Min-A	135	438	71	102	14	5	23	78	73	114	.233	.345	.445	118	14	11	73	10	2	2	.972	11	*O/1	1.9
1966	Min-A	70	168	34	37	6	1	8	19	30	34	.220	.348	.411	110	5	3	27	6	0	2	.967	-1	O	0.2
1967	Min-A	153	496	73	128	21	6	24	75	74	114	.258	.357	.470	132	27	22	87	6	4	-1	.978	-1	*O	1.5
1968	Min-A	145	469	63	116	16	8	22	52	52	98	.247	.325	.456	128	19	16	65	9	7	-2	.966	-4	*O1	0.5
1969	*Min-A	81	189	18	43	8	2	8	27	29	39	.228	.333	.418	107	2	2	24	2	4	-2	1.000	-3	O/1	-0.6
1970	*Min-A	47	72	15	15	5	0	1	7	14	20	.208	.345	.319	83	-1	-1	9	1	0	0	1.000	-3	O/1	-0.5
Total	13	1541	5032	811	1281	216	53	256	796	795	1033	.255	.360	.471	126	211	192	877	84	50	-5	.975	28	*O1	14.9

■ BEAU ALLRED

Allred, Dale Le Beau b: 6/4/65, Mesa, Ariz. BL/TL, 6', 190 lbs. Deb: 9/07/89

YEAR	TM/L	G	AB	R	H	2B	3B	HR	RBI	BB	SO	AVG	OBP	SLG	PRO+	BR	/A	RC	SB	CS	SBR	FA	FR	POS	TPR
1989	Cle-A	13	24	0	6	3	0	0	1	2	10	.250	.308	.375	90	-0	-0	3	0	0	0	1.000	1	/OD	0.1
1990	Cle-A	4	16	2	3	1	0	1	2	2	3	.188	.278	.438	98	-0	-0	2	0	0	0	.833	-1	/O	-0.1
1991	Cle-A	48	125	17	29	3	0	3	12	25	35	.232	.364	.328	92	-0	-0	17	2	2	-1	.972	2	O/D	0.0
Total	3	65	165	19	38	7	0	4	15	29	48	.230	.349	.345	93	-1	-1	22	2	2	-1	.969	2	/OD	0.0

■ MEL ALMADA

Almada, Baldomero Melo b: 2/7/13, Hwatabampo, Sonora, Mexico d: 8/13/88, Hermosillo, Mexico BL/TL, 6', 170 lbs. Deb: 9/08/33

YEAR	TM/L	G	AB	R	H	2B	3B	HR	RBI	BB	SO	AVG	OBP	SLG	PRO+	BR	/A	RC	SB	CS	SBR	FA	FR	POS	TPR
1933	Bos-A	14	44	11	15	0	0	1	3	11	3	.341	.473	.409	137	3	3	10	3	1	0	1.000	-0	O	0.2
1934	Bos-A	23	90	7	21	2	1	0	10	6	8	.233	.281	.278	42	-7	-8	7	3	2	-0	.985	4	O	-0.6
1935	Bos-A	151	607	85	176	27	9	3	59	55	34	.290	.350	.379	83	-10	-16	83	20	9	1	.968	-0	*O/1	-2.0
1936	Bos-A	96	320	40	81	16	4	1	21	24	15	.253	.305	.338	55	-22	-24	33	2	4	-2	.987	-2	O	-2.8
1937	Bos-A	32	110	17	26	6	2	1	9	15	6	.236	.328	.355	69	-5	-5	13	0	1	-1	.927	-6	O/1	-1.2
	Was-A	100	433	74	134	21	4	4	33	38	21	.309	.365	.404	98	-4	-1	66	12	4	1	.964	14	*O	1.0
	Yr	132	543	91	160	27	6	5	42	53	27	.295	.357	.394	91	-9	-7	79	12	5	1	.960	9	*O/1	-0.2
1938	Was-A	47	197	24	48	7	4	1	15	8	16	.244	.277	.335	56	-15	-13	19	4	1	1	.968	5	O	-0.8
	StL-A	102	436	77	149	22	2	3	37	38	22	.342	.398	.422	106	5	5	74	9	5	-0	.966	-1	*O	0.1
	Yr	149	633	101	197	29	6	4	52	46	38	.311	.362	.395	92	-10	-8	92	13	6	0	.967	4	*O	-0.7
1939	StL-A	42	134	17	32	2	1	1	7	10	8	.239	.292	.291	48	-10	-11	12	1	0	0	.987	-3	O	-1.3
	Bro-N	39	112	11	24	4	0	0	3	9	17	.214	.273	.250	40	-9	-10	8	2			.977	2	O	-0.9
Total	7	646	2483	363	706	107	27	15	197	214	150	.284	.342	.367	79	-74	-80	324	56	27		.970	13	O/1	-8.3

■ RAFAEL ALMEIDA

Almeida, Rafael D. "Mike" b: 7/30/1887, Havana, Cuba d: 3/68, Havana, Cuba BR/TR, 5'9", 164 lbs. Deb: 7/04/11

YEAR	TM/L	G	AB	R	H	2B	3B	HR	RBI	BB	SO	AVG	OBP	SLG	PRO+	BR	/A	RC	SB	CS	SBR	FA	FR	POS	TPR
1911	Cin-N	36	96	9	30	5	1	0	15	9	16	.313	.383	.385	120	2	3	16	3			.890	-2	3/2S	0.1
1912	Cin-N	16	59	9	13	4	3	0	10	5	8	.220	.281	.390	85	-2	-2	6	0			.891	-2	3	-0.3
1913	Cin-N	50	130	14	34	4	2	3	21	11	16	.262	.324	.392	104	0	0	17	4			.919	4	3/OS2	0.5
Total	3	102	285	32	77	13	6	3	46	25	40	.270	.335	.389	106	1	2	39	7			.904	-0	/3OS2	0.3

■ BILL ALMON

Almon, William Francis b: 11/21/52, Providence, R.I. BR/TR, 6'3", 190 lbs. Deb: 9/02/74

YEAR	TM/L	G	AB	R	H	2B	3B	HR	RBI	BB	SO	AVG	OBP	SLG	PRO+	BR	/A	RC	SB	CS	SBR	FA	FR	POS	TPR
1974	SD-N	16	38	4	12	1	0	0	3	2	9	.316	.350	.342	98	-0	-0	5	1	0	0	.915	-2	S	0.0
1975	SD-N	6	10	0	4	0	0	0	0	0	1	.400	.400	.400	131	0	0	2	0	0	0	1.000	1	/S	0.1
1976	SD-N	14	57	6	14	3	0	1	6	2	9	.246	.271	.351	82	-2	-2	6	3	1	0	.962	1	S	0.2
1977	SD-N	155	613	75	160	18	11	2	43	37	114	.261	.303	.336	79	-25	-17	61	20	9	1	.954	18	*S	1.9
1978	SD-N	138	405	39	102	19	2	0	21	33	74	.252	.308	.309	79	-14	-11	40	17	5	2	.933	0	*3S/2	-0.9
1979	SD-N	100	198	20	45	3	0	1	8	21	48	.227	.301	.258	57	-12	-11	16	6	5	-1	.985	16	2S/O	0.9
1980	Mon-N	18	38	2	10	1	1	0	3	1	5	.263	.282	.342	73	-1	-1	3	0	0	0	.911	-2	S/2	-0.3
	NY-N	48	112	13	19	3	2	0	4	8	27	.170	.225	.232	29	-11	-11	6	2	0	1	.967	9	S2/3	0.2
	Yr	66	150	15	29	4	3	0	7	9	32	.193	.239	.260	40	-12	-12	10	2	0	1	.948	6	S2/3	-0.1
1981	Chi-A	103	349	46	105	10	2	4	41	21	60	.301	.344	.375	109	3	4	46	16	6	1	.969	14	*S	3.1
1982	Chi-A	111	308	40	79	10	4	4	26	25	49	.256	.314	.354	83	-7	-7	34	10	8	-2	.949	20	*S/D	1.9
1983	Oak-A	143	451	45	120	29	1	4	63	26	67	.266	.309	.361	89	-10	-7	51	26	8	3	.941	-31	S31O/2D	-3.4
1984	Oak-A	106	211	24	47	11	0	7	16	10	42	.223	.258	.374	78	-8	-7	18	5	7	-3	1.000	-9	O1D/3CS	-2.1
1985	Pit-N	88	244	33	66	17	0	6	29	22	61	.270	.333	.414	109	2	3	32	10	7	-1	.987	-22	SO/13	-1.9
1986	Pit-N	102	196	29	43	7	2	7	27	30	38	.219	.323	.383	92	-2	-2	25	11	4	1	.983	-13	O3S/1	-1.5
1987	Pit-N	19	20	5	4	1	0	0	1	1	5	.200	.238	.250	29	-2	-2	1	0	0	0	.944	1	/SO3	-0.1
	NY-N	49	54	8	13	3	0	0	4	8	16	.241	.339	.296	74	-2	-2	6	1	0	0	.972	-3	S2/1O	-0.4
	Yr	68	74	13	17	4	0	0	5	9	21	.230	.313	.284	62	-4	-4	7	1	0	0	.963	-2	S2/O13	-0.5
1988	Phi-N	20	26	1	3	2	0	0	1	3	11	.115	.207	.192	15	-3	-3	1	0	0	0	.944	1	/3S1	-0.2
Total	15	1236	3330	390	846	138	25	36	296	250	636	.254	.307	.343	83	-95	-74	354	128	60	2	.956	-1	S3O2/1DC	-2.5

■ ROBERTO ALOMAR

Alomar, Roberto (Velazquez) b: 2/5/68, Ponce, P.R. BB/TR, 6', 184 lbs. Deb: 4/22/88 F

YEAR	TM/L	G	AB	R	H	2B	3B	HR	RBI	BB	SO	AVG	OBP	SLG	PRO+	BR	/A	RC	SB	CS	SBR	FA	FR	POS	TPR
1988	SD-N	143	545	84	145	24	6	9	41	47	83	.266	.328	.382	105	2	3	68	24	6	4	.980	17	*2	3.1
1989	SD-N	158	623	82	184	27	1	7	56	53	76	.295	.352	.376	108	7	7	85	42	17	2	.967	6	*2	2.1
1990	SD-N★	147	586	80	168	27	5	6	60	48	72	.287	.343	.381	98	-1	-1	76	24	7	3	.976	-2	*2/S	0.4
1991	*Tor-A★	161	637	88	188	41	11	9	69	57	86	.295	.357	.436	114	16	12	107	53	11	**9**	.981	-22	*2	0.3
1992	*Tor-A★	152	571	105	177	27	8	8	76	87	52	.310	.406	.427	128	29	26	111	49	9	9	.993	-25	*2/D	1.4
Total	5	761	2962	439	862	146	31	39	302	292	369	.291	.358	.401	111	53	47	448	192	50	28	.979	-27	2/SD	7.3

■ SANDY ALOMAR

Alomar, Santos Jr. (Velazquez) b: 6/18/66, Salinas, P.R. BR/TR, 6'5", 200 lbs. Deb: 9/30/88 F

YEAR	TM/L	G	AB	R	H	2B	3B	HR	RBI	BB	SO	AVG	OBP	SLG	PRO+	BR	/A	RC	SB	CS	SBR	FA	FR	POS	TPR
1988	SD-N	1	1	0	0	0	0	0	0	0	1	.000	.000	.000	-99	-0	-0	0	0	0	0	.000	0	H	0.0
1989	SD-N	7	19	1	4	1	0	1	6	3	3	.211	.318	.421	110	0	0	2	0	0	0	1.000	-0	/C	0.0
1990	Cle-A★	132	445	60	129	26	2	9	66	25	46	.290	.331	.418	109	4	4	60	4	1	1	.981	-13	*C	0.0
1991	Cle-A★	51	184	10	40	9	0	0	7	8	24	.217	.265	.266	47	-13	-13	12	0	4	-2	.987	2	C/D	-1.1
1992	Cle-A★	89	299	22	75	16	0	2	26	13	32	.251	.293	.324	72	-11	-11	27	3	3	-1	.996	-3	C/D	-1.1
Total	5	280	948	93	248	52	2	12	105	49	106	.262	.306	.359	85	-20	-21	101	7	8	-3	.988	-15	C/D	-2.2

■ SANDY ALOMAR

Alomar, Santos Sr. (Conde) b: 10/19/43, Salinas, P.R. BB/TR, 5'9", 155 lbs. Deb: 9/15/64 FC

YEAR	TM/L	G	AB	R	H	2B	3B	HR	RBI	BB	SO	AVG	OBP	SLG	PRO+	BR	/A	RC	SB	CS	SBR	FA	FR	POS	TPR
1964	Mil-N	19	53	3	13	1	0	0	6	0	11	.245	.245	.264	43	-4	-4	3	1	0	0	.967	8	S	0.6
1965	Mil-N	67	108	16	26	1	1	0	8	4	12	.241	.268	.269	51	-7	-7	7	12	5	1	.964	14	S2	1.0
1966	Atl-N	31	44	4	4	1	0	0	2	1	10	.091	.111	.114	-37	-8	-8	1	0	0	0	.981	3	2/S	-0.4
1967	NY-N	15	22	1	0	0	0	0	0	0	6	.000	.000	.000	-99	-6	-6	0	0	0	0	1.000	2	S/32	-0.3
	Chi-A	12	15	4	3	0	0	0	0	2	0	.200	.294	.200	50	-1	-1	1	2	0	1	.952	2	/S2	0.2
1968	Chi-A	133	363	41	92	8	2	0	12	20	42	.253	.294	.287	76	-10	-11	32	21	8	2	.958	-16	23/SO	-2.2
1969	Chi-A	22	58	8	13	2	0	0	4	4	6	.224	.274	.259	47	-4	-4	5	2	0	1	.980	3	2	0.1
	Cal-A	134	559	60	140	10	2	1	30	36	48	.250	.296	.281	65	-28	-25	50	18	3	4	.969	-10	*2	-2.1
	Yr	156	617	68	153	12	2	1	34	40	54	.248	.294	.279	63	-32	-29	54	20	3	4	.970	-7	*2	-2.0
1970	Cal-A★	162	672	82	169	18	2	2	36	49	65	.251	.303	.293	68	-31	-28	64	35	12	3	.979	9	*2S/3	-0.2
1971	Cal-A	162	689	77	179	24	3	4	42	41	60	.260	.301	.321	82	-22	-16	70	39	10	6	.989	21	*2S	2.8
1972	Cal-A	155	610	65	146	20	3	1	25	47	55	.239	.294	.287	78	-20	-16	52	20	12	-1	.977	3	*2/S	-0.6
1973	Cal-A	136	470	45	112	7	1	0	28	34	44	.238	.290	.257	60	-27	-23	39	25	10	2	.979	-8	*2S	-2.0
1974	Cal-A	46	54	12	12	0	1	0	1	2	8	.222	.250	.259	49	-4	-3	4	2	0	1	.977	9	S2/3OD	0.8

YEAR	TM/L	G	AB	R	H	2B	3B	HR	RBI	BB	SO	AVG	OBP	SLG	PRO+	BR	/A	RC	SB	CS	SBR	FA	FR	POS	TPR
	NY-A	76	279	35	75	8	0	1	27	14	25	.269	.304	.308	79	-9	-8	25	6	4	-1	.977	-12	2	-1.7
	Yr	122	333	47	87	8	1	1	28	16	33	.261	.295	.300	74	-12	-11	29	8	4	0	.976	-3	2S/3OD	-0.9
1975	NY-A	151	489	61	117	18	4	2	39	26	58	.239	.278	.305	66	-23	-22	44	28	6	5	**.985**	-12	*2/S	-2.2
1976	*NY-A	67	163	20	39	4	0	1	10	13	12	.239	.295	.282	70	-6	-6	14	12	7	-1	.970	-5	2/S31O	-1.0
1977	Tex-A	69	83	21	22	3	0	1	11	8	13	.265	.337	.337	84	-2	-2	10	4	3	-1	.973	13	D2/SO13	1.1
1978	Tex-A	24	29	3	6	1	0	0	1	1	7	.207	.233	.241	34	-3	-3	2	0	0	0	.975	5	/123SD	0.3
Total	15	1481	4760	558	1168	126	19	13	282	302	482	.245	.291	.288	68	-213	-192	421	227	80	20	.977	31	*2S/3D1O	-5.8

■ FELIPE ALOU Alou, Felipe Rojas (b: Felipe Rojas (Alou)) b: 5/12/35, Haina, D.R. BR/TR, 6', 195 lbs. Deb: 6/08/58 FMC

YEAR	TM/L	G	AB	R	H	2B	3B	HR	RBI	BB	SO	AVG	OBP	SLG	PRO+	BR	/A	RC	SB	CS	SBR	FA	FR	POS	TPR
1958	SF-N	75	182	21	46	9	2	4	16	19	34	.253	.327	.390	91	-3	-2	24	4	2	0	.985	-3	O	-0.8
1959	SF-N	95	247	38	68	13	2	10	33	17	38	.275	.322	.466	109	2	2	36	5	3	-0	.974	-6	O	-0.7
1960	SF-N	106	322	48	85	17	3	8	44	16	42	.264	.303	.410	99	-4	-2	39	10	2	2	.958	-4	O	-0.8
1961	SF-N	132	415	59	120	19	0	18	52	26	41	.289	.334	.465	113	5	6	62	11	4	1	.990	-1	*O	0.0
1962	*SF-N★	154	561	96	177	30	3	25	98	33	66	.316	.359	.513	133	23	24	103	10	7	-1	.971	-1	*O	1.3
1963	SF-N	157	565	75	159	31	9	20	82	27	87	.281	.321	.474	127	17	17	83	11	2	2	.986	2	*O	1.5
1964	Mil-N	121	415	60	105	26	3	9	51	30	41	.253	.310	.395	96	-2	-2	51	5	2	0	.975	-5	O1	-1.2
1965	Mil-N	143	555	80	165	29	2	23	78	31	63	.297	.340	.481	128	19	19	90	8	4	0	.980	-5	O1/3S	0.8
1966	Atl-N☆	154	666	**122**	**218**	32	6	31	74	24	51	.327	.362	.533	143	38	37	123	5	7	-3	.988	3	1O/3S	2.9
1967	Atl-N	140	574	76	157	26	3	15	43	32	50	.274	.320	.408	108	4	5	73	6	5	-1	.993	-12	1O	-1.8
1968	Atl-N★	160	662	72	**210**	37	5	11	57	48	56	.317	.367	.438	140	32	32	103	12	11	-3	.980	4	*O	2.8
1969	*Atl-N	123	476	54	134	13	1	5	32	23	23	.282	.320	.345	86	-9	-9	51	4	6	-2	.989	-2	*O	-2.1
1970	Oak-A	154	575	70	156	25	3	8	55	32	31	.271	.311	.367	89	-12	-9	63	10	5	0	.977	-3	*O/1	-2.1
1971	Oak-A	2	8	0	2	1	0	0	0	0	1	.250	.250	.375	77	-0	-0	1	0	0	0	1.000	1	/O	0.0
	NY-A	131	461	52	133	20	6	8	69	32	24	.289	.337	.410	118	6	9	59	5	5	-2	.985	-12	O1	-1.4
	Yr	133	469	52	135	21	6	8	69	32	25	.288	.336	.409	117	5	9	60	5	5	-2	.986	-11	O1	-1.4
1972	NY-A	120	324	33	90	18	1	6	37	22	27	.278	.328	.395	118	5	6	41	1	0	0	.990	1	1O	0.1
1973	NY-A	93	280	25	66	12	0	4	27	9	25	.236	.260	.321	65	-14	-13	22	0	1	-1	.988	-1	1O	-2.1
	Mon-N	19	48	4	10	1	0	1	4	2	4	.208	.240	.292	45	-4	-4	2	0	1	-1	1.000	3	O/1	-0.2
1974	Mil-A	3	3	0	0	0	0	0	0	0	2	.000	.000	.000	-99	-1	-1	0	0	0	0	.000	-1	/O	-0.2
Total	17	2082	7339	985	2101	359	49	206	852	423	706	.286	.330	.433	114	101	115	1028	107	67	-8	.979	-41	*O1/3S	-4.0

■ JESUS ALOU Alou, Jesus Maria Rojas (b: Jesus Maria Rojas (Alou)) b: 3/24/42, Haina, D.R. BR/TR, 6'2", 195 lbs. Deb: 9/10/63 FC

YEAR	TM/L	G	AB	R	H	2B	3B	HR	RBI	BB	SO	AVG	OBP	SLG	PRO+	BR	/A	RC	SB	CS	SBR	FA	FR	POS	TPR
1963	SF-N	16	24	3	6	1	0	0	5	0	3	.250	.280	.292	66	-1	-1	1	0	1	-1	.875	-1	O	-0.3
1964	SF-N	115	376	42	103	11	0	3	28	13	35	.274	.305	.327	77	-11	-12	35	6	6	-2	.973	-1	*O	-2.0
1965	SF-N	143	543	76	162	19	4	9	52	13	40	.298	.318	.398	98	-1	-3	61	8	5	-1	.980	1	*O	-0.9
1966	SF-N	110	370	41	96	13	1	1	20	9	22	.259	.281	.308	62	-18	-19	28	5	5	-2	.967	-8	*O	-3.5
1967	SF-N	129	510	55	149	15	4	5	30	14	39	.292	.316	.367	96	-4	-3	55	1	7	-4	.948	-7	*O	-2.3
1968	SF-N	120	419	26	110	15	4	0	39	9	23	.263	.280	.317	79	-11	-11	31	1	4	-2	.989	1	*O	-2.1
1969	Hou-N	115	452	49	112	19	4	5	34	15	30	.248	.278	.341	74	-18	-17	38	4	6	-2	.928	-1	*O	-2.9
1970	Hou-N	117	458	59	140	27	3	1	44	21	15	.306	.338	.384	97	-5	-3	55	3	2	-0	.962	-7	*O	-1.5
1971	Hou-N	122	433	41	121	21	4	2	40	13	17	.279	.307	.360	91	-8	-6	43	3	7	-3	.983	4	*O	-1.1
1972	Hou-N	52	93	8	29	4	1	0	11	7	5	.312	.366	.376	114	2	2	11	0	2	-1	.970	-1	O	-0.2
1973	Hou-N	28	55	7	13	2	0	1	8	1	6	.236	.276	.327	67	-3	-3	4	0	0	0	.941	-2	O	-0.5
	*Oak-A	36	108	10	33	3	0	1	11	2	6	.306	.318	.361	96	-2	-1	12	0	0	0	1.000	-0	O/D	-0.2
1974	*Oak-A	96	220	13	59	8	0	2	15	5	9	.268	.291	.332	84	-6	-5	19	0	0	0	1.000	-1	DO	-0.7
1975	NY-N	62	102	8	27	3	0	0	11	4	5	.265	.299	.294	68	-5	-4	8	0	1	-1	.963	-0	O	-0.6
1978	Hou-N	77	139	7	45	5	1	2	19	6	5	.324	.352	.417	123	2	4	19	0	0	0	.976	-4	O	-0.1
1979	Hou-N	42	43	3	11	4	0	0	10	6	7	.256	.347	.349	96	-0	-0	4	0	0	0	1.000	-0	/O1	-0.1
Total	15	1380	4345	448	1216	170	26	32	377	138	267	.280	.307	.353	87	-89	-82	426	31	46	-18	.968	-28	*O/D1	-19.0

■ MATTY ALOU Alou, Mateo Rojas (b: Mateo Rojas (Alou)) b: 12/22/38, Haina, D.R. BL/TL, 5'9", 160 lbs. Deb: 9/26/60 F

YEAR	TM/L	G	AB	R	H	2B	3B	HR	RBI	BB	SO	AVG	OBP	SLG	PRO+	BR	/A	RC	SB	CS	SBR	FA	FR	POS	TPR
1960	SF-N	4	3	1	1	0	0	0	0	0	0	.333	.333	.333	88	-0	-0	0	0	0	0	1.000	-0	/O	0.0
1961	SF-N	81	200	38	62	7	2	6	24	15	18	.310	.358	.455	118	4	5	32	3	2	-0	.978	-3	O	-0.1
1962	*SF-N	78	195	28	57	8	1	3	14	14	17	.292	.349	.390	100	-0	0	27	3	1	0	.976	-2	O	-0.4
1963	SF-N	63	76	4	11	1	0	0	2	2	13	.145	.177	.158	-3	-10	-10	2	0	1	-1	.952	1	O	-1.1
1964	SF-N	110	250	28	66	4	2	1	14	11	25	.264	.303	.308	71	-9	-9	23	5	3	-0	.976	-5	O	-1.9
1965	SF-N	117	324	37	75	12	2	2	18	17	28	.231	.274	.299	60	-17	-18	24	10	2	2	.986	-7	*O/P	-2.8
1966	Pit-N	141	535	86	183	18	9	2	27	24	44	**.342**	.375	.421	121	15	15	84	23	15	-2	.972	-7	*O	-0.1
1967	Pit-N	139	550	87	186	21	7	2	28	24	42	.338	.372	.413	124	17	17	85	16	10	-1	.989	-6	*O/1	0.3
1968	Pit-N★	146	558	59	185	28	4	0	52	27	26	.332	.365	.396	130	19	19	79	18	10	-1	.984	-5	*O	0.7
1969	Pit-N★	162	698	105	**231**	**41**	6	1	48	42	35	.331	.371	.411	121	17	19	109	22	8	2	.977	-1	*O	1.1
1970	*Pit-N	155	677	97	201	21	8	1	47	30	18	.297	.331	.356	86	-15	-14	79	19	11	-1	.975	0	*O	-2.3
1971	StL-N	149	609	85	192	28	6	7	74	34	27	.315	.355	.415	113	13	11	89	19	10	-0	.981	2	O1	0.2
1972	StL-N	108	404	46	127	17	2	3	31	24	23	.314	.354	.389	112	6	6	54	11	4	1	.988	-1	1O	-0.2
	*Oak-A	32	121	11	34	5	0	1	16	11	12	.281	.346	.347	112	1	2	15	2	1	0	1.000	-2	O/1	-0.2
1973	NY-A	123	497	59	147	22	1	2	28	30	43	.296	.340	.356	100	-2	-0	57	5	2	0	.974	-4	O1/D	-1.1
	StL-N	11	11	1	3	0	0	0	1	1	0	.273	.333	.273	70	-0	-0	1	0	0	0	1.000	1	/1O	0.0
1974	SD-N	48	81	8	16	3	0	0	3	5	6	.198	.244	.235	36	-7	-7	4	0	0	0	.947	-2	O/1	-1.0
Total	15	1667	5789	780	1777	236	50	31	427	311	377	.307	.346	.381	105	30	35	764	156	80	-1	.979	-41	*O1/DP	-8.9

■ MOISES ALOU Alou, Moises Rojas (b: Moises Rojas) b: 7/3/66, Atlanta, Ga. BR/TR, 6'3", 185 lbs. Deb: 7/26/90 F

YEAR	TM/L	G	AB	R	H	2B	3B	HR	RBI	BB	SO	AVG	OBP	SLG	PRO+	BR	/A	RC	SB	CS	SBR	FA	FR	POS	TPR
1990	Pit-N	2	5	0	1	0	0	0	0	0	0	.200	.200	.200	11	-1	-1	0	0	0	0	1.000	-0	/O	-0.1
	Mon-N	14	15	4	3	0	1	0	0	0	3	.200	.200	.333	46	-1	-1	1	0	0	0	1.000	-0	/O	-0.1
	Yr	16	20	4	4	0	1	0	0	0	3	.200	.200	.300	37	-2	-2	1	0	0	0	1.000	-0	/O	-0.2
1992	Mon-N	115	341	53	96	28	2	9	56	25	46	.282	.332	.455	121	8	9	53	16	2	4	.978	-3	*O	0.8
Total	2	131	361	57	100	28	3	9	56	25	49	.277	.326	.446	117	7	7	55	16	2	4	.979	-3	O	0.6

■ WHITEY ALPERMAN Alperman, Charles Augustus b: 11/11/1879, Etna, Pa. d: 12/25/42, Pittsburgh, Pa. BR/TR, 5'10", 180 lbs. Deb: 4/13/06

YEAR	TM/L	G	AB	R	H	2B	3B	HR	RBI	BB	SO	AVG	OBP	SLG	PRO+	BR	/A	RC	SB	CS	SBR	FA	FR	POS	TPR
1906	Bro-N	128	441	38	111	15	7	3	46	6		.252	.275	.338	99	-7	-3	48	13			.940	2	*2S/3	0.0
1907	Bro-N	141	558	44	130	23	**16**	2	39	13		.233	.263	.342	98	-10	-5	54	5			.953	14	*23S	1.0
1908	Bro-N	70	213	17	42	3	1	1	15	9		.197	.247	.235	56	-11	-10	13	2			.934	-5	2/3OS	-1.8
1909	Bro-N	111	420	35	104	19	12	1	41	2		.248	.262	.357	95	-7	-5	40	7			.931	9	*2	0.2
Total	4	450	1632	134	387	60	36	7	141	30		.237	.264	.331	92	-34	-24	155	27			.941	20	2/S3O	-0.6

■ TOM ALSTON Alston, Thomas Edison b: 1/31/31, Greensboro, N.C. BL/TR, 6'5", 210 lbs. Deb: 4/13/54

YEAR	TM/L	G	AB	R	H	2B	3B	HR	RBI	BB	SO	AVG	OBP	SLG	PRO+	BR	/A	RC	SB	CS	SBR	FA	FR	POS	TPR
1954	StL-N	66	244	28	60	14	2	4	34	24	41	.246	.319	.369	78	-8	-8	27	3	5	-2	.989	10	1	-0.4
1955	StL-N	13	8	0	1	0	0	0	0	0	0	.125	.125	.125	-33	-2	-2	0	0	0	0	1.000	0	/1	-0.1
1956	StL-N	3	2	0	0	0	0	0	0	0	0	.000	.000	.000	-99	-1	-1	0	0	0	0	1.000	0	/1	0.0
1957	StL-N	9	17	2	5	1	0	0	2	1	5	.294	.333	.353	83	-0	-0	2	0	0	0	.947	-1	/1	-0.2
Total	4	91	271	30	66	15	2	4	36	25	46	.244	.312	.358	74	-10	-11	30	3	5	-2	.987	9	/1	-0.7

■ WALTER ALSTON Alston, Walter Emmons "Smokey" b: 12/1/11, Venice, Ohio d: 10/1/84, Oxford, Ohio BR/TR, 6'2", 195 lbs. Deb: 9/27/36 MH

YEAR	TM/L	G	AB	R	H	2B	3B	HR	RBI	BB	SO	AVG	OBP	SLG	PRO+	BR	/A	RC	SB	CS	SBR	FA	FR	POS	TPR
1936	StL-N	1	1	0	0	0	0	0	0	0	1	.000	.000	.000	-99	-0	-0	0	0			.500	-0	/1	-0.1

YEAR	TM/L	G	AB	R	H	2B	3B	HR	RBI	BB	SO	AVG	OBP	SLG	PRO+	BR	/A	RC	SB	CS	SBR	FA	FR	POS	TPR

■ DELL ALSTON Alston, Wendell b: 9/22/52, Valhalla, N.Y. BL/TR, 6', 180 lbs. Deb: 5/17/77

1977	NY-A	22	40	10	13	4	0	1	4	3	4	.325	.372	.500	137	2	2	6	3	3	-1	1.000	0	D/O	0.1
1978	NY-A	3	3	0	0	0	0	0	0	0	2	.000	.000	.000	-99	-1	-1	0	0	0	0	.000	0	H	-0.1
	Oak-A	58	173	17	36	2	0	1	10	10	21	.208	.251	.237	40	-14	-13	10	11	10	-3	.956	-5	O/1D	-2.4
	Yr	61	176	17	36	2	0	1	10	10	23	.205	.247	.233	38	-15	-14	10	11	10	-3	.956	-5	O/1D	-2.5
1979	Cle-A	54	62	10	18	0	2	1	12	10	10	.290	.389	.403	114	2	2	10	4	4	-1	.969	-5	O	-0.5
1980	Cle-A	52	54	11	12	1	2	0	9	5	7	.222	.281	.315	72	-2	-2	5	2	4	-2	.947	-4	O/D	-0.8
Total	4	189	332	48	79	7	4	3	35	28	44	.238	.301	.310	71	-13	-12	30	20	21	-7	.957	-14	O/D1	-3.7

■ JESSE ALTENBURG Altenburg, Jesse Howard b: 1/2/1893, Ashley, Mich. d: 3/12/73, Lansing, Mich. BL/TR, 5'9", 158 lbs. Deb: 9/19/16

1916	Pit-N	8	14	2	6	1	1	0	0	1	1	.429	.467	.643	237	2	2	4	0			1.000	-2	/O	0.0
1917	Pit-N	11	17	1	3	0	0	0	3	0	4	.176	.176	.176	8	-2	-2	1	0			1.000	-1	/O	-0.3
Total	2	19	31	3	9	1	1	0	3	1	5	.290	.313	.387	112	0	0	5	0			1.000	-3	/O	-0.3

■ DAVE ALTIZER Altizer, David Tilden "Filipino" b: 11/6/1876, Pearl, Ill. d: 5/14/64, Pleasant Hill, Ill BL/TR, 5'10.5", 160 lbs. Deb: 5/29/06

1906	Was-A	115	433	56	111	9	5	1	27	35		.256	.322	.307	102	-0	2	58	37			.931	-21	*S/O	-1.7
1907	Was-A	147	540	60	145	15	5	2	42	34		.269	.315	.326	114	3	7	71	38			.927	-10	S1O	-0.3
1908	Was-A	67	205	19	46	1	1	0	18	13		.224	.274	.239	73	-7	-5	16	8			.959	-2	23/1S	-0.9
	Cle-A	29	89	11	19	1	2	0	5	7		.213	.278	.270	78	-2	-2	9	7			.952	4	O/S	0.1
	Yr	96	294	30	65	2	3	0	23	20		.221	.275	.248	75	-9	-7	26	15			.959	1	203/1S	-0.8
1909	Chi-A	116	382	47	89	6	7	1	20	39		.233	.330	.293	101	1	2	47	27			.949	8	O1	0.8
1910	Cin-N	3	10	3	6	0	0	0	0	3	0	.600	.692	.600	290	3	3	4	0			.933	-2	/S	0.1
1911	Cin-N	37	75	8	17	4	1	0	4	9	5	.227	.318	.307	78	-2	-2	8	2			.907	1	S/12O	0.0
Total	6	514	1734	204	433	36	21	4	116	140	5	.250	.316	.302	101	-6	5	215	119			.926	-22	SO1/23	-1.9

■ GEORGE ALTMAN Altman, George Lee b: 3/20/33, Goldsboro, N.C. BL/TR, 6'4", 200 lbs. Deb: 4/11/59

1959	Chi-N	135	420	54	103	14	4	12	47	34	80	.245	.312	.383	85	-10	-9	51	1	0	0	.990	4	*O	-1.1
1960	Chi-N	119	334	50	89	16	4	13	51	32	67	.266	.332	.455	114	5	6	51	4	3	-1	.993	-5	O1	-0.4
1961	Chi-N★	138	518	77	157	28	**12**	27	96	40	92	.303	.358	.560	137	27	26	105	6	2	1	.978	6	*O/1	2.4
1962	Chi-N★	147	534	74	170	27	5	22	74	62	89	.318	.394	.511	136	31	29	110	19	7	2	.972	1	*O1	2.2
1963	StL-N	135	464	62	127	18	7	9	47	47	93	.274	.343	.401	104	8	4	66	13	4	2	.979	1	*O	0.0
1964	NY-N	124	422	48	97	14	1	9	47	18	70	.230	.263	.332	68	-19	-18	35	4	2	0	.968	6	*O	-1.9
1965	Chi-N	90	196	24	46	7	1	4	23	19	36	.235	.302	.342	79	-5	-5	21	3	2	-0	.943	-5	O/1	-1.3
1966	Chi-N	88	185	19	41	6	0	5	17	14	37	.222	.276	.335	68	-8	-8	17	2	2	-1	.958	-4	O/1	-1.5
1967	Chi-N	15	18	1	2	2	0	0	1	2	8	.111	.200	.222	20	-2	-2	1	0	0	0	1.000	-1	/O1	-0.3
Total	9	991	3091	409	832	132	34	101	403	268	572	.269	.331	.432	105	29	22	456	52	22	2	.977	3	O/1	-1.9

■ JOE ALTOBELLI Altobelli, Joseph Salvatore b: 5/26/32, Detroit, Mich. BL/TL, 6', 185 lbs. Deb: 4/14/55 MC

1955	Cle-A	42	75	8	15	3	0	2	5	5	14	.200	.259	.320	53	-5	-5	6	0	1	-1	.992	-1	1	-0.8
1957	Cle-A	83	87	9	18	3	2	0	9	5	14	.207	.258	.287	49	-6	-6	7	3	2	-0	.994	-0	1/O	-0.8
1961	Min-A	41	95	10	21	2	1	3	14	13	14	.221	.315	.358	75	-3	-3	11	0	0		.951	-2	O/1	-0.7
Total	3	166	257	27	54	8	3	5	28	23	42	.210	.280	.323	60	-14	-15	24	3	3	-1	.993	-3	/1O	-2.3

■ NICK ALTROCK Altrock, Nicholas b: 9/15/1876, Cincinnati, Ohio d: 1/20/65, Washington, D.C. BB/TL, 5'10", 197 lbs. Deb: 7/14/1898 C

1898	Lou-N	11	29	4	7	0	0	0	2	2	2	.241	.313	.241	60	-1	-1	3	1			1.000	2	P	0.0
1902	Bos-A	3	8	0	0	0	0	0	0	0		.000	.000	.000	-97	-2	-2	0	0			.818	1	/P	0.0
1903	Bos-A	1	3	0	2	0	0	0	0	1		.667	.750	.667	311	1	1	2	0			1.000	1	/P	0.0
	Chi-A	13	30	6	9	0	0	0	3	3		.300	.364	.300	106	0	0	4	1			.935	3	P	0.0
	Yr	14	33	6	11	0	0	0	3	4		.333	.405	.333	128	1	1	5	1			.944	4	P	0.0
1904	Chi-A	41	111	13	22	1	0	1	8	4		.198	.239	.234	52	-6	-6	7	0			.969	4	P/1	0.0
1905	Chi-A	40	112	8	14	1	0	0	5	6		.125	.190	.134	4	-12	-11	3	0			.988	8	P/1	0.0
1906	*Chi-A	38	100	4	16	2	0	0	3	8		.160	.222	.180	27	-8	-8	5	2			.970	4	P/1	0.0
1907	Chi-A	30	72	7	13	0	0	0	2	3		.181	.234	.222	47	-4	-4	4	0			.958	5	P	0.0
1908	Chi-A	23	49	6	10	2	0	0	3	0		.204	.235	.245	57	-2	-2	3	1			.967	5	P	0.0
1909	Chi-A	1	3	0	0	0	0	0	0	0		.000	.000	.000	-99	-1	-1	0	0			1.000	0	/P	0.0
	Was-A	12	19	2	1	0	0	0	0	1		.053	.143	.053	-40	-3	-3	0	0			.905	-0	/PO	-0.2
	Yr	13	22	2	1	0	0	0	0	1		.045	.125	.045	-48	-4	-3	0	0			.920	-0	/PO	-0.2
1912	Was-A	1	1	0	0	0	0	0	0	0		.000	.000	.000	-99	-0	-0	0	0			.000	0	/P1	0.0
1913	Was-A	1	1	0	0	0	0	0	0	0		.000	.000	.000	-98	-0	-0	0	0			.833	0	/P	0.0
1914	Was-A	1	0	0	0	0	0	0	0	0		—	—	—	—	0	0	0	0			.000	-0	/P	0.0
1915	Was-A	1	1	0	0	0	0	0	0	0		.000	.000	.000	-98	-0	-0	0	0			.000	-0	/P	0.0
1918	Was-A	5	8	1	1	0	0	1	1	0		.125	.125	.500	90	-0	-0	1	0			.917	0	/P1	0.0
1919	Was-A	1	0	0	0	0	0	0	0	0		—	—	—	—	0	0	0	0			.000	0	/P	0.0
1924	Was-A	1	1	1	1	0	0	0	0	0		1.000	1.000	3.000	935	1	1	3	0	0	0	.667	-0	/P	0.0
1929	Was-A	1	1	0	1	0	0	0	0	0		1.000	1.000	1.000	413	0	0	1	0	0	0	.000	-0	/O	0.0
1931	Was-A	1	0	0	0	0	0	0	0	1		—	1.000	—	182	0	0	0	0	1	-1	.000	0	H	0.0
1933	Was-A	1	1	0	0	0	0	0	0	0		.000	.000	.000	-99	-0	-0	0	0			.000	0	H	0.0
Total	19	230	550	52	97	9	1	2	27	29	0	.176	.232	.207	39	-39	-37	34	5	1		.964	33	P/1O	-0.2

■ GEORGE ALUSIK Alusik, George Joseph b: 2/11/35, Ashley, Pa. BR/TR, 6'3.5", 175 lbs. Deb: 9/11/58

1958	Det-A	2	2	0	0	0	0	0	0	0	1	.000	.000	.000	-93	-1	-1	0	0	0	0	1.000	-0	/O	-0.1
1961	Det-A	15	14	0	2	0	0	0	2	1	4	.143	.200	.143	-6	-2	-2	1	0	0	0	.000	-0	/O	-0.3
1962	Det-A	2	2	0	0	0	0	0	0	0	0	.000	.000	.000	-97	-1	-1	0	0	0	0	.000	0	H	-0.1
	KC-A	90	209	29	57	10	1	11	35	16	29	.273	.327	.488	113	4	3	33	1	1	-0	.968	-3	O/1	-0.3
	Yr	92	211	29	57	10	1	11	35	16	29	.270	.325	.483	111	3	3	32	1	1	-0	.968	-3	O/1	-0.4
1963	KC-A	87	221	28	59	11	0	9	37	26	33	.267	.347	.439	114	6	5	33	0	1	-1	1.000	-3	O	-0.2
1964	KC-A	102	204	18	49	10	1	3	19	30	36	.240	.343	.343	89	-1	-2	25	0	0	0	.984	-4	O1	-0.9
Total	5	298	652	75	167	31	2	23	93	73	103	.256	.335	.416	102	5	2	91	1	2	-0	.985	-10	O/1	-1.9

■ LUIS ALVARADO Alvarado, Luis Cesar (Martinez) b: 1/15/49, LaJas, P.R. BR/TR, 5'9", 162 lbs. Deb: 9/13/68

1968	Bos-A	11	46	3	6	2	0	0	1	1	11	.130	.167	.174	3	-5	-6	1	0	0	0	.976	-4	S	-1.0
1969	Bos-A	6	5	0	0	0	0	0	0	0	0	.000	.000	.000	-95	-1	-1	0	0	1	-1	1.000	2	/S	0.0
1970	Bos-A	59	183	19	41	11	0	1	10	9	30	.224	.260	.301	51	-12	-13	13	1	2	-1	.929	5	3S	-0.7
1971	Chi-A	99	264	22	57	14	1	0	8	11	34	.216	.247	.277	47	-18	-19	18	1	2	-1	.959	15	S2	0.4
1972	Chi-A	103	254	30	54	4	1	4	29	13	36	.213	.254	.283	58	-13	-13	15	2	2	-0	.957	2	S2/3	-0.3
1973	Chi-A	80	203	21	47	7	2	0	20	4	20	.232	.250	.286	49	-14	-14	14	6	2	1	.980	5	2S3/D	-0.5
1974	Chi-A	8	10	1	1	0	0	0	0	0	1	.100	.100	.100	-41	-2	-2	0	0	0	0	.667	-1	/S23	-0.3
	StL-N	17	36	3	5	2	0	0	1	2	6	.139	.184	.194	6	-5	-5	1	0	0	0	.980	-1	/S	-0.5
	Cle-A	61	114	12	25	2	0	1	12	6	14	.219	.258	.237	44	-8	-8	7	1	1	-0	.972	11	2/SD	0.4
1976	StL-N	16	42	5	12	1	0	0	3	3	6	.286	.333	.310	82	-1	-1	5	0	0	0	.936	-9	2	-1.0
1977	NY-N	1	2	0	0	0	0	0	0	0	0	.000	.000	.000	-99	-1	-1	0	0	0	0	1.000	0	/2	0.0
	Det-A	2	1	0	0	0	0	0	0	0	0	.000	.000	.000	-95	-0	-0	0	0	0	0	.000	0	/3	0.0
Total	9	463	1160	116	248	43	4	5	84	49	160	.214	.248	.271	47	-79	-83	74	11	10	-3	.957	26	S2/3D	-3.5

YEAR	TM/L	G	AB	R	H	2B	3B	HR	RBI	BB	SO	AVG	OBP	SLG	PRO+	BR	/A	RC	SB	CS	SBR	FA	FR	POS	TPR

■ ORLANDO ALVAREZ Alvarez, Jesus Manuel Orlando (Monge) b: 2/28/52, Rio Grande, P.R. BR/TR, 6′, 165 lbs. Deb: 9/01/73

1973	LA-N	4	4	0	1	1	0	0	0	0	1	.250	.250	.500	108	-0	0	1	0	0	0	.000	0	H	0.0
1974	LA-N	2	1	0	0	0	0	0	0	0	0	.000	.000	.000	-99	-0	-0	0	0	0	0	1.000	0	/O	0.0
1975	LA-N	4	4	0	0	0	0	0	0	0	1	.000	.000	.000	-99	-1	-1	0	0	0	0	.000	0	H	-0.1
1976	Cal-A	15	42	4	7	1	0	2	8	0	3	.167	.167	.333	47	-3	-3	2	0	0	0	1.000	-1	O/D	-0.5
Total	4	25	51	4	8	2	0	2	8	0	5	.157	.157	.314	36	-5	-4	3	0	0	0	1.000	-1	/OD	-0.6

■ OSSIE ALVAREZ Alvarez, Oswaldo (Gonzalez) b: 10/19/33, Matanzas, Cuba BR/TR, 5′10″, 165 lbs. Deb: 4/19/58

1958	Was-A	87	196	20	41	3	0	0	5	16	26	.209	.269	.224	38	-16	-16	13	1	1	-0	.968	12	S2/3	0.1
1959	Det-A	8	2	0	1	0	0	0	0	0	1	.500	.500	.500	166	0	0	1	0	0	0	.000	0	H	0.0
Total	2	95	198	20	42	3	0	0	5	16	27	.212	.271	.227	39	-16	-16	13	1	1	-0		12	/S23	0.1

■ ROGELIO ALVAREZ Alvarez, Rogelio (Hernandez) b: 4/18/38, Pinar Del Rio, Cuba BR/TR, 5′11″, 183 lbs. Deb: 9/18/60

1960	Cin-N	3	9	1	1	0	0	0	0	0	3	.111	.111	.111	-38	-2	-2	0	0	0	0	1.000	-1	/1	-0.3
1962	Cin-N	14	28	1	6	0	0	0	2	1	10	.214	.241	.214	23	-3	-3	2	0	0	0	.973	-1	1	-0.4
Total	2	17	37	2	7	0	0	0	2	1	13	.189	.211	.189	8	-5	-5	2	0	0	0	.979	-1	/1	-0.7

■ MAX ALVIS Alvis, Roy Maxwell b: 2/2/38, Jasper, Tex. BR/TR, 5′11″, 187 lbs. Deb: 9/11/62

1962	Cle-A	12	51	1	11	2	0	3	2	13	.216	.245	.255	36	-5	-4	3	3	1	0	.935	-4	3	-0.8	
1963	Cle-A	158	602	81	165	32	7	22	67	36	109	.274	.326	.460	118	12	13	90	9	7	-2	.942	-5	*3	0.7
1964	Cle-A	107	381	51	96	14	3	18	53	29	77	.252	.315	.446	110	4	4	53	5	5	-2	.955	-7	*3	-0.6
1965	Cle-A★	159	604	88	149	24	2	21	61	47	121	.247	.311	.397	99	-1	-2	74	12	8	-1	.958	-19	*3	-2.7
1966	Cle-A	157	596	67	146	22	3	17	55	50	98	.245	.306	.378	95	-4	-4	66	4	7	-3	.958	-6	*3	-1.8
1967	Cle-A★	161	637	66	163	23	4	21	70	38	107	.256	.302	.403	106	3	3	73	3	10	-5	.965	-8	*3	-1.3
1968	Cle-A	131	452	38	101	17	3	8	37	41	91	.223	.294	.327	89	-7	-6	42	5	5	-2	.960	-17	*3	-2.8
1969	Cle-A	66	191	13	43	6	0	1	15	14	26	.225	.278	.272	53	-12	-12	13	1	1	-0	.973	-2	3/S	-1.5
1970	Mil-A	62	115	16	21	2	0	3	12	5	20	.183	.217	.278	35	-10	-10	5	1	2	-1	.909	2	3	-1.0
Total	9	1013	3629	421	895	142	22	111	373	262	662	.247	.304	.390	97	-19	-19	420	43	46	-15	.956	-64	3/S	-11.8

■ BILLY ALVORD Alvord, William Charles "Uncle Bill" b: 8/1863, St.Louis, Mo. 5′10″, 187 lbs. Deb: 4/30/1885

1885	StL-N	2	5	0	0	0	0	0	0	1	2	.000	.167	.000	-45	-1	-1	0				.714	-1	/3	-0.1
1889	KC-a	50	186	23	43	8	9	0	18	10	35	.231	.270	.371	79	-5	-7	20	3			.877	5	3/S2	0.0
1890	Tol-a	116	495	69	135	13	16	2		22		.273	.304	.376	100	-1	-3	64	21			.872	4	*3	0.4
1891	Cle-N	13	59	7	17	2	2	1	7	0	7	.288	.300	.441	112	1	0	8	0			.814	-2	3	-0.1
	Was-a	81	312	28	73	8	3	0	30	11	38	.234	.260	.279	59	-18	-16	24	3			.862	17	3	0.4
1893	Cle-N	3	12	2	2	0	0	0	2	0	1	.167	.167	.167	-10	-2	-2	0	0			.875	-2	/3	-0.3
Total	5	265	1069	129	270	31	30	3	57	44	83	.253	.283	.346	83	-26	-28	117	27			.865	22	3/2S	0.3

■ BRANT ALYEA Alyea, Garrabrant Ryerson b: 12/8/40, Passaic, N.J. BR/TR, 6′3″, 215 lbs. Deb: 9/11/65

1965	Was-A	8	13	3	3	0	0	2	6	1	4	.231	.286	.692	171	1	1	2	0	0	0	1.000	-1	/1O	0.0
1968	Was-A	53	150	18	40	11	1	6	23	10	39	.267	.317	.473	141	6	6	21	0	0	0	1.000	1	O	0.6
1969	Was-A	104	237	29	59	4	0	11	40	34	67	.249	.346	.405	115	3	5	32	1	3	-2	.938	-7	O/1	-0.8
1970	*Min-A	94	258	34	75	12	1	16	61	28	51	.291	.367	.531	143	15	15	46	3	3	-1	.980	-5	O	0.6
1971	Min-A	79	158	13	28	4	0	2	15	24	38	.177	.290	.241	50	-10	-10	11	1	1	-0	.962	-6	O	-2.0
1972	Oak-A	20	31	3	6	1	0	1	2	3	5	.194	.265	.323	78	-1	-1	3	0	0	0	1.000	1	/O	0.2
	StL-N	13	19	0	3	1	0	0	1	0	6	.158	.158	.211	4	-2	-2	1	0	0	0	1.000	1	/O	-0.2
Total	6	371	866	100	214	33	2	38	148	100	210	.247	.329	.421	113	12	13	115	5	7	-3	.972	-14	O/1	-1.6

■ JOEY AMALFITANO Amalfitano, John Joseph b: 1/23/34, San Pedro, Cal. BR/TR, 5′11″, 180 lbs. Deb: 5/03/54 MC

1954	NY-N	9	5	2	0	0	0	0	0	0	4	.000	.000	.000	-99	-1	-1	0	0	0	0	1.000	2	/32	0.1
1955	NY-N	36	22	8	5	1	1	0	1	2	2	.227	.292	.364	72	-1	-1	2	0	0	0	.957	12	/S3	1.0
1960	SF-N	106	328	42	91	15	3	1	27	26	31	.277	.336	.351	94	-5	-2	39	2	3	-1	.935	3	32/SO	0.2
1961	SF-N	109	384	64	98	11	4	2	23	44	59	.255	.332	.320	77	-13	-11	44	7	4	-0	.970	-22	2/3	-2.3
1962	Hou-N	117	380	44	90	12	5	1	27	45	43	.237	.319	.303	73	-16	-12	36	4	4	-1	.967	2	*2/3	-0.2
1963	SF-N	54	137	11	24	3	0	1	7	12	18	.175	.247	.219	36	-11	-11	6	2	6	-3	.980	-3	2/3	-1.6
1964	Chi-N	100	324	51	78	19	6	4	27	40	42	.241	.333	.373	95	0	0	38	2	7	-4	.964	2	2/1S	0.5
1965	Chi-N	67	96	13	26	4	0	0	8	12	14	.271	.364	.313	90	-0	-1	12	2	2	-1	.989	5	2/S	0.5
1966	Chi-N	41	38	8	6	2	0	0	3	4	10	.158	.238	.211	26	-4	-4	2	0	0	0	.977	1	2/3S	-0.2
1967	Chi-N	4	1	0	0	0	0	0	0	0	1	.000	.000	.000	-96	-0	-0	0	0	0	0	.000	0	H	-0.1
Total	10	643	1715	248	418	67	19	9	123	185	224	.244	.322	.321	78	-52	-46	180	19	26	-10	.970	2	2/3S10	-2.0

■ RICH AMARAL Amaral, Richard Louis b: 4/1/62, Visalia, Cal. BR/TR, 6′, 175 lbs. Deb: 5/27/91

1991	Sea-A	14	16	2	1	0	0	0	0	1	5	.063	.167	.063	-34	-3	-3	0	0	0	0	1.000	4	/23S1D	0.1
1992	Sea-A	35	100	9	24	3	0	1	7	5	16	.240	.276	.300	61	-5	-5	7	4	2	0	.955	2	3S/012	-0.3
Total	2	49	116	11	25	3	0	1	7	6	21	.216	.260	.267	47	-8	-8	8	4	2	0	.956	5	/S3201D	-0.2

■ RUBEN AMARO Amaro, Ruben Jr. b: 2/12/65, Philadelphia, Pa. BB/TR, 5′10″, 170 lbs. Deb: 6/08/91 F

1991	Cal-A	10	23	0	5	1	0	0	2	3	3	.217	.308	.261	59	-1	-1	2	0	0	0	1.000	-3	/O2D	-0.4
1992	Phi-N	126	374	43	82	15	6	7	34	37	54	.219	.305	.348	85	-8	-7	40	11	5	0	.992	0	*O	-1.0
Total	2	136	397	43	87	16	6	7	36	40	57	.219	.305	.343	83	-9	-8	41	11	5	0	.992	-3	O/2D	-1.4

■ RUBEN AMARO Amaro, Ruben Sr. (Mora) b: 1/6/36, Vera Cruz, Mexico BR/TR, 5′11″, 170 lbs. Deb: 6/29/58 FC

1958	StL-N	40	76	8	17	2	1	0	0	5	8	.224	.272	.276	44	-6	-6	5	0	1	-1	.948	3	S/2	-0.2
1960	Phi-N	92	264	25	61	9	1	0	16	21	32	.231	.293	.273	56	-16	-16	21	0	1	-1	.965	-8	S	-1.9
1961	Phi-N	135	381	34	98	14	9	1	32	53	59	.257	.351	.349	88	-6	-6	49	1	0	0	.970	14	*S/12	1.9
1962	Phi-N	79	226	24	55	10	0	0	19	30	28	.243	.335	.288	71	-9	-8	23	5	2	0	.968	6	S/1	0.5
1963	Phi-N	115	217	25	47	9	2	2	19	19	31	.217	.280	.304	69	-9	-9	18	0	1	-1	.950	2	S3/1	-0.4
1964	Phi-N	129	299	31	79	11	0	4	34	16	37	.264	.308	.341	84	-7	-6	30	1	6	-3	.971	-4	S1/230	-0.2
1965	Phi-N	118	184	26	39	7	0	0	15	27	22	.212	.316	.250	63	-8	-8	15	1	1	-0	.990	-3	1S/2	-0.8
1966	NY-A	14	23	0	5	0	0	0	3	0	2	.217	.217	.217	26	-2	-2	1	0	0	0	.977	5	S	0.4
1967	NY-A	130	417	31	93	12	0	1	17	43	49	.223	.297	.259	68	-17	-15	32	3	2	-0	.973	9	*S/31	0.5
1968	NY-A	47	41	3	5	1	0	0	0	9	6	.122	.280	.146	33	-3	-3	4	0	0	0	.962	-0	S1	-0.3
1969	Cal-A	41	27	4	6	0	0	0	1	4	6	.222	.323	.222	58	-1	-1	3	0	0	0	1.000	0	1/2S3	-0.1
Total	11	940	2155	211	505	75	13	8	156	227	280	.234	.310	.292	70	-84	-79	200	11	14	-5	.967	24	S1/320	-1.4

■ WAYNE AMBLER Ambler, Wayne Harper b: 11/8/15, Abington, Pa. BR/TR, 5′8.5″, 165 lbs. Deb: 6/04/37

1937	Phi-A	56	162	3	35	5	0	0	11	13	8	.216	.274	.247	33	-17	-16	12	1	0	0	.955	-4	2	-1.6
1938	Phi-A	120	393	42	92	21	2	0	38	48	31	.234	.317	.298	56	-27	-25	40	2	1	0	.942	-19	*S/2	-3.3
1939	Phi-A	95	227	15	48	13	0	0	24	22	25	.211	.281	.269	42	-20	-19	17	1	0	1	.954	-3	S2	-1.5
Total	3	271	782	60	175	39	2	0	73	83	64	.224	.298	.279	47	-64	-61	69	4	1	1	.946	-26	S/2	-6.4

■ ED AMELUNG Amelung, Edward Allen b: 4/13/59, Fullerton, Cal. BL/TL, 5′11″, 180 lbs. Deb: 7/28/84

1984	LA-N	34	46	7	10	0	0	0	4	2	4	.217	.250	.217	33	-4	-4	2	3	2	-0	1.000	-3	O	-0.8
1986	LA-N	8	11	0	1	0	0	0	0	2	4	.091	.091	.091	-53	-2	-2	0	0	0	0	1.000	-1	/O	-0.3
Total	2	42	57	7	11	0	0	0	4	2	8	.193	.220	.193	17	-6	-6	2	3	2	-0	1.000	-4	/O	-1.1

■ SANDY AMOROS

Amoros, Edmundo (Isasi) b: 1/30/30, Havana, Cuba d: 6/27/92, Miami, Fla. BL/TL, 5'7.5", 170 lbs. Deb: 8/22/52

YEAR	TM/L	G	AB	R	H	2B	3B	HR	RBI	BB	SO	AVG	OBP	SLG	PRO+	BR	/A	RC	SB	CS	SBR	FA	FR	POS	TPR
1952	*Bro-N	20	44	10	11	3	1	0	3	5	14	.250	.327	.364	90	-1	-1	6	1	0	0	1.000	-3	O	-0.4
1954	Bro-N	79	263	44	72	18	6	9	34	31	24	.274	.353	.490	113	6	5	45	1	4	-2	.987	5	O	0.4
1955	*Bro-N	119	388	59	96	16	7	10	51	55	45	.247	.350	.402	96	0	-1	57	10	5	0	.972	-1	*O	-0.7
1956	*Bro-N	114	292	53	76	11	8	16	58	59	51	.260	.386	.517	130	18	15	61	3	4	-2	.955	-10	O	-0.2
1957	Bro-N	106	238	40	66	7	1	7	26	46	42	.277	.401	.403	107	8	5	41	3	2	-0	.984	-1	O	0.0
1959	LA-N	5	5	1	1	0	0	0	1	0	1	.200	.200	.200	6	-1	-1	0	0	0	0	.000	0	H	-0.1
1960	LA-N	9	14	1	2	0	0	0	0	3	2	.143	.294	.143	23	-1	-1	1	0	0	0	1.000	0	/O	-0.1
	Det-A	65	67	7	10	0	0	1	7	12	10	.149	.278	.194	29	-6	-7	4	0	0	0	1.000	-1	O	-0.8
Total	7	517	1311	215	334	55	23	43	180	211	189	.255	.363	.430	105	23	14	215	18	15	-4	.976	-11	O	-1.9

■ ALF ANDERSON

Anderson, Alfred Walton b: 1/28/14, Gainesville, Ga. d: 6/23/85, Albany, Ga. BR/TR, 5'11", 165 lbs. Deb: 4/20/41

YEAR	TM/L	G	AB	R	H	2B	3B	HR	RBI	BB	SO	AVG	OBP	SLG	PRO+	BR	/A	RC	SB	CS	SBR	FA	FR	POS	TPR
1941	Pit-N	70	223	32	48	7	2	1	10	14	30	.215	.265	.278	53	-14	-14	17	2			.931	-6	S	-1.7
1942	Pit-N	54	166	24	45	4	1	0	7	18	19	.271	.342	.307	89	-1	-2	18	4			.942	-15	S	-1.6
1946	Pit-N	2	1	0	0	0	0	0	0	1	0	.000	.500	.000	47	0	0	0	0			.000	0	H	0.0
Total	3	126	390	56	93	11	3	1	17	33	49	.238	.300	.290	68	-15	-16	35	6			.936	-21	S	-3.3

■ ANDY ANDERSON

Anderson, Andy Holm b: 11/13/22, Bremerton, Wash. d: 7/18/82, Seattle, Wash. BR/TR, 5'11", 172 lbs. Deb: 5/10/48

YEAR	TM/L	G	AB	R	H	2B	3B	HR	RBI	BB	SO	AVG	OBP	SLG	PRO+	BR	/A	RC	SB	CS	SBR	FA	FR	POS	TPR
1948	StL-A	51	87	13	24	5	1	1	12	8	15	.276	.337	.391	91	-1	-1	10	0	0	0	.917	-2	2S/1	-0.2
1949	StL-A	71	136	10	17	3	0	1	5	14	21	.125	.207	.169	-0	-20	-21	5	0	1	-1	.957	-7	S/23	-2.6
Total	2	122	223	23	41	8	1	2	17	22	36	.184	.257	.256	35	-21	-22	15	0	1	-1	.946	-9	/S231	-2.8

■ BRADY ANDERSON

Anderson, Brady Kevin b: 1/18/64, Silver Spring, Md. BL/TL, 6'1", 170 lbs. Deb: 4/04/88

YEAR	TM/L	G	AB	R	H	2B	3B	HR	RBI	BB	SO	AVG	OBP	SLG	PRO+	BR	/A	RC	SB	CS	SBR	FA	FR	POS	TPR
1988	Bos-A	41	148	14	34	5	3	0	12	15	35	.230	.317	.304	72	-5	-5	16	4	2	0	.989	2	O	-0.5
	Bal-A	53	177	17	35	8	1	1	9	8	40	.198	.232	.271	42	-14	-14	11	6	4	-1	.981	5	O	-1.1
	Yr	94	325	31	69	13	4	1	21	23	75	.212	.273	.286	57	-19	-19	27	10	6	-1	.984	7	O	-1.6
1989	Bal-A	94	266	44	55	12	2	4	16	43	45	.207	.324	.312	82	-6	-5	31	16	4	2	.985	-2	O/D	-0.7
1990	Bal-A	89	234	24	54	5	2	3	24	31	46	.231	.333	.308	83	-5	-4	28	15	2	3	.987	2	OD	0.0
1991	Bal-A	113	256	40	59	12	3	2	27	38	44	.230	.341	.324	89	-4	-2	33	12	5	1	.981	-15	*O/D	-1.9
1992	Bal-A★	159	623	100	169	28	10	21	80	98	98	.271	.378	.449	131	28	28	118	53	16	6	.980	14	*O	4.5
Total	5	549	1704	239	406	70	21	31	168	233	308	.238	.339	.359	97	-6	-2	236	106	33	12	.983	6	O/D	0.3

■ DAVE ANDERSON

Anderson, David Carter b: 8/1/60, Louisville, Ky. BR/TR, 6'2", 185 lbs. Deb: 5/08/83

YEAR	TM/L	G	AB	R	H	2B	3B	HR	RBI	BB	SO	AVG	OBP	SLG	PRO+	BR	/A	RC	SB	CS	SBR	FA	FR	POS	TPR
1983	LA-N	61	115	12	19	4	2	1	2	12	15	.165	.244	.261	40	-9	-9	8	6	3	0	.969	3	S/3	-0.3
1984	LA-N	121	374	51	94	16	2	3	34	45	55	.251	.335	.329	88	-5	-5	44	15	5	2	.965	19	*S3	2.6
1985	*LA-N	77	221	24	44	6	0	4	18	35	42	.199	.311	.281	69	-9	-8	21	5	4	-1	.957	17	3S/2	1.0
1986	LA-N	92	216	31	53	9	0	1	15	22	39	.245	.315	.301	76	-8	-6	20	5	1	1	.976	9	3S/2	0.6
1987	LA-N	108	265	32	62	12	3	1	13	24	43	.234	.300	.313	64	-14	-13	26	9	5	-0	.977	6	S3/2	-0.3
1988	*LA-N	116	285	31	71	10	2	2	20	32	45	.249	.327	.319	89	-4	-3	30	4	2	0	.986	14	S32	1.8
1989	LA-N	87	140	15	32	2	0	1	14	17	26	.229	.312	.264	67	-6	-5	13	2	0	1	.990	0	S3/2	-0.3
1990	SF-N	60	100	14	35	5	1	1	6	3	20	.350	.369	.450	129	3	3	15	1	2	-1	1.000	-6	S2/13	-0.2
1991	SF-N	100	226	24	56	5	2	2	13	12	35	.248	.286	.314	71	-10	-9	18	2	4	-2	.956	-10	S13/2	-1.8
1992	LA-N	51	84	10	24	4	0	3	8	4	11	.286	.318	.440	114	1	1	9	0	4	-2	.974	2	3/S	0.1
Total	10	873	2026	244	490	73	12	19	143	206	331	.242	.313	.318	79	-61	-54	204	49	30	-3	.970	54	S3/21	3.2

■ DWAIN ANDERSON

Anderson, Dwain Cleaven b: 11/23/47, Oakland, Cal. BR/TR, 5'11", 165 lbs. Deb: 9/03/71

YEAR	TM/L	G	AB	R	H	2B	3B	HR	RBI	BB	SO	AVG	OBP	SLG	PRO+	BR	/A	RC	SB	CS	SBR	FA	FR	POS	TPR
1971	Oak-A	16	37	3	10	2	1	0	3	5	9	.270	.372	.378	115	1	1	5	0	1	-1	.968	-1	S/23	0.1
1972	Oak-A	3	7	2	0	0	0	0	0	1	4	.000	.125	.000	-64	-1	-1	0	0	0	0	1.000	-0	/S3	-0.2
	StL-N	57	135	12	36	4	1	1	8	8	23	.267	.313	.333	85	-3	-3	13	0	1	-1	.952	-3	S3/2	-0.3
1973	StL-N	18	17	5	2	0	0	0	0	4	4	.118	.286	.118	16	-2	-2	1	0	0	0	.500	-2	/SO	-0.4
	SD-N	53	107	11	13	0	0	0	3	14	29	.121	.223	.121	-2	-15	-13	4	2	0	1	.932	3	S/3	-0.7
	Yr	71	124	16	15	0	0	0	3	18	33	.121	.232	.121	1	-16	-15	5	2	0	1	.919	1	S/3O	-1.1
1974	Cle-A	2	3	0	1	0	0	0	0	0	1	.333	.333	.333	93	-0	-0	0	0	0	0	1.000	-1	/2	-0.1
Total	4	149	306	33	62	6	2	1	14	32	70	.203	.282	.245	52	-20	-18	23	2	2	-1	.940	-4	/S32O	-1.6

■ GOAT ANDERSON

Anderson, Edward John b: 1/13/1880, Cleveland, Ohio d: 3/15/23, South Bend, Ind. BL/TR, Deb: 4/11/07

YEAR	TM/L	G	AB	R	H	2B	3B	HR	RBI	BB	SO	AVG	OBP	SLG	PRO+	BR	/A	RC	SB	CS	SBR	FA	FR	POS	TPR
1907	Pit-N	127	413	73	85	3	1	1	12	80		.206	.343	.225	77	-5	-6	44	27			.953	-1	*O/2	-1.3

■ FERRELL ANDERSON

Anderson, Ferrell Jack "Andy" b: 1/9/18, Maple City, Kan. d: 3/12/78, Joplin, Mo. BR/TR, 6'1", 200 lbs. Deb: 4/16/46

YEAR	TM/L	G	AB	R	H	2B	3B	HR	RBI	BB	SO	AVG	OBP	SLG	PRO+	BR	/A	RC	SB	CS	SBR	FA	FR	POS	TPR
1946	Bro-N	79	199	19	51	10	0	2	14	18	21	.256	.330	.337	89	-3	-3	22	1			.964	-2	C	-0.2
1953	StL-N	18	35	1	10	2	0	0	1	0	4	.286	.286	.343	63	-2	-2	4	0	0	0	1.000	-1	C	-0.3
Total	2	97	234	20	61	12	0	2	15	18	25	.261	.324	.338	85	-5	-5	26	1	0		.968	-3	/C	-0.5

■ GEORGE ANDERSON

Anderson, George Jendrus "Andy" (Born George Andrew Jendrus)
b: 9/26/1889, Cleveland, Ohio d: 5/28/62, Cleveland, Ohio BL/TR, 5'8.5", 160 lbs. Deb: 5/26/14

YEAR	TM/L	G	AB	R	H	2B	3B	HR	RBI	BB	SO	AVG	OBP	SLG	PRO+	BR	/A	RC	SB	CS	SBR	FA	FR	POS	TPR
1914	Bro-F	98	364	58	115	13	3	3	24	31	50	.316	.376	.393	120	9	10	62	16			.946	4	O	1.0
1915	Bro-F	136	511	70	135	23	9	2	39	52	54	.264	.342	.356	106	4	4	72	20			.956	-8	*O	-1.1
1918	StL-N	35	132	20	39	4	5	0	6	15	7	.295	.380	.402	143	7	7	20	0			.956	-1	O	0.4
Total	3	269	1007	148	289	40	17	5	69	98	111	.287	.359	.375	116	20	21	154	36			.952	-5	O	0.3

■ SPARKY ANDERSON

Anderson, George Lee b: 2/22/34, Bridgewater, S.Dak BR/TR, 5'9", 170 lbs. Deb: 4/10/59 MC

YEAR	TM/L	G	AB	R	H	2B	3B	HR	RBI	BB	SO	AVG	OBP	SLG	PRO+	BR	/A	RC	SB	CS	SBR	FA	FR	POS	TPR
1959	Phi-N	152	477	42	104	9	3	0	34	42	53	.218	.283	.249	43	-38	-39	32	6	9	-4	.984	3	*2	-2.9

■ HAL ANDERSON

Anderson, Harold b: 2/10/04, St.Louis, Mo. d: 5/1/74, St.Louis, Mo. BR/TR, 5'11", 160 lbs. Deb: 4/12/32

YEAR	TM/L	G	AB	R	H	2B	3B	HR	RBI	BB	SO	AVG	OBP	SLG	PRO+	BR	/A	RC	SB	CS	SBR	FA	FR	POS	TPR
1932	Chi-A	9	32	4	8	0	0	0	2	0	1	.250	.250	.250	32	-3	-3	2	0	1	-1	1.000	0	/O	-0.4

■ HARRY ANDERSON

Anderson, Harry Walter b: 9/10/31, North East, Md. BL/TR, 6'3", 210 lbs. Deb: 4/18/57

YEAR	TM/L	G	AB	R	H	2B	3B	HR	RBI	BB	SO	AVG	OBP	SLG	PRO+	BR	/A	RC	SB	CS	SBR	FA	FR	POS	TPR
1957	Phi-N	118	400	53	107	15	4	17	61	36	61	.268	.337	.452	113	5	7	61	2	3	-1	.986	4	*O	0.3
1958	Phi-N	140	515	80	155	34	6	23	97	59	95	.301	.376	.524	137	26	27	100	0	2	-1	.975	-2	O1	1.7
1959	Phi-N	142	508	50	122	28	6	14	63	43	95	.240	.306	.402	85	-11	-12	62	1	1	-0	.980	18	*O	-0.1
1960	Phi-N	38	93	10	23	2	0	5	12	10	19	.247	.333	.430	107	1	1	13	0	0	0	1.000	-1	O1	-0.2
	Cin-N	42	66	6	11	3	0	1	9	11	20	.167	.286	.258	49	-4	-5	6	0	0	0	.990	-1	1/O	-0.7
	Yr	80	159	16	34	5	0	6	21	21	39	.214	.313	.358	82	-4	-4	19	0	0	0	.989	-2	1O	-0.9
1961	Cin-N	4	4	0	1	0	0	0	0	0	1	.250	.250	.250	33	-0	-0	0	0	0	0	.000	0	H	0.0
Total	5	484	1586	199	419	82	16	60	242	159	291	.264	.337	.450	109	16	18	242	3	6	-3	.982	19	O/1	1.0

■ JIM ANDERSON

Anderson, James Lea b: 2/23/57, Los Angeles, Cal. BR/TR, 6', 170 lbs. Deb: 7/02/78

YEAR	TM/L	G	AB	R	H	2B	3B	HR	RBI	BB	SO	AVG	OBP	SLG	PRO+	BR	/A	RC	SB	CS	SBR	FA	FR	POS	TPR
1978	Cal-A	48	108	6	21	7	0	0	7	11	16	.194	.269	.259	51	-7	-7	7	0	0	0	.955	3	S/2	0.0
1979	*Cal-A	96	234	33	58	13	1	3	23	17	31	.248	.302	.350	78	-8	-7	24	3	2	-0	.949	-1	S3/2C	-0.1
1980	Sea-A	116	317	46	72	7	0	8	30	27	39	.227	.294	.325	69	-13	-14	30	2	4	-2	.958	3	S3/2CD	-0.6
1981	Sea-A	70	162	12	33	7	0	2	19	17	29	.204	.283	.284	61	-7	-8	12	3	5	-2	.947	4	S/3	-0.1
1983	Tex-A	50	102	8	22	1	1	0	6	5	8	.216	.252	.245	38	-9	-8	6	1	2	-1	.962	6	S2/3OCD	-0.2
1984	Tex-A	39	47	2	5	0	0	0	1	4	7	.106	.176	.106	-19	-8	-8	1	0	0	0	.989	10	S/32	0.4
Total	6	419	970	107	211	35	2	13	86	81	130	.218	.281	.298	60	-52	-52	81	9	13	-5	.955	25	S/32DCO	-0.6

■ **JOHN ANDERSON** Anderson, John Joseph "Honest John" b: 12/14/1873, Sasbourg, Norway d: 7/23/49, Worcester, Mass. BB/TR, 6'2", 180 lbs. Deb: 9/08/1894

YEAR	TM/L	G	AB	R	H	2B	3B	HR	RBI	BB	SO	AVG	OBP	SLG	PRO+	BR	/A	RC	SB	CS	SBR	FA	FR	POS	TPR
1894	Bro-N	17	63	14	19	1	3	1	19	3	3	.302	.333	.460	98	-1	-0	12	7			.778	-5	O/3	-0.5
1895	Bro-N	102	419	76	120	11	14	9	87	12	29	.286	.314	.444	104	-5	1	68	24			.882	-6	*O	-1.0
1896	Bro-N	108	430	70	135	23	17	1	55	18	23	.314	.344	.453	118	5	9	82	37			.942	-3	O1	0.1
1897	Bro-N	117	492	93	160	28	12	4	85	17		.325	.355	.455	120	7	11	93	29			.936	0	*O/1	0.3
1898	Bro-N	6	21	1	3	2	0	0	2	1		.143	.217	.238	31	-2	-2	1	0			1.000	0	/O	-0.2
	Was-N	110	430	70	131	28	18	9	71	23		.305	.357	.516	150	24	24	88	18			.948	9	O1	2.4
	Bro-N	19	69	11	19	3	4	0	8	5		.275	.333	.435	120	1	1	11	2			.966	-1	O/1	0.0
	Yr	135	520	82	153	33	**22**	9	81	29		.294	.348	**.494**	141	23	24	99	20			.952	8	*O1	2.2
1899	Bro-N	117	439	65	118	18	7	4	92	27		.269	.317	.369	86	-9	-10	61	25			.933	-4	O1	-1.7
1901	Mil-A	138	576	90	190	46	7	8	99	24		.330	.360	.476	137	21	25	114	35			**.982**	5	*1O	2.5
1902	StL-A	126	524	60	149	29	6	4	85	21		.284	.316	.385	95	-6	-5	71	15			.985	-9	*1/O	-1.6
1903	StL-A	138	550	65	156	34	8	2	78	23		.284	.312	.385	112	5	6	73	16			.986	4	*1/O	0.8
1904	NY-A	143	558	62	155	27	12	3	82	23		.278	.308	.385	113	10	7	75	20			.956	-0	*O1	0.0
1905	NY-A	32	99	12	23	3	1	0	14	8		.232	.290	.283	74	-2	-3	11	9			.900	-2	O/1	-0.7
	Was-A	101	400	50	116	21	6	1	38	22		.290	.330	.380	130	10	12	59	22			.960	-0	O/1	0.7
	Yr	133	499	62	139	24	7	1	52	30		.279	.322	.361	117	8	9	70	31			.949	-2	*O/1	0.0
1906	Was-A	151	583	62	158	25	4	3	70	19		.271	.295	.343	105	-2	1	73	**39**			.953	5	*O	-0.2
1907	Was-A	87	333	33	96	12	4	0	44	34		.288	.358	.348	136	10	13	50	19			.983	-1	1O	1.1
1908	Chi-A	123	355	36	93	17	1	0	47	30		.262	.321	.315	109	3	4	43	21			.963	-6	O/1	-0.6
Total	14	1635	6341	870	1841	328	124	49	976	310	55	.290	.328	.404	114	70	95	985	338			1.000	-14	*O1/3	1.4

■ **KENT ANDERSON** Anderson, Kent McKay b: 8/12/63, Florence, S.C. BR/TR, 6'1", 180 lbs. Deb: 4/15/89 F

YEAR	TM/L	G	AB	R	H	2B	3B	HR	RBI	BB	SO	AVG	OBP	SLG	PRO+	BR	/A	RC	SB	CS	SBR	FA	FR	POS	TPR
1989	Cal-A	86	223	27	51	6	1	0	17	17	42	.229	.286	.265	57	-13	-12	17	1	2	-1	.972	14	S/23OD	0.6
1990	Cal-A	49	143	16	44	6	1	1	5	13	19	.308	.369	.385	113	2	3	20	0	2	-1	.964	13	S3/2	1.6
Total	2	135	366	43	95	12	2	1	22	30	61	.260	.319	.311	79	-10	-9	37	1	4	-2	.969	27	/S32OD	2.2

■ **MIKE ANDERSON** Anderson, Michael Allen b: 6/22/51, Florence, S.C. BR/TR, 6'2", 200 lbs. Deb: 9/02/71 F

YEAR	TM/L	G	AB	R	H	2B	3B	HR	RBI	BB	SO	AVG	OBP	SLG	PRO+	BR	/A	RC	SB	CS	SBR	FA	FR	POS	TPR
1971	Phi-N	26	89	11	22	5	1	2	5	13	28	.247	.343	.393	108	1	1	13	0	0	0	.986	2	O	0.2
1972	Phi-N	36	103	8	20	5	1	2	5	19	36	.194	.320	.320	80	-2	-2	12	1	0	0	.987	5	O	0.2
1973	Phi-N	87	193	32	49	9	1	9	28	19	53	.254	.324	.451	110	3	2	27	0	3	-2	.981	2	O	0.0
1974	Phi-N	145	395	35	99	22	2	5	34	37	75	.251	.315	.354	83	-7	-9	41	2	1	0	.980	3	*O/1	-1.1
1975	Phi-N	115	247	24	64	10	3	4	28	17	66	.259	.312	.372	86	-4	-5	27	1	2	-1	.977	-7	*O/1	-1.7
1976	StL-N	86	199	17	58	8	1	1	12	26	30	.291	.376	.357	108	3	3	27	1	1	-0	.982	2	O/1	0.3
1977	StL-N	94	154	18	34	4	1	4	17	14	31	.221	.286	.338	68	-7	-7	14	2	3	-1	.980	5	O	-0.5
1978	Bal-A	53	32	2	3	0	1	0	3	3	10	.094	.171	.156	-8	-5	-4	1	0	0	0	.962	-15	O	-2.1
1979	Phi-N	79	78	12	18	4	0	1	2	13	14	.231	.341	.321	79	-2	-2	9	1	2	-1	.973	6	O/P	0.3
Total	9	721	1490	159	367	67	11	28	134	161	343	.246	.321	.362	88	-20	-24	173	8	12	-5	.980	3	O/1P	-4.4

■ **ERNIE ANDRES** Andres, Ernest Henry "Junie" b: 1/11/18, Jeffersonville, Ind. BR/TR, 6'1", 200 lbs. Deb: 4/16/46

YEAR	TM/L	G	AB	R	H	2B	3B	HR	RBI	BB	SO	AVG	OBP	SLG	PRO+	BR	/A	RC	SB	CS	SBR	FA	FR	POS	TPR
1946	Bos-A	15	41	0	4	2	0	0	1	3	5	.098	.159	.146	-14	-6	-7	1	0	0	0	1.000	1	3	-0.6

■ **KIM ANDREW** Andrew, Kim Darrell b: 11/14/53, Glendale, Cal. BR/TR, 5'10", 160 lbs. Deb: 4/16/75

YEAR	TM/L	G	AB	R	H	2B	3B	HR	RBI	BB	SO	AVG	OBP	SLG	PRO+	BR	/A	RC	SB	CS	SBR	FA	FR	POS	TPR
1975	Bos-A	2	2	0	1	0	0	0	0	0	0	.500	.500	.500	169	0	0	1	0	0	0	1.000	-0	/2	0.0

■ **FRED ANDREWS** Andrews, Fred b: 5/4/52, Lafayette, La. BR/TR, 5'8", 163 lbs. Deb: 9/26/76

YEAR	TM/L	G	AB	R	H	2B	3B	HR	RBI	BB	SO	AVG	OBP	SLG	PRO+	BR	/A	RC	SB	CS	SBR	FA	FR	POS	TPR
1976	Phi-N	4	6	1	4	0	0	0	0	2	0	.667	.778	.667	304	2	2	4	1	1	-0	1.000	-1	/2	0.2
1977	Phi-N	12	23	3	4	0	1	0	2	1	5	.174	.208	.261	24	-2	-3	1	1	0	0	1.000	3	/2	0.1
Total	2	16	29	4	8	0	1	0	2	3	5	.276	.364	.345	90	-0	-0	5	2	1	0	1.000	2	/2	0.3

■ **ED ANDREWS** Andrews, George Edward b: 4/5/1859, Painesville, Ohio d: 8/12/34, W.Palm Beach, Fla. BR/TR, 5'8", 160 lbs. Deb: 5/01/1884 U

YEAR	TM/L	G	AB	R	H	2B	3B	HR	RBI	BB	SO	AVG	OBP	SLG	PRO+	BR	/A	RC	SB	CS	SBR	FA	FR	POS	TPR
1884	Phi-N	109	420	74	93	21	2	0	23	9	42	.221	.238	.281	66	-18	-15	29				.891	-22	*2	-3.1
1885	Phi-N	103	421	77	112	15	3	0	23	32	25	.266	.318	.316	108	3	4	43				.921	-0	*O/2	0.2
1886	Phi-N	107	437	93	109	15	4	2	28	31	35	.249	.299	.316	86	-6	-7	59	**56**			.903	4	*O/2	-0.4
1887	Phi-N	104	464	110	151	19	7	4	67	21	21	.325	.359	.422	112	11	6	93	57			.902	-4	*O/21	0.0
1888	Phi-N	124	528	75	126	14	4	3	44	21	41	.239	.272	.297	79	-10	-13	53	35			.903	-4	*O	-2.1
1889	Phi-N	10	39	10	11	1	0	0	7	2	4	.282	.317	.308	70	-1	-2	6	7			.808	-1	/O2	-0.2
	Ind-N	40	173	32	53	11	0	0	22	5	10	.306	.330	.370	95	-1	-2	24	7			.885	-3	O/2	-0.5
	Yr	50	212	42	64	12	0	0	29	7	14	.302	.327	.358	90	-2	-3	30	14			.867	-4	O/2	-0.7
1890	Bro-P	94	395	84	100	14	2	3	38	40	32	.253	.323	.322	70	-14	-19	49	21			.912	1	*O	-1.7
1891	Cin-a	83	356	47	75	7	4	0	26	33	35	.211	.279	.253	50	-20	-26	32	22			.961	17	O	-1.0
Total	8	774	3233	602	830	117	26	12	278	194	245	.257	.301	.320	83	-57	-72	389	205			.912	-13	O2/1	-8.8

■ **JIM ANDREWS** Andrews, James Pratt b: 6/5/1865, Shelburne Falls, Mass. d: 12/27/07, Chicago, Ill. Deb: 4/19/1890

YEAR	TM/L	G	AB	R	H	2B	3B	HR	RBI	BB	SO	AVG	OBP	SLG	PRO+	BR	/A	RC	SB	CS	SBR	FA	FR	POS	TPR
1890	Chi-N	53	202	32	38	4	2	3	17	23	41	.188	.278	.272	60	-9	-11	19	11			.900	1	O	-1.1

■ **MIKE ANDREWS** Andrews, Michael Jay b: 7/9/43, Los Angeles, Cal. BR/TR, 6'3", 195 lbs. Deb: 9/18/66 F

YEAR	TM/L	G	AB	R	H	2B	3B	HR	RBI	BB	SO	AVG	OBP	SLG	PRO+	BR	/A	RC	SB	CS	SBR	FA	FR	POS	TPR
1966	Bos-A	5	18	1	3	0	0	0	0	0	2	.167	.167	.167	-4	-2	-3	1	0	0	0	1.000	2	/2	0.0
1967	*Bos-A	142	494	79	130	20	0	8	40	62	72	.263	.348	.352	99	6	1	63	7	7	-2	.976	-6	*2/S	0.3
1968	Bos-A	147	536	77	145	22	1	7	45	81	57	.271	.369	.354	113	16	12	75	3	8	-4	.976	1	*2/S3	2.1
1969	Bos-A★	121	464	79	136	26	2	15	59	71	53	.293	.393	.455	129	24	21	88	1	1	-0	.972	5	*2	3.7
1970	Bos-A	151	589	91	149	28	1	17	65	81	63	.253	.346	.390	96	3	-2	84	2	1	0	.973	-30	*2	-2.0
1971	Chi-A	109	330	45	93	16	0	12	47	67	36	.282	.405	.439	135	20	18	62	3	5	-2	.956	-3	21	1.8
1972	Chi-A	148	505	58	111	18	0	7	50	70	78	.220	.317	.297	82	-8	-10	54	2	2	-1	.973	-14	*2/1	-1.9
1973	Chi-A	52	159	10	32	9	0	0	10	23	28	.201	.302	.258	57	-8	-9	12	0	1	-1	1.000	-3	D/123	-1.3
	*Oak-A	18	21	1	4	1	0	0	0	3	1	.190	.292	.238	53	-1	-1	1	0	0	0	.944	-1	/2D	-0.2
	Yr	70	180	11	36	10	0	0	10	26	29	.200	.301	.256	57	-9	-10	14	0	1	-1	.974	-4	D2/13	-1.5
Total	8	893	3116	441	803	140	4	66	316	458	390	.258	.356	.369	104	49	29	439	18	25	-10	.973	-49	2/1DS3	2.5

■ **ROB ANDREWS** Andrews, Robert Patrick b: 12/11/52, Santa Monica, Cal. BR/TR, 6', 185 lbs. Deb: 4/07/75 F

YEAR	TM/L	G	AB	R	H	2B	3B	HR	RBI	BB	SO	AVG	OBP	SLG	PRO+	BR	/A	RC	SB	CS	SBR	FA	FR	POS	TPR
1975	Hou-N	103	277	29	66	5	4	0	19	31	34	.238	.315	.285	73	-12	-9	27	12	5	1	.982	7	2/S	0.3
1976	Hou-N	109	410	42	105	8	5	0	23	33	27	.256	.312	.300	81	-13	-9	37	7	3	0	.977	8	*2/S	0.7
1977	SF-N	127	436	60	115	11	3	0	25	56	33	.264	.348	.303	76	-13	-12	49	5	6	-2	.964	-12	*2	-1.9
1978	SF-N	79	177	21	39	3	3	1	11	20	18	.220	.299	.288	67	-8	-7	17	5	1	1	.977	9	2/S	0.6
1979	SF-N	75	154	22	40	3	0	2	13	8	9	.260	.296	.318	73	-7	-6	14	4	1	1	.956	4	2/3	0.1
Total	5	493	1454	174	365	30	15	3	91	148	121	.251	.320	.298	76	-52	-43	143	33	16	0	.972	15	2/S3	-0.2

■ **STAN ANDREWS** Andrews, Stanley Joseph "Polo" (b: Stanley Joseph Andruskewicz) b: 4/17/17, Lynn, Mass. BR/TR, 5'11", 178 lbs. Deb: 6/11/39

YEAR	TM/L	G	AB	R	H	2B	3B	HR	RBI	BB	SO	AVG	OBP	SLG	PRO+	BR	/A	RC	SB	CS	SBR	FA	FR	POS	TPR
1939	Bos-N	13	26	1	6	0	0	0	1	1	2	.231	.259	.231	35	-2	-2	1	0			.857	-2	C	-0.3
1940	Bos-N	19	33	1	6	0	0	0	2	0	3	.182	.182	.182	1	-4	-4	1	1			.944	-1	C	-0.4
1944	Bro-N	4	8	1	1	0	0	0	1	1	2	.125	.222	.125	-1	-1	-1	0	0			1.000	-0	/C	-0.1
1945	Bro-N	21	49	5	8	0	1	0	2	5	4	.163	.255	.204	29	-5	-5	3	0			.948	2	C	-0.1
	Phi-N	13	33	3	11	2	0	1	6	1	5	.333	.353	.485	135	1	1	6	1			.950	-1	C	0.1
	Yr	34	82	8	19	2	1	1	8	6	9	.232	.292	.317	70	-4	-3	8	1			.949	1	C	0.0
Total	4	70	149	11	32	2	1	1	12	8	16	.215	.259	.262	46	-11	-11	11	2			.938	-1	/C	-0.8

YEAR	TM/L	G	AB	R	H	2B	3B	HR	RBI	BB	SO	AVG	OBP	SLG	PRO+	BR	/A	RC	SB	CS	SBR	FA	FR	POS	TPR

■ WALLY ANDREWS Andrews, William Walter b: 9/18/1859, Philadelphia, Pa. d: 1/20/40, Indianapolis, Ind. BR/TR, 6'3", 170 lbs. Deb: 5/22/1884

1884	Lou-a	14	49	10	10	5	1	0			4	.204	.264	.347	105	0	0	5				.950	-1	/13OS	-0.1
1888	Lou-a	26	93	12	18	6	3	0	6	13		.194	.292	.323	102	0	1	10	5			.997	2	1	0.0
Total	2	40	142	22	28	11	4	0	6	17		.197	.283	.331	103	0	1	15	5			.985	1	/13SO	-0.1

■ FRED ANDRUS Andrus, Frederick Hotham b: 8/23/1850, Washington, Mich. d: 11/10/37, Detroit, Mich. BR/TR, 6'2", 185 lbs. Deb: 7/25/1876

1876	Chi-N	8	36	6	11	3	0	0	2	0	5	.306	.306	.389	116	1	0	4				.714	-3	/O	-0.2
1884	Chi-N	1	5	3	1	0	0	0	0	1	0	.200	.333	.200	67	-0	-0	0				1.000	0	/P	0.0
Total	2	9	41	9	12	3	0	0	2	1	5	.293	.310	.366	110	1	0	5					-3	/OP	-0.2

■ BILL ANDRUS Andrus, William Morgan "Andy" b: 7/25/07, Beaumont, Tex. d: 3/12/82, Washington, D.C. BR/TR, 6', 185 lbs. Deb: 9/19/31

1931	Was-A	3	7	0	0	0	0	0	1	0	1	.000	.000	.000	-99	-2	-2	0	0	0	0	.750	-0	/3	-0.2
1937	Phi-N	3	2	0	0	0	0	0	0	0	2	.000	.000	.000	-93	-1	-1	0	0			.000	0	/3	-0.1
Total	2	6	9	0	0	0	0	0	1	0	3	.000	.000	.000	-98	-3	-3	0	0	0	0	.750	-0	/3	-0.3

■ WYMAN ANDRUS Andrus, Wyman W. b: 10/14/1858, Orono, Ontario, Can d: 6/17/35, Miles City, Mon. Deb: 9/15/1885

| 1885 | Pro-N | 1 | 4 | 0 | 0 | 0 | 0 | 0 | 0 | 1 | | .000 | .000 | .000 | -99 | -1 | -1 | 0 | | | | 1.000 | 1 | /3 | 0.0 |

■ TOM ANGLEY Angley, Thomas Samuel b: 10/2/04, Baltimore, Md. d: 10/26/52, Wichita, Kan. BL/TR, 5'8", 190 lbs. Deb: 4/23/29

| 1929 | Chi-N | 5 | 16 | 1 | 4 | 1 | 0 | 0 | 6 | 2 | 2 | .250 | .333 | .313 | 61 | -1 | -1 | 2 | 0 | | | .968 | 1 | /C | 0.1 |

■ PAT ANKENMAN Ankenman, Frederick Norman b: 12/23/12, Houston, Tex. d: 1/13/89, Houston, Tex. BR/TR, 5'4", 125 lbs. Deb: 4/16/36

1936	StL-N	1	3	0	0	0	0	0	0	0	3	.000	.000	.000	-99	-1	-1	0	0			.600	-1	/S	-0.2
1943	Bro-N	1	2	1	1	0	0	0	0	0	0	.500	.500	.500	189	0	0	1	0			1.000	1	/S	0.1
1944	Bro-N	13	24	1	6	1	0	0	3	0	2	.250	.250	.292	53	-2	-2	2	0			.971	0	2/S	-0.1
Total	3	15	29	2	7	1	0	0	3	0	5	.241	.241	.276	46	-2	-2	2	0			.800	-1	/2S	-0.2

■ BILL ANNIS Annis, William Perley b: 3/8/1857, Stoneham, Mass. d: 6/10/23, Kennebunkport, Me BR , 5'7", 150 lbs. Deb: 5/01/1884

| 1884 | Bos-N | 27 | 96 | 17 | 17 | 2 | 0 | 0 | 3 | 0 | 8 | .177 | .177 | .198 | 18 | -9 | -9 | 3 | | | | .897 | -3 | O | -1.2 |

■ CAP ANSON Anson, Adrian Constantine b: 4/11/1852, Marshalltown, Iowa d: 4/14/22, Chicago, Ill. BR/TR, 6', 227 lbs. Deb: 5/06/1871 MH

1871	Rok-n	25	120	29	39	11	4	0	16	2	1	.325	.336	.467	134	4	5	21	6					*3/C2O	0.2
1872	Ath-n	46	215	40	89	9	7	0	50	16	3	.414	.455	.521	199	26	25	52						*3	1.4
1873	Ath-n	52	254	53	101	9	2	0	36	5	1	.398	.409	.449	142	16	12	47						*13/C2O	0.9
1874	Ath-n	55	260	51	86	8	3	0		3		.331	.338	.385	119	8	4	35						13/OS	0.3
1875	Ath-n	69	324	84	105	17	4	1		6		.324	.336	.410	141	18	12	46						1OC/3M	1.1
1876	Chi-N	66	309	63	110	9	7	2	59	12	8	.356	.380	.450	157	24	19	54				.849	13	*3/C	2.9
1877	Chi-N	59	255	52	86	19	1	0	32	9	3	.337	.360	.420	129	13	8	39				.883	8	*3C	1.6
1878	Chi-N	60	261	55	89	12	2	0	40	13	1	.341	.372	.402	145	15	13	40				.825	-8	*O/23C	0.3
1879	Chi-N	51	227	40	72	20	1	0	34	2	2	.317	.323	.414	133	9	8	31				.975	0	1/M	0.6
1880	Chi-N	86	356	54	120	24	1	1	74	14	12	.337	.360	.419	154	23	20	55				.978	0	*1/3S2M	1.3
1881	Chi-N	84	343	67	137	21	7	1	82	26	4	.399	.442	.510	189	39	37	79				.975	7	*1/CSM	3.3
1882	Chi-N	82	348	69	126	29	8	1	83	20	7	.362	.397	.500	177	33	30	71				.949	-1	*1/CM	1.9
1883	Chi-N	98	413	70	127	36	5	0	68	18	9	.308	.336	.419	121	14	10	60				.964	3	*1/POCM	0.2
1884	Chi-N	112	475	108	159	30	3	21	102	29	13	.335	.373	.543	170	45	39	99				.956	-0	*1/CSPM	2.3
1885	*Chi-N	112	464	100	144	35	7	7	108	34	13	.310	.357	.461	142	32	22	78				.958	-4	*1/CM	0.5
1886	*Chi-N	125	504	117	187	35	11	10	147	55	19	.371	.433	.544	170	58	46	134	29			.963	8	*1CM	3.7
1887	Chi-N	122	472	107	164	33	13	7	102	60	18	.347	.422	.517	143	41	30	117	27			.973	10	*1/CM	2.3
1888	Chi-N	134	515	101	177	20	12	12	84	47	24	.344	.400	.499	175	51	46	117	28			.986	9	*1M	4.2
1889	Chi-N	134	518	100	161	32	7	7	117	86	19	.311	.414	.440	134	31	27	108	27			.982	9	*1M	2.4
1890	Chi-N	139	504	95	157	14	5	7	107	113	23	.312	.443	.401	143	39	36	105	29			.978	0	*1/C2M	2.6
1891	Chi-N	136	540	81	157	24	8	8	120	75	29	.291	.378	.409	132	23	23	92	17			.981	8	*1/CM	2.2
1892	Chi-N	146	559	62	152	25	9	1	74	67	30	.272	.354	.354	115	12	12	77	13			.973	-5	*1/M	0.0
1893	Chi-N	103	398	70	125	24	2	0	91	68	12	.314	.415	.384	117	12	13	71	13			.981	-4	*1/M	0.6
1894	Chi-N	83	340	82	132	28	4	5	99	40	15	.388	.457	.538	134	24	20	94	17			.990	3	1/2M	1.8
1895	Chi-N	122	474	87	159	23	6	2	91	55	23	.335	.408	.422	109	14	8	90	12			.985	-1	*1/M	0.8
1896	Chi-N	108	402	72	133	18	2	2	90	49	10	.331	.407	.400	111	11	9	78	24			.983	-1	*1C/M	0.8
1897	Chi-N	114	424	67	121	17	3	3	75	60		.285	.379	.361	92	-0	-3	65	11			.975	1	*1C/M	-0.1
Total	5 n	247	1173	277	420	54	19	1	102	32	5	.358	.375	.439	146	72	59	201	12					3/1OCS2	3.9
Total	22	2276	9101	1719	2995	528	124	97	1879	952	294	.329	.395	.446	139	562	470	1756	247			.974	57	*13/CO2PS	36.2

■ ERIC ANTHONY Anthony, Eric Todd b: 11/8/67, San Diego, Cal. BL/TL, 6'2", 195 lbs. Deb: 7/29/89

1989	Hou-N	25	61	7	11	2	0	4	9	7	16	.180	.286	.410	100	-0	-0	7	0	0	0	1.000	-1	O	-0.1
1990	Hou-N	84	239	26	46	8	0	10	29	29	78	.192	.285	.351	76	-9	-8	26	5	0	2	.970	-2	O	-1.0
1991	Hou-N	39	118	11	18	6	0	1	7	12	41	.153	.231	.229	31	-11	-10	7	1	0	0	.986	3	O	-0.9
1992	Hou-N	137	440	45	105	15	1	19	80	38	98	.239	.301	.407	105	-2	1	53	5	4	-1	.973	-6	*O	-1.0
Total	4	285	858	89	180	31	1	34	123	88	233	.210	.286	.367	86	-22	-17	93	11	4	1	.976	-6	O	-3.0

■ JOE ANTOLICK Antolick, Joseph b: 4/11/16, Hokendauqua, Pa. BR/TR, 6', 185 lbs. Deb: 9/20/44

| 1944 | Phi-N | 4 | 6 | 1 | 2 | 0 | 0 | 0 | 0 | 1 | 0 | .333 | .429 | .333 | 120 | 0 | 0 | 1 | 0 | | | 1.000 | 1 | /C | 0.1 |

■ JOHN ANTONELLI Antonelli, John Lawrence b: 7/15/15, Memphis, Tenn. d: 4/18/90, Memphis, Tenn. BR/TR, 5'10.5", 165 lbs. Deb: 9/16/44

1944	StL-N	8	21	0	4	1	0	0	1	0	4	.190	.190	.238	20	-2	-2	1	0			1.000	1	/132	-0.1
1945	StL-N	2	3	0	0	0	0	0	0	0	1	.000	.000	.000	-98	-1	-1	0	0			.667	-0	/3	-0.1
	Phi-N	125	504	50	129	27	2	1	28	24	24	.256	.292	.323	73	-21	-19	45	1			.959	-9	*32/1S	-2.4
	Yr	127	507	50	129	27	2	1	28	24	25	.254	.291	.321	72	-21	-20	45	1			.957	-9	*32/1S	-2.5
Total	2	135	528	50	133	28	2	1	29	24	29	.252	.287	.318	70	-24	-22	46	1			.958	-8	3/21S	-2.6

■ BILL ANTONELLO Antonello, William James b: 5/19/27, Brooklyn, N.Y. BR/TR, 5'11", 185 lbs. Deb: 4/30/53

| 1953 | Bro-N | 40 | 43 | 9 | 7 | 1 | 1 | 4 | 2 | 11 | | .163 | .200 | .302 | 28 | -5 | -5 | 2 | 0 | 0 | 0 | .964 | -6 | O | -1.0 |

■ LUIS APARICIO Aparicio, Luis Ernesto (Montiel) b: 4/29/34, Maracaibo, Venez. BR/TR, 5'9", 160 lbs. Deb: 4/17/56 H

1956	Chi-A	152	533	69	142	19	6	3	56	34	63	.266	.312	.341	71	-22	-23	59	21	4	4	.954	0	*S	-0.7
1957	Chi-A	143	575	82	148	22	6	3	41	52	55	.257	.319	.332	78	-17	-17	65	28	8	4	.972	-13	*S	-1.4
1958	Chi-A	145	557	76	148	20	9	2	40	35	38	.266	.310	.345	82	-15	-14	62	29	6	5	.973	9	*S	1.3
1959	*Chi-A	152	612	98	157	18	5	6	51	53	40	.257	.319	.332	80	-17	-16	70	56	13	9	.970	-4	*S	0.2
1960	Chi-A	153	600	86	166	20	7	2	61	43	39	.277	.326	.343	82	-15	-15	71	51	8	11	.979	30	*S	3.8
1961	Chi-A	156	625	90	170	24	4	6	45	38	33	.272	.315	.352	79	-20	-19	72	53	13	9	.962	6	*S	0.9
1962	Chi-A	153	581	72	140	23	9	7	40	32	36	.241	.282	.334	65	-29	-29	54	31	12	2	.973	10	*S	-0.4
1963	Bal-A	146	601	73	150	18	8	5	45	36	40	.250	.294	.331	77	-20	-19	62	40	6	8	.983	-5	*S	-0.6
1964	Bal-A	146	578	93	154	20	3	10	37	49	51	.266	.327	.363	92	-6	-6	71	57	17	7	.979	3	*S	1.5
1965	Bal-A	144	564	67	127	20	10	8	40	46	56	.225	.287	.339	76	-17	-19	57	26	7	4	.971	3	*S	-0.2
1966	*Bal-A	151	659	97	182	25	8	6	41	33	42	.276	.312	.366	95	-6	-5	74	25	11	5	.978	10	*S	2.2
1967	Bal-A	134	546	55	127	22	5	4	31	29	44	.233	.273	.313	73	-19	-19	47	18	5	2	.957	-20	*S	-2.6
1968	Chi-A	155	622	55	164	24	4	4	36	33	43	.264	.303	.334	92	-6	-7	61	17	11	-2	.977	25	*S	3.6

YEAR	TM/L	G	AB	R	H	2B	3B	HR	RBI	BB	SO	AVG	OBP	SLG	PRO+	BR	/A	RC	SB	CS	SBR	FA	FR	POS	TPR
1969	Chi-A	156	599	77	168	24	5	5	51	66	29	.280	.354	.362	96	2	-2	81	24	4	5	.976	29	*S	5.1
1970	Chi-A★	146	552	86	173	29	3	5	43	53	34	.313	.375	.404	110	12	9	85	8	3	1	.976	18	*S	4.6
1971	Bos-A★	125	491	56	114	23	0	4	45	35	43	.232	.286	.303	63	-22	-25	44	6	4	-1	.971	-18	*S	-3.1
1972	Bos-A†	110	436	47	112	26	3	3	39	26	28	.257	.302	.351	89	-4	-7	45	3	3	-1	.968	-17	*S	-1.0
1973	Bos-A	132	499	56	135	17	1	0	49	43	33	.271	.328	.309	76	-12	-16	53	13	1	3	.966	-17	*S	-1.2
Total	18	2599	10230	1335	2677	394	92	83	791	736	742	.262	.313	.343	82	-235	-246	1137	506	136	70	.972	51	*S	12.0

■ LUKE APPLING Appling, Lucius Benjamin b: 4/2/07, High Point, N.C. d: 1/3/91, Cumming, Ga. BR/TR, 5'10", 183 lbs. Deb: 9/10/30 MCH

YEAR	TM/L	G	AB	R	H	2B	3B	HR	RBI	BB	SO	AVG	OBP	SLG	PRO+	BR	/A	RC	SB	CS	SBR	FA	FR	POS	TPR
1930	Chi-A	6	26	2	8	2	0	0	2	0	0	.308	.308	.385	77	-1	-1	3	2	0	1	.879	-1	/S	-0.1
1931	Chi-A	96	297	36	69	13	4	1	28	29	27	.232	.303	.313	66	-16	-14	30	9	2	2	.900	-6	S/2	-1.0
1932	Chi-A	139	489	66	134	20	10	3	63	40	36	.274	.329	.374	87	-14	-9	60	9	8	-2	.929	18	S23	1.5
1933	Chi-A	151	612	90	197	36	10	6	85	56	29	.322	.379	.443	122	15	18	100	6	11	-5	.939	11	*S	3.3
1934	Chi-A	118	452	75	137	28	6	2	61	59	27	.303	.384	.405	100	4	2	73	3	1	0	.945	-9	*S/2	0.0
1935	Chi-A	153	525	94	161	28	6	1	71	122	40	.307	.437	.389	112	20	17	100	12	6	0	.958	**21**	*S	4.4
1936	Chi-A★	138	526	111	204	31	7	6	128	85	25	**.388**	.474	.508	137	40	37	131	10	6	-1	.951	15	*S	5.3
1937	Chi-A	154	574	98	182	42	8	4	77	86	28	.317	.407	.439	113	14	15	107	18	10	-1	.944	14	*S	3.5
1938	Chi-A	81	294	41	89	14	0	0	44	42	17	.303	.392	.350	85	-4	-5	42	1	3	-2	.953	1	S	0.1
1939	Chi-A☆	148	516	82	162	16	6	0	56	105	37	.314	.430	.368	103	11	9	90	16	9	-1	.951	-2	*S	1.8
1940	Chi-A★	150	566	96	197	27	13	0	79	69	35	.348	.420	.442	122	23	22	109	3	5	-2	.953	-2	*S	2.9
1941	Chi-A☆	154	592	93	186	26	8	1	57	82	32	.314	.399	.390	111	11	12	98	12	8	-1	.948	0	*S	2.2
1942	Chi-A	142	543	78	142	26	4	3	53	63	23	.262	.342	.341	94	-5	-3	70	17	5	2	.948	-7	*S	0.1
1943	Chi-A☆	155	585	63	192	33	2	3	80	90	29	**.328**	**.419**	.407	142	35	35	109	27	8	3	.957	7	*S	6.0
1945	Chi-A	18	57	12	21	2	2	1	10	12	7	.368	.478	.526	197	7	8	16	1	0	0	.930	-1	S	0.9
1946	Chi-A★	149	582	59	180	27	5	1	55	71	41	.309	.384	.378	118	13	15	88	6	4	-1	.951	7	*S	3.2
1947	Chi-A★	139	503	67	154	29	0	8	49	64	28	.306	.386	.412	126	16	18	81	8	6	-1	.949	-7	*S/3	1.8
1948	Chi-A	139	497	63	156	16	2	0	47	94	35	.314	.423	.354	112	12	14	82	10	4	1	.943	12	3S	2.8
1949	Chi-A	142	492	82	148	21	5	5	58	121	24	.301	.439	.394	125	22	25	90	7	12	-5	.964	-1	*S	2.7
1950	Chi-A	50	128	11	30	3	4	0	13	12	8	.234	.300	.320	61	-8	-8	12	2	0	1	.967	0	S1/2	-0.5
Total	20	2422	8856	1319	2749	440	102	45	1116	1302	528	.310	.399	.398	113	196	209	1493	179	108	-11	.948	73	*S/321	40.9

■ JACK ARAGON Aragon, Angel Valdes (Reyes) b: 11/20/15, Havana, Cuba d: 4/4/88, Clearwater, Fla. BR/TR, 5'10", 176 lbs. Deb: 8/13/41 F

YEAR	TM/L	G	AB	R	H	2B	3B	HR	RBI	BB	SO	AVG	OBP	SLG	PRO+	BR	/A	RC	SB	CS	SBR	FA	FR	POS	TPR
1941	NY-N	1	0	0	0	0	0	0	0	0	0	—	—	—	—	0	0	0	0			.000	0	R	0.0

■ ANGEL ARAGON Aragon, Angel (Valdes) "Pete" b: 8/2/1890, Havana, Cuba d: 1/24/52, New York, N.Y. BR/TR, 5'5", 150 lbs. Deb: 8/20/14 F

YEAR	TM/L	G	AB	R	H	2B	3B	HR	RBI	BB	SO	AVG	OBP	SLG	PRO+	BR	/A	RC	SB	CS	SBR	FA	FR	POS	TPR
1914	NY-A	6	7	1	1	0	0	0	0	1	2	.143	.333	.143	44	-0	-0	1	0			.000	-1	/O	-0.1
1916	NY-A	12	24	1	5	0	0	0	3	2	2	.208	.269	.208	43	-2	-2	2	2			.864	1	/3O	0.0
1917	NY-A	14	45	2	3	1	0	0	2	2	2	.067	.106	.089	-40	-8	-8	1	0			.933	1	/O3S	-0.8
Total	3	32	76	4	9	1	0	0	5	5	6	.118	.183	.132	-4	-10	-10	3	2			.921	2	/3OS	-0.9

■ MAURICE ARCHDEACON Archdeacon, Maurice John "Flash" b: 12/14/1898, St.Louis, Mo. d: 9/5/54, St.Louis, Mo. BL/TL, 5'8", 153 lbs. Deb: 9/17/23

YEAR	TM/L	G	AB	R	H	2B	3B	HR	RBI	BB	SO	AVG	OBP	SLG	PRO+	BR	/A	RC	SB	CS	SBR	FA	FR	POS	TPR
1923	Chi-A	22	87	23	35	5	1	0	4	6	8	.402	.441	.483	145	5	6	17	2	3	-1	.918	-2	O	0.1
1924	Chi-A	95	288	59	92	9	3	0	25	40	30	.319	.410	.372	106	3	5	47	11	7	-1	.958	-5	O	-0.6
1925	Chi-A	10	9	2	1	0	0	0	0	2	1	.111	.273	.111	0	-1	-1	0	0	0	0	1.000	-0	/O	-0.1
Total	3	127	384	84	128	14	4	0	29	48	39	.333	.413	.391	112	7	9	65	13	10	-2	.950	-7	/O	-0.6

■ JIMMY ARCHER Archer, James Patrick b: 5/13/1883, Dublin, Ireland d: 3/29/58, Milwaukee, Wis. BR/TR, 5'10", 168 lbs. Deb: 9/06/04

YEAR	TM/L	G	AB	R	H	2B	3B	HR	RBI	BB	SO	AVG	OBP	SLG	PRO+	BR	/A	RC	SB	CS	SBR	FA	FR	POS	TPR
1904	Pit-N	7	20	1	3	0	0	0	1	0		.150	.150	.150	-7	-2	-3	0	0			.919	0	/CO	-0.2
1907	*Det-A	18	42	6	5	0	0	0	0	4		.119	.196	.119	1	-5	-5	1	0			.975	2	C/2	-0.1
1909	Chi-N	80	261	31	60	9	2	1	30	12		.230	.266	.291	71	-9	-10	22	5			.960	-4	C	-0.7
1910	*Chi-N	98	313	36	81	17	6	2	41	14	49	.259	.293	.371	94	-5	-4	36	6			.970	3	C1	0.4
1911	Chi-N	116	387	41	98	18	5	4	41	18	43	.253	.288	.357	80	-12	-12	41	5			.977	-1	*C1/2	-0.3
1912	Chi-N	120	385	35	109	20	1	6	58	22	36	.283	.330	.387	96	-3	-3	51	7			.966	-5	*C	0.3
1913	Chi-N	111	368	38	98	14	7	2	44	19	27	.266	.311	.359	91	-5	-5	41	4			.969	2	*C/1	0.6
1914	Chi-N	79	248	17	64	9	2	0	19	9	9	.258	.284	.310	77	-8	-8	21	1			.973	5	C	0.4
1915	Chi-N	97	309	21	75	11	5	1	27	11	38	.243	.273	.320	79	-9	-9	27	5	6	-2	.977	-2	C/1	-0.6
1916	Chi-N	77	205	11	45	6	2	1	30	12	24	.220	.269	.283	63	-7	-10	18	3			.979	-3	C/3	-1.0
1917	Chi-N	2	2	0	0	0	0	0	0	0	1	.000	.000	.000	-93	-0	-0	0	0			.000	0	H	-0.1
1918	Pit-N	24	58	4	9	1	2	0	3	1	6	.155	.197	.241	32	-5	-5	3	0			.989	5	C/1	0.1
	Bro-N	9	22	3	6	0	1	0	0	1	5	.273	.304	.364	104	0	0	2	0			.968	1	/C	0.1
	Cin-N	9	26	2	7	1	0	0	2	1	3	.269	.296	.308	86	-1	-0	2	0			1.000	1	/C1	0.1
	Yr	42	106	9	22	2	3	0	5	3	14	.208	.243	.283	59	-5	-5	7	0			.987	7	C/1	0.3
Total	12	847	2646	246	660	106	33	17	296	124	241	.249	.288	.334	80	-71	-74	266	36	6		.971	4	C/1230	-1.0

■ GEORGE ARCHIE Archie, George Albert b: 4/27/14, Nashville, Tenn. BR/TR, 6', 170 lbs. Deb: 9/14/38

YEAR	TM/L	G	AB	R	H	2B	3B	HR	RBI	BB	SO	AVG	OBP	SLG	PRO+	BR	/A	RC	SB	CS	SBR	FA	FR	POS	TPR
1938	Det-A	3	2	1	0	0	0	0	0	0	1	.000	.000	.000	-95	-1	-1	0	0	0	0	.000	0	H	-0.1
1941	Was-A	105	379	45	102	20	4	3	48	30	42	.269	.324	.367	87	-10	-8	45	8	4	0	.936	-4	31	-1.2
	StL-A	9	29	3	11	3	0	0	5	7	3	.379	.500	.483	156	3	3	8	2	0	1	.975	0	/1	0.3
	Yr	114	408	48	113	23	4	3	53	37	45	.277	.339	.375	92	-7	-5	52	10	4	1	.936	-4	31	-0.9
1946	StL-A	4	11	1	2	1	0	0	0	0	1	.182	.182	.273	25	-1	-1	1	0	0	0	1.000	2	/1	0.0
Total	3	121	421	50	115	24	4	3	53	37	47	.273	.333	.371	90	-9	-6	53	10	4	1	.988	-2	/31	-1.0

■ JOSE ARCIA Arcia, Jose Raimundo (Orta) b: 8/22/43, Havana, Cuba BR/TR, 6'3", 170 lbs. Deb: 4/10/68

YEAR	TM/L	G	AB	R	H	2B	3B	HR	RBI	BB	SO	AVG	OBP	SLG	PRO+	BR	/A	RC	SB	CS	SBR	FA	FR	POS	TPR
1968	Chi-N	59	84	15	16	4	0	1	8	3	24	.190	.218	.274	44	-6	-6	5	0	0	0	1.000	2	O2/S3	-0.4
1969	SD-N	120	302	35	65	11	3	0	10	14	47	.215	.255	.272	49	-21	-20	20	14	7	0	.977	6	2S/3O1	-0.8
1970	SD-N	114	229	28	51	9	3	0	17	12	36	.223	.282	.288	55	-15	-14	18	3	6	-3	.955	12	S2/3O	0.1
Total	3	293	615	78	132	24	6	1	35	29	107	.215	.260	.278	51	-42	-40	43	17	13	-3	.950	20	S/2031	-1.1

■ DAN ARDELL Ardell, Daniel Miers b: 5/27/41, Seattle, Wash. BL/TL, 6'2", 190 lbs. Deb: 9/14/61

YEAR	TM/L	G	AB	R	H	2B	3B	HR	RBI	BB	SO	AVG	OBP	SLG	PRO+	BR	/A	RC	SB	CS	SBR	FA	FR	POS	TPR
1961	LA-A	7	4	1	1	0	0	0	0	1	2	.250	.400	.250	70	-0	-0	1	0	0	0	1.000	-0	/1	0.0

■ JOE ARDNER Ardner, Joseph A. "Old Hoss" b: 2/27/1858, Mt.Vernon, Ohio d: 9/15/35, Cleveland, Ohio BR/TR, 160 lbs. Deb: 5/01/1884

YEAR	TM/L	G	AB	R	H	2B	3B	HR	RBI	BB	SO	AVG	OBP	SLG	PRO+	BR	/A	RC	SB	CS	SBR	FA	FR	POS	TPR
1884	Cle-N	26	92	6	16	1	1	0	4	1	24	.174	.183	.207	21	-8	-8	4				.866	-5	2/3	-1.2
1890	Cle-N	84	323	28	72	13	1	0	35	17	40	.223	.266	.269	59	-17	-16	26	9			.920	-6	2	-1.6
Total	2	110	415	34	88	14	2	0	39	18	64	.212	.248	.255	51	-25	-25	30	9			.908	-11	2/3	-2.8

■ HANK ARFT Arft, Henry Irven "Bow Wow" b: 1/28/22, Manchester, Mo. BL/TL, 5'10.5", 190 lbs. Deb: 7/27/48

YEAR	TM/L	G	AB	R	H	2B	3B	HR	RBI	BB	SO	AVG	OBP	SLG	PRO+	BR	/A	RC	SB	CS	SBR	FA	FR	POS	TPR
1948	StL-A	69	248	25	59	10	3	5	38	45	43	.238	.355	.363	89	-3	-3	34	1	2	-1	.995	-1	1	-0.5
1949	StL-A	6	5	1	1	1	0	0	2	0	1	.200	.200	.400	55	-0	-0	0	0	0	0	.000	0	H	0.0
1950	StL-A	98	280	45	75	16	4	1	32	46	48	.268	.375	.364	87	-3	-5	43	3	2	-0	.995	2	1	-0.5
1951	StL-A	112	345	44	90	16	5	7	42	41	34	.261	.339	.397	96	-1	-2	48	4	6	-2	.989	8	1	-0.1
1952	StL-A	15	28	1	4	3	1	0	4	5	7	.143	.273	.321	63	-1	-2	3	0	0	0	.985	-0	1	-0.2
Total	5	300	906	116	229	46	13	13	118	137	133	.253	.352	.375	90	-8	-12	128	8	10	-4	.992	8	1	-1.3

■ ALEX ARIAS Arias, Alejandro b: 11/20/67, New York, N.Y. BR/TR, 6'3", 185 lbs. Deb: 5/12/92

YEAR	TM/L	G	AB	R	H	2B	3B	HR	RBI	BB	SO	AVG	OBP	SLG	PRO+	BR	/A	RC	SB	CS	SBR	FA	FR	POS	TPR
1992	Chi-N	32	99	14	29	6	0	0	7	11	13	.293	.375	.354	105	1	1	13	0	0	0	.967	-4	S	0.0

YEAR	TM/L	G	AB	R	H	2B	3B	HR	RBI	BB	SO	AVG	OBP	SLG	PRO+	BR	/A	RC	SB	CS	SBR	FA	FR	POS	TPR

■ BUZZ ARLETT
Arlett, Russell Loris   b: 1/3/1899, Elmhurst, Cal.   d: 5/16/64, Minneapolis, Minn.   BB/TR, 6'3.5", 225 lbs.   Deb: 4/14/31

| 1931 | Phi-N | 121 | 418 | 65 | 131 | 26 | 7 | 18 | 72 | 45 | 39 | .313 | .387 | .538 | 135 | 27 | 22 | 90 | 3 | | | .955 | 1 | O1 | 1.6 |

■ TONY ARMAS
Armas, Antonio Rafael (Machado)   b: 7/2/53, Anzoategui, Venez.   BR/TR, 6'1", 200 lbs.   Deb: 9/06/76

1976	Pit-N	4	6	0	2	0	0	0	1	0	2	.333	.333	.333	89	-0	-0	1	0	0	0	1.000	0	/O	0.0
1977	Oak-A	118	363	26	87	8	2	13	53	20	99	.240	.279	.380	79	-12	-11	37	1	2	-1	.981	9	*O/S	-0.7
1978	Oak-A	91	239	17	51	6	1	2	13	10	62	.213	.251	.272	50	-17	-15	16	1	2	-1	.991	3	O/D	-1.7
1979	Oak-A	80	278	29	69	9	3	11	34	16	67	.248	.292	.421	95	-5	-3	33	1	0	0	.976	7	O	0.1
1980	Oak-A	158	628	87	175	18	8	35	109	29	128	.279	.313	.500	128	13	18	89	5	3	-0	.975	18	*O	3.0
1981	*Oak-A★	109	440	51	115	24	3	22	76	19	115	.261	.295	.480	126	9	11	61	5	1	1	.993	12	*O	2.0
1982	Oak-A	138	536	58	125	19	2	28	89	33	128	.233	.279	.433	96	-8	-5	61	2	2	-1	.983	12	O/D	0.2
1983	Bos-A	145	574	77	125	23	2	36	107	29	131	.218	.258	.453	85	-10	-15	55	0	1	-1	.985	7	*O	-1.3
1984	Bos-A☆	157	639	107	171	29	5	43	123	32	156	.268	.304	.531	120	18	15	97	1	3	-2	.974	2	*OD	1.1
1985	Bos-A	103	385	50	102	17	5	23	64	18	90	.265	.301	.514	114	6	4	54	0	0	0	.983	-7	OD	-0.4
1986	*Bos-A	121	425	40	112	21	4	11	58	24	77	.264	.306	.409	92	-5	-5	49	0	3	-2	.969	-13	*O/D	-2.4
1987	Cal-A	28	81	8	16	3	1	3	9	1	11	.198	.207	.370	51	-6	-6	5	1	0	0	1.000	-4	O	-1.0
1988	Cal-A	120	368	42	100	20	2	13	49	22	87	.272	.313	.443	112	3	4	46	1	3	-2	.986	-9	*O/D	-0.9
1989	Cal-A	60	202	22	52	7	1	11	30	7	48	.257	.282	.465	109	1	1	26	0	0	0	.990	2	O/1D	0.2
Total	14	1432	5164	614	1302	204	39	251	815	260	1201	.252	.290	.453	103	-12	-6	629	18	20	-7	.981	38	*O/D1S	-1.8

■ ED ARMBRISTER
Armbrister, Edison Rosanda   b: 7/4/48, Nassau, Bahamas   BR/TR, 5'11", 160 lbs.   Deb: 8/31/73

1973	*Cin-N	18	37	5	8	3	1	1	5	2	8	.216	.256	.432	92	-1	-1	4	0	0	0	.917	0	O	-0.1
1974	Cin-N	9	7	0	2	0	0	0	0	1	1	.286	.375	.286	88	-0	-0	1	0	0	0	1.000	0	/O	0.0
1975	*Cin-N	59	65	9	12	1	0	0	2	5	19	.185	.254	.200	27	-6	-6	4	3	1	0	.867	-2	O	-0.9
1976	*Cin-N	73	78	20	23	3	2	2	7	6	22	.295	.345	.462	124	3	2	13	7	3	0	.972	4	O	0.6
1977	Cin-N	65	78	12	20	4	3	1	5	10	21	.256	.341	.423	102	0	0	9	5	6	-2	.903	1	O	-0.2
Total	5	224	265	46	65	11	6	4	19	24	71	.245	.310	.377	88	-4	-5	31	15	10	-2	.925	3	/O	-0.6

■ CHARLIE ARMBRUSTER
Armbruster, Charles A.   b: 8/30/1880, Cincinnati, Ohio   d: 10/7/64, Grants Pass, Ore.   BR/TR, 5'9", 180 lbs.   Deb: 7/17/05

1905	Bos-A	35	91	13	18	4	0	0	6	18		.198	.336	.242	84	-1	-1	9	3			.944	-6	C	-0.4
1906	Bos-A	72	201	9	29	6	1	0	6	25		.144	.242	.184	34	-14	-14	10	2			.955	1	C/1	-0.8
1907	Bos-A	23	60	2	6	1	0	0	0	8		.100	.206	.117	3	-6	-6	2	1			.935	2	C	-0.2
	Chi-A	1	3	0	0	0	0	0	0	1		.000	.250	.000	-20	-0	-0	0	0			1.000	1	/C	0.0
	Yr	24	63	2	6	1	0	0	0	9		.095	.208	.111	2	-7	-7	2	1			.940	3	C	-0.2
Total	3	131	355	24	53	11	1	0	12	52		.149	.262	.186	42	-22	-22	21	6			.949	-2	C/1	-1.4

■ HARRY ARMBRUSTER
Armbruster, Henry "Army"   b: 3/20/1882, Cincinnati, Ohio   d: 12/10/53, Cincinnati, Ohio   BL/TL, 5'10", 190 lbs.   Deb: 4/30/06

| 1906 | Phi-A | 91 | 265 | 40 | 63 | 6 | 3 | 2 | 24 | 43 | | .238 | .350 | .306 | 103 | 4 | 3 | 36 | 13 | | | .971 | 0 | O | 0.0 |

■ GEORGE ARMSTRONG
Armstrong, George Noble "Dodo"   b: 6/3/24, Orange, N.J.   BR/TR, 5'10", 190 lbs.   Deb: 4/26/46

| 1946 | Phi-A | 8 | 6 | 0 | 1 | 0 | 0 | 0 | 1 | 1 | | .167 | .286 | .333 | 73 | -0 | -0 | 1 | 0 | 0 | 0 | 1.000 | 1 | /C | 0.0 |

■ SAM ARMSTRONG
Armstrong, Samuel   b: 1850, Baltimore, Md.   6'2", 160 lbs.   Deb: 6/26/1871

| 1871 | Kek-n | 12 | 49 | 9 | 11 | 2 | 1 | 0 | | 5 | 0 | 1 | .224 | .224 | .306 | 50 | -3 | -3 | 3 | 0 | | | | | O | -0.2 |

■ HARRY ARNDT
Arndt, Harry J.   b: 2/12/1879, South Bend, Ind.   d: 3/24/21, South Bend, Ind.   TR ,   Deb: 7/02/02

1902	Det-A	10	34	4	5	0	1	0	7	6		.147	.275	.206	34	-3	-3	2	0			.958	0	O/1	-0.3
	Bal-A	68	248	41	63	7	4	2	28	35		.254	.353	.339	88	-1	-3	34	9			.872	1	O/23S	-0.6
	Yr	78	282	45	68	7	5	2	35	41		.241	.344	.323	82	-4	-6	36	9			.885	1	O/231S	-0.9
1905	StL-N	113	415	40	101	11	6	2	36	24		.243	.286	.313	81	-11	-10	43	13			.951	-14	2/O3S	-2.4
1906	StL-N	69	256	30	69	7	9	2	26	19		.270	.320	.391	127	5	7	35	5			.965	12	3/1O	2.2
1907	StL-N	11	32	3	6	1	0	0	2	1		.188	.212	.219	36	-2	-2	2	0			1.000	0	/13	-0.2
Total	4	271	985	118	244	26	20	6	99	85		.248	.310	.333	91	-13	-12	116	27			.952	-1	/203S1	-1.3

■ LARRY ARNDT
Arndt, Larry Wayne   b: 2/25/63, Fremont, Ohio   BR/TR, 6'1", 195 lbs.   Deb: 6/06/89

| 1989 | Oak-A | 2 | 6 | 1 | 1 | 0 | 0 | 0 | 1 | 0 | | .167 | .167 | .167 | -6 | -1 | -1 | 0 | 0 | 0 | 0 | 1.000 | 0 | /13 | -0.1 |

■ CHRIS ARNOLD
Arnold, Christopher Paul   b: 11/6/47, Long Beach, Cal.   BR/TR, 5'10", 160 lbs.   Deb: 9/07/71

1971	SF-N	6	13	2	3	0	0	1	3	1	2	.231	.286	.462	110	0	0	2	0	0	0	.917	-1	/2	-0.1
1972	SF-N	51	84	8	19	3	1	1	4	8	12	.226	.293	.321	74	-3	-3	7	0	1	-1	.970	3	3/2S	0.0
1973	SF-N	49	54	7	16	2	0	1	13	8	11	.296	.387	.389	111	1	1	8	0	0	0	.944	-5	/C23	-0.4
1974	SF-N	78	174	22	42	7	3	1	26	15	27	.241	.305	.333	75	-5	-6	19	1	1	-0	.974	-6	2/3S	-1.1
1975	SF-N	29	41	4	8	0	0	0	4	4	13	.195	.267	.195	28	-4	-4	2	0	0	0	.923	1	2/O	-0.4
1976	SF-N	60	69	4	15	0	1	0	5	6	16	.217	.280	.246	49	-4	-5	4	0	0	0	1.000	3	/231S	-0.1
Total	6	273	435	47	103	12	5	4	51	42	76	.237	.305	.315	72	-15	-16	42	1	2	-1	.971	-5	/23CSO1	-2.1

■ BILLY ARNOLD
Arnold, Willis S.   b: 3/2/1851, Middletown, Conn.   d: 1/17/1899, Albany, N.Y.   Deb: 4/26/1872

| 1872 | Man-n | 2 | 8 | 1 | 1 | 0 | 0 | 0 | | 0 | 0 | .125 | .125 | .125 | -24 | -1 | -1 | 0 | | | | | | /O | -0.1 |

■ MORRIE ARNOVICH
Arnovich, Morris "Snooker"   b: 11/16/10, Superior, Wis.   d: 7/20/59, Superior, Wis.   BR/TR, 5'10", 168 lbs.   Deb: 9/14/36

1936	Phi-N	13	48	4	15	3	0	1	7	1	3	.313	.353	.438	102	1	0	7	0			1.000	2	O	0.2
1937	Phi-N	117	410	60	119	27	4	10	60	34	32	.290	.349	.449	107	8	4	63	5			.972	7	*O	0.7
1938	Phi-N	139	502	47	138	29	0	4	72	42	37	.275	.333	.357	92	-7	-5	60	2			.983	17	*O	0.8
1939	Phi-N☆	134	491	68	159	25	5	5	67	58	28	.324	.397	.413	122	15	17	83	7			.983	15	*O	2.6
1940	Phi-N	39	141	13	28	2	1	0	12	14	15	.199	.276	.227	42	-11	-10	9	0			.959	3	O	-1.0
	*Cin-N	62	211	17	60	10	2	0	21	13	10	.284	.326	.351	86	-4	-4	23	1			1.000	2	O	-0.5
	Yr	101	352	30	88	12	3	0	33	27	25	.250	.305	.301	68	-15	-15	31	1			.983	5	O	-1.5
1941	NY-N	85	207	25	58	8	3	2	22	23	14	.280	.352	.377	103	2	1	27	0			.982	-4	O	-0.6
1946	NY-N	1	3	0	0	0	0	0	0	0	0	.000	.000	.000	-99	-1	-1	0	0			1.000	-0	/O	-0.1
Total	7	590	2013	234	577	104	12	22	261	185	139	.287	.350	.383	100	3	1	272	17			.981	42	O	2.1

■ TUG ARUNDEL
Arundel, John Thomas   b: 6/30/1862, Romulus, N.Y.   d: 9/5/12, Auburn, N.Y.   Deb: 5/23/1882

1882	Phi-a	1	5	0	0	0	0	0		0		.000	.000	.000	-90	-1	-1	0				.800	-0	/C	-0.1
1884	Tol-a	15	47	6	4	0	0	0		3		.085	.140	.085	-23	-6	-6	1				.946	8	C	0.3
1887	Ind-N	43	157	13	31	4	0	0	13	8	12	.197	.241	.223	32	-14	-13	11	8			.865	-5	C/O1	-1.3
1888	Was-N	17	51	2	10	1	0	0	3	5	10	.196	.268	.235	67	-2	-2	4	1			.840	-7	C	-0.7
Total	4	76	260	21	45	5	0	0	16	16	22	.173	.224	.196	27	-23	-22	15	9			.882	-5	/CO1	-1.8

■ RANDY ASADOOR
Asadoor, Randall Carl   b: 10/20/62, Fresno, Cal.   BR/TR, 6'1", 185 lbs.   Deb: 9/14/86

| 1986 | SD-N | 15 | 55 | 9 | 20 | 5 | 0 | 2 | 6 | 3 | 9 | .364 | .397 | .455 | 137 | 3 | 3 | 9 | 1 | 2 | -1 | .889 | 0 | 3/2 | 0.2 |

■ JIM ASBELL
Asbell, James Marion "Big Train"   b: 6/22/14, Dallas, Tex.   d: 7/6/67, San Mateo, Cal.   BR/TR, 6', 195 lbs.   Deb: 5/08/38

| 1938 | Chi-N | 17 | 33 | 6 | 6 | 2 | 0 | 0 | 3 | 9 | 11 | .182 | .250 | .242 | 35 | -3 | -3 | 2 | 0 | | | 1.000 | -1 | O | -0.4 |

■ CASPER ASBJORNSON
Asbjornson, Robert Anthony (Name Changed To Asby)   b: 6/19/09, Concord, Mass.   d: 1/21/70, Williamsport, Pa.   BR/TR, 6'1", 196 lbs.   Deb: 9/17/28

| 1928 | Bos-A | 6 | 16 | 0 | 3 | 1 | 0 | 0 | 1 | 1 | 1 | .188 | .235 | .250 | 28 | -2 | -2 | 1 | 0 | 0 | 0 | .917 | -2 | /C | -0.3 |

YEAR	TM/L	G	AB	R	H	2B	3B	HR	RBI	BB	SO	AVG	OBP	SLG	PRO+	BR	/A	RC	SB	CS	SBR	FA	FR	POS	TPR
1929	Bos-A	17	29	1	3	0	0	0	0	1	6	.103	.133	.103	-39	-6	-6	0	0	0	0	.897	-3	C	-0.7
1931	Cin-N	45	118	13	36	7	1	0	22	7	23	.305	.349	.381	102	-1	0	16	0			.981	-0	C	0.2
1932	Cin-N	29	58	5	10	2	0	1	4	0	15	.172	.186	.259	19	-7	-6	3	0			.961	0	C	-0.6
Total	4	97	221	19	52	10	1	1	27	9	45	.235	.272	.303	56	-15	-14	20	0	<u>0</u>		.960	-5	/C	-1.4

■ **RICHIE ASHBURN** Ashburn, Rich "Whitey" b: 3/19/27, Tilden, Neb. BL/TR, 5'10", 170 lbs. Deb: 4/20/48

YEAR	TM/L	G	AB	R	H	2B	3B	HR	RBI	BB	SO	AVG	OBP	SLG	PRO+	BR	/A	RC	SB	CS	SBR	FA	FR	POS	TPR
1948	Phi-N★	117	463	78	154	17	4	2	40	60	22	.333	.410	.400	122	16	17	82	**32**			.981	**18**	*O	2.8
1949	Phi-N	154	662	84	188	18	11	1	37	58	38	.284	.343	.349	88	-12	-10	82	9			.980	**25**	*O	0.7
1950	*Phi-N	151	594	84	180	25	**14**	2	41	63	32	.303	.372	.402	105	4	6	91	14			.988	8	*O	0.7
1951	Phi-N★	154	643	92	**221**	31	5	4	63	50	37	.344	.393	.426	122	19	21	118	29	6	5	.988	**32**	*O	5.1
1952	Phi-N	154	613	93	173	31	6	1	42	75	30	.282	.362	.357	101	2	3	86	16	11	-2	.980	15	*O	1.1
1953	Phi-N★	156	622	110	**205**	25	9	2	57	61	35	.330	.394	.408	110	11	12	109	14	6	1	.990	**26**	*O	3.1
1954	Phi-N	153	559	111	175	16	8	1	41	**125**	46	.313	**.442**	.376	116	22	22	107	11	8	-2	.984	17	*O	3.0
1955	Phi-N	140	533	91	180	32	9	3	42	105	36	**.338**	**.449**	.448	142	37	38	117	12	10	-2	.983	11	*O	4.0
1956	Phi-N	154	628	94	190	26	8	3	50	79	45	.303	.385	.384	110	10	11	101	10	1	2	.983	25	*O	3.1
1957	Phi-N	156	626	93	186	26	8	0	33	**94**	44	.297	.392	.364	108	9	12	95	13	10	-2	.987	**32**	*O	3.3
1958	Phi-N☆	152	615	98	**215**	24	**13**	2	33	**97**	48	**.350**	**.441**	.441	136	36	38	129	30	12	2	.984	22	*O	5.3
1959	Phi-N	153	564	86	150	16	2	1	20	79	42	.266	.362	.307	79	-12	-13	66	9	11	-4	.971	5	*O	-2.1
1960	Chi-N	151	547	99	159	16	5	0	40	**116**	50	.291	**.416**	.338	110	14	15	91	16	4	2	.976	1	*O	1.2
1961	Chi-N	109	307	49	79	7	4	0	19	55	27	.257	.375	.306	83	-5	-5	39	7	6	-2	.978	-8	O	-1.9
1962	NY-N★	135	389	60	119	7	3	7	28	81	39	.306	.426	.393	119	17	16	72	12	7	-1	.975	4	O/2	1.3
Total	15	2189	8365	1322	2574	317	109	29	586	1198	571	.308	.397	.382	111	169	182	1386	234	<u>92</u>		.983	234	*O/2	30.7

■ **ALAN ASHBY** Ashby, Alan Dean b: 7/8/51, Long Beach, Cal. BB/TR, 6'2", 190 lbs. Deb: 7/03/73

YEAR	TM/L	G	AB	R	H	2B	3B	HR	RBI	BB	SO	AVG	OBP	SLG	PRO+	BR	/A	RC	SB	CS	SBR	FA	FR	POS	TPR
1973	Cle-A	11	29	4	5	1	0	1	3	2	11	.172	.226	.310	49	-2	-2	2	0	0	0	.978	-2	C	-0.4
1974	Cle-A	10	7	1	1	0	0	0	0	1	2	.143	.250	.143	15	-1	-1	0	0	0	0	1.000	0	/C	0.0
1975	Cle-A	90	254	32	57	10	1	5	32	30	42	.224	.309	.331	81	-6	-6	26	3	2	-0	.990	3	C/13D	0.0
1976	Cle-A	89	247	26	59	5	1	4	32	27	49	.239	.314	.316	86	-4	-4	24	0	2	-1	.987	6	C/13	0.3
1977	Tor-A	124	396	25	83	16	3	2	29	50	51	.210	.301	.280	59	-21	-22	34	0	2	-1	.984	-7	*C	-2.6
1978	Tor-A	81	264	27	69	15	0	9	29	28	32	.261	.334	.420	109	4	3	35	1	1	-0	.986	-7	C	-0.2
1979	Hou-N	108	336	25	68	15	2	2	35	26	70	.202	.264	.277	51	-24	-22	24	0	0	0	.987	-1	*C	-2.0
1980	*Hou-N	116	352	30	90	19	2	3	48	35	40	.256	.323	.347	94	-6	-3	38	0	0	0	.991	2	*C	0.4
1981	*Hou-N	83	255	20	69	13	0	4	33	35	33	.271	.359	.369	112	3	5	34	0	2	-1	.982	7	C	1.4
1982	Hou-N	100	339	40	87	14	2	12	49	27	53	.257	.313	.416	111	0	3	44	2	0	1	.977	-5	C	0.3
1983	Hou-N	87	275	31	63	18	1	8	34	31	38	.229	.307	.389	98	-4	-1	31	0	0	0	.974	-13	C	-1.1
1984	Hou-N	66	191	16	50	7	0	4	27	20	22	.262	.335	.361	103	-1	1	24	0	0	0	.986	-3	C	0.1
1985	Hou-N	65	189	20	53	8	0	8	25	24	27	.280	.364	.450	130	7	8	29	0	0	0	.978	-0	C	1.1
1986	*Hou-N	120	315	24	81	15	0	7	38	39	56	.257	.339	.371	98	-1	-0	40	1	0	0	.985	-4	*C	0.2
1987	Hou-N	125	386	53	111	16	0	14	63	50	52	.288	.371	.438	118	8	10	61	0	1	-1	**.993**	-4	*C	1.3
1988	Hou-N	73	227	19	54	10	0	7	33	29	36	.238	.324	.374	104	0	1	28	0	0	0	.991	-10	C	-0.4
1989	Hou-N	22	61	4	10	1	1	0	3	7	8	.164	.261	.213	38	-5	-5	4	0	0	0	1.000	-3	C	-0.7
Total	17	1370	4123	397	1010	183	13	90	513	461	622	.245	.323	.361	93	-53	-35	478	7	10	-4	.986	-41	*C/13D	-2.3

■ **TUCKER ASHFORD** Ashford, Thomas Steven b: 12/4/54, Memphis, Tenn. BR/TR, 6'1", 195 lbs. Deb: 9/21/76

YEAR	TM/L	G	AB	R	H	2B	3B	HR	RBI	BB	SO	AVG	OBP	SLG	PRO+	BR	/A	RC	SB	CS	SBR	FA	FR	POS	TPR
1976	SD-N	4	5	0	3	1	0	0	0	1	0	.600	.667	.800	343	2	2	4	2	0	1	1.000	0	/3	0.2
1977	SD-N	81	249	25	54	18	0	3	24	21	35	.217	.280	.325	69	-14	-10	22	2	3	-1	.937	2	3S/2	-0.9
1978	SD-N	75	155	11	38	11	0	3	26	14	31	.245	.308	.374	97	-2	-1	18	1	0	0	.917	-16	321	-1.8
1980	Tex-A	15	32	2	4	0	0	0	3	3	3	.125	.200	.125	-9	-5	-5	1	0	0	0	.943	3	3/S	-0.2
1981	NY-A	3	0	0	0	0	0	0	0	0	0	—	—	—	—	0	0	0	0	0	0	.000	0	/2	0.0
1983	NY-N	35	56	3	10	0	1	0	2	7	4	.179	.270	.214	36	-5	-5	3	0	0	0	.957	-1	32/C	-0.6
1984	KC-A	9	13	1	2	1	0	0	0	1	2	.154	.214	.231	23	-1	-1	0	0	0	0	.909	0	/3	-0.1
Total	7	222	510	42	111	31	1	6	55	47	75	.218	.285	.318	70	-25	-20	48	5	3	-0	.936	-12	3/21SC	-3.4

■ **BILLY ASHLEY** Ashley, Billy Manual b: 7/11/70, Taylor, Mich. BR/TR, 6'7", 220 lbs. Deb: 9/01/92

YEAR	TM/L	G	AB	R	H	2B	3B	HR	RBI	BB	SO	AVG	OBP	SLG	PRO+	BR	/A	RC	SB	CS	SBR	FA	FR	POS	TPR
1992	LA-N	29	95	6	21	5	0	2	6	5	34	.221	.260	.337	69	-4	-4	8	0	0	0	.857	-3	O	-0.8

■ **TOM ASMUSSEN** Asmussen, Thomas William b: 9/26/1876, Chicago, Ill. d: 8/21/63, Arlington Heights Ill. TR , Deb: 8/10/07

YEAR	TM/L	G	AB	R	H	2B	3B	HR	RBI	BB	SO	AVG	OBP	SLG	PRO+	BR	/A	RC	SB	CS	SBR	FA	FR	POS	TPR
1907	Bos-N	2	5	0	0	0	0	0	0	0		.000	.000	.000	-99	-1	-1	0	0			1.000	-1	/C	-0.3

■ **KEN ASPROMONTE** Aspromonte, Kenneth Joseph b: 9/22/31, Brooklyn, N.Y. BR/TR, 6', 180 lbs. Deb: 9/02/57 FM

YEAR	TM/L	G	AB	R	H	2B	3B	HR	RBI	BB	SO	AVG	OBP	SLG	PRO+	BR	/A	RC	SB	CS	SBR	FA	FR	POS	TPR
1957	Bos-A	24	78	9	21	5	0	0	4	17	10	.269	.400	.333	97	1	1	11	0	1	-1	.965	-3	2	-0.1
1958	Bos-A	6	16	0	2	0	0	0	0	3	1	.125	.263	.125	10	-2	-2	1	0	0	0	.952	-3	/2	-0.5
	Was-A	92	253	15	57	9	1	5	27	25	28	.225	.297	.328	73	-10	-9	23	1	1	-0	.964	3	23/S	-0.2
	Yr	98	269	15	59	9	1	5	27	28	29	.219	.295	.316	69	-12	-11	24	1	1	-0	.963	-0	23/S	-0.7
1959	Was-A	70	225	31	55	12	0	2	14	26	39	.244	.323	.324	79	-6	-6	23	2	1	0	.960	-10	2S/1O	-1.1
1960	Was-A	4	3	0	0	0	0	0	0	0	1	.000	.000	.000	-99	-1	-1	0	0	0	0	.000	0	H	-0.1
	Cle-A	117	459	65	133	20	1	10	48	53	32	.290	.366	.403	111	6	8	69	4	1	1	.976	-12	23	0.4
	Yr	121	462	65	133	20	1	10	48	53	33	.288	.364	.400	110	5	7	69	4	1	1	.976	-12	23	0.3
1961	LA-A	66	238	29	53	10	0	2	14	33	21	.223	.322	.290	58	-11	-15	24	0	0	0	.970	18	2	1.0
	Cle-A	22	70	5	16	6	1	0	5	6	3	.229	.289	.343	70	-3	-3	6	0	0	0	.963	-2	2	-0.3
	Yr	88	308	34	69	16	1	2	19	39	24	.224	.315	.302	61	-14	-18	31	0	0	0	.969	17	2	0.7
1962	Cle-A	20	28	4	4	2	0	0	1	6	5	.143	.294	.214	41	-2	-2	2	0	0	0	1.000	-1	/23	-0.3
	Mil-N	34	79	11	23	2	0	0	7	6	5	.291	.349	.316	82	-2	-2	7	0	1	-1	1.000	-0	2/3	-0.1
1963	Chi-N	20	34	2	5	3	0	0	4	4	4	.147	.237	.235	35	-3	-3	2	0	0	0	.951	3	/21	0.1
Total	7	475	1483	171	369	69	3	19	124	179	149	.249	.332	.338	82	-33	-34	169	7	5	-1	.969	-7	2/3S1O	-1.2

■ **BOB ASPROMONTE** Aspromonte, Robert Thomas b: 6/19/38, Brooklyn, N.Y. BR/TR, 6'2", 185 lbs. Deb: 9/19/56 F

YEAR	TM/L	G	AB	R	H	2B	3B	HR	RBI	BB	SO	AVG	OBP	SLG	PRO+	BR	/A	RC	SB	CS	SBR	FA	FR	POS	TPR
1956	Bro-N	1	1	0	0	0	0	0	0	0	1	.000	.000	.000	-93	-0	-0	0	0	0	0	.000	0	H	0.0
1960	LA-N	21	55	1	10	1	0	1	6	0	6	.182	.196	.255	21	-6	-6	3	1	0	0	.933	-2	S/3	-0.7
1961	LA-N	47	58	7	14	3	0	0	2	4	12	.241	.290	.293	51	-4	-4	5	0	0	0	.917	0	/3S2	-0.4
1962	Hou-N	149	534	59	142	18	4	11	59	46	54	.266	.333	.376	97	-7	-2	67	4	5	-2	.967	1	*3S/2	0.0
1963	Hou-N	136	468	42	100	9	5	8	49	40	57	.214	.277	.306	72	-19	-16	38	3	1	0	.938	-16	*3/1	-3.5
1964	Hou-N	157	553	51	155	20	3	12	69	35	54	.280	.332	.392	109	2	6	69	6	7	-2	**.973**	-15	*3	-1.4
1965	Hou-N	152	578	53	152	15	2	5	52	38	54	.263	.312	.322	85	-16	-11	57	2	2	-1	.962	0	*3/1S	-1.6
1966	Hou-N	152	560	55	141	16	3	8	52	35	63	.252	.298	.334	81	-18	-14	50	0	4	-2	**.962**	-11	*3/1S	-3.2
1967	Hou-N	137	486	51	143	24	5	6	58	45	44	.294	.356	.401	121	11	13	67	2	2	-1	.963	-4	*3	0.7
1968	Hou-N	124	409	25	92	9	2	1	46	35	57	.225	.289	.264	68	-16	-15	30	1	0	0	.973	-0	3O/1S	-1.9
1969	*Atl-N	82	198	16	50	8	1	3	24	13	19	.253	.305	.348	82	-5	-5	21	0	1	-1	.975	-7	O3S/2	-1.4
1970	Atl-N	62	127	5	27	3	0	0	7	13	13	.213	.286	.236	39	-10	-11	9	0	0	0	.938	-0	3/S1O	-1.2
1971	NY-N	104	342	21	77	9	1	5	33	29	25	.225	.286	.301	67	-15	-15	27	0	2	-1	.965	-5	3	-2.3
Total	13	1324	4369	386	1103	135	26	60	457	333	459	.252	.310	.336	86	-103	-81	441	19	24	-9	.960	-58	*3/OS12	-16.9

■ **BRIAN ASSELSTINE** Asselstine, Brian Hanly b: 9/23/53, Santa Barbara, Cal BL/TR, 6'1", 175 lbs. Deb: 9/14/76

YEAR	TM/L	G	AB	R	H	2B	3B	HR	RBI	BB	SO	AVG	OBP	SLG	PRO+	BR	/A	RC	SB	CS	SBR	FA	FR	POS	TPR
1976	Atl-N	11	33	2	7	0	0	1	3	1	2	.212	.235	.303	49	-2	-2	3	0	0	0	1.000	-0	/O	-0.3

YEAR	TM/L	G	AB	R	H	2B	3B	HR	RBI	BB	SO	AVG	OBP	SLG	PRO+	BR	/A	RC	SB	CS	SBR	FA	FR	POS	TPR
1977	Atl-N	83	124	12	26	6	0	4	17	9	10	.210	.263	.355	57	-7	-8	12	1	0	0	.983	3	O	-0.6
1978	Atl-N	39	103	11	28	3	3	2	13	11	16	.272	.353	.417	103	2	1	16	2	1	0	.968	-1	O	-0.2
1979	Atl-N	8	10	1	1	0	0	0	0	1	2	.100	.182	.100	-20	-2	-2	0	0	0	0	1.000	-0	/O	-0.2
1980	Atl-N	87	218	18	62	13	1	3	25	11	37	.284	.322	.394	96	-1	-2	24	1	3	-2	.962	-6	O	-1.2
1981	Atl-N	56	86	8	22	5	0	2	10	5	7	.256	.297	.384	90	-1	-1	9	1	0	0	.958	-1	O	-0.3
Total	6	284	574	52	146	27	4	12	68	38	74	.254	.304	.378	83	-10	-15	63	5	4	-1	.971	-6	O	-2.8

■ JOE ASTROTH Astroth, Joseph Henry b: 9/1/22, East Alton, Ill. BR/TR, 5'9", 187 lbs. Deb: 8/13/45

YEAR	TM/L	G	AB	R	H	2B	3B	HR	RBI	BB	SO	AVG	OBP	SLG	PRO+	BR	/A	RC	SB	CS	SBR	FA	FR	POS	TPR
1945	Phi-A	10	17	1	1	0	0	0	1	0	1	.059	.111	.059	-50	-3	-3	0	0	0	0	.857	0	/C	-0.3
1946	Phi-A	4	7	0	1	0	0	0	0	0	2	.143	.143	.143	-20	-1	-1	0	0	0	0	.889	-0	/C	-0.1
1949	Phi-A	55	148	18	36	4	1	0	12	21	13	.243	.337	.284	67	-7	-6	15	1	0	0	.979	2	C	-0.2
1950	Phi-A	39	110	11	36	3	1	1	18	18	3	.327	.422	.400	113	3	3	18	0	0	0	.985	-6	C	-0.1
1951	Phi-A	64	187	30	46	10	2	2	19	18	13	.246	.312	.353	78	-6	-6	21	0	1	-1	.992	4	C	-0.1
1952	Phi-A	104	337	24	84	7	2	1	36	25	27	.249	.305	.291	62	-15	-18	27	2	2	-1	.992	-5	*C	-1.9
1953	Phi-A	82	260	28	77	15	2	3	24	27	12	.296	.367	.404	104	3	2	38	1	0	0	.987	7	C	1.3
1954	Phi-A	77	226	22	50	8	1	1	23	21	19	.221	.296	.279	58	-13	-13	20	0	0	0	.988	-2	C	-1.2
1955	KC-A	101	274	29	69	4	1	5	23	47	33	.252	.373	.328	89	-2	-2	35	2	3	-1	.989	-4	*C	-0.4
1956	KC-A	8	13	0	1	0	0	0	0	0	1	.077	.077	.077	-59	-3	-3	0	0	0	0	1.000	2	/C	-0.1
Total	10	544	1579	163	401	51	10	13	156	177	124	.254	.334	.324	77	-44	-48	175	6	6	-2	.987	-2	C	-3.1

■ CHARLIE ATHERTON Atherton, Charles Morgan Herbert "Prexy" b: 10/19/1873, New Brunswick, N.J d: 12/19/34, Vienna, Austria BR/TR, 5'10", 160 lbs. Deb: 5/30/1899

YEAR	TM/L	G	AB	R	H	2B	3B	HR	RBI	BB	SO	AVG	OBP	SLG	PRO+	BR	/A	RC	SB	CS	SBR	FA	FR	POS	TPR
1899	Was-N	65	242	28	60	5	6	0	23	21		.248	.313	.318	74	-9	-8	26	2			.890	-6	3/O	-1.3

■ ED ATKINSON Atkinson, Edward b: 1851, Baltimore, Md. Deb: 10/22/1873

YEAR	TM/L	G	AB	R	H	2B	3B	HR	RBI	BB	SO	AVG	OBP	SLG	PRO+	BR	/A	RC	SB	CS	SBR	FA	FR	POS	TPR
1873	Was-n	2	8	2	0	0	0	0	0	0	0	.000	.000	.000	-99	-2	-2	0						/O	-0.1

■ LEFTY ATKINSON Atkinson, Hubert Berley b: 6/4/04, Chicago, Ill. d: 2/12/61, Chicago, Ill. BL/TL, 5'6.5", 149 lbs. Deb: 8/05/27

YEAR	TM/L	G	AB	R	H	2B	3B	HR	RBI	BB	SO	AVG	OBP	SLG	PRO+	BR	/A	RC	SB	CS	SBR	FA	FR	POS	TPR
1927	Was-A	1	1	1	0	0	0	0	0	0	0	.000	.000	.000	-99	-0	-0	0	0	0	0	.000	0	H	0.0

■ DICK ATTREAU Attreau, Richard Gilbert b: 4/8/1897, Chicago, Ill. d: 7/5/64, Chicago, Ill. BL/TL, 6', 160 lbs. Deb: 9/14/26

YEAR	TM/L	G	AB	R	H	2B	3B	HR	RBI	BB	SO	AVG	OBP	SLG	PRO+	BR	/A	RC	SB	CS	SBR	FA	FR	POS	TPR
1926	Phi-N	17	61	9	14	1	1	0	5	6	5	.230	.299	.279	53	-4	-4	5	0			.989	-1	1	-0.6
1927	Phi-N	44	83	17	17	1	1	1	11	14	18	.205	.320	.277	60	-4	-4	8	1			.989	-2	1	-0.7
Total	2	61	144	26	31	2	2	1	16	20	23	.215	.311	.278	57	-8	-8	13	1			.989	-3	/1	-1.3

■ TOBY ATWELL Atwell, Maurice Dailey b: 3/8/24, Leesburg, Va. BL/TR, 5'9.5", 185 lbs. Deb: 4/15/52

YEAR	TM/L	G	AB	R	H	2B	3B	HR	RBI	BB	SO	AVG	OBP	SLG	PRO+	BR	/A	RC	SB	CS	SBR	FA	FR	POS	TPR
1952	Chi-N☆	107	362	36	105	16	3	2	31	40	22	.290	.362	.367	102	2	2	49	2	1	0	.977	-7	*C	0.0
1953	Chi-N	24	74	10	17	2	0	1	8	13	7	.230	.345	.297	68	-3	-3	9	0	0	0	.940	1	C	-0.1
	Pit-N	53	139	11	34	6	0	0	17	20	12	.245	.352	.288	70	-5	-5	14	0	0	0	.967	-3	C	-0.6
	Yr	77	213	21	51	8	0	1	25	33	19	.239	.349	.291	69	-8	-8	23	0	0	0	.957	-2	C	-0.7
1954	Pit-N	96	287	36	83	8	4	3	26	43	21	.289	.387	.376	101	2	2	42	2	3	-1	.990	-2	C	0.3
1955	Pit-N	71	207	21	44	8	0	1	18	40	16	.213	.343	.266	65	-9	-9	21	0	1	-1	.992	6	C	-0.2
1956	Pit-N	12	18	0	2	0	0	0	3	1	5	.111	.158	.111	-27	-3	-3	0	0	0	0	1.000	1	/C	-0.2
	Mil-N	15	30	2	5	1	0	2	7	4	1	.167	.265	.400	80	-1	-1	3	0	0	0	1.000	-1	C	-0.1
	Yr	27	48	2	7	1	0	2	10	5	6	.146	.226	.292	40	-4	-4	3	0	0	0	1.000	0	C	-0.3
Total	5	378	1117	116	290	41	7	9	110	161	84	.260	.357	.333	86	-18	-17	139	4	5	-2	.980	-5	C	-0.9

■ BILL ATWOOD Atwood, William Franklin b: 9/25/11, Rome, Ga. BR/TR, 5'11.5", 190 lbs. Deb: 4/15/36

YEAR	TM/L	G	AB	R	H	2B	3B	HR	RBI	BB	SO	AVG	OBP	SLG	PRO+	BR	/A	RC	SB	CS	SBR	FA	FR	POS	TPR
1936	Phi-N	71	192	21	58	9	2	2	29	11	15	.302	.346	.401	92	0	-2	27	0			.972	-1	C	-0.1
1937	Phi-N	87	279	27	68	15	1	2	32	30	27	.244	.317	.326	69	-9	-12	32	3			.968	-14	C	-2.2
1938	Phi-N	102	281	27	55	8	1	3	28	25	26	.196	.261	.263	46	-21	-20	19	0			.969	0	C	-1.6
1939	Phi-N	4	6	0	0	0	0	0	1	2	3	.000	.250	.000	-29	-1	-1	0	1			1.000	-0	/C	-0.1
1940	Phi-N	78	203	7	39	9	0	0	22	25	18	.192	.284	.236	47	-15	-14	14	0			.989	1	C	-0.8
Total	5	342	961	82	220	41	4	7	112	93	89	.229	.299	.302	63	-46	-50	92	4			.974	-14	C	-4.8

■ JAKE ATZ Atz, John Jacob (b: John Jacob Zimmerman) b: 7/1/1879, Washington, D.C. d: 5/22/45, New Orleans, La. BR/TR, 5'9.5", 160 lbs. Deb: 9/24/02

YEAR	TM/L	G	AB	R	H	2B	3B	HR	RBI	BB	SO	AVG	OBP	SLG	PRO+	BR	/A	RC	SB	CS	SBR	FA	FR	POS	TPR
1902	Was-A	3	10	1	1	0	0	0	0	0		.100	.100	.100	-44	-2	-2	0	0			1.000	0	/2	-0.1
1907	Chi-A	4	8	0	1	0	0	0	0	0		.125	.125	.125	-21	-1	-1	0	0			1.000	1	/3O	0.0
1908	Chi-A	83	206	24	40	3	0	0	27	31		.194	.311	.209	71	-5	-5	17	9			.936	-3	2S/3	-0.9
1909	Chi-A	119	381	39	90	18	3	0	22	38		.236	.309	.299	96	-3	-1	40	14			.954	-7	*2/OS	-1.2
Total	4	209	605	64	132	21	3	0	49	69		.218	.304	.263	83	-11	-9	58	23			.949	-9	2/SO3	-2.2

■ HARRY AUBREY Aubrey, Harry Herbert "Chub" b: 7/5/1880, St.Joseph, Mo. d: 9/18/53, Baltimore, Md. TR , Deb: 4/22/03

YEAR	TM/L	G	AB	R	H	2B	3B	HR	RBI	BB	SO	AVG	OBP	SLG	PRO+	BR	/A	RC	SB	CS	SBR	FA	FR	POS	TPR
1903	Bos-N	96	325	26	69	8	2	0	27	18		.212	.264	.249	49	-22	-21	25	7			.868	-10	S/2O	-2.6

■ RICK AUERBACH Auerbach, Frederick Steven b: 2/15/50, Woodland Hills, Cal BR/TR, 6', 165 lbs. Deb: 4/13/71

YEAR	TM/L	G	AB	R	H	2B	3B	HR	RBI	BB	SO	AVG	OBP	SLG	PRO+	BR	/A	RC	SB	CS	SBR	FA	FR	POS	TPR
1971	Mil-A	79	236	22	48	10	0	1	9	20	40	.203	.271	.258	51	-15	-15	17	3	2	-0	.963	-10	S	-1.7
1972	Mil-A	153	554	50	121	16	3	2	30	43	62	.218	.277	.269	64	-25	-24	42	24	8	2	.959	-21	*S	-2.4
1973	Mil-A	6	10	2	1	1	0	0	0	0	1	.100	.100	.200	-18	-2	-2	0	0	1	-1	.833	0	/S	-0.2
1974	*LA-N	45	73	12	25	0	0	1	4	8	9	.342	.407	.384	127	3	3	11	4	2	0	.950	2	S2/3	0.6
1975	LA-N	85	170	18	38	9	0	0	12	18	22	.224	.298	.276	63	-9	-8	13	3	2	-0	.960	-17	S/23	-2.0
1976	LA-N	36	47	7	6	0	0	0	1	6	6	.128	.226	.128	2	-6	-6	1	0	1	-1	.943	11	S/32	0.6
1977	Cin-N	33	45	5	7	2	0	0	3	4	7	.156	.224	.200	15	-5	-6	2	0	0	0	.976	6	2S	0.2
1978	Cin-N	63	55	17	18	6	0	2	5	7	12	.327	.413	.545	166	5	5	13	1	0	0	.971	10	S2/3	1.7
1979	*Cin-N	62	100	17	21	8	1	1	12	14	19	.210	.307	.340	76	-3	-3	11	0	1	-1	.933	7	3S/2	0.4
1980	Cin-N	24	33	5	11	1	1	1	4	3	5	.333	.389	.515	150	2	2	5	0	3	-2	1.000	-1	/S32	0.0
1981	Sea-A	38	84	12	13	3	0	1	6	4	15	.155	.202	.226	22	-8	-9	4	1	1	-0	.979	3	S	-0.3
Total	11	624	1407	167	309	56	5	9	86	127	198	.220	.287	.286	65	-64	-62	119	36	21	-2	.960	-9	S/23	-3.1

■ DAVE AUGUSTINE Augustine, David Ralph b: 11/28/49, Follansbee, W.Va. BR/TR, 6'2", 174 lbs. Deb: 9/03/73

YEAR	TM/L	G	AB	R	H	2B	3B	HR	RBI	BB	SO	AVG	OBP	SLG	PRO+	BR	/A	RC	SB	CS	SBR	FA	FR	POS	TPR
1973	Pit-N	11	7	1	2	1	0	0	0	0	1	.286	.286	.429	98	-0	-0	0	0	0	0	1.000	1	/O	0.1
1974	Pit-N	18	22	3	4	0	0	0	0	0	5	.182	.182	.182	2	-3	-3	0	0	1	-1	1.000	4	O	0.1
Total	2	29	29	4	6	1	0	0	0	0	6	.207	.207	.241	26	-3	-3	1	0	1	-1	1.000	5	/O	0.2

■ TEX AULDS Aulds, Leycester Doyle b: 12/28/20, Farmerville, La. BR/TR, 6'2", 185 lbs. Deb: 5/25/47

YEAR	TM/L	G	AB	R	H	2B	3B	HR	RBI	BB	SO	AVG	OBP	SLG	PRO+	BR	/A	RC	SB	CS	SBR	FA	FR	POS	TPR
1947	Bos-A	3	4	0	1	0	0	0	0	0	1	.250	.250	.250	37	-0	-0	0	0	0	0	1.000	0	/C	0.0

■ DOUG AULT Ault, Douglas Reagan b: 3/9/50, Beaumont, Tex. BR/TL, 6'3", 200 lbs. Deb: 9/09/76

YEAR	TM/L	G	AB	R	H	2B	3B	HR	RBI	BB	SO	AVG	OBP	SLG	PRO+	BR	/A	RC	SB	CS	SBR	FA	FR	POS	TPR
1976	Tex-A	9	20	0	6	1	0	0	0	1	3	.300	.333	.350	98	-0	-0	2	0	0	0	1.000	-1	/1D	-0.1
1977	Tor-A	129	445	44	109	22	3	11	64	39	68	.245	.311	.382	87	-8	-9	48	4	4	-1	.987	7	*1/D	-1.0
1978	Tor-A	54	104	10	25	1	1	3	7	17	14	.240	.352	.356	98	0	0	13	0	0	0	.979	-2	1/OD	-0.3
1980	Tor-A	64	144	12	28	5	1	3	15	14	23	.194	.275	.306	56	-8	-9	12	0	1	-1	1.000	3	1D/O	-0.8
Total	4	256	713	66	168	29	5	17	86	71	108	.236	.311	.362	82	-15	-18	75	4	5	-2	.988	8	1/DO	-2.2

■ HENRY AUSTIN Austin, Henry C. b: 1844, Brooklyn, N.Y. d: 9/3/1895, Amityville, N.Y. Deb: 4/28/1873

YEAR	TM/L	G	AB	R	H	2B	3B	HR	RBI	BB	SO	AVG	OBP	SLG	PRO+	BR	/A	RC	SB	CS	SBR	FA	FR	POS	TPR
1873	Res-n	23	101	10	25	3	3	0	11	0	4	.248	.248	.337	76	-4	-2	9						O	-0.1

■ JIMMY AUSTIN
Austin, James Philip "Pepper" b: 12/8/1879, Swansea, Wales d: 3/6/65, Laguna Beach, Cal. BB/TR, 5'7.5", 155 lbs. Deb: 4/19/09 MC

YEAR	TM/L	G	AB	R	H	2B	3B	HR	RBI	BB	SO	AVG	OBP	SLG	PRO+	BR	/A	RC	SB	CS	SBR	FA	FR	POS	TPR
1909	NY-A	136	437	37	101	11	5	1	39	32		.231	.285	.286	80	-10	-10	45	30			.928	13	*3S/2	0.8
1910	NY-A	133	432	46	94	11	4	2	36	47		.218	.305	.275	77	-8	-11	45	22			.942	4	*3	-0.4
1911	StL-A	148	541	84	141	25	11	2	45	69		.261	.351	.359	102	-0	3	79	26			.931	16	*3	2.0
1912	StL-A	149	536	57	135	14	8	2	44	38		.252	.306	.319	82	-15	-13	62	28			.911	-1	*3	-1.3
1913	StL-A	142	489	56	130	18	6	2	42	45	51	.266	.338	.339	101	-1	1	66	37			**.944**	7	*3M	1.0
1914	StL-A	130	466	55	111	16	4	0	30	40	59	.238	.300	.290	80	-13	-11	41	20	23	-8	.935	1	*3	-1.5
1915	StL-A	141	477	61	127	6	6	1	30	64	60	.266	.355	.310	103	2	4	59	18	15	-4	.917	10	*3	1.7
1916	StL-A	129	411	55	85	15	6	1	28	74	59	.207	.333	.280	89	-5	-3	47	19			.939	-7	*3	-0.6
1917	StL-A	127	455	61	109	18	8	0	19	50	46	.240	.319	.314	97	-3	-1	50	13			.947	3	*3/S	0.4
1918	StL-A	110	367	42	97	14	4	0	20	53	32	.264	.359	.324	109	4	6	49	18			.939	-17	S3M	-0.8
1919	StL-A	106	396	54	94	9	9	1	21	42	31	.237	.314	.313	74	-12	-13	40	8			.939	7	3	-0.3
1920	StL-A	83	280	38	76	11	3	1	32	31	15	.271	.352	.343	82	-5	-7	35	2	4	-2	.943	2	3	-0.2
1921	StL-A	27	66	8	18	2	1	0	2	4	7	.273	.324	.333	64	-3	-4	7	2	1	0	.938	-3	S/23	-0.5
1922	StL-A	15	31	6	9	3	1	0	1	3	2	.290	.353	.452	105	0	0	5	0	0	0	.957	-3	/32	-0.2
1923	StL-A	1	0	0	0	0	0	0	0	0	0	—	—	—	—	0	0	0	0	0	0	.000	0	/M	0.0
1925	StL-A	1	1	0	0	0	0	0	0	0	0	.000	.000	.000	-95	-0	-0	0	0	0	0	1.000	0	/3	0.0
1926	StL-A	1	2	1	1	1	0	0	1	0	0	.500	.500	1.000	272	0	0	1	1	0	0	1.000	0	/3	0.1
1929	StL-A	1	1	0	0	0	0	0	0	0	1	.000	.000	.000	-96	-0	-0	0	0	0	0	1.000	1	/3	0.0
Total	18	1580	5388	661	1328	174	76	13	390	592	363	.246	.326	.314	90	-71	-59	633	244	43		.933	33	*3S/2	0.2

■ CHICK AUTRY
Autry, Martin Gordon b: 3/5/03, Martindale, Tex. d: 1/26/50, Savannah, Ga. BR/TR, 6', 180 lbs. Deb: 4/20/24

YEAR	TM/L	G	AB	R	H	2B	3B	HR	RBI	BB	SO	AVG	OBP	SLG	PRO+	BR	/A	RC	SB	CS	SBR	FA	FR	POS	TPR
1924	NY-A	2	0	1	0	0	0	0	0	0	0	—	1.000	—	172	0	0	0	0	0	0	1.000	-0	/C	0.0
1926	Cle-A	3	7	1	1	0	0	0	0	1	0	.143	.250	.143	4	-1	-1	0	0	0	0	1.000	-0	/C	-0.1
1927	Cle-A	16	43	5	11	4	1	0	7	0	6	.256	.256	.395	66	-2	-2	4	0	0	0	.933	2	C	0.1
1928	Cle-A	22	60	6	18	6	1	1	9	1	7	.300	.311	.483	105	0	0	9	0	0	0	.972	0	C	0.2
1929	Chi-A	43	96	7	20	6	0	1	12	1	8	.208	.224	.302	35	-10	-10	6	0	0	0	.940	-4	C	-1.1
1930	Chi-A	34	71	1	18	1	1	0	5	4	8	.254	.293	.296	52	-5	-5	6	0	0	0	.992	8	C	0.4
Total	6	120	277	21	68	17	3	2	33	7	29	.245	.269	.350	59	-18	-18	26	0	0	0	.965	5	/C	-0.5

■ CHICK AUTRY
Autry, William Askew b: 1/2/1885, Humboldt, Tenn. d: 1/16/76, Santa Rosa, Cal. BL/TL, 5'11", 168 lbs. Deb: 9/18/07

YEAR	TM/L	G	AB	R	H	2B	3B	HR	RBI	BB	SO	AVG	OBP	SLG	PRO+	BR	/A	RC	SB	CS	SBR	FA	FR	POS	TPR
1907	Cin-N	7	25	3	5	0	0	0	0	1		.200	.231	.200	34	-2	-2	1	0			.929	-1	/O	-0.4
1909	Cin-N	9	33	3	6	2	0	0	4	2		.182	.229	.242	46	-2	-2	2	1			.956	0	/1	-0.2
	Bos-N	65	199	16	39	4	0	0	13	21		.196	.279	.216	51	-10	-11	15	5			.994	5	1/O	-0.8
	Yr	74	232	19	45	6	0	0	17	23		.194	.272	.220	51	-12	-13	17	6			.989	5	1/O	-1.0
Total	2	81	257	22	50	6	0	0	17	24		.195	.269	.218	49	-14	-15	18	6			.968	4	/1O	-1.4

■ EARL AVERILL
Averill, Earl Douglas b: 9/9/31, Cleveland, Ohio BR/TR, 5'10", 190 lbs. Deb: 4/19/56 F

YEAR	TM/L	G	AB	R	H	2B	3B	HR	RBI	BB	SO	AVG	OBP	SLG	PRO+	BR	/A	RC	SB	CS	SBR	FA	FR	POS	TPR
1956	Cle-A	42	93	12	22	6	0	3	14	14	25	.237	.343	.398	93	-1	-1	13	0	1	-1	.994	3	C	0.2
1958	Cle-A	17	55	2	10	1	0	2	7	4	7	.182	.250	.309	54	-4	-3	4	1	0	0	.863	0	3	-0.3
1959	Chi-N	74	186	22	44	10	0	10	34	15	39	.237	.300	.452	98	-1	-1	25	0	1	-1	.963	3	C3/O2	0.3
1960	Chi-N	52	102	14	24	4	0	1	13	11	16	.235	.316	.304	71	-4	-4	10	1	1	-0	.979	-9	C/3O	-1.2
	Chi-A	10	14	2	3	0	0	0	2	4	2	.214	.389	.214	68	-0	-0	2	0	0	0	1.000	2	/C	0.2
1961	LA-A	115	323	56	86	9	0	21	59	62	70	.266	.388	.489	119	16	11	64	1	0	0	.991	-7	C/O2	0.9
1962	LA-A	92	187	21	41	9	0	4	22	43	47	.219	.368	.332	93	-1	-0	26	0	0	0	1.000	-4	O/C	-0.6
1963	Phi-N	47	71	8	19	2	0	3	8	9	14	.268	.350	.423	123	2	2	11	0	0	0	.966	2	C/O13	0.4
Total	7	449	1031	137	249	41	0	44	159	162	220	.242	.349	.409	101	7	3	154	3	3	-1	.984	-10	C/O321	-0.1

■ EARL AVERILL
Averill, Howard Earl "Rock" b: 5/21/02, Snohomish, Wash. d: 8/16/83, Everett, Wash. BL/TR, 5'9.5", 172 lbs. Deb: 4/16/29 FH

YEAR	TM/L	G	AB	R	H	2B	3B	HR	RBI	BB	SO	AVG	OBP	SLG	PRO+	BR	/A	RC	SB	CS	SBR	FA	FR	POS	TPR
1929	Cle-A	151	597	110	198	43	13	18	96	63	53	.332	.398	.538	134	34	30	125	13	13	-4	.966	-4	*O	1.2
1930	Cle-A	139	534	102	181	33	8	19	119	56	48	.339	.404	.537	131	29	26	116	10	7	-1	.949	2	*O	1.6
1931	Cle-A	155	627	140	209	36	10	32	143	68	38	.333	.404	.576	147	48	43	144	9	9	-3	.976	0	*O	2.8
1932	Cle-A	153	631	116	198	37	14	32	124	75	40	.314	.392	.569	137	41	35	140	5	8	-3	.964	2	*O	2.1
1933	Cle-A★	151	599	83	180	39	16	11	92	54	29	.301	.363	.474	115	16	12	104	3	1	0	.971	2	*O	0.7
1934	Cle-A★	154	598	128	187	48	6	31	113	99	44	.313	.414	.569	149	46	44	145	5	3	-0	.970	9	*O	4.2
1935	Cle-A†	140	563	109	162	34	13	19	79	70	58	.288	.368	.496	119	16	15	105	8	4	0	.982	-2	*O	0.7
1936	Cle-A★	152	614	136	**232**	39	**15**	28	126	65	35	.378	.438	.627	159	56	56	168	3	3	-1	.969	-4	*O	3.9
1937	Cle-A★	156	609	121	182	33	11	21	92	88	65	.299	.387	.493	119	19	18	119	5	4	-1	.976	-8	*O	0.4
1938	Cle-A★	134	482	101	159	27	15	14	93	81	48	.330	.429	.535	143	32	33	115	5	2	0	.975	5	*O	3.1
1939	Cle-A	24	55	8	15	8	0	1	7	6	12	.273	.344	.473	111	0	1	9	0	1	-1	1.000	-2	O	-0.3
	Det-A	87	309	58	81	20	6	10	58	43	30	.262	.354	.463	100	3	-1	53	4	2	0	.976	-5	O	-0.8
	Yr	111	364	66	96	28	6	11	65	49	42	.264	.353	.464	102	3	0	62	4	3	-1	.977	-7	O	-1.1
1940	*Det-A	64	118	10	33	4	1	2	20	5	14	.280	.309	.381	71	-4	-6	14	0	0	0	.962	-5	O	-1.1
1941	Bos-N	8	17	2	2	0	0	0	2	1	4	.118	.211	.118	-6	-2	-2	1	0			1.000	1	/O	-0.2
Total	13	1668	6353	1224	2019	401	128	238	1164	774	518	.318	.395	.534	132	334	305	1358	70	57		.970	-8	*O	18.3

■ BOBBY AVILA
Avila, Roberto Francisco (Gonzalez) b: 4/2/24, Vera Cruz, Mexico BR/TR, 5'10", 175 lbs. Deb: 4/30/49

YEAR	TM/L	G	AB	R	H	2B	3B	HR	RBI	BB	SO	AVG	OBP	SLG	PRO+	BR	/A	RC	SB	CS	SBR	FA	FR	POS	TPR
1949	Cle-A	31	14	3	3	0	0	0	3	1	3	.214	.267	.214	29	-1	-1	1	0	0	0	1.000	11	/2	0.9
1950	Cle-A	80	201	39	60	10	2	1	21	29	17	.299	.390	.383	102	0	1	32	5	0	2	.983	-5	2/S	0.0
1951	Cle-A	141	542	76	165	21	3	10	58	60	31	.304	.374	.410	118	9	13	84	14	8	-1	.982	-1	*2	1.8
1952	Cle-A★	150	597	102	179	26	**11**	7	45	67	36	.300	.371	.415	127	15	20	93	12	10	-2	.966	-18	*2	0.8
1953	Cle-A	141	559	85	160	22	3	8	55	58	27	.286	.355	.379	101	-1	1	75	10	8	-2	**.986**	13	*2	2.1
1954	*Cle-A★	143	555	112	189	27	2	15	67	59	31	.341	.405	.477	139	32	30	109	9	7	-2	.976	8	*2/S	4.7
1955	Cle-A★	141	537	83	146	22	4	13	61	82	47	.272	.370	.400	103	7	4	81	1	4	-2	.982	-3	*2	1.0
1956	Cle-A	138	513	74	115	14	2	10	54	70	68	.224	.323	.318	68	-22	-23	57	17	4	3	.977	-10	*2	-1.8
1957	Cle-A	129	463	60	124	19	3	5	48	46	47	.268	.335	.354	89	-7	-6	55	2	4	-2	.983	-15	*23	-1.5
1958	Cle-A	113	375	54	95	21	3	5	30	55	45	.253	.350	.365	100	-0	1	50	5	7	-3	.986	-21	23	-1.7
1959	Bal-A	20	47	1	8	0	0	0	0	4	5	.170	.235	.170	14	-6	-5	1	0	0	0	1.000	-4	O/23	-1.0
	Bos-A	22	45	7	11	0	0	3	6	6	11	.244	.333	.444	107	1	0	6	0	0	0	.975	-2	2	-0.1
	Yr	42	92	8	19	0	0	3	6	10	16	.207	.284	.304	61	-5	-5	6	0	0	0	.967	-6	2O/3	-1.1
	Mil-N	51	172	29	41	3	2	3	19	24	31	.238	.332	.331	84	-5	-3	22	3	0	1	.967	-12	2	-1.0
Total	11	1300	4620	725	1296	185	35	80	467	561	399	.281	.360	.388	104	23	33	666	78	52	-8	.979	-57	*2/3OS	4.2

■ RAMON AVILES
Aviles, Ramon Antonio (Miranda) b: 1/22/52, Manati, P.R. BR/TR, 5'9", 155 lbs. Deb: 7/10/77

YEAR	TM/L	G	AB	R	H	2B	3B	HR	RBI	BB	SO	AVG	OBP	SLG	PRO+	BR	/A	RC	SB	CS	SBR	FA	FR	POS	TPR
1977	Bos-A	1	0	0	0	0	0	0	0	0	0	—	—	—	—	0	-0	0	0	0	0	1.000	0	/2	0.0
1979	Phi-N	27	61	7	17	2	0	0	12	8	8	.279	.371	.311	86	-1	-1	8	0	0	0	.977	-7	2	-0.7
1980	*Phi-N	51	101	12	28	6	0	2	9	10	9	.277	.342	.396	100	1	0	13	0	0	0	.944	-7	S2	-0.4
1981	*Phi-N	38	28	2	6	1	0	0	3	3	5	.214	.290	.250	52	-2	-2	2	0	0	0	1.000	4	23/S	0.3
Total	4	117	190	21	51	9	0	2	24	21	22	.268	.344	.347	88	-1	-2	24	0	0	0	.971	-10	/2S3	-0.8

■ BENNY AYALA
Ayala, Benigno (Felix) b: 2/7/51, Yauco, P.R. BR/TR, 6'1", 185 lbs. Deb: 8/27/74

YEAR	TM/L	G	AB	R	H	2B	3B	HR	RBI	BB	SO	AVG	OBP	SLG	PRO+	BR	/A	RC	SB	CS	SBR	FA	FR	POS	TPR
1974	NY-N	23	68	9	16	1	0	2	8	7	17	.235	.316	.338	84	-2	-1	7	0	0	0	.927	-1	O	-0.3
1976	NY-N	22	26	2	3	0	0	1	2	2	6	.115	.179	.231	16	-3	-3	1	0	1	-1	.889	1	/O	-0.3
1977	StL-N	1	3	0	1	0	0	0	0	0	1	.333	.333	.333	81	-0	-0	0	0	0	0	1.000	2	/O	0.2

YEAR	TM/L	G	AB	R	H	2B	3B	HR	RBI	BB	SO	AVG	OBP	SLG	PRO+	BR	/A	RC	SB	CS	SBR	FA	FR	POS	TPR
1979	*Bal-A	42	86	15	22	5	0	6	13	6	9	.256	.304	.523	123	2	2	13	0	0	0	.974	-3	OD	-0.1
1980	Bal-A	76	170	28	45	8	1	10	33	19	21	.265	.339	.500	128	6	6	28	0	0	0	1.000	-2	DO	0.3
1981	Bal-A	44	86	12	24	2	0	3	13	11	9	.279	.367	.407	123	3	3	13	0	1	-1	1.000	0	D/O	0.3
1982	Bal-A	64	128	17	39	6	0	6	24	5	14	.305	.331	.492	123	3	3	19	1	1	-0	.972	-5	OD/1	-0.2
1983	*Bal-A	47	104	12	23	7	0	4	13	9	18	.221	.283	.404	88	-2	-2	12	0	0	0	.953	-3	OD	-0.5
1984	Bal-A	60	118	9	25	6	0	4	24	8	24	.212	.262	.364	73	-5	-5	10	1	1	-0	1.000	-4	DO	-0.9
1985	Cle-A	46	76	10	19	7	0	2	15	4	17	.250	.287	.421	92	-1	-1	9	0	0	0	.917	-4	O/D	-0.5
Total	10	425	865	114	217	42	1	38	145	71	136	.251	.309	.434	104	1	2	113	2	4	-2	.958	-18	OD/1	-2.0

■ DICK AYLWARD Aylward, Richard John "Dandy" b: 6/4/25, Baltimore, Md. d: 6/11/83, Spring Valley, Cal. BR/TR, 6', 190 lbs. Deb: 5/01/53

YEAR	TM/L	G	AB	R	H	2B	3B	HR	RBI	BB	SO	AVG	OBP	SLG	PRO+	BR	/A	RC	SB	CS	SBR	FA	FR	POS	TPR
1953	Cle-A	4	3	0	0	0	0	0	0	0	1	.000	.000	.000	-99	-1	-1	0	0	0	0	1.000	-0	/C	-0.1

■ JOE AZCUE Azcue, Jose Joaquin (Lopez) b: 8/18/39, Cienfuegos, Cuba BR/TR, 6', 200 lbs. Deb: 8/03/60

YEAR	TM/L	G	AB	R	H	2B	3B	HR	RBI	BB	SO	AVG	OBP	SLG	PRO+	BR	/A	RC	SB	CS	SBR	FA	FR	POS	TPR
1960	Cin-N	14	31	1	3	0	0	0	3	2	6	.097	.152	.097	-30	-6	-6	0	0	1	-1	1.000	5	C	0.0
1962	KC-A	72	223	18	51	9	1	2	25	17	27	.229	.292	.305	59	-12	-13	20	1	0	0	.985	3	C	-0.8
1963	KC-A	2	4	0	0	0	0	0	0	0	1	.000	.000	.000	-96	-1	-1	0	0	0	0	1.000	0	/C	-0.1
	Cle-A	94	320	26	91	16	0	14	46	15	46	.284	.316	.466	117	6	6	42	1	1	-0	.992	5	C	1.4
	Yr	96	324	26	91	16	0	14	46	15	47	.281	.313	.460	114	5	5	42	1	1	-0	.992	5	C	1.3
1964	Cle-A	83	271	20	74	9	1	4	34	16	38	.273	.318	.358	88	-4	-4	30	0	2	-1	.993	-0	C	-0.2
1965	Cle-A	111	335	16	77	7	0	2	35	27	54	.230	.293	.269	60	-17	-17	24	2	1	0	.994	-1	*C	-1.4
1966	Cle-A	98	302	22	83	10	1	9	37	20	22	.275	.324	.404	108	3	3	38	0	2	-1	.989	-8	C	-0.1
1967	Cle-A	86	295	33	74	12	5	11	34	22	35	.251	.309	.437	117	6	6	37	0	3	-2	**.999**	5	C	1.5
1968	Cle-A★	115	357	23	100	10	0	4	42	28	33	.280	.332	.342	106	2	3	40	1	1	-0	**.996**	11	C	2.2
1969	Cle-A	7	24	1	7	0	0	1	1	4	3	.292	.393	.417	122	1	1	4	0	0	0	.980	2	/C	0.3
	Bos-A	19	51	7	11	2	0	0	3	4	5	.216	.273	.255	46	-4	-4	3	0	0	0	.981	3	C	0.0
	Cal-A	80	248	15	54	6	0	1	19	27	28	.218	.300	.254	59	-14	-12	17	0	1	-1	.992	5	C	-0.5
	Yr	106	323	23	72	8	0	2	23	35	36	.223	.303	.266	62	-16	-15	24	0	1	-1	.989	9	*C	-0.2
1970	Cal-A	114	351	19	85	13	1	2	25	24	40	.242	.294	.302	67	-17	-15	30	0	0	0	.991	-5	*C	-1.6
1972	Cal-A	3	2	0	0	0	0	0	0	0	1	.000	.000	.000	-99	-0	-0	0	0	0	0	1.000	1	/C	0.0
	Mil-A	11	14	0	2	0	0	0	0	1	5	.143	.200	.143	3	-2	-2	0	0	0	0	1.000	2	/C	0.0
	Yr	14	16	0	2	0	0	0	0	1	6	.125	.176	.125	-10	-2	-2	0	0	0	0	1.000	2	/C	0.0
Total	11	909	2828	201	712	94	9	50	304	207	344	.252	.307	.344	85	-59	-57	287	5	12	-6	.992	25	C	0.7

■ OSCAR AZOCAR Azocar, Oscar Gregorio (Azocar) b: 2/21/65, Soro, Venez. BL/TL, 6'1", 170 lbs. Deb: 7/17/90

YEAR	TM/L	G	AB	R	H	2B	3B	HR	RBI	BB	SO	AVG	OBP	SLG	PRO+	BR	/A	RC	SB	CS	SBR	FA	FR	POS	TPR
1990	NY-A	65	214	18	53	8	0	5	19	2	15	.248	.258	.355	70	-9	-9	20	7	0	2	.991	0	O/D	-0.9
1991	SD-N	38	57	5	14	2	0	0	9	1	9	.246	.271	.281	54	-3	-4	4	2	0	1	.875	-3	O/1	-0.6
1992	SD-N	99	168	15	32	6	0	0	8	9	12	.190	.232	.226	29	-15	-16	9	1	0	0	.942	-1	O	-1.9
Total	3	202	439	38	99	16	0	5	36	12	36	.226	.249	.296	52	-28	-29	34	10	0	3	.964	-4	O/1D	-3.4

■ CHARLIE BABB Babb, Charles Amos b: 2/20/1873, Milwaukie, Ore. d: 3/20/54, Portland, Ore. BB/TR, 5'10", 165 lbs. Deb: 4/17/03

YEAR	TM/L	G	AB	R	H	2B	3B	HR	RBI	BB	SO	AVG	OBP	SLG	PRO+	BR	/A	RC	SB	CS	SBR	FA	FR	POS	TPR
1903	NY-N	121	424	68	105	15	8	0	46	45		.248	.337	.321	85	-5	-8	56	22			.912	-2	*S/3	-0.4
1904	Bro-N	151	521	49	138	18	3	0	53	53		.265	.339	.311	104	3	4	69	34			.927	-3	*S	0.6
1905	Bro-N	75	235	27	44	8	2	0	17	27		.187	.290	.238	63	-11	-9	20	10			.923	-2	S1/32	-1.2
Total	3	347	1180	144	287	41	13	0	116	125		.243	.328	.300	89	-14	-12	146	66			.921	-7	S/132	-1.0

■ LOREN BABE Babe, Loren Rolland "Bee Bee" b: 1/11/28, Pisgah, Iowa d: 2/14/84, Omaha, Neb. BL/TR, 5'10", 180 lbs. Deb: 8/19/52 C

YEAR	TM/L	G	AB	R	H	2B	3B	HR	RBI	BB	SO	AVG	OBP	SLG	PRO+	BR	/A	RC	SB	CS	SBR	FA	FR	POS	TPR
1952	NY-A	12	21	1	2	1	0	0	0	4	4	.095	.240	.143	9	-3	-2	1	1	0	0	.909	2	/3	-0.1
1953	NY-A	5	18	2	6	1	0	2	6	0	2	.333	.333	.722	185	2	2	4	0	0	0	.920	3	/3	0.5
	Phi-A	103	343	34	77	16	2	0	20	35	20	.224	.300	.283	56	-20	-21	30	0	1	-1	.950	1	3/S	-2.3
	Yr	108	361	36	83	17	2	2	26	35	22	.230	.302	.305	62	-18	-20	34	0	1	-1	.948	5	3/S	-1.8
Total	2	120	382	37	85	18	2	2	26	39	26	.223	.298	.296	59	-21	-22	36	1	1	-0	.946	6	3/S	-1.9

■ CHARLIE BABINGTON Babington, Charles Percy b: 5/4/1895, Cranston, R.I. d: 3/22/57, Providence, R.I. BR/TR, 6', 170 lbs. Deb: 7/20/15

YEAR	TM/L	G	AB	R	H	2B	3B	HR	RBI	BB	SO	AVG	OBP	SLG	PRO+	BR	/A	RC	SB	CS	SBR	FA	FR	POS	TPR
1915	NY-N	28	33	5	8	3	1	0	2	0	4	.242	.265	.394	104	-0	-0	4	1			.909	-5	O/1	-0.6

■ SHOOTY BABITT Babitt, Mack Neal b: 3/9/59, Oakland, Cal. BR/TR, 5'8", 174 lbs. Deb: 4/09/81

YEAR	TM/L	G	AB	R	H	2B	3B	HR	RBI	BB	SO	AVG	OBP	SLG	PRO+	BR	/A	RC	SB	CS	SBR	FA	FR	POS	TPR
1981	Oak-A	54	156	10	40	1	3	0	14	13	13	.256	.314	.301	82	-4	-3	14	5	4	-1	.972	-17	2	-2.0

■ WALLY BACKMAN Backman, Walter Wayne b: 9/22/59, Hillsboro, Ore. BB/TR, 5'9", 160 lbs. Deb: 9/02/80

YEAR	TM/L	G	AB	R	H	2B	3B	HR	RBI	BB	SO	AVG	OBP	SLG	PRO+	BR	/A	RC	SB	CS	SBR	FA	FR	POS	TPR
1980	NY-N	27	93	12	30	1	1	0	9	11	14	.323	.400	.355	115	2	3	13	2	3	-1	1.000	-10	2/S	-0.7
1981	NY-N	26	36	5	10	2	0	0	0	4	7	.278	.350	.333	96	-0	-0	5	1	0	0	.946	-3	2/3	-0.3
1982	NY-N	96	261	37	71	13	2	3	22	49	47	.272	.387	.372	114	7	7	39	8	7	-2	.964	-11	2/3OS	-0.2
1983	NY-N	26	42	6	7	0	1	0	3	2	8	.167	.205	.214	16	-5	-5	2	0	0	0	1.000	-2	2/3	-0.7
1984	NY-N	128	436	68	122	19	2	1	26	56	63	.280	.362	.339	99	1	2	57	32	9	4	.981	-12	*2/S	-0.2
1985	NY-N	145	520	77	142	24	5	1	38	36	72	.273	.321	.344	88	-10	-8	61	30	12	2	**.989**	-9	*2/S	-1.1
1986	*NY-N	124	387	67	124	18	2	1	27	36	32	.320	.378	.385	114	7	8	59	13	7	-0	.966	-3	*2	0.9
1987	NY-N	94	300	43	75	6	1	1	23	25	43	.250	.308	.287	62	-17	-15	28	11	3	2	.983	-7	2	-1.7
1988	*NY-N	99	294	44	89	12	0	0	17	41	49	.303	.390	.344	118	7	8	42	9	5	-0	.989	-9	2	0.3
1989	Min-A	87	299	33	69	9	2	1	26	32	45	.231	.307	.284	63	-12	-15	28	1	1	-0	.982	-22	2/D	-3.5
1990	*Pit-N	104	315	62	92	21	3	2	28	42	53	.292	.377	.397	118	7	8	49	6	3	0	.920	-19	32	-1.0
1991	Phi-N	94	185	20	45	12	0	0	15	30	30	.243	.349	.308	87	-2	-2	22	3	2	-0	.981	-15	23	-1.7
1992	Phi-N	42	48	6	13	1	0	0	6	6	9	.271	.352	.292	85	-1	-1	5	1	0	0	.968	0	2/3	0.0
Total	13	1092	3216	480	889	138	19	10	240	370	472	.276	.352	.340	95	-17	-9	411	117	52	4	.980	-121	23/SOD	-9.9

■ EDDIE BACON Bacon, Edgar Suter b: 4/8/1895, Franklin Co., Ky. d: 10/2/63, Frankfurt, Ky. Deb: 8/13/17

YEAR	TM/L	G	AB	R	H	2B	3B	HR	RBI	BB	SO	AVG	OBP	SLG	PRO+	BR	/A	RC	SB	CS	SBR	FA	FR	POS	TPR
1917	Phi-A	4	6	1	3	1	0	0	2	0	0	.500	.500	.667	259	1	1	2	0			1.000	1	/P	0.0

■ ART BADER Bader, Arthur Herman b: 9/21/1886, St.Louis, Mo. d: 4/5/57, St.Louis, Mo. BR/TR, 5'10", 170 lbs. Deb: 8/02/04

YEAR	TM/L	G	AB	R	H	2B	3B	HR	RBI	BB	SO	AVG	OBP	SLG	PRO+	BR	/A	RC	SB	CS	SBR	FA	FR	POS	TPR
1904	StL-A	2	3	0	0	0	0	0	0	1		.000	.250	.000	-19	-0	-0	0	0			1.000	1	/O	0.0

■ RED BADGRO Badgro, Morris Hiram b: 12/1/02, Orilla, Wash. BL/TR, 6', 190 lbs. Deb: 6/20/29

YEAR	TM/L	G	AB	R	H	2B	3B	HR	RBI	BB	SO	AVG	OBP	SLG	PRO+	BR	/A	RC	SB	CS	SBR	FA	FR	POS	TPR
1929	StL-A	54	148	27	42	12	0	1	18	11	15	.284	.342	.385	84	-3	-4	20	1	0	0	.983	-4	O	-0.9
1930	StL-A	89	234	30	56	18	3	1	27	13	27	.239	.285	.355	59	-14	-16	23	3	5	-2	.952	0	O	-1.9
Total	2	143	382	57	98	30	3	2	45	24	42	.257	.307	.366	69	-17	-19	43	4	5	-2	.962	-4	/O	-2.8

■ CARLOS BAERGA Baerga, Carlos Obed (Ortiz) b: 11/4/68, Santurce, P.R. BB/TR, 5'11", 165 lbs. Deb: 4/14/90

YEAR	TM/L	G	AB	R	H	2B	3B	HR	RBI	BB	SO	AVG	OBP	SLG	PRO+	BR	/A	RC	SB	CS	SBR	FA	FR	POS	TPR
1990	Cle-A	108	312	46	81	17	2	7	47	16	57	.260	.304	.394	94	-3	-3	37	0	2	-1	.944	-9	3S/2	-1.2
1991	Cle-A	158	593	80	171	28	2	11	69	48	74	.288	.348	.398	105	5	4	82	3	2	-0	.944	11	32/S	1.7
1992	Cle-A★	161	657	92	205	32	1	20	105	35	76	.312	.359	.455	125	22	21	105	10	2	2	.979	8	*2/D	3.5
Total	3	427	1562	218	457	77	5	38	221	99	207	.293	.344	.421	111	23	22	224	13	6	0	.973	10	23/SD	4.0

■ JOSE BAEZ Baez, Jose Antonio (b: Jose Antonio Mota (Baez)) b: 12/31/53, San Cristobal, D.R. BR/TR, 5'8", 160 lbs. Deb: 4/06/77

YEAR	TM/L	G	AB	R	H	2B	3B	HR	RBI	BB	SO	AVG	OBP	SLG	PRO+	BR	/A	RC	SB	CS	SBR	FA	FR	POS	TPR
1977	Sea-A	91	305	39	79	14	1	1	17	19	20	.259	.305	.321	71	-12	-12	30	6	1	1	.973	9	2/3D	0.3
1978	Sea-A	23	50	8	8	0	1	0	2	6	7	.160	.250	.200	28	-5	-5	3	1	0	0	.978	12	2/3D	0.9
Total	2	114	355	47	87	14	2	1	19	25	27	.245	.297	.304	65	-17	-16	34	7	1	2	.974	21	/2D3	1.2

YEAR	TM/L	G	AB	R	H	2B	3B	HR	RBI	BB	SO	AVG	OBP	SLG	PRO+	BR	/A	RC	SB	CS	SBR	FA	FR	POS	TPR
■ **KEVIN BAEZ**	Baez, Kevin Richard b: 1/10/67, Brooklyn, N.Y. BR/TR, 6', 160 lbs. Deb: 9/03/90																								
1990	NY-N	5	12	0	2	1	0	0	0	0	0	.167	.167	.250	13	-1	-1	0	0	0	0	1.000	0	/S	-0.1
1992	NY-N	6	13	0	2	0	0	0	0	0	0	.154	.154	.154	-13	-2	-2	0	0	0	0	.889	1	/S	-0.1
Total	2	11	25	0	4	1	0	0	0	0	0	.160	.160	.200	-0	-3	-3	0	0	0	0	.933	1	/S	-0.2
■ **JEFF BAGWELL**	Bagwell, Jeffery Robert b: 5/27/68, Boston, Mass. BR/TR, 6', 195 lbs. Deb: 4/08/91																								
1991	Hou-N	156	554	79	163	26	4	15	82	75	116	.294	.391	.437	141	27	31	98	7	4	-0	.991	-1	*1	1.9
1992	Hou-N	162	586	87	160	34	6	18	96	84	97	.273	.375	.444	139	26	30	98	10	6	-1	.995	7	*1	2.7
Total	2	318	1140	166	323	60	10	33	178	159	213	.283	.383	.440	140	53	61	197	17	10	-1	.993	5	1	4.6
■ **BILL BAGWELL**	Bagwell, William Mallory "Big Bill" b: 2/24/1896, Choudrant, La. d: 10/5/76, Choudrant, La. BL/TL, 6'1", 175 lbs. Deb: 4/17/23																								
1923	Bos-N	56	93	8	27	4	2	2	10	6	12	.290	.333	.441	107	0	1	14	0	0	0	1.000	-3	O	-0.3
1925	Phi-A	36	50	4	15	2	1	0	10	2	2	.300	.327	.380	74	-2	-2	6	0	0	0	.667	-2	/O	-0.4
Total	2	92	143	12	42	6	3	2	20	8	14	.294	.331	.420	95	-2	-2	20	0	0	0	.973	-5	/O	-0.7
■ **FRANK BAHRET**	Bahret, Frank J. b: Baltimore, Md. Deb: 4/17/1884																								
1884	Bal-U	2	8	0	0	0	0	0		0		.000	.000	.000	-91	-2	-2	0				1.000	0	/O	-0.2
■ **GENE BAILEY**	Bailey, Arthur Eugene b: 11/25/1893, Pearsall, Tex. d: 11/14/73, Houston, Tex. BR/TR, 5'8", 160 lbs. Deb: 9/10/17																								
1917	Phi-A	5	12	1	1	0	0	0	0	1	1	.083	.154	.083	-28	-2	-2	0	0			.833	-1	/O	-0.4
1919	Bos-N	4	6	0	2	0	0	0	1	0	2	.333	.333	.333	105	-0	0	1	1			1.000	0	/O	0.0
1920	Bos-N	13	24	2	2	0	0	0	0	3	3	.083	.185	.083	-22	-4	-4	1	0	1	-1	.929	-2	/O	-0.7
	Bos-A	46	135	14	31	2	0	0	5	9	15	.230	.283	.244	42	-11	-10	9	2	7	-4	.986	-4	O	-2.1
1923	Bro-N	127	411	71	109	11	7	1	42	43	34	.265	.343	.333	81	-11	-9	49	9	7	-2	.959	2	*O/1	-1.5
1924	Bro-N	18	46	7	11	3	0	1	4	7	6	.239	.340	.370	93	-1	-0	6	1	0	0	1.000	1	O	0.0
Total	5	213	634	95	156	16	7	2	52	63	61	.246	.321	.303	69	-28	-26	66	13	15		.965	-5	O/1	-4.7
■ **FRED BAILEY**	Bailey, Frederick Middleton "Penny" b: 8/16/1895, Mt.Hope, W.Va. d: 8/16/72, Huntington, W.Va. BL/TL, 5'11", 150 lbs. Deb: 8/19/16																								
1916	Bos-N	6	10	0	1	0	0	0	1	0	3	.100	.100	.100	-40	-2	-2	0	0			1.000	-0	/O	-0.2
1917	Bos-N	50	110	9	21	2	1	1	5	9	25	.191	.270	.255	65	-5	-4	8	3			.962	-1	O	-0.8
1918	Bos-N	4	4	1	1	0	0	0	0	0	1	.250	.250	.250	55	-0	-0	0	0			.000	0	H	0.0
Total	3	60	124	10	23	2	1	1	6	9	29	.185	.257	.242	57	-7	-6	8	3			.963	-2	/O	-1.0
■ **BILL BAILEY**	Bailey, Harry Lewis b: 11/19/1881, Shawnee, Ohio d: 10/27/67, Seattle, Wash. BL/TR, 5'10.5", 170 lbs. Deb: 4/21/11																								
1911	NY-A	5	9	1	1	0	0	0	0	0		.111	.111	.111	-36	-2	-2	0	0			.000	0	/O3	-0.2
■ **MARK BAILEY**	Bailey, John Mark b: 11/4/61, Springfield, Mo. BB/TR, 6'5", 195 lbs. Deb: 4/27/84																								
1984	Hou-N	108	344	38	73	16	1	9	34	53	71	.212	.321	.343	93	-5	-2	40	0	1	-1	.983	-2	*C	0.1
1985	Hou-N	114	332	47	88	14	0	10	45	67	70	.265	.390	.398	124	12	13	51	0	2	-1	.979	-10	*C/1	0.7
1986	Hou-N	57	153	9	27	5	0	4	15	28	45	.176	.304	.288	66	-7	-7	13	1	1	-0	.989	2	C/1	-0.2
1987	Hou-N	35	64	5	13	1	0	0	3	10	21	.203	.311	.219	45	-5	-5	5	1	0	0	.985	-0	C	-0.3
1988	Hou-N	8	23	1	3	0	0	0	0	5	6	.130	.286	.130	24	-2	-2	1	0	1	-1	.981	-1	/C	-0.3
1990	SF-N	5	7	1	1	0	0	1	3	0	2	.143	.143	.571	90	-0	-0	1	0	0	0	1.000	-0	/C	-0.1
1992	SF-N	13	26	0	4	1	0	0	1	3	7	.154	.241	.192	26	-3	-2	1	0	0	0	1.000	-1	/C	-0.3
Total	7	340	949	101	209	37	1	24	101	166	222	.220	.338	.337	93	-10	-5	111	2	5	-2	.983	-13	C/1	-0.4
■ **ED BAILEY**	Bailey, Lonas Edgar b: 4/15/31, Strawberry Plains, Tenn. BL/TR, 6'2", 205 lbs. Deb: 9/26/53 F																								
1953	Cin-N	2	8	1	3	1	0	0	1	1	3	.375	.444	.500	145	1	1	2	0	0	0	1.000	-1	/C	0.0
1954	Cin-N	73	183	21	36	2	3	9	20	35	34	.197	.326	.388	83	-4	-5	26	1	0	0	.973	-12	C	-1.4
1955	Cin-N	21	39	3	8	1	1	1	4	4	10	.205	.326	.359	77	-1	-1	4	0	0	0	.962	3	C	0.2
1956	Cin-N★	118	383	59	115	8	2	28	75	52	50	.300	.388	.551	140	27	24	83	2	0	1	.984	4	*C	3.3
1957	Cin-N★	122	391	54	102	15	2	20	48	73	69	.261	.380	.463	117	16	12	72	5	3	-0	.991	-12	*C	0.4
1958	Cin-N	112	360	39	90	23	1	11	59	47	61	.250	.338	.411	92	-1	-4	51	2	2	-1	.988	-4	C	-0.3
1959	Cin-N	121	379	43	100	13	0	12	40	62	53	.264	.370	.393	101	4	2	58	2	0	1	.990	2	*C	1.1
1960	Cin-N★	133	441	52	115	19	3	13	67	59	70	.261	.351	.406	105	5	4	65	1	0	0	.990	-13	*C	-0.1
1961	Cin-N	12	43	4	13	4	0	0	2	3	5	.302	.348	.395	95	-0	-0	6	0	0	0	.967	-4	C	-0.4
	SF-N☆	107	340	39	81	9	1	13	51	42	41	.238	.329	.385	92	-5	-3	42	1	5	-3	.985	-1	*C/O	-0.2
	Yr	119	383	43	94	13	1	13	53	45	46	.245	.331	.386	93	-5	-4	48	1	5	-3	.984	-5	*C/O	-0.6
1962	*SF-N	96	254	32	59	9	1	17	45	42	42	.232	.354	.476	123	8	8	44	1	1	-0	.987	-5	C	0.6
1963	SF-N★	105	308	41	81	8	0	21	68	50	64	.263	.368	.494	147	19	19	54	0	6	-4	.987	-0	C	2.0
1964	Mil-N	95	271	30	71	10	1	5	34	34	39	.262	.346	.362	99	1	1	35	2	0	1	.982	-10	C	-0.5
1965	SF-N	24	28	1	3	0	0	0	3	6	7	.107	.265	.107	9	-3	-3	1	0	0	0	1.000	3	C/1	0.0
	Chi-N	66	150	13	38	6	0	5	23	34	28	.253	.391	.393	119	6	5	23	0	1	-1	.981	-5	C/1	0.2
	Yr	90	178	14	41	6	0	5	26	40	35	.230	.372	.348	102	3	2	23	0	1	-1	.984	-2	C/1	0.2
1966	Cal-A	5	3	0	0	0	0	0	0	1	1	.000	.250	.000	-22	-0	-0	0	0	0	0	.000	0	H	0.0
Total	14	1212	3581	432	915	128	15	155	540	545	577	.256	.358	.429	110	69	58	566	17	18	-6	.986	-54	*C/1O	4.9
■ **BOB BAILEY**	Bailey, Robert Sherwood b: 10/13/42, Long Beach, Cal. BR/TR, 6', 188 lbs. Deb: 9/14/62																								
1962	Pit-N	14	42	6	7	2	1	0	6	6	10	.167	.271	.262	44	-3	-3	3	1	1	-0	.921	0	3	-0.3
1963	Pit-N	154	570	60	130	15	3	12	45	58	98	.228	.305	.328	82	-12	-13	58	10	9	-2	.933	6	*3/S	-1.0
1964	Pit-N	143	530	73	149	26	3	11	51	44	78	.281	.337	.404	108	5	6	68	10	8	-2	.943	8	*3O/S	0.9
1965	Pit-N	159	626	87	160	28	3	11	49	70	93	.256	.330	.363	95	-3	-3	72	10	14	-5	.939	-15	*3O	-3.0
1966	Pit-N	126	380	51	106	19	3	13	46	47	65	.279	.361	.447	123	13	13	60	5	3	-0	.956	1	3O	1.2
1967	LA-N	116	322	21	73	8	2	4	28	40	50	.227	.314	.301	84	-9	-6	29	5	5	-2	.941	2	3O/1S	-0.7
1968	LA-N	105	322	24	73	9	3	8	39	38	69	.227	.310	.348	105	-1	2	35	1	2	-1	.953	-2	3/SO	-0.1
1969	Mon-N	111	358	46	95	16	6	9	53	40	76	.265	.341	.419	111	5	5	49	3	3	-1	.992	5	1O/3	0.2
1970	Mon-N	131	352	77	101	19	3	28	84	72	70	.287	.409	.597	166	34	34	86	5	3	-0	.953	-13	3O1	1.7
1971	Mon-N	157	545	65	137	21	4	14	83	97	105	.251	.364	.382	111	11	11	78	13	7	-0	**.960**	-11	*3O/1	-0.4
1972	Mon-N	143	489	55	114	10	4	16	57	59	112	.233	.317	.368	92	-4	-5	56	6	7	-2	.938	-8	*3/O1	-1.7
1973	Mon-N	151	513	77	140	25	4	26	86	88	99	.273	.380	.489	134	29	26	90	5	8	-3	.956	-4	*3/O	1.9
1974	Mon-N	152	507	69	142	20	2	20	73	100	107	.280	.400	.446	129	28	24	89	4	7	-3	.974	-19	O3	-0.1
1975	Mon-N	106	227	23	62	5	0	5	30	46	38	.273	.398	.361	107	6	5	34	4	4	-1	.979	-6	O/3	-0.4
1976	Cin-N	69	124	17	37	6	1	6	23	16	26	.298	.379	.508	146	8	8	22	0	0	0	.974	-2	O3	0.5
1977	Cin-N	49	79	9	20	2	1	2	11	12	10	.253	.352	.380	94	-0	-0	11	1	1	-0	.975	0	1/O	-0.2
	Bos-A	2	2	0	0	0	0	0	0	0	1	.000	.000	.000	-90	-1	-1	0	0	0	0	.000	0	H	-0.1
1978	Bos-A	43	94	12	18	3	0	4	9	19	19	.191	.333	.351	84	-0	-2	12	2	1	0	1.000	0	D/3O	-0.2
Total	17	1931	6082	772	1564	234	43	189	773	852	1126	.257	.350	.403	111	106	101	852	85	83	-24	.946	-58	*3O1/DS	-1.8
■ **BOB BAILOR**	Bailor, Robert Michael b: 7/10/51, Connellsville, Pa. BR/TR, 5'11", 170 lbs. Deb: 9/06/75 C																								
1975	Bal-A	5	7	0	1	0	0	0	0	1	0	.143	.250	.143	14	-1	-1	0	0	0	0	1.000	2	/S2	0.1
1976	Bal-A	9	6	2	2	0	1	0	0	0	0	.333	.333	.667	200	1	1	1	0	1	-1	.000	-0	/SD	0.0
1977	Tor-A	122	496	62	154	21	5	5	32	17	26	.310	.336	.403	99	-0	-1	66	15	6	1	.988	1	OS/D	0.4
1978	Tor-A	154	621	74	164	29	7	1	52	38	21	.264	.312	.338	81	-14	-16	66	5	6	-2	.964	15	*O3/S	-0.9
1979	Tor-A	130	414	50	95	11	5	1	38	36	27	.229	.300	.287	59	-23	-23	37	14	8	-1	.987	1	*O/3	-2.7
1980	Tor-A	117	347	44	82	14	2	1	16	36	33	.236	.312	.297	65	-15	-17	33	12	8	-1	.991	12	OS3/P2D	-0.8

YEAR	TM/L	G	AB	R	H	2B	3B	HR	RBI	BB	SO	AVG	OBP	SLG	PRO+	BR	/A	RC	SB	CS	SBR	FA	FR	POS	TPR
1981	NY-N	51	81	11	23	3	1	0	8	8	11	.284	.356	.346	101	0	0	10	2	0	1	.955	-2	S2O/3	0.1
1982	NY-N	110	376	44	104	14	1	0	31	20	17	.277	.317	.319	79	-11	-10	41	20	3	4	.984	-22	S23	-2.4
1983	NY-N	118	340	33	85	8	0	1	30	20	23	.250	.294	.282	61	-18	-18	28	18	3	4	.969	-6	S23/O	-1.3
1984	LA-N	65	131	11	36	4	0	0	8	8	1	.275	.317	.305	76	-4	-4	13	3	1	0	.944	10	23S	0.8
1985	*LA-N	74	118	8	29	3	1	0	7	3	5	.246	.270	.288	58	-7	-7	9	1	0	0	.962	15	32/SO	0.9
Total	11	955	2937	339	775	107	23	9	222	187	164	.264	.312	.325	76	-92	-95	305	90	36	5	.980	26	OS23/DP	-5.8

■ HAROLD BAINES Baines, Harold Douglass b: 3/15/59, Easton, Md. BL/TL, 6'2", 195 lbs. Deb: 4/10/80

YEAR	TM/L	G	AB	R	H	2B	3B	HR	RBI	BB	SO	AVG	OBP	SLG	PRO+	BR	/A	RC	SB	CS	SBR	FA	FR	POS	TPR
1980	Chi-A	141	491	55	125	23	6	13	49	19	65	.255	.284	.405	87	-11	-11	50	2	4	-2	.963	-7	*O/D	-2.4
1981	Chi-A	82	280	42	80	11	7	10	41	12	41	.286	.320	.482	131	9	9	41	6	2	1	.985	-0	O/D	0.7
1982	Chi-A	161	608	89	165	29	8	25	105	49	95	.271	.326	.469	115	11	11	91	10	3	1	.980	2	*O	1.0
1983	*Chi-A	156	596	76	167	33	2	20	99	49	85	.280	.336	.443	108	9	6	85	7	5	-1	.973	0	*O	0.1
1984	Chi-A	147	569	72	173	28	10	29	94	54	75	.304	.364	**.541**	141	35	31	109	1	2	-1	.981	0	*O	2.6
1985	Chi-A★	160	640	86	198	29	3	22	113	42	89	.309	.353	.467	118	19	15	98	1	1	-0	.994	7	*O/D	1.7
1986	Chi-A★	145	570	72	169	29	2	21	88	38	89	.296	.343	.465	114	12	10	87	2	1	0	.984	12	*O/D	1.8
1987	Chi-A★	132	505	59	148	26	4	20	93	46	82	.293	.353	.479	115	13	11	84	0	0	0	1.000	-1	*D/O	0.9
1988	Chi-A	158	599	55	166	39	1	13	81	67	109	.277	.351	.411	113	11	11	83	0	0	0	.882	-1	*D/O	1.0
1989	Chi-A★	96	333	55	107	20	1	13	56	60	52	.321	.426	.505	165	29	31	72	0	1	-1	.981	-0	DO	2.9
	Tex-A	50	172	18	49	9	0	3	16	13	27	.285	.335	.390	102	1	0	21	0	2	-1	.667	-0	D/O	-0.1
	Yr	146	505	73	156	29	1	16	72	73	79	.309	.397	.465	144	30	31	93	0	3	-2	.964	-1	*DO	2.8
1990	Tex-A	103	321	41	93	10	1	13	44	47	63	.290	.380	.449	131	14	14	53	0	1	-1	.833	0	D/O	1.4
	*Oak-A	32	94	11	25	5	0	3	21	20	17	.266	.395	.415	132	4	5	15	0	2	-1	.000	0	D	0.4
	Yr	135	415	52	118	15	1	16	65	67	80	.284	.384	.441	131	18	19	69	0	3	-2	.833	0	*D/O	1.8
1991	Oak-A★	141	488	76	144	25	1	20	90	72	67	.295	.387	.473	145	26	29	89	0	1	-1	.923	-2	*DO	2.7
1992	*Oak-A	140	478	58	121	18	0	16	76	59	61	.253	.335	.391	107	2	4	62	1	3	-2	.964	-5	*DO	-0.2
Total	13	1844	6744	865	1930	334	46	241	1066	647	1017	.286	.350	.457	120	183	178	1042	30	28	-8	.978	6	*OD	14.5

■ AL BAIRD Baird, Albert Wells b: 6/2/1895, Cleburne, Tex. d: 11/27/76, Shreveport, La. BR/TR, 5'9", 160 lbs. Deb: 9/10/17

YEAR	TM/L	G	AB	R	H	2B	3B	HR	RBI	BB	SO	AVG	OBP	SLG	PRO+	BR	/A	RC	SB	CS	SBR	FA	FR	POS	TPR
1917	NY-N	10	24	1	7	0	0	0	4	2	2	.292	.346	.292	100	-0	0	3	2			1.000	2	/2S	0.2
1919	NY-N	38	83	8	20	1	0	0	5	5	9	.241	.284	.253	63	-4	-4	6	3			.898	8	2/S3	0.6
Total	2	48	107	9	27	1	0	0	9	7	11	.252	.298	.262	71	-4	-4	9	5			.921	10	/2S3	0.8

■ DOUG BAIRD Baird, Howard Douglas b: 9/27/1891, St.Charles, Mo. d: 6/13/67, Thomasville, Ga. BR/TR, 5'9.5", 148 lbs. Deb: 4/18/15

YEAR	TM/L	G	AB	R	H	2B	3B	HR	RBI	BB	SO	AVG	OBP	SLG	PRO+	BR	/A	RC	SB	CS	SBR	FA	FR	POS	TPR
1915	Pit-N	145	512	49	112	26	12	1	53	37	88	.219	.277	.322	82	-13	-12	51	29	12	2	.939	-1	*3O/2	-0.8
1916	Pit-N	128	430	41	93	10	7	1	28	24	49	.216	.263	.279	66	-17	-18	32	20	16	-4	.933	-5	32O	-2.7
1917	Pit-N	43	135	17	35	6	1	0	18	20	19	.259	.355	.319	104	2	1	18	8			.935	-4	3/2	-0.2
	StL-N	104	364	38	92	19	12	0	24	23	52	.253	.301	.371	108	1	3	45	18			.941	13	*3/O	2.0
	Yr	147	499	55	127	25	13	0	42	43	71	.255	.316	.357	107	3	4	63	26			.940	9	*3/2O	1.8
1918	StL-N	82	316	41	78	12	8	2	25	25	42	.247	.304	.354	104	-0	1	40	25			.967	16	3/SO	2.0
1919	Phi-N	66	242	33	61	13	3	2	30	22	28	.252	.317	.355	95	1	-1	30	13			.950	11	3	1.3
	StL-N	16	33	4	7	0	1	0	4	2	3	.212	.257	.273	63	-2	-1	3	2			.773	-4	/32O	-0.5
	Bro-N	20	60	6	11	0	1	0	8	1	10	.183	.197	.217	24	-6	-6	3	3			1.000	1	3	-0.5
	Yr	102	335	43	79	13	5	2	42	25	41	.236	.291	.322	81	-7	-8	36	18			.946	8	3/2O	0.3
1920	Bro-N	6	6	1	2	0	0	0	1	2	1	.333	.556	.333	154	1	1	2	0	0	0	.800	-0	/3	0.1
	NY-N	7	8	0	1	0	0	0	0	1	3	.125	.222	.125	1	-1	-1	0	0	0	0	1.000	2	/3	0.1
	Yr	13	14	1	3	0	0	0	1	3	4	.214	.389	.214	76	-0	-0	2	0	0	0	.929	1	/3	0.2
Total	6	617	2106	230	492	86	45	6	191	157	295	.234	.291	.326	88	-33	-33	223	118	28		.944	28	3/O2S	0.8

■ CHARLIE BAKER Baker, Charles A. b: 1856, Westboro, Mass. d: 1/15/37, Manchester, N.H. Deb: 8/01/1884

YEAR	TM/L	G	AB	R	H	2B	3B	HR	RBI	BB	SO	AVG	OBP	SLG	PRO+	BR	/A	RC	SB	CS	SBR	FA	FR	POS	TPR
1884	CP-U	15	57	5	8	2	0	1		0		.140	.140	.228	23	-4	-4	2				.722	-1	O/S2	-0.5

■ CHUCK BAKER Baker, Charles Joseph b: 12/6/52, Seattle, Wash. BR/TR, 5'11", 180 lbs. Deb: 4/07/78

YEAR	TM/L	G	AB	R	H	2B	3B	HR	RBI	BB	SO	AVG	OBP	SLG	PRO+	BR	/A	RC	SB	CS	SBR	FA	FR	POS	TPR
1978	SD-N	44	58	8	12	1	0	0	3	2	15	.207	.233	.224	31	-6	-5	3	0	0	0	.952	14	2S	1.0
1980	SD-N	9	22	0	3	1	0	0	0	0	4	.136	.136	.182	-13	-3	-3	1	0	0	0	.963	2	/S	-0.1
1981	Min-A	40	66	6	12	0	3	0	6	1	8	.182	.194	.273	31	-6	-6	3	0	0	0	.969	7	S/23D	0.3
Total	3	93	146	14	27	2	3	0	9	3	27	.185	.201	.240	25	-15	-14	7	0	0	0	.962	22	/S2D3	1.2

■ DAVE BAKER Baker, David Glenn b: 11/25/57, Lacona, Iowa BL/TR, 6', 185 lbs. Deb: 9/12/82 F

YEAR	TM/L	G	AB	R	H	2B	3B	HR	RBI	BB	SO	AVG	OBP	SLG	PRO+	BR	/A	RC	SB	CS	SBR	FA	FR	POS	TPR
1982	Tor-A	9	20	3	5	1	0	0	2	3	3	.250	.400	.300	88	0	-0	3	0	0	0	.808	1	/3	0.0

■ DEL BAKER Baker, Delmer David b: 5/3/1892, Sherwood, Ore. d: 9/11/73, San Antonio, Tex. BR/TR, 5'11.5", 176 lbs. Deb: 4/16/14 MC

YEAR	TM/L	G	AB	R	H	2B	3B	HR	RBI	BB	SO	AVG	OBP	SLG	PRO+	BR	/A	RC	SB	CS	SBR	FA	FR	POS	TPR
1914	Det-A	44	70	4	15	2	1	0	1	6	9	.214	.276	.271	63	-3	-3	5	0	2	-1	.920	-6	C	-0.9
1915	Det-A	68	134	16	33	3	3	0	15	15	15	.246	.327	.313	87	-1	-2	16	3	1	0	.940	-5	C	-0.3
1916	Det-A	61	98	7	15	4	0	0	6	11	8	.153	.245	.194	31	-8	-8	6	2			.975	-2	C	-0.9
Total	3	173	302	27	63	9	4	0	22	32	32	.209	.289	.265	63	-12	-14	27	5	3		.948	-12	C	-2.1

■ DOUG BAKER Baker, Douglas Lee b: 4/3/61, Fullerton, Cal. BB/TR, 5'9", 165 lbs. Deb: 7/02/84 F

YEAR	TM/L	G	AB	R	H	2B	3B	HR	RBI	BB	SO	AVG	OBP	SLG	PRO+	BR	/A	RC	SB	CS	SBR	FA	FR	POS	TPR
1984	*Det-A	43	108	15	20	4	1	0	12	7	22	.185	.241	.241	34	-10	-10	7	3	0	1	.969	2	S/2D	-0.4
1985	Det-A	15	27	4	5	1	0	0	1	0	9	.185	.185	.222	11	-3	-3	1	0	0	0	.960	-3	S/2	-0.5
1986	Det-A	13	24	1	3	1	0	0	0	2	7	.125	.192	.167	-1	-3	-3	1	0	0	0	.970	2	S/2D	-0.1
1987	Det-A	8	1	0	0	0	0	0	0	0	1	.000	.000	.000	-99	-0	-0	0	0	0	0	1.000	3	/S23	0.2
1988	Min-A	11	7	1	0	0	0	0	0	0	5	.000	.000	.000	-97	-2	-2	0	0	0	0	1.000	1	/S23	0.0
1989	Min-A	43	78	17	23	5	1	0	9	9	18	.295	.382	.385	109	2	1	13	0	0	0	.982	-3	2S/D	-0.1
1990	Min-A	3	1	0	0	0	0	0	0	0	0	.000	.000	.000	-94	-0	-0	0	0	0	0	1.000	1	/2	0.0
Total	7	136	246	38	51	11	2	0	22	18	62	.207	.270	.268	49	-17	-17	22	3	0	1	.973	4	/S2D3	-0.9

■ GENE BAKER Baker, Eugene Walter b: 6/15/25, Davenport, Iowa BR/TR, 6'1", 170 lbs. Deb: 9/20/53 C

YEAR	TM/L	G	AB	R	H	2B	3B	HR	RBI	BB	SO	AVG	OBP	SLG	PRO+	BR	/A	RC	SB	CS	SBR	FA	FR	POS	TPR
1953	Chi-N	7	22	1	5	1	0	0	0	1	4	.227	.261	.273	39	-2	-2	2	1	0	0	.917	-3	/2	-0.4
1954	Chi-N	135	541	68	149	32	5	13	61	47	55	.275	.336	.425	96	-3	-4	76	4	5	-2	.967	-3	*2	0.0
1955	Chi-N★	154	609	82	163	29	7	11	52	49	57	.268	.324	.392	89	-10	-10	76	9	7	-2	.967	7	*2	0.8
1956	Chi-N	140	546	65	141	23	3	12	57	39	54	.258	.311	.377	85	-13	-11	62	4	3	-1	.969	17	*2	1.7
1957	Chi-N	12	44	4	11	3	1	1	10	6	3	.250	.353	.432	111	1	1	7	0	0	0	.867	-4	3	-0.3
	Pit-N	111	365	36	97	19	4	2	36	29	29	.266	.322	.356	84	-9	-8	41	3	2	-0	.955	-4	3S2	-0.7
	Yr	123	409	40	108	22	5	3	46	35	32	.264	.325	.364	87	-8	-7	48	3	2	-0	.942	-7	3S2	-1.0
1958	Pit-N	29	56	3	14	2	1	0	7	8	6	.250	.344	.321	80	-2	-1	6	0	0	0	1.000	-1	3/2	-0.2
1960	*Pit-N	33	37	5	9	0	0	0	4	2	9	.243	.282	.243	45	-3	-3	3	0	0	0	1.000	2	/32	-0.1
1961	Pit-N	9	10	1	1	0	0	0	0	3	2	.100	.308	.100	15	-1	-1	0	0	0	0	1.000	1	/3	0.0
Total	8	630	2230	265	590	109	21	39	227	184	219	.265	.323	.385	88	-42	-39	272	21	17	-4	.968	12	2/3S	0.8

■ FLOYD BAKER Baker, Floyd Wilson b: 10/10/16, Luray, Va. BL/TR, 5'9", 160 lbs. Deb: 5/04/43 C

YEAR	TM/L	G	AB	R	H	2B	3B	HR	RBI	BB	SO	AVG	OBP	SLG	PRO+	BR	/A	RC	SB	CS	SBR	FA	FR	POS	TPR
1943	StL-A	22	46	5	8	2	0	0	4	6	4	.174	.269	.217	42	-3	-3	3	0	1	-1	.961	0	S/3	-0.3
1944	*StL-A	44	97	10	17	3	0	0	5	11	5	.175	.259	.206	32	-8	-9	6	2	0	1	.979	-3	2S	-1.0
1945	Chi-A	82	208	22	52	8	0	0	19	23	12	.250	.325	.288	81	-5	-5	22	3	2	-0	.971	2	32	-0.2
1946	Chi-A	9	24	2	6	1	0	0	3	2	3	.250	.308	.292	71	-1	-1	2	0	0	0	.962	1	/3	0.1
1947	Chi-A	105	371	61	98	12	3	0	22	66	28	.264	.375	.313	96	-1	1	49	9	7	-2	.980	18	*3/2S	1.9

YEAR	TM/L	G	AB	R	H	2B	3B	HR	RBI	BB	SO	AVG	OBP	SLG	PRO+	BR	/A	RC	SB	CS	SBR	FA	FR	POS	TPR
1948	Chi-A	104	335	47	72	8	3	0	18	73	26	.215	.359	.257	68	-13	-12	35	4	10	-5	.961	13	32/S	-0.4
1949	Chi-A	125	388	38	101	15	4	1	40	84	32	.260	.392	.327	94	-1	1	59	3	1	0	**.977**	12	*3/S2	1.1
1950	Chi-A	83	186	26	59	7	0	0	11	32	10	.317	.417	.355	102	2	3	30	1	1	-0	.987	3	3/2O	0.4
1951	Chi-A	82	133	24	35	6	1	0	14	25	12	.263	.380	.323	93	-0	-0	18	0	1	-1	.924	-1	3/2S	-0.2
1952	Was-A	79	263	27	69	8	0	0	33	30	17	.262	.342	.293	81	-7	-6	30	1	0	0	.994	-16	2/S3	-1.8
1953	Was-A	9	7	0	0	0	0	0	0	1	0	.000	.222	.000	-37	-1	-1	0	0	0	0	.000	-0	/3	-0.2
	Bos-A	81	172	22	47	4	2	0	24	24	10	.273	.365	.320	82	-2	-3	21	0	2	-1	.963	1	32	-0.4
	Yr	90	179	22	47	4	2	0	24	25	10	.263	.359	.307	78	-4	-5	21	0	2	-1	.952	0	32	-0.6
1954	Bos-A	21	20	1	4	2	0	0	3	0	1	.200	.200	.300	32	-2	-2	1	0	0	0	.889	1	/32	-0.1
	Phi-N	23	22	0	5	0	0	0	0	5	4	.227	.370	.227	60	-1	-1	2	0	0	0	1.000	4	/32	0.3
1955	Phi-N	5	8	0	0	0	0	0	0	0	1	.000	.000	.000	-99	-2	-2	0	0	0	0	1.000	1	/3	-0.1
Total	13	874	2280	285	573	76	13	1	196	382	165	.251	.360	.297	82	-47	-41	279	23	25	-8	.971	34	32/SO	-0.9

■ FRANK BAKER Baker, Frank b: 1/11/44, Bartow, Fla. BL/TR, 5'10", 180 lbs. Deb: 7/27/69

YEAR	TM/L	G	AB	R	H	2B	3B	HR	RBI	BB	SO	AVG	OBP	SLG	PRO+	BR	/A	RC	SB	CS	SBR	FA	FR	POS	TPR
1969	Cle-A	52	172	21	44	5	3	3	15	14	34	.256	.316	.372	89	-2	-3	20	2	1	0	.950	1	O	-0.5
1971	Cle-A	73	181	18	38	12	1	1	23	12	34	.210	.263	.304	55	-10	-12	13	1	3	-2	.985	-6	O	-2.4
Total	2	125	353	39	82	17	4	4	38	26	68	.232	.289	.337	71	-12	-14	33	3	4	-2	.966	-6	/O	-2.9

■ FRANK BAKER Baker, Frank Watts b: 10/29/46, Meridian, Miss. BL/TR, 6'2", 178 lbs. Deb: 8/09/70

YEAR	TM/L	G	AB	R	H	2B	3B	HR	RBI	BB	SO	AVG	OBP	SLG	PRO+	BR	/A	RC	SB	CS	SBR	FA	FR	POS	TPR
1970	NY-A	35	117	6	27	4	1	0	11	14	26	.231	.323	.282	72	-5	-4	11	1	2	-1	.973	4	S	0.4
1971	NY-A	43	79	9	11	2	0	0	2	16	22	.139	.284	.165	32	-7	-6	5	3	0	1	.949	11	S	0.9
1973	*Bal-A	44	63	10	12	1	2	1	11	7	7	.190	.271	.317	66	-3	-3	6	0	0	0	.964	4	S/213	0.3
1974	*Bal-A	24	29	3	5	1	0	0	0	3	5	.172	.250	.207	34	-2	-2	1	0	0	0	.842	2	S/23	0.0
Total	4	146	288	28	55	8	3	1	24	40	60	.191	.294	.250	56	-17	-15	24	4	2	0	.953	20	S/231	1.6

■ GEORGE BAKER Baker, George F. b: 1859, St.Louis, Mo. Deb: 5/24/1883

YEAR	TM/L	G	AB	R	H	2B	3B	HR	RBI	BB	SO	AVG	OBP	SLG	PRO+	BR	/A	RC	SB	CS	SBR	FA	FR	POS	TPR
1883	Bal-a	7	22	0	5	0	0	0		0		.227	.227	.227	45	-1	-1	1				.667	-3	/SCO	-0.3
1884	StL-U	80	317	39	52	6	0	0		5		.164	.177	.183	21	-25	-27	11				**.897**	16	C/2O3S	-0.4
1885	StL-N	38	131	5	16	0	0	0	5	9	28	.122	.179	.122	-1	-14	-13	3				.865	-11	C/3O2	-2.0
1886	KC-N	1	4	1	1	0	0	0	0	0	1	.250	.250	.250	49	-0	-0	0	0			.889	-0	/C	0.0
Total	4	126	474	45	74	6	0	0	5	14	29	.156	.180	.169	17	-41	-41	15	0			.887	3	C/O3S2	-2.7

■ HOWARD BAKER Baker, Howard Francis b: 3/1/1888, Bridgeport, Conn. d: 1/16/64, Bridgeport, Conn. BR/TR, 5'11", 175 lbs. Deb: 8/11/12

YEAR	TM/L	G	AB	R	H	2B	3B	HR	RBI	BB	SO	AVG	OBP	SLG	PRO+	BR	/A	RC	SB	CS	SBR	FA	FR	POS	TPR
1912	Cle-A	11	30	1	5	0	0	0	2	5		.167	.286	.167	29	-3	-3	1	0			.964	-1	3	-0.4
1914	Chi-A	15	47	4	13	1	1	0	5	3	8	.277	.320	.340	100	-0	-0	5	2	1	0	.879	-4	3	-0.5
1915	Chi-A	2	2	0	0	0	0	0	0	0	2	.000	.000	.000	-97	-0	-0	0	0			.000	0	H	-0.1
	NY-N	1	3	0	0	0	0	0	0	0	0	.000	.000	.000	-99	-1	-1	0	0			1.000	0	/3	-0.1
Total	3	29	82	5	18	1	1	0	7	8	10	.220	.289	.256	61	-4	-4	7	2	1		.922	-6	/3	-1.1

■ JACK BAKER Baker, Jack Edward b: 5/4/50, Birmingham, Ala. BR/TR, 6'5", 225 lbs. Deb: 9/11/76

YEAR	TM/L	G	AB	R	H	2B	3B	HR	RBI	BB	SO	AVG	OBP	SLG	PRO+	BR	/A	RC	SB	CS	SBR	FA	FR	POS	TPR
1976	Bos-A	12	23	1	3	0	0	1	2	1	5	.130	.167	.261	21	-2	-3	1	0	0	0	.981	-0	/1D	-0.3
1977	Bos-A	2	3	0	0	0	0	0	0	0	1	.000	.000	.000	-90	-1	-1	0	0	0	0	.857	0	/1	-0.1
Total	2	14	26	1	3	0	0	1	2	1	6	.115	.148	.231	8	-3	-3	1	0	0	0	.966	-0	/1D	-0.4

■ JESSE BAKER Baker, Jesse (b: Michael Myron Silverman) b: 3/4/1895, Cleveland, Ohio d: 7/29/76, W.Los Angeles, Cal. BR/TR, 5'4", 140 lbs. Deb: 9/14/19

YEAR	TM/L	G	AB	R	H	2B	3B	HR	RBI	BB	SO	AVG	OBP	SLG	PRO+	BR	/A	RC	SB	CS	SBR	FA	FR	POS	TPR
1919	Was-A	1	0	0	0	0	0	0	1	0	0	—	—	—	—	0	0	0	0			1.000	0	/S	0.0

■ FRANK BAKER Baker, John Franklin "Home Run" b: 3/13/1886, Trappe, Md. d: 6/28/63, Trappe, Md. BL/TR, 5'11", 173 lbs. Deb: 9/21/08 H

YEAR	TM/L	G	AB	R	H	2B	3B	HR	RBI	BB	SO	AVG	OBP	SLG	PRO+	BR	/A	RC	SB	CS	SBR	FA	FR	POS	TPR
1908	Phi-A	9	31	5	9	3	0	0	2	0		.290	.290	.387	112	0	0	4	0			1.000	2	/3	0.3
1909	Phi-A	148	541	73	165	27	**19**	4	85	26		.305	.343	.447	146	27	26	90	20			.920	-8	*3	2.6
1910	*Phi-A	146	561	83	159	25	15	2	74	34		.283	.329	.392	127	14	15	79	21			.920	6	*3	2.7
1911	*Phi-A	148	592	96	198	42	14	**11**	115	40		.334	.379	.508	149	33	35	127	38			**.942**	-1	*3	3.5
1912	Phi-A	149	577	116	200	40	21	**10**	**130**	50		.347	.404	.541	176	49	52	140	40			.941	10	*3	6.1
1913	*Phi-A	149	564	116	190	34	9	**12**	**117**	63	31	.337	.413	.493	169	46	48	122	34			.921	8	*3	6.0
1914	*Phi-A	150	570	84	182	23	10	**9**	89	53	37	.319	.380	.442	153	31	34	95	19	20	-6	.955	10	*3	4.6
1916	NY-A	100	360	46	97	23	2	10	52	36	30	.269	.344	.428	129	13	12	58	15			.940	2	3	1.9
1917	NY-A	146	553	57	156	24	2	6	71	48	27	.282	.345	.365	116	10	10	72	18			.949	11	*3	2.6
1918	NY-A	126	504	65	154	24	5	6	62	38	13	.306	.357	.409	128	17	16	74	8			**.972**	11	*3	3.2
1919	NY-A	141	567	70	166	22	1	10	83	44	18	.293	.346	.388	105	4	3	77	13			.955	-2	*3	0.7
1921	*NY-A	94	330	46	97	16	2	9	71	26	12	.294	.353	.436	98	-1	-2	51	8	5	-1	.959	-2	3	0.2
1922	*NY-A	69	234	30	65	12	3	7	36	15	14	.278	.327	.444	97	-1	-2	33	1	3	-2	.962	-10	3	-0.9
Total	13	1575	5984	887	1838	315	103	96	987	473	182	.307	.363	.442	136	243	246	1020	235	28		.943	37	*3	33.5

■ DUSTY BAKER Baker, Johnnie B b: 6/15/49, Riverside, Cal. BR/TR, 6'2", 187 lbs. Deb: 9/07/68 C

YEAR	TM/L	G	AB	R	H	2B	3B	HR	RBI	BB	SO	AVG	OBP	SLG	PRO+	BR	/A	RC	SB	CS	SBR	FA	FR	POS	TPR
1968	Atl-N	6	5	0	2	0	0	0	0	0	1	.400	.400	.400	140	0	0	1	0	0	0	.000	0	/O	0.0
1969	Atl-N	3	7	0	0	0	0	0	0	0	3	.000	.000	.000	-99	-2	-2	0	0	0	0	1.000	-0	/O	-0.2
1970	Atl-N	13	24	3	7	0	0	0	4	2	4	.292	.346	.292	69	-1	-1	2	0	0	0	.800	-0	O	-0.1
1971	Atl-N	29	62	2	14	2	0	0	4	1	14	.226	.238	.258	38	-5	-5	3	0	1	-1	1.000	1	O	-0.6
1972	Atl-N	127	446	62	143	27	2	17	76	45	68	.321	.388	.504	139	30	25	85	4	7	-3	.989	9	*O	2.7
1973	Atl-N	159	604	101	174	29	4	21	99	67	72	.288	.364	.454	116	21	15	103	24	3	5	.983	4	*O	1.8
1974	Atl-N	149	574	80	147	35	0	20	69	71	87	.256	.339	.422	107	8	5	83	18	7	1	.981	-4	*O	-0.4
1975	Atl-N	142	494	63	129	18	2	19	72	67	57	.261	.349	.421	109	9	6	74	12	7	-1	.990	-10	*O	-1.0
1976	LA-N	112	384	36	93	13	0	4	39	31	54	.242	.300	.307	74	-14	-13	33	2	4	-2	.996	-7	*O	-2.8
1977	*LA-N	153	533	86	155	26	1	30	86	58	89	.291	.367	.512	134	24	25	99	2	6	-3	.987	-14	*O	0.2
1978	*LA-N	149	522	62	137	24	1	11	66	47	66	.262	.327	.375	96	-3	-3	66	12	3	2	.985	-4	*O	-1.1
1979	LA-N	151	554	86	152	29	1	23	88	56	70	.274	.342	.455	117	11	12	84	11	4	1	.990	5	*O	1.2
1980	LA-N	153	579	80	170	26	4	29	97	43	66	.294	.346	.503	137	24	25	96	12	10	-2	.991	-2	*O	1.6
1981	*LA-N★	103	400	48	128	17	3	9	49	29	43	.320	.367	.445	134	15	16	63	10	7	-1	.990	-2	*O	1.0
1982	LA-N★	147	570	80	171	19	1	23	88	56	62	.300	.366	.458	132	22	24	96	17	10	-1	.975	-11	*O	0.8
1983	*LA-N	149	531	71	138	25	1	15	73	72	59	.260	.350	.395	107	6	6	78	7	1	2	.981	-6	*O	-0.3
1984	SF-N	100	243	31	71	7	2	3	32	40	27	.292	.392	.374	120	7	8	39	4	1	1	.974	-1	O	0.6
1985	Oak-A	111	343	48	92	15	1	14	52	50	47	.268	.361	.440	128	9	13	54	2	1	0	.993	-5	1OD	0.4
1986	Oak-A	83	242	25	58	8	0	4	19	27	37	.240	.316	.322	80	-8	-6	24	0	1	-1	1.000	-3	OD/1	-1.1
Total	19	2039	7117	964	1981	320	23	242	1013	762	926	.278	.351	.432	116	153	152	1084	137	73	-3	.985	-51	*O/1D	2.7

■ KIRTLEY BAKER Baker, Kirtley "Whitey" b: 6/24/1869, Aurora, Ind. d: 4/15/27, Covington, Ky. BR/TR, 5'9", 160 lbs. Deb: 5/07/1890

YEAR	TM/L	G	AB	R	H	2B	3B	HR	RBI	BB	SO	AVG	OBP	SLG	PRO+	BR	/A	RC	SB	CS	SBR	FA	FR	POS	TPR
1890	Pit-N	26	68	6	10	0	0	0	0	10	6	.147	.275	.147	29	-6	-5	3	1			.878	-0	P	0.0
1893	Bal-N	19	57	9	17	1	1	0	6	8	6	.298	.385	.351	96	0	-0	8	1			.930	5	P/O	0.2
1894	Bal-N	2	4	0	0	0	0	0	0	0	1	.000	.000	.000	-96	-1	-1	0	0			1.000	1	/OP	0.0
1898	Was-N	6	18	3	5	0	1	0	3	3		.278	.381	.389	121	1	1	3	0			1.000	-1	/P	0.0
1899	Was-N	12	19	1	3	0	0	0	1	1		.158	.200	.158	-1	-3	-3	1	0			.862	2	P	0.0
Total	5	65	166	19	35	1	2	0	10	22	13	.211	.311	.241	58	-9	-8	15	2			.895	7	/PO	0.2

■ PHIL BAKER Baker, Philip b: 9/19/1856, Philadelphia, Pa. d: 6/4/40, Washington, D.C. BL/TL, 5'8", 152 lbs. Deb: 5/01/1883

YEAR	TM/L	G	AB	R	H	2B	3B	HR	RBI	BB	SO	AVG	OBP	SLG	PRO+	BR	/A	RC	SB	CS	SBR	FA	FR	POS	TPR
1883	Bal-a	28	121	22	33	2	1	1		8		.273	.318	.331	106	1	1	13				.883	-7	CO/S	-0.4

YEAR	TM/L	G	AB	R	H	2B	3B	HR	RBI	BB	SO	AVG	OBP	SLG	PRO+	BR	/A	RC	SB	CS	SBR	FA	FR	POS	TPR
1884	Was-U	86	371	75	107	12	5	1		11		.288	.309	.356	128	9	11	42				.955	-10	1OC	-0.1
1886	Was-N	81	325	37	72	6	5	1	34	20	32	.222	.267	.280	70	-13	-10	29	16			.967	-7	1O/C	-2.2
Total	3	195	817	134	212	20	11	3	34	39	32	.259	.293	.322	101	-3	2	84	16			.963	-24	/1OCS	-2.7

■ TRACY BAKER Baker, Tracy Lee b: 11/7/1891, Pendleton, Ore. d: 3/14/75, Placerville, Cal. BR/TR, 6'1", 180 lbs. Deb: 6/19/11

YEAR	TM/L	G	AB	R	H	2B	3B	HR	RBI	BB	SO	AVG	OBP	SLG	PRO+	BR	/A	RC	SB	CS	SBR	FA	FR	POS	TPR
1911	Bos-A	1	0	0	0	0	0	0	0	0		—	—	—	—	0	0	0	0			1.000	-0	/1	0.0

■ BILL BAKER Baker, William Presley b: 2/22/11, Paw Creek, N.C. BR/TR, 6', 200 lbs. Deb: 5/04/40 C

YEAR	TM/L	G	AB	R	H	2B	3B	HR	RBI	BB	SO	AVG	OBP	SLG	PRO+	BR	/A	RC	SB	CS	SBR	FA	FR	POS	TPR
1940	*Cin-N	27	69	5	15	1	1	0	7	4	8	.217	.260	.261	44	-5	-5	4	2			1.000	4	C	0.0
1941	Cin-N	2	1	0	0	0	0	0	0	1	1	.000	.500	.000	49	0	0	0	0			1.000	0	/C	0.0
	Pit-N	35	67	5	15	3	0	0	6	11	0	.224	.333	.269	71	-2	-2	7	0			.967	0	C	0.0
	Yr	37	68	5	15	3	0	0	6	12	1	.221	.338	.265	71	-2	-2	7	0			.967	0	C	0.0
1942	Pit-N	18	17	1	2	0	0	0	2	1	0	.118	.167	.118	-16	-2	-3	0	0			1.000	1	C	-0.1
1943	Pit-N	63	172	12	47	6	3	1	26	22	6	.273	.365	.360	106	3	2	23	3			.979	0	C	0.7
1946	Pit-N	53	113	7	27	4	0	1	8	12	6	.239	.312	.301	72	-4	-4	11	0			.965	-6	C/1	-0.9
1948	StL-N	45	119	13	35	10	1	0	15	15	7	.294	.373	.395	102	2	1	17	1			.994	-1	C	0.2
1949	StL-N	20	30	2	4	1	0	0	4	2	2	.133	.188	.167	-4	-4	-5	1	0			1.000	-2	C	-0.6
Total	7	263	588	45	145	25	5	2	68	68	30	.247	.328	.316	79	-13	-16	63	6			.983	-3	C/1	-0.7

■ JOHN BALAZ Balaz, John Lawrence b: 11/24/50, Toronto, Ont., Can. BR/TR, 6'3", 180 lbs. Deb: 9/10/74

YEAR	TM/L	G	AB	R	H	2B	3B	HR	RBI	BB	SO	AVG	OBP	SLG	PRO+	BR	/A	RC	SB	CS	SBR	FA	FR	POS	TPR
1974	Cal-A	14	42	4	10	0	0	1	5	2	10	.238	.289	.310	76	-2	-1	4	0	0	0	1.000	-1	O	-0.3
1975	Cal-A	45	120	10	29	8	1	1	10	5	25	.242	.272	.350	80	-4	-3	12	0	0	0	1.000	-0	OD	-0.5
Total	2	59	162	14	39	8	1	2	15	7	35	.241	.276	.340	79	-6	-5	16	0	0	0	1.000	-1	/OD	-0.8

■ STEVE BALBONI Balboni, Stephen Charles b: 1/16/57, Brockton, Mass. BR/TR, 6'3", 225 lbs. Deb: 4/22/81

YEAR	TM/L	G	AB	R	H	2B	3B	HR	RBI	BB	SO	AVG	OBP	SLG	PRO+	BR	/A	RC	SB	CS	SBR	FA	FR	POS	TPR
1981	NY-A	4	7	2	2	1	1	0	2	1	4	.286	.375	.714	211	1	1	2	0	0	0	1.000	0	/1D	0.1
1982	NY-A	33	107	8	20	2	1	2	4	6	34	.187	.230	.280	40	-9	-9	7	0	0	0	.990	-1	1/D	-1.1
1983	NY-A	32	86	8	20	2	0	5	17	8	23	.233	.298	.430	101	-1	-0	11	0	0	0	.984	-1	1/D	-0.2
1984	*KC-A	126	438	58	107	23	2	28	77	45	139	.244	.320	.498	122	12	11	69	0	0	0	.987	-5	*1/D	-0.1
1985	*KC-A	160	600	74	146	28	2	36	88	52	166	.243	.309	.477	111	7	7	86	1	1	-0	.993	-8	*1	-1.1
1986	KC-A	138	512	54	117	25	1	29	88	43	146	.229	.290	.451	96	-4	-5	67	0	0	0	.987	-6	*1	-2.0
1987	KC-A	121	386	44	80	11	1	24	60	34	97	.207	.275	.427	80	-11	-13	43	0	0	0	.989	1	1D	-1.5
1988	KC-A	21	63	2	9	2	0	2	5	1	20	.143	.156	.270	17	-7	-7	3	0	0	0	.980	-1	1/D	-0.9
	Sea-A	97	350	44	88	15	1	21	61	23	67	.251	.299	.480	110	5	3	48	0	1	-1	.994	-1	D1	-0.2
	Yr	118	413	46	97	17	1	23	66	24	87	.235	.279	.448	96	-2	-4	49	0	1	-1	.991	-2	D1	-1.1
1989	NY-A	110	300	33	71	12	2	17	59	25	67	.237	.302	.460	113	3	4	39	0	0	0	.994	-2	D1	0.1
1990	NY-A	116	266	24	51	6	0	17	34	35	91	.192	.293	.406	93	-3	-3	33	0	0	0	.984	-3	D1	-0.8
Total	10	958	3115	351	711	127	11	181	495	273	854	.228	.294	.450	100	-6	-10	408	1	2	-1	.989	-26	1D	-7.7

■ BOBBY BALCENA Balcena, Robert Rudolph b: 8/1/25, San Pedro, Cal. d: 1/4/90, San Pedro, Cal. BR/TL, 5'7", 160 lbs. Deb: 9/16/56

YEAR	TM/L	G	AB	R	H	2B	3B	HR	RBI	BB	SO	AVG	OBP	SLG	PRO+	BR	/A	RC	SB	CS	SBR	FA	FR	POS	TPR
1956	Cin-N	7	2	2	0	0	0	0	0	0	1	.000	.000	.000	-94	-1	-1	0	0	0	0	1.000	-1	/O	-0.1

■ LADY BALDWIN Baldwin, Charles Busted b: 4/8/1859, Ormel, N.Y. d: 3/7/37, Hastings, Mich. BL/TL, 5'11", 160 lbs. Deb: 9/30/1884

YEAR	TM/L	G	AB	R	H	2B	3B	HR	RBI	BB	SO	AVG	OBP	SLG	PRO+	BR	/A	RC	SB	CS	SBR	FA	FR	POS	TPR
1884	Mil-U	7	27	6	6	3	0	0		0		.222	.222	.333	158	-0	1	2				.778	0	/OP	0.1
1885	Det-N	31	124	12	30	6	3	0	18	6	22	.242	.277	.339	98	-0	-0	12				.879	1	PO	-0.1
1886	Det-N	57	204	25	41	6	3	0	25	18	44	.201	.266	.260	59	-9	-10	15	3			.969	3	P/O	0.0
1887	*Det-N	24	85	15	23	0	1	0	7	10	6	.271	.354	.294	81	-1	-2	11	4			.926	1	P	0.0
1888	Det-N	6	23	5	6	0	0	0	3	3	3	.261	.346	.261	98	0	0	2	0			1.000	-0	/PO	0.0
1890	Bro-N	2	3	1	0	0	0	0	0	1	1	.000	.250	.000	-24	-0	-0	0	0			.625	0	/P	0.0
	Buf-P	7	28	4	8	1	0	0	2	2	1	.286	.333	.321	84	-1	-0	3	0			1.000	-0	/P	0.0
Total	6	134	494	68	114	16	7	0	55	40	77	.231	.290	.291	78	-13	-12	45	7			.934	6	P/O	0.0

■ KID BALDWIN Baldwin, Clarence Geoghan b: 11/1/1864, Newport, Ky. d: 7/12/1897, Cincinnati, Ohio BR/TR, 5'6", 147 lbs. Deb: 7/27/1884

YEAR	TM/L	G	AB	R	H	2B	3B	HR	RBI	BB	SO	AVG	OBP	SLG	PRO+	BR	/A	RC	SB	CS	SBR	FA	FR	POS	TPR
1884	KC-U	50	191	19	37	6	3	0		4		.194	.210	.257	66	-8	-4	11				.885	0	CO/23	0.0
	CP-U	1	1	0	1	0	0	0		0		1.000	1.000	1.000	582	0	0	1				1.000	-0	/C	0.0
	Yr	51	192	19	38	6	3	0		4		.198	.214	.260	68	-8	-4	11				.885	0	CO/23	0.0
1885	Cin-a	34	126	9	17	1	0	1		3		.135	.155	.167	3	-13	-14	3				.863	-2	C/O2P3	-1.2
1886	Cin-a	87	315	41	72	8	7	3		8		.229	.252	.327	80	-7	-9	30	12			.891	-6	C3/O	-0.6
1887	Cin-a	96	388	46	98	15	10	1		6		.253	.271	.351	73	-14	-16	41	13			.874	-2	*C/O	-0.7
1888	Cin-a	67	271	27	59	11	3	1	25	3		.218	.235	.292	67	-9	-11	20	4			.918	-2	C/O1	-0.6
1889	Cin-a	60	223	34	55	14	2	1	34	5	32	.247	.273	.341	74	-8	-9	23	7			.912	2	C/O31	-0.2
1890	Cin-N	22	72	5	11	0	0	0	10	3	6	.153	.187	.153	0	-9	-9	2	2			.902	3	C/O	-0.4
	Phi-a	24	90	5	21	1	2	0		4		.233	.274	.289	69	-4	-3	8	2			.887	1	C/3	0.0
Total	7	441	1677	186	371	56	27	7	69	36	38	.221	.243	.299	65	-72	-75	140	40			.893	-6	C/O321P	-3.7

■ FRANK BALDWIN Baldwin, Frank De Witt b: 12/25/28, High Bridge, N.J. BR/TR, 5'11", 195 lbs. Deb: 4/22/53

YEAR	TM/L	G	AB	R	H	2B	3B	HR	RBI	BB	SO	AVG	OBP	SLG	PRO+	BR	/A	RC	SB	CS	SBR	FA	FR	POS	TPR
1953	Cin-N	16	20	0	2	0	0	0	0	1	9	.100	.143	.100	-35	-4	-4	0	0	0	0	1.000	-1	/C	-0.5

■ HENRY BALDWIN Baldwin, Henry Clay "Ted" b: 6/13/1894, Chadds Ford, Pa. d: 2/24/64, West Chester, Pa. BR/TR, 5'11", 180 lbs. Deb: 5/22/27

YEAR	TM/L	G	AB	R	H	2B	3B	HR	RBI	BB	SO	AVG	OBP	SLG	PRO+	BR	/A	RC	SB	CS	SBR	FA	FR	POS	TPR
1927	Phi-N	6	16	1	5	0	0	0	1	1	2	.313	.353	.313	78	-0	-0	2	0			.857	-2	/S3	-0.2

■ JEFF BALDWIN Baldwin, Jeffrey Allen b: 9/5/65, Milford, Del. BL/TL, 6'1", 180 lbs. Deb: 5/22/90

YEAR	TM/L	G	AB	R	H	2B	3B	HR	RBI	BB	SO	AVG	OBP	SLG	PRO+	BR	/A	RC	SB	CS	SBR	FA	FR	POS	TPR
1990	Hou-N	7	8	1	0	0	0	0	0	1	2	.000	.111	.000	-69	-2	-2	0	0	0	0	1.000	-1	/O	-0.3

■ REGGIE BALDWIN Baldwin, Reginald Conrad b: 8/19/54, River Rouge, Mich. BR/TR, 6'1", 195 lbs. Deb: 5/25/78

YEAR	TM/L	G	AB	R	H	2B	3B	HR	RBI	BB	SO	AVG	OBP	SLG	PRO+	BR	/A	RC	SB	CS	SBR	FA	FR	POS	TPR
1978	Hou-N	38	67	5	17	5	0	1	11	3	3	.254	.286	.373	89	-2	-1	6	0	0	0	.955	-1	C	-0.2
1979	Hou-N	14	20	0	4	1	0	0	1	0	1	.200	.200	.250	23	-2	-2	1	0	0	0	1.000	-1	/C1	-0.3
Total	2	52	87	5	21	6	0	1	12	3	4	.241	.267	.345	74	-4	-3	7	0	0	0	.956	-2	/C1	-0.5

■ BILLY BALDWIN Baldwin, Robert Harvey b: 6/9/51, Tazewell, Va. BL/TL, 6', 175 lbs. Deb: 7/29/75

YEAR	TM/L	G	AB	R	H	2B	3B	HR	RBI	BB	SO	AVG	OBP	SLG	PRO+	BR	/A	RC	SB	CS	SBR	FA	FR	POS	TPR
1975	Det-A	30	95	8	21	3	0	4	8	5	14	.221	.260	.379	75	-3	-4	10	2	1	0	.983	2	O/D	-0.3
1976	NY-N	9	22	4	6	1	1	1	5	1	2	.273	.304	.545	146	1	1	4	0	0	0	.929	1	/O	0.2
Total	2	39	117	12	27	4	1	5	13	6	16	.231	.268	.410	87	-2	-3	13	2	1	0	.972	3	/OD	-0.1

■ MIKE BALENTI Balenti, Michael Richard b: 7/3/1886, Calumet, Okla. d: 8/4/55, Altus, Okla. BR/TR, 5'11", 175 lbs. Deb: 7/19/11

YEAR	TM/L	G	AB	R	H	2B	3B	HR	RBI	BB	SO	AVG	OBP	SLG	PRO+	BR	/A	RC	SB	CS	SBR	FA	FR	POS	TPR
1911	Cin-N	8	8	2	2	0	0	0	0	0	1	.250	.250	.250	42	-1	-1	1	3			.857	0	/SO	0.0
1913	StL-A	70	211	17	38	2	4	0	11	6	32	.180	.206	.227	28	-20	-19	10	3			.923	1	S/O	-1.6
Total	2	78	219	19	40	2	4	0	11	6	33	.183	.208	.228	28	-21	-20	12	6			.922	1	/SO	-1.6

■ LEE BALES Bales, Wesley Owen b: 12/4/44, Los Angeles, Cal. BB/TR, 5'10.5", 165 lbs. Deb: 8/07/66

YEAR	TM/L	G	AB	R	H	2B	3B	HR	RBI	BB	SO	AVG	OBP	SLG	PRO+	BR	/A	RC	SB	CS	SBR	FA	FR	POS	TPR
1966	Atl-N	12	16	4	1	0	0	0	0	0	5	.063	.063	.063	-64	-3	-4	0	0	0	0	1.000	3	/23	0.0
1967	Hou-N	19	27	4	3	0	0	0	2	8	7	.111	.314	.111	28	-2	-2	2	1	1	-0	.944	-2	/2S	-0.4
Total	2	31	43	8	4	0	0	0	2	8	12	.093	.235	.093	-3	-6	-6	2	1	1	-0	.978	1	/23S	-0.4

■ ART BALL Ball, Arthur Clark b: 4/1876, Kentucky d: 12/26/15, Chicago, Ill. TR, Deb: 8/01/1894

YEAR	TM/L	G	AB	R	H	2B	3B	HR	RBI	BB	SO	AVG	OBP	SLG	PRO+	BR	/A	RC	SB	CS	SBR	FA	FR	POS	TPR
1894	StL-N	1	3	0	1	0	0	0	0	0	1	.333	.333	.333	63	-0	-0	0	0			.667	-1	/2	-0.1

YEAR	TM/L	G	AB	R	H	2B	3B	HR	RBI	BB	SO	AVG	OBP	SLG	PRO+	BR	/A	RC	SB	CS	SBR	FA	FR	POS	TPR
1898	Bal-N	32	81	7	15	2	0	0	8	7		.185	.258	.210	34	-7	-7	5	2			.906	9	3S/2O	0.3
Total	2	33	84	7	16	2	0	0	8	7	1	.190	.261	.214	35	-7	-7	6	2			.929	8	/3S2O	0.2

■ NEAL BALL Ball, Cornelius b: 4/22/1881, Grand Haven, Mich. d: 10/15/57, Bridgeport, Conn. BR/TR, 5′7″, 145 lbs. Deb: 9/12/07

YEAR	TM/L	G	AB	R	H	2B	3B	HR	RBI	BB	SO	AVG	OBP	SLG	PRO+	BR	/A	RC	SB	CS	SBR	FA	FR	POS	TPR
1907	NY-A	15	44	5	9	1	1	0	4	1		.205	.222	.273	53	-2	-3	3	1			.817	-3	S/2	-0.6
1908	NY-A	132	446	34	110	16	2	0	38	21		.247	.282	.291	86	-7	-8	45	32			.898	-6	*S/2	-1.3
1909	NY-A	8	29	5	6	1	1	0	3	3		.207	.281	.310	86	-0	-0	3	2			.917	-3	/2	-0.5
	Cle-A	96	324	29	83	13	2	1	25	17		.256	.295	.318	90	-3	-4	36	17			.914	-11	S	-1.6
	Yr	104	353	34	89	14	3	1	28	20		.252	.294	.317	90	-4	-5	39	19			.914	-14	S/2	-2.1
1910	Cle-A	53	119	13	25	3	1	0	12	9		.210	.266	.252	61	-5	-5	9	4			.927	-2	S/2O3	-0.7
1911	Cle-A	116	412	45	122	14	9	3	45	27		.296	.339	.396	104	1	1	62	21			.945	6	23/S	0.4
1912	Cle-A	40	132	12	30	4	1	0	14	9		.227	.277	.273	55	-7	-8	12	7			.938	0	2	-0.9
	*Bos-A	18	45	10	9	2	0	0	6	3		.200	.250	.244	40	-3	-4	4	5			.927	-4	2	-0.8
	Yr	58	177	22	39	6	1	0	20	12		.220	.270	.266	51	-11	-12	16	12			.936	-3	2	-1.7
1913	Bos-A	23	58	9	10	2	0	0	4	9	13	.172	.294	.207	46	-4	-4	4	3			.902	-2	2/S3	-0.5
Total	7	501	1609	162	404	56	17	4	151	99	13	.251	.296	.314	83	-31	-36	178	92			.902	-25	S2/3O	-6.5

■ JIM BALL Ball, James Chandler b: 2/22/1884, Hartford, Md. d: 4/7/63, Glendale, Cal. BR/TR, 5′11″, 175 lbs. Deb: 9/21/07

YEAR	TM/L	G	AB	R	H	2B	3B	HR	RBI	BB	SO	AVG	OBP	SLG	PRO+	BR	/A	RC	SB	CS	SBR	FA	FR	POS	TPR
1907	Bos-N	10	36	3	6	2	0	0	3	2		.167	.211	.222	36	-3	-3	2	0			.963	-2	C	-0.4
1908	Bos-N	6	15	1	1	0	0	0	0	1		.067	.125	.067	-39	-2	-2	0	0			.917	-1	/C	-0.3
Total	2	16	51	4	7	2	0	0	3	3		.137	.185	.176	14	-5	-5	2	0			.949	-2	/C	-0.7

■ PELHAM BALLENGER Ballenger, Pelham Ashby b: 2/6/1894, Gilreath Mill, S.C. d: 12/8/48, Greenville, County S.C. BR/TR, 5′11″, 160 lbs. Deb: 5/07/28

YEAR	TM/L	G	AB	R	H	2B	3B	HR	RBI	BB	SO	AVG	OBP	SLG	PRO+	BR	/A	RC	SB	CS	SBR	FA	FR	POS	TPR
1928	Was-A	3	9	0	1	0	0	0	0	0	1	.111	.111	.111	-42	-2	-2	0	0	0	0	1.000	1	/3	0.0

■ HAL BAMBERGER Bamberger, Harold Earl "Dutch" b: 10/29/24, Lebanon, Pa. BL/TR, 6′, 173 lbs. Deb: 9/15/48

YEAR	TM/L	G	AB	R	H	2B	3B	HR	RBI	BB	SO	AVG	OBP	SLG	PRO+	BR	/A	RC	SB	CS	SBR	FA	FR	POS	TPR
1948	NY-N	7	12	0	1	0	0	0	0	1	2	.083	.154	.083	-34	-2	-2	0	0			1.000	-0	/O	-0.3

■ STUD BANCKER Bancker, John b: Philadelphia, Pa. Deb: 4/21/1875

YEAR	TM/L	G	AB	R	H	2B	3B	HR	RBI	BB	SO	AVG	OBP	SLG	PRO+	BR	/A	RC	SB	CS	SBR	FA	FR	POS	TPR
1875	NH-n	19	72	3	11	0	0	0		0		.153	.153	.153	7	-7	-5	2						C/2S3	-0.4

■ DAVE BANCROFT Bancroft, David James "Beauty" b: 4/20/1891, Sioux City, Iowa d: 10/9/72, Superior, Wis. BB/TR, 5′9.5″, 160 lbs. Deb: 4/14/15 MCH

YEAR	TM/L	G	AB	R	H	2B	3B	HR	RBI	BB	SO	AVG	OBP	SLG	PRO+	BR	/A	RC	SB	CS	SBR	FA	FR	POS	TPR
1915	*Phi-N	153	563	85	143	18	2	7	30	77	62	.254	.346	.330	104	6	5	64	15	27	-12	.928	5	*S	1.2
1916	Phi-N	142	477	53	101	10	0	3	33	74	57	.212	.323	.252	75	-9	-11	46	15			.933	25	*S	2.4
1917	Phi-N	127	478	56	116	22	5	4	43	44	42	.243	.307	.335	93	-2	-4	52	14			.936	**28**	*S/2O	3.3
1918	Phi-N	125	499	69	132	19	4	0	26	54	36	.265	.338	.319	94	2	-2	55	11			.928	18	*S	2.4
1919	Phi-N	92	335	45	91	13	7	0	25	31	30	.272	.333	.352	99	3	0	41	8			.951	10	S	1.7
1920	Phi-N	42	171	23	51	7	2	0	5	9	12	.298	.337	.363	96	0	-1	19	1	7	-4	.981	9	S	0.9
	NY-N	108	442	79	132	29	7	0	31	33	32	.299	.349	.396	115	8	8	61	7	5	-1	.946	30	*S	4.8
	Yr	150	613	102	183	36	9	0	36	42	44	.299	.346	.387	109	8	7	80	8	12	-5	**.955**	**39**	*S	5.7
1921	*NY-N	153	606	121	193	26	15	6	67	66	23	.318	.389	.441	119	18	18	106	17	10	-1	.960	17	*S	4.8
1922	*NY-N	156	651	117	209	41	5	4	60	79	27	.321	.397	.418	109	13	12	111	16	11	-2	.941	22	*S	4.5
1923	*NY-N	107	444	80	135	33	3	1	31	62	23	.304	.391	.399	110	8	9	72	8	7	-2	.936	**21**	S2	3.6
1924	Bos-N	79	319	49	89	11	1	2	21	37	24	.279	.356	.339	91	-5	-3	40	4	4	-1	.961	-5	SM	0.0
1925	Bos-N	128	479	75	153	29	8	2	49	64	22	.319	.400	.426	122	10	17	85	7	4	-0	**.945**	10	*SM	3.7
1926	Bos-N	127	453	70	141	18	6	1	44	64	29	.311	.399	.384	122	10	16	72	3			.956	-3	*S/3M	2.6
1927	Bos-N	111	375	44	91	13	4	1	31	43	36	.243	.322	.307	75	-15	-12	38	5			.939	6	*S/3M	0.5
1928	Bro-N	149	515	47	127	19	5	0	51	59	20	.247	.326	.303	66	-25	-24	53	7			.948	4	*S	-0.2
1929	Bro-N	104	358	35	99	11	3	1	44	29	11	.277	.331	.332	66	-19	-18	40	7			.955	-0	*S	-0.6
1930	NY-N	10	17	0	1	1	0	0	0	2	1	.059	.158	.118	-33	-4	-4	0	0			.966	1	/S	-0.2
Total	16	1913	7182	1048	2004	320	77	32	591	827	487	.279	.355	.358	98	-1	8	954	145	75		.944	198	*S/23O	35.4

■ CHRIS BANDO Bando, Christopher Michael b: 2/4/56, Cleveland, Ohio BB/TR, 6′, 195 lbs. Deb: 8/13/81 F

YEAR	TM/L	G	AB	R	H	2B	3B	HR	RBI	BB	SO	AVG	OBP	SLG	PRO+	BR	/A	RC	SB	CS	SBR	FA	FR	POS	TPR
1981	Cle-A	21	47	3	10	3	0	0	6	2	2	.213	.245	.277	51	-3	-3	3	0	0	0	.967	-2	C/D	-0.5
1982	Cle-A	66	184	13	39	6	1	3	16	24	30	.212	.303	.304	68	-8	-8	17	0	0	0	.990	-6	C/3	-1.2
1983	Cle-A	48	121	15	31	3	0	4	15	15	19	.256	.338	.380	94	-0	-1	15	0	1	-1	.995	-2	C	-0.2
1984	Cle-A	75	220	38	64	11	0	12	41	33	35	.291	.383	.505	141	13	13	41	1	2	-1	.982	-4	C/13D	1.1
1985	Cle-A	73	173	11	24	4	1	0	13	22	21	.139	.236	.173	14	-20	-20	7	0	1	-1	.986	-3	C	-2.1
1986	Cle-A	92	254	28	68	9	0	2	26	22	49	.268	.329	.327	81	-7	-6	27	0	1	-1	.990	-10	C	-1.2
1987	Cle-A	89	211	20	46	9	0	5	16	12	28	.218	.260	.332	55	-14	-14	17	0	0	0	.990	-2	C	-1.1
1988	Cle-A	32	72	6	9	1	0	1	8	8	12	.125	.222	.181	14	-8	-8	3	0	0	0	.979	1	C	-0.6
	Det-A	1	0	0	0	0	0	0	0	0	0	—	—	—	—	0	0	0	0	0	0	.000	0	/C	0.0
	Yr	33	72	6	9	1	0	1	8	8	12	.125	.222	.181	14	-8	-8	3	0	0	0	.979	1	C	-0.6
1989	Oak-A	1	2	0	1	0	0	0	1	0	1	.500	.500	.500	189	0	0	1	0	0	0	1.000	1	/C	0.1
Total	9	498	1284	134	292	46	2	27	142	138	197	.227	.303	.329	73	-47	-47	131	1	5	-3	.987	-28	C/3D1	-5.7

■ SAL BANDO Bando, Salvatore Leonard b: 2/13/44, Cleveland, O. BR/TR, 6′, 205 lbs. Deb: 9/03/66 FC

YEAR	TM/L	G	AB	R	H	2B	3B	HR	RBI	BB	SO	AVG	OBP	SLG	PRO+	BR	/A	RC	SB	CS	SBR	FA	FR	POS	TPR
1966	KC-A	11	24	1	7	1	1	0	1	1	3	.292	.320	.417	113	0	0	3	0	0	0	.933	4	/3	0.5
1967	KC-A	47	130	11	25	3	2	0	6	16	24	.192	.295	.246	64	-6	-5	11	1	0	0	.959	8	3	0.3
1968	Oak-A	162	605	67	152	25	5	9	67	51	78	.251	.317	.354	108	2	5	69	13	4	2	.964	-12	*3/O	-0.5
1969	Oak-A★	162	609	106	171	25	3	31	113	111	82	.281	.401	.484	153	41	45	124	1	4	-2	.954	-13	*3	3.1
1970	Oak-A	155	502	93	132	20	2	20	75	118	88	.263	.409	.430	137	27	30	94	6	10	-4	.954	-22	*3	0.3
1971	*Oak-A	153	538	75	146	23	1	24	94	86	55	.271	.380	.452	137	27	28	93	3	7	-3	.971	-17	*3	0.7
1972	*Oak-A★	152	535	64	126	20	3	15	77	78	55	.236	.342	.368	118	10	13	70	3	1	0	.960	6	*3/2	1.9
1973	*Oak-A★	162	592	97	170	**32**	3	29	98	82	84	.287	.378	.498	153	36	40	**113**	4	2	0	.949	-23	*3/D	1.6
1974	*Oak-A	146	498	84	121	21	2	22	103	86	79	.243	.360	.426	134	18	22	80	2	3	-1	.946	-13	*3/D	0.7
1975	*Oak-A	160	562	64	129	24	1	15	78	87	80	.230	.338	.356	98	-1	1	73	7	1	2	.967	-16	*3	-1.4
1976	Oak-A	158	550	75	132	18	2	27	84	76	74	.240	.337	.427	128	16	18	84	20	6	2	.962	-5	*3/SD	1.6
1977	Mil-A	159	580	65	145	27	3	17	82	75	89	.250	.339	.395	99	0	0	81	4	2	0	.966	-2	*3D/2S	-0.3
1978	Mil-A	152	540	85	154	20	6	17	78	72	52	.285	.375	.439	128	22	22	92	3	2	-0	.968	12	*3D/1	3.2
1979	Mil-A	130	476	57	117	14	3	9	43	57	42	.246	.330	.345	82	-11	-11	54	2	0	1	.963	-9	*3D/1P2	-2.0
1980	Mil-A	78	254	28	50	12	1	5	31	29	35	.197	.282	.311	64	-13	-12	22	5	3	-0	.934	-4	3D/1	-1.8
1981	*Mil-A	32	65	10	13	4	0	2	9	6	3	.200	.268	.354	82	-2	-2	6	1	1	-0	.967	0	3/1D	-0.2
Total	16	2019	7060	982	1790	289	38	242	1039	1031	923	.254	.355	.408	120	165	193	1069	75	46	-5	.959	-104	*3/D1S2PO	7.7

■ JEFF BANISTER Banister, Jeffery Todd b: 1/15/65, Weatherford, Okla. BR/TR, 6′2″, 200 lbs. Deb: 7/23/91

YEAR	TM/L	G	AB	R	H	2B	3B	HR	RBI	BB	SO	AVG	OBP	SLG	PRO+	BR	/A	RC	SB	CS	SBR	FA	FR	POS	TPR
1991	Pit-N	1	1	0	1	0	0	0	0	0	0	1.000	1.000	1.000	471	0	0	1	0	0	0	.000	0	/H	0.0

■ ERNIE BANKS Banks, Ernest b: 1/31/31, Dallas, Tex. BR/TR, 6′1″, 180 lbs. Deb: 9/17/53 CH

YEAR	TM/L	G	AB	R	H	2B	3B	HR	RBI	BB	SO	AVG	OBP	SLG	PRO+	BR	/A	RC	SB	CS	SBR	FA	FR	POS	TPR
1953	Chi-N	10	35	3	11	1	1	2	6	4	5	.314	.385	.571	142	2	2	8	0	0	0	.981	3	S	0.5
1954	Chi-N	154	593	70	163	19	7	19	79	40	50	.275	.328	.427	94	-6	-7	80	6	10	-4	.959	-1	*S	0.1
1955	Chi-N★	154	596	98	176	29	9	44	117	45	72	.295	.347	.596	145	34	35	117	9	3	1	**.972**	5	*S	5.3
1956	Chi-N☆	139	538	82	160	25	8	28	85	52	62	.297	.359	.530	137	25	27	99	6	9	-4	.962	-16	*S	1.9
1957	Chi-N★	156	594	113	169	34	6	43	102	70	85	.285	.363	.579	150	39	40	123	8	4	0	.975	-17	*S3	3.4
1958	Chi-N★	154	617	119	193	23	11	**47**	**129**	52	87	.313	.370	**.614**	157	46	47	135	4	4	-1	.960	-2	*S	5.7

YEAR	TM/L	G	AB	R	H	2B	3B	HR	RBI	BB	SO	AVG	OBP	SLG	PRO+	BR	/A	RC	SB	CS	SBR	FA	FR	POS	TPR
1959	Chi-N★	155	589	97	179	25	6	45	**143**	64	72	.304	.379	.596	156	44	45	126	2	4	-2	**.985**	6	*S	**6.2**
1960	Chi-N★	156	597	94	162	32	7	**41**	117	71	69	.271	.353	.554	145	34	35	113	1	3	-2	**.977**	11	*S	**5.7**
1961	Chi-N★	138	511	75	142	22	4	29	80	54	75	.278	.349	.507	122	16	15	88	1	2	-1	.965	12	*SO/1	3.3
1962	Chi-N★	154	610	87	164	20	6	37	104	30	71	.269	.311	.503	110	9	6	89	5	1	1	.993	0	*1/3	-0.3
1963	Chi-N	130	432	41	98	20	1	18	64	39	73	.227	.297	.403	94	-1	-4	50	0	3	-2	.993	-2	*1	-1.4
1964	Chi-N	157	591	67	156	29	6	23	95	36	84	.264	.310	.450	107	7	4	77	1	2	-1	.994	11	*1	0.8
1965	Chi-N★	163	612	79	162	25	3	28	106	55	64	.265	.331	.453	116	14	12	87	3	5	-2	.992	-7	*1	-0.6
1966	Chi-N	141	511	52	139	23	7	15	75	29	59	.272	.317	.432	105	3	3	66	0	1	-1	.992	2	*1/3	-0.5
1967	Chi-N★	151	573	68	158	26	4	23	95	27	93	.276	.312	.455	112	10	7	74	2	2	-1	.993	1	*1	-0.2
1968	Chi-N	150	552	71	136	27	0	32	83	27	67	.246	.288	.469	116	13	9	72	2	0	1	.996	-1	*1	-0.3
1969	Chi-N★	155	565	60	143	19	2	23	106	42	101	.253	.313	.416	91	0	-8	71	0	0	0	**.997**	1	*1	-2.1
1970	Chi-N	72	222	25	56	6	2	12	44	20	33	.252	.317	.459	94	1	-3	32	0	0	0	.993	-2	1	-1.0
1971	Chi-N	39	83	4	16	2	0	3	6	6	14	.193	.247	.325	53	-4	-6	7	0	0	0	1.000	1	1	-0.8
Total	19	2528	9421	1305	2583	407	90	512	1636	763	1236	.274	.333	.500	122	288	261	1513	50	53	-17	.994	4	*1S/30	25.7

■ GEORGE BANKS Banks, George Edward b: 9/24/38, Pacolet Mills, S.C. d: 3/1/85, Spartanburg, S.C. BR/TR, 5'11", 185 lbs. Deb: 4/15/62

YEAR	TM/L	G	AB	R	H	2B	3B	HR	RBI	BB	SO	AVG	OBP	SLG	PRO+	BR	/A	RC	SB	CS	SBR	FA	FR	POS	TPR
1962	Min-A	63	103	22	26	0	2	4	15	21	27	.252	.384	.408	109	3	2	16	0	0	0	.962	-3	O/3	-0.1
1963	Min-A	25	71	5	11	4	0	3	8	9	21	.155	.259	.338	65	-3	-4	6	0	0	0	.910	2	3	-0.2
1964	Min-A	1	1	0	0	0	0	0	0	0	1	.000	.000	.000	-99	-0	-0	0	0	0	0	.000	0	H	0.0
	Cle-A	9	17	6	5	1	0	2	3	6	6	.294	.478	.706	226	3	3	6	0	0	0	1.000	-1	/O23	0.3
	Yr	10	18	6	5	1	0	2	3	6	7	.278	.458	.667	210	3	3	6	0	0	0	1.000	-1	/O23	0.3
1965	Cle-A	4	5	0	1	1	0	0	0	1	3	.200	.333	.400	107	0	0	0	0	1	-1	1.000	0	/3	0.0
1966	Cle-A	4	4	0	1	0	0	0	1	0	1	.250	.250	.250	44	-0	-0	0	0	0	0	.000	0	H	0.0
Total	5	106	201	33	44	6	2	9	27	37	59	.219	.346	.403	102	2	1	30	0	1	-1	.919	-1	/3O2	0.0

■ BILL BANKSTON Bankston, Wilborn Everett b: 5/25/1893, Barnesville, Ga. d: 2/26/70, Griffin, Ga. BL/TR, 5'11", 180 lbs. Deb: 8/15/15

YEAR	TM/L	G	AB	R	H	2B	3B	HR	RBI	BB	SO	AVG	OBP	SLG	PRO+	BR	/A	RC	SB	CS	SBR	FA	FR	POS	TPR
1915	Phi-A	11	36	6	5	1	1	1	2	2	5	.139	.205	.306	55	-2	-2	2	1			.882	-1	/O	-0.3

■ JIM BANNING Banning, James M. b: 1866, New York, N.Y. BL/TR, 5'6", 150 lbs. Deb: 9/27/1888

YEAR	TM/L	G	AB	R	H	2B	3B	HR	RBI	BB	SO	AVG	OBP	SLG	PRO+	BR	/A	RC	SB	CS	SBR	FA	FR	POS	TPR
1888	Was-N	1	0	0	0	0	0	0	0	0	0	—	—	—	—	0	0	0	0			1.000	-0	/C	0.0
1889	Was-N	2	1	0	0	0	0	0	0	0	0	.000	.000	.000	-99	-0	-0	0	0			1.000	1	/C	0.1
Total	2	3	1	0	0	0	0	0	0	0	0	.000	.000	.000	-99	-0	-0	0	0			1.000	1	/C	0.1

■ ALAN BANNISTER Bannister, Alan b: 9/3/51, Montebello, Cal. BR/TR, 5'11", 175 lbs. Deb: 7/13/74

YEAR	TM/L	G	AB	R	H	2B	3B	HR	RBI	BB	SO	AVG	OBP	SLG	PRO+	BR	/A	RC	SB	CS	SBR	FA	FR	POS	TPR
1974	Phi-N	26	25	4	3	0	0	0	1	3	7	.120	.241	.120	3	-3	-3	1	0	0	0	1.000	0	/OS	-0.3
1975	Phi-N	24	61	10	16	3	1	0	0	1	9	.262	.274	.344	68	-3	-3	5	2	2	-1	1.000	4	O/2S	0.0
1976	Chi-A	73	145	19	36	6	2	0	8	14	21	.248	.319	.317	86	-2	-2	17	12	4	1	.988	-2	OS/23D	-0.4
1977	Chi-A	139	560	87	154	20	3	3	57	54	49	.275	.341	.338	86	-10	-9	66	4	3	-1	.936	-34	*S/2O	-2.9
1978	Chi-A	49	107	16	24	3	2	0	8	11	12	.224	.303	.290	67	-4	-5	9	3	3	-1	1.000	-3	DO/S2	-0.9
1979	Chi-A	136	506	71	144	28	8	2	55	43	40	.285	.344	.383	96	-2	-2	69	22	6	3	.963	-24	2O3/1D	-2.1
1980	Chi-A	45	130	16	25	6	0	0	9	12	16	.192	.261	.238	38	-11	-11	8	5	2	0	1.000	-2	O3	-1.4
	Cle-A	81	262	41	86	17	4	1	32	28	25	.328	.393	.435	126	10	10	46	9	2	2	.968	-17	2O/3S	-0.4
	Yr	126	392	57	111	23	4	1	41	40	41	.283	.350	.370	97	-1	-1	52	14	4	2	.981	-19	O23/S	-1.8
1981	Cle-A	68	232	36	61	11	1	1	17	16	19	.263	.310	.332	86	-4	-4	27	16	2	4	.986	-14	O2/1S	-1.4
1982	Cle-A	101	348	40	93	16	1	4	41	42	41	.267	.348	.353	94	-2	-2	47	18	5	2	.991	-11	O2/S3D	-1.0
1983	Cle-A	117	377	51	100	25	4	5	45	31	43	.265	.326	.393	93	-2	-4	48	6	6	-2	.969	-14	O2/1D	-2.1
1984	Hou-N	9	20	2	4	2	0	0	0	2	2	.200	.273	.300	65	-1	-1	2	0	0	0	.947	-1	/SO	-0.2
	Tex-A	47	112	20	33	2	1	2	9	21	17	.295	.410	.384	118	4	4	20	3	0	1	.959	-12	2/O13D	-0.7
1985	Tex-A	57	122	17	32	4	1	1	6	14	17	.262	.338	.336	84	-2	-2	15	8	2	1	1.000	-2	DO2/31	-0.3
Total	12	972	3007	430	811	143	28	19	288	292	318	.270	.337	.355	90	-32	-35	381	108	37	10	.983	-133	O2S/D31	-14.1

■ JIMMY BANNON Bannon, James Henry "Foxy Grandpa" b: 5/5/1871, Amesbury, Mass. d: 3/24/48, Glen Rock, N.J. BR/TR, 5'5", 160 lbs. Deb: 6/15/1893 F

YEAR	TM/L	G	AB	R	H	2B	3B	HR	RBI	BB	SO	AVG	OBP	SLG	PRO+	BR	/A	RC	SB	CS	SBR	FA	FR	POS	TPR
1893	StL-N	26	107	9	36	3	4	0	15	4	5	.336	.366	.439	115	2	2	21	8			.795	-6	O/SP	-0.4
1894	Bos-N	128	494	130	166	29	10	13	114	62	42	.336	.414	.514	115	20	12	128	47			.873	18	*O/P	1.7
1895	Bos-N	123	489	101	171	35	5	6	74	54	31	.350	.420	.479	124	25	18	114	28			.879	10	*O/P	1.5
1896	Bos-N	89	343	52	86	9	5	0	50	32	23	.251	.316	.306	63	-16	-20	40	16			.901	1	O/2S3	-2.1
Total	4	366	1433	292	459	76	24	19	253	152	101	.320	.390	.447	106	31	12	303	99			.877	24	O/S23P	0.7

■ TOM BANNON Bannon, Thomas Edward "Ward Six" b: 5/8/1869, Amesbury, Mass. d: 1/26/50, Lynn, Mass. BR/TR, 5'8", 175 lbs. Deb: 5/10/1895 F

YEAR	TM/L	G	AB	R	H	2B	3B	HR	RBI	BB	SO	AVG	OBP	SLG	PRO+	BR	/A	RC	SB	CS	SBR	FA	FR	POS	TPR
1895	NY-N	37	159	33	43	6	2	0	8	7	8	.270	.301	.333	67	-8	-8	23	20			.894	2	O1	-0.6
1896	NY-N	2	7	1	1	1	0	0	0	1	1	.143	.250	.286	44	-1	-1	1	0			.500	-1	/O	-0.2
Total	2	39	166	34	44	7	2	0	8	8	9	.265	.299	.331	66	-9	-8	23	20			.878	1	/O1	-0.8

■ WALTER BARBARE Barbare, Walter Lawrence "Dinty" b: 8/11/1891, Greenville, S.C. d: 10/28/65, Greenville, S.C. BR/TR, 6', 162 lbs. Deb: 9/17/14

YEAR	TM/L	G	AB	R	H	2B	3B	HR	RBI	BB	SO	AVG	OBP	SLG	PRO+	BR	/A	RC	SB	CS	SBR	FA	FR	POS	TPR
1914	Cle-A	15	52	6	16	2	2	0	5	2	5	.308	.345	.423	126	2	1	7	1	4	-2	.933	0	3/S	0.0
1915	Cle-A	77	246	15	47	3	1	0	11	10	27	.191	.235	.211	33	-20	-21	14	6	5	-1	.960	7	3/1	-1.3
1916	Cle-A	13	48	3	11	1	0	0	3	4	9	.229	.288	.250	58	-2	-3	4	0			.977	1	3	-0.1
1918	Bos-A	13	29	2	5	3	0	0	2	0	1	.172	.172	.276	36	-2	-2	2	1			.826	-4	3/S	-0.7
1919	Pit-N	85	293	34	80	11	5	1	34	18	18	.273	.317	.355	98	0	-1	36	11			.961	-7	3/2	-0.5
1920	Pit-N	57	186	9	51	5	2	0	12	9	11	.274	.308	.323	79	-5	-5	18	5	3	-0	.923	-5	S2/3	-0.8
1921	Bos-N	134	550	66	166	22	7	0	49	24	28	.302	.331	.367	89	-12	-8	68	11	4	1	.957	-17	*S/23	-1.2
1922	Bos-N	106	373	38	86	5	4	0	40	21	22	.231	.272	.265	41	-34	-31	28	2	0	1	.966	2	231	-2.4
Total	8	500	1777	173	462	52	21	1	156	88	121	.260	.297	.315	71	-73	-70	177	37	16		.959	-21	3S/21	-7.0

■ RED BARBARY Barbary, Donald Odell b: 6/20/20, Simpsonville, S.C BR/TR, 6'3", 190 lbs. Deb: 5/22/43

YEAR	TM/L	G	AB	R	H	2B	3B	HR	RBI	BB	SO	AVG	OBP	SLG	PRO+	BR	/A	RC	SB	CS	SBR	FA	FR	POS	TPR
1943	Was-A	1	1	0	0	0	0	0	0	0	0	.000	.000	.000	-99	-0	-0	0	0	0	0	.000	0	H	0.0

■ JAP BARBEAU Barbeau, William Joseph b: 6/10/1882, New York, N.Y. d: 9/10/69, Milwaukee, Wis. BR/TR, 5'5", 140 lbs. Deb: 9/27/05

YEAR	TM/L	G	AB	R	H	2B	3B	HR	RBI	BB	SO	AVG	OBP	SLG	PRO+	BR	/A	RC	SB	CS	SBR	FA	FR	POS	TPR
1905	Cle-A	11	37	1	10	1	1	0	2	1		.270	.289	.351	102	-0	-0	4	1			.905	1	2	0.1
1906	Cle-A	42	129	8	25	5	3	0	12	9		.194	.257	.279	69	-5	-5	11	5			.830	-7	3/S	-1.2
1909	Pit-N	91	350	60	77	16	3	0	25	37		.220	.302	.283	75	-7	-10	35	19			.891	-21	3	-3.2
	StL-N	48	175	23	44	3	0	0	5	28		.251	.370	.269	105	2	3	23	14			.901	-11	3	-0.7
	Yr	139	525	83	121	19	3	0	30	65		.230	.326	.278	85	-5	-7	58	33			.895	-31	*3	-3.9
1910	StL-N	7	21	4	4	0	1	0	2	3	3	.190	.292	.286	71	-1	-1	2	0			.917	2	/32	0.2
Total	4	199	712	96	160	25	8	0	46	78	3	.225	.311	.282	83	-11	-13	75	39			.884	-35	3/2S	-4.8

■ DAVE BARBEE Barbee, David Monroe b: 5/7/05, Greensboro, N.C. d: 7/1/68, Albermarle, N.C. BR/TR, 5'11.5", 178 lbs. Deb: 7/29/26

YEAR	TM/L	G	AB	R	H	2B	3B	HR	RBI	BB	SO	AVG	OBP	SLG	PRO+	BR	/A	RC	SB	CS	SBR	FA	FR	POS	TPR
1926	Phi-A	19	47	7	8	1	1	1	5	2	4	.170	.220	.298	32	-5	-5	3	0	0	0	1.000	0	O	-0.6
1932	Pit-N	97	327	37	84	22	6	5	55	18	38	.257	.300	.407	89	-6	-5	40	1			.975	4	O	-0.7
Total	2	116	374	44	92	23	7	6	60	20	42	.246	.290	.393	82	-11	-11	44	1	0		.977	4	/O	-1.3

■ CHARLIE BARBER Barber, Charles D. b: 1854, Philadelphia, Pa. d: 11/23/10, Philadelphia, Pa. BR/TR, Deb: 4/17/1884

YEAR	TM/L	G	AB	R	H	2B	3B	HR	RBI	BB	SO	AVG	OBP	SLG	PRO+	BR	/A	RC	SB	CS	SBR	FA	FR	POS	TPR
1884	Cin-U	55	204	38	41	1	4	0		11		.201	.242	.245	60	-7	-10	12				.837	4	3	-0.5

■ TURNER BARBER Barber, Tyrus Turner b: 7/9/1893, Lavinia, Tenn. d: 10/20/68, Milan, Tenn. BL/TR, 5'11", 170 lbs. Deb: 8/19/15

YEAR	TM/L	G	AB	R	H	2B	3B	HR	RBI	BB	SO	AVG	OBP	SLG	PRO+	BR	/A	RC	SB	CS	SBR	FA	FR	POS	TPR
1915	Was-A	20	53	9	16	1	1	0	6	6	7	.302	.383	.358	120	2	1	7	0	3	-2	.952	-2	O	-0.3

YEAR	TM/L	G	AB	R	H	2B	3B	HR	RBI	BB	SO	AVG	OBP	SLG	PRO+	BR	/A	RC	SB	CS	SBR	FA	FR	POS	TPR
1916	Was-A	15	33	3	7	0	1	1	5	2	3	.212	.257	.364	87	-1	-1	3	0			.833	-3	O	-0.4
1917	Chi-N	7	28	2	6	1	0	0	2	2	8	.214	.267	.250	55	-1	-2	2	1			1.000	1	/O	-0.2
1918	*Chi-N	55	123	11	29	3	2	0	10	9	16	.236	.293	.293	77	-3	-3	11	3			.940	-8	O/1	-1.4
1919	Chi-N	76	230	26	72	9	4	0	21	14	17	.313	.355	.387	122	6	6	33	7			.949	-4	O	-0.3
1920	Chi-N	94	340	27	90	10	5	0	50	9	26	.265	.290	.324	74	-11	-12	31	5	6	-2	.988	-7	1O/2	-2.6
1921	Chi-N	127	452	73	142	14	4	1	54	41	24	.314	.379	.369	99	1	1	64	5	9	-4	.970	2	*O	-1.0
1922	Chi-N	84	226	35	70	7	4	0	29	30	9	.310	.391	.376	97	1	0	35	7	4	-0	.953	-6	O1	-0.9
1923	Bro-N	13	46	3	10	2	0	0	8	2	2	.217	.250	.261	36	-4	-4	3	0	1	-1	1.000	-2	O	-0.7
Total	9	491	1531	189	442	47	21	2	185	115	112	.289	.343	.351	93	-10	-13	189	28	23		.959	-29	O/12	-7.8

■ BRET BARBERIE
Barberie, Bret Edward b: 8/16/67, Long Beach, Cal. BB/TR, 5'11", 185 lbs. Deb: 6/16/91

YEAR	TM/L	G	AB	R	H	2B	3B	HR	RBI	BB	SO	AVG	OBP	SLG	PRO+	BR	/A	RC	SB	CS	SBR	FA	FR	POS	TPR
1991	Mon-N	57	136	16	48	12	2	2	18	20	22	.353	.443	.515	171	13	14	31	0	0	0	.931	-2	S23/1	1.4
1992	Mon-N	111	285	26	66	11	0	1	24	47	62	.232	.356	.281	83	-4	-4	33	9	5	-0	.932	5	32/S	0.2
Total	2	168	421	42	114	23	2	3	42	67	84	.271	.384	.356	111	9	10	64	9	5	-0	.941	3	/32S1	1.6

■ JIM BARBIERI
Barbieri, James Patrick b: 9/15/41, Schenectady, N.Y. BL/TR, 5'7", 155 lbs. Deb: 7/05/66

YEAR	TM/L	G	AB	R	H	2B	3B	HR	RBI	BB	SO	AVG	OBP	SLG	PRO+	BR	/A	RC	SB	CS	SBR	FA	FR	POS	TPR
1966	*LA-N	39	82	9	23	5	0	0	3	9	7	.280	.352	.341	102	-0	0	11	2	0	1	.939	0	O	0.0

■ GEORGE BARCLAY
Barclay, George Oliver "Deerfoot" b: 5/16/1876, Millville, Pa. d: 4/3/09, Philadelphia, Pa. TR, 5'10", 162 lbs. Deb: 4/17/02

YEAR	TM/L	G	AB	R	H	2B	3B	HR	RBI	BB	SO	AVG	OBP	SLG	PRO+	BR	/A	RC	SB	CS	SBR	FA	FR	POS	TPR
1902	StL-N	137	543	79	163	14	2	3	53	31		.300	.346	.350	119	9	12	79	30			.904	-7	*O	-0.5
1903	StL-N	108	419	37	104	10	8	0	42	15		.248	.276	.310	69	-19	-17	41	12			.901	-8	*O	-3.1
1904	StL-N	103	375	41	75	7	4	1	28	12		.200	.235	.248	52	-22	-21	27	14			.947	-6	*O	-3.5
	Bos-N	24	93	5	21	3	1	0	10	2		.226	.258	.280	69	-4	-3	8	3			.935	-3	O	-0.8
	Yr	127	468	46	96	10	5	1	38	14		.205	.239	.254	55	-26	-24	35	17			.945	-9	*O	-4.3
1905	Bos-N	29	108	5	19	1	0	0	7	2		.176	.205	.185	17	-11	-11	5	2			.854	-5	O	-1.8
Total	4	401	1538	167	382	35	15	4	140	62		.248	.285	.298	79	-47	-40	159	61			.911	-29	O	-9.7

■ JESSE BARFIELD
Barfield, Jesse Lee b: 10/29/59, Joliet, Ill. BR/TR, 6'1", 205 lbs. Deb: 9/03/81

YEAR	TM/L	G	AB	R	H	2B	3B	HR	RBI	BB	SO	AVG	OBP	SLG	PRO+	BR	/A	RC	SB	CS	SBR	FA	FR	POS	TPR
1981	Tor-A	25	95	7	22	3	2	2	9	4	19	.232	.270	.368	77	-2	-3	8	4	3	-1	1.000	5	O	0.1
1982	Tor-A	139	394	54	97	13	2	18	58	42	79	.246	.323	.426	95	2	-3	54	1	4	-2	.963	-6	*O/D	-1.4
1983	Tor-A	128	388	58	98	13	3	27	68	22	110	.253	.300	.510	111	7	4	55	2	5	-2	.966	4	*O/D	0.3
1984	Tor-A	110	320	51	91	14	1	14	49	35	81	.284	.359	.466	122	11	10	55	8	2	1	.952	6	O/D	1.5
1985	*Tor-A	155	539	94	156	34	9	27	84	66	143	.289	.371	.536	141	33	31	106	22	8	2	.989	22	*O	4.8
1986	Tor-A★	158	589	107	170	35	2	**40**	108	69	146	.289	.371	.559	145	39	37	122	8	8	-2	.992	21	*O	**4.9**
1987	Tor-A	159	590	89	155	25	3	28	84	58	141	.263	.332	.458	104	5	3	87	3	5	-2	.992	16	*O	1.2
1988	Tor-A	137	468	62	114	21	5	18	56	41	108	.244	.306	.425	102	0	0	60	7	3	0	.988	13	*O/D	0.9
1989	Tor-A	21	80	8	16	4	0	5	11	5	28	.200	.256	.438	94	-1	-1	9	0	2	-1	.979	3	O	0.0
	NY-A	129	441	71	106	19	1	18	56	82	122	.240	.362	.410	119	12	13	70	5	3	-0	.972	9	*O	1.9
	Yr	150	521	79	122	23	1	23	67	87	150	.234	.347	.415	115	11	12	78	5	5	-2	.973	12	*O	1.9
1990	NY-A	153	476	69	117	21	2	25	78	82	150	.246	.362	.456	127	19	18	84	4	3	-1	.973	9	*O	2.3
1991	NY-A	84	284	37	64	12	0	17	48	36	80	.225	.313	.447	107	2	2	38	1	0	0	1.000	11	O	1.2
1992	NY-A	30	95	8	13	2	0	2	7	9	27	.137	.212	.221	21	-10	-10	4	1	1	-0	.966	0	O	-1.2
Total	12	1428	4759	715	1219	216	30	241	716	551	1234	.256	.338	.466	116	117	101	749	66	47	-8	.980	114	*O/D	16.5

■ AL BARKER
Barker, Alfred L b: 1/18/1839, Rockford, Ill. d: 9/15/12, Rockford, Ill. Deb: 6/01/1871

YEAR	TM/L	G	AB	R	H	2B	3B	HR	RBI	BB	SO	AVG	OBP	SLG	PRO+	BR	/A	RC	SB	CS	SBR	FA	FR	POS	TPR
1871	Rok-n	1	4	0	1	0	0	0	2	1	0	.250	.400	.250	97	0	0	0	0					/O	0.0

■ RAY BARKER
Barker, Raymond Herrell "Buddy" b: 3/12/36, Martinsburg.W.Va. BL/TR, 6', 192 lbs. Deb: 9/13/60

YEAR	TM/L	G	AB	R	H	2B	3B	HR	RBI	BB	SO	AVG	OBP	SLG	PRO+	BR	/A	RC	SB	CS	SBR	FA	FR	POS	TPR
1960	Bal-A	5	6	0	0	0	0	0	0	0	3	.000	.000	.000	-99	-2	-2	0	0	0	0	.000	-0	/O	-0.2
1965	Cle-A	11	6	0	0	0	0	0	0	2	2	.000	.250	.000	-22	-1	-1	0	0	0	0	1.000	-0	/1	-0.1
	NY-A	98	205	21	52	11	0	7	31	20	46	.254	.329	.410	109	2	2	28	1	0	0	.991	6	1/3	0.7
	Yr	109	211	21	52	11	0	7	31	22	48	.246	.326	.398	105	1	1	28	1	0	0	.991	6	1/3	0.6
1966	NY-A	61	75	11	14	5	0	3	13	4	20	.187	.228	.373	72	-3	-3	7	0	0	0	.987	5	1	0.1
1967	NY-A	17	26	2	2	0	0	0	0	3	5	.077	.172	.077	-25	-4	-4	0	0	0	0	.961	1	1	-0.4
Total	4	192	318	34	68	16	0	10	44	29	76	.214	.286	.358	84	-8	-7	35	1	0	0	.987	12	1/3O	0.1

■ RED BARKLEY
Barkley, John Duncan b: 9/19/13, Childress, Tex. BR/TR, 5'11", 160 lbs. Deb: 9/02/37

YEAR	TM/L	G	AB	R	H	2B	3B	HR	RBI	BB	SO	AVG	OBP	SLG	PRO+	BR	/A	RC	SB	CS	SBR	FA	FR	POS	TPR
1937	StL-A	31	101	9	27	6	0	0	14	14	17	.267	.357	.327	73	-4	-4	13	1	0	0	.969	-4	2	-0.5
1939	Bos-N	12	11	1	0	0	0	0	0	1	2	.000	.083	.000	-82	-3	-3	0	0			.842	4	/S3	0.1
1943	Bro-N	20	51	6	16	3	0	0	7	4	7	.314	.364	.373	113	1	1	7	1			.894	-3	S	-0.1
Total	3	63	163	16	43	9	0	0	21	19	26	.264	.341	.319	75	-6	-6	20	2	0		.882	-3	/2S3	-0.5

■ SAM BARKLEY
Barkley, Samuel E b: 5/24/1858, Wheeling, W.Va. d: 4/20/12, Wheeling, W.Va. BR/TR, 5'11.5", Deb: 5/01/1884 M

YEAR	TM/L	G	AB	R	H	2B	3B	HR	RBI	BB	SO	AVG	OBP	SLG	PRO+	BR	/A	RC	SB	CS	SBR	FA	FR	POS	TPR
1884	Tol-a	104	435	71	133	**39**	9	1		22		.306	.342	.444	152	26	24	68				.930	25	*2/C	**4.6**
1885	*StL-a	106	418	67	112	18	10	3		25		.268	.312	.380	115	10	7	51				.921	15	*21	2.1
1886	Pit-a	122	478	77	127	31	8	1		58		.266	.345	.370	127	15	16	70	22			.936	-4	*2/O1	1.4
1887	Pit-N	89	340	44	76	10	4	1	35	30	24	.224	.294	.285	67	-16	-12	31	6			.979	-5	12	-1.8
1888	KC-a	116	482	67	104	21	6	4	51	26		.216	.262	.309	80	-8	-13	44	15			.938	-7	*2/M	-1.4
1889	KC-a	45	176	36	50	6	2	0	23	15	20	.284	.340	.341	91	-1	-2	24	8			.923	-12	2/1	-1.0
Total	6	582	2329	362	602	125	39	10	109	176	44	.258	.314	.359	108	27	19	288	51			.929	12	2/1OC	3.9

■ TOM BARLOW
Barlow, Thomas H. Deb: 5/02/1872

YEAR	TM/L	G	AB	R	H	2B	3B	HR	RBI	BB	SO	AVG	OBP	SLG	PRO+	BR	/A	RC	SB	CS	SBR	FA	FR	POS	TPR
1872	Atl-n	37	170	34	56	2	0	0	10	3	2	.329	.341	.341	94	2	-4	20						*C/S	-0.4
1873	Atl-n	55	271	48	74	2	2	1	13	4	0	.273	.284	.306	82	-9	-3	24						*C/2S	-0.2
1874	Har-n	32	156	37	44	4	1	0		1		.282	.287	.321	89	-1	-3	15						S	-0.3
1875	NH-n	1	5	1	1	0	0	0		0		.200	.200	.200	44	-0	-0	0						/S	0.0
	Atl-n	1	4	0	0	0	0	0		0		.000	.000	.000	-99	-1	-1	0						/2	-0.1
	Yr	2	9	1	1	0	0	0		0		.111	.111	.111	-26	-1	-1	0						/S2	-0.1
Total	4 n	126	606	120	175	8	3	1		8		.289	.298	.317	86	-9	-10	59						/CS2	-1.0

■ BRUCE BARMES
Barmes, Bruce Raymond "Squeaky" b: 10/23/29, Vincennes, Ind. BL/TR, 5'8", 165 lbs. Deb: 9/13/53

YEAR	TM/L	G	AB	R	H	2B	3B	HR	RBI	BB	SO	AVG	OBP	SLG	PRO+	BR	/A	RC	SB	CS	SBR	FA	FR	POS	TPR
1953	Was-A	5	5	1	1	0	0	0	0	0	0	.200	.200	.200	8	-1	-1	0	0	0	0	1.000	0	/O	-0.1

■ BABE BARNA
Barna, Herbert Paul b: 3/2/15, Clarksburg, W.Va. d: 5/18/72, Charleston, W.Va. BL/TR, 6'2", 210 lbs. Deb: 9/16/37

YEAR	TM/L	G	AB	R	H	2B	3B	HR	RBI	BB	SO	AVG	OBP	SLG	PRO+	BR	/A	RC	SB	CS	SBR	FA	FR	POS	TPR
1937	Phi-A	14	36	10	14	2	0	2	9	2	6	.389	.421	.611	159	3	3	9	1	0	0	.800	-2	/O1	0.1
1938	Phi-A	9	30	4	4	0	0	0	2	3	5	.133	.212	.133	-12	-5	-5	1	0	0	0	.917	-1	/O	-0.6
1941	NY-N	10	42	5	9	3	0	1	5	2	6	.214	.250	.357	68	-2	-2	4	0			1.000	1	O	-0.2
1942	NY-N	104	331	39	85	8	7	6	58	38	48	.257	.333	.378	107	3	3	44	3			.983	-5	O	-0.6
1943	NY-N	40	113	11	23	5	1	1	12	16	9	.204	.302	.292	72	-4	-4	11	3			.984	-1	O	-0.7
	Bos-A	30	112	19	19	4	1	2	10	15	24	.170	.268	.277	58	-6	-6	9	2	1	0	.940	-4	O	-1.3
Total	5	207	664	88	154	22	9	12	96	76	98	.232	.311	.346	88	-11	-11	78	9	1		.969	-13	O/1	-3.3

■ RED BARNES
Barnes, Emile Deering b: 12/25/03, Suggsville, Ala. d: 7/3/59, Mobile, Ala. BL/TR, 5'10.5", 158 lbs. Deb: 9/29/27

YEAR	TM/L	G	AB	R	H	2B	3B	HR	RBI	BB	SO	AVG	OBP	SLG	PRO+	BR	/A	RC	SB	CS	SBR	FA	FR	POS	TPR
1927	Was-A	3	11	5	4	1	0	0	0	1	3	.364	.417	.455	127	0	0	2	0	0	0	1.000	0	/O	0.0
1928	Was-A	114	417	82	127	22	15	6	51	55	38	.305	.391	.472	127	16	17	80	7	3	0	.978	4	*O	1.3
1929	Was-A	72	130	16	26	5	2	1	15	13	12	.200	.273	.292	45	-11	-11	11	1	0	0	.877	-6	O	-1.7

YEAR	TM/L	G	AB	R	H	2B	3B	HR	RBI	BB	SO	AVG	OBP	SLG	PRO+	BR	/A	RC	SB	CS	SBR	FA	FR	POS	TPR
1930	Was-A	12	12	1	2	1	0	0	0	0	3	.167	.167	.250	4	-2	-2	0				.000	0	H	-0.2
	Chi-A	85	266	48	66	12	7	1	31	26	20	.248	.317	.357	73	-12	-11	31	4	2	0	.939	-0	O	-1.4
	Yr	97	278	49	68	13	7	1	31	26	23	.245	.311	.353	70	-14	-12	32	4	2	0	.939	-0	O	-1.6
Total	4	286	836	152	225	41	24	8	97	95	76	.269	.347	.404	95	-8	-6	125	12	5	1	.953	-2	O	-2.0
■ EPPIE BARNES Barnes, Everett Duane b: 12/1/1900, Ossining, N.Y. d: 11/17/80, Mineola, N.Y. BL/TL, 5'9", 175 lbs. Deb: 9/25/23																									
1923	Pit-N	2	2	0	1	0	0	0	0	0	1	.500	.500	.500	161	0	0	0	0	0	0	1.000	0	/1	0.1
1924	Pit-N	2	5	0	0	0	0	0	0	0	1	.000	.000	.000	-98	-1	-1	0	0	0	0	1.000	0	/1	-0.1
Total	2	4	7	0	1	0	0	0	0	0	2	.143	.143	.143	-23	-1	-1	0	0	0	0	1.000	1	/1	0.0
■ HONEY BARNES Barnes, John Francis b: 1/29/1900, Fulton, N.Y. d: 6/18/81, Lockport, N.Y. BL/TR, 5'10", 175 lbs. Deb: 4/20/26																									
1926	NY-A	1	0	0	0	0	0	0	0	1	0	—	1.000	—	179	0	0	0	0	0	0	.000	0	/C	0.0
■ LUTE BARNES Barnes, Luther Owens b: 4/28/47, Forest City, Iowa BR/TR, 5'10", 160 lbs. Deb: 8/06/72																									
1972	NY-N	24	72	5	17	2	2	0	6	6	4	.236	.295	.319	76	-2	-2	6	0	1	-1	.959	1	2/S	-0.1
1973	NY-N	3	2	2	1	0	0	0	1	0	1	.500	.500	.500	181	0	0	1	0	0	0	.000	0	H	0.0
Total	2	27	74	7	18	2	2	0	7	6	5	.243	.300	.324	79	-2	-2	7	0	1	-1	.956	1	2S	-0.1
■ ROSS BARNES Barnes, Roscoe Charles b: 5/8/1850, Lima, N.Y. d: 2/5/15, Chicago, Ill. BR/TR, 5'8.5", 145 lbs. Deb: 5/05/1871 U																									
1871	Bos-n	31	157	66	63	10	9	0	34	13	1	.401	.447	.580	186	19	18	47	11					2S/3	1.0
1872	Bos-n	45	230	81	97	28	2	1	44	9	4	.422	.444	.574	200	29	27	64						*2	1.7
1873	Bos-n	60	322	125	137	28	10	3	61	18	2	.425	.456	.602	193	43	37	94						*23	2.4
1874	Bos-n	51	259	72	89	12	4	0		8		.344	.363	.421	141	14	11	41						*2	0.7
1875	Bos-n	78	393	114	142	22	6	1		7		.361	.373	.455	178	32	30	68						*2	2.4
1876	Chi-N	66	322	126	138	21	14	1	59	20	8	.429	.462	.590	222	50	44	90				.910	5	*2/P	4.2
1877	Chi-N	22	92	16	25	1	0	0	5	7	4	.272	.323	.283	83	-0	-2	9				.838	-2	*2	-0.9
1879	Cin-N	77	323	55	86	9	2	1	30	16	25	.266	.301	.316	109	2	4	31				.864	-1	*S2	0.7
1881	Bos-N	69	295	42	80	14	1	0	17	16	16	.271	.309	.325	104	0	2	30				.854	-0	*S/2	0.6
Total	5 n	265	1361	458	528	100	31	5	139	55	7	.388	.412	.518	180	138	123	314						2S/3	8.2
Total	4	234	1032	239	329	45	17	2	111	59	53	.319	.356	.401	143	51	48	160				.859	-5	S2/P	4.6
■ SAM BARNES Barnes, Samuel Thomas b: 12/18/1899, Suggsville, Ala. d: 2/19/81, Montgomery, Ala. BL/TR, 5'8", 150 lbs. Deb: 9/14/21																									
1921	Det-A	7	11	2	2	1	0	0		2	1	.182	.357	.273	63	-1	-1	1	0	0	0	.944	2	/2	0.1
■ BILL BARNES Barnes, William H. b: Indianapolis, Ind. Deb: 9/27/1884																									
1884	StP-U	8	30	2	6	1	0	0			0	.200	.200	.233	85	-2	0	1				.727	-2	/O	-0.1
■ SKEETER BARNES Barnes, William Henry b: 3/3/57, Cincinnati, Ohio BR/TR, 5'10", 180 lbs. Deb: 9/06/83																									
1983	Cin-N	15	34	5	7	0	0	1	4	7	3	.206	.372	.294	84	-0	-0	4	2	2	-1	1.000	-0	/13	-0.2
1984	Cin-N	32	42	5	5	0	0	1	3	4	6	.119	.196	.190	8	-5	-5	2	0	0	0	1.000	0	3/O	-0.6
1985	Mon-N	19	26	0	4	1	0	0	0	0	2	.154	.154	.192	-4	-4	-3	0	0	1	-1	1.000	1	/3O1	-0.3
1987	StL-N	4	4	1	1	0	0	0	3	0	0	.250	.250	1.000	208	1	1	1	0	0	0	.000	0	/3	0.1
1989	Cin-N	5	3	1	0	0	0	0	0	0	0	.000	.000	.000	-97	-1	-1	0	0	1	-1	.000	0	H	-0.1
1991	Det-A	75	159	28	46	13	2	5	17	7	24	.289	.327	.491	121	4	4	24	10	7	-1	1.000	-1	O3/12D	0.1
1992	Det-A	95	165	27	45	8	1	3	25	10	18	.273	.322	.388	97	-1	-1	20	3	1	0	.919	2	310/2D	0.1
Total	7	245	433	67	108	22	3	11	52	30	53	.249	.304	.390	91	-6	-6	51	15	12	-3	.934	2	/3012D	-0.9
■ ED BARNEY Barney, Edmund J. b: 1/23/1890, Amery, Wis. d: 10/4/67, Rice Lake, Wis. BL/TR, 5'10.5", 178 lbs. Deb: 7/22/15																									
1915	NY-A	11	36	1	7	0	0	0	8	3	6	.194	.256	.194	35	-3	-3	2	1			1.000	-0	O	-0.4
	Pit-N	32	99	16	27	1	2	0	5	11	12	.273	.363	.323	110	2	2	13	7	3	0	.972	2	O	0.3
1916	Pit-N	45	137	16	27	2	4	0	9	23	15	.197	.313	.226	66	-4	-4	13	8			.964	5	O	-0.2
Total	2	88	272	33	61	5	2	0	22	37	33	.224	.324	.257	78	-6	-6	29	17	4		.971	7	/O	-0.3
■ CLYDE BARNHART Barnhart, Clyde Lee "Pooch" b: 12/29/1895, Buck Valley, Pa. d: 1/21/80, Hagerstown, Md. BR/TR, 5'10", 155 lbs. Deb: 9/22/20 F																									
1920	Pit-N	12	46	5	15				5	1	2	.326	.340	.500	135	2	2	8	1	0		.971	0	3	0.3
1921	Pit-N	124	449	66	116	15	13	3	62	32	36	.258	.312	.370	78	-13	-15	53	3	3	-1	.956	-19	*3	-2.6
1922	Pit-N	75	209	30	69	7	5	1	38	25	7	.330	.402	.426	112	5	5	37	3	2	-0	.918	-12	3O	-0.6
1923	Pit-N	114	327	60	106	25	13	9	72	47	21	.324	.409	.563	151	26	24	74	5	7	-3	.985	3	O	1.9
1924	Pit-N	102	344	49	95	6	11	3	51	30	17	.276	.338	.384	91	-3	-4	46	8	4	0	.970	3	O	-0.8
1925	*Pit-N	142	539	85	175	32	11	4	114	59	25	.325	.391	.447	106	12	7	96	9	5	-0	.962	1	*O	-0.2
1926	Pit-N	76	203	26	39	3	0	0	10	23	13	.192	.278	.207	30	-19	-20	13	1			.991	-4	O	-2.8
1927	*Pit-N	108	360	65	115	23	4	3	54	37	19	.319	.384	.431	110	10	6	59	2			.978	4	O	0.4
1928	Pit-N	61	196	18	58	6	2	4	30	11	9	.296	.333	.408	89	-2	-3	26	3			.971	-2	O/3	-0.8
Total	9	814	2673	404	788	121	61	27	436	265	149	.295	.360	.416	100	17	1	412	35	21		.973	-27	O3	-5.2
■ VIC BARNHART Barnhart, Victor Dee b: 9/1/22, Hagerstown, Md. BR/TR, 6', 188 lbs. Deb: 10/01/44 F																									
1944	Pit-N	1	2	0	1	0	0	0	0	1	1	.500	.667	.500	222	1	1	1				.889	1	/S	0.2
1945	Pit-N	71	201	21	54	7	0	0	19	9	11	.269	.300	.303	65	-9	-10	17	2	0		.928	8	S/3	0.2
1946	Pit-N	2	1	0	0	0	0	0	0	0	0	.000	.000	.000	-98	-0	-0	0	0			.000	0	H	0.0
Total	3	74	204	21	55	7	0	0	19	10	12	.270	.304	.304	67	-9	-10	17	2			.927	9	/S3	0.4
■ BILLY BARNIE Barnie, William Harrison "Bald Billy" b: 1/26/1853, New York, N.Y. d: 7/15/1900, Hartford, Conn. 5'7", 157 lbs. Deb: 5/07/1874 MU																									
1874	Har-n	45	188	21	34	3	2	0			0	.181	.181	.218	25	-15	-17	8						CO/S	-1.2
1875	Wes-n	10	36	4	4	1	0	0			0	.111	.111	.139	-13	-4	-4	1						/CO	-0.3
	Mut-n	9	35	1	5	1	0	0			0	.143	.143	.171	8	-3	-3	1						/CO	-0.3
	Yr	19	71	4	9	2	0	0			0	.127	.127	.155	-3	-7	-8	1						CO	-0.6
1883	Bal-a	17	55	7	11	0	0	0		2		.200	.228	.200	38	-4	-4	3				.846	-2	C/OSM	-0.2
1886	Bal-a	2	6	0	0	0	0	0		1		.000	.143	.000	-54	-1	-1	0				.000	-1	/OC	-0.2
Total	2 n	64	259	25	43	5	2	0			0	.166	.166	.201	18	-22	-24	9	0					/COS	-1.8
Total	2	19	61	7	11	0	0	0		3		.180	.219	.180	29	-5	-5	0				.848	-3	/COS	-0.6
■ DICK BARONE Barone, Richard Anthony b: 10/13/32, San Jose, Cal. BR/TR, 5'9", 165 lbs. Deb: 9/22/60																									
1960	Pit-N	3	6	0	0	0	0	0	0	0	0	.000	.000	.000	-99	-2	-2	0	0	0	0	.875	-0	/S	-0.2
■ SCOTTY BARR Barr, Hyder Edward b: 10/6/1886, Bristol, Tenn. d: 12/2/34, Ft.Worth, Tex. BR/TR, 6', 175 lbs. Deb: 8/22/08																									
1908	Phi-A	19	56	4	8	2	0	0	1	3		.143	.200	.179	22	-5	-5	2	0			.923	-7	2/31O	-1.4
1909	Phi-A	22	51	5	4	1	0	0	1	11		.078	.254	.098	12	-5	-5	2	2			.947	-1	O/1	-0.7
Total	2	41	107	9	12	3	0	0	2	14		.112	.228	.140	18	-9	-10	4	2			.947	-8	/O213	-2.1
■ CUNO BARRAGAN Barragan, Facundo b: 6/20/32, Sacramento, Cal. BR/TR, 5'11", 180 lbs. Deb: 9/01/61																									
1961	Chi-N	10	28	3	6	0	0	1	2	2	7	.214	.267	.321	54	-2	-2	2	0	0	0	1.000	-1	C	-0.3
1962	Chi-N	58	134	11	27	6	1	0	12	21	28	.201	.310	.261	53	-8	-9	11	0	2	-1	.971	-7	C	-1.5
1963	Chi-N	1	1	0	0	0	0	0	0	0	0	.000	.000	.000	-95	-0	-0	0	0	0	0	1.000	-0	/C	0.0
Total	3	69	163	14	33	6	1	1	14	23	36	.202	.301	.270	53	-10	-11	13	0	2	-1	.975	-8	/C	-1.8

YEAR	TM/L	G	AB	R	H	2B	3B	HR	RBI	BB	SO	AVG	OBP	SLG	PRO+	BR	/A	RC	SB	CS	SBR	FA	FR	POS	TPR
■ GERMAN BARRANCA	Barranca, German (Costales) b: 10/19/56, Veracruz, Mex. BL/TR, 6', 160 lbs. Deb: 9/02/79																								
1979	KC-A	5	5	3	3	1	0	0	0	0	0	.600	.600	.800	269	1	1	2	3	1	0	1.000	3	/23	0.4
1980	KC-A	7	0	3	0	0	0	0	0	0	0	—	—	—	—	0	0	0	0	0	0	.000	0	/R	0.0
1981	Cin-N	9	6	2	2	0	0	0	1	0	0	.333	.333	.333	88	-0	-0	1	0	0	0	.000	0	/H	0.0
1982	Cin-N	46	51	11	13	1	3	0	2	2	9	.255	.283	.392	85	-1	-1	6	2	0	1	.824	-1	/2	-0.2
Total	4	67	62	19	18	2	3	0	3	2	9	.290	.313	.419	101	0	-0	9	5	1	1	.893	2	/23	0.2
■ JIMMY BARRETT	Barrett, James Erigena b: 3/28/1875, Athol, Mass. d: 10/24/21, Detroit, Mich. BL/TR, 5'9", 170 lbs. Deb: 9/13/1899																								
1899	Cin-N	26	92	30	34	2	4	0	10	18		.370	.477	.478	160	9	9	24	4			.936	-2	O	0.4
1900	Cin-N	137	545	114	172	11	7	5	42	72		.316	.400	.389	121	17	19	106	44			.929	4	*O	1.2
1901	Det-A	135	542	110	159	16	9	4	65	76		.293	.385	.378	107	12	8	92	26			.940	15	*O	1.1
1902	Det-A	136	509	93	154	19	6	4	44	74		.303	.397	.387	116	16	15	91	24			.961	8	*O	1.2
1903	Det-A	136	517	95	163	13	10	2	31	**74**		.315	**.407**	.391	145	30	32	98	27			.955	7	*O	3.1
1904	Det-A	162	624	83	167	10	5	0	31	**79**		.268	.353	.300	111	9	11	74	15			.971	12	*O	1.5
1905	Det-A	20	67	2	17	1	0	0	3	6		.254	.324	.269	88	-1	-1	6	0			1.000	-3	O	-0.5
1906	Cin-N	5	12	1	0	0	0	0	0	2		.000	.143	.000	-53	-2	-2	0	0			1.000	0	/O	-0.3
1907	Bos-A	106	390	52	95	11	6	1	28	38		.244	.314	.310	100	0	1	41	3			.966	4	O	0.1
1908	Bos-A	3	8	0	1	0	0	0	1	1		.125	.222	.125	13	-1	-1	0	0			1.000	-1	/O	-0.2
Total	10	866	3306	580	962	83	47	16	255	440		.291	.379	.359	117	90	91	533	143			.954	44	O	7.6
■ JOHNNY BARRETT	Barrett, John Joseph "Jack" b: 12/18/15, Lowell, Mass. d: 8/17/74, Seabrook Beach, N.H. BL/TL, 5'10.5", 170 lbs. Deb: 4/14/42																								
1942	Pit-N	111	332	56	82	11	6	0	26	48	42	.247	.347	.316	92	-0	-1	40	10			.973	6	O	0.0
1943	Pit-N	130	290	41	67	12	3	1	32	32	23	.231	.316	.303	77	-7	-8	30	5			.988	-11	O	-2.5
1944	Pit-N	149	568	99	153	24	**19**	7	83	86	56	.269	.366	.415	115	16	13	93	**28**			.972	-1	*O	0.4
1945	Pit-N	142	507	97	130	29	4	15	67	79	68	.256	.357	.418	111	11	8	81	25			.976	-2	*O	-0.1
1946	Pit-N	32	71	7	12	3	0	0	6	8	11	.169	.253	.211	32	-6	-6	4	1			.919	-3	O	-1.1
	Bos-N	24	43	3	10	3	0	0	6	12	1	.233	.400	.302	100	1	1	6	0			.962	-3	O	-0.3
	Yr	56	114	10	22	6	0	0	12	20	12	.193	.313	.246	59	-5	-6	10	1			.937	-6	O	-1.4
Total	5	588	1811	303	454	82	32	23	220	265	201	.251	.349	.369	100	14	6	255	69			.974	-15	O	-3.6
■ MARTY BARRETT	Barrett, Martin F. b: 11/1860, Port Henry, N.Y. d: 1/29/10, Holyoke, Mass. BR/TR, 5'9", 170 lbs. Deb: 6/24/1884																								
1884	Bos-N	3	6	0	0	0	0	0	0	0	4	.000	.000	.000	-99	-1	-1	0				.900	-1	/C	-0.2
	Ind-a	5	13	1	1	1	0	0		1		.077	.143	.154	-2	-1	-1	0				.808	-3	/CO	-0.4
Total	1	8	19	1	1	1	0	0	0	1	4	.053	.100	.105	-34	-3	-3	0				.833	-4	/CO	-0.6
■ MARTY BARRETT	Barrett, Martin Glenn b: 6/23/58, Arcadia, Cal. BR/TR, 5'10", 176 lbs. Deb: 9/06/82 F																								
1982	Bos-A	8	18	0	1	0	0	0	0	0	1	.056	.056	.056	-66	-4	-4	0	0	0	0	1.000	5	/2	0.1
1983	Bos-A	33	44	7	10	1	1	0	2	3	1	.227	.277	.295	54	-3	-3	4	0	0	0	.984	4	2/D	0.2
1984	Bos-A	139	475	56	144	23	3	3	45	42	25	.303	.361	.383	101	5	2	66	5	3	-0	**.987**	0	*2	0.7
1985	Bos-A	156	534	59	142	26	0	5	56	56	50	.266	.338	.343	84	-8	-11	62	7	5	-1	.987	15	*2	0.8
1986	*Bos-A	158	625	94	179	39	4	4	60	65	31	.286	.355	.381	100	1	1	87	15	7	0	.982	-3	*2	0.5
1987	Bos-A	137	559	72	164	23	0	3	43	51	38	.293	.354	.351	85	-8	-10	74	15	2	3	**.988**	**32**	*2	3.0
1988	*Bos-A	150	612	83	173	28	1	1	65	40	35	.283	.334	.337	85	-9	-12	69	7	3	0	.990	2	*2	-0.4
1989	Bos-A	86	336	31	86	18	0	1	27	32	12	.256	.324	.318	77	-7	-10	35	4	1	1	.975	1	2/D	-0.6
1990	*Bos-A	62	159	15	36	4	0	0	13	15	13	.226	.297	.252	53	-9	-10	13	4	0	1	.992	9	2/3D	0.1
1991	SD-N	12	16	1	3	1	0	1	3	0	3	.188	.235	.438	83	-0	-0	2	0	0	0	1.000	1	/23	0.0
Total	10	941	3378	418	938	163	9	18	314	304	209	.278	.340	.347	86	-43	-58	412	57	21	5	.986	66	2/D3	4.4
■ BOB BARRETT	Barrett, Robert Schley "Jumbo" b: 1/27/1899, Atlanta, Ga. d: 1/18/82, Atlanta, Ga. BR/TR, 5'11", 175 lbs. Deb: 4/30/23																								
1923	Chi-N	3	3	0	1	0	0	0	0	0	0	.333	.333	.333	76	-0	-0	0	0	0	0	.000	0	H	0.0
1924	Chi-N	54	133	12	32	2	3	5	21	7	29	.241	.279	.414	82	-4	-4	15	1	0	0	.943	-1	21/3	-0.5
1925	Chi-N	14	32	1	10	1	0	0	7	1	4	.313	.333	.344	72	-1	-1	3	1	2	-1	1.000	-3	/32	-0.5
	Bro-N	1	1	0	0	0	0	0	1	0	0	.000	.000	.000	-99	-0	-0	0	0	0	0	.000	0	H	0.0
	Yr	15	33	1	10	1	0	0	8	1	4	.303	.324	.333	67	-2	-2	3	1	2	-1	1.000	-3	/32	-0.5
1927	Bro-N	99	355	29	92	10	2	5	38	14	22	.259	.289	.341	68	-17	-17	34	1			.920	-8	3	-2.0
1929	Bos-A	68	126	15	34	10	0	0	19	10	6	.270	.324	.349	75	-5	-5	15	3	1	0	.938	6	3/12O	0.2
Total	5	239	650	57	169	23	5	10	86	32	61	.260	.296	.357	72	-27	-27	68	6	3		.924	-6	3/21O	-2.8
■ TOM BARRETT	Barrett, Thomas Loren b: 4/2/60, San Fernando, Cal. BB/TR, 5'9", 157 lbs. Deb: 7/02/88 F																								
1988	Phi-N	36	54	5	11	1	0	0	3	7	8	.204	.306	.222	53	-3	-3	4	0	0	0	.959	2	2	-0.1
1989	Phi-N	14	27	3	6	0	0	0	1	1	7	.222	.250	.222	36	-2	-2	2	0	0	0	.978	4	/2	0.2
1992	Bos-A	4	3	1	0	0	0	0	0	2	0	.000	.400	.000	20	-0	-0	0	0	0	0	1.000	1	/2	0.0
Total	3	54	84	9	17	1	0	0	4	10	15	.202	.295	.214	47	-5	-5	6	0	0	0	.970	7	/2	0.1
■ BILL BARRETT	Barrett, William b: Washington, D.C. Deb: 7/08/1871																								
1871	Kek-n	1	5	1	1	1	0	0	1	0	0	.200	.200	.400	66	-0	-0	0	0					/C3	0.0
1872	Oly-n	1	4	0	0	0	0	0	0	0	0	.000	.000	.000	-99	-1	-1	0						/C	-0.1
	Atl-n	8	35	6	7	2	0	0	1	0	1	.200	.200	.257	34	-2	-4	2						/O	-0.2
	Yr	9	39	6	7	2	0	0	1	0	1	.179	.179	.231	22	-3	-5	2						/OC	-0.3
1873	Bal-n	1	4	0	1	0	0	0	0	0	0	.250	.250	.250	48	-0	-0	0						/SO	-0.1
Total	3 n	11	48	7	9	3	0	0	2	0	1	.188	.188	.250	28	-4	-5	2						/OCS3	-0.4
■ BILL BARRETT	Barrett, William Joseph "Whispering Bill" b: 5/28/1900, Cambridge, Mass. d: 1/26/51, Cambridge, Mass. BR/TR, 6', 175 lbs. Deb: 5/13/21																								
1921	Phi-A	14	30	3	7	2	1	0	3	0	5	.233	.233	.367	51	-2	-2	2	0	0	0	.925	2	/SP31	0.1
1923	Chi-A	44	162	17	44	7	2	2	23	9	24	.272	.310	.377	81	-5	-5	20	12	3	2	.940	0	O/3	-0.5
1924	Chi-A	119	406	52	110	18	5	2	56	30	38	.271	.326	.355	78	-15	-14	47	15	10	-2	.904	-15	SO/3	-2.1
1925	Chi-A	81	245	44	89	23	3	3	40	24	27	.363	.420	.518	145	14	16	52	5	6	-2	.943	-7	2O/S3	0.6
1926	Chi-A	111	368	46	113	31	4	6	61	25	26	.307	.353	.462	115	4	6	59	9	7	-2	.969	-6	*O/1	-0.7
1927	Chi-A	147	556	62	159	35	9	4	83	52	46	.286	.347	.403	96	-5	-3	72	20	13	-2	.963	7	*O	-0.8
1928	Chi-A	76	235	34	65	11	2	3	26	14	30	.277	.320	.379	84	-6	-6	29	8	3	1	.988	-5	O2	-1.1
1929	Chi-A	3	1	0	0	0	0	0	0	2	0	.000	.667	.000	87	0	0	0	0	0	0	.000	0	H	0.0
	Bos-A	111	370	57	100	23	4	3	35	51	38	.270	.363	.378	93	-4	-2	53	11	8	-2	.974	4	*O/3	-0.7
	Yr	114	371	57	100	23	4	3	35	53	38	.270	.365	.377	94	-3	-2	54	11	8	-2	.974	4	*O/3	-0.7
1930	Bos-A	6	18	3	3	1	0	0	1	1	3	.167	.211	.222	10	-2	-2	1	0	0	0	1.000	-1	/O	-0.4
	Was-A	6	4	0	0	0	0	0	0	1	2	.000	.200	.000	-44	-1	-1	0	0	0	0	1.000	-0	/O	-0.1
	Yr	12	22	3	3	1	0	0	1	2	5	.136	.208	.182	-0	-3	-3	1	0	0	0	1.000	-1	/O	-0.5
Total	9	718	2395	318	690	151	30	23	328	209	239	.288	.347	.405	97	-23	-14	335	80	50	-6	.964	-21	O/S23P1	-5.7
■ JOSE BARRIOS	Barrios, Jose Manuel b: 6/26/57, New York, N.Y. BR/TR, 6'4", 195 lbs. Deb: 4/23/82																								
1982	SF-N	10	19	2	3	0	0	0	0	1	4	.158	.200	.158	1	-2	-2	0	0	0	0	1.000	-1	/1	-0.4
■ BARRON	Barron Deb: 6/19/1874																								
1874	Bal-n	17	78	6	20	0	0	0		0		.256	.256	.256	64	-3	-3	5						O	-0.2

■ **RED BARRON** Barron, David Irenus b: 6/21/1900, Clarksville, Ga. d: 10/4/82, Atlanta, Ga. BR/TR, 5'11.5", 185 lbs. Deb: 6/10/29

YEAR	TM/L	G	AB	R	H	2B	3B	HR	RBI	BB	SO	AVG	OBP	SLG	PRO+	BR	/A	RC	SB	CS	SBR	FA	FR	POS	TPR
1929	Bos-N	10	21	3	4	1	0	0	1	1	4	.190	.227	.238	16	-3	-3	1	2			.929	1	/O	-0.2

■ **FRANK BARROWS** Barrows, Franklin L. b: 10/22/1846, Hudson, Ohio d: 2/6/22, Fitchburg, Mass. Deb: 5/20/1871

YEAR	TM/L	G	AB	R	H	2B	3B	HR	RBI	BB	SO	AVG	OBP	SLG	PRO+	BR	/A	RC	SB	CS	SBR	FA	FR	POS	TPR
1871	Bos-n	18	86	13	13	2	1	0	11	0	0	.151	.151	.198	-1	-11	-12	3	1					O/2	-0.7

■ **CUKE BARROWS** Barrows, Roland b: 10/20/1883, Gray, Maine d: 2/10/55, Gorham, Maine BL/TR, 5'8", 158 lbs. Deb: 9/18/09

YEAR	TM/L	G	AB	R	H	2B	3B	HR	RBI	BB	SO	AVG	OBP	SLG	PRO+	BR	/A	RC	SB	CS	SBR	FA	FR	POS	TPR
1909	Chi-A	5	20	1	3	0	0	0	2	0		.150	.190	.150	8	-2	-2	1	0			.923	2	/O	-0.1
1910	Chi-A	6	20	0	4	0	0	0	1	3		.200	.304	.200	61	-1	-1	1	0			.875	-1	/O	-0.3
1911	Chi-A	13	46	5	9	2	0	0	4	7		.196	.315	.239	57	-3	-2	4	2			1.000	-2	O	-0.5
1912	Chi-A	8	13	0	3	0	0	0	2	2		.231	.333	.231	64	-1	-0	2	1			1.000	-0	/O	-0.1
Total	4	32	99	6	19	2	0	0	9	12		.192	.292	.212	50	-6	-5	8	3			.950	-2	/O	-1.0

■ **SHAD BARRY** Barry, John C. b: 10/27/1878, Newburgh, N.Y. d: 11/27/36, Los Angeles, Cal. BR/TR, Deb: 5/30/1899

YEAR	TM/L	G	AB	R	H	2B	3B	HR	RBI	BB	SO	AVG	OBP	SLG	PRO+	BR	/A	RC	SB	CS	SBR	FA	FR	POS	TPR
1899	Was-N	78	247	31	71	7	5	1	33	12		.287	.328	.368	92	-4	-3	35	11			.946	-16	O1S3/2	-1.7
1900	Bos-N	81	254	40	66	10	7	1	37	13		.260	.301	.366	74	-7	-11	32	9			.956	-16	OS21/3	-2.5
1901	Bos-N	11	40	3	7	2	0	0	6	2		.175	.233	.225	30	-3	-4	2	1			.926	-0	O	-0.5
	Phi-N	67	252	35	62	10	0	1	22	15		.246	.294	.298	70	-9	-10	28	13			.903	-12	23O/S	-2.1
	Yr	78	292	38	69	12	0	1	28	17		.236	.285	.288	65	-12	-14	30	14			.903	-12	2O3/S	-2.6
1902	Phi-N	138	543	65	156	20	6	3	58	44		.287	.344	.363	118	11	11	77	14			.939	-5	*O/1	-0.3
1903	Phi-N	138	550	75	152	24	5	1	60	30		.276	.321	.344	93	-8	-6	72	26			.970	-2	*O1/3	-1.4
1904	Phi-N	35	122	15	25	2	0	0	3	11		.205	.281	.221	58	-6	-5	9	2			.979	13	O/3	0.6
	Chi-N	73	263	29	69	7	2	1	26	17		.262	.310	.316	93	-2	-2	31	12			.917	-1	O13/S2	-0.5
	Yr	108	385	44	94	9	2	1	29	28		.244	.300	.286	83	-8	-7	40	14			.955	12	O13/S2	0.1
1905	Chi-N	27	104	10	22	2	0	0	10	5		.212	.255	.231	43	-7	-7	8	5			.982	1	1	-0.8
	Cin-N	125	494	90	160	11	12	1	56	33		.324	.367	.401	117	17	10	83	16			.982	-7	*1/O	-0.1
	Yr	152	598	100	182	13	12	1	66	38		.304	.348	.371	105	10	3	90	21			.982	-7	*1/O	-0.9
1906	Cin-N	73	279	38	80	10	5	1	33	26		.287	.350	.369	119	8	6	42	11			.993	1	1O	0.5
	StL-N	62	237	26	59	9	1	0	12	15		.249	.296	.295	89	-4	-3	24	6			.930	-7	O1/3	-1.3
	Yr	135	516	64	139	19	6	1	45	41		.269	.326	.335	106	3	3	65	17			.922	-6	O1/3	-0.8
1907	StL-N	81	294	30	73	5	2	0	19	28		.248	.318	.279	90	-4	-3	30	4			.963	-6	O	-1.4
1908	StL-N	74	268	24	61	8	1	0	11	19		.228	.286	.265	80	-7	-6	23	9			.967	-1	O/S	-1.1
	NY-N	37	67	5	10	1	1	0	5	9		.149	.260	.194	43	-4	-4	4	1			.971	-6	O	-1.3
	Yr	111	335	29	71	9	2	0	16	28		.212	.281	.251	71	-11	-10	27	10			.968	-7	*O/S	-2.4
Total	10	1100	4014	516	1073	128	47	10	391	279		.267	.320	.330	93	-28	-36	501	140			.955	-64	O1/23S	-13.9

■ **JACK BARRY** Barry, John Joseph b: 4/26/1887, Meriden, Conn. d: 4/23/61, Shrewsbury, Mass. BR/TR, 5'9", 158 lbs. Deb: 7/13/08 M

YEAR	TM/L	G	AB	R	H	2B	3B	HR	RBI	BB	SO	AVG	OBP	SLG	PRO+	BR	/A	RC	SB	CS	SBR	FA	FR	POS	TPR
1908	Phi-A	40	135	13	30	4	3	0	8	10		.222	.291	.296	85	-1	-2	13	5			.966	-11	2S/3	-1.5
1909	Phi-A	124	409	56	88	11	2	1	23	44		.215	.307	.259	77	-8	-9	40	17			.927	-31	*S	-4.4
1910	*Phi-A	145	487	64	126	19	5	3	60	52		.259	.336	.337	112	7	7	61	14			.916	-22	*S	-1.0
1911	*Phi-A	127	442	73	117	18	7	1	63	38		.265	.333	.344	91	-7	-5	62	30			**.944**	-7	*S	-0.3
1912	Phi-A	140	483	75	126	19	9	0	55	47		.261	.335	.337	96	-4	-2	63	22			.925	-6	*S	0.4
1913	*Phi-A	134	455	62	125	20	6	3	85	44	32	.275	.349	.365	112	5	7	64	15			.953	-8	*S	1.2
1914	*Phi-A	140	467	57	113	12	0	0	42	53	34	.242	.324	.268	81	-11	-8	48	22	13	-1	.947	5	*S	0.7
1915	Phi-A	54	194	16	43	6	2	0	15	15	9	.222	.284	.273	69	-8	-7	16	6	5	-1	.952	-4	S	-0.9
	*Bos-A	78	248	30	65	13	2	0	26	24	11	.262	.342	.331	104	1	2	32	0			.962	-4	2	-0.2
	Yr	132	442	46	108	19	4	0	41	39	20	.244	.317	.305	89	-7	-6	48	6	5	-1	.962	-9	2S	-1.1
1916	Bos-A	94	330	28	67	6	1	0	20	17	24	.203	.277	.227	52	-19	-19	27	8			.974	2	2	-1.6
1917	Bos-A	116	388	45	83	9	0	2	30	47	27	.214	.305	.253	71	-12	-12	39	12			**.974**	-11	*2M	-1.9
1919	Bos-A	31	108	13	26	5	1	0	2	5	5	.241	.293	.306	72	-5	-4	11	2			.922	-7	2	-1.0
Total	11	1223	4146	532	1009	142	38	10	429	396	142	.243	.321	.303	88	-62	-53	476	153	18		.935	-105	S2/3	-10.5

■ **RICH BARRY** Barry, Richard Donovan b: 9/12/40, Berkeley, Cal. BR/TR, 6'4", 205 lbs. Deb: 7/04/69

YEAR	TM/L	G	AB	R	H	2B	3B	HR	RBI	BB	SO	AVG	OBP	SLG	PRO+	BR	/A	RC	SB	CS	SBR	FA	FR	POS	TPR
1969	Phi-N	20	32	4	6	1	0	0	0	5	6	.188	.316	.219	54	-2	-2	2	0	0	0	.938	-0	/O	-0.2

■ **DICK BARTELL** Bartell, Richard William "Rowdy Richard" b: 11/22/07, Chicago, Ill. BR/TR, 5'9", 160 lbs. Deb: 10/02/27 C

YEAR	TM/L	G	AB	R	H	2B	3B	HR	RBI	BB	SO	AVG	OBP	SLG	PRO+	BR	/A	RC	SB	CS	SBR	FA	FR	POS	TPR
1927	Pit-N	1	2	0	0	0	0	0	0	2	0	.000	.500	.000	41	0	0	0	0			1.000	0	/S	0.0
1928	Pit-N	72	233	27	71	8	4	1	36	21	18	.305	.377	.386	96	1	-1	34	4			.974	2	2S/3	0.5
1929	Pit-N	143	610	101	184	40	13	2	57	40	29	.302	.347	.420	87	-11	-14	86	11			.953	4	S2	0.2
1930	Pit-N	129	475	69	152	32	13	4	75	39	34	.320	.378	.467	102	2	2	82	8			.941	6	*S	1.9
1931	Phi-N	135	554	88	160	43	7	0	34	27	38	.289	.325	.392	85	-7	-13	72	6			.948	3	*S/2	0.4
1932	Phi-N	154	614	118	189	48	7	1	53	64	47	.308	.379	.414	101	13	3	102	8			.963	10	*S	2.6
1933	Phi-N★	152	587	78	159	25	5	1	37	56	46	.271	.340	.336	83	-3	-13	73	6			.951	9	*S	0.7
1934	Phi-N	146	604	102	187	30	4	0	37	64	59	.310	.384	.373	91	6	-5	92	13			.954	14	*S	1.7
1935	NY-N	137	539	60	141	28	4	14	53	37	52	.262	.316	.406	94	-6	-5	72	5			.954	10	*S	1.2
1936	*NY-N	145	510	71	152	31	3	8	42	40	36	.298	.355	.418	109	5	6	79	6			.956	**45**	*S	**5.7**
1937	*NY-N★	128	516	91	158	38	2	14	62	40	38	.306	.367	.469	124	18	17	92	5			.958	**38**	*S	6.1
1938	NY-N	127	481	67	126	26	1	9	49	55	60	.262	.347	.376	98	0	-0	67	4			.952	22	*S	3.2
1939	Chi-N	105	336	37	80	24	2	3	34	42	25	.238	.335	.348	82	-7	-8	41	6			.943	-5	*S/3	-0.4
1940	*Det-A	139	528	76	123	24	3	7	53	76	53	.233	.335	.330	67	-20	-27	65	12	2	2	.953	12	*S	-0.1
1941	Det-A	5	12	0	2	1	0	0	1	2	2	.167	.333	.250	51	-1	-1	1	0	1	-1	.920	1	/S	-0.1
	NY-N	104	373	44	113	20	0	5	35	52	29	.303	.394	.397	121	13	13	60	6			.959	-10	3S	0.6
1942	NY-N	90	316	53	77	10	3	5	24	44	34	.244	.351	.342	102	3	2	41	4			.965	1	3S	0.6
1943	NY-N	99	337	48	91	14	0	5	28	47	27	.270	.371	.356	110	6	6	47	5			.980	18	3S	2.9
1946	NY-N	5	2	0	0	0	0	0	0	0	0	.000	.000	.000	-99	-1	-1	0	0			1.000	1	/32	0.0
Total	18	2016	7629	1130	2165	442	71	79	710	748	627	.284	.355	.391	96	13	-36	1107	109	3		.953	178	*S32	27.7

■ **TONY BARTIROME** Bartirome, Anthony Joseph b: 5/9/32, Pittsburgh, Pa. BL/TL, 5'10", 155 lbs. Deb: 4/19/52 C

YEAR	TM/L	G	AB	R	H	2B	3B	HR	RBI	BB	SO	AVG	OBP	SLG	PRO+	BR	/A	RC	SB	CS	SBR	FA	FR	POS	TPR
1952	Pit-N	124	355	32	78	10	3	0	16	26	37	.220	.273	.265	48	-24	-25	28	3	3	-1	.989	2	*1	-2.9

■ **BOYD BARTLEY** Bartley, Boyd Owen b: 2/11/20, Chicago, Ill. BR/TR, 5'8.5", 165 lbs. Deb: 5/30/43

YEAR	TM/L	G	AB	R	H	2B	3B	HR	RBI	BB	SO	AVG	OBP	SLG	PRO+	BR	/A	RC	SB	CS	SBR	FA	FR	POS	TPR
1943	Bro-N	9	21	0	1	0	0	0	1	1	3	.048	.091	.048	-59	-4	-4	0	0			.897	2	/S	-0.2

■ **IRV BARTLING** Bartling, Irving Henry b: 6/27/14, Bay City, Mich. d: 6/12/73, Westland, Mich. BR/TR, 6', 175 lbs. Deb: 9/08/38

YEAR	TM/L	G	AB	R	H	2B	3B	HR	RBI	BB	SO	AVG	OBP	SLG	PRO+	BR	/A	RC	SB	CS	SBR	FA	FR	POS	TPR
1938	Phi-A	14	46	5	8	1	1	0	5	3	7	.174	.224	.239	17	-6	-6	3	0	0	0	.914	-3	S/3	-0.7

■ **HARRY BARTON** Barton, Harry Lamb b: 1/20/1875, Chester, Pa. d: 1/25/55, Upland, Pa. BB/TR, 5'6.5", 155 lbs. Deb: 4/15/05

YEAR	TM/L	G	AB	R	H	2B	3B	HR	RBI	BB	SO	AVG	OBP	SLG	PRO+	BR	/A	RC	SB	CS	SBR	FA	FR	POS	TPR
1905	Phi-A	29	60	5	10	2	1	0	3	3		.167	.206	.233	39	-4	-4	4	2			.954	-6	C/13O	-1.0

■ **BOB BARTON** Barton, Robert Wilbur b: 7/30/41, Norwood, O. BR/TR, 6', 175 lbs. Deb: 9/17/65

YEAR	TM/L	G	AB	R	H	2B	3B	HR	RBI	BB	SO	AVG	OBP	SLG	PRO+	BR	/A	RC	SB	CS	SBR	FA	FR	POS	TPR
1965	SF-N	4	7	1	4	0	0	0	1	0	0	.571	.571	.571	217	1	1	2	0	0	0	1.000	1	/C	0.2
1966	SF-N	43	91	1	16	2	1	0	3	5	5	.176	.219	.220	22	-9	-10	4	0	0	0	.994	7	C	-0.1
1967	SF-N	7	19	0	4	0	0	0	1	0	2	.211	.250	.211	34	-2	-2	1	0	0	0	1.000	1	/C	-0.1
1968	SF-N	46	92	4	24	2	0	0	5	7	18	.261	.313	.283	80	-2	-2	9	0	0	0	.995	12	C	1.3
1969	SF-N	49	106	5	18	2	0	0	1	9	19	.170	.241	.189	22	-11	-11	5	0	0	0	.985	1	C	-0.9

YEAR	TM/L	G	AB	R	H	2B	3B	HR	RBI	BB	SO	AVG	OBP	SLG	PRO+	BR	/A	RC	SB	CS	SBR	FA	FR	POS	TPR
1970	SD-N	61	188	15	41	6	0	4	16	15	37	.218	.279	.314	61	-11	-10	16	1	1	-0	.995	7	C	-0.1
1971	SD-N	121	376	23	94	17	2	5	23	35	49	.250	.317	.346	94	-6	-3	36	0	5	-3	.981	14	*C	1.3
1972	SD-N	29	88	1	17	1	0	0	9	2	19	.193	.211	.205	20	-9	-9	4	2	0	1	.989	1	C	-0.7
1973	Cin-N	3	1	0	0	0	0	0	0	1	0	.000	.500	.000	52	0	0	0	0	0	0	1.000	1	/C	0.1
1974	SD-N	30	81	4	19	1	0	0	7	13	19	.235	.340	.247	69	-3	-3	8	0	0	0	.981	10	C	0.8
Total	10	393	1049	54	237	31	3	9	66	87	168	.226	.288	.287	65	-52	-48	85	3	6	-3	.987	53	C	1.8

■ VINCE BARTON Barton, Vincent David b: 2/1/08, Edmonton, Alberta, Canada d: 9/13/73, Toronto, Ont., Can BL/TR, 6', 180 lbs. Deb: 7/17/31

YEAR	TM/L	G	AB	R	H	2B	3B	HR	RBI	BB	SO	AVG	OBP	SLG	PRO+	BR	/A	RC	SB	CS	SBR	FA	FR	POS	TPR
1931	Chi-N	66	239	45	57	10	1	13	50	21	40	.238	.323	.452	104	1	1	36	1			.964	-4	O	-0.7
1932	Chi-N	36	134	19	30	2	3	3	15	8	22	.224	.273	.351	67	-7	-6	13	0			1.000	-2	O	-1.0
Total	2	102	373	64	87	12	4	16	65	29	62	.233	.306	.416	91	-5	-5	50	1			.976	-6	/O	-1.7

■ DAVE BARTOSCH Bartosch, David Robert b: 3/24/17, St.Louis, Mo. BR/TR, 6'1", 190 lbs. Deb: 4/28/45

YEAR	TM/L	G	AB	R	H	2B	3B	HR	RBI	BB	SO	AVG	OBP	SLG	PRO+	BR	/A	RC	SB	CS	SBR	FA	FR	POS	TPR
1945	StL-N	24	47	9	12	1	0	0	1	6	3	.255	.340	.277	71	-2	-2	5	0			.964	1	O	-0.2

■ MONTY BASGALL Basgall, Romanus b: 2/8/22, Pfeifer, Kan. BR/TR, 5'10.5", 175 lbs. Deb: 4/19/48 C

YEAR	TM/L	G	AB	R	H	2B	3B	HR	RBI	BB	SO	AVG	OBP	SLG	PRO+	BR	/A	RC	SB	CS	SBR	FA	FR	POS	TPR
1948	Pit-N	38	51	12	11	1	0	2	6	3	5	.216	.259	.353	63	-3	-3	5	0			1.000	6	2	0.3
1949	Pit-N	107	308	25	67	9	1	2	26	31	32	.218	.291	.273	51	-21	-22	25	1			.972	-7	2/3	-2.5
1951	Pit-N	55	153	15	32	5	2	0	9	12	14	.209	.271	.268	44	-12	-12	10	0	0	0	.969	11	2	0.0
Total	3	200	512	52	110	15	3	4	41	46	51	.215	.282	.279	50	-35	-37	40	1	0		.973	9	2/3	-2.2

■ AL BASHANG Bashang, Albert C. b: 8/22/1888, Cincinnati, Ohio d: 6/23/67, Cincinnati, Ohio BB/TR, 5'8", 150 lbs. Deb: 7/30/12

YEAR	TM/L	G	AB	R	H	2B	3B	HR	RBI	BB	SO	AVG	OBP	SLG	PRO+	BR	/A	RC	SB	CS	SBR	FA	FR	POS	TPR
1912	Det-A	6	12	3	1	0	0	0	0	3		.083	.267	.083	2	-1	-1	0	0			1.000	-1	/O	-0.3
1918	Bro-N	2	5	0	1	0	0	0	0	0	0	.200	.200	.200	22	-0	-0	0	0			1.000	0	/O	0.0
Total	2	8	17	3	2	0	0	0	0	3	0	.118	.250	.118	8	-2	-2	0	0			1.000	-1	/O	-0.3

■ WALT BASHORE Bashore, Walter Franklin (b: Walter Franklin Beshore) b: 10/6/09, Harrisburg, Pa. d: 9/26/84, Sebring, Fla. BR/TR, 6', 170 lbs. Deb: 7/14/36

YEAR	TM/L	G	AB	R	H	2B	3B	HR	RBI	BB	SO	AVG	OBP	SLG	PRO+	BR	/A	RC	SB	CS	SBR	FA	FR	POS	TPR
1936	Phi-N	10	10	1	2	0	0	0	0	1	3	.200	.273	.200	26	-1	-1	1	0			1.000	-3	/O3	-0.4

■ EDDIE BASINSKI Basinski, Edwin Frank "Bazooka" or "Fiddler" b: 11/4/22, Buffalo, N.Y. BR/TR, 6'1", 172 lbs. Deb: 5/20/44

YEAR	TM/L	G	AB	R	H	2B	3B	HR	RBI	BB	SO	AVG	OBP	SLG	PRO+	BR	/A	RC	SB	CS	SBR	FA	FR	POS	TPR
1944	Bro-N	39	105	13	27	4	1	0	9	6	10	.257	.310	.314	77	-3	-3	11	1			.960	-2	2/S	-0.3
1945	Bro-N†	108	336	30	88	9	4	0	33	11	33	.262	.293	.313	69	-15	-14	29	0			.926	-10	*S/2	-1.7
1947	Pit-N	56	161	15	32	6	2	4	17	18	27	.199	.279	.335	61	-9	-10	15	0			.972	-1	2	-0.8
Total	3	203	602	58	147	19	7	4	59	35	70	.244	.292	.319	68	-27	-27	55	1			.925	-13	S/2	-2.8

■ JOHN BASS Bass, John E. b: 1850, Baltimore, Md. 5'6", 150 lbs. Deb: 5/04/1871

YEAR	TM/L	G	AB	R	H	2B	3B	HR	RBI	BB	SO	AVG	OBP	SLG	PRO+	BR	/A	RC	SB	CS	SBR	FA	FR	POS	TPR
1871	Cle-n	22	89	18	27	1	**10**	3	18	3	4	.303	.326	.640	179	7	9	19	0					*3	0.5
1872	Atl-n	2	7	0	1	1	0	0	1	0	0	.143	.143	.286	24	-1	-1	0						/O	-0.1
1877	Har-N	1	4	1	1	0	0	0	0	0	0	.250	.250	.250	65	-0	-0	0				.000	-1	/O	-0.1
Total	2 n	24	96	18	28	2	10	3	19	3	4	.292	.313	.615	166	7	8	19						/3O	0.4

■ KEVIN BASS Bass, Kevin Charles b: 5/12/59, Menlo Park, Cal. BB/TR, 6', 183 lbs. Deb: 4/09/82

YEAR	TM/L	G	AB	R	H	2B	3B	HR	RBI	BB	SO	AVG	OBP	SLG	PRO+	BR	/A	RC	SB	CS	SBR	FA	FR	POS	TPR
1982	Mil-A	18	9	4	0	0	0	0	0	1	1	.000	.100	.000	-74	-2	-2	0	0	0	0	1.000	-5	O/D	-0.8
	Hou-N	12	24	2	1	0	0	0	1	0	8	.042	.042	.042	-83	-6	-5	0	0	0	0	.917	-0	/O	-0.6
1983	Hou-N	88	195	25	46	7	3	2	18	6	27	.236	.259	.333	67	-10	-9	16	2	2	-1	.945	-5	O	-1.7
1984	Hou-N	121	331	33	86	17	5	2	29	6	57	.260	.279	.360	84	-10	-8	32	5	5	-2	.975	-2	O	-1.4
1985	Hou-N	150	539	72	145	27	5	16	68	31	63	.269	.316	.427	109	3	4	71	19	8	1	**.997**	6	*O	0.8
1986	*Hou-N★	157	591	83	184	33	5	20	79	38	72	.311	.359	.486	134	23	25	97	22	13	-1	.984	4	*O	2.3
1987	Hou-N	157	592	83	168	31	5	19	85	53	77	.284	.347	.449	113	7	10	90	21	8	2	.987	10	*O	1.6
1988	Hou-N	157	541	57	138	27	2	14	72	42	65	.255	.316	.390	106	0	3	66	31	6	6	.979	2	*O	0.7
1989	Hou-N	87	313	42	94	19	4	5	44	29	44	.300	.362	.435	131	11	12	51	11	4	1	.985	9	O	2.1
1990	SF-N	61	214	25	54	9	1	7	32	14	26	.252	.304	.402	96	-3	-2	25	2	2	-1	.968	-5	O	-0.9
1991	SF-N	124	361	43	84	10	4	10	40	36	56	.233	.309	.366	92	-5	-4	39	7	4	-0	.977	-1	*O	-0.8
1992	SF-N	89	265	25	71	11	3	7	30	16	53	.268	.312	.411	109	0	2	31	7	7	-2	.983	-5	O	-0.8
	NY-N	46	137	15	37	12	2	2	9	7	17	.270	.306	.431	107	1	1	18	7	2	1	.987	1	O	0.2
	Yr	135	402	40	108	23	5	9	39	23	70	.269	.310	.418	108	1	3	49	14	9	-1	.985	-5	*O	-0.6
Total	11	1267	4112	509	1108	203	39	104	507	279	566	.269	.321	.414	107	9	27	536	134	61	4	.982	8	*O/D	0.7

■ RANDY BASS Bass, Randy William b: 3/13/54, Lawton, Okla. BL/TR, 6'1", 210 lbs. Deb: 9/03/77

YEAR	TM/L	G	AB	R	H	2B	3B	HR	RBI	BB	SO	AVG	OBP	SLG	PRO+	BR	/A	RC	SB	CS	SBR	FA	FR	POS	TPR
1977	Min-A	9	19	0	2	0	0	0	0	0	5	.105	.105	.105	-43	-4	-4	0	0	0	0	.000	0	/D	-0.4
1978	KC-A	2	2	0	0	0	0	0	0	0	0	.000	.000	.000	-97	-1	-1	0	0	0	0	.000	0	H	-0.1
1979	Mon-N	2	1	0	0	0	0	0	0	0	0	.000	.000	.000	-99	-0	-0	0	0	0	0	1.000	-0	/1	0.0
1980	SD-N	19	49	5	14	0	1	3	8	7	7	.286	.386	.510	157	3	4	10	0	0	0	.985	-1	1	0.2
1981	SD-N	69	176	13	37	4	1	4	20	20	28	.210	.294	.313	78	-6	-5	15	0	1	-1	.993	2	1	-0.7
1982	SD-N	13	30	1	6	0	0	1	8	2	4	.200	.273	.300	63	-2	-1	3	0	0	0	1.000	-1	/1	-0.2
	Tex-A	16	48	5	10	2	0	1	6	1	7	.208	.240	.313	53	-3	-3	4	0	0	0	1.000	-0	/1D	-0.4
Total	6	130	325	24	69	6	2	9	42	30	51	.212	.287	.326	76	-12	-10	32	0	1	-1	.993	-0	/1D	-1.6

■ DOC BASS Bass, Williams Capers (Also Played One Game In 1918 Under Name Of Johnson)
b: 12/4/1899, Macon, Ga. d: 1/12/70, Macon, Ga. BL/TL, 5'10", 165 lbs. Deb: 7/29/18

YEAR	TM/L	G	AB	R	H	2B	3B	HR	RBI	BB	SO	AVG	OBP	SLG	PRO+	BR	/A	RC	SB	CS	SBR	FA	FR	POS	TPR
1918	Bos-N	2	1	1	1	0	0	0	0	0	0	1.000	1.000	1.000	533	0	0	2	1			.000	0	/H	0.1

■ CHARLEY BASSETT Bassett, Charles Edwin b: 2/9/1863, Central Falls, R.I. d: 5/28/42, Pawtucket, R.I. BR/TR, 5'10", 150 lbs. Deb: 7/22/1884

YEAR	TM/L	G	AB	R	H	2B	3B	HR	RBI	BB	SO	AVG	OBP	SLG	PRO+	BR	/A	RC	SB	CS	SBR	FA	FR	POS	TPR
1884	Pro-N	27	79	10	11	2	1	0	6	4	15	.139	.181	.190	17	-7	-7	3				.815	0	3/SO2	-0.6
1885	Pro-N	82	285	21	41	8	2	0	16	19	60	.144	.197	.186	26	-23	-21	11				.900	5	2S3/C	-1.3
1886	KC-N	90	342	41	89	19	8	2	32	36	43	.260	.331	.380	109	7	3	46	6			.886	8	S/3	1.1
1887	Ind-N	119	452	41	104	14	6	1	47	25	31	.230	.278	.294	63	-23	-21	45	25			**.931**	16	*2	-0.1
1888	Ind-N	128	481	58	116	20	3	2	60	32	41	.241	.297	.308	93	-2	-3	52	24			.922	-16	*2	-1.4
1889	Ind-N	127	477	64	117	12	5	4	68	37	38	.245	.304	.317	73	-16	-17	52	15			.937	11	*2	0.0
1890	NY-N	100	410	52	98	13	8	0	54	29	25	.239	.300	.310	80	-11	-11	43	14			**.952**	12	*2	0.7
1891	NY-N	130	524	60	136	19	8	4	68	36	29	.260	.312	.349	98	-5	-1	64	16			**.908**	8	*3/2	1.2
1892	NY-N	35	130	9	27	2	3	0	16	6	10	.208	.254	.269	61	-6	-6	9	0			.938	9	2/3	0.4
	Lou-N	79	313	36	67	5	5	2	35	15	19	.214	.250	.281	67	-15	-11	27	16			.861	-0	3/2	-0.8
	Yr	114	443	45	94	7	8	2	51	21	29	.212	.251	.278	65	-21	-18	36	16			.858	9	32	-0.4
Total	9	917	3493	392	806	114	49	15	402	239	311	.231	.285	.304	77	-101	-96	351	116			.932	53	23S/OC	-0.8

■ JOHNNY BASSLER Bassler, John Landis b: 6/3/1895, Mechanics Grove, Pa. d: 6/29/79, Santa Monica, Cal BL/TR, 5'9", 170 lbs. Deb: 7/11/13 C

YEAR	TM/L	G	AB	R	H	2B	3B	HR	RBI	BB	SO	AVG	OBP	SLG	PRO+	BR	/A	RC	SB	CS	SBR	FA	FR	POS	TPR
1913	Cle-A	1	2	0	0	0	0	0	0	0	0	.000	.000	.000	-97	-0	-1	0	0			.500	-1	/C	-0.2
1914	Cle-A	43	77	5	14	1	1	0	6	15	8	.182	.323	.221	61	-3	-3	6	3	2	-0	.946	-1	C/3O	-0.3
1921	Det-A	119	388	37	119	18	5	0	56	58	16	.307	.401	.379	101	3	3	63	2	1	0	.975	2	*C	1.1
1922	Det-A	121	372	41	120	14	0	0	41	62	12	.323	.422	.360	109	7	9	62	2	1	0	.980	-3	*C	1.2
1923	Det-A	135	383	45	114	12	3	0	49	76	13	.298	.414	.345	103	5	6	61	2	2	-1	.988	12	*C	2.3
1924	Det-A	124	379	43	131	20	3	1	68	62	11	.346	.441	.422	125	17	18	76	2	1	0	.979	-4	*C	2.0
1925	Det-A	121	344	40	96	19	3	0	52	74	6	.279	.408	.352	96	1	2	56	1	1	-0	.983	-8	*C	0.0
1926	Det-A	66	174	20	53	8	1	0	22	45	6	.305	.447	.362	111	7	6	33	0	0	0	1.000	2	C	1.2
1927	Det-A	81	200	19	57	7	0	0	24	45	9	.285	.416	.320	92	1	1	30	1	0	0	.974	-2	C	0.4

YEAR	TM/L	G	AB	R	H	2B	3B	HR	RBI	BB	SO	AVG	OBP	SLG	PRO+	BR	/A	RC	SB	CS	SBR	FA	FR	POS	TPR
Total	9	811	2319	250	704	99	16	1	318	437	81	.304	.416	.361	104	37	42	387	13	8		.980	-1	C/O3	7.7

■ CHARLIE BASTIAN
Bastian, Charles J. b: 7/4/1860, Philadelphia, Pa. d: 1/18/32, Pennsauken, N.J. BR/TR, 5'6.5", 145 lbs. Deb: 8/18/1884

YEAR	TM/L	G	AB	R	H	2B	3B	HR	RBI	BB	SO	AVG	OBP	SLG	PRO+	BR	/A	RC	SB	CS	SBR	FA	FR	POS	TPR
1884	Wil-U	17	60	6	12	1	3	2		3		.200	.238	.417	114	1	1	6				.907	10	2/PS	1.0
	KC-U	11	46	6	9	3	0	1		4		.196	.260	.326	112	-0	1	4				.950	-1	2	0.1
	Yr	28	106	12	21	4	3	3		7		.198	.248	.377	112	1	2	10				.923	10	2/PS	1.1
1885	Phi-N	103	389	63	65	11	5	4	29	35	82	.167	.236	.252	59	-17	-16	24				.890	6	*S	-0.8
1886	Phi-N	105	373	46	81	9	11	2	38	33	73	.217	.281	.316	81	-8	-9	42	29			**.945**	-5	*2S/3	-0.9
1887	Phi-N	60	221	33	47	11	1	1	21	19	29	.213	.284	.285	57	-11	-14	22	11			.921	-13	2S/3	-2.2
1888	Phi-N	80	275	30	53	4	1	1	17	27	41	.193	.282	.225	62	-9	-11	21	12			.945	12	23/S	0.3
1889	Chi-N	46	155	19	21	0	0	0	10	25	46	.135	.256	.135	11	-17	-19	6	1			.919	6	S/2	-0.9
1890	Chi-P	80	283	38	54	10	5	0	29	33	37	.191	.287	.261	46	-20	-23	23	4			.880	-10	S2/3	-2.3
1891	Cin-a	1	4	0	0	0	0	0	0	0	0	.000	.000	.000	-92	-1	-1	0	0			1.000	1	/2	0.0
	Phi-N	1	0	0	0	0	0	0	0	0	0	—	—	—	—	0	0	0	0			1.000	0	/S	0.0
Total	8	504	1806	241	342	49	26	11	144	179	308	.189	.268	.264	59	-84	-90	148	57			.892	7	S2/3P	-5.7

■ EMIL BATCH
Batch, Emil "Heinie" or "Ace" b: 1/21/1880, Brooklyn, N.Y. d: 8/23/26, Brooklyn, N.Y. BR/TR, 5'7", 170 lbs. Deb: 9/13/04

YEAR	TM/L	G	AB	R	H	2B	3B	HR	RBI	BB	SO	AVG	OBP	SLG	PRO+	BR	/A	RC	SB	CS	SBR	FA	FR	POS	TPR
1904	Bro-N	28	94	9	24	1	2	2	7	1		.255	.263	.372	98	-1	-1	11	6			.880	-2	3	-0.2
1905	Bro-N	145	568	64	143	20	11	5	49	26		.252	.285	.352	97	-9	-4	65	21			.887	-8	*3	-0.8
1906	Bro-N	59	203	23	52	7	6	0	11	15		.256	.311	.350	115	1	3	24	3			.964	1	O/3	0.1
1907	Bro-N	116	388	38	96	10	3	0	31	23		.247	.291	.289	89	-9	-5	38	7			.937	-3	*O/32S	-1.3
Total	4	348	1253	134	315	38	22	7	98	65		.251	.289	.334	98	-18	-8	139	37			.886	-11	3O/S2	-2.2

■ JOHN BATEMAN
Bateman, John Alvin b: 7/21/42, Killeen, Tex. BR/TR, 6'3", 220 lbs. Deb: 4/19/63

YEAR	TM/L	G	AB	R	H	2B	3B	HR	RBI	BB	SO	AVG	OBP	SLG	PRO+	BR	/A	RC	SB	CS	SBR	FA	FR	POS	TPR
1963	Hou-N	128	404	23	85	8	6	10	59	13	103	.210	.251	.334	71	-18	-15	33	0	0	0	.971	2	*C	-1.0
1964	Hou-N	74	221	18	42	8	0	5	19	17	48	.190	.251	.294	56	-14	-12	14	0	1	-1	.987	6	C	-0.4
1965	Hou-N	45	142	15	28	3	1	7	14	12	37	.197	.260	.380	83	-5	-3	11	0	1	-1	.985	0	C	-0.2
1966	Hou-N	131	433	39	121	24	3	17	70	20	74	.279	.319	.467	123	8	11	58	0	0	0	.981	1	*C	2.1
1967	Hou-N	76	252	16	48	9	0	2	17	17	53	.190	.247	.250	44	-19	-18	14	0	0	0	.989	1	C	-1.4
1968	Hou-N	111	350	28	87	19	0	4	33	23	46	.249	.301	.337	93	-4	-3	31	1	1	-0	.985	-2	*C	0.1
1969	Mon-N	74	235	16	49	4	0	8	19	12	44	.209	.250	.328	60	-13	-13	17	0	2	-1	.985	-0	C	-1.2
1970	Mon-N	139	520	51	123	21	5	15	68	28	75	.237	.277	.383	75	-20	-20	51	8	4	0	.983	-2	*C	-1.5
1971	Mon-N	139	492	34	119	17	3	10	56	19	87	.242	.276	.350	76	-17	-17	40	1	0	0	.985	-9	*C	-2.2
1972	Mon-N	18	29	0	7	1	0	0	3	3	4	.241	.313	.276	67	-1	-1	2	0	0	0	1.000	-2	/C	-0.3
	Phi-N	82	252	10	56	9	0	3	17	8	39	.222	.249	.294	52	-16	-16	17	0	1	-1	.972	1	C	-1.4
	Yr	100	281	10	63	10	0	3	20	11	43	.224	.256	.292	54	-17	-18	20	0	1	-1	.973	-1	C	-1.7
Total	10	1017	3330	250	765	123	18	81	375	172	610	.230	.273	.350	77	-118	-109	289	10	10	-3	.982	-3	C	-7.4

■ CHARLIE BATES
Bates, Charles William b: 9/17/07, Philadelphia, Pa. d: 1/29/80, Topeka, Kan. BR/TR, 5'10", 165 lbs. Deb: 9/22/27

YEAR	TM/L	G	AB	R	H	2B	3B	HR	RBI	BB	SO	AVG	OBP	SLG	PRO+	BR	/A	RC	SB	CS	SBR	FA	FR	POS	TPR
1927	Phi-A	9	38	5	9	2	2	0	2	3	5	.237	.293	.395	73	-1	-2	4	3	1	0	.857	-0	/O	-0.2

■ DEL BATES
Bates, Delbert Oakley b: 6/12/40, Seattle, Wash. BL/TR, 6'2", 195 lbs. Deb: 5/06/70

YEAR	TM/L	G	AB	R	H	2B	3B	HR	RBI	BB	SO	AVG	OBP	SLG	PRO+	BR	/A	RC	SB	CS	SBR	FA	FR	POS	TPR
1970	Phi-N	22	60	1	8	2	0	0	1	6	15	.133	.257	.167	16	-7	-7	3	0	1	-1	.992	-4	C	-1.0

■ BUD BATES
Bates, Hubert Edgar b: 3/16/12, Los Angeles, Cal. d: 4/29/87, Long Beach, Cal. BR/TR, 6', 165 lbs. Deb: 9/16/39

YEAR	TM/L	G	AB	R	H	2B	3B	HR	RBI	BB	SO	AVG	OBP	SLG	PRO+	BR	/A	RC	SB	CS	SBR	FA	FR	POS	TPR
1939	Phi-N	15	58	8	15	2	0	1	2	2	8	.259	.283	.345	70	-3	-3	5	1			.978	3	O	0.0

■ JOHNNY BATES
Bates, John William b: 8/21/1882, Steubenville, Ohio d: 2/10/49, Steubenville, Ohio BL/TL, 5'7", 168 lbs. Deb: 4/12/06

YEAR	TM/L	G	AB	R	H	2B	3B	HR	RBI	BB	SO	AVG	OBP	SLG	PRO+	BR	/A	RC	SB	CS	SBR	FA	FR	POS	TPR
1906	Bos-N	140	504	52	127	21	5	6	54	36		.252	.313	.349	110	3	5	61	9			.958	-10	*O	-1.4
1907	Bos-N	126	447	52	116	18	12	2	49	39		.260	.329	.367	118	9	9	60	11			.979	-2	*O	0.2
1908	Bos-N	127	445	48	115	14	6	1	29	35		.258	.315	.324	106	2	3	53	25			.948	-4	*O	-0.6
1909	Bos-N	63	236	27	68	15	3	1	23	20		.288	.354	.390	125	8	7	37	15			.945	5	O	1.0
	Phi-N	77	266	43	78	11	1	1	15	28		.293	.365	.353	122	8	7	43	22			.959	-2	O	0.3
	Yr	140	502	70	146	26	4	2	38	48		.291	.360	.371	123	16	14	81	37			.952	3	*O	1.3
1910	Phi-N	135	498	91	152	26	11	3	61	61	49	.305	.385	.420	130	23	20	93	31			.954	12	*O	2.7
1911	Cin-N	148	518	89	151	24	13	1	61	103	59	.292	.415	.394	131	24	27	99	33			.966	5	*O	2.4
1912	Cin-N	81	239	45	69	12	7	1	29	47	16	.289	.406	.410	127	10	11	45	10			.950	7	O	1.4
1913	Cin-N	131	407	63	113	13	7	6	51	67	30	.278	.387	.388	122	14	15	67	21			.946	4	*O	1.4
1914	Cin-N	58	155	29	39	7	5	2	15	28	17	.252	.380	.400	128	7	7	25	4			.913	-6	O	-0.2
	Chi-N	9	8	2	1	0	0	0	1	1	1	.125	.300	.125	28	-1	-1	0	0			1.000	-0	/O	-0.1
	Yr	67	163	31	40	7	5	2	16	29	18	.245	.376	.387	124	7	6	25	4			.917	-6	O	-0.3
	Bal-F	59	190	24	58	6	3	1	29	38	18	.305	.429	.384	128	11	10	36	6			.950	-1	O	0.6
Total	9	1154	3913	565	1087	167	73	25	417	503	190	.278	.367	.377	122	118	119	619	187			.955	9	*O	7.7

■ RAY BATES
Bates, Raymond b: 2/8/1890, Paterson, N.J. d: 8/15/70, Tucson, Ariz. BR/TR, 6', 165 lbs. Deb: 5/31/13

YEAR	TM/L	G	AB	R	H	2B	3B	HR	RBI	BB	SO	AVG	OBP	SLG	PRO+	BR	/A	RC	SB	CS	SBR	FA	FR	POS	TPR
1913	Cle-A	27	30	4	5	0	2	0	4	3	9	.167	.265	.300	63	-1	-2	3	3			.905	-0	3/O	-0.2
1917	Phi-A	127	485	47	115	20	7	2	66	21	39	.237	.277	.320	83	-12	-12	45	12			.933	6	*3	-0.3
Total	2	154	515	51	120	20	9	2	70	24	48	.233	.277	.318	82	-14	-13	48	15			.932	6	3/O	-0.5

■ BILLY BATES
Bates, William Derrick b: 12/7/63, Houston, Tex. BL/TR, 5'7", 155 lbs. Deb: 8/17/89

YEAR	TM/L	G	AB	R	H	2B	3B	HR	RBI	BB	SO	AVG	OBP	SLG	PRO+	BR	/A	RC	SB	CS	SBR	FA	FR	POS	TPR
1989	Mil-A	7	14	3	3	0	0	0	0	0	1	.214	.214	.214	21	-1	-1	0	2	0	1	.938	4	/2	0.3
1990	Mil-A	14	29	6	3	1	0	0	2	4	7	.103	.212	.138	-0	-4	-4	2	4	0	1	.962	3	2	0.0
	*Cin-N	8	5	2	0	0	0	0	0	0	2	.000	.000	.000	-96	-1	-1	-0	2	1	0	1.000	1	/2	0.0
Total	2	29	48	11	6	1	0	0	2	4	10	.125	.192	.146	-4	-7	-7	2	8	1	2	.953	8	/2	0.3

■ BILL BATHE
Bathe, William David b: 10/14/60, Downey, Cal. BR/TR, 6'2", 200 lbs. Deb: 4/12/86

YEAR	TM/L	G	AB	R	H	2B	3B	HR	RBI	BB	SO	AVG	OBP	SLG	PRO+	BR	/A	RC	SB	CS	SBR	FA	FR	POS	TPR
1986	Oak-A	39	103	9	19	3	0	5	11	2	20	.184	.208	.359	55	-7	-6	7	0	0	0	.991	1	C	-0.4
1989	*SF-N	30	32	3	9	1	0	0	6	0	7	.281	.281	.313	72	-1	-1	3	0	0	0	1.000	-1	/C	-0.2
1990	SF-N	52	48	3	11	0	1	3	12	7	12	.229	.327	.458	118	1	1	7	0	0	0	1.000	-1	/C	0.0
Total	3	121	183	15	39	4	1	8	29	9	39	.213	.254	.377	75	-8	-7	17	0	0	0	.992	-1	/C	-0.6

■ RAFAEL BATISTA
Batista, Rafael (Sanchez) b: 10/20/47, San Pedro De Macoris, D.R. BL/TL, 6'1", 195 lbs. Deb: 6/17/73

YEAR	TM/L	G	AB	R	H	2B	3B	HR	RBI	BB	SO	AVG	OBP	SLG	PRO+	BR	/A	RC	SB	CS	SBR	FA	FR	POS	TPR
1973	Hou-N	12	15	2	4	0	0	0	2	1	6	.267	.313	.267	62	-1	-1	1	0	0	0	1.000	-0	/1	-0.1
1975	Hou-N	10	10	0	3	1	0	0	0	0	4	.300	.300	.400	100	-0	-0	1	0	0	0	.000	0	H	0.0
Total	2	22	25	2	7	1	0	0	2	1	10	.280	.308	.320	76	-1	-1	2	0	0	0	.750	-0	/1	-0.1

■ KEVIN BATISTE
Batiste, Kevin Wade b: 10/21/66, Galveston, Tex. BR/TR, 6'2", 175 lbs. Deb: 6/13/89

YEAR	TM/L	G	AB	R	H	2B	3B	HR	RBI	BB	SO	AVG	OBP	SLG	PRO+	BR	/A	RC	SB	CS	SBR	FA	FR	POS	TPR
1989	Tor-A	6	8	1	2	0	0	0	0	0	5	.250	.250	.250	42	-1	-1	1	0	0	0	1.000	-1	/O	-0.1

■ KIM BATISTE
Batiste, Kimothy Emil b: 3/15/68, New Orleans, La. BR/TR, 6', 175 lbs. Deb: 9/08/91

YEAR	TM/L	G	AB	R	H	2B	3B	HR	RBI	BB	SO	AVG	OBP	SLG	PRO+	BR	/A	RC	SB	CS	SBR	FA	FR	POS	TPR
1991	Phi-N	10	27	2	6	0	0	0	1	1	8	.222	.250	.222	34	-2	-2	1	0	1	-1	.970	1	/S	-0.1
1992	Phi-N	44	136	9	28	4	0	1	10	4	18	.206	.229	.257	38	-11	-11	7	0	0	0	.922	-8	S	-1.8
Total	2	54	163	11	34	4	0	1	11	5	26	.209	.232	.252	37	-14	-13	8	0	1	-1	.930	-7	/S	-1.9

■ BILL BATSCH
Batsch, William McKinley b: 5/18/1892, Mingo Junction, O. d: 12/31/63, Canton, Ohio BR/TR, 5'10.5", 168 lbs. Deb: 9/09/16

YEAR	TM/L	G	AB	R	H	2B	3B	HR	RBI	BB	SO	AVG	OBP	SLG	PRO+	BR	/A	RC	SB	CS	SBR	FA	FR	POS	TPR
1916	Pit-N	1	0	0	0	0	0	0	0	1	0	—	1.000	—	218	0	0	0	0			.000	0	H	0.0

YEAR	TM/L	G	AB	R	H	2B	3B	HR	RBI	BB	SO	AVG	OBP	SLG	PRO+	BR	/A	RC	SB	CS	SBR	FA	FR	POS	TPR
■ **LARRY BATTAM** Battam, Lawrence J. b: 5/1/1878, Brooklyn, N.Y. d: 1/27/38, Brooklyn, N.Y. 5′11″, Deb: 9/28/1895																									
1895	NY-N	2	4	0	1	0	0	0	0	2	1	.250	.500	.250	102	0	0	1	0			.667	-1	/3	0.0
■ **GEORGE BATTEN** Batten, George Burnett b: 10/7/1891, Haddonfield, N.J. d: 8/4/72, New Port Richey, Fla. BR/TR, 5′11″, 165 lbs. Deb: 9/28/12																									
1912	NY-A	1	3	0	0	0	0	0	0	0		.000	.000	.000	-94	-1	-1	0	0			1.000	-1	/2	-0.2
■ **EARL BATTEY** Battey, Earl Jesse b: 1/5/35, Los Angeles, Cal. BR/TR, 6′1″, 205 lbs. Deb: 9/10/55																									
1955	Chi-A	5	7	1	2	0	0	0	0	1	1	.286	.444	.286	97	0	0	1	0	0	0	1.000	2	/C	0.2
1956	Chi-A	4	4	1	1	0	0	0	0	1	1	.250	.400	.250	74	-0	-0	0	0	0	0	.800	-1	/C	-0.1
1957	Chi-A	48	115	12	20	2	3	3	6	11	38	.174	.246	.322	54	-8	-8	8	0	2	-1	.989	6	C	-0.2
1958	Chi-A	68	168	24	38	8	0	8	26	24	34	.226	.330	.417	106	1	1	24	1	0	0	.988	2	C	0.6
1959	Chi-A	26	64	9	14	1	2	2	7	8	13	.219	.306	.391	91	-1	-1	8	0	0	0	.990	4	C	0.4
1960	Was-A	137	466	49	126	24	2	15	60	48	68	.270	.349	.427	110	6	6	67	4	5	-2	.982	5	*C	1.8
1961	Min-A	133	460	70	139	24	1	17	55	53	66	.302	.378	.470	118	17	13	78	3	3	-1	.993	7	*C	2.5
1962	Min-A★	148	522	58	146	20	3	11	57	57	48	.280	.351	.393	96	0	-2	70	0	0	0	.991	6	*C	1.0
1963	Min-A★	147	508	64	145	17	1	26	84	61	75	.285	.371	.476	133	25	24	89	0	0	0	.994	1	*C	3.1
1964	Min-A	131	405	33	110	17	1	12	52	51	49	.272	.354	.407	111	7	7	54	1	1	-0	.990	-5	*C	0.7
1965	*Min-A★	131	394	36	117	22	2	6	60	50	23	.297	.379	.409	119	14	12	63	0	0	0	.986	-8	*C	1.1
1966	Min-A★	115	364	30	93	12	1	4	34	43	30	.255	.339	.327	87	-2	-5	39	4	1	1	.995	6	*C	0.9
1967	Min-A	48	109	6	18	3	1	0	8	13	24	.165	.254	.211	36	-8	-9	6	0	0	0	.987	-2	C	-1.1
Total	13	1141	3586	393	969	150	17	104	449	421	470	.270	.351	.409	106	50	38	508	13	12	-3	.990	23	*C	10.9
■ **JOE BATTIN** Battin, Joseph V. b: 11/11/1851, Philadelphia, Pa. d: 12/10/37, Akron, Ohio BR/TR, Deb: 8/11/1871 MU																									
1871	Cle-n	1	3	0	0	0	0	0	0	1	0	.000	.250	.000	-21	-0	-0	0	0					/O	0.0
1873	Ath-n	1	5	4	3	0	0	0	2	1	0	.600	.667	.600	257	1	1	2						/O	0.1
1874	Ath-n	51	226	40	52	11	1	0		1		.230	.233	.288	60	-9	-12	16						*2/OS	-1.1
1875	StL-n	67	284	31	71	7	3	0		0		.250	.250	.296	97	-3	1	22						*2/3	0.0
1876	StL-N	64	283	34	85	11	4	0	46	6	6	.300	.315	.367	134	8	10	34				**.867**	14	*3/2	2.2
1877	StL-N	57	226	28	45	3	7	1	22	6	17	.199	.220	.288	62	-10	-9	15				.823	-3	32/OP	-0.9
1882	Pit-a	34	133	13	28	5	1	1		3		.211	.228	.286	76	-4	-3	9				.876	21	3	1.7
1883	Pit-a	98	388	42	83	9	6	1		11		.214	.236	.276	67	-15	-12	26				**.891**	29	*3/PM	1.4
1884	Pit-a	43	158	10	28	1	2	0		3		.177	.198	.209	34	-11	-11	7				.919	8	3M	-0.3
	CP-U	18	69	8	13	2	0	0		0		.188	.188	.217	37	-4	-4	3				.908	11	3M	0.6
	Bal-U	17	59	3	6	1	0	0		0		.102	.102	.119	-23	-7	-8	1				.813	2	3	-0.6
	Yr	35	128	11	19	3	0	0		0		.148	.148	.172	8	-12	-13	3				.868	13	3	0.0
1890	Syr-a	29	119	15	25	2	1	0		8		.210	.260	.244	56	-7	-5	10	8			.794	-4	3	-0.8
Total	4 n	120	518	75	126	18	4	0	2	3		.243	.248	.293	80	-11	-11	39	0					2/O3S	-1.0
Total	6	360	1435	153	313	34	21	3	68	37	23	.218	.238	.277	69	-52	-43	103	8			.870	77	3/2OP	3.3
■ **JIM BATTLE** Battle, James Milton b: 3/26/01, Bailey, Tex. d: 9/30/65, Chico, Cal. BR/TR, 6′1″, 170 lbs. Deb: 9/09/27																									
1927	Chi-A	6	8	1	3	0	1	0	0	0	1	.375	.375	.625	160	1	1	2	0	0	0	1.000	-1	/3S	0.0
■ **MATT BATTS** Batts, Matthew Daniel b: 10/16/21, San Antonio, Tex. BR/TR, 5′11″, 200 lbs. Deb: 9/10/47																									
1947	Bos-A	7	16	3	8	1	0	1	5	1	1	.500	.529	.750	236	3	3	7	0	0	0	1.000	-1	/C	0.3
1948	Bos-A	46	118	13	37	12	0	1	24	15	9	.314	.391	.441	115	4	3	21	0	0	0	.986	-1	C	0.4
1949	Bos-A	60	157	23	38	9	1	3	31	25	22	.242	.350	.369	84	-2	-4	22	1	0	0	.977	2	C	0.1
1950	Bos-A	75	238	27	65	15	3	4	34	18	19	.273	.327	.412	80	-5	-8	31	0	0	0	.994	3	C	-0.3
1951	Bos-A	11	29	1	4	1	0	0	2	1	2	.138	.167	.172	-8	-4	-5	1	0	0	0	.975	-0	C	-0.5
	StL-A	79	248	26	75	17	1	5	31	21	21	.302	.357	.440	111	4	3	38	2	0	1	.960	-8	C	-0.2
	Yr	90	277	27	79	18	1	5	33	22	23	.285	.338	.412	98	-0	-1	38	2	0	1	.962	-9	C	-0.7
1952	Det-A	56	173	11	41	4	1	3	13	14	22	.237	.298	.324	72	-7	-7	17	1	0	0	.983	3	C	-0.1
1953	Det-A	116	374	38	104	24	3	6	43	24	36	.278	.322	.406	97	-4	-3	48	2	3	-1	.986	-14	*C	-1.3
1954	Det-A	12	21	1	6	1	0	0	5	2	4	.286	.348	.333	89	-0	-0	3	0	0	0	.967	1	/C	0.1
	Chi-A	55	158	16	36	7	1	3	19	17	15	.228	.303	.342	74	-5	-6	15	0	1	-1	.992	7	C	0.2
	Yr	67	179	17	42	8	1	3	24	19	19	.235	.308	.341	76	-6	-6	17	0	1	-1	.989	8	C	0.3
1955	Cin-N	26	71	4	18	4	1	0	13	4	11	.254	.293	.338	63	-3	-4	6	0	0	0	.986	-1	C	-0.5
1956	Cin-N	3	2	0	0	0	0	0	0	1	1	.000	.333	.000	0	-0	-0	0	0	0	0	.000	0	H	0.0
Total	10	546	1605	163	432	95	11	26	220	143	163	.269	.330	.391	89	-20	-28	208	6	4	-1	.983	-10	C	-1.8
■ **HANK BAUER** Bauer, Henry Albert b: 7/31/22, E.St.Louis, Ill. BR/TR, 6′, 192 lbs. Deb: 9/06/48 MC																									
1948	NY-A	19	50	6	9	1	1	1	9	6	13	.180	.268	.300	51	-4	-4	5	1	0	0	.964	-1	O	-0.5
1949	*NY-A	103	301	56	82	6	6	10	45	37	42	.272	.354	.432	107	2	2	47	2	2	-1	.977	-9	O	-1.1
1950	*NY-A	113	415	72	133	16	2	13	70	35	41	.320	.380	.463	118	9	10	75	2	3	-1	.987	-1	*O	0.3
1951	*NY-A	118	348	53	103	19	3	10	54	42	39	.296	.373	.454	128	11	13	60	5	2	0	.990	-5	*O	0.4
1952	*NY-A★	141	553	86	162	31	6	17	74	50	61	.293	.355	.463	134	18	22	91	6	7	-2	.984	3	*O	1.7
1953	*NY-A★	133	437	77	133	20	6	10	57	59	45	.304	.394	.446	131	18	20	81	2	3	-1	.992	0	*O	1.4
1954	NY-A★	114	377	73	111	16	5	12	54	40	42	.294	.362	.459	128	11	13	63	4	4	-1	.989	-6	*O	0.2
1955	*NY-A	139	492	97	137	20	5	20	53	56	65	.278	.362	.461	122	13	14	86	8	4	0	.981	4	*O/C	1.2
1956	*NY-A	147	539	96	130	18	7	26	84	59	72	.241	.318	.445	103	-3	-0	77	4	2	0	.969	-8	*O	-1.6
1957	*NY-A	137	479	70	124	22	**9**	18	65	42	64	.259	.324	.455	112	5	6	71	7	2	1	.986	-7	*O	-0.8
1958	*NY-A	128	452	62	121	22	6	12	50	32	56	.268	.318	.423	106	-0	2	60	3	2	-0	.980	-9	*O	-1.3
1959	NY-A	114	341	44	81	20	0	9	39	33	54	.238	.309	.375	90	-7	-5	41	4	2	0	.972	-13	*O	-2.3
1960	KC-A	95	255	30	70	15	0	3	31	21	36	.275	.332	.369	89	-4	-4	30	1	0	0	.978	-6	O	-1.3
1961	KC-A	43	106	11	28	3	1	3	18	9	8	.264	.322	.396	91	-2	-2	14	1	0	0	.958	-7	OM	-1.0
Total	14	1544	5145	833	1424	229	57	164	703	521	638	.277	.347	.439	114	68	87	801	50	33	-5	.982	-65	*O/C	-4.7
■ **PADDY BAUMANN** Baumann, Charles John b: 12/20/1885, Indianapolis, Ind. d: 11/20/69, Indianapolis, Ind. BR/TR, 5′9″, 160 lbs. Deb: 8/10/11																									
1911	Det-A	26	94	8	24	2	4	0	11	6		.255	.307	.362	82	-2	-3	11	1			.956	6	2/O	0.2
1912	Det-A	16	42	3	11	1	0	0	7	6		.262	.354	.286	86	-1	-0	6	4			.786	-2	/32O	-0.2
1913	Det-A	50	191	31	57	7	4	1	22	16	18	.298	.353	.393	120	4	4	28	4			.943	-7	2	-0.4
1914	Det-A	3	11	1	0	0	0	0	0	2	1	.000	.154	.000	-52	-2	-2	0	0			1.000	-1	/2	-0.4
1915	NY-A	76	219	30	64	13	1	2	28	28	32	.292	.380	.388	130	9	9	33	9	10	-3	.978	-2	23/O	0.5
1916	NY-A	79	237	35	68	5	3	1	25	19	16	.287	.352	.346	108	3	2	33	10			.958	-7	O3/2	-0.6
1917	NY-A	49	110	10	24	2	1	0	8	4	9	.218	.246	.255	52	-7	-7	7	2			.941	-12	2/O3	-2.1
Total	7	299	904	118	248	30	13	4	101	81	76	.274	.340	.350	103	4	3	117	30	10		.953	-26	2/3O	-3.0
■ **JIM BAUMER** Baumer, James Sloan b: 1/29/31, Tulsa, Okla. BR/TR, 6′2″, 185 lbs. Deb: 9/14/49																									
1949	Chi-A	8	10	2	4	1	1	0	2	2	1	.400	.571	.700	243	2	2	5	0	0	0	.938	1	/S	0.3
1961	Cin-N	10	24	0	3	0	0	0	0	0	9	.125	.125	.125	-33	-5	-5	0	0	0	0	1.000	-0	/2	-0.4
Total	2	18	34	2	7	1	1	0	2	2	10	.206	.289	.294	55	-2	-2	5	0	0	0	.953	1	/2S	-0.1
■ **JOHN BAUMGARTNER** Baumgartner, John Edward b: 5/29/31, Birmingham, Ala. BR/TR, 6′1″, 190 lbs. Deb: 4/14/53																									
1953	Det-A	7	27	3	5	0	0	0	2	0	5	.185	.185	.185	0	-4	-4	1	0	0	0	.913	-1	/3	-0.4

YEAR	TM/L	G	AB	R	H	2B	3B	HR	RBI	BB	SO	AVG	OBP	SLG	PRO+	BR	/A	RC	SB	CS	SBR	FA	FR	POS	TPR
■ **FRANK BAUMHOLTZ** Baumholtz, Frank Conrad b: 10/7/18, Midvale, Ohio BL/TL, 5'10.5", 175 lbs. Deb: 4/15/47																									
1947	Cin-N	151	643	96	182	32	9	5	45	56	53	.283	.341	.384	93	-7	-7	88	6			.977	-5	*O	-1.9
1948	Cin-N	128	415	57	123	19	5	4	30	27	32	.296	.344	.395	103	-1	1	57	8			.987	3	*O	-0.2
1949	Cin-N	27	81	12	19	5	3	1	8	6	8	.235	.295	.407	86	-2	-2	10	0			.964	2	O	-0.1
	Chi-N	58	164	15	37	4	2	1	15	9	21	.226	.270	.293	52	-12	-11	14	2			.986	-4	O	-1.7
	Yr	85	245	27	56	9	5	2	23	15	29	.229	.279	.331	64	-13	-13	24	2			.976	-3	O	-1.8
1951	Chi-N	146	560	62	159	28	10	2	50	49	36	.284	.346	.380	94	-3	-5	74	5	4	-1	.975	-7	*O	-1.7
1952	Chi-N	103	409	59	133	17	4	4	35	27	27	.325	.371	.416	116	10	9	64	5	7	-3	.974	3	*O	0.5
1953	Chi-N	133	520	75	159	36	7	3	25	42	36	.306	.359	.419	100	2	0	82	3	3	-1	.980	-3	*O	-0.8
1954	Chi-N	90	303	38	90	12	6	4	28	20	15	.297	.343	.416	95	-2	-2	42	1	3	-2	.988	-10	O	-1.6
1955	Chi-N	105	280	23	81	12	5	1	27	16	24	.289	.330	.379	88	-5	-5	33	0	1	-1	.993	2	O	-0.6
1956	Phi-N	76	100	13	27	0	0	0	9	6	6	.270	.318	.270	61	-5	-5	8	0	2	-1	.962	-0	O	-0.7
1957	Phi-N	2	2	0	0	0	0	0	0	0	0	.000	.000	.000	-99	-1	-1	0	0	0	0	.000	0	H	-0.1
Total	10	1019	3477	450	1010	165	51	25	272	258	258	.290	.342	.389	95	-26	-26	470	30	20		.980	-20	O	-8.9
■ **JIM BAXES** Baxes, Dimitrios Speros b: 7/5/28, San Francisco, Cal BR/TR, 6'1", 190 lbs. Deb: 4/11/59 F																									
1959	LA-N	11	33	4	10	1	0	2	5	4	7	.303	.395	.515	130	2	2	6	1	0	0	.952	7	3	0.8
	Cle-A	77	247	35	59	11	0	15	34	21	47	.239	.299	.466	111	1	2	30	0	1	-1	.956	-13	23	-0.8
Total	1	88	280	39	69	12	0	17	39	25	54	.246	.310	.471	113	3	4	36	1	1	-0	.931	-7	/23	0.0
■ **MIKE BAXES** Baxes, Michael b: 12/18/30, San Francisco, Cal BR/TR, 5'10", 175 lbs. Deb: 4/17/56 F																									
1956	KC-A	73	106	9	24	3	1	1	5	18	15	.226	.339	.302	70	-4	-4	12	0	1	-1	.944	4	S/2	0.2
1958	KC-A	73	231	31	49	10	1	0	8	21	24	.212	.286	.264	52	-15	-15	17	1	6	-3	.969	-4	2/S	-1.9
Total	2	146	337	40	73	13	2	1	13	39	39	.217	.303	.276	58	-19	-19	29	1	7	-4	.946	-0	/S2	-1.7
■ **JOHN BAXTER** Baxter, John Morris b: 7/27/1876, Chippewa Falls, Wis. d: 8/7/26, Portland, Ore. 6'3", Deb: 4/19/07																									
1907	StL-N	6	21	1	4	0	0	0	0	0		.190	.190	.190	20	-2	-2	1	0			.921	-1	/1	-0.3
■ **HARRY BAY** Bay, Harry Elbert "Deerfoot" b: 1/17/1878, Pontiac, Ill. d: 3/20/52, Peoria, Ill. BL/TL, 5'8", 138 lbs. Deb: 7/23/01																									
1901	Cin-N	41	157	25	33	1	2	1	3	13		.210	.275	.261	60	-9	-7	13	4			.953	-1	O	-1.1
1902	Cin-N	6	16	3	6	0	0	0	1	2		.375	.474	.375	148	1	1	3	0			.778	0	/O	0.1
	Cle-A	108	455	71	132	10	5	0	23	36		.290	.343	.334	92	-6	-4	64	22			**.973**	4	*O	-0.7
1903	Cle-A	140	579	94	169	15	12	1	35	29		.292	.329	.364	110	5	7	89	**45**			.950	-3	*O	-0.5
1904	Cle-A	132	506	69	122	12	9	3	36	43		.241	.307	.318	99	-0	-0	64	**38**			**.987**	7	*O	-0.1
1905	Cle-A	144	552	90	166	18	10	0	22	36		.301	.349	.370	126	17	16	89	36			.970	1	*O	1.1
1906	Cle-A	68	280	47	77	8	3	0	14	26		.275	.337	.325	109	3	3	39	17			.979	-3	O	-0.3
1907	Cle-A	34	95	14	17	1	1	0	7	10		.179	.271	.211	54	-4	-5	8	7			.968	0	O	-0.6
1908	Cle-A	2	0	0	0	0	0	0	0	0		—	—	—	—	0	0	0	0			.000	0	R	0.0
Total	8	675	2640	413	722	65	42	5	141	195		.273	.328	.336	103	7	12	369	169			.968	6	O	-2.1
■ **DICK BAYLESS** Bayless, Harry Owen b: 9/6/1883, Joplin, Mo. d: 12/16/20, Santa Rita, N.M. BL/TR, 5'9", 178 lbs. Deb: 9/09/08																									
1908	Cin-N	19	71	7	16	1	0	1	3	6		.225	.304	.282	90	-1	-1	6	0			.946	3	O	0.1
■ **DON BAYLOR** Baylor, Don Edward b: 6/28/49, Austin, Tex. BR/TR, 6'1", 195 lbs. Deb: 9/18/70 C																									
1970	Bal-A	8	17	4	4	0	0	0	4	2	3	.235	.316	.235	54	-1	-1	1	1	1	-0	1.000	0	/O	-0.2
1971	Bal-A	1	2	0	0	0	0	0	1	2	1	.000	.600	.000	83	0	0	0	0	0	0	1.000	0	/O	0.1
1972	Bal-A	102	320	33	81	13	3	11	38	29	50	.253	.332	.416	118	8	7	47	24	2	6	.975	-9	O/1	0.1
1973	*Bal-A	118	405	64	116	20	4	11	51	35	48	.286	.362	.437	125	13	14	65	32	9	4	.981	-1	*O/1D	1.2
1974	*Bal-A	137	489	66	133	22	1	10	59	43	56	.272	.343	.382	112	6	8	65	29	12	2	.978	-17	*O/1D	-1.5
1975	Bal-A	145	524	79	148	21	6	25	76	53	64	.282	.363	.489	148	26	30	90	32	17	-1	.982	-2	*O/1D	2.2
1976	Oak-A	157	595	85	147	25	1	15	68	58	72	.247	.334	.368	110	5	8	80	52	12	8	.981	-9	O1D	0.0
1977	Cal-A	154	561	87	141	27	0	25	75	62	76	.251	.339	.433	113	7	10	81	26	12	1	.966	-1	OD1	0.5
1978	Cal-A	158	591	103	151	26	0	34	99	56	71	.255	.338	.472	131	19	22	93	22	9	1	.974	-2	*DO1	1.9
1979	*Cal-A★	162	628	**120**	186	33	3	36	**139**	71	51	.296	.377	.530	147	37	40	126	22	12	-1	.976	2	OD/1	3.5
1980	Cal-A	90	340	39	85	12	2	5	51	24	32	.250	.320	.341	83	-8	-7	36	6	6	-2	.969	3	OD	-0.8
1981	Cal-A	103	377	52	90	18	1	17	66	42	51	.239	.326	.427	116	7	7	51	3	3	-1	1.000	1	D/1O	0.8
1982	*Cal-A	157	608	80	160	24	1	24	93	57	69	.263	.333	.424	106	5	5	84	10	4	1	.000	0	*D	0.6
1983	NY-A	144	534	82	162	33	3	21	85	40	53	.303	.366	.494	139	25	27	96	17	7	1	1.000	-0	*D/O1	2.7
1984	NY-A	134	493	84	129	29	1	27	89	38	68	.262	.343	.489	132	18	20	83	1	1	-0	.889	-1	*D/O	1.9
1985	NY-A	142	477	70	110	24	1	23	91	52	90	.231	.336	.430	111	6	7	70	0	4	-2	.000	0	*D	0.5
1986	*Bos-A	160	585	93	139	23	1	31	94	62	111	.238	.346	.439	112	11	10	91	3	5	-2	.986	-1	*D1/O	0.6
1987	Bos-A	108	339	64	81	8	0	16	57	40	47	.239	.360	.404	100	2	1	52	5	2	0	.000	0	D	0.1
	*Min-A	20	49	3	14	1	0	0	6	5	12	.286	.397	.306	87	-0	-0	6	0	1	-1	.000	0	D	-0.1
	Yr	128	388	67	95	9	0	16	63	45	59	.245	.364	.392	98	2	1	58	5	3	-0	.000	0	*D	0.0
1988	*Oak-A	92	264	28	58	7	0	7	34	34	44	.220	.335	.326	89	-4	-2	30	0	1	-1	.000	0	D	-0.3
Total	19	2292	8198	1236	2135	366	28	338	1276	805	1069	.260	.346	.436	119	181	206	1247	285	120	14	.977	-37	*DO1	13.8
■ **JACK BEACH** Beach, Stonewall Jackson b: 1862, Alexandria, Va. d: 7/23/1896, Alexandria, Va. Deb: 5/01/1884																									
1884	Was-a	8	31	3	3	2	0	0		0		.097	.097	.161	-18	-4	-3	0				.667	-1	/O	-0.4
■ **JOHNNY BEALL** Beall, John Woolf b: 3/12/1882, Beltsville, Md. d: 6/14/26, Beltsville, Md. BL/TR, 6', 180 lbs. Deb: 4/17/13																									
1913	Cle-A	6	6	0	1	0	0	0	1	0	2	.167	.167	.167	-2	-1	-1	0	0			.000	0	H	-0.1
	Chi-A	17	60	10	16	0	1	2	3	0	0	.267	.279	.400	99	-1	-1	6	1			.953	1	O	-0.1
	Yr	23	66	10	17	0	1	2	4	0	2	.258	.269	.379	89	-1	-1	6	1			.953	1	O	-0.2
1915	Cin-N	10	34	3	8	1	0	0	3	5	10	.235	.350	.265	86	-0	-0	3	0	1	-1	.960	1	O	0.0
1916	Cin-N	6	21	3	7	2	0	1	4	3	7	.333	.417	.571	207	3	3	5	1			1.000	1	/O	0.4
1918	StL-N	19	49	2	11	1	0	0	6	3	6	.224	.269	.245	59	-2	-2	4	0			1.000	-1	O	-0.5
Total	4	58	170	18	43	4	1	3	17	11	25	.253	.306	.341	95	-2	-1	19	2	1		.972	2	/O	-0.3
■ **BOB BEALL** Beall, Robert Brooks b: 4/24/48, Portland, Ore. BB/TL, 5'11", 180 lbs. Deb: 5/12/75																									
1975	Atl-N	20	31	2	7	2	0	0	1	6	9	.226	.351	.290	77	-1	-1	4	0	0	0	.984	-0	/1	-0.1
1978	Atl-N	108	185	29	45	8	0	1	16	36	27	.243	.369	.303	81	-1	-3	22	4	5	-2	.987	0	1/O	-0.8
1979	Atl-N	17	15	1	2	2	0	0	1	3	4	.133	.278	.267	46	-1	-1	1	0	0	0	1.000	0	/1	-0.1
1980	Pit-N	3	3	0	0	0	0	0	0	0	1	.000	.000	.000	-99	-1	-1	0	0	0	0	.000	0	/H	-0.1
Total	4	148	234	32	54	12	0	1	18	45	41	.231	.357	.295	76	-3	-6	28	4	5	-2	.987	0	/1O	-1.1
■ **TOMMY BEALS** Beals, Thomas L. (a.k.a. W.Thomas In 1871-1873) b: Hartford, Conn. d: 10/2/15, San Francisco, Cal. BR , 5'5", 144 lbs. Deb: 7/27/1871																									
1871	Oly-n	10	36	6	7	0	0	0	1	2	0	.194	.237	.194	27	-3	-3	2	2					/O2	-0.2
1872	Oly-n	9	36	7	12	0	2	0	5	1	1	.333	.351	.444	151	2	2	6						/2SO	0.1
1873	Was-n	37	169	35	46	8	6	0	20	1	1	.272	.276	.391	97	-1	-0	19						2C/O	-0.1
1874	Bos-n	19	97	20	19	3	4	0		0		.196	.196	.309	55	-4	-5	6						2/O	-0.4
1875	Bos-n	36	164	41	42	1	5	0		2		.256	.265	.323	99	0	-1	14						2O	-0.1
1880	Chi-N	13	46	4	7	0	0	0	3	1	6	.152	.170	.152	10	-4	-4	1				.889	-6	O/2	-1.0
Total	5 n	111	502	109	126	12	17	0	26	6	2	.251	.260	.343	87	-7	-7	47						/2OCS	-0.7

YEAR	TM/L	G	AB	R	H	2B	3B	HR	RBI	BB	SO	AVG	OBP	SLG	PRO+	BR	/A	RC	SB	CS	SBR	FA	FR	POS	TPR
■ **CHARLIE BEAMON**					Beamon, Charles Alfonzo Jr.		b: 12/4/53, Oakland, Cal.		BL/TL, 6'1", 183 lbs.		Deb: 9/11/78		F												
1978	Sea-A	10	11	2	2	0	0	0	1	1	1	.182	.250	.182	23	-1	-1	1	0	0	0	1.000	1	/1D	0.0
1979	Sea-A	27	25	5	5	1	0	0	0	0	5	.200	.200	.240	18	-3	-3	1	1	0	0	1.000	-0	/1O	-0.3
1981	Tor-A	8	15	1	3	1	0	0	0	2	2	.200	.294	.267	59	-1	-1	1	0	0	0	1.000	-0	/D1	-0.1
Total	3	45	51	8	10	2	0	0	0	3	8	.196	.241	.235	32	-5	-5	3	1	0	0	1.000	1	/D1O	-0.4
■ **JOE BEAN**				Bean, Joseph William		b: 3/18/1874, Boston, Mass.		d: 2/15/61, Atlanta, Ga.		BR/TR, 5'8", 138 lbs.		Deb: 4/28/02												
1902	NY-N	48	176	13	39	2	1	0	5	5		.222	.247	.244	52	-10	-10	14	9			.889	-9	S	-1.8
■ **BILL BEAN**				Bean, William Daro		b: 5/11/64, Santa Ana, Cal.		BL/TL, 6' ", 185 lbs.		Deb: 4/25/87													
1987	Det-A	26	66	6	17	2	0	0	4	5	11	.258	.310	.288	63	-4	-3	6	1	1	-0	1.000	0	O	-0.4
1988	Det-A	10	11	2	2	0	1	0	0	0	2	.182	.182	.364	51	-1	-1	1	0	0	0	1.000	-1	/O1D	-0.2
1989	Det-A	9	11	0	0	0	0	0	0	2	3	.000	.214	.000	-36	-2	-2	0	0	0	0	.833	-3	/O1	-0.5
	LA-N	51	71	7	14	4	0	0	3	4	10	.197	.250	.254	45	-5	-5	4	0	2	-1	1.000	-9	O	-1.7
Total	3	96	159	15	33	6	1	0	7	11	26	.208	.267	.258	47	-12	-11	11	1	3	-2	.991	-13	/O1D	-2.8
■ **BILLY BEANE**				Beane, William Lamar		b: 3/29/62, Orlando, Fla.		BR/TR, 6'4", 195 lbs.		Deb: 9/13/84													
1984	NY-N	5	10	0	1	0	0	0	0	0	2	.100	.100	.100	-44	-2	-2	0	0	1	-1	1.000	-2	/O	-0.4
1985	NY-N	8	8	0	2	1	0	0	1	0	3	.250	.250	.375	74	-0	-0	1	0	0	0	1.000	-1	/O	-0.1
1986	Min-A	80	183	20	39	6	0	3	15	11	54	.213	.258	.295	49	-13	-13	12	2	3	-1	1.000	-5	O/D	-2.1
1987	Min-A	12	15	1	4	0	1	0	1	0	6	.267	.267	.400	71	-1	-1	2	0	0	0	1.000	-2	/O	-0.2
1988	Det-A	6	6	1	1	0	0	0	0	0	2	.167	.167	.167	-7	-1	-1	0	0	0	0	1.000	-2	/O	-0.3
1989	Oak-A	37	79	8	19	5	0	0	11	0	13	.241	.241	.304	54	-5	-5	5	3	1	0	1.000	-2	O/1C3D	-0.7
Total	6	148	301	30	66	14	3	6	35	11	80	.219	.247	.296	48	-22	-22	20	5	5	-2	1.000	-11	/O/D13C	-3.8
■ **TED BEARD**				Beard, Cramer Theodore		b: 1/7/21, Woodsboro, Md.		BL/TL, 5'8", 165 lbs.		Deb: 9/05/48													
1948	Pit-N	25	81	15	16	1	3	0	7	12	18	.198	.316	.284	62	-4	-4	8	5			1.000	2	O	-0.4
1949	Pit-N	14	24	1	2	0	0	0	1	2	2	.083	.154	.083	-34	-5	-5	0	0			.900	-3	O	-0.8
1950	Pit-N	61	177	32	41	6	2	4	12	27	45	.232	.333	.356	79	-4	-5	22	3			.983	2	O	-0.5
1951	Pit-N	22	48	7	9	1	0	1	3	6	14	.188	.291	.271	51	-3	-3	4	0	0	0	1.000	-2	O	-0.5
1952	Pit-N	15	44	5	8	2	1	0	3	7	9	.182	.294	.273	57	-2	-3	4	2	0	1	1.000	0	O	-0.2
1957	Chi-A	38	78	15	16	1	0	0	7	18	14	.205	.354	.218	59	-3	-3	7	3	2	-0	.974	-1	O	-0.6
1958	Chi-A	19	22	5	2	0	0	1	2	6	5	.091	.286	.227	44	-2	-2	2	3	0	1	1.000	-4	O	-0.5
Total	7	194	474	80	94	11	6	6	35	78	107	.198	.315	.285	61	-24	-25	49	16	2		.987	-5	O	-3.5
■ **OLLIE BEARD**				Beard, Oliver Perry		b: 5/2/1862, Lexington, Ky.		d: 5/28/29, Cincinnati, Ohio		BR/TR, 5'11", 180 lbs.		Deb: 4/17/1889										
1889	Cin-a	141	558	96	159	13	14	1	77	35	39	.285	.328	.364	96	-1	-4	80	36			.896	20	*S	2.0
1890	Cin-N	122	492	64	132	17	15	3	72	44	13	.268	.331	.382	110	5	6	74	30			.897	1	*S/3	1.2
1891	Lou-a	68	257	35	62	4	5	0	24	33	9	.241	.330	.296	83	-5	-5	28	7			.879	7	3/S	0.4
Total	3	331	1307	195	353	34	34	4	173	112	61	.270	.330	.357	99	-2	-3	182	73			.896	28	S/3	3.6
■ **LEW BEASLEY**				Beasley, Lewis Paige		b: 8/27/48, Sparta, Va.		BL/TR, 5'10", 172 lbs.		Deb: 5/21/77												
1977	Tex-A	25	32	5	7	1	0	0	3	2	2	.219	.265	.250	41	-3	-3	2	1	1	-0	.833	-6	O/SD	-0.9
■ **DAVE BEATLE**				Beatle, David		b: 1861, New York, N.Y.		6'2", 200 lbs.		Deb: 6/17/1884													
1884	Det-N	1	3	0	0	0	0	0	0	0	2	.000	.000	.000	-99	-1	-1	0				.500	-1	/OC	-0.1
■ **DESMOND BEATTY**				Beatty, Aloysius Desmond "Desperate"		b: 4/7/1893, Baltimore, Md.		d: 10/6/69, Norway, Maine		BR/TR, 5'8.5", 158 lbs.		Deb: 9/28/14									
1914	NY-N	2	3	0	0	0	0	0	1	0		.000	.000	.000	-99	-1	-1	0				.400	-1	/S3	-0.1
■ **JIM BEAUCHAMP**				Beauchamp, James Edward		b: 8/21/39, Vinita, Okla.		BR/TR, 6'2", 205 lbs.		Deb: 9/22/63		C										
1963	StL-N	4	3	0	0	0	0	0	0	0	2	.000	.000	.000	-91	-1	-1	0	0	0	0	.000	0	H	-0.1
1964	Hou-N	23	55	6	9	2	0	2	4	5	16	.164	.246	.309	58	-3	-3	4	0	0	0	.913	-1	O/1	-0.5
1965	Hou-N	24	53	5	10	1	0	0	4	5	11	.189	.259	.208	36	-5	-4	3	0	2	-1	1.000	1	/O1	-0.5
	Mil-N	4	3	0	0	0	0	0	0	1	1	.000	.250	.000	-23	-0	-0	0	0	1	-1	1.000	-0	/1	-0.1
	Yr	28	56	5	10	1	0	0	4	6	12	.179	.258	.196	32	-5	-5	2	0	3	-2	1.000	1	/O1	-0.6
1967	Atl-N	4	3	0	0	0	0	0	1	0		.000	.000	.000	-99	-1	-1	0				.000	0	H	-0.1
1968	Cin-N	31	57	10	15	2	0	2	14	4	19	.263	.311	.404	107	1	0	7	0	0	0	1.000	2	O/1	0.2
1969	Cin-N	43	60	8	15	1	0	1	8	5	13	.250	.308	.317	71	-2	-2	6	0	0	0	1.000	2	/O1	-0.3
1970	Hou-N	31	26	3	5	0	0	1	4	3	7	.192	.276	.308	59	-2	-2	2	0	1	-1	1.000	0	O	-0.2
	StL-N	44	58	8	15	2	0	1	6	8	11	.259	.348	.345	85	-1	-1	8	2	0	1	1.000	2	O/1	0.1
	Yr	75	84	11	20	2	0	2	10	11	18	.238	.326	.333	78	-3	-3	10	2	1	0	1.000	2	O/1	-0.1
1971	StL-N	77	162	24	38	8	3	2	16	9	26	.235	.279	.358	76	-5	-6	16	3	1	0	.982	-2	1/O	-1.1
1972	NY-N	58	120	10	29	1	0	5	19	7	33	.242	.289	.375	90	-2	-2	13	0	0	0	.979	-3	1/O	-0.8
1973	*NY-N	50	61	5	17	1	0	1	14	7	11	.279	.353	.328	91	-1	0	8	1	0	0	.969	-1	1/O	-0.2
Total	10	393	661	79	153	18	4	14	90	54	150	.231	.292	.334	76	-21	-22	66	6	5	-1	.980	3	1/O	-3.6
■ **GINGER BEAUMONT**				Beaumont, Clarence Howeth		b: 7/23/1876, Rochester, Wis.		d: 4/10/56, Burlington, Wis.		BL/TR, 5'8", 190 lbs.		Deb: 4/21/1899									
1899	Pit-N	111	437	90	154	15	8	3	38	41		.352	.416	.444	137	23	23	97	31			.924	6	*O/1	1.9
1900	*Pit-N	138	567	105	158	14	9	5	50	40		.279	.331	.362	90	-8	-8	81	27			.944	-12	*O	-2.8
1901	Pit-N	133	558	120	185	14	5	8	72	44		.332	.382	.418	128	23	21	107	36			.943	-5	*O	0.6
1902	Pit-N	130	541	100	193	21	6	0	67	39		**.357**	.403	.418	148	34	32	109	33			.975	0	*O	2.4
1903	*Pit-N	141	613	**137**	**209**	30	6	7	68	44		.341	.389	.444	133	29	26	119	23			.948	-7	*O	1.0
1904	Pit-N	153	615	97	**185**	12	12	3	54	34		.301	.338	.374	117	13	11	92	28			.968	-4	*O	-0.2
1905	Pit-N	103	384	60	126	12	8	3	40	22		.328	.365	.424	132	15	14	70	21			.972	0	*O	1.0
1906	Pit-N	80	310	48	82	9	3	2	32	19		.265	.311	.332	97	-0	-2	35	1			.945	-5	*O	-1.2
1907	Bos-N	150	580	67	**187**	19	14	4	62	37		.322	.366	.424	148	30	30	103	25			.962	5	*O	3.3
1908	Bos-N	125	476	66	127	20	6	2	52	42		.267	.328	.347	117	8	9	58	13			.965	-1	*O	0.4
1909	Bos-N	123	407	35	107	11	4	0	60	35		.263	.321	.310	92	-2	-4	45	12			.969	1	*O	-0.8
1910	*Chi-N	76	172	30	46	5	1	2	22	28	14	.267	.373	.343	110	3	3	24	4			.957	-4	O	-0.3
Total	12	1463	5660	955	1759	182	82	39	617	425	14	.311	.362	.393	123	168	155	939	254			.956	-26	*O/1	5.3
■ **E. P. BEAVENS**				Beavens, E. P. (a.k.a. E. P. Bevens)		b: 1848, Troy, N.Y.		TR, 5'8", 138 lbs.		Deb: 5/09/1871											
1871	Tro-n	3	15	7	6	0	0	0	5	0		.400	.400	.400	129	1	1	3	2					/2	0.0
1872	Atl-n	10	45	6	10	2	0	0	3	1	0	.222	.239	.267	47	-2	-4	3						/2SO	-0.3
Total	2 n	13	60	13	16	2	0	0	8	1		.267	.279	.300	66	-2	-3	6						/2OS	-0.3
■ **BUCK BECANNON**				Becannon, James Melvin		b: 8/22/1859, New York, N.Y.		d: 11/5/23, New York, N.Y.		5'10", 165 lbs.		Deb: 10/15/1884									
1884	*NY-a	1	3	0	0	0	0	0	0	0		.000	.000	.000	-99	-1	-1	0				1.000	0	/P	0.0
1885	NY-a	10	33	3	10	0	0	0	0	1		.303	.343	.303	118	0	1	4				.947	0	P	0.0
1887	NY-N	1	5	0	0	0	0	0	0	0	2	.000	.000	.000	-99	-1	-1	0				.667	0	/3	-0.2
Total	3	12	41	3	10	0	0	0	0	1	2	.244	.279	.244	71	-2	-1	4	0			.952	0	P3	-0.2
■ **GEORGE BECHTEL**				Bechtel, George A.		b: 1848, Philadelphia, Pa.		5'11", 165 lbs.		Deb: 5/20/1871											
1871	Ath-n	20	94	24	33	9	1	1	21	2	2	.351	.365	.500	147	5	6	19	4					O/P3	0.4

YEAR	TM/L	G	AB	R	H	2B	3B	HR	RBI	BB	SO	AVG	OBP	SLG	PRO+	BR	/A	RC	SB	CS	SBR	FA	FR	POS	TPR
1872	Mut-n	51	246	60	74	11	2	0	39	6	3	.301	.317	.362	116	3	6	31						*O/1	0.7
1873	Phi-n	53	258	53	63	12	1	1	38	9	1	.244	.270	.310	68	-9	-11	22						*O/P	-0.6
1874	Phi-n	32	151	29	44	5	4	1		2		.291	.301	.397	116	3	2	18						O/P	0.3
1875	Cen-n	14	62	12	17	5	0	0		0		.274	.274	.355	126	1	2	6						P	0.0
	Ath-n	35	164	33	46	5	2	0		1		.280	.285	.335	102	2	-1	16						O/P	0.0
	Yr	49	226	45	63	10	2	0		1		.279	.282	.341	108	3	1	22						OP	0.0
1876	Lou-N	14	55	2	10	1	0	0	2	0	1	.182	.182	.200	23	-4	-6	2				.882	-2	O	-0.7
	NY-N	2	10	2	3	0	0	0	0	0	0	.300	.300	.300	115	-0	0	1				.429	-1	/O	-0.1
	Yr	16	65	4	13	1	0	0	2	0	1	.200	.200	.215	34	-4	-5	3				.750	-3	O	-0.8
Total	5 n	205	975	211	277	47	10	3	98	20	6	.284	.298	.362	103	5	3	114						O/P31	0.8

■ CLYDE BECK

Beck, Clyde Eugene "Jersey" b: 1/6/1900, Bassett, Cal. d: 7/15/88, Temple City, Cal. BR/TR, 5'10", 176 lbs. Deb: 5/19/26

YEAR	TM/L	G	AB	R	H	2B	3B	HR	RBI	BB	SO	AVG	OBP	SLG	PRO+	BR	/A	RC	SB	CS	SBR	FA	FR	POS	TPR
1926	Chi-N	30	81	10	16	0	0	1	4	7	15	.198	.261	.235	34	-7	-8	5	0			.993	12	2	0.5
1927	Chi-N	117	391	44	101	20	5	2	44	43	37	.258	.332	.350	83	-9	-9	46	0			.969	22	23/S	1.7
1928	Chi-N	131	483	72	124	18	4	3	52	58	58	.257	.341	.329	77	-16	-15	56	3			.958	-1	3S/2	-0.6
1929	Chi-N	54	190	28	40	7	0	0	9	19	24	.211	.282	.247	32	-20	-20	14	3			.978	5	3S	-1.1
1930	Chi-N	83	244	32	52	7	0	6	34	36	32	.213	.314	.316	53	-19	-19	26	2			.953	0	S2/3	-1.1
1931	Cin-N	53	136	17	21	4	2	0	19	21	14	.154	.272	.213	34	-13	-12	10	1			.960	-2	3/S	-1.1
Total	6	468	1525	203	354	56	11	12	162	184	180	.232	.317	.307	63	-83	-82	156	9			.959	36	32S	-1.7

■ ERVE BECK

Beck, Ervin Thomas "Dutch" b: 7/19/1878, Toledo, Ohio d: 12/23/16, Toledo, Ohio BR/TR, 5'10", 168 lbs. Deb: 9/19/1899

YEAR	TM/L	G	AB	R	H	2B	3B	HR	RBI	BB	SO	AVG	OBP	SLG	PRO+	BR	/A	RC	SB	CS	SBR	FA	FR	POS	TPR
1899	Bro-N	8	24	2	4	2	0	0	2	0		.167	.167	.250	13	-3	-3	1	0			.931	-2	/2S	-0.5
1901	Cle-A	135	539	78	156	26	8	6	79	23		.289	.320	.401	103	-2	1	74	7			.927	-11	*2	-0.4
1902	Cin-N	48	187	19	57	10	3	1	20	3		.305	.323	.406	114	4	2	26	2			.936	-5	2/1O	-0.2
	Det-A	41	162	23	48	4	0	2	22	4		.296	.313	.358	84	-3	-4	20	3			.971	1	1/O	-0.3
Total	3	232	912	122	265	42	11	9	123	30		.291	.315	.390	99	-5	-4	121	12			.929	-17	2/1OS	-1.4

■ FRANK BECK

Beck, Frank J. b: 1862, Poughkeepsie, N.Y. TR , Deb: 5/02/1884

YEAR	TM/L	G	AB	R	H	2B	3B	HR	RBI	BB	SO	AVG	OBP	SLG	PRO+	BR	/A	RC	SB	CS	SBR	FA	FR	POS	TPR
1884	Pit-a	3	12	1	4	1	0	0		0		.333	.333	.417	144	1	1	2				1.000	0	/P	0.0
	Bal-U	5	20	1	2	1	0	0		0		.100	.100	.150	-15	-2	-3	0				.500	-1	/OP	-0.3
Total	1	8	32	2	6	2	0	0		0		.188	.188	.250	42	-2	-2	2				1.000	-1	/PO	-0.3

■ FRED BECK

Beck, Frederick Thomas b: 11/17/1886, Havana, Ill. d: 3/12/62, Havana, Ill. BL/TL, 6'1", 180 lbs. Deb: 4/14/09

YEAR	TM/L	G	AB	R	H	2B	3B	HR	RBI	BB	SO	AVG	OBP	SLG	PRO+	BR	/A	RC	SB	CS	SBR	FA	FR	POS	TPR
1909	Bos-N	96	334	20	66	4	6	3	27	17		.198	.245	.272	58	-16	-18	23	5			.966	4	O1	-1.8
1910	Bos-N	154	571	52	157	32	9	**10**	64	19	55	.275	.307	.415	105	3	-0	73	8			.963	2	*O1	-0.5
1911	Cin-N	41	87	7	16	1	2	2	20	1	13	.184	.193	.310	41	-8	-7	5	2			1.000	-2	O/1	-1.0
	Phi-N	66	210	26	59	8	3	3	25	17	21	.281	.346	.390	105	1	1	29	3			.957	-5	O	-0.8
	Yr	107	297	33	75	9	5	5	45	18	34	.253	.304	.367	88	-6	-6	34	5			.966	-7	O/1	-1.8
1914	Chi-F	157	555	51	155	23	4	11	77	44	66	.279	.341	.395	116	6	10	81	9			.982	-13	*1	-0.7
1915	Chi-F	121	373	35	83	9	3	5	38	24	38	.223	.277	.303	75	-14	-12	34	4			.992	-6	*1	-2.3
Total	5	635	2130	191	536	77	27	34	251	122	193	.252	.301	.361	93	-28	-26	247	31			.984	-20	1O	-7.1

■ ZINN BECK

Beck, Zinn Bertram b: 9/30/1885, Steubenville, O. d: 3/19/81, W.Palm Beach, Fla. BR/TR, 5'10.5", 160 lbs. Deb: 9/14/13

YEAR	TM/L	G	AB	R	H	2B	3B	HR	RBI	BB	SO	AVG	OBP	SLG	PRO+	BR	/A	RC	SB	CS	SBR	FA	FR	POS	TPR
1913	StL-N	10	30	4	5	1	0	0	2	4	10	.167	.265	.200	34	-2	-2	2	1			.833	0	/S3	-0.2
1914	StL-N	137	457	42	106	15	11	3	45	28	32	.232	.282	.333	84	-11	-11	45	14			.935	10	*3S	0.5
1915	StL-N	70	223	21	52	9	4	0	15	12	31	.233	.282	.309	79	-6	-6	18	3	10	-5	.935	0	3/S2	-0.9
1916	StL-N	62	184	8	41	7	1	0	10	14	21	.223	.281	.272	71	-6	-6	15	3			.910	-6	3/12	-1.2
1918	NY-A	11	8	0	0	0	0	0	1	0	1	.000	.000	.000	-98	-2	-2	-0	0			1.000	0	/13	-0.2
Total	5	290	902	75	204	32	16	3	73	58	95	.226	.279	.307	76	-28	-27	80	21	10		.932	4	3/S12	-2.0

■ HEINE BECKENDORF

Beckendorf, Henry Ward b: 6/15/1884, New York, N.Y. d: 9/15/49, Jackson Heights, N.Y. BR/TR, 5'9", 174 lbs. Deb: 4/16/09

YEAR	TM/L	G	AB	R	H	2B	3B	HR	RBI	BB	SO	AVG	OBP	SLG	PRO+	BR	/A	RC	SB	CS	SBR	FA	FR	POS	TPR
1909	Det-A	15	27	1	7	1	0	0	1	2		.259	.310	.296	88	-0	-0	3	0			.957	-0	C	0.0
1910	Det-A	3	7	0	3	0	0	0	2	1		.429	.500	.429	179	1	1	1	0			.909	-1	/C	0.0
	Was-A	37	103	8	15	1	0	0	10	5		.146	.207	.155	14	-10	-10	4	0			.991	1	C	-0.6
	Yr	40	110	8	18	1	0	0	12	6		.164	.227	.173	26	-9	-9	5	0			.988	0	C	-0.6
Total	2	55	137	9	25	2	0	0	13	8		.182	.243	.197	39	-10	-9	8	0			.983	-0	/C	-0.6

■ BEALS BECKER

Becker, David Beals b: 7/5/1886, ElDorado, Kan. d: 8/16/43, Huntington Park, Cal. BL/TL, 5'9", 170 lbs. Deb: 4/19/08

YEAR	TM/L	G	AB	R	H	2B	3B	HR	RBI	BB	SO	AVG	OBP	SLG	PRO+	BR	/A	RC	SB	CS	SBR	FA	FR	POS	TPR
1908	Pit-N	20	65	4	10	0	1	0	0	2		.154	.191	.185	20	-6	-6	2	2			1.000	-1	O	-0.8
	Bos-N	43	171	13	47	3	1	0	7	7		.275	.303	.304	96	-1	-1	17	7			.941	-4	O	-0.8
	Yr	63	236	17	57	3	2	0	7	9		.242	.272	.271	75	-7	-7	19	9			.958	-5	O	-1.6
1909	Bos-N	152	562	60	138	15	6	6	24	47		.246	.305	.326	91	-4	-7	64	21			.932	-2	*O	-1.6
1910	NY-N	80	126	18	36	2	4	3	24	14	25	.286	.357	.437	131	5	5	23	11			.972	-3	O/1	0.1
1911	*NY-N	88	172	28	45	11	1	1	20	26	22	.262	.359	.355	97	1	-0	28	19			.975	-5	O	-0.7
1912	*NY-N	125	402	66	106	18	8	6	58	54	35	.264	.354	.393	101	3	1	66	30			.958	-1	*O	-0.5
1913	Cin-N	30	108	11	32	5	3	0	14	6	12	.296	.333	.398	109	1	1	14	0			.971	2	O	0.2
	Phi-N	88	306	53	99	19	10	9	44	22	30	.324	.369	.539	151	21	19	62	11			.983	-2	O/1	1.5
	Yr	118	414	64	131	24	13	9	58	28	42	.316	.360	.502	140	22	20	75	11			.980	0	*O/1	1.7
1914	Phi-N	138	514	76	167	25	5	9	66	37	59	.325	.370	.446	133	25	21	87	16			.947	9	*O	2.6
1915	*Phi-N	112	338	38	83	16	4	11	35	26	48	.246	.301	.414	114	5	4	40	12	15	-5	.943	-8	O	-1.4
Total	8	876	2764	367	763	114	43	45	292	241	231	.276	.335	.397	112	48	37	403	129	15		.955	-13	O/1	-1.4

■ HEINZ BECKER

Becker, Heinz Reinhard "Dutch" b: 8/26/15, Berlin, Germany d: 11/11/91, Dallas, Tex. BB/TR, 6'2", 200 lbs. Deb: 4/21/43

YEAR	TM/L	G	AB	R	H	2B	3B	HR	RBI	BB	SO	AVG	OBP	SLG	PRO+	BR	/A	RC	SB	CS	SBR	FA	FR	POS	TPR
1943	Chi-N	24	69	5	10	0	0	0	2	9	6	.145	.244	.145	14	-7	-7	3	0			.983	1	1	-0.8
1945	*Chi-N	67	133	25	38	8	2	2	27	17	16	.286	.375	.421	124	4	4	22	0			1.000	-2	1	0.1
1946	Chi-N	9	7	0	2	0	0	0	1	1	1	.286	.375	.286	91	-0	-0	1	0			.000	0	H	0.0
	Cle-A	50	147	15	44	10	1	0	17	23	18	.299	.401	.381	127	5	6	25	1	0	0	.995	0	1	0.5
1947	Cle-A	2	2	0	0	0	0	0	0	0	1	.000	.000	.000	-99	-1	-1	0	0	0	0	.000	0	H	-0.1
Total	4	152	358	45	94	18	3	2	47	50	42	.263	.359	.346	102	1	3	50	1	0		.994	-0	/1	-0.3

■ JOE BECKER

Becker, Joseph Edward b: 6/25/08, St.Louis, Mo. BR/TR, 6'1", 180 lbs. Deb: 5/10/36 C

YEAR	TM/L	G	AB	R	H	2B	3B	HR	RBI	BB	SO	AVG	OBP	SLG	PRO+	BR	/A	RC	SB	CS	SBR	FA	FR	POS	TPR
1936	Cle-A	22	50	5	9	3	1	1	11	5	4	.180	.255	.340	45	-5	-5	4	0	0	0	.977	-4	C	-0.8
1937	Cle-A	18	33	3	11	2	1	0	2	3	4	.333	.405	.455	116	1	1	6	0	0	0	.949	-1	C	0.1
Total	2	40	83	8	20	5	2	1	13	8	8	.241	.315	.386	73	-4	-4	11	0	0	0	.964	-5	/C	-0.7

■ MARTY BECKER

Becker, Martin Henry b: 12/25/1893, Tiffin, Ohio d: 9/25/57, Cincinnati, Ohio BB/TL, 5'8.5", 155 lbs. Deb: 9/08/15

YEAR	TM/L	G	AB	R	H	2B	3B	HR	RBI	BB	SO	AVG	OBP	SLG	PRO+	BR	/A	RC	SB	CS	SBR	FA	FR	POS	TPR
1915	NY-N	17	52	5	13	2	0	0	3	2	9	.250	.278	.288	76	-2	-2	6	3			.917	0	O	-0.1

■ GLENN BECKERT

Beckert, Glenn Alfred b: 10/12/40, Pittsburgh, Pa. BR/TR, 6'1", 190 lbs. Deb: 4/12/65

YEAR	TM/L	G	AB	R	H	2B	3B	HR	RBI	BB	SO	AVG	OBP	SLG	PRO+	BR	/A	RC	SB	CS	SBR	FA	FR	POS	TPR
1965	Chi-N	154	614	73	147	21	3	3	30	28	52	.239	.276	.298	60	-31	-33	47	6	8	-3	.973	9	*2	-1.4
1966	Chi-N	153	656	73	188	23	7	1	59	26	36	.287	.318	.348	84	-13	-14	73	10	4	1	.970	-20	*2/S	-2.4
1967	Chi-N	146	597	91	167	32	3	5	40	30	25	.280	.314	.369	91	-5	-8	68	10	3	1	.968	4	*2	0.8
1968	Chi-N	155	643	**98**	189	28	4	4	37	31	20	.294	.328	.369	102	6	2	79	8	4	0	.977	6	*2	2.0
1969	Chi-N★	131	543	69	158	22	1	1	37	24	24	.291	.328	.341	78	-9	-17	60	6	0	2	.965	6	*2	0.2
1970	Chi-N★	143	591	99	170	15	6	3	36	32	22	.288	.324	.349	72	-17	-25	66	4	1	1	.970	10	*2/O	-0.3

YEAR	TM/L	G	AB	R	H	2B	3B	HR	RBI	BB	SO	AVG	OBP	SLG	PRO+	BR	/A	RC	SB	CS	SBR	FA	FR	POS	TPR
1971	Chi-N★	131	530	80	181	18	5	2	42	24	24	.342	.370	.406	104	13	4	76	3	2	-0	.986	-3	*2	1.3
1972	Chi-N★	120	474	51	128	22	2	3	43	23	17	.270	.307	.344	76	-10	-16	47	2	1	0	.976	11	*2	0.2
1973	Chi-N	114	372	38	95	13	0	0	29	30	15	.255	.314	.290	64	-15	-18	32	0	2	-1	.984	-12	2	-2.8
1974	SD-N	64	172	11	44	1	0	0	7	11	8	.256	.301	.262	61	-9	-8	14	0	0	0	.938	-17	2/3	-2.5
1975	SD-N	9	16	2	6	1	0	0	0	1	0	.375	.412	.438	145	1	1	3	0	0	0	1.000	-1	/3	0.0
Total	11	1320	5208	685	1473	196	31	22	360	260	243	.283	.319	.345	81	-89	-133	565	49	25	-0	.973	-7	*2/3OS	-4.9

■ JAKE BECKLEY Beckley, Jacob Peter "Eagle Eye" b: 8/4/1867, Hannibal, Mo. d: 6/25/18, Kansas City, Mo. BL/TL, 5'10", 200 lbs. Deb: 6/20/1888 H

YEAR	TM/L	G	AB	R	H	2B	3B	HR	RBI	BB	SO	AVG	OBP	SLG	PRO+	BR	/A	RC	SB	CS	SBR	FA	FR	POS	TPR
1888	Pit-N	71	283	35	97	15	3	0	27	7	22	.343	.363	.417	163	15	18	51	20			.979	-3	1	0.9
1889	Pit-N	123	522	91	157	24	10	9	97	29	29	.301	.345	.437	132	11	19	84	11			.982	2	*1/O	1.2
1890	Pit-P	121	516	109	167	38	**22**	9	120	42	32	.324	.381	.535	158	30	38	115	18			.976	-0	*1	2.5
1891	Pit-N	133	554	94	162	20	19	4	73	44	46	.292	.353	.419	130	18	20	89	13			.982	13	*1	2.3
1892	Pit-N	151	614	102	145	21	19	10	96	31	44	.236	.288	.381	103	-0	-0	78	30			.978	21	*1	1.3
1893	Pit-N	131	542	108	164	32	19	5	106	54	26	.303	.386	.459	129	20	22	105	15			.986	11	*1	2.4
1894	Pit-N	131	533	121	183	36	18	7	120	43	16	.343	.412	.518	126	21	22	127	21			.978	5	*1	2.2
1895	Pit-N	129	530	104	174	31	19	5	110	24	20	.328	.381	.487	132	18	23	110	20			.978	-7	*1	1.6
1896	Pit-N	59	217	44	55	7	5	3	32	22	28	.253	.349	.373	96	-2	-0	33	8			.982	-1	1/O2	-0.1
	NY-N	46	182	37	55	8	4	5	38	9	7	.302	.352	.473	122	4	5	35	11			.982	-1	1/O	0.4
	Yr	105	399	81	110	15	9	8	70	31	35	.276	.351	.419	108	2	4	68	19			.982	-2	*1/O2	0.3
1897	NY-N	17	68	8	17	2	3	1	11	2		.250	.301	.412	90	-2	-1	9	2			.973	2	1	0.1
	Cin-N	97	365	76	126	17	9	7	76	18		.345	.395	.499	127	17	13	83	23			.979	-3	*1	0.9
	Yr	114	433	84	143	19	12	8	87	20		.330	.380	.485	121	16	12	92	25			.978	-1	*1	1.0
1898	Cin-N	118	459	86	135	20	12	4	72	28		.294	.344	.416	110	9	4	71	6			.983	-1	*1	0.3
1899	Cin-N	134	513	87	171	27	16	3	99	40		.333	.393	.466	133	24	23	106	20			.986	5	*1	2.5
1900	Cin-N	141	558	98	190	26	10	2	94	40		.341	.389	.434	130	20	22	107	23			.980	6	*1	2.5
1901	Cin-N	140	580	78	178	36	13	3	79	28		.307	.346	.429	133	16	21	92	4			.977	-4	*1	1.5
1902	Cin-N	129	531	82	175	23	7	5	69	34		.330	.375	.427	135	28	23	94	15			.983	-3	*1/P	1.8
1903	Cin-N	120	459	85	150	29	10	2	81	42		.327	.384	.447	123	22	14	91	23			.976	4	*1	1.5
1904	StL-N	142	551	72	179	22	9	1	67	35		.325	.374	.403	147	26	29	93	17			.988	-12	*1	1.5
1905	StL-N	134	514	48	147	20	10	1	57	30		.286	.333	.370	113	5	7	70	12			.982	-8	*1	-0.5
1906	StL-N	87	320	29	79	16	6	0	44	13		.247	.283	.334	97	-4	-3	33	3			.987	-4	1	-1.1
1907	StL-N	32	115	6	24	3	0	0	7	1		.209	.222	.235	45	-8	-7	7	0			.988	-2	1	-1.2
Total	20	2386	9526	1600	2930	473	243	86	1575	616	270	.308	.361	.435	126	289	311	1684	315			.981	19	*1/OP2	24.5

■ JULIO BECQUER Becquer, Julio (Villegas) b: 12/20/31, Havana, Cuba BL/TL, 5'11.5", 178 lbs. Deb: 9/13/55

YEAR	TM/L	G	AB	R	H	2B	3B	HR	RBI	BB	SO	AVG	OBP	SLG	PRO+	BR	/A	RC	SB	CS	SBR	FA	FR	POS	TPR
1955	Was-A	10	14	1	3	0	0	0	1	0	1	.214	.214	.214	16	-2	-2	1	0	0	0	1.000	1	/1	-0.1
1957	Was-A	105	186	14	42	6	2	2	22	10	29	.226	.269	.312	59	-11	-11	13	3	3	-1	1.000	-0	1	-1.4
1958	Was-A	86	164	10	39	3	0	0	12	8	21	.238	.273	.256	47	-12	-11	10	1	2	-1	.994	6	1/O	-0.9
1959	Was-A	108	220	20	59	12	5	1	26	8	17	.268	.297	.382	85	-5	-5	22	3	2	-0	.990	2	1	-0.6
1960	Was-A	110	298	41	75	15	7	4	35	12	35	.252	.283	.389	81	-9	-9	27	1	3	-2	.989	-3	1/P	-1.9
1961	LA-A	11	8	0	0	0	0	0	0	1	5	.000	.111	.000	-61	-2	-2	0	0	0	0	1.000	0	/1	-0.2
	Min-A	57	84	13	20	1	2	5	18	2	12	.238	.256	.476	86	-2	-2	9	0	1	-1	1.000	-1	1/OP	-0.4
	Yr	68	92	13	20	1	2	5	18	3	17	.217	.242	.435	72	-4	-4	9	0	1	-1	1.000	-0	1/OP	-0.6
1963	Min-A	1	0	1	0	0	0	0	0	0	0	—	—	—	—	0	0	0	0	0	0	.000	0	H	0.0
Total	7	488	974	100	238	37	16	12	114	41	120	.244	.277	.352	70	-43	-42	82	8	11	-4	.993	5	1/OP	-5.5

■ HOWIE BEDELL Bedell, Howard William b: 9/29/35, Clearfield, Pa. BL/TR, 6'1", 185 lbs. Deb: 4/10/62 C

YEAR	TM/L	G	AB	R	H	2B	3B	HR	RBI	BB	SO	AVG	OBP	SLG	PRO+	BR	/A	RC	SB	CS	SBR	FA	FR	POS	TPR
1962	Mil-N	58	138	15	27	1	2	0	2	11	22	.196	.255	.232	33	-13	-13	9	1	0	0	.955	-3	O	-1.7
1968	Phi-N	9	7	0	1	0	0	0	1	1	0	.143	.250	.143	20	-1	-1	0	0	0	0	.000	0	H	-0.1
Total	2	67	145	15	28	1	2	0	3	12	22	.193	.255	.228	32	-14	-13	9	1	0	0	.960	-3	/O	-1.8

■ GENE BEDFORD Bedford, William Eugene b: 12/2/1896, Dallas, Tex. d: 10/6/77, San Antonio, Tex. BB/TR, 5'8", 170 lbs. Deb: 6/25/25

YEAR	TM/L	G	AB	R	H	2B	3B	HR	RBI	BB	SO	AVG	OBP	SLG	PRO+	BR	/A	RC	SB	CS	SBR	FA	FR	POS	TPR
1925	Cle-A	2	3	1	0	0	0	0	0	0	1	.000	.000	.000	-99	-1	-1	0	0	0	0	1.000	-1	/2	-0.2

■ ED BEECHER Beecher, Edward "Scrap Iron" b: 5/1876, Indiana Deb: 9/26/1897

YEAR	TM/L	G	AB	R	H	2B	3B	HR	RBI	BB	SO	AVG	OBP	SLG	PRO+	BR	/A	RC	SB	CS	SBR	FA	FR	POS	TPR
1897	StL-N	3	12	1	4	0	0	0	1	0		.333	.333	.333	78	-0	-0	2	1			1.000	-0	/O	-0.1
1898	Cle-N	8	25	1	5	2	0	0	0	0		.200	.200	.280	38	-2	-2	2	0			.846	-2	/O	-0.4
Total	2	11	37	2	9	2	0	0	1	0		.243	.243	.297	51	-3	-2	3	1			.895	-2	/O	-0.5

■ ED BEECHER Beecher, Edward H. b: 7/2/1860, Guilford, Conn. d: 9/12/35, Hartford, Conn. BL/TL, 5'10", 185 lbs. Deb: 6/28/1887

YEAR	TM/L	G	AB	R	H	2B	3B	HR	RBI	BB	SO	AVG	OBP	SLG	PRO+	BR	/A	RC	SB	CS	SBR	FA	FR	POS	TPR
1887	Pit-N	41	169	15	41	8	0	2	22	7	8	.243	.281	.325	74	-7	-5	18	8			.915	5	O	-0.1
1889	Was-N	42	179	20	53	9	0	0	30	5	4	.296	.319	.346	93	-3	-2	21	3			.861	-1	O/1	-0.4
1890	Buf-P	126	536	69	159	22	10	3	90	29	23	.297	.341	.392	106	-3	5	78	14			.810	-5	*O/P	-0.3
1891	Was-a	58	235	35	57	11	3	2	28	27	9	.243	.333	.340	100	-1	1	33	17			.824	3	O	0.2
	Phi-a	16	71	9	15	2	4	0	7	3	4	.211	.243	.352	70	-3	-3	8	7			1.000	-1	O	-0.4
	Yr	74	306	44	72	13	7	2	35	30	13	.235	.314	.343	93	-4	-3	41	24			.845	2	O	-0.2
Total	4	283	1190	148	325	52	17	7	177	71	48	.273	.322	.363	96	-18	-5	159	49			.843	1	O/1P	-1.0

■ JODIE BEELER Beeler, Joseph Sam b: 11/26/21, Dallas, Tex. BR/TR, 6', 170 lbs. Deb: 9/21/44

YEAR	TM/L	G	AB	R	H	2B	3B	HR	RBI	BB	SO	AVG	OBP	SLG	PRO+	BR	/A	RC	SB	CS	SBR	FA	FR	POS	TPR
1944	Cin-N	3	3	0	0	0	0	0	0	0	2	.000	.000	.000	-99	-1	-1	0	0			.000	-1	/23	-0.2

■ GENE BEGLEY Begley, Eugene T. b: 6/7/1861, Brooklyn, N.Y. Deb: 9/11/1886

YEAR	TM/L	G	AB	R	H	2B	3B	HR	RBI	BB	SO	AVG	OBP	SLG	PRO+	BR	/A	RC	SB	CS	SBR	FA	FR	POS	TPR
1886	NY-N	5	16	1	2	0	0	0	1	1	3	.125	.176	.125	-7	-2	-2	1	1			.864	-1	/CO	-0.2

■ JIM BEGLEY Begley, James Lawrence "Imp" b: 9/19/02, San Francisco, Cal. d: 2/20/57, San Francisco, Cal BR/TR, 5'6", 145 lbs. Deb: 5/28/24

YEAR	TM/L	G	AB	R	H	2B	3B	HR	RBI	BB	SO	AVG	OBP	SLG	PRO+	BR	/A	RC	SB	CS	SBR	FA	FR	POS	TPR
1924	Cin-N	2	5	1	1	0	0	0	0	2	0	.200	.429	.200	75	-0	-0	1	0	0	0	.933	1	/2	0.1

■ STEVE BEHEL Behel, Stephen Arnold Douglas b: 11/6/1860, Earlville, Ill. d: 2/15/45, Los Angeles, Cal. Deb: 9/27/1884

YEAR	TM/L	G	AB	R	H	2B	3B	HR	RBI	BB	SO	AVG	OBP	SLG	PRO+	BR	/A	RC	SB	CS	SBR	FA	FR	POS	TPR
1884	Mil-U	9	33	5	8	1	0	0		3		.242	.306	.273	179	0	3	3				1.000	-1	/O	0.1
1886	NY-a	59	224	32	46	5	2	0		22		.205	.279	.246	70	-8	-6	20	16			.858	-4	O	-1.0
Total	2	68	257	37	54	6	2	0		25		.210	.283	.249	78	-8	-4	23	16			.865	-5	/O	-0.9

■ OLLIE BEJMA Bejma, Alojzy Frank b: 9/12/07, South Bend, Ind. BR/TR, 5'10", 165 lbs. Deb: 4/24/34

YEAR	TM/L	G	AB	R	H	2B	3B	HR	RBI	BB	SO	AVG	OBP	SLG	PRO+	BR	/A	RC	SB	CS	SBR	FA	FR	POS	TPR
1934	StL-A	95	262	39	71	16	3	2	29	40	36	.271	.376	.378	87	-1	-4	40	3	2	-0	.952	-12	S23/O	-1.3
1935	StL-A	64	198	18	38	8	2	2	26	27	21	.192	.289	.283	46	-15	-17	18	1	0	0	.952	-4	2/S3	-1.6
1936	StL-A	67	139	19	36	2	3	2	18	27	21	.259	.380	.360	81	-3	-4	21	0	0	0	.963	-12	2/3S	-1.2
1939	Chi-A	90	307	52	77	9	3	8	44	36	27	.251	.331	.378	79	-9	-10	39	1	3	-2	.981	-14	2/S3	-2.0
Total	4	316	906	128	222	35	11	14	117	130	105	.245	.343	.354	75	-28	-35	118	5	5	-2	.967	-42	2/S3O	-6.1

■ MARK BELANGER Belanger, Mark Henry b: 6/8/44, Pittsfield, Mass. BR/TR, 6'1", 170 lbs. Deb: 8/07/65

YEAR	TM/L	G	AB	R	H	2B	3B	HR	RBI	BB	SO	AVG	OBP	SLG	PRO+	BR	/A	RC	SB	CS	SBR	FA	FR	POS	TPR
1965	Bal-A	11	3	1	1	0	0	0	0	0	0	.333	.333	.333	88	-0	-0	0	0	1	-1	1.000	3	/S	0.2
1966	Bal-A	8	19	2	3	1	0	0	0	0	3	.158	.158	.211	5	-2	-2	1	0	0	0	1.000	4	/S	0.2
1967	Bal-A	69	184	19	32	5	0	1	10	12	46	.174	.224	.217	31	-16	-16	10	6	1	1	.952	7	S2/3	-0.4
1968	Bal-A	145	472	40	98	13	0	2	21	40	114	.208	.275	.248	59	-22	-22	35	10	1	2	.969	12	*S	0.8
1969	*Bal-A	150	530	76	152	17	4	2	50	53	54	.287	.354	.345	95	-1	-2	66	14	6	1	.968	-10	*S	0.5
1970	*Bal-A	145	459	53	100	6	5	1	36	52	65	.218	.304	.259	56	-26	-26	42	13	2	3	.970	8	*S	-0.1

YEAR	TM/L	G	AB	R	H	2B	3B	HR	RBI	BB	SO	AVG	OBP	SLG	PRO+	BR	/A	RC	SB	CS	SBR	FA	FR	POS	TPR
1971	*Bal-A	150	500	67	133	19	4	0	35	73	48	.266	.367	.320	97	1	1	63	10	8	-2	.978	-0	*S	2.0
1972	Bal-A	113	285	36	53	9	1	2	16	18	53	.186	.239	.246	43	-20	-20	18	6	3	0	.975	21	*S	1.3
1973	*Bal-A	154	470	60	106	15	1	0	27	49	54	.226	.305	.262	61	-23	-22	41	13	6	0	.971	3	*S	0.0
1974	*Bal-A	155	493	54	111	14	4	5	36	51	69	.225	.300	.300	75	-16	-14	49	17	7	1	**.984**	9	*S	1.7
1975	Bal-A	152	442	44	100	11	1	3	27	36	53	.226	.286	.276	63	-23	-20	40	16	4	2	.978	**28**	*S	2.6
1976	Bal-A★	153	522	66	141	22	2	1	40	51	64	.270	.337	.326	101	-2	2	60	27	17	-2	.982	16	*S	3.6
1977	Bal-A	144	402	39	83	13	4	2	30	43	68	.206	.288	.274	58	-25	-22	34	15	8	-0	**.985**	21	*S	1.3
1978	Bal-A	135	348	39	74	13	0	0	16	40	55	.213	.305	.250	61	-18	-15	29	6	6	-2	**.985**	**34**	*S	3.1
1979	*Bal-A	101	198	28	33	6	2	0	9	29	33	.167	.276	.217	36	-18	-17	15	5	1	1	.990	3	S	-0.6
1980	Bal-A	113	268	37	61	7	3	0	22	12	25	.228	.261	.276	48	-19	-19	20	6	3	0	.975	-1	*S	-1.0
1981	Bal-A	64	139	9	23	3	2	1	10	12	25	.165	.242	.237	39	-11	-11	8	2	1	0	.973	5	S	-0.2
1982	LA-N	54	50	6	12	1	0	0	4	5	10	.240	.309	.260	62	-2	-2	4	1	0	0	.953	8	S/2	0.7
Total	18	2016	5784	676	1316	175	33	20	389	576	839	.228	.302	.280	68	-245	-229	533	167	75	5	.977	169	*S/23	15.7

■ WAYNE BELARDI Belardi, Carroll Wayne b: 9/5/30, St.Helena, Cal. BL/TL, 6'1", 185 lbs. Deb: 4/18/50

YEAR	TM/L	G	AB	R	H	2B	3B	HR	RBI	BB	SO	AVG	OBP	SLG	PRO+	BR	/A	RC	SB	CS	SBR	FA	FR	POS	TPR
1950	Bro-N	10	10	0	0	0	0	0	0	0	4	.000	.000	.000	-98	-3	-3	0	0			1.000	-0	/1	-0.3
1951	Bro-N	3	3	1	1	0	1	0	0	0	2	.333	.333	1.000	240	1	1	1	0	0	0	.000	0	H	0.1
1953	*Bro-N	69	163	19	39	3	2	11	34	16	40	.239	.311	.485	101	0	-0	26	0	0	0	.984	-0	1	-0.2
1954	Bro-N	11	9	0	2	0	0	0	1	2	3	.222	.364	.222	55	-0	-1	1	0	0	0	.000	0	H	-0.1
	Det-A	88	250	27	58	7	1	11	24	33	34	.232	.333	.400	102	-0	0	35	1	0	0	.988	2	1	-0.1
1955	Det-A	3	3	0	0	0	0	0	0	0	1	.000	.000	.000	-99	-1	-1	0	0	0	0	.000	0	H	-0.1
1956	Det-A	79	154	24	43	3	1	6	15	15	13	.279	.373	.429	111	3	3	25	0	0	0	.988	-1	1/O	0.0
Total	6	263	592	71	143	13	5	28	74	66	97	.242	.332	.422	100	-1	-1	88	1	0		.987	0	1/O	-0.7

■ KEVIN BELCHER Belcher, Kevin Donnell b: 8/8/67, Waco, Tex. BR/TR, 6', 170 lbs. Deb: 9/03/90

YEAR	TM/L	G	AB	R	H	2B	3B	HR	RBI	BB	SO	AVG	OBP	SLG	PRO+	BR	/A	RC	SB	CS	SBR	FA	FR	POS	TPR
1990	Tex-A	16	15	4	2	1	0	0	0	2	6	.133	.235	.200	23	-2	-2	1	0	0	0	1.000	-2	/O	-0.3

■ IRA BELDEN Belden, Ira Allison b: 4/16/1874, Cleveland, Ohio d: 7/15/16, Lakewood, Ohio BL/TR, 5'11", 175 lbs. Deb: 9/17/1897

YEAR	TM/L	G	AB	R	H	2B	3B	HR	RBI	BB	SO	AVG	OBP	SLG	PRO+	BR	/A	RC	SB	CS	SBR	FA	FR	POS	TPR
1897	Cle-N	8	30	5	8	0	2	0	4	2		.267	.333	.400	88	-0	-1	4	0			1.000	2	/O	0.0

■ CHARLIE BELL Bell, Charles C. b: 8/12/1868, Cincinnati, Ohio d: 2/7/37, Cincinnati, Ohio TR, Deb: 10/13/1889 F

YEAR	TM/L	G	AB	R	H	2B	3B	HR	RBI	BB	SO	AVG	OBP	SLG	PRO+	BR	/A	RC	SB	CS	SBR	FA	FR	POS	TPR
1889	KC-a	2	6	1	1	1	0	0	3	2	2	.167	.375	.333	99	0	0	1	0			.000	-0	/OP	-0.1
1891	Lou-a	10	28	3	1	0	0	0	0	6	8	.036	.206	.036	-29	-4	-4	0	0			.783	-2	P	0.0
	Cin-a	1	4	1	2	0	0	0	1	0	0	.500	.500	.500	175	0	0	1	0			1.000	0	/P	0.0
	Yr	11	32	4	3	0	0	0	1	6	8	.094	.237	.094	-3	-4	-4	1	0			.815	-1	P	0.0
Total	2	13	38	5	4	1	0	0	4	8	10	.105	.261	.132	15	-4	-4	2	0			.844	-1	/PO	-0.1

■ BUDDY BELL Bell, David Gus b: 8/27/51, Pittsburgh, Pa. BR/TR, 6'2", 185 lbs. Deb: 4/15/72 F

YEAR	TM/L	G	AB	R	H	2B	3B	HR	RBI	BB	SO	AVG	OBP	SLG	PRO+	BR	/A	RC	SB	CS	SBR	FA	FR	POS	TPR
1972	Cle-A	132	466	49	119	21	1	9	36	34	29	.255	.310	.363	96	-1	-2	52	5	6	-2	.990	7	*O/3	-0.3
1973	Cle-A★	156	631	86	169	23	7	14	59	49	47	.268	.327	.393	100	1	-1	76	7	15	-7	.958	24	*3/O	1.6
1974	Cle-A	116	423	51	111	15	1	7	46	35	29	.262	.323	.352	95	-3	-3	46	1	3	-2	.963	4	*3/D	-0.1
1975	Cle-A	153	553	66	150	20	4	10	59	51	72	.271	.334	.376	100	0	0	69	6	5	-1	.950	-3	*3	-0.5
1976	Cle-A	159	604	75	170	26	2	7	60	44	49	.281	.332	.366	105	3	4	71	3	8	-4	.956	5	*3/1	0.4
1977	Cle-A	129	479	64	140	23	4	11	64	45	63	.292	.354	.426	115	8	10	68	1	8	-5	.960	13	*3O	1.6
1978	Cle-A	142	556	71	157	27	8	6	62	39	43	.282	.329	.392	103	1	2	65	1	3	-2	.970	28	*3/D	2.7
1979	Tex-A	162	670	89	200	42	3	18	101	30	45	.299	.331	.451	110	6	7	95	5	4	-1	.969	12	*3S	2.0
1980	Tex-A★	129	490	76	161	24	4	17	83	40	39	.329	.379	.498	143	25	27	88	3	1	0	**.981**	22	*3/S	4.6
1981	Tex-A★	97	360	44	106	16	1	10	64	42	30	.294	.373	.428	137	15	17	58	3	3	-1	.961	**30**	3/S	4.5
1982	Tex-A★	148	537	62	159	27	2	13	67	70	50	.296	.379	.426	127	17	21	87	5	4	-1	**.976**	**34**	*3/S	5.0
1983	Tex-A	156	618	75	171	35	3	14	66	50	48	.277	.335	.411	106	3	5	78	3	5	-2	.967	16	*3	1.6
1984	Tex-A★	148	553	88	174	36	5	11	83	63	54	.315	.388	.458	129	26	24	95	2	1	0	.958	21	*3	4.2
1985	Tex-A	84	313	33	74	13	3	4	32	33	21	.236	.311	.335	76	-10	-10	31	3	2	-0	.942	13	3	0.1
	Cin-N	67	247	28	54	15	2	6	36	34	27	.219	.313	.368	86	-3	-5	27	0	1	-1	.946	-9	3	-1.6
1986	Cin-N	155	568	89	158	29	3	20	75	73	49	.278	.365	.445	117	18	15	91	2	8	-4	.975	1	*3/2	0.9
1987	Cin-N	143	522	74	148	19	2	17	70	71	39	.284	.370	.425	105	9	6	84	4	1	1	**.979**	-17	*3	-1.2
1988	Cin-N	21	54	3	10	0	0	0	3	7	3	.185	.279	.185	34	-4	-5	3	0	0	0	.968	0	3/1	-0.5
	Hou-N	74	269	24	68	10	1	7	37	19	29	.253	.302	.375	97	-3	-2	29	1	1	-0	.924	-11	3/1	-1.5
	Yr	95	323	27	78	10	1	7	40	26	32	.241	.298	.344	86	-7	-6	32	1	1	-0	.931	-11	3/1	-2.0
1989	Tex-A	34	82	4	15	4	0	0	3	7	10	.183	.247	.232	35	-7	-7	4	0	0	0	1.000	1	D/31	-0.6
Total	18	2405	8995	1151	2514	425	56	201	1106	836	776	.279	.343	.406	108	102	103	1218	55	79	-31	.964	191	*3O/SD12	22.9

■ GUS BELL Bell, David Russell b: 11/15/28, Louisville, Ky. BL/TR, 6'2", 196 lbs. Deb: 5/30/50 F

YEAR	TM/L	G	AB	R	H	2B	3B	HR	RBI	BB	SO	AVG	OBP	SLG	PRO+	BR	/A	RC	SB	CS	SBR	FA	FR	POS	TPR
1950	Pit-N	111	422	62	119	22	11	8	53	28	46	.282	.333	.443	99	0	-2	63	4			.977	6	*O	0.0
1951	Pit-N	149	600	80	167	27	**12**	16	89	42	41	.278	.330	.443	103	3	1	88	1	4	-2	.986	3	*O	-0.3
1952	Pit-N	131	468	53	117	21	5	16	59	36	72	.250	.306	.419	97	-2	-4	61	1	4	-2	.972	-7	*O	-1.9
1953	Cin-N★	151	610	102	183	37	5	30	105	48	72	.300	.354	.525	124	21	20	113	0	2	-1	.977	14	*O	2.6
1954	Cin-N★	153	619	104	185	38	7	17	101	48	58	.299	.353	.465	108	9	7	100	5	3	-0	.986	2	*O	0.2
1955	Cin-N	154	610	88	188	30	6	27	104	54	57	.308	.364	.510	122	24	20	114	4	4	-1	.987	-8	*O	0.3
1956	Cin-N★	150	603	82	176	31	4	29	84	50	66	.292	.349	.501	117	20	15	105	6	2	1	.986	-7	*O	0.1
1957	Cin-N★	121	510	65	149	20	3	13	61	30	54	.292	.335	.420	95	0	-4	70	0	1	-1	.988	0	*O	-1.2
1958	Cin-N	112	385	42	97	16	2	10	46	36	40	.252	.318	.382	80	-9	-12	46	2	3	-1	**.996**	-2	*O	-2.1
1959	Cin-N	148	580	59	170	27	2	19	115	29	44	.293	.329	.445	101	2	-0	81	2	3	-1	**.996**	7	*O	-0.2
1960	Cin-N	143	515	65	135	19	5	12	62	29	40	.262	.303	.388	86	-10	-11	60	4	3	-1	.988	0	*O	-1.8
1961	*Cin-N	103	235	27	60	10	1	3	33	18	21	.255	.308	.345	72	-9	-9	25	1	1	-0	.991	-3	O	-1.6
1962	NY-N	30	101	8	15	2	0	1	6	10	7	.149	.225	.198	14	-12	-12	5	0	1	-1	.979	2	O	-1.3
	Mil-N	79	214	28	61	11	3	5	24	12	17	.285	.323	.435	104	-0	1	30	0	0	0	.987	-5	O	-0.7
	Yr	109	315	36	76	13	3	6	30	22	24	.241	.291	.359	74	-12	-12	33	0	1	-1	.984	-3	O	-2.0
1963	Mil-N	3	3	0	1	0	0	0	0	0	0	.333	.333	.333	94	0	-0	0	0	0	0	.000	0	H	0.0
1964	Mil-N	3	3	0	0	0	0	0	0	0	1	.000	.000	.000	-99	-1	-1	0	0	0	0	.000	0	H	-0.1
Total	15	1741	6478	865	1823	311	66	206	942	470	636	.281	.333	.445	102	37	9	962	30	31		.985	2	*O	-8.0

■ DEREK BELL Bell, Derek Nathaniel b: 12/11/68, Tampa, Fla. BR/TR, 6'2", 200 lbs. Deb: 6/28/91

YEAR	TM/L	G	AB	R	H	2B	3B	HR	RBI	BB	SO	AVG	OBP	SLG	PRO+	BR	/A	RC	SB	CS	SBR	FA	FR	POS	TPR
1991	Tor-A	18	28	5	4	0	0	0	1	6	5	.143	.314	.143	30	-2	-2	2	3	2	-0	.889	-3	O	-0.6
1992	*Tor-A	61	161	23	39	6	3	2	15	15	34	.242	.326	.354	86	-2	-3	19	7	2	1	1.000	-1	O/D	-0.4
Total	2	79	189	28	43	6	3	2	16	21	39	.228	.324	.323	78	-4	-5	21	10	4	1	.984	-4	/OD	-1.0

■ FERN BELL Bell, Fern Lee "Danny" b: 1/21/13, Ada, Okla. BR/TR, 6', 180 lbs. Deb: 4/17/39

YEAR	TM/L	G	AB	R	H	2B	3B	HR	RBI	BB	SO	AVG	OBP	SLG	PRO+	BR	/A	RC	SB	CS	SBR	FA	FR	POS	TPR
1939	Pit-N	83	262	44	75	5	8	2	34	42	18	.286	.385	.389	110	5	5	42	2			.975	0	O/3	0.3
1940	Pit-N	6	3	0	0	0	0	0	1	1	1	.000	.250	.000	-26	-0	-0	0	0			.000	0	H	0.0
Total	2	89	265	44	75	5	8	2	35	43	19	.283	.383	.385	109	4	5	42	2				0	/O3	0.3

■ FRANK BELL Bell, Frank Gustav b: 1863, Cincinnati, Ohio d: 4/14/1891, Cincinnati, Ohio Deb: 7/07/1885 F

YEAR	TM/L	G	AB	R	H	2B	3B	HR	RBI	BB	SO	AVG	OBP	SLG	PRO+	BR	/A	RC	SB	CS	SBR	FA	FR	POS	TPR
1885	Bro-a	10	29	5	5	0	1	0		0		.172	.200	.241	40	-2	-2	1				.739	-2	/CO3	-0.3

■ **JAY BELL** Bell, Jay Stuart b: 12/11/65, Eglin A.F.B., Fla. BR/TR, 6'1", 180 lbs. Deb: 9/29/86

YEAR	TM/L	G	AB	R	H	2B	3B	HR	RBI	BB	SO	AVG	OBP	SLG	PRO+	BR	/A	RC	SB	CS	SBR	FA	FR	POS	TPR
1986	Cle-A	5	14	3	5	2	0	1	4	2	3	.357	.438	.714	211	2	2	5	0	0	0	.778	-0	/2D	0.2
1987	Cle-A	38	125	14	27	9	1	2	13	8	31	.216	.269	.352	62	-7	-7	13	2	0	1	.947	3	S	-0.1
1988	Cle-A	73	211	23	46	5	1	2	21	21	53	.218	.292	.280	59	-11	-11	18	4	2	0	.965	-13	S/D	-1.9
1989	Pit-N	78	271	33	70	13	3	2	27	19	47	.258	.309	.351	91	-4	-3	28	5	3	-0	.968	-15	S	-1.3
1990	*Pit-N	159	583	93	148	28	7	7	52	65	109	.254	.332	.362	94	-7	-4	72	10	6	-1	.970	-3	*S	0.6
1991	*Pit-N	157	608	96	164	32	8	16	67	52	99	.270	.331	.428	114	9	10	85	10	6	-1	.968	8	*S	3.0
1992	*Pit-N	159	632	87	167	36	6	9	55	55	103	.264	.327	.383	102	0	1	80	7	5	-1	.973	17	*S	3.1
Total	7	669	2444	349	627	125	26	39	239	222	445	.257	.322	.377	96	-18	-12	301	38	22	-2	.968	-3	S/D2	3.6

■ **RUDY BELL** Bell, John (b: Rudolph Fred Baerwald) b: 1/1/1881, Wausau, Wis. d: 7/28/55, Albuquerque, N.M. BR/TR, 5'8.5", 158 lbs. Deb: 9/16/07

YEAR	TM/L	G	AB	R	H	2B	3B	HR	RBI	BB	SO	AVG	OBP	SLG	PRO+	BR	/A	RC	SB	CS	SBR	FA	FR	POS	TPR
1907	NY-A	17	52	4	11	2	1	0	3	3		.212	.268	.288	72	-1	-2	6	4			.897	-1	O	-0.4

■ **GEORGE BELL** Bell, Jorge (Mathey) b: 10/21/59, San Pedro De Macoris, D.R. BR/TR, 6'1", 190 lbs. Deb: 4/09/81 F

YEAR	TM/L	G	AB	R	H	2B	3B	HR	RBI	BB	SO	AVG	OBP	SLG	PRO+	BR	/A	RC	SB	CS	SBR	FA	FR	POS	TPR
1981	Tor-A	60	163	19	38	2	1	5	12	5	27	.233	.256	.350	69	-6	-7	14	3	2	-0	.969	1	O/D	-0.8
1983	Tor-A	39	112	5	30	5	4	2	17	4	17	.268	.305	.438	96	-0	-1	13	1	1	-0	.954	-2	O/D	-0.4
1984	Tor-A	159	606	85	177	39	4	26	87	24	86	.292	.328	.498	121	18	15	95	11	2	2	.971	-1	*O/3D	1.2
1985	*Tor-A	157	607	87	167	28	6	28	95	43	90	.275	.331	.479	116	14	12	97	21	6	3	.968	8	*O/3	1.8
1986	Tor-A	159	641	101	198	38	6	31	108	41	62	.309	.352	.532	133	30	28	113	7	8	-3	.966	7	*OD/3	2.6
1987	Tor-A★	156	610	111	188	32	4	47	**134**	39	75	.308	.357	.605	146	40	38	125	5	1	1	.960	0	*O/23D	3.2
1988	Tor-A	156	614	78	165	27	5	24	97	34	66	.269	.308	.446	108	5	4	78	4	2	0	.946	-7	*O/D	-0.8
1989	*Tor-A	153	613	88	182	41	2	18	104	33	60	.297	.337	.458	124	16	17	89	4	3	-1	.963	-4	*OD	0.9
1990	Tor-A★	142	562	67	149	25	0	21	86	32	80	.265	.308	.422	100	-0	-1	70	3	2	-0	.979	4	*OD	0.0
1991	Chi-N★	149	558	63	159	27	0	25	86	32	62	.285	.328	.468	116	14	11	81	2	6	-3	.962	-5	*O	0.0
1992	Chi-A	155	627	74	160	27	0	25	112	31	97	.255	.297	.418	101	-4	-2	68	5	2	0	.964	-2	*DO	-0.4
Total	11	1485	5713	778	1613	291	32	252	938	318	722	.282	.325	.477	117	125	114	845	66	35	-1	.964	-0	*OD/32	7.3

■ **JUAN BELL** Bell, Juan (Mathey) b: 3/29/68, San Pedro De Macoris, D.R. BR/TR, 5'11", 172 lbs. Deb: 9/06/89 F

YEAR	TM/L	G	AB	R	H	2B	3B	HR	RBI	BB	SO	AVG	OBP	SLG	PRO+	BR	/A	RC	SB	CS	SBR	FA	FR	POS	TPR
1989	Bal-A	8	4	2	0	0	0	0	0	0	1	.000	.000	.000	-99	-1	-1	0	1	0	0	1.000	2	/2SD	0.1
1990	Bal-A	5	2	1	0	0	0	0	0	0	1	.000	.000	.000	-99	-1	-1	0	0	0	0	1.000	1	/SD	0.0
1991	Bal-A	100	209	26	36	9	2	1	15	8	51	.172	.203	.249	25	-22	-21	11	0	0	0	.973	-1	2S/OD	-2.1
1992	Phi-N	46	147	12	30	3	1	1	8	18	29	.204	.295	.259	58	-8	-8	13	5	0	2	.972	4	S	0.1
Total	4	159	362	41	66	12	3	2	23	26	82	.182	.239	.249	37	-31	-30	24	6	0	2	.974	5	/2SDO	-1.9

■ **KEVIN BELL** Bell, Kevin Robert b: 7/13/55, Los Angeles, Cal. BR/TR, 6', 195 lbs. Deb: 6/16/76

YEAR	TM/L	G	AB	R	H	2B	3B	HR	RBI	BB	SO	AVG	OBP	SLG	PRO+	BR	/A	RC	SB	CS	SBR	FA	FR	POS	TPR
1976	Chi-A	68	230	24	57	7	6	5	20	18	56	.248	.305	.396	104	1	0	28	2	1	0	.970	3	3/D	0.3
1977	Chi-A	9	28	4	5	1	0	1	6	3	8	.179	.258	.321	57	-2	-2	3	0	0	0	.909	0	/S3O	-0.1
1978	Chi-A	54	68	9	13	0	0	2	5	5	19	.191	.257	.279	50	-4	-5	5	1	0	0	.946	11	3/D	0.7
1979	Chi-A	70	200	20	49	8	1	4	22	15	43	.245	.298	.355	75	-7	-7	20	2	4	-2	.923	12	3/S	0.3
1980	Chi-A	92	191	16	34	5	2	1	11	29	37	.178	.286	.241	46	-14	-14	15	0	0	0	.925	7	3/SD	-0.8
1982	Oak-A	4	9	1	3	1	0	0	0	0	2	.333	.333	.444	117	0	0	1	0	0	0	.857	0	/3D	0.0
Total	6	297	726	74	161	22	9	13	64	70	165	.222	.292	.331	73	-26	-26	72	5	5	-2	.940	33	3/SDO	0.4

■ **LES BELL** Bell, Lester Rowland b: 12/14/01, Harrisburg, Pa. d: 12/26/85, Hershey, Pa. BR/TR, 5'11", 165 lbs. Deb: 9/18/23

YEAR	TM/L	G	AB	R	H	2B	3B	HR	RBI	BB	SO	AVG	OBP	SLG	PRO+	BR	/A	RC	SB	CS	SBR	FA	FR	POS	TPR
1923	StL-N	15	51	5	19	2	1	0	9	9	7	.373	.467	.451	146	4	4	12	1	0	0	.917	-1	S	0.4
1924	StL-N	17	57	5	14	3	2	1	5	3	7	.246	.295	.421	91	-1	-1	7	0	0	0	.905	-4	S	-0.3
1925	StL-N	153	586	80	167	29	9	11	88	43	47	.285	.334	.422	89	-8	-10	82	4	5	-2	.924	-1	*3/S	-0.2
1926	*StL-N	155	581	85	189	33	14	17	100	54	62	.325	.383	.518	135	32	29	112	9			.950	-22	*3	1.6
1927	StL-N	115	390	48	101	26	6	9	65	34	63	.259	.320	.426	95	-2	-4	52	5			.904	-14	*3S	-1.3
1928	Bos-N	153	591	58	164	36	7	10	91	40	45	.277	.323	.413	96	-9	-5	77	1			.948	5	*3	0.8
1929	Bos-N	139	483	58	144	23	5	9	72	50	42	.298	.364	.422	98	-4	-1	74	4			.953	-20	*3/2S	-1.5
1930	Chi-N	74	248	35	69	15	4	5	47	24	27	.278	.342	.431	85	-6	-6	36	1			.948	-0	3/1	-0.3
1931	Chi-N	75	252	30	71	17	1	4	32	19	22	.282	.332	.405	95	-1	-2	35	0			.944	4	3	0.6
Total	9	896	3239	404	938	184	49	66	509	276	322	.290	.346	.438	102	3	3	486	25	5		.939	-53	3/S12	-0.2

■ **MIKE BELL** Bell, Michael Allen b: 4/22/68, Lewiston, N.J. BL/TL, 6'1", 175 lbs. Deb: 5/02/90

YEAR	TM/L	G	AB	R	H	2B	3B	HR	RBI	BB	SO	AVG	OBP	SLG	PRO+	BR	/A	RC	SB	CS	SBR	FA	FR	POS	TPR
1990	Atl-N	36	45	8	11	5	1	1	5	2	9	.244	.292	.467	99	0	-0	4	0	1	-1	.981	1	1	-0.1
1991	Atl-N	17	30	4	4	0	0	1	1	2	7	.133	.188	.233	17	-3	-4	1	1	0	0	.975	-0	1	-0.4
Total	2	53	75	12	15	5	1	2	6	4	16	.200	.250	.373	67	-3	-4	5	1	1	-0	.979	1	/1	-0.5

■ **BEAU BELL** Bell, Roy Chester b: 8/20/07, Bellville, Tex. d: 9/14/77, College Station, Tex. BR/TR, 6'2", 185 lbs. Deb: 4/16/35

YEAR	TM/L	G	AB	R	H	2B	3B	HR	RBI	BB	SO	AVG	OBP	SLG	PRO+	BR	/A	RC	SB	CS	SBR	FA	FR	POS	TPR
1935	StL-A	76	220	20	55	8	2	3	17	16	16	.250	.304	.345	65	-11	-12	23	1	1	-0	.918	-5	O1/3	-2.0
1936	StL-A	155	616	100	212	40	12	11	123	60	55	.344	.403	.502	119	21	18	126	4	1	1	.974	-2	*O1	0.8
1937	StL-A☆	156	642	82	**218**	**51**	8	14	117	53	54	.340	.391	.509	124	23	23	127	2	2	-1	.984	3	*O1/3	1.6
1938	StL-A	147	526	91	138	35	3	13	84	71	46	.262	.350	.414	91	-8	-8	79	1	3	-2	.979	4	*O/1	-0.9
1939	StL-A	11	32	4	7	1	0	1	5	4	3	.219	.324	.344	69	-1	-2	4	0	0	0	1.000	-0	/O	-0.2
	Det-A	54	134	14	32	4	2	0	24	24	16	.239	.358	.299	65	-5	-7	15	0	1	-1	1.000	1	O	-0.7
	Yr	65	166	18	39	5	2	1	29	28	19	.235	.352	.307	66	-7	-8	19	0	1	-1	1.000	1	O	-0.9
1940	Cle-A	120	444	55	124	22	2	4	58	34	41	.279	.332	.365	83	-13	-11	55	2	2	-1	.971	-2	O1	-1.9
1941	Cle-A	48	104	12	20	4	3	0	9	10	8	.192	.270	.288	50	-8	-7	8	1	2	-1	1.000	-3	O1	-1.3
Total	7	767	2718	378	806	165	32	46	437	272	239	.297	.362	.432	99	-2	-6	437	11	12	-4	.976	-5	O/13	-4.6

■ **TERRY BELL** Bell, Terence William b: 10/27/62, Dayton, Ohio BR/TR, 6', 195 lbs. Deb: 9/03/86

YEAR	TM/L	G	AB	R	H	2B	3B	HR	RBI	BB	SO	AVG	OBP	SLG	PRO+	BR	/A	RC	SB	CS	SBR	FA	FR	POS	TPR
1986	KC-A	8	3	0	0	0	0	0	0	2	1	.000	.400	.000	20	-0	-0	0	0	0	0	1.000	-0	/C	0.0
1987	Atl-N	1	1	0	0	0	0	0	0	0	1	.000	.000	.000	-95	-0	-0	0	0	0	0	.000	0	/H	0.0
Total	2	9	4	0	0	0	0	0	0	2	2	.000	.333	.000	-0	-0	-0	0	0	0	0		-0	/C	0.0

■ **ZEKE BELLA** Bella, John b: 8/23/30, Greenwich, Conn. BR/TL, 5'11", 185 lbs. Deb: 9/11/57

YEAR	TM/L	G	AB	R	H	2B	3B	HR	RBI	BB	SO	AVG	OBP	SLG	PRO+	BR	/A	RC	SB	CS	SBR	FA	FR	POS	TPR
1957	NY-A	5	10	0	1	0	0	0	0	1	2	.100	.182	.100	-21	-2	-2	0	0	0	0	1.000	1	/O	-0.1
1959	KC-A	47	82	10	17	2	1	1	9	9	14	.207	.293	.293	60	-4	-4	6	0	0	0	1.000	-3	O/1	-0.9
Total	2	52	92	10	18	2	1	1	9	10	16	.196	.282	.272	52	-6	-6	7	0	0	0	1.000	-3	/O1	-1.0

■ **STEVE BELLAN** Bellan, Esteban Enrique b: 1850, Cuba d: 8/8/32, Havana, Cuba 5'6", 154 lbs. Deb: 5/09/1871

YEAR	TM/L	G	AB	R	H	2B	3B	HR	RBI	BB	SO	AVG	OBP	SLG	PRO+	BR	/A	RC	SB	CS	SBR	FA	FR	POS	TPR
1871	Tro-n	29	128	26	32	3	3	0	23	9	2	.250	.299	.320	77	-3	-4	14	4					*3/S	-0.4
1872	Tro-n	23	118	22	30	4	1	0	16	0	0	.254	.254	.305	70	-4	-4	10						/S3O	-0.3
1873	Mut-n	8	32	4	7	2	0	0	3	2	0	.219	.265	.281	61	-1	-1	2						/32	-0.1
Total	3 n	60	278	52	69	9	4	0	42	11	2	.248	.277	.309	73	-9	-9	26						/3SO2	-0.8

■ **ALBERT BELLE** Belle, Albert Jojuan "Joey" b: 8/25/66, Shreveport, La. BR/TR, 6'1", 190 lbs. Deb: 7/15/89

YEAR	TM/L	G	AB	R	H	2B	3B	HR	RBI	BB	SO	AVG	OBP	SLG	PRO+	BR	/A	RC	SB	CS	SBR	FA	FR	POS	TPR
1989	Cle-A	62	218	22	49	8	4	7	37	12	55	.225	.272	.394	84	-5	-5	22	2	2	-1	.979	1	OD	-0.7
1990	Cle-A	9	23	1	4	0	0	1	3	1	6	.174	.208	.304	42	-2	-2	1	0	0	0	.000	-0	/OD	-0.2
1991	Cle-A	123	461	60	130	31	2	28	95	25	99	.282	.326	.540	134	19	19	71	3	1	0	.952	3	OD	2.0
1992	Cle-A	153	585	81	152	23	1	34	112	52	128	.260	.324	.477	121	15	14	87	8	2	1	.969	-4	*DO	1.0
Total	4	347	1287	164	335	62	7	70	247	90	288	.260	.314	.483	118	27	25	182	13	5	1	.963	-0	OD	2.1

YEAR	TM/L	G	AB	R	H	2B	3B	HR	RBI	BB	SO	AVG	OBP	SLG	PRO+	BR	/A	RC	SB	CS	SBR	FA	FR	POS	TPR
■ RAFAEL BELLIARD	Belliard, Rafael Leonidas (Matias) b: 10/24/61, Pueblo Nuevo, D.R. BR/TR, 5'6", 160 lbs. Deb: 9/06/82																								
1982	Pit-N	9	2	3	1	0	0	0	0	0	0	.500	.500	.500	175	0	0	1	1	0	0	1.000	3	/S	0.3
1983	Pit-N	4	1	1	0	0	0	0	0	0	1	.000	.000	.000	-98	-0	-0	0	0	0	0	1.000	1	/S	0.1
1984	Pit-N	20	22	3	5	0	0	0	0	0	1	.227	.227	.227	28	-2	-2	1	4	1	1	.889	1	S/2	0.0
1985	Pit-N	17	20	1	4	0	0	0	1	0	5	.200	.200	.200	12	-2	-2	1	0	0	0	.947	6	S	0.4
1986	Pit-N	117	309	33	72	5	2	0	31	26	54	.233	.299	.262	55	-18	-19	26	12	2	2	.970	13	S2	0.4
1987	Pit-N	81	203	26	42	4	3	1	15	20	25	.207	.288	.271	49	-15	-15	17	5	1	1	.979	6	S/2	-0.3
1988	Pit-N	122	286	28	61	0	4	0	11	26	47	.213	.288	.241	54	-16	-16	21	7	1	2	**.977**	-12	*S/2	-2.0
1989	Pit-N	67	154	10	33	4	0	0	8	8	22	.214	.253	.240	43	-12	-11	10	5	2	0	.978	7	S2/3	-0.1
1990	Pit-N	47	54	10	11	3	0	0	6	5	13	.204	.283	.259	52	-4	-3	4	1	2	-1	1.000	5	2S/3	0.1
1991	*Atl-N	149	353	36	88	9	2	0	27	22	63	.249	.297	.286	61	-16	-19	31	3	1	0	.967	26	*S	1.6
1992	*Atl-N	144	285	20	60	6	1	0	14	14	43	.211	.255	.239	37	-22	-25	17	0	1	-1	.969	**27**	*S/2	0.8
Total	11	777	1689	171	377	31	12	1	113	121	274	.223	.281	.258	50	-107	-112	128	38	11	5	.970	82	S/23	1.3
■ JACK BELLMAN	Bellman, John Hutchins "Happy Jack" b: 3/4/1864, Taylorsville, Ky. d: 12/8/31, Louisville, Ky. Deb: 4/23/1889																								
1889	StL-a	1	2	1	1	0	0	0	0	1	0	.500	.667	.500	211	1	0	1	0			1.000	-0	/C	0.0
■ ROB BELLOIR	Belloir, Robert Edward b: 7/13/48, Heidelberg, Ger. BR/TR, 5'10", 155 lbs. Deb: 8/02/75																								
1975	Atl-N	43	105	11	23	2	1	0	9	7	8	.219	.268	.257	45	-8	-8	7	0	0	0	.922	-2	S/2	-0.7
1976	Atl-N	30	60	5	12	2	0	0	4	5	7	.200	.262	.233	39	-5	-5	4	0	0	0	.929	-1	S3/2	-0.6
1977	Atl-N	6	1	2	0	0	0	0	0	0	0	.000	.000	.000	-89	-0	-0	0	0	0	0	1.000	2	/S	0.2
1978	Atl-N	2	1	0	1	1	0	0	0	0	0	1.000	1.000	2.000	647	1	1	2	0	0	0	1.000	-0	/S3	0.1
Total	4	81	167	18	36	5	1	0	13	12	15	.216	.268	.257	45	-12	-13	13	0	0	0	.924	-2	/S32	-1.0
■ ESTEBAN BELTRE	Beltre, Esteban (Valera) b: 12/26/67, Ingenio Quisqueya, D.R. BR/TR, 5'10", 155 lbs. Deb: 9/03/91																								
1991	Chi-A	8	6	0	1	0	0	0	0	1	1	.167	.286	.167	29	-1	-1	1	1	0	0	1.000	-1	/S	-0.1
1992	Chi-A	49	110	21	21	2	0	1	10	3	18	.191	.212	.236	26	-11	-11	5	1	0	0	.924	-1	S/D	-0.9
Total	2	57	116	21	22	2	0	1	10	4	19	.190	.217	.233	26	-12	-11	6	2	0	1	.926	-1	/SD	-1.0
■ HARRY BEMIS	Bemis, Harry Parker b: 2/1/1874, Farmington, N.H. d: 5/23/47, Cleveland, Ohio BR/TR, 5'6.5", 155 lbs. Deb: 4/23/02																								
1902	Cle-A	93	317	42	99	12	7	1	29	19		.312	.366	.404	118	6	8	50	3			.964	7	C/O2	2.2
1903	Cle-A	92	314	31	82	20	3	1	41	8		.261	.295	.354	96	-3	-2	35	5			**.988**	-7	C1/2	-0.2
1904	Cle-A	97	336	35	76	11	6	0	25	8		.226	.259	.295	76	-10	-10	29	6			.958	-3	C1/2	-0.4
1905	Cle-A	70	226	27	66	13	3	0	28	13		.292	.344	.376	127	7	7	32	3			.972	-5	C/231	0.9
1906	Cle-A	93	297	28	82	13	5	2	30	12		.276	.311	.374	116	4	4	39	8			.963	-9	C	0.3
1907	Cle-A	65	172	12	43	7	0	0	19	7		.250	.283	.291	83	-3	-4	17	5			.957	-7	C/1	-0.8
1908	Cle-A	91	277	23	62	9	1	0	33	7		.224	.253	.264	68	-10	-10	22	14			.964	-6	C/1	-1.1
1909	Cle-A	42	123	4	23	2	3	0	13	0		.187	.194	.252	39	-9	-9	6	2			.971	-0	C	-0.8
1910	Cle-A	61	167	12	36	5	1	1	16	5		.216	.238	.275	60	-8	-8	12	3			.961	-4	C	-0.9
Total	9	704	2229	214	569	92	29	5	234	79		.255	.292	.329	92	-26	-24	242	49			.966	-36	C/123O	-0.8
■ FREDDIE BENAVIDES	Benavides, Alfredo b: 4/7/66, Laredo, Tex. BR/TR, 6'2", 180 lbs. Deb: 5/14/91																								
1991	Cin-N	24	63	11	18	1	0	0	3	1	15	.286	.308	.302	69	-2	-3	6	1	0	0	.974	3	S/2	0.2
1992	Cin-N	74	173	14	40	10	1	1	17	10	34	.231	.277	.318	65	-7	-8	15	0	1	-1	1.000	4	2S/3	-0.3
Total	2	98	236	25	58	11	1	1	20	11	49	.246	.285	.314	66	-10	-11	21	1	1	-0	.957	7	/S23	-0.1
■ JOHNNY BENCH	Bench, Johnny Lee b: 12/7/47, Oklahoma City, Okla. BR/TR, 6'1", 208 lbs. Deb: 8/28/67 H																								
1967	Cin-N	26	86	7	14	3	1	1	6	5	19	.163	.209	.256	29	-8	-9	4	0	1	-1	.995	5	C	-0.3
1968	Cin-N★	154	564	67	155	40	2	15	82	31	96	.275	.315	.433	115	14	10	71	1	5	-3	.991	6	*C	2.7
1969	Cin-N★	148	532	83	156	23	1	26	90	49	86	.293	.357	.487	128	23	20	92	6	6	-2	.992	-3	*C	2.4
1970	*Cin-N★	158	605	97	177	35	4	**45**	**148**	54	102	.293	.351	.587	146	36	35	121	5	2	0	.986	7	*CO1/3	4.8
1971	Cin-N★	149	562	80	134	19	2	27	61	49	83	.238	.300	.423	105	-0	1	66	2	1	0	.988	-1	*C1O/3	0.5
1972	*Cin-N★	147	538	87	145	22	2	**40**	**125**	100	84	.270	.386	.541	**171**	44	48	110	6	6	-2	.993	-4	*CO/13	4.9
1973	*Cin-N★	152	557	83	141	17	3	25	104	83	83	.253	.350	.429	121	12	15	82	4	1	1	.995	-1	*CO/13	2.0
1974	Cin-N★	160	621	108	174	38	2	33	**129**	80	90	.280	.365	.507	144	33	35	114	5	4	-1	.993	-5	*C3/1	3.5
1975	*Cin-N★	142	530	83	150	39	1	28	110	65	108	.283	.363	.519	140	29	28	101	11	0	3	.989	4	*CO/1	4.1
1976	*Cin-N★	135	465	62	109	24	1	16	74	81	95	.234	.350	.394	108	8	7	69	13	2	3	**.997**	-3	*C/O1	1.1
1977	Cin-N★	142	494	67	136	34	2	31	109	58	95	.275	.353	.540	133	23	22	92	2	4	-2	.987	-12	*C/O13	1.2
1978	Cin-N†	120	393	52	102	17	1	23	73	50	83	.260	.345	.483	129	14	14	65	4	2	0	.989	-8	*C1/O	0.9
1979	*Cin-N†	130	464	73	128	19	0	22	80	67	73	.276	.367	.459	123	16	16	79	4	2	0	.986	-7	*C/1	1.4
1980	Cin-N★	114	360	52	90	12	0	24	68	41	64	.250	.330	.483	124	11	11	57	4	2	0	.991	-17	*C	-0.3
1981	Cin-N	52	178	14	55	8	0	8	25	17	21	.309	.369	.489	139	9	9	31	0	2	-1	.983	-2	1/C	0.4
1982	Cin-N	119	399	44	103	16	0	13	38	37	58	.258	.321	.396	98	-1	-2	48	1	2	-1	.917	-17	*3/1C	-2.4
1983	Cin-N★	110	310	32	79	15	2	12	54	24	38	.255	.308	.432	100	0	-1	37	0	1	-1	.933	-12	31/CO	-1.7
Total	17	2158	7658	1091	2048	381	24	389	1376	891	1278	.267	.345	.476	127	264	259	1240	68	43	-5	.990	-69	*C31O	25.2
■ ART BENEDICT	Benedict, Arthur Melville b: 3/31/1862, Cornwall, Ill. d: 1/20/48, Denver, Colo. BR/TR, Deb: 5/14/1883																								
1883	Phi-N	3	15	3	4	1	0	0	4	0	4	.267	.267	.333	89	-0	-0	1				.571	-5	/2	-0.4
■ BRUCE BENEDICT	Benedict, Bruce Edwin b: 8/18/55, Birmingham, Ala. BR/TR, 6'1", 190 lbs. Deb: 8/18/78																								
1978	Atl-N	22	52	3	13	2	0	0	1	6	6	.250	.328	.288	66	-2	-2	5	0	0	0	.990	2	C	0.0
1979	Atl-N	76	204	14	46	11	0	0	15	33	18	.225	.333	.279	64	-8	-10	20	1	3	-2	.984	1	C	-0.8
1980	Atl-N	120	359	18	91	14	1	2	34	28	36	.253	.309	.315	72	-12	-13	34	3	3	-1	.988	3	*C	-0.8
1981	Atl-N★	90	295	26	78	12	1	5	35	33	21	.264	.344	.363	98	1	-0	37	1	1	-0	.986	6	C	1.0
1982	*Atl-N	118	386	34	95	11	1	3	44	37	40	.246	.317	.303	71	-12	-14	37	4	4	-1	**.993**	2	*C	-0.9
1983	Atl-N★	134	423	43	126	13	1	2	43	61	24	.298	.388	.348	98	6	2	57	1	3	-2	.992	9	*C	1.6
1984	Atl-N	95	300	26	67	8	1	4	25	34	25	.223	.304	.297	65	-12	-14	27	1	2	-1	.991	1	C	-1.0
1985	Atl-N	70	208	12	42	6	0	0	20	22	12	.202	.281	.231	42	-15	-16	13	0	1	-1	.989	-2	C	-1.7
1986	Atl-N	64	160	11	36	10	1	0	13	15	10	.225	.299	.300	62	-7	-8	13	1	0	0	.993	-3	C	-0.9
1987	Atl-N	37	95	4	14	1	0	1	5	17	15	.147	.277	.189	25	-10	-10	6	0	1	-1	.989	4	C	-0.5
1988	Atl-N	90	236	11	57	7	0	0	19	19	26	.242	.298	.271	61	-10	-12	20	0	2	-1	.989	8	C	0.0
1989	Atl-N	66	160	12	31	3	0	1	6	23	18	.194	.299	.231	52	-9	-9	13	0	0	0	.995	16	C	1.0
Total	12	982	2878	214	696	98	6	18	260	328	251	.242	.322	.299	71	-90	-108	282	12	20	-8	.990	47	C	-3.0
■ JOE BENES	Benes, Joseph Anthony "Bananas" b: 1/8/01, Long Island City, N.Y. d: 3/7/75, Elmhurst, N.J. BR/TR, 5'8.5", 158 lbs. Deb: 5/09/31																								
1931	StL-N	10	12	1	2	0	0	0	0	2	1	.167	.333	.167	37	-1	-1	1	0			1.000	1	/S23	0.0
■ BENNY BENGOUGH	Bengough, Bernard Oliver b: 7/27/1898, Niagara Falls, N.Y. d: 12/22/68, Philadelphia, Pa. BR/TR, 5'7.5", 168 lbs. Deb: 5/18/23 C																								
1923	NY-A	19	53	1	7	2	0	0	3	4	2	.132	.193	.170	-4	-8	-8	2	0	0	0	.973	1	C	-0.7
1924	NY-A	11	16	4	5	1	1	0	3	2	0	.313	.389	.500	128	1	1	3	0	0	0	1.000	3	C	0.4
1925	NY-A	95	283	17	73	14	2	0	23	19	9	.258	.305	.322	60	-18	-17	28	0	2	-1	**.993**	6	C	-0.7
1926	NY-A	36	84	9	32	6	0	0	14	7	4	.381	.435	.452	134	4	4	17	1	0	0	.973	8	C	1.4
1927	*NY-A	31	85	6	21	3	3	0	10	4	4	.247	.281	.353	66	-5	-5	7	0	3	-2	.986	12	C	0.6
1928	*NY-A	58	161	12	43	3	1	0	9	7	8	.267	.302	.298	60	-10	-9	15	0	0	0	.992	6	C	0.1
1929	NY-A	23	62	5	12	2	1	0	7	0	2	.194	.194	.258	16	-8	-7	3	0	0	0	.982	-5	C	-1.0

YEAR	TM/L	G	AB	R	H	2B	3B	HR	RBI	BB	SO	AVG	OBP	SLG	PRO+	BR	/A	RC	SB	CS	SBR	FA	FR	POS	TPR
1930	NY-A	44	102	10	24	4	2	0	12	3	8	.235	.257	.314	46	-9	-8	8	1	0	0	.990	9	C	0.3
1931	StL-A	40	140	6	35	4	1	0	12	4	4	.250	.271	.293	46	-11	-11	10	0	3	-2	.986	-1	C	-1.1
1932	StL-A	54	139	13	35	7	1	0	15	12	4	.252	.311	.317	60	-8	-9	14	0	1	-1	.989	6	C	-0.1
Total	10	411	1125	83	287	46	12	0	108	62	45	.255	.295	.317	59	-71	-70	107	2	9	-5	.988	45	C	-0.8

■ JUAN BENIQUEZ Beniquez, Juan Jose (Torres) b: 5/13/50, San Sebastian, P.R. BR/TR, 5'11", 165 lbs. Deb: 9/04/71

YEAR	TM/L	G	AB	R	H	2B	3B	HR	RBI	BB	SO	AVG	OBP	SLG	PRO+	BR	/A	RC	SB	CS	SBR	FA	FR	POS	TPR
1971	Bos-A	16	57	8	17	2	0	0	4	3	4	.298	.333	.333	83	-1	-1	6	3	1	0	.895	-8	S	-0.7
1972	Bos-A	33	99	10	24	4	1	1	8	7	11	.242	.292	.333	81	-2	-2	10	2	0	1	.900	5	S	0.7
1974	Bos-A	106	389	60	104	14	3	5	33	25	61	.267	.313	.357	86	-4	-7	41	19	11	-1	.978	2	O/D	-1.1
1975	*Bos-A	78	254	43	74	14	4	2	17	25	26	.291	.359	.402	106	5	2	34	7	10	-4	.991	1	OD3	-0.2
1976	Tex-A	145	478	49	122	14	4	0	33	39	56	.255	.315	.301	79	-11	-12	47	17	6	2	.986	20	*O/2	0.4
1977	Tex-A	123	424	56	114	19	6	10	50	43	43	.269	.338	.413	102	2	1	55	26	18	-3	.988	7	*O	0.0
1978	Tex-A	127	473	61	123	17	3	11	50	20	59	.260	.294	.378	88	-9	-9	48	10	12	-4	.972	-0	*O	-2.0
1979	NY-A	62	142	19	36	6	1	4	17	9	17	.254	.307	.394	90	-3	-2	16	3	3	-1	.981	-6	O/3	-1.0
1980	Sea-A	70	237	26	54	10	0	6	21	17	25	.228	.280	.346	70	-10	-10	20	2	3	-1	.957	1	O/D	-1.4
1981	Cal-A	58	166	18	30	5	0	3	13	15	16	.181	.253	.265	49	-11	-11	11	2	1	0	.959	-7	O/D	-2.0
1982	*Cal-A	112	196	25	52	11	2	3	24	15	21	.265	.321	.388	93	-2	-2	25	3	0	1	.983	-27	*O	-2.9
1983	Cal-A	92	315	44	96	15	0	3	34	15	29	.305	.344	.381	100	-0	0	39	4	2	0	.968	-8	O/D	-1.0
1984	Cal-A	110	354	60	119	17	0	8	39	18	43	.336	.373	.452	128	13	13	55	0	3	-2	.971	-12	O	-0.3
1985	Cal-A	132	411	54	125	13	5	8	42	34	46	.304	.364	.418	114	8	9	59	4	3	-1	1.000	-15	O1D/3S	-1.1
1986	Bal-A	113	343	48	103	15	0	6	36	40	49	.300	.378	.397	113	7	7	51	2	3	-1	.963	-6	O3D1	-0.2
1987	KC-A	57	174	14	41	7	0	3	26	11	26	.236	.285	.328	60	-10	-10	14	0	0	0	1.000	-4	OD/13	-1.5
	Tor-A	39	81	6	23	5	1	5	21	5	13	.284	.333	.556	127	3	3	14	0	0	0	.875	-2	D/O1	0.1
	Yr	96	255	20	64	12	1	8	47	16	39	.251	.300	.400	82	-6	-7	28	0	0	0	.976	-6	DO/13	-1.4
1988	Tor-A	27	58	9	17	2	0	1	8	8	6	.293	.379	.379	112	1	1	8	0	0	0	.000	-0	D/O	0.1
Total	17	1500	4651	610	1274	190	30	79	476	349	551	.274	.329	.379	95	-22	-30	553	104	76	-14	.977	-60	*OD/13S2	-14.1

■ STAN BENJAMIN Benjamin, Alfred Stanley b: 5/20/14, Framingham, Mass. BR/TR, 6'2", 194 lbs. Deb: 9/16/39

YEAR	TM/L	G	AB	R	H	2B	3B	HR	RBI	BB	SO	AVG	OBP	SLG	PRO+	BR	/A	RC	SB	CS	SBR	FA	FR	POS	TPR
1939	Phi-N	12	50	4	7	2	1	0	2	1	6	.140	.157	.220	0	-7	-7	1	1			.867	-0	/O3	-0.8
1940	Phi-N	8	9	1	2	0	0	0	1	1	1	.222	.300	.222	48	-1	-1	1	0			1.000	1	/O	0.0
1941	Phi-N	129	480	47	113	20	7	3	27	20	81	.235	.266	.325	68	-23	-21	39	17			.980	-4	*O/123	-3.3
1942	Phi-N	78	210	24	47	8	3	2	8	10	27	.224	.262	.319	73	-9	-8	18	5			.976	-3	O1	-1.4
1945	Cle-A	14	21	1	7	2	0	0	3	0	0	.333	.333	.429	126	0	0	3	0	1	-1	1.000	2	/O	0.1
Total	5	241	770	77	176	32	11	5	41	32	115	.229	.260	.318	66	-39	-36	61	23	1		.975	-5	O/132	-5.4

■ MIKE BENJAMIN Benjamin, Michael Paul b: 11/22/65, Euclid, Ohio BR/TR, 6'3", 195 lbs. Deb: 7/07/89

YEAR	TM/L	G	AB	R	H	2B	3B	HR	RBI	BB	SO	AVG	OBP	SLG	PRO+	BR	/A	RC	SB	CS	SBR	FA	FR	POS	TPR
1989	SF-N	14	6	6	1	0	0	0	0	0	1	.167	.167	.167	-5	-1	-1	0	0	0	0	1.000	2	/S	0.1
1990	SF-N	22	56	7	12	3	1	2	3	3	10	.214	.254	.411	83	-2	-2	5	1	0	0	.988	5	S	0.5
1991	SF-N	54	106	12	13	3	0	2	8	7	26	.123	.191	.208	13	-13	-12	5	3	0	1	.984	16	S/3	0.7
1992	SF-N	40	75	4	13	2	1	1	3	4	15	.173	.215	.267	38	-6	-6	4	1	0	0	.991	5	S/3	0.1
Total	4	130	243	29	39	8	2	5	14	14	52	.160	.212	.272	36	-22	-21	15	5	0	2	.987	27	S/3	1.4

■ IKE BENNERS Benners, Isaac B. b: Philadelphia, Pa. BL , 175 lbs. Deb: 5/01/1884

YEAR	TM/L	G	AB	R	H	2B	3B	HR	RBI	BB	SO	AVG	OBP	SLG	PRO+	BR	/A	RC	SB	CS	SBR	FA	FR	POS	TPR
1884	Bro-a	49	189	25	38	11	5	1		7		.201	.237	.328	84	-3	-3	15				.815	-5	O	-0.9
	Wil-U	6	22	0	1	0	0	0		1		.045	.087	.045	-53	-3	-4	0				.750	0	/O	-0.3
Total	1	55	211	25	39	11	5	1		8		.185	.222	.299	70	-6	-7	15				.806	-5	/O	-1.2

■ CHARLIE BENNETT Bennett, Charles Wesley b: 11/21/1854, New Castle, Pa. d: 2/24/27, Detroit, Mich. BR/TR, 5'11", 180 lbs. Deb: 5/01/1878

YEAR	TM/L	G	AB	R	H	2B	3B	HR	RBI	BB	SO	AVG	OBP	SLG	PRO+	BR	/A	RC	SB	CS	SBR	FA	FR	POS	TPR
1878	Mil-N	49	184	16	45	9	0	1	12	10	26	.245	.284	.310	89	-1	-2	17				.831	-13	CO	-1.5
1880	Wor-N	51	193	20	44	9	3	0	18	10	30	.228	.266	.306	86	-1	-3	16				.913	-0	C/O	-0.3
1881	Det-N	76	299	44	90	18	7	7	64	18	37	.301	.341	.478	149	18	17	50				**.962**	18	*C/3O	**3.4**
1882	Det-N	84	342	43	103	16	10	5	51	20	33	.301	.340	.450	151	19	19	54				.945	7	*C3/2S1	2.5
1883	Det-N	92	371	56	113	34	7	5	55	26	59	.305	.350	.474	155	21	24	63				**.944**	-3	*C2O	2.2
1884	Det-N	90	341	37	90	18	6	3	40	36	40	.264	.334	.378	132	10	13	44				.917	-5	*C/OS321	1.4
1885	Det-N	91	349	49	94	24	13	5	60	47	37	.269	.356	.456	161	25	24	58				.919	-1	CO3	2.7
1886	Det-N	72	235	37	57	13	5	4	34	48	29	.243	.371	.391	128	11	10	37	4			**.955**	12	C/OS	2.6
1887	*Det-N	46	160	26	39	6	5	3	20	30	22	.244	.363	.400	110	4	3	26	7			.951	2	C/O1	0.8
1888	Det-N	74	258	32	68	12	4	5	29	31	40	.264	.347	.399	140	12	12	38	4			**.966**	7	C/1	2.5
1889	Bos-N	82	247	42	57	8	2	4	28	21	43	.231	.296	.328	71	-8	-11	27	7			**.955**	11	C	0.6
1890	Bos-N	85	281	59	60	17	2	3	40	72	56	.214	.377	.320	98	6	2	37	6			**.959**	10	C	1.7
1891	Bos-N	75	256	35	55	9	3	5	39	42	61	.215	.332	.332	85	-0	-5	30	3			**.960**	14	C	1.3
1892	*Bos-N	35	114	19	23	4	0	1	16	27	23	.202	.355	.263	82	0	-2	13	6			.948	1	C	0.2
1893	Bos-N	60	191	34	40	6	0	4	27	40	36	.209	.352	.304	71	-5	-8	23	5			.953	-3	C	-0.5
Total	15	1062	3821	549	978	203	67	55	533	478	572	.256	.340	.387	119	111	93	532	42			.942	57	C/O32S1	19.6

■ HERSCHEL BENNETT Bennett, Herschel Emmett b: 9/21/1896, Elwood, Mo. d: 9/9/64, Springfield, Mo. BL/TR, 5'9.5", 160 lbs. Deb: 4/19/23

YEAR	TM/L	G	AB	R	H	2B	3B	HR	RBI	BB	SO	AVG	OBP	SLG	PRO+	BR	/A	RC	SB	CS	SBR	FA	FR	POS	TPR
1923	StL-A	5	4	0	0	0	0	0	0	1	1	.000	.200	.000	-42	-1	-1	0	0	0	0	1.000	-0	/O	-0.1
1924	StL-A	41	94	16	31	4	3	1	11	3	6	.330	.364	.468	107	1	1	16	1	0	0	.966	-4	O	-0.4
1925	StL-A	93	298	46	83	11	6	2	37	18	16	.279	.324	.376	73	-11	-13	34	4	8	-4	.916	-2	O	-2.2
1926	StL-A	80	225	33	60	14	2	1	26	22	21	.267	.337	.360	78	-6	-7	28	2	1	0	.950	3	O	-0.8
1927	StL-A	93	256	40	68	12	2	3	30	14	21	.266	.311	.363	72	-10	-11	28	6	2	1	.946	1	O	-1.3
Total	5	312	877	135	242	41	13	7	104	58	65	.276	.327	.376	77	-27	-32	107	13	11	-3	.937	-1	O	-4.8

■ FRED BENNETT Bennett, James Fred "Red" b: 3/15/02, Atkins, Ark. d: 5/12/57, Atkins, Ark. BR/TR, 5'9", 185 lbs. Deb: 4/13/28

YEAR	TM/L	G	AB	R	H	2B	3B	HR	RBI	BB	SO	AVG	OBP	SLG	PRO+	BR	/A	RC	SB	CS	SBR	FA	FR	POS	TPR
1928	StL-A	7	8	0	2	1	0	0	0	0	2	.250	.250	.375	60	-0	-1	1	0	0	0	1.000	0	/O	-0.1
1931	Pit-N	32	89	6	25	5	0	1	7	7	4	.281	.333	.371	90	-1	-1	11	0			.951	-2	O	-0.5
Total	2	39	97	6	27	6	0	1	7	7	6	.278	.327	.371	87	-2	-2	12	0	0		.953	-2	/O	-0.6

■ JOE BENNETT Bennett, Joseph Rosenblum b: 7/2/1900, New York, N.Y. d: 7/11/87, Morro Bay, Cal. BR/TR, 5'9", 168 lbs. Deb: 7/05/23

YEAR	TM/L	G	AB	R	H	2B	3B	HR	RBI	BB	SO	AVG	OBP	SLG	PRO+	BR	/A	RC	SB	CS	SBR	FA	FR	POS	TPR
1923	Phi-N	1	0	0	0	0	0	0	0	0	0	—	—	—	—	0	0	0	0	0	0	1.000	0	/3	0.0

■ PUG BENNETT Bennett, Justin Titus b: 2/20/1874, Ponca, Neb. d: 9/12/35, Kirkland, Wash. BR/TR, 5'11", 165 lbs. Deb: 4/12/06

YEAR	TM/L	G	AB	R	H	2B	3B	HR	RBI	BB	SO	AVG	OBP	SLG	PRO+	BR	/A	RC	SB	CS	SBR	FA	FR	POS	TPR
1906	StL-N	153	595	66	156	16	7	1	34	56		.262	.331	.318	107	3	5	74	20			.948	-7	*2	0.0
1907	StL-N	87	324	20	72	8	2	0	21	21		.222	.272	.259	69	-13	-11	26	7			.939	-15	2/3	-3.2
Total	2	240	919	86	228	24	9	1	55	77		.248	.310	.297	94	-10	-6	100	27			.945	-22	2/3	-3.2

■ VERN BENSON Benson, Vernon Adair b: 9/19/24, Granite Quarry, N.C. BL/TR, 5'11", 180 lbs. Deb: 7/31/43 MC

YEAR	TM/L	G	AB	R	H	2B	3B	HR	RBI	BB	SO	AVG	OBP	SLG	PRO+	BR	/A	RC	SB	CS	SBR	FA	FR	POS	TPR
1943	Phi-A	2	2	0	0	0	0	0	0	0	0	.000	.000	.000	-99	-0	-0	0	0	0	0	.000	0	H	-0.1
1946	Phi-A	7	5	1	0	0	0	0	0	1	3	.000	.167	.000	-51	-1	-1	0	0	0	0	1.000	-0	/O	-0.1
1951	StL-N	13	46	8	12	3	1	1	7	6	8	.261	.346	.435	108	1	1	8	0	0	0	.950	0	/3O	0.1
1952	StL-N	20	47	6	9	2	0	2	5	5	9	.191	.269	.362	73	-2	-2	5	0	0	0	.889	-1	3	-0.3
1953	StL-N	13	4	2	0	0	0	0	0	1	2	.000	.200	.000	-42	-1	-1	0	0	0	0	.000	0	H	-0.1
Total	5	55	104	17	21	5	1	3	12	13	22	.202	.291	.356	75	-4	-4	13	0	0	0	.911	-0	/3O	-0.5

YEAR	TM/L	G	AB	R	H	2B	3B	HR	RBI	BB	SO	AVG	OBP	SLG	PRO+	BR	/A	RC	SB	CS	SBR	FA	FR	POS	TPR
■ JACK BENTLEY	Bentley, John Needles b: 3/8/1895, Sandy Spring, Md. d: 10/24/69, Olney, Md. BL/TL, 5′11.5″, 200 lbs. Deb: 9/06/13																								
1913	Was-A	3	3	0	0	0	0	0	0	0	0	.000	.000	.000	-98	-1	-1	0	0			1.000	0	/P	0.0
1914	Was-A	30	40	7	11	2	0	0	4	0	5	.275	.275	.325	77	-1	-1	4	0			.930	-1	P	0.0
1915	Was-A	4	2	0	0	0	0	0	0	0	1	.000	.000	.000	-98	-0	-0	0	0			.750	-0	/P	0.0
1916	Was-A	2	0	0	0	0	0	0	0	0	0	—	—	—	—	0	0	0	0			1.000	0	/P	0.0
1923	*NY-N	52	89	9	38	6	2	1	14	3	4	.427	.446	.573	169	8	8	22	0	0	0	.977	-1	P	0.0
1924	*NY-N	46	98	12	26	5	1	0	6	3	13	.265	.287	.337	68	-5	-4	9	0	0	0	.979	-1	P	0.0
1925	NY-N	64	99	10	30	5	2	3	18	9	11	.303	.361	.485	119	2	2	17	0	0	0	.930	-2	P/O1	-0.1
1926	Phi-N	75	240	19	62	12	3	2	27	5	4	.258	.273	.358	66	-11	-13	22	0			.993	-2	1/P	-1.7
	NY-N	3	4	0	1	0	0	0	0	0	0	.250	.250	.250	35	-0	-0	0	0			.000	-0	/P	0.0
	Yr	78	244	19	63	12	3	2	27	5	4	.258	.273	.357	65	-12	-13	23	0			.993	-2	1/P	-1.7
1927	NY-N	8	9	1	2	0	0	1	2	1	1	.222	.300	.556	125	0	0	1	0			.750	-0	/P1	0.0
Total	9	287	584	58	170	30	8	7	71	21	39	.291	.316	.406	91	-8	-9	77	0	0		.949	-6	P/1O	-1.8
■ BUTCH BENTON	Benton, Alfred Lee b: 8/24/57, Tampa, Fla. BR/TR, 6′1″, 190 lbs. Deb: 9/14/78																								
1978	NY-N	4	4	1	2	0	0	0	2	0	0	.500	.600	.500	218	1	1	1	0	0	0	1.000	0	/C	0.1
1980	NY-N	12	21	0	1	0	0	0	0	2	4	.048	.167	.048	-39	-4	-4	0	0	0	0	.935	-1	/C	-0.5
1982	Chi-N	4	7	0	1	0	0	0	1	0	1	.143	.143	.143	-19	-1	-1	0	0	0	0	1.000	2	/C	0.1
1985	Cle-A	31	67	5	12	4	0	0	7	3	9	.179	.214	.239	24	-7	-7	3	0	0	0	.957	-3	C	-0.9
Total	4	51	99	6	16	4	0	0	10	5	14	.162	.217	.202	16	-11	-11	5	0	0	0	.959	-2	/C	-1.2
■ RABBIT BENTON	Benton, Stanley W. "Stan" b: 9/29/01, Canal City, Ky. d: 6/7/84, Mesquite, Tex. BR/TR, 5′7″, 150 lbs. Deb: 9/13/22																								
1922	Phi-N	6	19	1	4	1	0	0	3	2	1	.211	.286	.263	39	-2	-2	2	0	0	0	.889	0	/2	-0.1
■ TODD BENZINGER	Benzinger, Todd Eric b: 2/11/63, Dayton, Ky. BB/TR, 6′1″, 185 lbs. Deb: 6/21/87																								
1987	Bos-A	73	223	36	62	11	1	8	43	22	41	.278	.348	.444	105	3	2	34	5	4	-1	.987	8	O/1	0.7
1988	*Bos-A	120	405	47	103	28	1	13	70	22	80	.254	.294	.425	95	-2	-4	48	2	3	-1	.991	-4	1O/D	-1.6
1989	Cin-N	161	628	79	154	28	3	17	76	44	120	.245	.297	.381	89	-8	-10	70	3	7	-3	.995	-13	*1	-4.2
1990	*Cin-N	118	376	35	95	14	2	5	46	19	69	.253	.296	.340	71	-13	-15	38	3	4	-2	.992	-2	1O	-2.7
1991	Cin-N	51	123	7	23	3	2	1	11	10	20	.187	.248	.268	43	-9	-10	9	2	0	1	.986	-1	1O	-1.2
	KC-A	78	293	29	86	15	3	2	40	17	46	.294	.339	.386	99	-0	-0	36	2	6	-3	.996	-5	1/D	-1.3
1992	LA-N	121	293	24	70	16	2	4	31	15	54	.239	.276	.348	77	-10	-10	26	2	4	-2	.989	-0	O1	-1.5
Total	6	722	2341	257	593	115	14	50	317	149	430	.253	.301	.378	86	-40	-47	260	19	28	-11	.994	-17	1O/D	-11.8
■ JOHNNY BERARDINO	Berardino, John "Bernie" b: 5/1/17, Los Angeles, Cal. BR/TR, 6′, 180 lbs. Deb: 4/22/39																								
1939	StL-A	126	468	42	120	24	5	5	58	37	36	.256	.314	.361	71	-20	-22	53	6	2	1	.958	4	*2/3S	-1.0
1940	StL-A	142	523	71	135	31	4	16	85	32	46	.258	.301	.424	84	-13	-15	64	6	8	-3	.939	13	*S2/3	0.6
1941	StL-A	128	469	48	127	30	4	5	89	41	27	.271	.332	.384	86	-8	-10	57	3	5	-2	.954	-14	*S/3	-1.7
1942	StL-A	29	74	11	21	6	0	1	10	4	2	.284	.329	.405	104	0	0	11	3	1	0	.950	0	/S312	0.1
1946	StL-A	144	582	70	154	29	5	5	68	34	58	.265	.306	.357	81	-13	-16	61	2	4	-2	.972	-2	*2	-1.1
1947	StL-A	90	306	29	80	22	1	1	20	44	26	.261	.358	.350	95	-0	-1	40	6	5	-1	.977	-9	2	-0.5
1948	Cle-A	66	147	19	28	5	1	2	10	27	16	.190	.328	.279	64	-7	-7	14	0	1	-1	.988	4	21S/3	-0.3
1949	Cle-A	50	116	11	23	6	1	0	13	14	14	.198	.295	.267	50	-9	-8	10	0	1	-1	.935	-1	3/2S	-0.9
1950	Cle-A	4	5	1	2	0	0	0	3	1	0	.400	.500	.400	137	0	0	1	0	0	0	1.000	1	/23	0.1
	Pit-N	40	131	12	27	3	1	1	12	19	11	.206	.307	.267	51	-9	-9	11	0			.964	3	2/3	-0.5
1951	StL-A	39	119	13	27	7	1	0	13	17	18	.227	.324	.303	68	-5	-5	12	1	1	-0	.917	-7	3/21O	-1.2
1952	Cle-A	35	32	5	3	0	0	0	2	10	8	.094	.310	.094	17	-3	-3	2	0	1	-1	.960	2	/2S31	-0.2
	Pit-N	19	56	2	8	4	0	0	4	4	6	.143	.200	.214	14	-7	-7	2	0	0	0	.960	6	2	0.0
Total	11	912	3028	334	755	167	23	36	387	284	268	.249	.316	.355	77	-93	-102	339	27	29		.968	1	2S/31O	-6.6
■ LOU BERBERET	Berberet, Louis Joseph b: 11/20/29, Long Beach, Cal. BL/TR, 5′11″, 212 lbs. Deb: 9/17/54																								
1954	NY-A	5	5	1	2	0	0	0	3	1	1	.400	.500	.400	154	0	0	1	0	0	0	1.000	1	/C	0.2
1955	NY-A	2	5	1	2	0	0	0	2	1	0	.400	.500	.400	147	0	0	1	0	0	0	1.000	1	/C	0.1
1956	Was-A	95	207	25	54	6	3	4	27	46	33	.261	.402	.377	107	4	4	33	0	0	0	.997	-1	C	0.6
1957	Was-A	99	264	24	69	11	2	7	36	41	38	.261	.365	.398	110	4	4	37	0	1	-1	**1.000**	-3	C	0.4
1958	Was-A	5	6	0	1	0	0	0	0	4	1	.167	.500	.167	94	0	0	1	0	0	0	.917	1	/C	0.1
	Bos-A	57	167	11	35	5	3	2	18	31	32	.210	.337	.311	74	-4	-5	18	0	2	-1	.984	-6	C	-1.0
	Yr	62	173	11	36	5	3	2	18	35	33	.208	.344	.306	76	-3	-5	19	0	2	-1	.981	-5	C	-0.9
1959	Det-A	100	338	38	73	8	2	13	44	35	59	.216	.290	.367	75	-10	-13	36	0	0	0	.989	-11	C	-1.8
1960	Det-A	85	232	18	45	4	0	5	23	41	31	.194	.318	.276	60	-11	-12	22	2	0	1	.993	-0	C	-0.8
Total	7	448	1224	118	281	34	10	31	153	200	195	.230	.341	.350	86	-16	-20	150	2	3	-1	.992	-17	C	-2.2
■ MOE BERG	Berg, Morris b: 3/2/02, New York, N.Y. d: 5/29/72, Belleville, N.J. BR/TR, 6′1″, 185 lbs. Deb: 7/04/23 C																								
1923	Bro-N	49	129	9	24	3	2	0	6	2	5	.186	.198	.240	16	-16	-15	6	1	0	0	.906	-6	S/2	-1.7
1926	Chi-A	41	113	4	25	6	0	0	7	6	9	.221	.261	.274	41	-10	-10	8	0	2	-1	.948	6	S/23	-0.2
1927	Chi-A	35	69	4	17	4	0	0	4	4	10	.246	.288	.304	55	-5	-5	6	0	0	0	.952	-4	2C/S3	-0.7
1928	Chi-A	76	224	25	55	16	0	0	29	14	25	.246	.302	.317	64	-12	-12	23	2	1	0	.990	5	C	0.0
1929	Chi-A	107	352	32	101	7	0	0	47	17	16	.287	.323	.307	64	-19	-18	36	5	1	1	.982	-3	*C	-1.0
1930	Chi-A	20	61	4	7	3	0	0	7	1	5	.115	.129	.164	-27	-12	-11	1	0	0	0	.986	-1	C	-1.0
1931	Cle-A	10	13	1	1	1	0	0	0	1	1	.077	.143	.154	-21	-2	-2	0	0	0	0	.889	0	/C	-0.2
1932	Was-A	75	195	16	46	8	1	1	26	8	13	.236	.266	.303	48	-16	-15	16	1	1	-0	1.000	7	C	-0.5
1933	Was-A	40	65	8	12	3	0	2	9	4	5	.185	.232	.323	46	-5	-5	5	0	0	0	1.000	3	C	-0.1
1934	Was-A	33	86	5	21	4	0	0	6	6	4	.244	.301	.291	55	-6	-5	8	2	0	1	.988	-4	C	-0.7
	Cle-A	29	97	4	25	3	1	0	9	1	7	.258	.265	.309	47	-8	-8	8	0	0	0	.980	5	C	-0.2
	Yr	62	183	9	46	7	1	0	15	7	11	.251	.283	.301	51	-14	-13	16	2	0	1	.983	1	C	-0.9
1935	Bos-A	38	98	13	28	5	0	2	12	5	3	.286	.320	.398	79	-3	-3	12	0	0	0	.991	2	C	0.0
1936	Bos-A	39	125	9	30	4	1	0	19	2	6	.240	.264	.288	34	-13	-14	10	0	0	0	.986	12	C	0.0
1937	Bos-A	47	141	13	36	3	1	0	20	5	4	.255	.281	.291	43	-12	-13	12	0	0	0	.979	3	C	-0.8
1938	Bos-A	10	12	0	4	0	0	0	0	0	1	.333	.333	.333	64	-1	-1	1	0	0	0	1.000	1	/C1	0.0
1939	Bos-A	14	33	3	9	1	0	1	5	2	3	.273	.314	.394	77	-1	-1	4	0	0	0	.965	4	C	0.3
Total	15	663	1813	150	441	71	6	6	206	78	117	.243	.278	.299	49	-140	-139	156	11	5	0	.986	29	C/S231	-6.8
■ AUGIE BERGAMO	Bergamo, August Samuel b: 2/14/17, Detroit, Mich. d: 8/19/74, Grosse Pointe City, Mich. BL/TL, 5′9″, 165 lbs. Deb: 4/25/44																								
1944	*StL-N	80	192	35	55	6	3	2	19	35	23	.286	.399	.380	118	7	6	32	0			.988	-7	O/1	-0.3
1945	StL-N	94	304	51	96	17	2	3	44	43	21	.316	.401	.414	124	12	11	55	0			.969	-1	O/1	0.6
Total	2	174	496	86	151	23	5	5	63	78	44	.304	.400	.401	122	19	18	88	0			.975	-9	O/1	0.3
■ MARTY BERGEN	Bergen, Martin b: 10/25/1871, N.Brookfield, Mass d: 1/19/1900, N.Brookfield, Mass TR , 5′10″, 170 lbs. Deb: 4/17/1896 F																								
1896	Bos-N	65	245	39	66	6	4	4	37	11	22	.269	.309	.376	77	-7	-10	31	6			.920	6	C/1	0.2
1897	*Bos-N	87	327	47	81	11	3	2	45	18		.248	.295	.318	58	-19	-22	33	5			.963	4	C/O	-0.8
1898	Bos-N	120	446	62	125	16	5	3	60	13		.280	.302	.359	85	-8	-12	53	9			.962	2	*C/1	0.2
1899	Bos-N	72	260	32	67	11	3	1	34	10		.258	.290	.335	65	-11	-15	27	4			.955	3	C	-0.5
Total	4	344	1278	180	339	44	15	10	176	52	22	.265	.299	.347	72	-45	-58	145	24			.954	14	C/1O	-0.9

■ BILL BERGEN Bergen, William Aloysius b: 6/13/1878, N.Brookfield, Mass. d: 12/19/43, Worcester, Mass. BR/TR, 6', 184 lbs. Deb: 5/06/01 F

YEAR	TM/L	G	AB	R	H	2B	3B	HR	RBI	BB	SO	AVG	OBP	SLG	PRO+	BR	/A	RC	SB	CS	SBR	FA	FR	POS	TPR
1901	Cin-N	87	308	15	55	6	4	1	17	8		.179	.199	.234	27	-30	-27	16	2			.970	-5	C	-2.3
1902	Cin-N	89	322	19	58	8	3	0	36	14		.180	.214	.224	32	-25	-28	17	2			.959	15	C	-0.4
1903	Cin-N	58	207	21	47	4	2	0	19	7		.227	.252	.266	43	-14	-17	15	2			.980	2	C	-0.9
1904	Bro-N	96	329	17	60	4	2	0	12	9		.182	.204	.207	28	-28	-27	16	3			.959	14	C/1	-0.3
1905	Bro-N	79	247	12	47	3	2	0	22	7		.190	.213	.219	31	-22	-20	14	4			.954	12	C	-0.1
1906	Bro-N	103	353	9	56	3	3	0	19	7		.159	.175	.184	13	-36	-33	13	2			.977	5	*C	-2.0
1907	Bro-N	51	138	2	22	3	0	0	14	1		.159	.165	.181	9	-15	-14	5	1			.968	3	C	-0.8
1908	Bro-N	99	302	8	53	8	2	0	15	5		.175	.189	.215	30	-25	-23	13	1			**.989**	16	C	0.1
1909	Bro-N	112	346	16	48	1	1	1	15	10		.139	.163	.156	-1	-41	-40	10	4			.976	22	*C	-0.9
1910	Bro-N	89	249	11	40	2	1	0	14	6	39	.161	.180	.177	4	-30	-30	9	0			.981	18	C	-0.4
1911	Bro-N	84	227	8	30	3	1	0	10	14	42	.132	.183	.154	-6	-32	-31	7	2			**.981**	15	C	-0.9
Total	11	947	3028	138	516	45	21	2	193	88	81	.170	.194	.201	20	-298	-290	134	23			.972	117	C/1	-8.9

■ CLARENCE BERGER Berger, Clarence Edward b: 11/1/1894, E.Cleveland, Ohio d: 6/30/59, Washington, D.C. BL/TR, 6', 185 lbs. Deb: 9/23/14

YEAR	TM/L	G	AB	R	H	2B	3B	HR	RBI	BB	SO	AVG	OBP	SLG	PRO+	BR	/A	RC	SB	CS	SBR	FA	FR	POS	TPR
1914	Pit-N	6	13	2	1	0	0	0	0	1	4	.077	.143	.077	-36	-2	-2	0	0			1.000	-2	/O	-0.5

■ JOHNNY BERGER Berger, John Henne b: 8/27/01, Philadelphia, Pa. d: 5/7/79, Lake Charles, La. BR/TR, 5'9", 165 lbs. Deb: 4/20/22

YEAR	TM/L	G	AB	R	H	2B	3B	HR	RBI	BB	SO	AVG	OBP	SLG	PRO+	BR	/A	RC	SB	CS	SBR	FA	FR	POS	TPR
1922	Phi-A	2	1	0	1	0	0	0	0	0	0	1.000	1.000	1.000	412	0	0	1	1	0	0	1.000	1	/C	0.1
1927	Was-A	9	15	1	4	0	0	0	1	2	3	.267	.353	.267	63	-1	-1	1	0	0	0	.926	0	/C	0.0
Total	2	11	16	1	5	0	0	0	1	2	3	.313	.389	.313	85	-0	-0	3	1	0	0	.935	1	/C	0.1

■ TUN BERGER Berger, John Henry b: 12/6/1867, Pittsburgh, Pa. d: 6/10/07, Pittsburgh, Pa. TR , 204 lbs. Deb: 5/09/1890

YEAR	TM/L	G	AB	R	H	2B	3B	HR	RBI	BB	SO	AVG	OBP	SLG	PRO+	BR	/A	RC	SB	CS	SBR	FA	FR	POS	TPR
1890	Pit-N	104	391	64	104	18	4	0	40	35	23	.266	.337	.332	110	-1	7	49	11			.912	-7	OSC/23	0.2
1891	Pit-N	43	134	15	32	2	1	1	14	12	10	.239	.315	.291	81	-3	-3	14	4			.920	-13	C2/SO	-1.2
1892	Was-N	26	97	9	14	2	1	0	3	7	9	.144	.210	.186	21	-9	-9	5	3			.872	-11	S/C	-1.7
Total	3	173	622	88	150	22	6	1	57	54	42	.241	.313	.301	89	-13	-5	67	18			.837	-30	/SCO23	-2.7

■ JOE BERGER Berger, Joseph August "Fats" b: 12/20/1886, St.Louis, Mo. d: 3/6/56, Rock Island, Ill. BR/TR, 5'10.5", 170 lbs. Deb: 4/11/13

YEAR	TM/L	G	AB	R	H	2B	3B	HR	RBI	BB	SO	AVG	OBP	SLG	PRO+	BR	/A	RC	SB	CS	SBR	FA	FR	POS	TPR
1913	Chi-A	79	223	27	48	6	2	2	20	36	28	.215	.330	.287	82	-4	-4	23	5			.959	3	2/S3	-0.2
1914	Chi-A	48	148	11	23	3	1	0	3	13	9	.155	.224	.189	25	-14	-13	6	2	8	-4	.922	-2	S2/3	-2.0
Total	2	127	371	38	71	9	3	2	23	49	37	.191	.289	.248	60	-18	-18	29	7	8		.956	1	/2S3	-2.2

■ BOZE BERGER Berger, Louis William b: 5/13/10, Baltimore, Md. BR/TR, 6'2", 180 lbs. Deb: 8/17/32

YEAR	TM/L	G	AB	R	H	2B	3B	HR	RBI	BB	SO	AVG	OBP	SLG	PRO+	BR	/A	RC	SB	CS	SBR	FA	FR	POS	TPR
1932	Cle-A	1	1	0	0	0	0	0	0	0	1	.000	.000	.000	-94	-0	-0	0	0	0	0	1.000	1	/S	0.1
1935	Cle-A	124	461	62	119	27	5	5	43	34	97	.258	.310	.371	74	-18	-19	53	7	5	-1	.964	13	*2/S13	0.2
1936	Cle-A	28	52	1	9	2	0	0	3	1	14	.173	.189	.212	-1	-8	-8	2	0	0	0	.959	4	/123S	-0.4
1937	Chi-A	52	130	19	31	5	0	5	13	15	24	.238	.322	.392	79	-5	-5	17	1	1	-0	.931	-1	3/2S	-0.4
1938	Chi-A	118	470	60	102	15	3	3	36	43	80	.217	.284	.281	41	-43	-44	40	4	1	1	.946	-10	S2/3	-4.2
1939	Bos-A	20	30	4	9	2	0	0	2	1	10	.300	.323	.367	73	-1	-1	4	0	0	0	.947	1	S/32	0.0
Total	6	343	1144	146	270	51	8	13	97	94	226	.236	.296	.329	57	-75	-78	116	12	7	-1	.954	9	2/S31	-4.7

■ WALLY BERGER Berger, Walter Antone b: 10/10/05, Chicago, Ill. d: 11/30/88, Redondo Beach, Cal BR/TR, 6'2", 198 lbs. Deb: 4/15/30

YEAR	TM/L	G	AB	R	H	2B	3B	HR	RBI	BB	SO	AVG	OBP	SLG	PRO+	BR	/A	RC	SB	CS	SBR	FA	FR	POS	TPR
1930	Bos-N	151	555	98	172	27	14	38	119	54	69	.310	.375	.614	139	27	30	124	3			.966	4	*O	2.1
1931	Bos-N	156	617	94	199	44	8	19	84	55	70	.323	.380	.512	143	32	34	122	13			.977	11	*O/1	3.4
1932	Bos-N	145	602	90	185	34	6	17	73	33	66	.307	.346	.468	121	13	16	98	5			**.993**	5	*O1	1.2
1933	Bos-N★	137	528	84	165	37	8	27	106	41	77	.313	.365	.566	**177**	40	45	113	2			.977	4	*O	4.3
1934	Bos-N★	150	615	92	183	35	8	34	121	49	65	.298	.352	.546	148	29	35	119	2			.978	1	*O	2.8
1935	Bos-N★	150	589	91	174	39	4	**34**	**130**	50	80	.295	.355	.548	151	30	36	115	3			.965	9	*O	3.8
1936	Bos-N☆	138	534	88	154	23	3	25	91	53	84	.288	.361	.483	134	18	23	95	1			.966	7	*O	2.4
1937	Bos-N	30	113	14	31	9	1	5	22	11	33	.274	.344	.504	140	4	5	21	0			1.000	-2	O	0.2
	*NY-N	59	199	40	58	11	2	12	43	18	30	.291	.359	.548	141	11	11	39	3			.965	-2	O	0.7
	Yr	89	312	54	89	20	3	17	65	29	63	.285	.354	.532	141	15	16	60	3			.976	-4	O	0.9
1938	NY-N	16	32	5	6	0	0	0	4	2	4	.188	.235	.188	17	-4	-4	2	0			1.000	1	/O	-0.3
	Cin-N	99	407	74	125	23	4	16	56	29	44	.307	.356	.501	137	17	18	73	2			.966	-3	O	1.2
	Yr	115	439	79	131	23	4	16	60	31	48	.298	.347	.478	128	13	15	74	2			.970	-2	*O	0.9
1939	*Cin-N	97	329	36	85	15	1	14	44	36	63	.258	.341	.438	107	3	3	50	1			.970	-8	O	-0.8
1940	Cin-N	2	2	0	0	0	0	0	0	0	1	.000	.000	.000	-99	-1	-1	0	0			.000	0	H	-0.1
	Phi-N	20	41	3	13	2	0	1	5	4	8	.317	.378	.439	130	1	2	7	1			.947	-2	O/1	-0.1
	Yr	22	43	3	13	2	0	1	5	4	9	.302	.362	.419	119	1	1	6	1			.947	-2	O/1	-0.2
Total	11	1350	5163	809	1550	299	59	242	898	435	694	.300	.359	.522	140	222	255	977	36			.974	26	*O/1	20.8

■ JOHN BERGH Bergh, John Baptist b: 10/8/1857, Boston, Mass. d: 4/16/1883, Boston, Mass. Deb: 8/05/1876

YEAR	TM/L	G	AB	R	H	2B	3B	HR	RBI	BB	SO	AVG	OBP	SLG	PRO+	BR	/A	RC	SB	CS	SBR	FA	FR	POS	TPR
1876	Phi-N	1	4	0	0	0	0	0	0	0	2	.000	.000	.000	-99	-1	-1	0				1.000	-0	/OC	-0.1
1880	Bos-N	11	40	2	8	3	0	0	0	2	5	.200	.238	.275	76	-1	-1	3				.844	-3	C	-0.4
Total	2	12	44	2	8	3	0	0	0	2	7	.182	.217	.250	59	-2	-2	3				.841	-4	/CO	-0.5

■ MARTY BERGHAMMER Berghammer, Martin Andrew "Pepper" b: 6/18/1888, Elliott, Pa. d: 12/21/57, Pittsburgh, Pa. BL/TR, 5'9", 172 lbs. Deb: 9/08/11

YEAR	TM/L	G	AB	R	H	2B	3B	HR	RBI	BB	SO	AVG	OBP	SLG	PRO+	BR	/A	RC	SB	CS	SBR	FA	FR	POS	TPR
1911	Chi-A	2	5	0	0	0	0	0	0	0		.000	.167	.000	-54	-1	-1	0	0			1.000	-0	/2	-0.1
1913	Cin-N	74	188	25	41	4	1	1	13	10	29	.218	.269	.266	53	-12	-11	17	16			.909	5	S2	-0.3
1914	Cin-N	77	112	15	25	2	0	0	6	10	18	.223	.287	.241	56	-6	-6	8	4			.906	7	S2	0.2
1915	Pit-F	132	469	96	114	10	6	0	33	83	44	.243	.371	.290	96	2	3	64	26			**.943**	-16	*S	-0.2
Total	4	285	774	136	180	16	7	1	52	103	91	.233	.335	.275	79	-16	-16	90	46			.931	-5	S/2	-0.4

■ AL BERGMAN Bergman, Alfred Henry "Dutch" b: 9/27/1890, Peru, Ind. d: 6/20/61, Fort Wayne, Ind. BR/TR, 5'7", 155 lbs. Deb: 8/29/16

YEAR	TM/L	G	AB	R	H	2B	3B	HR	RBI	BB	SO	AVG	OBP	SLG	PRO+	BR	/A	RC	SB	CS	SBR	FA	FR	POS	TPR
1916	Cle-A	8	14	2	3	0	1	0	0	2	4	.214	.313	.357	95	-0	-0	2	0			.889	-2	/2	-0.2

■ DAVE BERGMAN Bergman, David Bruce b: 6/6/53, Evanston, Ill. BL/TL, 6'1.5", 185 lbs. Deb: 8/26/75

YEAR	TM/L	G	AB	R	H	2B	3B	HR	RBI	BB	SO	AVG	OBP	SLG	PRO+	BR	/A	RC	SB	CS	SBR	FA	FR	POS	TPR
1975	NY-A	7	17	0	0	0	0	0	0	2	4	.000	.105	.000	-70	-4	-4	0	0	0	0	.917	0	/O	-0.4
1977	NY-A	5	4	1	1	0	0	0	1	0	0	.250	.250	.250	37	-0	-0	0	0	0	0	1.000	-1	/O1	-0.1
1978	Hou-N	104	186	15	43	5	1	0	12	39	32	.231	.364	.269	86	-3	-1	20	2	0	1	.993	-2	1O	-0.6
1979	Hou-N	13	15	4	6	0	0	1	2	0	3	.400	.400	.600	179	1	1	4	0	0	0	1.000	-0	/1	0.1
1980	*Hou-N	90	78	12	20	6	1	0	3	10	10	.256	.341	.359	104	-0	0	10	1	0	0	.995	3	1/O	0.3
1981	Hou-N	6	6	1	1	0	0	1	1	0	0	.167	.167	.667	134	0	0	1	0	0	0	1.000	0	/1	0.1
	SF-N	63	145	16	37	9	0	3	13	19	18	.255	.341	.379	106	1	1	19	2	0	1	.992	2	1O	0.2
	Yr	69	151	17	38	9	0	4	14	19	18	.252	.335	.391	108	1	2	20	2	0	1	.992	2	1O	0.3
1982	SF-N	100	121	22	33	3	1	4	14	18	11	.273	.367	.413	118	3	3	20	3	0	1	.991	1	1/O	0.4
1983	SF-N	90	140	16	40	4	1	6	24	24	21	.286	.394	.457	140	7	8	25	2	1	0	.994	3	1/O	0.9
1984	*Det-A	120	271	42	74	8	5	7	44	33	40	.273	.358	.417	115	6	6	41	3	4	-2	.989	8	*1/O	0.8
1985	Det-A	69	140	8	25	2	0	3	7	14	15	.179	.253	.257	41	-12	-11	9	0	0	0	.991	1	1/OD	-1.2
1986	Det-A	65	130	14	30	6	1	1	9	21	16	.231	.338	.315	79	-3	-3	15	0	0	0	.986	2	1/OD	-0.3
1987	*Det-A	91	172	25	47	7	3	6	22	30	23	.273	.384	.453	127	6	7	32	0	1	-1	.992	-1	1/OD	0.2
1988	Det-A	116	289	37	85	14	0	5	35	38	34	.294	.376	.394	121	7	9	43	0	2	-1	.990	-0	1DO	0.3
1989	Det-A	137	385	38	103	13	1	7	37	44	44	.268	.346	.361	102	1	2	50	1	3	-2	.993	5	*1/OD	-0.3
1990	Det-A	100	205	21	57	10	1	2	26	33	17	.278	.378	.366	108	4	4	29	3	2	-0	.995	-3	D1/O	-0.1

YEAR	TM/L	G	AB	R	H	2B	3B	HR	RBI	BB	SO	AVG	OBP	SLG	PRO+	BR	/A	RC	SB	CS	SBR	FA	FR	POS	TPR
1991	Det-A	86	194	23	46	10	1	7	29	35	40	.237	.354	.407	108	3	3	30	1	1	-0	.997	-1	1D/O	0.0
1992	Det-A	87	181	17	42	3	0	1	10	20	19	.232	.308	.265	61	-9	-9	16	1	0	0	.986	-2	1D/O	-1.4
Total	17	1349	2679	312	690	100	16	54	289	380	347	.258	.351	.367	102	9	16	364	19	14	-3	.992	15	1DO	-1.1
■ **FRANK BERKELBACH** Berkelbach, Francis P. b: Philadelphia, Pa. 6′, 182 lbs. Deb: 7/04/1884																									
1884	Cin-a	6	25	3	6	0	1	0		0		.240	.296	.320	99	0	-0	2				.667	-2	/O	-0.1
■ **NATE BERKENSTOCK** Berkenstock, Nathan b: 1831, Pennsylvania d: 2/23/1900, Philadelphia, Pa. Deb: 10/30/1871																									
1871	Ath-n	1	4	0	0	0	0	0	0	0	3	.000	.000	.000	-99	-1	-1	0	0					/O	-0.1
■ **BOB BERMAN** Berman, Robert Leon b: 1/24/1899, New York, N.Y. d: 8/2/88, Bridgeport, Conn. BR/TR, 5′8″, 147 lbs. Deb: 6/04/18																									
1918	Was-A	2	0	0	0	0	0	0	0	0	0	—	—	—	—	0	0	0	0			1.000	1	/C	0.1
■ **CURT BERNARD** Bernard, Curtis Henry b: 2/18/1878, Parkersburg, W.Va. d: 4/10/55, Culver City, Cal. BL/TR, 5′10″, 150 lbs. Deb: 9/17/00																									
1900	NY-N	20	71	9	18	2	0	0	8	6		.254	.329	.282	73	-3	-2	7	1			.929	-2	O/S	-0.5
1901	NY-N	23	76	11	17	0	2	0	6	7		.224	.289	.276	67	-3	-3	7	2			.800	-1	O/2S3	-0.5
Total	2	43	147	20	35	2	2	0	14	13		.238	.309	.279	70	-6	-5	14	3			.857	-3	/O2S3	-1.0
■ **TONY BERNAZARD** Bernazard, Antonio (Garcia) b: 8/24/56, Caguas, P.R. BB/TR, 5′9″, 160 lbs. Deb: 7/13/79																									
1979	Mon-N	22	40	11	12	2	0	1	8	15	12	.300	.500	.425	156	5	5	9	1	2	-1	.982	-1	2	0.3
1980	Mon-N	82	183	26	41	7	1	5	18	17	41	.224	.290	.355	79	-5	-5	19	9	2	2	.976	2	2S	0.2
1981	Chi-A	106	384	53	106	14	4	6	34	54	66	.276	.368	.380	118	10	11	56	4	4	-1	.987	-1	*2/S	1.6
1982	Chi-A	137	540	90	138	25	9	11	56	67	88	.256	.340	.396	101	2	2	78	11	0	3	.985	25	*2	3.7
1983	Chi-A	59	233	30	61	16	2	2	26	17	45	.262	.312	.373	85	-4	-5	27	2	1	0	.976	-2	2	-0.4
	Sea-A	80	300	35	80	18	1	6	30	38	52	.267	.353	.393	101	3	1	44	21	8	2	.971	1	2	0.8
	Yr	139	533	65	141	34	3	8	56	55	97	.265	.336	.385	94	-1	-4	71	23	9	2	.973	-1	*2	0.4
1984	Cle-A	140	439	44	97	15	4	2	38	43	70	.221	.293	.287	60	-22	-23	37	20	13	-2	.971	-11	*2/D	-3.1
1985	Cle-A	153	500	73	137	26	3	11	59	69	72	.274	.363	.404	111	8	9	75	17	9	-0	.978	-29	*2/S	-1.5
1986	Cle-A	146	562	88	169	28	4	17	73	53	77	.301	.367	.456	125	18	19	96	17	8	0	.979	1	*2	2.6
1987	Cle-A	79	293	39	70	12	1	11	30	25	49	.239	.301	.399	83	-7	-8	35	7	4	-0	.983	-16	2	-1.9
	Oak-A	61	214	34	57	14	1	3	19	30	30	.266	.357	.383	103	-0	2	29	4	4	-1	.953	-18	2/D	-1.5
	Yr	140	507	73	127	26	2	14	49	55	79	.250	.325	.393	91	-8	-6	65	11	8	-2	.971	-34	*2/D	-3.4
1991	Det-A	6	12	0	2	0	0	0	0	0	4	.167	.167	.167	-7	-2	-2	0	0	0	0	.900	1	/2D	0.0
Total	10	1071	3700	523	970	177	30	75	391	428	606	.262	.341	.387	100	4	5	508	113	55	1	.978	-48	2/SD	0.8
■ **JUAN BERNHARDT** Bernhardt, Juan Ramon (Coradin) b: 8/31/53, San Pedro De Macoris, D.R. BR/TR, 5′11″, 160 lbs. Deb: 7/10/76																									
1976	NY-A	10	21	1	4	1	0	0	1	0	4	.190	.190	.238	25	-2	-2	1	0	0	0	.800	-1	/O3D	-0.3
1977	Sea-A	89	305	32	74	9	2	7	30	5	26	.243	.260	.354	66	-15	-15	25	2	3	-1	.982	-1	D3/1	-1.7
1978	Sea-A	54	165	13	38	9	0	2	12	9	10	.230	.274	.321	67	-7	-7	14	1	1	-0	.989	-0	13/D	-1.0
1979	Sea-A	1	1	0	1	0	0	0	0	0	0	1.000	1.000	1.000	434	0	0	1	0	0	0	.000	0	/H	0.0
Total	4	154	492	46	117	19	2	9	43	14	40	.238	.263	.339	66	-24	-24	41	3	4	-2	.965	-2	/D31O	-3.0
■ **CARLOS BERNIER** Bernier, Carlos (Rodriguez) b: 1/28/29, Juana Diaz, P.R. d: 4/6/89, Juana Diaz, P.R. BR/TR, 5′9″, 180 lbs. Deb: 4/22/53																									
1953	Pit-N	105	310	48	66	7	8	3	31	51	53	.213	.332	.316	70	-13	-12	32	15	14	-4	.970	5	O	-1.4
■ **JOHNNY BERO** Bero, John George b: 12/22/22, Gary, W.Va. d: 5/11/85, Gardena, Cal. BL/TR, 6′, 170 lbs. Deb: 9/26/48																									
1948	Det-A	4	9	2	0	0	0	0	0	1	1	.000	.100	.000	-70	-2	-2	0	0	0	0	1.000	-1	/2	-0.3
1951	StL-A	61	160	24	34	5	0	5	17	26	30	.213	.323	.338	76	-5	-5	19	1	1	-0	.954	-9	S/2	-1.1
Total	2	65	169	26	34	5	0	5	17	27	31	.201	.311	.320	69	-7	-8	19	1	1	-0	1.000	-10	/S2	-1.4
■ **DALE BERRA** Berra, Dale Anthony b: 12/13/56, Ridgewood, N.J. BR/TR, 6′, 190 lbs. Deb: 8/22/77 F																									
1977	Pit-N	17	40	0	7	1	0	0	3	1	8	.175	.195	.200	6	-5	-5	2	0	0	0	.973	3	3	-0.3
1978	Pit-N	56	135	16	28	2	0	6	14	13	20	.207	.287	.356	75	-4	-5	14	3	1	0	.908	1	3/S	-0.4
1979	Pit-N	44	123	11	26	5	0	3	15	11	17	.211	.276	.325	61	-6	-7	10	0	0	0	.940	1	S3	-0.5
1980	Pit-N	93	245	21	54	8	2	6	31	16	52	.220	.271	.343	69	-10	-11	22	2	0	1	.968	2	3S/2	-0.6
1981	Pit-N	81	232	21	56	12	0	2	27	17	34	.241	.302	.319	74	-7	-8	24	11	1	3	.976	2	3S2	-0.1
1982	Pit-N	156	529	64	139	25	5	10	61	33	83	.263	.311	.386	91	-5	-7	59	6	6	-2	.961	-2	*S/3	0.3
1983	Pit-N	161	537	51	135	25	1	10	52	61	84	.251	.328	.358	88	-7	-9	63	8	5	-1	.963	16	*S	2.3
1984	Pit-N	136	450	31	100	16	0	9	52	34	78	.222	.278	.318	67	-20	-20	38	1	3	-2	.955	-2	*S/3	-1.1
1985	NY-A	48	109	8	25	5	1	1	8	7	20	.229	.276	.321	64	-6	-5	9	1	1	-0	.917	4	3/S	-0.1
1986	NY-A	42	108	10	25	7	0	2	13	9	14	.231	.297	.352	77	-4	-4	12	0	0	0	.972	-1	S3/D	-0.3
1987	Hou-N	19	45	3	8	3	0	0	2	8	12	.178	.302	.244	49	-3	-3	4	0	0	0	.963	-3	S/2	-0.4
Total	11	853	2553	236	603	109	9	49	278	210	422	.236	.297	.344	76	-78	-84	258	32	17	-1	.959	21	S3/2D	-1.2
■ **YOGI BERRA** Berra, Lawrence Peter b: 5/12/25, St.Louis, Mo. BL/TR, 5′8″, 194 lbs. Deb: 9/22/46 FMCH																									
1946	NY-A	7	22	3	8	1	0	2	4	1	1	.364	.391	.682	193	3	3	6	0	0	0	1.000	2	/C	0.5
1947	*NY-A	83	293	41	82	15	3	11	54	13	12	.280	.310	.464	115	3	3	41	0	1	-1	.972	-6	CO	-0.1
1948	NY-A☆	125	469	70	143	24	10	14	98	25	24	.305	.341	.488	120	9	10	77	3	3	-1	.979	-9	CO	0.2
1949	*NY-A★	116	415	59	115	20	2	20	91	22	25	.277	.323	.480	111	2	2	65	2	1	0	.989	11	*C	1.9
1950	*NY-A★	151	597	116	192	30	6	28	124	55	12	.322	.383	.533	136	26	28	125	4	2	0	.985	1	*C	3.4
1951	*NY-A★	141	547	92	161	19	4	27	88	44	20	.294	.350	.492	131	17	19	92	5	4	-1	.984	9	*C	3.2
1952	*NY-A★	142	534	97	146	17	1	30	98	66	24	.273	.358	.478	139	21	25	95	2	3	-1	.992	2	*C	3.4
1953	*NY-A★	137	503	80	149	23	5	27	108	50	32	.296	.363	.523	142	24	26	98	0	3	-2	.986	3	*C	3.3
1954	NY-A★	151	584	88	179	28	6	22	125	56	29	.307	.371	.488	139	26	28	107	0	1	-1	.990	-0	*C/3	3.5
1955	*NY-A★	147	541	84	147	20	3	27	108	60	20	.272	.352	.470	121	13	14	90	1	0	0	.984	-0	*C	1.9
1956	*NY-A★	140	521	93	155	29	2	30	105	65	29	.298	.381	.534	144	28	30	108	3	2	-0	.986	7	*C/O	4.1
1957	*NY-A★	134	482	74	121	14	2	24	82	57	24	.251	.331	.438	110	5	6	69	1	2	-1	.995	16	*C/O	2.6
1958	*NY-A★	122	433	60	115	17	3	22	90	35	35	.266	.323	.471	120	8	10	67	3	0	1	**1.000**	6	CO/1	2.1
1959	NY-A★	131	472	64	134	25	1	19	69	43	38	.284	.349	.462	125	13	15	77	1	2	-1	**.997**	7	*C/O	2.7
1960	*NY-A★	120	359	46	99	14	1	15	62	38	23	.276	.350	.446	120	7	9	55	2	1	0	.989	-10	CO	0.1
1961	*NY-A★	119	395	62	107	11	0	22	61	35	28	.271	.333	.466	117	5	8	62	2	0	1	.988	3	OC	0.7
1962	*NY-A★	86	232	25	52	8	0	10	35	24	18	.224	.302	.388	87	-6	-5	26	0	1	-1	.990	8	CO	0.2
1963	*NY-A	64	147	20	43	6	0	8	28	15	17	.293	.362	.497	139	7	7	26	1	0	0	.988	8	C	1.8
1965	NY-N	4	9	1	2	0	0	0	0	0	3	.222	.222	.222	27	-1	-1	0	0	0	0	.941	1	/C	0.0
Total	19	2120	7555	1175	2150	321	49	358	1430	704	414	.285	.350	.482	126	209	238	1284	30	26	-7	.989	57	*CO/13	35.5
■ **DENNIS BERRAN** Berran, Dennis Martin b: 10/8/1887, Merrimac, Mass. d: 4/28/43, Boston, Mass. BL/TL, Deb: 8/11/12																									
1912	Chi-A	2	4	1	1	0	0	0	0	0		.250	.250	.250	44	-0	-0	0	0			1.000	-1	/O	-0.1
■ **RAY BERRES** Berres, Raymond Frederick b: 8/31/07, Kenosha, Wis. BR/TR, 5′9″, 170 lbs. Deb: 4/24/34 C																									
1934	Bro-N	39	79	7	17	4	0	0	3	1	16	.215	.225	.266	32	-8	-7	5	0			.969	-2	C	-0.8
1936	Bro-N	105	267	16	64	10	1	1	13	14	35	.240	.280	.296	55	-17	-17	21	1			.988	23	*C	0.9
1937	Pit-N	2	6	0	1	0	0	0	0	0	0	.167	.167	.167	-9	-1	-1	0	0			1.000	1	/C	0.0
1938	Pit-N	40	100	7	23	2	0	0	6	8	10	.230	.287	.250	48	-7	-7	7	0			.993	4	C	-0.1
1939	Pit-N	81	231	22	53	6	1	0	16	11	25	.229	.267	.264	44	-18	-18	15	1			.993	-2	C	-1.6
1940	Pit-N	21	32	2	6	0	0	0	2	1	1	.188	.212	.188	11	-4	-4	1	0			.980	3	C	-0.1

YEAR	TM/L	G	AB	R	H	2B	3B	HR	RBI	BB	SO	AVG	OBP	SLG	PRO+	BR	/A	RC	SB	CS	SBR	FA	FR	POS	TPR
	Bos-N	85	229	12	44	4	1	0	14	18	19	.192	.251	.218	32	-21	-20	13	0			.981	1	C	-1.4
	Yr	106	261	14	50	4	1	0	16	19	20	.192	.246	.215	29	-25	-24	14	0			.981	3	*C	-1.5
1941	Bos-N	120	279	21	56	10	0	1	19	17	20	.201	.247	.247	41	-23	-21	15	2			**.995**	9	*C	-0.4
1942	NY-N	12	32	0	6	0	0	0	1	2	3	.188	.235	.188	24	-3	-3	1	0			.973	-2	C	-0.4
1943	NY-N	20	28	1	4	1	0	0	0	1	2	.143	.172	.179	1	-4	-4	1	0			.981	4	C	0.1
1944	NY-N	16	17	4	8	0	0	1	2	1	0	.471	.526	.647	230	3	3	5	0			1.000	0	C	0.4
1945	NY-N	20	30	4	5	0	0	0	2	2	3	.167	.219	.167	8	-4	-4	1	0			1.000	1	C	-0.2
Total	11	561	1330	96	287	37	3	3	78	76	134	.216	.260	.255	43	-106	-102	87	4			.989	40	C	-3.6

■ GERONIMO BERROA

Berroa, Geronimo Emiliano Letta (b: Geronimo Emiliano Letta (Berroa)) b: 3/18/65, Santo Domingo, D.R. BR/TR, 6', 165 lbs. Deb: 4/05/89

YEAR	TM/L	G	AB	R	H	2B	3B	HR	RBI	BB	SO	AVG	OBP	SLG	PRO+	BR	/A	RC	SB	CS	SBR	FA	FR	POS	TPR
1989	Atl-N	81	136	7	36	4	0	2	9	7	32	.265	.301	.338	80	-3	-4	13	0	1	-1	.971	1	O	-0.4
1990	Atl-N	7	4	0	0	0	0	0	0	1	1	.000	.200	.000	-38	-1	-1	0	0	0	0	1.000	-1	/O	-0.2
1992	Cin-N	13	15	2	4	1	0	0	0	2	1	.267	.389	.333	101	0	0	2	0	1	-1	1.000	0	/O	0.0
Total	3	101	155	9	40	5	0	2	9	10	34	.258	.307	.329	79	-4	-4	15	0	2	-1	.973	0	/O	-0.6

■ KEN BERRY

Berry, Allen Kent b: 5/10/41, Kansas City, Mo. BR/TR, 5'11", 180 lbs. Deb: 9/09/62

YEAR	TM/L	G	AB	R	H	2B	3B	HR	RBI	BB	SO	AVG	OBP	SLG	PRO+	BR	/A	RC	SB	CS	SBR	FA	FR	POS	TPR
1962	Chi-A	3	6	2	2	0	0	0	0	0	0	.333	.333	.333	80	-0	-0	1	0	0	0	1.000	1	/O	0.0
1963	Chi-A	4	5	2	1	0	0	0	0	1	1	.200	.333	.200	55	-0	-0	0	0	0	0	.857	-0	/O2	0.0
1964	Chi-A	12	32	4	12	1	0	1	4	5	3	.375	.459	.500	171	3	3	7	0	1	-1	1.000	-3	O	0.0
1965	Chi-A	157	472	51	103	17	4	12	42	28	96	.218	.269	.347	79	-17	-14	45	4	2	0	.980	3	*O	-1.7
1966	Chi-A	147	443	50	120	20	2	8	34	28	63	.271	.317	.379	106	-1	3	51	7	10	-4	.991	-9	*O	-1.8
1967	Chi-A★	147	485	49	117	14	4	7	41	46	68	.241	.311	.330	93	-6	-4	49	9	8	-2	.992	-15	*O	-3.1
1968	Chi-A	153	504	49	127	21	2	7	32	25	64	.252	.289	.343	90	-7	-7	46	6	6	-2	.981	3	*O	-1.6
1969	Chi-A	130	297	25	69	12	2	4	18	24	50	.232	.296	.327	71	-11	-12	27	1	2	-1	**1.000**	-5	*O	-2.4
1970	Chi-A	141	463	45	128	12	2	7	50	43	61	.276	.346	.356	90	-3	-5	54	6	4	-1	.988	6	*O	-0.7
1971	Cal-A	111	298	29	66	17	0	3	22	18	33	.221	.273	.309	69	-14	-12	23	3	2	-0	.988	2	*O	-1.5
1972	Cal-A	119	409	41	118	15	3	5	39	35	47	.289	.348	.377	122	8	10	56	5	3	-0	**1.000**	14	*O	2.1
1973	Cal-A	136	415	48	118	11	2	3	36	26	50	.284	.328	.342	96	-6	-2	41	1	6	-3	**.997**	3	*O	-0.8
1974	Mil-A	98	267	21	64	9	2	1	24	18	26	.240	.295	.300	72	-10	-10	24	3	1	0	.995	-3	OD	-1.6
1975	Cle-A	25	40	6	8	1	0	0	1	1	7	.200	.238	.225	31	-4	-4	2	0	1	-1	.926	-2	O/D	-0.7
Total	14	1383	4136	422	1053	150	23	58	343	298	569	.255	.309	.344	90	-67	-54	425	45	46	-14	.989	-5	*O/D2	-13.8

■ CHARLIE BERRY

Berry, Charles Francis b: 10/18/02, Philipsburg, N.J. d: 9/6/72, Evanston, Ill. BR/TR, 6', 185 lbs. Deb: 6/15/25 FUC

YEAR	TM/L	G	AB	R	H	2B	3B	HR	RBI	BB	SO	AVG	OBP	SLG	PRO+	BR	/A	RC	SB	CS	SBR	FA	FR	POS	TPR
1925	Phi-A	10	14	1	3	1	0	0	3	0	2	.214	.214	.286	24	-2	-2	1	0	0	0	.900	-1	/C	-0.2
1928	Bos-A	80	177	18	46	7	3	1	19	21	19	.260	.342	.350	84	-4	-4	22	1	1	-0	.959	-9	C	-0.8
1929	Bos-A	77	207	19	50	11	4	1	21	15	29	.242	.302	.348	69	-11	-10	21	2	4	-2	.983	3	C	-0.3
1930	Bos-A	88	256	31	74	9	6	6	35	16	22	.289	.331	.441	98	-3	-2	38	2	0	1	.988	7	C	1.2
1931	Bos-A	111	357	41	101	16	2	6	49	29	38	.283	.337	.389	96	-5	-3	48	4	0	1	.985	-3	*C	0.2
1932	Bos-A	10	32	0	6	3	0	0	6	3	2	.188	.257	.281	40	-3	-3	2	0	0	0	.944	-1	C	-0.3
	Chi-A	72	226	33	69	15	6	4	31	21	23	.305	.364	.478	124	5	7	40	3	0	1	.981	-2	C	1.0
	Yr	82	258	33	75	18	6	4	37	24	25	.291	.351	.453	114	2	4	42	3	0	1	.977	-2	C	0.7
1933	Chi-A	86	271	25	69	8	3	2	28	17	16	.255	.301	.328	70	-13	-12	27	0	0	0	.987	-8	C	-1.5
1934	Phi-A	99	269	14	72	10	2	0	34	22	23	.268	.323	.320	69	-13	-12	29	1	0	0	.987	-0	C	-0.7
1935	Phi-A	62	190	14	48	7	3	3	29	10	20	.253	.290	.368	70	-9	-9	20	0	0	0	.987	-1	C	-0.7
1936	Phi-A	13	17	0	1	1	0	0	1	6	2	.059	.304	.118	8	-2	-2	1	0	0	0	.971	1	C	-0.1
1938	Phi-A	1	2	0	0	0	0	0	0	0	0	.000	.000	.000	-99	-1	-1	0	0	0	0	1.000	0	/C	0.0
Total	11	709	2018	196	539	88	29	23	256	160	196	.267	.322	.374	83	-62	-51	251	13	5	1	.982	-12	C	-2.2

■ CHARLIE BERRY

Berry, Charles Joseph b: 9/6/1860, Elizabeth, N.J. d: 1/22/40, Phillipsburg, N.J. BR/TR, 5'11", 175 lbs. Deb: 4/30/1884 F

YEAR	TM/L	G	AB	R	H	2B	3B	HR	RBI	BB	SO	AVG	OBP	SLG	PRO+	BR	/A	RC	SB	CS	SBR	FA	FR	POS	TPR
1884	Alt-U	7	25	2	6	0	0	0		0		.240	.240	.240	62	-1	-1	1				.862	-6	/2	-0.7
	KC-U	29	118	15	29	6	1	1		1		.246	.252	.339	113	-0	2	10				.887	3	2/O3	0.5
	CP-U	7	27	4	3	2	0	0		0		.111	.111	.185	-1	-3	-3	1				.833	1	/2	-0.2
	Yr	43	170	21	38	8	1	1		1		.224	.228	.300	84	-4	-2	12				.871	-3	2/O3	-0.4

■ CLAUDE BERRY

Berry, Claude Elzy "Admiral" b: 2/14/1880, Losantville, Ind. d: 2/1/74, Richmond, Ind. BR/TR, 5'7", 165 lbs. Deb: 4/22/04

YEAR	TM/L	G	AB	R	H	2B	3B	HR	RBI	BB	SO	AVG	OBP	SLG	PRO+	BR	/A	RC	SB	CS	SBR	FA	FR	POS	TPR
1904	Chi-A	3	1	1	0	0	0	0	0	1		.000	.500	.000	68	0	0	0	0			1.000	1	/C	0.1
1906	Phi-A	10	30	2	7	0	0	0	2	2		.233	.281	.233	60	-1	-1	2	1			.938	6	C	0.5
1907	Phi-A	8	19	2	4	2	0	0	1	2		.211	.286	.316	90	-0	-0	2	0			.944	-2	/C	-0.2
1914	Pit-F	124	411	35	98	18	9	2	36	26	50	.238	.284	.341	78	-13	-13	44	6			.970	1	*C	-0.1
1915	Pit-F	100	292	32	56	11	1	1	26	29	42	.192	.269	.247	52	-17	-17	23	7			.980	-0	C	-1.0
Total	5	245	753	72	165	31	10	3	65	60	92	.219	.279	.299	68	-32	-31	72	14			.971	4	C	-0.7

■ NEIL BERRY

Berry, Cornelius John b: 1/11/22, Kalamazoo, Mich. BR/TR, 5'10", 170 lbs. Deb: 4/20/48

YEAR	TM/L	G	AB	R	H	2B	3B	HR	RBI	BB	SO	AVG	OBP	SLG	PRO+	BR	/A	RC	SB	CS	SBR	FA	FR	POS	TPR
1948	Det-A	87	256	46	68	8	1	0	16	37	23	.266	.358	.305	75	-7	-8	31	1	3	-2	.930	4	S2	-0.2
1949	Det-A	109	329	38	78	9	1	0	18	27	24	.237	.299	.271	51	-23	-23	27	4	2	0	.970	-0	2/S	-1.9
1950	Det-A	39	40	9	10	1	0	0	7	6	11	.250	.348	.275	59	-2	-2	5	0	0	0	.944	2	S/23	0.1
1951	Det-A	67	157	17	36	5	2	0	9	10	15	.229	.275	.287	52	-11	-11	13	4	2	0	.944	8	S2/3	0.0
1952	Det-A	73	189	22	43	4	3	0	13	22	19	.228	.311	.280	65	-8	-9	17	1	3	-2	.965	4	S/3	-0.3
1953	StL-A	57	99	14	28	1	2	0	11	9	10	.283	.343	.333	82	-2	-2	11	1	2	-1	.825	-1	32/S	-0.4
	Chi-A	5	8	1	1	0	0	0	0	1	1	.125	.222	.125	-4	-1	-1	0	0	0	0	1.000	2	/2	0.1
	Yr	62	107	15	29	1	2	0	11	10	11	.271	.333	.318	75	-3	-4	11	1	2	-1	.825	1	32/S	-0.3
1954	Bal-A	5	9	1	1	0	0	0	0	1	2	.111	.200	.111	-14	-1	-1	0	0	0	0	1.000	0	/S	-0.1
Total	7	442	1087	148	265	28	9	0	74	113	105	.244	.317	.286	62	-56	-58	104	11	12	-4	.949	19	S2/3	-2.7

■ JOE BERRY

Berry, Joseph Howard Jr. "Nig" b: 12/31/1894, Philadelphia, Pa. d: 4/29/76, Philadelphia, Pa. BB/TR, 5'10.5", 159 lbs. Deb: 7/18/21 F

YEAR	TM/L	G	AB	R	H	2B	3B	HR	RBI	BB	SO	AVG	OBP	SLG	PRO+	BR	/A	RC	SB	CS	SBR	FA	FR	POS	TPR
1921	NY-N	9	6	0	2	0	1	0	2	1	1	.333	.429	.667	185	1	1	2	0	0	0	.875	0	/2	0.1
1922	NY-N	6	0	0	0	0	0	0	0	0	0	—	—	—	—	0	0	0	0	0	0	.000	0	R	0.0
Total	2	15	6	0	2	0	1	0	2	1	1	.333	.429	.667	185	1	1	2	0	0	0	.968	0	/2	0.1

■ JOE BERRY

Berry, Joseph Howard Sr. "Hodge" b: 9/10/1872, Wheeling, W.Va. d: 3/13/61, Allenwood, N.J. BB/TR, 5'9", 172 lbs. Deb: 9/04/02 F

YEAR	TM/L	G	AB	R	H	2B	3B	HR	RBI	BB	SO	AVG	OBP	SLG	PRO+	BR	/A	RC	SB	CS	SBR	FA	FR	POS	TPR
1902	Phi-N	1	4	0	1	0	0	0	1	1		.250	.400	.250	101	0	0	1	1			1.000	-1	/C	-0.1

■ SEAN BERRY

Berry, Sean Robert b: 3/22/66, Santa Monica, Cal. BR/TR, 5'11", 200 lbs. Deb: 9/17/90

YEAR	TM/L	G	AB	R	H	2B	3B	HR	RBI	BB	SO	AVG	OBP	SLG	PRO+	BR	/A	RC	SB	CS	SBR	FA	FR	POS	TPR
1990	KC-A	8	23	2	5	1	1	0	4	2	5	.217	.280	.348	76	-1	-1	2	0	0	0	.944	1	/3	0.0
1991	KC-A	31	60	5	8	3	0	0	1	5	23	.133	.212	.183	10	-7	-7	2	0	0	0	.970	8	3	0.1
1992	Mon-N	24	57	5	19	1	0	1	4	1	11	.333	.345	.404	112	1	1	8	2	1	0	.879	-3	3	-0.2
Total	3	63	140	12	32	5	1	1	9	8	39	.229	.275	.300	61	-7	-7	12	2	1	0	.941	6	/3	-0.1

■ TOM BERRY

Berry, Thomas Haney b: 12/31/1842, Chester, Pa. d: 6/6/15, Chester, Pa. 5'6", 140 lbs. Deb: 9/02/1871

YEAR	TM/L	G	AB	R	H	2B	3B	HR	RBI	BB	SO	AVG	OBP	SLG	PRO+	BR	/A	RC	SB	CS	SBR	FA	FR	POS	TPR
1871	Ath-n	1	4	0	1	0	0	0	0	0	0	.250	.250	.250	45	-0	-0	0	0					/O	0.0

■ DAMON BERRYHILL

Berryhill, Damon Scott b: 12/3/63, South Laguna, Cal. BB/TR, 6' ", 210 lbs. Deb: 9/05/87

YEAR	TM/L	G	AB	R	H	2B	3B	HR	RBI	BB	SO	AVG	OBP	SLG	PRO+	BR	/A	RC	SB	CS	SBR	FA	FR	POS	TPR
1987	Chi-N	12	28	2	5	1	0	0	1	3	5	.179	.258	.214	26	-3	-3	1	0	1	-1	.909	-4	C	-0.7
1988	Chi-N	95	309	19	80	19	1	7	38	17	56	.259	.298	.395	93	-2	-4	33	1	0	0	.982	-3	C	0.0
1989	Chi-N	91	334	37	86	13	0	5	41	16	54	.257	.295	.341	76	-8	-11	31	1	0	0	.992	-12	C	-1.9

YEAR	TM/L	G	AB	R	H	2B	3B	HR	RBI	BB	SO	AVG	OBP	SLG	PRO+	BR	/A	RC	SB	CS	SBR	FA	FR	POS	TPR
1990	Chi-N	17	53	6	10	4	0	1	9	5	14	.189	.259	.321	54	-3	-4	4	0	0	0	.978	-3	C	-0.6
1991	Chi-N	62	159	13	30	7	0	5	14	11	41	.189	.246	.327	57	-9	-10	12	1	2	-1	.967	-6	C	-1.6
	Atl-N	1	1	0	0	0	0	0	0	0	1	.000	.000	.000	-94	-0	-0	0	0	0	0	1.000	0	/C	0.0
	Yr	63	160	13	30	7	0	5	14	11	42	.188	.244	.325	56	-9	-10	12	1	2	-1	.967	-6	C	-1.6
1992	*Atl-N	101	307	21	70	16	1	10	43	17	67	.228	.271	.384	77	-8	-11	31	0	2	-1	.998	-8	C	-1.6
Total	6	379	1191	98	281	60	2	28	146	69	238	.236	.280	.360	76	-33	-42	113	3	5	-2	.985	-35	C	-6.4

■ HARRY BERTE

Berte, Harry Thomas b: 5/10/1872, Covington, Ky. d: 5/6/52, Los Angeles, Cal. TR, Deb: 9/17/03

YEAR	TM/L	G	AB	R	H	2B	3B	HR	RBI	BB	SO	AVG	OBP	SLG	PRO+	BR	/A	RC	SB	CS	SBR	FA	FR	POS	TPR
1903	StL-N	4	15	1	5	0	0	0	1	1		.333	.375	.333	106	0	0	2	0			.778	-4	/2S	-0.4

■ DICK BERTELL

Bertell, Richard George b: 11/21/35, Oak Park, Ill. BR/TR, 6'0.5", 200 lbs. Deb: 9/22/60

YEAR	TM/L	G	AB	R	H	2B	3B	HR	RBI	BB	SO	AVG	OBP	SLG	PRO+	BR	/A	RC	SB	CS	SBR	FA	FR	POS	TPR
1960	Chi-N	5	15	0	2	0	0	0	2	3	1	.133	.278	.133	17	-2	-2	1	0	0	0	1.000	-1	/C	-0.3
1961	Chi-N	92	267	20	73	7	1	2	33	15	33	.273	.312	.330	70	-11	-12	26	0	0	0	.982	4	C	-0.4
1962	Chi-N	77	215	19	65	6	2	2	18	13	30	.302	.345	.377	90	-2	-3	27	0	1	-1	.986	-13	C	-1.4
1963	Chi-N	100	322	15	75	7	2	2	14	24	41	.233	.286	.286	62	-14	-16	25	0	2	-1	.988	16	C	0.3
1964	Chi-N	112	353	29	84	11	3	4	35	33	67	.238	.307	.320	74	-10	-12	34	2	1	0	.981	-5	*C	-1.2
1965	Chi-N	34	84	6	18	2	0	0	7	11	10	.214	.305	.238	54	-5	-5	7	0	0	0	.981	3	C	-0.1
	SF-N	22	48	1	9	1	0	0	3	7	5	.188	.291	.208	42	-3	-4	3	0	0	0	.992	2	C	-0.1
	Yr	56	132	7	27	3	0	0	10	18	15	.205	.300	.227	50	-8	-8	10	0	0	0	.986	5	C	-0.2
1967	Chi-N	2	6	1	1	0	1	0	0	0	1	.167	.167	.500	80	-0	-0	1	0	0	0	1.000	0	/C	0.0
Total	7	444	1310	91	327	34	9	10	112	106	188	.250	.307	.312	70	-47	-53	124	2	4	-2	.985	7	C	-3.2

■ HARRY BERTHRONG

Berthrong, Henry W. b: 1/1/1844, Mumford, N.Y. d: 4/28/28, Chelsea, Mass. TR, 5'6.5", 140 lbs. Deb: 5/05/1871

YEAR	TM/L	G	AB	R	H	2B	3B	HR	RBI	BB	SO	AVG	OBP	SLG	PRO+	BR	/A	RC	SB	CS	SBR	FA	FR	POS	TPR
1871	Oly-n	17	73	17	17	1	1	0	8	4	2	.233	.273	.274	61	-4	-3	6	3					O/23	-0.2

■ RENO BERTOIA

Bertoia, Reno Peter b: 1/8/35, St.Vito Udine, Italy BR/TR, 5'11.5", 185 lbs. Deb: 9/22/53

YEAR	TM/L	G	AB	R	H	2B	3B	HR	RBI	BB	SO	AVG	OBP	SLG	PRO+	BR	/A	RC	SB	CS	SBR	FA	FR	POS	TPR
1953	Det-A	1	1	0	0	0	0	0	0	0	1	.000	.000	.000	-99	-0	-0	0	0	0	0	.500	-0	/2	-0.1
1954	Det-A	54	37	13	6	2	0	1	2	5	9	.162	.262	.297	54	-3	-2	3	1	0	0	.969	17	2/3S	1.5
1955	Det-A	38	68	13	14	2	1	1	10	5	11	.206	.260	.309	54	-5	-5	6	0	0	0	.923	7	3/2S	0.2
1956	Det-A	22	66	7	12	2	0	1	5	6	12	.182	.260	.258	37	-6	-6	4	0	0	0	.982	10	2/3	0.5
1957	Det-A	97	295	28	81	16	2	4	28	19	43	.275	.327	.383	91	-3	-4	36	2	3	-1	.953	-19	3/S2	-2.3
1958	Det-A	86	240	28	56	6	0	6	27	20	35	.233	.298	.333	68	-9	-11	25	5	2	0	.950	4	3/SO	-0.6
1959	Was-A	90	308	33	73	10	0	8	29	29	48	.237	.305	.347	79	-9	-9	30	2	5	-2	.971	-11	2/3S	-1.7
1960	Was-A	121	460	44	122	17	7	4	45	26	58	.265	.316	.359	83	-12	-11	50	3	5	-2	.961	-0	*32	-1.3
1961	Min-A	35	104	17	22	2	0	1	8	20	12	.212	.339	.260	59	-5	-6	10	0	0	0	.900	-5	3	-1.1
	KC-A	39	120	12	29	2	0	0	13	9	15	.242	.295	.258	49	-8	-8	9	1	0	0	.942	5	3/2	-0.3
	Det-A	24	46	6	10	1	0	1	4	3	8	.217	.265	.304	50	-3	-3	4	2	0	1	.931	0	3/2S	-0.2
	Yr	98	270	35	61	5	0	2	25	32	35	.226	.308	.267	54	-17	-18	24	3	0	1	.923	-1	32/S	-1.6
1962	Det-A	5	0	3	0	0	0	0	0	0	0	—	—	—	—	0	0	0	0	0	0	1.000	1	/2S3	0.1
Total	10	612	1745	204	425	60	10	27	171	142	252	.244	.306	.336	73	-63	-66	177	16	15	-4	.949	8	32/SO	-5.3

■ BOB BESCHER

Bescher, Robert Henry b: 2/25/1884, London, Ohio d: 11/29/42, London, Ohio BB/TL, 6'1", 200 lbs. Deb: 9/05/08

YEAR	TM/L	G	AB	R	H	2B	3B	HR	RBI	BB	SO	AVG	OBP	SLG	PRO+	BR	/A	RC	SB	CS	SBR	FA	FR	POS	TPR
1908	Cin-N	32	114	16	31	5	5	0	17	9		.272	.336	.404	140	4	5	18	10			1.000	4	O	0.8
1909	Cin-N	124	446	73	107	17	6	1	34	56		.240	.335	.312	102	2	3	63	**54**			.953	-0	*O	-0.3
1910	Cin-N	150	589	95	147	20	10	4	48	81	75	.250	.344	.338	104	1	4	91	**70**			.947	2	*O	-0.2
1911	Cin-N	153	599	106	165	32	10	1	45	102	78	.275	.385	.367	115	13	16	114	**80**			.954	-8	*O	0.0
1912	Cin-N	145	548	**120**	154	29	11	4	38	83	61	.281	.381	.396	116	12	14	107	**67**			.963	4	*O	1.0
1913	Cin-N	141	511	86	132	22	11	1	37	**94**	68	.258	.377	.350	109	10	10	77	38			.968	4	*O	0.8
1914	NY-N	135	512	82	138	23	4	6	35	45	48	.270	.336	.365	112	5	7	70	36			.960	9	*O	1.1
1915	StL-N	130	486	71	128	15	7	4	34	52	53	.263	.342	.348	109	6	6	61	27	19	-3	.971	-1	*O	-0.5
1916	StL-N	151	561	78	132	24	8	6	43	60	50	.235	.316	.339	102	1	2	67	39	12	5	.953	0	*O	-0.1
1917	StL-N	42	110	10	17	1	1	1	8	20	13	.155	.290	.209	56	-5	-5	8	3			.984	-3	O	-1.1
1918	Cle-A	25	60	12	20	2	1	0	6	17	5	.333	.487	.400	153	7	6	13	3			.969	-0	O	0.5
Total	11	1228	4536	749	1171	190	74	28	345	619	451	.258	.353	.351	109	56	68	690	427	31		.960	9	*O	2.0

■ BESTICK

Bestick b: New York, N.Y. Deb: 6/10/1872

YEAR	TM/L	G	AB	R	H	2B	3B	HR	RBI	BB	SO	AVG	OBP	SLG	PRO+	BR	/A	RC	SB	CS	SBR	FA	FR	POS	TPR
1872	Eck-n	4	14	0	3	0	0	0	1	0	0	.214	.214	.214	38	-1	-1	1						/C	-0.1

■ JIM BESWICK

Beswick, James William b: 2/12/58, Wilkinsburg, Pa. BB/TR, 6'1", 180 lbs. Deb: 8/09/78

YEAR	TM/L	G	AB	R	H	2B	3B	HR	RBI	BB	SO	AVG	OBP	SLG	PRO+	BR	/A	RC	SB	CS	SBR	FA	FR	POS	TPR
1978	SD-N	17	20	2	1	0	0	0	0	1	7	.050	.095	.050	-63	-4	-4	0	0	0	0	1.000	1	/O	-0.4

■ FRANK BETCHER

Betcher, Franklin Lyle (b: Franklin Lyle Bettger)
b: 2/15/1888, Philadelphia, Pa. d: 11/27/81, Wynnewood, Pa. BB/TR, 5'11", 173 lbs. Deb: 5/21/10

YEAR	TM/L	G	AB	R	H	2B	3B	HR	RBI	BB	SO	AVG	OBP	SLG	PRO+	BR	/A	RC	SB	CS	SBR	FA	FR	POS	TPR
1910	StL-N	35	89	7	18	2	0	0	6	7	14	.202	.276	.225	48	-6	-6	6	1			.928	0	S/32O	-0.5

■ BILL BETHEA

Bethea, William Lamar "Spot" b: 1/1/42, Houston, Tex. BR/TR, 6', 175 lbs. Deb: 9/13/64

YEAR	TM/L	G	AB	R	H	2B	3B	HR	RBI	BB	SO	AVG	OBP	SLG	PRO+	BR	/A	RC	SB	CS	SBR	FA	FR	POS	TPR
1964	Min-A	10	30	4	5	1	0	0	2	4	4	.167	.265	.200	31	-3	-3	2	0	0	0	1.000	-1	/2S	-0.3

■ LARRY BETTENCOURT

Bettencourt, Lawrence Joseph b: 9/22/05, Newark, Cal. d: 9/15/78, New Orleans, La. BR/TR, 5'11", 195 lbs. Deb: 6/02/28

YEAR	TM/L	G	AB	R	H	2B	3B	HR	RBI	BB	SO	AVG	OBP	SLG	PRO+	BR	/A	RC	SB	CS	SBR	FA	FR	POS	TPR
1928	StL-A	67	159	30	45	9	4	4	24	22	19	.283	.377	.465	117	5	4	29	2	1	0	.946	-11	3/OC	-0.4
1931	StL-A	74	206	27	53	9	2	3	26	31	35	.257	.357	.364	87	-2	-3	28	4	3	-1	.963	-2	O	-0.9
1932	StL-A	27	30	4	4	1	0	1	3	7	6	.133	.297	.267	45	-2	-3	3	1	0	0	1.000	-0	/O3	-0.3
Total	3	168	395	61	102	19	6	8	53	60	60	.258	.360	.397	95	0	-2	60	7	4	-0	.966	-13	/O3C	-1.6

■ BRUNO BETZEL

Betzel, Christian Frederick Albert John Henry David
b: 12/6/1894, Chattanooga, Ohio d: 2/7/65, W.Hollywood, Fla. BR/TR, 5'9", 158 lbs. Deb: 9/03/14

YEAR	TM/L	G	AB	R	H	2B	3B	HR	RBI	BB	SO	AVG	OBP	SLG	PRO+	BR	/A	RC	SB	CS	SBR	FA	FR	POS	TPR
1914	StL-N	7	9	2	0	0	0	0	0	1	1	.000	.100	.000	-70	-2	-2	0	0			1.000	2	/23	0.0
1915	StL-N	117	367	42	92	12	4	0	27	18	48	.251	.291	.305	80	-9	-9	33	10	13	-5	.937	5	*3/2S	-0.5
1916	StL-N	142	510	49	119	15	11	1	37	39	77	.233	.288	.312	85	-10	-10	47	22	16	-3	.960	28	*23/O	2.3
1917	StL-N	106	328	24	71	4	3	1	17	20	47	.216	.266	.256	62	-15	-14	24	9			.962	12	2O/3	0.0
1918	StL-N	76	230	18	51	6	7	0	13	12	16	.222	.260	.309	76	-8	-7	20	8			.914	-2	3O2	-0.9
Total	5	448	1444	135	333	37	25	2	94	90	189	.231	.278	.295	76	-44	-42	124	49	29		.956	46	23/OS	0.9

■ KURT BEVACQUA

Bevacqua, Kurt Anthony b: 1/23/47, Miami Beach, Fla. BR/TR, 6'1", 185 lbs. Deb: 6/22/71

YEAR	TM/L	G	AB	R	H	2B	3B	HR	RBI	BB	SO	AVG	OBP	SLG	PRO+	BR	/A	RC	SB	CS	SBR	FA	FR	POS	TPR
1971	Cle-A	55	137	9	28	3	1	3	13	4	28	.204	.227	.307	46	-9	-11	9	0	0	0	.971	-9	2/O3S	-1.9
1972	Cle-A	19	35	2	4	0	0	1	1	3	10	.114	.184	.200	14	-4	-4	1	0	0	0	.900	-1	O/3	-0.6
1973	KC-A	99	276	39	71	8	3	2	40	25	42	.257	.321	.330	78	-6	-8	29	2	3	-1	.935	-11	32DO/1	-2.1
1974	Pit-N	18	35	1	4	1	0	0	0	2	10	.114	.162	.143	-15	-5	-5	0	0	0	0	.955	-0	/3O	-0.6
	KC-A	39	90	10	19	0	0	0	3	9	20	.211	.290	.211	43	-6	-7	6	1	1	-0	.987	-4	13/2SD	-1.1
1975	Mil-A	104	258	30	59	14	0	2	24	26	45	.229	.302	.306	72	-9	-9	24	3	4	-2	.948	1	32/S1D	-0.8
1976	Mil-A	12	7	3	1	0	0	0	0	0	0	.143	.143	.143	-17	-1	-1	0	0	0	0	1.000	2	/2D	0.1
1977	Tex-A	39	96	13	32	7	2	5	28	6	13	.333	.373	.604	159	8	7	18	0	1	-1	1.000	-7	O3/12D	0.0
1978	Tex-A	90	248	21	55	12	0	6	30	18	31	.222	.274	.343	72	-10	-10	22	1	2	-1	.877	-4	3D2/1	-1.5
1979	SD-N	114	297	23	75	12	4	1	34	38	25	.253	.337	.330	88	-6	-4	31	2	5	-2	.954	-3	32/1O	-1.0
1980	SD-N	62	71	4	19	6	1	0	12	6	1	.268	.325	.380	102	-0	0	9	1	1	-0	.929	-3	3/O21	-0.4
	Pit-N	22	43	1	7	1	0	0	4	6	7	.163	.280	.186	32	-4	-4	2	0	0	0	.958	0	/31	-0.4

YEAR	TM/L	G	AB	R	H	2B	3B	HR	RBI	BB	SO	AVG	OBP	SLG	PRO+	BR	/A	RC	SB	CS	SBR	FA	FR	POS	TPR
	Yr	84	114	5	26	7	1	0	16	12	8	.228	.307	.307	75	-4	-4	11	1	1	-0	.947	-3	3/O12	-0.8
1981	Pit-N	29	27	2	7	1	0	1	4	4	6	.259	.355	.407	112	1	1	4	0	0	0	.941	1	/23	0.2
1982	SD-N	64	123	15	31	9	0	0	24	17	22	.252	.343	.325	93	-2	-1	14	2	0	1	.989	-2	1/O3	-0.3
1983	SD-N	74	156	17	38	7	0	2	24	18	33	.244	.322	.327	83	-4	-3	16	0	3	-2	.995	0	13O	-0.7
1984	*SD-N	59	80	7	16	3	0	1	9	14	19	.200	.326	.275	71	-3	-3	7	0	0	0	1.000	-2	13/O	-0.5
1985	SD-N	71	138	17	33	6	0	3	25	25	17	.239	.356	.348	99	0	1	18	0	0	0	.946	-2	3/1O	-0.2
Total	15	970	2117	214	499	90	11	27	275	221	329	.236	.309	.327	78	-60	-60	210	12	20	-8	.938	-42	321/ODS	-11.8
■ HAL BEVAN Bevan, Joseph Harold b: 11/15/30, New Orleans, La. d: 10/5/68, New Orleans, La. BR/TR, 6'2", 198 lbs. Deb: 4/24/52																									
1952	Bos-A	1	1	0	0	0	0	0	0	0	0	.000	.000	.000	-93	-0	-0	0	0	0	0	.000	0	/3	0.0
	Phi-A	8	17	1	6	0	0	0	4	0	1	.353	.353	.353	91	-0	-0	2	2	0	1	1.000	1	/3	0.1
	Yr	9	18	1	6	0	0	0	4	0	1	.333	.333	.333	81	-0	-0	2	2	0	1	1.000	1	/3	0.1
1955	KC-A	3	3	0	0	0	0	0	0	0	0	.000	.000	.000	-99	-1	-1	0	0	0	0	1.000	0	/3	-0.1
1961	Cin-N	3	3	1	1	0	0	1	1	0	2	.333	.333	1.333	311	1	1	1	0	0	0	.000	0	H	0.1
Total	3	15	24	2	7	0	0	1	5	0	3	.292	.292	.417	89	-0	-1	3	2	0	1	1.000	1	/3	0.1
■ MONTE BEVILLE Beville, Henry Monte b: 2/24/1875, Dublin, Ind. d: 1/24/55, Grand Rapids, Mich BL/TR, 5'11", 180 lbs. Deb: 4/24/03																									
1903	NY-A	82	258	23	50	14	1	0	29	16		.194	.246	.256	48	-15	-17	18	4			.960	-11	C/1	-2.2
1904	NY-A	9	22	2	6	2	0	0	2	2		.273	.333	.364	115	1	0	3	0			.906	-2	/1C	-0.1
	Det-A	54	174	14	36	5	1	0	13	8		.207	.246	.247	58	-9	-8	12	2			.957	-3	C1	-0.9
	Yr	63	196	16	42	7	1	0	15	10		.214	.256	.260	65	-8	-8	15	2			.950	-5	C1	-1.0
Total	2	145	454	39	92	21	2	0	44	26		.203	.251	.258	55	-23	-25	33	6			.957	-16	C/1	-3.2
■ BUDDY BIANCALANA Biancalana, Roland Americo b: 2/2/60, Larkspur, Cal. BB/TR, 5'11", 160 lbs. Deb: 9/12/82																									
1982	KC-A	3	2	0	1	0	1	0	0	1	0	.500	.667	1.500	474	1	1	1	0	0	0	1.000	3	/S	0.3
1983	KC-A	6	15	2	3	0	0	0	0	0	7	.200	.200	.200	10	-2	-2	1	1	0	0	.914	4	/S	0.3
1984	*KC-A	66	134	18	26	6	1	2	9	6	44	.194	.229	.299	44	-10	-10	9	1	2	-1	.946	6	S2/D	-0.2
1985	*KC-A	81	138	21	26	5	1	1	6	17	34	.188	.277	.261	48	-10	-10	10	1	4	-2	.961	11	S/2D	0.3
1986	KC-A	100	190	24	46	4	4	2	8	15	50	.242	.298	.337	71	-7	-8	20	5	1	1	.946	2	S2	0.1
1987	KC-A	37	47	4	10	1	0	1	7	1	10	.213	.229	.298	37	-4	-4	3	0	0	0	.886	4	S2/D	0.1
	Hou-N	18	24	1	1	0	0	0	0	1	12	.042	.080	.042	-69	-6	-6	0	0	0	0	.889	-1	S/2	-0.6
Total	6	311	550	70	113	16	7	6	30	41	157	.205	.261	.293	50	-38	-39	44	8	7	-2	.945	28	S/2D	0.3
■ TOMMY BIANCO Bianco, Thomas Anthony b: 12/16/52, Rockville Cntr, N.Y BB/TR, 5'11", 190 lbs. Deb: 5/28/75																									
1975	Mil-A	18	34	6	6	1	0	0	0	3	7	.176	.263	.206	34	-3	-3	2	0	0	0	.941	-1	/31D	-0.4
■ HANK BIASATTI Biasatti, Henry Arcado b: 1/14/22, Beano, Italy BL/TL, 5'11", 175 lbs. Deb: 4/23/49																									
1949	Phi-A	21	24	6	2	2	0	0	2	8	5	.083	.313	.167	30	-2	-2	2	0	0	0	.979	-1	/1	-0.3
■ DANTE BICHETTE Bichette, Alphonse Dante b: 11/18/63, W.Palm Beach, Fla. BR/TR, 6'3", 215 lbs. Deb: 9/05/88																									
1988	Cal-A	21	46	1	12	2	0	0	8	0	7	.261	.261	.304	59	-3	-2	4	0	0	0	.979	-2	O	-0.5
1989	Cal-A	48	138	13	29	7	0	3	15	6	24	.210	.243	.326	60	-8	-8	11	3	0	1	.990	6	O/D	-0.2
1990	Cal-A	109	349	40	89	15	1	15	53	16	79	.255	.293	.433	103	-1	-0	42	5	2	0	.965	-4	*O	-0.7
1991	Mil-A	134	445	53	106	18	3	15	59	22	107	.238	.276	.393	85	-12	-11	45	14	8	-1	.976	11	*O/3	-0.3
1992	Mil-A	112	387	37	111	27	2	5	41	16	74	.287	.320	.406	104	-0	1	46	18	7	1	.990	-2	*O/D	-0.2
Total	5	424	1365	144	347	69	6	38	176	60	291	.254	.289	.397	92	-24	-20	148	40	17	2	.979	8	O/D3	-1.9
■ OSCAR BIELASKI Bielaski, Oscar b: 3/21/1847, Washington, D.C. d: 11/8/11, Washington, D.C. BR/TR, 5'10.5", 170 lbs. Deb: 4/24/1872																									
1872	Nat-n	10	46	13	9	0	0	0	2	0	0	.196	.196	.196	18	-4	-6	2						O	-0.4
1873	Was-n	38	173	35	49	2	3	0	20	4	5	.283	.299	.329	88	-3	-2	17						*O	-0.1
1874	Bal-n	27	113	18	27	1	0	0		2		.239	.252	.248	60	-5	-5	7						O/12	-0.3
1875	Chi-n	51	196	21	49	2	0	0		2		.250	.258	.260	79	-4	-4	13						*O	-0.3
1876	Chi-N	32	139	24	29	3	0	0	10	2	3	.209	.220	.230	45	-7	-10	7				.763	-2	O	-1.1
Total	4 n	126	528	87	134	5	3	0	22	8	5	.254	.265	.275	72	-16	-17	40						O/21	-1.1
■ LOU BIERBAUER Bierbauer, Louis W. b: 9/28/1865, Erie, Pa. d: 1/31/26, Erie, Pa. BL/TR, 5'8", 140 lbs. Deb: 4/17/1886																									
1886	Phi-a	137	522	56	118	17	5	2		21		.226	.256	.289	71	-17	-18	45	19			.910	-3	*2/CSP	-1.3
1887	Phi-a	126	530	74	144	19	7	1		13		.272	.289	.340	77	-17	-17	65	40			.921	-8	*2/P	-1.8
1888	Phi-a	134	535	83	143	20	9	0	80	25		.267	.301	.338	109	4	4	66	34			.916	22	*23/P	2.8
1889	Phi-a	130	549	80	167	27	7	7	105	29	30	.304	.344	.417	120	11	12	87	17			.941	37	*2/C	4.6
1890	Bro-P	133	589	128	180	31	11	7	99	40	15	.306	.350	.431	103	6	-0	97	16			.931	25	*2	2.5
1891	Pit-N	121	500	60	103	13	6	1	47	28	19	.206	.252	.262	53	-31	-29	37	12			.929	-2	*2	-2.3
1892	Pit-N	152	649	81	153	20	9	8	65	25	29	.236	.264	.331	81	-17	-18	61	11			.950	32	*2	1.5
1893	Pit-N	128	528	84	150	19	11	4	94	36	12	.284	.335	.384	94	-7	-5	73	11			**.959**	16	*2	1.1
1894	Pit-N	130	525	86	159	19	13	3	107	26	9	.303	.337	.406	81	-18	-17	82	19			.938	9	*2	-0.2
1895	Pit-N	117	466	53	120	13	11	0	69	19	8	.258	.290	.333	65	-27	-23	53	18			.946	14	*2	-0.2
1896	Pit-N	59	258	33	74	10	6	0	39	5	7	.287	.300	.372	82	-9	-7	32	7			.966	12	2	0.7
1897	StL-N	12	46	1	10	0	0	0	1	0		.217	.217	.217	15	-6	-5	3	2			.921	-2	2	-0.6
1898	StL-N	4	9	0	0	0	0	0	0	1		.000	.100	.000	-69	-2	-2	0	0			.429	-0	/2S3	-0.2
Total	13	1383	5706	819	1521	208	95	33	706	268	129	.267	.301	.354	85	-130	-126	701	206			.935	151	*2/3CPS	6.6
■ CHARLIE BIERMAN Bierman, Charles S. b: 1845, Hoboken, N.J. d: 2/14/1879, Hoboken, N.J. 6', 180 lbs. Deb: 6/21/1871																									
1871	Kek-n	1	2	0	0	0	0	0	0	1	0	.000	.333	.000	6	-0	-0	0	0					/1	0.0
■ CARSON BIGBEE Bigbee, Carson Lee "Skeeter" b: 3/31/1895, Waterloo, Ore. d: 10/17/64, Portland, Ore. BL/TR, 5'9", 157 lbs. Deb: 8/25/16 F																									
1916	Pit-N	43	164	17	41	3	6	0	3	7	14	.250	.285	.341	91	-2	-2	19	8			.946	-5	2O/3	-0.8
1917	Pit-N	133	469	46	112	11	6	0	21	37	16	.239	.301	.288	78	-10	-11	46	19			.961	-3	*O2/S	-2.2
1918	Pit-N	92	310	47	79	11	3	1	19	42	10	.255	.344	.319	99	2	1	40	19			.958	0	O	-0.4
1919	Pit-N	125	478	61	132	11	4	2	27	37	26	.276	.332	.328	95	0	-2	59	31			.971	18	*O	0.8
1920	Pit-N	137	550	78	154	19	15	4	32	45	28	.280	.341	.391	106	7	5	74	31	15	0	.971	6	*O	0.1
1921	Pit-N	147	632	100	204	23	17	3	42	41	19	.323	.364	.427	106	8	6	94	21	20	-6	.977	16	*O	0.5
1922	Pit-N	150	614	113	215	29	15	5	99	56	13	.350	.405	.471	124	24	23	116	24	15	-2	.956	17	*O	2.6
1923	Pit-N	123	499	79	149	18	7	0	54	43	15	.299	.355	.363	88	-6	-8	65	10	9	-2	.990	10	*O	-0.8
1924	Pit-N	89	282	42	74	4	1	0	15	26	12	.262	.331	.284	65	-12	-13	29	15	7	0	.943	0	O	-1.7
1925	*Pit-N	66	126	31	30	7	0	0	8	7	8	.238	.278	.294	43	-10	-11	10	2	2	-1	.942	-6	O	-1.9
1926	Pit-N	42	68	15	15	3	1	2	4	3	0	.221	.264	.382	69	-3	-3	7	2			.966	-3	O	-0.8
Total	11	1147	4192	629	1205	139	75	17	324	344	161	.287	.345	.369	96	-2	-16	558	182	68		.966	50	*O/2S3	-4.6
■ LYLE BIGBEE Bigbee, Lyle Randolph "Al" b: 8/22/1893, Sweet Home, Ore. d: 8/5/42, Portland, Ore. BL/TR, 6', 180 lbs. Deb: 4/15/20 F																									
1920	Phi-A	38	75	5	14	2	0	1	8	9	12	.187	.282	.253	42	-6	-6	6	1	0	0	.857	-2	OP	-0.7
1921	Pit-N	5	2	0	0	0	0	0	0	0	1	.000	.000	.000	-97	-1	-1	0	0	0	0	1.000	-0	/P	0.0
Total	2	43	77	5	14	2	0	1	8	9	13	.182	.276	.247	39	-7	-7	6	1	0	0	1.000	-2	/PO	-0.7
■ ELLIOT BIGELOW Bigelow, Elliot Allardice "Babe" or "Gilly" b: 10/13/1897, Tarpon Springs, Fla. d: 8/10/33, Tampa, Fla. BL/TL, 5'11", 185 lbs. Deb: 4/18/29																									
1929	Bos-A	100	211	23	60	16	0	1	26	23	18	.284	.357	.374	91	-3	-2	28	1	4	-2	.944	-10	O	-1.7

■ CRAIG BIGGIO

Biggio, Craig Alan b: 12/14/65, Smithtown, N.Y. BR/TR, 5'11", 185 lbs. Deb: 6/26/88

YEAR	TM/L	G	AB	R	H	2B	3B	HR	RBI	BB	SO	AVG	OBP	SLG	PRO+	BR	/A	RC	SB	CS	SBR	FA	FR	POS	TPR
1988	Hou-N	50	123	14	26	6	1	3	5	7	29	.211	.254	.350	74	-5	-4	11	6	1	1	.991	16	C	1.6
1989	Hou-N	134	443	64	114	21	2	13	60	49	64	.257	.339	.402	115	7	9	65	21	3	5	.990	-6	*C/O	1.5
1990	Hou-N	150	555	53	153	24	2	4	42	53	79	.276	.342	.348	93	-6	-4	68	25	11	1	.985	-7	*CO	-0.5
1991	Hou-N★	149	546	79	161	23	4	4	46	53	71	.295	.359	.374	113	6	10	79	19	6	2	.990	-14	*C/2O	0.6
1992	Hou-N★	162	613	96	170	32	3	6	39	94	95	.277	.380	.369	120	14	19	95	38	15	2	.984	-21	*2	0.4
Total	5	645	2280	306	624	106	12	30	192	256	338	.274	.352	.370	108	16	28	318	109	36	11	.989	-33	C2/O	3.6

■ PETE BIGLER

Bigler, Ivan Edward b: 12/13/1892, Bradford, Ohio d: 4/1/75, Coldwater, Mich. BR/TR, 5'9", 150 lbs. Deb: 5/06/17

YEAR	TM/L	G	AB	R	H	2B	3B	HR	RBI	BB	SO	AVG	OBP	SLG	PRO+	BR	/A	RC	SB	CS	SBR	FA	FR	POS	TPR
1917	StL-A	1	0	0	0	0	0	0	0	0	0	—	—	—	—	0	0	0	0			.000	0	/R	0.0

■ GEORGE BIGNELL

Bignell, George William b: 7/18/1858, Taunton, Mass. d: 1/16/25, Providence, R.I. Deb: 9/27/1884

YEAR	TM/L	G	AB	R	H	2B	3B	HR	RBI	BB	SO	AVG	OBP	SLG	PRO+	BR	/A	RC	SB	CS	SBR	FA	FR	POS	TPR
1884	Mil-U	4	9	4	2	0	0	0		1		.222	.300	.222	146	-0	1	1				.951	3	/C	0.3

■ LARRY BIITTNER

Biittner, Lawrence David b: 7/27/45, Pocahontas, Ia. BL/TL, 6'2", 205 lbs. Deb: 7/17/70

YEAR	TM/L	G	AB	R	H	2B	3B	HR	RBI	BB	SO	AVG	OBP	SLG	PRO+	BR	/A	RC	SB	CS	SBR	FA	FR	POS	TPR
1970	Was-A	2	2	0	0	0	0	0	0	0	0	.000	.000	.000	-99	-1	-1	0	0	0	0	.000	0	H	-0.1
1971	Was-A	66	171	12	44	4	1	0	16	16	20	.257	.324	.292	80	-5	-4	16	1	0	0	.940	-0	O/1	-0.7
1972	Tex-A	137	382	34	99	18	1	3	31	29	37	.259	.315	.335	98	-3	-1	40	1	3	-2	.991	-1	1O	-1.2
1973	Tex-A	83	258	19	65	8	2	1	12	20	21	.252	.308	.310	78	-9	-7	24	1	0	0	.980	1	O1/D	-1.0
1974	Mon-N	18	26	2	7	1	0	0	3	0	2	.269	.269	.308	58	-1	-2	2	0	0	0	1.000	1	/O	-0.1
1975	Mon-N	121	346	34	109	13	5	3	28	34	33	.315	.376	.408	113	9	7	51	2	1	0	.972	-1	O	0.2
1976	Mon-N	11	32	2	6	1	0	0	1	0	3	.188	.188	.219	14	-4	-4	1	0	0	0	.947	1	/O	-0.4
	Chi-N	78	192	21	47	13	1	0	17	10	6	.245	.286	.323	66	-7	-9	17	0	2	-1	.985	6	1O	-0.8
	Yr	89	224	23	53	14	1	0	18	10	9	.237	.272	.308	59	-11	-13	17	0	2	-1	.985	6	1O	-1.2
1977	Chi-N	138	493	74	147	28	1	12	62	35	36	.298	.346	.432	97	5	-2	70	2	1	0	.987	2	1O/P	-0.6
1978	Chi-N	120	343	32	88	15	1	4	50	23	37	.257	.305	.341	72	-9	-14	35	0	1	-1	.987	5	1O	-1.5
1979	Chi-N	111	272	35	79	13	3	3	50	21	23	.290	.341	.393	91	-0	-3	34	1	1	-0	.925	-3	O1	-1.0
1980	Chi-N	127	273	21	68	12	2	1	34	18	33	.249	.300	.319	68	-10	-12	25	1	3	-2	.996	0	1O	-1.7
1981	Cin-N	42	61	1	13	4	0	0	8	4	4	.213	.262	.279	52	-4	-4	4	0	0	0	1.000	1	/1O	-0.4
1982	Cin-N	97	184	18	57	9	2	2	24	17	16	.310	.374	.413	118	5	5	27	1	0	0	.978	0	O1	0.4
1983	Tex-A	66	116	5	32	5	1	0	18	9	16	.276	.328	.336	85	-2	-2	13	0	0	0	.987	2	1/OD	-0.1
Total	14	1217	3151	310	861	144	20	29	354	236	287	.273	.326	.359	87	-37	-54	358	10	12	-4	.970	13	O1/DP	-9.0

■ DANN BILARDELLO

Bilardello, Dann James b: 5/26/59, Santa Cruz, Cal. BR/TR, 6', 190 lbs. Deb: 4/11/83

YEAR	TM/L	G	AB	R	H	2B	3B	HR	RBI	BB	SO	AVG	OBP	SLG	PRO+	BR	/A	RC	SB	CS	SBR	FA	FR	POS	TPR
1983	Cin-N	109	298	27	71	18	0	9	38	15	49	.238	.277	.389	80	-8	-9	30	2	1	0	.991	-1	*C	-0.7
1984	Cin-N	68	182	16	38	7	0	2	10	19	34	.209	.287	.280	57	-9	-10	14	0	1	-1	.992	1	C	-0.8
1985	Cin-N	42	102	6	17	0	0	1	9	4	15	.167	.206	.196	12	-12	-12	3	0	0	0	.986	8	C	-0.3
1986	Mon-N	79	191	12	37	5	0	4	17	14	32	.194	.249	.283	47	-14	-14	13	1	0	0	.982	2	C	-0.9
1989	Pit-N	33	80	11	18	6	0	2	8	2	18	.225	.244	.375	77	-3	-3	6	1	2	-1	.970	5	C	0.3
1990	Pit-N	19	37	1	2	0	0	0	3	4	10	.054	.146	.054	-44	-7	-7	1	0	0	0	1.000	3	C	-0.3
1991	SD-N	15	26	4	7	2	1	0	5	3	4	.269	.345	.423	111	1	0	4	0	0	0	1.000	5	C	0.6
1992	SD-N	17	33	2	4	1	0	0	1	4	8	.121	.216	.152	6	-4	-4	1	0	0	0	1.000	5	C	0.2
Total	8	382	949	79	194	39	1	18	91	65	170	.204	.258	.305	55	-57	-60	73	4	4	-1	.988	28	C	-1.9

■ STEVE BILKO

Bilko, Stephen Thomas b: 11/13/28, Nanticoke, Pa. d: 3/7/78, Wilkes-Barre, Pa. BR/TR, 6'1", 230 lbs. Deb: 9/22/49

YEAR	TM/L	G	AB	R	H	2B	3B	HR	RBI	BB	SO	AVG	OBP	SLG	PRO+	BR	/A	RC	SB	CS	SBR	FA	FR	POS	TPR
1949	StL-N	6	17	3	5	2	0	0	2	5	6	.294	.455	.412	128	1	1	4	0			1.000	0	/1	0.1
1950	StL-N	10	33	1	6	1	0	0	2	4	10	.182	.270	.212	27	-3	-4	2	0			.989	0	/1	-0.3
1951	StL-N	21	72	5	16	4	0	2	12	9	10	.222	.309	.361	79	-2	-2	9	0	0	0	.984	-0	1	-0.3
1952	StL-N	20	72	7	19	6	1	1	6	4	15	.264	.303	.417	97	-1	-1	9	0	0	0	.995	4	1	0.3
1953	StL-N	154	570	72	143	23	3	21	84	70	125	.251	.334	.412	93	-6	-6	79	0	1	-1	.991	7	*1	-0.5
1954	StL-N	8	14	1	2	0	0	0	1	3	1	.143	.294	.143	18	-2	-2	0	0	0	0	1.000	2	/1	0.0
	Chi-N	47	92	11	22	8	1	4	12	11	24	.239	.320	.478	104	0	0	12	0	0	0	1.000	6	1	0.5
	Yr	55	106	12	24	8	1	4	13	14	25	.226	.317	.434	92	-1	-2	12	0	0	0	1.000	8	1	0.5
1958	Cin-N	31	87	12	23	4	2	4	17	10	20	.264	.340	.494	111	2	1	13	0	0	0	.995	-1	1	-0.1
	LA-N	47	101	13	21	1	2	7	18	8	37	.208	.266	.465	86	-2	-3	11	0	0	0	.995	2	1	-0.2
	Yr	78	188	25	44	5	4	11	35	18	57	.234	.301	.479	98	-0	-1	24	0	0	0	.995	0	1	-0.3
1960	Det-A	78	222	20	46	11	2	9	25	27	31	.207	.293	.396	82	-5	-6	25	0	1	-1	.991	0	1	-1.1
1961	LA-A	114	294	49	82	16	1	20	59	58	81	.279	.398	.544	134	21	17	65	1	1	-0	.989	3	1/O	1.2
1962	LA-A	64	164	26	47	9	1	8	38	25	35	.287	.387	.500	141	9	10	32	1	1	-0	.995	-1	1	0.5
Total	10	600	1738	220	432	85	13	76	276	234	395	.249	.339	.444	103	13	6	262	2	4		.992	22	1/O	0.1

■ JOSH BILLINGS

Billings, John Augustus b: 11/30/1891, Grantville, Kan. d: 12/30/81, Santa Monica, Cal. BR/TR, 5'11", 165 lbs. Deb: 9/09/13

YEAR	TM/L	G	AB	R	H	2B	3B	HR	RBI	BB	SO	AVG	OBP	SLG	PRO+	BR	/A	RC	SB	CS	SBR	FA	FR	POS	TPR
1913	Cle-A	1	3	0	0	0	0	0	0	0	3	.000	.000	.000	-97	-1	-1	0	0			.857	0	/C	0.0
1914	Cle-A	11	8	2	2	1	0	0	0	1	1	.250	.333	.375	109	0	0	1	1			.813	2	/C	0.3
1915	Cle-A	8	21	2	4	1	0	0	0	0	6	.190	.190	.238	28	-2	-2	1	1			1.000	-1	/CO	-0.3
1916	Cle-A	22	31	2	5	0	0	0	1	2	11	.161	.212	.161	12	-3	-4	1	1			.981	3	C	0.0
1917	Cle-A	66	129	8	23	3	2	0	9	8	21	.178	.243	.233	42	-9	-10	8	2			.974	2	C	-0.5
1918	Cle-A	2	3	0	1	0	0	0	0	0	0	.333	.333	.333	92	-0	-0	0	0			1.000	-0	/C	0.0
1919	StL-A	38	76	9	15	1	1	0	3	1	12	.197	.218	.237	27	-7	-8	4	0			.982	5	C/1	-0.1
1920	StL-A	66	155	19	43	5	2	0	11	11	10	.277	.353	.335	81	-3	-4	20	1	0	0	.967	-5	C	-0.6
1921	StL-A	20	46	2	10	0	0	0	4	0	7	.217	.217	.217	11	-6	-6	2	0	0	0	.982	2	C	-0.4
1922	StL-A	5	7	0	3	1	0	0	1	0	0	.429	.429	.571	153	1	1	2	0	0	0	1.000	0	/C	0.1
1923	StL-A	4	9	0	0	0	0	0	0	0	2	.000	.000	.000	-95	-3	-3	0	0	0	0	.917	0	/C	-0.2
Total	11	243	488	44	106	12	5	0	29	23	73	.217	.268	.262	47	-33	-36	40	5	0		.964	8	C/1O	-1.7

■ DICK BILLINGS

Billings, Richard Arlin b: 12/4/42, Detroit, Mich. BR/TR, 6'1", 195 lbs. Deb: 9/11/68

YEAR	TM/L	G	AB	R	H	2B	3B	HR	RBI	BB	SO	AVG	OBP	SLG	PRO+	BR	/A	RC	SB	CS	SBR	FA	FR	POS	TPR
1968	Was-A	12	33	3	6	1	0	1	3	5	13	.182	.289	.303	82	-1	-1	3	0	0	0	.929	0	/O3	-0.1
1969	Was-A	27	37	3	5	0	0	0	0	6	8	.135	.256	.135	13	-4	-4	1	0	1	-1	1.000	-0	/O3	-0.5
1970	Was-A	11	24	3	6	2	0	1	1	2	3	.250	.308	.458	114	0	0	3	0	0	0	1.000	-2	/C	-0.1
1971	Was-A	116	349	32	86	14	0	6	48	21	54	.246	.299	.338	85	-10	-7	34	2	5	-2	.992	-3	CO/3	-1.2
1972	Tex-A	133	469	41	119	15	1	5	58	29	77	.254	.300	.322	89	-9	-7	42	1	5	-3	.981	-5	CO/31	-1.4
1973	Tex-A	81	280	17	50	11	0	3	32	20	43	.179	.238	.250	39	-23	-22	15	1	1	-0	.975	-19	C/O1D	-4.0
1974	Tex-A	16	31	2	7	1	0	0	0	4	6	.226	.314	.258	68	-1	-1	3	2	0	1	1.000	1	C/OD	0.1
	StL-N	1	5	0	1	0	0	0	0	0	1	.200	.200	.200	12	-1	-1	0	0	0	0	1.000	0	/C	0.0
1975	StL-N	3	3	0	0	0	0	0	0	0	2	.000	.000	.000	-97	-1	-1	0	0	0	0	.000	0	H	-0.1
Total	8	400	1231	101	280	44	1	16	142	87	207	.227	.283	.304	73	-49	-43	102	6	12	-5	.984	-27	C/O31D	-7.3

■ GEORGE BINKS

Binks, George Alvin "Bingo" (b: George Alvin Binkowski) b: 7/11/16, Chicago, Ill. BL/TL, 6', 175 lbs. Deb: 9/23/44

YEAR	TM/L	G	AB	R	H	2B	3B	HR	RBI	BB	SO	AVG	OBP	SLG	PRO+	BR	/A	RC	SB	CS	SBR	FA	FR	POS	TPR
1944	Was-A	5	12	0	3	0	0	0	0	0	1	.250	.250	.250	45	-1	-1	1	0	0	0	1.000	-1	/O	-0.2
1945	Was-A	145	550	62	153	32	6	6	81	34	52	.278	.324	.391	117	3	8	69	11	7	-1	.977	4	*O1	0.4
1946	Was-A	65	134	13	26	3	0	0	12	6	16	.194	.229	.216	26	-14	-13	7	1	0	0	1.000	-0	O	-1.5
1947	Phi-A	104	333	33	86	19	4	2	34	23	36	.258	.308	.357	83	-8	-9	38	8	2	1	.965	1	O1	-1.1
1948	Phi-A	17	41	2	4	1	0	0	2	2	2	.098	.140	.122	-30	-8	-8	1	1	0	0	1.000	-2	O	-1.0
	StL-A	15	23	2	5	0	0	0	1	2	1	.217	.280	.217	32	-2	-2	2	0	0	0	1.000	-1	/O1	-0.4

YEAR	TM/L	G	AB	R	H	2B	3B	HR	RBI	BB	SO	AVG	OBP	SLG	PRO+	BR	/A	RC	SB	CS	SBR	FA	FR	POS	TPR
	Yr	32	64	4	9	1	0	0	3	4	3	.141	.191	.156	-7	-10	-10	2	1	0	0	1.000	-3	O/1	-1.4
Total	5	351	1093	112	277	55	10	8	130	67	108	.253	.299	.344	86	-29	-24	117	21	9	1	.977	1	O/1	-3.8
■ **STEVE BIRAS**	Biras, Stephen Alexander b: 2/26/22, E.St.Louis, Ill. d: 4/21/65, St.Louis, Mo. BR/TR, 5'11", 185 lbs. Deb: 9/15/44																								
1944	Cle-A	2	2	0	2	0	0	0	2	0	0	1.000	1.000	1.000	491	1	1	2	0	0	0	.667	0	/2	0.1
■ **JUD BIRCHALL**	Birchall, Adoniram Judson b: 1858, Germantown, Pa. d: 12/22/1887, Philadelphia, Pa. Deb: 5/02/1882																								
1882	Phi-a	75	338	65	89	12	1	0		8		.263	.280	.305	87	-1	-7	30				.860	0	*O/2	-0.7
1883	Phi-a	96	449	95	108	10	1	1		19		.241	.271	.274	70	-11	-17	34				.809	6	*O	-1.1
1884	Phi-a	54	221	36	57	2	2	0		4		.258	.287	.285	84	-2	-5	19				.838	3	O/3	-0.2
Total	3	225	1008	196	254	24	4	1		31		.252	.278	.287	79	-15	-29	82				.832	9	O/32	-2.0
■ **FRANK BIRD**	Bird, Frank Zepherin "Dodo" b: 3/10/1869, Spencer, Mass. d: 5/20/58, Worcester, Mass. BR/TR, 5'10", 195 lbs. Deb: 4/16/1892																								
1892	StL-N	17	50	9	10	3	1	1	1	6	11	.200	.286	.360	102	-0	0	6	2			.920	-5	C	-0.3
■ **GEORGE BIRD**	Bird, George Raymond b: 6/23/1850, Stillman Valley, Ill. d: 11/9/40, Rockford, Ill. BR/TR, 5'9", 150 lbs. Deb: 5/06/1871																								
1871	Rok-n	25	106	19	28	2	5	0	13	3	2	.264	.284	.377	92	-2	-0	12	1					*O	0.0
■ **DAVE BIRDSALL**	Birdsall, David Solomon b: 7/16/1838, New York, N.Y. d: 12/30/1896, Boston, Mass. BR/TR, 5'9", 126 lbs. Deb: 5/05/1871																								
1871	Bos-n	29	152	51	46	3	3	0	24	4	4	.303	.321	.362	93	-1	-2	20	6					*O/C	-0.1
1872	Bos-n	16	76	11	14	3	0	0	14	1	0	.184	.195	.224	27	-6	-7	3						C/O	-0.6
1873	Bos-n	3	12	4	1	0	0	0	1	0	0	.083	.083	.083	-47	-2	-2	0						/O	-0.2
Total	3 n	48	240	66	61	6	3	0	39	5	4	.254	.269	.304	65	-9	-11	23						/OC	-0.9
■ **JOE BIRMINGHAM**	Birmingham, Joseph Leo "Dode" b: 8/6/1884, Elmira, N.Y. d: 4/24/46, Tampico, Mexico BR/TR, 5'10", 185 lbs. Deb: 9/12/06 M																								
1906	Cle-A	10	41	5	13	2	1	0	6	1		.317	.333	.415	136	1	1	6	2			1.000	1	/O3	0.3
1907	Cle-A	136	476	55	112	10	9	1	33	16		.235	.265	.300	80	-12	-12	46	23			.949	12	*O/S	-0.5
1908	Cle-A	122	413	32	88	10	1	2	38	19		.213	.253	.257	65	-16	-16	30	15			.957	6	*O/S	-1.7
1909	Cle-A	100	343	29	99	10	5	1	38	19		.289	.333	.356	113	6	5	44	12			.948	4	O	0.6
1910	Cle-A	104	367	41	84	11	2	0	35	23		.229	.284	.270	72	-11	-12	33	18			.961	14	*O/3	-0.3
1911	Cle-A	125	447	55	136	18	5	2	51	15		.304	.334	.380	98	-2	-3	61	16			.973	8	*O3	0.0
1912	Cle-A	107	369	49	94	19	3	1	45	26		.255	.311	.331	81	-9	-10	43	15			.952	5	O/1M	-1.0
1913	Cle-A	47	131	16	37	9	1	0	15	8	22	.282	.324	.366	99	-0	-1	18	7			.974	-3	OM	-0.5
1914	Cle-A	19	47	2	6	0	0	0	4	2	5	.128	.163	.128	-12	-6	-7	1	0	1	-1	1.000	-2	OM	-1.1
Total	9	770	2634	284	669	89	27	7	265	129	27	.254	.295	.316	85	-48	-54	282	108	1		.958	45	O/31S	-4.2
■ **JOHN BISCHOFF**	Bischoff, John George "Smiley" b: 10/28/1894, Granite City, Ill. d: 12/28/81, Granite City, Ill. BR/TR, 5'7", 165 lbs. Deb: 4/18/25																								
1925	Chi-A	7	11	1	1	0	0	0	0	1	5	.091	.167	.091	-35	-2	-2	0	0	0	0	1.000	-0	/C	-0.2
	Bos-A	41	133	13	37	9	1	1	16	6	11	.278	.309	.383	75	-6	-6	15	1	2	-1	.952	-3	C	-0.7
	Yr	48	144	14	38	9	1	1	16	7	16	.264	.298	.361	67	-8	-8	15	1	2	-1	.955	-3	C	-0.9
1926	Bos-A	59	127	6	33	11	2	0	19	15	16	.260	.343	.378	91	-2	-2	16	1	3	-2	.974	-1	C	-0.2
Total	2	107	271	20	71	20	3	1	35	22	32	.262	.320	.369	78	-10	-9	32	2	5	-2	.964	-4	/C	-1.1
■ **FRANK BISHOP**	Bishop, Frank H. b: 9/21/1860, Belvidere, Ill. d: 6/18/29, Chicago, Ill. Deb: 5/27/1884																								
1884	CP-U	4	16	1	3	1	0	0		0		.188	.188	.250	47	-1	-1	1				.667	-2	/3S	-0.2
■ **MAX BISHOP**	Bishop, Max Frederick "Tilly" or "Camera Eye" b: 9/5/1899, Waynesboro, Pa. d: 2/24/62, Waynesboro, Pa. BL/TR, 5'8.5", 165 lbs. Deb: 4/15/24																								
1924	Phi-A	91	294	52	75	13	2	2	21	54	30	.255	.380	.333	84	-4	-5	41	4	3	-1	.969	6	2	0.1
1925	Phi-A	105	368	66	103	18	4	4	27	87	37	.280	.420	.383	98	7	3	65	5	9	-4	.957	5	*2	0.6
1926	Phi-A	122	400	77	106	20	2	0	33	116	41	.265	.431	.325	94	8	4	67	4	5	-2	**.987**	0	*2	0.6
1927	Phi-A	117	372	80	103	15	1	0	22	105	28	.277	.442	.323	95	9	5	60	8	6	-1	.967	3	*2	1.0
1928	Phi-A	126	472	104	149	27	5	6	50	97	36	.316	.435	.432	125	25	23	95	9	9	-3	**.978**	-11	*2	1.3
1929	*Phi-A	129	475	102	110	19	6	3	36	**128**	44	.232	.398	.316	83	-3	-6	70	1	4	-2	.970	-26	*2	-2.7
1930	*Phi-A	130	441	117	111	27	6	10	38	128	60	.252	.426	.408	108	16	12	88	3	2	-0	.976	-6	*2	1.1
1931	*Phi-A	130	497	115	146	30	4	5	37	112	51	.294	.426	.400	111	20	15	94	3	1	0	.984	-0	*2	2.2
1932	Phi-A	114	409	89	104	24	2	5	37	110	43	.254	.412	.359	98	7	4	69	2	2	-1	**.988**	-9	*2	0.0
1933	Phi-A	117	391	80	115	27	1	4	42	106	46	.294	.446	.399	124	21	21	78	1	5	-3	.975	-13	*2	1.1
1934	Bos-A	97	253	65	66	13	1	1	22	82	22	.261	.445	.332	96	7	4	46	3	2	-0	.990	0	21	0.5
1935	Bos-A	60	122	19	28	3	1	1	14	28	14	.230	.377	.295	71	-3	-4	16	0	2	-1	.978	-5	21/S	-0.8
Total	12	1338	4494	966	1216	236	35	41	379	1153	452	.271	.423	.366	102	109	77	789	43	50	-17	.976	-56	*2/1S	5.0
■ **MIKE BISHOP**	Bishop, Michael b: 11/5/58, Santa Maria, Cal. BR/TR, 6'2", 188 lbs. Deb: 4/16/83																								
1983	NY-N	3	8	2	1	1	0	0	0	3	4	.125	.364	.250	74	-0	-0	1	0	0	0	.944	-0	/C	0.0
■ **RIVINGTON BISLAND**	Bisland, Rivington Martin b: 2/17/1890, New York, N.Y. d: 1/11/73, Salzburg, Austria BR/TR, 5'9", 155 lbs. Deb: 9/13/12																								
1912	Pit-N	1	1	0	0	0	0	0	0	0	0	.000	.000	.000	-99	-0	-0	0	0			.000	0	H	0.0
1913	StL-A	12	44	3	6	0	0	0	3	2	5	.136	.191	.136	-4	-6	-6	1	0			.963	-5	S	-1.1
1914	Cle-A	18	57	9	6	1	0	0	2	6	2	.105	.190	.123	-5	-7	-8	1	2	5	-2	.962	-0	S/3	-1.0
Total	3	31	102	12	12	1	0	0	5	8	7	.118	.189	.127	-6	-13	-13	2	2	5		.962	-5	/S3	-2.1
■ **DEL BISSONETTE**	Bissonette, Adelphia Louis b: 9/6/1899, Winthrop, Me. d: 6/9/72, Augusta, Maine BL/TL, 5'11", 180 lbs. Deb: 4/11/28 MC																								
1928	Bro-N	155	587	90	188	30	13	25	106	70	75	.320	.396	.543	145	36	38	125	5			.987	-4	*1	2.0
1929	Bro-N	116	431	68	121	28	10	12	75	46	58	.281	.351	.476	105	1	2	71	2			.987	-9	*1	-1.7
1930	Bro-N	146	572	102	192	33	13	16	113	56	66	.336	.396	.523	121	18	19	115	4			.987	-9	*1	-0.4
1931	Bro-N	152	587	90	170	19	14	12	87	59	53	.290	.354	.431	111	8	9	93	4			.990	-7	*1	-1.2
1933	Bro-N	35	114	9	28	7	0	1	10	2	17	.246	.259	.333	71	-5	-4	9	2			.988	0	1	-0.8
Total	5	604	2291	359	699	117	50	66	391	233	269	.305	.371	.486	119	59	63	412	17			.988	-28	1	-2.1
■ **RED BITTMAN**	Bittman, Henry Peter b: 7/22/1862, Cincinnati, Ohio d: 11/8/29, Cincinnati, Ohio Deb: 10/10/1889																								
1889	KC-a	4	14	2	4	0	0	0	2	1	1	.286	.333	.286	75	-0	-0	2	1			1.000	1	/2	0.1
■ **GEORGE BJORKMAN**	Bjorkman, George Anton b: 8/26/56, Ontario, Cal. BR/TR, 6'2", 190 lbs. Deb: 7/10/83																								
1983	Hou-N	29	75	8	17	4	0	2	14	16	29	.227	.370	.360	110	1	2	11	0	0	0	.993	-3	C	0.0
■ **JOHN BLACK**	Black, John Falcnor "Jack" (b: John Falcnor Haddow) b: 2/23/1890, Covington, Ky. d: 3/20/62, Rutherford, N.J. BR/TR, 6'1", 185 lbs. Deb: 6/20/11																								
1911	StL-A	54	186	13	28	4	0	0	7	10		.151	.202	.172	5	-24	-23	7	4			.972	0	1	-2.3
■ **BILL BLACK**	Black, John William "Jigger" b: 8/12/1899, Philadelphia, Pa. d: 1/14/68, Philadelphia, Pa. BL/TR, 5'11", 168 lbs. Deb: 5/04/24																								
1924	Chi-A	6	5	0	1	0	0	0	0	0	0	.200	.200	.200	3	-1	-1	0	0	0	0	.000	0	/2	-0.1
■ **BOB BLACK**	Black, Robert Benjamin b: 12/10/1862, Cincinnati, Ohio d: 3/21/33, Sioux City, Iowa Deb: 8/17/1884																								
1884	KC-U	38	146	25	36	14	2	1		10		.247	.295	.390	149	5	8	17				.784	-1	OP/2S	0.2
■ **ETHAN BLACKABY**	Blackaby, Ethan Allen b: 7/24/40, Cincinnati, O. BL/TL, 5'11", 190 lbs. Deb: 9/06/62																								
1962	Mil-N	6	13	0	2	1	0	0	0	1	8	.154	.214	.231	20	-1	-1	1	0	0	0	1.000	-1	/O	-0.2
1964	Mil-N	9	12	0	1	0	0	0	1	1	2	.083	.154	.083	-31	-2	-2	0	0	0	0	.500	-1	/O	-0.3
Total	2	15	25	0	3	1	0	0	1	2	10	.120	.185	.160	-4	-4	-4	1	0	0	0	.800	-2	/O	-0.5

EARL BLACKBURN
Blackburn, Earl Stuart b: 11/1/1892, Leesville, Ohio d: 8/3/66, Mansfield, Ohio BR/TR, 5'11", 180 lbs. Deb: 9/17/12

YEAR	TM/L	G	AB	R	H	2B	3B	HR	RBI	BB	SO	AVG	OBP	SLG	PRO+	BR	/A	RC	SB	CS	SBR	FA	FR	POS	TPR
1912	Pit-N	1	0	0	0	0	0	0	0	0	0	—	—	—	—	0	0	0	0			1.000	0	/C	0.0
	Cin-N	1	0	0	0	0	0	0	0	1	0	—	1.000	—	191	0	0	0	0			1.000	0	/C	0.1
	Yr	2	0	0	0	0	0	0	0	1	0	—	1.000	—	190	0	0	0	0			1.000	0	/C	0.1
1913	Cin-N	17	27	1	7	0	0	0	3	2	5	.259	.310	.259	64	-1	-1	3	2			.848	-1	C	-0.1
1915	Bos-N	3	6	0	1	0	0	0	0	2	1	.167	.375	.167	70	-0	-0	0	0			1.000	-0	/C	0.0
1916	Bos-N	47	110	12	30	4	4	0	7	9	21	.273	.328	.382	123	2	3	15	2			.972	-1	C	0.5
1917	Chi-N	2	2	0	0	0	0	0	0	0	0	.000	.000	.000	-93	-0	-0	0	0			.000	0	H	-0.1
Total	5	71	145	13	38	4	4	0	10	14	27	.262	.327	.345	107	1	1	18	4			.954	-2	/C	0.4

LENA BLACKBURNE
Blackburne, Russell Aubrey "Slats"
b: 10/23/1886, Clifton Heights, Pa. d: 2/29/68, Riverside, N.J. BR/TR, 5'11", 160 lbs. Deb: 4/14/10 MC

YEAR	TM/L	G	AB	R	H	2B	3B	HR	RBI	BB	SO	AVG	OBP	SLG	PRO+	BR	/A	RC	SB	CS	SBR	FA	FR	POS	TPR
1910	Chi-A	75	242	16	42	3	1	0	10	19		.174	.245	.194	39	-17	-16	13	4			.911	19	S	0.7
1912	Chi-A	5	1	0	0	0	0	0	0	1		.000	.500	.000	48	0	0	1	1			.800	1	/S3	0.1
1914	Chi-A	144	474	52	105	10	5	1	35	66	58	.222	.324	.270	80	-10	-9	49	25	15	-1	.963	1	*2	-1.1
1915	Chi-A	96	283	33	61	5	1	0	25	35	34	.216	.304	.240	61	-12	-13	25	13	11	-3	.949	-10	3/S	-2.4
1918	Cin-N	125	435	34	99	8	10	1	45	25	30	.228	.271	.299	75	-14	-13	36	6			.938	10	*S	0.2
1919	Bos-N	31	80	5	21	3	1	0	4	6	7	.262	.322	.325	99	-0	-0	9	3			.948	3	3/12S	0.5
	Phi-N	72	291	32	58	10	5	2	19	10	22	.199	.228	.289	51	-17	-19	20	2			.933	6	3/1	-1.1
	Yr	103	371	37	79	13	6	2	23	16	29	.213	.249	.296	61	-17	-18	30	5			.937	10	3/12S	-0.6
1927	Chi-A	1	1	1	1	0	0	0	1	0	0	1.000	1.000	1.000	431	0	0	1	0	0	0	.000	0	H	0.0
1929	Chi-A	1	0	0	0	0	0	0	0	0	0	—	—	—	—	0	0	0	0	0	0	.000	0	/PM	0.0
Total	8	550	1807	173	387	39	23	4	139	162	151	.214	.284	.268	67	-69	-70	154	54	26		.927	30	S32/1P	-3.1

GEORGE BLACKERBY
Blackerby, George Franklin b: 11/10/03, Luther, Okla. d: 5/30/87, Wichita Falls, Tex. BR/TR, 6'1", 176 lbs. Deb: 8/10/28

YEAR	TM/L	G	AB	R	H	2B	3B	HR	RBI	BB	SO	AVG	OBP	SLG	PRO+	BR	/A	RC	SB	CS	SBR	FA	FR	POS	TPR
1928	Chi-A	30	83	8	21	0	0	0	12	4	10	.253	.287	.253	44	-7	-7	6	2	1	0	.953	-1	O	-0.9

FRED BLACKWELL
Blackwell, Fredrick William " b: 9/7/1891, Bowling Green, Ky. d: 12/8/75, Morgantown, Ky. BL/TR, 5'11.5", 160 lbs. Deb: 9/25/17

YEAR	TM/L	G	AB	R	H	2B	3B	HR	RBI	BB	SO	AVG	OBP	SLG	PRO+	BR	/A	RC	SB	CS	SBR	FA	FR	POS	TPR
1917	Pit-N	3	10	1	2	0	0	0	2	0	3	.200	.200	.200	22	-1	-1	0	0			1.000	0	/C	-0.1
1918	Pit-N	8	13	1	2	0	0	0	4	3	4	.154	.313	.154	42	-1	-1	1	0			.926	0	/C	0.0
1919	Pit-N	24	65	3	14	3	0	0	4	3	9	.215	.261	.262	55	-3	-4	5	0			.964	-0	C	-0.2
Total	3	35	88	5	18	3	0	0	10	6	16	.205	.263	.239	50	-5	-5	6	0			.961	0	/C	-0.3

TIM BLACKWELL
Blackwell, Timothy P b: 8/19/52, San Diego, Cal. BB/TR, 5'11", 180 lbs. Deb: 7/03/74

YEAR	TM/L	G	AB	R	H	2B	3B	HR	RBI	BB	SO	AVG	OBP	SLG	PRO+	BR	/A	RC	SB	CS	SBR	FA	FR	POS	TPR
1974	Bos-A	44	122	9	30	1	1	0	8	10	21	.246	.308	.270	63	-5	-6	10	1	1	-0	.971	2	C	-0.2
1975	Bos-A	59	132	15	26	3	2	0	6	19	13	.197	.303	.250	53	-7	-8	11	0	0	0	.984	8	C/D	0.1
1976	Phi-N	4	8	0	2	0	0	0	1	0	1	.250	.250	.250	41	-1	-1	1	0	0	0	1.000	1	/C	0.0
1977	Phi-N	1	0	1	0	0	0	0	0	0	0	—	—	—	—	0	0	0	0	0	0	1.000	0	/C	0.0
	Mon-N	16	22	3	2	1	0	0	0	2	7	.091	.167	.136	-18	-4	-4	0	0	0	0	.925	-1	C	-0.4
	Yr	17	22	4	2	1	0	0	0	2	7	.091	.167	.136	-18	-4	-4	0	0	0	0	.929	-1	C	-0.4
1978	Chi-N	49	103	8	23	3	0	0	7	23	17	.223	.370	.252	68	-2	-4	11	0	0	0	.987	7	C	0.5
1979	Chi-N	63	122	8	20	3	1	0	12	32	25	.164	.342	.205	48	-7	-8	11	0	0	0	.975	1	C	-0.6
1980	Chi-N	103	320	24	87	16	4	5	30	41	62	.272	.355	.394	101	4	2	46	0	1	-1	.982	17	*C	2.2
1981	Chi-N	58	158	21	37	10	2	1	11	23	23	.234	.331	.342	87	-1	-2	19	2	1	0	.993	2	C	0.1
1982	Mon-N	23	42	2	8	2	1	0	3	3	11	.190	.244	.286	47	-3	-3	3	0	0	0	.985	2	C	-0.1
1983	Mon-N	6	15	0	3	1	0	0	2	1	3	.200	.250	.267	43	-1	-1	1	0	0	0	.935	1	/C	-0.1
Total	10	426	1044	91	238	40	11	6	80	154	183	.228	.329	.305	73	-26	-35	113	3	3	-1	.981	40	C/D	1.5

RAY BLADES
Blades, Francis Raymond b: 8/6/1896, Mt.Vernon, Ill. d: 5/18/79, Lincoln, Ill. BR/TR, 5'7.5", 163 lbs. Deb: 8/19/22 MC

YEAR	TM/L	G	AB	R	H	2B	3B	HR	RBI	BB	SO	AVG	OBP	SLG	PRO+	BR	/A	RC	SB	CS	SBR	FA	FR	POS	TPR
1922	StL-N	37	130	27	39	2	4	3	21	25	21	.300	.428	.446	132	6	7	26	3	3	-1	.931	-1	O/S3	0.4
1923	StL-N	98	317	48	78	21	5	5	44	37	46	.246	.342	.391	95	-3	-2	45	4	2	0	.967	6	O/3	-0.1
1924	StL-N	131	456	86	142	21	13	11	68	35	38	.311	.373	.487	131	18	19	81	7	9	-3	.956	-3	*O/23	0.6
1925	StL-N	122	462	112	158	37	8	12	57	59	47	.342	.423	.535	140	31	30	105	6	8	-3	.979	11	*O/3	2.8
1926	StL-N	107	416	81	127	17	12	8	43	62	57	.305	.409	.462	129	22	20	80	6			.980	4	*O	1.6
1927	StL-N	61	180	33	57	8	5	2	29	28	22	.317	.414	.450	127	9	8	34	3			.914	-13	O	-0.7
1928	*StL-N	51	85	9	20	7	1	1	19	20	26	.235	.393	.376	100	1	1	14	0			.972	-2	O	-0.2
1930	*StL-N	45	101	26	40	6	2	4	25	21	15	.396	.504	.614	163	13	12	32	1			.957	-3	O	0.7
1931	*StL-N	35	67	10	19	4	0	1	5	10	7	.284	.392	.388	106	2	1	11	1			.871	-4	O	-0.4
1932	StL-N	80	201	35	46	10	1	3	29	34	31	.229	.340	.333	80	-4	-5	25	2			.975	-5	O/3	-1.3
Total	10	767	2415	467	726	133	51	50	340	331	310	.301	.395	.460	123	95	92	453	33	22		.963	-10	O/32S	3.4

RICK BLADT
Bladt, Richard Alan b: 12/9/46, Santa Cruz, Cal. BR/TR, 6'1", 160 lbs. Deb: 6/15/69

YEAR	TM/L	G	AB	R	H	2B	3B	HR	RBI	BB	SO	AVG	OBP	SLG	PRO+	BR	/A	RC	SB	CS	SBR	FA	FR	POS	TPR
1969	Chi-N	10	13	1	2	0	0	0	1	0	5	.154	.154	.154	-12	-2	-2	0	0	0	0	1.000	2	/O	0.0
1975	NY-A	52	117	13	26	3	1	1	11	11	8	.222	.295	.291	68	-5	-5	11	6	2	1	.973	-2	O	-0.8
Total	2	62	130	14	28	3	1	1	12	11	13	.215	.282	.277	59	-7	-7	11	6	2	1	.976	-0	/O	-0.8

RAE BLAEMIRE
Blaemire, Rae Bertrum b: 2/8/11, Gary, Ind. d: 12/23/75, Champaign, Ill. BR/TR, 6', 178 lbs. Deb: 9/13/41

YEAR	TM/L	G	AB	R	H	2B	3B	HR	RBI	BB	SO	AVG	OBP	SLG	PRO+	BR	/A	RC	SB	CS	SBR	FA	FR	POS	TPR
1941	NY-N	2	5	0	2	0	0	0	0	0	0	.400	.400	.400	123	0	0	1	0			1.000	-0	/C	0.0

FOOTSIE BLAIR
Blair, Clarence Vick b: 7/13/1900, Interprise, Okla. d: 7/1/82, Texarkana, Tex. BL/TR, 6'1", 180 lbs. Deb: 4/28/29

YEAR	TM/L	G	AB	R	H	2B	3B	HR	RBI	BB	SO	AVG	OBP	SLG	PRO+	BR	/A	RC	SB	CS	SBR	FA	FR	POS	TPR
1929	*Chi-N	26	72	10	23	5	0	1	8	3	4	.319	.347	.431	91	-1	-1	10	1			.897	1	/312	0.0
1930	Chi-N	134	578	97	158	24	12	6	59	20	58	.273	.306	.388	66	-33	-33	66	9			.958	8	*23	-1.6
1931	Chi-N	86	240	31	62	19	4	3	29	14	26	.258	.302	.408	88	-4	-5	30	1			.956	-6	21/3	-0.9
Total	3	246	890	138	243	48	16	10	96	37	88	.273	.308	.397	73	-38	-39	106	11			.958	4	2/13	-2.5

BUDDY BLAIR
Blair, Louis Nathan b: 9/10/10, Columbia, Miss. BL/TR, 6', 186 lbs. Deb: 4/14/42

YEAR	TM/L	G	AB	R	H	2B	3B	HR	RBI	BB	SO	AVG	OBP	SLG	PRO+	BR	/A	RC	SB	CS	SBR	FA	FR	POS	TPR
1942	Phi-A	137	484	48	135	26	8	5	66	30	30	.279	.325	.397	103	-0	0	59	1	6	-3	.931	-7	*3	-0.8

PAUL BLAIR
Blair, Paul L b: 2/1/44, Cushing, Okla. BR/TR, 6', 171 lbs. Deb: 9/09/64

YEAR	TM/L	G	AB	R	H	2B	3B	HR	RBI	BB	SO	AVG	OBP	SLG	PRO+	BR	/A	RC	SB	CS	SBR	FA	FR	POS	TPR
1964	Bal-A	8	1	0	0	0	0	0	0	0	1	.000	.000	.000	-99	-0	-0	0	0	1	-1	1.000	-2	/O	-0.3
1965	Bal-A	119	364	49	85	19	2	5	25	32	52	.234	.303	.338	80	-9	-10	38	8	5	-1	.992	3	*O	-1.3
1966	*Bal-A	133	303	35	84	20	2	6	33	15	36	.277	.311	.416	109	2	2	37	5	6	-2	.990	-11	*O	-1.5
1967	Bal-A	151	552	72	162	27	**12**	11	64	50	68	.293	.357	.446	137	24	25	87	8	6	-1	.985	21	*O	4.1
1968	Bal-A	141	421	48	89	22	1	7	38	37	60	.211	.278	.318	80	-10	-10	39	4	2	0	.993	0	*O/3	-1.8
1969	*Bal-A★	150	625	102	178	32	5	26	76	40	72	.285	.330	.477	122	16	16	97	20	6	2	.988	25	*O	3.5
1970	*Bal-A	133	480	79	128	24	2	18	65	56	93	.267	.347	.438	114	10	9	74	24	11	1	.990	19	*O/3	2.3
1971	*Bal-A	141	516	75	135	24	8	10	44	32	94	.262	.306	.397	99	-3	-3	60	14	11	-2	.991	2	*O	-1.0
1972	Bal-A	142	477	47	111	20	8	8	49	25	78	.233	.271	.358	84	-10	-11	41	7	8	-3	.991	9	*O	-1.2
1973	*Bal-A★	146	500	73	140	25	3	10	64	43	72	.280	.337	.402	108	4	5	67	18	8	1	.990	7	*O/D	0.7
1974	*Bal-A	151	552	77	144	27	4	17	62	43	59	.261	.317	.417	113	5	7	73	27	9	3	.985	7	*O	1.2
1975	Bal-A	140	440	51	96	13	4	5	31	25	82	.218	.260	.300	62	-25	-22	34	17	11	-2	.991	-2	*O/1D	-3.1
1976	Bal-A	145	375	29	74	16	0	3	16	22	49	.197	.246	.264	52	-24	-22	23	15	6	1	.979	-8	*O/D	-3.5
1977	*NY-A	83	164	20	43	4	3	4	25	9	16	.262	.309	.396	91	-2	-2	18	3	2	-0	.969	-13	O/D	-1.7
1978	*NY-A	75	125	10	22	5	0	2	13	9	17	.176	.231	.264	40	-10	-10	7	1	1	-0	.989	-15	O/2S3	-2.8
1979	NY-A	2	5	0	1	0	0	0	0	0	1	.200	.200	.200	8	-1	-1	0	0	0	0	1.000	0	/O	0.0

YEAR	TM/L	G	AB	R	H	2B	3B	HR	RBI	BB	SO	AVG	OBP	SLG	PRO+	BR	/A	RC	SB	CS	SBR	FA	FR	POS	TPR
	Cin-N	75	140	7	21	4	1	2	15	11	27	.150	.212	.236	22	-15	-15	7	0	0	0	.992	8	O	-0.9
1980	NY-A	12	2	2	0	0	0	0	0	0	0	.000	.000	.000	-99	-1	-1	0	0	0	0	1.000	-4	O	-0.5
Total	17	1947	6042	776	1513	282	55	134	620	449	877	.250	.305	.382	96	-49	-42	702	171	93	-5	.988	47	*O/23SD1	-7.8
■ WALTER BLAIR	Blair, Walter Allen "Heavy" b: 10/13/1883, Landrus, Pa. d: 8/20/48, Lewisburg, Pa. BR/TR, 6', 185 lbs. Deb: 9/17/07 M																								
1907	NY-A	7	22	1	4	0	0	0	1	2		.182	.250	.182	35	-1	-2	1	0			.922	2	/C	0.0
1908	NY-A	76	211	9	40	5	1	1	13	11		.190	.237	.237	53	-11	-11	13	4			.956	-14	C/O1	-2.3
1909	NY-A	42	110	5	23	2	2	0	11	7		.209	.269	.264	68	-4	-4	8	2			.964	-8	C	-1.0
1910	NY-A	6	22	2	5	0	1	0	2	0		.227	.227	.318	67	-1	-1	2	0			.970	-2	/C	-0.3
1911	NY-A	85	222	18	43	9	2	0	26	16		.194	.257	.252	40	-17	-19	16	2			.970	4	C/1	-0.8
1914	Buf-F	128	378	22	92	11	2	0	33	32	64	.243	.304	.283	66	-16	-17	36	6			.984	5	*C	-0.1
1915	Buf-F	98	290	23	65	15	3	2	20	18	32	.224	.274	.317	72	-10	-11	27	4			**.981**	4	CM	0.0
Total	7	442	1255	80	272	42	11	3	106	86	96	.217	.272	.275	60	-60	-65	102	18			.974	-9	C/O1	-4.5
■ HARRY BLAKE	Blake, Harry Cooper b: 6/16/1874, Portsmouth, Ohio d: 10/14/19, Chicago, Ill. BR/TR, 5'7", 165 lbs. Deb: 7/07/1894																								
1894	Cle-N	73	296	51	78	15	4	1	51	30	22	.264	.335	.351	65	-16	-18	37	1			.932	2	O	-1.6
1895	*Cle-N	84	315	50	87	10	1	3	45	30	33	.276	.341	.343	74	-9	-13	43	11			.898	-2	O	-1.7
1896	*Cle-N	104	383	66	92	12	5	1	43	46	30	.240	.322	.305	64	-17	-21	43	10			.944	2	*O/S	-2.3
1897	Cle-N	32	117	17	30	3	1	1	15	12		.256	.331	.325	70	-4	-5	15	5			.989	4	O	-0.3
1898	Cle-N	136	474	65	116	18	7	0	58	69		.245	.342	.312	89	-6	-5	59	12			.952	8	*O/1	-0.6
1899	StL-N	97	292	50	70	9	4	2	41	43		.240	.341	.318	80	-6	-7	39	16			.979	-2	O/2S1C	-1.3
Total	6	526	1877	299	473	67	22	8	253	230	85	.252	.336	.324	74	-58	-69	237	55			.948	12	O/21SC	-7.8
■ LINC BLAKELY	Blakely, Lincoln Howard b: 2/12/12, Oakland, Cal. d: 9/28/76, Oakland, Cal. BR/TR, 6', 180 lbs. Deb: 4/29/34																								
1934	Cin-N	34	102	11	23	1	1	0	10	5	14	.225	.269	.255	42	-8	-8	6	1			.987	3	O	-0.6
■ BOB BLAKISTON	Blakiston, Robert J. (b: Robert J. Blackstone) b: 10/2/1855, San Francisco, Cal. d: 12/25/18, San Francisco, Cal 5'8.5", 180 lbs. Deb: 5/02/1882																								
1882	Phi-a	72	281	40	64	4	1	0		9		.228	.252	.249	62	-9	-13	18				.855	0	O3/2	-1.1
1883	Phi-a	44	167	26	41	3	3	0		9		.246	.284	.299	81	-2	-4	15				.857	-4	O/13	-0.8
1884	Phi-a	32	128	21	33	6	0	0		11		.258	.336	.305	106	2	1	13				.902	2	O/312S	0.2
	Ind-a	6	18	0	4	1	0	0		1		.222	.263	.278	81	-0	-0	1				.884	-1	/1O	-0.1
	Yr	38	146	21	37	7	0	0		12		.253	.327	.301	104	2	1	15				.902	1	O/132S	0.1
Total	3	154	594	87	142	14	4	0		30		.239	.280	.276	78	-9	-17	47				.872	-2	O/312S	-1.8
■ JOHNNY BLANCHARD	Blanchard, John Edwin b: 2/26/33, Minneapolis, Minn. BL/TR, 6'1", 198 lbs. Deb: 9/25/55																								
1955	NY-A	1	3	0	0	0	0	0	0	1	0	.000	.250	.000	-29	-1	-1	0	0	0	0	1.000	0	/C	0.0
1959	NY-A	49	59	6	10	1	0	2	4	7	12	.169	.258	.288	51	-4	-4	4	0	0	0	.963	-2	C/O1	-0.6
1960	*NY-A	53	99	8	24	3	1	4	14	6	17	.242	.292	.414	94	-2	-1	12	0	0	0	.988	10	C	0.9
1961	*NY-A	93	243	38	74	10	1	21	54	27	28	.305	.383	.613	170	20	22	56	1	0	0	.990	-2	CO	2.2
1962	*NY-A	93	246	33	57	7	0	13	39	28	32	.232	.313	.419	98	-2	-1	33	0	0	0	.987	-7	OC/1	-1.1
1963	*NY-A	76	218	22	49	4	0	16	45	26	30	.225	.307	.463	114	3	3	31	0	0	0	.987	-9	O	-0.9
1964	*NY-A	77	161	18	41	8	0	7	28	24	24	.255	.351	.435	115	4	4	24	1	0	0	.984	-3	CO/1	0.1
1965	NY-A	12	34	1	5	1	0	1	3	7	3	.147	.293	.265	60	-2	-2	3	0	0	0	.961	-1	C	-0.2
	KC-A	52	120	10	24	2	0	2	11	8	16	.200	.256	.267	49	-8	-8	8	0	0	0	1.000	-10	OC	-2.0
	Yr	64	154	11	29	3	0	3	14	15	19	.188	.265	.266	52	-10	-10	11	0	0	0	.971	-11	CO	-2.2
	Mil-N	10	10	1	1	0	0	1	2	2	1	.100	.250	.400	79	-0	-0	1	0	0	0	.000	0	/O	0.0
Total	8	516	1193	137	285	36	2	67	200	136	163	.239	.320	.441	109	8	12	173	2	0	1	.987	-25	OC/1	-1.6
■ DAMASO BLANCO	Blanco, Damaso (Caripe) b: 12/11/41, Curiepe, Venez. BR/TR, 5'10", 165 lbs. Deb: 5/26/72																								
1972	SF-N	39	20	5	7	1	0	0	2	4	3	.350	.458	.400	144	2	1	4	2	1	0	.889	6	3/S2	0.8
1973	SF-N	28	12	4	0	0	0	0	0	1	2	.000	.077	.000	-74	-3	-3	0	0	0	0	1.000	2	/3S2	-0.1
1974	SF-N	5	1	0	0	0	0	0	0	0	1	.000	.000	.000	-96	-0	-0	0	1	0	0	.000	0	H	0.0
Total	3	72	33	9	7	1	0	0	2	5	6	.212	.316	.242	58	-2	-2	4	3	1	0	.929	8	/3S2	0.7
■ OSSIE BLANCO	Blanco, Oswaldo Carlos (Diaz) b: 9/8/45, Caracas, Venez. BR/TR, 6', 185 lbs. Deb: 5/26/70																								
1970	Chi-A	34	66	4	13	0	0	0	8	3	14	.197	.232	.197	19	-7	-7	3	0	1	-1	.993	-1	1/O	-1.1
1974	Cle-A	18	36	1	7	0	0	0	2	7	4	.194	.326	.194	53	-2	-2	2	0	3	-2	.992	-1	1/D	-0.6
Total	2	52	102	5	20	0	0	0	10	10	18	.196	.268	.196	31	-9	-9	5	0	4	-2	.993	-2	/1DO	-1.7
■ COONIE BLANK	Blank, Frank Ignatz b: 10/18/1892, St.Louis, Mo. d: 12/8/61, St.Louis, Mo. BR/TR, 5'11", 165 lbs. Deb: 8/15/09																								
1909	StL-N	1	2	0	0	0	0	0	0	0		.000	.000	.000	-99	-0	-0	0	0			1.000	-0	/C	-0.1
■ CLIFF BLANKENSHIP	Blankenship, Clifford Douglas b: 4/10/1880, Columbus, Ga. d: 4/26/56, Oakland, Cal. BR/TR, 5'10.5", 165 lbs. Deb: 4/17/05																								
1905	Cin-N	19	56	8	11	1	1	0	7	4		.196	.250	.250	44	-4	-4	4	1			.960	-2	1	-0.7
1907	Was-A	37	102	4	23	2	0	0	6	3		.225	.248	.245	62	-5	-4	7	3			.991	0	C/1	-0.3
1909	Was-A	39	60	4	15	1	0	0	9	0		.250	.250	.267	66	-3	-2	4	2			.907	-9	C/O	-1.2
Total	3	95	218	16	49	4	1	0	22	7		.225	.249	.252	58	-11	-11	16	6			.964	-11	/C1O	-2.2
■ LANCE BLANKENSHIP	Blankenship, Lance Robert b: 12/6/63, Portland, Ore. BR/TR, 6', 190 lbs. Deb: 9/04/88																								
1988	Oak-A	10	3	1	0	0	0	0	0	0	1	.000	.000	.000	-99	-1	-1	0	0	1	-1	1.000	0	/2D	-0.1
1989	*Oak-A	58	125	22	29	5	1	1	4	8	31	.232	.278	.312	68	-6	-5	12	5	1	1	1.000	3	O2D	-0.1
1990	*Oak-A	86	136	18	26	3	0	0	10	20	23	.191	.295	.213	46	-10	-9	9	3	1	0	.947	-2	3O2/1D	-1.1
1991	Oak-A	90	185	33	46	8	0	3	21	23	42	.249	.341	.341	95	-2	-1	24	12	3	2	.983	8	2O3/D	0.9
1992	*Oak-A	123	349	59	84	24	1	3	34	82	57	.241	.394	.341	112	8	10	55	21	7	2	.992	-3	2O/1D	1.0
Total	5	367	798	133	185	40	2	7	69	133	154	.232	.348	.313	90	-10	-5	100	41	13	5	.990	6	2O/3D1	0.6
■ LARVELL BLANKS	Blanks, Larvell b: 1/28/50, Del Rio, Tex. BR/TR, 5'8", 167 lbs. Deb: 7/19/72																								
1972	Atl-N	33	85	10	28	5	0	1	7	7	12	.329	.380	.424	117	3	2	13	0	0	0	1.000	6	2/S3	1.0
1973	Atl-N	17	18	1	4	0	0	0	0	1	3	.222	.263	.222	33	-2	-2	1	0	0	0	.000	-3	/32S	-0.4
1974	Atl-N	3	8	0	2	0	0	0	1	0	0	.250	.250	.250	38	-1	-1	1	0	0	0	.889	-0	/S	-0.1
1975	Atl-N	141	471	49	110	13	3	3	38	38	43	.234	.294	.293	61	-23	-25	40	4	3	-1	.960	-12	*S2	-2.6
1976	Cle-A	104	328	45	92	8	7	5	41	30	31	.280	.341	.393	116	6	6	41	1	2	-1	.977	-20	S2/3D	-0.6
1977	Cle-A	105	322	43	92	10	4	6	38	19	37	.286	.327	.398	100	-2	-1	42	3	0	1	.960	-25	S32/D	-1.8
1978	Cle-A	70	193	19	49	10	0	2	20	10	16	.254	.291	.337	77	-6	-6	18	0	0	0	.926	-10	S2/3D	-1.0
1979	Tex-A	68	120	13	24	5	0	1	15	11	9	.200	.267	.267	45	-9	-9	9	0	0	0	.972	-9	S2	-1.4
1980	Atl-N	88	221	23	45	6	0	2	12	16	27	.204	.257	.258	43	-16	-17	14	1	2	-1	.947	7	S3/2	-0.9
Total	9	629	1766	203	446	57	14	20	172	132	178	.253	.306	.335	78	-51	-52	179	9	7	-2	.957	-66	S2/3D	-7.8
■ DON BLASINGAME	Blasingame, Don Lee b: 3/16/32, Corinth, Miss. BL/TR, 5'10", 165 lbs. Deb: 9/20/55																								
1955	StL-N	5	16	4	6	1	0	0	0	6	0	.375	.545	.438	165	2	2	4	1	1	-0	.955	2	/2S	0.4
1956	StL-N	150	587	94	153	22	7	0	27	72	52	.261	.344	.322	81	-14	-14	70	8	8	-2	.986	22	2S/3	1.8
1957	StL-N	154	650	108	176	25	7	8	58	71	49	.271	.343	.368	89	-7	-8	87	21	9	1	.984	26	*2	3.1
1958	StL-N★	143	547	71	150	19	10	2	36	57	47	.274	.344	.356	83	-10	-13	69	20	5	3	.964	-1	*2	-0.1
1959	StL-N	150	615	90	178	26	7	1	24	67	42	.289	.361	.359	87	-4	-9	83	15	15	-5	.979	21	*2	1.8
1960	SF-N	136	523	72	123	12	8	2	31	49	53	.235	.303	.300	70	-24	-20	52	14	2	3	.979	-13	*2	-1.8

YEAR	TM/L	G	AB	R	H	2B	3B	HR	RBI	BB	SO	AVG	OBP	SLG	PRO+	BR	/A	RC	SB	CS	SBR	FA	FR	POS	TPR
1961	SF-N	3	1	1	0	0	0	0	0	2	1	.000	.667	.000	100	0	0	0	0	0	0	.000	0	H	0.0
	*Cin-N	123	450	59	100	18	4	1	21	39	38	.222	.287	.287	52	-30	-31	38	4	3	-1	.972	-19	*2	-3.8
	Yr	126	451	60	100	18	4	1	21	41	39	.222	.289	.286	53	-30	-30	39	4	3	-1	.972	-19	*2	-3.8
1962	Cin-N	141	494	77	139	9	7	2	35	63	44	.281	.365	.340	88	-4	-6	66	4	3	-1	.976	-10	*2	-0.2
1963	Cin-N	18	31	4	5	2	0	0	0	7	5	.161	.316	.226	57	-1	-2	3	0	1	-1	.974	0	2/3	-0.1
	Was-A	69	254	29	65	10	2	2	12	24	18	.256	.320	.335	84	-5	-5	29	3	2	-0	.991	1	2	0.2
1964	Was-A	143	506	56	135	17	2	1	34	40	44	.267	.321	.314	78	-15	-14	54	8	5	-1	.977	-30	*2	-3.6
1965	Was-A	129	403	47	90	8	8	1	18	35	45	.223	.289	.290	66	-18	-17	36	5	4	-1	.984	1	*2	-1.0
1966	Was-A	68	200	18	43	9	0	1	11	18	21	.215	.280	.275	61	-10	-10	17	2	1	0	.984	-1	2/S	-0.8
	KC-A	12	19	1	3	0	0	0	1	2	3	.158	.238	.158	17	-2	-2	1	0	1	-1	1.000	-1	/2	-0.3
	Yr	80	219	19	46	9	0	1	12	20	24	.210	.276	.265	57	-12	-12	17	2	2	-1	.985	-2	2/S	-1.1
Total	12	1444	5296	731	1366	178	62	21	308	552	462	.258	.330	.327	78	-142	-149	610	105	60	-4	.979	-3	*2/S3	-4.4

■ JOHNNY BLATNIK Blatnik, John Louis b: 3/10/21, Bridgeport, Ohio BR/TR, 6', 195 lbs. Deb: 4/21/48

YEAR	TM/L	G	AB	R	H	2B	3B	HR	RBI	BB	SO	AVG	OBP	SLG	PRO+	BR	/A	RC	SB	CS	SBR	FA	FR	POS	TPR
1948	Phi-N	121	415	56	108	27	8	6	45	31	77	.260	.315	.407	96	-5	-4	51	3			.946	-1	*O	-1.0
1949	Phi-N	6	8	3	1	0	0	0	0	4	1	.125	.417	.125	53	-0	-0	1	0			1.000	-0	/O	-0.1
1950	Phi-N	4	4	0	1	0	0	0	0	2	3	.250	.500	.250	106	0	0	1	0			1.000	-0	/O	0.0
	StL-N	7	20	0	3	0	0	0	1	3	2	.150	.261	.150	11	-3	-3	1	0			.875	-2	/O	-0.5
	Yr	11	24	0	4	0	0	0	1	5	5	.167	.310	.167	29	-2	-2	1	0			.900	-2	/O	-0.5
Total	3	138	447	59	113	27	8	6	46	40	83	.253	.317	.389	91	-7	-6	54	3			.945	-3	O	-1.6

■ BUDDY BLATTNER Blattner, Robert Garnett b: 2/8/20, St.Louis, Mo. BR/TR, 6'0.5", 180 lbs. Deb: 4/18/42

YEAR	TM/L	G	AB	R	H	2B	3B	HR	RBI	BB	SO	AVG	OBP	SLG	PRO+	BR	/A	RC	SB	CS	SBR	FA	FR	POS	TPR
1942	StL-N	19	23	3	1	0	0	0	1	3	6	.043	.185	.043	-29	-4	-4	0	0			.900	-0	S/2	-0.4
1946	NY-N	126	420	63	107	18	6	11	49	56	52	.255	.351	.405	113	8	8	63	12			.976	1	*2/1	1.7
1947	NY-N	55	153	28	40	9	2	0	13	21	19	.261	.351	.346	85	-3	-3	20	4			.947	-3	23	-0.4
1948	NY-N	8	20	3	4	1	0	0	0	3	2	.200	.304	.250	51	-1	-1	2	2			1.000	2	/2	0.1
1949	Phi-N	64	97	15	24	6	0	5	21	19	17	.247	.371	.464	126	3	4	18	0			.981	-10	23/S	-0.6
Total	5	272	713	112	176	34	8	16	84	102	96	.247	.347	.384	102	4	3	103	18			.971	-11	2/3S1	0.4

■ JEFF BLAUSER Blauser, Jeffrey Michael b: 11/8/65, Los Gatos, Cal. BR/TR, 6'1", 180 lbs. Deb: 7/05/87

YEAR	TM/L	G	AB	R	H	2B	3B	HR	RBI	BB	SO	AVG	OBP	SLG	PRO+	BR	/A	RC	SB	CS	SBR	FA	FR	POS	TPR
1987	Atl-N	51	165	11	40	6	3	2	15	18	34	.242	.328	.352	76	-4	-6	19	7	3	0	.962	10	S	0.9
1988	Atl-N	18	67	7	16	3	1	2	7	2	11	.239	.271	.403	87	-1	-1	7	0	1	-1	.967	3	/2S	0.2
1989	Atl-N	142	456	63	123	24	2	12	46	38	101	.270	.327	.410	107	5	4	62	5	2	0	.929	-17	32S/O	-1.0
1990	Atl-N	115	386	46	104	24	3	8	39	35	70	.269	.338	.409	99	2	-0	54	3	5	-2	.961	-3	S2/3O	0.3
1991	*Atl-N	129	352	49	91	14	3	11	54	54	59	.259	.360	.409	109	9	6	54	5	6	-2	.948	-36	S23	-2.8
1992	*Atl-N	123	343	61	90	19	3	14	46	46	82	.262	.356	.458	119	13	10	59	5	5	-2	.968	-47	*S2/3	-3.4
Total	6	578	1769	237	464	90	15	49	207	193	357	.262	.340	.413	104	24	12	255	25	22	-6	.960	-89	S23/O	-5.8

■ MARV BLAYLOCK Blaylock, Marvin Edward b: 9/30/29, Ft.Smith, Ark. BL/TL, 6'1.5", 175 lbs. Deb: 9/26/50

YEAR	TM/L	G	AB	R	H	2B	3B	HR	RBI	BB	SO	AVG	OBP	SLG	PRO+	BR	/A	RC	SB	CS	SBR	FA	FR	POS	TPR
1950	NY-N	1	1	0	0	0	0	0	0	0	0	.000	.000	.000	-99	-0	-0	0	0			.000	0	H	0.0
1955	Phi-N	113	259	30	54	7	7	3	24	31	43	.208	.296	.324	66	-13	-13	27	6	1	1	.991	3	1/O	-1.2
1956	Phi-N	136	460	61	117	14	8	10	50	50	86	.254	.330	.385	93	-5	-4	60	5	1	1	.992	-5	*1/O	-1.7
1957	Phi-N	37	26	5	4	0	0	2	4	3	8	.154	.313	.385	89	-0	-0	4	0	0	0	1.000	0	1/O	0.0
Total	4	287	746	96	175	21	15	15	78	84	137	.235	.317	.363	83	-19	-17	90	11	2		.992	-2	1/O	-2.9

■ CURT BLEFARY Blefary, Curtis Le Roy b: 7/5/43, Brooklyn, N.Y. BL/TR, 6'2", 195 lbs. Deb: 4/14/65

YEAR	TM/L	G	AB	R	H	2B	3B	HR	RBI	BB	SO	AVG	OBP	SLG	PRO+	BR	/A	RC	SB	CS	SBR	FA	FR	POS	TPR
1965	Bal-A	144	462	72	120	23	4	22	70	88	73	.260	.382	.470	138	27	26	87	4	2	0	.979	2	*O	2.3
1966	*Bal-A	131	419	73	107	14	3	23	64	73	56	.255	.373	.468	142	24	25	77	1	4	-2	.976	-3	*O1	1.4
1967	Bal-A	155	554	69	134	19	5	22	81	73	94	.242	.339	.413	122	15	16	81	4	4	-1	.968	13	*O1	2.2
1968	Bal-A	137	451	50	90	8	1	15	39	65	66	.200	.306	.322	90	-4	-4	49	6	3	0	.962	-9	OC1	-1.8
1969	Hou-N	155	542	66	137	26	7	12	67	77	79	.253	.350	.393	110	7	8	77	8	7	-2	.987	6	*1/O	0.0
1970	NY-A	99	269	34	57	6	0	9	37	43	37	.212	.327	.335	87	-6	-4	31	1	3	-2	.972	-11	O/1	-2.1
1971	NY-A	21	36	4	7	1	0	1	2	3	5	.194	.256	.306	62	-2	-2	3	0	0	0	.875	-1	/O1	-0.3
	*Oak-A	50	101	15	22	2	0	5	12	15	15	.218	.325	.386	103	0	0	13	0	1	-1	.975	-5	CO/32	-0.5
	Yr	71	137	19	29	3	0	6	14	18	20	.212	.308	.365	93	-2	-1	16	0	1	-1	.958	-5	OC/312	-0.8
1972	Oak-A	8	11	1	5	2	0	0	1	0	1	.455	.455	.636	234	2	2	3	0	0	0	.000	-0	/12O	0.1
	SD-N	74	102	10	20	3	0	3	9	19	18	.196	.322	.314	88	-2	-1	11	0	0	0	.982	-7	C/13O	-0.9
Total	8	974	2947	394	699	104	20	112	382	456	444	.237	.345	.400	115	61	65	432	24	24	-7	.972	-14	O1/C32	0.4

■ IKE BLESSITT Blessitt, Isaiah b: 9/30/49, Detroit, Mich. BR/TR, 5'11", 185 lbs. Deb: 9/07/72

YEAR	TM/L	G	AB	R	H	2B	3B	HR	RBI	BB	SO	AVG	OBP	SLG	PRO+	BR	/A	RC	SB	CS	SBR	FA	FR	POS	TPR
1972	Det-A	4	5	0	0	0	0	0	0	0	2	.000	.000	.000	-97	-1	-1	0	0	0	0	1.000	-0	/O	-0.2

■ NED BLIGH Bligh, Edwin Forrest b: 6/30/1864, Brooklyn, N.Y. d: 4/18/1892, Brooklyn, N.Y. BR/TR, 5'11", 172 lbs. Deb: 6/26/1886

YEAR	TM/L	G	AB	R	H	2B	3B	HR	RBI	BB	SO	AVG	OBP	SLG	PRO+	BR	/A	RC	SB	CS	SBR	FA	FR	POS	TPR
1886	Bal-a	3	9	0	0	0	0	0		1		.000	.100	.000	-69	-2	-2	0	0			.833	-2	/C	-0.3
1888	Cin-a	3	5	0	0	0	0	0	0	0		.000	.000	.000	-95	-1	-1	0	0			1.000	-1	/CO	-0.2
1889	Col-a	28	93	6	13	1	1	0	5	4	14	.140	.200	.172	8	-11	-10	4	2			.927	-3	C	-0.9
1890	Col-a	8	29	2	6	2	0	0		2		.207	.258	.276	64	-2	-1	2	0			.933	2	/C	0.1
	*Lou-a	24	73	9	15	0	0	1		9		.205	.293	.247	63	-3	-3	6	1			.921	-0	C	-0.1
	Yr	32	102	11	21	2	0	1		11		.206	.283	.255	63	-5	-4	8	1			.925	1	C	0.0
Total	4	66	209	17	34	3	1	1	5	16	14	.163	.232	.201	29	-19	-17	12	3			.923	-5	/CO	-1.4

■ ELMER BLISS Bliss, Elmer Ward b: 3/9/1875, Penfield, Pa. d: 3/18/62, Bradford, Pa. BL/TR, 6', 180 lbs. Deb: 9/28/03

YEAR	TM/L	G	AB	R	H	2B	3B	HR	RBI	BB	SO	AVG	OBP	SLG	PRO+	BR	/A	RC	SB	CS	SBR	FA	FR	POS	TPR
1903	NY-A	1	3	0	0	0	0	0	0	0		.000	.000	.000	-94	-1	-1	0	0			.000	-0	/P	0.0
1904	NY-A	1	1	0	0	0	0	0	0	0		.000	.000	.000	-96	-0	-0	0	0			.000	-0	/O	-0.1
Total	2	2	4	0	0	0	0	0	0	0		.000	.000	.000	-94	-1	-1	0	0				-1	/OP	-0.1

■ FRANK BLISS Bliss, Frank Eugene b: 12/10/1852, Chicago, Ill. d: 1/8/29, Nashville, Tenn. Deb: 6/20/1878

YEAR	TM/L	G	AB	R	H	2B	3B	HR	RBI	BB	SO	AVG	OBP	SLG	PRO+	BR	/A	RC	SB	CS	SBR	FA	FR	POS	TPR
1878	Mil-N	2	8	1	1	0	0	0	0	0	0	.125	.125	.125	-17	-1	-1	0				1.000	-0	/3C	-0.1

■ JACK BLISS Bliss, John Joseph Albert b: 1/9/1882, Vancouver, Wash. d: 10/23/68, Temple City, Cal. BR/TR, 5'9", 185 lbs. Deb: 5/10/08

YEAR	TM/L	G	AB	R	H	2B	3B	HR	RBI	BB	SO	AVG	OBP	SLG	PRO+	BR	/A	RC	SB	CS	SBR	FA	FR	POS	TPR
1908	StL-N	44	136	9	29	4	0	1	5	8		.213	.267	.265	74	-5	-4	11	3			.992	5	C	0.5
1909	StL-N	35	113	12	25	2	1	1	8	12		.221	.307	.283	89	-2	-1	11	2			.951	1	C	0.3
1910	StL-N	16	33	2	2	0	0	0	3	4	8	.061	.162	.061	-36	-6	-5	0	0			.980	-1	C	-0.6
1911	StL-N	97	258	36	59	6	4	1	27	42	25	.229	.341	.295	81	-6	-5	28	5			.952	-9	C/S	-0.6
1912	StL-N	49	114	11	28	3	1	0	18	19	14	.246	.372	.289	84	-2	-1	14	3			.973	-6	C	-0.3
Total	5	241	654	70	143	15	6	3	61	85	47	.219	.318	.274	76	-20	-17	64	13			.966	-10	C/S	-0.7

■ BRUNO BLOCK Block, James John (b: James John Blochowicz)
b: 3/13/1885, Wisconsin Rapids, Wis. d: 8/6/37, S.Milwaukee, Wis. BR/TR, 5'9", 185 lbs. Deb: 8/05/07

YEAR	TM/L	G	AB	R	H	2B	3B	HR	RBI	BB	SO	AVG	OBP	SLG	PRO+	BR	/A	RC	SB	CS	SBR	FA	FR	POS	TPR
1907	Was-A	24	57	3	8	2	1	0	2	2		.140	.169	.211	23	-5	-5	2	0			.949	-6	C	-1.0
1910	Chi-A	55	152	12	32	1	1	0	9	13		.211	.273	.230	60	-7	-6	11	3			.964	1	C	-0.1
1911	Chi-A	39	115	11	35	6	1	1	18	6		.304	.339	.400	109	0	1	15	0			.972	-3	C	0.2
1912	Chi-A	46	136	8	35	5	6	0	26	7		.257	.294	.382	96	-2	-1	16	1			.980	2	C	0.4
1914	Chi-F	44	105	8	21	4	1	0	14	11	17	.200	.276	.257	55	-6	-6	8	1			.966	0	C	-0.3
Total	5	208	565	42	131	18	10	1	69	39	17	.232	.281	.304	76	-20	-17	52	5			.969	-5	C	-0.8

YEAR	TM/L	G	AB	R	H	2B	3B	HR	RBI	BB	SO	AVG	OBP	SLG	PRO+	BR	/A	RC	SB	CS	SBR	FA	FR	POS	TPR
■ **CY BLOCK**	Block, Seymour b: 5/4/19, Brooklyn, N.Y. BR/TR, 6′, 180 lbs. Deb: 9/07/42																								
1942	Chi-N	9	33	6	12	1	1	0	4	3	3	.364	.417	.455	161	2	2	6	2			.917	-2	/32	0.0
1945	*Chi-N	2	7	1	1	0	0	0	1	0	0	.143	.143	.143	-21	-1	-1	0	0			1.000	1	/23	0.0
1946	Chi-N	6	13	2	3	0	0	0	0	4	0	.231	.412	.231	86	0	0	2	0			1.000	1	/3	0.1
Total	3	17	53	9	16	1	1	0	5	7	3	.302	.383	.358	118	1	1	8	2			.947	-0	/32	0.1
■ **TERRY BLOCKER**	Blocker, Terry Fennell b: 8/18/59, Columbia, S.C. BL/TL, 6′2″, 195 lbs. Deb: 4/11/85																								
1985	NY-N	18	15	1	1	0	0	0	0	1	2	.067	.125	.067	-46	-3	-3	0	0	0	0	1.000	-1	/O	-0.4
1988	Atl-N	66	198	13	42	4	2	2	10	10	20	.212	.250	.283	50	-12	-13	13	1	1	-0	.994	4	O	-1.2
1989	Atl-N	26	31	1	7	1	0	0	1	1	5	.226	.250	.258	44	-2	-2	2	1	0	0	1.000	-2	/OP	-0.4
Total	3	110	244	15	50	5	2	2	11	12	27	.205	.242	.266	44	-17	-18	15	2	1	0	.994	1	/OP	-2.0
■ **WES BLOGG**	Blogg, Wesley C. b: 1855, Norfolk, Va. d: 3/10/1897, Deb: 6/20/1883																								
1883	Pit-a	9	34	0	5	0	0	0		0		.147	.147	.147	-5	-4	-4	1				.881	-1	/CO	-0.4
■ **RON BLOMBERG**	Blomberg, Ronald Mark "Boomer" b: 8/23/48, Atlanta, Ga. BL/TR, 6′1″, 205 lbs. Deb: 9/10/69																								
1969	NY-A	4	6	0	3	0	0	0	0	1	0	.500	.571	.500	210	1	1	2	0	0	0	1.000	-0	/O	0.1
1971	NY-A	64	199	30	64	6	2	7	31	14	23	.322	.366	.477	146	9	10	33	2	4	-2	.970	-5	O	0.2
1972	NY-A	107	299	36	80	22	1	14	49	38	26	.268	.356	.488	155	18	19	53	0	2	-1	.985	-8	1	0.3
1973	NY-A	100	301	45	99	13	1	12	57	34	25	.329	.397	.498	156	20	22	60	2	0	1	.980	1	D1	2.0
1974	NY-A	90	264	39	82	11	2	10	48	29	33	.311	.383	.481	151	16	17	49	2	1	0	1.000	0	DO	1.7
1975	NY-A	34	106	18	27	8	2	4	17	13	10	.255	.336	.481	132	4	4	17	0	0	0	1.000	0	D/O	0.4
1976	NY-A	1	2	0	0	0	0	0	0	0	0	.000	.000	.000	-99	-0	-0	0	0	0	0	.000	0	/D	-0.1
1978	Chi-A	61	156	16	36	7	0	5	22	11	17	.231	.281	.372	81	-4	-4	17	0	0	0	.986	-1	D/1	-0.6
Total	8	461	1333	184	391	67	8	52	224	140	134	.293	.363	.473	142	64	68	231	6	7	-2	.983	-14	D1/O	4.0
■ **JOE BLONG**	Blong, Joseph Myles b: 9/17/1853, St.Louis, Mo. d: 9/16/1892, St.Louis, Mo. BR/TR, Deb: 5/04/1875																								
1875	RS-n	16	68	3	10	2	0	0		0		.147	.147	.176	13	-6	-5	2						P/O	0.1
1876	StL-N	62	264	30	62	7	4	0	30	2	9	.235	.241	.292	81	-6	-4	19				.895	1	*O/P	-0.3
1877	StL-N	58	218	17	47	8	3	0	13	4	22	.216	.230	.280	63	-10	-8	14				.835	-3	*OP	-0.7
Total	2	120	482	47	109	15	7	0	43	6	31	.226	.236	.286	72	-16	-12	33				.867	-2	O/P	-1.0
■ **JIMMY BLOODWORTH**	Bloodworth, James Henry b: 7/26/17, Tallahassee, Fla. BR/TR, 5′11″, 180 lbs. Deb: 9/14/37																								
1937	Was-A	15	50	3	11	2	1	0	8	5	8	.220	.291	.300	51	-4	-4	4	0	1	-1	.946	-1	2	-0.4
1939	Was-A	83	318	34	92	24	1	4	40	10	26	.289	.313	.409	90	-9	-6	37	3	1	0	.972	14	2/O	1.1
1940	Was-A	119	469	47	115	17	8	11	70	16	71	.245	.272	.386	73	-24	-20	46	3	1	0	.978	13	21/3	-0.1
1941	Was-A	142	506	59	124	24	3	7	66	41	58	.245	.303	.346	75	-22	-19	54	1	1	-0	.971	**35**	*2/3S	2.4
1942	Det-A	137	533	62	129	23	1	13	57	35	63	.242	.295	.362	78	-13	-18	54	2	8	-4	.972	10	*2/S	-0.4
1943	Det-A	129	474	41	114	23	4	6	52	29	59	.241	.289	.344	79	-11	-15	39	4	7	-3	.972	17	*2	0.7
1946	Det-A	76	249	25	61	8	1	5	36	12	26	.245	.285	.345	71	-9	-11	22	3	3	-1	.974	-1	2	-0.8
1947	Pit-N	88	316	27	79	9	0	7	48	16	39	.250	.290	.345	66	-15	-16	30	1			.979	-14	2	-2.5
1949	Cin-N	134	452	40	118	27	1	9	59	27	36	.261	.304	.385	83	-12	-12	51	1			.981	-3	21/3	-1.2
1950	Cin-N	4	14	1	3	1	0	0	1	2	0	.214	.313	.286	58	-1	-1	1	0			1.000	-3	/2	-0.4
	*Phi-N	54	96	6	22	2	0	0	13	6	12	.229	.275	.250	40	-8	-8	7	0			1.000	-2	2/13	-0.9
	Yr	58	110	7	25	3	0	0	14	8	12	.227	.280	.255	42	-9	-9	8	0			1.000	-5	2/13	-1.3
1951	Phi-N	21	42	2	6	0	0	0	1	3	9	.143	.200	.143	-6	-6	-6	1	1	0	0	1.000	-1	/21	-0.6
Total	11	1002	3519	347	874	160	20	62	451	202	407	.248	.292	.358	74	-134	-135	346	19	22		.975	64	2/13OS	-3.1
■ **BUD BLOOMFIELD**	Bloomfield, Clyde Stalcup b: 1/5/36, Oklahoma City, Okla. BR/TR, 5′11.5″, 175 lbs. Deb: 9/25/63																								
1963	StL-N	1	0	0	0	0	0	0	0	0	0	—	—	—	—	0	0	0	0	0	0	.000	0	/3	0.0
1964	Min-A	7	7	1	1	0	0	0	0	0	0	.143	.143	.143	-20	-1	-1	0	0	0	0	1.000	1	/2S	0.0
Total	2	8	7	1	1	0	0	0	0	0	0	.143	.143	.143	-20	-1	-1	0	0	0	0		1	/2S3	0.0
■ **JACK BLOTT**	Blott, John Leonard b: 8/24/02, Girard, Ohio d: 6/11/64, Ann Arbor, Mich. BR/TR, 6′, 210 lbs. Deb: 7/30/24																								
1924	Cin-N	2	1	0	0	0	0	0	0	0	0	.000	.000	.000	-99	-0	-0	0	0	0	0	1.000	-0	/C	0.0
■ **MIKE BLOWERS**	Blowers, Michael Roy b: 4/24/65, Wurzburg, Germany BR/TR, 6′2″, 190 lbs. Deb: 9/01/89																								
1989	NY-A	13	38	2	10	0	0	0	3	3	13	.263	.317	.263	66	-2	-2	3	0	0	0	.852	-3	3	-0.4
1990	NY-A	48	144	16	27	4	0	5	21	12	50	.188	.255	.319	59	-8	-8	12	1	0	0	.899	-8	3/D	-1.6
1991	NY-A	15	35	3	7	0	0	1	1	4	3	.200	.282	.286	57	-2	-2	3	0	0	0	.870	-3	3	-0.5
1992	Sea-A	31	73	7	14	3	0	1	2	6	20	.192	.253	.274	47	-5	-5	5	0	0	0	.984	6	3/1	0.0
Total	4	107	290	28	58	7	0	7	27	25	86	.200	.266	.297	57	-17	-17	22	1	0	0	.915	-9	3/1D	-2.5
■ **BERT BLUE**	Blue, Bird Wayne b: 12/9/1877, Bettsville, Ohio d: 9/2/29, Detroit, Mich. BR/TR, 6′3″, 200 lbs. Deb: 6/15/08																								
1908	StL-A	11	24	2	9	1	2	0	1	3		.375	.444	.583	232	3	3	6	0			.942	1	/C	0.5
	Phi-A	6	18	2	3	0	0	0	1	0		.167	.167	.167	8	-2	-2	0	0			1.000	1	/C	0.0
	Yr	17	42	4	12	1	2	0	2	3		.286	.333	.405	136	2	2	6	0			.967	2	C	0.5
■ **LU BLUE**	Blue, Luzerne Atwell b: 3/5/1897, Washington, D.C. d: 7/28/58, Alexandria, Va. BB/TL, 5′10″, 165 lbs. Deb: 4/14/21																								
1921	Det-A	153	585	103	180	33	11	5	75	103	47	.308	.416	.427	117	18	19	107	13	17	-6	.990	-7	*1	0.2
1922	Det-A	145	584	131	175	31	9	6	45	82	48	.300	.392	.414	114	12	14	100	8	5	-1	.991	0	*1	0.7
1923	Det-A	129	504	100	143	27	7	1	46	96	40	.284	.402	.371	106	8	9	81	9	11	-4	.992	5	*1	0.3
1924	Det-A	108	395	81	123	26	7	2	53	64	26	.311	.413	.428	119	12	13	75	9	4	0	.986	3	*1	1.0
1925	Det-A	150	532	91	163	18	9	3	94	83	29	.306	.403	.391	104	5	6	92	19	5	3	.988	0	*1	0.1
1926	Det-A	128	429	92	123	24	14	1	52	90	18	.287	.413	.415	115	14	13	81	13	7	-0	.985	-5	*1/O	0.1
1927	Det-A	112	365	71	95	17	9	1	42	71	28	.260	.384	.364	94	-0	-1	53	13	7	-0	.984	-2	*1	-0.9
1928	StL-A	154	549	116	154	32	11	14	80	105	43	.281	.400	.455	120	22	20	107	12	7	-1	.989	2	*1	0.7
1929	StL-A	151	573	111	168	40	10	6	61	126	32	.293	.422	.429	115	23	20	114	12	6	0	.994	-3	*1	0.2
1930	StL-A	117	425	85	100	27	5	4	42	81	44	.235	.363	.351	79	-10	-12	60	12	7	-1	.987	0	*1	-2.1
1931	Chi-A	155	589	119	179	23	15	1	62	127	60	.304	.430	.399	126	24	30	113	13	3	2	.990	-3	*1	1.3
1932	Chi-A	112	373	51	93	21	2	0	43	64	21	.249	.364	.316	83	-10	-6	49	17	6	2	.986	9	*1	-0.4
1933	Bro-N	1	1	0	0	0	0	0	0	0	0	.000	.000	.000	-99	-0	-0	0	0			1.000	-0	/1	0.0
Total	13	1615	5904	1151	1696	319	109	44	695	1092	436	.287	.402	.401	109	119	125	1031	150	85		.989	1	*1/O	1.2
■ **OSSIE BLUEGE**	Bluege, Oswald Louis b: 10/24/1900, Chicago, Ill. d: 10/14/85, Edina, Minn. BR/TR, 5′11″, 162 lbs. Deb: 4/24/22 FMC																								
1922	Was-A	19	61	5	12	1	0	0	2	7	7	.197	.300	.213	37	-6	-5	5	1	0	0	.925	-3	3/S	-0.7
1923	Was-A	109	379	48	93	15	7	2	42	48	53	.245	.343	.338	84	-10	-8	48	5	3	-0	.936	4	*3/2	0.5
1924	*Was-A	117	402	59	113	15	4	2	49	39	36	.281	.358	.353	86	-9	-7	53	7	5	-1	.943	-12	*32/S	-1.1
1925	*Was-A	145	522	77	150	27	4	4	79	59	56	.287	.362	.377	89	-9	-7	73	16	13	-3	.953	1	*3/S	0.0
1926	Was-A	139	487	69	132	19	8	3	65	70	46	.271	.368	.361	93	-5	-3	69	12	9	-2	.952	-19	*3/S	-1.4
1927	Was-A	146	503	71	138	21	10	1	66	57	47	.274	.354	.362	87	-9	-8	64	15	5	2	.961	15	*3	1.4
1928	Was-A	146	518	78	154	33	7	2	75	46	27	.297	.364	.400	101	1	1	79	18	6	2	.960	12	*3/2	2.2
1929	Was-A	64	220	35	65	6	0	5	31	19	15	.295	.354	.391	91	-3	-3	31	6	4	-1	.967	2	32S	0.2
1930	Was-A	134	476	64	138	27	7	3	69	51	40	.290	.368	.395	93	-3	-4	73	15	8	-0	.964	-1	*3	0.3
1931	Was-A	152	570	82	155	25	7	8	98	50	39	.272	.336	.382	88	-10	-10	74	16	10	-1	**.960**	-5	*3/S	-0.7

YEAR	TM/L	G	AB	R	H	2B	3B	HR	RBI	BB	SO	AVG	OBP	SLG	PRO+	BR	/A	RC	SB	CS	SBR	FA	FR	POS	TPR
1932	Was-A	149	507	64	131	22	4	5	64	83	41	.258	.367	.347	87	-8	-7	71	9	7	-2	.970	6	*3	0.8
1933	*Was-A	140	501	63	131	14	0	6	71	55	34	.261	.338	.325	77	-16	-15	58	6	7	-2	.965	-8	*3	-1.6
1934	Was-A	99	285	39	70	9	2	0	11	23	15	.246	.306	.291	57	-19	-17	27	2	1	0	.950	8	3S/2O	-0.6
1935	Was-A★	100	320	44	84	14	3	0	34	37	21	.262	.341	.325	75	-12	-11	37	2	2	-1	.967	1	S3/2	-0.6
1936	Was-A	90	319	43	92	12	1	1	55	38	16	.288	.375	.342	83	-9	-7	44	5	3	-0	.993	0	2S3	-0.1
1937	Was-A	42	127	12	36	4	2	1	13	13	9	.283	.355	.370	87	-3	-2	17	1	1	-0	.952	2	S/13	0.1
1938	Was-A	58	184	25	48	12	1	0	21	21	11	.261	.340	.337	75	-8	-6	22	3	1	0	.990	1	2S/13	-0.2
1939	Was-A	18	59	5	9	0	0	0	3	7	2	.153	.242	.153	3	-9	-8	2	1	0	0	.989	1	1/2S3	-0.7
Total	18	1867	6440	883	1751	276	67	43	848	723	515	.272	.352	.356	85	-147	-126	847	140	85	-9	.957	4	*3S2/1O	-2.2
■ **OTTO BLUEGE**	Bluege, Otto Adam "Squeaky" b: 7/20/09, Chicago, Ill. d: 6/28/77, Chicago, Ill. BR/TR, 5'10", 154 lbs. Deb: 4/12/32 F																								
1932	Cin-N	1	0	1	0	0	0	0	0	0	0	—	—	—	—	0	0	0	0			.000	0	R	0.0
1933	Cin-N	108	291	17	62	6	2	0	18	26	29	.213	.278	.247	52	-18	-17	19	0			.937	-9	S2/3	-2.1
Total	2	109	291	18	62	6	2	0	18	26	29	.213	.278	.247	52	-18	-17	19	0				-9	/S23	-2.1
■ **RED BLUHM**	Bluhm, Harvey Fred b: 6/27/1894, Cleveland, Ohio d: 5/7/52, Flint, Mich. BR/TR, 5'11", 165 lbs. Deb: 7/03/18																								
1918	Bos-A	1	1	0	0	0	0	0	0	0	0	.000	.000	.000	-99	-0	-0	0	0			.000	0	H	0.0
■ **CHET BOAK**	Boak, Chester Robert b: 6/19/35, New Castle, Pa. d: 11/28/83, Emporium, Pa. BR/TR, 6', 180 lbs. Deb: 9/18/60																								
1960	KC-A	5	13	1	2	0	0	0	1	0	2	.154	.214	.154	1	-2	-2	1	0	0	0	.957	1	/2	-0.1
1961	Was-A	5	7	0	0	0	0	0	0	1	1	.000	.125	.000	-64	-2	-2	0	1	0	0	1.000	-1	/2	-0.2
Total	2	10	20	1	2	0	0	0	1	1	3	.100	.182	.100	-22	-3	-3	1	1	0	0	.962	0	/2	-0.3
■ **FREDERICK BOARDMAN**	Boardman, Frederick Deb: 8/29/1874																								
1874	Bal-n	1	3	0	1	0	0	0		0		.333	.333	.333	114	0	0	0						/O	0.0
■ **RANDY BOBB**	Bobb, Mark Randall b: 1/1/48, Los Angeles, Cal. d: 6/13/82, Carnelian Bay, Cal BR/TR, 6'1", 185 lbs. Deb: 8/15/68																								
1968	Chi-N	7	8	0	1	0	0	0	0	1	2	.125	.222	.125	6	-1	-1	0	0	0	0	1.000	0	/C	-0.1
1969	Chi-N	3	2	0	0	0	0	0	0	0	1	.000	.000	.000	-89	-1	-1	0	0	0	0	1.000	1	/C	0.0
Total	2	10	10	0	1	0	0	0	0	1	3	.100	.182	.100	-14	-1	-1	0	0	0	0	1.000	1	/C	-0.1
■ **JOHN BOCCABELLA**	Boccabella, John Dominic b: 6/29/41, San Francisco, Cal BR/TR, 6'1", 200 lbs. Deb: 9/02/63																								
1963	Chi-N	24	74	7	14	4	1	1	5	6	21	.189	.250	.311	57	-4	-4	5	0	1	-1	.996	-1	1	-0.7
1964	Chi-N	9	23	4	9	2	1	0	6	0	3	.391	.391	.565	159	2	2	5	0	0	0	1.000	-0	/1O	0.1
1965	Chi-N	6	12	2	4	0	0	2	4	1	2	.333	.385	.833	227	2	2	4	0	0	0	1.000	-0	/1O	0.1
1966	Chi-N	75	206	22	47	9	0	6	25	14	39	.228	.277	.359	74	-7	-7	19	0	1	-1	.981	0	O1/C	-1.1
1967	Chi-N	25	35	0	6	1	1	0	8	3	7	.171	.256	.257	45	-2	-3	2	0	0	0	1.000	0	/O1C	-0.3
1968	Chi-N	7	14	0	1	0	0	0	1	2	2	.071	.188	.071	-19	-2	-2	0	0	0	0	1.000	-0	/CO	-0.3
1969	Mon-N	40	86	4	9	2	0	1	6	6	30	.105	.172	.163	-6	-12	-12	2	1	0	0	1.000	1	C	-1.1
1970	Mon-N	61	145	18	39	3	1	5	17	11	24	.269	.321	.407	94	-2	-2	18	0	1	-1	.993	10	1C/3	0.6
1971	Mon-N	74	177	15	39	11	0	3	15	14	26	.220	.281	.333	73	-6	-7	15	0	1	-1	.979	-1	C1/3	-1.0
1972	Mon-N	83	207	14	47	8	1	1	10	9	29	.227	.263	.290	56	-12	-12	15	1	2	-1	.983	8	C/13	-0.4
1973	Mon-N	118	403	25	94	13	0	7	46	26	57	.233	.281	.318	63	-19	-21	33	1	1	-0	.980	1	*C/1	-1.6
1974	SF-N	29	80	6	11	3	0	0	5	4	6	.138	.179	.175	-1	-11	-11	2	0	0	0	.991	-2	C	-1.3
Total	12	551	1462	117	320	56	5	26	148	96	246	.219	.269	.317	62	-74	-77	122	3	7	-3	.984	15	C1/O3	-7.0
■ **MILT BOCEK**	Bocek, Milton Frank b: 7/16/12, Chicago, Ill. BR/TR, 6'1", 185 lbs. Deb: 9/03/33																								
1933	Chi-A	11	22	3	8	1	0	1	3	4	6	.364	.462	.545	173	2	2	6	0	0	0	1.000	-2	/O	0.0
1934	Chi-A	19	38	3	8	1	0	0	3	5	5	.211	.302	.237	39	-3	-3	3	0	0	0	1.000	2	O	-0.1
Total	2	30	60	6	16	2	0	1	6	9	11	.267	.362	.350	86	-1	-1	9	0	0	0	1.000	1	/O	-0.1
■ **BRUCE BOCHTE**	Bochte, Bruce Anton b: 11/12/50, Pasadena, Cal. BL/TL, 6'3", 200 lbs. Deb: 7/19/74																								
1974	Cal-A	57	196	24	53	4	1	5	26	18	23	.270	.335	.378	111	1	3	24	6	3	0	.985	-4	O1	-0.5
1975	Cal-A	107	375	41	107	19	3	3	48	45	43	.285	.365	.376	118	6	9	53	3	4	-2	.987	-7	*1/D	-0.6
1976	Cal-A	146	466	53	120	17	1	2	49	64	53	.258	.350	.311	101	-1	3	52	4	5	-2	.988	-2	O1/D	-0.9
1977	Cal-A	25	100	12	29	4	0	2	8	7	4	.290	.336	.390	101	-0	0	12	3	2	-0	1.000	2	O/D	0.1
	Cle-A	112	392	52	119	19	1	5	43	40	38	.304	.368	.395	112	5	7	54	3	2	-0	.966	5	O1/D	0.7
	Yr	137	492	64	148	23	1	7	51	47	42	.301	.362	.394	110	5	7	67	6	4	-1	.974	7	*O1/D	0.8
1978	Sea-A	140	486	58	128	25	3	11	51	60	47	.263	.346	.395	108	6	6	67	3	4	-2	.984	-4	OD/1	-0.4
1979	Sea-A★	150	554	81	175	38	6	16	100	67	64	.316	.392	.493	134	29	28	100	2	2	-1	.991	5	*1	2.3
1980	Sea-A	148	520	62	156	34	4	13	78	72	81	.300	.385	.456	128	23	22	90	2	3	-1	.996	6	*1D	1.8
1981	Sea-A	99	335	39	87	16	0	6	30	47	53	.260	.354	.361	102	4	3	44	1	3	-2	.995	-5	1O/D	-0.9
1982	Sea-A	144	509	58	151	21	0	12	70	67	71	.297	.382	.409	114	14	12	79	8	5	-1	.988	-5	O1D	0.2
1984	Oak-A	148	469	58	124	23	0	5	52	52	59	.264	.338	.345	96	-6	-1	54	2	5	-2	.993	-13	*1/D	-2.5
1985	Oak-A	137	424	48	125	17	1	14	60	49	58	.295	.368	.439	129	12	16	67	3	1	0	.990	-9	*1	0.1
1986	Oak-A	125	407	57	104	13	1	6	43	65	68	.256	.358	.337	98	-3	1	52	3	2	-0	.991	2	*1/D	-0.5
Total	12	1538	5233	643	1478	250	21	100	658	653	662	.282	.363	.396	114	91	109	749	43	41	-12	.992	-30	*1O/D	-1.1
■ **BRUCE BOCHY**	Bochy, Bruce Douglas b: 4/16/55, Landes De Bussac, France BR/TR, 6'4", 210 lbs. Deb: 7/19/78																								
1978	Hou-N	54	154	8	41	8	0	3	15	11	35	.266	.315	.377	100	-2	-0	16	0	0	0	.974	3	C	0.3
1979	Hou-N	56	129	11	28	4	0	1	6	13	25	.217	.294	.271	59	-8	-7	10	0	0	0	.970	-1	C	-0.7
1980	*Hou-N	22	22	0	4	1	0	0	0	5	7	.182	.357	.227	72	-1	-0	2	0	0	0	1.000	-2	C/1	-0.3
1982	NY-N	17	49	4	15	4	0	2	8	4	6	.306	.358	.510	141	2	3	9	0	0	0	.961	4	C/1	0.7
1983	SD-N	23	42	2	9	1	1	0	3	0	9	.214	.214	.286	39	-4	-3	2	0	0	0	1.000	2	C	-0.1
1984	*SD-N	37	92	10	21	5	1	4	15	3	21	.228	.253	.435	90	-2	-2	9	0	1	-1	.988	5	C	0.4
1985	SD-N	48	112	16	30	2	0	6	13	6	30	.268	.305	.446	109	1	1	15	0	0	0	.988	1	C	0.3
1986	SD-N	63	127	16	32	9	0	8	22	14	23	.252	.326	.512	130	4	4	21	1	0	0	.991	3	C	1.0
1987	SD-N	38	75	8	12	3	0	2	11	11	21	.160	.267	.280	47	-6	-6	5	0	1	-1	.962	-4	C	-0.9
Total	9	358	802	75	192	37	2	26	93	67	177	.239	.300	.388	92	-14	-11	89	1	2	-1	.979	9	C/1	0.7
■ **EDDIE BOCKMAN**	Bockman, Joseph Edward b: 7/26/20, Santa Ana, Cal. BR/TR, 5'9", 175 lbs. Deb: 9/11/46																								
1946	NY-A	4	12	2	1	1	0	0	0	1	4	.083	.154	.167	-10	-2	-2	0	0	0	0	.933	1	/3	0.0
1947	Cle-A	46	66	8	17	2	2	1	14	5	17	.258	.310	.394	97	-1	-1	9	0	0	0	.946	9	3/2SO	0.8
1948	Pit-N	70	176	23	42	7	1	4	23	17	35	.239	.309	.358	79	-5	-6	19	2			.962	8	3/2	0.2
1949	Pit-N	79	220	21	49	6	1	6	19	23	31	.223	.296	.341	69	-9	-10	23	3			.959	6	3/2	-0.5
Total	4	199	474	54	109	16	4	11	56	46	87	.230	.299	.350	74	-17	-18	51	5	0		.958	24	3/2OS	0.5
■ **PING BODIE**	Bodie, Frank Stephan (b: Francesco Stephano Pezzolo) b: 10/8/1887, San Francisco, Cal. d: 12/17/61, San Francisco, Cal BR/TR, 5'8", 195 lbs. Deb: 4/22/11																								
1911	Chi-A	145	551	75	159	27	13	4	97	49		.289	.348	.407	114	6	9	82	14			.969	7	*O2	0.8
1912	Chi-A	138	472	58	139	24	7	5	72	43		.294	.358	.407	123	11	13	73	12			.969	-12	*O	-0.6
1913	Chi-A	127	406	39	107	14	8	8	48	35	57	.264	.325	.397	112	4	4	54	5			.968	-5	*O	-0.6
1914	Chi-A	107	327	21	75	9	5	3	29	21	35	.229	.278	.315	79	-10	-9	32	12	11	-3	.959	-2	O	-2.1
1917	Phi-A	148	557	51	162	28	11	7	74	53	40	.291	.356	.418	138	22	23	86	13			.963	5	*O/1	2.2
1918	NY-A	91	324	36	83	12	6	3	46	27	24	.256	.319	.358	102	1	-0	39	6			.971	4	O	-0.1

YEAR	TM/L	G	AB	R	H	2B	3B	HR	RBI	BB	SO	AVG	OBP	SLG	PRO+	BR	/A	RC	SB	CS	SBR	FA	FR	POS	TPR
1919	NY-A	134	475	45	132	27	8	6	59	36	46	.278	.334	.406	107	3	3	67	15			.959	-8	*O	-1.5
1920	NY-A	129	471	63	139	26	12	7	79	40	30	.295	.350	.446	106	5	3	70	6	14	-7	.968	-10	*O	-2.2
1921	NY-A	31	87	5	15	2	2	0	12	8	8	.172	.242	.241	23	-10	-11	5	0	1	-1	.944	-6	O	-1.8
Total	9	1050	3670	393	1011	169	72	43	516	312	240	.275	.335	.396	110	32	35	508	83	26		.965	-27	O/21	-5.9
■ **TONY BOECKEL** Boeckel, Norman Doxie b: 8/25/1892, Los Angeles, Cal. d: 2/16/24, Torrey Pines, Cal. BR/TR, 5'10.5", 175 lbs. Deb: 7/23/17																									
1917	Pit-N	64	219	16	58	11	1	0	23	8	31	.265	.297	.324	87	-3	-4	22	6			.935	-4	3	-0.7
1919	Pit-N	45	152	18	38	9	2	0	16	18	20	.250	.333	.336	97	1	0	20	11			.930	-8	3	-0.7
	Bos-N	95	365	42	91	11	5	1	26	35	13	.249	.317	.315	94	-4	-2	38	10			.960	-4	3	-0.2
	Yr	140	517	60	129	20	7	1	42	53	33	.250	.322	.321	95	-3	-2	58	21			.951	-12	*3	-0.9
1920	Bos-N	153	582	70	156	28	5	3	62	38	50	.268	.314	.349	94	-8	-5	62	18	15	-4	.936	-7	*3/S2	-0.8
1921	Bos-N	153	592	93	185	20	13	10	84	52	41	.313	.370	.441	120	12	16	95	20	15	-3	.933	-12	*3	1.2
1922	Bos-N	119	402	61	116	19	6	6	47	35	32	.289	.349	.410	99	-3	-1	58	14	8	-1	.952	-11	*3	-0.4
1923	Bos-N	148	568	72	169	32	4	7	79	51	31	.298	.357	.405	105	1	4	83	11	8	-2	.939	-10	*3/S	0.6
Total	6	777	2880	372	813	130	36	27	337	237	218	.282	.339	.381	102	-4	10	378	90	46		.941	-55	3/S2	-1.0
■ **LEN BOEHMER** Boehmer, Leonard Joseph Stephen b: 6/28/41, Flint Hill, Mo. BR/TR, 6'1", 192 lbs. Deb: 6/18/67																									
1967	Cin-N	2	3	0	0	0	0	0	0	0	0	.000	.000	.000	-90	-1	-1	0	0	0	0	1.000	-0	/2	-0.1
1969	NY-A	45	108	5	19	4	0	0	7	8	10	.176	.233	.213	26	-11	-10	5	0	1	-1	.995	1	1/32S	-1.2
1971	NY-A	3	5	0	0	0	0	0	0	0	0	.000	.000	.000	-99	-1	-1	0	0	0	0	1.000	-0	/3	-0.2
Total	3	50	116	5	19	4	0	0	7	8	10	.164	.218	.198	18	-13	-12	5	0	1	-1	.933	1	/132S	-1.5
■ **TERRY BOGENER** Bogener, Terry Wayne b: 9/28/55, Hannibal, Mo. BL/TL, 6', 193 lbs. Deb: 6/14/82																									
1982	Tex-A	24	60	6	13	2	1	1	4	4	8	.217	.288	.333	74	-2	-2	6	2	0	1	1.000	-4	O/D	-0.5
■ **WADE BOGGS** Boggs, Wade Anthony b: 6/15/58, Omaha, Neb. BL/TR, 6'2", 197 lbs. Deb: 4/10/82																									
1982	Bos-A	104	338	51	118	14	1	5	44	35	21	.349	.410	.441	126	17	14	61	1	0	0	.994	18	13/OD	2.8
1983	Bos-A	153	582	100	210	44	7	5	74	92	36	**.361**	**.449**	.486	147	**51**	45	130	3	3	-1	.947	8	*3	4.9
1984	Bos-A	158	625	109	203	31	4	6	55	89	44	.325	.409	.416	123	29	25	110	3	2	-0	.959	21	*3/D	4.3
1985	Bos-A★	161	653	107	**240**	42	3	8	78	96	61	**.368**	**.452**	.478	149	55	51	143	2	1	0	.965	8	*3	5.5
1986	*Bos-A★	149	580	107	207	47	2	8	71	**105**	44	**.357**	**.455**	.486	156	52	51	133	0	4	-2	.953	-1	*3	4.3
1987	Bos-A★	147	551	108	200	40	6	24	89	105	48	**.363**	**.467**	.588	**173**	**67**	**64**	**154**	1	3	-2	.965	3	*3/1D	**6.0**
1988	*Bos-A★	155	584	**128**	214	**45**	6	5	58	**125**	34	**.366**	**.480**	.490	165	**66**	**62**	**140**	2	3	-1	.971	-5	*3/D	5.5
1989	Bos-A★	156	621	**113**	205	**51**	7	3	54	107	51	.330	**.434**	.449	141	47	41	122	2	6	-3	.958	-4	*3/D	3.6
1990	*Bos-A★	155	619	89	187	44	5	6	63	87	68	.302	.389	.418	120	24	20	103	0	0	0	.946	-22	*3/D	-0.1
1991	Bos-A★	144	546	93	181	42	2	8	51	89	32	.332	.425	.460	138	37	33	107	1	2	-1	.968	1	*3	3.4
1992	Bos-A★	143	514	62	133	22	4	7	50	74	31	.259	.356	.358	96	3	-1	67	1	3	-2	.952	-1	*3D	-0.3
Total	11	1625	6213	1067	2098	422	47	85	687	1004	470	.338	.432	.462	140	445	407	1270	16	27	-11	.959	26	*3/1DO	39.9
■ **CHARLIE BOHN** Bohn, Charles b: 1857, Cleveland, Ohio d: 8/1/03, Cleveland, Ohio Deb: 6/20/1882																									
1882	Lou-a	4	13	0	2	0	0	0		0		.154	.154	.154	4	-1	-1	0				.667	1	/OP	0.0
■ **SAM BOHNE** Bohne, Samuel Arthur (b: Samuel Arthur Cohen) b: 10/22/1896, San Francisco, Cal d: 5/23/77, Palo Alto, Cal. BR/TR, 5'8.5", 175 lbs. Deb: 9/09/16																									
1916	StL-N	14	38	3	9	0	0	0	0	4	6	.237	.310	.237	69	-1	-1	4	3			.870	-4	S	-0.5
1921	Cin-N	153	613	98	175	28	16	3	44	54	38	.285	.347	.398	101	-2	1	83	26	22	-5	.973	8	*23	1.0
1922	Cin-N	112	383	53	105	14	5	3	51	39	18	.274	.344	.360	83	-10	-9	49	13	8	-1	.958	11	2S	0.5
1923	Cin-N	139	539	77	136	18	10	3	47	48	37	.252	.316	.340	74	-21	-19	56	16	19	-7	.975	5	23/S1	-1.5
1924	Cin-N	100	349	42	89	15	9	4	46	18	24	.255	.293	.384	81	-11	-10	39	9	6	-1	.941	-9	2S3	-1.5
1925	Cin-N	73	214	24	55	9	1	2	24	14	14	.257	.303	.336	65	-12	-11	22	6	4	-1	.933	-8	S2/013	-1.4
1926	Cin-N	25	54	8	11	0	2	0	5	4	8	.204	.259	.278	46	-4	-4	4	1			.931	-3	S	-0.5
	Bro-N	47	125	4	25	3	2	1	11	12	9	.200	.270	.280	49	-9	-9	10	1			.965	11	23	0.3
	Yr	72	179	12	36	3	4	1	16	16	17	.201	.267	.279	48	-13	-13	14	2			.965	8	2S3	-0.2
Total	7	663	2315	309	605	87	45	16	228	193	154	.261	.321	.359	81	-70	-62	266	75	59		.966	11	2S3/01	-3.6
■ **BRUCE BOISCLAIR** Boisclair, Bruce Armand b: 12/9/52, Putnam, Conn. BL/TL, 6'2", 190 lbs. Deb: 9/11/74																									
1974	NY-N	7	12	0	3	1	0	0	1	1	4	.250	.308	.333	81	-0	-0	1	0	0	0	.923	2	/O	0.2
1976	NY-N	110	286	42	82	13	3	2	13	28	55	.287	.350	.374	112	2	4	38	9	5	-0	.981	0	O/1	0.2
1977	NY-N	127	307	41	90	21	1	4	44	31	57	.293	.360	.407	110	3	5	46	6	4	-1	.959	-7	O/1	-0.6
1978	NY-N	107	214	24	48	7	1	4	15	23	43	.224	.300	.322	77	-7	-7	21	3	3	-1	.983	1	O/1	-0.9
1979	NY-N	59	98	7	18	5	1	0	4	3	24	.184	.216	.255	29	-10	-9	5	0	2	-1	1.000	0	O/1	-1.2
Total	5	410	917	114	241	47	6	10	77	86	183	.263	.327	.360	94	-13	-7	111	18	14	-3	.975	-4	O/1	-2.3
■ **BOB BOKEN** Boken, Robert Anthony b: 2/23/08, Maryville, Ill. d: 10/6/88, Las Vegas, Nev. BR/TR, 6'2", 165 lbs. Deb: 4/25/33																									
1933	Was-A	55	133	19	37	5	2	3	26	9	16	.278	.324	.414	95	-2	-1	18	0	0	0	.969	-2	23S	-0.1
1934	Was-A	11	27	5	6	1	1	0	6	3	1	.222	.300	.333	66	-2	-1	3	2	0	1	.864	1	/32	0.1
	Chi-A	81	297	30	70	9	1	3	40	15	32	.236	.275	.303	47	-23	-24	25	2	1	0	.929	-10	2S	-2.8
	Yr	92	324	35	76	10	2	3	46	18	33	.235	.277	.306	49	-25	-26	28	4	1	1	.929	-9	2S/3	-2.7
Total	2	147	457	54	113	15	4	6	72	27	49	.247	.291	.337	62	-26	-27	46	4	1	1	.941	-11	/2S3	-2.8
■ **BOLAND** Boland Deb: 9/04/1875																									
1875	Atl-n	1	4	0	0	0	0	0		0		.000	.000	.000	-99	-1	-1	0						/O	-0.1
■ **ED BOLAND** Boland, Edward John b: 4/18/08, Long Island City, N.Y. BL/TL, 5'10", 165 lbs. Deb: 9/18/34																									
1934	Phi-N	8	30	2	9	1	1	0	5	0	2	.300	.300	.400	76	-1	-1	4	1			.778	-2	/O	-0.3
1935	Phi-N	30	47	5	10	0	0	0	4	4	6	.213	.275	.213	30	-4	-5	3	1			.833	-3	O	-0.8
1944	Was-A	19	59	4	16	4	0	0	14	0	6	.271	.271	.339	77	-2	-2	5	0	0	0	.889	-1	O	-0.4
Total	3	57	136	11	35	5	1	0	23	4	14	.257	.279	.309	59	-7	-8	12	2	0		.852	-5	/O	-1.5
■ **CHARLIE BOLD** Bold, Charles Dickens "Dutch" b: 10/27/1894, Karlskrona, Sweden d: 7/29/78, Chelsea, Mass. BR/TR, 6'2", 185 lbs. Deb: 8/24/14																									
1914	StL-A	2	1	0	0	0	0	0	0	0	1	.000	.000	.000	-99	-0	-0	0	0			.500	-0	/1	-0.1
■ **CARL BOLES** Boles, Carl Theodore b: 10/31/34, Center Point, Ark. BR/TR, 5'11", 185 lbs. Deb: 8/02/62																									
1962	SF-N	19	24	4	9	0	0	0	1	0	6	.375	.375	.375	104	0	0	3	0	0	0	.833	-1	/O	-0.1
■ **JOE BOLEY** Boley, John Peter (b: John Peter Bolinsky) b: 7/19/1896, Mahanoy City, Pa. d: 12/30/62, Mahanoy City, Pa. BR/TR, 5'11", 170 lbs. Deb: 4/12/27																									
1927	Phi-A	118	370	49	115	18	8	1	52	26	14	.311	.361	.411	95	-0	-3	52	8	5	-1	.951	-11	*S	-0.3
1928	Phi-A	132	425	49	112	20	3	0	49	32	11	.264	.317	.325	67	-19	-21	46	5	1	1	.949	-17	*S	-2.2
1929	*Phi-A	91	303	36	76	17	6	2	47	24	16	.251	.310	.366	71	-13	-14	36	1	0	0	.963	-10	S/3	-1.3
1930	*Phi-A	121	420	41	116	22	2	4	55	32	26	.276	.335	.367	74	-14	-17	53	0	0	0	**.970**	-7	*S	-1.0
1931	*Phi-A	67	224	26	51	9	3	0	20	15	13	.228	.282	.295	49	-16	-18	19	1	1	-0	.954	-13	S/2	-2.4
1932	Phi-A	10	34	2	7	2	0	0	4	1	4	.206	.229	.265	26	-4	-4	2	0	1	-1	.897	-7	S	-1.0
	Cle-A	1	4	0	1	0	0	0	0	0	0	.250	.250	.250	28	-0	-0	0	0	0	0	.000	0	/S	0.0
	Yr	11	38	2	8	2	0	0	4	1	4	.211	.231	.263	27	-4	-4	2	0	1	-1	.897	-7	S	-1.0
Total	6	540	1780	203	478	88	22	7	227	130	84	.269	.323	.354	72	-66	-77	208	15	8	-0	.957	-64	S/23	-8.2

YEAR	TM/L	G	AB	R	H	2B	3B	HR	RBI	BB	SO	AVG	OBP	SLG	PRO+	BR	/A	RC	SB	CS	SBR	FA	FR	POS	TPR
■ **JIM BOLGER**	Bolger, James Cyril "Dutch" b: 2/23/32, Cincinnati, Ohio BR/TR, 6'2", 180 lbs. Deb: 6/24/50																								
1950	Cin-N	2	1	0	0	0	0	0	0	0	0	.000	.000	.000	-99	-0	-0	0	0			.000	-1	/O	-0.1
1951	Cin-N	2	0	1	0	0	0	0	0	0	0	—	—	—	—	0	0	0	1	0	0	1.000	0	R	0.0
1954	Cin-N	5	3	1	1	0	0	0	0	0	1	.333	.333	.333	72	-0	-0	0	0	0	0	.000	-1	/O	-0.1
1955	Chi-N	64	160	19	33	5	4	0	7	9	17	.206	.257	.287	45	-13	-13	11	2	2	-1	.955	-3	O	-1.8
1957	Chi-N	112	273	28	75	4	1	5	29	10	36	.275	.308	.352	78	-9	-9	27	0	1	-1	.987	2	O/3	-1.0
1958	Chi-N	84	120	15	27	4	1	1	11	9	20	.225	.285	.300	56	-8	-8	10	0	1	-1	.940	-6	O	-1.5
1959	Cle-A	8	7	0	0	0	0	0	0	1	1	.000	.125	.000	-65	-2	-2	0	0	0	0	.000	0	H	-0.2
	Phi-N	35	48	1	4	1	0	0	1	3	8	.083	.137	.104	-34	-9	-9	0	0	0	0	.938	-1	/O	-1.1
Total	7	312	612	65	140	14	6	6	48	32	83	.229	.274	.301	54	-41	-40	49	3	4		.966	-9	O/3	-5.8
■ **FRANK BOLLING**	Bolling, Frank Elmore b: 11/16/31, Mobile, Ala. BR/TR, 6'1", 175 lbs. Deb: 4/13/54 F																								
1954	Det-A	117	368	46	87	15	2	6	38	36	51	.236	.304	.337	77	-13	-12	38	3	5	-2	.974	-29	*2	-3.8
1956	Det-A	102	366	53	103	21	7	7	45	42	51	.281	.359	.434	108	4	4	60	6	2	1	.978	-15	*2	-0.2
1957	Det-A	146	576	72	149	27	6	15	40	57	64	.259	.328	.405	96	-2	-3	73	4	9	-4	.980	-3	*2	0.2
1958	Det-A	154	610	91	164	25	4	14	75	54	54	.269	.332	.392	92	-1	-7	81	6	4	-1	**.985**	8	*2	1.2
1959	Det-A	127	459	56	122	18	3	13	55	45	37	.266	.341	.403	98	2	-1	65	2	2	-1	.987	-1	*2	0.7
1960	Det-A	139	536	64	136	20	4	9	59	40	48	.254	.308	.356	77	-16	-18	58	7	4	-0	.978	-5	*2	-1.0
1961	Mil-N★	148	585	86	153	16	4	15	56	57	62	.262	.330	.379	93	-10	-5	70	7	3	0	**.988**	1	*2	1.2
1962	Mil-N★	122	406	45	110	17	4	9	43	35	45	.271	.335	.399	99	-2	-1	55	2	2	-1	**.989**	-9	*2	0.1
1963	Mil-N	142	542	73	132	18	2	5	43	41	47	.244	.300	.312	77	-16	-15	52	2	1	0	.981	-5	*2	-0.7
1964	Mil-N	120	352	35	70	11	1	5	34	21	44	.199	.248	.278	48	-24	-25	24	0	1	-1	**.985**	-9	*2	-2.8
1965	Mil-N	148	535	55	141	26	3	7	50	24	41	.264	.295	.363	84	-12	-12	54	0	4	-2	.976	-16	*2	-1.9
1966	Atl-N	75	227	16	48	7	0	1	18	10	14	.211	.248	.256	40	-18	-18	14	1	1	-0	.983	-15	2	-3.2
Total	12	1540	5562	692	1415	221	40	106	556	462	558	.254	.315	.366	85	-108	-114	643	40	38	-11	.982	-98	*2	-10.2
■ **JACK BOLLING**	Bolling, John Edward b: 2/20/17, Mobile, Ala. BL/TL, 5'11", 168 lbs. Deb: 6/10/39																								
1939	Phi-N	69	211	27	61	11	0	3	13	11	10	.289	.324	.384	92	-3	-3	25	6			.982	2	1	-0.6
1944	Bro-N	56	131	21	46	14	1	1	25	14	4	.351	.418	.496	159	10	10	27	0			.991	1	1	1.0
Total	2	125	342	48	107	25	1	4	38	25	14	.313	.361	.427	118	7	8	52	6			.985	3	/1	0.4
■ **MILT BOLLING**	Bolling, Milton Joseph b: 8/9/30, Mississippi City, Miss. BR/TR, 6'1", 180 lbs. Deb: 9/10/52 F																								
1952	Bos-A	11	36	4	8	1	0	1	3	3	5	.222	.282	.333	66	-2	-2	3	0	1	-1	.984	6	S	0.4
1953	Bos-A	109	323	30	85	12	1	5	28	23	41	.263	.318	.353	77	-9	-11	37	1	4	-2	.956	5	*S	-0.1
1954	Bos-A	113	370	42	92	20	3	6	36	47	55	.249	.340	.368	84	-3	-8	49	2	4	-2	.946	15	*S/3	1.5
1955	Bos-A	6	5	0	1	0	0	0	0	0	1	.200	.200	.200	7	-1	-1	0	0	0	0	.800	0	/S	-0.1
1956	Bos-A	45	118	19	25	3	2	3	8	18	20	.212	.321	.347	68	-4	-6	14	0	1	-1	.947	-8	S3/2	-1.3
1957	Bos-A	1	1	0	0	0	0	0	0	0	0	.000	.000	.000	-95	-0	-0	0	0	0	0	.000	0	H	0.0
	Was-A	91	277	29	63	12	1	4	19	18	59	.227	.279	.321	64	-14	-14	22	2	2	-1	.982	8	2S/3	0.0
	Yr	92	278	29	63	12	1	4	19	18	59	.227	.279	.320	64	-15	-14	22	2	2	-1	.982	8	2S/3	0.0
1958	Det-A	24	31	3	6	2	0	0	0	5	7	.194	.306	.258	53	-2	-2	3	0	0	0	.946	2	S/23	0.1
Total	7	400	1161	127	280	50	7	19	94	114	188	.241	.314	.345	74	-34	-44	129	5	12	-6	.952	28	S/23	0.5
■ **DON BOLLWEG**	Bollweg, Donald Raymond b: 2/12/21, Wheaton, Ill. BL/TL, 6'1", 190 lbs. Deb: 9/28/50																								
1950	StL-N	4	11	1	2	0	0	0	1	1	1	.182	.250	.182	15	-1	-1	0	0			1.000	-1	/1	-0.2
1951	StL-N	6	9	1	1	1	0	0	2	0	1	.111	.111	.222	-13	-1	-1	0	0	0	0	.941	-1	/1	-0.2
1953	*NY-A	70	155	24	46	6	4	6	24	21	31	.297	.384	.503	143	8	9	33	1	0	0	.983	-4	1	0.4
1954	Phi-A	103	268	35	60	15	3	5	24	35	33	.224	.320	.358	85	-5	-5	33	1	0	0	.978	2	1	-0.7
1955	KC-A	12	9	1	1	0	0	0	2	3	2	.111	.333	.111	23	-1	-1	0	0	0	0	1.000	-0	/1	-0.1
Total	5	195	452	62	110	22	7	11	53	60	68	.243	.337	.396	100	-1	-0	67	2	0		.980	-3	1	-0.8
■ **CECIL BOLTON**	Bolton, Cecil Glenford "Glenn" b: 2/13/04, Booneville, Miss. BL/TR, 6'4", 195 lbs. Deb: 9/21/28																								
1928	Cle-A	4	13	1	2	0	2	0	0	2	2	.154	.267	.462	87	-0	-0	2	0	0	0	.955	-1	/1	-0.2
■ **CLIFF BOLTON**	Bolton, William Clifton b: 4/10/07, High Point, N.C. d: 4/21/79, Lexington, N.C. BL/TR, 5'9", 160 lbs. Deb: 4/20/31																								
1931	Was-A	23	43	3	11	1	1	0	6	1	5	.256	.273	.326	56	-3	-3	4	0	0	0	.947	-6	C	-0.7
1933	*Was-A	33	39	4	16	1	1	0	6	6	3	.410	.500	.487	164	4	4	10	0	0	0	.889	-2	/CO	0.3
1934	Was-A	42	148	12	40	9	1	1	17	11	9	.270	.321	.365	80	-5	-5	18	2	0	1	.981	-3	C	-0.5
1935	Was-A	110	375	47	114	18	11	2	55	58	13	.304	.399	.427	117	9	11	67	0	1	-1	.971	-23	*C	-0.6
1936	Was-A	86	289	41	84	18	4	2	51	25	12	.291	.349	.401	90	-7	-5	41	1	2	-1	.979	-3	C	-0.4
1937	Det-A	27	57	6	15	2	0	1	7	8	6	.263	.354	.351	76	-2	-2	8	0	0	0	.982	0	C	-0.1
1941	Was-A	14	11	0	0	0	0	0	1	1	2	.000	.083	.000	-80	-3	-3	0	0	0	0	1.000	0	/C	-0.3
Total	7	335	962	113	280	49	18	6	143	110	50	.291	.366	.398	98	-7	-2	147	3	3	-1	.974	-36	C/O	-2.3
■ **TOMMY BOND**	Bond, Thomas Henry b: 4/2/1856, Granard, Ireland d: 1/24/41, Boston, Mass. BR/TR, 5'7.5", 160 lbs. Deb: 5/05/1874 MU																								
1874	Atl-n	55	247	25	54	11	0	0		1		.219	.222	.263	61	-12	-7	15						*P	0.0
1875	Har-n	71	289	32	78	12	3	0		0		.270	.270	.332	102	2	-0	27						PO/12	0.4
1876	Har-N	45	182	18	50	8	0	0	21	0	4	.275	.275	.319	90	-1	-3	16				.887	5	P	0.0
1877	Bos-N	61	259	32	59	4	3	0	30	1	15	.228	.231	.266	54	-13	-14	16				.937	3	*P/O	-0.1
1878	Bos-N	59	236	22	50	4	1	0	23	0	9	.212	.212	.237	44	-13	-16	12				.941	1	*P/O	-0.1
1879	Bos-N	65	257	35	62	3	1	0	21	6	8	.241	.259	.261	70	-8	-8	18				.957	5	*P/O1	-0.2
1880	Bos-N	76	282	27	62	4	1	0	24	8	14	.220	.241	.241	66	-10	-9	17				.940	13	*PO/31	0.0
1881	Bos-N	3	10	0	2	0	0	0	0	0	0	.200	.200	.200	27	-1	-1	0				1.000	1	/P	0.0
1882	Wor-N	8	30	1	4	0	0	0	2	2	3	.133	.188	.133	5	-3	-3	1				.714	-3	/OPM	-0.5
1884	Bos-U	37	162	21	48	8	0	0		4		.296	.313	.346	125	4	4	18				.863	1	PO/3	-0.1
	Ind-a	7	23	0	3	1	1	0		0		.130	.130	.261	27	-2	-2	1				.700	-2	/PO	-0.1
Total	2 n	126	536	57	132	23	3	0		1		.246	.248	.300	84	-11	-8	41						/PO21	0.4
Total	8	361	1441	156	340	32	7	0	121	21	53	.236	.247	.268	68	-46	-51	99				.927	24	P/O31	-1.1
■ **WALT BOND**	Bond, Walter Franklin b: 10/19/37, Denmark, Tenn. d: 9/14/67, Houston, Tex. BL/TR, 6'7", 228 lbs. Deb: 4/19/60																								
1960	Cle-A	40	131	19	29	2	1	5	18	13	14	.221	.306	.366	84	-4	-3	15	4	1	1	1.000	2	O	-0.2
1961	Cle-A	38	52	7	9	1	1	2	7	6	10	.173	.271	.346	65	-3	-3	5	1	0	0	1.000	-1	O	-0.4
1962	Cle-A	12	50	10	19	3	0	6	17	4	9	.380	.426	.800	228	8	8	17	1	0	0	1.000	-0	O	0.7
1964	Hou-N	148	543	63	138	16	7	20	85	38	90	.254	.312	.420	110	2	6	70	2	2	-1	.989	-11	1O	-1.3
1965	Hou-N	117	407	46	107	17	2	7	47	42	51	.263	.339	.366	106	0	3	52	2	1	0	.983	-4	1O	-0.6
1967	Min-A	10	16	4	5	1	0	1	5	3	1	.313	.421	.563	174	2	2	4	0	0	0	.875	0	/O	0.2
Total	6	365	1199	149	307	40	11	41	179	106	175	.256	.325	.410	110	6	14	163	10	4	1	.974	-13	O1	-1.6
■ **BARRY BONDS**	Bonds, Barry Lamar b: 7/24/64, Riverside, Cal. BL/TL, 6'1", 185 lbs. Deb: 5/30/86 F																								
1986	Pit-N	113	413	72	92	26	3	16	48	65	102	.223	.331	.416	102	3	2	64	36	7	7	.983	15	*O	2.0
1987	Pit-N	150	551	99	144	34	9	25	59	54	88	.261	.331	.492	114	10	9	93	32	10	4	.986	20	*O	2.7
1988	Pit-N	144	538	97	152	30	5	24	58	72	82	.283	.369	.491	147	32	32	100	17	11	-2	.980	5	*O	3.3
1989	Pit-N	159	580	96	144	34	6	19	58	93	93	.248	.353	.426	126	18	20	92	32	10	4	.984	20	*O	4.2
1990	*Pit-N★	151	519	104	156	32	3	33	114	93	83	.301	.410	**.565**	**172**	**48**	**51**	**128**	52	13	8	.983	15	*O	**7.1**
1991	*Pit-N	153	510	95	149	28	5	25	116	107	73	.292	**.419**	.514	**163**	**45**	**47**	**118**	43	13	5	.991	14	*O	**6.4**

YEAR	TM/L	G	AB	R	H	2B	3B	HR	RBI	BB	SO	AVG	OBP	SLG	PRO+	BR	/A	RC	SB	CS	SBR	FA	FR	POS	TPR
1992	*Pit-N★	140	473	**109**	147	36	5	34	103	**127**	69	.311	**.461**	**.624**	**207**	**72**	**73**	**148**	39	8	7	.991	11	*O	**9.0**
Total	7	1010	3584	672	984	220	36	176	556	611	590	.275	.383	.503	147	227	233	743	251	72	32	.985	99	O	34.7
■ BOBBY BONDS	Bonds, Bobby Lee b: 3/15/46, Riverside, Cal. BR/TR, 6'1", 190 lbs. Deb: 6/25/68 FC																								
1968	SF-N	81	307	55	78	10	5	9	35	38	84	.254	.338	.407	123	9	9	46	16	7	1	.978	6	O	1.2
1969	SF-N	158	622	**120**	161	25	6	32	90	81	187	.259	.353	.473	132	24	26	114	45	4	**11**	.978	11	*O	4.0
1970	SF-N	157	663	134	200	36	10	26	78	77	189	.302	.376	.504	135	31	32	134	48	10	**8**	.969	11	*O	4.2
1971	*SF-N★	155	619	110	178	32	4	33	102	62	137	.288	.357	.512	146	34	35	115	26	8	3	**.994**	7	*O	3.9
1972	SF-N	153	626	118	162	29	5	26	80	60	137	.259	.329	.446	116	13	12	96	44	6	**10**	.978	10	*O	2.7
1973	SF-N★	160	643	**131**	182	34	4	39	96	87	148	.283	.372	.530	141	40	37	130	43	17	3	.970	8	*O	4.2
1974	SF-N	150	567	97	145	22	8	21	71	95	134	.256	.366	.434	118	19	16	100	41	11	6	.966	7	*O	2.2
1975	NY-A★	145	529	93	143	26	3	32	85	89	137	.270	.378	.512	154	35	37	103	30	17	-1	.987	7	*OD	3.8
1976	Cal-A	99	378	48	100	10	3	10	54	41	90	.265	.341	.386	120	6	9	50	30	15	0	.977	5	O/D	1.1
1977	Cal-A	158	592	103	156	23	9	37	115	74	141	.264	.347	.520	138	26	29	107	41	18	2	.986	5	*OD	2.9
1978	Chi-A	26	90	8	25	4	0	2	8	10	10	.278	.350	.389	107	1	1	13	6	2	1	.956	1	O/D	0.1
	Tex-A	130	475	85	126	15	4	29	82	69	110	.265	.361	.497	139	24	24	82	37	20	-1	.970	5	*OD	2.4
	Yr	156	565	93	151	19	4	31	90	79	120	.267	.359	.480	133	25	25	95	43	22	-0	.968	5	*OD	2.5
1979	Cle-A	146	538	93	148	24	1	25	85	74	135	.275	.371	.463	123	19	18	92	34	23	-4	.979	11	*OD	2.0
1980	StL-N	86	231	37	47	5	3	5	24	33	74	.203	.308	.316	72	-7	-8	25	15	5	2	.967	-5	O	-1.5
1981	Chi-N	45	163	26	35	7	1	6	19	24	44	.215	.323	.380	95	-0	-1	19	5	6	-2	.982	0	O	-0.5
Total	14	1849	7043	1258	1886	302	66	332	1024	914	1757	.268	.356	.471	129	274	276	1224	461	169	37	.977	89	*O/D	32.7
■ GEORGE BONE	Bone, George Drummond b: 8/28/1876, New Haven, Conn. d: 5/26/18, West Haven, Conn. BB/TR, 5'7", 152 lbs. Deb: 9/18/01																								
1901	Mil-A	12	43	6	13	2	0	0	6	4		.302	.362	.349	103	-0	0	6	0			.869	-2	S	-0.1
■ NINO BONGIOVANNI	Bongiovanni, Anthony Thomas b: 12/21/11, Pike's Peak, La. BL/TL, 5'10", 175 lbs. Deb: 4/23/38																								
1938	Cin-N	2	7	0	2	1	0	0	0	0	0	.286	.286	.429	97	-0	-0	1	0			1.000	0	/O	0.0
1939	*Cin-N	66	159	17	41	6	0	0	16	9	8	.258	.298	.296	60	-9	-9	15	0			.989	1	O	-0.9
Total	2	68	166	17	43	7	0	0	16	9	8	.259	.297	.301	61	-9	-9	15	0			.990	1	/O	-0.9
■ JUAN BONILLA	Bonilla, Juan Guillermo b: 2/12/55, Santurce, P.R. BR/TR, 5'9", 170 lbs. Deb: 4/09/81																								
1981	SD-N	99	369	30	107	13	2	1	25	25	23	.290	.338	.344	101	-3	0	41	4	9	-4	.976	-11	2	-1.0
1982	SD-N	45	182	21	51	6	2	0	8	11	15	.280	.325	.335	90	-4	-2	20	0	1	-1	.975	-8	2	-0.9
1983	SD-N	152	556	55	132	17	4	4	45	50	40	.237	.304	.304	71	-23	-21	50	3	0	1	.986	-15	*2	-2.9
1985	NY-A	8	16	0	2	1	0	0	2	0	3	.125	.125	.188	-16	-3	-2	0	0	0	0	.955	1	/2	-0.1
1986	Bal-A	102	284	33	69	10	1	1	18	25	21	.243	.311	.296	67	-13	-12	25	0	0	0	.981	-9	23/D	-1.9
1987	NY-A	23	55	6	14	3	0	1	3	5	6	.255	.317	.364	81	-2	-1	6	0	0	0	.965	1	2/3D	0.0
Total	6	429	1462	145	375	50	9	7	101	116	108	.256	.315	.317	79	-46	-39	142	7	10	-4	.980	-41	2/3D	-6.8
■ BOBBY BONILLA	Bonilla, Roberto Martin Antonio b: 2/23/63, New York, N.Y. BB/TR, 6'3", 230 lbs. Deb: 4/09/86																								
1986	Chi-A	75	234	27	63	10	2	2	26	33	49	.269	.362	.355	93	-0	-1	32	4	1	1	.989	-1	O1	-0.5
	Pit-N	63	192	28	46	6	2	1	17	29	39	.240	.342	.307	79	-4	-5	21	4	4	-1	.974	-7	O/13	-1.6
1987	Pit-N	141	466	58	140	33	3	15	77	39	64	.300	.357	.481	119	12	12	78	3	5	-2	.932	-20	3O/1	-1.2
1988	Pit-N★	159	584	87	160	32	7	24	100	85	82	.274	.370	.476	143	32	33	106	3	5	-2	.935	-1	*3	3.1
1989	Pit-N★	163	616	96	173	37	10	24	86	76	93	.281	.361	.490	146	32	35	108	8	8	-2	.929	6	*3/1O	4.1
1990	*Pit-N★	160	625	112	175	39	7	32	120	45	103	.280	.329	.518	135	22	25	104	4	3	-1	.961	-2	*O3/1	2.0
1991	*Pit-N★	157	577	102	174	**44**	6	18	100	90	67	.302	.398	.492	151	39	41	114	2	4	-2	.989	3	*O3/1	4.1
1992	NY-N	128	438	62	109	23	0	19	70	66	73	.249	.349	.432	121	12	12	66	4	3	-1	.992	7	*O/1	1.7
Total	7	1046	3732	572	1040	224	37	135	596	463	570	.279	.360	.467	131	146	152	629	32	33	-10	.979	-16	O3/1	11.7
■ LUTHER BONIN	Bonin, Ernest Luther "Bonnie" b: 1/13/1888, Green Hill, Ind. d: 1/3/65, Sycamore, Ohio BL/TR, 5'9.5", 178 lbs. Deb: 4/13/13																								
1913	StL-A	1	1	0	0	0	0	0	0	0	0	.000	.000	.000	-99	-0	-0	0	0			.000	0	H	0.0
1914	Buf-F	20	76	6	14	4	1	0	4	7	11	.184	.253	.263	46	-5	-6	6	3			.970	1	O	-0.6
Total	2	21	77	6	14	4	1	0	4	7	11	.182	.250	.260	44	-6	-6	6	3				1	/O	-0.6
■ BARRY BONNELL	Bonnell, Robert Barry b: 10/27/53, Clermont County, O. BR/TR, 6'3", 200 lbs. Deb: 5/04/77																								
1977	Atl-N	100	360	41	108	11	0	1	45	37	32	.300	.368	.339	81	-3	-8	45	7	5	-1	.989	10	O3	-0.2
1978	Atl-N	117	304	36	73	11	3	1	16	20	30	.240	.287	.306	59	-14	-18	23	12	6	0	.984	9	*O3	-1.2
1979	Atl-N	127	375	47	97	20	3	12	45	26	55	.259	.312	.424	92	-2	-5	46	8	7	-2	.983	-18	*O/3	-3.0
1980	Tor-A	130	463	55	124	22	4	13	56	37	59	.268	.325	.417	97	0	-2	59	3	4	-2	.973	6	*O/D	-0.3
1981	Tor-A	66	227	21	50	7	4	4	28	12	25	.220	.262	.339	68	-9	-10	18	4	3	-1	.975	2	O	-1.2
1982	Tor-A	140	437	59	128	26	3	6	49	32	51	.293	.345	.407	97	4	-2	63	14	2	3	.979	-18	*O/3D	-2.0
1983	Tor-A	121	377	49	120	21	3	10	54	33	52	.318	.373	.469	123	16	13	64	10	7	-1	.986	-13	*O/3D	-0.4
1984	Sea-A	110	363	42	96	15	4	8	48	25	51	.264	.315	.394	96	-3	-2	43	5	2	0	.994	-11	O3/1D	-1.6
1985	Sea-A	48	111	9	27	8	0	1	10	6	19	.243	.282	.342	70	-5	-5	10	1	2	-1	.976	-1	O/1D	-0.7
1986	Sea-A	17	51	4	10	2	0	0	4	1	13	.196	.212	.235	21	-6	-6	2	0	1	-1	.941	1	/O1D	-0.6
Total	10	976	3068	363	833	143	24	56	355	229	387	.272	.325	.389	89	-21	-46	374	64	39	-4	.982	-32	O/3D1	-11.2
■ FRANK BONNER	Bonner, Frank J b: 8/20/1869, Lowell, Mass. d: 12/31/05, Kansas City, Mo. BR/TR, 5'7.5", 169 lbs. Deb: 4/26/1894																								
1894	*Bal-N	33	118	27	38	10	2	0	24	17	5	.322	.412	.441	103	2	1	27	12			.904	-15	2/O3S	-1.0
1895	Bal-N	11	42	9	14	1	1	0	7	5	1	.333	.404	.405	108	1	1	9	4			.742	-5	3	-0.3
	StL-N	15	59	3	8	0	1	1	8	1	8	.136	.164	.220	-1	-9	-9	3	2			.656	-5	3/OC	-1.2
	Yr	26	101	12	22	1	2	1	15	6	9	.218	.269	.297	47	-8	-8	10	6			.698	-10	3/OC	-1.5
1896	Bro-N	9	34	8	6	2	0	0	5	2	8	.176	.263	.235	35	-3	-3	2	1			.915	-1	/2	-0.3
1899	Was-N	85	347	41	95	20	4	2	44	18		.274	.313	.372	89	-7	-7	44	6			.940	2	2	0.0
1902	Cle-A	34	132	14	37	6	0	0	14	5		.280	.312	.326	80	-4	-3	14	1			.907	-10	2	-1.2
	Phi-A	11	44	2	8	0	0	0	3	0		.182	.200	.182	6	-6	-6	2	0			.933	3	2	-0.2
	Yr	45	176	16	45	6	0	0	17	5		.256	.284	.290	60	-10	-9	15	1			.915	-7	2	-1.4
1903	Bos-N	48	173	11	38	5	0	1	10	7		.220	.262	.266	53	-11	-10	13	2			.957	-4	2S	-1.2
Total	6	246	949	115	244	44	8	4	115	55	22	.257	.305	.333	73	-37	-36	114	28			.931	-35	2/S3OC	-5.4
■ BOBBY BONNER	Bonner, Robert Averill b: 8/12/56, Uvalde, Tex. BR/TR, 6', 185 lbs. Deb: 9/12/80																								
1980	Bal-A	4	4	1	0	0	0	0	1	0	0	.000	.000	.000	-99	-1	-1	0	0	0	0	.889	1	/S	0.0
1981	Bal-A	10	27	6	8	2	0	0	2	1	4	.296	.321	.370	99	-0	-0	4	1	0	0	.976	1	/S	0.2
1982	Bal-A	41	77	8	13	3	1	0	5	3	12	.169	.200	.234	19	-9	-9	3	0	0	0	.959	-5	S/2	-1.2
1983	Bai-A	6	0	0	0	0	0	0	0	0	0	—	—	—	—	0	0	0	0	0	0	1.000	-0	/2D	0.0
Total	4	61	108	15	21	5	1	0	8	4	16	.194	.223	.259	34	-10	-10	7	1	0	0	.960	-4	/S2D	-1.0
■ ZEKE BONURA	Bonura, Henry John b: 9/20/08, New Orleans, La. d: 3/9/87, New Orleans, La. BR/TR, 6', 210 lbs. Deb: 4/17/34																								
1934	Chi-A	127	510	86	154	35	4	27	110	64	31	.302	.380	.545	132	25	23	106	0	2	-1	**.996**	5	*1	1.4
1935	Chi-A	138	550	107	162	34	4	21	92	57	28	.295	.364	.485	115	13	11	99	4	0	1	.994	2	*1	0.0
1936	Chi-A	148	587	120	194	39	7	12	138	94	29	.330	.426	.482	119	25	22	126	4	2	0	**.996**	12	*1	1.7
1937	Chi-A	116	447	79	154	41	2	19	100	49	24	.345	.412	.573	146	30	30	107	5	1	1	.989	-2	*1	1.5
1938	Was-A	137	540	72	156	27	3	22	114	44	29	.289	.346	.472	111	0	6	88	2	2	-1	**.993**	3	*1	-0.6
1939	NY-N	123	455	75	146	26	6	11	85	46	22	.321	.388	.477	130	20	20	80	1			.992	5	*1	1.2

YEAR	TM/L	G	AB	R	H	2B	3B	HR	RBI	BB	SO	AVG	OBP	SLG	PRO+	BR	/A	RC	SB	CS	SBR	FA	FR	POS	TPR
1940	Was-A	79	311	41	85	16	3	3	45	40	13	.273	.358	.373	96	-4	-1	45	2	0	1	.982	-4	1	-1.2
	Chi-N	49	182	20	48	14	0	4	20	10	4	.264	.302	.407	96	-2	-2	18	1			.991	5	1	-0.1
Total	7	917	3582	600	1099	232	29	119	704	404	180	.307	.380	.487	121	108	109	670	19	7		.992	27	1	3.9
■ EVERETT BOOE Booe, Everett Little b: 9/28/1891, Mocksville, N.C. d: 5/21/69, Kenedy, Tex. BL/TR, 5'8.5", 165 lbs. Deb: 4/13/13																									
1913	Pit-N	29	80	9	16	0	2	0	2	6	9	.200	.256	.250	47	-6	-5	5	2			1.000	-1	O	-0.7
1914	Ind-F	20	31	5	7	1	0	0	6	7	6	.226	.368	.258	72	-0	-1	5	4			.778	-2	/OS	-0.2
	Buf-F	76	241	29	54	9	2	0	14	21	50	.224	.289	.278	60	-12	-13	23	8			.959	-4	O/S32	-1.9
	Yr	96	272	34	61	10	2	0	20	28	56	.224	.299	.276	62	-12	-14	28	12			.944	-5	OS/32	-2.1
Total	2	125	352	43	77	10	4	0	22	34	65	.219	.289	.270	59	-18	-19	33	14			.959	-6	/OS32	-2.8
■ BUDDY BOOKER Booker, Richard Lee b: 5/28/42, Lynchburg, Va. BL/TR, 5'10", 170 lbs. Deb: 6/04/66																									
1966	Cle-A	18	28	6	6	1	0	2	5	2	6	.214	.267	.464	105	0	0	3	0	0	0	.964	-5	C	-0.5
1968	Chi-A	5	5	0	0	0	0	0	0	1	2	.000	.167	.000	-46	-1	-1	0	0	0	0	1.000	-1	/C	-0.2
Total	2	23	33	6	6	1	0	2	5	3	8	.182	.250	.394	83	-1	-1	3	0	0	0	.967	-6	/C	-0.7
■ ROD BOOKER Booker, Roderick Stewart b: 9/4/58, Los Angeles, Cal. BL/TR, 6' ", 175 lbs. Deb: 4/29/87																									
1987	StL-N	44	47	9	13	1	1	0	8	7	7	.277	.370	.340	88	-0	-1	7	2	0	1	.960	3	2/3S	0.4
1988	StL-N	18	35	6	12	3	0	0	3	4	3	.343	.410	.429	140	2	2	6	2	2	-1	.889	-3	3/2	-0.1
1989	StL-N	10	8	1	2	0	0	0	0	0	1	.250	.250	.250	42	-1	-1	1	0	0	0	.867	2	/23	0.2
1990	Phi-N	73	131	19	29	5	2	0	10	15	26	.221	.301	.290	64	-6	-6	10	3	1	0	.976	-6	S23	-1.0
1991	Phi-N	28	53	3	12	1	0	0	7	1	7	.226	.241	.245	37	-4	-4	3	0	0	0	1.000	-2	S/3	-0.6
Total	5	173	274	38	68	10	3	0	28	27	44	.248	.316	.307	72	-10	-10	27	7	3	0	.985	-5	/S23	-1.1
■ AL BOOL Bool, Albert J. b: 8/24/1897, Lincoln, Neb. d: 9/27/81, Lincoln, Neb. BR/TR, 5'11", 180 lbs. Deb: 9/29/28																									
1928	Was-A	2	7	0	1	0	0	0	1	0	0	.143	.143	.143	-25	-1	-1	0	0	0	0	1.000	0	/C	-0.1
1930	Pit-N	78	216	30	56	12	4	7	46	25	29	.259	.336	.449	87	-5	-5	32	0			.967	-1	C	0.0
1931	Bos-N	49	85	5	16	1	0	0	6	9	13	.188	.266	.200	28	-9	-8	5	0			.989	-2	C	-0.8
Total	3	129	308	35	73	13	4	7	53	34	42	.237	.313	.373	71	-15	-14	38	0	0		.973	-2	C	-0.9
■ BRET BOONE Boone, Bret Robert b: 4/6/69, ElCajon, Cal. BR/TR, 5'10", 180 lbs. Deb: 8/19/92 F																									
1992	Sea-A	33	129	15	25	4	0	4	15	4	34	.194	.224	.318	50	-9	-9	8	1	1	-0	.965	-0	2/3	-0.9
■ IKE BOONE Boone, Isaac Morgan b: 2/17/1897, Samantha, Ala. d: 8/1/58, Northport, Ala. BL/TR, 6', 195 lbs. Deb: 4/22/22 F																									
1922	NY-N	2	2	0	1	0	0	0	0	0	1	.500	.500	.500	157	0	0	0	0	0	0	.000	0	H	0.0
1923	Bos-A	5	15	1	4	0	1	0	2	1	0	.267	.313	.400	86	-0	-0	2	0	1	-1	.929	0	/O	-0.1
1924	Bos-A	128	487	72	164	31	4	13	98	54	32	.337	.404	.497	131	22	22	99	2	2	-1	.976	-7	*O	0.6
1925	Bos-A	133	476	79	157	34	5	9	68	60	19	.330	.406	.479	124	18	18	94	1	4	-2	.941	-7	*O	0.1
1927	Chi-A	29	53	10	12	4	0	1	11	3	4	.226	.268	.358	63	-3	-3	5	0	0	0	1.000	-2	O	-0.5
1930	Bro-N	40	101	13	30	9	1	3	13	14	8	.297	.383	.495	111	2	2	19	0			.960	-2	O	-0.1
1931	Bro-N	6	5	0	1	0	0	0	0	1	1	.200	.333	.200	47	-0	-0	0	0			.000	0	H	0.0
1932	Bro-N	13	21	2	3	1	0	0	2	5	2	.143	.308	.190	38	-2	-2	2	0			1.000	-1	/O	-0.3
Total	8	356	1160	177	372	79	11	26	194	138	67	.321	.394	.475	121	36	37	221	3	7		.960	-18	O	-0.3
■ LUKE BOONE Boone, Lute Joseph "Danny" b: 5/6/1890, Pittsburgh, Pa. d: 7/29/82, Pittsburgh, Pa. BR/TR, 5'9", 160 lbs. Deb: 9/09/13																									
1913	NY-A	6	12	3	4	0	0	0	1	3	1	.333	.467	.333	134	1	1	2	0			.857	-1	/S	0.0
1914	NY-A	106	370	34	82	8	2	0	21	31	41	.222	.285	.254	63	-17	-17	26	10	18	-8	.960	23	2/3O	-0.2
1915	NY-A	130	431	44	88	12	2	5	43	41	53	.204	.285	.276	68	-17	-17	35	14	17	-6	.965	**21**	*2S/3	0.0
1916	NY-A	46	124	14	23	4	0	1	8	8	10	.185	.252	.242	47	-8	-8	10	7			.973	7	3S/2	0.1
1918	Pit-N	27	91	7	18	3	0	0	3	8	6	.198	.263	.231	49	-5	-6	6	1			.921	-0	S/2	-0.5
Total	5	315	1028	102	215	27	4	6	76	91	111	.209	.282	.261	63	-46	-47	79	32	35		.964	50	2/S3O	-0.6
■ RAY BOONE Boone, Raymond Otis "Ike" b: 7/27/23, San Diego, Cal. BR/TR, 6'1", 188 lbs. Deb: 9/03/48 F																									
1948	*Cle-A	6	5	0	2	1	0	0	1	0	1	.400	.400	.600	168	0	0	1	0	0	0	.889	1	/S	0.2
1949	Cle-A	86	258	39	65	4	4	4	26	38	17	.252	.352	.345	87	-5	-4	32	0	2	-1	.947	2	S	0.1
1950	Cle-A	109	365	53	110	14	6	7	58	56	27	.301	.397	.430	116	8	10	65	4	3	-1	.945	-9	*S	0.7
1951	Cle-A	151	544	65	127	14	1	12	51	48	36	.233	.302	.329	75	-23	-19	55	5	3	-0	.957	-7	*S	-1.6
1952	Cle-A	103	316	57	83	8	2	7	45	53	33	.263	.372	.367	113	4	7	45	0	1	-1	.941	-10	S/32	0.3
1953	Cle-A	34	112	21	27	1	2	4	21	24	21	.241	.375	.393	110	2	2	18	1	2	-1	.952	-1	S	0.3
	Det-A	101	385	73	120	16	6	22	93	48	47	.312	.395	.556	156	29	29	89	2	1	0	.958	1	3/S	2.8
	Yr	135	497	94	147	17	8	26	114	72	68	.296	.390	.519	146	30	32	106	3	3	-1	.958	0	3S	3.1
1954	Det-A★	148	543	76	160	19	7	20	85	71	53	.295	.378	.466	133	23	24	95	4	2	0	.964	2	*3/S	2.3
1955	Det-A	135	500	61	142	22	7	20	**116**	50	49	.284	.350	.476	123	12	14	80	1	1	-0	.953	-5	*3	0.8
1956	Det-A★	131	481	77	148	14	6	25	81	77	46	.308	.406	.518	142	30	30	103	0	0	0	.959	-7	*3	2.5
1957	Det-A	129	462	48	126	25	3	12	65	57	47	.273	.356	.418	108	7	6	68	1	1	-0	.990	-10	*1/3	-1.2
1958	Det-A	39	114	16	27	4	1	6	20	14	13	.237	.326	.447	103	1	0	16	0	2	-1	.988	-1	1	-0.4
	Chi-A	77	246	25	60	12	1	7	41	18	33	.244	.298	.386	89	-5	-4	27	1	1	-0	.986	-2	1	-1.1
	Yr	116	360	41	87	16	2	13	61	32	46	.242	.307	.406	93	-4	-4	43	1	3	-2	.986	-3	1	-1.5
1959	Chi-A	9	21	3	5	0	0	1	5	7	5	.238	.429	.381	126	1	1	5	1	0	0	.955	0	/1	0.1
	KC-A	61	132	19	36	6	0	2	12	27	17	.273	.396	.364	108	3	3	21	1	0	0	.983	1	1/3	0.2
	Yr	70	153	22	41	6	0	3	17	34	22	.268	.401	.366	111	4	4	25	2	0	1	.980	1	1/3	0.3
	Mil-N	13	15	3	3	0	0	1	2	4	2	.200	.368	.400	114	0	0	2	0	0	0	1.000	-0	/1	0.0
1960	Mil-N	7	12	3	3	1	0	0	4	5	1	.250	.471	.333	135	1	1	2	0	0	0	1.000	0	/1	0.1
	Bos-A	34	78	6	16	1	0	1	11	11	15	.205	.303	.256	51	-5	-5	6	0	0	0	.994	-0	1	-0.7
Total	13	1373	4589	645	1260	162	46	151	737	608	463	.275	.363	.429	115	84	95	731	21	19	-5	.958	-46	3S1/2	5.4
■ BOB BOONE Boone, Robert Raymond b: 11/19/47, San Diego, Cal. BR/TR, 6'2", 202 lbs. Deb: 9/10/72 F																									
1972	Phi-N	16	51	4	14	1	0	1	4	5	7	.275	.339	.353	95	-0	-0	6	1	0	0	.936	-6	C	-0.6
1973	Phi-N	145	521	42	136	20	2	10	61	41	36	.261	.315	.365	86	-9	-11	60	3	4	-2	.990	6	*C	0.0
1974	Phi-N	146	488	41	118	24	3	3	52	35	29	.242	.298	.322	70	-18	-20	45	3	1	0	.976	-7	*C	-2.1
1975	Phi-N	97	289	28	71	14	2	2	20	32	14	.246	.323	.329	78	-7	-8	30	1	3	-2	.990	1	C/3	-0.6
1976	*Phi-N★	121	361	40	98	18	2	4	54	45	44	.271	.354	.366	101	3	2	45	2	5	-2	.993	-9	*C/1	-0.8
1977	*Phi-N	132	440	55	125	26	4	11	66	42	54	.284	.349	.436	105	6	3	66	5	5	-2	.989	3	*C/3	0.8
1978	*Phi-N★	132	435	48	123	18	4	12	62	46	37	.283	.353	.425	115	10	9	62	2	5	-2	**.991**	-9	*C/1O	0.1
1979	Phi-N★	119	398	38	114	21	3	9	58	49	33	.286	.367	.422	111	9	7	61	1	4	-2	.988	-12	*C/3	-0.3
1980	*Phi-N	141	480	34	110	23	1	9	55	48	41	.229	.301	.338	74	-14	-17	48	3	4	-2	.979	5	*C	-1.0
1981	*Phi-N	76	227	19	48	7	0	4	24	22	16	.211	.281	.295	61	-11	-12	18	2	2	-1	.985	-2	C	-1.3
1982	*Cal-A	143	472	42	121	17	0	7	58	39	34	.256	.313	.337	79	-14	-14	51	0	2	-1	.989	7	*C	-0.2
1983	Cal-A★	142	468	46	120	18	0	9	52	24	42	.256	.293	.353	77	-15	-15	44	4	3	-1	.980	4	*C	-0.5
1984	Cal-A	139	450	33	91	16	1	3	32	25	45	.202	.244	.262	40	-37	-36	28	3	3	-1	.984	7	*C	-2.3
1985	Cal-A	150	460	37	114	17	0	5	55	37	35	.248	.308	.317	72	-17	-17	45	1	2	-1	.987	5	*C	-0.6
1986	*Cal-A	144	442	48	98	12	2	7	49	43	30	.222	.291	.305	63	-23	-22	39	1	0	0	.988	12	*C	-0.1
1987	Cal-A	128	389	42	94	18	0	3	33	35	36	.242	.306	.311	66	-20	-18	37	0	2	-1	.983	0	*C/D	-1.0
1988	Cal-A	122	352	38	104	17	0	5	39	29	26	.295	.352	.386	110	4	5	47	2	2	-1	.986	-6	*C	0.6
1989	KC-A	131	405	33	111	13	2	1	43	49	37	.274	.355	.323	93	-2	-2	47	3	2	-0	.991	5	*C	1.0

YEAR	TM/L	G	AB	R	H	2B	3B	HR	RBI	BB	SO	AVG	OBP	SLG	PRO+	BR	/A	RC	SB	CS	SBR	FA	FR	POS	TPR
1990	KC-A	40	117	11	28	3	0	0	9	17	12	.239	.336	.265	71	-4	-4	11	1	1	-0	.985	2	C	0.0
Total	19	2264	7245	679	1838	303	26	105	826	663	608	.254	.318	.346	82	-160	-170	790	38	50	-19	.986	6	*C/13DO	-8.9
■ **BOOTH** Booth Deb: 5/01/1875																									
1875	NH-n	1	2	0	0	0	0	0		0		.000	.000	.000	-99	-0	-0	0						/S	0.0
■ **AMOS BOOTH** Booth, Amos Smith "Darling" b: 9/14/1853, Cincinnati, O. d: 7/1/21, Miamisburg, Ohio BR/TR, Deb: 4/25/1876																									
1876	Cin-N	63	272	31	71	3	0	0	14	9	11	.261	.285	.272	101	-4	3	22				.760	-18	3CS/OP	-1.3
1877	Cin-N	44	157	16	27	2	1	0	13	12	10	.172	.231	.197	41	-11	-8	7				.853	-5	SCP2/3O	-0.8
1880	Cin-N	1	2	0	0	0	0	0	0	0	0	.000	.000	.000	-99	-0	-0	0				.000	0	/3	0.0
1882	Bal-a	1	3	0	0	0	0	0		0		.000	.000	.000	-99	-1	-1	0				1.000	0	/3	-0.1
	Lou-a	1	4	0	0	0	0	0		0		.000	.000	.000	-99	-1	-1	0				1.000	-1	/2	-0.1
	Yr	2	7	0	0	0	0	0		0		.000	.000	.000	-99	-1	-1	0				1.000	-1	/32	-0.2
Total	4	110	438	47	98	5	1	0	27	21	21	.224	.259	.240	73	-16	-7	29				.746	-23	/CS3P2O	-2.3
■ **EDDIE BOOTH** Booth, Edward H. b: Brooklyn, N.Y. Deb: 4/26/1872																									
1872	Man-n	24	118	24	40	3	2	0	15	0	1	.339	.339	.398	134	3	5	16						2/O	0.2
	Atl-n	15	62	11	18	5	0	0	8	0	0	.290	.290	.371	87	0	-2	6						O/2	-0.2
	Yr	39	180	35	58	8	2	0	23	0	1	.322	.322	.389	114	3	2	22						2O	0.0
1873	Res-n	18	72	11	21	2	2	0	4	0	2	.292	.292	.375	103	-1	1	8						O/2	0.1
	Atl-n	16	69	8	14	3	1	0	7	3	0	.203	.236	.275	56	-4	-3	5						O	-0.1
	Yr	34	141	19	35	5	3	0	11	3	2	.248	.264	.326	80	-5	-2	12						O/2	0.0
1874	Atl-n	44	187	24	47	2	4	1		3		.251	.263	.321	96	-3	1	16						*O	0.1
1875	Mut-n	68	278	33	55	3	4	0		1		.198	.201	.237	48	-13	-16	14						*O/2	-1.3
1876	NY-N	57	228	17	49	2	1	0	7	2	4	.215	.222	.232	59	-11	-7	12				.764	-5	*O/2P	-1.0
Total	4 n	185	786	111	195	18	13	1	34	7	3	.248	.255	.308	81	-17	-14	65						O/2D	-1.2
■ **FRENCHY BORDAGARAY** Bordagaray, Stanley George b: 1/3/10, Coalinga, Cal. BR/TR, 5'7.5", 175 lbs. Deb: 4/17/34																									
1934	Chi-A	29	87	12	28	3	1	0	2	3	8	.322	.344	.379	84	-2	-2	11	1	2	-1	.938	-1	O	-0.4
1935	Bro-N	120	422	69	119	19	6	1	39	17	29	.282	.319	.363	85	-10	-9	51	18			.980	1	*O	-1.2
1936	Bro-N	125	372	63	117	21	3	4	31	17	42	.315	.346	.419	104	2	2	54	12			.991	0	O2/3	-0.1
1937	StL-N	96	300	43	88	11	4	1	37	15	25	.293	.331	.367	88	-5	-5	37	11			.942	-9	3O	-1.4
1938	StL-N	81	156	19	44	5	1	0	21	8	9	.282	.325	.327	76	-4	-5	17	2			.959	0	O/3	-0.6
1939	*Cin-N	63	122	19	24	5	1	0	12	9	10	.197	.252	.254	36	-11	-11	8	3			1.000	-6	O/2	-1.8
1941	*NY-A	36	73	10	19	1	0	0	4	6	8	.260	.325	.274	61	-4	-4	7	1	0	0	.967	-3	O	-0.7
1942	Bro-N	48	58	11	14	2	0	0	5	3	3	.241	.279	.276	62	-3	-3	4	2			1.000	-4	O	-0.8
1943	Bro-N	89	268	47	81	18	2	0	19	30	15	.302	.379	.384	120	8	8	42	6			.989	-15	O3	-0.9
1944	Bro-N	130	501	85	141	26	4	6	51	36	22	.281	.331	.385	103	-0	1	64	3			.945	-20	3O	-2.0
1945	Bro-N	113	273	32	70	9	6	2	49	29	15	.256	.328	.355	91	-4	-3	33	7			.886	-11	3O	-1.4
Total	11	930	2632	410	745	120	28	14	270	173	186	.283	.331	.366	91	-32	-33	329	66	2		.982	-66	O3/2	-11.3
■ **PAT BORDERS** Borders, Patrick Lance b: 5/14/63, Columbus, Ohio BR/TR, 6'2", 190 lbs. Deb: 4/06/88																									
1988	Tor-A	56	154	15	42	6	3	5	21	3	24	.273	.287	.448	102	-0	-0	18	0	0	0	.973	2	C/23D	0.4
1989	*Tor-A	94	241	22	62	11	1	3	29	11	45	.257	.292	.349	81	-7	-6	23	2	1	0	.980	0	CD	-0.3
1990	Tor-A	125	346	36	99	24	2	15	49	18	57	.286	.321	.497	123	10	9	48	0	1	-1	.993	0	*C/D	1.5
1991	*Tor-A	105	291	22	71	17	0	5	36	11	45	.244	.274	.354	70	-12	-13	27	0	0	0	.993	13	*C	0.5
1992	*Tor-A	138	480	47	116	26	2	13	53	33	75	.242	.293	.385	85	-9	-11	53	1	1	-0	.991	5	*C	0.1
Total	5	518	1512	142	390	84	8	41	188	76	246	.258	.295	.405	92	-17	-22	168	3	3	-1	.989	21	C/D32	2.2
■ **MIKE BORDICK** Bordick, Michael Todd b: 7/21/65, Marquette, Mich. BR/TR, 5'11", 170 lbs. Deb: 4/11/90																									
1990	*Oak-A	25	14	0	1	0	0	0	0	1	4	.071	.133	.071	-43	-3	-3	0	0	0	0	1.000	-0	3/S2	-0.3
1991	Oak-A	90	235	21	56	5	1	0	21	14	37	.238	.290	.268	59	-14	-12	19	3	4	-2	.972	-4	S/23	-1.1
1992	*Oak-A	154	504	62	151	19	4	3	48	40	59	.300	.362	.371	110	5	7	69	12	6	0	.987	7	2S	2.2
Total	3	269	753	83	208	24	5	3	69	55	100	.276	.335	.333	91	-12	-7	88	15	10	-2	.970	3	S2/3	0.8
■ **GLENN BORGMANN** Borgmann, Glenn Dennis b: 5/25/50, Paterson, N.J. BR/TR, 6'4", 210 lbs. Deb: 7/01/72																									
1972	Min-A	56	175	11	41	4	0	3	14	25	25	.234	.330	.309	86	-1	-2	18	0	0	0	.965	-1	C	-0.1
1973	Min-A	12	34	7	9	2	0	0	9	6	10	.265	.375	.324	95	0	0	5	0	0	0	1.000	-2	C	-0.2
1974	Min-A	128	345	33	87	8	1	3	45	39	44	.252	.330	.307	81	-6	-8	36	2	1	0	**.997**	-1	*C	-0.4
1975	Min-A	125	352	34	73	15	2	2	33	47	59	.207	.304	.278	64	-15	-16	31	0	1	-1	.989	-2	*C	-1.4
1976	Min-A	24	65	10	16	3	0	1	6	19	7	.246	.417	.338	119	3	3	11	1	1	-0	.976	2	C	0.5
1977	Min-A	17	43	12	11	1	0	2	7	11	9	.256	.407	.419	128	2	2	8	0	0	0	1.000	2	C	0.4
1978	Min-A	49	123	16	26	4	1	3	15	18	17	.211	.312	.333	80	-3	-3	15	0	0	0	.990	5	C/D	0.3
1979	Min-A	31	70	4	14	3	0	0	8	12	11	.200	.317	.243	52	-4	-5	6	1	0	0	.993	7	C	0.3
1980	Chi-A	32	87	10	19	2	0	2	14	14	9	.218	.327	.310	76	-3	-3	10	0	0	0	1.000	2	C	0.0
Total	9	474	1294	137	296	42	4	16	151	191	191	.229	.329	.304	79	-26	-31	140	4	3	-1	.989	10	C/D	-0.6
■ **BOB BORKOWSKI** Borkowski, Robert Vilarian b: 1/27/26, Dayton, Ohio BR/TR, 6', 182 lbs. Deb: 4/22/50																									
1950	Chi-N	85	256	27	70	7	4	4	29	16	30	.273	.319	.379	84	-7	-6	29	1			.975	1	O/1	-0.8
1951	Chi-N	58	89	9	14	1	0	0	10	3	16	.157	.185	.169	-4	-13	-13	2	0	0	0	.933	-4	O	-1.8
1952	Cin-N	126	377	42	95	11	4	4	24	26	53	.252	.300	.334	76	-13	-13	39	1	3	-2	.991	-6	*O/1	-2.5
1953	Cin-N	94	249	32	67	11	1	7	29	21	41	.269	.328	.406	89	-4	-4	34	0	1	-1	.982	-7	O/1	-1.3
1954	Cin-N	73	162	13	43	12	1	1	19	8	18	.265	.304	.370	73	-6	-7	15	0	2	-1	1.000	0	O/1	-0.9
1955	Cin-N	25	18	1	3	1	0	0	1	1	2	.167	.211	.222	14	-2	-2	1	0	0	0	1.000	-4	O/1	-0.6
	Bro-N	9	19	2	2	0	0	0	0	1	6	.105	.150	.105	-30	-4	-4	0	0	0	0	1.000	-3	/O	-0.7
	Yr	34	37	3	5	1	0	0	1	2	8	.135	.179	.162	-8	-6	-6	1	0	0	0	1.000	-6	O/1	-1.3
Total	6	470	1170	126	294	43	10	16	112	76	166	.251	.299	.346	71	-48	-49	120	2	6		.982	-22	O/1	-8.6
■ **RED BOROM** Borom, Edward Jones b: 10/30/15, Spartanburg, S.C. BL/TR, 5'11", 180 lbs. Deb: 4/23/44																									
1944	Det-A	7	14	1	1	0	0	0	1	2	2	.071	.188	.071	-23	-2	-2	0	0	0	0	.950	1	/2S	-0.1
1945	*Det-A	55	130	19	35	4	0	0	9	7	8	.269	.307	.300	72	-4	-5	13	4	2	0	.966	5	2/3S	0.2
Total	2	62	144	20	36	4	0	0	10	9	10	.250	.294	.278	62	-6	-7	13	4	2	0	.964	6	/23S	0.1
■ **STEVE BOROS** Boros, Stephen b: 9/3/36, Flint, Mich. BR/TR, 6', 185 lbs. Deb: 6/19/57 MC																									
1957	Det-A	24	41	4	6	1	0	0	2	1	8	.146	.167	.171	-7	-6	-6	1	0	0	0	.906	3	/3S	-0.3
1958	Det-A	6	2	0	0	0	0	0	0	0	0	.000	.000	.000	-93	-1	-1	0	0	0	0	1.000	2	/2	0.1
1961	Det-A	116	396	51	107	18	2	5	62	68	42	.270	.388	.364	99	4	3	61	4	2	0	.953	-21	*3	-1.7
1962	Det-A	116	356	46	81	14	1	16	47	53	62	.228	.333	.407	95	-1	-3	50	3	1	0	.931	-15	*3/2	-1.6
1963	Chi-N	41	90	9	19	5	1	3	7	12	19	.211	.304	.389	93	-0	-1	11	0	2	-1	.975	-2	1O	-0.6
1964	Cin-N	117	370	31	95	12	3	2	31	47	43	.257	.344	.322	86	-4	-6	41	4	1	1	.961	4	*3	-0.3
1965	Cin-N	2	0	0	0	0	0	0	0	0	0	—	—	—	—	0	0	0	0	0	0	1.000	0	/3	0.0
Total	7	422	1255	141	308	50	7	26	149	181	174	.245	.346	.359	90	-7	-13	164	11	6	-0	.948	-30	3/1O2S	-4.4
■ **BABE BORTON** Borton, William Baker b: 8/14/1888, Marion, Ill. d: 7/29/54, Berkeley, Cal. BL/TL, 6', 178 lbs. Deb: 9/02/12																									
1912	Chi-A	31	105	15	39	3	1	0	17	8		.371	.416	.419	143	5	6	19	1			.997	0	1	0.6

YEAR	TM/L	G	AB	R	H	2B	3B	HR	RBI	BB	SO	AVG	OBP	SLG	PRO+	BR	/A	RC	SB	CS	SBR	FA	FR	POS	TPR
1913	Chi-A	28	80	9	22	5	0	0	13	23	5	.275	.442	.338	130	5	5	12	1			.991	-2	1	0.3
	NY-A	33	108	8	14	2	0	0	11	18	19	.130	.260	.148	20	-10	-10	5	1			.978	4	1	-0.7
	Yr	61	188	17	36	7	0	0	24	41	24	.191	.342	.229	68	-5	-5	16	2			.984	3	1	-0.4
1915	StL-F	159	549	**97**	157	20	14	3	83	**92**	64	.286	.395	.390	124	26	22	96	17			.993	-10	*1	0.9
1916	StL-A	66	98	10	22	1	2	1	12	19	13	.224	.350	.306	102	0	1	11	1			.991	-1	1	-0.1
Total	4	317	940	139	254	31	17	4	136	160	101	.270	.381	.352	113	26	23	144	21			.991	-8	1	1.0

■ DON BOSCH Bosch, Donald John b: 7/15/42, San Francisco, Cal BB/TR, 5'10", 160 lbs. Deb: 9/19/66

YEAR	TM/L	G	AB	R	H	2B	3B	HR	RBI	BB	SO	AVG	OBP	SLG	PRO+	BR	/A	RC	SB	CS	SBR	FA	FR	POS	TPR
1966	Pit-N	3	2	0	0	0	0	0	0	0	0	.000	.000	.000	-99	-1	-1	0	0	0	0	.000	0	/O	-0.1
1967	NY-N	44	93	7	13	0	1	0	2	5	24	.140	.184	.161	-0	-12	-12	3	3	1	0	1.000	3	O	-1.1
1968	NY-N	50	111	14	19	1	0	3	7	9	33	.171	.233	.261	48	-7	-7	6	0	2	-1	.974	6	O	-0.4
1969	Mon-N	49	112	13	20	5	0	1	4	8	20	.179	.233	.250	35	-10	-10	7	1	0	0	.964	1	O	-1.1
Total	4	146	318	34	52	6	1	4	13	22	77	.164	.218	.226	28	-29	-29	16	4	3	-1	.979	9	O	-2.7

■ RICK BOSETTI Bosetti, Richard Alan b: 8/5/53, Redding, Cal. BR/TR, 5'11", 185 lbs. Deb: 9/09/76

YEAR	TM/L	G	AB	R	H	2B	3B	HR	RBI	BB	SO	AVG	OBP	SLG	PRO+	BR	/A	RC	SB	CS	SBR	FA	FR	POS	TPR
1976	Phi-N	13	18	6	5	1	0	0	0	1	3	.278	.316	.333	82	-0	-0	2	3	0	1	1.000	1	/O	0.2
1977	StL-N	41	69	12	16	0	0	0	3	6	11	.232	.303	.232	47	-5	-5	5	4	4	-1	1.000	3	O	-0.4
1978	Tor-A	136	568	61	147	25	5	5	42	30	65	.259	.300	.347	80	-15	-16	58	6	10	-4	.986	25	*O	-0.1
1979	Tor-A	162	619	59	161	35	2	8	65	22	70	.260	.289	.362	73	-23	-24	58	13	12	-3	.974	17	*O	-1.7
1980	Tor-A	53	188	24	40	7	1	4	18	15	29	.213	.278	.324	62	-9	-10	16	4	6	-2	.985	-1	O	-1.6
1981	Tor-A	25	47	5	11	2	0	0	4	2	6	.234	.265	.277	53	-3	-3	3	0	2	-1	1.000	-2	O/D	-0.7
	*Oak-A	9	19	4	2	0	0	0	1	3	3	.105	.227	.105	-2	-2	-2	1	0	0	0	1.000	-0	/OD	-0.3
	Yr	34	66	9	13	2	0	0	5	5	9	.197	.254	.227	38	-5	-5	3	0	2	-1	1.000	-2	O/D	-1.0
1982	Oak-A	6	15	1	3	0	0	0	0	0	1	.200	.200	.200	11	-2	-2	0	0	0	0	1.000	1	/O	-0.1
Total	7	445	1543	172	385	70	8	17	133	79	188	.250	.290	.338	71	-60	-63	143	30	34	-11	.982	45	O/D	-4.7

■ THAD BOSLEY Bosley, Thaddis b: 9/17/56, Oceanside, Cal. BL/TL, 6'3", 175 lbs. Deb: 6/29/77

YEAR	TM/L	G	AB	R	H	2B	3B	HR	RBI	BB	SO	AVG	OBP	SLG	PRO+	BR	/A	RC	SB	CS	SBR	FA	FR	POS	TPR
1977	Cal-A	58	212	19	63	10	2	0	19	16	32	.297	.349	.363	98	-1	-0	27	5	4	-1	.963	1	O	-0.2
1978	Chi-A	66	219	25	59	5	1	2	13	13	32	.269	.310	.329	79	-6	-6	20	12	11	-3	.975	0	O	-1.2
1979	Chi-A	36	77	13	24	1	1	1	8	9	14	.312	.384	.390	109	1	1	12	4	1	1	.967	1	O	0.2
1980	Chi-A	70	147	12	33	2	0	2	14	10	27	.224	.274	.279	52	-10	-10	10	3	2	-0	.958	-7	O	-1.8
1981	*Mil-A	42	105	11	24	2	0	0	3	6	13	.229	.270	.248	53	-7	-6	7	2	1	0	.966	-6	O/D	-1.3
1982	Sea-A	22	46	3	8	1	0	0	2	4	8	.174	.240	.196	21	-5	-5	2	3	1	0	1.000	-5	O	-1.1
1983	Chi-N	43	72	12	21	4	1	2	12	10	12	.292	.378	.458	125	3	3	13	1	1	-0	1.000	-0	O	0.2
1984	*Chi-N	55	98	17	29	2	2	2	14	13	22	.296	.378	.418	113	3	2	17	5	1	1	.976	-4	O	-0.1
1985	Chi-N	108	180	25	59	6	3	7	27	20	29	.328	.395	.511	137	12	10	37	5	1	1	.988	-7	O	0.3
1986	Chi-N	87	120	15	33	4	1	1	9	18	24	.275	.370	.350	92	1	-1	17	3	0	1	.969	-10	O	-1.0
1987	KC-A	80	140	13	39	6	1	1	16	9	26	.279	.322	.357	78	-4	-4	16	0	0	0	.966	-6	OD	-1.0
1988	KC-A	15	21	1	4	0	0	0	2	2	6	.190	.261	.190	28	-2	-2	1	0	0	0	1.000	-2	/OD	-0.4
	Cal-A	35	75	9	21	5	0	0	7	6	12	.280	.333	.347	93	-1	-1	9	1	1	-0	.965	-1	O/D	-0.2
	Yr	50	96	10	25	5	0	0	9	8	18	.260	.317	.313	78	-3	-3	10	1	1	-0	.967	-3	O/D	-0.6
1989	Tex-A	37	40	5	9	2	0	1	9	3	11	.225	.279	.350	75	-1	-1	4	2	0	1	1.000	0	/OD	-0.1
1990	Tex-A	30	29	3	4	0	0	1	3	4	7	.138	.242	.241	36	-3	-3	2	1	0	0	1.000	-3	/OD	-0.5
Total	14	784	1581	183	430	50	12	20	158	143	275	.272	.333	.357	89	-18	-22	194	47	24	-0	.972	-47	O/D	-8.2

■ HARLEY BOSS Boss, Elmer Harley "Lefty" b: 11/19/08, Hodge, La. d: 5/15/64, Nashville, Tenn. BL/TL, 5'11.5", 185 lbs. Deb: 7/19/28

YEAR	TM/L	G	AB	R	H	2B	3B	HR	RBI	BB	SO	AVG	OBP	SLG	PRO+	BR	/A	RC	SB	CS	SBR	FA	FR	POS	TPR
1928	Was-A	12	12	1	3	0	0	0	2	3	1	.250	.400	.250	75	-0	-0	1	0	0	0	.970	-1	/1	-0.1
1929	Was-A	28	66	9	18	2	1	0	6	2	6	.273	.294	.333	61	-4	-4	6	0	0	0	.977	0	1	-0.5
1930	Was-A	3	3	0	0	0	0	0	0	0	0	.000	.000	.000	-99	-1	-1	0	0	0	0	1.000	-0	/1	-0.1
1933	Cle-A	112	438	54	118	17	7	1	53	25	27	.269	.310	.347	71	-17	-20	46	2	5	-2	.994	6	*1	-2.5
Total	4	155	519	64	139	19	8	1	61	30	34	.268	.309	.341	69	-22	-25	54	2	5	-2	.992	5	1	-3.2

■ HENRY BOSTICK Bostick, Henry Landers (b: Henry Lipschitz) b: 1/12/1895, Boston, Mass. d: 9/16/68, Denver, Colo. BR/TR, Deb: 5/18/15

YEAR	TM/L	G	AB	R	H	2B	3B	HR	RBI	BB	SO	AVG	OBP	SLG	PRO+	BR	/A	RC	SB	CS	SBR	FA	FR	POS	TPR
1915	Phi-A	2	7	0	0	0	0	0	2	1	1	.000	.125	.000	-65	-1	-1	0	0			1.000	-1	/3	-0.3

■ LYMAN BOSTOCK Bostock, Lyman Wesley b: 11/22/50, Birmingham, Ala. d: 9/23/78, Gary, Ind. BL/TR, 6'1", 180 lbs. Deb: 4/08/75

YEAR	TM/L	G	AB	R	H	2B	3B	HR	RBI	BB	SO	AVG	OBP	SLG	PRO+	BR	/A	RC	SB	CS	SBR	FA	FR	POS	TPR
1975	Min-A	98	369	52	104	21	5	0	29	28	42	.282	.332	.366	95	-1	-2	44	2	3	-1	.985	-3	O/D	-1.1
1976	Min-A	128	474	75	153	21	9	4	60	33	37	.323	.368	.430	130	19	18	71	12	6	0	.988	6	*O	1.9
1977	Min-A	153	593	104	199	36	12	14	90	51	59	.336	.394	.508	146	36	37	116	16	7	1	.989	4	*O	3.5
1978	Cal-A	147	568	74	168	24	4	5	71	59	36	.296	.364	.379	113	8	11	72	15	12	-3	.989	11	*O/D	1.3
Total	4	526	2004	305	624	102	30	23	250	171	174	.311	.368	.427	124	62	63	303	45	28	-3	.988	18	O/D	5.6

■ DARYL BOSTON Boston, Daryl Lamont b: 1/4/63, Cincinnati, Ohio BL/TL, 6'3", 193 lbs. Deb: 5/13/84

YEAR	TM/L	G	AB	R	H	2B	3B	HR	RBI	BB	SO	AVG	OBP	SLG	PRO+	BR	/A	RC	SB	CS	SBR	FA	FR	POS	TPR
1984	Chi-A	35	83	8	14	3	1	0	3	4	20	.169	.207	.229	20	-9	-9	5	6	0	2	.910	-6	O/D	-1.5
1985	Chi-A	95	232	20	53	13	1	3	15	14	44	.228	.272	.332	62	-12	-13	20	8	6	-1	.989	-6	O/D	-2.2
1986	Chi-A	56	199	29	53	11	3	5	22	21	33	.266	.336	.427	103	2	1	28	9	5	-0	.969	5	O/D	0.3
1987	Chi-A	103	337	51	87	21	2	10	29	25	68	.258	.309	.421	89	-5	-6	43	12	6	0	.991	-0	O/D	-0.8
1988	Chi-A	105	281	37	61	12	2	15	31	21	44	.217	.272	.434	95	-3	-3	32	9	3	1	.951	-3	O/D	-0.7
1989	Chi-A	101	218	34	55	3	4	5	23	24	31	.252	.326	.372	99	-1	-0	29	7	2	1	.971	-7	O/D	-0.8
1990	Chi-A	5	1	0	0	0	0	0	0	0	0	.000	.000	.000	-99	-0	-0	0	1	0	0	.000	-0	/OD	0.0
	NY-N	115	366	65	100	21	2	12	45	28	50	.273	.328	.440	110	4	4	52	18	7	1	.986	-5	*O	-0.2
1991	NY-N	137	255	40	70	16	4	4	21	30	42	.275	.351	.416	116	5	5	38	15	8	-0	.981	-17	*O	-1.4
1992	NY-N	130	289	37	72	14	2	11	35	38	60	.249	.342	.426	117	6	7	43	12	6	0	.993	-6	O	-0.1
Total	9	882	2261	321	565	114	21	65	224	205	392	.250	.314	.405	96	-13	-15	290	97	43	3	.976	-44	O/D	-7.4

■ KEN BOSWELL Boswell, Kenneth George b: 2/23/46, Austin, Tex. BL/TR, 6', 172 lbs. Deb: 9/18/67

YEAR	TM/L	G	AB	R	H	2B	3B	HR	RBI	BB	SO	AVG	OBP	SLG	PRO+	BR	/A	RC	SB	CS	SBR	FA	FR	POS	TPR
1967	NY-N	11	40	2	9	3	0	1	4	1	5	.225	.244	.375	76	-1	-1	3	0	0	0	.971	2	/23	0.1
1968	NY-N	75	284	37	74	7	2	4	11	16	27	.261	.302	.342	93	-3	-3	29	7	2	1	.965	-1	2	0.1
1969	*NY-N	102	362	48	101	14	7	3	32	36	47	.279	.348	.381	102	2	1	47	7	3	0	.959	-15	2	-0.7
1970	NY-N	105	351	32	89	13	2	5	44	41	32	.254	.335	.345	82	-8	-8	39	5	4	-1	.996	-15	*2	-1.6
1971	NY-N	116	392	46	107	20	1	5	40	36	31	.273	.337	.367	101	0	1	48	5	2	0	.973	-29	*2	-2.1
1972	NY-N	100	355	35	75	9	1	9	33	32	35	.211	.276	.318	70	-15	-14	29	2	2	-1	.990	-31	2	-4.5
1973	*NY-N	76	110	12	25	2	1	2	14	12	11	.227	.303	.318	74	-4	-4	11	0	0	0	.973	0	3/2	-0.4
1974	NY-N	96	222	19	48	6	1	2	15	18	19	.216	.278	.279	57	-13	-13	16	0	1	-1	1.000	7	23/O	-0.6
1975	Hou-N	86	178	16	43	8	2	0	21	30	12	.242	.354	.309	92	-2	-1	19	0	3	-2	.991	-10	23	-1.1
1976	Hou-N	91	126	12	33	8	1	0	18	8	8	.262	.306	.341	92	-3	-2	11	1	0	0	.933	-5	3/2O	-0.7
1977	Hou-N	72	97	7	21	1	1	0	12	10	12	.216	.290	.247	50	-7	-6	6	0	0	0	1.000	-3	2/3	-0.8
Total	11	930	2517	266	625	91	19	31	244	240	239	.248	.316	.337	85	-55	-49	259	27	17	-2	.979	-101	2/3O	-12.3

■ JOHN BOTTARINI Bottarini, John Charles b: 9/14/08, Crockett, Cal. d: 10/8/76, Jemez Springs, N.M. BR/TR, 6', 190 lbs. Deb: 4/22/37

YEAR	TM/L	G	AB	R	H	2B	3B	HR	RBI	BB	SO	AVG	OBP	SLG	PRO+	BR	/A	RC	SB	CS	SBR	FA	FR	POS	TPR
1937	Chi-N	26	40	3	11	3	0	1	7	5	10	.275	.370	.425	111	1	1	7	0			1.000	1	C/O	0.2

■ JIM BOTTOMLEY Bottomley, James Leroy "Sunny Jim" b: 4/23/1900, Oglesby, Ill. d: 12/11/59, St.Louis, Mo. BL/TL, 6', 180 lbs. Deb: 8/18/22 MCH

YEAR	TM/L	G	AB	R	H	2B	3B	HR	RBI	BB	SO	AVG	OBP	SLG	PRO+	BR	/A	RC	SB	CS	SBR	FA	FR	POS	TPR
1922	StL-N	37	151	29	49	8	5	5	35	6	13	.325	.358	.543	136	6	7	29	3	1	0	.986	-3	1	0.3
1923	StL-N	134	523	79	194	34	14	8	94	45	44	.371	.425	.535	155	39	41	117	4	6	-2	.986	-12	*1	1.8

YEAR	TM/L	G	AB	R	H	2B	3B	HR	RBI	BB	SO	AVG	OBP	SLG	PRO+	BR	/A	RC	SB	CS	SBR	FA	FR	POS	TPR
1924	StL-N	137	528	87	167	31	12	14	111	35	35	.316	.362	.500	131	20	21	94	5	4	-1	.982	-12	*1/2	0.0
1925	StL-N	153	619	92	**227**	**44**	12	21	128	47	36	.367	.413	.578	147	46	43	145	3	4	-2	.987	-4	*1	2.7
1926	*StL-N	154	603	98	180	**40**	14	19	**120**	58	52	.299	.364	.506	127	25	22	109	4			.989	-15	*1	-0.3
1927	StL-N	152	574	95	174	31	15	19	124	74	49	.303	.387	.509	134	31	29	112	8			.989	-11	*1	0.7
1928	*StL-N	149	576	123	187	42	**20**	**31**	**136**	71	54	.325	.402	.628	163	53	51	142	10			.987	-14	*1	2.3
1929	StL-N	146	560	108	176	31	12	29	137	70	54	.314	.391	.568	133	29	28	122	3			.991	-6	*1	0.7
1930	*StL-N	131	487	92	148	33	7	15	97	44	36	.304	.368	.493	102	4	1	86	5			.990	-14	*1	-2.2
1931	*StL-N	108	382	73	133	34	5	9	75	34	24	.348	.403	.534	144	26	24	84	3			.987	-3	1	1.2
1932	StL-N	91	311	45	92	16	3	11	48	25	32	.296	.350	.473	115	8	7	52	2			.986	-3	1	-0.2
1933	Cin-N	145	549	57	137	23	9	13	83	42	28	.250	.311	.395	102	-0	1	68	3			.991	-9	*1	-2.3
1934	Cin-N	142	556	72	158	31	11	11	78	33	40	.284	.324	.439	105	0	2	80	1			.989	-4	*1	-1.3
1935	Cin-N	107	399	44	103	21	1	1	49	18	24	.258	.294	.323	68	-19	-18	37	3			.992	-3	1	-3.0
1936	StL-A	140	544	72	162	39	11	12	95	44	55	.298	.354	.476	100	0	-2	92	0	0	0	.992	-10	*1	-2.2
1937	StL-A	65	109	11	26	7	0	1	12	18	15	.239	.346	.330	71	-4	-5	14	1	0	0	.995	1	1M	-0.5
Total	16	1991	7471	1177	2313	465	151	219	1422	664	591	.310	.369	.500	124	262	252	1384	58	15		.988	-120	*1/2	-2.3

■ ED BOUCHEE

Bouchee, Edward Francis b: 3/7/33, Livingston, Mont. BL/TL, 6'1", 205 lbs. Deb: 9/19/56

YEAR	TM/L	G	AB	R	H	2B	3B	HR	RBI	BB	SO	AVG	OBP	SLG	PRO+	BR	/A	RC	SB	CS	SBR	FA	FR	POS	TPR
1956	Phi-N	9	22	0	6	2	0	0	1	5	6	.273	.407	.364	112	1	1	4	0	0	0	1.000	-0	/1	0.0
1957	Phi-N	154	574	78	168	35	8	17	76	84	91	.293	.396	.470	136	29	31	110	1	0	0	.988	4	*1	2.6
1958	Phi-N	89	334	55	86	19	5	9	39	51	74	.257	.356	.425	107	3	4	51	1	0	0	.993	0	1	-0.1
1959	Phi-N	136	499	75	142	29	4	15	74	70	74	.285	.378	.449	117	15	14	85	0	4	-2	.986	-0	*1	0.2
1960	Phi-N	22	65	1	17	4	0	0	8	9	11	.262	.360	.323	89	-1	-1	8	0	0	0	.994	1	1	-0.1
	Chi-N	98	299	33	71	11	1	5	44	45	51	.237	.341	.331	86	-5	-4	37	2	0	1	.991	-0	1	-1.1
	Yr	120	364	34	88	15	1	5	52	54	62	.242	.344	.330	86	-6	-5	46	2	0	1	.992	1	*1	-1.2
1961	Chi-N	112	319	49	79	12	3	12	38	58	77	.248	.372	.417	108	6	5	53	1	4	-2	.983	1	*1	-0.3
1962	NY-N	50	87	7	14	2	0	3	10	18	17	.161	.305	.287	59	-5	-5	8	0	0	0	.976	4	1	-0.2
Total	7	670	2199	298	583	114	21	61	290	340	401	.265	.370	.419	112	43	45	357	5	8	-3	.988	9	1	1.0

■ AL BOUCHER

Boucher, Alexander Francis "Bo" b: 11/13/1881, Franklin, Mass. d: 6/23/74, Torrance, Cal. BR/TR, 5'8.5", 156 lbs. Deb: 4/16/14

YEAR	TM/L	G	AB	R	H	2B	3B	HR	RBI	BB	SO	AVG	OBP	SLG	PRO+	BR	/A	RC	SB	CS	SBR	FA	FR	POS	TPR
1914	StL-F	147	516	62	119	26	4	2	49	52	88	.231	.304	.308	70	-17	-21	56	13			.916	-4	*3	-2.1

■ MEDRIC BOUCHER

Boucher, Medric Charles Francis b: 3/12/1886, St.Louis, Mo. d: 3/12/74, Martinez, Cal. BR/TR, 5'10", 165 lbs. Deb: 6/03/14

YEAR	TM/L	G	AB	R	H	2B	3B	HR	RBI	BB	SO	AVG	OBP	SLG	PRO+	BR	/A	RC	SB	CS	SBR	FA	FR	POS	TPR
1914	Bal-F	16	16	2	5	1	1	0	2	1	1	.313	.353	.500	137	1	1	3	0			.950	0	/C1O	0.1
	Pit-F	1	1	0	0	0	0	0	0	0	0	.000	.000	.000	-99	-0	-0	0	0			.000	0	H	0.0
	Yr	17	17	2	5	1	1	0	2	1	1	.294	.333	.471	124	0	0	3	0			.950	0	/C1O	0.1

■ LOU BOUDREAU

Boudreau, Louis b: 7/17/17, Harvey, Ill. BR/TR, 5'11", 185 lbs. Deb: 9/09/38 MH

YEAR	TM/L	G	AB	R	H	2B	3B	HR	RBI	BB	SO	AVG	OBP	SLG	PRO+	BR	/A	RC	SB	CS	SBR	FA	FR	POS	TPR
1938	Cle-A	1	1	0	0	0	0	0	0	1	0	.000	.500	.000	36	0	0	0	0	0	0	.000	0	/3	0.0
1939	Cle-A	53	225	42	58	15	4	0	19	28	24	.258	.340	.360	82	-7	-6	28	2	1	0	.953	8	S	0.6
1940	Cle-A★	155	627	97	185	46	10	9	101	73	39	.295	.370	.443	113	10	12	103	6	3	0	**.968**	12	*S	3.5
1941	Cle-A★	148	579	95	149	**45**	8	10	56	85	57	.257	.355	.415	108	3	7	92	9	4	0	**.966**	13	*S	3.0
1942	Cle-A★	147	506	57	143	18	10	2	58	75	39	.283	.379	.370	118	10	14	73	7	16	-8	**.965**	-0	*SM	1.5
1943	Cle-A☆	152	539	69	154	32	7	3	67	90	31	.286	.388	.388	135	22	26	87	4	7	-3	**.970**	**28**	*S/CM	**6.5**
1944	Cle-A☆	150	584	91	191	**45**	5	3	67	73	39	**.327**	.406	.437	146	33	36	112	11	3	2	**.978**	26	*S/CM	**7.7**
1945	Cle-A†	97	345	50	106	24	1	3	48	35	20	.307	.374	.409	133	12	14	53	0	4	-2	.983	1	SM	2.1
1946	Cle-A	140	515	51	151	30	6	6	62	40	14	.293	.345	.410	118	6	10	72	6	7	-2	**.970**	16	*SM	3.3
1947	Cle-A★	150	538	79	165	**45**	3	4	67	67	10	.307	.388	.424	129	20	21	95	1	0	0	**.982**	17	*SM	4.7
1948	*Cle-A★	152	560	116	199	34	6	18	106	98	9	.355	.453	.534	166	53	55	143	3	2	-0	**.975**	9	*S/CM	**6.8**
1949	Cle-A	134	475	53	135	20	3	4	60	70	10	.284	.381	.364	100	0	2	68	0	1	-1	.982	5	S3/12M	1.1
1950	Cle-A	81	260	23	70	13	2	1	29	31	5	.269	.349	.346	81	-8	-7	32	1	2	-1	.986	0	S/123M	-0.3
1951	Bos-A	82	273	37	73	18	1	5	47	30	12	.267	.353	.396	93	1	-3	39	1	0	0	.951	-1	S3/1	0.0
1952	Bos-A	4	2	1	0	0	0	0	2	0	0	.000	.000	.000	-93	-1	-1	0	0	0	0	1.000	-0	/S3M	-0.1
Total	15	1646	6029	861	1779	385	66	68	789	796	309	.295	.380	.415	121	154	181	996	51	50	-15	.973	134	*S/312C	40.4

■ CHRIS BOURJOS

Bourjos, Christopher b: 10/16/55, Chicago, Ill. BR/TR, 6', 185 lbs. Deb: 8/31/80

YEAR	TM/L	G	AB	R	H	2B	3B	HR	RBI	BB	SO	AVG	OBP	SLG	PRO+	BR	/A	RC	SB	CS	SBR	FA	FR	POS	TPR
1980	SF-N	13	22	4	5	1	0	1	2	2	7	.227	.292	.409	96	-0	-0	2	0	0	0	1.000	-1	/O	-0.1

■ RAFAEL BOURNIGAL

Bournigal, Rafael Antonio b: 5/12/66, Azua, D.R. BR/TR, 5'11", 160 lbs. Deb: 9/01/92

YEAR	TM/L	G	AB	R	H	2B	3B	HR	RBI	BB	SO	AVG	OBP	SLG	PRO+	BR	/A	RC	SB	CS	SBR	FA	FR	POS	TPR
1992	LA-N	10	20	1	3	1	0	0	0	1	2	.150	.227	.200	22	-2	-2	1	0	0	0	.967	2	/S	0.1

■ PAT BOURQUE

Bourque, Patrick Daniel b: 3/23/47, Worcester, Mass. BL/TL, 6', 210 lbs. Deb: 9/06/71

YEAR	TM/L	G	AB	R	H	2B	3B	HR	RBI	BB	SO	AVG	OBP	SLG	PRO+	BR	/A	RC	SB	CS	SBR	FA	FR	POS	TPR
1971	Chi-N	14	37	3	7	0	1	1	3	3	9	.189	.250	.324	54	-2	-3	3	0	0	0	.957	2	1	-0.1
1972	Chi-N	11	27	3	7	1	0	0	5	2	2	.259	.310	.296	66	-1	-1	3	0	0	0	1.000	1	/1	-0.1
1973	Chi-N	57	139	11	29	6	0	7	20	16	21	.209	.299	.403	86	-2	-3	18	1	1	-0	.986	5	1	-0.1
	*Oak-A	23	42	8	8	4	1	2	9	15	10	.190	.404	.476	155	3	4	9	0	0	0	1.000	-1	D/1	0.3
1974	Oak-A	73	96	6	22	4	0	1	16	15	20	.229	.333	.302	90	-2	-1	10	0	2	-1	.988	-1	1/D	-0.4
	Min-A	23	64	5	14	2	0	1	8	7	11	.219	.296	.297	68	-2	-3	6	0	0	0	.987	3	1	-0.1
	Yr	96	160	11	36	6	0	2	24	22	31	.225	.319	.300	82	-4	-3	16	0	2	-1	.988	2	1/D	-0.5
Total	4	201	405	36	87	17	2	12	61	58	73	.215	.316	.356	87	-5	-7	48	1	3	-2	.985	11	1/D	-0.5

■ LARRY BOWA

Bowa, Lawrence Robert b: 12/6/45, Sacramento, Cal. BB/TR, 5'10", 155 lbs. Deb: 4/07/70 MC

YEAR	TM/L	G	AB	R	H	2B	3B	HR	RBI	BB	SO	AVG	OBP	SLG	PRO+	BR	/A	RC	SB	CS	SBR	FA	FR	POS	TPR
1970	Phi-N	145	547	50	137	17	6	0	34	21	48	.250	.278	.303	57	-35	-33	45	24	13	-1	.979	-21	*S/2	-3.8
1971	Phi-N	159	650	74	162	18	5	0	25	36	61	.249	.294	.292	66	-28	-28	59	28	11	2	**.987**	10	*S	0.5
1972	Phi-N	152	579	67	145	11	**13**	1	31	32	51	.250	.292	.320	72	-20	-22	54	17	9	-0	**.987**	5	*S	0.4
1973	Phi-N	122	446	42	94	11	3	0	23	24	31	.211	.253	.249	38	-36	-38	28	10	6	-1	.979	-0	*S	-2.4
1974	Phi-N★	162	669	97	184	19	10	1	36	23	52	.275	.300	.338	75	-21	-24	69	39	11	5	**.984**	-16	*S	-1.5
1975	Phi-N★	136	583	79	178	18	9	2	38	24	32	.305	.335	.377	94	-3	-6	75	24	6	4	.962	-12	*S	0.1
1976	*Phi-N★	156	624	71	155	15	9	0	49	32	31	.248	.285	.301	65	-28	-30	55	30	8	4	.975	-14	*S	-2.2
1977	*Phi-N	154	624	93	175	19	3	4	41	32	32	.280	.316	.340	73	-21	-25	70	32	3	8	.983	1	*S	0.2
1978	*Phi-N★	156	654	78	192	31	5	3	43	24	40	.294	.320	.370	91	-8	-9	80	27	5	5	**.986**	2	*S	1.9
1979	Phi-N★	147	539	74	130	17	11	0	31	61	32	.241	.319	.314	71	-19	-21	57	20	9	1	**.991**	-13	*S	-1.7
1980	*Phi-N	147	540	57	144	16	4	2	39	24	28	.267	.302	.322	70	-19	-22	53	21	6	3	.975	-13	*S	-1.7
1981	*Phi-N	103	360	34	102	14	3	0	31	26	17	.283	.332	.339	87	-4	-6	40	16	7	1	.975	-10	*S	-0.6
1982	Chi-N	142	499	50	123	15	7	0	29	39	38	.246	.302	.305	68	-19	-21	47	8	3	1	.973	-30	*S	-4.0
1983	Chi-N	147	499	73	133	20	5	2	43	35	30	.267	.315	.339	77	-13	-16	56	7	3	0	**.984**	15	*S	1.4
1984	*Chi-N	133	391	33	87	14	2	0	17	28	24	.223	.274	.269	49	-24	-28	30	10	4	1	.974	7	*S	-1.0
1985	Chi-N	72	195	13	48	6	4	0	13	11	20	.246	.286	.318	62	-8	-11	18	5	1	1	.970	12	S	0.7
	NY-N	14	19	2	2	1	0	0	2	2	2	.105	.190	.158	-2	-3	-3	1	0	0	0	.882	1	/S2	-0.2
	Yr	86	214	15	50	7	4	0	15	13	22	.234	.278	.304	57	-11	-13	19	5	1	1	.965	12	S/2	0.5
Total	16	2247	8418	987	2191	262	99	15	525	474	569	.260	.301	.320	71	-310	-341	836	318	105	32	.980	-76	*S/2	-13.9

■ BENNY BOWCOCK

Bowcock, Benjamin James b: 10/28/1879, Fall River, Mass. d: 6/16/61, New Bedford, Mass BR/TR, 5'7", 150 lbs. Deb: 9/18/03

YEAR	TM/L	G	AB	R	H	2B	3B	HR	RBI	BB	SO	AVG	OBP	SLG	PRO+	BR	/A	RC	SB	CS	SBR	FA	FR	POS	TPR
1903	StL-A	14	50	7	16	3	1	1	10	3		.320	.358	.480	154	3	3	9	1			.885	-7	2	-0.4

YEAR	TM/L	G	AB	R	H	2B	3B	HR	RBI	BB	SO	AVG	OBP	SLG	PRO+	BR	/A	RC	SB	CS	SBR	FA	FR	POS	TPR

■ TIM BOWDEN Bowden, David Timon b: 8/15/1891, Mcdonough, Ga. d: 10/25/49, Emory, Ga. BL/TR, 5'10", 175 lbs. Deb: 9/17/14

| 1914 | StL-A | 7 | 9 | 0 | 2 | 0 | 0 | 0 | 0 | 1 | 6 | .222 | .300 | .222 | 59 | -0 | -0 | 1 | 0 | | | 1.000 | -1 | /O | -0.1 |

■ CHICK BOWEN Bowen, Emmons Joseph b: 7/26/1897, New Haven, Conn. d: 8/9/48, New Haven, Conn. BR/TR, 5'7", 165 lbs. Deb: 9/15/19

| 1919 | NY-N | 3 | 5 | 0 | 1 | 0 | 0 | 0 | 1 | 1 | 2 | .200 | .333 | .200 | 63 | -0 | -0 | 0 | 0 | | | 1.000 | -0 | /O | -0.1 |

■ SAM BOWEN Bowen, Samuel Thomas b: 9/18/52, Brunswick, Ga. BR/TR, 5'9", 170 lbs. Deb: 8/25/77

1977	Bos-A	3	2	0	0	0	0	0	0	0	2	.000	.000	.000	-90	-1	-1	0	0	0	0	1.000	-1	/O	-0.1
1978	Bos-A	6	7	3	1	0	0	1	1	1	2	.143	.250	.571	112	0	0	1	0	0	0	1.000	-2	/O	-0.2
1980	Bos-A	7	13	0	2	0	0	0	2	3	3	.154	.267	.154	17	-1	-1	1	1	0	0	1.000	1	/O	0.0
Total	3	16	22	3	3	0	0	1	3	7	.136	.240	.273	38	-2	-2	2	1	0	0	1.000	-1	/O	-0.3

■ SAM BOWENS Bowens, Samuel Edward b: 3/23/39, Wilmington, N.C. BR/TR, 6'1.5", 195 lbs. Deb: 9/07/63

1963	Bal-A	15	48	8	16	3	1	9	4	5	.333	.385	.500	149	3	3	9	1	1	-0	.952	-1	O	0.1
1964	Bal-A	139	501	58	132	25	2	22	71	42	99	.263	.325	.453	114	8	9	71	4	3	-1	.981	-0	*O	0.2
1965	Bal-A	84	203	16	33	4	1	7	20	10	41	.163	.202	.296	39	-17	-17	10	7	1	2	.982	-2	O	-2.2
1966	Bal-A	89	243	26	51	9	1	6	20	17	52	.210	.275	.329	74	-9	-8	21	9	3	1	.960	-0	O	-1.1
1967	Bal-A	62	120	13	22	2	1	5	12	11	43	.183	.258	.342	76	-4	-4	10	3	4	-2	.977	-0	O	-0.9
1968	Was-A	57	115	14	22	4	0	4	7	11	39	.191	.262	.330	81	-3	-3	11	0	0	-0	.957	-1	O	-0.6
1969	Was-A	33	57	6	11	1	0	4	5	4	14	.193	.258	.211	34	-5	-5	3	1	1	-0	.971	-5	O	-1.2
Total	7	479	1287	141	287	48	6	45	143	100	293	.223	.284	.375	87	-26	-25	136	25	13	-0	.974	-12	O	-5.7

■ FRANK BOWERMAN Bowerman, Frank Eugene "Mike" b: 12/5/1868, Romeo, Mich. d: 11/30/48, Romeo, Mich. BR/TR, 6'2", 190 lbs. Deb: 8/24/1895 M

1895	Bal-N	1	1	0	0	0	0	0	0	0	0	.000	.000	.000	-97	-0	-0	0	0			1.000	0	/C	0.0
1896	Bal-N	4	16	0	2	0	0	0	4	1	0	.125	.176	.125	-19	-3	-3	0	0			.900	0	/C1	-0.2
1897	*Bal-N	38	130	16	41	5	0	1	21	1		.315	.331	.377	86	-3	-3	18	3			.948	3	C	0.3
1898	Bal-N	5	16	5	7	1	0	0	1	2		.438	.526	.500	191	2	2	5	1			.950	0	/C	0.3
	Pit-N	69	241	17	66	6	3	0	29	7		.274	.297	.324	79	-8	-7	25	4			.946	4	C/1	0.3
	Yr	74	257	22	73	7	3	0	30	9		.284	.313	.335	87	-5	-5	30	5			.946	5	C/1	0.6
1899	Pit-N	109	424	49	110	16	10	3	53	11		.259	.286	.366	79	-15	-14	50	10			.948	12	C1	0.4
1900	NY-N	80	270	25	65	5	3	1	42	6		.241	.268	.293	57	-17	-15	25	10			.929	13	C/S	0.4
1901	NY-N	59	191	20	38	5	3	0	14	7		.199	.231	.257	43	-14	-13	13	3			.950	13	C/2S31	0.4
1902	NY-N	107	367	38	93	14	6	0	26	13		.253	.279	.324	87	-7	-7	38	12			.956	2	C/1	0.5
1903	NY-N	64	210	22	58	6	2	1	31	6		.276	.303	.338	80	-5	-6	24	5			.977	0	C/1O	0.2
1904	NY-N	93	289	38	67	11	4	2	27	16		.232	.286	.318	83	-5	-6	30	7			.976	-3	C/12P	-0.1
1905	NY-N	98	297	37	80	8	1	3	41	12		.269	.322	.333	94	-2	-2	36	6			.982	-3	C1/2	0.1
1906	NY-N	103	285	23	65	7	3	1	42	15		.228	.272	.284	72	-9	-10	25	5			.984	3	C1	-0.1
1907	NY-N	96	311	31	81	8	2	0	32	17		.260	.307	.299	87	-4	-5	35	11			.990	-5	C1	-0.5
1908	Bos-N	86	254	16	58	8	1	1	25	13		.228	.274	.280	78	-7	-6	20	4			.971	-3	C1	-0.5
1909	Bos-N	33	99	6	21	2	0	0	4	2		.212	.228	.232	41	-7	-7	5	0			.928	1	CM	-0.5
Total	15	1045	3401	343	852	102	38	13	392	129		.251	.286	.314	77	-103	-104	347	81			.963	39	C1/2S3PO	0.8

■ BILLY BOWERS Bowers, Grover Bill b: 3/25/23, Parkin, Ark. BL/TR, 5'9.5", 176 lbs. Deb: 4/24/49

| 1949 | Chi-A | 26 | 78 | 5 | 15 | 2 | 1 | 0 | 6 | 4 | 5 | .192 | .232 | .244 | 27 | -9 | -8 | 4 | 1 | 1 | -0 | .980 | 0 | O | -0.9 |

■ STEW BOWERS Bowers, Stewart Cole "Doc" b: 2/26/15, New Freedom, Pa. BB/TR, 6', 170 lbs. Deb: 8/05/35

1935	Bos-A	11	5	1	1	0	0	0	0	1	2	.200	.333	.200	38	-0	-0	0	0	0	0	.875	0	P	0.0
1936	Bos-A	6	0	1	0	0	0	0	0	0	0	—	—	—	—	-0	-0	0	0	0	0	.000	-0	/P	0.0
1937	Bos-A	1	0	1	0	0	0	0	0	0	0	—	—	—	—	0	0	0	0	0	0	.000	0	R	0.0
Total	3	18	5	3	1	0	0	0	0	1	2	.200	.333	.200	38	-0	-0	0	0	0	0	.875	-0	/P	0.0

■ FRANK BOWES Bowes, Frank M. b: 1865, Bath, N.Y. d: 1/21/1895, New York, N.Y. TR, 5'9", 160 lbs. Deb: 4/17/1890

| 1890 | Bro-a | 61 | 232 | 28 | 51 | 5 | 2 | 0 | | 7 | | .220 | .246 | .259 | 52 | -15 | -13 | 18 | 11 | | | .813 | -9 | CO3/1S | -1.8 |

■ WELDON BOWLIN Bowlin, Lois Weldon "Hoss" b: 12/10/40, Paragould, Ark. BR/TR, 5'9", 155 lbs. Deb: 9/27/67

| 1967 | KC-A | 2 | 5 | 0 | 1 | 0 | 0 | 0 | 0 | 0 | 0 | .200 | .200 | .200 | 19 | -1 | -0 | 0 | 0 | 0 | 0 | 1.000 | 0 | /3 | 0.0 |

■ STEVE BOWLING Bowling, Stephen Shaddon b: 6/26/52, Tulsa, Okla. BR/TR, 6', 185 lbs. Deb: 9/07/76

1976	Mil-A	14	42	4	7	2	0	0	2	2	5	.167	.205	.214	23	-4	-4	2	0	0	0	.975	1	O/D	-0.3
1977	Tor-A	89	194	19	40	8	1	1	13	37	42	.206	.333	.273	67	-8	-8	18	2	3	-1	.987	-0	O	-1.2
Total	2	103	236	23	47	10	1	1	15	39	47	.199	.313	.263	60	-12	-12	20	2	3	-1	.985	1	O/D	-1.5

■ ELMER BOWMAN Bowman, Elmari Wilhelm "Big Bow" b: 3/19/1897, Proctor, Vt. d: 12/17/85, Los Angeles, Cal. BR/TR, 6'0.5", 193 lbs. Deb: 8/03/20

| 1920 | Was-A | 2 | 1 | 1 | 0 | 0 | 0 | 0 | 0 | 1 | 0 | .000 | .500 | .000 | 42 | 0 | 0 | 0 | 0 | 0 | 0 | .000 | 0 | H | 0.0 |

■ ERNIE BOWMAN Bowman, Ernest Ferrell b: 7/28/35, Johnson City, Tenn. BR/TR, 5'10", 160 lbs. Deb: 4/12/61

1961	SF-N	38	38	10	8	0	2	0	2	1	8	.211	.231	.316	45	-3	-3	3	2	0	1	.885	3	2S/3	0.1
1962	*SF-N	46	42	9	8	1	0	1	4	1	10	.190	.227	.286	37	-4	-4	2	0	1	-1	1.000	3	23S	-0.1
1963	SF-N	81	125	10	23	3	0	0	4	0	15	.184	.184	.208	13	-14	-14	4	1	2	-1	.952	4	S23	-1.0
Total	3	165	205	29	39	4	2	1	10	2	33	.190	.202	.244	24	-21	-20	9	3	3	-1	.950	9	/S23	-1.0

■ JOE BOWMAN Bowman, Joseph Emil b: 6/17/10, Kansas City, Kan. d: 11/22/90, Kansas City, Mo. BL/TR, 6'2", 190 lbs. Deb: 4/18/32

1932	Phi-A	7	1	0	1	0	0	0	0	0	0	1.000	1.000	1.000	405	0	0	1	0	0	0	.875	1	/P	0.0
1934	NY-N	31	29	4	5	1	0	0	4	2	3	.172	.226	.241	26	-3	-3	2	0			1.000	0	P	0.0
1935	Phi-N	49	67	6	13	1	1	1	7	4	7	.194	.239	.284	36	-6	-7	5	1			.947	-1	P/O	0.0
1936	Phi-N	44	77	9	15	1	0	0	6	6	14	.195	.253	.208	23	-8	-9	4	0			.886	-2	P	0.0
1937	Pit-N	35	47	3	10	1	0	0	4	5	9	.213	.288	.234	43	-4	-4	3	0			1.000	0	P	0.0
1938	Pit-N	18	21	5	7	0	1	0	1	1	3	.333	.364	.429	116	-0	-0	2	0			.909	-1	P	0.0
1939	Pit-N	70	96	9	33	8	1	0	18	5	9	.344	.382	.448	124	3	3	17	0			1.000	0	P	0.0
1940	Pit-N	57	90	11	22	5	1	1	14	14	14	.244	.352	.356	96	-0	-0	12	0			.981	0	P	0.0
1941	Pit-N	22	31	4	8	1	0	0	1	1	2	.258	.281	.290	61	-2	-2	2	0			1.000	0	P	0.0
1944	Bos-A	59	100	7	20	5	2	0	16	5	19	.200	.238	.290	51	-7	-7	7	1	0	0	.935	-2	P	0.0
1945	Bos-A	9	9	0	2	0	0	0	1	1	1	.222	.300	.222	51	-1	-1	1	0	0	0	1.000	-0	/P	0.0
	Cin-N	29	71	4	5	2	1	0	3	2	9	.070	.096	.127	-39	-13	-13	1	1			.927	-2	P	0.0
Total	11	430	639	62	141	24	8	2	75	46	90	.221	.275	.293	55	-39	-40	58	3	0		.958	-8	P/O	0.0

■ BOB BOWMAN Bowman, Robert Leroy b: 5/10/31, Laytonville, Cal. BR/TR, 6'1", 195 lbs. Deb: 4/16/55

1955	Phi-N	3	3	0	0	0	0	0	0	0	0	.000	.000	.000	-99	-1	-1	0	0	0	0	1.000	-0	/O	-0.1
1956	Phi-N	6	16	2	3	0	1	1	2	0	6	.188	.188	.500	78	-1	-1	2	0	0	0	.833	-1	O	-0.2
1957	Phi-N	99	237	31	63	8	2	6	23	27	50	.266	.356	.392	104	1	2	35	0	0	0	.929	-2	O	-0.4
1958	Phi-N	91	184	31	53	11	2	8	24	16	30	.288	.345	.500	122	5	5	31	0	1	-1	.988	-6	O	-0.3
1959	Phi-N	57	79	7	10	0	0	2	5	5	23	.127	.179	.203	1	-11	-11	3	0	0	0	1.000	-1	O/P	-1.3
Total	5	256	519	71	129	19	5	17	54	48	109	.249	.319	.403	93	-7	-6	70	0	1	-1	.965	-10	O/P	-2.3

■ BILL BOWMAN Bowman, William G. b: 1869, Chicago, Ill. d: 4/6/18, Arlington Heights, Ill. 5'11", 180 lbs. Deb: 6/18/1891

| 1891 | Chi-N | 15 | 45 | 2 | 4 | 1 | 0 | 0 | 5 | 5 | 9 | .089 | .196 | .111 | -9 | -6 | -6 | 1 | 0 | | | .915 | -5 | C | -0.9 |

■ **RED BOWSER** Bowser, James H. b: Greensburg, Pa. d: 5/22/43, Moundsville, W.Va. Deb: 9/13/10

YEAR	TM/L	G	AB	R	H	2B	3B	HR	RBI	BB	SO	AVG	OBP	SLG	PRO+	BR	/A	RC	SB	CS	SBR	FA	FR	POS	TPR
1910	Chi-A	1	2	0	0	0	0	0	0	0		.000	.000	.000	-99	-0	-0	0	0			.000	0	/O	-0.1

■ **FRANK BOYD** Boyd, Frank Jay b: 4/2/1868, West Middletown, Pa d: 12/16/37, Oil City, Pa. BR/TR, Deb: 5/18/1893

YEAR	TM/L	G	AB	R	H	2B	3B	HR	RBI	BB	SO	AVG	OBP	SLG	PRO+	BR	/A	RC	SB	CS	SBR	FA	FR	POS	TPR
1893	Cle-N	2	5	3	1	1	0	0	3	1	0	.200	.333	.400	91	-0	-0	1	0			1.000	-0	/C	0.0

■ **JAKE BOYD** Boyd, Jacob Henry b: 1/19/1874, Martinsburg, W.Va. d: 8/12/32, Gettysburg, Pa. TL, 160 lbs. Deb: 9/20/1894

YEAR	TM/L	G	AB	R	H	2B	3B	HR	RBI	BB	SO	AVG	OBP	SLG	PRO+	BR	/A	RC	SB	CS	SBR	FA	FR	POS	TPR
1894	Was-N	6	21	1	3	0	0	0	1	1	4	.143	.182	.143	-21	-4	-4	1	2			.833	1	/OP	-0.1
1895	Was-N	51	157	29	42	5	1	1	16	20	28	.268	.375	.331	86	-2	-2	21	2			.786	-14	OP2/S3	-1.4
1896	Was-N	4	13	1	1	0	0	0	1	1	1	.077	.200	.077	-24	-2	-2	0	0			.909	0	/P	0.0
Total	3	61	191	31	46	5	1	1	18	22	33	.241	.344	.293	67	-9	-8	22	4			.794	-13	/OP2S3	-1.5

■ **BOB BOYD** Boyd, Robert Richard "The Rope" b: 10/1/26, Potts Camp, Miss. BL/TL, 5'10", 170 lbs. Deb: 9/08/51

YEAR	TM/L	G	AB	R	H	2B	3B	HR	RBI	BB	SO	AVG	OBP	SLG	PRO+	BR	/A	RC	SB	CS	SBR	FA	FR	POS	TPR
1951	Chi-A	12	18	3	3	0	1	0	4	3	3	.167	.286	.278	54	-1	-1	2	0	0	0	1.000	-1	/1	-0.2
1953	Chi-A	55	165	20	49	6	2	3	23	13	11	.297	.352	.412	103	1	1	23	1	4	-2	1.000	-2	1O	-0.5
1954	Chi-A	29	56	10	10	3	0	0	5	4	3	.179	.233	.232	27	-6	-6	3	2	0	1	.955	-1	O1	-0.8
1956	Bal-A	70	225	28	70	8	3	2	11	30	14	.311	.395	.400	119	4	7	35	0	5	-3	.990	-7	1/O	-0.7
1957	Bal-A	141	485	73	154	16	8	4	34	55	31	.318	.389	.408	126	14	18	80	2	4	-2	.991	-3	*1/O	0.5
1958	Bal-A	125	401	58	124	21	5	7	36	25	24	.309	.353	.439	123	8	11	62	1	1	-0	.994	-2	1	0.3
1959	Bal-A	128	415	42	110	20	2	3	41	29	14	.265	.315	.345	83	-11	-10	44	3	1	0	.985	-9	*1	-2.6
1960	Bal-A	71	82	9	26	5	2	0	9	6	5	.317	.364	.427	114	1	2	12	0	0	0	1.000	-0	1	0.1
1961	KC-A	26	48	7	11	2	0	0	9	1	2	.229	.245	.271	38	-4	-4	2	0	2	-1	1.000	-1	/1	-0.7
	Mil-N	36	41	3	10	0	0	0	3	1	7	.244	.262	.244	38	-4	-3	3	0	0	0	1.000	1	/1	-0.2
Total	9	693	1936	253	567	81	23	19	175	167	114	.293	.351	.388	105	3	13	266	9	17	-8	.991	-24	1/O	-4.8

■ **BILL BOYD** Boyd, William J. b: 12/22/1852, New York, N.Y. d: 9/30/12, Jamaica, N.Y. Deb: 4/22/1872 MU

YEAR	TM/L	G	AB	R	H	2B	3B	HR	RBI	BB	SO	AVG	OBP	SLG	PRO+	BR	/A	RC	SB	CS	SBR	FA	FR	POS	TPR
1872	Mut-n	35	164	26	44	6	1	1	32	6	7	.268	.294	.335	100	-1	1	17						*3/SO	-0.1
1873	Atl-n	50	228	31	63	10	5	1	30	2	2	.276	.283	.377	103	-2	3	25						*O/3	0.2
1874	Har-n	26	116	22	41	9	4	0		2		.353	.364	.500	164	9	8	22						3O	0.6
1875	Atl-n	36	148	14	44	8	2	1		1		.297	.302	.399	161	6	9	18						2O/3P1M	0.7
Total	4 n	147	656	93	192	33	12	3		11		.293	.304	.393	125	11	21	82						/O321PS	1.4

■ **CLETE BOYER** Boyer, Cletis Leroy b: 2/9/37, Cassville, Mo. BR/TR, 6', 182 lbs. Deb: 6/05/55 FC

YEAR	TM/L	G	AB	R	H	2B	3B	HR	RBI	BB	SO	AVG	OBP	SLG	PRO+	BR	/A	RC	SB	CS	SBR	FA	FR	POS	TPR
1955	KC-A	47	79	3	19	1	0	0	6	3	17	.241	.268	.253	40	-7	-7	5	0	0	0	.963	6	S32	0.0
1956	KC-A	67	129	15	28	3	1	1	4	11	24	.217	.284	.279	49	-10	-10	10	1	1	-0	.971	18	2/3	1.0
1957	KC-A	10	0	0	0	0	0	0	0	0	0	—	—	—	—	0	0	0	0	0	0	.000	0	/23	0.0
1959	NY-A	47	114	4	20	2	0	0	3	6	23	.175	.217	.193	14	-13	-13	5	1	0	0	.990	6	S3	-0.5
1960	*NY-A	124	393	54	95	20	1	14	46	23	85	.242	.289	.405	90	-10	-7	44	2	3	-1	.967	28	3S	2.1
1961	*NY-A	148	504	61	113	19	5	11	55	63	83	.224	.313	.347	80	-17	-13	55	1	3	-2	.967	**30**	*3S/O	1.7
1962	*NY-A	158	566	85	154	24	1	18	68	51	106	.272	.335	.413	104	-0	2	76	3	2	-0	.964	**36**	*3	4.0
1963	*NY-A	152	557	59	140	20	3	12	54	33	91	.251	.296	.363	84	-13	-12	60	4	2	0	.954	22	*3/S2	1.1
1964	*NY-A	147	510	43	111	10	5	8	52	36	93	.218	.271	.304	59	-28	-29	41	6	1	1	.968	19	*3S	-0.9
1965	NY-A	148	514	69	129	23	6	18	58	39	79	.251	.306	.424	106	2	3	63	4	1	1	.968	**26**	*3/S	2.7
1966	NY-A	144	500	59	120	22	4	14	57	46	48	.240	.307	.384	101	-2	-0	60	6	0	2	.966	20	3S	2.7
1967	Atl-N	154	572	63	140	18	3	26	96	39	81	.245	.295	.423	105	1	1	68	6	3	0	**.970**	5	*3/S	0.6
1968	Atl-N	71	273	19	62	7	2	4	17	16	32	.227	.275	.311	75	-8	-8	22	2	0	1	.981	-0	3	-0.9
1969	*Atl-N	144	496	57	124	16	1	14	57	55	87	.250	.330	.371	96	-2	-3	58	3	7	-3	**.965**	3	*3	-0.3
1970	Atl-N	134	475	44	117	14	1	16	62	41	71	.246	.308	.381	79	-12	-16	53	2	5	-2	.954	12	*3/S	-0.6
1971	Atl-N	30	98	10	24	1	0	6	19	8	11	.245	.302	.449	101	1	-0	13	0	0	0	.961	3	3/S	0.2
Total	16	1725	5780	645	1396	200	33	162	654	470	931	.242	.301	.372	87	-119	-111	635	41	28	-5	.965	233	*3S/2O	12.9

■ **KEN BOYER** Boyer, Kenton Lloyd b: 5/20/31, Liberty, Mo. d: 9/7/82, St.Louis, Mo. BR/TR, 6'2", 200 lbs. Deb: 4/12/55 FMC

YEAR	TM/L	G	AB	R	H	2B	3B	HR	RBI	BB	SO	AVG	OBP	SLG	PRO+	BR	/A	RC	SB	CS	SBR	FA	FR	POS	TPR
1955	StL-N	147	530	78	140	27	2	18	62	37	67	.264	.313	.425	94	-6	-6	67	22	17	-4	.952	4	*3S	-0.5
1956	StL-N★	150	595	91	182	30	2	26	98	38	65	.306	.349	.494	123	18	18	97	8	3	1	.961	9	*3	3.0
1957	StL-N	142	544	79	144	18	3	19	62	44	77	.265	.321	.414	94	-4	-5	70	12	8	-1	**.996**	4	*O3	-0.7
1958	StL-N	150	570	101	175	21	9	23	90	49	53	.307	.365	.496	121	20	17	100	11	6	-0	.962	23	*3/OS	4.1
1959	StL-N★	149	563	86	174	18	5	28	94	67	77	.309	.384	.508	127	29	24	112	12	6	0	.956	14	*3S	3.8
1960	StL-N★	151	552	95	168	26	10	32	97	56	77	.304	.373	.562	139	38	32	111	8	7	-2	.959	13	*3	4.3
1961	StL-N★	153	589	109	194	26	11	24	95	68	91	.329	.400	.533	132	38	31	126	6	3	0	.951	13	*3	4.4
1962	StL-N★	160	611	92	178	27	5	24	98	75	104	.291	.370	.470	113	21	13	105	12	7	-1	.956	4	*3	1.8
1963	StL-N★	159	617	86	176	28	2	24	111	70	90	.285	.360	.454	121	26	20	98	1	0	0	.925	-13	*3	0.8
1964	*StL-N★	162	628	100	185	30	10	24	**119**	70	85	.295	.367	.489	128	32	26	107	3	5	-2	.951	3	*3	2.6
1965	StL-N	144	535	71	139	18	2	13	75	57	73	.260	.332	.374	90	-0	-6	64	2	7	-4	**.968**	-11	*3	-2.6
1966	NY-N	136	496	62	132	28	2	14	61	30	64	.266	.308	.415	101	-2	-0	59	4	3	-1	.951	11	*3/1	0.7
1967	NY-N	56	166	17	39	7	2	3	13	26	22	.235	.339	.355	100	0	1	20	2	1	0	.949	-2	3/1	-0.3
	Chi-A	57	180	17	47	5	1	4	21	7	25	.261	.289	.367	96	-2	-2	18	0	2	-1	.957	1	31	-0.3
1968	Chi-A	10	24	0	3	0	0	0	0	1	6	.125	.160	.125	-13	-3	-3	0	0	0	0	.900	-1	/31	-0.5
	LA-N	83	221	20	60	7	2	6	41	16	34	.271	.324	.403	127	4	6	29	2	2	-1	.922	-4	31	0.0
1969	LA-N	25	34	0	7	2	0	0	4	2	7	.206	.250	.265	48	-3	-2	2	0	0	0	.971	-0	/1	-0.3
Total	15	2034	7455	1104	2143	318	68	282	1141	713	1017	.287	.351	.462	115	207	162	1184	105	77	-15	.952	69	*3O/1S	20.3

■ **DOE BOYLAND** Boyland, Dorian Scott b: 1/6/55, Chicago, Ill. BL/TL, 6'4", 200 lbs. Deb: 9/04/78

YEAR	TM/L	G	AB	R	H	2B	3B	HR	RBI	BB	SO	AVG	OBP	SLG	PRO+	BR	/A	RC	SB	CS	SBR	FA	FR	POS	TPR
1978	Pit-N	6	8	1	2	0	0	0	1	0	1	.250	.250	.250	38	-1	-1	1	0	0	0	1.000	-0	/1	-0.1
1979	Pit-N	4	3	0	0	0	0	0	0	0	2	.000	.000	.000	-96	-1	-1	0	0	0	0	.000	0	/H	-0.1
1981	Pit-N	11	8	0	0	0	0	0	0	1	3	.000	.111	.000	-64	-2	-2	0	0	0	0	.000	0	/H	-0.2
Total	3	21	19	1	2	0	0	0	1	1	6	.105	.150	.105	-26	-3	-3	1	0	0	0		-0	/1	-0.4

■ **EDDIE BOYLE** Boyle, Edward J. b: 5/8/1874, Cincinnati, Ohio d: 2/9/41, Cincinnati, Ohio BR/TR, 6'3", 200 lbs. Deb: 4/17/1896 F

YEAR	TM/L	G	AB	R	H	2B	3B	HR	RBI	BB	SO	AVG	OBP	SLG	PRO+	BR	/A	RC	SB	CS	SBR	FA	FR	POS	TPR
1896	Lou-N	3	9	0	0	0	0	0	0	2	2	.000	.182	.000	-51	-2	-2	0	0			.938	1	/C	-0.1
	Pit-N	2	5	0	0	0	0	0	0	0	1	.000	.000	.000	-99	-1	-1	0	0			.833	-0	/C	-0.1
	Yr	5	14	0	0	0	0	0	0	2	3	.000	.125	.000	-67	-3	-3	0	0			.909	0	/C	-0.2

■ **HENRY BOYLE** Boyle, Henry J. "Handsome Henry" b: 9/20/1860, Philadelphia, Pa. d: 5/25/32, Philadelphia, Pa. TR, Deb: 7/09/1884

YEAR	TM/L	G	AB	R	H	2B	3B	HR	RBI	BB	SO	AVG	OBP	SLG	PRO+	BR	/A	RC	SB	CS	SBR	FA	FR	POS	TPR
1884	StL-U	65	262	41	68	10	3	4		9		.260	.284	.366	114	5	3	28				.885	5	OP/3S21	0.7
1885	StL-N	72	258	24	52	9	1	1	21	13	38	.202	.240	.256	64	-11	-9	16				.907	-4	PO/2	-0.7
1886	StL-N	30	108	8	27	2	2	1	13	5	19	.250	.283	.333	93	-2	-1	10	0			.852	1	P/O	0.0
1887	Ind-N	41	141	17	27	9	1	2	13	9	18	.191	.250	.312	59	-8	-7	12	2			.912	-5	P/O	-0.2
1888	Ind-N	37	125	13	18	2	0	1	6	6	31	.144	.189	.184	20	-11	-11	5	1			.933	3	P/1	0.0
1889	Ind-N	46	155	17	38	10	0	1	17	9	23	.245	.291	.329	73	-6	-6	16	4			.958	-5	P/3	0.0
Total	6	291	1049	120	230	42	7	10	70	51	129	.219	.258	.301	75	-33	-31	87	7			.912	-5	P/O321S	-0.2

■ **JIM BOYLE** Boyle, James John b: 1/19/04, Cincinnati, Ohio d: 12/24/58, Cincinnati, Ohio BR/TR, 6', 180 lbs. Deb: 6/20/26 F

YEAR	TM/L	G	AB	R	H	2B	3B	HR	RBI	BB	SO	AVG	OBP	SLG	PRO+	BR	/A	RC	SB	CS	SBR	FA	FR	POS	TPR
1926	NY-N	1	0	0	0	0	0	0	0	0	0	—	—	—	—	0	0	0	0			.000	0	/C	0.0

■ **JACK BOYLE** Boyle, John Anthony "Honest Jack" b: 3/22/1866, Cincinnati, Ohio d: 1/7/13, Cincinnati, Ohio BR/TR, 6'4", 190 lbs. Deb: 10/08/1886 F

YEAR	TM/L	G	AB	R	H	2B	3B	HR	RBI	BB	SO	AVG	OBP	SLG	PRO+	BR	/A	RC	SB	CS	SBR	FA	FR	POS	TPR
1886	Cin-a	1	5	0	1	0	0	0		0		.200	.200	.200	26	-0	-0	0	0			.769	-0	/C	0.0
1887	*StL-a	88	350	48	66	3	1	2		20		.189	.237	.220	26	-33	-39	20	7			**.897**	-11	C/O13	-3.5
1888	*StL-a	71	257	33	62	8	1	1	23	13		.241	.286	.292	79	-3	-7	25	11			**.932**	14	C/O	1.2
1889	StL-a	99	347	54	85	11	4	4	42	21	42	.245	.301	.334	73	-8	-16	37	5			.947	5	C3/O12	-0.3
1890	Chi-P	100	369	56	96	9	5	1	49	44	29	.260	.347	.320	77	-9	-12	46	11			.940	-4	C3S/1O	-0.8
1891	StL-a	123	439	78	123	18	8	5	79	47	36	.280	.365	.392	104	12	0	72	19			.936	-14	CS/3O21	-0.4
1892	NY-N	120	436	52	80	8	8	0	32	36	40	.183	.252	.239	51	-26	-25	29	10			.922	14	C1/OS	-0.7
1893	Phi-N	116	504	105	144	29	9	4	81	41	30	.286	.351	.403	102	1	1	81	22			.988	6	*1/C2	0.4
1894	Phi-N	114	495	98	149	21	10	4	88	45	26	.301	.363	.408	89	-10	-8	85	21			.983	1	*1/32	-0.4
1895	Phi-N	133	565	90	143	17	4	0	67	35	23	.253	.302	.297	56	-36	-36	59	13			.973	-6	*1	-3.2
1896	Phi-N	40	145	17	43	4	1	1	28	6	7	.297	.346	.359	89	-2	-2	20	3			.920	-6	C1	-0.5
1897	Phi-N	75	288	37	73	9	1	2	36	19		.253	.306	.313	65	-15	-14	30	3			.962	-9	C1	-1.5
1898	Phi-N	6	22	0	2	0	1	0	3	1		.091	.130	.182	-11	-3	-3	1	0			.919	-0	/1C	-0.3
Total	13	1086	4222	668	1067	137	53	24	528	328	233	.253	.315	.327	74	-134	-161	505	125			.929	-10	C1/3SO2	-10.0

■ **JACK BOYLE** Boyle, John Bellew b: 7/9/1889, Morris, Ill. d: 4/3/71, Ft.Lauderdale, Fla. BL/TR, 5'11.5", 165 lbs. Deb: 6/28/12

YEAR	TM/L	G	AB	R	H	2B	3B	HR	RBI	BB	SO	AVG	OBP	SLG	PRO+	BR	/A	RC	SB	CS	SBR	FA	FR	POS	TPR
1912	Phi-N	15	25	4	7	1	0	0	2	1	5	.280	.308	.320	67	-1	-1	2	0			.905	5	/3S	0.4

■ **BUZZ BOYLE** Boyle, Ralph Francis b: 2/9/08, Cincinnati, Ohio d: 11/12/78, Cincinnati, Ohio BL/TL, 5'11.5", 170 lbs. Deb: 9/11/29 F

YEAR	TM/L	G	AB	R	H	2B	3B	HR	RBI	BB	SO	AVG	OBP	SLG	PRO+	BR	/A	RC	SB	CS	SBR	FA	FR	POS	TPR
1929	Bos-N	17	57	8	15	2	1	1	2	6	11	.263	.333	.386	81	-2	-2	7	2			1.000	-0	O	-0.3
1930	Bos-N	1	1	0	0	0	0	0	0	0	1	.000	.000	.000	-99	-0	-0	0	0			.000	-1	/O	-0.1
1933	Bro-N	93	338	38	101	13	4	0	31	16	24	.299	.331	.361	102	-1	0	42	7			.975	-6	O	-1.1
1934	Bro-N	128	472	88	144	26	10	7	48	51	44	.305	.376	.447	126	14	17	84	8			.970	11	*O	2.2
1935	Bro-N	127	475	51	129	17	9	4	44	43	45	.272	.332	.371	90	-7	-6	62	7			.963	3	*O	-0.8
Total	5	366	1343	185	389	58	24	12	125	116	125	.290	.347	.395	105	3	9	196	24			.970	6	O	-0.1

■ **GIBBY BRACK** Brack, Gilbert Herman b: 3/29/08, Chicago, Ill. d: 1/20/60, Greenville, Tex. BR/TR, 5'9", 170 lbs. Deb: 4/23/37

YEAR	TM/L	G	AB	R	H	2B	3B	HR	RBI	BB	SO	AVG	OBP	SLG	PRO+	BR	/A	RC	SB	CS	SBR	FA	FR	POS	TPR
1937	Bro-N	112	372	60	102	27	9	5	38	44	93	.274	.351	.435	111	6	6	60	9			.969	1	*O	0.3
1938	Bro-N	40	56	10	12	2	1	1	6	4	14	.214	.267	.339	64	-3	-3	5	1			1.000	2	O	-0.1
	Phi-N	72	282	40	81	20	4	4	28	18	30	.287	.332	.429	111	2	3	41	2			.964	-2	O	-0.1
	Yr	112	338	50	93	22	5	5	34	22	44	.275	.321	.414	102	-0	-0	46	3			.969	-0	O	-0.2
1939	Phi-N	91	270	40	78	21	4	6	41	26	49	.289	.351	.463	121	6	7	45	1			.959	-4	O1	-0.1
Total	3	315	980	150	273	70	18	16	113	92	186	.279	.341	.436	111	12	13	151	13			.967	-4	O/1	0.0

■ **BUDDY BRADFORD** Bradford, Charles William b: 7/25/44, Mobile, Ala. BR/TR, 5'11", 191 lbs. Deb: 9/09/66

YEAR	TM/L	G	AB	R	H	2B	3B	HR	RBI	BB	SO	AVG	OBP	SLG	PRO+	BR	/A	RC	SB	CS	SBR	FA	FR	POS	TPR
1966	Chi-A	14	28	3	4	0	0	0	0	2	6	.143	.200	.143	0	-4	-3	1	0	0	0	.833	-3	/O	-0.7
1967	Chi-A	24	20	6	2	1	0	0	1	1	7	.100	.143	.150	-14	-3	-3	1	1	0	0	.900	-4	O	-0.8
1968	Chi-A	103	281	32	61	11	0	5	24	23	67	.217	.281	.310	78	-7	-8	24	8	4	0	.965	-12	O	-2.8
1969	Chi-A	93	273	36	70	8	2	11	27	34	75	.256	.347	.421	109	5	4	42	5	2	0	.961	-13	O	-1.4
1970	Chi-A	32	91	8	17	3	0	2	8	10	30	.187	.267	.286	51	-6	-6	6	1	2	-1	.979	-4	O	-1.3
	Cle-A	75	163	25	32	6	1	7	23	21	43	.196	.292	.374	79	-4	-5	16	0	1	-1	.984	-4	O/3	-1.3
	Yr	107	254	33	49	9	1	9	31	31	73	.193	.283	.343	69	-10	-12	22	1	3	-2	.982	-8	O/3	-2.6
1971	Cle-A	20	38	4	6	2	1	0	3	6	10	.158	.273	.263	48	-2	-3	3	0	0	0	.930	-0	O	-0.4
	Cin-N	79	100	17	20	3	0	2	12	14	23	.200	.316	.290	74	-3	-3	10	4	2	0	.986	3	O	-0.2
1972	Chi-A	35	48	13	13	2	0	2	8	4	13	.271	.340	.438	127	2	2	6	3	2	-0	1.000	-5	O	-0.5
1973	Chi-A	53	168	24	40	3	1	8	15	17	43	.238	.316	.411	100	0	-0	20	4	5	-2	.992	4	O	0.0
1974	Chi-A	39	96	16	32	2	0	5	10	13	11	.333	.418	.510	162	8	8	20	1	2	-1	.980	-3	O/D	0.3
1975	Chi-A	25	58	8	9	3	1	2	15	8	22	.155	.290	.345	78	-2	-2	6	3	2	-0	.966	-2	O/D	-0.5
	StL-N	50	81	12	22	1	0	4	15	12	24	.272	.366	.432	117	2	2	12	0	2	-1	.935	1	O	0.1
1976	Chi-A	55	160	20	35	5	2	4	14	19	37	.219	.309	.350	92	-1	-1	20	6	0	2	.978	-3	O/D	-0.5
Total	11	697	1605	224	363	50	8	52	175	184	411	.226	.313	.364	91	-14	-19	185	36	24	-4	.971	-46	O/D3	-10.0

■ **VIC BRADFORD** Bradford, Henry Victor b: 3/5/15, Brownsville, Tenn. BR/TR, 6'2", 190 lbs. Deb: 5/01/43

YEAR	TM/L	G	AB	R	H	2B	3B	HR	RBI	BB	SO	AVG	OBP	SLG	PRO+	BR	/A	RC	SB	CS	SBR	FA	FR	POS	TPR
1943	NY-N	6	5	1	1	0	0	0	1	1	1	.200	.333	.200	55	-0	-0	0	0			1.000	0	/O	0.0

■ **AL BRADLEY** Bradley, Al 5'10", 185 lbs. Deb: 5/21/1884

YEAR	TM/L	G	AB	R	H	2B	3B	HR	RBI	BB	SO	AVG	OBP	SLG	PRO+	BR	/A	RC	SB	CS	SBR	FA	FR	POS	TPR
1884	Was-U	1	3	0	0	0	0	0		2		.000	.400	.000	47	0	0	0				1.000	0	/O	0.0

■ **GEORGE BRADLEY** Bradley, George Washington "Grin" b: 7/13/1852, Reading, Pa. d: 10/2/31, Philadelphia, Pa. BR/TR, 5'10.5", 175 lbs. Deb: 5/04/1875

YEAR	TM/L	G	AB	R	H	2B	3B	HR	RBI	BB	SO	AVG	OBP	SLG	PRO+	BR	/A	RC	SB	CS	SBR	FA	FR	POS	TPR
1875	StL-n	60	254	28	62	8	3	0		1		.244	.247	.299	97	-3	1	19						*P/3O	0.5
1876	StL-N	64	265	29	66	7	6	0	28	3	12	.249	.257	.321	97	-2	-0	22				.919	1	*P	0.0
1877	Chi-N	55	214	31	52	7	3	0	12	6	19	.243	.264	.304	70	-5	-9	18				.950	-2	*P3/1O	-0.4
1879	Tro-N	63	251	36	62	9	5	0	23	1	20	.247	.250	.323	93	-3	-1	21				.867	7	P/31OS	0.2
1880	Pro-N	82	309	32	70	7	6	0	23	5	38	.227	.239	.288	80	-7	-6	22				.858	19	*3P/O1	1.5
1881	Det-N	1	4	0	0	0	0	0	0	0	0	.000	.000	.000	-96	-1	-1	0				.667	-1	/S	-0.2
	Cle-N	60	241	21	60	10	1	2	18	4	25	.249	.261	.324	88	-5	-3	21				.865	-9	3/PSO	-0.9
	Yr	61	245	21	60	10	1	2	18	4	25	.245	.257	.318	84	-6	-4	21				.865	-10	3/SPO	-1.1
1882	Cle-N	30	115	16	21	5	0	0	6	4	16	.183	.210	.226	41	-7	-7	6				.897	3	P/O1	-0.4
1883	Cle-N	4	16	0	5	0	1	0	1	0	1	.313	.313	.438	126	0	0	2				.792	-0	/S	0.0
	Phi-a	76	312	47	73	8	5	1		8		.234	.253	.301	72	-8	-12	24				.779	3	3PO/1	-0.4
1884	Cin-U	58	226	31	43	4	7	0		7		.190	.215	.270	58	-9	-11	13				.912	-0	PO/S1	-0.6
1886	Phi-a	13	48	1	4	0	1	0		1		.083	.102	.125	-28	-7	-7	1	2			.849	1	S	-0.5
1888	Bal-a	1	3	0	0	0	0	0	0	0		.000	.000	.000	-99	-1	-1	0	0			.600	-1	/S	-0.1
Total	10	507	2004	244	456	57	35	3	111	39	131	.228	.242	.295	74	-55	-57	150	2			.896	22	P3/OS1	-1.8

■ **GEORGE BRADLEY** Bradley, George Washington b: 4/1/14, Greenwood, Ark. d: 10/19/82, Lawrenceburg, Tenn BR/TR, 6'1.5", 185 lbs. Deb: 4/28/46

YEAR	TM/L	G	AB	R	H	2B	3B	HR	RBI	BB	SO	AVG	OBP	SLG	PRO+	BR	/A	RC	SB	CS	SBR	FA	FR	POS	TPR
1946	StL-A	4	12	2	2	1	0	0	3	0	1	.167	.167	.250	15	-1	-1	0	0	0	0	1.000	-1	/O	-0.2

■ **HUGH BRADLEY** Bradley, Hugh Frederick "Corns" b: 5/23/1885, Grafton, Mass. d: 1/26/49, Worcester, Mass. BR/TR, 5'10", 175 lbs. Deb: 4/25/10

YEAR	TM/L	G	AB	R	H	2B	3B	HR	RBI	BB	SO	AVG	OBP	SLG	PRO+	BR	/A	RC	SB	CS	SBR	FA	FR	POS	TPR
1910	Bos-A	32	83	8	14	6	2	0	7	5		.169	.216	.289	57	-4	-5	6	2			.995	-2	1/CO	-0.8
1911	Bos-A	12	41	9	13	2	0	1	4	2		.317	.364	.439	125	1	1	7	1			.993	1	1	0.2
1912	Bos-A	40	137	16	26	11	1	1	19	15		.190	.275	.307	63	-6	-7	13	3			.989	0	1	-0.8
1914	Pit-F	118	427	41	131	20	6	0	61	27	27	.307	.359	.382	112	6	7	65	7			.990	-0	*1	0.4
1915	Pit-F	26	66	3	18	4	1	0	6	4	5	.273	.314	.364	100	-0	-0	8	2			.952	-3	O	-0.4
	Bro-F	37	126	7	31	3	2	0	18	4	9	.246	.269	.302	68	-5	-5	13	6			.996	2	1/OC	-0.4
	New-F	12	33	0	5	0	0	0	2	2	3	.152	.243	.152	18	-3	-3	2	2			.986	-2	/1	-0.5
	Yr	75	225	10	54	7	3	0	26	10	17	.240	.278	.298	70	-9	-9	23	10			.994	-2	1O/C	-1.3
Total	5	277	913	84	238	46	12	2	117	59	44	.261	.314	.344	90	-13	-13	113	23			.991	-3	1/OC	-2.3

■ **JACK BRADLEY** Bradley, John Thomas b: 9/20/1893, Denver, Colo. d: 3/18/69, Tulsa, Okla. BR/TR, 5'11", 175 lbs. Deb: 6/18/16

YEAR	TM/L	G	AB	R	H	2B	3B	HR	RBI	BB	SO	AVG	OBP	SLG	PRO+	BR	/A	RC	SB	CS	SBR	FA	FR	POS	TPR
1916	Cle-A	2	3	0	0	0	0	0	0	0	1	.000	.000	.000	-94	-1	-1	0	0			1.000	-0	/C	-0.1

■ **MARK BRADLEY** Bradley, Mark Allen b: 12/3/56, Elizabethtown, Ky. BR/TR, 6'1", 180 lbs. Deb: 9/03/81

YEAR	TM/L	G	AB	R	H	2B	3B	HR	RBI	BB	SO	AVG	OBP	SLG	PRO+	BR	/A	RC	SB	CS	SBR	FA	FR	POS	TPR
1981	LA-N	9	6	2	1	1	0	0	0	0	1	.167	.167	.333	41	-1	-0	0	0	0	0	1.000	1	/O	0.1

YEAR	TM/L	G	AB	R	H	2B	3B	HR	RBI	BB	SO	AVG	OBP	SLG	PRO+	BR	/A	RC	SB	CS	SBR	FA	FR	POS	TPR
1982	LA-N	8	3	1	1	0	0	0	0	0	0	.333	.333	.333	89	-0	-0	0	0	0	0	1.000	0	/O	0.0
1983	NY-N	73	104	10	21	4	0	3	5	11	35	.202	.278	.327	68	-5	-5	9	4	2	0	1.000	1	O	-0.5
Total	3	90	113	13	23	5	0	3	5	11	36	.204	.274	.327	67	-5	-5	10	4	2	0	1.000	2	/O	-0.4

■ PHIL BRADLEY
Bradley, Philip Poole b: 3/11/59, Bloomington, Ind. BR/TR, 6', 185 lbs. Deb: 9/02/83

YEAR	TM/L	G	AB	R	H	2B	3B	HR	RBI	BB	SO	AVG	OBP	SLG	PRO+	BR	/A	RC	SB	CS	SBR	FA	FR	POS	TPR
1983	Sea-A	23	67	8	18	2	0	0	5	8	5	.269	.347	.299	77	-2	-2	8	3	1	0	.974	-6	O/D	-0.8
1984	Sea-A	124	322	49	97	12	4	0	24	34	61	.301	.373	.363	106	3	4	46	21	8	2	.992	-11	*O/D	-0.8
1985	Sea-A★	159	641	100	192	33	8	26	88	55	129	.300	.366	.498	133	29	29	116	22	9	1	.986	6	*O	3.0
1986	Sea-A	143	526	88	163	27	4	12	50	77	134	.310	.406	.445	130	26	26	99	21	12	-1	.996	1	*O	2.1
1987	Sea-A	158	603	101	179	38	10	14	67	84	119	.297	.390	.463	119	24	19	113	40	10	6	.983	1	*O	2.0
1988	Phi-N	154	569	77	150	30	5	11	56	54	106	.264	.344	.392	109	9	8	78	11	9	-2	.990	9	*O	1.0
1989	Bal-A	144	545	83	151	23	10	11	55	70	103	.277	.367	.417	124	16	18	87	20	6	2	.990	-2	*O/D	1.5
1990	Bal-A	72	289	39	78	9	1	4	26	30	35	.270	.353	.349	100	-0	1	36	10	4	1	.987	2	O/D	0.2
	Chi-A	45	133	20	30	5	1	0	5	20	26	.226	.344	.278	78	-3	-3	15	7	3	0	.973	-4	O/D	-0.8
	Yr	117	422	59	108	14	2	4	31	50	61	.256	.350	.327	93	-3	-2	51	17	7	1	.982	-2	*O/D	-0.6
Total	8	1022	3695	565	1058	179	43	78	376	432	718	.286	.371	.421	118	103	100	598	155	62	9	.988	-3	O/D	7.4

■ SCOTT BRADLEY
Bradley, Scott William b: 3/22/60, Glen Ridge, N.J. BL/TR, 5'11", 185 lbs. Deb: 9/09/84

YEAR	TM/L	G	AB	R	H	2B	3B	HR	RBI	BB	SO	AVG	OBP	SLG	PRO+	BR	/A	RC	SB	CS	SBR	FA	FR	POS	TPR
1984	NY-A	9	21	3	6	1	0	0	2	1	1	.286	.318	.333	84	-1	-0	2	0	0	0	1.000	-1	/OC	-0.1
1985	NY-A	19	49	4	8	2	1	0	1	1	5	.163	.196	.245	20	-5	-5	2	0	0	0	.923	-1	/CD	-0.6
1986	Chi-A	9	21	3	6	0	0	0	0	1	0	.286	.375	.286	81	-0	-0	2	0	2	-1	.000	-0	/OD	-0.2
	Sea-A	68	199	17	60	8	3	5	28	12	7	.302	.347	.447	113	4	4	27	1	0	0	.990	-13	C/D	-0.6
	Yr	77	220	20	66	8	3	5	28	13	7	.300	.350	.432	110	3	3	28	1	2	-1	.990	-14	C/DO	-0.8
1987	Sea-A	102	342	34	95	15	1	5	43	15	18	.278	.314	.371	77	-10	-12	36	0	1	-1	.983	-6	C/3OD	-1.3
1988	Sea-A	103	335	45	86	17	1	4	33	17	16	.257	.297	.349	77	-9	-11	32	1	1	-0	.991	4	C/O31	-0.1
1989	Sea-A	103	270	21	74	16	0	3	37	21	23	.274	.329	.367	93	-2	-3	32	1	1	-0	.993	3	C/1OD	0.4
1990	Sea-A	101	233	11	52	9	0	1	28	15	20	.223	.270	.275	52	-15	-15	17	0	1	-1	.995	1	C/31D	-1.2
1991	Sea-A	83	172	10	35	7	0	0	11	19	19	.203	.283	.244	47	-12	-12	13	0	0	0	.993	-5	C/31D	-1.4
1992	Sea-A	2	1	0	0	0	0	0	0	1	1	.000	.500	.000	51	0	0	0	0	0	0	1.000	1	/C	0.1
	Cin-N	5	5	1	2	0	0	0	1	1	0	.400	.500	.400	150	0	0	1	0	0	0	1.000	-1	/C	0.0
Total	9	604	1648	149	424	75	6	18	184	104	110	.257	.306	.343	76	-49	-55	165	3	6	-3	.990	-19	C/D3O1	-5.0

■ BILL BRADLEY
Bradley, William Joseph b: 2/13/1878, Cleveland, Ohio d: 3/11/54, Cleveland, Ohio BR/TR, 6', 185 lbs. Deb: 8/26/1899 M

YEAR	TM/L	G	AB	R	H	2B	3B	HR	RBI	BB	SO	AVG	OBP	SLG	PRO+	BR	/A	RC	SB	CS	SBR	FA	FR	POS	TPR
1899	Chi-N	35	129	26	40	6	1	2	18	12		.310	.378	.419	122	3	4	23	4			.884	-4	3/S	0.1
1900	Chi-N	122	444	63	125	21	8	5	49	27		.282	.330	.399	104	-1	1	65	14			.882	17	*31	1.7
1901	Cle-A	133	516	95	151	28	13	1	55	26		.293	.336	.403	109	2	5	77	15			**.930**	10	*3/P	1.5
1902	Cle-A	137	550	104	187	39	12	11	77	27		.340	.375	.515	151	31	34	114	11			.923	12	*3	4.3
1903	Cle-A	136	536	101	168	36	22	6	68	25		.313	.348	.496	154	31	32	104	21			.924	12	*3	4.6
1904	Cle-A	154	609	94	183	32	8	5	83	26		.300	.334	.404	134	21	22	95	23			**.955**	9	*3	3.8
1905	Cle-A	146	541	63	145	34	6	0	51	27		.268	.321	.353	112	8	7	72	22			**.945**	13	*3M	2.8
1906	Cle-A	82	302	32	83	16	2	2	25	18		.275	.324	.361	116	5	5	42	13			.966	5	3	1.4
1907	Cle-A	139	498	48	111	20	1	0	34	35		.223	.286	.267	76	-12	-13	50	20			**.938**	5	*3	-0.4
1908	Cle-A	148	548	70	133	24	7	1	46	29		.243	.297	.318	99	-1	-1	61	18			.939	-31	*3S	-3.1
1909	Cle-A	95	334	30	62	6	3	0	22	19		.186	.236	.222	43	-21	-23	20	8			.957	-11	3/12	-3.5
1910	Cle-A	61	214	12	42	3	0	0	12	10		.196	.236	.210	39	-15	-15	12	6			.956	-1	3	-1.6
1914	Bro-F	7	6	1	3	1	0	0	3	0	0	.500	.500	.667	232	1	1	2	0			.000	0	HM	0.1
1915	KC-F	66	203	15	38	9	1	0	9	9	18	.187	.225	.241	39	-16	-15	13	6			.949	-6	3	-2.1
Total	14	1461	5430	754	1471	275	84	33	552	290	18	.271	.317	.371	108	36	44	753	181			.933	28	*3/S12P	9.6

■ DALLAS BRADSHAW
Bradshaw, Dallas Carl "Windy" b: 11/23/1895, Wolf Creek, Ill. d: 12/11/39, Herrin, Ill. BL/TR, 5'7", 145 lbs. Deb: 6/05/17

YEAR	TM/L	G	AB	R	H	2B	3B	HR	RBI	BB	SO	AVG	OBP	SLG	PRO+	BR	/A	RC	SB	CS	SBR	FA	FR	POS	TPR
1917	Phi-A	2	4	0	0	0	0	0	0	0	1	.000	.000	.000	-99	-1	-1	0	0			1.000	1	/2	0.0

■ GEORGE BRADSHAW
Bradshaw, George Thomas b: 9/12/24, Salisbury, N.C. BR/TR, 6'2", 185 lbs. Deb: 8/10/52

YEAR	TM/L	G	AB	R	H	2B	3B	HR	RBI	BB	SO	AVG	OBP	SLG	PRO+	BR	/A	RC	SB	CS	SBR	FA	FR	POS	TPR
1952	Was-A	10	23	3	5	2	0	0	6	1	2	.217	.280	.304	65	-1	-1	2	0	0	0	.917	-3	/C	-0.4

■ BRADY
Brady Deb: 9/25/1875

YEAR	TM/L	G	AB	R	H	2B	3B	HR	RBI	BB	SO	AVG	OBP	SLG	PRO+	BR	/A	RC	SB	CS	SBR	FA	FR	POS	TPR
1875	Chi-n	1	4	1	1	0	1	0		0		.250	.250	.750	230	1	1	1						/O	0.0

■ BRIAN BRADY
Brady, Brian Phelan b: 7/11/62, Elmhurst, N.Y. BL/TL, 5'11", 185 lbs. Deb: 4/16/89

YEAR	TM/L	G	AB	R	H	2B	3B	HR	RBI	BB	SO	AVG	OBP	SLG	PRO+	BR	/A	RC	SB	CS	SBR	FA	FR	POS	TPR
1989	Cal-A	2	2	0	1	1	0	0	1	0	1	.500	.500	1.000	319	1	1	1	0	0	0	.000	-0	/O	0.0

■ CLIFF BRADY
Brady, Clifford Francis b: 3/6/1897, St.Louis, Mo. d: 9/25/74, Belleville, Ill. BR/TR, 5'5.5", 140 lbs. Deb: 8/08/20

YEAR	TM/L	G	AB	R	H	2B	3B	HR	RBI	BB	SO	AVG	OBP	SLG	PRO+	BR	/A	RC	SB	CS	SBR	FA	FR	POS	TPR
1920	Bos-A	53	180	16	41	5	1	0	12	13	12	.228	.284	.267	48	-14	-13	14	0	1	-1	.974	17	2	0.5

■ BOB BRADY
Brady, Robert Jay b: 11/8/22, Lewistown, Pa. BL/TR, 6'1", 175 lbs. Deb: 8/24/46

YEAR	TM/L	G	AB	R	H	2B	3B	HR	RBI	BB	SO	AVG	OBP	SLG	PRO+	BR	/A	RC	SB	CS	SBR	FA	FR	POS	TPR
1946	Bos-N	3	5	0	1	0	0	0	0	1	1	.200	.333	.200	52	-0	-0	0	0			.857	0	/C	0.0
1947	Bos-N	1	1	0	0	0	0	0	0	0	0	.000	.000	.000	-99	-0	-0	0	0			.000	0	H	0.0
Total	2	4	6	0	1	0	0	0	0	1	1	.167	.286	.167	29	-1	-1	0	0				0	/C	0.0

■ STEVE BRADY
Brady, Stephen A. b: 7/14/1851, Worcester, Mass. d: 11/1/17, Hartford, Conn. 5'9.5", 165 lbs. Deb: 7/23/1874 F

YEAR	TM/L	G	AB	R	H	2B	3B	HR	RBI	BB	SO	AVG	OBP	SLG	PRO+	BR	/A	RC	SB	CS	SBR	FA	FR	POS	TPR
1874	Har-n	27	115	19	38	5	2	0		3		.330	.347	.409	133	5	4	17						3/O	0.3
1875	Was-n	21	90	6	13	1	1	0		0		.144	.144	.178	11	-8	-7	2						2/O1	-0.6
1883	NY-a	97	432	69	117	12	6	0		11		.271	.289	.326	94	-1	-4	42				.961	3	*1O	-0.8
1884	*NY-a	112	485	102	122	11	3	1		21		.252	.283	.293	93	-5	-3	41				.918	1	*O/12	-0.3
1885	NY-a	108	434	60	128	14	5	3		25		.295	.342	.371	139	14	19	56				.879	-6	*O/123	1.0
1886	NY-a	124	466	56	112	8	5	0		35		.240	.298	.279	86	-8	-5	45	16			.830	-5	*O/1	-1.1
Total	2 n	48	205	25	51	6	3	0		3		.249	.260	.307	85	-3	-3	19	0					/32O1	-0.3
Total	4	441	1817	287	479	45	19	4		92		.264	.302	.316	102	-0	8	184	16			.875	-6	O/123	-1.2

■ TOM BRADY
Brady, Thomas A. b: Hartford, Conn. d: 8/27/22, Hartford, Conn. Deb: 9/25/1875 F

YEAR	TM/L	G	AB	R	H	2B	3B	HR	RBI	BB	SO	AVG	OBP	SLG	PRO+	BR	/A	RC	SB	CS	SBR	FA	FR	POS	TPR
1875	Har-n	1	4	0	0	0	0	0		0		.000	.000	.000	-95	-1	-1	0						/O	-0.1

■ BOBBY BRAGAN
Bragan, Robert Randall "Nig" b: 10/30/17, Birmingham, Ala. BR/TR, 5'10.5", 175 lbs. Deb: 4/16/40 MC

YEAR	TM/L	G	AB	R	H	2B	3B	HR	RBI	BB	SO	AVG	OBP	SLG	PRO+	BR	/A	RC	SB	CS	SBR	FA	FR	POS	TPR
1940	Phi-N	132	474	36	105	14	1	7	44	28	34	.222	.265	.300	58	-29	-27	37	2			.936	1	*S/3	-1.5
1941	Phi-N	154	557	37	140	19	3	4	69	26	29	.251	.285	.318	72	-23	-21	48	7			.944	-7	*S/23	-1.7
1942	Phi-N	109	335	17	73	12	2	2	15	20	21	.218	.264	.284	63	-17	-15	24	0			.939	9	SC/23	0.0
1943	Bro-N	74	220	17	58	7	2	2	24	15	16	.264	.311	.341	88	-4	-4	23	0			.973	4	C3	0.5
1944	Bro-N	94	266	26	71	8	4	0	17	13	14	.267	.304	.327	79	-8	-8	25	2			.954	-0	SC/32	-0.3
1947	*Bro-N	25	36	3	7	2	0	0	3	7	3	.194	.326	.250	53	-2	-2	4	1			1.000	4	C	0.2
1948	Bro-N	9	12	0	2	0	0	0	0	1	0	.167	.231	.167	9	-2	-2	1	0			1.000	-0	/C	-0.2
Total	7	597	1900	136	456	62	12	15	172	110	117	.240	.282	.309	69	-86	-79	160	12			.941	10	SC/32	-3.0

■ GLENN BRAGGS
Braggs, Glenn Erick b: 10/17/62, San Bernardino, Cal BR/TR, 6'3", 210 lbs. Deb: 7/18/86

YEAR	TM/L	G	AB	R	H	2B	3B	HR	RBI	BB	SO	AVG	OBP	SLG	PRO+	BR	/A	RC	SB	CS	SBR	FA	FR	POS	TPR
1986	Mil-A	58	215	19	51	8	2	4	18	11	47	.237	.278	.349	67	-10	-10	20	1	1	-0	.910	1	O/D	-1.1
1987	Mil-A	132	505	67	136	28	7	13	77	47	96	.269	.336	.430	98	1	-1	69	12	5	1	.972	14	*O/D	0.9
1988	Mil-A	72	272	30	71	14	0	10	42	14	60	.261	.309	.423	102	0	0	34	6	4	-1	.978	4	OD	0.2

YEAR	TM/L	G	AB	R	H	2B	3B	HR	RBI	BB	SO	AVG	OBP	SLG	PRO+	BR	/A	RC	SB	CS	SBR	FA	FR	POS	TPR
1989	Mil-A	144	514	77	127	12	3	15	66	42	111	.247	.309	.370	91	-7	-6	58	17	5	2	.972	-0	*OD	-0.8
1990	Mil-A	37	113	17	28	5	0	3	13	12	21	.248	.336	.372	98	-0	-0	15	5	3	-0	.965	2	O/D	0.1
	*Cin-N	72	201	22	60	9	1	6	28	26	43	.299	.387	.443	122	8	7	35	3	4	-2	.968	6	O	1.0
1991	Cin-N	85	250	36	65	10	0	11	39	23	46	.260	.327	.432	108	3	2	36	11	3	2	.966	-2	O	0.0
1992	Cin-N	92	266	40	63	16	3	8	38	36	48	.237	.332	.410	104	3	2	35	3	1	0	.946	-9	O	-0.9
Total	7	692	2336	308	601	102	16	70	321	211	472	.257	.325	.405	98	-1	-7	302	58	26	2	.963	16	O/D	-0.6

■ DAVE BRAIN Brain, David Leonard b: 1/24/1879, Hereford, England d: 5/25/59, Los Angeles, Cal. BR/TR, 5'10", 170 lbs. Deb: 4/24/01

YEAR	TM/L	G	AB	R	H	2B	3B	HR	RBI	BB	SO	AVG	OBP	SLG	PRO+	BR	/A	RC	SB	CS	SBR	FA	FR	POS	TPR
1901	Chi-A	5	20	2	7	1	0	0	5	1		.350	.381	.400	120	0	1	3	0			.909	1	/2	0.1
1903	StL-N	119	464	44	107	8	15	1	60	25		.231	.270	.319	70	-21	-19	47	21			.908	10	S3	-0.5
1904	StL-N	127	488	57	130	24	12	7	72	17		.266	.291	.408	121	6	8	66	18			.927	3	S3O2/1	1.4
1905	StL-N	44	158	11	36	4	5	1	17	8		.228	.269	.335	83	-4	-4	16	4			.910	-9	S/3O	-1.3
	Pit-N	85	307	31	79	17	6	3	46	15		.257	.296	.381	99	-1	-2	39	8			.923	6	3/S	0.7
	Yr	129	465	42	115	21	11	4	63	23		.247	.287	.366	94	-5	-6	55	12			.929	-3	3S/O	-0.6
1906	Bos-N	139	525	43	131	19	5	5	45	29		.250	.293	.333	98	-5	-3	58	11			.917	26	*3	3.0
1907	Bos-N	133	509	60	142	24	9	**10**	56	29		.279	.324	.420	134	17	17	75	10			.916	25	*3/O	5.0
1908	Cin-N	16	55	4	6	0	0	0	1	8		.109	.222	.109	7	-5	-5	1	0			.947	-1	O	-0.8
	NY-N	11	17	2	3	0	0	0	1	2		.176	.263	.176	39	-1	-1	1	1			.867	-3	/2O3S	-0.4
	Yr	27	72	6	9	0	0	0	2	10		.125	.232	.125	15	-7	-7	2	1			.947	-3	O/23S	-1.2
Total	7	679	2543	254	641	97	52	27	303	134		.252	.292	.363	101	-14	-8	307	73			.913	58	3S/O21	7.2

■ ASA BRAINARD Brainard, Asa "Count" b: 1841, Albany, N.Y. d: 12/29/1888, Denver, Colo. TR , 5'8.5", 150 lbs. Deb: 5/05/1871

YEAR	TM/L	G	AB	R	H	2B	3B	HR	RBI	BB	SO	AVG	OBP	SLG	PRO+	BR	/A	RC	SB	CS	SBR	FA	FR	POS	TPR
1871	Oly-n	30	134	24	30	4	0	0	21	7	2	.224	.262	.254	52	-8	-7	10	4					*P	0.0
1872	Oly-n	9	41	8	16	3	0	0	6	0	0	.390	.390	.463	170	3	3	8						/P	0.0
	Man-n	6	25	2	5	0	0	0	0	1	0	.200	.231	.200	36	-2	-2	1						/2P	-0.1
	Yr	15	66	10	21	3	0	0	6	1	0	.318	.328	.364	119	1	2	8						P/2	-0.1
1873	Bal-n	16	69	18	18	2	0	0	8	0	2	.261	.261	.290	62	-3	-3	5						P/O2	0.1
1874	Bal-n	46	198	19	50	5	0	0		2		.253	.260	.278	72	-6	-6	15						P2/O	0.1
Total	4 n	107	467	71	119	14	0	0		10		.255	.270	.285	71	-17	-14	39						/P2O	0.1

■ FRED BRAINERD Brainerd, Frederick F. b: 2/17/1892, Champaign, Ill. d: 4/17/59, Galveston, Tex. BR/TR, 6', 176 lbs. Deb: 10/06/14

YEAR	TM/L	G	AB	R	H	2B	3B	HR	RBI	BB	SO	AVG	OBP	SLG	PRO+	BR	/A	RC	SB	CS	SBR	FA	FR	POS	TPR
1914	NY-N	2	5	1	1	0	0	0	0	1	0	.200	.333	.200	62	-0	-0	1	0			.923	1	/2	0.1
1915	NY-N	91	249	31	50	7	2	1	21	21	44	.201	.266	.257	62	-12	-11	17	6	7	-2	.988	7	13/S2O	-0.7
1916	NY-N	2	7	0	0	0	0	0	0	0	0	.000	.000	.000	-99	-2	-2	0	0			.625	-1	/3	-0.3
Total	3	95	261	32	51	7	2	1	21	22	44	.195	.261	.249	58	-14	-12	17	6	7		.857	7	/13S2O	-0.9

■ ART BRAMHALL Bramhall, Arthur Washington b: 2/22/09, Oak Park, Ill. d: 9/4/85, Madison, Wis. BR/TR, 5'11", 170 lbs. Deb: 4/18/35

YEAR	TM/L	G	AB	R	H	2B	3B	HR	RBI	BB	SO	AVG	OBP	SLG	PRO+	BR	/A	RC	SB	CS	SBR	FA	FR	POS	TPR
1935	Phi-N	2	1	0	0	0	0	0	0	0	0	.000	.000	.000	-91	-0	-0	0	0			1.000	1	/S3	0.0

■ AL BRANCATO Brancato, Albert "Bronk" b: 5/29/19, Philadelphia, Pa. BR/TR, 5'9.5", 188 lbs. Deb: 9/07/39

YEAR	TM/L	G	AB	R	H	2B	3B	HR	RBI	BB	SO	AVG	OBP	SLG	PRO+	BR	/A	RC	SB	CS	SBR	FA	FR	POS	TPR
1939	Phi-A	21	68	12	14	5	0	1	8	8	4	.206	.299	.324	60	-4	-4	7	1	0	0	.939	-1	3/S	-0.4
1940	Phi-A	107	298	42	57	11	2	1	23	28	36	.191	.265	.252	36	-29	-28	20	3	1	0	.949	0	S3	-2.1
1941	Phi-A	144	530	60	124	20	9	2	49	59	49	.234	.311	.317	68	-26	-24	54	1	5	-3	.915	-19	*S/3	-3.4
1945	Phi-A	10	34	3	4	1	0	0	0	1	3	.118	.143	.147	-16	-5	-5	1	0	0	0	.959	-1	S	-0.6
Total	4	282	930	117	199	37	11	4	80	96	92	.214	.290	.290	54	-64	-61	81	5	6	-2	.927	-21	S/3	-6.5

■ RON BRAND Brand, Ronald George b: 1/13/40, Los Angeles, Cal. BR/TR, 5'8", 170 lbs. Deb: 5/26/63

YEAR	TM/L	G	AB	R	H	2B	3B	HR	RBI	BB	SO	AVG	OBP	SLG	PRO+	BR	/A	RC	SB	CS	SBR	FA	FR	POS	TPR
1963	Pit-N	46	66	8	19	2	0	1	7	10	11	.288	.390	.364	118	2	2	10	0	0	0	.968	9	C/23	1.2
1965	Hou-N	117	391	27	92	6	3	2	37	19	34	.235	.281	.281	63	-21	-18	28	10	5	0	.988	-7	*C/3O	-2.1
1966	Hou-N	56	123	12	30	2	0	0	10	9	13	.244	.306	.260	64	-6	-5	9	0	2	-1	.986	-5	C/2O3	-1.0
1967	Hou-N	84	215	22	52	8	1	0	18	23	17	.242	.321	.288	78	-6	-5	21	4	0	1	.998	-2	C/2O	-0.3
1968	Hou-N	43	81	7	13	2	0	0	4	9	11	.160	.261	.185	36	-6	-6	5	1	1	-0	1.000	3	C/3O	-0.2
1969	Mon-N	103	287	19	74	12	0	0	20	30	19	.258	.330	.300	77	-8	-8	27	2	3	-1	.985	-7	C/O	-1.3
1970	Mon-N	72	126	10	30	2	3	0	9	9	16	.238	.289	.302	59	-7	-7	12	2	1	0	.952	-5	S3/CO2	-1.1
1971	Mon-N	47	56	3	12	0	0	0	1	3	5	.214	.254	.214	34	-5	-5	3	1	1	-0	.957	4	S/3OC2	0.0
Total	8	568	1345	108	322	34	7	3	106	112	126	.239	.305	.282	68	-57	-52	114	20	13	-2	.988	-11	C/S3O2	-4.8

■ JACKIE BRANDT Brandt, John George b: 4/28/34, Omaha, Neb. BR/TR, 5'11", 170 lbs. Deb: 4/21/56

YEAR	TM/L	G	AB	R	H	2B	3B	HR	RBI	BB	SO	AVG	OBP	SLG	PRO+	BR	/A	RC	SB	CS	SBR	FA	FR	POS	TPR
1956	StL-N	27	42	9	12	3	0	1	3	4	5	.286	.362	.429	111	1	1	6	0	1	-1	1.000	-3	O	-0.4
	NY-N	98	351	45	105	16	8	11	47	17	31	.299	.332	.484	116	7	7	55	3	4	-2	.989	-6	O	-0.5
	Yr	125	393	54	117	19	8	12	50	21	36	.298	.335	.478	116	7	8	61	3	5	-2	.990	-9	*O	-0.9
1958	SF-N	18	52	7	13	1	0	0	3	6	5	.250	.328	.269	62	-3	-3	5	1	0	0	1.000	-0	O	-0.3
1959	SF-N	137	429	63	116	16	5	12	57	35	69	.270	.325	.415	98	-3	-2	58	11	4	1	.984	-7	*O3/12	-1.3
1960	Bal-A	145	511	73	130	24	6	15	65	47	69	.254	.321	.413	98	-3	-2	69	5	3	-0	.983	-10	*O/31	-2.0
1961	Bal-A★	139	516	93	153	18	5	16	72	62	51	.297	.373	.444	120	13	15	85	10	2	2	.974	-16	*O/3	-0.7
1962	Bal-A	143	505	76	129	29	5	19	75	55	64	.255	.333	.446	113	5	8	76	9	3	1	.976	9	*O/3	1.0
1963	Bal-A	142	451	49	112	15	5	15	61	34	85	.248	.301	.404	98	-4	-2	51	4	5	-2	.986	-7	*O/3	-1.9
1964	Bal-A	137	523	66	127	25	1	13	47	45	104	.243	.306	.369	87	-9	-9	59	1	4	-2	.981	16	*O	-0.2
1965	Bal-A	96	243	35	59	17	0	8	24	21	40	.243	.303	.412	99	-0	-1	30	1	2	-1	.961	-6	O	-1.1
1966	Phi-N	82	164	16	41	6	1	1	15	17	36	.250	.320	.317	78	-4	-4	16	0	2	-1	.988	0	O	-0.8
1967	Phi-N	16	19	1	2	1	0	0	1	0	6	.105	.105	.158	-25	-3	-3	0	0	0	0	1.000	-0	/O	-0.4
	Hou-N	41	89	7	21	4	1	1	15	8	9	.236	.299	.337	85	-2	-2	9	0	0	0	.991	-1	1/O3	-0.4
	Yr	57	108	8	23	5	1	1	16	8	15	.213	.267	.306	65	-5	-5	9	0	0	0	.991	-2	1/O3	-0.8
Total	11	1221	3895	540	1020	175	37	112	485	351	574	.262	.325	.412	101	-7	1	520	45	30	-4	.980	-32	*O/312	-9.0

■ OTIS BRANNAN Brannan, Otis Owen b: 3/13/1899, Greenbrier, Ark. d: 6/6/67, Little Rock, Ark. BL/TR, 5'9", 160 lbs. Deb: 4/11/28

YEAR	TM/L	G	AB	R	H	2B	3B	HR	RBI	BB	SO	AVG	OBP	SLG	PRO+	BR	/A	RC	SB	CS	SBR	FA	FR	POS	TPR
1928	StL-A	135	483	68	118	18	3	10	66	60	19	.244	.333	.356	79	-13	-15	59	3	9	-5	.964	-8	*2	-2.4
1929	StL-A	23	51	4	15	1	0	1	8	4	4	.294	.345	.373	82	-1	-1	7	0	0	0	.975	-1	2	-0.2
Total	2	158	534	72	133	19	3	11	74	64	23	.249	.334	.358	79	-14	-16	66	3	9	-5	.966	-9	2	-2.6

■ MIKE BRANNOCK Brannock, Michael J. b: 1853, Guelph, Ont., Canada 5'8", 162 lbs. Deb: 10/21/1871

YEAR	TM/L	G	AB	R	H	2B	3B	HR	RBI	BB	SO	AVG	OBP	SLG	PRO+	BR	/A	RC	SB	CS	SBR	FA	FR	POS	TPR
1871	Chi-n	3	14	2	1	0	0	0	0	0	0	.071	.071	.071	-53	-3	-3	0	0					/3	-0.2
1875	Chi-n	2	9	2	1	0	0	0		0		.111	.111	.111	-23	-1	-1	0						/3	-0.1
Total	2 n	5	23	4	2	0	0	0		0		.087	.087	.087	-43	-4	-4	0						/3	-0.3

■ DUD BRANOM Branom, Edgar Dudley b: 11/30/1897, Sulphur Springs, Tex. d: 2/4/80, Sun City, Ariz. BL/TL, 6'1", 190 lbs. Deb: 4/12/27

YEAR	TM/L	G	AB	R	H	2B	3B	HR	RBI	BB	SO	AVG	OBP	SLG	PRO+	BR	/A	RC	SB	CS	SBR	FA	FR	POS	TPR
1927	Phi-A	30	94	8	22	1	0	0	13	2	5	.234	.250	.245	27	-10	-11	6	2	1	0	.973	-0	1	-1.2

■ KITTY BRANSFIELD Bransfield, William Edward b: 1/7/1875, Worcester, Mass. d: 5/1/47, Worcester, Mass. BR/TR, 5'11", 207 lbs. Deb: 8/22/1898 U

YEAR	TM/L	G	AB	R	H	2B	3B	HR	RBI	BB	SO	AVG	OBP	SLG	PRO+	BR	/A	RC	SB	CS	SBR	FA	FR	POS	TPR
1898	Bos-N	5	9	2	2	0	1	0	1	0		.222	.222	.444	85	-0	-0	1	0			.889	-1	/C1	-0.1
1901	Pit-N	139	566	92	167	26	16	0	91	29		.295	.335	.398	109	7	5	86	23			.981	-10	*1	-0.7
1902	Pit-N	102	413	49	126	21	8	0	69	17		.305	.334	.395	120	10	9	65	23			.984	-6	*1	0.1
1903	*Pit-N	127	505	69	134	23	7	2	57	33		.265	.314	.350	87	-8	-10	63	13			.981	6	*1	-0.6
1904	Pit-N	139	520	47	116	17	9	0	60	22		.223	.259	.290	68	-19	-21	45	11			.981	-3	*1	-2.9
1905	Phi-N	151	580	55	150	23	9	3	76	27		.259	.294	.345	94	-9	-6	70	27			.985	-1	*1	-1.2

YEAR	TM/L	G	AB	R	H	2B	3B	HR	RBI	BB	SO	AVG	OBP	SLG	PRO+	BR	/A	RC	SB	CS	SBR	FA	FR	POS	TPR
1906	Phi-N	140	524	47	144	28	5	1	60	16		.275	.300	.353	104	-0	-0	62	12			.980	-2	*1	-0.7
1907	Phi-N	94	348	25	81	15	2	0	38	14		.233	.262	.287	74	-12	-12	30	8			.978	-3	1	-1.9
1908	Phi-N	144	527	53	160	25	7	3	71	23		.304	.335	.395	129	17	15	79	30			.986	-1	*1	1.4
1909	Phi-N	140	527	47	154	27	6	1	59	18		.292	.319	.372	113	6	6	68	17			**.989**	7	*1	1.3
1910	Phi-N	123	427	39	102	17	4	3	52	20	34	.239	.275	.319	71	-16	-18	40	10			.982	-4	*1	-2.4
1911	Phi-N	23	43	4	11	1	1	0	3	0	5	.256	.256	.326	61	-2	-2	4	1			.987	0	/1	-0.2
	Chi-N	3	10	0	4	2	0	0	0	2	2	.400	.500	.600	207	2	2	3	0			1.000	-0	/1	0.1
	Yr	26	53	4	15	3	1	0	3	2	7	.283	.309	.377	91	-1	-1	6	1			.991	-0	1	-0.1
Total	12	1330	4999	529	1351	225	75	13	637	221	41	.270	.304	.353	97	-24	-33	614	175			.983	-18	*1/C	-7.8
■ JEFF BRANSON Branson, Jeffery Glenn b: 1/26/67, Waynesboro, Miss. BL/TR, 6', 180 lbs. Deb: 4/17/92																									
1992	Cin-N	72	115	12	34	7	1	0	15	5	16	.296	.325	.374	93	-1	-1	13	0	1	-1	.946	2	2/3S	0.0
■ MARSHALL BRANT Brant, Marshall Lee b: 9/17/55, Garberville, Cal. BR/TR, 6'5", 185 lbs. Deb: 10/01/80																									
1980	NY-A	3	6	0	0	0	0	0	0	0	3	.000	.000	.000	-99	-2	-2	0	0	0	0	1.000	0	/1D	-0.1
1983	Oak-A	5	14	2	2	0	0	0	2	0	3	.143	.143	.143	-22	-2	-2	0	0	0	0	.905	-1	/1D	-0.4
Total	2	8	20	2	2	0	0	0	2	0	6	.100	.100	.100	-47	-4	-4	0	0	0	0	.935	-1	/1D	-0.5
■ MICKEY BRANTLEY Brantley, Michael Charles b: 6/17/61, Catskill, N.Y. BR/TR, 5'10", 180 lbs. Deb: 8/09/86																									
1986	Sea-A	27	102	12	20	3	2	3	7	10	21	.196	.268	.353	67	-5	-5	9	1	1	-0	.983	0	O	-0.6
1987	Sea-A	92	351	52	106	23	2	14	54	24	44	.302	.347	.499	115	10	7	62	13	4	2	.982	-6	O/D	0.0
1988	Sea-A	149	577	76	152	25	4	15	56	26	64	.263	.298	.399	89	-7	-10	66	18	7	1	.982	-5	*O/D	-1.8
1989	Sea-A	34	108	14	17	5	0	0	8	7	7	.157	.209	.204	16	-12	-12	5	2	2	-1	1.000	1	O/D	-1.3
Total	4	302	1138	154	295	56	8	32	125	67	136	.259	.302	.407	89	-14	-20	142	34	14	2	.984	-9	O/D	-3.7
■ ROY BRASHEAR Brashear, Roy Parks b: 1/3/1874, Ashtabula, Ohio d: 4/20/51, Los Angeles, Cal. BR/TR, 5'11", 205 lbs. Deb: 4/25/02 F																									
1902	StL-N	110	388	36	107	8	2	1	40	32		.276	.333	.314	104	0	2	46	9			.980	-9	12O/S	-0.8
1903	Phi-N	20	75	9	17	3	0	0	4	6		.227	.284	.267	59	-4	-4	7	2			.918	-4	2/1	-0.7
Total	2	130	463	45	124	11	2	1	44	38		.268	.325	.307	96	-4	-1	53	11			.978	-13	/12OS	-1.5
■ JOE BRATCHER Bratcher, Joseph Warlick "Goobers" b: 7/22/1898, Grand Saline, Tex d: 10/13/77, Fort Worth, Tex. BL/TR, 5'8.5", 140 lbs. Deb: 8/26/24																									
1924	StL-N	4	1	1	0	0	0	0	0	0	0	.000	.000	.000	-99	-0	-0	0	0	0	0	.000	-1	/O	-0.1
■ FRED BRATSCHI Bratschi, Frederick Oscar "Fritz" b: 1/16/1892, Alliance, Ohio d: 1/10/62, Massillon, Ohio BR/TR, 5'10", 170 lbs. Deb: 7/24/21																									
1921	Chi-A	16	28	0	8	1	0	0	3	0	2	.286	.286	.321	55	-2	-2	2	0	0	0	1.000	1	/O	-0.1
1926	Bos-A	72	167	12	46	10	1	0	19	14	15	.275	.335	.347	81	-5	-5	20	0	1	-1	.949	-7	O	-1.4
1927	Bos-A	1	1	0	0	0	0	0	0	0	0	.000	.000	.000	-99	-0	-0	0	0	0	0	.000	0	H	0.0
Total	3	89	196	12	54	11	1	0	22	14	17	.276	.327	.342	76	-8	-7	22	0	1	-1	.956	-6	/O	-1.5
■ STEVE BRAUN Braun, Stephen Russell b: 5/8/48, Trenton, N.J. BL/TR, 5'10", 180 lbs. Deb: 4/06/71 C																									
1971	Min-A	128	343	51	87	12	2	5	35	48	50	.254	.354	.344	95	1	-0	44	8	3	1	.933	-13	32S/O	-1.1
1972	Min-A	121	402	40	116	21	0	2	50	45	38	.289	.363	.356	109	8	6	51	4	5	-2	.970	-12	32S/O	-0.8
1973	Min-A	115	361	46	102	28	5	6	42	74	48	.283	.409	.438	133	22	20	68	4	3	-1	.941	-11	*3/O	0.8
1974	Min-A	129	453	53	127	12	1	8	40	56	51	.280	.362	.364	105	7	5	62	4	4	-1	.964	2	*O3	0.1
1975	Min-A	136	453	70	137	18	3	11	45	66	55	.302	.392	.428	129	21	20	79	0	2	-1	.971	-2	*O/132D	1.2
1976	Min-A	122	417	73	120	12	3	3	61	67	43	.288	.388	.353	114	13	11	63	12	4	1	.971	-3	DO3	0.8
1977	Sea-A	139	451	51	106	19	1	5	31	80	59	.235	.353	.315	84	-7	-7	54	8	3	1	.975	5	*OD/3	-0.5
1978	Sea-A	32	74	11	17	4	0	3	15	9	5	.230	.313	.405	101	-0	0	9	1	0	0	1.000	-1	D/O	0.0
	*KC-A	64	137	16	36	10	1	0	14	28	16	.263	.388	.350	106	3	3	21	3	2	-0	.964	-5	O3	-0.5
	Yr	96	211	27	53	14	1	3	29	37	21	.251	.363	.370	105	3	3	30	4	2	0	.967	-6	OD3	-0.5
1979	KC-A	58	116	15	31	2	0	4	10	22	11	.267	.384	.388	107	2	2	19	0	0	0	1.000	1	OD/3	0.2
1980	KC-A	14	23	0	1	0	0	0	1	2	2	.043	.120	.043	-53	-5	-5	0	0	0	0	1.000	-2	/OD	-0.7
	Tor-A	37	55	4	15	2	0	1	9	8	5	.273	.365	.364	96	0	-0	7	0	0	0	1.000	0	D/3	0.0
	Yr	51	78	4	16	2	0	1	10	10	7	.205	.295	.269	54	-5	-5	6	0	0	0	1.000	-2	D/O3	-0.7
1981	StL-N	44	46	9	9	2	1	0	2	15	7	.196	.393	.283	92	1	0	7	1	0	0	1.000	1	O/3	0.1
1982	*StL-N	58	62	6	17	4	0	0	4	11	10	.274	.384	.339	103	1	1	8	0	0	0	1.000	-3	/O3	-0.2
1983	StL-N	78	92	8	25	2	1	3	7	21	7	.272	.407	.413	128	4	4	17	0	1	-1	1.000	-2	O/3	0.2
1984	StL-N	86	98	6	27	3	1	0	16	17	17	.276	.383	.327	104	1	1	14	0	0	0	1.000	-5	O/3	-0.4
1985	*StL-N	64	67	7	16	4	0	1	6	10	9	.239	.346	.343	94	-0	-0	9	0	0	0	1.000	-2	O	-0.2
Total	15	1425	3650	466	989	155	19	52	388	579	433	.271	.373	.367	108	72	61	532	45	27	-3	.973	-51	O3D/2S1	-1.0
■ ANGEL BRAVO Bravo, Angel Alfonso (Urdaneta) b: 8/4/42, Maracaibo, Venez. BL/TL, 5'8", 150 lbs. Deb: 6/06/69																									
1969	Chi-A	27	90	10	26	4	2	1	3	3	5	.289	.319	.411	98	0	-0	12	2	0	1	.978	-4	O	-0.6
1970	*Cin-N	65	65	10	18	1	1	0	3	9	13	.277	.365	.323	86	-1	-1	8	0	1	-1	.947	0	O	-0.2
1971	Cin-N	5	5	0	1	0	0	0	0	0	1	.200	.200	.200	14	-1	-1	0	0	0	0	.000	0	H	-0.1
	SD-N	52	58	6	9	2	0	0	6	8	12	.155	.269	.190	34	-5	-5	3	0	1	-1	.833	-2	/O	-0.8
	Yr	57	63	6	10	2	0	0	6	8	13	.159	.264	.190	33	-6	-5	4	0	1	-1	.833	-2	/O	-0.9
Total	3	149	218	26	54	7	3	1	12	20	31	.248	.317	.321	77	-6	-7	24	2	2	-1	.957	-6	/O	-1.7
■ BUSTER BRAY Bray, Clarence Wilbur b: 4/1/13, Birmingham, Ala. d: 9/4/82, Evansville, Ind. BL/TL, 6', 170 lbs. Deb: 4/18/41																									
1941	Bos-N	4	11	2	1	1	0	0	1	1	2	.091	.167	.182	-2	-2	-1	0	0			1.000	-0	/O	-0.2
■ FRANK BRAZILL Brazill, Frank Leo b: 8/11/1899, Spangler, Pa. d: 11/3/76, Oakland, Cal. BL/TR, 5'11.5", 175 lbs. Deb: 4/13/21																									
1921	Phi-A	66	177	17	48	3	1	0	19	23	21	.271	.361	.299	70	-7	-7	20	2	4	-2	.984	-1	1/3	-1.0
1922	Phi-A	6	13	0	1	0	0	0	1	0	1	.077	.077	.077	-58	-3	-3	0	0	0	0	.750	-2	/3	-0.5
Total	2	72	190	17	49	3	1	0	20	23	22	.258	.344	.284	62	-10	-10	20	2	4	-2	.892	-3	/13	-1.5
■ SID BREAM Bream, Sidney Eugene b: 8/3/60, Carlisle, Pa. BL/TL, 6'4", 220 lbs. Deb: 9/01/83																									
1983	LA-N	15	11	0	2	0	0	0	2	2	2	.182	.308	.182	39	-1	-1	1	0	0	0	1.000	-0	/1	-0.1
1984	LA-N	27	49	2	9	3	0	0	6	6	9	.184	.273	.245	47	-3	-3	4	1	0	0	1.000	2	1	-0.2
1985	LA-N	24	53	4	7	0	0	3	6	7	10	.132	.233	.302	50	-4	-4	4	0	0	0	.994	2	1	-0.3
	Pit-N	26	95	14	27	7	0	3	15	11	14	.284	.358	.453	127	3	3	14	0	2	-1	.992	2	1	0.2
	Yr	50	148	18	34	7	0	6	21	18	24	.230	.313	.399	100	-1	-0	18	0	2	-1	.993	4	1	-0.1
1986	Pit-N	154	522	73	140	37	5	16	77	60	73	.268	.345	.450	115	12	10	79	13	7	-0	.989	23	*1/O	2.4
1987	Pit-N	149	516	64	142	25	3	13	65	49	69	.275	.338	.411	97	-2	-3	66	9	8	-2	.988	11	*1	-0.4
1988	Pit-N	148	462	50	122	37	0	10	65	47	64	.264	.333	.409	114	7	8	61	9	9	-3	.995	21	*1	1.7
1989	Pit-N	19	36	3	8	3	0	0	4	12	10	.222	.417	.306	113	1	1	5	0	4	-2	.992	-0	1	-0.2
1990	*Pit-N	147	389	39	105	23	2	15	67	48	65	.270	.353	.455	125	11	13	64	8	4	0	.993	10	*1	1.4
1991	*Atl-N	91	265	32	67	12	0	11	45	25	31	.253	.317	.423	100	2	-0	33	0	3	-2	.996	-0	1	-0.7
1992	*Atl-N	125	372	30	97	25	1	10	61	46	51	.261	.344	.414	105	7	3	57	6	0	2	.989	-3	*1	-0.5
Total	10	925	2770	311	726	172	11	81	413	313	398	.262	.338	.420	107	33	28	387	46	37	-8	.991	66	1/O	3.3
■ JIM BREAZEALE Breazeale, James Leo b: 10/3/49, Houston, Tex. BL/TR, 6'2", 210 lbs. Deb: 9/13/69																									
1969	Atl-N	2	1	1	0	0	0	0	0	2	0	.000	.667	.000	101	0	0	0	0	0	0	.833	-0	/1	0.0
1971	Atl-N	10	21	1	4	0	0	1	3	0	3	.190	.190	.333	43	-2	-2	1	0	0	0	1.000	-0	/1	-0.2
1972	Atl-N	52	85	10	21	2	0	5	17	6	12	.247	.297	.447	100	1	-0	10	0	1	-1	1.000	-2	1/3	-0.4

YEAR	TM/L	G	AB	R	H	2B	3B	HR	RBI	BB	SO	AVG	OBP	SLG	PRO+	BR	/A	RC	SB	CS	SBR	FA	FR	POS	TPR
1978	Chi-A	25	72	8	15	3	0	3	13	8	10	.208	.287	.375	84	-2	-2	8	0	0	0	.992	-3	1/D	-0.6
Total	4	89	179	20	40	5	0	9	33	16	25	.223	.287	.402	88	-2	-3	20	0	1	-1	.993	-5	/1D3	-1.2
■ DANNY BREEDEN	Breeden, Danny Richard b: 6/27/42, Albany, Ga. BR/TR, 5'11.5", 185 lbs. Deb: 7/24/69 F																								
1969	Cin-N	3	8	0	1	0	0	0	1	0	3	.125	.125	.125	-28	-1	-1	0	0	0	0	.941	0	/C	-0.1
1971	Chi-N	25	65	3	10	1	0	0	4	9	18	.154	.267	.169	23	-6	-7	4	0	0	0	.975	4	C	-0.2
Total	2	28	73	3	11	1	0	0	5	9	21	.151	.253	.164	18	-7	-9	4	0	0	0	.972	5	/C	-0.3
■ HAL BREEDEN	Breeden, Harold Noel b: 6/28/44, Albany, Ga. BR/TL, 6'2", 200 lbs. Deb: 4/07/71 F																								
1971	Chi-N	23	36	1	5	1	0	1	2	2	7	.139	.184	.250	19	-4	-4	2	0	0	0	.982	1	/1	-0.4
1972	Mon-N	42	87	6	20	2	0	3	10	7	15	.230	.287	.356	80	-2	-2	9	0	0	0	.994	-1	1/O	-0.5
1973	Mon-N	105	258	36	71	10	6	15	43	29	45	.275	.353	.535	138	14	13	47	0	1	-1	.991	3	1	1.1
1974	Mon-N	79	190	14	47	13	0	2	20	24	35	.247	.332	.347	85	-2	-4	21	0	1	-1	.987	1	1	-0.7
1975	Mon-N	24	37	4	5	2	0	0	1	7	5	.135	.273	.189	29	-3	-4	2	0	0	0	.989	-0	1	-0.5
Total	5	273	608	61	148	28	6	21	76	69	107	.243	.323	.413	99	2	-1	81	0	2	-1	.990	4	1/O	-1.0
■ MARV BREEDING	Breeding, Marvin Eugene b: 3/8/34, Decatur, Ala. BR/TR, 6', 175 lbs. Deb: 4/19/60																								
1960	Bal-A	152	551	69	147	25	2	3	43	35	80	.267	.314	.336	77	-19	-18	59	10	4	1	.977	5	*2	0.2
1961	Bal-A	90	244	32	51	8	0	1	16	14	33	.209	.252	.254	36	-22	-22	16	5	2	0	.970	7	2	-0.7
1962	Bal-A	95	240	27	59	10	1	2	18	8	41	.246	.273	.321	62	-14	-13	21	2	2	-1	.977	21	2/S3	1.3
1963	Was-A	58	197	20	54	7	2	1	14	7	21	.274	.299	.345	80	-5	-5	20	1	1	-0	.914	-9	32/S	-1.3
	LA-N	20	36	6	6	0	0	0	1	2	5	.167	.211	.167	11	-4	-4	2	1	0	0	.972	-4	2/S3	-0.7
Total	4	415	1268	154	317	50	5	7	92	66	180	.250	.289	.314	65	-64	-61	118	19	9	0	.975	20	2/3S	-1.2
■ HERB BREMER	Bremer, Herbert Frederick b: 10/26/13, Chicago, Ill. d: 11/28/79, Columbus, Ga. BR/TR, 6', 195 lbs. Deb: 9/16/37																								
1937	StL-N	11	33	2	7	1	0	0	3	2	4	.212	.257	.242	36	-3	-3	2	0			.979	-0	C	-0.3
1938	StL-N	50	151	14	33	5	1	2	14	9	36	.219	.262	.305	53	-9	-10	13	1			.977	3	C	-0.5
1939	StL-N	9	9	0	1	0	0	0	1	0	2	.111	.111	.111	-38	-2	-2	0	0			1.000	1	/C	-0.1
Total	3	70	193	16	41	6	1	2	18	11	42	.212	.255	.285	45	-14	-15	15	1			.979	3	/C	-0.9
■ SAM BRENEGAN	Brenegan, Olaf Selmar b: 9/1/1890, Galesville, Wis. d: 4/20/56, Galesville, Wis. BL/TR, 6'2", 185 lbs. Deb: 4/24/14																								
1914	Pit-N	1	0	0	0	0	0	0	0	0	0	—	—	—	—	0	0	0	0			.000	-0	/C	0.0
■ BOB BRENLY	Brenly, Robert Earl b: 2/25/54, Coshocton, Ohio BR/TR, 6'2", 210 lbs. Deb: 8/14/81 C																								
1981	SF-N	19	45	5	15	2	1	1	4	6	4	.333	.423	.489	161	4	4	9	0	1	-1	.964	-4	C/3O	0.0
1982	SF-N	65	180	26	51	4	1	4	15	18	26	.283	.352	.383	106	2	2	25	6	2	1	.961	0	C/3	0.5
1983	SF-N	104	281	36	63	12	2	7	34	37	48	.224	.319	.356	89	-5	-4	30	10	7	-1	.983	2	C1/O	0.0
1984	SF-N★	145	506	74	147	28	0	20	80	48	52	.291	.355	.464	133	19	21	79	6	9	-4	.986	-18	*C1/O	0.4
1985	SF-N	133	440	41	97	16	1	19	56	57	62	.220	.313	.391	100	-3	-0	55	1	4	-2	.984	-7	*C31	-0.4
1986	SF-N	149	472	60	116	26	0	16	62	74	97	.246	.352	.403	113	6	9	71	10	6	-1	**.995**	-7	*C31	0.6
1987	*SF-N	123	375	55	100	19	1	18	51	47	85	.267	.353	.467	121	8	10	63	10	7	-1	.988	9	*C/13	2.5
1988	SF-N	73	206	13	39	7	0	5	22	20	40	.189	.268	.296	64	-10	-9	17	1	2	-1	.984	-4	C	-1.0
1989	Tor-A	48	88	9	15	3	1	1	6	10	17	.170	.255	.261	47	-6	-6	6	1	0	0	.975	2	DC/1	-0.4
	SF-N	12	22	2	4	2	0	0	3	1	7	.182	.217	.273	40	-2	-2	1	0	0	0	1.000	0	C	-0.1
Total	9	871	2615	321	647	119	7	91	333	318	438	.247	.333	.403	107	12	24	356	45	38	-9	.984	-25	C/13DO	2.1
■ JACK BRENNAN	Brennan, John Gottlieb (b: John Gottlieb Dorn) b: 1862, St.Louis, Mo. d: 10/18/04, Philadelphia, Pa. Deb: 7/14/1884																								
1884	StL-U	56	231	38	50	6	1	0		12		.216	.255	.251	69	-6	-8	15				.891	-3	CO/3S	-0.6
1885	StL-N	3	10	0	1	0	0	0	1	1	1	.100	.182	.100	-7	-1	-1	0				.750	-1	/O3	-0.2
1888	KC-a	34	118	5	20	2	0	0	6	3		.169	.203	.186	26	-9	-10	5	3			.884	-3	C/O3	-1.0
1889	Phi-a	31	113	12	25	4	0	0	15	10	15	.221	.285	.257	57	-6	-6	9	1			.818	-4	C/O23	-0.7
1890	Cle-P	59	233	32	59	3	7	0	26	13	29	.253	.304	.326	76	-10	-7	26	8			.845	-4	C3/O	-0.6
Total	5	183	705	87	155	15	8	0	48	39	45	.220	.267	.264	61	-33	-32	55	12			.869	-15	C/O32S	-3.1
■ BILL BRENZEL	Brenzel, William Richard b: 3/3/10, Oakland, Cal. d: 6/12/79, Oakland, Cal. BR/TR, 5'10", 173 lbs. Deb: 4/13/32																								
1932	Pit-N	9	24	0	1	1	0	0	2	0	4	.042	.042	.083	-69	-6	-6	0	0			1.000	2	/C	-0.3
1934	Cle-A	15	51	4	11	3	0	0	3	2	1	.216	.245	.275	33	-5	-5	4	0	0	0	1.000	3	C	-0.2
1935	Cle-A	52	142	12	31	5	1	0	14	6	10	.218	.250	.268	33	-14	-14	10	2	2	-1	.975	-7	C	-1.9
Total	3	76	217	16	43	9	1	0	19	8	15	.198	.227	.249	23	-25	-25	13	2	2		.985	-2	/C	-2.4
■ ROGER BRESNAHAN	Bresnahan, Roger Philip "The Duke Of Tralee" b: 6/11/1879, Toledo, Ohio d: 12/4/44, Toledo, Ohio BR/TR, 5'9", 200 lbs. Deb: 8/27/1897 MCH																								
1897	Was-N	6	16	1	6	0	0	0	3	1		.375	.412	.375	109	0	0	3	0			1.000	-1	/PO	0.0
1900	Chi-N	2	2	0	0	0	0	0	0	0		.000	.000	.000	-99	-1	-1	0	0			.000	-0	/C	-0.1
1901	Bal-A	86	295	40	79	9	9	1	32	23		.268	.321	.369	87	-4	-6	40	10			.919	-19	C/O3P2	-1.6
1902	Bal-A	65	235	30	64	8	6	4	34	21		.272	.335	.409	101	1	-0	37	12			.880	-8	3CO	-0.7
	NY-N	51	178	16	51	9	3	1	22	16		.287	.352	.388	129	6	6	28	6			.946	-0	OC/1S3	0.7
1903	NY-N	113	406	87	142	30	8	4	55	61		.350	.438	.493	159	37	34	106	34			.965	0	O1C/3	2.9
1904	NY-N	109	402	81	114	22	7	5	33	58		.284	.379	.410	138	23	21	70	13			.954	0	O1/S23	1.6
1905	*NY-N	104	331	58	100	18	3	0	46	50		.302	.406	.375	131	17	16	57	11			.970	-1	C/O	2.4
1906	NY-N	124	405	69	114	22	4	0	43	81		.281	.414	.356	138	25	24	73	25			.974	5	CO	3.8
1907	NY-N	110	328	57	83	9	7	4	38	61		.253	.380	.360	128	15	14	53	15			.986	-7	C/1O3	1.7
1908	NY-N	140	449	70	127	25	3	1	54	**83**		.283	.400	.359	136	27	24	72	14			.985	-18	*C	2.2
1909	StL-N	72	234	27	57	4	1	0	23	46		.244	.370	.269	105	3	4	28	11			.960	-6	C/23M	0.3
1910	StL-N	88	234	35	65	15	3	0	27	55	17	.278	.419	.368	135	12	14	42	13			.961	-9	C/OPM	1.1
1911	StL-N	81	227	22	63	17	8	3	41	45	19	.278	.404	.463	146	14	15	44	4			.968	-2	C/2M	2.0
1912	StL-N	48	108	8	36	7	2	1	15	14	9	.333	.419	.463	145	7	7	22	4			.974	7	CM	1.6
1913	Chi-N	69	162	20	37	5	2	1	21	21	11	.228	.324	.302	79	-4	-4	18	7			.963	-3	C	-0.3
1914	Chi-N	101	248	42	69	10	4	0	24	49	20	.278	.401	.351	125	10	10	40	14			.978	-3	C2/O	1.5
1915	Chi-N	77	221	19	45	8	1	1	19	29	23	.204	.296	.262	70	-7	-7	22	19	3	**4**	.982	3	CM	0.5
Total	17	1446	4481	682	1252	218	71	26	530	714	99	.279	.385	.377	125	181	172	754	212	3		.971	-62	CO/312PS	19.6
■ RUBE BRESSLER	Bressler, Raymond Bloom b: 10/23/1894, Coder, Pa. d: 11/7/66, Cincinnati, Ohio BR/TL, 6', 187 lbs. Deb: 4/24/14																								
1914	Phi-A	29	51	6	11	1	1	0	4	6	7	.216	.310	.275	79	-1	-1	5	0			.941	-2	P	0.0
1915	Phi-A	33	55	9	8	0	1	1	4	9	13	.145	.277	.236	56	-3	-3	4	0			.900	0	P	0.0
1916	Phi-A	4	5	1	1	0	1	0	1	0	0	.200	.200	.600	147	0	0	1	0			1.000	-0	/P	0.0
1917	Cin-N	3	5	0	1	0	0	0	0	0	2	.200	.200	.200	24	-0	-0	0	0			1.000	-0	/P	0.0
1918	Cin-N	23	62	10	17	5	0	0	6	5	4	.274	.328	.355	110	1	1	7	0			.982	2	P/O	-0.1
1919	Cin-N	61	165	22	34	3	4	2	17	23	15	.206	.311	.309	89	-2	-2	17	2			.965	1	OP	-0.5
1920	Cin-N	21	30	4	8	1	0	0	3	1	4	.267	.290	.300	71	-1	-1	3	1	0	0	1.000	-1	P/O1	-0.2
1921	Cin-N	109	323	41	99	18	6	1	54	39	20	.307	.385	.409	115	6	8	52	5	5	-2	.953	-6	O/1	-0.6
1922	Cin-N	52	53	7	14	0	2	0	8	4	4	.264	.316	.340	70	-2	-2	6	1	0	0	1.000	-2	/1O	-0.3
1923	Cin-N	54	119	25	33	3	1	0	18	20	4	.277	.399	.319	93	-0	0	17	3	1	0	.983	-3	1/O	-0.3
1924	Cin-N	115	383	41	133	14	13	4	49	22	20	.347	.389	.483	134	17	18	69	9	10	-3	.990	4	1O	1.2
1925	Cin-N	97	319	43	111	17	6	4	61	40	16	.348	.424	.476	133	16	17	66	9	5	-0	.982	-3	1O	0.8

YEAR	TM/L	G	AB	R	H	2B	3B	HR	RBI	BB	SO	AVG	OBP	SLG	PRO+	BR	/A	RC	SB	CS	SBR	FA	FR	POS	TPR
1926	Cin-N	86	297	58	106	15	9	1	51	37	20	.357	.433	.478	149	20	21	61	3			.970	-4	O/1	1.2
1927	Cin-N	124	467	43	136	14	8	3	77	32	22	.291	.338	.375	94	-6	-4	58	4			.972	7	*O	-0.5
1928	Bro-N	145	501	78	148	29	13	4	70	80	33	.295	.398	.429	118	15	16	88	2			**.985**	-6	*O	0.1
1929	Bro-N	136	456	72	145	22	8	9	77	67	27	.318	.406	.461	117	12	14	86	4			.954	3	*O	0.8
1930	Bro-N	109	335	53	100	12	8	3	52	51	19	.299	.394	.409	96	-1	-0	56	4			.995	6	O/1	0.0
1931	Bro-N	67	153	22	43	4	5	0	26	11	10	.281	.329	.373	89	-3	-2	19	0			.982	-4	O/1	-0.9
1932	Phi-N	27	83	9	19	6	1	0	6	2	5	.229	.247	.325	47	-6	-7	7	0			1.000	3	O	-0.5
	StL-N	10	19	0	3	0	0	0	2	0	1	.158	.158	.158	-14	-3	-3	1	0			1.000	-0	/O	-0.4
	Yr	37	102	9	22	6	1	0	8	2	6	.216	.231	.294	37	-9	-10	7	0			1.000	3	O	-0.9
Total	19	1305	3881	544	1170	164	87	32	586	449	246	.301	.378	.413	110	58	69	623	47	21		.971	-4	O1P	-0.2

■ EDDIE BRESSOUD
Bressoud, Edward Francis b: 5/2/32, Los Angeles, Cal. BR/TR, 6′1″, 175 lbs. Deb: 6/14/56

YEAR	TM/L	G	AB	R	H	2B	3B	HR	RBI	BB	SO	AVG	OBP	SLG	PRO+	BR	/A	RC	SB	CS	SBR	FA	FR	POS	TPR
1956	NY-N	49	163	15	37	4	2	0	9	12	20	.227	.284	.276	52	-11	-11	13	1	0	0	.950	-9	S	-1.7
1957	NY-N	49	127	11	34	2	2	5	10	4	19	.268	.301	.433	94	-1	-1	16	0	1	-1	.940	1	S3	0.2
1958	SF-N	66	137	19	36	5	3	0	8	14	22	.263	.331	.343	81	-4	-4	16	0	1	-1	.966	-2	2/3S	-0.3
1959	SF-N	104	315	36	79	17	2	9	26	28	55	.251	.312	.403	91	-6	-5	40	0	0	0	.974	-6	S/123	-0.3
1960	SF-N	116	386	37	87	19	6	9	43	35	72	.225	.293	.376	87	-10	-8	41	1	2	-1	.960	6	*S	0.6
1961	SF-N	59	114	14	24	6	0	3	11	11	23	.211	.280	.342	66	-6	-5	9	1	1	-0	.964	-9	S/32	-1.3
1962	Bos-A	153	599	79	166	40	9	14	68	46	118	.277	.331	.444	103	4	2	85	2	3	-1	.965	25	*S	3.8
1963	Bos-A	140	497	61	129	23	6	20	60	52	93	.260	.332	.451	113	11	9	75	1	1	-0	.962	-9	*S	1.0
1964	Bos-A☆	158	566	86	166	41	3	15	55	72	99	.293	.374	.456	123	24	20	99	1	1	-0	.972	-14	*S	1.9
1965	Bos-A	107	296	29	67	11	1	8	25	29	77	.226	.298	.351	79	-6	-9	32	0	1	-1	.963	-5	S/3O	-0.9
1966	NY-N	133	405	48	91	15	5	10	49	47	107	.225	.307	.360	87	-8	-7	45	2	2	-1	.960	8	S3/12	0.7
1967	*StL-N	52	67	8	9	1	1	1	1	9	18	.134	.237	.224	33	-6	-6	4	0	0	0	.929	-4	S/3	-0.9
Total	12	1186	3672	443	925	184	40	94	365	359	723	.252	.321	.401	96	-20	-24	474	9	13	-5	.963	-19	*S/231O	2.8

■ JIM BRETON
Breton, John Frederick b: 7/15/1891, Chicago, Ill. d: 5/30/73, Beloit, Wis. BR/TR, 5′10.5″, 178 lbs. Deb: 8/25/13

YEAR	TM/L	G	AB	R	H	2B	3B	HR	RBI	BB	SO	AVG	OBP	SLG	PRO+	BR	/A	RC	SB	CS	SBR	FA	FR	POS	TPR
1913	Chi-A	12	30	1	5	1	1	0	2	1	5	.167	.194	.267	35	-3	-3	1	0			.938	3	/S3	0.0
1914	Chi-A	81	231	21	49	7	2	0	24	24	42	.212	.292	.260	67	-9	-9	20	9	6	-1	.910	3	3	-0.5
1915	Chi-A	16	36	3	5	1	0	0	1	5	9	.139	.262	.167	27	-3	-3	3	2	1	0	.882	-2	3/2S	-0.5
Total	3	109	297	25	59	9	3	0	27	30	56	.199	.279	.249	59	-15	-15	24	11	7		.906	4	/3S2	-1.0

■ GEORGE BRETT
Brett, George Howard b: 5/15/53, Glen Dale, W.Va. BL/TR, 6′, 200 lbs. Deb: 8/02/73 F

YEAR	TM/L	G	AB	R	H	2B	3B	HR	RBI	BB	SO	AVG	OBP	SLG	PRO+	BR	/A	RC	SB	CS	SBR	FA	FR	POS	TPR
1973	KC-A	13	40	2	5	2	0	0	0	0	5	.125	.125	.175	-15	-6	-6	1	0	0	0	.974	3	3	-0.4
1974	KC-A	133	457	49	129	21	5	2	47	21	38	.282	.314	.363	89	-4	-7	50	8	5	-1	.948	-9	*3/S	-1.9
1975	KC-A	159	634	84	**195**	35	**13**	11	89	46	49	.308	.356	.456	125	22	20	102	13	10	-2	.949	-6	*3/S	1.1
1976	*KC-A★	159	645	94	**215**	34	**14**	7	67	49	36	**.333**	.381	.462	145	36	36	**114**	21	11	-0	.948	3	*3/S	4.0
1977	*KC-A★	139	564	105	176	32	13	22	88	55	24	.312	.375	.532	143	33	33	108	14	12	-3	.957	17	*3/SD	4.5
1978	*KC-A★	128	510	79	150	**45**	8	9	62	39	35	.294	.345	.467	123	16	15	83	23	7	3	.961	5	*3/S	2.2
1979	KC-A★	154	645	119	**212**	42	**20**	23	107	51	36	.329	.378	.563	147	43	41	134	17	10	-1	.944	14	*3/1	5.0
1980	*KC-A†	117	449	87	175	33	9	24	118	58	22	**.390**	**.461**	**.664**	**203**	**65**	**64**	**135**	15	6	1	.955	4	*3/1	**6.5**
1981	*KC-A★	89	347	42	109	27	7	6	43	27	23	.314	.365	.484	144	18	19	60	14	6	1	.946	-9	3	0.9
1982	KC-A★	144	552	101	166	32	9	21	82	71	51	.301	.381	.505	141	32	32	107	6	1	1	.959	-6	*3O	2.3
1983	KC-A★	123	464	90	144	38	2	25	93	57	39	.310	.387	**.563**	157	36	36	100	0	1	-1	.919	-25	*31O/D	0.8
1984	*KC-A★	104	377	42	107	21	3	13	69	38	37	.284	.349	.459	121	11	10	58	0	2	-1	.949	-4	*3	0.4
1985	*KC-A★	155	550	108	184	38	5	30	112	103	49	.335	.442	**.585**	**178**	**63**	**63**	**146**	9	1	2	.967	12	*3/D	7.2
1986	KC-A†	124	441	70	128	28	4	16	73	80	45	.290	.404	.481	137	27	26	89	1	2	-1	.952	-2	*3/SD	2.0
1987	KC-A	115	427	71	124	18	2	22	78	72	47	.290	.394	.496	131	23	21	85	6	3	0	.993	-5	1D3	0.9
1988	KC-A★	157	589	90	180	42	3	24	103	82	51	.306	.393	.509	149	41	40	119	14	3	2	.992	-9	*1D/S	2.3
1989	KC-A	124	457	67	129	26	3	12	80	59	47	.282	.368	.431	125	16	16	71	14	4	2	.998	4	*1D/O	1.3
1990	KC-A	142	544	82	179	**45**	7	14	87	56	63	**.329**	.392	.515	154	37	38	106	9	2	2	.993	-1	*1D/O3	3.1
1991	KC-A	131	505	77	129	40	2	10	61	58	75	.255	.332	.402	102	1	1	65	2	0	1	.989	-1	*D1	0.0
1992	KC-A	152	592	55	169	35	5	7	61	35	69	.285	.332	.397	102	2	1	74	8	6	-1	.987	0	*D1/3	-0.1
Total	20	2562	9789	1514	3005	634	134	298	1520	1057	841	.307	.376	.490	137	513	499	1807	194	92	3	.951	-17	*31D/OS	42.1

■ TONY BREWER
Brewer, Anthony Bruce b: 11/25/57, Shreveport, La. BR/TR, 5′11″, 190 lbs. Deb: 8/01/84 F

YEAR	TM/L	G	AB	R	H	2B	3B	HR	RBI	BB	SO	AVG	OBP	SLG	PRO+	BR	/A	RC	SB	CS	SBR	FA	FR	POS	TPR
1984	LA-N	24	37	3	4	1	0	1	4	4	9	.108	.195	.216	16	-4	-4	2	1	0	0	1.000	-2	O	-0.6

■ MIKE BREWER
Brewer, Michael Quinn b: 10/24/59, Shreveport, La. BR/TR, 6′5″, 190 lbs. Deb: 6/11/86 F

YEAR	TM/L	G	AB	R	H	2B	3B	HR	RBI	BB	SO	AVG	OBP	SLG	PRO+	BR	/A	RC	SB	CS	SBR	FA	FR	POS	TPR
1986	KC-A	12	18	0	3	1	0	0	0	2	6	.167	.250	.222	29	-2	-2	1	0	1	-1	1.000	-2	/OD	-0.4

■ ROD BREWER
Brewer, Rodney Lee b: 2/24/66, Eustis, Fla. BL/TL, 6′3″, 210 lbs. Deb: 9/05/90

YEAR	TM/L	G	AB	R	H	2B	3B	HR	RBI	BB	SO	AVG	OBP	SLG	PRO+	BR	/A	RC	SB	CS	SBR	FA	FR	POS	TPR
1990	StL-N	14	25	4	6	1	0	0	2	0	4	.240	.240	.280	42	-2	-2	1	0	0	0	.981	1	/1	-0.2
1991	StL-N	19	13	0	1	0	0	0	1	0	5	.077	.077	.077	-56	-3	-3	0	0	0	0	1.000	-0	1/O	-0.3
1992	StL-N	29	103	11	31	6	0	0	10	8	12	.301	.357	.359	105	1	1	13	0	1	-1	1.000	1	1/O	-0.1
Total	3	62	141	15	38	7	0	0	13	8	21	.270	.313	.319	79	-4	-4	15	0	1	-1	.997	2	/1O	-0.6

■ CHARLIE BREWSTER
Brewster, Charles Lawrence b: 12/27/16, Marthaville, La. BR/TR, 5′8.5″, 175 lbs. Deb: 5/02/43

YEAR	TM/L	G	AB	R	H	2B	3B	HR	RBI	BB	SO	AVG	OBP	SLG	PRO+	BR	/A	RC	SB	CS	SBR	FA	FR	POS	TPR
1943	Cin-N	7	8	0	1	0	0	0	0	0	1	.125	.125	.125	-28	-1	-1	0	0			1.000	-0	/2	-0.1
	Phi-N	49	159	13	35	2	0	0	12	10	19	.220	.275	.233	49	-11	-10	11	1			.901	-20	S	-3.0
	Yr	56	167	13	36	2	0	0	12	10	20	.216	.268	.228	45	-12	-11	11	1			.901	-20	S/2	-3.1
1944	Chi-N	10	44	4	11	2	0	0	2	5	7	.250	.327	.295	76	-1	-1	4	0			.903	0	S	0.0
1946	Cle-A	3	2	0	0	0	0	0	0	1	1	.000	.333	.000	-1	-0	-0	0	0	0	0	1.000	0	/S	0.0
Total	3	69	213	17	47	4	0	0	14	16	28	.221	.281	.239	52	-13	-13	15	1	0		.902	-20	/S2	-3.1

■ FRITZ BRICKELL
Brickell, Fritz Darrell b: 3/19/35, Wichita, Kan. d: 10/15/65, Wichita, Kan. BR/TR, 5′5.5″, 157 lbs. Deb: 4/30/58 F

YEAR	TM/L	G	AB	R	H	2B	3B	HR	RBI	BB	SO	AVG	OBP	SLG	PRO+	BR	/A	RC	SB	CS	SBR	FA	FR	POS	TPR
1958	NY-A	2	0	0	0	0	0	0	0	0	0	—	—	—	—	0	0	0	0	0	0	1.000	0	/2	0.0
1959	NY-A	18	39	4	10	1	0	1	4	1	10	.256	.275	.359	75	-2	-1	4	0	0	0	.925	0	S/2	0.0
1961	LA-A	21	49	3	6	0	0	0	3	6	9	.122	.218	.122	-6	-7	-8	1	0	0	0	.901	0	S	-0.7
Total	3	41	88	7	16	1	0	1	7	7	19	.182	.242	.227	26	-9	-9	5	0	0	0	.911	0	/S2	-0.7

■ FRED BRICKELL
Brickell, George Frederick b: 11/9/06, Saffordville, Kan. d: 4/8/61, Wichita, Kan. BL/TR, 5′7″, 160 lbs. Deb: 8/19/26 F

YEAR	TM/L	G	AB	R	H	2B	3B	HR	RBI	BB	SO	AVG	OBP	SLG	PRO+	BR	/A	RC	SB	CS	SBR	FA	FR	POS	TPR
1926	Pit-N	24	55	11	19	3	1	0	4	3	6	.345	.400	.436	119	2	2	9	0			.920	-0	O	0.1
1927	*Pit-N	32	21	6	6	1	0	1	4	1	0	.286	.318	.476	103	0	-0	3	0			1.000	-1	/O	0.0
1928	Pit-N	81	202	34	65	4	4	3	41	20	18	.322	.383	.426	107	4	3	33	5			.958	1	O	0.1
1929	Pit-N	60	118	13	37	4	2	0	17	7	12	.314	.352	.381	80	-3	-4	15	3			1.000	0	O	-0.5
1930	Pit-N	68	219	36	65	9	3	1	14	15	20	.297	.342	.379	74	-9	-9	28	3			.951	-4	O	-1.5
	Phi-N	53	240	33	59	12	6	0	17	13	21	.246	.290	.346	49	-19	-21	24	1			.963	5	O	-1.9
	Yr	121	459	69	124	21	9	1	31	28	41	.270	.315	.362	61	-28	-30	51	4			.958	0	*O	-3.4
1931	Phi-N	130	514	77	130	14	5	1	31	42	39	.253	.316	.305	63	-22	-28	52	5			.978	4	*O	-3.3
1932	Phi-N	45	66	9	22	6	1	0	2	4	5	.333	.389	.455	112	3	2	12	2			.935	-0	O	0.1
1933	Phi-N	8	13	2	4	1	1	0	1	1	0	.308	.357	.538	136	1	1	3	0			1.000	1	/O	0.1
Total	8	501	1448	221	407	54	23	6	131	106	121	.281	.335	.363	75	-44	-55	178	19			.967	5	O	-6.8

YEAR	TM/L	G	AB	R	H	2B	3B	HR	RBI	BB	SO	AVG	OBP	SLG	PRO+	BR	/A	RC	SB	CS	SBR	FA	FR	POS	TPR

■ GEORGE BRICKLEY   Brickley, George Vincent b: 7/19/1894, Everett, Mass. d: 2/23/47, Everett, Mass. BR/TR, 5'9", 180 lbs. Deb: 9/26/13

| 1913 | Phi-A | 5 | 12 | 0 | 2 | 0 | 1 | 0 | 0 | 0 | 4 | .167 | .231 | .333 | 66 | -1 | -1 | 1 | 0 | | | 1.000 | -1 | /O | -0.2 |

■ JIM BRIDEWESER   Brideweser, James Ehrenfeld b: 2/13/27, Lancaster, Ohio d: 8/25/89, El Toro, Cal. BR/TR, 6', 165 lbs. Deb: 9/29/51

1951	NY-A	2	8	1	3	0	0	0	0	0	1	.375	.375	.375	107	0	0	1	0	0	0	.818	0	/S	0.0
1952	NY-A	42	38	12	10	0	0	0	2	3	5	.263	.317	.263	67	-2	-2	3	0	0	0	.935	2	S/23	0.1
1953	NY-A	7	3	3	3	0	1	0	3	1	0	1.000	1.000	1.667	631	2	2	5	0	0	0	.833	0	/S	0.3
1954	Bal-A	73	204	18	54	7	2	0	12	15	27	.265	.318	.319	81	-7	-5	20	1	1	-0	.944	-12	S2	-1.3
1955	Chi-A	34	58	6	12	3	2	0	4	3	7	.207	.246	.328	52	-4	-4	4	0	0	0	.949	6	S/32	0.3
1956	Chi-A	10	11	0	2	1	0	0	1	0	3	.182	.250	.273	37	-1	-1	1	0	0	0	.938	0	S	-0.1
	Det-A	70	156	23	34	4	0	0	10	20	19	.218	.307	.244	47	-11	-12	13	3	1	0	.987	14	S2/3	0.6
	Yr	80	167	23	36	5	0	0	11	20	22	.216	.303	.246	46	-12	-13	13	3	1	0	.979	14	S2/3	0.5
1957	Bal-A	91	142	16	38	7	1	1	18	21	15	.268	.362	.352	102	-0	1	19	2	0	1	.943	5	S/32	1.1
Total	7	329	620	79	156	22	6	1	50	63	77	.252	.323	.311	75	-23	-20	66	6	2	1	.946	15	S/23	1.0

■ ROCKY BRIDGES   Bridges, Everett Lamar b: 8/7/27, Refugio, Tex. BR/TR, 5'8", 175 lbs. Deb: 4/17/51 C

1951	Bro-N	63	134	13	34	7	0	1	15	10	10	.254	.306	.328	69	-6	-6	12	0	0	0	.871	3	32/S	-0.2
1952	Bro-N	51	56	9	11	3	0	0	2	7	9	.196	.286	.250	49	-4	-4	4	0	1	-1	.986	12	2S/3	0.8
1953	Cin-N	122	432	52	98	13	2	1	21	37	42	.227	.288	.273	47	-33	-33	35	6	3	0	.976	11	*2/S3	-1.6
1954	Cin-N	53	52	4	12	1	0	0	2	7	7	.231	.322	.250	50	-3	-4	4	0	1	-1	1.000	0	S23	0.7
1955	Cin-N	95	168	20	48	4	0	1	18	15	19	.286	.344	.327	75	-4	-6	19	1	1	-0	.965	7	3S/2	0.1
1956	Cin-N	71	19	9	4	0	0	0	1	4	3	.211	.348	.211	52	-1	-1	1	1	2	-1	.966	8	3/2SO	0.6
1957	Cin-N	5	1	1	0	0	0	0	0	1	1	.000	.500	.000	46	-0	0	0	0	0	0	1.000	-1	/2S3	-0.1
	Was-A	120	391	40	89	17	2	3	47	40	32	.228	.303	.304	67	-18	-17	34	0	2	-1	.971	29	*S2/3	2.2
1958	Was-A☆	116	377	38	99	14	3	5	28	27	32	.263	.317	.355	86	-8	-7	38	0	3	-2	.976	3	*S/23	0.4
1959	Det-A	116	381	38	102	16	3	3	35	30	35	.268	.323	.349	80	-8	-11	40	1	2	-1	.952	-6	*S/2	-0.8
1960	Det-A	10	5	0	1	0	0	0	0	0	0	.200	.200	.200	8	-1	-1	0	0	0	0	1.000	3	/3S	0.2
	Cle-A	10	27	1	9	0	0	0	3	1	2	.333	.357	.333	91	-0	-0	3	0	0	0	1.000	3	/S3	0.3
	Yr	20	32	1	10	0	0	0	3	1	2	.313	.333	.313	76	-1	-1	3	0	0	0	1.000	6	3S	0.5
	StL-N	3	0	0	0	0	0	0	0	0	0	—	—	—	—	0	0	0	0	0	0	1.000	1	/2	0.1
1961	LA-A	84	229	20	55	5	1	2	15	26	37	.240	.320	.297	59	-10	-14	23	1	0	0	.988	10	2S3	0.3
Total	11	919	2272	245	562	80	11	16	187	205	229	.247	.312	.313	67	-96	-103	215	10	15	-6	.968	95	S23/O	3.0

■ AL BRIDWELL   Bridwell, Albert Henry b: 1/4/1884, Friendship, Ohio d: 1/23/69, Portsmouth, Ohio BL/TR, 5'9", 170 lbs. Deb: 4/16/05

1905	Cin-N	82	254	17	64	3	1	0	17	19		.252	.309	.272	67	-8	-11	26	8			.944	0	30/2S1	-1.0
1906	Bos-N	120	459	41	104	9	1	0	22	44		.227	.297	.251	73	-14	-13	39	6			.930	17	*S/O	0.9
1907	Bos-N	140	509	49	111	8	2	0	26	61		.218	.309	.242	73	-13	-13	46	17			.942	7	*S	-0.3
1908	NY-N	147	467	53	133	14	1	0	46	52		.285	.363	.319	113	12	9	63	20			.933	11	*S	2.7
1909	NY-N	145	476	59	140	11	5	0	55	67		.294	.386	.338	123	17	16	75	32			.940	2	*S	2.3
1910	NY-N	142	492	74	136	15	7	0	48	73	23	.276	.374	.335	107	8	7	68	14			.946	6	*S	2.0
1911	NY-N	76	263	28	71	10	1	0	31	33	10	.270	.358	.316	86	-3	-4	33	8			.917	6	S	0.7
	Bos-N	51	182	29	53	5	0	0	10	33	8	.291	.403	.319	95	3	1	25	2			.950	-11	S	-0.7
	Yr	127	445	57	124	15	1	0	41	66	18	.279	.377	.317	90	-0	-3	59	10			.929	-5	*S	0.0
1912	Bos-N	31	106	6	25	5	1	0	14	5	5	.236	.270	.302	55	-7	-7	9	2			.936	-6	S	-1.0
1913	Chi-N	136	405	35	97	6	6	1	37	74	28	.240	.358	.291	86	-3	-4	47	12			.948	2	*S	1.1
1914	StL-F	117	381	46	90	6	5	1	33	71	18	.236	.359	.286	80	-4	-7	47	9			.944	-11	*S2	-1.0
1915	StL-F	65	175	20	40	3	2	0	19	25	21	.229	.328	.269	72	-4	-5	16	8			.952	1	23/1	-0.3
Total	11	1252	4169	457	1064	95	32	2	348	557	98	.255	.347	.295	90	-17	-30	499	136			.939	23	*S/2301	5.4

■ BUNNY BRIEF   Brief, Anthony Vincent (b: Antonio Bordetzki) b: 7/3/1892, Remus, Mich. d: 2/10/63, Milwaukee, Wis. BR/TR, 6', 185 lbs. Deb: 9/22/12

1912	StL-A	15	42	9	13	3	0	0	5	6		.310	.408	.381	131	2	2	8	2			.826	-1	/O1	0.0
1913	StL-A	85	258	24	56	11	6	1	26	21	46	.217	.284	.318	78	-9	-8	24	3			.986	-1	1/O	-1.0
1915	Chi-A	48	154	13	33	6	2	2	17	16	28	.214	.305	.318	84	-3	-3	16	8	6	-1	.986	-2	1	-0.8
1917	Pit-N	36	115	15	25	5	1	2	11	15	21	.217	.318	.330	96	0	-0	14	4			.988	2	1	0.0
Total	4	184	569	61	127	25	9	5	59	58	95	.223	.306	.325	87	-9	-9	62	17	6		.987	-2	1/O	-1.8

■ CHARLIE BRIGGS   Briggs, Charles R. b: 1861, Batavia, Ill. 5'7", 170 lbs. Deb: 5/02/1884

| 1884 | CP-U | 49 | 182 | 29 | 31 | 8 | 2 | 1 | | 11 | | .170 | .218 | .253 | 59 | -7 | -7 | 10 | | | | .814 | -5 | O2/S | -1.1 |

■ DAN BRIGGS   Briggs, Dan Lee b: 11/18/52, Scotia, Cal. BL/TL, 6', 180 lbs. Deb: 9/10/75

1975	Cal-A	13	31	3	7	1	0	1	3	2	6	.226	.273	.355	82	-1	-1	2	0	2	-1	.953	-1	/10D	-0.4
1976	Cal-A	77	248	19	53	13	2	1	14	13	47	.214	.256	.294	65	-13	-11	17	0	3	-2	.993	-0	1O/D	-1.8
1977	Cal-A	59	74	6	12	2	0	1	4	8	14	.162	.244	.230	31	-7	-7	4	0	0	0	.993	0	1O	-0.7
1978	Cle-A	15	49	4	8	0	1	1	1	4	9	.163	.226	.265	38	-4	-4	3	0	0	0	1.000	2	O	-0.3
1979	SD-N	104	227	34	47	4	3	8	30	18	45	.207	.280	.357	77	-9	-7	23	2	1	0	.986	5	1O	-0.6
1981	Mon-N	9	11	0	1	0	0	0	0	0	3	.091	.091	.091	-48	-2	-2	0	0	1	-1	1.000	1	1/O	-0.2
1982	Chi-N	48	48	1	6	0	0	0	1	0	9	.125	.143	.125	-24	-8	-8	1	0	0	0	.875	1	O/1	-0.8
Total	7	325	688	67	134	20	6	12	53	45	133	.195	.251	.294	56	-44	-40	50	2	7	-4	.989	8	1O/D	-4.8

■ GRANT BRIGGS   Briggs, Grant b: 3/16/1865, Pittsburgh, Pa. d: 5/31/28, Pittsburgh, Pa. Deb: 4/17/1890

1890	Syr-a	86	316	44	57	6	5	0		16		.180	.222	.231	39	-26	-21	18	7			.928	-4	CO/3S	-1.9
1891	Lou-a	1	4	0	1	0	0	0	0	0	0	.250	.250	.250	46	-0	-0	0	0			1.000	-0	/C	0.0
1892	StL-N	22	55	2	4	1	0	0	1	5	16	.073	.164	.091	-23	-8	-7	1	2			.902	-9	C/O	-1.5
1895	Lou-N	1	3	0	0	0	0	0	0	0	1	.000	.000	.000	-99	-1	-1	0	0			1.000	-1	/C	-0.1
Total	4	110	378	46	62	7	5	0	1	21	17	.164	.212	.209	29	-35	-29	20	9			.925	-13	/CO3S	-3.5

■ JOHN BRIGGS   Briggs, John Edward b: 3/10/44, Paterson, N.J. BL/TL, 6'1", 195 lbs. Deb: 4/17/64

1964	Phi-N	61	66	16	17	2	0	1	6	9	12	.258	.347	.333	94	-0	-0	8	1	1	-0	.957	1	O/1	0.0
1965	Phi-N	93	229	47	54	9	4	4	23	42	44	.236	.354	.362	104	2	3	33	3	2	-0	.982	-2	O	-0.2
1966	Phi-N	81	255	43	72	13	5	10	23	41	55	.282	.382	.490	140	15	15	50	3	2	-0	.977	-7	O	0.4
1967	Phi-N	106	332	47	77	12	4	9	30	41	72	.232	.316	.373	96	-1	-2	40	3	5	-2	.979	-5	O	-1.4
1968	Phi-N	110	338	36	86	13	1	7	31	58	72	.254	.365	.361	119	10	10	49	8	5	-1	.968	-3	O1	0.1
1969	Phi-N	124	361	51	86	20	3	12	46	64	78	.238	.353	.410	116	7	9	56	9	6	-1	.971	1	*O/1	0.3
1970	Phi-N	110	341	43	92	15	7	9	47	39	65	.270	.345	.434	110	3	4	48	5	4	-0	.980	5	O/1	0.3
1971	Phi-N	10	22	3	4	1	0	0	3	6	2	.182	.357	.227	69	-1	-1	2	0	0	0	.846	-1	/O	-0.2
	Mil-A	125	375	51	99	11	1	21	59	71	79	.264	.383	.467	141	21	22	71	1	2	-0	.958	1	O1	1.4
1972	Mil-A	135	418	58	111	14	1	21	65	54	67	.266	.351	.455	141	20	20	67	1	2	-1	.980	-2	*O1	1.2
1973	Mil-A	142	488	72	120	20	7	18	57	87	83	.246	.362	.426	124	16	17	80	15	9	-1	.968	7	*O/D	1.7
1974	Mil-A	144	554	72	140	30	8	17	73	71	102	.253	.338	.428	120	13	14	82	9	7	-2	.973	5	*O/D	1.2
1975	Mil-A	28	74	12	22	1	0	3	5	20	13	.297	.447	.432	149	6	6	15	0	2	-0	.962	2	O/D	0.6
	Min-A	87	264	44	61	9	2	7	39	60	41	.231	.373	.360	106	5	4	41	6	2	-1	.983	7	1O/D	0.8
	Yr	115	338	56	83	10	2	10	44	80	54	.246	.390	.376	115	11	11	56	6	4	-1	.983	9	O1/D	1.4
Total	12	1366	4117	601	1041	170	43	139	507	663	785	.253	.357	.416	121	116	121	643	64	49	-10	.973	10	*O1/D	6.2

YEAR	TM/L	G	AB	R	H	2B	3B	HR	RBI	BB	SO	AVG	OBP	SLG	PRO+	BR	/A	RC	SB	CS	SBR	FA	FR	POS	TPR
■ HARRY BRIGHT Bright, Harry James b: 9/22/29, Kansas City, Mo. BR/TR, 6', 190 lbs. Deb: 8/07/58																									
1958	Pit-N	15	24	4	6	1	0	1	3	1	6	.250	.280	.417	84	-1	-1	3	0	0	0	1.000	0	/3	0.0
1959	Pit-N	40	48	4	12	1	0	3	8	5	10	.250	.321	.458	105	0	0	7	0	0	0	1.000	-2	/O32	-0.2
1960	Pit-N	4	4	0	0	0	0	0	0	0	2	.000	.000	.000	-99	-1	-1	0	0	0	0	.000	0	H	-0.1
1961	Was-A	72	183	20	44	6	0	4	21	19	23	.240	.312	.339	75	-7	-6	18	0	2	-1	.928	7	3/C2	0.0
1962	Was-A	113	392	55	107	15	4	17	67	26	51	.273	.321	.462	109	3	3	54	2	1	0	.989	-1	1/C3	-0.4
1963	Cin-N	1	1	0	0	0	0	0	0	0	1	.000	.000	.000	-97	-0	-0	0	0	0	0	1.000	-0	/1	0.0
	*NY-A	60	157	15	37	7	0	7	23	13	31	.236	.298	.414	98	-1	-1	19	0	0	0	.985	-5	13	-0.7
1964	NY-A	4	5	0	1	0	0	0	0	1	1	.200	.333	.200	52	-0	-0	0	0	0	0	1.000	-0	/1	-0.1
1965	Chi-N	27	25	1	7	1	0	0	4	0	8	.280	.280	.320	67	-1	-1	2	0	0	0	.000	0	H	-0.1
Total	8	336	839	99	214	31	4	32	126	65	133	.255	.311	.416	96	-8	-7	104	2	3	-1	.988	-1	1/3CO2	-1.6
■ GREG BRILEY Briley, Gregory "Peewee" b: 5/24/65, Greenville, N.C. BL/TR, 5'9", 175 lbs. Deb: 6/27/88																									
1988	Sea-A	13	36	6	9	2	0	1	4	5	6	.250	.341	.389	100	0	0	5	0	1	-1	.929	-2	O	-0.3
1989	Sea-A	115	394	52	105	22	4	13	52	39	82	.266	.340	.442	115	9	8	59	11	5	0	.958	-5	*O2/D	0.1
1990	Sea-A	125	337	40	83	18	2	5	29	37	48	.246	.323	.356	89	-4	-5	41	16	4	2	.989	-4	*O/D	-0.9
1991	Sea-A	139	381	39	99	17	3	2	26	27	51	.260	.309	.336	78	-11	-11	39	23	11	0	.980	-17	*O/23D	-3.0
1992	Sea-A	86	200	18	55	10	0	5	12	4	31	.275	.293	.400	92	-3	-3	23	9	2	2	.967	-9	OD/23	-1.1
Total	5	478	1348	155	351	69	9	26	123	112	218	.260	.320	.383	94	-9	-11	167	59	23	4	.974	-36	O/D23	-5.2
■ BILL BRINKER Brinker, William Hutchinson "Dode" b: 8/30/1883, Warrensburg, Mo. d: 2/5/65, Arcadia, Cal. BB/TR, 6'1", 190 lbs. Deb: 4/24/12																									
1912	Phi-N	9	18	1	4	1	0	0	2	2	3	.222	.300	.278	55	-1	-1	1	0			.778	-1	/3O	-0.2
■ CHUCK BRINKMAN Brinkman, Charles Ernest b: 9/16/44, Cincinnati, O. BR/TR, 6'1", 185 lbs. Deb: 7/10/69 F																									
1969	Chi-A	14	15	2	1	0	0	0	0	1	5	.067	.125	.067	-43	-3	-3	0	0	0	0	1.000	1	C	-0.2
1970	Chi-A	9	20	4	5	1	0	0	0	3	3	.250	.348	.300	77	-0	-1	2	0	0	0	.974	1	/C	0.1
1971	Chi-A	15	20	0	4	0	0	0	1	3	5	.200	.304	.200	44	-1	-1	1	0	0	0	1.000	2	C	0.1
1972	Chi-A	35	52	1	7	0	0	0	0	4	7	.135	.196	.135	-0	-6	-6	1	0	0	0	.985	7	C	0.2
1973	Chi-A	63	139	13	26	6	0	1	10	11	37	.187	.252	.252	41	-11	-11	9	0	0	0	.987	10	C	0.0
1974	Chi-A	8	14	1	2	0	0	0	0	1	3	.143	.200	.143	-0	-2	-2	0	0	0	0	1.000	-1	/C	-0.3
	Pit-N	4	7	1	1	0	0	0	1	0	0	.143	.143	.143	-21	-1	-1	0	0	0	0	1.000	-0	/C	-0.1
Total	6	148	267	22	46	7	0	1	12	23	60	.172	.241	.210	28	-25	-26	15	0	0	0	.988	20	C	-0.2
■ ED BRINKMAN Brinkman, Edwin Albert b: 12/8/41, Cincinnati, O. BR/TR, 6', 170 lbs. Deb: 9/06/61 FC																									
1961	Was-A	4	11	0	1	0	0	0	0	1	1	.091	.167	.091	-30	-2	-2	0	0	0	0	.889	0	/3	-0.2
1962	Was-A	54	133	8	22	7	1	0	4	11	28	.165	.229	.233	25	-14	-14	6	1	0	0	.942	2	S3	-0.9
1963	Was-A	145	514	44	117	20	3	7	45	31	86	.228	.277	.319	67	-23	-23	46	5	3	-0	.950	7	*S	-0.7
1964	Was-A	132	447	54	100	20	3	8	34	26	99	.224	.273	.336	68	-20	-20	41	2	2	-1	.969	-3	*S	-1.5
1965	Was-A	154	444	35	82	13	2	5	35	38	82	.185	.252	.257	46	-32	-31	28	1	2	-1	.964	4	*S	-2.1
1966	Was-A	158	582	42	133	18	9	7	48	29	105	.229	.265	.326	70	-24	-23	45	7	9	-3	.965	12	*S	-0.1
1967	Was-A	109	320	21	60	9	2	1	18	24	58	.188	.253	.237	47	-21	-20	20	1	3	-2	**.979**	14	*S	0.1
1968	Was-A	77	193	12	36	3	0	0	6	19	31	.187	.259	.202	43	-13	-13	10	0	0	0	.967	3	S/2O	-0.4
1969	Was-A	151	576	71	153	18	5	2	43	50	42	.266	.330	.325	88	-12	-8	59	2	2	-1	.976	15	*S	2.3
1970	Was-A	158	625	63	164	17	2	1	40	60	41	.262	.332	.301	79	-19	-15	62	8	9	-3	.974	31	*S	3.3
1971	Det-A	159	527	40	120	18	2	1	37	44	54	.228	.296	.275	60	-25	-28	42	1	4	-2	.980	12	*S	0.2
1972	*Det-A	156	516	42	105	19	1	6	49	38	51	.203	.262	.279	59	-25	-27	37	0	0	0	**.990**	2	*S	-0.3
1973	Det-A★	162	515	55	122	16	4	7	40	34	79	.237	.285	.324	67	-20	-24	44	0	1	-1	.968	-13	*S	-1.8
1974	Det-A	153	502	55	111	15	3	14	54	29	71	.221	.268	.347	73	-17	-19	45	2	0	1	.972	13	*S/3	1.4
1975	StL-N	28	75	6	18	4	0	1	6	7	10	.240	.313	.333	77	-2	-2	7	0	0	0	.948	0	S	0.0
	Tex-A	1	2	0	0	0	0	0	0	0	1	.000	.000	.000	-99	-1	-1	0	0	0	0	1.000	-0	/3	-0.1
	NY-A	44	63	2	11	4	1	0	2	3	6	.175	.224	.270	40	-5	-5	3	0	0	0	.933	-3	S/23	-0.6
	Yr	45	65	2	11	4	1	0	2	3	7	.169	.217	.262	36	-6	-6	3	0	0	0	.933	-3	S/32	-0.7
Total	15	1845	6045	550	1355	201	38	60	461	444	845	.224	.282	.300	65	-276	-275	497	30	35	-12	.970	94	*S/32O	-1.4
■ LEON BRINKOPF Brinkopf, Leon Clarence b: 10/20/26, Cape Girardeau, Mo BR/TR, 5'11.5", 185 lbs. Deb: 4/18/52																									
1952	Chi-N	9	22	1	4	0	0	0	2	4	5	.182	.308	.182	38	-2	-2	2	0	0	0	.955	-2	/S	-0.4
■ FATTY BRIODY Briody, Charles F. "Alderman" b: 8/13/1858, Lansingburg, N.Y. d: 6/22/03, Chicago, Ill. TR , 5'8.5", 190 lbs. Deb: 6/16/1880																									
1880	Tro-N	1	4	0	0	0	0	0	0	0	0	.000	.000	.000	-95	-1	-1	0				.700	-1	/C	-0.2
1882	Cle-N	53	194	30	50	13	0	0	13	9	13	.258	.291	.325	100	-1	0	19				.902	2	C	0.3
1883	Cle-N	40	145	23	34	5	1	0	10	3	13	.234	.250	.283	62	-7	-6	11				.900	4	C/213	-0.1
1884	Cle-N	43	148	17	25	6	0	1	12	6	19	.169	.201	.230	34	-11	-12	7				.922	10	C/O	0.2
	Cin-U	22	89	11	30	2	2	0		1		.337	.344	.404	141	5	3	13				.943	17	C	1.8
1885	StL-N	62	215	14	42	9	0	1	17	12	23	.195	.238	.251	62	-10	-8	13				.893	-9	C/O32	-1.1
1886	KC-N	56	215	14	51	10	3	0	29	3	35	.237	.248	.312	65	-8	-10	17	0			.919	1	C/O1	-0.3
1887	Det-N	33	128	24	29	6	1	1	26	9	10	.227	.283	.313	64	-6	-6	13	6			.907	6	C	0.2
1888	KC-a	13	48	1	10	1	0	0	8	1		.208	.224	.229	45	-3	-3	3	0			.896	-4	C	-0.5
Total	8	323	1186	134	271	52	7	3	115	44	113	.228	.257	.292	70	-40	-42	95	6			.910	25	C/2013	0.3
■ GEORGE BRISTOW Bristow, George T. b: 5/1870, Paw Paw, Ill. TR , Deb: 4/15/1899																									
1899	Cle-N	3	8	0	1	1	0	0	0	0		.125	.222	.250	32	-1	-1	0	0			1.000	0	/O	-0.1
■ BERNARDO BRITO Brito, Bernardo b: 12/4/63, San Cristobal, D.R. BR/TR, 6'1", 190 lbs. Deb: 9/15/92																									
1992	Min-A	8	14	1	2	1	0	0	2	0	4	.143	.143	.214	-1	-2	-2	0	0	1	-1	.750	-1	/OD	-0.4
■ GUS BRITTAIN Brittain, August Schuster b: 11/29/09, Wilmington, N.C. d: 2/16/74, Wilmington, N.C. BR/TR, 5'10", 192 lbs. Deb: 7/22/37																									
1937	Cin-N	3	6	0	1	0	0	0	0	0	3	.167	.167	.167	-10	-1	-1	0	0			1.000	-0	/C	-0.1
■ GIL BRITTON Britton, Stephen Gilbert b: 9/21/1891, Parsons, Kan. d: 6/20/83, Parsons, Kan. BR/TR, 5'10", 160 lbs. Deb: 9/20/13																									
1913	Pit-N	3	12	0	0	0	0	0	0	0	2	.000	.000	.000	-99	-3	-3	0	0			.824	-1	/S	-0.4
■ GREG BROCK Brock, Gregory Allen b: 6/14/57, McMinnville, Ore. BL/TR, 6'3", 205 lbs. Deb: 9/01/82																									
1982	LA-N	18	17	1	2	1	0	0	1	1	5	.118	.167	.176	-4	-2	-2	1	0	0	0	1.000	-0	/1	-0.3
1983	*LA-N	146	455	64	102	14	2	20	66	83	81	.224	.345	.396	105	4	5	64	5	1	1	.991	5	*1	0.3
1984	LA-N	88	271	33	61	6	0	14	34	39	37	.225	.323	.402	104	1	1	37	8	0	2	.995	7	1	0.7
1985	*LA-N	129	438	64	110	19	0	21	66	54	72	.251	.333	.438	118	8	9	65	4	2	0	.994	2	*1	0.4
1986	LA-N	115	325	33	76	13	0	16	52	37	60	.234	.312	.422	108	-1	2	42	2	5	-2	.996	12	1	0.6
1987	Mil-A	141	532	81	159	29	3	13	85	57	63	.299	.373	.438	111	12	10	88	5	4	-1	.993	4	*1	0.2
1988	Mil-A	115	364	53	77	16	1	6	50	63	48	.212	.333	.310	81	-7	-8	39	6	2	1	.993	9	*1/D	-0.7
1989	Mil-A	107	373	40	99	16	0	12	52	43	49	.265	.346	.405	112	6	6	53	6	1	1	.995	-5	*1/D	-0.5
1990	Mil-A	123	367	42	91	23	0	7	50	43	45	.248	.330	.368	96	-2	-2	46	4	2	0	.995	-4	*1	-1.4
1991	Mil-A	31	60	9	17	4	0	1	6	14	9	.283	.419	.400	131	3	3	11	1	1	-0	1.000	-1	1	0.1
Total	10	1013	3202	420	794	141	6	110	462	434	469	.248	.340	.399	105	21	25	446	41	18	2	.994	29	1/D	-0.6

YEAR	TM/L	G	AB	R	H	2B	3B	HR	RBI	BB	SO	AVG	OBP	SLG	PRO+	BR	/A	RC	SB	CS	SBR	FA	FR	POS	TPR
■ JOHN BROCK Brock, John Roy b: 10/16/1896, Hamilton, Ill. d: 10/27/51, Clayton, Mo. BR/TR, 5'6.5", 165 lbs. Deb: 8/10/17																									
1917	StL-N	7	15	4	6	1	0	0	2	0	2	.400	.400	.467	170	1	1	3	2			.944	-1	/C	0.1
1918	StL-N	27	52	9	11	2	0	0	4	3	10	.212	.255	.250	56	-3	-3	4	5			.951	-2	C/O	-0.3
Total	2	34	67	13	17	3	0	0	6	3	12	.254	.286	.299	81	-2	-2	8	7			.949	-2	/CO	-0.2
■ LOU BROCK Brock, Louis Clark b: 6/18/39, ElDorado, Ark. BL/TL, 5'11.5", 170 lbs. Deb: 9/10/61 H																									
1961	Chi-N	4	11	1	1	0	0	0	0	1	3	.091	.167	.091	-29	-2	-2	0	0	0	0	.750	-0	/O	-0.3
1962	Chi-N	123	434	73	114	24	7	9	35	35	96	.263	.322	.412	92	-3	-5	58	16	7	1	.965	-4	*O	-1.5
1963	Chi-N	148	547	79	141	19	11	9	37	31	122	.258	.302	.382	91	-4	-7	64	24	12	0	.973	11	*O	-0.4
1964	Chi-N	52	215	30	54	9	2	2	14	13	40	.251	.300	.340	77	-6	-7	23	10	3	1	.959	-0	O	-0.9
	*StL-N	103	419	81	146	21	9	12	44	27	87	.348	.391	.527	143	30	26	86	33	15	1	.949	0	*O	2.3
	Yr	155	634	111	200	30	11	14	58	40	127	.315	.360	.464	121	24	19	107	43	18	2	.953	-0	*O	1.4
1965	StL-N	155	631	107	182	35	8	16	69	45	116	.288	.345	.445	110	17	10	99	63	27	3	.959	1	*O	0.7
1966	StL-N	156	643	94	183	24	12	15	46	31	134	.285	.321	.429	106	4	4	91	**74**	18	**11**	.936	-2	*O	0.6
1967	*StL-N★	159	689	**113**	206	32	12	21	76	24	109	.299	.328	.472	128	21	21	106	**52**	18	5	.956	-1	*O	1.9
1968	*StL-N	159	660	92	184	**46**	**14**	6	51	46	124	.279	.329	.418	125	17	18	98	**62**	12	**11**	.952	-5	*O	1.8
1969	StL-N	157	655	97	195	33	10	12	47	50	115	.298	.349	.434	118	15	15	105	**53**	14	8	.949	-7	*O	0.7
1970	StL-N	155	664	114	202	29	5	13	57	60	99	.304	.363	.422	107	9	7	105	51	15	6	.962	-8	*O	-0.2
1971	StL-N★	157	640	**126**	200	37	7	7	61	76	107	.313	.386	.425	125	27	24	114	**64**	19	**8**	.951	-11	*O	1.3
1972	StL-N☆	153	621	81	193	26	8	3	42	47	93	.311	.360	.393	115	11	12	93	**63**	18	8	.952	-7	*O	0.7
1973	StL-N	160	650	110	193	29	8	7	63	71	112	.297	.366	.398	112	12	12	101	**70**	20	9	.963	-7	*O	0.7
1974	StL-N★	153	635	105	194	25	7	3	48	61	88	.306	.368	.381	111	9	10	98	**118**	33	**16**	.967	-3	*O	1.6
1975	StL-N★	136	528	78	163	27	6	3	47	38	64	.309	.359	.400	106	7	5	79	56	16	7	.966	-2	*O	0.5
1976	StL-N	133	498	73	150	24	5	4	67	35	75	.301	.348	.394	109	6	6	65	56	19	5	.983	-7	*O	-0.1
1977	StL-N	141	489	69	133	22	6	2	46	30	74	.272	.317	.354	81	-14	-13	52	35	24	-4	.954	-20	*O	-4.3
1978	StL-N	92	298	31	66	9	0	0	12	17	29	.221	.263	.252	45	-22	-21	21	17	5	2	.975	-11	O	-3.7
1979	StL-N★	120	405	56	123	15	4	5	38	23	43	.304	.346	.398	101	1	1	54	21	12	-1	.958	-14	O	-1.9
Total	19	2616	10332	1610	3023	486	141	149	900	761	1730	.293	.344	.410	109	135	114	1512	938	307	97	.959	-98	*O	-0.5
■ MATT BRODERICK Broderick, Matthew Thomas b: 12/1/1877, Lattimer, Pa. d: 2/26/40, Freeland, Pa. BR/TR, 5'6.5", 135 lbs. Deb: 5/01/03																									
1903	Bro-N	2	2	0	0	0	0	0	0	0		.000	.000	.000	-99	-1	-1	0	0			1.000	0	/2	0.0
■ STEVE BRODIE Brodie, Walter Scott b: 9/11/1868, Warronton, Va. d: 10/30/35, Baltimore, Md. BL/TR, 5'11", 180 lbs. Deb: 4/21/1890																									
1890	Bos-N	132	514	77	152	19	9	0	67	66	20	.296	.387	.368	114	18	11	87	29			**.953**	3	*O	0.9
1891	Bos-N	133	523	84	136	13	6	2	78	63	39	.260	.351	.319	87	1	-9	69	25			.951	10	*O	-0.3
1892	StL-N	154	602	85	152	10	9	4	60	52	31	.252	.316	.319	99	-4	0	71	28			.943	8	*O2/3	0.3
1893	StL-N	107	469	71	149	16	8	2	79	33	16	.318	.376	.399	108	6	5	88	41			.951	9	*O	0.8
	Bal-N	25	97	18	35	7	2	0	19	12	2	.361	.446	.474	145	7	7	25	8			.963	-3	O	0.2
	Yr	132	566	89	184	23	10	2	98	45	18	.325	.389	.412	114	13	12	112	49			.953	6	*O	1.0
1894	*Bal-N	129	573	134	210	25	11	3	113	18	8	.366	.399	.464	105	9	4	128	42			.950	-6	*O	-0.8
1895	*Bal-N	131	528	85	184	27	10	2	134	26	15	.348	.394	.449	116	15	12	111	35			.965	5	*O	0.6
1896	*Bal-N	132	516	98	153	19	11	2	87	36	17	.297	.363	.388	98	1	-1	84	25			.972	11	*O	-0.1
1897	Pit-N	100	370	47	108	7	12	2	53	25		.292	.348	.392	99	-3	-1	57	11			**.983**	-0	*O	-0.7
1898	Pit-N	42	156	15	41	5	0	0	21	6		.263	.303	.295	73	-6	-5	16	3			.958	3	O	-0.5
	Bal-N	23	98	12	30	3	2	0	19	5		.306	.346	.378	105	1	0	14	3			.923	3	O	0.1
	Yr	65	254	27	71	8	2	0	40	11		.280	.320	.327	86	-5	-5	30	6			.946	6	O	-0.4
1899	Bal-N	137	531	82	164	26	1	3	87	31		.309	.373	.379	101	6	1	86	19			**.979**	1	*O	-0.7
1901	Bal-A	83	306	41	95	6	6	2	41	25		.310	.376	.389	107	6	4	51	9			.963	-3	O	-0.5
1902	NY-N	109	416	37	117	8	2	3	42	22		.281	.328	.332	104	2	2	51	11			.953	7	*O	0.1
Total	12	1437	5699	886	1726	191	89	25	900	420	148	.303	.364	.381	104	56	31	938	289			.959	48	*O/23	-0.6
■ RICO BROGNA Brogna, Rico Joseph b: 4/18/70, Turners Falls, Mass BL/TL, 6'2", 202 lbs. Deb: 8/08/92																									
1992	Det-A	9	26	3	5	1	0	1	3	3	5	.192	.276	.346	72	-1	-1	3	0	0	0	.982	1	/1D	-0.1
■ JACK BROHAMER Brohamer, John Anthony b: 2/26/50, Maywood, Cal. BL/TR, 5'10", 165 lbs. Deb: 4/18/72																									
1972	Cle-A	136	527	49	123	13	2	5	35	27	46	.233	.272	.294	66	-21	-23	42	3	2	-0	.977	6	*2/3	-1.1
1973	Cle-A	102	300	29	66	12	1	4	29	32	23	.220	.295	.307	69	-12	-13	28	0	2	-1	.971	17	2	0.8
1974	Cle-A	101	315	33	85	11	1	2	30	26	22	.270	.331	.330	92	-3	-3	36	2	1	0	.987	-4	2	-0.3
1975	Cle-A	69	217	15	53	5	0	6	16	14	14	.244	.290	.350	80	-6	-6	21	2	2	-1	.976	4	2	0.0
1976	Chi-A	119	354	33	89	12	2	7	40	44	28	.251	.339	.356	103	2	2	43	1	3	-2	.984	18	*2/3	2.7
1977	Chi-A	59	152	26	39	10	3	2	20	21	8	.257	.351	.401	105	1	1	23	0	0	0	.923	2	32/D	0.4
1978	Bos-A	81	244	34	57	14	1	1	25	25	13	.234	.305	.311	67	-8	-12	23	1	3	-2	.974	-3	3D2	-1.6
1979	Bos-A	64	192	25	51	7	1	1	11	15	15	.266	.319	.328	71	-7	-8	18	0	3	-2	.982	0	23	-0.8
1980	Bos-A	21	57	5	18	2	0	1	6	4	3	.316	.361	.404	104	1	0	8	0	0	0	.900	-1	3/2D	-0.1
	Cle-A	53	142	13	32	5	1	1	15	14	6	.225	.295	.296	62	-7	-7	12	0	1	-1	.979	-4	2/D	-0.9
	Yr	74	199	18	50	7	1	2	21	18	9	.251	.313	.327	74	-6	-7	19	0	1	-1	.981	-5	23/D	-1.0
Total	9	805	2500	262	613	91	12	30	227	222	178	.245	.309	.327	79	-60	-67	253	9	17	-8	.979	33	23/D	-0.9
■ HERMAN BRONKIE Bronkie, Herman Charles "Dutch" b: 3/31/1885, S.Manchester, Conn d: 5/27/68, Somers, Conn. BR/TR, 5'9", 165 lbs. Deb: 9/20/10																									
1910	Cle-A	5	9	1	2	0	0	0	0	1		.222	.300	.222	63	-0	-0	1	1			.625	-1	/3S	-0.2
1911	Cle-A	2	6	0	1	0	0	0	0	0		.167	.167	.167	-7	-1	-1	0	0			1.000	-1	/3	-0.2
1912	Cle-A	6	16	1	0	0	0	0	0	1		.000	.059	.000	-80	-4	-4	0	0			.917	2	/3	-0.2
1914	Chi-N	1	1	1	1	1	0	0	1	0	0	1.000	1.000	2.000	786	1	1	2	0			.000	-0	/3	0.0
1918	StL-N	18	68	7	15	3	0	1	7	2	4	.221	.243	.309	70	-3	-3	5	0			.984	-1	3	-0.3
1919	StL-A	67	196	23	50	6	4	0	14	23	23	.255	.336	.327	84	-3	-4	22	2			.939	4	32/1	0.2
1922	StL-A	23	64	7	18	4	1	0	2	6	7	.281	.343	.375	84	-1	-2	8	0	2	-1	.917	-0	3	-0.2
Total	7	122	360	40	87	14	5	1	24	33	34	.242	.307	.317	75	-11	-12	38	3	2		.931	2	/321S	-0.9
■ TOM BROOKENS Brookens, Thomas Dale b: 8/10/53, Chambersburg, Pa. BR/TR, 5'10", 170 lbs. Deb: 7/10/79																									
1979	Det-A	60	190	23	50	5	2	4	21	11	40	.263	.310	.374	81	-5	-5	23	10	3	1	.945	11	32	0.7
1980	Det-A	151	509	64	140	25	9	10	66	32	71	.275	.319	.418	98	-1	-2	64	13	11	-3	.931	4	*3/2SD	-0.3
1981	Det-A	71	239	19	58	10	1	4	25	14	43	.243	.290	.343	79	-6	-7	23	5	3	-0	.952	-4	3	-1.4
1982	Det-A	140	398	40	92	15	3	9	58	27	63	.231	.280	.352	72	-16	-16	36	5	9	-4	.939	10	*32/SO	-1.1
1983	Det-A	138	332	50	71	13	3	6	32	29	46	.214	.281	.325	68	-15	-14	32	10	4	1	.928	5	*3S2/D	-0.8
1984	*Det-A	113	224	32	55	11	4	5	26	19	33	.246	.307	.397	94	-2	-2	27	6	6	-2	.969	20	3S2/D	1.8
1985	Det-A	156	485	54	115	34	6	7	47	27	78	.237	.277	.375	77	-17	-16	50	14	5	1	.943	3	*3/S2CD	-1.4
1986	Det-A	98	281	42	76	11	2	3	25	20	42	.270	.321	.356	84	-6	-6	32	11	8	-2	.955	2	32SD/O	-0.5
1987	*Det-A	143	444	59	107	15	3	13	59	33	63	.241	.296	.376	80	-15	-13	49	7	4	-0	.954	2	*3S2	-1.0
1988	Det-A	136	441	62	107	23	5	5	38	44	74	.243	.316	.351	90	-8	-5	49	4	4	-1	.952	-3	*3/S2	-1.1
1989	NY-A	66	168	14	38	6	0	4	14	11	27	.226	.274	.333	71	-7	-7	14	1	3	-2	.926	-4	3/S2OD	-1.2
1990	Cle-A	64	154	18	41	7	2	1	20	14	25	.266	.327	.357	92	-2	-2	18	0	0	0	.923	4	32/S1D	0.3
Total	12	1336	3865	477	950	175	40	71	431	281	605	.246	.299	.367	83	-99	-95	417	86	60	-10	.943	49	*32S/DO1C	-6.0

YEAR	TM/L	G	AB	R	H	2B	3B	HR	RBI	BB	SO	AVG	OBP	SLG	PRO+	BR	/A	RC	SB	CS	SBR	FA	FR	POS	TPR
■ HARRY BROOKS Brooks, Harry Frank b: 11/30/1865, Philadelphia d: 12/5/45, Philadelphia, Pa. Deb: 7/24/1886																									
1886	NY-a	1	1	0	0	0	0	0		0		.000	.000	.000	-99	-0	-0	0	0			.500	-1	/OP	0.0
■ HUBIE BROOKS Brooks, Hubert b: 9/24/56, Los Angeles, Cal. BR/TR, 6', 200 lbs. Deb: 9/04/80																									
1980	NY-N	24	81	8	25	2	1	1	10	5	9	.309	.364	.395	115	1	2	12	1	1	-0	.966	-1	3	0.0
1981	NY-N	98	358	34	110	21	2	4	38	23	65	.307	.351	.411	117	7	7	50	9	5	-0	.924	-2	3/OS	0.4
1982	NY-N	126	457	40	114	21	2	2	40	28	76	.249	.300	.317	73	-17	-16	43	6	3	0	.931	-8	*3	-2.9
1983	NY-N	150	586	53	147	18	4	5	58	24	96	.251	.285	.321	68	-26	-26	51	6	4	-1	.950	3	*3/2	-2.6
1984	NY-N	153	561	61	159	23	2	16	73	48	79	.283	.342	.417	114	9	10	75	6	5	-1	.929	-18	*3S	-0.9
1985	Mon-N	156	605	67	163	34	7	13	100	34	79	.269	.314	.413	108	-0	4	71	6	9	-4	.958	-34	*S	-2.0
1986	Mon-N★	80	306	50	104	18	5	14	58	25	60	.340	.393	.569	164	25	25	65	4	2	0	.958	-14	S	1.9
1987	Mon-N★	112	430	57	113	22	3	14	72	24	72	.263	.303	.426	88	-7	-9	54	4	3	-1	.953	-26	*S	-2.7
1988	Mon-N	151	588	61	164	35	2	20	90	35	108	.279	.321	.447	113	12	9	78	7	3	0	.968	-2	*O	0.3
1989	Mon-N	148	542	56	145	30	1	14	70	39	108	.268	.321	.404	105	3	3	65	6	11	-5	.964	-2	*O	-0.8
1990	LA-N	153	568	74	151	28	1	20	91	33	108	.266	.313	.424	104	-1	1	71	2	5	-2	.964	-3	*O	-0.8
1991	NY-N	103	357	48	85	11	1	16	50	44	62	.238	.327	.409	106	3	3	49	3	1	0	.972	-1	*O	0.0
1992	Cal-A	82	306	28	66	13	0	8	36	12	46	.216	.248	.337	63	-16	-16	22	3	3	-1	.986	-0	D/1	-1.8
Total	13	1536	5745	637	1546	276	31	147	786	374	968	.269	.318	.405	101	-8	-4	704	63	55	-14	.966	-108	O3S/D21	-11.9
■ MANDY BROOKS Brooks, Jonathan Joseph (b: Jonathan Joseph Brozek) b: 8/18/1897, Milwaukee, Wis. d: 6/17/62, Kirkwood, Mo. BR/TR, 5'9", 165 lbs. Deb: 5/30/25																									
1925	Chi-N	90	349	55	98	25	7	14	72	19	28	.281	.322	.513	108	3	2	57	10	3	1	.977	5	O	0.2
1926	Chi-N	26	48	7	9	1	0	1	6	5	5	.188	.278	.271	48	-3	-4	4	0			1.000	-2	O	-0.7
Total	2	116	397	62	107	26	7	15	78	24	33	.270	.316	.484	101	-1	-2	61	10	3wa		.979	2	O	-0.5
■ BOBBY BROOKS Brooks, Robert b: 11/1/45, Los Angeles, Cal. BR/TR, 5'8.5", 165 lbs. Deb: 9/01/69																									
1969	Oak-A	29	79	13	19	5	0	3	10	20	24	.241	.400	.418	135	4	4	15	0	2	-1	1.000	0	O	0.3
1970	Oak-A	7	18	2	6	1	0	2	5	1	7	.333	.368	.722	201	2	2	4	0	1	-1	1.000	-1	/O	0.0
1972	Oak-A	15	39	4	7	0	0	0	5	8	8	.179	.319	.179	54	-2	-2	2	0	1	-1	.930	2	O	-0.1
1973	Cal-A	4	7	0	1	0	0	0	0	0	3	.143	.143	.143	-21	-1	-1	0	0	0	0	.000	-0	/O	-0.1
Total	4	55	143	19	33	6	0	5	20	29	42	.231	.364	.378	116	3	4	21	0	4	-2	.964	1	/O	0.1
■ SCOTT BROSIUS Brosius, Scott David b: 8/15/66, Hillsboro, Ore. BR/TR, 6'1", 185 lbs. Deb: 8/07/91																									
1991	Oak-A	36	68	9	16	5	0	2	4	3	11	.235	.268	.397	86	-2	-2	7	3	1	0	1.000	-1	2O/3D	-0.2
1992	Oak-A	38	87	13	19	2	0	4	13	3	13	.218	.261	.379	80	-3	-3	9	3	0	1	1.000	-7	O3/1SD	-0.9
Total	2	74	155	22	35	7	0	6	17	6	24	.226	.264	.387	83	-5	-4	16	6	1	1	1.000	-8	/O321DS	-1.1
■ SIG BROSKIE Broskie, Sigmund Theodore "Chops" b: 3/23/11, Iselin, Pa. d: 5/17/75, Canton, Ohio BR/TR, 5'11.5", 200 lbs. Deb: 9/11/40																									
1940	Bos-N	11	22	1	6	1	0	0	4	1	2	.273	.304	.318	76	-1	-1	2	0			.935	0	C	0.0
■ TONY BROTTEM Brottem, Anton Christian b: 4/30/1892, Halstad, Minn. d: 8/5/29, Chicago, Ill. BR/TR, 6'0.5", 176 lbs. Deb: 4/17/16																									
1916	StL-N	26	33	3	6	1	0	0	4	3	10	.182	.250	.212	43	-2	-2	2	1			.950	-1	C/O	-0.3
1918	StL-N	2	4	0	0	0	0	0	0	1	0	.000	.200	.000	-39	-1	-1	0	0			1.000	1	/1	0.0
1921	Was-A	4	7	1	1	0	0	0	0	2	1	.143	.333	.143	26	-1	-1	0	0	0	0	1.000	1	/C	0.1
	Pit-N	30	91	6	22	2	0	0	9	3	11	.242	.266	.264	40	-8	-8	6	0	1	-1	.983	-2	C	-0.9
Total	3	62	135	10	29	3	0	0	13	9	22	.215	.264	.237	38	-11	-11	9	1	1		.977	-1	/C1O	-1.1
■ CAL BROUGHTON Broughton, Cecil Calvert b: 12/28/1860, Magnolia, Wis. d: 3/15/39, Evansville, Wis. BR/TR, Deb: 5/02/1883																									
1883	Cle-N	4	10	2	2	0	0	0	1	2	2	.200	.333	.200	68	-0	-0	1				.950	-0	/C	0.0
	Bal-a	9	32	1	6	0	0	0		1		.188	.212	.188	29	-2	-3	1				.825	-2	/CO	-0.3
1884	Mil-U	11	39	5	12	5	0	0		0		.308	.308	.436	275	2	5	5				.937	-1	/CO	0.3
1885	StL-a	4	17	1	1	0	0	0		0		.059	.059	.059	-60	-3	-3	0				.889	-1	/C	-0.4
	NY-a	11	41	1	6	1	0	0		1		.146	.167	.171	9	-4	-4	1				.860	-2	C	-0.4
	Yr	15	58	2	7	1	0	0		1		.121	.136	.138	-13	-7	-7	1				.867	-3	C	-0.8
1888	Det-N	1	4	0	0	0	0	0	0	0	0	.000	.000	.000	-99	-1	-1	0	0			1.000	1	/C	0.0
Total	4	40	143	10	27	6	0	0	1	4	2	.189	.211	.231	50	-9	-6	9	0			.887	-5	/CO	-0.8
■ MARK BROUHARD Brouhard, Mark Steven b: 5/22/56, Burbank.Cal. BR/TR, 6'1", 210 lbs. Deb: 4/12/80																									
1980	Mil-A	45	125	17	29	6	0	5	16	7	24	.232	.278	.400	86	-3	-3	13	1	0	0	.964	0	DO1	-0.3
1981	Mil-A	60	186	19	51	6	3	2	20	7	41	.274	.308	.371	100	-2	-1	19	1	1	-0	.990	1	O/D	-0.1
1982	*Mil-A	40	108	16	29	4	1	4	10	9	17	.269	.336	.435	117	1	2	14	0	3	-2	.986	2	O/D	0.2
1983	Mil-A	56	185	25	51	10	1	7	23	9	39	.276	.316	.454	118	2	4	23	0	4	-2	.991	2	OD	0.2
1984	Mil-A	66	197	20	47	7	0	6	22	16	36	.239	.302	.365	87	-4	-3	21	0	3	-2	.983	4	O/D	-0.3
1985	Mil-A	37	108	11	28	7	2	1	13	5	26	.259	.298	.389	87	-2	-2	12	0	0	0	.964	-3	O/D	-0.6
Total	6	304	909	108	235	40	7	25	104	53	183	.259	.307	.400	99	-8	-3	103	2	11	-6	.983	7	O/D1	-0.9
■ ART BROUTHERS Brouthers, Arthur H. b: 11/25/1882, Montgomery, Ala. d: 9/28/59, Charleston, S.C. TR , 6'1", Deb: 4/14/06																									
1906	Phi-A	37	144	18	30	5	1	0	14	5		.208	.235	.257	53	-8	-8	11	4			.900	-4	3/2	-1.3
■ DAN BROUTHERS Brouthers, Dennis Joseph "Big Dan" b: 5/8/1858, Sylvan Lake, N.Y. d: 8/2/32, E.Orange, N.J. BL/TL, 6'2", 207 lbs. Deb: 6/23/1879 H																									
1879	Tro-N	39	168	17	46	12	1	4	17	1	18	.274	.278	.429	138	5	6	21				.926	-5	1/P	0.1
1880	Tro-N	3	12	0	2	0	0	0	1	1	0	.167	.231	.167	35	-1	-1	0				.893	-1	/1	-0.2
1881	Buf-N	65	270	60	86	18	9	**8**	45	18	22	.319	.361	**.541**	182	24	25	54				.797	-5	O1	1.5
1882	Buf-N	84	351	71	**129**	23	11	6	63	21	7	**.368**	**.403**	**.547**	**198**	**39**	**38**	**79**				**.974**	1	*1	2.7
1883	Buf-N	98	425	85	**159**	41	**17**	3	**97**	16	17	**.374**	**.397**	**.572**	**186**	**44**	**43**	**99**				.961	2	*1/3P	3.0
1884	Buf-N	94	398	82	130	22	15	14	79	33	20	.327	.378	**.563**	**186**	41	39	87				.964	0	*1/3	2.6
1885	Buf-N	98	407	87	146	32	11	7	59	34	10	.359	.408	**.543**	199	47	45	92				.975	-2	*1	2.9
1886	Det-N	121	489	139	181	**40**	15	**11**	72	66	16	.370	.445	**.581**	**204**	**66**	**64**	139	21			.968	-8	*1	3.7
1887	*Det-N	123	500	**153**	169	**36**	20	12	101	71	9	.338	**.426**	.562	**169**	52	49	138	34			.969	-4	*1	2.7
1888	Det-N	129	522	**118**	160	**33**	11	9	66	68	13	.307	.399	.464	177	48	**48**	113	34			.971	-2	*1	3.4
1889	Bos-N	126	485	105	181	26	9	7	118	66	6	**.373**	.462	.507	163	**51**	46	127	22			.974	1	*1	3.3
1890	Bos-P	123	460	117	152	36	9	1	97	99	17	.330	**.466**	.454	139	40	33	113	28			.963	2	*1	2.3
1891	Bos-a	130	486	117	170	26	19	5	109	87	20	**.350**	**.471**	**.512**	**188**	**59**	**60**	135	31			.978	-7	*1	4.0
1892	Bro-N	152	588	121	**197**	30	20	5	**124**	84	30	**.335**	.432	.480	**185**	**58**	**62**	**138**	31			.982	12	*1	**6.1**
1893	Bro-N	77	282	57	95	21	11	2	59	52	10	.337	.450	.511	165	25	28	71	9			.986	3	1	2.4
1894	*Bal-N	123	525	137	182	39	23	9	128	67	9	.347	.425	.560	132	32	27	146	38			.976	-2	*1	2.0
1895	Bal-N	5	23	2	6	2	0	0	5	1	1	.261	.292	.348	64	-1	-1	3	0			1.000	0	/1	-0.1
	Lou-N	24	97	13	30	10	1	2	15	11	2	.309	.380	.495	135	4	5	19	1			.953	-2	1	0.2
	Yr	29	120	15	36	12	1	2	20	12	3	.300	.364	.467	121	2	3	21	1			.960	-2	1	0.1
1896	Phi-N	57	218	42	75	13	3	1	41	44	11	.344	.462	.445	144	17	17	49	7			.983	-3	1	1.3
1904	NY-N	2	5	0	0	0	0	0	0	0		.000	.000	.000	-96	-1	-1	0	0			1.000	-0	/1	-0.2
Total	19	1673	6711	1523	2296	460	205	106	1296	840	238	.342	.423	.519	171	648	631	1624	256			.971	-18	*1/OP3	43.7
■ JOE BROVIA Brovia, Joseph John "Ox" b: 2/18/22, Davenport, Cal. BL/TR, 6'3", 195 lbs. Deb: 7/03/55																									
1955	Cin-N	21	18	0	2	0	0	0	4	1	6	.111	.158	.111	-25	-3	-3	0	0	0	0	.000	0	H	-0.3

YEAR	TM/L	G	AB	R	H	2B	3B	HR	RBI	BB	SO	AVG	OBP	SLG	PRO+	BR	/A	RC	SB	CS	SBR	FA	FR	POS	TPR

■ FRANK BROWER   Brower, Frank Willard "Turkeyfoot" b: 3/26/1893, Gainesville, Va.   d: 11/20/60, Baltimore, Md.   BL/TR, 6'2", 180 lbs.   Deb: 8/14/20

1920	Was-A	36	119	21	37	7	2	1	13	9	11	.311	.374	.429	115	2	3	19	1	1	-0	.900	-0	O/13	0.1
1921	Was-A	83	203	31	53	12	3	1	35	18	7	.261	.330	.365	81	-7	-6	25	1	1	-0	.917	3	O/1	-0.6
1922	Was-A	139	471	61	138	20	6	9	71	52	25	.293	.375	.418	112	5	9	76	8	6	-1	.978	-4	*O/1	-0.5
1923	Cle-A	126	397	77	113	25	8	16	66	62	32	.285	.392	.509	136	21	21	82	6	5	-1	.988	-3	*1/O	1.1
1924	Cle-A	66	107	16	30	10	1	3	20	27	9	.280	.434	.477	133	7	7	24	1	1	-0	.990	-1	1/PO	0.3
Total	5	450	1297	206	371	74	20	30	205	168	84	.286	.379	.443	117	28	33	227	17	14	-3	.952	-4	O1/P3	0.4

■ LOUIS BROWER   Brower, Louis Lester b: 7/1/1900, Cleveland, Ohio   BR/TR, 5'10", 155 lbs.   Deb: 6/13/31

| 1931 | Det-A | 21 | 62 | 3 | 10 | 1 | 0 | 0 | 6 | 8 | 5 | .161 | .278 | .177 | 21 | -7 | -7 | 4 | 1 | 0 | 0 | .886 | -7 | S/2 | -1.2 |

■ BOB BROWER   Brower, Robert Richard b: 1/10/60, Jamaica, N.Y.   BR/TR, 5'11", 185 lbs.   Deb: 9/03/86

1986	Tex-A	21	9	3	1	1	0	0	0	3	1	.111	.111	.222	-12	-1	-1	-0	1	2	-1	1.000	-5	O/D	-0.8
1987	Tex-A	127	303	63	79	10	3	14	46	36	66	.261	.339	.452	107	3	3	47	15	9	-1	.964	-13	*O/D	-1.3
1988	Tex-A	82	201	29	45	7	0	1	11	27	38	.224	.316	.274	65	-8	-9	18	10	5	0	.972	-7	OD	-1.8
1989	NY-A	26	69	9	16	3	0	2	3	6	11	.232	.293	.362	85	-2	-1	7	3	1	0	.970	2	O/D	0.1
Total	4	256	582	104	141	21	3	17	60	69	118	.242	.323	.376	89	-8	-9	73	29	17	-2	.968	-24	O/D	-3.8

■ BROWN   Brown   Deb: 7/29/1874

| 1874 | Bal-n | 2 | 9 | 0 | 0 | 0 | 0 | 0 | 0 | | | .000 | .000 | .000 | -99 | -2 | -2 | 0 | | | | | | /S | -0.2 |

■ CURTIS BROWN   Brown, Curtis b: 9/14/45, Sacramento, Cal.   BR/TR, 5'11", 180 lbs.   Deb: 5/27/73   F

| 1973 | Mon-N | 1 | 4 | 0 | 0 | 0 | 0 | 0 | 0 | 0 | 0 | .000 | .000 | .000 | -97 | -1 | -1 | 0 | 0 | 0 | 0 | 1.000 | 0 | /O | -0.1 |

■ DARRELL BROWN   Brown, Darrell Wayne b: 10/29/55, Oklahoma City, Okla.   BB/TR, 6', 184 lbs.   Deb: 4/11/81

1981	Det-A	16	4	4	1	0	0	0	0	0	1	.250	.250	.250	43	-0	-0	1	0	1	0	1.000	-2	/OD	-0.2
1982	Oak-A	8	18	2	6	0	1	0	3	1	2	.333	.368	.444	128	1	1	3	1	0	0	1.000	-1	/OD	0.0
1983	Min-A	91	309	40	84	6	2	0	22	10	28	.272	.297	.304	64	-14	-16	26	3	3	-1	.995	-4	O/D	-2.3
1984	Min-A	95	260	36	71	9	3	1	19	14	16	.273	.310	.342	77	-7	-8	27	4	1	1	.993	4	OD	-0.5
Total	4	210	591	82	162	15	6	1	44	25	47	.274	.305	.325	71	-21	-24	57	9	4	0	.994	-3	O/D	-3.0

■ DELOS BROWN   Brown, Delos Hight b: 10/4/1892, Anna, Ill.   d: 12/21/64, Carbondale, Ill.   BR/TR, 5'9", 160 lbs.   Deb: 6/12/14

| 1914 | Chi-A | 1 | 1 | 0 | 0 | 0 | 0 | 0 | 0 | 0 | 1 | .000 | .000 | .000 | -99 | -0 | -0 | 0 | 0 | | | .000 | 0 | H | 0.0 |

■ DRUMMOND BROWN   Brown, Drummond Nicol b: 1/31/1885, Los Angeles, Cal.   d: 1/27/27, Parkville, Mo.   BR/TR, 6', 180 lbs.   Deb: 4/25/13

1913	Bos-N	15	34	3	11	1	0	1	2	9	9	.324	.361	.441	126	1	1	5	0			.960	-4	C	-0.2
1914	KC-F	31	58	4	11	3	0	0	5	7	6	.190	.277	.241	50	-4	-4	5	1			.954	5	C/1	0.3
1915	KC-F	77	227	13	55	10	1	1	26	12	23	.242	.289	.308	79	-7	-6	23	3			.961	-2	C/1	-0.4
Total	3	123	319	20	77	14	1	2	33	21	38	.241	.294	.310	79	-10	-9	33	4			.960	-1	C/1	-0.3

■ EARL BROWN   Brown, Earl James "Snitz" b: 3/5/11, Louisville, Ky.   BL/TL, 6', 175 lbs.   Deb: 9/12/35

1935	Pit-N	9	32	6	8	2	0	0	6	2	8	.250	.294	.313	61	-2	-2	3	0			1.000	0	/1	-0.3
1936	Pit-N	8	23	7	7	1	2	0	3	1	4	.304	.333	.522	124	1	1	3	0			1.000	0	/O1	0.1
1937	Phi-N	105	332	42	97	19	3	6	52	21	41	.292	.342	.422	98	2	1	48	4			.980	1	O1	-0.5
1938	Phi-N	21	74	4	19	4	0	0	8	5	11	.257	.304	.311	71	-3	-3	7	0			.978	-0	1/O	-0.3
Total	4	143	461	59	131	26	5	6	69	29	64	.284	.332	.401	93	-2	-5	60	4			.983	1	/O1	-1.2

■ ED BROWN   Brown, Edward P. b: Chicago, Ill.   TR ,   Deb: 8/19/1882

1882	StL-a	17	60	4	11	0	0	0			4	.183	.234	.183	41	-3	-4	3				.808	-2	O/2P	-0.5
1884	Tol-a	42	153	13	27	3	0	0			2	.176	.187	.196	26	-12	-12	6				.815	-8	3/OCP	-1.8
Total	2	59	213	17	38	3	0	0			6	.178	.201	.192	30	-15	-16	8				.815	-10	/3OP2C	-2.3

■ EDDIE BROWN   Brown, Edward William "Glass Arm Eddie" b: 7/17/1891, Milligan, Neb.   d: 9/10/56, Vallejo, Cal.   BR/TR, 6'3", 190 lbs.   Deb: 9/26/20

1920	NY-N	3	8	1	1	1	0	0	0	0	3	.125	.125	.250	6	-1	-1	0	0	0	0	1.000	0	/O	-0.1
1921	NY-N	70	128	16	36	6	2	0	12	4	11	.281	.324	.359	80	-4	-4	15	1	0	0	.956	-3	O	-0.8
1924	Bro-N	114	455	56	140	30	4	5	78	26	15	.308	.345	.424	108	3	3	65	3	5	-2	.975	2	*O	-0.3
1925	Bro-N	153	618	88	189	39	11	5	99	22	18	.306	.332	.429	95	-8	-6	86	3	4	-2	.972	8	*O	-0.9
1926	Bos-N	153	612	71	**201**	31	8	2	84	23	20	.328	.355	.415	117	5	12	86	5			.965	8	*O	0.9
1927	Bos-N	155	558	64	171	35	6	2	75	28	20	.306	.340	.401	106	-3	3	73	11			.980	3	O/1	-0.3
1928	Bos-N	142	523	45	140	28	2	2	59	24	22	.268	.305	.340	72	-25	-21	53	6			.960	-4	*O/1	-3.3
Total	7	790	2902	341	878	170	33	16	407	127	109	.303	.334	.400	99	-33	-12	379	29	9		.970	13	O/1	-4.8

■ RANDY BROWN   Brown, Edwin Randolph b: 8/29/44, Leesburg, Fla.   BL/TR, 5'7", 170 lbs.   Deb: 9/11/69

1969	Cal-A	13	25	3	4	1	0	0	6	1		.160	.323	.200	52	-1	-1	2	0	0	0	1.000	-1	C/O	-0.2
1970	Cal-A	5	4	0	0	0	0	0	0	0	0	.000	.000	.000	-99	-1	-1	0	0	0	0	1.000	-0	/C	-0.1
Total	2	18	29	3	4	1	0	0	6	1		.138	.286	.172	32	-3	-2	2	0	0	0	1.000	-1	/CO	-0.3

■ FRED BROWN   Brown, Fred Herbert b: 4/12/1879, Ossipee, N.H.   d: 2/3/55, Somersworth, N.H.   BR/TR, 5'10.5", 190 lbs.   Deb: 5/04/01

1901	Bos-N	7	14	1	2	0	0	0	2	0		.143	.143	.143	-16	-2	-2	0	0			1.000	0	/O	-0.2
1902	Bos-N	2	6	1	2	1	0	0	0	0		.333	.333	.500	155	0	0	1	0			1.000	0	/O	0.0
Total	2	9	20	2	4	1	0	0	2	0		.200	.200	.250	31	0	0	1	0			1.000	0	/O	-0.2

■ IKE BROWN   Brown, Isaac b: 4/13/42, Memphis, Tenn.   BR/TR, 6'1", 205 lbs.   Deb: 6/17/69

1969	Det-A	70	170	24	39	4	3	5	12	26	43	.229	.338	.376	96	0	-1	21	2	3	-1	.962	-6	23/OS	-0.5
1970	Det-A	56	94	17	27	5	0	4	15	13	26	.287	.380	.468	132	4	4	17	0	0	0	.935	-3	2/O3	0.3
1971	Det-A	59	110	20	28	1	0	5	19	19	25	.255	.364	.482	133	6	5	19	0	1	-1	1.000	-1	1/O23S	0.3
1972	*Det-A	51	84	12	21	3	0	2	10	17	23	.250	.376	.357	115	2	2	11	1	2	-1	1.000	-1	O1/2S3	0.3
1973	Det-A	42	76	12	22	2	1	1	9	15	13	.289	.407	.382	115	3	2	12	0	1	-1	.983	-2	1O/3D	-0.1
1974	Det-A	2	2	0	0	0	0	0	0	0	0	.000	.000	.000	-97	-1	-1	0	0	0	0	1.000	0	/3	0.0
Total	6	280	536	85	137	15	4	20	65	90	130	.256	.366	.410	115	16	13	80	3	7	-3	.956	-9	/2103SD	0.2

■ JIM BROWN   Brown, James Donaldson "Don" or "Moose" b: 3/31/1897, Laurel, Md.   BR/TR, 6', 178 lbs.   Deb: 9/13/15

1915	StL-N	1	2	0	1	0	0	0	0	2	1	.500	.750	.500	281	1	1	1	0			1.000	-0	/O	0.1
1916	Phi-A	14	42	6	10	2	1	1	5	4	9	.238	.304	.405	119	0	1	6	0			.895	-1	O	-0.1
Total	2	15	44	6	11	2	1	1	5	6	10	.250	.340	.409	131	1	1	6	0			.900	-2	/O	0.0

■ JIMMY BROWN   Brown, James Roberson b: 4/25/10, Jamesville, N.C.   d: 12/29/77, Bath, N.C.   BB/TR, 5'8.5", 165 lbs.   Deb: 4/23/37   C

1937	StL-N	138	525	86	145	20	9	2	53	27	29	.276	.313	.360	81	-13	-15	58	10			.964	-14	*2S/3	-2.0
1938	StL-N	108	382	50	115	12	6	0	38	27	9	.301	.350	.364	91	-1	-4	50	7			.968	1	2S3	0.2
1939	StL-N	147	645	88	192	31	8	3	51	32	18	.298	.335	.384	87	-7	-12	83	4			.957	-5	*S2	-0.5
1940	StL-N	107	454	56	127	14	0	0	30	24	15	.280	.317	.335	76	-12	-15	48	9			.977	-22	23S	-3.3
1941	StL-N	132	549	81	168	28	9	3	56	45	22	.306	.363	.406	109	12	7	83	2			.965	3	*32	1.4
1942	*StL-N★	145	606	75	155	28	4	1	71	52	11	.256	.315	.320	80	-11	-16	63	4			.970	-12	23S	-2.4
1943	StL-N	34	110	8	20	4	2	0	8	6	2	.182	.224	.255	37	-9	-10	7	0			.978	2	2/3S	-0.6
1946	Pit-N	79	241	23	58	12	4	0	12	18	5	.241	.293	.266	58	-13	-13	18	3			.960	-2	S2/3	-1.3
Total	8	890	3512	465	980	146	42	9	319	231	110	.279	.326	.352	84	-55	-78	411	39			.968	-50	23S	-8.5

YEAR	TM/L	G	AB	R	H	2B	3B	HR	RBI	BB	SO	AVG	OBP	SLG	PRO+	BR	/A	RC	SB	CS	SBR	FA	FR	POS	TPR
■ JIM BROWN	Brown, James W. H. b: 12/12/1860, Clinton Co., Pa. d: 4/6/08, Williamsport, Pa. Deb: 4/17/1884																								
1884	Alt-U	21	88	12	22	2	2	1		1		.250	.258	.352	103	0	0	8				.615	-3	OP	-0.3
	NY-N	1	3	0	0	0	0	0	0	0	1	.000	.000	.000	-98	-1	-1	0				.333	-0	/P	0.0
	StP-U	6	16	5	5	4	0	0		1		.313	.353	.563	378	2	3	3				.706	0	/P1O	0.0
1886	Phi-a	1	3	0	0	0	0	0		0		.000	.000	.000	-99	-1	-1	0	0			1.000	-0	/P	0.0
Total	2	29	110	17	27	6	2	1	0	2	1	.245	.259	.364	114	1	2	11	0			.741	-4	/PO1	-0.3
■ JARVIS BROWN	Brown, Jarvis Ardel b: 3/26/67, Waukegan, Ill. BR/TR, 5'7", 165 lbs. Deb: 7/02/91																								
1991	*Min-A	38	37	10	8	0	0	0	0	2	8	.216	.256	.216	31	-3	-4	3	7	1	2	.955	-11	O/D	-1.3
1992	Min-A	35	15	8	1	0	0	0	0	2	4	.067	.222	.067	-15	-2	-2	0	2	2	-1	.952	-10	O/D	-1.4
Total	2	73	52	18	9	0	0	0	0	4	12	.173	.246	.173	18	-6	-6	3	9	3	1	.953	-21	/OD	-2.7
■ JAKE BROWN	Brown, Jerald Ray b: 3/22/48, Sumrall, Miss. d: 12/18/81, Houston, Tex. BR/TR, 6'2", 200 lbs. Deb: 5/17/75																								
1975	SF-N	41	43	6	9	3	0	0	4	5	13	.209	.292	.279	57	-2	-3	4	0	0	0	.857	0	O	-0.3
■ CHRIS BROWN	Brown, John Christopher b: 8/15/61, Jackson, Miss. BR/TR, 6'2", 210 lbs. Deb: 9/03/84																								
1984	SF-N	23	84	6	24	7	0	1	11	9	19	.286	.362	.405	119	2	2	12	2	1	0	.900	-2	3	0.0
1985	SF-N	131	432	50	117	20	3	16	61	38	78	.271	.345	.442	125	10	13	61	2	3	-1	**.971**	5	*3	1.6
1986	SF-N★	116	416	57	132	16	3	7	49	33	43	.317	.380	.421	127	12	15	65	13	9	-2	.933	-14	*3/S	-0.3
1987	SF-N	38	132	17	32	6	0	6	17	9	16	.242	.306	.424	95	-2	-1	14	1	3	-2	.905	-2	3/S	-0.5
	SD-N	44	155	17	36	3	0	6	23	11	30	.232	.296	.368	77	-6	-5	16	3	1	0	.942	-4	3	-0.9
	Yr	82	287	34	68	9	0	12	40	20	46	.237	.300	.394	86	-8	-6	30	4	4	-1	.923	-6	3/S	-1.4
1988	SD-N	80	247	14	58	6	0	2	19	19	49	.235	.297	.283	69	-10	-9	20	0	0	0	.949	5	3	-0.6
1989	Det-A	17	57	3	11	3	0	0	4	1	17	.193	.207	.246	28	-6	-5	2	0	0	0	.909	-1	3	-0.7
Total	6	449	1523	164	410	61	6	38	184	120	252	.269	.335	.392	105	1	9	190	21	17	-4	.943	-13	3/S	-1.4
■ LINDSAY BROWN	Brown, John Lindsay "Red" b: 7/22/11, Mason, Tex. d: 1/1/67, San Antonio, Tex. BR/TR, 5'10", 160 lbs. Deb: 7/13/37																								
1937	Bro-N	48	115	16	31	3	1	0	6	3	17	.270	.288	.313	62	-6	-6	10	1			.937	6	S	0.2
■ JOE BROWN	Brown, Joseph E. b: 4/4/1859, Warren, Pa. d: 6/28/1888, Warren, Pa. Deb: 8/16/1884																								
1884	Chi-N	15	61	6	13	1	0	0	3	0	15	.213	.213	.230	36	-4	-5	3				.750	-3	/OP1C	-0.5
1885	Bal-a	5	19	2	3	0	0	0		0		.158	.158	.158	1	-2	-2	0				1.000	0	/P2	0.0
Total	2	20	80	8	16	1	0	0	3	0	15	.200	.200	.213	29	-6	-7	4				.895	-3	/PO2C1	-0.5
■ LARRY BROWN	Brown, Larry Leslie b: 3/1/40, Shinnston, W.Va. BR/TR, 5'11", 165 lbs. Deb: 7/06/63 F																								
1963	Cle-A	74	247	28	63	6	0	5	18	22	27	.255	.319	.340	85	-5	-5	27	4	3	-1	.938	-8	S2	-0.9
1964	Cle-A	115	335	33	77	12	1	12	40	24	55	.230	.285	.379	84	-8	-8	34	1	2	-1	.981	11	*2/S	1.0
1965	Cle-A	124	438	52	111	22	2	8	40	38	62	.253	.316	.368	93	-4	-4	51	5	7	-3	.977	3	S2	0.5
1966	Cle-A	105	340	29	78	12	0	3	17	36	58	.229	.309	.291	73	-11	-11	30	0	1	-1	.961	-4	S2	-0.7
1967	Cle-A	152	485	38	110	16	2	7	37	53	62	.227	.311	.311	84	-9	-9	48	4	4	-1	.967	1	*S	0.6
1968	Cle-A	154	495	43	116	18	3	6	35	43	46	.234	.302	.319	90	-7	-6	47	1	1	-0	.966	-14	*S	-0.6
1969	Cle-A	132	469	48	112	10	2	4	24	44	43	.239	.305	.294	66	-19	-21	43	5	3	-0	.959	-17	*S3/2	-2.9
1970	Cle-A	72	155	17	40	5	2	0	15	20	14	.258	.343	.316	79	-3	-4	17	1	0	0	.950	-2	S32	-0.3
1971	Cle-A	13	50	4	11	1	0	0	5	3	3	.220	.278	.240	44	-3	-4	3	0	0	0	.980	-6	S	-0.9
	Oak-A	70	189	14	37	2	1	1	9	7	19	.196	.228	.233	31	-17	-17	9	1	2	-1	.959	4	S23	-1.0
	Yr	83	239	18	48	3	1	1	14	10	22	.201	.239	.234	35	-21	-21	12	1	2	-1	.965	-2	S23	-1.9
1972	Oak-A	47	142	11	26	2	0	0	4	13	8	.183	.252	.197	37	-11	-10	6	0	0	0	.974	-8	2/3	-1.8
1973	*Bal-A	17	28	4	7	0	0	1	5	5	4	.250	.364	.357	104	0	0	4	0	0	0	.880	-2	3/2	-0.2
1974	Tex-A	54	76	10	15	2	0	0	5	9	13	.197	.282	.224	48	-5	-5	4	0	0	0	.931	8	3/2S	0.3
Total	12	1129	3449	331	803	108	13	47	254	317	414	.233	.301	.313	76	-102	-103	324	22	23	-7	.964	-34	S23	-6.9
■ LEON BROWN	Brown, Leon b: 11/16/49, Sacramento, Cal. BR/TR, 6', 185 lbs. Deb: 5/19/76 F																								
1976	NY-N	64	70	11	15	3	0	0	2	4	4	.214	.257	.257	49	-5	-5	3	2	4	-2	1.000	6	O	-0.1
■ LEW BROWN	Brown, Lewis J. "Blower" b: 2/1/1858, Leominster, Mass. d: 1/16/1889, Boston, Mass. BR/TR, 5'10.5", 185 lbs. Deb: 6/17/1876																								
1876	Bos-N	45	195	23	41	6	6	2	21	3	22	.210	.222	.333	82	-3	-4	15				.856	-2	C/O	-0.4
1877	Bos-N	58	221	27	56	12	8	1	31	6	33	.253	.273	.394	104	2	0	24				.897	15	*C/1	1.6
1878	Pro-N	58	243	44	74	21	6	1	43	7	37	.305	.324	.453	153	13	13	37				.880	3	*C1/OP	1.5
1879	Pro-N	53	229	23	59	13	4	2	38	4	24	.258	.270	.376	112	2	3	24				.847	-4	C/O	0.0
	Chi-N	6	21	2	6	1	0	0	3	1	4	.286	.318	.333	109	0	0	2				.974	0	/1	0.0
	Yr	59	250	25	65	14	4	2	41	5	28	.260	.275	.372	112	3	3	26				.847	-4	C/O1	0.0
1881	Det-N	27	108	16	26	3	1	3	14	3	16	.241	.261	.370	93	-1	-1	11				.959	-1	1	-0.4
	Pro-N	18	75	9	18	3	1	0	10	4	13	.240	.278	.307	85	-1	-1	7				.833	-4	O/1	-0.5
	Yr	45	183	25	44	6	2	3	24	7	29	.240	.268	.344	90	-2	-2	17				.960	-4	1O	-0.9
1883	Bos-N	14	54	5	13	4	1	0	9	3	6	.241	.281	.352	89	-1	-1	5				.943	-2	1	-0.3
	Lou-a	14	60	6	11	2	1	0		1		.183	.197	.250	46	-4	-3	3				.891	-2	1/C	-0.6
1884	Bos-U	85	325	50	75	18	3	1		13		.231	.260	.314	95	-2	-1	27				.914	13	C1/OP	1.1
Total	7	378	1531	205	379	83	31	10	169	45	155	.248	.269	.362	104	6	6	155				.884	17	C1/OP	2.0
■ MARTY BROWN	Brown, Marty Leo b: 1/23/63, Lawton, Okla. BR/TR, 6'1", 190 lbs. Deb: 9/04/88																								
1988	Cin-N	10	16	0	3	1	0	0	2	1	2	.188	.235	.250	38	-1	-1	1	0	1	-1	1.000	1	/3	-0.1
1989	Cin-N	16	30	2	5	1	0	0	4	4	9	.167	.265	.200	34	-2	-3	2	0	0	0	.913	2	3	-0.1
1990	Bal-A	9	15	1	3	0	0	0	0	1	7	.200	.250	.200	28	-1	-1	1	0	0	0	1.000	0	/23D	-0.1
Total	3	35	61	3	11	2	0	0	6	6	18	.180	.254	.213	34	-5	-5	3	0	1	-1	.943	3	/3D2	-0.3
■ MIKE BROWN	Brown, Michael Charles b: 12/29/59, San Francisco, Cal. BR/TR, 6'2", 195 lbs. Deb: 7/21/83																								
1983	Cal-A	31	104	12	24	5	1	3	9	7	20	.231	.279	.385	81	-3	-3	11	1	0	0	.949	-2	O	-0.5
1984	Cal-A	62	148	19	42	8	3	7	22	13	23	.284	.342	.520	136	6	7	22	0	2	-1	.968	-6	O/D	-0.1
1985	Cal-A	60	153	23	41	9	1	4	20	7	21	.268	.304	.418	96	-1	-1	16	0	1	-1	1.000	-3	O/D	-0.5
	Pit-N	57	205	29	68	18	2	5	33	22	27	.332	.396	.512	154	14	15	40	2	2	-1	.938	-2	O	1.0
1986	Pit-N	87	243	18	53	7	0	4	26	27	32	.218	.296	.296	62	-12	-12	20	2	3	-1	.973	-4	O	-2.1
1988	Cal-A	18	50	4	11	2	0	0	3	1	12	.220	.235	.260	40	-4	-4	3	0	0	0	.946	-1	O	-0.5
Total	5	315	903	105	239	49	7	23	113	77	135	.265	.323	.411	102	1	1	112	5	8	-3	.964	-17	O/D	-2.7
■ OLIVER BROWN	Brown, Oliver S. b: 1849, Brooklyn, N.Y. d: 9/23/32, Brooklyn, N.Y. Deb: 8/01/1872																								
1872	Atl-n	4	16	0	1	0	0	0	0	0	1	.063	.063	.063	-52	-3	-3	0						/O	-0.2
1875	Atl-n	3	10	0	0	0	0	0		0		.000	.000	.000	-99	-2	-2	0						/1	-0.2
Total	2 n	7	26	0	1	0	0	0		0		.038	.038	.038	-71	-5	-5	0						/O1	-0.4
■ OLLIE BROWN	Brown, Ollie Lee "Downtown" b: 2/11/44, Tuscaloosa, Ala. BR/TR, 6'3", 200 lbs. Deb: 9/10/65 F																								
1965	SF-N	6	10	0	2	1	0	0	0	0	2	.200	.200	.300	38	-1	-1	1	0	0	0	1.000	0	/O	-0.1
1966	SF-N	115	348	32	81	7	1	7	33	33	66	.233	.303	.319	71	-12	-13	30	2	5	-2	.978	-3	*O	-2.4
1967	SF-N	120	412	44	110	12	1	13	53	25	65	.267	.315	.396	104	1	1	47	0	2	-1	.985	-4	*O	-1.0
1968	SF-N	40	95	7	22	4	0	0	11	3	23	.232	.270	.274	64	-4	-4	7	1	0	0	1.000	-3	O	-0.9
1969	SD-N	151	568	76	150	18	3	20	61	44	97	.264	.320	.412	108	2	4	73	10	6	-1	.976	5	*O	0.0

YEAR	TM/L	G	AB	R	H	2B	3B	HR	RBI	BB	SO	AVG	OBP	SLG	PRO+	BR	/A	RC	SB	CS	SBR	FA	FR	POS	TPR
1970	SD-N	139	534	79	156	34	1	23	89	34	78	.292	.335	.489	123	11	14	82	5	3	-0	.964	4	*O	1.0
1971	SD-N	145	484	36	132	16	0	9	55	52	74	.273	.347	.362	108	2	5	61	3	3	-1	.982	3	*O	0.1
1972	SD-N	23	70	3	12	2	0	0	3	5	9	.171	.227	.200	24	-7	-7	3	0	0	0	1.000	-0	O	-0.8
	Oak-A	20	54	5	13	1	0	1	4	6	14	.241	.317	.315	93	-1	-0	6	1	1	-0	1.000	-2	O	-0.4
	Mil-A	66	179	21	50	8	0	3	25	17	24	.279	.345	.374	116	3	4	20	0	2	-1	.992	7	O/3	0.8
	Yr	86	233	26	63	9	0	4	29	23	38	.270	.339	.361	111	3	3	26	1	3	-2	.994	5	O/3	0.4
1973	Mil-A	97	296	28	83	10	1	7	32	33	53	.280	.356	.392	113	5	5	42	4	1	1	1.000	-1	D/O	0.5
1974	Hou-N	27	69	8	15	1	0	3	6	4	15	.217	.260	.362	76	-3	-3	6	0	0	0	1.000	0	O	-0.3
	Phi-N	43	99	11	24	5	2	4	13	6	20	.242	.286	.455	101	-0	-1	11	0	1	-1	.921	-4	O	-0.6
	Yr	70	168	19	39	6	2	7	19	10	35	.232	.275	.417	91	-3	-3	17	0	1	-1	.961	-4	O	-0.9
1975	Phi-N	84	145	19	44	12	0	6	26	15	29	.303	.369	.510	137	8	7	28	1	1	-0	1.000	-2	O	0.3
1976	*Phi-N	92	209	30	53	10	1	5	30	33	33	.254	.355	.383	106	3	3	31	2	1	0	.949	-0	O	0.0
1977	*Phi-N	53	70	5	17	3	1	1	13	4	14	.243	.284	.357	68	-3	-3	6	1	1	-0	1.000	-1	O	-0.5
Total	13	1221	3642	404	964	144	11	102	454	314	616	.265	.326	.394	103	3	11	455	30	27	-7	.977	-1	O/D3	-4.3

■ OSCAR BROWN

Brown, Oscar Lee b: 2/8/46, Long Beach, Cal. BR/TR, 6', 175 lbs. Deb: 9/03/69 F

1969	Atl-N	7	4	2	1	0	0	0	0	0	1	.250	.250	.250	40	-0	-0	0	0	0	0	1.000	0	/O	0.0
1970	Atl-N	28	47	6	18	2	1	1	7	7	7	.383	.473	.532	159	5	5	11	0	2	-1	.960	-1	O	0.2
1971	Atl-N	27	43	4	9	4	0	0	5	3	8	.209	.261	.302	56	-2	-3	4	0	0	0	1.000	1	O	-0.2
1972	Atl-N	76	164	19	37	5	1	3	16	4	29	.226	.244	.323	55	-9	-11	11	0	2	-1	.899	4	O	-1.1
1973	Atl-N	22	58	3	12	3	0	0	0	3	10	.207	.246	.259	37	-5	-5	4	0	0	0	1.000	1	O	-0.5
Total	5	160	316	34	77	14	2	4	28	17	55	.244	.284	.339	68	-11	-14	30	0	4	-2	.939	5	O	-1.6

■ DICK BROWN

Brown, Richard Ernest b: 1/17/35, Shinnston, W.Va. d: 4/17/70, Baltimore, Md. BR/TR, 6'3", 190 lbs. Deb: 6/20/57 F

1957	Cle-A	34	114	10	30	4	0	4	22	4	23	.263	.288	.404	88	-3	-2	13	1	1	-0	.986	1	C	0.0
1958	Cle-A	68	173	20	41	5	0	7	20	14	27	.237	.305	.387	91	-3	-2	21	1	0	0	.987	6	C	0.6
1959	Cle-A	48	141	15	31	7	0	5	16	11	39	.220	.290	.376	85	-4	-3	16	0	0	0	.996	3	C	0.2
1960	Chi-A	16	43	4	7	0	0	3	5	3	11	.163	.217	.372	57	-3	-3	3	0	0	0	.986	3	C	0.1
1961	Det-A	93	308	32	82	12	2	16	45	22	57	.266	.315	.474	105	2	1	42	0	2	-1	.990	-1	C	0.4
1962	Det-A	134	431	40	104	12	0	12	40	21	66	.241	.280	.353	67	-20	-22	40	0	1	-1	.994	3	*C	-1.5
1963	Bal-A	59	171	13	42	7	0	2	13	15	35	.246	.310	.322	79	-5	-4	18	1	0	0	.986	6	C	0.4
1964	Bal-A	88	230	24	59	6	0	8	32	12	45	.257	.296	.387	89	-4	-4	24	2	0	1	.988	4	C	0.3
1965	Bal-A	96	255	17	59	9	1	5	30	17	53	.231	.282	.333	73	-9	-9	22	2	2	-1	.983	10	C	0.4
Total	9	636	1866	175	455	62	3	62	223	119	356	.244	.293	.380	82	-48	-49	199	7	6	-2	.989	35	C	0.9

■ BOBBY BROWN

Brown, Robert William "Doc" b: 10/25/24, Seattle, Wash. BL/TR, 6'1", 180 lbs. Deb: 9/22/46

1946	NY-A	7	24	1	8	1	0	0	1	4	0	.333	.429	.375	124	1	1	4	0	0	0	1.000	-4	/S3	-0.2
1947	*NY-A	69	150	21	45	6	1	1	18	21	9	.300	.390	.373	114	3	4	23	0	2	-1	.932	-11	3S/O	-0.9
1948	NY-A	113	363	62	109	19	5	3	48	48	16	.300	.383	.405	111	6	6	60	0	1	-1	.946	-18	3S2/O	-1.0
1949	*NY-A	104	343	61	97	14	4	6	61	38	18	.283	.359	.399	101	-0	-0	50	4	3	-1	.949	-4	3/O	-0.6
1950	*NY-A	95	277	33	74	4	2	4	37	39	18	.267	.360	.339	82	-8	-6	35	3	1	0	.958	-4	3	-1.0
1951	*NY-A	103	313	44	84	15	2	6	51	47	18	.268	.369	.387	108	3	5	49	1	1	-0	.955	-5	3	-0.1
1952	NY-A	29	89	6	22	2	0	1	14	9	6	.247	.323	.303	80	-3	-2	9	1	1	-0	.894	3	3	0.0
1954	NY-A	28	60	5	13	1	0	1	7	8	3	.217	.309	.283	65	-3	-3	5	0	1	-1	1.000	-0	3	-0.4
Total	8	548	1619	233	452	62	14	22	237	214	88	.279	.367	.376	100	-0	4	234	9	10	-3	.948	-43	3/S2O	-4.2

■ BOBBY BROWN

Brown, Rogers Lee b: 5/24/54, Norfolk, Va. BB/TR, 6'1", 205 lbs. Deb: 4/05/79

1979	Tor-A	4	10	1	0	0	0	0	0	2	1	.000	.167	.000	-50	-2	-2	0	0	0	0	1.000	-0	/O	-0.2
	NY-A	30	68	7	17	3	1	0	3	2	17	.250	.271	.324	61	-4	-4	6	2	1	0	.949	-3	O	-0.7
	Yr	34	78	8	17	3	1	0	3	4	18	.218	.256	.282	46	-6	-6	6	2	1	0	.955	-3	O	-0.9
1980	*NY-A	137	412	65	107	12	5	14	47	29	82	.260	.308	.415	98	-3	-2	52	27	8	3	.972	-1	*O/D	-0.4
1981	*NY-A	31	62	5	14	1	0	0	6	5	15	.226	.284	.242	53	-4	-4	5	4	2	0	.949	-2	O/D	-0.6
1982	Sea-A	79	245	29	59	7	1	4	17	17	32	.241	.290	.327	67	-10	-11	25	28	6	5	.968	3	O/D	-0.5
1983	SD-N	57	225	40	60	5	3	5	22	23	38	.267	.335	.382	102	-1	0	31	27	9	3	.963	-6	O	-0.5
1984	*SD-N	85	171	28	43	7	2	3	29	11	33	.251	.297	.368	86	-4	-4	18	16	4	2	.971	-2	O	-0.5
1985	SD-N	79	84	8	13	3	0	0	6	5	20	.155	.202	.190	11	-10	-10	3	6	4	-1	1.000	-7	O	-1.9
Total	7	502	1277	183	313	38	12	26	130	94	238	.245	.297	.355	80	-37	-36	140	110	34	13	.968	-18	O/D	-5.3

■ SAM BROWN

Brown, Samuel Wakefield b: 5/21/1878, Webster, Pa. d: 11/8/31, Mount Pleasant, Pa. BR/TR, Deb: 4/21/06

1906	Bos-N	71	231	12	48	6	1	0	20	13		.208	.256	.242	57	-12	-11	17	4			.970	-1	CO3/12	-1.0
1907	Bos-N	70	208	17	40	6	0	0	14	12		.192	.250	.221	48	-12	-12	13	0			.970	7	C/1	0.0
Total	2	141	439	29	88	12	1	0	34	25		.200	.253	.232	53	-24	-24	29	4			.970	6	/CO312	-1.0

■ TOMMY BROWN

Brown, Thomas Michael "Buckshot" b: 12/6/27, Brooklyn, N.Y. BR/TR, 6'1", 170 lbs. Deb: 8/03/44

1944	Bro-N	46	146	17	24	4	0	0	8	8	17	.164	.208	.192	13	-17	-16	6	0			.925	-9	S	-2.4
1945	Bro-N	57	196	13	48	3	4	2	19	6	16	.245	.267	.332	66	-10	-10	17	3			.918	-4	S/O	-1.0
1947	Bro-N	15	34	3	8	1	0	0	2	1	6	.235	.257	.265	37	-3	-3	2	0			1.000	2	/3OS	-0.2
1948	Bro-N	54	145	18	35	4	0	2	20	7	17	.241	.281	.310	58	-8	-9	12	1			.936	-1	3/1	-1.0
1949	*Bro-N	41	89	14	27	2	0	3	18	6	8	.303	.347	.427	102	1	0	13	0			.931	-2	O	-0.3
1950	Bro-N	48	86	15	25	2	1	8	20	11	9	.291	.378	.616	153	7	6	19	0			.917	0	O	0.6
1951	Bro-N	11	25	2	4	2	0	0	1	2	4	.160	.222	.240	24	-3	-3	1	0	0	0	.909	0	/O	-0.3
	Phi-N	78	196	24	43	2	1	10	32	15	21	.219	.278	.393	80	-7	-6	19	1	2	-1	.966	-12	O21/3	-2.0
	Yr	89	221	26	47	4	1	10	33	17	25	.213	.272	.376	73	-9	-9	21	1	2	-1	.957	-11	O21/3	-2.3
1952	Phi-N	18	25	2	4	1	0	1	2	4	3	.160	.276	.320	65	-1	-1	3	0	0	0	1.000	-1	/1O	-0.2
	Chi-N	61	200	24	64	11	0	3	24	12	24	.320	.358	.420	114	4	4	29	1	2	-1	.911	-19	S2/1	-1.4
	Yr	79	225	26	68	12	0	4	26	16	27	.302	.349	.409	109	3	2	32	1	2	-1	.911	-20	S2/1O	-1.6
1953	Chi-N	65	138	19	27	7	1	2	13	13	17	.196	.279	.304	51	-10	-10	11	1	0	0	.903	-6	S/O	-1.4
Total	9	494	1280	151	309	39	7	31	159	85	142	.241	.292	.355	74	-47	-48	132	7	4		.916	-52	S/O321	-9.6

■ TOM BROWN

Brown, Thomas Tarlton b: 9/21/1860, Liverpool, England d: 10/25/27, Washington, D.C. BL/TR, 5'10", 168 lbs. Deb: 7/06/1882 MU

1882	Bal-a	45	181	30	55	5	2	1		6		.304	.326	.370	146	6	8	22				.728	-0	O/P	0.8
1883	Col-a	97	420	69	115	12	7	5		20		.274	.307	.371	128	8	13	49				.805	-2	*O/P	1.0
1884	Col-a	107	451	93	123	9	11	5		24		.273	.315	.375	138	13	19	55				.847	-6	*O/P	1.1
1885	Pit-a	108	437	81	134	16	12	4		34		.307	.366	.426	155	26	27	70				.828	-3	*O/P	2.0
1886	Pit-a	115	460	106	131	11	11	1		56		.285	.365	.363	131	18	18	74	30			.837	6	*O/P	1.9
1887	Pit-N	47	192	30	47	3	4	0	6	11	40	.245	.289	.302	70	-9	-7	21	12			.870	5	O	-0.2
	Ind-N	36	140	20	25	3	0	2	9	8	25	.179	.228	.243	33	-13	-12	11	13			.813	-2	O	-1.2
	Yr	83	332	50	72	6	4	2	15	19	65	.217	.263	.277	54	-21	-18	32	25			.851	3	O	-1.4
1888	Bos-N	107	420	62	104	10	7	9	49	30	68	.248	.299	.369	112	7	6	62	46			.896	-3	*O	0.0
1889	Bos-N	90	362	93	84	10	5	2	24	59	56	.232	.341	.304	78	-6	-10	61	63			.901	3	O	-0.9
1890	Bos-P	128	543	146	150	23	14	4	61	86	84	.276	.378	.392	101	8	1	113	79			.911	4	*O	0.1
1891	Bos-a	137	589	**177**	**189**	30	**21**	5	71	70	96	.321	.397	.469	153	38	39	**155**	**106**			.878	-10	*O	2.1
1892	Lou-N	153	660	105	150	16	8	2	45	47	94	.227	.284	.285	80	-21	-13	77	78			.919	19	*O	-0.1
1893	Lou-N	122	529	104	127	15	7	5	54	56	63	.240	.319	.323	78	-21	-13	77	**66**			.929	27	*O	0.6

YEAR	TM/L	G	AB	R	H	2B	3B	HR	RBI	BB	SO	AVG	OBP	SLG	PRO+	BR	/A	RC	SB	CS	SBR	FA	FR	POS	TPR
1894	Lou-N	129	536	122	136	22	14	9	57	60	73	.254	.332	.397	82	-22	-14	96	66			.912	3	*O	-1.6
1895	StL-N	83	350	72	76	11	4	1	31	48	44	.217	.315	.280	57	-22	-21	43	34			.950	8	O	-1.6
	Was-N	34	134	25	32	8	3	2	16	18	16	.239	.329	.388	87	-3	-3	20	8			.909	-7	O	-1.0
	Yr	117	484	97	108	19	7	3	47	66	60	.223	.319	.310	65	-25	-24	63	42			.942	2	*O	-2.6
1896	Was-N	116	435	87	128	17	6	2	59	58	49	.294	.385	.375	103	4	4	77	28			.928	-5	*O	-0.8
1897	Was-N	116	469	91	137	17	2	5	45	52		.292	.364	.369	94	-3	-3	75	25			.928	1	*O/M	-0.9
1898	Was-N	16	55	8	9	1	0	0	2	5		.164	.233	.182	19	-6	-6	3	3			.925	0	O/M	-0.6
Total	17	1786	7363	1521	1952	239	138	64	529	748	708	.265	.337	.361	103	4	34	1161	657			.890	38	*O/P	0.7

■ TOM BROWN
Brown, Thomas William b: 12/12/40, Laureldale, Pa. BB/TL, 6'1", 190 lbs. Deb: 4/08/63

YEAR	TM/L	G	AB	R	H	2B	3B	HR	RBI	BB	SO	AVG	OBP	SLG	PRO+	BR	/A	RC	SB	CS	SBR	FA	FR	POS	TPR
1963	Was-A	61	116	8	17	4	0	1	4	11	45	.147	.227	.207	23	-12	-12	6	2	1	0	1.000	-2	O1	-1.6

■ WILLARD BROWN
Brown, Willard "Big Bill" or "California"
b: 1866, San Francisco, Cal. d: 12/20/1897, San Francisco, Cal BR/TR, 6'2", 190 lbs. Deb: 5/10/1887

YEAR	TM/L	G	AB	R	H	2B	3B	HR	RBI	BB	SO	AVG	OBP	SLG	PRO+	BR	/A	RC	SB	CS	SBR	FA	FR	POS	TPR
1887	NY-N	49	170	17	37	3	2	0	25	10	15	.218	.273	.259	52	-11	-10	15	10			.914	-0	C/3O	-0.5
1888	*NY-N	20	59	4	16	1	0	0	6	1	8	.271	.283	.288	86	-1	-1	5	1			.893	3	C	0.4
1889	*NY-N	40	139	16	36	10	0	1	29	9	9	.259	.318	.353	88	-2	-2	18	6			.846	-5	C/O	-0.4
1890	NY-P	60	230	47	64	8	4	4	43	13	13	.278	.320	.400	86	-3	-7	32	5			.900	-5	CO/132	-0.8
1891	Phi-N	115	441	62	107	20	4	0	50	34	35	.243	.303	.306	77	-11	-13	44	7			**.989**	5	*1C/O	-1.0
1893	Bal-N	7	32	5	4	3	0	0	5	1	3	.125	.152	.219	-1	-5	-5	1	0			.985	-0	/1	-0.4
	Lou-N	111	461	80	140	23	7	1	85	50	32	.304	.373	.390	114	4	10	72	9			.989	-2	*1/C	0.5
	Yr	118	493	85	144	26	7	1	90	51	35	.292	.360	.379	106	-1	5	72	9			**.988**	-2	*1/C	0.1
1894	Lou-N	13	48	5	10	2	0	0	9	5	7	.208	.283	.250	33	-5	-5	4	1			.977	4	1	0.0
	StL-N	3	9	0	1	0	0	0	0	0	2	.111	.111	.111	-46	-2	-2	0	0			1.000	0	/1	-0.1
	Yr	16	57	5	11	2	0	0	9	5	9	.193	.258	.228	20	-7	-7	4	1			.982	4	1	-0.1
Total	7	418	1589	236	415	70	17	6	252	123	124	.261	.319	.338	84	-37	-34	192	39			.987	1	1C/032	-2.3

■ WILLARD BROWN
Brown, Willard Jessie b: 6/26/15, Shreveport, La. BR/TR, 5'11.5", 200 lbs. Deb: 7/19/47

YEAR	TM/L	G	AB	R	H	2B	3B	HR	RBI	BB	SO	AVG	OBP	SLG	PRO+	BR	/A	RC	SB	CS	SBR	FA	FR	POS	TPR
1947	StL-A	21	67	4	12	3	0	1	6	0	7	.179	.179	.269	23	-7	-7	2	2	2	-1	1.000	0	O	-0.9

■ GATES BROWN
Brown, William James b: 5/2/39, Crestline, O. BL/TR, 5'11", 220 lbs. Deb: 6/19/63 C

YEAR	TM/L	G	AB	R	H	2B	3B	HR	RBI	BB	SO	AVG	OBP	SLG	PRO+	BR	/A	RC	SB	CS	SBR	FA	FR	POS	TPR
1963	Det-A	55	82	16	22	3	1	2	14	8	13	.268	.341	.402	104	1	1	11	2	1	0	1.000	4	O	0.4
1964	Det-A	123	426	65	116	22	6	15	54	31	53	.272	.328	.458	114	8	7	64	11	4	1	.981	8	*O	1.2
1965	Det-A	96	227	33	58	14	2	10	43	17	33	.256	.307	.467	115	4	4	34	6	0	2	.973	2	O	0.6
1966	Det-A	88	169	27	45	5	1	7	27	18	19	.266	.344	.432	119	5	4	26	3	0	1	.980	-3	O	0.1
1967	Det-A	51	91	17	17	1	1	2	9	13	15	.187	.288	.286	68	-3	-3	8	0	0	0	1.000	-2	O	-0.6
1968	*Det-A	67	92	15	34	7	2	6	15	12	4	.370	.442	.685	231	15	15	28	0	0	0	1.000	-1	O/1	1.4
1969	Det-A	60	93	13	19	1	2	1	6	5	17	.204	.253	.290	49	-6	-7	7	0	0	0	.906	1	O	-0.7
1970	Det-A	81	124	18	28	3	0	3	24	20	14	.226	.338	.323	82	-2	-2	15	0	0	0	.950	-1	O	-0.5
1971	Det-A	82	195	37	66	2	3	11	29	21	17	.338	.408	.549	163	18	17	44	4	2	0	.986	-6	O	0.9
1972	*Det-A	103	252	33	58	5	0	10	31	26	28	.230	.307	.369	97	-0	-1	29	3	0	1	.977	2	O	-0.1
1973	Det-A	125	377	48	89	11	1	12	50	52	41	.236	.330	.366	90	-1	-5	44	1	1	-0	1.000	-1	*D/O	-0.6
1974	Det-A	73	99	7	24	2	0	4	17	10	15	.242	.312	.384	96	-0	-1	12	0	0	0	.000	0	D	-0.1
1975	Det-A	47	35	1	6	2	0	1	3	9	6	.171	.356	.314	87	-0	-0	4	0	0	0	.000	0	H	0.0
Total	13	1051	2262	330	582	78	19	84	322	242	275	.257	.333	.420	109	37	28	324	30	8	4	.977	3	OD/1	2.0

■ BILL BROWN
Brown, William Verna "Verna" b: 7/8/1893, Coleman, Tex. d: 5/13/65, Lubbock, Tex. BL/TL, 5'8", 185 lbs. Deb: 8/15/12

YEAR	TM/L	G	AB	R	H	2B	3B	HR	RBI	BB	SO	AVG	OBP	SLG	PRO+	BR	/A	RC	SB	CS	SBR	FA	FR	POS	TPR
1912	StL-A	9	20	0	4	0	0	0	1	0		.200	.200	.200	15	-2	-2	1	0			.909	-2	/O	-0.4

■ BYRON BROWNE
Browne, Byron Ellis b: 12/27/42, St.Joseph, Mo. BR/TR, 6'2", 200 lbs. Deb: 9/09/65

YEAR	TM/L	G	AB	R	H	2B	3B	HR	RBI	BB	SO	AVG	OBP	SLG	PRO+	BR	/A	RC	SB	CS	SBR	FA	FR	POS	TPR
1965	Chi-N	4	6	0	0	0	0	0	0	0	2	.000	.000	.000	-98	-2	-2	0	0	0	0	.667	-0	/O	-0.2
1966	Chi-N	120	419	46	102	15	7	16	51	40	143	.243	.317	.427	103	2	2	57	3	3	-1	.967	-3	*O	-0.8
1967	Chi-N	10	19	3	3	2	0	0	2	4	5	.158	.304	.263	61	-1	-1	2	1	1	-0	1.000	-0	/O	-0.2
1968	Hou-N	10	13	0	3	0	0	0	1	4	6	.231	.412	.231	99	0	0	1	0	0	0	1.000	2	/O	0.2
1969	StL-N	22	53	9	12	0	1	1	7	11	14	.226	.359	.321	92	-0	-0	6	0	0	0	1.000	4	O	0.3
1970	Phi-N	104	270	29	67	17	2	10	36	33	72	.248	.330	.437	107	1	2	36	1	2	-1	.975	-3	O	-0.5
1971	Phi-N	58	68	5	14	3	0	3	5	8	23	.206	.289	.382	89	-1	-1	8	0	0	0	1.000	-1	O	-0.3
1972	Phi-N	21	21	2	4	0	0	0	0	1	8	.190	.227	.190	19	-2	-2	1	0	0	0	1.000	-1	/O	-0.3
Total	8	349	869	94	205	37	10	30	102	101	273	.236	.319	.405	98	-2	-2	111	5	6	-2	.973	-3	O	-1.8

■ GEORGE BROWNE
Browne, George Edward b: 1/12/1876, Richmond, Va. d: 12/9/20, Hyde Park, N.Y. BL/TR, 5'10.5", 160 lbs. Deb: 9/27/01

YEAR	TM/L	G	AB	R	H	2B	3B	HR	RBI	BB	SO	AVG	OBP	SLG	PRO+	BR	/A	RC	SB	CS	SBR	FA	FR	POS	TPR
1901	Phi-N	8	26	2	5	1	0	0	4	1		.192	.250	.231	39	-2	-2	2	2			1.000	-1	/O	-0.4
1902	Phi-N	70	281	41	73	7	1	0	26	16		.260	.304	.292	84	-5	-5	30	11			.910	8	O	-0.3
	NY-N	53	216	30	69	9	5	0	14	9		.319	.352	.407	135	8	8	37	13			.895	-0	O	0.4
	Yr	123	497	71	142	16	6	0	40	25		.286	.325	.342	106	3	3	66	24			.904	7	*O	0.1
1903	NY-N	141	591	105	185	20	3	3	45	43		.313	.363	.372	106	8	5	94	27			.918	-4	*O	-0.8
1904	NY-N	150	596	**99**	169	16	5	4	39	39		.284	.328	.347	104	6	3	80	24			.925	-5	*O	-1.2
1905	*NY-N	127	536	95	157	16	14	4	43	20		.293	.322	.397	112	7	6	80	26			.915	-9	*O	-1.0
1906	NY-N	122	477	61	126	10	4	0	38	27		.264	.304	.302	87	-7	-8	58	32			.934	-5	*O	-2.1
1907	NY-N	127	458	54	119	11	10	5	37	31		.260	.307	.360	106	3	2	59	15			.941	-9	*O	-1.4
1908	Bos-N	138	536	61	122	10	6	1	34	36		.228	.276	.274	77	-15	-14	45	17			.950	4	*O	-1.8
1909	Chi-N	12	39	7	8	0	1	0	1	5		.205	.295	.256	70	-1	-1	4	3			.944	-2	O	-0.4
	Was-A	103	393	40	107	15	5	1	16	17		.272	.308	.344	111	1	3	45	13			.935	-2	*O	-0.4
1910	Was-A	7	22	1	4	0	0	0	0	1		.182	.217	.182	26	-2	-2	1	0			.667	-2	/O	-0.4
	Chi-A	30	112	17	27	4	1	0	4	12		.241	.315	.295	95	-1	-0	12	5			.952	-4	O	-0.6
	Yr	37	134	18	31	4	1	0	4	13		.231	.299	.276	84	-3	-2	12	5			.917	-5	O	-1.0
1911	Bro-N	8	12	1	4	0	0	0	2	1	1	.333	.385	.333	106	0	0	2	2			1.000	-0	/O	0.0
1912	Phi-N	6	5	0	1	0	0	0	0	1	0	.200	.333	.200	45	-0	-0	0	0			.000	0	H	0.0
Total	12	1102	4300	614	1176	119	55	18	303	259	1	.273	.317	.339	100	-0	-7	549	190			.927	-32	*O	-10.4

■ JERRY BROWNE
Browne, Jerome Austin b: 2/13/66, Christiansted, V.I. BB/TR, 5'10", 170 lbs. Deb: 9/06/86

YEAR	TM/L	G	AB	R	H	2B	3B	HR	RBI	BB	SO	AVG	OBP	SLG	PRO+	BR	/A	RC	SB	CS	SBR	FA	FR	POS	TPR
1986	Tex-A	12	24	6	10	2	0	0	3	1	4	.417	.440	.500	151	2	2	4	0	2	-1	.923	-1	/2	0.0
1987	Tex-A	132	454	63	123	16	6	1	38	61	50	.271	.360	.339	87	-6	-7	59	27	17	-2	.980	-17	*2/D	-1.9
1988	Tex-A	73	214	26	49	9	2	1	17	25	32	.229	.310	.304	71	-7	-8	20	7	5	-1	.958	-25	2/D	-3.2
1989	Cle-A	153	598	83	179	31	4	5	45	68	64	.299	.372	.390	113	13	12	90	14	6	1	.979	-48	*2/D	-3.1
1990	Cle-A	140	513	92	137	26	5	6	50	72	46	.267	.359	.372	105	5	6	72	12	7	-1	.985	-21	*2	-1.3
1991	Cle-A	107	290	28	66	5	2	1	29	27	29	.228	.296	.269	57	-16	-16	24	2	4	-2	.964	-10	2O3/D	-2.8
1992	*Oak-A	111	324	43	93	12	2	3	40	40	40	.287	.372	.364	111	5	6	46	3	3	-1	.965	-10	3O2/SD	-0.5
Total	7	728	2417	341	657	101	21	17	222	294	265	.272	.353	.352	96	-5	-5	316	65	44	-7	.977	-131	2/3ODS	-12.8

■ PIDGE BROWNE
Browne, Prentice Almont b: 3/21/29, Peekskill, N.Y. BL/TL, 6'1", 190 lbs. Deb: 4/13/62

YEAR	TM/L	G	AB	R	H	2B	3B	HR	RBI	BB	SO	AVG	OBP	SLG	PRO+	BR	/A	RC	SB	CS	SBR	FA	FR	POS	TPR
1962	Hou-N	65	100	8	21	4	2	1	10	13	9	.210	.301	.320	72	-5	-4	8	0	0	0	.983	1	1	-0.4

■ PETE BROWNING
Browning, Louis Rogers "The Gladiator" b: 6/17/1861, Louisville, Ky. d: 9/10/05, Louisville, Ky. BR/TR, 6', 180 lbs. Deb: 5/02/1882

YEAR	TM/L	G	AB	R	H	2B	3B	HR	RBI	BB	SO	AVG	OBP	SLG	PRO+	BR	/A	RC	SB	CS	SBR	FA	FR	POS	TPR
1882	Lou-a	69	288	67	109	17	3	5		26		**.378**	**.430**	**.510**	**229**	**35**	**38**	**65**				.890	12	2S3	**4.6**

YEAR	TM/L	G	AB	R	H	2B	3B	HR	RBI	BB	SO	AVG	OBP	SLG	PRO+	BR	/A	RC	SB	CS	SBR	FA	FR	POS	TPR
1883	Lou-a	84	358	95	121	15	9	4		23		.338	.378	.464	183	27	32	64				.861	-8	OS3/21	2.1
1884	Lou-a	103	447	101	150	33	8	4		13		.336	.357	.472	180	33	36	77				.806	-9	3O1/2P	2.2
1885	Lou-a	112	481	98	**174**	34	10	9		25		**.362**	**.393**	.530	193	**48**	**49**	**103**				.900	5	*O	**4.5**
1886	Lou-a	112	467	86	159	29	6	2		30		**.340**	.389	.441	153	32	28	92	26			.791	-10	*O	1.3
1887	Lou-a	134	547	137	220	35	16	4		55		.402	.464	.547	180	62	60	191	103			.868	-3	*O	4.4
1888	Lou-a	99	383	58	120	22	8	3	72	37		.313	.380	.436	168	28	29	79	36			.888	-1	*O	2.3
1889	Lou-a	83	324	39	83	19	5	2	32	34	30	.256	.327	.364	101	-1	0	47	21			.882	-3	O	-0.4
1890	Cle-P	118	493	112	184	**40**	8	5	93	75	36	**.373**	.459	.517	**177**	47	**55**	136	35			.893	4	*O	**4.3**
1891	Pit-N	50	203	35	59	14	1	4	28	27	31	.291	.377	.429	140	10	10	35	4			.904	5	O	1.3
	Cin-N	55	216	29	74	10	3	0	33	24	23	.343	.413	.417	143	13	13	43	12			.924	-1	O	0.9
	Yr	105	419	64	133	24	4	4	61	51	54	.317	.395	.422	142	23	23	78	16			.913	5	*O	2.2
1892	Lou-N	21	77	10	19	4	0	0	4	12	7	.247	.348	.299	107	0	1	10	5			.911	-1	O	0.0
	Cin-N	83	307	47	93	12	5	3	52	40	25	.303	.383	.404	142	16	16	52	8			.917	-2	O/1	1.0
	Yr	104	384	57	112	16	5	3	56	52	32	.292	.376	.383	135	16	18	62	13			.916	-3	*O/1	1.0
1893	Lou-N	57	220	38	78	11	3	1	37	44	15	.355	.466	.445	157	17	21	51	8			.881	-3	O	1.2
1894	StL-N	2	7	1	1	0	0	0	0	0	0	.143	.143	.143	-30	-1	-1	0	0			1.000	-1	/O	-0.2
	Bro-N	1	2	1	2	0	0	0	2	1	0	1.000	1.000	1.000	417	1	1	2	0			1.000	-0	/O	0.1
	Yr	3	9	2	3	0	0	0	2	1	0	.333	.400	.333	82	-0	-0	1	0			1.000	-1	/O	-0.1
Total	13	1183	4820	954	1646	295	85	46	353	466	167	.341	.403	.467	166	368	388	1048	258			.883	-16	O/32S1P	29.6

■ BILL BRUBAKER

Brubaker, Wilbur Lee b: 11/7/10, Cleveland, Ohio d: 4/2/78, Laguna Hills, Cal. BR/TR, 6'2", 185 lbs. Deb: 9/08/32 F

YEAR	TM/L	G	AB	R	H	2B	3B	HR	RBI	BB	SO	AVG	OBP	SLG	PRO+	BR	/A	RC	SB	CS	SBR	FA	FR	POS	TPR
1932	Pit-N	7	24	3	10	3	0	0	4	3	4	.417	.481	.542	178	3	3	6	1			.909	-0	/3	0.3
1933	Pit-N	2	2	0	0	0	0	0	0	0	0	.000	.000	.000	-99	-1	-1	0	0			1.000	0	/3	0.0
1934	Pit-N	3	6	0	2	1	0	0	1	1	0	.333	.429	.500	144	0	0	1	0			1.000	1	/3	0.1
1935	Pit-N	6	11	1	0	0	0	0	0	2	5	.000	.154	.000	-53	-2	-2	0	0			.889	-0	/3	-0.3
1936	Pit-N	145	554	77	160	27	4	6	102	50	96	.289	.352	.384	96	-1	-2	76	5			.940	-15	*3	-1.2
1937	Pit-N	120	413	57	105	20	4	6	48	47	51	.254	.335	.366	90	-5	-5	52	2			.952	2	*3/S1	0.0
1938	Pit-N	45	112	18	33	5	0	3	19	9	14	.295	.347	.420	109	1	1	16	2			.875	-1	3/1SO	0.0
1939	Pit-N	100	345	41	80	23	1	7	43	29	51	.232	.297	.365	78	-12	-11	36	3			.950	10	23/S	0.3
1940	Pit-N	38	78	8	15	3	1	0	7	8	16	.192	.267	.256	45	-6	-6	6	0			.955	6	3/S1	0.0
1943	Bos-N	13	19	3	8	3	0	0	1	2	2	.421	.476	.579	207	3	3	5	0			.778	-1	/31	0.2
Total	10	479	1564	208	413	85	10	22	225	151	239	.264	.333	.373	90	-19	-20	200	13			.938	2	3/21SO	-0.6

■ LOU BRUCE

Bruce, Louis R. b: 1/16/1877, St.Regis, N.Y. d: 2/9/68, Ilion, N.Y. BL/TR, 5'5", 145 lbs. Deb: 6/22/04

YEAR	TM/L	G	AB	R	H	2B	3B	HR	RBI	BB	SO	AVG	OBP	SLG	PRO+	BR	/A	RC	SB	CS	SBR	FA	FR	POS	TPR
1904	Phi-A	30	101	9	27	3	0	0	8	5		.267	.302	.297	86	-1	-2	11	2			.969	-2	O/P23	-0.6

■ EARLE BRUCKER

Brucker, Earle Francis Jr. b: 8/29/25, Los Angeles, Cal. BL/TR, 6'2", 210 lbs. Deb: 10/02/48 F

YEAR	TM/L	G	AB	R	H	2B	3B	HR	RBI	BB	SO	AVG	OBP	SLG	PRO+	BR	/A	RC	SB	CS	SBR	FA	FR	POS	TPR
1948	Phi-A	2	6	0	1	1	0	0	0	1	1	.167	.286	.333	64	-0	-0	1	0	0	0	1.000	-0	/C	-0.1

■ EARLE BRUCKER

Brucker, Earle Francis Sr. b: 5/6/01, Albany, N.Y. d: 5/8/81, San Diego, Cal. BR/TR, 5'11", 175 lbs. Deb: 4/19/37 FMC

YEAR	TM/L	G	AB	R	H	2B	3B	HR	RBI	BB	SO	AVG	OBP	SLG	PRO+	BR	/A	RC	SB	CS	SBR	FA	FR	POS	TPR
1937	Phi-A	102	317	40	82	16	5	6	37	48	30	.259	.356	.397	91	-5	-4	47	1	2	-1	.971	-6	C	-0.6
1938	Phi-A	53	171	26	64	21	1	3	35	19	16	.374	.437	.561	152	13	14	42	1	1	-0	.986	-2	C/1	1.2
1939	Phi-A	62	172	18	50	15	1	3	31	24	16	.291	.381	.442	112	3	3	28	0	1	-1	1.000	-5	C	0.0
1940	Phi-A	23	46	3	9	1	1	0	2	6	3	.196	.288	.261	44	-4	-4	3	0	0	0	.966	2	C	-0.1
1943	Phi-A	1	1	0	0	0	0	0	0	0	0	.000	.000	.000	-99	-0	-0	0	0	0	0	.000	0	H	0.0
Total	5	241	707	87	205	53	8	12	105	97	65	.290	.376	.438	108	7	9	120	2	4	-2		-11	C/1	0.5

■ J. T. BRUETT

Bruett, Joseph Timothy b: 10/8/67, Milwaukee, Wis. BL/TL, 5'11", 175 lbs. Deb: 6/03/92

YEAR	TM/L	G	AB	R	H	2B	3B	HR	RBI	BB	SO	AVG	OBP	SLG	PRO+	BR	/A	RC	SB	CS	SBR	FA	FR	POS	TPR
1992	Min-A	56	76	7	19	4	0	0	2	6	12	.250	.313	.303	71	-3	-3	8	6	3	0	.979	-12	O/D	-1.6

■ FRANK BRUGGY

Bruggy, Frank Leo b: 5/4/1891, Elizabeth, N.J. d: 4/5/59, Elizabeth, N.J. BR/TR, 5'11", 195 lbs. Deb: 4/13/21

YEAR	TM/L	G	AB	R	H	2B	3B	HR	RBI	BB	SO	AVG	OBP	SLG	PRO+	BR	/A	RC	SB	CS	SBR	FA	FR	POS	TPR
1921	Phi-N	96	277	28	86	11	2	5	28	23	37	.310	.370	.419	100	4	1	44	6	2	1	.953	-9	C/1	-0.3
1922	Phi-A	53	111	10	31	7	0	0	9	6	11	.279	.322	.342	71	-4	-5	12	1	2	-1	.925	-2	C	-0.6
1923	Phi-A	54	105	4	22	3	0	1	6	4	9	.210	.245	.267	34	-10	-10	7	1	1	-0	.950	0	C/1	-0.9
1924	Phi-A	50	113	9	30	6	0	0	8	8	15	.265	.314	.319	63	-6	-6	12	4	0	1	.928	-8	C	-1.0
1925	Cin-N	6	14	2	3	0	0	0	1	2	0	.214	.313	.214	38	-1	-1	1	0	0	0	.870	-0	/C	-0.1
Total	5	259	620	53	172	27	2	6	52	43	72	.277	.329	.356	76	-18	-22	76	12	5	1	.941	-18	C/1	-2.9

■ JACOB BRUMFIELD

Brumfield, Jacob Donnell b: 5/27/65, Bogalusa, La. BR/TR, 6', 170 lbs. Deb: 4/06/92

YEAR	TM/L	G	AB	R	H	2B	3B	HR	RBI	BB	SO	AVG	OBP	SLG	PRO+	BR	/A	RC	SB	CS	SBR	FA	FR	POS	TPR
1992	Cin-N	24	30	6	4	0	0	0	2	2	4	.133	.212	.133	-0	-4	-4	2	6	0	2	1.000	-2	O	-0.5

■ MIKE BRUMLEY

Brumley, Anthony Michael b: 4/9/63, Oklahoma City, Okla. BB/TR, 5'10", 165 lbs. Deb: 6/16/87 F

YEAR	TM/L	G	AB	R	H	2B	3B	HR	RBI	BB	SO	AVG	OBP	SLG	PRO+	BR	/A	RC	SB	CS	SBR	FA	FR	POS	TPR
1987	Chi-N	39	104	8	21	2	2	1	9	10	30	.202	.278	.288	49	-7	-8	9	7	1	2	.965	4	S/2	0.0
1989	Det-A	92	212	33	42	5	2	1	11	14	45	.198	.251	.255	44	-16	-15	14	8	4	0	.980	-8	S23/OD	-2.0
1990	Sea-A	62	147	19	33	5	4	0	7	10	22	.224	.274	.313	63	-7	-7	12	2	0	1	.983	-2	S/23OD	-0.6
1991	Bos-A	63	118	16	25	5	0	0	5	10	22	.212	.273	.254	45	-8	-9	9	2	0	1	.950	13	S3/2OD	0.6
1992	Bos-A	2	1	0	0	0	0	0	0	0	0	.000	.000	.000	-95	-0	-0	0	0	0	0	.000	0	/H	0.0
Total	5	258	582	76	121	17	8	2	32	44	119	.208	.266	.275	49	-39	-40	45	19	5	3	.971	8	S/23DO	-2.0

■ MIKE BRUMLEY

Brumley, Tony Mike b: 7/10/38, Granite, Okla. BL/TR, 5'10", 195 lbs. Deb: 4/18/64 F

YEAR	TM/L	G	AB	R	H	2B	3B	HR	RBI	BB	SO	AVG	OBP	SLG	PRO+	BR	/A	RC	SB	CS	SBR	FA	FR	POS	TPR
1964	Was-A	136	426	36	104	19	2	2	35	40	54	.244	.310	.312	74	-14	-14	40	1	1	-0	.991	-13	*C	-2.3
1965	Was-A	79	216	15	45	4	0	3	15	20	33	.208	.282	.269	58	-12	-11	16	1	1	-0	.990	2	C	-0.7
1966	Was-A	9	18	1	2	1	0	0	0	0	2	.111	.111	.167	-22	-3	-3	0	0	0	0	1.000	-1	/C	-0.4
Total	3	224	660	52	151	24	2	5	50	60	89	.229	.296	.294	67	-29	-28	57	2	2	-1	.991	-12	C	-3.4

■ GLENN BRUMMER

Brummer, Glenn Edward b: 11/23/54, Olney, Ill. BR/TR, 6', 200 lbs. Deb: 5/25/81

YEAR	TM/L	G	AB	R	H	2B	3B	HR	RBI	BB	SO	AVG	OBP	SLG	PRO+	BR	/A	RC	SB	CS	SBR	FA	FR	POS	TPR
1981	StL-N	21	30	2	6	1	0	0	2	1	2	.200	.226	.233	30	-3	-3	2	0	0	0	1.000	2	C	-0.1
1982	*StL-N	35	64	4	15	4	0	0	8	0	12	.234	.234	.297	47	-5	-5	5	2	0	1	.970	3	C	-0.1
1983	StL-N	45	87	7	24	7	0	0	9	10	11	.276	.351	.356	96	-0	-0	10	1	3	-2	.978	0	C	0.0
1984	StL-N	28	58	3	12	0	0	1	3	3	7	.207	.246	.259	43	-4	-4	3	0	0	0	.973	4	C	0.0
1985	Tex-A	49	108	7	30	4	0	0	5	11	22	.278	.355	.315	84	-2	-2	11	1	5	-3	.989	-4	C/OD	-0.7
Total	5	178	347	23	87	16	0	1	27	25	54	.251	.305	.305	70	-14	-14	30	4	8	-4	.981	5	C/DO	-0.9

■ TOM BRUNANSKY

Brunansky, Thomas Andrew b: 8/20/60, Covina, Cal. BR/TR, 6'4", 211 lbs. Deb: 4/09/81

YEAR	TM/L	G	AB	R	H	2B	3B	HR	RBI	BB	SO	AVG	OBP	SLG	PRO+	BR	/A	RC	SB	CS	SBR	FA	FR	POS	TPR
1981	Cal-A	11	33	7	5	0	0	3	6	8	10	.152	.317	.424	112	1	1	5	1	0	0	.938	3	O	0.3
1982	Min-A	127	463	77	126	30	1	20	46	71	101	.272	.378	.471	128	22	20	84	1	2	-1	.986	13	*O	2.8
1983	Min-A	151	542	70	123	24	5	28	82	61	95	.227	.310	.445	101	2	-0	72	2	5	-2	.985	18	*O/D	1.1
1984	Min-A	155	567	75	144	21	0	32	85	57	94	.254	.322	.460	109	9	6	81	4	5	-2	.984	5	*O/D	0.4
1985	Min-A★	157	567	71	137	28	4	27	90	71	86	.242	.326	.448	103	7	2	83	5	3	-0	.984	5	*O	0.2
1986	Min-A	157	593	69	152	28	1	23	75	53	98	.256	.318	.423	97	-1	-3	78	12	4	1	.982	8	*O/D	0.1
1987	*Min-A	155	532	83	138	22	2	32	85	74	104	.259	.354	.489	116	16	13	90	11	11	-3	.990	-2	*OD	0.3
1988	Min-A	14	49	5	9	1	0	1	6	7	11	.184	.286	.265	54	-3	-3	4	1	2	-1	.864	-2	O/D	-0.7
	StL-N	143	523	69	128	22	4	22	79	79	82	.245	.348	.428	121	16	15	79	16	6	1	**.996**	4	*O	1.7
1989	StL-N	158	556	67	133	29	3	20	85	59	107	.239	.314	.410	102	3	1	70	5	9	-4	.977	4	*O/1	-0.3
1990	StL-N	19	57	5	9	3	0	1	2	12	10	.158	.314	.263	60	-3	-3	6	0	0	0	.950	1	O	-0.2

YEAR	TM/L	G	AB	R	H	2B	3B	HR	RBI	BB	SO	AVG	OBP	SLG	PRO+	BR	/A	RC	SB	CS	SBR	FA	FR	POS	TPR
	*Bos-A	129	461	61	123	24	5	15	71	54	105	.267	.347	.438	113	11	9	67	5	10	-5	.982	10	*O/D	1.1
1991	Bos-A	142	459	54	105	24	1	16	70	49	72	.229	.307	.390	87	-6	-9	56	1	2	-1	.989	3	*O/D	-1.0
1992	Bos-A	138	458	47	122	31	3	15	74	66	96	.266	.359	.445	118	15	12	73	2	5	-2	.980	3	O1D	0.9
Total	12	1656	5860	760	1454	287	29	255	856	721	1071	.248	.334	.438	108	89	61	847	66	64	-19	.983	70	*O/D1	6.7
■ **ARLO BRUNSBERG** Brunsberg, Arlo Adolph b: 8/15/40, Fertile, Minn. BL/TR, 6', 195 lbs. Deb: 9/23/66																									
1966	Det-A	2	3	1	1	1	0	0	0	0	0	.333	.500	.667	227	1	1	1	0	0	0	1.000	-1	/C	0.0
■ **BOB BRUSH** Brush, Robert b: 3/8/1875, Osage, Iowa d: 4/2/44, San Bernardino, Cal. Deb: 4/20/07																									
1907	Bos-N	2	2	0	0	0	0	0	0	0		.000	.000	.000	-99	-0	-0	0	0			1.000	-0	/1	-0.1
■ **BILL BRUTON** Bruton, William Haron b: 12/22/25, Panola, Ala. BL/TR, 6'0.5", 169 lbs. Deb: 4/13/53																									
1953	Mil-N	151	613	82	153	18	14	1	41	44	100	.250	.306	.330	70	-31	-25	65	**26**	11	1	.979	8	*O	-2.1
1954	Mil-N	142	567	89	161	20	7	4	30	40	78	.284	.336	.365	88	-14	-10	73	**34**	13	2	.981	1	*O	-1.2
1955	Mil-N	149	636	106	175	30	12	9	47	43	72	.275	.325	.403	97	-8	-4	86	**25**	11	1	.968	15	*O	0.5
1956	Mil-N	147	525	73	143	23	**15**	8	56	26	63	.272	.308	.419	99	-6	-2	66	8	6	-1	.969	3	*O	-0.9
1957	Mil-N	79	306	41	85	16	9	5	30	19	35	.278	.322	.438	110	0	3	44	11	4	1	.981	1	O	0.0
1958	*Mil-N	100	325	47	91	11	3	3	28	27	37	.280	.339	.360	93	-6	-3	41	4	1	1	.977	-7	O	-1.4
1959	Mil-N	133	478	72	138	22	6	6	41	35	54	.289	.339	.397	104	-3	2	64	13	5	1	.991	4	*O	0.0
1960	Mil-N	151	629	**112**	180	27	**13**	12	54	41	97	.286	.332	.428	115	4	10	89	22	13	-1	.986	4	*O	0.5
1961	Det-A	160	596	99	153	15	5	17	63	61	66	.257	.329	.384	87	-9	-11	79	22	6	3	.988	12	*O	-0.5
1962	Det-A	147	561	90	156	27	5	16	74	55	67	.278	.348	.430	104	6	4	84	14	7	0	.983	19	*O	1.4
1963	Det-A	145	524	84	134	21	8	8	48	59	70	.256	.331	.372	93	-2	-4	67	14	7	0	.991	10	*O	-0.1
1964	Det-A	106	296	42	82	11	5	5	33	32	54	.277	.348	.399	105	3	3	42	14	5	1	.987	-1	O	0.0
Total	12	1610	6056	937	1651	241	102	94	545	482	793	.273	.329	.393	96	-65	-38	801	207	89	9	.981	68	*O	-3.8
■ **ED BRUYETTE** Bruyette, Edward T. b: 8/31/1874, Wanawa, Wis. d: 8/5/40, Peshastin, Wash. BL/TR, 5'10", 170 lbs. Deb: 8/06/01																									
1901	Mil-A	26	82	7	15	3	0	0	4	12		.183	.295	.220	46	-6	-5	6	1			.778	-6	O/2S3	-1.2
■ **BILLY BRYAN** Bryan, William Ronald b: 12/4/38, Morgan, Ga. BL/TR, 6'4", 200 lbs. Deb: 9/12/61																									
1961	KC-A	9	19	2	3	0	0	1	2	2	7	.158	.238	.316	47	-2	-2	1	0	0	0	1.000	-2	/C	-0.3
1962	KC-A	25	74	5	11	2	1	2	7	5	32	.149	.203	.284	28	-8	-8	5	0	0	0	.976	-3	C	-1.0
1963	KC-A	24	65	11	11	1	1	3	7	9	22	.169	.270	.354	70	-2	-3	6	0	0	0	.981	5	C	0.3
1964	KC-A	93	220	19	53	9	2	13	36	16	69	.241	.292	.477	107	2	1	29	0	0	0	.991	-9	C	-0.6
1965	KC-A	108	325	36	82	11	5	14	51	29	87	.252	.317	.446	116	5	6	47	0	0	0	.984	-6	C	0.5
1966	KC-A	32	76	0	10	4	0	0	7	6	17	.132	.195	.184	10	-9	-9	3	0	0	0	.965	-1	C/1	-1.0
	NY-A	27	69	5	15	2	0	4	5	5	19	.217	.270	.420	99	-1	-0	8	0	0	0	.988	-0	C/1	0.0
	Yr	59	145	5	25	6	0	4	12	11	36	.172	.231	.297	52	-10	-9	10	0	0	0	.975	-2	C/1	-1.0
1967	NY-A	16	12	1	2	0	0	1	2	5	3	.167	.412	.417	151	1	1	3	0	0	0	1.000	1	/C	0.2
1968	Was-A	40	108	7	22	3	0	3	8	14	27	.204	.301	.315	90	-2	-1	11	0	1	-1	.983	-4	C	-0.4
Total	8	374	968	86	209	32	9	41	125	91	283	.216	.285	.395	91	-14	-14	112	0	1	-1	.984	-18	C/1	-2.3
■ **DEREK BRYANT** Bryant, Derek Roszell b: 10/9/51, Lexington, Ky. BR/TR, 5'11", 185 lbs. Deb: 4/24/79																									
1979	Oak-A	39	106	8	19	2	1	0	13	10	10	.179	.250	.217	29	-11	-10	6	0	0	0	1.000	-2	O/D	-1.3
■ **DON BRYANT** Bryant, Donald Ray b: 7/13/41, Jasper, Fla. BR/TR, 6'5", 200 lbs. Deb: 7/17/66 C																									
1966	Chi-N	13	26	2	8	2	0	0	4	1	4	.308	.357	.385	105	0	0	4	1	0	0	.978	0	C	0.1
1969	Hou-N	31	59	2	11	1	0	1	6	4	13	.186	.250	.254	42	-5	-4	4	0	0	0	.993	3	C	-0.1
1970	Hou-N	15	24	2	5	0	0	0	3	1	8	.208	.240	.208	22	-3	-3	1	0	0	0	.957	-0	C	-0.3
Total	3	59	109	6	24	3	0	1	13	6	25	.220	.274	.275	53	-7	-7	9	1	0	0	.983	3	/C	-0.3
■ **G. BRYANT** Bryant, G. Deb: 8/06/1885																									
1885	Det-N	1	4	0	0	0	0	0	1	0	2	.000	.000	.000	-99	-1	-1	0				1.000	-1	/2	-0.2
■ **RALPH BRYANT** Bryant, Ralph Wendell b: 5/20/61, Fort Gaines, Ga. BL/TR, 6'2", 200 lbs. Deb: 9/08/85																									
1985	LA-N	6	6	0	2	0	0	0	1	0	2	.333	.333	.333	90	-0	-0	1	0	0	0	.000	-1	/O	-0.1
1986	LA-N	27	75	15	19	4	2	6	13	5	25	.253	.309	.600	156	4	4	13	0	1	-1	.953	-1	O	0.2
1987	LA-N	46	69	7	17	2	1	2	10	10	24	.246	.350	.391	99	-0	0	10	2	1	0	.917	-3	O	-0.4
Total	3	79	150	22	38	6	3	8	24	15	51	.253	.329	.493	125	4	4	24	2	2	-1	.940	-5	/O	-0.3
■ **STEVE BRYE** Brye, Stephen Robert b: 2/4/49, Alameda, Cal. BR/TR, 6', 190 lbs. Deb: 9/03/70																									
1970	Min-A	9	11	1	2	1	0	0	2	2	4	.182	.308	.273	60	-1	-1	1	0	0	0	1.000	-2	/O	-0.2
1971	Min-A	28	107	10	24	1	0	3	11	7	15	.224	.272	.318	65	-5	-5	9	3	1	0	.966	1	O	-0.6
1972	Min-A	100	253	18	61	9	3	0	12	17	38	.241	.292	.300	73	-7	-9	22	3	1	0	.994	2	O	-1.0
1973	Min-A	92	278	39	73	9	5	6	33	35	43	.263	.345	.396	104	3	2	38	3	5	-2	.986	1	O/D	-0.2
1974	Min-A	135	488	52	138	32	1	2	41	22	59	.283	.320	.365	93	-3	-5	54	1	3	-2	**.997**	1	*O	-1.1
1975	Min-A	86	246	41	62	13	1	9	34	21	37	.252	.316	.423	105	2	1	32	2	1	0	.983	-3	O/D	-0.4
1976	Min-A	87	258	33	68	11	0	2	23	13	31	.264	.299	.329	82	-6	-6	24	1	2	-1	.987	-13	O/D	-2.5
1977	Mil-A	94	241	27	60	14	3	7	28	16	39	.249	.298	.419	93	-3	-3	30	1	0	0	1.000	-1	O/D	-0.6
1978	Pit-N	66	115	16	27	7	0	1	9	11	10	.235	.307	.322	73	-4	-4	12	2	1	0	.983	0	O	-0.6
Total	9	697	1997	237	515	97	13	30	193	144	276	.258	.311	.365	89	-23	-30	222	16	14	-4	.991	-13	O/D	-7.2
■ **HAL BUBSER** Bubser, Harold Fred b: 9/28/1895, Chicago, Ill. d: 6/22/59, Melrose Park, Ill BR/TR, 5'11", 170 lbs. Deb: 4/15/22																									
1922	Chi-A	3	3	0	0	0	0	0	0	0	2	.000	.000	.000	-99	-1	-1	0	0	0	0	.000	0	H	-0.1
■ **JOHNNY BUCHA** Bucha, John George b: 1/22/25, Allentown, Pa. BR/TR, 5'11", 190 lbs. Deb: 5/02/48																									
1948	StL-N	2	1	0	0	0	0	0	0	1	0	.000	.500	.000	43	0	0	0	0			1.000	-0	/C	0.0
1950	StL-N	22	36	1	5	1	0	0	1	4	7	.139	.225	.167	5	-5	-5	1	0			.959	0	C	-0.5
1953	Det-A	60	158	17	35	9	0	1	14	20	14	.222	.309	.297	65	-8	-7	16	1	1	-0	.984	-4	C	-1.0
Total	3	84	195	18	40	10	0	1	15	25	21	.205	.295	.272	53	-13	-13	17	1	1		.980	-4	/C	-1.5
■ **JERRY BUCHEK** Buchek, Gerald Peter b: 5/9/42, St.Louis, Mo. BR/TR, 5'11", 185 lbs. Deb: 6/30/61																									
1961	StL-N	31	90	6	12	2	0	0	9	0	28	.133	.152	.156	-16	-15	-16	1	0	0	0	.912	-6	S	-2.1
1963	StL-N	3	4	0	1	0	0	0	0	0	2	.250	.250	.250	41	-0	-0	0	0	0	0	1.000	0	/S	0.0
1964	*StL-N	35	30	7	6	0	2	0	1	3	11	.200	.273	.333	64	-1	-2	3	0	0	0	.929	7	S/23	0.6
1965	StL-N	55	166	17	41	8	3	3	21	13	46	.247	.302	.386	84	-2	-4	19	1	0	0	.994	10	2S/3	1.1
1966	StL-N	100	284	23	67	10	4	4	25	23	71	.236	.293	.342	75	-9	-9	26	0	5	-3	.974	-13	2S/3	-2.0
1967	NY-N	124	411	35	97	11	2	14	41	26	101	.236	.285	.375	89	-8	-7	41	3	5	-2	.977	4	23/S	0.1
1968	NY-N	73	192	8	35	4	0	1	11	10	53	.182	.234	.219	36	-15	-15	9	1	1	-0	.935	1	32/O	-1.7
Total	7	421	1177	96	259	35	11	22	108	75	312	.220	.271	.325	67	-50	-53	98	5	11	-5	.978	3	2S/3O	-4.0
■ **JIM BUCHER** Bucher, James Quinter b: 3/11/11, Manassas, Va. BL/TR, 5'11", 170 lbs. Deb: 4/18/34																									
1934	Bro-N	47	84	12	19	5	2	0	8	4	7	.226	.261	.333	61	-5	-5	7	1			.920	-1	2/3	-0.5
1935	Bro-N	123	473	72	143	22	1	7	58	10	33	.302	.317	.397	93	-7	-6	58	4			.950	-11	23O	-1.4
1936	Bro-N	110	370	49	93	12	8	2	41	29	27	.251	.306	.343	74	-13	-14	40	5			.910	-8	32O	-2.0
1937	Bro-N	125	380	44	96	11	2	4	37	20	18	.253	.295	.324	67	-17	-18	37	5			.951	-14	23/O	-2.7

YEAR	TM/L	G	AB	R	H	2B	3B	HR	RBI	BB	SO	AVG	OBP	SLG	PRO+	BR	/A	RC	SB	CS	SBR	FA	FR	POS	TPR
1938	StL-N	17	57	7	13	3	1	0	7	2	2	.228	.254	.316	53	-4	-4	4	0			.955	-4	2/3	-0.7
1944	Bos-A	80	277	39	76	9	2	4	31	19	13	.274	.326	.365	98	-1	-1	33	3	3	-1	.958	-9	32	-1.0
1945	Bos-A	52	151	19	34	4	3	0	11	7	13	.225	.264	.291	60	-8	-8	11	1	3	-2	.940	-2	3/2	-1.1
Total	7	554	1792	242	474	66	19	17	193	91	113	.265	.302	.351	78	-56	-55	192	19	6		.939	-48	32/O	-9.4

■ **KEVIN BUCKLEY** Buckley, Kevin John b: 1/16/59, Quincy, Mass. BR/TR, 6′1″, 200 lbs. Deb: 9/04/84

YEAR	TM/L	G	AB	R	H	2B	3B	HR	RBI	BB	SO	AVG	OBP	SLG	PRO+	BR	/A	RC	SB	CS	SBR	FA	FR	POS	TPR
1984	Tex-A	5	7	1	2	1	0	0	0	2	4	.286	.444	.429	138	1	1	2	0	0	0	.000	0	/D	0.1

■ **DICK BUCKLEY** Buckley, Richard D. b: 9/21/1858, Troy, N.Y. d: 12/12/29, Pittsburgh, Pa. TR, 5′10″, 195 lbs. Deb: 4/20/1888

YEAR	TM/L	G	AB	R	H	2B	3B	HR	RBI	BB	SO	AVG	OBP	SLG	PRO+	BR	/A	RC	SB	CS	SBR	FA	FR	POS	TPR
1888	Ind-N	71	260	28	71	9	3	5	22	6	24	.273	.289	.388	114	4	3	31	4			.898	-21	C3/O1	-1.2
1889	Ind-N	68	260	35	67	11	0	8	41	15	32	.258	.301	.392	92	-3	-4	33	5			.877	-21	C3/O1	-1.7
1890	NY-N	70	266	39	68	11	0	2	26	23	35	.256	.324	.320	90	-3	-3	29	3			.931	9	C/3	1.0
1891	NY-N	75	253	23	55	9	1	4	31	11	30	.217	.258	.308	69	-11	-10	21	3			.958	19	C/3	1.3
1892	StL-N	121	410	43	93	17	4	5	52	22	34	.227	.275	.324	87	-10	-7	39	7			.937	-7	*C/1	-0.6
1893	StL-N	9	23	2	4	1	0	0	1	0	0	.174	.174	.217	5	-3	-3	1	0			.914	1	/C	-0.1
1894	StL-N	29	89	5	16	1	2	1	3	6	3	.180	.240	.270	24	-11	-11	7	1			.936	3	C/1	-0.5
	Phi-N	43	160	18	47	7	3	1	26	6	13	.294	.327	.394	77	-7	-6	22	0			.966	4	C/1	0.1
	Yr	72	249	23	63	8	5	2	29	12	16	.253	.295	.349	57	-18	-18	29	1			.954	7	C/1	-0.4
1895	Phi-N	38	112	20	28	6	1	0	14	9	17	.250	.333	.321	71	-5	-5	14	2			.919	7	C	0.4
Total	8	524	1833	213	449	72	14	26	216	98	188	.245	.291	.342	82	-49	-46	198	25			.931	-6	C/31O	-1.3

■ **BILL BUCKNER** Buckner, William Joseph b: 12/14/49, Vallejo, Cal. BL/TL, 6′, 185 lbs. Deb: 9/21/69

YEAR	TM/L	G	AB	R	H	2B	3B	HR	RBI	BB	SO	AVG	OBP	SLG	PRO+	BR	/A	RC	SB	CS	SBR	FA	FR	POS	TPR
1969	LA-N	1	1	0	0	0	0	0	0	0	0	.000	.000	.000	-99	-0	-0	0	0	0	0	.000	0	H	0.0
1970	LA-N	28	68	6	13	3	1	0	4	3	7	.191	.225	.265	32	-7	-6	4	0	1	-1	1.000	1	O/1	-0.6
1971	LA-N	108	358	37	99	15	1	5	41	11	18	.277	.307	.366	96	-5	-3	40	4	1	1	.994	0	O1	-0.7
1972	LA-N	105	383	47	122	14	3	5	37	17	13	.319	.349	.410	118	7	8	52	10	3	1	.992	-2	O1	0.2
1973	LA-N	140	575	68	158	20	0	8	46	17	34	.275	.299	.351	83	-17	-14	58	12	2	2	.998	-7	1O	-2.9
1974	*LA-N	145	580	83	182	30	3	7	58	30	24	.314	.352	.412	118	9	12	81	31	13	2	.976	-7	*O/1	0.0
1975	LA-N	92	288	30	70	11	2	6	31	17	15	.243	.290	.358	82	-9	-8	27	8	3	1	.986	0	O	-1.0
1976	LA-N	154	642	76	193	28	4	7	60	26	26	.301	.329	.389	105	1	2	82	28	9	3	.985	-2	*O/1	-0.3
1977	Chi-N	122	426	40	121	27	0	11	60	21	23	.284	.319	.425	88	-3	-8	52	7	5	-1	.990	-0	1	-1.5
1978	Chi-N	117	446	47	144	26	1	5	74	18	17	.323	.349	.419	102	7	1	59	7	5	-1	.995	8	*1	0.2
1979	Chi-N	149	591	72	168	34	7	14	66	30	28	.284	.321	.437	96	2	-5	78	9	4	0	.995	18	*1	0.5
1980	Chi-N	145	578	69	187	41	3	10	68	30	18	**.324**	.357	.457	117	18	13	90	1	2	-1	.993	4	1O	1.0
1981	Chi-N★	106	421	45	131	**35**	3	10	75	26	16	.311	.353	.480	129	17	15	65	5	2	0	.984	1	*1	1.1
1982	Chi-N	161	657	93	201	34	5	15	105	36	26	.306	.347	.441	116	15	13	98	15	5	2	.993	16	*1	2.2
1983	Chi-N	153	626	79	175	**38**	6	16	66	25	30	.280	.313	.436	101	2	-2	83	12	4	1	.992	21	*1O	1.2
1984	Chi-N	21	43	3	9	0	0	0	2	1	1	.209	.244	.209	26	-4	-4	2	0	0	0	1.000	2	/1O	-0.3
	Bos-A	114	439	51	122	21	2	11	67	24	38	.278	.323	.410	97	0	-2	55	2	2	-1	.986	5	*1	-0.6
1985	Bos-A	162	673	89	201	46	3	16	110	30	36	.299	.330	.447	106	8	5	96	18	4	3	.992	25	*1	2.2
1986	*Bos-A	153	629	73	168	39	2	18	102	40	25	.267	.315	.421	98	-3	-3	76	6	4	-1	.989	20	*1D	0.6
1987	Bos-A	75	286	23	78	6	1	2	42	13	19	.273	.304	.322	65	-14	-15	25	1	3	-2	.991	3	1	-1.8
	Cal-A	57	183	16	56	12	1	3	32	9	7	.306	.339	.432	106	0	1	26	1	0	0	1.000	-0	D/1	0.1
	Yr	132	469	39	134	18	2	5	74	22	26	.286	.318	.365	80	-13	-13	51	2	3	-1	.992	3	1D	-1.7
1988	Cal-A	19	43	1	9	0	0	0	9	4	0	.209	.277	.209	39	-3	-3	3	2	0	1	1.000	0	D/1	-0.2
	KC-A	89	242	18	62	14	0	3	34	13	19	.256	.294	.351	79	-7	-7	24	3	1	0	.994	-0	D1	-0.9
	Yr	108	285	19	71	14	0	3	43	17	19	.249	.291	.330	73	-10	-10	27	5	1	1	.994	0	D1	-1.1
1989	KC-A	79	176	7	38	4	1	1	16	6	11	.216	.242	.267	43	-13	-13	11	1	0	0	.985	-0	1D	-1.5
1990	Bos-A	22	43	4	8	0	0	1	3	3	2	.186	.239	.256	37	-4	-4	3	0	0	0	1.000	-0	1	-0.5
Total	22	2517	9397	1077	2715	498	49	174	1208	450	453	.289	.324	.408	99	-2	-27	1190	183	73	11	.992	106	*1OD	-3.5

■ **MARK BUDASKA** Budaska, Mark David b: 12/27/52, Sharon, Pa. BB/TL, 6′, 180 lbs. Deb: 6/06/78

YEAR	TM/L	G	AB	R	H	2B	3B	HR	RBI	BB	SO	AVG	OBP	SLG	PRO+	BR	/A	RC	SB	CS	SBR	FA	FR	POS	TPR
1978	Oak-A	4	4	0	1	1	0	0	0	1	2	.250	.400	.500	160	0	0	1	0	0	0	.500	-1	/O	-0.1
1981	Oak-A	9	32	3	5	1	0	0	2	4	10	.156	.250	.188	29	-3	-3	2	0	1	-1	.000	0	/D	-0.4
Total	2	13	36	3	6	2	0	0	2	5	12	.167	.268	.222	44	-3	-2	2	0	1	-1		-1	/DO	-0.5

■ **BUDD** Budd Deb: 9/10/1890

YEAR	TM/L	G	AB	R	H	2B	3B	HR	RBI	BB	SO	AVG	OBP	SLG	PRO+	BR	/A	RC	SB	CS	SBR	FA	FR	POS	TPR
1890	Cle-P	1	4	0	0	0	0	0	0	0	3	.000	.000	.000	-99	-1	-1	0	0			1.000	-0	/O	-0.1

■ **DON BUDDIN** Buddin, Donald Thomas b: 5/5/34, Turbeville, S.C. BR/TR, 5′11″, 178 lbs. Deb: 4/17/56

YEAR	TM/L	G	AB	R	H	2B	3B	HR	RBI	BB	SO	AVG	OBP	SLG	PRO+	BR	/A	RC	SB	CS	SBR	FA	FR	POS	TPR
1956	Bos-A	114	377	49	90	24	0	5	37	65	62	.239	.357	.342	76	-6	-13	49	2	0	1	.953	14	*S	1.0
1958	Bos-A	136	497	74	118	25	2	12	43	82	106	.237	.350	.368	92	1	-4	66	0	4	-2	.958	15	*S	2.1
1959	Bos-A	151	485	75	117	24	1	10	53	92	99	.241	.368	.357	95	3	0	72	6	1	1	.949	-17	*S	-0.3
1960	Bos-A	124	428	62	105	21	5	6	36	62	59	.245	.342	.360	87	-5	-7	53	4	2	0	.951	-5	*S	-0.2
1961	Bos-A	115	339	58	89	22	3	6	42	72	45	.263	.395	.398	110	9	8	58	2	1	0	.956	-1	*S	1.6
1962	Hou-N	40	80	10	13	4	1	2	10	17	17	.162	.316	.313	75	-3	-2	8	0	0	0	.952	3	S/3	0.3
	Det-A	31	83	14	19	3	0	0	4	20	16	.229	.385	.265	76	-1	-2	11	1	0	0	.978	-2	S/23	-0.2
Total	6	711	2289	342	551	123	12	41	225	410	404	.241	.360	.359	90	-3	-20	317	15	8	-0	.954	7	S/32	4.3

■ **STEVE BUECHELE** Buechele, Steven Bernard b: 9/26/61, Lancaster, Cal. BR/TR, 6′2″, 190 lbs. Deb: 7/19/85

YEAR	TM/L	G	AB	R	H	2B	3B	HR	RBI	BB	SO	AVG	OBP	SLG	PRO+	BR	/A	RC	SB	CS	SBR	FA	FR	POS	TPR
1985	Tex-A	69	219	22	48	6	3	6	21	14	38	.219	.272	.356	70	-9	-10	18	3	2	-0	.969	6	3/2	-0.4
1986	Tex-A	153	461	54	112	19	2	18	54	35	98	.243	.303	.410	90	-6	-8	54	5	8	-3	.968	19	*32/O	0.6
1987	Tex-A	136	363	45	86	20	0	13	50	28	66	.237	.293	.399	81	-10	-11	42	2	2	-1	.964	3	*32/O	-0.9
1988	Tex-A	155	503	68	126	21	4	16	58	65	79	.250	.342	.404	105	6	5	71	2	4	-2	.962	8	*3/2	1.0
1989	Tex-A	155	486	60	114	22	2	16	59	36	107	.235	.294	.387	89	-7	-8	50	1	3	-2	.969	15	*32/SD	0.7
1990	Tex-A	91	251	30	54	10	0	7	30	27	63	.215	.296	.339	77	-8	-8	26	1	0	0	.966	6	3/2	-0.1
1991	Tex-A	121	416	58	111	17	2	18	66	39	69	.267	.337	.447	117	8	9	60	0	4	-2	**.991**	20	*32/S	2.7
	*Pit-N	31	114	16	28	5	1	4	19	10	28	.246	.317	.412	105	0	1	14	0	1	-1	.956	3	3	0.3
1992	Pit-N	80	285	27	71	14	1	8	43	34	61	.249	.333	.389	105	2	2	37	0	2	-1	.957	6	3	0.8
	Chi-N	65	239	25	66	9	3	1	21	18	44	.276	.340	.351	94	-1	-2	29	1	1	-0	.960	-2	3/2	-0.4
	Yr	145	524	52	137	23	4	9	64	52	105	.261	.336	.372	100	1	1	66	1	3	-2	.958	4	*3/2	0.4
Total	8	1056	3337	405	816	143	18	107	421	306	653	.245	.314	.394	94	-26	-29	402	15	27	-12	.968	84	3/2SOD	4.3

■ **CHARLIE BUELOW** Buelow, Charles John b: 1/12/1877, Dubuque, Iowa d: 5/4/51, Dubuque, Iowa BR/TR, Deb: 6/01/01

YEAR	TM/L	G	AB	R	H	2B	3B	HR	RBI	BB	SO	AVG	OBP	SLG	PRO+	BR	/A	RC	SB	CS	SBR	FA	FR	POS	TPR
1901	NY-N	22	72	3	8	4	0	0	4	2		.111	.147	.167	-10	-10	-10	2	0			.853	3	3/2	-0.7

■ **FRITZ BUELOW** Buelow, Frederick William b: 2/13/1876, Berlin, Germany d: 12/27/33, Detroit, Mich. BR/TR, 5′10.5″, 170 lbs. Deb: 9/28/1899

YEAR	TM/L	G	AB	R	H	2B	3B	HR	RBI	BB	SO	AVG	OBP	SLG	PRO+	BR	/A	RC	SB	CS	SBR	FA	FR	POS	TPR
1899	StL-N	7	15	4	7	0	2	0	2	2		.467	.556	.733	247	3	3	6	0			1.000	-2	/CO	0.1
1900	StL-N	6	17	2	4	0	0	0	3	0		.235	.235	.235	30	-2	-2	1	0			.864	-2	/CO	-0.3
1901	Det-A	70	231	28	52	5	5	2	29	11		.225	.269	.316	59	-12	-14	22	2			.967	5	C	-0.2
1902	Det-A	66	224	23	50	5	2	2	29	9		.223	.253	.290	49	-15	-16	18	3			.927	0	C/1	-0.9
1903	Det-A	63	192	24	41	3	6	1	13	6		.214	.249	.307	68	-8	-7	17	4			.961	1	C/1	-0.1
1904	Det-A	42	136	6	15	1	1	0	5	8		.110	.160	.132	-7	-16	-16	4	2			.975	1	C	-1.1
	Cle-A	42	119	11	21	4	1	0	5	11		.176	.252	.227	52	-6	-6	8	2			.979	2	C	0.0
	Yr	84	255	17	36	5	2	0	10	19		.141	.204	.176	21	-22	-22	12	4			.977	3	C	-1.1

YEAR	TM/L	G	AB	R	H	2B	3B	HR	RBI	BB	SO	AVG	OBP	SLG	PRO+	BR	/A	RC	SB	CS	SBR	FA	FR	POS	TPR
1905	Cle-A	75	239	11	41	4	1	1	18	6		.172	.198	.209	29	-19	-20	12	7			.963	-7	C/O13	-2.3
1906	Cle-A	34	86	7	14	2	0	0	7	9		.163	.250	.186	38	-6	-6	5	0			.938	3	C/1	-0.1
1907	StL-A	26	75	9	11	1	0	0	1	7		.147	.220	.160	22	-6	-6	3	0			.983	1	C	-0.4
Total	9	431	1334	125	256	25	18	6	112	69		.192	.238	.251	46	-88	-89	97	20			.960	2	C/O13	-5.3

■ **ART BUES** Bues, Arthur Frederick b: 3/3/1888, Milwaukee, Wis. d: 11/7/54, Whitefish Bay, Wis. BR/TR, 5'11", 184 lbs. Deb: 4/17/13

YEAR	TM/L	G	AB	R	H	2B	3B	HR	RBI	BB	SO	AVG	OBP	SLG	PRO+	BR	/A	RC	SB	CS	SBR	FA	FR	POS	TPR
1913	Bos-N	2	1	0	0	0	0	0	0	0	1	.000	.000	.000	-98	-0	-0	0	0			.000	0	/23	0.0
1914	Chi-N	14	45	3	10	1	1	0	4	5	6	.222	.300	.289	76	-1	-1	4	1			.968	-2	3	-0.4
Total	2	16	46	3	10	1	1	0	4	5	7	.217	.294	.283	72	-2	-2	4	1			.968	-2	/32	-0.4

■ **CHARLIE BUFFINTON** Buffinton, Charles G. b: 6/14/1861, Fall River, Mass. d: 9/23/07, Fall River, Mass. BR/TR, 6'1", 180 lbs. Deb: 5/17/1882 M

YEAR	TM/L	G	AB	R	H	2B	3B	HR	RBI	BB	SO	AVG	OBP	SLG	PRO+	BR	/A	RC	SB	CS	SBR	FA	FR	POS	TPR
1882	Bos-N	15	50	5	13	1	0	0	4	2	3	.260	.288	.280	83	-1	-1	4				.615	-1	/OP1	-0.2
1883	Bos-N	86	341	28	81	8	3	1	26	6	24	.238	.251	.287	62	-15	-16	25				.756	-7	OP/1	-1.4
1884	Bos-N	87	352	48	94	18	3	1	39	16	12	.267	.299	.344	102	0	1	37				.946	-1	PO1	-0.5
1885	Bos-N	82	338	26	81	12	3	1	33	3	26	.240	.246	.302	79	-9	-8	26				.912	-0	PO1	-1.0
1886	Bos-N	44	176	27	51	4	1	1	30	6	12	.290	.313	.341	103	-0	1	20	3			.968	-6	1P/O	-0.7
1887	Phi-N	66	269	34	72	12	1	1	46	11	3	.268	.299	.331	72	-8	-11	30	8			.931	2	PO1	-0.9
1888	Phi-N	46	160	14	29	4	1	0	12	7	5	.181	.216	.219	38	-10	-11	8	1			.939	9	P/O	0.0
1889	Phi-N	47	154	16	32	2	0	0	21	9	5	.208	.256	.221	32	-13	-15	9	0			.916	1	P/O	0.0
1890	Phi-P	42	150	24	41	3	2	1	24	9	3	.273	.319	.340	76	-5	-5	17	1			.864	0	P/O1M	-0.1
1891	Bos-a	58	181	16	34	2	1	1	16	19	15	.188	.269	.227	45	-13	-12	11	0			.934	3	PO/1	-0.5
1892	Bal-N	13	43	7	15	1	1	0	4	3	6	.349	.391	.419	143	2	2	8	1			.892	2	P	0.0
Total	11	586	2214	245	543	67	16	7	255	91	114	.245	.276	.299	72	-72	-77	195	14			.916	2	PO/1	-5.3

■ **DON BUFORD** Buford, Donald Alvin b: 2/2/37, Linden, Tex. BB/TR, 5'8", 165 lbs. Deb: 9/14/63 C

YEAR	TM/L	G	AB	R	H	2B	3B	HR	RBI	BB	SO	AVG	OBP	SLG	PRO+	BR	/A	RC	SB	CS	SBR	FA	FR	POS	TPR
1963	Chi-A	12	42	9	12	1	2	0	5	5	7	.286	.362	.405	116	1	1	6	1	0	0	.955	-5	/32	-0.3
1964	Chi-A	135	442	62	116	14	6	4	30	46	62	.262	.339	.348	94	-4	-2	54	12	7	-1	.968	-16	23	-1.3
1965	Chi-A	155	586	93	166	22	5	10	47	67	76	.283	.361	.389	120	12	16	87	17	7	1	.981	3	*23	3.2
1966	Chi-A	163	607	85	148	26	7	8	52	69	71	.244	.324	.349	100	-4	1	74	51	22	2	.939	1	*32O	0.4
1967	Chi-A	156	535	61	129	10	9	4	32	65	51	.241	.324	.316	93	-5	-3	58	34	21	-2	.948	4	*32/O	0.1
1968	Bal-A	130	426	65	120	13	4	15	46	57	46	.282	.372	.437	144	24	24	74	27	12	1	1.000	-6	O2/3	2.0
1969	*Bal-A	144	554	99	161	31	3	11	64	96	62	.291	.400	.417	128	25	25	97	19	18	-5	.983	-4	*O2/3	0.9
1970	*Bal-A	144	504	99	137	15	2	17	66	109	55	.272	.409	.411	125	24	23	97	16	8	0	.987	6	*O/23	2.3
1971	*Bal-A★	122	449	**99**	130	19	4	19	54	89	62	.290	.415	.477	153	34	35	97	15	7	0	.987	3	*O	3.4
1972	Bal-A	125	408	46	84	6	2	5	22	69	83	.206	.326	.267	76	-8	-9	40	8	3	1	.989	-1	*O	-1.7
Total	10	1286	4553	718	1203	157	44	93	418	672	575	.264	.364	.379	115	98	109	686	200	105	-3	.988	-15	O23	9.0

■ **JAY BUHNER** Buhner, Jay Campbell b: 8/13/64, Louisville, Ky. BR/TR, 6'3", 205 lbs. Deb: 9/11/87

YEAR	TM/L	G	AB	R	H	2B	3B	HR	RBI	BB	SO	AVG	OBP	SLG	PRO+	BR	/A	RC	SB	CS	SBR	FA	FR	POS	TPR
1987	NY-A	7	22	0	5	2	0	0	1	1	6	.227	.261	.318	53	-2	-1	2	0	0	0	1.000	0	/O	-0.2
1988	NY-A	25	69	8	13	0	0	3	13	3	25	.188	.253	.319	60	-4	-4	6	0	0	0	.964	1	O	-0.4
	Sea-A	60	192	28	43	13	1	10	25	25	68	.224	.323	.458	111	4	3	29	1	1	-0	.993	9	O	1.0
	Yr	85	261	36	56	13	1	13	38	28	93	.215	.305	.421	98	-0	-1	34	1	1	-0	.985	10	O	0.6
1989	Sea-A	58	204	27	56	15	1	9	33	19	55	.275	.342	.490	128	8	7	34	1	4	-2	.966	1	O	0.5
1990	Sea-A	51	163	16	45	12	0	7	33	17	50	.276	.359	.479	131	7	7	27	2	2	-1	.966	-4	OD	0.1
1991	Sea-A	137	406	64	99	14	4	27	77	53	117	.244	.340	.498	128	15	15	68	0	1	-1	.981	6	*O	1.7
1992	Sea-A	152	543	69	132	16	3	25	79	71	146	.243	.337	.422	110	8	8	77	0	6	-4	.994	11	*O	1.2
Total	6	490	1599	212	393	72	9	81	261	189	467	.246	.334	.454	116	37	34	242	4	14	-7	.984	23	O/D	3.9

■ **HARRY BUKER** Buker, Henry L. "Happy" b: 1859, Chicago, Ill. d: 8/10/1899, Chicago, Ill. Deb: 6/11/1884

YEAR	TM/L	G	AB	R	H	2B	3B	HR	RBI	BB	SO	AVG	OBP	SLG	PRO+	BR	/A	RC	SB	CS	SBR	FA	FR	POS	TPR
1884	Det-N	30	111	5	15	1	0	0	3	4	15	.135	.165	.144	-2	-13	-12	3				.867	1	SO	-0.9

■ **GEORGE BULLARD** Bullard, George Donald "Curly" b: 10/24/28, Lynn, Mass. BR/TR, 5'9.5", 165 lbs. Deb: 9/17/54

YEAR	TM/L	G	AB	R	H	2B	3B	HR	RBI	BB	SO	AVG	OBP	SLG	PRO+	BR	/A	RC	SB	CS	SBR	FA	FR	POS	TPR
1954	Det-A	4	1	0	0	0	0	0	0	0	0	.000	.000	.000	-99	-0	-0	0	0	0	0	.800	2	/S	0.1

■ **SIM BULLAS** Bullas, Simeon Edward b: 4/10/1861, Cleveland, Ohio d: 1/14/08, Cleveland, Ohio 5'7.5", 150 lbs. Deb: 5/02/1884

YEAR	TM/L	G	AB	R	H	2B	3B	HR	RBI	BB	SO	AVG	OBP	SLG	PRO+	BR	/A	RC	SB	CS	SBR	FA	FR	POS	TPR
1884	Tol-a	13	45	4	4	0	1	0		1		.089	.109	.133	-20	-6	-6	1				.909	-6	C/O	-1.0

■ **SCOTT BULLETT** Bullett, Scott Douglas b: 12/25/68, Martinsburg, W.Va. BB/TL, 6'2", 200 lbs. Deb: 9/03/91

YEAR	TM/L	G	AB	R	H	2B	3B	HR	RBI	BB	SO	AVG	OBP	SLG	PRO+	BR	/A	RC	SB	CS	SBR	FA	FR	POS	TPR
1991	Pit-N	11	4	2	0	0	0	0	0	0	3	.000	.200	.000	-40	-1	-1	0	1	1	-0	1.000	-1	/O	-0.2

■ **BUD BULLING** Bulling, Terry Charles "Terry" b: 12/15/52, Lynwood, Cal. BR/TR, 6'1", 200 lbs. Deb: 7/03/77

YEAR	TM/L	G	AB	R	H	2B	3B	HR	RBI	BB	SO	AVG	OBP	SLG	PRO+	BR	/A	RC	SB	CS	SBR	FA	FR	POS	TPR
1977	Min-A	15	32	2	5	1	0	0	5	5	5	.156	.270	.188	28	-3	-3	2	0	0	0	.952	-0	C/D	-0.3
1981	Sea-A	62	154	15	38	3	0	2	15	21	20	.247	.341	.305	84	-2	-3	18	0	0	0	.977	-3	C	-0.3
1982	Sea-A	56	154	17	34	7	0	1	8	19	16	.221	.306	.286	62	-7	-8	13	2	1	0	.991	7	C	0.1
1983	Sea-A	5	5	0	0	0	0	0	0	0	0	.000	.000	.000	-96	-1	-1	0	0	0	0	1.000	1	/C	0.0
Total	4	138	345	34	77	11	0	3	28	45	41	.223	.315	.281	66	-13	-15	33	2	1	0	.983	6	C/D	-0.5

■ **ERIC BULLOCK** Bullock, Eric Gerald b: 2/16/60, Los Angeles, Cal. BL/TL, 5'11", 185 lbs. Deb: 8/26/85

YEAR	TM/L	G	AB	R	H	2B	3B	HR	RBI	BB	SO	AVG	OBP	SLG	PRO+	BR	/A	RC	SB	CS	SBR	FA	FR	POS	TPR
1985	Hou-N	18	25	3	7	2	0	0	2	1	3	.280	.308	.360	89	-1	-0	2	0	1	-1	.750	-2	/O	-0.3
1986	Hou-N	6	21	0	1	0	0	0	1	0	3	.048	.048	.048	-76	-5	-5	0	2	0	1	.875	-1	/O	-0.6
1988	Min-A	16	17	3	5	0	0	0	3	3	1	.294	.400	.294	95	0	0	3	1	0	0	.875	-1	/OD	-0.1
1989	Phi-N	6	4	1	0	0	0	0	0	0	2	.000	.000	.000	-99	-1	-1	0	0	0	0	1.000	-1	/O	-0.2
1990	Mon-N	4	2	0	1	0	0	0	0	0	0	.500	.500	.500	183	0	0	1	0	0	0	.000	0	/H	0.0
1991	Mon-N	73	72	6	16	4	0	1	6	9	13	.222	.309	.319	78	-2	-2	7	6	1	1	1.000	-1	/O1	-0.2
1992	Mon-N	8	5	0	0	0	0	0	0	0	1	.000	.000	.000	-99	-1	-1	0	0	0	0	.000	0	/H	-0.1
Total	7	131	146	13	30	6	0	1	12	13	23	.205	.270	.267	52	-9	-9	13	9	2	2	.892	-5	/O1D	-1.5

■ **AL BUMBRY** Bumbry, Alonza Benjamin (b: Alonza Benjamin Bumbrey) b: 4/21/47, Fredericksburg, Va. BL/TR, 5'8", 175 lbs. Deb: 9/05/72 C

YEAR	TM/L	G	AB	R	H	2B	3B	HR	RBI	BB	SO	AVG	OBP	SLG	PRO+	BR	/A	RC	SB	CS	SBR	FA	FR	POS	TPR
1972	Bal-A	9	11	5	4	0	1	0	0	0	0	.364	.364	.545	164	1	1	2	1	1	-0	1.000	0	/O	0.1
1973	*Bal-A	110	356	73	120	15	**11**	7	34	34	49	.337	.399	.500	153	24	25	72	23	10	1	.978	-10	O/D	1.2
1974	*Bal-A	94	270	35	63	10	3	1	19	21	46	.233	.291	.304	74	-10	-9	25	12	4	1	.953	-1	O/D	-1.1
1975	Bal-A	114	349	47	94	19	4	2	32	32	81	.269	.338	.364	105	-1	2	47	16	3	3	1.000	-2	DO/3	0.2
1976	Bal-A	133	450	71	113	15	7	9	36	43	76	.251	.318	.376	109	1	4	57	42	10	7	.989	-12	*OD	-0.6
1977	Bal-A	133	518	74	164	31	3	4	41	45	88	.317	.373	.411	121	11	15	83	19	8	1	.991	-10	*O	0.1
1978	Bal-A	33	114	21	27	5	2	2	6	17	15	.237	.346	.368	108	1	1	15	5	3	-0	.985	-2	O	-0.2
1979	*Bal-A	148	569	80	162	29	1	7	49	43	74	.285	.338	.376	96	-6	-3	76	37	12	4	.982	-3	*O	-0.8
1980	Bal-A★	160	645	118	205	29	9	9	53	78	75	.318	.394	.433	128	26	27	118	44	11	7	.990	15	*O	4.1
1981	Bal-A	101	392	61	107	18	2	1	27	51	51	.273	.360	.337	102	3	3	49	22	15	-2	.992	4	*O	0.1
1982	Bal-A	150	562	77	147	20	4	5	40	44	77	.262	.315	.338	80	-15	-15	60	10	5	0	.986	8	*O/D	-1.1
1983	*Bal-A	124	378	63	104	14	4	3	31	31	33	.275	.330	.357	91	-5	-4	47	12	5	1	.988	-11	*OD	-1.8
1984	Bal-A	119	344	47	93	12	1	3	24	25	35	.270	.320	.337	84	-8	-7	35	9	5	-0	.988	-6	O/D	-1.6
1985	SD-N	68	95	6	19	3	0	1	10	7	9	.200	.255	.263	46	-7	-7	6	2	0	1	.939	-2	O	-0.9
Total	14	1496	5053	778	1422	220	52	54	402	471	709	.281	.345	.378	104	14	33	692	254	92	21	.986	-31	*O/D3	-2.3

■ **JOSH BUNCE** Bunce, Joshua b: 5/10/1847, Brooklyn, N.Y. d: 4/28/12, Brooklyn, N.Y. Deb: 8/27/1877

YEAR	TM/L	G	AB	R	H	2B	3B	HR	RBI	BB	SO	AVG	OBP	SLG	PRO+	BR	/A	RC	SB	CS	SBR	FA	FR	POS	TPR
1877	Har-N	1	4	0	0	0	0	0	0	0	0	.000	.000	.000	-99	-1	-1	0				1.000	-0	/O	-0.1

YEAR	TM/L	G	AB	R	H	2B	3B	HR	RBI	BB	SO	AVG	OBP	SLG	PRO+	BR	/A	RC	SB	CS	SBR	FA	FR	POS	TPR
■ NELSON BURBRINK Burbrink, Nelson Edward b: 12/28/21, Cincinnati, Ohio BR/TR, 5'10", 195 lbs. Deb: 6/05/55																									
1955	StL-N	58	170	11	47	8	1	0	15	14	13	.276	.335	.335	79	-5	-5	19	1	1	-0	.979	-1	C	-0.4
■ AL BURCH Burch, Albert William b: 10/7/1883, Albany, N.Y. d: 10/5/26, Brooklyn, N.Y. BL/TR, 5'8.5", 160 lbs. Deb: 6/19/06																									
1906	StL-N	91	335	40	89	5	1	0	11	37		.266	.339	.287	100	-0	1	40	15			.934	1	O	-0.3
1907	StL-N	48	154	18	35	3	1	0	5	17		.227	.304	.260	80	-4	-3	15	7			.922	0	O	-0.5
	Bro-N	40	120	12	35	2	2	0	12	11		.292	.351	.342	128	2	4	17	5			.890	2	O/2	0.5
	Yr	88	274	30	70	5	3	0	17	28		.255	.325	.296	100	-1	0	31	12			.908	2	O/2	0.0
1908	Bro-N	123	456	45	111	8	4	2	18	33		.243	.294	.292	91	-7	-5	43	15			.971	13	*O	0.3
1909	Bro-N	152	601	80	163	20	6	1	30	51		.271	.329	.329	108	3	5	76	38			.955	6	*O/1	0.6
1910	Bro-N	103	352	41	83	8	3	1	20	22	30	.236	.281	.284	67	-16	-15	31	13			.957	-1	O1	-2.1
1911	Bro-N	54	167	18	38	2	3	0	7	15	22	.228	.291	.275	61	-9	-8	14	3			.972	2	O/2	-0.9
Total	6	611	2185	254	554	48	20	4	103	186	52	.254	.312	.299	92	-31	-21	236	96			.950	22	O/12	-2.4
■ ERNIE BURCH Burch, Earnest W. b: 1856, Dekalb Co., Ill. BL , Deb: 8/15/1884																									
1884	Cle-N	32	124	9	26	4	0	0	7	5	24	.210	.240	.242	50	-7	-7	7				.899	4	O	-0.3
1886	Bro-a	113	456	78	119	22	6	2		39		.261	.321	.349	110	6	5	58	16			.884	-13	*O	-0.9
1887	Bro-a	49	188	47	55	4	4	2		29		.293	.395	.388	120	7	6	36	15			.899	1	O	0.5
Total	3	194	768	134	200	30	10	4	7	73	24	.260	.328	.341	104	6	4	101	31			.891	-8	O	-0.7
■ BOB BURDA Burda, Edward Robert b: 7/16/38, St.Louis, Mo. BL/TL, 5'11", 180 lbs. Deb: 8/25/62																									
1962	StL-N	7	14	0	1	0	0	0	0	3	1	.071	.235	.071	-12	-2	-2	1	1	0	0	.917	0	/O	-0.2
1965	SF-N	31	27	0	3	0	0	0	5	5	6	.111	.250	.111	6	-3	-3	1	0	0	0	.969	-1	1/O	-0.4
1966	SF-N	37	43	3	7	3	0	0	2	2	5	.163	.200	.233	19	-5	-5	2	0	0	0	1.000	-0	/1O	-0.6
1969	SF-N	97	161	20	37	8	0	6	27	21	12	.230	.319	.391	100	-1	-0	21	0	1	-1	.995	0	1O	-0.3
1970	SF-N	28	23	1	6	0	0	0	3	5	2	.261	.414	.261	86	-0	-0	3	0	0	0	.933	-1	/1O	-0.1
	Mil-A	78	222	19	55	9	0	4	20	16	17	.248	.307	.342	78	-7	-7	24	1	0	0	.987	-7	O/1	-1.8
1971	StL-N	65	71	6	21	0	0	1	12	10	11	.296	.390	.338	104	1	1	10	0	0	0	1.000	0	1/O	0.1
1972	Bos-A	45	73	4	12	1	0	2	9	8	11	.164	.247	.260	48	-4	-5	4	0	0	0	.992	-0	1/O	-0.7
Total	7	388	634	53	142	21	0	13	78	70	65	.224	.306	.319	74	-20	-21	64	2	1	0	.992	-8	1/O	-4.0
■ JACK BURDOCK Burdock, John Joseph "Black Jack" b: 4/1852, Brooklyn, N.Y. d: 11/28/31, Brooklyn, N.Y. BR/TR, 5'9.5", 158 lbs. Deb: 5/02/1872 MU																									
1872	Atl-n	37	174	26	45	2	1	0	15	1	1	.259	.263	.282	58	-6	-13	13						*S/C2	-0.9
1873	Atl-n	55	245	56	62	9	2	2	33	7	4	.253	.274	.331	86	-7	-1	23						*2/C	-0.4
1874	Mut-n	61	272	45	76	16	3	2		1		.279	.282	.382	106	3	1	30						*3	0.1
1875	Har-n	74	347	72	102	14	5	0		5		.294	.304	.363	123	10	7	39						*2/3	0.5
1876	Har-N	69	309	66	80	9	1	0	23	13	16	.259	.289	.294	87	-1	-5	27				.895	1	*2/3	-0.4
1877	Har-N	58	277	35	72	6	0	0	9	2	16	.260	.265	.282	81	-9	-4	21				**.903**	7	*2/3	0.4
1878	Bos-N	60	246	37	64	12	6	0	25	3	17	.260	.269	.358	97	1	-2	24				**.918**	**21**	*2	2.2
1879	Bos-N	84	359	64	86	10	3	0	36	9	28	.240	.258	.284	77	-8	-9	27				.911	10	*2	0.6
1880	Bos-N	86	356	58	90	17	4	2	35	8	26	.253	.269	.340	108	2	3	33				**.923**	12	*2	1.9
1881	Bos-N	73	282	36	67	12	4	1	24	7	18	.238	.256	.319	84	-7	-5	24				.911	-11	*2/S	-1.2
1882	Bos-N	83	319	36	76	6	7	0	27	9	24	.238	.259	.301	79	-7	-7	25				**.932**	3	*2	-0.2
1883	Bos-N	96	400	80	132	27	8	5	88	14	35	.330	.353	.475	145	23	21	69				.921	-1	*2/M	1.9
1884	Bos-N	87	361	65	97	14	4	6	49	15	52	.269	.298	.380	112	4	5	42				**.922**	1	*2/3	0.7
1885	Bos-N	45	169	18	24	5	0	0	7	8	18	.142	.181	.172	15	-16	-15	5				.917	-4	2	-1.7
1886	Bos-N	59	221	26	48	6	1	0	25	11	27	.217	.254	.253	57	-12	-11	15	3			.904	-8	2	-1.5
1887	Bos-N	65	237	36	61	6	0	0	29	18	22	.257	.320	.283	70	-8	-9	28	19			.882	-19	2	-2.2
1888	Bos-N	22	79	5	16	0	0	0	4	2	5	.203	.232	.203	40	-5	-5	4	1			.903	0	2	-0.4
	Bro-a	70	246	15	30	1	2	1	8	8		.122	.166	.154	5	-25	-25	8	9			.904	2	2	-2.0
1891	Bro-N	3	12	1	1	0	0	0	1	1	1	.083	.154	.083	-30	-2	-2	0	0			1.000	-1	/2	-0.2
Total	4 n	227	1038	199	285	41	11	4	48	14	5	.275	.284	.347	97	-1	-6	105	3					2/3SC	-0.7
Total	14	960	3873	578	944	131	40	15	390	128	305	.244	.270	.310	84	-70	-70	354	32			.912	13	2/3S	-2.1
■ JOE BURG Burg, Joseph Peter b: 6/4/1882, Chicago, Ill. d: 4/28/69, Joliet, Ill. BR/TR, 5'9", 150 lbs. Deb: 9/26/10																									
1910	Bos-N	13	46	7	15	0	1	0	10	7	12	.326	.415	.370	124	2	2	9	5			.867	3	3/S	0.5
■ SMOKY BURGESS Burgess, Forrest Harrill b: 2/6/27, Caroleen, N.C. d: 9/15/91, Asheville, N.C. BL/TR, 5'8", 187 lbs. Deb: 4/19/49																									
1949	Chi-N	46	56	4	15	0	0	1	12	4	4	.268	.317	.321	73	-2	-2	6	0			1.000	1	/C	-0.1
1951	Chi-N	94	219	21	55	4	2	2	20	21	12	.251	.317	.315	69	-9	-9	21	2	0	1	.980	-3	C	-0.9
1952	Phi-N	110	371	49	110	27	2	6	56	49	21	.296	.380	.429	125	13	13	65	3	1	0	.978	-6	*C	1.4
1953	Phi-N	102	312	31	91	17	5	4	36	37	17	.292	.370	.417	105	3	3	48	3	2	-0	**.993**	-8	C	-0.1
1954	Phi-N★	108	345	41	127	27	5	4	46	42	11	.368	.437	.510	146	25	25	75	1	5	-3	.975	-8	C	1.8
1955	Phi-N	7	21	4	4	2	0	1	1	3	1	.190	.292	.429	90	-0	-0	2	0	0	0	1.000	1	/C	0.0
	Cin-N	116	421	67	129	15	3	20	77	47	35	.306	.377	.499	123	18	15	78	1	1	-0	.986	-9	*C	0.9
	Yr	123	442	71	133	17	3	21	78	50	36	.301	.373	.495	122	18	15	80	1	1	-0	.987	-9	*C	0.9
1956	Cin-N	90	229	28	63	10	0	12	39	26	18	.275	.349	.476	112	6	4	37	0	1	-1	1.000	-2	C	0.4
1957	Cin-N	90	205	29	58	14	1	14	39	24	16	.283	.358	.566	134	12	10	41	0	0	0	.988	-5	C	0.7
1958	Cin-N	99	251	28	71	12	1	6	31	22	20	.283	.343	.410	93	-1	-2	34	0	0	0	.988	4	C	0.5
1959	Pit-N★	114	377	41	112	28	5	11	59	31	16	.297	.354	.485	122	11	11	62	0	0	0	.984	-17	*C	0.0
1960	*Pit-N★	110	337	33	99	15	2	7	39	35	13	.294	.360	.412	110	6	5	50	0	1	-1	**.994**	1	C	1.1
1961	Pit-N★	100	323	37	98	17	3	12	52	30	16	.303	.366	.486	123	11	11	57	1	0	0	**.991**	-14	C	0.2
1962	Pit-N	103	360	38	118	19	2	13	61	31	19	.328	.381	.500	134	17	17	68	0	1	-1	.988	-11	*C	0.9
1963	Pit-N	91	264	20	74	10	1	6	37	24	14	.280	.343	.394	111	4	4	32	0	1	-1	.990	-11	C	-0.6
1964	Pit-N☆	68	171	9	42	3	1	2	17	13	14	.246	.303	.310	73	-6	-6	14	2	1	0	.992	-8	C	-1.2
	Chi-A	7	5	1	1	0	0	1	1	2	0	.200	.429	.800	239	1	1	2	0	0	0	.000	0	H	0.1
1965	Chi-A	80	77	2	22	4	0	2	24	11	7	.286	.375	.416	132	3	3	12	0	0	0	1.000	-0	/C	0.4
1966	Chi-A	79	67	0	21	5	0	0	15	11	8	.313	.418	.388	143	4	4	12	0	0	0	1.000	-0	/C	0.4
1967	Chi-A	77	60	2	8	1	0	2	11	14	8	.133	.307	.250	69	-2	-2	5	0	0	0	.000	0	H	-0.2
Total	18	1691	4471	485	1318	230	33	126	673	477	270	.295	.364	.446	116	112	105	722	13	14		.988	-96	*C	5.7
■ TOM BURGESS Burgess, Thomas Roland "Tim" b: 9/1/27, London, Ont., Can. BL/TL, 6', 180 lbs. Deb: 4/17/54 C																									
1954	StL-N	17	21	2	1	1	0	0	1	3	9	.048	.167	.095	-29	-4	-4	0	0	0	0	.750	-1	/O	-0.6
1962	LA-A	87	143	17	28	7	1	2	13	36	20	.196	.358	.301	82	-3	-2	18	2	0	1	.997	-3	1/O	-0.6
Total	2	104	164	19	29	8	1	2	14	39	29	.177	.335	.274	67	-7	-6	19	2	0	1	.857	-4	/1O	-1.2
■ BILL BURGO Burgo, William Ross b: 11/5/19, Johnstown, Pa. d: 10/19/88, Morgan City, La. BR/TR, 5'8", 185 lbs. Deb: 9/22/43																									
1943	Phi-A	17	70	12	26	4	2	1	9	4	1	.371	.421	.529	178	7	7	16	0	2	-1	.979	2	O	0.7
1944	Phi-A	27	88	6	21	2	0	1	3	7	3	.239	.316	.295	76	-3	-2	8	1	3	-2	.955	2	O	-0.3
Total	2	44	158	18	47	6	2	2	12	11	4	.297	.362	.399	121	4	4	23	1	5	-3	.965	4	/O	0.4
■ BILL BURICH Burich, William Max b: 5/29/18, Calumet, Mich. BR/TR, 6', 180 lbs. Deb: 4/15/42																									
1942	Phi-N	25	80	3	23	1	0	0	7	6	13	.287	.337	.300	92	-1	-1	8	2			.917	-5	S/3	-0.5
1946	Phi-N	2	1	1	0	0	0	0	0	0	0	.000	.000	.000	-99	-0	-0	0	0			.000	0	/3	0.0
Total	2	27	81	4	23	1	0	0	7	6	13	.284	.333	.296	89	-1	-1	8	2			1.000	-5	/S3	-0.5

YEAR	TM/L	G	AB	R	H	2B	3B	HR	RBI	BB	SO	AVG	OBP	SLG	PRO+	BR	/A	RC	SB	CS	SBR	FA	FR	POS	TPR

■ MACK BURK Burk, Mack Edwin b: 4/21/35, Nacogdoches, Tex. BR/TR, 6'4", 180 lbs. Deb: 5/25/56

1956	Phi-N	15	1	3	1	0	0	0	0	0	0	1.000	1.000	1.000	449	0	0	1	0	0	0	1.000	5	/C	0.5
1958	Phi-N	1	1	0	0	0	0	0	0	0	1	.000	.000	.000	-99	-0	-0	0	0	0	0	.000	0	H	0.0
Total	2	16	2	3	1	0	0	0	0	0	1	.500	.500	.500	171	0	0	1	0	0	0		5	/C	0.5

■ CHRIS BURKAM Burkam, Chauncey De Pew b: 10/13/1892, Benton Harbor, Mich. d: 5/9/64, Kalamazoo, Mich. BL/TR, 5'11", 175 lbs. Deb: 6/24/15

| 1915 | StL-A | 1 | 1 | 0 | 0 | 0 | 0 | 0 | 0 | 0 | 1 | .000 | .000 | .000 | -99 | -0 | -0 | 0 | | | | .000 | 0 | H | 0.0 |

■ DAN BURKE Burke, Daniel L. b: 10/25/1868, Abington, Mass. d: 3/20/33, Taunton, Mass. BR/TR, 5'10", 190 lbs. Deb: 4/18/1890

1890	Roc-a	32	102	14	22	1	0	0		17		.216	.333	.225	73	-3	-2	9	2			.944	-5	O/C1	-0.7
	Syr-a	9	20	1	0	0	0	0		5		.000	.231	.000	-33	-3	-3	0	0			.900	3	/C	0.1
	Yr	41	122	15	22	1	0	0		22		.180	.315	.189	55	-6	-4	8	2			.944	-2	OC/1	-0.6
1892	Bos-N	1	4	0	0	0	0	0	0	0	2	.000	.000	.000	-92	-1	-1	0	0			.900	1	/C	0.0
Total	2	42	126	15	22	1	0	0	0	22	2	.175	.307	.183	51	-7	-5	9	2			.892	-2	/OC1	-0.6

■ EDDIE BURKE Burke, Edward D. b: 10/6/1866, Northumberland, Pa. d: 11/26/07, Utica, N.Y. BL/TR, 5'6", 161 lbs. Deb: 4/19/1890

1890	Phi-N	100	430	85	113	16	11	4	50	49	40	.263	.349	.379	112	8	7	72	38			.904	4	*O/2	0.7
	Pit-N	31	124	17	26	5	2	1	7	14	9	.210	.295	.306	87	-4	-1	13	6			.911	0	O	-0.1
	Yr	131	554	102	139	21	13	5	57	63	49	.251	.337	.363	107	5	6	85	44			.906	4	*O/2	0.6
1891	Mil-a	35	144	31	34	9	0	2	21	12	19	.236	.337	.340	80	-0	-5	19	7			.918	3	O	-0.3
1892	Cin-N	15	41	6	6	1	0	0	4	9	4	.146	.300	.171	45	-2	-2	3	2			1.000	-3	O/3	-0.5
	NY-N	89	363	81	94	10	5	6	41	46	37	.259	.350	.364	120	9	10	62	42			.857	-3	2O	0.6
	Yr	104	404	87	100	11	5	6	45	55	41	.248	.345	.344	112	7	7	65	44			.857	-6	2O/3	0.1
1893	NY-N	135	537	122	150	23	10	9	80	51	32	.279	.369	.410	108	7	7	104	54			.912	2	*O	0.2
1894	*NY-N	136	566	121	172	23	11	4	77	37	35	.304	.357	.405	86	-14	-13	97	34			.933	-4	*O	-2.1
1895	NY-N	39	167	38	43	6	2	1	12	7	9	.257	.299	.335	67	-9	-8	22	14			.914	2	O	-0.8
	Cin-N	56	228	52	61	8	6	1	25	22	14	.268	.343	.368	82	-5	-7	36	19			.899	2	O	-0.7
	Yr	95	395	90	104	14	8	2	37	29	23	.263	.325	.354	76	-14	-15	58	33			.905	4	O	-1.5
1896	Cin-N	122	521	120	177	24	9	1	52	41	29	.340	.382	.426	110	14	8	111	53			.935	3	*O	0.1
1897	Cin-N	95	387	71	103	17	1	1	41	29		.266	.327	.323	67	-15	-20	50	22			.940	7	*O	-1.7
Total	8	853	3508	744	979	142	57	30	410	317	228	.279	.352	.378	95	-11	-25	590	291			.921	14	O/23	-4.6

■ FRANK BURKE Burke, Frank Aloysius b: 2/16/1880, Carbon, Co., Pa. d: 9/17/46, Los Angeles, Cal. TR, Deb: 9/14/06

1906	NY-N	8	9	2	3	1	0	1		1	1	.333	.400	.667	228	1	1	3	1			.667	-2	/O	0.0
1907	Bos-N	43	129	6	23	0	1	0	8	11		.178	.243	.194	37	-9	-9	8	3			.955	-4	O	-1.6
Total	2	51	138	8	26	1	2	0	9	12		.188	.253	.225	50	-8	-8	10	4			.942	-5	/O	-1.6

■ GLENN BURKE Burke, Glenn Lawrence b: 11/16/52, Oakland, Cal. BR/TR, 6', 195 lbs. Deb: 4/09/76

1976	LA-N	25	46	9	11	2	0	0	5	3	8	.239	.300	.283	67	-2	-2	4	3	2	-0	.971	1	O	-0.2
1977	*LA-N	83	169	16	43	8	0	1	13	5	22	.254	.280	.320	61	-10	-9	15	13	5	1	.971	1	O	-1.0
1978	LA-N	16	19	2	4	0	0	0	2	0	4	.211	.211	.211	18	-2	-2	1	0	0	-0	1.000	-0	O	-0.7
	Oak-A	78	200	19	47	6	1	1	14	10	26	.235	.271	.290	61	-11	-10	14	15	8	-0	.987	1	O/1D	-1.7
1979	Oak-A	23	89	4	19	2	1	0	4	4	10	.213	.247	.258	39	-8	-7	5	3	1	0	1.000	1	O	-0.7
Total	4	225	523	50	124	18	2	2	38	22	70	.237	.271	.291	56	-33	-31	38	35	16	1	.983	-2	O/D1	-3.8

■ JIMMY BURKE Burke, James Timothy "Sunset Jimmy" b: 10/12/1874, St.Louis, Mo. d: 3/26/42, St.Louis, Mo. BR/TR, 5'7", 160 lbs. Deb: 10/06/1898 MC

1898	Cle-N	13	38	1	4	0	0	0	1	2		.105	.150	.132	-19	-6	-6	1	1			.853	-4	3	-1.0
1899	StL-N	2	6	1	2	0	0	0	0	1		.333	.429	.333	108	0	1	1	0			.923	1	/2	0.1
1901	Mil-A	64	233	24	48	8	0	0	26	17		.206	.266	.240	43	-18	-17	18	6			.860	-7	3	-2.1
	Chi-A	42	148	20	39	5	0	0	21	12		.264	.327	.297	76	-5	-4	19	11			.867	-2	S3	-0.3
	Yr	106	381	44	87	13	0	0	47	29		.228	.290	.262	56	-23	-21	37	17			.859	-9	3S	-2.4
	Pit-N	14	51	4	10	0	0	0	4	4		.196	.268	.196	35	-4	-4	3	0			.877	3	3	-0.1
1902	Pit-N	60	203	24	60	12	2	0	26	17		.296	.356	.374	121	6	5	32	9			.895	-5	2O/3S	0.1
1903	StL-N	115	431	55	123	13	3	0	42	23		.285	.326	.329	90	-7	-5	58	28			.911	6	32/O	0.2
1904	StL-N	118	406	37	92	10	3	0	37	15		.227	.266	.266	70	-16	-14	37	17			.897	-7	*3	-1.8
1905	StL-N	122	431	34	97	9	5	1	30	21		.225	.275	.276	67	-19	-17	39	15			.924	3	*3M	-1.0
Total	7	550	1947	200	475	58	13	1	187	112		.244	.295	.289	74	-69	-61	207	87			.899	-13	3/2SO	-5.9

■ JOHN BURKE Burke, John Patrick b: 1/27/1877, Hazelton, Pa. d: 8/4/50, Jersey City, N.J. BR/TR, Deb: 6/27/02

| 1902 | NY-N | 4 | 13 | 0 | 2 | 0 | 0 | 0 | 0 | 0 | | .154 | .154 | .154 | -5 | -2 | -2 | 0 | 0 | | | 1.000 | -1 | /PO | -0.2 |

■ JOE BURKE Burke, Joseph A. b: Cincinnati, Ohio 5'7", 160 lbs. Deb: 9/26/1890

1890	StL-a	2	6	3	4	0	0	0		1		.667	.750	.667	283	2	2	3	0			.750	-0	/3	0.1
1891	Cin-a	1	4	0	1	0	0	0	1	0	2	.250	.250	.250	41	-0	-0	0	0			1.000	1	/2	0.1
Total	2	3	10	3	5	0	0	0	1	1	2	.500	.583	.500	196	2	2	3	0			1	/32	0.2

■ LEO BURKE Burke, Leo Patrick b: 5/6/34, Hagerstown, Md. BR/TR, 5'10", 190 lbs. Deb: 9/07/58

1958	Bal-A	7	11	4	5	0	1	0	4	1	2	.455	.500	.818	271	2	2	5	0	0	0	1.000	-2	/O3	0.1
1959	Bal-A	5	10	0	2	0	0	0	1	0	5	.200	.273	.200	33	-1	-1	0	0	0	0	1.000	-2	/23	-0.3
1961	LA-A	6	5	0	0	0	0	0	0	0	1	.000	.000	.000	-90	-1	-1	0	0	0	0	.000	0	H	-0.1
1962	LA-A	19	64	8	17	1	0	4	14	5	11	.266	.329	.469	115	1	1	10	0	0	0	.958	-1	O/3S	-0.3
1963	StL-N	30	49	6	10	2	1	1	5	4	12	.204	.264	.347	68	-2	-2	4	0	0	0	1.000	-0	O/3	-0.3
	Chi-N	27	49	4	9	0	0	2	7	4	13	.184	.245	.306	55	-3	-3	3	0	1	-1	.925	3	2/1	0.0
	Yr	57	98	10	19	2	1	3	12	8	25	.194	.255	.327	61	-4	-5	8	0	1	-1	1.000	3	O2/31	-0.3
1964	Chi-N	59	103	11	27	3	1	1	14	7	31	.262	.315	.340	81	-2	-3	11	0	0	0	1.000	-1	0/231C	-0.4
1965	Chi-N	12	10	0	2	0	0	0	0	0	4	.200	.200	.200	13	-1	-1	0	0	0	0	1.000	0	/CO	-0.1
Total	7	165	301	33	72	7	2	9	45	21	79	.239	.295	.365	81	-7	-8	34	0	2	-1	.985	-3	/0231CS	-1.1

■ LES BURKE Burke, Leslie Kingston "Buck" b: 12/18/02, Lynn, Mass. d: 5/6/75, Danvers, Mass. BL/TR, 5'9", 168 lbs. Deb: 5/02/23

1923	Det-A	7	10	2	1	0	0	0	2	0	1	.100	.100	.100	-48	-2	-2	0	0	0	0	.500	-1	/32	-0.3
1924	Det-A	72	241	30	61	10	4	0	17	22	20	.253	.321	.328	69	-12	-11	26	2	4	-2	.957	-6	2/S	-1.7
1925	Det-A	77	180	32	52	6	3	0	24	17	8	.289	.357	.356	82	-5	-4	25	4	1	1	.962	2	2	-0.1
1926	Det-A	38	75	9	17	1	0	0	4	7	3	.227	.301	.240	42	-6	-6	6	1	2	-1	.942	4	2/3S	-0.3
Total	4	194	506	73	131	17	7	0	47	46	32	.259	.327	.320	67	-25	-24	56	7	7	-2	.958	-1	2/3S	-2.4

■ MIKE BURKE Burke, Michael E. b: Cincinnati, Ohio d: 6/9/1889, Albany, N.Y. BR/TR, 6', 190 lbs. Deb: 5/01/1879

| 1879 | Cin-N | 28 | 117 | 13 | 26 | 3 | 0 | 0 | 8 | 2 | 5 | .222 | .235 | .248 | 63 | -5 | -4 | 7 | | | | .786 | -8 | S/O3 | -1.0 |

■ PAT BURKE Burke, Patrick Edward b: 5/13/01, St.Louis, Mo. d: 7/7/65, St.Louis, Mo. BR/TR, 5'10.5", 170 lbs. Deb: 9/23/24

| 1924 | StL-A | 1 | 3 | 0 | 0 | 0 | 0 | 0 | 0 | 0 | 1 | .000 | .000 | .000 | -94 | -1 | -1 | 0 | 0 | 0 | 0 | .000 | 0 | /3 | -0.1 |

■ WALTER BURKE Burke, Walter R. b: California d: 3/3/11, Memphis, Tenn. 6', 200 lbs. Deb: 6/10/1882

1882	Buf-N	1	4	0	0	0	0	0	0	0	0	.000	.000	.000	-98	-1	-1	0				1.000	1	/OP	-0.1
1883	Buf-N	1	5	0	1	0	0	0	1	0	3	.200	.200	.200	22	-0	-0	0				.000	-1	/OP	-0.1
1884	Bos-U	47	184	21	41	8	3	0		6		.223	.247	.299	85	-3	-3	14				.841	-4	PO	-0.1

YEAR	TM/L	G	AB	R	H	2B	3B	HR	RBI	BB	SO	AVG	OBP	SLG	PRO+	BR	/A	RC	SB	CS	SBR	FA	FR	POS	TPR
1887	Det-N	2	8	1	2	0	0	0	1	0	1	.250	.250	.250	39	-1	-1	1	0			.750	-1	/PO	0.0
Total	4	51	201	22	44	8	3	0	2	6	5	.219	.242	.289	77	-5	-5	15	0			.848	-5	/PO	-0.3
■ JESSE BURKETT	Burkett, Jesse Cail "Crab" b: 12/4/1868, Wheeling, W.Va. d: 5/27/53, Worcester, Mass. BL/TL, 5'8", 155 lbs. Deb: 4/22/1890 CH																								
1890	NY-N	101	401	67	124	23	13	4	60	33	52	.309	.366	.461	143	20	20	75	14			.824	3	OP	1.4
1891	Cle-N	40	167	29	45	7	4	0	13	23	19	.269	.358	.359	107	3	2	22	1			.892	-3	O	-0.2
1892	*Cle-N	145	608	119	167	15	14	6	66	67	59	.275	.348	.375	116	15	12	94	36			.904	3	*O	0.7
1893	Cle-N	125	511	145	178	25	15	6	82	98	23	.348	.459	.491	146	45	39	137	39			.849	-8	*O	2.1
1894	Cle-N	125	523	138	187	27	14	8	94	84	27	.358	.447	.509	127	30	26	136	28			.915	-4	*O/P	1.0
1895	*Cle-N	131	550	153	**225**	22	13	5	83	74	31	**.409**	.486	.524	154	56	50	165	41			.884	-3	*O	2.9
1896	*Cle-N	133	586	**160**	**240**	27	16	6	72	49	19	**.410**	.461	.541	157	56	51	166	34			.926	-2	*O	3.2
1897	Cle-N	127	517	129	198	28	7	2	60	76		.383	.468	.476	142	42	37	133	28			.949	-2	*O	2.2
1898	Cle-N	150	624	114	213	18	9	0	42	69		.341	.415	.399	135	30	31	114	19			.938	-8	*O	1.2
1899	StL-N	141	558	116	221	21	8	7	71	67		.396	.463	.500	160	52	50	145	25			.938	-3	*O/2	3.2
1900	StL-N	141	559	88	203	11	15	7	68	62		.363	.429	.474	150	39	40	133	32			.934	4	*O	3.0
1901	StL-N	142	601	**142**	**226**	20	15	10	75	59		**.376**	**.440**	.509	**184**	**59**	**63**	**151**	27			.923	-1	*O	5.0
1902	StL-A	138	553	97	169	29	9	5	52	71		.306	.389	.418	125	20	21	102	23			.924	6	*O/PS3	1.6
1903	StL-A	132	515	73	151	20	7	3	40	52		.293	.361	.377	125	15	17	79	17			.941	-4	*O	0.5
1904	StL-A	147	575	72	156	15	10	2	27	78		.271	.362	.343	132	19	23	78	12			.942	5	*O	2.2
1905	Bos-A	148	573	78	147	12	13	4	47	67		.257	.339	.344	115	12	12	74	13			.929	-1	*O	0.4
Total	16	2066	8421	1720	2850	320	182	75	952	1029	230	.338	.415	.446	141	514	493	1803	389			.917	-18	*O/P3S2	30.4
■ ELLIS BURKS	Burks, Ellis Rena b: 9/11/64, Vicksburg, Miss. BR/TR, 6'2", 200 lbs. Deb: 4/30/87																								
1987	Bos-A	133	558	94	152	30	2	20	59	41	98	.272	.324	.441	98	-1	-3	85	27	6	5	.988	14	*O/D	1.1
1988	*Bos-A	144	540	93	159	37	5	18	92	62	89	.294	.370	.481	131	27	24	99	25	9	2	.977	12	*O/D	3.3
1989	Bos-A	97	399	73	121	19	6	12	61	36	52	.303	.368	.471	127	18	15	71	21	5	3	.977	7	O/D	2.3
1990	*Bos-A†	152	588	89	174	33	8	21	89	48	82	.296	.350	.486	126	23	20	92	9	11	-4	.994	2	*O/D	1.4
1991	Bos-A	130	474	56	119	33	3	14	56	39	81	.251	.316	.422	97	0	-3	60	6	11	-5	.993	-3	*O/D	-1.3
1992	Bos-A	66	235	35	60	8	3	8	30	25	48	.255	.330	.417	103	2	1	32	5	2	0	.984	-7	O/D	-0.8
Total	6	722	2794	440	785	160	27	93	387	251	450	.281	.344	.457	114	70	54	440	93	44	2	.986	25	O/D	6.0
■ RICK BURLESON	Burleson, Richard Paul "Rooster" b: 4/29/51, Lynwood, Cal. BR/TR, 5'10", 165 lbs. Deb: 5/04/74 C																								
1974	Bos-A	114	384	36	109	22	0	4	44	21	34	.284	.324	.372	93	-1	-4	43	3	3	-1	.957	-5	S2/3	0.2
1975	*Bos-A	158	580	66	146	25	1	6	62	45	44	.252	.309	.329	74	-15	-21	58	8	5	-1	.963	-1	*S	-0.6
1976	Bos-A	152	540	75	157	27	1	7	42	60	37	.291	.367	.383	107	15	7	76	14	9	-1	.957	-7	*S	1.8
1977	Bos-A★	154	663	80	194	36	7	3	52	47	69	.293	.341	.382	87	-3	-13	83	13	12	-3	.970	12	*S	1.3
1978	Bos-A†	145	626	75	155	32	5	5	49	40	71	.248	.297	.339	71	-18	-27	60	8	8	-2	.981	19	*S	0.9
1979	Bos-A★	153	627	93	174	32	5	5	60	35	54	.278	.319	.368	80	-14	-18	72	9	5	-0	**.980**	22	*S	2.0
1980	Bos-A	155	644	89	179	29	2	8	51	62	51	.278	.343	.366	90	-4	-8	76	12	13	-4	.974	26	*S	3.1
1981	Cal-A★	109	430	53	126	17	1	5	33	42	38	.293	.360	.372	111	7	7	58	4	6	-2	.979	21	*S	3.8
1982	Cal-A	11	45	4	7	1	0	0	2	6	3	.156	.255	.178	21	-5	-5	2	0	0	0	.986	7	S	0.4
1983	Cal-A	33	119	22	34	7	0	0	11	12	12	.286	.351	.345	93	-1	-1	13	0	2	-1	.969	-0	S	0.1
1984	Cal-A	7	4	2	0	0	0	0	0	0	2	.000	.000	.000	-99	-1	-1	0	0	0	0	.000	0	/H	-0.1
1986	*Cal-A	93	271	35	77	14	0	5	29	33	32	.284	.364	.391	107	3	3	40	1	3	-2	.984	-7	DS/23	-0.2
1987	Bal-A	62	206	26	43	14	1	2	14	17	30	.209	.279	.316	59	-13	-12	17	0	2	-1	.977	-1	2/D	-1.1
Total	13	1346	5139	656	1401	256	23	50	449	420	477	.273	.331	.361	87	-49	-91	599	72	68	-19	.971	86	*S/2D3	11.6
■ HERCULES BURNETT	Burnett, Hercules H. b: 8/13/1865, Louisville, Ky. d: 10/4/36, Louisville, Ky. BR , Deb: 6/26/1888																								
1888	Lou-a	1	4	1	0	0	0	0	0	1		.000	.200	.000	-32	-1	-1	0	1			.667	-0	/O	-0.1
1895	Lou-N	5	17	6	7	0	1	2	3	2	2	.412	.474	.882	264	3	4	8	2			.769	-0	/O1	0.2
Total	2	6	21	7	7	0	1	2	3	3	2	.333	.417	.714	214	3	3	8	3			.750	-1	/O1	0.1
■ JOHNNY BURNETT	Burnett, John Henderson b: 11/1/04, Bartow, Fla. d: 8/13/59, Tampa, Fla. BL/TR, 5'11", 175 lbs. Deb: 5/07/27																								
1927	Cle-A	17	8	5	0	0	0	0	0	0	3	.000	.000	.000	-99	-2	-2	0	1	0	0	.833	5	/2	0.2
1928	Cle-A	3	10	3	5	0	0	0	1	0	1	.500	.500	.500	162	1	1	2	0	0	0	.867	0	/S	0.1
1929	Cle-A	19	33	2	5	1	0	0	2	1	2	.152	.200	.182	-1	-5	-5	1	0	0	0	.923	6	S/2	0.1
1930	Cle-A	54	170	28	53	13	0	0	20	17	8	.312	.378	.388	91	-1	-2	26	2	2	-1	.973	-5	3S	-0.3
1931	Cle-A	111	427	85	128	25	5	1	52	39	25	.300	.360	.389	92	-2	-5	61	5	2	0	.938	-15	S23/O	-1.0
1932	Cle-A	129	512	81	152	23	5	4	53	46	27	.297	.359	.385	87	-5	-10	72	2	5	-2	.946	-22	*S2	-2.2
1933	Cle-A	83	261	39	71	11	2	1	29	23	14	.272	.333	.341	76	-8	-9	31	3	2	-0	.938	-5	S23	-1.0
1934	Cle-A	72	208	28	61	11	2	3	30	18	11	.293	.352	.409	94	-1	-2	30	1	1	-0	.981	-8	3/S2O	-0.7
1935	StL-A	70	206	17	46	10	1	0	26	19	16	.223	.289	.282	46	-16	-17	18	1	0	0	.939	-6	3S2	-1.9
Total	9	558	1835	288	521	94	15	9	213	163	107	.284	.345	.366	81	-38	-51	241	15	12	-3	.935	-49	S32/O	-6.7
■ JACK BURNETT	Burnett, John P. b: 12/2/1889, Missouri d: 9/8/29, Taft, Cal. Deb: 7/02/07																								
1907	StL-N	59	206	18	49	8	4	0	12	15		.238	.296	.316	95	-2	-2	22	5			.955	-4	O	-0.9
■ C.B. BURNS	Burns, Charles Birmingham b: 5/15/1879, Bay View, Md. d: 6/6/68, Havre De Grace, Md BR/TR, 6', 175 lbs. Deb: 8/19/02																								
1902	Bal-A	1	1	0	1	0	0	0	0	0		1.000	1.000	1.000	436	0	0	1	0			.000	0	H	0.0
■ ED BURNS	Burns, Edward James b: 10/31/1888, San Francisco, Cal d: 6/1/42, Monterey, Cal. BR/TR, 5'6", 165 lbs. Deb: 6/25/12																								
1912	StL-N	1	1	0	0	0	0	0	1	0	0	.000	.000	.000	-99	-0	-0	0	0			.000	0	/C	0.0
1913	Phi-N	17	30	3	6	3	0	0	3	6	3	.200	.351	.300	83	-0	-0	4	2			.980	-4	C	-0.3
1914	Phi-N	70	139	8	36	3	4	0	16	20	12	.259	.352	.338	99	2	0	18	5			.947	-2	C	0.2
1915	*Phi-N	67	174	11	42	5	0	0	16	20	12	.241	.327	.270	81	-3	-3	16	1			.981	-6	C	-0.5
1916	Phi-N	78	219	14	51	8	1	0	14	16	18	.233	.294	.279	74	-6	-7	20	3			.981	-12	C/SO	-1.5
1917	Phi-N	20	49	2	10	1	0	0	6	1	5	.204	.220	.224	35	-4	-4	3	2			.971	-1	C	-0.5
1918	Phi-N	68	184	10	38	1	1	0	9	20	9	.207	.288	.223	53	-9	-10	12	1			.981	-4	C	-1.1
Total	7	321	796	48	183	21	6	0	65	83	59	.230	.308	.271	73	-20	-24	72	14			.974	-29	C/OS	-3.7
■ GEORGE BURNS	Burns, George Henry "Tioga George" b: 1/31/1893, Niles, Ohio d: 1/7/78, Kirkland, Wash. BR/TR, 6'1.5", 180 lbs. Deb: 4/14/14																								
1914	Det-A	137	478	55	139	22	5	5	57	32	56	.291	.351	.389	119	12	10	70	23	13	-1	.982	-5	*1	0.1
1915	Det-A	105	392	49	99	18	3	5	50	22	51	.253	.301	.352	91	-4	-7	45	9	3	1	.986	-4	*1	-1.3
1916	Det-A	135	479	60	137	22	6	4	73	22	30	.286	.327	.382	109	5	3	66	12			.985	-10	*1	-1.2
1917	Det-A	119	407	42	92	14	10	1	40	15	33	.226	.264	.317	77	-13	-13	34	3			.990	-4	*1	-2.3
1918	Phi-A	130	505	61	**178**	22	9	6	70	23	25	.352	.390	.467	157	33	32	91	8			.983	6	*1/O	3.6
1919	Phi-A	126	470	63	139	29	9	8	57	19	18	.296	.339	.447	118	10	9	72	15			.980	2	1O	0.7
1920	Phi-A	22	60	1	14	3	0	1	7	6	7	.233	.313	.333	71	-2	-3	7	4	0	1	.958	1	O	-0.2
	*Cle-A	44	56	7	15	4	1	0	13	4	3	.268	.339	.375	86	-1	-1	8	1	0	0	.979	1	1/O	0.0
	Yr	66	116	8	29	7	1	1	20	10	10	.250	.326	.353	78	-3	-4	15	5	0	2	.958	1	O1	-0.2
1921	Cle-A	84	244	52	88	21	4	0	49	13	19	.361	.398	.480	121	8	8	46	2	1	0	.990	2	1	0.7
1922	Bos-A	147	558	71	171	32	5	12	73	20	28	.306	.341	.446	104	1	1	85	8	2	1	.987	-1	*1	-0.4
1923	Bos-A	146	551	91	181	47	5	7	82	45	33	.328	.386	.470	124	19	18	100	9	7	-2	.990	-1	*1	0.8
1924	Cle-A	129	462	64	143	37	5	4	68	29	27	.310	.370	.437	106	4	4	77	14	5	1	.987	8	*1	0.5
1925	Cle-A	127	488	69	164	41	4	6	79	24	24	.336	.371	.473	112	8	7	83	16	11	-2	.989	-1	*1	-0.2

YEAR	TM/L	G	AB	R	H	2B	3B	HR	RBI	BB	SO	AVG	OBP	SLG	PRO+	BR	/A	RC	SB	CS	SBR	FA	FR	POS	TPR
1926	Cle-A	151	603	97	**216**	**64**	3	4	114	28	33	.358	.394	.494	129	25	24	116	13	7	-0	.988	1	*1	1.5
1927	Cle-A	140	549	84	175	51	2	3	78	42	27	.319	.375	.435	109	8	7	84	13	11	-3	.990	3	*1	-0.2
1928	Cle-A	82	209	29	52	12	1	5	30	17	11	.249	.323	.388	85	-5	-5	26	2	3	-1	.984	2	1	-0.8
	NY-A	4	4	1	2	0	0	0	0	0	1	.500	.500	.500	169	0	0	1	0	0	0	1.000	-0	/1	0.0
	Yr	86	213	30	54	12	1	5	30	17	12	.254	.326	.390	87	-4	-4	27	2	3	-1	.985	2	1	-0.8
1929	NY-A	9	9	0	0	0	0	0	0	0	4	.000	.000	.000	-99	-3	-3	0	0	0	0	.000	0	H	-0.2
	*Phi-A	29	49	5	13	5	0	1	11	2	3	.265	.294	.429	81	-1	-2	6	1	0	0	1.000	-0	1	-0.2
	Yr	38	58	5	13	5	0	1	11	2	7	.224	.250	.362	55	-4	-4	5	1	0	0	1.000	-0	1	-0.4
Total	16	1866	6573	901	2018	444	72	72	951	363	433	.307	.354	.429	112	104	93	1017	153	63		.987	0	*1/O	0.9
■ GEORGE BURNS	Burns, George Joseph b: 11/24/1889, Utica, N.Y. d: 8/15/66, Gloversville, N.Y. BR/TR, 5'7", 160 lbs. Deb: 10/03/11 C																								
1911	NY-N	6	17	2	1	0	0	0	0	1	0	.059	.111	.059	-50	-3	-4	0	0			1.000	-2	/O	-0.6
1912	NY-N	29	51	11	15	4	0	0	3	8	8	.294	.400	.373	109	1	1	10	7			1.000	-4	O	-0.4
1913	*NY-N	150	605	81	173	37	4	2	54	58	74	.286	.352	.370	106	6	5	88	40			.963	7	*O	0.5
1914	NY-N	154	561	**100**	170	35	10	3	60	89	53	.303	.403	.417	149	34	36	**113**	**62**			.950	8	*O	4.0
1915	NY-N	155	622	83	169	27	14	3	51	56	57	.272	.333	.375	121	10	14	79	27	20	-4	.960	-6	*O	-0.4
1916	NY-N	155	623	**105**	174	24	8	5	41	63	47	.279	.346	.368	126	15	19	82	37	26	-5	.962	3	*O	1.0
1917	*NY-N	152	597	**103**	180	25	13	5	45	**75**	55	.302	.380	.412	148	32	34	**102**	40			.974	5	*O	3.4
1918	NY-N	119	465	80	135	22	6	4	51	43	37	.290	.354	.389	129	15	16	74	40			.965	9	*O	2.0
1919	NY-N	139	534	**86**	162	30	9	2	46	**82**	37	.303	**.396**	.404	142	30	31	**96**	**40**			**.990**	1	*O	2.4
1920	NY-N	154	631	**115**	181	35	9	6	46	**76**	48	.287	.365	.399	121	18	18	91	22	22	-7	.983	1	*O	0.2
1921	*NY-N	149	605	111	181	28	9	4	61	**80**	24	.299	.386	.395	107	10	9	93	19	20	-6	.972	3	*O/3	-0.5
1922	Cin-N	156	631	104	180	20	10	1	53	78	38	.285	.366	.353	88	-10	-9	83	30	23	-5	.976	6	*O	-1.8
1923	Cin-N	154	614	99	168	27	13	3	45	**101**	46	.274	.376	.375	101	2	4	90	12	14	-5	.960	-1	*O	-1.2
1924	Cin-N	93	336	43	86	19	2	2	33	29	21	.256	.315	.342	77	-11	-11	36	3	6	-3	.963	1	O	-1.8
1925	Phi-N	88	349	65	102	29	1	1	22	33	20	.292	.353	.390	82	-5	-9	47	4	8	-4	.990	0	O	-1.7
Total	15	1853	7241	1188	2077	362	108	41	611	872	565	.287	.366	.384	115	143	156	1085	383	139		.970	32	*O/3	5.1
■ JIM BURNS	Burns, James M. b: Quincy, Ill. 5'7", 168 lbs. Deb: 9/25/1888																								
1888	KC-a	15	66	13	20	0	0	0	4	1		.303	.343	.303	104	1	0	9	6			.853	2	O	0.1
1889	KC-a	134	579	103	176	23	11	5	97	20	68	.304	.335	.408	107	8	2	100	56			.913	-7	*O/3	-0.7
1891	Was-a	20	82	15	26	6	0	0	10	6	10	.317	.378	.390	129	2	3	13	2			.771	-4	O/S	-0.1
Total	3	169	727	131	222	29	11	5	111	27	78	.305	.341	.396	109	11	5	123	64			.897	-9	O/S3	-0.7
■ JACK BURNS	Burns, John Irving "Slug" b: 8/31/07, Cambridge, Mass. d: 4/18/75, Brighton, Mass. BL/TL, 5'10.5", 175 lbs. Deb: 9/17/30 C																								
1930	StL-A	8	30	5	9	3	0	0	2	5	5	.300	.400	.400	100	0	0	5	0	0	0	1.000	1	/1	0.0
1931	StL-A	144	570	75	148	27	7	4	70	42	58	.260	.312	.353	72	-22	-25	63	19	12	-2	.993	18	*1	-2.0
1932	StL-A	150	617	111	188	33	8	11	70	61	43	.305	.368	.438	102	7	2	100	17	11	-2	.992	4	*1	-0.7
1933	StL-A	144	556	89	160	43	4	7	71	56	51	.288	.353	.417	97	2	-3	81	11	11	-3	.992	3	*1	-1.6
1934	StL-A	154	612	86	157	28	8	13	73	62	47	.257	.327	.392	78	-15	-23	81	9	3	1	.992	-0	*1	-3.3
1935	StL-A	143	549	77	157	28	1	5	67	68	49	.286	.366	.368	86	-6	-10	78	3	2	-0	.992	-8	*1	-3.1
1936	StL-A	9	14	2	3	1	0	0	1	3	1	.214	.353	.286	58	-1	-1	2	0	0	0	1.000	0	/1	-0.1
	Det-A	138	558	96	158	36	3	4	63	79	45	.283	.375	.380	87	-10	-10	82	4	8	-4	.994	1	*1	-2.3
	Yr	147	572	98	161	37	3	4	64	82	46	.281	.374	.378	86	-11	-11	84	4	8	-4	.994	1	*1	-2.4
Total	7	890	3506	541	980	199	31	44	417	376	299	.280	.351	.392	87	-44	-69	493	63	47	-9	.992	19	1	-13.1
■ JACK BURNS	Burns, John Joseph b: 5/13/1880, Avoca, Pa. d: 6/24/57, Waterford, Conn. BR/TR, 5'10", 160 lbs. Deb: 9/11/03																								
1903	Det-A	11	37	2	10	0	0	0	3	1		.270	.325	.270	83	-1	-1	4	0			.981	1	2	0.0
1904	Det-A	4	16	3	2	0	0	0	1	1		.125	.176	.125	-4	-2	-2	1	1			.952	-1	/2	-0.4
Total	2	15	53	5	12	0	0	0	4	2		.226	.281	.226	58	-3	-2	4	1			.973	-1	/2	-0.4
■ JOE BURNS	Burns, Joseph Francis b: 3/26/1889, Ipswich, Mass. d: 7/12/87, Beverly, Ma. BL/TL, 5'11", 170 lbs. Deb: 6/19/10																								
1910	Cin-N	1	1	0	1	0	0	0	0	0	0	1.000	1.000	1.000	506	0	0	2	1			.000	0	H	0.0
1913	Det-A	4	13	0	5	0	0	0	1	2	4	.385	.500	.385	162	1	1	2	0			1.000	-1	/O	0.1
Total	2	5	14	0	6	0	0	0	1	2	4	.429	.529	.429	184	2	2	4	1				-1	/O	0.1
■ JOE BURNS	Burns, Joseph Francis b: 2/25/1900, Trenton, N.J. d: 1/7/86, Trenton, N.J. BR/TR, 6', 175 lbs. Deb: 4/18/24																								
1924	Chi-A	8	19	1	2	0	0	0	0	0	2	.105	.105	.105	-47	-4	-4	0	0	0	0	.933	-2	/C	-0.5
■ JOE BURNS	Burns, Joseph James b: 6/17/16, Bryn Mawr, Pa. d: 6/24/74, Bryn Mawr, Pa. BR/TR, 5'10.5", 175 lbs. Deb: 4/24/43																								
1943	Bos-N	52	135	12	28	3	0	1	5	8	25	.207	.262	.252	49	-9	-9	8	2			.933	-1	3/O	-1.0
1944	Phi-A	28	75	5	18	2	0	1	8	4	8	.240	.278	.307	68	-3	-3	7	0	1	-1	.919	-8	3/2	-1.2
1945	Phi-A	31	90	7	23	1	1	0	3	4	17	.256	.287	.289	68	-4	-4	7	0	1	-1	1.000	-4	O/31	-1.0
Total	3	111	300	24	69	6	1	2	16	16	50	.230	.274	.277	60	-16	-16	22	2	2			-12	/3O21	-3.2
■ PAT BURNS	Burns, Patrick Deb: 8/11/1884																								
1884	Bal-a	6	25	3	5	2	1	0		3		.200	.286	.360	108	0	0	3				.953	-1	/1	-0.1
	Bal-U	1	4	0	2	0	0	0		0		.500	.500	.500	217	1	0	1				.917	-0	/1	0.0
Total	1	7	29	3	7	2	1	0		3		.241	.313	.379	122	1	1	4				.947	-1	/1	-0.1
■ DICK BURNS	Burns, Richard Simon b: 12/26/1863, Holyoke, Mass. d: 11/11/37, Holyoke, Mass. BL/TL, 140 lbs. Deb: 5/03/1883																								
1883	Det-N	37	140	11	26	7	1	0	5	2	22	.186	.197	.250	36	-11	-10	7				.758	-6	OP	-1.0
1884	Cin-U	79	350	84	107	17	**12**	4		5		.306	.315	.457	147	20	16	52				.827	-3	OP/S	0.3
1885	StL-N	14	54	2	12	2	1	0	4	3	8	.222	.263	.296	86	-1	-1	4				.682	-3	O/P	-0.5
Total	3	130	544	97	145	26	14	4	9	10	30	.267	.280	.388	112	8	5	63				.785	-12	/OPS	-1.2
■ TOM BURNS	Burns, Thomas Everett b: 3/30/1857, Honesdale, Pa. d: 3/19/02, Jersey City, N.J. BR/TR, 5'7", 152 lbs. Deb: 5/01/1880 MU																								
1880	Chi-N	85	333	47	103	17	3	0	43	12	23	.309	.333	.378	133	14	11	43				.864	-24	*S/3CP	-0.8
1881	Chi-N	84	342	41	95	20	3	4	42	14	22	.278	.306	.389	112	6	4	42				.870	-5	*S/32	0.4
1882	Chi-N	84	355	55	88	23	6	0	48	15	28	.248	.278	.346	95	-0	-3	35				.911	0	2S	0.0
1883	Chi-N	97	405	69	119	37	7	2	67	13	31	.294	.316	.435	118	12	8	57				.872	-1	*S2/O	0.8
1884	Chi-N	83	343	54	84	14	2	7	44	13	50	.245	.272	.359	89	-2	-6	34				.838	-2	*S/3	-0.6
1885	*Chi-N	111	445	82	121	23	9	7	71	16	48	.272	.297	.411	111	12	3	56				.844	-2	*S/2	0.3
1886	*Chi-N	112	445	64	123	18	10	3	65	14	40	.276	.298	.382	92	2	-8	57	15			.890	13	*3	0.7
1887	Chi-N	115	424	57	112	20	10	3	60	34	32	.264	.320	.380	84	-3	-12	63	32			.872	21	*3/O	0.9
1888	Chi-N	134	483	60	115	12	6	3	70	26	49	.238	.281	.306	83	-5	-10	52	34			.905	17	*3	0.9
1889	Chi-N	136	525	64	127	27	6	4	66	32	57	.242	.288	.339	73	-18	-22	58	18			.880	3	*3	-1.3
1890	Chi-N	139	538	86	149	17	6	5	86	57	45	.277	.348	.359	104	6	3	85	44			.898	2	*3	0.9
1891	Chi-N	59	243	36	55	8	1	1	17	21	21	.226	.288	.280	67	-10	-10	25	18			.892	-2	3/SO	-0.8
1892	Pit-N	12	39	7	8	0	0	0	4	3	8	.205	.262	.205	43	-3	-3	2	1			.690	-5	/3OM	-0.7
Total	13	1251	4920	722	1299	236	69	39	683	270	454	.264	.303	.364	96	12	-44	610	162			.886	16	3S/2OCP	0.7
■ OYSTER BURNS	Burns, Thomas P. b: 9/6/1864, Philadelphia, Pa. d: 11/11/28, Brooklyn, N.Y. BR/TR, 5'8", 183 lbs. Deb: 8/18/1884																								
1884	Wil-U	2	7	0	1	0	1	0		1		.143	.250	.429	122	0	0	1				.778	-0	/S	0.0
	Bal-a	35	131	34	39	2	6	6		7		.298	.348	.542	182	12	12	25				.826	-5	O2/P3	0.6

YEAR	TM/L	G	AB	R	H	2B	3B	HR	RBI	BB	SO	AVG	OBP	SLG	PRO+	BR	/A	RC	SB	CS	SBR	FA	FR	POS	TPR
1885	Bal-a	78	321	47	74	11	6	5		16		.231	.280	.349	102	0	1	32				.908	-0	OPS/321	0.1
1887	Bal-a	140	551	122	188	33	**19**	9		63		.341	.414	.519	172	46	52	146	58			.841	-19	*S3/P2	2.8
1888	Bal-a	79	325	54	97	18	9	4	42	24		.298	.349	.446	162	20	21	60	23			.855	-5	OS/P32	1.4
	Bro-a	52	204	40	58	9	6	2	25	14		.284	.339	.417	146	10	10	37	21			.851	-13	SO/2	-0.2
	Yr	131	529	94	155	27	15	6	67	38		.293	.345	.435	155	30	31	97	44			.847	-18	OS/P23	1.2
1889	*Bro-a	131	504	105	153	19	13	5	100	68	26	.304	.391	.423	134	24	24	98	32			.920	-8	*OS	1.1
1890	*Bro-N	119	472	102	134	22	12	**13**	**128**	51	42	.284	.359	.464	141	23	23	88	21			.941	-3	*O/3	1.4
1891	Bro-N	123	470	75	134	24	13	4	83	53	30	.285	.358	.417	128	16	16	80	21			.922	2	*O/S3	1.3
1892	Bro-N	141	542	88	171	27	18	4	96	65	42	.315	.395	.454	165	39	42	113	33			.937	-13	*O/3S	2.2
1893	Bro-N	109	415	68	112	22	8	7	60	36	16	.270	.334	.412	104	-2	2	63	14			.932	-1	*O/S	-0.4
1894	Bro-N	125	505	106	179	32	14	5	107	44	18	.354	.409	.503	130	17	24	120	30			.949	-4	*O	0.9
1895	Bro-N	20	76	7	14	0	1	0	7	8	2	.184	.271	.211	29	-8	-7	4	0			.918	1	O	-0.6
	NY-N	33	114	21	35	5	3	1	25	14	6	.307	.388	.430	115	2	3	24	10			.870	-5	O/1	-0.3
	Yr	53	190	28	49	5	4	1	32	22	8	.258	.341	.342	82	-6	-4	26	10			.893	-3	O/1	-0.9
Total	11	1187	4637	869	1389	224	129	65	673	464	182	.300	.368	.446	138	199	222	891	263			.920	-73	OS/3P21	10.3

■ ALEX BURR

Burr, Alexander Thomson b: 11/1/1893, Chicago, Ill. d: 11/1/18, France BR/TR, 6'3.5", 190 lbs. Deb: 4/21/14

YEAR	TM/L	G	AB	R	H	2B	3B	HR	RBI	BB	SO	AVG	OBP	SLG	PRO+	BR	/A	RC	SB	CS	SBR	FA	FR	POS	TPR
1914	NY-A	1	0	0	0	0	0	0	0	0	0	—	—	—	—	0	0	0	0			.000	-1	/O	-0.1

■ BUSTER BURRELL

Burrell, Frank Andrew b: 12/22/1866, Weymouth, Mass. d: 5/8/62, Weymouth, Mass. BR/TR, 5'10", 165 lbs. Deb: 8/01/1891

YEAR	TM/L	G	AB	R	H	2B	3B	HR	RBI	BB	SO	AVG	OBP	SLG	PRO+	BR	/A	RC	SB	CS	SBR	FA	FR	POS	TPR
1891	NY-N	15	53	1	5	0	0	0	1	3	12	.094	.158	.094	-26	-8	-8	1	2			.856	-5	C/O	-1.1
1895	Bro-N	12	28	7	4	0	0	1	5	4	3	.143	.250	.250	33	-3	-3	2	0			.838	-2	C	-0.3
1896	Bro-N	62	206	19	62	11	3	0	23	15	13	.301	.348	.383	100	-2	0	29	1			.928	-10	C	-0.2
1897	Bro-N	33	103	15	25	2	0	2	18	10		.243	.310	.320	70	-5	-4	11	1			.884	-4	C/1	-0.4
Total	4	122	390	42	96	13	3	3	47	32	28	.246	.305	.318	71	-18	-14	43	4			.896	-20	C/1O	-2.0

■ LARRY BURRIGHT

Burright, Larry Allen "Possum" b: 7/10/37, Roseville, Ill. BR/TR, 5'11", 170 lbs. Deb: 4/12/62

YEAR	TM/L	G	AB	R	H	2B	3B	HR	RBI	BB	SO	AVG	OBP	SLG	PRO+	BR	/A	RC	SB	CS	SBR	FA	FR	POS	TPR
1962	LA-N	115	249	35	51	6	5	4	30	21	67	.205	.267	.317	60	-16	-14	20	4	3	-1	.962	14	*2/S	0.7
1963	NY-N	41	100	9	22	2	1	0	3	8	25	.220	.291	.260	59	-5	-5	8	1	0	0	.946	12	S2/3	1.0
1964	NY-N	3	7	0	0	0	0	0	0	0	0	.000	.000	.000	-99	-2	-2	0	0	0	0	1.000	4	/2	0.3
Total	3	159	356	44	73	8	6	4	33	29	92	.205	.269	.295	56	-23	-21	29	5	3	-0	.964	30	2/S3	2.0

■ PAUL BURRIS

Burris, Paul Robert b: 7/21/23, Hickory, N.C. BR/TR, 6', 190 lbs. Deb: 10/02/48

YEAR	TM/L	G	AB	R	H	2B	3B	HR	RBI	BB	SO	AVG	OBP	SLG	PRO+	BR	/A	RC	SB	CS	SBR	FA	FR	POS	TPR
1948	Bos-N	2	4	0	2	0	0	0	0	0	0	.500	.500	.500	174	0	0	1	0			1.000	1	/C	0.1
1950	Bos-N	10	23	1	4	1	0	0	3	1	2	.174	.208	.217	13	-3	-3	1	0			1.000	1	/C	-0.1
1952	Bos-N	55	168	14	37	4	0	2	21	7	19	.220	.256	.280	50	-12	-11	10	0	0	0	1.000	-4	C	-1.4
1953	Mil-N	2	1	0	0	0	0	0	0	0	0	.000	.000	.000	-99	-0	-0	0	0	0	0	1.000	-0	/C	0.0
Total	4	69	196	15	43	5	0	2	24	8	21	.219	.254	.276	47	-15	-14	12	0	0		1.000	-2	/C	-1.4

■ HENRY BURROUGHS

Burroughs, Henry F. b: 1845, Detroit, Mich. 5'8", 147 lbs. Deb: 5/05/1871

YEAR	TM/L	G	AB	R	H	2B	3B	HR	RBI	BB	SO	AVG	OBP	SLG	PRO+	BR	/A	RC	SB	CS	SBR	FA	FR	POS	TPR
1871	Oly-n	12	63	11	15	2	3	1	14	1	1	.238	.250	.413	91	-1	-0	7	0					/O3	0.0
1872	Oly-n	2	7	1	1	1	0	0	0	1	0	.143	.250	.286	68	-0	-0	1						/O	0.0
Total	2 n	14	70	12	16	3	3	1	14	2	1	.229	.250	.400	89	-1	-1	7						/O3	0.0

■ JEFF BURROUGHS

Burroughs, Jeffrey Alan b: 3/7/51, Long Beach, Cal. BR/TR, 6'1", 200 lbs. Deb: 7/20/70

YEAR	TM/L	G	AB	R	H	2B	3B	HR	RBI	BB	SO	AVG	OBP	SLG	PRO+	BR	/A	RC	SB	CS	SBR	FA	FR	POS	TPR
1970	Was-A	6	12	1	2	0	0	0	1	2	5	.167	.286	.167	29	-1	-1	1	0	0	0	1.000	-0	/O	-0.1
1971	Was-A	59	181	20	42	9	0	5	25	22	55	.232	.319	.365	99	-2	-0	22	1	0	0	.966	-5	O	-0.8
1972	Tex-A	22	65	4	12	1	0	1	3	5	22	.185	.243	.246	48	-4	-4	3	0	2	-1	.935	-1	O/1	-0.8
1973	Tex-A	151	526	71	147	17	1	30	85	67	88	.279	.362	.487	143	25	28	95	0	0	0	.975	13	*O/1D	3.4
1974	Tex-A★	152	554	84	167	33	2	25	**118**	91	104	.301	.405	.504	164	**45**	**47**	113	2	3	-1	.972	-8	*O/1D	3.2
1975	Tex-A	152	585	81	132	20	0	29	94	79	155	.226	.319	.409	105	3	3	76	4	4	-1	.966	-8	*O/D	-1.3
1976	Tex-A	158	604	71	143	22	2	18	86	69	93	.237	.317	.369	98	0	-1	69	0	0	0	.987	-2	*O/D	-1.0
1977	Atl-N	154	579	91	157	19	1	41	114	86	126	.271	.365	.520	120	28	19	114	4	1	1	.974	-9	*O	0.5
1978	Atl-N☆	153	488	72	147	30	6	23	77	**117**	92	.301	**.436**	.529	151	50	43	116	1	2	-1	.975	-9	*O	2.9
1979	Atl-N	116	397	49	89	14	1	11	47	73	75	.224	.349	.348	84	-3	-7	50	2	2	-1	.963	-6	*O	-1.9
1980	Atl-N	99	278	35	73	14	0	13	51	35	57	.263	.349	.453	118	8	7	45	1	1	-0	.977	-8	O	-0.4
1981	Sea-A	89	319	32	81	13	1	10	41	41	64	.254	.339	.395	107	5	3	43	0	1	-1	.985	-9	O/D	-0.9
1982	Oak-A	113	285	42	79	13	2	16	48	45	61	.277	.376	.505	146	16	18	54	1	3	-2	.981	-5	DO	1.0
1983	Oak-A	121	401	43	108	15	1	10	56	47	79	.269	.346	.387	108	1	5	51	0	2	-1	.000	0	*D	0.3
1984	Oak-A	58	71	5	15	1	0	2	8	18	23	.211	.371	.310	97	-0	1	9	0	0	0	1.000	-2	D/O	-0.1
1985	*Tor-A	86	191	19	49	9	3	6	28	34	36	.257	.369	.429	115	6	5	30	0	1	-1	.000	0	D	0.4
Total	16	1689	5536	720	1443	230	20	240	882	831	1135	.261	.359	.439	120	177	164	892	16	22	-8	.974	-58	*OD/1	4.4

■ DICK BURRUS

Burrus, Maurice Lennon b: 1/29/1898, Hatteras, N.C. d: 2/2/72, Elizabeth City, N.C BL/TL, 5'11", 175 lbs. Deb: 6/23/19

YEAR	TM/L	G	AB	R	H	2B	3B	HR	RBI	BB	SO	AVG	OBP	SLG	PRO+	BR	/A	RC	SB	CS	SBR	FA	FR	POS	TPR
1919	Phi-A	70	194	17	50	3	4	0	8	9	25	.258	.294	.314	70	-8	-8	18	2			.986	-4	1O	-1.5
1920	Phi-A	71	135	11	25	8	0	0	10	5	7	.185	.225	.244	24	-15	-15	7	0	3	-2	.989	-2	1/O	-1.9
1925	Bos-N	152	588	82	200	41	4	5	87	51	29	.340	.396	.449	126	15	22	104	8	9	-3	**.990**	1	*1	1.0
1926	Bos-N	131	486	59	131	21	1	3	61	37	16	.270	.324	.335	85	-15	-9	53	4			.991	12	*1	-0.5
1927	Bos-N	72	220	22	70	8	3	0	32	17	10	.318	.370	.382	110	1	3	31	3			.972	1	1	0.1
1928	Bos-N	64	137	15	37	6	0	3	13	19	8	.270	.367	.380	101	-0	1	20	1			.977	-2	1	-0.4
Total	6	560	1760	206	513	87	12	11	211	138	95	.291	.347	.373	97	-22	-6	231	18	12		.986	7	1/O	-3.2

■ FRANK BURT

Burt, Frank J. b: Camden, N.J. Deb: 5/02/1882

YEAR	TM/L	G	AB	R	H	2B	3B	HR	RBI	BB	SO	AVG	OBP	SLG	PRO+	BR	/A	RC	SB	CS	SBR	FA	FR	POS	TPR
1882	Bal-a	10	36	2	4	2	1	0		1		.111	.135	.222	20	-3	-3	1				.815	-1	O	-0.3

■ ELLIS BURTON

Burton, Ellis Narrington b: 8/12/36, Los Angeles, Cal. BB/TR, 5'11", 165 lbs. Deb: 9/18/58

YEAR	TM/L	G	AB	R	H	2B	3B	HR	RBI	BB	SO	AVG	OBP	SLG	PRO+	BR	/A	RC	SB	CS	SBR	FA	FR	POS	TPR
1958	StL-N	8	30	5	7	0	1	2	4	3	8	.233	.324	.500	110	0	0	4	0	1	-1	1.000	-0	/O	-0.1
1960	StL-N	29	28	5	6	1	0	0	2	4	14	.214	.313	.250	52	-2	-2	2	0	2	-1	1.000	-7	O	-1.1
1963	Cle-A	26	31	6	6	3	0	1	1	4	4	.194	.286	.387	87	-1	-1	3	0	0	0	1.000	-4	O	-0.5
	Chi-N	93	322	45	74	16	1	12	41	36	59	.230	.315	.398	98	2	-0	41	6	3	0	.975	-10	O	-1.6
1964	Chi-N	42	105	12	20	3	2	2	7	17	22	.190	.303	.314	71	-3	-4	11	4	0	1	.981	-2	O	-0.6
1965	Chi-N	17	40	6	7	1	0	0	4	1	10	.175	.195	.200	11	-5	-5	2	1	0	0	1.000	1	O	-0.4
Total	5	215	556	79	120	24	4	17	59	65	117	.216	.304	.365	85	-8	-11	64	11	6	-0	.981	-22	O	-4.3

■ JIM BUSBY

Busby, James Franklin b: 1/8/27, Kenedy, Tex. BR/TR, 6'1", 175 lbs. Deb: 4/23/50 C

YEAR	TM/L	G	AB	R	H	2B	3B	HR	RBI	BB	SO	AVG	OBP	SLG	PRO+	BR	/A	RC	SB	CS	SBR	FA	FR	POS	TPR
1950	Chi-A	18	48	5	10	0	0	0	4	1	5	.208	.224	.208	12	-6	-6	2	0	2	-1	.964	-1	O	-0.8
1951	Chi-A★	143	477	59	135	15	2	5	68	40	46	.283	.344	.354	91	-7	-6	58	26	11	1	.982	3	*O	-0.6
1952	Chi-A	16	39	5	5	0	0	0	0	2	7	.128	.171	.128	-16	-6	-6	1	0	2	-1	1.000	-0	O	-0.9
	Was-A	129	512	58	125	24	4	2	47	22	48	.244	.281	.318	69	-24	-22	44	5	6	-2	.993	14	*O	-1.7
	Yr	145	551	63	130	24	4	2	47	24	55	.236	.273	.305	62	-30	-29	44	5	8	-3	.994	13	*O	-2.6
1953	Was-A	150	586	68	183	28	7	6	82	38	45	.312	.358	.415	111	6	8	90	13	6	0	.988	**19**	*O	2.1
1954	Was-A	155	628	83	187	22	7	7	80	43	56	.298	.346	.389	107	-0	4	88	17	2	**4**	.988	12	*O	1.4
1955	Was-A	47	191	23	44	6	2	6	14	13	22	.230	.279	.377	79	-8	-6	20	5	0	2	.993	2	O	-0.5
	Chi-A	99	337	38	82	13	4	1	27	25	37	.243	.296	.315	62	-17	-19	32	7	3	0	.984	2	O	-2.0
	Yr	146	528	61	126	19	6	7	41	38	59	.239	.290	.337	68	-25	-25	52	12	3	2	.987	5	*O	-2.5

YEAR	TM/L	G	AB	R	H	2B	3B	HR	RBI	BB	SO	AVG	OBP	SLG	PRO+	BR	/A	RC	SB	CS	SBR	FA	FR	POS	TPR
1956	Cle-A	135	494	72	116	17	3	12	50	43	47	.235	.301	.354	71	-21	-22	52	8	3	1	.989	5	*O	-2.3
1957	Cle-A	30	74	9	14	2	1	2	4	1	8	.189	.200	.324	41	-6	-6	4	0	1	-1	.978	-3	O	-1.2
	Bal-A	86	288	31	72	10	1	3	19	23	36	.250	.305	.323	77	-11	-9	30	6	3	0	.984	10	O	-0.4
	Yr	116	362	40	86	12	2	5	23	24	44	.238	.285	.323	69	-17	-15	33	6	4	-1	.983	6	*O	-1.6
1958	Bal-A	113	215	32	51	7	2	3	19	24	37	.237	.322	.330	84	-5	-4	24	6	4	-1	**.995**	-9	*O/3	-1.7
1959	Bos-A	61	102	16	23	8	0	1	5	5	18	.225	.269	.333	61	-5	-6	8	0	1	-1	.980	-6	O	-1.3
1960	Bos-A	1	0	0	0	0	0	0	0	0	0	—	—	—	—	0	0	0	0	0	0	.000	-0	/O	0.0
	Bal-A	79	159	25	41	7	1	0	12	20	14	.258	.341	.314	79	-4	-4	17	2	3	-1	.985	-5	O	-1.3
	Yr	80	159	25	41	7	1	0	12	20	14	.258	.341	.314	79	-4	-4	17	2	3	-1	.985	-6	O	-1.3
1961	Bal-A	75	89	15	23	3	1	0	6	8	10	.258	.320	.315	72	-4	-3	10	2	0	1	.987	-16	O	-2.1
1962	Hou-N	15	11	2	2	0	0	0	1	2	3	.182	.308	.182	38	-1	-1	1	0	1	-1	1.000	-0	O/C	-0.2
Total	13	1352	4250	541	1113	162	35	48	438	310	439	.262	.316	.350	82	-121	-109	481	97	48	0	.988	25	*O/C3	-13.5

■ PAUL BUSBY

Busby, Paul Miller "Red" b: 8/25/18, Waynesboro, Miss. BL/TR, 6'1", 175 lbs. Deb: 9/14/41

YEAR	TM/L	G	AB	R	H	2B	3B	HR	RBI	BB	SO	AVG	OBP	SLG	PRO+	BR	/A	RC	SB	CS	SBR	FA	FR	POS	TPR
1941	Phi-N	10	16	3	5	0	0	0	2	0	1	.313	.313	.313	79	-1	-0	2	0			1.000	-1	/O	-0.1
1943	Phi-N	26	40	13	10	1	0	0	5	2	1	.250	.286	.275	65	-2	-2	3	2			1.000	0	O	-0.2
Total	2	36	56	16	15	1	0	0	7	2	2	.268	.293	.286	69	-2	-2	5	2			1.000	-1	/O	-0.3

■ ED BUSCH

Busch, Edgar John b: 11/16/17, Lebanon, Ill. d: 1/17/87, St.Clair Co., Ill. BR/TR, 5'10", 175 lbs. Deb: 9/30/43

YEAR	TM/L	G	AB	R	H	2B	3B	HR	RBI	BB	SO	AVG	OBP	SLG	PRO+	BR	/A	RC	SB	CS	SBR	FA	FR	POS	TPR
1943	Phi-A	4	17	2	5	0	0	0	0	1	2	.294	.368	.294	95	-0	-0	2	0	1	-1	.941	-3	/S	-0.3
1944	Phi-A	140	484	41	131	11	3	0	40	29	17	.271	.313	.306	78	-14	-13	44	5	3	-0	.940	-30	*S2/3	-3.6
1945	Phi-A	126	416	37	104	10	3	0	35	32	9	.250	.305	.288	73	-14	-14	37	2	3	-1	.952	1	*S/231	-0.6
Total	3	270	917	80	240	21	6	0	75	62	28	.262	.311	.298	76	-29	-28	82	7	7	-2	.946	-32	S/231	-4.5

■ DONIE BUSH

Bush, Owen Joseph b: 10/8/1887, Indianapolis, Ind. d: 3/28/72, Indianapolis, Ind. BB/TR, 5'6", 140 lbs. Deb: 9/18/08 M

YEAR	TM/L	G	AB	R	H	2B	3B	HR	RBI	BB	SO	AVG	OBP	SLG	PRO+	BR	/A	RC	SB	CS	SBR	FA	FR	POS	TPR
1908	Det-A	20	68	13	20	1	1	0	4	7		.294	.360	.338	122	2	2	9	2			.938	-3	S	-0.1
1909	*Det-A	157	532	114	145	18	2	0	33	**88**		.273	.380	.314	114	17	14	89	53			.925	4	*S	2.4
1910	Det-A	142	496	90	130	13	4	3	34	**78**		.262	.365	.323	108	12	8	78	49			**.940**	9	*S/3	2.5
1911	Det-A	150	561	126	130	18	5	1	36	**98**		.232	.349	.287	74	-12	-17	73	40			.925	17	*S	1.0
1912	Det-A	144	511	107	118	14	8	2	38	**117**		.231	.377	.301	98	3	5	72	35			.929	29	*S	4.6
1913	Det-A	153	597	98	150	19	10	1	40	80	32	.251	.344	.322	96	-2	-1	77	44			.938	2	*S	1.6
1914	Det-A	157	596	97	150	18	4	0	32	**112**	54	.252	.373	.295	98	7	5	71	35	26	-5	.944	**34**	*S	5.0
1915	Det-A	155	561	99	128	12	8	1	44	118	44	.228	.364	.283	89	2	-2	65	35	27	-6	.937	9	*S	1.4
1916	Det-A	145	550	73	124	5	9	0	34	75	42	.225	.319	.267	74	-14	-16	57	19			.954	-15	*S	-2.6
1917	Det-A	147	581	**112**	163	18	3	0	24	80	40	.281	.370	.322	111	11	11	78	34			.932	-18	*S	0.0
1918	Det-A	128	500	74	117	10	3	0	22	79	31	.234	.340	.266	86	-7	-5	48	9			.931	-20	*S	-2.2
1919	Det-A	129	509	82	124	11	6	0	26	75	36	.244	.343	.289	80	-12	-10	57	22			.943	-12	*S	-1.5
1920	Det-A	141	506	85	133	18	5	1	33	73	32	.263	.357	.324	83	-11	-9	66	15	7	0	.938	-17	*S	-1.3
1921	Det-A	104	402	72	113	6	5	0	27	45	23	.281	.355	.321	74	-15	-14	48	8	11	-4	.949	-5	S2	-1.4
	Was-A	23	84	15	18	1	0	0	2	12	4	.214	.313	.226	41	-7	-7	7	2	2	-1	.932	-4	S	-0.9
	Yr	127	486	87	131	7	5	0	29	57	27	.270	.347	.305	69	-22	-21	55	10	13	-5	.946	-10	*S2	-2.3
1922	Was-A	41	134	17	32	4	1	0	7	21	7	.239	.342	.284	68	-6	-5	14	1	1	-0	.957	-2	3/2	-0.5
1923	Was-A	10	22	6	9	0	0	0	0	0	1	.409	.409	.409	122	0	1	3	0	1	-1	.813	-2	/32M	-0.1
Total	16	1946	7210	1280	1804	186	74	9	436	1158	346	.250	.356	.300	91	-32	-40	911	403	75		.936	5	*S/32	7.9

■ RANDY BUSH

Bush, Robert Randall b: 10/5/58, Dover, Del. BL/TL, 6'1", 186 lbs. Deb: 5/01/82

YEAR	TM/L	G	AB	R	H	2B	3B	HR	RBI	BB	SO	AVG	OBP	SLG	PRO+	BR	/A	RC	SB	CS	SBR	FA	FR	POS	TPR
1982	Min-A	55	119	13	29	6	1	4	13	8	28	.244	.308	.412	93	-1	-1	16	0	0	0	1.000	-1	D/O	-0.3
1983	Min-A	124	373	43	93	24	3	11	56	34	51	.249	.324	.418	99	1	-1	50	0	1	-1	1.000	1	*D/1	-0.1
1984	Min-A	113	311	46	69	17	1	11	43	31	60	.222	.301	.389	85	-5	-7	38	1	2	-1	1.000	-0	D/1	-0.8
1985	Min-A	97	234	26	56	13	3	10	35	24	30	.239	.323	.449	103	3	1	36	3	0	1	.969	-6	OD/1	-0.5
1986	Min-A	130	357	50	96	19	7	7	45	39	63	.269	.348	.420	105	4	3	53	5	3	-0	.977	-7	*O/1D	-0.7
1987	*Min-A	122	293	46	74	10	2	11	46	43	49	.253	.354	.413	99	2	0	45	10	3	1	.982	-8	O/1D	-0.9
1988	Min-A	136	394	51	103	20	3	14	51	58	49	.261	.369	.434	120	14	13	64	8	6	-1	.979	-6	*O/1D	0.2
1989	Min-A	141	391	60	103	17	4	14	54	48	73	.263	.348	.435	112	10	7	54	5	8	-3	.986	-9	*O1/D	-0.9
1990	Min-A	73	181	17	44	8	0	6	18	21	27	.243	.341	.387	97	1	-0	24	0	3	-2	1.000	-2	OD/1	-0.5
1991	*Min-A	93	165	21	50	10	1	6	23	24	25	.303	.401	.485	137	11	10	31	0	2	-1	1.000	-5	O1D	0.3
1992	Min-A	100	182	14	39	8	1	2	22	11	37	.214	.267	.302	57	-10	-11	14	1	1	-0	1.000	-3	OD/1	-1.5
Total	11	1184	3000	387	756	152	26	96	406	341	492	.252	.338	.416	102	29	13	425	33	29	-8	.983	-47	OD/1	-5.7

■ DOC BUSHONG

Bushong, Albert John b: 9/15/1856, Philadelphia, Pa. d: 8/19/08, Brooklyn, N.Y. BR/TR, 5'11", 165 lbs. Deb: 7/19/1875

YEAR	TM/L	G	AB	R	H	2B	3B	HR	RBI	BB	SO	AVG	OBP	SLG	PRO+	BR	/A	RC	SB	CS	SBR	FA	FR	POS	TPR
1875	Atl-n	1	5	0	3	0	1	0		0		.600	.600	1.000	509	2	2	3						/C	0.1
1876	Phi-N	5	21	4	1	0	0	0	1	0	0	.048	.048	.048	-69	-4	-4	0				.769	-1	/C	-0.4
1880	Wor-N	41	146	13	25	3	0	0	19	1	16	.171	.177	.192	23	-11	-13	5				.918	16	C/O3	0.4
1881	Wor-N	76	275	35	64	7	4	0	21	21	23	.233	.287	.287	77	-5	-7	23				.918	11	*C	0.6
1882	Wor-N	69	253	20	40	4	1	1	15	5	17	.158	.174	.194	18	-22	-23	9				.897	-3	*C	-2.2
1883	Cle-N	63	215	15	37	5	0	0	9	7	19	.172	.198	.195	21	-20	-20	9				.909	15	C	0.0
1884	Cle-N	62	203	24	48	6	1	0	10	17	11	.236	.295	.276	78	-4	-5	17				.886	0	C/O	0.1
1885	*StL-a	85	300	42	80	13	5	0		11		.267	.297	.343	100	1	-1	31				.932	14	*C/3	1.8
1886	*StL-a	107	386	56	86	8	0	1		31		.223	.281	.251	66	-13	-16	31	12			**.942**	16	*C/1	1.0
1887	*StL-a	53	201	35	51	4	0	0		11		.254	.299	.274	56	-10	-14	21	14			.927	7	C/O3	-0.2
1888	Bro-a	69	253	23	53	5	1	0	16	5		.209	.231	.237	53	-13	-13	16	9			.915	-7	C	-1.3
1889	*Bro-a	25	84	15	13	1	0	0	8	9	7	.155	.237	.167	17	-9	-9	4	2			.894	-1	C	-0.7
1890	*Bro-N	16	55	5	13	2	0	0	7	6	4	.236	.311	.273	72	-2	-2	5	2			.913	-1	C/O	-0.2
Total	12	671	2392	287	511	58	12	2	106	124	97	.214	.254	.250	56	-111	-126	172	39			.916	65	C/O31	-1.1

■ JOE BUSKEY

Buskey, Joseph Henry "Jazzbow" b: 12/18/02, Cumberland, Md. d: 4/11/49, Cumberland, Md. BR/TR, 5'10", 175 lbs. Deb: 4/19/26

YEAR	TM/L	G	AB	R	H	2B	3B	HR	RBI	BB	SO	AVG	OBP	SLG	PRO+	BR	/A	RC	SB	CS	SBR	FA	FR	POS	TPR
1926	Phi-N	5	8	1	0	0	0	0	0	1	1	.000	.111	.000	-65	-2	-2	0	0			.810	-0	/S	-0.2

■ MIKE BUSKEY

Buskey, Michael Thomas b: 1/13/49, San Francisco, Cal. BR/TR, 5'11", 160 lbs. Deb: 9/02/77

YEAR	TM/L	G	AB	R	H	2B	3B	HR	RBI	BB	SO	AVG	OBP	SLG	PRO+	BR	/A	RC	SB	CS	SBR	FA	FR	POS	TPR
1977	Phi-N	6	7	1	2	0	1	0	1	0	1	.286	.375	.571	143	0	0	2	0	0	0	.882	2	/S	0.2

■ RAY BUSSE

Busse, Raymond Edward b: 9/25/48, Daytona Beach, Fla. BR/TR, 6'4", 175 lbs. Deb: 7/24/71

YEAR	TM/L	G	AB	R	H	2B	3B	HR	RBI	BB	SO	AVG	OBP	SLG	PRO+	BR	/A	RC	SB	CS	SBR	FA	FR	POS	TPR
1971	Hou-N	10	34	2	5	3	0	0	4	2	9	.147	.194	.235	22	-4	-3	2	0	0	0	.929	-2	/S3	-0.6
1973	StL-N	24	70	6	10	4	2	2	5	5	21	.143	.200	.343	48	-5	-5	3	0	1	-1	.898	-2	S	-0.6
	Hou-N	15	17	1	1	0	0	0	0	1	12	.059	.111	.059	-52	-3	-3	0	0	0	0	1.000	1	/S3	-0.2
	Yr	39	87	7	11	4	2	2	5	6	33	.126	.183	.287	28	-9	-9	3	0	1	-1	.906	-1	S/3	-0.8
1974	Hou-N	19	34	3	7	1	0	0	0	3	12	.206	.270	.235	44	-3	-2	2	0	0	0	.864	-0	/3	-0.3
Total	3	68	155	12	23	8	2	2	9	11	54	.148	.205	.265	31	-15	-15	7	0	1	-1	.908	-3	/S3	-1.7

■ HANK BUTCHER

Butcher, Henry Joseph b: 7/12/1886, Chicago, Ill. d: 12/28/79, Hazel Crest, Ill. BR/TR, 5'10", 180 lbs. Deb: 7/08/11

YEAR	TM/L	G	AB	R	H	2B	3B	HR	RBI	BB	SO	AVG	OBP	SLG	PRO+	BR	/A	RC	SB	CS	SBR	FA	FR	POS	TPR
1911	Cle-A	38	133	21	32	7	3	1	11	11		.241	.303	.361	84	-3	-3	17	9			.984	0	O	-0.5
1912	Cle-A	26	82	9	16	4	1	1	10	6		.195	.250	.305	57	-5	-5	6	1			.920	1	O	-0.5
Total	2	64	215	30	48	11	4	2	21	17		.223	.283	.340	74	-8	-8	23	10			.956	2	/O	-1.0

YEAR	TM/L	G	AB	R	H	2B	3B	HR	RBI	BB	SO	AVG	OBP	SLG	PRO+	BR	/A	RC	SB	CS	SBR	FA	FR	POS	TPR

■ SAL BUTERA　　Butera, Salvatore Philip　b: 9/25/52, Richmond Hill, N.Y　BR/TR, 6', 190 lbs.　Deb: 4/10/80

1980	Min-A	34	85	4	23	1	0	0	2	3	6	.271	.303	.282	57	-4	-5	7	0	0	0	.950	-1	C/D	-0.6
1981	Min-A	62	167	13	40	7	1	0	18	22	14	.240	.328	.293	75	-4	-5	16	0	0	0	.970	5	C/1D	0.2
1982	Min-A	54	126	9	32	2	0	0	8	17	12	.254	.347	.270	70	-4	-4	12	0	0	0	.988	6	C	0.3
1983	Det-A	4	5	1	1	0	0	0	0	0	0	.200	.200	.200	11	-1	-1	0	0	0	0	.929	1	/C	0.1
1984	Mon-N	3	3	0	0	0	0	0	0	1	0	.000	.250	.000	-26	-0	-0	0	0	0	0	1.000	1	/C	0.0
1985	Mon-N	67	120	11	24	1	0	3	12	13	12	.200	.284	.283	63	-6	-6	11	0	0	0	.984	0	C/P	-0.4
1986	Cin-N	56	113	14	27	6	1	2	16	21	10	.239	.358	.363	95	1	-0	15	0	0	0	.979	1	C/P	0.3
1987	Cin-N	5	11	1	2	0	0	1	2	1	0	.182	.250	.455	78	-0	-0	1	0	0	0	.920	1	C	0.1
	*Min-A	51	111	7	19	5	0	1	12	7	16	.171	.220	.243	22	-12	-13	5	0	0	0	.983	1	C	-1.0
1988	Tor-A	23	60	3	14	2	1	1	6	1	9	.233	.246	.350	65	-3	-3	5	0	0	0	.991	3	C	0.1
Total	9	359	801	63	182	24	3	8	76	86	85	.227	.304	.295	65	-35	-38	71	0	0	0	.978	17	C/DP1	-0.9

■ ED BUTKA　　Butka, Edward Luke "Babe"　b: 1/7/16, Canonsburg, Pa.　BR/TR, 6'3", 193 lbs.　Deb: 9/26/43

1943	Was-A	3	9	0	3	1	0	0	1	0	3	.333	.333	.444	132	0	0	1	0	0	0	1.000	1	/1	0.1
1944	Was-A	15	41	1	8	1	0	0	1	2	11	.195	.233	.220	31	-4	-4	2	0	0	0	.972	0	1	-0.4
Total	2	18	50	1	11	2	0	0	2	2	14	.220	.250	.260	48	-4	-3	4	0	0	0	.977	1	/1	-0.3

■ ART BUTLER　　Butler, Arthur Edward (b: Arthur Edward Bouthillier)　b: 12/19/1887, Fall River, Mass.　d: 10/7/84, Fall River, Mass.　BR/TR, 5'9", 160 lbs.　Deb: 4/14/11

1911	Bos-N	27	68	11	12	2	0	0	2	6	6	.176	.263	.206	30	-6	-7	4	0			.930	-3	3/2S	-1.0
1912	Pit-N	43	154	19	42	4	2	1	17	15	13	.273	.337	.344	88	-3	-2	19	2			.960	-22	2	-2.6
1913	Pit-N	82	214	40	60	9	3	0	20	32	14	.280	.379	.350	114	4	5	31	9			.919	-12	2S/3O	-0.5
1914	StL-N	86	274	29	55	12	3	1	24	39	23	.201	.311	.277	76	-7	-7	28	14			.927	-19	S/O	-2.1
1915	StL-N	130	469	73	119	12	5	1	31	47	34	.254	.323	.307	91	-4	-4	52	26	14	-1	.916	-34	*S/2	-3.2
1916	StL-N	86	110	9	23	5	0	0	7	7	12	.209	.256	.255	57	-6	-5	8	3			.882	-6	O/2S3	-1.4
Total	6	454	1289	181	311	44	13	3	101	146	102	.241	.323	.303	85	-22	-20	141	54	14		.919	-96	S/2O3	-10.8

■ BRETT BUTLER　　Butler, Brett Morgan　b: 6/15/57, Los Angeles, Cal.　BL/TL, 5'10", 160 lbs.　Deb: 8/20/81

1981	Atl-N	40	126	17	32	2	3	0	4	19	17	.254	.352	.317	89	-1	-1	17	9	1	2	.987	-0	O	-0.1
1982	*Atl-N	89	240	35	52	2	0	0	7	25	35	.217	.291	.225	44	-17	-18	19	21	8	2	1.000	-6	O	-2.5
1983	Atl-N	151	549	84	154	21	13	5	37	54	56	.281	.347	.393	98	4	-1	75	39	23	-2	.987	8	*O	0.0
1984	Cle-A	159	602	108	162	25	9	3	49	86	62	.269	.364	.355	98	3	2	86	52	22	2	.991	15	*O	1.4
1985	Cle-A	152	591	106	184	28	14	5	50	63	42	.311	.379	.431	122	19	19	100	47	20	2	.998	22	*O/D	3.7
1986	Cle-A	161	587	92	163	17	14	4	51	70	65	.278	.359	.375	102	2	3	84	32	15	1	.993	9	*O	0.7
1987	Cle-A	137	522	91	154	25	8	9	41	91	55	.295	.401	.425	119	18	18	97	33	16	0	.990	15	*O	2.7
1988	SF-N	157	568	109	163	27	9	6	43	97	64	.287	.395	.398	134	25	28	99	43	20	1	.988	6	*O	3.2
1989	*SF-N	154	594	100	168	22	4	4	36	59	69	.283	.351	.354	105	3	5	78	31	16	-0	.986	14	*O	1.6
1990	SF-N	160	622	108	192	20	9	3	44	90	62	.309	.401	.384	122	19	22	108	51	19	4	.986	7	*O	3.0
1991	LA-N★	161	615	112	182	13	5	2	38	108	79	.296	.402	.343	114	16	17	93	38	28	-5	1.000	12	*O	2.1
1992	LA-N	157	553	86	171	14	11	3	39	95	67	.309	.413	.391	131	26	27	99	41	21	-0	.995	7	*O	2.7
Total	12	1678	6169	1048	1777	216	99	44	439	857	673	.288	.377	.377	111	117	122	956	437	209	6	.992	104	*O/D	18.5

■ FRANK BUTLER　　Butler, Frank Dean "Stuffy" or "Goldbrick"　b: 7/18/1860, Savannah, Ga.　d: 7/10/45, Jacksonville, Fla　BL/TL,　Deb: 7/30/1895

| 1895 | NY-N | 5 | 22 | 5 | 6 | 1 | 0 | 2 | 1 | 1 | 1 | .273 | .304 | .318 | 64 | -1 | -1 | 2 | | | | 1.000 | -1 | /O | -0.2 |

■ KID BUTLER　　Butler, Frank Edward　b: 5/1861, Boston, Mass.　d: 4/9/21, S.Boston, Mass.　Deb: 5/20/1884

| 1884 | Bos-U | 71 | 255 | 36 | 43 | 15 | 0 | 0 | | 12 | | .169 | .206 | .227 | 47 | -14 | -13 | 12 | | | | .810 | -6 | O2/S3 | -1.7 |

■ JOHN BUTLER　　Butler, John Albert (a.k.a. Frederick King In 1901)　b: 7/26/1879, Boston, Mass.　d: 2/2/50, Boston, Mass.　BR/TR, 5'7", 170 lbs.　Deb: 9/28/01

1901	Mil-A	1	3	0	0	0	0	0	0	1		.000	.250	.000	-28	-0	-0	0	0			1.000	-1	/C	-0.1
1904	StL-N	12	37	0	6	1	0	0	1	4		.162	.244	.189	36	-3	-3	2	0			.968	-2	/C	-0.4
1906	Bro-N	1	0	0	0	0	0	0	0	0		—	—	—	0	0	0	0	0			1.000	0	/C	0.0
1907	Bro-N	30	79	6	10	1	0	0	2	9		.127	.216	.139	13	-8	-7	3	0			.946	-5	C/O	-1.1
Total	4	44	119	6	16	2	0	0	3	14		.134	.226	.151	19	-11	-10	5	0			.953	-8	/CO	-1.6

■ JOHNNY BUTLER　　Butler, John Stephen "Trolley Line"　b: 3/20/1893, Fall River, Kan.　d: 4/29/67, Seal Beach, Cal.　BR/TR, 6', 175 lbs.　Deb: 4/18/26　C

1926	Bro-N	147	501	54	135	27	5	1	68	54	44	.269	.346	.349	89	-7	-6	62	6			.949	-7	*S3/2	0.0
1927	Bro-N	149	521	39	124	13	6	2	57	34	33	.238	.292	.298	58	-31	-31	46	9			.959	-2	S3	-2.0
1928	Chi-N	62	174	17	47	7	0	0	16	19	7	.270	.352	.310	75	-6	-5	20	2			.950	10	3/S	0.7
1929	StL-N	17	55	5	9	1	1	0	5	4	5	.164	.220	.218	9	-8	-8	3	0			.964	1	/3S	-0.6
Total	4	375	1251	115	315	48	12	3	146	111	89	.252	.320	.317	70	-52	-51	130	17			.954	2	S3/2	-1.9

■ DICK BUTLER　　Butler, Richard H.　b: Brooklyn, N.Y.　Deb: 6/16/1897

1897	Lou-N	10	38	3	7	0	0	0	2	0		.184	.184	.184	-3	-6	-5	2	1			.818	-2	C	-0.6
1899	Was-N	12	36	4	10	0	1	0	1	2		.278	.316	.333	79	-1	-1	4	1			.892	-4	C	-0.4
Total	2	22	74	7	17	0	1	0	3	2		.230	.250	.257	37	-7	-6	6	2			.852	-6	/C	-1.0

■ BILL BUTLER　　Butler, William J.　b: 1861, New Orleans, La.　Deb: 6/29/1884

| 1884 | Ind-a | 9 | 31 | 7 | 7 | 3 | 2 | 0 | | 1 | | .226 | .250 | .452 | 130 | 1 | 1 | 4 | | | | .700 | -2 | /O | -0.1 |

■ KID BUTLER　　Butler, Willis Everett　b: 8/9/1887, Franklin, Pa.　d: 2/22/64, Richmond, Cal.　BR/TR, 5'11", 155 lbs.　Deb: 4/30/07

| 1907 | StL-A | 20 | 59 | 4 | 13 | 2 | 0 | 0 | 6 | 2 | | .220 | .246 | .254 | 60 | -3 | -3 | 4 | 1 | | | .940 | -1 | 2/3S | -0.4 |

■ FRANK BUTTERY　　Buttery, Frank　b: 5/13/1851, Silver Mine, Conn.　d: 12/16/02, Silver Mine, Conn.　Deb: 4/26/1872

| 1872 | Man-n | 18 | 93 | 18 | 25 | 0 | 0 | 0 | 8 | 0 | 2 | .269 | .269 | .269 | 70 | -4 | -2 | 7 | | | | | | /P3O | -0.1 |

■ JOE BUZAS　　Buzas, Joseph John　b: 10/2/19, Alpha, N.J.　BR/TR, 6'1", 180 lbs.　Deb: 4/17/45

| 1945 | NY-A | 30 | 65 | 8 | 17 | 2 | 1 | 0 | 6 | 2 | 5 | .262 | .284 | .323 | 73 | -2 | -3 | 6 | 2 | 0 | 1 | .898 | -3 | S | -0.4 |

■ BURLEY BYERS　　Byers, Burley (b: Christopher A. Bayer)　b: 12/19/1875, Louisville, Ky.　d: 5/30/33, Louisville, Ky.　175 lbs.　Deb: 6/17/1899

| 1899 | Lou-N | 1 | 3 | 0 | 0 | 0 | 0 | 0 | 0 | 0 | | .000 | .000 | .000 | -99 | -1 | -1 | 0 | 0 | | | .600 | -1 | /S | -0.2 |

■ BILL BYERS　　Byers, James William　b: 10/3/1877, Bridgeton, Ind.　d: 9/8/48, Baltimore, Md.　BR/TR, 5'7",　Deb: 4/15/04

| 1904 | StL-N | 19 | 60 | 3 | 13 | 0 | 0 | 0 | 4 | 1 | | .217 | .230 | .217 | 40 | -4 | -4 | 3 | 0 | | | .971 | -1 | C/1 | -0.4 |

■ RANDY BYERS　　Byers, Randell Parker　b: 10/2/64, Bridgeton, N.J.　BL/TR, 6'2", 180 lbs.　Deb: 9/07/87

1987	SD-N	10	16	1	5	1	0	0	1	0	5	.313	.353	.375	96	-0	-0	2	1	0	0	1.000	0	/O	0.0
1988	SD-N	11	10	0	2	1	0	0	0	0	5	.200	.200	.300	42	-1	-1	1	0	0	0	1.000	-1	/O	-0.2
Total	2	21	26	1	7	2	0	0	1	0	10	.269	.296	.346	77	-1	-1	3	1	0	0	1.000	-1	/O	-0.2

■ SAMMY BYRD　　Byrd, Samuel Dewey "Babe Ruth's Legs"　b: 10/15/07, Bremen, Ga.　d: 5/11/81, Mesa, Ariz.　BR/TR, 5'10.5", 175 lbs.　Deb: 5/11/29

1929	NY-A	62	170	32	53	12	0	5	28	28	18	.312	.409	.471	135	7	9	33	1	4	-2	.950	-0	O	0.3
1930	NY-A	92	218	46	62	12	2	6	31	30	18	.284	.371	.440	110	2	3	38	5	1	5	.992	-12	O	-1.0
1931	NY-A	115	248	51	67	18	2	3	32	29	26	.270	.349	.395	101	-2	0	36	5	0	2	.974	-13	O	-1.4
1932	*NY-A	105	209	49	62	12	1	8	30	30	20	.297	.385	.478	129	7	9	39	1	2	-1	.964	-18	O	-1.2

YEAR	TM/L	G	AB	R	H	2B	3B	HR	RBI	BB	SO	AVG	OBP	SLG	PRO+	BR	/A	RC	SB	CS	SBR	FA	FR	POS	TPR
1933	NY-A	85	107	26	30	6	1	2	11	15	12	.280	.369	.411	113	1	2	17	0	1	-1	.987	-16	O	-1.5
1934	NY-A	106	191	32	47	8	0	3	23	18	22	.246	.318	.335	73	-9	-7	21	1	2	-1	**.988**	-13	*O	-2.2
1935	Cin-N	121	416	51	109	25	4	9	52	37	51	.262	.322	.406	97	-4	-2	56	4			.970	3	*O	-0.3
1936	Cin-N	59	141	17	35	8	0	2	13	11	11	.248	.303	.348	80	-5	-4	15	0			.989	-1	O	-0.6
Total	8	745	1700	304	465	101	10	38	220	198	178	.274	.350	.412	104	-2	11	255	17	10		.975	-71	O	-7.9

■ **BOBBY BYRNE** Byrne, Robert Matthew b: 12/31/1884, St.Louis, Mo. d: 12/31/64, Wayne, Pa. BR/TR, 5'7.5", 145 lbs. Deb: 4/11/07

YEAR	TM/L	G	AB	R	H	2B	3B	HR	RBI	BB	SO	AVG	OBP	SLG	PRO+	BR	/A	RC	SB	CS	SBR	FA	FR	POS	TPR
1907	StL-N	149	559	55	143	11	5	0	29	35		.256	.304	.293	91	-8	-6	61	21			.920	22	*3/S	2.3
1908	StL-N	127	439	27	84	7	1	0	14	23		.191	.238	.212	46	-27	-25	27	16			.925	9	*3/S	-1.4
1909	StL-N	105	421	61	90	13	6	1	33	46		.214	.302	.280	86	-9	-6	42	21			.922	16	*3	1.5
	*Pit-N	46	168	31	43	6	2	0	7	32		.256	.387	.315	109	6	4	24	8			.987	5	3	1.2
	Yr	151	589	92	133	19	8	1	40	78		.226	.327	.290	93	-3	-2	65	29			.939	21	*3	2.7
1910	Pit-N	148	602	101	**178**	**43**	12	2	52	66	27	.296	.366	.417	121	21	16	104	36			.929	-7	*3	1.4
1911	Pit-N	153	598	96	155	24	17	2	52	67	41	.259	.342	.366	95	-1	-5	82	23			.930	-3	*3	-0.5
1912	Pit-N	130	528	99	152	31	11	3	35	54	40	.288	.358	.405	110	6	7	83	20			**.948**	-23	*3	-1.5
1913	Pit-N	113	448	54	121	22	0	1	47	29	28	.270	.322	.326	89	-9	-6	49	10			.940	-11	*3	-1.6
	Phi-N	19	58	9	13	1	0	1	4	5	3	.224	.308	.293	69	-2	-2	6	2			.963	3	3	0.0
	Yr	132	506	63	134	23	0	2	51	34	31	.265	.320	.322	86	-11	-9	54	12			.943	-9	*3	-1.6
1914	Phi-N	126	467	61	127	12	1	0	26	45	44	.272	.339	.302	85	-4	-7	49	9			.934	-3	*23	-1.1
1915	*Phi-N	105	387	50	81	6	4	0	21	39	28	.209	.290	.245	62	-16	-17	28	4	12	-6	**.969**	-7	*3	-2.8
1916	Phi-N	48	141	22	33	10	1	0	9	14	7	.234	.308	.319	89	-1	-2	17	6			.933	3	3	0.3
1917	Phi-N	13	14	1	5	0	0	0	0	1	2	.357	.400	.357	128	1	1	2	0			1.000	-1	/3	-0.1
	Chi-A	1	1	0	0	0	0	0	0	0	0	.000	.000	.000	-98	-0	-0	0	0			1.000	0	/2	0.0
Total	11	1283	4831	667	1225	186	60	10	329	456	220	.254	.324	.323	91	-45	-48	572	176	12		.934	3	*32/S	-2.3

■ **JIM BYRNES** Byrnes, James Joseph b: 1/5/1880, San Francisco, Cal. d: 7/31/41, San Francisco, Cal BR/TR, 5'9", 150 lbs. Deb: 4/19/06

YEAR	TM/L	G	AB	R	H	2B	3B	HR	RBI	BB	SO	AVG	OBP	SLG	PRO+	BR	/A	RC	SB	CS	SBR	FA	FR	POS	TPR
1906	Phi-A	10	23	2	4	0	1	0	0	0		.174	.174	.261	35	-2	-2	1	0			.889	-0	/C	-0.1

■ **MILT BYRNES** Byrnes, Milton John "Skippy" b: 11/15/16, St.Louis, Mo. d: 2/1/79, St.Louis, Mo. BL/TL, 5'10.5", 170 lbs. Deb: 4/21/43

YEAR	TM/L	G	AB	R	H	2B	3B	HR	RBI	BB	SO	AVG	OBP	SLG	PRO+	BR	/A	RC	SB	CS	SBR	FA	FR	POS	TPR
1943	StL-A	129	429	58	120	28	7	4	50	53	49	.280	.362	.406	122	13	12	65	1	4	-2	**.997**	8	*O	1.3
1944	*StL-A	128	407	63	120	20	4	4	45	68	50	.295	.396	.393	119	16	13	67	1	7	-4	.976	-6	*O	-0.2
1945	StL-A	133	442	53	110	29	4	8	59	78	84	.249	.363	.387	112	12	9	69	1	3	-2	.988	5	*O/1	0.6
Total	3	390	1278	174	350	77	15	16	154	199	183	.274	.373	.395	117	41	35	201	3	14	-8	.987	8	O/1	1.7

■ **PUTSY CABALLERO** Caballero, Ralph Joseph b: 11/5/27, New Orleans, La. BR/TR, 5'10", 170 lbs. Deb: 9/14/44

YEAR	TM/L	G	AB	R	H	2B	3B	HR	RBI	BB	SO	AVG	OBP	SLG	PRO+	BR	/A	RC	SB	CS	SBR	FA	FR	POS	TPR
1944	Phi-N	4	4	0	0	0	0	0	0	0	1	.000	.000	.000	-99	-1	-1	0	0			.889	2	/3	0.1
1945	Phi-N	9	1	1	0	0	0	0	1	0	0	.000	.000	.000	-99	-0	-0	0	0			.857	2	/3	0.2
1947	Phi-N	2	7	2	1	0	0	0	0	1	0	.143	.250	.143	7	-1	-1	0	0			1.000	-0	/23	-0.1
1948	Phi-N	113	351	33	86	12	1	0	19	24	18	.245	.293	.285	58	-21	-20	29	7			.962	6	32	-1.4
1949	Phi-N	29	68	8	19	3	0	0	3	0	3	.279	.279	.324	63	-4	-4	6	0			.981	4	2/S	0.1
1950	*Phi-N	46	24	12	4	0	0	0	0	2	2	.167	.231	.167	7	-3	-3	1	1			.950	9	/23S	0.6
1951	Phi-N	84	161	15	30	3	2	1	11	12	7	.186	.243	.248	33	-15	-15	9	1	2	-1	.985	9	2/3S	-0.5
1952	Phi-N	35	42	10	10	3	0	0	6	2	3	.238	.273	.310	62	-2	-2	2	1	0	0	.857	2	/S23	0.1
Total	8	322	658	81	150	21	3	1	40	41	34	.228	.273	.274	49	-48	-46	47	10	2		.968	35	23/S	-0.9

■ **ENOS CABELL** Cabell, Enos Milton b: 10/8/49, Fort Riley, Kan. BR/TR, 6'5", 185 lbs. Deb: 9/17/72

YEAR	TM/L	G	AB	R	H	2B	3B	HR	RBI	BB	SO	AVG	OBP	SLG	PRO+	BR	/A	RC	SB	CS	SBR	FA	FR	POS	TPR
1972	Bal-A	3	5	0	0	0	0	0	1	0	0	.000	.000	.000	-97	-1	-1	0	0	0	0	1.000	-0	/1	-0.2
1973	Bal-A	32	47	12	10	2	0	1	3	3	7	.213	.260	.319	63	-2	-2	3	1	3	-2	.991	-1	1/3	-0.6
1974	*Bal-A	80	174	24	42	4	2	3	17	7	20	.241	.271	.339	77	-6	-6	14	5	3	-0	.995	2	103/2D	-0.6
1975	Hou-N	117	348	43	92	17	6	2	43	18	53	.264	.306	.365	92	-8	-5	38	12	3	2	.973	1	O13	-0.5
1976	Hou-N	144	586	85	160	13	7	2	43	29	79	.273	.310	.329	89	-15	-9	61	35	8	6	.958	-9	*3/1	-1.4
1977	Hou-N	150	625	101	176	36	7	16	68	27	55	.282	.315	.438	109	-2	4	82	42	22	-1	.948	-6	*3/1S	-0.4
1978	Hou-N	162	660	92	195	31	8	7	71	22	80	.295	.323	.398	109	-1	4	81	33	15	1	.958	-16	*31/S	-1.4
1979	Hou-N	155	603	60	164	30	5	6	67	21	68	.272	.300	.368	86	-17	-13	60	37	18	0	.957	-23	*31	-4.0
1980	*Hou-N	152	604	69	167	23	8	2	55	26	84	.276	.307	.351	90	-14	-9	61	21	13	-2	.927	-20	*3/1	-3.4
1981	SF-N	96	396	41	101	20	1	2	36	10	47	.255	.275	.326	71	-16	-16	33	6	7	-2	.987	-1	13	-2.5
1982	Det-A	125	464	45	121	17	3	2	37	15	48	.261	.285	.323	67	-21	-22	41	15	6	1	.992	-8	13/O	-3.4
1983	Det-A	121	392	62	122	23	5	5	46	16	41	.311	.340	.434	114	5	6	51	4	8	-4	.997	7	*1/3SD	0.4
1984	Hou-N	127	436	52	135	17	3	8	44	21	47	.310	.343	.417	121	6	10	56	8	11	-4	.993	-1	*1	-0.1
1985	Hou-N	60	143	20	35	8	1	2	14	16	15	.245	.321	.357	92	-2	-1	16	3	1	0	.994	-1	1	-0.5
	*LA-N	57	192	20	56	11	0	0	22	14	21	.292	.340	.349	96	-2	-1	24	6	2	1	.920	-2	31/O	-0.3
	Yr	117	335	40	91	19	1	2	36	30	36	.272	.332	.352	94	-4	-2	40	9	3	1	.993	-3	13/O	-0.8
1986	LA-N	107	277	27	71	11	0	2	29	14	26	.256	.297	.318	75	-12	-9	26	10	4	1	.987	0	1O/3	-1.3
Total	15	1688	5952	753	1647	263	56	60	596	259	691	.277	.309	.370	93	-108	-68	646	238	124	-3	.944	-76	31O/DS2	-20.2

■ **AL CABRERA** Cabrera, Alfredo A. b: 1883, Canary Islands d: Havana, Cuba TR , Deb: 5/16/13

YEAR	TM/L	G	AB	R	H	2B	3B	HR	RBI	BB	SO	AVG	OBP	SLG	PRO+	BR	/A	RC	SB	CS	SBR	FA	FR	POS	TPR
1913	StL-N	1	2	0	0	0	0	0	0	0	0	.000	.000	.000	-99	-1	-1	0	0			.000	0	/S	-0.1

■ **FRANCISCO CABRERA** Cabrera, Francisco (Paulino) b: 10/10/66, Santo Domingo, D.R. BR/TR, 6'4", 195 lbs. Deb: 7/24/89

YEAR	TM/L	G	AB	R	H	2B	3B	HR	RBI	BB	SO	AVG	OBP	SLG	PRO+	BR	/A	RC	SB	CS	SBR	FA	FR	POS	TPR
1989	Tor-A	3	12	1	2	1	0	0	0	1	3	.167	.231	.250	36	-1	-1	1	0	0	0	.000	0	/D	-0.1
	Atl-N	4	14	0	3	2	0	0	0	0	3	.214	.214	.357	59	-1	-1	1	0	0	0	1.000	-1	/1C	-0.2
1990	Atl-N	63	137	14	38	5	1	7	25	5	21	.277	.303	.482	106	2	1	19	1	0	0	.990	-2	1/C	-0.3
1991	*Atl-N	44	95	7	23	6	0	4	23	6	20	.242	.287	.432	94	-0	-1	10	1	1	-0	.987	-3	C1	-0.4
1992	*Atl-N	12	10	2	3	0	0	2	3	1	1	.300	.364	.900	228	2	2	3	0	0	0	.000	0	/C	0.2
Total	4	126	268	24	69	14	1	13	51	13	48	.257	.292	.463	101	1	-1	34	2	1	0	.987	-5	/1CD	-0.8

■ **CRAIG CACEK** Cacek, Craig Thomas b: 9/10/54, Hollywood, Cal. BR/TR, 6'1", 200 lbs. Deb: 6/18/77

YEAR	TM/L	G	AB	R	H	2B	3B	HR	RBI	BB	SO	AVG	OBP	SLG	PRO+	BR	/A	RC	SB	CS	SBR	FA	FR	POS	TPR
1977	Hou-N	7	20	0	1	0	0	0	1	1	3	.050	.095	.050	-66	-5	-4	0	0	0	0	.981	-1	/1	-0.6

■ **CHARLIE CADY** Cady, Charles B. b: 12/1865, Chicago, Ill. d: 6/7/09, Kankakee, Ill. 5'11", 180 lbs. Deb: 9/05/1883

YEAR	TM/L	G	AB	R	H	2B	3B	HR	RBI	BB	SO	AVG	OBP	SLG	PRO+	BR	/A	RC	SB	CS	SBR	FA	FR	POS	TPR
1883	Cle-N	3	11	0	0	0	0	0	0	1	5	.000	.083	.000	-73	-2	-2	0				1.000	-1	/OP	-0.2
1884	CP-U	6	20	4	2	1	1	0		1		.100	.143	.250	31	-1	-1	1				.909	-0	/PO	-0.1
	KC-U	2	3	0	0	0	0	0		0		.000	.000	.000	-99	-1	-1	0				.600	-2	/C2	-0.2
	Yr	8	23	4	2	1	1	0		1		.087	.125	.217	14	-2	-2	1				.909	-2	/POC2	-0.3
Total	2	11	34	4	2	1	1	0	0	2	5	.059	.111	.147	-17	-4	-4	1				.917	-3	/PO2C	-0.5

■ **HICK CADY** Cady, Forrest Leroy b: 1/26/1886, Bishop Hill, Ill. d: 3/3/46, Cedar Rapids, Iowa BR/TR, 6'2", 179 lbs. Deb: 4/26/12

YEAR	TM/L	G	AB	R	H	2B	3B	HR	RBI	BB	SO	AVG	OBP	SLG	PRO+	BR	/A	RC	SB	CS	SBR	FA	FR	POS	TPR
1912	*Bos-A	47	135	19	35	13	2	0	9	10		.259	.324	.385	98	0	-1	17	0			.990	11	C/1	1.4
1913	Bos-A	40	96	10	24	5	2	0	6	5	14	.250	.294	.344	84	-2	-2	10	1			.992	8	C	0.9
1914	Bos-A	61	159	14	41	6	1	0	8	12	22	.258	.310	.308	86	-3	-3	16	2	1	0	.971	-3	C	-0.1
1915	*Bos-A	78	205	25	57	10	2	0	17	19	25	.278	.342	.346	109	1	2	25	0	2	-1	.980	-2	C	0.5
1916	*Bos-A	78	162	5	31	6	3	0	13	15	16	.191	.264	.265	59	-8	-8	12	0			.967	-13	C/1	-2.0
1917	Bos-A	17	46	4	7	1	1	0	2	1	6	.152	.170	.217	18	-5	-5	2	0			.959	1	C	-0.3
1919	Phi-N	34	98	6	21	6	0	1	19	4	8	.214	.252	.306	63	-4	-5	8	1			.984	-7	C	-1.1
Total	7	355	901	83	216	47	11	1	74	66	91	.240	.297	.320	82	-21	-22	89	4	3		.979	-5	C/1	-0.7

YEAR	TM/L	G	AB	R	H	2B	3B	HR	RBI	BB	SO	AVG	OBP	SLG	PRO+	BR	/A	RC	SB	CS	SBR	FA	FR	POS	TPR

■ TOM CAFEGO   Cafego, Thomas   b: 8/21/11, Whipple, W.Va.   d: 10/29/61, Detroit, Mich.   BL/TR, 5'10", 160 lbs.   Deb: 9/03/37

| 1937 | StL-A | 4 | 4 | 1 | 0 | 0 | 0 | 0 | 0 | 0 | 1 | .000 | .000 | .000 | -99 | -1 | -1 | 0 | 0 | 0 | 0 | .500 | -1 | /O | -0.2 |

■ JOE CAFFIE   Caffie, Joseph Clifford "Rabbit"   b: 2/14/31, Ramer, Ala.   BL/TR, 5'10.5", 180 lbs.   Deb: 9/13/56

1956	Cle-A	12	38	7	13	0	0	2	4	1	4	8	.342	.432	.342	104	1	1	6	3	2	-0	1.000	1	O	0.1
1957	Cle-A	32	89	14	24	2	1	3	10	4	11	.270	.301	.416	95	-1	-1	11	0	1	-1	.976	-0	O	-0.3
Total	2	44	127	21	37	2	1	3	11	8	19	.291	.343	.394	99	-0	-0	17	3	3	-1	.984	1	/O	-0.2

■ BEN CAFFYN   Caffyn, Benjamin Thomas   b: 2/10/1880, Peoria, Ill.   d: 11/22/42, Peoria, Ill.   BL/TL,   Deb: 8/21/06

| 1906 | Cle-A | 30 | 103 | 16 | 20 | 4 | 0 | 0 | 3 | 12 | | .194 | .291 | .233 | 66 | -4 | -3 | 8 | 2 | | | .909 | -4 | O | -1.0 |

■ WAYNE CAGE   Cage, Wayne Levell   b: 11/23/51, Monroe, La.   BL/TL, 6'4", 205 lbs.   Deb: 4/22/78

1978	Cle-A	36	98	11	24	6	1	4	13	9	28	.245	.308	.449	112	1	1	13	1	2	-1	.988	1	D1	0.1
1979	Cle-A	29	56	6	13	2	0	1	6	5	16	.232	.295	.321	66	-3	-3	5	0	2	-1	1.000	1	/1D	-0.3
Total	2	65	154	17	37	8	1	5	19	14	44	.240	.304	.403	94	-2	-2	17	1	4	-2	.992	2	/D1	-0.2

■ JOHN CAHILL   Cahill, John Patrick Francis "Patsy"   b: 4/30/1865, San Francisco, Cal   d: 10/31/01, Pleasanton, Cal.   BR/TR, 5'7.5", 168 lbs.   Deb: 5/31/1884

1884	Col-a	59	210	28	46	3	3	0		6		.219	.248	.262	75	-7	-4	14				.843	-0	O/SP	-0.5
1886	StL-N	125	463	43	92	17	6	1	32	9	79	.199	.214	.268	49	-30	-26	31	16			.866	2	*O/PS3	-2.5
1887	Ind-N	68	263	22	54	4	3	0	26	9	5	.205	.234	.243	35	-23	-21	24	34			.826	-6	O/3PS	-2.3
Total	3	252	936	93	192	24	12	1	58	24	84	.205	.227	.260	50	-60	-52	68	50			.851	-5	O/3PS	-5.3

■ TOM CAHILL   Cahill, Thomas H.   b: 10/1868, Fall River, Mass.   d: 12/25/1894, Scranton, Pa.   Deb: 4/09/1891

| 1891 | Lou-a | 120 | 433 | 70 | 111 | 18 | 7 | 3 | 47 | 41 | 51 | .256 | .329 | .351 | 99 | -2 | -1 | 64 | 39 | | | .931 | -3 | CSO/23 | 0.3 |

■ BOB CAIN   Cain, Robert Max "Sugar"   b: 10/16/24, Longford, Kan.   BL/TL, 6', 165 lbs.   Deb: 9/18/49

1949	Chi-A	6	3	0	0	0	0	0	0	0	1	.000	.000	.000	-99	-1	-1	0	0	0	0	1.000	-0	/P	0.0
1950	Chi-A	35	61	7	12	2	0	0	2	3	15	.197	.234	.230	20	-8	-7	4	0	0	0	.974	0	P	0.0
1951	Chi-A	4	9	1	3	1	0	0	0	0	3	.333	.333	.444	111	0	0	1	0	0	0	1.000	-0	/P	0.0
	Det-A	35	53	9	13	3	0	0	9	6	9	.245	.322	.302	69	-2	-2	5	0	0	0	.972	0	P	0.0
	Yr	39	62	10	16	4	0	0	9	6	12	.258	.324	.323	75	-2	-2	7	0	0	0	.975	-0	P	0.0
1952	StL-A	35	58	7	8	0	1	0	1	4	14	.138	.194	.172	2	-8	-8	2	0	0	0	.966	-2	P	0.0
1953	StL-A	34	30	3	6	2	0	0	2	1	3	.200	.226	.267	32	-3	-3	2	0	0	0	1.000	-2	P	0.0
1954	Chi-A	1	0	1	0	0	0	0	0	0	0	—	—	—	—	0	0	0	0	0	0	.000	0	R	0.0
Total	6	150	214	28	42	8	1	0	14	14	45	.196	.246	.243	31	-21	-21	14	0	0	0	.975	-4	P	0.0

■ GEORGE CAITHAMER   Caithamer, George Theodore "Sidel"   b: 7/22/10, Chicago, Ill.   d: 6/1/54, Chicago, Ill.   BR/TR, 5'7.5", 160 lbs.   Deb: 9/17/34

| 1934 | Chi-A | 5 | 19 | 1 | 6 | 1 | 0 | 0 | 3 | 1 | 5 | .316 | .350 | .368 | 83 | -0 | -0 | 2 | 0 | 0 | 0 | .958 | -1 | /C | -0.1 |

■ IVAN CALDERON   Calderon, Ivan (Perez)   b: 3/19/62, Fajardo, P.R.   BR/TR, 6'1", 220 lbs.   Deb: 8/10/84

1984	Sea-A	11	24	2	5	1	0	1	2	2	5	.208	.269	.375	77	-1	-1	2	1	0	0	1.000	-1	O	-0.1
1985	Sea-A	67	210	37	60	16	4	8	28	19	45	.286	.351	.514	132	9	9	34	4	2	0	.981	1	O/1D	0.8
1986	Sea-A	37	131	13	31	5	0	2	13	6	33	.237	.275	.321	61	-7	-7	12	3	1	0	.937	-1	O	-0.9
	Chi-A	13	33	3	10	2	1	0	2	3	6	.303	.361	.424	109	-1	0	5	0	0	0	.900	-0	/OD	0.0
	Yr	50	164	16	41	7	1	2	15	9	39	.250	.293	.341	71	-6	-7	17	3	1	0	.932	-1	O/D	-0.9
1987	Chi-A	144	542	93	159	38	2	28	83	60	109	.293	.365	.526	129	25	23	102	10	5	0	.984	5	*O/D	2.2
1988	Chi-A	73	264	40	56	14	0	14	35	34	66	.212	.302	.424	101	-0	-0	33	4	4	-1	.954	2	O/D	-0.2
1989	Chi-A	157	622	83	178	34	9	14	87	43	94	.286	.335	.437	119	12	14	87	7	1	2	.978	0	*OD1	1.1
1990	Chi-A	158	607	85	166	44	2	14	74	51	79	.273	.331	.422	111	6	8	76	32	16	0	.975	4	*OD/1	0.9
1991	Mon-N★	134	470	69	141	22	3	19	75	53	64	.300	.375	.481	141	24	25	85	31	16	-0	.974	5	*O/1	2.8
1992	Mon-N	48	170	19	45	14	2	3	24	14	22	.265	.324	.424	111	2	2	22	1	2	-1	.988	0	O	0.1
Total	9	842	3073	444	851	190	23	103	422	285	523	.277	.341	.454	119	71	73	458	93	47	-0	.974	16	O/D1	6.7

■ SAM CALDERONE   Calderone, Samuel Francis   b: 2/6/26, Beverly, N.J.   BR/TR, 5'10.5", 185 lbs.   Deb: 4/19/50

1950	NY-N	34	67	9	20	1	0	1	12	2	5	.299	.319	.358	77	-2	-2	7	0			.972	-4	C	-0.5
1953	NY-N	35	45	4	10	2	0	0	8	1	4	.222	.239	.267	31	-4	-5	3	0	0	0	.966	-1	C	-0.4
1954	Mil-N	22	29	3	11	2	0	0	5	4	4	.379	.455	.448	146	2	2	6	0	0	0	1.000	3	C	0.5
Total	3	91	141	16	41	5	0	1	25	7	13	.291	.324	.348	76	-5	-5	16	0	0	0	.978	-2	/C	-0.4

■ BRUCE CALDWELL   Caldwell, Bruce   b: 2/8/06, Ashton, R.I.   d: 2/15/59, West Haven, Conn.   BR/TR, 6', 195 lbs.   Deb: 6/30/28

1928	Cle-A	18	27	2	6	1	1	0	3	2	2	.222	.300	.333	66	-1	-1	3	1	0	0	1.000	-2	O/1	-0.3
1932	Bro-N	7	11	2	1	0	0	0	2	2	2	.091	.231	.091	-10	-2	-2	0	0			.875	-1	/1	-0.3
Total	2	25	38	4	7	1	1	0	5	4	4	.184	.279	.263	44	-3	-3	3	1	0		.900	-3	/O1	-0.6

■ RAY CALDWELL   Caldwell, Raymond Benjamin "Rube" or "Sum"   b: 4/26/1888, Corydon, Pa.   d: 8/17/67, Salamanca, N.Y.   BL/TR, 6'2", 190 lbs.   Deb: 9/09/10

1910	NY-A	6	6	0	0	0	0	0	0	0		.000	.000	.000	-95	-1	-1	0	0			1.000	-0	/P	0.0
1911	NY-A	59	147	14	40	4	1	0	17	11		.272	.323	.313	73	-4	-6	16	5			.953	-3	PO	-0.1
1912	NY-A	44	76	18	18	1	2	0	6	5		.237	.284	.303	64	-3	-4	7	4			.938	1	P/O	-0.1
1913	NY-A	59	97	10	28	3	2	0	11	3	15	.289	.310	.361	96	-1	-1	11	3			1.000	-1	P/O	-0.1
1914	NY-A	59	113	9	22	4	0	0	10	7	24	.195	.248	.230	44	-8	-8	7	2	1	0	.967	-4	P/1	-0.3
1915	NY-A	72	144	27	35	4	1	4	20	9	32	.243	.288	.368	96	-2	-2	15	4	3	-1	.988	3	P	0.0
1916	NY-A	45	93	6	19	2	0	0	4	2	17	.204	.221	.226	34	-8	-8	5	1			.960	-3	P/O	-0.2
1917	NY-A	63	124	12	32	6	1	2	12	16	16	.258	.343	.371	117	3	3	16	2			.973	-3	P/O	-0.2
1918	NY-A	65	151	14	44	10	0	1	18	13	23	.291	.352	.377	113	3	3	20	2			.977	-2	PO	0.1
1919	Bos-A	33	48	5	13	1	1	0	4	0	9	.271	.271	.333	73	-2	-2	4	0			.950	-2	P/O	-0.1
	Cle-A	6	23	4	8	4	0	0	2	0	4	.348	.348	.522	134	1	1	4	0			.900	-1	/P	0.0
	Yr	39	71	9	21	5	1	0	6	0	13	.296	.296	.394	97	-1	-1	8	0			.933	-3	P/O	-0.1
1920	*Cle-A	41	89	17	19	3	0	0	7	10	7	.213	.300	.247	45	-7	-7	7	0	2	-1	.917	-3	P	0.0
1921	Cle-A	38	53	2	11	0	0	1	3	2	5	.208	.236	.340	45	-5	-5	4	0	0	0	.930	-0	P	0.0
Total	12	590	1164	138	289	46	8	8	114	78	158	.248	.297	.322	78	-34	-36	117	23	6		.960	-20	P/O1	-0.7

■ JACK CALHOUN   Calhoun, John Charles "Red"   b: 12/14/1879, Pittsburgh, Pa.   d: 2/27/47, Cincinnati, Ohio   BR/TR, 6', 185 lbs.   Deb: 6/27/02

| 1902 | StL-N | 20 | 64 | 3 | 10 | 2 | 1 | 0 | 8 | 8 | | .156 | .260 | .219 | 50 | -4 | -3 | 4 | 1 | | | .972 | -3 | 3/1O | -0.6 |

■ BILL CALHOUN   Calhoun, William Davitte "Mary"   b: 6/23/1890, Rockmart, Ga.   d: 2/11/55, Sandersville, Ga.   BL/TR, 6', 180 lbs.   Deb: 4/24/13

| 1913 | Bos-N | 6 | 13 | 0 | 1 | 0 | 0 | 0 | 0 | 0 | 3 | .077 | .077 | .077 | -55 | -3 | -3 | 0 | 0 | | | .970 | -0 | /1 | -0.3 |

■ MARTY CALLAGHAN   Callaghan, Martin Francis   b: 6/9/1900, Norwood, Mass.   d: 6/23/75, Norfolk, Mass.   BL/TL, 5'10", 157 lbs.   Deb: 4/13/22

1922	Chi-N	74	175	31	45	7	4	0	20	17	17	.257	.326	.343	71	-7	-7	20	2	3	-1	.946	-9	O	-2.0
1923	Chi-N	61	129	18	29	1	3	0	14	8	18	.225	.275	.279	47	-10	-10	9	2	2	0	.969	-4	O	-1.7
1928	Cin-N	81	238	29	69	11	4	0	24	27	10	.290	.362	.370	93	-2	-2	33	5			.980	-4	O	-1.0
1930	Cin-N	79	225	28	62	9	2	0	16	19	25	.276	.335	.333	66	-13	-11	25	1			.986	3	O	-1.1
Total	4	295	767	106	205	28	13	0	74	71	70	.267	.328	.338	72	-32	-31	87	10	8		.973	-14	O	-5.8

■ DAVE CALLAHAN   Callahan, David Joseph   b: 7/20/1888, Ottawa, Ill.   d: 10/28/69, Ottawa, Ill.   BL/TR, 5'10", 165 lbs.   Deb: 9/14/10

| 1910 | Cle-A | 13 | 44 | 6 | 8 | 1 | 0 | 0 | 2 | 4 | | .182 | .265 | .205 | 47 | -3 | -3 | 4 | 5 | | | 1.000 | 0 | O | -0.3 |

YEAR	TM/L	G	AB	R	H	2B	3B	HR	RBI	BB	SO	AVG	OBP	SLG	PRO+	BR	/A	RC	SB	CS	SBR	FA	FR	POS	TPR
1911	Cle-A	6	16	1	4	0	1	0	0	1		.250	.294	.375	85	-0	-0	2	0			1.000	0	/O	0.0
Total	2	19	60	7	12	1	1	0	2	5		.200	.273	.250	58	-3	-3	5	5			1.000	1	/O	-0.3
■ ED CALLAHAN	Callahan, Edward Joseph b: 12/11/1857, Boston, Mass. d: 2/5/47, New York, N.Y. Deb: 7/19/1884																								
1884	StL-U	1	3	0	0	0	0	0		0		.000	.000	.000	-97	-1	-1	0				1.000	0	/O	0.0
	KC-U	3	11	0	4	0	0	0		0		.364	.364	.364	168	0	1	1				.800	1	/S	0.1
	Bos-U	4	13	2	5	0	0	0		1		.385	.429	.385	180	1	1	2				.750	-1	/O	0.0
	Yr	8	27	2	9	0	0	0		1		.333	.357	.333	142	1	1	3				.778	0	/OS	0.1
■ NIXEY CALLAHAN	Callahan, James Joseph b: 3/18/1874, Fitchburg, Mass. d: 10/4/34, Boston, Mass. BR/TR, 5'10.5", 180 lbs. Deb: 5/12/1894 M																								
1894	Phi-N	9	21	4	5	0	0	0	0	0	7	.238	.238	.238	17	-3	-3	1	0			.923	1	/P	0.0
1897	Chi-N	94	360	60	105	18	6	3	47	10		.292	.320	.400	86	-7	-9	52	12			.918	5	2POS/3	-0.3
1898	Chi-N	43	164	27	43	7	5	0	22	4		.262	.280	.366	85	-4	-4	18	3			.947	-1	P/OS21	-0.3
1899	Chi-N	47	150	21	39	4	3	0	18	8		.260	.306	.327	76	-6	-5	19	9			.904	3	P/OS2	-0.3
1900	Chi-N	32	115	16	27	3	2	0	9	6		.235	.273	.296	59	-7	-6	11	5			.975	6	P	0.0
1901	Chi-A	45	118	15	39	7	3	1	19	10		.331	.383	.466	138	5	6	26	10			.944	4	P/32	0.0
1902	Chi-A	70	218	27	51	7	2	0	13	6		.234	.261	.284	53	-15	-13	19	4			.941	2	PO/S	-0.9
1903	Chi-A	118	439	47	128	26	5	2	56	20		.292	.324	.387	118	6	8	66	24			.895	-6	*3/OPM	0.3
1904	Chi-A	132	482	66	126	23	2	0	54	39		.261	.318	.317	106	1	4	63	29			.977	-17	*O2M	-2.0
1905	Chi-A	96	345	50	94	18	6	1	43	29		.272	.336	.368	129	9	11	54	26			.956	-8	O	-0.1
1911	Chi-A	120	466	64	131	13	5	3	60	15		.281	.306	.350	86	-12	-10	63	45			.963	-9	*O	-2.6
1912	Chi-A	111	408	45	111	9	7	1	52	12		.272	.298	.336	84	-11	-10	47	19			.939	-15	*OM	-3.1
1913	Chi-A	6	9	0	2	0	0	0	1	0	2	.222	.222	.222	30	-1	-1	0	0			1.000	-0	/OM	-0.1
Total	13	923	3295	442	901	135	46	11	394	159	9	.273	.311	.352	94	-44	-33	439	186			.953	-35	OP3/2S1	-9.4
■ JIM CALLAHAN	Callahan, James Timothy "Red" (b: James Timothy Callaghan) b: 1/12/1879, Allegheny Co., Pa. d: 3/9/68, Carnegie, Pa. BR/TR, 5'9", 145 lbs. Deb: 5/25/02																								
1902	NY-N	1	4	0	0	0	0	0	0	1		.000	.200	.000	-38	-1	-1	0	0			.000	-0	/O	-0.1
■ LEO CALLAHAN	Callahan, Leo David b: 8/9/1890, Jamaica Plain, Mass d: 5/2/82, Erie, Pa. BL/TL, 5'8", 142 lbs. Deb: 4/09/13																								
1913	Bro-N	33	41	6	7	3	1	0	3	4	5	.171	.244	.293	52	-3	-3	3	0			.857	-2	/O	-0.5
1919	Phi-N	81	235	26	54	14	4	1	9	29	19	.230	.317	.336	90	-1	-2	26	5			.950	1	O	-0.6
Total	2	114	276	32	61	17	5	1	12	33	24	.221	.306	.330	84	-3	-5	29	5			.941	-1	/O	-1.1
■ PAT CALLAHAN	Callahan, Patrick Henry b: 10/15/1866, Cleveland, Ohio d: 2/4/40, Louisville, Ky. Deb: 5/01/1884																								
1884	Ind-a	61	258	38	67	8	5	2		8		.260	.282	.353	111	2	3	26				.812	-7	3	-0.3
■ WESLEY CALLAHAN	Callahan, Wesley Leroy b: 7/3/1888, Lyons, Ind. d: 9/13/53, Dayton, Ohio BR/TR, 5'7.5", 155 lbs. Deb: 9/07/13																								
1913	StL-N	7	14	0	4	0	0	0	1	2	2	.286	.375	.286	91	-0	-0	2	1			.920	1	/S	0.1
■ FRANK CALLAWAY	Callaway, Frank Burnett b: 2/26/1898, Knoxville, Tenn. d: 8/21/87, Knoxville, Tenn. BR/TR, 6', 170 lbs. Deb: 9/17/21																								
1921	Phi-A	14	50	7	12	1	1	0	4	2	11	.240	.283	.300	49	-4	-4	5	1	0	0	.878	-5	S	-0.7
1922	Phi-A	29	48	5	13	0	2	0	4	0	13	.271	.271	.354	60	-3	-3	4	0	0	0	.880	1	2/3S	-0.1
Total	2	43	98	12	25	1	3	0	8	2	24	.255	.277	.327	54	-7	-7	9	1	0	0	.889	-4	/S23	-0.8
■ JOHNNY CALLISON	Callison, John Wesley b: 3/12/39, Qualls, Okla. BL/TR, 5'10", 175 lbs. Deb: 9/09/58																								
1958	Chi-A	18	64	10	19	4	2	1	12	6	14	.297	.357	.469	128	2	2	11	1	0	0	.976	3	O	0.4
1959	Chi-A	49	104	12	18	3	0	3	12	13	20	.173	.271	.288	54	-7	-6	7	0	1	-1	.983	-3	O	-1.2
1960	Phi-N	99	288	36	75	11	5	9	30	45	70	.260	.360	.427	114	7	7	46	0	4	-2	.989	1	O	0.1
1961	Phi-N	138	455	74	121	20	11	9	47	69	76	.266	.366	.418	109	6	7	74	10	4	1	.967	1	*O	0.2
1962	Phi-N★	157	603	107	181	26	**10**	23	83	54	96	.300	.363	.491	131	22	24	110	10	3	1	.980	25	*O	4.1
1963	Phi-N	157	626	96	178	36	11	26	78	50	111	.284	.339	.502	140	29	30	107	8	3	1	.994	21	*O	4.6
1964	Phi-N★	162	654	101	179	30	10	31	104	36	95	.274	.318	.492	126	19	19	103	6	3	0	.988	18	*O	3.1
1965	Phi-N☆	160	619	93	162	25	**16**	32	101	57	117	.262	.330	.509	135	25	26	105	6	5	-1	.982	18	*O	3.7
1966	Phi-N	155	612	93	169	**40**	7	11	55	56	83	.276	.340	.418	109	8	8	86	8	8	-2	.990	5	*O	0.4
1967	Phi-N	149	556	62	145	30	5	14	64	55	63	.261	.331	.408	109	7	7	72	6	12	-5	.977	8	*O	0.2
1968	Phi-N	121	398	46	97	18	4	14	40	42	70	.244	.321	.415	119	9	9	54	4	3	-1	**1.000**	2	*O	0.6
1969	Phi-N	134	495	66	131	29	5	16	64	49	73	.265	.335	.440	119	9	11	74	2	1	0	.990	14	*O	1.8
1970	Chi-N	147	477	65	126	23	2	19	68	60	63	.264	.350	.440	98	7	-1	75	7	2	1	.973	-2	*O	-0.9
1971	Chi-N	103	290	27	61	12	1	8	38	36	55	.210	.302	.341	71	-7	-12	31	2	1	0	.982	-4	O	-2.2
1972	NY-A	92	275	28	71	10	0	9	34	18	34	.258	.304	.393	110	1	2	33	3	0	1	.992	-3	O	-0.3
1973	NY-A	45	136	10	24	4	0	1	10	4	24	.176	.200	.228	21	-14	-14	5	1	1	-0	.960	-2	OD	-1.8
Total	16	1886	6652	926	1757	321	89	226	840	650	1064	.264	.333	.441	114	123	120	992	74	51	-8	.984	102	*O/D	12.8
■ JACK CALVO	Calvo, Jacinto (Gonzalez) (Born Jacinto Del Calvo) b: 6/11/1894, Havana, Cuba d: 6/15/65, Miami, Fla. BL/TL, 5'10", 156 lbs. Deb: 5/09/13																								
1913	Was-A	17	33	5	8	0	0	1	2	1	4	.242	.265	.333	73	-1	-1	3	0			.900	-2	O	-0.4
1920	Was-A	17	23	5	1	0	1	0	2	2	2	.043	.120	.130	-35	-5	-4	0	0	0	0	1.000	-4	O	-0.8
Total	2	34	56	10	9	0	1	1	4	3	6	.161	.203	.250	27	-6	-6	4	0	0		.938	-6	/O	-1.2
■ HANK CAMELLI	Camelli, Henry Richard b: 12/12/14, Gloucester, Mass. BR/TR, 5'11", 190 lbs. Deb: 10/03/43																								
1943	Pit-N	1	3	1	0	0	0	0	0	1	0	.000	.250	.000	-24	-0	-0	0	0			1.000	0	/C	0.0
1944	Pit-N	63	125	14	37	5	1	1	10	18	12	.296	.385	.376	110	3	2	18	0			.959	4	C	0.9
1945	Pit-N	1	2	0	0	0	0	0	0	1	0	.000	.333	.000	-3	-0	-0	0	0			1.000	-0	/C	0.0
1946	Pit-N	42	96	8	20	2	2	0	5	8	9	.208	.269	.271	52	-6	-6	7	0			.971	4	C	-0.1
1947	Bos-N	52	150	10	29	8	1	1	11	18	18	.193	.280	.280	50	-11	-11	11	0			.977	6	C	-0.1
Total	5	159	376	33	86	15	4	2	26	46	39	.229	.313	.306	70	-15	-15	36	0			.970	14	C	0.7
■ JACK CAMERON	Cameron, John William "Happy Jack" b: 9/1884, Nova Scotia, Can. d: 8/17/51, Boston, Mass. Deb: 9/13/06																								
1906	Bos-N	18	61	3	11	0	0	0	4	2		.180	.206	.180	21	-6	-5	2	0			.852	-1	O/P	-0.8
■ DOLPH CAMILLI	Camilli, Adolph Louis b: 4/23/07, San Francisco, Cal BL/TL, 5'10", 185 lbs. Deb: 9/09/33 F																								
1933	Chi-N	16	58	8	13	2	1	2	7	4	11	.224	.274	.397	90	-1	-1	6	3			.994	2	1	-0.1
1934	Chi-N	32	120	17	33	8	0	4	19	5	25	.275	.315	.442	102	-0	-0	18	1			.988	2	1	-0.1
	Phi-N	102	378	52	100	20	3	12	68	48	69	.265	.350	.429	95	4	-3	59	3			.985	-4	*1	-1.5
	Yr	134	498	69	133	28	3	16	87	53	94	.267	.342	.432	96	4	-3	77	4			.986	-2	*1	-1.6
1935	Phi-N	156	602	88	157	23	5	25	83	65	113	.261	.336	.440	97	5	-3	93	9			.987	-1	*1	-2.1
1936	Phi-N	151	530	106	167	29	13	28	102	116	84	.315	.441	.577	156	58	50	148	5			.988	-10	*1	2.5
1937	Phi-N	131	475	101	161	23	7	27	80	90	82	.339	**.446**	.587	165	55	49	137	6			**.994**	4	*1	3.8
1938	Bro-N	146	509	106	128	25	11	24	100	**119**	101	.251	.393	.485	137	31	30	110	6			.995	-1	*1	1.2
1939	Bro-N★	157	565	105	164	30	12	26	104	**110**	107	.290	.409	.524	144	42	39	128	1			.990	10	*1	3.2
1940	Bro-N	142	512	92	147	29	13	23	96	89	83	.287	.397	.529	145	39	34	114	9			.992	-4	*1	1.7
1941	*Bro-N†	149	529	92	151	29	6	**34**	**120**	104	115	.285	.407	.556	162	**50**	**47**	**128**	3			.989	3	*1	3.9
1942	Bro-N	150	524	89	132	23	7	26	109	97	85	.252	.372	.471	144	32	30	97	10			.992	-1	*1	2.2
1943	Bro-N	95	353	56	87	15	6	6	43	65	48	.246	.365	.374	113	8	8	52	2			.992	-0	1	0.3
1945	Bos-A	63	198	24	42	5	2	2	19	35	38	.212	.330	.288	78	-4	-5	21	2	0	1	.991	2	1	-0.6
Total	12	1490	5353	936	1482	261	86	239	950	947	961	.277	.388	.492	134	319	277	1111	60	0		.990	2	*1	14.4

■ **DOUG CAMILLI** Camilli, Douglas Joseph b: 9/22/36, Philadelphia, Pa. BR/TR, 5'11", 195 lbs. Deb: 9/25/60 FC

YEAR	TM/L	G	AB	R	H	2B	3B	HR	RBI	BB	SO	AVG	OBP	SLG	PRO+	BR	/A	RC	SB	CS	SBR	FA	FR	POS	TPR
1960	LA-N	6	24	4	8	2	0	1	3	1	4	.333	.385	.542	141	2	1	5	0	0	0	.980	0	/C	0.2
1961	LA-N	13	30	3	4	0	0	3	4	1	9	.133	.161	.433	47	-2	-3	2	0	0	0	.986	2	C	0.0
1962	LA-N	45	88	16	25	5	2	4	22	12	21	.284	.370	.523	145	4	5	16	0	0	0	.983	-5	C	0.1
1963	LA-N	49	117	9	19	1	1	3	10	11	22	.162	.234	.265	47	-9	-8	7	0	0	0	.977	8	C	0.2
1964	LA-N	50	123	1	22	3	0	0	10	8	19	.179	.229	.203	25	-12	-11	6	0	0	0	.990	8	C	-0.1
1965	Was-A	75	193	13	37	6	1	3	18	16	34	.192	.257	.280	53	-12	-12	14	0	0	0	.980	1	C	-0.8
1966	Was-A	44	107	5	22	4	0	2	8	3	19	.206	.234	.299	53	-7	-7	7	0	0	0	.990	4	C	-0.1
1967	Was-A	30	82	5	15	1	0	2	5	4	16	.183	.221	.268	46	-6	-5	5	0	0	0	.993	0	C	-0.4
1969	Was-A	1	3	0	1	0	0	0	0	0	2	.333	.333	.333	92	-0	-0	0	0	0	0	1.000	-0	/C	0.0
Total	9	313	767	56	153	22	4	18	80	56	146	.199	.257	.309	61	-42	-39	61	0	0	0	.984	19	C	-0.9

■ **LOU CAMILLI** Camilli, Louis Steven b: 9/24/46, ElPaso, Tex. BB/TR, 5'10", 170 lbs. Deb: 8/09/69

YEAR	TM/L	G	AB	R	H	2B	3B	HR	RBI	BB	SO	AVG	OBP	SLG	PRO+	BR	/A	RC	SB	CS	SBR	FA	FR	POS	TPR
1969	Cle-A	13	14	0	0	0	0	0	0	0	3	.000	.000	.000	-97	-4	-4	-0	0	0	0	1.000	3	3	0.0
1970	Cle-A	16	15	0	0	0	0	0	0	2	2	.000	.118	.000	-62	-3	-3	0	0	0	0	1.000	-1	/S23	-0.4
1971	Cle-A	39	81	5	16	2	0	0	0	8	10	.198	.270	.222	37	-6	-7	5	0	0	0	.938	1	S2	-0.4
1972	Cle-A	39	41	2	6	2	0	0	3	3	8	.146	.205	.195	19	-4	-4	2	0	0	0	1.000	-2	/S2	-0.6
Total	4	107	151	7	22	4	0	0	3	13	23	.146	.213	.172	11	-17	-18	7	0	0	0	.951	2	/S23	-1.4

■ **KEN CAMINITI** Caminiti, Kenneth Gene b: 4/21/63, Hanford, Cal. BB/TR, 6', 200 lbs. Deb: 7/16/87

YEAR	TM/L	G	AB	R	H	2B	3B	HR	RBI	BB	SO	AVG	OBP	SLG	PRO+	BR	/A	RC	SB	CS	SBR	FA	FR	POS	TPR
1987	Hou-N	63	203	10	50	7	1	3	23	12	44	.246	.288	.335	67	-10	-10	19	0	0	0	.949	3	3	-0.7
1988	Hou-N	30	83	5	15	2	0	1	7	5	18	.181	.227	.241	36	-7	-7	4	0	0	0	.948	-0	3	-0.8
1989	Hou-N	161	585	71	149	31	3	10	72	51	93	.255	.318	.369	99	-3	-1	70	4	1	1	.954	13	*3	1.4
1990	Hou-N	153	541	52	131	20	2	4	51	48	97	.242	.304	.309	71	-22	-21	50	9	4	0	.945	-11	*3	-3.1
1991	Hou-N	152	574	65	145	30	3	13	80	46	85	.253	.314	.383	101	-5	-1	65	4	5	-2	.948	8	*3	0.7
1992	Hou-N	135	506	68	149	31	2	13	62	44	68	.294	.352	.441	131	15	18	76	10	4	1	.966	-9	*3	1.1
Total	6	694	2492	271	639	121	11	44	295	206	405	.256	.315	.367	95	-33	-20	283	27	14	-0	.952	4	3	-1.4

■ **HOWIE CAMP** Camp, Howard Lee "Red" b: 7/1/1893, Mumford, Ala. d: 5/8/60, Eastaboga, Ala. BL/TR, 5'9", 169 lbs. Deb: 9/19/17

YEAR	TM/L	G	AB	R	H	2B	3B	HR	RBI	BB	SO	AVG	OBP	SLG	PRO+	BR	/A	RC	SB	CS	SBR	FA	FR	POS	TPR
1917	NY-A	5	21	3	6	1	0	0	0	1	2	.286	.318	.333	98	-0	-0	2	0			.857	1	/O	0.0

■ **LEW CAMP** Camp, Llewellyn Robert b: 2/22/1868, Columbus, Ohio d: 10/1/48, Omaha, Neb. BL/TR, 6', 175 lbs. Deb: 8/26/1892 F

YEAR	TM/L	G	AB	R	H	2B	3B	HR	RBI	BB	SO	AVG	OBP	SLG	PRO+	BR	/A	RC	SB	CS	SBR	FA	FR	POS	TPR
1892	StL-N	42	145	19	30	3	1	2	13	17	27	.207	.294	.283	80	-4	-3	16	12			.780	-16	3/O	-1.6
1893	Chi-N	38	156	37	41	7	7	2	17	19	19	.263	.347	.436	111	2	2	35	30			.847	-10	3O/2S	-0.6
1894	Chi-N	8	33	1	6	2	0	0	1	1	6	.182	.206	.242	8	-5	-5	2	0			.830	-2	/2	-0.6
Total	3	88	334	57	77	12	8	4	31	37	52	.231	.311	.350	87	-7	-6	53	42			.801	-28	/32OS	-2.8

■ **ROY CAMPANELLA** Campanella, Roy b: 11/19/21, Philadelphia, Pa. BR/TR, 5'8", 200 lbs. Deb: 4/20/48 H

YEAR	TM/L	G	AB	R	H	2B	3B	HR	RBI	BB	SO	AVG	OBP	SLG	PRO+	BR	/A	RC	SB	CS	SBR	FA	FR	POS	TPR
1948	Bro-N	83	279	32	72	11	3	9	45	36	45	.258	.345	.416	102	2	1	42	3			.981	10	C	1.6
1949	*Bro-N★	130	436	65	125	22	2	22	82	67	36	.287	.385	.498	130	22	20	86	3			.985	5	*C	3.1
1950	Bro-N★	126	437	70	123	19	3	31	89	55	51	.281	.364	.551	134	22	21	84	1			.985	-4	*C	2.2
1951	Bro-N★	143	505	90	164	33	1	33	108	53	51	.325	.393	.590	158	42	40	114	1	2	-1	.986	8	*C	5.3
1952	*Bro-N★	128	468	73	126	18	1	22	97	57	59	.269	.352	.453	120	14	13	72	8	4	0	**.994**	-7	*C	1.3
1953	*Bro-N★	144	519	103	162	26	3	41	**142**	67	58	.312	.395	.611	154	43	41	128	4	2	0	.989	3	*C	4.8
1954	Bro-N★	111	397	43	82	14	3	19	51	42	49	.207	.286	.401	74	-15	-17	42	1	4	-2	.989	-3	*C	-1.6
1955	*Bro-N†	123	446	81	142	20	1	32	107	56	41	.318	.402	.583	153	37	35	101	2	3	-1	.992	1	*C	3.9
1956	*Bro-N★	124	388	39	85	6	1	20	73	66	61	.219	.334	.394	88	-2	-6	49	1	0	0	.985	3	*C	0.2
1957	Bro-N	103	330	31	80	9	0	13	62	34	50	.242	.321	.388	81	-5	-9	40	1	0	0	**.993**	16	*C	1.1
Total	10	1215	4205	627	1161	178	18	242	856	533	501	.276	.362	.500	123	159	139	759	25	15		.988	32	*C	21.9

■ **BERT CAMPANERIS** Campaneris, Dagoberto (Blanco) "Campy" (b: Dagoberto Campaneria (Blanco))
b: 3/9/42, Pueblo Nuevo, Cuba BR/TR, 5'10", 160 lbs. Deb: 7/23/64

YEAR	TM/L	G	AB	R	H	2B	3B	HR	RBI	BB	SO	AVG	OBP	SLG	PRO+	BR	/A	RC	SB	CS	SBR	FA	FR	POS	TPR
1964	KC-A	67	269	27	69	14	3	4	22	15	41	.257	.306	.375	86	-5	-5	32	10	2	2	.981	-6	SO/3	-0.9
1965	KC-A	144	578	67	156	23	**12**	6	42	41	71	.270	.328	.382	103	1	2	76	**51**	19	4	.938	-14	*SO/PC123	-0.3
1966	KC-A	142	573	82	153	29	10	5	42	25	72	.267	.303	.379	98	-5	-3	70	**52**	10	**10**	.971	-17	*S	0.3
1967	KC-A	147	601	85	149	29	6	3	32	36	82	.248	.298	.331	89	-11	-9	64	**55**	16	**7**	.954	-19	*S	-0.7
1968	Oak-A★	159	642	87	**177**	25	9	4	38	50	69	.276	.332	.361	116	8	11	82	**62**	22	**5**	.956	1	*S/O	3.8
1969	Oak-A	135	547	71	142	15	2	2	25	30	62	.260	.303	.305	74	-22	-19	59	62	8	**14**	.967	-5	*S	0.3
1970	Oak-A	147	603	97	168	28	4	22	64	36	73	.279	.323	.448	115	6	9	91	**42**	10	7	.973	-10	*S	2.4
1971	*Oak-A	134	569	80	143	18	4	5	47	29	64	.251	.290	.323	75	-21	-19	56	34	7	6	.960	-5	*S	-0.1
1972	*Oak-A☆	149	625	85	150	25	2	8	32	32	88	.240	.279	.325	84	-17	-14	59	**52**	14	**7**	.977	7	*S	2.4
1973	*Oak-A★	151	601	89	150	17	6	4	46	50	79	.250	.311	.318	82	-17	-14	63	34	10	4	.969	-7	*S	0.3
1974	*Oak-A★	134	527	77	153	18	8	2	41	47	81	.290	.348	.366	113	4	9	70	34	15	1	.966	-9	*S/D	1.9
1975	*Oak-A★	137	509	69	135	15	3	4	46	50	71	.265	.339	.330	92	-6	-4	60	24	12	0	.962	-31	*S	-2.1
1976	Oak-A	149	536	67	137	14	1	1	52	63	80	.256	.337	.291	89	-8	-5	64	54	12	**9**	.969	-6	*S	1.7
1977	Tex-A★	150	552	77	140	19	7	5	46	47	86	.254	.317	.341	78	-15	-16	60	27	20	-4	.968	18	*S	1.4
1978	Tex-A	98	269	30	50	5	3	1	17	20	36	.186	.247	.238	37	-22	-22	19	22	4	4	.954	4	S/D	-0.4
1979	Tex-A	8	9	2	1	0	0	0	0	1	3	.111	.200	.111	-14	-1	-1	0	1	0	0	.962	4	/S	0.3
	*Cal-A	85	239	27	56	4	4	0	15	19	32	.234	.296	.285	59	-14	-13	21	12	4	1	.957	4	S	0.0
	Yr	93	248	29	57	4	4	0	15	20	35	.230	.293	.278	57	-15	-14	21	13	4	2	.957	7	S	0.3
1980	Cal-A	77	210	32	53	8	1	2	18	14	33	.252	.302	.329	75	-8	-7	21	10	5	0	.957	-5	S/2D	-0.6
1981	Cal-A	55	82	11	21	2	1	1	10	5	10	.256	.299	.341	84	-2	-2	9	5	2	0	.900	-2	3/S2	-0.4
1983	NY-A	60	143	19	46	5	0	0	11	8	9	.322	.358	.357	101	-0	0	16	6	7	-2	.964	-3	23	-0.4
Total	19	2328	8684	1181	2249	313	86	79	646	618	1142	.259	.313	.342	89	-154	-123	992	649	199	75	.964	-102	*S/3O2D1C	8.9

■ **AL CAMPANIS** Campanis, Alexander Sebastian (b: Alessandro Campani) b: 11/2/16, Cos, Greece BB/TR, 6', 185 lbs. Deb: 9/23/43 F

YEAR	TM/L	G	AB	R	H	2B	3B	HR	RBI	BB	SO	AVG	OBP	SLG	PRO+	BR	/A	RC	SB	CS	SBR	FA	FR	POS	TPR
1943	Bro-N	7	20	3	2	0	0	0	0	4	5	.100	.250	.100	3	-2	-2	1	0			1.000	4	/2	0.2

■ **JIM CAMPANIS** Campanis, James Alexander b: 2/9/44, New York, N.Y. BR/TR, 6', 195 lbs. Deb: 9/20/66 F

YEAR	TM/L	G	AB	R	H	2B	3B	HR	RBI	BB	SO	AVG	OBP	SLG	PRO+	BR	/A	RC	SB	CS	SBR	FA	FR	POS	TPR
1966	LA-N	1	1	0	0	0	0	0	0	0	0	.000	.000	.000	-99	-0	-0	0	0	0	0	1.000	0	/C	0.0
1967	LA-N	41	62	3	10	1	0	2	2	9	14	.161	.268	.274	60	-4	-3	5	0	0	0	.990	-0	C	-0.3
1968	LA-N	4	11	0	1	0	0	0	0	1	2	.091	.167	.091	-23	-2	-2	0	0	0	0	.960	1	/C	0.0
1969	KC-A	30	83	4	13	5	0	0	5	5	19	.157	.205	.217	18	-9	-9	3	0	0	0	.982	3	C	-0.5
1970	KC-A	31	54	6	7	0	0	2	2	4	14	.130	.203	.241	22	-6	-6	2	0	0	0	.986	1	C/O	-0.5
1973	Pit-N	6	6	0	1	0	0	0	0	0	0	.167	.167	.167	-8	-1	-1	0	0	0	0	.000	0	H	-0.1
Total	6	113	217	13	32	6	0	4	9	19	49	.147	.219	.230	27	-21	-21	10	0	0	0	.983	5	/CO	-1.4

■ **COUNT CAMPAU** Campau, Charles Columbus b: 10/17/1863, Detroit, Mich. d: 4/3/38, New Orleans, La. BL/TR, 5'11", 160 lbs. Deb: 7/07/1888 M

YEAR	TM/L	G	AB	R	H	2B	3B	HR	RBI	BB	SO	AVG	OBP	SLG	PRO+	BR	/A	RC	SB	CS	SBR	FA	FR	POS	TPR
1888	Det-N	70	251	28	51	5	3	1	18	19	36	.203	.259	.259	68	-9	-9	24	27			.933	-4	O	-1.4
1890	StL-a	75	314	68	101	9	12	**9**		26		.322	.374	.513	144	22	15	75	36			.934	3	O/31M	1.4
1894	Was-N	2	7	1	1	0	0	0	0	1	4	.143	.250	.143	-2	-1	-1	0	0			1.000	-0	/O	-0.1
Total	3	147	572	97	153	14	15	10	18	46	40	.267	.322	.397	112	13	6	100	63			.934	-1	O/13	-0.1

■ **VIN CAMPBELL** Campbell, Arthur Vincent b: 1/30/1888, St.Louis, Mo. d: 11/16/69, Towson, Md. BL/TR, 6', 185 lbs. Deb: 6/06/08

YEAR	TM/L	G	AB	R	H	2B	3B	HR	RBI	BB	SO	AVG	OBP	SLG	PRO+	BR	/A	RC	SB	CS	SBR	FA	FR	POS	TPR
1908	Chi-N	1	1	0	0	0	0	0	0	0		.000	.000	.000	-96	-0	-0	0	0			.000	0	H	0.0

YEAR	TM/L	G	AB	R	H	2B	3B	HR	RBI	BB	SO	AVG	OBP	SLG	PRO+	BR	/A	RC	SB	CS	SBR	FA	FR	POS	TPR
1910	Pit-N	97	282	42	92	9	5	4	21	26	23	.326	.391	.436	133	15	12	55	17			.895	-4	O	0.5
1911	Pit-N	42	93	12	29	3	1	0	10	8	7	.312	.366	.366	101	1	0	14	6			.923	-3	O	-0.3
1912	Bos-N	145	624	102	185	32	9	3	48	32	44	.296	.334	.391	96	-4	-5	87	19			.938	0	*O	-1.2
1914	Ind-F	134	544	92	173	23	11	7	44	37	47	.318	.368	.439	116	20	12	101	26			.925	-6	*O	0.1
1915	New-F	127	525	78	163	18	10	1	44	29	35	.310	.352	.389	125	11	14	83	24			.947	-5	*O	0.3
Total	6	546	2069	326	642	85	36	15	167	132	156	.310	.357	.408	114	41	34	341	92			.929	-17	O	-0.6
■ **BRUCE CAMPBELL**	Campbell, Bruce Douglas b: 10/20/09, Chicago, Ill. BL/TR, 6'1", 185 lbs. Deb: 9/12/30																								
1930	Chi-A	5	10	4	5	1	1	0	5	1	2	.500	.545	.800	245	2	2	4	0	0	0	1.000	-0	/O	0.2
1931	Chi-A	4	17	4	7	2	0	2	5	0	4	.412	.444	.882	256	3	3	7	0	0	0	.900	-0	/O	0.3
1932	Chi-A	7	18	3	4	1	0	0	2	0	2	.222	.222	.278	31	-2	-2	1	0	1	-1	1.000	-1	/O	-0.3
	StL-A	139	593	83	169	35	11	14	85	40	102	.285	.336	.452	97	0	-5	90	7	5	-1	.935	6	*O	-0.8
	Yr	146	611	86	173	36	11	14	87	40	104	.283	.333	.447	95	-2	-6	90	7	6	-2	.935	5	*O	-1.1
1933	StL-A	148	567	87	157	38	8	16	106	69	77	.277	.357	.457	108	11	6	95	10	4	1	.950	-1	*O	-0.2
1934	StL-A	138	481	62	134	25	6	9	74	51	64	.279	.350	.412	88	-3	-9	71	5	4	-1	.935	3	*O	-1.1
1935	Cle-A	80	308	56	100	26	3	7	54	31	33	.325	.390	.497	126	12	12	60	2	1	0	.992	-5	O	0.3
1936	Cle-A	76	172	35	64	15	2	6	30	19	17	.372	.440	.587	150	14	14	45	2	1	0	.960	-4	O	0.7
1937	Cle-A	134	448	82	135	42	11	4	61	67	49	.301	.392	.471	116	12	12	85	4	5	-2	.978	-2	*O	0.4
1938	Cle-A	133	511	90	148	27	12	12	72	53	57	.290	.360	.460	106	2	3	85	11	7	-1	.967	-0	*O	-0.1
1939	Cle-A	130	450	84	129	23	13	8	72	67	48	.287	.383	.449	116	9	11	81	7	6	-2	.942	-3	*O	0.3
1940	*Det-A	103	297	56	84	15	5	8	44	45	28	.283	.381	.448	104	7	3	51	2	7	-4	.959	-2	O	-0.6
1941	Det-A	141	512	72	141	28	10	15	93	68	67	.275	.364	.457	105	11	4	90	3	3	-1	.976	-8	*O	-1.2
1942	Was-A	122	378	41	105	17	5	5	63	37	34	.278	.344	.389	107	3	3	51	0	6	-4	.955	-1	O	-0.6
Total	13	1360	4762	759	1382	295	87	106	766	548	584	.290	.367	.455	108	81	57	815	53	50	-14	.956	-19	*O	-2.7
■ **SOUP CAMPBELL**	Campbell, Clarence b: 3/7/15, Sparta, Va. BL/TR, 6'1", 188 lbs. Deb: 4/21/40																								
1940	Cle-A	35	62	8	14	1	0	0	2	7	12	.226	.304	.242	45	-5	-5	5	0	0	0	1.000	-2	O	-0.7
1941	Cle-A	104	328	36	82	10	4	3	35	31	21	.250	.317	.332	75	-13	-11	32	1	9	-5	.981	2	O	-1.9
Total	2	139	390	44	96	11	4	3	37	38	33	.246	.315	.318	70	-18	-16	37	1	9	-5	.984	0	/O	-2.6
■ **DAVE CAMPBELL**	Campbell, David Wilson b: 1/14/42, Manistee, Mich. BR/TR, 6', 185 lbs. Deb: 9/17/67																								
1967	Det-A	2	2	0	0	0	0	0	0	0	1	.000	.000	.000	-97	-0	-0	0	0	0	0	.500	-0	/1	-0.1
1968	Det-A	9	8	1	1	0	0	1	2	1	3	.125	.222	.500	111	0	0	1	0	0	0	1.000	0	/2	0.1
1969	Det-A	32	39	4	4	1	0	0	2	4	15	.103	.205	.128	-5	-5	-6	1	0	1	-1	.967	-2	1/23	-0.8
1970	SD-N	154	581	71	127	28	2	12	40	40	115	.219	.270	.336	64	-33	-30	54	18	6	2	.974	12	*2	-0.4
1971	SD-N	108	365	38	83	14	2	7	29	37	75	.227	.299	.334	85	-10	-7	38	9	6	-1	.968	-2	23/S1O	-0.5
1972	SD-N	33	100	6	24	5	0	0	3	11	12	.240	.315	.290	79	-3	-2	8	0	4	-2	.988	4	3/2	-0.1
1973	SD-N	33	98	2	22	3	0	0	8	7	15	.224	.276	.255	52	-7	-6	6	1	1	-0	.979	-1	2/13	-0.6
	StL-N	13	21	1	0	0	0	0	1	1	6	.000	.045	.000	-87	-5	-5	0	0	0	0	.933	-3	/2	-0.8
	Hou-N	9	15	1	4	2	0	0	2	0	4	.267	.267	.400	83	-0	-0	2	0	0	0	1.000	2	/31O	0.2
	Yr	55	134	4	26	5	0	0	11	8	25	.194	.239	.231	33	-12	-12	7	1	1	-0	.975	-2	2/31O	-1.2
1974	Hou-N	35	23	4	2	1	0	0	2	1	8	.087	.125	.130	-30	-4	-4	1	1	0	0	.895	6	/213O	0.2
Total	8	428	1252	128	267	54	4	20	89	102	254	.213	.274	.311	64	-69	-62	110	29	18	-2	.923	17	2/31OS	-2.8
■ **JIM CAMPBELL**	Campbell, James Robert b: 6/24/37, Palo Alto, Cal. BR/TR, 6', 190 lbs. Deb: 7/17/62																								
1962	Hou-N	27	86	6	19	4	0	3	6	6	23	.221	.272	.372	77	-4	-3	8	0	0	0	.970	6	C	0.4
1963	Hou-N	55	158	9	35	3	0	4	19	10	40	.222	.268	.316	72	-7	-6	12	0	0	0	.979	-2	C	-0.7
Total	2	82	244	15	54	7	0	7	25	16	63	.221	.269	.336	74	-11	-9	20	0	0	0		4	/C	-0.3
■ **JIM CAMPBELL**	Campbell, James Robert b: 1/10/43, Hartsville, S.C. BL/TR, 6', 205 lbs. Deb: 4/11/70																								
1970	StL-N	13	13	0	3	0	0	0	1	0	3	.231	.231	.231	24	-1	-1	1	0	0	0	.000	0	H	-0.1
■ **JOE CAMPBELL**	Campbell, Joseph Earl b: 3/10/44, Louisville, Ky. BR/TR, 6'1", 175 lbs. Deb: 5/03/67																								
1967	Chi-N	1	3	0	0	0	0	0	0	0	3	.000	.000	.000	-96	-1	-1	0	0	0	0	.000	0	/O	-0.1
■ **MARC CAMPBELL**	Campbell, Marc Thaddeus b: 11/29/1884, Punxsutawney, Pa. d: 2/13/46, New Bethlehem, Pa. BL/TR, 5'10", 155 lbs. Deb: 9/30/07																								
1907	Pit-N	2	4	0	1	0	0	0	1	1		.250	.400	.250	103	0	0	0	0			.889	0	/S	0.0
■ **MAT CAMPBELL**	Campbell, Mathew b: New Jersey Deb: 4/28/1873 F																								
1873	Res-n	21	82	9	12	0	0	0	3	3	6	.146	.176	.146	-4	-10	-9	2						1/SO	-0.6
■ **PAUL CAMPBELL**	Campbell, Paul McLaughlin b: 9/1/17, Paw Creek, N.C. BL/TL, 5'10", 185 lbs. Deb: 4/15/41																								
1941	Bos-A	1	0	0	0	0	0	0	0	0	0	—	—	—	—	0	0	0	0	0	0	.000	0	R	0.0
1942	Bos-A	26	15	4	1	0	0	0	0	1	5	.067	.125	.067	-44	-3	-3	0	1	0	0	1.000	-2	/O	-0.5
1946	*Bos-A	28	26	3	3	1	0	0	0	2	7	.115	.179	.154	-6	-4	-4	1	0	0	0	1.000	-0	/1	-0.4
1948	Det-A	59	83	15	22	1	1	1	11	1	10	.265	.274	.337	60	-5	-5	8	0	0	0	.969	3	1	-0.2
1949	Det-A	87	255	38	71	15	4	3	30	24	32	.278	.343	.404	97	-2	-2	38	3	3	-1	.988	-3	1	-0.6
1950	Det-A	3	1	1	0	0	0	0	0	0	0	.000	.000	.000	-97	-0	-0	0	0	0	0	.000	0	H	0.0
Total	6	204	380	61	97	17	5	4	41	28	54	.255	.308	.358	76	-14	-14	47	4	3	-1	.984	-2	1/O	-1.7
■ **RON CAMPBELL**	Campbell, Ronald Thomas b: 4/5/40, Chattanooga, Tenn. BR/TR, 6'1", 180 lbs. Deb: 9/01/64																								
1964	Chi-N	26	92	7	25	6	1	1	10	1	21	.272	.280	.391	83	-2	-2	10	0	1	-1	.941	14	2	1.3
1965	Chi-N	2	2	0	0	0	0	0	0	0	0	.000	.000	.000	-98	-1	-1	0	0	0	0	.000	0	H	-0.1
1966	Chi-N	24	60	4	13	1	0	0	4	6	5	.217	.288	.233	46	-4	-4	4	1	1	-0	.980	4	S/3	0.0
Total	3	52	154	11	38	7	1	1	14	7	26	.247	.280	.325	67	-6	-7	13	1	2	-1		18	/2S3	1.2
■ **SAM CAMPBELL**	Campbell, Samuel b: Philadelphia, Pa. Deb: 10/11/1890																								
1890	Phi-a	2	5	0	0	0	0	0		1		.000	.167	.000	-51	-1	-1	0	0			.833	-2	/2	-0.3
■ **GILLY CAMPBELL**	Campbell, William Gilthorpe b: 2/13/08, Kansas City, Kan. d: 2/21/73, Los Angeles, Cal. BL/TR, 5'7.5", 182 lbs. Deb: 4/25/33																								
1933	Chi-N	46	89	11	25	3	1	1	10	7	4	.281	.347	.371	105	1	1	12	0			.949	-2	C	0.0
1935	Cin-N	88	218	26	56	7	0	3	30	42	7	.257	.379	.330	95	-0	1	30	3			.986	0	C/1O	0.3
1936	Cin-N	89	235	28	63	13	1	1	40	43	14	.268	.384	.345	104	1	3	35	2			.984	6	C/1	1.2
1937	Cin-N	18	40	3	11	2	0	0	2	5	1	.275	.356	.325	90	-1	-0	5	0			.967	-1	C	0.0
1938	Bro-N	54	126	10	31	5	0	0	11	19	9	.246	.354	.286	76	-3	-3	13	0			.958	-0	C	-0.2
Total	5	295	708	78	186	30	2	5	93	116	35	.263	.371	.332	96	-2	1	95	5			.975	4	C/1O	1.3
■ **FRANK CAMPOS**	Campos, Francisco Jose (Lopez) b: 5/11/24, Havana, Cuba BL/TL, 5'11", 180 lbs. Deb: 9/11/51																								
1951	Was-A	8	26	4	11	3	1	0	3	0	1	.423	.423	.615	182	3	3	7	0	0	0	1.000	-2	/O	0.1
1952	Was-A	53	112	9	29	6	1	0	8	1	13	.259	.278	.330	71	-5	-5	11	0	0	0	.978	-2	O	-0.8
1953	Was-A	10	9	0	1	0	0	0	2	1	0	.111	.200	.111	-14	-1	-1	0	0	0	0	.000	0	H	-0.1
Total	3	71	147	13	41	9	2	0	13	2	14	.279	.298	.367	86	-4	-3	18	0	0	0	.981	-4	/O	-0.8
■ **SIL CAMPUSANO**	Campusano, Silvestre (Diaz) b: 12/31/65, Santo Domingo, D.R. BR/TR, 6', 175 lbs. Deb: 4/04/88																								
1988	Tor-A	73	142	14	31	10	2	2	12	9	33	.218	.284	.359	78	-4	-4	16	0	0	0	.934	-10	O/D	-1.6
1990	Phi-N	66	85	10	18	1	1	2	9	6	16	.212	.272	.318	62	-5	-5	8	1	0	0	.976	-13	O	-1.9

YEAR	TM/L	G	AB	R	H	2B	3B	HR	RBI	BB	SO	AVG	OBP	SLG	PRO+	BR	/A	RC	SB	CS	SBR	FA	FR	POS	TPR
1991	Phi-N	15	35	2	4	0	0	1	2	1	10	.114	.139	.200	-6	-5	-5	1	0	0	0	1.000	-1	O	-0.6
Total	3	154	262	26	53	11	3	5	23	16	59	.202	.261	.324	62	-14	-14	24	1	0	0	.953	-24	O/D	-4.1

■ GEORGE CANALE

Canale, George Anthony b: 8/11/65, Memphis, Tenn. BL/TR, 6'1", 190 lbs. Deb: 9/03/89

YEAR	TM/L	G	AB	R	H	2B	3B	HR	RBI	BB	SO	AVG	OBP	SLG	PRO+	BR	/A	RC	SB	CS	SBR	FA	FR	POS	TPR
1989	Mil-A	13	26	5	5	1	0	1	3	2	3	.192	.250	.346	67	-1	-1	2	0	1	-1	.989	-0	1	-0.3
1990	Mil-A	10	13	4	1	1	0	0	0	2	6	.077	.200	.154	0	-2	-2	0	0	1	-1	1.000	1	/1D	-0.2
1991	Mil-A	21	34	6	6	2	0	3	10	8	6	.176	.333	.500	130	1	1	4	0	0	0	.983	3	1	0.3
Total	3	44	73	15	12	4	0	4	13	12	15	.164	.282	.384	85	-2	-2	7	0	2	-1	.988	3	/1D	-0.2

■ JIM CANAVAN

Canavan, James Edward b: 11/26/1866, New Bedford, Mass. d: 5/27/49, New Bedford, Mass. BR/TR, 5'8", 160 lbs. Deb: 4/08/1891

YEAR	TM/L	G	AB	R	H	2B	3B	HR	RBI	BB	SO	AVG	OBP	SLG	PRO+	BR	/A	RC	SB	CS	SBR	FA	FR	POS	TPR
1891	Cin-a	101	426	74	97	13	14	7	66	27	44	.228	.282	.373	82	-8	-14	52	21			.860	-11	*S	-1.7
	Mil-a	35	142	33	38	2	4	3	21	16	10	.268	.342	.401	96	2	-2	22	7			.864	-2	2S	-0.2
	Yr	136	568	107	135	15	18	10	87	43	54	.238	.297	.380	86	-6	-17	74	28			.860	-13	*S2	-1.9
1892	Chi-N	118	439	48	73	10	11	0	32	48	48	.166	.248	.239	48	-27	-27	35	33			.923	-2	*2/OS	-2.6
1893	Cin-N	121	461	65	104	13	7	5	64	51	20	.226	.305	.317	65	-22	-24	55	31			.931	-1	*O/23	-2.5
1894	Cin-N	101	356	77	97	16	9	13	70	62	25	.272	.380	.478	103	4	1	72	13			.904	-2	*O/S321	-0.6
1897	Bro-N	63	240	25	52	9	3	2	34	26		.217	.296	.304	62	-15	-12	25	9			.909	-21	2	-2.6
Total	5	539	2064	322	461	63	48	30	287	230	147	.223	.304	.344	75	-65	-79	262	114			.920	-40	O2S/31	-10.2

■ CASEY CANDAELE

Candaele, Casey Todd b: 1/12/61, Lompoc, Cal. BB/TR, 5'9", 165 lbs. Deb: 6/05/86

YEAR	TM/L	G	AB	R	H	2B	3B	HR	RBI	BB	SO	AVG	OBP	SLG	PRO+	BR	/A	RC	SB	CS	SBR	FA	FR	POS	TPR
1986	Mon-N	30	104	9	24	4	1	0	6	5	15	.231	.266	.288	53	-7	-7	6	3	5	-2	.983	-2	2/3	-1.0
1987	Mon-N	138	449	62	122	23	4	1	23	38	28	.272	.331	.347	78	-12	-14	51	7	10	-4	.985	-1	2OS/1	-1.7
1988	Mon-N	36	116	9	20	5	1	0	4	10	11	.172	.238	.233	34	-10	-10	6	1	0	0	.988	1	2	-0.8
	Hou-N	21	31	2	5	3	0	0	1	1	6	.161	.188	.258	28	-3	-3	1	0	1	-1	1.000	1	2/O3	-0.3
	Yr	57	147	11	25	8	1	0	5	11	17	.170	.228	.238	33	-13	-13	7	1	1	-0	.990	2	2/O3	-1.1
1990	Hou-N	130	262	30	75	8	6	3	22	31	42	.286	.364	.397	112	4	5	38	7	5	-1	1.000	-14	O2S/3	-1.0
1991	Hou-N	151	461	44	121	20	7	4	50	40	49	.262	.321	.362	97	-5	-2	55	9	3	1	.982	5	*2O3	0.7
1992	Hou-N	135	320	19	68	12	1	1	18	24	36	.213	.274	.266	57	-19	-17	25	7	1	2	.968	-5	S3O/2	-1.8
Total	6	641	1743	175	435	75	20	9	124	149	187	.250	.311	.331	79	-52	-48	183	34	25	-5	.986	-14	2OS/31	-5.9

■ JOHN CANGELOSI

Cangelosi, John Anthony b: 3/10/63, Brooklyn, N.Y. BB/TL, 5'8", 150 lbs. Deb: 6/03/85

YEAR	TM/L	G	AB	R	H	2B	3B	HR	RBI	BB	SO	AVG	OBP	SLG	PRO+	BR	/A	RC	SB	CS	SBR	FA	FR	POS	TPR
1985	Chi-A	5	2	2	0	0	0	0	0	0	1	.000	.333	.000	1	-0	-0	0	0	0	0	1.000	-2	/OD	-0.2
1986	Chi-A	137	438	65	103	16	3	2	32	71	61	.235	.351	.299	77	-10	-12	55	50	17	5	.969	-5	*O/D	-1.6
1987	Pit-N	104	182	44	50	8	3	4	18	46	33	.275	.429	.418	125	9	9	39	21	6	3	.962	-4	O	0.7
1988	Pit-N	75	118	18	30	4	1	0	8	17	16	.254	.353	.305	92	-1	-1	15	9	4	0	.963	-2	O/P	-0.3
1989	Pit-N	112	160	18	35	4	2	0	9	35	20	.219	.369	.269	88	-1	-0	19	11	8	-2	.973	-6	O	-1.0
1990	Pit-N	58	76	13	15	2	0	0	1	11	12	.197	.307	.224	50	-5	-5	6	7	2	1	1.000	-1	O	-0.5
1992	Tex-A	73	85	12	16	2	0	1	6	18	16	.188	.330	.247	66	-3	-3	8	6	5	-1	.964	-13	O/D	-1.9
Total	7	564	1061	172	249	36	9	7	74	198	159	.235	.363	.305	86	-11	-11	143	104	42	6	.969	-32	O/DP	-4.8

■ RIP CANNELL

Cannell, Virgin Wirt b: 1/23/1880, S.Bridgton, Maine d: 8/26/48, Bridgton, Maine BL/TR, 5'10.5", 180 lbs. Deb: 4/14/04

YEAR	TM/L	G	AB	R	H	2B	3B	HR	RBI	BB	SO	AVG	OBP	SLG	PRO+	BR	/A	RC	SB	CS	SBR	FA	FR	POS	TPR
1904	Bos-N	100	346	32	81	5	1	0	18	23		.234	.286	.254	70	-13	-11	30	10			.897	-11	O	-2.9
1905	Bos-N	154	567	52	140	14	4	0	36	51		.247	.311	.286	80	-14	-12	59	17			.935	-8	*O	-2.9
Total	2	254	913	84	221	19	5	0	54	74		.242	.302	.274	77	-26	-23	88	27			.923	-19	O	-5.8

■ CHRIS CANNIZZARO

Cannizzaro, Christopher John b: 5/3/38, Oakland, Cal. BR/TR, 6', 190 lbs. Deb: 4/17/60 C

YEAR	TM/L	G	AB	R	H	2B	3B	HR	RBI	BB	SO	AVG	OBP	SLG	PRO+	BR	/A	RC	SB	CS	SBR	FA	FR	POS	TPR
1960	StL-N	7	9	0	2	0	0	0	1	1	3	.222	.300	.222	42	-1	-1	1	0	0	0	1.000	1	/C	0.1
1961	StL-N	6	2	0	1	0	0	0	0	0	0	.500	.500	.500	151	0	0	1	0	0	0	1.000	1	/C	0.1
1962	NY-N	59	133	9	32	2	1	0	9	19	26	.241	.340	.271	65	-6	-6	13	1	1	-0	.973	2	C/O	-0.3
1963	NY-N	16	33	4	8	1	0	0	4	1	8	.242	.265	.273	54	-2	-2	3	0	0	0	1.000	-1	C	-0.2
1964	NY-N	60	164	11	51	10	0	0	10	14	28	.311	.369	.372	112	2	3	21	0	5	-3	.988	2	C	0.4
1965	NY-N	114	251	17	46	8	2	0	7	28	60	.183	.270	.231	44	-18	-17	16	0	2	-1	.977	12	*C	-0.2
1968	Pit-N	25	58	5	14	2	2	1	7	9	13	.241	.343	.397	123	2	2	8	0	0	0	.976	-0	C	0.3
1969	SD-N☆	134	418	23	92	14	3	4	33	42	81	.220	.291	.297	68	-19	-17	34	0	1	-1	.988	-14	*C	-2.6
1970	SD-N	111	341	27	95	13	3	5	42	48	49	.279	.369	.378	105	2	4	47	2	7	-4	.980	-16	*C	-1.0
1971	SD-N	21	63	2	12	1	0	1	8	11	10	.190	.320	.254	69	-3	-2	4	0	0	0	.992	-2	C	-0.3
	Chi-N	71	197	18	42	8	1	5	23	28	24	.213	.314	.340	74	-4	-7	19	0	0	0	.983	-11	C	-1.7
	Yr	92	260	20	54	9	1	6	31	39	34	.208	.316	.319	73	-6	-9	24	0	0	0	.985	-12	C	-2.0
1972	LA-N	73	200	14	48	6	0	2	18	31	38	.240	.342	.300	86	-3	-3	22	0	1	-1	.983	-8	C	-0.9
1973	LA-N	17	21	0	4	0	0	0	3	3	3	.190	.292	.190	38	-2	-2	1	0	0	0	1.000	-0	C	-0.2
1974	SD-N	26	60	2	11	1	0	0	4	6	11	.183	.258	.200	31	-6	-5	3	0	0	0	.979	5	C	0.1
Total	13	740	1950	132	458	66	12	18	169	241	354	.235	.321	.309	77	-56	-53	192	3	17	-9	.983	-27	C/O	-6.4

■ JOE CANNON

Cannon, Joseph Jerome b: 7/13/53, Camp Lejune, N.C. BL/TR, 6'3", 193 lbs. Deb: 9/22/77

YEAR	TM/L	G	AB	R	H	2B	3B	HR	RBI	BB	SO	AVG	OBP	SLG	PRO+	BR	/A	RC	SB	CS	SBR	FA	FR	POS	TPR
1977	Hou-N	9	17	3	2	2	0	0	1	0	5	.118	.118	.235	-9	-3	-2	0	1	1	-0	1.000	0	/O	-0.3
1978	Hou-N	8	18	1	4	0	0	0	1	0	1	.222	.222	.222	26	-2	-2	1	0	1	-1	.778	-1	/O	-0.3
1979	Tor-A	61	142	14	30	1	1	1	5	1	34	.211	.217	.254	26	-15	-15	8	12	2	2	1.000	-4	O	-1.8
1980	Tor-A	70	50	16	4	0	0	0	4	0	14	.080	.098	.080	-48	-10	-10	0	2	2	-1	.968	-10	O/D	-2.2
Total	4	148	227	34	40	3	1	1	11	1	54	.176	.183	.211	7	-29	-29	9	15	6	1	.977	-15	/OD	-4.6

■ JOSE CANSECO

Canseco, Jose (Capas) b: 7/2/64, Havana, Cuba BR/TR, 6'3", 240 lbs. Deb: 9/02/85 F

YEAR	TM/L	G	AB	R	H	2B	3B	HR	RBI	BB	SO	AVG	OBP	SLG	PRO+	BR	/A	RC	SB	CS	SBR	FA	FR	POS	TPR
1985	Oak-A	29	96	16	29	3	0	5	13	4	31	.302	.330	.490	130	2	3	15	1	1	-0	.951	-0	O	0.2
1986	Oak-A☆	157	600	85	144	29	1	33	117	65	175	.240	.322	.457	118	6	13	89	15	7	0	.958	-3	*O/D	0.4
1987	Oak-A	159	630	81	162	35	3	31	113	50	157	.257	.314	.470	111	2	8	91	15	3	3	.975	11	*OD	1.6
1988	*Oak-A★	158	610	120	187	34	0	**42**	**124**	78	128	.307	.394	**.569**	**172**	54	57	136	40	16	2	.978	8	*OD	**6.2**
1989	*Oak-A†	65	227	40	61	9	1	17	57	23	69	.269	.341	.542	151	13	14	41	6	3	0	.976	4	O/D	1.6
1990	*Oak-A★	131	481	83	132	14	2	37	101	72	158	.274	.375	.543	160	34	37	98	19	10	-0	.995	5	OD	3.9
1991	Oak-A	154	572	115	152	32	1	**44**	122	78	152	.266	.363	.556	159	38	42	116	26	6	4	.965	-3	*OD	4.1
1992	Oak-A†	97	366	66	90	11	0	22	72	48	104	.246	.338	.456	126	10	11	52	5	7	-3	.988	4	OD	1.1
	Tex-A	22	73	8	17	4	0	4	15	15	24	.233	.385	.452	138	4	4	14	1	0	0	.970	1	O/D	0.5
	Yr	119	439	74	107	15	0	26	87	63	128	.244	.346	.456	128	13	16	67	6	7	-2	.985	5	OD	1.6
Total	8	972	3655	614	974	171	8	235	734	433	998	.266	.351	.511	141	163	189	652	128	53	7	.974	26	OD	19.6

■ OZZIE CANSECO

Canseco, Osvaldo (Capas) b: 7/2/64, Havana, Cuba BR/TR, 6'2", 220 lbs. Deb: 7/18/90 F

YEAR	TM/L	G	AB	R	H	2B	3B	HR	RBI	BB	SO	AVG	OBP	SLG	PRO+	BR	/A	RC	SB	CS	SBR	FA	FR	POS	TPR
1990	Oak-A	9	19	1	2	1	0	0	1	1	10	.105	.150	.158	-14	-3	-3	0	0	0	0	1.000	-0	/OD	-0.3
1992	StL-N	9	29	7	8	5	0	0	3	7	4	.276	.417	.448	147	2	2	6	0	0	0	.889	-2	/O	0.0
Total	2	18	48	8	10	6	0	0	4	8	14	.208	.321	.333	87	-1	-1	6	0	0	0	.917	-2	/OD	-0.3

■ BART CANTZ

Cantz, Bartholomew L. b: 1/29/1860, Philadelphia, Pa. d: 2/12/43, Philadelphia, Pa. Deb: 7/25/1888

YEAR	TM/L	G	AB	R	H	2B	3B	HR	RBI	BB	SO	AVG	OBP	SLG	PRO+	BR	/A	RC	SB	CS	SBR	FA	FR	POS	TPR
1888	Bal-a	37	126	7	21	2	1	0	9	2		.167	.180	.198	24	-11	-10	5	0			.904	-9	C/O	-1.5
1889	Bal-a	20	69	6	12	2	0	0	8	4	14	.174	.219	.203	21	-7	-7	4	2			.860	-7	C/O	-1.1
1890	Phi-a	5	22	1	1	0	0	0		0		.045	.045	.045	-75	-5	-5	0	0			.893	-3	/C	-0.6
Total	3	62	217	14	34	4	1	0	17	6	14	.157	.179	.184	13	-22	-22	8	2			.890	-19	/CO	-3.2

■ NICK CAPRA

Capra, Nick Lee b: 3/8/58, Denver, Colo. BR/TR, 5'8", 165 lbs. Deb: 9/06/82

YEAR	TM/L	G	AB	R	H	2B	3B	HR	RBI	BB	SO	AVG	OBP	SLG	PRO+	BR	/A	RC	SB	CS	SBR	FA	FR	POS	TPR
1982	Tex-A	13	15	2	4	0	0	1	1	3	4	.267	.421	.467	151	1	1	3	2	1	0	1.000	1	/O	0.2
1983	Tex-A	8	2	2	0	0	0	0	0	0	0	.000	.000	.000	-99	-1	-1	0	0	0	0	.000	-2	/O	-0.2
1985	Tex-A	8	8	1	1	0	0	0	0	0	0	.125	.125	.125	-31	-1	-1	0	0	0	0	1.000	-1	/O	-0.3
1988	KC-A	14	29	3	4	1	0	0	0	2	3	.138	.194	.172	3	-4	-4	1	1	0	0	1.000	-2	O/D	-0.6
1991	Tex-A	2	0	1	0	0	0	0	0	1	0	—	1.000	—	205	0	0	0	0	0	0	1.000	-0	/O	0.0
Total	5	45	54	9	9	1	0	1	1	6	7	.167	.262	.241	41	-4	-4	4	3	1	0	1.000	-5	/OD	-0.9

■ PAT CAPRI

Capri, Patrick Nicholas b: 11/27/18, New York, N.Y. d: 6/14/89, New York.N.Y. BR/TR, 6'0.5", 170 lbs. Deb: 7/16/44

YEAR	TM/L	G	AB	R	H	2B	3B	HR	RBI	BB	SO	AVG	OBP	SLG	PRO+	BR	/A	RC	SB	CS	SBR	FA	FR	POS	TPR
1944	Bos-N	7	1	1	0	0	0	0	0	0	1	.000	.000	.000	-96	-0	-0	0	0			1.000	3	/2	0.3

■ RALPH CAPRON

Capron, Ralph Earl b: 6/16/1889, Minneapolis, Minn d: 9/19/80, Los Angeles, Cal. BL/TR, 5'11.5", 165 lbs. Deb: 4/25/12

YEAR	TM/L	G	AB	R	H	2B	3B	HR	RBI	BB	SO	AVG	OBP	SLG	PRO+	BR	/A	RC	SB	CS	SBR	FA	FR	POS	TPR
1912	Pit-N	1	0	0	0	0	0	0	0	0	0	—	—	—	—	0	0	0	0			.000	0	R	0.0
1913	Phi-N	2	1	1	0	0	0	0	0	0	0	.000	.000	.000	-96	-0	-0	0	0			.000	-1	/O	-0.1
Total	2	3	1	1	0	0	0	0	0	0	0	.000	.000	.000	-96	-0	-0	0	0				-1	/O	-0.1

■ JOHN CARBINE

Carbine, John C. b: 10/12/1855, Syracuse, N.Y. d: 9/11/15, Chicago, Ill. 6', 187 lbs. Deb: 5/08/1875

YEAR	TM/L	G	AB	R	H	2B	3B	HR	RBI	BB	SO	AVG	OBP	SLG	PRO+	BR	/A	RC	SB	CS	SBR	FA	FR	POS	TPR
1875	Wes-n	10	36	0	3	0	0	0		0		.083	.083	.083	-40	-5	-5	0						1	-0.5
1876	Lou-N	7	25	3	4	0	0	0	1	0	0	.160	.160	.160	6	-2	-3	1				.878	-0	/1O	-0.3

■ BERNIE CARBO

Carbo, Bernardo b: 8/5/47, Detroit, Mich. BL/TR, 6', 175 lbs. Deb: 9/02/69

YEAR	TM/L	G	AB	R	H	2B	3B	HR	RBI	BB	SO	AVG	OBP	SLG	PRO+	BR	/A	RC	SB	CS	SBR	FA	FR	POS	TPR
1969	Cin-N	4	3	0	0	0	0	0	0	0	2	.000	.000	.000	-95	-1	-1	0	0	0	0	.000	0	H	-0.1
1970	*Cin-N	125	365	54	113	19	3	21	63	94	77	.310	.456	.551	168	40	40	100	10	4	1	.979	-8	*O	2.7
1971	Cin-N	106	310	33	68	20	1	5	20	54	56	.219	.339	.339	94	-2	-1	38	2	1	0	.982	-6	O	-1.2
1972	Cin-N	19	21	2	3	0	0	0	0	6	3	.143	.357	.143	50	-1	-1	2	0	0	0	1.000	0	/O	-0.1
	StL-N	99	302	42	78	13	1	7	34	57	56	.258	.385	.377	119	9	10	47	0	1	-1	.967	3	O/3	0.9
	Yr	118	323	44	81	13	1	7	34	63	59	.251	.383	.362	115	8	9	48	0	1	-1	.969	3	O/3	0.8
1973	StL-N	111	308	42	88	18	0	8	40	58	52	.286	.401	.422	128	14	14	56	2	0	1	.978	2	O	1.3
1974	Bos-A	117	338	40	84	20	0	12	61	58	90	.249	.365	.414	116	12	9	52	4	3	-1	.994	-1	OD	0.4
1975	Bos-A	107	319	64	82	21	3	15	50	83	69	.257	.412	.483	140	25	22	68	2	4	-2	.976	-1	OD	1.6
1976	Bos-A	17	55	5	13	4	0	2	6	8	17	.236	.333	.418	106	1	1	8	1	0	0	1.000	-0	D/O	0.1
	Mil-A	69	183	20	43	7	0	3	15	33	55	.235	.352	.322	100	1	1	22	1	2	-1	1.000	4	OD	0.3
	Yr	86	238	25	56	11	0	5	21	41	72	.235	.348	.345	102	2	2	30	2	2	-1	1.000	3	DO	0.4
1977	Bos-A	86	228	36	66	6	1	15	34	47	72	.289	.411	.522	136	18	14	51	1	2	-1	.951	2	O/D	1.3
1978	Bos-A	17	46	7	12	3	0	1	6	8	8	.261	.370	.391	103	1	0	6	1	1	-0	1.000	1	/OD	0.1
	Cle-A	60	174	21	50	8	0	4	16	20	31	.287	.364	.402	117	4	4	25	1	0	0	1.000	-2	D/O	0.3
	Yr	77	220	28	62	11	0	5	22	28	39	.282	.365	.400	113	5	5	31	2	1	0	1.000	-0	DO	0.4
1979	StL-N	52	64	6	18	1	0	3	12	10	22	.281	.378	.438	121	2	2	12	1	0	0	1.000	-3	O	-0.1
1980	StL-N	14	11	0	2	0	0	0	0	1	0	.182	.250	.182	22	-1	-1	1	0	0	0	.000	0	H	-0.1
	Pit-N	7	6	0	2	0	0	0	1	1	1	.333	.429	.333	114	0	0	1	0	0	0	.000	0	/H	0.0
	Yr	21	17	0	4	0	0	0	1	2	1	.235	.316	.235	55	-1	-1	2	0	0	0	.000	0		-0.1
Total	12	1010	2733	372	722	140	9	96	358	538	611	.264	.389	.427	125	125	114	489	26	18	-3	.978	-8	OD/3	7.4

■ JOSE CARDENAL

Cardenal, Jose Rosario Domec (b: Jose Rosario Domec (Cardenal)) b: 10/7/43, Matanzas, Cuba BR/TR, 5'10", 150 lbs. Deb: 4/14/63

YEAR	TM/L	G	AB	R	H	2B	3B	HR	RBI	BB	SO	AVG	OBP	SLG	PRO+	BR	/A	RC	SB	CS	SBR	FA	FR	POS	TPR
1963	SF-N	9	5	1	1	0	0	0	2	1	1	.200	.333	.200	58	-0	-0	0	0	1	-1	.000	0	/O	-0.1
1964	SF-N	20	15	3	0	0	0	0	0	2	3	.000	.118	.000	-62	-3	-3	0	2	0	1	.909	2	O	-0.1
1965	Cal-A	134	512	58	128	23	2	11	57	27	72	.250	.290	.367	87	-11	-9	54	37	17	1	.964	10	*O/32	-0.5
1966	Cal-A	154	561	67	155	15	3	16	48	34	69	.276	.322	.399	109	4	5	72	24	11	1	.992	12	*O	1.2
1967	Cal-A	108	381	40	90	13	5	6	27	15	63	.236	.269	.344	83	-10	-9	35	10	5	0	.986	0	*O	-1.5
1968	Cle-A	157	583	78	150	21	7	7	44	39	74	.257	.306	.353	101	-1	-0	65	40	18	1	.974	13	*O	0.6
1969	Cle-A	146	557	75	143	26	3	11	45	49	58	.257	.317	.373	89	-6	-9	67	36	6	7	.982	11	*O/3	0.2
1970	StL-N	148	552	73	162	32	6	10	74	45	70	.293	.348	.428	104	4	3	81	26	9	2	.969	-5	*O	-0.6
1971	StL-N	89	301	37	73	12	4	7	48	29	35	.243	.309	.379	90	-3	-4	35	12	3	2	.969	7	O	0.1
	Mil-A	53	198	20	51	10	0	3	32	13	20	.258	.307	.354	88	-4	-4	21	9	5	-0	.979	7	O	0.0
1972	Chi-N	143	533	96	155	24	6	17	70	55	58	.291	.358	.454	117	20	14	83	25	14	-1	.971	-5	*O	0.2
1973	Chi-N	145	522	80	158	33	2	11	68	58	62	.303	.378	.437	116	19	14	86	19	7	2	.980	-4	*O	0.6
1974	Chi-N	143	542	75	159	35	3	13	72	56	67	.293	.361	.441	118	16	14	84	23	9	2	.965	7	*O	1.7
1975	Chi-N	154	574	85	182	30	2	9	68	77	50	.317	.402	.423	124	25	22	103	34	12	3	.976	10	*O	3.0
1976	Chi-N	136	521	64	156	25	2	8	47	32	39	.299	.341	.401	101	6	1	71	23	14	-2	.981	0	*O	-0.6
1977	Chi-N	100	226	33	54	12	1	3	18	28	30	.239	.325	.341	71	-6	-10	24	5	4	-1	.989	-8	O/2S	-2.1
1978	*Phi-N	87	201	27	50	12	0	4	33	23	16	.249	.326	.368	93	-2	-2	23	2	3	-1	.990	-5	1O	-1.1
1979	Phi-N	29	48	4	10	3	0	0	9	8	8	.208	.321	.271	61	-2	-2	4	1	0	0	1.000	-2	O/1	-0.4
	NY-N	11	37	8	11	4	0	2	4	6	3	.297	.409	.568	170	3	4	10	1	0	0	1.000	-1	/O1	0.2
	Yr	40	85	12	21	7	0	2	13	14	11	.247	.360	.400	106	1	1	13	2	0	1	1.000	-3	O/1	-0.2
1980	NY-N	26	42	4	7	1	0	0	4	6	4	.167	.271	.190	32	-4	-4	2	0	1	-1	1.000	-0	/O1	-0.5
	*KC-A	25	53	8	18	2	0	0	5	5	5	.340	.397	.377	112	1	1	9	0	0	0	.970	-3	O	-0.2
Total	18	2017	6964	936	1913	333	46	138	775	608	807	.275	.335	.395	102	46	21	928	329	139	15	.976	48	*O/132S	0.1

■ LEO CARDENAS

Cardenas, Leonardo Lazaro (Alfonso) "Chico" b: 12/17/38, Matanzas, Cuba BR/TR, 5'10", 163 lbs. Deb: 7/25/60

YEAR	TM/L	G	AB	R	H	2B	3B	HR	RBI	BB	SO	AVG	OBP	SLG	PRO+	BR	/A	RC	SB	CS	SBR	FA	FR	POS	TPR
1960	Cin-N	48	142	13	33	2	4	1	12	6	32	.232	.264	.324	59	-8	-8	12	0	0	0	.958	7	S	0.2
1961	*Cin-N	74	198	23	61	18	1	5	24	15	39	.308	.357	.485	119	6	5	33	1	0	0	.973	-5	S	0.5
1962	Cin-N	153	589	77	173	31	4	10	60	39	99	.294	.343	.411	98	1	-2	79	2	5	-2	.972	-7	*S	0.3
1963	Cin-N	158	565	42	133	22	4	7	48	23	101	.235	.270	.326	69	-22	-24	46	3	5	-2	**.972**	-3	*S	-2.0
1964	Cin-N★	163	597	61	150	32	2	9	69	41	110	.251	.302	.357	82	-12	-15	63	4	4	-1	.960	-10	*S	-1.5
1965	Cin-N★	156	557	65	160	25	11	11	57	60	100	.287	.358	.431	113	16	11	81	1	4	-2	.975	-1	*S	2.0
1966	Cin-N★	160	568	59	145	25	4	20	81	45	87	.255	.311	.419	93	-0	-6	69	9	4	0	**.980**	-15	*S	-0.6
1967	Cin-N	108	379	30	97	14	3	2	21	34	77	.256	.320	.325	76	-7	-12	38	4	5	-2	.971	-10	*S	-1.4
1968	Cin-N★	137	452	45	106	13	2	7	41	36	83	.235	.294	.319	79	-9	-12	39	2	1	0	.955	-23	*S	-2.4
1969	*Min-A	160	578	67	162	24	4	10	70	66	96	.280	.358	.388	106	8	6	78	5	6	-2	.965	**34**	*S	5.6
1970	*Min-A	160	588	67	145	34	4	11	65	42	101	.247	.301	.374	84	-13	-14	65	2	5	-2	.978	3	*S	0.6
1971	Min-A☆	153	554	59	146	25	4	18	75	51	69	.264	.327	.421	107	6	4	73	3	3	-1	**.985**	-0	*S	2.4
1972	Cal-A	150	551	25	123	11	2	6	42	35	73	.223	.272	.283	69	-24	-21	41	1	2	-1	.970	3	*S	0.4
1973	Cle-A	72	195	9	42	4	0	0	12	13	42	.215	.264	.236	41	-15	-15	11	1	4	-2	.964	-8	S/3	-1.9
1974	Tex-A	34	92	5	25	3	0	0	7	2	14	.272	.287	.304	72	-4	-3	8	1	0	0	1.000	2	3S/D	0.0
1975	Tex-A	55	102	15	24	2	0	1	5	14	12	.235	.328	.284	75	-3	-3	11	0	0	0	.956	11	3/S2	0.8
Total	16	1941	6707	662	1725	285	49	118	689	522	1135	.257	.313	.367	88	-80	-107	748	39	48	-17	.971	-22	*S/3D2	3.0

■ ROD CAREW

Carew, Rodney Cline b: 10/1/45, Gatun, C.Z. BL/TR, 6', 182 lbs. Deb: 4/11/67 CH

YEAR	TM/L	G	AB	R	H	2B	3B	HR	RBI	BB	SO	AVG	OBP	SLG	PRO+	BR	/A	RC	SB	CS	SBR	FA	FR	POS	TPR
1967	Min-A★	137	514	66	150	22	7	8	51	37	91	.292	.342	.409	112	13	8	68	5	9	-4	.976	-10	*2	0.3
1968	Min-A★	127	461	46	126	27	2	1	42	26	71	.273	.314	.347	95	-1	-3	49	12	4	1	.968	-14	*2/S	-1.0
1969	*Min-A★	123	458	79	152	30	4	8	56	37	72	**.332**	.386	.467	135	22	21	83	19	8	1	.970	-17	*2	1.5
1970	*Min-A†	51	191	27	70	12	3	4	28	11	28	.366	.407	.524	153	14	13	39	4	6	-2	.961	-11	2/1	0.4
1971	Min-A★	147	577	88	177	16	10	2	48	45	81	.307	.358	.380	106	7	5	73	6	7	-2	.976	-25	*2/3	-1.2
1972	Min-A★	142	535	61	170	21	6	0	51	43	60	**.318**	.371	.379	118	16	13	75	12	6	0	.978	-0	*2	2.4

YEAR	TM/L	G	AB	R	H	2B	3B	HR	RBI	BB	SO	AVG	OBP	SLG	PRO+	BR	/A	RC	SB	CS	SBR	FA	FR	POS	TPR
1973	Min-A★	149	580	98	**203**	30	**11**	6	62	62	55	**.350**	.415	.471	143	39	36	113	41	16	3	.984	7	*2	**5.5**
1974	Min-A★	153	599	86	**218**	30	5	3	55	74	49	**.364**	**.435**	.446	148	45	42	**118**	38	16	2	.960	9	*2	**6.1**
1975	Min-A★	143	535	89	192	24	4	14	80	64	40	**.359**	**.428**	.497	158	44	43	118	35	9	5	.973	4	*21/D	5.7
1976	Min-A★	156	605	97	200	29	12	9	90	67	52	.331	.398	.463	147	**40**	38	111	49	22	2	.989	-2	*1/2	2.9
1977	Min-A★	155	616	**128**	**239**	38	**16**	14	100	69	55	**.388**	**.452**	.570	**179**	**67**	**68**	**160**	23	13	-1	.994	6	*1/2D	**6.2**
1978	Min-A★	152	564	85	188	26	10	5	70	78	62	**.333**	**.415**	.441	138	34	32	105	27	7	4	.989	1	*1/2O	2.9
1979	*Cal-A†	110	409	78	130	15	3	3	44	73	46	.318	.421	.391	125	16	18	73	18	8	1	.988	-7	*1/D	0.5
1980	Cal-A★	144	540	74	179	34	7	3	59	59	38	.331	.398	.437	132	23	25	92	23	15	-2	.994	-4	*1D	1.2
1981	Cal-A★	93	364	57	111	17	1	2	21	45	45	.305	.381	.374	118	10	10	53	16	9	-1	.995	-1	1/D	0.4
1982	*Cal-A†	138	523	88	167	25	5	3	44	67	49	.319	.399	.403	121	18	18	83	10	17	-7	.992	1	*1	0.5
1983	Cal-A★	129	472	66	160	24	2	2	44	57	48	.339	.411	.411	128	20	21	78	6	7	-2	.994	-9	1D/2	0.4
1984	Cal-A★	93	329	42	97	8	1	3	31	40	39	.295	.371	.353	102	2	3	44	4	3	-1	.981	-4	1/D	-0.7
1985	Cal-A	127	443	69	124	17	3	2	39	64	47	.280	.372	.345	99	1	2	60	5	5	-2	.994	-8	*1	-1.5
Total	19	2469	9315	1424	3053	445	112	92	1015	1018	1028	.328	.395	.429	131	431	414	1595	353	187	-6	.991	-85	*12/DS3O	32.5

■ ANDY CAREY

Carey, Andrew Arthur b: 10/18/31, Oakland, Cal. BR/TR, 6'1", 195 lbs. Deb: 5/02/52

YEAR	TM/L	G	AB	R	H	2B	3B	HR	RBI	BB	SO	AVG	OBP	SLG	PRO+	BR	/A	RC	SB	CS	SBR	FA	FR	POS	TPR
1952	NY-A	16	40	6	6	0	0	0	1	3	10	.150	.209	.150	1	-5	-5	1	0	0	0	.889	-1	3/S	-0.6
1953	NY-A	51	81	14	26	5	0	4	8	9	12	.321	.389	.531	152	5	5	17	2	1	0	.988	8	3/S2	1.3
1954	NY-A	122	411	60	124	14	6	8	65	43	38	.302	.377	.423	123	11	13	64	5	5	-2	.967	17	*3	2.6
1955	*NY-A	135	510	73	131	19	**11**	7	47	44	51	.257	.317	.378	88	-11	-10	60	3	3	-1	.954	14	*3	0.2
1956	*NY-A	132	422	54	100	18	2	7	50	45	53	.237	.313	.339	75	-17	-15	45	9	6	-1	.947	-3	*3	-1.7
1957	*NY-A	85	247	30	63	6	5	6	33	15	42	.255	.311	.393	92	-4	-3	29	2	2	-1	.977	3	3	0.1
1958	*NY-A	102	315	39	90	19	4	12	45	34	43	.286	.366	.486	137	14	15	57	1	2	-1	.961	10	3	2.6
1959	NY-A	41	101	11	26	1	0	3	9	7	17	.257	.306	.356	84	-3	-2	10	1	1	-0	.916	2	3	-0.1
1960	NY-A	4	3	1	1	0	0	0	1	0	1	.333	.333	.333	86	-0	-0	0	0	0	0	1.000	-1	/3O	-0.1
	KC-A	102	343	30	80	14	4	12	53	26	52	.233	.289	.402	84	-8	-9	36	0	0	0	.975	-0	3	-1.0
	Yr	106	346	31	81	14	4	12	54	26	53	.234	.290	.402	85	-9	-9	36	0	0	0	.975	-1	3/O	-1.1
1961	KC-A	39	123	20	30	6	2	3	11	15	23	.244	.336	.398	95	-1	-1	17	0	0	0	.944	-1	3	-0.2
	Chi-A	56	143	21	38	12	3	0	14	11	24	.266	.327	.392	93	-2	-2	19	0	1	-1	.961	-5	3	-0.7
	Yr	95	266	41	68	18	5	3	25	26	47	.256	.331	.395	94	-3	-2	36	0	1	-1	.953	-6	3	-0.9
1962	LA-N	53	111	12	26	5	1	2	13	16	23	.234	.336	.351	90	-2	-1	14	0	0	0	.932	1	3	0.0
Total	11	938	2850	371	741	119	38	64	350	268	389	.260	.329	.396	97	-23	-14	369	23	21	-6	.958	45	3/SO2	2.4

■ SCOOPS CAREY

Carey, George C. b: 12/4/1870, E.Liverpool, Ohio d: 12/17/16, E.Liverpool, Ohio BR/TR, 175 lbs. Deb: 4/26/1895

YEAR	TM/L	G	AB	R	H	2B	3B	HR	RBI	BB	SO	AVG	OBP	SLG	PRO+	BR	/A	RC	SB	CS	SBR	FA	FR	POS	TPR
1895	*Bal-N	123	490	59	128	21	6	1	75	27	32	.261	.305	.335	65	-25	-27	53	2			**.987**	-6	*1/OS3	-2.5
1898	Lou-N	8	32	1	6	1	1	0	1	1		.188	.212	.281	42	-3	-3	2	0			.961	0	/1	-0.2
1902	Was-A	120	452	46	142	35	11	0	60	20		.314	.350	.440	117	10	9	73	3			**.989**	4	*1	1.0
1903	Was-A	48	183	8	37	3	2	0	23	4		.202	.223	.240	38	-13	-14	10	0			.977	-3	1	-1.9
Total	4	299	1157	114	313	60	20	1	159	52	32	.271	.308	.360	80	-31	-34	139	5			.986	-6	1/3SO	-3.6

■ MAX CAREY

Carey, Max George "Scoops" (b: Maximilian Carnarius)
b: 1/11/1890, Terre Haute, Ind. d: 5/30/76, Miami, Fla. BB/TR, 5'11.5", 170 lbs. Deb: 10/03/10 MCH

YEAR	TM/L	G	AB	R	H	2B	3B	HR	RBI	BB	SO	AVG	OBP	SLG	PRO+	BR	/A	RC	SB	CS	SBR	FA	FR	POS	TPR
1910	Pit-N	2	6	2	3	0	1	0	2	2	1	.500	.625	.833	307	2	2	3	0			1.000	2	/O	0.3
1911	Pit-N	129	427	77	110	15	10	5	43	44	75	.258	.337	.375	95	-1	-3	64	27			.975	7	*O	-0.3
1912	Pit-N	150	587	114	177	23	8	5	66	61	79	.302	.372	.394	111	9	10	104	45			.968	9	*O	1.0
1913	Pit-N	154	620	**99**	172	23	10	5	49	55	67	.277	.339	.371	107	2	6	92	**61**			.961	15	*O	1.4
1914	Pit-N	156	593	76	144	25	**17**	1	31	59	56	.243	.313	.347	101	-3	-0	72	38			.966	11	*O	0.4
1915	Pit-N	140	564	76	143	26	5	3	27	57	58	.254	.326	.333	101	1	2	66	**36**	17	1	.982	13	*O	1.0
1916	Pit-N	154	599	90	158	23	11	7	42	59	58	.264	.337	.374	117	13	13	87	**63**	19	**8**	.983	**30**	*O	4.7
1917	Pit-N	155	588	82	174	21	12	1	51	58	38	.296	.369	.378	125	22	20	94	**46**			.979	25	*O	4.0
1918	Pit-N	126	468	70	128	14	6	3	48	**62**	25	.274	.363	.348	113	12	10	76	**58**			.958	19	*O	2.4
1919	Pit-N	66	244	41	75	10	2	0	9	25	24	.307	.376	.365	119	8	7	38	18			.947	2	O	0.5
1920	Pit-N	130	485	74	140	18	4	1	35	59	31	.289	.369	.348	104	7	5	72	**52**	10	**10**	.967	1	*O	0.6
1921	Pit-N	140	521	85	161	34	4	7	56	70	30	.309	.395	.430	115	16	14	95	37	12	4	.957	16	*O	2.3
1922	Pit-N	155	629	140	207	28	12	10	70	**80**	26	.329	.408	.459	122	24	23	131	**51**	2	**14**	.969	20	*O	4.2
1923	Pit-N	153	610	120	188	32	**19**	6	63	73	28	.308	.388	.452	119	20	18	117	**51**	8	**11**	.962	20	*O	3.6
1924	Pit-N	149	599	113	178	30	9	8	55	58	17	.297	.366	.417	108	9	8	97	**49**	13	**7**	.965	9	*O	1.3
1925	*Pit-N	133	542	109	186	39	13	5	44	66	19	.343	.418	.491	123	28	22	118	**46**	11	**7**	.950	9	*O	2.8
1926	Pit-N	86	324	46	72	14	5	0	28	30	14	.222	.288	.296	55	-19	-22	28	10			.943	4	O	-2.3
	Bro-N	27	100	18	26	3	1	0	7	8	5	.260	.315	.310	70	-4	-4	10	0			.933	-1	O	-0.7
	Yr	113	424	64	98	17	6	0	35	38	19	.231	.294	.300	58	-24	-26	38	10			.941	3	*O	-3.0
1927	Bro-N	144	538	70	143	30	10	1	54	64	18	.266	.345	.364	90	-7	-7	69	32			.970	6	*O	-1.0
1928	Bro-N	108	296	41	73	11	0	2	19	47	24	.247	.354	.304	74	-10	-9	34	18			.986	-12	O	-2.7
1929	Bro-N	19	23	2	7	0	0	0	1	3	2	.304	.407	.304	81	-0	-0	3	0			1.000	-1	/O	-0.1
Total	20	2476	9363	1545	2665	419	159	70	800	1040	695	.285	.361	.386	107	128	113	1472	738	92		.966	199	*O	23.4

■ ROGER CAREY

Carey, Roger J. Deb: 7/09/1887

YEAR	TM/L	G	AB	R	H	2B	3B	HR	RBI	BB	SO	AVG	OBP	SLG	PRO+	BR	/A	RC	SB	CS	SBR	FA	FR	POS	TPR
1887	NY-N	1	4	0	0	0	0	0	2	0	1	.000	.000	.000	-99	-1	-1	0	0			.800	1	/2	0.0

■ TOM CAREY

Carey, Thomas Francis Aloysius "Scoops" b: 10/11/06, Hoboken, N.J. d: 2/21/70, Rochester, N.Y. BR/TR, 5'8.5", 170 lbs. Deb: 7/19/35 C

YEAR	TM/L	G	AB	R	H	2B	3B	HR	RBI	BB	SO	AVG	OBP	SLG	PRO+	BR	/A	RC	SB	CS	SBR	FA	FR	POS	TPR
1935	StL-A	76	296	29	86	18	4	0	42	13	11	.291	.320	.378	77	-9	-11	35	0	2	-1	.961	-1	2	-0.7
1936	StL-A	134	488	58	133	27	6	1	57	27	25	.273	.315	.359	64	-27	-29	55	2	1	0	.967	-1	*2/S	-1.8
1937	StL-A	130	487	54	134	24	1	1	40	21	26	.275	.306	.335	61	-29	-29	49	1	2	-1	.983	2	2S/3	-1.8
1939	Bos-A	54	161	17	39	6	2	0	20	3	9	.242	.265	.304	44	-14	-14	12	0	0	0	1.000	6	2S	-0.6
1940	Bos-A	43	62	4	20	4	0	0	7	2	1	.323	.344	.387	86	-1	-1	8	0	0	0	.953	5	S/23	0.4
1941	Bos-A	25	21	7	4	0	0	0	0	0	0	.190	.190	.190	1	-3	-3	1	0	0	0	1.000	4	/2S3	0.1
1942	Bos-A	1	1	0	1	0	0	0	1	0	0	1.000	1.000	1.000	448	0	0	1	0	0	0	1.000	-0	/2	0.0
1946	Bos-A	3	5	0	1	0	0	0	0	0	1	.200	.200	.200	11	-1	-1	0	0	0	0	.900	1	/2	0.1
Total	8	466	1521	169	418	79	13	2	167	66	73	.275	.308	.348	63	-83	-89	162	3	5	-2	.973	17	2/S3	-4.3

■ TOM CAREY

Carey, Thomas John (b: J. J. Norton) b: 1849, Brooklyn, N.J. d: 2/13/1899, Los Angeles, Cal. BR/TR, 5'8", 145 lbs. Deb: 5/04/1871 M

YEAR	TM/L	G	AB	R	H	2B	3B	HR	RBI	BB	SO	AVG	OBP	SLG	PRO+	BR	/A	RC	SB	CS	SBR	FA	FR	POS	TPR
1871	Kek-n	19	87	16	20	2	0	0	10	2	1	.230	.247	.253	43	-6	-7	7	5					2/S	-0.5
1872	Bal-n	42	197	43	58	7	1	2	27	0	2	.294	.294	.371	99	1	-1	23						2/S3O1	-0.2
1873	Bal-n	56	290	76	97	18	3	2	55	1	2	.334	.337	.438	127	9	9	43						*2/3SM	0.2
1874	Mut-n	64	286	54	82	10	3	1		2		.287	.292	.353	101	1	-0	30						*S2M	-0.2
1875	Har-n	86	382	63	101	6	2	0		2		.264	.268	.291	89	-3	-6	31						*S	-0.8
1876	Har-N	68	289	51	78	7	0	0	26	3	4	.270	.277	.294	84	-3	-6	24				.882	-1	*S	-0.7
1877	Har-N	60	274	38	70	3	2	1	20	0	9	.255	.255	.292	81	-9	-4	21				.826	-6	*S	-0.8
1878	Pro-N	61	253	33	60	10	3	0	24	0	14	.237	.237	.300	76	-7	-7	18				.874	1	*S	-0.2
1879	Cle-N	80	335	30	80	14	1	0	32	5	20	.239	.250	.287	77	-8	-8	25				.864	-3	*S	-0.6
Total	5 n	267	1242	252	358	43	9	5	92	7	5	.288	.292	.349	99	2	-5	134						S2/3O1	-1.5
Total	4	269	1151	152	288	34	6	1	102	8	47	.250	.255	.293	79	-26	-25	88				.862	-9	S	-2.3

YEAR	TM/L	G	AB	R	H	2B	3B	HR	RBI	BB	SO	AVG	OBP	SLG	PRO+	BR	/A	RC	SB	CS	SBR	FA	FR	POS	TPR
Total	3	79	287	34	49	6	1	0	1	19	8	.171	.232	.199	29	-26	-22	20	19			.853	-2	/O32	-2.2

■ **PAT CARROLL** Carroll, Patrick b: 1853, Philadelphia, Pa. d: 2/14/16, Philadelphia, Pa. Deb: 5/10/1884

YEAR	TM/L	G	AB	R	H	2B	3B	HR	RBI	BB	SO	AVG	OBP	SLG	PRO+	BR	/A	RC	SB	CS	SBR	FA	FR	POS	TPR
1884	Alt-U	11	49	4	13	1	0	0		1		.265	.280	.286	90	-0	-1	4				.920	-4	/CO	-0.3
	Phi-U	5	19	1	3	1	0	0		0		.158	.158	.211	25	-1	-1	1				.839	3	/C	0.2
	Yr	16	68	5	16	2	0	0		1		.235	.246	.265	74	-2	-2	5				.877	-1	C/O	-0.1

■ **DOC CARROLL** Carroll, Ralph Arthur "Red" b: 12/28/1891, Worcester, Mass. d: 6/27/83, Worcester, Mass. BR/TR, 6', 170 lbs. Deb: 6/27/16

YEAR	TM/L	G	AB	R	H	2B	3B	HR	RBI	BB	SO	AVG	OBP	SLG	PRO+	BR	/A	RC	SB	CS	SBR	FA	FR	POS	TPR
1916	Phi-A	10	22	1	2	0	0	0	0	1	8	.091	.167	.091	-24	-3	-3	1	0			.942	0	C	-0.3

■ **CLIFF CARROLL** Carroll, Samuel Clifford b: 10/18/1859, Clay Grove, Iowa d: 6/12/23, Portland, Ore. BB/TR, 5'8", 163 lbs. Deb: 8/03/1882

YEAR	TM/L	G	AB	R	H	2B	3B	HR	RBI	BB	SO	AVG	OBP	SLG	PRO+	BR	/A	RC	SB	CS	SBR	FA	FR	POS	TPR
1882	Pro-N	10	41	4	5	0	0	0	2	0	4	.122	.122	.122	-21	-5	-5	1				1.000	1	O	-0.4
1883	Pro-N	58	238	37	63	12	3	1	20	4	28	.265	.277	.353	87	-3	-4	24				.902	5	O	0.0
1884	*Pro-N	113	452	90	118	16	4	3	54	29	39	.261	.306	.334	104	1	3	47				.904	2	*O	0.2
1885	Pro-N	104	426	62	99	12	3	1	40	29	29	.232	.281	.282	86	-8	-5	35				.886	4	*O	-0.4
1886	Was-N	111	433	73	99	11	6	2	22	44	26	.229	.300	.296	87	-8	-4	49	31			.862	-1	*O	-0.7
1887	Was-N	103	420	79	104	17	4	4	37	17	30	.248	.291	.336	79	-14	-10	54	40			.902	1	*O	-0.9
1888	Pit-N	5	20	1	0	0	0	0	0	0	8	.000	.000	.000	-99	-4	-4	0	2			.667	-1	/O	-0.6
1890	Chi-N	136	582	134	166	16	6	7	65	53	34	.285	.352	.369	108	10	6	90	34			.936	15	*O	1.4
1891	Chi-N	130	515	87	132	20	8	7	80	50	42	.256	.340	.367	108	6	6	77	31			.915	-5	*O	-0.3
1892	StL-N	101	407	82	111	14	8	4	49	47	22	.273	.363	.376	132	14	17	68	30			.901	4	*O	1.5
1893	Bos-N	120	438	80	98	7	5	2	54	88	28	.224	.360	.276	67	-14	-20	55	29			.917	2	*O	-2.0
Total	11	991	3972	729	995	125	47	31	423	361	290	.251	.320	.329	94	-26	-23	499	197			.905	25	O	-2.2

■ **TOM CARROLL** Carroll, Thomas Edward b: 9/17/36, Jamaica, N.Y. BR/TR, 6'3", 186 lbs. Deb: 5/07/55

YEAR	TM/L	G	AB	R	H	2B	3B	HR	RBI	BB	SO	AVG	OBP	SLG	PRO+	BR	/A	RC	SB	CS	SBR	FA	FR	POS	TPR
1955	*NY-A	14	6	3	2	0	0	0	0	0	2	.333	.333	.333	81	-0	-0	1	0	0	0	.875	4	/S	0.4
1956	NY-A	36	17	11	6	0	0	0	0	1	3	.353	.389	.353	100	-0	0	3	1	0	0	.857	7	3/S	0.7
1959	KC-A	14	7	1	1	0	0	0	1	0	1	.143	.143	.143	-21	-1	-1	0	0	0	0	1.000	4	/S3	0.3
Total	3	64	30	15	9	0	0	0	1	1	6	.300	.323	.300	69	-1	-1	3	1	0	0	.962	15	/3S	1.4

■ **KID CARSEY** Carsey, Wilfred b: 10/22/1870, New York, N.Y. d: 3/29/60, Miami, Fla. BL/TR, 5'7", 168 lbs. Deb: 4/08/1891

YEAR	TM/L	G	AB	R	H	2B	3B	HR	RBI	BB	SO	AVG	OBP	SLG	PRO+	BR	/A	RC	SB	CS	SBR	FA	FR	POS	TPR
1891	Was-a	61	187	25	28	5	2	0	15	19	38	.150	.236	.198	27	-18	-16	9	2			.922	5	P/OS	-0.2
1892	Phi-N	44	131	8	20	2	1	1	10	9	24	.153	.207	.206	26	-12	-12	6	1			.888	2	P/O	-0.1
1893	Phi-N	39	145	12	27	1	1	0	10	5	14	.186	.229	.207	17	-17	-17	8	2			.925	2	P	0.0
1894	Phi-N	35	125	30	34	2	2	0	18	16	11	.272	.359	.320	68	-6	-6	16	3			.937	2	P	0.0
1895	Phi-N	44	141	24	41	2	0	0	20	15	12	.291	.363	.305	75	-4	-4	18	2			.878	-1	P	0.0
1896	Phi-N	27	81	13	18	2	2	0	7	11	12	.222	.315	.296	64	-4	-4	9	1			.908	1	P	0.0
1897	Phi-N	4	13	1	3	0	0	0	1	0		.231	.231	.231	23	-1	-1	1	0			1.000	-0	/P	0.0
	StL-N	13	43	2	13	2	2	0	5	1		.302	.318	.442	101	-0	-0	7	1			.917	1	P	0.0
	Yr	17	56	3	16	2	2	0	6	1		.286	.298	.393	83	-2	-2	7	1			.930	1	P	0.0
1898	StL-N	38	105	8	21	0	1	1	10	10		.200	.270	.248	47	-7	-7	9	3			.935	-6	P2/O	-1.0
1899	Cle-N	11	36	5	10	0	0	0	4	3		.278	.333	.278	74	-1	-1	3	0			.879	3	P/S	0.1
	Was-N	4	11	1	0	0	0	0	0	0		.000	.000	.000	-99	-3	-3	0	0			.923	1	/P	0.0
	NY-N	5	18	2	6	1	0	0	1	2		.333	.400	.389	121	0	1	4	2			.667	-1	/3S	0.0
	Yr	20	65	8	16	1	0	0	5	5		.246	.300	.262	58	-4	-3	6	2			.891	3	P/S3	0.1
1901	Bro-N	2	2	0	0	0	0	0	0	0		.000	.000	.000	-97	-0	-1	0	0			1.000	-0	/P	0.0
Total	10	327	1038	131	221	17	11	2	101	91	111	.213	.281	.256	48	-74	-72	89	17			.911	7	P/O2S3	-1.2

■ **KIT CARSON** Carson, Walter Lloyd b: 11/15/12, Colton, Cal. d: 6/21/83, Long Beach, Cal. BL/TL, 6', 180 lbs. Deb: 7/21/34

YEAR	TM/L	G	AB	R	H	2B	3B	HR	RBI	BB	SO	AVG	OBP	SLG	PRO+	BR	/A	RC	SB	CS	SBR	FA	FR	POS	TPR
1934	Cle-A	5	18	4	5	2	1	0	1	2	3	.278	.350	.500	115	0	0	3	0	0	0	1.000	-1	/O	-0.1
1935	Cle-A	16	22	1	5	2	0	0	1	2	6	.227	.292	.318	57	-1	-1	2	0	1	-1	1.000	-0	/O	-0.2
Total	2	21	40	5	10	4	1	0	2	4	9	.250	.318	.400	83	-1	-1	5	0	1	-1	1.000	-2	/O	-0.3

■ **FRANK CARSWELL** Carswell, Frank Willis "Tex" or "Wheels" b: 11/6/19, Palestine, Tex. BR/TR, 6', 195 lbs. Deb: 4/17/53

YEAR	TM/L	G	AB	R	H	2B	3B	HR	RBI	BB	SO	AVG	OBP	SLG	PRO+	BR	/A	RC	SB	CS	SBR	FA	FR	POS	TPR
1953	Det-A	16	15	2	4	0	0	0	2	3	1	.267	.389	.267	81	-0	-0	2	0	0	0	1.000	-1	/O	-0.1

■ **GARY CARTER** Carter, Gary Edmund b: 4/8/54, Culver City, Cal. BR/TR, 6'2", 215 lbs. Deb: 9/16/74

YEAR	TM/L	G	AB	R	H	2B	3B	HR	RBI	BB	SO	AVG	OBP	SLG	PRO+	BR	/A	RC	SB	CS	SBR	FA	FR	POS	TPR
1974	Mon-N	9	27	5	11	0	1	1	6	1	2	.407	.429	.593	174	3	3	7	2	0	1	1.000	-1	/CO	0.3
1975	Mon-N★	144	503	58	136	20	1	17	68	72	83	.270	.363	.416	111	11	9	80	5	2	0	.974	-18	OC/3	-1.0
1976	Mon-N	91	311	31	68	8	1	6	38	30	43	.219	.289	.309	67	-12	-14	28	0	2	-1	.994	5	CO	-1.0
1977	Mon-N	154	522	86	148	29	2	31	84	58	103	.284	.361	.525	138	24	26	98	5	5	-2	.990	3	*C/O	3.2
1978	Mon-N	157	533	76	136	27	1	20	72	62	70	.255	.338	.422	113	8	9	77	10	6	-1	.989	10	*C/1	2.3
1979	Mon-N★	141	505	74	143	26	5	22	75	40	62	.283	.342	.485	124	14	15	82	3	2	-0	.989	13	*C	3.3
1980	Mon-N★	154	549	76	145	25	5	29	101	58	78	.264	.336	.486	127	18	18	89	3	2	-0	**.993**	14	*C	3.9
1981	*Mon-N★	100	374	48	94	20	2	16	68	35	35	.251	.317	.444	113	6	5	51	1	5	-3	.993	2	*C/1	0.9
1982	Mon-N★	154	557	91	163	32	1	29	97	78	64	.293	.385	.510	146	37	35	107	2	5	-2	.991	14	*C	5.5
1983	Mon-N★	145	541	63	146	37	3	17	79	51	57	.270	.341	.444	116	11	11	80	1	1	-0	**.995**	10	*C/1	2.8
1984	Mon-N★	159	596	75	175	32	1	27	**106**	64	57	.294	.368	.487	145	30	33	108	2	2	-1	.993	-5	*C1	3.4
1985	NY-N†	149	555	83	156	17	1	32	100	69	46	.281	.367	.488	141	28	29	97	1	1	-0	.992	5	*C/1O	4.2
1986	*NY-N★	132	490	81	125	14	2	24	105	62	63	.255	.346	.439	118	10	12	72	1	0	0	.991	6	*C/1O3	2.7
1987	NY-N★	139	523	55	123	18	2	20	83	42	73	.235	.293	.392	84	-17	-13	58	0	0	0	.991	-0	*C/1O	-0.4
1988	*NY-N★	130	455	39	110	16	2	11	46	34	52	.242	.304	.358	94	-6	-4	50	0	2	-1	.990	-3	*C1/3	0.0
1989	NY-N	50	153	14	28	8	0	2	15	12	15	.183	.242	.275	50	-11	-10	10	0	0	0	.980	-2	C/1	-1.0
1990	SF-N	92	244	24	62	10	0	9	27	25	31	.254	.326	.406	104	-0	1	33	1	1	-0	.992	-3	C/1	0.1
1991	LA-N	101	248	22	61	14	0	6	26	22	26	.246	.325	.375	98	-1	-0	28	2	2	-1	.988	3	C1	0.6
1992	Mon-N	95	285	24	62	18	1	5	29	33	37	.218	.303	.340	82	-7	-6	29	0	4	-2	.989	1	C/1	-0.3
Total	19	2296	7971	1025	2092	371	31	324	1225	848	997	.262	.338	.439	116	145	158	1185	39	42	-14	.991	53	*CO/13	29.5

■ **HOWIE CARTER** Carter, John Howard b: 10/13/04, New York, N.Y. BR/TR, 5'10", 154 lbs. Deb: 6/21/26

YEAR	TM/L	G	AB	R	H	2B	3B	HR	RBI	BB	SO	AVG	OBP	SLG	PRO+	BR	/A	RC	SB	CS	SBR	FA	FR	POS	TPR
1926	Cin-N	5	1	0	0	0	0	0	0	0	0	.000	.000	.000	-99	-0	-0	0	0			1.000	0	/2S	0.0

■ **JOE CARTER** Carter, Joseph b: 3/7/60, Oklahoma City, Okla. BR/TR, 6'3", 215 lbs. Deb: 7/30/83

YEAR	TM/L	G	AB	R	H	2B	3B	HR	RBI	BB	SO	AVG	OBP	SLG	PRO+	BR	/A	RC	SB	CS	SBR	FA	FR	POS	TPR
1983	Chi-N	23	51	6	9	1	1	0	1	0	21	.176	.176	.235	13	-6	-6	2	1	0	0	1.000	0	O	-0.7
1984	Cle-A	66	244	32	67	6	1	13	41	11	48	.275	.309	.467	109	3	2	34	2	4	-2	.956	1	O/1	0.0
1985	Cle-A	143	489	64	128	27	0	15	59	25	74	.262	.300	.409	93	-6	-6	60	24	6	4	.983	-1	*O1/23D	-0.8
1986	Cle-A	162	663	108	200	36	9	29	**121**	32	95	.302	.339	.514	130	23	25	116	29	7	5	.976	-6	*O1	1.5
1987	Cle-A	149	588	83	155	27	2	32	106	27	105	.264	.306	.480	103	1	1	87	31	6	6	.983	-8	1O/D	-0.9
1988	Cle-A	157	621	85	168	36	6	27	98	35	82	.271	.317	.478	116	13	11	96	27	5	5	.985	14	*O	2.5
1989	Cle-A	162	651	84	158	32	4	35	105	39	112	.243	.294	.465	109	6	5	89	13	5	1	.978	-1	*O1/D	-0.1
1990	SD-N	162	634	79	147	27	1	24	115	48	93	.232	.293	.391	86	-13	-14	72	22	6	3	.988	9	*O1	-0.7
1991	*Tor-A★	162	638	89	174	42	3	33	108	49	112	.273	.334	.503	124	22	19	108	20	9	1	.974	3	*OD	1.9
1992	*Tor-A★	158	622	97	164	30	7	34	119	36	109	.264	.315	.498	119	17	13	94	12	5	1	.971	6	*OD/1	1.6
Total	10	1344	5201	727	1370	264	34	242	873	302	851	.263	.311	.467	110	59	50	757	181	53	23	.978	16	*O1/D32	4.3

YEAR	TM/L	G	AB	R	H	2B	3B	HR	RBI	BB	SO	AVG	OBP	SLG	PRO+	BR	/A	RC	SB	CS	SBR	FA	FR	POS	TPR
■ **BLACKIE CARTER** Carter, Otis Leonard b: 9/30/02, Langley, S.C. d: 9/10/76, Greenville, S.C. BR/TR, 5'10", 175 lbs. Deb: 10/03/25																									
1925	NY-N	1	4	0	0	0	0	0	0	0	1	.000	.000	.000	-99	-1	-1	0	0	0	0	1.000	1	/O	-0.1
1926	NY-N	5	17	4	4	1	0	1	1	1	0	.235	.278	.471	100	-0	-0	2	0			.917	0	/O	0.0
Total	2	6	21	4	4	1	0	1	1	1	1	.190	.227	.381	61	-1	-1	2	0	0		.929	1	/O	-0.1
■ **STEVE CARTER** Carter, Steven Jerome b: 12/3/64, Charlottesville, Va. BL/TR, 6'4", 201 lbs. Deb: 4/16/89																									
1989	Pit-N	9	16	2	2	1	0	1	3	2	5	.125	.222	.375	70	-1	-1	1	0	0	0	1.000	-1	/O	-0.2
1990	Pit-N	5	5	0	1	0	0	0	0	0	1	.200	.200	.200	11	-1	-1	0	0	0	0	1.000	-1	/O	-0.2
Total	2	14	21	2	3	1	0	1	3	2	6	.143	.217	.333	56	-1	-1	2	0	0	0	1.000	-2	/O	-0.4
■ **ED CARTWRIGHT** Cartwright, Edward Charles "Jumbo" b: 10/6/1859, Johnstown, Pa. d: 9/3/33, St.Petersburg, Fla BR/TR, 5'10", 220 lbs. Deb: 7/10/1890																									
1890	StL-a	75	300	70	90	12	4	8		29		.300	.367	.447	125	15	8	60	26			.976	-1	1	0.3
1894	Was-N	132	507	88	149	35	13	12	106	57	43	.294	.374	.485	111	5	8	107	31			.973	-2	*1	0.6
1895	Was-N	122	472	95	156	34	17	3	90	54	41	.331	.400	.494	134	22	23	116	50			.984	14	*1	3.2
1896	Was-N	133	499	76	138	15	10	1	62	54	44	.277	.350	.353	87	-8	-8	74	28			.978	-0	*1	-0.5
1897	Was-N	33	124	19	29	4	0	0	15	8		.234	.286	.266	46	-10	-10	12	9			.963	2	1	-0.6
Total	5	495	1902	348	562	100	44	24	273	202	128	.295	.368	.432	108	24	22	369	144			.977	14	1	3.0
■ **RICO CARTY** Carty, Ricardo Adolfo Jacobo (b: Ricardo Adolfo Jacobo (Carty)) b: 9/1/39, San Pedro De Macoris, D.R. BR/TR, 6'3", 200 lbs. Deb: 9/15/63																									
1963	Mil-N	2	2	0	0	0	0	0	0	0	2	.000	.000	.000	-99	-1	-1	0	0	0	0	.000	0	H	-0.1
1964	Mil-N	133	455	72	150	28	4	22	88	43	78	.330	.391	.554	162	37	37	94	1	2	-1	.978	-8	*O	2.4
1965	Mil-N	83	271	37	84	18	1	10	35	17	44	.310	.357	.494	136	13	13	44	1	4	-2	.958	-4	O	0.4
1966	Atl-N	151	521	73	170	25	2	15	76	60	74	.326	.396	.468	137	29	28	94	4	6	-2	.971	-1	*OC/13	2.1
1967	Atl-N	134	444	41	113	16	2	15	64	49	70	.255	.330	.401	110	5	6	55	4	3	-1	.959	-1	*O/1	-0.2
1969	*Atl-N	104	304	47	104	15	0	16	58	32	28	.342	.405	.549	164	26	26	61	0	2	-1	.952	-9	O	1.2
1970	Atl-N★	136	478	84	175	23	3	25	101	77	46	**.366**	**.456**	.584	167	54	51	125	1	2	-1	.974	-6	*O	3.6
1972	Atl-N	86	271	31	75	12	2	6	29	44	33	.277	.378	.402	111	9	6	42	0	0	0	.979	-5	O	-0.2
1973	Tex-A	86	306	24	71	12	0	3	33	36	39	.232	.315	.301	77	-10	-8	30	2	0	1	1.000	-2	OD	-1.2
	Chi-N	22	70	4	15	0	0	1	8	6	10	.214	.276	.257	45	-5	-5	4	0	0	0	.947	-1	O	-0.8
	Oak-A	7	8	1	2	1	0	1	1	2	1	.250	.400	.750	230	1	1	3	0	0	0	.000	0	/D	0.1
1974	Cle-A	33	91	6	33	5	0	1	16	5	9	.363	.396	.451	144	5	5	15	0	0	0	.985	-2	D/1	0.3
1975	Cle-A	118	383	57	118	19	1	18	64	45	31	.308	.384	.504	149	25	25	70	2	2	-1	.990	-1	D1O	2.1
1976	Cle-A	152	552	67	171	34	0	13	83	67	45	.310	.384	.442	143	30	31	92	1	1	-0	1.000	-2	*D1/O	2.9
1977	Cle-A	127	461	50	129	23	1	15	80	56	51	.280	.358	.432	118	10	12	68	1	2	-1	1.000	1	*D/1	1.1
1978	Tor-A	104	387	51	110	16	0	20	68	36	41	.284	.345	.481	127	14	13	64	1	1	-0	.000	0	*D	1.3
	Oak-A	41	141	19	39	5	1	11	31	21	16	.277	.370	.560	167	11	12	27	0	0	0	.000	0	D	1.2
	Yr	145	528	70	149	21	1	31	99	57	57	.282	.352	.502	138	25	25	91	1	1	-0	.000	0	*D	2.5
1979	Tor-A	132	461	48	118	26	0	12	55	46	45	.256	.325	.390	91	-5	-6	54	3	1	0	.000	0	*D	-0.6
Total	15	1651	5606	712	1677	278	17	204	890	642	663	.299	.372	.464	132	248	243	941	21	26	-9	.970	-40	OD/1C3	15.6
■ **BOB CARUTHERS** Caruthers, Robert Lee "Parisian Bob" b: 1/5/1864, Memphis, Tenn. d: 8/5/11, Peoria, Ill. BL/TR, 5'7", 138 lbs. Deb: 9/07/1884 MU																									
1884	StL-a	23	82	15	21	2	0	2		4		.256	.291	.354	108	1	1	9				.750	-6	OP	-0.5
1885	*StL-a	60	222	37	50	10	2	1		20		.225	.289	.302	85	-2	-4	20				.902	-0	P/O	-0.1
1886	*StL-a	87	317	91	106	21	14	4		64		.334	.448	.527	198	42	39	89	26			.897	-6	PO/2	1.2
1887	*StL-a	98	364	102	130	23	11	8		66		.357	.463	.547	166	44	36	118	49			.903	9	OP/1	1.8
1888	Bro-a	94	335	58	77	10	5	5	53	45		.230	.328	.334	116	7	8	45	23			.899	1	OP	0.2
1889	*Bro-a	59	172	45	43	8	3	2	31	44	17	.250	.408	.366	123	8	8	30	9			.968	0	P/O1	-0.1
1890	*Bro-N	71	238	46	63	7	4	1	29	47	18	.265	.397	.340	117	8	8	38	13			.860	-4	OP	-0.4
1891	Bro-N	56	171	24	48	5	3	2	23	25	13	.281	.372	.380	122	5	6	26	4			.940	-3	PO/2	-0.2
1892	StL-N	143	513	76	142	16	8	3	69	86	29	.277	.386	.357	134	21	25	82	24			.892	-11	*OP/21M	0.6
1893	Chi-N	1	3	0	0	0	0	0	0	0	1	.000	.000	.000	-99	-1	-1	0	0			1.000	-0	/O	-0.1
	Cin-N	13	48	14	14	2	0	1	8	16	1	.292	.477	.396	132	4	4	11	4			.857	-1	O	0.2
	Yr	14	51	14	14	2	0	1	8	16	2	.275	.456	.373	121	3	3	11	4			.862	-1	O	0.1
Total	10	705	2465	508	694	104	50	29	213	417	79	.282	.391	.400	137	138	129	468	152			.875	-22	OP/12	2.6
■ **PAUL CASANOVA** Casanova, Paulino (Ortiz) b: 12/21/41, Colon, Matanzas, Cuba BR/TR, 6'4", 200 lbs. Deb: 9/18/65																									
1965	Was-A	5	13	2	4	1	0	0	1	1	3	.308	.357	.385	112	0	0	2	0	0	0	.938	-2	/C	-0.2
1966	Was-A	122	429	45	109	16	5	13	44	14	78	.254	.279	.406	95	-5	-4	46	1	2	-1	.981	-10	*C	-0.8
1967	Was-A☆	141	528	47	131	19	1	9	53	17	65	.248	.274	.339	84	-14	-12	44	1	1	-0	.984	-5	*C	-1.0
1968	Was-A	96	322	19	63	6	0	4	25	7	52	.196	.213	.252	42	-24	-23	16	0	1	-1	.989	-9	C	-3.1
1969	Was-A	124	379	26	82	9	2	4	37	18	52	.216	.257	.282	54	-25	-23	26	0	0	0	.992	-6	*C	-2.4
1970	Was-A	104	328	25	75	17	3	6	30	10	47	.229	.254	.354	69	-16	-15	28	0	0	0	.988	-1	*C	-1.1
1971	Was-A	94	311	19	63	9	1	5	26	14	52	.203	.239	.286	51	-22	-20	19	0	3	-2	.985	-4	C	-2.5
1972	Atl-N	49	136	8	28	3	0	2	10	4	28	.206	.229	.272	38	-11	-12	6	0	1	-1	.975	-6	C	-1.9
1973	Atl-N	82	236	18	51	7	0	7	18	11	36	.216	.254	.335	58	-13	-15	18	0	2	-1	.977	6	C	-0.8
1974	Atl-N	42	104	5	21	0	0	0	8	5	17	.202	.239	.202	23	-10	-11	5	0	0	0	.986	-1	C	-1.1
Total	10	859	2786	214	627	87	12	50	252	101	430	.225	.254	.319	64	-140	-134	210	2	10	-5	.985	-38	C	-14.9
■ **GEORGE CASE** Case, George Washington b: 11/11/15, Trenton, N.J. d: 1/23/89, Trenton, N.J. BR/TR, 6', 183 lbs. Deb: 9/08/37 C																									
1937	Was-A	22	90	14	26	6	2	0	11	3	5	.289	.312	.400	82	-3	-3	11	2	1	0	.945	-0	O	-0.4
1938	Was-A	107	433	69	132	27	3	2	40	39	28	.305	.362	.395	96	-7	-2	63	11	6	-0	.964	-4	*O	-0.9
1939	Was-A☆	128	530	103	160	20	7	2	35	56	36	.302	.369	.377	98	-6	0	80	**51**	17	**5**	.955	3	*O	0.3
1940	Was-A	154	656	109	192	29	5	5	56	52	39	.293	.349	.375	94	-11	-5	94	**35**	10	**5**	.970	1	*O	-0.7
1941	Was-A	153	649	95	176	32	8	2	53	51	37	.271	.325	.354	84	-19	-15	82	**33**	9	**5**	.975	15	*O	-0.5
1942	Was-A	125	513	101	164	26	2	5	43	44	30	.320	.377	.407	122	14	15	88	**44**	6	**10**	.951	-2	*O	1.7
1943	Was-A★	141	613	**102**	180	36	5	1	52	41	27	.294	.341	.374	113	6	8	88	**61**	14	**10**	.985	1	*O	1.3
1944	Was-A†	119	464	63	116	14	2	2	32	49	22	.250	.326	.302	83	-11	-9	50	49	18	4	.970	6	*O	-0.5
1945	Was-A†	123	504	72	148	19	5	1	31	49	27	.294	.360	.357	118	6	11	68	30	16	-1	.979	13	*O	1.7
1946	Cle-A	118	484	46	109	23	4	1	22	34	38	.225	.280	.295	65	-26	-22	43	**28**	11	**2**	.983	-4	*O	-3.2
1947	Was-A	36	80	11	12	1	0	0	2	8	8	.150	.227	.162	10	-10	-9	4	5	1	1	.963	0	O	-1.0
Total	11	1226	5016	785	1415	233	43	21	377	426	297	.282	.341	.358	95	-67	-32	670	349	109	39	.970	30	*O	-2.2
■ **DENNIS CASEY** Casey, Dennis Patrick b: 3/30/1858, Binghamton, N.Y. d: 1/19/09, Binghamton, N.Y. BL/TR, 5'9", 164 lbs. Deb: 8/18/1884 F																									
1884	Wil-U	2	8	1	2	1	0	0		0		.250	.250	.375	106	0	0	1				1.000	-0	/O	0.0
	Bal-a	37	149	20	37	7	4	3		5		.248	.273	.409	118	3	2	17				.898	-1	O	0.1
1885	Bal-a	63	264	50	76	10	5	3		21		.288	.347	.398	140	12	12	37				.821	-5	O	0.5
Total	2	102	421	71	115	18	9	6		26		.273	.320	.401	132	15	15	55				.847	-6	O	0.6
■ **DOC CASEY** Casey, James Patrick b: 3/15/1870, Lawrence, Mass. d: 12/31/36, Detroit, Mich. BB/TR, 5'6", 157 lbs. Deb: 9/14/1898																									
1898	Was-N	28	112	13	31	2	0	0	15	3		.277	.302	.295	71	-4	-4	15	15			.893	-3	3/SC	-0.6
1899	Was-N	9	34	3	4	2	0	0	2	2		.118	.167	.176	-6	-5	-5	1	1			.853	-1	/3	-0.5
	Bro-N	134	525	75	141	14	8	1	43	25		.269	.313	.331	75	-17	-19	65	27			.892	-19	*3	-3.3
	Yr	143	559	78	145	16	8	1	45	27		.259	.304	.322	70	-22	-24	66	28			.889	-19	*3	-3.8
1900	Bro-N	1	3	0	1	0	0	0	1	0		.333	.500	.333	125	0	0	1	0			1.000	0	/3	0.0

YEAR	TM/L	G	AB	R	H	2B	3B	HR	RBI	BB	SO	AVG	OBP	SLG	PRO+	BR	/A	RC	SB	CS	SBR	FA	FR	POS	TPR
1901	Det-A	128	540	105	153	16	9	2	46	32		.283	.335	.357	88	-6	-9	79	34			.887	5	*3	-0.3
1902	Det-A	132	520	69	142	18	7	3	55	44		.273	.338	.352	90	-5	-7	72	22			.904	1	*3	-0.4
1903	Chi-N	112	435	56	126	8	3	1	40	19		.290	.324	.329	89	-8	-6	54	11			.915	-19	*3	-2.3
1904	Chi-N	136	548	71	147	20	4	1	43	18		.268	.300	.325	93	-5	-5	64	21			.911	-10	*3/C	-1.2
1905	Chi-N	144	526	66	122	21	10	1	56	41		.232	.295	.316	79	-12	-14	59	22			**.949**	-9	*3/S	-1.9
1906	Bro-N	149	571	71	133	17	8	0	34	52		.233	.303	.291	93	-9	-4	61	22			.919	-17	*3	-1.8
1907	Bro-N	141	527	55	122	19	3	0	19	34		.231	.281	.279	82	-15	-11	51	16			.955	-6	*3	-1.5
Total	10	1114	4341	584	1122	137	52	9	354	270		.258	.310	.320	85	-87	-85	521	191			.915	-76	*3/CS	-13.8

■ JOE CASEY

Casey, Joseph Felix b: 8/15/1887, Boston, Mass. d: 6/2/66, Melrose, Mass. BR/TR, 5'9", 180 lbs. Deb: 10/01/09

YEAR	TM/L	G	AB	R	H	2B	3B	HR	RBI	BB	SO	AVG	OBP	SLG	PRO+	BR	/A	RC	SB	CS	SBR	FA	FR	POS	TPR
1909	Det-A	3	5	1	0	0	0	0	0	1		.000	.167	.000	-45	-1	-1	0	0			1.000	2	/C	0.1
1910	Det-A	23	62	3	12	3	0	0	2	2		.194	.231	.242	45	-4	-4	4	1			.964	6	C	0.4
1911	Det-A	15	33	2	5	0	0	0	3	3		.152	.222	.152	5	-4	-4	1	0			.956	-3	C/O	-0.7
1918	Was-A	9	17	3	4	0	0	0	2	2	2	.235	.316	.235	68	-1	-1	1	0			1.000	2	/C	0.2
Total	4	50	117	9	21	3	0	0	7	8	2	.179	.238	.205	32	-9	-10	6	1			.970	6	/CO	0.0

■ BOB CASEY

Casey, Orrin Robinson b: 1/26/1859, Adolphustown, Ontario, Canada 5'11", 190 lbs. Deb: 7/17/1882

YEAR	TM/L	G	AB	R	H	2B	3B	HR	RBI	BB	SO	AVG	OBP	SLG	PRO+	BR	/A	RC	SB	CS	SBR	FA	FR	POS	TPR
1882	Det-N	9	39	5	9	2	1	1	7	0	15	.231	.231	.410	101	-0	-0	4				.667	-5	/32	-0.4

■ DAVE CASH

Cash, David b: 6/11/48, Utica, N.Y. BR/TR, 5'11", 175 lbs. Deb: 9/13/69

YEAR	TM/L	G	AB	R	H	2B	3B	HR	RBI	BB	SO	AVG	OBP	SLG	PRO+	BR	/A	RC	SB	CS	SBR	FA	FR	POS	TPR
1969	Pit-N	18	61	8	17	3	1	0	4	9	9	.279	.371	.361	108	1	1	9	2	0	1	.990	5	2	0.8
1970	*Pit-N	64	210	30	66	7	6	1	28	17	25	.314	.368	.419	113	3	4	30	5	2	0	.974	6	2	1.4
1971	*Pit-N	123	478	79	138	17	4	2	34	46	33	.289	.351	.354	101	1	1	61	13	5	1	.987	6	*23/S	1.7
1972	*Pit-N	99	425	58	120	22	4	3	30	22	31	.282	.318	.374	98	-3	-2	48	9	9	-3	.992	28	2	3.0
1973	Pit-N	116	436	59	118	21	2	2	31	38	36	.271	.329	.342	88	-8	-6	49	2	5	-2	.979	6	23	0.2
1974	Phi-N★	162	687	89	206	26	11	2	58	46	33	.300	.352	.378	100	4	1	93	20	8	1	.977	**29**	*2	4.0
1975	Phi-N★	162	699	111	**213**	40	3	4	57	56	34	.305	.360	.388	103	7	4	100	13	6	0	.981	9	*2	2.3
1976	*Phi-N★	160	666	92	189	14	**12**	1	56	54	13	.284	.339	.345	92	-4	-6	75	10	12	-4	**.988**	-2	*2	-0.2
1977	Mon-N	153	650	91	188	42	7	0	43	52	33	.289	.344	.375	96	-6	-4	82	21	12	-1	.986	-11	*2	-0.5
1978	Mon-N	159	658	66	166	26	3	3	43	37	29	.252	.292	.315	70	-27	-26	58	12	6	0	**.986**	-30	*2	-4.8
1979	Mon-N	76	187	24	60	11	1	2	19	12	12	.321	.362	.422	114	3	4	27	7	4	-0	.971	-6	2	0.0
1980	SD-N	130	397	25	90	14	2	1	23	35	21	.227	.289	.280	63	-21	-18	30	6	5	-1	.987	4	*2	-1.0
Total	12	1422	5554	732	1571	243	56	21	426	424	309	.283	.336	.358	93	-50	-49	661	120	74	-8	.984	43	*2/3S	6.9

■ NORM CASH

Cash, Norman Dalton b: 11/10/34, Justiceburg, Tex. d: 10/12/86, Beaver Island, Mich. BL/TL, 6', 190 lbs. Deb: 6/18/58

YEAR	TM/L	G	AB	R	H	2B	3B	HR	RBI	BB	SO	AVG	OBP	SLG	PRO+	BR	/A	RC	SB	CS	SBR	FA	FR	POS	TPR
1958	Chi-A	13	8	2	2	0	0	0	0	0	1	.250	.250	.250	39	-1	-1	1	0	0	0	1.000	-1	/O	-0.2
1959	*Chi-A	58	104	16	25	0	1	4	16	18	9	.240	.378	.375	109	2	2	17	1	1	-0	.984	-1	1	-0.1
1960	Det-A	121	353	64	101	16	3	18	63	65	58	.286	.406	.501	140	24	22	79	4	2	0	.991	-2	1/O	1.3
1961	Det-A★	159	535	119	**193**	22	8	41	132	124	85	**.361**	**.488**	.662	198	**86**	**84**	**178**	11	5	0	.992	5	*1	7.3
1962	Det-A	148	507	94	123	16	2	39	89	104	82	.243	.385	.513	134	30	28	104	6	3	0	.992	7	*1/O	2.5
1963	Det-A	147	493	67	133	19	1	26	79	89	76	.270	.388	.471	135	29	27	94	2	3	-1	.994	2	*1	2.2
1964	Det-A	144	479	63	123	15	5	23	83	70	66	.257	.355	.453	121	16	15	78	2	1	0	**.997**	4	*1	1.3
1965	Det-A	142	467	79	124	23	1	30	82	77	62	.266	.374	.512	147	31	30	91	6	6	-2	.992	5	*1	2.8
1966	Det-A★	160	603	98	168	18	3	32	93	66	91	.279	.354	.478	133	28	27	101	2	1	0	.988	4	*1	2.1
1967	Det-A	152	488	64	118	16	5	22	72	81	100	.242	.354	.430	127	20	19	78	3	2	-0	**.995**	9	*1	2.1
1968	*Det-A	127	411	50	108	15	1	25	63	39	70	.263	.331	.487	141	21	20	63	1	1	-0	.992	9	*1	2.3
1969	Det-A	142	483	81	135	15	4	22	74	63	80	.280	.370	.464	126	21	18	85	2	1	0	.994	6	*1	1.4
1970	Det-A	130	370	58	96	18	2	15	53	72	58	.259	.387	.441	127	16	16	64	0	1	-1	.989	2	*1	0.8
1971	Det-A★	135	452	72	128	10	3	32	91	59	86	.283	.375	.531	148	32	30	93	1	0	0	.992	-0	*1	1.9
1972	*Det-A★	137	440	51	114	16	0	22	61	50	64	.259	.340	.445	128	17	16	66	0	2	-1	.993	-0	*1	0.4
1973	Det-A	121	363	51	95	19	0	19	40	47	73	.262	.359	.471	124	16	12	63	1	0	0	.991	2	*1/D	0.7
1974	Det-A	53	149	17	34	3	2	7	12	19	30	.228	.327	.416	109	2	2	21	1	1	-0	.985	-1	1	-0.2
Total	17	2089	6705	1046	1820	241	41	377	1103	1043	1091	.271	.377	.488	138	390	366	1278	43	30	-5	.992	50	*1/OD	28.6

■ RON CASH

Cash, Ronald Forrest b: 11/20/49, Atlanta, Ga. BR/TR, 6', 180 lbs. Deb: 9/04/73

YEAR	TM/L	G	AB	R	H	2B	3B	HR	RBI	BB	SO	AVG	OBP	SLG	PRO+	BR	/A	RC	SB	CS	SBR	FA	FR	POS	TPR
1973	Det-A	14	39	8	16	1	1	0	6	5	5	.410	.477	.487	161	4	4	9	0	0	0	.900	-2	/O3	0.2
1974	Det-A	20	62	6	14	2	0	0	5	0	11	.226	.226	.258	38	-5	-5	3	0	1	-1	.979	-1	1/3	-0.9
Total	2	34	101	14	30	3	1	0	11	5	16	.297	.330	.347	89	-1	-1	12	0	1	-1	.950	-3	/13O	-0.7

■ ED CASKIN

Caskin, Edward James b: 12/30/1851, Danvers, Mass. d: 10/9/24, Danvers, Mass. BR/TR, 5'9.5", 165 lbs. Deb: 5/01/1879

YEAR	TM/L	G	AB	R	H	2B	3B	HR	RBI	BB	SO	AVG	OBP	SLG	PRO+	BR	/A	RC	SB	CS	SBR	FA	FR	POS	TPR
1879	Tro-N	70	304	32	78	13	2	0	21	2	14	.257	.261	.313	95	-4	-1	25				.902	6	SC/2	0.8
1880	Tro-N	82	333	36	75	5	4	0	28	7	24	.225	.241	.264	68	-10	-12	22				.885	7	*S/C	0.0
1881	Tro-N	63	234	33	53	7	1	0	21	13	29	.226	.267	.265	65	-8	-10	17				.906	1	*S	-0.5
1883	NY-N	95	383	47	91	11	2	1	40	14	25	.238	.264	.285	68	-15	-14	30				.855	-5	*S2/C	-1.5
1884	NY-N	100	351	49	81	11	1	1	40	34	55	.231	.299	.276	80	-6	-7	30				.883	5	*S/C	-0.1
1885	StL-N	71	262	31	47	3	0	0	12	12	22	.179	.215	.191	34	-19	-17	11				.884	-4	3/CS	-1.8
1886	NY-N	1	4	1	2	0	0	0	1	0	1	.500	.500	.500	203	0	0	1	0			1.000	-1	/S	0.0
Total	7	482	1871	229	427	50	10	2	163	82	170	.228	.261	.269	70	-61	-61	136	0			.883	9	S/3C2	-3.1

■ HARRY CASSADY

Cassady, Harry Delbert (b: Harry Delbert Cassaday)
b: 7/20/1880, Belleflower, Ill. d: 4/19/69, Fresno, Cal. BL/TL, 5'8", 145 lbs. Deb: 8/08/04

YEAR	TM/L	G	AB	R	H	2B	3B	HR	RBI	BB	SO	AVG	OBP	SLG	PRO+	BR	/A	RC	SB	CS	SBR	FA	FR	POS	TPR
1904	Pit-N	12	44	8	9	0	0	0	3	2		.205	.239	.205	37	-3	-3	3	2			.867	-1	O	-0.5
1905	Was-A	10	30	1	4	0	0	0	1	0		.133	.133	.133	-16	-4	-4	1	0			1.000	0	/O	-0.4
Total	2	22	74	9	13	0	0	0	4	2		.176	.197	.176	17	-7	-7	3	2			.933	-1	/O	-0.9

■ JOHN CASSIDY

Cassidy, John P. b: 1857, Brooklyn, N.Y. d: 7/2/1891, Brooklyn, N.Y. BR/TL, 5'8", 168 lbs. Deb: 4/24/1875

YEAR	TM/L	G	AB	R	H	2B	3B	HR	RBI	BB	SO	AVG	OBP	SLG	PRO+	BR	/A	RC	SB	CS	SBR	FA	FR	POS	TPR
1875	Atl-n	41	165	14	29	3	2	1		1		.176	.181	.236	49	-9	-6	7						PO/1	0.1
	NH-n	6	22	3	3	1	0	0		0		.136	.136	.182	10	-2	-1	1						/1	-0.1
	Yr	47	187	17	32	4	2	1		1		.171	.176	.230	45	-11	-7	8						P1O	0.0
1876	Har-N	12	47	6	13	2	0	0	8	1	0	.277	.292	.319	95	0	-0	4				1.000	1	/O1	0.0
1877	Har-N	60	251	43	95	10	5	0	27	3	3	.378	.386	.458	184	18	22	45				.722	-5	*O/P	1.3
1878	Chi-N	60	256	33	68	7	1	0	29	9	11	.266	.291	.301	89	-1	-4	23				.810	8	*O/C	0.2
1879	Tro-N	9	37	4	7	1	0	0	1	2	4	.189	.231	.216	52	-2	-2	2				.889	-2	/O1	-0.4
1880	Tro-N	83	352	40	89	14	8	0	29	12	34	.253	.277	.338	102	3	0	34				.880	-2	*O/2	-0.3
1881	Tro-N	85	370	57	82	13	3	1	11	18	21	.222	.258	.281	66	-12	-15	27				.872	-9	*O/S	-2.5
1882	Tro-N	29	121	14	21	3	1	0	9	3	16	.174	.194	.215	32	-9	-8	5				.778	-9	O3	-1.6
1883	Pro-N	89	366	46	87	16	5	0	42	9	38	.238	.256	.309	69	-13	-14	30				.864	1	*O/21	-1.2
1884	Bro-a	106	433	57	109	11	6	2		19		.252	.286	.319	99	0	-0	41				.847	-8	*O/3S	-0.9
1885	Bro-a	54	221	36	47	6	2	1		8		.213	.250	.271	66	-8	-8	15				.852	-7	O	-1.5
Total	10	587	2454	336	618	83	31	4	156	84	127	.252	.278	.316	89	-25	-30	227				.845	-31	O/31S2PC	-6.9

■ JOE CASSIDY

Cassidy, Joseph Phillip b: 2/8/1883, Chester, Pa. d: 3/25/06, Chester, Pa. BR/TR, Deb: 4/18/04

YEAR	TM/L	G	AB	R	H	2B	3B	HR	RBI	BB	SO	AVG	OBP	SLG	PRO+	BR	/A	RC	SB	CS	SBR	FA	FR	POS	TPR
1904	Was-A	152	581	63	140	12	**19**	1	33	15		.241	.265	.332	90	-9	-8	59	17			.937	12	SO3	0.6
1905	Was-A	151	576	67	124	16	4	1	43	25		.215	.250	.262	65	-25	-22	47	23			.934	**33**	*S	1.5
Total	2	303	1157	130	264	28	23	2	76	40		.228	.258	.297	78	-34	-31	106	40			.935	45	S/O3	2.1

YEAR	TM/L	G	AB	R	H	2B	3B	HR	RBI	BB	SO	AVG	OBP	SLG	PRO+	BR	/A	RC	SB	CS	SBR	FA	FR	POS	TPR

■ PETE CASSIDY Cassidy, Peter Francis b: 4/8/1873, Wilmington, Del. d: 7/9/29, Wilmington, Del. BR/TR, 5'10", 165 lbs. Deb: 4/18/1896

1896	Lou-N	49	184	16	39	1	1	0	12	7	7	.212	.256	.228	31	-18	-17	13	5			.973	-7	1S	-2.0
1899	Bro-N	6	20	2	3	1	0	0	4	1		.150	.261	.200	27	-2	-2	1	1			1.000	-4	/3S	-0.6
	Was-N	46	178	21	56	13	0	3	32	9		.315	.361	.438	120	4	4	31	5			.970	-2	1/3S	0.3
	Yr	52	198	23	59	14	0	3	36	10		.298	.350	.414	110	2	2	32	6			.970	-6	1/3S	-0.3
Total	2	101	382	39	98	15	1	3	48	17	7	.257	.306	.325	72	-16	-15	45	11			.972	-13	/1S3	-2.3

■ JACK CASSINI Cassini, Jack Dempsey "Gabby" or "Scat" b: 10/26/19, Dearborn, Mich. BR/TR, 5'10", 175 lbs. Deb: 4/19/49

| 1949 | Pit-N | 8 | 0 | 3 | 0 | 0 | 0 | 0 | 0 | 0 | 0 | — | — | — | — | 0 | 0 | 0 | 0 | | | .000 | 0 | R | 0.0 |

■ JIM CASTIGLIA Castiglia, James Vincent b: 9/30/18, Passaic, N.J. BL/TR, 5'11", 200 lbs. Deb: 4/14/42

| 1942 | Phi-A | 16 | 18 | 2 | 7 | 0 | 0 | 0 | 2 | 1 | 3 | .389 | .421 | .389 | 129 | 1 | 1 | 3 | 0 | 0 | 0 | .875 | -1 | /C | 0.0 |

■ PETE CASTIGLIONE Castiglione, Peter Paul b: 2/13/21, Greenwich, Conn. BR/TR, 5'11", 175 lbs. Deb: 9/10/47

1947	Pit-N	13	50	6	14	0	0	0	1	2	5	.280	.308	.280	55	-3	-3	4	0			.970	1	S	-0.2
1948	Pit-N	4	0	0	0	0	0	0	0	0	0	.000	.000	.000	-98	-1	-1	0	1			1.000	1	/S	0.0
1949	Pit-N	118	448	57	120	20	2	6	43	20	43	.268	.299	.362	74	-16	-17	49	2			.957	-1	3S/O	-2.0
1950	Pit-N	94	263	29	67	10	3	3	22	23	23	.255	.317	.350	73	-9	-11	29	1			.970	-17	3S/21	-2.6
1951	Pit-N	132	482	62	126	19	4	7	42	34	28	.261	.311	.361	78	-14	-16	55	2	2	-1	.957	4	3S	-1.2
1952	Pit-N	67	214	27	57	9	1	4	18	17	8	.266	.323	.374	90	-2	-3	27	3	3	-1	.951	6	3/1O	0.1
1953	Pit-N	45	159	14	33	2	1	4	21	5	14	.208	.236	.308	41	-14	-14	11	1	1	-0	.978	4	3	-1.1
	StL-N	67	52	9	9	2	0	0	3	2	5	.173	.204	.212	9	-7	-7	2	0	0	-0	.967	8	3/2S	0.1
	Yr	112	211	23	42	4	1	4	24	7	19	.199	.228	.284	33	-21	-21	13	1	1	-0	.976	12	3/2S	-1.0
1954	StL-N	5	0	1	0	0	0	0	0	0	0					0	0	0	0			1.000	0	/3	0.0
Total	8	545	1670	205	426	62	11	24	150	103	126	.255	.300	.349	71	-66	-71	178	10	6		.960	4	3/S210	-6.9

■ VINNY CASTILLA Castilla, Vinicio (Soria) b: 7/4/67, Oaxaca, Mexico BR/TR, 6'1", 175 lbs. Deb: 9/01/91

1991	Atl-N	12	5	1	1	0	0	0	0	0	2	.200	.200	.200	12	-1	-1	0	0	0	0	1.000	1	S	0.1
1992	Atl-N	9	16	1	4	1	0	0	1	1	4	.250	.333	.313	77	-0	-0	2	0	0	0	.875	0	/3S	0.0
Total	2	21	21	2	5	1	0	0	1	1	6	.238	.304	.286	63	-1	-1	2	0	0	0	1.000	2	/S3	0.1

■ TONY CASTILLO Castillo, Anthony b: 6/14/57, San Jose, Cal. BR/TR, 6'4", 190 lbs. Deb: 9/22/78

| 1978 | SD-N | 5 | 8 | 0 | 1 | 0 | 0 | 0 | 1 | 0 | 2 | .125 | .125 | .125 | -33 | -1 | -1 | 0 | 0 | 0 | 0 | .950 | 1 | /C | 0.0 |

■ BRAULIO CASTILLO Castillo, Braulio Robinson Medrano (b: Braulio Robinson Medrano (Castillo))
 b: 5/13/68, Elias Pina, D.R. BR/TR, 6', 160 lbs. Deb: 8/18/91

1991	Phi-N	28	52	3	9	3	0	2	1	1	15	.173	.189	.231	18	-6	-6	2	1	1	-0	.977	-2	O	-0.8
1992	Phi-N	28	76	12	15	3	1	2	7	4	15	.197	.237	.342	63	-4	-4	6	1	0	0	.956	-2	O	-0.6
Total	2	56	128	15	24	6	1	2	9	5	30	.188	.218	.297	44	-10	-10	8	2	1	0	.966	-4	/O	-1.4

■ MANNY CASTILLO Castillo, Esteban Manuel Antonio (Cabrera) b: 4/1/57, Santo Domingo, D.R. BB/TR, 5'9", 160 lbs. Deb: 9/01/80

1980	KC-A	7	10	1	2	0	0	0	0	0	0	.200	.200	.200	10	-1	-1	0	0	0	0	1.000	2	/32D	0.0
1982	Sea-A	138	506	49	130	29	1	3	49	22	35	.257	.291	.336	70	-20	-22	46	2	8	-4	.938	-24	*3/2	-5.4
1983	Sea-A	91	203	13	42	6	3	0	24	7	20	.207	.237	.266	37	-17	-18	12	1	1	-0	.971	8	31/2PD	-1.1
Total	3	236	719	63	174	35	4	3	73	29	55	.242	.274	.314	59	-38	-41	58	3	9	-5	.949	-15	3/21DP	-6.5

■ JUAN CASTILLO Castillo, Juan (Bryas) b: 1/25/62, San Pedro De Macoris, D.R. BB/TR, 5'11", 162 lbs. Deb: 4/12/86

1986	Mil-A	26	54	6	9	0	0	0	5	5	12	.167	.250	.204	24	-6	-6	3	1	1	-0	1.000	5	2/S3OD	-0.1
1987	Mil-A	116	321	44	72	11	4	3	28	33	76	.224	.303	.312	62	-17	-18	33	15	7	0	.973	-6	2S/3	-1.8
1988	Mil-A	54	90	10	20	0	0	0	2	3	14	.222	.247	.222	32	-8	-8	5	2	0	1	.932	7	23S/OD	-1.8
1989	Mil-A	3	4	0	0	0	0	0	3	0	2	.000	.000	.000	-99	-1	-1	0	0	0	0	1.000	1	/2	0.0
Total	4	199	469	60	101	11	5	3	38	41	104	.215	.284	.279	51	-31	-33	41	18	8	1	.972	6	2/S3DO	-1.9

■ MARTY CASTILLO Castillo, Martin Horace b: 1/16/57, Long Beach, Cal. BR/TR, 6'1", 190 lbs. Deb: 8/19/81

1981	Det-A	6	8	1	1	0	0	0	0	0	2	.125	.125	.125	-27	-1	-1	0	0	0	0	1.000	2	/3CO	0.1
1982	Det-A	5	0	0	0	0	0	0	0	0	0	—	—	—		0	0	0	0	0	0	1.000	-0	/C	0.0
1983	Det-A	67	119	10	23	4	0	2	10	7	22	.193	.238	.277	42	-10	-9	8	2	0	0	.990	4	3C	-0.5
1984	*Det-A	70	141	16	33	5	2	4	17	10	33	.234	.285	.383	83	-4	-3	15	1	0	0	.970	2	C3/D	-0.5
1985	Det-A	57	84	4	10	2	0	2	5	2	19	.119	.140	.214	-5	-12	-12	2	0	2	-0	.977	7	C3	-0.5
Total	5	201	352	31	67	11	2	8	32	19	76	.190	.232	.301	46	-27	-26	25	3	2	-0	.978	15	3/CDO	-0.9

■ CARMEN CASTILLO Castillo, Monte Carmelo b: 6/8/58, San Pedro De Macoris, D.R. BR/TR, 6'1", 190 lbs. Deb: 7/17/82

1982	Cle-A	47	120	11	25	4	0	2	11	6	17	.208	.258	.292	51	-8	-8	9	0	0	0	.978	-3	O/D	-1.2
1983	Cle-A	23	36	9	10	2	1	2	3	4	6	.278	.366	.472	124	1	1	6	1	1	0	.929	1	O/D	0.0
1984	Cle-A	87	211	36	55	9	2	10	36	21	32	.261	.333	.464	116	5	4	30	1	3	-2	.933	-6	O/D	-0.5
1985	Cle-A	67	184	27	45	5	1	11	25	11	40	.245	.298	.462	105	0	1	24	3	0	1	.953	-2	O/D	-0.2
1986	Cle-A	85	205	34	57	9	0	8	32	9	48	.278	.312	.439	103	-0	0	25	2	1	0	.939	-2	O/D	-0.2
1987	Cle-A	89	220	27	55	17	0	11	31	16	52	.250	.301	.477	101	-0	-0	33	1	1	-0	1.000	-1	DO	-0.2
1988	Cle-A	66	176	12	48	8	0	4	14	5	31	.273	.297	.386	87	-3	-3	19	6	2	1	.933	-6	O/D	-1.0
1989	Min-A	94	218	23	56	13	3	8	33	15	40	.257	.303	.454	105	3	1	29	1	2	0	.976	-3	DO	-0.5
1990	Min-A	64	137	11	30	4	0	0	12	3	23	.219	.241	.248	35	-12	-13	9	0	1	-1	.923	-5	DO	-1.9
1991	Min-A	9	12	0	2	1	0	0	0	0	2	.167	.231	.333	52	-1	-1	1	0	0	0	1.000	-1	/OD	-0.2
Total	10	631	1519	190	383	71	8	55	197	90	291	.252	.300	.418	93	-14	-18	184	15	11	-2	.953	-30	OD	-5.9

■ JOHN CASTINO Castino, John Anthony b: 10/23/54, Evanston, Ill. BR/TR, 5'11", 175 lbs. Deb: 4/06/79

1979	Min-A	148	393	49	112	13	8	5	52	27	72	.285	.333	.397	92	-3	-5	52	5	2	-0	.963	18	*3/S	1.2
1980	Min-A	150	546	67	165	17	7	13	64	29	67	.302	.337	.430	101	5	0	75	7	5	-1	.961	28	*3S	2.6
1981	Min-A	101	381	41	102	13	9	6	36	18	52	.268	.303	.396	94	-1	-4	45	4	5	-2	.975	11	3/2	0.4
1982	Min-A	117	410	48	99	12	6	6	37	36	51	.241	.306	.344	76	-12	-14	41	2	5	-2	.995	4	23/OD	-0.8
1983	Min-A	142	563	83	156	30	4	11	57	62	54	.277	.350	.403	103	3	3	81	0	0	0	.990	7	*2/3D	1.6
1984	Min-A	8	27	5	12	1	0	0	3	5	2	.444	.531	.481	174	4	3	6	0	0	0	1.000	-1	/3	0.2
Total	6	666	2320	293	646	86	34	41	249	177	298	.278	.331	.398	95	-1	-15	300	22	19	-5	.967	67	32/SOD	5.2

■ VINCE CASTINO Castino, Vincent Charles b: 10/11/17, Willisville, Ill. d: 3/6/67, Sacramento, Cal. BR/TR, 5'9", 175 lbs. Deb: 6/24/43

1943	Chi-A	33	101	14	23	1	0	2	16	12	11	.228	.310	.297	78	-3	-3	10	0	0		.971	-9	C	-1.1
1944	Chi-A	29	78	8	18	5	0	0	3	10	13	.231	.326	.295	79	-2	-2	8	0	1		.990	1	C	0.0
1945	Chi-A	26	36	2	8	1	0	0	4	3	7	.222	.282	.250	56	-2	-2	2	0	0		.951	-2	C	-0.4
Total	3	88	215	24	49	7	0	2	23	25	31	.228	.311	.288	75	-7	-6	20	0	1	-1	.976	-11	/C	-1.5

■ DON CASTLE Castle, Donald Hardy b: 2/1/50, Kokomo, Ind. BL/TL, 6'1", 205 lbs. Deb: 9/11/73

| 1973 | Tex-A | 4 | 13 | 0 | 4 | 1 | 0 | 0 | 2 | 1 | 3 | .308 | .357 | .385 | 114 | 0 | 0 | 1 | 0 | 0 | 0 | .000 | 0 | /D | 0.0 |

■ JOHN CASTLE Castle, John Francis b: 6/1/1883, Honey Brook, Pa. d: 4/13/29, Philadelphia, Pa. 5'10.5", Deb: 4/30/10

| 1910 | Phi-N | 3 | 4 | 1 | 1 | 0 | 0 | 0 | 0 | 0 | 0 | .250 | .250 | .250 | 44 | -0 | -0 | 0 | 1 | | | .000 | -1 | /O | -0.1 |

YEAR	TM/L	G	AB	R	H	2B	3B	HR	RBI	BB	SO	AVG	OBP	SLG	PRO+	BR	/A	RC	SB	CS	SBR	FA	FR	POS	TPR
■ FOSTER CASTLEMAN	Castleman, Foster Ephraim b: 1/1/31, Nashville, Tenn. BR/TR, 6', 175 lbs. Deb: 8/04/54																								
1954	NY-N	13	12	0	3	0	0	0	1	0	3	.250	.308	.250	47	-1	-1	1	0	0	0	.000	0	/3	-0.1
1955	NY-N	15	28	3	6	1	0	2	4	2	4	.214	.267	.464	89	-1	-1	4	0	0	0	1.000	-3	/23	-0.3
1956	NY-N	124	385	33	87	16	3	14	45	15	50	.226	.259	.392	72	-16	-16	37	2	1	0	.947	7	*3/S2	-0.8
1957	NY-N	18	37	7	6	2	0	1	1	2	8	.162	.205	.297	33	-4	-4	2	0	0	0	.867	-2	/32S	-0.6
1958	Bal-A	98	200	15	34	5	0	3	14	16	34	.170	.242	.240	35	-18	-17	12	2	0	1	.964	-19	S/23O	-3.1
Total	5	268	662	58	136	24	3	20	65	35	99	.205	.252	.341	60	-40	-38	55	4	1	1	.944	-17	3/S2O	-4.9
■ LOUIS CASTRO	Castro, Louis Manuel "Jud" b: 1877, Colombia, South America d: Venezuela BR/TR, 5'7", Deb: 4/23/02																								
1902	Phi-A	42	143	18	35	8	1	1	15	4		.245	.270	.336	64	-7	-8	14	2			.916	-16	2/OS	-2.2
■ DANNY CATER	Cater, Danny Anderson b: 2/25/40, Austin, Tex. BR/TR, 5'11.5", 180 lbs. Deb: 4/14/64																								
1964	Phi-N	60	152	13	45	9	1	1	13	7	15	.296	.327	.388	102	-0	0	18	1	0	0	.981	1	O/13	0.0
1965	Chi-A	142	514	74	139	18	4	14	55	33	65	.270	.318	.403	110	1	5	61	3	3	-1	.978	-9	*O3/1	-1.2
1966	Chi-A	21	60	3	11	1	1	0	4	0	10	.183	.197	.233	25	-6	-5	3	3	1	0	.909	-3	O	-1.0
	KC-A	116	425	47	124	16	3	7	52	28	37	.292	.337	.393	113	5	6	53	1	4	-2	.994	-5	13O	-0.7
	Yr	137	485	50	135	17	4	7	56	28	47	.278	.320	.373	102	-1	1	55	4	5	-2	.994	-8	13O	-1.7
1967	KC-A	142	529	55	143	17	4	4	46	34	56	.270	.319	.340	98	-3	-2	54	4	5	-2	.916	-15	3O1	-2.6
1968	Oak-A	147	504	53	146	28	3	6	62	35	43	.290	.338	.393	127	12	14	61	8	7	-2	**.995**	-4	*1O/2	-0.1
1969	Oak-A	152	584	64	153	24	2	10	76	28	40	.262	.298	.361	87	-14	-11	55	1	4	-2	.992	6	*1O/2	-1.9
1970	NY-A	155	582	64	175	26	5	6	76	34	44	.301	.341	.393	108	1	5	74	4	2	0	.992	-4	*13/O	-1.0
1971	NY-A	121	428	39	118	16	5	4	50	19	25	.276	.310	.364	96	-6	-4	42	0	3	-2	.995	8	13	-0.4
1972	Bos-A	92	317	32	75	17	1	8	39	15	33	.237	.275	.372	87	-5	-6	28	0	1	-1	.993	6	1	-1.0
1973	Bos-A	63	195	30	61	12	0	1	24	10	22	.313	.350	.390	102	2	0	25	0	0	0	.997	1	13/D	-0.1
1974	Bos-A	56	126	14	31	5	0	5	20	10	13	.246	.312	.405	98	1	-1	15	1	0	0	1.000	1	1D	0.0
1975	StL-N	22	35	3	8	2	0	0	2	1	3	.229	.250	.286	47	-3	-3	3	0	0	0	.981	0	1	-0.3
Total	12	1289	4451	491	1229	191	29	66	519	254	406	.276	.318	.377	102	-16	-1	492	26	30	-10	.994	-18	1O3/D2	-10.3
■ ELI CATES	Cates, Eli Eldo b: 1/26/1877, Greensfork, Ind. d: 5/29/64, Richmond, Ind. BR/TR, 5'9.5", 175 lbs. Deb: 4/20/08																								
1908	Was-A	40	59	5	11	1	1	0	3	6		.186	.273	.237	72	-2	-1	4	0			.907	-0	P/2	-0.1
■ TED CATHER	Cather, Theodore P b: 5/20/1889, Chester, Pa. d: 4/9/45, Elkton, Md. BR/TR, 5'10.5", 178 lbs. Deb: 9/23/12																								
1912	StL-N	5	19	4	8	1	1	0	2	0	4	.421	.421	.579	176	2	2	5	1			.944	2	/O	0.3
1913	StL-N	67	183	16	39	8	4	0	12	9	24	.213	.250	.301	58	-11	-10	15	7			.915	-7	O/P1	-2.0
1914	StL-N	39	99	11	27	7	0	0	13	3	15	.273	.294	.343	90	-2	-2	11	4			.981	0	O	-0.3
	*Bos-N	50	145	19	43	11	2	0	27	7	28	.297	.338	.400	120	3	3	21	7			.953	-9	O	-0.8
	Yr	89	244	30	70	18	2	0	40	10	43	.287	.320	.377	108	1	1	32	11			.966	-9	O	-1.1
1915	Bos-N	40	102	10	21	3	1	2	18	15	19	.206	.319	.314	96	-1	-0	11	2	4	-2	.902	-7	O	-1.2
Total	4	201	548	60	138	30	8	2	72	34	90	.252	.300	.347	91	-8	-7	62	21	4		.938	-21	O/1P	-4.0
■ HOWDY CATON	Caton, James Howard "Buster" b: 7/16/1896, Zanesville, Ohio d: 1/8/48, Zanesville, Ohio BR/TR, 5'6", 165 lbs. Deb: 9/17/17																								
1917	Pit-N	14	57	6	12	1	2	0	4	6	7	.211	.286	.298	77	-1	-2	5	0			.895	-2	S	-0.4
1918	Pit-N	80	303	37	71	5	7	0	17	32	16	.234	.312	.297	83	-4	-6	31	12			.928	-7	S	-1.0
1919	Pit-N	39	102	13	18	1	2	0	5	12	10	.176	.263	.225	46	-6	-7	7	2			.927	-11	S3/O	-1.9
1920	Pit-N	98	352	29	83	11	5	0	27	33	19	.236	.305	.295	71	-12	-13	32	4	9	-4	.929	-22	S	-3.4
Total	4	231	814	85	184	18	16	0	53	83	52	.226	.301	.287	72	-24	-27	74	18	9		.926	-43	S/3O	-6.7
■ TOM CATTERSON	Catterson, Thomas Henry b: 8/25/1884, Warwick, R.I. d: 2/5/20, Portland, Maine BL/TL, 5'10", 170 lbs. Deb: 9/19/08																								
1908	Bro-N	19	68	5	13	1	1	1	2	5		.191	.257	.279	74	-2	-2	5	0			.976	0	O	-0.3
1909	Bro-N	9	18	0	4	0	0	0	1	3		.222	.333	.222	75	-0	-0	1	0			.833	-2	/O	-0.3
Total	2	28	86	5	17	1	1	1	3	8		.198	.274	.267	75	-3	-2	6	0			.957	-2	/O	-0.6
■ JAKE CAULFIELD	Caulfield, John Joseph b: 11/23/17, Los Angles, Cal. d: 12/16/86, San Francisco, Cal BR/TR, 5'11", 170 lbs. Deb: 4/24/46																								
1946	Phi-A	44	94	13	26	8	0	0	10	4	11	.277	.306	.362	87	-2	-2	10	0	0	0	.929	-6	S/3	-0.7
■ WAYNE CAUSEY	Causey, James Wayne b: 12/26/36, Ruston, La. BL/TR, 5'10.5", 175 lbs. Deb: 6/05/55																								
1955	Bal-A	68	175	14	34	2	1	1	9	17	25	.194	.269	.234	39	-16	-14	12	0	1	-1	.912	-8	3/2S	-2.3
1956	Bal-A	53	88	7	15	0	1	1	4	8	23	.170	.240	.227	26	-10	-9	5	0	0	0	.980	2	3/2	-0.6
1957	Bal-A	14	10	2	2	0	0	0	1	5	2	.200	.500	.200	105	1	1	2	0	0	0	.960	3	/23	0.4
1961	KC-A	104	312	37	86	14	1	8	49	37	28	.276	.352	.404	101	1	1	46	0	0	0	.955	20	3S/2	2.2
1962	KC-A	117	305	40	77	14	1	4	38	41	30	.252	.345	.344	84	-5	-6	38	2	0	1	.953	2	S3/2	0.1
1963	KC-A	139	554	72	155	32	4	8	44	56	54	.280	.346	.395	103	6	3	77	4	2	0	.978	5	*S/3	1.8
1964	KC-A	157	604	82	170	31	4	8	49	88	65	.281	.379	.386	110	14	12	90	0	1	-1	.967	-1	*S2/3	2.2
1965	KC-A	144	513	48	134	17	8	3	34	61	48	.261	.342	.343	97	-2	-1	63	1	3	-2	.972	-19	S23	-1.5
1966	KC-A	28	79	1	18	0	0	0	5	7	6	.228	.291	.228	53	-5	-4	5	1	0	0	.871	-6	3S	-1.0
	Chi-A	78	164	23	40	8	2	0	13	24	13	.244	.340	.317	97	-1	0	20	2	0	1	.980	-16	2/S3	-1.3
	Yr	106	243	24	58	8	2	0	18	31	19	.239	.325	.288	83	-6	-4	25	3	0	1	.980	-21	23S	-2.3
1967	Chi-A	124	292	21	66	10	3	1	28	32	35	.226	.305	.291	80	-8	-7	27	2	5	-2	.978	-8	2/S	-1.3
1968	Chi-A	59	100	8	18	2	0	0	7	14	7	.180	.287	.200	49	-6	-6	7	0	0	0	.971	-13	2	-2.0
	Cal-A	4	11	0	0	0	0	0	0	0	1	.000	.000	.000	-99	-3	-3	0	0	0	0	1.000	1	/2	-0.2
	Yr	63	111	8	18	2	0	0	7	14	8	.162	.262	.180	36	-8	-8	6	0	0	0	.975	-13	2	-2.2
	Atl-N	16	37	2	4	0	1	1	4	0	4	.108	.108	.243	3	-4	-4	1	0	0	0	1.000	-4	/2S3	-1.0
Total	11	1105	3244	357	819	130	26	35	285	390	341	.252	.335	.341	90	-37	-37	394	12	12	-4	.969	-42	S23	-4.5
■ JOHN CAVANAUGH	Cavanaugh, John J. b: 6/5/1900, Scranton, Pa. d: 1/14/61, New Brunswick, N.J BR/TR, 5'9", 158 lbs. Deb: 7/07/19																								
1919	Phi-N	1	1	0	0	0	0	0	0	0	1	.000	.000	.000	-93	-0	-0	0	0			.000	0	/3	0.0
■ PHIL CAVARRETTA	Cavarretta, Philip Joseph b: 7/19/16, Chicago, Ill. BL/TL, 5'11.5", 175 lbs. Deb: 9/16/34 MC																								
1934	Chi-N	7	21	5	8	0	1	1	6	2	3	.381	.435	.619	182	2	2	6	1			1.000	1	/1	0.3
1935	*Chi-N	146	589	85	162	28	12	8	82	39	61	.275	.322	.404	93	-6	-6	79	4			.986	2	*1	-2.0
1936	Chi-N	124	458	55	125	18	1	9	56	17	36	.273	.306	.376	81	-12	-13	53	8			.987	-2	*1	-2.6
1937	Chi-N	106	329	43	94	18	7	5	56	32	35	.286	.349	.429	106	4	3	50	7			.972	-1	O1	-0.5
1938	*Chi-N	92	268	29	64	11	4	1	28	14	27	.239	.287	.321	65	-12	-13	25	4			.962	-7	O1	-2.5
1939	Chi-N	22	55	4	15	3	1	0	0	4	3	.273	.322	.364	82	-1	-1	6	2			.991	-1	1/O	-0.4
1940	Chi-N	65	193	34	54	11	4	2	22	31	18	.280	.388	.409	122	6	7	33	3			.991	-1	1	0.1
1941	Chi-N	107	346	46	99	18	4	6	40	53	28	.286	.384	.413	129	13	14	58	2			.992	-8	O1	0.0
1942	Chi-N	136	482	59	130	28	4	3	54	71	42	.270	.365	.363	118	10	12	71	7			.989	6	O1	1.2
1943	Chi-N	143	530	93	154	27	9	8	73	75	42	.291	.382	.421	134	23	24	89	3			.987	-11	*1/O	0.5
1944	Chi-N★	152	614	106	**197**	35	15	5	82	67	42	.321	.390	.451	137	30	31	111	4			.992	-7	*1O	1.6
1945	*Chi-N†	132	498	94	177	34	10	6	97	81	34	**.355**	**.449**	.500	167	46	48	119	5			.993	-1	*1O	3.7
1946	Chi-N★	139	510	89	150	28	10	8	78	88	54	.294	.401	.435	140	28	29	92	2			.967	1	O1	2.4
1947	Chi-N★	127	459	56	144	22	5	2	63	58	35	.314	.391	.397	114	8	11	76	2			.977	-0	*O1	0.4
1948	Chi-N	111	334	41	93	16	5	3	40	35	29	.278	.349	.383	102	-1	1	48	4			.998	1	1O	-0.1
1949	Chi-N	105	360	46	106	22	4	8	49	45	31	.294	.374	.444	122	10	11	62	2			.993	9	1O	1.8
1950	Chi-N	82	256	49	70	11	1	10	31	40	31	.273	.376	.441	115	6	6	45	1			.986	-1	1/O	0.4

YEAR	TM/L	G	AB	R	H	2B	3B	HR	RBI	BB	SO	AVG	OBP	SLG	PRO+	BR	/A	RC	SB	CS	SBR	FA	FR	POS	TPR
1951	Chi-N	89	206	24	64	7	1	6	28	27	28	.311	.393	.442	122	8	7	39	0	0	0	.994	4	1M	0.8
1952	Chi-N	41	63	7	15	1	1	1	8	9	3	.238	.333	.333	84	-1	-1	8	0	0	0	.991	1	1M	-0.1
1953	Chi-N	27	21	3	6	3	0	0	3	6	3	.286	.444	.429	126	1	1	5	0	0	0	.000	0	HM	0.1
1954	Chi-A	71	158	21	50	6	0	3	24	26	12	.316	.419	.411	124	7	7	31	4	0	1	.993	-4	1/O	0.2
1955	Chi-A	6	4	1	0	0	0	0	0	0	1	.000	.000	.000	-97	-1	-1	0	0	0	0	1.000	-0	/1	-0.1
Total	22	2030	6754	990	1977	347	99	95	920	820	598	.293	.372	.416	118	170	178	1106	65	0		.990	-21	*1O	5.2

■ IKE CAVENEY Caveney, James Christopher b: 12/10/1894, San Francisco, Cal d: 7/6/49, San Francisco, Cal BR/TR, 5'9", 168 lbs. Deb: 4/12/22

YEAR	TM/L	G	AB	R	H	2B	3B	HR	RBI	BB	SO	AVG	OBP	SLG	PRO+	BR	/A	RC	SB	CS	SBR	FA	FR	POS	TPR
1922	Cin-N	118	394	41	94	12	9	3	54	29	33	.239	.301	.338	66	-21	-20	41	6	6	-2	.934	-6	*S	-1.5
1923	Cin-N	138	488	58	135	21	9	4	63	26	41	.277	.315	.381	84	-13	-12	58	5	4	-1	.942	-0	*S	0.0
1924	Cin-N	95	337	36	92	19	1	4	32	14	21	.273	.310	.371	83	-9	-9	38	2	3	-1	.924	3	S/2	0.3
1925	Cin-N	115	358	38	89	9	5	2	47	28	31	.249	.303	.318	60	-22	-21	36	2	0	1	.941	9	*S	-0.1
Total	4	466	1577	173	410	61	24	13	196	97	126	.260	.307	.354	74	-66	-61	174	15	13	-3	.936	6	S/2	-1.3

■ ANDUJAR CEDENO Cedeno, Andujar (Domastorg) b: 8/21/69, LaRomana, D.R. BR/TR, 6'1", 170 lbs. Deb: 9/02/90

YEAR	TM/L	G	AB	R	H	2B	3B	HR	RBI	BB	SO	AVG	OBP	SLG	PRO+	BR	/A	RC	SB	CS	SBR	FA	FR	POS	TPR
1990	Hou-N	7	8	0	0	0	0	0	0	0	5	.000	.000	.000	-99	-2	-2	0	0	0	0	.833	-0	/S	-0.3
1991	Hou-N	67	251	27	61	13	2	9	36	9	74	.243	.272	.418	97	-4	-2	27	4	3	-1	.930	-14	S	-1.3
1992	Hou-N	71	220	15	38	13	2	2	13	14	71	.173	.232	.277	46	-17	-15	15	2	0	1	.959	-2	S	-1.3
Total	3	145	479	42	99	26	4	11	49	23	150	.207	.249	.347	70	-23	-20	42	6	3	0	.944	-16	S	-2.9

■ CESAR CEDENO Cedeno, Cesar (Encarnacion) b: 2/25/51, Santo Domingo, D.R. BR/TR, 6'2", 195 lbs. Deb: 6/20/70

YEAR	TM/L	G	AB	R	H	2B	3B	HR	RBI	BB	SO	AVG	OBP	SLG	PRO+	BR	/A	RC	SB	CS	SBR	FA	FR	POS	TPR
1970	Hou-N	90	355	46	110	21	4	7	42	15	57	.310	.341	.451	115	4	6	53	17	4	3	.968	-0	O	0.4
1971	Hou-N	161	611	85	161	**40**	6	10	81	25	102	.264	.296	.398	97	-6	-5	70	20	9	1	.989	-7	*O/1	-2.0
1972	Hou-N★	139	559	103	179	**39**	8	22	82	56	62	.320	.387	.537	163	43	44	115	55	21	4	.981	5	*O	4.9
1973	Hou-N★	139	525	86	168	35	2	25	70	41	79	.320	.377	.537	151	34	34	102	56	15	8	.981	10	*O	4.7
1974	Hou-N★	160	610	95	164	29	5	26	102	64	103	.269	.342	.461	129	17	20	99	57	17	7	.993	11	*O	3.2
1975	Hou-N	131	500	93	144	31	3	13	63	62	52	.288	.374	.440	135	18	22	85	50	17	5	.982	-0	*O	2.2
1976	Hou-N★	150	575	89	171	26	5	18	83	55	51	.297	.360	.454	143	22	28	94	58	15	8	.980	3	*O	3.4
1977	Hou-N	141	530	92	148	36	8	14	71	47	50	.279	.350	.457	126	10	17	89	61	14	10	**.997**	5	*O	2.6
1978	Hou-N	50	192	31	54	8	2	7	23	15	24	.281	.333	.453	127	4	6	31	23	2	6	.987	6	O	1.6
1979	Hou-N	132	470	57	123	27	4	6	54	64	52	.262	.354	.374	105	1	4	63	30	13	1	.981	-5	1O	-0.7
1980	*Hou-N	137	499	71	154	32	8	10	73	66	72	.309	.390	.465	150	27	31	93	48	15	5	.977	-0	*O	3.2
1981	*Hou-N	82	306	42	83	19	0	5	34	24	31	.271	.326	.382	106	-0	2	37	12	7	-1	.991	-1	1O	-0.4
1982	Cin-N	138	492	52	142	35	1	8	57	41	41	.289	.348	.413	110	8	7	67	16	11	-2	.990	-3	*O/1	-0.1
1983	Cin-N	98	332	40	77	16	0	9	39	33	53	.232	.307	.361	82	-7	-9	38	13	9	-2	.993	-3	O1	-1.7
1984	Cin-N	110	380	59	105	24	2	10	47	25	54	.276	.323	.429	105	4	2	52	19	3	4	.980	-2	O1	0.0
1985	Cin-N	83	220	24	53	12	0	3	30	19	35	.241	.310	.336	77	-6	-7	23	9	5	-0	.990	-1	O1	-1.1
	*StL-N	28	76	14	33	4	1	6	19	5	7	.434	.469	.750	238	13	13	26	5	1	1	.993	-4	1/O	0.9
	Yr	111	296	38	86	16	1	9	49	24	42	.291	.350	.443	116	8	6	45	14	6	1	.993	-4	1O	-0.2
1986	LA-N	37	78	5	18	2	1	0	6	7	13	.231	.294	.282	64	-4	-4	7	1	1	-0	.944	-4	O	-0.9
Total	17	2006	7310	1084	2087	436	60	199	976	664	938	.285	.350	.443	124	180	212	1144	550	179	58	.985	10	*O1	20.2

■ ORLANDO CEPEDA Cepeda, Orlando Manuel (Penne) "Baby Bull" or "Cha Cha" b: 9/17/37, Ponce, P.R. BR/TR, 6'2", 210 lbs. Deb: 4/15/58 C

YEAR	TM/L	G	AB	R	H	2B	3B	HR	RBI	BB	SO	AVG	OBP	SLG	PRO+	BR	/A	RC	SB	CS	SBR	FA	FR	POS	TPR
1958	SF-N	148	603	88	188	**38**	4	25	96	29	84	.312	.346	.512	126	18	20	97	15	11	-2	.989	-3	*1	0.6
1959	SF-N★	151	605	92	192	35	4	27	105	33	100	.317	.358	.522	134	25	26	110	23	9	2	.984	-8	*1O/3	1.1
1960	SF-N★	151	569	81	169	36	3	24	96	34	91	.297	.345	.497	135	20	24	95	15	6	1	.983	0	O1	1.6
1961	SF-N★	152	585	105	182	28	4	**46**	**142**	39	91	.311	.363	.609	158	41	44	118	12	8	-1	.997	-5	1O	2.6
1962	*SF-N★	162	625	105	191	26	1	35	114	37	97	.306	.350	.518	132	24	25	108	10	4	1	.991	-8	*1/O	0.8
1963	SF-N☆	156	579	100	183	33	4	34	97	37	70	.316	.367	.563	166	45	46	113	8	3	1	.985	-8	*1/O	3.5
1964	SF-N★	142	529	75	161	27	2	31	97	43	83	.304	.366	.539	148	35	33	101	9	4	0	.986	-4	*1/O	2.5
1965	SF-N	33	34	1	6	1	0	1	5	3	9	.176	.243	.294	49	-2	-2	2	0	0	0	1.000	0	/1O	-0.2
1966	SF-N	19	49	5	14	2	0	3	15	4	11	.286	.352	.510	132	2	2	9	0	1	-1	.778	-2	/O1	-0.2
	StL-N	123	452	65	137	24	0	17	58	34	68	.303	.369	.469	130	19	19	75	9	8	-2	.989	-6	*1	0.2
	Yr	142	501	70	151	26	0	20	73	38	79	.301	.367	.473	130	22	21	83	9	9	-3	.990	-9	*1/O	0.0
1967	*StL-N★	151	563	91	183	37	0	25	**111**	62	75	.325	.403	.524	166	47	48	118	11	2	2	.993	-0	*1	4.3
1968	*StL-N	157	600	71	149	26	2	16	73	43	96	.248	.308	.378	107	3	4	68	8	6	-1	.988	-5	*1	-1.6
1969	*Atl-N	154	573	74	147	28	2	22	88	55	76	.257	.327	.428	109	6	6	79	12	5	1	.994	3	*1	-0.3
1970	Atl-N	148	567	87	173	33	0	34	111	47	75	.305	.368	.543	133	31	26	108	6	5	-1	.992	3	*1	1.5
1971	Atl-N	71	250	31	69	10	1	14	44	22	29	.276	.335	.492	124	9	8	35	3	6	-3	.992	2	1	0.1
1972	Atl-N	28	84	6	25	3	0	4	9	7	17	.298	.352	.476	122	3	3	14	0	0	0	1.000	1	1	0.2
	Oak-A	3	3	0	0	0	0	0	0	0	0	.000	.000	.000	-99	-1	-1	0	0	0	0	.000	0	H	-0.1
1973	Bos-A	142	550	51	159	25	0	20	86	50	81	.289	.352	.444	116	16	12	79	0	2	-1	.000	0	*D	1.1
1974	KC-A	33	107	3	23	5	0	1	18	9	16	.215	.282	.290	61	-5	-6	8	1	0	0	.000	0	D	-0.6
Total	17	2124	7927	1131	2351	417	27	379	1365	588	1169	.297	.353	.499	133	337	337	1338	142	80	-5	.990	-40	*1OD/3	17.1

■ ED CERMAK Cermak, Edward Hugo b: 3/10/1882, Cleveland, Ohio d: 11/22/11, Cleveland, Ohio BR/TR, 5'11", 170 lbs. Deb: 9/09/01

YEAR	TM/L	G	AB	R	H	2B	3B	HR	RBI	BB	SO	AVG	OBP	SLG	PRO+	BR	/A	RC	SB	CS	SBR	FA	FR	POS	TPR
1901	Cle-A	1	4	0	0	0	0	0	0	0		.000	.000	.000	-99	-1	-1	0	0			1.000	1	/O	0.0

■ RICK CERONE Cerone, Richard Aldo b: 5/19/54, Newark, N.J. BR/TR, 5'11", 192 lbs. Deb: 8/17/75

YEAR	TM/L	G	AB	R	H	2B	3B	HR	RBI	BB	SO	AVG	OBP	SLG	PRO+	BR	/A	RC	SB	CS	SBR	FA	FR	POS	TPR
1975	Cle-A	7	12	1	3	1	0	0	0	1	0	.250	.308	.333	81	-0	-0	1	0	0	0	1.000	-1	/C	-0.1
1976	Cle-A	7	16	1	2	0	0	0	1	0	2	.125	.125	.125	-27	-3	-2	0	0	0	0	.963	0	/CD	-0.2
1977	Tor-A	31	100	7	20	4	0	1	10	6	12	.200	.245	.270	40	-8	-8	6	0	0	0	.994	-2	C	-0.9
1978	Tor-A	88	282	25	63	8	2	3	20	23	32	.223	.284	.298	63	-13	-14	23	0	3	-2	.992	-0	C/D	-1.5
1979	Tor-A	136	469	47	112	27	4	7	61	37	40	.239	.296	.358	75	-17	-17	50	1	4	-2	.980	-8	*C	-2.2
1980	*NY-A	147	519	70	144	30	4	14	85	32	56	.277	.327	.432	108	3	4	70	1	3	-2	.990	6	*C	1.4
1981	*NY-A	71	234	23	57	13	2	2	21	12	24	.244	.280	.342	80	-7	-7	20	0	2	-1	.992	-6	C	-1.1
1982	NY-A	89	300	29	68	10	0	5	28	19	27	.227	.275	.310	61	-16	-16	23	0	2	-1	.989	-8	C	-2.2
1983	NY-A	80	246	18	54	7	0	2	22	15	29	.220	.267	.272	51	-17	-16	18	0	0	0	.991	-0	C/3	-1.3
1984	NY-A	38	120	8	25	3	0	2	13	9	15	.208	.269	.283	55	-8	-7	9	1	0	0	.996	3	C	-0.2
1985	Atl-N	96	282	15	61	9	0	3	25	29	25	.216	.292	.280	57	-14	-16	20	0	3	-2	.986	-8	C	-2.3
1986	Mil-A	68	216	22	56	14	0	4	18	15	28	.259	.310	.380	84	-4	-5	25	1	1	-0	.991	7	C	0.6
1987	NY-A	113	284	28	69	12	1	4	23	30	46	.243	.324	.335	76	-10	-9	31	0	1	-1	**.998**	4	*C/P1	0.1
1988	Bos-A	84	264	31	71	13	1	3	27	20	32	.269	.328	.360	89	-3	-4	31	0	0	0	**1.000**	-5	C/D	-0.3
1989	Bos-A	102	296	28	72	16	1	4	48	34	40	.243	.325	.345	84	-4	-6	33	0	0	0	.984	3	C/OD	0.1
1990	NY-A	49	139	12	42	6	0	2	11	5	13	.302	.326	.388	99	-0	-1	17	0	0	0	.995	-3	C/2D	-0.2
1991	NY-N	90	227	18	62	13	0	2	16	30	24	.273	.360	.357	103	2	2	29	1	1	-0	.987	-2	C	0.4
1992	Mon-N	33	63	10	17	4	0	1	7	3	5	.270	.313	.381	96	-0	-0	7	1	2	-1	1.000	1	C	0.0
Total	18	1329	4069	393	998	190	15	59	436	320	450	.245	.304	.343	78	-120	-124	413	6	22	-11	.990	-19	*C/D1P2O3	-9.9

■ BOB CERV Cerv, Robert Henry b: 5/5/26, Weston, Neb. BR/TR, 6', 202 lbs. Deb: 8/01/51

YEAR	TM/L	G	AB	R	H	2B	3B	HR	RBI	BB	SO	AVG	OBP	SLG	PRO+	BR	/A	RC	SB	CS	SBR	FA	FR	POS	TPR
1951	NY-A	12	28	4	6	1	0	0	2	4	6	.214	.313	.250	55	-2	-2	2	0	0	0	.875	-1	/O	-0.3
1952	NY-A	36	87	11	21	3	2	1	8	9	22	.241	.313	.356	91	-2	-1	10	0	1	-1	1.000	-2	O	-0.5
1953	NY-A	8	6	0	0	0	0	0	0	1	1	.000	.143	.000	-61	-1	-1	0	0	0	0	.000	0	H	-0.1
1954	NY-A	56	100	14	26	6	0	5	13	11	17	.260	.333	.470	122	2	2	14	0	2	-1	.897	-5	O	-0.5

YEAR	TM/L	G	AB	R	H	2B	3B	HR	RBI	BB	SO	AVG	OBP	SLG	PRO+	BR	/A	RC	SB	CS	SBR	FA	FR	POS	TPR
1955	*NY-A	55	85	17	29	4	2	3	22	7	16	.341	.411	.541	157	6	7	20	4	0	1	1.000	-4	O	0.4
1956	*NY-A	54	115	16	35	5	6	3	25	18	13	.304	.398	.530	148	7	8	24	0	1	-1	.984	-4	O	0.1
1957	KC-A	124	345	35	94	14	2	11	44	20	57	.272	.314	.420	97	-2	-2	42	1	1	-0	.964	-7	O	-1.5
1958	KC-A★	141	515	93	157	20	7	38	104	50	82	.305	.372	.592	158	41	40	106	3	3	-1	.985	20	*O	5.2
1959	KC-A	125	463	61	132	22	4	20	87	35	87	.285	.339	.479	120	13	11	72	3	2	-0	.980	6	*O	1.1
1960	KC-A	23	78	14	20	1	1	6	12	10	17	.256	.341	.526	130	3	3	14	0	0	0	.977	3	O	0.5
	*NY-A	87	216	32	54	11	1	8	28	30	36	.250	.349	.421	114	2	4	32	0	0	0	.982	4	O/1	0.5
	Yr	110	294	46	74	12	2	14	40	40	53	.252	.347	.449	119	6	7	46	0	0	0	.980	6	O/1	1.0
1961	LA-A	18	57	3	9	3	0	2	6	1	8	.158	.172	.316	25	-6	-7	2	0	0	0	.944	-2	O	-1.0
	NY-A	57	118	17	32	5	1	6	20	12	17	.271	.344	.483	125	3	4	18	1	0	0	.983	1	O/1	0.3
	Yr	75	175	20	41	8	1	8	26	13	25	.234	.291	.429	91	-3	-3	19	1	0	0	.974	-1	O/1	-0.7
1962	NY-A	14	17	1	2	1	0	0	0	2	3	.118	.250	.176	18	-2	-2	1	0	0	0	1.000	-0	/O	-0.2
	Hou-N	19	31	2	7	0	0	2	3	2	10	.226	.273	.419	89	-1	-1	3	0	0	0	.833	-1	/O	-0.1
Total	12	829	2261	320	624	96	26	105	374	212	392	.276	.343	.481	122	62	63	361	12	10	-2	.976	7	O/1	3.9

■ RON CEY

Cey, Ronald Charles b: 2/15/48, Tacoma, Wash. BR/TR, 5'10", 185 lbs. Deb: 9/03/71

YEAR	TM/L	G	AB	R	H	2B	3B	HR	RBI	BB	SO	AVG	OBP	SLG	PRO+	BR	/A	RC	SB	CS	SBR	FA	FR	POS	TPR
1971	LA-N	2	2	0	0	0	0	0	0	0	2	.000	.000	.000	-99	-1	-1	0	0	0	0	.000	0	H	-0.1
1972	LA-N	11	37	3	10	1	0	1	3	7	10	.270	.400	.378	125	1	2	6	0	0	0	.900	-2	3	-0.1
1973	LA-N	152	507	60	124	18	4	15	80	74	77	.245	.343	.385	106	2	5	66	1	1	-0	.961	16	*3	2.1
1974	*LA-N★	159	577	88	151	20	2	18	97	76	68	.262	.355	.397	115	9	12	82	1	1	-0	.959	17	*3	2.8
1975	LA-N★	158	566	72	160	29	2	25	101	78	74	.283	.376	.473	141	27	30	101	5	2	0	.960	-4	*3	2.7
1976	LA-N★	145	502	69	139	18	3	23	80	89	74	.277	.389	.462	144	29	30	92	0	4	-2	.965	11	*3	4.0
1977	*LA-N★	153	564	77	136	22	3	30	110	93	106	.241	.351	.450	114	11	11	92	3	4	-2	.964	17	*3	2.5
1978	*LA-N★	159	555	84	150	32	0	23	84	96	96	.270	.384	.452	134	27	27	99	2	5	-2	.966	5	*3	2.9
1979	LA-N★	150	487	77	137	20	1	28	81	86	85	.281	.391	.499	143	29	30	97	3	3	-1	**.977**	-1	*3	2.8
1980	LA-N	157	551	81	140	25	0	28	77	69	92	.254	.342	.452	122	14	16	84	2	2	-1	.972	7	*3	2.0
1981	*LA-N	85	312	42	90	15	2	13	50	40	55	.288	.375	.474	145	16	18	55	0	2	-1	.941	7	3	2.4
1982	LA-N	150	556	62	141	23	1	24	79	57	99	.254	.327	.428	113	6	8	76	3	2	-0	.963	11	*3	1.6
1983	Chi-N	159	581	73	160	33	1	24	90	62	85	.275	.350	.460	117	17	14	90	0	0	0	.955	-21	*3	-0.9
1984	*Chi-N	146	505	71	121	27	0	25	97	61	108	.240	.329	.442	105	9	3	74	3	2	-0	**.967**	-20	*3	-1.9
1985	Chi-N	145	500	64	116	18	2	22	63	58	106	.232	.317	.408	91	0	-6	65	1	1	-0	.943	-7	*3	-1.7
1986	Chi-N	97	256	42	70	21	0	13	36	44	66	.273	.386	.508	134	16	14	53	0	0	0	.952	-6	3	0.6
1987	Oak-A	45	104	12	23	6	0	4	11	22	32	.221	.362	.394	108	1	2	16	0	0	0	.982	-1	D/13	0.0
Total	17	2073	7162	977	1868	328	21	316	1139	1012	1235	.261	.357	.445	121	216	215	1149	24	29	-10	.961	30	*3/D1	21.7

■ ELIO CHACON

Chacon, Elio (Rodirguez) b: 10/26/36, Caracas, Venez. d: 4/24/92, Caracas, Venez. BR/TR, 5'9", 160 lbs. Deb: 4/20/60

YEAR	TM/L	G	AB	R	H	2B	3B	HR	RBI	BB	SO	AVG	OBP	SLG	PRO+	BR	/A	RC	SB	CS	SBR	FA	FR	POS	TPR
1960	Cin-N	49	116	14	21	1	0	0	7	14	23	.181	.275	.190	29	-11	-11	8	7	1	2	.980	5	2/O	-0.1
1961	*Cin-N	61	132	26	35	4	2	2	5	21	22	.265	.374	.371	97	1	0	20	1	4	-2	.989	3	2/O	0.5
1962	NY-N	118	368	49	87	10	3	2	27	76	64	.236	.369	.296	80	-6	-7	44	12	7	-1	.961	-3	*S/23	-0.1
Total	3	228	616	89	143	15	5	4	39	111	109	.232	.353	.292	74	-17	-18	71	20	12	-1	.985	6	S/2O3	0.3

■ CHET CHADBOURNE

Chadbourne, Chester James "Pop" b: 10/28/1884, Parkman, Me. d: 6/21/43, Los Angeles, Cal. BL/TR, 5'9", 170 lbs. Deb: 9/17/06

YEAR	TM/L	G	AB	R	H	2B	3B	HR	RBI	BB	SO	AVG	OBP	SLG	PRO+	BR	/A	RC	SB	CS	SBR	FA	FR	POS	TPR
1906	Bos-A	11	43	7	13	1	0	0	3	3		.302	.348	.326	112	1	1	5	1			.926	3	2/S	0.4
1907	Bos-A	10	38	0	11	0	0	0	1	7		.289	.400	.289	122	1	1	5	1			1.000	-0	O	0.1
1914	KC-F	147	581	92	161	22	8	1	37	69	49	.277	.359	.348	106	3	6	91	42			.965	9	*O	0.9
1915	KC-F	152	587	75	133	16	9	1	35	62	29	.227	.307	.290	79	-17	-14	65	29			**.979**	1	*O	-2.2
1918	Bos-N	27	104	9	27	2	1	0	6	5	5	.260	.300	.298	86	-2	-2	11	5			.925	-3	O	-0.7
Total	5	347	1353	183	345	41	18	2	82	146	83	.255	.333	.316	93	-14	-7	178	78			.969	10	O/2S	-1.5

■ DAVE CHALK

Chalk, David Lee b: 8/30/50, Del Rio, Tex. BR/TR, 5'10", 175 lbs. Deb: 9/04/73

YEAR	TM/L	G	AB	R	H	2B	3B	HR	RBI	BB	SO	AVG	OBP	SLG	PRO+	BR	/A	RC	SB	CS	SBR	FA	FR	POS	TPR
1973	Cal-A	24	69	14	16	2	0	0	6	9	13	.232	.329	.261	74	-3	-2	6	0	0	0	.962	2	S	0.2
1974	Cal-A★	133	465	44	117	9	3	5	31	30	57	.252	.307	.316	84	-12	-9	41	10	10	-3	.938	-2	S3	-0.2
1975	Cal-A☆	149	513	59	140	24	2	3	56	66	49	.273	.358	.345	107	2	6	64	6	9	-4	.976	6	*3	0.9
1976	Cal-A	142	438	39	95	14	1	0	33	49	62	.217	.310	.253	71	-17	-13	36	0	0	0	.971	5	*S3	0.3
1977	Cal-A	149	519	58	144	27	2	3	45	52	69	.277	.349	.355	96	-4	-1	65	12	8	-1	.948	-3	*3/2S	-0.6
1978	Cal-A	135	470	42	119	12	0	1	34	38	34	.253	.318	.285	74	-17	-15	43	5	8	-3	.955	-20	S23/D	-2.5
1979	Tex-A	9	8	0	2	0	0	0	0	0	0	.250	.250	.250	36	-1	-1	0	0	0	0	1.000	-0	/S2	-0.1
	Oak-A	66	212	15	47	6	0	2	13	29	14	.222	.318	.278	66	-10	-9	20	2	1	0	.988	-17	2S3	-2.1
	Yr	75	220	15	49	6	0	2	13	29	14	.223	.316	.277	65	-11	-10	20	2	1	0	.988	-17	2S3	-2.2
1980	*KC-A	69	167	19	42	10	1	1	20	18	27	.251	.332	.341	84	-3	-3	19	1	1	-0	.964	-3	32/SD	-0.7
1981	KC-A	27	49	2	11	3	0	0	5	4	2	.224	.283	.286	65	-2	-2	4	0	1	-1	.955	-2	32/S	-0.4
Total	9	903	2910	292	733	107	9	15	243	295	327	.252	.328	.310	85	-67	-49	299	36	38	-12	.962	-34	3S2/D	-5.2

■ JOE CHAMBERLAIN

Chamberlain, Joseph Jeremiah b: 5/10/10, San Francisco, Cal d: 1/28/83, San Francisco, Cal. BR/TR, 6'1", 175 lbs. Deb: 4/17/34

YEAR	TM/L	G	AB	R	H	2B	3B	HR	RBI	BB	SO	AVG	OBP	SLG	PRO+	BR	/A	RC	SB	CS	SBR	FA	FR	POS	TPR
1934	Chi-A	43	141	13	34	5	1	2	17	6	38	.241	.272	.333	54	-10	-10	13	1	1	-0	.896	-6	S3/2	-1.4

■ WES CHAMBERLAIN

Chamberlain, Wesley Polk b: 4/13/66, Chicago, Ill. BR/TR, 6'2", 210 lbs. Deb: 8/31/90

YEAR	TM/L	G	AB	R	H	2B	3B	HR	RBI	BB	SO	AVG	OBP	SLG	PRO+	BR	/A	RC	SB	CS	SBR	FA	FR	POS	TPR
1990	Phi-N	18	46	9	13	3	0	2	4	1	9	.283	.298	.478	110	0	0	7	4	0	1	.958	-1	O	0.1
1991	Phi-N	101	383	51	92	16	3	13	50	31	73	.240	.300	.399	96	-3	-3	45	9	4	0	.985	5	O	0.0
1992	Phi-N	76	275	26	71	18	0	9	41	10	55	.258	.287	.422	99	-2	-2	32	4	0	1	.971	-1	O	-0.3
Total	3	195	704	86	176	37	3	24	95	42	137	.250	.295	.413	98	-5	-4	84	17	4	3	.978	4	O	-0.2

■ AL CHAMBERS

Chambers, Albert Eugene b: 3/24/61, Harrisburg, Pa. BL/TL, 6'4", 217 lbs. Deb: 7/23/83

YEAR	TM/L	G	AB	R	H	2B	3B	HR	RBI	BB	SO	AVG	OBP	SLG	PRO+	BR	/A	RC	SB	CS	SBR	FA	FR	POS	TPR
1983	Sea-A	31	67	11	14	3	0	1	7	18	20	.209	.376	.299	85	-0	-1	9	0	1	-1	1.000	-1	D/O	-0.2
1984	Sea-A	22	49	4	11	1	0	1	4	3	12	.224	.269	.306	60	-3	-3	4	2	1	0	.947	-2	O/D	-0.5
1985	Sea-A	4	4	0	0	0	0	0	0	0	2	.000	.000	.000	-99	-1	-1	0	0	0	0	.000	0	/H	-0.1
Total	3	57	120	15	25	4	0	2	11	21	34	.208	.326	.292	71	-4	-4	13	2	2	-1	.955	-3	/DO	-0.8

■ CHRIS CHAMBLISS

Chambliss, Carroll Christopher b: 12/26/48, Dayton, O. BL/TR, 6'1", 215 lbs. Deb: 5/28/71 C

YEAR	TM/L	G	AB	R	H	2B	3B	HR	RBI	BB	SO	AVG	OBP	SLG	PRO+	BR	/A	RC	SB	CS	SBR	FA	FR	POS	TPR
1971	Cle-A	111	415	49	114	20	4	9	48	40	83	.275	.341	.407	102	6	2	58	2	0	1	.992	-5	*1	-1.4
1972	Cle-A	121	466	51	136	27	2	6	44	26	63	.292	.329	.397	112	8	6	59	3	4	-2	.993	-6	*1	-1.3
1973	Cle-A	155	572	70	156	30	2	11	53	58	76	.273	.343	.390	104	5	4	74	4	8	-4	.991	7	*1	-0.5
1974	Cle-A	17	67	8	22	4	0	0	7	5	5	.328	.375	.388	121	2	2	9	0	1	-1	.982	-2	1	-0.2
	NY-A	110	400	38	97	16	3	6	43	23	43	.243	.284	.343	82	-11	-10	38	0	0	0	.992	7	*1	-1.1
	Yr	127	467	46	119	20	3	6	50	28	48	.255	.297	.349	87	-10	-8	47	0	1	-1	.990	5	*1	-1.3
1975	NY-A	150	562	66	171	38	4	9	72	29	50	.304	.340	.434	121	11	13	77	0	1	-1	.991	3	*1	0.5
1976	*NY-A★	156	641	79	188	32	6	17	96	27	80	.293	.325	.441	124	15	16	90	1	0	0	.994	-2	*1/D	0.4
1977	*NY-A	157	600	90	172	32	6	17	90	45	73	.287	.338	.445	113	9	10	85	4	0	1	.989	-5	*1	-0.3
1978	*NY-A	162	625	81	171	26	3	12	90	41	60	.274	.323	.382	100	-3	-1	79	2	1	0	**.997**	4	*1/D	-0.6
1979	NY-A	149	554	61	155	27	3	18	63	34	53	.280	.327	.437	106	2	3	78	3	2	-0	.995	0	*1D	-0.5
1980	Atl-N	158	602	83	170	37	2	18	72	49	73	.282	.340	.440	113	12	10	90	7	3	0	.993	-2	*1	-0.1
1981	Atl-N	107	404	44	110	25	2	8	51	44	41	.272	.345	.403	109	6	5	56	4	1	1	.997	7	*1	0.7
1982	*Atl-N	157	534	57	144	25	2	20	86	57	57	.270	.340	.436	111	11	8	79	7	3	0	.993	14	*1	1.6
1983	Atl-N	131	447	59	125	24	3	20	78	63	68	.280	.369	.481	124	20	16	78	2	7	-4	.996	0	*1	0.6
1984	Atl-N	135	389	47	100	14	0	9	44	58	54	.257	.355	.362	95	3	-1	51	1	2	-1	.993	2	*1	-0.7

YEAR	TM/L	G	AB	R	H	2B	3B	HR	RBI	BB	SO	AVG	OBP	SLG	PRO+	BR	/A	RC	SB	CS	SBR	FA	FR	POS	TPR
1985	Atl-N	101	170	16	40	7	0	3	21	18	22	.235	.309	.329	74	-5	-6	17	0	0	0	.997	2	1	-0.6
1986	Atl-N	97	122	13	38	8	0	2	14	15	24	.311	.387	.426	117	4	4	20	0	2	-1	.993	-2	1	0.0
1988	NY-A	1	1	0	0	0	0	0	0	0	1	.000	.000	.000	-99	-0	-0	0	0	0	0	.000	0	/H	0.0
Total	17	2175	7571	912	2109	392	42	185	972	632	926	.279	.336	.415	108	94	80	1036	40	35	-9	.993	25	*1/D	-3.5

■ MIKE CHAMPION

Champion, Robert Michael b: 2/10/55, Montgomery, Ala. BR/TR, 6', 185 lbs. Deb: 9/14/76

YEAR	TM/L	G	AB	R	H	2B	3B	HR	RBI	BB	SO	AVG	OBP	SLG	PRO+	BR	/A	RC	SB	CS	SBR	FA	FR	POS	TPR
1976	SD-N	11	38	4	9	2	0	1	2	1	3	.237	.256	.368	82	-1	-1	3	0	0	0	.940	-4	2	-0.4
1977	SD-N	150	507	35	116	14	6	1	43	27	85	.229	.271	.286	55	-36	-30	39	3	3	-1	.974	-26	*2	-4.8
1978	SD-N	32	53	3	12	0	2	0	4	5	13	.226	.293	.302	72	-2	-2	5	0	0	0	.932	2	2/3	0.1
Total	3	193	598	42	137	16	8	2	49	33	101	.229	.272	.293	58	-40	-33	47	3	3	-1	.968	-28	2/3	-5.1

■ FRANK CHANCE

Chance, Frank Leroy "Husk" or "The Peerless Leader"
b: 9/9/1877, Fresno, Cal. d: 9/15/24, Los Angeles, Cal. BR/TR, 6', 190 lbs. Deb: 4/29/1898 MH

YEAR	TM/L	G	AB	R	H	2B	3B	HR	RBI	BB	SO	AVG	OBP	SLG	PRO+	BR	/A	RC	SB	CS	SBR	FA	FR	POS	TPR
1898	Chi-N	53	147	32	41	4	3	1	14	7		.279	.338	.367	102	0	0	21	7			.950	-5	CO/1	-0.4
1899	Chi-N	64	192	37	55	6	2	1	22	15		.286	.351	.354	96	-1	-1	28	10			.950	-3	C/O1	0.0
1900	Chi-N	56	149	26	44	9	3	0	13	15		.295	.413	.396	129	6	7	30	8			.932	2	C/1	1.2
1901	Chi-N	69	241	38	67	12	4	0	36	29		.278	.376	.361	119	6	7	44	27			.932	-6	OC/1	0.0
1902	Chi-N	75	240	39	69	9	4	1	31	35		.287	.396	.371	141	13	13	47	27			.969	-4	1C/O	1.2
1903	Chi-N	125	441	83	144	24	10	2	81	78		.327	.439	.440	155	34	36	118	**67**			.972	-3	*1/C	2.9
1904	Chi-N	124	451	89	140	16	10	6	49	36		.310	.382	.430	151	28	28	93	42			.990	12	*1/C	3.8
1905	Chi-N	118	392	92	124	16	12	2	70	78		.316	**.449**	.434	157	37	35	98	38			.990	2	*1M	3.4
1906	*Chi-N	136	474	**103**	151	24	10	3	71	70		.319	**.418**	.430	156	39	36	114	**57**			.989	-1	*1M	3.4
1907	*Chi-N	111	382	58	112	19	2	1	49	51		.293	.395	.361	129	19	17	71	35			**.992**	7	*1M	2.4
1908	*Chi-N	129	452	65	123	27	4	2	55	37		.272	.338	.363	119	12	10	64	27			.989	4	*1M	1.4
1909	Chi-N	93	324	53	88	16	4	0	46	30		.272	.341	.346	110	5	4	48	29			.994	-2	1M	0.2
1910	*Chi-N	88	295	54	88	12	8	0	36	37	15	.298	.395	.393	131	13	13	52	16			.996	-2	1M	1.2
1911	Chi-N	31	88	23	21	6	3	1	17	25	13	.239	.432	.409	136	6	6	20	9			.990	-2	1M	0.4
1912	Chi-N	2	5	2	1	0	0	0	0	3	0	.200	.500	.200	96	0	0	1	1			1.000	-0	/1M	0.0
1913	NY-A	12	24	3	5	0	0	0	6	8	1	.208	.406	.208	81	0	0	3	1			1.000	1	/1M	0.0
1914	NY-A	1	0	0	0	0	0	0	0	0	0	—	—	—	—	0	0	0	0			1.000	-0	/1M	0.0
Total	17	1287	4297	797	1273	200	79	20	596	554	29	.296	.394	.394	135	218	212	852	401			.987	1	1C/O	21.1

■ BOB CHANCE

Chance, Robert b: 9/10/40, Statesboro, Ga. BL/TR, 6'2", 219 lbs. Deb: 9/04/63

YEAR	TM/L	G	AB	R	H	2B	3B	HR	RBI	BB	SO	AVG	OBP	SLG	PRO+	BR	/A	RC	SB	CS	SBR	FA	FR	POS	TPR
1963	Cle-A	16	52	5	15	4	0	2	7	1	10	.288	.302	.481	116	1	1	7	0	1	-1	.909	-2	O	-0.3
1964	Cle-A	120	390	45	109	16	1	14	75	40	101	.279	.351	.433	118	9	9	58	3	3	-1	.988	-12	1O	-0.9
1965	Was-A	72	199	20	51	9	0	4	14	18	44	.256	.318	.362	94	-2	-2	23	0	1	-1	.988	-2	1/O	-0.7
1966	Was-A	37	57	1	10	3	0	1	8	2	23	.175	.203	.281	38	-5	-5	3	0	0	0	.974	-2	1	-0.7
1967	Was-A	27	42	5	9	2	0	3	7	7	13	.214	.340	.476	144	2	2	8	0	0	0	1.000	-0	1	0.2
1969	Cal-A	5	7	0	1	0	0	0	1	0	4	.143	.143	.143	-21	-1	-1	0	0	0	0	.909	-0	/1	-0.2
Total	6	277	747	76	195	34	1	24	112	68	195	.261	.326	.406	106	4	5	98	3	5	-2	.987	-18	1/O	-2.6

■ DARREL CHANEY

Chaney, Darrel Lee b: 3/9/48, Hammond, Ind. BB/TR, 6'1", 190 lbs. Deb: 4/11/69

YEAR	TM/L	G	AB	R	H	2B	3B	HR	RBI	BB	SO	AVG	OBP	SLG	PRO+	BR	/A	RC	SB	CS	SBR	FA	FR	POS	TPR
1969	Cin-N	93	209	21	40	5	2	0	15	24	75	.191	.278	.234	43	-15	-16	15	1	0	0	.947	-12	S	-2.2
1970	*Cin-N	57	95	7	22	3	0	1	4	3	26	.232	.263	.295	49	-7	-7	8	1	1	-0	.941	5	S2/3	0.0
1971	Cin-N	10	24	2	3	0	0	0	1	1	3	.125	.160	.125	-19	-4	-4	0	0	1	-1	1.000	-1	/S23	-0.4
1972	*Cin-N	83	196	29	49	7	2	2	19	29	28	.250	.347	.337	101	-0	1	24	1	3	-2	.963	-7	S23	-0.1
1973	*Cin-N	105	227	27	41	7	1	0	14	26	50	.181	.268	.220	39	-19	-18	15	4	3	-1	.964	12	S23	0.2
1974	Cin-N	117	135	27	27	6	1	2	16	26	33	.200	.329	.304	79	-3	-3	14	1	2	-1	.952	17	32S	1.5
1975	*Cin-N	71	160	18	35	6	0	2	26	14	38	.219	.282	.294	59	-9	-9	14	3	0	1	.961	17	S23	1.2
1976	Atl-N	153	496	42	125	20	8	1	50	54	92	.252	.327	.331	82	-8	-11	54	5	7	-3	.950	-0	*S/23	0.4
1977	Atl-N	74	209	22	42	7	2	3	15	17	44	.201	.261	.297	44	-15	-18	15	0	0	0	.979	4	S2	-0.9
1978	Atl-N	89	245	27	55	9	1	3	20	25	48	.224	.296	.306	62	-10	-13	24	1	0	0	.976	-6	S/32	-1.1
1979	Atl-N	63	117	15	19	5	0	0	10	19	34	.162	.279	.205	32	-10	-11	8	2	1	0	.945	-3	S/23C	-1.2
Total	11	915	2113	237	458	75	17	14	190	238	471	.217	.297	.288	61	-101	-110	191	19	18	-5	.959	26	S23/C	-2.6

■ LES CHANNELL

Channell, Lester Clark "Goat" or "Gint" b: 3/3/1886, Crestline, Ohio d: 5/8/54, Denver, Colo. BL/TL, 6', 180 lbs. Deb: 5/11/10

YEAR	TM/L	G	AB	R	H	2B	3B	HR	RBI	BB	SO	AVG	OBP	SLG	PRO+	BR	/A	RC	SB	CS	SBR	FA	FR	POS	TPR
1910	NY-A	6	19	3	6	0	0	0	3	2		.316	.381	.316	112	0	0	3	2			1.000	-1	/O	-0.1
1914	NY-A	1	1	0	1	1	0	0	0	0	0	1.000	1.000	2.000	803	1	1	2	0			.000	0	H	0.1
Total	2	7	20	3	7	1	0	0	3	2	0	.350	.409	.400	145	1	1	5	2				-1	/O	0.0

■ CHARLIE CHANT

Chant, Charles Joseph b: 8/7/51, Bell, Cal. BR/TR, 6', 190 lbs. Deb: 9/12/75

YEAR	TM/L	G	AB	R	H	2B	3B	HR	RBI	BB	SO	AVG	OBP	SLG	PRO+	BR	/A	RC	SB	CS	SBR	FA	FR	POS	TPR
1975	Oak-A	5	5	1	0	0	0	0	0	0	0	.000	.000	.000	-99	-1	-1	0	0	0	0	1.000	-2	/OD	-0.3
1976	StL-N	15	14	0	2	0	0	0	0	0	4	.143	.143	.143	-19	-2	-2	0	0	0	0	1.000	2	O	0.0
Total	2	20	19	1	2	0	0	0	0	0	4	.105	.105	.105	-40	-3	-3	0	0	0	0	1.000	0	/OD	-0.3

■ ED CHAPLIN

Chaplin, Bert Edgar (b: Bert Edgar Chapman) b: 9/25/1893, Pelzer, S.C. d: 8/15/78, Sanford, Fla. BL/TR, 5'7", 158 lbs. Deb: 9/04/20

YEAR	TM/L	G	AB	R	H	2B	3B	HR	RBI	BB	SO	AVG	OBP	SLG	PRO+	BR	/A	RC	SB	CS	SBR	FA	FR	POS	TPR
1920	Bos-A	4	5	2	1	1	0	0	1	4	1	.200	.556	.400	163	1	1	2	0	0	0	.900	-1	/C	0.1
1921	Bos-A	3	2	0	0	0	0	0	0	0	1	.000	.000	.000	-99	-1	-1	0	0	0	0	1.000	0	/C	0.0
1922	Bos-A	28	69	8	13	1	1	0	6	9	9	.188	.282	.232	35	-6	-6	5	2	1	0	.960	-3	C	-0.8
Total	3	35	76	10	14	2	1	0	7	13	11	.184	.303	.237	43	-6	-6	7	2	1	0	.953	-3	/C	-0.7

■ CALVIN CHAPMAN

Chapman, Calvin Louis b: 12/20/10, Courtland, Miss. d: 4/1/83, Batesville, Miss. BL/TR, 5'9", 160 lbs. Deb: 9/10/35

YEAR	TM/L	G	AB	R	H	2B	3B	HR	RBI	BB	SO	AVG	OBP	SLG	PRO+	BR	/A	RC	SB	CS	SBR	FA	FR	POS	TPR
1935	Cin-N	15	53	6	18	1	0	0	3	4	5	.340	.386	.358	105	0	1	8	2			.949	-3	S/2	-0.1
1936	Cin-N	96	219	35	54	7	3	1	22	16	19	.247	.301	.320	72	-10	-8	22	5			.961	-14	O2/3	-2.1
Total	2	111	272	41	72	8	3	1	25	20	24	.265	.317	.327	78	-10	-8	30	7			.968	-16	/O2S3	-2.2

■ GLENN CHAPMAN

Chapman, Glenn Justice "Pete" b: 1/21/06, Cambridge City, Ind. d: 11/5/88, Richmond, Ind. BR/TR, 5'11.5", 170 lbs. Deb: 4/18/34

YEAR	TM/L	G	AB	R	H	2B	3B	HR	RBI	BB	SO	AVG	OBP	SLG	PRO+	BR	/A	RC	SB	CS	SBR	FA	FR	POS	TPR
1934	Bro-N	67	93	19	26	5	1	1	10	7	19	.280	.330	.387	96	-1	-1	12	1			1.000	-7	O2	-0.8

■ HARRY CHAPMAN

Chapman, Harry E. b: 10/26/1887, Severance, Kan. d: 10/21/18, Nevada, Mo. BR/TR, 5'11", 160 lbs. Deb: 10/06/12

YEAR	TM/L	G	AB	R	H	2B	3B	HR	RBI	BB	SO	AVG	OBP	SLG	PRO+	BR	/A	RC	SB	CS	SBR	FA	FR	POS	TPR
1912	Chi-N	1	4	1	1	0	1	0	1	0	0	.250	.250	.750	169	0	0	1	1			1.000	1	/C	0.1
1913	Cin-N	2	2	0	1	0	0	0	0	0	1	.500	.500	.500	187	0	0	0	0			.000	0	H	0.0
1914	StL-F	64	181	16	38	2	1	0	14	13	27	.210	.270	.232	41	-13	-14	13	2			.973	-4	C/12O	-1.4
1915	StL-F	62	186	19	37	6	3	1	29	22	24	.199	.284	.280	62	-8	-9	17	4			.989	8	C	0.4
1916	StL-A	18	31	2	3	0	0	0	0	2	5	.097	.152	.097	-27	-5	-5	1	0			.981	2	C	-0.2
Total	5	147	404	38	80	8	5	1	44	37	57	.198	.269	.250	49	-25	-27	32	7			.982	7	C/O21	-1.1

■ JACK CHAPMAN

Chapman, John Curtis "Death To Flying Things" b: 5/8/1843, Brooklyn, N.Y. d: 6/10/16, Brooklyn, N.Y. TR , 5'11", 170 lbs. Deb: 5/05/1874 M

YEAR	TM/L	G	AB	R	H	2B	3B	HR	RBI	BB	SO	AVG	OBP	SLG	PRO+	BR	/A	RC	SB	CS	SBR	FA	FR	POS	TPR
1874	Atl-n	53	238	32	64	7	3	0		5		.269	.284	.324	105	-2	3	22						*O/1	0.3
1875	StL-n	43	195	28	44	6	3	0		1		.226	.230	.287	85	-4	-1	13						O	-0.1
1876	Lou-N	17	67	4	16	1	0	0	5	1	3	.239	.250	.254	58	-2	-4	4				.750	-4	O/3M	-0.7
Total	2 n	96	433	60	108	13	6	0		6		.249	.260	.307	96	-6	2	36						/O1	0.2

■ JOHN CHAPMAN

Chapman, John Joseph b: 10/15/1899, Centralia, Pa. d: 11/3/53, Philadelphia, Pa. BR/TR, 5'10.5", 175 lbs. Deb: 6/28/24

YEAR	TM/L	G	AB	R	H	2B	3B	HR	RBI	BB	SO	AVG	OBP	SLG	PRO+	BR	/A	RC	SB	CS	SBR	FA	FR	POS	TPR
1924	Phi-A	19	71	7	20	4	1	0	7	4	8	.282	.329	.366	78	-2	-2	9	0	0	0	.958	-10	S	-1.0

YEAR	TM/L	G	AB	R	H	2B	3B	HR	RBI	BB	SO	AVG	OBP	SLG	PRO+	BR	/A	RC	SB	CS	SBR	FA	FR	POS	TPR
■ KELVIN CHAPMAN Chapman, Kelvin Keith b: 6/2/56, Willits, Cal. BR/TR, 5'11", 173 lbs. Deb: 4/05/79																									
1979	NY-N	35	80	7	12	1	2	0	4	5	15	.150	.200	.213	13	-10	-9	4	0	0	0	.980	-4	2/3	-1.2
1984	NY-N	75	197	27	57	13	0	3	23	19	30	.289	.358	.401	115	4	4	26	8	7	-2	.979	1	2/3	0.5
1985	NY-N	62	144	16	25	3	0	0	7	9	15	.174	.232	.194	21	-15	-15	7	5	4	-1	.970	-6	2/3	-2.2
Total	3	172	421	50	94	17	2	3	34	33	60	.223	.286	.295	64	-21	-20	36	13	11	-3	.976	-9	2/3	-2.9
■ RAY CHAPMAN Chapman, Raymond Johnson b: 1/15/1891, Beaver Dam, Ky. d: 8/17/20, New York, N.Y. BR/TR, 5'10", 170 lbs. Deb: 8/30/12																									
1912	Cle-A	31	109	29	34	6	3	0	19	10		.312	.375	.422	124	4	3	22	10			.904	-10	S	-0.4
1913	Cle-A	141	508	78	131	19	7	3	39	46	51	.258	.322	.341	91	-5	-6	66	29			.936	-9	*S/O	-0.3
1914	Cle-A	106	375	59	103	16	10	2	42	48	48	.275	.358	.387	119	11	9	58	24	9	2	.913	-15	S2	0.3
1915	Cle-A	154	570	101	154	14	17	3	67	70	82	.270	.353	.370	114	12	10	84	36	15	2	.944	9	*S	3.5
1916	Cle-A	109	346	50	80	10	5	0	27	50	46	.231	.330	.289	81	-5	-7	41	21	14	-2	.935	13	S32	0.9
1917	Cle-A	156	563	98	170	28	13	2	36	61	65	.302	.370	.409	128	25	20	105	52			.938	**24**	*S	5.6
1918	Cle-A	128	446	**84**	119	19	8	1	32	**84**	46	.267	.390	.352	113	17	12	74	30			.936	6	*S/O	2.5
1919	Cle-A	115	433	75	130	23	10	3	53	31	38	.300	.351	.420	109	8	5	72	18			.944	-0	*S	1.2
1920	Cle-A	111	435	97	132	27	8	3	49	52	38	.303	.380	.423	109	9	7	72	13	9	-2	.959	12	*S	2.6
Total	9	1051	3785	671	1053	162	81	17	364	452	414	.278	.358	.377	110	76	52	595	233	47		.939	30	S/23O	15.9
■ SAM CHAPMAN Chapman, Samuel Blake b: 4/11/16, Tiburon, Cal. BR/TR, 6'1", 190 lbs. Deb: 5/16/38																									
1938	Phi-A	114	406	60	105	17	7	17	63	55	94	.259	.353	.461	105	0	2	67	3	4	-2	.952	-2	*O	-0.4
1939	Phi-A	140	498	74	134	24	6	15	64	51	62	.269	.338	.432	98	-5	-3	73	11	4	1	.955	4	*O1	-0.3
1940	Phi-A	134	508	88	140	26	3	23	75	46	96	.276	.337	.474	110	4	6	78	2	6	-3	.963	4	*O	0.0
1941	Phi-A	143	552	97	178	29	9	25	106	47	49	.322	.378	.543	145	30	32	110	6	9	-4	.967	14	*O	3.3
1945	Phi-A	9	30	3	6	2	0	0	1	2	4	.200	.250	.267	50	-2	-2	2	0	0	0	1.000	-1	/O	-0.4
1946	Phi-A★	146	545	77	142	22	5	20	67	54	66	.261	.327	.429	111	6	6	73	1	3	-2	.970	10	*O	0.8
1947	Phi-A	149	551	84	139	18	5	14	83	65	70	.252	.331	.379	95	-3	-4	71	3	4	-2	.987	12	*O	-0.2
1948	Phi-A	123	445	58	115	18	6	13	70	55	50	.258	.341	.413	100	-1	-1	63	6	1	1	.982	7	*O	0.1
1949	Phi-A	154	589	89	164	24	4	24	108	80	68	.278	.367	.455	121	12	15	97	3	4	-2	.979	11	*O	1.7
1950	Phi-A	144	553	93	139	20	6	23	95	68	79	.251	.338	.434	98	-5	-4	83	3	3	-1	.978	10	*O	0.0
1951	Phi-A	18	65	7	11	1	0	0	5	12	12	.169	.299	.185	32	-6	-6	4	0	0	0	.957	-1	O	-0.8
	Cle-A	94	246	24	56	9	1	6	36	27	32	.228	.304	.346	80	-9	-7	27	3	0	1	.985	-18	O/1	-2.6
	Yr	112	311	31	67	10	1	6	41	39	44	.215	.303	.312	69	-15	-13	31	3	0	1	.978	-19	*O/1	-3.4
Total	11	1368	4988	754	1329	210	52	180	773	562	682	.266	.342	.438	107	22	33	749	41	38	-11	.972	53	*O/1	1.2
■ BEN CHAPMAN Chapman, William Benjamin b: 12/25/08, Nashville, Tenn. BR/TR, 6', 190 lbs. Deb: 4/15/30 MC																									
1930	NY-A	138	513	74	162	31	10	10	81	43	58	.316	.371	.474	118	9	13	91	14	6	1	.912	-6	32	1.3
1931	NY-A	149	600	120	189	28	11	17	122	75	77	.315	.396	.483	138	27	32	119	**61**	23	**5**	.963	8	*O2	3.3
1932	*NY-A	151	581	101	174	41	15	10	107	71	55	.299	.381	.473	126	17	22	107	**38**	18	1	.949	-3	*O	1.0
1933	NY-A★	147	565	112	176	36	4	9	98	72	45	.312	.393	.437	127	18	23	99	**27**	18	-3	.975	11	*O	2.2
1934	NY-A★	149	588	82	181	21	**13**	5	86	67	68	.308	.381	.413	113	6	11	94	26	16	-2	.967	8	*O	1.1
1935	NY-A★	140	553	118	160	38	8	8	74	61	39	.289	.361	.430	110	3	7	87	17	10	-1	.964	17	*O	1.6
1936	NY-A	36	139	19	37	14	3	1	21	15	20	.266	.338	.432	92	-3	-2	20	1	2	-1	.965	2	O	-0.2
	Was-A	97	401	91	133	36	7	4	60	69	18	.332	.431	.486	133	19	23	89	19	7	2	.959	4	O	2.1
	Yr	133	540	110	170	50	10	5	81	84	38	.315	.408	.472	123	16	20	109	20	9	1	.961	7	*O	1.9
1937	Was-A	35	130	23	34	7	1	0	12	26	7	.262	.385	.331	86	-3	-2	20	8	0	2	.957	-1	O	-0.2
	Bos-A	113	423	76	130	23	11	7	57	57	35	.307	.391	.463	110	10	8	79	27	12	1	.985	9	*O/S	1.2
	Yr	148	553	99	164	30	12	7	69	83	42	.297	.389	.432	105	7	6	99	**35**	12	**3**	.978	7	*O/S	1.0
1938	Bos-A	127	480	92	163	40	8	6	80	65	33	.340	.418	.494	122	22	18	102	13	6	0	.966	6	*O/3	1.9
1939	Cle-A	149	545	101	158	31	9	6	82	87	30	.290	.390	.413	109	7	10	91	18	6	2	.971	-4	*O	0.2
1940	Cle-A	143	548	82	157	40	6	4	50	78	45	.286	.377	.403	105	4	6	85	13	7	-0	.964	2	*O	0.0
1941	Was-A	28	110	9	28	6	0	1	10	10	6	.255	.317	.336	76	-4	-4	10	2	2	-1	.983	1	O	-0.5
	Chi-A	57	190	26	43	9	1	2	19	19	14	.226	.297	.316	63	-11	-10	19	2	2	-1	.992	1	O	-1.2
	Yr	85	300	35	71	15	1	3	29	29	20	.237	.304	.323	68	-15	-14	29	4	4	-1	.989	2	O	-1.7
1944	Bro-N	20	38	11	14	4	0	0	11	5	4	.368	.442	.474	161	3	3	9	1			.900	-2	P	0.0
1945	Bro-N	13	22	2	3	0	0	0	3	2	1	.136	.208	.136	-3	-3	-3	1	0			.938	1	P	0.0
	Phi-N	24	51	4	16	2	0	0	4	2	1	.314	.340	.353	95	-1	-0	5	0			.933	-3	O/3PM	-0.4
	Yr	37	73	6	19	2	0	0	7	4	2	.260	.299	.288	65	-4	-3	5	0			.941	-3	PO/3	-0.4
1946	Phi-N	1	1	1	0	0	0	0	0	0	0	.000	.000	.000	-99	-0	-0	0	0			.000	0	/PM	0.0
Total	15	1717	6478	1144	1958	407	107	90	977	824	556	.302	.383	.440	115	120	155	1127	287	135		.967	50	*O/32PS	13.4
■ FRED CHAPMAN Chapman, William Fred "Chappie" b: 7/17/16, Liberty, S.C. BR/TR, 6'1", 185 lbs. Deb: 9/15/39																									
1939	Phi-A	15	49	5	14	1	1	0	1	1	3	.286	.300	.347	66	-3	-3	5	1	0	0	.899	-4	S	-0.4
1940	Phi-A	26	69	6	11	1	0	0	4	6	10	.159	.227	.174	6	-10	-9	3	1	1	-0	.862	-5	S	-1.3
1941	Phi-A	35	69	1	11	1	0	0	4	4	15	.159	.205	.174	1	-10	-10	2	1	2	-1	.917	-2	S/32	-1.1
Total	3	76	187	12	36	3	1	0	9	11	28	.193	.237	.219	20	-22	-22	11	3	3	-1	.889	-11	/S32	-2.8
■ HARRY CHAPPAS Chappas, Harry Perry b: 10/26/57, Mt.Ranier, Md. BB/TR, 5'3", 150 lbs. Deb: 9/07/78																									
1978	Chi-A	20	75	11	20	1	0	0	6	6	11	.267	.329	.280	72	-2	-3	8	1	2	-1	1.000	0	S	-0.1
1979	Chi-A	26	59	9	17	1	0	1	4	5	5	.288	.354	.356	92	-0	-0	7	1	1	-0	.929	3	S	0.3
1980	Chi-A	26	50	6	8	2	0	0	2	4	10	.160	.236	.200	21	-5	-5	2	0	2	-1	.981	-1	S/2D	-0.6
Total	3	72	184	26	45	4	0	1	12	15	26	.245	.312	.283	65	-8	-8	17	2	5	-2	.967	1	/SD2	-0.4
■ LARRY CHAPPELL Chappell, La Verne Ashford b: 2/19/1890, McClusky, Ill. d: 11/8/18, San Francisco, Cal. BL/TR, 6', 186 lbs. Deb: 7/18/13																									
1913	Chi-A	60	208	20	48	8	1	0	15	18	22	.231	.295	.279	69	-8	-8	18	7			.952	-1	O	-1.3
1914	Chi-A	21	39	3	9	0	0	0	1	4	11	.231	.302	.231	61	-2	-2	3	0			.929	-2	/O	-0.4
1915	Chi-A	1	1	0	0	0	0	0	0	0	0	.000	.000	.000	-97	-0	-0	0	0			.000	0	H	0.0
1916	Cle-A	3	2	0	0	0	0	0	0	1	0	.000	.333	.000	1	-0	-0	0	1			.000	0	H	0.0
	Bos-N	20	53	4	12	1	1	0	9	2	8	.226	.268	.283	72	-2	-2	4	1			.957	-2	O	-0.5
1917	Bos-N	4	2	0	0	0	0	0	1	0	1	.000	.000	.000	-99	-0	-0	0	0			.000	-1	/O	-0.1
Total	5	109	305	27	69	9	2	0	26	25	42	.226	.289	.269	66	-13	-12	26	9			.951	-6	/O	-2.3
■ JOE CHARBONEAU Charboneau, Joseph b: 6/17/55, Belvidere, Ill. BR/TR, 6'2", 205 lbs. Deb: 4/11/80																									
1980	Cle-A	131	453	76	131	17	2	23	87	49	70	.289	.362	.488	130	19	19	72	2	4	-2	.963	1	OD	1.5
1981	Cle-A	48	138	14	29	7	1	4	18	7	22	.210	.248	.362	75	-5	-5	11	1	0	0	.963	-2	OD	-0.8
1982	Cle-A	22	56	7	12	2	1	2	9	5	7	.214	.290	.393	86	-1	-1	6	0	0	0	.955	-3	O/D	-0.5
Total	3	201	647	97	172	26	4	29	114	61	99	.266	.333	.453	115	12	12	90	3	4	-2	.962	-4	O/D	0.2
■ ED CHARLES Charles, Edwin Douglas b: 4/29/33, Daytona Beach, Fla. BR/TR, 5'10", 170 lbs. Deb: 4/11/62																									
1962	KC-A	147	535	81	154	24	7	17	74	54	70	.288	.358	.454	113	12	10	89	20	4	4	.964	4	*3/2	2.0
1963	KC-A	158	603	82	161	28	2	15	79	58	79	.267	.336	.395	100	4	1	77	15	8	-0	.949	-8	*3	-0.8
1964	KC-A	150	557	69	134	25	2	16	63	64	92	.241	.323	.379	92	-4	-6	66	12	7	-1	.954	-15	*3	-2.4
1965	KC-A	134	480	55	129	19	7	8	56	44	72	.269	.335	.387	106	3	4	64	13	4	2	.971	-1	*3/2S	0.2
1966	KC-A	118	385	52	110	18	8	9	42	30	53	.286	.337	.444	127	11	12	56	12	5	1	.963	-6	*3/1O	0.5
1967	KC-A	19	61	5	15	1	0	0	5	12	13	.246	.378	.262	95	0	0	7	1	0	0	.966	-0	3	0.1

YEAR	TM/L	G	AB	R	H	2B	3B	HR	RBI	BB	SO	AVG	OBP	SLG	PRO+	BR	/A	RC	SB	CS	SBR	FA	FR	POS	TPR
	NY-N	101	323	32	77	13	2	3	31	24	58	.238	.305	.319	80	-9	-8	33	4	1	1	.944	9	3	0.0
1968	NY-N	117	369	41	102	11	1	15	53	28	57	.276	.331	.434	127	12	12	52	5	4	-1	.954	1	*3/1	1.3
1969	*NY-N	61	169	21	35	8	1	3	18	18	31	.207	.287	.320	68	-7	-7	15	4	2	0	.946	-0	3	-0.8
Total	8	1005	3482	438	917	147	30	86	421	332	525	.263	.332	.397	104	23	18	458	86	35	5	.957	-15	3/12OS	0.1

■ CHAPPY CHARLES Charles, Raymond (b: Charles Shuh Achenbach) b: 3/25/1881, Phillipsburg, N.J. d: 8/4/59, Bethlehem, Pa. BR/TR, 5'11", 175 lbs. Deb: 4/15/08

YEAR	TM/L	G	AB	R	H	2B	3B	HR	RBI	BB	SO	AVG	OBP	SLG	PRO+	BR	/A	RC	SB	CS	SBR	FA	FR	POS	TPR
1908	StL-N	121	454	39	93	14	3	1	17	19		.205	.238	.256	61	-22	-20	31	15			.921	-12	2S3	-3.7
1909	StL-N	99	339	33	80	7	3	0	29	31		.236	.309	.274	87	-7	-4	31	7			.918	-2	2S/3	-0.8
	Cin-N	13	43	3	11	2	0	0	5	4		.256	.319	.302	94	-0	-0	5	2			.932	-3	2/S	-0.4
	Yr	112	382	36	91	9	3	0	34	35		.238	.310	.277	87	-7	-5	36	9			.920	-5	2S/3	-1.2
1910	Cin-N	4	15	1	2	0	1	0	0	0	1	.133	.133	.267	17	-2	-2	0	0			.818	-2	/S	-0.3
Total	3	237	851	76	186	23	7	1	51	54	1	.219	.270	.266	72	-31	-26	68	24			.920	-18	2/S3	-5.2

■ MIKE CHARTAK Chartak, Michael George "Shotgun" b: 4/28/16, Brooklyn, N.Y. d: 7/25/67, Cedar Rapids, Ia. BL/TL, 6'2", 180 lbs. Deb: 9/13/40

YEAR	TM/L	G	AB	R	H	2B	3B	HR	RBI	BB	SO	AVG	OBP	SLG	PRO+	BR	/A	RC	SB	CS	SBR	FA	FR	POS	TPR
1940	NY-A	11	15	2	2	1	0	0	3	5	5	.133	.350	.200	49	-1	-1	2	0	0	0	1.000	-1	/O	-0.2
1942	NY-A	5	5	0	0	0	0	0	0	0	0	.000	.000	.000	-99	-1	-1	0	0	0	0	.000	0	H	-0.1
	Was-A	24	92	11	20	4	2	1	8	14	16	.217	.321	.337	86	-2	-2	10	0	1	-1	.926	-0	O	-0.4
	StL-A	73	237	37	59	11	2	9	43	40	27	.249	.362	.426	119	7	7	39	3	3	-1	.974	7	O	1.0
	Yr	102	334	48	79	15	4	10	51	54	43	.237	.346	.395	107	4	4	48	3	4	-2	.962	7	O	0.5
1943	StL-A	108	344	38	88	16	2	10	37	39	55	.256	.333	.401	112	6	5	47	1	3	-2	.970	-4	O1	-0.5
1944	*StL-A	35	72	8	17	2	1	1	7	6	9	.236	.304	.333	77	-2	-2	8	0	0	0	1.000	0	1/O	-0.3
Total	4	256	765	96	186	34	7	21	98	104	112	.243	.337	.388	105	7	5	105	4	7	-3	.967	3	O/1	-0.5

■ HAL CHASE Chase, Harold Homer "Prince Hal" b: 2/13/1883, Los Gatos, Cal. d: 5/18/47, Colusa, Cal. BR/TL, 6', 175 lbs. Deb: 4/14/05 M

YEAR	TM/L	G	AB	R	H	2B	3B	HR	RBI	BB	SO	AVG	OBP	SLG	PRO+	BR	/A	RC	SB	CS	SBR	FA	FR	POS	TPR
1905	NY-A	128	465	60	116	16	6	3	49	15		.249	.277	.329	83	-6	-11	52	22			.976	-9	*1/S2	-2.7
1906	NY-A	151	597	84	193	23	10	0	76	13		.323	.339	.395	118	18	11	94	28			.980	-3	*1/2	0.4
1907	NY-A	125	498	72	143	23	3	2	68	19		.287	.313	.357	105	6	2	68	32			.973	1	*1/O	-0.1
1908	NY-A	106	405	50	104	11	3	1	36	15		.257	.283	.306	91	-5	-5	42	27			.980	-4	1/2O3P	-1.3
1909	NY-A	118	474	60	134	17	3	4	63	20		.283	.317	.357	112	5	5	61	25			.978	-2	*1/S	0.2
1910	NY-A	130	524	67	152	20	5	3	73	16		.290	.312	.365	106	5	1	71	40			.981	-4	*1M	-0.3
1911	NY-A	133	527	82	166	32	7	3	62	21		.315	.342	.419	105	6	1	87	36			.974	-2	*1/O2M	-0.1
1912	NY-A	131	522	61	143	21	9	4	58	17		.274	.299	.372	86	-8	-13	67	33			.979	-5	*1/2	-1.9
1913	NY-A	39	146	15	31	2	4	0	9	11	13	.212	.268	.281	60	-8	-8	12	5			.982	-5	1/2O	-1.4
	Chi-A	102	384	49	110	11	10	2	39	16	41	.286	.320	.383	107	1	1	48	9			.976	1	*1	0.1
	Yr	141	530	64	141	13	14	2	48	27	54	.266	.305	.355	94	-7	-6	59	14			.977	-4	*1/2O	-1.3
1914	Chi-A	58	206	27	55	10	5	0	20	23	19	.267	.343	.364	114	3	3	28	9	4	0	.981	2	1	0.5
	Buf-F	75	291	43	101	19	9	3	48	6	31	.347	.365	.505	143	15	15	59	10			.980	-1	1	1.3
1915	Buf-F	145	567	85	165	31	10	**17**	89	20	50	.291	.316	.471	127	17	15	95	23			.983	0	*1/O	1.3
1916	Cin-N	142	542	66	**184**	29	12	4	82	19	48	**.339**	.363	.459	**155**	30	31	93	22	11	0	.986	-7	1O2	2.2
1917	Cin-N	152	602	71	167	28	15	4	86	15	49	.277	.296	.394	115	5	7	72	21			.983	-3	*1	-0.1
1918	Cin-N	74	259	30	78	12	6	2	38	13	15	.301	.339	.417	133	8	9	37	5			.980	-2	1/O	0.4
1919	NY-N	110	408	58	116	17	7	5	45	17	40	.284	.318	.397	115	6	6	54	16			.984	-1	*1	0.1
Total	15	1919	7417	980	2158	322	124	57	941	276	306	.291	.319	.391	111	98	72	1039	363	15		.980	-45	*1/O2SP3	-1.4

■ BUSTER CHATHAM Chatham, Charles L b: 12/25/01, West, Tex. d: 12/15/75, Waco, Tex. BR/TR, 5'5", 150 lbs. Deb: 6/01/30

YEAR	TM/L	G	AB	R	H	2B	3B	HR	RBI	BB	SO	AVG	OBP	SLG	PRO+	BR	/A	RC	SB	CS	SBR	FA	FR	POS	TPR
1930	Bos-N	112	404	48	108	20	11	5	56	37	41	.267	.332	.408	80	-15	-13	54	8			.920	-14	3S	-1.8
1931	Bos-N	17	44	4	10	1	0	1	3	6	6	.227	.320	.318	75	-2	-1	5	0			.762	-6	/S3	-0.6
Total	2	129	448	52	118	21	11	6	59	43	47	.263	.331	.400	80	-17	-14	59	8			.924	-20	/3S	-2.4

■ JIM CHATTERTON Chatterton, James M. b: 10/14/1864, Brooklyn, N.Y. d: 12/15/44, Tewksbury, Mass. Deb: 6/07/1884

YEAR	TM/L	G	AB	R	H	2B	3B	HR	RBI	BB	SO	AVG	OBP	SLG	PRO+	BR	/A	RC	SB	CS	SBR	FA	FR	POS	TPR
1884	KC-U	4	15	4	2	1	0	0		2		.133	.235	.200	56	-1	-0	1				1.000	0	/O1P	-0.1

■ OSSIE CHAVARRIA Chavarria, Osvaldo (Quijano) b: 8/5/40, Colon, Panama BR/TR, 5'11", 155 lbs. Deb: 4/14/66

YEAR	TM/L	G	AB	R	H	2B	3B	HR	RBI	BB	SO	AVG	OBP	SLG	PRO+	BR	/A	RC	SB	CS	SBR	FA	FR	POS	TPR
1966	KC-A	86	191	26	46	10	0	2	10	18	43	.241	.306	.325	84	-4	-4	19	3	2	-0	.939	-5	OS2/13	-0.8
1967	KC-A	38	59	2	6	2	0	0	4	7	16	.102	.209	.136	4	-7	-7	2	1	0	0	1.000	2	2/3OS	-0.4
Total	2	124	250	28	52	12	0	2	14	25	59	.208	.283	.280	65	-11	-10	21	4	2	0	.990	-2	/2OS31	-1.2

■ HARRY CHEEK Cheek, Harry G. b: 1879, Sedalia, Mo. d: 6/25/56, Paramas, N.J. TR, Deb: 5/12/10

YEAR	TM/L	G	AB	R	H	2B	3B	HR	RBI	BB	SO	AVG	OBP	SLG	PRO+	BR	/A	RC	SB	CS	SBR	FA	FR	POS	TPR
1910	Phi-N	2	4	1	2	1	0	0	0	0	0	.500	.500	.750	255	1	1	1	0			1.000	-1	/C	0.0

■ PAUL CHERVINKO Chervinko, Paul b: 7/28/10, Trauger, Pa. d: 6/3/76, Danville, Ill. BR/TR, 5'8", 185 lbs. Deb: 5/30/37

YEAR	TM/L	G	AB	R	H	2B	3B	HR	RBI	BB	SO	AVG	OBP	SLG	PRO+	BR	/A	RC	SB	CS	SBR	FA	FR	POS	TPR
1937	Bro-N	30	48	1	7	0	1	0	2	3	16	.146	.196	.188	5	-6	-6	2	0			1.000	0	C	-0.6
1938	Bro-N	12	27	0	4	0	0	0	3	2	0	.148	.207	.148	-1	-4	-4	1	0			.974	0	C	-0.3
Total	2	42	75	1	11	0	1	0	5	5	16	.147	.200	.173	3	-10	-10	2	0			.990	1	/C	-0.9

■ CUPID CHILDS Childs, Clarence Algernon b: 8/14/1867, Calvert Co., Md. d: 11/8/12, Baltimore, Md. BL/TR, 5'8", 185 lbs. Deb: 4/23/1888

YEAR	TM/L	G	AB	R	H	2B	3B	HR	RBI	BB	SO	AVG	OBP	SLG	PRO+	BR	/A	RC	SB	CS	SBR	FA	FR	POS	TPR
1888	Phi-N	2	4	0	0	0	0	0	0	0	0	.000	.000	.000	-95	-1	-1	0	0			.857	0	/2	-0.1
1890	Syr-a	126	493	109	170	**33**	14	2		72		.345	.434	.481	193	47	**55**	130	56			.928	12	*2/S	**6.4**
1891	Cle-N	141	551	120	155	21	12	2	83	97	32	.281	.395	.374	122	23	20	99	39			.910	-12	*2	1.2
1892	*Cle-N	145	558	**136**	177	14	11	3	53	117	20	.317	**.443**	.398	151	47	43	113	26			.938	-6	*2	3.6
1893	Cle-N	124	485	145	158	19	10	3	65	120	12	.326	.463	.425	131	36	30	109	23			.926	10	*2	3.4
1894	Cle-N	118	479	143	169	21	12	2	52	107	11	.353	.475	.459	124	30	26	116	17			.916	-3	*2	2.1
1895	*Cle-N	119	462	96	133	15	3	4	90	74	24	.288	.393	.359	92	2	-4	76	20			.921	10	*2	1.0
1896	*Cle-N	132	498	106	177	24	9	1	106	100	18	.355	.467	.446	136	39	33	120	25			.942	**42**	*2	6.9
1897	Cle-N	114	444	105	150	15	9	1	61	74		.338	.435	.419	119	21	16	96	25			.944	17	*2	3.3
1898	Cle-N	110	413	90	119	9	4	1	31	69		.288	.395	.337	112	9	10	62	9			.931	9	*2	2.4
1899	StL-N	125	464	73	123	11	11	1	48	74		.265	.369	.343	93	-0	-2	66	11			.934	-12	*2	-0.6
1900	Chi-N	137	531	67	128	14	5	0	44	57		.241	.323	.286	71	-21	-18	58	15			.935	16	*2	0.4
1901	Chi-N	63	236	24	61	9	0	0	21	30		.258	.357	.297	94	-1	0	27	3			.939	9	2	1.2
Total	13	1456	5618	1214	1720	205	100	20	654	991	117	.306	.416	.389	121	230	210	1073	269			.930	92	*2/S	31.2

■ PETE CHILDS Childs, Peter Pierre b: 11/15/1871, Philadelphia, Pa. d: 2/15/22, Philadelphia, Pa. TR, Deb: 4/24/01

YEAR	TM/L	G	AB	R	H	2B	3B	HR	RBI	BB	SO	AVG	OBP	SLG	PRO+	BR	/A	RC	SB	CS	SBR	FA	FR	POS	TPR
1901	StL-N	29	79	12	21	1	0	0	8	14		.266	.389	.278	101	1	1	9	0			.907	-6	2/OS	-0.4
	Chi-N	60	210	23	48	5	1	0	14	26		.229	.319	.262	72	-7	-6	20	4			.959	13	2	0.9
	Yr	89	289	35	69	6	1	0	22	40		.239	.339	.266	80	-6	-5	29	4			.947	7	2/OS	0.5
1902	Phi-N	123	403	25	78	5	0	0	25	34		.194	.260	.206	44	-26	-26	25	6			.945	-9	*2	-3.2
Total	2	212	692	60	147	11	1	0	47	74		.212	.294	.231	59	-32	-30	54	10			.946	-2	2/OS	-2.7

■ PEARCE CHILES Chiles, Pearce Nuget "What's The Use" b: 5/28/1867, Deepwater, Mo. BR/TR, 5'11", 185 lbs. Deb: 4/18/1899

YEAR	TM/L	G	AB	R	H	2B	3B	HR	RBI	BB	SO	AVG	OBP	SLG	PRO+	BR	/A	RC	SB	CS	SBR	FA	FR	POS	TPR
1899	Phi-N	97	338	57	108	28	7	2	76	16		.320	.352	.462	127	8	10	59	6			.944	-16	O12	-0.7
1900	Phi-N	33	111	13	24	6	2	1	23	6		.216	.256	.333	63	-6	-6	11	4			.987	-3	12/O	-0.8
Total	2	130	449	70	132	34	9	3	99	22		.294	.328	.430	111	2	4	70	10			.947	-19	/O12	-1.5

■ RICH CHILES Chiles, Richard Francis b: 11/22/49, Sacramento, Cal. BL/TL, 5'11", 170 lbs. Deb: 9/20/71

YEAR	TM/L	G	AB	R	H	2B	3B	HR	RBI	BB	SO	AVG	OBP	SLG	PRO+	BR	/A	RC	SB	CS	SBR	FA	FR	POS	TPR
1971	Hou-N	67	119	12	27	5	1	2	15	6	20	.227	.270	.336	73	-5	-5	10	0	1	-1	1.000	-3	O	-1.0

YEAR	TM/L	G	AB	R	H	2B	3B	HR	RBI	BB	SO	AVG	OBP	SLG	PRO+	BR	/A	RC	SB	CS	SBR	FA	FR	POS	TPR
1972	Hou-N	9	11	0	3	1	0	0	2	1	1	.273	.333	.364	100	-0	0	1	0	0	0	1.000	0	/O	0.0
1973	NY-N	8	25	2	3	2	0	0	1	0	2	.120	.120	.200	-13	-4	-4	0	0	0	0	1.000	3	/O	-0.2
1976	Hou-N	5	4	1	2	1	0	0	0	0	0	.500	.500	.750	276	1	1	2	0	0	0	1.000	0	/O	0.1
1977	Min-A	108	261	31	69	16	1	3	36	23	17	.264	.329	.368	91	-4	-3	32	0	1	-1	.946	-2	DO	-0.7
1978	Min-A	87	198	22	53	12	0	1	22	20	25	.268	.341	.343	91	-1	-2	22	1	2	-1	.965	-2	O/D	-0.7
Total	6	284	618	68	157	37	2	6	76	50	65	.254	.315	.350	85	-13	-12	67	1	4	-2	.972	-4	O/D	-2.5

■ DINO CHIOZZA Chiozza, Dino Joseph "Dynamo" b: 6/30/12, Memphis, Tenn. d: 4/23/72, Memphis, Tenn. BL/TR, 6', 170 lbs. Deb: 7/14/35 F

YEAR	TM/L	G	AB	R	H	2B	3B	HR	RBI	BB	SO	AVG	OBP	SLG	PRO+	BR	/A	RC	SB	CS	SBR	FA	FR	POS	TPR
1935	Phi-N	2	0	1	0	0	0	0	0	0	0	—	—	—	—	0	0	0	0			1.000	-0	/S	0.0

■ LOU CHIOZZA Chiozza, Louis Peo b: 5/17/10, Tallulah, La. d: 2/28/71, Memphis, Tenn. BL/TR, 6', 172 lbs. Deb: 4/17/34 F

YEAR	TM/L	G	AB	R	H	2B	3B	HR	RBI	BB	SO	AVG	OBP	SLG	PRO+	BR	/A	RC	SB	CS	SBR	FA	FR	POS	TPR
1934	Phi-N	134	484	66	147	28	5	0	44	34	35	.304	.357	.382	86	-1	-9	68	9			.938	-24	23O	-2.7
1935	Phi-N	124	472	71	134	26	6	3	47	33	44	.284	.333	.383	84	-5	-12	64	5			.947	3	*2/3	0.0
1936	Phi-N	144	572	83	170	32	6	1	48	37	39	.297	.346	.379	87	-3	-11	80	17			.972	1	O23	-1.1
1937	*NY-N	117	439	49	102	11	2	4	29	20	30	.232	.266	.294	51	-30	-30	36	6			.939	2	3O/2	-2.7
1938	NY-N	57	179	15	42	7	2	3	17	12	7	.235	.283	.346	72	-7	-7	18	5			.944	-8	2O/3	-1.4
1939	NY-N	40	142	19	38	3	1	3	12	9	10	.268	.311	.366	81	-4	-4	17	3			.915	-3	3/S	-0.6
Total	6	616	2288	303	633	107	22	14	197	145	165	.277	.324	.361	78	-50	-73	283	45			.943	-30	23O/S	-8.5

■ WALT CHIPPLE Chipple, Walter John (b: Walter John Chlipala) b: 9/26/18, Utica, N.Y. d: 6/8/88, Tonawanda, N.Y. BR/TR, 6'0.5", 168 lbs. Deb: 4/17/45

YEAR	TM/L	G	AB	R	H	2B	3B	HR	RBI	BB	SO	AVG	OBP	SLG	PRO+	BR	/A	RC	SB	CS	SBR	FA	FR	POS	TPR
1945	Was-A	18	44	4	6	0	0	0	5	5	6	.136	.224	.136	6	-5	-5	1	0	1	-1	.978	3	O	-0.3

■ TOM CHISM Chism, Thomas Raymond b: 5/9/55, Chester, Pa. BL/TL, 6'1", 195 lbs. Deb: 9/13/79

YEAR	TM/L	G	AB	R	H	2B	3B	HR	RBI	BB	SO	AVG	OBP	SLG	PRO+	BR	/A	RC	SB	CS	SBR	FA	FR	POS	TPR
1979	Bal-A	6	3	0	0	0	0	0	0	0	0	.000	.000	.000	-99	-1	-1	0	0	0	0	1.000	-0	/1	-0.1

■ HARRY CHITI Chiti, Harry b: 11/16/32, Kincaid, Ill. BR/TR, 6'3", 225 lbs. Deb: 9/27/50

YEAR	TM/L	G	AB	R	H	2B	3B	HR	RBI	BB	SO	AVG	OBP	SLG	PRO+	BR	/A	RC	SB	CS	SBR	FA	FR	POS	TPR
1950	Chi-N	3	6	0	2	0	0	0	0	0	0	.333	.333	.333	77	-0	-0	1	0			1.000	-1	/C	-0.1
1951	Chi-N	9	31	1	11	2	0	0	5	2	2	.355	.394	.419	117	1	1	4	0	0	0	.913	0	/C	0.1
1952	Chi-N	32	113	14	31	5	0	5	13	5	8	.274	.305	.451	106	1	0	15	0	1	-1	.984	6	C	0.7
1955	Chi-N	113	338	24	78	6	1	11	41	25	68	.231	.286	.352	68	-16	-16	33	0	0	0	.984	1	*C	-1.1
1956	Chi-N	72	203	17	43	6	4	4	18	19	35	.212	.283	.340	68	-10	-9	18	0	0	0	.981	2	C	-0.5
1958	KC-A	103	295	32	79	11	3	9	44	18	48	.268	.316	.417	98	-1	-1	37	3	2	-0	.987	3	C	0.6
1959	KC-A	55	162	20	44	11	1	5	25	17	26	.272	.344	.444	113	3	3	22	0	1	-1	.988	2	C	0.7
1960	KC-A	58	190	16	42	7	0	5	28	17	33	.221	.288	.337	68	-9	-9	18	1	0	0	.983	-1	C	-0.6
	Det-A	37	104	9	17	0	0	2	5	10	12	.163	.237	.221	24	-11	-11	4	0	3	-2	.984	1	C	-1.0
	Yr	95	294	25	59	7	0	7	33	27	45	.201	.270	.296	52	-20	-20	21	1	3	-2	.984	1	C	-1.6
1961	Det-A	5	12	0	1	0	0	0	0	1	2	.083	.154	.083	-34	-2	-2	0	0	0	0	1.000	1	/C	-0.1
1962	NY-N	15	41	2	8	1	0	0	0	1	8	.195	.233	.220	22	-4	-5	2	0	0	0	.971	-1	C	-0.5
Total	10	502	1495	135	356	49	9	41	179	115	242	.238	.296	.365	77	-48	-50	153	4	7		.983	13	C	-1.8

■ FELIX CHOUINARD Chouinard, Felix George b: 10/5/1887, Hines, Ill. d: 4/28/55, Hines, Ill. BR/TR, 5'7", 150 lbs. Deb: 9/11/10

YEAR	TM/L	G	AB	R	H	2B	3B	HR	RBI	BB	SO	AVG	OBP	SLG	PRO+	BR	/A	RC	SB	CS	SBR	FA	FR	POS	TPR
1910	Chi-A	24	82	6	16	3	2	0	9	8		.195	.275	.280	77	-2	-2	7	4			.962	4	O/2	0.1
1911	Chi-A	14	17	3	3	0	0	0	0	0		.176	.176	.176	-2	-2	-2	1	0			.857	1	/2O	-0.1
1914	Pit-F	9	30	2	9	1	0	1	3	0	4	.300	.300	.433	108	0	0	4	1			.917	-1	/2OS	-0.1
	Bro-F	32	79	7	20	1	2	0	8	4	13	.253	.289	.316	73	-3	-3	9	3			.929	-1	O	-0.4
	Bal-F	5	9	3	4	0	0	0	1	0	1	.444	.444	.444	148	1	1	2	0			1.000	-0	/O	0.0
	Yr	46	118	12	33	2	2	1	12	4	18	.280	.303	.356	87	-2	-2	15	4			.941	-1	O/2S	-0.5
1915	Bro-F	4	4	1	2	0	0	0	2	0	0	.500	.500	.500	196	0	0	1	0			1.000	-1	/O	0.0
Total	4	88	221	22	54	5	4	1	23	12	18	.244	.286	.317	79	-7	-6	24	8			.948	3	/O2S	-0.5

■ HARRY CHOZEN Chozen, Harry b: 9/27/15, Winnebago, Minn. BR/TR, 5'9.5", 190 lbs. Deb: 9/21/37

YEAR	TM/L	G	AB	R	H	2B	3B	HR	RBI	BB	SO	AVG	OBP	SLG	PRO+	BR	/A	RC	SB	CS	SBR	FA	FR	POS	TPR
1937	Cin-N	1	4	0	1	0	0	0	0	0	0	.250	.250	.250	38	-0	-0	0	0			.833	-0	/C	-0.1

■ NEIL CHRISLEY Chrisley, Barbra O'Neil b: 12/16/31, Calhoun Falls, S.C BL/TR, 6'3", 187 lbs. Deb: 4/15/57

YEAR	TM/L	G	AB	R	H	2B	3B	HR	RBI	BB	SO	AVG	OBP	SLG	PRO+	BR	/A	RC	SB	CS	SBR	FA	FR	POS	TPR
1957	Was-A	26	51	6	8	2	1	0	3	7	7	.157	.259	.235	36	-5	-4	4	0	0	0	.810	-1	O	-0.6
1958	Was-A	105	233	19	50	7	4	5	26	16	18	.215	.265	.343	67	-11	-11	19	1	3	-2	.992	1	O/3	-1.5
1959	Det-A	65	106	7	14	3	0	6	11	12	10	.132	.227	.330	48	-8	-8	8	0	0	0	1.000	-2	O	-1.2
1960	Det-A	96	220	27	56	10	3	5	24	19	26	.255	.317	.395	89	-3	-4	28	2	0	1	.981	2	O/1	-0.3
1961	Mil-N	10	9	1	2	0	0	0	0	1	1	.222	.300	.222	44	-1	-1	1	0	0	0	.000	0	H	-0.1
Total	5	302	619	60	130	22	8	16	64	55	62	.210	.277	.349	69	-27	-28	60	3	3	-1	.975	-0	O/13	-3.7

■ LLOYD CHRISTENBURY Christenbury, Lloyd Reid "Low" b: 10/19/1893, Mecklenburg Co., N.C. d: 12/13/44, Birmingham, Ala. BL/TR, 5'7", 165 lbs. Deb: 9/20/19

YEAR	TM/L	G	AB	R	H	2B	3B	HR	RBI	BB	SO	AVG	OBP	SLG	PRO+	BR	/A	RC	SB	CS	SBR	FA	FR	POS	TPR
1919	Bos-N	7	31	5	9	1	0	0	4	2	2	.290	.333	.323	102	-0	0	3	0			.941	1	/O	0.1
1920	Bos-N	65	106	17	22	2	2	0	14	13	12	.208	.300	.264	66	-5	-4	9	0	1	-1	.895	-7	O/S23	-1.2
1921	Bos-N	62	125	34	44	6	2	3	16	21	7	.352	.449	.504	161	10	11	28	3	4	-2	.914	-13	2/S3	-0.2
1922	Bos-N	71	152	22	38	5	2	1	13	18	11	.250	.337	.329	76	-6	-5	17	2	4	-2	.946	0	O/23	-0.8
Total	4	205	414	78	113	14	6	4	47	54	32	.273	.362	.365	101	-0	3	58	5	9		.936	-18	/O2S3	-2.1

■ BRUCE CHRISTENSEN Christensen, Bruce Ray b: 2/22/48, Madison, Wis. BL/TR, 5'11", 160 lbs. Deb: 7/17/71

YEAR	TM/L	G	AB	R	H	2B	3B	HR	RBI	BB	SO	AVG	OBP	SLG	PRO+	BR	/A	RC	SB	CS	SBR	FA	FR	POS	TPR
1971	Cal-A	29	63	4	17	1	0	0	3	6	5	.270	.333	.286	83	-2	-1	6	0	1	-1	.988	2	S	0.3

■ JOHN CHRISTENSEN Christensen, John Lawrence b: 9/5/60, Downey, Cal. BR/TR, 6'3", 205 lbs. Deb: 9/13/84

YEAR	TM/L	G	AB	R	H	2B	3B	HR	RBI	BB	SO	AVG	OBP	SLG	PRO+	BR	/A	RC	SB	CS	SBR	FA	FR	POS	TPR
1984	NY-N	5	11	2	3	2	0	0	3	1	2	.273	.333	.455	121	0	0	1	0	1	-1	.500	-2	/O	-0.2
1985	NY-N	51	113	10	21	4	1	3	13	19	23	.186	.303	.319	76	-4	-3	11	1	2	-1	.956	-6	O	-1.1
1987	Sea-A	53	132	19	32	6	1	2	12	12	28	.242	.306	.348	69	-5	-6	14	2	0	1	1.000	-3	O/D	-0.9
1988	Min-A	23	38	5	10	4	0	0	5	3	5	.263	.349	.368	98	0	0	5	0	0	0	1.000	-3	O/D	-0.3
Total	4	132	294	36	66	16	2	5	33	35	58	.224	.311	.344	77	-8	-9	32	3	3	-1	.977	-13	O/D	-2.5

■ CUCKOO CHRISTENSEN Christensen, Walter Niels "Seacap" b: 10/24/1899, San Francisco, Cal d: 12/20/84, Menlo Park, Cal. BL/TL, 5'6.5", 156 lbs. Deb: 4/13/26

YEAR	TM/L	G	AB	R	H	2B	3B	HR	RBI	BB	SO	AVG	OBP	SLG	PRO+	BR	/A	RC	SB	CS	SBR	FA	FR	POS	TPR
1926	Cin-N	114	329	41	115	15	7	0	41	40	18	.350	.426	.438	136	17	19	62	8			.978	-10	O	0.3
1927	Cin-N	57	185	25	47	6	0	0	16	20	16	.254	.330	.286	68	-8	-7	18	4			.957	-3	O	-1.3
Total	2	171	514	66	162	21	7	0	57	60	34	.315	.392	.383	112	9	11	80	12			.970	-13	O	-1.0

■ BOB CHRISTIAN Christian, Robert Charles b: 10/17/45, Chicago, Ill. d: 2/20/74, San Diego, Cal. BR/TR, 5'10", 180 lbs. Deb: 9/02/68

YEAR	TM/L	G	AB	R	H	2B	3B	HR	RBI	BB	SO	AVG	OBP	SLG	PRO+	BR	/A	RC	SB	CS	SBR	FA	FR	POS	TPR
1968	Det-A	3	3	0	1	1	0	0	0	0	0	.333	.333	.667	191	0	0	1	0	0	0	1.000	-0	/1O	0.0
1969	Chi-A	39	129	11	28	4	0	3	16	10	19	.217	.279	.318	63	-6	-7	12	3	0	1	.958	0	O	-0.8
1970	Chi-A	12	15	3	4	0	0	1	3	1	4	.267	.313	.467	108	0	0	2	0	0	0	1.000	-1	/O	-0.1
Total	3	54	147	14	33	5	0	4	19	11	23	.224	.283	.340	70	-6	-6	15	3	0	1	.959	-1	/O1	-0.9

■ MARK CHRISTMAN Christman, Marquette Joseph b: 10/21/13, Maplewood, Mo. d: 10/9/76, St.Louis, Mo. BR/TR, 5'11", 180 lbs. Deb: 4/20/38

YEAR	TM/L	G	AB	R	H	2B	3B	HR	RBI	BB	SO	AVG	OBP	SLG	PRO+	BR	/A	RC	SB	CS	SBR	FA	FR	POS	TPR
1938	Det-A	95	318	35	79	6	4	1	44	27	21	.248	.307	.302	50	-23	-26	31	5	2	0	.983	9	3S	-1.3
1939	Det-A	6	16	0	4	2	0	0	0	0	2	.250	.250	.375	54	-1	-1	1	0	0	0	.900	-1	/3	-0.2
	StL-A	79	222	27	48	6	3	0	20	20	10	.216	.281	.270	41	-20	-20	16	2	1	0	.960	21	S/2	0.5
	Yr	85	238	27	52	8	3	0	20	20	12	.218	.279	.277	42	-21	-22	17	2	1	0	.960	20	S/32	0.3

YEAR	TM/L	G	AB	R	H	2B	3B	HR	RBI	BB	SO	AVG	OBP	SLG	PRO+	BR	/A	RC	SB	CS	SBR	FA	FR	POS	TPR
1943	StL-A	98	336	31	91	11	5	2	35	19	19	.271	.318	.351	94	-3	-3	38	0	3	-2	.991	-0	3S12	-0.4
1944	*StL-A	148	547	56	148	25	1	6	83	47	37	.271	.332	.353	90	-3	-7	64	5	2	0	**.972**	4	*3/1	-0.1
1945	StL-A†	78	289	32	80	7	4	4	34	19	19	.277	.328	.370	98	0	-1	36	1	0	0	.973	-3	3	-0.2
1946	StL-A	128	458	40	118	22	2	1	41	22	29	.258	.295	.321	68	-18	-20	41	0	2	-1	.975	9	3S	-0.9
1947	Was-A	110	374	27	83	15	2	1	33	32	16	.222	.287	.281	60	-21	-20	30	4	4	-1	.978	-10	*S/2	-2.7
1948	Was-A	120	409	38	106	17	2	1	40	25	19	.259	.303	.318	67	-21	-19	37	0	3	-2	.969	-32	*S/32	-4.7
1949	Was-A	49	112	8	24	2	0	3	18	8	7	.214	.273	.313	56	-8	-8	9	0	0	0	.967	3	3/1S2	-0.5
Total	9	911	3081	294	781	113	23	19	348	219	179	.253	.306	.324	71	-117	-126	302	17	17	-5	.975	-0	3S/12	-10.5

■ STEVE CHRISTMAS
Christmas, Stephen Randall b: 12/9/57, Orlando, Fla. BL/TR, 6', 190 lbs. Deb: 9/01/83

YEAR	TM/L	G	AB	R	H	2B	3B	HR	RBI	BB	SO	AVG	OBP	SLG	PRO+	BR	/A	RC	SB	CS	SBR	FA	FR	POS	TPR
1983	Cin-N	9	17	0	1	0	0	0	1	1	3	.059	.111	.059	-50	-3	-4	0	0	0	0	1.000	-0	/C	-0.4
1984	Chi-A	12	11	1	4	1	0	1	4	0	2	.364	.364	.727	185	1	1	3	0	0	0	1.000	0	/C	0.1
1986	Chi-N	3	9	0	1	1	0	0	2	0	1	.111	.111	.222	-10	-1	-1	0	0	0	0	1.000	-0	/C1	-0.2
Total	3	24	37	1	6	2	0	1	7	1	6	.162	.184	.297	30	-4	-4	3	0	0	0	1.000	-0	/C1	-0.5

■ JOE CHRISTOPHER
Christopher, Joseph O'Neal b: 12/13/35, Frederiksted, V.I. BR/TR, 5'10", 176 lbs. Deb: 5/26/59

YEAR	TM/L	G	AB	R	H	2B	3B	HR	RBI	BB	SO	AVG	OBP	SLG	PRO+	BR	/A	RC	SB	CS	SBR	FA	FR	POS	TPR
1959	Pit-N	15	12	6	0	0	0	0	0	1	4	.000	.077	.000	-78	-3	-3	0	0	0	0	1.000	-3	/O	-0.6
1960	*Pit-N	50	56	21	13	2	0	1	3	5	8	.232	.295	.321	68	-2	-2	6	1	0	0	1.000	-2	O	-0.5
1961	Pit-N	76	186	25	49	7	3	0	14	18	24	.263	.328	.333	76	-6	-6	19	6	4	-1	.978	-2	O	-1.1
1962	NY-N	119	271	36	66	10	2	6	32	35	42	.244	.339	.362	87	-4	-5	36	11	3	2	.972	-0	O	-0.7
1963	NY-N	64	149	19	33	5	1	1	8	13	21	.221	.297	.289	68	-6	-6	13	1	3	-2	.983	-3	O	-1.3
1964	NY-N	154	543	78	163	26	8	16	76	48	92	.300	.363	.466	135	23	24	88	6	5	-1	.974	-1	*O	1.6
1965	NY-N	148	437	38	109	18	3	5	40	35	82	.249	.314	.339	87	-9	-7	46	4	4	-1	.989	-7	*O	-2.2
1966	Bos-A	12	13	1	1	0	0	0	0	2	4	.077	.200	.077	-15	-2	-2	0	0	0	0	1.000	-1	/O	-0.3
Total	8	638	1667	224	434	68	17	29	173	157	277	.260	.331	.374	96	-9	-7	208	29	19	-3	.979	-19	O	-5.1

■ LOYD CHRISTOPHER
Christopher, Loyd Eugene b: 12/31/19, Richmond, Cal. d: 9/5/91, Richmond, Cal. BR/TR, 6'2", 190 lbs. Deb: 4/20/45 F

YEAR	TM/L	G	AB	R	H	2B	3B	HR	RBI	BB	SO	AVG	OBP	SLG	PRO+	BR	/A	RC	SB	CS	SBR	FA	FR	POS	TPR
1945	Bos-A	8	14	4	4	0	0	0	4	3	2	.286	.412	.286	101	0	0	2	0	0	0	1.000	-1	/O	-0.1
	Chi-N	1	0	0	0	0	0	0	0	0	0	—	—	—	—	0	0	0	0			.000	-0	/O	0.0
1947	Chi-A	7	23	1	5	0	1	0	0	2	4	.217	.280	.304	65	-1	-1	1	0	1	-1	1.000	1	/O	-0.1
Total	2	16	37	5	9	0	1	0	4	5	6	.243	.333	.297	80	-1	-1	3	0	1		1.000	0	/O	-0.2

■ HI CHURCH
Church, Hiram Lincoln b: Central Square, N.Y. Deb: 8/23/1890

YEAR	TM/L	G	AB	R	H	2B	3B	HR	RBI	BB	SO	AVG	OBP	SLG	PRO+	BR	/A	RC	SB	CS	SBR	FA	FR	POS	TPR
1890	Bro-a	3	9	1	1	0	0	0		0		.111	.111	.111	-35	-1	-1	0	0			1.000	-1	/O	-0.2

■ JOHN CHURRY
Churry, John b: 11/26/1900, Johnstown, Pa. d: 2/8/70, Zanesville, Ohio BR/TR, 5'9", 172 lbs. Deb: 5/24/24

YEAR	TM/L	G	AB	R	H	2B	3B	HR	RBI	BB	SO	AVG	OBP	SLG	PRO+	BR	/A	RC	SB	CS	SBR	FA	FR	POS	TPR
1924	Chi-N	6	7	0	1	1	0	0	0	2	0	.143	.333	.286	67	-0	-0	1	0	0	0	1.000	0	/C	0.0
1925	Chi-N	3	6	1	3	0	0	0	1	0	0	.500	.500	.500	154	1	1	1	0	0	0	1.000	-0	/C	0.0
1926	Chi-N	2	4	0	0	0	0	0	0	1	2	.000	.200	.000	-42	-1	-1	0	0			1.000	0	/C	-0.1
1927	Chi-N	1	1	0	1	0	0	0	0	0	0	1.000	1.000	1.000	436	0	0	1	0			1.000	0	/C	0.1
Total	4	12	18	1	5	1	0	0	1	3	2	.278	.381	.333	89	-0	-0	3	0	0		1.000	0	/C	0.0

■ LARRY CIAFFONE
Ciaffone, Lawrence Thomas "Symphony Larry" b: 8/17/24, Brooklyn, N.Y. d: 12/14/91, Brooklyn, N.Y. BR/TR, 5'9.5", 185 lbs. Deb: 4/17/51

YEAR	TM/L	G	AB	R	H	2B	3B	HR	RBI	BB	SO	AVG	OBP	SLG	PRO+	BR	/A	RC	SB	CS	SBR	FA	FR	POS	TPR
1951	StL-N	5	5	0	0	0	0	0	0	1	2	.000	.167	.000	-51	-1	-1	0	0	0	0	1.000	-0	/O	-0.1

■ ARCHI CIANFROCCO
Cianfrocco, Angelo Dominic b: 10/6/66, Rome, N.Y. BR/TR, 6'5", 200 lbs. Deb: 4/08/92

YEAR	TM/L	G	AB	R	H	2B	3B	HR	RBI	BB	SO	AVG	OBP	SLG	PRO+	BR	/A	RC	SB	CS	SBR	FA	FR	POS	TPR
1992	Mon-N	86	232	25	56	5	2	6	30	11	66	.241	.279	.358	79	-7	-7	24	3	0	1	.993	1	13/O	-0.8

■ DARRYL CIAS
Cias, Darryl Richard b: 4/23/57, New York, N.Y. BR/TR, 5'11", 190 lbs. Deb: 4/27/83

YEAR	TM/L	G	AB	R	H	2B	3B	HR	RBI	BB	SO	AVG	OBP	SLG	PRO+	BR	/A	RC	SB	CS	SBR	FA	FR	POS	TPR
1983	Oak-A	19	18	1	6	1	0	0	1	2	4	.333	.400	.389	126	1	1	3	1	0	0	.967	-0	C	0.1

■ JOE CICERO
Cicero, Joseph Francis "Dode" b: 11/18/10, Atlantic City, N.J d: 3/30/83, Clearwater, Fla. BR/TR, 5'8", 167 lbs. Deb: 9/20/29

YEAR	TM/L	G	AB	R	H	2B	3B	HR	RBI	BB	SO	AVG	OBP	SLG	PRO+	BR	/A	RC	SB	CS	SBR	FA	FR	POS	TPR
1929	Bos-A	10	32	6	10	2	2	0	4	0	2	.313	.313	.500	108	0	0	5	0	0	0	1.000	-1	/O	-0.1
1930	Bos-A	18	30	5	5	1	2	0	4	1	5	.167	.194	.333	32	-3	-3	2	0	0	0	.000	-2	/O3	-0.5
1945	Phi-A	12	19	3	3	0	0	0	0	1	6	.158	.238	.158	16	-2	-2	1	0	0	0	1.000	-2	/O	-0.5
Total	3	40	81	14	18	3	4	0	8	2	13	.222	.250	.358	60	-5	-5	8	0	0	0	1.000	-4	/O3	-1.1

■ TED CIESLAK
Cieslak, Thaddeus Walter b: 11/22/16, Milwaukee, Wis. BR/TR, 5'10", 175 lbs. Deb: 4/18/44

YEAR	TM/L	G	AB	R	H	2B	3B	HR	RBI	BB	SO	AVG	OBP	SLG	PRO+	BR	/A	RC	SB	CS	SBR	FA	FR	POS	TPR
1944	Phi-N	85	220	18	54	10	0	2	11	21	17	.245	.314	.318	81	-6	-5	22	1			.877	-15	3/O	-2.1

■ AL CIHOCKI
Cihocki, Albert Joseph b: 5/7/24, Nanticoke, Pa. BR/TR, 5'11", 185 lbs. Deb: 4/17/45

YEAR	TM/L	G	AB	R	H	2B	3B	HR	RBI	BB	SO	AVG	OBP	SLG	PRO+	BR	/A	RC	SB	CS	SBR	FA	FR	POS	TPR
1945	Cle-A	92	283	21	60	9	3	0	24	11	48	.212	.241	.265	49	-20	-18	19	2	1	0	.946	1	S32	-1.4

■ ED CIHOCKI
Cihocki, Edward Joseph "Cy" b: 5/9/07, Wilmington, Del. d: 11/9/87, Newark, Del. BR/TR, 5'8", 163 lbs. Deb: 5/29/32

YEAR	TM/L	G	AB	R	H	2B	3B	HR	RBI	BB	SO	AVG	OBP	SLG	PRO+	BR	/A	RC	SB	CS	SBR	FA	FR	POS	TPR
1932	Phi-A	1	1	0	0	0	0	0	0	0	0	.000	.000	.000	-97	-0	-0	0	0	0	0	.000	0	H	0.0
1933	Phi-A	33	97	6	14	2	3	0	9	7	16	.144	.202	.227	13	-12	-13	5	0	0	0	.904	-2	S/23	-1.3
Total	2	34	98	6	14	2	3	0	9	7	16	.143	.200	.224	12	-13	-13	5	0	0	0		-2	/S32	-1.3

■ GINO CIMOLI
Cimoli, Gino Nicholas b: 12/18/29, San Francisco, Cal. BR/TR, 6'2", 200 lbs. Deb: 4/19/56

YEAR	TM/L	G	AB	R	H	2B	3B	HR	RBI	BB	SO	AVG	OBP	SLG	PRO+	BR	/A	RC	SB	CS	SBR	FA	FR	POS	TPR
1956	*Bro-N	73	36	3	4	1	0	0	4	1	8	.111	.135	.139	-24	-6	-7	1	1	0	0	.946	-18	O	-2.6
1957	Bro-N★	142	532	88	156	22	5	10	57	39	86	.293	.346	.410	93	2	-5	76	3	1	0	.979	-3	*O	-1.5
1958	LA-N	109	325	35	80	6	3	9	27	18	49	.246	.292	.366	71	-13	-14	30	3	3	-1	.974	-8	*O	-2.9
1959	StL-N	143	519	61	145	40	7	8	72	37	83	.279	.330	.430	94	-1	-5	70	7	0	2	.979	5	*O	-0.5
1960	*Pit-N	101	307	36	82	14	4	0	28	32	43	.267	.338	.339	85	-5	-5	35	1	0	0	.964	-7	O	-1.7
1961	Pit-N	21	67	4	20	3	1	0	6	2	13	.299	.319	.373	83	-2	-2	7	0	0	0	.971	-0	O	-0.3
	Mil-N	37	117	12	23	5	0	3	4	11	15	.197	.266	.316	57	-8	-7	10	1	0	0	.985	-2	O	-1.0
	Yr	58	184	16	43	8	1	3	10	13	28	.234	.284	.337	67	-10	-9	17	1	0	0	.980	-2	O	-1.3
1962	KC-A	152	550	67	151	20	**15**	10	71	40	89	.275	.326	.420	96	-2	-4	74	2	1	0	.968	-9	*O	-2.1
1963	KC-A	145	529	56	139	19	11	4	48	39	72	.263	.316	.363	86	-7	-10	60	3	1	0	.985	2	*O	-1.5
1964	KC-A	4	9	1	0	0	0	0	0	0	1	.000	.000	.000	-97	-2	-2	0	0	0	0	1.000	-0	/O	-0.3
	Bal-A	38	58	6	8	3	2	0	3	2	13	.138	.167	.259	16	-7	-7	2	0	0	0	.893	-9	O	-1.7
	Yr	42	67	7	8	3	2	0	3	2	14	.119	.145	.224	1	-9	-9	2	0	0	0	.912	-9	O	-2.0
1965	Cal-A	4	5	1	0	0	0	0	1	0	2	.000	.000	.000	-99	-1	-1	0	0	0	0	1.000	0	/O	-0.1
Total	10	969	3054	370	808	133	48	44	321	221	474	.265	.317	.383	85	-52	-69	365	21	6	3	.974	-49	O	-16.2

■ FRANK CIPRIANI
Cipriani, Frank Dominick b: 4/14/41, Buffalo, N.Y. BR/TR, 6', 180 lbs. Deb: 9/08/61

YEAR	TM/L	G	AB	R	H	2B	3B	HR	RBI	BB	SO	AVG	OBP	SLG	PRO+	BR	/A	RC	SB	CS	SBR	FA	FR	POS	TPR
1961	KC-A	13	36	2	9	0	0	0	2	2	4	.250	.289	.250	46	-3	-3	3	0	0	0	1.000	-1	O	-0.4

■ GEORGE CISAR
Cisar, George Joseph b: 8/25/12, Chicago, Ill. BR/TR, 6', 175 lbs. Deb: 9/09/37

YEAR	TM/L	G	AB	R	H	2B	3B	HR	RBI	BB	SO	AVG	OBP	SLG	PRO+	BR	/A	RC	SB	CS	SBR	FA	FR	POS	TPR
1937	Bro-N	20	29	8	6	0	0	0	4	2	6	.207	.258	.207	27	-3	-3	1	3			1.000	-3	O	-0.6

■ BILL CISSELL
Cissell, Chalmer William b: 1/3/04, Perryville, Mo. d: 3/15/49, Chicago, Ill. BR/TR, 5'11", 170 lbs. Deb: 4/11/28

YEAR	TM/L	G	AB	R	H	2B	3B	HR	RBI	BB	SO	AVG	OBP	SLG	PRO+	BR	/A	RC	SB	CS	SBR	FA	FR	POS	TPR
1928	Chi-A	125	443	66	115	22	3	1	60	29	41	.260	.307	.330	68	-21	-20	46	18	6	2	.938	-2	*S	-0.6
1929	Chi-A	152	618	83	173	27	12	5	62	28	53	.280	.312	.387	80	-21	-20	72	25	17	-3	.937	-3	*S	-0.7
1930	Chi-A	141	562	82	152	28	9	2	48	28	32	.270	.307	.363	72	-27	-24	62	16	9	-1	.948	-11	*23S	-2.5
1931	Chi-A	109	409	42	90	13	5	1	46	16	26	.220	.256	.284	44	-35	-32	31	18	6	2	.944	-10	S2/3	-2.9

YEAR	TM/L	G	AB	R	H	2B	3B	HR	RBI	BB	SO	AVG	OBP	SLG	PRO+	BR	/A	RC	SB	CS	SBR	FA	FR	POS	TPR
1932	Chi-A	12	43	7	11	1	1	1	5	1	0	.256	.273	.395	76	-2	-2	5	0	0	0	.928	0	S	-0.1
	Cle-A	131	541	78	173	35	6	6	93	28	25	.320	.354	.440	98	3	-2	80	18	15	-4	.964	11	*2/S	1.1
	Yr	143	584	85	184	36	7	7	98	29	25	.315	.349	.437	97	1	-4	85	18	15	-4	.964	11	*2S	1.0
1933	Cle-A	112	409	53	94	21	3	6	33	31	29	.230	.284	.340	62	-22	-24	39	6	6	-2	.947	-7	2S/3	-2.6
1934	Bos-A	102	416	71	111	13	4	4	44	28	23	.267	.315	.346	66	-19	-23	46	11	4	1	.959	-4	2/S3	-1.9
1937	Phi-A	34	117	15	31	7	0	1	14	17	10	.265	.358	.350	81	-3	-3	16	0	0	0	.962	3	2	0.2
1938	NY-N	38	149	19	40	6	0	2	18	6	11	.268	.297	.349	76	-5	-5	14	1			.977	9	2/3	0.6
Total	9	956	3707	516	990	173	43	29	423	212	250	.267	.308	.360	73	-153	-156	412	113	63		.958	-14	2S/3	-9.4

■ MOOSE CLABAUGH Clabaugh, John William b: 11/13/01, Albany, Mo. d: 7/11/84, Tucson, Arizona BL/TR, 6', 185 lbs. Deb: 8/30/26

1926	Bro-N	11	14	2	1	1	0	0	1	0	1	.071	.133	.143	-26	-3	-2	0	0			.600	-1	/O	-0.3

■ BOBBY CLACK Clack, Robert S. "Gentlemanly Bob" (b: Robert S. Clark) b: 6/1850, England d: 10/22/33, Danvers, Mass. BR/TR, 5'9", 153 lbs. Deb: 5/15/1874

1874	Atl-n	33	134	22	23	2	0	0		2		.172	.184	.187	21	-12	-9	5						O/1	-0.7
1875	Atl-n	17	59	1	6	0	0	0		0		.102	.102	.102	-34	-7	-6	1						O	-0.5
1876	Cin-N	32	118	10	19	0	1	0	5	5	12	.161	.195	.178	29	-9	-6	4				.736	0	O/213P	-0.5
Total	2 n	50	193	23	29	2	0	0		2		.150	.159	.161	5	-19	-15	5						/O1D	-1.2

■ DANNY CLAIRE Claire, David Matthew b: 11/17/1897, Ludington, Mich. d: 1/7/56, Las Vegas, Nev. BR/TR, 5'8", 164 lbs. Deb: 9/17/20

1920	Det-A	3	7	1	1	0	0	0	0	0	0	.143	.143	.143	-25	-1	-1	0	0	0	0	.800	-0	/S	-0.1

■ AL CLANCY Clancy, Albert Harrison b: 8/14/1888, Santa Fe, N.Mex. d: 10/17/51, Las Cruces, N.Mex. BR/TR, 5'10.5", 175 lbs. Deb: 6/20/11

1911	StL-A	3	5	0	0	0	0	0	0	0		.000	.167	.000	-54	-1	-1	0	0			.800	0	/3	-0.1

■ BUD CLANCY Clancy, John William b: 9/15/1900, Odell, Ill. d: 9/26/68, Ottumwa, Iowa BL/TL, 6', 170 lbs. Deb: 8/29/24

1924	Chi-A	13	35	5	9	1	0	0	6	3	2	.257	.316	.286	58	-2	-2	3	3	2	-0	.947	-2	/1	-0.4
1925	Chi-A	4	3	0	0	0	0	0	0	1	0	.000	.250	.000	-34	-1	-1	0	0	0	0	.000	0	H	-0.1
1926	Chi-A	12	38	3	13	2	2	0	7	1	1	.342	.375	.500	131	1	1	7	0	0	0	.991	0	1	0.1
1927	Chi-A	130	464	46	139	21	2	3	53	24	24	.300	.337	.373	86	-11	-10	56	4	3	-1	.991	0	*1	-1.7
1928	Chi-A	130	487	64	132	19	11	2	37	42	25	.271	.331	.368	85	-12	-11	60	6	9	-4	.991	5	*1	-2.0
1929	Chi-A	92	290	36	82	14	6	3	45	16	19	.283	.320	.403	86	-7	-7	38	3	1	0	.991	2	1	-1.1
1930	Chi-A	68	234	28	57	8	3	3	27	12	18	.244	.286	.342	61	-15	-14	23	3	1	0	.995	-3	1	-2.1
1932	Bro-N	53	196	14	60	4	2	0	16	6	13	.306	.327	.347	83	-5	-5	22	0			.996	3	1	-0.6
1934	Phi-N	20	49	8	12	0	0	1	7	6	4	.245	.339	.306	65	-2	-2	6	0			1.000	-1	1	-0.4
Total	9	522	1796	204	504	69	26	12	198	111	106	.281	.325	.368	81	-54	-49	215	19	16		.992	4	1	-8.3

■ BILL CLANCY Clancy, William Edward b: 4/12/1879, Redfield, N.Y. d: 2/10/48, Oriskany, N.Y. BR/TR, 6'2", 180 lbs. Deb: 4/14/05

1905	Pit-N	56	227	23	52	11	3	2	34	4		.229	.246	.330	70	-9	-10	20	3			.983	-4	1/O	-1.6

■ UKE CLANTON Clanton, Eucal "Cat" b: 2/19/1898, Powell, Mo. d: 2/24/60, Antlers, Okla. BL/TL, 5'8", 165 lbs. Deb: 9/21/22

1922	Cle-A	1	1	0	0	0	0	0	0	0	1	.000	.000	.000	-99	-0	-0	0	0	0	0	.500	-0	/1	-0.1

■ AARON CLAPP Clapp, Aaron Bronson b: 7/1856, Ithaca, N.Y. d: 1/13/14, Sayre, Pa. TR , 5'8", 175 lbs. Deb: 5/01/1879 F

1879	Tro-N	36	146	24	39	9	3	0	18	6	10	.267	.296	.370	126	3	4	16				.935	-4	1O	-0.1

■ JOHN CLAPP Clapp, John Edgar b: 7/17/1851, Ithaca, N.Y. d: 12/18/04, Ithaca, N.Y. BR/TR, 5'7", 194 lbs. Deb: 4/26/1872 FM

1872	Man-n	19	97	30	32	8	0	1	12	1	0	.330	.337	.443	147	4	5	15						CM	0.3
1873	Ath-n	45	204	36	62	11	2	1	28	2	2	.304	.311	.392	98	1	-2	25						*C/S2O	-0.3
1874	Ath-n	39	165	46	48	8	4	3		1		.291	.295	.442	121	5	3	22						CO/S	0.3
1875	Ath-n	60	291	65	77	7	8	0		8		.265	.284	.344	104	5	-0	29						C	0.2
1876	StL-N	64	298	60	91	4	2	0	29	8	2	.305	.324	.332	125	6	8	33				.874	9	*C/O2	1.7
1877	StL-N	60	255	47	81	6	6	0	34	8	6	.318	.338	.388	135	8	10	34				.887	-6	*CO/1	0.5
1878	Ind-N	63	263	42	80	10	2	0	29	13	8	.304	.337	.357	148	8	13	32				.890	-7	*O1/CS2M	0.4
1879	Buf-N	70	292	47	77	12	5	1	36	11	11	.264	.290	.349	107	3	2	30				.906	-9	*C/OM	-0.5
1880	Cin-N	80	323	33	91	16	4	1	20	21	10	.282	.326	.365	135	12	12	39				.897	17	*COM	2.9
1881	Cle-N	68	261	47	66	12	2	0	25	**35**	6	.253	.341	.314	113	4	6	29				.890	-5	COM	0.3
1883	NY-N	20	73	6	13	0	0	0	5	5	4	.178	.231	.178	27	-6	-6	3				.895	5	C/OM	0.0
Total	4 n	163	757	177	219	34	14	5	40	12	2	.289	.300	.391	111	16	6	91						C/OS2	0.5
Total	7	425	1765	282	499	60	21	2	178	101	47	.283	.322	.344	122	35	46	201				.892	4	CO/1S2	5.3

■ DENNY CLARE Clare, Dennis J. b: 1/1853, Brooklyn, N.Y. d: 11/26/28, Brooklyn, N.Y. Deb: 9/14/1872

1872	Atl-n	2	7	1	1	0	0	0	0	0	0	.143	.143	.143	-10	-1	-1	0						/2	-0.1

■ DOUG CLAREY Clarey, Douglas William b: 4/20/54, Los Angeles, Cal. BR/TR, 6', 180 lbs. Deb: 4/20/76

1976	StL-N	9	4	2	1	0	0	1	2	0	1	.250	.250	1.000	240	1	1	1	0	0	0	1.000	0	/2	0.1

■ ALLIE CLARK Clark, Alfred Aloysius b: 6/16/23, S.Amboy, N.J. BR/TR, 6', 185 lbs. Deb: 8/05/47

1947	*NY-A	24	67	9	25	5	0	1	14	5	2	.373	.417	.493	154	5	5	12	0	0	0	1.000	0	O	0.4
1948	*Cle-A	81	271	43	84	5	2	9	38	23	13	.310	.364	.443	117	5	5	41	0	2	-1	.982	-6	O/31	-0.5
1949	Cle-A	35	74	8	13	4	0	1	9	4	7	.176	.218	.270	29	-8	-8	4	0	0	0	1.000	-4	O/1	-1.3
1950	Cle-A	59	163	19	35	6	1	6	21	11	10	.215	.264	.374	64	-10	-10	12	0	1	-1	.987	-3	O	-1.4
1951	Cle-A	3	10	3	3	2	0	1	3	1	2	.300	.364	.800	221	1	1	3	0	0	0	1.000	-1	/O	0.1
	Phi-A	56	161	20	40	10	1	4	22	15	7	.248	.320	.398	91	-2	-2	20	2	0	1	.984	-1	O3	-0.4
	Yr	59	171	23	43	12	1	5	25	16	9	.251	.323	.421	98	-1	-1	23	2	0	1	.985	-1	O3	-0.3
1952	Phi-A	71	186	23	51	12	0	7	29	10	19	.274	.315	.452	105	2	0	24	0	2	-1	.988	-3	O/1	-0.6
1953	Phi-A	20	74	6	15	4	0	3	13	3	5	.203	.234	.378	61	-4	-5	6	0	0	0	1.000	-0	O	-0.6
	Chi-A	9	15	0	1	0	0	0	0	0	5	.067	.067	.067	-62	-3	-3	-0	0	0	0	1.000	-0	/1O	-0.4
	Yr	29	89	6	16	4	0	3	13	3	10	.180	.207	.326	40	-8	-8	5	0	0	0	1.000	-1	O/1	-1.0
Total	7	358	1021	131	267	48	4	32	149	72	70	.262	.312	.410	92	-16	-16	123	2	5	-2	.988	-19	O/31	-4.7

■ DAD CLARK Clark, Alfred Robert "Fred" b: 7/16/1873, San Francisco, Cal. d: 7/26/56, Ogden, Utah BL/TL, 5'11", 170 lbs. Deb: 7/03/02

1902	Chi-N	12	43	1	8	1	0	0	2	4		.186	.255	.209	45	-3	-3	3	1			.938	-2	1	-0.5

■ EARL CLARK Clark, Bailey Earl b: 11/6/07, Washington, D.C. d: 1/16/38, Washington, D.C. BR/TR, 5'10", 160 lbs. Deb: 8/17/27

1927	Bos-N	13	44	6	12	1	0	0	3	2	4	.273	.304	.295	66	-2	-2	4	0			1.000	-1	O	-0.3
1928	Bos-N	28	112	18	34	9	1	0	10	4	8	.304	.339	.402	98	-1	-1	15	0			.987	-1	O	-0.3
1929	Bos-N	84	279	43	88	13	3	1	30	12	30	.315	.346	.394	86	-7	-6	37	6			.978	4	O	-0.6
1930	Bos-N	82	233	29	69	11	3	3	28	7	22	.296	.320	.408	77	-10	-9	29	3			.977	1	O	-1.0
1931	Bos-N	16	50	8	11	2	0	0	4	7	4	.220	.316	.260	58	-3	-3	5	1			.970	1	O	-0.3
1932	Bos-N	50	44	11	11	2	0	0	4	2	7	.250	.283	.295	58	-3	-2	4	1			1.000	-2	O	-0.5
1933	Bos-N	7	23	3	8	1	0	0	1	2	1	.348	.400	.391	138	1	1	4	0			1.000	-1	/O	0.0
1934	StL-A	13	41	4	7	2	0	0	1	1	3	.171	.190	.220	5	-6	-6	2	0	0	0	1.000	1	/O	-0.6
Total	8	293	826	122	240	41	7	4	81	37	79	.291	.324	.372	78	-32	-27	98	11	0		.981	2	O	-3.6

■ DANNY CLARK Clark, Daniel Curran b: 1/18/1894, Meridian, Miss. d: 5/23/37, Meridian, Miss. BL/TR, 5'9", 167 lbs. Deb: 4/12/22

1922	Det-A	83	185	31	54	11	3	3	26	15	11	.292	.345	.432	105	-0	1	28	1	0	0	.945	-6	2/O3	-0.4

YEAR	TM/L	G	AB	R	H	2B	3B	HR	RBI	BB	SO	AVG	OBP	SLG	PRO+	BR	/A	RC	SB	CS	SBR	FA	FR	POS	TPR
1924	Bos-A	104	325	36	90	23	3	2	54	51	19	.277	.378	.385	97	-0	-0	49	4	7	-3	.943	-6	3	-0.2
1927	StL-N	58	72	8	17	2	2	0	13	8	7	.236	.313	.319	67	-3	-3	7	0			.929	1	/O	-0.3
Total	3	245	582	75	161	36	8	5	93	74	37	.277	.360	.392	96	-3	-3	85	5	7		.943	-11	/32O	-0.9

■ DAVE CLARK
Clark, David Earl b: 9/3/62, Tupelo, Miss. BL/TR, 6'2", 200 lbs. Deb: 9/03/86

YEAR	TM/L	G	AB	R	H	2B	3B	HR	RBI	BB	SO	AVG	OBP	SLG	PRO+	BR	/A	RC	SB	CS	SBR	FA	FR	POS	TPR
1986	Cle-A	18	58	10	16	1	0	3	9	7	11	.276	.354	.448	119	1	2	10	1	0	0	1.000	1	O/D	0.2
1987	Cle-A	29	87	11	18	5	0	3	12	2	24	.207	.225	.368	53	-6	-6	6	1	0	0	1.000	0	OD	-0.6
1988	Cle-A	63	156	11	41	4	1	3	18	17	28	.263	.335	.359	92	-1	-1	17	0	2	-1	.947	-4	DO	-0.7
1989	Cle-A	102	253	21	60	12	0	8	29	30	63	.237	.318	.379	94	-1	-2	29	0	2	-1	.964	-5	DO	-0.8
1990	Chi-N	84	171	22	47	4	2	5	20	8	40	.275	.307	.409	89	-2	-3	21	7	1	2	1.000	-2	O	-0.5
1991	KC-A	11	10	1	2	0	0	0	1	1	1	.200	.273	.200	33	-1	-1	1	0	0	0	.000	-0	/OD	-0.1
1992	Pit-N	23	33	3	7	0	0	2	7	6	8	.212	.333	.394	107	0	0	5	0	0	0	1.000	-1	/O	-0.1
Total	7	330	768	79	191	26	3	24	96	71	175	.249	.312	.384	90	-9	-12	88	9	5	-0	.984	-12	OD	-2.6

■ GLEN CLARK
Clark, Glen Ester b: 3/7/41, Austin, Tex. BB/TR, 6'1", 190 lbs. Deb: 6/03/67

YEAR	TM/L	G	AB	R	H	2B	3B	HR	RBI	BB	SO	AVG	OBP	SLG	PRO+	BR	/A	RC	SB	CS	SBR	FA	FR	POS	TPR
1967	Atl-N	4	4	0	0	0	0	0	0	0	1	.000	.000	.000	-99	-1	-1	0	0	0	0	.000	0	H	-0.1

■ PEP CLARK
Clark, Harry b: 3/20/1883, Union City, Ohio d: 6/8/65, Milwaukee, Wis. BR/TR, 5'7.5", 175 lbs. Deb: 9/11/03

YEAR	TM/L	G	AB	R	H	2B	3B	HR	RBI	BB	SO	AVG	OBP	SLG	PRO+	BR	/A	RC	SB	CS	SBR	FA	FR	POS	TPR
1903	Chi-A	15	65	7	20	4	2	0	9	2		.308	.338	.431	135	2	2	11	5			.877	-0	3	0.2

■ JACK CLARK
Clark, Jack Anthony b: 11/10/55, New Brighton, Pa. BR/TR, 6'2", 205 lbs. Deb: 9/12/75

YEAR	TM/L	G	AB	R	H	2B	3B	HR	RBI	BB	SO	AVG	OBP	SLG	PRO+	BR	/A	RC	SB	CS	SBR	FA	FR	POS	TPR
1975	SF-N	8	17	3	4	0	0	0	2	1	2	.235	.278	.235	42	-1	-1	1	1	0	0	1.000	-0	/O3	-0.1
1976	SF-N	26	102	14	23	6	2	2	10	8	18	.225	.282	.382	85	-2	-2	12	6	2	1	.987	3	O	0.0
1977	SF-N	136	413	64	104	17	4	13	51	49	73	.252	.334	.407	98	-1	-1	58	12	4	1	.975	4	*O	0.0
1978	SF-N★	156	592	90	181	46	8	25	98	50	72	.306	.363	.537	155	36	39	109	15	11	-2	.982	10	*O	4.2
1979	SF-N★	143	527	84	144	25	2	26	86	63	95	.273	.352	.476	133	17	21	88	11	8	-2	.982	5	*O/3	1.9
1980	SF-N	127	437	77	124	20	8	22	82	74	52	.284	.390	.517	155	31	32	87	2	5	-2	.967	-4	*O	2.3
1981	SF-N	99	385	60	103	19	2	17	53	45	45	.268	.346	.460	129	13	14	59	1	1	-0	.981	5	O	1.6
1982	SF-N	157	563	90	154	30	3	27	103	90	91	.274	.375	.481	138	30	30	98	6	9	-4	.980	-3	*O	2.0
1983	SF-N	135	492	82	132	25	0	20	66	74	79	.268	.365	.441	126	16	18	80	5	3	-0	.967	7	*O/1	2.1
1984	SF-N	57	203	33	65	9	1	11	44	43	29	.320	.439	.537	179	22	22	47	1	1	-0	.990	1	O/1	2.1
1985	*StL-N★	126	442	71	124	26	3	22	87	83	88	.281	.397	.502	151	32	32	89	1	4	-2	.988	-11	*1O	1.2
1986	StL-N	65	232	34	55	12	2	9	23	45	61	.237	.363	.422	117	6	6	38	1	1	-0	.995	-7	1	-0.5
1987	*StL-N★	131	419	93	120	23	1	35	106	**136**	139	.286	**.461**	**.597**	**174**	**54**	**53**	127	1	2	-1	.989	-8	*1/O	3.4
1988	NY-A	150	496	81	120	14	0	27	93	113	141	.242	.385	.433	130	23	24	88	3	2	-0	.951	-1	*DO1	2.1
1989	SD-N	142	455	76	110	19	1	26	94	**132**	145	.242	.413	.459	149	36	36	95	6	2	1	.988	1	*1O	2.8
1990	SD-N	115	334	59	89	12	1	25	62	**104**	91	.266	.443	.533	166	37	36	84	4	3	-1	.994	-3	*1	2.5
1991	Bos-A	140	481	75	120	18	1	28	87	96	133	.249	.378	.466	126	23	20	86	0	2	-1	.000	0	*D	1.9
1992	Bos-A	81	257	32	54	11	0	5	33	56	87	.210	.356	.311	84	-2	-4	33	1	1	-0	.992	-1	D1	-0.5
Total	18	1994	6847	1118	1826	332	39	340	1180	1262	1441	.267	.383	.476	138	367	374	1279	77	61	-14	.978	-0	*O1D/3	29.0

■ JIM CLARK
Clark, James (b: James Petrosky) b: 9/21/27, Bagley, Pa. BR/TR, 5'9", 150 lbs. Deb: 8/17/48

YEAR	TM/L	G	AB	R	H	2B	3B	HR	RBI	BB	SO	AVG	OBP	SLG	PRO+	BR	/A	RC	SB	CS	SBR	FA	FR	POS	TPR
1948	Was-A	9	12	1	3	0	0	0	0	0	2	.250	.250	.250	34	-1	-1	1	0	0	0	1.000	-0	/S3	-0.1

■ JIM CLARK
Clark, James Edward b: 4/30/47, Kansas City, Kan. BR/TR, 6'1", 190 lbs. Deb: 7/16/71

YEAR	TM/L	G	AB	R	H	2B	3B	HR	RBI	BB	SO	AVG	OBP	SLG	PRO+	BR	/A	RC	SB	CS	SBR	FA	FR	POS	TPR
1971	Cle-A	13	18	2	3	0	1	0	0	2	7	.167	.250	.278	45	-1	-1	1	0	0	0	1.000	0	/O1	-0.2

■ JIM CLARK
Clark, James Francis b: 12/26/1887, Brooklyn, N.Y. d: 3/20/69, Beaumont, Tex. BR/TR, 5'11", 175 lbs. Deb: 9/02/11

YEAR	TM/L	G	AB	R	H	2B	3B	HR	RBI	BB	SO	AVG	OBP	SLG	PRO+	BR	/A	RC	SB	CS	SBR	FA	FR	POS	TPR
1911	StL-N	14	18	2	3	0	1	0	3	3	4	.167	.286	.278	60	-1	-1	2	2			1.000	-3	/O	-0.4
1912	StL-N	2	1	0	0	0	0	0	0	0	1	.000	.000	.000	-99	-0	-0	0	0			.000	0	H	0.0
Total	2	16	19	2	3	0	1	0	3	3	5	.158	.273	.263	51	-1	-1	2	2				-3	/O	-0.4

■ JERALD CLARK
Clark, Jerald Dwayne b: 8/10/63, Crockett, Tex. BR/TR, 6'4", 189 lbs. Deb: 9/19/88 F

YEAR	TM/L	G	AB	R	H	2B	3B	HR	RBI	BB	SO	AVG	OBP	SLG	PRO+	BR	/A	RC	SB	CS	SBR	FA	FR	POS	TPR
1988	SD-N	6	15	0	3	1	0	0	3	0	4	.200	.200	.267	33	-1	-1	1	0	0	0	1.000	1	/O	0.0
1989	SD-N	17	41	5	8	2	0	1	7	3	9	.195	.250	.317	61	-2	-2	3	0	1	-1	.947	-1	O	-0.4
1990	SD-N	53	101	12	27	4	1	5	11	5	24	.267	.302	.475	109	1	1	14	0	0	0	1.000	-1	1O	-0.1
1991	SD-N	118	369	26	84	16	0	10	47	31	90	.228	.298	.352	80	-9	-10	38	2	1	0	.994	-3	O1	-1.7
1992	SD-N	146	496	45	120	22	6	12	58	22	97	.242	.280	.383	83	-11	-13	53	3	0	1	.990	12	*O1	-0.3
Total	5	340	1022	88	242	45	7	28	126	61	224	.237	.286	.377	83	-22	-26	108	5	2	0	.989	9	O/1	-2.5

■ CAP CLARK
Clark, John Carrol b: 9/19/06, Snow Camp, N.C. d: 2/16/57, Fayetteville, N.C. BL/TR, 5'11", 180 lbs. Deb: 4/23/38

YEAR	TM/L	G	AB	R	H	2B	3B	HR	RBI	BB	SO	AVG	OBP	SLG	PRO+	BR	/A	RC	SB	CS	SBR	FA	FR	POS	TPR
1938	Phi-N	52	74	11	19	1	1	0	4	9	10	.257	.337	.297	78	-2	-2	8	0			.936	-3	C	-0.4

■ MEL CLARK
Clark, Melvin Earl b: 7/7/26, Letart, W.Va. BR/TR, 6', 180 lbs. Deb: 9/11/51

YEAR	TM/L	G	AB	R	H	2B	3B	HR	RBI	BB	SO	AVG	OBP	SLG	PRO+	BR	/A	RC	SB	CS	SBR	FA	FR	POS	TPR
1951	Phi-N	10	31	2	10	1	0	1	3	0	3	.323	.323	.452	108	0	0	4	0	1	-1	1.000	-1	/O	-0.1
1952	Phi-N	47	155	20	52	6	4	1	15	6	13	.335	.364	.445	125	4	5	25	2	1	0	1.000	4	O/3	0.7
1953	Phi-N	60	198	31	59	10	4	0	19	11	17	.298	.338	.389	89	-3	-3	24	1	0	0	.991	1	O	-0.3
1954	Phi-N	83	233	26	56	9	7	1	24	17	21	.240	.292	.352	67	-12	-12	21	0	1	-1	.961	2	O	-1.2
1955	Phi-N	10	32	3	5	3	0	0	1	3	4	.156	.229	.250	27	-3	-3	2	0	0	0	1.000	3	/O	-0.1
1957	Det-A	5	7	0	0	0	0	0	1	0	3	.000	.000	.000	-97	-2	-2	0	0	0	0	1.000	0	/O	-0.2
Total	6	215	656	82	182	29	15	3	63	37	61	.277	.318	.381	85	-16	-15	75	3	3	-1	.983	10	O/3	-1.2

■ SPIDER CLARK
Clark, Owen F. b: 9/16/1867, Brooklyn, N.Y. d: 2/8/1892, Brooklyn, N.Y. TR, 5'10", 150 lbs. Deb: 5/02/1889

YEAR	TM/L	G	AB	R	H	2B	3B	HR	RBI	BB	SO	AVG	OBP	SLG	PRO+	BR	/A	RC	SB	CS	SBR	FA	FR	POS	TPR
1889	Was-N	38	145	19	37	7	2	3	22	6	18	.255	.285	.393	96	-3	-1	19	8			.887	6	CS/O32	0.5
1890	Buf-P	69	260	45	69	11	1	1	25	20	16	.265	.325	.327	83	-9	-5	31	8			.938	-4	OC2/13SP	-0.6
Total	2	107	405	64	106	18	3	4	47	26	34	.262	.311	.351	87	-11	-6	50	16			.952	2	/OC2S13P	-0.1

■ PHIL CLARK
Clark, Phillip Benjamin b: 5/6/68, Crockett, Tex. BR/TR, 6', 180 lbs. Deb: 5/27/92 F

YEAR	TM/L	G	AB	R	H	2B	3B	HR	RBI	BB	SO	AVG	OBP	SLG	PRO+	BR	/A	RC	SB	CS	SBR	FA	FR	POS	TPR
1992	Det-A	23	54	3	22	4	0	1	5	6	9	.407	.467	.537	178	6	6	13	1	0	0	.931	-1	O/D	0.5

■ BOBBY CLARK
Clark, Robert Cale b: 6/13/55, Sacramento, Cal. BR/TR, 6', 190 lbs. Deb: 8/21/79

YEAR	TM/L	G	AB	R	H	2B	3B	HR	RBI	BB	SO	AVG	OBP	SLG	PRO+	BR	/A	RC	SB	CS	SBR	FA	FR	POS	TPR
1979	*Cal-A	19	54	8	16	2	2	1	5	5	11	.296	.356	.463	123	1	2	8	1	1	-0	.978	2	O	0.3
1980	Cal-A	78	261	26	60	10	1	5	23	11	42	.230	.266	.333	65	-14	-13	21	0	1	-1	.982	8	O	-0.8
1981	Cal-A	34	88	12	22	2	1	4	19	7	18	.250	.305	.432	110	1	1	11	0	0	0	1.000	0	O	0.0
1982	*Cal-A	102	90	11	19	1	0	2	8	0	29	.211	.211	.289	36	-8	-8	5	1	0	0	1.000	-29	*O	-3.8
1983	Cal-A	76	212	17	49	9	1	5	21	9	45	.231	.262	.354	68	-10	-10	18	0	0	0	1.000	-11	O/3D	-2.2
1984	Mil-A	58	169	17	44	7	2	2	16	16	35	.260	.328	.361	94	-2	-1	17	1	5	-3	.981	-10	O	-1.6
1985	Mil-A	29	93	6	21	3	0	0	8	7	19	.226	.280	.258	49	-6	-6	6	1	1	-0	1.000	1	O	-0.7
Total	7	396	967	97	231	34	7	19	100	55	199	.239	.282	.347	74	-38	-35	87	4	8	-4	.990	-39	O/D3	-8.8

■ BOB CLARK
Clark, Robert H. b: 3/18/1863, Covington, Ky. d: 8/21/19, Covington, Ky. BR/TR, 5'10", 175 lbs. Deb: 4/17/1886

YEAR	TM/L	G	AB	R	H	2B	3B	HR	RBI	BB	SO	AVG	OBP	SLG	PRO+	BR	/A	RC	SB	CS	SBR	FA	FR	POS	TPR
1886	Bro-a	71	269	37	58	8	2	0		17		.216	.262	.260	65	-11	-11	23	14			.864	-13	COS	-1.7
1887	Bro-a	48	177	24	47	3	1	0		7		.266	.297	.294	66	-8	-8	20	15			.871	-1	C/O	-0.4
1888	Bro-a	45	150	23	36	5	3	1	20	9		.240	.292	.333	103	0	1	18	11			.884	-2	C/O1	0.2
1889	*Bro-a	53	182	32	50	5	2	0	22	26	7	.275	.368	.324	100	1	1	29	18			.870	7	C	1.1
1890	*Bro-N	43	151	24	33	3	3	0	15	15	8	.219	.306	.278	72	-5	-5	16	10			.836	-14	C/O	-1.4

YEAR	TM/L	G	AB	R	H	2B	3B	HR	RBI	BB	SO	AVG	OBP	SLG	PRO+	BR	/A	RC	SB	CS	SBR	FA	FR	POS	TPR
1891	Cin-N	16	54	2	6	0	0	0	3	6	9	.111	.213	.111	-3	-7	-7	2	3			.868	-5	C	-1.0
1893	Lou-N	12	28	3	3	1	0	0	3	5	5	.107	.242	.143	5	-4	-3	1	0			.947	-2	C/OS	-0.4
Total	7	288	1011	145	233	25	11	1	63	85	29	.230	.296	.280	73	-32	-32	110	71			.867	-30	C/OS1	-3.6

■ RON CLARK Clark, Ronald Bruce b: 1/14/43, Ft.Worth, Tex. BR/TR, 5'10", 175 lbs. Deb: 9/11/66 C

1966	Min-A	5	1	1	1	0	0	0	1	0	0	1.000	1.000	1.000	448	0	0	1	0	0	0	.000	0	/3	0.0
1967	Min-A	20	60	7	10	3	1	2	11	4	9	.167	.219	.350	61	-3	-3	4	0	0	0	.891	-1	3	-0.5
1968	Min-A	104	227	14	42	5	1	1	13	16	44	.185	.245	.229	42	-15	-16	14	3	2	-0	.932	-8	3S2	-2.3
1969	Min-A	5	8	0	1	0	0	0	0	0	0	.125	.125	.125	-29	-1	-1	0	0	0	0	1.000	-1	/3	-0.2
	Sea-A	57	163	9	32	5	0	0	12	13	29	.196	.260	.227	38	-14	-13	11	1	0	0	.966	-9	S3/21	-1.9
	Yr	62	171	9	33	5	0	0	12	13	29	.193	.254	.222	35	-15	-15	10	1	0	0	.966	-10	S3/21	-2.1
1971	Oak-A	2	1	0	0	0	0	0	0	1	0	.000	.500	.000	53	0	0	0	0	0	0	.000	0	H	0.0
1972	Oak-A	14	15	1	4	2	0	0	1	2	4	.267	.353	.400	130	0	1	2	0	0	0	1.000	0	2/3	0.1
	Mil-A	22	54	8	10	1	1	2	5	5	11	.185	.254	.352	81	-2	-1	5	0	0	0	.963	5	23	0.5
	Yr	36	69	9	14	3	1	2	6	7	15	.203	.276	.362	92	-1	-1	6	0	0	0	.974	6	23	0.6
1975	Phi-N	1	1	0	0	0	0	0	0	0	1	.000	.000	.000	-96	-0	-0	0	0	0	0	.000	0	H	0.0
Total	7	230	530	40	100	16	3	5	43	41	98	.189	.251	.258	49	-34	-35	35	4	2	0	.904	-13	/3S21	-4.3

■ ROY CLARK Clark, Roy Elliott "Pepper" b: 5/11/1874, New Haven, Conn. d: 11/1/25, Bridgeport, Conn. BL/TR, 5'8", 170 lbs. Deb: 4/19/02

1902	NY-N	21	76	4	11	1	0	0	3	1		.145	.156	.158	-3	-9	-9	3	5			.962	-3	O	-1.4

■ WILL CLARK Clark, William Nuschler b: 3/13/64, New Orleans, La. BL/TL, 6'2", 190 lbs. Deb: 4/08/86

1986	SF-N	111	408	66	117	27	2	11	41	34	76	.287	.346	.444	122	8	11	62	4	7	-3	.989	-2	*1	-0.1
1987	*SF-N	150	529	89	163	29	5	35	91	49	98	.308	.372	.580	155	34	38	109	5	17	-9	.991	2	*1	2.1
1988	SF-N★	162	575	102	162	31	6	29	**109**	**100**	129	.282	.392	.508	163	**44**	**47**	**120**	9	1	2	.993	-3	*1	3.5
1989	*SF-N★	159	588	**104**	196	38	9	23	111	74	103	.333	.412	.546	177	56	58	**136**	8	3	1	.994	0	*1	4.8
1990	SF-N★	154	600	91	177	25	5	19	95	62	97	.295	.364	.448	127	18	21	101	8	2	1	.992	1	*1	1.1
1991	SF-N★	148	565	84	170	32	7	29	116	51	91	.301	.361	**.536**	154	35	37	110	4	2	0	**.997**	3	*1	3.1
1992	SF-N★	144	513	69	154	40	1	16	73	73	82	.300	.392	.476	152	32	35	98	12	7	-1	.993	-0	*1	2.6
Total	7	1028	3778	605	1139	222	35	162	636	443	676	.301	.379	.507	151	227	246	737	50	39	-8	.993	2	1	17.1

■ WILLIE CLARK Clark, William Otis "Wee Willie" b: 8/16/1872, Pittsburgh, Pa. d: 11/13/32, Pittsburgh, Pa. Deb: 6/20/1895

1895	NY-N	23	88	9	23	3	2	0	16	5	6	.261	.301	.341	69	-4	-4	10	1			.974	1	1	-0.2
1896	NY-N	72	247	38	72	12	4	0	33	15	12	.291	.352	.372	96	-2	-1	36	8			.975	-4	1	-0.4
1897	NY-N	116	431	63	122	17	12	1	75	37		.283	.352	.385	97	-4	-1	67	18			.984	2	*1/O3	0.1
1898	Pit-N	57	209	29	64	9	7	1	31	22		.306	.378	.431	134	8	9	35	0			.984	0	1	0.9
1899	Pit-N	80	298	49	85	13	10	0	44	35		.285	.379	.396	113	6	6	51	11			.989	1	1	0.7
Total	5	348	1273	188	366	54	35	2	199	114	18	.288	.359	.390	104	4	9	199	38			.983	0	1/O3	1.1

■ BILL CLARK Clark, William Winfield b: 4/11/1875, Circleville, Ohio d: 4/15/59, Los Angeles, Cal. BR/TR, 5'10", 175 lbs. Deb: 7/12/1897

1897	Lou-N	4	16	2	3	0	0	0	2	1		.188	.235	.188	13	-2	-2	1	1			.810	-1	/23	-0.3

■ ARTIE CLARKE Clarke, Arthur Franklin b: 5/6/1865, Providence, R.I. d: 11/14/49, Brookline, Mass. BR/TR, 5'8", 155 lbs. Deb: 4/19/1890

1890	NY-N	101	395	55	89	12	8	0	49	32	38	.225	.290	.296	73	-14	-14	48	44			.908	-3	CO32/S	-1.2
1891	NY-N	48	174	17	33	2	2	0	21	15	16	.190	.254	.224	43	-13	-12	11	5			.916	-12	C/3O	-1.8
Total	2	149	569	72	122	14	10	0	70	47	54	.214	.279	.274	64	-26	-25	59	49			.912	-15	/CO32S	-3.0

■ FRED CLARKE Clarke, Fred Clifford "Cap" b: 10/3/1872, Winterset, Iowa d: 8/14/60, Winfield, Kan. BL/TR, 5'10.5", 165 lbs. Deb: 6/30/1894 FMH

1894	Lou-N	75	310	54	83	11	7	7	48	25	27	.268	.330	.416	86	-11	-7	52	25			.885	4	O	-0.6
1895	Lou-N	132	550	96	191	21	5	4	82	34	24	.347	.396	.425	121	12	18	111	40			.881	11	*O	1.5
1896	Lou-N	131	517	96	168	15	18	9	79	43	34	.325	.392	.476	135	22	26	113	34			.908	0	*O	1.3
1897	Lou-N	128	518	120	202	30	13	6	67	45		.390	.462	.533	**168**	49	52	158	57			.926	6	*OM	4.1
1898	Lou-N	149	599	116	184	23	12	3	47	48		.307	.373	.401	124	17	19	108	40			.940	6	*OM	1.3
1899	Lou-N	148	602	122	206	23	9	5	70	49		.342	.406	.435	131	27	27	131	49			.964	1	*O/SM	1.5
1900	Pit-N	106	399	84	110	15	12	3	32	51		.276	.368	.396	110	7	6	69	21			.944	3	*OM	0.1
1901	Pit-N	129	527	118	171	24	15	6	60	51		.324	.395	.461	144	33	31	109	23			.970	2	*O/S3M	2.2
1902	Pit-N	113	459	103	145	27	14	2	53	51		.316	.408	.449	**159**	37	35	99	29			.958	-1	*OM	2.8
1903	*Pit-N	104	427	88	150	**32**	15	5	70	41		.351	.413	**.532**	**164**	37	35	106	21			.962	-8	*O/SM	2.0
1904	Pit-N	72	278	51	85	7	11	0	25	22		.306	.367	.410	137	13	12	48	11			.979	0	OM	0.9
1905	Pit-N	141	525	95	157	18	15	2	51	55		.299	.367	.402	126	19	17	91	24			.976	4	*OM	1.5
1906	Pit-N	118	417	69	129	14	**13**	1	39	40		.309	.371	.412	139	21	19	75	18			.974	6	*OM	2.2
1907	Pit-N	148	501	97	145	18	13	2	59	68		.289	.382	.389	140	26	26	93	37			**.987**	6	*OM	2.9
1908	Pit-N	151	551	83	146	18	15	2	53	65		.265	.349	.363	127	18	18	79	24			.973	10	*OM	2.5
1909	*Pit-N	152	550	97	158	16	11	3	68	**80**		.287	.384	.373	124	25	20	92	31			**.987**	7	*OM	2.3
1910	Pit-N	123	429	57	113	23	9	2	63	53	23	.263	.350	.373	105	6	3	62	12			.967	3	*OM	0.0
1911	Pit-N	110	392	73	127	25	13	5	49	53	27	.324	.407	.492	146	27	25	82	10			.970	0	*OM	2.0
1913	Pit-N	9	13	0	1	1	0	0	0	0	0	.077	.077	.154	-37	-2	-2	0	0			1.000	-1	/OM	-0.3
1914	Pit-N	2	2	0	0	0	0	0	0	0	0	.000	.000	.000	-99	-0	-0	0	0			.000	0	HM	-0.1
1915	Pit-N	1	2	0	1	0	0	0	0	0	0	.500	.500	.500	206	0	0	1	0			.000	-1	/OM	0.0
Total	21	2242	8568	1619	2672	361	220	67	1015	874	135	.312	.386	.429	132	383	379	1678	506			.952	58	*O/S3	30.1

■ HARRY CLARKE Clarke, Harry Corson b: 1861, d: 3/3/23, Long Beach, Cal. Deb: 8/28/1889

1889	Was-N	1	3	0	0	0	0	0	0	0	1	.000	.000	.000	-99	-1	-1	0	0			1.000	1	/O	0.1

■ HENRY CLARKE Clarke, Henry Tefft b: 8/28/1875, Bellevue, Neb. d: 3/28/50, Colorado Springs, Colo. BR/TR, Deb: 6/26/1897

1897	Cle-N	7	25	3	7	0	0	0	3	2		.280	.333	.280	60	-1	-1	2	0			.714	-1	/PO	-0.1
1898	Chi-N	2	4	0	1	0	0	0	0	1		.250	.400	.250	87	0	0	0	0			.000	-1	/OP	-0.1
Total	2	9	29	3	8	0	0	0	3	3		.276	.344	.276	64	-1	-1	3	0			.750	-2	/PO	-0.2

■ HORACE CLARKE Clarke, Horace Meredith b: 6/2/40, Frederiksted, St.Croix, V.I. BB/TR, 5'9", 178 lbs. Deb: 5/13/65

1965	NY-A	51	108	13	28	1	0	1	9	6	6	.259	.298	.296	70	-4	-4	10	2	1	0	.923	3	3/2S	-0.2
1966	NY-A	96	312	37	83	10	4	6	28	27	24	.266	.326	.381	107	1	2	40	5	3	-0	.970	-19	S2/3	-1.1
1967	NY-A	143	588	74	160	17	0	3	29	42	64	.272	.321	.316	92	-8	-5	64	21	4	4	**.990**	15	*2	2.5
1968	NY-A	148	579	52	133	6	1	2	26	23	46	.230	.259	.254	58	-31	-29	39	20	7	2	.984	**30**	*2	1.2
1969	NY-A	156	641	82	183	26	7	4	48	53	41	.285	.340	.367	101	-2	1	83	33	13	2	.982	-4	*2	1.2
1970	NY-A	158	686	81	172	24	2	4	46	35	35	.251	.289	.309	68	-33	-29	62	23	7	3	.979	-7	*2	-2.1
1971	NY-A	159	625	76	156	23	7	2	41	64	43	.250	.321	.318	87	-14	-10	66	17	7	1	.981	-3	*2	0.2
1972	NY-A	147	547	65	132	20	2	3	37	56	44	.241	.316	.302	87	-9	-7	56	18	6	2	.985	6	*2	1.0
1973	NY-A	148	590	60	155	21	0	2	35	47	48	.263	.319	.308	80	-17	-14	56	11	10	-3	.979	8	*2	0.0
1974	NY-A	24	47	3	11	1	0	0	1	4	5	.234	.294	.255	61	-2	-2	4	1	0	0	1.000	-6	2/D	-0.7
	SD-N	42	90	5	17	1	0	0	4	8	6	.189	.255	.200	30	-8	-8	5	0	0	0	.978	-4	2	-1.2
Total	10	1272	4813	548	1230	150	23	27	304	365	362	.256	.310	.313	82	-128	-106	482	151	58	11	.983	19	*2/S3D	0.8

■ NIG CLARKE Clarke, Jay Justin b: 12/15/1882, Amherstburg, Ont., Canada d: 6/15/49, River Rouge, Mich BL/TR, 5'8", 165 lbs. Deb: 4/26/05

1905	Cle-A	5	9	2	1	1	0	0	1	1		.111	.200	.222	33	-1	-1	0	0			1.000	-2	/C	-0.2

YEAR	TM/L	G	AB	R	H	2B	3B	HR	RBI	BB	SO	AVG	OBP	SLG	PRO+	BR	/A	RC	SB	CS	SBR	FA	FR	POS	TPR
	Det-A	3	7	1	3	0	0	1	1	0		.429	.500	.857	326	2	2	3	0			1.000	1	/C	0.3
	Cle-A	37	114	9	23	5	1	0	8	10		.202	.266	.263	67	-4	-4	8	0			.961	-1	C	-0.2
	Yr	45	130	12	27	6	1	1	10	11		.208	.275	.292	79	-3	-3	11	0			.965	-2	C	-0.1
1906	Cle-A	57	179	22	64	12	4	1	21	13		.358	.404	.486	181	16	16	37	3			.982	-0	C	2.2
1907	Cle-A	120	390	44	105	19	6	3	33	35		.269	.333	.372	124	11	10	51	3			.961	-11	*C	1.1
1908	Cle-A	97	290	34	70	8	6	1	27	30		.241	.315	.321	106	3	2	31	6			.969	-8	C	0.3
1909	Cle-A	55	164	15	45	4	2	0	14	9		.274	.316	.323	98	0	-1	17	1			.952	-3	C	0.1
1910	Cle-A	21	58	4	9	2	0	0	2	8		.155	.258	.190	40	-4	-4	3	0			.974	3	C	0.1
1911	StL-A	82	256	22	55	10	1	0	18	26		.215	.287	.262	56	-16	-14	20	2			.926	-5	C/1	-1.2
1919	Phi-N	26	62	4	15	3	0	0	2	4	5	.242	.299	.290	72	-2	-2	5	1			.969	0	C	0.0
1920	Pit-N	3	7	0	0	0	0	0	0	2	4	.000	.222	.000	-32	-1	-1	0	0	0	0	1.000	1	/C	0.0
Total	9	506	1536	157	390	64	20	6	127	138	9	.254	.318	.333	102	4	4	177	16	0		.960	-24	C/1	2.5

■ JOSH CLARKE Clarke, Joshua Baldwin "Pepper" b: 3/8/1879, Winfield, Kan. d: 7/2/62, Ventura, Cal. BL/TR, 5'10", 180 lbs. Deb: 6/15/1898 F

YEAR	TM/L	G	AB	R	H	2B	3B	HR	RBI	BB	SO	AVG	OBP	SLG	PRO+	BR	/A	RC	SB	CS	SBR	FA	FR	POS	TPR
1898	Lou-N	6	18	0	3	0	0	0	0	1		.167	.211	.167	9	-2	-2	1	0			.917	-1	/O	-0.3
1905	StL-N	50	167	31	43	3	2	3	18	27		.257	.361	.353	117	4	4	25	8			.942	-8	O2/S	-0.5
1908	Cle-A	131	492	70	119	8	4	1	21	76		.242	.348	.280	104	7	7	61	37			.963	-3	*O	-0.2
1909	Cle-A	4	12	1	0	0	0	0	0	2		.000	.143	.000	-52	-2	-2	0	0			.600	-2	/O	-0.5
1911	Bos-N	32	120	16	28	7	3	1	4	29	22	.233	.387	.367	103	3	2	19	6			.938	4	O	0.4
Total	5	223	809	118	193	18	9	5	43	135	22	.239	.351	.302	102	9	8	106	51			.949	-9	O/2S	-1.1

■ GREY CLARKE Clarke, Richard Grey "Noisy" b: 9/26/12, Fulton, Ala. BR/TR, 5'9", 183 lbs. Deb: 4/19/44

YEAR	TM/L	G	AB	R	H	2B	3B	HR	RBI	BB	SO	AVG	OBP	SLG	PRO+	BR	/A	RC	SB	CS	SBR	FA	FR	POS	TPR
1944	Chi-A	63	169	14	44	10	1	0	27	22	6	.260	.352	.331	97	-0	0	19	0	4	-2	.941	1	3	-0.1

■ SUMPTER CLARKE Clarke, Sumpter Mills b: 10/18/1897, Savannah, Ga. d: 3/16/62, Knoxville, Tenn. BR/TR, 5'11", 170 lbs. Deb: 9/27/20 F

YEAR	TM/L	G	AB	R	H	2B	3B	HR	RBI	BB	SO	AVG	OBP	SLG	PRO+	BR	/A	RC	SB	CS	SBR	FA	FR	POS	TPR
1920	Chi-N	1	3	0	1	0	0	0	0	0	1	.333	.333	.333	90	-0	-0	0	0	0	0	1.000	-0	/3	0.0
1923	Cle-A	1	3	0	0	0	0	0	0	0	0	.000	.000	.000	-99	-1	-1	0	0	0	0	1.000	-0	/O	-0.1
1924	Cle-A	35	104	17	24	6	1	0	11	6	12	.231	.273	.308	49	-8	-8	9	0	0	0	1.000	-5	O	-1.5
Total	3	37	110	17	25	6	1	0	11	6	13	.227	.267	.300	46	-9	-9	9	0	0	0	1.000	-6	/O3	-1.6

■ TOMMY CLARKE Clarke, Thomas Aloysius b: 5/9/1888, New York, N.Y. d: 8/14/45, Corona, N.Y. BR/TR, 5'11", 175 lbs. Deb: 8/26/09

YEAR	TM/L	G	AB	R	H	2B	3B	HR	RBI	BB	SO	AVG	OBP	SLG	PRO+	BR	/A	RC	SB	CS	SBR	FA	FR	POS	TPR
1909	Cin-N	18	52	8	13	3	2	0	10	6		.250	.328	.385	122	1	1	8	3			.965	5	C	0.8
1910	Cin-N	64	151	19	42	6	5	1	20	19	17	.278	.370	.404	131	5	6	23	1			.971	-1	C	1.0
1911	Cin-N	86	203	20	49	6	7	1	25	25	22	.241	.328	.355	94	-3	-2	26	4			.970	2	C/1	0.7
1912	Cin-N	72	146	19	41	7	2	0	22	28	14	.281	.400	.356	111	3	4	25	9			.983	5	C	1.3
1913	Cin-N	114	330	29	87	11	8	1	38	39	40	.264	.345	.355	100	1	1	39	2			.979	-9	*C	0.1
1914	Cin-N	113	313	30	82	13	7	2	25	31	30	.262	.332	.367	105	3	2	39	6			.973	-4	*C	0.7
1915	Cin-N	96	226	23	65	7	2	0	21	33	22	.288	.381	.336	116	7	6	32	7	3	0	.981	-4	C	0.8
1916	Cin-N	78	177	10	42	10	1	0	17	24	20	.237	.328	.305	97	-0	0	20	8			.965	-10	C	-0.7
1917	Cin-N	58	110	11	32	3	3	1	13	11	12	.291	.361	.400	139	4	5	16	2			.991	-5	C	0.2
1918	Chi-N	1	0	0	0	0	0	0	0	0	0	—	—	—	—	0	0	0	0			.000	0	/C	0.0
Total	10	700	1708	169	453	66	37	6	191	216	177	.265	.351	.358	109	21	23	227	42	3		.975	-22	C/1	4.9

■ BOILERYARD CLARKE Clarke, William Jones b: 10/18/1868, New York, N.Y. d: 7/29/59, Princeton, N.J. BR/TR, 5'11.5", 170 lbs. Deb: 5/01/1893

YEAR	TM/L	G	AB	R	H	2B	3B	HR	RBI	BB	SO	AVG	OBP	SLG	PRO+	BR	/A	RC	SB	CS	SBR	FA	FR	POS	TPR
1893	Bal-N	49	183	23	32	1	3	1	24	19	14	.175	.274	.230	35	-17	-17	12	2			.909	-3	C1	-1.4
1894	Bal-N	28	100	18	24	8	0	1	19	16	14	.240	.361	.350	71	-4	-5	14	2			.903	-2	C/1	-0.4
1895	*Bal-N	67	241	38	70	15	3	0	35	13	18	.290	.350	.378	87	-4	-5	36	8			.938	6	C/1	0.6
1896	Bal-N	80	300	48	89	14	7	2	71	14	12	.297	.345	.410	99	-0	-1	47	7			.948	-11	C1	-0.4
1897	*Bal-N	64	241	32	65	7	1	1	38	9		.270	.320	.320	69	-11	-11	27	5			.939	-15	C/1	-1.7
1898	Bal-N	82	285	26	69	5	2	0	27	4		.242	.289	.274	60	-14	-15	24	2			.962	3	C1	-0.5
1899	Bos-N	60	223	25	50	3	2	2	32	10		.224	.270	.283	47	-15	-18	19	2			.940	-1	C	-1.3
1900	Bos-N	81	270	35	85	5	2	1	30	9		.315	.344	.359	84	-2	-7	35	0			.928	8	C/1	0.7
1901	Was-A	110	422	58	118	15	5	3	54	23		.280	.335	.360	94	-4	-3	56	7			.952	-9	*C/1	-0.1
1902	Was-A	87	291	31	78	16	0	6	40	23		.268	.334	.385	98	-1	-1	39	1			**.972**	-3	C	0.5
1903	Was-A	126	465	35	111	14	6	2	38	15		.239	.273	.308	73	-15	-16	44	12			.981	-11	1C	-2.5
1904	Was-A	85	275	23	58	8	1	0	17	17		.211	.269	.247	65	-11	-10	21	5			.977	0	C1	-0.5
1905	NY-N	31	50	2	9	0	0	1	4	4		.180	.241	.240	43	-3	-4	3	1			.973	-1	1C	-0.4
Total	13	950	3346	394	858	111	32	20	429	176	58	.256	.311	.327	76	-101	-113	378	54			.947	-38	C1	-7.4

■ STU CLARKE Clarke, William Stuart b: 1/24/06, San Francisco, Cal d: 8/26/85, Hayward, Cal. BR/TR, 5'8.5", 160 lbs. Deb: 7/17/29

YEAR	TM/L	G	AB	R	H	2B	3B	HR	RBI	BB	SO	AVG	OBP	SLG	PRO+	BR	/A	RC	SB	CS	SBR	FA	FR	POS	TPR
1929	Pit-N	57	178	20	47	5	7	2	21	19	21	.264	.338	.404	81	-5	-6	24	3			.919	-8	S3/2	-0.8
1930	Pit-N	4	9	2	4	0	1	0	2	1	0	.444	.500	.667	178	1	1	3	0			1.000	-1	/2	0.0
Total	2	61	187	22	51	5	8	2	23	20	21	.273	.346	.417	86	-4	-4	27	3			1.000	-9	/S32	-0.8

■ BUZZ CLARKSON Clarkson, James Buster b: 3/13/18, Hopkins, S.C. d: 1/18/89, Jeannette, Pa. BR/TR, 5'11", 210 lbs. Deb: 4/30/52

YEAR	TM/L	G	AB	R	H	2B	3B	HR	RBI	BB	SO	AVG	OBP	SLG	PRO+	BR	/A	RC	SB	CS	SBR	FA	FR	POS	TPR
1952	Bos-N	14	25	3	5	0	0	0	1	3	3	.200	.286	.200	38	-2	-2	2	0	0	0	.938	-2	/S3	-0.4

■ ELLIS CLARY Clary, Ellis "Cat" b: 9/11/16, Valdosta, Ga. BR/TR, 5'8", 160 lbs. Deb: 6/07/42 C

YEAR	TM/L	G	AB	R	H	2B	3B	HR	RBI	BB	SO	AVG	OBP	SLG	PRO+	BR	/A	RC	SB	CS	SBR	FA	FR	POS	TPR
1942	Was-A	76	240	34	66	9	0	0	16	45	25	.275	.394	.313	101	3	3	35	2	0	1	.969	-17	2/3	-0.9
1943	Was-A	73	254	36	65	19	1	0	19	44	31	.256	.370	.339	112	4	5	35	8	4	0	.945	-8	3/S	-0.2
	StL-A	23	69	15	19	2	0	0	5	11	6	.275	.375	.304	98	1	0	9	1	2	-1	.972	-1	3/2	-0.1
	Yr	96	323	51	84	21	1	0	24	55	37	.260	.371	.331	109	5	6	43	9	6	-1	.949	-9	3/2S	-0.3
1944	*StL-A	25	49	6	13	1	1	0	4	12	9	.265	.410	.327	106	2	1	8	1	0	0	1.000	-1	3/2	0.0
1945	StL-A	26	38	6	8	1	0	1	2	2	3	.211	.250	.316	61	-2	-2	3	0	2	-1	.947	3	3/2	0.0
Total	4	223	650	97	171	32	2	1	46	114	74	.263	.376	.323	103	7	8	89	12	8	-1	.953	-25	3/2S	-1.2

■ DAIN CLAY Clay, Dain Elmer "Sniffy" or "Ding-A-Ling" b: 7/10/19, Hicksville, Ohio BR/TR, 5'10.5", 160 lbs. Deb: 6/12/43

YEAR	TM/L	G	AB	R	H	2B	3B	HR	RBI	BB	SO	AVG	OBP	SLG	PRO+	BR	/A	RC	SB	CS	SBR	FA	FR	POS	TPR
1943	Cin-N	49	93	19	25	2	4	0	9	8	14	.269	.333	.376	106	0	1	12	1			.936	-9	O	-1.0
1944	Cin-N	110	356	51	89	15	0	0	17	17	18	.250	.290	.292	67	-17	-15	31	8			.993	-2	O	-2.2
1945	Cin-N	153	656	81	184	29	2	1	50	37	58	.280	.321	.335	84	-16	-14	71	19			.989	6	*O	-1.7
1946	Cin-N	121	435	52	99	17	0	2	22	53	40	.228	.318	.280	73	-15	-14	43	11			**.988**	7	*O	-1.3
Total	4	433	1540	203	397	63	6	3	98	115	130	.258	.314	.312	79	-48	-42	157	39			.987	3	O	-6.2

■ BILL CLAY Clay, Frederick C. b: 11/23/1874, Baltimore, Md. d: 10/12/17, York, Pa. TR , Deb: 8/08/02

YEAR	TM/L	G	AB	R	H	2B	3B	HR	RBI	BB	SO	AVG	OBP	SLG	PRO+	BR	/A	RC	SB	CS	SBR	FA	FR	POS	TPR
1902	Phi-N	3	8	1	2	0	0	0	1	0		.250	.250	.250	54	-0	-0	1	0			.750	-1	/O	-0.2

■ ROYCE CLAYTON Clayton, Royce Spencer b: 1/2/70, Burbank, Cal. BR/TR, 6', 175 lbs. Deb: 9/20/91

YEAR	TM/L	G	AB	R	H	2B	3B	HR	RBI	BB	SO	AVG	OBP	SLG	PRO+	BR	/A	RC	SB	CS	SBR	FA	FR	POS	TPR
1991	SF-N	9	26	0	3	1	0	0	2	1	6	.115	.148	.154	-15	-4	-4	0	0	0	0	.880	-6	/S	-1.0
1992	SF-N	98	321	31	72	7	4	4	24	26	63	.224	.282	.308	71	-14	-12	26	8	4	0	.973	-9	S/3	-1.5
Total	2	107	347	31	75	8	4	4	26	27	69	.216	.273	.297	64	-18	-16	27	8	4	0	.968	-15	S/3	-2.5

■ CHET CLEMENS Clemens, Chester Spurgeon b: 5/10/17, San Fernando, Cal. BR/TR, 6', 175 lbs. Deb: 9/13/39

YEAR	TM/L	G	AB	R	H	2B	3B	HR	RBI	BB	SO	AVG	OBP	SLG	PRO+	BR	/A	RC	SB	CS	SBR	FA	FR	POS	TPR
1939	Bos-N	9	23	2	5	0	0	0	1	1	3	.217	.250	.217	29	-2	-2	1	1			.867	-1	/O	-0.3
1944	Bos-N	19	17	7	3	1	1	0	2	2	2	.176	.263	.353	69	-1	-1	2	0			1.000	-2	/O	-0.3
Total	2	28	40	9	8	1	1	0	3	3	5	.200	.256	.275	46	-3	-3	3	1			.905	-3	/O	-0.6

■ CLEM CLEMENS
Clemens, Clement Lambert "Count" (b: Clement Lambert Ulatowski)
b: 11/21/1886, Chicago, Ill. d: 11/2/67, St.Petersburg, Fla. BR/TR, 5'11", 176 lbs. Deb: 5/15/14

YEAR	TM/L	G	AB	R	H	2B	3B	HR	RBI	BB	SO	AVG	OBP	SLG	PRO+	BR	/A	RC	SB	CS	SBR	FA	FR	POS	TPR
1914	Chi-F	13	27	4	4	0	0	0	2	3	0	.148	.233	.148	10	-3	-3	1	0			.950	-1	/C	-0.3
1915	Chi-F	11	22	3	3	1	0	0	3	1	0	.136	.174	.182	5	-3	-3	1	0			1.000	-1	/C2	-0.3
1916	Chi-N	10	15	0	0	0	0	0	0	1	6	.000	.063	.000	-72	-3	-3	0	0			.941	1	/C	-0.2
Total	3	34	64	7	7	1	0	0	5	5	6	.109	.174	.125	-12	-9	-9	2	0			.962	-0	/C2	-0.8

■ DOUG CLEMENS
Clemens, Douglas Horace b: 6/9/39, Leesport, Pa. BL/TR, 6', 180 lbs. Deb: 10/02/60

YEAR	TM/L	G	AB	R	H	2B	3B	HR	RBI	BB	SO	AVG	OBP	SLG	PRO+	BR	/A	RC	SB	CS	SBR	FA	FR	POS	TPR
1960	StL-N	1	0	0	0	0	0	0	0	0	0	—	—	—	—	0	0	0	0	0	0	1.000	0	/O	0.0
1961	StL-N	6	12	1	2	1	0	0	0	3	1	.167	.333	.250	53	-1	-1	1	0	0	0	.667	-1	/O	-0.2
1962	StL-N	48	93	12	22	1	1	1	12	17	19	.237	.355	.301	71	-2	-4	11	0	0	0	.974	-3	O	-0.8
1963	StL-N	5	6	1	1	0	0	1	2	1	2	.167	.286	.667	151	0	0	1	0	0	0	1.000	1	/O	0.1
1964	StL-N	33	78	8	16	4	3	1	9	6	16	.205	.271	.372	73	-2	-3	8	0	0	0	.970	-1	O	-0.5
	Chi-N	54	140	23	39	10	2	2	12	18	22	.279	.365	.421	116	4	4	22	0	0	0	.923	1	O	0.3
	Yr	87	218	31	55	14	5	3	21	24	38	.252	.332	.404	100	2	0	30	0	0	0	.937	0	O	-0.2
1965	Chi-N	128	340	36	75	11	0	4	26	38	53	.221	.303	.288	66	-14	-15	29	5	8	-3	.981	-8	*O	-3.2
1966	Phi-N	79	121	10	31	1	0	1	15	16	25	.256	.353	.289	81	-2	-2	14	1	0	0	1.000	1	O/1	-0.2
1967	Phi-N	69	73	2	13	5	0	0	4	8	15	.178	.268	.247	48	-5	-5	5	0	0	0	1.000	-2	O	-0.7
1968	Phi-N	29	57	6	12	1	1	2	8	7	13	.211	.297	.368	99	-0	-0	6	0	0	0	1.000	0	O	-0.1
Total	9	452	920	99	211	34	7	12	88	114	166	.229	.319	.321	78	-22	-26	98	6	8	-3	.969	-12	O/1	-5.3

■ BOB CLEMENS
Clemens, Robert Baxter b: 8/9/1886, Mt.Hebron, Mo. d: 4/5/64, Marshall, Mo. BR/TR, 5'9", 163 lbs. Deb: 9/17/14

YEAR	TM/L	G	AB	R	H	2B	3B	HR	RBI	BB	SO	AVG	OBP	SLG	PRO+	BR	/A	RC	SB	CS	SBR	FA	FR	POS	TPR
1914	StL-A	7	13	1	3	0	1	0	3	2	1	.231	.375	.385	133	1	1	1	0	2	-1	.750	-1	/O	-0.2

■ WALLY CLEMENT
Clement, Wallace Oakes b: 7/21/1881, Auburn, Me. d: 11/1/53, Coral Gables, Fla. BL/TR, 5'11", 175 lbs. Deb: 8/17/08

YEAR	TM/L	G	AB	R	H	2B	3B	HR	RBI	BB	SO	AVG	OBP	SLG	PRO+	BR	/A	RC	SB	CS	SBR	FA	FR	POS	TPR
1908	Phi-N	16	36	0	8	3	0	0	1	0		.222	.222	.306	66	-1	-2	3	2			1.000	4	/O	0.2
1909	Phi-N	3	3	0	0	0	0	0	0	0		.000	.000	.000	-99	-1	-1	0	0			.000	0	H	-0.1
	Bro-N	92	340	35	88	8	4	0	17	18		.259	.296	.306	90	-6	-5	35	11			.965	4	O	-0.5
	Yr	95	343	35	88	8	4	0	17	18		.257	.294	.303	88	-7	-5	34	11			.965	4	O	-0.6
Total	2	111	379	35	96	11	4	0	18	18		.253	.287	.303	86	-8	-7	38	13			.970	8	/O	-0.4

■ ROBERTO CLEMENTE
Clemente, Roberto (Walker) "Bob" b: 8/18/34, Carolina, P.R. d: 12/31/72, San Juan, P.R. BR/TR, 5'11", 175 lbs. Deb: 4/17/55 H

YEAR	TM/L	G	AB	R	H	2B	3B	HR	RBI	BB	SO	AVG	OBP	SLG	PRO+	BR	/A	RC	SB	CS	SBR	FA	FR	POS	TPR
1955	Pit-N	124	474	48	121	23	11	5	47	18	60	.255	.285	.382	76	-18	-17	46	2	5	-2	.978	12	*O	-1.3
1956	Pit-N	147	543	66	169	30	7	7	60	13	58	.311	.332	.431	105	1	3	72	6	6	-2	.957	2	*O/23	-0.4
1957	Pit-N	111	451	42	114	17	7	4	30	23	45	.253	.289	.348	72	-19	-18	41	0	4	-2	.979	13	*O	-1.3
1958	Pit-N	140	519	69	150	24	10	6	50	31	41	.289	.329	.408	96	-5	-3	67	8	2	1	.982	25	*O	1.6
1959	Pit-N	105	432	60	128	17	7	4	50	15	51	.296	.324	.396	91	-6	-6	52	2	3	-1	.948	9	*O	-0.3
1960	*Pit-N★	144	570	89	179	22	6	16	94	39	72	.314	.360	.458	121	17	16	87	4	5	-2	.971	3	*O	1.1
1961	Pit-N★	146	572	100	201	30	10	23	89	35	59	**.351**	.392	.559	148	39	38	119	4	1	1	.969	13	*O	4.3
1962	Pit-N★	144	538	95	168	28	9	10	74	35	73	.312	.355	.454	115	11	11	81	6	4	-1	.973	13	*O	1.4
1963	Pit-N★	152	600	77	192	23	8	17	76	31	64	.320	.357	.470	135	26	26	94	12	2	2	.958	-5	*O	1.7
1964	Pit-N★	155	622	95	**211**	40	7	12	87	51	87	**.339**	.391	.484	145	37	37	118	5	2	0	.968	8	*O	4.0
1965	Pit-N★	152	589	91	194	21	14	10	65	43	78	**.329**	.380	.463	136	28	28	101	8	0	2	.968	10	*O	3.5
1966	Pit-N★	154	638	105	202	31	11	29	119	46	109	.317	.363	.536	146	38	38	119	7	5	-1	.965	16	*O	4.6
1967	Pit-N★	147	585	103	**209**	26	10	23	110	41	103	**.357**	.402	.554	170	**52**	**52**	**126**	9	1	2	.970	9	*O	5.8
1968	Pit-N	132	502	74	146	18	12	18	57	51	77	.291	.357	.482	152	30	31	82	2	3	-1	.984	11	*O	3.8
1969	Pit-N★	138	507	87	175	20	**12**	19	91	56	73	.345	.413	.544	170	45	46	109	4	1	1	.980	6	*O	4.6
1970	*Pit-N★	108	412	65	145	22	10	14	60	38	66	.352	.409	.556	159	32	33	93	3	0	1	.966	5	*O	3.3
1971	*Pit-N★	132	522	82	178	29	8	13	86	26	65	.341	.372	.502	146	29	29	90	1	2	-1	.993	8	*O	3.2
1972	*Pit-N†	102	378	68	118	19	7	10	60	29	49	.312	.361	.479	140	17	18	61	0	0	0	1.000	5	O	1.9
Total	18	2433	9454	1416	3000	440	166	240	1305	621	1230	.317	.362	.475	130	354	362	1557	83	46	-3	.973	162	*O/23	41.5

■ ED CLEMENTS
Clements, Edward b: Philadelphia, Pa. Deb: 6/24/1890

YEAR	TM/L	G	AB	R	H	2B	3B	HR	RBI	BB	SO	AVG	OBP	SLG	PRO+	BR	/A	RC	SB	CS	SBR	FA	FR	POS	TPR
1890	Pit-N	1	1	0	0	0	0	0	0	0	0	.000	.000	.000	-99	-0	-0	0	0			.400	-0	/S	-0.1

■ JACK CLEMENTS
Clements, John J. b: 7/24/1864, Philadelphia, Pa. d: 5/23/41, Norristown, Pa. BL/TL, 5'8.5", 204 lbs. Deb: 4/22/1884 M

YEAR	TM/L	G	AB	R	H	2B	3B	HR	RBI	BB	SO	AVG	OBP	SLG	PRO+	BR	/A	RC	SB	CS	SBR	FA	FR	POS	TPR
1884	Phi-U	41	177	37	50	13	2	3		9		.282	.317	.429	162	9	11	25				.764	1	OC/S	1.1
	Phi-N	9	30	3	7	0	0	0	0	4	8	.233	.324	.233	82	-1	-0	2				.827	1	/C	0.1
1885	Phi-N	52	188	14	36	11	3	1	14	2	30	.191	.200	.298	61	-9	-8	11				.891	-8	CO	-1.2
1886	Phi-N	54	185	15	38	5	1	0	11	7	34	.205	.234	.243	45	-12	-12	12	4			.930	12	C/O	0.4
1887	Phi-N	66	246	48	69	13	7	1	47	9	24	.280	.317	.402	95	-0	-3	34	7			.940	9	C/3S	1.0
1888	Phi-N	86	326	26	80	8	4	1	32	10	36	.245	.276	.304	82	-5	-7	29	3			.927	-1	C/O	0.0
1889	Phi-N	78	310	51	88	17	1	4	35	29	21	.284	.347	.384	97	2	-2	43	3			.916	-7	C	-0.2
1890	Phi-N	97	381	64	120	23	8	7	74	45	30	.315	.392	.472	150	26	24	76	10			.944	2	C/1M	3.0
1891	Phi-N	107	423	58	131	29	4	4	75	43	19	.310	.380	.426	133	20	18	71	3			.927	-5	*C/1	2.0
1892	Phi-N	109	402	50	106	25	6	8	76	43	40	.264	.339	.415	130	14	14	61	7			.950	6	*C	2.5
1893	Phi-N	94	376	64	107	20	3	17	80	39	29	.285	.360	.489	127	12	12	69	3			.942	-12	*C/1	0.7
1894	Phi-N	45	159	26	55	6	5	3	36	24	7	.346	.455	.503	136	10	11	41	6			.946	-3	C	0.9
1895	Phi-N	88	322	64	127	27	2	13	75	22	7	.394	.446	.612	173	34	34	92	3			.969	-10	*C	2.5
1896	Phi-N	57	184	35	66	5	7	5	45	17	14	.359	.427	.543	159	15	15	45	2			.966	-3	C	1.5
1897	Phi-N	55	185	18	44	4	2	6	36	12		.238	.305	.378	82	-6	-5	23	3			.962	-3	C	-0.3
1898	StL-N	99	335	39	86	19	5	3	41	21		.257	.314	.370	94	-3	-4	41	1			**.971**	-6	C	-0.2
1899	Cle-N	4	12	1	3	0	0	0	0	0		.250	.308	.250	58	-1	-1	1	0			.938	0	/C	0.0
1900	Bos-N	16	42	6	13	1	0	1	10	3		.310	.370	.405	101	1	0	6	0			.948	1	C	0.2
Total	17	1157	4283	619	1226	226	60	77	687	339	299	.286	.347	.421	118	106	97	683	55			.937	-27	*C/O13S	14.0

■ VERNE CLEMONS
Clemons, Verne James "Stinger" or "Tubby" b: 9/8/1891, Clemons, Iowa d: 5/5/59, Bay Pines, Fla. BR/TR, 5'9.5", 190 lbs. Deb: 4/22/16

YEAR	TM/L	G	AB	R	H	2B	3B	HR	RBI	BB	SO	AVG	OBP	SLG	PRO+	BR	/A	RC	SB	CS	SBR	FA	FR	POS	TPR
1916	StL-A	4	7	0	1	1	0	0	0	0	1	.143	.143	.286	30	-1	-1	0	0			.889	0	/C	0.0
1919	StL-N	88	239	14	63	13	2	2	22	26	13	.264	.336	.360	116	3	5	29	4			.982	2	C	1.4
1920	StL-N	112	338	17	95	10	6	1	36	30	12	.281	.340	.355	103	0	2	42	1	1	-0	.977	-6	*C	0.2
1921	StL-N	117	341	29	109	16	2	2	48	33	17	.320	.380	.396	108	4	5	53	0	0	0	.985	-4	*C	0.6
1922	StL-N	71	160	9	41	4	0	0	15	18	5	.256	.331	.281	62	-9	-8	16	1	0	0	.996	3	C	-0.3
1923	StL-N	57	130	6	37	9	1	0	13	10	11	.285	.345	.369	90	-2	-2	17	0	0	0	.981	5	C	0.5
1924	StL-N	25	56	3	18	3	0	0	6	2	3	.321	.345	.375	94	-1	-0	7	0	0	0	.983	-2	C	-0.1
Total	7	474	1271	78	364	56	11	5	140	119	62	.286	.348	.360	99	-5	1	164	6	1		.983	-2	C	2.3

■ DONN CLENDENON
Clendenon, Donn Alvin b: 7/15/35, Neosho, Mo. BR/TR, 6'3.5", 210 lbs. Deb: 9/22/61

YEAR	TM/L	G	AB	R	H	2B	3B	HR	RBI	BB	SO	AVG	OBP	SLG	PRO+	BR	/A	RC	SB	CS	SBR	FA	FR	POS	TPR
1961	Pit-N	9	35	7	11	1	1	0	2	5	10	.314	.400	.400	113	1	1	6	0	0	0	1.000	0	/O	0.0
1962	Pit-N	80	222	39	67	8	5	7	28	26	58	.302	.378	.477	128	9	9	42	16	4	2	.990	-2	1O	0.5
1963	Pit-N	154	563	65	155	28	7	15	57	39	136	.275	.328	.430	116	11	11	75	22	13	-1	.991	7	*1	1.0
1964	Pit-N	133	457	53	129	23	8	12	64	26	96	.282	.324	.446	115	8	8	62	12	8	-1	.989	-1	*1	0.1
1965	Pit-N	162	612	89	184	32	14	14	96	48	128	.301	.356	.467	129	24	23	99	9	9	-3	.984	2	*1/3	1.5
1966	Pit-N	155	571	80	171	22	10	28	98	52	142	.299	.360	.520	141	31	31	102	8	7	-2	.985	-1	*1	1.8
1967	Pit-N	131	478	46	119	15	2	13	56	34	107	.249	.300	.370	90	-6	-7	49	4	4	-1	.988	4	*1	-1.2

YEAR	TM/L	G	AB	R	H	2B	3B	HR	RBI	BB	SO	AVG	OBP	SLG	PRO+	BR	/A	RC	SB	CS	SBR	FA	FR	POS	TPR
1968	Pit-N	158	584	63	150	20	6	17	87	47	163	.257	.313	.399	114	8	9	72	10	3	1	.990	10	*1	0.9
1969	Mon-N	38	129	14	31	6	1	4	14	6	32	.240	.274	.395	85	-3	-3	11	0	2	-1	.987	3	1O	-0.3
	*NY-N	72	202	31	51	5	0	12	37	19	62	.252	.323	.455	113	4	3	30	3	2	-0	.984	-4	1/O	-0.5
	Yr	110	331	45	82	11	1	16	51	25	94	.248	.304	.432	103	1	-0	40	3	4	-2	.985	-0	1O	-0.8
1970	NY-N	121	396	65	114	18	3	22	97	39	91	.288	.353	.515	129	15	15	68	4	1	1	.991	-2	*1	0.5
1971	NY-N	88	263	29	65	10	0	11	37	21	78	.247	.305	.411	103	-0	0	29	1	2	-1	.985	-2	1	-0.9
1972	StL-N	61	136	13	26	4	0	4	9	17	37	.191	.281	.309	68	-6	-6	10	1	2	-1	.986	3	1	-0.6
Total	12	1362	4648	594	1273	192	57	159	682	379	1140	.274	.331	.442	117	94	94	657	90	57	-7	.988	18	*1/O3	2.8

■ ELMER CLEVELAND

Cleveland, Elmer Ellsworth b: 9/15/1862, Washington, D.C. d: 10/8/13, Zimmerman, Pa. BR/TR, Deb: 8/29/1884

YEAR	TM/L	G	AB	R	H	2B	3B	HR	RBI	BB	SO	AVG	OBP	SLG	PRO+	BR	/A	RC	SB	CS	SBR	FA	FR	POS	TPR
1884	Cin-U	29	115	24	37	9	2	0		4		.322	.345	.435	150	7	6	18				.843	2	3	0.7
1888	NY-N	9	34	6	8	0	2	2	5	3	1	.235	.297	.529	163	2	2	6	1			.667	-7	/3	-0.4
	Pit-N	30	108	10	24	2	1	2	11	5	23	.222	.270	.315	95	-1	-0	10	3			.831	-9	3	-0.9
	Yr	39	142	16	32	2	3	4	16	8	24	.225	.276	.366	112	1	2	16	4			.806	-15	3	-1.3
1891	Col-a	12	41	12	7	0	0	0	4	12	9	.171	.370	.171	62	-1	-1	4	4			.843	3	3	0.3
Total	3	80	298	52	76	11	5	4	20	24	33	.255	.317	.366	120	7	7	38	8			.830	-10	/3	-0.3

■ STAN CLIBURN

Cliburn, Stanley Gene b: 12/19/56, Jackson, Miss. BR/TR, 6', 195 lbs. Deb: 5/06/80 F

YEAR	TM/L	G	AB	R	H	2B	3B	HR	RBI	BB	SO	AVG	OBP	SLG	PRO+	BR	/A	RC	SB	CS	SBR	FA	FR	POS	TPR
1980	Cal-A	54	56	7	10	2	0	2	6	3	9	.179	.220	.321	48	-4	-4	4	0	0	0	.971	5	C	0.2

■ HARLOND CLIFT

Clift, Harlond Benton "Darkie" b: 8/12/12, ElReno, Okla. d: 4/27/92, Yakima, Wash. BR/TR, 5'11", 180 lbs. Deb: 4/17/34

YEAR	TM/L	G	AB	R	H	2B	3B	HR	RBI	BB	SO	AVG	OBP	SLG	PRO+	BR	/A	RC	SB	CS	SBR	FA	FR	POS	TPR
1934	StL-A	147	572	104	149	30	10	14	56	84	100	.260	.357	.421	92	0	-7	91	7	2	1	.929	-16	*3	-1.6
1935	StL-A	137	475	101	140	26	4	11	69	83	39	.295	.406	.436	113	15	12	89	0	3	-2	.934	-6	*3/2	0.9
1936	StL-A	152	576	145	174	40	11	20	73	115	68	.302	.424	.514	127	31	28	134	12	4	1	.951	3	*3	3.2
1937	StL-A☆	155	571	103	175	36	7	29	118	98	80	.306	.413	.546	139	36	35	134	8	5	-1	.947	**41**	*3	**7.2**
1938	StL-A	149	534	119	155	25	7	34	118	118	67	.290	.423	.554	143	38	38	133	10	5	0	**.962**	14	*3	4.8
1939	StL-A	151	526	90	142	25	2	15	84	**111**	55	.270	.402	.411	106	11	9	97	4	3	-1	.953	12	*3	2.0
1940	StL-A	150	523	92	143	29	5	20	87	104	62	.273	.396	.463	119	20	18	103	9	8	-2	**.959**	4	*3	2.1
1941	StL-A	154	584	108	149	33	9	17	84	113	93	.255	.376	.430	109	13	10	102	6	4	-1	.959	1	*3	1.3
1942	StL-A	143	541	108	148	39	4	7	55	106	48	.274	.394	.399	122	21	20	95	6	4	-1	.941	-1	*3/S	2.1
1943	StL-A	105	379	43	88	11	3	3	25	54	37	.232	.329	.301	83	-6	-7	40	5	4	-1	.950	19	*3	1.3
	Was-A	8	30	4	9	0	0	0	4	5	3	.300	.417	.300	115	1	1	4	0	0	0	.968	-1	/3	0.1
	Yr	113	409	47	97	11	3	3	29	59	40	.237	.336	.301	85	-5	-6	44	5	4	-1	.951	18	*3	1.4
1944	Was-A	12	44	4	7	3	0	0	3	3	3	.159	.213	.227	27	-4	-4	2	0	0	0	.842	-3	3	-0.7
1945	Was-A	119	375	49	79	12	0	8	53	76	58	.211	.349	.307	99	-1	3	48	2	1	0	.934	-4	*3	0.2
Total	12	1582	5730	1070	1558	309	62	178	829	1070	713	.272	.390	.441	115	173	155	1072	69	43	-5	.948	63	*3/2S	22.9

■ FLEA CLIFTON

Clifton, Herman Earl b: 12/12/09, Cincinnati, Ohio BR/TR, 5'10", 160 lbs. Deb: 4/29/34

YEAR	TM/L	G	AB	R	H	2B	3B	HR	RBI	BB	SO	AVG	OBP	SLG	PRO+	BR	/A	RC	SB	CS	SBR	FA	FR	POS	TPR
1934	Det-A	16	16	3	1	0	0	0	1	1	2	.063	.118	.063	-52	-4	-4	0	0	0	0	1.000	2	/32	-0.2
1935	*Det-A	43	110	15	28	5	0	0	9	5	13	.255	.293	.300	56	-8	-7	10	2	1	0	.934	-1	3/2S	-0.6
1936	Det-A	13	26	5	5	1	0	0	1	4	3	.192	.300	.231	33	-3	-3	2	0	1	-1	.926	-0	/S32	-0.3
1937	Det-A	15	43	4	5	1	0	0	2	7	10	.116	.240	.140	-2	-7	-7	2	3	0	1	.958	-0	/3S2	-0.5
Total	4	87	195	27	39	7	0	0	13	17	28	.200	.268	.236	30	-21	-20	14	5	2	0	.937	-0	/3S2	-1.6

■ MONK CLINE

Cline, John P. b: 3/3/1858, Ohio d: 9/23/16, Louisville, Ky. BL/TL, 5'4", 150 lbs. Deb: 7/04/1882

YEAR	TM/L	G	AB	R	H	2B	3B	HR	RBI	BB	SO	AVG	OBP	SLG	PRO+	BR	/A	RC	SB	CS	SBR	FA	FR	POS	TPR
1882	Bal-a	44	172	18	38	6	2	0		3		.221	.234	.279	79	-5	-3	12				.825	6	O/S23	0.3
1884	Lou-a	94	396	91	115	16	7	2		27		.290	.342	.381	145	17	20	53				.875	6	*O/S	2.2
1885	Lou-a	2	9	0	2	1	0	0		0		.222	.222	.333	76	-0	-0	1				1.000	-1	/O3	-0.1
1888	KC-a	73	293	45	69	13	2	0	19	20		.235	.289	.294	84	-3	-6	34	29			.883	5	O/23	-0.2
1891	Lou-a	21	76	13	23	3	1	0	12	19	3	.303	.442	.368	138	5	5	14	2			.906	-3	O	0.1
Total	5	234	946	167	247	39	12	2	31	69	3	.261	.315	.334	113	14	16	113	31			.867	14	O/S23	2.3

■ TY CLINE

Cline, Tyrone Alexander b: 6/15/39, Hampton, S.C. BL/TL, 6'0.5", 170 lbs. Deb: 9/14/60

YEAR	TM/L	G	AB	R	H	2B	3B	HR	RBI	BB	SO	AVG	OBP	SLG	PRO+	BR	/A	RC	SB	CS	SBR	FA	FR	POS	TPR
1960	Cle-A	7	26	2	8	1	1	0	2	0	4	.308	.308	.423	99	-0	-0	3	0	0	0	1.000	2	/O	0.1
1961	Cle-A	12	43	9	9	2	1	0	1	6	1	.209	.333	.302	73	-2	-1	5	1	0	0	1.000	-2	O	-0.4
1962	Cle-A	118	375	53	93	15	5	2	28	28	50	.248	.309	.331	74	-15	-13	39	5	4	-1	.992	3	*O	-1.7
1963	Mil-N	72	174	17	41	2	1	0	10	10	31	.236	.285	.259	58	-9	-9	14	2	1	0	.992	9	O	-0.3
1964	Mil-N	101	116	22	35	4	2	1	13	8	22	.302	.362	.397	113	2	2	18	0	1	-1	.982	5	O/1	0.6
1965	Mil-N	123	220	27	42	5	3	0	10	16	50	.191	.246	.241	37	-18	-18	14	2	2	-1	.969	8	O/1	-1.4
1966	Chi-N	7	17	3	6	0	0	0	2	0	2	.353	.353	.353	96	-0	-0	2	1	0	0	1.000	-0	/O	0.0
	Atl-N	42	71	12	18	0	0	0	6	3	11	.254	.303	.254	56	-4	-4	5	2	1	0	1.000	0	O/1	-0.5
	Yr	49	88	15	24	0	0	0	8	3	13	.273	.312	.273	63	-4	-4	7	3	1	0	1.000	0	O/1	-0.5
1967	Atl-N	10	8	0	0	0	0	0	0	0	3	.000	.111	.000	-66	-2	-2	0	0	0	0	1.000	0	/O	-0.2
	SF-N	64	122	18	33	5	5	0	4	9	13	.270	.326	.393	106	1	1	16	2	1	0	1.000	-1	O	-0.1
	Yr	74	130	18	33	5	5	0	4	9	16	.254	.312	.369	96	-1	-1	16	2	1	0	1.000	-1	O	-0.3
1968	SF-N	116	291	37	65	6	3	1	28	11	26	.223	.254	.275	59	-15	-15	20	0	2	-1	.971	-0	O1	-2.4
1969	Mon-N	101	209	26	50	5	3	2	12	32	22	.239	.346	.321	87	-2	-2	25	4	3	-1	.988	1	O1	-0.5
1970	Mon-N	2	2	0	1	0	0	0	0	0	0	.500	.500	.500	169	0	0	1	0	0	0	.000	0	H	0.0
	*Cin-N	48	63	13	17	7	1	0	8	12	11	.270	.387	.413	114	2	2	11	1	2	-1	.966	1	O/1	0.1
	Yr	50	65	13	18	7	1	0	8	12	11	.277	.390	.415	115	2	2	11	1	2	-1	.966	1	O/1	0.1
1971	Cin-N	69	97	12	19	1	0	0	1	18	16	.196	.333	.206	57	-5	-4	8	2	2	-1	1.000	-2	O/1	-0.8
Total	12	892	1834	251	437	53	25	6	125	153	262	.238	.304	.304	72	-66	-64	180	22	19	-5	.986	24	O/1	-7.5

■ GENE CLINES

Clines, Eugene Anthony b: 10/6/46, San Pablo, Cal. BR/TR, 5'9", 170 lbs. Deb: 6/28/70 C

YEAR	TM/L	G	AB	R	H	2B	3B	HR	RBI	BB	SO	AVG	OBP	SLG	PRO+	BR	/A	RC	SB	CS	SBR	FA	FR	POS	TPR
1970	Pit-N	31	37	4	15	2	0	0	3	2	5	.405	.436	.459	143	2	2	7	2	1	0	1.000	-1	/O	0.1
1971	*Pit-N	97	273	52	84	12	4	1	24	22	36	.308	.366	.392	115	6	6	42	15	6	1	.981	6	O	1.0
1972	*Pit-N	107	311	52	104	15	6	0	17	16	47	.334	.371	.421	127	10	10	47	12	6	0	.958	-3	O	0.4
1973	Pit-N	110	304	42	80	11	3	1	23	26	36	.263	.327	.329	84	-7	-6	30	8	7	-2	.968	-0	O	-1.2
1974	*Pit-N	107	276	29	62	5	1	0	14	30	40	.225	.310	.250	60	-15	-13	23	14	2	3	.989	7	O	-0.6
1975	NY-N	82	203	25	46	6	3	0	10	11	21	.227	.270	.286	57	-13	-12	15	4	4	-1	.982	6	O	-1.0
1976	Tex-A	116	446	52	123	12	3	0	38	16	52	.276	.307	.316	81	-10	-11	39	11	9	-2	.987	3	*OD	-1.6
1977	Chi-N	101	239	27	70	12	2	3	41	25	25	.293	.362	.397	93	2	-2	34	1	2	-1	.986	-10	O	-1.5
1978	Chi-N	109	229	31	59	10	2	0	17	21	28	.258	.323	.319	71	-6	-9	24	4	3	-1	.978	-3	O	-1.6
1979	Chi-N	10	10	0	2	0	0	0	0	0	1	.200	.200	.200	9	-1	-1	0	0	0	0	.000	0	/H	-0.1
Total	10	870	2328	314	645	85	24	5	187	169	291	.277	.331	.341	88	-32	-36	260	71	40	-3	.979	4	O/D	-6.1

■ BILLY CLINGMAN

Clingman, William Frederick b: 11/21/1869, Cincinnati, Ohio d: 5/14/58, Cincinnati, Ohio BB/TR, 5'11", 150 lbs. Deb: 9/09/1890

YEAR	TM/L	G	AB	R	H	2B	3B	HR	RBI	BB	SO	AVG	OBP	SLG	PRO+	BR	/A	RC	SB	CS	SBR	FA	FR	POS	TPR
1890	Cin-N	7	27	2	7	1	0	0	5	1	0	.259	.286	.296	72	-1	-1	2	0			.892	-1	/S2	-0.1
1891	Cin-a	1	5	0	1	1	0	0	0	0	0	.200	.200	.400	67	-0	-0	0	0			.667	-1	/2	-0.1
1895	Pit-N	106	382	69	99	16	4	0	45	41	43	.259	.334	.322	76	-15	-11	50	19			.887	14	*3	0.3
1896	Lou-N	121	423	57	99	10	2	2	37	57	51	.234	.329	.281	66	-20	-17	47	19			.925	24	*3	0.8
1897	Lou-N	113	395	59	90	14	7	2	47	37		.228	.302	.314	65	-22	-19	44	14			**.947**	**29**	*3	1.1
1898	Lou-N	154	538	65	138	12	6	0	50	51		.257	.327	.301	82	-13	-11	61	15			.914	15	3S/O2	0.7
1899	Lou-N	109	366	67	96	15	4	2	44	46		.262	.349	.342	90	-4	-4	51	13			.916	-4	*S	0.0
1900	Chi-N	47	159	15	33	6	0	0	11	17		.208	.292	.245	51	-11	-10	14	6			.872	-14	S	-1.9

YEAR	TM/L	G	AB	R	H	2B	3B	HR	RBI	BB	SO	AVG	OBP	SLG	PRO+	BR	/A	RC	SB	CS	SBR	FA	FR	POS	TPR
1901	Was-A	137	480	66	116	10	7	2	55	42		.242	.308	.304	71	-19	-18	51	10			**.932**	18	*S	1.0
1903	Cle-A	21	64	10	18	1	1	0	7	11		.281	.387	.328	118	2	2	9	2			.932	-0	2/S3	0.3
Total	10	816	2839	410	697	86	31	8	301	303	94	.246	.323	.306	74	-103	-90	329	98			.919	79	3S/2O	2.1

■ JIM CLINTON

Clinton, James Lawrence "Big Jim" b: 8/10/1850, New York, N.Y. d: 9/3/21, Brooklyn, N.Y. BR/TR, 5'8.5", 174 lbs. Deb: 5/18/1872 MU

YEAR	TM/L	G	AB	R	H	2B	3B	HR	RBI	BB	SO	AVG	OBP	SLG	PRO+	BR	/A	RC	SB	CS	SBR	FA	FR	POS	TPR
1872	Eck-n	25	97	13	23	3	1	0	7	0	2	.237	.237	.289	72	-4	-1	7						/3/OS2CM	-0.2
1873	Res-n	9	38	5	9	1	0	0	3	0	0	.237	.237	.263	51	-2	-2	2						/3	-0.2
1874	Atl-n	2	11	3	2	1	0	0		0		.182	.182	.273	48	-1	-0	1						/2O	0.0
1875	Atl-n	22	81	3	10	0	0	0		0		.123	.123	.123	-16	-9	-7	1						P/O12	-0.1
1876	Lou-N	16	65	8	22	2	0	0	0	0	0	.338	.338	.369	115	2	1	8				.783	1	O/1P	0.1
1882	Wor-N	26	98	9	16	2	0	0	3	7	13	.163	.219	.184	30	-7	-8	4				.734	-4	O	-1.0
1883	Bal-a	94	399	69	125	16	8	0		27		.313	.357	.393	137	19	17	57				.842	5	*O/2	1.8
1884	Bal-a	104	437	82	118	12	6	4		29		.270	.334	.352	122	14	11	53				.807	-1	*O/2	0.8
1885	Cin-a	105	408	48	97	5	5	0		15		.238	.277	.275	76	-10	-11	32				.877	-0	*O	-1.3
1886	Bal-a	23	83	8	15	1	0	0		4		.181	.227	.193	34	-6	-6	4	3			.894	-0	O	-0.6
Total	4 n	58	227	24	44	5	1	0	10	0	2	.194	.194	.225	38	-16	-11	11	0					/3PO21SC	-0.5
Total	6	368	1490	224	393	38	19	4	3	82	13	.264	.311	.323	102	12	4	159	3			.838	0	O/2P1	-0.2

■ LOU CLINTON

Clinton, Luciean Louis b: 10/13/37, Ponca City, Okla. BR/TR, 6'1", 185 lbs. Deb: 4/22/60

YEAR	TM/L	G	AB	R	H	2B	3B	HR	RBI	BB	SO	AVG	OBP	SLG	PRO+	BR	/A	RC	SB	CS	SBR	FA	FR	POS	TPR
1960	Bos-A	96	298	37	68	17	5	6	37	20	66	.228	.283	.379	75	-10	-12	29	4	3	-1	.966	2	O	-1.5
1961	Bos-A	17	51	4	13	2	1	0	3	2	10	.255	.283	.333	63	-3	-3	5	0	0	0	1.000	3	O	0.0
1962	Bos-A	114	398	63	117	24	10	18	75	34	79	.294	.351	.540	132	18	17	75	2	1	0	.979	1	*O	1.2
1963	Bos-A	148	560	71	130	23	7	22	77	49	118	.232	.295	.416	94	-4	-6	65	0	0	0	.982	11	*O	-0.3
1964	Bos-A	37	120	15	31	4	3	3	6	9	33	.258	.310	.417	95	-0	-1	15	1	0	0	1.000	5	O	0.3
	LA-A	91	306	30	76	18	0	9	38	31	40	.248	.320	.395	108	-1	3	40	3	0	1	.985	3	O	0.2
	Yr	128	426	45	107	22	3	12	44	40	73	.251	.317	.401	104	-1	2	55	4	0	1	.990	7	*O	0.5
1965	Cal-A	89	222	29	54	12	3	1	8	23	37	.243	.317	.338	88	-4	-3	23	2	3	-1	.983	-2	O	-0.9
	KC-A	1	1	0	0	0	0	0	0	0	0	.000	.000	.000	-99	-0	-0	0	0	0	0	.000	-0	/O	-0.1
	Cle-A	12	34	2	6	1	0	1	2	3	7	.176	.243	.294	51	-2	-2	3	0	0	0	.941	-0	/O	-0.3
	Yr	102	257	31	60	13	3	2	10	26	44	.233	.306	.331	83	-6	-6	26	2	3	-1	.977	-2	O	-1.3
1966	NY-A	80	159	18	35	10	2	5	21	16	27	.220	.291	.403	101	-1	-0	19	0	0	0	.976	-6	O	-0.9
1967	NY-A	6	4	1	2	1	0	0	2	1	1	.500	.600	.750	308	1	1	2	0	0	0	.000	-0	/O	0.1
Total	8	691	2153	270	532	112	31	65	269	188	418	.247	.310	.418	99	-6	-7	275	12	7	-1	.980	16	O	-2.2

■ ED CLOUGH

Clough, Edgar George "Big Ed" or "Spec" b: 10/28/06, Wiconisco, Pa. d: 1/30/44, Harrisburg, Pa. BL/TL, 6', 188 lbs. Deb: 8/28/24

YEAR	TM/L	G	AB	R	H	2B	3B	HR	RBI	BB	SO	AVG	OBP	SLG	PRO+	BR	/A	RC	SB	CS	SBR	FA	FR	POS	TPR
1924	StL-N	7	14	0	1	0	0	0	1	0	3	.071	.071	.071	-63	-3	-3	0	0	0	0	1.000	0	/O	-0.3
1925	StL-N	3	4	0	1	0	0	0	0	0	0	.250	.250	.250	28	-0	-0	0	0	0	0	1.000	-0	/P	0.0
1926	StL-N	1	1	0	0	0	0	0	0	0	0	.000	.000	.000	-96	-0	-0	0	0			.000	-0	/P	0.0
Total	3	11	19	0	2	0	0	0	1	0	3	.105	.105	.105	-44	-4	-4	0	0	0		1.000	0	/OP	-0.3

■ OTIS CLYMER

Clymer, Otis Edgar b: 1/27/1876, Pine Grove, Pa. d: 2/27/26, St.Paul, Minn. BB/TR, 5'11", 180 lbs. Deb: 4/14/05

YEAR	TM/L	G	AB	R	H	2B	3B	HR	RBI	BB	SO	AVG	OBP	SLG	PRO+	BR	/A	RC	SB	CS	SBR	FA	FR	POS	TPR
1905	Pit-N	96	365	74	108	11	5	0	23	19		.296	.332	.353	102	2	0	52	23			.986	-2	O/1	-0.6
1906	Pit-N	11	45	7	11	0	1	0	1	3		.244	.292	.289	78	-1	-1	4	1			.900	-1	O	-0.3
1907	Pit-N	22	66	8	15	2	0	0	4	5		.227	.311	.258	77	-1	-1	7	4			.923	-3	O/1	-0.5
	Was-A	57	206	30	65	5	5	1	16	18		.316	.379	.403	162	12	13	40	18			.912	-4	O/1	0.9
1908	Was-A	110	368	32	93	11	4	1	35	20		.253	.291	.313	105	-2	1	38	19			.933	-7	O2/3	-1.1
1909	Was-A	45	138	11	27	5	2	0	6	17		.196	.284	.261	76	-4	-3	12	7			.922	-4	O	-1.0
1913	Chi-N	30	105	16	24	5	1	0	7	14	18	.229	.319	.295	76	-3	-3	12	9			.933	-2	O	-0.6
	Bos-N	14	37	4	12	3	1	0	6	3	3	.324	.375	.459	135	2	2	7	2			.880	-2	O	-0.1
	Yr	44	142	20	36	8	2	0	13	17	21	.254	.333	.338	91	-1	-1	18	11			.918	-4	O	-0.7
Total	6	385	1330	182	355	42	19	2	98	99	21	.267	.321	.332	106	3	8	172	83			.939	-24	O/213	-3.3

■ BILL CLYMER

Clymer, William Johnston "Derby Day Bill" b: 12/18/1873, Philadelphia, Pa. d: 12/26/36, Philadelphia, Pa. Deb: 6/26/1891 C

YEAR	TM/L	G	AB	R	H	2B	3B	HR	RBI	BB	SO	AVG	OBP	SLG	PRO+	BR	/A	RC	SB	CS	SBR	FA	FR	POS	TPR
1891	Phi-a	3	11	0	0	0	0	0	0	1	2	.000	.154	.000	-53	-2	-2	0	1			.867	-2	/S	-0.3

■ PETE COACHMAN

Coachman, Bobby Dean b: 11/11/61, Cottonwood, Ala. BR/TR, 5'9", 175 lbs. Deb: 8/18/90

YEAR	TM/L	G	AB	R	H	2B	3B	HR	RBI	BB	SO	AVG	OBP	SLG	PRO+	BR	/A	RC	SB	CS	SBR	FA	FR	POS	TPR
1990	Cal-A	16	45	3	14	3	0	0	5	1	7	.311	.354	.378	107	0	0	6	0	1	-1	.958	1	/32D	0.1

■ GIL COAN

Coan, Gilbert Fitzgerald b: 5/18/22, Monroe, N.C. BL/TR, 6', 180 lbs. Deb: 4/27/46

YEAR	TM/L	G	AB	R	H	2B	3B	HR	RBI	BB	SO	AVG	OBP	SLG	PRO+	BR	/A	RC	SB	CS	SBR	FA	FR	POS	TPR
1946	Was-A	59	134	17	28	3	2	3	9	7	37	.209	.269	.328	70	-6	-6	12	2	2	-1	.969	-2	O	-1.0
1947	Was-A	11	42	5	21	3	2	0	3	5	6	.500	.553	.667	245	8	8	17	2	1	0	1.000	1	O	0.8
1948	Was-A	138	513	56	119	13	9	7	60	41	78	.232	.298	.333	70	-25	-23	55	23	9	2	.970	12	*O	-1.7
1949	Was-A	111	358	36	78	7	8	3	25	29	58	.218	.278	.307	56	-25	-24	32	9	6	-1	.975	2	O	-2.7
1950	Was-A	104	366	58	111	17	4	7	50	28	46	.303	.359	.429	106	-0	2	60	10	5	0	.970	-3	O	-0.4
1951	Was-A	135	538	85	163	25	7	9	62	39	62	.303	.357	.426	113	7	8	85	8	5	-1	.965	**22**	*O	2.4
1952	Was-A	107	332	50	68	11	6	5	20	32	35	.205	.277	.319	68	-16	-15	32	9	4	0	.984	0	O	-1.9
1953	Was-A	68	168	28	33	1	4	2	17	22	23	.196	.301	.286	60	-9	-9	17	7	0	**2**	1.000	4	O	-0.5
1954	Bal-A	94	265	29	74	11	1	2	20	16	17	.279	.323	.351	91	-6	-4	31	9	4	0	.968	-4	O	-1.0
1955	Bal-A	61	130	18	31	7	1	1	11	13	15	.238	.313	.331	79	-5	-4	14	4	2	0	.983	-4	O	-0.9
	Chi-A	17	17	0	3	0	0	0	1	0	5	.176	.176	.176	-5	-2	-3	1	0	0	0	1.000	-1	/O	-0.3
	Yr	78	147	18	34	7	1	1	12	13	20	.231	.298	.313	68	-7	-7	14	4	2	0	.984	-5	O	-1.2
	NY-N	9	13	0	2	0	0	0	0	0	1	.154	.154	.154	-18	-2	-2	0	0	0	0	1.000	-2	/O	-0.5
1956	NY-N	4	1	2	0	0	0	0	0	0	1	.000	.000	.000	-99	-0	-0	0	0	0	0	.000	0	H	0.0
Total	11	918	2877	384	731	98	44	39	278	232	384	.254	.316	.359	84	-83	-70	355	83	38	2	.973	24	O	-7.7

■ JOE COBB

Cobb, Joseph Stanley (b: Joseph Stanley Serafin) b: 1/24/1895, Hudson, Pa. d: 12/24/47, Allentown, Pa. BR/TR, 5'9", 170 lbs. Deb: 4/25/18

YEAR	TM/L	G	AB	R	H	2B	3B	HR	RBI	BB	SO	AVG	OBP	SLG	PRO+	BR	/A	RC	SB	CS	SBR	FA	FR	POS	TPR
1918	Det-A	1	0	0	0	0	0	0	0	1	0	—	1.000	—	210	0	0	0	0			.000	0	H	0.0

■ TY COBB

Cobb, Tyrus Raymond "The Georgia Peach" b: 12/18/1886, Narrows, Ga. d: 7/17/61, Atlanta, Ga. BL/TR, 6'1", 175 lbs. Deb: 8/30/05 MH

YEAR	TM/L	G	AB	R	H	2B	3B	HR	RBI	BB	SO	AVG	OBP	SLG	PRO+	BR	/A	RC	SB	CS	SBR	FA	FR	POS	TPR
1905	Det-A	41	150	19	36	6	0	1	15	10		.240	.287	.300	86	-2	-2	14	2			.958	2	O	-0.3
1906	Det-A	98	358	45	113	15	5	1	34	19		.316	.355	.394	131	14	13	61	23			.961	6	O	1.5
1907	*Det-A	150	605	97	**212**	28	14	5	**119**	24		**.350**	.380	**.468**	**164**	**44**	**42**	**130**	**49**			.961	11	*O	5.2
1908	*Det-A	150	581	88	**188**	**36**	**20**	4	**108**	34		**.324**	.367	**.475**	**166**	**44**	**41**	**114**	39			.944	4	*O	4.4
1909	*Det-A	156	573	**116**	**216**	33	10	**9**	**107**	48		**.377**	**.431**	**.517**	**190**	**63**	**61**	**159**	**76**			.946	3	*O	**6.4**
1910	Det-A	140	506	**106**	194	35	13	8	91	64		.383	**.456**	**.551**	**202**	68	64	**156**	65			.958	9	*O	7.2
1911	Det-A	146	591	**147**	**248**	**47**	**24**	8	**127**	44		**.420**	.467	**.621**	**193**	**78**	**74**	**207**	**83**			.957	11	*O	**7.4**
1912	Det-A	140	553	120	**226**	30	23	7	83	43		**.409**	.456	**.584**	**203**	67	**70**	173	61			.940	1	*O	6.2
1913	Det-A	122	428	70	167	18	16	4	67	58	31	**.390**	**.467**	.535	**196**	52	53	124	51			.947	3	*O	5.3
1914	Det-A	98	345	69	127	22	11	2	57	57	22	.368	.466	.513	188	42	41	89	35	17	0	.949	-10	O	3.0
1915	Det-A	156	563	**144**	**208**	31	13	3	99	118	43	**.369**	**.486**	.487	**182**	**72**	**68**	**155**	**96**	38	6	.951	-3	*O	**6.6**
1916	Det-A	145	542	**113**	201	31	10	5	68	78	39	.371	.452	.493	177	58	55	**136**	**68**	24	**6**	.953	-2	*O/1	5.7
1917	Det-A	152	588	107	**225**	**44**	**24**	6	102	61	34	**.383**	**.444**	**.570**	**210**	**74**	**75**	**164**	**55**			.973	13	*O	**8.5**
1918	Det-A	111	421	83	161	19	**14**	3	64	41	21	**.382**	**.440**	**.515**	**196**	**44**	**46**	**105**	34			.975	2	O1/P23	4.6
1919	Det-A	124	497	92	**191**	36	13	1	70	38	22	**.384**	.429	.515	168	42	43	116	28			.973	-2	*O	3.4
1920	Det-A	112	428	86	143	28	8	2	63	58	28	.334	.416	.451	133	20	22	82	14	10	-2	.966	-7	*O	0.4

YEAR	TM/L	G	AB	R	H	2B	3B	HR	RBI	BB	SO	AVG	OBP	SLG	PRO+	BR	/A	RC	SB	CS	SBR	FA	FR	POS	TPR
1921	Det-A	128	507	124	197	37	16	12	101	56	19	.389	.452	.596	167	50	51	134	22	15	-2	.970	13	*OM	4.8
1922	Det-A	137	526	99	211	42	16	4	99	55	24	.401	.462	.565	172	52	55	133	9	13	-5	.980	4	*OM	4.2
1923	Det-A	145	556	103	189	40	7	6	88	66	14	.340	.413	.469	135	27	28	108	9	10	-3	.969	5	*OM	1.9
1924	Det-A	155	625	115	211	38	10	4	78	85	18	.338	.418	.450	126	25	26	121	23	14	-2	**.986**	5	*OM	1.8
1925	Det-A	121	415	97	157	31	12	12	102	65	12	.378	.468	.598	**171**	45	46	118	13	9	-2	.948	-2	*O/PM	3.3
1926	Det-A	79	233	48	79	18	5	4	62	26	2	.339	.408	.511	137	13	13	49	9	4	0	.950	-5	OM	0.4
1927	Phi-A	134	490	104	175	32	7	5	93	67	12	.357	.440	.482	131	31	27	97	22	16	-3	.969	-5	*O	1.1
1928	Phi-A	95	353	54	114	27	4	1	40	34	16	.323	.389	.431	112	8	7	58	5	8	-3	.964	-1	O	-0.2
Total	24	3035	11434	2246	4189	724	295	117	1937	1249	357	.366	.433	.512	167	1032	1017	2803	891	178		.961	56	*O/1P32	92.8

■ DAVE COBLE

Coble, David Lamar b: 12/24/12, Monroe, N.C. d: 10/15/71, Orlando, Fla. BR/TR, 6'1", 183 lbs. Deb: 5/01/39

YEAR	TM/L	G	AB	R	H	2B	3B	HR	RBI	BB	SO	AVG	OBP	SLG	PRO+	BR	/A	RC	SB	CS	SBR	FA	FR	POS	TPR
1939	Phi-N	15	25	2	7	1	0	0	0	0	3	.280	.280	.320	63	-1	-1	2	0			.938	-1	C	-0.2

■ GEORGE COCHRAN

Cochran, George Leslie b: 2/12/1889, Rusk, Tex. d: 5/21/60, Harbor City, Cal. TR , Deb: 7/29/18

YEAR	TM/L	G	AB	R	H	2B	3B	HR	RBI	BB	SO	AVG	OBP	SLG	PRO+	BR	/A	RC	SB	CS	SBR	FA	FR	POS	TPR
1918	Bos-A	24	60	7	7	0	0	0	3	10	6	.117	.264	.117	15	-6	-6	2	3			.960	-4	3/S	-1.0

■ DAVE COCHRANE

Cochrane, David Carter b: 1/31/63, Riverside, Cal. BB/TR, 6'2", 180 lbs. Deb: 9/02/86

YEAR	TM/L	G	AB	R	H	2B	3B	HR	RBI	BB	SO	AVG	OBP	SLG	PRO+	BR	/A	RC	SB	CS	SBR	FA	FR	POS	TPR
1986	Chi-A	19	62	4	12	2	0	1	2	5	22	.194	.254	.274	42	-5	-5	4	0	0	0	.872	-3	3/S	-0.8
1989	Sea-A	54	102	13	24	4	1	3	7	14	27	.235	.333	.382	98	0	-0	13	0	2	-1	.905	-13	S/132OC	-1.5
1990	Sea-A	15	20	0	3	0	0	0	0	0	8	.150	.150	.150	-16	-3	-3	0	0	0	0	1.000	0	/S13C	-0.3
1991	Sea-A	65	178	16	44	13	0	2	22	9	38	.247	.287	.354	76	-6	-6	18	0	1	-1	.969	-14	OC3/1D	-2.1
1992	Sea-A	65	152	10	38	5	0	2	12	12	34	.250	.309	.322	76	-5	-5	16	1	0	0	.879	-8	OC3/1SD2	-1.2
Total	5	218	514	43	121	24	1	8	43	40	129	.235	.294	.333	73	-18	-19	50	1	3	-2	.925	-38	/O3CS12D	-5.9

■ MICKEY COCHRANE

Cochrane, Gordon Stanley b: 4/6/03, Bridgewater, Mass. d: 6/28/62, Lake Forest, Ill. BL/TR, 5'10.5", 180 lbs. Deb: 4/14/25 MCH

YEAR	TM/L	G	AB	R	H	2B	3B	HR	RBI	BB	SO	AVG	OBP	SLG	PRO+	BR	/A	RC	SB	CS	SBR	FA	FR	POS	TPR
1925	Phi-A	134	420	69	139	21	5	6	55	44	19	.331	.397	.448	107	9	5	76	7	4	-0	.984	-10	*C	0.2
1926	Phi-A	120	370	50	101	8	9	8	47	56	15	.273	.369	.408	97	2	-1	60	5	2	0	.975	12	*C	1.7
1927	Phi-A	126	432	80	146	20	6	12	80	50	7	.338	.409	.495	127	22	18	84	9	6	-1	.986	3	*C	2.7
1928	Phi-A	131	468	92	137	26	12	10	57	76	25	.293	.395	.464	122	19	17	89	7	7	-2	.966	2	*C	2.7
1929	*Phi-A	135	514	113	170	37	8	7	95	69	8	.331	.412	.475	123	23	20	103	7	6	-2	.983	8	*C	3.7
1930	*Phi-A	130	487	110	174	42	5	10	85	55	18	.357	.424	.526	133	30	27	111	5	0	2	**.993**	6	*C	4.1
1931	*Phi-A	122	459	87	160	31	6	17	89	56	21	.349	.423	.553	146	37	33	108	2	3	-1	.986	10	*C	4.5
1932	Phi-A	139	518	118	152	35	4	23	112	100	22	.293	.412	.510	132	31	28	115	0	1	-1	**.993**	10	*C/O	4.2
1933	Phi-A	130	429	104	138	30	4	15	60	106	22	.322	**.459**	.515	156	42	41	109	8	6	-1	.989	-7	*C	3.8
1934	*Det-A★	129	437	74	140	32	1	2	76	78	26	.320	.428	.412	117	16	16	83	8	4	0	.988	-4	*CM	1.6
1935	*Det-A☆	115	411	93	131	33	3	5	47	96	15	.319	.452	.450	139	27	29	91	5	5	-2	.989	-5	*CM	2.6
1936	Det-A	44	126	24	34	8	0	2	17	46	15	.270	.465	.381	111	6	5	27	1	1	-0	.983	-9	CM	-0.1
1937	Det-A	27	98	27	30	10	1	2	12	25	4	.306	.452	.490	134	7	7	23	0	1	-1	1.000	-2	CM	0.5
Total	13	1482	5169	1041	1652	333	64	119	832	857	217	.320	.419	.478	127	269	244	1079	64	46	-8	.985	14	*C/O	32.2

■ JIM COCKMAN

Cockman, James b: 4/26/1873, Guelph, Ont., Can. d: 9/28/47, Guelph, Ont., Can. BR/TR, 5'6", 145 lbs. Deb: 9/28/05

YEAR	TM/L	G	AB	R	H	2B	3B	HR	RBI	BB	SO	AVG	OBP	SLG	PRO+	BR	/A	RC	SB	CS	SBR	FA	FR	POS	TPR
1905	NY-A	13	38	5	4	0	0	0	2	4		.105	.190	.105	-5	-4	-5	1	2			.875	-2	3	-0.8

■ JACK COFFEY

Coffey, John Francis b: 1/28/1887, New York, N.Y. d: 2/14/66, Bronx, N.Y. BR/TR, 5'11", 178 lbs. Deb: 6/23/09

YEAR	TM/L	G	AB	R	H	2B	3B	HR	RBI	BB	SO	AVG	OBP	SLG	PRO+	BR	/A	RC	SB	CS	SBR	FA	FR	POS	TPR
1909	Bos-N	73	257	21	48	4	4	0	20	11		.187	.229	.233	41	-17	-19	14	2			.896	-12	S	-3.3
1918	Det-A	22	67	7	14	0	2	0	4	8	6	.209	.303	.269	75	-2	-2	6	2			.957	0	2	0.0
	Bos-A	15	44	5	7	1	0	1	2	3	2	.159	.213	.250	40	-3	-3	3	2			.955	2	3/2	-0.1
	Yr	37	111	12	21	1	2	1	6	11	8	.189	.268	.261	62	-6	-5	9	4			.959	2	23	-0.1
Total	2	110	368	33	69	5	6	1	26	22	8	.188	.241	.242	47	-23	-24	22	6				-9	/S23	-3.4

■ FRANK COGGINS

Coggins, Franklin b: 5/22/44, Griffin, Ga. BB/TR, 6'2", 187 lbs. Deb: 9/10/67

YEAR	TM/L	G	AB	R	H	2B	3B	HR	RBI	BB	SO	AVG	OBP	SLG	PRO+	BR	/A	RC	SB	CS	SBR	FA	FR	POS	TPR
1967	Was-A	19	75	9	23	3	0	1	8	2	17	.307	.325	.387	114	1	1	9	1	0	0	.964	3	2	0.6
1968	Was-A	62	171	15	30	6	1	0	7	9	33	.175	.217	.222	34	-14	-13	8	1	1	-0	.953	4	2	-0.8
1972	Chi-N	6	1	1	0	0	0	0	0	1	0	.000	.500	.000	48	0	0	0	0	0	0	.000	0	H	0.0
Total	3	87	247	25	53	9	1	1	15	12	50	.215	.251	.271	59	-13	-12	17	2	1	0	.957	7	/2	-0.2

■ RICH COGGINS

Coggins, Richard Allen b: 12/7/50, Indianapolis, Ind. BL/TL, 5'8", 170 lbs. Deb: 8/29/72

YEAR	TM/L	G	AB	R	H	2B	3B	HR	RBI	BB	SO	AVG	OBP	SLG	PRO+	BR	/A	RC	SB	CS	SBR	FA	FR	POS	TPR
1972	Bal-A	16	39	5	13	4	0	0	1	1	6	.333	.350	.436	129	1	1	5	0	2	-1	1.000	2	O	0.2
1973	*Bal-A	110	389	54	124	19	9	7	41	28	24	.319	.365	.468	134	16	16	65	17	9	-0	.987	-3	*O/D	0.9
1974	*Bal-A	113	411	53	100	13	3	4	32	29	31	.243	.301	.319	81	-11	-10	42	26	6	4	.984	-7	*O	-1.9
1975	Mon-N	13	37	1	10	3	1	0	4	1	7	.270	.289	.405	87	-1	-1	4	0	0	0	1.000	-1	O	-0.2
	NY-A	51	107	7	24	1	0	1	6	7	16	.224	.272	.262	53	-7	-6	8	3	3	-1	.970	-3	O/D	-1.2
1976	NY-A	7	4	1	1	0	0	0	1	0	1	.250	.250	.250	47	-0	-0	0	1	0	0	1.000	-0	/O	0.0
	Chi-A	32	96	4	15	2	0	0	5	6	15	.156	.206	.177	13	-10	-11	4	3	1	0	1.000	-4	O/D	-1.6
	Yr	39	100	5	16	2	0	0	6	6	16	.160	.208	.180	14	-11	-11	4	4	1	1	1.000	-4	O/D	-1.6
Total	5	342	1083	125	287	42	13	12	90	72	100	.265	.314	.361	94	-12	-10	129	50	21	2	.986	-17	O/D	-3.8

■ ED COGSWELL

Cogswell, Edward b: 2/25/1854, England d: 7/27/1888, Fitchburg, Mass. BR/TR, 5'8", 150 lbs. Deb: 7/11/1879

YEAR	TM/L	G	AB	R	H	2B	3B	HR	RBI	BB	SO	AVG	OBP	SLG	PRO+	BR	/A	RC	SB	CS	SBR	FA	FR	POS	TPR
1879	Bos-N	49	236	51	76	8	1	1	18	8	5	.322	.344	.377	135	9	9	31				.967	1	1	0.7
1880	Tro-N	47	209	41	63	7	3	0	13	11	10	.301	.336	.364	130	8	7	26				.961	1	1	0.4
1882	Wor-N	13	51	10	7	1	0	0	1	6	6	.137	.228	.157	26	-4	-4	2				.937	-1	1	-0.6
Total	3	109	496	102	146	16	4	1	32	25	21	.294	.328	.349	121	13	11	59				.960	1	1	0.5

■ ALTA COHEN

Cohen, Alta Albert "Schoolboy" b: 12/25/08, New York, N.Y. BL/TL, 5'10.5", 170 lbs. Deb: 4/15/31

YEAR	TM/L	G	AB	R	H	2B	3B	HR	RBI	BB	SO	AVG	OBP	SLG	PRO+	BR	/A	RC	SB	CS	SBR	FA	FR	POS	TPR
1931	Bro-N	1	3	1	2	0	0	0	0	0	0	.667	.667	.667	261	1	1	1	0			1.000	1	/O	0.2
1932	Bro-N	9	32	1	5	1	0	0	1	3	7	.156	.229	.188	14	-4	-4	2	0			.850	1	/O	-0.4
1933	Phi-N	19	32	6	6	1	0	0	1	6	4	.188	.316	.219	49	-2	-2	2	0			1.000	-0	/O	-0.3
Total	3	29	67	8	13	2	0	0	2	9	11	.194	.289	.224	42	-5	-5	5	0			.925	2	/O	-0.5

■ ANDY COHEN

Cohen, Andrew Howard b: 10/25/04, Baltimore, Md. d: 10/29/88, ElPaso, Tex. BR/TR, 5'8", 155 lbs. Deb: 6/06/26 FMC

YEAR	TM/L	G	AB	R	H	2B	3B	HR	RBI	BB	SO	AVG	OBP	SLG	PRO+	BR	/A	RC	SB	CS	SBR	FA	FR	POS	TPR
1926	NY-N	32	35	4	9	0	1	0	8	1	2	.257	.278	.314	60	-2	-2	3	0			.792	2	2S/3	0.0
1928	NY-N	129	504	64	138	24	7	9	59	31	17	.274	.318	.403	87	-11	-11	63	3			.969	3	*2/S3	-0.4
1929	NY-N	101	347	40	102	12	2	5	47	11	15	.294	.319	.383	73	-15	-15	41	3			.964	12	2/S3	0.1
Total	3	262	886	108	249	36	10	14	114	43	34	.281	.317	.392	81	-28	-28	106	6			.964	16	2/S3	-0.3

■ JIMMIE COKER

Coker, Jimmie Goodwin b: 3/28/36, Holly Hill, S.C. d: 10/29/91, Throckmorton, Tex. BR/TR, 5'11", 195 lbs. Deb: 9/11/58

YEAR	TM/L	G	AB	R	H	2B	3B	HR	RBI	BB	SO	AVG	OBP	SLG	PRO+	BR	/A	RC	SB	CS	SBR	FA	FR	POS	TPR
1958	Phi-N	2	6	0	1	0	0	0	0	0	0	.167	.167	.167	-12	-1	-1	0	0	0	0	1.000	0	/C	-0.1
1960	Phi-N	81	252	18	54	5	3	6	34	23	45	.214	.290	.329	69	-11	-11	24	0	3	-2	.982	2	C	-0.6
1961	Phi-N	11	25	3	10	1	0	1	4	7	4	.400	.531	.560	193	4	4	9	1	0	0	.984	0	C	0.5
1962	Phi-N	5	3	0	0	0	0	0	1	1	2	.000	.250	.000	-27	-1	-1	0	0	0	0	.000	0	H	-0.1
1963	SF-N	4	5	0	1	0	0	0	0	1	2	.200	.333	.200	58	-0	-0	0	0	0	0	1.000	-1	/C	-0.1
1964	Cin-N	11	32	3	10	2	0	1	4	3	5	.313	.371	.469	130	1	1	5	0	0	0	1.000	2	C	0.4
1965	Cin-N	24	61	3	15	2	0	2	9	8	16	.246	.333	.377	93	0	-0	8	0	0	0	.993	5	C	0.6
1966	Cin-N	50	111	9	28	3	0	4	14	8	5	.252	.303	.387	83	-2	-3	13	0	1	-1	.979	5	C/O	0.3
1967	Cin-N	45	97	8	18	2	1	2	4	4	20	.186	.218	.289	39	-7	-8	5	0	1	-1	.976	-0	C	-0.9
Total	9	233	592	44	137	15	4	16	70	55	99	.231	.301	.351	77	-16	-19	64	1	5	-3	.983	14	C/O	0.0

YEAR	TM/L	G	AB	R	H	2B	3B	HR	RBI	BB	SO	AVG	OBP	SLG	PRO+	BR	/A	RC	SB	CS	SBR	FA	FR	POS	TPR

■ ROCKY COLAVITO   Colavito, Rocco Domenico b: 8/10/33, New York, N.Y.   BR/TR, 6'3", 190 lbs.   Deb: 9/10/55 C

1955	Cle-A	5	9	3	4	2	0	0	0	0	2	.444	.444	.667	189	1	1	3	0	0	0	1.000	2	/O	0.3
1956	Cle-A	101	322	55	89	11	4	21	65	49	46	.276	.375	.531	134	16	15	67	0	1	-1	.968	-1	O	0.9
1957	Cle-A	134	461	66	116	26	0	25	84	71	80	.252	.353	.471	124	14	15	76	1	6	-3	.962	12	*O	1.7
1958	Cle-A	143	489	80	148	26	3	41	113	84	89	.303	.407	**.620**	183	53	54	122	0	2	-1	.981	2	*O1/P	4.9
1959	Cle-A★	154	588	90	151	24	0	**42**	111	71	86	.257	.339	.512	135	22	25	101	3	3	-1	.985	12	*O	2.8
1960	Det-A	145	555	67	138	18	1	35	87	53	80	.249	.319	.474	108	6	5	78	3	6	-3	.976	7	*O	0.2
1961	Det-A★	163	583	129	169	30	2	45	140	113	75	.290	.407	.580	156	52	49	141	1	2	-1	.975	10	*O	4.8
1962	Det-A★	161	601	90	164	30	2	37	112	96	68	.273	.375	.514	132	31	29	117	2	0	1	.992	18	*O	3.7
1963	Det-A	160	597	91	162	29	2	22	91	84	78	.271	.362	.437	119	20	17	95	0	0	0	.988	7	*O	1.7
1964	KC-A★	160	588	89	161	31	2	34	102	83	56	.274	.368	.507	136	33	31	110	3	1	0	.973	3	*O	2.7
1965	Cle-A★	162	592	92	170	25	2	26	**108**	**93**	63	.287	.387	.468	140	35	34	**110**	1	1	-0	**1.000**	4	*O	3.2
1966	Cle-A★	151	533	68	127	13	0	30	72	76	81	.238	.337	.432	119	14	14	74	2	1	0	.982	7	*O	1.5
1967	Cle-A	63	191	10	46	9	0	5	21	24	31	.241	.329	.366	104	2	1	23	2	2	-1	.962	-4	O	-0.6
	Chi-A	60	190	20	42	4	1	3	29	25	10	.221	.312	.300	85	-4	-3	19	1	1	-0	.977	-7	O	-1.4
	Yr	123	381	30	88	13	1	8	50	49	41	.231	.320	.333	95	-2	-2	42	3	3	-1	.970	-11	*O	-2.0
1968	LA-N	40	113	8	23	3	0	3	11	15	18	.204	.297	.310	89	-2	-1	9	0	1	-1	1.000	-2	O	-0.6
	NY-A	39	91	13	20	2	2	5	13	14	17	.220	.330	.451	139	4	4	14	0	0	0	.933	-4	O/P	-0.2
Total	14	1841	6503	971	1730	283	21	374	1159	951	880	.266	.362	.489	132	297	290	1157	19	27	-11	.980	66	*O/1P	25.6

■ MIKE COLBERN   Colbern, Michael Malloy b: 4/19/55, Santa Monica, Cal.   BR/TR, 6'3", 205 lbs.   Deb: 7/18/78

1978	Chi-A	48	141	11	38	5	1	2	20	1	36	.270	.285	.362	80	-4	-4	14	0	1	-1	.969	0	C/D	-0.4
1979	Chi-A	32	83	5	20	5	1	0	8	4	25	.241	.276	.325	61	-5	-5	8	0	0	0	.971	3	C	-0.1
Total	2	80	224	16	58	10	2	2	28	5	61	.259	.281	.348	73	-9	-9	22	0	1	-1	.970	3	/CD	-0.5

■ CRAIG COLBERT   Colbert, Craig Charles b: 2/13/65, Iowa City, Iowa   BR/TR, 6', 190 lbs.   Deb: 4/06/92

| 1992 | SF-N | 49 | 126 | 10 | 29 | 5 | 2 | 1 | 16 | 9 | 22 | .230 | .281 | .325 | 75 | -5 | -4 | 10 | 1 | 0 | 0 | .994 | -7 | C/32 | -1.0 |

■ NATE COLBERT   Colbert, Nathan b: 4/9/46, St.Louis, Mo.   BR/TR, 6'2", 209 lbs.   Deb: 4/14/66

1966	Hou-N	19	7	3	0	0	0	0	0	0	4	.000	.000	.000	-99	-2	-2	0	0	0	0	.000	0	H	-0.2
1968	Hou-N	20	53	5	8	1	0	0	4	1	23	.151	.167	.170	1	-6	-6	1	1	1	-0	.952	-1	O/1	-0.9
1969	SD-N	139	483	64	123	20	9	24	66	45	123	.255	.322	.482	128	12	15	72	6	4	-1	.990	1	*1	0.5
1970	SD-N	156	572	84	148	17	6	38	86	56	150	.259	.329	.509	126	14	17	93	3	5	-2	.991	-8	*1/3	-0.7
1971	SD-N★	156	565	81	149	25	3	27	84	63	119	.264	.342	.462	135	18	23	87	5	2	0	.993	1	*1	1.0
1972	SD-N★	151	563	87	141	27	2	38	111	70	127	.250	.333	.508	147	25	30	95	15	6	1	.996	7	*1	2.6
1973	SD-N★	145	529	73	143	25	2	22	80	54	146	.270	.347	.450	130	13	18	80	9	8	-2	.992	3	*1	0.7
1974	SD-N	119	368	53	76	16	0	14	54	62	108	.207	.323	.364	96	-4	-2	46	10	2	2	.988	6	1O	0.0
1975	Det-A	45	156	16	23	4	2	4	18	17	52	.147	.231	.276	41	-12	-13	9	0	2	-1	.982	-4	1/D	-2.2
	Mon-N	38	81	10	14	4	1	4	11	5	31	.173	.230	.395	68	-4	-4	7	0	0	0	.988	-1	1/D	-0.6
1976	Mon-N	14	40	5	8	2	0	2	6	9	16	.200	.347	.400	107	1	1	6	3	1	0	1.000	1	/O1	0.1
	Oak-A	2	5	0	0	0	0	0	1	0	3	.000	.167	.000	-50	-1	-1	0	0	0	0	.000	0	/D	-0.1
Total	10	1004	3422	481	833	141	25	173	520	383	902	.243	.324	.451	120	55	75	497	52	31	-3	.991	4	1/OD3	0.2

■ GREG COLBRUNN   Colbrunn, Gregory Joseph b: 7/26/69, Fontana, Cal.   BR/TR, 6', 190 lbs.   Deb: 7/09/92

| 1992 | Mon-N | 52 | 168 | 12 | 45 | 8 | 0 | 2 | 18 | 6 | 34 | .268 | .301 | .351 | 85 | -4 | -4 | 18 | 3 | 2 | -0 | .992 | -1 | 1 | -0.9 |

■ ALEX COLE   Cole, Alexander b: 8/17/65, Fayetteville, N.C.   BL/TL, 6'2", 170 lbs.   Deb: 7/27/90

1990	Cle-A	63	227	43	68	5	4	0	13	28	38	.300	.379	.357	107	3	3	37	40	9	7	.961	2	O/D	1.0
1991	Cle-A	122	387	58	114	17	3	0	21	58	47	.295	.388	.354	106	6	6	55	27	17	-2	.970	1	*O/D	0.2
1992	Cle-A	41	97	11	20	1	0	0	5	10	21	.206	.287	.216	42	-7	-7	7	9	2	2	.971	-4	O/D	-1.0
	*Pit-N	64	205	33	57	3	7	0	10	18	46	.278	.336	.361	99	-1	-0	25	7	4	-0	.989	-1	O	-0.3
Total	3	290	916	145	259	26	14	0	49	114	152	.283	.364	.342	98	-2	2	125	83	32	6	.971	-3	O/D	-0.1

■ DICK COLE   Cole, Richard Roy b: 5/6/26, Long Beach, Cal.   BR/TR, 6'2", 175 lbs.   Deb: 4/27/51 C

1951	StL-N	15	36	4	7	1	0	0	3	6	5	.194	.310	.222	45	-3	-3	3	0	0	0	.969	5	2	0.2
	Pit-N	42	106	9	25	4	0	1	11	15	9	.236	.331	.302	69	-4	-4	11	0	1	-1	.981	-2	2/S	-0.6
	Yr	57	142	13	32	5	0	1	14	21	14	.225	.325	.282	63	-6	-7	14	0	1	-1	.978	2	2/S	-0.4
1953	Pit-N	97	235	29	64	13	1	0	23	38	26	.272	.374	.336	87	-3	-3	32	2	2	-1	.965	-3	S/21	-0.2
1954	Pit-N	138	486	40	131	22	5	1	40	41	48	.270	.326	.342	75	-18	-17	52	0	0	0	.949	-11	S32	-2.3
1955	Pit-N	77	239	16	54	8	3	0	21	18	22	.226	.286	.285	53	-16	-16	19	0	0	0	.935	1	32S	-1.2
1956	Pit-N	72	99	7	21	2	1	0	9	11	9	.212	.291	.253	49	-7	-7	7	0	0	0	.947	-8	32/S	-1.4
1957	Mil-N	15	14	1	1	0	0	0	0	3	5	.071	.235	.071	-13	-2	-2	0	0	0	0	.952	0	2/13	-0.1
Total	6	456	1215	106	303	50	10	2	107	132	124	.249	.324	.312	69	-53	-51	125	2	3	-1	.961	-19	S23/1	-5.6

■ STU COLE   Cole, Stewart Bryan b: 2/7/66, Charlotte, N.C.   BR/TR, 6'1", 175 lbs.   Deb: 9/05/91

| 1991 | KC-A | 9 | 7 | 1 | 1 | 0 | 0 | 0 | 0 | 2 | 2 | .143 | .333 | .143 | 37 | -1 | -1 | 1 | 0 | 0 | 0 | 1.000 | 0 | /2SD | 0.0 |

■ WILLIS COLE   Cole, Willis Russell b: 1/6/1882, Milton Junction, Wis.   d: 10/11/65, Madison, Wis.   BR/TR, 5'8", 170 lbs.   Deb: 8/22/09

1909	Chi-A	46	165	17	39	7	3	0	16	16		.236	.308	.315	101	-1	0	17	3			.889	-4	O	-0.6
1910	Chi-A	22	80	6	14	2	1	0	2	4		.175	.224	.225	42	-6	-5	4	0			.974	1	O	-0.6
Total	2	68	245	23	53	9	4	0	18	20		.216	.281	.286	82	-6	-5	21	3			.912	-3	/O	-1.2

■ CHOO CHOO COLEMAN   Coleman, Clarence b: 8/25/37, Orlando, Fla.   BL/TR, 5'9", 165 lbs.   Deb: 4/16/61

1961	Phi-N	34	47	3	6	1	0	0	4	2	8	.128	.180	.149	-12	-8	-7	1	0	0	0	.977	-1	C	-0.8
1962	NY-N	55	152	24	38	7	2	6	17	11	24	.250	.305	.441	96	-1	-1	19	2	4	-2	.995	-9	C	-1.0
1963	NY-N	106	247	22	44	0	0	3	9	24	49	.178	.264	.215	39	-19	-19	15	5	5	-2	.969	4	C/O	-1.6
1966	NY-N	6	16	2	3	0	0	0	0	0	4	.188	.188	.188	5	-2	-2	1	0	0	0	.963	0	/C	-0.2
Total	4	201	462	51	91	8	2	9	30	37	85	.197	.267	.281	52	-29	-30	36	7	9	-3	.977	-6	C/O	-3.6

■ CURT COLEMAN   Coleman, Curtis Hancock b: 2/18/1887, Salem, Ore.   d: 7/1/80, Newport, Ore.   BL/TR, 5'11", 180 lbs.   Deb: 4/13/12

| 1912 | NY-A | 12 | 37 | 8 | 9 | 4 | 0 | 0 | 4 | 7 | | .243 | .364 | .351 | 99 | 0 | 0 | 5 | 0 | | | .865 | -1 | 3 | -0.1 |

■ DAVE COLEMAN   Coleman, David Lee b: 10/26/50, Dayton, Ohio   BR/TR, 6'3", 195 lbs.   Deb: 4/13/77

| 1977 | Bos-A | 11 | 12 | 1 | 0 | 0 | 0 | 0 | 0 | 1 | 3 | .000 | .077 | .000 | -69 | -3 | -3 | 0 | 0 | 0 | 0 | 1.000 | -3 | /O | -0.7 |

■ JERRY COLEMAN   Coleman, Gerald Francis b: 9/14/24, San Jose, Cal.   BR/TR, 6', 170 lbs.   Deb: 4/20/49 M

1949	*NY-A	128	447	54	123	21	5	2	42	63	44	.275	.367	.358	92	-4	-4	62	8	6	-1	**.981**	1	*2/S	0.2
1950	*NY-A★	153	522	69	150	19	6	6	69	67	38	.287	.372	.381	96	-4	-2	79	3	2	-0	.977	-15	*2/S	-1.0
1951	NY-A	121	362	48	90	11	2	3	43	31	36	.249	.315	.315	73	-15	-13	37	6	1	1	.968	3	2S	-0.3
1952	NY-A	11	42	6	17	2	1	0	4	5	4	.405	.468	.500	180	4	4	10	0	1	-1	.971	3	2	0.7
1953	NY-A	8	10	1	2	0	0	0	0	0	2	.200	.200	.200	9	-1	-1	0	0	1	-1	1.000	-1	2	0.1
1954	NY-A	107	300	39	65	7	1	3	21	26	29	.217	.279	.277	54	-20	-18	24	0	0	1	.977	**18**	2S/3	-0.5
1955	*NY-A	43	96	12	22	5	0	1	9	11	11	.229	.321	.281	64	-5	-5	9	1	2	-1	.966	-2	S2/3	-0.5
1956	*NY-A	80	183	15	47	5	1	0	18	12	33	.257	.306	.295	61	-11	-10	16	1	2	-1	.979	17	2S3	0.9
1957	*NY-A	72	157	23	42	7	2	2	12	20	21	.268	.354	.376	101	0	1	20	1	1	-0	.969	5	23/S	0.8

YEAR	TM/L	G	AB	R	H	2B	3B	HR	RBI	BB	SO	AVG	OBP	SLG	PRO+	BR	/A	RC	SB	CS	SBR	FA	FR	POS	TPR
Total	9	723	2119	267	558	77	18	16	217	235	218	.263	.341	.339	83	-55	-48	257	22	15	-2	.976	31	2S/3	1.5

■ GORDY COLEMAN

Coleman, Gordon Calvin b: 7/5/34, Rockville, Md. BL/TR, 6'2", 218 lbs. Deb: 9/19/59

YEAR	TM/L	G	AB	R	H	2B	3B	HR	RBI	BB	SO	AVG	OBP	SLG	PRO+	BR	/A	RC	SB	CS	SBR	FA	FR	POS	TPR
1959	Cle-A	6	15	5	8	0	1	0	2	1	2	.533	.563	.667	245	3	3	6	0	0	0	.955	0	/1	0.3
1960	Cin-N	66	251	26	68	10	1	6	32	12	32	.271	.309	.390	89	-4	-4	31	1	1	-0	.998	7	1	-0.3
1961	*Cin-N	150	520	63	149	27	4	26	87	45	67	.287	.346	.504	120	15	14	88	1	3	-2	.991	7	*1	0.7
1962	Cin-N	136	476	73	132	13	1	28	86	36	68	.277	.332	.485	113	9	7	73	2	3	-1	.989	-1	*1	-0.4
1963	Cin-N	123	365	38	90	20	2	14	59	29	51	.247	.306	.427	105	3	2	47	1	0	0	.987	1	*1	-0.1
1964	Cin-N	89	198	18	48	6	2	5	27	13	30	.242	.292	.369	82	-4	-5	20	2	0	1	.990	4	1	-0.3
1965	Cin-N	108	325	39	98	19	0	14	57	24	38	.302	.351	.489	125	14	11	55	0	0	0	.991	-1	1	0.6
1966	Cin-N	91	227	20	57	7	0	5	37	16	45	.251	.300	.348	73	-6	-9	24	2	1	0	.986	-1	1	-1.4
1967	Cin-N	4	7	0	0	0	0	0	0	1	0	.000	.125	.000	-55	-1	-2	0	0	0	0	1.000	0	/1	-0.2
Total	9	773	2384	282	650	102	11	98	387	177	333	.273	.326	.448	106	29	18	344	9	8	-2	.990	16	1	-1.1

■ JOHN COLEMAN

Coleman, John Francis b: 3/6/1863, Saratoga Spgs., N.Y d: 5/31/22, Detroit, Mich. BL/TR, 5'9.5", 170 lbs. Deb: 5/01/1883

YEAR	TM/L	G	AB	R	H	2B	3B	HR	RBI	BB	SO	AVG	OBP	SLG	PRO+	BR	/A	RC	SB	CS	SBR	FA	FR	POS	TPR
1883	Phi-N	90	354	33	83	12	8	0	32	15	39	.234	.266	.314	83	-10	-5	30				.886	10	PO/2	0.6
1884	Phi-N	43	171	16	42	7	2	0	22	8	20	.246	.279	.310	89	-3	-2	15				.844	2	OP/1	-0.1
	Phi-a	28	107	16	22	2	3	2		5		.206	.241	.336	83	-1	-2	9				.743	-1	O/P1	-0.4
1885	Phi-a	96	398	71	119	15	11	3		25		.299	.345	.415	134	19	15	58				.844	-1	*O/P	1.0
1886	Phi-a	121	492	67	121	18	16	0		33		.246	.296	.348	102	1	0	60	28			.862	2	*O/1P2	-0.1
	Pit-a	11	43	3	15	2	1	0		2		.349	.378	.442	159	3	3	8	1			.786	-2	O	0.0
	Yr	132	535	70	136	20	17	0		35		.254	.302	.355	107	4	3	68	29			.858	-1	*O/1P2	-0.1
1887	Pit-N	115	475	75	139	21	11	2	54	31	40	.293	.337	.396	111	3	8	74	25			.899	1	*O/1	0.5
1888	Pit-N	116	438	49	101	11	4	0	26	29	52	.231	.285	.274	87	-9	-4	39	15			.928	2	O1	-0.7
1889	Phi-a	6	19	1	1	0	0	0	1	1	3	.053	.100	.053	-56	-4	-4	0	1			.929	0	/PO	-0.1
1890	Pit-N	3	11	1	2	0	0	0	0	3	0	.182	.357	.182	69	-0	-0	1	1			1.000	-1	/OP	-0.1
Total	8	629	2508	332	645	88	56	7	135	152	154	.257	.302	.345	102	-2	9	295	71				11	OP/12	0.6

■ ED COLEMAN

Coleman, Parke Edward b: 12/1/01, Canby, Ore. d: 8/5/64, Oregon City, Ore. BL/TR, 6'2", 200 lbs. Deb: 4/15/32

YEAR	TM/L	G	AB	R	H	2B	3B	HR	RBI	BB	SO	AVG	OBP	SLG	PRO+	BR	/A	RC	SB	CS	SBR	FA	FR	POS	TPR
1932	Phi-A	26	73	13	25	7	1	1	13	1	6	.342	.351	.507	115	2	1	13	1	0	0	1.000	1	O	0.1
1933	Phi-A	102	388	48	109	26	3	6	68	19	51	.281	.318	.410	91	-6	-7	50	0	0	0	.948	-1	O	-1.2
1934	Phi-A	101	329	53	92	14	6	14	60	29	34	.280	.342	.486	116	4	6	55	0	1	-1	.980	-2	O	0.0
1935	Phi-A	10	13	0	1	0	0	0	0	0	3	.077	.077	.077	-61	-3	-3	0	0	0	0	.000	-0	/O	-0.3
	StL-A	108	397	66	114	15	9	17	71	53	41	.287	.373	.499	118	13	10	75	0	2	-1	.974	-3	*O	0.3
	Yr	118	410	66	115	15	9	17	71	53	44	.280	.364	.485	113	10	7	74	0	2	-1	.974	-3	*O	0.0
1936	StL-A	92	137	13	40	5	4	2	34	15	17	.292	.366	.431	93	-1	-2	22	0	0	0	.939	-3	O	-0.4
Total	5	439	1337	193	381	67	23	40	246	117	152	.285	.345	.459	105	8	6	215	1	3	-2	.966	-8	O	-1.5

■ RAY COLEMAN

Coleman, Raymond Leroy b: 6/4/22, Dunsmuir, Cal. BL/TR, 5'11", 170 lbs. Deb: 4/22/47

YEAR	TM/L	G	AB	R	H	2B	3B	HR	RBI	BB	SO	AVG	OBP	SLG	PRO+	BR	/A	RC	SB	CS	SBR	FA	FR	POS	TPR
1947	StL-A	110	343	34	89	9	7	2	30	26	32	.259	.314	.344	81	-9	-9	33	2	5	-2	.984	-2	O	-1.9
1948	StL-A	17	29	2	5	0	1	0	2	2	5	.172	.226	.241	24	-3	-3	1	1	0	0	.889	-1	/O	-0.4
	Phi-A	68	210	32	51	6	6	0	21	31	17	.243	.340	.329	78	-6	-6	23	4	3	-1	.978	2	O	-0.8
	Yr	85	239	34	56	6	7	0	23	33	22	.234	.327	.318	72	-9	-10	24	5	3	-0	.972	1	O	-1.2
1950	StL-A	117	384	54	104	25	6	8	55	32	37	.271	.330	.430	90	-6	-8	52	7	5	-1	.985	3	O	-0.9
1951	StL-A	91	341	41	96	16	5	5	55	24	32	.282	.329	.402	94	-3	-4	43	3	4	-2	.975	1	O	-0.7
	Chi-A	51	181	21	50	8	7	3	21	15	14	.276	.332	.448	112	1	2	26	2	3	-1	.980	-3	O	-0.4
	Yr	142	522	62	146	24	12	8	76	39	46	.280	.330	.418	100	-1	-2	69	5	7	-3	.977	-2	*O	-1.1
1952	Chi-A	85	195	19	42	7	1	2	14	13	17	.215	.264	.292	54	-12	-12	15	0	0	0	.978	-7	O	-2.2
	StL-A	20	46	5	9	3	0	0	1	5	4	.196	.288	.261	52	-3	-3	4	0	0	0	1.000	-2	O	-0.6
	Yr	105	241	24	51	10	1	2	15	18	21	.212	.269	.286	54	-15	-15	19	0	0	0	.982	-9	O	-2.8
Total	5	559	1729	208	446	74	33	20	199	148	158	.258	.318	.374	84	-40	-44	198	19	20	-6	.980	-9	O	-7.9

■ BOB COLEMAN

Coleman, Robert Hunter b: 9/26/1890, Huntingburg, Ind. d: 7/16/59, Boston, Mass. BR/TR, 6'2", 190 lbs. Deb: 6/13/13 MC

YEAR	TM/L	G	AB	R	H	2B	3B	HR	RBI	BB	SO	AVG	OBP	SLG	PRO+	BR	/A	RC	SB	CS	SBR	FA	FR	POS	TPR
1913	Pit-N	24	50	5	9	2	0	0	9	7	8	.180	.281	.220	46	-3	-3	3	0			.978	-3	C	-0.5
1914	Pit-N	73	150	11	40	4	1	1	14	15	32	.267	.333	.327	101	-0	0	17	3			.977	2	C	0.7
1916	Cle-A	19	28	3	6	2	0	0	4	7	6	.214	.371	.286	92	0	0	3	0			.972	-3	C	-0.2
Total	3	116	228	19	55	8	1	1	27	29	46	.241	.327	.298	87	-4	-3	23	3			.976	-4	C	-0.0

■ VINCE COLEMAN

Coleman, Vincent Maurice b: 9/22/61, Jacksonville, Fla. BB/TR, 6', 170 lbs. Deb: 4/18/85

YEAR	TM/L	G	AB	R	H	2B	3B	HR	RBI	BB	SO	AVG	OBP	SLG	PRO+	BR	/A	RC	SB	CS	SBR	FA	FR	POS	TPR
1985	*StL-N	151	636	107	170	20	10	1	40	50	115	.267	.321	.335	84	-14	-13	79	**110**	25	**18**	.979	9	*O	0.9
1986	StL-N	154	600	94	139	13	8	0	29	60	98	.232	.304	.280	63	-30	-29	67	**107**	14	**24**	.972	9	*O	-0.2
1987	*StL-N	151	623	121	180	14	10	3	43	70	126	.289	.364	.358	90	-5	-6	96	**109**	22	**20**	.970	9	*O	1.7
1988	StL-N★	153	616	77	160	20	10	3	38	49	111	.260	.315	.339	87	-9	-10	71	**81**	27	8	.971	5	*O	-0.2
1989	StL-N★	145	563	94	143	21	9	2	28	50	90	.254	.317	.334	84	-10	-12	70	**65**	10	**14**	.962	-5	*O	-0.7
1990	StL-N	124	497	73	145	18	9	6	39	35	88	.292	.341	.400	103	2	2	74	**77**	17	**13**	.981	8	*O	2.0
1991	NY-N	72	278	45	71	7	5	1	17	39	47	.255	.347	.327	91	-2	-2	35	37	14	3	.979	0	O	-0.1
1992	NY-N	71	229	37	63	11	1	2	21	27	41	.275	.357	.358	104	2	2	32	24	9	2	.991	-1	O	0.1
Total	8	1021	4042	648	1071	124	62	18	255	380	716	.265	.330	.340	86	-66	-69	525	610	138	100	.974	34	O	3.5

■ CAD COLES

Coles, Cadwallader Jones b: 1/17/1885, Rock Hill, S.C. d: 6/30/42, Miami, Fla. BL/TR, 6'0.5", 174 lbs. Deb: 4/16/14

YEAR	TM/L	G	AB	R	H	2B	3B	HR	RBI	BB	SO	AVG	OBP	SLG	PRO+	BR	/A	RC	SB	CS	SBR	FA	FR	POS	TPR
1914	KC-F	78	194	17	49	7	3	1	25	5	30	.253	.271	.335	75	-8	-7	20	6			.889	-7	O/1	-1.6

■ CHUCK COLES

Coles, Charles Edward b: 6/27/31, Fredericktown, Pa BL/TL, 5'9", 180 lbs. Deb: 9/19/58

YEAR	TM/L	G	AB	R	H	2B	3B	HR	RBI	BB	SO	AVG	OBP	SLG	PRO+	BR	/A	RC	SB	CS	SBR	FA	FR	POS	TPR
1958	Cin-N	5	11	0	2	1	0	0	2	2	6	.182	.308	.273	52	-1	-1	1	0	0	0	1.000	1	/O	0.0

■ DARNELL COLES

Coles, Darnell b: 6/2/62, San Bernardino, Cal BR/TR, 6'1", 185 lbs. Deb: 9/04/83

YEAR	TM/L	G	AB	R	H	2B	3B	HR	RBI	BB	SO	AVG	OBP	SLG	PRO+	BR	/A	RC	SB	CS	SBR	FA	FR	POS	TPR
1983	Sea-A	27	92	9	26	7	0	1	6	7	12	.283	.333	.391	95	-0	-1	8	0	3	-2	.941	-3	3	-0.6
1984	Sea-A	48	143	15	23	3	1	0	6	17	26	.161	.259	.196	28	-14	-13	8	2	1	0	.918	-3	3/OD	-1.8
1985	Sea-A	27	59	8	14	4	0	1	5	9	17	.237	.348	.356	93	-0	-0	8	0	1	-1	.918	1	S/3OD	0.1
1986	Det-A	142	521	67	142	30	2	20	86	45	84	.273	.337	.453	113	9	9	81	6	2	1	.938	-5	*3/SOD	0.1
1987	Det-A	53	149	14	27	5	1	4	15	15	23	.181	.265	.309	54	-11	-10	13	0	1	-1	.847	-5	3/1OSD	-1.6
	Pit-N	40	119	20	27	8	0	6	24	19	20	.227	.338	.445	105	1	1	17	1	3	-2	1.000	-5	O3/1	-0.7
1988	Pit-N	68	211	20	49	13	1	5	36	20	41	.232	.308	.374	96	-1	-1	25	1	1	-0	.990	-3	O/13	-0.7
	Sea-A	55	195	32	57	10	1	10	34	17	26	.292	.361	.508	134	10	9	35	3	2	-0	.986	-3	O/1D	0.4
1989	Sea-A	146	535	54	135	21	3	10	59	27	61	.252	.296	.359	81	-12	-15	54	5	4	-1	.975	7	O31D	-1.1
1990	Sea-A	37	107	9	23	5	1	2	16	4	17	.215	.250	.336	62	-6	-6	9	0	0	0	.970	1	O/31D	-0.5
	Det-A	52	108	13	22	2	0	1	4	12	21	.204	.283	.250	50	-7	-7	7	0	4	-2	1.000	-1	DO/3	-1.1
	Yr	89	215	22	45	7	1	3	20	16	38	.209	.267	.293	56	-13	-13	16	0	4	-2	.977	-0	OD3/1	-1.6
1991	SF-N	11	14	1	3	0	0	0	0	0	2	.214	.214	.214	22	-1	-1	0	0	0	0	.000	-1	/O1	-0.3
1992	Cin-N	55	141	16	44	11	2	3	18	3	15	.312	.326	.482	120	4	3	22	1	0	0	1.000	1	31/O	0.4
Total	10	761	2394	278	592	119	12	63	309	195	365	.247	.311	.386	91	-29	-32	288	19	22	-8	.922	-21	3O/D1S	-7.4

■ CHRIS COLETTA

Coletta, Christopher Michael b: 8/2/44, Brooklyn, N.Y. BL/TL, 5'11", 190 lbs. Deb: 8/15/72

YEAR	TM/L	G	AB	R	H	2B	3B	HR	RBI	BB	SO	AVG	OBP	SLG	PRO+	BR	/A	RC	SB	CS	SBR	FA	FR	POS	TPR
1972	Cal-A	14	30	5	9	1	0	1	7	1	4	.300	.323	.433	131	1	1	4	0	0	0	1.000	-2	/O	-0.2

YEAR	TM/L	G	AB	R	H	2B	3B	HR	RBI	BB	SO	AVG	OBP	SLG	PRO+	BR	/A	RC	SB	CS	SBR	FA	FR	POS	TPR

■ ED COLGAN   Colgan, William H.   b: E.St.Louis, Ill.   d: 8/8/1895, Great Falls, Mont.   180 lbs.   Deb: 5/03/1884

| 1884 | Pit-a | 48 | 161 | 10 | 25 | 4 | 1 | 0 | 3 | | | .155 | .171 | .193 | 20 | -13 | -14 | 5 | | | | .906 | 2 | C/O | -0.7 |

■ BILL COLIVER   Coliver, William J.   b: 1867, Detroit, Mich.   d: 3/24/1888, Detroit, Mich.   Deb: 7/04/1885

| 1885 | Bos-N | 1 | 4 | 0 | 0 | 0 | 0 | 0 | 0 | 0 | 1 | .000 | .000 | .000 | -99 | -1 | -1 | 0 | | | | .000 | -0 | /O | -0.1 |

■ COLLINS   Collins   Deb: 9/12/1892

| 1892 | StL-N | 1 | 2 | 0 | 0 | 0 | 0 | 0 | 0 | 0 | 0 | .000 | .000 | .000 | -99 | -0 | -0 | 0 | | | | 1.000 | 0 | /O | 0.0 |

■ CHUB COLLINS   Collins, Charles Augustine   b: 10/12/1857, Dundas, Ont., Canad   d: 5/20/14, Dundas, Ont., Can.   Deb: 5/01/1884

1884	Buf-N	45	169	24	30	6	0	0	20	14	36	.178	.240	.213	42	-10	-11	9				.914	0	2/S	-0.9
	Ind-a	38	138	18	31	3	1	0		9		.225	.272	.261	79	-3	-3	10				.886	-8	2	-0.9
1885	Det-N	14	55	8	10	0	2	0	6	0	11	.182	.182	.255	40	-4	-4	3				.792	-8	S	-1.1
Total	2	97	362	50	71	9	3	0	26	23	47	.196	.244	.238	55	-17	-18	22				.901	-16	/2S	-2.9

■ WILSON COLLINS   Collins, Cyril Wilson   b: 5/7/1889, Pulaski, Tenn.   d: 2/28/41, Knoxville, Tenn.   BR/TR, 5'9.5", 165 lbs.   Deb: 5/12/13

1913	Bos-N	16	3	3	1	0	0	0	0	0	1	.333	.333	.333	89	-0	-0	0	0			1.000	-4	/O	-0.4
1914	Bos-N	27	35	5	9	0	0	0	1	2	8	.257	.297	.257	66	-1	-1	3	0			.917	-4	O	-0.7
Total	2	43	38	8	10	0	0	0	1	2	9	.263	.300	.263	68	-2	-1	3	0			.926	-8	/O	-1.1

■ DAN COLLINS   Collins, Daniel Thomas   b: 7/12/1854, St.Louis, Mo.   d: 9/21/1883, New Orleans, La.   Deb: 6/08/1874

| 1874 | Chi-n | 3 | 12 | 1 | 1 | 0 | 0 | 0 | | | | .083 | .083 | .083 | -46 | -2 | -2 | 0 | | | | | | /POS | -0.1 |
| 1876 | Lou-N | 7 | 28 | 3 | 4 | 1 | 0 | 0 | 9 | 0 | 2 | .143 | .143 | .179 | 5 | -3 | -3 | 1 | | | | .909 | 1 | /O | -0.3 |

■ DAVE COLLINS   Collins, David S   b: 10/20/52, Rapid City, S.D.   BB/TL, 5'11", 175 lbs.   Deb: 6/07/75 C

1975	Cal-A	93	319	41	85	13	4	3	29	36	55	.266	.343	.361	106	0	3	42	24	10	1	.988	4	OD	0.5
1976	Cal-A	99	365	45	96	12	1	4	28	40	55	.263	.336	.334	103	-1	2	43	32	19	-2	.994	3	OD	0.4
1977	Sea-A	120	402	46	96	9	3	5	28	33	66	.239	.301	.313	69	-17	-17	41	25	10	2	.985	0	OD	-1.8
1978	Cin-N	102	102	13	22	1	0	0	7	15	18	.216	.316	.225	54	-6	-6	7	7	7	-2	.969	2	O	-0.6
1979	*Cin-N	122	396	59	126	16	4	3	35	27	48	.318	.365	.402	108	5	5	58	16	9	-1	.976	-13	O1	-1.4
1980	Cin-N	144	551	94	167	20	4	3	35	53	68	.303	.367	.370	106	6	6	84	79	21	11	.986	-7	*O	0.5
1981	Cin-N	95	360	63	98	18	6	3	23	41	41	.272	.356	.381	107	5	5	52	26	10	2	.977	-5	O	-0.2
1982	NY-A	111	348	41	88	12	3	3	25	28	49	.253	.318	.330	80	-10	-9	37	13	8	-1	.992	-5	O1/D	-1.9
1983	Tor-A	118	402	55	109	12	4	1	34	43	67	.271	.345	.328	81	-6	-9	51	31	7	5	.989	6	*O1/D	-0.7
1984	Tor-A	128	441	59	136	24	15	2	44	33	41	.308	.369	.444	119	14	12	81	60	14	10	.991	1	*O1/D	2.0
1985	Oak-A	112	379	52	95	16	4	0	29	29	37	.251	.306	.346	84	-11	-8	42	29	8	4	.978	6	O	-0.1
1986	Det-A	124	419	44	113	18	2	1	27	44	49	.270	.342	.329	84	-8	-8	49	27	12	1	.995	3	OD	-0.7
1987	Cin-N	57	85	19	25	5	0	0	5	11	12	.294	.388	.353	94	0	-0	14	9	0	3	1.000	5	O	0.1
1988	Cin-N	99	174	12	41	6	2	0	14	11	27	.236	.289	.293	65	-7	-8	16	7	2	1	.965	-4	O/1	-1.3
1989	Cin-N	78	106	12	25	4	0	0	7	10	17	.236	.302	.274	63	-5	-5	9	3	1	0	1.000	2	O	-0.3
1990	StL-N	99	58	12	13	3	0	0	3	13	10	.224	.366	.241	70	-2	-2	7	7	1	2	1.000	-6	1O	-0.6
Total	16	1701	4907	667	1335	187	52	32	373	467	660	.272	.340	.351	93	-42	-39	633	395	139	35	.986	-12	*O1D	-6.0

■ EDDIE COLLINS   Collins, Edward Trowbridge Jr.   b: 11/23/16, Lansdowne, Pa.   BL/TR, 5'10", 175 lbs.   Deb: 7/04/39 F

1939	Phi-A	32	21	6	5	1	0	0			3	.238	.238	.286	34	-2	-2	1	1	0	0	1.000	0	/O2	-0.2
1941	Phi-A	80	219	29	53	6	3	0	12	20	24	.242	.305	.297	61	-13	-12	21	2	1	0	.968	-0	O	-1.5
1942	Phi-A	20	34	6	8	2	0	0	4	4	2	.235	.316	.294	72	-1	-1	4	1	0	0	.800	-4	/O	-0.5
Total	3	132	274	41	66	9	3	0	16	24	29	.241	.302	.296	61	-16	-15	26	4	1	1	.959	-4	/O2	-2.2

■ EDDIE COLLINS   Collins, Edward Trowbridge Sr. "Cocky" (a.k.a. Edward T. Sullivan in 1906)   b: 5/2/1887, Millerton, N.Y.   d: 3/25/51, Boston, Mass.   BL/TR, 5'9", 175 lbs.   Deb: 9/17/06   FMCH

1906	Phi-A	6	15	2	3	0	0	0	0	0		.200	.200	.200	25	-1	-1	1	0			.900	-0	/S23	-0.2
1907	Phi-A	14	20	0	5	0	0	0	2	0		.250	.250	.250	58	-1	-1	1	0			.833	1	/S	-0.2
1908	Phi-A	102	330	39	90	18	7	1	40	16		.273	.312	.379	117	8	5	42	8			.944	-12	2SO	-0.7
1909	Phi-A	153	572	104	198	30	10	3	56	62		.346	.416	.449	170	49	48	134	67			**.967**	8	*2/S	5.8
1910	*Phi-A	153	583	81	188	16	15	3	81	49		.322	.381	.417	151	33	34	122	81			**.972**	**36**	*2	7.1
1911	*Phi-A	132	493	92	180	22	13	3	73	62		.365	.451	.481	163	43	44	124	38			.967	3	*2	4.3
1912	Phi-A	153	543	**137**	189	25	11	0	64	101		.348	.450	.435	159	44	44	136	63			.955	15	*2	5.7
1913	*Phi-A	148	534	**125**	184	23	13	3	73	85	37	.345	.441	.453	166	46	47	126	55			.965	16	*2	6.3
1914	*Phi-A	152	526	122	181	23	14	2	85	97	31	**.344**	**.452**	.452	**179**	52	54	120	58	30	-1	**.970**	3	*2	5.7
1915	Chi-A	155	521	118	173	22	10	4	77	**119**	27	.332	.460	.436	163	52	50	116	46	30	-4	**.974**	13	*2	6.3
1916	Chi-A	155	545	87	168	14	17	0	52	86	36	.308	.405	.396	139	31	30	99	40	21	-1	**.976**	-6	*2	3.1
1917	*Chi-A	156	564	91	163	18	12	0	67	89	16	.289	.389	.363	127	24	22	98	53			.969	-26	*2	0.5
1918	Chi-A	97	330	51	91	8	2	2	30	73	13	.276	.407	.330	121	14	13	54	22			.974	-1	2	2.1
1919	*Chi-A	140	518	87	165	19	7	4	80	68	27	.319	.400	.405	126	21	20	97	**33**			.974	3	*2	3.1
1920	Chi-A	153	602	117	224	38	13	3	76	69	19	.372	.438	.493	146	42	42	133	19	8	1	**.976**	10	*2	5.6
1921	Chi-A	139	526	79	177	20	10	2	58	66	11	.337	.412	.424	115	14	15	94	12	10	-2	**.968**	27	*2	3.9
1922	Chi-A	154	598	92	194	20	12	1	69	73	16	.324	.401	.403	110	12	12	101	20	12	-1	**.976**	-10	*2	0.5
1923	Chi-A	145	505	89	182	22	5	5	67	84	8	.360	.455	.453	141	34	35	109	**49**	29	-3	.975	-4	*2	2.9
1924	Chi-A	152	556	108	194	27	7	6	86	89	16	.349	.441	.455	136	30	33	119	**42**	17	2	**.977**	-7	*2M	2.8
1925	Chi-A	118	425	80	147	26	3	3	80	87	8	.346	.461	.442	137	26	29	96	19	6	2	.970	-9	*2M	2.2
1926	Chi-A	106	375	66	129	32	4	1	62	62	8	.344	.441	.459	140	22	24	80	13	8	-1	.973	-6	*2M	1.9
1927	Phi-A	95	226	50	76	12	1	1	15	56	9	.336	.468	.412	123	14	12	46	6	2	1	.965	-7	2/S	0.7
1928	Phi-A	36	33	3	10	3	0	0	7	4	4	.303	.378	.394	100	0	0	5	0	0	0	.000	-2	/2S	-0.1
1929	Phi-A	9	7	0	0	0	0	0	0	2	0	.000	.222	.000	-37	-1	-1	0	0	0	0	.000	0	H	-0.1
1930	Phi-A	3	2	1	1	0	0	0	0	0	0	.500	.500	.500	148	0	0	0	0	0	0	.000	0	H	0.0
Total	25	2826	9949	1821	3312	438	186	47	1300	1499	286	.333	.424	.428	142	605	614	2056	744	173		.970	43	*2/SO3	69.4

■ HUB COLLINS   Collins, Hubert B.   b: 4/15/1864, Louisville, Ky.   d: 5/21/1892, Brooklyn, N.Y.   BR/TR, 5'8", 160 lbs.   Deb: 9/04/1886

1886	Lou-a	27	101	12	29	3	2	0		5		.287	.321	.356	108	1	0	14	7			.885	-2	0/3S21	-0.2
1887	Lou-a	130	559	122	162	22	8	1		39		.290	.338	.363	96	-2	-4	95	71			.887	-8	*02/1S3	-1.1
1888	Lou-a	116	485	117	149	26	11	2	50	41		.307	.366	.419	158	29	31	99	62			.890	13	O2S	3.8
	Bro-a	12	42	16	13	5	1	0	3	9		.310	.442	.476	199	5	5	13	9			.897	-3	2	0.3
Yr		128	527	133	162	**31**	12	2	53	50		.307	.373	.423	162	35	36	112	71			.890	10	O2S	**4.1**
1889	*Bro-a	138	560	139	149	18	3	2	73	80	41	.266	.365	.320	97	2	2	91	65			.929	-2	*2	0.6
1890	*Bro-N	129	510	**148**	142	32	7	3	69	85	47	.278	.385	.386	127	21	20	111	85			.945	5	*2	2.9
1891	Bro-N	107	435	82	120	16	5	3	31	59	63	.276	.365	.356	113	9	9	70	32			.910	-22	2O	-1.0
1892	Bro-N	21	87	17	26	5	1	0	17	14	13	.299	.396	.379	142	4	5	15	4			.925	-2	O	0.2
Total	7	680	2779	653	790	127	38	11	243	332	164	.284	.365	.369	118	70	69	509	335			.928	-21	2O/S13	5.5

■ HUGH COLLINS   Collins, Hugh   150 lbs.   Deb: 8/01/1887

| 1887 | NY-a | 1 | 4 | 0 | 1 | 0 | 0 | 0 | | 0 | | .250 | .250 | .250 | 43 | -0 | -0 | 0 | 0 | | | .000 | -0 | /C | -0.1 |

■ RIPPER COLLINS   Collins, James Anthony   b: 3/30/04, Altoona, Pa.   d: 4/15/70, New Haven, Conn.   BB/TL, 5'9", 165 lbs.   Deb: 4/18/31 C

| 1931 | *StL-N | 89 | 279 | 34 | 84 | 20 | 10 | 4 | 59 | 18 | 24 | .301 | .350 | .487 | 118 | 8 | 7 | 48 | 1 | | | .995 | 5 | 1/O | 0.5 |

YEAR	TM/L	G	AB	R	H	2B	3B	HR	RBI	BB	SO	AVG	OBP	SLG	PRO+	BR	/A	RC	SB	CS	SBR	FA	FR	POS	TPR
1932	StL-N	149	549	82	153	28	8	21	91	38	67	.279	.329	.474	110	8	6	87	4			.999	-5	1O	-0.9
1933	StL-N	132	493	66	153	26	7	10	68	38	49	.310	.363	.452	125	20	17	81	7			.994	3	*1	0.8
1934	*StL-N	154	600	116	200	40	12	**35**	128	57	50	.333	.393	**.615**	155	53	48	148	2			.991	8	*1	4.1
1935	StL-N★	150	578	109	181	36	10	23	122	65	45	.313	.385	.529	138	35	32	125	0			.987	1	*1	1.6
1936	StL-N★	103	277	48	81	15	3	13	48	48	30	.292	.399	.509	143	18	18	61	1			.990	-2	1/O	0.9
1937	Chi-N★	115	456	77	125	16	5	16	71	32	46	.274	.329	.436	102	3	0	64	2			.991	1	*1	-1.2
1938	*Chi-N	143	490	78	131	22	8	13	61	54	48	.267	.344	.424	107	7	5	73	1			**.996**	10	*1	0.0
1941	Pit-N	49	62	5	13	2	2	0	11	6	14	.210	.279	.306	65	-3	-3	6	0			.947	-0	1/O	-0.4
Total	9	1084	3784	615	1121	205	65	135	659	356	373	.296	.360	.492	125	149	130	694	18			.992	19	1/O	5.4

■ JIMMY COLLINS Collins, James Joseph b: 1/16/1870, Buffalo, N.Y. d: 3/6/43, Buffalo, N.Y. BR/TR, 5'9", 178 lbs. Deb: 4/19/1895 MH

YEAR	TM/L	G	AB	R	H	2B	3B	HR	RBI	BB	SO	AVG	OBP	SLG	PRO+	BR	/A	RC	SB	CS	SBR	FA	FR	POS	TPR
1895	Bos-N	11	38	10	8	3	0	1	8	4	4	.211	.302	.368	69	-2	-2	4	0			.714	-2	O	-0.4
	Lou-N	96	373	65	104	17	5	6	49	33	16	.279	.352	.399	102	-3	2	58	12			.926	21	3O/2S	1.8
	Yr	107	411	75	112	20	5	7	57	37	20	.273	.347	.397	98	-4	-0	63	12			.926	19	3O/2S	1.4
1896	Bos-N	84	304	48	90	10	9	1	46	30	12	.296	.374	.398	100	3	0	51	10			.909	21	3/S	1.9
1897	*Bos-N	134	529	103	183	28	13	6	132	41		.346	.400	.482	125	24	18	111	14			.917	21	*3	3.6
1898	Bos-N	152	597	107	196	35	5	**15**	111	40		.328	.377	.479	138	32	27	117	12			.932	15	*3	4.0
1899	Bos-N	151	599	98	166	28	11	5	92	40		.277	.335	.386	89	-3	-12	84	12			.943	21	*3	0.9
1900	Bos-N	142	586	104	178	25	5	6	95	34		.304	.352	.394	94	4	-7	93	23			.935	10	*3/S	0.4
1901	Bos-A	138	564	108	187	42	16	6	94	34		.332	.375	.495	142	28	30	116	19			.914	14	*3M	4.0
1902	Bos-A	108	429	71	138	21	10	6	61	24		.322	.362	.459	123	14	12	82	18			**.954**	9	*3M	2.1
1903	*Bos-A	130	540	88	160	33	17	5	72	24		.296	.329	.448	125	19	15	90	23			**.952**	12	*3M	3.0
1904	Bos-A	156	631	85	171	33	13	3	67	27		.271	.306	.379	110	10	6	82	19			.945	7	*3M	1.9
1905	Bos-A	131	508	66	140	26	5	4	65	37		.276	.330	.370	121	12	11	71	18			.923	6	*3M	2.4
1906	Bos-A	37	142	17	39	8	4	1	16	4		.275	.295	.408	120	2	2	18	1			.911	3	3M	0.6
1907	Bos-A	41	158	13	46	8	0	0	10	10		.291	.333	.342	117	3	3	21	4			.874	-7	3	-0.3
	Phi-A	100	365	38	100	22	0	0	35	24		.274	.331	.334	110	5	4	44	4			.904	-2	3	0.6
	Yr	141	523	51	146	30	0	0	45	34		.279	.332	.337	112	8	7	65	8			.895	-10	*3	0.3
1908	Phi-A	115	433	34	94	14	3	0	30	20		.217	.258	.263	65	-15	-18	31	5			.928	-7	*3	-2.3
Total	14	1726	6796	1055	2000	353	116	65	983	426	32	.294	.344	.409	112	134	93	1073	194			.929	140	*3/OS2	24.2

■ ZIP COLLINS Collins, John Edgar b: 5/2/1892, Brooklyn, N.Y. d: 12/19/83, Manassas, Va. BL/TL, 5'11", 152 lbs. Deb: 7/31/14

YEAR	TM/L	G	AB	R	H	2B	3B	HR	RBI	BB	SO	AVG	OBP	SLG	PRO+	BR	/A	RC	SB	CS	SBR	FA	FR	POS	TPR
1914	Pit-N	49	182	14	44	2	0	0	15	8	10	.242	.277	.253	61	-9	-9	13	3			.962	1	O	-1.1
1915	Pit-N	101	354	51	104	8	5	1	23	24	38	.294	.340	.353	112	4	5	44	6	7	-2	.942	5	O	0.4
	Bos-N	5	14	3	4	1	1	0	0	2	1	.286	.375	.500	171	1	1	3	1			1.000	0	/O	0.2
	Yr	106	368	54	108	9	6	1	23	26	39	.293	.342	.359	114	5	6	47	7	7	-2	.944	6	O	0.6
1916	Bos-N	93	268	39	56	1	6	1	18	18	42	.209	.261	.269	66	-12	-11	21	4			.947	-6	O	-2.3
1917	Bos-N	9	27	3	4	0	1	0	2	0	4	.148	.148	.222	14	-3	-3	1	0			1.000	1	/O	-0.3
1921	Phi-A	24	71	14	20	5	1	0	5	6	5	.282	.354	.380	87	-1	-1	9	1	2	-1	.915	0	O	-0.3
Total	5	281	916	124	232	17	14	2	63	58	100	.253	.301	.309	85	-20	-17	92	15	9		.946	1	O	-3.4

■ SHANO COLLINS Collins, John Francis b: 12/4/1885, Charlestown, Mass. d: 9/10/55, Newton, Mass. BR/TR, 6', 185 lbs. Deb: 4/21/10 FM

YEAR	TM/L	G	AB	R	H	2B	3B	HR	RBI	BB	SO	AVG	OBP	SLG	PRO+	BR	/A	RC	SB	CS	SBR	FA	FR	POS	TPR
1910	Chi-A	97	315	29	62	10	8	1	24	25		.197	.258	.289	74	-11	-10	26	10			.949	4	O1	-1.0
1911	Chi-A	106	370	48	97	16	12	4	48	20		.262	.309	.403	101	-3	-1	50	14			.978	4	1/2O	0.2
1912	Chi-A	153	579	75	168	34	10	2	81	29		.290	.330	.394	110	2	5	83	26			.969	3	*O1	0.1
1913	Chi-A	148	535	53	128	26	9	1	47	32	60	.239	.286	.327	80	-16	-15	55	22			.949	1	*O	-2.2
1914	Chi-A	154	598	61	164	34	9	3	65	27	49	.274	.312	.376	108	2	3	71	30	24	-5	.970	9	*O	-0.1
1915	Chi-A	153	576	73	148	24	17	2	85	28	50	.257	.298	.368	96	-4	-6	70	38	19	0	.963	2	*O1	-1.1
1916	Chi-A	143	527	74	128	28	12	0	42	59	51	.243	.323	.342	98	-1	-1	65	16			.959	8	*O/1	-0.1
1917	*Chi-A	82	252	38	59	13	3	1	14	10	27	.234	.269	.321	78	-7	-8	24	14			.992	-2	O	-1.4
1918	Chi-A	103	365	30	100	18	11	1	56	17	19	.274	.310	.392	111	3	2	45	7			.973	14	O/1	1.2
1919	*Chi-A	63	179	21	50	6	3	1	16	7	11	.279	.317	.363	90	-3	-3	21	3			.957	1	O/1	-0.5
1920	Chi-A	133	495	70	150	21	10	1	63	23	24	.303	.339	.392	93	-6	-6	65	12	9	-2	.988	-9	*1O	-1.9
1921	Bos-A	141	542	63	155	29	12	4	69	18	38	.286	.314	.406	85	-16	-14	68	15	8	-0	.966	4	*O/1	-2.0
1922	Bos-A	135	472	33	128	24	7	1	52	7	30	.271	.289	.358	68	-24	-23	46	7	9	-3	.951	-7	*O/1	-4.1
1923	Bos-A	97	342	41	79	10	5	0	18	11	29	.231	.265	.289	46	-27	-28	25	7	8	-3	.953	-2	O	-3.7
1924	Bos-A	89	240	37	70	17	5	0	28	18	17	.292	.349	.404	94	-3	-3	33	4	6	-2	.957	-10	O1	-1.8
1925	Bos-A	2	3	1	1	0	0	0	1	0	0	.333	.333	.333	70	-0	-0	0	0	0	0	.000	-1	/O	-0.1
Total	16	1799	6390	747	1687	310	133	22	709	331	405	.264	.306	.364	90	-114	-108	748	225	83		.962	19	*O1/2	-18.5

■ JOE COLLINS Collins, Joseph Edward (b: Joseph Edward Kollonige) b: 12/3/22, Scranton, Pa. d: 8/30/89, Union, N.J. BL/TL, 6', 185 lbs. Deb: 9/25/48

YEAR	TM/L	G	AB	R	H	2B	3B	HR	RBI	BB	SO	AVG	OBP	SLG	PRO+	BR	/A	RC	SB	CS	SBR	FA	FR	POS	TPR
1948	NY-A	5	5	0	1	1	0	0	2	0	1	.200	.200	.400	58	-0	-0	0	0	0	0	.000	0	H	0.0
1949	NY-A	7	10	2	1	0	0	0	4	6	2	.100	.438	.100	46	-0	-0	1	0	0	0	.920	-1	/1	-0.2
1950	*NY-A	108	205	47	48	8	3	8	28	31	34	.234	.335	.420	95	-3	-2	31	5	0	2	.987	0	1/O	-0.2
1951	*NY-A	125	262	52	75	8	5	9	48	34	23	.286	.368	.458	127	8	9	44	9	7	-2	.987	4	*1O	0.8
1952	*NY-A	122	428	69	120	16	8	18	59	55	47	.280	.364	.481	142	18	22	77	4	2	0	.990	-3	*1	1.6
1953	*NY-A	127	387	72	104	11	2	17	44	59	36	.269	.365	.439	121	9	11	65	2	6	-3	.989	1	*1/O	0.4
1954	NY-A	130	343	67	93	20	2	12	46	51	37	.271	.365	.446	126	10	12	58	2	2	-1	.992	1	*1	0.8
1955	*NY-A	105	278	40	65	9	1	13	45	44	32	.234	.343	.414	104	1	1	40	0	2	-1	.998	5	1O	0.2
1956	*NY-A	100	262	38	59	5	3	7	43	34	33	.225	.316	.347	78	-10	-8	30	3	1	0	.990	2	O1	-1.0
1957	*NY-A	79	149	17	30	1	0	2	10	24	18	.201	.312	.248	56	-9	-8	12	2	1	0	.987	-3	1O	-1.3
Total	10	908	2329	404	596	79	24	86	329	338	263	.256	.351	.421	112	25	36	360	27	21	-5	.990	7	1O	1.1

■ KEVIN COLLINS Collins, Kevin Michael "Casey" b: 8/4/46, Springfield, Mass. BL/TR, 6'2", 190 lbs. Deb: 9/01/65

YEAR	TM/L	G	AB	R	H	2B	3B	HR	RBI	BB	SO	AVG	OBP	SLG	PRO+	BR	/A	RC	SB	CS	SBR	FA	FR	POS	TPR
1965	NY-N	11	23	3	4	1	0	0	0	1	9	.174	.208	.217	21	-2	-2	1	0	1	-1	1.000	-1	/3S	-0.5
1967	NY-N	4	10	1	1	0	0	0	0	0	3	.100	.100	.100	-43	-2	-2	0	1	0	0	1.000	-0	/2	-0.2
1968	NY-N	58	154	12	31	5	2	1	13	7	37	.201	.236	.279	54	-9	-9	10	0	1	-1	.955	-7	3/2S	-1.8
1969	NY-N	16	40	1	6	3	0	1	2	3	10	.150	.209	.300	40	-3	-3	3	0	0	0	.925	3	3	-0.1
	Mon-N	52	96	5	23	5	1	2	12	8	16	.240	.298	.375	87	-2	-2	11	0	0	0	1.000	-7	23	-0.9
	Yr	68	136	6	29	8	1	3	14	11	26	.213	.272	.353	73	-5	-5	13	0	0	0	.917	-4	32	-1.0
1970	Det-A	25	24	2	5	1	0	1	3	1	10	.208	.240	.375	67	-1	-1	2	0	0	0	1.000	0	/1	-0.1
1971	Det-A	35	41	6	11	2	1	1	4	0	12	.268	.268	.439	94	-0	-1	4	0	0	0	1.000	1	/3O2	0.0
Total	6	201	388	30	81	17	4	6	34	20	97	.209	.248	.320	62	-20	-20	31	1	2	-1	.944	-11	/32SO1	-3.6

■ ORTH COLLINS Collins, Orth Stein "Buck" b: 4/27/1880, Lafayette, Ind. d: 12/13/49, Ft.Lauderdale, Fla BL/TR, 6', 150 lbs. Deb: 6/01/04

YEAR	TM/L	G	AB	R	H	2B	3B	HR	RBI	BB	SO	AVG	OBP	SLG	PRO+	BR	/A	RC	SB	CS	SBR	FA	FR	POS	TPR
1904	NY-A	5	17	3	6	1	1	0	1	1		.353	.389	.529	181	2	2	4	0			1.000	2	/O	0.4
1909	Was-A	8	7	0	0	0	0	0	0	0		.000	.000	.000	-99	-2	-2	0	0			1.000	-1	/OP	-0.2
Total	2	13	24	3	6	1	1	0	1	1		.250	.280	.375	104	0	0	4	0			1.000	1	/OP	0.2

■ RIP COLLINS Collins, Robert Joseph b: 9/18/09, Pittsburgh, Pa. d: 4/19/69, Pittsburgh, Pa. BR/TR, 5'11", 176 lbs. Deb: 4/28/40

YEAR	TM/L	G	AB	R	H	2B	3B	HR	RBI	BB	SO	AVG	OBP	SLG	PRO+	BR	/A	RC	SB	CS	SBR	FA	FR	POS	TPR
1940	Chi-N	47	120	11	25	3	0	1	14	14	18	.208	.296	.258	55	-7	-7	9	4			.951	-3	C	-0.7
1944	NY-A	3	3	0	1	0	0	0	0	1	0	.333	.500	.333	136	0	0	1	0	0	0	1.000	0	/C	0.1
Total	2	50	123	11	26	3	0	1	14	15	18	.211	.302	.260	58	-7	-7	10	4	0		.953	-2	/C	-0.6

YEAR	TM/L	G	AB	R	H	2B	3B	HR	RBI	BB	SO	AVG	OBP	SLG	PRO+	BR	/A	RC	SB	CS	SBR	FA	FR	POS	TPR
■ **PAT COLLINS** Collins, Tharon Leslie b: 9/13/1896, Sweet Sprgs., Mo. d: 5/20/60, Kansas City, Kan. BR/TR, 5'9", 178 lbs. Deb: 9/05/19																									
1919	StL-A	11	21	2	3	1	0	0	1	4	2	.143	.280	.190	32	-2	-2	1	0			.929	-1	/C	-0.2
1920	StL-A	23	28	5	6	1	0	0	6	3	5	.214	.290	.250	43	-2	-2	2	0	0	0	1.000	-2	/C	-0.4
1921	StL-A	58	111	9	27	3	0	1	10	16	17	.243	.339	.297	60	-6	-7	12	1	0	0	.961	-1	C	-0.6
1922	StL-A	63	127	14	39	6	0	8	23	21	21	.307	.405	.543	140	9	8	28	0	1	-1	.980	6	C/1	1.4
1923	StL-A	85	181	9	32	8	0	3	30	15	45	.177	.240	.271	32	-18	-19	13	0	0	0	.980	-1	C	-1.8
1924	StL-A	32	54	9	17	2	0	1	11	11	14	.315	.431	.407	110	2	1	10	0	1	-1	.969	-1	C	0.1
1926	*NY-A	102	290	41	83	11	3	7	35	73	55	.286	.433	.417	124	14	14	59	3	2	-0	.971	2	*C	2.2
1927	*NY-A	92	251	38	69	9	3	7	36	54	24	.275	.407	.418	118	8	9	45	0	1	-1	.976	-7	C	0.7
1928	*NY-A	70	136	18	30	5	0	6	14	35	16	.221	.380	.390	106	2	2	23	0	0	0	.977	-5	C	0.2
1929	Bos-N	7	5	1	0	0	0	0	2	3	1	.000	.375	.000	2	-1	-1	1	0			1.000	1	/C	0.1
Total	10	543	1204	146	306	46	6	33	168	235	200	.254	.378	.385	98	5	4	194	4	5		.974	-7	C/1	1.7
■ **BILL COLLINS** Collins, William J. b: 1863, Dublin, Ireland d: 6/8/1893, New York, N.Y. BR , Deb: 10/05/1889																									
1889	Phi-a	1	4	0	1	0	0	0	1	1	0	.250	.400	.250	90	0	0	1	1			.800	-1	/C	0.0
1890	Phi-a	1	1	0	0	0	0	0		0		.000	.000	.000	-99	-0	-0	0	0			.500	-0	/S	0.0
1891	Cle-N	2	3	0	0	0	0	0	0	0	0	.000	.000	.000	-96	-1	-1	0	0			.000	1	/OC	0.0
Total	3	4	8	0	1	0	0	0	1	1	0	.125	.222	.125	2	-1	-1	1	1			.867	0	/COS	0.0
■ **BILL COLLINS** Collins, William Shirley b: 3/27/1882, Chesterton, Ind. d: 6/26/61, San Bernadino, Cal. BB/TR, 6', 170 lbs. Deb: 4/14/10																									
1910	Bos-N	151	584	67	141	6	7	3	40	43	48	.241	.308	.291	72	-18	-22	63	36			**.977**	13	*O	-1.7
1911	Bos-N	17	44	8	6	1	1	0	8	1	8	.136	.156	.205	0	-6	-6	2	4			1.000	0	O/3	-0.7
	Chi-N	7	3	2	1	1	0	0	0	1	0	.333	.500	.667	225	1	1	1	0			1.000	-2	/O	-0.1
	Yr	24	47	10	7	2	1	0	8	2	8	.149	.184	.234	16	-5	-6	3	4			1.000	-2	O/3	-0.8
1913	Bro-N	32	95	8	18	1	0	0	4	8	11	.189	.267	.200	33	-8	-8	5	2			.921	-3	O	-1.3
1914	Buf-F	21	47	6	7	2	2	0	2	1	8	.149	.167	.277	24	-5	-5	2	0			.864	-1	O	-0.6
Total	4	228	773	91	173	11	10	3	54	54	75	.224	.287	.276	61	-37	-41	74	42			.966	7	O/3	-4.4
■ **FRANK COLMAN** Colman, Frank Lloyd b: 3/2/18, London, Ont., Canada d: 2/19/83, London, Ont., Can. BL/TL, 5'11", 188 lbs. Deb: 9/12/42																									
1942	Pit-N	10	37	2	5	0	0	1	2	2	2	.135	.179	.216	15	-4	-4	2	0			1.000	1	/O	-0.4
1943	Pit-N	32	59	9	16	2	2	0	4	8	7	.271	.358	.373	108	1	1	9	0			1.000	0	O	0.0
1944	Pit-N	99	226	30	61	9	5	6	53	25	27	.270	.345	.434	113	5	4	34	0			.964	-3	O/1	-0.1
1945	Pit-N	77	153	18	32	11	1	4	30	9	16	.209	.253	.373	70	-7	-7	14	0			.993	-1	1O	-1.0
1946	Pit-N	26	53	3	9	3	0	1	6	2	7	.170	.214	.283	39	-4	-5	3	0			1.000	0	/O1	-0.5
	NY-A	5	15	2	4	0	0	1	5	1	1	.267	.313	.467	114	0	0	2	0	0	0	1.000	-0	/O	0.0
1947	NY-A	22	28	2	3	0	0	2	6	2	6	.107	.167	.321	34	-3	-3	2	0	0	0	1.000	-1	/O	-0.4
Total	6	271	571	66	130	25	8	15	106	49	66	.228	.291	.378	85	-11	-14	65	0	0		.980	-4	O/1	-2.4
■ **CRIS COLON** Colon, Cristobal b: 1/3/69, LaGuaira, Venez. BB/TR, 6'2", 180 lbs. Deb: 9/18/92																									
1992	Tex-A	14	36	5	6	0	0	0	1	1	8	.167	.189	.167	0	-5	-5	1	0	0	0	.946	3	S	-0.1
■ **BOB COLUCCIO** Coluccio, Robert Pasquali b: 10/2/51, Centralia, Wash. BR/TR, 5'11", 183 lbs. Deb: 4/15/73																									
1973	Mil-A	124	438	65	98	21	8	15	58	54	92	.224	.313	.411	105	1	2	58	13	6	0	.992	10	*OD	0.7
1974	Mil-A	138	394	42	88	13	4	6	31	43	61	.223	.305	.322	81	-10	-9	40	15	9	-1	.989	0	*O/D	-1.5
1975	Mil-A	22	62	8	12	0	1	1	5	11	11	.194	.324	.274	70	-2	-2	5	1	4	-2	1.000	1	O	-0.5
	Chi-A	61	161	22	33	4	2	4	13	13	34	.205	.269	.329	67	-7	-7	15	4	0	1	.980	-5	O/D	-1.4
	Yr	83	223	30	45	4	3	5	18	24	45	.202	.285	.314	68	-9	-9	20	5	4	-1	.987	-5	O/D	-1.9
1977	Chi-A	20	37	4	10	0	0	0	7	6	2	.270	.372	.270	79	-1	-1	4	0	2	-1	1.000	-2	O	-0.5
1978	StL-N	5	3	0	0	0	0	0	0	1	2	.000	.250	.000	-25	-0	-0	0	0	0	0	1.000	0	/O	0.0
Total	5	370	1095	141	241	38	15	26	114	128	202	.220	.306	.353	87	-19	-18	122	33	21	-3	.990	3	O/D	-3.2
■ **EARLE COMBS** Combs, Earle Bryan "The Kentucky Colonel" b: 5/14/1899, Pebworth, Ky. d: 7/21/76, Richmond, Ky. BL/TR, 6', 185 lbs. Deb: 4/16/24 CH																									
1924	NY-A	24	35	10	14	5	0	0	2	4	2	.400	.462	.543	159	3	3	8	0	1	-1	1.000	-3	O	-0.1
1925	NY-A	150	593	117	203	36	13	3	61	65	43	.342	.411	.462	123	20	22	112	12	13	-4	.979	4	*O	1.1
1926	*NY-A	145	606	113	181	31	12	8	55	47	23	.299	.352	.429	105	1	2	92	8	6	-1	.970	1	*O	-0.8
1927	*NY-A	152	648	137	**231**	36	**23**	6	64	62	31	.356	.414	.511	143	37	40	131	15	6	1	.968	2	*O	3.1
1928	*NY-A	149	626	118	194	33	**21**	7	56	77	33	.310	.387	.463	127	21	24	114	10	8	-2	.980	8	*O	2.0
1929	NY-A	142	586	119	202	33	15	3	65	69	32	.345	.414	.468	135	25	31	115	11	7	-1	.966	-4	*O	1.6
1930	NY-A	137	532	129	183	30	**22**	7	82	74	26	.344	.424	.523	145	33	37	120	16	10	-1	.969	-4	*O	2.0
1931	NY-A	138	563	120	179	31	13	5	58	68	34	.318	.394	.446	128	18	23	103	11	3	2	.974	-0	*O	1.4
1932	*NY-A	144	591	143	190	32	10	9	65	81	16	.321	.405	.455	129	22	27	110	3	9	-5	.967	-7	*O	0.5
1933	NY-A	122	417	86	125	22	16	5	64	47	19	.300	.372	.465	128	12	16	73	6	4	-1	.975	-4	*O	0.5
1934	NY-A	63	251	47	80	13	5	2	25	40	9	.319	.412	.434	127	8	11	48	3	1	0	.993	-2	O	0.6
1935	NY-A	89	298	47	84	7	4	3	35	36	10	.282	.359	.362	92	-5	-3	40	1	3	-2	.993	-4	O	-1.0
Total	12	1455	5746	1186	1866	309	154	58	632	670	278	.325	.397	.462	127	196	232	1066	96	71	-14	.974	-14	*O	10.9
■ **MERL COMBS** Combs, Merrill Russell b: 12/11/19, Los Angeles, Cal. d: 7/8/81, Riverside, Cal. BL/TR, 6', 172 lbs. Deb: 9/12/47 C																									
1947	Bos-A	17	68	8	15	1	0	1	6	9	9	.221	.329	.279	65	-2	-3	7	0	0	0	1.000	4	3	0.1
1949	Bos-A	14	24	5	5	1	0	0	1	9	0	.208	.424	.250	75	-0	-0	4	0	0	0	.923	-0	/3S	-0.1
1950	Bos-A	1	0	0	0	0	0	0	0	1	0	—	1.000	—	158	0	0	0	0	0	0	.000	0	H	0.0
	Was-A	37	102	19	25	1	0	0	6	22	16	.245	.379	.255	68	-4	-3	12	0	0	0	.966	-1	S	-0.2
	Yr	38	102	19	25	1	0	0	6	23	16	.245	.384	.255	69	-4	-3	12	0	0	0	.966	-1	S	-0.2
1951	Cle-A	19	28	2	5	2	0	0	2	2	3	.179	.233	.250	32	-3	-3	2	0	0	0	.960	5	S	0.3
1952	Cle-A	52	139	11	23	1	1	1	10	14	15	.165	.242	.209	28	-14	-13	8	0	1	-1	.972	9	S/2	-0.2
Total	5	140	361	45	73	6	1	2	25	57	43	.202	.314	.241	52	-23	-22	32	0	1	-1	.968	17	/S32	-0.1
■ **WAYNE COMER** Comer, Harry Wayne b: 2/3/44, Shenandoah, Va. BR/TR, 5'10", 175 lbs. Deb: 9/17/67																									
1967	Det-A	4	3	0	1	0	0	0	0	0	0	.333	.333	.333	95	-0	-0	0	0	0	0	.000	-0	/O	0.0
1968	*Det-A	48	48	8	6	0	1	1	3	2	7	.125	.160	.229	16	-5	-5	1	0	0	0	1.000	-5	O/C	-1.2
1969	Sea-A	147	481	88	118	18	1	15	54	82	79	.245	.356	.380	108	6	7	70	18	7	1	.980	3	*O/C3	0.4
1970	Mil-A	13	17	1	1	0	0	0	1	0	3	.059	.059	.059	-67	-4	-4	0	0	0	0	1.000	-1	/O	-0.5
	Was-A	77	129	21	30	4	0	0	8	22	16	.233	.349	.264	75	-4	-3	14	4	1	1	.960	-10	O/3	-1.5
	Yr	90	146	22	31	4	0	0	9	22	19	.212	.320	.240	59	-8	-7	13	4	1	1	.962	-11	O/3	-2.0
1972	Det-A	27	9	1	1	0	0	0	1	0	1	.111	.111	.111	-33	-1	-1	0	0	1	-1	1.000	-5	O	-0.9
Total	5	316	687	119	157	22	2	16	67	106	106	.229	.333	.336	90	-8	-7	85	22	9	1	.978	-18	O/3C	-3.7
■ **CHARLIE COMISKEY** Comiskey, Charles Albert "Commy" or "The Old Roman" b: 8/15/1859, Chicago, Ill. d: 10/26/31, Eagle River, Wis. BR/TR, 6', 180 lbs. Deb: 5/02/1882 MH																									
1882	StL-a	78	329	58	80	9	5	1		4		.243	.252	.310	85	-4	-6	26				.967	-1	*1/P	-1.4
1883	StL-a	96	401	87	118	17	9	2		11		.294	.313	.397	120	11	8	51				.963	-2	*1/OM	-0.3
1884	StL-a	108	460	76	110	17	6	2		5		.239	.255	.315	85	-6	-9	38				.969	2	*1/2PM	-1.7
1885	*StL-a	83	340	68	87	15	7	2		14		.256	.293	.359	103	3	0	37				.969	1	*1M	-0.7
1886	*StL-a	131	578	95	147	15	9	3		10		.254	.267	.327	83	-10	-14	63	41			.975	4	*1/2OM	-2.2
1887	*StL-a	125	538	139	180	22	5	4		27		.335	.374	.416	111	16	5	131	117			.976	3	*1/2OM	-0.2
1888	*StL-a	137	576	102	157	22	5	6	83	12		.273	.292	.359	100	5	-4	84	72			.970	-6	*1/O2M	-1.9

YEAR	TM/L	G	AB	R	H	2B	3B	HR	RBI	BB	SO	AVG	OBP	SLG	PRO+	BR	/A	RC	SB	CS	SBR	FA	FR	POS	TPR
1889	StL-a	137	587	105	168	28	10	3	102	19	19	.286	.312	.383	88	-3	-15	93	65			.970	-1	*1/O2PM	-2.1
1890	Chi-P	88	377	53	92	11	3	0	59	14	17	.244	.277	.289	51	-26	-28	41	34			.965	-2	1M	-2.8
1891	StL-a	141	580	86	152	16	2	3	93	33	25	.262	.310	.312	70	-15	-29	70	41			.980	3	*1/OM	-2.8
1892	Cin-N	141	551	61	125	14	6	3	71	32	16	.227	.274	.290	73	-19	-18	53	30			.984	1	*1M	-2.1
1893	Cin-N	64	259	38	57	12	1	0	26	11	2	.220	.257	.274	42	-22	-23	21	9			.979	-6	1M	-2.5
1894	Cin-N	61	220	26	58	8	0	0	33	5	5	.264	.289	.300	42	-20	-22	23	10			.972	-4	1/OM	-2.0
Total	13	1390	5796	994	1531	206	68	29	467	197	84	.264	.293	.338	83	-90	-154	731	419			.973	-8	*1/2OP	-22.7

■ JIM COMMAND Command, James Dalton "Igor" b: 10/15/28, Grand Rapids, Mich BL/TR, 6'2", 200 lbs. Deb: 6/20/54

YEAR	TM/L	G	AB	R	H	2B	3B	HR	RBI	BB	SO	AVG	OBP	SLG	PRO+	BR	/A	RC	SB	CS	SBR	FA	FR	POS	TPR
1954	Phi-N	9	18	1	4	1	0	1	6	2	4	.222	.300	.444	91	-0	-0	3	0	0	0	.929	-0	/3	-0.1
1955	Phi-N	5	5	0	0	0	0	0	0	0	0	.000	.000	.000	-99	-1	-1	0	0	0	0	.000	0	H	-0.1
Total	2	14	23	1	4	1	0	1	6	2	4	.174	.240	.348	52	-2	-2	3	0	0	0		-0	/3	-0.2

■ ADAM COMOROSKY Comorosky, Adam b: 12/9/05, Swoyersville, Pa. d: 3/2/51, Swoyersville, Pa. BR/TR, 5'10", 167 lbs. Deb: 9/13/26

YEAR	TM/L	G	AB	R	H	2B	3B	HR	RBI	BB	SO	AVG	OBP	SLG	PRO+	BR	/A	RC	SB	CS	SBR	FA	FR	POS	TPR
1926	Pit-N	8	15	2	4	1	1	0	0	1	2	.267	.313	.467	102	0	-0	2	1			1.000	-1	/O	-0.2
1927	Pit-N	18	61	5	14	1	0	0	4	3	1	.230	.266	.246	35	-5	-6	4	0			.978	2	O	-0.5
1928	Pit-N	51	176	22	52	6	3	2	34	15	6	.295	.354	.398	92	-1	-2	25	1			.968	-1	O	-0.5
1929	Pit-N	127	473	86	152	26	11	6	97	40	22	.321	.377	.461	104	5	3	80	19			.963	0	*O	-0.5
1930	Pit-N	152	597	112	187	47	**23**	12	119	51	33	.313	.371	.529	114	12	12	114	14			.969	1	*O	0.2
1931	Pit-N	99	350	37	85	12	1	1	48	34	28	.243	.310	.291	63	-18	-17	34	11			.978	3	O	-2.1
1932	Pit-N	108	370	54	106	18	4	4	46	25	20	.286	.337	.389	96	-3	-2	50	7			.981	7	O	0.0
1933	Pit-N	64	162	18	46	8	1	1	15	4	9	.284	.301	.364	89	-3	-3	16	2			1.000	-1	O	-0.5
1934	Cin-N	127	446	46	115	12	6	0	40	34	23	.258	.315	.312	70	-19	-18	44	1			.970	1	*O	-2.2
1935	Cin-N	59	137	22	34	3	1	2	14	7	14	.248	.290	.328	68	-7	-6	13	1			.953	-2	O	-0.9
Total	10	813	2787	404	795	134	51	28	417	214	158	.285	.339	.400	91	-38	-38	382	57			.972	9	O	-7.2

■ PETE COMPTON Compton, Anna Sebastian "Bash" b: 9/28/1889, San Marcos, Tex. d: 2/3/78, Kansas City, Mo. BL/TL, 5'11", 170 lbs. Deb: 9/06/11

YEAR	TM/L	G	AB	R	H	2B	3B	HR	RBI	BB	SO	AVG	OBP	SLG	PRO+	BR	/A	RC	SB	CS	SBR	FA	FR	POS	TPR
1911	StL-A	28	107	9	29	4	0	0	5	8		.271	.322	.308	79	-3	-3	11	2			.917	1	O	-0.3
1912	StL-A	103	268	26	75	6	4	2	30	22		.280	.339	.354	102	-1	1	36	11			.925	1	O	-0.2
1913	StL-A	63	100	14	18	5	2	2	17	13	13	.180	.274	.330	79	-3	-3	9	2			.862	-4	O	-0.9
1915	StL-F	2	8	0	2	0	0	0	3	0	0	.250	.250	.250	45	-1	-1	1	0			1.000	-1	/O	-0.1
	Bos-N	35	116	10	28	7	1	1	12	8	11	.241	.290	.345	96	-1	-1	13	4	1	1	.971	0	O	-0.1
1916	Bos-N	34	98	13	20	2	0	0	8	7	7	.204	.264	.224	53	-6	-5	7	5			.939	-2	O	-1.0
	Pit-N	5	16	1	1	0	0	0	0	2	5	.063	.211	.063	-14	-2	-2	0	0			.917	0	/O	-0.3
	Yr	39	114	14	21	2	0	0	8	9	12	.184	.256	.202	43	-8	-7	8	5			.936	-2	O	-1.3
1918	NY-N	21	60	5	13	0	1	0	5	5	4	.217	.277	.250	62	-3	-3	4	2			.971	-1	O	-0.5
Total	6	291	773	78	186	24	8	5	80	65	40	.241	.303	.312	83	-20	-16	81	26	1		.933	-6	O	-3.4

■ MIKE COMPTON Compton, Michael Lynn b: 8/15/44, Stamford, Tex. BR/TR, 5'10", 180 lbs. Deb: 4/17/70

YEAR	TM/L	G	AB	R	H	2B	3B	HR	RBI	BB	SO	AVG	OBP	SLG	PRO+	BR	/A	RC	SB	CS	SBR	FA	FR	POS	TPR
1970	Phi-N	47	110	8	18	0	1	1	7	9	22	.164	.240	.209	22	-12	-12	6	0	0	0	.986	8	C	-0.2

■ CLINT CONATSER Conatser, Clinton Astor "Connie" b: 7/24/21, Los Angeles, Cal. BR/TR, 5'11", 182 lbs. Deb: 4/21/48

YEAR	TM/L	G	AB	R	H	2B	3B	HR	RBI	BB	SO	AVG	OBP	SLG	PRO+	BR	/A	RC	SB	CS	SBR	FA	FR	POS	TPR
1948	*Bos-N	90	224	30	62	9	3	3	23	32	27	.277	.370	.384	106	2	3	34	0			.974	-9	O	-0.9
1949	Bos-N	53	152	10	40	6	0	3	16	14	19	.263	.325	.362	89	-3	-2	17	0			.951	0	O	-0.4
Total	2	143	376	40	102	15	3	6	39	46	46	.271	.352	.375	99	-1	0	51	0			.965	-8	O	-1.3

■ DAVE CONCEPCION Concepcion, David Ismael (Benitez) b: 6/17/48, Aragua, Venez. BR/TR, 6'1", 180 lbs. Deb: 4/06/70

YEAR	TM/L	G	AB	R	H	2B	3B	HR	RBI	BB	SO	AVG	OBP	SLG	PRO+	BR	/A	RC	SB	CS	SBR	FA	FR	POS	TPR
1970	*Cin-N	101	265	38	69	6	3	1	19	23	45	.260	.326	.317	73	-10	-10	27	10	2	2	.945	-8	S/2	-0.6
1971	Cin-N	130	327	24	67	4	4	1	20	18	51	.205	.246	.251	42	-25	-25	19	9	3	1	.974	-4	*S2/3O	-1.7
1972	*Cin-N	119	378	40	79	13	2	2	29	32	65	.209	.274	.270	58	-22	-20	27	13	6	0	.969	3	*S/32	-0.2
1973	Cin-N†	89	328	39	94	18	3	8	46	21	55	.287	.331	.433	116	4	6	47	22	5	4	.974	2	S/O	2.4
1974	Cin-N	160	594	70	167	25	1	14	82	44	79	.281	.337	.397	106	3	4	80	41	6	9	.963	9	*S/O	4.3
1975	*Cin-N★	140	507	62	139	23	1	5	49	39	51	.274	.328	.353	88	-8	-9	59	33	6	6	.977	8	*S/3	2.0
1976	*Cin-N★	152	576	74	162	28	7	9	69	49	68	.281	.339	.401	107	6	5	77	21	10	0	.968	17	*S	4.1
1977	Cin-N★	156	572	59	155	26	3	8	64	46	77	.271	.325	.369	84	-11	-13	69	29	7	5	**.986**	8	*S	1.7
1978	Cin-N★	153	565	75	170	33	4	6	67	51	83	.301	.360	.405	113	10	10	82	23	10	1	.969	-5	*S	2.7
1979	*Cin-N†	149	590	91	166	25	3	16	84	64	73	.281	.352	.415	108	7	7	85	19	7	2	.967	14	*S	4.0
1980	Cin-N★	156	622	72	162	31	8	5	77	37	107	.260	.303	.360	84	-14	-14	65	12	2	2	.978	-13	*S/2	-0.7
1981	Cin-N★	106	421	57	129	28	0	5	67	37	61	.306	.364	.409	117	10	10	60	4	5	-2	.960	4	*S	2.4
1982	Cin-N★	147	572	48	164	25	4	5	53	45	61	.287	.339	.371	96	-1	-2	68	13	6	0	.977	13	*S/13	2.5
1983	Cin-N	143	528	54	123	22	0	1	47	56	81	.233	.307	.280	61	-25	-27	43	14	9	-1	.979	-22	*S/31	-3.9
1984	Cin-N	154	531	46	130	26	1	4	58	52	72	.245	.312	.320	75	-15	-18	56	22	6	3	.978	-35	*S3/1	-4.3
1985	Cin-N	155	560	59	141	19	2	7	48	50	67	.252	.316	.330	77	-14	-17	54	16	12	-2	.962	-32	*S/3	-3.9
1986	Cin-N	90	311	42	81	13	2	3	30	26	43	.260	.318	.344	79	-7	-9	33	13	2	3	.965	-2	S123	-0.4
1987	Cin-N	104	279	32	89	15	0	1	33	28	24	.319	.381	.384	99	2	1	39	4	3	-1	.992	0	213/S	0.2
1988	Cin-N	84	197	11	39	9	0	0	8	18	23	.198	.265	.244	45	-13	-14	13	3	2	-0	.994	1	21S/3P	-1.3
Total	19	2488	8723	993	2326	389	48	101	950	736	1186	.267	.325	.357	88	-122	-135	1005	321	109	31	.971	-42	*S23/1OP	9.3

■ ONIX CONCEPCION Concepcion, Onix Cardona (Cardona) b: 10/5/57, Dorado, P.R. BR/TR, 5'6", 180 lbs. Deb: 8/30/80

YEAR	TM/L	G	AB	R	H	2B	3B	HR	RBI	BB	SO	AVG	OBP	SLG	PRO+	BR	/A	RC	SB	CS	SBR	FA	FR	POS	TPR
1980	*KC-A	12	15	1	2	0	0	0	2	0	1	.133	.133	.133	-26	-3	-3	0	0	0	0	.833	1	/S	-0.2
1981	KC-A	2	0	0	0	0	0	0	0	0	0	—	—	—	—	0	0	0	0	0	0	.000	0	/S	0.0
1982	KC-A	74	205	17	48	9	1	0	15	5	18	.234	.256	.288	49	-14	-14	14	2	1	0	.948	-2	S2/D	-1.1
1983	KC-A	80	219	22	53	11	3	0	20	12	12	.242	.284	.320	66	-10	-10	20	10	3	1	.913	1	32S/D	-0.6
1984	*KC-A	90	287	36	81	9	2	1	23	14	33	.282	.322	.338	82	-6	-7	31	9	6	-1	.972	3	S/23	0.4
1985	*KC-A	131	314	32	64	5	1	2	20	16	29	.204	.256	.245	38	-26	-27	19	4	4	-1	.959	5	*S/2	-1.2
1987	Pit-N	1	1	0	1	0	0	0	0	0	0	1.000	1.000	1.000	429	0	0	1	0	0	0	.000	0	/H	0.0
Total	7	390	1041	108	249	34	7	3	80	47	93	.239	.279	.294	58	-60	-60	86	25	14	-1	.960	8	S/23D	-2.7

■ RAMON CONDE Conde, Ramon Luis (Roman) "Wito" b: 12/29/34, Juana Diaz, P.R. BR/TR, 5'8", 172 lbs. Deb: 7/17/62

YEAR	TM/L	G	AB	R	H	2B	3B	HR	RBI	BB	SO	AVG	OBP	SLG	PRO+	BR	/A	RC	SB	CS	SBR	FA	FR	POS	TPR
1962	Chi-A	14	16	0	0	0	0	0	1	3	3	.000	.158	.000	-54	-4	-3	0	0	0	0	.889	-1	/3	-0.4

■ FRED CONE Cone, Joseph Frederick b: 5/1848, Rockford, Ill. d: 4/13/09, Chicago, Ill. 5'9.5", 171 lbs. Deb: 5/05/1871

YEAR	TM/L	G	AB	R	H	2B	3B	HR	RBI	BB	SO	AVG	OBP	SLG	PRO+	BR	/A	RC	SB	CS	SBR	FA	FR	POS	TPR
1871	Bos-n	19	77	17	20	3	1	0	16	8	2	.260	.329	.325	86	-1	-1	12	12					O	0.0

■ BUNK CONGALTON Congalton, William Millar b: 1/24/1875, Guelph, Ont., Can. d: 8/16/37, Cleveland, Ohio BL/TL, 5'11", 190 lbs. Deb: 4/18/02

YEAR	TM/L	G	AB	R	H	2B	3B	HR	RBI	BB	SO	AVG	OBP	SLG	PRO+	BR	/A	RC	SB	CS	SBR	FA	FR	POS	TPR
1902	Chi-N	45	179	14	40	3	0	1	24	7		.223	.253	.257	59	-9	-9	13	3			.987	0	O	-1.2
1905	Cle-A	12	47	4	17	0	0	0	5	2		.362	.388	.362	136	2	2	8	3			.923	-1	O	0.0
1906	Cle-A	117	419	51	134	13	5	3	50	24		.320	.361	.396	139	17	18	69	12			.957	-9	*O	0.4
1907	Cle-A	9	22	2	4	0	0	0	2	4		.182	.308	.182	56	-1	-1	1	0			1.000	0	/O	-0.1
	Bos-A	124	496	44	142	11	8	2	47	20		.286	.318	.353	115	6	7	63	13			.969	-2	*O	0.0
	Yr	133	518	46	146	11	8	2	49	24		.282	.317	.346	112	6	6	64	13			.971	-2	*O	-0.1
Total	4	307	1163	115	337	27	13	6	128	57		.290	.326	.351	115	16	17	154	31			.967	-12	O	-0.9

■ TONY CONIGLIARO Conigliaro, Anthony Richard b: 1/7/45, Revere, Mass. d: 2/24/90, Salem, Mass. BR/TR, 6'3", 185 lbs. Deb: 4/16/64 F

YEAR	TM/L	G	AB	R	H	2B	3B	HR	RBI	BB	SO	AVG	OBP	SLG	PRO+	BR	/A	RC	SB	CS	SBR	FA	FR	POS	TPR
1964	Bos-A	111	404	69	117	21	2	24	52	35	78	.290	.354	.530	135	22	19	72	2	4	-2	.973	3	*O	1.6

YEAR	TM/L	G	AB	R	H	2B	3B	HR	RBI	BB	SO	AVG	OBP	SLG	PRO+	BR	/A	RC	SB	CS	SBR	FA	FR	POS	TPR
1965	Bos-A	138	521	82	140	21	5	**32**	82	51	116	.269	.340	.512	131	25	21	91	4	2	0	.976	14	*O	3.0
1966	Bos-A	150	558	77	148	26	7	28	93	52	112	.265	.333	.487	120	22	16	91	0	2	-1	.973	-0	*O	0.8
1967	Bos-A★	95	349	59	100	11	5	20	67	27	58	.287	.346	.519	141	21	18	62	4	6	-2	.983	3	O	1.6
1969	Bos-A	141	506	57	129	21	3	20	82	48	111	.255	.324	.427	103	4	1	68	2	4	-2	.981	-8	*O	-1.6
1970	Bos-A	146	560	89	149	20	1	36	116	43	93	.266	.327	.498	116	16	11	90	4	2	0	.977	3	*O	0.7
1971	Cal-A	74	266	23	59	18	0	4	15	23	52	.222	.286	.335	81	-9	-7	23	3	3	-1	.994	6	O	-0.6
1975	Bos-A	21	57	8	7	1	0	2	9	8	9	.123	.231	.246	32	-5	-6	4	1	0	0	.000	0	D	-0.6
Total	8	876	3221	464	849	139	23	166	516	287	629	.264	.330	.476	118	97	74	501	20	23	-8	.979	21	O/D	4.9

■ **BILLY CONIGLIARO** Conigliaro, William Michael b: 8/15/47, Revere, Mass. BR/TR, 6', 190 lbs. Deb: 4/11/69 F

YEAR	TM/L	G	AB	R	H	2B	3B	HR	RBI	BB	SO	AVG	OBP	SLG	PRO+	BR	/A	RC	SB	CS	SBR	FA	FR	POS	TPR
1969	Bos-A	32	80	14	23	6	2	4	7	9	23	.287	.367	.563	149	6	5	17	1	1	-0	.926	-7	O	-0.3
1970	Bos-A	114	398	59	108	16	3	18	58	35	73	.271	.341	.462	112	10	6	59	3	7	-3	.968	0	*O	-0.2
1971	Bos-A	101	351	42	92	26	1	11	33	25	68	.262	.311	.436	102	3	0	45	3	2	-0	.983	4	*O	-0.1
1972	Mil-A	52	191	22	44	6	2	7	16	8	54	.230	.261	.393	95	-3	-2	18	1	0	0	.992	6	O	0.2
1973	*Oak-A	48	110	5	22	2	2	0	14	9	26	.200	.261	.255	48	-8	-7	8	1	0	0	1.000	-2	O/2	-1.0
Total	5	347	1130	142	289	56	10	40	128	86	244	.256	.313	.429	103	8	2	147	9	10	-3	.980	2	O/2	-1.4

■ **JEFF CONINE** Conine, Jeffrey Guy b: 6/27/66, Tacoma, Wash. BR/TR, 6'1", 205 lbs. Deb: 9/16/90

YEAR	TM/L	G	AB	R	H	2B	3B	HR	RBI	BB	SO	AVG	OBP	SLG	PRO+	BR	/A	RC	SB	CS	SBR	FA	FR	POS	TPR
1990	KC-A	9	20	3	5	2	0	0	2	2	5	.250	.318	.350	88	-0	-0	2	0	0	0	.977	0	/1	-0.1
1992	KC-A	28	91	10	23	5	2	0	9	8	23	.253	.313	.352	85	-2	-2	10	0	0	0	1.000	-2	O/1	-0.5
Total	2	37	111	13	28	7	2	0	11	10	28	.252	.314	.351	86	-2	-2	12	0	0	0	.988	-2	/O1	-0.6

■ **JOCKO CONLAN** Conlan, John Bertrand b: 12/6/1899, Chicago, Ill. d: 4/16/89, Scottsdale, Ariz. BL/TL, 5'7.5", 165 lbs. Deb: 7/06/34 UH

YEAR	TM/L	G	AB	R	H	2B	3B	HR	RBI	BB	SO	AVG	OBP	SLG	PRO+	BR	/A	RC	SB	CS	SBR	FA	FR	POS	TPR
1934	Chi-A	63	225	35	56	11	3	0	16	19	7	.249	.310	.324	62	-12	-13	24	2	2	-1	.955	-3	O	-1.8
1935	Chi-A	65	140	20	40	7	1	0	15	14	6	.286	.355	.350	81	-3	-4	18	3	3	-1	.961	-3	O	-0.8
Total	2	128	365	55	96	18	4	0	31	33	13	.263	.327	.334	69	-15	-17	41	5	5	-2	.957	-6	/O	-2.6

■ **JOCKO CONLON** Conlon, Arthur Joseph b: 12/10/1897, Woburn, Mass. d: 8/5/87, Falmouth, Mass. BR/TR, 5'7", 145 lbs. Deb: 4/17/23

YEAR	TM/L	G	AB	R	H	2B	3B	HR	RBI	BB	SO	AVG	OBP	SLG	PRO+	BR	/A	RC	SB	CS	SBR	FA	FR	POS	TPR
1923	Bos-N	59	147	23	32	3	0	0	17	11	11	.218	.299	.238	45	-12	-11	11	0	3	-2	.955	1	2/S3	-1.0

■ **BERT CONN** Conn, Albert Thomas b: 9/22/1879, Philadelphia, Pa. d: 11/2/44, Philadelphia, Pa. TR , Deb: 9/16/1898

YEAR	TM/L	G	AB	R	H	2B	3B	HR	RBI	BB	SO	AVG	OBP	SLG	PRO+	BR	/A	RC	SB	CS	SBR	FA	FR	POS	TPR
1898	Phi-N	1	3	1	1	0	1	0	1	0		.333	.333	1.000	291	1	1	1	0			1.000	-0	/P	0.0
1900	Phi-N	6	9	4	3	1	0	0	1	0		.333	.333	.444	115	0	0	1	0			.667	-1	/P	0.0
1901	Phi-N	5	18	2	4	1	0	0	0	0		.222	.263	.278	56	-1	-1	1	0			.880	-1	/2	-0.2
Total	3	12	30	7	8	2	1	0	2	0		.267	.290	.400	96	-0	-0	4	0			.714	-2	/2P	-0.2

■ **FRITZIE CONNALLY** Connally, Fritzie Lee b: 5/19/58, Bryan, Tex. BR/TR, 6'3", 210 lbs. Deb: 9/09/83

YEAR	TM/L	G	AB	R	H	2B	3B	HR	RBI	BB	SO	AVG	OBP	SLG	PRO+	BR	/A	RC	SB	CS	SBR	FA	FR	POS	TPR
1983	Chi-N	8	10	0	1	0	0	0	0	0	5	.100	.100	.100	-42	-2	-2	0	0	0	0	1.000	0	/3	-0.2
1985	Bal-A	50	112	16	26	4	0	3	15	19	21	.232	.348	.348	94	-1	-0	15	0	0	0	.976	-3	3/1D	-0.4
Total	2	58	122	16	27	4	0	3	15	19	26	.221	.331	.328	83	-3	-2	15	0	0	0	.977	-3	/31D	-0.6

■ **BRUCE CONNATSER** Connatser, Broadus Milburn b: 9/19/02, Sevierville, Tenn d: 1/27/71, Terre Haute, Ind. BR/TR, 5'11.5", 170 lbs. Deb: 9/15/31

YEAR	TM/L	G	AB	R	H	2B	3B	HR	RBI	BB	SO	AVG	OBP	SLG	PRO+	BR	/A	RC	SB	CS	SBR	FA	FR	POS	TPR
1931	Cle-A	12	49	5	14	3	0	0	4	2	3	.286	.327	.347	73	-2	-2	6	0	0	0	1.000	1	1	-0.2
1932	Cle-A	23	60	8	14	3	1	0	4	4	8	.233	.281	.317	51	-4	-5	6	1	0	0	1.000	0	1	-0.5
Total	2	35	109	13	28	6	1	0	8	6	11	.257	.302	.330	61	-6	-7	11	1	0	0	1.000	2	/1	-0.7

■ **FRANK CONNAUGHTON** Connaughton, Frank Henry b: 1/1/1869, Clinton, Mass. d: 12/1/42, Boston, Mass. BR/TR, 5'9", 165 lbs. Deb: 5/29/1894

YEAR	TM/L	G	AB	R	H	2B	3B	HR	RBI	BB	SO	AVG	OBP	SLG	PRO+	BR	/A	RC	SB	CS	SBR	FA	FR	POS	TPR
1894	Bos-N	46	171	42	59	9	2	2	33	16	8	.345	.407	.456	102	3	0	34	3			.892	-3	S/CO	0.0
1896	NY-N	88	315	53	82	3	2	2	43	25	7	.260	.319	.302	68	-15	-13	39	22			.892	3	SO	-0.9
1906	Bos-N	12	44	3	9	0	0	0	1	3		.205	.271	.205	50	-2	-2	3	1			.918	-3	S/2	-0.5
Total	3	146	530	98	150	12	4	4	77	44	15	.283	.344	.343	79	-14	-15	76	26			.894	-3	/SOC2	-1.4

■ **GENE CONNELL** Connell, Eugene Joseph b: 5/10/06, Hazelton, Pa. d: 8/31/37, Waverly, N.Y. BR/TR, 6'0.5", 180 lbs. Deb: 7/04/31 F

YEAR	TM/L	G	AB	R	H	2B	3B	HR	RBI	BB	SO	AVG	OBP	SLG	PRO+	BR	/A	RC	SB	CS	SBR	FA	FR	POS	TPR
1931	Phi-N	6	12	1	3	0	0	0	0	0	3	.250	.250	.250	32	-1	-1	1	0			1.000	-1	/C	-0.2

■ **JOE CONNELL** Connell, Joseph Bernard b: 1/16/02, Bethlehem, Pa. d: 9/21/77, Trexlertown, Pa. BL/TR, 5'8", 165 lbs. Deb: 6/15/26 F

YEAR	TM/L	G	AB	R	H	2B	3B	HR	RBI	BB	SO	AVG	OBP	SLG	PRO+	BR	/A	RC	SB	CS	SBR	FA	FR	POS	TPR
1926	NY-N	2	1	1	0	0	0	0	0	0	0	.000	.000	.000	-99	-0	-0	0	0			.000	0	H	0.0

■ **PETE CONNELL** Connell, Peter J. b: Brooklyn, N.Y. Deb: 9/03/1886

YEAR	TM/L	G	AB	R	H	2B	3B	HR	RBI	BB	SO	AVG	OBP	SLG	PRO+	BR	/A	RC	SB	CS	SBR	FA	FR	POS	TPR
1886	NY-a	1	5	0	0	0	0	0		0		.000	.000	.000	-99	-1	-1	0	0			.667	-1	/3	-0.2

■ **TERRY CONNELL** Connell, Terence G. b: 6/17/1855, Philadelphia, Pa. d: 3/25/24, Philadelphia, Pa. Deb: 6/20/1874

YEAR	TM/L	G	AB	R	H	2B	3B	HR	RBI	BB	SO	AVG	OBP	SLG	PRO+	BR	/A	RC	SB	CS	SBR	FA	FR	POS	TPR
1874	Chi-n	1	4	0	0	0	0	0		0		.000	.000	.000	-99	-1	-1	0						/C	-0.1

■ **TOM CONNELLY** Connelly, Thomas Martin b: 10/20/1897, Chicago, Ill. d: 2/18/41, Hines, Ill. BL/TR, 5'11.5", 165 lbs. Deb: 9/24/20

YEAR	TM/L	G	AB	R	H	2B	3B	HR	RBI	BB	SO	AVG	OBP	SLG	PRO+	BR	/A	RC	SB	CS	SBR	FA	FR	POS	TPR
1920	NY-A	1	1	0	0	0	0	0	0	0	0	.000	.000	.000	-97	-0	-0	0	0	0	0	.000	0	H	0.0
1921	NY-A	4	5	0	1	0	0	0	0	1	0	.200	.333	.200	38	-0	-0	0	0	0	0	1.000	0	/O	-0.1
Total	2	5	6	0	1	0	0	0	0	1	0	.167	.286	.167	18	-1	-1	0	0	0	0		0	/O	-0.1

■ **ED CONNOLLY** Connolly, Edward Joseph Sr. b: 7/17/08, Brooklyn, N.Y. d: 11/12/63, Pittsfield, Mass. BR/TR, 5'8.5", 180 lbs. Deb: 9/20/29 F

YEAR	TM/L	G	AB	R	H	2B	3B	HR	RBI	BB	SO	AVG	OBP	SLG	PRO+	BR	/A	RC	SB	CS	SBR	FA	FR	POS	TPR
1929	Bos-A	5	8	0	0	0	0	0	0	0	2	.000	.000	.000	-99	-2	-2	0	0	0	0	.889	-1	/C	-0.3
1930	Bos-A	27	48	1	9	2	0	0	7	4	3	.188	.250	.229	23	-6	-5	3	0	0	0	1.000	-1	C	-0.4
1931	Bos-A	42	93	3	7	1	0	0	3	5	18	.075	.131	.086	-44	-19	-19	1	0	0	0	.981	-1	C	-1.7
1932	Bos-A	75	222	9	50	8	4	0	21	20	27	.225	.289	.297	54	-16	-15	20	0	1	-1	.957	4	C	-0.7
Total	4	149	371	13	66	11	4	0	31	29	50	.178	.239	.229	23	-43	-41	24	0	1	-1	.895	1	C	-3.1

■ **RED CONNOLLY** Connolly, John M. b: 1863, New York, N.Y. d: 3/2/1896, New York, N.Y. Deb: 7/01/1886

YEAR	TM/L	G	AB	R	H	2B	3B	HR	RBI	BB	SO	AVG	OBP	SLG	PRO+	BR	/A	RC	SB	CS	SBR	FA	FR	POS	TPR
1886	StL-N	2	7	0	0	0	0	0	0	0	3	.000	.000	.000	-99	-2	-2	0	0			.000	-1	/O	-0.2

■ **JOE CONNOLLY** Connolly, Joseph Aloysius b: 2/12/1888, N.Smithfield, R.I. d: 9/1/43, Springfield, R.I. BL/TR, 5'7.5", 165 lbs. Deb: 4/10/13

YEAR	TM/L	G	AB	R	H	2B	3B	HR	RBI	BB	SO	AVG	OBP	SLG	PRO+	BR	/A	RC	SB	CS	SBR	FA	FR	POS	TPR
1913	Bos-N	126	427	79	120	18	11	5	57	66	47	.281	.379	.410	123	16	15	72	18			.954	-8	*O	0.2
1914	*Bos-N	120	399	64	122	28	10	9	65	49	36	.306	.393	.494	164	31	31	80	12			.974	-5	*O	2.3
1915	Bos-N	104	305	48	91	14	8	0	23	39	35	.298	.387	.397	144	15	17	48	13	12	-3	.971	-4	O	0.7
1916	Bos-N	62	110	11	25	5	2	0	12	14	13	.227	.320	.309	98	-0	0	13	5			.980	-1	O	-0.2
Total	4	412	1241	202	358	65	31	14	157	168	131	.288	.380	.425	139	61	63	212	48	12		.967	-17	O	3.0

■ **JOE CONNOLLY** Connolly, Joseph George "Coaster Joe" b: 6/4/1896, San Francisco, Cal d: 3/30/60, San Francisco, Cal BR/TR, 6', 170 lbs. Deb: 10/01/21

YEAR	TM/L	G	AB	R	H	2B	3B	HR	RBI	BB	SO	AVG	OBP	SLG	PRO+	BR	/A	RC	SB	CS	SBR	FA	FR	POS	TPR
1921	NY-N	2	4	0	0	0	0	0	0	1	1	.000	.200	.000	-42	-1	-1	0	0	0	0	1.000	-0	/O	-0.1
1922	Cle-A	12	45	6	11	2	1	0	6	5	8	.244	.320	.333	70	-2	-2	5	1	0	0	.972	2	O	-0.1
1923	Cle-A	52	109	25	33	10	1	3	25	13	7	.303	.377	.495	129	4	4	20	1	2	-1	.957	-10	O	-0.8
1924	Bos-A	14	10	1	1	0	0	0	1	2	2	.100	.250	.100	-8	-2	-2	0	0	0	0	1.000	-1	/O	-0.2
Total	4	80	168	32	45	12	2	3	32	21	18	.268	.349	.417	100	-0	-0	26	2	2	-1	.966	-9	/O	-1.2

■ **BUD CONNOLLY** Connolly, Mervin Thomas "Mike" b: 5/25/01, San Francisco, Cal d: 6/12/64, Berkeley, Cal. BR/TR, 5'8", 154 lbs. Deb: 5/03/25

YEAR	TM/L	G	AB	R	H	2B	3B	HR	RBI	BB	SO	AVG	OBP	SLG	PRO+	BR	/A	RC	SB	CS	SBR	FA	FR	POS	TPR
1925	Bos-A	43	107	12	28	7	1	0	21	23	9	.262	.392	.346	88	-1	-1	15	0	3	-2	.950	-11	S/3	-0.9

YEAR	TM/L	G	AB	R	H	2B	3B	HR	RBI	BB	SO	AVG	OBP	SLG	PRO+	BR	/A	RC	SB	CS SBR	FA	FR	POS	TPR

■ TOM CONNOLLY Connolly, Thomas Francis "Blackie" or "Ham" b: 12/30/1892, Boston, Mass. d: 5/14/66, Boston, Mass. BL/TR, 5'11", 175 lbs. Deb: 5/12/15

| 1915 | Was-A | 50 | 141 | 14 | 26 | 3 | 2 | 0 | 7 | 14 | 19 | .184 | .268 | .234 | 49 | -9 | -9 | 9 | 5 | 4 -1 | .970 | -7 | 3O/S | -1.7 |

■ NED CONNOR Connor, Edward b: 1850, New York 5'9", 156 lbs. Deb: 5/18/1871

| 1871 | Tro-n | 7 | 33 | 6 | 7 | 0 | 0 | 0 | 2 | 0 | 0 | .212 | .212 | .212 | 22 | -3 | -3 | 2 | 0 | | | | /1O2 | -0.2 |

■ JIM CONNOR Connor, James Matthew (b: James Matthew O'Connor) b: 5/11/1863, Port Jervis, N.Y. d: 9/3/50, Providence, R.I. BR/TR, Deb: 7/11/1892

1892	Chi-N	9	34	0	2	0	0	0	0	1	7	.059	.111	.059	-47	-6	-6	0	0		.917	-6	/2	-1.1
1897	Chi-N	77	285	40	83	10	5	3	38	24		.291	.355	.393	94	-1	-3	45	10		.936	22	2	2.0
1898	Chi-N	138	505	51	114	9	9	0	67	42		.226	.289	.279	63	-24	-24	47	11		.946	-4	*2	-1.8
1899	Chi-N	69	234	26	48	7	1	0	24	18		.205	.265	.244	41	-19	-18	18	6		.942	6	23	-0.9
Total	4	293	1058	117	247	26	15	3	129	85	7	.233	.296	.295	64	-51	-52	110	27		.942	18	2/3	-1.8

■ JOE CONNOR Connor, Joseph Francis b: 12/8/1874, Waterbury, Conn. d: 11/8/57, Waterbury, Conn. BR/TR, 6'2", 185 lbs. Deb: 9/09/1895 F

1895	StL-N	2	7	0	0	0	0	0	1	0	2	.000	.000	.000	-99	-2	-2	0	0		1.000	1	/3	-0.1
1900	Bos-N	7	19	2	4	0	0	0	4	2		.211	.286	.211	34	-2	-2	1	1		.971	2	/C	0.1
1901	Mil-A	38	102	10	28	3	1	1	9	6		.275	.321	.353	91	-2	-1	14	4		.949	-2	C/23O	0.2
	Cle-A	37	121	13	17	3	1	0	6	7		.140	.200	.182	7	-15	-15	5	2		.942	0	C/OS	-1.0
	Yr	75	223	23	45	6	2	1	15	13		.202	.255	.260	45	-17	-16	17	6		.946	1	C/O23S	-0.8
1905	NY-A	8	22	4	5	1	0	0	2	3		.227	.320	.273	80	-0	-0	3	1		.978	2	/C1	0.2
Total	4	92	271	29	54	7	2	1	22	18	2	.199	.257	.251	43	-21	-20	23	8		.952	6	/CO31S2	-0.6

■ ROGER CONNOR Connor, Roger b: 7/1/1857, Waterbury, Conn. d: 1/4/31, Waterbury, Conn. BL/TL, 6'3", 220 lbs. Deb: 5/01/1880 FMH

1880	Tro-N	83	340	53	113	18	8	3	47	13	21	.332	.357	.459	166	25	23	57			.821	-10	*3	1.5
1881	Tro-N	85	367	55	107	17	6	2	31	15	20	.292	.319	.387	115	9	6	46			.950	2	*1	0.0
1882	Tro-N	81	349	65	115	22	**18**	4	42	13	20	.330	.354	.530	188	30	32	67			.951	3	1O3	2.7
1883	NY-N	98	409	80	146	28	15	1	50	25	16	.357	.394	.506	173	35	35	84			.958	3	*1	2.4
1884	NY-N	116	477	98	151	28	4	4	82	38	32	.317	.367	.417	143	26	24	75			.860	3	2O3	2.5
1885	NY-N	110	455	102	**169**	23	15	1	65	51	8	**.371**	**.435**	.495	**203**	52	53	100			.975	3	*1	**4.0**
1886	NY-N	118	485	105	172	29	**20**	7	71	41	15	.355	.405	.540	158	49	48	116	17		.973	10	*1	3.9
1887	NY-N	127	471	113	134	26	22	17	104	75	50	.285	.392	.541	166	38	43	120	43		**.993**	5	*1	2.9
1888	*NY-N	134	481	98	140	15	17	14	71	**73**	44	.291	.389	.480	**181**	45	46	103	27		.982	1	*1/2	3.4
1889	*NY-N	131	496	117	157	32	17	13	**130**	93	46	.317	.426	**.528**	168	47	47	124	21		.977	-8	*1/3	2.6
1890	NY-P	123	484	133	169	24	15	**14**	103	88	22	.349	.450	**.548**	155	49	41	132	22		**.985**	11	*1	3.6
1891	NY-N	129	479	112	139	29	13	7	94	83	39	.290	.399	.449	156	32	36	99	27		.983	1	*1	2.7
1892	Phi-N	155	564	123	166	**37**	11	12	73	116	39	.294	.420	.463	170	52	52	122	22		**.985**	-6	*1	3.6
1893	NY-N	135	511	111	156	25	8	11	105	91	26	.305	.413	.450	131	26	25	108	24		.974	2	*1/3	2.0
1894	NY-N	22	82	10	24	7	0	1	14	8	0	.293	.356	.415	87	-2	-2	14	2		.976	2	1/O	0.0
	StL-N	99	380	83	122	28	25	7	79	51	17	.321	.410	.582	138	22	22	100	17		.974	5	*1	2.1
	Yr	121	462	93	146	35	25	8	93	59	17	.316	.400	.552	130	21	21	113	19		.974	7	*1	2.1
1895	StL-N	103	398	78	131	29	9	8	77	63	10	.329	.423	.508	143	26	27	92	9		.986	4	*1	2.7
1896	StL-N	126	483	71	137	21	9	11	72	52	13	.284	.356	.433	114	6	9	80	10		**.988**	13	*1M	2.0
1897	StL-N	22	83	13	19	3	1	1	12	9	5	.229	.333	.325	76	-3	-3	10	3		.984	-0	1	-0.2
Total	18	1997	7794	1620	2467	441	233	138	1322	1002	449	.317	.397	.486	155	563	564	1648	244		.978	42	*13/2O	44.4

■ JERRY CONNORS Connors, Jeremiah b: Philadelphia, Pa. Deb: 7/11/1882

| 1892 | Phi-N | 1 | 3 | 0 | 0 | 0 | 0 | 0 | 0 | 0 | 1 | .000 | .000 | .000 | -99 | -1 | -1 | 0 | 0 | | .000 | -0 | /O | -0.1 |

■ JOE CONNORS Connors, Joseph P. b: Paterson, N.J. Deb: 5/03/1884

1884	Alt-U	3	11	0	1	0	0	0		0		.091	.091	.091	-38	-2	-2	0			1.000	-0	/P3O	-0.1
	KC-U	3	11	2	1	0	0	0		1		.091	.167	.091	-12	-1	-1	0			1.000	0	/OP	0.0
	Yr	6	22	2	2	0	0	0		1		.091	.130	.091	-25	-3	-3	0			.750	0	/PO3	-0.1

■ CHUCK CONNORS Connors, Kevin Joseph Aloysius b: 4/10/21, Brooklyn, N.Y. d: 11/10/92 Los Angeles, Cal. BL/TL, 6'5", 190 lbs. Deb: 5/01/49

1949	Bro-N	1	1	0	0	0	0	0	0	0	0	.000	.000	.000	-96	-0	-0	0	0		.000	0	H	0.0
1951	Chi-N	66	201	16	48	5	1	2	18	12	25	.239	.282	.303	56	-12	-13	19	4	0 1	.984	-1	1	-1.5
Total	2	67	202	16	48	5	1	2	18	12	25	.238	.280	.302	56	-12	-13	19	4	0		-1	/1	-1.5

■ MERV CONNORS Connors, Mervyn James b: 1/23/14, Berkeley, Cal. BR/TR, 6'2", 192 lbs. Deb: 9/04/37

1937	Chi-A	28	103	12	24	4	1	2	12	14	19	.233	.325	.350	70	-5	-5	12	2	1 0	.926	-3	3	-0.7
1938	Chi-A	24	62	14	22	4	0	6	13	9	17	.355	.437	.710	178	8	7	19	0	0 0	.979	0	1	0.5
Total	2	52	165	26	46	8	1	8	25	23	36	.279	.367	.485	111	3	3	32	2	1 0		-3	/31	-0.2

■ BEN CONROY Conroy, Bernard Patrick b: 3/14/1871, Philadelphia, Pa. d: 11/25/37, Philadelphia, Pa. 160 lbs. Deb: 4/21/1890

| 1890 | Phi-a | 117 | 404 | 45 | 69 | 13 | 1 | 0 | | 45 | | .171 | .262 | .208 | 42 | -29 | -27 | 27 | 17 | | .893 | -6 | S2/O | -2.3 |

■ WID CONROY Conroy, William Edward b: 4/5/1877, Camden, N.J. d: 12/6/59, Mt.Holly, N.J. BR/TR, 5'9", 158 lbs. Deb: 4/25/01 C

1901	Mil-A	131	503	74	129	20	6	5	64	36		.256	.316	.350	89	-11	-7	65	21		.922	20	*S3	2.0
1902	Pit-N	99	365	55	89	10	6	1	47	24		.244	.299	.312	86	-5	-7	39	10		.925	8	S/O	0.7
1903	NY-A	126	503	74	137	23	12	1	45	32		.272	.322	.372	101	5	1	74	33		.919	3	*3/S	0.6
1904	NY-A	140	489	58	119	18	12	1	52	43		.243	.311	.335	100	3	1	64	30		.944	4	*3S/O	0.9
1905	NY-A	101	385	55	105	19	11	2	25	32		.273	.329	.395	116	12	7	60	25		.928	7	3OS1/2	1.6
1906	NY-A	148	567	67	139	17	10	4	54	47		.245	.303	.332	90	-1	-7	70	32		.968	-1	OS/3	-1.3
1907	NY-A	140	530	58	124	12	11	3	51	30		.234	.276	.315	82	-8	-12	60	41		.955	12	*OS	-0.5
1908	NY-A	141	531	44	126	22	3	1	39	14		.237	.258	.296	79	-13	-14	46	23		.939	13	*32O	-0.1
1909	Was-A	139	488	44	119	13	4	1	20	37		.244	.298	.293	91	-7	-5	51	24		.938	-0	*32/OS	-0.2
1910	Was-A	103	351	36	89	11	3	1	27	30		.254	.314	.311	100	-2	0	38	11		.961	2	3O/2	0.1
1911	Was-A	106	349	40	81	11	4	2	28	20		.232	.282	.304	64	-18	-17	33	12		.930	6	3O/2	-1.1
Total	11	1374	5061	605	1257	176	82	22	452	345		.248	.300	.329	91	-45	-60	600	262		.934	72	3SO/21	3.1

■ BILL CONROY Conroy, William Frederick "Pep" b: 1/9/1899, Chicago, Ill. d: 1/23/70, Chicago, Ill. BR/TR, 5'8.5", 160 lbs. Deb: 4/18/23

| 1923 | Was-A | 18 | 60 | 6 | 8 | 2 | 0 | 2 | 4 | 9 | | .133 | .188 | .233 | 11 | -8 | -8 | 3 | 0 | 0 0 | .926 | -2 | 3/1O | -0.9 |

■ BILL CONROY Conroy, William Gordon b: 2/26/15, Bloomington, Ill. BR/TR, 6', 185 lbs. Deb: 9/21/35

1935	Phi-A	1	4	0	1	1	0	0	1	0		.250	.400	.500	133	0	0	1	0	0 0	1.000	1	/C	0.1
1936	Phi-A	1	2	0	1	0	0	0	0	1		.500	.500	.500	151	0	0	0	0	0 0	1.000	-0	/C	0.0
1937	Phi-A	26	60	4	12	1	1	0	3	7	9	.200	.284	.250	36	-6	-6	5	1	0 0	1.000	-1	C/1	-0.5
1942	Bos-A	83	250	22	50	4	2	4	20	40	47	.200	.315	.280	66	-10	-11	26	2	0 1	.971	-1	C	-0.4
1943	Bos-A	39	89	13	16	5	0	1	6	18	19	.180	.336	.270	77	-2	-2	9	0	0 0	.969	2	C	0.2
1944	Bos-A	19	47	6	10	2	0	0	4	11	9	.213	.362	.255	79	-1	-1	5	0	0 0	.972	-0	C	0.0
Total	6	169	452	45	90	13	3	5	33	77	85	.199	.322	.274	66	-18	-19	46	3	0 1		1	C/1	-0.6

■ BILLY CONSOLO Consolo, William Angelo b: 8/18/34, Cleveland, Ohio BR/TR, 5'11", 180 lbs. Deb: 4/20/53 C

| 1953 | Bos-A | 47 | 65 | 9 | 14 | 2 | 0 | 2 | 6 | 23 | | .215 | .239 | .323 | 48 | -5 | -5 | 5 | 1 | 2 -1 | .808 | 10 | 32 | 0.4 |
| 1954 | Bos-A | 91 | 242 | 23 | 55 | 7 | 1 | 1 | 11 | 33 | 69 | .227 | .325 | .277 | 59 | -10 | -14 | 24 | 2 | 1 0 | .953 | -3 | S32 | -1.3 |

YEAR	TM/L	G	AB	R	H	2B	3B	HR	RBI	BB	SO	AVG	OBP	SLG	PRO+	BR	/A	RC	SB	CS	SBR	FA	FR	POS	TPR
1955	Bos-A	8	18	4	4	0	0	0	0	5	4	.222	.391	.222	63	-0	-1	2	0	0	0	.889	-3	/2	-0.3
1956	Bos-A	48	11	13	2	0	0	0	1	3	5	.182	.357	.182	41	-1	-1	1	0	0	0	.920	12	2	1.0
1957	Bos-A	68	196	26	53	6	1	4	19	23	48	.270	.347	.372	91	-1	-2	25	1	3	-2	.933	12	S2/3	1.3
1958	Bos-A	46	72	13	9	2	1	0	5	6	14	.125	.192	.181	3	-10	-10	2	0	0	0	.925	7	2S/3	-0.2
1959	Bos-A	10	14	3	3	1	0	0	0	2	5	.214	.313	.286	63	-1	-1	1	0	0	0	.818	-2	/S	-0.2
	Was-A	79	202	25	43	5	3	0	10	36	54	.213	.332	.267	67	-8	-8	21	1	0	0	.952	10	S/2	0.9
	Yr	89	216	28	46	6	3	0	10	38	59	.213	.331	.269	66	-9	-9	22	1	0	0	.948	9	S/2	0.7
1960	Was-A	100	174	23	36	4	2	3	15	25	29	.207	.310	.305	68	-8	-8	17	1	1	-0	.938	-1	S2/3	-0.5
1961	Min-A	11	5	1	0	0	0	0	0	0	1	.000	.000	.000	-95	-1	-1	0	0	0	0	1.000	0	/2S3	-0.1
1962	Phi-N	13	5	3	2	0	0	0	0	0	1	.400	.400	.400	119	0	0	1	0	0	0	.000	0	/3	0.0
	LA-A	28	20	4	2	0	0	0	0	3	11	.100	.217	.100	-12	-3	-3	1	2	0	1	.917	3	3/S2	0.1
	KC-A	54	154	11	37	4	2	0	16	23	33	.240	.339	.292	70	-5	-6	16	1	3	-2	.950	-1	S	-0.5
	Yr	82	174	15	39	4	2	0	16	26	44	.224	.325	.270	62	-9	-9	17	3	3	-1	.944	2	S3/2	-0.4
Total	10	603	1178	158	260	31	11	9	83	161	297	.221	.316	.289	63	-53	-59	116	9	10	-3	.945	45	S2/3	0.6

■ CHARLIE CONWAY
Conway, Charles Connell b: 4/28/1886, Youngstown, Ohio d: 9/12/68, Youngstown, Ohio BR/TR, Deb: 4/15/11

YEAR	TM/L	G	AB	R	H	2B	3B	HR	RBI	BB	SO	AVG	OBP	SLG	PRO+	BR	/A	RC	SB	CS	SBR	FA	FR	POS	TPR
1911	Was-A	2	3	0	1	0	1	0	0	0		.333	.333	1.000	272	1	1	1	0			.000	-1	/O	0.0

■ JACK CONWAY
Conway, Jack Clements b: 7/30/19, Bryan, Tex. BR/TR, 5′11.5″, 175 lbs. Deb: 9/09/41

YEAR	TM/L	G	AB	R	H	2B	3B	HR	RBI	BB	SO	AVG	OBP	SLG	PRO+	BR	/A	RC	SB	CS	SBR	FA	FR	POS	TPR
1941	Cle-A	2	2	0	1	0	0	0	1	0	0	.500	.500	.500	174	0	0	1	0	0	0	1.000	1	/S	0.1
1946	Cle-A	68	258	24	58	6	2	0	18	20	36	.225	.281	.264	56	-16	-14	20	2	2	-1	.955	-7	2S/3	-1.9
1947	Cle-A	34	50	3	9	2	0	0	5	3	8	.180	.226	.220	25	-5	-5	2	0	0	0	.877	0	S/23	-0.4
1948	NY-N	24	49	8	12	2	1	1	3	5	10	.245	.315	.388	89	-1	-1	6	0			.985	6	2/S3	0.6
Total	4	128	359	35	80	10	3	1	27	28	54	.223	.279	.276	57	-22	-20	28	2	2		.962	0	/2S3	-1.6

■ OWEN CONWAY
Conway, Owen Sylvester b: 10/23/1890, New York, N.Y. d: 3/12/42, Philadelphia, Pa. TR , Deb: 6/21/15

YEAR	TM/L	G	AB	R	H	2B	3B	HR	RBI	BB	SO	AVG	OBP	SLG	PRO+	BR	/A	RC	SB	CS	SBR	FA	FR	POS	TPR
1915	Phi-A	4	15	2	1	0	0	0	0	0	3	.067	.067	.067	-62	-3	-3	0	0			.750	1	/3	-0.2

■ PETE CONWAY
Conway, Peter J. b: 10/30/1866, Burmont, Pa. d: 1/13/03, Clifton Heights, Pa. BR/TR, 5′10.5″, Deb: 8/10/1885 F

YEAR	TM/L	G	AB	R	H	2B	3B	HR	RBI	BB	SO	AVG	OBP	SLG	PRO+	BR	/A	RC	SB	CS	SBR	FA	FR	POS	TPR
1885	Buf-N	29	90	7	10	5	0	1	7	5	28	.111	.158	.200	15	-8	-9	3				.889	-1	P/OS1	-0.2
1886	KC-N	51	194	22	47	8	2	1	18	5	34	.242	.261	.320	71	-6	-8	17	3			.857	-1	OP	-0.4
	Det-N	12	43	10	8	1	0	2	3	1	8	.186	.205	.349	64	-2	-2	3	0			.846	-1	P/O	0.0
	Yr	63	237	32	55	9	2	3	21	6	42	.232	.251	.325	70	-8	-10	21	3			.826	-1	PO	-0.4
1887	*Det-N	24	95	16	22	5	1	1	7	2	9	.232	.247	.337	60	-5	-5	8	0			.979	2	P/O	-0.2
1888	Det-N	45	167	28	46	4	2	3	23	8	25	.275	.320	.377	124	4	4	21	1			.938	2	P/O	0.0
1889	Pit-N	3	10	2	1	0	0	1	2	1	3	.100	.182	.400	68	-1	-0	1	1			.875	-0	/PO	0.0
Total	5	164	599	85	134	23	5	9	60	22	107	.224	.255	.324	74	-17	-20	54	5			.907	2	P/O1S	-0.8

■ RIP CONWAY
Conway, Richard Daniel b: 4/18/1896, White Bear, Minn. d: 12/3/71, St.Paul, Minn. BL/TR, 5′6″, 160 lbs. Deb: 4/16/18

YEAR	TM/L	G	AB	R	H	2B	3B	HR	RBI	BB	SO	AVG	OBP	SLG	PRO+	BR	/A	RC	SB	CS	SBR	FA	FR	POS	TPR
1918	Bos-N	14	24	4	4	0	0	0	2	2	4	.167	.231	.167	23	-2	-2	1	1			.810	-4	/23	-0.6

■ BILL CONWAY
Conway, William F. b: 11/28/1861, Lowell, Mass. d: 12/28/43, Somerville, Mass. BR/TR, 5′8″, 170 lbs. Deb: 7/28/1884 F

YEAR	TM/L	G	AB	R	H	2B	3B	HR	RBI	BB	SO	AVG	OBP	SLG	PRO+	BR	/A	RC	SB	CS	SBR	FA	FR	POS	TPR
1884	Phi-N	1	4	0	0	0	0	0	0	0	1	.000	.000	.000	-99	-1	-1	0				1.000	0	/C	-0.1
1886	Bal-a	7	14	4	2	0	0	0		7		.143	.429	.143	87	0	1	1	0			.925	-3	/C	-0.2
Total	2	8	18	4	2	0	0	0	0	7	1	.111	.360	.111	54	-0	-0	1	0			.936	-3	/C	-0.3

■ ED CONWELL
Conwell, Edward James "Irish" b: 1/29/1890, Chicago, Ill. d: 5/1/26, Norwood Park, Ill. BR/TR, 5′11″, 155 lbs. Deb: 9/22/11

YEAR	TM/L	G	AB	R	H	2B	3B	HR	RBI	BB	SO	AVG	OBP	SLG	PRO+	BR	/A	RC	SB	CS	SBR	FA	FR	POS	TPR
1911	StL-N	1	1	0	0	0	0	0	0	0	1	.000	.000	.000	-99	-0	-0	0	0			.000	-0	/3	-0.1

■ HERB CONYERS
Conyers, Herbert Leroy b: 1/8/21, Cowgill, Mo. d: 9/16/64, Cleveland, Ohio BL/TR, 6′5″, 210 lbs. Deb: 4/18/50

YEAR	TM/L	G	AB	R	H	2B	3B	HR	RBI	BB	SO	AVG	OBP	SLG	PRO+	BR	/A	RC	SB	CS	SBR	FA	FR	POS	TPR
1950	Cle-A	7	9	2	3	0	0	1	1	1	2	.333	.400	.667	175	1	1	3	1	0	0	1.000	-0	/1	0.1

■ DALE COOGAN
Coogan, Dale Roger b: 8/14/30, Los Angeles, Cal. d: 3/8/89, Mission Viejo, Cal. BL/TL, 6′1″, 190 lbs. Deb: 4/22/50

YEAR	TM/L	G	AB	R	H	2B	3B	HR	RBI	BB	SO	AVG	OBP	SLG	PRO+	BR	/A	RC	SB	CS	SBR	FA	FR	POS	TPR
1950	Pit-N	53	129	19	31	6	1	1	13	17	24	.240	.338	.326	73	-4	-5	15	0			.980	2	1	-0.3

■ DAN COOGAN
Coogan, Daniel George b: 2/16/1875, Philadelphia, Pa. d: 10/28/42, Philadelphia, Pa. 128 lbs. Deb: 4/25/1895

YEAR	TM/L	G	AB	R	H	2B	3B	HR	RBI	BB	SO	AVG	OBP	SLG	PRO+	BR	/A	RC	SB	CS	SBR	FA	FR	POS	TPR
1895	Was-N	26	77	9	17	2	1	0	7	13	6	.221	.333	.273	60	-4	-4	8	1			.746	-11	S/CO3	-1.1

■ JIM COOK
Cook, James Fitchie b: 11/10/1879, Dundee, Ill. d: 6/17/49, St.Louis, Mo. BR/TR, 5′9″, 163 lbs. Deb: 7/02/03

YEAR	TM/L	G	AB	R	H	2B	3B	HR	RBI	BB	SO	AVG	OBP	SLG	PRO+	BR	/A	RC	SB	CS	SBR	FA	FR	POS	TPR
1903	Chi-N	8	26	3	4	1	0	0	2	2		.154	.241	.192	25	-3	-2	1	1			1.000	-2	/O21	-0.4

■ DOC COOK
Cook, Luther Almus b: 6/24/1886, Witt, Tex. d: 6/30/73, Lawrenceburg, Tenn. BL/TR, 6′, 170 lbs. Deb: 8/07/13

YEAR	TM/L	G	AB	R	H	2B	3B	HR	RBI	BB	SO	AVG	OBP	SLG	PRO+	BR	/A	RC	SB	CS	SBR	FA	FR	POS	TPR
1913	NY-A	20	72	9	19	2	1	0	1	10	4	.264	.369	.319	102	1	1	9	1			.939	1	O	0.1
1914	NY-A	132	470	59	133	11	3	1	40	44	60	.283	.356	.326	105	4	4	53	26	32	-11	.949	-5	*O	-2.0
1915	NY-A	132	476	70	129	16	5	2	33	62	43	.271	.364	.338	111	8	8	63	29	18	-2	.959	1	*O	0.0
1916	NY-A	4	10	0	1	0	0	0	1	0	2	.100	.100	.100	-39	-2	-2	0	0			1.000	-1	/O	-0.3
Total	4	288	1028	138	282	29	9	3	75	116	109	.274	.359	.329	106	11	11	125	56	50		.953	-4	O	-2.2

■ PAUL COOK
Cook, Paul b: 5/5/1863, Caledonia, N.Y. d: 5/25/05, Rochester, N.Y. BR/TR, Deb: 9/13/1884

YEAR	TM/L	G	AB	R	H	2B	3B	HR	RBI	BB	SO	AVG	OBP	SLG	PRO+	BR	/A	RC	SB	CS	SBR	FA	FR	POS	TPR
1884	Phi-N	3	12	0	1	0	0	0	0	0	2	.083	.083	.083	-50	-2	-2	0				.818	-2	/C	-0.3
1886	Lou-a	66	262	28	54	5	2	0		10		.206	.235	.240	48	-15	-17	17	6			.945	-9	1C/O	-2.6
1887	Lou-a	61	223	34	55	4	2	0		11		.247	.294	.283	62	-11	-11	24	15			.916	-10	C/1	-1.4
1888	Lou-a	57	185	20	34	2	0	0	13	5		.184	.222	.195	37	-13	-12	10	9			.901	-14	C/OS	-2.0
1889	Lou-a	81	286	34	65	10	1	0	15	15	48	.227	.287	.269	62	-14	-13	26	11			.925	5	C/OS1	-0.2
1890	Bro-P	58	218	32	55	3	3	0	31	14	18	.252	.303	.294	58	-12	-14	22	7			.890	-0	C1/O	-1.0
1891	Lou-a	45	153	21	35	3	1	0	23	11	17	.229	.285	.261	60	-8	-8	13	4			.909	-9	C1	-1.3
	StL-a	7	25	3	5	0	0	0	1	1	2	.200	.259	.200	29	-2	-3	1	0			.921	3	/C	0.1
	Yr	52	178	24	40	3	1	0	24	12	19	.225	.281	.253	55	-10	-10	14	4			.912	-6	C1	-1.2
Total	7	378	1364	172	304	27	9	0	83	67	87	.223	.270	.256	54	-76	-80	113	52			.906	-35	C/1OS	-8.7

■ CLIFF COOK
Cook, Raymond Clifford b: 8/20/36, Dallas, Tex. BR/TR, 6′, 188 lbs. Deb: 9/09/59

YEAR	TM/L	G	AB	R	H	2B	3B	HR	RBI	BB	SO	AVG	OBP	SLG	PRO+	BR	/A	RC	SB	CS	SBR	FA	FR	POS	TPR
1959	Cin-N	9	21	3	8	2	1	0	5	2	8	.381	.435	.571	161	2	2	6	1	0	0	.909	1	/3	0.3
1960	Cin-N	54	149	9	31	7	0	3	13	8	51	.208	.248	.315	52	-10	-10	12	0	0	0	.954	4	3/O	-0.7
1961	Cin-N	4	5	0	0	0	0	0	0	0	4	.000	.000	.000	-99	-1	-1	0	0	0	0	1.000	0	/3	-0.1
1962	Cin-N	6	5	0	0	0	0	0	0	0	2	.000	.000	.000	-97	-1	-1	0	0	0	0	1.000	-0	/3	-0.2
	NY-N	40	112	12	26	6	1	2	9	4	34	.232	.277	.357	68	-5	-5	12	1	0	0	.875	-8	3O	-1.3
	Yr	46	117	12	26	6	1	2	9	4	36	.222	.266	.342	61	-7	-7	11	1	0	0	.878	-8	3O	-1.5
1963	NY-N	50	106	9	15	2	1	2	8	12	37	.142	.229	.236	34	-9	-9	6	0	1	-1	1.000	1	O/31	-1.0
Total	5	163	398	33	80	17	3	7	35	26	136	.201	.255	.312	54	-25	-26	35	2	1	0	.937	-2	/3O1	-3.0

■ DUSTY COOKE
Cooke, Allen Lindsey b: 6/23/07, Swepsonville, N.C d: 11/21/87, Raleigh, N.C. BL/TR, 6′1″, 205 lbs. Deb: 4/15/30 MC

YEAR	TM/L	G	AB	R	H	2B	3B	HR	RBI	BB	SO	AVG	OBP	SLG	PRO+	BR	/A	RC	SB	CS	SBR	FA	FR	POS	TPR
1930	NY-A	92	216	43	55	12	3	6	29	32	61	.255	.353	.421	100	-1	0	32	4	6	-2	.978	-6	O	-1.1
1931	NY-A	27	39	10	13	1	0	1	6	8	11	.333	.447	.436	141	2	3	9	4	1	1	1.000	-1	O	0.2
1932	NY-A	3	0	1	0	0	0	0	0	1	0	—	1.000	—	191	0	0	0	0	0	0	.000	0	H	0.0
1933	Bos-A	119	454	86	133	35	10	5	54	67	71	.293	.386	.447	121	14	15	81	7	5	-1	.956	-18	*O	-1.0
1934	Bos-A	74	168	34	41	8	5	1	26	36	25	.244	.377	.369	87	-1	-3	26	7	2	1	.976	-4	O	-0.7

YEAR	TM/L	G	AB	R	H	2B	3B	HR	RBI	BB	SO	AVG	OBP	SLG	PRO+	BR	/A	RC	SB	CS	SBR	FA	FR	POS	TPR
1935	Bos-A	100	294	51	90	18	6	3	34	46	24	.306	.400	.439	109	9	6	52	6	8	-3	.972	-6	O	-0.6
1936	Bos-A	111	341	58	93	20	3	6	47	72	48	.273	.401	.402	93	2	-2	60	4	3	-1	.972	2	O	-0.4
1938	Cin-N	82	233	41	64	15	1	2	33	28	36	.275	.355	.373	103	1	2	33	0			.963	3	O	0.3
Total	8	608	1745	324	489	109	28	24	229	290	276	.280	.384	.416	106	26	21	294	32	25		.969	-30	O	-3.3

■ FRED COOKE
Cooke, Frederick B. b: Paulding, Ohio Deb: 7/30/1897

YEAR	TM/L	G	AB	R	H	2B	3B	HR	RBI	BB	SO	AVG	OBP	SLG	PRO+	BR	/A	RC	SB	CS	SBR	FA	FR	POS	TPR
1897	Cle-N	5	17	2	5	2	0	0	3	3		.294	.400	.412	109	0	0	3	0			.857	1	/O	0.1

■ SCOTT COOLBAUGH
Coolbaugh, Scott Robert b: 6/13/66, Binghamton, N.Y. BR/TR, 5'11", 185 lbs. Deb: 9/02/89

YEAR	TM/L	G	AB	R	H	2B	3B	HR	RBI	BB	SO	AVG	OBP	SLG	PRO+	BR	/A	RC	SB	CS	SBR	FA	FR	POS	TPR
1989	Tex-A	25	51	7	14	1	0	2	7	4	12	.275	.327	.412	105	0	0	6	0	0	0	.958	5	3/D	0.5
1990	Tex-A	67	180	21	36	6	0	2	13	15	47	.200	.265	.267	49	-12	-12	14	1	0	0	.941	7	3	-0.5
1991	SD-N	60	180	12	39	8	1	2	15	19	45	.217	.295	.306	67	-7	-8	15	0	3	-2	.952	4	3	-0.6
Total	3	152	411	40	89	15	1	6	35	38	104	.217	.286	.302	64	-19	-20	35	1	3	-2	.948	15	3/D	-0.6

■ DUFF COOLEY
Cooley, Duff Gordan "Dick" b: 3/14/1873, Dallas, Tex. d: 8/9/37, Dallas, Tex. BL/TR, 5'11", 158 lbs. Deb: 7/27/1893

YEAR	TM/L	G	AB	R	H	2B	3B	HR	RBI	BB	SO	AVG	OBP	SLG	PRO+	BR	/A	RC	SB	CS	SBR	FA	FR	POS	TPR
1893	StL-N	29	107	20	37	2	3	0	21	8	9	.346	.391	.421	117	3	3	21	8			.947	-9	OC/S	-0.5
1894	StL-N	54	206	35	61	3	1	1	21	12	16	.296	.335	.335	63	-12	-12	27	7			.833	-11	O3/S1	-2.0
1895	StL-N	132	563	106	191	9	20	7	75	36	29	.339	.382	.464	121	15	16	113	27			.936	11	*O/3SC	1.4
1896	StL-N	40	166	29	51	5	3	0	13	7	3	.307	.335	.373	92	-3	-2	26	12			.959	-1	O	-0.5
	Phi-N	64	287	63	88	6	4	2	22	18	16	.307	.348	.376	94	-3	-2	46	18			.901	-5	O	-1.1
	Yr	104	453	92	139	11	7	2	35	25	19	.307	.343	.375	93	-6	-4	72	30			.923	-5	*O	-1.6
1897	Phi-N	133	566	124	186	14	13	4	40	51		.329	.386	.420	116	11	13	108	31			.960	7	*O/1	0.9
1898	Phi-N	149	629	123	196	24	12	4	55	48		.312	.364	.407	126	16	20	103	17			.943	4	*O	1.2
1899	Phi-N	94	406	75	112	15	8	1	31	29		.276	.330	.360	92	-6	-4	55	15			.971	-5	1O/2	-0.9
1900	Pit-N	66	249	30	50	8	1	0	22	14		.201	.243	.241	34	-23	-23	19	9			.989	-5	1	-2.6
1901	Bos-N	63	240	27	62	13	3	0	27	14		.258	.302	.338	78	-5	-8	28	5			.943	2	O1	-1.0
1902	Bos-N	135	548	73	162	26	8	0	58	34		.296	.339	.372	118	11	11	82	27			.952	-6	*O/1	-0.4
1903	Bos-N	138	553	76	160	26	10	1	70	44		.289	.342	.378	110	3	6	83	27			.952	-5	*O1	-0.7
1904	Bos-N	122	467	41	127	18	7	5	70	24		.272	.312	.373	116	5	7	60	14			.976	-7	*O/1	-0.8
1905	Det-A	97	377	25	93	11	9	1	32	26		.247	.297	.332	99	-1	-1	42	7			.959	7	O	0.2
Total	13	1316	5364	847	1576	180	102	26	557	365	73	.294	.341	.380	104	12	24	812	224			.945	-22	*O1/3CS2	-6.8

■ CECIL COOMBS
Coombs, Cecil Lysander b: 3/18/1888, Moweaqua, Ill. d: 11/25/75, Fort Worth, Tex. BR/TR, 5'9", 160 lbs. Deb: 8/07/14

YEAR	TM/L	G	AB	R	H	2B	3B	HR	RBI	BB	SO	AVG	OBP	SLG	PRO+	BR	/A	RC	SB	CS	SBR	FA	FR	POS	TPR
1914	Chi-A	7	23	1	4	1	0	0	1	1	7	.174	.208	.217	28	-2	-2	1	0	1	-1	1.000	1	/O	-0.2

■ JACK COOMBS
Coombs, John Wesley "Colby Jack" b: 11/18/1882, LeGrand, Iowa d: 4/15/57, Palestine, Tex. BB/TR, 6', 185 lbs. Deb: 7/05/06 MC

YEAR	TM/L	G	AB	R	H	2B	3B	HR	RBI	BB	SO	AVG	OBP	SLG	PRO+	BR	/A	RC	SB	CS	SBR	FA	FR	POS	TPR
1906	Phi-A	24	67	9	16	2	0	0	3	1		.239	.261	.269	64	-3	-3	5	2			.968	0	P	0.0
1907	Phi-A	24	48	4	8	0	0	1	4	0		.167	.167	.229	26	-4	-4	2	1			.979	0	P	0.0
1908	Phi-A	78	220	24	56	9	5	1	23	9		.255	.287	.355	101	1	-0	24	6			.990	6	OP/1	0.5
1909	Phi-A	37	83	4	14	4	0	0	10	4		.169	.216	.217	36	-6	-6	4	1			.973	-0	P	0.0
1910	*Phi-A	46	132	20	29	3	0	0	9	7		.220	.270	.242	61	-6	-6	9	3			.990	-5	P	0.0
1911	*Phi-A	52	141	31	45	6	1	2	23	8		.319	.356	.418	118	2	3	22	5			.913	-3	P	0.0
1912	Phi-A	56	110	10	28	2	0	0	13	14		.255	.344	.273	80	-3	-2	11	1			1.000	-1	P	0.0
1913	Phi-A	2	3	1	1	1	0	0	0	0	2	.333	.333	.667	196	0	0	1	0			.500	-0	/P	0.0
1914	Phi-A	5	11	0	3	1	0	0	2	1	1	.273	.333	.364	114	0	0	1	0	1	-1	1.000	-1	/PO	-0.1
1915	Bro-N	29	75	8	21	1	1	0	5	2	17	.280	.299	.320	86	-1	-1	7	0	1	-1	.980	-4	P	0.0
1916	*Bro-N	27	61	2	11	2	0	0	3	2	10	.180	.206	.213	28	-5	-5	3	0			1.000	-6	P	0.0
1917	Bro-N	32	44	4	10	0	1	0	2	4	9	.227	.292	.273	72	-1	-1	4	1			.971	-3	P	0.0
1918	Bro-N	46	113	6	19	3	2	0	3	7	5	.168	.223	.230	38	-8	-8	6	1			.962	-7	PO	-0.8
1920	Det-A	2	2	0	0	0	0	0	0	0	0	.000	.000	.000	-99	-1	-1	0	0	0	0	1.000	-0	/P	0.0
Total	14	460	1110	123	261	34	10	4	100	59	44	.235	.278	.295	74	-34	-35	98	21	2		.966	-23	P/O1	-0.4

■ WILLIAM COON
Coon, William K. b: 3/21/1855, Pennsylvania d: 8/30/15, Burlington, N.J. Deb: 9/04/1875

YEAR	TM/L	G	AB	R	H	2B	3B	HR	RBI	BB	SO	AVG	OBP	SLG	PRO+	BR	/A	RC	SB	CS	SBR	FA	FR	POS	TPR
1875	Ath-n	3	12	1	2	0	0	0		0		.167	.167	.167	14	-1	-1	0						/C	-0.1
1876	Phi-N	54	220	30	50	5	1	0	22	2	4	.227	.234	.259	65	-8	-8	14				.761	-15	OC/32P	-2.0

■ JIMMY COONEY
Cooney, James Edward "Scoops" b: 8/24/1894, Cranston, R.I. d: 8/7/91, Warwick, R.I. BR/TR, 5'11", 160 lbs. Deb: 9/22/17 F

YEAR	TM/L	G	AB	R	H	2B	3B	HR	RBI	BB	SO	AVG	OBP	SLG	PRO+	BR	/A	RC	SB	CS	SBR	FA	FR	POS	TPR
1917	Bos-A	11	36	4	8	1	0	0	3	6	2	.222	.333	.250	79	-1	-1	4	0			1.000	5	2/S	0.5
1919	NY-N	5	14	3	3	0	0	0	1	0	0	.214	.214	.214	29	-1	-1	1	0			1.000	-1	/S2	-0.2
1924	StL-N	110	383	44	113	20	8	1	57	20	20	.295	.330	.397	96	-4	-3	48	12	10	-2	.969	1	S/32	0.7
1925	StL-N	54	187	27	51	11	2	0	18	4	5	.273	.292	.353	62	-10	-11	18	1	3	-2	.976	-11	S2/O	-1.9
1926	Chi-N	141	513	52	129	18	5	1	47	23	10	.251	.288	.312	61	-28	-29	45	11			**.972**	19	*S	0.5
1927	Chi-N	33	132	16	32	2	0	0	6	8	7	.242	.286	.258	46	-10	-10	10	1			.973	-2	S	-0.9
	Phi-N	76	259	33	70	12	1	0	15	13	9	.270	.305	.324	68	-12	-12	25	4			.980	17	S	1.1
	Yr	109	391	49	102	14	1	0	21	21	16	.261	.299	.302	61	-21	-22	35	5			**.978**	15	*S	0.2
1928	Bos-N	18	51	2	7	0	0	0	3	2	5	.137	.170	.137	-20	-9	-8	1	1			.982	2	S/2	-0.6
Total	7	448	1575	181	413	64	16	2	150	76	58	.262	.298	.327	67	-74	-75	153	30	13		.974	30	S/23O	-0.8

■ JIMMY COONEY
Cooney, James Joseph b: 7/9/1865, Cranston, R.I. d: 7/1/03, Cranston, R.I. BB/TR, 5'9", 155 lbs. Deb: 4/19/1890 F

YEAR	TM/L	G	AB	R	H	2B	3B	HR	RBI	BB	SO	AVG	OBP	SLG	PRO+	BR	/A	RC	SB	CS	SBR	FA	FR	POS	TPR
1890	Chi-N	135	574	114	156	19	10	4	52	73	23	.272	.360	.361	108	11	7	93	45			**.936**	1	*S/C	1.4
1891	Chi-N	118	465	84	114	15	3	0	42	48	17	.245	.318	.290	80	-11	-11	51	21			**.917**	8	*S	0.4
1892	Chi-N	65	238	18	41	1	0	0	20	23	5	.172	.248	.176	30	-19	-19	13	10			.912	-8	S	-2.3
	Was-N	6	25	5	4	0	1	0	4	4	3	.160	.276	.240	60	-1	-1	2	1			.862	-3	/S	-0.4
	Yr	71	263	23	45	1	1	0	24	27	8	.171	.251	.183	33	-20	-21	15	11			.908	-11	S	-2.7
Total	3	324	1302	221	315	35	14	4	118	148	48	.242	.324	.300	84	-20	-24	159	77			.923	-2	S/C	-0.9

■ JOHNNY COONEY
Cooney, John Walter b: 3/18/01, Cranston, R.I. d: 7/8/86, Sarasota, Fla. BR/TL, 5'10", 165 lbs. Deb: 4/19/21 FMC

YEAR	TM/L	G	AB	R	H	2B	3B	HR	RBI	BB	SO	AVG	OBP	SLG	PRO+	BR	/A	RC	SB	CS	SBR	FA	FR	POS	TPR
1921	Bos-N	8	5	0	1	0	0	0	0	0	1	.200	.200	.200	7	-1	-1	0	0	0	0	1.000	0	/P	0.0
1922	Bos-N	4	8	0	0	0	0	0	0	0	1	.000	.000	.000	-99	-2	-2	0	0	0	0	1.000	0	/P	0.0
1923	Bos-N	42	66	7	25	1	0	0	3	4	2	.379	.414	.394	119	2	2	11	0	1	-1	1.000	0	PO/1	0.2
1924	Bos-N	55	130	10	33	2	1	0	4	9	5	.254	.302	.285	61	-7	-7	11	0	4	-2	.962	0	PO/1	-0.4
1925	Bos-N	54	103	17	33	7	0	0	13	3	6	.320	.346	.388	96	-2	-1	14	1	0	0	.949	0	P/1O	-0.1
1926	Bos-N	64	126	17	38	3	2	0	18	13	7	.302	.367	.357	105	-0	1	17	6			.996	5	1P/O	0.3
1927	Bos-N	10	1	3	0	0	0	0	0	0	0	.000	.000	.000	-99	-0	-0	0	0			.000	0	H	0.0
1928	Bos-N	33	41	2	7	0	0	0	2	4	3	.171	.244	.171	11	-5	-5	2	0			1.000	2	P/1O	-0.2
1929	Bos-N	41	72	10	23	4	1	0	6	3	3	.319	.355	.403	91	-1	-1	10	1			1.000	2	OP	-0.1
1930	Bos-N	4	3	0	0	0	0	0	0	0	0	.000	.000	.000	-99	-1	-1	0	0			1.000	1	/P	0.0
1935	Bro-N	10	29	3	9	0	1	0	1	3	2	.310	.375	.379	106	0	0	5	0			1.000	-1	O	-0.1
1936	Bro-N	130	507	71	143	17	5	0	30	24	15	.282	.315	.335	74	-18	-18	54	3			**.994**	8	*O	-1.6
1937	Bro-N	120	430	61	126	18	5	0	37	22	10	.293	.327	.358	85	-8	-9	49	5			.976	6	*O/1	-0.7
1938	Bos-N	120	432	45	117	25	5	0	17	22	12	.271	.308	.352	90	-12	-6	47	2			.982	-10	*O1	-2.1
1939	Bos-N	118	368	39	101	8	1	2	27	21	8	.274	.317	.318	77	-15	-11	37	2			.992	-6	*O/1	-2.1
1940	Bos-N	108	365	40	116	14	3	0	21	25	9	.318	.363	.373	109	2	5	50	4			.992	-1	O/1	-0.1
1941	Bos-N	123	442	52	141	25	2	0	29	27	15	.319	.358	.385	114	5	7	59	3			**.996**	4	*O/1	0.5
1942	Bos-N	74	198	23	41	6	0	0	7	23	5	.207	.290	.237	56	-11	-10	15	2			.984	-14	O1	-3.0

YEAR	TM/L	G	AB	R	H	2B	3B	HR	RBI	BB	SO	AVG	OBP	SLG	PRO+	BR	/A	RC	SB	CS	SBR	FA	FR	POS	TPR
1943	Bro-N	37	34	7	7	0	0	0	2	4	3	.206	.289	.206	44	-2	-2	2	1			1.000	-0	/1O	-0.3
1944	Bro-N	7	4	0	3	0	0	0	1	0	0	.750	.750	.750	329	1	1	2	0			1.000	-0	/O	0.1
	NY-A	10	8	1	1	0	0	0	1	1	0	.125	.222	.125	1	-1	-1	0	0	0	0	1.000	-0	/O	-0.2
Total	20	1172	3372	408	965	130	26	2	219	208	107	.286	.329	.342	87	-77	-60	383	30	5		.988	-6	OP/1	-9.9

■ PHIL COONEY

Cooney, Philip Clarence (b: Philip Clarence Cohen) b: 9/14/1882, New York, N.Y. d: 10/6/57, New York, N, Y. BL/TR, 5'8", 155 lbs. Deb: 9/27/05

YEAR	TM/L	G	AB	R	H	2B	3B	HR	RBI	BB	SO	AVG	OBP	SLG	PRO+	BR	/A	RC	SB	CS	SBR	FA	FR	POS	TPR
1905	NY-A	1	3	0	0	0	0	0	0	0		.000	.000	.000	-90	-1	-1	0	0			1.000	-0	/3	-0.1

■ BILL COONEY

Cooney, William A. "Cush" b: 4/7/1883, Boston, Mass. d: 11/6/28, Roxbury, Mass. TR , Deb: 9/22/09

YEAR	TM/L	G	AB	R	H	2B	3B	HR	RBI	BB	SO	AVG	OBP	SLG	PRO+	BR	/A	RC	SB	CS	SBR	FA	FR	POS	TPR
1909	Bos-N	5	10	0	3	0	0	0	0	0		.300	.300	.300	82	-0	-0	1	0			.500	-0	/P2S	0.0
1910	Bos-N	8	12	2	3	0	0	0	1	2	0	.250	.357	.250	74	-0	-0	1	0			.000	-1	/O	-0.1
Total	2	13	22	2	6	0	0	0	1	2	0	.273	.333	.273	78	-0	-1	2	0				-1	/POS2	-0.1

■ CECIL COOPER

Cooper, Cecil Celester b: 12/20/49, Brenham, Tex. BL/TL, 6'2", 190 lbs. Deb: 9/08/71

YEAR	TM/L	G	AB	R	H	2B	3B	HR	RBI	BB	SO	AVG	OBP	SLG	PRO+	BR	/A	RC	SB	CS	SBR	FA	FR	POS	TPR
1971	Bos-A	14	42	9	13	4	1	0	3	5	4	.310	.396	.452	130	2	2	8	1	0	0	.988	-2	1	-0.1
1972	Bos-A	12	17	0	4	1	0	0	2	2	5	.235	.316	.294	78	-0	-0	2	0	0	0	1.000	-1	/1	-0.1
1973	Bos-A	30	101	12	24	2	0	3	11	7	12	.238	.287	.347	73	-3	-4	10	1	2	-1	.984	-0	1	-0.7
1974	Bos-A	121	414	55	114	24	1	8	43	32	74	.275	.329	.396	101	4	0	54	2	5	-2	.983	-1	1D	-0.8
1975	*Bos-A	106	305	49	95	17	6	14	44	19	33	.311	.358	.544	140	19	16	57	1	4	-2	.995	2	D1	1.4
1976	Bos-A	123	451	66	127	22	6	15	78	16	62	.282	.308	.457	109	10	3	64	7	1	2	.994	-1	1D	-0.1
1977	Mil-A	160	643	86	193	31	7	20	78	28	110	.300	.329	.463	113	10	10	93	13	8	-1	.992	5	*1D	0.5
1978	Mil-A	107	407	60	127	23	2	13	54	32	72	.312	.362	.474	133	17	17	69	3	4	-2	.988	2	1D	1.3
1979	Mil-A★	150	590	83	182	**44**	1	24	106	56	77	.308	.368	.508	134	27	27	110	15	3	3	.993	-8	*1D	1.3
1980	Mil-A★	153	622	96	219	33	4	25	**122**	39	42	.352	.392	.539	157	43	45	126	17	6	2	**.997**	4	*1D	4.2
1981	*Mil-A	106	416	70	133	**35**	1	12	60	28	30	.320	.367	.495	154	24	26	70	5	4	-1	.992	-0	*1/D	2.0
1982	*Mil-A★	155	654	104	205	38	3	32	121	32	53	.313	.345	.528	145	29	34	118	2	3	-1	.997	-1	*1/D	2.3
1983	Mil-A★	160	661	106	203	37	3	30	**126**	37	63	.307	.345	.508	142	26	32	110	2	1	0	.993	-10	*1/D	1.3
1984	Mil-A	148	603	63	166	28	3	11	67	27	59	.275	.309	.386	95	-8	-5	70	8	2	1	.991	3	*1D	-0.9
1985	Mil-A★	154	631	82	185	39	8	16	99	30	77	.293	.327	.456	112	9	9	86	10	3	1	.986	-2	*1D	0.1
1986	Mil-A	134	542	46	140	24	1	12	75	41	87	.258	.312	.373	83	-11	-14	60	1	2	-1	.988	-4	1D	-2.5
1987	Mil-A	63	250	25	62	13	0	6	36	17	51	.248	.296	.372	74	-9	-10	27	1	1	-0	.000	0	D	-1.0
Total	17	1896	7349	1012	2192	415	47	241	1125	448	911	.298	.340	.466	121	186	189	1134	89	49	-3	.992	-13	*1D	8.2

■ CLAUDE COOPER

Cooper, Claude William b: 4/1/1892, Troupe, Tex. d: 1/21/74, Plainview, Tex. BL/TL, 5'9", 158 lbs. Deb: 4/14/13

YEAR	TM/L	G	AB	R	H	2B	3B	HR	RBI	BB	SO	AVG	OBP	SLG	PRO+	BR	/A	RC	SB	CS	SBR	FA	FR	POS	TPR
1913	*NY-N	27	30	11	9	4	0	0	4	4	6	.300	.382	.433	132	1	1	6	3			.895	-5	O	-0.4
1914	Bro-F	113	399	56	96	14	11	2	25	26	60	.241	.294	.346	82	-11	-10	50	25			.926	-1	*O	-1.6
1915	Bro-F	153	527	75	155	26	12	2	63	77	78	.294	.388	.400	133	24	24	98	31			.958	18	*O1	3.8
1916	Phi-N	56	104	9	20	2	0	0	11	7	15	.192	.250	.212	41	-7	-7	6	1			.945	-3	O/1	-1.3
1917	Phi-N	24	29	5	3	1	0	0	1	5	4	.103	.235	.138	15	-3	-3	1	0			.923	-4	O	-0.9
Total	5	373	1089	156	283	47	23	4	104	119	163	.260	.338	.356	103	5	5	161	60			.943	5	O/1	-0.4

■ GARY COOPER

Cooper, Gary Clifton b: 8/13/64, Lynwood, Cal. BR/TR, 6'1", 200 lbs. Deb: 9/15/91

YEAR	TM/L	G	AB	R	H	2B	3B	HR	RBI	BB	SO	AVG	OBP	SLG	PRO+	BR	/A	RC	SB	CS	SBR	FA	FR	POS	TPR
1991	Hou-N	9	16	1	4	1	0	0	2	3	6	.250	.368	.313	99	-0	0	2	0	0	0	.833	-2	/3	-0.2

■ GARY COOPER

Cooper, Gary Nathaniel b: 12/22/56, Savannah, Ga. BB/TR, 6'3", 175 lbs. Deb: 8/25/80

YEAR	TM/L	G	AB	R	H	2B	3B	HR	RBI	BB	SO	AVG	OBP	SLG	PRO+	BR	/A	RC	SB	CS	SBR	FA	FR	POS	TPR
1980	Atl-N	21	2	3	0	0	0	0	0	0	1	.000	.000	.000	-97	-1	-1	-1	2	1	0	1.000	3	O	0.2

■ PAT COOPER

Cooper, Orge Patterson b: 11/26/17, Albemarle, N.C. BR/TR, 6'3", 180 lbs. Deb: 5/11/46

YEAR	TM/L	G	AB	R	H	2B	3B	HR	RBI	BB	SO	AVG	OBP	SLG	PRO+	BR	/A	RC	SB	CS	SBR	FA	FR	POS	TPR
1946	Phi-A	1	0	0	0	0	0	0	0	0	0	—	—	—	—	0	0	0	0	0	0	.000	-0	/P	0.0
1947	Phi-A	13	16	0	4	2	0	0	3	0	5	.250	.250	.375	71	-1	-1	2	0	0	0	1.000	-0	/1	-0.1
Total	2	14	16	0	4	2	0	0	3	0	5	.250	.250	.375	71	-1	-1	2	0	0	0		-0	/1P	-0.1

■ SCOTT COOPER

Cooper, Scott Kendrick b: 10/13/67, St.Louis, Mo. BL/TR, 6'3", 200 lbs. Deb: 9/05/90

YEAR	TM/L	G	AB	R	H	2B	3B	HR	RBI	BB	SO	AVG	OBP	SLG	PRO+	BR	/A	RC	SB	CS	SBR	FA	FR	POS	TPR
1990	Bos-A	2	1	0	0	0	0	0	0	0	1	.000	.000	.000	-96	-0	-0	0	0	0	0	.000	0	/H	0.0
1991	Bos-A	14	35	6	16	4	2	0	7	2	2	.457	.486	.686	210	6	5	12	0	0	0	.933	2	3	0.8
1992	Bos-A	123	337	34	93	21	0	5	33	37	33	.276	.348	.383	99	2	0	46	1	1	-0	.990	9	13/2SD	0.6
Total	3	139	373	40	109	25	2	5	40	39	36	.292	.359	.410	109	8	5	58	1	1	-0	.963	11	/13DS2	1.4

■ WALKER COOPER

Cooper, William Walker "Walk" b: 1/8/15, Atherton, Mo. d: 4/11/91, Scottsdale, Ariz. BR/TR, 6'3", 210 lbs. Deb: 9/25/40 FC

YEAR	TM/L	G	AB	R	H	2B	3B	HR	RBI	BB	SO	AVG	OBP	SLG	PRO+	BR	/A	RC	SB	CS	SBR	FA	FR	POS	TPR
1940	StL-N	6	19	3	6	1	0	0	2	2	2	.316	.381	.368	102	0	0	3	1			1.000	-0	/C	0.0
1941	StL-N	68	200	19	49	9	1	1	20	13	14	.245	.291	.315	66	-8	-10	17	1			.966	4	C	-0.1
1942	*StL-N★	125	438	58	123	32	7	7	65	29	29	.281	.327	.434	113	10	6	57	4			.972	3	*C	1.9
1943	*StL-N★	122	449	52	143	30	4	9	81	19	19	.318	.349	.463	128	17	14	69	1			.975	-3	*C	2.1
1944	*StL-N★	112	397	56	126	25	5	13	72	20	19	.317	.352	.504	136	18	17	65	4			.980	4	C	2.7
1945	StL-N	4	18	3	7	0	0	0	1	0	1	.389	.389	.389	114	0	0	3	0			.966	1	/C	0.2
1946	NY-N★	87	280	29	75	10	1	8	46	17	12	.268	.310	.396	99	-1	-2	32	0			.972	-12	C	-1.0
1947	NY-N★	140	515	79	157	24	8	35	122	24	43	.305	.339	.586	141	26	25	97	2			.979	-9	*C	2.4
1948	NY-N★	91	290	40	77	12	0	16	54	28	29	.266	.332	.472	115	5	5	42	1			.979	-13	C	-0.2
1949	NY-N	42	147	14	31	4	2	4	21	7	8	.211	.261	.347	62	-8	-8	11	0			.982	-2	C	-0.8
	Cin-N	82	307	34	86	9	2	16	62	21	24	.280	.330	.479	113	5	4	46	0			.978	-3	C	0.6
	Yr	124	454	48	117	13	4	20	83	28	32	.258	.308	.436	97	-4	-4	56	0			.979	-5	*C	-0.2
1950	Cin-N	15	47	3	9	3	0	0	4	0	5	.191	.191	.255	16	-6	-6	2	0			.972	1	C	-0.4
	Bos-N	102	337	52	111	19	3	14	60	30	26	.329	.389	.528	148	18	21	69	1			.973	-5	C	2.0
	Yr	117	384	55	120	22	3	14	64	30	31	.313	.367	.495	132	13	16	69	1			.973	-4	*C	1.6
1951	Bos-N	109	342	42	107	14	1	18	59	28	18	.313	.367	.518	145	16	19	64	1	1	-0	.981	-2	C	2.1
1952	Bos-N	102	349	33	82	12	1	10	55	22	32	.235	.282	.361	80	-12	-10	36	1	0	0	.983	-4	C	-1.0
1953	Mil-N	53	137	12	30	6	0	3	16	12	15	.219	.287	.328	64	-8	-7	12	1	0	0	.983	-5	C	-1.0
1954	Pit-N	14	15	0	3	2	0	0	1	2	1	.200	.294	.333	64	-1	-1	1	0	0	0	1.000	-0	/C	-0.1
	Chi-N	57	158	21	49	10	2	7	32	21	23	.310	.398	.532	138	9	9	32	0	0	0	.978	-2	C	0.9
	Yr	71	173	21	52	12	2	7	33	23	24	.301	.389	.514	132	9	8	33	0	0	0	.978	-2	C	0.8
1955	Chi-N	54	111	11	31	8	1	7	15	6	19	.279	.322	.559	128	4	4	19	0	0	0	.961	-11	C	-0.6
1956	StL-N	40	68	5	18	5	1	2	14	3	8	.265	.296	.456	98	-0	-0	8	0	0	0	.984	-3	C	-0.3
1957	StL-N	48	78	7	21	5	1	3	10	5	10	.269	.313	.474	106	1	0	9	0	0	0	.957	-2	C	-0.1
Total	18	1473	4702	573	1341	240	40	173	812	309	357	.285	.332	.464	116	84	82	695	18	1		.977	-63	*C	9.3

■ JOEY CORA

Cora, Jose Manuel (Amaro) b: 5/14/65, Caguas, P.R. BB/TR, 5'8", 150 lbs. Deb: 4/06/87

YEAR	TM/L	G	AB	R	H	2B	3B	HR	RBI	BB	SO	AVG	OBP	SLG	PRO+	BR	/A	RC	SB	CS	SBR	FA	FR	POS	TPR
1987	SD-N	77	241	23	57	7	2	0	13	28	26	.237	.319	.282	63	-13	-12	22	15	11	-2	.975	-2	2/S	-1.3
1989	SD-N	12	19	5	6	1	0	0	1	1	0	.316	.350	.368	105	0	0	3	1	0	0	.960	2	/S32	0.3
1990	SD-N	51	100	12	27	3	0	0	2	6	9	.270	.311	.300	68	-4	-4	10	8	3	1	.833	-3	S2/C	-0.6
1991	Chi-A	100	228	37	55	2	3	0	18	20	21	.241	.316	.276	67	-10	-9	22	11	6	-0	.970	-9	2/SD	-1.7
1992	Chi-A	68	122	27	30	7	1	0	9	22	13	.246	.378	.320	100	1	1	18	10	3	1	.984	5	2D/S3	0.8
Total	5	308	710	104	175	20	6	0	43	77	69	.246	.329	.292	73	-26	-24	75	45	23	-0	.971	-8	2/SD3C	-2.5

■ GENE CORBETT

Corbett, Eugene Louis b: 10/25/13, Winona, Minn. BL/TR, 6'1.5", 190 lbs. Deb: 9/19/36

YEAR	TM/L	G	AB	R	H	2B	3B	HR	RBI	BB	SO	AVG	OBP	SLG	PRO+	BR	/A	RC	SB	CS	SBR	FA	FR	POS	TPR
1936	Phi-N	6	21	1	3	0	0	0	2	2	3	.143	.217	.143	-1	-3	-3	1	0			1.000	-1	/1	-0.4

YEAR	TM/L	G	AB	R	H	2B	3B	HR	RBI	BB	SO	AVG	OBP	SLG	PRO+	BR	/A	RC	SB	CS	SBR	FA	FR	POS	TPR
1937	Phi-N	7	12	4	4	2	0	0	1	0	0	.333	.333	.500	114	0	0	2	0			.800	-1	/32	-0.1
1938	Phi-N	24	75	7	6	1	0	2	7	6	11	.080	.148	.173	-12	-12	-11	2	0			.995	-1	1	-1.5
Total	3	37	108	12	13	3	0	2	10	8	14	.120	.181	.204	5	-14	-14	5	0			.996	-2	/132	-2.0
■ CLAUDE CORBITT	Corbitt, Claude Elliott b: 7/21/15, Sunbury, N.C. d: 5/1/78, Cincinnati, Ohio BR/TR, 5'10", 170 lbs. Deb: 9/23/45																								
1945	Bro-N	2	4	1	2	0	0	0	0	1	0	.500	.600	.500	209	1	1	1	0			1.000	0	/3	0.1
1946	Cin-N	82	274	25	68	10	1	1	16	23	13	.248	.309	.303	77	-9	-8	27	3			.947	-13	S	-1.8
1948	Cin-N	87	258	24	66	11	0	0	18	14	16	.256	.297	.298	64	-14	-13	24	4			.973	-8	23S	-1.8
1949	Cin-N	44	94	10	17	1	0	0	3	9	1	.181	.252	.191	20	-10	-11	5	1			.984	-6	S2/3	-1.5
Total	4	215	630	60	153	22	1	1	37	47	30	.243	.297	.286	63	-33	-31	57	8			.956	-26	S/23	-5.0
■ ART CORCORAN	Corcoran, Arthur Andrew "Bunny" b: 11/23/1894, Roxbury, Mass. d: 7/27/58, Chelsea, Mass. TR , Deb: 9/09/15																								
1915	Phi-A	1	4	0	0	0	0	0	0	0	2	.000	.000	.000	-99	-1	-1	0	0			1.000	-0	/3	-0.1
■ JOHN CORCORAN	Corcoran, John A. b: 1873, Cincinnati, Ohio d: 11/2/01, Cincinnati, Ohio TL , Deb: 9/17/1895																								
1895	Pit-N	6	20	0	3	0	0	0	1	0	2	.150	.150	.150	-23	-4	-3	0	0			.895	-1	/S3	-0.4
■ JACK CORCORAN	Corcoran, John H. b: 1860, Lowell, Mass. Deb: 5/01/1884																								
1884	Bro-a	52	185	17	39	4	3	0		8		.211	.251	.265	70	-6	-6	13				.873	-9	C/O2SP	-1.0
■ LARRY CORCORAN	Corcoran, Lawrence J. b: 8/10/1859, Brooklyn, N.Y. d: 10/14/1891, Newark, N.J. BL/TB, 120 lbs. Deb: 5/01/1880 F																								
1880	Chi-N	72	286	41	66	11	1	0	25	10	33	.231	.257	.276	76	-5	-8	21				.957	3	*P/OS	-0.3
1881	Chi-N	47	189	25	42	8	0	0	9	5	22	.222	.242	.265	57	-9	-10	12				.893	-1	P/SO	0.0
1882	Chi-N	40	169	23	35	10	2	1	24	6	18	.207	.234	.308	69	-5	-6	12				.919	1	P/3	0.0
1883	Chi-N	68	263	40	55	12	7	0	25	6	62	.209	.227	.308	57	-12	-15	19				.906	-3	PO/S2	-0.6
1884	Chi-N	64	251	43	61	3	4	1	19	10	33	.243	.272	.299	73	-6	-9	21				.882	7	P/OS	-0.1
1885	Chi-N	7	22	6	6	1	0	0	4	6	1	.273	.429	.318	126	2	1	3				.905	0	/PS	0.0
	NY-N	3	14	3	5	0	0	0	2	0	1	.357	.357	.357	133	0	0	2				1.000	1	/P	0.0
	Yr	10	36	9	11	1	0	0	6	6	2	.306	.405	.333	128	2	1	5				.935	1	P/S	0.0
1886	NY-N	1	4	0	0	0	0	0	0	0	2	.000	.000	.000	-99	-1	-1	0	0			.000	-1	/O	-0.2
	Was-N	21	81	9	15	2	1	0	3	7	14	.185	.250	.235	51	-5	-4	6	3			.619	-3	O/SP	-0.6
	Yr	22	85	9	15	2	1	0	3	7	16	.176	.239	.224	44	-6	-5	5	3			.591	-3	O/SP	-0.8
1887	Ind-N	3	10	2	2	0	0	0	0	2	1	.200	.333	.200	55	-1	-0	1	2			1.000	-0	/OP	0.0
Total	8	326	1289	192	287	47	15	2	111	52	187	.223	.253	.287	67	-42	-51	97	5			.910	4	P/OS23	-1.8
■ MICKEY CORCORAN	Corcoran, Michael Joseph b: 8/26/1882, Buffalo, N.Y. d: 12/9/50, Buffalo, N.Y. BR/TR, 5'8", 165 lbs. Deb: 9/15/10																								
1910	Cin-N	14	46	3	10	3	0	0	7	5	9	.217	.308	.283	76	-2	-1	4	0			.911	-1	2	-0.2
■ TOMMY CORCORAN	Corcoran, Thomas William "Corky" b: 1/4/1869, New Haven, Conn. d: 6/25/60, Plainfield, Conn. BR/TR, 5'9", 164 lbs. Deb: 4/19/1890 U																								
1890	Pit-P	123	503	80	117	14	13	1	61	38	45	.233	.289	.318	69	-27	-19	60	43			.884	4	*S	-0.7
1891	Phi-a	133	511	84	130	11	15	7	71	29	56	.254	.307	.376	95	-4	-6	70	30			**.911**	12	*S	1.1
1892	Bro-N	151	613	77	145	11	6	1	74	34	51	.237	.281	.279	74	-22	-18	61	39			**.925**	-2	*S	-1.3
1893	Bro-N	115	459	61	126	11	10	2	58	27	12	.275	.318	.355	84	-14	-10	58	14			.907	14	*S	0.7
1894	Bro-N	129	576	123	173	21	20	5	92	25	17	.300	.329	.432	90	-17	-10	96	33			.904	-4	*S	-0.5
1895	Bro-N	127	535	81	142	17	10	2	69	23	11	.265	.299	.346	74	-26	-19	64	17			.924	18	*S	0.4
1896	Bro-N	132	532	63	154	15	7	3	73	15	13	.289	.310	.361	83	-18	-13	67	16			.926	24	*S	1.3
1897	Cin-N	109	445	76	128	30	5	3	57	13		.288	.311	.398	81	-11	-16	62	15			.913	5	S2	-0.6
1898	Cin-N	153	619	80	155	28	15	2	87	26		.250	.283	.354	77	-17	-23	71	19			.932	14	*S	-0.3
1899	Cin-N	137	537	91	149	11	8	0	81	28		.277	.316	.328	75	-18	-19	69	32			.931	4	*S2	-0.4
1900	Cin-N	127	523	64	128	21	9	1	54	22		.245	.278	.325	68	-26	-24	58	27			.921	-4	*S/2	-1.7
1901	Cin-N	31	115	14	24	3	3	0	15	11		.209	.278	.287	69	-5	-4	11	6			.919	4	S	0.3
1902	Cin-N	138	538	54	136	18	4	0	54	11		.253	.269	.301	69	-17	-23	51	20			.926	-13	*S/2	-2.9
1903	Cin-N	115	459	61	113	18	7	2	73	12		.246	.267	.329	63	-20	-27	45	12			.943	6	*S	-1.5
1904	Cin-N	150	578	55	133	17	9	2	74	19		.230	.257	.301	67	-20	-26	52	19			**.936**	2	*S	-2.1
1905	Cin-N	151	605	70	150	21	11	2	85	23		.248	.275	.329	72	-17	-25	66	28			**.952**	20	*S	-0.2
1906	Cin-N	117	430	29	89	13	1	1	33	19		.207	.242	.249	51	-24	-26	30	8			.941	8	*S	-1.6
1907	NY-N	62	226	21	60	9	2	0	24	7		.265	.288	.323	89	-3	-4	25	9			.939	-5	2	-1.1
Total	18	2200	8804	1184	2252	289	155	34	1135	382	205	.256	.289	.335	75	-305	-311	1015	387			.924	107	*S2	-11.1
■ TIM CORCORAN	Corcoran, Timothy Michael b: 3/19/53, Glendale, Cal. BL/TL, 5'11", 175 lbs. Deb: 5/18/77																								
1977	Det-A	55	103	13	29	3	0	3	15	6	9	.282	.321	.398	90	-1	-2	12	0	1	-1	1.000	-0	O/D	-0.3
1978	Det-A	116	324	37	86	13	1	1	27	24	27	.265	.326	.321	80	-7	-8	33	3	2	-0	.985	-6	*O/D	-1.9
1979	Det-A	18	22	4	5	1	0	0	6	4	2	.227	.346	.273	67	-1	-1	2	1	1	-0	1.000	-1	/O1	-0.3
1980	Det-A	84	153	20	44	7	1	3	18	22	10	.288	.381	.405	113	4	4	23	0	2	-1	.985	-2	1O/D	-0.1
1981	Min-A	22	51	4	9	3	0	0	4	6	7	.176	.263	.235	42	-4	-4	3	0	0	0	1.000	1	1/D	-0.4
1983	Phi-N	3	0	0	0	0	0	0	0	0	0	—	—	—	—	0	0	0	0	0	0	1.000	-0	/1	0.0
1984	Phi-N	102	208	30	71	13	1	5	36	37	27	.341	.443	.486	158	19	18	45	0	1	-1	.997	-4	1O	1.1
1985	Phi-N	103	182	11	39	6	1	0	22	29	20	.214	.322	.258	63	-8	-8	16	0	0	0	.993	-2	1/O	-1.4
1986	NY-N	6	7	1	0	0	0	0	0	2	0	.000	.222	.000	-34	-1	-1	0	0	0	0	1.000	0	/1	-0.1
Total	9	509	1050	120	283	46	4	12	128	130	102	.270	.354	.355	96	2	-2	136	4	7	-3	.993	-15	1O/D	-3.4
■ WIL CORDERO	Cordero, Wilfredo b: 10/3/71, Mayaguez, P.R. BR/TR, 6'2", 185 lbs. Deb: 7/24/92																								
1992	Mon-N	45	126	17	38	4	1	2	8	9	31	.302	.353	.397	113	2	2	17	0	0	0	.949	-6	S/2	-0.2
■ FRED COREY	Corey, Frederick Harrison b: 1857, S.Kingston, R.I. d: 11/27/12, Providence, R.I. BR/TR, Deb: 5/01/1878																								
1878	Pro-N	7	21	3	3	0	0	0	1	0	2	.143	.143	.143	-6	-2	-2	0				1.000	0	/P21	-0.1
1880	Wor-N	41	138	11	24	8	1	0	6	4	27	.174	.197	.246	45	-7	-9	7				.759	-11	OP/S31	-1.3
1881	Wor-N	51	203	22	45	8	4	0	10	5	10	.222	.240	.300	65	-7	-9	15				.827	2	OP/S	-0.3
1882	Wor-N	64	255	33	63	7	12	0	29	5	31	.247	.262	.369	97	-0	-1	25				.847	-13	SPO/31	-1.2
1883	Phi-a	71	298	45	77	16	2	1		12		.258	.287	.336	92	-0	-4	29				.799	-2	3PO/2SC	-0.6
1884	Phi-a	104	439	64	121	17	16	5		17		.276	.306	.421	129	17	13	58				**.887**	13	*3	2.4
1885	Phi-a	94	384	61	94	14	8	1		17		.245	.282	.331	90	-2	-5	37				.872	8	*3/SP	0.4
Total	7	432	1738	239	427	70	43	7	46	60	70	.246	.273	.348	94	-2	-17	172				.863	-4	3/POS21C	-0.7
■ MARK COREY	Corey, Mark Mundell b: 11/3/55, Tucumcari, N.Mex. BR/TR, 6'2", 200 lbs. Deb: 9/01/79																								
1979	Bal-A	13	13	1	2	0	0	0	1	0	4	.154	.154	.154	-17	-2	-2	0	1	0	0	1.000	-3	O	-0.4
1980	Bal-A	36	36	7	10	2	0	1	2	5	7	.278	.366	.417	115	1	1	6	0	1	-1	1.000	-10	O	-1.0
1981	Bal-A	10	8	2	0	0	0	0	0	2	2	.000	.200	.000	-38	-1	-1	0	0	0	0	1.000	-2	/O	-0.4
Total	3	59	57	10	12	2	0	1	3	7	13	.211	.297	.298	65	-3	-3	6	1	1	-0	1.000	-15	/O	-1.8
■ CHUCK CORGAN	Corgan, Charles Howard b: 12/4/02, Wagoner, Okla. d: 6/13/28, Wagoner, Okla. BB/TR, 5'11", 180 lbs. Deb: 9/19/25																								
1925	Bro-N	14	47	4	8	1	1	0	0	3	9	.170	.220	.234	16	-6	-6	3	0	0	0	.908	4	S	0.0
1927	Bro-N	19	57	3	15	1	0	0	1	4	4	.263	.311	.281	59	-3	-3	5	0			.969	-1	2/S	-0.3
Total	2	33	104	7	23	2	1	0	1	7	13	.221	.270	.260	40	-9	-9	8	0	0		.900	3	/S2	-0.3

YEAR	TM/L	G	AB	R	H	2B	3B	HR	RBI	BB	SO	AVG	OBP	SLG	PRO+	BR	/A	RC	SB	CS	SBR	FA	FR	POS	TPR
■ **ROY CORHAN**						Corhan, Roy George "Irish"		b: 10/21/1887, Indianapolis, Ind.			d: 11/24/58, San Francisco, Cal			BR/TR, 5'9.5", 165 lbs.			Deb: 4/20/11								
1911	Chi-A	43	131	14	28	6	2	0	8	15		.214	.304	.290	68	-6	-5	12	2			.924	11	S	0.8
1916	StL-N	92	295	30	62	6	3	0	18	20	31	.210	.265	.251	59	-14	-14	24	15			.917	1	S	-0.9
Total	2	135	426	44	90	12	5	0	26	35	31	.211	.277	.263	62	-20	-19	36	17			.920	12	S	-0.1
■ **POP CORKHILL**						Corkhill, John Stewart		b: 4/11/1858, Parkesburg, Pa.			d: 4/4/21, Pennsauken, N.J.			BL/TR, 5'10", 180 lbs.			Deb: 5/01/1883								
1883	Cin-a	88	375	53	81	10	8	2		3		.216	.222	.301	64	-14	-17	26				**.930**	1	*O/S21	-1.4
1884	Cin-a	110	452	85	124	13	11	4		6		.274	.290	.378	114	8	5	51				**.934**	10	*OS/13P	1.2
1885	Cin-a	112	440	64	111	10	8	1		7		.252	.275	.318	88	-5	-7	40				.938	17	*O3/1SP	0.7
1886	Cin-a	129	540	81	143	9	7	5		23		.265	.302	.335	98	-0	-3	64	24			.919	-0	*O3/1SP	-0.5
1887	Cin-a	128	541	79	168	19	11	5		14		.311	.333	.414	107	5	3	87	30			**.952**	15	*O/P	1.3
1888	Cin-a	118	490	68	133	11	9	1	74	15		.271	.299	.337	101	3	-1	59	27			.958	7	*O/P12	0.2
	Bro-a	19	71	17	27	4	3	1	19	4		.380	.429	.563	222	9	9	19	3			.980	2	O	0.9
	Yr	137	561	85	160	15	12	2	93	19		.285	.316	.365	116	12	8	76	30			.961	8	*O/P12	1.1
1889	*Bro-a	138	537	91	134	21	9	8	78	42	24	.250	.308	.367	93	-6	-6	69	22			**.949**	12	*O/S1	0.3
1890	Bro-N	51	204	23	46	4	2	1	21	15	11	.225	.279	.279	64	-9	-9	18	6			.977	4	O/1	-0.7
1891	Phi-a	83	349	50	73	7	7	0	31	26	15	.209	.268	.269	54	-20	-22	29	12			.956	7	O	-1.6
	Cin-N	1	4	0	0	0	0	0	0	0	1	.000	.000	.000	-99	-1	-1	0				1.000	1	/O	-0.4
	Pit-N	41	145	16	33	1	1	3	20	7	10	.228	.268	.310	72	-6	-5	14	7			.935	2	O	-0.4
	Yr	42	149	16	33	1	1	3	20	7	11	.221	.261	.302	67	-7	-6	14	7			.939	3	O	-0.4
1892	Pit-N	68	256	23	47	1	4	0	25	12	19	.184	.229	.219	37	-19	-20	15	6			.953	7	O	-1.4
Total	10	1086	4404	650	1120	110	80	31	268	174	80	.254	.288	.337	89	-55	-73	489	137			.947	83	*O/1PS32	-1.4
■ **PAT CORRALES**						Corrales, Patrick		b: 3/20/41, Los Angeles, Cal.			BR/TR, 6', 195 lbs.			Deb: 8/02/64		MC								
1964	Phi-N	2	1	1	0	0	0	0	0	1	0	.000	.500	.000	55	0	0	0	0	0	0	.000	0	H	0.0
1965	Phi-N	63	174	16	39	8	1	2	15	25	42	.224	.325	.316	83	-4	-3	19	0	0	0	.982	-3	C	-0.4
1966	StL-N	28	72	5	13	2	0	0	3	2	17	.181	.224	.208	21	-8	-8	3	1	0	0	.975	9	C	0.3
1968	Cin-N	20	56	3	15	4	0	0	6	6	16	.268	.349	.339	101	1	0	7	0	0	0	.991	0	C	0.2
1969	Cin-N	29	72	10	19	5	0	1	5	8	17	.264	.346	.375	97	0	-0	9	0	1	-1	.986	3	C	0.4
1970	*Cin-N	43	106	9	25	5	1	1	10	8	22	.236	.289	.330	65	-5	-5	9	0	0	0	.983	5	C	0.1
1971	Cin-N	40	94	6	17	2	0	0	6	6	17	.181	.230	.202	24	-9	-9	5	0	0	0	.980	1	C	-0.8
1972	Cin-N	2	1	0	0	0	0	0	0	2	0	.000	.667	.000	110	0	0	0	0	0	0	1.000	1	/C	0.2
	SD-N	44	119	6	23	0	0	0	6	11	26	.193	.267	.193	35	-10	-9	7	0	0	0	.993	3	C	-0.5
	Yr	46	120	6	23	0	0	0	6	13	26	.192	.293	.192	38	-10	-9	7	0	0	0	.993	4	C	-0.3
1973	SD-N	29	72	7	15	2	1	0	3	6	10	.208	.278	.264	55	-5	-4	6	0	0	0	.986	-1	C	-0.4
Total	9	300	767	63	166	28	3	4	54	75	167	.216	.292	.276	61	-39	-38	64	1	1	-0	.984	18	C	-0.9
■ **VIC CORRELL**						Correll, Victor Crosby		b: 2/5/46, Washington, D.C.			BR/TR, 5'10", 185 lbs.			Deb: 10/04/72										
1972	Bos-A	1	4	1	2	0	0	0	1	0	1	.500	.500	.500	188	0	0	1	0	0	0	1.000	1	/C	0.1
1974	Atl-N	73	202	20	48	15	1	4	29	21	38	.238	.332	.381	92	-1	-2	25	0	0	0	.988	6	C	0.6
1975	Atl-N	103	325	37	70	12	1	11	39	42	66	.215	.307	.360	82	-7	-9	34	0	2	-1	.973	-2	C	-0.8
1976	Atl-N	69	200	26	45	6	2	5	16	21	37	.225	.302	.350	80	-4	-6	20	0	1	-1	.981	3	C	-0.2
1977	Atl-N	54	144	16	30	7	0	7	16	22	33	.208	.317	.403	82	-2	-4	18	2	3	-1	.973	2	C	-0.2
1978	Cin-N	52	105	9	25	7	0	1	8	8	17	.238	.292	.333	74	-4	-4	8	0	0	0	.980	1	C	-0.3
1979	Cin-N	48	133	14	31	12	0	1	15	14	26	.233	.311	.346	78	-4	-4	14	0	0	0	.992	7	C	0.4
1980	Cin-N	10	19	1	8	1	0	0	3	0	2	.421	.421	.474	149	1	1	4	0	0	0	.919	-0	C	0.1
Total	8	410	1132	124	259	60	4	29	125	128	220	.229	.312	.366	83	-20	-27	125	2	6	-4	.979	18	C	-0.3
■ **PHIL CORRIDAN**						Corridan, Philip		Deb: 7/16/1884																	
1884	CP-U	2	7	1	1	0	0	0		0	0	.143	.143	.143	-3	-1	-1	0				.800	-1	/2O	-0.1
■ **JOHN CORRIDEN**						Corriden, John Michael Jr.		b: 10/6/18, Logansport, Ind.			BB/TR, 5'6", 160 lbs.			Deb: 4/20/46		F								
1946	Bro-N	1	0	1	0	0	0	0	0	0	0	—	—	—	—	0	0	0	0	0	0	.000	0	R	0.0
■ **RED CORRIDEN**						Corriden, John Michael Sr.		b: 9/4/1887, Logansport, Ind.			d: 9/28/59, Indianapolis, Ind			BR/TR, 5'9", 165 lbs.			Deb: 9/08/10		FMC					
1910	StL-A	26	84	19	13	3	0	1	4	13		.155	.297	.226	68	-3	-2	8	5			.902	4	S3	0.3
1912	Det-A	38	138	22	28	6	0	0	5	15		.203	.286	.246	54	-8	-8	11	4			.929	-4	3/2S	-1.1
1913	Chi-N	46	97	13	17	3	0	2	9	10	14	.175	.252	.268	48	-7	-7	7	4			.907	-1	S/23	-0.6
1914	Chi-N	107	318	42	73	9	5	3	29	35	33	.230	.323	.318	91	-3	-3	37	13			.894	-33	S/32	-3.0
1915	Chi-N	6	3	1	0	0	0	0	0	2	1	.000	.571	.000	79	1	1	0	0			.667	-1	/3O	0.0
Total	5	223	640	97	131	21	5	6	47	75	48	.205	.304	.281	74	-20	-19	63	26			.896	-35	S/32O	-4.4
■ **JESS CORTAZZO**						Cortazzo, John Francis		b: 9/26/04, Wilmerding, Pa.			d: 3/4/63, Pittsburgh, Pa.			BR/TR, 5'3.5", 142 lbs.			Deb: 9/01/23							
1923	Chi-A	1	1	0	0	0	0	0	0	0	0	.000	.000	.000	-99	-0	-0	0	0	0	0	.000	0	H	0.0
■ **JOE COSCARART**						Coscarart, Joseph Marvin		b: 11/18/09, Escondido, Cal.			BR/TR, 6', 185 lbs.			Deb: 4/26/35		F								
1935	Bos-N	86	284	30	67	11	2	1	29	16	28	.236	.277	.299	59	-18	-15	23	2			.962	-4	3S2	-1.5
1936	Bos-N	104	367	28	90	11	2	2	44	19	37	.245	.292	.302	64	-20	-17	31	0			.935	2	3/S2	-1.2
Total	2	190	651	58	157	22	4	3	73	35	65	.241	.285	.301	62	-38	-32	55	2			.943	-3	3/S2	-2.7
■ **PETE COSCARART**						Coscarart, Peter Joseph		b: 6/16/13, Escondido, Cal.			BR/TR, 5'11.5", 175 lbs.			Deb: 4/26/38		F							
1938	Bro-N	32	79	10	12	3	0	0	6	9	18	.152	.256	.190	24	-8	-8	5	0			.955	1	2	-0.6
1939	Bro-N	115	419	59	116	22	2	4	43	46	56	.277	.354	.368	91	-2	-4	58	10			.960	-8	*2/3S	-0.6
1940	Bro-N★	143	506	55	120	24	4	9	58	53	59	.237	.311	.354	78	-12	-16	56	5			.958	-32	*2	-3.9
1941	*Bro-N	43	62	13	8	1	0	0	5	7	12	.129	.217	.145	3	-8	-8	2	1			.948	5	2/S	-0.2
1942	Pit-N	133	487	57	111	12	4	3	29	38	56	.228	.288	.287	67	-19	-21	42	2			.952	-18	*S2	-3.4
1943	Pit-N	133	491	57	119	19	6	0	48	46	48	.242	.307	.305	75	-14	-16	47	4			.961	-4	2S/3	-1.3
1944	Pit-N	139	554	89	146	30	4	4	42	41	57	.264	.315	.354	85	-9	-12	62	10			.967	-7	*2/SO	-1.2
1945	Pit-N	123	392	59	95	17	2	8	38	55	55	.242	.341	.357	91	-2	-4	50	2			.978	21	*2/3	2.3
1946	Pit-N	3	2	0	1	1	0	0	0	0	0	.500	.500	1.000	312	1	1	1	0			.000	0	/S	0.1
Total	9	864	2992	399	728	129	22	28	269	295	361	.243	.314	.329	78	-75	-89	322	34			.963	-41	2S/3O	-8.8
■ **RAY COSEY**						Cosey, Donald Ray		b: 2/15/56, San Raphael, Cal.			BL/TL, 5'10", 185 lbs.			Deb: 4/14/80										
1980	Oak-A	9	9	0	1	0	0	0	0	0	0	.111	.111	.111	-42	-2	-2	0	0	0	0	.000	0	/H	-0.2
■ **DAN COSTELLO**						Costello, Daniel Francis "Dashing Dan"		b: 9/9/1891, Jessup, Pa.			d: 3/26/36, Pittsburgh, Pa.			BL/TR, 6'0.5", 185 lbs.			Deb: 7/02/13					
1913	NY-A	2	2	1	1	0	0	0	0	0	0	.500	.500	.500	192	0	0	0	0			.000	0	H	0.0
1914	Pit-N	21	64	7	19	1	0	0	5	8	16	.297	.375	.313	110	1	1	8	2			.970	-1	O	-0.1
1915	Pit-N	71	125	16	27	4	1	0	11	7	23	.216	.258	.264	59	-6	-6	10	7	1	2	.893	-5	O/1	-1.2
1916	Pit-N	60	159	11	38	1	3	0	8	6	23	.239	.267	.283	68	-6	-6	13	3			.976	-2	O	-1.2
Total	4	154	350	35	85	6	4	0	24	21	62	.243	.286	.283	73	-11	-11	32	12	1		.959	-9	/O1	-2.5
■ **TIM COSTO**						Costo, Timothy Roger		b: 2/16/69, Melrose Park, Ill.			BR/TR, 6'5", 220 lbs.			Deb: 9/18/92										
1992	Cin-N	12	36	3	8	2	0	0	2	5	6	.222	.317	.278	67	-1	-1	3	0	0	0	1.000	0	1	-0.2

YEAR	TM/L	G	AB	R	H	2B	3B	HR	RBI	BB	SO	AVG	OBP	SLG	PRO+	BR	/A	RC	SB	CS	SBR	FA	FR	POS	TPR

■ HENRY COTE Cote, Henry Joseph b: 2/19/1864, Troy, N.Y. d: 4/28/40, Troy, N.Y. Deb: 9/16/1894

1894	Lou-N	10	31	7	9	2	2	0	3	5	6	.290	.389	.484	119	1	1	7	2			.918	5	C	0.5
1895	Lou-N	10	33	10	10	0	0	0	5	3	3	.303	.361	.303	79	-1	-1	5	2			.872	-3	C	-0.2
Total	2	20	64	17	19	2	2	0	8	8	9	.297	.375	.391	99	-0	-0	11	4			.900	2	/C	0.3

■ PETE COTE Cote, Warren Peter b: 8/30/02, Cambridge, Mass. d: 10/17/87, Middleton, Mass. BR/TR, 5'6", 148 lbs. Deb: 6/18/26

| 1926 | NY-N | 2 | 1 | 0 | 0 | 0 | 0 | 0 | 0 | 0 | 0 | .000 | .000 | .000 | -99 | -0 | -0 | 0 | 0 | | | .000 | 0 | H | 0.0 |

■ ED COTTER Cotter, Edward Chrsitopher b: 7/4/04, Hartford, Conn. d: 6/14/59, Hartford, Conn. BR/TR, 6', 185 lbs. Deb: 6/12/26

| 1926 | Phi-N | 17 | 26 | 3 | 8 | 0 | 1 | 0 | 1 | 4 | 4 | .308 | .333 | .385 | 88 | -0 | -0 | 3 | 1 | | | .833 | 0 | /3S | 0.0 |

■ HOOKS COTTER Cotter, Harvey Louis b: 5/22/1900, Holden, Mo. d: 8/6/55, Los Angeles, Cal. BL/TL, 5'10", 160 lbs. Deb: 4/15/22

1922	Chi-N	1	1	0	1	0	0	0	0	0	0	1.000	1.000	2.000	644	1	1	2	0	0	0	.000	0	H	0.1
1924	Chi-N	98	310	39	81	16	4	4	33	36	31	.261	.338	.377	91	-3	-4	40	3	5	-2	.989	4	1	-0.7
Total	2	99	311	39	82	17	4	4	33	36	31	.264	.340	.383	92	-3	-3	42	3	5	-2		4	/1	-0.6

■ DICK COTTER Cotter, Richard Raphael b: 10/12/1889, Manchester, N.H. d: 4/4/45, Brooklyn, N.Y. BR/TR, 5'11", 172 lbs. Deb: 8/17/11

1911	Phi-N	20	46	2	13	0	0	0	5	5	7	.283	.353	.283	78	-1	-1	5	1			.975	-2	C	-0.1
1912	Chi-N	26	54	6	15	0	2	0	10	6	13	.278	.361	.352	96	-0	-0	7	1			.954	-3	C	-0.2
Total	2	46	100	8	28	0	2	0	15	11	20	.280	.357	.320	87	-1	-1	12	2			.964	-5	/C	-0.3

■ TOM COTTER Cotter, Thomas B. b: 9/30/1866, Waltham, Mass. d: 11/22/06, Brookline, Mass. BR/TR, 5'10.5", 149 lbs. Deb: 9/03/1891

| 1891 | Bos-a | 6 | 12 | 1 | 3 | 0 | 0 | 0 | 4 | 1 | 2 | .250 | .308 | .250 | 63 | -1 | -1 | 1 | 0 | | | .938 | -1 | /CO | -0.1 |

■ CHUCK COTTIER Cottier, Charles Keith b: 1/8/36, Delta, Colo. BR/TR, 5'10.5", 175 lbs. Deb: 4/17/59 MC

1959	Mil-N	10	24	1	3	1	0	0	1	3	7	.125	.222	.167	6	-3	-3	1	0	0	0	.976	1	2	-0.2
1960	Mil-N	95	229	29	52	8	0	3	19	14	21	.227	.278	.301	63	-13	-11	20	1	0	0	.968	17	2	1.3
1961	Det-A	10	7	2	2	0	0	0	1	1	1	.286	.375	.286	77	-0	-0	1	0	0	0	.889	2	/S2	0.1
	Was-A	101	337	37	79	14	4	2	34	30	51	.234	.299	.318	66	-17	-16	34	9	1	2	.982	15	*2	1.2
	Yr	111	344	39	81	14	4	2	35	31	52	.235	.301	.317	66	-17	-16	35	9	1	2	.982	17	*2/S	1.3
1962	Was-A	136	443	50	107	14	6	6	40	44	57	.242	.313	.341	76	-15	-14	49	14	8	-1	.981	21	*2	1.8
1963	Was-A	113	337	30	69	16	4	5	21	24	63	.205	.258	.320	61	-18	-18	28	2	1	0	.963	11	2S/3	0.1
1964	Was-A	73	137	16	23	6	2	3	10	19	33	.168	.269	.307	60	-7	-7	12	2	0	1	.982	14	2/3S	1.0
1965	Was-A	7	1	1	0	0	0	0	0	0	0	.000	.000	.000	-99	-0	-0	0	0	0	0	.000	0	H	0.0
1968	Cal-A	33	67	2	13	4	1	0	1	2	5	.194	.217	.284	53	-4	-4	4	0	0	0	.963	3	3/2	-0.2
1969	Cal-A	2	2	0	0	0	0	0	0	0	0	.000	.000	.000	-99	-1	-1	0	0	0	0	1.000	-0	/2	-0.1
Total	9	580	1584	168	348	63	17	19	127	137	248	.220	.284	.317	65	-79	-75	150	28	10	2	.976	81	2/S3	5.0

■ HENRY COTTO Cotto, Henry b: 1/5/61, New York, N.Y. BR/TR, 6'2", 178 lbs. Deb: 4/05/84

1984	*Chi-N	105	146	24	40	5	0	0	8	10	23	.274	.325	.308	72	-4	-5	16	9	3	1	.984	-12	O	-1.9
1985	NY-A	34	56	4	17	1	0	1	6	3	12	.304	.339	.375	98	-0	-0	7	1	1	-0	.977	-7	O	-0.8
1986	NY-A	35	80	11	17	3	0	1	6	2	17	.213	.232	.287	41	-7	-7	5	3	0	1	1.000	-7	O/D	-0.8
1987	NY-A	68	149	21	35	10	0	5	20	6	35	.235	.269	.403	76	-6	-6	14	4	2	0	.989	-8	O	-1.4
1988	Sea-A	133	386	50	100	18	1	8	33	23	53	.259	.306	.373	85	-6	-9	46	27	3	6	.992	-5	*O/D	-1.0
1989	Sea-A	100	295	44	78	11	3	9	33	12	44	.264	.300	.407	94	-2	-3	35	10	4	1	.988	-7	O/D	-1.1
1990	Sea-A	127	355	40	92	14	3	4	33	22	52	.259	.310	.349	83	-8	-8	38	21	3	5	.990	-9	*O/D	-1.5
1991	Sea-A	66	177	35	54	6	2	6	23	10	27	.305	.349	.463	123	5	5	28	16	3	3	.981	-5	O/D	0.2
1992	Sea-A	108	294	42	76	11	1	5	27	14	49	.259	.294	.354	80	-8	-8	34	23	2	6	1.000	-10	O/D	-1.4
Total	9	776	1938	271	509	79	9	39	189	102	312	.263	.304	.373	86	-36	-41	222	114	21	22	.990	-63	O/D	-9.7

■ DENNIS COUGHLIN Coughlin, Dennis F. Deb: 4/27/1872

| 1872 | Nat-n | 8 | 38 | 5 | 12 | 0 | 0 | 0 | 6 | 0 | 0 | .316 | .316 | .316 | 81 | -0 | -2 | 4 | | | | | | /OS2 | -0.1 |

■ ED COUGHLIN Coughlin, Edward E. b: 8/5/1861, Hartford, Conn. d: 12/25/52, Hartford, Conn. Deb: 5/15/1884

| 1884 | Buf-N | 1 | 4 | 0 | 1 | 0 | 0 | 0 | 1 | 0 | 2 | .250 | .250 | .250 | 56 | -0 | -0 | 0 | | | | .750 | 0 | /OP | 0.0 |

■ BILL COUGHLIN Coughlin, William Paul "Scranton Bill" b: 7/12/1878, Scranton, Pa. d: 5/7/43, Scranton, Pa. BR/TR, 5'9", 140 lbs. Deb: 8/09/1899

1899	Was-N	6	24	2	3	0	1	0	3	1		.125	.160	.208	1	-3	-3	1	1			.818	-1	/3	-0.4
1901	Was-A	137	506	75	139	17	13	6	68	25		.275	.317	.395	98	-4	-3	71	16			.922	0	*3	-0.1
1902	Was-A	123	469	84	141	27	4	6	71	26		.301	.348	.414	109	6	5	80	29			.926	12	3S2	1.9
1903	Was-A	125	473	56	116	18	3	1	31	9		.245	.267	.302	69	-17	-18	48	30			.952	4	*3/S2	-1.3
1904	Was-A	65	265	28	73	15	4	0	17	9		.275	.307	.362	113	3	3	35	10			.939	2	3	0.8
	Det-A	56	206	22	47	6	0	0	17	5		.228	.257	.257	65	-9	-8	14	1			.929	-3	3	-1.1
	Yr	121	471	50	120	21	4	0	34	14		.255	.285	.316	92	-6	-5	48	11			.935	-1	*3	-0.3
1905	Det-A	137	489	48	123	20	6	0	44	34		.252	.309	.317	98	-0	-1	57	16			.914	-10	*3	-0.6
1906	Det-A	147	498	54	117	15	5	2	60	36		.235	.293	.297	83	-8	-10	58	31			.940	-11	*3	-1.7
1907	*Det-A	134	519	80	126	10	2	0	46	35		.243	.301	.270	79	-9	-11	51	15			.930	-10	*3	-1.9
1908	*Det-A	119	405	32	87	5	1	0	23	23		.215	.269	.232	61	-16	-18	29	10			.941	-15	*3	-3.3
Total	9	1049	3854	481	972	133	39	15	380	203		.252	.299	.319	87	-58	-63	442	159			.931	-31	3/S2	-7.7

■ MARLAN COUGHTRY Coughtry, James Marlan b: 9/11/34, Hollywood, Cal. BL/TR, 6'1", 170 lbs. Deb: 9/02/60

1960	Bos-A	15	19	3	3	0	0	0	0	5	8	.158	.333	.158	36	-1	-2	1	0	0	0	.909	1	2/3	0.0
1962	LA-A	11	22	0	4	0	0	0	2	0	6	.182	.182	.182	-2	-3	-3	1	0	0	0	.867	3	/32	0.0
	KC-A	6	11	1	2	0	0	0	1	4	3	.182	.400	.182	61	-0	-0	1	0	0	0	.917	1	/3	0.1
	Cle-A	3	2	1	1	0	0	0	1	1	1	.500	.667	.500	226	1	1	1	0	0	0	.000	0	H	0.1
	Yr	20	35	2	7	0	0	0	4	5	10	.200	.300	.200	38	-3	-3	3	0	0	0	.889	4	/32	0.2
Total	2	35	54	5	10	0	0	0	4	10	18	.185	.313	.185	37	-4	-4	4	0	0	0	.915	6	/23	0.2

■ BOB COULSON Coulson, Robert Jackson b: 6/17/1887, Courtney, Pa. d: 9/11/53, Washington, Pa. BR/TR, 5'10.5", 175 lbs. Deb: 8/04/08

1908	Cin-N	8	18	3	6	1	1	0	1	3		.333	.429	.500	202	2	2	4	0			1.000	1	/O	0.3
1910	Bro-N	25	89	14	22	3	4	1	13	6	14	.247	.302	.404	109	0	0	13	9			.922	0	O	0.0
1911	Bro-N	146	521	52	122	23	7	0	50	42	78	.234	.301	.305	73	-21	-18	57	32			.968	1	*O	-2.5
1914	Pit-F	18	64	7	13	1	0	0	3	7	10	.203	.282	.219	44	-5	-4	5	2			.931	-2	O	-0.8
Total	4	197	692	76	163	28	12	1	67	58	102	.236	.303	.315	78	-24	-20	79	43			.960	0	O	-3.0

■ CHIP COULTER Coulter, Thomas Lee b: 6/5/45, Steubenville, O. BB/TR, 5'10", 172 lbs. Deb: 9/18/69

| 1969 | StL-N | 6 | 19 | 3 | 6 | 1 | 1 | 0 | 4 | 2 | 6 | .316 | .381 | .474 | 138 | 1 | 1 | 3 | 0 | 1 | -1 | .960 | -0 | /2 | 0.1 |

■ CLINT COURTNEY Courtney, Clinton Dawson "Scrap Iron" b: 3/16/27, Hall Summit, La. d: 6/16/75, Rochester, N.Y. BL/TR, 5'8", 180 lbs. Deb: 9/29/51 C

1951	NY-A	1	2	0	0	0	0	0	0	0	1	.000	.333	.000	-5	-0	-0	0	0	0	0	.800	0	/C	0.0
1952	StL-A	119	413	38	118	24	3	5	50	39	26	.286	.349	.395	104	3	2	58	0	2	-1	**.996**	3	*C	1.0
1953	StL-A	106	355	28	89	12	2	4	19	25	20	.251	.302	.330	69	-15	-16	33	0	1	-1	.980	-5	*C	-1.7
1954	Bal-A	122	397	25	107	18	3	4	37	30	7	.270	.326	.360	95	-7	-4	46	0	1	0	.990	-3	*C	-0.1
1955	Chi-A	19	37	7	14	3	0	1	10	7	0	.378	.477	.541	168	4	4	8	0	0	0	1.000	-1	C	0.3
	Was-A	75	238	26	71	8	4	2	30	19	9	.298	.353	.391	105	-0	1	33	0	0	0	.983	-14	C	-1.0
	Yr	94	275	33	85	11	4	3	40	26	9	.309	.371	.411	114	4	5	42	0	0	0	.985	-15	C	-0.7

YEAR	TM/L	G	AB	R	H	2B	3B	HR	RBI	BB	SO	AVG	OBP	SLG	PRO+	BR	/A	RC	SB	CS	SBR	FA	FR	POS	TPR
1956	Was-A	101	283	31	85	20	3	5	44	20	10	.300	.365	.445	113	5	5	43	0	5	-3	.979	-15	C	-1.0
1957	Was-A	91	232	23	62	14	1	6	27	16	11	.267	.346	.414	108	2	3	33	0	0	0	.994	-1	C	0.4
1958	Was-A	134	450	46	113	18	0	8	62	48	23	.251	.335	.344	89	-7	-6	52	1	5	-3	.991	-3	*C	-0.4
1959	Was-A	72	189	19	44	4	1	2	18	20	19	.233	.310	.296	68	-8	-8	18	0	1	-1	.987	-13	C	-1.9
1960	Bal-A	83	154	14	35	3	0	1	12	30	14	.227	.380	.266	79	-3	-2	18	0	1	-1	.975	4	C	0.4
1961	KC-A	1	1	0	0	0	0	0	0	0	0	.000	.000	.000	-99	-0	-0	0	0	0	0	.000	0	H	0.0
	Bal-A	22	45	3	12	2	0	0	4	10	3	.267	.400	.311	95	0	0	6	0	0	0	1.000	1	C	0.2
	Yr	23	46	3	12	2	0	0	4	10	3	.261	.393	.304	91	-0	-0	6	0	0	0	1.000	1	C	0.2
Total	11	946	2796	260	750	126	17	38	313	264	143	.268	.341	.366	94	-26	-21	349	3	16	-9	.987	-45	C	-3.8
■ **ERNIE COURTNEY**	Courtney, Edward Ernest b: 1/20/1875, Des Moines, Iowa d: 2/29/20, Buffalo, N.Y. BL/TR, 5'10", Deb: 4/17/02																								
1902	Bos-N	48	165	23	36	3	0	0	17	13		.218	.295	.236	64	-6	-6	13	3			.974	-1	O/S	-1.0
	Bal-A	1	4	3	2	0	1	0	1	1		.500	.600	1.000	324	1	1	2	0			1.000	0	/3	0.1
1903	NY-A	25	79	7	21	3	3	1	8	7		.266	.341	.418	119	3	2	12	1			.916	-2	S/21	0.1
	Det-A	23	74	7	17	0	0	0	6	5		.230	.305	.230	64	-3	-3	6	1			.938	-4	3/S	-0.6
	Yr	48	153	14	38	3	3	1	14	12		.248	.324	.327	94	-0	-1	18	2			.921	-6	S3/21	-0.5
1905	Phi-N	155	601	77	165	14	7	2	77	47		.275	.334	.331	103	-0	3	77	17			.923	-17	*3	-0.9
1906	Phi-N	116	398	53	94	12	2	0	42	45		.236	.315	.276	85	-6	-6	38	6			.923	-11	31/OS	-1.6
1907	Phi-N	130	440	42	107	17	4	2	43	55		.243	.335	.314	105	3	4	51	6			.907	-8	31/O2S	-0.3
1908	Phi-N	60	160	14	29	3	0	0	6	15		.181	.260	.200	46	-9	-10	9	1			.915	-7	31/2S	-1.8
Total	6	558	1921	226	471	52	17	5	200	188		.245	.321	.298	91	-17	-14	208	35			.920	-49	3/1OS2	-6.0
■ **DEE COUSINEAU**	Cousineau, Edward Thomas b: 12/16/1898, Watertown, Mass. d: 7/14/51, Watertown, Mass. BR/TR, 6', 170 lbs. Deb: 10/06/23																								
1923	Bos-N	1	2	1	2	0	0	0	2	0	0	1.000	1.000	1.000	447	1	1	2	0	0	0	.000	0	/C	0.1
1924	Bos-N	3	2	0	0	0	0	0	0	0	0	.000	.000	.000	-99	-1	-1	0	0	0	0	.500	-1	/C	-0.1
1925	Bos-N	1	0	0	0	0	0	0	0	0	0	—	—	—	—	0	0	0	0	0	0	.000	0	/C	0.0
Total	3	5	4	1	2	0	0	0	2	0	0	.500	.500	.500	174	0	0	2	0	0	0	.500	-1	/C	0.0
■ **JACK COVENEY**	Coveney, John Patrick b: 6/10/1880, S.Natick, Mass. d: 3/28/61, Wayland, Mass. BR/TR, 5'9", 175 lbs. Deb: 9/19/03																								
1903	StL-N	4	14	0	2	0	0	0	0	0		.143	.143	.143	-19	-2	-2	0	0			.923	1	/C	-0.1
■ **SAM COVINGTON**	Covington, Clarence Otto b: 12/17/1892, Henryville, Tenn. d: 1/4/63, Denison, Tex. BL/TR, 6'1", 190 lbs. Deb: 8/25/13 F																								
1913	StL-A	20	60	3	9	0	1	0	4	4	6	.150	.203	.183	14	-7	-6	3	3			.994	3	1	-0.4
1917	Bos-N	17	66	8	13	2	0	1	10	5	5	.197	.264	.273	69	-3	-2	5	1			.994	0	1	-0.3
1918	Bos-N	3	3	0	1	0	0	0	0	0	0	.333	.333	.333	108	0	0	0	0			.000	0	H	0.0
Total	3	40	129	11	23	2	1	1	14	9	11	.178	.237	.233	43	-9	-9	8	4			.994	3	/1	-0.7
■ **WES COVINGTON**	Covington, John Wesley b: 3/27/32, Laurinburg, N.C. BL/TR, 6'1", 205 lbs. Deb: 4/19/56																								
1956	Mil-N	75	138	17	39	4	0	2	16	16	20	.283	.361	.355	100	-1	0	19	1	0	0	.979	-3	O	-0.4
1957	*Mil-N	96	328	51	93	4	8	21	65	29	44	.284	.345	.537	143	14	17	61	4	1	1	.981	0	O	1.3
1958	*Mil-N	90	294	43	97	12	1	24	74	20	35	.330	.382	.622	175	24	27	68	0	0	0	.953	-4	O	1.9
1959	Mil-N	103	373	38	104	17	3	7	45	26	41	.279	.331	.397	101	-4	-0	46	0	1	-1	.962	-3	O	-0.8
1960	Mil-N	95	281	25	70	16	1	10	35	15	37	.249	.290	.420	99	-4	-2	31	1	2	-1	.964	-5	O	-1.1
1961	Mil-N	9	21	3	4	1	0	0	0	2	4	.190	.261	.238	36	-2	-2	1	0	0	0	1.000	-2	/O	-0.4
	Chi-A	22	59	5	17	1	0	4	15	4	5	.288	.333	.508	123	2	2	9	0	0	0	.900	-1	O	0.0
	KC-A	17	44	3	7	0	0	1	6	4	7	.159	.260	.227	31	-4	-4	3	0	0	0	1.000	-2	O	-0.7
	Yr	39	103	8	24	1	0	5	21	8	12	.233	.301	.388	83	-3	-3	11	0	0	0	.941	-3	O	-0.7
	Phi-N	57	165	23	50	9	0	7	26	15	17	.303	.361	.485	124	5	5	28	0	0	0	.950	-5	O	-0.2
1962	Phi-N	116	304	36	86	12	1	9	44	19	44	.283	.329	.418	102	-1	0	40	0	0	0	.944	-10	O	-1.4
1963	Phi-N	119	353	46	107	24	1	17	64	26	56	.303	.354	.521	150	21	21	63	1	0	0	.937	-11	*O	0.7
1964	Phi-N	129	339	37	95	18	0	13	58	38	50	.280	.358	.448	127	12	12	55	0	0	0	.972	-12	*O	-0.4
1965	Phi-N	101	235	27	58	10	1	15	45	26	47	.247	.324	.489	128	7	8	37	0	0	0	.968	-3	O	0.3
1966	Chi-N	9	11	0	1	0	0	0	0	1	2	.091	.167	.091	-26	-2	-2	0	0	0	0	1.000	0	/O	-0.2
	*LA-N	37	33	1	4	0	1	1	6	6	5	.121	.293	.273	63	-2	-1	3	0	0	0	1.000	-0	/O	-0.2
	Yr	46	44	1	5	0	1	1	6	7	7	.114	.264	.227	41	-4	-3	3	0	0	0	1.000	-0	/O	-0.4
Total	11	1075	2978	355	832	128	17	131	499	247	414	.279	.339	.466	123	65	83	463	7	4	-0	.961	-61	O	-1.6
■ **BILLY COWAN**	Cowan, Billy Rolland b: 8/28/38, Calhoun City, Miss. BR/TR, 6', 170 lbs. Deb: 9/09/63																								
1963	Chi-N	14	36	1	9	1	1	1	2	0	11	.250	.250	.417	84	-1	-1	3	0	1	-1	.917	-1	O	-0.3
1964	Chi-N	139	497	52	120	16	4	19	50	18	128	.241	.269	.404	83	-10	-12	53	12	3	2	.968	-9	*O	-2.7
1965	NY-N	82	156	16	28	8	2	3	9	4	45	.179	.205	.314	45	-12	-11	9	3	2	-0	1.000	3	O/2S	-1.1
	Mil-N	19	27	4	5	1	0	0	0	0	9	.185	.185	.222	14	-3	-3	1	0	0	0	1.000	-0	O	-0.4
	Yr	101	183	20	33	9	2	3	9	4	54	.180	.202	.301	41	-15	-14	11	3	2	-0	1.000	3	O/2S	-1.5
1967	Phi-N	34	59	11	9	0	0	3	6	4	14	.153	.206	.305	44	-4	-4	4	1	0	0	1.000	-2	O/23	-0.8
1969	NY-A	32	48	5	8	0	0	1	3	3	9	.167	.216	.229	25	-5	-5	2	0	0	0	1.000	-2	O	-0.7
	Cal-A	28	56	10	17	1	0	4	10	3	9	.304	.350	.536	152	3	3	10	0	0	0	1.000	-0	O/1	0.3
	Yr	60	104	15	25	1	0	5	13	6	18	.240	.288	.394	93	-2	-1	11	0	0	0	1.000	-2	O/1	-0.4
1970	Cal-A	68	134	20	37	9	1	5	25	11	29	.276	.336	.470	124	3	4	21	0	1	-1	.929	-6	O1/3	-0.5
1971	Cal-A	74	174	12	48	8	0	4	20	7	41	.276	.304	.391	103	-2	-0	20	1	1	-0	1.000	-2	O/1	-0.5
1972	Cal-A	3	3	0	0	0	0	0	0	0	2	.000	.000	.000	-99	-1	-1	0	0	0	0	.000	0	H	-0.1
Total	8	493	1190	131	281	44	8	40	125	50	297	.236	.269	.387	83	-31	-31	124	17	8	0	.977	-18	O/132S	-6.8
■ **AL COWENS**	Cowens, Alfred Edward b: 10/25/51, Los Angeles, Cal. BR/TR, 6'2", 200 lbs. Deb: 4/06/74																								
1974	KC-A	110	269	28	65	7	1	1	25	23	38	.242	.304	.286	67	-10	-12	23	5	0	2	.988	-9	*O/3D	-2.4
1975	KC-A	120	328	44	91	13	8	4	42	28	36	.277	.342	.402	107	4	3	44	12	7	-1	.978	-10	*O/D	-1.1
1976	*KC-A	152	581	71	154	23	6	3	59	26	50	.265	.300	.341	87	-10	-11	57	23	16	-3	.986	5	*O/D	-1.5
1977	*KC-A	162	606	98	189	32	14	23	112	41	64	.312	.363	.525	138	31	30	109	16	12	-2	.982	3	*O/D	2.4
1978	*KC-A	132	485	63	133	24	8	5	63	31	54	.274	.326	.388	97	-1	-2	62	14	6	1	.990	2	*O/3D	-0.5
1979	KC-A	136	516	69	152	18	7	9	73	40	44	.295	.349	.409	102	3	1	71	10	8	-2	.986	-0	*O	-0.6
1980	Cal-A	34	119	11	27	5	0	1	17	12	21	.227	.303	.294	66	-6	-5	11	1	2	-1	1.000	1	O/D	-0.7
	Det-A	108	403	58	113	15	3	5	42	37	40	.280	.342	.370	93	-2	-3	51	5	6	-2	.986	2	*O/D	-0.8
	Yr	142	522	69	140	20	3	6	59	49	61	.268	.333	.352	87	-8	-9	61	6	8	-3	.989	3	*O/D	-1.5
1981	Det-A	85	253	27	66	11	4	1	18	22	36	.261	.322	.348	90	-2	-3	29	3	3	-1	.994	-6	O	-1.3
1982	Sea-A	146	560	72	151	39	8	20	78	46	81	.270	.326	.475	114	11	9	84	11	7	-1	.987	7	*O/D	1.1
1983	Sea-A	110	356	39	73	19	2	7	35	23	38	.205	.257	.329	58	-20	-22	28	10	2	2	.985	2	OD	-2.1
1984	Sea-A	139	524	60	145	34	2	15	78	27	83	.277	.315	.435	106	2	3	66	9	5	-0	.987	-2	*O/D	-0.4
1985	Sea-A	122	452	59	120	32	5	14	69	30	56	.265	.313	.451	105	3	2	56	0	0	0	.967	2	*O/D	0.0
1986	Sea-A	28	82	5	15	4	0	0	6	3	18	.183	.212	.232	20	-9	-9	4	1	0	0	.971	-0	O/D	-1.0
Total	13	1584	5534	704	1494	276	68	108	717	389	659	.270	.322	.403	98	-6	-18	694	120	74	-8	.985	-5	*O/D3	-8.9
■ **DICK COX**	Cox, Elmer Joseph b: 9/30/1897, Pasadena, Cal. d: 6/1/66, Morro Bay, Cal. BR/TR, 5'7.5", 158 lbs. Deb: 4/16/25																								
1925	Bro-N	122	434	68	143	23	10	7	64	37	29	.329	.382	.477	121	12	13	79	4	3	-1	.968	-4	*O	0.1
1926	Bro-N	124	398	53	118	17	4	1	45	46	20	.296	.375	.367	102	2	3	56	6			.964	-8	*O	-1.2
Total	2	246	832	121	261	40	14	8	109	83	49	.314	.379	.424	112	14	16	135	10	3		.966	-12	O	-1.1

■ FRANK COX Cox, Francis Bernhard "Runt" b: 8/29/1857, Waltham, Mass. d: 6/24/28, Hartford, Conn. 5'6", Deb: 8/13/1884

YEAR	TM/L	G	AB	R	H	2B	3B	HR	RBI	BB	SO	AVG	OBP	SLG	PRO+	BR	/A	RC	SB	CS	SBR	FA	FR	POS	TPR
1884	Det-N	27	102	6	13	3	1	0	4	2	36	.127	.144	.176	0	-11	-10	3				.812	-4	S	-1.2

■ JIM COX Cox, James Charles b: 5/28/50, Bloomington, Ill. BR/TR, 5'11", 175 lbs. Deb: 7/19/73

YEAR	TM/L	G	AB	R	H	2B	3B	HR	RBI	BB	SO	AVG	OBP	SLG	PRO+	BR	/A	RC	SB	CS	SBR	FA	FR	POS	TPR
1973	Mon-N	9	15	1	2	1	0	0	0	1	4	.133	.188	.200	7	-2	-2	1	0	0	0	.950	-1	/2	-0.2
1974	Mon-N	77	236	29	52	9	1	2	26	23	36	.220	.292	.292	61	-11	-13	20	2	3	-1	.968	15	2	0.4
1975	Mon-N	11	27	1	7	1	0	1	5	1	2	.259	.286	.407	87	-0	-1	2	1	0	0	1.000	0	/2	0.0
1976	Mon-N	13	29	2	5	0	1	0	2	2	2	.172	.226	.241	31	-3	-3	1	0	0	0	.958	1	2	-0.1
Total	4	110	307	33	66	11	2	3	33	27	44	.215	.281	.293	58	-16	-18	24	3	3	-1	.969	16	/2	0.1

■ JEFF COX Cox, Jeffrey Lindon b: 11/9/55, Los Angeles, Cal. BR/TR, 5'11", 170 lbs. Deb: 7/01/80

YEAR	TM/L	G	AB	R	H	2B	3B	HR	RBI	BB	SO	AVG	OBP	SLG	PRO+	BR	/A	RC	SB	CS	SBR	FA	FR	POS	TPR
1980	Oak-A	59	169	20	36	3	0	0	9	14	23	.213	.273	.231	43	-14	-12	12	8	5	-1	.979	-16	2	-2.5
1981	Oak-A	2	0	0	0	0	0	0	0	0	0	—	—	—	—	0	0	0	0	0	0	1.000	1	/2	0.1
Total	2	61	169	20	36	3	0	0	9	14	23	.213	.273	.231	43	-14	-12	12	8	5	-1	.979	-15	/2	-2.4

■ LARRY COX Cox, Larry Eugene b: 9/11/47, Bluffton, Ohio d: 2/17/90, Bellefontaine, Ohio BR/TR, 5'11", 190 lbs. Deb: 4/18/73 C

YEAR	TM/L	G	AB	R	H	2B	3B	HR	RBI	BB	SO	AVG	OBP	SLG	PRO+	BR	/A	RC	SB	CS	SBR	FA	FR	POS	TPR
1973	Phi-N	1	0	0	0	0	0	0	0	0	0	—	—	—	—	0	0	0	0	0	0	1.000	-0	/C	0.0
1974	Phi-N	30	53	5	9	2	0	0	4	4	9	.170	.241	.208	25	-5	-5	3	0	0	0	.990	0	C	-0.5
1975	Phi-N	11	5	0	1	0	0	0	1	1	0	.200	.333	.200	49	-0	-0	0	1	0	0	1.000	-0	C	0.0
1977	Sea-A	35	93	6	23	6	0	2	6	10	12	.247	.320	.376	90	-1	-1	11	1	1	-0	.970	-1	C	-0.2
1978	Chi-N	59	121	10	34	5	0	2	18	12	16	.281	.346	.372	90	0	-1	15	0	0	0	.967	2	C	0.1
1979	Sea-A	100	293	32	63	11	3	4	36	22	39	.215	.270	.314	56	-18	-19	24	2	1	0	.981	-2	C	-1.7
1980	Sea-A	105	243	18	49	6	2	4	20	19	36	.202	.260	.292	50	-17	-17	17	1	2	-1	**.993**	12	*C	-0.3
1981	Tex-A	5	13	0	3	1	0	0	0	0	4	.231	.231	.308	57	-1	-1	1	0	0	0	1.000	3	/C	0.3
1982	Chi-N	2	4	1	0	0	0	0	0	2	1	.000	.333	.000	1	-0	-0	0	0	0	0	1.000	1	/C	0.1
Total	9	348	825	72	182	31	5	12	85	70	117	.221	.282	.314	61	-42	-45	71	5	4	-1	.983	15	C	-2.2

■ BOBBY COX Cox, Robert Joseph b: 5/21/41, Tulsa, Okla. BR/TR, 5'11", 180 lbs. Deb: 4/14/68 MC

YEAR	TM/L	G	AB	R	H	2B	3B	HR	RBI	BB	SO	AVG	OBP	SLG	PRO+	BR	/A	RC	SB	CS	SBR	FA	FR	POS	TPR
1968	NY-A	135	437	33	100	15	1	7	41	41	85	.229	.302	.316	90	-6	-5	42	3	2	-0	.957	-5	*3	-1.1
1969	NY-A	85	191	17	41	7	1	2	17	34	41	.215	.336	.293	80	-5	-4	19	0	1	-1	.935	11	3/2	0.8
Total	2	220	628	50	141	22	2	9	58	75	126	.225	.313	.309	87	-11	-9	61	3	3	-1	.950	6	3/2	-0.3

■ BILLY COX Cox, William Richard b: 8/29/19, Newport, Pa. d: 3/30/78, Harrisburg, Pa. BR/TR, 5'10", 150 lbs. Deb: 9/20/41

YEAR	TM/L	G	AB	R	H	2B	3B	HR	RBI	BB	SO	AVG	OBP	SLG	PRO+	BR	/A	RC	SB	CS	SBR	FA	FR	POS	TPR
1941	Pit-N	10	37	4	10	3	1	0	2	3	2	.270	.325	.405	105	0	0	5	1			.943	2	S	0.3
1946	Pit-N	121	411	32	119	22	6	2	36	26	15	.290	.333	.387	101	1	-0	54	4			.935	-16	*S	-1.0
1947	Pit-N	132	529	75	145	30	7	15	54	29	28	.274	.313	.442	96	-4	-6	74	5			.968	-13	*S	-1.1
1948	Bro-N	88	237	36	59	13	2	3	15	38	19	.249	.353	.359	90	-1	-3	31	3			.958	-4	3/S2	-0.7
1949	*Bro-N	100	390	48	91	18	2	8	40	30	18	.233	.290	.351	68	-17	-19	39	5			.964	9	*3	-1.2
1950	Bro-N	119	451	62	116	17	2	8	44	35	24	.257	.311	.357	74	-17	-18	48	6			**.957**	12	*32/S	-0.6
1951	Bro-N	142	455	62	127	25	4	9	51	37	30	.279	.336	.411	98	-1	-2	64	5	5	-2	.967	-8	*3/S	-1.3
1952	*Bro-N	116	455	56	118	12	3	6	34	25	32	.259	.301	.338	76	-15	-15	43	10	12	-4	.970	-9	*3S/2	-3.0
1953	*Bro-N	100	327	44	95	18	1	10	44	37	21	.291	.363	.443	106	4	3	54	2	2	-1	.974	-2	3/S2	-0.1
1954	Bro-N	77	226	26	53	9	2	2	17	21	13	.235	.300	.319	59	-13	-14	21	0	0	0	.961	2	32/S	-1.2
1955	Bal-A	53	194	25	41	7	2	3	14	17	16	.211	.275	.314	63	-12	-10	16	1	2	-1	.969	-9	32/S	-2.0
Total	11	1058	3712	470	974	174	32	66	351	298	218	.262	.318	.380	85	-73	-82	448	42	21		.965	-36	3S/2	-11.9

■ TED COX Cox, William Ted b: 1/24/55, Oklahoma City, Okla BR/TR, 6'3", 195 lbs. Deb: 9/18/77

YEAR	TM/L	G	AB	R	H	2B	3B	HR	RBI	BB	SO	AVG	OBP	SLG	PRO+	BR	/A	RC	SB	CS	SBR	FA	FR	POS	TPR
1977	Bos-A	13	58	11	21	3	1	1	6	3	6	.362	.393	.500	127	3	2	12	0	0	0	.000	0	D	0.2
1978	Cle-A	82	227	14	53	7	0	1	19	16	30	.233	.287	.278	60	-12	-12	18	0	1	-1	.980	-5	O3D/1S	-2.0
1979	Cle-A	78	189	17	40	6	0	4	22	14	27	.212	.273	.307	56	-12	-12	14	3	4	-2	.964	0	3O/2	-1.4
1980	Sea-A	83	247	17	60	9	0	2	23	19	25	.243	.297	.304	64	-12	-12	21	0	0	0	.945	-2	3	-1.5
1981	Tor-A	16	50	6	15	4	0	2	9	5	10	.300	.364	.500	138	3	3	9	0	1	-1	.897	-4	3/1D	-0.3
Total	5	272	771	65	189	29	1	10	79	57	98	.245	.300	.324	71	-29	-31	75	3	6	-3	.947	-11	3/OD12S	-5.0

■ TOOTS COYNE Coyne, Martin Albert b: 10/20/1894, St.Louis, Mo. d: 9/18/39, St.Louis, Mo. TR , Deb: 9/28/14

YEAR	TM/L	G	AB	R	H	2B	3B	HR	RBI	BB	SO	AVG	OBP	SLG	PRO+	BR	/A	RC	SB	CS	SBR	FA	FR	POS	TPR
1914	Phi-A	1	2	0	0	0	0	0	0	0	2	.000	.000	.000	-99	-0	-0	0	0			1.000	-0	/3	-0.1

■ ESTEL CRABTREE Crabtree, Estel Crayton "Crabby" b: 8/19/03, Crabtree, Ohio d: 1/4/67, Logan, Ohio BL/TR, 6', 168 lbs. Deb: 4/18/29 C

YEAR	TM/L	G	AB	R	H	2B	3B	HR	RBI	BB	SO	AVG	OBP	SLG	PRO+	BR	/A	RC	SB	CS	SBR	FA	FR	POS	TPR
1929	Cin-N	1	1	0	0	0	0	0	0	0	0	.000	.000	.000	-99	-0	-0	0	0			.000	0	H	0.0
1931	Cin-N	117	443	70	119	12	12	4	37	23	33	.269	.309	.377	89	-11	-8	53	3			.974	10	*O/31	-0.5
1932	Cin-N	108	402	38	110	14	9	2	35	23	26	.274	.316	.368	86	-9	-8	48	2			.990	9	O	-0.5
1933	StL-N	23	34	6	9	3	0	0	3	2	3	.265	.306	.353	83	-1	-1	4	1			.947	-0	/O	-0.1
1941	StL-N	77	167	27	57	6	3	5	28	26	24	.341	.439	.503	154	15	14	39	1			1.000	-8	O/3	0.4
1942	StL-N	10	9	1	3	2	0	0	2	1	3	.333	.400	.556	166	1	1	2	0			.000	0	H	0.1
1943	Cin-N	95	254	25	70	12	0	2	26	25	17	.276	.345	.346	101	0	1	29	1			.939	-5	O	-0.8
1944	Cin-N	58	98	7	28	4	1	0	11	13	3	.286	.369	.347	106	1	1	12	0			1.000	-4	O/1	-0.4
Total	8	489	1408	174	396	53	25	13	142	113	109	.281	.339	.382	100	-4	0	186	8			.976	1	O/31	-1.8

■ HARRY CRAFT Craft, Harry Francis "Wildfire" b: 4/19/15, Ellisville, Miss. BR/TR, 6'1", 185 lbs. Deb: 9/19/37 MC

YEAR	TM/L	G	AB	R	H	2B	3B	HR	RBI	BB	SO	AVG	OBP	SLG	PRO+	BR	/A	RC	SB	CS	SBR	FA	FR	POS	TPR
1937	Cin-N	10	42	7	13	2	1	0	4	1	3	.310	.326	.405	102	-0	-0	5	0			1.000	0	O	0.0
1938	Cin-N	151	612	70	165	28	9	15	83	29	46	.270	.305	.418	100	-5	-3	77	3			.983	16	*O	0.9
1939	*Cin-N	134	502	58	129	20	7	13	67	27	54	.257	.299	.402	86	-11	-11	61	5			.981	3	*O	-1.3
1940	*Cin-N	115	422	47	103	18	5	6	48	17	46	.244	.277	.353	72	-17	-17	41	2			**.997**	6	*O/1	-1.7
1941	Cin-N	119	413	48	103	15	2	10	59	33	43	.249	.308	.368	90	-6	-7	46	4			.983	2	*O	-1.2
1942	Cin-N	37	113	7	20	2	1	0	6	3	11	.177	.205	.212	22	-11	-11	5	0			.987	1	O	-1.3
Total	6	566	2104	237	533	85	25	44	267	110	203	.253	.294	.380	85	-51	-49	236	14			.986	28	O/1	-4.6

■ ROD CRAIG Craig, Rodney Paul b: 1/12/58, Los Angeles, Cal. BB/TR, 6'1", 195 lbs. Deb: 9/11/79

YEAR	TM/L	G	AB	R	H	2B	3B	HR	RBI	BB	SO	AVG	OBP	SLG	PRO+	BR	/A	RC	SB	CS	SBR	FA	FR	POS	TPR
1979	Sea-A	16	52	9	20	8	1	0	6	1	5	.385	.396	.577	156	4	4	12	1	1	-0	.923	-2	O	0.1
1980	Sea-A	70	240	30	57	15	1	3	20	17	35	.237	.293	.346	74	-9	-9	22	3	6	-3	.987	-2	O	-1.6
1982	Cle-A	49	65	7	15	2	0	0	1	4	6	.231	.275	.262	49	-5	-4	4	3	1	0	.966	-4	O/D	-0.9
1986	Chi-A	10	10	3	2	0	0	0	0	2	2	.200	.333	.200	48	-1	-1	1	0	0	0	.000	-1	/O	-0.1
Total	4	145	367	49	94	25	2	3	27	24	48	.256	.305	.360	80	-10	-10	39	7	8	-3	.977	-9	O/D	-2.5

■ DOC CRAMER Cramer, Roger Maxwell "Flit" b: 7/22/05, Beach Haven, N.J. d: 9/9/90, Manahawkin, N.J. BL/TR, 6'2", 185 lbs. Deb: 9/18/29 C

YEAR	TM/L	G	AB	R	H	2B	3B	HR	RBI	BB	SO	AVG	OBP	SLG	PRO+	BR	/A	RC	SB	CS	SBR	FA	FR	POS	TPR
1929	Phi-A	2	6	0	0	0	0	0	0	0	2	.000	.000	.000	-97	-2	-2	0	0	0	0	1.000	1	/O	-0.1
1930	Phi-A	30	82	12	19	1	1	0	6	2	8	.232	.250	.268	30	-9	-9	5	0	0	0	.927	-2	O/S	-1.2
1931	*Phi-A	65	223	37	58	8	2	2	20	11	15	.260	.301	.341	64	-11	-12	23	2	1	0	.979	1	O	-1.4
1932	Phi-A	92	384	73	129	27	6	3	46	17	27	.336	.367	.461	109	7	5	64	3	1	0	.976	8	O	0.7
1933	Phi-A	152	661	109	195	27	8	8	75	36	24	.295	.331	.396	91	-9	-10	86	5	4	-1	.971	5	*O	-1.4
1934	Phi-A	153	649	99	202	29	9	6	46	40	35	.311	.353	.411	100	-4	-1	93	1	5	-3	.985	5	*O	-0.4
1935	Phi-A★	149	644	96	214	37	4	3	70	37	34	.332	.373	.416	105	4	4	99	6	7	-2	.975	4	*O	0.0
1936	Bos-A	154	643	99	188	31	7	0	41	49	20	.292	.347	.362	71	-25	-30	82	4	6	-2	.975	16	*O	-2.0
1937	Bos-A☆	133	560	90	171	22	11	0	51	35	14	.305	.351	.384	82	-13	-16	76	8	6	-1	.969	6	*O	-1.4
1938	Bos-A★	148	658	116	198	36	8	0	71	51	19	.301	.354	.380	80	-16	-21	87	4	9	-4	.986	9	*O/P	-1.9

YEAR	TM/L	G	AB	R	H	2B	3B	HR	RBI	BB	SO	AVG	OBP	SLG	PRO+	BR	/A	RC	SB	CS	SBR	FA	FR	POS	TPR
1939	Bos-A★	137	589	110	183	30	6	0	56	36	17	.311	.352	.382	85	-11	-14	77	3	3	-1	.984	2	*O	-1.7
1940	Bos-A☆	150	661	94	**200**	27	12	1	51	36	29	.303	.340	.384	84	-13	-16	86	3	5	-2	.969	-5	*O	-3.0
1941	Was-A	154	660	93	180	25	6	2	66	37	15	.273	.317	.338	77	-26	-22	71	4	1	1	.984	-7	*O	-3.7
1942	Det-A	151	630	71	166	26	4	0	43	43	18	.263	.314	.317	72	-19	-25	63	4	4	-1	.981	-0	*O	-3.6
1943	Det-A	140	606	79	182	18	4	1	43	31	13	.300	.335	.348	93	-1	-6	73	4	3	-1	.989	1	*O	-1.4
1944	Det-A	143	578	69	169	20	9	2	42	37	21	.292	.337	.369	96	0	-3	74	6	5	-1	.980	-8	*O	-2.1
1945	*Det-A†	141	541	62	149	22	8	6	58	36	21	.275	.324	.379	97	1	-3	65	2	9	-5	**.991**	-8	*O	-2.5
1946	Det-A	68	204	26	60	8	2	1	26	15	8	.294	.342	.368	93	-1	-2	26	3	0	1	1.000	-6	O	-1.0
1947	Det-A	73	157	21	42	2	2	2	30	20	5	.268	.350	.344	91	-1	-2	17	0	4	-2	.965	-2	O	-0.8
1948	Det-A	4	4	1	0	0	0	0	1	3	0	.000	.429	.000	19	-0	-0	0	0	0	0	1.000	-0	/O	0.0
Total	20	2239	9140	1357	2705	396	109	37	842	572	345	.296	.340	.375	87	-146	-184	1168	62	73	-25	.979	19	*O/PS	-28.9

■ DICK CRAMER
Cramer, William B. b: Brooklyn, N.Y. d: 8/12/1885, Camden, N.J. Deb: 5/12/1883

YEAR	TM/L	G	AB	R	H	2B	3B	HR	RBI	BB	SO	AVG	OBP	SLG	PRO+	BR	/A	RC	SB	CS	SBR	FA	FR	POS	TPR
1883	NY-N	2	6	0	0	0	0	0	0	1	5	.000	.143	.000	-52	-1	-1	0				.000	-1	/O	-0.2

■ DEL CRANDALL
Crandall, Delmar Wesley b: 3/5/30, Ontario, Cal. BR/TR, 6'1", 195 lbs. Deb: 6/17/49 MC

YEAR	TM/L	G	AB	R	H	2B	3B	HR	RBI	BB	SO	AVG	OBP	SLG	PRO+	BR	/A	RC	SB	CS	SBR	FA	FR	POS	TPR
1949	Bos-N	67	228	21	60	10	1	4	34	9	18	.263	.291	.368	80	-8	-7	22	2			.982	7	C	0.4
1950	Bos-N	79	255	21	56	11	0	4	37	13	24	.220	.257	.310	52	-20	-17	20	0			.967	3	C/1	-1.2
1953	Mil-N†	116	382	55	104	13	1	15	51	33	47	.272	.330	.429	102	-3	0	53	2	1	0	.986	15	*C	1.9
1954	Mil-N☆	138	463	60	112	18	2	21	64	40	56	.242	.306	.425	94	-10	-6	57	0	3	-2	.989	14	*C	1.2
1955	Mil-N★	133	440	61	104	15	2	26	62	40	56	.236	.303	.457	103	-3	0	58	2	1	0	.985	-2	*C	0.3
1956	Mil-N†	112	311	37	74	14	2	16	48	35	30	.238	.317	.450	110	1	3	44	1	2	-1	**.996**	3	*C	0.9
1957	*Mil-N	118	383	45	97	11	2	15	46	30	38	.253	.309	.410	98	-5	-2	45	1	2	-1	.987	-8	*C/O1	-0.7
1958	*Mil-N★	131	427	50	116	23	1	18	63	48	38	.272	.351	.457	122	7	12	66	4	1	1	**.990**	6	*C	2.5
1959	Mil-N★	150	518	65	133	19	2	21	72	46	48	.257	.321	.423	105	-4	2	65	5	1	1	**.994**	6	*C	1.8
1960	Mil-N★	142	537	81	158	14	1	19	77	34	36	.294	.341	.430	118	6	11	74	4	6	-2	.988	-15	*C	0.3
1961	Mil-N	15	30	3	6	3	0	0	1	1	0	.200	.226	.300	40	-3	-2	2	0	0	0	1.000	-2	/C	-0.4
1962	Mil-N★	107	350	35	104	12	3	8	45	27	24	.297	.351	.417	108	3	4	46	3	4	-2	**.994**	-4	C/1	0.2
1963	Mil-N	86	259	18	52	4	0	3	28	18	22	.201	.253	.251	46	-18	-18	14	1	4	-2	.991	5	C/1	-1.4
1964	SF-N	69	195	12	45	8	1	3	11	22	21	.231	.309	.328	78	-5	-5	18	0	3	-2	.993	13	C	0.8
1965	Pit-N	60	140	11	30	2	0	2	10	14	10	.214	.290	.271	59	-7	-7	11	1	0	0	.996	5	C	0.0
1966	Cle-A	50	108	10	25	2	0	4	8	14	9	.231	.320	.361	95	-1	-1	12	0	0	0	.991	15	C	1.8
Total	16	1573	5026	585	1276	179	18	179	657	424	477	.254	.315	.404	97	-69	-33	607	26	28		.989	61	*C/1O	8.4

■ DOC CRANDALL
Crandall, James Otis b: 10/8/1887, Wadena, Ind. d: 8/17/51, Bell, Cal. BR/TR, 5'10.5", 180 lbs. Deb: 4/24/08

YEAR	TM/L	G	AB	R	H	2B	3B	HR	RBI	BB	SO	AVG	OBP	SLG	PRO+	BR	/A	RC	SB	CS	SBR	FA	FR	POS	TPR
1908	NY-N	34	72	8	16	4	0	2	6	4		.222	.263	.361	94	-0	-1	7	0			.985	-2	P/2	0.0
1909	NY-N	30	41	4	10	0	1	1	1	1		.244	.262	.366	93	-1	-1	4	0			.941	2	P	0.0
1910	NY-N	45	73	10	25	2	4	1	13	5	7	.342	.385	.521	163	5	5	15	0			.984	-2	P/S	0.0
1911	*NY-N	61	113	12	27	1	4	2	21	8	16	.239	.295	.372	83	-3	-3	13	2			.958	-0	P/S2	-0.3
1912	*NY-N	50	80	9	25	6	2	0	19	6	7	.313	.360	.438	114	2	1	13	0			.957	0	P/21	0.0
1913	*NY-N	31	25	4	7	2	1	0	2	1	5	.280	.308	.440	111	0	0	3	0			1.000	1	P/2	0.1
	StL-N	2	2	0	0	0	0	0	0	0	2	.000	.000	.000	-99	-1	-1	0	0			.000	0	H	-0.1
	*NY-N	15	22	3	8	2	0	0	2	2	3	.364	.417	.455	148	1	1	4	0			1.000	1	P	0.0
	Yr	48	49	7	15	4	1	0	4	3	10	.306	.346	.429	120	1	1	7	0			1.000	2	P/2	0.0
1914	StL-F	118	278	40	86	16	5	2	41	58	32	.309	.429	.424	136	19	17	54	3			.926	-18	2P/SO	-0.5
1915	StL-F	84	141	18	40	2	2	1	19	27	15	.284	.406	.348	116	6	5	22	4			.958	1	P	0.0
1916	StL-A	16	12	0	1	0	0	0	0	2	4	.083	.214	.083	-11	-2	-1	0	0			.000	-0	/P	0.0
1918	Bos-N	14	28	1	8	0	0	0	2	4	3	.286	.375	.286	107	0	0	3	0			1.000	0	/PO	0.0
Total	10	500	887	109	253	35	19	9	126	118	94	.285	.371	.398	118	28	24	137	9			.962	-17	P/2SO1	-0.8

■ ED CRANE
Crane, Edward Nicholas "Cannon-Ball" b: 5/1862, Boston, Mass. d: 9/19/1896, Rochester, N.Y. BR/TR, 5'10.5", 204 lbs. Deb: 4/17/1884

YEAR	TM/L	G	AB	R	H	2B	3B	HR	RBI	BB	SO	AVG	OBP	SLG	PRO+	BR	/A	RC	SB	CS	SBR	FA	FR	POS	TPR
1884	Bos-U	101	428	83	122	23	6	12		14		.285	.308	.451	156	23	24	61				.826	-5	OC/1P	1.7
1885	Pro-N	1	2	0	0	0	0	0	0	1	1	.000	.333	.000	16	-0	-0	0				.500	0	/O	0.0
	Buf-N	13	51	5	14	0	1	2	9	3	8	.275	.315	.431	135	2	2	7				.769	-3	O	-0.1
	Yr	14	53	5	14	0	1	2	9	4	9	.264	.316	.415	131	2	2	7				.750	-2	O	-0.1
1886	Was-N	80	292	20	50	11	3	0	20	13	54	.171	.207	.229	34	-23	-21	16	8			.866	3	OP/C	-1.6
1888	*NY-N	12	37	3	6	2	0	1	2	3	11	.162	.225	.297	68	-1	-1	3	1			.867	1	P	0.0
1889	*NY-N	29	103	16	21	1	0	2	11	13	21	.204	.293	.272	60	-5	-5	10	6			.762	-4	P/1	0.0
1890	NY-P	43	146	27	46	5	4	0	16	10	26	.315	.363	.404	98	1	-1	24	5			.846	-3	P	0.0
1891	Cin-a	34	110	13	17	0	0	1	7	8	28	.155	.212	.182	13	-12	-14	5	4			.822	-2	P/O	-0.1
	Cin-N	15	46	3	5	0	0	0	2	3	12	.109	.163	.109	-19	-7	-7	1	3			.906	0	P	0.0
1892	NY-N	48	163	20	40	1	1	0	14	11	30	.245	.297	.264	73	-5	-5	14	2			.821	-1	P/O	-0.1
1893	NY-N	12	26	8	12	1	0	0	3	7	0	.462	.576	.500	189	4	4	8	0			.889	-1	P/1O	0.0
	Bro-N	3	5	1	2	1	0	0	0	0	0	.400	.400	.600	174	0	0	1	0			.500	-1	/PO	0.0
	Yr	15	31	9	14	2	0	0	3	7	0	.452	.553	.516	189	5	5	9	0			.850	-2	P/O1	0.0
Total	9	391	1409	199	335	45	15	18	84	86	191	.238	.283	.329	87	-24	-24	150	29			.842	-15	PO/C1	-0.2

■ FRED CRANE
Crane, Frederic William Hotchkiss b: 11/4/1840, Saybrook, Conn. d: 4/27/25, Brooklyn, N.Y. Deb: 5/26/1873

YEAR	TM/L	G	AB	R	H	2B	3B	HR	RBI	BB	SO	AVG	OBP	SLG	PRO+	BR	/A	RC	SB	CS	SBR	FA	FR	POS	TPR
1873	Res-n	1	4	0	1	0	0	0	1	0	0	.250	.250	.250	52	-0	-0	0						/2	0.0
1875	Atl-n	21	80	7	17	1	0	0		0		.213	.213	.225	59	-4	-2	4						1/O	-0.2
Total	2 n	22	84	7	18	1	0	0		0		.214	.214	.226	59	-4	-2	4						/1O2	-0.2

■ SAM CRANE
Crane, Samuel Byren "Lucky" or "Red" b: 9/13/1894, Harrisburg, Pa. d: 11/12/55, Philadelphia, Pa. BR/TR, 5'11.5", 154 lbs. Deb: 10/02/14

YEAR	TM/L	G	AB	R	H	2B	3B	HR	RBI	BB	SO	AVG	OBP	SLG	PRO+	BR	/A	RC	SB	CS	SBR	FA	FR	POS	TPR
1914	Phi-A	2	6	0	0	0	0	0	0	2	3	.000	.250	.000	-25	-1	-1	0	0			.929	1	/S	0.0
1915	Phi-A	8	23	3	2	2	0	0	1	0	4	.087	.087	.174	-23	-4	-3	0	0			.900	2	/S2	-0.1
1916	Phi-A	2	4	1	1	0	0	0	0	2	1	.250	.500	.250	132	0	0	1	0			1.000	-0	/S	0.0
1917	Was-A	32	95	6	17	2	0	0	4	4	14	.179	.212	.200	26	-9	-8	4	0			.889	-4	S	-1.3
1920	Cin-N	54	144	20	31	4	0	0	9	7	9	.215	.261	.243	46	-10	-10	9	5	4	-1	.945	-9	S3/2O	-1.9
1921	Cin-N	73	215	20	50	10	2	0	16	14	14	.233	.292	.298	59	-13	-12	19	2	5	-2	.953	-17	S/3O	-2.5
1922	Bro-N	3	8	1	2	1	0	0	0	0	1	.250	.333	.375	83	-0	-0	1	0	0	0	.875	2	/S	0.2
Total	7	174	495	51	103	19	2	0	30	29	46	.208	.262	.255	46	-36	-34	34	7	9		.931	-25	S/32O	-5.6

■ SAM CRANE
Crane, Samuel Newhall b: 1/2/1854, Springfield, Mass. d: 6/26/25, New York, N.Y. BR/TR, Deb: 5/01/1880 M

YEAR	TM/L	G	AB	R	H	2B	3B	HR	RBI	BB	SO	AVG	OBP	SLG	PRO+	BR	/A	RC	SB	CS	SBR	FA	FR	POS	TPR
1880	Buf-N	10	31	4	4	0	0	0	2	1	8	.129	.156	.129	-2	-3	-3	1				.866	-2	2/OM	-0.5
1883	NY-a	96	349	57	82	8	5	0		13		.235	.262	.287	74	-9	-11	27				.859	-11	*2/O	-1.8
1884	Cin-U	80	309	56	72	9	3	1		11		.233	.259	.291	80	-4	-8	24				.858	-9	*2M	-1.4
1885	Det-N	68	245	23	47	4	6	1	20	13	45	.192	.233	.269	62	-10	-10	16				.908	-5	2	-1.2
1886	Det-N	47	185	24	26	2	2	1	12	8	34	.141	.176	.189	11	-19	-20	8	8			.903	1	2/SO	-1.7
	StL-N	39	116	10	20	3	1	0	7	13	27	.172	.256	.216	48	-7	-6	8	6			.897	-11	2	-1.4
	Yr	86	301	34	46	5	3	1	19	21	61	.153	.208	.199	25	-27	-26	16	14			.900	-10	2/SO	-3.1
1887	Was-N	7	30	6	9	1	1	0	1	1	6	.300	.323	.400	107	-0	0	6	5			.865	-1	/S	0.0
1890	NY-N	2	6	0	0	0	0	0	0	0	1	.000	.000	.000	-99	-1	-1	0	1			.778	-1	/1O	-0.2
	Pit-N	22	82	3	16	3	0	0	3	0	5	.195	.205	.232	32	-7	-6	5	5			.880	3	2/SO	-0.1
	NY-N	2	6	0	0	0	0	0	0	0	1	.000	.000	.000	-99	-1	-1	0	0			1.000	1	/2	-0.1

YEAR	TM/L	G	AB	R	H	2B	3B	HR	RBI	BB	SO	AVG	OBP	SLG	PRO+	BR	/A	RC	SB	CS	SBR	FA	FR	POS	TPR
	Yr	26	94	3	16	3	0	0	3	0	7	.170	.179	.202	13	-10	-9	5	6			.883	3	2/SO1	-0.4
Total	7	373	1359	183	276	30	18	3	45	60	127	.203	.237	.258	57	-64	-68	94	25			.878	-34	2/SO1	-8.4
■ **GAVVY CRAVATH**	Cravath, Clifford Carlton "Cactus" b: 3/23/1881, Escondido, Cal. d: 5/23/63, Laguna Beach, Cal. BR/TR, 5'10.5", 186 lbs. Deb: 4/18/08 MC																								
1908	Bos-A	94	277	43	71	10	11	1	34	38		.256	.354	.383	136	13	12	40	6			.925	-2	O/1	0.9
1909	Chi-A	19	50	7	9	0	0	1	8	19		.180	.406	.240	109	2	2	6	3			.944	-2	O	-0.1
	Was-A	4	6	0	0	0	0	0	1	1		.000	.143	.000	-57	-1	-1	0	0			1.000	1	/O	0.0
	Yr	23	56	7	9	0	0	1	9	20		.161	.382	.214	93	1	1	6	3			.947	-2	O	-0.1
1912	Phi-N	130	436	63	124	30	9	11	70	47	77	.284	.358	.470	118	14	10	78	15			.966	5	*O	0.9
1913	Phi-N	147	525	78	**179**	34	14	**19**	**128**	55	63	.341	.407	**.568**	**169**	**50**	**48**	**120**	10			.958	-4	*O	3.9
1914	Phi-N	149	499	76	149	27	8	**19**	100	83	72	.299	.402	.499	**157**	**43**	**39**	103	14			.930	3	*O	3.8
1915	*Phi-N	150	522	**89**	149	31	7	**24**	**115**	**86**	77	.285	**.393**	**.510**	**170**	**47**	**46**	**105**	11	9	-2	.946	9	*O	**5.0**
1916	Phi-N	137	448	70	127	21	8	11	70	64	89	.283	**.379**	.440	146	29	27	80	9			.966	-3	*O	2.0
1917	Phi-N	140	503	70	141	29	16	**12**	83	70	57	.280	.369	.473	151	35	32	88	6			.946	-3	*O	2.4
1918	Phi-N	121	426	43	99	27	5	**8**	54	54	46	.232	.320	.376	105	6	3	51	7			.931	-4	*O	-0.8
1919	Phi-N	83	214	34	73	18	5	**12**	45	35	21	.341	.438	.640	207	**32**	30	61	8			.914	-5	OM	2.4
1920	Phi-N	46	45	2	13	5	0	1	11	9	12	.289	.407	.467	144	3	3	9	0	0	0	.667	-2	/OM	0.1
Total	11	1220	3951	575	1134	232	83	119	719	561	514	.287	.380	.478	149	273	251	742	89	9		.944	-6	*O/1	20.5
■ **BILL CRAVER**	Craver, William H. b: 6/1844, Troy, N.Y. d: 6/17/01, Troy, N.Y. BR/TR, 5'9", 160 lbs. Deb: 5/09/1871 M																								
1871	Tro-n	27	118	26	38	8	1	0	26	3	0	.322	.339	.407	112	2	2	19	6					2/SC1M	0.0
1872	Bal-n	35	180	55	50	5	3	0	24	5	2	.278	.297	.339	91	-1	-3	20						C/O32M	-0.1
1873	Bal-n	41	196	45	57	7	4	0	27	2	3	.291	.298	.367	95	-1	-1	21						CS/O1	-0.2
1874	Phi-n	55	267	68	94	13	11	0		4		.352	.362	.483	161	19	17	48						*2/CM	1.2
1875	Cen-n	14	65	8	18	5	2	0		0		.277	.277	.415	148	2	3	8						/S31M	0.2
	Ath-n	54	260	71	83	11	11	2		4		.319	.330	.469	156	18	14	41						2/C	1.1
	Yr	68	325	79	101	16	**13**	2		4		.311	.319	.458	155	21	17	49						2/S31C	1.3
1876	NY-N	56	246	24	55	4	0	0	22	2	7	.224	.230	.240	65	-11	-6	14				.814	-23	2C/S	-2.5
1877	Lou-N	57	238	33	63	5	2	0	29	5	11	.265	.280	.303	71	-4	-11	21				.904	-1	*S	-0.9
Total	5 n	226	1086	273	340	49	32	2	77	18	5	.313	.324	.423	129	39	32	157						2/CSO31	2.2
Total	2	113	484	57	118	9	2	0	51	7	18	.244	.255	.271	69	-15	-17	35				.897	-23	/S2C	-3.4
■ **PAT CRAWFORD**	Crawford, Clifford Rankin b: 1/28/02, Society Hill, S.C. BL/TR, 5'11", 170 lbs. Deb: 4/18/29																								
1929	NY-N	65	57	13	17	3	0	3	24	11	5	.298	.412	.509	127	3	3	12	1			1.000	-0	/13	0.2
1930	NY-N	25	76	11	21	3	2	3	17	7	2	.276	.345	.487	100	-0	-0	13	0			.966	-4	2/1	-0.3
	Cin-N	76	224	24	65	7	1	3	26	23	10	.290	.359	.371	81	-8	-6	30	2			.969	-8	21	-1.2
	Yr	101	300	35	86	10	3	6	43	30	12	.287	.355	.400	86	-8	-6	43	2			.968	-12	21	-1.5
1933	StL-N	91	224	24	60	8	2	0	21	14	9	.268	.317	.321	78	-5	-6	23	1			.986	3	12/3	-0.6
1934	*StL-N	61	70	3	19	2	0	0	16	5	3	.271	.320	.300	63	-3	-4	7	0			.900	2	/32	-0.2
Total	4	318	651	75	182	23	5	9	104	60	29	.280	.344	.372	85	-14	-13	85	4			.969	-8	/213	-2.1
■ **FORREST CRAWFORD**	Crawford, Forrest A. b: 5/10/1881, Rockdale, Tex. d: 3/29/08, Austin, Tex. BL/TR, Deb: 7/30/06																								
1906	StL-N	45	145	8	30	3	1	0	11	7		.207	.243	.241	54	-8	-8	9	1			.927	-10	S/3	-1.8
1907	StL-N	7	22	0	5	0	0	0	3	2		.227	.292	.227	65	-1	-1	2	0			.912	-1	/S	-0.2
Total	2	52	167	8	35	3	1	0	14	9		.210	.250	.240	55	-9	-8	11	1			.924	-10	/S3	-2.0
■ **GEORGE CRAWFORD**	Crawford, George Deb: 10/08/1890																								
1890	Phi-a	5	17	1	2	0	0	0		0		.118	.118	.118	-30	-3	-3	0	1			1.000	1	/OS	-0.2
■ **GLENN CRAWFORD**	Crawford, Glenn Martin "Shorty" b: 12/2/13, North Branch, Mich. d: 1/2/72, Saginaw, Mich. BL/TR, 5'9", 165 lbs. Deb: 4/22/45																								
1945	StL-N	4	3	0	0	0	0	0	0	1	0	.000	.250	.000	-26	-0	-0	0	0			.000	-1	/O	-0.1
	Phi-N	82	302	41	89	13	2	2	24	36	15	.295	.372	.371	110	4	5	45	5			.976	-2	OS2	0.4
	Yr	86	305	41	89	13	2	2	24	37	15	.292	.370	.367	108	3	4	45	5			.976	-2	OS2	0.3
1946	Phi-N	1	1	0	0	0	0	0	0	0	0	.000	.000	.000	-99	-0	-0	0	0			.000	0	H	0.0
Total	2	87	306	41	89	13	2	2	24	37	15	.291	.369	.366	108	3	4	45	5				-2	/OS2	0.3
■ **KEN CRAWFORD**	Crawford, Kenneth Daniel b: 10/31/1894, South Bend, Ind. d: 11/11/76, Pittsburgh, Pa. BL/TR, 5'9", 145 lbs. Deb: 9/06/15																								
1915	Bal-F	23	82	4	20	2	1	0	7	1	18	.244	.253	.293	58	-4	-5	6	0			.978	-2	1/O	-0.8
■ **JAKE CRAWFORD**	Crawford, Rufus b: 3/20/28, Campbell, Mo. BR/TR, 6'1.5", 185 lbs. Deb: 9/07/52																								
1952	StL-A	7	11	1	2	1	0	0	0	1	5	.182	.250	.273	44	-1	-1	1	1	0	0	1.000	-0	/O	-0.1
■ **SAM CRAWFORD**	Crawford, Samuel Earl "Wahoo Sam" b: 4/18/1880, Wahoo, Neb. d: 6/15/68, Hollywood, Cal. BL/TL, 6', 190 lbs. Deb: 9/10/1899 H																								
1899	Cin-N	31	127	25	39	3	7	1	20	2		.307	.318	.465	111	1	1	21	6			.970	2	O	0.1
1900	Cin-N	101	389	68	101	15	15	7	59	28		.260	.314	.429	107	0	2	59	14			.948	12	*O	0.5
1901	Cin-N	131	515	91	170	20	16	**16**	104	37		.330	.378	.524	172	37	42	110	13			.923	3	*O	3.4
1902	Cin-N	140	555	92	185	18	**22**	3	78	47		.333	.386	.461	147	39	32	108	16			.932	4	*O	2.8
1903	Det-A	137	550	88	184	23	**25**	4	89	25		.335	.366	.489	159	35	36	110	18			.960	4	*O	3.2
1904	Det-A	150	562	49	143	22	16	2	73	44		.254	.309	.361	115	7	9	72	20			.973	4	*O	0.5
1905	Det-A	154	575	73	171	38	10	6	75	50		.297	.357	.430	148	31	31	99	22			**.988**	11	*O1	3.9
1906	Det-A	145	563	65	166	25	16	2	72	38		.295	.341	.407	130	21	19	89	24			.984	1	*O1	1.5
1907	*Det-A	144	582	**102**	188	34	17	4	81	37		.323	.366	.460	158	39	37	108	18			.965	8	*O/1	4.2
1908	*Det-A	152	591	102	184	33	16	**7**	80	37		.311	.354	.457	157	38	35	100	15			.970	-8	*O1	2.4
1909	*Det-A	156	589	83	185	**35**	14	6	97	47		.314	.366	.452	151	37	34	108	30			.965	-7	*O1	2.4
1910	Det-A	154	588	83	170	26	**19**	5	**120**	37		.289	.332	.423	128	21	17	89	20			.963	-11	*O/1	-0.1
1911	Det-A	146	574	109	217	36	14	7	115	61		.378	.438	.526	160	52	48	147	37			.975	-12	*O	2.8
1912	Det-A	149	581	81	189	30	21	4	109	42		.325	.373	.470	145	28	30	116	41			.984	-17	*O	0.6
1913	Det-A	153	609	78	193	32	**23**	9	83	52	28	.317	.371	.489	154	36	37	110	13			.964	-10	*O1	2.1
1914	Det-A	157	582	74	183	22	**26**	8	**104**	69	31	.314	.388	.483	157	42	40	113	25	16	-2	.977	-8	*O	2.6
1915	Det-A	156	612	81	183	31	**19**	4	**112**	66	29	.299	.367	.431	132	27	24	101	24	14	-1	.974	-14	*O	0.1
1916	Det-A	100	322	41	92	11	13	0	42	37	10	.286	.359	.401	124	11	9	51	10			.978	-10	O/1	-0.6
1917	Det-A	61	104	6	18	4	0	2	12	4	6	.173	.204	.269	44	-7	-7	6	0			.988	-3	1/O	-1.2
Total	19	2517	9570	1391	2961	458	309	97	1525	760	104	.309	.362	.452	143	494	475	1715	366	30		.965	-50	*O1	31.2
■ **WILLIE CRAWFORD**	Crawford, Willie Murphy b: 9/7/46, Los Angeles, Cal. BL/TL, 6'1", 205 lbs. Deb: 9/16/64																								
1964	LA-N	10	16	3	5	1	0	0	0	1	7	.313	.353	.375	113	0	0	2	1	1	-0	1.000	0	/O	0.0
1965	*LA-N	52	27	10	4	0	0	0	0	2	8	.148	.207	.148	2	-3	-3	1	2	0	1	1.000	3	/O	0.0
1966	LA-N	6	0	1	0	0	0	0	0	0	0	—	—	—	—	0	0	0	0	0	0	.000	0	R	0.0
1967	LA-N	4	4	0	1	0	0	0	0	1	3	.250	.400	.250	98	0	0	1	0	0	0	.000	-0	/O	0.0
1968	LA-N	61	175	25	44	12	1	4	14	20	64	.251	.335	.400	130	4	6	24	1	3	-2	.966	1	O	0.3
1969	LA-N	129	389	64	96	17	5	11	41	49	85	.247	.331	.401	112	2	5	52	4	5	-2	.973	-6	*O	-0.8
1970	LA-N	109	299	48	70	8	6	8	40	33	88	.234	.314	.381	89	-7	-5	36	4	4	-1	.960	4	O	-0.5
1971	LA-N	114	342	64	96	16	6	9	40	28	49	.281	.337	.442	126	8	10	51	5	2	0	.981	-9	O	-0.3
1972	LA-N	96	243	28	61	7	3	8	27	35	55	.251	.350	.403	116	5	6	34	4	2	0	.983	-5	O	-0.2
1973	LA-N	145	457	75	135	26	2	14	66	78	91	.295	.399	.453	142	25	27	88	12	5	1	.978	0	*O	2.3

YEAR	TM/L	G	AB	R	H	2B	3B	HR	RBI	BB	SO	AVG	OBP	SLG	PRO+	BR	/A	RC	SB	CS	SBR	FA	FR	POS	TPR
1974	*LA-N	139	468	73	138	23	4	11	61	64	88	.295	.380	.432	132	18	20	77	7	8	-3	.966	-8	*O	0.5
1975	LA-N	124	373	46	98	15	2	9	46	49	43	.263	.348	.386	108	2	4	52	5	5	-2	.990	-6	*O	-0.7
1976	StL-N	120	392	49	119	17	5	9	50	37	53	.304	.365	.441	127	14	14	62	2	1	0	.982	-2	*O	0.8
1977	Hou-N	42	114	14	29	3	0	2	18	16	10	.254	.346	.333	91	-2	-1	14	0	0	0	.959	-5	O	-0.7
	Oak-A	59	136	7	25	7	1	1	16	18	20	.184	.279	.272	52	-9	-9	10	0	0	0	.978	2	OD	-0.8
Total	14	1210	3435	507	921	152	35	86	419	431	664	.268	.351	.408	117	56	74	505	47	36	-8	.975	-28	O/D	-0.1
■ **GEORGE CREAMER**	Creamer, George W. (b: George W. Triebel) b: 1855, Philadelphia, Pa. d: 6/27/1886, Philadelphia, Pa. BR/TR, 6'2", Deb: 5/01/1878 M																								
1878	Mil-N	50	193	30	41	7	3	0	15	5	15	.212	.232	.280	63	-7	-8	13				.839	-5	2O/3	-1.1
1879	Syr-N	15	60	3	13	2	0	0	3	1	2	.217	.230	.250	65	-3	-2	4				.825	-10	2/SO	-1.0
1880	Wor-N	85	306	40	61	6	3	0	27	4	21	.199	.210	.239	47	-15	-18	16				.883	-7	*2	-2.0
1881	Wor-N	80	309	42	64	9	2	0	25	11	27	.207	.234	.249	49	-16	-19	18				.904	-9	*2	-2.3
1882	Wor-N	81	286	27	65	16	6	1	29	14	24	.227	.263	.336	88	-3	-4	26				.907	11	*2	0.8
1883	Pit-a	91	369	54	94	7	9	0		20		.255	.293	.322	103	-0	2	36				.897	9	*2	1.1
1884	Pit-a	98	339	38	62	8	5	0		16		.183	.224	.236	52	-17	-18	18				**.937**	16	*2M	0.1
Total	7	500	1862	234	400	55	28	1	99	71	89	.215	.244	.276	68	-61	-66	131				.901	6	2/O3S	-4.4
■ **BIRDIE CREE**	Cree, William Franklin b: 10/23/1882, Khedive, Pa. d: 11/8/42, Sunbury, Pa. BR/TR, 5'6", 150 lbs. Deb: 9/17/08																								
1908	NY-A	21	78	5	21	0	2	0	4	7		.269	.345	.321	115	2	2	9	1			1.000	1	O	0.2
1909	NY-A	104	343	48	90	6	3	2	27	30		.262	.338	.315	105	3	3	40	10			.949	-7	O/S23	-0.7
1910	NY-A	134	467	58	134	19	16	4	73	40		.287	.353	.422	135	22	19	79	28			.955	-12	*O	0.1
1911	NY-A	137	520	90	181	30	22	4	88	56		.348	.415	.513	149	40	35	129	48			.964	0	*O/S2	2.8
1912	NY-A	50	190	25	63	11	6	0	22	20		.332	.409	.453	138	12	10	39	12			.948	5	O	1.2
1913	NY-A	145	534	51	145	25	6	1	63	50	51	.272	.338	.346	100	0	0	68	22			**.988**	-4	*O	-1.1
1914	NY-A	77	275	45	85	18	5	0	40	30	24	.309	.389	.411	141	14	14	43	4	9	-4	.976	7	O	1.5
1915	NY-A	74	196	23	42	8	2	0	15	36	22	.214	.353	.276	88	-1	-1	20	7	8	-3	.945	-3	O	-1.0
Total	8	742	2603	345	761	117	62	11	332	269	97	.292	.368	.398	124	92	82	427	132	17		.965	-13	O/S23	3.0
■ **CONNIE CREEDEN**	Creeden, Cornelius Stephen b: 7/21/15, Danvers, Mass. d: 11/30/69, Santa Ana, Cal. BL/TL, 6'1", 200 lbs. Deb: 4/28/43																								
1943	Bos-N	5	4	0	1	0	0	0	1	1	0	.250	.400	.250	91	0	0	1	0			.000	0	H	0.0
■ **PAT CREEDEN**	Creeden, Patrick Francis "Whoops" b: 5/23/06, Newburyport, Mass. d: 4/20/92, Brockton, Mass. BL/TR, 5'8", 175 lbs. Deb: 4/14/31																								
1931	Bos-A	5	8	0	0	0	0	0	0	1	3	.000	.111	.000	-73	-2	-2	0	0	0	0	.846	0	/2	-0.2
■ **MARTY CREEGAN**	Creegan, Martin b: San Francisco, Cal. Deb: 4/17/1884																								
1884	Was-U	9	33	4	5	0	0	0		1		.152	.176	.152	12	-3	-3	1				.667	-1	/OC31	-0.3
■ **GUS CREELY**	Creely, August L. b: 6/6/1870, Florissant, Mo. d: 4/22/34, St.Louis, Mo. 5'6", 150 lbs. Deb: 10/09/1890																								
1890	StL-a	4	15	0	0	0	0	0		0		.000	.000	.000	-88	-4	-4	0	1			.769	-3	/S	-0.6
■ **PETE CREGAN**	Cregan, Peter James "Peekskill Pete" b: 4/13/1875, Kingston, N.Y. d: 5/18/45, New York, N.Y. BR/TR, 5'7.5", 150 lbs. Deb: 9/08/1899																								
1899	NY-N	1	2	0	0	0	0	0	0	0		.000	.000	.000	-99	-1	-1	0	0			1.000	-0	/O	-0.1
1903	Cin-N	6	19	0	2	0	0	0	0	1		.105	.190	.105	-13	-3	-3	1	0			.769	-1	/O	-0.5
Total	2	7	21	0	2	0	0	0	0	1		.095	.174	.095	-21	-3	-4	1	0			.786	-2	/O	-0.6
■ **BERNIE CREGER**	Creger, Bernard Odell b: 3/21/27, Wytheville, Va. BR/TR, 6', 175 lbs. Deb: 4/29/47																								
1947	StL-N	15	16	3	3	1	0	0	0	1	3	.188	.235	.250	28	-2	-2	1	1			.828	-3	S	-0.5
■ **CREEPY CRESPI**	Crespi, Frank Angelo Joseph b: 2/16/18, St.Louis, Mo. d: 3/1/90, Florissant, Mo. BR/TR, 5'8.5", 175 lbs. Deb: 9/14/38																								
1938	StL-N	7	19	2	5	2	0	0	1	2	7	.263	.333	.368	88	-0	-0	2	0			.813	-2	/S	-0.2
1939	StL-N	15	29	3	5	1	0	0	6	3	6	.172	.250	.207	23	-3	-3	2	0			.962	-0	/2S	-0.3
1940	StL-N	3	11	2	3	1	0	0	0	1	2	.273	.333	.364	87	-0	-0	1	1			1.000	-1	/3S	-0.1
1941	StL-N	146	560	85	156	24	2	4	46	57	58	.279	.355	.350	93	1	-4	72	3			.962	0	*2	0.7
1942	*StL-N	93	292	33	71	4	2	0	35	27	29	.243	.309	.271	65	-10	-13	26	4			.967	-5	2/S	-1.4
Total	5	264	911	125	240	32	4	4	88	90	102	.263	.336	.321	82	-13	-21	104	8			.963	-7	2/S3	-1.3
■ **LOU CRIGER**	Criger, Louis b: 2/3/1872, Elkhart, Ind. d: 5/14/34, Tucson, Ariz. BR/TR, 5'10", 165 lbs. Deb: 9/21/1896																								
1896	Cle-N	2	5	0	0	0	0	0	0	1	0	.000	.167	.000	-50	-1	-1	0	1			1.000	1	/C	0.0
1897	Cle-N	39	138	15	31	4	1	0	22	23		.225	.340	.268	58	-7	-8	15	5			.937	-1	C/1	-0.4
1898	Cle-N	84	287	43	80	13	4	1	32	40		.279	.375	.362	113	6	6	42	2			.957	16	C	2.8
1899	StL-N	77	258	39	66	4	5	2	44	28		.256	.333	.333	81	-6	-7	35	14			.949	2	C	0.1
1900	StL-N	80	288	31	78	8	6	2	38	4		.271	.286	.361	79	-10	-10	32	5			.953	6	C/3	0.3
1901	Bos-A	76	268	26	62	6	3	0	24	11		.231	.270	.276	52	-18	-17	23	7			.967	21	C/1	1.0
1902	Bos-A	83	266	32	68	16	6	0	28	27		.256	.324	.361	87	-4	-5	35	7			.965	14	C/O	1.7
1903	*Bos-A	96	317	41	61	7	10	3	31	26		.192	.256	.306	65	-12	-14	28	5			.979	23	C	1.9
1904	Bos-A	98	299	34	63	10	5	2	34	27		.211	.283	.298	79	-5	-7	27	1			.981	19	C	2.5
1905	Bos-A	109	313	33	62	6	7	1	36	54		.198	.322	.272	88	-2	-2	31	5			.972	6	*C	1.6
1906	Bos-A	7	17	0	3	1	0	0	1	1		.176	.222	.235	44	-1	-1	1	1			.981	5	/C	0.4
1907	Bos-A	75	226	12	41	4	0	0	14	19		.181	.251	.199	44	-14	-13	13	2			.978	0	C	-0.7
1908	Bos-A	84	237	12	45	4	2	0	25	13		.190	.232	.224	47	-13	-14	13	1			.980	13	C	0.7
1909	StL-A	74	212	15	36	1	1	0	9	25		.170	.261	.184	44	-13	-12	12	2			.986	8	C	0.3
1910	NY-A	27	69	3	13	2	0	0	4	10		.188	.291	.217	56	-3	-3	4	0			.993	-1	C	-0.2
1912	StL-A	1	2	1	0	0	0	0	0	0		.000	.000	.000	-99	-1	-1	0	0			1.000	1	/C	0.0
Total	16	1012	3202	337	709	86	50	11	342	309	0	.221	.294	.290	72	-103	-108	311	58			.971	131	C/1O3	12.0
■ **DAVE CRIPE**	Cripe, David Gordon b: 4/7/51, Ramona, Cal. BR/TR, 6', 180 lbs. Deb: 9/10/78																								
1978	KC-A	7	13	1	2	0	0	0	1	0	2	.154	.154	.154	-13	-2	-2	0	0	0	0	1.000	-2	/3	-0.4
■ **DAVE CRISCIONE**	Criscione, David Gerald b: 9/2/51, Dunkirk, N.Y. BR/TR, 5'8", 185 lbs. Deb: 7/17/77																								
1977	Bal-A	7	9	1	3	0	0	1	1	0	1	.333	.333	.667	176	1	1	2	0	0	0	1.000	-1	/C	0.0
■ **TONY CRISCOLA**	Criscola, Anthony Paul b: 7/9/15, Walla Walla, Wash. BL/TR, 5'11.5", 180 lbs. Deb: 4/15/42																								
1942	StL-A	91	158	17	47	9	2	1	13	8	13	.297	.331	.399	103	0	0	22	2	2	-1	.955	-14	O	-1.7
1943	StL-A	29	52	4	8	0	0	0	1	8	7	.154	.267	.154	24	-5	-5	3	0	0	0	.960	-2	O	-0.8
1944	Cin-N	64	157	14	36	3	2	0	14	14	12	.229	.297	.274	64	-8	-7	13	0			.977	2	O	-0.8
Total	3	184	367	35	91	12	4	1	28	30	32	.248	.307	.311	75	-12	-12	38	2	2		.966	-15	O	-3.3
■ **PAT CRISHAM**	Crisham, Patrick J. b: 6/4/1877, Amesbury, Mass. d: 6/12/15, Syracuse, N.Y. 6', 168 lbs. Deb: 5/05/1899																								
1899	Bal-N	53	172	23	50	5	3	0	20	4		.291	.311	.355	78	-5	-6	21	4			.979	-5	1C	-0.8
■ **JOE CRISP**	Crisp, Joseph Shelby b: 7/8/1889, Higginsville, Mo. d: 2/5/39, Kansas City, Mo. BR/TR, 6'4", 200 lbs. Deb: 9/02/10																								
1910	StL-A	1	1	0	0	0	0	0	0	0		.000	.000	.000	-99	-0	-0	0	0			1.000	-0	/C	0.0
1911	StL-A	1	1	0	1	0	0	0	0	0		1.000	1.000	1.000	477	0	0	1	0			.000	0	/H	0.0
Total	2	2	2	0	1	0	0	0	0	0		.500	.500	.500	206	0	0	1	0				-0	/C	0.0

YEAR	TM/L	G	AB	R	H	2B	3B	HR	RBI	BB	SO	AVG	OBP	SLG	PRO+	BR	/A	RC	SB	CS	SBR	FA	FR	POS	TPR

■ DODE CRISS Criss, Dode b: 3/12/1885, Sherman, Miss. d: 9/8/55, Sherman, Miss. BL/TR, 6'2", 200 lbs. Deb: 4/20/08

1908	StL-A	64	82	15	28	6	0	0	14	9		.341	.407	.415	166	6	6	14	1			.933	-1	O/P1	0.5
1909	StL-A	35	48	2	14	6	1	0	7	0		.292	.306	.458	152	2	2	6	0			1.000	-1	P	0.0
1910	StL-A	70	91	11	21	4	2	1	11	11		.231	.320	.352	118	1	2	11	2			.983	-1	1/P	0.1
1911	StL-A	58	83	10	21	3	1	2	15	11		.253	.347	.386	109	1	1	11	0			.956	-2	1/P	-0.1
Total	4	227	304	38	84	19	4	3	47	31		.276	.349	.395	133	10	11	42	3			.964	-5	/P1O	0.5

■ CHES CRIST Crist, Chester Arthur "Squak" b: 2/10/1882, Cozaddale, Ohio d: 1/7/57, Cincinnati, Ohio BR/TR, 5'11", 165 lbs. Deb: 5/18/06

| 1906 | Phi-N | 6 | 11 | 1 | 0 | 0 | 0 | 0 | 0 | 0 | | .000 | .083 | .000 | -74 | -2 | -2 | 0 | 0 | | | .800 | -3 | /C | -0.6 |

■ HUGHIE CRITZ Critz, Hugh Melville b: 9/17/1900, Starkville, Miss. d: 1/10/80, Greenwood, Miss. BR/TR, 5'8", 147 lbs. Deb: 5/31/24

1924	Cin-N	102	413	67	133	15	14	3	35	19	18	.322	.352	.448	115	7	7	63	19	11	-1	.956	2	2/S	1.0
1925	Cin-N	144	541	74	150	14	8	2	51	34	17	.277	.321	.344	72	-24	-22	59	13	13	-4	.970	22	*2	-0.2
1926	Cin-N	155	607	96	164	24	14	3	79	39	25	.270	.316	.371	87	-14	-12	70	7			.981	24	*2	1.6
1927	Cin-N	113	396	50	110	10	8	4	49	16	18	.278	.306	.374	84	-11	-10	44	7			.969	-2	*2	-0.8
1928	Cin-N	153	640	95	190	21	11	5	52	37	24	.296	.335	.387	90	-12	-10	81	18			.971	-17	*2	-2.3
1929	Cin-N	107	425	55	105	17	9	1	50	27	21	.247	.292	.336	58	-31	-27	41	9			.974	4	*2/S	-1.8
1930	Cin-N	28	104	15	24	3	2	0	11	6	6	.231	.273	.298	40	-11	-10	8	1			.987	-3	2	-1.0
	NY-N	124	558	93	148	17	11	4	50	24	26	.265	.296	.357	58	-40	-38	57	7			.972	5	*2	-2.3
	Yr	152	662	108	172	20	13	4	61	30	32	.260	.292	.347	55	-50	-48	65	8			.974	2	*2	-3.3
1931	NY-N	66	238	33	69	7	2	4	17	8	17	.290	.313	.387	89	-5	-5	29	4			.984	0	2	0.0
1932	NY-N	151	659	90	182	32	7	2	50	34	27	.276	.313	.355	81	-19	-17	74	3			.974	1	*2	-0.8
1933	*NY-N	133	558	68	137	18	5	2	33	23	24	.246	.279	.306	68	-24	-23	48	4			.982	47	*2	3.3
1934	NY-N	137	571	77	138	17	1	6	40	19	24	.242	.269	.306	55	-38	-36	47	3			.978	25	*2	-0.2
1935	NY-N	65	219	19	41	0	3	2	14	3	10	.187	.198	.242	18	-25	-25	10	2			.966	3	2	-1.8
Total	12	1478	5930	832	1591	195	95	38	531	289	257	.268	.303	.352	74	-247	-228	631	97	24		.974	111	*2/S	-5.3

■ DAVEY CROCKETT Crockett, Daniel Solomon b: 10/5/1875, Roanoke, Va. d: 2/23/61, Charlottesville, Va. BL/TR, 6'1", 175 lbs. Deb: 7/11/01

| 1901 | Det-A | 28 | 102 | 10 | 29 | 2 | 2 | 0 | 14 | 6 | | .284 | .336 | .343 | 85 | -1 | -2 | 13 | 1 | | | .968 | -0 | 1 | -0.3 |

■ ART CROFT Croft, Arthur F. b: 1/23/1855, St.Louis, Mo. d: 3/16/1884, St.Louis, Mo. Deb: 5/04/1875

1875	RS-n	19	75	5	15	3	0	0				.200	.200	.240	57	-4	-2	4						O	-0.2
1877	StL-N	54	220	23	51	5	2	0	27	1	15	.232	.235	.273	63	-10	-8	14				.971	-3	10/2	-1.1
1878	Ind-N	60	222	22	35	6	0	0	16	5	23	.158	.176	.185	22	-19	-15	7				.963	-1	*1/O	-1.7
Total	2	114	442	45	86	11	2	0	43	6	38	.195	.205	.229	43	-29	-23	22				.965	-4	/1O2	-2.8

■ HARRY CROFT Croft, Henry T. b: 8/1/1875, Chicago, Ill. d: 12/11/33, Oak Park, Ill. Deb: 5/19/1899

1899	Lou-N	2	2	0	0	0	0	0	0	0	0	.000	.000	.000	-99	-1	-1	0	0			.000	0		0.0
	Phi-N	2	7	0	1	0	0	0	0	0	1	.143	.250	.143	9	-1	-1	0	0			1.000	-1	/2	-0.2
	Yr	4	9	0	1	0	0	0	0	0	1	.111	.200	.111	-14	-1	-1	0	0			1.000	-1	/2	-0.2
1901	Chi-N	3	12	1	4	0	0	0	4	0		.333	.333	.333	97	-0	-0	1	0			1.000	2	/O	0.2
Total	2	7	21	1	5	0	0	0	4	1		.238	.273	.238	47	-2	-1	2	0				1	/O2	0.0

■ FRED CROLIUS Crolius, Fred Joseph b: 12/16/1876, Jersey City, N.J. d: 8/25/60, Ormond Beach, Fla. Deb: 4/19/01

1901	Bos-N	49	200	22	48	4	1	1	13	9		.240	.306	.285	66	-7	-9	20	6			.850	-8	O	-2.0
1902	Pit-N	9	38	4	10	2	1	0	7	0		.263	.263	.368	91	-1	-1	4	0			1.000	-0	/O	-0.2
Total	2	58	238	26	58	6	2	1	20	9		.244	.300	.298	70	-7	-10	24	6			.868	-8	/O	-2.2

■ WARREN CROMARTIE Cromartie, Warren Livingston b: 9/29/53, Miami Beach, Fla. BL/TL, 6', 192 lbs. Deb: 9/06/74

1974	Mon-N	8	17	2	3	0	0	0	3	3		.176	.300	.176	34	-1	-1	1	1	0		1.000	-0	/O	-0.2
1976	Mon-N	33	81	8	17	1	0	0	2	1	5	.210	.220	.222	25	-8	-8	3	1	2	-1	.943	-2	O	-1.2
1977	Mon-N	155	620	64	175	41	7	5	50	33	40	.282	.323	.395	94	-8	-6	77	10	3	1	.976	2	*O	-0.9
1978	Mon-N	159	607	77	180	32	6	10	56	33	60	.297	.340	.418	112	8	8	82	8	8	-2	.978	16	*O/1	1.5
1979	Mon-N	158	659	84	181	46	5	8	46	38	78	.275	.315	.396	94	-8	-7	79	8	7	-2	.976	12	*O	-0.4
1980	Mon-N	162	597	74	172	33	5	14	70	51	64	.288	.346	.430	112	15	12	80	8	8	-2	.991	-4	*1/O	-0.5
1981	*Mon-N	99	358	41	109	19	2	6	42	39	21	.304	.373	.419	123	12	11	55	2	3	-1	.992	-4	10	0.2
1982	Mon-N	144	497	59	126	24	3	14	62	69	60	.254	.348	.398	106	7	5	71	3	0	1	.979	6	*O/1	0.9
1983	Mon-N	120	360	37	100	26	2	3	43	43	48	.278	.356	.386	106	4	4	49	8	3	1	.973	8	*O/1	1.0
1991	KC-A	69	131	13	41	7	2	1	20	15	18	.313	.384	.420	122	4	4	21	3	1	-2	.996	-4	1/OD	-0.3
Total	10	1107	3927	459	1104	229	32	61	391	325	403	.281	.339	.402	105	20	22	517	50	37	-7	.977	29	O1/D	0.1

■ NED CROMPTON Crompton, Edward b: 2/12/1889, Liverpool, England d: 9/28/50, Aspinwall, Pa. BL/TL, 5'10.5", 175 lbs. Deb: 9/13/09

1909	StL-A	17	63	7	10	2	1	0	4	3		.159	.254	.222	54	-3	-3	4	1			.909	1	O	-0.3
1910	Cin-N	1	2	0	0	0	0	0	0	0	2	.000	.000	.000	-99	-1	-0	0	0			.000	-1	/O	-0.1
Total	2	18	65	7	10	2	1	0	4	2	2	.154	.247	.215	49	-4	-3	4	1			.909	1	/O	-0.4

■ HERB CROMPTON Crompton, Herbert Bryan "Workhorse" b: 11/7/11, Taylor Ridge, Ill. d: 8/5/63, Moline, Ill. BR/TR, 6', 185 lbs. Deb: 4/26/37

1937	Was-A	2	3	0	1	0	0	0	0	0	0	.333	.333	.333	72	-0	-0	0	0	0	0	1.000	0	/C	0.0
1945	NY-A	36	99	6	19	3	0	0	12	2	7	.192	.208	.222	24	-10	-10	4	0	0	0	.984	1	C	-0.9
Total	2	38	102	6	20	3	0	0	12	2	7	.196	.212	.225	25	-10	-10	4	0	0	0	.984	1	/C	-0.9

■ CHRIS CRON Cron, Christopher John b: 3/31/64, Albuquerque, N.Mex. BR/TR, 6'2", 200 lbs. Deb: 8/15/91

1991	Cal-A	6	15	0	2	0	0	0	0	2	5	.133	.235	.133	5	-2	-2	1	0	0	0	1.000	2	/1D	-0.1
1992	Chi-A	6	10	0	0	0	0	0	0	0	4	.000	.000	.000	-99	-3	-3	0	0	0	0	.923	-1	/1O	-0.3
Total	2	12	25	0	2	0	0	0	0	2	9	.080	.148	.080	-35	-5	-4	1	0	0	0	.980	1	/1OD	-0.4

■ DAN CRONIN Cronin, Daniel T. b: 4/1857, S.Boston, Mass. d: 11/30/1885, Boston, Mass. 5'8", 170 lbs. Deb: 7/08/1884

1884	CP-U	1	4	1	1	0	0	0			0	.250	.250	.250	70	-0	-0	0				.200	-2	/2	-0.2
	StL-U	1	5	0	0	0	0	0			0	.000	.000	.000	-97	-1	-1	0				.000	-1	/O	-0.2
	Yr	2	9	1	1	0	0	0			0	.111	.111	.111	-24	-1	-1	0				.000	-3	/2O	-0.4

■ JIM CRONIN Cronin, James John b: 8/7/05, Richmond, Cal. d: 6/10/83, Concord, Cal. BB/TR, 5'10.5", 150 lbs. Deb: 7/04/29

| 1929 | Phi-A | 25 | 56 | 7 | 13 | 2 | 1 | 0 | 4 | 5 | 7 | .232 | .295 | .304 | 52 | -4 | -4 | 5 | 0 | 0 | 0 | .966 | 5 | 2/S3 | 0.2 |

■ JOE CRONIN Cronin, Joseph Edward b: 10/12/06, San Francisco, Cal d: 9/7/84, Osterville, Mass. BR/TR, 5'11.5", 180 lbs. Deb: 4/29/26 MH

1926	Pit-N	38	83	9	22	2	0	1	11	6	15	.265	.315	.337	72	-3	-3	9	0			.977	0	2/S	0.3
1927	Pit-N	12	22	2	5	1	0	0	3	2	3	.227	.292	.273	48	-1	-2	2	0			1.000	-4	/2S1	-0.5
1928	Was-A	63	227	23	55	10	4	0	25	22	27	.242	.309	.322	66	-11	-11	25	4	0	1	.953	8	S	0.5
1929	Was-A	145	494	72	139	29	8	8	61	85	37	.281	.388	.421	107	8	8	84	5	9	-4	.923	6	*S/2	2.6
1930	Was-A	154	587	127	203	41	9	13	126	72	36	.346	.422	.513	135	34	33	129	17	10	-1	.923	26	*S	6.7
1931	Was-A	156	611	103	187	44	13	12	126	81	52	.306	.391	.480	127	25	25	116	10	9	-2	.950	13	*S	4.6
1932	Was-A	143	557	95	177	43	18	6	116	66	45	.318	.393	.492	129	23	24	109	7	5	-1	.959	6	*S	3.8
1933	*Was-A★	152	602	89	186	45	11	5	118	87	49	.309	.398	.445	124	22	23	111	5	4	-1	.960	10	*SM	4.0
1934	Was-A★	127	504	68	143	30	9	7	101	53	28	.284	.353	.421	103	-1	-1	78	8	0	2	.951	18	*SM	2.7
1935	Bos-A★	144	556	70	164	37	14	9	95	63	40	.295	.370	.460	106	11	11	96	3	3	-1	.949	-13	*S/1M	-0.1

YEAR	TM/L	G	AB	R	H	2B	3B	HR	RBI	BB	SO	AVG	OBP	SLG	PRO+	BR	/A	RC	SB	CS	SBR	FA	FR	POS	TPR
1936	Bos-A	81	295	36	83	22	4	2	43	32	21	.281	.354	.403	82	-6	-9	43	1	3	-2	.930	-2	S3M	-0.7
1937	Bos-A★	148	570	102	175	40	4	18	110	84	73	.307	.402	.486	118	21	18	116	5	3	-0	.958	-13	*SM	1.4
1938	Bos-A★	143	530	98	172	**51**	5	17	94	91	60	.325	.428	.536	134	35	31	126	7	5	-1	.954	7	*SM	4.3
1939	Bos-A★	143	520	97	160	33	3	19	107	87	48	.308	.407	.492	124	24	21	104	6	6	-2	.959	6	*SM	3.5
1940	Bos-A	149	548	104	156	35	6	24	111	83	65	.285	.380	.502	122	22	18	112	7	5	-1	.948	2	*S/3M	3.0
1941	Bos-A★	143	518	98	161	38	8	16	95	82	55	.311	.406	.508	137	31	29	107	1	4	-2	.958	-8	*S3/OM	2.7
1942	Bos-A	45	79	7	24	3	0	4	24	15	21	.304	.415	.494	150	6	6	16	0	1	-1	.865	-1	3/1SM	0.5
1943	Bos-A	59	77	8	24	4	0	5	29	11	4	.312	.398	.558	176	7	7	17	0	0	0	.968	0	3M	0.8
1944	Bos-A	76	191	24	46	7	0	5	28	34	19	.241	.358	.356	106	2	2	25	1	4	-2	.981	-2	1M	-0.4
1945	Bos-A	3	8	1	3	0	0	0	1	3	2	.375	.545	.375	165	1	1	2	0	0	0	1.000	1	/3M	0.2
Total	20	2124	7579	1233	2285	515	118	170	1424	1059	700	.301	.390	.468	119	250	229	1426	87	71		.951	68	*S/312O	39.9

■ BILL CRONIN Cronin, William Patrick "Crungy" b: 12/26/02, W.Newton, Mass. d: 10/26/66, Newton, Mass. BR/TR, 5'9", 167 lbs. Deb: 7/04/28

YEAR	TM/L	G	AB	R	H	2B	3B	HR	RBI	BB	SO	AVG	OBP	SLG	PRO+	BR	/A	RC	SB	CS	SBR	FA	FR	POS	TPR
1928	Bos-N	3	2	1	0	0	0	0	0	1	0	.000	.333	.000	-6	-0	-0	0	0			1.000	-0	/C	0.0
1929	Bos-N	6	9	0	1	0	0	0	0	0	0	.111	.111	.111	-47	-2	-2	0	0			1.000	1	/C	-0.1
1930	Bos-N	66	178	19	45	9	1	0	17	4	8	.253	.277	.315	44	-17	-16	15	0			.983	7	C	-0.3
1931	Bos-N	51	107	8	22	6	1	0	10	7	5	.206	.267	.280	49	-8	-7	8	0			.941	1	C	-0.4
Total	4	126	296	28	68	15	2	0	27	12	13	.230	.269	.294	43	-27	-25	24	0			.968	9	C	-0.8

■ TOM CROOKE Crooke, Thomas Aloysius b: 7/26/1884, Washington, D.C. d: 4/5/29, Quantico, Va. BR/TR, 6', 180 lbs. Deb: 9/29/09

YEAR	TM/L	G	AB	R	H	2B	3B	HR	RBI	BB	SO	AVG	OBP	SLG	PRO+	BR	/A	RC	SB	CS	SBR	FA	FR	POS	TPR
1909	Was-A	3	7	2	2	1	0	0	2	2		.286	.444	.429	184	1	1	2	1			.969	-1	/1	0.0
1910	Was-A	8	21	1	4	1	0	0	1	1		.190	.227	.238	48	-1	-1	1	0			1.000	-0	/1	-0.2
Total	2	11	28	3	6	2	0	0	3	3		.214	.290	.286	85	-1	-0	3	1			.988	-1	/1	-0.2

■ JACK CROOKS Crooks, John Charles b: 11/9/1865, St.Paul, Minn. d: 2/2/18, St.Louis, Mo. BR/TR, 5'10", 170 lbs. Deb: 9/26/1889 M

YEAR	TM/L	G	AB	R	H	2B	3B	HR	RBI	BB	SO	AVG	OBP	SLG	PRO+	BR	/A	RC	SB	CS	SBR	FA	FR	POS	TPR
1889	Col-a	12	43	13	14	2	3	0	7	10	4	.326	.463	.512	190	5	6	15	10			.987	5	2	0.9
1890	Col-a	135	485	86	107	5	4	1		96		.221	.357	.254	89	-4	1	66	57			.937	-4	*2/3O	0.5
1891	Col-a	138	519	110	127	19	13	0	46	103	47	.245	.379	.331	113	10	15	86	50			**.957**	20	*2	3.5
1892	StL-N	128	445	82	95	7	4	7	38	**136**	52	.213	.400	.294	119	17	20	63	23			.929	-7	*23/OM	1.5
1893	StL-N	128	448	93	106	10	9	1	48	**121**	37	.237	.408	.306	93	4	3	70	31			.908	4	*3/SC	0.8
1895	Was-N	117	409	80	114	19	8	6	57	68	39	.279	.392	.408	110	8	9	83	36			**.956**	12	*2	2.2
1896	Was-N	25	84	20	24	3	0	3	20	16	8	.286	.406	.429	122	3	3	17	2			.916	-2	2/3	0.2
	Lou-N	39	122	19	29	5	1	2	15	20	8	.238	.354	.344	90	-2	-1	18	8			.925	4	2	0.5
	Yr	64	206	39	53	8	1	5	35	36	16	.257	.376	.379	104	2	2	35	10			.922	2	2/3	0.7
1898	StL-N	72	225	33	52	4	2	1	20	40		.231	.359	.280	82	-3	-3	26	3			.959	8	2/3SO	0.8
Total	8	794	2780	536	668	74	44	21	251	610	195	.240	.385	.321	104	37	54	445	220			.946	40	23/SOC	10.9

■ ED CROSBY Crosby, Edward Carlton b: 5/26/49, Long Beach, Cal. BL/TR, 6'2", 180 lbs. Deb: 7/12/70

YEAR	TM/L	G	AB	R	H	2B	3B	HR	RBI	BB	SO	AVG	OBP	SLG	PRO+	BR	/A	RC	SB	CS	SBR	FA	FR	POS	TPR
1970	StL-N	38	95	9	24	4	1	0	6	7	5	.253	.311	.316	67	-4	-4	10	0	0	0	.954	-1	S/32	-0.2
1972	StL-N	101	276	27	60	9	1	0	19	18	27	.217	.270	.257	51	-18	-17	18	1	1	-0	.979	-6	S23	-1.9
1973	StL-N	22	39	4	5	2	1	0	1	4	4	.128	.209	.231	22	-4	-4	2	0	0	0	.938	-3	/S23	-0.7
	*Cin-N	36	51	4	11	1	1	0	5	7	12	.216	.333	.275	74	-2	-1	5	0	1	-1	.953	5	S/2	0.5
	Yr	58	90	8	16	3	2	0	6	11	16	.178	.282	.256	52	-6	-6	7	0	1	-1	.950	2	S2/3	-0.2
1974	Cle-A	37	86	11	18	3	0	0	6	6	12	.209	.261	.244	46	-6	-6	6	0	1	-1	.926	-10	3S/2	-1.6
1975	Cle-A	61	128	12	30	3	0	0	7	13	14	.234	.305	.258	60	-6	-6	9	0	4	-2	.974	4	S23	-0.2
1976	Cle-A	2	2	0	1	0	0	0	0	0	0	.500	.500	.500	195	0	0	1	0	0	0	1.000	1	/3D	0.1
Total	6	297	677	67	149	22	4	0	44	55	74	.220	.284	.264	55	-40	-39	50	1	7	-4	.964	-11	S/23D	-4.0

■ FRANKIE CROSETTI Crosetti, Frank Peter Joseph "Crow" b: 10/4/10, San Francisco, Cal. BR/TR, 5'10", 165 lbs. Deb: 4/12/32 C

YEAR	TM/L	G	AB	R	H	2B	3B	HR	RBI	BB	SO	AVG	OBP	SLG	PRO+	BR	/A	RC	SB	CS	SBR	FA	FR	POS	TPR
1932	*NY-A	116	398	47	96	20	9	5	57	51	51	.241	.335	.374	88	-10	-6	53	3	2	-0	.937	-5	S3/2	-0.3
1933	NY-A	136	451	71	114	20	5	9	60	55	40	.253	.337	.379	95	-7	-3	61	4	1	1	.936	-8	*S	-0.1
1934	NY-A	138	554	85	147	22	10	11	67	61	58	.265	.344	.401	98	-8	-2	78	5	6	-2	.945	-10	*S3/2	-0.6
1935	NY-A	87	305	49	78	17	6	8	50	41	27	.256	.351	.430	107	0	3	48	3	1	0	.963	-7	S	0.1
1936	*NY-A★	151	632	137	182	35	7	15	78	90	83	.288	.387	.437	107	4	8	113	18	7	1	.948	-8	*S	0.9
1937	*NY-A	149	611	127	143	29	5	11	49	86	105	.234	.340	.352	74	-23	-24	79	13	7	-0	.948	2	*S	-1.1
1938	*NY-A	157	631	113	166	35	3	9	55	106	97	.263	.382	.371	90	-7	-6	98	**27**	12	1	.948	18	*S	2.2
1939	*NY-A☆	152	656	109	153	25	5	10	56	65	81	.233	.315	.332	67	-34	-33	71	11	7	-1	**.968**	8	*S	-1.2
1940	NY-A	145	546	84	106	23	4	4	31	72	77	.194	.299	.273	52	-40	-37	47	14	8	-1	.954	-14	*S	-3.8
1941	NY-A	50	148	13	33	2	2	1	22	18	14	.223	.320	.284	62	-8	-8	13	0	2	-1	.944	10	S3	0.3
1942	*NY-A	74	285	50	69	5	5	4	23	31	31	.242	.335	.337	91	-3	-3	35	1	1	-0	.951	-3	3/S2	-0.4
1943	*NY-A	95	348	36	81	8	1	2	20	36	47	.233	.317	.279	74	-10	-10	33	4	4	-1	.946	3	S	-0.2
1944	NY-A	55	197	20	47	4	2	5	30	11	21	.239	.299	.355	84	-4	-5	20	3	0	1	.960	-9	S	-0.9
1945	NY-A	130	441	57	105	12	0	4	48	59	65	.238	.341	.293	81	-6	-9	52	7	1	2	.946	-8	*S	-0.6
1946	NY-A	28	59	4	17	3	0	0	3	8	2	.288	.382	.339	101	1	1	8	0	3	-2	.940	7	S	0.7
1947	NY-A	3	1	0	0	0	0	0	0	0	0	.000	.000	.000	-99	-0	-0	0	0	0	0	.000	0	/2S	0.0
1948	NY-A	17	14	4	4	0	1	0	0	2	0	.286	.375	.429	115	0	0	3	0	0	0	1.000	0	/2S	0.1
Total	17	1683	6277	1006	1541	260	65	98	649	792	799	.245	.341	.354	84	-155	-134	812	113	62	-3	.949	-24	*S3/2	-4.9

■ AMOS CROSS Cross, Amos C. b: 1861, Czechoslovakia d: 7/16/1888, Cleveland, Ohio Deb: 4/22/1885 F

YEAR	TM/L	G	AB	R	H	2B	3B	HR	RBI	BB	SO	AVG	OBP	SLG	PRO+	BR	/A	RC	SB	CS	SBR	FA	FR	POS	TPR
1885	Lou-a	35	130	11	37	2	1	0		0		.285	.290	.315	94	-1	-1	12				.936	-1	C	0.0
1886	Lou-a	74	283	51	78	14	6	1		44		.276	.375	.378	131	14	11	46	13			.910	-16	C1/SO	-0.2
1887	Lou-a	8	28	0	3	0	0	0		1		.107	.138	.107	-30	-5	-5	0	0			.808	-4	/C1O	-0.8
Total	3	117	441	62	118	16	7	1		45		.268	.338	.342	110	8	5	59	13			.916	-22	/C1OS	-1.0

■ CLARENCE CROSS Cross, Clarence (b: Clarence Crause) b: 3/4/1856, St.Louis, Mo. d: 6/23/31, Seattle, Wash. Deb: 5/05/1884

YEAR	TM/L	G	AB	R	H	2B	3B	HR	RBI	BB	SO	AVG	OBP	SLG	PRO+	BR	/A	RC	SB	CS	SBR	FA	FR	POS	TPR
1884	Alt-U	2	7	1	4	1	0	0		2		.571	.667	.714	362	2	2	3				.500	-2	/3	0.0
	Phi-U	2	9	0	2	0	0	0		0		.222	.222	.222	55	-0	-0	0				.545	-2	/S	-0.2
	KC-U	25	93	13	20	1	0	0		6		.215	.263	.226	76	-3	-1	6				.836	3	S/3	0.2
	Yr	29	109	14	26	2	0	0		8		.239	.291	.257	98	-1	1	8				.813	-1	S/3	0.0
1887	NY-a	16	55	9	11	2	1	0		2		.200	.267	.273	55	-3	-3	4	0			.833	-3	S/3	-0.5
Total	2	45	164	23	37	4	1	0		10		.226	.282	.262	81	-5	-2	14	0			.818	-4	/S3	-0.5

■ FRANK CROSS Cross, Frank Atwell "Mickey" b: 1/20/1873, Cleveland, Ohio d: 11/2/32, Geauga Lake, Ohio TR, Deb: 5/20/01 F

YEAR	TM/L	G	AB	R	H	2B	3B	HR	RBI	BB	SO	AVG	OBP	SLG	PRO+	BR	/A	RC	SB	CS	SBR	FA	FR	POS	TPR
1901	Cle-A	1	5	0	3	0	0	0	0	0		.600	.600	.600	243	1	1	2	0			.000	-0	/O	0.0

■ JEFF CROSS Cross, Joffre James b: 8/28/18, Tulsa, Okla. BR/TR, 5'11", 160 lbs. Deb: 9/27/42

YEAR	TM/L	G	AB	R	H	2B	3B	HR	RBI	BB	SO	AVG	OBP	SLG	PRO+	BR	/A	RC	SB	CS	SBR	FA	FR	POS	TPR
1942	StL-N	1	4	0	1	0	0	0	1	0	0	.250	.250	.250	43	-0	-0	0	0			1.000	-1	/S	-0.1
1946	StL-N	49	69	17	15	3	0	0	6	10	8	.217	.316	.261	62	-3	-3	6	4			.970	6	S/23	0.3
1947	StL-N	51	49	4	5	1	0	0	3	10	6	.102	.254	.122	3	-7	-7	2	0			.947	5	3S/2	-0.1
1948	StL-N	2	0	0	0	0	0	0	0	0	0	—	—	—	—	0	0	0	0			.000	0	R	0.0
	Chi-N	16	20	1	2	0	0	0	0	0	4	.100	.100	.100	-48	-4	-4	0	0			.786	-4	/S2	-0.7
	Yr	18	20	1	2	0	0	0	0	0	4	.100	.100	.100	-47	-4	-4	0	0			.786	-4	/S2	-0.7
Total	4	119	142	22	23	4	0	0	10	20	18	.162	.265	.190	26	-14	-15	9	4			.932	7	/S32	-0.6

■ LAVE CROSS Cross, Lafayette Napoleon b: 5/12/1866, Milwaukee, Wis. d: 9/6/27, Toledo, Ohio BR/TR, 5'8.5", 155 lbs. Deb: 4/23/1887 FM

YEAR	TM/L	G	AB	R	H	2B	3B	HR	RBI	BB	SO	AVG	OBP	SLG	PRO+	BR	/A	RC	SB	CS	SBR	FA	FR	POS	TPR
1887	Lou-a	54	203	32	54	8	3	0		15		.266	.320	.335	83	-4	-5	27	15			.916	-3	CO	-0.3
1888	Lou-a	47	181	20	41	3	0	0	15	2		.227	.239	.243	58	-9	-8	13	10			.929	1	CO/S	-0.4
1889	Phi-a	55	199	22	44	8	2	0	23	14	9	.221	.272	.281	60	-11	-10	19	11			.934	19	C	1.2
1890	Phi-P	63	245	42	73	7	8	3	47	12	6	.298	.331	.429	101	0	-1	37	5			.885	2	CO	0.4
1891	Phi-a	110	402	66	121	20	14	5	52	38	23	.301	.366	.458	134	18	16	74	14			.971	-4	OC3/S2	1.4
1892	Phi-N	140	541	84	149	15	10	4	69	39	16	.275	.328	.362	111	6	6	72	18			.921	-2	3CO2/S	0.8
1893	Phi-N	96	415	81	124	17	6	4	78	26	7	.299	.342	.398	98	-2	-2	64	18			.974	16	C3OS/1	1.4
1894	Phi-N	119	529	123	204	34	9	7	125	29	7	.386	.421	.524	132	24	26	130	21			.919	21	*3C/S2	3.7
1895	Phi-N	125	535	95	145	26	9	2	101	35	8	.271	.319	.364	77	-18	-19	73	21			**.940**	33	*3	1.3
1896	Phi-N	106	406	63	104	23	5	1	73	32	14	.256	.312	.345	76	-15	-14	49	8			.937	14	3S/2OC	0.2
1897	Phi-N	88	344	37	89	17	5	3	51	10		.259	.282	.363	71	-17	-15	40	10			.912	3	32/OS	-0.8
1898	StL-N	151	602	71	191	28	8	3	79	28		.317	.348	.405	113	10	8	94	14			**.945**	18	*3/S	2.5
1899	Cle-N	38	154	15	44	5	0	1	20	8		.286	.325	.338	88	-4	-2	18	2			.955	4	3M	0.2
	StL-N	103	403	61	122	14	5	4	64	17		.303	.333	.392	96	-2	-4	58	11			.960	29	*3	2.4
	Yr	141	557	76	166	19	5	5	84	25		.298	.330	.377	94	-6	-6	76	13			**.959**	33	*3	2.6
1900	StL-N	16	61	6	18	1	0	0	6	1		.295	.306	.311	71	-2	-2	7	1			.962	1	3	-0.1
	*Bro-N	117	461	73	135	14	6	4	67	25		.293	.332	.375	90	-4	-8	66	20			.943	2	*3	-0.5
	Yr	133	522	79	153	15	6	4	73	26		.293	.329	.368	88	-7	-10	73	21			**.945**	4	*3	-0.6
1901	Phi-A	100	424	82	139	28	12	2	73	19		.328	.358	.465	122	14	11	81	23			.919	5	*3	1.5
1902	Phi-A	137	559	90	191	39	8	0	108	27		.342	.374	.440	120	18	15	105	25			.942	7	*3	2.1
1903	Phi-A	137	559	60	163	22	4	2	90	10		.292	.304	.356	93	-3	-6	67	14			.950	-3	*3/1	-0.7
1904	Phi-A	155	607	73	176	31	10	1	71	13		.290	.309	.379	112	10	7	78	10			.936	-10	*3	0.2
1905	*Phi-A	147	587	69	156	29	5	0	77	26		.266	.299	.332	99	-1	-2	64	8			.928	-9	*3	-0.7
1906	Was-A	130	494	55	130	14	6	1	46	28		.263	.303	.322	101	-3	-0	57	19			**.952**	-4	*3	0.0
1907	Was-A	41	161	13	32	8	0	0	10	10		.199	.246	.248	63	-8	-6	11	3			.978	7	3	0.2
Total	21	2275	9072	1333	2645	411	135	47	1345	464	90	.292	.328	.382	100	-5	-17	1304	301			.938	147	*3CO/S21	16.0

■ MONTE CROSS Cross, Montford Montgomery b: 8/31/1869, Philadelphia, Pa. d: 6/21/34, Philadelphia, Pa. BR/TR, 6'2", 180 lbs. Deb: 9/27/1892 U

YEAR	TM/L	G	AB	R	H	2B	3B	HR	RBI	BB	SO	AVG	OBP	SLG	PRO+	BR	/A	RC	SB	CS	SBR	FA	FR	POS	TPR
1892	Bal-N	15	50	5	8	0	0	0	2	4	10	.160	.222	.160	17	-5	-5	2	2			.864	-3	S	-0.7
1894	Pit-N	13	43	14	19	1	5	2	13	5	4	.442	.520	.837	227	9	9	22	6			.924	2	S	0.9
1895	Pit-N	108	393	67	101	14	13	3	54	38	38	.257	.327	.382	89	-10	-6	64	39			.883	-13	*S/2	-1.1
1896	StL-N	125	427	66	104	10	6	6	52	58	48	.244	.342	.337	85	-10	-7	66	40			.892	-12	*S	-1.2
1897	StL-N	131	462	59	132	17	11	4	55	62		.286	.379	.396	107	4	6	87	38			.920	28	*S	3.2
1898	Phi-N	149	525	68	135	25	5	1	50	55		.257	.337	.330	95	-5	-2	68	20			.907	14	*S	1.7
1899	Phi-N	154	557	85	143	25	6	3	65	56		.257	.335	.339	88	-11	-7	77	26			.909	2	*S	0.5
1900	Phi-N	131	466	59	94	11	3	3	62	51		.202	.289	.258	52	-30	-30	42	19			.928	-3	*S	-2.0
1901	Phi-N	139	483	49	95	14	1	1	44	52		.197	.281	.236	50	-29	-30	41	24			.924	-16	*S	-3.5
1902	Phi-A	137	497	72	115	22	2	3	59	32		.231	.289	.302	61	-24	-27	52	17			.927	11	*S	-0.8
1903	Phi-A	137	470	44	116	21	2	3	45	49		.247	.326	.319	90	-2	-4	62	31			.940	8	*S/2	1.0
1904	Phi-A	153	503	33	95	23	4	1	38	46		.189	.266	.256	63	-18	-21	42	19			.937	-16	*S	-3.7
1905	*Phi-A	79	252	28	67	17	2	0	24	19		.266	.330	.349	114	5	4	35	8			.929	-5	S/2	0.1
1906	Phi-A	134	445	32	89	23	3	1	40	50		.200	.288	.272	74	-11	-13	45	22			.938	4	*S	-0.5
1907	Phi-A	77	248	37	51	9	5	0	18	39		.206	.316	.282	89	-1	-2	30	17			.954	13	S	1.4
Total	15	1682	5821	718	1364	232	68	31	621	616	100	.234	.316	.314	80	-138	-135	737	328			.920	15	*S/2	-4.7

■ FRANK CROSSIN Crossin, Frank Patrick b: 6/15/1891, Avondale, Pa. d: 12/6/65, Kingston, Pa. BR/TR, 5'10", 160 lbs. Deb: 9/24/12

YEAR	TM/L	G	AB	R	H	2B	3B	HR	RBI	BB	SO	AVG	OBP	SLG	PRO+	BR	/A	RC	SB	CS	SBR	FA	FR	POS	TPR
1912	StL-A	8	22	2	5	0	0	0	2	1		.227	.261	.227	41	-2	-2	1	1			.920	-5	/C	-0.6
1913	StL-A	4	4	1	1	0	0	0	0	1	1	.250	.500	.250	124	0	0	1	0			.857	-1	/C	0.0
1914	StL-A	43	90	5	11	1	1	0	5	10	10	.122	.225	.156	15	-9	-9	4	3			.934	-1	C	-0.7
Total	3	55	116	8	17	1	1	0	7	12	11	.147	.244	.172	25	-11	-10	6	4			.930	-6	/C	-1.3

■ JOE CROTTY Crotty, Joseph P. b: 12/24/1860, Cincinnati, O. d: 6/22/26, Minneapolis, Minn BR/TR, Deb: 5/04/1882

YEAR	TM/L	G	AB	R	H	2B	3B	HR	RBI	BB	SO	AVG	OBP	SLG	PRO+	BR	/A	RC	SB	CS	SBR	FA	FR	POS	TPR
1882	Lou-a	5	20	1	2	0	0	0		0		.100	.100	.100	-34	-3	-3	0				.882	-0	/C	-0.3
	StL-a	8	28	2	4	1	0	0		3		.143	.226	.179	37	-2	-2	1				.882	-1	/CO	-0.3
	Yr	13	48	3	6	1	0	0		3		.125	.176	.146	10	-4	-4	1				.882	-2	C/O	-0.6
1884	Cin-U	21	84	11	22	4	2	1		1		.262	.271	.393	113	2	1	9				.896	-7	C	-0.4
1885	Lou-a	39	129	14	20	2	0	0		3		.155	.193	.171	17	-12	-12	4				.931	1	C/1	-0.7
1886	NY-a	14	47	6	8	0	1	0		4		.170	.250	.213	49	-3	-2	3	3			.933	-3	C	-0.3
Total	4	87	308	34	56	7	3	1		11		.182	.220	.234	48	-17	-18	18	3			.915	-10	/C1O	-2.0

■ JACK CROUCH Crouch, Jack Albert "Roxy" b: 6/12/03, Salisbury, N.C. d: 8/25/72, Leesburg, Fla. BR/TR, 5'9", 165 lbs. Deb: 9/18/30

YEAR	TM/L	G	AB	R	H	2B	3B	HR	RBI	BB	SO	AVG	OBP	SLG	PRO+	BR	/A	RC	SB	CS	SBR	FA	FR	POS	TPR
1930	StL-A	6	14	1	2	1	0	0	1	1	3	.143	.200	.214	5	-2	-2	1	0	0	0	1.000	1	/C	-0.1
1931	StL-A	8	12	0	0	0	0	0	1	0	4	.000	.000	.000	-97	-3	-4	0	0	0	0	.895	1	/C	-0.3
1933	StL-A	19	30	1	5	0	0	1	5	2	6	.167	.219	.267	26	-3	-3	2	0	0	0	1.000	-1	/C	-0.3
	Cin-N	10	16	5	2	0	0	0	1	0	0	.125	.222	.125	1	-2	-2	1	1			1.000	2	/C	0.0
Total	3	43	72	7	9	1	0	1	8	3	13	.125	.182	.181	-3	-11	-11	3	1	0		.976	3	/C	-0.7

■ FRANK CROUCHER Croucher, Frank Donald "Dingle" b: 7/23/14, San Antonio, Tex. d: 5/21/80, Houston, Tex. BR/TR, 5'11", 165 lbs. Deb: 4/18/39

YEAR	TM/L	G	AB	R	H	2B	3B	HR	RBI	BB	SO	AVG	OBP	SLG	PRO+	BR	/A	RC	SB	CS	SBR	FA	FR	POS	TPR
1939	Det-A	97	324	38	87	15	0	5	40	16	42	.269	.303	.361	64	-16	-19	33	2	2	-1	.934	-8	S/2	-1.9
1940	*Det-A	37	57	3	6	0	0	0	2	4	5	.105	.164	.105	-26	-11	-12	1	0	0	0	.936	-2	S/23	-1.2
1941	Det-A	136	489	51	124	21	4	2	39	33	72	.254	.305	.325	61	-24	-30	50	2	0	1	.935	-3	*S	-2.2
1942	Was-A	26	65	2	18	1	1	0	5	3	9	.277	.309	.323	79	-2	-2	6	0	0	0	.950	5	2	0.4
Total	4	296	935	94	235	37	5	7	86	56	128	.251	.296	.324	58	-52	-63	90	4	2	0	.934	-8	S/23	-4.9

■ BUCK CROUSE Crouse, Clyde Elsworth b: 1/6/1897, Anderson, Ind. d: 10/23/83, Muncie, Ind. BL/TR, 5'8", 158 lbs. Deb: 8/01/23

YEAR	TM/L	G	AB	R	H	2B	3B	HR	RBI	BB	SO	AVG	OBP	SLG	PRO+	BR	/A	RC	SB	CS	SBR	FA	FR	POS	TPR
1923	Chi-A	23	70	6	18	2	1	1	7	3	4	.257	.297	.357	73	-3	-3	7	0	0	0	.955	-2	C	-0.4
1924	Chi-A	94	305	30	79	10	1	1	44	23	12	.259	.319	.308	64	-17	-16	32	3	2	-0	.945	1	C	-0.9
1925	Chi-A	54	131	18	46	7	0	2	25	12	4	.351	.410	.450	125	4	5	24	1	2	-1	.952	-2	C	0.4
1926	Chi-A	49	135	10	32	4	1	0	17	14	7	.237	.309	.281	57	-9	-8	13	0	0	0	.985	3	C	-0.3
1927	Chi-A	85	222	22	53	11	0	0	20	21	10	.239	.307	.288	57	-14	-14	20	4	1	1	.972	7	C	-0.1
1928	Chi-A	78	218	17	55	5	2	2	20	19	14	.252	.315	.321	68	-10	-10	22	3	4	-2	.959	-1	C	-0.7
1929	Chi-A	45	107	11	29	7	0	2	12	5	7	.271	.316	.393	82	-3	-3	14	2	0	1	.979	6	C	0.6
1930	Chi-A	42	118	14	30	8	1	0	15	17	10	.254	.348	.339	78	-4	-3	15	1	1	-0	.979	7	C	0.6
Total	8	470	1306	128	342	54	6	8	160	114	68	.262	.326	.331	72	-57	-52	146	14	10	-2	.964	18	C	-0.8

■ DON CROW Crow, Donald Le Roy b: 8/18/58, Yakima, Wash. BR/TR, 6'4", 200 lbs. Deb: 7/25/82

YEAR	TM/L	G	AB	R	H	2B	3B	HR	RBI	BB	SO	AVG	OBP	SLG	PRO+	BR	/A	RC	SB	CS	SBR	FA	FR	POS	TPR
1982	LA-N	4	4	0	0	0	0	0	0	0	3	.000	.000	.000	-99	-1	-1	0	0	0	0	1.000	1	/C	0.0

■ GEORGE CROWE Crowe, George Daniel "Big George" b: 3/22/23, Whiteland, Ind. BL/TL, 6'2", 212 lbs. Deb: 4/16/52

YEAR	TM/L	G	AB	R	H	2B	3B	HR	RBI	BB	SO	AVG	OBP	SLG	PRO+	BR	/A	RC	SB	CS	SBR	FA	FR	POS	TPR
1952	Bos-N	73	217	25	56	13	1	4	20	18	25	.258	.329	.382	100	-1	-0	28	0	1	-1	.985	2	1	-0.1
1953	Mil-N	47	42	6	12	2	0	2	6	2	7	.286	.333	.476	115	0	1	7	0	0	0	1.000	0	/1	0.1
1955	Mil-N	104	303	41	85	12	4	15	55	45	44	.281	.375	.495	135	13	15	59	1	0	0	.989	2	1	1.2
1956	Cin-N	77	144	22	36	2	1	10	23	11	28	.250	.312	.486	104	2	0	22	0	0	0	.988	2	1	0.1

YEAR	TM/L	G	AB	R	H	2B	3B	HR	RBI	BB	SO	AVG	OBP	SLG	PRO+	BR	/A	RC	SB	CS	SBR	FA	FR	POS	TPR
1957	Cin-N	133	494	71	134	20	1	31	92	32	62	.271	.317	.504	108	9	5	77	1	1	-0	.989	-2	*1	-0.4
1958	Cin-N☆	111	345	31	95	12	5	7	61	41	51	.275	.352	.400	94	-0	-2	50	1	0	0	.992	-3	1/2	-1.0
1959	StL-N	77	103	14	31	6	0	8	29	5	12	.301	.333	.592	132	5	4	18	0	0	0	1.000	2	1	0.6
1960	StL-N	73	72	5	17	3	0	4	13	5	16	.236	.286	.444	89	-1	-1	8	0	0	0	1.000	0	/1	-0.2
1961	StL-N	7	7	0	1	0	0	0	0	0	1	.143	.143	.143	-22	-1	-1	0	0	0	0	.000	0	H	-0.1
Total	9	702	1727	215	467	70	12	81	299	159	246	.270	.335	.466	109	26	20	269	3	2	-0	.990	4	1/2	0.2

■ ED CROWLEY
Crowley, Edgar Jewel b: 8/20/06, Watkinsville, Ga. d: 4/14/70, Birmingham, Ala. BR/TR, 6'1", 180 lbs. Deb: 6/21/28

YEAR	TM/L	G	AB	R	H	2B	3B	HR	RBI	BB	SO	AVG	OBP	SLG	PRO+	BR	/A	RC	SB	CS	SBR	FA	FR	POS	TPR
1928	Was-A	2	1	0	0	0	0	0	0	0	0	.000	.000	.000	-99	-0	-0	0	0	0	0	.000	-0	/3	-0.1

■ JOHN CROWLEY
Crowley, John A. b: 1/12/1862, Lawrence, Mass. d: 9/23/1896, Lawrence, Mass. 5'10", 164 lbs. Deb: 5/01/1884

YEAR	TM/L	G	AB	R	H	2B	3B	HR	RBI	BB	SO	AVG	OBP	SLG	PRO+	BR	/A	RC	SB	CS	SBR	FA	FR	POS	TPR
1884	Phi-N	48	168	26	41	7	3	0	19	15	21	.244	.306	.321	102	-0	1	17				.832	-23	C	-1.6

■ TERRY CROWLEY
Crowley, Terrence Michael b: 2/16/47, Staten Island, N.Y. BL/TL, 6', 180 lbs. Deb: 9/04/69 C

YEAR	TM/L	G	AB	R	H	2B	3B	HR	RBI	BB	SO	AVG	OBP	SLG	PRO+	BR	/A	RC	SB	CS	SBR	FA	FR	POS	TPR
1969	Bal-A	7	18	2	6	0	0	0	3	1	4	.333	.368	.333	97	-0	-0	2	0	0	0	1.000	0	/1O	0.0
1970	*Bal-A	83	152	25	39	5	0	5	20	35	26	.257	.396	.388	116	5	5	25	2	0	1	.973	-5	O1	-0.2
1971	Bal-A	18	23	2	4	0	0	0	1	3	4	.174	.269	.174	28	-2	-2	1	0	0	0	1.000	-2	/O1	-0.4
1972	Bal-A	97	247	30	57	10	0	11	29	32	26	.231	.321	.405	112	5	4	32	0	0	0	.990	-7	O1	-0.7
1973	*Bal-A	54	131	16	27	4	0	3	15	16	14	.206	.297	.305	71	-5	-5	12	0	0	0	.867	-1	DO/1	-0.6
1974	Cin-N	84	125	11	30	12	0	1	20	10	16	.240	.301	.360	86	-3	-3	13	1	0	0	1.000	-1	O/1	-0.4
1975	*Cin-N	66	71	8	19	6	0	1	11	7	6	.268	.333	.394	100	0	-0	8	0	0	0	1.000	2	/1O	0.2
1976	Atl-N	7	6	0	0	0	0	0	1	0	0	.000	.000	.000	-94	-2	-2	-0	0	0	0	.000	0	H	-0.2
	Bal-A	33	61	5	15	1	0	0	5	7	11	.246	.333	.262	81	-2	-1	6	0	0	0	1.000	1	D/1	-0.1
1977	Bal-A	18	22	3	8	1	0	1	9	1	3	.364	.391	.545	162	2	2	5	0	0	0	1.000	-0	/1D	0.2
1978	Bal-A	62	95	9	24	2	0	0	12	8	12	.253	.317	.274	72	-4	-3	8	0	0	0	1.000	0	D/O1	-0.3
1979	*Bal-A	61	63	8	20	5	1	1	8	14	13	.317	.449	.476	155	5	6	14	0	0	0	1.000	-0	D/1	0.5
1980	Bal-A	92	233	33	67	8	0	12	50	29	21	.288	.366	.476	130	9	10	40	0	0	0	1.000	1	D/1	1.1
1981	Bal-A	68	134	12	33	6	0	4	25	29	12	.246	.380	.381	120	5	5	21	0	0	0	1.000	0	D/1	0.5
1982	Bal-A	65	93	8	22	2	0	3	17	21	9	.237	.377	.355	103	1	1	13	0	0	0	.988	0	D1	0.1
1983	Mon-N	50	44	2	8	0	0	0	3	9	4	.182	.333	.182	47	-3	-3	3	0	0	0	1.000	-1	/1	-0.4
Total	15	865	1518	174	379	62	1	42	229	222	181	.250	.348	.375	104	12	13	202	3	0	1	.980	-11	DO/1	-0.7

■ BILL CROWLEY
Crowley, William Michael b: 4/8/1857, Philadelphia, Pa. d: 7/14/1891, Gloucester, N.J. BR/TR, 5'7.5", 159 lbs. Deb: 4/26/1875

YEAR	TM/L	G	AB	R	H	2B	3B	HR	RBI	BB	SO	AVG	OBP	SLG	PRO+	BR	/A	RC	SB	CS	SBR	FA	FR	POS	TPR
1875	Phi-n	9	37	4	3	0	0	0		1		.081	.105	.081	-33	-5	-5	0						/O312	-0.4
1877	Lou-N	61	238	30	67	9	3	1	23	4	13	.282	.293	.357	88	1	-5	26				.849	9	*O/SC32	0.1
1879	Buf-N	60	261	41	75	9	5	0	30	6	14	.287	.303	.360	115	5	4	29				.809	-1	OC/12	0.1
1880	Buf-N	85	354	57	95	16	4	0	20	19	23	.268	.306	.336	115	7	6	37				.824	1	*OC	0.5
1881	Bos-N	72	279	33	71	12	0	0	31	14	15	.254	.290	.297	89	-4	-3	25				.880	-1	*O	-0.5
1883	Phi-a	23	96	16	24	4	3	0		3		.250	.273	.354	92	-0	-1	10				.810	-2	O/1	-0.3
	Cle-N	11	41	3	12	5	0	0	5	1	7	.293	.310	.415	119	1	1	5				.923	-3	O	-0.2
1884	Bos-N	108	407	50	110	14	6	6	61	33	74	.270	.325	.378	121	10	10	51				.870	-5	*O	0.3
1885	Buf-N	92	344	29	83	14	1	1	36	21	32	.241	.285	.297	85	-4	-6	30				.874	-5	*O	-1.2
Total	7	512	2020	259	537	83	22	8	206	101	178	.266	.301	.341	103	14	6	213				.853	-6	O/C12S3	-1.2

■ WALTON CRUISE
Cruise, Walton Edwin b: 5/6/1890, Childersburg, Ala. d: 1/9/75, Sylacauga, Ala. BL/TR, 6', 175 lbs. Deb: 4/14/14

YEAR	TM/L	G	AB	R	H	2B	3B	HR	RBI	BB	SO	AVG	OBP	SLG	PRO+	BR	/A	RC	SB	CS	SBR	FA	FR	POS	TPR
1914	StL-N	95	256	20	58	9	3	4	28	25	42	.227	.303	.332	90	-4	-3	26	3			.976	-3	O	-1.0
1916	StL-N	3	3	0	2	0	0	0	0	1	0	.667	.750	.667	339	1	1	2	0			1.000	-1	/O	0.0
1917	StL-N	153	529	70	156	20	10	5	59	38	73	.295	.343	.399	131	16	18	76	16			.965	-14	*O	-0.4
1918	StL-N	70	240	34	65	5	4	6	39	30	26	.271	.359	.400	136	10	11	35	2			.964	-7	O	-0.1
1919	StL-N	9	21	0	2	1	0	0	0	1	6	.095	.136	.143	-17	-3	-3	0	0			.833	-2	/O1	-0.5
	Bos-N	73	241	23	52	7	0	1	21	17	29	.216	.267	.257	61	-12	-11	18	8			.978	-5	O	-2.3
	Yr	82	262	23	54	8	0	1	21	18	35	.206	.257	.248	55	-15	-14	18	8			.971	-7	O/1	-2.8
1920	Bos-N	91	288	40	80	7	5	1	21	31	26	.278	.352	.347	106	1	3	37	5	3	-0	.950	-7	O	-1.1
1921	Bos-N	108	344	47	119	16	7	8	55	48	24	.346	.429	.503	154	24	27	75	10	8	-2	.963	-6	*O/1	1.3
1922	Bos-N	104	352	51	98	15	10	4	46	44	20	.278	.360	.412	103	-0	2	54	4	4	-1	.948	-0	*O/1	-0.6
1923	Bos-N	21	38	4	8	2	0	0	0	3	2	.211	.268	.263	42	-3	-3	3	1	0	0	.952	-0	/O	-0.3
1924	Bos-N	9	9	4	4	1	0	1	3	0	2	.444	.444	.889	260	2	2	3	0	0	0	.000	0	H	0.2
Total	10	736	2321	293	644	83	39	30	272	238	250	.277	.348	.386	114	32	43	329	49	15		.962	-45	O/1	-4.8

■ GENE CRUMLING
Crumling, Eugene Leon b: 4/5/22, Wrightsville, Pa. BR/TR, 6', 180 lbs. Deb: 9/11/45

YEAR	TM/L	G	AB	R	H	2B	3B	HR	RBI	BB	SO	AVG	OBP	SLG	PRO+	BR	/A	RC	SB	CS	SBR	FA	FR	POS	TPR
1945	StL-N	6	12	0	1	0	0	0	1	0	1	.083	.083	.083	-52	-2	-2	0	0			1.000	2	/C	-0.1

■ BUDDY CRUMP
Crump, Arthur Elliott b: 11/29/01, Norfolk, Va. d: 9/7/76, Raleigh, N.C. BL/TL, 5'10", 156 lbs. Deb: 9/28/24

YEAR	TM/L	G	AB	R	H	2B	3B	HR	RBI	BB	SO	AVG	OBP	SLG	PRO+	BR	/A	RC	SB	CS	SBR	FA	FR	POS	TPR
1924	NY-N	1	4	0	0	0	0	0	1	0	1	.000	.000	.000	-99	-1	-1	0	0	0	0	.500	-1	/O	-0.2

■ PRESS CRUTHERS
Cruthers, Charles Preston b: 9/8/1890, Marshallton, Del. d: 12/27/76, Kenosha, Wis. BR/TR, 5'9", 152 lbs. Deb: 9/29/13

YEAR	TM/L	G	AB	R	H	2B	3B	HR	RBI	BB	SO	AVG	OBP	SLG	PRO+	BR	/A	RC	SB	CS	SBR	FA	FR	POS	TPR
1913	Phi-A	3	12	0	3	1	0	0	0	0	0	.250	.250	.333	72	-1	-0	1	0			.923	-3	/2	-0.4
1914	Phi-A	4	15	1	3	0	1	0	0	0	4	.200	.200	.333	63	-1	-1	1	0	1	-1	1.000	2	/2	0.0
Total	2	7	27	1	6	1	1	0	0	0	4	.222	.222	.333	67	-1	-1	2	0	1		.973	-1	/2	-0.4

■ TOMMY CRUZ
Cruz, Cirilo (Dilan) b: 2/15/51, Arroyo, P.R. BL/TL, 5'9", 165 lbs. Deb: 9/04/73 F

YEAR	TM/L	G	AB	R	H	2B	3B	HR	RBI	BB	SO	AVG	OBP	SLG	PRO+	BR	/A	RC	SB	CS	SBR	FA	FR	POS	TPR
1973	StL-N	3	0	1	0	0	0	0	0	0	0	—	—	—	—	0	0	0	0	0	0	.000	0	/O	0.0
1977	Chi-A	4	2	1	0	0	0	0	0	0	0	.000	.000	.000	-99	-1	-1	0	0	0	0	1.000	-1	/O	-0.1
Total	2	7	2	2	0	0	0	0	0	0	0	.000	.000	.000	-99	-1	-1	0	0	0	0	1.000	-1	/O	-0.1

■ HECTOR CRUZ
Cruz, Hector Louis (Dilan) "Heity" b: 4/2/53, Arroyo, P.R. BR/TR, 5'11", 170 lbs. Deb: 8/11/73 F

YEAR	TM/L	G	AB	R	H	2B	3B	HR	RBI	BB	SO	AVG	OBP	SLG	PRO+	BR	/A	RC	SB	CS	SBR	FA	FR	POS	TPR
1973	StL-N	11	11	1	0	0	0	0	0	1	3	.000	.083	.000	-75	-3	-3	0	0	0	0	1.000	1	/O	-0.2
1975	StL-N	23	48	7	7	2	2	0	6	2	4	.146	.180	.271	23	-5	-5	2	0	0	0	.800	-2	3/O	-0.8
1976	StL-N	151	526	54	120	17	1	13	71	42	119	.228	.288	.338	77	-17	-17	50	1	0	0	.934	-21	*3	-4.2
1977	StL-N	118	339	50	80	19	2	6	42	46	56	.236	.329	.357	85	-7	-6	41	4	3	-1	.964	-6	*O/3	-1.7
1978	Chi-N	30	76	8	18	5	0	2	9	3	6	.237	.266	.382	70	-2	-3	6	0	0	0	1.000	1	O/3	-0.3
	SF-N	79	197	19	44	8	1	6	24	21	39	.223	.301	.365	89	-4	-3	20	0	2	-1	.978	-1	O3	-0.7
	Yr	109	273	27	62	13	1	8	33	24	45	.227	.292	.370	83	-7	-7	27	0	2	-1	.983	1	O3	-1.0
1979	SF-N	16	25	2	3	0	0	0	1	3	7	.120	.214	.120	-7	-4	-3	1	0	0	0	1.000	-1	/O3	-0.5
	*Cin-N	74	182	24	44	10	2	4	27	31	39	.242	.352	.385	100	1	1	24	0	1	-1	.984	6	O	0.4
	Yr	90	207	26	47	10	2	4	28	34	46	.227	.336	.353	89	-3	-3	24	0	1	-1	.985	4	O/3	-0.1
1980	Cin-N	52	75	5	16	4	1	1	5	8	16	.213	.289	.333	73	-3	-3	7	0	0	0	.955	1	O	-0.2
1981	Chi-N	53	109	15	25	5	0	7	15	17	24	.229	.333	.468	120	3	3	17	2	2	-1	.925	-4	3O	-0.2
1982	Chi-N	17	19	1	4	1	0	0	0	2	4	.211	.286	.263	53	-1	-1	1	0	0	0	1.000	-1	/O	-0.2
Total	9	624	1607	186	361	71	9	39	200	176	317	.225	.303	.353	81	-41	-42	170	7	8	-3	.975	-27	O3	-8.6

■ HENRY CRUZ
Cruz, Henry (Acosta) b: 2/27/52, Christiansted, V.I. BL/TL, 6', 175 lbs. Deb: 4/18/75

YEAR	TM/L	G	AB	R	H	2B	3B	HR	RBI	BB	SO	AVG	OBP	SLG	PRO+	BR	/A	RC	SB	CS	SBR	FA	FR	POS	TPR
1975	LA-N	53	94	8	25	3	1	0	5	7	6	.266	.317	.319	80	-3	-2	10	1	1	-0	.960	-1	O	-0.4
1976	LA-N	49	88	8	16	2	1	4	14	9	11	.182	.258	.364	76	-3	-3	8	0	2	-1	.976	-0	O	-0.6
1977	Chi-A	16	21	3	6	0	0	2	5	1	3	.286	.318	.571	137	1	1	4	0	0	0	.833	-3	/O	-0.2

YEAR	TM/L	G	AB	R	H	2B	3B	HR	RBI	BB	SO	AVG	OBP	SLG	PRO+	BR	/A	RC	SB	CS	SBR	FA	FR	POS	TPR
1978	Chi-A	53	77	13	17	2	1	2	10	8	11	.221	.302	.351	82	-2	-2	8	0	1	-1	1.000	-5	O/D	-0.8
Total	4	171	280	32	64	7	3	8	34	25	31	.229	.294	.361	84	-7	-6	29	1	4	-2	.974	-8	O/D	-2.0
■ JOSE CRUZ	Cruz, Jose (Dilan) b: 8/8/47, Arroyo, P.R. BL/TL, 6', 175 lbs. Deb: 9/19/70 F																								
1970	StL-N	6	17	2	6	1	0	0	1	4	0	.353	.500	.412	144	2	2	4	0	0	0	1.000	1	/O	0.2
1971	StL-N	83	292	46	80	13	2	9	27	49	35	.274	.380	.425	123	12	11	49	6	3	0	.975	-2	O	0.6
1972	StL-N	117	332	33	78	14	4	2	23	36	54	.235	.312	.319	81	-8	-8	35	9	3	1	.979	-1	*O	-1.4
1973	StL-N	132	406	51	92	22	5	10	57	51	66	.227	.314	.379	92	-5	-5	50	10	4	1	.979	-4	*O	-1.4
1974	StL-N	107	161	24	42	4	3	5	20	20	27	.261	.343	.416	112	2	3	23	4	2	0	.975	2	O/1	0.4
1975	Hou-N	120	315	44	81	15	2	9	49	52	44	.257	.364	.403	121	6	9	49	6	3	0	.980	2	O	0.9
1976	Hou-N	133	439	49	133	21	5	4	61	53	46	.303	.378	.401	133	13	18	70	28	11	2	.972	6	*O	2.2
1977	Hou-N	157	579	87	173	31	10	17	87	69	67	.299	.373	.475	138	21	28	104	44	23	-1	.973	2	*O	2.4
1978	Hou-N	153	565	79	178	34	9	10	83	57	57	.315	.378	.460	144	25	30	102	37	9	6	.975	-0	*O/1	3.0
1979	Hou-N	157	558	73	161	33	7	9	72	72	66	.289	.370	.421	122	13	17	91	36	14	2	.959	1	*O	1.4
1980	*Hou-N☆	160	612	79	185	29	7	11	91	60	66	.302	.365	.426	130	17	22	97	36	11	4	.969	6	*O	2.8
1981	*Hou-N	107	409	53	109	16	5	13	55	35	49	.267	.324	.425	117	5	7	54	5	7	-3	.984	5	*O	0.6
1982	Hou-N	155	570	62	157	27	2	9	68	60	67	.275	.345	.377	110	2	8	75	21	11	-0	.964	9	*O	1.3
1983	Hou-N	160	594	85	**189**	28	8	14	92	65	86	.318	.386	.463	143	28	33	109	30	16	-1	.979	3	*O	3.1
1984	Hou-N	160	600	96	187	28	13	12	95	73	68	.312	.386	.462	148	31	36	111	22	8	2	.976	13	*O	4.7
1985	Hou-N★	141	544	69	163	34	4	9	79	43	74	.300	.351	.426	120	11	13	81	16	5	2	.971	10	*O	2.2
1986	*Hou-N	141	479	48	133	22	4	10	72	55	86	.278	.352	.403	111	6	7	68	3	4	-2	.984	6	*O	0.7
1987	Hou-N	126	365	47	88	17	4	11	38	36	65	.241	.309	.400	90	-8	-6	47	4	1	1	.984	6	O	-0.2
1988	NY-A	38	80	9	16	2	0	1	7	8	8	.200	.273	.262	51	-5	-5	5	0	1	-1	.889	-2	D/O	-0.8
Total	19	2353	7917	1036	2251	391	94	165	1077	898	1031	.284	.358	.420	122	169	220	1223	317	136	14	.974	63	*O/D1	22.7
■ JULIO CRUZ	Cruz, Julio Luis b: 12/2/54, Brooklyn, N.Y. BB/TR, 5'9", 165 lbs. Deb: 7/04/77																								
1977	Sea-A	60	199	25	51	3	1	1	7	24	29	.256	.336	.296	75	-6	-6	22	15	6	1	.983	2	2/D	0.1
1978	Sea-A	147	550	77	129	14	1	1	25	69	66	.235	.321	.269	68	-21	-21	58	59	10	**12**	**.987**	8	*2/SD	0.9
1979	Sea-A	107	414	70	112	16	2	1	29	62	61	.271	.366	.326	87	-4	-5	59	49	9	9	.979	17	*2	2.7
1980	Sea-A	119	422	66	88	9	3	2	16	59	49	.209	.307	.258	56	-24	-24	42	45	7	9	.983	1	*2/D	-0.7
1981	Sea-A	94	352	57	90	12	3	2	24	39	40	.256	.335	.324	87	-3	-5	45	43	8	**8**	.982	8	2/S	1.8
1982	Sea-A	154	549	83	133	22	5	8	49	57	71	.242	.317	.344	79	-13	-15	66	46	13	6	.987	4	*2/S3D	0.3
1983	Sea-A	61	181	24	46	10	1	2	12	20	22	.254	.335	.354	86	-2	-3	25	33	6	6	.984	7	2/D	1.2
	*Chi-A	99	334	47	84	9	4	1	40	29	44	.251	.315	.311	71	-12	-13	35	24	6	4	.983	10	2	0.5
	Yr	160	515	71	130	19	5	3	52	49	66	.252	.322	.326	76	-14	-16	60	57	12	10	.983	17	*2/D	1.7
1984	Chi-A	143	415	42	92	14	4	5	43	45	58	.222	.298	.311	66	-17	-20	40	14	6	1	.976	22	*2	0.8
1985	Chi-A	91	234	28	46	2	3	0	15	32	40	.197	.299	.231	46	-16	-17	17	8	5	-1	.982	13	2/D	-0.2
1986	Chi-A	81	209	38	45	2	0	0	19	42	28	.215	.347	.225	58	-10	-11	20	7	2	1	.985	2	2/D	-0.6
Total	10	1156	3859	557	916	113	27	23	279	478	508	.237	.324	.299	71	-129	-141	430	343	78	56	.983	93	*2/DS3	6.8
■ TODD CRUZ	Cruz, Todd Ruben b: 11/23/55, Highland Park, Mich BR/TR, 6', 175 lbs. Deb: 9/04/78																								
1978	Phi-N	3	4	0	2	0	0	0	2	0	0	.500	.500	.500	178	0	0	1	0	1	-1	1.000	2	/S	0.1
1979	KC-A	55	118	9	24	7	0	2	15	3	19	.203	.230	.314	44	-9	-10	8	0	1	-1	.974	4	S/3	-0.3
1980	Cal-A	18	40	5	11	3	0	1	5	5	8	.275	.356	.425	116	1	1	6	0	0	0	.860	-6	S/32O	-0.4
	Chi-A	90	293	23	68	11	1	2	18	9	54	.232	.260	.297	52	-19	-19	22	2	1	0	.956	5	S	-0.4
	Yr	108	333	28	79	14	1	3	23	14	62	.237	.272	.312	60	-19	-18	28	2	1	0	.948	-1	*S/32O	-0.8
1982	Sea-A	136	492	44	113	20	2	16	57	12	95	.230	.248	.376	67	-23	-24	37	2	10	-5	.963	19	*S	0.2
1983	Sea-A	65	216	21	41	4	2	7	21	7	56	.190	.222	.324	46	-16	-17	15	1	3	-2	.964	21	S	0.8
	*Bal-A	81	221	16	46	9	1	3	27	15	52	.208	.262	.299	55	-14	-14	14	3	4	-2	.942	5	3/2	-1.1
	Yr	146	437	37	87	13	3	10	48	22	108	.199	.242	.311	51	-30	-30	29	4	7	-3	.942	25	3S/2	-0.3
1984	Bal-A	96	142	15	31	4	0	3	9	8	33	.218	.265	.310	60	-8	-8	11	1	4	-2	.955	11	3/PD	0.1
Total	6	544	1526	133	336	58	6	34	154	59	317	.220	.253	.333	59	-88	-90	113	9	24	-12	.960	60	S3/2DPO	-1.0
■ MIKE CUBBAGE	Cubbage, Michael Lee b: 7/21/50, Charlottesville, Va. BL/TR, 6', 180 lbs. Deb: 4/07/74 MC																								
1974	Tex-A	9	15	0	0	0	0	0	0	0	4	.000	.000	.000	-99	-4	-4	0	0	0	0	1.000	2	/32	-0.2
1975	Tex-A	58	143	12	32	6	0	4	21	18	14	.224	.311	.350	87	-3	-2	17	0	0	0	.962	2	2/3D	0.1
1976	Tex-A	14	32	2	7	0	0	0	0	7	7	.219	.359	.219	70	-1	-1	3	0	0	0	1.000	-0	/23D	-0.1
	Min-A	104	342	40	89	19	5	3	49	42	37	.260	.346	.371	107	5	4	44	1	1	-0	.940	2	3/2D	0.6
	Yr	118	374	42	96	19	5	3	49	49	44	.257	.347	.358	104	4	3	47	1	1	-0	.940	2	*3/D2	0.5
1977	Min-A	129	417	60	110	16	5	9	55	37	49	.264	.324	.391	95	-4	-3	53	1	4	-2	.952	9	*3/D	0.2
1978	Min-A	125	394	40	111	12	7	7	57	40	44	.282	.349	.401	108	6	5	56	3	1	0	.971	2	*3/2	0.6
1979	Min-A	94	243	26	67	10	1	2	23	39	26	.276	.376	.350	94	1	-1	33	1	8	-5	.928	-12	3D/12	-1.7
1980	Min-A	103	285	29	70	9	0	8	42	23	37	.246	.304	.361	76	-7	-10	32	0	1	-1	.996	7	13/2D	-0.7
1981	NY-N	67	80	9	17	2	2	1	4	9	15	.213	.292	.325	76	-3	-3	8	0	0	0	.963	1	3	-0.2
Total	8	703	1951	218	503	74	20	34	251	215	233	.258	.333	.369	94	-9	-14	245	6	15	-7	.952	12	3/12D	-1.4
■ AL CUCCINELLO	Cuccinello, Alfred Edward b: 11/26/14, Long Island City, N.Y. BR/TR, 5'10", 165 lbs. Deb: 5/17/35 F																								
1935	NY-N	54	165	27	41	7	1	4	20	1	20	.248	.262	.376	70	-8	-7	15	0			.951	6	2/3	0.2
■ TONY CUCCINELLO	Cuccinello, Anthony Francis "Cooch" or "Chick" b: 11/8/07, Long Island City, N.Y. BR/TR, 5'7", 160 lbs. Deb: 4/15/30 FC																								
1930	Cin-N	125	443	64	138	22	5	10	78	47	44	.312	.380	.451	105	1	4	75	5			.920	-19	*32/S	-0.7
1931	Cin-N	154	575	67	181	39	11	2	93	54	28	.315	.374	.431	123	13	18	96	1			.969	5	*2	3.2
1932	Bro-N	154	597	76	168	32	6	12	77	46	47	.281	.337	.415	103	1	2	86	5			.973	19	*2	2.9
1933	Bro-N★	134	485	58	122	31	4	9	65	44	40	.252	.316	.388	105	-0	2	57	4			.977	-19	*23	-0.9
1934	Bro-N	140	528	59	138	32	2	14	94	49	45	.261	.325	.409	100	-4	-0	73	0			.974	12	*23	1.8
1935	Bro-N	102	360	49	105	20	3	8	53	40	35	.292	.366	.431	116	7	8	57	3			.977	6	23	1.9
1936	Bos-N	150	565	68	174	26	3	7	86	58	49	.308	.374	.402	116	9	14	89	1			.971	22	*2	4.5
1937	Bos-N	152	575	77	156	36	4	11	80	61	40	.271	.341	.405	112	2	8	83	2			.967	-10	*2	0.9
1938	Bos-N☆	147	555	62	147	25	2	9	76	52	32	.265	.331	.366	102	-6	1	67	4			.974	-26	*2	-1.6
1939	Bos-N	81	310	42	95	17	1	2	40	26	26	.306	.360	.387	109	1	4	43	5			.970	-4	2	0.5
1940	Bos-N	34	126	14	34	9	0	0	19	8	9	.270	.319	.341	87	-3	-2	13	1			.978	1	3	0.0
	NY-N	88	307	26	64	9	2	5	36	16	42	.208	.248	.300	50	-21	-22	21	1			.987	5	23	-1.3
	Yr	122	433	40	98	18	2	5	55	24	51	.226	.269	.312	60	-24	-24	34	2			.971	6	32	-1.3
1942	Bos-N	40	104	8	21	3	0	1	8	9	11	.202	.265	.260	55	-6	-6	7	1			.907	-4	32	-0.9
1943	Bos-N	13	19	0	0	0	0	0	2	3	1	.000	.136	.000	-60	-4	-4	0	0			.929	0	/32S	-0.4
	Chi-A	34	103	5	28	5	0	2	11	13	13	.272	.353	.379	114	2	2	15	3	1	0	.965	-2	3	0.1
1944	Chi-A	38	130	5	34	3	0	0	17	8	16	.262	.304	.285	70	-5	-5	12	0	0	0	.959	-2	3/2	-0.7
1945	Chi-A†	118	402	50	124	25	3	2	49	45	19	.308	.379	.400	130	14	15	64	6	2	1	.936	-5	*3	1.5
Total	15	1704	6184	730	1729	334	46	94	884	579	497	.280	.343	.394	105	-1	40	857	42	3		.973	-18	*23/S	10.8
■ JIM CUDWORTH	Cudworth, James Alaric "Cuddy" b: 8/22/1858, Fairhaven, Mass. d: 12/21/43, Middleboro, Mass. BR/TR, 6', 165 lbs. Deb: 7/27/1884																								
1884	KC-U	32	116	7	17	3	1	0		2		.147	.161	.190	21	-10	-7	4				.963	2	1O/P	-0.6
■ MANUEL CUETO	Cueto, Manuel "Potato" b: 2/8/1892, Guanajay, Cuba d: 6/29/42, Regla, Havana, Cuba BR/TR, 5'5", 157 lbs. Deb: 6/25/14																								
1914	StL-F	19	43	2	4	0	0	0	2	5	0	.093	.188	.093	-18	-7	-7	1	0			.941	-1	3/S2	-0.8

YEAR	TM/L	G	AB	R	H	2B	3B	HR	RBI	BB	SO	AVG	OBP	SLG	PRO+	BR	/A	RC	SB	CS	SBR	FA	FR	POS	TPR
1917	Cin-N	56	140	10	28	3	0	1	11	16	17	.200	.287	.243	66	-6	-5	11	4			.963	-1	O/2C	-0.8
1918	Cin-N	47	108	14	32	5	1	0	14	19	5	.296	.406	.361	137	6	6	18	4			.929	-14	O2/SC	-0.8
1919	Cin-N	29	88	10	22	2	0	0	4	10	4	.250	.340	.273	88	-1	-1	10	5			.982	4	O/3	0.1
Total	4	151	379	36	86	10	1	1	31	50	26	.227	.323	.266	81	-8	-7	40	13			.964	-12	/O2SC3	-2.3

■ JOHN CUFF Cuff, John J. b: 6/1864, Jersey City, N, J. Deb: 9/11/1884

YEAR	TM/L	G	AB	R	H	2B	3B	HR	RBI	BB	SO	AVG	OBP	SLG	PRO+	BR	/A	RC	SB	CS	SBR	FA	FR	POS	TPR
1884	Bal-U	3	11	1	1	1	0	0		1		.091	.167	.182	16	-1	-1	0				.920	0	/C	0.0

■ LEON CULBERSON Culberson, Delbert Leon "Lee" b: 8/6/19, Hall's Station, Ga. d: 9/17/89, Rome, Ga. BR/TR, 5'11", 180 lbs. Deb: 5/16/43

YEAR	TM/L	G	AB	R	H	2B	3B	HR	RBI	BB	SO	AVG	OBP	SLG	PRO+	BR	/A	RC	SB	CS	SBR	FA	FR	POS	TPR
1943	Bos-A	81	312	36	85	16	6	3	34	31	35	.272	.338	.391	111	5	4	46	14	0	4	.978	6	O	1.0
1944	Bos-A	75	282	41	67	11	5	2	21	20	20	.238	.288	.333	78	-9	-9	27	6	4	-1	.979	-3	O	-1.7
1945	Bos-A	97	331	26	91	21	6	6	45	20	37	.275	.316	.429	113	4	4	41	4	3	-1	.967	5	O	0.3
1946	*Bos-A	59	179	34	56	10	1	3	18	16	19	.313	.369	.430	116	5	4	29	3	2	-0	.967	-7	O/3	-0.5
1947	Bos-A	47	84	10	20	1	0	0	11	12	10	.238	.354	.250	65	-3	-4	9	1	1	-0	.974	-4	O/3	-0.9
1948	Was-A	12	29	1	5	0	0	0	2	8	5	.172	.351	.172	43	-2	-2	2	0	0	0	1.000	-3	O	-0.5
Total	6	371	1217	148	324	59	18	14	131	107	126	.266	.327	.379	100	1	-2	153	28	10	2	.974	-6	O/3	-2.3

■ JOHN CULLEN Cullen, John J. b: 3/E,Cal. Deb: 8/18/1884

YEAR	TM/L	G	AB	R	H	2B	3B	HR	RBI	BB	SO	AVG	OBP	SLG	PRO+	BR	/A	RC	SB	CS	SBR	FA	FR	POS	TPR
1884	Wil-U	9	31	2	6	0	0	0		1		.194	.219	.194	39	-2	-2	1				.750	-1	/OS	-0.3

■ TIM CULLEN Cullen, Timothy Leo b: 2/16/42, San Francisco, Cal. BR/TR, 6'1", 185 lbs. Deb: 8/08/66

YEAR	TM/L	G	AB	R	H	2B	3B	HR	RBI	BB	SO	AVG	OBP	SLG	PRO+	BR	/A	RC	SB	CS	SBR	FA	FR	POS	TPR
1966	Was-A	18	34	8	8	1	0	0	0	2	8	.235	.278	.265	57	-2	-2	3	0	0	0	.889	1	/32	0.0
1967	Was-A	124	402	35	95	7	0	2	31	40	47	.236	.307	.269	74	-13	-12	35	4	5	-2	.951	15	S23/O	1.1
1968	Chi-A	72	155	16	31	7	0	2	13	15	23	.200	.275	.284	69	-6	-6	12	0	0	0	.966	6	2	0.3
	Was-A	47	114	8	31	4	2	1	16	7	12	.272	.325	.368	113	1	2	14	0	0	0	.968	-1	S2/3	0.4
	Yr	119	269	24	62	11	2	3	29	22	35	.230	.296	.320	87	-4	-4	26	0	0	0	.965	5	2S/3	0.7
1969	Was-A	119	249	22	52	7	0	1	15	14	27	.209	.257	.249	44	-19	-18	14	1	1	-0	.981	12	*2/S3	-0.1
1970	Was-A	123	262	22	56	10	2	1	18	31	38	.214	.304	.279	65	-13	-11	22	3	2	-0	**.994**	27	*2/S	2.2
1971	Was-A	125	403	34	77	13	4	2	26	33	47	.191	.252	.258	47	-29	-27	26	2	0	1	.997	21	2S	0.7
1972	*Oak-A	72	142	10	37	8	1	0	15	5	17	.261	.286	.331	88	-3	-3	13	0	1	-1	.952	-1	2/3S	-0.2
Total	7	700	1761	155	387	57	9	9	134	147	219	.220	.283	.278	65	-85	-76	138	10	9	-2	.979	79	2S/3O	4.4

■ ROY CULLENBINE Cullenbine, Roy Joseph b: 10/18/13, Nashville, Tenn. d: 5/28/91, Mt.Clemens, Mich. BB/TR, 6'1", 190 lbs. Deb: 4/19/38

YEAR	TM/L	G	AB	R	H	2B	3B	HR	RBI	BB	SO	AVG	OBP	SLG	PRO+	BR	/A	RC	SB	CS	SBR	FA	FR	POS	TPR
1938	Det-A	25	67	12	19	1	3	0	9	12	9	.284	.392	.388	91	-0	-1	11	2	0	1	1.000	-0	O	-0.1
1939	Det-A	75	179	31	43	9	2	6	23	34	29	.240	.362	.413	91	-0	-2	29	0	1	-1	.902	-5	O/1	-0.9
1940	Bro-N	22	61	8	11	1	0	1	9	23	11	.180	.405	.246	78	0	-0	8	2			1.000	1	O	-0.1
	StL-A	86	257	41	59	11	2	7	31	50	34	.230	.359	.370	87	-3	-4	38	0	1	-1	.975	-2	O/1	-1.0
1941	StL-A★	149	501	82	159	29	9	9	98	121	43	.317	.452	.465	138	38	36	120	6	4	-1	.964	1	*O1	2.7
1942	StL-A	38	109	15	21	7	1	2	14	30	20	.193	.367	.330	95	1	1	16	0	1	-1	.930	1	O/1	-0.1
	Was-A	64	241	30	69	19	0	2	35	44	18	.286	.396	.390	123	9	9	41	1	2	-1	.966	8	O3	1.5
	*NY-A	21	77	16	28	7	0	2	17	18	2	.364	.484	.532	190	10	10	22	0	1	-1	.980	2	O/1	1.1
	Yr	123	427	61	118	33	1	6	66	92	40	.276	.405	.400	127	19	20	77	1	4	-2	.959	11	O3/1	2.5
1943	Cle-A	138	488	66	141	24	4	8	56	96	58	.289	.407	.404	146	27	31	89	3	4	-2	.981	3	*O1	2.7
1944	Cle-A☆	154	571	98	162	34	5	16	80	87	49	.284	.380	.445	141	28	30	102	4	4	-1	.967	-2	*O	2.0
1945	Cle-A	8	13	3	1	1	0	0	0	11	0	.077	.500	.154	97	1	1	2	0	0	0	1.000	-2	/O3	-0.1
	*Det-A	146	523	80	145	27	5	18	93	102	36	.277	.398	.451	137	34	30	103	2	0	1	.980	13	*O	3.7
	Yr	154	536	83	146	28	5	18	93	**113**	36	.272	.402	.444	137	35	31	106	2	0	1	.980	11	*O/3	3.6
1946	Det-A	113	328	63	110	21	0	15	56	88	39	.335	.477	.537	172	42	39	95	3	0	1	.965	1	O1	3.8
1947	Det-A	142	464	82	104	18	1	24	78	137	51	.224	.401	.422	125	24	22	91	3	2	-0	.989	16	*1	3.3
Total	10	1181	3879	627	1072	209	32	110	599	853	399	.276	.408	.432	132	211	202	769	26	20		.969	34	O1/3	18.5

■ DICK CULLER Culler, Richard Broadus b: 1/15/15, High Point, N.C. d: 6/16/64, Chapel Hill, N.C. BR/TR, 5'9.5", 155 lbs. Deb: 9/19/36

YEAR	TM/L	G	AB	R	H	2B	3B	HR	RBI	BB	SO	AVG	OBP	SLG	PRO+	BR	/A	RC	SB	CS	SBR	FA	FR	POS	TPR
1936	Phi-A	9	38	3	9	0	0	0	1	1	3	.237	.256	.237	23	-5	-4	2	0	0	0	.946	-3	/2S	-0.7
1943	Chi-A	53	148	9	32	5	1	0	11	16	11	.216	.297	.264	65	-6	-6	11	4	5	-2	.950	11	32/S	0.4
1944	Bos-N	8	28	2	2	0	0	0	0	4	2	.071	.188	.071	-24	-5	-5	0	0			.904	2	/S	-0.2
1945	Bos-N	136	527	87	138	12	1	2	30	50	35	.262	.328	.300	75	-16	-17	54	7			.954	-8	*S/3	-1.5
1946	Bos-N	134	482	70	123	15	3	0	33	62	18	.255	.342	.299	82	-9	-10	51	7			.948	-8	*S	-1.1
1947	Bos-N	77	214	20	53	5	1	0	19	19	15	.248	.309	.280	59	-13	-12	19	1			.967	3	S	-0.6
1948	Chi-N	48	89	4	15	2	0	0	5	13	3	.169	.275	.191	29	-9	-8	5	0			.968	16	S/2	0.9
1949	NY-N	7	1	0	0	0	0	0	0	1	0	.000	.500	.000	45	0	0	0	0			.889	2	/S	0.2
Total	8	472	1527	195	372	39	6	2	99	166	87	.244	.320	.281	68	-62	-62	144	19	5		.954	14	S/32	-2.6

■ NICK CULLOP Cullop, Henry Nicholas "Tomato Face" b: 10/16/1900, St.Louis, Mo. d: 12/8/78, Westerville, Ohio BR/TR, 6', 200 lbs. Deb: 4/14/26

YEAR	TM/L	G	AB	R	H	2B	3B	HR	RBI	BB	SO	AVG	OBP	SLG	PRO+	BR	/A	RC	SB	CS	SBR	FA	FR	POS	TPR
1926	NY-A	2	2	0	1	0	0	0	0	0	1	.500	.500	.500	164	0	0	0	0	0	0	.000	0	H	0.0
1927	Was-A	15	23	2	5	2	0	0	1	1	6	.217	.250	.304	44	-2	-2	2	0	0	0	1.000	-1	/O1	-0.3
	Cle-A	32	68	9	16	2	3	1	8	9	19	.235	.333	.397	88	-1	-1	8	0	4	-2	.982	3	O/P	-0.2
	Yr	47	91	11	21	4	3	1	9	10	25	.231	.314	.374	78	-3	-3	9	0	4	-2	.984	2	O/1P	-0.5
1929	Bro-N	13	41	7	8	2	2	1	5	8	7	.195	.327	.415	84	-1	-1	6	0			1.000	-1	O/1	-0.2
1930	Cin-N	7	22	2	4	0	0	1	5	1	9	.182	.217	.318	29	-3	-3	1	0			1.000	0	/O	-0.2
1931	Cin-N	104	334	29	88	23	7	8	48	21	86	.263	.309	.446	107	-1	1	47	1			.968	0	O	-0.4
Total	5	173	490	49	122	29	12	11	67	40	128	.249	.308	.424	96	-8	-5	64	1	4		.975	2	O/1P	-1.3

■ WIL CULMER Culmer, Wilfred Hillard b: 11/11/58, Nassau, Bahamas BR/TR, 6'4", 210 lbs. Deb: 4/12/83

YEAR	TM/L	G	AB	R	H	2B	3B	HR	RBI	BB	SO	AVG	OBP	SLG	PRO+	BR	/A	RC	SB	CS	SBR	FA	FR	POS	TPR
1983	Cle-A	7	19	0	2	0	0	0	1	0	4	.105	.105	.105	-40	-4	-4	0	0	1	-1	1.000	-1	/OD	-0.6

■ BENNY CULP Culp, Benjamin Baldy b: 1/19/14, Philadelphia, Pa. BR/TR, 5'9", 175 lbs. Deb: 9/17/42 C

YEAR	TM/L	G	AB	R	H	2B	3B	HR	RBI	BB	SO	AVG	OBP	SLG	PRO+	BR	/A	RC	SB	CS	SBR	FA	FR	POS	TPR
1942	Phi-N	1	0	0	0	0	0	0	0	0	0	—	—	—	—	0	0	0	0			.500	-0	/C	0.0
1943	Phi-N	10	24	4	5	1	0	0	2	3	3	.208	.296	.250	61	-1	-1	2	0			.958	-3	C	-0.3
1944	Phi-N	4	2	1	0	0	0	0	0	0	0	.000	.000	.000	-99	-1	-1	0	0			1.000	1	/C	0.0
Total	3	15	26	5	5	1	0	0	2	3	3	.192	.276	.231	49	-2	-2	2	0			.926	-2	/C	-0.3

■ JACK CUMMINGS Cummings, John William b: 4/1/04, Pittsburgh, Pa. d: 10/5/62, W.Mifflin, Pa. BR/TR, 6', 195 lbs. Deb: 9/11/26

YEAR	TM/L	G	AB	R	H	2B	3B	HR	RBI	BB	SO	AVG	OBP	SLG	PRO+	BR	/A	RC	SB	CS	SBR	FA	FR	POS	TPR
1926	NY-N	7	16	3	5	3	0	0	4	4	2	.313	.450	.500	157	1	1	4	0			.958	0	/C	0.2
1927	NY-N	43	80	8	29	6	1	2	14	5	10	.363	.407	.538	151	6	6	17	0			.974	-5	C	0.2
1928	NY-N	33	27	4	9	2	0	2	9	3	4	.333	.400	.630	165	2	2	7	0			.833	0	/C	0.2
1929	NY-N	3	3	0	1	0	0	0	0	0	0	.333	.333	.333	66	-0	-0	0	0			1.000	-0	/C	0.0
	Bos-N	3	6	0	1	0	0	0	1	0	2	.167	.167	.167	-18	-1	-1	0	0			.667	-1	/C	-0.2
	Yr	6	9	0	2	0	0	0	1	0	2	.222	.222	.222	11	-1	-1	0	0			.714	-1	/C	-0.2
Total	4	89	132	15	45	11	1	4	28	12	18	.341	.400	.530	145	8	8	28	0			.947	-6	/C	0.4

■ GEORGE CUNNINGHAM Cunningham, George Harold b: 7/13/1894, Sturgeon Lake, Minn. d: 3/10/72, Chattanooga, Tenn. BR/TR, 5'11", 185 lbs. Deb: 4/14/16

YEAR	TM/L	G	AB	R	H	2B	3B	HR	RBI	BB	SO	AVG	OBP	SLG	PRO+	BR	/A	RC	SB	CS	SBR	FA	FR	POS	TPR
1916	Det-A	35	41	7	11	2	2	0	3	8	12	.268	.388	.415	136	2	2	7	0			.948	1	P	0.0
1917	Det-A	44	34	5	6	0	0	1	3	3	13	.176	.243	.265	55	-2	-2	2	0			.922	0	P	0.0
1918	Det-A	56	112	11	25	4	1	0	2	16	34	.223	.320	.277	84	-2	-2	11	2			.923	-6	PO	-0.8
1919	Det-A	26	23	4	5	0	0	0	5	9	8	.217	.438	.217	89	0	0	2	0			.857	0	P	0.0

YEAR	TM/L	G	AB	R	H	2B	3B	HR	RBI	BB	SO	AVG	OBP	SLG	PRO+	BR	/A	RC	SB	CS	SBR	FA	FR	POS	TPR
1921	Det-A	1	0	0	0	0	0	0	0	0	0	—	—	—	—	0	0	0	0	0	0	1.000	-0	/O	0.0
Total	5	162	210	27	47	6	3	1	13	36	67	.224	.337	.295	91	-2	-1	22	2	0		.923	-4	P/O	-0.8
■ JOE CUNNINGHAM	Cunningham, Joseph Robert b: 8/27/31, Paterson, N.J. BL/TL, 6'1", 190 lbs. Deb: 6/30/54 C																								
1954	StL-N	85	310	40	88	11	3	11	50	43	40	.284	.375	.445	112	6	6	55	1	1	-0	.989	2	1	0.4
1956	StL-N	4	3	1	0	0	0	0	0	1	1	.000	.250	.000	-25	-1	-1	0	0	0	0	1.000	-0	/1	-0.1
1957	StL-N	122	261	50	83	15	0	9	52	56	29	.318	.447	.479	146	22	21	61	3	3	-1	1.000	-3	1O	1.3
1958	StL-N	131	337	61	105	20	3	12	57	82	23	.312	.450	.496	144	29	27	80	4	4	-1	.997	-6	1O	1.4
1959	StL-N★	144	458	65	158	28	6	7	60	88	47	.345	**.456**	.478	140	38	34	104	2	6	-3	.972	-7	*O1	1.6
1960	StL-N	139	492	68	138	28	3	6	39	59	59	.280	.364	.386	97	6	0	70	1	7	-4	.950	-7	*O1	-1.9
1961	StL-N	113	322	60	92	11	2	7	40	53	32	.286	.404	.398	104	9	5	58	1	0	0	.964	-12	O1	-1.2
1962	Chi-A	149	526	91	155	32	7	8	70	101	59	.295	.415	.428	128	25	26	102	3	3	-1	**.994**	-6	*1/O	0.9
1963	Chi-A	67	210	32	60	12	1	1	31	33	23	.286	.393	.367	116	6	6	33	1	0	0	.989	-7	1	-0.3
1964	Chi-A	40	108	13	27	7	0	0	10	14	15	.250	.352	.315	90	-1	-1	13	0	1	-1	.996	-1	1	-0.3
	Was-A	49	126	15	27	4	0	0	7	23	13	.214	.344	.246	68	-4	-4	12	0	1	-1	.997	-4	1	-1.1
	Yr	89	234	28	54	11	0	0	17	37	28	.231	.348	.278	78	-6	-5	25	0	2	-1	.997	-5	1	-1.4
1965	Was-A	95	201	29	46	9	1	3	20	46	27	.229	.375	.328	103	3	3	27	0	1	-1	.986	-4	1	-0.5
1966	Was-A	3	8	0	1	0	0	0	0	0	1	.125	.125	.125	-28	-1	-1	0	0	0	0	1.000	1	/1	0.0
Total	12	1141	3362	525	980	177	26	64	436	599	369	.291	.406	.417	119	136	121	614	16	27	-11	.993	-54	1O	0.2
■ RAY CUNNINGHAM	Cunningham, Raymond Lee b: 1/17/08, Mesquite, Tex. BR/TR, 5'7.5", 150 lbs. Deb: 9/16/31																								
1931	StL-N	3	4	0	0	0	0	0	1	0	0	.000	.000	.000	-96	-1	-1	0	0			1.000	1	/3	0.0
1932	StL-N	11	22	4	4	1	0	0	0	3	4	.182	.280	.227	37	-2	-2	2	0			1.000	3	/32	0.1
Total	2	14	26	4	4	1	0	0	1	3	4	.154	.241	.192	18	-3	-3	2	0			1.000	4	/32	0.1
■ BILL CUNNINGHAM	Cunningham, William Aloysius b: 7/30/1895, San Francisco, Cal. d: 9/26/53, Colusa, Cal. BR/TR, 5'8", 155 lbs. Deb: 7/14/21 C																								
1921	NY-N	40	76	10	21	2	1	1	12	3	3	.276	.313	.368	79	-2	-2	8	0	1	-1	1.000	-4	O	-0.8
1922	*NY-N	85	229	37	75	15	2	2	33	7	9	.328	.350	.437	101	0	-0	33	4	5	-2	.988	-4	O/3	-0.9
1923	*NY-N	79	203	22	55	7	1	5	27	10	9	.271	.305	.389	83	-6	-5	24	5	2	0	.992	-7	O/2	-1.4
1924	Bos-N	114	437	44	119	15	8	1	40	32	27	.272	.326	.350	85	-11	-9	51	8	5	-1	.970	6	*O	-1.1
Total	4	318	945	113	270	39	12	9	112	52	48	.286	.326	.381	88	-19	-17	116	17	13	-3	.982	-8	O/23	-4.2
■ BILL CUNNINGHAM	Cunningham, William James b: 6/9/1888, Schenectady, N.Y. d: 2/21/46, Schenectady, N.Y. BR/TR, 5'9", 170 lbs. Deb: 9/12/10																								
1910	Was-A	21	74	3	22	5	1	0	14	12		.297	.402	.392	156	5	5	14	4			.957	-4	2	0.0
1911	Was-A	94	331	34	63	10	5	3	37	19		.190	.239	.278	45	-26	-25	25	10			.932	-13	2	-4.0
1912	Was-A	8	27	5	5	1	0	1	8	3		.185	.267	.333	71	-1	-1	3	2			.962	-3	/2S	-0.4
Total	3	123	432	42	90	16	6	4	59	34		.208	.271	.301	64	-22	-21	41	16			.938	-20	2/S	-4.4
■ DOC CURLEY	Curley, Walter James b: 3/12/1874, Upton, Mass. d: 9/23/20, Framingham, Mass. BR/TR, Deb: 9/12/1899																								
1899	Chi-N	10	37	7	4	0	1	0	2	3		.108	.233	.162	9	-5	-4	2	0			.907	-5	2	-0.9
■ PETE CURREN	Curren, Peter b: Baltimore, Md. Deb: 9/12/1876																								
1876	Phi-N	3	12	5	4	1	0	0	2	0	0	.333	.333	.417	150	1	1	2				.588	-1	/CO	0.0
■ PERRY CURRIN	Currin, Perry Gilmore b: 9/27/28, Washington, D.C. BL/TR, 6', 175 lbs. Deb: 6/29/47																								
1947	StL-A	3	2	0	0	0	0	0	0	1	0	.000	.333	.000	-3	-0	-0	0	0	0	0	1.000	1	/S	0.1
■ TONY CURRY	Curry, George Anthony b: 12/22/38, Nassau, Bahamas BL/TL, 5'11", 185 lbs. Deb: 4/12/60																								
1960	Phi-N	95	245	26	64	14	2	6	34	16	53	.261	.309	.408	94	-2	-2	31	0	2	-1	.925	-8	O	-1.4
1961	Phi-N	15	36	3	7	2	0	0	3	1	8	.194	.216	.250	24	-4	-4	2	0	0	0	.833	-1	/O	-0.5
1966	Cle-A	19	16	4	2	0	0	0	3	3	8	.125	.263	.125	16	-2	-2	1	0	0	0	.000	0	H	-0.2
Total	3	129	297	33	73	16	2	6	40	20	69	.246	.296	.374	82	-8	-8	34	0	2	-1	.915	-8	/O	-2.1
■ JIM CURRY	Curry, James E. b: 3/10/1893, Camden, N.J. d: 8/2/38, Lakeland, N.J. BR/TR, 5'11", 160 lbs. Deb: 10/02/09																								
1909	Phi-A	1	4	1	1	0	0	0	0	0		.250	.250	.250	57	-0	-0	0	0			1.000	-1	/2	-0.1
1911	NY-A	4	11	3	2	0	0	0	0	1		.182	.250	.182	20	-1	-1	1	0			.773	-1	/2	-0.3
1918	Det-A	5	20	1	5	1	0	0	0	0	0	.250	.286	.300	80	-1	-1	2	0			.952	-3	/2	-0.3
Total	3	10	35	5	8	1	0	0	0	1	0	.229	.270	.257	56	-2	-2	2	0			.867	-5	/2	-0.7
■ CHAD CURTIS	Curtis, Chad David b: 11/6/68, Marion, Ind. BR/TR, 5'10", 175 lbs. Deb: 4/08/92																								
1992	Cal-A	139	441	59	114	16	2	10	46	51	71	.259	.343	.372	102	1	2	58	43	18	2	.978	-3	*O/D	-0.2
■ GENE CURTIS	Curtis, Eugene Holmes "Eude" b: 5/5/1883, Bethany, W.Va. d: 1/1/19, Steubenville, Ohio BR/TR, 6'3", 220 lbs. Deb: 9/21/03																								
1903	Pit-N	5	19	2	8	1	0	0	3	1		.421	.450	.474	159	2	1	4	0			.833	-0	/O	0.1
■ FRED CURTIS	Curtis, Frederick Marion b: 10/30/1880, Beaver Lake, Mich. d: 4/5/39, Minneapolis, Minn. BR/TR, 6'1", Deb: 7/24/05																								
1905	NY-A	2	9	0	2	1	0	0	2	1		.222	.300	.333	91	0	-0	1	1			1.000	-0	/1	0.0
■ HARRY CURTIS	Curtis, Harry Albert b: 2/19/1883, Portland, Maine d: 8/1/51, Evanston, Ill. TR , 5'10.5", 170 lbs. Deb: 8/28/07																								
1907	NY-N	6	9	2	2	0	0	0	1	2		.222	.364	.222	81	-0	-0	1	2			.909	0	/C	0.0
■ JIM CURTIS	Curtis, James D. b: 12/27/1861, Coldwater, Mich. d: 2/14/45, N.Adams, Mass. BL , 5'8.5", 157 lbs. Deb: 7/15/1891																								
1891	Cin-N	27	108	11	29	3	3	1	13	9	19	.269	.331	.380	108	1	1	15	3			.862	-0	O	0.0
	Was-a	29	103	17	26	3	2	0	12	13	16	.252	.347	.320	99	-0	0	12	2			.797	-1	O	-0.2
Total	1	56	211	28	55	6	5	1	25	22	35	.261	.339	.351	103	1	1	27	5			.829	-2	/O	-0.2
■ GUY CURTRIGHT	Curtright, Guy Paxton b: 10/18/12, Holliday, Mo. BR/TR, 5'11", 200 lbs. Deb: 4/21/43																								
1943	Chi-A	138	488	67	142	20	7	3	48	69	60	.291	.382	.379	123	16	16	74	13	12	-3	.972	-2	*O	0.5
1944	Chi-A	72	198	22	50	8	2	2	23	23	21	.253	.330	.343	94	-2	-1	23	4	3	-1	.948	1	O	-0.3
1945	Chi-A	98	324	51	91	15	7	4	32	39	29	.281	.358	.407	125	9	10	49	3	4	-2	.986	1	O	0.6
1946	Chi-A	23	55	7	11	2	0	0	5	11	14	.200	.333	.236	63	-2	-2	4	0	1	-1	1.000	1	O	-0.3
Total	4	331	1065	147	294	45	16	9	108	142	124	.276	.363	.374	115	21	23	150	20	20	-6	.973	2	O	0.5
■ TONY CUSICK	Cusick, Andrew Daniel "Andy" b: 1860, Fall River, Mass. d: 8/6/29, Chicago, Ill. BR/TR, 5'9.5", 190 lbs. Deb: 8/21/1884																								
1884	Wil-U	11	34	0	5	0	0	0		1		.147	.171	.147	8	-3	-3	1				.871	-0	/CSO23	-0.2
	Phi-N	9	29	2	4	0	0	0	1	0	3	.138	.138	.138	-14	-4	-3	1				.930	4	/C	0.1
1885	Phi-N	39	141	12	25	1	0	0	5	1	24	.177	.183	.184	19	-12	-12	5				.808	-3	C/O	-1.1
1886	Phi-N	29	104	10	23	5	1	0	4	3	14	.221	.243	.288	61	-5	-5	8	1			.891	-6	C/O1	-0.7
1887	Phi-N	7	24	3	7	1	0	0	5	3	1	.292	.393	.333	100	0	0	3	0			.643	-3	/C12	-0.3
Total	4	95	332	27	64	7	1	0	15	8	42	.193	.214	.220	37	-24	-24	17	1			.844	-9	/CO1S23	-2.2
■ JACK CUSICK	Cusick, John Peter b: 6/12/28, Weehawken, N.J. d: 11/17/89, Edgewood, N.J. BR/TR, 6', 170 lbs. Deb: 4/24/51																								
1951	Chi-N	65	164	16	29	3	2	2	16	17	29	.177	.254	.256	37	-15	-15	11	2	1	0	.953	-2	S	-1.4
1952	Bos-N	49	78	5	13	1	0	0	6	6	9	.167	.226	.179	14	-9	-9	2	0	1	-1	.969	-2	S/3	-1.0
Total	2	114	242	21	42	4	2	2	22	23	38	.174	.245	.231	30	-24	-24	13	2	2	-1	.958	-4	/S3	-2.4

■ NED CUTHBERT Cuthbert, Edgar Edward b: 6/20/1845, Philadelphia, Pa. d: 2/6/05, St.Louis, Mo. BR/TR, 5'6", 140 lbs. Deb: 5/20/1871 MU

YEAR	TM/L	G	AB	R	H	2B	3B	HR	RBI	BB	SO	AVG	OBP	SLG	PRO+	BR	/A	RC	SB	CS	SBR	FA	FR	POS	TPR
1871	Ath-n	28	150	47	37	7	5	3	30	10	2	.247	.294	.420	103	0	1	24	16					*O/C	0.1
1872	Ath-n	47	258	82	90	9	0	1	47	6	10	.349	.364	.395	133	10	10	41						*O	0.9
1873	Phi-n	51	278	78	77	5	3	2	32	2	4	.277	.282	.338	79	-6	-8	30						*O	-0.3
1874	Chi-n	58	293	65	81	6	1	1		7		.276	.293	.314	93	-2	-2	28						*O/C	-0.1
1875	StL-n	68	318	68	77	9	2	0		3		.242	.249	.283	92	-5	-0	23						*O/C	0.0
1876	StL-N	63	283	46	70	10	1	0	25	7	4	.247	.266	.290	90	-4	-2	22				.843	-8	*O	-1.0
1877	Cin-N	12	56	6	10	5	0	0	2	1	2	.179	.193	.268	49	-4	-3	3				.830	4	O	0.1
1882	StL-a	60	233	28	52	16	5	0		17		.223	.276	.335	101	2	0	22				.896	-4	*OM	-0.4
1883	StL-a	21	71	3	12	1	0	0		4		.169	.213	.183	27	-5	-6	3				.794	-1	O/1	-0.6
1884	Bal-U	44	168	29	34	5	0	0		10		.202	.247	.232	57	-6	-9	10				.750	-5	O	-1.3
Total	5 n	252	1297	340	362	36	11	7	109	28	16	.279	.294	.340	99	-3	-1	146						O/C	0.6
Total	5	200	811	112	178	37	6	0	27	39	6	.219	.255	.280	77	-18	-19	60				.833	-14	O/1	-3.2

■ GEORGE CUTSHAW Cutshaw, George William "Clancy" b: 7/27/1887, Wilmington, Ill. d: 8/22/73, San Diego, Cal. BR/TR, 5'9", 160 lbs. Deb: 4/25/12

YEAR	TM/L	G	AB	R	H	2B	3B	HR	RBI	BB	SO	AVG	OBP	SLG	PRO+	BR	/A	RC	SB	CS	SBR	FA	FR	POS	TPR
1912	Bro-N	102	357	41	100	14	4	0	28	31	16	.280	.341	.342	91	-6	-4	47	16			.958	8	2/3S	0.2
1913	Bro-N	147	592	72	158	23	13	7	80	39	22	.267	.315	.385	97	-2	-4	80	39			.957	18	*2	1.2
1914	Bro-N	153	583	69	150	22	12	2	78	30	32	.257	.297	.346	89	-8	-10	67	34			.959	28	*2	1.8
1915	Bro-N	154	566	68	139	18	9	0	62	34	35	.246	.293	.309	81	-13	-14	53	28	23	-5	**.971**	17	*2	0.0
1916	*Bro-N	154	581	58	151	21	4	2	63	25	32	.260	.292	.320	85	-9	-11	58	27	20	-4	.958	8	*2	-0.2
1917	Bro-N	135	487	42	126	17	7	4	49	21	26	.259	.292	.347	93	-4	-5	54	22			.963	-9	*2	-0.9
1918	Pit-N	126	463	56	132	16	10	5	68	27	18	.285	.326	.395	115	9	7	66	25			.964	-3	*2	1.4
1919	Pit-N	139	512	49	124	15	8	3	51	30	22	.242	.287	.320	79	-11	-14	54	36			**.980**	-11	*2	-2.0
1920	Pit-N	131	488	56	123	16	8	0	47	23	10	.252	.287	.318	71	-17	-19	44	17	14	-3	.968	1	*2	-1.8
1921	Pit-N	98	350	46	119	18	4	0	53	11	11	.340	.362	.414	102	2	1	52	14	5	1	.951	-15	2	-1.1
1922	Det-A	132	499	57	133	14	8	2	61	20	13	.267	.300	.339	68	-25	-23	52	11	5	0	.972	9	*2	-1.0
1923	Det-A	45	143	15	32	1	2	0	13	9	5	.224	.279	.259	43	-12	-12	12	2	1	0	.988	12	2/3	0.1
Total	12	1516	5621	629	1487	195	89	25	653	300	242	.265	.305	.344	86	-96	-106	639	271	68		.965	61	*2/3S	-2.3

■ KIKI CUYLER Cuyler, Hazen Shirley b: 8/30/1899, Harrisville, Mich. d: 2/11/50, Ann Arbor, Mich. BR/TR, 5'10.5", 180 lbs. Deb: 9/29/21 CH

YEAR	TM/L	G	AB	R	H	2B	3B	HR	RBI	BB	SO	AVG	OBP	SLG	PRO+	BR	/A	RC	SB	CS	SBR	FA	FR	POS	TPR
1921	Pit-N	1	3	0	0	0	0	0	0	0	1	.000	.000	.000	-97	-1	-1	0	0	0	0	1.000	-0	/O	-0.1
1922	Pit-N	1	0	0	0	0	0	0	0	0	0	—	—	—	—	0	0	0	0	0	0	.000	0	R	0.0
1923	Pit-N	11	40	4	10	1	1	0	2	5	3	.250	.348	.325	77	-1	-1	4	2	3	-1	.931	-1	O	-0.4
1924	Pit-N	117	466	94	165	27	16	9	85	30	62	.354	.402	.539	147	32	31	101	32	11	3	.943	5	*O	3.1
1925	*Pit-N	153	617	**144**	220	43	**26**	18	102	58	56	.357	.423	.598	148	53	47	158	41	13	5	.967	7	*O	4.4
1926	Pit-N	157	614	**113**	197	31	15	8	92	50	66	.321	.380	.459	119	22	17	105	**35**			.968	13	*O	1.9
1927	Pit-N	85	285	60	88	13	7	3	31	37	36	.309	.394	.435	114	10	7	49	20			.980	1	O	0.4
1928	Chi-N	133	499	92	142	25	9	17	79	51	61	.285	.359	.473	117	11	12	84	**37**			.982	6	*O	0.9
1929	*Chi-N	139	509	111	183	29	7	15	102	66	56	.360	.438	.532	139	33	33	118	**43**			.974	-0	*O	2.2
1930	Chi-N	156	642	155	228	50	17	13	134	72	49	.355	.428	.547	133	37	36	148	**37**			.980	12	*O	3.2
1931	Chi-N	154	613	100	202	37	12	9	88	72	54	.330	.404	.473	133	32	31	122	13			.970	-4	*O	1.6
1932	*Chi-N	110	446	58	130	19	9	10	77	29	43	.291	.340	.442	109	5	5	68	9			.969	-7	*O	-0.9
1933	Chi-N	70	262	37	83	13	3	5	35	21	29	.317	.376	.447	135	12	12	43	4			.978	-7	O	0.1
1934	Chi-N★	142	559	80	189	**42**	8	6	69	31	62	.338	.377	.474	129	20	22	101	15			.971	0	*O	1.6
1935	Chi-N	45	157	22	42	5	1	4	18	10	16	.268	.331	.389	92	-2	-2	21	3			.981	-1	O	-0.4
	Cin-N	62	223	36	56	8	3	2	22	27	18	.251	.337	.341	85	-5	-4	28	5			.985	-3	O	-0.8
	Yr	107	380	58	98	13	4	6	40	37	34	.258	.335	.361	88	-6	-5	49	8			.983	-3	O	-1.2
1936	Cin-N	144	567	96	185	29	11	7	74	47	67	.326	.380	.453	132	19	23	102	16			.974	-4	*O	1.3
1937	Cin-N	117	406	48	110	12	4	0	32	36	50	.271	.333	.320	82	-11	-9	43	10			.973	-8	*O	-2.0
1938	Bro-N	82	253	45	69	10	8	2	23	34	23	.273	.363	.399	107	4	3	39	6			.993	0	O	0.2
Total	18	1879	7161	1295	2299	394	157	128	1065	676	752	.321	.386	.474	125	270	263	1336	328	27		.972	12	*O	16.3

■ MILT CUYLER Cuyler, Milton b: 10/7/68, Macon, Ga. BB/TR, 5'10", 175 lbs. Deb: 9/06/90

YEAR	TM/L	G	AB	R	H	2B	3B	HR	RBI	BB	SO	AVG	OBP	SLG	PRO+	BR	/A	RC	SB	CS	SBR	FA	FR	POS	TPR
1990	Det-A	19	51	8	13	3	1	0	8	5	10	.255	.321	.353	88	-1	-1	5	1	2	-1	.976	0	O	-0.2
1991	Det-A	154	475	77	122	15	7	3	33	52	92	.257	.336	.337	86	-7	-8	61	41	10	6	.986	8	*O	0.3
1992	Det-A	89	291	39	70	11	1	3	28	10	62	.241	.275	.316	64	-14	-14	25	8	5	-1	.983	-0	O	-1.8
Total	3	262	817	124	205	29	9	6	69	67	164	.251	.315	.330	78	-22	-23	92	50	17	5	.984	8	O	-1.7

■ AL CYPERT Cypert, Alfred Boyd "Cy" b: 8/8/1889, Little Rock, Ark. d: 1/9/73, Washington, D.C. BR/TR, 5'10.5", 150 lbs. Deb: 6/27/14

YEAR	TM/L	G	AB	R	H	2B	3B	HR	RBI	BB	SO	AVG	OBP	SLG	PRO+	BR	/A	RC	SB	CS	SBR	FA	FR	POS	TPR
1914	Cle-A	1	1	0	0	0	0	0	0	0	1	.000	.000	.000	-96	-0	-0	0	0			.000	0	/3	0.0

■ PAUL DADE Dade, Lonnie Paul b: 12/7/51, Seattle, Wash. BR/TR, 6', 195 lbs. Deb: 9/12/75

YEAR	TM/L	G	AB	R	H	2B	3B	HR	RBI	BB	SO	AVG	OBP	SLG	PRO+	BR	/A	RC	SB	CS	SBR	FA	FR	POS	TPR
1975	Cal-A	11	30	5	6	4	0	0	1	6	7	.200	.333	.333	96	-0	-0	4	0	0	0	1.000	1	/O3D	0.0
1976	Cal-A	13	9	2	1	0	0	0	1	3	3	.111	.333	.111	36	-1	-0	0	0	0	0	.750	0	/O23D	0.0
1977	Cle-A	134	461	65	134	15	3	3	45	32	58	.291	.339	.356	93	-6	-4	54	16	8	0	.989	-7	O3/2D	-1.5
1978	Cle-A	93	307	37	78	12	1	3	20	34	45	.254	.332	.329	88	-5	-4	35	12	9	-2	.962	2	O/D	-0.8
1979	Cle-A	44	170	22	48	4	1	3	18	12	22	.282	.330	.371	88	-3	-3	21	12	6	0	.962	2	O/3D	-0.2
	SD-N	76	283	38	78	19	2	1	19	14	48	.276	.314	.367	91	-6	-4	32	13	5	1	.949	7	3/O	0.3
1980	SD-N	68	53	17	10	0	0	0	3	12	10	.189	.338	.189	54	-3	-2	4	4	5	-2	.846	4	3/O2	-0.1
Total	6	439	1313	186	355	54	7	10	107	113	193	.270	.331	.345	89	-23	-18	151	57	33	-3	.970	7	O3/D2	-2.3

■ ANGELO DAGRES Dagres, Angelo George "Junior" b: 8/22/34, Newburyport, Mass. BL/TL, 5'11", 175 lbs. Deb: 9/11/55

YEAR	TM/L	G	AB	R	H	2B	3B	HR	RBI	BB	SO	AVG	OBP	SLG	PRO+	BR	/A	RC	SB	CS	SBR	FA	FR	POS	TPR
1955	Bal-A	8	15	5	4	0	0	0	3	1	2	.267	.313	.267	61	-1	-1	2	0	0	0	.818	-1	/O	-0.2

■ BILL DAHLEN Dahlen, William Frederick "Bad Bill" b: 1/5/1870, Nelliston, N.Y. d: 12/5/50, Brooklyn, N.Y. BR/TR, 5'9", 180 lbs. Deb: 4/22/1891 M

YEAR	TM/L	G	AB	R	H	2B	3B	HR	RBI	BB	SO	AVG	OBP	SLG	PRO+	BR	/A	RC	SB	CS	SBR	FA	FR	POS	TPR
1891	Chi-N	135	549	114	143	18	13	9	76	67	60	.260	.348	.390	117	12	12	84	21			.887	9	3OS	2.2
1892	Chi-N	143	581	114	169	23	19	5	58	45	56	.291	.347	.422	133	22	21	109	60			.909	25	S3/O2	4.7
1893	Chi-N	116	485	113	146	28	15	5	64	58	30	.301	.381	.452	125	16	17	98	31			.892	3	*SO2/3	1.9
1894	Chi-N	121	502	149	179	32	14	15	107	76	33	.357	.444	.566	137	37	31	149	42			.898	32	S3	**5.0**
1895	Chi-N	129	516	106	131	19	10	7	62	61	51	.254	.344	.370	81	-10	-16	81	38			.904	35	*S/O	2.0
1896	Chi-N	125	474	137	167	30	19	9	74	64	36	.352	.438	.553	156	44	40	142	51			.915	25	*S	5.7
1897	Chi-N	75	276	67	80	18	8	6	40	43		.290	.399	.478	126	13	11	62	15			.930	28	S	3.4
1898	Chi-N	142	521	96	151	35	8	1	79	58		.290	.385	.393	124	18	18	94	27			.921	25	*S	**4.6**
1899	Bro-N	121	428	87	121	22	7	4	76	67		.283	.398	.395	115	14	12	81	29			.941	19	*S3	3.5
1900	*Bro-N	133	483	87	125	16	11	1	69	73		.259	.364	.344	90	-0	-5	74	31			.938	19	*S	2.3
1901	Bro-N	131	511	69	136	17	9	4	82	30		.266	.309	.358	91	-5	-7	66	23			.929	14	*S/2	1.7
1902	Bro-N	138	527	67	139	25	8	2	74	43		.264	.329	.353	110	6	6	71	20			.916	-6	*S	0.9
1903	Bro-N	138	474	71	124	17	9	1	64	82		.262	.373	.342	108	6	8	76	34			**.948**	18	*S	3.0
1904	NY-N	145	523	70	140	26	2	2	**80**	44		.268	.325	.337	100	3	0	75	47			.930	28	*S	3.4
1905	*NY-N	148	520	67	126	20	4	7	81	62		.242	.336	.337	99	2	1	74	37			.948	20	*S/O	2.4
1906	NY-N	143	471	63	113	18	3	1	49	76		.240	.354	.297	101	6	5	58	16			.938	0	*S	1.1
1907	NY-N	143	464	40	96	20	1	0	34	51		.207	.288	.254	68	-15	-17	40	11			.941	7	*S	-0.6
1908	Bos-N	144	524	50	125	23	2	3	48	35		.239	.295	.307	94	-5	-4	51	10			.952	**38**	*S	4.2
1909	Bos-N	69	197	22	46	6	1	2	16	29		.234	.332	.305	93	0	-1	21	4			.908	9	S/23	1.0

YEAR	TM/L	G	AB	R	H	2B	3B	HR	RBI	BB	SO	AVG	OBP	SLG	PRO+	BR	/A	RC	SB	CS	SBR	FA	FR	POS	TPR
1910	Bro-N	3	2	0	0	0	0	0	0	0	0	.000	.000	.000	-99	-1	-0	-0	0			.000	0	HM	-0.1
1911	Bro-N	1	3	0	0	0	0	0	0	0	3	.000	.000	.000	-99	-1	-1	0	0			1.000	2	/SM	0.1
Total	21	2443	9031	1589	2457	413	163	84	1233	1064	269	.272	.357	.382	110	163	133	1505	547			.927	349	*S3/O2	52.4

■ BABE DAHLGREN

Dahlgren, Ellsworth Tenney b: 6/15/12, San Francisco, Cal. BR/TR, 6', 190 lbs. Deb: 4/16/35 C

YEAR	TM/L	G	AB	R	H	2B	3B	HR	RBI	BB	SO	AVG	OBP	SLG	PRO+	BR	/A	RC	SB	CS	SBR	FA	FR	POS	TPR
1935	Bos-A	149	525	77	138	27	7	9	63	56	67	.263	.337	.392	83	-10	-15	71	6	5	-1	.988	-7	*1	-3.7
1936	Bos-A	16	57	6	16	3	1	1	7	7	1	.281	.359	.421	87	-1	-1	9	2	1	0	.980	-1	1	-0.3
1937	NY-A	1	1	0	0	0	0	0	0	0	0	.000	.000	.000	-99	-0	-0	0	0	0	0	.000	0	H	0.0
1938	NY-A	27	43	8	8	1	0	0	1	1	7	.186	.205	.209	4	-6	-6	2	0	0	0	.826	-1	/31	-0.7
1939	*NY-A	144	531	71	125	18	6	15	89	57	54	.235	.312	.377	76	-21	-20	61	2	3	-1	.991	-7	*1	-4.1
1940	NY-A	155	568	51	150	24	4	12	73	46	54	.264	.325	.384	86	-15	-12	69	1	1	-0	.990	-10	*1	-3.5
1941	Bos-N	44	166	20	39	8	1	7	30	16	13	.235	.306	.422	108	0	1	20	0			.993	2	1/3	0.1
	Chi-N	99	359	50	101	20	1	16	59	43	39	.281	.360	.476	139	15	17	62	2			.991	-8	1	0.1
	Yr	143	525	70	140	28	2	23	89	59	52	.267	.343	.459	129	16	18	82	2			.992	-6	*1/3	0.2
1942	Chi-N	17	56	4	12	1	0	0	6	4	2	.214	.267	.232	48	-4	-3	3	0			.986	1	1	-0.4
	StL-A	2	2	0	0	0	0	0	0	0	0	.000	.000	.000	-99	-1	-1	0	0	0	0	.000	0	H	-0.1
	Bro-N	17	19	2	1	0	0	0	0	4	5	.053	.217	.053	-19	-3	-3	0	0			1.000	1	1	-0.2
1943	Phi-N★	136	508	55	146	19	2	5	56	50	39	.287	.354	.362	111	5	7	62	2			.988	-23	13S/C	-1.8
1944	Pit-N	158	599	67	173	28	7	12	101	47	56	.289	.347	.419	110	11	8	84	2			.987	8	*1	0.7
1945	Pit-N	144	531	57	133	24	8	5	75	51	51	.250	.318	.354	84	-10	-13	57	1			**.996**	1	*1	-2.2
1946	StL-A	28	80	2	14	1	0	0	9	8	13	.175	.250	.188	22	-8	-9	4	0	1	-1	.981	1	1	-1.0
Total	12	1137	4045	470	1056	174	37	82	569	390	401	.261	.329	.383	92	-47	-49	505	18	11		.990	-44	*1/3SC	-17.1

■ JOHN DAILEY

Dailey, John G. b: Brooklyn, N.Y. Deb: 7/12/1875

YEAR	TM/L	G	AB	R	H	2B	3B	HR	RBI	BB	SO	AVG	OBP	SLG	PRO+	BR	/A	RC	SB	CS	SBR	FA	FR	POS	TPR
1875	Was-n	27	106	17	20	3	5	0		0		.189	.189	.311	72	-3	-2	6						S/32	-0.3
	Atl-n	2	8	3	1	0	0	0		0		.125	.125	.125	-15	-1	-1	0						/1O	-0.1
	Yr	29	114	20	21	3	5	0		0		.184	.184	.298	67	-4	-3	6						S/3210	-0.4

■ VINCE DAILEY

Dailey, Vincent Perry b: 12/25/1864, Osceola, Pa. d: 11/14/19, Hornell, N.Y. 6', 200 lbs. Deb: 4/21/1890

YEAR	TM/L	G	AB	R	H	2B	3B	HR	RBI	BB	SO	AVG	OBP	SLG	PRO+	BR	/A	RC	SB	CS	SBR	FA	FR	POS	TPR
1890	Cle-N	64	246	41	71	5	7	0	32	33	23	.289	.373	.366	120	6	7	41	17			.859	1	O/P	0.5

■ CON DAILY

Daily, Cornelius F. b: 9/11/1864, Blackstone, Mass. d: 6/14/28, Brooklyn, N.Y. BL, 6', 192 lbs. Deb: 6/09/1884 F

YEAR	TM/L	G	AB	R	H	2B	3B	HR	RBI	BB	SO	AVG	OBP	SLG	PRO+	BR	/A	RC	SB	CS	SBR	FA	FR	POS	TPR
1884	Phi-U	2	8	0	0	0	0	0		0		.000	.000	.000	-99	-2	-2	0				.857	-1	/C	-0.2
1885	Pro-N	60	223	20	58	6	1	0	19	12	20	.260	.298	.296	96	-2	-0	20				.876	-1	C/1O	0.2
1886	Bos-N	50	180	25	43	4	2	0	21	19	29	.239	.312	.283	85	-3	-2	17	2			.911	-11	C/O	-0.7
1887	Bos-N	36	120	12	19	5	0	0	13	9	8	.158	.229	.200	21	-12	-12	7	7			.889	-2	C	-1.0
1888	Ind-N	57	202	14	44	6	1	0	14	10	28	.218	.255	.257	64	-8	-8	17	15			.893	-1	C/O312	-0.6
1889	Ind-N	62	219	35	55	6	2	0	26	28	21	.251	.347	.297	81	-4	-5	28	14			.887	-12	C/O13	-1.1
1890	Bro-P	46	168	20	42	6	3	0	35	15	14	.250	.315	.321	68	-7	-9	19	6			.879	-7	C/1O	-1.0
1891	Bro-N	60	206	25	66	10	1	0	30	15	13	.320	.378	.379	124	6	6	33	7			.925	-0	C/OS1	1.0
1892	Bro-N	80	278	38	65	10	1	0	28	38	21	.234	.328	.277	88	-4	-2	32	18			.943	-2	CO	0.1
1893	Bro-N	61	215	33	57	4	2	1	32	20	12	.265	.342	.316	81	-6	-5	28	13			.935	-1	C/O	-0.1
1894	Bro-N	67	234	40	60	14	7	0	32	31	22	.256	.351	.376	83	-9	-5	35	8			.930	-2	C/1	-0.1
1895	Bro-N	40	142	17	30	3	2	1	11	10	18	.211	.268	.282	47	-12	-10	12	3			.956	-3	C/O	-0.7
1896	Chi-N	9	27	1	2	0	0	0	1	1	2	.074	.107	.074	-49	-6	-6	0	1			.969	-2	/C	-0.6
Total	13	630	2222	280	541	74	22	2	262	208	208	.243	.314	.299	77	-67	-59	250	94			.912	-42	C/O13S2	-4.8

■ ED DAILY

Daily, Edward M. b: 9/7/1862, Providence, R.I. d: 10/21/1891, Washington, D.C. BR/TR, 5'10.5", 174 lbs. Deb: 5/04/1885 F

YEAR	TM/L	G	AB	R	H	2B	3B	HR	RBI	BB	SO	AVG	OBP	SLG	PRO+	BR	/A	RC	SB	CS	SBR	FA	FR	POS	TPR
1885	Phi-N	50	184	22	38	8	2	1	13	0	25	.207	.207	.288	60	-9	-8	11				.891	-4	P	0.0
1886	Phi-N	79	309	40	70	17	1	4	50	7	34	.227	.244	.327	72	-11	-11	31	23			.827	5	OP	-0.5
1887	Phi-N	26	106	18	30	11	1	1	17	3	9	.283	.303	.434	98	0	-1	17	8			.659	-6	O/P	-0.7
	Was-N	78	311	39	78	6	10	2	36	14	27	.251	.285	.354	82	-9	-7	40	26			.855	-5	O/P	-1.2
	Yr	104	417	57	108	17	11	3	53	17	36	.259	.290	.374	87	-9	-8	56	34			.812	-11	O/P	-1.9
1888	Was-N	110	453	56	102	8	4	7	39	7	42	.225	.239	.307	79	-13	-10	45	44			.912	4	*O/P1	-0.9
1889	Col-a	136	578	105	148	22	8	3	70	38	65	.256	.303	.337	89	-13	-8	79	60			.854	-3	*O/P	-1.2
1890	Bro-a	91	394	68	94	15	7	1		24		.239	.284	.320	83	-11	-9	51	49			.892	6	OP	-0.4
	NY-N	4	15	1	2	1	0	0	1	0	4	.133	.133	.200	-2	-2	-2	0	0			.500	0	/OP	-0.1
	*Lou-a	23	80	24	20	0	2	0		13		.250	.355	.300	98	0	0	13	13			.925	1	PO	-0.1
1891	Lou-a	22	64	10	16	2	0	0	8	8	6	.250	.342	.281	83	-1	-1	8	4			.884	0	P/O	0.0
	Was-a	21	79	13	18	2	0	0	6	11	10	.228	.322	.253	71	-3	-2	9	8			.719	-4	O	-0.6
	Yr	43	143	23	34	4	0	0	14	19	16	.238	.331	.266	76	-4	-3	17	12			.750	-3	OP	-0.6
Total	7	640	2573	396	616	92	35	19	240	125	222	.239	.276	.325	81	-71	-58	304	235			.857	-6	OP/1	-5.7

■ GEORGE DAISEY

Daisey, George K. b: Altoona, Pa. 5'11", 190 lbs. Deb: 5/31/1884

YEAR	TM/L	G	AB	R	H	2B	3B	HR	RBI	BB	SO	AVG	OBP	SLG	PRO+	BR	/A	RC	SB	CS	SBR	FA	FR	POS	TPR
1884	Alt-U	1	4	0	0	0	0	0		0		.000	.000	.000	-99	-1	-1	0				.000	-1	/O	-0.1

■ PETE DALENA

Dalena, Peter Martin b: 6/26/60, Fresno, Cal. BL/TR, 5'11", 200 lbs. Deb: 7/07/89

YEAR	TM/L	G	AB	R	H	2B	3B	HR	RBI	BB	SO	AVG	OBP	SLG	PRO+	BR	/A	RC	SB	CS	SBR	FA	FR	POS	TPR
1989	Cle-A	5	7	0	1	1	0	0	0	0	3	.143	.143	.286	18	-1	-1	0	0	0	0	.000	0	/D	-0.1

■ JOHN DALEY

Daley, John Francis b: 5/25/1887, Pittsburgh, Pa. d: 8/31/88, Mansfield, Ohio BR/TR, 5'7.5", 155 lbs. Deb: 7/19/12

YEAR	TM/L	G	AB	R	H	2B	3B	HR	RBI	BB	SO	AVG	OBP	SLG	PRO+	BR	/A	RC	SB	CS	SBR	FA	FR	POS	TPR
1912	StL-A	18	52	7	9	0	0	1	3	9		.173	.317	.231	60	-2	-2	5	4			.833	-4	S	-0.5

■ JUD DALEY

Daley, Judson Lawrence b: 3/14/1884, S.Coventry, Conn. d: 1/26/67, Gasden, Ala. BL/TR, 5'8", 172 lbs. Deb: 9/19/11

YEAR	TM/L	G	AB	R	H	2B	3B	HR	RBI	BB	SO	AVG	OBP	SLG	PRO+	BR	/A	RC	SB	CS	SBR	FA	FR	POS	TPR
1911	Bro-N	19	65	8	15	2	1	0	7	2	8	.231	.286	.292	65	-3	-3	6	2			.952	2	O	-0.2
1912	Bro-N	61	199	22	51	9	1	1	13	24	17	.256	.342	.327	87	-4	-3	24	2			.947	2	O	-0.4
Total	2	80	264	30	66	11	2	1	20	26	25	.250	.329	.318	82	-7	-6	30	4			.949	3	/O	-0.6

■ PETE DALEY

Daley, Peter Harvey b: 1/14/30, Grass Valley, Cal. BR/TR, 6', 195 lbs. Deb: 5/03/55

YEAR	TM/L	G	AB	R	H	2B	3B	HR	RBI	BB	SO	AVG	OBP	SLG	PRO+	BR	/A	RC	SB	CS	SBR	FA	FR	POS	TPR
1955	Bos-A	17	50	4	11	2	1	0	5	3	6	.220	.264	.300	47	-4	-4	4	0	0	0	1.000	3	C	0.0
1956	Bos-A	59	187	22	50	11	3	5	29	18	30	.267	.338	.439	92	0	-3	25	1	0	0	.992	-10	C	-1.0
1957	Bos-A	78	191	17	43	10	0	3	25	16	31	.225	.288	.325	64	-9	-10	16	0	0	0	**1.000**	-2	C	-1.0
1958	Bos-A	27	56	10	18	2	1	2	8	7	11	.321	.397	.500	136	4	3	10	0	0	0	.990	2	C	0.6
1959	Bos-A	65	169	9	38	7	0	1	11	13	31	.225	.280	.284	53	-10	-11	14	1	1	-0	.996	3	C	-0.6
1960	KC-A	73	228	19	60	10	2	5	25	16	41	.263	.311	.390	88	-4	-4	26	0	0	0	.990	-5	C/O	-0.5
1961	Was-A	72	203	12	39	7	1	2	17	14	37	.192	.244	.266	37	-19	-18	11	0	1	-1	.988	7	C	-0.9
Total	7	391	1084	93	259	49	8	18	120	87	187	.239	.297	.349	71	-41	-48	106	2	2	-1	.993	-2	C/O	-3.4

■ TOM DALEY

Daley, Thomas Francis "Pete" b: 11/13/1884, Dubois, Pa. d: 12/2/34, Los Angeles, Cal. BL/TR, 5'5", 168 lbs. Deb: 8/29/08

YEAR	TM/L	G	AB	R	H	2B	3B	HR	RBI	BB	SO	AVG	OBP	SLG	PRO+	BR	/A	RC	SB	CS	SBR	FA	FR	POS	TPR
1908	Cin-N	14	46	5	5	0	0	0	1	3		.109	.180	.109	-8	-5	-5	1	1			1.000	-0	O	-0.7
1913	Phi-A	62	141	13	36	2	1	0	11	13	28	.255	.327	.284	81	-3	-3	14	4			.963	-1	O	-0.6
1914	Phi-A	28	86	17	22	1	3	0	7	12	14	.256	.347	.337	110	1	1	9	4	7	-3	1.000	2	O	-0.1
	NY-A	69	191	36	48	6	4	0	9	38	13	.251	.378	.325	112	5	5	25	8	8	-2	.958	6	O	0.6
	Yr	97	277	53	70	7	7	0	16	50	27	.253	.369	.329	111	5	6	35	12	15	-5	.969	7	O	0.5
1915	NY-A	10	8	2	2	0	0	0	1	2	2	.250	.400	.250	95	0	0	1	1			1.000	-0	/O	0.0
Total	4	183	472	73	113	9	8	0	29	68	57	.239	.340	.292	92	-3	-2	51	18	15		.970	6	O	-0.8

YEAR	TM/L	G	AB	R	H	2B	3B	HR	RBI	BB	SO	AVG	OBP	SLG	PRO+	BR	/A	RC	SB	CS	SBR	FA	FR	POS	TPR
■ DOM DALLESSANDRO	Dallessandro, Nicholas Dominic "Dim Dom" b: 10/3/13, Reading, Pa. d: 4/29/88, Indianapolis, Ind. BL/TL, 5'6", 168 lbs. Deb: 4/24/37																								
1937	Bos-A	68	147	18	34	7	1	0	11	27	16	.231	.351	.293	61	-7	-8	17	2	1	0	.965	-5	O	-1.3
1940	Chi-N	107	287	33	77	19	6	1	36	34	13	.268	.348	.387	104	1	2	40	4			.969	-3	O	-0.4
1941	Chi-N	140	486	73	132	36	2	6	85	68	37	.272	.362	.391	116	9	11	72	3			.987	-2	*O	0.2
1942	Chi-N	96	264	30	69	12	4	4	43	36	18	.261	.350	.383	119	5	6	35	4			.986	-2	O	0.2
1943	Chi-N	87	176	13	39	8	3	1	31	40	14	.222	.369	.318	101	2	2	24	1			.967	-4	O	-0.4
1944	Chi-N	117	381	53	116	19	4	8	74	61	29	.304	.400	.438	137	20	20	70	1			.982	-2	*O	1.3
1946	Chi-N	65	89	4	20	2	2	1	9	23	12	.225	.384	.326	104	1	2	12	1			.971	-3	O	-0.2
1947	Chi-N	66	115	18	33	7	1	1	14	21	11	.287	.397	.391	115	3	3	18	0			1.000	-2	O	0.0
Total	8	746	1945	242	520	110	23	22	303	310	150	.267	.369	.381	112	34	39	287	16	1		.980	-22	O	-0.6
■ ABNER DALRYMPLE	Dalrymple, Abner Frank b: 9/9/1857, Warren, Ill. d: 1/25/39, Warren, Ill. BL/TR, 5'10.5", 175 lbs. Deb: 5/01/1878																								
1878	Mil-N	61	271	52	96	10	4	0	15	6	29	.354	.368	.421	149	16	14	43				.832	7	*O	1.6
1879	Chi-N	71	333	47	97	25	1	0	23	4	29	.291	.300	.372	113	7	4	38				.728	-13	*O	-1.2
1880	Chi-N	86	382	**91**	**126**	25	12	0	36	3	18	.330	.335	.458	157	25	22	60				.859	4	*O	2.3
1881	Chi-N	82	362	72	117	22	4	1	37	15	22	.323	.350	.414	133	16	14	54				.835	-7	*O	0.5
1882	Chi-N	84	397	96	117	25	11	1	36	14	18	.295	.319	.421	129	15	12	55				.877	0	*O	1.1
1883	Chi-N	80	363	78	108	24	4	2	37	11	29	.298	.318	.402	111	7	4	48				.826	-1	*O	0.2
1884	Chi-N	111	521	111	161	18	9	22	69	14	39	.309	.327	.505	146	32	26	88				.882	1	*O	2.2
1885	*Chi-N	113	492	109	135	27	12	**11**	61	46	42	.274	.336	.445	131	28	17	76				.879	-1	*O	1.3
1886	*Chi-N	82	331	62	77	7	12	3	26	33	44	.233	.302	.353	86	-0	-8	41	16			.952	4	O	-0.6
1887	Pit-N	92	358	45	76	18	5	2	31	45	43	.212	.311	.307	79	-11	-7	44	29			.900	4	*O	-0.4
1888	Pit-N	57	227	19	50	9	2	0	14	6	28	.220	.247	.278	74	-8	-6	18	7			.909	-2	O	-1.0
1891	Mil-a	32	135	31	42	7	5	1	22	7	18	.311	.345	.459	110	5	0	24	6			.909	-1	O	-0.1
Total	12	951	4172	813	1202	217	81	43	407	204	359	.288	.323	.410	121	131	91	588	58			.863	-4	O	5.9
■ CLAY DALRYMPLE	Dalrymple, Clayton Errol b: 12/3/36, Chico, Cal. BL/TR, 6', 199 lbs. Deb: 4/24/60																								
1960	Phi-N	82	158	11	43	6	2	4	21	15	21	.272	.347	.411	106	2	2	22	0	0	0	.966	-5	C	-0.1
1961	Phi-N	129	378	23	83	11	1	5	42	30	30	.220	.284	.294	54	-25	-24	30	0	2	-1	.978	0	*C	-2.0
1962	Phi-N	123	370	40	102	13	3	11	54	70	32	.276	.396	.416	122	13	14	65	1	3	-2	.987	-12	*C	0.5
1963	Phi-N	142	452	40	114	15	3	10	40	45	55	.252	.327	.365	100	-0	1	54	0	2	-1	.981	1	*C	0.6
1964	Phi-N	127	382	36	91	16	3	6	46	39	40	.238	.309	.343	84	-8	-7	41	0	1	-1	.991	3	*C	0.0
1965	Phi-N	103	301	14	64	5	5	4	23	34	37	.213	.293	.302	69	-12	-12	27	0	1	-1	.993	18	*C	1.0
1966	Phi-N	114	331	30	81	13	3	4	39	60	57	.245	.365	.338	97	1	1	46	0	0	0	.993	-4	*C	0.4
1967	Phi-N	101	268	12	46	7	1	3	21	36	49	.172	.272	.239	47	-18	-18	18	1	2	-1	.994	20	C	0.7
1968	Phi-N	85	241	19	50	9	1	3	26	22	57	.207	.277	.290	70	-9	-9	19	1	2	-1	.990	-3	C	-0.9
1969	*Bal-A	37	80	8	19	1	1	3	6	13	8	.237	.344	.387	103	1	1	10	0	0	0	1.000	2	C	0.3
1970	Bal-A	13	32	4	7	1	0	1	3	7	4	.219	.359	.344	94	-0	-0	4	0	0	0	1.000	6	C	0.6
1971	Bal-A	23	49	6	10	1	0	1	6	16	13	.204	.409	.286	101	1	1	8	0	0	0	.971	2	C	0.4
Total	12	1079	3042	243	710	98	23	55	327	387	403	.233	.324	.335	85	-54	-51	343	3	13	-7	.987	27	*C	1.5
■ BILL DALRYMPLE	Dalrymple, William Dunn b: 2/7/1891, Baltimore, Md. d: 7/14/67, San Diego, Cal. TR , Deb: 7/06/15																								
1915	StL-A	3	2	0	0	0	0	0	0	0	0	.000	.000	.000	-99	-0	-0	0	0			1.000	0	/3	0.0
■ JACK DALTON	Dalton, Talbot Percy b: 7/3/1885, Henderson, Tenn. BR/TR, 5'10.5", 187 lbs. Deb: 6/20/10																								
1910	Bro-N	77	273	33	62	9	4	1	21	26	30	.227	.304	.300	79	-8	-7	27	5			.966	3	O	-0.8
1914	Bro-N	128	442	65	141	13	8	1	45	53	39	.319	.396	.391	131	20	19	74	19			.965	-3	*O	1.2
1915	Buf-F	132	437	68	128	17	3	2	46	50	38	.293	.368	.359	112	9	8	72	28			.966	-5	*O	-0.3
1916	Det-A	8	11	1	2	0	0	0	0	0	5	.182	.182	.182	9	-1	-1	0	0			1.000	-1	/O	-0.3
Total	4	345	1163	167	333	39	15	4	112	129	112	.286	.362	.356	111	20	19	174	52			.966	-7	O	-0.2
■ BERT DALY	Daly, Albert Joseph b: 4/8/1881, Bayonne, N.J. d: 9/3/52, Bayonne, N.J. BR/TR, 5'9", 170 lbs. Deb: 8/07/03																								
1903	Phi-A	10	21	2	4	0	2	0	4	1		.190	.227	.381	76	-1	-1	2	0			.700	-4	/23S	-0.5
■ SUN DALY	Daly, James J. b: 1/6/1865, Rutland, Vt. d: 4/30/38, Albany, N.Y. Deb: 9/30/1892																								
1892	Bal-N	13	48	5	12	0	2	0	7	1	4	.250	.265	.333	80	-1	-1	4	0			.923	0	O	-0.2
■ JOE DALY	Daly, Joseph John b: 9/21/1868, Conshohocken, Pa. d: 3/21/43, Philadelphia, Pa. TR , 5'8", 157 lbs. Deb: 9/19/1890 F																								
1890	Phi-a	21	75	8	21	4	1	0		3		.280	.308	.360	101	-0	-0	9	1			.900	-6	O/C	-0.5
1891	Cle-N	1	3	0	0	0	0	0	0	0	2	.000	.000	.000	-96	-1	-1	0	0			1.000	0	/O	-0.1
1892	Bos-N	1	0	0	0	0	0	0	0	0	0	—	—	—	—	0	0	0	0			1.000	0	/C	0.0
Total	3	23	78	8	21	4	1	0	0	3	2	.269	.296	.346	93	-1	-1	9	1			.909	-6	/OC	-0.6
■ TOM DALY	Daly, Thomas Daniel b: 12/12/1891, St.John, N.B., Can. d: 11/7/46, Medford, Mass. BR/TR, 5'11.5", 171 lbs. Deb: 9/23/13 C																								
1913	Chi-A	1	3	0	0	0	0	0	0	0	0	.000	.000	.000	-99	-1	-1	0	0			1.000	1	/C	0.0
1914	Chi-A	62	133	13	31	2	0	0	8	7	13	.233	.271	.248	57	-7	-7	9	3	4	-2	.909	-10	O/3C1	-2.2
1915	Chi-A	29	47	5	9	1	0	0	3	5	9	.191	.269	.213	43	-3	-3	3	0			.958	-3	C/1	-0.5
1916	Cle-A	31	73	3	16	1	1	0	8	1	2	.219	.230	.260	45	-5	-5	4	0			.982	-2	C/O	-0.6
1918	Chi-N	1	1	0	0	0	0	0	0	0	0	.000	.000	.000	-98	-0	-0	0	0			.667	-0	/C	0.0
1919	Chi-N	25	50	4	11	0	1	0	1	2	5	.220	.250	.260	53	-3	-3	3	0			.956	-2	C	-0.5
1920	Chi-N	44	90	12	28	6	0	0	13	2	6	.311	.333	.378	102	0	0	11	1	1	-0	.981	-3	C	-0.2
1921	Chi-N	51	143	12	34	7	1	0	22	8	8	.238	.278	.301	53	-10	-10	12	1	2	-1	.973	4	C	-0.4
Total	8	244	540	49	129	17	3	0	55	25	43	.239	.274	.281	59	-28	-29	42	5	7		.972	-15	C/O31	-4.4
■ TOM DALY	Daly, Thomas Peter "Tido" b: 2/7/1866, Philadelphia, Pa. d: 10/29/38, Brooklyn, N.Y. BB/TR, 5'7", 170 lbs. Deb: 4/30/1887 F																								
1887	Chi-N	74	256	45	53	10	4	2	17	22	25	.207	.270	.301	53	-14	-19	29	29			**.935**	33	C/OS21	1.6
1888	Chi-N	65	219	34	42	2	6	0	29	10	26	.192	.230	.256	53	-10	-12	16	10			.939	20	C/O	1.3
1889	Was-N	71	250	39	75	13	5	1	40	38	28	.300	.394	.404	133	10	12	48	18			.917	3	C/12OS	1.7
1890	*Bro-N	82	292	55	71	9	4	5	43	32	43	.243	.326	.353	100	0	-0	41	20			.953	7	C1/O	1.1
1891	Bro-N	58	200	29	50	11	5	2	27	21	34	.250	.327	.385	110	2	2	28	7			.881	-6	C1S/O	-0.2
1892	Bro-N	124	446	76	114	15	6	4	51	64	61	.256	.355	.343	118	9	12	68	34			.897	-11	3OC2	0.4
1893	Bro-N	126	470	94	136	21	14	8	70	76	65	.289	.388	.445	129	16	20	96	32			.915	-18	23	0.4
1894	Bro-N	123	492	135	168	22	10	8	82	77	42	.341	.436	.476	131	20	28	128	51			.908	-19	*2	1.1
1895	Bro-N	120	455	89	128	17	8	2	68	52	52	.281	.359	.367	97	-6	1	73	28			.930	-19	*2	-0.9
1896	Bro-N	67	224	43	63	13	6	3	29	33	25	.281	.385	.433	125	6	9	46	19			.909	-3	2/C	0.8
1898	Bro-N	23	73	11	24	3	1	0	11	14		.329	.443	.397	142	5	5	16	6			.993	3	2	0.8
1899	Bro-N	141	498	95	156	24	9	5	88	69		.313	.409	.428	127	23	21	108	43			.929	16	*2	4.0
1900	*Bro-N	97	343	72	107	17	3	4	55	46		.312	.404	.414	119	14	11	71	27			.921	-9	2/1O	0.5
1901	Bro-N	133	520	88	164	**38**	10	3	90	42		.315	.371	.444	132	23	21	101	31			.944	11	*2	3.7
1902	Chi-A	137	489	57	110	22	3	1	54	55		.225	.305	.288	68	-22	-19	52	19			.957	-15	*2	-2.8
1903	Chi-A	43	150	20	31	11	0	0	19	20		.207	.304	.280	80	-4	-3	16	6			.948	-13	2	-1.5
	Cin-N	80	307	42	90	14	9	1	38	16		.293	.332	.407	100	3	-2	45	5			.937	-10	2	-0.9
Total	16	1564	5684	1024	1582	262	103	49	811	687	401	.278	.362	.387	109	77	87	981	385			.931	-31	*2C3/O1S	11.1

YEAR	TM/L	G	AB	R	H	2B	3B	HR	RBI	BB	SO	AVG	OBP	SLG	PRO+	BR	/A	RC	SB	CS	SBR	FA	FR	POS	TPR
■ **BILL DAM**	Dam, Elbridge Rust b: 4/4/1885, Cambridge, Mass. d: 6/22/30, Quincy, Mass. Deb: 8/23/09																								
1909	Bos-N	1	2	1	1	1	0	0	0	1		.500	.667	1.000	398	1	1	1	0			1.000	-0	/O	0.1
■ **JACK DAMASKA**	Damaska, Jack Lloyd b: 8/21/37, Beaver Falls, Pa. BR/TR, 5'11", 168 lbs. Deb: 7/03/63																								
1963	StL-N	5	5	1	1	0	0	0	1	0	4	.200	.200	.200	14	-1	-1	0	0	0	0	.000	0	/2O	-0.1
■ **HARRY DAMRAU**	Damrau, Harry Robert (Also Known As Arthur Lee Whitehorn) b: 9/11/1890, Newburgh, N.Y. d: 8/21/57, Staten Island, N.Y BR/TR, 5'10", 178 lbs. Deb: 9/17/15																								
1915	Phi-A	16	56	4	11	1	0	0	3	5	17	.196	.262	.214	44	-4	-4	3	1	1	-0	.870	-4	3	-0.8
■ **JAKE DANIEL**	Daniel, Handley Jacob b: 4/22/11, Roanoke, Ala. BL/TL, 5'11", 175 lbs. Deb: 7/24/37																								
1937	Bro-N	12	27	3	5	1	0	0	3	3	4	.185	.267	.222	34	-2	-2	2	0			1.000	-0	/1	-0.3
■ **BERT DANIELS**	Daniels, Bernard Elmer b: 10/13/1882, Danville, Ill. d: 6/6/58, Cedar Grove, N.J. BR/TR, 5'9.5", 180 lbs. Deb: 6/25/10																								
1910	NY-A	95	356	68	90	13	8	1	17	41		.253	.356	.343	112	10	7	58	41			.957	3	O/31	0.7
1911	NY-A	131	462	74	132	16	9	2	31	48		.286	.375	.372	102	7	3	80	40			.941	1	*O	-0.3
1912	NY-A	135	496	72	136	25	11	2	41	51		.274	.363	.381	106	9	5	82	37			.945	5	*O	0.3
1913	NY-A	94	320	52	69	13	5	0	22	44	36	.216	.343	.287	85	-4	-4	38	27			.966	1	O	-0.7
1914	Cin-N	71	269	29	59	9	7	0	19	19	40	.219	.276	.305	70	-10	-11	25	14			.974	0	O	-1.5
Total	5	526	1903	295	486	76	40	5	130	203	76	.255	.349	.345	98	13	0	283	159			.953	10	O/31	-1.5
■ **TONY DANIELS**	Daniels, Frederick Clinton b: 12/28/24, Gastonia, N.C. BR/TR, 5'9.5", 185 lbs. Deb: 6/12/45																								
1945	Phi-N	76	230	15	46	3	2	0	10	12	22	.200	.249	.230	35	-21	-20	13	1			.955	7	2/3	-0.8
■ **JACK DANIELS**	Daniels, Harold Jack "Sour Mash Jack" b: 12/21/27, Chester, Pa. BL/TL, 5'10", 165 lbs. Deb: 4/18/52																								
1952	Bos-N	106	219	31	41	5	1	2	14	28	30	.187	.288	.247	51	-14	-13	18	3	3	-1	.977	-9	O	-2.7
■ **KAL DANIELS**	Daniels, Kalvoski b: 8/20/63, Vienna, Ga. BL/TR, 5'11", 195 lbs. Deb: 4/09/86																								
1986	Cin-N	74	181	34	58	10	4	6	23	22	30	.320	.400	.519	145	13	12	40	15	2	3	.967	-0	O	1.4
1987	Cin-N	108	368	73	123	24	1	26	64	60	62	.334	.429	.617	166	40	37	100	26	8	3	.968	3	O	4.0
1988	Cin-N	140	495	95	144	29	1	18	64	87	94	.291	**.400**	.463	141	33	31	98	27	6	5	.982	4	*O	3.7
1989	Cin-N	44	133	26	29	11	0	2	9	36	28	.218	.392	.346	109	4	4	21	6	4	-1	1.000	2	O	0.4
	LA-N	11	38	7	13	2	0	2	8	7	5	.342	.444	.553	187	4	4	10	3	0	1	1.000	0	O	0.5
	Yr	55	171	33	42	13	0	4	17	43	33	.246	.403	.392	125	9	8	31	9	4	0	1.000	2	O	0.9
1990	LA-N	130	450	81	133	23	1	27	94	68	104	.296	.392	.531	156	32	34	96	4	3	-1	.987	2	*O	3.3
1991	LA-N	137	461	54	115	15	1	17	73	63	116	.249	.341	.397	109	5	6	65	6	1	1	.979	1	*O	0.5
1992	LA-N	35	104	9	24	5	0	2	8	10	30	.231	.304	.337	82	-3	-2	9	0	0	0	.964	-2	O/1	-0.6
	Chi-N	48	108	12	27	6	0	4	17	12	24	.250	.331	.417	108	1	1	14	0	2	-1	1.000	-2	O	-0.2
	Yr	83	212	21	51	11	0	6	25	22	54	.241	.318	.377	95	-1	-1	23	0	2	-1	.984	-4	O/1	-0.8
Total	7	727	2338	391	666	125	8	104	360	365	493	.285	.385	.479	137	130	127	454	87	26	11	.980	8	O/1	13.0
■ **LAW DANIELS**	Daniels, Lawrence Long b: 7/14/1862, Newton, Mass. d: 1/7/29, Waltham, Mass. BR/TR, 5'10", 170 lbs. Deb: 4/25/1887																								
1887	Bal-a	48	165	23	41	5	1	0		8		.248	.287	.291	67	-8	-6	16	7			.845	-8	CO/12S3	-1.0
1888	KC-a	61	218	32	45	2	0	2	28	14		.206	.264	.243	62	-8	-10	20	20			.855	-2	OC/3S	-0.9
Total	2	109	383	55	86	7	1	2	28	22		.225	.274	.264	64	-16	-16	36	27			.859	-10	/CO13S2	-1.9
■ **BUCK DANNER**	Danner, Henry Frederick b: 6/8/1891, Dedham, Mass. d: 9/21/49, Boston, Mass. BR/TR, 5'6", 135 lbs. Deb: 9/17/15																								
1915	Phi-A	3	12	1	3	0	0	0	0	0	1	.250	.250	.250	51	-1	-1	1	1			.750	-3	/S	-0.3
■ **HARRY DANNING**	Danning, Harry "Harry The Horse" b: 9/6/11, Los Angeles, Cal. BR/TR, 6'1", 190 lbs. Deb: 7/30/33 F																								
1933	NY-N	3	2	0	0	0	0	0	0	1	0	.000	.333	.000	2	-0	-0	0	0			1.000	0	/C	0.0
1934	NY-N	53	97	8	32	7	0	1	7	1	9	.330	.337	.433	107	0	1	12	1			.989	-0	C	0.1
1935	NY-N	65	152	16	37	11	1	2	20	9	16	.243	.286	.368	76	-6	-5	16	0			.978	3	C	-0.1
1936	*NY-N	32	69	3	11	2	2	0	4	1	5	.159	.183	.246	15	-8	-8	2	0			.988	2	C	-0.6
1937	*NY-N	93	292	30	84	12	4	8	51	18	20	.288	.331	.438	106	2	2	42	0			.982	-5	C	0.1
1938	NY-N☆	120	448	59	137	26	3	9	60	23	40	.306	.345	.438	113	7	7	66	1			.984	-8	*C	0.5
1939	NY-N☆	135	520	79	163	28	5	16	74	35	42	.313	.359	.479	122	15	15	87	4			.991	7	*C	2.9
1940	NY-N★	140	524	65	157	34	4	13	91	35	31	.300	.349	.454	119	13	13	79	3			.980	7	*C	3.0
1941	NY-N★	130	459	58	112	22	4	7	56	30	25	.244	.292	.355	80	-12	-14	46	1			.993	7	*C/1	0.4
1942	NY-N	119	408	45	114	20	3	1	34	34	29	.279	.335	.350	100	0	0	46	3			.979	-5	*C	0.5
Total	10	890	2971	363	847	162	26	57	397	187	217	.285	.330	.415	104	12	9	395	13			.985	8	C/1	6.8
■ **IKE DANNING**	Danning, Ike b: 1/20/05, Los Angeles, Cal. d: 3/30/83, Santa Monica, Cal BR/TR, 5'10", 160 lbs. Deb: 9/21/28 F																								
1928	StL-A	2	6	0	3	0	0	0	1	1	2	.500	.571	.500	178	1	1	2	0	0	0	.917	1	/C	0.1
■ **FATS DANTONIO**	Dantonio, John James b: 12/31/19, New Orleans, La. BR/TR, 5'8", 165 lbs. Deb: 9/18/44																								
1944	Bro-N	3	7	0	1	0	0	0	0	0	1	.143	.143	.143	-20	-1	-1	0	0			.846	0	/C	-0.1
1945	Bro-N	47	128	12	32	6	1	0	12	11	6	.250	.309	.313	74	-5	-4	13	3			.929	-5	C	-0.8
Total	2	50	135	12	33	6	1	0	12	11	7	.244	.301	.304	69	-6	-6	13	3			.923	-5	/C	-0.9
■ **BABE DANZIG**	Danzig, Harold P. b: 4/30/1887, Binghamton, N.Y. d: 7/14/31, San Francisco, Cal. BR/TR, 6'2", 205 lbs. Deb: 4/12/09																								
1909	Bos-A	6	13	0	2	0	0	0	0	2		.154	.313	.154	47	-1	-1	1	0			.960	-1	/1	-0.2
■ **CLIFF DAPPER**	Dapper, Clifford Roland b: 1/2/20, Los Angeles, Cal. BR/TR, 6'2", 190 lbs. Deb: 4/19/42																								
1942	Bro-N	8	17	2	8	1	0	1	9	2	2	.471	.526	.706	255	3	3	7	0			1.000	-0	/C	0.4
■ **CLIFF DARINGER**	Daringer, Clifford Clarence "Shanty" b: 4/10/1885, Hayden, Ind. d: 12/26/71, Sacramento, Cal. BL/TR, 5'7.5", 155 lbs. Deb: 4/20/14 F																								
1914	KC-F	64	160	12	42	2	1	0	16	11	7	.262	.322	.287	77	-5	-4	19	9			.944	6	S32	0.4
■ **ROLLA DARINGER**	Daringer, Rolla Harrison b: 11/15/1888, N.Vernon, Ind. d: 5/23/74, Seymour, Ind. BL/TR, 5'10", 155 lbs. Deb: 9/19/14 F																								
1914	StL-N	2	4	1	2	1	0	0	0	1	2	.500	.600	.750	304	1	1	2	0			.667	-1	/S	0.0
1915	StL-N	10	23	3	2	0	0	0	0	9	5	.087	.344	.087	33	-1	-1	1	0	1	-1	.947	-3	S	-0.5
Total	2	12	27	4	4	1	0	0	0	10	7	.148	.378	.185	72	-0	-0	3	0	1		.927	-4	/S	-0.5
■ **ALVIN DARK**	Dark, Alvin Ralph "Blackie" b: 1/7/22, Comanche, Okla. BR/TR, 5'11", 185 lbs. Deb: 7/14/46 MC																								
1946	Bos-N	15	13	0	3	3	0	0	1	0	3	.231	.231	.462	93	-0	-0	1	0			.905	2	S/O	0.2
1948	*Bos-N	137	543	85	175	39	6	3	48	24	36	.322	.353	.433	114	8	9	84	4			.963	-12	*S	0.4
1949	Bos-N	130	529	74	146	23	5	3	53	31	43	.276	.317	.355	85	-15	-12	59	5			.961	-4	*S/3	-0.6
1950	NY-N	154	587	79	164	36	5	16	67	39	60	.279	.331	.440	100	-1	-1	85	9			.962	-15	*S	-0.4
1951	*NY-N★	156	646	114	196	**41**	7	14	69	42	39	.303	.352	.454	114	12	12	104	12	7	-1	.944	1	*S	2.3
1952	NY-N☆	151	589	92	177	29	3	14	73	47	39	.301	.357	.431	117	14	13	92	6	6	-2	.965	3	*S	2.6
1953	NY-N	155	647	126	194	41	6	23	88	28	34	.300	.335	.488	109	8	7	102	7	2	1	.967	8	*S2O/3P	2.4
1954	*NY-N★	154	644	98	189	26	6	20	70	27	40	.293	.327	.446	98	-3	-3	89	5	3	-0	.956	4	*S	1.3
1955	NY-N	115	475	77	134	20	3	9	45	22	32	.282	.321	.394	88	-8	-9	60	2	1	0	.962	-14	*S	-1.2
1956	NY-N	48	206	19	52	12	0	2	17	8	13	.252	.284	.340	67	-10	-10	19	0	0	0	.961	-5	S	-1.1
	StL-N	100	413	54	118	14	7	4	37	21	33	.286	.323	.383	89	-7	-7	50	3	1	0	.959	-2	S	0.0
	Yr	148	619	73	170	26	7	6	54	29	46	.275	.310	.368	82	-16	-16	69	3	1	0	.960	-7	*S	-1.1

YEAR	TM/L	G	AB	R	H	2B	3B	HR	RBI	BB	SO	AVG	OBP	SLG	PRO+	BR	/A	RC	SB	CS	SBR	FA	FR	POS	TPR
1957	StL-N	140	583	80	169	25	8	4	64	29	56	.290	.328	.381	88	-9	-10	72	3	4	-2	.965	6	*S/3	0.8
1958	StL-N	18	64	7	19	0	0	1	5	2	6	.297	.318	.344	72	-2	-3	6	0	0	0	.943	-3	/S3	-0.5
	Chi-N	114	464	54	137	16	4	3	43	29	23	.295	.343	.366	89	-7	-6	57	1	1	-0	.949	-3	*3	-0.9
	Yr	132	528	61	156	16	4	4	48	31	29	.295	.340	.364	87	-10	-9	63	1	1	-0	.948	-6	*3/S	-1.4
1959	Chi-N	136	477	60	126	22	9	6	45	55	50	.264	.344	.386	95	-3	-3	66	1	1	-0	.948	-2	*3/1S	-0.5
1960	Phi-N	55	198	29	48	5	1	3	14	19	14	.242	.315	.323	75	-6	-6	20	1	1	-0	.953	-8	3/1	-1.5
	Mil-N	50	141	16	42	6	2	1	18	7	13	.298	.336	.390	106	-0	1	18	0	0	0	.960	-1	O1/32	-0.2
	Yr	105	339	45	90	11	3	4	32	26	27	.265	.323	.351	88	-7	-5	38	1	1	-0	.954	-8	3O1/2	-1.7
Total	14	1828	7219	1064	2089	358	72	126	757	430	534	.289	.334	.411	98	-31	-29	987	59	27		.960	-43	*S3/O21P	3.1
■ DELL DARLING Darling, Conrad b: 12/21/1861, Erie, Pa. d: 11/20/04, Erie, Pa. BR/TR, 5'8", 170 lbs. Deb: 7/03/1883																									
1883	Buf-N	6	18	1	3	0	0	0	1	2	5	.167	.250	.167	29	-1	-1	1				.875	-2	/C	-0.3
1887	Chi-N	38	141	28	45	7	4	3	20	22	18	.319	.411	.489	134	10	7	37	19			.786	2	OC	0.9
1888	Chi-N	20	75	12	16	3	1	2	7	3	12	.213	.253	.360	89	-0	-1	7	0			.932	3	C	0.3
1889	Chi-N	36	120	14	23	1	1	0	7	25	22	.192	.331	.217	53	-6	-7	11	5			.960	4	C	0.0
1890	Chi-P	58	221	45	57	12	4	2	39	29	28	.258	.352	.376	92	-1	-3	32	5			.957	-9	1S/CO23	-1.0
1891	StL-a	17	53	9	7	1	3	0	9	10	11	.132	.270	.264	48	-3	-4	4	0			.894	2	C/2S	-0.1
Total	6	175	628	109	151	24	13	7	83	91	96	.240	.340	.354	89	-1	-10	91	29			.923	-1	C/1OS23	-0.2
■ JACK DARRAGH Darragh, James S. b: 7/17/1866, Ebensburg, Pa. d: 8/12/39, Rochester, Pa. Deb: 5/13/1891																									
1891	Lou-a	1	2	0	1	0	0	0	0	0	0	.500	.500	.500	193	0	0	1	0			1.000	0	/1	0.0
■ BOBBY DARWIN Darwin, Arthur Bobby Lee b: 2/16/43, Los Angeles, Cal. BR/TR, 6'2", 200 lbs. Deb: 9/30/62																									
1962	LA-A	1	1	0	0	0	0	0	0	0	1	.000	.000	.000	-99	-0	-0	0	0	0	0	.000	-0	/P	0.0
1969	LA-N	6	0	1	0	0	0	0	0	0	0	—	—	—	—	0	0	0	0	0	0	.000	-0	/P	0.0
1971	LA-N	11	20	2	5	1	0	1	4	2	9	.250	.318	.450	123	0	0	3	0	0	0	1.000	0	/O	0.0
1972	Min-A	145	513	48	137	20	2	22	80	38	145	.267	.327	.442	122	16	13	67	2	3	-1	.980	4	*O	1.1
1973	Min-A	145	560	69	141	20	2	18	90	46	137	.252	.312	.391	93	-3	-6	64	5	2	0	.980	2	*O/D	-1.0
1974	Min-A	152	575	67	152	13	7	25	94	37	127	.264	.324	.442	114	12	9	80	1	3	-2	.970	-2	*O	-0.1
1975	Min-A	48	169	26	37	6	0	5	18	18	44	.219	.309	.343	82	-3	-4	17	2	0	1	.969	-4	OD	-0.8
	Mil-A	55	186	19	46	6	2	8	23	11	54	.247	.300	.430	104	0	0	24	4	1	1	.978	1	O/D	0.0
	Yr	103	355	45	83	12	2	13	41	29	98	.234	.304	.389	94	-3	-4	41	6	1	1	.975	-3	OD	-0.8
1976	Mil-A	25	73	6	18	3	1	1	5	6	16	.247	.321	.356	100	-0	0	8	0	0	0	.977	-1	O/D	-0.2
	Bos-A	43	106	9	19	5	2	3	13	2	35	.179	.216	.349	57	-5	-7	8	1	0	0	.964	-2	OD	-1.0
	Yr	68	179	15	37	8	3	4	18	8	51	.207	.260	.352	73	-6	-7	16	1	0	0	.972	-3	OD	-1.2
1977	Bos-A	4	9	1	2	1	0	0	1	0	4	.222	.222	.333	44	-1	-1	0	0	0	0	.500	-0	/OD	-0.1
	Chi-N	11	12	2	2	1	0	0	0	0	5	.167	.167	.250	9	-2	-2	1	0	0	0	.000	0	/O	-0.2
Total	9	646	2224	250	559	76	16	83	328	160	577	.251	.312	.412	103	14	4	272	15	9	-1	.976	-2	O/DP	-2.3
■ DOUG DASCENZO Dascenzo, Douglas Craig b: 6/30/64, Cleveland, Ohio BB/TL, 5'7", 150 lbs. Deb: 9/02/88																									
1988	Chi-N	26	75	9	16	3	0	0	4	9	4	.213	.298	.253	57	-4	-4	6	6	1	1	1.000	2	O	-0.1
1989	Chi-N	47	139	20	23	1	0	1	12	13	13	.165	.237	.194	23	-13	-15	7	6	3	0	1.000	-2	O	-1.9
1990	Chi-N	113	241	27	61	9	5	1	26	21	18	.253	.316	.344	76	-6	-8	27	15	6	1	1.000	-18	*O/P	-2.7
1991	Chi-N	118	239	40	61	11	0	1	18	24	26	.255	.328	.314	78	-5	-7	26	14	7	0	.985	-19	O/P	-2.9
1992	Chi-N	139	376	37	96	13	4	0	20	27	32	.255	.305	.311	73	-12	-13	36	6	8	-3	.978	-17	*O	-3.9
Total	5	443	1070	133	257	37	9	3	80	94	93	.240	.303	.300	67	-41	-47	102	47	25	-1	.990	-53	O/P	-11.5
■ WALLY DASHIELL Dashiell, John Wallace b: 5/9/02, Jewett, Tex. d: 5/20/72, Pensacola, Fla. BR/TR, 5'9.5", 170 lbs. Deb: 4/20/24																									
1924	Chi-A	1	2	0	0	0	0	0	0	0	0	.000	.000	.000	-99	-1	-1	0	0	0	0	.667	-1	/S	-0.1
■ JEFF DATZ Datz, Jeffrey William b: 11/28/59, Camden, N.J. BR/TR, 6'4", 220 lbs. Deb: 9/05/89																									
1989	Det-A	7	10	0	2	0	0	0	0	1	1	.200	.333	.200	55	-1	-0	1	0	0	0	1.000	0	/CD	0.0
■ HARRY DAUBERT Daubert, Harry "Jake" b: 6/19/1892, Columbus, Ohio d: 1/8/44, Detroit, Mich. BR/TR, 6', 160 lbs. Deb: 9/04/15																									
1915	Pit-N	1	1	0	0	0	0	0	0	0	1	.000	.000	.000	-99	-0	-0	0	0			.000	0	H	0.0
■ JAKE DAUBERT Daubert, Jacob Ellsworth b: 4/7/1884, Shamokin, Pa. d: 10/9/24, Cincinnati, Ohio BL/TL, 5'10.5", 160 lbs. Deb: 4/14/10																									
1910	Bro-N	144	552	67	146	15	15	8	50	47	53	.264	.328	.389	112	4	6	79	23			.989	-3	*1	0.4
1911	Bro-N	149	573	89	176	17	8	5	45	51	56	.307	.366	.391	117	9	12	94	32			.989	2	*1	1.3
1912	Bro-N	145	559	81	172	19	16	3	66	48	45	.308	.369	.415	119	11	14	95	29			**.993**	0	*1	1.1
1913	Bro-N	139	508	76	178	17	7	2	52	44	40	**.350**	.405	.423	133	25	24	94	25			.991	3	*1	2.6
1914	Bro-N	126	474	89	156	17	7	6	45	30	34	**.329**	.375	.432	137	22	21	85	25			.993	-6	*1	1.3
1915	Bro-N	150	544	62	164	21	8	2	47	57	48	.301	.369	.381	125	19	18	81	11	13	-5	.993	9	*1	2.0
1916	*Bro-N	127	478	75	151	16	7	3	33	38	39	.316	.371	.397	132	21	19	80	21	7	2	**.993**	4	*1	2.3
1917	Bro-N	125	468	59	122	4	4	2	30	51	30	.261	.341	.299	94	1	-1	53	11			.991	6	*1	0.1
1918	Bro-N	108	396	50	122	12	**15**	2	47	27	18	.308	.360	.429	141	18	18	63	10			.991	0	*1	1.6
1919	*Cin-N	140	537	79	148	10	12	2	44	35	23	.276	.322	.350	105	1	3	66	11			.989	-2	*1	-0.4
1920	Cin-N	142	553	97	168	28	13	4	48	47	29	.304	.362	.423	127	18	19	83	11	13	-5	.990	-9	*1	0.2
1921	Cin-N	136	516	69	158	18	12	2	64	24	16	.306	.341	.399	100	-4	-1	70	12	6	0	.993	2	*1	-0.2
1922	Cin-N	156	610	114	205	15	**22**	12	66	56	21	.336	.395	.492	130	25	26	115	14	17	-6	**.994**	-0	*1	1.3
1923	Cin-N	125	500	63	146	27	10	2	54	40	20	.292	.349	.398	99	-2	-1	68	11	12	-4	.993	6	*1	-0.5
1924	Cin-N	102	405	47	114	14	9	1	31	28	17	.281	.331	.368	88	-7	-7	48	5	10	-5	.990	7	*1	-1.0
Total	15	2014	7673	1117	2326	250	165	56	722	623	489	.303	.360	.401	117	159	170	1174	251	78		.991	19	*1	12.1
■ RICH DAUER Dauer, Richard Fremont b: 7/27/52, San Bernardino, Cal. BR/TR, 6', 180 lbs. Deb: 9/11/76 C																									
1976	Bal-A	11	39	0	4	0	0	0	3	1	3	.103	.146	.103	-28	-6	-6	1	0	0	0	1.000	-3	2	-0.9
1977	Bal-A	96	304	38	74	15	1	5	25	20	28	.243	.294	.349	79	-11	-9	30	1	0	0	.982	6	2/3D	0.3
1978	Bal-A	133	459	57	121	23	0	6	46	26	22	.264	.303	.353	89	-10	-7	44	0	4	-2	.998	3	23/D	-0.1
1979	*Bal-A	142	479	63	123	20	0	9	61	36	36	.257	.310	.355	82	-14	-12	51	0	1	-1	.979	-5	*23	-1.2
1980	Bal-A	152	557	71	158	32	0	2	63	46	19	.284	.342	.352	91	-6	-6	64	3	2	-0	.991	-4	*23	-0.2
1981	Bal-A	96	369	41	97	27	0	4	38	27	18	.263	.318	.369	98	-1	-1	44	0	0	0	**.989**	-14	2/3	-1.0
1982	Bal-A	158	558	75	156	24	2	8	57	50	34	.280	.340	.373	96	-3	-2	70	0	1	-1	.987	-36	*23	-3.4
1983	*Bal-A	140	459	49	108	19	0	5	41	47	29	.235	.309	.309	72	-17	-16	42	1	1	-0	.988	-29	*23	-4.0
1984	Bal-A	127	397	29	101	26	0	2	24	24	23	.254	.297	.335	76	-14	-13	36	1	3	-2	.980	-19	*2/3	-2.9
1985	Bal-A	85	208	25	42	7	0	2	14	20	7	.202	.275	.264	50	-14	-14	14	0	1	-1	.990	5	23/1	-0.8
Total	10	1140	3829	448	984	193	3	43	372	297	219	.257	.313	.343	83	-98	-86	396	6	13	-6	.987	-96	23/D1	-14.2
■ DOC DAUGHERTY Daugherty, Harold Ray b: 10/12/27, Paris, Pa. BR/TR, 6', 180 lbs. Deb: 4/22/51																									
1951	Det-A	1	1	0	0	0	0	0	0	0	1	.000	.000	.000	-99	-0	-0	0	0	0	0	.000	0	H	0.0
■ JACK DAUGHERTY Daugherty, John Michael b: 7/3/60, Hialeah, Fla. BB/TL, 6' ", 188 lbs. Deb: 9/01/87																									
1987	Mon-N	11	10	1	1	1	0	0	1	0	3	.100	.100	.200	-22	-2	-2	0	0	0	0	1.000	0	/1	-0.2
1989	Tex-A	52	106	15	32	4	2	1	10	11	21	.302	.373	.406	117	3	3	17	2	1	0	1.000	1	1/OD	0.2
1990	Tex-A	125	310	36	93	20	2	6	47	22	49	.300	.350	.435	118	7	7	48	0	0	0	.982	-3	O1D	0.2
1991	Tex-A	58	144	8	28	3	2	1	11	16	23	.194	.275	.264	51	-10	-9	12	1	0	0	.981	-4	O1/D	-1.5

YEAR	TM/L	G	AB	R	H	2B	3B	HR	RBI	BB	SO	AVG	OBP	SLG	PRO+	BR	/A	RC	SB	CS	SBR	FA	FR	POS	TPR
1992	Tex-A	59	127	13	26	9	0	0	9	16	21	.205	.299	.276	64	-6	-6	11	2	1	0	.939	-4	OD/1	-1.1
Total	5	305	697	73	180	37	6	8	78	65	117	.258	.325	.363	92	-7	-7	88	5	2	0	.973	-11	O/1D	-2.4

■ BOB DAUGHTERS

Daughters, Robert Francis "Red" b: 8/5/14, Cincinnati, Ohio d: 8/22/88, Southbury, Conn. BR/TR, 6'2", 185 lbs. Deb: 4/24/37

YEAR	TM/L	G	AB	R	H	2B	3B	HR	RBI	BB	SO	AVG	OBP	SLG	PRO+	BR	/A	RC	SB	CS	SBR	FA	FR	POS	TPR
1937	Bos-A	1	0	1	0	0	0	0	0	0	0	—	—	—	—	0	0	0	0	0	0	.000	0	R	0.0

■ DARREN DAULTON

Daulton, Darren Arthur b: 1/3/62, Arkansas City, Kan. BL/TR, 6'2", 195 lbs. Deb: 9/25/83

YEAR	TM/L	G	AB	R	H	2B	3B	HR	RBI	BB	SO	AVG	OBP	SLG	PRO+	BR	/A	RC	SB	CS	SBR	FA	FR	POS	TPR
1983	Phi-N	2	3	1	1	0	0	0	0	1	1	.333	.500	.333	137	0	0	1	0	0	0	1.000	-0	/C	0.0
1985	Phi-N	36	103	14	21	3	1	4	11	16	37	.204	.311	.369	87	-1	-2	13	3	0	1	.994	0	C	0.1
1986	Phi-N	49	138	18	31	4	0	8	21	38	41	.225	.395	.428	123	7	6	26	2	3	-1	.985	-4	C	0.4
1987	Phi-N	53	129	10	25	6	0	3	13	16	37	.194	.283	.310	55	-8	-9	13	0	0	0	.991	1	C/1	-0.6
1988	Phi-N	58	144	13	30	6	0	1	12	17	26	.208	.292	.271	61	-7	-7	12	2	1	0	.977	-6	C/1	-1.1
1989	Phi-N	131	368	29	74	12	2	8	44	52	58	.201	.303	.310	76	-11	-11	37	2	1	0	.984	-11	*C	-1.7
1990	Phi-N	143	459	62	123	30	1	12	57	72	72	.268	.370	.416	116	12	12	76	7	1	2	.989	-9	*C	1.4
1991	Phi-N	89	285	36	56	12	0	12	42	41	66	.196	.302	.365	88	-5	-5	34	5	0	2	.985	-17	C	-1.6
1992	Phi-N★	145	485	80	131	32	5	27	**109**	88	103	.270	.389	.524	157	38	38	107	11	2	2	.987	-14	*C	3.7
Total	9	706	2114	263	492	105	9	75	309	341	441	.233	.343	.397	106	24	23	319	32	8	5	.987	-59	C/1	0.6

■ YO-YO DAVALILLO

Davalillo, Pompeyo Antonio (Romero) b: 6/30/31, Caracas, Venez. BR/TR, 5'3", 140 lbs. Deb: 8/01/53 F

YEAR	TM/L	G	AB	R	H	2B	3B	HR	RBI	BB	SO	AVG	OBP	SLG	PRO+	BR	/A	RC	SB	CS	SBR	FA	FR	POS	TPR
1953	Was-A	19	58	10	17	1	0	0	2	1	7	.293	.305	.310	68	-3	-3	6	1	0	0	.935	2	S	0.0

■ VIC DAVALILLO

Davalillo, Victor Jose (Romero) b: 7/31/36, Cabimas, Venez. BL/TL, 5'7", 155 lbs. Deb: 4/09/63 F

YEAR	TM/L	G	AB	R	H	2B	3B	HR	RBI	BB	SO	AVG	OBP	SLG	PRO+	BR	/A	RC	SB	CS	SBR	FA	FR	POS	TPR
1963	Cle-A	90	370	44	108	18	5	7	36	16	41	.292	.323	.424	108	3	3	50	3	3	-1	.988	17	O	1.5
1964	Cle-A	150	577	64	156	26	2	6	51	34	77	.270	.312	.354	85	-12	-12	65	21	11	-0	.986	16	*O	-0.3
1965	Cle-A★	142	505	67	152	19	1	5	40	35	50	.301	.346	.372	103	3	2	68	26	7	4	.988	15	*O	1.6
1966	Cle-A	121	344	42	86	6	4	3	19	24	37	.250	.299	.317	77	-10	-10	32	8	6	-1	.986	0	*O	-1.6
1967	Cle-A	139	359	47	103	17	5	2	22	10	30	.287	.308	.379	101	-0	-1	39	6	7	-2	.986	-8	*O	-1.7
1968	Cle-A	51	180	15	43	2	3	2	13	3	19	.239	.255	.317	74	-6	-6	13	8	6	-1	.967	2	O	-0.9
	Cal-A	93	339	34	101	15	4	1	18	15	34	.298	.328	.375	117	4	5	41	17	10	-1	.995	6	O	0.7
	Yr	144	519	49	144	17	7	3	31	18	53	.277	.303	.355	102	-2	-1	54	25	16	-2	.987	8	*O	-0.2
1969	Cal-A	33	71	10	11	1	1	0	1	6	5	.155	.231	.197	22	-8	-7	4	3	0	1	1.000	-2	O/1	-1.0
	StL-N	63	98	15	26	3	0	2	10	7	8	.265	.314	.357	87	-2	-2	10	1	1	-0	1.000	1	O/P	-0.2
1970	StL-N	111	183	29	57	14	3	1	33	13	19	.311	.357	.437	109	3	2	28	4	1	1	.972	1	O	0.2
1971	*Pit-N	99	295	48	84	14	6	1	33	11	31	.285	.315	.383	97	-2	-2	36	10	2	2	.983	1	O1	-0.3
1972	*Pit-N	117	368	59	117	19	2	4	28	26	44	.318	.368	.413	124	10	11	59	14	1	4	.979	-2	O/1	0.9
1973	Pit-N	59	83	9	15	1	0	1	3	2	7	.181	.200	.229	19	-9	-9	3	0	2	-1	.977	2	1O	-0.9
	*Oak-A	38	64	5	12	1	0	0	4	3	4	.188	.224	.203	22	-7	-6	3	0	0	0	.967	-2	O/1D	-0.9
1974	Oak-A	17	23	0	4	0	0	0	1	2	2	.174	.240	.174	22	-2	-2	1	0	0	0	1.000	-2	/OD	-0.5
1977	*LA-N	24	48	3	15	2	0	0	4	0	6	.313	.313	.354	79	-2	-1	5	0	0	0	1.000	-2	O	-0.3
1978	LA-N	75	77	15	24	1	1	1	11	3	7	.312	.338	.390	103	0	0	10	2	1	0	1.000	0	O/1	0.0
1979	LA-N	29	27	2	7	1	0	0	2	2	0	.259	.310	.296	67	-1	-1	3	2	0	1	1.000	0	/O	-0.1
1980	LA-N	7	6	1	1	0	0	0	0	0	1	.167	.167	.167	-7	-1	-1	0	0	0	0	1.000	-0	/1	-0.1
Total	16	1458	4017	509	1122	160	37	36	329	212	422	.279	.317	.364	94	-38	-35	472	125	58	3	.986	43	*O/1DP	-3.9

■ JERRY DaVANON

DaVanon, Frank Gerald b: 8/21/45, Oceanside, Cal. BR/TR, 5'11", 175 lbs. Deb: 4/11/69

YEAR	TM/L	G	AB	R	H	2B	3B	HR	RBI	BB	SO	AVG	OBP	SLG	PRO+	BR	/A	RC	SB	CS	SBR	FA	FR	POS	TPR
1969	SD-N	24	59	4	8	1	0	0	3	3	12	.136	.177	.153	-7	-8	-8	1	0	3	-2	.932	0	2/S	-0.9
	StL-N	16	40	7	12	3	0	1	7	6	8	.300	.391	.450	135	2	2	7	0	0	0	.958	1	S	0.4
	Yr	40	99	11	20	4	0	1	10	9	20	.202	.269	.273	53	-6	-6	6	0	3	-2	.959	1	S2	-0.5
1970	StL-N	11	18	2	2	1	0	0	0	2	5	.111	.200	.167	-1	-3	-3	1	0	0	0	1.000	3	/32	0.0
1971	Bal-A	38	81	14	19	5	0	0	4	12	20	.235	.340	.296	82	-2	-1	8	0	0	0	.970	-3	2S/31	-0.3
1973	Cal-A	41	49	6	12	3	0	0	2	3	9	.245	.288	.306	73	-2	-2	4	1	2	-1	.927	5	S2/3	0.4
1974	StL-N	30	40	4	6	1	0	0	4	4	5	.150	.261	.175	24	-4	-4	2	0	1	-1	.840	-2	S/32O	-0.6
1975	Hou-N	32	97	15	27	4	2	1	10	16	7	.278	.386	.392	125	3	4	16	2	0	1	.944	2	S/23	0.9
1976	Hou-N	61	107	19	31	3	3	1	20	21	12	.290	.411	.402	144	6	7	18	0	2	-1	.980	3	2S/3	1.2
1977	StL-N	9	8	2	0	0	0	0	0	1	2	.000	.111	.000	-68	-2	-2	0	0	0	0	.923	1	/2	0.0
Total	8	262	499	73	117	21	5	3	50	68	80	.234	.332	.315	86	-10	-7	56	3	8	-4	.936	12	S/2301	1.1

■ JIM DAVENPORT

Davenport, James Houston b: 8/17/33, Siluria, Ala. BR/TR, 5'11", 175 lbs. Deb: 4/15/58 MC

YEAR	TM/L	G	AB	R	H	2B	3B	HR	RBI	BB	SO	AVG	OBP	SLG	PRO+	BR	/A	RC	SB	CS	SBR	FA	FR	POS	TPR
1958	SF-N	134	434	70	111	22	3	12	41	33	64	.256	.319	.403	92	-7	-6	57	1	3	-2	.960	-4	*3/S	-1.0
1959	SF-N	123	469	65	121	16	3	6	38	28	65	.258	.303	.343	73	-19	-18	50	0	1	-1	**.978**	-3	*3/S	-2.1
1960	SF-N	112	363	43	91	15	3	6	38	26	58	.251	.308	.358	87	-9	-7	39	0	2	-1	**.961**	-1	*3/S	-0.9
1961	SF-N	137	436	64	121	28	4	12	65	45	65	.278	.348	.443	112	5	7	67	4	3	-1	**.965**	8	*3	1.5
1962	*SF-N★	144	485	83	144	25	5	14	58	45	76	.297	.359	.456	119	11	12	76	2	5	-2	.952	4	*3	1.6
1963	SF-N	147	460	40	116	19	3	4	36	32	87	.252	.301	.333	83	-11	-10	46	5	2	0	.962	1	*32/S	-0.7
1964	SF-N	116	297	24	70	10	6	2	26	29	46	.236	.304	.330	77	-8	-9	29	2	0	1	.979	-3	S32	-0.7
1965	SF-N	106	271	29	68	14	3	4	31	21	47	.251	.307	.369	87	-4	-5	30	0	0	0	.949	-21	3S2	-2.5
1966	SF-N	111	305	42	76	6	2	9	30	22	40	.249	.302	.370	83	-6	-7	33	1	1	-0	.961	-18	S32/1	-2.2
1967	SF-N	124	295	42	81	10	3	5	30	39	50	.275	.367	.380	116	7	7	41	1	4	-2	1.000	1	3S2	0.9
1968	SF-N	113	272	27	61	1	1	1	17	26	32	.224	.292	.246	63	-12	-11	19	0	3	-2	.960	-7	3S/2	-2.2
1969	SF-N	112	303	20	73	10	1	2	42	29	37	.241	.307	.300	72	-11	-11	27	0	1	-1	.967	1	*3/1SO	-1.0
1970	SF-N	22	37	3	9	1	0	0	4	7	6	.243	.364	.270	73	-1	-1	4	0	0	0	1.000	-3	3	-0.4
Total	13	1501	4427	552	1142	177	37	77	456	382	673	.258	.320	.367	90	-65	-57	519	16	25	-10	.964	-43	*3S2/10	-9.7

■ ANDRE DAVID

David, Andre Anter b: 5/18/58, Hollywood, Cal. BL/TL, 6', 170 lbs. Deb: 6/29/84

YEAR	TM/L	G	AB	R	H	2B	3B	HR	RBI	BB	SO	AVG	OBP	SLG	PRO+	BR	/A	RC	SB	CS	SBR	FA	FR	POS	TPR
1984	Min-A	33	48	5	12	2	0	1	5	7	11	.250	.357	.354	93	0	-0	6	0	0	0	1.000	-3	O/D	-0.4
1986	Min-A	5	5	0	1	0	0	0	0	0	2	.200	.333	.200	48	-0	-0	0	0	0	0	.000	0	/D	0.0
Total	2	38	53	5	13	2	0	1	5	7	13	.245	.355	.340	89	-0	-1	6	0	0	0		-3	/OD	-0.4

■ CLAUDE DAVIDSON

Davidson, Claude Boucher "Davey" b: 10/13/1896, Boston, Mass. d: 4/18/56, Weymouth, Mass. BL/TR, 5'11", 155 lbs. Deb: 4/25/18

YEAR	TM/L	G	AB	R	H	2B	3B	HR	RBI	BB	SO	AVG	OBP	SLG	PRO+	BR	/A	RC	SB	CS	SBR	FA	FR	POS	TPR
1918	Phi-A	31	81	4	15	1	0	0	4	5	9	.185	.233	.198	29	-7	-7	4	0			.943	-7	2/O3	-1.5
1919	Was-A	2	7	1	3	0	0	0	0	1	1	.429	.500	.429	163	1	1	2	0			1.000	-0	/3	0.1
Total	2	33	88	5	18	1	0	0	4	6	10	.205	.255	.216	41	-6	-6	6	0			1.000	-7	/2O3	-1.4

■ HOMER DAVIDSON

Davidson, Homer Hurd "Divvy" b: 10/14/1884, Cleveland, Ohio d: 7/26/48, Detroit, Mich. BR/TR, 5'10.5", 155 lbs. Deb: 4/25/08

YEAR	TM/L	G	AB	R	H	2B	3B	HR	RBI	BB	SO	AVG	OBP	SLG	PRO+	BR	/A	RC	SB	CS	SBR	FA	FR	POS	TPR
1908	Cle-A	9	4	2	0	0	0	0	0	0		.000	.000	.000	-99	-1	-1	-0	1			1.000	2	/CO	0.1

■ MARK DAVIDSON

Davidson, John Mark b: 2/15/61, Knoxville, Tenn. BR/TR, 6'2", 190 lbs. Deb: 6/20/86

YEAR	TM/L	G	AB	R	H	2B	3B	HR	RBI	BB	SO	AVG	OBP	SLG	PRO+	BR	/A	RC	SB	CS	SBR	FA	FR	POS	TPR
1986	Min-A	36	68	5	8	3	0	0	2	6	22	.118	.189	.162	-3	-10	-10	2	2	3	-1	.980	-4	O/D	-1.6
1987	*Min-A	102	150	32	40	4	1	1	14	13	26	.267	.325	.327	71	-5	-6	17	9	2	2	1.000	-14	O/D	-1.9
1988	Min-A	100	106	22	23	7	0	1	10	10	20	.217	.291	.311	67	-4	-5	9	3	3	-1	.955	-16	O/3D	-2.3
1989	Hou-N	33	65	7	13	2	1	1	5	7	14	.200	.278	.308	70	-3	-3	6	1	0	0	1.000	-3	O	-0.6
1990	Hou-N	57	130	12	38	5	1	1	11	10	18	.292	.343	.369	99	-1	-0	16	0	3	-2	.981	-2	O	-0.5
1991	Hou-N	85	142	10	27	6	0	2	15	12	28	.190	.263	.275	54	-9	-8	11	0	0	0	1.000	-11	O	-2.1
Total	6	413	661	88	149	27	3	6	57	58	128	.225	.291	.303	64	-32	-32	60	15	11	-2	.983	-49	O/D3	-9.0

YEAR	TM/L	G	AB	R	H	2B	3B	HR	RBI	BB	SO	AVG	OBP	SLG	PRO+	BR	/A	RC	SB	CS	SBR	FA	FR	POS	TPR
■ BILL DAVIDSON	Davidson, William Simpson b: 5/10/1884, Lafayette, Ind. d: 5/23/54, Lincoln, Neb. BR/TR, 5'10", 170 lbs. Deb: 9/29/09																								
1909	Chi-N	2	7	2	1	0	0	0	0	1		.143	.250	.143	22	-1	-1	0	1			1.000	-0	/O	-0.1
1910	Bro-N	136	509	48	121	13	7	0	34	24	54	.238	.277	.291	68	-23	-22	48	27			.961	-7	*O	-3.7
1911	Bro-N	87	292	33	68	3	4	1	26	16	21	.233	.275	.281	58	-18	-16	27	18			.956	-5	O	-2.5
Total	3	225	808	83	190	16	11	1	60	41	75	.235	.276	.286	64	-42	-38	75	46			.959	-12	O	-6.3
■ CHICK DAVIES	Davies, Lloyd Garrison b: 3/6/1892, Peabody, Mass. d: 9/5/73, Middletown, Conn. BL/TL, 5'8", 145 lbs. Deb: 7/11/14																								
1914	Phi-A	19	46	6	11	3	1	0	5	5	13	.239	.314	.348	103	-0	0	6	1			.926	0	O/P	0.0
1915	Phi-A	56	132	13	24	5	3	0	11	14	31	.182	.270	.265	62	-7	-6	10	2	4	-2	.973	4	O/P	-0.6
1925	NY-N	4	6	1	0	0	0	0	0	0	1	.000	.000	.000	-99	-2	-2	0	0	0	0	1.000	0	/PO	-0.1
1926	NY-N	38	18	4	4	0	0	0	1	3	5	.222	.333	.222	53	-1	-1	1	0			.938	1	P	0.0
Total	4	117	202	24	39	8	4	0	17	22	50	.193	.279	.272	65	-10	-9	17	3	4		.938	6	/PO	-0.7
■ LEFTY DAVIS	Davis, Alphonzo De Ford b: 2/4/1875, Nashville, Tenn. d: 2/4/19, Collins, N.Y. BL/TL, 5'10", 170 lbs. Deb: 4/18/01																								
1901	Bro-N	25	91	11	19	2	0	0	7	10		.209	.287	.231	50	-5	-6	7	4			.822	-5	O/2	-1.2
	Pit-N	87	335	87	105	8	11	2	33	56		.313	.415	.421	139	21	20	70	22			.975	7	O	2.0
	Yr	112	426	98	124	10	11	2	40	66		.291	.389	.380	120	16	14	76	26			.942	2	*O/2	0.8
1902	Pit-N	59	232	52	65	7	3	0	20	35		.280	.379	.336	117	8	7	39	19			.945	-2	O	0.0
1903	NY-A	104	372	54	88	10	0	0	25	43		.237	.319	.263	72	-9	-12	38	11			.906	-7	*O/S	-2.7
1907	Cin-N	73	266	28	61	5	5	1	25	23		.229	.293	.297	82	-5	-6	27	9			.972	5	O	-0.4
Total	4	348	1296	232	338	32	19	3	110	167		.261	.348	.322	98	10	3	182	65			.939	-2	O/S2	-2.3
■ ALVIN DAVIS	Davis, Alvin Glenn b: 9/9/60, Riverside, Cal. BL/TR, 6'1", 195 lbs. Deb: 4/11/84																								
1984	Sea-A★	152	567	80	161	34	3	27	116	97	78	.284	.395	.497	147	38	39	117	5	4	-1	.992	-4	*1/D	2.4
1985	Sea-A	155	578	78	166	33	1	18	78	90	71	.287	.385	.441	125	23	23	101	1	2	-1	.992	-5	*1	0.7
1986	Sea-A	135	479	66	130	18	1	18	72	76	68	.271	.375	.426	116	14	13	78	0	3	-2	.986	1	*1D	0.4
1987	Sea-A	157	580	86	171	37	2	29	100	72	84	.295	.375	.516	126	28	23	111	0	0	0	.994	-7	*1	0.5
1988	Sea-A	140	478	67	141	24	1	18	69	95	53	.295	.416	.462	139	34	31	95	1	1	-0	.994	-6	*1D	1.5
1989	Sea-A	142	498	84	152	30	1	21	95	101	49	.305	.428	.496	155	44	42	109	0	1	-1	.992	-3	*1D	2.8
1990	Sea-A	140	494	63	140	21	0	17	68	85	68	.283	.393	.429	128	23	22	87	0	2	-1	.994	-1	D1	1.6
1991	Sea-A	145	462	39	102	15	1	12	69	56	78	.221	.305	.335	77	-14	-14	48	0	3	-2	1.000	-1	*D1	-1.8
1992	Cal-A	40	104	5	26	8	0	0	16	13	9	.250	.333	.327	87	-2	-2	12	0	0	0	.995	-0	1/D	-0.3
Total	9	1206	4240	568	1189	220	10	160	683	685	558	.280	.384	.450	127	186	176	757	7	16	-8	.992	-26	1D	7.8
■ BILL DAVIS	Davis, Arthur Willard b: 6/6/42, Graceville, Minn. BL/TL, 6'7", 215 lbs. Deb: 9/16/65																								
1965	Cle-A	10	10	0	3	1	0	0	0	0	1	.300	.300	.400	96	-0	-0	1	0	0	0	.000	0	H	0.0
1966	Cle-A	23	38	2	6	1	0	1	4	6	9	.158	.273	.263	55	-2	-2	3	0	0	0	.981	0	/1	-0.3
1969	SD-N	31	57	1	10	1	0	0	1	8	18	.175	.288	.193	39	-5	-4	3	0	0	0	.992	-1	1	-0.7
Total	3	64	105	3	19	3	0	1	5	14	28	.181	.283	.238	50	-7	-6	8	0	0	0	.988	-1	/1	-1.0
■ BROCK DAVIS	Davis, Bryshear Barnett b: 10/19/43, Oakland, Cal. BL/TL, 5'10", 168 lbs. Deb: 4/09/63																								
1963	Hou-N	34	55	7	11	2	0	1	2	4	10	.200	.254	.291	60	-3	-3	4	0	0	0	.864	-0	O	-0.4
1964	Hou-N	1	3	0	0	0	0	0	0	1	1	.000	.250	.000	-24	-0	-0	0	0	0	0	1.000	0	/O	-0.1
1966	Hou-N	10	27	2	4	1	0	0	1	5	4	.148	.281	.185	35	-2	-2	2	1	0	0	1.000	0	/O	-0.2
1970	Chi-N	6	3	0	0	0	0	0	0	0	1	.000	.000	.000	-89	-1	-1	0	0	0	0	.000	0	/O	-0.1
1971	Chi-N	106	301	22	77	7	5	0	28	35	34	.256	.337	.312	74	-5	-10	33	0	6	-4	.982	-0	O	-2.0
1972	Mil-A	85	154	17	49	2	0	0	12	12	23	.318	.367	.331	111	2	2	18	6	4	-1	.970	-5	O	-0.5
Total	6	242	543	48	141	12	5	1	43	57	73	.260	.332	.306	79	-10	-14	58	7	10	-4	.973	-5	O	-3.3
■ CHILI DAVIS	Davis, Charles Theodore b: 1/17/60, Kingston, Jamaica BB/TR, 6'3", 195 lbs. Deb: 4/10/81																								
1981	SF-N	8	15	1	2	0	0	0	0	1	2	.133	.188	.133	-8	-2	-2	0	2	0	1	1.000	-0	/O	-0.2
1982	SF-N	154	641	86	167	27	6	19	76	45	115	.261	.311	.410	100	-2	-1	79	24	13	-1	.972	10	*O	0.4
1983	SF-N	137	486	54	113	21	2	11	59	55	108	.233	.311	.352	86	-11	-9	52	10	12	-4	.976	5	*O	-1.3
1984	SF-N★	137	499	87	157	21	6	21	81	42	74	.315	.369	.507	149	28	30	89	12	8	-1	.971	8	*O	3.3
1985	SF-N	136	481	53	130	25	2	13	56	62	74	.270	.354	.412	119	9	12	68	15	7	0	.980	13	*O	2.2
1986	SF-N★	153	526	71	146	28	3	13	70	84	96	.278	.378	.416	125	16	19	83	16	13	-3	.972	-2	*O	1.0
1987	*SF-N	149	500	80	125	22	1	24	76	72	109	.250	.347	.442	113	5	9	78	16	9	-1	.975	-13	*O	-0.9
1988	Cal-A	158	600	81	161	29	3	21	93	56	118	.268	.331	.432	115	9	11	82	9	10	-3	.942	-4	*O/D	-0.1
1989	Cal-A	154	560	81	152	24	1	22	90	61	109	.271	.343	.436	120	13	14	80	3	0	1	.979	-4	*O/D	0.7
1990	Cal-A	113	412	58	109	17	1	12	58	61	89	.265	.359	.398	114	8	9	59	1	2	-1	.965	-3	DO	0.4
1991	*Min-A	153	534	84	148	34	1	29	93	95	117	.277	.387	.507	139	35	31	107	5	6	-2	1.000	-0	*D/O	2.8
1992	Min-A	138	444	63	128	27	2	12	66	73	76	.288	.392	.439	128	22	20	78	4	5	-2	1.000	-1	*D/O1	1.7
Total	12	1590	5698	799	1538	275	28	197	818	707	1087	.270	.352	.432	118	129	142	854	117	85	-16	.971	9	*OD/1	10.0
■ DOUG DAVIS	Davis, Douglas Raymond b: 9/24/62, Bloomsburg, Pa. BR/TR, 6', 180 lbs. Deb: 7/08/88																								
1988	Cal-A	6	12	1	0	0	0	0	0	0	3	.000	.077	.000	-79	-3	-3	0	0	0	0	1.000	-3	/C3	-0.6
1992	Tex-A	1	1	0	1	0	0	0	0	0	0	1.000	1.000	1.000	477	0	0	1	0	0	0	.000	0	/C	0.0
Total	2	7	13	1	1	0	0	0	0	0	3	.077	.143	.077	-38	-2	-2	1	0	0	0	1.000	-3	/C3	-0.6
■ ERIC DAVIS	Davis, Eric Keith b: 5/29/62, Los Angeles, Cal. BR/TR, 6'3", 175 lbs. Deb: 5/19/84																								
1984	Cin-N	57	174	33	39	10	1	10	30	24	48	.224	.322	.466	114	4	3	28	10	2	2	.992	1	O	0.5
1985	Cin-N	56	122	26	30	3	3	8	18	7	39	.246	.287	.516	114	2	2	19	16	3	3	.987	-6	O	-0.2
1986	Cin-N	132	415	97	115	15	3	27	71	68	100	.277	.380	.523	140	27	24	95	80	11	17	.975	-9	*O	3.0
1987	Cin-N★	129	474	120	139	23	4	37	100	84	134	.293	.401	.593	152	41	38	124	50	6	11	.990	28	*O	**7.1**
1988	Cin-N	135	472	81	129	18	3	26	93	65	124	.273	.365	.489	138	27	24	90	35	3	9	.981	-0	*O	3.1
1989	Cin-N★	131	462	74	130	14	2	34	101	68	116	.281	.375	.541	154	35	33	91	21	7	2	.984	2	*O	3.6
1990	*Cin-N	127	453	84	118	26	2	24	86	60	100	.260	.350	.486	122	16	14	81	21	3	5	.993	7	*O	2.3
1991	Cin-N	89	285	39	67	10	0	11	33	48	92	.235	.355	.386	104	4	3	44	14	2	3	.985	6	O	1.1
1992	LA-N	76	267	21	61	8	1	5	32	36	71	.228	.327	.322	86	-5	-4	31	19	1	5	.961	-5	O	-0.6
Total	9	932	3124	575	828	127	19	182	564	460	824	.265	.362	.493	131	152	138	603	266	38	57	.984	24	O	19.9
■ GEORGE DAVIS	Davis, George Stacey b: 8/23/1870, Cohoes, N.Y. d: 10/17/40, Philadelphia, Pa. BB/TR, 5'9", 180 lbs. Deb: 4/19/1890 M																								
1890	Cle-N	136	526	98	139	22	9	6	73	53	34	.264	.336	.375	111	6	7	75	22			.946	12	*O/2S	1.3
1891	Cle-N	136	570	115	165	35	12	3	89	53	29	.289	.354	.409	119	17	13	100	42			.931	14	*O3/P	2.1
1892	*Cle-N	144	597	95	144	27	12	5	82	58	51	.241	.312	.352	98	1	-2	79	36			.914	-10	3OS/2	-1.0
1893	NY-N	133	549	112	195	22	27	11	119	42	20	.355	.410	.554	157	42	41	143	37			.884	0	*3/S	3.6
1894	*NY-N	122	477	120	168	26	19	8	91	66	10	.352	.435	.537	136	28	29	133	40			.908	-1	*3	2.2
1895	NY-N	110	430	108	146	36	9	5	101	55	12	.340	.417	.500	141	25	27	113	48			.881	15	312/OM	3.4
1896	NY-N	124	494	98	158	25	12	6	99	50	24	.320	.387	.455	127	17	19	109	48			.917	11	3S/O1	2.8
1897	NY-N	130	519	112	183	31	10	10	**136**	41		.353	.406	.509	145	29	32	137	65			.926	22	*S	4.8
1898	NY-N	121	486	80	149	20	5	2	86	32		.307	.351	.381	113	5	7	77	26			.933	**36**	*S	4.5
1899	NY-N	108	416	68	140	21	5	1	57	37		.337	.393	.418	127	13	16	85	34			**.945**	**46**	*S	**6.2**
1900	NY-N	114	426	69	136	20	4	3	61	35		.319	.375	.406	121	9	12	78	29			**.944**	29	*SM	4.5
1901	NY-N	130	491	69	148	26	7	7	65	40		.301	.356	.426	131	16	18	87	27			.939	23	*S3M	4.9
1902	Chi-A	132	485	76	145	27	7	3	93	65		.299	.387	.402	124	15	18	91	31			**.951**	-2	*S/1	2.3

YEAR	TM/L	G	AB	R	H	2B	3B	HR	RBI	BB	SO	AVG	OBP	SLG	PRO+	BR	/A	RC	SB	CS	SBR	FA	FR	POS	TPR
1903	NY-N	4	15	2	4	0	0	0	1	1		.267	.313	.267	63	-1	-1	1	0			.870	-2	/S	-0.2
1904	Chi-A	152	563	75	142	27	15	1	69	43		.252	.311	.359	116	7	10	76	32			.937	17	*S	3.4
1905	Chi-A	151	550	74	153	29	1	1	55	60		.278	.353	.340	126	15	17	84	31			**.948**	16	*S	**4.0**
1906	*Chi-A	133	484	63	134	26	6	0	80	41		.277	.338	.355	121	10	12	70	27			.946	10	*S/2	2.8
1907	Chi-A	132	466	59	111	16	2	1	52	47		.238	.313	.288	95	-3	-1	50	15			.949	9	*S	1.3
1908	Chi-A	128	419	41	91	14	1	0	26	41		.217	.298	.255	81	-8	-7	41	22			.960	4	2S/1	-0.4
1909	Chi-A	28	68	5	9	1	0	0	2	10		.132	.253	.147	28	-5	-5	4	4			.986	1	1/2	-0.5
Total	20	2368	9031	1539	2660	451	163	73	1437	870	180	.295	.361	.405	122	239	263	1634	616			.940	250	*S302/1P	52.0

■ KIDDO DAVIS

Davis, George Willis b: 2/12/02, Bridgeport, Conn. d: 3/4/83, Bridgeport, Conn. BR/TR, 5′11″, 178 lbs. Deb: 6/15/26

YEAR	TM/L	G	AB	R	H	2B	3B	HR	RBI	BB	SO	AVG	OBP	SLG	PRO+	BR	/A	RC	SB	CS	SBR	FA	FR	POS	TPR
1926	NY-A	1	0	0	0	0	0	0	0	0	0	—	—	—	—	0	0	0	0	0	0	.000	-0	/O	0.0
1932	Phi-N	137	576	100	178	39	6	5	57	44	56	.309	.359	.424	98	8	-1	90	16			.975	14	*O	0.5
1933	*NY-N	126	434	61	112	20	4	7	37	25	30	.258	.298	.371	92	-6	-5	47	10			.988	-10	*O	-2.3
1934	StL-N	16	33	6	10	3	0	1	4	3	1	.303	.361	.485	117	1	1	6	1			.960	1	/O	0.1
	Phi-N	100	393	50	115	25	5	3	48	27	28	.293	.338	.405	86	-1	-8	55	1			.991	17	*O	0.5
	Yr	116	426	56	125	28	5	4	52	30	29	.293	.340	.411	89	-0	-7	60	2			.988	18	*O	0.6
1935	NY-N	47	91	16	24	7	1	2	6	10	4	.264	.343	.429	108	1	1	14	2			.977	-1	O	-0.1
1936	*NY-N	47	67	6	16	1	0	0	5	6	5	.239	.301	.254	51	-4	-4	6	0			1.000	-1	O	-0.6
1937	NY-N	56	76	20	20	10	0	0	9	10	7	.263	.356	.395	103	1	0	11	1			.932	-10	O	-1.0
	Cin-N	40	136	19	35	6	0	1	5	16	6	.257	.340	.324	85	-3	-2	16	1			.959	2	O	-0.2
	Yr	96	212	39	55	16	0	1	14	26	13	.259	.346	.349	90	-3	-2	27	2			.951	-8	O	-1.2
1938	Cin-N	5	18	3	5	1	0	0	0	1	4	.278	.316	.333	81	-1	-0	2	0			1.000	-1	/O	-0.1
Total	8	575	1824	281	515	112	16	19	171	142	141	.282	.336	.393	92	-5	-19	246	32	0		.980	10	O	-3.2

■ GERRY DAVIS

Davis, Gerald Edward b: 12/25/58, Trenton, N.J. BR/TR, 6′, 185 lbs. Deb: 9/20/83

YEAR	TM/L	G	AB	R	H	2B	3B	HR	RBI	BB	SO	AVG	OBP	SLG	PRO+	BR	/A	RC	SB	CS	SBR	FA	FR	POS	TPR
1983	SD-N	5	15	3	5	2	0	0	1	3	4	.333	.444	.467	158	1	1	3	1	0	0	1.000	0	/O	0.2
1985	SD-N	44	58	10	17	3	1	0	2	5	7	.293	.349	.379	105	0	0	7	0	0	0	.952	-4	O	-0.4
Total	2	49	73	13	22	5	1	0	3	8	11	.301	.370	.397	117	2	2	11	1	0	0	.967	-3	/O	-0.2

■ GLENN DAVIS

Davis, Glenn Earle b: 3/28/61, Jacksonville, Fla. BR/TR, 6′3″, 210 lbs. Deb: 9/02/84

YEAR	TM/L	G	AB	R	H	2B	3B	HR	RBI	BB	SO	AVG	OBP	SLG	PRO+	BR	/A	RC	SB	CS	SBR	FA	FR	POS	TPR
1984	Hou-N	18	61	6	13	5	0	2	8	4	12	.213	.262	.393	88	-2	-1	7	0	0	0	.988	2	1	0.0
1985	Hou-N	100	350	51	95	11	0	20	64	27	68	.271	.336	.474	128	10	11	53	0	0	0	.985	-2	1/O	0.4
1986	*Hou-N★	158	574	91	152	32	3	31	101	64	72	.265	.348	.493	133	22	24	100	3	1	0	.992	2	*1	1.5
1987	Hou-N	151	578	70	145	35	2	27	93	47	84	.251	.313	.458	105	-1	2	80	4	1	1	.991	3	*1	-0.6
1988	Hou-N	152	561	78	152	26	0	30	99	53	77	.271	.346	.478	140	24	26	91	4	3	-1	**.996**	0	*1	1.4
1989	Hou-N★	158	581	87	156	26	1	34	89	69	123	.269	.353	.492	144	29	31	102	4	2	0	.992	3	*1	2.3
1990	Hou-N	93	327	44	82	15	4	22	64	46	54	.251	.357	.523	143	17	18	62	8	3	1	.995	-3	1	0.9
1991	Bal-A	49	176	29	40	9	1	10	28	16	29	.227	.310	.460	115	2	3	27	4	0	1	.976	4	1D	0.5
1992	Bal-A	106	398	46	110	15	2	13	48	37	65	.276	.341	.422	113	6	6	56	1	0	0	1.000	-0	*D/1	0.6
Total	9	985	3606	502	945	174	13	189	594	363	584	.262	.339	.475	128	107	121	577	28	10	2	.992	8	1D/O	7.0

■ HARRY DAVIS

Davis, Harry Albert "Stinky" b: 5/7/08, Shreveport, La. BL/TL, 5′10.5″, 160 lbs. Deb: 4/13/32

YEAR	TM/L	G	AB	R	H	2B	3B	HR	RBI	BB	SO	AVG	OBP	SLG	PRO+	BR	/A	RC	SB	CS	SBR	FA	FR	POS	TPR
1932	Det-A	141	590	92	159	32	13	4	74	60	53	.269	.339	.388	84	-11	-14	80	12	7	-1	.989	-5	*1	-2.9
1933	Det-A	66	173	24	37	8	2	0	14	22	8	.214	.303	.283	55	-11	-11	16	2	3	-1	.978	-5	1	-2.0
1937	StL-A	120	450	89	124	25	3	3	35	71	26	.276	.374	.364	86	-7	-7	65	7	6	-2	.991	-4	*1/O	-2.4
Total	3	327	1213	205	320	65	18	7	123	153	87	.264	.347	.364	81	-28	-33	161	21	16	-3	.988	-14	1/O	-7.3

■ HARRY DAVIS

Davis, Harry H (b: Harry Davis) "Jasper" b: 7/19/1873, Philadelphia, Pa. d: 8/11/47, Philadelphia, Pa. BR/TR, 5′10″, 180 lbs. Deb: 9/21/1895 M

YEAR	TM/L	G	AB	R	H	2B	3B	HR	RBI	BB	SO	AVG	OBP	SLG	PRO+	BR	/A	RC	SB	CS	SBR	FA	FR	POS	TPR
1895	NY-N	7	24	1	7	0	1	0	6	2	0	.292	.346	.375	90	-0	-0	4	1			.957	0	/1	0.0
1896	NY-N	64	233	43	64	11	10	2	50	31	20	.275	.372	.433	117	5	6	45	16			.883	-4	O1	-0.1
	Pit-N	44	168	24	32	5	6	0	23	13	21	.190	.257	.292	48	-13	-12	16	9			.966	1	1O/S	-1.0
	Yr	108	401	67	96	16	16	2	73	44	41	.239	.325	.374	89	-8	-6	59	25			.973	-3	1O/S	-1.1
1897	Pit-N	111	429	70	131	10	**28**	2	63	26		.305	.359	.473	123	9	12	83	21			.965	-12	13O/S	0.0
1898	Pit-N	58	222	31	65	9	13	1	24	12		.293	.332	.464	130	6	7	38	7			.980	-2	1/O	0.4
	Lou-N	37	138	18	30	5	2	1	16	7		.217	.255	.304	61	-8	-7	13	6			.967	0	1/2O	-0.7
	Was-N	1	3	0	0	0	0	0	0	0		.000	.000	.000	-99	-1	-1	0	0			.875	-0	/1	-0.1
	Yr	96	363	49	95	14	15	2	40	19		.262	.300	.399	102	-2	-1	49	13			.974	-2	1/O2	-0.4
1899	Was-N	18	64	3	12	2	3	0	8	8		.188	.288	.313	65	-3	-3	7	2			.988	-1	1	-0.4
1901	Phi-A	117	496	92	152	28	10	8	76	23		.306	.338	.452	113	10	7	85	21			.976	9	*1	1.2
1902	Phi-A	133	561	89	172	**43**	8	6	92	30		.307	.344	.444	112	11	8	98	28			.984	7	*1/O	1.2
1903	Phi-A	106	420	77	125	28	7	6	55	24		.298	.343	.440	128	17	14	74	24			.972	-1	*1/O	1.2
1904	Phi-A	102	404	54	125	21	11	**10**	62	23		.309	.350	.490	156	28	25	76	12			.983	-1	*1	2.4
1905	*Phi-A	150	607	**93**	173	**47**	6	**8**	**83**	43		.285	.334	.422	137	25	24	101	36			.985	1	*1	2.2
1906	Phi-A	145	551	94	161	42	7	**12**	**96**	49		.292	.355	.459	150	33	32	101	23			.975	-0	*1	2.9
1907	Phi-A	149	582	84	155	**37**	8	**8**	87	42		.266	.318	.399	125	17	15	83	20			.977	4	*1	1.7
1908	Phi-A	147	513	65	127	23	9	5	62	61		.248	.332	.357	116	15	11	68	20			.986	1	*1	1.0
1909	Phi-A	149	530	73	142	22	11	4	75	51		.268	.338	.374	122	15	14	73	20			.988	-5	*1	0.8
1910	*Phi-A	139	492	61	122	19	4	1	41	53		.248	.332	.309	102	2	3	57	17			.986	-4	*1	-0.2
1911	*Phi-A	57	183	27	36	9	1	1	22	24		.197	.297	.273	60	-10	-9	16	2			.977	2	1	-0.7
1912	Cle-A	2	5	0	0	0	0	0	0	0		.000	.000	.000	-97	-1	-1	0	0			.941	0	/1M	-0.1
1913	Phi-A	7	17	2	6	2	0	0	4	1	4	.353	.389	.471	155	1	1	3	0			1.000	1	/1	0.2
1914	Phi-A	5	7	0	3	0	0	0	2	1	0	.429	.556	.429	204	1	1	1	0	2	-1	1.000	-0	/1	0.0
1915	Phi-A	5	3	0	1	0	0	0	4	0	0	.333	.333	.333	103	-0	-0	0	0			.000	0	/1	0.0
1916	Phi-A	1	0	0	0	0	0	0	0	1	0	—	1.000	—	213	0	0	0	0			.000	0	H	0.0
1917	Phi-A	1	1	0	0	0	0	0	0	0	0	.000	.000	.000	-99	-0	-0	0	0			.000	0	H	0.0
Total	22	1755	6653	1001	1841	363	145	75	951	525	45	.277	.335	.409	119	158	145	1042	285	2		.980	-6	*1/O32S	11.9

■ TOMMY DAVIS

Davis, Herman Thomas b: 3/21/39, Brooklyn, N.Y. BR/TR, 6′2″, 205 lbs. Deb: 9/22/59 C

YEAR	TM/L	G	AB	R	H	2B	3B	HR	RBI	BB	SO	AVG	OBP	SLG	PRO+	BR	/A	RC	SB	CS	SBR	FA	FR	POS	TPR
1959	LA-N	1	1	0	0	0	0	0	0	0	1	.000	.000	.000	-93	-0	-0	0	0	0	0	.000	0	H	0.0
1960	LA-N	110	352	43	97	18	1	11	44	13	35	.276	.305	.426	92	-2	-5	45	6	2	1	.975	-0	O/3	-0.9
1961	LA-N	132	460	60	128	13	2	15	58	32	53	.278	.328	.413	87	-4	-9	59	10	4	1	.973	-2	O3	-1.4
1962	LA-N★	163	665	120	**230**	27	9	27	**153**	33	65	**.346**	.379	.535	151	37	42	129	18	6	2	.961	-5	*O3	3.1
1963	*LA-N★	146	556	69	181	19	3	16	88	29	59	**.326**	.363	.457	144	24	28	86	15	10	-2	.969	-11	*O3	1.0
1964	LA-N	152	592	70	163	20	5	14	86	29	68	.275	.314	.397	106	-2	3	69	11	8	-2	.982	4	*O	-0.2
1965	LA-N	17	60	3	15	1	1	0	9	2	4	.250	.274	.300	66	-3	-3	3	2	1	0	1.000	-1	O	-0.5
1966	*LA-N	100	313	27	98	11	1	3	27	16	36	.313	.347	.383	111	1	4	38	3	3	-1	.972	-7	O/3	-0.8
1967	NY-N	154	577	72	174	32	0	16	73	31	71	.302	.345	.440	125	16	17	84	9	3	1	.975	-9	*O/1	0.2
1968	Chi-A	132	456	30	122	5	3	8	50	16	48	.268	.292	.344	91	-5	-6	42	4	2	0	.962	-4	*O/1	-1.9
1969	Sea-A	123	454	52	123	29	1	6	80	30	46	.271	.322	.379	97	-4	-3	53	19	4	3	.967	-7	*O/1	-1.3
	Hou-N	24	79	2	19	3	0	1	9	8	9	.241	.318	.316	80	-2	-2	8	1	1	-0	1.000	-2	O	-0.6
1970	Hou-N	57	213	24	60	12	2	3	30	7	25	.282	.305	.399	91	-5	-4	25	8	3	1	.949	-5	O	-1.0
	Chi-N	11	42	4	11	2	0	2	8	1	1	.262	.279	.452	83	-1	-1	5	0	0	0	.938	-2	O	-0.3
	Yr	68	255	28	71	14	2	5	38	8	26	.278	.300	.408	89	-5	-5	31	8	3	1	.947	-6	O	-1.3
	Oak-A	66	200	17	58	9	1	1	27	8	18	.290	.321	.360	91	-4	-3	21	2	4	-2	.963	-7	O/1	-1.5

YEAR	TM/L	G	AB	R	H	2B	3B	HR	RBI	BB	SO	AVG	OBP	SLG	PRO+	BR	/A	RC	SB	CS	SBR	FA	FR	POS	TPR
1971	*Oak-A	79	219	26	71	8	1	3	42	15	19	.324	.368	.411	123	6	6	31	7	1	2	.989	2	1O/23	0.6
1972	Chi-N	15	26	3	7	1	0	0	6	2	3	.269	.321	.308	72	-1	-1	2	0	1	-1	1.000	-1	/1O	-0.3
	Bal-A	26	82	9	21	3	0	0	6	6	18	.256	.307	.293	77	-2	-2	7	2	0	1	1.000	0	O/1	-0.3
1973	*Bal-A	137	552	53	169	20	3	7	89	30	56	.306	.343	.391	107	4	4	72	11	3	2	.971	-0	*D/1	0.5
1974	*Bal-A	158	626	67	181	20	1	11	84	34	49	.289	.329	.377	106	1	3	73	6	2	1	.000	0	*D	0.4
1975	Bal-A	116	460	43	130	14	1	6	57	23	52	.283	.317	.357	96	-7	-3	49	2	0	1	.000	0	*D	-0.3
1976	Cal-A	72	219	16	58	5	0	3	26	15	18	.265	.315	.329	95	-3	-2	20	0	1	-1	1.000	-0	D/1	-0.2
	KC-A	8	19	1	5	0	0	0	0	1	0	.263	.300	.263	65	-1	-1	1	0	0	0	.000	0	/D	-0.1
	Yr	80	238	17	63	5	0	3	26	16	18	.265	.314	.324	92	-4	-2	21	0	1	-1	1.000	-0	D/H1	-0.3
Total	18	1999	7223	811	2121	272	35	153	1052	381	754	.294	.332	.405	109	44	65	923	136	59	5	.970	-56	*OD3/12	-5.8

■ **IKE DAVIS** Davis, Isaac Marion b: 6/14/1895, Pueblo, Col. d: 4/2/84, Tucson, Ariz. BR/TR, 5'7", 140 lbs. Deb: 4/23/19

YEAR	TM/L	G	AB	R	H	2B	3B	HR	RBI	BB	SO	AVG	OBP	SLG	PRO+	BR	/A	RC	SB	CS	SBR	FA	FR	POS	TPR
1919	Was-A	8	14	0	0	0	0	0	0	0	6	.000	.000	.000	-99	-4	-4	0	0			.857	-2	/S	-0.6
1924	Chi-A	10	33	5	8	1	1	0	4	2	5	.242	.286	.333	61	-2	-2	3	0	0	0	.940	1	S	0.0
1925	Chi-A	146	562	105	135	31	9	0	61	71	58	.240	.333	.327	72	-27	-22	66	19	14	-3	.937	8	*S	-0.1
Total	3	164	609	110	143	32	10	0	65	73	69	.235	.324	.320	68	-33	-28	69	19	14		.936	8	S	-0.7

■ **IRA DAVIS** Davis, J. Ira "Slats" b: 7/8/1870, Philadelphia, Pa. d: 12/21/42, Brooklyn, N.Y. 162 lbs. Deb: 4/22/1899

YEAR	TM/L	G	AB	R	H	2B	3B	HR	RBI	BB	SO	AVG	OBP	SLG	PRO+	BR	/A	RC	SB	CS	SBR	FA	FR	POS	TPR
1899	NY-N	6	17	3	4	1	1	0	2	0		.235	.235	.412	79	-1	-1	2	1			.750	-0	/S1	-0.1

■ **JACKE DAVIS** Davis, Jacke Sylvesta b: 3/5/36, Carthage, Tex. BR/TR, 5'11", 160 lbs. Deb: 4/19/62

YEAR	TM/L	G	AB	R	H	2B	3B	HR	RBI	BB	SO	AVG	OBP	SLG	PRO+	BR	/A	RC	SB	CS	SBR	FA	FR	POS	TPR
1962	Phi-N	48	75	9	16	0	1	1	6	4	20	.213	.253	.280	44	-6	-6	5	1	0	0	.926	-1	O	-0.8

■ **JUMBO DAVIS** Davis, James J. b: 9/5/1861, New York, N.Y. d: 2/14/21, St.Louis, Mo. BL/TR, 5'11", 195 lbs. Deb: 7/27/1884 U

YEAR	TM/L	G	AB	R	H	2B	3B	HR	RBI	BB	SO	AVG	OBP	SLG	PRO+	BR	/A	RC	SB	CS	SBR	FA	FR	POS	TPR
1884	KC-U	7	29	3	6	0	0	0		0		.207	.207	.207	46	-2	-1	1				.633	-2	/3	-0.3
1886	Bal-a	60	216	23	42	5	2	1		11		.194	.240	.250	56	-11	-10	16	12			.848	5	3	-0.4
1887	Bal-a	130	485	81	150	23	**19**	8		28		.309	.353	.485	143	20	25	103	49			.826	4	3S	2.5
1888	KC-a	121	491	70	131	22	8	3	61	20		.267	.304	.363	109	8	3	68	42			.843	30	*3/S	3.2
1889	KC-a	62	241	40	64	4	3	0	30	17	35	.266	.319	.307	76	-6	-8	32	25			.803	-0	3	-0.5
	StL-a	2	4	1	0	0	0	0	0	1	1	.000	.200	.000	-35	-1	-1	0	0			1.000	-0	/SO	-0.1
	Yr	64	245	41	64	4	3	0	30	18	36	.261	.317	.302	74	-6	-9	32	25			.803	-1	3/SO	-0.6
1890	StL-a	21	71	8	18	3	1	0		9		.254	.338	.324	85	-0	-2	10	5			.731	-1	3	-0.2
	Bro-a	38	142	33	43	9	2	2		15		.303	.385	.437	150	8	9	28	10			.845	-5	3	0.5
	Yr	59	213	41	61	12	3	2		24		.286	.369	.399	126	8	7	38	15			.800	-6	3	0.3
1891	Was-a	12	44	7	14	3	2	0	9	7	5	.318	.412	.477	165	3	4	12	8			.820	-2	3	0.2
Total	7	453	1723	266	468	69	37	14	100	108	41	.272	.322	.379	110	20	19	272	151			.824	28	3/SO	4.9

■ **JODY DAVIS** Davis, Jody Richard b: 11/12/56, Gainesville, Ga. BR/TR, 6'3", 210 lbs. Deb: 4/21/81

YEAR	TM/L	G	AB	R	H	2B	3B	HR	RBI	BB	SO	AVG	OBP	SLG	PRO+	BR	/A	RC	SB	CS	SBR	FA	FR	POS	TPR
1981	Chi-N	56	180	14	46	5	1	4	21	21	28	.256	.337	.361	94	-0	-1	21	0	1	-1	.972	-1	C	-0.1
1982	Chi-N	130	418	41	109	20	2	12	52	36	92	.261	.321	.404	99	0	-1	55	0	1	-1	.984	8	*C	1.1
1983	Chi-N	151	510	56	138	31	2	24	84	33	93	.271	.317	.480	113	10	7	72	0	2	-1	.984	-14	*C	-0.1
1984	*Chi-N★	150	523	55	134	25	2	19	94	47	99	.256	.319	.421	97	3	-3	63	5	6	-2	.984	4	*C	0.7
1985	Chi-N	142	482	47	112	30	0	17	58	48	83	.232	.302	.400	85	-4	-11	57	1	0	0	.990	-1	*C	-0.5
1986	Chi-N★	148	528	61	132	27	2	21	74	41	110	.250	.304	.428	92	-2	-7	66	0	1	-1	.992	4	*C/1	0.6
1987	Chi-N	125	428	57	106	12	2	19	51	52	91	.248	.332	.418	93	-2	-4	58	1	2	-1	.989	-3	*C	0.1
1988	Chi-N	88	249	19	57	9	0	6	33	29	51	.229	.312	.337	83	-4	-5	25	0	3	-2	.995	-4	C	-0.7
	Atl-N	2	8	2	2	0	0	1	3	0	1	.250	.250	.625	137	0	0	1	0	0	0	1.000	1	/C	0.1
	Yr	90	257	21	59	9	0	7	36	29	52	.230	.310	.346	84	-4	-5	27	0	3	-2	.995	-4	C	-0.6
1989	Atl-N	78	231	12	39	5	0	4	19	23	61	.169	.247	.242	39	-18	-19	13	0	0	0	.985	-9	C/1	-2.6
1990	Atl-N	12	28	0	2	0	0	0	1	3	3	.071	.161	.071	-32	-5	-5	0	0	0	0	1.000	1	/1C	-0.5
Total	10	1082	3585	364	877	164	11	127	490	333	712	.245	.310	.403	91	-22	-49	432	7	16	-8	.987	-15	*C/1	-1.9

■ **JOHN DAVIS** Davis, John Humphrey "Red" b: 7/15/15, Laurel Run, Pa. BR/TR, 5'11", 172 lbs. Deb: 9/09/41

YEAR	TM/L	G	AB	R	H	2B	3B	HR	RBI	BB	SO	AVG	OBP	SLG	PRO+	BR	/A	RC	SB	CS	SBR	FA	FR	POS	TPR
1941	NY-N	21	70	8	15	3	0	0	5	8	12	.214	.295	.257	55	-4	-4	6	0			.970	1	3	-0.2

■ **CRASH DAVIS** Davis, Lawrence Columbus b: 7/14/19, Canon, Ga. BR/TR, 6', 173 lbs. Deb: 6/15/40

YEAR	TM/L	G	AB	R	H	2B	3B	HR	RBI	BB	SO	AVG	OBP	SLG	PRO+	BR	/A	RC	SB	CS	SBR	FA	FR	POS	TPR
1940	Phi-A	23	67	4	18	1	1	0	9	3	10	.269	.310	.313	63	-4	-4	7	1	0	0	.963	4	2/S	0.1
1941	Phi-A	39	105	8	23	3	0	0	8	11	16	.219	.293	.248	45	-8	-8	9	0	0	0	.952	2	21	-0.5
1942	Phi-A	86	272	31	61	8	1	2	26	21	30	.224	.282	.283	60	-15	-15	22	1	0	0	.965	-6	2S/1	-1.6
Total	3	148	444	43	102	12	2	2	43	35	56	.230	.289	.279	57	-27	-26	37	2	0	1	.961	0	/2S1	-2.0

■ **MARK DAVIS** Davis, Mark Anthony b: 11/25/64, San Diego, Cal. BR/TR, 6', 180 lbs. Deb: 7/02/91 F

YEAR	TM/L	G	AB	R	H	2B	3B	HR	RBI	BB	SO	AVG	OBP	SLG	PRO+	BR	/A	RC	SB	CS	SBR	FA	FR	POS	TPR
1991	Cal-A	3	2	0	0	0	0	0	0	0	0	.000	.000	.000	-99	-1	-1	0	0	0	0	.500	-1	/O	-0.2

■ **MIKE DAVIS** Davis, Michael Dwayne b: 6/11/59, San Diego, Cal. BL/TL, 6'3", 185 lbs. Deb: 4/10/80 F

YEAR	TM/L	G	AB	R	H	2B	3B	HR	RBI	BB	SO	AVG	OBP	SLG	PRO+	BR	/A	RC	SB	CS	SBR	FA	FR	POS	TPR
1980	Oak-A	51	95	11	20	2	1	1	8	7	14	.211	.265	.284	54	-6	-6	7	2	1	0	1.000	1	O/1D	-0.6
1981	*Oak-A	17	20	0	1	1	0	0	0	2	4	.050	.136	.100	-33	-3	-3	0	0	0	0	1.000	-0	/O1D	-0.4
1982	Oak-A	23	75	12	30	4	0	1	10	2	8	.400	.416	.493	155	5	5	15	3	2	-0	.946	-1	O/1	0.3
1983	Oak-A	128	443	61	122	24	4	8	62	27	74	.275	.324	.402	105	-1	2	56	32	15	1	.974	9	*O/D	0.8
1984	Oak-A	134	382	47	88	18	3	9	46	31	66	.230	.290	.364	85	-11	-8	40	14	9	-1	.961	-1	*O/D	-1.4
1985	Oak-A	154	547	92	157	34	1	24	82	50	99	.287	.349	.484	135	18	24	91	24	10	1	.979	2	*O	2.1
1986	Oak-A	142	489	77	131	28	3	19	55	34	91	.268	.317	.454	115	3	8	72	27	4	6	.973	2	*O	1.1
1987	Oak-A	139	494	69	131	32	1	22	72	42	94	.265	.324	.468	114	3	8	72	19	7	2	.942	-7	*OD	-0.1
1988	*LA-N	108	281	29	55	11	2	2	17	25	59	.196	.261	.270	55	-17	-16	20	7	3	0	.961	-9	O	-2.9
1989	LA-N	67	173	21	43	7	1	5	19	16	28	.249	.312	.387	101	-0	-0	20	6	5	-1	.987	-3	O	-0.6
Total	10	963	2999	419	778	161	16	91	371	236	537	.259	.316	.415	105	-10	14	395	134	56	7	.968	-8	O/D1	-1.7

■ **ODIE DAVIS** Davis, Odie Ernest b: 8/13/55, San Antonio, Tex. BR/TR, 6'1", 178 lbs. Deb: 9/03/80

YEAR	TM/L	G	AB	R	H	2B	3B	HR	RBI	BB	SO	AVG	OBP	SLG	PRO+	BR	/A	RC	SB	CS	SBR	FA	FR	POS	TPR
1980	Tex-A	17	8	0	1	0	0	0	0	0	2	.125	.125	.125	-32	-1	-1	0	0	0	0	.880	5	S/3	0.3

■ **OTIS DAVIS** Davis, Otis Allen "Scat" b: 9/24/20, Charleston, Ark. BL/TL, 6', 160 lbs. Deb: 4/22/46

YEAR	TM/L	G	AB	R	H	2B	3B	HR	RBI	BB	SO	AVG	OBP	SLG	PRO+	BR	/A	RC	SB	CS	SBR	FA	FR	POS	TPR
1946	Bro-N	1	0	1	0	0	0	0	0	0	0	—	—	—	—	0	0	0	0			1.000	0	R	0.0

■ **DICK DAVIS** Davis, Richard Earl b: 9/25/53, Long Beach, Cal. BR/TR, 6'3", 195 lbs. Deb: 7/12/77

YEAR	TM/L	G	AB	R	H	2B	3B	HR	RBI	BB	SO	AVG	OBP	SLG	PRO+	BR	/A	RC	SB	CS	SBR	FA	FR	POS	TPR
1977	Mil-A	22	51	7	14	2	0	0	6	1	8	.275	.288	.314	64	-3	-3	4	0	0	0	1.000	-2	O/D	-0.5
1978	Mil-A	69	218	28	54	10	1	5	26	7	23	.248	.278	.372	81	-6	-6	20	2	5	-2	1.000	-1	DO	-1.1
1979	Mil-A	91	335	51	89	13	1	12	41	16	46	.266	.299	.418	91	-5	-5	38	3	3	-1	.973	-0	DO	-0.8
1980	Mil-A	106	365	50	99	26	2	4	30	11	43	.271	.298	.386	89	-8	-6	40	5	3	-0	.971	-2	DO	-1.0
1981	*Phi-N	45	96	12	32	6	1	2	19	8	13	.333	.390	.479	139	6	5	18	1	2	-1	.974	-2	O	0.1
1982	Phi-N	28	68	5	19	3	1	2	7	2	9	.279	.300	.441	103	0	-0	8	1	0	0	1.000	-1	O	-0.1
	Tor-A	3	7	0	2	0	0	0	2	0	1	.286	.286	.286	53	-0	-0	1	0	0	0	1.000	0	/OD	-0.1
	Pit-N	39	77	7	14	2	1	2	10	5	9	.182	.232	.312	49	-5	-6	6	1	0	0	.971	-2	O	-0.8
Total	6	403	1217	160	323	62	7	27	141	50	152	.265	.298	.394	89	-22	-21	134	13	13	-4	.981	-11	OD	-4.3

■ **BRANDY DAVIS** Davis, Robert Brandon b: 9/10/28, Newark, Del. BR/TR, 6', 170 lbs. Deb: 4/15/52 C

YEAR	TM/L	G	AB	R	H	2B	3B	HR	RBI	BB	SO	AVG	OBP	SLG	PRO+	BR	/A	RC	SB	CS	SBR	FA	FR	POS	TPR
1952	Pit-N	55	95	14	17	1	1	0	1	11	28	.179	.264	.211	32	-8	-9	7	9	2	2	.932	-3	O	-1.1

YEAR	TM/L	G	AB	R	H	2B	3B	HR	RBI	BB	SO	AVG	OBP	SLG	PRO+	BR	/A	RC	SB	CS	SBR	FA	FR	POS	TPR
1953	Pit-N	12	39	5	8	2	0	0	2	0	3	.205	.205	.256	20	-5	-5	2	0	2	-1	.955	0	/O	-0.6
Total	2	67	134	19	25	3	1	0	3	11	31	.187	.248	.224	29	-13	-13	9	9	4	0	.938	-3	/O	-1.7

■ BOB DAVIS

Davis, Robert John Eugene b: 3/1/52, Pryor, Okla. BR/TR, 6', 180 lbs. Deb: 4/06/73

YEAR	TM/L	G	AB	R	H	2B	3B	HR	RBI	BB	SO	AVG	OBP	SLG	PRO+	BR	/A	RC	SB	CS	SBR	FA	FR	POS	TPR
1973	SD-N	5	11	1	1	0	0	0	0	0	5	.091	.091	.091	-54	-2	-2	0	0	0	0	.941	2	/C	0.0
1975	SD-N	43	128	6	30	3	2	0	7	11	31	.234	.310	.289	71	-5	-5	12	0	0	0	.986	3	C	0.0
1976	SD-N	51	83	7	17	0	1	0	5	5	13	.205	.250	.229	40	-7	-6	5	0	0	0	.965	4	C	-0.2
1977	SD-N	48	94	9	17	2	0	1	10	5	24	.181	.238	.234	30	-10	-8	5	0	0	0	.975	-1	C	-0.9
1978	SD-N	19	40	3	8	1	0	0	2	1	5	.200	.220	.225	26	-4	-4	1	0	1	-1	.960	-2	C	-0.7
1979	Tor-A	32	89	6	11	2	0	1	8	6	15	.124	.188	.180	-0	-13	-13	2	0	0	0	.984	-2	C	-1.3
1980	Tor-A	91	218	18	47	11	0	4	19	12	25	.216	.260	.321	56	-13	-14	17	0	0	0	.983	-2	C	-1.4
1981	Cal-A	1	2	0	0	0	0	0	0	0	0	.000	.000	.000	-99	-1	-1	0	0	0	0	1.000	-0	/C	-0.1
Total	8	290	665	50	131	19	3	6	51	40	118	.197	.250	.262	42	-54	-52	42	0	1	-1	.955	1	C	-4.6

■ RON DAVIS

Davis, Ronald Everette b: 10/21/41, Roanoke Rapids, N.C d: 9/5/92, Houston, Tex. BR/TR, 6', 180 lbs. Deb: 8/01/62

YEAR	TM/L	G	AB	R	H	2B	3B	HR	RBI	BB	SO	AVG	OBP	SLG	PRO+	BR	/A	RC	SB	CS	SBR	FA	FR	POS	TPR
1962	Hou-N	6	14	1	3	0	0	0	1	1	7	.214	.267	.214	33	-1	-1	1	1	0	0	1.000	0	/O	-0.1
1966	Hou-N	48	194	21	48	10	1	2	19	13	26	.247	.308	.340	86	-5	-3	20	2	2	-1	.982	6	O	-0.1
1967	Hou-N	94	285	31	73	19	1	7	38	17	48	.256	.303	.404	104	-1	1	34	5	3	-0	.976	-2	O	-0.6
1968	Hou-N	52	217	22	46	10	1	1	12	13	48	.212	.269	.281	67	-9	-9	16	0	4	-2	.971	5	O	-1.0
	*StL-N	33	79	11	14	4	2	0	5	5	17	.177	.226	.278	51	-5	-5	5	1	0	0	.979	3	O	-0.3
	Yr	85	296	33	60	14	3	1	17	18	65	.203	.258	.280	63	-14	-13	21	1	4	-2	.973	8	O	-1.3
1969	Pit-N	62	64	10	15	1	1	0	4	7	14	.234	.310	.281	68	-3	-3	6	0	0	0	.933	0	O	-0.4
Total	5	295	853	96	199	44	6	10	79	56	160	.233	.288	.334	82	-24	-20	83	9	9	-3	.974	12	O	-2.5

■ STEVE DAVIS

Davis, Steven Michael b: 12/30/53, Oakland, Cal. BR/TR, 6'1", 200 lbs. Deb: 9/23/79

YEAR	TM/L	G	AB	R	H	2B	3B	HR	RBI	BB	SO	AVG	OBP	SLG	PRO+	BR	/A	RC	SB	CS	SBR	FA	FR	POS	TPR
1979	Chi-N	3	4	0	0	0	0	0	1	0	0	.000	.000	.000	-91	-1	-1	0	0	0	0	1.000	0	/23	-0.1

■ TOD DAVIS

Davis, Thomas Oscar b: 7/24/24, Los Angeles, Cal. d: 12/31/78, W.Covina, Cal. BR/TR, 6'2", 190 lbs. Deb: 4/27/49

YEAR	TM/L	G	AB	R	H	2B	3B	HR	RBI	BB	SO	AVG	OBP	SLG	PRO+	BR	/A	RC	SB	CS	SBR	FA	FR	POS	TPR
1949	Phi-A	31	75	7	20	0	1	1	6	9	16	.267	.345	.333	83	-2	-2	10	0	0	0	.912	-1	S3/2	-0.2
1951	Phi-A	11	15	0	1	0	0	0	0	1	3	.067	.125	.067	-46	-3	-3	0	0	0	0	1.000	-0	/23	-0.3
Total	2	42	90	7	21	0	1	1	6	10	19	.233	.310	.289	61	-5	-5	10	0	0	0	.966	-1	/S32	-0.5

■ TRENCH DAVIS

Davis, Trench Neal b: 9/12/60, Baltimore, Md. BL/TL, 6'3", 171 lbs. Deb: 6/04/85

YEAR	TM/L	G	AB	R	H	2B	3B	HR	RBI	BB	SO	AVG	OBP	SLG	PRO+	BR	/A	RC	SB	CS	SBR	FA	FR	POS	TPR
1985	Pit-N	2	7	1	1	0	0	0	0	0	0	.143	.143	.143	-20	-1	-1	0	1	0	0	.667	-1	/O	-0.2
1986	Pit-N	15	23	2	3	0	0	0	1	0	4	.130	.130	.130	-27	-4	-4	0	0	0	0	.917	-0	/O	-0.5
1987	Atl-N	6	3	0	0	0	0	0	0	0	1	.000	.000	.000	-95	-1	-1	0	0	0	0	.000	0	/H	-0.1
Total	3	23	33	3	4	0	0	0	1	0	5	.121	.121	.121	-32	-6	-6	0	1	0	0	.867	-1	/O	-0.8

■ SPUD DAVIS

Davis, Virgil Lawrence b: 12/20/04, Birmingham, Ala. d: 8/14/84, Birmingham, Ala. BR/TR, 6'1", 197 lbs. Deb: 4/30/28 MC

YEAR	TM/L	G	AB	R	H	2B	3B	HR	RBI	BB	SO	AVG	OBP	SLG	PRO+	BR	/A	RC	SB	CS	SBR	FA	FR	POS	TPR
1928	StL-N	2	5	1	1	0	0	0	1	1	0	.200	.333	.200	42	-0	-0	0	0			.750	-1	/C	-0.1
	Phi-N	67	163	16	46	2	0	3	18	15	11	.282	.343	.350	79	-4	-5	19	0			.980	3	C	0.2
	Yr	69	168	17	47	2	0	3	19	16	11	.280	.342	.345	78	-5	-5	20	0			.971	2	C	0.1
1929	Phi-N	98	263	31	90	18	0	7	48	19	17	.342	.391	.490	110	7	4	49	1			.961	-12	C	-0.1
1930	Phi-N	106	329	41	103	16	1	14	65	17	20	.313	.349	.495	94	-0	-4	54	1			.986	-2	C	0.1
1931	Phi-N	120	393	30	128	32	1	4	51	36	28	.326	.382	.443	112	12	8	68	0			.994	1	*C	1.7
1932	Phi-N	125	402	44	135	23	5	14	70	40	39	.336	.399	.522	130	26	20	86	1			.987	-3	*C	2.2
1933	Phi-N	141	495	51	173	28	3	9	65	32	24	.349	.395	.473	130	30	23	89	2			.983	-11	*C	2.0
1934	*StL-N	107	347	45	104	22	4	9	65	34	27	.300	.366	.464	113	10	7	58	0			.988	1	C	1.2
1935	StL-N	102	315	28	100	24	2	1	60	33	30	.317	.386	.416	111	8	6	54	0			**.992**	-5	C/1	0.5
1936	StL-N	112	363	24	99	26	2	4	59	35	34	.273	.342	.388	97	-2	-2	48	0			.985	-13	*C/3	-1.0
1937	Cin-N	76	209	19	56	10	1	3	33	23	15	.268	.341	.368	97	-2	-1	26	0			.980	12	C	1.4
1938	Cin-N	12	36	3	6	1	0	0	1	5	6	.167	.286	.194	35	-3	-3	2	0			.962	0	C	-0.2
	Phi-N	70	215	11	53	7	0	2	23	14	14	.247	.293	.307	67	-10	-10	17	1			.980	-12	C	-1.9
	Yr	82	251	14	59	8	0	2	24	19	20	.235	.292	.291	62	-13	-12	19	1			.977	-12	C	-2.1
1939	Phi-N	87	202	10	62	8	1	0	23	24	20	.307	.383	.356	103	1	2	29	0			**1.000**	-2	C	0.3
1940	Pit-N	99	285	23	93	14	1	5	39	35	20	.326	.404	.435	132	13	14	48	0			.967	-6	C	1.4
1941	Pit-N	57	107	3	27	4	1	0	6	11	11	.252	.322	.308	78	-3	-3	10	0			1.000	-2	C	-0.2
1944	Pit-N	54	93	6	28	7	0	2	14	10	8	.301	.369	.441	122	3	3	15	0			.966	-1	C	0.3
1945	Pit-N	23	33	2	8	2	0	0	6	2	2	.242	.306	.303	67	-1	-2	3	0			.968	-0	C	-0.1
Total	16	1458	4255	388	1312	244	22	77	647	386	326	.308	.369	.430	108	84	58	676	6			.984	-55	*C/13	7.7

■ BUTCH DAVIS

Davis, Wallace McArthur b: 6/19/58, Martin Co., N.C. BR/TR, 6', 190 lbs. Deb: 8/23/83

YEAR	TM/L	G	AB	R	H	2B	3B	HR	RBI	BB	SO	AVG	OBP	SLG	PRO+	BR	/A	RC	SB	CS	SBR	FA	FR	POS	TPR
1983	KC-A	33	122	13	42	2	6	2	18	4	19	.344	.365	.508	137	6	6	21	4	3	-1	.977	2	O	0.6
1984	KC-A	41	116	11	17	3	0	2	12	10	19	.147	.214	.224	21	-12	-13	5	4	3	-1	.959	-1	O/D	-1.5
1987	Pit-N	7	7	3	1	1	0	0	0	1	3	.143	.250	.286	41	-1	-1	1	0	0	0	1.000	0	/O	0.0
1988	Bal-A	13	25	2	6	1	0	0	0	0	8	.240	.240	.280	46	-2	-2	1	1	0	0	1.000	-0	O/D	-0.2
1989	Bal-A	5	6	1	1	1	0	0	0	0	3	.167	.167	.333	39	-1	-0	0	0	0	0	1.000	-1	/OD	-0.1
1991	LA-N	1	1	0	0	0	0	0	0	0	0	.000	.000	.000	-99	-0	-0	0	0	0	0	.000	0	/H	0.0
Total	6	100	277	30	67	8	6	4	30	15	52	.242	.281	.357	75	-10	-10	28	9	6	-1	.973	0	/OD	-1.2

■ WILLIE DAVIS

Davis, William Henry b: 4/15/40, Mineral Springs, Ark. BL/TL, 6'2.5", 181 lbs. Deb: 9/08/60

YEAR	TM/L	G	AB	R	H	2B	3B	HR	RBI	BB	SO	AVG	OBP	SLG	PRO+	BR	/A	RC	SB	CS	SBR	FA	FR	POS	TPR
1960	LA-N	22	88	12	28	6	1	2	10	4	12	.318	.348	.477	116	3	2	12	3	5	-2	.981	1	O	0.0
1961	LA-N	128	339	56	86	19	6	12	45	27	46	.254	.318	.451	93	-0	-4	49	12	5	1	.983	-7	*O	-1.6
1962	LA-N	157	600	103	171	18	**10**	21	85	42	72	.285	.338	.453	117	7	12	92	32	7	5	.963	6	*O	1.4
1963	*LA-N	156	515	60	126	19	8	9	60	25	61	.245	.284	.365	92	-11	-7	51	25	11	1	.978	9	*O	-0.4
1964	LA-N	157	613	91	180	23	7	12	77	22	59	.294	.319	.413	112	2	7	82	42	13	5	.983	19	*O	2.5
1965	*LA-N	142	558	52	133	24	3	10	57	14	81	.238	.266	.346	76	-23	-18	51	25	9	2	.967	3	*O	-2.1
1966	*LA-N	153	624	74	177	31	6	11	61	15	68	.284	.305	.405	104	-5	0	76	21	10	0	.970	3	*O	-0.4
1967	LA-N	143	569	65	146	27	9	6	41	29	65	.257	.296	.367	97	-9	-4	62	20	6	2	.971	0	*O	-0.9
1968	LA-N	160	643	86	161	24	10	7	31	31	88	.250	.286	.351	98	-9	-4	68	36	10	5	.973	2	*O	-0.7
1969	LA-N	129	498	66	155	23	8	11	59	33	39	.311	.359	.456	136	17	21	79	24	10	1	.979	-0	*O	1.5
1970	LA-N	146	593	92	181	23	**16**	8	93	29	54	.305	.339	.438	111	4	7	88	38	14	3	.992	10	*O	1.3
1971	LA-N★	158	641	84	198	33	10	10	74	23	47	.309	.333	.438	124	12	16	88	20	8	1	.981	5	*O	1.5
1972	LA-N	149	615	81	178	22	7	19	79	27	61	.289	.320	.441	117	9	11	87	20	3	4	.987	5	*O	1.3
1973	LA-N★	152	599	82	171	29	9	16	77	29	62	.285	.324	.444	116	6	10	86	17	5	2	.980	-2	*O	0.3
1974	Mon-N	153	611	86	180	27	9	12	89	27	69	.295	.328	.427	104	5	2	85	25	7	3	.969	-3	*O	-0.5
1975	Tex-A	42	169	16	42	8	2	5	17	4	25	.249	.270	.408	90	-3	-3	18	13	5	1	.990	-1	O	-0.5
	StL-N	98	350	41	102	19	6	6	50	14	27	.291	.326	.431	105	3	1	50	10	1	2	.970	3	O	0.4
1976	SD-N	141	493	61	132	18	10	5	46	19	34	.268	.298	.375	98	-8	-4	56	14	2	3	.992	2	*O	-0.4
1979	*Cal-A	43	56	9	14	2	1	0	2	4	7	.250	.300	.321	70	-3	-2	5	1	0	0	1.000	-1	/OD	-0.3
Total	18	2429	9174	1217	2561	395	138	182	1053	418	977	.279	.314	.412	106	-2	42	1186	398	131	41	.978	53	*O/D	2.4

■ ANDRE DAWSON

Dawson, Andre Fernando b: 7/10/54, Miami, Fla. BR/TR, 6'3", 195 lbs. Deb: 9/11/76

YEAR	TM/L	G	AB	R	H	2B	3B	HR	RBI	BB	SO	AVG	OBP	SLG	PRO+	BR	/A	RC	SB	CS	SBR	FA	FR	POS	TPR
1976	Mon-N	24	85	9	20	4	1	0	7	5	13	.235	.278	.306	63	-4	-4	7	1	2	-1	.969	2	O	-0.5
1977	Mon-N	139	525	64	148	26	9	19	65	34	93	.282	.328	.474	116	7	9	82	21	7	2	.989	3	*O	0.8

YEAR	TM/L	G	AB	R	H	2B	3B	HR	RBI	BB	SO	AVG	OBP	SLG	PRO+	BR	/A	RC	SB	CS	SBR	FA	FR	POS	TPR
1978	Mon-N	157	609	84	154	24	8	25	72	30	128	.253	.301	.442	106	1	2	80	28	11	2	.988	14	*O	1.2
1979	Mon-N	155	639	90	176	24	12	25	92	27	115	.275	.311	.468	111	5	6	91	35	10	5	.988	-2	*O	0.2
1980	Mon-N	151	577	96	178	41	7	17	87	44	69	.308	.364	.492	137	27	27	105	34	9	5	.986	11	*O	3.9
1981	*Mon-N★	103	394	71	119	21	3	24	64	35	50	.302	.369	.553	157	29	28	83	26	4	5	.980	13	*O	4.5
1982	Mon-N★	148	608	107	183	37	7	23	83	34	96	.301	.346	.498	131	25	23	106	39	10	6	.982	14	*O	4.0
1983	Mon-N★	159	633	104	**189**	36	10	32	113	38	81	.299	.347	.539	143	32	33	113	25	11	1	.980	6	*O	3.6
1984	Mon-N	138	533	73	132	23	6	17	86	41	80	.248	.304	.409	103	-3	0	65	13	5	1	.975	16	*O	1.3
1985	Mon-N	139	529	65	135	27	2	23	91	29	92	.255	.299	.444	112	1	5	67	13	4	2	.973	-4	*O	-0.2
1986	Mon-N	130	496	65	141	32	2	20	78	37	79	.284	.341	.478	125	14	15	75	18	12	-2	.986	-0	*O	0.9
1987	Chi-N★	153	621	90	178	24	2	**49**	**137**	32	103	.287	.329	.568	127	25	22	111	11	3	2	.986	6	*O	2.4
1988	Chi-N★	157	591	78	179	31	8	24	79	37	73	.303	.348	.504	136	30	27	100	12	4	1	.989	1	*O	2.6
1989	*Chi-N★	118	416	62	105	18	6	21	77	35	62	.252	.312	.476	114	10	7	55	8	5	-1	.987	5	*O	0.9
1990	Chi-N★	147	529	72	164	28	5	27	100	42	65	.310	.363	.535	134	30	25	101	16	2	4	.981	-0	*O	2.6
1991	Chi-N★	149	563	69	153	21	4	31	104	22	80	.272	.305	.488	114	11	8	79	4	5	-2	.988	-1	*O	0.2
1992	Chi-N	143	542	60	150	27	2	22	90	30	70	.277	.319	.456	114	10	9	75	6	2	1	.992	-1	*O	0.6
Total	17	2310	8890	1259	2504	444	94	399	1425	552	1349	.282	.330	.487	123	251	241	1396	310	106	29	.984	82	*O	29.0

■ BOOTS DAY

Day, Charles Frederick b: 8/31/47, Ilion, N.Y. BL/TL, 5'9", 160 lbs. Deb: 6/15/69

YEAR	TM/L	G	AB	R	H	2B	3B	HR	RBI	BB	SO	AVG	OBP	SLG	PRO+	BR	/A	RC	SB	CS	SBR	FA	FR	POS	TPR
1969	StL-N	11	6	1	0	0	0	0	0	1	1	.000	.143	.000	-57	-1	-1	0	0	0	0	.000	0	/O	-0.1
1970	Chi-N	11	8	2	2	0	0	0	0	0	3	.250	.250	.250	31	-1	-1	0	0	0	0	.875	1	/O	0.0
	Mon-N	41	108	14	29	4	0	0	5	6	18	.269	.307	.306	65	-5	-5	10	3	2	-0	.987	4	O	-0.3
	Yr	52	116	16	31	4	0	0	5	6	21	.267	.303	.302	61	-6	-6	10	3	2	-0	.976	6	O	-0.3
1971	Mon-N	127	371	53	105	10	2	4	33	33	39	.283	.343	.353	97	-1	-1	47	9	4	0	.982	-1	*O	-0.7
1972	Mon-N	128	386	32	90	7	4	0	30	29	44	.233	.288	.272	59	-20	-21	31	3	6	-3	.979	-11	*O	-4.2
1973	Mon-N	101	207	36	57	7	0	4	28	21	28	.275	.342	.367	93	-1	-2	26	0	3	-2	1.000	-1	O	-0.7
1974	Mon-N	52	65	8	12	0	0	0	2	5	8	.185	.243	.185	20	-7	-7	3	0	0	0	1.000	-1	O	-0.8
Total	6	471	1151	146	295	28	6	8	98	95	141	.256	.314	.312	75	-35	-38	117	15	15	-5	.983	-7	O	-6.8

■ BRIAN DAYETT

Dayett, Brian Kelly b: 1/22/57, New London, Conn. BR/TR, 5'10", 180 lbs. Deb: 9/11/83

YEAR	TM/L	G	AB	R	H	2B	3B	HR	RBI	BB	SO	AVG	OBP	SLG	PRO+	BR	/A	RC	SB	CS	SBR	FA	FR	POS	TPR
1983	NY-A	11	29	3	6	0	1	0	5	2	4	.207	.258	.276	49	-2	-2	2	0	0	0	1.000	1	/O	-0.1
1984	NY-A	64	127	14	31	8	0	4	23	9	14	.244	.299	.402	96	-2	-1	15	0	0	0	.988	-9	O/D	-1.1
1985	Chi-N	22	26	1	6	0	0	1	4	0	6	.231	.259	.346	61	-1	-2	2	0	0	0	1.000	-2	O	-0.4
1986	Chi-N	24	67	7	18	4	0	4	11	6	10	.269	.329	.507	118	2	2	10	0	1	-1	1.000	-4	O	-0.3
1987	Chi-N	97	177	20	49	14	1	5	25	20	37	.277	.350	.452	106	3	2	29	0	0	0	1.000	-13	O	-1.2
Total	5	218	426	45	110	26	2	14	68	37	71	.258	.320	.427	99	-0	-1	58	0	1	-1	.995	-26	O/D	-3.1

■ CHARLIE DEAL

Deal, Charles Albert b: 10/30/1891, Wilkinsburg, Pa. d: 9/16/79, Covina, Cal. BR/TR, 6', 160 lbs. Deb: 7/19/12

YEAR	TM/L	G	AB	R	H	2B	3B	HR	RBI	BB	SO	AVG	OBP	SLG	PRO+	BR	/A	RC	SB	CS	SBR	FA	FR	POS	TPR
1912	Det-A	42	142	13	32	4	2	0	11	9		.225	.272	.282	60	-8	-7	12	4			.942	10	3	0.3
1913	Det-A	16	50	3	11	0	2	0	3	1	7	.220	.235	.300	57	-3	-3	4	2			.862	2	3	-0.1
	Bos-N	10	36	6	11	1	0	0	3	2	1	.306	.359	.333	96	0	-0	5	1			.935	-6	2	-0.7
1914	*Bos-N	79	257	17	54	13	2	0	23	20	23	.210	.270	.276	63	-12	-12	21	4			.948	-5	3/S	-1.6
1915	StL-F	65	223	21	72	12	4	1	27	12	16	.323	.357	.426	123	7	6	40	10			.951	5	3	1.4
1916	StL-A	23	74	7	10	1	0	0	10	6	8	.135	.200	.149	5	-9	-8	3	4			.970	-2	3/2	-1.0
	Chi-N	2	8	2	2	1	0	0	3	0	0	.250	.250	.375	82	-0	-0	1	0			1.000	2	/3	0.2
1917	Chi-N	135	449	46	114	11	3	0	47	19	18	.254	.284	.292	71	-13	-16	41	10			.957	7	*3	-0.9
1918	*Chi-N	119	414	43	99	9	3	2	34	21	13	.239	.279	.290	72	-13	-14	37	11			.942	-2	*3	-1.6
1919	Chi-N	116	405	37	117	23	5	2	52	12	12	.289	.316	.385	110	4	4	52	11			**.973**	7	*3	1.7
1920	Chi-N	129	450	48	108	10	5	3	39	20	14	.240	.285	.304	68	-18	-19	39	5	8	-3	**.973**	10	*3	-0.7
1921	Chi-N	115	422	52	122	19	8	3	66	13	9	.289	.310	.393	85	-10	-10	50	3	5	-2	**.973**	14	*3	0.9
Total	10	851	2930	295	752	104	34	11	318	135	121	.257	.293	.327	79	-75	-81	304	65	13		.958	41	3/2S	-2.1

■ LINDSAY DEAL

Deal, Fred Lindsay b: 9/3/11, Lenoir, N.C. d: 4/18/79, Little Rock, Ark. BL/TR, 6', 175 lbs. Deb: 9/13/39

YEAR	TM/L	G	AB	R	H	2B	3B	HR	RBI	BB	SO	AVG	OBP	SLG	PRO+	BR	/A	RC	SB	CS	SBR	FA	FR	POS	TPR
1939	Bro-N	4	7	0	0	0	0	0	0	0	2	.000	.000	.000	-97	-2	-2	0	0			1.000	0	/O	-0.2

■ SNAKE DEAL

Deal, John Wesley b: 1/21/1879, Lancaster, Pa. d: 5/9/44, Harrisburg, Pa. BR/TR, 6', 164 lbs. Deb: 7/09/06

YEAR	TM/L	G	AB	R	H	2B	3B	HR	RBI	BB	SO	AVG	OBP	SLG	PRO+	BR	/A	RC	SB	CS	SBR	FA	FR	POS	TPR
1906	Cin-N	65	231	13	48	4	3	0	21	6		.208	.228	.251	48	-14	-15	18	15			.985	2	1	-1.7

■ PAT DEALY

Dealy, Patrick E. b: Burlington, Vt. d: 12/16/24, Buffalo, N.Y. BR/TR, 5'8", 145 lbs. Deb: 9/30/1884

YEAR	TM/L	G	AB	R	H	2B	3B	HR	RBI	BB	SO	AVG	OBP	SLG	PRO+	BR	/A	RC	SB	CS	SBR	FA	FR	POS	TPR
1884	StP-U	5	15	2	2	0	0	0		0		.133	.133	.133	-18	-2	-1	0				.871	3	/CO	0.2
1885	Bos-N	35	130	18	29	4	1	1	9	2	14	.223	.235	.292	72	-4	-4	9				.903	0	C/3OS1	-0.1
1886	Bos-N	15	46	9	15	1	1	0	3	4	4	.326	.380	.391	140	2	2	9	5			.929	-2	C/O	0.2
1887	Was-N	58	212	33	55	8	2	1	18	8	8	.259	.293	.330	78	-7	-5	32	36			.931	-7	CS/O3	-0.9
1890	Syr-a	18	66	9	12	1	0	0		5		.182	.250	.197	38	-5	-4	4	4			.900	-6	C/3O	-0.8
Total	5	131	469	71	113	14	4	2	30	19	26	.241	.275	.301	76	-17	-12	55	45			.914	-12	/CS3O1	-1.4

■ CHUBBY DEAN

Dean, Alfred Lovill b: 8/24/16, Mt.Airy, N.C. d: 12/21/70, Riverside, Cal. BL/TL, 5'11", 181 lbs. Deb: 4/14/36

YEAR	TM/L	G	AB	R	H	2B	3B	HR	RBI	BB	SO	AVG	OBP	SLG	PRO+	BR	/A	RC	SB	CS	SBR	FA	FR	POS	TPR
1936	Phi-A	111	342	41	98	21	3	1	48	24	24	.287	.337	.374	77	-14	-12	44	3	2	-0	.989	-1	1	-1.9
1937	Phi-A	104	309	36	81	14	4	2	31	42	10	.262	.350	.353	79	-10	-9	41	2	1	0	.991	-2	1/P	-1.9
1938	Phi-A	16	20	3	6	2	0	0	1	1	4	.300	.333	.400	85	-1	-0	3	0	0	0	1.000	1	/P	0.0
1939	Phi-A	80	77	12	27	4	0	0	19	8	4	.351	.412	.403	111	1	2	12	0	0	0	.935	1	P	0.0
1940	Phi-A	67	90	6	26	2	0	0	6	16	9	.289	.396	.311	88	-1	-1	13	0	0	0	.976	1	P/1	0.0
1941	Phi-A	27	37	0	9	2	0	0	9	4	3	.243	.317	.297	65	-2	-2	4	0	0	0	1.000	0	P/1	0.0
	Cle-A	17	25	2	4	1	0	0	2	3	2	.160	.250	.200	21	-3	-3	1	0	0	0	1.000	1	/P	0.0
	Yr	44	62	2	13	3	0	0	11	7	5	.210	.290	.258	48	-5	-4	5	0	0	0	1.000	1	P/1	0.0
1942	Cle-A	70	101	4	27	1	0	0	7	11	7	.267	.339	.277	79	-3	-2	10	0	0	0	.939	-3	P	0.0
1943	Cle-A	41	46	2	9	0	0	0	5	6	2	.196	.288	.196	45	-3	-3	3	0	0	0	.929	-1	P	0.0
Total	8	533	1047	106	287	47	7	3	128	115	65	.274	.347	.341	79	-34	-31	129	5	3	-0	.964	-5	P1	-3.8

■ TOMMY DEAN

Dean, Tommy Douglas b: 8/30/45, Iuka, Miss. BR/TR, 6', 165 lbs. Deb: 9/17/67

YEAR	TM/L	G	AB	R	H	2B	3B	HR	RBI	BB	SO	AVG	OBP	SLG	PRO+	BR	/A	RC	SB	CS	SBR	FA	FR	POS	TPR
1967	LA-N	12	28	1	4	1	0	0	2	0	9	.143	.143	.179	-9	-4	-4	1	0	0	0	.981	6	S	0.3
1969	SD-N	101	273	14	48	9	2	2	9	27	54	.176	.252	.245	42	-22	-21	17	0	3	-2	.978	4	S/2	-1.0
1970	SD-N	61	158	18	35	5	1	2	13	11	29	.222	.272	.304	56	-10	-10	13	2	0	1	.974	6	S	0.2
1971	SD-N	41	70	2	8	0	0	0	1	4	13	.114	.162	.114	-22	-11	-10	2	1	0	0	.969	6	S3/2	-0.2
Total	4	215	529	35	95	15	3	4	25	42	105	.180	.241	.242	36	-47	-44	33	3	3	-1	.976	23	S/32	-0.7

■ HARRY DEANE

Deane, John Henry b: 5/6/1846, Trenton, N.J. d: 5/31/25, Indianapolis, Ind. 5'7", 150 lbs. Deb: 7/20/1871 M

YEAR	TM/L	G	AB	R	H	2B	3B	HR	RBI	BB	SO	AVG	OBP	SLG	PRO+	BR	/A	RC	SB	CS	SBR	FA	FR	POS	TPR
1871	Kek-n	6	22	3	4	0	1	0	2	2	0	.182	.250	.273	49	-1	-1	2	0					/OM	-0.1
1874	Bal-n	47	204	29	50	9	2	0		4		.245	.260	.309	81	-4	-4	17						*O/2	-0.2
Total	2 n	53	226	32	54	9	3	0		6		.239	.259	.305	77	-6	-6	18						/O2	-0.3

■ BUDDY DEAR

Dear, Paul Stanford b: 12/1/05, Norfolk, Va. BR/TR, 5'8", 143 lbs. Deb: 9/09/27

YEAR	TM/L	G	AB	R	H	2B	3B	HR	RBI	BB	SO	AVG	OBP	SLG	PRO+	BR	/A	RC	SB	CS	SBR	FA	FR	POS	TPR
1927	Was-A	2	1	1	0	0	0	0	0	0	0	.000	.000	.000	-99	-0	-0	0	0	0	0	.000	0	/2	0.0

■ CHARLIE DeARMOND

DeArmond, Charles Hommer "Hummer" b: 2/13/1877, Okeana, Ohio d: 12/17/33, Morning Sun, Ohio BR/TR, 5'10", 165 lbs. Deb: 9/19/03

YEAR	TM/L	G	AB	R	H	2B	3B	HR	RBI	BB	SO	AVG	OBP	SLG	PRO+	BR	/A	RC	SB	CS	SBR	FA	FR	POS	TPR
1903	Cin-N	11	39	10	11	2	1	0	7	3		.282	.349	.385	98	0	-0	6	1			.878	-1	3	-0.1

YEAR	TM/L	G	AB	R	H	2B	3B	HR	RBI	BB	SO	AVG	OBP	SLG	PRO+	BR	/A	RC	SB	CS	SBR	FA	FR	POS	TPR

■ JOHN DEASLEY   Deasley, John   b: 1/1861, Philadelphia, Pa.   d: 12/25/10, Philadelphia, Pa.   Deb: 6/17/1884   F

1884	Was-U	31	134	20	29	1	1	0		3		.216	.234	.239	62	-5	-5	8				.836	0	S	-0.4
	KC-U	13	40	3	7	2	0	0		2		.175	.214	.225	56	-2	-1	2				.833	-0	S	-0.1
	Yr	44	174	23	36	3	1	0		5		.207	.229	.236	61	-7	-6	10				.835	0	S	-0.5

■ PAT DEASLEY   Deasley, Thomas H.   b: 11/17/1857, Ireland   d: 4/1/43, Philadelphia, Pa.   BR/TR, 5'8.5", 154 lbs.   Deb: 5/18/1881   F

1881	Bos-N	43	147	13	35	5	2	0	8	5	10	.238	.263	.299	80	-4	-3	12				.914	-4	C/OS1	-0.6
1882	Bos-N	67	264	36	70	8	0	0	29	7	22	.265	.284	.295	86	-4	-4	23				.958	2	*CO/S	-0.1
1883	StL-a	58	206	27	53	2	1	0		6		.257	.278	.277	75	-5	-6	16				.930	8	C/O	0.4
1884	StL-a	75	254	27	52	5	4	0		7		.205	.235	.256	60	-10	-11	16				.919	14	*C/O1	0.8
1885	NY-N	54	207	22	53	5	1	0	24	9	20	.256	.287	.290	88	-3	-3	18				.935	7	C/OS	0.8
1886	NY-N	41	143	18	38	6	1	0	17	4	12	.266	.286	.322	84	-3	-3	14	2			.925	7	CO	0.5
1887	NY-N	30	118	12	37	5	0	0	23	9	7	.314	.367	.356	109	1	2	17	3			.867	-13	C/3S	-0.8
1888	Was-N	34	127	6	20	1	0	0	4	2	18	.157	.171	.165	9	-13	-12	4	2			.922	8	C/OS2	-0.1
Total	8	402	1466	161	358	37	9	0	105	49	89	.244	.271	.282	75	-40	-40	119	7			.927	27	C/OS312	0.9

■ HANK DeBERRY   DeBerry, John Herman   b: 12/29/1894, Savannah, Tenn.   d: 9/10/51, Savannah, Tenn.   BR/TR, 5'11", 195 lbs.   Deb: 9/12/16

1916	Cle-A	15	33	7	9	4	0	0	4	6	9	.273	.385	.394	126	2	1	5	0			1.000	-3	C	-0.1
1917	Cle-A	25	33	3	9	2	0	0	1	2	7	.273	.333	.333	96	0	-0	3	0			.968	1	/C	0.1
1922	Bro-N	85	259	29	78	10	1	3	35	20	9	.301	.354	.382	91	-4	-3	36	4	1	1	.971	-2	C	-0.1
1923	Bro-N	78	235	21	67	11	6	1	48	20	12	.285	.346	.396	98	-2	-1	33	2	1	0	.971	8	C	1.0
1924	Bro-N	77	218	20	53	10	3	3	26	20	11	.243	.307	.358	80	-7	-6	24	0	1	-1	.993	23	C	1.9
1925	Bro-N	67	193	26	50	8	4	2	24	16	8	.259	.322	.342	72	-9	-8	22	2	2	-1	.981	19	C	1.3
1926	Bro-N	48	115	6	33	11	0	0	13	8	5	.287	.333	.383	94	-1	-1	14	0			.976	8	C	0.9
1927	Bro-N	68	201	15	47	3	2	1	21	17	8	.234	.294	.284	55	-13	-13	17	1			.988	23	C	1.5
1928	Bro-N	82	258	19	65	8	2	0	23	18	15	.252	.301	.298	58	-16	-16	23	3			.977	18	C	0.9
1929	Bro-N	68	210	13	55	11	1	1	25	17	15	.262	.317	.338	64	-12	-12	23	1			.991	9	C	0.0
1930	Bro-N	35	95	11	28	3	0	0	14	4	10	.295	.323	.326	58	-6	-6	10	0			.978	12	C	0.7
Total	11	648	1850	170	494	81	16	11	234	148	119	.267	.323	.346	76	-68	-64	210	13	5		.982	113	C	8.1

■ ADAM DEBUS   Debus, Adam Joseph   b: 10/7/1892, Chicago, Ill.   d: 5/13/77, Chicago, Ill.   BR/TR, 5'10.5", 150 lbs.   Deb: 7/14/17

| 1917 | Pit-N | 38 | 131 | 9 | 30 | 5 | 4 | 0 | 7 | 7 | 14 | .229 | .279 | .328 | 83 | -2 | -3 | 12 | 2 | | | .898 | -6 | S3 | -0.9 |

■ DOUG DeCINCES   DeCinces, Douglas Vernon   b: 8/29/50, Burbank, Cal.   BR/TR, 6'2", 194 lbs.   Deb: 9/09/73

1973	Bal-A	10	18	2	2	0	0	0	3	1	5	.111	.158	.111	-23	-3	-3	0	0	0	0	.895	3	/32S	0.0
1974	Bal-A	1	1	0	0	0	0	0	0	1	0	.000	.500	.000	55	0	0	0	0	0	0	1.000	0	/3	0.0
1975	Bal-A	61	167	20	42	6	3	4	23	13	32	.251	.309	.395	105	-1	0	20	0	1	-1	.947	3	3S2/1	0.4
1976	Bal-A	129	440	36	103	17	2	11	42	29	68	.234	.285	.357	93	-8	-5	43	8	4	0	.941	-1	*321/SD	-0.7
1977	Bal-A	150	522	63	135	28	3	19	69	64	86	.259	.342	.433	117	7	11	75	8	8	-2	.958	10	*3/12D	1.7
1978	Bal-A	142	511	72	146	37	1	28	80	46	81	.286	.347	.526	152	27	30	89	7	7	-2	.975	10	*32	3.8
1979	*Bal-A	120	422	67	97	27	1	16	61	54	68	.230	.322	.412	100	-3	-0	56	5	3	-0	.964	-3	*3	-0.4
1980	Bal-A	145	489	64	122	23	2	16	64	49	83	.249	.322	.403	98	-2	-2	59	11	6	-0	.960	25	*3/1	2.0
1981	Bal-A	100	346	49	91	23	2	13	55	41	32	.263	.343	.454	128	12	12	51	0	3	-2	.942	-2	*3/1O	0.7
1982	*Cal-A	153	575	94	173	42	5	30	97	66	80	.301	.374	.548	149	38	38	113	7	5	-1	.961	21	*3/S	5.3
1983	Cal-A★	95	370	49	104	19	3	18	65	32	56	.281	.338	.495	127	12	13	59	2	0	1	.955	9	3D	2.0
1984	Cal-A	146	547	77	147	23	3	20	82	53	79	.269	.333	.431	111	7	7	77	4	1	1	.964	-6	*3/D	0.0
1985	Cal-A	120	427	50	104	22	1	20	78	47	71	.244	.321	.440	107	3	3	55	1	4	-2	.958	-10	*3/D	-1.0
1986	*Cal-A	140	512	69	131	20	3	26	96	52	74	.256	.327	.459	112	7	8	72	2	2	-1	.955	-8	*3/SD	-0.4
1987	Cal-A	133	453	65	106	23	0	16	63	70	87	.234	.339	.391	96	-4	-1	61	3	4	-2	.948	-3	*3/1SD	-0.7
	StL-N	4	9	1	2	2	0	0	1	0	2	.222	.222	.444	70	-0	-0	1	0	0	0	.833	1	/3	0.1
Total	15	1649	5809	778	1505	312	29	237	879	618	904	.259	.330	.445	116	91	111	832	58	48	-11	.958	49	*3/2D1SO	12.8

■ HARRY DECKER   Decker, Earl Harry   b: 9/3/1854, Lockport, Ill.   BR/TR, 5'11", 180 lbs.   Deb: 8/23/1884

1884	Ind-a	4	15	1	4	1	0	0		1		.267	.313	.333	117	0	0	2				.870	-3	/C	-0.3
	KC-U	23	75	8	10	2	0	0		5		.133	.188	.160	21	-6	-4	2				.813	2	OC	-0.2
1886	Det-N	14	54	2	12	1	0	0	5	2	9	.222	.250	.241	48	-3	-3	3	0			.871	4	C/O	0.2
	Was-N	7	23	0	5	1	1	0	2	1	5	.217	.250	.348	85	-1	-0	2	0			.946	1	/C3S	0.1
	Yr	21	77	2	17	2	1	0	7	3	14	.221	.250	.273	59	-4	-4	5	0			.886	5	C/3OS	0.3
1889	Phi-N	11	30	4	3	0	0	0	2	2	5	.100	.156	.100	-25	-5	-5	1	1			.857	-1	/2CO	-0.5
1890	Phi-N	5	19	5	7	1	0	0	2	4	1	.368	.478	.421	162	2	2	6	4			.938	-1	/1OC	-0.2
	Pit-N	92	354	52	97	14	3	5	38	26	36	.274	.324	.373	119	1	8	46	8			.909	-26	C1/O2S	-1.2
	Yr	97	373	57	104	15	3	5	40	30	37	.279	.333	.375	122	3	9	52	12			.909	-27	C1/O2S	-1.2
Total	4	156	570	72	138	20	4	5	49	41	56	.242	.293	.318	91	-11	-4	62	13			.903	-25	C/O12S3	-1.9

■ FRANK DECKER   Decker, Frank   b: 2/26/1856, St.Louis, Mo.   d: 2/5/40, St.Louis, Mo.   BR/TR,   Deb: 6/25/1879

1879	Syr-N	3	10	0	1	0	0	0	0	0	3	.100	.100	.100	-38	-1	-1	0				.714	-2	/CO1	-0.3
1882	StL-a	2	8	0	2	0	0	0	0	0	0	.250	.250	.250	66	-0	-0	1				.813	-0	/2	0.0
Total	2	5	18	0	3	0	0	0	0	0	3	.167	.167	.167	12	-2	-2	1					-2	/2C1O	-0.3

■ GEORGE DECKER   Decker, George A "Gentleman George"   b: 6/1/1869, York, Pa.   d: 6/7/09, Patton, Cal.   BL/TL, 6'1", 180 lbs.   Deb: 7/11/1892

1892	Chi-N	78	291	32	66	6	6	2	28	20	49	.227	.277	.306	77	-8	-9	28	9			.876	-12	O2	-2.1
1893	Chi-N	81	328	57	89	9	8	2	48	24	22	.271	.325	.366	86	-8	-7	47	22			.878	-9	O12/S	-1.4
1894	Chi-N	91	384	74	120	17	6	8	92	24	17	.313	.361	.451	91	-3	-7	73	23			.974	-8	10/32S	-1.3
1895	Chi-N	73	297	51	82	9	7	2	41	17	22	.276	.324	.374	76	-9	-12	41	11			.910	-7	O1/3S2	-1.9
1896	Chi-N	107	421	68	118	23	11	5	61	23	14	.280	.318	.423	92	-4	-7	65	20			.928	-3	O1	-1.3
1897	Chi-N	111	428	72	124	12	7	5	63	24		.290	.333	.386	86	-8	-10	61	11			.925	-3	O1/2	-1.6
1898	StL-N	76	286	26	74	10	0	1	45	20		.259	.314	.304	76	-8	-9	30	4			.980	-7	1	-1.6
	Lou-N	42	148	27	44	4	3	0	19	9		.297	.342	.365	104	0	1	22	9			.993	-1	1/O	-0.1
	Yr	118	434	53	118	14	3	1	64	29		.272	.323	.325	85	-8	-9	52	13			.984	-9	*1/O	-1.7
1899	Lou-N	38	135	13	36	8	0	1	18	12		.267	.336	.348	88	-2	-2	19	3			.968	-2	1	-0.4
	Was-N	4	9	0	0	0	0	0	0	0		.000	.000	.000	-99	-2	-2	0	0			.955	-1	/1O	-0.3
	Yr	42	144	13	36	8	0	1	18	12		.250	.316	.326	77	-5	-5	18	3			.967	-3	1/O	-0.7
Total	8	701	2727	420	753	98	49	25	415	173	124	.276	.324	.376	85	-53	-66	386	112			.900	-53	O1/23S	-12.0

■ STEVE DECKER   Decker, Steven Michael   b: 10/25/65, Rock Island, Ill.   BR/TR, 6'3", 205 lbs.   Deb: 9/18/90

1990	SF-N	15	54	5	16	2	0	3	8	1	10	.296	.309	.500	123	1	1	8	0	0	0	.989	2	C	0.4
1991	SF-N	79	233	11	48	7	1	5	24	16	44	.206	.266	.309	63	-12	-11	18	0	1	-1	.984	-3	C	-1.1
1992	SF-N	15	43	3	7	1	0	0	1	6	7	.163	.280	.186	36	-4	-3	3	0	0	0	1.000	3	C	0.0
Total	3	109	330	19	71	10	1	8	33	23	61	.215	.275	.324	70	-15	-13	29	0	1	-1	.987	2	C	-0.7

■ ARTIE DEDE   Dede, Arthur Richard   b: 7/12/1895, Brooklyn, N.Y.   d: 9/6/71, Keene, N.H.   BR/TR, 5'9", 155 lbs.   Deb: 10/04/16

| 1916 | Bro-N | 1 | 1 | 0 | 0 | 0 | 0 | 0 | 0 | 0 | 0 | .000 | .000 | .000 | -97 | -0 | -0 | 0 | | | | 1.000 | -0 | /C | -0.1 |

■ ROD DEDEAUX   Dedeaux, Raoul Martial   b: 2/17/15, New Orleans, La.   BR/TR, 5'11", 160 lbs.   Deb: 9/28/35

| 1935 | Bro-N | 2 | 4 | 0 | 1 | 0 | 0 | 0 | 1 | 0 | 0 | .250 | .250 | .250 | 36 | -0 | -0 | 0 | 0 | | | .857 | 0 | /S | 0.0 |

YEAR	TM/L	G	AB	R	H	2B	3B	HR	RBI	BB	SO	AVG	OBP	SLG	PRO+	BR	/A	RC	SB	CS	SBR	FA	FR	POS	TPR

■ **JIM DEE**   Dee, James D.   b: Buffalo, N.Y.   Deb: 7/30/1884

| | 1884 | Pit-a | 12 | 40 | 0 | 5 | 0 | 0 | 0 | | 0 | 1 | .125 | .146 | .125 | -9 | -5 | -5 | 1 | | | | .860 | 1 | S | -0.3 |

■ **SHORTY DEE**   Dee, Maurice Leo   b: 10/4/1889, Halifax, N.S., Can.   d: 8/12/71, Jamaica Plain, Mass.   BR/TR, 5'6", 155 lbs.   Deb: 9/14/15

| | 1915 | StL-A | 1 | 3 | 1 | 0 | 0 | 0 | 0 | 0 | 0 | 1 | .000 | .250 | .000 | -26 | -0 | -0 | 0 | 0 | 1 | -1 | .500 | -1 | /S | -0.3 |

■ **ROB DEER**   Deer, Robert George   b: 9/29/60, Orange, Cal.   BR/TR, 6'3", 210 lbs.   Deb: 9/04/84

1984	SF-N	13	24	5	4	0	0	3	3	7	10	.167	.375	.542	160	2	2	5	1	1	-0	.905	0	/O	0.2
1985	SF-N	78	162	22	30	5	1	8	20	23	71	.185	.286	.377	88	-4	-3	19	0	1	-1	.982	-4	O1	-1.0
1986	Mil-A	134	466	75	108	17	3	33	86	72	179	.232	.338	.494	119	14	12	82	5	2	0	.974	8	*O/1	1.5
1987	Mil-A	134	474	71	113	15	2	28	80	86	186	.238	.361	.456	112	11	9	85	12	4	1	.974	8	*O1/D	1.3
1988	Mil-A	135	492	71	124	24	0	23	85	51	153	.252	.331	.441	113	9	8	74	9	5	-0	.990	7	*O/D	1.1
1989	Mil-A	130	466	72	98	18	2	26	65	60	158	.210	.306	.425	105	1	2	59	4	8	-4	.972	5	*O/D	0.0
1990	Mil-A	134	440	57	92	15	1	27	69	64	147	.209	.315	.432	108	3	4	64	2	3	-1	.970	9	*O1/D	0.8
1991	Det-A	134	448	64	80	14	2	25	64	89	175	.179	.315	.386	91	-4	-5	60	1	3	-2	.978	11	*O/D	0.2
1992	Det-A	110	393	66	97	20	1	32	64	51	131	.247	.328	.547	142	21	21	73	4	2	0	.983	5	*O/D	2.4
Total	9	1002	3365	503	746	128	12	205	536	503	1210	.222	.328	.450	112	55	51	522	38	29	-6	.977	49	O/1D	6.5

■ **CHARLIE DEES**   Dees, Charles Henry   b: 6/24/35, Birmingham, Ala.   BL/TL, 6'1", 173 lbs.   Deb: 5/26/63

1963	LA-A	60	202	23	62	11	1	3	27	11	31	.307	.367	.416	126	5	7	30	3	3	-1	.986	-2	1	0.1
1964	LA-A	26	26	3	2	1	0	0	1	1	4	.077	.143	.115	-30	-4	-4	0	1	2	-1	.981	0	1	-0.5
1965	Cal-A	12	32	1	5	0	0	0	1	1	8	.156	.182	.156	-3	-4	-4	1	1	2	-1	.986	-1	/1	-0.7
Total	3	98	260	27	69	12	1	3	29	13	43	.265	.323	.354	95	-3	-2	31	5	7	-3	.986	-3	/1	-1.1

■ **TONY DeFATE**   DeFate, Clyde Herbert   b: 2/22/1895, Kansas City, Mo.   d: 9/3/63, New Orleans, La.   BR/TR, 5'8.5", 158 lbs.   Deb: 4/18/17

1917	StL-N	14	14	0	2	0	0	0	1	4	5	.143	.143	.143	50	-1	-1	1	0			1.000	-1	/32	-0.1
	Det-A	3	2	1	0	0	0	0	0	0	1	.000	.000	.000	-99	-0	-0	0				1.000	-0	/2	-0.1
Total	1	17	16	1	2	0	0	0	1	4	6	.125	.300	.125	33	-1	-1	1	0			1.000	-1	/32	-0.2

■ **ARTURO DeFREITAS**   DeFreitas, Arturo Marcelino (Simon)   b: 4/26/53, San Pedro De Macoris, D.R.   BR/TR, 6'2", 195 lbs.   Deb: 9/07/78

1978	Cin-N	9	19	1	4	1	0	1	2	1	4	.211	.250	.421	84	-1	-1	2	0	0	0	1.000	0	/1	-0.1
1979	Cin-N	23	34	2	7	2	0	0	4	0	16	.206	.206	.265	27	-3	-3	2	0	0	0	.974	-1	/1O	-0.5
Total	2	32	53	3	11	3	0	1	6	1	20	.208	.222	.321	47	-4	-4	4	0	0	0	.988	-1	/1O	-0.6

■ **RUBE DeGROFF**   DeGroff, Edward Arthur   b: 9/2/1879, Hyde Park, N.Y.   d: 12/17/55, Poughkeepsie, N.Y.   BL, 5'11",   Deb: 9/22/05

1905	StL-N	15	56	3	14	2	1	0	5	5	5	.250	.311	.321	92	-1	-1	6	1			.909	0	O	-0.1
1906	StL-N	1	4	1	0	0	0	0	0	0	0	.000	.000	.000	-99	-1	-1	0	0			.000	-0	/O	-0.2
Total	2	16	60	4	14	2	1	0	5	5	5	.233	.292	.300	80	-2	-1	6	1			.909	-0	/O	-0.3

■ **HERMAN DEHLMAN**   Dehlman, Herman J. "Dutch"   b: 1850, Catasauqua, Pa.   d: 3/13/1885, Wilkes-Barre, Pa.   Deb: 5/02/1872

1872	Atl-n	37	164	30	36	3	0	0	15	3	1	.220	.234	.238	39	-10	-16	10						*1	-1.0
1873	Atl-n	54	221	50	52	5	2	0	17	9	7	.235	.265	.276	67	-11	-6	18						*1	-0.1
1874	Atl-n	53	216	40	50	5	1	0		7		.231	.256	.264	74	-8	-3	15						*1	-0.3
1875	StL-n	67	254	42	57	12	2	0		11		.224	.257	.287	97	-3	1	19						*1	0.1
1876	StL-N	64	245	40	45	6	0	0	9	9	10	.184	.213	.208	43	-15	-13	11				.958	0	*1	-1.2
1877	StL-N	32	119	24	22	4	0	0	11	7	21	.185	.230	.218	44	-7	-7	6				.931	-3	1/O	-0.9
Total	4 n	211	855	162	195	25	5	0	32	30	8	.228	.254	.269	70	-31	-24	62						1/D	-1.3
Total	2	96	364	64	67	10	0	0	20	16	31	.184	.218	.212	43	-22	-19	17				.950	-3	/1O	-2.1

■ **JIM DEIDEL**   Deidel, James Lawrence   b: 6/6/49, Denver, Col.   BR/TR, 6'2", 195 lbs.   Deb: 5/31/74

| 1974 | NY-A | 2 | 2 | 0 | 0 | 0 | 0 | 0 | 0 | 0 | 0 | .000 | .000 | .000 | -99 | -1 | -0 | 0 | 0 | 0 | 0 | 1.000 | 1 | /C | 0.1 |

■ **PEP DEININGER**   Deininger, Otto Charles   b: 10/10/1877, Wasseralfingen, Germany   d: 9/25/50, Boston, Mass.   BL/TL, 5'8.5", 180 lbs.   Deb: 4/26/02

1902	Bos-A	2	6	0	2	1	1	0	0	0		.333	.333	.833	210	1	1	2	0			1.000	-1	/P	0.0
1908	Phi-N	1	0	0	0	0	0	0	0	0		—	—	—	—	0	0	0	0			.000	-1	/O	-0.1
1909	Phi-N	55	169	22	44	9	0	0	16	11		.260	.309	.314	93	-2	-2	18	5			.989	-2	O/2	-0.6
Total	3	58	175	22	46	10	1	0	16	11		.263	.310	.331	97	-1	-1	19	5			.989	-3	/OP2	-0.7

■ **PAT DEISEL**   Deisel, Edward   b: 4/29/1876, Ripley, Ohio   d: 4/17/48, Cincinnati, Ohio   BR/TR, 5'5", 145 lbs.   Deb: 8/21/02

1902	Bro-N	1	3	0	2	0	0	0	1	1		.667	.750	.667	335	1	1	2	0			1.000	0	/C	0.1
1903	Cin-N	2	0	0	0	0	0	0	0	0	1	—	1.000	—	175	0	0	0	0			.000	0	/C	0.0
Total	2	3	3	0	2	0	0	0	1	2		.667	.800	.667	341	1	1	2	0			1.000	0	/C	0.1

■ **BILL DEITRICK**   Deitrick, William Alexander   b: 4/20/02, Hanover Co., Va.   d: 5/6/46, Bethesda, Md.   BR/TR, 5'10", 160 lbs.   Deb: 9/19/27

1927	Phi-N	5	6	1	1	0	0	0	0	0		.167	.167	.167	-10	-1	-1	0	0			.750	-1	/S	-0.2
1928	Phi-N	52	100	13	20	6	0	0	7	17	10	.200	.322	.260	52	-6	-7	9	1			1.000	-2	O/S	-0.9
Total	2	57	106	14	21	6	0	0	7	17	10	.198	.315	.255	49	-7	-8	9	1			.895	-3	/OS	-1.1

■ **MIKE DEJAN**   Dejan, Michael Dan   b: 1/13/15, Cleveland, Ohio   d: 2/2/53, W.Los Angeles, Cal.   BL/TL, 6'1", 185 lbs.   Deb: 7/13/40

| 1940 | Cin-N | 12 | 16 | 1 | 3 | 0 | 1 | 0 | 2 | 3 | | .188 | .316 | .313 | 73 | -1 | -1 | 2 | 0 | | | 1.000 | -0 | /O | -0.1 |

■ **IVAN DeJESUS**   DeJesus, Ivan (Alvarez)   b: 1/9/53, Santurce, P.R.   BR/TR, 5'11", 175 lbs.   Deb: 9/13/74

1974	LA-N	3	3	1	1	0	0	0	0	0	2	.333	.333	.333	91	-0	-0	0	0	0	0	1.000	-1	/S	-0.1
1975	LA-N	63	87	10	16	2	1	0	2	11	15	.184	.276	.230	43	-7	-6	6	1	2	-1	.974	7	S	0.3
1976	LA-N	22	41	4	7	2	1	0	2	4	9	.171	.244	.268	46	-3	-3	4	0	1	-1	.950	5	S/3	0.3
1977	Chi-N	155	624	91	166	31	7	3	40	56	90	.266	.330	.353	75	-14	-23	75	24	12	0	.962	**36**	*S	3.0
1978	Chi-N	160	619	**104**	172	24	7	3	35	74	78	.278	.357	.354	88	-1	-8	84	41	12	5	.967	13	*S	3.1
1979	Chi-N	160	636	92	180	26	10	5	52	59	82	.283	.346	.379	89	-1	-9	83	24	20	-5	.959	0	*S	0.4
1980	Chi-N	157	618	78	160	26	3	3	33	60	81	.259	.328	.325	77	-13	-18	72	44	16	4	.969	8	*S	1.2
1981	Chi-N	106	403	49	78	8	4	0	13	46	61	.194	.276	.233	44	-28	-30	30	21	9	1	.959	10	*S	-0.9
1982	Phi-N	161	536	53	128	21	5	3	59	54	70	.239	.311	.313	73	-17	-19	55	14	4	2	.973	-8	*S/3	-1.1
1983	*Phi-N	158	497	60	126	15	7	4	45	53	77	.254	.325	.336	85	-10	-10	56	11	4	1	.966	-14	*S	-0.8
1984	Phi-N	144	435	40	112	13	3	0	35	43	76	.257	.327	.306	77	-11	-12	43	12	5	1	.951	-21	*S	-2.2
1985	StL-N	59	72	11	16	5	0	0	7	4	16	.222	.263	.292	55	-4	-4	7	2	2	-1	1.000	2	3S	-0.2
1986	NY-A	7	4	1	0	0	0	0	0	0	1	.000	.200	.000	-40	-1	-1	0	0	0	0	.900	-1	/S	-0.1
1987	SF-N	9	10	0	2	0	0	0	2	0	3	.200	.200	.200	7	-1	-1	1	0	0	-1	.840	2	/S	-0.1
1988	Det-A	7	17	1	3	0	0	0	0	1	4	.176	.222	.176	14	-2	-2	1	0	0	0	.893	1	/S	-0.1
Total	15	1371	4602	595	1167	175	48	21	324	466	664	.254	.324	.326	76	-111	-145	514	194	88	5	.963	40	*S/3	2.9

■ **MARK DeJOHN**   DeJohn, Mark Stephen   b: 9/18/53, Middletown, Conn.   BB/TR, 5'11", 170 lbs.   Deb: 4/28/82

| 1982 | Det-A | 24 | 21 | 1 | 4 | 2 | 0 | 1 | 4 | 4 | | .190 | .320 | .286 | 68 | -1 | -1 | 3 | 1 | 0 | 0 | .978 | 6 | S/32 | 0.6 |

■ **BILL DeKONING**   DeKoning, William Callahan   b: 12/19/18, Brooklyn, N.Y.   d: 7/26/79, Palm Harbor, Fla.   BR/TR, 5'11", 185 lbs.   Deb: 5/27/45

| 1945 | NY-N | 3 | 1 | 0 | 0 | 0 | 0 | 0 | 0 | 0 | 1 | .000 | .000 | .000 | -99 | -0 | -0 | 0 | 0 | | | 1.000 | -0 | /C | 0.0 |

■ ED DELAHANTY Delahanty, Edward James "Big Ed" b: 10/30/1867, Cleveland, Ohio d: 7/2/03, Niagara Falls, N.Y BR/TR, 6'1", 170 lbs. Deb: 5/22/1888 FH

YEAR	TM/L	G	AB	R	H	2B	3B	HR	RBI	BB	SO	AVG	OBP	SLG	PRO+	BR	/A	RC	SB	CS	SBR	FA	FR	POS	TPR
1888	Phi-N	74	290	40	66	12	2	1	31	12	26	.228	.261	.293	74	-7	-9	33	38			.872	-10	2O	-1.7
1889	Phi-N	56	246	37	72	13	3	0	27	14	17	.293	.333	.370	90	-1	-4	38	19			.956	-13	O2/S	-1.4
1890	Cle-P	115	517	107	154	26	13	3	64	24	30	.298	.339	.416	112	0	8	83	25			.830	-7	S2O/31	0.4
1891	Phi-N	128	543	92	132	19	9	5	86	33	50	.243	.296	.339	84	-10	-12	63	25			.909	1	*O1/2	-1.4
1892	Phi-N	123	477	79	146	30	**21**	6	91	31	32	.306	.360	**.495**	160	31	32	98	29			.944	10	*O/3	3.4
1893	Phi-N	132	595	145	219	35	18	**19**	**146**	47	20	.368	.423	**.583**	169	**55**	**55**	**167**	37			.948	31	*O2/1	**6.4**
1894	Phi-N	114	489	147	199	39	18	4	131	60	16	.407	.478	.585	161	48	50	151	21			.925	16	*O1/3S2	4.6
1895	Phi-N	116	480	149	194	**49**	10	11	106	86	31	.404	**.500**	.617	**189**	**68**	**68**	176	46			.944	2	*O/S23	4.9
1896	Phi-N	123	499	131	198	**44**	17	**13**	**126**	62	22	.397	.472	**.631**	**194**	**66**	**67**	170	37			.952	15	*O1/2	6.1
1897	Phi-N	129	530	109	200	40	15	5	96	60		.377	.444	.538	162	45	47	142	26			.970	9	*O/1	3.9
1898	Phi-N	144	548	115	183	36	9	4	92	77		.334	.426	.454	159	40	**44**	**135**	**58**			.964	6	*O	3.6
1899	Phi-N	146	581	135	**238**	**55**	9	9	**137**	55		**.410**	.464	**.582**	**193**	**68**	**71**	**175**	30			.969	0	*O	5.4
1900	Phi-N	131	539	82	174	32	10	2	109	41		.323	.378	.430	124	16	17	98	16			.981	-3	*1	1.2
1901	Phi-N	139	542	106	192	**38**	16	8	108	65		.354	.427	.528	173	53	52	139	29			.949	-5	O1	3.8
1902	Was-A	123	473	103	178	**43**	14	10	93	62		**.376**	**.454**	**.590**	**186**	**57**	**57**	**137**	16			.961	2	*O1	4.8
1903	Was-A	42	156	22	52	11	1	1	21	12		.333	.388	.436	144	9	9	28	3			.962	2	O/1	0.8
Total	16	1835	7505	1599	2597	522	185	101	1464	741	244	.346	.412	.505	154	539	551	1833	455			.951	56	*O12/S3	44.8

■ FRANK DELAHANTY Delahanty, Frank George "Pudgie" b: 1/29/1883, Cleveland, Ohio d: 7/22/66, Cleveland, Ohio BR/TR, 5'9", 160 lbs. Deb: 8/23/05 F

YEAR	TM/L	G	AB	R	H	2B	3B	HR	RBI	BB	SO	AVG	OBP	SLG	PRO+	BR	/A	RC	SB	CS	SBR	FA	FR	POS	TPR
1905	NY-A	9	27	0	6	1	0	0	2	1		.222	.250	.259	55	-1	-2	2	0			.932	-1	/1O	-0.3
1906	NY-A	92	307	37	73	11	8	2	41	16		.238	.278	.345	86	-3	-6	35	11			.954	3	O	-0.8
1907	Cle-A	15	52	3	9	0	1	0	4	4		.173	.232	.212	41	-3	-3	3	2			.917	-0	O	-0.5
1908	NY-A	37	125	12	32	1	2	0	10	10		.256	.316	.296	98	0	-0	14	9			.957	-1	O	-0.3
1914	Buf-F	79	274	29	55	4	7	2	27	23	19	.201	.265	.288	56	-16	-16	28	21			.976	-6	O	-2.7
	Pit-F	41	159	25	38	4	4	1	7	11	11	.239	.297	.333	80	-5	-4	19	7			.984	-3	O/2	-0.9
	Yr	120	433	54	93	8	11	3	34	34	30	.215	.277	.305	65	-20	-21	47	28			.979	-8	*O/2	-3.6
1915	Pit-F	14	42	3	10	1	0	0	3	1	0	.238	.256	.262	53	-3	-3	3	0			1.000	1	O	-0.3
Total	6	287	986	109	223	22	22	5	94	66	30	.226	.278	.308	73	-30	-35	104	50			.964	-7	O/12	-5.8

■ JIM DELAHANTY Delahanty, James Christopher b: 6/20/1879, Cleveland, Ohio d: 10/17/53, Cleveland, Ohio BR/TR, 5'10.5", 170 lbs. Deb: 4/19/01 F

YEAR	TM/L	G	AB	R	H	2B	3B	HR	RBI	BB	SO	AVG	OBP	SLG	PRO+	BR	/A	RC	SB	CS	SBR	FA	FR	POS	TPR
1901	Chi-N	17	63	4	12	2	0	0	4	3		.190	.239	.222	36	-5	-5	5	5			.877	-1	3/2	-0.6
1902	NY-N	7	26	3	6	1	0	0	3	1		.231	.259	.269	64	-1	-1	2	0			.917	-1	/O	-0.2
1904	Bos-N	142	499	56	142	27	8	3	60	27		.285	.333	.389	128	12	15	72	16			.888	1	*32/OP	1.9
1905	Bos-N	125	461	50	119	11	8	5	55	28		.258	.315	.349	100	-2	-0	57	12			.962	-7	*O/P	-1.4
1906	Cin-N	115	379	63	106	21	4	1	39	45		.280	.364	.364	122	13	11	61	21			.903	-19	*3/SO	-0.5
1907	StL-A	33	95	8	21	3	0	0	6	5		.221	.275	.253	69	-3	-3	9	6			.889	-1	3/O2	-0.4
	Was-A	108	404	44	118	18	7	2	54	36		.292	.363	.386	151	18	22	66	18			.941	-13	23/O1	1.0
	Yr	141	499	52	139	21	7	2	60	41		.279	.347	.361	134	15	19	74	24			.942	-14	23O/1	0.6
1908	Was-A	83	287	33	91	11	4	1	30	24		.317	.374	.394	163	16	18	48	16			.963	3	2	2.3
1909	Was-A	90	302	18	67	13	5	1	21	23		.222	.290	.308	93	-4	-2	28	4			.956	-3	2	-0.8
	*Det-A	46	150	29	38	10	1	0	20	17		.253	.364	.333	115	5	4	22	9			.943	-7	2	-0.5
	Yr	136	452	47	105	23	6	1	41	40		.232	.316	.316	101	1	1	50	13			.951	-10	*2	-1.3
1910	Det-A	106	378	67	111	16	2	3	45	43		.294	.379	.370	126	17	14	59	15			.940	-14	*2	-0.2
1911	Det-A	144	542	83	184	30	14	3	94	56		.339	.411	.463	137	33	29	110	15			.978	-10	123	1.7
1912	Det-A	79	266	34	76	14	1	0	41	42		.286	.397	.346	117	7	8	41	9			.930	-5	2O	0.1
1914	Bro-F	74	214	28	62	13	5	0	15	25	21	.290	.372	.397	120	6	6	36	4			.957	-19	2/1	-1.4
1915	Bro-F	17	25	0	6	1	0	0	2	3	3	.240	.345	.280	85	-0	-0	3	1			.857	-1	/2	-0.1
Total	13	1186	4091	520	1159	191	59	19	489	378	24	.283	.356	.373	122	111	114	618	151			.946	-95	23O/1SP	0.9

■ JOE DELAHANTY Delahanty, Joseph Nicholas b: 10/18/1875, Cleveland, Ohio d: 1/9/36, Cleveland, Ohio BR/TR, 5'9", 168 lbs. Deb: 9/30/07 F

YEAR	TM/L	G	AB	R	H	2B	3B	HR	RBI	BB	SO	AVG	OBP	SLG	PRO+	BR	/A	RC	SB	CS	SBR	FA	FR	POS	TPR
1907	StL-N	7	22	3	7	0	0	1	2	0		.318	.318	.455	147	1	1	4	3			.933	-1	/O	0.0
1908	StL-N	140	499	37	127	14	11	1	44	32		.255	.309	.333	110	2	5	54	11			.977	-5	*O	-0.6
1909	StL-N	123	411	28	88	16	4	2	54	42		.214	.292	.287	85	-10	-7	37	10			.985	-16	O2	-2.9
Total	3	270	932	68	222	30	15	4	100	74		.238	.301	.315	100	-7	-1	96	24			.978	-21	O/2	-3.5

■ TOM DELAHANTY Delahanty, Thomas James b: 3/9/1872, Cleveland, Ohio d: 1/10/51, Sanford, Fla. BL/TR, 5'8", 175 lbs. Deb: 9/29/1894 F

YEAR	TM/L	G	AB	R	H	2B	3B	HR	RBI	BB	SO	AVG	OBP	SLG	PRO+	BR	/A	RC	SB	CS	SBR	FA	FR	POS	TPR
1894	Phi-N	1	4	0	1	0	0	0	0	0	1	.250	.250	.250	23	-0	-0	0	0			.875	0	/2	0.0
1896	Cle-N	16	56	11	13	4	0	0	4	8	4	.232	.338	.304	68	-2	-3	7	4			.823	-1	3	-0.3
	Pit-N	1	3	1	1	0	0	0	0	0	0	.333	.333	.333	81	-0	-0	0	0			.750	-1	/S	-0.1
	Yr	17	59	12	14	4	0	0	4	8	4	.237	.338	.305	69	-2	-3	8	4			.823	-2	3/S	-0.4
1897	Lou-N	1	4	1	1	1	0	0	2	0		.250	.250	.500	99	-0	-0	1	0			.333	-2	/2	-0.2
Total	3	19	67	13	16	5	0	0	6	8	5	.239	.329	.313	68	-3	-3	9	4			.727	-4	/32S	-0.6

■ MIKE de la HOZ de la Hoz, Miguel Angel (Piloto) b: 10/2/38, Havana, Cuba BR/TR, 5'11", 175 lbs. Deb: 7/22/60

YEAR	TM/L	G	AB	R	H	2B	3B	HR	RBI	BB	SO	AVG	OBP	SLG	PRO+	BR	/A	RC	SB	CS	SBR	FA	FR	POS	TPR
1960	Cle-A	49	160	20	41	6	2	6	23	9	12	.256	.300	.431	98	-2	-1	19	0	0	0	.950	-15	S/3	-1.3
1961	Cle-A	61	173	20	45	10	0	3	23	7	10	.260	.297	.370	79	-6	-5	18	0	0	0	.969	3	2S3	0.0
1962	Cle-A	12	12	0	1	0	0	0	0	0	3	.083	.083	.083	-57	-3	-3	0	0	0	0	1.000	-0	/2	-0.3
1963	Cle-A	67	150	15	40	10	0	5	25	9	29	.267	.313	.433	107	1	1	20	0	0	0	.962	4	2/3SO	0.9
1964	Mil-N	78	189	25	55	7	1	4	12	14	22	.291	.346	.402	109	3	2	25	1	1	-0	.968	-4	23/S	0.0
1965	Mil-N	81	176	15	45	3	2	2	11	8	21	.256	.296	.330	75	-6	-6	16	0	1	-1	.963	-10	S32/1	-1.6
1966	Atl-N	71	110	11	24	3	0	2	7	5	18	.218	.252	.300	52	-7	-7	8	0	1	-1	.950	-2	3/2S	-1.1
1967	Atl-N	74	143	10	29	3	0	3	14	4	14	.203	.224	.287	46	-10	-10	8	1	0	0	1.000	-4	23/S	-1.5
1969	Cin-N	1	1	0	0	0	0	0	0	0	1	.000	.000	.000	-95	-0	-0	0	0	0	0	.000	0	H	0.0
Total	9	494	1114	116	280	42	5	25	115	56	130	.251	.292	.365	82	-30	-29	114	2	3	-1	.936	-28	32S/O1	-4.9

■ BILL DeLANCEY DeLancey, William Pinkney b: 11/28/11, Greensboro, N.C. d: 11/28/46, Phoenix, Ariz. BL/TR, 5'11.5", 185 lbs. Deb: 9/11/32

YEAR	TM/L	G	AB	R	H	2B	3B	HR	RBI	BB	SO	AVG	OBP	SLG	PRO+	BR	/A	RC	SB	CS	SBR	FA	FR	POS	TPR
1932	StL-N	8	26	1	5	0	2	0	2	2	1	.192	.250	.346	57	-2	-2	2	0			.930	1	/C	-0.1
1934	*StL-N	93	253	41	80	18	3	13	40	41	37	.316	.414	.565	150	22	20	62	1			.980	5	C	2.7
1935	StL-N	103	301	37	84	14	5	6	41	42	34	.279	.369	.419	107	6	4	50	0			.971	-2	C	0.6
1940	StL-N	15	18	0	4	0	0	0	2	0	2	.222	.222	.222	22	-2	-2	1	0			.929	1	C	-0.1
Total	4	219	598	79	173	32	10	19	85	85	74	.289	.380	.472	121	24	20	115	1			.972	4	C	3.1

■ BILL DELANEY Delaney, William L. b: 3/4/1863, Cincinnati, O. d: 3/1/42, Canton, Ohio BR/TR, Deb: 8/21/1890

YEAR	TM/L	G	AB	R	H	2B	3B	HR	RBI	BB	SO	AVG	OBP	SLG	PRO+	BR	/A	RC	SB	CS	SBR	FA	FR	POS	TPR
1890	Cle-N	36	116	16	22	1	1	1	7	21	19	.190	.314	.241	66	-4	-4	11	5			.926	-10	2	-1.0

■ JESUS De La ROSA De La Rosa, Jesus (b: Jesus De Los Santos (De La Rosa)) b: 8/5/53, Santo Domingo, D.R BR/TR, 6'1", 153 lbs. Deb: 8/02/75

YEAR	TM/L	G	AB	R	H	2B	3B	HR	RBI	BB	SO	AVG	OBP	SLG	PRO+	BR	/A	RC	SB	CS	SBR	FA	FR	POS	TPR
1975	Hou-N	3	3	1	1	1	0	0	0	0	0	.333	.333	.667	186	0	0	1	0	0	0	.000	0	H	0.0

■ PUCHY DELGADO Delgado, Luis Felipe (Robles) b: 2/2/54, Hatillo, P.R. BB/TL, 5'11", 170 lbs. Deb: 9/06/77

YEAR	TM/L	G	AB	R	H	2B	3B	HR	RBI	BB	SO	AVG	OBP	SLG	PRO+	BR	/A	RC	SB	CS	SBR	FA	FR	POS	TPR
1977	Sea-A	13	22	4	4	0	0	0	2	1	8	.182	.217	.182	10	-3	-3	1	0	0	0	1.000	-2	O	-0.5

■ BOBBY Del GRECO Del Greco, Robert George b: 4/7/33, Pittsburgh, Pa. BR/TR, 5'11", 190 lbs. Deb: 4/16/52

YEAR	TM/L	G	AB	R	H	2B	3B	HR	RBI	BB	SO	AVG	OBP	SLG	PRO+	BR	/A	RC	SB	CS	SBR	FA	FR	POS	TPR
1952	Pit-N	99	341	34	74	14	2	1	20	38	70	.217	.301	.279	60	-17	-18	30	6	5	-1	.977	6	O	-1.8
1956	Pit-N	14	20	4	4	0	0	2	3	3	3	.200	.304	.500	114	0	0	3	0	0	0	1.000	-2	/O3	-0.2

YEAR	TM/L	G	AB	R	H	2B	3B	HR	RBI	BB	SO	AVG	OBP	SLG	PRO+	BR	/A	RC	SB	CS	SBR	FA	FR	POS	TPR
	StL-N	102	270	29	58	16	2	5	18	32	50	.215	.312	.344	76	-9	-9	31	1	1	-0	.987	-9	O	-2.3
	Yr	116	290	33	62	16	2	7	21	35	53	.214	.311	.355	79	-9	-8	34	1	1	-0	.987	-10	*O/3	-2.5
1957	Chi-N	20	40	2	8	2	0	0	3	10	17	.200	.360	.250	69	-1	-1	5	1	0	0	.967	-2	O	-0.3
	NY-A	8	7	3	3	0	0	0	0	2	2	.429	.556	.429	175	1	1	2	1	0	0	1.000	-2	/O	-0.1
1958	NY-A	12	5	1	1	0	0	0	0	1	1	.200	.333	.200	52	-0	-0	0	0	1	-1	1.000	-4	O	-0.5
1960	Phi-N	100	300	48	71	16	4	10	26	54	64	.237	.355	.417	110	5	5	46	1	5	-3	.970	12	O	1.0
1961	Phi-N	41	112	14	29	5	0	2	11	12	17	.259	.346	.357	88	-2	-2	14	0	0	0	1.000	3	O/23	0.0
	KC-A	74	239	34	55	14	1	5	21	30	31	.230	.319	.360	81	-6	-7	29	1	0	0	.983	5	O	-0.5
1962	KC-A	132	338	61	86	21	1	9	38	49	62	.254	.370	.402	105	5	4	55	4	1	1	.984	0	*O	-0.1
1963	KC-A	121	306	40	65	7	1	8	29	40	52	.212	.313	.320	75	-8	-10	32	1	2	-1	.981	-6	*O/3	-2.3
1965	Phi-N	8	4	1	0	0	0	0	0	0	3	.000	.000	.000	-99	-1	-1	0	0	0	0	.000	0	/O	-0.1
Total	9	731	1982	271	454	95	11	42	169	271	372	.229	.331	.352	85	-33	-37	247	16	15	-4	.981	1	O/32	-7.2

■ JUAN DELIS Delis, Juan Francisco b: 2/27/28, Santiago, Cuba BR/TR, 5'11", 170 lbs. Deb: 4/16/55

YEAR	TM/L	G	AB	R	H	2B	3B	HR	RBI	BB	SO	AVG	OBP	SLG	PRO+	BR	/A	RC	SB	CS	SBR	FA	FR	POS	TPR
1955	Was-A	54	132	12	25	3	1	0	11	3	15	.189	.219	.227	21	-15	-14	6	1	2	-1	.918	-2	3/O2	-1.7

■ EDDIE DELKER Delker, Edward Alberts b: 4/17/07, DeAlto, Pa. BR/TR, 5'10.5", 170 lbs. Deb: 4/28/29

YEAR	TM/L	G	AB	R	H	2B	3B	HR	RBI	BB	SO	AVG	OBP	SLG	PRO+	BR	/A	RC	SB	CS	SBR	FA	FR	POS	TPR
1929	StL-N	22	40	5	6	0	1	0	3	2	12	.150	.227	.200	7	-6	-6	2	0			.750	-2	/S23	-0.7
1931	StL-N	1	2	0	1	1	0	0	2	0	0	.500	.500	1.000	283	1	0	1	0			1.000	-0	/3	0.0
1932	StL-N	20	42	1	5	4	0	0	2	8	7	.119	.260	.214	28	-4	-4	3	0			1.000	4	2/3S	0.1
	Phi-N	30	62	7	10	1	1	1	7	6	14	.161	.235	.258	29	-6	-7	4	0			.925	-2	2	-0.8
	Yr	50	104	8	15	5	1	1	9	14	21	.144	.246	.240	29	-10	-11	7	0			.946	3	2/3S	-0.7
1933	Phi-N	25	41	6	7	3	1	0	1	0	12	.171	.171	.293	27	-4	-4	2	0			.968	6	2/3	0.2
Total	4	98	187	19	29	9	3	1	15	16	45	.155	.229	.251	26	-19	-21	12	0			.952	6	/23S	-1.2

■ BERT DELMAS Delmas, Albert Charles b: 5/20/11, San Francisco, Cal d: 12/4/79, Huntington Beach, Cal. BL/TR, 5'11", 165 lbs. Deb: 9/10/33

YEAR	TM/L	G	AB	R	H	2B	3B	HR	RBI	BB	SO	AVG	OBP	SLG	PRO+	BR	/A	RC	SB	CS	SBR	FA	FR	POS	TPR
1933	Bro-N	12	28	4	7	0	0	0	0	1	7	.250	.276	.250	53	-2	-2	2	0			.912	-3	2	-0.5

■ LUIS De Los SANTOS De Los Santos, Luis Manuel (Martinez) b: 12/29/66, San Cristobal, D.R. BR/TR, 6'5", 205 lbs. Deb: 9/07/88

YEAR	TM/L	G	AB	R	H	2B	3B	HR	RBI	BB	SO	AVG	OBP	SLG	PRO+	BR	/A	RC	SB	CS	SBR	FA	FR	POS	TPR
1988	KC-A	11	22	1	2	1	1	0	1	4	4	.091	.231	.227	29	-2	-2	1	0	0	0	1.000	-0	/1D	-0.3
1989	KC-A	28	87	6	22	3	1	0	6	5	14	.253	.293	.310	71	-3	-3	8	0	0	0	.986	0	1	-0.5
1991	Det-A	16	30	1	5	2	0	0	0	2	4	.167	.219	.233	25	-3	-3	1	0	0	0	1.000	-0	/O13D	-0.4
Total	3	55	139	8	29	6	2	0	7	11	22	.209	.267	.281	53	-9	-9	10	0	0	0	.988	-1	/1DO3	-1.2

■ GARTON Del SAVIO Del Savio, Garton Orville b: 11/26/13, New York, N.Y. BR/TR, 5'9.5", 165 lbs. Deb: 4/24/43

YEAR	TM/L	G	AB	R	H	2B	3B	HR	RBI	BB	SO	AVG	OBP	SLG	PRO+	BR	/A	RC	SB	CS	SBR	FA	FR	POS	TPR
1943	Phi-N	4	11	0	1	0	0	0	0	1	0	.091	.167	.091	-26	-2	-2	0	0			.857	0	/S	-0.1

■ JIM DELSING Delsing, James Henry b: 11/13/25, Rudolph, Wis. BL/TR, 5'10", 175 lbs. Deb: 4/21/48

YEAR	TM/L	G	AB	R	H	2B	3B	HR	RBI	BB	SO	AVG	OBP	SLG	PRO+	BR	/A	RC	SB	CS	SBR	FA	FR	POS	TPR
1948	Chi-A	20	63	5	12	0	0	0	5	5	12	.190	.261	.190	22	-7	-7	3	0	0	0	1.000	-1	O	-0.9
1949	NY-A	9	20	5	7	1	0	1	3	1	2	.350	.381	.550	145	1	1	4	0	0	0	1.000	-2	/O	-0.1
1950	NY-A	12	10	2	4	0	0	0	2	2	0	.400	.500	.400	137	1	1	2	0	0	0	.000	0	H	0.1
	StL-A	69	209	25	55	5	2	0	15	20	23	.263	.328	.306	61	-11	-12	21	1	4	-2	.994	2	O	-1.4
	Yr	81	219	27	59	5	2	0	17	22	23	.269	.336	.311	65	-11	-12	23	1	4	-2	.994	2	O	-1.3
1951	StL-A	131	449	59	112	20	2	8	45	56	39	.249	.338	.356	85	-7	-9	52	2	9	-5	.983	9	*O	-0.9
1952	StL-A	93	298	34	76	13	6	1	34	25	29	.255	.323	.349	85	-5	-6	33	3	3	-1	.986	-1	O	-1.2
	Det-A	33	113	14	31	2	1	3	15	11	8	.274	.344	.389	103	1	0	16	1	0	0	.958	-0	O	-0.1
	Yr	126	411	48	107	15	7	4	49	36	37	.260	.329	.360	90	-5	-6	49	4	3	-1	.979	-1	*O	-1.3
1953	Det-A	138	479	77	138	26	6	11	62	66	39	.288	.380	.436	121	14	15	84	1	3	-2	.992	-2	*O	0.7
1954	Det-A	122	371	39	92	24	2	6	38	49	38	.248	.337	.372	96	-3	-2	48	4	4	-1	**.996**	-0	*O	-0.8
1955	Det-A	114	356	49	85	15	2	10	60	48	40	.239	.331	.376	92	-5	-4	47	2	0	1	.995	-5	*O	-1.3
1956	Det-A	10	12	0	0	0	0	0	0	3	3	.000	.250	.000	-29	-2	-2	0	0	0	0	1.000	-1	/O	-0.3
	Chi-A	55	41	11	5	3	0	0	2	10	13	.122	.294	.195	31	-4	-4	3	1	0	0	.957	-8	O	-1.2
	Yr	65	53	11	5	3	0	0	2	13	16	.094	.284	.151	17	-6	-6	4	1	0	0	.962	-8	O	-1.5
1960	KC-A	16	40	2	10	3	0	0	5	3	5	.250	.302	.325	69	-2	-2	4	0	0	0	1.000	1	O	-0.1
Total	10	822	2461	322	627	112	21	40	286	299	251	.255	.340	.366	91	-30	-31	320	15	23	-9	.989	-8	O	-7.5

■ JOE DeMAESTRI DeMaestri, Joseph Paul "Oats" b: 12/9/28, San Francisco, Cal. BR/TR, 6', 174 lbs. Deb: 4/19/51

YEAR	TM/L	G	AB	R	H	2B	3B	HR	RBI	BB	SO	AVG	OBP	SLG	PRO+	BR	/A	RC	SB	CS	SBR	FA	FR	POS	TPR
1951	Chi-A	56	74	8	15	0	2	1	3	5	11	.203	.253	.297	49	-6	-5	5	0	4	-2	.959	6	S2/3	-0.1
1952	StL-A	81	186	13	42	9	1	1	18	8	25	.226	.258	.301	54	-12	-12	14	0	1	-1	.939	2	S/23	-0.7
1953	Phi-A	111	420	53	107	17	3	6	35	24	39	.255	.297	.352	72	-16	-18	42	0	1	-1	.964	-16	*S	-2.7
1954	Phi-A	146	539	49	124	16	3	8	40	20	63	.230	.262	.315	57	-33	-33	42	1	4	-2	.965	-6	*S/23	-3.1
1955	KC-A	123	457	42	114	14	1	6	37	20	47	.249	.285	.324	63	-24	-25	39	3	5	-2	.964	-12	*S	-2.9
1956	KC-A	133	434	41	101	16	1	6	39	25	73	.233	.279	.316	57	-28	-28	37	3	3	-1	.964	6	*S/2	-1.3
1957	KC-A☆	135	461	44	113	14	6	9	33	22	82	.245	.282	.360	73	-18	-18	44	6	1	1	**.980**	-7	*S	-1.2
1958	KC-A	139	442	32	97	11	1	6	38	16	84	.219	.248	.290	47	-32	-33	29	1	0	0	**.980**	11	*S	-1.1
1959	KC-A	118	352	31	86	16	5	6	34	28	65	.244	.307	.369	83	-8	-8	38	1	0	0	.957	5	*S	0.5
1960	*NY-A	49	35	8	8	1	0	0	2	0	9	.229	.229	.257	33	-3	-3	2	0	0	0	.952	7	2S	0.5
1961	NY-A	30	41	1	6	0	0	0	2	0	13	.146	.146	.146	-23	-7	-7	1	0	0	0	.981	7	S/23	0.1
Total	11	1121	3441	322	813	114	23	49	281	168	511	.236	.275	.325	62	-186	-192	293	15	19	-7	.967	4	*S/23	-12.0

■ FRANK DEMAREE Demaree, Joseph Franklin (b: Joseph Franklin Dimaria)
b: 6/10/10, Winters, Cal. d: 8/30/58, Los Angeles, Cal. BR/TR, 5'11.5", 185 lbs. Deb: 7/22/32

YEAR	TM/L	G	AB	R	H	2B	3B	HR	RBI	BB	SO	AVG	OBP	SLG	PRO+	BR	/A	RC	SB	CS	SBR	FA	FR	POS	TPR
1932	*Chi-N	23	56	4	14	3	0	0	6	2	7	.250	.288	.304	60	-3	-3	5	0			1.000	-1	O	-0.5
1933	Chi-N	134	515	68	140	24	6	6	51	22	42	.272	.304	.377	94	-5	-5	59	4			.965	0	*O	-1.2
1935	*Chi-N	107	385	60	125	19	4	2	66	26	23	.325	.369	.410	108	5	5	58	6			.973	-2	O	0.0
1936	Chi-N★	154	605	93	212	34	3	16	96	49	30	.350	.400	.496	137	34	32	119	4			.968	-2	*O	2.3
1937	Chi-N★	154	615	104	199	36	6	17	115	57	31	.324	.382	.485	129	28	25	112	6			.980	2	*O	2.1
1938	*Chi-N	129	476	63	130	15	7	8	62	45	34	.273	.341	.384	96	-0	-2	62	1			.972	-8	*O	-1.4
1939	NY-N	150	560	68	170	27	2	11	79	66	40	.304	.381	.418	114	13	12	89	2			.986	-1	*O	0.7
1940	NY-N	121	460	68	139	18	6	7	61	45	39	.302	.364	.413	113	9	9	71	5			.980	-6	*O	-0.3
1941	NY-N	16	35	3	6	0	0	0	1	4	1	.171	.256	.171	22	-4	-4	1	0			1.000	-0	O	-0.5
	Bos-N	48	113	20	26	5	2	2	15	12	5	.230	.304	.363	91	-2	-2	12	2			1.000	-4	O	-0.7
	Yr	64	148	23	32	5	2	2	16	16	6	.216	.293	.318	74	-6	-5	13	2			1.000	-5	O	-1.2
1942	Bos-N	64	187	18	42	5	0	3	24	17	10	.225	.289	.299	74	-7	-6	15	2			1.000	4	O	-0.5
1943	*StL-N	39	86	5	25	2	0	0	9	8	4	.291	.351	.314	89	-1	-1	9	1			1.000	-3	O	-0.6
1944	StL-A	16	51	4	13	2	0	0	6	6	3	.255	.333	.294	76	-1	-1	6	0	0	0	.969	-1	O	-0.3
Total	12	1155	4144	578	1241	190	36	72	591	359	269	.299	.357	.415	110	67	59	616	33	0		.978	-22	*O	-0.9

■ BILLY DeMARS DeMars, William Lester "Kid" b: 8/26/25, Brooklyn, N.Y. BR/TR, 5'10", 160 lbs. Deb: 5/18/48 C

YEAR	TM/L	G	AB	R	H	2B	3B	HR	RBI	BB	SO	AVG	OBP	SLG	PRO+	BR	/A	RC	SB	CS	SBR	FA	FR	POS	TPR
1948	Phi-A	18	29	3	5	0	0	0	1	5	3	.172	.294	.172	26	-3	-3	2	0	0	0	.927	4	/S23	0.1
1950	StL-A	61	178	25	44	5	1	0	13	22	13	.247	.330	.287	57	-11	-12	17	0	1	-1	.933	-7	S/3	-1.5
1951	StL-A	1	4	1	1	0	0	0	0	1	0	.250	.400	.250	76	-0	-0	1	0	0	0	1.000	-0	/S	0.0
Total	3	80	211	29	50	5	1	0	14	28	16	.237	.326	.270	53	-14	-15	20	0	1	-1	.933	-4	/S32	-1.4

■ **JOHN DeMERIT** DeMerit, John Stephen "Thumper" b: 1/8/36, West Bend, Wis. BR/TR, 6'1.5", 195 lbs. Deb: 6/18/57

YEAR	TM/L	G	AB	R	H	2B	3B	HR	RBI	BB	SO	AVG	OBP	SLG	PRO+	BR	/A	RC	SB	CS	SBR	FA	FR	POS	TPR
1957	*Mil-N	33	34	8	5	0	0	0	1	0	8	.147	.147	.147	-22	-6	-5	1	1	0	0	1.000	-3	O	-0.8
1958	Mil-N	3	3	1	2	0	0	0	0	0	0	.667	.667	.667	278	1	1	1	0	0	0	1.000	-1	/O	0.0
1959	Mil-N	11	5	4	1	0	0	0	0	1	2	.200	.333	.200	51	-0	-0	0	0	0	0	1.000	-0	/O	-0.1
1961	Mil-N	32	74	5	12	3	0	2	5	5	19	.162	.225	.284	36	-7	-7	5	0	0	0	1.000	2	O	-0.6
1962	NY-N	14	16	3	3	0	0	1	1	2	4	.188	.278	.375	72	-1	-1	2	0	0	0	1.000	-1	/O	-0.1
Total	5	93	132	21	23	3	0	3	7	8	33	.174	.227	.265	32	-13	-12	9	1	0	0	1.000	-3	/O	-1.6

■ **DON DEMETER** Demeter, Donald Lee b: 6/25/35, Oklahoma City, Okla BR/TR, 6'4", 190 lbs. Deb: 9/18/56

YEAR	TM/L	G	AB	R	H	2B	3B	HR	RBI	BB	SO	AVG	OBP	SLG	PRO+	BR	/A	RC	SB	CS	SBR	FA	FR	POS	TPR
1956	Bro-N	3	3	1	1	0	0	1	1	0	1	.333	.333	1.333	297	1	1	1	0	0	0	1.000	-0	/O	0.0
1958	LA-N	43	106	11	20	2	0	5	8	5	32	.189	.225	.349	48	-8	-9	8	2	3	-1	1.000	-4	O	-1.6
1959	*LA-N	139	371	55	95	11	1	18	70	16	87	.256	.298	.437	86	-5	-9	45	5	6	-2	.983	-6	*O	-2.2
1960	LA-N	64	168	23	46	7	1	9	29	8	34	.274	.311	.488	108	3	1	25	0	1	-1	.989	-8	O	-1.0
1961	LA-N	15	29	3	5	0	0	1	2	3	6	.172	.250	.276	36	-3	-3	2	0	0	0	.950	1	O	-0.2
	Phi-N	106	382	54	98	18	4	20	68	19	74	.257	.300	.482	105	0	1	54	2	1	0	.995	11	O1	0.5
	Yr	121	411	57	103	18	4	21	70	22	80	.251	.297	.467	99	-2	-2	55	2	1	0	.990	12	O1	0.3
1962	Phi-N	153	550	85	169	24	3	29	107	41	93	.307	.366	.520	139	26	28	101	2	7	-4	.937	-6	*3O/1	1.6
1963	Phi-N	154	515	63	133	20	2	22	83	31	93	.258	.308	.433	112	6	7	66	1	4	-2	**1.000**	-5	*O31	-0.6
1964	Det-A	134	441	57	113	22	1	22	80	17	85	.256	.292	.460	104	1	1	58	4	1	1	1.000	-2	O1	-0.6
1965	Det-A	122	389	50	108	16	4	16	58	23	65	.278	.328	.463	121	10	10	56	4	2	0	.988	-2	O1	0.3
1966	Det-A	32	99	12	21	5	0	5	12	3	19	.212	.235	.414	81	-3	-3	8	1	0	0	.985	5	O/1	0.1
	Bos-A	73	226	31	66	13	1	9	29	5	42	.292	.310	.478	111	6	3	33	1	0	0	.982	-2	O/1	-0.1
	Yr	105	325	43	87	18	1	14	41	8	61	.268	.287	.458	102	3	0	40	2	0	1	.984	3	O/1	0.0
1967	Bos-A	20	43	7	12	5	0	1	4	3	11	.279	.326	.465	122	2	1	7	0	0	0	1.000	-1	O/3	0.0
	Cle-A	51	121	15	25	4	0	5	12	6	16	.207	.256	.364	80	-3	-3	10	0	0	0	.985	-2	O/3	-0.7
	Yr	71	164	22	37	9	0	6	16	9	27	.226	.274	.390	92	-2	-2	17	0	0	0	.988	-3	O/3	-0.7
Total	11	1109	3443	467	912	147	17	163	563	180	658	.265	.309	.459	108	32	25	474	22	25	-8	.990	-21	O31	-4.5

■ **STEVE DEMETER** Demeter, Stephen b: 1/27/35, Homer City, Pa. BR/TR, 5'9.5", 185 lbs. Deb: 7/29/59 C

YEAR	TM/L	G	AB	R	H	2B	3B	HR	RBI	BB	SO	AVG	OBP	SLG	PRO+	BR	/A	RC	SB	CS	SBR	FA	FR	POS	TPR
1959	Det-A	11	18	1	2	1	0	0	1	0	1	.111	.111	.167	-24	-3	-3	0	0	0	0	.909	1	/3	-0.2
1960	Cle-A	4	5	0	0	0	0	0	0	0	1	.000	.000	.000	-99	-1	-1	0	0	0	0	1.000	0	/3	-0.1
Total	2	15	23	1	2	1	0	0	1	0	2	.087	.087	.130	-40	-4	-5	0	0	0	0	.933	1	/3	-0.3

■ **RAY DEMMITT** Demmitt, Charles Raymond b: 2/2/1884, Illiopolis, Ill. d: 2/19/56, Glen Ellyn, Ill. BL/TR, 5'8", 170 lbs. Deb: 4/12/09

YEAR	TM/L	G	AB	R	H	2B	3B	HR	RBI	BB	SO	AVG	OBP	SLG	PRO+	BR	/A	RC	SB	CS	SBR	FA	FR	POS	TPR
1909	NY-A	123	427	68	105	12	12	4	30	55		.246	.340	.358	120	11	11	57	16			.908	5	*O	1.3
1910	StL-A	10	23	4	4	1	0	0	2	3		.174	.296	.217	65	-1	-1	2	0			1.000	1	/O	0.0
1914	Det-A	1	0	0	0	0	0	0	0	0	0	—	—	—	—	0	0	0	0			.000	0	R	0.0
	Chi-A	146	515	63	133	13	12	2	46	61	48	.258	.344	.342	108	5	6	60	12	20	-8	.953	-5	*O	-1.5
	Yr	147	515	63	133	13	12	2	46	61	48	.258	.344	.342	108	5	6	60	12	20	-8	.953	-5	*O	-1.5
1915	Chi-A	9	6	0	0	0	0	0	0	1	2	.000	.143	.000	-55	-1	-1	0	0			1.000	-1	/O	-0.2
1917	StL-A	14	53	6	15	1	2	0	7	0	8	.283	.296	.377	109	-0	0	6	1			1.000	-3	O	-0.4
1918	StL-A	116	405	45	114	23	5	1	61	38	35	.281	.346	.370	120	7	9	55	10			.951	7	*O	1.1
1919	StL-A	79	202	19	48	11	2	1	19	14	27	.238	.290	.327	71	-8	-8	19	3			.868	-7	O	-2.0
Total	7	498	1631	205	419	61	33	8	165	172	120	.257	.334	.349	108	14	15	199	42	20		.934	-3	O	-1.7

■ **GENE DeMONTREVILLE** DeMontreville, Eugene Napoleon b: 3/26/1874, St.Paul, Minn. d: 2/18/35, Memphis, Tenn. BR/TR, 5'8", 165 lbs. Deb: 8/20/1894 F

YEAR	TM/L	G	AB	R	H	2B	3B	HR	RBI	BB	SO	AVG	OBP	SLG	PRO+	BR	/A	RC	SB	CS	SBR	FA	FR	POS	TPR
1894	Pit-N	2	8	0	2	0	0	0	0	1	4	.250	.333	.250	44	-1	-1	1	0			.889	-1	/S	-0.1
1895	Was-N	12	46	7	10	1	3	0	9	3	4	.217	.265	.370	65	-3	-3	6	5			.929	4	S	0.1
1896	Was-N	133	533	94	183	24	5	8	77	29	27	.343	.381	.452	121	15	15	106	28			.890	16	*S	3.0
1897	Was-N	133	566	92	193	27	8	3	93	21		.341	.366	.433	111	7	7	104	30			.886	10	*S2	1.8
1898	Bal-N	151	567	93	186	19	2	0	86	52		.328	.394	.369	117	16	15	106	49			.944	0	*2S	2.2
1899	Chi-N	82	310	43	87	6	3	0	40	17		.281	.328	.319	80	-9	-8	44	26			.902	9	S	0.7
	Bal-N	60	240	40	67	13	4	1	36	10		.279	.313	.379	85	-4	-6	36	21			.961	9	2	0.5
	Yr	142	550	83	154	19	7	1	76	27		.280	.322	.345	83	-14	-14	80	47			.902	18	S2	1.2
1900	Bro-N	69	234	34	57	8	1	0	28	10		.244	.286	.286	55	-13	-15	26	21			.952	2	2S/301	-1.0
1901	Bos-N	140	577	83	173	14	4	5	72	17		.300	.320	.364	90	-3	-10	80	25			**.954**	6	*23	0.1
1902	Bos-N	124	481	51	125	16	5	0	53	12		.260	.279	.314	82	-11	-12	53	23			.940	-17	*2S	-2.6
1903	Was-A	12	44	0	12	2	0	0	3	0		.273	.273	.318	75	-1	-1	4	0			.931	-4	2/S	-0.6
1904	StL-A	4	9	0	1	0	0	0	0	2		.111	.273	.111	25	-1	-1	0	0			1.000	-1	/2	-0.1
Total	11	922	3615	537	1096	130	35	17	497	174	35	.303	.340	.373	97	-8	-19	566	228			.948	31	2S/310	4.0

■ **LEE DeMONTREVILLE** DeMontreville, Leon b: 9/23/1879, St.Paul, Minn. d: 3/22/62, Pelham Manor, N.Y. BR/TR, 5'7", 140 lbs. Deb: 7/10/03 F

YEAR	TM/L	G	AB	R	H	2B	3B	HR	RBI	BB	SO	AVG	OBP	SLG	PRO+	BR	/A	RC	SB	CS	SBR	FA	FR	POS	TPR
1903	StL-N	26	70	8	17	3	1	0	7	8		.243	.338	.314	89	-1	-1	9	3			.901	-3	S/2O	-0.3

■ **RICK DEMPSEY** Dempsey, John Rikard b: 9/13/49, Fayetteville, Tenn. BR/TR, 6', 190 lbs. Deb: 9/23/69

YEAR	TM/L	G	AB	R	H	2B	3B	HR	RBI	BB	SO	AVG	OBP	SLG	PRO+	BR	/A	RC	SB	CS	SBR	FA	FR	POS	TPR
1969	Min-A	5	6	1	3	1	0	0	0	1	0	.500	.571	.667	240	1	1	2	0	0	0	.833	-1	/C	0.0
1970	Min-A	5	7	1	0	0	0	0	0	1	1	.000	.125	.000	-62	-2	-2	0	0	0	0	.923	0	/C	-0.2
1971	Min-A	6	13	2	4	1	0	0	0	1	1	.308	.357	.385	107	0	0	2	0	0	0	.944	2	/C	0.2
1972	Min-A	25	40	0	8	1	0	0	0	6	8	.200	.304	.225	56	-2	-2	3	0	0	0	.986	-1	C	-0.3
1973	NY-A	6	11	0	2	0	0	0	0	1	3	.182	.250	.182	24	-1	-1	0	0	0	0	.818	-2	/C	-0.3
1974	NY-A	43	109	12	26	3	0	2	12	8	7	.239	.291	.321	78	-3	-3	9	1	0	0	.978	4	C/OD	0.3
1975	NY-A	71	145	18	38	8	0	1	11	21	15	.262	.355	.338	100	0	1	18	0	0	0	.977	3	CD/O3	0.3
1976	NY-A	21	42	1	5	0	0	0	2	5	4	.119	.213	.119	-1	-5	-5	1	0	0	0	1.000	2	/CO	-0.3
	Bal-A	59	174	11	37	2	0	0	10	13	17	.213	.275	.224	50	-11	-10	11	1	1	-0	.987	5	C/O	-0.4
	Yr	80	216	12	42	2	0	0	12	18	21	.194	.263	.204	40	-16	-15	13	1	1	-0	.988	7	C/O	-0.7
1977	Bal-A	91	270	27	61	7	4	3	34	34	34	.226	.317	.315	78	-9	-7	27	2	3	-1	.977	-2	C	-0.8
1978	Bal-A	136	441	41	114	25	0	6	32	48	54	.259	.331	.356	99	-3	0	53	7	3	0	.985	-5	*C	-0.1
1979	*Bal-A	124	368	48	88	23	0	6	41	38	37	.239	.310	.351	81	-11	-10	39	0	1	-1	.990	19	*C	1.3
1980	Bal-A	119	362	51	95	26	3	9	40	36	45	.262	.334	.425	108	3	3	50	3	1	0	.987	9	*C/O1D	1.7
1981	Bal-A	92	251	24	54	10	1	6	15	32	36	.215	.306	.335	85	-5	-5	26	0	1	-1	**.998**	3	C/D	0.1
1982	Bal-A	125	344	35	88	15	1	5	36	46	37	.256	.344	.349	91	-3	-3	42	0	3	-2	.991	0	*C/D	0.0
1983	*Bal-A	128	347	33	80	16	2	4	32	40	54	.231	.315	.323	78	-11	-10	36	1	1	-0	**.997**	21	*C	1.5
1984	Bal-A	109	330	37	76	11	0	11	34	40	58	.230	.315	.364	89	-5	-4	37	1	2	-1	.992	-4	*C	-0.5
1985	Bal-A	132	362	54	92	19	0	12	52	50	87	.254	.346	.406	108	3	5	55	0	1	-1	.987	-11	*C	0.0
1986	Bal-A	122	327	42	68	15	1	13	29	45	78	.208	.309	.379	87	-6	-6	41	1	0	0	.990	5	*C	0.6
1987	Cle-A	60	141	16	25	10	0	1	9	23	29	.177	.297	.270	51	-10	-10	12	0	0	0	.984	1	C	-0.5
1988	*LA-N	77	167	25	42	13	0	7	30	25	44	.251	.349	.455	133	6	7	27	1	0	0	.989	5	C	1.7
1989	LA-N	79	151	16	27	7	0	4	16	30	37	.179	.319	.305	80	-3	-3	16	1	0	0	.984	3	C	0.3
1990	LA-N	62	128	13	25	5	0	2	15	23	29	.195	.318	.281	68	-5	-5	11	1	0	0	.992	0	C	-0.2
1991	Mil-A	61	147	15	34	5	0	4	21	23	20	.231	.335	.347	91	-2	-1	16	0	2	-1	.993	5	C/P1	0.5
1992	Bal-A	8	9	2	1	0	0	0	0	2	1	.111	.273	.111	11	-1	-1	0	0	0	0	1.000	-1	/C	-0.2
Total	24	1766	4692	525	1093	223	12	96	471	592	736	.233	.321	.347	88	-85	-70	537	20	19	-5	.988	60	*C/OD1P3	4.7

YEAR	TM/L	G	AB	R	H	2B	3B	HR	RBI	BB	SO	AVG	OBP	SLG	PRO+	BR	/A	RC	SB	CS	SBR	FA	FR	POS	TPR

■ TOD DENNEHEY Dennehey, Thomas Francis b: 5/12/1899, Philadelphia, Pa. d: 8/8/77, Philadelphia, Pa. BL/TL, 5'10", 180 lbs. Deb: 4/21/23

YEAR	TM/L	G	AB	R	H	2B	3B	HR	RBI	BB	SO	AVG	OBP	SLG	PRO+	BR	/A	RC	SB	CS	SBR	FA	FR	POS	TPR
1923	Phi-N	9	24	4	7	2	0	0	2	1	3	.292	.320	.375	74	-1	-1	3	0	0	0	1.000	-1	/O	-0.2

■ OTTO DENNING Denning, Otto George "Dutch" b: 12/28/12, Hays, Kan. d: 5/25/92, Chicago, Ill. BR/TR, 6', 180 lbs. Deb: 4/15/42

YEAR	TM/L	G	AB	R	H	2B	3B	HR	RBI	BB	SO	AVG	OBP	SLG	PRO+	BR	/A	RC	SB	CS	SBR	FA	FR	POS	TPR
1942	Cle-A	92	214	15	45	14	0	1	19	18	14	.210	.275	.290	62	-12	-10	18	0	0	0	**.992**	-2	C/O	-0.8
1943	Cle-A	37	129	8	31	6	0	0	13	5	1	.240	.269	.287	67	-6	-6	9	3	1	0	.966	-3	1	-1.1
Total	2	129	343	23	76	20	0	1	32	23	15	.222	.272	.289	64	-18	-16	27	3	1	0		-6	/C1O	-1.9

■ JERRY DENNY Denny, Jeremiah Dennis (b: Jeremiah Dennis Eldridge)
b: 3/16/1859, New York, N.Y. d: 8/16/27, Houston, Tex. BR/TR, 5'11.5", 180 lbs. Deb: 5/02/1881

YEAR	TM/L	G	AB	R	H	2B	3B	HR	RBI	BB	SO	AVG	OBP	SLG	PRO+	BR	/A	RC	SB	CS	SBR	FA	FR	POS	TPR
1881	Pro-N	85	320	38	77	16	2	1	24	5	44	.241	.252	.313	78	-9	-8	26				.840	6	*3	-0.1
1882	Pro-N	84	329	54	81	10	9	2	42	4	46	.246	.255	.350	92	-3	-3	30				.861	13	*3	1.0
1883	Pro-N	98	393	73	108	26	8	8	55	9	48	.275	.291	.443	116	8	7	52				**.876**	10	*3	1.4
1884	*Pro-N	110	439	57	109	22	9	6	59	14	58	.248	.272	.380	105	1	2	46				.874	-2	*3/12C	0.0
1885	Pro-N	83	318	40	71	14	4	3	24	12	53	.223	.252	.321	88	-6	-4	26				.869	-0	*3	-0.2
1886	StL-N	119	475	58	122	24	6	9	62	14	68	.257	.278	.389	108	-1	4	57	16			.895	23	*3/S	2.6
1887	Ind-N	122	510	86	165	34	12	11	97	13	22	.324	.344	.502	139	21	24	101	29			.889	23	*3/SO2	4.0
1888	Ind-N	126	524	92	137	27	7	12	63	9	79	.261	.277	.408	116	9	8	70	32			.894	25	*3S/2OP	3.3
1889	Ind-N	133	578	96	163	24	0	18	112	27	63	.282	.314	.417	103	1	-1	85	22			**.913**	12	*3/2S	1.4
1890	NY-N	114	437	50	93	18	7	3	42	28	62	.213	.270	.307	69	-18	-18	40	11			.889	5	*3/S2	-0.7
1891	NY-N	4	16	0	4	1	0	0	1	0	3	.250	.250	.313	68	-1	-1	2	2			.700	-3	/3	-0.3
	Cle-N	36	138	17	31	5	0	0	21	12	23	.225	.291	.261	60	-6	-7	12	3			.884	-3	3/O	-0.8
	Phi-N	19	73	5	21	1	1	0	11	4	6	.288	.325	.329	90	-1	-1	8	1			.977	-1	1/3	-0.2
	Yr	59	227	22	56	7	1	0	33	16	32	.247	.299	.286	70	-8	-9	22	6			.876	-8	31/O	-1.3
1893	Lou-N	44	175	22	43	5	4	1	22	9	15	.246	.283	.337	71	-9	-7	18	4			.920	1	S/3	-0.4
1894	Lou-N	60	221	26	61	11	7	0	32	13	12	.276	.325	.389	78	-10	-7	33	10			.874	3	3	-0.3
Total	13	1237	4946	714	1286	238	76	74	667	173	602	.260	.287	.384	100	-24	-13	606	130			.882	110	*3/S12OPC	10.7

■ DREW DENSON Denson, Andrew b: 11/16/65, Cincinnati, Ohio BB/TR, 6'5", 210 lbs. Deb: 9/13/89

YEAR	TM/L	G	AB	R	H	2B	3B	HR	RBI	BB	SO	AVG	OBP	SLG	PRO+	BR	/A	RC	SB	CS	SBR	FA	FR	POS	TPR
1989	Atl-N	12	36	1	9	1	0	0	5	3	9	.250	.308	.278	67	-1	-2	3	1	0	0	.988	2	1	0.0

■ BUCKY DENT Dent, Russell Earl (b: Russell Earl O'Dey) b: 11/25/51, Savannah, Ga. BR/TR, 5'11", 181 lbs. Deb: 6/01/73 MC

YEAR	TM/L	G	AB	R	H	2B	3B	HR	RBI	BB	SO	AVG	OBP	SLG	PRO+	BR	/A	RC	SB	CS	SBR	FA	FR	POS	TPR
1973	Chi-A	40	117	17	29	2	0	0	10	10	18	.248	.313	.265	62	-5	-6	10	2	3	-1	.963	5	S/23	0.3
1974	Chi-A	154	496	55	136	15	3	5	45	28	48	.274	.317	.347	89	-6	-8	54	3	4	-2	.972	9	*S	2.0
1975	Chi-A★	157	602	52	159	29	4	3	58	36	48	.264	.306	.341	81	-15	-16	60	2	4	-2	**.981**	27	*S	2.7
1976	Chi-A	158	562	44	138	18	4	2	52	43	45	.246	.301	.302	77	-16	-16	52	3	5	-2	.976	-6	*S	-0.5
1977	*NY-A	158	477	54	118	18	4	8	49	39	28	.247	.306	.352	80	-14	-13	52	1	1	-0	.974	-11	*S	-0.8
1978	*NY-A	123	379	40	92	11	1	5	40	23	24	.243	.290	.317	72	-15	-14	34	3	1	0	.981	-8	*S	-0.7
1979	NY-A	141	431	47	99	14	2	2	32	37	30	.230	.292	.285	58	-26	-25	39	0	0	0	.977	32	*S	2.2
1980	*NY-A★	141	489	57	128	26	2	5	52	48	37	.262	.330	.354	89	-8	-7	59	0	3	-2	**.982**	13	*S	2.1
1981	NY-A★	73	227	20	54	11	0	7	27	19	17	.238	.302	.379	97	-2	-1	27	0	1	-1	.970	-2	S	0.4
1982	NY-A	59	160	11	27	1	1	0	9	8	11	.169	.208	.188	10	-20	-19	6	0	0	0	.962	17	S	0.2
	Tex-A	46	146	16	32	9	0	1	14	13	10	.219	.283	.301	64	-8	-7	13	0	0	0	.980	-2	S	-0.5
	Yr	105	306	27	59	10	1	1	23	21	21	.193	.245	.242	35	-27	-26	18	0	0	0	.970	15	*S	-0.3
1983	Tex-A	131	417	36	99	15	2	2	34	23	31	.237	.279	.297	60	-23	-22	34	3	7	-3	**.979**	-8	*S/D	-2.2
1984	KC-A	11	9	2	3	0	0	0	1	1	2	.333	.400	.333	105	0	0	1	0	0	0	1.000	-1	/S3	0.0
Total	12	1392	4512	451	1114	169	23	40	423	328	349	.247	.300	.321	74	-157	-154	442	17	29	-12	.976	66	*S/32D	5.2

■ SAM DENTE Dente, Samuel Joseph "Blackie" b: 4/26/22, Harrison, N.J. BR/TR, 5'11", 175 lbs. Deb: 7/10/47

YEAR	TM/L	G	AB	R	H	2B	3B	HR	RBI	BB	SO	AVG	OBP	SLG	PRO+	BR	/A	RC	SB	CS	SBR	FA	FR	POS	TPR
1947	Bos-A	46	168	14	39	4	2	0	11	19	15	.232	.310	.280	60	-8	-9	15	0	1	-1	.939	-3	3	-1.4
1948	StL-A	98	267	26	72	11	2	0	22	22	8	.270	.328	.326	72	-10	-11	29	1	3	-2	.958	-2	S/3	-1.1
1949	Was-A	153	590	48	161	24	4	1	53	31	24	.273	.309	.332	71	-27	-26	58	4	4	-1	.957	-9	*S	-2.5
1950	Was-A	155	603	56	144	20	5	2	59	39	19	.239	.286	.299	52	-47	-42	49	1	1	-0	.952	1	*S2	-2.9
1951	Was-A	88	273	21	65	8	1	0	29	25	10	.238	.302	.275	58	-16	-16	22	3	0	1	.962	3	S2/3	-0.7
1952	Chi-A	62	145	12	32	0	1	0	11	5	8	.221	.257	.234	37	-12	-12	8	0	0	0	.942	2	S3/2O1	-1.0
1953	Chi-A	2	0	0	0	0	0	0	0	0	0	—	—	—	—	0	0	0	0	0	0	.000	0	/S	0.0
1954	*Cle-A	68	169	18	45	7	1	1	19	14	4	.266	.322	.337	79	-4	-5	18	0	0	0	.971	-3	S/2	-0.4
1955	Cle-A	73	105	10	27	4	0	0	10	12	8	.257	.333	.295	68	-4	-5	11	0	0	0	.976	7	S3/2	0.5
Total	9	745	2320	205	585	78	16	4	214	167	96	.252	.303	.305	62	-129	-126	211	9	9	-3	.958	-5	S/32O1	-9.5

■ MIKE DePANGHER DePangher, Michael Anthony b: 9/11/1858, Marysville, Cal. d: 7/7/15, San Francisco, Cal 5'8", 190 lbs. Deb: 8/01/1884

YEAR	TM/L	G	AB	R	H	2B	3B	HR	RBI	BB	SO	AVG	OBP	SLG	PRO+	BR	/A	RC	SB	CS	SBR	FA	FR	POS	TPR
1884	Phi-N	4	10	0	2	0	0	0	0	1	3	.200	.273	.200	54	-1	-0	1				.920	1	/C	0.0

■ TONY DePHILLIPS DePhillips, Anthony Andrew b: 9/20/12, New York, N.Y. BR/TR, 6'2", 185 lbs. Deb: 4/25/43

YEAR	TM/L	G	AB	R	H	2B	3B	HR	RBI	BB	SO	AVG	OBP	SLG	PRO+	BR	/A	RC	SB	CS	SBR	FA	FR	POS	TPR
1943	Cin-N	35	20	0	2	1	0	0	2	1	5	.100	.143	.150	-16	-3	-3	1	0			.981	5	C	0.3

■ GENE DERBY Derby, Eugene A. b: 2/1860, New Hampshire d: 10/12/28, Buffalo, N.Y. Deb: 9/03/1885

YEAR	TM/L	G	AB	R	H	2B	3B	HR	RBI	BB	SO	AVG	OBP	SLG	PRO+	BR	/A	RC	SB	CS	SBR	FA	FR	POS	TPR
1885	Bal-a	10	31	4	4	0	0	0		1		.129	.182	.129	1	-3	-3	1				.952	1	/CO	-0.2

■ BOB DERNIER Dernier, Robert Eugene b: 1/5/57, Kansas City, Mo. BR/TR, 6', 165 lbs. Deb: 9/07/80

YEAR	TM/L	G	AB	R	H	2B	3B	HR	RBI	BB	SO	AVG	OBP	SLG	PRO+	BR	/A	RC	SB	CS	SBR	FA	FR	POS	TPR
1980	Phi-N	10	7	5	4	0	0	0	1	1	0	.571	.625	.571	224	1	1	4	3	0	1	1.000	2	/O	0.4
1981	Phi-N	10	4	0	3	0	0	0	0	0	0	.750	.750	.750	313	1	1	2	2	1	0	1.000	1	/O	0.2
1982	Phi-N	122	370	56	92	10	2	4	21	36	69	.249	.317	.319	77	-10	-11	41	42	12	5	.981	6	*O	-0.2
1983	*Phi-N	122	221	41	51	10	0	1	15	18	21	.231	.289	.290	61	-12	-11	22	35	7	6	.988	11	*O	0.4
1984	*Chi-N	143	536	94	149	26	5	3	32	63	60	.278	.356	.362	94	3	-3	75	45	17	3	.986	5	*O	0.1
1985	Chi-N	121	469	63	119	20	3	1	21	40	44	.254	.316	.316	70	-14	-20	51	31	8	5	.972	9	*O	-1.0
1986	Chi-N	108	324	32	73	14	1	4	18	22	41	.225	.275	.312	57	-17	-20	30	27	2	7	.987	1	*O	-1.6
1987	Chi-N	93	199	38	63	4	4	8	21	19	19	.317	.379	.497	125	8	7	37	16	7	1	.989	-12	O	-0.5
1988	Phi-N	68	166	19	48	3	1	1	10	9	19	.289	.330	.337	90	-2	-2	19	13	6	0	.980	-4	O	-0.8
1989	Phi-N	107	187	26	32	5	0	1	13	14	28	.171	.229	.214	27	-18	-18	10	4	3	-1	.970	-13	O	-3.5
Total	10	904	2483	374	634	92	16	23	152	222	301	.255	.318	.333	77	-58	-75	290	218	63	28	.982	6	O	-6.5

■ CLAUD DERRICK Derrick, Claud Lester "Deek" b: 6/11/1886, Burton, Ga. d: 7/15/74, Clayton, Ga. BR/TR, 6', 175 lbs. Deb: 9/08/10

YEAR	TM/L	G	AB	R	H	2B	3B	HR	RBI	BB	SO	AVG	OBP	SLG	PRO+	BR	/A	RC	SB	CS	SBR	FA	FR	POS	TPR
1910	Phi-A	2	1	0	0	0	0	0	0	0		.000	.000	.000	-99	-0	-0	0	0			.500	-0	/S	-0.1
1911	Phi-A	36	100	14	23	1	2	0	5	7		.230	.294	.280	61	-5	-5	11	7			.960	1	2/S13	-0.4
1912	Phi-A	21	58	7	14	0	1	0	7	5		.241	.313	.276	71	-2	-2	6	1			.884	1	S	0.0
1913	NY-A	23	65	7	19	1	0	1	7	5	8	.292	.352	.354	106	1	1	8	2			.874	0	S/32	0.2
1914	Cin-N	3	6	2	2	1	0	0	1	0	0	.333	.333	.500	142	0	0	1	1			.889	0	/S	0.1
	Chi-N	28	96	5	21	3	1	0	13	5	13	.219	.257	.271	57	-5	-5	7	2			.895	3	/S	-0.1
	Yr	31	102	7	23	4	1	0	14	5	13	.225	.262	.284	62	-5	-5	8	3			.894	3	S	0.0
Total	5	113	326	35	79	6	4	1	33	22	21	.242	.298	.294	72	-12	-12	33	13			.892	4	/S231	-0.3

■ MIKE DERRICK Derrick, James Michael b: 9/19/43, Columbia, S.C. BL/TR, 6', 190 lbs. Deb: 4/09/70

YEAR	TM/L	G	AB	R	H	2B	3B	HR	RBI	BB	SO	AVG	OBP	SLG	PRO+	BR	/A	RC	SB	CS	SBR	FA	FR	POS	TPR
1970	Bos-A	24	33	3	7	1	0	0	5	0	11	.212	.212	.242	23	-3	-4	1	0	1	-1	1.000	0	/O1	-0.4

■ RUSS DERRY Derry, Alva Russell b: 10/7/16, Princeton, Mo. BL/TR, 6'1", 180 lbs. Deb: 7/04/44

YEAR	TM/L	G	AB	R	H	2B	3B	HR	RBI	BB	SO	AVG	OBP	SLG	PRO+	BR	/A	RC	SB	CS	SBR	FA	FR	POS	TPR
1944	NY-A	38	114	14	29	3	0	4	14	20	19	.254	.366	.386	111	3	2	19	1	0	0	.949	-1	O	0.0
1945	NY-A	78	253	37	57	6	2	13	45	31	49	.225	.312	.419	107	3	1	34	1	0	0	.978	0	O	-0.2
1946	Phi-A	69	184	17	38	8	5	0	14	27	54	.207	.311	.304	73	-6	-6	20	0	0	0	.985	4	O	-0.5
1949	StL-N	2	2	0	0	0	0	0	0	0	2	.000	.000	.000	-96	-1	-1	0	0			.000	0	H	-0.1
Total	4	187	553	68	124	17	7	17	73	78	124	.224	.322	.373	95	-2	-3	72	2	0		.976	3	O	-0.8

■ JOE DeSA DeSa, Joseph b: 7/27/59, Honolulu, Hawaii d: 12/20/86, San Juan, P.R. BL/TL, 5'11", 170 lbs. Deb: 9/06/80

YEAR	TM/L	G	AB	R	H	2B	3B	HR	RBI	BB	SO	AVG	OBP	SLG	PRO+	BR	/A	RC	SB	CS	SBR	FA	FR	POS	TPR
1980	StL-N	7	11	0	3	0	0	0	0	0	2	.273	.273	.273	51	-1	-1	1	0	0	0	1.000	-0	/1O	-0.1
1985	Chi-A	28	44	5	8	2	0	2	7	3	6	.182	.234	.364	58	-3	-3	4	0	0	0	1.000	1	/1OD	-0.2
Total	2	35	55	5	11	2	0	2	7	3	8	.200	.241	.345	57	-3	-3	4	0	0	0	1.000	0	/1DO	-0.3

■ GENE DESAUTELS Desautels, Eugene Abraham "Red" b: 6/13/07, Worcester, Mass. BR/TR, 5'11", 170 lbs. Deb: 6/22/30

YEAR	TM/L	G	AB	R	H	2B	3B	HR	RBI	BB	SO	AVG	OBP	SLG	PRO+	BR	/A	RC	SB	CS	SBR	FA	FR	POS	TPR
1930	Det-A	42	126	13	24	4	2	0	9	7	9	.190	.239	.254	25	-15	-15	8	2	0	1	.996	9	C	-0.2
1931	Det-A	3	11	1	1	0	0	0	1	0	1	.091	.091	.091	-50	-2	-2	0	0	0	0	1.000	-1	/C	-0.3
1932	Det-A	28	72	8	17	2	0	0	2	13	11	.236	.360	.264	62	-3	-4	8	0	0	0	.984	4	C	0.1
1933	Det-A	30	42	5	6	1	0	0	4	4	6	.143	.234	.167	8	-6	-6	2	0	0	0	.976	2	C	-0.3
1937	Bos-A	96	305	33	74	10	3	0	27	36	26	.243	.325	.295	55	-19	-21	31	1	2	-1	**.993**	4	C	-1.2
1938	Bos-A	108	333	47	97	16	2	2	48	57	31	.291	.396	.369	89	-1	-4	53	1	1	-0	.985	6	*C	0.6
1939	Bos-A	76	226	26	55	14	0	0	21	33	13	.243	.340	.305	64	-11	-12	27	3	1	0	.994	10	C	0.2
1940	Bos-A	71	222	19	50	7	1	0	17	32	13	.225	.328	.266	54	-13	-15	21	0	1	-1	.992	-3	C	-1.3
1941	Cle-A	66	189	20	38	5	1	1	17	14	12	.201	.260	.254	38	-17	-16	14	1	0	0	.997	6	C	-0.5
1942	Cle-A	62	162	14	40	5	0	0	9	12	13	.247	.303	.278	68	-8	-6	15	1	0	0	.975	-8	C	-1.1
1943	Cle-A	68	185	14	38	6	1	0	19	11	16	.205	.250	.249	49	-13	-12	12	2	0	1	.982	2	C	-0.6
1945	Cle-A	10	9	1	1	0	0	0	0	1	1	.111	.200	.111	-9	-1	-1	0	0	0	0	1.000	0	C	-0.1
1946	Phi-A	52	130	10	28	3	1	0	13	12	16	.215	.282	.254	51	-9	-8	10	1	1	-0	.989	2	C	-0.5
Total	13	712	2012	211	469	73	11	3	187	232	168	.233	.315	.285	58	-118	-122	201	12	6	0	.989	31	C	-5.2

■ DELINO DeSHIELDS DeShields, Delino Lamont b: 1/15/69, Seaford, Del. BL/TR, 6'1", 170 lbs. Deb: 4/09/90

YEAR	TM/L	G	AB	R	H	2B	3B	HR	RBI	BB	SO	AVG	OBP	SLG	PRO+	BR	/A	RC	SB	CS	SBR	FA	FR	POS	TPR
1990	Mon-N	129	499	69	144	28	6	4	45	66	96	.289	.376	.393	116	10	13	75	42	22	-1	.981	-8	*2	0.7
1991	Mon-N	151	563	83	134	15	4	10	51	95	151	.238	.350	.332	94	-2	-1	74	56	23	3	.962	-22	*2	-1.7
1992	Mon-N	135	530	82	155	19	8	7	56	54	108	.292	.361	.398	115	11	12	80	46	15	5	.976	-22	*2	-0.3
Total	3	415	1592	234	433	62	18	21	152	215	355	.272	.362	.373	108	19	23	229	144	60	7	.972	-52	2	-1.3

■ ORESTES DESTRADE Destrade, Orestes (Cucuas) b: 5/8/62, Santiago, Cuba BB/TR, 6'4", 210 lbs. Deb: 9/11/87

YEAR	TM/L	G	AB	R	H	2B	3B	HR	RBI	BB	SO	AVG	OBP	SLG	PRO+	BR	/A	RC	SB	CS	SBR	FA	FR	POS	TPR
1987	NY-A	9	19	5	5	0	0	0	1	5	5	.263	.417	.263	87	-0	-0	2	0	0	0	1.000	-0	/1D	0.0
1988	Pit-N	36	47	2	7	1	0	1	3	5	17	.149	.231	.234	34	-4	-4	3	0	0	0	1.000	-1	/1	-0.6
Total	2	45	66	7	12	1	0	1	4	10	22	.182	.289	.242	51	-4	-4	5	0	0	0	1.000	-1	/1D	-0.6

■ BOB DETHERAGE Detherage, Robert Wayne b: 9/20/54, Springfield, Mo. BR/TR, 6', 180 lbs. Deb: 4/11/80

YEAR	TM/L	G	AB	R	H	2B	3B	HR	RBI	BB	SO	AVG	OBP	SLG	PRO+	BR	/A	RC	SB	CS	SBR	FA	FR	POS	TPR
1980	KC-A	20	26	2	8	2	0	1	7	1	4	.308	.333	.500	124	1	1	4	1	1	-0	1.000	-7	O	-0.7

■ GEORGE DETORE Detore, George Francis b: 11/11/06, Utica, N.Y. BR/TR, 5'8", 170 lbs. Deb: 9/14/30

YEAR	TM/L	G	AB	R	H	2B	3B	HR	RBI	BB	SO	AVG	OBP	SLG	PRO+	BR	/A	RC	SB	CS	SBR	FA	FR	POS	TPR
1930	Cle-A	3	12	0	2	1	0	0	2	0	2	.167	.167	.250	4	-2	-2	1	0	0	0	.750	-2	/3	-0.3
1931	Cle-A	30	56	3	15	6	0	0	7	8	2	.268	.359	.375	88	-0	-1	7	0	2	-1	.958	4	3S/2	0.3
Total	2	33	68	3	17	7	0	0	9	8	4	.250	.329	.353	74	-2	-3	8	0	2	-1	.929	2	/3S2	0.0

■ DUCKY DETWEILER Detweiler, Robert Sterling b: 2/15/19, Trumbauersville, Pa. BR/TR, 5'11", 178 lbs. Deb: 9/12/42

YEAR	TM/L	G	AB	R	H	2B	3B	HR	RBI	BB	SO	AVG	OBP	SLG	PRO+	BR	/A	RC	SB	CS	SBR	FA	FR	POS	TPR
1942	Bos-N	12	44	3	14	2	1	0	5	2	7	.318	.348	.409	123	1	1	6	0			.929	-4	3	-0.3
1946	Bos-N	1	1	0	0	0	0	0	0	0	0	.000	.000	.000	-99	-0	-0	0	0			.000	0	H	0.0
Total	2	13	45	3	14	2	1	0	5	2	7	.311	.340	.400	118	1	1	6	0				-4	/3	-0.3

■ MIKE DEVEREAUX Devereaux, Michael b: 4/10/63, Casper, Wyo. BR/TR, 6' ", 195 lbs. Deb: 9/02/87

YEAR	TM/L	G	AB	R	H	2B	3B	HR	RBI	BB	SO	AVG	OBP	SLG	PRO+	BR	/A	RC	SB	CS	SBR	FA	FR	POS	TPR
1987	LA-N	19	54	7	12	3	0	0	4	3	10	.222	.263	.278	45	-4	-4	4	3	1	0	1.000	-2	O	-0.6
1988	LA-N	30	43	4	5	1	0	0	2	2	10	.116	.156	.140	-15	-6	-6	1	0	1	-1	1.000	-5	O	-1.3
1989	Bal-A	122	391	55	104	14	3	8	46	36	60	.266	.331	.379	103	-0	1	49	22	11	0	.983	-4	*O/D	-0.5
1990	Bal-A	108	367	48	88	18	1	12	49	28	48	.240	.294	.392	93	-6	-4	38	13	12	-3	.983	6	*O/D	-0.4
1991	Bal-A	149	608	82	158	27	10	19	59	47	115	.260	.315	.431	109	2	5	80	16	9	-1	.993	12	*O	1.2
1992	Bal-A	156	653	76	180	29	11	24	107	44	94	.276	.325	.464	119	14	14	94	10	8	-2	.989	5	*O	1.4
Total	6	584	2116	272	547	92	25	63	267	160	337	.259	.313	.415	104	-1	6	266	64	42	-6	.988	12	O/D	-0.2

■ JIM DEVINE Devine, Walter James b: 10/5/1858, Brooklyn, N.Y. d: 1/11/05, Syracuse, N.Y. TL , Deb: 5/08/1883

YEAR	TM/L	G	AB	R	H	2B	3B	HR	RBI	BB	SO	AVG	OBP	SLG	PRO+	BR	/A	RC	SB	CS	SBR	FA	FR	POS	TPR
1883	Bal-a	2	9	4	2	0	0	0		0		.222	.222	.222	42	-1	-1	0				.500	-1	/PO	0.0
1886	NY-N	1	3	0	0	0	0	0	0	0	1	.000	.000	.000	-99	-1	-1	0	0			.000	-0	/O	-0.1
Total	2	3	12	4	2	0	0	0	0	0	1	.167	.167	.167	6	-1	-1	0	0			—	-1	/OP	-0.1

■ MICKEY DEVINE Devine, William Patrick b: 5/9/1892, Albany, N.Y. d: 10/1/37, Albany, N.Y. BR/TR, 5'10", 165 lbs. Deb: 8/02/18

YEAR	TM/L	G	AB	R	H	2B	3B	HR	RBI	BB	SO	AVG	OBP	SLG	PRO+	BR	/A	RC	SB	CS	SBR	FA	FR	POS	TPR
1918	Phi-N	4	8	0	1	1	0	0	0	0	1	.125	.125	.250	13	-1	-1	0	0			.909	0	/C	-0.1
1920	Bos-A	8	12	1	2	0	0	0	0	1	2	.167	.231	.167	7	-2	-2	1	1	0	0	.955	1	/C	0.0
1925	NY-N	21	33	6	9	3	0	0	4	2	3	.273	.314	.364	76	-1	-1	4	0	0	0	.933	2	C/3	0.1
Total	3	33	53	7	12	4	0	0	4	3	6	.226	.268	.302	51	-4	-4	5	1	0		.936	2	/C3	0.0

■ BERNIE DeVIVEIROS DeViveiros, Bernard John b: 4/19/01, Oakland, Cal. BR/TR, 5'7", 160 lbs. Deb: 9/13/24

YEAR	TM/L	G	AB	R	H	2B	3B	HR	RBI	BB	SO	AVG	OBP	SLG	PRO+	BR	/A	RC	SB	CS	SBR	FA	FR	POS	TPR
1924	Chi-A	1	1	0	0	0	0	0	0	0	0	.000	.000	.000	-99	-0	-0	0	0	0	0	.333	-1	/S	-0.1
1927	Det-A	24	22	4	5	1	0	0	2	2	8	.227	.292	.273	46	-2	-2	2	1	0	0	.913	0	S/3	-0.1
Total	2	25	23	4	5	1	0	0	2	2	8	.217	.280	.261	40	-2	-2	2	1	0	0	.846	-1	/S3	-0.2

■ ART DEVLIN Devlin, Arthur McArthur b: 10/16/1879, Washington, D.C. d: 9/18/48, Jersey City, N.J. BR/TR, 6', 175 lbs. Deb: 4/14/04 C

YEAR	TM/L	G	AB	R	H	2B	3B	HR	RBI	BB	SO	AVG	OBP	SLG	PRO+	BR	/A	RC	SB	CS	SBR	FA	FR	POS	TPR
1904	NY-N	130	474	81	133	16	8	1	66	62		.281	.369	.354	119	16	13	79	33			.907	7	*3	2.6
1905	*NY-N	153	525	74	129	14	7	2	61	66		.246	.342	.310	93	-0	-2	79	**59**			.932	5	*3	0.9
1906	NY-N	148	498	76	149	23	8	2	65	74		.299	.394	.390	142	29	27	102	54			.944	**28**	*3	6.5
1907	NY-N	143	491	61	136	16	2	1	54	63		.277	.373	.324	115	14	12	80	38			.940	0	*3/S	1.9
1908	NY-N	157	534	59	135	18	4	2	45	62		.253	.345	.313	105	9	6	65	19			**.947**	13	*3	2.8
1909	NY-N	143	491	61	130	19	8	0	56	65		.265	.362	.336	115	12	11	70	26			.934	16	*3	3.5
1910	NY-N	147	493	71	128	17	5	2	67	62	32	.260	.353	.327	98	1	1	69	28			.933	5	*3	1.0
1911	NY-N	95	260	42	71	16	2	0	25	42	19	.273	.386	.350	103	4	3	40	9			.944	2	3/12S	0.6
1912	Bos-N	124	436	59	126	18	8	0	54	51	37	.289	.367	.367	99	2	1	62	11			.992	-1	1S3/O	0.1
1913	Bos-N	73	210	19	48	7	5	0	12	29	17	.229	.328	.310	81	-4	-5	23	8			.973	8	3	0.4
Total	10	1313	4412	603	1185	164	57	10	505	576	105	.269	.363	.338	109	83	69	668	285			.938	83	*3/1S20	20.3

■ JIM DEVLIN Devlin, James Alexander b: 1849, Philadelphia, Pa. d: 10/10/1883, Philadelphia, Pa. BR/TR, 5'11", 175 lbs. Deb: 4/21/1873

YEAR	TM/L	G	AB	R	H	2B	3B	HR	RBI	BB	SO	AVG	OBP	SLG	PRO+	BR	/A	RC	SB	CS	SBR	FA	FR	POS	TPR
1873	Phi-n	23	99	18	24	4	4	0	9	2	4	.242	.257	.364	78	-2	-3	9						1/3SO	-0.2
1874	Chi-n	45	203	26	59	5	1	0		2		.291	.298	.325	97	-0	-1	20						1O/3	0.0
1875	Chi-n	69	315	60	92	18	5	0		5		.292	.303	.381	134	11	10	37						1P/O	0.8
1876	Lou-N	68	298	38	94	14	1	0	28	1	11	.315	.318	.369	109	8	0	36				.941	2	*P/1	0.0

YEAR	TM/L	G	AB	R	H	2B	3B	HR	RBI	BB	SO	AVG	OBP	SLG	PRO+	BR	/A	RC	SB	CS	SBR	FA	FR	POS	TPR
1877	Lou-N	61	268	38	72	6	3	1	27	7	27	.269	.287	.325	78	-2	-9	26				.933	2	*P	0.0
Total	3 n	137	617	104	175	27	10	0	9	9	4	.284	.294	.360	111	8	6	67						/1PO3S	0.6
Total	2	129	566	76	166	20	4	1	55	8	38	.293	.303	.348	94	6	-9	61				.937	4	P/1	0.0

■ **JIM DEVLIN** Devlin, James Raymond b: 8/25/22, Plains, Pa. BL/TR, 5'11.5", 165 lbs. Deb: 4/27/44

YEAR	TM/L	G	AB	R	H	2B	3B	HR	RBI	BB	SO	AVG	OBP	SLG	PRO+	BR	/A	RC	SB	CS	SBR	FA	FR	POS	TPR
1944	Cle-A	1	1	0	0	0	0	0	0	0	0	.000	.000	.000	-99	-0	-0	0	0	0	0	1.000	0	/C	0.0

■ **REX DeVOGT** DeVogt, Rex Eugene b: 1/4/1888, Clare, Mich. d: 11/9/35, Alma, Mich. BR/TR, 5'9", 170 lbs. Deb: 4/17/13

YEAR	TM/L	G	AB	R	H	2B	3B	HR	RBI	BB	SO	AVG	OBP	SLG	PRO+	BR	/A	RC	SB	CS	SBR	FA	FR	POS	TPR
1913	Bos-N	3	6	0	0	0	0	0	0	0	3	.000	.000	.000	-98	-2	-2	0	0			.941	1	/C	0.0

■ **JOSH DEVORE** Devore, Joshua D. b: 11/13/1887, Murray City, Ohio d: 10/6/54, Chillicothe, Ohio BL/TL, 5'6", 160 lbs. Deb: 9/25/08

YEAR	TM/L	G	AB	R	H	2B	3B	HR	RBI	BB	SO	AVG	OBP	SLG	PRO+	BR	/A	RC	SB	CS	SBR	FA	FR	POS	TPR
1908	NY-N	5	6	1	1	0	0	0	2	1		.167	.286	.167	43	-0	-0	1	1			1.000	-1	/O	-0.1
1909	NY-N	22	28	6	4	1	0	0	1	2		.143	.250	.179	33	-2	-2	2	3			.824	-4	O	-0.7
1910	NY-N	133	490	92	149	11	10	2	27	46	67	.304	.371	.380	119	12	12	84	43			.929	-12	*O	-0.6
1911	*NY-N	149	565	96	158	19	10	3	50	81	69	.280	.376	.365	104	8	6	99	61			.934	1	*O	-0.1
1912	*NY-N	106	327	66	90	14	6	2	37	51	43	.275	.381	.373	104	5	3	56	27			.918	-8	O	-0.9
1913	NY-N	16	21	4	4	0	1	0	1	3	4	.190	.320	.286	73	-1	-1	3	6			1.000	-2	/O	-0.3
	Cin-N	66	217	30	58	6	4	3	14	12	21	.267	.309	.373	95	-2	-2	29	17			.920	-3	O	-0.8
	Phi-N	23	39	9	11	1	0	0	5	4	7	.282	.364	.308	89	-0	-0	4	0			.889	-3	O	-0.4
	Yr	105	277	43	73	7	5	3	20	19	32	.264	.318	.357	92	-3	-3	37	23			.919	-9	O	-1.5
1914	Phi-N	30	53	5	16	2	0	0	7	4	5	.302	.351	.340	99	0	-0	6	0			.947	2	/O	0.2
	*Bos-N	51	128	22	29	4	0	1	5	18	14	.227	.327	.281	82	-2	-2	12	2			.915	-8	O	-1.3
	Yr	81	181	27	45	6	0	1	12	22	19	.249	.333	.298	87	-2	-2	19	2			.923	-6	O	-1.1
Total	7	601	1874	331	520	58	31	11	149	222	230	.277	.361	.359	103	18	13	297	160			.925	-38	O	-5.0

■ **AL DeVORMER** DeVormer, Albert E. b: 8/19/1891, Grand Rapids, Mich d: 8/29/66, Grand Rapids, Mich BR/TR, 6'0.5", 175 lbs. Deb: 8/04/18

YEAR	TM/L	G	AB	R	H	2B	3B	HR	RBI	BB	SO	AVG	OBP	SLG	PRO+	BR	/A	RC	SB	CS	SBR	FA	FR	POS	TPR
1918	Chi-A	8	19	2	5	2	0	0	0	0	4	.263	.263	.368	90	-0	-0	2	1			1.000	-2	/CO	-0.2
1921	*NY-A	22	49	6	17	4	0	0	7	2	4	.347	.373	.429	102	0	0	8	2	0	1	.950	-1	C	0.1
1922	NY-A	24	59	8	12	4	1	0	11	1	6	.203	.217	.305	34	-6	-6	4	0	0	0	.968	-1	C/1	-0.6
1923	Bos-A	74	209	20	54	7	3	0	18	6	21	.258	.282	.321	58	-13	-13	19	3	0	1	.979	0	C/1	-0.9
1927	NY-N	68	141	14	35	3	1	2	21	11	11	.248	.312	.326	71	-6	-6	14	1			.953	-4	C/1	-0.8
Total	5	196	477	50	123	20	5	2	57	20	46	.258	.292	.333	65	-25	-25	48	7	0		.967	-7	C/1O	-2.4

■ **WALT DEVOY** Devoy, Walter Joseph b: 3/14/1886, St.Louis, Mo. d: 12/17/53, St.Louis, Mo. 5'11", 165 lbs. Deb: 9/13/09

YEAR	TM/L	G	AB	R	H	2B	3B	HR	RBI	BB	SO	AVG	OBP	SLG	PRO+	BR	/A	RC	SB	CS	SBR	FA	FR	POS	TPR
1909	StL-A	19	69	7	17	3	1	0	8	3		.246	.278	.319	95	-1	-1	7	4			.944	-2	O/1	-0.3

■ **JEFF DeWILLIS** DeWillis, Jeffrey Allen b: 4/13/65, Houston, Tex. BR/TR, 6'2", 170 lbs. Deb: 4/19/87

YEAR	TM/L	G	AB	R	H	2B	3B	HR	RBI	BB	SO	AVG	OBP	SLG	PRO+	BR	/A	RC	SB	CS	SBR	FA	FR	POS	TPR
1987	Tor-A	13	25	2	3	1	0	1	2	2	12	.120	.185	.280	21	-3	-3	1	0	0	0	.964	2	C	-0.1

■ **CHARLIE DEXTER** Dexter, Charles Dana b: 6/15/1876, Evansville, Ind. d: 6/9/34, Cedar Rapids, Iowa BR/TR, 5'7", 155 lbs. Deb: 4/17/1896

YEAR	TM/L	G	AB	R	H	2B	3B	HR	RBI	BB	SO	AVG	OBP	SLG	PRO+	BR	/A	RC	SB	CS	SBR	FA	FR	POS	TPR
1896	Lou-N	107	402	65	112	18	7	3	37	17	34	.279	.318	.381	89	-9	-7	57	21			.903	-3	CO	-0.7
1897	Lou-N	76	257	43	72	12	5	2	46	21		.280	.342	.389	96	-3	-2	39	12			.907	-5	OC3/S	-0.5
1898	Lou-N	112	421	76	132	13	5	1	66	26		.314	.363	.375	114	6	7	77	44			.958	-1	O/2C	0.1
1899	Lou-N	80	295	47	76	7	1	1	33	21		.258	.316	.298	69	-12	-12	38	21			.942	3	O/S	-1.3
1900	Chi-N	40	125	7	25	5	0	2	20	1		.200	.213	.288	39	-11	-10	9	2			.943	7	CO/2	-0.2
1901	Chi-N	116	460	46	123	9	5	1	66	16		.267	.302	.315	82	-12	-10	52	22			.982	3	13O2/C	-0.8
1902	Chi-N	69	266	30	60	12	0	2	26	19		.226	.290	.293	82	-6	-5	29	13			.853	-13	31O	-2.1
	Bos-N	48	183	33	47	3	0	1	18	16		.257	.323	.290	88	-2	-2	24	16			.901	-3	S2/O3	-0.4
	Yr	117	449	63	107	15	0	3	44	35		.238	.303	.292	85	-8	-7	52	29			.854	-16	31S2O	-2.5
1903	Bos-N	123	457	82	102	15	1	3	34	61		.223	.323	.280	76	-14	-12	55	32			.941	-10	*O/SC	-2.6
Total	8	771	2866	429	749	94	24	16	346	198	34	.261	.318	.328	85	-64	-53	378	183			.942	-22	OC/312S	-8.5

■ **ALEX DIAZ** Diaz, Alexis b: 10/5/68, Brooklyn, N.Y. BB/TR, 5'11", 175 lbs. Deb: 7/25/92

YEAR	TM/L	G	AB	R	H	2B	3B	HR	RBI	BB	SO	AVG	OBP	SLG	PRO+	BR	/A	RC	SB	CS	SBR	FA	FR	POS	TPR
1992	Mil-A	22	9	5	1	0	0	0	1	0	0	.111	.111	.111	-38	-2	-2	-0	3	2	-0	1.000	-4	O/D	-0.7

■ **BO DIAZ** Diaz, Baudilio Jose (Seijas) b: 3/23/53, Cua, Venezuela d: 11/23/90, Caracas, Venez. BR/TR, 5'11", 190 lbs. Deb: 9/06/77

YEAR	TM/L	G	AB	R	H	2B	3B	HR	RBI	BB	SO	AVG	OBP	SLG	PRO+	BR	/A	RC	SB	CS	SBR	FA	FR	POS	TPR
1977	Bos-A	2	1	0	0	0	0	0	0	0	1	.000	.000	.000	-90	-0	-0	0	0	0	0	1.000	1	/C	0.0
1978	Cle-A	44	127	12	30	4	0	2	11	4	17	.236	.260	.315	61	-7	-7	10	0	0	0	.971	-1	C	-0.7
1979	Cle-A	15	32	0	5	2	0	0	1	2	6	.156	.206	.219	15	-4	-4	1	0	0	0	.958	4	C	0.0
1980	Cle-A	76	207	15	47	11	2	3	32	7	27	.227	.252	.343	61	-11	-12	14	1	0	0	.989	3	C	-0.6
1981	Cle-A★	63	182	25	57	19	0	7	38	13	23	.313	.362	.533	157	12	12	32	2	2	-1	.975	-3	C/D	1.1
1982	Phi-N	144	525	69	151	29	1	18	85	36	87	.288	.337	.450	116	11	10	72	3	6	-3	.989	-9	*C	0.4
1983	*Phi-N	136	471	49	111	17	0	15	64	38	57	.236	.295	.367	84	-12	-11	49	1	4	-2	.986	14	*C	0.7
1984	Phi-N	27	75	5	16	4	0	1	9	5	13	.213	.262	.307	58	-4	-4	5	0	0	0	.992	-0	C	-0.4
1985	Phi-N	26	76	9	16	5	1	2	16	6	7	.211	.268	.382	78	-2	-3	6	0	0	0	.972	2	C	0.0
	Cin-N	51	161	12	42	8	0	3	15	15	18	.261	.328	.366	89	-1	-2	19	0	0	0	.988	9	C	0.9
	Yr	77	237	21	58	13	1	5	31	21	25	.245	.309	.371	86	-4	-5	25	0	0	0	.983	11	C	0.9
1986	Cin-N	134	474	50	129	21	0	10	56	40	52	.272	.329	.380	91	-4	-6	59	1	1	-0	.984	-6	*C	-0.4
1987	Cin-N★	140	496	49	134	28	1	15	82	19	73	.270	.304	.421	86	-9	-11	59	1	0	0	.992	-6	*C	-0.8
1988	Cin-N	92	315	26	69	9	0	10	35	7	41	.219	.238	.343	63	-15	-17	20	0	2	-1	.990	-3	C	-1.6
1989	Cin-N	43	132	6	27	5	0	1	8	6	7	.205	.239	.265	43	-10	-10	7	0	2	-1	.984	-0	C	-1.0
Total	13	993	3274	327	834	162	5	87	452	198	429	.255	.300	.387	87	-56	-65	354	9	17	-8	.986	3	C/D	-2.4

■ **CARLOS DIAZ** Diaz, Carlos Francisco b: 12/24/64, Elizabeth, N.J. BR/TR, 6'3", 195 lbs. Deb: 5/08/90

YEAR	TM/L	G	AB	R	H	2B	3B	HR	RBI	BB	SO	AVG	OBP	SLG	PRO+	BR	/A	RC	SB	CS	SBR	FA	FR	POS	TPR
1990	Tor-A	9	3	1	1	0	0	0	0	0	2	.333	.333	.333	85	-0	-0	0	0	0	0	1.000	2	/C	0.2

■ **EDGAR DIAZ** Diaz, Edgar (Serrano) b: 2/8/64, Santurce, P.R. BR/TR, 6', 155 lbs. Deb: 9/16/86

YEAR	TM/L	G	AB	R	H	2B	3B	HR	RBI	BB	SO	AVG	OBP	SLG	PRO+	BR	/A	RC	SB	CS	SBR	FA	FR	POS	TPR
1986	Mil-A	5	13	0	3	0	0	0	0	1	3	.231	.286	.231	41	-1	-1	1	0	0	0	.875	-1	/S	-0.1
1990	Mil-A	86	218	27	59	2	2	0	14	21	32	.271	.338	.298	80	-5	-5	23	3	2	-0	.950	-2	S2/3D	-0.2
Total	2	91	231	27	62	2	2	0	14	22	35	.268	.335	.294	78	-6	-6	24	3	2	-0	.946	-2	/S23D	-0.3

■ **MARIO DIAZ** Diaz, Mario Rafael (Torres) b: 1/10/62, Humacao, P.R. BR/TR, 5'10", 160 lbs. Deb: 9/12/87

YEAR	TM/L	G	AB	R	H	2B	3B	HR	RBI	BB	SO	AVG	OBP	SLG	PRO+	BR	/A	RC	SB	CS	SBR	FA	FR	POS	TPR
1987	Sea-A	11	23	4	7	0	1	0	3	0	4	.304	.304	.391	79	-1	-1	3	0	0	0	.972	4	S	0.3
1988	Sea-A	28	72	6	22	5	0	0	9	3	5	.306	.333	.375	94	-0	-1	8	0	0	0	.985	-4	S/213	-0.3
1989	Sea-A	52	74	9	10	0	0	1	7	7	7	.135	.210	.176	9	-9	-9	3	0	0	0	.930	-9	S2/3	-1.7
1990	NY-N	16	22	0	3	1	0	0	1	0	3	.136	.136	.182	-13	-3	-3	1	0	0	0	.958	2	S/2	-0.2
1991	Tex-A	96	182	24	48	7	0	1	22	15	18	.264	.320	.319	79	-5	-5	18	0	1	-1	.962	-3	S2/3D	-0.5
1992	Tex-A	19	31	2	7	1	0	0	1	1	2	.226	.250	.258	44	-2	-2	1	0	1	-1	.975	1	S/23	-0.1
Total	6	222	404	45	97	14	1	2	43	26	39	.240	.286	.295	61	-21	-21	34	0	2	-1	.962	-9	S/23D1	-2.5

■ **MIKE DIAZ** Diaz, Michael Anthony b: 4/15/60, San Francisco, Cal. BR/TR, 6'2", 195 lbs. Deb: 9/15/83

YEAR	TM/L	G	AB	R	H	2B	3B	HR	RBI	BB	SO	AVG	OBP	SLG	PRO+	BR	/A	RC	SB	CS	SBR	FA	FR	POS	TPR
1983	Chi-N	6	7	2	2	1	0	0	1	0	0	.286	.286	.429	91	-0	-0	1	0	0	0	1.000	-0	/C	-0.1
1986	Pit-N	97	209	22	56	9	0	12	36	19	43	.268	.335	.483	120	6	5	33	0	1	-1	.966	-5	O1/3C	-0.2
1987	Pit-N	103	241	28	58	8	2	16	48	31	42	.241	.335	.490	114	5	4	40	1	0	0	.960	-6	O1/C	-0.4
1988	Pit-N	47	74	6	17	3	0	0	5	16	13	.230	.367	.270	87	-1	-0	8	0	0	0	1.000	-5	O/1C	-0.6
	Chi-A	40	152	12	36	6	0	3	12	5	30	.237	.266	.336	67	-7	-7	12	0	1	-1	.987	-2	1/D	-1.3

YEAR	TM/L	G	AB	R	H	2B	3B	HR	RBI	BB	SO	AVG	OBP	SLG	PRO+	BR	/A	RC	SB	CS	SBR	FA	FR	POS	TPR
Total	4	293	683	70	169	27	2	31	102	71	128	.247	.324	.429	103	3	2	94	1	2	-1	.988	-18	/1OC3D	-2.6

■ PAUL DICKEN Dicken, Paul Franklin b: 10/2/43, Deland, Fla. BR/TR, 6'5", 195 lbs. Deb: 6/07/64

YEAR	TM/L	G	AB	R	H	2B	3B	HR	RBI	BB	SO	AVG	OBP	SLG	PRO+	BR	/A	RC	SB	CS	SBR	FA	FR	POS	TPR
1964	Cle-A	11	11	0	0	0	0	0	0	0	5	.000	.000	.000	-99	-3	-3	0	0	0	0	.000	0	H	-0.3
1966	Cle-A	2	2	0	0	0	0	0	0	0	1	.000	.000	.000	-99	-1	-1	0	0	0	0	.000	0	H	-0.1
Total	2	13	13	0	0	0	0	0	0	0	6	.000	.000	.000	-99	-3	-3	0	0	0	0		0		-0.4

■ BUTTERCUP DICKERSON Dickerson, Lewis Pessano b: 10/11/1858, Tyaskin, Md. d: 7/23/20, Baltimore, Md. BL/TR, 5'6", 140 lbs. Deb: 7/15/1878

YEAR	TM/L	G	AB	R	H	2B	3B	HR	RBI	BB	SO	AVG	OBP	SLG	PRO+	BR	/A	RC	SB	CS	SBR	FA	FR	POS	TPR
1878	Cin-N	29	123	17	38	5	1	0	9	0	7	.309	.309	.366	134	2	4	14				.877	-1	O	0.1
1879	Cin-N	81	350	73	102	18	**14**	2	57	3	27	.291	.297	.440	147	14	16	47				.801	-4	*O	0.8
1880	Tro-N	30	119	15	23	2	2	0	10	2	3	.193	.207	.244	49	-6	-7	6				.903	6	O/S	-0.1
	Wor-N	31	133	22	39	8	6	0	20	1	2	.293	.299	.444	136	6	5	18				.852	-2	O	0.2
	Yr	61	252	37	62	10	8	0	30	3	5	.246	.255	.349	96	0	-2	23				.883	4	O/S	0.1
1881	Wor-N	80	367	48	116	18	6	1	31	8	8	.316	.331	.406	123	12	9	51				.892	10	*O	1.6
1883	Pit-a	85	355	62	88	15	1	0		17		.248	.282	.296	91	-5	-2	30				.798	0	*O/S2	-0.2
1884	StL-U	46	211	49	77	15	1	0		8		.365	.388	.445	175	17	16	37				.895	5	O/3	1.8
	Bal-a	13	56	9	12	2	1	0		4		.214	.290	.286	88	-0	-1	5				.941	-2	O/3	-0.3
	Lou-a	8	28	6	4	0	2	1		3		.143	.226	.393	105	0	0	3				.813	-1	/O	0.0
	Yr	21	84	15	16	2	3	1		7		.190	.269	.321	94	-0	-0	7				.879	-3	O/3	-0.3
1885	Buf-N	5	21	1	1	1	0	0	0	1	4	.048	.091	.095	-38	-3	-3	0				1.000	1	/O	-0.3
Total	7	408	1763	302	500	84	34	4	127	47	51	.284	.303	.377	121	38	38	211				.854	12	O/S32	3.6

■ GEORGE DICKEY Dickey, George Willard "Skeets" b: 7/10/15, Kensett, Ark. d: 6/16/76, Dewitt, Ark. BB/TR, 6'2", 180 lbs. Deb: 9/21/35 F

YEAR	TM/L	G	AB	R	H	2B	3B	HR	RBI	BB	SO	AVG	OBP	SLG	PRO+	BR	/A	RC	SB	CS	SBR	FA	FR	POS	TPR
1935	Bos-A	5	11	1	0	0	0	0	1	1	3	.000	.083	.000	-72	-3	-3	0	0	0	0	1.000	-1	/C	-0.4
1936	Bos-A	10	23	0	1	1	0	0	0	2	3	.043	.120	.087	-46	-6	-6	0	0	0	0	.912	0	C	-0.5
1941	Chi-A	32	55	6	11	1	0	2	8	5	7	.200	.267	.327	57	-4	-4	5	0	0	0	1.000	1	C	-0.2
1942	Chi-A	59	116	6	27	3	0	1	17	9	11	.233	.288	.284	63	-6	-6	10	0	0	0	.918	-4	C	-0.8
1946	Chi-A	37	78	8	15	1	0	0	1	12	13	.192	.300	.205	45	-6	-5	5	0	2	-1	1.000	2	C	-0.3
1947	Chi-A	83	211	15	47	6	0	1	27	34	25	.223	.331	.265	69	-8	-7	22	4	2	0	.985	2	C	-0.1
Total	6	226	494	36	101	12	0	4	54	63	62	.204	.294	.253	53	-32	-31	41	4	4	-1	.974	-0	C	-2.3

■ BILL DICKEY Dickey, William Malcolm b: 6/6/07, Bastrop, La. BL/TR, 6'1.5", 185 lbs. Deb: 8/15/28 FMCH

YEAR	TM/L	G	AB	R	H	2B	3B	HR	RBI	BB	SO	AVG	OBP	SLG	PRO+	BR	/A	RC	SB	CS	SBR	FA	FR	POS	TPR
1928	NY-A	10	15	1	3	1	1	0	2	0	2	.200	.200	.400	56	-1	-1	1	0	0	0	1.000	-1	/C	-0.2
1929	NY-A	130	447	60	145	30	6	10	65	14	16	.324	.346	.485	120	6	10	73	4	3	-1	.979	1	*C	2.0
1930	NY-A	109	366	55	124	25	7	5	65	21	14	.339	.375	.486	122	8	11	67	7	1	2	.977	-12	*C	0.8
1931	NY-A	130	477	65	156	17	10	6	78	39	20	.327	.378	.442	122	10	14	80	2	1	0	**.996**	4	*C	2.5
1932	*NY-A	108	423	66	131	20	4	15	84	34	13	.310	.361	.482	123	9	12	72	2	4	-2	.987	-2	*C	1.4
1933	NY-A☆	130	478	58	152	24	8	14	97	47	14	.318	.381	.490	138	19	23	89	3	4	-2	.993	0	*C	2.8
1934	NY-A★	104	395	56	127	24	4	12	72	38	18	.322	.384	.494	134	14	18	74	0	3	-2	.986	-2	*C	1.8
1935	NY-A	120	448	54	125	26	6	14	81	35	11	.279	.339	.458	111	1	5	70	1	1	-0	**.995**	-2	*C	0.9
1936	*NY-A★	112	423	99	153	26	8	22	107	46	16	.362	.428	.617	161	35	38	111	0	2	-1	.976	0	*C	3.7
1937	*NY-A★	140	530	87	176	35	2	29	133	73	22	.332	.417	.570	145	37	37	128	3	2	-0	.991	12	*C	5.1
1938	*NY-A★	132	454	84	142	27	4	27	115	75	22	.313	.412	.568	144	30	31	111	3	0	1	.987	4	*C	3.7
1939	*NY-A★	128	480	98	145	23	3	24	105	77	37	.302	.403	.512	135	24	26	104	5	0	2	**.989**	8	*C	3.8
1940	NY-A★	106	372	45	92	11	1	9	54	48	32	.247	.336	.355	83	-11	-9	46	0	3	-2	.994	-1	*C	-0.3
1941	*NY-A★	109	348	35	99	15	5	7	71	45	17	.284	.371	.417	110	5	5	56	2	1	0	**.994**	1	*C	1.4
1942	*NY-A†	82	268	28	79	13	1	2	37	26	11	.295	.359	.373	108	2	3	34	2	2	-1	.976	3	C	1.2
1943	*NY-A☆	85	242	29	85	18	2	4	33	41	12	.351	.445	.492	173	24	24	57	2	1	0	.994	-1	C	2.9
1946	NY-A★	54	134	10	35	8	0	2	10	19	12	.261	.357	.366	101	1	1	17	0	1	-1	.987	10	CM	1.3
Total	17	1789	6300	930	1969	343	72	202	1209	678	289	.313	.382	.486	128	216	247	1193	36	29	-7	.988	24	*C	34.8

■ JOHNNY DICKSHOT Dickshot, John Oscar "Ugly" (b: John Oscar Dicksus) b: 1/24/10, Waukegan, Ill. BR/TR, 6', 195 lbs. Deb: 4/16/36

YEAR	TM/L	G	AB	R	H	2B	3B	HR	RBI	BB	SO	AVG	OBP	SLG	PRO+	BR	/A	RC	SB	CS	SBR	FA	FR	POS	TPR
1936	Pit-N	9	9	2	2	0	0	0	1	1	2	.222	.300	.222	42	-1	-1	1	0			.000	-1	/O	-0.1
1937	Pit-N	82	264	42	67	8	4	3	33	26	36	.254	.323	.348	82	-6	-6	29	0			.950	-3	O	-1.1
1938	Pit-N	29	35	3	8	0	0	0	4	8	5	.229	.372	.229	68	-1	-1	4	3			1.000	-1	O	-0.3
1939	NY-N	10	34	3	8	0	0	0	5	5	3	.235	.333	.235	55	-2	-2	3	0			1.000	-1	O	-0.3
1944	Chi-A	62	162	18	41	8	5	0	15	13	10	.253	.313	.364	94	-2	-2	20	2	0	1	.974	-3	O	-0.6
1945	Chi-A	130	486	74	147	19	10	4	58	48	41	.302	.366	.407	128	15	16	75	18	3	**4**	.971	1	*O	1.5
Total	6	322	990	142	273	35	19	7	116	101	97	.276	.345	.371	104	3	5	131	23	3		.968	-7	O	-0.9

■ BOB DIDIER Didier, Robert Daniel b: 2/16/49, Hattiesburg, Miss. BB/TR, 6', 190 lbs. Deb: 4/07/69 C

YEAR	TM/L	G	AB	R	H	2B	3B	HR	RBI	BB	SO	AVG	OBP	SLG	PRO+	BR	/A	RC	SB	CS	SBR	FA	FR	POS	TPR
1969	*Atl-N	114	352	30	90	16	1	0	32	34	39	.256	.321	.307	76	-10	-10	36	1	3	-2	.994	-2	*C	-0.9
1970	Atl-N	57	168	9	25	2	1	0	7	12	11	.149	.210	.173	3	-23	-24	6	1	0	0	.988	1	C	-2.1
1971	Atl-N	51	155	9	34	4	1	0	5	6	17	.219	.248	.258	41	-12	-13	10	0	0	0	1.000	3	C	-0.9
1972	Atl-N	13	40	5	12	2	1	0	5	2	4	.300	.349	.400	103	1	0	6	0	0	0	1.000	2	C	0.2
1973	Det-A	7	22	3	10	1	0	0	1	3	0	.455	.520	.500	177	3	3	6	0	0	0	1.000	2	/C	0.5
1974	Bos-A	5	14	0	1	0	0	0	1	2	1	.071	.188	.071	-22	-2	-2	0	0	0	0	.968	1	/C	-0.1
Total	6	247	751	56	172	25	4	0	51	59	72	.229	.287	.273	55	-43	-47	64	2	3	-1	.994	6	C	-3.3

■ ERNIE DIEHL Diehl, Ernest Guy b: 10/2/1877, Cincinnati, Ohio d: 11/6/58, Miami, Fla. BR/TR, 6'1", 190 lbs. Deb: 5/31/03

YEAR	TM/L	G	AB	R	H	2B	3B	HR	RBI	BB	SO	AVG	OBP	SLG	PRO+	BR	/A	RC	SB	CS	SBR	FA	FR	POS	TPR
1903	Pit-N	1	3	0	1	0	0	0	0	0		.333	.333	.333	88	-0	-0	0	0			.000	-1	/O	-0.1
1904	Pit-N	12	37	6	6	0	0	0	4	6		.162	.311	.162	47	-2	-2	3	3			1.000	1	/OS	-0.1
1906	Bos-N	3	11	1	5	0	1	0	0	0		.455	.455	.636	247	2	2	3	0			1.000	0	/OS	0.2
1909	Bos-N	1	4	1	2	1	0	0	0	0		.500	.500	.750	274	1	1	1	0			.800	1	/O	0.1
Total	4	17	55	8	14	1	1	0	4	6		.255	.349	.309	102	1	0	8	3			.944	2	/OS	0.1

■ CHUCK DIERING Diering, Charles Edward Allen b: 2/5/23, St.Louis, Mo. BR/TR, 5'10", 165 lbs. Deb: 4/15/47

YEAR	TM/L	G	AB	R	H	2B	3B	HR	RBI	BB	SO	AVG	OBP	SLG	PRO+	BR	/A	RC	SB	CS	SBR	FA	FR	POS	TPR
1947	StL-N	105	74	22	16	3	1	2	11	19	22	.216	.383	.365	95	1	0	12	3			1.000	-22	O	-2.2
1948	StL-N	7	7	2	0	0	0	0	0	2	2	.000	.222	.000	-33	-1	-1	0	1			1.000	-1	/O	-0.2
1949	StL-N	131	369	60	97	21	8	3	38	35	49	.263	.328	.388	87	-5	-7	49	1			.987	-2	*O	-1.4
1950	StL-N	89	204	34	51	12	0	3	18	35	38	.250	.360	.353	84	-2	-4	28	1			.989	-1	O	-0.7
1951	StL-N	64	85	9	22	5	1	0	8	6	15	.259	.308	.341	74	-3	-3	9	0	1	-1	1.000	-8	O	-1.3
1952	NY-N	41	23	2	4	1	1	0	2	4	3	.174	.296	.304	66	-1	-1	2	0	2	-1	1.000	-10	O	-1.3
1954	Bal-A	128	418	35	108	14	1	2	29	56	57	.258	.351	.311	89	-8	-4	46	3	7	-3	.983	13	*O	0.1
1955	Bal-A	137	371	38	95	16	2	3	31	57	45	.256	.355	.334	93	-6	-2	45	5	8	-3	.976	3	*O3S	-0.5
1956	Bal-A	50	97	15	18	4	0	1	4	23	19	.186	.342	.258	65	-5	-4	10	2	5	-2	1.000	-4	O/3	-1.1
Total	9	752	1648	217	411	76	14	14	141	237	250	.249	.346	.338	86	-31	-26	201	16	23		.987	-31	O/3S	-8.6

■ DICK DIETZ Dietz, Richard Allen b: 9/18/41, Crawfordsville, Ind. BR/TR, 6'1", 195 lbs. Deb: 6/18/66

YEAR	TM/L	G	AB	R	H	2B	3B	HR	RBI	BB	SO	AVG	OBP	SLG	PRO+	BR	/A	RC	SB	CS	SBR	FA	FR	POS	TPR
1966	SF-N	13	23	1	1	0	0	0	0	0	9	.043	.083	.043	-62	-5	-5	0	0	0	0	1.000	-1	/C	-0.6
1967	SF-N	56	120	10	27	3	0	4	19	25	44	.225	.363	.350	106	2	2	16	0	1	-1	.983	0	C	0.4
1968	SF-N	98	301	21	82	14	2	6	38	34	68	.272	.348	.392	122	9	9	42	1	1	-0	.976	-8	C	0.7
1969	SF-N	79	244	28	56	8	1	11	35	53	53	.230	.373	.406	120	8	8	38	0	0	0	.973	-5	C	0.7
1970	SF-N★	148	493	82	148	36	2	22	107	109	106	.300	.430	.515	154	41	42	113	0	1	-1	.984	-18	*C	3.0
1971	*SF-N	142	453	58	114	19	0	19	72	97	86	.252	.388	.419	131	21	22	79	1	3	-2	.982	-12	*C	1.4

YEAR	TM/L	G	AB	R	H	2B	3B	HR	RBI	BB	SO	AVG	OBP	SLG	PRO+	BR	/A	RC	SB	CS	SBR	FA	FR	POS	TPR
1972	LA-N	27	56	4	9	1	0	1	6	14	11	.161	.329	.232	63	-2	-2	5	2	0	1	1.000	3	C	0.3
1973	Atl-N	83	139	22	41	8	1	3	24	49	25	.295	.479	.432	143	14	13	32	0	0	0	.989	1	1C	1.2
Total	8	646	1829	226	478	89	6	66	301	381	402	.261	.392	.425	130	87	88	326	4	6	-2	.980	-40	C/1	7.1
■ **ROY DIETZEL**	Dietzel, Leroy Louis b: 1/9/31, Baltimore, Md. BR/TR, 6', 190 lbs. Deb: 9/02/54																								
1954	Was-A	9	21	1	5	0	0	0	1	5	4	.238	.385	.238	78	-0	-0	2	0	0	0	.960	-2	/23	-0.2
■ **JAY DIFANI**	Difani, Clarence Joseph b: 12/21/23, Crystal City, Mo. BR/TR, 6', 170 lbs. Deb: 4/23/48																								
1948	Was-A	2	2	0	0	0	0	0	0	0	2	.000	.000	.000	-99	-1	-1	0	0	0	0	.000	0	H	-0.1
1949	Was-A	2	1	0	1	1	0	0	0	0	0	1.000	1.000	2.000	699	1	1	2	0	0	0	1.000	0	/2	0.1
Total	2	4	3	0	1	1	0	0	0	0	2	.333	.333	.667	166	0	0	2	0	0	0		0	/2	0.0
■ **STEVE DIGNAN**	Dignan, Stephen E. b: 5/16/1859, Boston, Mass. d: 7/11/1881, Boston, Mass. Deb: 6/01/1880																								
1880	Bos-N	8	34	4	11	1	0	0	4	0	3	.324	.324	.353	133	1	1	4				.684	0	/O	0.1
	Wor-N	3	10	1	3	0	1	0	2	0	1	.300	.300	.500	153	1	1	2				.750	-1	/O	0.0
	Yr	11	44	5	14	1	1	0	6	0	4	.318	.318	.386	137	2	2	6				.696	-1	O	0.1
■ **DON DILLARD**	Dillard, David Donald b: 1/8/37, Greenville, S.C. BL/TR, 6'1", 200 lbs. Deb: 4/24/59																								
1959	Cle-A	10	10	0	4	0	0	0	1	0	2	.400	.400	.400	125	0	0	2	0	0	0	.000	0	H	0.0
1960	Cle-A	6	7	0	1	0	0	0	0	1	3	.143	.250	.143	9	-1	-1	0	0	0	0	.000	-0	/O	-0.1
1961	Cle-A	74	147	27	40	5	0	7	17	15	28	.272	.340	.449	112	2	2	23	0	0	0	1.000	-4	O	-0.3
1962	Cle-A	95	174	22	40	5	1	5	14	11	25	.230	.276	.356	71	-8	-7	16	0	1	-1	.965	-10	O	-2.0
1963	Mil-N	67	119	9	28	6	4	1	12	5	21	.235	.272	.378	86	-3	-2	11	0	2	-1	.951	1	O	-0.4
1965	Mil-N	20	19	1	3	0	0	1	3	0	6	.158	.158	.316	30	-2	-2	0	0	0	0	.000	0	/O	-0.2
Total	6	272	476	59	116	16	5	14	47	32	85	.244	.293	.387	86	-12	-10	53	0	3	-2	.976	-14	O	-3.0
■ **PAT DILLARD**	Dillard, Robert Lee b: 6/12/1874, Chattanooga, Tenn d: 7/22/07, Denver, Colo. BL/TR, 6', 180 lbs. Deb: 4/21/00																								
1900	StL-N	57	183	24	42	5	2	0	12	13		.230	.284	.279	56	-11	-11	17	7			.942	-5	O3/S	-1.6
■ **STEVE DILLARD**	Dillard, Stephen Bradley b: 2/8/51, Memphis, Tenn. BR/TR, 6'1", 180 lbs. Deb: 9/28/75																								
1975	Bos-A	1	5	2	2	0	0	0	0	0	0	.400	.400	.400	117	0	0	1	1	0	0	1.000	1	/2	0.1
1976	Bos-A	57	167	22	46	14	0	1	15	17	20	.275	.342	.377	99	2	-0	20	6	4	-1	.918	-4	32S/D	-0.3
1977	Bos-A	66	141	22	34	7	0	1	13	7	13	.241	.277	.312	54	-8	-10	12	4	3	-1	.967	8	2/SD	0.0
1978	Det-A	56	130	21	29	5	2	0	7	6	11	.223	.257	.292	53	-8	-8	9	1	2	-1	.958	17	2/D	0.9
1979	Chi-N	89	166	31	47	6	1	5	24	17	24	.283	.353	.422	101	2	0	25	1	0	0	.988	9	2/3	1.3
1980	Chi-N	100	244	31	55	8	1	4	27	20	54	.225	.287	.316	63	-11	-13	22	2	2	-1	.908	2	32/S	-1.0
1981	Chi-N	53	119	18	26	7	1	2	11	8	20	.218	.268	.345	70	-5	-5	11	0	0	0	.974	3	2/3S	-0.1
1982	Chi-A	16	41	1	7	3	1	0	5	1	5	.171	.190	.293	30	-4	-4	2	0	1	-1	.959	3	2	-0.1
Total	8	438	1013	148	246	50	6	13	102	76	147	.243	.297	.343	73	-30	-40	102	15	12	-3	.973	37	2/3SD	0.8
■ **PICKLES DILLHOEFER**	Dillhoefer, William Martin b: 10/13/1894, Cleveland, Ohio d: 2/23/22, St.Louis, Mo. BR/TR, 5'7", 154 lbs. Deb: 4/16/17																								
1917	Chi-N	42	95	3	12	1	1	0	8	2	9	.126	.144	.158	-7	-12	-13	3	1			.985	8	C	-0.3
1918	Phi-N	8	11	0	1	0	0	0	0	1	1	.091	.167	.091	-19	-2	-2	0	2			.923	-1	/C	-0.2
1919	StL-N	45	108	11	23	3	2	0	12	8	6	.213	.267	.278	68	-5	-4	9	5			.967	-5	C	-0.7
1920	StL-N	76	224	26	59	8	3	0	13	13	7	.263	.304	.326	84	-6	-5	22	2	1	0	.953	-0	C	-0.1
1921	StL-N	76	162	19	39	4	4	0	15	11	7	.241	.289	.315	61	-9	-9	15	2	1	0	.953	2	C	-0.5
Total	5	247	600	59	134	16	10	0	48	35	30	.223	.266	.283	58	-33	-32	49	12	2		.961	4	C	-1.8
■ **BOB DILLINGER**	Dillinger, Robert Bernard "Duke" b: 9/17/18, Glendale, Cal. BR/TR, 5'11.5", 170 lbs. Deb: 4/16/46																								
1946	StL-A	83	225	33	63	6	3	0	11	19	30	.280	.341	.333	85	-3	-4	27	8	1	**2**	.922	-3	3/S	-0.5
1947	StL-A	137	571	70	168	23	6	3	37	56	38	.294	.361	.371	102	4	2	80	**34**	13	**2**	.958	2	*3	0.8
1948	StL-A	153	644	110	**207**	34	10	2	44	65	34	.321	.385	.415	110	12	10	105	**28**	11	2	.955	-16	*3	-0.6
1949	StL-A★	137	544	68	176	22	13	1	51	51	40	.324	.385	.417	108	9	6	87	**20**	14	-2	.938	-25	*3	-2.3
1950	Phi-A	84	356	55	110	21	9	3	41	31	20	.309	.366	.444	109	3	4	57	5	3	-0	.957	-2	3	0.0
	Pit-N	58	222	23	64	8	2	1	9	13	22	.288	.328	.356	77	-6	-7	24	4			.957	2	3	-0.7
1951	Pit-N	12	43	3	10	3	0	0	0	1	0	.233	.250	.302	47	-3	-3	2	2	0	1	.963	-2	3	-0.5
	Chi-A	89	299	39	90	6	4	0	20	15	17	.301	.337	.348	87	-6	-6	34	5	5	-2	.930	-6	3	-1.4
Total	6	753	2904	401	888	123	47	10	213	251	201	.306	.363	.391	100	9	1	417	106	47		.948	-50	3/S	-5.2
■ **POP DILLON**	Dillon, Frank Edward b: 10/17/1873, Normal, Ill. d: 9/12/31, Pasadena, Cal. BL/TR, Deb: 9/08/1899																								
1899	Pit-N	30	121	21	31	5	0	0	20	5		.256	.286	.298	60	-7	-7	12	5			.988	1	1	-0.5
1900	Pit-N	5	18	3	2	1	0	0	1	0		.111	.111	.167	-24	-3	-3	0	0			.981	1	/1	-0.2
1901	Det-A	74	281	40	81	14	6	1	42	15		.288	.324	.391	94	-1	-3	42	14			.979	3	1	-0.2
1902	Det-A	66	243	21	50	6	3	0	22	16		.206	.255	.255	41	-19	-20	17	2			.976	5	1	-1.5
	Bal-A	2	7	1	2	0	1	0	0	2		.286	.444	.571	172	1	1	2	0			.960	0	/1	0.1
	Yr	68	250	22	52	6	4	0	22	18		.208	.261	.264	45	-18	-19	19	2			.975	6	1	-1.4
1904	Bro-N	135	511	60	132	18	6	0	31	40		.258	.313	.317	98	-3	-1	57	13			.982	3	*1	-0.1
Total	5	312	1181	146	298	44	16	1	116	78		.252	.299	.319	79	-32	-33	131	34			.980	14	1	-2.4
■ **JOHN DILLON**	Dillon, John Deb: 5/98/1875 F																								
1875	RS-n	1	1	0	0	0	0	0		0		.000	.000	.000	-99	-0	-0	0						/S	0.0
■ **PACKY DILLON**	Dillon, Packard Andrew b: St.Louis, Mo. d: 1/8/1890, Guelph, Ont., Canada Deb: 5/04/1875 F																								
1875	RS-n	3	13	1	3	1	0	0		0		.231	.231	.308	93	-0	-0	1						/C	0.0
■ **MIGUEL DILONE**	Dilone, Miguel Angel (Reyes) b: 11/1/54, Santiago, D.R. BB/TR, 6', 160 lbs. Deb: 9/02/74																								
1974	Pit-N	12	2	3	0	0	0	0	0	1	0	.000	.333	.000	-1	-0	-0	0	2	0	1	1.000	1	/O	0.2
1975	Pit-N	18	6	8	0	0	0	0	0	0	1	.000	.000	.000	-99	-2	-2	-0	2	2	-1	1.000	2	/O	0.0
1976	Pit-N	16	17	7	4	0	0	0	0	0	0	.235	.235	.235	34	-1	-1	1	5	1	1	1.000	2	/O	0.1
1977	Pit-N	29	44	5	6	0	0	0	0	2	3	.136	.174	.136	-15	-7	-7	2	12	0	4	1.000	1	O	-0.3
1978	Oak-A	135	258	34	59	8	0	1	14	23	30	.229	.294	.271	63	-13	-12	21	50	23	1	.985	-7	OD/3	-2.1
1979	Oak-A	30	91	15	17	1	2	1	6	6	7	.187	.237	.275	40	-8	-7	5	6	5	-1	.959	-2	O	-1.1
	Chi-N	43	36	14	11	0	0	0	1	2	5	.306	.342	.306	71	-1	-1	4	15	5	2	1.000	4	O	0.3
1980	Cle-A	132	528	82	180	30	9	0	40	28	45	.341	.376	.432	120	15	15	89	61	18	8	.973	-0	*OD	1.7
1981	Cle-A	72	269	33	78	5	5	0	19	18	28	.290	.334	.346	98	-1	-1	31	29	10	3	.971	6	OD	0.6
1982	Cle-A	104	379	50	89	12	3	3	25	25	36	.235	.286	.306	63	-19	-19	35	33	5	7	.964	-3	O/D	-1.8
1983	Cle-A	32	68	15	13	3	1	0	7	10	5	.191	.295	.265	53	-4	-4	6	5	1	1	1.000	1	O	-0.3
	Chi-A	4	3	1	0	0	0	0	0	0	0	.000	.000	.000	-96	-1	-1	0	1	0	0	1.000	-1	/OD	-0.1
	Yr	36	71	16	13	3	1	0	7	10	5	.183	.284	.254	47	-5	-5	6	6	1	1	1.000	0	O/D	-0.4
	Pit-N	7	0	1	0	0	0	0	0	0	0	—	—	—	—	0	0	0	2	0	1	.000	0	/R	0.1
1984	Mon-N	88	169	28	47	8	2	1	10	17	18	.278	.348	.367	106	1	1	26	27	2	7	.987	1	O	0.9
1985	Mon-N	51	84	10	16	0	2	0	6	6	11	.190	.244	.238	38	-7	-7	4	7	3	0	.974	-2	O	-0.9
	SD-N	27	46	8	10	0	1	0	1	4	8	.217	.280	.261	53	-3	-3	4	10	3	1	.917	-2	O	-0.4
	Yr	78	130	18	26	0	3	0	7	10	19	.200	.257	.246	43	-10	-9	8	17	6	2	.952	-4	O	-1.3
Total	12	800	2000	314	530	67	25	6	129	142	197	.265	.316	.333	81	-53	-49	229	267	78	33	.975	0	O/D3	-3.1

■ DOM DiMAGGIO DiMaggio, Dominic Paul "The Little Professor" b: 2/12/17, San Francisco, Cal. BR/TR, 5'9", 168 lbs. Deb: 4/16/40 F

YEAR	TM/L	G	AB	R	H	2B	3B	HR	RBI	BB	SO	AVG	OBP	SLG	PRO+	BR	/A	RC	SB	CS	SBR	FA	FR	POS	TPR
1940	Bos-A	108	418	81	126	32	6	8	46	41	46	.301	.367	.464	109	8	6	73	7	6	-2	.977	10	O	0.9
1941	Bos-A★	144	584	117	165	37	6	8	58	90	57	.283	.385	.408	107	11	9	101	13	6	0	.964	6	*O	0.6
1942	Bos-A☆	151	622	110	178	36	8	14	48	70	52	.286	.364	.437	121	20	17	103	16	10	-1	.987	17	*O	2.5
1946	*Bos-A★	142	534	85	169	24	7	7	73	66	58	.316	.393	.427	122	22	18	92	10	6	-1	.985	7	*O	1.9
1947	Bos-A	136	513	75	145	21	5	8	71	74	62	.283	.376	.390	105	11	6	80	10	6	-1	.977	19	*O	1.8
1948	Bos-A	155	648	127	185	40	4	9	87	101	58	.285	.383	.401	104	10	6	110	10	2	2	.981	16	*O	1.4
1949	Bos-A★	145	605	126	186	34	5	8	60	96	55	.307	.404	.420	110	18	12	110	9	7	-2	.977	14	*O	1.7
1950	Bos-A★	141	588	**131**	193	30	**11**	7	70	82	68	.328	.414	.452	111	21	13	117	**15**	4	**2**	.983	9	*O	1.6
1951	Bos-A★	146	639	**113**	189	34	4	12	72	73	53	.296	.370	.418	103	12	3	101	4	7	-3	.973	3	*O	-0.3
1952	Bos-A★	128	486	81	143	20	1	6	33	57	61	.294	.371	.377	100	7	2	70	6	8	-3	.975	0	*O	-0.6
1953	Bos-A	3	3	0	1	0	0	0	0	0	1	.333	.333	.333	76	-0	-0	0	0	0	0	.000	0	H	0.0
Total	11	1399	5640	1046	1680	308	57	87	618	750	571	.298	.383	.419	109	140	92	958	100	62	-7	.978	101	*O	11.5

■ JOE DiMAGGIO DiMaggio, Joseph Paul "Joltin' Joe" or "The Yankee Clipper" b: 11/25/14, Martinez, Cal. BR/TR, 6'2", 193 lbs. Deb: 5/03/36 FCH

YEAR	TM/L	G	AB	R	H	2B	3B	HR	RBI	BB	SO	AVG	OBP	SLG	PRO+	BR	/A	RC	SB	CS	SBR	FA	FR	POS	TPR
1936	*NY-A★	138	637	132	206	44	**15**	29	125	24	39	.323	.352	.576	130	19	23	127	4	0	1	.978	15	*O	2.9
1937	*NY-A★	151	621	**151**	215	35	15	**46**	167	64	37	.346	.412	**.673**	168	61	61	173	3	0	1	.962	11	*O	6.1
1938	*NY-A★	145	599	129	194	32	13	32	140	59	21	.324	.386	.581	140	33	33	136	6	1	1	.963	4	*O	3.0
1939	*NY-A★	120	462	108	176	32	6	30	126	52	20	**.381**	.448	.671	**185**	56	57	139	3	0	1	.986	8	*O	**5.6**
1940	NY-A★	132	508	93	179	28	9	31	133	61	30	**.352**	.425	.626	**176**	51	54	135	1	2	-1	.978	1	*O	4.4
1941	*NY-A★	139	541	122	193	43	11	30	**125**	76	13	.357	.440	.643	186	64	65	162	4	2	0	.978	10	*O	6.3
1942	*NY-A★	154	610	123	186	29	13	21	114	68	36	.305	.376	.498	148	34	36	120	4	2	0	.981	2	*O	3.0
1946	NY-A☆	132	503	81	146	20	8	25	95	59	24	.290	.367	.511	142	28	27	96	1	0	0	.982	4	*O	2.6
1947	*NY-A★	141	534	97	168	31	10	20	97	64	32	.315	.391	.522	154	37	37	112	3	0	1	**.997**	-13	*O	1.8
1948	NY-A★	153	594	110	190	26	11	**39**	**155**	67	30	.320	.396	.598	164	49	49	140	1	1	-0	.972	4	*O	4.3
1949	*NY-A★	76	272	58	94	14	6	14	67	55	18	.346	.459	.596	178	32	32	76	0	1	-1	.985	-1	O	2.5
1950	*NY-A★	139	525	114	158	33	10	32	122	80	33	.301	.394	**.585**	152	35	38	125	0	0	0	.976	1	*O/1	3.0
1951	*NY-A☆	116	415	72	109	22	4	12	71	61	36	.263	.365	.422	117	8	10	65	0	0	0	.990	4	*O	1.0
Total	13	1736	6821	1390	2214	389	131	361	1537	790	369	.325	.398	.579	156	507	522	1606	30	9	4	.978	51	*O/1	46.5

■ VINCE DiMAGGIO DiMaggio, Vincent Paul b: 9/6/12, Martinez, Cal. d: 10/3/86, N.Hollywood, Cal. BR/TR, 5'11", 183 lbs. Deb: 4/19/37 F

YEAR	TM/L	G	AB	R	H	2B	3B	HR	RBI	BB	SO	AVG	OBP	SLG	PRO+	BR	/A	RC	SB	CS	SBR	FA	FR	POS	TPR
1937	Bos-N	132	493	56	126	18	4	13	69	39	111	.256	.311	.387	98	-9	-3	61	8			.982	16	*O	0.8
1938	Bos-N	150	540	71	123	28	3	14	61	65	134	.228	.313	.369	96	-10	-3	68	11			.973	13	*O/2	0.6
1939	Cin-N	8	14	1	1	1	0	0	2	2	10	.071	.188	.143	-10	-2	-2	0	0			1.000	-0	/O	-0.2
1940	Cin-N	2	4	2	1	0	0	0	0	1	0	.250	.400	.250	82	-0	-0	0	0			1.000	0	/O	0.0
	Pit-N	110	356	59	103	26	0	19	54	37	83	.289	.364	.522	143	19	20	68	11			.979	-2	*O	1.3
	Yr	112	360	61	104	26	0	19	54	38	83	.289	.365	.519	142	19	20	68	11			.979	-2	*O	1.3
1941	Pit-N	151	528	73	141	27	5	21	100	68	100	.267	.354	.456	128	18	19	88	10			.976	7	*O	1.7
1942	Pit-N	143	496	57	118	22	3	15	75	52	87	.238	.311	.385	101	1	-1	59	10			.978	**20**	*O	1.3
1943	Pit-N★	157	580	64	144	41	2	15	88	70	126	.248	.329	.403	107	7	5	80	11			.985	15	*O/S	1.3
1944	Pit-N★	109	342	41	82	20	4	9	50	33	83	.240	.307	.401	94	-2	-4	42	6			.984	-6	*O/3	-1.5
1945	Phi-N	127	452	64	116	25	3	19	84	43	91	.257	.321	.451	117	6	7	67	12			.994	10	*O	1.1
1946	Phi-N	6	19	1	4	1	0	0	1	0	7	.211	.211	.263	35	-2	-2	1	0			1.000	-1	/O	-0.3
	NY-N	15	25	2	0	0	0	0	0	2	5	.000	.074	.000	-78	-6	-6	0	0			.967	-1	O	-0.8
	Yr	21	44	3	4	1	0	0	1	2	12	.091	.130	.114	-31	-8	-8	0	0			.975	-2	O	-1.1
Total	10	1110	3849	491	959	209	24	125	584	412	837	.249	.324	.413	108	21	31	535	79			.981	71	*O/3S2	5.3

■ MIKE DIMMEL Dimmel, Michael Wayne b: 10/16/54, Albert Lea, Minn. BR/TR, 6', 180 lbs. Deb: 9/02/77

YEAR	TM/L	G	AB	R	H	2B	3B	HR	RBI	BB	SO	AVG	OBP	SLG	PRO+	BR	/A	RC	SB	CS	SBR	FA	FR	POS	TPR
1977	Bal-A	25	5	8	0	0	0	0	0	0	1	.000	.000	.000	-99	-1	-1	0	1	0	0	1.000	-6	O	-0.7
1978	Bal-A	8	0	2	0	0	0	0	0	0	0	—	—	—	—	0	0	0	0	1	-1	.667	-3	/O	-0.4
1979	StL-N	6	3	1	1	0	0	0	0	0	0	.333	.333	.333	82	-0	-0	0	0	1	-1	1.000	0	/O	0.0
Total	3	39	8	11	1	0	0	0	0	0	1	.125	.125	.125	-33	-1	-1	0	1	2	-1	.952	-8	/O	-1.1

■ KERRY DINEEN Dineen, Kerry Michael b: 7/1/52, Englewood, N.J. BL/TL, 5'11", 165 lbs. Deb: 6/14/75

YEAR	TM/L	G	AB	R	H	2B	3B	HR	RBI	BB	SO	AVG	OBP	SLG	PRO+	BR	/A	RC	SB	CS	SBR	FA	FR	POS	TPR
1975	NY-A	7	22	3	8	1	0	0	1	2	1	.364	.417	.409	138	1	1	4	0	0	0	1.000	0	/O	0.1
1976	NY-A	4	7	0	2	0	0	0	1	1	2	.286	.375	.286	96	0	0	1	1	1	-0	.900	-0	/O	-0.1
1978	Phi-N	5	8	0	2	1	0	0	0	1	0	.250	.333	.375	97	-0	-0	1	0	0	0	1.000	-0	/O	0.0
Total	3	16	37	3	12	2	0	0	2	4	3	.324	.390	.378	121	1	1	5	1	1	-0	.967	-0	/O	0.0

■ VANCE DINGES Dinges, Vance George b: 5/29/15, Elizabeth, N.J. d: 10/4/90, Harrisonburg, Va. BL/TL, 6'2", 175 lbs. Deb: 4/17/45

YEAR	TM/L	G	AB	R	H	2B	3B	HR	RBI	BB	SO	AVG	OBP	SLG	PRO+	BR	/A	RC	SB	CS	SBR	FA	FR	POS	TPR
1945	Phi-N†	109	397	46	114	15	4	1	36	35	17	.287	.346	.353	97	-3	-1	49	5			.986	-1	O1	-0.8
1946	Phi-N	50	104	7	32	5	1	1	10	9	12	.308	.363	.404	121	2	3	15	2			.985	-0	1/O	0.1
Total	2	159	501	53	146	20	5	2	46	44	29	.291	.350	.363	102	-0	1	64	7			.986	-1	/1O	-0.7

■ BOB DiPIETRO DiPietro, Robert Louis Paul b: 9/1/27, San Francisco, Cal BR/TR, 5'11", 185 lbs. Deb: 9/23/51

YEAR	TM/L	G	AB	R	H	2B	3B	HR	RBI	BB	SO	AVG	OBP	SLG	PRO+	BR	/A	RC	SB	CS	SBR	FA	FR	POS	TPR
1951	Bos-A	4	11	0	1	0	0	0	0	1	1	.091	.167	.091	-26	-2	-2	0	0	0	0	.833	0	/O	-0.2

■ GARY DISARCINA Disarcina, Gary Thomas b: 11/19/67, Malden, Mass. BR/TR, 6'1", 170 lbs. Deb: 9/23/89

YEAR	TM/L	G	AB	R	H	2B	3B	HR	RBI	BB	SO	AVG	OBP	SLG	PRO+	BR	/A	RC	SB	CS	SBR	FA	FR	POS	TPR
1989	Cal-A	2	0	0	0	0	0	0	0	0	0	—	—	—	—	0	0	0	0	0	0	.000	0	/S	0.0
1990	Cal-A	18	57	8	8	1	1	0	0	3	10	.140	.183	.193	5	-7	-7	2	1	0	0	.940	2	S/2	-0.4
1991	Cal-A	18	57	5	12	2	0	0	3	3	4	.211	.274	.246	45	-4	-4	4	0	0	0	.915	-1	S/23	-0.4
1992	Cal-A	157	518	48	128	19	0	3	42	20	50	.247	.284	.301	65	-25	-24	41	9	7	-2	.967	12	*S	-0.2
Total	4	195	632	61	148	22	1	3	45	26	64	.234	.274	.286	58	-36	-35	47	10	7	-1	.962	13	S/23	-1.0

■ BENNY DISTEFANO Distefano, Benito James b: 1/23/62, Brooklyn, N.Y. BL/TL, 6'1", 195 lbs. Deb: 5/18/84

YEAR	TM/L	G	AB	R	H	2B	3B	HR	RBI	BB	SO	AVG	OBP	SLG	PRO+	BR	/A	RC	SB	CS	SBR	FA	FR	POS	TPR
1984	Pit-N	45	78	10	13	1	2	3	9	5	13	.167	.226	.346	59	-5	-5	5	0	1	-1	.946	1	O1	-0.5
1986	Pit-N	31	39	3	7	1	0	1	5	1	5	.179	.200	.282	31	-4	-4	2	0	0	0	1.000	-1	/O1	-0.5
1988	Pit-N	16	29	6	10	3	1	1	6	3	4	.345	.406	.621	194	3	3	7	0	0	0	1.000	-0	/1O	0.3
1989	Pit-N	96	154	12	38	8	0	2	15	17	30	.247	.333	.338	96	-1	-0	17	1	0	0	.981	-3	1/CO	-0.6
1992	Hou-N	52	60	4	14	0	2	0	7	5	14	.233	.303	.300	76	-2	-2	6	0	0	0	1.000	-0	O/1	-0.3
Total	5	240	360	35	82	13	5	7	42	31	66	.228	.298	.350	85	-8	-7	37	1	1	-0	.985	-3	/1OC	-1.6

■ DUTCH DISTEL Distel, George Adam b: 4/15/1896, Madison, Ind. d: 2/12/67, Madison, Ind. BR/TR, 5'9", 165 lbs. Deb: 6/21/18

YEAR	TM/L	G	AB	R	H	2B	3B	HR	RBI	BB	SO	AVG	OBP	SLG	PRO+	BR	/A	RC	SB	CS	SBR	FA	FR	POS	TPR
1918	StL-N	8	17	3	3	1	1	0	1	2	3	.176	.263	.353	90	-0	-0	2	0			.900	-2	/2SO	-0.2

■ JACK DITTMER Dittmer, John Douglas b: 1/10/28, Elkader, Iowa BL/TR, 6'1", 175 lbs. Deb: 6/17/52

YEAR	TM/L	G	AB	R	H	2B	3B	HR	RBI	BB	SO	AVG	OBP	SLG	PRO+	BR	/A	RC	SB	CS	SBR	FA	FR	POS	TPR
1952	Bos-N	93	326	26	63	7	2	7	41	26	26	.193	.255	.291	53	-22	-21	24	1	0	0	.982	6	2	-1.0
1953	Mil-N	138	504	54	134	22	1	9	63	18	35	.266	.293	.367	75	-22	-18	53	1	0	0	.965	-29	*2	-3.8
1954	Mil-N	66	192	22	47	8	0	6	20	19	17	.245	.322	.380	88	-5	-3	24	0	1	-1	.977	-3	2	-0.4
1955	Mil-N	38	72	4	9	1	1	1	4	4	15	.125	.171	.208	0	-10	-10	3	0	0	0	.977	-2	2	-1.0
1956	Mil-N	44	102	8	25	4	0	1	6	8	8	.245	.300	.314	69	-5	-4	10	0	0	0	.979	3	2	0.0
1957	Det-A	16	22	3	5	1	0	0	2	2	1	.227	.292	.273	54	-1	-1	2	0	0	0	1.000	-1	/32	-0.2
Total	6	395	1218	117	283	43	4	24	136	77	102	.232	.281	.333	66	-66	-58	116	2	1	0	.974	-26	2/3	-6.4

YEAR	TM/L	G	AB	R	H	2B	3B	HR	RBI	BB	SO	AVG	OBP	SLG	PRO+	BR	/A	RC	SB	CS	SBR	FA	FR	POS	TPR
■ MOXIE DIVIS	Divis, Edward G. b: 1/16/1894, Cleveland, Ohio d: 12/19/55, Lakewood, Ohio Deb: 8/04/16																								
1916	Phi-A	3	6	0	1	0	0	0	1	0	2	.167	.167	.167	0	-1	-1	0	0			1.000	1	/O	0.0
■ LEO DIXON	Dixon, Leo Moses b: 9/4/1894, Chicago, Ill. d: 4/11/84, Chicago, Ill. BR/TR, 5'11", 170 lbs. Deb: 4/14/25																								
1925	StL-A	76	205	27	46	11	1	1	19	24	42	.224	.318	.302	55	-13	-15	21	3	2	-0	.981	9	C	-0.2
1926	StL-A	33	89	7	17	3	1	0	8	11	14	.191	.294	.247	40	-7	-8	7	1	4	-2	.977	4	C	-0.4
1927	StL-A	36	103	6	20	3	1	0	12	7	6	.194	.245	.243	26	-11	-12	6	0	1	-1	.937	3	C	-0.7
1929	Cin-N	14	30	0	5	2	0	0	2	3	7	.167	.242	.233	19	-4	-4	2	0			1.000	4	C	0.1
Total	4	159	427	40	88	19	3	1	41	45	69	.206	.291	.272	43	-36	-38	36	4	7		.971	21	C	-1.2
■ WALT DOANE	Doane, Walter Rudolph b: 3/12/1887, Bellevue, Idaho d: 10/19/35, W.Brandywine, Pa. BL/TR, 6', 165 lbs. Deb: 9/20/09																								
1909	Cle-A	4	9	1	1	0	0	0	0	1		.111	.200	.111	-1	-1	-1	0	0			.778	1	/OP	0.0
1910	Cle-A	6	7	0	2	1	0	0	2	1		.286	.375	.429	150	0	0	1	0			.750	-1	/P	0.0
Total	2	10	16	1	3	1	0	0	2	2		.188	.278	.250	64	-1	-1	1	0			.800	-0	/PO	0.0
■ DAN DOBBEK	Dobbek, Daniel John b: 12/6/34, Ontonagon, Mich. BL/TR, 6', 195 lbs. Deb: 9/09/59																								
1959	Was-A	16	60	8	15	1	2	1	5	5	13	.250	.308	.383	89	-1	-1	7	0	0	0	1.000	1	O	-0.1
1960	Was-A	110	248	32	54	8	2	10	30	35	41	.218	.317	.387	90	-4	-4	31	4	3	-1	.973	-8	O	-1.5
1961	Min-A	72	125	12	21	3	1	4	14	13	18	.168	.257	.304	47	-9	-10	10	1	2	-1	.985	-9	O	-2.1
Total	3	198	433	52	90	12	5	15	49	53	72	.208	.299	.363	77	-14	-15	48	5	5	-2	.980	-16	O	-3.7
■ JOHN DOBBS	Dobbs, John Gordon b: 6/3/1876, Chattanooga, Tenn. d: 9/9/34, Charlotte, N.C. BL/TR, 5'9.5", 170 lbs. Deb: 4/20/01																								
1901	Cin-N	109	435	71	119	17	4	2	27	36		.274	.336	.345	105	-1	3	60	19			.948	-6	*O/3	-1.0
1902	Cin-N	63	256	39	76	7	3	1	16	19		.297	.345	.359	107	5	2	37	7			.963	8	O	0.6
	Chi-N	59	235	31	71	8	2	0	35	18		.302	.357	.353	123	6	6	33	3			.977	1	O	0.3
	Yr	122	491	70	147	15	5	1	51	37		.299	.351	.356	114	11	9	70	10			.970	8	*O	0.9
1903	Chi-N	16	61	8	14	1	1	0	4	7		.230	.329	.279	76	-2	-2	6	0			1.000	1	O	-0.2
	Bro-N	111	414	61	98	15	7	2	59	48		.237	.320	.321	86	-8	-7	53	23			.966	4	*O	-0.9
	Yr	127	475	69	112	16	8	2	63	55		.236	.321	.316	85	-10	-8	59	23			.970	4	*O	-1.1
1904	Bro-N	101	363	36	90	16	2	0	30	28		.248	.302	.303	90	-5	-4	39	11			.936	0	O/2S	-1.0
1905	Bro-N	123	460	59	117	21	4	2	36	31		.254	.304	.330	97	-7	-2	54	15			.938	-6	*O	-1.5
Total	5	582	2224	305	585	85	23	7	207	187		.263	.324	.331	98	-12	-3	281	78			.954	0	O/3S2	-3.7
■ LARRY DOBY	Doby, Lawrence Eugene b: 12/13/24, Camden, S.C. BL/TR, 6'1", 182 lbs. Deb: 7/05/47 MC																								
1947	Cle-A	29	32	3	5	1	0	0	2	1	11	.156	.182	.188	3	-4	-4	1	0	0	0	1.000	-1	/21S	-0.5
1948	*Cle-A	121	439	83	132	23	9	14	66	54	77	.301	.384	.490	135	19	20	84	9	9	-3	.955	3	*O	1.4
1949	Cle-A★	147	547	106	153	25	3	24	85	91	90	.280	.389	.468	129	21	22	104	10	9	-2	.976	-7	*O	0.5
1950	Cle-A★	142	503	110	164	25	5	25	102	98	71	.326	**.442**	.545	**156**	**42**	**44**	**130**	8	6	-1	.987	-6	*O	2.9
1951	Cle-A★	134	447	84	132	27	5	20	69	101	81	.295	.428	.512	**163**	37	41	108	4	1	1	.977	-1	*O	3.4
1952	Cle-A★	140	519	**104**	143	26	8	**32**	104	90	111	.276	.383	**.541**	**166**	38	42	116	5	2	0	.986	11	*O	**4.8**
1953	Cle-A★	149	513	92	135	18	5	29	102	96	121	.263	.385	.487	138	26	28	105	3	2	-0	.984	-7	*O	1.5
1954	*Cle-A★	153	577	94	157	18	4	**32**	**126**	85	94	.272	.368	.484	130	25	23	108	3	1	0	.995	6	*O	2.4
1955	Cle-A☆	131	491	91	143	17	5	26	75	61	100	.291	.372	.505	129	22	20	95	2	0	1	.994	3	*O	1.8
1956	Chi-A	140	504	89	135	22	3	24	102	102	105	.268	.395	.466	125	22	21	100	0	1	-1	.987	6	*O	1.8
1957	Chi-A	119	416	57	120	27	2	14	79	56	79	.288	.376	.464	127	17	16	71	2	3	-1	.985	-4	*O	0.5
1958	Cle-A	89	247	41	70	10	1	13	45	26	49	.283	.352	.490	132	9	10	41	0	2	-1	1.000	1	O	0.7
1959	Det-A	18	55	5	12	3	1	0	4	8	9	.218	.317	.309	69	-2	-2	6	0	0	0	.960	-1	O	-0.4
	Chi-A	21	58	1	14	1	1	0	9	2	13	.241	.267	.293	54	-4	-4	5	1	0	0	.955	-1	O/1	-0.5
	Yr	39	113	6	26	4	2	0	13	10	22	.230	.293	.301	62	-6	-6	11	1	0	0	.957	-1	O/1	-0.9
Total	13	1533	5348	960	1515	243	52	253	970	871	1011	.283	.387	.490	137	267	278	1074	47	36	-8	.983	3	*O/21S	20.3
■ ORAN DODD	Dodd, Oran A. b: 9/14/1889, Bagwell, Tex. d: 3/31/29, Newport, Ark. BR/TR, 5'8", 150 lbs. Deb: 7/26/12																								
1912	Pit-N	5	9	0	0	0	0	0	1	1	3	.000	.100	.000	-73	-2	-2	0	0			1.000	0	/32	-0.2
■ TOM DODD	Dodd, Thomas Marion b: 8/15/58, Portland, Ore. BR/TR, 6', 190 lbs. Deb: 7/25/86																								
1986	Bal-A	8	13	1	3	0	0	1	2	2	2	.231	.375	.462	128	1	1	2	0	0	0	.000	-0	/3D	0.0
■ JOHN DODGE	Dodge, John Lewis b: 4/27/1889, Bolivar, Tenn. d: 6/19/16, Mobile, Ala. BR/TR, 5'11.5", 165 lbs. Deb: 8/29/12																								
1912	Phi-N	30	92	3	11	1	0	0	3	4	11	.120	.156	.130	-20	-15	-16	2	2			1.000	8	3/2S	-0.9
1913	Phi-N	3	3	0	1	0	0	0	0	2	0	.333	.600	.333	164	1	1	1	0			1.000	-1	/S	0.0
	Cin-N	94	323	35	78	8	8	4	45	10	34	.241	.269	.353	77	-11	-11	32	11			.908	0	3	-1.0
	Yr	97	326	35	79	8	8	4	45	12	34	.242	.274	.353	78	-11	-10	33	11			.908	-1	3/S	-1.0
Total	2	127	418	38	90	9	8	4	48	16	45	.215	.248	.304	55	-26	-27	35	13			.926	7	3/2S	-1.9
■ PAT DODSON	Dodson, Patrick Neal b: 10/11/59, Santa Monica, Cal. BL/TL, 6'4", 210 lbs. Deb: 9/05/86																								
1986	Bos-A	9	12	3	5	2	0	1	3	3	3	.417	.533	.833	264	3	3	6	0	0	0	1.000	-1	/1	0.2
1987	Bos-A	26	42	4	7	3	0	2	6	8	13	.167	.300	.381	77	-1	-1	5	0	0	0	1.000	-1	1/D	-0.3
1988	Bos-A	17	45	5	8	3	1	1	1	6	17	.178	.275	.356	72	-2	-2	5	0	0	0	1.000	2	1	-0.1
Total	3	52	99	12	20	8	1	4	10	17	33	.202	.319	.424	97	0	-0	16	0	0	0	1.000	0	/1D	-0.2
■ BOBBY DOERR	Doerr, Robert Pershing b: 4/7/18, Los Angeles, Cal. BR/TR, 5'11", 175 lbs. Deb: 4/20/37 CH																								
1937	Bos-A	55	147	22	33	5	1	2	14	18	25	.224	.313	.313	56	-9	-10	15	2	4	-2	.973	4	2	-0.5
1938	Bos-A	145	509	70	147	26	7	5	80	59	39	.289	.363	.397	86	-7	-11	74	5	10	-5	.968	6	*2	-0.1
1939	Bos-A	127	525	75	167	28	2	12	73	38	32	.318	.365	.448	103	5	2	78	1	10	-6	.976	**27**	*2	2.8
1940	Bos-A	151	595	87	173	37	10	22	105	57	53	.291	.353	.497	113	14	10	104	10	5	0	.977	18	*2	3.6
1941	Bos-A★	132	500	74	141	28	4	16	93	43	43	.282	.339	.450	105	3	2	78	1	3	-2	.971	-6	*2	0.3
1942	Bos-A☆	144	545	71	158	35	5	15	102	67	55	.290	.369	.455	127	22	19	95	4	4	-1	**.975**	11	*2	3.9
1943	Bos-A★	155	604	78	163	32	3	16	75	62	59	.270	.339	.412	117	13	12	86	8	8	-2	**.990**	15	*2	3.5
1944	Bos-A★	125	468	95	152	30	10	15	81	58	31	.325	.399	**.528**	166	38	39	103	5	2	0	.976	4	*2	5.1
1946	*Bos-A★	151	583	95	158	34	9	18	116	66	67	.271	.346	.453	115	16	12	90	5	6	-2	**.986**	**27**	*2	4.8
1947	Bos-A★	146	561	79	145	23	10	17	95	59	47	.258	.329	.426	101	5	-0	74	3	3	-1	.981	**24**	*2	3.4
1948	Bos-A★	140	527	94	150	23	6	27	111	83	49	.285	.386	.505	129	26	22	107	3	2	-0	.993	8	*2	3.7
1949	Bos-A	139	541	91	167	30	9	18	109	75	33	.309	.393	.497	126	26	20	101	2	2	-1	.980	**28**	*2	5.2
1950	Bos-A★	149	586	103	172	29	**11**	27	120	67	42	.294	.367	.519	114	19	10	109	3	4	-2	**.988**	9	*2	2.2
1951	Bos-A★	106	402	60	116	21	2	13	73	57	33	.289	.378	.448	112	13	8	71	2	1	0	.981	6	*2	1.9
Total	14	1865	7093	1094	2042	381	89	223	1247	809	608	.288	.362	.461	114	181	135	1185	54	64	-22	.980	181	*2	39.8
■ JOHN DOHERTY	Doherty, John Michael b: 8/22/51, Woburn, Mass. BL/TL, 5'11", 185 lbs. Deb: 6/01/74																								
1974	Cal-A	74	223	20	57	14	1	3	15	8	13	.256	.281	.368	91	-5	-3	23	2	1	0	.991	-1	1/D	-0.8
1975	Cal-A	30	94	7	19	3	0	1	12	8	12	.202	.265	.266	54	-6	-5	7	1	1	-0	.983	-1	1/D	-0.8
Total	2	104	317	27	76	17	1	4	27	16	25	.240	.276	.338	80	-11	-9	29	3	2	-0		-2	/1D	-1.6
■ COZY DOLAN	Dolan, Albert J. (b: James Alberts) b: 12/23/1889, Chicago, Ill. d: 12/10/58, Chicago, Ill. BR/TR, 5'10", 160 lbs. Deb: 8/15/09 C																								
1909	Cin-N	3	6	2	1	0	0	0	0	2		.167	.375	.167	69	-0	-0	1	0			.750	-1	/3	-0.1
1911	NY-A	19	69	19	21	1	2	0	6	8		.304	.385	.377	106	1	1	14	12			.947	-1	3	0.0

YEAR	TM/L	G	AB	R	H	2B	3B	HR	RBI	BB	SO	AVG	OBP	SLG	PRO+	BR	/A	RC	SB	CS	SBR	FA	FR	POS	TPR
1912	NY-A	18	60	15	12	1	3	0	11	5		.200	.273	.317	64	-3	-3	7	5			.768	-6	3	-1.0
	Phi-N	11	50	8	14	2	2	0	7	1	10	.280	.294	.400	83	-1	-1	6	3			.872	-1	3	-0.2
1913	Phi-N	55	126	15	33	4	0	0	8	1	21	.262	.273	.294	59	-6	-7	12	9			.905	-7	OS/231	-1.5
	Pit-N	35	133	22	27	5	2	0	9	15	14	.203	.289	.271	63	-7	-6	13	14			.937	-2	3	-0.8
	Yr	90	259	37	60	9	2	0	17	16	35	.232	.282	.282	61	-13	-13	25	23			.932	-9	3OS/21	-2.3
1914	StL-N	126	421	76	101	16	3	4	32	55	74	.240	.335	.321	96	-1	-0	57	42			.955	-8	O3	-1.2
1915	StL-N	111	322	53	90	14	9	2	38	34	37	.280	.356	.398	127	11	11	49	17	11	-2	.929	-11	O	-0.6
1922	NY-N	1	0	0	0	0	0	0	0	0	0	—	—	—	—	0	0	0	0	0	0	.000	0	R	0.0
Total	7	379	1187	210	299	43	21	6	111	121	156	.252	.328	.339	95	-5	-6	159	102	11		.940	-36	O3/S21	-5.4

■ JOE DOLAN Dolan, Joseph b: 2/24/1873, Baltimore, Md. d: 3/24/38, Omaha, Neb. TR , 5'10", 155 lbs. Deb: 8/11/1896

1896	Lou-N	44	165	14	35	2	1	3	18	9	12	.212	.253	.291	46	-13	-12	14	6			.940	9	S	-0.1
1897	Lou-N	36	133	10	28	2	2	0	7	8		.211	.271	.256	41	-12	-11	11	6			.849	-4	S2	-1.1
1899	Phi-N	61	222	27	57	6	3	1	30	11		.257	.298	.324	73	-9	-8	23	3			.915	-11	2	-1.5
1900	Phi-N	74	257	39	51	7	3	1	27	16		.198	.259	.261	44	-20	-20	21	10			.931	3	32S	-1.4
1901	Phi-N	10	37	0	3	0	0	0	2	2		.081	.128	.081	-38	-6	-7	0	0			.973	-3	2	-1.0
	Phi-A	98	338	50	73	21	2	1	38	26		.216	.280	.299	58	-18	-20	31	3			.881	17	S3/2O	0.1
Total	5	323	1152	140	247	38	11	6	122	72	12	.214	.269	.282	51	-79	-78	101	28			.902	10	S2/3O	-5.0

■ BIDDY DOLAN Dolan, Leon Mark b: 7/9/1881, Onalaska, Wis. d: 7/15/50, Indianapolis, Ind BR/TR, 6', Deb: 4/16/14

1914	Ind-F	32	103	13	23	4	2	1	15	12	13	.223	.316	.330	76	-2	-4	14	5			.979	1	1	-0.4

■ COZY DOLAN Dolan, Patrick Henry b: 12/3/1872, Cambridge, Mass. d: 3/29/07, Louisville, Ky. BL/TL, 5'10", 160 lbs. Deb: 8/09/1892

1892	Was-N	5	13	1	3	0	0	0	1	2	5	.231	.333	.231	75	-0	-0	1	0			1.000	-1	/P	0.0
1895	Bos-N	26	83	12	20	4	1	0	7	6	7	.241	.300	.313	56	-5	-6	9	3			.949	3	P/O	-0.1
1896	Bos-N	6	14	4	2	0	0	0	0	0	1	.143	.143	.143	-22	-2	-3	0	0			.765	-0	/P	0.0
1900	Chi-N	13	48	5	13	1	0	0	2	2		.271	.300	.292	66	-2	-2	5	2			.826	-2	O	-0.4
1901	Chi-N	43	171	29	45	1	2	0	16	7		.263	.296	.292	74	-6	-5	16	3			.878	2	O	-0.7
	Bro-N	66	253	33	66	11	1	0	29	17		.261	.307	.312	78	-6	-7	28	7			.967	-2	O	-1.3
	Yr	109	424	62	111	12	3	0	45	24		.262	.303	.304	76	-13	-13	44	10			.931	0	*O	-2.0
1902	Bro-N	141	592	72	166	16	7	1	54	33		.280	.324	.336	103	2	1	75	24			.936	-9	*O	-1.8
1903	Chi-A	27	104	16	27	5	1	0	7	6		.260	.313	.327	96	-1	-0	12	5			.971	2	1/O	0.1
	Cin-N	93	385	64	111	20	3	0	58	28		.288	.340	.356	89	-1	-7	52	11			.937	-7	O	-1.9
1904	Cin-N	129	465	88	132	8	10	6	51	39		.284	.341	.383	114	13	8	71	19			.939	-4	*O1	-0.3
1905	Cin-N	22	77	7	18	2	1	0	4	7		.234	.306	.286	69	-2	-3	8	2			.965	-4	1/O	-0.8
	Bos-N	112	433	44	119	11	7	3	48	27		.275	.322	.353	104	0	1	58	21			.946	4	*O/P1	0.0
	Yr	134	510	51	137	13	8	3	52	34		.269	.319	.343	98	-2	-2	66	23			.931	0	*O1/P	-0.8
1906	Bos-N	152	549	54	136	20	4	0	39	55		.248	.318	.299	95	-4	-2	61	17			.928	-2	*O/2P1	-1.1
Total	10	835	3187	429	858	99	37	10	316	229	13	.269	.322	.333	94	-16	-26	397	114			.931	-18	O/1P2	-8.3

■ TOM DOLAN Dolan, Thomas J. b: 1/10/1859, New York, N.Y. d: 1/16/13, St.Louis, Mo. BR/TR, Deb: 9/30/1879

1879	Chi-N	1	4	0	0	0	0	0	0	0	2	.000	.000	.000	-94	-1	-1	0				1.000	1	/C	0.0
1882	Buf-N	22	89	12	14	0	1	0	8	2	11	.157	.176	.180	14	-8	-8	3				.941	-8	C/O3	-1.5
1883	StL-a	81	295	32	63	9	2	1		9		.214	.237	.268	59	-12	-15	19				.957	12	CO/P	0.0
1884	StL-a	35	137	19	36	6	2	0		6		.263	.299	.336	106	1	1	14				.873	-6	C/O	-0.2
	StL-U	19	69	9	13	3	0	0		4		.188	.233	.232	56	-3	-3	4				.897	11	C/3O	0.7
1885	StL-N	3	9	1	2	0	0	0	0	2	1	.222	.364	.222	99	0	0	1				.810	-1	/C	0.0
1886	StL-N	15	44	8	11	3	0	0	1	7	9	.250	.353	.318	113	1	1	6	2			.928	6	C	0.8
	Bal-a	38	125	13	19	3	2	0		8		.152	.203	.208	31	-10	-9	7	8			.918	-6	C/O	-1.1
1888	StL-a	11	36	1	7	1	0	0	1	1		.194	.216	.222	39	-2	-3	2	1			.914	-0	C	-0.2
Total	7	225	808	95	165	25	7	1	10	39	23	.204	.242	.256	59	-34	-38	56	11			.916	8	C/O3P	-1.5

■ LESTER DOLE Dole, Lester Carrington b: 7/8/1855, Meriden, Conn. d: 12/10/18, Concord, N.H. 5'11", Deb: 5/27/1875

1875	NH-n	1	4	1	2	0	0	0		0		.500	.500	.500	283	1	1	1						/O	0.1

■ FRANK DOLJACK Doljack, Frank Joseph "Dolie" b: 10/5/07, Cleveland, Ohio d: 1/23/48, Cleveland, Ohio BR/TR, 5'11", 175 lbs. Deb: 9/04/30

1930	Det-A	20	74	10	19	5	1	3	17	2	11	.257	.286	.473	87	-2	-2	9	0	1	-1	.930	0	O	-0.3
1931	Det-A	63	187	20	52	13	3	4	20	15	17	.278	.335	.444	100	0	-1	28	3	2	-0	.925	3	O	-0.1
1932	Det-A	8	26	5	10	1	0	1	7	2	2	.385	.429	.538	143	2	2	6	1	0	0	1.000	-2	/O	0.0
1933	Det-A	42	147	18	42	5	2	0	22	14	13	.286	.348	.347	83	-3	-3	17	2	6	-3	.941	2	O	-0.6
1934	*Det-A	56	120	15	28	7	1	1	19	13	15	.233	.313	.333	67	-6	-6	13	2	1	0	.943	-3	O/1	-0.9
1943	Cle-A	3	7	0	0	0	0	0	0	1	2	.000	.125	.000	-66	-1	-1	0	0	0	0	1.000	-1	/O	-0.2
Total	6	192	561	68	151	31	7	9	85	47	60	.269	.329	.398	87	-10	-12	73	8	10	-4	.934	-0	O/1	-2.1

■ ART DOLL Doll, Arthur James "Moose" b: 5/7/13, Chicago, Ill. d: 4/28/78, Calumet City, Ill. BR/TR, 6'1", 190 lbs. Deb: 9/21/35

1935	Bos-N	3	10	0	1	0	0	0	0	0	1	.100	.100	.100	-50	-2	-2	0	0			.867	0	/C	-0.2
1936	Bos-N	1	2	0	0	0	0	0	0	0	2	.000	.000	.000	-99	-1	-1	0	0			1.000	-0	/P	0.0
1938	Bos-N	3	1	0	1	0	0	0	0	0	0	1.000	1.000	1.000	501	0	0	1	0			1.000	0	/P	0.0
Total	3	7	13	0	2	0	0	0	0	0	3	.154	.154	.154	-18	-2	-2	1	0			1.000	0	/PC	-0.2

■ SHE DONAHUE Donahue, Charles Michael b: 6/29/1877, Oswego, N.Y. d: 8/28/47, New York, N.Y. BR/TR, 5'9", Deb: 4/29/04

1904	StL-N	4	15	1	4	0	0	0	2	0		.267	.267	.267	68	-1	-1	2	3			.846	-3	/2S	-0.4
	Phi-N	58	200	21	43	4	0	0	14	3		.215	.227	.235	44	-14	-13	13	7			.857	-17	S3/12	-3.0
	Yr	62	215	22	47	4	0	0	16	3		.219	.229	.237	46	-14	-13	15	10			.852	-20	S3/21	-3.4

■ JIM DONAHUE Donahue, James Augustus b: 1/8/1862, Lockport, Ill. d: 4/19/35, Lockport, Ill. BR/TR, 6', 175 lbs. Deb: 4/19/1886

1886	NY-a	49	186	14	37	0	0	0		10		.199	.251	.199	45	-12	-10	10	1			.803	-2	OC	-1.0
1887	NY-a	60	220	33	62	4	1	1		21		.282	.350	.323	94	-2	-0	28	6			.890	-8	C/O132	-0.3
1888	KC-a	88	337	29	79	11	3	1	28	21		.234	.281	.294	82	-5	-8	32	12			.902	-11	CO/32	-1.2
1889	KC-a	67	252	30	59	5	4	0	32	21	20	.234	.293	.286	63	-11	-13	25	12			.887	-8	CO3	-1.5
1891	Col-a	77	280	27	61	4	3	0	35	31	18	.218	.298	.254	64	-14	-11	22	2			.942	3	C/O1	-0.1
Total	5	341	1275	133	298	24	11	2	95	104	38	.234	.295	.275	71	-42	-42	117	33			.911	-25	C/O312	-4.1

■ JIGGS DONAHUE Donahue, John Augustus b: 7/13/1879, Springfield, Ohio d: 7/19/13, Columbus, Ohio BL/TL, 6'1", 178 lbs. Deb: 9/10/00 F

1900	Pit-N	3	10	1	2	0	1	0	3	0		.200	.200	.400	63	-1	-1	1	1			.889	-1	/CO	-0.2
1901	Pit-N	2	0	0	0	0	0	0	0	0		—	—	—	—	0	0	0	0			.000	-1	/CO	-0.1
	Mil-A	37	107	10	34	5	4	0	16	10		.318	.387	.439	135	4	5	20	4			.933	-2	C1	0.4
1902	StL-A	30	89	11	21	1	1	1	7	12		.236	.327	.303	76	-3	-2	10	2			.956	-1	C/1	-0.1
1904	Chi-A	102	367	46	91	9	7	1	48	25		.248	.298	.319	99	-2	-0	43	18			.979	7	*1	0.5
1905	Chi-A	149	533	71	153	22	4	1	76	44		.287	.346	.349	126	13	16	81	32			**.988**	8	*1	2.0
1906	*Chi-A	154	556	70	143	17	7	1	57	48		.257	.320	.318	103	1	3	74	36			**.988**	9	*1	0.7
1907	Chi-A	157	609	75	158	16	4	0	68	28		.259	.295	.299	93	-8	-5	65	27			**.994**	21	*1	1.2
1908	Chi-A	93	304	22	62	8	2	0	22	25		.204	.271	.243	69	-10	-10	24	14			.994	5	1	-0.7
1909	Chi-A	2	4	0	0	0	0	0	2	1		.000	.200	.000	-38	-1	-1	0	0			1.000	-0	/1	-0.1
	Was-A	84	283	13	67	12	1	0	28	22		.237	.294	.286	87	-5	-4	27	9			.984	-4	1	-0.9

YEAR	TM/L	G	AB	R	H	2B	3B	HR	RBI	BB	SO	AVG	OBP	SLG	PRO+	BR	/A	RC	SB	CS	SBR	FA	FR	POS	TPR
	Yr	86	287	13	67	12	1	0	30	23		.233	.293	.282	86	-6	-4	27	9			.984	-4	1	-1.0
Total	9	813	2862	319	731	90	31	4	327	215		.255	.311	.313	100	-11	0	345	143			.987	39	1/CO	2.7
■ JOHN DONAHUE	Donahue, John Frederick "Jiggs" b: 4/19/1894, Roxbury, Mass. d: 10/3/49, Boston, Mass. BB/TR, 5'8", 170 lbs. Deb: 9/25/23																								
1923	Bos-A	10	36	5	10	4	0	0	1	4	5	.278	.350	.389	94	-0	-0	5	0	1	-1	1.000	3	/O	0.2
■ PAT DONAHUE	Donahue, Patrick William b: 11/8/1884, Springfield, Ohio d: 1/31/66, Springfield, Ohio BR/TR, 6', 175 lbs. Deb: 5/29/08 F																								
1908	Bos-A	35	86	8	17	2	0	1	6	9		.198	.289	.256	75	-2	-2	6	0			.959	0	C/1	0.0
1909	Bos-A	64	176	14	42	4	1	2	25	17		.239	.309	.307	93	-1	-1	18	2			.982	-3	C	0.1
1910	Bos-A	2	4	0	0	0	0	0	0	0		.000	.000	.000	-98	-1	-1	0	0			1.000	0	/C	-0.1
	Phi-A	14	34	2	5	0	0	0	4	3		.147	.237	.147	21	-3	-3	2	1			1.000	3	C	0.2
	Cle-A	2	6	0	1	0	0	0	0	0		.167	.167	.167	4	-1	-1	0	0			1.000	-1	/C1	-0.1
	Phi-A	1	1	0	0	0	0	0	0	0		.000	.000	.000	-99	-0	-0	0	0			1.000	1	/C	0.0
	Yr	19	45	2	6	0	0	0	4	3		.133	.204	.133	6	-5	-5	2	1			1.000	4	C/1	0.0
Total	3	118	307	24	65	6	1	3	35	29		.212	.288	.267	75	-7	-8	26	3			.978	1	C/1	0.1
■ TIM DONAHUE	Donahue, Timothy Cornelius "Bridget" b: 6/8/1870, Raynham, Mass. d: 6/12/02, Taunton, Mass. BL/TR, 5'11", 180 lbs. Deb: 7/28/1891																								
1891	Bos-a	4	7	0	0	0	0	0	0	0	5	.000	.000	.000	-99	-2	-2	0	0			.833	-1	/C	-0.2
1895	Chi-N	63	219	29	59	9	1	2	36	20	25	.269	.339	.347	74	-7	-9	29	5			.915	-2	C	-0.4
1896	Chi-N	57	188	27	41	10	1	0	20	11	15	.218	.276	.282	47	-14	-15	19	11			.937	5	C	-0.3
1897	Chi-N	58	188	28	45	7	3	0	21	9		.239	.281	.309	54	-12	-14	18	3			.947	7	C/S1	-0.1
1898	Chi-N	122	396	52	87	12	3	0	39	49		.220	.318	.265	68	-15	-15	42	17			.962	6	*C	0.3
1899	Chi-N	92	278	39	69	9	3	0	29	34		.248	.345	.302	80	-7	-6	35	10			.951	5	C/1	0.6
1900	Chi-N	67	216	21	51	10	1	0	17	19		.236	.313	.292	70	-9	-8	24	8			.928	-9	C/2	-1.0
1902	Was-A	3	8	0	2	0	0	0	1	0		.250	.250	.250	38	-1	-1	1	0			1.000	0	/C	0.0
Total	8	466	1500	196	354	57	12	2	163	142	45	.236	.314	.294	66	-67	-69	166	54			.943	10	C/1S2	-1.1
■ JOHN DONALDSON	Donaldson, John David b: 5/5/43, Charlotte, N.C. BL/TR, 5'11", 165 lbs. Deb: 8/26/66																								
1966	KC-A	15	30	4	4	0	0	0	1	3	4	.133	.212	.133	2	-4	-4	1	1	0	0	1.000	-2	/2	-0.6
1967	KC-A	105	377	27	104	16	5	0	28	37	39	.276	.344	.345	107	3	4	47	6	3	0	.982	-18	*2/S	-0.8
1968	Oak-A	127	363	37	80	9	2	2	27	45	44	.220	.310	.273	82	-9	-7	32	5	5	-2	.971	-4	2/3S	-0.7
1969	Oak-A	12	13	1	1	0	0	0	0	2	4	.077	.200	.077	-21	-2	-2	0	0	0	0	.857	0	/2	-0.2
	Sea-A	95	338	22	79	8	3	1	19	36	36	.234	.307	.284	67	-15	-14	32	6	1	1	.974	-1	2/3S	-0.6
	Yr	107	351	23	80	8	3	1	19	38	40	.228	.303	.276	64	-17	-16	32	6	1	1	.972	-0	2/3S	-0.8
1970	Oak-A	41	89	4	22	2	1	1	11	9	6	.247	.316	.326	80	-3	-2	9	1	0	0	.986	-3	2/S3	-0.3
1974	Oak-A	10	15	1	2	0	0	0	0	0	0	.133	.133	.133	-25	-2	-2	0	0	0	0	.962	1	/23	-0.1
Total	6	405	1225	96	292	35	11	4	86	132	133	.238	.314	.295	81	-31	-27	121	19	9	0	.976	-26	2/3S	-3.3
■ LEN DONDERO	Dondero, Leonard Peter "Mike" b: 9/12/03, Newark, Cal. BR/TR, 5'11", 178 lbs. Deb: 4/21/29																								
1929	StL-A	19	31	2	6	0	0	1	8	0	4	.194	.194	.290	22	-4	-4	2	0	0	0	.857	-3	3/2	-0.6
■ MIKE DONLIN	Donlin, Michael Joseph "Turkey Mike" b: 5/30/1878, Peoria, Ill. d: 9/24/33, Hollywood, Cal. BL/TL, 5'9", 170 lbs. Deb: 7/19/1899																								
1899	StL-N	66	266	49	86	9	6	6	27	17		.323	.366	.470	126	9	8	55	20			.873	-7	O1/SP	-0.3
1900	StL-N	78	276	40	90	8	6	10	48	14		.326	.361	.507	139	12	13	57	14			.922	-4	O1	0.5
1901	Bal-A	121	476	107	162	23	13	5	67	53		.340	.409	.475	138	30	26	109	33			.918	9	O1	2.6
1902	Cin-N	34	143	30	41	5	4	0	9	9		.287	.333	.378	109	3	1	22	9			.877	-1	O/PS	-0.2
1903	Cin-N	126	496	110	174	25	18	7	67	56		.351	.420	.516	150	**43**	35	122	26			.900	-2	*O/1	2.4
1904	Cin-N	60	236	42	84	11	7	1	38	18		.356	.406	.475	158	20	17	56	21			.872	-3	O/1	1.2
	NY-N	42	132	17	37	7	3	2	14	10		.280	.336	.424	129	5	4	20	1			.918	-7	O	-0.4
	Yr	102	368	59	121	18	10	3	52	28		.329	.381	.457	148	25	22	75	22			.886	-9	O/1	0.8
1905	*NY-N	150	606	**124**	216	31	16	7	80	56		.356	.413	.495	167	52	50	142	33			.934	-12	*O	3.2
1906	NY-N	37	121	15	38	5	1	1	14	11		.314	.371	.397	137	5	5	22	9			.929	-6	O/1	-0.3
1908	NY-N	155	593	71	198	26	13	6	106	23		.334	.364	.452	153	37	34	108	30			.977	0	*O	3.2
1911	NY-N	12	12	3	4	0	0	1	1	0	1	.333	.333	.583	150	1	1	3	2			1.000	-1	/O	-0.1
	Bos-N	56	222	33	70	16	1	2	34	22	17	.315	.377	.423	115	7	4	38	7			.912	-3	O	-0.1
	Yr	68	234	36	74	16	1	3	35	22	18	.316	.375	.432	117	8	5	41	9			.913	-4	O	-0.2
1912	Pit-N	77	244	27	77	9	8	2	35	20	16	.316	.370	.443	124	7	7	43	8			.982	-2	O	0.2
1914	NY-N	35	31	1	5	1	1	1	3	3	5	.161	.235	.355	77	-1	-1	2	0			.000	0	H	-0.1
Total	12	1049	3854	669	1282	176	97	51	543	312	39	.333	.385	.468	142	228	205	799	213			.924	-37	O/1PS	11.8
■ JIM DONNELLY	Donnelly, James B. b: 7/19/1865, New Haven, Conn. d: 3/5/15, Meriden, Conn. BR/TR, Deb: 7/11/1884																								
1884	KC-U	6	23	2	3	1	0	0		1		.130	.167	.174	18	-2	-1	1				.536	-4	/3C	-0.5
	Ind-a	40	134	22	34	2	2	0		5		.254	.301	.299	102	0	1	12				.850	-5	3/SO2	-0.3
1885	Det-N	56	211	24	49	4	3	1	22	10	29	.232	.267	.294	81	-4	-4	17				.850	-3	3/1	-0.6
1886	KC-N	113	438	51	88	11	3	0	38	36	57	.201	.262	.240	50	-24	-28	32	16			.845	0	*3	-2.3
1887	Was-N	117	425	51	85	9	6	1	46	16	26	.200	.234	.256	39	-35	-32	36	42			.867	16	*3/S	-1.2
1888	Was-N	122	428	43	86	9	4	0	23	20	16	.201	.242	.241	59	-20	-17	36	44			.875	-5	*3/S	-2.0
1889	Was-N	4	13	3	2	0	0	0	0	2	0	.154	.267	.154	21	-1	-1	1	1			.667	-2	/3	-0.2
1890	StL-a	11	42	11	14	0	0	0		8		.333	.451	.333	118	3	2	9	5			.795	-3	3	-0.1
1891	Col-a	17	54	6	13	0	0	0	9	13	5	.241	.388	.241	89	-0	0	8	7			.855	3	3	0.3
1896	Bal-N	106	396	70	130	14	10	0	71	34	11	.328	.387	.414	112	8	7	82	38			.884	-2	*3	0.6
1897	Pit-N	44	161	22	31	4	0	0	14	16		.193	.270	.217	31	-16	-15	14	14			.920	2	3	-1.1
	NY-N	23	85	19	16	3	0	0	11	9		.188	.266	.224	31	-9	-8	7	6			.869	-6	3	-1.2
	Yr	67	246	41	47	7	0	0	25	25		.191	.268	.220	31	-25	-23	21	20			.905	-4	3	-2.3
1898	StL-N	1	1	0	1	0	0	0	0	0		1.000	1.000	1.000	463	0	0	1	0			.500	0	/3	0.0
Total	11	660	2411	324	552	57	28	2	234	170	144	.229	.284	.278	66	-100	-97	257	173			.862	-8	3/SO21C	-8.6
■ JOHN DONNELLY	Donnelly, John b: Elizabeth, N.J. Deb: 4/14/1873 F																								
1873	Was-n	30	137	15	35	3	0	0	17	1	0	.255	.261	.277	60	-7	-6	10						S2/O3	-0.5
1874	Phi-n	6	22	2	5	0	0	0		0		.227	.227	.227	44	-1	-1	1						/SO2	-0.1
Total	2 n	36	159	17	40	3	0	0		1		.252	.256	.270	58	-8	-7	11						/S2O3	-0.6
■ PETE DONNELLY	Donnelly, Peter J. b: Philadelphia, Pa. d: 10/1/1890, Jersey City.N.J. Deb: 5/13/1871 F																								
1871	Kek-n	9	34	7	7	1	1	0	3	1	2	.206	.229	.294	48	-2	-2	2	0					/O3	-0.1
■ CHRIS DONNELS	Donnels, Chris Barton b: 4/21/66, Los Angeles, Cal. BL/TR, 6', 185 lbs. Deb: 5/07/91																								
1991	NY-N	37	89	7	20	2	0	0	5	14	19	.225	.330	.247	65	-4	-4	8	1	1	-0	1.000	3	13	-0.2
1992	NY-N	45	121	8	21	4	0	0	6	17	25	.174	.275	.207	39	-9	-9	8	1	0	0	.941	4	32	-0.6
Total	2	82	210	15	41	6	0	0	11	31	44	.195	.299	.224	50	-13	-13	16	2	1	0	.940	6	/312	-0.8
■ JOE DONOHUE	Donohue, Joseph F. b: 1869, Syracuse, N.Y. Deb: 8/24/1891																								
1891	Phi-N	6	22	2	7	1	0	0	2	1	3	.318	.375	.364	115	1	0	3	0			1.000	-0	/OS	0.0
■ TOM DONOHUE	Donohue, Thomas James b: 11/15/52, Mineola, N.Y. BR/TR, 6', 185 lbs. Deb: 4/06/79																								
1979	Cal-A	38	107	13	24	3	1	3	14	3	29	.224	.259	.355	66	-6	-5	10	2	0	1	.981	-3	C	-0.6
1980	Cal-A	84	218	18	41	4	1	2	14	7	63	.188	.217	.243	26	-22	-22	12	5	1	1	.986	-10	C	-2.8

YEAR	TM/L	G	AB	R	H	2B	3B	HR	RBI	BB	SO	AVG	OBP	SLG	PRO+	BR	/A	RC	SB	CS	SBR	FA	FR	POS	TPR
Total	2	122	325	31	65	7	2	5	28	10	92	.200	.231	.280	40	-28	-27	23	7	1	2	.985	-12	C	-3.4

■ FRED DONOVAN Donovan, Frederick Maurice b: 7/4/1864, New Hampshire d: 3/7/16, Bloomington, Ill. BR/TR, Deb: 6/23/1895

YEAR	TM/L	G	AB	R	H	2B	3B	HR	RBI	BB	SO	AVG	OBP	SLG	PRO+	BR	/A	RC	SB	CS	SBR	FA	FR	POS	TPR
1895	Cle-N	3	12	1	1	0	0	0	1	1	2	.083	.154	.083	-35	-2	-3	0	0			.938	-0	/C	-0.2

■ JERRY DONOVAN Donovan, Jeremiah Francis b: 9/3/1876, Lock Haven, Pa. d: 6/27/38, St.Petersburg, Fla. BR/TR, Deb: 4/12/06 F

YEAR	TM/L	G	AB	R	H	2B	3B	HR	RBI	BB	SO	AVG	OBP	SLG	PRO+	BR	/A	RC	SB	CS	SBR	FA	FR	POS	TPR
1906	Phi-N	61	166	11	33	4	0	0	15	6		.199	.236	.223	43	-11	-11	10	2			.955	-4	C/SO	-1.2

■ MIKE DONOVAN Donovan, Michael Berchman b: 10/18/1881, Brooklyn, N.Y. d: 2/3/38, New York, N.Y. BR/TR, 5'8", 155 lbs. Deb: 5/29/04

YEAR	TM/L	G	AB	R	H	2B	3B	HR	RBI	BB	SO	AVG	OBP	SLG	PRO+	BR	/A	RC	SB	CS	SBR	FA	FR	POS	TPR
1904	Cle-A	2	2	0	0	0	0	0	0	0		.000	.000	.000	-99	-0	-0	0	0			.000	0	/S	0.0
1908	NY-A	5	19	2	5	1	0	0	2	0		.263	.263	.316	87	-0	-0	1	0			1.000	1	/3	0.1
Total	2	7	21	2	5	1	0	0	2	0		.238	.238	.286	69	-1	-1	1	0				1	/3S	0.1

■ PATSY DONOVAN Donovan, Patrick Joseph b: 3/16/1865, County Cork, Ireland d: 12/25/53, Lawrence, Mass. BL/TL, 5'11.5", 175 lbs. Deb: 4/19/1890 M

YEAR	TM/L	G	AB	R	H	2B	3B	HR	RBI	BB	SO	AVG	OBP	SLG	PRO+	BR	/A	RC	SB	CS	SBR	FA	FR	POS	TPR
1890	Bos-N	32	140	17	36	0	0	0	9	8	17	.257	.307	.257	62	-6	-7	14	10			.891	-5	O	-1.2
	*Bro-N	28	105	17	23	5	1	0	8	5	5	.219	.268	.286	63	-5	-5	9	3			1.000	2	O	-0.4
	Yr	60	245	34	59	5	1	0	17	13	22	.241	.290	.269	62	-11	-12	23	13			.952	-3	O	-1.6
1891	Lou-a	105	439	73	141	10	3	2	53	30	18	.321	.375	.371	118	10	11	73	27			.912	5	*O	1.0
	Was-a	17	70	9	14	1	0	0	3	4	5	.200	.243	.214	35	-6	-5	4	1			.857	-2	O	-0.7
	Yr	122	509	82	155	11	3	2	56	34	23	.305	.358	.350	107	4	5	75	28			.907	2	*O	0.3
1892	Was-N	40	163	29	39	3	3	0	12	11	13	.239	.295	.294	83	-4	-3	19	16			.844	1	O	-0.4
	Pit-N	90	388	77	114	15	3	2	26	20	16	.294	.333	.363	112	5	5	62	40			.872	-3	O	-0.2
	Yr	130	551	106	153	18	6	2	38	31	29	.278	.322	.343	104	1	2	81	56			.862	-2	*O	-0.6
1893	Pit-N	113	499	114	158	5	8	2	56	42	8	.317	.373	.371	102	1	2	88	46			.937	-1	*O	-0.3
1894	Pit-N	132	576	145	174	21	10	4	76	33	12	.302	.345	.394	80	-20	-19	97	41			.932	8	*O	-1.5
1895	Pit-N	125	519	114	160	17	6	1	58	47	19	.308	.375	.370	100	-2	3	88	36			.961	-5	*O	-1.0
1896	Pit-N	131	573	113	183	20	5	3	59	35	18	.319	.370	.387	106	2	6	103	48			.954	7	*O	0.2
1897	Pit-N	120	479	82	154	16	7	0	57	25		.322	.360	.384	100	-3	0	81	34			.949	1	*OM	-0.7
1898	Pit-N	147	610	112	184	16	9	0	37	34		.302	.346	.357	104	1	2	93	41			.928	0	*O	-0.7
1899	Pit-N	121	531	82	156	11	7	1	55	17		.294	.322	.347	84	-13	-13	70	26			.941	-12	*OM	-3.1
1900	StL-N	126	503	78	159	11	1	0	61	38		.316	.368	.342	97	-1	-0	83	**45**			.951	-5	*O	-1.3
1901	StL-N	130	531	92	161	23	5	1	73	27		.303	.343	.371	113	4	8	81	28			.979	4	*OM	0.2
1902	StL-N	126	502	70	158	12	4	0	35	28		.315	.363	.355	127	13	15	80	34			.959	10	*OM	1.8
1903	StL-N	105	410	63	134	15	3	0	39	25		.327	.370	.378	117	7	9	70	25			.952	-1	*OM	0.2
1904	Was-A	125	436	30	100	6	0	0	19	24		.229	.271	.243	64	-18	-17	36	17			.963	9	*OM	-1.7
1906	Bro-N	7	21	1	5	0	0	0	0	0		.238	.238	.238	53	-1	-1	1	0			1.000	-1	/OM	-0.2
1907	Bro-N	1	1	0	0	0	0	0	0	0		.000	.000	.000	-99	-0	-0	0	0			1.000	0	/OM	0.0
Total	17	1821	7496	1318	2253	207	75	16	736	453	131	.301	.347	.355	99	-35	-9	1154	518			.941	13	*O	-10.0

■ TOM DONOVAN Donovan, Thomas Joseph b: 1/1/1873, West Troy, N.Y. d: 3/25/33, Watervliet, N.Y. BR/TR, 6'2", 168 lbs. Deb: 9/10/01 F

YEAR	TM/L	G	AB	R	H	2B	3B	HR	RBI	BB	SO	AVG	OBP	SLG	PRO+	BR	/A	RC	SB	CS	SBR	FA	FR	POS	TPR
1901	Cle-A	18	71	9	18	3	1	0	5	0		.254	.254	.324	62	-4	-4	6	1			.862	-1	O/P	-0.5

■ BILL DONOVAN Donovan, William Edward "Wild Bill" b: 10/13/1876, Lawrence, Mass. d: 12/9/23, Forsyth, N.Y. BR/TR, 5'11", 190 lbs. Deb: 4/22/1898 M

YEAR	TM/L	G	AB	R	H	2B	3B	HR	RBI	BB	SO	AVG	OBP	SLG	PRO+	BR	/A	RC	SB	CS	SBR	FA	FR	POS	TPR
1898	Was-N	39	103	11	17	2	2	2	8	4		.165	.211	.282	41	-8	-8	7	2			.933	1	OP/S2	-0.5
1899	Bro-N	5	13	2	3	1	0	0	0	0		.231	.231	.308	46	-1	-1	1	0			.857	-0	/P	0.0
1900	Bro-N	5	13	0	0	0	0	0	2	0		.000	.000	.000	-94	-3	-4	0	0			1.000	1	/P	0.0
1901	Bro-N	46	135	16	23	3	0	2	13	8		.170	.217	.237	31	-12	-12	8	1			.927	-1	P	0.0
1902	Bro-N	48	161	16	28	3	2	1	16	9		.174	.222	.236	41	-11	-11	10	7			.948	2	P/1O2	-0.3
1903	Det-A	40	124	11	30	3	2	0	12	4		.242	.266	.298	71	-5	-4	12	3			.938	-2	P/S2O	0.1
1904	Det-A	46	140	12	38	2	1	1	6	3		.271	.287	.321	95	-2	-1	14	2			.967	-3	P/1O	-0.4
1905	Det-A	44	130	16	25	4	0	0	5	12		.192	.266	.223	55	-6	-6	12	8			.933	-0	P/O2	0.1
1906	Det-A	28	91	5	11	0	1	0	0	1		.121	.130	.143	-14	-12	-12	3	6			.949	-1	P/2O	-0.2
1907	*Det-A	37	109	20	29	7	2	0	19	6		.266	.304	.367	110	1	1	14	4			.945	-6	P	0.0
1908	*Det-A	30	82	5	13	1	0	0	2	10		.159	.250	.171	36	-5	-6	4	2			.917	-6	P	0.0
1909	*Det-A	22	45	6	9	0	0	0	1	2		.200	.250	.200	41	-3	-3	3	0			.974	-2	P	0.0
1910	Det-A	26	69	6	10	1	0	0	2	5		.145	.203	.159	13	-7	-7	2	0			.955	-6	P	0.0
1911	Det-A	24	60	11	12	3	1	1	6	11		.200	.324	.333	79	-1	-2	7	1			.935	-5	P	0.0
1912	Det-A	6	13	3	1	0	0	0	0	1		.077	.143	.077	-38	-2	-2	0	0			1.000	-2	/P1O	-0.3
1915	NY-A	10	12	1	1	0	0	0	0	1	6	.083	.154	.083	-29	-2	-2	0	0			1.000	-1	/PM	0.0
1916	NY-A	1	0	0	0	0	0	0	0	0	0	—	—	—	—	0	0	0	0			.000	-0	/PM	0.0
1918	Det-A	2	2	1	1	0	0	0	1	0	0	.500	.500	.500	210	0	0	0	0			1.000	-0	/P	0.0
Total	18	459	1302	142	251	30	11	7	93	77	6	.193	.241	.249	49	-79	-81	98	36			.958	-30	P/O12S	-1.5

■ RED DOOIN Dooin, Charles Sebastian b: 6/12/1879, Cincinnati, Ohio d: 5/14/52, Rochester, N.Y. BR/TR, 5'9.5", 165 lbs. Deb: 4/18/02 M

YEAR	TM/L	G	AB	R	H	2B	3B	HR	RBI	BB	SO	AVG	OBP	SLG	PRO+	BR	/A	RC	SB	CS	SBR	FA	FR	POS	TPR
1902	Phi-N	94	333	20	77	7	3	0	35	10		.231	.260	.270	64	-15	-15	27	8			.950	4	C/O	-0.2
1903	Phi-N	62	188	18	41	5	1	0	14	8		.218	.254	.255	47	-14	-13	15	9			.940	-4	C/1O	-1.1
1904	Phi-N	108	355	41	86	11	4	6	36	8		.242	.261	.346	91	-7	-5	37	15			.938	8	C/1O3	1.3
1905	Phi-N	113	380	45	95	13	5	0	36	10		.250	.269	.311	76	-14	-12	37	12			.965	8	*C/3	0.7
1906	Phi-N	113	351	25	86	19	1	0	32	13		.245	.274	.305	81	-9	-9	35	15			.948	-11	*C	-1.0
1907	Phi-N	101	313	18	66	8	4	0	14	15		.211	.249	.262	61	-15	-14	24	10			.959	2	C/2O	-0.4
1908	Phi-N	133	435	28	108	17	4	0	41	17		.248	.283	.306	85	-7	-8	43	20			.966	12	*C	1.8
1909	Phi-N	141	468	42	105	14	1	2	38	21		.224	.264	.271	65	-20	-20	37	14			.958	4	*C	-0.3
1910	Phi-N	103	331	30	80	13	4	0	30	22	17	.242	.289	.305	71	-12	-13	31	10			.956	-4	C/OM	-0.8
1911	Phi-N	74	247	18	81	15	1	1	16	14	12	.328	.366	.409	115	5	5	39	6			.967	5	CM	1.6
1912	Phi-N	69	184	20	43	9	0	0	22	5	12	.234	.262	.283	46	-13	-15	15	8			.958	0	CM	-0.9
1913	Phi-N	55	129	6	33	4	1	0	13	3	9	.256	.273	.302	62	-6	-7	10	1			.962	4	CM	0.1
1914	Phi-N	53	118	10	21	2	0	1	8	4	14	.178	.205	.220	25	-11	-12	6	4			.967	-0	C/OM	-1.0
1915	Cin-N	10	31	2	10	0	0	0	0	2	5	.323	.364	.323	106	0	0	4	1			.915	-4	C	-0.3
	NY-N	46	124	9	27	2	2	0	9	3	15	.218	.236	.266	55	-7	-7	8	0	2	-1	.964	1	C	-0.5
	Yr	56	155	11	37	2	2	0	9	5	20	.239	.262	.277	66	-7	-6	11	1	2	-1	.956	-3	C	-0.8
1916	NY-N	15	17	1	2	0	0	0	0	0	3	.118	.118	.118	-29	-3	-2	0	0			.972	0	C	-0.2
Total	15	1290	4004	333	961	139	31	10	344	155	87	.240	.271	.298	72	-146	-148	369	133	2		.957	26	*C/O132	-1.2

■ MICKEY DOOLAN Doolan, Michael Joseph "Doc" (b: Michael Joseph Doolittle)
b: 5/7/1880, Ashland, Pa. d: 11/1/51, Orlando, Fla. BR/TR, 5'10.5", 170 lbs. Deb: 4/14/05 C

YEAR	TM/L	G	AB	R	H	2B	3B	HR	RBI	BB	SO	AVG	OBP	SLG	PRO+	BR	/A	RC	SB	CS	SBR	FA	FR	POS	TPR
1905	Phi-N	136	492	53	125	27	11	1	48	24		.254	.292	.360	97	-6	-3	59	17			.935	-9	*S	-1.0
1906	Phi-N	154	535	41	123	19	7	1	55	27		.230	.270	.297	77	-16	-16	51	16			.930	6	*S	-0.6
1907	Phi-N	145	509	33	104	19	7	1	47	25		.204	.243	.275	63	-24	-23	40	18			.929	14	*S	-0.5
1908	Phi-N	129	445	29	104	25	4	2	49	17		.234	.265	.321	84	-8	-10	39	5			.939	0	*S	-0.8
1909	Phi-N	147	493	39	108	12	10	1	35	37		.219	.276	.290	75	-15	-15	43	10			.939	**24**	*S	1.3
1910	Phi-N	148	536	58	141	31	6	2	57	35	56	.263	.315	.354	92	-5	-7	64	16			**.948**	21	*S	2.0
1911	Phi-N	146	512	51	122	23	6	1	49	44	65	.238	.301	.313	71	-20	-21	52	14			.936	20	*S	0.9
1912	Phi-N	146	532	47	137	26	6	1	62	34	59	.258	.305	.335	70	-20	-24	56	6			.950	8	*S	-0.4
1913	Phi-N	151	518	32	113	12	6	1	43	29	68	.218	.262	.270	50	-33	-35	40	17			.941	17	*S/2	-0.5
1914	Bal-F	145	486	58	119	23	6	1	53	40	47	.245	.311	.323	78	-12	-14	63	30			**.949**	**29**	*S	2.8

YEAR	TM/L	G	AB	R	H	2B	3B	HR	RBI	BB	SO	AVG	OBP	SLG	PRO+	BR	/A	RC	SB	CS	SBR	FA	FR	POS	TPR
1915	Bal-F	119	404	41	75	13	7	2	21	24	39	.186	.238	.267	47	-27	-28	31	10			.946	32	*S	1.4
	Chi-F	24	86	9	23	1	1	0	9	2	7	.267	.292	.302	79	-3	-2	10	5			.914	0	S	0.0
	Yr	143	490	50	98	14	8	2	30	26	46	.200	.248	.273	52	-30	-31	40	15			.941	**32**	*S	1.4
1916	Chi-N	28	70	4	15	2	1	0	5	8	7	.214	.295	.271	67	-2	-3	6	0			.918	3	S	0.1
	NY-N	18	51	4	12	3	1	1	3	2	4	.235	.264	.392	106	-0	0	6	1			.975	2	S/2	0.3
	Yr	46	121	8	27	5	2	1	8	10	11	.223	.282	.322	82	-2	-3	12	1			.939	4	S/2	0.4
1918	Bro-N	92	308	14	55	8	2	0	18	22	24	.179	.233	.218	38	-23	-23	18	8			**.968**	10	2	-0.8
Total	13	1728	5977	513	1376	244	81	15	554	370	376	.230	.279	.306	72	-211	-224	578	173			.940	177	*S/2	4.2
■ HARRY DOOMS	Dooms, Henry E. "Jack" b: 1/30/1867, St.Louis, Mo. d: 12/14/1899, St.Louis, Mo. Deb: 8/07/1892																								
1892	Lou-N	1	4	0	0	0	0	0	0	1	3	.000	.200	.000	-41	-1	-1	0	0			.000	-1	/O	-0.1
■ TOM DORAN	Doran, Thomas J. "Long Tom" b: 12/2/1880, Westchester Co., N.Y. d: 6/22/10, New York, N.Y. BL/TR, 5'11", 152 lbs. Deb: 4/19/04																								
1904	Bos-A	12	32	1	4	0	1	0	0	4		.125	.243	.188	35	-2	-2	2	1			.898	-5	C	-0.7
1905	Bos-A	3	3	0	0	0	0	0	0	0		.000	.000	.000	-99	-1	-1	0	0			1.000	0	/C	0.0
	Det-A	34	94	8	15	3	0	0	4	8		.160	.248	.191	40	-6	-6	6	2			.962	-6	C	-1.0
	Yr	37	97	8	15	3	0	0	4	8		.155	.241	.186	36	-7	-7	6	2			.963	-6	C	-1.0
1906	Bos-A	2	3	1	0	0	0	0	0	0		.000	.000	.000	-99	-1	-1	0	0			1.000	-0	/C	-0.1
Total	3	51	132	10	19	3	1	0	4	12		.144	.236	.182	33	-10	-10	8	3			.949	-11	/C	-1.8
■ BILL DORAN	Doran, William Donald b: 5/28/58, Cincinnati, Ohio BB/TR, 5'11", 175 lbs. Deb: 9/06/82																								
1982	Hou-N	26	97	11	27	3	0	0	6	4	11	.278	.307	.309	79	-4	-3	10	5	0	2	.975	-3	2	-0.3
1983	Hou-N	154	535	70	145	12	7	8	39	86	67	.271	.372	.364	112	7	11	76	12	12	-4	.979	5	*2	2.0
1984	Hou-N	147	548	92	143	18	11	4	41	66	69	.261	.343	.356	104	-1	4	70	21	12	-1	.986	6	*2S	1.5
1985	Hou-N	148	578	84	166	31	6	14	59	71	69	.287	.365	.434	126	18	20	92	23	15	-2	.980	7	*2	3.2
1986	*Hou-N	145	550	92	152	29	3	6	37	81	57	.276	.371	.373	109	7	9	81	42	19	1	.974	-42	*2	-2.7
1987	Hou-N	162	625	82	177	23	3	16	79	82	64	.283	.369	.406	109	7	10	99	31	11	3	**.992**	-16	*2/S	0.4
1988	Hou-N	132	480	66	119	18	1	7	53	65	60	.248	.339	.333	97	-2	0	59	17	4	3	**.987**	-3	*2	0.5
1989	Hou-N	142	507	65	111	25	2	8	58	59	63	.219	.303	.323	82	-13	-11	54	22	3	5	.980	-27	*2	-3.1
1990	Hou-N	109	344	49	99	21	2	6	32	71	53	.288	.410	.413	131	16	17	65	18	9	0	.989	-11	2	0.9
	Cin-N	17	59	10	22	8	0	1	5	8	5	.373	.448	.559	168	6	6	16	5	0	2	.985	1	2/3	0.9
	Yr	126	403	59	121	29	2	7	37	79	58	.300	.415	.434	137	22	23	81	23	9	2	.988	-10	*2/3	1.8
1991	Cin-N	111	361	51	101	12	2	6	35	46	39	.280	.361	.374	103	5	3	51	5	4	-1	.981	-14	2/O1	-1.1
1992	Cin-N	132	387	48	91	16	2	8	47	64	40	.235	.344	.349	92	-0	-2	48	7	4	-0	.988	-9	*21	-1.2
Total	11	1425	5071	720	1353	216	39	84	491	703	597	.267	.357	.374	107	45	64	722	208	93	7	.983	-106	*2/1SO3	1.0
■ BILL DORAN	Doran, William James b: 6/14/1898, San Francisco, Cal. d: 3/9/78, Santa Monica, Cal. BL/TR, 5'11.5", 175 lbs. Deb: 6/23/22																								
1922	Cle-A	3	2	0	1	0	0	0	0	1	0	.500	.667	.500	206	0	0	1	0	0	0	.000	0	/3	0.0
■ JERRY DORGAN	Dorgan, Jeremiah F. b: 1856, Meriden, Conn. d: 6/10/1891, New Haven, Conn. BL/TR, Deb: 7/08/1880 F																								
1880	Wor-N	10	35	2	7	1	0	0	1	0	1	.200	.200	.229	41	-2	-2	2				.750	-3	/OC	-0.5
1882	Phi-a	44	181	25	51	9	1	0		4		.282	.297	.343	103	3	-0	19				.880	-1	CO/3	0.0
1884	Ind-a	34	141	22	42	6	1	0		2		.298	.317	.355	125	3	4	16				.793	-2	O/C	0.1
	Bro-a	4	13	2	4	0	0	0		0		.308	.308	.308	104	0	0	1				.921	2	/C	0.2
	Yr	38	154	24	46	6	1	0		2		.299	.316	.351	123	3	4	18				.793	-0	O/C	0.3
1885	Det-N	39	161	23	46	6	2	0	24	8	10	.286	.320	.348	115	3	3	18				.857	-3	O	-0.1
Total	4	131	531	74	150	22	4	0	25	14	11	.282	.303	.339	108	6	4	56				.817	-7	/OC3	-0.3
■ MIKE DORGAN	Dorgan, Michael Cornelius b: 10/2/1853, Middletown, Conn. d: 4/26/09, Syracuse, N.Y. BR/TR, 5'9", 180 lbs. Deb: 5/08/1877 FM																								
1877	StL-N	60	266	45	82	9	7	0	23	9	13	.308	.331	.395	135	8	10	36				.824	-8	*OC/3S2	0.0
1879	Syr-N	59	270	38	72	11	5	1	17	4	13	.267	.277	.356	120	2	6	27				.954	-5	1O3/SCP2	0.0
1880	Pro-N	79	321	45	79	10	1	0	31	10	18	.246	.269	.283	90	-4	-3	25				.858	2	*O/3PM	-0.3
1881	Wor-N	51	220	36	61	5	0	0	18	8	4	.277	.303	.300	85	-2	-4	20				.953	1	1O/SM	-0.6
	Det-N	8	34	5	8	1	0	0	5	1	0	.235	.257	.265	62	-1	-2	2				1.000	-0	/O31	-0.2
	Yr	59	254	41	69	6	0	0	23	9	4	.272	.297	.295	82	-4	-6	23				.897	0	O1/S3	-0.8
1883	NY-N	64	261	32	61	11	3	0	27	2	23	.234	.240	.299	63	-12	-11	19				.847	-5	O/CP	-1.5
1884	NY-N	83	341	61	94	11	6	1	48	13	27	.276	.302	.352	103	2	0	37				.851	1	OP/C2	0.0
1885	NY-N	89	347	60	113	17	8	0	46	11	24	.326	.346	.421	149	17	18	52				.905	-2	*O/1	1.2
1886	NY-N	118	442	61	129	19	4	2	79	29	37	.292	.335	.367	112	7	6	59	9			.888	-8	*O/1	-0.4
1887	NY-N	71	283	41	73	10	0	0	34	15	20	.258	.302	.293	71	-12	-9	33	22			.870	-2	O/1	-1.0
1890	Syr-a	33	139	19	30	8	0	0		16		.216	.301	.273	80	-5	-2	14	8			.900	-2	O	-0.5
Total	10	715	2924	443	802	112	34	4	328	118	179	.274	.303	.340	103	0	10	325	39			.867	-30	O/1CP3S2	-3.3
■ CHARLIE DORMAN	Dorman, Charles William "Slats" b: 4/23/1898, San Francisco, Cal d: 11/15/28, San Francisco, Cal BR/TR, 6'2", 185 lbs. Deb: 5/14/23																								
1923	Chi-A	1	2	0	1	0	0	0	0	0	0	.500	.500	.500	166	0	0	0	0	0	0	1.000	-0	/C	0.0
■ RED DORMAN	Dorman, Dwight Dexter "Curlie" b: 10/3/05, Jacksonville, Ill. d: 12/7/74, Anaheim, Cal. BR/TR, 5'10.5", 180 lbs. Deb: 8/21/28																								
1928	Cle-A	25	77	12	28	6	0	0	11	9	6	.364	.430	.442	128	4	4	15	1	0	0	.915	-3	O	0.0
■ BRIAN DORSETT	Dorsett, Brian Richard b: 4/9/61, Terre Haute, Ind. BR/TR, 6'3", 215 lbs. Deb: 9/08/87																								
1987	Cle-A	5	11	2	3	0	0	1	3	0	3	.273	.333	.545	127	0	0	2	0	0	0	1.000	-2	/C	-0.1
1988	Cal-A	7	11	0	1	0	0	0	2	1	5	.091	.167	.091	-26	-2	-2	0	0	0	0	1.000	1	/C	-0.1
1989	NY-A	8	22	3	8	1	0	0	4	1	3	.364	.391	.409	127	1	1	4	0	0	0	1.000	-0	/C	0.1
1990	NY-A	14	35	2	5	2	0	0	0	2	4	.143	.189	.200	9	-4	-4	1	0	0	0	1.000	-1	/CD	-0.5
1991	SD-N	11	12	0	1	0	0	0	1	0	3	.083	.083	.083	-51	-2	-2	0	0	0	0	1.000	0	/1	-0.2
Total	5	45	91	7	18	3	0	1	10	4	18	.198	.240	.264	40	-7	-7	7	0	0	0	1.000	-3	/CD1	-0.8
■ JERRY DORSEY	Dorsey, Jeremiah b: 1885, Oakland, Cal. BL/TL, 5'11", 175 lbs. Deb: 9/23/11																								
1911	Pit-N	2	6	0	0	0	0	0	0	0	1	.000	.000	.000	-96	-2	-2	0	0			1.000	0	/O	-0.1
■ JERRY DORSEY	Dorsey, Michael Jeremiah b: 1854, Canada d: 11/3/38, Auburn, N.Y. Deb: 7/09/1884																								
1884	Bal-U	1	3	0	0	0	0	0		0		.000	.000	.000	-91	-1	-1	0				.000	-0	/OP	-0.1
■ HERM DOSCHER	Doscher, John Henry Sr. b: 12/20/1852, New York, N.Y. d: 3/20/34, Buffalo, N.Y. BR/TR, 5'10", 182 lbs. Deb: 9/04/1872 FU																								
1872	Atl-n	6	25	4	9	1	0	0	5	0	1	.360	.360	.400	114	1	0	4						/O	0.0
1873	Atl-n	1	6	1	1	0	0	0	1	0	0	.167	.167	.167	-2	-1	-1	0						/O	0.0
1875	Was-n	22	81	5	15	2	0	0		0		.185	.185	.210	38	-5	-5	3						3/S	-0.4
1879	Tro-N	47	191	16	42	8	0	0	18	2	10	.220	.228	.262	65	-8	-6	12				.806	-4	3	-0.8
	Chi-N	3	11	1	2	0	0	0	1	0	3	.182	.182	.182	19	-1	-1	0				.700	-1	/3	-0.2
	Yr	50	202	17	44	8	0	0	19	2	13	.218	.225	.257	62	-9	-7	12				.800	-5	3	-1.0
1881	Cle-N	5	19	2	4	0	0	0	0	0	2	.211	.211	.211	35	-1	-1	1				.895	-0	/3	-0.1
1882	Cle-N	25	104	7	25	2	0	0	10	0	11	.240	.240	.260	62	-5	-4	7				.857	-2	3/OS	-0.5
Total	3 n	29	112	10	25	3	0	0	6	0	1	.223	.223	.250	57	-5	-5	7						/3OS	-0.4
Total	3	80	325	26	73	10	0	0	29	2	26	.225	.229	.255	61	-15	-12	20				.823	-7	/3OS	-1.6

YEAR	TM/L	G	AB	R	H	2B	3B	HR	RBI	BB	SO	AVG	OBP	SLG	PRO+	BR	/A	RC	SB	CS	SBR	FA	FR	POS	TPR
■ **DUTCH DOTTERER** Dotterer, Henry John b: 11/11/31, Syracuse, N.Y. BR/TR, 6', 209 lbs. Deb: 9/25/57																									
1957	Cin-N	4	12	0	1	0	0	0	2	1	2	.083	.154	.083	-32	-2	-2	0	0	0	0	1.000	-1	/C	-0.3
1958	Cin-N	11	28	1	7	1	0	1	2	2	4	.250	.300	.393	77	-1	-1	3	0	0	0	.981	4	/C	0.3
1959	Cin-N	52	161	21	43	7	0	2	17	16	23	.267	.333	.348	79	-4	-5	19	0	0	0	.992	-0	C	-0.2
1960	Cin-N	33	79	4	18	5	0	2	11	13	10	.228	.337	.367	91	-1	-1	10	0	1	-1	.979	1	C	0.1
1961	Was-A	7	19	1	5	2	0	0	1	3	5	.263	.364	.368	98	-0	0	3	0	0	0	1.000	2	/C	0.2
Total	5	107	299	27	74	15	0	5	33	35	44	.247	.326	.348	79	-8	-9	36	0	1	-1	.988	7	C	0.1
■ **CHARLIE DOUGHERTY** Dougherty, Charles William b: 2/7/1862, Darlington, Wis. d: 2/18/25, Milwaukee, Wis. Deb: 4/17/1884																									
1884	Alt-U	23	85	6	22	5	0	0		2		.259	.276	.318	99	-0	-0	8				.854	0	2/OS	0.0
■ **PATSY DOUGHERTY** Dougherty, Patrick Henry b: 10/27/1876, Andover, N.Y. d: 4/30/40, Bolivar, N.Y. BL/TR, 6'2", 190 lbs. Deb: 4/19/02																									
1902	Bos-A	108	438	77	150	12	6	0	34	42		.342	.411	.397	121	17	15	82	20			.899	-9	*O/3	-0.1
1903	*Bos-A	139	590	**107**	**195**	19	12	4	59	33		.331	.372	.424	131	27	24	**111**	35			.952	4	*O	1.9
1904	Bos-A	49	195	33	53	5	4	0	4	25		.272	.355	.338	113	5	4	28	10			.925	0	O	0.1
	NY-A	106	452	80	128	13	10	6	22	19		.283	.316	.396	119	11	9	62	11			.925	-8	*O	-0.6
	Yr	155	647	**113**	181	18	14	6	26	44		.280	.329	.379	118	17	13	90	21			.925	-8	*O	-0.5
1905	NY-A	116	418	56	110	9	6	3	29	28		.263	.317	.335	96	3	-2	52	17			.898	-6	*O/3	-1.4
1906	NY-A	12	52	3	10	2	0	0	4	0		.192	.192	.231	29	-4	-5	2	0			1.000	2	O	-0.4
	*Chi-A	75	253	30	59	9	4	1	27	19		.233	.295	.312	93	-3	-2	29	11			.985	-2	O	-0.8
	Yr	87	305	33	69	11	4	1	31	19		.226	.278	.298	81	-7	-7	31	11			.987	1	O	-1.2
1907	Chi-A	148	533	69	144	17	2	1	59	36		.270	.322	.315	107	2	4	68	33			.946	-7	*O	-0.9
1908	Chi-A	138	482	68	134	11	6	0	45	58		.278	.367	.326	128	17	18	76	**47**			.947	-15	*O	-0.3
1909	Chi-A	139	491	71	140	23	13	1	55	51		.285	.359	.391	143	21	24	82	36			.942	-16	*O	0.3
1910	Chi-A	127	443	45	110	8	6	1	43	41		.248	.318	.300	98	-3	-1	48	22			.923	-13	*O	-2.2
1911	Chi-A	76	211	39	61	10	9	0	32	26		.289	.380	.422	128	7	8	41	19			.933	-6	O	0.0
Total	10	1233	4558	678	1294	138	78	17	413	378		.284	.346	.360	117	102	96	681	261			.935	-75	*O/3	-4.4
■ **JOHN DOUGLAS** Douglas, John Franklin b: 9/14/17, Thayer, W.Va. d: 2/11/84, Miami, Fla. BL/TL, 6'2.5", 195 lbs. Deb: 4/21/45																									
1945	Bro-N	5	9	0	0	0	0	0	0	2	4	.000	.182	.000	-47	-2	-2	0	0			.971	-1	/1	-0.3
■ **ASTYANAX DOUGLASS** Douglass, Astyanax Saunders b: 9/19/1899, Covington, Tex. d: 1/26/75, ElPaso, Tex. BL/TR, 6'1", 190 lbs. Deb: 7/30/21																									
1921	Cin-N	4	7	1	1	0	0	0	0	0	1	.143	.143	.143	-25	-1	-1	0	0	0	0	1.000	0	/C	-0.1
1925	Cin-N	7	17	1	3	0	0	0	1	1	3	.176	.222	.176	3	-2	-2	1	0	0	0	.889	-1	/C	-0.3
Total	2	11	24	2	4	0	0	0	1	1	4	.167	.200	.167	-4	-4	-4	1	0	0	0	.926	-0	/C	-0.4
■ **KLONDIKE DOUGLASS** Douglass, William Bingham b: 5/10/1872, Boston, Pa. d: 12/13/53, Bend, Ore. BL/TR, 6', 200 lbs. Deb: 4/23/1896																									
1896	StL-N	81	296	42	78	6	4	1	28	35	15	.264	.351	.321	83	-7	-5	41	18			.894	-7	O/CS	-1.4
1897	StL-N	125	516	77	170	15	3	6	50	52		.329	.403	.405	116	12	14	92	12			.948	-17	CO1/3S	0.1
1898	Phi-N	146	582	105	150	26	4	2	48	55		.258	.333	.326	93	-7	-3	74	18			.976	2	*1	-0.2
1899	Phi-N	77	275	26	70	6	6	0	27	10		.255	.296	.320	71	-12	-11	29	7			.970	-5	C/31O	-1.0
1900	Phi-N	50	160	23	48	9	4	0	25	13		.300	.360	.406	112	2	3	27	7			.934	-4	C/3	0.2
1901	Phi-N	51	173	14	56	6	1	0	23	11		.324	.371	.370	113	4	3	29	10			.979	2	C/1O	0.8
1902	Phi-N	109	408	37	95	12	3	0	37	23		.233	.274	.277	70	-15	-15	35	6			.986	-8	1CO	-2.3
1903	Phi-N	105	377	43	96	5	4	1	36	28		.255	.306	.297	75	-13	-12	39	6			.985	-1	1	-1.4
1904	Phi-N	3	10	1	3	0	0	0	1	0		.300	.364	.300	110	0	0	1	0			.970	-0	/1	0.0
Total	9	747	2797	368	766	85	29	10	275	227	<u>15</u>	.274	.337	.336	91	-36	-26	366	84			.981	-38	1CO/3S	-5.2
■ **TAYLOR DOUTHIT** Douthit, Taylor Lee b: 4/22/01, Little Rock, Ark. d: 5/28/86, Fremont, Cal. BR/TR, 5'11.5", 175 lbs. Deb: 9/14/23																									
1923	StL-N	9	27	3	5	0	2	0	0	0	4	.185	.185	.333	35	-3	-3	2	1	0	0	1.000	-0	/O	-0.3
1924	StL-N	53	173	24	48	13	1	0	13	16	19	.277	.349	.364	93	-2	-1	23	4	3	-1	.976	2	O	-0.3
1925	StL-N	30	73	13	20	3	1	1	8	2	6	.274	.312	.384	75	-3	-3	9	0	0	0	.981	-1	O	-0.5
1926	*StL-N	139	530	96	163	20	4	3	52	55	46	.308	.375	.377	99	4	1	76	23			.958	18	*O	0.9
1927	StL-N	130	488	81	128	29	6	5	50	52	45	.262	.336	.377	88	-6	-8	62	6			.964	8	*O	-0.9
1928	*StL-N	154	648	111	191	35	3	3	43	84	36	.295	.384	.372	97	2	1	95	11			.984	24	*O	1.4
1929	StL-N	150	613	128	206	42	7	9	62	79	49	.336	.416	.471	118	21	20	120	8			.974	4	*O	1.3
1930	*StL-N	154	664	109	201	41	10	7	93	60	38	.303	.364	.426	87	-10	-13	102	4			.964	8	*O	-1.4
1931	StL-N	36	133	21	44	11	2	1	21	11	9	.331	.386	.466	123	5	5	25	1			.972	0	O	0.2
	Cin-N	95	374	42	98	9	1	0	24	42	24	.262	.340	.291	76	-13	-10	40	4			.983	5	O	-1.2
	Yr	131	507	63	142	20	3	1	45	53	33	.280	.352	.337	89	-8	-6	64	5			.980	5	*O	-1.0
1932	Cin-N	96	333	28	81	12	1	0	25	31	29	.243	.311	.285	64	-17	-15	32	3			.985	1	O	-2.0
1933	Cin-N	1	0	1	0	0	0	0	0	0	0	—	—	—	—	0	0	0	0			.000	0	R	0.0
	Chi-N	27	71	8	16	5	0	0	5	11	7	.225	.329	.296	80	-2	-1	6	2			.930	-0	O	-0.3
	Yr	28	71	9	16	5	0	0	5	11	7	.225	.329	.296	80	-2	-1	6	2			.930	-0	O	-0.3
Total	11	1074	4127	665	1201	220	38	29	396	443	312	.291	.364	.384	93	-22	-29	592	67	<u>3</u>		.972	69	*O	-3.1
■ **CLARENCE DOW** Dow, Clarence G. b: 10/11/1854, Charlestown, Mass. d: 3/11/1893, West Somerville, Mass. Deb: 9/22/1884																									
1884	Bos-U	1	6	1	2	0	0	0		0		.333	.333	.333	128	0	0	1				.333	-1	/O	0.0
■ **JOHN DOWD** Dowd, John Leo (b: John Leo O'Dowd) b: 1/3/1891, Weymouth, Mass. d: 1/31/81, Ft.Lauderdale, Fla BR/TR, 5'8", 170 lbs. Deb: 7/03/12																									
1912	NY-A	10	31	1	6	1	0	0	0	6		.194	.342	.226	60	-1	-1	2	0			.840	-6	S	-0.6
■ **SNOOKS DOWD** Dowd, Raymond Bernard b: 12/20/1897, Springfield, Mass. d: 4/4/62, Northampton, Mass. BR/TR, 5'8", 163 lbs. Deb: 4/27/19																									
1919	Det-A	1	0	0	0	0	0	0	0	0	0	—	—	—	—	0	0	0	0			.000	0	R	0.0
	Phi-A	13	18	4	3	0	0	0	6	0	5	.167	.167	.167	-6	-3	-3	1	2			.800	1	/2S3O	-0.2
	Yr	14	18	4	3	0	0	0	6	0	5	.167	.167	.167	-6	-3	-3	1	2			.800	1	/2S3O	-0.2
1926	Bro-N	2	8	0	0	0	0	0	0	0	0	.000	.000	.000	-99	-2	-2	0	0			1.000	-2	/2	-0.5
Total	2	16	26	4	3	0	0	0	6	0	5	.115	.115	.115	-36	-5	-5	1	2			.875	-1	/2SO3	-0.7
■ **TOMMY DOWD** Dowd, Thomas Jefferson "Buttermilk Tommy" b: 4/20/1869, Holyoke, Mass. d: 7/2/33, Holyoke, Mass. BR/TR, 5'8", 173 lbs. Deb: 4/08/1891 M																									
1891	Bos-a	4	11	1	1	0	0	0	0	0	1	.091	.091	.091	-48	-2	-2	0	0			.000	-2	/O	-0.3
	Was-a	112	464	66	120	9	10	1	44	19	44	.259	.291	.328	83	-14	-11	57	39			.885	-17	*2/O	-2.0
	Yr	116	475	67	121	9	10	1	44	19	45	.255	.286	.322	80	-16	-13	56	39			.885	-19	*2/O	-2.3
1892	Was-N	144	584	94	142	9	10	1	50	34	49	.243	.286	.298	81	-16	-14	65	49			.891	-33	2O3/S	-4.2
1893	StL-N	132	581	114	164	18	7	1	54	49	23	.282	.340	.343	83	-13	-14	90	59			.944	3	*O/2	-1.4
1894	StL-N	123	524	92	142	16	8	4	62	54	33	.271	.341	.355	70	-25	-25	77	31			.930	-7	*O/23	-3.1
1895	StL-N	129	505	95	163	19	17	7	74	30	31	.323	.364	.469	117	10	11	100	30			.927	-7	*O3/2	-0.4
1896	StL-N	126	521	93	138	17	11	5	46	42	19	.265	.322	.369	87	-13	-9	78	40			.920	-13	2OM	-1.9
1897	StL-N	35	145	25	38	9	1	0	9	6		.262	.291	.338	67	-8	-7	18	11			.915	-6	O/2M	-1.3
	Phi-N	91	391	68	114	14	4	0	43	19		.292	.324	.348	79	-13	-12	56	30			.919	-6	O2	-1.9
	Yr	126	536	93	152	23	5	0	52	25		.284	.316	.345	76	-21	-19	75	41			.918	-12	*O2	-3.2
1898	StL-N	139	586	70	143	17	7	0	32	30		.244	.287	.297	66	-26	-28	58	16			.920	-17	*O2	-5.0
1899	Cle-N	147	605	81	168	17	6	2	35	48		.278	.334	.336	90	-13	-7	80	28			.954	-2	*O	-1.8
1901	Bos-A	138	594	104	159	18	7	3	52	38		.268	.315	.337	82	-16	-14	76	33			.937	1	*O/13	-2.1
Total	10	1320	5511	903	1492	163	88	24	501	369	<u>200</u>	.271	.319	.345	83	-149	-130	755	366			.933	-106	O2/3S1	-25.4

YEAR	TM/L	G	AB	R	H	2B	3B	HR	RBI	BB	SO	AVG	OBP	SLG	PRO+	BR	/A	RC	SB	CS	SBR	FA	FR	POS	TPR

■ **KEN DOWELL**   Dowell, Kenneth Allen   b: 1/19/61, Sacramento, Cal.   BR/TR, 5'9", 160 lbs.   Deb: 6/24/87

| 1987 | Phi-N | 15 | 39 | 4 | 5 | 0 | 0 | 0 | 1 | 2 | 5 | .128 | .171 | .128 | -19 | -7 | -7 | 1 | 0 | 0 | 0 | 1.000 | 0 | S | -0.6 |

■ **JOE DOWIE**   Dowie, Joseph E.   b: 7/1865, New Orleans, La.   5'8", 150 lbs.   Deb: 7/10/1889

| 1889 | Bal-a | 20 | 75 | 12 | 17 | 5 | 0 | 0 | 8 | 3 | 10 | .227 | .266 | .293 | 60 | -4 | -4 | 7 | 5 | | | .947 | 0 | O | -0.4 |

■ **RED DOWNEY**   Downey, Alexander Cummings   b: 2/6/1889, Aurora, Ind.   d: 7/10/49, Detroit, Mich.   BL/TL, 5'11", 174 lbs.   Deb: 9/15/09

| 1909 | Bro-N | 19 | 78 | 7 | 20 | 1 | 0 | 0 | 8 | 2 | | .256 | .275 | .269 | 71 | -3 | -3 | 7 | 4 | | | 1.000 | -1 | O | -0.5 |

■ **TOM DOWNEY**   Downey, Thomas Edward   b: 1/1/1884, Lewiston, Me.   d: 8/3/61, Passaic, N.J.   BR/TR, 5'10", 178 lbs.   Deb: 5/07/09

1909	Cin-N	119	416	39	96	9	6	1	32	32		.231	.287	.288	79	-11	-10	40	16			.909	-7	*S/C	-1.7
1910	Cin-N	111	378	43	102	9	3	2	32	34	28	.270	.335	.325	97	-3	-1	46	12			.879	-7	S3	-0.5
1911	Cin-N	111	360	50	94	16	7	0	36	44	38	.261	.345	.344	97	-3	-1	46	10			.906	-12	S/2310	-0.6
1912	Phi-N	54	171	27	50	6	3	1	23	21	20	.292	.370	.380	99	2	-0	26	3			.893	-3	3/S	-0.2
	Chi-N	13	22	4	4	0	2	0	4	1	5	.182	.217	.364	58	-1	-1	2	0			.792	1	/S32	0.0
	Yr	67	193	31	54	6	5	1	27	22	25	.280	.353	.378	95	0	-1	28	3			.892	-2	3/S2	-0.2
1914	Buf-F	151	541	69	118	20	3	4	42	40	55	.218	.273	.277	56	-31	-32	54	35			.962	13	*2S/3	-2.0
1915	Buf-F	92	282	24	56	9	1	1	19	26	26	.199	.269	.248	51	-17	-17	23	11			.930	2	23/S1	-1.5
Total	6	651	2170	256	520	69	25	7	188	198	<u>172</u>	.240	.306	.304	77	-64	-64	238	87			.901	-12	S23/10C	-6.5

■ **BRIAN DOWNING**   Downing, Brian Jay   b: 10/9/50, Los Angeles, Cal.   BR/TR, 5'10", 194 lbs.   Deb: 5/31/73

1973	Chi-A	34	73	5	13	1	0	2	4	10	17	.178	.277	.274	54	-4	-5	6	0	0	0	1.000	0	OC/3D	-0.4
1974	Chi-A	108	293	41	66	12	1	10	39	51	72	.225	.344	.375	104	4	3	38	0	1	-1	.994	-7	CO/D	-0.3
1975	Chi-A	138	420	58	101	12	1	7	41	76	75	.240	.361	.324	93	0	-1	54	13	4	2	.990	2	*C/D	0.9
1976	Chi-A	104	317	38	81	14	0	3	30	40	55	.256	.341	.328	96	-0	-1	39	7	3	0	.988	-12	CD	-1.0
1977	Chi-A	69	169	28	48	4	2	4	25	34	21	.284	.410	.402	123	7	7	30	1	2	-1	.983	-7	C/OD	-0.3
1978	Cal-A	133	412	42	105	15	0	7	46	52	47	.255	.347	.342	98	-1	1	49	3	2	-0	.993	-7	*C/D	-0.3
1979	*Cal-A★	148	509	87	166	27	3	12	75	77	57	.326	.420	.462	142	30	33	99	3	3	-1	.985	-21	CD	1.5
1980	Cal-A	30	93	5	27	6	0	2	25	12	12	.290	.371	.419	119	2	3	13	0	2	-1	1.000	-4	CD	-0.2
1981	Cal-A	93	317	47	79	14	0	9	41	46	35	.249	.351	.379	110	5	5	43	1	1	-0	.990	-9	OC/D	-0.4
1982	*Cal-A	158	623	109	175	37	2	28	84	86	58	.281	.373	.482	132	29	29	114	2	1	0	1.000	2	*O	2.6
1983	Cal-A	113	403	68	99	15	1	19	53	62	59	.246	.353	.462	115	9	9	63	1	2	-1	.994	-0	OD	0.6
1984	Cal-A	156	539	65	148	28	2	23	91	70	66	.275	.365	.462	128	21	21	89	0	4	-2	1.000	1	*OD	1.6
1985	Cal-A	150	520	80	137	23	1	20	85	78	61	.263	.373	.427	119	16	16	86	3	3	-0	.992	1	*OD	1.3
1986	*Cal-A	152	513	90	137	27	4	20	95	90	84	.267	.394	.462	131	25	26	96	4	4	-1	.989	1	*DO	2.1
1987	Cal-A	155	567	110	154	29	3	29	77	**106**	85	.272	.401	.487	139	32	35	117	5	5	-2	1.000	0	*DO	2.8
1988	Cal-A	135	484	80	117	18	2	25	64	81	63	.242	.366	.442	129	19	20	81	3	4	-2	.000	0	*D	1.9
1989	Cal-A	142	544	59	154	25	2	14	59	56	87	.283	.356	.414	118	12	14	83	0	2	-1	.000	0	*D	1.3
1990	Cal-A	96	330	47	90	18	2	14	51	50	45	.273	.378	.467	138	17	17	59	0	0	0	.000	0	*D	1.8
1991	Tex-A	123	407	76	113	17	2	17	49	58	70	.278	.378	.455	132	18	19	73	1	1	-0	.000	0	*D	2.0
1992	Tex-A	107	320	53	89	18	0	10	39	62	58	.278	.408	.428	139	18	19	61	1	0	0	.000	0	D	2.0
Total	20	2344	7853	1188	2099	360	28	275	1073	1197	1127	.267	.373	.425	122	256	271	1293	50	44	-11	.995	-51	DOC/3	20.6

■ **RED DOWNS**   Downs, Jerome Willis   b: 8/22/1883, Neola, Iowa   d: 10/19/39, Council Bluffs, Ia   BR/TR, 5'11", 155 lbs.   Deb: 5/02/07

1907	Det-A	105	374	28	82	13	5	1	42	13		.219	.249	.289	69	-13	-14	30	3			.930	-25	2O/S3	-4.6
1908	*Det-A	84	289	29	64	10	3	1	35	5		.221	.237	.287	68	-10	-12	20	2			.925	1	2/3	-1.3
1912	Bro-N	9	32	2	8	3	0	0	3	1	5	.250	.273	.344	71	-2	-1	4	3			.881	-1	/2	-0.3
	Chi-N	43	95	9	25	4	1	0	14	9	17	.263	.327	.400	99	-1	-0	14	5			.907	2	2/S3	0.2
	Yr	52	127	11	33	7	1	0	17	10	22	.260	.314	.386	92	-2	-2	18	8			.896	2	2/S3	-0.1
Total	3	241	790	68	179	30	11	3	94	28	<u>22</u>	.227	.256	.304	73	-25	-28	67	13			.924	-24	2/OS3	-6.0

■ **TOM DOWSE**   Dowse, Thomas Joseph   b: 8/12/1866, Ireland   d: 12/14/46, Riverside, Cal.   BR/TR, 5'11", 175 lbs.   Deb: 4/21/1890

1890	Cle-N	40	159	20	33	2	1	0	9	12	22	.208	.267	.233	49	-10	-10	11	3			.870	-3	O1/CP	-1.2
1891	Col-a	55	201	24	45	7	0	0	22	13	22	.224	.278	.259	59	-11	-10	15	2			.919	-6	C/O	-1.0
1892	Lou-N	41	145	10	21	2	0	0	7	2	15	.145	.173	.159	2	-17	-15	4	1			.918	2	C1/O2	-1.1
	Cin-N	1	4	0	0	0	0	0	0	0	0	.000	.000	.000	-99	-1	-1	0	0			1.000	-1	/C	-0.2
	Phi-N	16	54	3	10	0	0	0	6	2	4	.185	.228	.185	27	-5	-5	3	1			.973	-1	C	-0.4
	Was-N	7	27	5	7	1	0	0	3	0	3	.259	.259	.296	71	-1	-1	2	0			.800	0	/OC	-0.1
	Yr	65	230	18	38	3	0	0	15	4	22	.165	.193	.178	14	-24	-22	9	2			.931	-3	C1/O2	-1.8
Total	3	160	590	62	116	12	1	0	46	29	66	.197	.243	.220	40	-45	-41	35	7			.921	-9	C/O12P	-4.0

■ **BRIAN DOYLE**   Doyle, Brian Reed   b: 1/26/55, Glasgow, Ky.   BL/TR, 5'10", 160 lbs.   Deb: 4/30/78   F

1978	*NY-A	39	52	6	10	0	0	0	0	0	3	.192	.192	.192	79	-6	-6	1	0	3	-2	.989	13	2/S3	0.6
1979	NY-A	20	32	2	4	2	0	0	5	3	1	.125	.200	.188	5	-4	-4	1	0	0	0	.944	1	2/3	-0.3
1980	NY-A	34	75	8	13	1	0	1	5	6	7	.173	.235	.227	27	-8	-7	4	1	1	-0	.953	5	2S/3	-0.1
1981	Oak-A	17	40	2	5	0	0	0	3	1	2	.125	.146	.125	-22	-6	-6	1	0	1	-1	1.000	1	2	-0.5
Total	4	110	199	18	32	3	0	1	13	10	13	.161	.201	.191	10	-24	-24	7	1	5	-3	.977	20	/2S3	-0.3

■ **CONNY DOYLE**   Doyle, Cornelius J.   b: 9/26/1857, Holyoke, Mass.   d: 10/6/38, W.Springfield, Mass   5'10", 185 lbs.   Deb: 6/23/1883

1883	Phi-N	16	68	3	15	3	2	0		0	15	.221	.221	.324	69	-3	-2	5				.788	-1	O	-0.3
1884	Pit-a	15	58	8	17	3	2	0		2		.293	.317	.414	137	2	2	8				.818	-1	O/S	0.1
Total	2	31	126	11	32	6	4	0	3	2	15	.254	.266	.365	101	-1	-0	13				.800	-3	/OS	-0.2

■ **DANNY DOYLE**   Doyle, Howard James   b: 1/24/17, Mcloud, Okla.   BB/TR, 6'1", 195 lbs.   Deb: 9/14/43

| 1943 | Bos-A | 13 | 43 | 2 | 9 | 1 | 0 | 0 | 6 | 9 | | .209 | .320 | .233 | 62 | -2 | -2 | 3 | 0 | 1 | -1 | .964 | -2 | C | -0.4 |

■ **JIM DOYLE**   Doyle, James Francis   b: 12/25/1881, Detroit, Mich.   d: 2/1/12, Syracuse, N.Y.   BR/TR, 5'10", 168 lbs.   Deb: 5/04/10

1910	Cin-N	7	13	1	2	2	0	0	1	0	2	.154	.154	.308	36	-1	-1	1	0			.875	-1	/3O	-0.3
1911	Chi-N	130	472	69	133	23	12	5	62	40	54	.282	.340	.413	110	5	5	73	19			.922	10	*3	1.6
Total	2	137	485	70	135	25	12	5	63	40	56	.278	.336	.410	108	4	4	73	19			.921	8	3/O	1.3

■ **JEFF DOYLE**   Doyle, Jeffrey Donald   b: 10/2/56, Havre, Mont.   BB/TR, 5'9", 160 lbs.   Deb: 9/13/83

| 1983 | StL-N | 13 | 37 | 4 | 11 | 1 | 2 | 0 | 2 | 1 | 3 | .297 | .316 | .432 | 105 | 0 | 0 | 4 | 0 | 0 | 0 | .966 | 1 | 2 | 0.2 |

■ **JACK DOYLE**   Doyle, John Joseph "Dirty Jack"   b: 10/25/1869, Killorgin, Ireland   d: 12/31/58, Holyoke, Mass.   BR/TR, 5'9", 155 lbs.   Deb: 8/27/1889   MU

1889	Col-a	11	36	6	10	1	1	0	3	6	6	.278	.381	.361	120	1	1	9	9			.897	-3	/CO2	-0.1
1890	Col-a	77	298	47	80	17	7	2		13		.268	.299	.393	114	0	3	44	27			.887	-6	CS/O23	0.2
1891	Cle-N	69	250	43	69	14	4	0	43	26	44	.276	.351	.364	106	4	2	41	24			.897	-3	CO3/S	0.2
1892	Cle-N	24	88	17	26	4	1	1	14	6	10	.295	.340	.398	120	2	2	14	5			.875	-1	O/C1S	0.1
	NY-N	90	366	61	109	22	1	5	55	18	30	.298	.336	.404	128	10	10	65	42			.864	-18	2CO3/S	-0.4
	Yr	114	454	78	135	26	2	6	69	24	40	.297	.337	.403	126	12	12	79	47			.890	-18	C2O3/S1	-0.3
1893	NY-N	82	318	56	102	17	5	1	51	27	12	.321	.383	.415	114	6	6	67	40			.919	-3	CO/S3	1.0
1894	*NY-N	105	422	90	155	30	8	3	100	35		.367	.420	.498	124	13	16	109	42			.968	-2	12/3CM	0.2
1895	NY-N	82	319	52	100	21	3	1	66	24	12	.313	.365	.408	104	1	2	62	35			.974	-11	*1/2	0.3
1896	*Bal-N	118	487	116	165	29	4	1	101	42	15	.339	.400	.421	117	14	13	115	73			.974	-11	*1/2	0.3

YEAR	TM/L	G	AB	R	H	2B	3B	HR	RBI	BB	SO	AVG	OBP	SLG	PRO+	BR	/A	RC	SB	CS	SBR	FA	FR	POS	TPR
1897	*Bal-N	114	460	91	163	29	4	2	87	29		.354	.394	.448	122	14	14	108	62			.979	5	*1	1.6
1898	Was-N	43	177	26	54	2	2	2	26	7		.305	.335	.373	103	0	0	26	9			.963	-2	1/2M	-0.2
	NY-N	82	297	42	84	15	3	1	43	12		.283	.317	.364	98	-3	-2	40	14			.860	-0	O1S/3C	-0.4
	Yr	125	474	68	138	17	5	3	69	19		.291	.324	.367	100	-3	-1	66	23			.970	-2	1OS/23C	-0.6
1899	NY-N	118	448	55	134	15	7	3	76	33		.299	.353	.384	106	1	3	75	35			.976	6	*1/C	0.9
1900	NY-N	133	505	69	135	24	1	1	66	34		.267	.317	.325	81	-16	-12	65	34			.971	6	*1	-0.6
1901	Chi-N	75	285	21	66	9	2	0	39	7		.232	.263	.277	59	-16	-14	24	8			.973	7	1	-0.8
1902	NY-N	49	186	21	56	13	0	1	19	10		.301	.340	.387	125	5	5	29	12			.991	3	1	0.8
	Was-A	78	312	52	77	15	2	1	20	29		.247	.315	.317	75	-10	-10	35	6			.929	-11	2/1OC	-1.9
1903	Bro-N	139	524	84	164	27	6	0	91	54		.313	.380	.387	123	14	17	94	34			.981	2	*1	1.5
1904	Bro-N	8	22	2	5	1	0	0	2	6		.227	.414	.273	117	1	1	3	1			1.000	1	/1	0.2
	Phi-N	66	236	20	52	10	3	1	22	19		.220	.281	.301	83	-6	-5	22	4			.977	4	1/2	-0.2
	Yr	74	258	22	57	11	3	1	24	25		.221	.295	.298	87	-5	-4	25	5			.980	5	1/2	0.0
1905	NY-A	1	3	0	0	0	0	0	0	0		.000	.000	.000	-90	-1	-1	0	0			.833	-1	/1	-0.2
Total	17	1564	6039	971	1806	315	64	26	924	437	132	.299	.351	.385	107	38	53	1047	516			.975	-21	*1CO2/S3	3.5

■ JOE DOYLE
Doyle, Joseph K. b: Cincinnati, Ohio Deb: 4/20/1872

YEAR	TM/L	G	AB	R	H	2B	3B	HR	RBI	BB	SO	AVG	OBP	SLG	PRO+	BR	/A	RC	SB	CS	SBR	FA	FR	POS	TPR
1872	Nat-n	9	42	7	12	0	0	0	8	0	0	.286	.286	.286	66	-1	-3	4						/S23	-0.2

■ LARRY DOYLE
Doyle, Lawrence Joseph "Laughing Larry" b: 7/31/1886, Caseyville, Ill. d: 3/1/74, Saranac Lake, N.Y. BL/TR, 5'10", 165 lbs. Deb: 7/22/07

YEAR	TM/L	G	AB	R	H	2B	3B	HR	RBI	BB	SO	AVG	OBP	SLG	PRO+	BR	/A	RC	SB	CS	SBR	FA	FR	POS	TPR
1907	NY-N	69	227	16	59	3	0	0	16	20		.260	.320	.273	83	-3	-4	22	3			.917	-22	2	-3.1
1908	NY-N	104	377	65	116	16	9	0	33	22		.308	.352	.398	133	16	14	60	17			.935	-10	*2	0.3
1909	NY-N	147	570	86	**172**	27	11	6	49	45		.302	.360	.419	140	26	25	96	31			.940	-18	*2	0.5
1910	NY-N	151	575	97	164	21	14	8	69	71	26	.285	.369	.412	128	20	20	101	39			.930	-17	*2	0.0
1911	*NY-N	143	526	102	163	25	**25**	13	77	71	39	.310	.397	.527	153	39	37	124	38			.944	-24	*2	1.0
1912	*NY-N	143	558	98	184	33	8	10	90	56	20	.330	.393	.471	132	27	25	116	36			.948	-8	*2	1.3
1913	*NY-N	132	482	67	135	25	6	5	73	59	29	.280	.364	.388	114	11	10	78	38			.955	-9	*2	-0.1
1914	NY-N	145	539	87	140	19	8	5	63	58	25	.260	.343	.353	111	6	8	69	17			.959	-19	*2	-1.3
1915	NY-N	150	591	86	**189**	**40**	10	4	70	32	28	**.320**	.358	.442	150	27	31	94	22	18	-4	.947	-7	*2	2.4
1916	NY-N	113	441	55	118	24	10	2	47	27	23	.268	.316	.381	120	6	8	60	17			.960	16	*2	3.1
	Chi-N	9	38	6	15	5	1	1	7	1	1	.395	.410	.658	203	5	5	11	2			.982	5	/2	1.0
	Yr	122	479	61	133	29	11	3	54	28	24	.278	.323	.403	127	11	13	70	19			.962	20	*2	4.1
1917	Chi-N	135	476	48	121	19	5	6	61	48	28	.254	.323	.353	99	4	0	56	5			.952	-2	*2	0.5
1918	NY-N	75	257	38	67	7	4	3	36	37	10	.261	.354	.354	118	6	7	34	10			.969	-12	2	-0.1
1919	NY-N	113	381	61	110	14	10	7	52	31	17	.289	.350	.433	136	16	16	59	12			.956	2	*2	2.5
1920	NY-N	137	471	48	134	21	2	4	50	47	28	.285	.352	.363	107	4	5	61	11	9	-2	.967	-26	*2	-2.0
Total	14	1766	6509	960	1887	299	123	74	793	625	274	.290	.357	.408	126	210	207	1041	298	27		.949	-152	*2	6.0

■ DENNY DOYLE
Doyle, Robert Dennis b: 1/17/44, Glasgow, Ky. BL/TR, 5'9", 175 lbs. Deb: 4/07/70 F

YEAR	TM/L	G	AB	R	H	2B	3B	HR	RBI	BB	SO	AVG	OBP	SLG	PRO+	BR	/A	RC	SB	CS	SBR	FA	FR	POS	TPR
1970	Phi-N	112	413	43	86	10	7	2	16	33	64	.208	.267	.281	48	-31	-30	31	6	5	-1	.978	-16	*2	-4.0
1971	Phi-N	95	342	34	79	12	1	3	24	19	31	.231	.281	.298	64	-16	-16	29	4	2	0	.967	4	2	-0.5
1972	Phi-N	123	442	33	110	14	2	1	26	31	33	.249	.298	.296	68	-17	-19	38	6	7	-2	.982	-9	*2	-2.6
1973	Phi-N	116	370	45	101	9	3	3	26	31	32	.273	.329	.338	83	-7	-8	41	1	3	-2	.974	9	*2	0.5
1974	Cal-A	147	511	47	133	19	2	1	34	25	49	.260	.296	.311	79	-17	-13	46	6	7	-2	.983	16	*2/S	0.8
1975	Cal-A	8	15	0	1	0	0	0	0	1	1	.067	.125	.067	-48	-3	-3	0	0	0	0	.926	2	/23	-0.1
	*Bos-A	89	310	50	96	21	2	4	36	14	11	.310	.342	.429	107	6	3	43	5	7	-3	.974	-31	2/3S	-2.8
	Yr	97	325	50	97	21	2	4	36	15	12	.298	.331	.412	102	3	0	42	5	7	-3	.970	-29	2/3S	-2.9
1976	Bos-A	117	432	51	108	15	5	0	26	22	39	.250	.286	.308	66	-15	-21	37	8	5	-1	.977	-25	*2	-4.2
1977	Bos-A	137	455	54	109	13	6	2	49	29	50	.240	.291	.308	57	-23	-30	40	2	4	-2	.979	-10	*2	-3.2
Total	8	944	3290	357	823	113	28	16	237	205	310	.250	.296	.316	70	-123	-137	305	38	40	-13	.977	-61	2/3S	-16.1

■ D. J. DOZIER
Dozier, William Henry b: 9/21/65, Norfolk, Va. BR/TR, 6', 202 lbs. Deb: 5/06/92

YEAR	TM/L	G	AB	R	H	2B	3B	HR	RBI	BB	SO	AVG	OBP	SLG	PRO+	BR	/A	RC	SB	CS	SBR	FA	FR	POS	TPR
1992	NY-N	25	47	4	9	2	0	0	2	4	19	.191	.269	.234	44	-3	-3	4	4	0	1	.971	0	O	-0.2

■ DRAKE
Drake Deb: 6/29/1884

YEAR	TM/L	G	AB	R	H	2B	3B	HR	RBI	BB	SO	AVG	OBP	SLG	PRO+	BR	/A	RC	SB	CS	SBR	FA	FR	POS	TPR
1884	Was-a	2	7	0	2	1	0	0		0		.286	.286	.429	150	0	0	1				.000	-1	/O	-0.1

■ DELOS DRAKE
Drake, Delos Daniel b: 12/3/1886, Girard, Ohio d: 10/3/65, Findlay, Ohio BR/TL, 5'11.5", 170 lbs. Deb: 4/30/11

YEAR	TM/L	G	AB	R	H	2B	3B	HR	RBI	BB	SO	AVG	OBP	SLG	PRO+	BR	/A	RC	SB	CS	SBR	FA	FR	POS	TPR
1911	Det-A	95	315	37	88	9	9	1	36	17		.279	.324	.375	90	-3	-5	44	20			.942	-10	O/1	-1.9
1914	StL-F	138	514	51	129	18	8	3	42	31	57	.251	.295	.335	75	-15	-19	59	17			.957	-1	*O1	-2.6
1915	StL-F	102	343	32	91	23	4	1	41	23	27	.265	.313	.364	94	-1	-3	43	6			.974	-5	O/1	-1.3
Total	3	335	1172	120	308	50	21	5	119	71	84	.263	.308	.354	85	-20	-27	146	43			.959	-16	O/1	-5.8

■ LARRY DRAKE
Drake, Larry Francis b: 5/4/21, McKinney, Tex. d: 7/14/85, Houston, Tex. BL/TR, 6'1.5", 195 lbs. Deb: 7/20/45

YEAR	TM/L	G	AB	R	H	2B	3B	HR	RBI	BB	SO	AVG	OBP	SLG	PRO+	BR	/A	RC	SB	CS	SBR	FA	FR	POS	TPR
1945	Phi-A	1	2	0	0	0	0	0	0	0	2	.000	.000	.000	-99	-1	-1	0	0	0	0	1.000	-0	/O	-0.1
1948	Was-A	4	7	0	2	0	0	0	1	1	3	.286	.375	.286	79	-0	-0	1	0	0	0	1.000	-0	/O	-0.1
Total	2	5	9	0	2	0	0	0	1	1	5	.222	.300	.222	44	-1	-1	1	0	0	0	1.000	-0	/O	-0.2

■ SAMMY DRAKE
Drake, Samuel Harrison b: 10/7/34, Little Rock, Ark. BB/TR, 5'11", 175 lbs. Deb: 4/17/60 F

YEAR	TM/L	G	AB	R	H	2B	3B	HR	RBI	BB	SO	AVG	OBP	SLG	PRO+	BR	/A	RC	SB	CS	SBR	FA	FR	POS	TPR
1960	Chi-N	15	15	5	1	0	0	0	0	1	4	.067	.125	.067	-46	-3	-3	0	0	0	0	1.000	-1	/32	-0.4
1961	Chi-N	13	5	1	0	0	0	0	0	1	1	.000	.167	.000	-50	-1	-1	0	0	0	0	1.000	1	/O	0.0
1962	NY-N	25	52	2	10	0	0	0	7	6	12	.192	.276	.192	28	-5	-5	3	0	0	0	.977	-2	2/3	-0.7
Total	3	53	72	8	11	0	0	0	7	8	17	.153	.237	.153	8	-9	-9	3	0	0	0	.917	-2	/23O	-1.1

■ SOLLY DRAKE
Drake, Solomon Louis b: 10/23/30, Little Rock, Ark. BB/TR, 6', 170 lbs. Deb: 4/17/56 F

YEAR	TM/L	G	AB	R	H	2B	3B	HR	RBI	BB	SO	AVG	OBP	SLG	PRO+	BR	/A	RC	SB	CS	SBR	FA	FR	POS	TPR
1956	Chi-N	65	215	29	55	9	1	2	15	23	35	.256	.331	.335	81	-6	-5	26	9	5	-0	.993	2	O	-0.6
1959	LA-N	9	8	2	2	0	0	0	0	1	3	.250	.333	.250	54	-0	-1	1	1	0	0	.667	-1	/O	-0.2
	Phi-N	67	62	10	9	1	0	0	3	8	15	.145	.243	.161	10	-8	-8	3	5	5	-2	1.000	-10	O	-2.0
	Yr	76	70	12	11	1	0	0	3	9	18	.157	.253	.171	15	-8	-8	3	6	5	-1	.974	-11	O	-2.2
Total	2	141	285	41	66	10	1	2	18	32	53	.232	.311	.295	64	-14	-14	29	15	10	-2	.989	-9	/O	-2.8

■ JAKE DRAUBY
Drauby, Jacob C. b: 1865, Harrisburg, Pa. 5'10", 163 lbs. Deb: 10/03/1892

YEAR	TM/L	G	AB	R	H	2B	3B	HR	RBI	BB	SO	AVG	OBP	SLG	PRO+	BR	/A	RC	SB	CS	SBR	FA	FR	POS	TPR
1892	Was-N	10	34	3	7	0	1	0	3	2	12	.206	.250	.265	59	-2	-2	2	0			.763	-2	3	-0.3

■ BILL DREESEN
Dreesen, William Richard b: 7/26/04, New York, N.Y. d: 11/9/71, Mt.Vernon, N.Y. BL/TR, 5'7.5", 160 lbs. Deb: 5/01/31

YEAR	TM/L	G	AB	R	H	2B	3B	HR	RBI	BB	SO	AVG	OBP	SLG	PRO+	BR	/A	RC	SB	CS	SBR	FA	FR	POS	TPR
1931	Bos-N	48	180	38	40	10	4	1	10	23	23	.222	.310	.339	77	-6	-6	20	1			.910	-8	3	-1.0

■ BILL DRESCHER
Drescher, William Clayton "Dutch" b: 5/23/21, Congers, N.Y. d: 5/15/68, Haverstraw, N.Y. BL/TR, 6'2", 190 lbs. Deb: 4/19/44

YEAR	TM/L	G	AB	R	H	2B	3B	HR	RBI	BB	SO	AVG	OBP	SLG	PRO+	BR	/A	RC	SB	CS	SBR	FA	FR	POS	TPR
1944	NY-A	4	7	0	1	0	0	0	0	0	0	.143	.143	.143	-18	-1	-1	0	0	0	0	.875	0	/C	-0.1
1945	NY-A	48	126	10	34	3	1	0	15	8	5	.270	.313	.310	77	-3	-4	12	0	2	-1	.991	-8	C	-1.2
1946	NY-A	5	6	0	2	1	0	0	1	0	0	.333	.333	.500	129	0	0	1	0	0	0	1.000	1	/C	0.1
Total	3	57	139	10	37	4	1	0	16	8	5	.266	.306	.309	75	-4	-5	13	0	2	-1	.985	-7	/C	-1.2

■ CHUCK DRESSEN
Dressen, Charles Walter b: 9/20/1898, Decatur, Ill. d: 8/10/66, Detroit, Mich. BR/TR, 5'5.5", 146 lbs. Deb: 4/17/25 MC

YEAR	TM/L	G	AB	R	H	2B	3B	HR	RBI	BB	SO	AVG	OBP	SLG	PRO+	BR	/A	RC	SB	CS	SBR	FA	FR	POS	TPR
1925	Cin-N	76	215	35	59	8	2	3	19	12	4	.274	.319	.372	78	-8	-7	26	5	3	-0	.951	2	3/2O	-0.3
1926	Cin-N	127	474	76	126	27	11	4	48	49	31	.266	.338	.395	99	-2	-1	63	0			.966	17	*3/SO	2.3

YEAR	TM/L	G	AB	R	H	2B	3B	HR	RBI	BB	SO	AVG	OBP	SLG	PRO+	BR	/A	RC	SB	CS	SBR	FA	FR	POS	TPR
1927	Cin-N	144	548	78	160	36	10	2	55	71	32	.292	.376	.405	113	9	11	85	7			**.967**	12	*3/S	3.0
1928	Cin-N	135	498	72	145	26	3	1	59	43	22	.291	.355	.361	89	-8	-7	64	10			.938	-2	*3	-0.1
1929	Cin-N	110	401	49	98	22	3	1	36	41	21	.244	.321	.322	63	-25	-22	42	8			.932	-20	3/2	-3.5
1930	Cin-N	33	19	0	4	0	0	0	1	1	3	.211	.250	.211	14	-3	-3	1	0			1.000	3	3/2	0.0
1931	Cin-N	5	15	0	1	0	0	0	0	1	1	.067	.125	.067	-50	-3	-3	0	0			.846	-0	/3	-0.3
1933	NY-N	16	45	3	10	4	0	0	3	1	4	.222	.239	.311	57	-3	-3	3	0			.972	0	3	-0.2
Total	8	646	2215	313	603	123	29	11	221	219	118	.272	.343	.369	89	-43	-34	285	30	<u>3</u>		.953	12	3/2OS	0.9

■ LEE DRESSEN Dressen, Lee August b: 7/23/1889, Ellinwodd, Kan. d: 6/30/31, Diller, Neb. BL/TL, 6', 165 lbs. Deb: 4/21/14

YEAR	TM/L	G	AB	R	H	2B	3B	HR	RBI	BB	SO	AVG	OBP	SLG	PRO+	BR	/A	RC	SB	CS	SBR	FA	FR	POS	TPR
1914	StL-N	46	103	16	24	2	1	0	7	11	20	.233	.307	.272	73	-3	-3	9	2			.982	-1	1	-0.5
1918	Det-A	31	107	10	19	1	2	0	3	21	10	.178	.323	.224	68	-3	-3	9	2			.988	-3	1	-0.9
Total	2	77	210	26	43	3	3	0	10	32	30	.205	.316	.248	71	-7	-6	18	4			.985	-5	/1	-1.4

■ CAMERON DREW Drew, Cameron Steward b: 2/12/64, Boston, Mass. BL/TR, 6'5", 230 lbs. Deb: 9/09/88

YEAR	TM/L	G	AB	R	H	2B	3B	HR	RBI	BB	SO	AVG	OBP	SLG	PRO+	BR	/A	RC	SB	CS	SBR	FA	FR	POS	TPR
1988	Hou-N	7	16	1	3	0	1	0	1	0	1	.188	.188	.313	43	-1	-1	1	0	0	0	1.000	0	/O	-0.1

■ DAVE DREW Drew, David Deb: 5/14/1884

YEAR	TM/L	G	AB	R	H	2B	3B	HR	RBI	BB	SO	AVG	OBP	SLG	PRO+	BR	/A	RC	SB	CS	SBR	FA	FR	POS	TPR
1884	Phi-U	2	9	1	4	0	0	0		0		.444	.444	.444	217	1	1	2				.000	-0	/P2S	0.1
	Was-U	13	53	8	16	1	2	0		1		.302	.315	.396	144	2	2	7				.806	1	/S1O	0.2
	Yr	15	62	9	20	1	2	0		1		.323	.333	.403	154	3	3	9				.813	1	/S1P2O	0.3

■ FRANK DREWS Drews, Frank John b: 5/25/16, Buffalo, N.Y. d: 4/22/72, Buffalo, N.Y. BR/TR, 5'10", 175 lbs. Deb: 8/13/44

YEAR	TM/L	G	AB	R	H	2B	3B	HR	RBI	BB	SO	AVG	OBP	SLG	PRO+	BR	/A	RC	SB	CS	SBR	FA	FR	POS	TPR
1944	Bos-N	46	141	14	29	9	1	0	10	25	14	.206	.329	.284	71	-4	-5	15	0			.959	1	2	-0.2
1945	Bos-N	49	147	13	30	4	1	0	19	16	18	.204	.282	.245	47	-10	-10	12	0			.976	5	2	-0.3
Total	2	95	288	27	59	13	2	0	29	41	32	.205	.306	.264	59	-14	-15	26	0			.967	5	/2	-0.5

■ DAN DRIESSEN Driessen, Daniel b: 7/29/51, Hilton Head, S.C. BL/TR, 5'11", 190 lbs. Deb: 6/09/73

YEAR	TM/L	G	AB	R	H	2B	3B	HR	RBI	BB	SO	AVG	OBP	SLG	PRO+	BR	/A	RC	SB	CS	SBR	FA	FR	POS	TPR
1973	*Cin-N	102	366	49	110	15	2	4	47	24	37	.301	.347	.385	108	1	3	48	8	3	1	.946	-10	31/O	-0.7
1974	Cin-N	150	470	63	132	23	6	7	56	48	62	.281	.349	.400	111	6	6	66	10	5	0	.915	-20	*31/O	-1.6
1975	*Cin-N	88	210	38	59	8	1	7	38	35	30	.281	.389	.429	124	9	8	36	10	3	1	.986	-3	1O	0.3
1976	*Cin-N	98	219	32	54	11	1	7	44	43	32	.247	.370	.402	116	7	6	35	14	1	4	.997	-2	1O	0.5
1977	Cin-N	151	536	75	161	31	4	17	91	64	85	.300	.378	.468	123	20	19	95	31	13	2	.994	-3	*1	0.8
1978	Cin-N	153	524	68	131	23	3	16	70	75	79	.250	.348	.397	108	7	7	76	28	9	3	**.996**	3	*1	0.4
1979	*Cin-N	150	515	72	129	24	3	18	75	62	77	.250	.334	.414	102	2	2	74	11	5	0	.993	-3	*1	-1.0
1980	Cin-N	154	524	81	139	36	1	14	74	**93**	68	.265	.382	.418	123	20	20	88	19	6	2	.995	-4	*1	0.9
1981	Cin-N	82	233	35	55	14	0	7	33	40	31	.236	.353	.386	108	4	3	33	2	4	-2	.995	-5	1	-0.8
1982	Cin-N	149	516	64	139	25	1	17	57	82	62	.269	.372	.421	119	17	15	85	11	6	-0	**.998**	-7	*1	0.1
1983	Cin-N	122	386	57	107	17	1	12	57	75	51	.277	.395	.420	121	16	15	66	6	4	-1	**.996**	-2	*1	0.6
1984	Cin-N	81	218	27	61	13	0	7	28	37	25	.280	.384	.436	124	10	8	38	2	1	0	.991	-4	1	0.2
	Mon-N	51	169	20	43	11	0	9	32	17	15	.254	.323	.479	128	4	5	24	0	1	-1	.995	-2	1	0.1
	Yr	132	387	47	104	24	0	16	60	54	40	.269	.358	.455	126	14	14	63	2	2	-1	.992	-5	*1	0.3
1985	Mon-N	91	312	31	78	18	0	6	25	33	29	.250	.326	.365	99	-3	-1	36	2	2	-1	.997	3	1	-0.4
	SF-N	54	181	22	42	8	0	3	22	17	22	.232	.302	.326	79	-6	-5	19	0	0	0	.998	-2	1	-1.0
	Yr	145	493	53	120	26	0	9	47	50	51	.243	.317	.351	92	-9	-5	55	2	2	-1	.997	1	*1	-1.4
1986	SF-N	15	16	2	3	2	0	0	0	4	4	.188	.350	.313	89	-0	-0	2	0	0	0	1.000	1	/1	0.0
	Hou-N	17	24	5	7	1	0	1	3	5	2	.292	.414	.458	144	2	2	5	0	0	0	1.000	-0	1	0.1
	Yr	32	40	7	10	3	0	1	3	9	6	.250	.388	.400	122	1	2	7	0	0	0	1.000	0	1	0.1
1987	*StL-N	24	60	5	14	2	0	1	11	7	8	.233	.313	.317	66	-3	-3	6	0	0	0	.993	-0	1	-0.4
Total	15	1732	5479	746	1464	282	23	153	763	761	719	.267	.359	.411	113	111	111	830	154	63	8	.995	-60	*13/O	-1.9

■ LEW DRILL Drill, Lewis L b: 5/9/1877, Browerville, Minn. d: 7/4/69, St.Paul, Minn. BR/TR, 5'6", 186 lbs. Deb: 4/23/02

YEAR	TM/L	G	AB	R	H	2B	3B	HR	RBI	BB	SO	AVG	OBP	SLG	PRO+	BR	/A	RC	SB	CS	SBR	FA	FR	POS	TPR
1902	Was-A	38	123	21	34	7	2	1	16	16		.276	.369	.390	109	2	2	19	0			.919	-10	C/2O3	-0.5
	Bal-A	2	8	2	2	0	0	0	0	0		.250	.250	.250	37	-1	-1	1	0			1.000	1	/C1	0.0
	Was-A	33	98	12	24	3	2	0	13	10		.245	.327	.316	78	-3	-3	12	5			.926	-4	C/O2	-0.4
	Yr	73	229	35	60	10	4	1	29	26		.262	.347	.354	94	-1	-1	32	5			.924	-14	C/O231	-0.9
1903	Was-A	51	154	11	39	9	3	0	23	15		.253	.331	.351	103	1	1	20	4			.966	-4	C/1	0.2
1904	Was-A	46	142	17	38	7	2	1	11	21		.268	.381	.366	139	7	8	22	3			.934	-7	CO	0.4
	Det-A	51	160	7	39	6	1	0	13	20		.244	.335	.294	103	1	1	17	2			.950	-8	C/1	-0.1
	Yr	97	302	24	77	13	3	1	24	41		.255	.357	.328	120	8	9	39	5			.944	-14	CO/1	0.3
1905	Det-A	72	211	17	55	9	0	0	24	32		.261	.366	.303	112	5	5	28	7			.970	-2	C	1.1
Total	4	293	896	87	231	41	10	2	100	114		.258	.352	.333	108	14	14	119	21			.953	-34	C/O123	0.7

■ JIM DRISCOLL Driscoll, James Bernard b: 5/14/44, Medford, Mass. BL/TR, 5'11", 175 lbs. Deb: 6/17/70

YEAR	TM/L	G	AB	R	H	2B	3B	HR	RBI	BB	SO	AVG	OBP	SLG	PRO+	BR	/A	RC	SB	CS	SBR	FA	FR	POS	TPR
1970	Oak-A	21	52	2	10	0	0	1	2	2	15	.192	.236	.250	35	-5	-4	3	0	0	0	.967	-3	/2S	-0.6
1972	Tex-A	15	18	0	0	0	0	0	0	2	3	.000	.100	.000	-72	-4	-4	0	0	0	0	.900	1	/23	-0.3
Total	2	36	70	2	10	0	0	1	2	4	18	.143	.200	.186	9	-8	-8	3	0	0	0	.950	-1	/2S3	-0.9

■ DENNY DRISCOLL Driscoll, John F. b: 11/19/1855, Lowell, Mass. d: 7/11/1886, Lowell, Mass. BL/TL, 5'10.5", 160 lbs. Deb: 7/01/1880

YEAR	TM/L	G	AB	R	H	2B	3B	HR	RBI	BB	SO	AVG	OBP	SLG	PRO+	BR	/A	RC	SB	CS	SBR	FA	FR	POS	TPR
1880	Buf-N	18	65	1	10	1	0	0	4	1	7	.154	.167	.169	14	-6	-6	2				.895	-2	O/P	-0.6
1882	Pit-a	23	80	12	11	2	0	1		3		.138	.169	.200	25	-6	-6	3				.885	-4	P	0.0
1883	Pit-a	41	148	19	27	2	1	0		4		.182	.204	.209	35	-11	-10	6				.890	4	P/O3	-0.2
1884	Lou-a	13	48	5	9	1	0	0		2		.188	.220	.208	45	-3	-3	2				.816	2	P/O	-0.1
1885	Buf-N	7	19	2	3	0	0	0	0	2	5	.158	.238	.158	29	-1	-1	1				.719	-5	/2	-0.6
Total	5	102	360	39	60	6	1	1	<u>4</u>	12	<u>12</u>	.167	.194	.197	30	-27	-25	14				.872	-5	/PO23	-1.5

■ PADDY DRISCOLL Driscoll, John Leo b: 1/11/1895, Evanston, Ill. d: 6/29/68, Chicago, Ill. BR/TR, 5'8.5", 155 lbs. Deb: 6/12/17

YEAR	TM/L	G	AB	R	H	2B	3B	HR	RBI	BB	SO	AVG	OBP	SLG	PRO+	BR	/A	RC	SB	CS	SBR	FA	FR	POS	TPR
1917	Chi-N	13	28	2	3	1	0	0	3	2	6	.107	.167	.143	-4	-3	-4	1	2			.882	2	/23S	-0.1

■ MIKE DRISSEL Drissel, Michael F. b: 12/19/1864, St.Louis, Mo. d: 2/26/13, St.Louis, Mo. BR/TR, 5'11", Deb: 9/05/1885

YEAR	TM/L	G	AB	R	H	2B	3B	HR	RBI	BB	SO	AVG	OBP	SLG	PRO+	BR	/A	RC	SB	CS	SBR	FA	FR	POS	TPR
1885	StL-a	6	20	0	1	0	0	0		0		.050	.050	.050	-65	-4	-4	0				.971	-0	/C	-0.3

■ WALT DROPO Dropo, Walter "Moose" b: 1/30/23, Moosup, Conn. BR/TR, 6'5", 220 lbs. Deb: 4/19/49

YEAR	TM/L	G	AB	R	H	2B	3B	HR	RBI	BB	SO	AVG	OBP	SLG	PRO+	BR	/A	RC	SB	CS	SBR	FA	FR	POS	TPR
1949	Bos-A	11	41	3	6	2	0	0	1	3	7	.146	.205	.195	6	-6	-6	1	0	0	0	1.000	-1	1	-0.7
1950	Bos-A★	136	559	101	180	28	8	34	**144**	45	75	.322	.378	.583	130	32	24	122	0	0	0	.988	-4	*1	1.6
1951	Bos-A	99	360	37	86	14	0	11	57	38	52	.239	.312	.369	76	-9	-14	40	0	0	0	.987	-1	1	-1.9
1952	Bos-A	37	132	13	35	7	1	6	27	11	22	.265	.331	.470	112	3	2	18	0	0	0	.994	-1	1	-0.1
	Det-A	115	459	56	128	17	3	23	70	26	63	.279	.320	.479	120	9	9	66	2	2	-1	.989	-1	*1	0.3
	Yr	152	591	69	163	24	4	29	97	37	85	.276	.323	.477	118	12	11	84	2	2	-1	.990	-2	*1	0.2
1953	Det-A	152	606	61	150	30	3	13	96	29	69	.248	.289	.371	78	-22	-21	61	2	0	1	.990	12	*1	-1.5
1954	Det-A	107	320	27	90	14	2	4	44	24	41	.281	.331	.375	95	-3	-3	37	0	1	-1	.996	1	1	-0.7
1955	Chi-A	141	453	55	127	15	2	19	79	42	71	.280	.344	.448	109	6	4	66	0	1	-1	.995	-5	*1	-0.9
1956	Chi-A	125	361	42	96	13	1	8	52	37	51	.266	.339	.374	87	-6	-7	44	1	0	0	**.993**	-3	*1	-1.6
1957	Chi-A	93	223	24	57	2	0	13	49	16	40	.256	.305	.439	101	-1	-1	26	0	1	-1	.987	2	1	-0.3
1958	Chi-A	28	52	3	10	1	0	2	8	5	11	.192	.276	.327	67	-3	-2	4	0	0	0	1.000	1	1	-0.3
	Cin-N	63	162	18	47	7	2	7	31	12	31	.290	.343	.488	111	3	2	25	0	0	0	1.000	1	1	0.1

YEAR	TM/L	G	AB	R	H	2B	3B	HR	RBI	BB	SO	AVG	OBP	SLG	PRO+	BR	/A	RC	SB	CS	SBR	FA	FR	POS	TPR
1959	Cin-N	26	39	4	4	1	0	1	2	4	7	.103	.205	.205	9	-5	-5	1	0	0	0	1.000	2	1	-0.4
	Bal-A	62	151	17	42	9	0	6	21	12	20	.278	.331	.457	117	2	3	21	0	0	0	.990	-2	1/3	-0.1
1960	Bal-A	79	179	16	48	8	0	4	21	20	19	.268	.345	.380	97	-1	-1	22	0	1	-1	.993	-1	1/3	-0.6
1961	Bal-A	14	27	1	7	0	0	1	2	4	3	.259	.355	.370	96	-0	-0	3	0	0	0	1.000	1	1	0.0
Total	13	1288	4124	478	1113	168	22	152	704	328	582	.270	.327	.432	100	0	-15	559	5	6	-2	.992	-1	*1/3	-7.1

■ KEITH DRUMRIGHT Drumright, Keith Alan b: 10/21/54, Springfield, Mo. BL/TR, 5'10", 170 lbs. Deb: 9/01/78

YEAR	TM/L	G	AB	R	H	2B	3B	HR	RBI	BB	SO	AVG	OBP	SLG	PRO+	BR	/A	RC	SB	CS	SBR	FA	FR	POS	TPR
1978	Hou-N	17	55	5	9	0	0	0	2	3	4	.164	.207	.164	5	-7	-6	2	0	1	-1	.944	-1	2	-0.8
1981	*Oak-A	31	86	8	25	1	1	0	11	4	4	.291	.322	.326	91	-1	-1	9	0	0	0	.989	-5	2/D	-0.6
Total	2	48	141	13	34	1	1	0	13	7	8	.241	.277	.262	58	-8	-7	10	0	1	-1	.969	-6	/2D	-1.4

■ JEAN DUBUC Dubuc, Jean Joseph Octave Arthur "Chauncey" b: 9/15/1888, St.Johnsbury, Vt. d: 8/28/58, Fort Myers, Fla. BR/TR, 5'10.5", 185 lbs. Deb: 6/25/08 C

YEAR	TM/L	G	AB	R	H	2B	3B	HR	RBI	BB	SO	AVG	OBP	SLG	PRO+	BR	/A	RC	SB	CS	SBR	FA	FR	POS	TPR
1908	Cin-N	15	29	2	4	1	0	0	2	0		.138	.138	.172	-1	-3	-3	1	0			.943	1	P	0.0
1909	Cin-N	19	18	1	3	0	0	0	0	2		.167	.250	.167	30	-1	-1	1	0			.844	0	P	0.0
1912	Det-A	40	108	16	29	6	2	1	9	3		.269	.295	.389	98	-1	-1	12	0			.972	4	P/O	0.0
1913	Det-A	68	135	17	36	5	3	2	11	2	17	.267	.277	.393	97	-2	-2	14	1			.953	6	P/O	-0.2
1914	Det-A	71	124	9	28	8	1	1	11	7	11	.226	.273	.331	79	-3	-4	12	1			.942	3	P	0.0
1915	Det-A	60	112	7	23	2	1	0	14	8	15	.205	.258	.241	47	-7	-8	7	0			.969	1	P	0.0
1916	Det-A	52	78	3	20	0	2	0	7	7	12	.256	.318	.308	85	-1	-1	8	0			.952	4	P	0.0
1918	*Bos-A	5	6	0	1	0	0	0	0	1	2	.167	.286	.167	37	-0	-0	0	0			1.000	-0	/P	0.0
1919	NY-N	37	42	2	6	1	1	0	2	0	6	.143	.143	.214	7	-5	-5	1	0			.964	2	P	0.0
Total	9	367	652	57	150	23	10	4	56	30	63	.230	.266	.314	72	-25	-26	57	2			.952	22	P/O	-0.2

■ ROB DUCEY Ducey, Robert Thomas b: 5/24/65, Toronto, Ont., Can. BL/TR, 6'2", 175 lbs. Deb: 5/01/87

YEAR	TM/L	G	AB	R	H	2B	3B	HR	RBI	BB	SO	AVG	OBP	SLG	PRO+	BR	/A	RC	SB	CS	SBR	FA	FR	POS	TPR
1987	Tor-A	34	48	12	9	1	0	1	6	8	10	.188	.304	.271	53	-3	-3	5	2	0	1	1.000	-7	O/D	-0.9
1988	Tor-A	27	54	15	17	4	1	0	6	5	7	.315	.373	.426	123	2	2	9	1	0	0	1.000	-6	O/D	-0.4
1989	Tor-A	41	76	5	16	4	0	0	7	9	25	.211	.294	.263	59	-4	-4	6	2	1	0	1.000	-2	O/D	-0.6
1990	Tor-A	19	53	7	16	5	0	0	7	7	15	.302	.393	.396	119	2	2	9	1	1	-0	1.000	-0	O	0.1
1991	*Tor-A	39	68	8	16	2	2	1	4	6	26	.235	.297	.368	80	-2	-2	8	2	0	1	.892	-4	O/D	-0.5
1992	Tor-A	23	21	3	1	1	0	0	0	0	10	.048	.048	.095	-58	-4	-5	0	0	1	-1	1.000	-3	O/D	-0.9
	Cal-A	31	59	4	14	3	0	0	2	5	12	.237	.297	.288	65	-3	-3	5	2	3	-1	.944	-1	O/D	-0.5
	Yr	54	80	7	15	4	0	0	2	5	22	.188	.235	.237	32	-7	-7	4	2	4	-2	.957	-4	O/D	-1.4
Total	6	214	379	54	89	20	3	2	32	40	105	.235	.310	.319	74	-12	-13	41	10	6	-1	.976	-22	O/D	-3.7

■ JOHN DUDRA Dudra, John Joseph b: 5/27/16, Assumption, Ill. d: 10/24/65, Pana, Ill. BR/TR, 5'11.5", 175 lbs. Deb: 9/07/41

YEAR	TM/L	G	AB	R	H	2B	3B	HR	RBI	BB	SO	AVG	OBP	SLG	PRO+	BR	/A	RC	SB	CS	SBR	FA	FR	POS	TPR
1941	Bos-N	14	25	3	9	3	1	0	3	3	4	.360	.429	.560	185	3	3	6	0			.933	0	/231S	0.3

■ PAT DUFF Duff, Patrick Henry b: 5/6/1875, Providence, R.I. d: 9/11/25, Providence, R.I. TR , Deb: 4/16/06

YEAR	TM/L	G	AB	R	H	2B	3B	HR	RBI	BB	SO	AVG	OBP	SLG	PRO+	BR	/A	RC	SB	CS	SBR	FA	FR	POS	TPR
1906	Was-A	1	1	0	0	0	0	0	0	0		.000	.000	.000	-99	-0	-0	0	0			.000	0	H	0.0

■ CHARLIE DUFFEE Duffee, Charles Edward "Home Run" b: 1/27/1866, Mobile, Ala. d: 12/24/1894, Mobile, Ala. BR/TR, Deb: 4/17/1889

YEAR	TM/L	G	AB	R	H	2B	3B	HR	RBI	BB	SO	AVG	OBP	SLG	PRO+	BR	/A	RC	SB	CS	SBR	FA	FR	POS	TPR
1889	StL-a	137	509	93	124	15	12	15	86	60	81	.244	.327	.409	98	6	-5	77	21			.936	18	*O/32	0.8
1890	StL-a	98	378	68	104	11	7	3		37		.275	.344	.365	98	5	-3	56	20			.951	10	O3/S	0.5
1891	Col-a	137	552	86	166	28	4	10	90	42	36	.301	.353	.420	132	15	20	99	41			.927	11	*O/3S	2.3
1892	Was-N	132	492	64	122	12	11	6	51	36	33	.248	.302	.354	103	-1	1	63	28			.913	19	*O/31	1.3
1893	Cin-N	4	12	3	2	1	0	0	0	5	0	.167	.412	.250	78	-0	-0	1	0			.400	-2	/O	-0.2
Total	5	508	1943	314	518	67	34	34	227	180	150	.267	.332	.389	108	25	12	295	110			.927	56	O/31S2	4.7

■ ED DUFFY Duffy, Edward Charles b: 1844, Ireland d: 6/21/1889, Brooklyn, N.Y. TR , 5'7.5", 152 lbs. Deb: 5/08/1871

YEAR	TM/L	G	AB	R	H	2B	3B	HR	RBI	BB	SO	AVG	OBP	SLG	PRO+	BR	/A	RC	SB	CS	SBR	FA	FR	POS	TPR
1871	Chi-n	26	121	30	28	5	0	0	15	3	2	.231	.250	.273	45	-8	-11	11	11					S/3	-0.7

■ FRANK DUFFY Duffy, Frank Thomas b: 10/14/46, Oakland, Cal. BR/TR, 6'1", 180 lbs. Deb: 9/04/70

YEAR	TM/L	G	AB	R	H	2B	3B	HR	RBI	BB	SO	AVG	OBP	SLG	PRO+	BR	/A	RC	SB	CS	SBR	FA	FR	POS	TPR
1970	Cin-N	6	11	1	2	2	0	0	0	1	2	.182	.250	.364	62	-1	-1	1	1	0	0	1.000	1	/S	0.1
1971	Cin-N	13	16	0	3	1	0	0	1	1	2	.188	.235	.250	38	-1	-1	1	0	0	0	.944	5	S	0.4
	*SF-N	21	28	4	5	0	0	0	2	0	10	.179	.179	.179	1	-4	-4	1	0	0	0	.968	5	/S23	0.2
	Yr	34	44	4	8	1	0	0	3	1	12	.182	.200	.205	15	-5	-5	2	0	0	0	.955	10	S/23	0.6
1972	Cle-A	130	385	23	92	16	4	3	27	31	54	.239	.297	.325	82	-7	-9	36	6	2	1	.977	3	*S	1.2
1973	Cle-A	116	361	34	95	16	4	8	50	25	41	.263	.314	.396	97	-1	-2	41	6	6	-2	**.986**	12	*S	2.3
1974	Cle-A	158	549	62	128	18	0	8	48	30	64	.233	.273	.310	68	-24	-23	45	7	8	-3	.980	-8	*S	-1.4
1975	Cle-A	146	482	44	117	22	2	1	47	27	60	.243	.286	.303	66	-22	-22	39	10	10	-3	.977	14	*S	0.4
1976	Cle-A	133	392	38	83	11	2	2	30	29	50	.212	.270	.265	58	-21	-21	29	10	0	3	**.983**	11	*S	0.7
1977	Cle-A	122	334	30	67	13	2	4	31	21	47	.201	.248	.287	47	-26	-24	24	8	3	1	.967	3	*S	-1.0
1978	Bos-A	64	104	12	27	5	0	0	4	6	11	.260	.306	.308	66	-4	-5	10	1	1	-0	.960	6	3S2/D	0.4
1979	Bos-A	6	3	0	0	0	0	0	0	0	1	.000	.000	.000	-95	-1	-1	0	0	0	0	1.000	1	/21	0.0
Total	10	915	2665	248	619	104	14	26	240	171	342	.232	.281	.311	69	-111	-112	227	49	30	-3	.977	53	S/32D1	3.3

■ HUGH DUFFY Duffy, Hugh b: 11/26/1866, Cranston, R.I. d: 10/19/54, Boston, Mass. BR/TR, 5'7", 168 lbs. Deb: 6/23/1888 MCH

YEAR	TM/L	G	AB	R	H	2B	3B	HR	RBI	BB	SO	AVG	OBP	SLG	PRO+	BR	/A	RC	SB	CS	SBR	FA	FR	POS	TPR
1888	Chi-N	71	298	60	84	10	4	7	41	9	32	.282	.305	.413	121	9	6	43	13			.910	5	O/S3	0.9
1889	Chi-N	136	584	144	172	21	7	12	89	46	30	.295	.348	.416	109	10	5	105	52			.894	-15	*OS	-1.1
1890	Chi-P	138	596	**161**	**191**	36	16	7	82	59	20	.320	.384	.470	124	24	19	**141**	78			.917	13	*O	2.2
1891	Bos-a	127	536	134	180	20	8	9	**110**	61	29	.336	.408	.453	152	35	36	137	85			.917	0	*O/3S	2.7
1892	*Bos-N	147	612	125	184	28	12	5	81	60	37	.301	.364	.410	125	26	18	113	51			.942	-9	*O/3	0.2
1893	Bos-N	131	560	147	203	23	7	6	118	50	13	.363	.416	.461	125	28	20	129	44			.953	-2	*O	0.9
1894	Bos-N	125	539	160	**237**	**51**	16	**18**	**145**	66	15	**.440**	.502	**.694**	174	**77**	**68**	**217**	48			.927	5	*O/S	4.9
1895	Bos-N	130	531	110	187	30	6	9	100	63	16	.352	.425	.482	126	30	22	131	42			.945	6	*O	1.4
1896	Bos-N	131	527	97	158	16	8	5	113	52	19	.300	.365	.389	95	1	-4	94	39			.957	1	*O/2S	-1.1
1897	*Bos-N	134	550	130	187	25	10	**11**	129	52		.340	.403	.482	125	26	20	128	41			.975	-1	*O/2S	0.9
1898	Bos-N	152	568	97	169	13	3	8	108	59		.298	.365	.373	106	9	5	92	29			.956	2	*O/31C	-0.4
1899	Bos-N	147	588	103	164	29	7	5	102	39		.279	.327	.378	85	-7	-16	84	26			.970	-4	*O	-2.8
1900	Bos-N	55	181	27	55	5	4	2	31	16		.304	.360	.409	100	3	-1	32	11			.957	-1	O/2	-0.5
1901	Mil-A	79	285	40	86	15	9	2	45	16		.302	.341	.439	121	5	7	49	12			.967	-6	OM	-0.4
1904	Phi-N	18	46	10	13	1	1	0	5	13		.283	.441	.348	150	4	4	9	3			.850	-3	OM	0.0
1905	Phi-N	15	40	7	12	2	1	0	3	1		.300	.317	.400	118	0	1	5	0			.909	1	/OM	0.1
1906	Phi-N	1	1	0	0	0	0	0	0	0		.000	.000	.000	-99	-0	-0	0	0			.000	0	HM	0.0
Total	17	1737	7042	1552	2282	325	119	106	1302	662	211	.324	.384	.449	122	279	210	1508	574			.943	-9	*O/S23C1	7.9

■ JOE DUGAN Dugan, Joseph Anthony "Jumping Joe" b: 5/12/1897, Mahanoy City, Pa. d: 7/7/82, Norwood, Mass. BR/TR, 5'11", 160 lbs. Deb: 7/05/17

YEAR	TM/L	G	AB	R	H	2B	3B	HR	RBI	BB	SO	AVG	OBP	SLG	PRO+	BR	/A	RC	SB	CS	SBR	FA	FR	POS	TPR
1917	Phi-A	43	134	9	26	8	0	0	16	3	16	.194	.229	.254	48	-9	-9	8	0			.917	1	S/2	-0.7
1918	Phi-A	121	411	26	80	11	3	3	34	16	55	.195	.230	.258	47	-28	-28	25	4			.930	17	S2	-0.6
1919	Phi-A	104	387	25	105	17	2	1	30	11	30	.271	.300	.333	77	-12	-13	40	9			.929	1	S/23	-0.6
1920	Phi-A	123	491	65	158	40	5	3	60	19	51	.322	.351	.442	108	5	4	73	5	8	-3	.948	-1	3S2	0.6
1921	Phi-A	119	461	54	136	22	6	10	58	28	45	.295	.342	.434	96	-4	-4	69	5	1	1	.953	-25	*3	-1.9
1922	Bos-A	84	341	45	98	22	3	3	38	9	28	.287	.308	.396	83	-10	-10	40	2	3	-1	.943	-9	3S	-1.3
	*NY-A	60	252	44	72	9	1	3	25	13	21	.286	.331	.365	79	-7	-8	31	1	0	0	.967	-10	3	-1.2
	Yr	144	593	89	170	31	4	6	63	22	49	.287	.318	.383	81	-17	-18	72	3	3	-1	.954	-19	*3S	-2.5

YEAR	TM/L	G	AB	R	H	2B	3B	HR	RBI	BB	SO	AVG	OBP	SLG	PRO+	BR	/A	RC	SB	CS	SBR	FA	FR	POS	TPR
1923	*NY-A	146	644	111	182	30	7	7	67	25	41	.283	.311	.384	81	-19	-20	76	4	2	0	**.974**	-12	*3	-1.9
1924	NY-A	148	610	105	184	31	7	3	56	31	32	.302	.341	.390	88	-12	-12	81	1	3	-2	.962	-15	*3/2	-1.6
1925	NY-A	102	404	50	118	19	4	0	31	19	20	.292	.330	.359	76	-16	-15	47	2	4	-2	.970	7	3	-0.2
1926	*NY-A	123	434	39	125	19	5	1	64	25	16	.288	.328	.362	81	-13	-12	52	2	4	-2	.955	-16	*3	-2.2
1927	*NY-A	112	387	44	104	24	3	2	43	27	37	.269	.321	.362	79	-14	-12	43	1	4	-2	.938	-19	*3	-2.7
1928	*NY-A	94	312	33	86	15	0	6	34	16	15	.276	.317	.381	85	-8	-7	38	1	0	0	.952	-18	3/2	-2.0
1929	Bos-N	60	125	14	38	10	0	0	15	8	8	.304	.346	.384	84	-4	-3	16	1			.918	-9	3/S2O	-1.0
1931	Det-A	8	17	1	4	0	0	0	0	0	3	.235	.235	.235	23	-2	-2	1	0	0	0	.900	-1	/3	-0.2
Total	14	1447	5410	665	1516	277	46	42	571	250	418	.280	.317	.372	82	-154	-151	641	37	29		.957	-107	*3S/2O	-17.5

■ BILL DUGAN

Dugan, William H. b: 1864, New York, N.Y. d: 7/24/21, New York, N.Y. Deb: 8/05/1884 F

YEAR	TM/L	G	AB	R	H	2B	3B	HR	RBI	BB	SO	AVG	OBP	SLG	PRO+	BR	/A	RC	SB	CS	SBR	FA	FR	POS	TPR
1884	Ric-a	9	28	4	2	1	0	0		0		.071	.103	.107	-31	-4	-4	0				.889	-3	/C	-0.5
	KC-U	3	6	0	0	0	0	0		0		.000	.000	.000	-99	-1	-1	0				.400	-1	/O	-0.2
Total	1	12	34	4	2	1	0	0		0		.059	.086	.088	-44	-5	-5	0					-4	/CO	-0.7

■ GUS DUGAS

Dugas, Augustin Joseph b: 3/24/07, St.Jean Dematha, Que., Canada BL/TL, 5'9", 165 lbs. Deb: 9/17/30

YEAR	TM/L	G	AB	R	H	2B	3B	HR	RBI	BB	SO	AVG	OBP	SLG	PRO+	BR	/A	RC	SB	CS	SBR	FA	FR	POS	TPR
1930	Pit-N	9	31	8	9	2	0	0	1	7	4	.290	.421	.355	90	-0	-0	5	0			.864	-1	/O	-0.2
1932	Pit-N	55	97	13	23	3	3	3	12	7	11	.237	.288	.423	90	-2	-2	12	0			.952	-3	O	-0.5
1933	Phi-N	37	71	4	12	3	0	0	9	1	9	.169	.181	.211	10	-8	-9	2	0			.984	-0	1/O	-1.1
1934	Was-A	24	19	2	1	1	0	0	1	3	3	.053	.182	.105	-25	-4	-4	0	0	0	0	1.000	-0	/O	-0.4
Total	4	125	218	27	45	9	3	3	23	18	27	.206	.267	.317	54	-14	-14	20	0	0		.926	-4	/O1	-2.2

■ DAN DUGDALE

Dugdale, Daniel Edward b: 10/28/1864, Peoria, Ill. d: 3/9/34, Seattle, Wash. 5'8", 180 lbs. Deb: 5/20/1886

YEAR	TM/L	G	AB	R	H	2B	3B	HR	RBI	BB	SO	AVG	OBP	SLG	PRO+	BR	/A	RC	SB	CS	SBR	FA	FR	POS	TPR
1886	KC-N	12	40	4	7	0	0	0	2	2	13	.175	.214	.175	18	-4	-4	2	1			.884	-2	/CO	-0.5
1894	Was-N	38	134	19	32	4	2	0	16	13	14	.239	.306	.299	49	-11	-11	15	7			.874	-5	C/3O	-1.0
Total	2	50	174	23	39	4	2	0	18	15	27	.224	.286	.270	43	-15	-15	17	8			.877	-7	/CO3	-1.5

■ OSCAR DUGEY

Dugey, Oscar Joseph "Jake" b: 10/25/1887, Palestine, Tex. d: 1/1/66, Dallas, Tex. BR/TR, 5'8", 160 lbs. Deb: 9/13/13 C

YEAR	TM/L	G	AB	R	H	2B	3B	HR	RBI	BB	SO	AVG	OBP	SLG	PRO+	BR	/A	RC	SB	CS	SBR	FA	FR	POS	TPR
1913	Bos-N	5	8	1	2	0	0	0	0	1	1	.250	.333	.250	67	-0	-0	1	0			.500	-1	/32S	-0.1
1914	Bos-N	58	109	17	21	2	0	1	10	10	15	.193	.267	.239	51	-7	-6	9	10			.933	-2	O2/3	-1.0
1915	*Phi-N	42	39	4	6	1	0	0	0	7	5	.154	.283	.179	41	-2	-3	2	2	1	0	.941	3	2	0.0
1916	Phi-N	41	50	9	11	3	0	0	1	9	8	.220	.339	.280	88	-0	-0	6	3			.967	3	2	0.3
1917	Phi-N	44	72	12	14	4	1	0	9	4	9	.194	.237	.278	55	-4	-4	5	2			.871	0	2/O	-0.4
1920	Bos-N	5	0	2	0	0	0	0	0	0	0	—	—	—	—	0	0	0	0	0	0	.000	0	R	0.0
Total	6	195	278	45	54	10	1	1	20	31	38	.194	.277	.248	58	-13	-14	23	17	1		.915	3	/2O3S	-1.2

■ JIM DUGGAN

Duggan, James Elmer "Mer" b: 6/3/1884, Whiteland, Ind. d: 12/5/51, Indianapolis, Ind. BL/TL, 5'10", 165 lbs. Deb: 6/29/11

YEAR	TM/L	G	AB	R	H	2B	3B	HR	RBI	BB	SO	AVG	OBP	SLG	PRO+	BR	/A	RC	SB	CS	SBR	FA	FR	POS	TPR
1911	StL-A	1	4	1	0	0	0	0	1	1		.000	.200	.000	-44	-1	-1	0	0			1.000	0	/1	-0.1

■ TOM DUNBAR

Dunbar, Thomas Jerome b: 11/24/59, Graniteville, S.C. BL/TL, 6'2", 192 lbs. Deb: 9/07/83

YEAR	TM/L	G	AB	R	H	2B	3B	HR	RBI	BB	SO	AVG	OBP	SLG	PRO+	BR	/A	RC	SB	CS	SBR	FA	FR	POS	TPR
1983	Tex-A	12	24	3	6	0	0	0	3	5	7	.250	.379	.250	79	-0	-0	3	3	1	0	.875	-3	/OD	-0.3
1984	Tex-A	34	97	9	25	2	0	2	10	6	16	.258	.301	.340	75	-3	-3	10	1	0	0	.939	-3	O/D	-0.6
1985	Tex-A	45	104	7	21	4	0	1	5	12	9	.202	.291	.269	54	-6	-6	7	0	3	-2	.933	-3	DO	-1.2
Total	3	91	225	19	52	6	0	3	18	23	32	.231	.305	.298	66	-10	-10	20	4	4	-1	.929	-9	/OD	-2.1

■ DAVE DUNCAN

Duncan, David Edwin b: 9/26/45, Dallas, Tex. BR/TR, 6'2", 200 lbs. Deb: 5/06/64 C

YEAR	TM/L	G	AB	R	H	2B	3B	HR	RBI	BB	SO	AVG	OBP	SLG	PRO+	BR	/A	RC	SB	CS	SBR	FA	FR	POS	TPR
1964	KC-A	25	53	2	9	0	1	1	5	2	20	.170	.200	.264	27	-5	-5	3	0	0	0	.981	3	C	-0.2
1967	KC-A	34	101	9	19	4	0	5	11	4	50	.188	.219	.376	75	-4	-4	8	0	1	-1	.979	-6	C	-1.0
1968	Oak-A	82	246	15	47	4	0	7	28	25	68	.191	.268	.293	73	-9	-8	19	1	2	-1	.987	0	C	-0.4
1969	Oak-A	58	127	11	16	3	0	3	22	19	41	.126	.240	.220	31	-12	-11	7	0	0	0	.982	-12	C	-2.2
1970	Oak-A	86	232	21	60	7	0	10	29	22	38	.259	.323	.418	107	0	1	31	0	0	0	.978	3	C	0.8
1971	*Oak-A☆	103	363	39	92	13	1	15	40	28	77	.253	.309	.419	106	1	2	47	1	1	-0	.984	3	*C	0.9
1972	*Oak-A	121	403	39	88	13	0	19	59	34	68	.218	.287	.392	106	-1	1	43	0	2	-1	.993	2	*C	0.7
1973	Cle-A	95	344	43	80	11	1	17	43	35	86	.233	.309	.419	101	1	-0	44	3	3	-1	.988	-1	C/D	0.2
1974	Cle-A	136	425	45	85	10	1	16	46	42	91	.200	.275	.341	77	-14	-13	38	0	4	-2	.976	-8	*C/1D	-1.9
1975	Bal-A	96	307	30	63	7	0	12	41	16	82	.205	.247	.345	70	-15	-13	25	0	0	0	.982	-7	C	-1.6
1976	Bal-A	93	284	20	58	7	0	4	17	25	56	.204	.271	.271	63	-15	-12	21	0	0	0	.985	-11	C	-2.2
Total	11	929	2885	274	617	79	4	109	341	252	677	.214	.280	.357	85	-72	-62	285	5	13	-6	.984	-32	C/D1	-6.9

■ JIM DUNCAN

Duncan, James William b: 7/1/1871, Saltsburg, Pa. d: 10/16/01, Foxburg, Pa. BR/TR, 5'8", 140 lbs. Deb: 7/18/1899

YEAR	TM/L	G	AB	R	H	2B	3B	HR	RBI	BB	SO	AVG	OBP	SLG	PRO+	BR	/A	RC	SB	CS	SBR	FA	FR	POS	TPR
1899	Was-N	15	47	5	11	2	0	0	5	4		.234	.294	.277	58	-3	-3	4	1			.940	-1	C	-0.2
	Cle-N	31	105	9	24	2	3	2	9	4		.229	.257	.362	74	-5	-4	10	0			.971	-4	1C	-0.7
	Yr	46	152	14	35	4	3	2	14	8		.230	.269	.336	69	-8	-7	14	1			.904	-5	C1	-0.9

■ PAT DUNCAN

Duncan, Louis Baird b: 10/6/1893, Coalton, Ohio d: 7/17/60, Columbus, Ohio BR/TR, 5'9", 170 lbs. Deb: 7/16/15

YEAR	TM/L	G	AB	R	H	2B	3B	HR	RBI	BB	SO	AVG	OBP	SLG	PRO+	BR	/A	RC	SB	CS	SBR	FA	FR	POS	TPR
1915	Pit-N	3	5	0	1	0	0	0	0	0	1	.200	.200	.200	22	-0	-0	0	0			1.000	-0	/O	-0.1
1919	*Cin-N	31	90	9	22	3	3	2	17	8	7	.244	.306	.411	118	1	2	12	2			.982	-1	O	-0.1
1920	Cin-N	154	576	75	170	16	11	2	83	42	42	.295	.350	.372	109	6	7	74	18	18	-5	.964	5	*O	-0.5
1921	Cin-N	145	532	57	164	27	10	2	60	44	33	.308	.367	.408	110	4	8	76	7	18	-9	.971	9	*O	-0.3
1922	Cin-N	151	607	94	199	44	12	8	94	40	31	.328	.370	.479	120	14	16	97	12	28	-13	.971	3	*O	-0.5
1923	Cin-N	147	566	92	185	26	8	7	83	30	27	.327	.363	.438	113	8	9	87	15	13	-3	**.993**	-1	*O	-0.4
1924	Cin-N	96	319	34	86	21	6	2	37	20	23	.270	.313	.392	89	-6	-6	37	1	7	-4	.927	-14	O	-2.9
Total	7	727	2695	361	827	137	50	23	374	184	164	.307	.355	.420	110	27	36	383	55	84		.970	1	O	-4.8

■ MARIANO DUNCAN

Duncan, Mariano (Nalasco) b: 3/13/63, San Pedro De Macoris, D.R. BB/TR, 6', 185 lbs. Deb: 4/09/85

YEAR	TM/L	G	AB	R	H	2B	3B	HR	RBI	BB	SO	AVG	OBP	SLG	PRO+	BR	/A	RC	SB	CS	SBR	FA	FR	POS	TPR
1985	*LA-N	142	562	74	137	24	6	6	39	38	113	.244	.295	.340	79	-18	-16	60	38	8	7	.954	-8	*S2	-0.5
1986	LA-N	109	407	47	93	7	0	8	30	30	78	.229	.285	.305	67	-21	-17	38	48	13	7	.951	-2	*S	-0.3
1987	LA-N	76	261	31	56	8	1	6	18	17	62	.215	.268	.322	57	-17	-16	24	11	1	3	.930	-1	S/2O	-0.9
1989	LA-N	49	84	9	21	5	1	0	8	0	15	.250	.267	.333	72	-3	-3	7	3	3	-1	.943	-0	S/2O	-0.4
	Cin-N	45	174	23	43	10	1	3	13	8	36	.247	.292	.368	85	-3	-4	19	6	2	1	.955	-7	S/2	-0.8
	Yr	94	258	32	64	15	2	3	21	8	51	.248	.284	.357	81	-7	-7	26	9	5	-0	.952	-8	S2/O	-1.2
1990	*Cin-N	125	435	67	133	22	**11**	10	55	24	67	.306	.348	.476	119	13	11	69	13	7	-0	.973	1	*2S/O	1.4
1991	Cin-N	100	333	46	86	7	4	12	40	12	57	.258	.290	.411	92	-3	-5	40	5	4	-1	.974	-6	2S/O	-1.0
1992	Phi-N	142	574	71	153	40	3	8	50	17	108	.267	.294	.389	92	-8	-8	64	23	3	5	.976	-23	O2S/3	-2.5
Total	7	788	2830	368	722	123	27	53	253	146	536	.255	.297	.374	86	-61	-58	320	147	41	20	.951	-47	S2/O3	-5.0

■ TAYLOR DUNCAN

Duncan, Taylor McDowell b: 5/12/53, Memphis, Tenn. BR/TR, 6', 170 lbs. Deb: 9/15/77

YEAR	TM/L	G	AB	R	H	2B	3B	HR	RBI	BB	SO	AVG	OBP	SLG	PRO+	BR	/A	RC	SB	CS	SBR	FA	FR	POS	TPR
1977	StL-N	8	12	2	4	0	0	1	2	2	1	.333	.429	.583	172	1	1	3	0	0	0	1.000	-2	/3	-0.1
1978	Oak-A	104	319	25	82	15	2	2	37	19	38	.257	.299	.335	82	-10	-8	32	1	2	-1	.953	-21	32/SD	-3.2
Total	2	112	331	27	86	15	2	3	39	21	39	.260	.304	.344	86	-8	-6	35	1	2	-1	.953	-23	/32DS	-3.3

■ VERN DUNCAN

Duncan, Vernon Van Duke b: 1/6/1890, Clayton, N.C. d: 6/1/54, Daytona Beach, Fla BL/TR, 5'9", 155 lbs. Deb: 9/11/13

YEAR	TM/L	G	AB	R	H	2B	3B	HR	RBI	BB	SO	AVG	OBP	SLG	PRO+	BR	/A	RC	SB	CS	SBR	FA	FR	POS	TPR
1913	Phi-N	8	12	3	5	1	0	0	1	0	3	.417	.417	.500	155	1	1	2	0			1.000	-0	/O	0.1
1914	Bal-F	157	557	99	160	20	8	2	53	67	55	.287	.375	.363	107	10	8	87	13			.914	-3	*O/32	-0.2
1915	Bal-F	146	531	68	142	18	4	2	43	54	40	.267	.337	.328	93	-2	-4	71	19			.965	-0	*O3/2	-1.0
Total	3	311	1100	170	307	39	12	4	97	121	98	.279	.357	.347	101	9	5	160	32			.939	-3	O/32	-1.1

YEAR	TM/L	G	AB	R	H	2B	3B	HR	RBI	BB	SO	AVG	OBP	SLG	PRO+	BR	/A	RC	SB	CS	SBR	FA	FR	POS	TPR

■ GUS DUNDON
Dundon, Augustus Joseph   b: 7/10/1874, Columbus, Ohio   d: 9/1/40, Pittsburgh, Pa.   BR/TR, 5'10", 165 lbs.   Deb: 4/14/04

1904	Chi-A	108	373	40	85	9	3	0	36	30		.228	.292	.268	81	-8	-7	37	19			.973	-15	*2/3S	-2.1
1905	Chi-A	106	364	30	70	7	3	0	22	23		.192	.248	.228	54	-20	-18	26	14			.983	13	*2/S	-0.5
1906	Chi-A	33	96	7	13	1	0	0	4	11		.135	.224	.146	17	-9	-9	4	4			.921	7	2S	-0.1
Total	3	247	833	77	168	17	6	0	62	64		.202	.265	.236	62	-37	-33	68	37			.972	5	2/3S	-2.7

■ ED DUNDON
Dundon, Edward Joseph "Dummy"   b: 7/10/1859, Columbus, Ohio   d: 8/18/1893, Columbus, Ohio   TR ,   Deb: 6/02/1883

1883	Col-a	26	93	8	15	1	0	0			3	.161	.188	.172	18	-8	-7	3				.804	0	P/O2	-0.2
1884	Col-a	26	86	6	12	2	2	0			5	.140	.196	.209	37	-6	-5	4				.966	3	OP/1	-0.1
Total	2	52	179	14	27	3	2	0			8	.151	.191	.190	27	-14	-12	7				.866	4	/PO12	-0.3

■ SAM DUNGAN
Dungan, Samuel Morrison   b: 1/29/1866, Ferndale, Cal.   d: 3/16/39, Santa Ana, Cal.   BR, 5'11", 180 lbs.   Deb: 4/12/1892

1892	Chi-N	113	433	46	123	19	7	0	53	36	19	.284	.346	.360	114	8	7	61	15			.905	-6	*O	-0.3
1893	Chi-N	107	465	86	138	23	7	2	64	29	8	.297	.350	.389	100	-2	-1	69	11			.920	4	*O	-0.2
1894	Chi-N	10	39	5	9	2	0	0	3	7	1	.231	.348	.282	52	-3	-3	4	1			1.000	0	/O	-0.3
	Lou-N	8	32	6	11	1	0	0	3	4	1	.344	.417	.375	101	-0	0	6	2			.941	0	/O	0.0
	Yr	18	71	11	20	3	0	0	6	11	2	.282	.378	.324	72	-3	-3	10	3			.971	1	O	-0.3
1900	Chi-N	6	15	1	4	0	0	0	1	1		.267	.313	.267	63	-1	-1	1	0			.800	-1	/O	-0.2
1901	Was-A	138	559	70	179	26	12	1	73	40		.320	.368	.415	118	13	14	92	9			.947	-5	*O1	0.1
Total	5	382	1543	214	464	71	26	3	197	116	29	.301	.356	.386	108	15	17	233	38			.924	-8	O/1	-0.9

■ LEE DUNHAM
Dunham, Leland Huffield   b: 6/9/02, Atlanta, Ill.   d: 5/11/61, Atlanta, Ill.   BL/TL, 5'11", 185 lbs.   Deb: 4/17/26

| 1926 | Phi-N | 5 | 4 | 0 | 1 | 0 | 0 | 0 | 1 | 0 | 1 | .250 | .250 | .250 | 33 | -0 | -0 | 0 | 0 | | | 1.000 | -0 | /1 | 0.0 |

■ FRED DUNLAP
Dunlap, Frederick C. "Sure Shot"   b: 5/21/1859, Philadelphia, Pa.   d: 12/1/02, Philadelphia, Pa.   BR/TR, 5'8", 165 lbs.   Deb: 5/01/1880   M

1880	Cle-N	85	373	61	103	27	9	4	30	7	32	.276	.289	.429	143	15	16	47				.911	8	*2	2.7
1881	Cle-N	80	351	60	114	25	4	3	24	18	24	.325	.358	.444	159	20	23	57				.909	8	*2/3	2.9
1882	Cle-N	84	364	68	102	19	4	0	28	23	26	.280	.323	.354	121	7	9	43				.900	18	*2M	2.5
1883	Cle-N	93	396	81	129	34	2	4	37	22	21	.326	.361	.452	147	21	22	66				.911	8	*2/O	2.7
1884	StL-U	101	449	160	185	39	8	13			29	.412	.448	.621	249	72	70	128				.926	31	*2/OPM	8.6
1885	StL-N	106	423	70	114	11	5	2	25	41	24	.270	.334	.333	124	9	13	48				.934	26	*2M	3.9
1886	StL-N	71	285	53	76	15	2	3	32	28	30	.267	.332	.365	119	5	7	38	7			.931	16	2/O	2.4
	Det-N	51	196	32	56	8	3	4	37	16	21	.286	.340	.418	126	7	6	33	13			.918	3	2	1.0
	Yr	122	481	85	132	23	5	7	69	44	51	.274	.335	.387	122	11	13	71	20			.926	19	*2/O	3.4
1887	*Det-N	65	272	60	72	13	10	5	45	25	12	.265	.327	.441	109	4	3	45	15			.948	24	2/P	2.4
1888	Pit-N	82	321	41	84	12	1	4	36	16	30	.262	.303	.333	114	2	5	41	24			.940	12	2	2.0
1889	Pit-N	121	451	59	106	19	0	2	65	46	33	.235	.309	.290	77	-18	-10	48	21			.950	-6	*2M	-0.9
1890	Pit-N	17	64	9	11	1	1	0	3	7	6	.172	.264	.219	48	-4	-3	4	2			.874	-3	2	-0.5
	NY-P	1	4	1	2	0	0	0	0	0	0	.500	.500	.500	156	0	0	1	0			1.000	-1	/2	0.0
1891	Was-a	8	25	4	5	1	1	0	4	5	4	.200	.355	.320	101	0	0	4	3			.818	-3	/2	-0.2
Total	12	965	3974	759	1159	224	53	41	366	283	263	.292	.340	.406	136	141	160	604	85			.924	137	2/OP3	29.5

■ GRANT DUNLAP
Dunlap, Grant Lester "Snap"   b: 12/20/23, Stockton, Cal.   BR/TR, 6'2", 180 lbs.   Deb: 4/21/53

| 1953 | StL-N | 16 | 17 | 2 | 6 | 0 | 1 | 1 | 3 | 0 | 2 | .353 | .353 | .647 | 154 | 1 | 1 | 3 | 0 | 0 | 0 | .000 | -0 | /O | 0.1 |

■ BILL DUNLAP
Dunlap, William James   b: 5/1/09, Palmer, Mass.   d: 11/29/80, Reading, Pa.   BR/TR, 5'11", 170 lbs.   Deb: 9/02/29

1929	Bos-N	10	29	6	12	0	1	1	4	4	4	.414	.485	.586	171	3	3	8	0			.889	-1	/O	0.1
1930	Bos-N	16	29	3	2	1	0	0	0	0	6	.069	.069	.103	-61	-7	-7	0	0			1.000	-1	/O	-0.8
Total	2	26	58	9	14	1	1	1	4	4	10	.241	.290	.345	57	-4	-4	8	0			.939	-2	/O	-0.7

■ JACK DUNLEAVY
Dunleavy, John Francis   b: 9/14/1879, Harrison, N.J.   d: 4/12/44, S.Norwalk, Conn.   TL , 5'6", 167 lbs.   Deb: 5/30/03

1903	StL-N	61	193	23	48	3	3	0	10	13		.249	.306	.295	74	-7	-6	22	10			.972	6	OP	-0.1
1904	StL-N	51	172	23	40	7	3	1	14	16		.233	.305	.326	100	-1	0	20	8			.987	1	O/P	-0.2
1905	StL-N	119	435	52	105	8	8	1	25	55		.241	.328	.303	92	-4	-3	51	15			.962	2	*O/2	-0.7
Total	3	231	800	98	193	18	14	2	49	84		.241	.318	.306	89	-12	-9	93	33			.969	9	O/P2	-1.0

■ GEORGE DUNLOP
Dunlop, George Henry   b: 7/19/1888, Meriden, Conn.   d: 12/12/72, Meriden, Conn.   BR/TR, 5'10", 170 lbs.   Deb: 9/09/13

1913	Cle-A	7	17	3	4	1	0	0	0	0	5	.235	.235	.294	53	-1	-1	1	0			.923	1	/S3	0.0
1914	Cle-A	1	3	0	0	0	0	0	0	1	1	.000	.250	.000	-23	-0	-0	0	0			1.000	-1	/S	-0.2
Total	2	8	20	3	4	1	0	0	0	1	6	.200	.238	.250	42	-1	-2	1	0			.929	0	/S3	-0.2

■ JACK DUNN
Dunn, John Joseph   b: 10/6/1872, Meadville, Pa.   d: 10/22/28, Towson, Md.   BR/TR, 5'9",   Deb: 5/06/1897

1897	Bro-N	36	131	20	29	4	0	0	17	4		.221	.244	.252	33	-13	-12	9	2			.911	-1	P/203S	-0.4
1898	Bro-N	51	167	21	41	0	1	0	19	7		.246	.280	.257	54	-10	-10	13	3			.939	-1	P/OS3	-0.2
1899	Bro-N	43	122	21	30	2	1	0	16	3		.246	.270	.279	49	-8	-9	10	3			.963	3	P/S	0.0
1900	Bro-N	10	26	2	6	0	0	0	1	1		.231	.259	.231	34	-2	-2	2	0			.960	1	P	0.0
	Phi-N	10	33	3	10	1	0	0	5	0		.303	.303	.333	76	-1	-1	4	1			.920	-1	P	0.0
	Yr	20	59	5	16	1	0	0	6	1		.271	.288	.288	56	-3	-4	5	1			.940	1	P	0.0
1901	Phi-N	2	1	1	1	0	0	0	0	1		1.000	1.000	1.000	472	1	1	1	0			1.000	-0	/P	0.0
	Bal-A	96	362	41	90	9	4	0	36	21		.249	.301	.296	63	-16	-19	38	10			.872	-8	3S/P20	-2.2
1902	NY-N	100	342	26	72	11	1	0	14	20		.211	.254	.248	56	-18	-18	28	13			.962	-10	OS3/P2	-2.9
1903	NY-N	78	257	35	62	15	1	0	37	15		.241	.288	.307	67	-10	-12	28	12			.907	-7	S32/O	-1.6
1904	NY-N	64	181	27	56	12	2	1	19	11		.309	.349	.414	130	7	6	31	11			.914	-8	3S/20P	-0.1
Total	8	490	1622	197	397	54	10	1	164	83		.245	.286	.292	65	-72	-76	164	55			.890	-32	3P/SO2	-7.4

■ JOE DUNN
Dunn, Joseph Edward   b: 3/11/1885, Springfield, Ohio   d: 3/19/44, Springfield, Ohio   BR/TR, 5'9", 160 lbs.   Deb: 9/12/08

1908	Bro-N	20	64	3	11	3	0	0	5	0		.172	.172	.219	26	-6	-5	2	0			.957	7	C	0.4
1909	Bro-N	10	25	1	4	1	0	0	2	0		.160	.192	.200	22	-2	-2	1	0			.952	-2	/C	-0.3
Total	2	30	89	4	15	4	0	0	7	0		.169	.178	.213	25	-8	-8	3	0			.956	6	/C	0.1

■ RON DUNN
Dunn, Ronald Ray   b: 1/24/50, Oklahoma City, Okla   BR/TR, 5'11", 180 lbs.   Deb: 9/03/74

1974	Chi-N	23	68	6	20	7	0	2	15	12	8	.294	.400	.485	141	5	4	12	0	0	0	.917	-7	2/3	-0.2
1975	Chi-N	32	44	2	7	3	0	1	6	6	17	.159	.260	.295	52	-3	-3	4	0	0	0	.957	-0	3/O2	-0.3
Total	2	55	112	8	27	10	0	3	21	18	25	.241	.346	.411	106	2	1	16	0	0	0	.918	-7	/23O	-0.5

■ STEVE DUNN
Dunn, Stephen   b: 12/21/1858, London, Ont., Can.   d: 5/5/33, London, Ont., Can.   Deb: 9/27/1884

| 1884 | StP-U | 9 | 32 | 4 | 8 | 2 | 0 | 0 | | | 0 | .250 | .250 | .313 | 164 | -0 | 2 | 3 | | | | .972 | 1 | /13 | 0.2 |

■ SHAWON DUNSTON
Dunston, Shawon Donnell   b: 3/21/63, Brooklyn, N.Y.   BR/TR, 6'1", 175 lbs.   Deb: 4/09/85

1985	Chi-N	74	250	40	65	12	4	4	18	19	42	.260	.312	.388	85	-2	-5	31	11	3	2	.958	13	S	1.7
1986	Chi-N	150	581	66	145	37	3	17	68	21	114	.250	.279	.411	82	-12	-17	64	13	11	-3	.961	20	*S	1.5
1987	Chi-N	95	346	40	85	18	3	5	22	10	68	.246	.269	.358	62	-18	-20	32	12	3	2	.969	5	S	-0.5
1988	Chi-N☆	155	575	69	143	23	6	9	56	16	108	.249	.272	.355	76	-17	-20	55	30	9	4	.973	6	*S	0.2
1989	*Chi-N	138	471	52	131	20	6	9	60	30	86	.278	.323	.403	99	3	-1	59	19	11	-1	.972	7	*S	1.6
1990	Chi-N★	146	545	73	143	22	8	17	66	15	87	.262	.286	.426	87	-8	-12	65	25	5	5	.970	6	*S	0.9

YEAR	TM/L	G	AB	R	H	2B	3B	HR	RBI	BB	SO	AVG	OBP	SLG	PRO+	BR	/A	RC	SB	CS	SBR	FA	FR	POS	TPR
1991	Chi-N	142	492	59	128	22	7	12	50	23	64	.260	.299	.407	92	-4	-7	59	21	6	3	.968	-6	*S	0.1
1992	Chi-N	18	73	8	23	3	1	0	2	3	13	.315	.342	.384	103	0	0	9	2	3	-1	.986	-5	S	-0.5
Total	8	918	3333	407	863	157	38	73	342	137	582	.259	.291	.395	84	-58	-82	374	133	51	9	.968	47	S	5.0

■ DAN DURAN
Duran, Daniel James b: 3/16/54, Palo Alto, Cal. BL/TL, 5'11", 190 lbs. Deb: 4/17/81

YEAR	TM/L	G	AB	R	H	2B	3B	HR	RBI	BB	SO	AVG	OBP	SLG	PRO+	BR	/A	RC	SB	CS	SBR	FA	FR	POS	TPR
1981	Tex-A	13	16	1	4	0	0	0	0	1	1	.250	.294	.250	61	-1	-1	1	0	0	0	1.000	-1	/O1	-0.2

■ KID DURBIN
Durbin, Blaine Alphonsus b: 9/10/1886, Kansas d: 9/11/43, Kirkwood, Mo. BL/TL, 5'8", 155 lbs. Deb: 4/24/07

YEAR	TM/L	G	AB	R	H	2B	3B	HR	RBI	BB	SO	AVG	OBP	SLG	PRO+	BR	/A	RC	SB	CS	SBR	FA	FR	POS	TPR
1907	Chi-N	11	18	2	6	0	0	0	0	1		.333	.368	.333	113	0	0	2	0			1.000	0	/PO	0.0
1908	Chi-N	14	28	3	7	1	0	0	0	2		.250	.323	.286	91	-0	-0	3	0			1.000	-3	O	-0.4
1909	Cin-N	6	5	1	1	0	0	0	0	1		.200	.333	.200	66	-0	-0	0	0			.000	0	H	0.0
	Pit-N	1	0	0	0	0	0	0	0	0		—	—	—	—	0	0	0	0			.000	0	R	0.0
	Yr	7	5	1	1	0	0	0	0	1		.200	.333	.200	65	-0	-0	0	0			.000	0		0.0
Total	3	32	51	6	14	1	0	0	0	4		.275	.339	.294	96	0	-0	5	0			1.000	-2	/OP	-0.4

■ JOE DURHAM
Durham, Joseph Vann "Pop" b: 7/31/31, Newport News, Va. BR/TR, 6'1", 186 lbs. Deb: 9/10/54

YEAR	TM/L	G	AB	R	H	2B	3B	HR	RBI	BB	SO	AVG	OBP	SLG	PRO+	BR	/A	RC	SB	CS	SBR	FA	FR	POS	TPR
1954	Bal-A	10	40	4	9	0	0	1	3	4	7	.225	.295	.300	68	-2	-2	4	0	0	0	.917	-1	O	-0.3
1957	Bal-A	77	157	19	29	2	0	4	17	16	42	.185	.260	.274	49	-12	-11	11	1	1	-0	1.000	-11	O	-2.6
1959	StL-N	6	5	2	0	0	0	0	0	0	1	.000	.000	.000	-94	-1	-1	0	0	0	0	1.000	0	/O	-0.1
Total	3	93	202	25	38	2	0	5	20	20	50	.188	.261	.272	49	-15	-14	15	1	1	-0	.979	-12	/O	-3.0

■ LEON DURHAM
Durham, Leon b: 7/31/57, Cincinnati, Ohio BL/TL, 6'2", 210 lbs. Deb: 5/27/80

YEAR	TM/L	G	AB	R	H	2B	3B	HR	RBI	BB	SO	AVG	OBP	SLG	PRO+	BR	/A	RC	SB	CS	SBR	FA	FR	POS	TPR
1980	StL-N	96	303	42	82	15	4	8	42	18	55	.271	.314	.426	101	1	-0	40	8	5	-1	.987	4	O/1	0.0
1981	Chi-N	87	328	42	95	14	6	10	35	27	53	.290	.344	.460	121	10	9	50	25	11	1	.970	-4	O/1	0.3
1982	Chi-N☆	148	539	84	168	33	7	22	90	66	77	.312	.389	.521	148	38	36	108	28	14	0	.963	-9	*O/1	2.4
1983	Chi-N★	100	337	58	87	18	8	12	55	66	83	.258	.384	.466	128	17	15	64	12	6	0	.966	-6	O/1	0.6
1984	*Chi-N	137	473	86	132	30	4	23	96	69	86	.279	.372	.505	132	28	23	90	16	8	0	.994	6	*1	2.2
1985	Chi-N	153	542	58	153	32	2	21	75	64	99	.282	.358	.465	116	20	13	90	7	6	-2	.995	3	*1	0.5
1986	Chi-N	141	484	66	127	18	7	20	65	67	98	.262	.353	.452	112	14	9	78	8	7	-2	.995	-7	*1	-0.9
1987	Chi-N	131	439	70	120	22	1	27	63	51	92	.273	.349	.513	120	15	12	79	2	2	-1	.990	-9	*1	-0.6
1988	Chi-N	24	73	10	16	6	1	3	6	9	20	.219	.305	.452	110	1	1	10	0	1	-1	.995	1	1	-0.1
	Cin-N	21	51	4	11	3	0	1	2	5	12	.216	.286	.333	74	-2	-2	5	0	0	0	.993	-1	1	-0.4
	Yr	45	124	14	27	9	1	4	8	14	32	.218	.297	.403	95	-0	-1	15	0	1	-1	.994	-0	1	-0.5
1989	StL-N	29	18	2	1	1	0	0	1	2	4	.056	.190	.111	-11	-3	-3	0	0	1	-1	.961	1	1	-0.3
Total	10	1067	3587	522	992	192	40	147	530	444	679	.277	.358	.475	122	140	113	615	106	61	-5	.994	-22	1O	3.7

■ BOBBY DURNBAUGH
Durnbaugh, Robert Eugene "Scroggy" b: 1/15/33, Dayton, Ohio BR/TR, 5'8", 170 lbs. Deb: 9/22/57

YEAR	TM/L	G	AB	R	H	2B	3B	HR	RBI	BB	SO	AVG	OBP	SLG	PRO+	BR	/A	RC	SB	CS	SBR	FA	FR	POS	TPR
1957	Cin-N	2	1	0	0	0	0	0	0	0	0	.000	.000	.000	-93	-0	-0	0	0	0	0	.500	-0	/S	0.0

■ GEORGE DURNING
Durning, George Dewey b: 5/9/1898, Philadelphia, Pa. d: 4/18/86, Tampa, Fla. BR/TR, 5'11", 175 lbs. Deb: 9/12/25

YEAR	TM/L	G	AB	R	H	2B	3B	HR	RBI	BB	SO	AVG	OBP	SLG	PRO+	BR	/A	RC	SB	CS	SBR	FA	FR	POS	TPR
1925	Phi-N	5	14	3	5	0	0	0	1	2	1	.357	.438	.357	97	0	0	2	0	0	0	1.000	2	/O	0.2

■ LEO DUROCHER
Durocher, Leo Ernest "Lippy" b: 7/27/05, W.Springfield, Mass. d: 10/7/91, Palm Springs, Cal. BR/TR, 5'10", 160 lbs. Deb: 10/02/25 MC

YEAR	TM/L	G	AB	R	H	2B	3B	HR	RBI	BB	SO	AVG	OBP	SLG	PRO+	BR	/A	RC	SB	CS	SBR	FA	FR	POS	TPR
1925	NY-A	2	1	1	0	0	0	0	0	0	0	.000	.000	.000	-99	-0	-0	0	0	0	0	.000	0	H	0.0
1928	*NY-A	102	296	46	80	8	6	0	31	22	52	.270	.327	.338	77	-11	-9	33	1	4	-2	.948	12	2S	0.5
1929	NY-A	106	341	53	84	4	5	0	32	34	33	.246	.320	.287	62	-21	-17	34	3	1	0	.958	**26**	S2	1.9
1930	Cin-N	119	354	31	86	15	3	3	32	20	45	.243	.287	.328	51	-30	-27	33	0			.959	10	*S2	-0.5
1931	Cin-N	121	361	26	82	11	5	1	29	18	32	.227	.264	.294	53	-26	-23	29	0			.965	-4	*S	-1.7
1932	Cin-N	143	457	43	99	22	5	1	33	36	40	.217	.275	.293	55	-30	-28	39	3			.960	-14	*S	-3.0
1933	Cin-N	16	51	6	11	1	0	1	3	4	5	.216	.273	.294	63	-3	-2	4	0			.953	6	S	0.4
	StL-N	123	395	45	102	18	4	2	41	26	32	.258	.306	.339	80	-8	-11	40	3			.961	-1	*S	-0.3
	Yr	139	446	51	113	19	4	3	44	30	37	.253	.302	.334	78	-11	-13	44	3			**.960**	5	*S	0.1
1934	*StL-N	146	500	62	130	26	5	3	70	33	40	.260	.308	.350	71	-17	-21	53	2			.957	1	*S	-1.2
1935	StL-N	143	513	62	136	23	5	8	78	29	46	.265	.304	.376	79	-14	-16	57	4			.963	9	*S	0.0
1936	StL-N★	136	510	57	146	22	3	1	58	29	47	.286	.327	.347	82	-13	-13	56	3			**.971**	-11	*S	-1.4
1937	StL-N	135	477	46	97	11	3	1	47	38	36	.203	.262	.245	38	-40	-42	30	6			.959	-11	*S	-4.4
1938	Bro-N★	141	479	41	105	18	5	1	56	47	30	.219	.293	.284	58	-26	-28	42	3			**.966**	-5	*S	-2.2
1939	Bro-N	116	390	42	108	21	6	1	34	27	24	.277	.325	.369	83	-8	-10	46	2			.957	-7	*S/3M	-0.8
1940	Bro-N☆	62	160	10	37	9	1	1	14	12	13	.231	.285	.319	62	-7	-9	14	1			.959	1	S/2M	-0.4
1941	Bro-N	18	42	2	12	1	0	0	6	1	3	.286	.302	.310	70	-2	-2	4	0			.917	-0	S/2M	-0.1
1943	Bro-N	6	18	1	4	0	0	0	1	1	2	.222	.263	.222	41	-1	-1	1	0			1.000	2	/SM	0.1
1945	Bro-N	2	5	1	1	0	0	0	2	0	0	.200	.200	.200	11	-1	-1	0	0			1.000	1	/2M	0.0
Total	17	1637	5350	575	1320	210	56	24	567	377	480	.247	.299	.320	66	-257	-260	513	31	5		.961	16	*S/23	-13.1

■ RED DURRETT
Durrett, Elmer Cable b: 2/3/21, Sherman, Tex. d: 1/17/92, Waxahachie, Tex. BL/TL, 5'10", 170 lbs. Deb: 9/14/44

YEAR	TM/L	G	AB	R	H	2B	3B	HR	RBI	BB	SO	AVG	OBP	SLG	PRO+	BR	/A	RC	SB	CS	SBR	FA	FR	POS	TPR
1944	Bro-N	11	32	3	5	1	0	1	1	7	10	.156	.308	.281	68	-1	-1	3	0			.933	1	/O	0.0
1945	Bro-N	8	16	2	2	0	0	0	0	3	3	.125	.263	.125	10	-2	-2	1	0			1.000	-1	/O	-0.3
Total	2	19	48	5	7	1	0	1	1	10	13	.146	.293	.229	48	-3	-3	4	0			.947	1	/O	-0.3

■ CEDRIC DURST
Durst, Cedric Montgomery b: 8/23/1896, Austin, Tex. d: 2/16/71, San Diego, Cal. BL/TL, 5'11", 160 lbs. Deb: 5/30/22

YEAR	TM/L	G	AB	R	H	2B	3B	HR	RBI	BB	SO	AVG	OBP	SLG	PRO+	BR	/A	RC	SB	CS	SBR	FA	FR	POS	TPR
1922	StL-A	15	12	5	4	1	0	0	0	0	1	.333	.333	.417	91	-0	-0	2	0	0	0	.857	-2	/O	-0.2
1923	StL-A	45	85	12	18	2	0	5	11	8	14	.212	.280	.412	76	-3	-4	10	0	0	0	1.000	-2	O/1	-0.7
1926	StL-A	80	219	32	52	7	5	3	16	22	19	.237	.310	.356	70	-9	-11	24	0	5	-3	.980	2	O/1	-1.5
1927	*NY-A	65	129	18	32	4	3	0	25	6	7	.248	.281	.326	59	-8	-8	11	0	3	-2	.980	-7	O/1	-1.8
1928	*NY-A	74	135	18	34	2	1	2	10	7	9	.252	.289	.326	63	-8	-7	13	1	0	0	.983	-3	O/1	-1.1
1929	NY-A	92	202	32	52	3	3	4	31	15	25	.257	.309	.361	77	-9	-7	23	3	2	-0	.987	-0	O/1	-1.0
1930	NY-A	8	19	0	3	1	0	0	5	0	1	.158	.158	.211	-8	-3	-3	1	0	0	0	1.000	-0	/O	-0.3
	Bos-A	102	302	29	74	19	5	1	24	17	24	.245	.290	.351	64	-18	-16	31	3	1	0	.968	-2	O	-2.1
	Yr	110	321	29	77	20	5	1	29	17	25	.240	.282	.343	60	-21	-19	32	3	1	0	.970	-2	O	-2.4
Total	7	481	1103	146	269	39	17	15	122	75	100	.244	.294	.351	67	-59	-56	114	7	11	-5	.979	-15	O/1	-8.7

■ ERV DUSAK
Dusak, Ervin Frank "Four Sack" b: 7/29/20, Chicago, Ill. BR/TR, 6'2", 185 lbs. Deb: 9/18/41

YEAR	TM/L	G	AB	R	H	2B	3B	HR	RBI	BB	SO	AVG	OBP	SLG	PRO+	BR	/A	RC	SB	CS	SBR	FA	FR	POS	TPR
1941	StL-N	6	14	1	2	0	0	0	3	2	6	.143	.250	.143	12	-2	-2	1	1			1.000	1	/O	-0.1
1942	StL-N	12	27	4	5	3	0	0	3	3	7	.185	.267	.296	60	-1	-1	2	0			1.000	0	/O3	-0.2
1946	*StL-N	100	275	38	66	9	1	9	42	33	63	.240	.321	.378	94	-1	-3	34	7			.993	3	O3/2	-0.2
1947	StL-N	111	328	56	93	7	3	6	28	50	34	.284	.378	.378	97	2	0	50	1			.970	1	O/3	-0.3
1948	StL-N	114	311	60	65	9	2	6	19	49	55	.209	.317	.309	66	-12	-15	34	3			.992	-5	O2/3PS	-2.2
1949	StL-N	1	0	1	0	0	0	0	0	0	0	—	—	—	—	0	0	0	0			.000	0	R	0.0
1950	StL-N	23	12	0	1	1	0	0	0	0	3	.083	.083	.167	-34	-2	-2	0	0			1.000	0	P/O	-0.1
1951	StL-N	5	2	1	1	0	0	1	1	0	1	.500	.500	2.000	537	1	1	2	0	0	0	1.000	0	/P	0.0
	Pit-N	21	39	6	12	3	0	1	7	3	11	.308	.357	.462	115	1	1	7	0	0	0	1.000	-6	O/P23	-0.5
	Yr	26	41	7	13	3	0	2	8	3	12	.317	.364	.537	136	2	2	8	0	0	0	1.000	-6	O/P23	-0.5
1952	Pit-N	20	27	1	6	0	0	1	3	2	8	.222	.276	.333	66	-1	-1	2	0	0	0	.818	-2	O	-0.3
Total	9	413	1035	168	251	32	6	24	106	142	188	.243	.334	.355	84	-16	-22	132	12	0		.981	-6	O/23PS	-3.9

YEAR	TM/L	G	AB	R	H	2B	3B	HR	RBI	BB	SO	AVG	OBP	SLG	PRO+	BR	/A	RC	SB	CS	SBR	FA	FR	POS	TPR
■ AL DWIGHT	Dwight, Albert Ward b: 1/4/1856, New York, N.Y. d: 2/20/03, San Francisco, Cal Deb: 6/19/1884																								
1884	KC-U	12	43	8	10	2	0	0		2		.233	.267	.279	97	-1	0	3				.953	-1	C/O2	0.0
■ JIM DWYER	Dwyer, James Edward b: 1/3/50, Evergreen Park, Ill. BL/TL, 5'10", 175 lbs. Deb: 6/10/73																								
1973	StL-N	28	57	7	11	1	1	0	0	1	5	.193	.207	.246	25	-6	-6	2	0	0	0	1.000	1	O	-0.6
1974	StL-N	74	86	13	24	1	0	2	11	11	16	.279	.367	.360	105	1	1	12	0	0	0	1.000	1	O/1	0.2
1975	StL-N	21	31	4	6	1	0	0	1	4	6	.194	.286	.226	42	-2	-2	2	0	0	0	1.000	1	/O	-0.2
	Mon-N	60	175	22	50	7	1	3	20	23	30	.286	.369	.389	106	3	2	28	4	1	1	.959	-1	O	0.0
	Yr	81	206	26	56	8	1	3	21	27	36	.272	.356	.364	96	1	-0	30	4	1	1	.966	0	O	-0.2
1976	Mon-N	50	92	7	17	3	1	0	5	11	10	.185	.272	.239	44	-6	-7	6	0	0	0	.970	-3	O	-1.1
	NY-N	11	13	2	2	0	0	0	0	2	1	.154	.267	.154	23	-1	-1	1	0	0	0	1.000	-0	/O	-0.1
	Yr	61	105	9	19	3	1	0	5	13	11	.181	.271	.229	42	-8	-8	7	0	0	0	.972	-3	O	-1.2
1977	StL-N	13	31	3	7	1	0	0	2	4	5	.226	.351	.258	68	-1	-1	3	0	0	0	1.000	-1	O	-0.2
1978	StL-N	34	65	8	14	3	0	1	4	9	3	.215	.320	.308	77	-2	-2	7	1	0	0	.952	-3	O	-0.5
	SF-N	73	173	22	39	9	2	5	22	28	29	.225	.333	.387	105	0	1	25	6	0	2	.987	2	O1	0.3
	Yr	107	238	30	53	12	2	6	26	37	32	.223	.330	.366	97	-1	-1	33	7	0	2	.979	-1	O1	-0.2
1979	Bos-A	76	113	19	30	7	0	2	14	17	9	.265	.366	.381	96	1	-0	15	3	1	0	.981	-1	1O	-0.2
1980	Bos-A	93	260	41	74	11	1	9	38	28	23	.285	.359	.438	111	6	5	41	3	2	-0	.975	-3	OD/1	-0.1
1981	Bal-A	68	134	16	30	0	1	3	10	20	19	.224	.325	.306	83	-2	-2	14	0	2	-1	.977	-11	O/1D	-1.6
1982	Bal-A	71	148	28	45	4	3	6	15	27	24	.304	.411	.493	148	11	11	33	2	0	1	.976	-8	O/1D	0.3
1983	*Bal-A	100	196	37	56	17	1	8	38	31	29	.286	.383	.505	145	12	12	39	1	1	-0	.966	-7	OD/1	0.3
1984	Bal-A	76	161	22	41	9	1	2	21	23	24	.255	.348	.360	98	-0	0	21	0	2	-1	.966	-4	O/D	-0.6
1985	Bal-A	101	233	35	58	8	3	7	36	37	31	.249	.354	.399	109	3	4	33	0	3	-2	.993	-3	O/D	-0.3
1986	Bal-A	94	160	18	39	13	1	8	31	23	31	.244	.346	.488	126	5	6	27	0	2	-1	1.000	-0	OD/1	0.4
1987	Bal-A	92	241	54	66	7	1	15	33	37	57	.274	.373	.498	132	10	11	46	4	1	1	1.000	-1	DO	0.9
1988	Bal-A	35	53	3	12	0	0	0	3	12	11	.226	.369	.226	73	-1	-1	5	0	0	0	1.000	-0	D/O	-0.1
	Min-A	20	41	6	12	1	0	2	15	13	8	.293	.473	.463	159	5	4	10	0	0	0	.000	0	D	0.4
	Yr	55	94	9	24	1	0	2	18	25	19	.255	.417	.330	113	3	3	15	0	0	0	1.000	-0	D/O	0.3
1989	Min-A	88	225	34	71	11	0	3	23	28	23	.316	.391	.404	117	8	6	36	2	0	1	.000	-0	D/O	0.7
	Mon-N	13	10	1	3	1	0	0	2	1	1	.300	.364	.400	116	0	0	2	0	0	0	.000	0	H	0.0
1990	Min-A	37	63	7	12	0	0	1	5	12	7	.190	.320	.238	55	-3	-4	5	0	0	0	1.000	-0	D/O	-0.4
Total	18	1328	2761	409	719	115	17	77	349	402	402	.260	.357	.398	107	39	37	417	26	15	-1	.979	-40	OD/1	-2.5
■ JOHN DWYER	Dwyer, John E. Deb: 5/16/1882																								
1882	Cle-N	1	3	0	0	0	0	0	1	0	0	.000	.000	.000	-99	-1	-1	0				.000	-1	/OC	-0.2
■ DOUBLE JOE DWYER	Dwyer, Joseph Michael b: 3/27/04, Orange, N.J. BL/TL, 5'9", 186 lbs. Deb: 4/20/37																								
1937	Cin-N	12	11	2	3	0	0	0	1	1	0	.273	.333	.273	70	-0	-0	1	0			.000	0	H	0.0
■ JERRY DYBZINSKI	Dybzinski, Jerome Matthew b: 7/7/55, Cleveland, Ohio BR/TR, 6'2", 180 lbs. Deb: 4/11/80																								
1980	Cle-A	114	248	32	57	11	1	1	23	13	35	.230	.274	.294	55	-15	-15	21	4	1	1	.971	21	S2/3D	1.3
1981	Cle-A	48	57	10	17	0	0	0	6	5	8	.298	.355	.298	91	-1	-0	8	7	1	2	.970	8	S/23D	1.1
1982	Cle-A	80	212	19	49	6	2	0	22	21	25	.231	.309	.278	63	-10	-10	18	3	5	-2	.957	17	S/3	1.1
1983	*Chi-A	127	256	30	59	10	1	1	32	18	29	.230	.286	.289	57	-14	-15	21	11	4	1	.966	1	*S/3	-0.5
1984	Chi-A	94	132	17	31	5	1	1	10	13	12	.235	.313	.311	70	-5	-5	14	7	2	1	.974	18	S3/2D	1.7
1985	Pit-N	5	4	0	0	0	0	0	0	0	0	.000	.000	.000	-99	-1	-1	0	0	0	0	.900	1	/S	0.0
Total	6	468	909	108	213	32	5	3	93	70	109	.234	.296	.290	61	-46	-48	81	32	13	2	.966	67	S/32D	4.7
■ JIM DYCK	Dyck, James Robert b: 2/3/22, Omaha, Neb. BR/TR, 6'2", 205 lbs. Deb: 9/27/51																								
1951	StL-A	4	15	1	1	0	0	0	0	1	1	.067	.125	.067	-46	-3	-3	0	0	0	0	1.000	0	/3	-0.3
1952	StL-A	122	402	60	108	22	3	15	64	50	68	.269	.354	.450	119	12	10	67	0	4	-2	.962	9	3O	1.4
1953	StL-A	112	334	38	71	15	1	9	27	38	40	.213	.299	.344	72	-13	-14	33	3	2	-0	.981	-6	O3	-2.3
1954	Cle-A	2	1	0	1	0	0	0	1	1	0	1.000	1.000	1.000	441	1	1	1	0	0	0	.000	0	H	0.1
1955	Bal-A	61	197	32	55	13	1	2	22	28	21	.279	.372	.386	112	2	4	29	1	0	0	.989	-0	O3	0.2
1956	Bal-A	11	23	3	5	2	0	0	0	10	5	.217	.455	.304	112	1	1	4	0	0	0	.923	-0	/O	0.1
	Cin-N	18	11	5	1	0	0	0	0	3	5	.091	.286	.091	7	-1	-1	0	0	0	0	1.000	0	/13	-0.1
Total	6	330	983	139	242	52	5	26	114	131	140	.246	.339	.389	98	-2	-3	135	4	6	-2	.982	3	O3/1	-0.9
■ BEN DYER	Dyer, Benjamin Franklin b: 2/13/1893, Chicago, Ill. d: 8/7/59, Kenosha, Wis. BR/TR, 5'10", 170 lbs. Deb: 5/23/14																								
1914	NY-N	7	4	1	1	0	0	0	0	0	1	.250	.250	.250	50	-0	-0	0	1			1.000	1	/S2	0.1
1915	NY-N	7	19	4	4	0	1	0	0	4	3	.211	.375	.316	117	1	1	2	0			.889	-0	/3S	0.1
1916	Det-A	4	14	4	4	1	0	0	1	1	1	.286	.333	.357	104	0	0	2	0			1.000	-2	/S	-0.2
1917	Det-A	30	67	6	14	5	0	0	0	2	17	.209	.232	.284	57	-4	-4	5	3			.846	2	S/3	-0.1
1918	Det-A	13	18	1	5	0	0	0	2	0	6	.278	.278	.278	71	-1	-1	1	0			1.000	0	/P1O2	-0.1
1919	Det-A	44	85	11	21	4	0	0	15	8	19	.247	.312	.294	72	-3	-3	8	0			.953	6	3S/O	0.4
Total	6	105	207	27	49	10	1	0	18	15	47	.237	.291	.295	74	-7	-7	18	4			.937	7	/3SO1P2	0.2
■ DUFFY DYER	Dyer, Don Robert b: 8/15/45, Dayton, Ohio BR/TR, 6', 195 lbs. Deb: 9/21/68 C																								
1968	NY-N	1	3	0	1	0	0	0	0	1	1	.333	.500	.333	153	0	0	1	0	0	0	1.000	0	/C	0.1
1969	*NY-N	29	74	5	19	3	1	3	12	4	22	.257	.295	.446	103	0	-0	9	0	0	0	.991	-1	C	0.0
1970	NY-N	59	148	8	31	1	0	2	12	21	32	.209	.308	.257	53	-9	-9	12	1	1	-0	.991	2	C	-0.6
1971	NY-N	59	169	13	39	7	1	2	18	14	45	.231	.293	.320	75	-6	-6	16	1	0	0	.992	0	C	-0.4
1972	NY-N	94	325	33	75	17	3	8	36	28	71	.231	.302	.375	94	-4	-3	36	0	1	-1	.993	18	C/O	1.9
1973	NY-N	70	189	9	35	6	1	1	9	13	40	.185	.245	.243	36	-16	-16	11	0	1	-1	.994	-1	C	-1.7
1974	NY-N	63	142	14	30	1	1	0	10	18	15	.211	.304	.232	53	-9	-8	10	0	0	0	.982	-4	C	-1.1
1975	*Pit-N	48	132	8	30	5	2	3	16	6	22	.227	.266	.364	74	-5	-5	12	0	0	0	.990	6	C	0.2
1976	Pit-N	69	184	12	41	8	0	3	9	29	35	.223	.338	.315	85	-2	-3	21	0	0	0	.994	7	C	0.6
1977	Pit-N	94	270	27	65	11	1	3	19	54	49	.241	.373	.322	86	-2	-3	36	6	0	2	**.996**	5	C	0.6
1978	Pit-N	58	175	7	37	8	1	0	13	18	32	.211	.296	.269	56	-9	-10	14	2	1	0	.991	6	C	-0.3
1979	Mon-N	28	74	4	18	6	0	1	8	9	17	.243	.325	.365	89	-1	-1	9	0	0	0	.993	7	C	0.6
1980	Det-A	48	108	11	20	1	0	4	11	13	34	.185	.273	.306	57	-6	-7	9	0	0	0	.986	3	CD	-0.3
1981	Det-A	2	0	0	0	0	0	0	0	0	0	—	—	—	—	0	0	0	0	0	0	.000	0	/C	0.0
Total	14	722	1993	151	441	74	11	30	173	228	415	.221	.307	.315	73	-71	-71	195	10	4	1	.992	46	C/DO	-0.4
■ EDDIE DYER	Dyer, Edwin Hawley b: 10/11/1900, Morgan City, La. d: 4/20/64, Houston, Tex. BL/TL, 5'11.5", 168 lbs. Deb: 7/08/22 M																								
1922	StL-N	6	3	1	1	1	0	0	0	0	0	.333	.333	.667	159	0	0	1	0	0	0	1.000	0	/P	0.0
1923	StL-N	35	45	17	12	3	0	2	5	3	5	.267	.313	.467	105	-0	0	7	1	0	0	1.000	-1	/OP	-0.1
1924	StL-N	50	76	8	18	2	3	0	8	3	8	.237	.266	.342	63	-4	-4	7	1	0	0	.909	1	P/O	-0.1
1925	StL-N	31	31	4	3	1	0	0	0	3	1	.097	.176	.129	-20	-6	-6	1	1	1	-0	.917	0	P	0.0
1926	StL-N	6	2	1	1	0	0	0	0	0	0	.500	.500	.500	164	0	0	0	0			1.000	0	/P	0.0
1927	StL-N	1	0	0	0	0	0	0	0	1	0	—	1.000	—	181	0	0	0	0			.000	-0	/P	0.0
Total	6	129	157	31	35	7	3	2	13	10	14	.223	.269	.344	61	-9	-9	16	3	1		.921	-0	/PO	-0.2
■ JIMMY DYKES	Dykes, James Joseph b: 11/10/1896, Philadelphia, Pa. d: 6/15/76, Philadelphia, Pa. BR/TR, 5'9", 185 lbs. Deb: 5/06/18 MC																								
1918	Phi-A	59	186	13	35	3	3	0	13	19	32	.188	.267	.237	51	-11	-11	13	3			.940	10	2/3	0.3

YEAR	TM/L	G	AB	R	H	2B	3B	HR	RBI	BB	SO	AVG	OBP	SLG	PRO+	BR	/A	RC	SB	CS	SBR	FA	FR	POS	TPR
1919	Phi-A	17	49	4	9	1	0	0	1	7	11	.184	.286	.204	38	-4	-4	3	0			.945	6	2	0.3
1920	Phi-A	142	546	81	140	25	4	8	35	55	73	.256	.334	.361	83	-12	-13	68	6	9	-4	.957	17	*23	0.6
1921	Phi-A	155	613	88	168	32	13	16	77	60	75	.274	.353	.447	102	1	1	99	6	5	-1	.954	25	*2	2.7
1922	Phi-A	145	501	66	138	23	7	12	68	55	98	.275	.359	.421	100	2	0	79	6	2	1	.945	-8	*3/2	0.4
1923	Phi-A	124	416	50	105	28	1	4	43	35	40	.252	.318	.353	76	-15	-16	48	6	4	-1	.964	4	*2S/3	-0.9
1924	Phi-A	110	410	68	128	26	6	3	50	38	59	.312	.372	.427	105	3	3	65	1	4	-2	.961	16	23/S	1.8
1925	Phi-A	122	465	93	150	32	11	5	55	46	49	.323	.393	.471	111	13	8	88	3	1	0	.944	10	32/S	2.2
1926	Phi-A	124	429	54	123	32	5	1	44	49	34	.287	.370	.392	93	0	-3	66	6	2	1	.950	**26**	32/S	2.8
1927	Phi-A	121	417	61	135	33	6	3	60	44	23	.324	.394	.453	113	12	9	73	2	3	-1	.989	-3	13/SO2P	0.0
1928	Phi-A	85	242	39	67	11	0	5	30	27	21	.277	.361	.384	93	-1	-2	36	2	1	0	.982	-2	2S3/1O	0.0
1929	*Phi-A	119	401	76	131	34	6	13	79	51	25	.327	.412	.539	138	26	24	91	8	3	1	.928	-11	S32	2.2
1930	*Phi-A	125	435	69	131	28	4	6	73	74	53	.301	.414	.425	109	13	9	82	3	3	-1	.960	-13	*3/O	0.3
1931	*Phi-A	101	355	48	97	28	2	3	46	49	47	.273	.371	.389	94	1	-2	54	1	2	-1	.974	-2	3S	0.2
1932	Phi-A	153	558	71	148	29	5	7	90	77	65	.265	.358	.373	87	-7	-10	80	8	2	1	**.980**	-5	*3S/2	-0.3
1933	Chi-A★	151	554	49	144	22	6	1	68	69	37	.260	.354	.327	85	-12	-9	67	3	7	-3	.953	-1	*3	-0.4
1934	Chi-A☆	127	456	52	122	17	4	7	82	64	28	.268	.363	.368	86	-6	-8	65	1	1	-0	.944	-5	312M	-1.0
1935	Chi-A	117	403	45	116	24	2	4	61	59	28	.288	.381	.387	97	1	-0	63	4	3	-1	.953	-5	31/2M	-0.4
1936	Chi-A	127	435	62	116	16	3	7	60	61	36	.267	.362	.366	77	-13	-15	61	1	3	-2	.951	-6	*3M	-1.7
1937	Chi-A	30	85	10	26	5	0	1	23	9	7	.306	.372	.400	95	-1	-1	13	0	0	0	.993	0	13M	-0.1
1938	Chi-A	26	89	9	27	4	2	2	13	10	8	.303	.374	.461	105	1	1	16	0	0	0	.941	1	2/S3M	0.3
1939	Chi-A	2	1	0	0	0	0	0	0	0	0	.000	.000	.000	-97	-0	-0	0	0	0	0	.667	0	/3M	0.0
Total	22	2282	8046	1108	2256	453	90	108	1071	958	849	.280	.365	.399	96	-7	-40	1230	70	55		.952	57	*321S/OP	9.3

■ LENNY DYKSTRA Dykstra, Leonard Kyle b: 2/10/63, Santa Ana, Cal. BL/TL, 5'10", 167 lbs. Deb: 5/03/85

YEAR	TM/L	G	AB	R	H	2B	3B	HR	RBI	BB	SO	AVG	OBP	SLG	PRO+	BR	/A	RC	SB	CS	SBR	FA	FR	POS	TPR
1985	NY-N	83	236	40	60	9	3	1	19	30	24	.254	.341	.331	91	-3	-2	30	15	2	3	.994	4	O	0.4
1986	*NY-N	147	431	77	127	27	7	8	45	58	55	.295	.378	.445	130	16	18	80	31	7	5	.990	4	*O	2.4
1987	NY-N	132	431	86	123	37	3	10	43	40	67	.285	.352	.455	118	7	10	74	27	7	4	.988	1	*O	1.1
1988	*NY-N	126	429	57	116	19	3	8	33	30	43	.270	.323	.385	107	1	3	56	30	8	4	.996	7	*O	1.2
1989	NY-N	56	159	27	43	12	1	3	13	23	15	.270	.370	.415	130	6	7	28	13	1	3	.984	2	O	1.1
	Phi-N	90	352	39	78	20	3	4	19	37	38	.222	.297	.330	79	-10	-10	35	17	11	-2	.991	7	O	-0.7
	Yr	146	511	66	121	32	4	7	32	60	53	.237	.321	.356	95	-4	-3	62	30	12	2	.988	9	*O	0.4
1990	Phi-N★	149	590	106	**192**	35	3	9	60	89	48	.325	.420	.441	137	34	34	121	33	5	7	.987	20	*O	5.8
1991	Phi-N	63	246	48	73	13	5	3	12	37	20	.297	.391	.427	131	11	11	47	24	4	5	.977	8	O	2.3
1992	Phi-N	85	345	53	104	18	0	6	39	40	32	.301	.379	.406	123	11	12	60	30	5	6	.989	13	O	3.0
Total	8	931	3219	533	916	190	28	52	283	384	342	.285	.365	.409	118	74	83	532	220	50	36	.989	65	O	16.6

■ JOHN DYLER Dyler, John F. b: 6/1852, Louisville, Ky. Deb: 7/22/1882 U

YEAR	TM/L	G	AB	R	H	2B	3B	HR	RBI	BB	SO	AVG	OBP	SLG	PRO+	BR	/A	RC	SB	CS	SBR	FA	FR	POS	TPR
1882	Lou-a	1	4	0	0	0	0	0		0		.000	.000	.000	-99	-1	-1	0				.000	-0	/O	-0.1

■ DON EADDY Eaddy, Donald Johnson b: 2/16/34, Grand Rapids, Mich BR/TR, 5'11", 165 lbs. Deb: 4/24/59

YEAR	TM/L	G	AB	R	H	2B	3B	HR	RBI	BB	SO	AVG	OBP	SLG	PRO+	BR	/A	RC	SB	CS	SBR	FA	FR	POS	TPR
1959	Chi-N	15	1	3	0	0	0	0	0	0	1	.000	.000	.000	-99	-0	-0	0	0	0	0	.500	3	/3	0.3

■ TRUCK EAGAN Eagan, Charles Eugene b: 8/10/1877, San Francisco, Cal d: 3/19/49, San Francisco, Cal BR/TR, 5'11", 190 lbs. Deb: 5/01/01

YEAR	TM/L	G	AB	R	H	2B	3B	HR	RBI	BB	SO	AVG	OBP	SLG	PRO+	BR	/A	RC	SB	CS	SBR	FA	FR	POS	TPR
1901	Pit-N	4	12	0	1	0	0	0	2	0		.083	.083	.083	-50	-2	-2	0	1			.923	-1	/S	-0.3
	Cle-A	5	18	2	3	0	1	0	2	1		.167	.211	.278	36	-2	-2	1	0			1.000	0	/23	-0.1
Total	1	9	30	2	4	0	1	0	4	1		.133	.161	.200	2	-4	-4	1	1			.944	-1	/2S3	-0.4

■ BILL EAGAN Eagan, William "Bad Bill" b: 6/1/1869, Camden, N.J. d: 2/14/05, Denver, Colo. Deb: 4/08/1891

YEAR	TM/L	G	AB	R	H	2B	3B	HR	RBI	BB	SO	AVG	OBP	SLG	PRO+	BR	/A	RC	SB	CS	SBR	FA	FR	POS	TPR
1891	StL-a	83	302	49	65	11	4	4	43	44	54	.215	.321	.318	74	-5	-13	38	21			.929	20	2	0.9
1893	Chi-N	6	19	3	5	0	0	0	2	5	5	.263	.417	.263	86	-0	0	4	4			.912	0	/2	0.0
1898	Pit-N	19	61	14	20	2	3	0	5	8		.328	.453	.459	165	6	6	14	1			.914	3	2	0.9
Total	3	108	382	66	90	13	7	4	50	57	59	.236	.348	.338	88	1	-7	56	26			.925	23	2	1.8

■ BILL EAGLE Eagle, William Lycurgus b: 7/25/1877, Rockville, Md. d: 4/27/51, Churchton, Md. Deb: 8/20/1898

YEAR	TM/L	G	AB	R	H	2B	3B	HR	RBI	BB	SO	AVG	OBP	SLG	PRO+	BR	/A	RC	SB	CS	SBR	FA	FR	POS	TPR
1898	Was-N	4	13	0	4	1	0	0	2	0		.308	.308	.385	98	-0	-0	2	0			.750	0	/O	0.0

■ CHARLIE EAKLE Eakle, Charles Emory b: 9/27/1887, Maryland d: 6/15/59, Baltimore, Md. Deb: 8/20/15

YEAR	TM/L	G	AB	R	H	2B	3B	HR	RBI	BB	SO	AVG	OBP	SLG	PRO+	BR	/A	RC	SB	CS	SBR	FA	FR	POS	TPR
1915	Bal-F	2	7	0	2	1	0	0	0	0	0	.286	.286	.429	105	0	-0	1	1			.600	-2	/2	-0.3

■ HOWARD EARL Earl, Howard J. "Slim Jim" b: 2/27/1869, Massachusetts d: 12/22/16, North Bay, N.Y. 6'2", 180 lbs. Deb: 4/19/1890

YEAR	TM/L	G	AB	R	H	2B	3B	HR	RBI	BB	SO	AVG	OBP	SLG	PRO+	BR	/A	RC	SB	CS	SBR	FA	FR	POS	TPR
1890	Chi-N	92	384	57	95	10	3	7	51	18	47	.247	.285	.344	81	-9	-11	43	17			.861	-4	O2/S1	-1.2
1891	Mil-a	31	129	21	32	5	2	1	17	5	13	.248	.281	.341	67	-4	-8	14	3			.978	-1	O/1	-0.9
Total	2	123	513	78	127	15	5	8	68	23	60	.248	.284	.343	77	-13	-19	57	20			.904	-5	/O21S	-2.1

■ SCOTT EARL Earl, William Scott b: 9/18/60, Seymour, Ind. BR/TR, 5'11", 165 lbs. Deb: 9/10/84

YEAR	TM/L	G	AB	R	H	2B	3B	HR	RBI	BB	SO	AVG	OBP	SLG	PRO+	BR	/A	RC	SB	CS	SBR	FA	FR	POS	TPR
1984	Det-A	14	35	3	4	0	1	0	1	0	9	.114	.114	.171	-22	-6	-6	1	1	0	0	.959	1	2	-0.4

■ BILLY EARLE Earle, William Moffat "The Little Globetrotter"
b: 11/10/1867, Philadelphia, Pa. d: 5/30/46, Omaha, Neb. BR/TR, 5'10.5", 170 lbs. Deb: 4/27/1889

YEAR	TM/L	G	AB	R	H	2B	3B	HR	RBI	BB	SO	AVG	OBP	SLG	PRO+	BR	/A	RC	SB	CS	SBR	FA	FR	POS	TPR
1889	Cin-a	53	169	37	45	4	7	4	31	30	24	.266	.386	.444	134	9	8	40	26			.776	-2	OC/1	0.6
1890	StL-a	22	73	16	17	3	1	0		7		.233	.317	.301	74	-1	-3	9	6			.955	5	C/OS32	0.3
1892	Pit-N	5	13	5	7	2	0	0	3	4	1	.538	.647	.692	307	4	4	7	2			.909	-1	/C	0.3
1893	Pit-N	27	95	21	24	4	4	2	15	7	6	.253	.304	.442	101	-1	-1	13	1			.959	1	C	0.2
1894	Lou-N	21	65	10	23	1	0	0	7	9	3	.354	.432	.369	104	0	1	12	2			.954	3	C/123O	0.5
	Bro-N	14	50	13	17	6	0	0	6	6	2	.340	.421	.460	123	1	2	12	4			.930	-2	C/2	0.1
	Yr	35	115	23	40	7	0	0	13	15	5	.348	.427	.409	112	2	3	24	6			.944	1	C/213O	0.6
Total	5	142	465	102	133	20	12	6	62	63	36	.286	.378	.419	116	13	12	94	41			.929	4	C/O123S	2.0

■ JAKE EARLY Early, Jacob Willard b: 5/19/15, King's Mountain, N.C. d: 5/31/85, Melbourne, Fla. BL/TR, 5'11", 168 lbs. Deb: 5/04/39

YEAR	TM/L	G	AB	R	H	2B	3B	HR	RBI	BB	SO	AVG	OBP	SLG	PRO+	BR	/A	RC	SB	CS	SBR	FA	FR	POS	TPR
1939	Was-A	32	84	8	22	7	2	0	14	5	14	.262	.303	.393	83	-3	-2	10	0	0	0	.963	-1	C	-0.2
1940	Was-A	80	206	26	53	8	4	5	14	23	22	.257	.335	.408	98	-3	-1	29	0	1	-1	.969	5	C	0.8
1941	Was-A	104	355	42	102	20	7	10	54	24	38	.287	.338	.468	117	4	6	57	0	1	-1	.965	-11	*C	0.3
1942	Was-A	104	353	31	72	14	2	3	46	37	37	.204	.281	.280	59	-20	-19	30	0	0	0	.981	-2	C	-1.4
1943	Was-A★	126	423	37	109	23	3	5	60	53	43	.258	.346	.362	111	4	6	57	5	3	-0	.980	-8	*C	0.7
1946	Was-A	64	189	13	38	6	0	4	18	23	27	.201	.288	.296	67	-9	-8	17	0	0	0	.960	2	C	-0.3
1947	StL-A	87	214	25	48	9	3	3	19	54	34	.224	.381	.336	98	2	2	32	0	1	-1	.989	-3	C	0.3
1948	Was-A	97	246	22	54	7	2	1	28	36	33	.220	.322	.276	62	-13	-12	25	2	1	0	.991	2	C	-0.5
1949	Was-A	53	138	12	34	4	0	1	11	26	11	.246	.370	.297	79	-3	-3	17	0	1	-1	.973	-4	C	-0.4
Total	9	747	2208	216	532	98	23	32	264	281	259	.241	.330	.350	89	-41	-32	275	7	8	-3	.976	-19	C	-0.7

■ MIKE EASLER Easler, Michael Anthony b: 11/29/50, Cleveland, Ohio BL/TR, 6'1", 196 lbs. Deb: 9/05/73 C

YEAR	TM/L	G	AB	R	H	2B	3B	HR	RBI	BB	SO	AVG	OBP	SLG	PRO+	BR	/A	RC	SB	CS	SBR	FA	FR	POS	TPR
1973	Hou-N	6	7	1	0	0	0	0	0	2	4	.000	.222	.000	-34	-1	-1	0	0	0	0	.500	-1	/O	-0.2
1974	Hou-N	15	15	0	1	0	0	0	0	0	5	.067	.067	.067	-65	-3	-3	0	0	0	0	.000	0	H	-0.3
1975	Hou-N	5	5	0	0	0	0	0	0	0	1	.000	.000	.000	-99	-1	-1	0	0	0	0	.000	0	H	-0.1
1976	Cal-A	21	54	6	13	1	1	0	4	2	11	.241	.268	.296	69	-2	-2	4	1	1	-0	.000	0	D	-0.3
1977	Pit-N	10	18	3	8	2	0	1	5	0	1	.444	.444	.722	202	3	2	6	0	0	0	1.000	-0	/O	0.2

YEAR	TM/L	G	AB	R	H	2B	3B	HR	RBI	BB	SO	AVG	OBP	SLG	PRO+	BR	/A	RC	SB	CS	SBR	FA	FR	POS	TPR
1979	*Pit-N	55	54	8	15	1	1	2	11	8	13	.278	.371	.444	116	2	1	9	0	1	-1	.000	0	/O	0.1
1980	Pit-N	132	393	66	133	27	3	21	74	43	65	.338	.404	.583	170	37	36	88	5	9	-4	.986	-8	*O	2.1
1981	Pit-N★	95	339	43	97	18	5	7	42	24	45	.286	.333	.431	112	6	5	44	4	7	-3	.980	6	O	0.5
1982	Pit-N	142	475	52	131	27	2	15	58	40	85	.276	.340	.436	112	9	7	69	1	1	-0	.973	-3	*O	0.1
1983	Pit-N	115	381	44	117	17	2	10	54	22	64	.307	.350	.441	115	8	7	57	4	2	0	.965	-7	*O	-0.3
1984	Bos-A	156	601	87	188	31	5	27	91	58	134	.313	.377	.516	138	36	32	118	1	1	-0	.976	2	*D1	3.2
1985	Bos-A	155	568	71	149	29	4	16	74	53	129	.262	.329	.412	97	1	-2	75	0	1	-1	.914	-2	*DO	-0.6
1986	NY-A	146	490	64	148	26	2	14	78	49	87	.302	.365	.449	122	14	15	76	3	2	-0	.958	-0	*DO	1.4
1987	Phi-N	33	110	7	31	4	0	1	10	6	20	.282	.319	.345	74	-4	-4	12	0	1	-1	.981	2	O	-0.4
	NY-A	65	167	13	47	6	0	4	21	14	32	.281	.341	.389	94	-2	-1	22	1	0	0	1.000	-1	DO	-0.2
Total	14	1151	3677	465	1078	189	25	118	522	321	696	.293	.353	.454	118	102	91	581	20	26	-10	.974	-12	OD/1	5.2

■ **DAMION EASLEY** Easley, Jacinto Damion b: 11/11/69, New York, N.Y. BR/TR, 5'11", 155 lbs. Deb: 8/13/92

YEAR	TM/L	G	AB	R	H	2B	3B	HR	RBI	BB	SO	AVG	OBP	SLG	PRO+	BR	/A	RC	SB	CS	SBR	FA	FR	POS	TPR
1992	Cal-A	47	151	14	39	5	0	1	12	8	26	.258	.309	.311	75	-5	-5	15	9	5	-0	.970	8	3/S	0.3

■ **CARL EAST** East, Carlton William b: 8/27/1894, Marietta, Ga. d: 1/15/53, Whitesburg, Ga. BL/TR, 6'2", 178 lbs. Deb: 8/24/15

YEAR	TM/L	G	AB	R	H	2B	3B	HR	RBI	BB	SO	AVG	OBP	SLG	PRO+	BR	/A	RC	SB	CS	SBR	FA	FR	POS	TPR
1915	StL-A	1	1	0	0	0	0	0	0	0	0	.000	.000	.000	-99	-0	-0	0	0			.000	-0	/P	0.0
1924	Was-A	2	6	1	2	1	0	0	2	2	1	.333	.500	.500	163	1	1	2	0	0	0	.800	-0	/O	0.0
Total	2	3	7	1	2	1	0	0	2	2	1	.286	.444	.429	134	0	0	2	0	0		.975	-1	/OP	0.0

■ **HARRY EAST** East, Henry H. b: 4/1863, St.Louis, Mo. Deb: 6/17/1882

YEAR	TM/L	G	AB	R	H	2B	3B	HR	RBI	BB	SO	AVG	OBP	SLG	PRO+	BR	/A	RC	SB	CS	SBR	FA	FR	POS	TPR
1882	Bal-a	1	4	0	0	0	0	0		0		.000	.000	.000	-99	-1	-1	0				.600	-0	/3	-0.1

■ **LUKE EASTER** Easter, Luscious Luke b: 8/4/15, Jonestown, Miss. d: 3/29/79, Euclid, Ohio BL/TR, 6'4.5", 240 lbs. Deb: 8/11/49 C

YEAR	TM/L	G	AB	R	H	2B	3B	HR	RBI	BB	SO	AVG	OBP	SLG	PRO+	BR	/A	RC	SB	CS	SBR	FA	FR	POS	TPR
1949	Cle-A	21	45	6	10	3	0	0	2	8	6	.222	.340	.289	68	-2	-2	4	0	1	-1	1.000	-4	O	-0.6
1950	Cle-A	141	540	96	151	20	4	28	107	70	95	.280	.373	.487	123	14	16	100	0	3	-2	.991	-3	*1O	0.8
1951	Cle-A	128	486	65	131	12	5	27	103	37	71	.270	.333	.481	125	9	13	77	0	1	-1	.988	-7	*1	0.0
1952	Cle-A	127	437	63	115	10	3	31	97	44	84	.263	.337	.513	144	17	21	79	1	1	-0	.983	4	*1	2.1
1953	Cle-A	68	211	26	64	9	0	7	31	15	35	.303	.361	.445	120	5	5	30	0	2	-1	.981	-2	1	0.0
1954	Cle-A	6	6	0	1	0	0	0	0	0	2	.167	.167	.167	-8	-1	-1	0	0	0	0	.000	0	H	-0.1
Total	6	491	1725	256	472	54	12	93	340	174	293	.274	.350	.481	126	42	53	290	1	8	-5	.986	-12	1/O	2.2

■ **HENRY EASTERDAY** Easterday, Henry P. b: 9/16/1864, Philadelphia, Pa. d: 3/30/1895, Philadelphia, Pa. BR/TR, 5'6", 145 lbs. Deb: 6/23/1884

YEAR	TM/L	G	AB	R	H	2B	3B	HR	RBI	BB	SO	AVG	OBP	SLG	PRO+	BR	/A	RC	SB	CS	SBR	FA	FR	POS	TPR
1884	Phi-U	28	115	12	28	5	0	0		5		.243	.275	.287	97	-1	0	9				.875	6	S	0.6
1888	KC-a	115	401	42	76	7	6	3	37	31		.190	.256	.259	64	-13	-17	33	23			**.888**	26	*S	1.1
1889	Col-a	95	324	43	56	5	8	4	34	41	57	.173	.270	.275	60	-18	-15	27	10			.890	12	S/23	0.2
1890	Col-a	58	197	25	31	5	1	1		23		.157	.249	.208	39	-15	-13	12	5			.879	6	S	-0.3
	Phi-a	19	68	17	10	1	0	1		10		.147	.256	.206	39	-5	-5	5	4			.860	-2	S	-0.5
	Lou-a	7	24	2	2	0	0	0		2		.083	.185	.083	-20	-3	-3	1	1			.886	1	/S3	-0.2
	Yr	84	289	44	43	6	1	2		35		.149	.245	.197	34	-24	-21	17	10			.875	5	S/3	-1.0
Total	4	322	1129	141	203	23	15	9	71	112	57	.180	.259	.251	58	-56	-53	87	43			.884	50	S/23	0.9

■ **PAUL EASTERLING** Easterling, Paul b: 9/28/05, Reidsville, Ga. BR/TR, 5'11", 180 lbs. Deb: 4/11/28

YEAR	TM/L	G	AB	R	H	2B	3B	HR	RBI	BB	SO	AVG	OBP	SLG	PRO+	BR	/A	RC	SB	CS	SBR	FA	FR	POS	TPR
1928	Det-A	43	114	17	37	7	1	3	12	8	24	.325	.374	.482	122	4	3	21	2	1	0	.921	-2	O	-0.1
1930	Det-A	29	79	7	16	6	0	1	14	6	18	.203	.259	.316	44	-7	-7	6	0	1	-1	1.000	-2	O	-1.0
1938	Phi-A	4	7	1	2	0	0	0	0	1	2	.286	.375	.286	70	-0	-0	1	0	0	0	.750	-0	/O	0.0
Total	3	76	200	25	55	13	1	4	26	15	44	.275	.329	.410	88	-4	-4	28	2	2	-1	.938	-4	/O	-1.1

■ **TED EASTERLY** Easterly, Theodore Harrison b: 4/20/1885, Lincoln, Neb. d: 7/6/51, Clearlake Highlands, Cal. BL/TR, 5'8", 165 lbs. Deb: 4/17/09

YEAR	TM/L	G	AB	R	H	2B	3B	HR	RBI	BB	SO	AVG	OBP	SLG	PRO+	BR	/A	RC	SB	CS	SBR	FA	FR	POS	TPR
1909	Cle-A	98	287	32	75	14	10	1	27	13		.261	.293	.390	111	3	2	34	8			.965	0	C	1.1
1910	Cle-A	110	363	34	111	16	6	0	55	21		.306	.344	.383	126	10	10	51	10			.953	-27	CO	-1.4
1911	Cle-A	99	287	34	93	19	5	1	37	8		.324	.345	.436	116	5	4	45	6			.910	-12	OC	-0.8
1912	Cle-A	65	186	17	55	4	0	2	21	7		.296	.328	.349	91	-2	-3	22	3			.958	-4	C	-0.2
	Chi-A	30	55	5	20	2	0	0	14	2		.364	.386	.400	129	2	2	9	1			.964	-4	C/O	-0.1
	Yr	95	241	22	75	6	0	2	35	9		.311	.341	.361	100	-0	-1	31	4			.959	-8	C/O	-0.3
1913	Chi-A	60	97	3	23	1	0	0	8	4	9	.237	.267	.247	51	-6	-6	7	2			.976	2	C	-0.2
1914	KC-F	134	436	58	146	20	12	1	67	31	25	.335	.384	.443	141	19	22	81	10			.969	-18	*C	1.5
1915	KC-F	110	309	32	84	12	5	3	32	21	15	.272	.320	.372	108	0	2	39	2			.969	4	C	1.4
Total	7	706	2020	215	607	88	38	8	261	107	49	.300	.338	.394	116	32	33	288	42			.964	-60	C/O	1.3

■ **ROY EASTERWOOD** Easterwood, Roy Charles "Shag" b: 1/12/15, Waxahachie, Tex. d: 8/24/84, Graham, Tex. BR/TR, 6'0.5", 196 lbs. Deb: 4/21/44

YEAR	TM/L	G	AB	R	H	2B	3B	HR	RBI	BB	SO	AVG	OBP	SLG	PRO+	BR	/A	RC	SB	CS	SBR	FA	FR	POS	TPR
1944	Chi-N	17	33	1	7	2	0	1	2	1	11	.212	.235	.364	67	-2	-2	2	0			1.000	-1	C	-0.2

■ **JOHN EASTON** Easton, John David "Goose" b: 3/4/33, Trenton, N.J. BR/TR, 6'2", 185 lbs. Deb: 6/19/55

YEAR	TM/L	G	AB	R	H	2B	3B	HR	RBI	BB	SO	AVG	OBP	SLG	PRO+	BR	/A	RC	SB	CS	SBR	FA	FR	POS	TPR
1955	Phi-N	1	0	0	0	0	0	0	0	0	0	—	—	—	—	0	0	0	0	0	0	.000	0	R	0.0
1959	Phi-N	3	3	0	0	0	0	0	0	0	3	.000	.000	.000	-98	-1	-1	0	0	0	0	.000	0	H	-0.1
Total	2	4	3	0	0	0	0	0	0	0	3	.000	.000	.000	-98	-1	-1	0	0	0	0		0		-0.1

■ **EDDIE EAYRS** Eayrs, Edwin b: 11/10/1890, Blackstone, Mass. d: 11/30/69, Warwick, R.I. BL/TL, 5'7", 160 lbs. Deb: 6/30/13

YEAR	TM/L	G	AB	R	H	2B	3B	HR	RBI	BB	SO	AVG	OBP	SLG	PRO+	BR	/A	RC	SB	CS	SBR	FA	FR	POS	TPR
1913	Pit-N	4	6	0	1	0	0	0	0	0	1	.167	.167	.167	-5	-1	-1	0	0			.667	-0	/P	0.0
1920	Bos-N	87	244	31	80	5	2	1	24	30	18	.328	.410	.377	133	10	12	40	4	3	-1	.950	-4	O/P	0.1
1921	Bos-N	15	15	0	1	0	0	0	1	0	4	.067	.067	.067	-68	-3	-3	0	0	0	0	.000	-0	/P	0.0
	Bro-N	8	6	1	1	0	0	0	1	2	0	.167	.375	.167	47	-0	-0	1	0	0	0	.000	-1	/O	-0.1
	Yr	23	21	1	2	0	0	0	2	2	4	.095	.174	.095	-27	-4	-4	0	0	0	0	.000	-1	/PO	-0.1
Total	3	114	271	32	83	5	2	1	26	32	23	.306	.388	.351	116	6	7	41	4	3		.950	-5	/OP	0.0

■ **HI EBRIGHT** Ebright, Hiram C. "Buck" b: 6/12/1859, Lancaster Co., Pa d: 10/24/16, Milwaukee, Wis. BR/TR, Deb: 4/24/1889

YEAR	TM/L	G	AB	R	H	2B	3B	HR	RBI	BB	SO	AVG	OBP	SLG	PRO+	BR	/A	RC	SB	CS	SBR	FA	FR	POS	TPR
1889	Was-N	16	59	7	15	2	2	1	6	3	8	.254	.302	.407	105	-0	0	8	1			.875	4	/COS	0.4

■ **JOHNNY ECHOLS** Echols, John Gresham b: 1/9/17, Atlanta, Ga. d: 11/13/72, Atlanta, Ga. BR/TR, 5'10.5", 175 lbs. Deb: 5/24/39

YEAR	TM/L	G	AB	R	H	2B	3B	HR	RBI	BB	SO	AVG	OBP	SLG	PRO+	BR	/A	RC	SB	CS	SBR	FA	FR	POS	TPR
1939	StL-N	2	0	0	0	0	0	0	0	0	0	—	—	—	—	0	0	0	0			.000	0	R	0.0

■ **OX ECKHARDT** Eckhardt, Oscar George b: 12/23/01, Yorktown, Tex. d: 4/22/51, Yorktown, Tex. BL/TR, 6'1", 185 lbs. Deb: 4/16/32

YEAR	TM/L	G	AB	R	H	2B	3B	HR	RBI	BB	SO	AVG	OBP	SLG	PRO+	BR	/A	RC	SB	CS	SBR	FA	FR	POS	TPR
1932	Bos-N	8	8	1	2	0	0	0	1	0	1	.250	.250	.250	36	-1	-1	0	0			.000	0	H	-0.1
1936	Bro-N	16	44	5	8	1	0	1	6	5	2	.182	.265	.273	45	-3	-3	4	0			1.000	1	O	-0.3
Total	2	24	52	6	10	1	0	1	7	5	3	.192	.263	.269	43	-4	-4	4	0				1	/O	-0.4

■ **CHARLIE EDEN** Eden, Charles M. b: 1/18/1855, Lexington, Ky. d: 9/17/20, Cincinnati, Ohio BR/TR, Deb: 8/17/1877

YEAR	TM/L	G	AB	R	H	2B	3B	HR	RBI	BB	SO	AVG	OBP	SLG	PRO+	BR	/A	RC	SB	CS	SBR	FA	FR	POS	TPR
1877	Chi-N	15	55	9	12	0	1	0	5	3	6	.218	.259	.255	56	-2	-3	4				.679	-2	O	-0.5
1879	Cle-N	81	353	40	96	**31**	7	3	34	6	20	.272	.284	.425	131	11	11	44				.808	-4	*O/1C	0.3
1884	Pit-a	32	122	12	33	7	4	1		7		.270	.341	.418	147	7	7	18				.759	-4	O/P	0.2
1885	Pit-a	98	405	57	103	18	6	0		17		.254	.298	.328	102	0	1	41				.814	-16	*O/P3	-1.4
Total	4	226	935	118	244	56	18	4	39	33	26	.261	.296	.372	116	16	16	106				.793	-25	O/P13C	-1.4

■ **MIKE EDEN** Eden, Edward Michael b: 5/22/49, Fort Clayton, Canal Zone BB/TR, 5'10", 170 lbs. Deb: 8/02/76

YEAR	TM/L	G	AB	R	H	2B	3B	HR	RBI	BB	SO	AVG	OBP	SLG	PRO+	BR	/A	RC	SB	CS	SBR	FA	FR	POS	TPR
1976	Atl-N	5	8	0	0	0	0	0	1	0	0	.000	.000	.000	-94	-2	-2	0	0	0	0	1.000	1	/2	-0.2

YEAR	TM/L	G	AB	R	H	2B	3B	HR	RBI	BB	SO	AVG	OBP	SLG	PRO+	BR	/A	RC	SB	CS	SBR	FA	FR	POS	TPR
1978	Chi-A	10	17	1	2	0	0	0	0	4	0	.118	.286	.118	17	-2	-2	1	0	0	0	.905	-0	/S2	-0.1
Total	2	15	25	1	2	0	0	0	1	4	0	.080	.207	.080	-16	-4	-4	1	0	0	0	1.000	0	/2S	-0.3

■ STUMP EDINGTON

Edington, Jacob Frank b: 7/4/1891, Roleen, Ind. d: 11/11/69, Bastrop, La. BL/TL, 5'8", 170 lbs. Deb: 6/20/12

1912	Pit-N	15	53	4	16	0	2	0	12	3	1	.302	.339	.377	97	-0	-0	7	0			1.000	1	O	0.0

■ DAVE EDLER

Edler, David Delmar b: 8/5/56, Sioux City, Iowa BR/TR, 6', 185 lbs. Deb: 9/04/80

1980	Sea-A	28	89	11	20	1	0	3	9	8	16	.225	.289	.337	70	-4	-4	8	2	3	-1	.965	4	3	-0.2
1981	Sea-A	29	78	7	11	3	0	0	5	11	13	.141	.256	.179	26	-7	-7	4	3	3	-1	.884	-3	3/S	-1.2
1982	Sea-A	40	104	14	29	2	2	2	18	11	13	.279	.348	.394	100	1	0	14	4	2	0	.922	3	3/OD	0.2
1983	Sea-A	29	63	2	12	1	1	1	4	5	11	.190	.261	.286	49	-4	-5	4	3	3	-1	.875	-2	3/1OD	-0.8
Total	4	126	334	34	72	7	3	6	36	35	53	.216	.294	.308	66	-14	-16	30	12	11	-3	.922	2	/3D1OS	-2.0

■ BOB EDMONDSON

Edmondson, Robert E. b: 4/30/1879, Paris, Ky. d: 8/14/31, Lawrence, Kan. BR/TR, 5'11", 185 lbs. Deb: 9/15/06

1906	Was-A	3	3	1	1	0	0	0	0	0		.333	.333	.333	115	0	0	0	0			1.000	-0	/PO	0.0
1908	Was-A	26	80	5	15	4	1	0	2	7		.188	.261	.262	77	-3	-2	5	0			.878	-2	O	-0.5
Total	2	29	83	6	16	4	1	0	2	7		.193	.264	.265	78	-3	-2	6	0			.878	-2	/OP	-0.5

■ EDDIE EDMONSON

Edmonson, Earl Edward b: 11/20/1889, Hopewell, Pa. d: 5/10/71, Leesburg, Fla. BL/TR, 6', 175 lbs. Deb: 10/04/13

1913	Cle-A	2	5	0	0	0	0	0	0	0	0	.000	.000	.000	-97	-1	-1	0	0			1.000	-1	/1O	-0.2

■ EDWARDS

Edwards TR , Deb: 9/17/15

1915	Phi-A	2	5	0	0	0	0	0	0	0	3	.000	.000	.000	-99	-1	-1	0	0			1.000	-1	/2	-0.3

■ BRUCE EDWARDS

Edwards, Charles Bruce "Bull" b: 7/15/23, Quincy, Ill. d: 4/25/75, Sacramento, Cal. BR/TR, 5'7", 194 lbs. Deb: 6/23/46

1946	Bro-N	92	292	24	78	13	5	1	25	34	20	.267	.348	.356	99	0	0	37	1			.982	6	C	1.2
1947	*Bro-N★	130	471	53	139	15	8	9	80	49	55	.295	.364	.418	103	5	3	73	2			.983	5	*C	1.6
1948	Bro-N	96	286	36	79	17	2	8	54	26	28	.276	.341	.434	105	3	1	41	4			.984	-8	CO3/1	-0.4
1949	*Bro-N	64	148	24	31	3	0	8	25	25	15	.209	.324	.392	87	-2	-3	19	0			.990	-3	C/O3	-0.4
1950	Bro-N	50	142	16	26	4	1	8	16	13	22	.183	.256	.394	67	-7	-8	13	1			.980	-4	C/1	-1.0
1951	Bro-N	17	36	6	9	2	0	1	8	1	3	.250	.270	.389	74	-1	-1	4	0	0	0	1.000	0	/C	-0.1
	Chi-N	51	141	19	33	9	2	3	17	16	14	.234	.316	.390	87	-2	-3	17	1	2	-1	.962	-3	C/1	-0.6
	Yr	68	177	25	42	11	2	4	25	17	17	.237	.308	.390	85	-4	-4	21	1	2	-1	.971	-3	C/1	-0.7
1952	Chi-N	50	94	7	23	2	2	1	12	8	12	.245	.304	.340	77	-3	-3	9	0	0	0	.989	-3	C/2	-0.5
1954	Chi-N	4	3	1	0	0	0	0	1	2	2	.000	.400	.000	15	-0	-0	0	0	0	0	.000	0	H	0.0
1955	Was-A	30	57	5	10	2	0	0	3	16	6	.175	.356	.211	58	-3	-2	5	0	1	-1	.980	7	C/3	0.4
1956	Cin-N	7	5	0	1	0	0	0	0	0	2	.200	.200	.200	8	-1	-1	0	0	0	0	.000	-1	/C23	-0.1
Total	10	591	1675	191	429	67	20	39	241	190	179	.256	.335	.390	93	-11	-17	217	9	3		.982	-3	C/O312	0.1

■ DAVE EDWARDS

Edwards, David Leonard b: 2/24/54, Los Angeles, Cal. BR/TR, 6', 177 lbs. Deb: 9/11/78 F

1978	Min-A	15	44	7	11	3	0	1	3	7	13	.250	.377	.386	113	1	1	7	1	1	-0	.950	1	O	0.1
1979	Min-A	96	229	42	57	8	0	8	35	24	45	.249	.323	.389	88	-3	-4	29	6	3	0	.983	-4	O	-1.1
1980	Min-A	81	200	26	50	9	1	2	20	12	51	.250	.296	.335	68	-8	-9	19	2	1	0	.932	-6	O/D	-1.8
1981	SD-N	58	112	13	24	4	1	2	13	11	24	.214	.285	.321	77	-4	-3	10	3	1	0	.970	2	O	-0.2
1982	SD-N	71	55	7	10	2	0	1	2	1	14	.182	.196	.273	32	-5	-5	2	0	0	0	.944	3	O/1	-0.3
Total	5	321	640	95	152	26	2	14	73	55	147	.237	.302	.350	77	-19	-21	67	12	6	0	.958	-4	O/D1	-3.3

■ HANK EDWARDS

Edwards, Henry Albert b: 1/29/19, Elmwood Place, O. d: 6/22/88, Santa Ana, Cal. BL/TL, 6', 190 lbs. Deb: 9/10/41

1941	Cle-A	16	68	10	15	1	1	1	6	2	4	.221	.243	.309	47	-6	-5	5	0	0	0	.929	-1	O	-0.7
1942	Cle-A	13	48	6	12	2	1	0	7	5	8	.250	.321	.333	89	-1	-1	6	2	1	0	.968	-1	O	-0.3
1943	Cle-A	92	297	38	82	18	6	3	28	30	34	.276	.343	.407	127	6	9	41	4	8	-4	.983	-5	O	-0.4
1946	Cle-A	124	458	62	138	33	**16**	10	54	43	48	.301	.361	.509	151	23	27	88	1	3	-2	.968	1	*O	2.1
1947	Cle-A	108	393	54	102	12	3	15	59	31	55	.260	.315	.420	106	-0	1	53	1	3	-2	.990	-7	*O	-1.3
1948	Cle-A	55	160	27	43	9	2	3	18	18	18	.269	.346	.406	102	-0	0	24	1	1	-0	.987	-3	O	-0.5
1949	Cle-A	5	15	3	4	0	0	1	1	1	2	.267	.313	.467	107	-0	-0	2	0	0	0	1.000	-1	/O	-0.1
	Chi-N	58	176	25	51	8	4	7	21	19	22	.290	.359	.500	131	6	7	31	0			.988	-4	O	0.1
1950	Chi-N	41	110	13	40	11	1	2	21	10	13	.364	.417	.536	150	8	8	25	0			.976	-3	O	0.4
1951	Bro-N	35	31	1	7	3	0	0	3	4	9	.226	.314	.323	70	-1	-1	3	0	0	0	.000	0	H	-0.1
	Cin-N	41	127	14	40	9	1	3	20	13	17	.315	.379	.472	126	5	5	22	0	2	-1	.985	-3	O	-0.1
	Yr	76	158	15	47	12	1	3	23	17	26	.297	.366	.443	115	4	3	25	0	2	-1	.985	-3	O	-0.2
1952	Cin-N	74	184	24	52	7	6	6	28	19	22	.283	.350	.484	129	7	7	31	0	3	-2	.988	-4	O	-0.1
	Chi-A	8	18	2	6	0	0	0	1	0	2	.333	.333	.333	85	-0	-0	2	0	0	0	1.000	0	/O	0.0
1953	StL-A	65	106	6	21	3	0	0	9	13	10	.198	.286	.226	39	-9	-9	8	0	1	-1	1.000	-1	O	-1.1
Total	11	735	2191	285	613	116	41	51	276	208	264	.280	.343	.440	119	38	46	340	9	22		.981	-31	O	-2.1

■ DOC EDWARDS

Edwards, Howard Rodney b: 12/10/36, Red Jacket, W.Va. BR/TR, 6'2", 215 lbs. Deb: 4/21/62 MC

1962	Cle-A	53	143	13	39	6	0	3	9	9	14	.273	.325	.378	91	-2	-2	18	0	0	0	.992	9	C	0.8
1963	Cle-A	10	31	6	8	2	0	0	0	2	6	.258	.303	.323	76	-1	-1	3	0	0	0	.988	5	C	0.4
	KC-A	71	240	16	60	12	0	6	35	11	23	.250	.289	.375	81	-5	-7	24	0	1	-1	.987	-6	C	-1.1
	Yr	81	271	22	68	14	0	6	35	13	29	.251	.290	.369	81	-6	-8	28	0	1	-1	.987	-1	C	-0.7
1964	KC-A	97	294	25	66	10	0	5	28	13	40	.224	.265	.310	57	-16	-17	21	0	1	-1	.986	1	C/1	-1.4
1965	KC-A	6	20	1	3	0	0	0	0	1	2	.150	.190	.150	-2	-3	-3	0	0	0	0	1.000	-0	/C	-0.3
	NY-A	45	100	3	19	3	0	1	9	13	14	.190	.289	.250	55	-6	-6	6	1	2	-1	.986	2	C	-0.3
	Yr	51	120	4	22	3	0	1	9	14	16	.183	.274	.233	46	-8	-8	6	1	2	-1	.988	2	C	-0.6
1970	Phi-N	35	78	5	21	0	0	0	6	4	10	.269	.313	.269	59	-4	-4	6	0	0	0	.970	6	C	0.3
Total	5	317	906	69	216	33	0	15	87	53	109	.238	.287	.325	68	-38	-39	79	1	4	-2	.986	17	C/1	-1.6

■ JOHNNY EDWARDS

Edwards, John Alban b: 6/10/38, Columbus, Ohio BL/TR, 6'4", 220 lbs. Deb: 6/27/61

1961	*Cin-N	52	145	14	27	5	0	2	14	18	28	.186	.280	.262	45	-11	-12	11	1	0	0	.982	-4	C	-1.2
1962	Cin-N	133	452	47	115	28	5	8	50	45	70	.254	.323	.392	88	-6	-8	58	1	1	-0	.987	12	*C	0.9
1963	Cin-N★	148	495	46	128	19	4	11	67	45	93	.259	.325	.380	99	2	0	61	1	5	-3	**.995**	13	*C	1.7
1964	Cin-N★	126	423	47	119	23	1	7	55	34	65	.281	.336	.390	100	2	1	56	1	2	-1	.992	23	*C	2.9
1965	Cin-N☆	114	371	47	99	22	2	17	51	50	45	.267	.355	.474	123	16	13	64	0	0	0	.990	5	*C	2.4
1966	Cin-N	98	282	24	54	8	0	6	39	31	42	.191	.272	.284	50	-17	-20	21	1	3	-2	.992	9	C	-0.8
1967	Cin-N	80	209	10	43	6	0	2	20	16	28	.206	.262	.263	46	-13	-16	14	1	4	-2	.990	15	C	0.0
1968	*StL-N	85	230	14	55	9	1	3	29	16	20	.239	.291	.326	86	-4	-4	21	1	1	-0	.992	1	C	0.1
1969	Hou-N	151	496	52	115	20	6	6	50	53	69	.232	.309	.333	81	-13	-12	49	2	1	0	**.994**	5	*C	0.1
1970	Hou-N	140	458	46	101	16	4	7	49	51	63	.221	.300	.319	69	-22	-20	44	1	0	0	**.995**	13	*C	0.0
1971	Hou-N	106	317	18	74	13	4	1	23	26	38	.233	.292	.309	72	-12	-11	30	1	1	-0	**.995**	8	*C	0.0
1972	Hou-N	108	332	33	89	16	2	5	40	50	39	.268	.366	.373	113	6	7	47	2	4	-2	.988	-8	*C	0.1
1973	Hou-N	79	250	24	61	10	2	5	27	19	23	.244	.303	.360	83	-6	-6	27	1	0	0	.989	-1	C	-0.4
1974	Hou-N	50	117	8	26	7	1	1	10	11	12	.222	.295	.325	76	-4	-4	11	1	1	-0	.989	5	C	0.3
Total	14	1470	4577	430	1106	202	32	81	524	465	635	.242	.314	.353	85	-84	-92	515	15	23	-9	.992	97	*C	6.1

YEAR	TM/L	G	AB	R	H	2B	3B	HR	RBI	BB	SO	AVG	OBP	SLG	PRO+	BR	/A	RC	SB	CS	SBR	FA	FR	POS	TPR
■ MARSHALL EDWARDS	Edwards, Marshall Lynn b: 8/27/52, Fort Lewis, Wash. BL/TL, 5'9", 157 lbs. Deb: 4/11/81 F																								
1981	*Mil-A	40	58	10	14	1	1	0	4	0	2	.241	.241	.293	56	-4	-3	4	6	2	1	.979	-9	O/D	-1.2
1982	*Mil-A	69	178	24	44	4	1	2	14	4	8	.247	.264	.315	62	-10	-9	14	10	4	1	.984	-2	O/D	-1.1
1983	Mil-A	51	74	14	22	1	1	0	5	1	9	.297	.307	.338	84	-2	-2	6	5	5	-2	1.000	-3	O/D	-0.7
Total	3	160	310	48	80	6	3	2	23	5	19	.258	.270	.316	66	-16	-14	24	21	11	-0	.987	-13	O/D	-3.0
■ MIKE EDWARDS	Edwards, Michael Lewis b: 8/27/52, Fort Lewis, Wash. BR/TR, 5'10", 154 lbs. Deb: 9/10/77 F																								
1977	Pit-N	7	6	1	0	0	0	0	0	0	3	.000	.143	.000	-56	-1	-1	-0	0	2	-1	1.000	3	/2	0.1
1978	Oak-A	142	414	48	113	16	2	1	23	16	32	.273	.303	.329	82	-13	-10	37	27	21	-5	.964	-28	*2/SD	-3.5
1979	Oak-A	122	400	35	93	12	2	1	23	15	37	.233	.264	.280	49	-30	-27	27	10	6	-1	.962	-14	*2/S	-3.3
1980	Oak-A	46	59	10	14	0	0	0	3	1	5	.237	.250	.237	37	-5	-5	3	1	1	-0	.971	4	2/OD	0.0
Total	4	317	879	94	220	28	4	2	49	32	77	.250	.281	.298	63	-49	-43	68	38	30	-7	.964	-34	2/SDO	-6.7
■ BEN EGAN	Egan, Arthur Augustus b: 11/20/1883, Augusta, N.Y. d: 2/18/68, Sherrill, N.Y. BR/TR, 6', 195 lbs. Deb: 9/29/08 C																								
1908	Phi-A	2	6	1	1	1	0	0	0	1		.167	.286	.333	95	0	-0	1	0			.933	0	/C	0.0
1912	Phi-A	49	138	9	24	3	4	0	13	6		.174	.208	.254	33	-13	-12	7	3			.958	4	C	-0.5
1914	Cle-A	29	88	7	20	2	1	0	11	3	20	.227	.277	.273	63	-4	-4	7	0	1	-1	.975	4	C	0.2
1915	Cle-A	42	120	4	13	3	0	0	6	8	14	.108	.164	.133	-11	-16	-17	3	0			.970	8	C	-0.6
Total	4	122	352	21	58	9	5	0	30	18	34	.165	.212	.219	27	-33	-33	18	3	1		.966	16	C	-0.9
■ JIM EGAN	Egan, James K. "Troy Terrier" b: 1858, Derby, Conn. d: 9/26/1884, New Haven, Conn. TL , Deb: 5/15/1882																								
1882	Tro-N	30	115	15	23	3	2	0	10	1	21	.200	.207	.261	51	-6	-6	6				.625	-8	OP/C	-0.8
■ DICK EGAN	Egan, Richard Joseph b: 6/23/1884, Portland, Ore. d: 7/7/47, Oakland, Cal. BR/TR, 5'11", 162 lbs. Deb: 9/15/08																								
1908	Cin-N	18	68	8	14	3	1	0	5	2		.206	.229	.279	64	-3	-3	6	7			.891	-3	2	-0.7
1909	Cin-N	127	480	59	132	14	3	2	53	37		.275	.329	.329	105	2	3	66	39			.950	24	*2S	2.7
1910	Cin-N	135	474	70	116	11	5	0	46	53	38	.245	.322	.289	82	-12	-9	59	41			.961	-11	*2/S	-2.4
1911	Cin-N	153	558	80	139	11	5	1	56	59	50	.249	.322	.292	75	-20	-17	65	37			.949	10	*2	-1.0
1912	Cin-N	149	507	69	125	14	5	0	52	56	26	.247	.324	.294	72	-20	-18	58	24			**.973**	3	*2	-1.9
1913	Cin-N	60	195	15	55	7	3	0	22	15	13	.282	.333	.349	95	-1	-1	25	6			.972	-5	2S/3	-0.5
1914	Bro-N	106	337	30	76	10	3	1	21	22	25	.226	.273	.282	64	-15	-16	28	8			.914	-9	S3/O21	-1.9
1915	Bro-N	3	3	0	0	0	0	0	0	0	0	.000	.000	.000	-98	-1	-1	0	0			.000	0	H	-0.1
	Bos-N	83	220	20	57	9	1	0	21	28	18	.259	.343	.309	102	0	2	24	3	4	-2	.974	-2	O2S/13	-0.2
	Yr	86	223	20	57	9	1	0	21	28	18	.256	.339	.305	100	-0	1	24	3	4	-2	.974	-2	O2S/13	-0.3
1916	Bos-N	83	238	23	53	8	3	0	16	19	21	.223	.280	.282	76	-8	-6	21	2			.949	-21	2S/3	-3.0
Total	9	917	3080	374	767	87	29	4	292	291	191	.249	.315	.300	82	-77	-67	353	167	4		.956	-14	2S/O31	-9.0
■ TOM EGAN	Egan, Thomas Patrick b: 6/9/46, Los Angeles, Cal. BR/TR, 6'4", 218 lbs. Deb: 5/27/65																								
1965	Cal-A	18	38	3	10	0	1	0	1	3	12	.263	.317	.316	82	-1	-1	4	0	0	0	1.000	-0	C	0.0
1966	Cal-A	7	11	0	0	0	0	0	0	1	5	.000	.083	.000	-76	-2	-2	0	0	0	0	1.000	2	/C	0.0
1967	Cal-A	1	1	0	0	0	0	0	0	0	0	.000	.000	.000	-99	-0	-0	0	0	0	0	1.000	0	/C	0.0
1968	Cal-A	16	43	2	5	1	0	1	4	2	15	.116	.156	.209	10	-5	-5	1	0	0	0	1.000	2	C	-0.2
1969	Cal-A	46	120	7	17	1	0	5	16	17	41	.142	.254	.275	50	-9	-8	9	0	1	-1	.985	6	C	0.0
1970	Cal-A	79	210	14	50	6	0	4	20	14	67	.238	.289	.324	71	-9	-8	20	0	0	0	.988	-1	C	-0.6
1971	Chi-A	85	251	29	60	11	1	10	34	26	94	.239	.320	.410	102	1	1	35	1	0	0	.986	3	C/1	0.7
1972	Chi-A	50	141	8	27	3	0	2	9	4	48	.191	.224	.255	42	-10	-10	7	0	0	0	.986	3	C	-0.6
1974	Cal-A	43	94	4	11	0	0	0	4	8	40	.117	.194	.117	-9	-13	-12	3	1	0	0	.996	16	C	0.5
1975	Cal-A	28	70	7	16	3	1	0	3	5	14	.229	.280	.300	69	-3	-3	6	0	0	0	.965	4	C	0.2
Total	10	373	979	74	196	25	3	22	91	80	336	.200	.267	.299	62	-51	-49	83	2	1	0	.987	35	C/1	-0.0
■ ELMER EGGERT	Eggert, Elmer Albert "Mose" b: 1/29/02, Rochester, N.Y. d: 4/9/71, Rochester, N.Y. BR/TR, 5'9", 160 lbs. Deb: 4/27/27																								
1927	Bos-A	5	3	0	0	0	0	0	0	1	1	.000	.250	.000	-31	-1	-1	0	0	0	0	.000	0	/2	-0.1
■ DAVE EGGLER	Eggler, David Daniel b: 4/30/1851, Brooklyn, N.Y. d: 4/5/02, Buffalo, N.Y. BR/TR, 5'9", 165 lbs. Deb: 5/18/1871																								
1871	Mut-n	33	147	37	47	7	3	0	18	4	3	.320	.338	.408	124	2	6	26	14					*O	0.5
1872	Mut-n	56	287	**95**	**97**	20	0	0	19	8	9	.338	.356	.408	144	11	15	47						*O	1.4
1873	Mut-n	53	268	82	90	16	5	0	34	5	2	.336	.348	.433	129	9	10	42						*O/3	0.8
1874	Phi-n	58	296	71	96	14	7	0		6		.324	.338	.419	135	13	11	43						*O/2	0.9
1875	Ath-n	66	293	66	89	15	7	0		2		.304	.308	.403	130	12	7	37						*O	0.7
1876	Phi-N	39	174	28	52	4	0	0	19	2	4	.299	.307	.322	111	2	2	18				.913	5	O	0.6
1877	Chi-N	33	136	20	36	3	0	0	20	1	5	.265	.270	.287	67	-4	-6	11				.861	3	O	-0.4
1879	Buf-N	78	317	41	66	5	7	0	27	11	41	.208	.235	.268	64	-11	-12	20				.919	-6	*O	-2.0
1883	Bal-a	53	202	15	38	2	0	0		1		.188	.192	.198	25	-16	-17	8				.916	1	O	-1.5
	Buf-N	38	153	13	38	2	1	0	13	2	29	.248	.258	.275	61	-7	-7	11				.845	-1	O	-0.8
1884	Buf-N	63	241	25	47	3	1	0	20	6	54	.195	.215	.216	35	-17	-19	11				.887	1	O	-1.7
1885	Buf-N	6	24	0	2	0	0	0	0	2	4	.083	.154	.083	-21	-3	-3	0				.938	1	/O	-0.3
Total	5 n	266	1291	351	419	72	22	0	71	25	14	.325	.337	.414	133	48	49	195						O/23	4.3
Total	6	310	1247	142	279	19	9	0	99	25	137	.224	.239	.253	56	-57	-63	80				.894	3	O	-6.1
■ RED EHRET	Ehret, Philip Sydney b: 8/31/1868, Louisville, Ky. d: 7/28/40, Cincinnati, Ohio BR/TR, 6', 175 lbs. Deb: 7/07/1888																								
1888	KC-a	17	63	4	12	4	0	0	4	1		.190	.203	.254	45	-4	-4	4	1			.750	-4	O/P21	-0.7
1889	Lou-a	67	258	27	65	6	6	1	31	4	23	.252	.263	.333	72	-11	-10	24	4			.891	-1	PO/S32	-0.6
1890	*Lou-a	43	146	11	31	2	1	0		1		.212	.218	.240	37	-12	-11	8	1			.859	-3	P	0.0
1891	Lou-a	26	91	9	22	2	1	0	9	5	15	.242	.281	.286	65	-4	-4	8	3			.871	0	P	0.0
1892	Pit-N	40	132	12	34	2	0	0	19	7	22	.258	.295	.273	73	-4	-4	11	1			.855	-4	P	0.0
1893	Pit-N	40	136	16	24	3	0	1	17	10	18	.176	.233	.221	22	-15	-15	7	1			.893	1	P	0.0
1894	Pit-N	46	135	6	23	4	1	0	11	8	22	.170	.217	.215	5	-21	-21	8	0			.859	-1	P	0.0
1895	StL-N	37	96	13	21	2	1	1	9	6	12	.219	.265	.292	45	-8	-8	8	0			.848	0	P	0.0
1896	Cin-N	34	102	10	20	2	0	1	20	10	12	.196	.268	.245	35	-9	-10	8	2			.923	1	P/1	0.0
1897	Cin-N	34	66	6	13	2	0	0	6	4		.197	.254	.227	26	-7	-8	5	2			.957	-1	P	0.0
1898	Lou-N	13	40	3	9	3	1	0	4	1		.225	.262	.350	76	-2	-1	4	0			.800	-1	P	0.0
Total	11	397	1265	117	274	32	11	4	130	57	124	.217	.252	.269	45	-96	-96	95	15			.882	-12	P/O123S	-1.3
■ HACK EIBEL	Eibel, Henry Hack b: 12/6/1893, Brooklyn, N.Y. d: 10/16/45, Macon, Ga. BL/TL, 5'11", 220 lbs. Deb: 6/13/12																								
1912	Cle-A	1	3	0	0	0	0	0	0	0		.000	.000	.000	-97	-1	-1	0	0			.000	-0	/O	-0.1
1920	Bos-A	29	43	4	8	2	0	0	6	3	6	.186	.239	.233	26	-5	-4	2	1	1	-0	.800	-2	/OP1	-0.6
Total	2	30	46	4	8	2	0	0	6	3	6	.174	.224	.217	19	-5	-5	2	1	1		.800	-2	/OP1	-0.7
■ IKE EICHRODT	Eichrodt, Frederick George b: 1/6/03, Chicago, Ill. d: 7/14/65, Indianapolis, Ind BR/TR, 5'11.5", 167 lbs. Deb: 9/07/25																								
1925	Cle-A	15	52	4	12	3	1	0	4	2	7	.231	.259	.327	48	-4	-4	4	0	0	0	.938	-2	O	-0.7
1926	Cle-A	37	80	14	25	7	1	0	7	2	11	.313	.329	.425	95	-1	-1	11	1	0	0	.976	-4	O	-0.5
1927	Cle-A	85	267	24	59	19	2	0	25	16	25	.221	.265	.307	48	-21	-21	21	2	3	-1	.979	1	O	-2.5
1931	Chi-A	34	117	9	25	5	1	0	15	1	8	.214	.220	.274	31	-12	-11	7	0	0	0	1.000	-5	O	-1.7
Total	4	171	516	51	121	34	5	0	51	21	51	.234	.264	.320	52	-39	-38	43	3	3	-1	.979	-9	O	-5.4

■ JIM EISENREICH
Eisenreich, James Michael b: 4/18/59, St.Cloud, Minn. BL/TL, 5'11", 195 lbs. Deb: 4/06/82

YEAR	TM/L	G	AB	R	H	2B	3B	HR	RBI	BB	SO	AVG	OBP	SLG	PRO+	BR	/A	RC	SB	CS	SBR	FA	FR	POS	TPR
1982	Min-A	34	99	10	30	6	0	2	9	11	13	.303	.378	.424	117	3	3	17	0	0	0	.973	-1	O	0.1
1983	Min-A	2	7	1	2	1	0	0	0	1	1	.286	.375	.429	116	0	0	1	0	0	0	1.000	1	/O	0.1
1984	Min-A	12	32	1	7	1	0	0	3	2	4	.219	.265	.250	41	-2	-3	2	2	0	1	1.000	-1	/OD	-0.3
1987	KC-A	44	105	10	25	8	2	4	21	7	13	.238	.286	.467	93	-1	-2	13	1	1	-0	.000	0	D	-0.2
1988	KC-A	82	202	26	44	8	1	1	19	6	31	.218	.240	.282	45	-15	-15	14	9	3	1	.965	-8	OD	-2.4
1989	KC-A	134	475	64	139	33	7	9	59	37	44	.293	.344	.448	122	13	13	73	27	8	3	.989	-11	*OD	0.2
1990	KC-A	142	496	61	139	29	7	5	51	42	51	.280	.338	.397	106	3	4	64	12	14	-5	**.996**	-9	*O/D	-1.4
1991	KC-A	135	375	47	113	22	3	2	47	20	35	.301	.338	.392	101	0	0	48	5	3	-0	.973	-17	*O1/D	-2.0
1992	KC-A	113	353	31	95	13	3	2	28	24	36	.269	.316	.340	83	-8	-8	37	11	6	-0	.995	-2	O/D	-1.3
Total	9	698	2144	251	594	121	23	25	237	150	228	.277	.325	.390	98	-7	-8	270	67	35	-1	.986	-48	O/D1	-7.2

■ ELAND
Eland Deb: 4/14/1873

YEAR	TM/L	G	AB	R	H	2B	3B	HR	RBI	BB	SO	AVG	OBP	SLG	PRO+	BR	/A	RC	SB	CS	SBR	FA	FR	POS	TPR
1873	Mar-n	1	3	0	0	0	0	0	0	0	0	.000	.000	.000	-99	-1	-1	0						/O	0.0

■ KID ELBERFELD
Elberfeld, Norman Arthur "The Tabasco Kid" b: 4/13/1875, Pomeroy, Ohio d: 1/13/44, Chattanooga, Tenn. BR/TR, 5'7", 158 lbs. Deb: 5/30/1898 M

YEAR	TM/L	G	AB	R	H	2B	3B	HR	RBI	BB	SO	AVG	OBP	SLG	PRO+	BR	/A	RC	SB	CS	SBR	FA	FR	POS	TPR
1898	Phi-N	14	38	1	9	4	0	0	7	5		.237	.420	.342	124	2	2	6	0			.795	-5	3	-0.3
1899	Cin-N	41	138	23	36	4	2	0	22	15		.261	.378	.319	90	-0	-1	19	5			.878	-4	S3	-0.3
1901	Det-A	121	432	76	133	21	11	3	76	57		.308	.397	.428	123	19	16	86	23			.907	23	*S	4.3
1902	Det-A	130	488	70	127	17	6	1	64	55		.260	.348	.326	86	-6	-7	65	19			.921	9	*S	0.9
1903	Det-A	35	132	29	45	5	3	0	19	11		.341	.412	.424	156	9	9	26	6			.932	6	S/3	1.7
	NY-A	90	349	49	100	18	5	0	45	22		.287	.340	.367	105	5	3	51	16			.914	7	S	1.4
	Yr	125	481	78	145	23	8	0	64	33		.301	.360	.383	119	14	12	77	22			.919	13	*S/3	3.1
1904	NY-A	122	445	55	117	13	5	2	46	37		.263	.335	.328	105	6	4	58	18			.933	15	*S	2.5
1905	NY-A	111	390	48	102	18	2	0	53	23		.262	.318	.318	91	1	-4	49	18			.908	-6	*S	-0.8
1906	NY-A	99	346	59	106	11	5	2	31	30		.306	.368	.384	123	15	11	58	19			.925	-4	S	1.1
1907	NY-A	120	447	61	121	17	6	0	51	36		.271	.336	.336	106	8	4	60	22			.930	11	*S	2.0
1908	NY-A	19	56	11	11	3	0	0	5	6		.196	.328	.250	88	-0	-0	5	1			.916	-3	SM	-0.3
1909	NY-A	106	379	47	90	9	5	0	26	28		.237	.314	.288	89	-3	-4	41	23			.943	-2	S3	-0.4
1910	Was-A	127	455	53	114	9	2	2	42	35		.251	.322	.292	97	-3	-0	49	19			**.943**	-10	*32/S	-0.8
1911	Was-A	127	404	58	110	19	4	0	47	65		.272	.405	.339	110	10	11	66	24			.957	10	23	2.0
1914	Bro-N	30	62	7	14	1	0	0	1	2	4	.226	.304	.242	62	-3	-3	4	0			.901	-4	S/2	-0.6
Total	14	1292	4561	647	1235	169	56	10	535	427	4	.271	.352	.339	104	60	41	645	213			.920	45	S3/2	12.4

■ GEORGE ELDER
Elder, George Rezin b: 3/10/21, Lebanon, Ky. BL/TR, 5'11", 180 lbs. Deb: 7/22/49

YEAR	TM/L	G	AB	R	H	2B	3B	HR	RBI	BB	SO	AVG	OBP	SLG	PRO+	BR	/A	RC	SB	CS	SBR	FA	FR	POS	TPR
1949	StL-A	41	44	9	11	3	0	0	2	4	11	.250	.313	.318	64	-2	-2	5	0	0	0	1.000	-1	O	-0.4

■ LEE ELIA
Elia, Lee Constantine b: 7/16/37, Philadelphia, Pa. BR/TR, 5'11", 175 lbs. Deb: 4/23/66 MC

YEAR	TM/L	G	AB	R	H	2B	3B	HR	RBI	BB	SO	AVG	OBP	SLG	PRO+	BR	/A	RC	SB	CS	SBR	FA	FR	POS	TPR
1966	Chi-A	80	195	16	40	5	2	3	22	15	39	.205	.269	.297	67	-9	-8	14	0	1	-1	.954	4	S	0.1
1968	Chi-N	15	17	1	3	0	0	0	3	0	6	.176	.222	.176	20	-2	-2	1	0	0	0	1.000	-1	/S23	-0.3
Total	2	95	212	17	43	5	2	3	25	15	45	.203	.265	.288	63	-11	-10	15	0	1	-1	.954	3	/S32	-0.2

■ PETE ELKO
Elko, Peter "Piccolo Pete" b: 6/17/18, Wilkes-Barre, Pa. BR/TR, 5'11", 185 lbs. Deb: 9/17/43

YEAR	TM/L	G	AB	R	H	2B	3B	HR	RBI	BB	SO	AVG	OBP	SLG	PRO+	BR	/A	RC	SB	CS	SBR	FA	FR	POS	TPR
1943	Chi-N	9	30	1	4	0	0	0	0	4	5	.133	.235	.133	8	-3	-3	1	0			.852	-2	/3	-0.5
1944	Chi-N	7	22	2	5	1	0	0	0	0	0	.227	.227	.273	40	-2	-2	1	0			1.000	-0	/3	-0.2
Total	2	16	52	3	9	1	0	0	0	4	5	.173	.232	.192	22	-5	-5	2	0			.902	-2	/3	-0.7

■ ROY ELLAM
Ellam, Roy "Whitey" or "Slippery" b: 2/8/1886, W.Conshohocken, Pa. d: 10/28/48, Conshohocken, Pa. BR/TR, 5'10.5", 203 lbs. Deb: 9/18/09

YEAR	TM/L	G	AB	R	H	2B	3B	HR	RBI	BB	SO	AVG	OBP	SLG	PRO+	BR	/A	RC	SB	CS	SBR	FA	FR	POS	TPR
1909	Cin-N	10	21	4	4	0	1	1	4	7		.190	.393	.429	156	2	2	4	1			.895	-1	/S	0.1
1918	Pit-N	26	77	9	10	1	1	0	2	17	17	.130	.302	.169	43	-4	-4	5	2			.924	-8	S	-1.3
Total	2	36	98	13	14	1	2	1	6	24	17	.143	.323	.224	67	-2	-3	9	3			.917	-10	/S	-1.2

■ FRANK ELLERBE
Ellerbe, Francis Rogers "Governor" b: 12/25/1895, Marion Co., S.C. d: 7/8/88, Latta, S.C. BR/TR, 5'10.5", 165 lbs. Deb: 8/28/19

YEAR	TM/L	G	AB	R	H	2B	3B	HR	RBI	BB	SO	AVG	OBP	SLG	PRO+	BR	/A	RC	SB	CS	SBR	FA	FR	POS	TPR
1919	Was-A	28	105	13	29	4	1	0	16	2	15	.276	.290	.333	75	-4	-4	12	5			.945	-4	S	-0.7
1920	Was-A	101	336	38	98	14	2	0	36	19	23	.292	.331	.345	82	-10	-9	39	5	4	-1	.934	-5	3S/O	-1.0
1921	Was-A	10	10	1	2	0	1	0	1	0	2	.200	.200	.400	52	-1	-1	1	0	0	0	.000	0	H	-0.1
	StL-A	105	430	65	124	20	12	2	49	22	42	.288	.327	.405	81	-10	-14	56	1	6	-3	.953	2	*3	-0.7
	Yr	115	440	66	126	20	13	2	50	22	44	.286	.325	.405	81	-11	-14	56	1	6	-3	.953	2	*3	-0.8
1922	StL-A	91	342	42	84	16	3	1	33	25	37	.246	.303	.319	60	-19	-21	35	1	0	0	.955	16	3	0.2
1923	StL-A	18	49	6	9	0	0	0	1	1	5	.184	.200	.184	1	-7	-7	2	0	1	-1	.967	-3	3	-1.0
1924	StL-A	21	61	7	12	3	0	0	2	2	3	.197	.222	.246	19	-7	-8	3	0	1	-1	.953	3	3	-0.4
	Cle-A	46	120	7	31	1	3	1	14	1	10	.258	.270	.342	56	-8	-8	11	0	0	0	.975	5	3/2	-0.1
	Yr	67	181	14	43	4	3	1	16	3	13	.238	.254	.309	44	-16	-16	14	0	1	-1	.967	8	3/2	-0.5
Total	6	420	1453	179	389	58	22	4	152	72	137	.268	.306	.346	68	-67	-72	158	12	12		.952	14	3/S2O	-3.8

■ JOE ELLICK
Ellick, Joseph J. b: 4/3/1854, Cincinnati, Ohio d: 4/21/23, Kansas City, Kan. 5'10", 162 lbs. Deb: 5/13/1875 MU

YEAR	TM/L	G	AB	R	H	2B	3B	HR	RBI	BB	SO	AVG	OBP	SLG	PRO+	BR	/A	RC	SB	CS	SBR	FA	FR	POS	TPR
1875	RS-n	7	27	1	6	1	0	0		0		.222	.222	.259	73	-1	-0	2						/3OS	0.0
1878	Mil-N	3	13	2	2	0	0	0	1	0	1	.154	.154	.154	1	-1	-1	0				.769	-3	/C3P	-0.4
1880	Wor-N	5	18	1	1	0	0	0	0	1	2	.056	.105	.056	-40	-3	-3	0				.882	0	/3	-0.3
1884	CP-U	92	394	71	93	11	0	0		16		.236	.266	.264	80	-8	-8	28				.903	-2	OS/2M	-0.9
	KC-U	2	8	0	0	0	0	0		0		.000	.000	.000	-99	-2	-1	0				.778	-1	/2O	-0.2
	Bal-U	7	27	2	4	0	0	0		2		.148	.207	.148	20	-2	-3	1				.714	-1	/SO	-0.3
	Yr	101	429	73	97	11	0	0		18		.226	.257	.252	73	-12	-12	28				.894	-3	OS/2	-1.4
Total	3	109	460	76	100	11	0	0	1	19	3	.217	.248	.241	66	-16	-16	30				.889	-6	/OS32CP	-2.1

■ LARRY ELLIOT
Elliot, Lawrence Lee b: 3/5/38, San Diego, Cal. BL/TL, 6'2", 200 lbs. Deb: 4/19/62

YEAR	TM/L	G	AB	R	H	2B	3B	HR	RBI	BB	SO	AVG	OBP	SLG	PRO+	BR	/A	RC	SB	CS	SBR	FA	FR	POS	TPR
1962	Pit-N	8	10	2	3	0	0	1	2	0	1	.300	.300	.600	135	0	0	2	0	0	0	1.000	0	/O	0.0
1963	Pit-N	4	4	0	0	0	0	0	0	0	3	.000	.000	.000	-99	-1	-1	0	0	0	0	.000	0	H	-0.1
1964	NY-N	80	224	27	51	8	0	9	22	28	55	.228	.322	.384	100	-0	0	27	1	2	-1	.985	1	O	-0.3
1966	NY-N	65	199	24	49	14	2	5	32	17	46	.246	.306	.412	100	-1	-0	25	0	1	-1	.912	-1	O	-0.5
Total	4	157	437	53	103	22	2	15	56	45	105	.236	.311	.398	99	-2	-1	54	1	3	-2	.956	-0	O	-0.9

■ ALLEN ELLIOTT
Elliott, Allen Clifford "Ace" b: 12/25/1897, St.Louis, Mo. d: 5/6/79, St.Louis, Mo. BL/TR, 6', 170 lbs. Deb: 6/14/23

YEAR	TM/L	G	AB	R	H	2B	3B	HR	RBI	BB	SO	AVG	OBP	SLG	PRO+	BR	/A	RC	SB	CS	SBR	FA	FR	POS	TPR
1923	Chi-N	53	168	21	42	8	2	2	29	2	12	.250	.267	.357	63	-9	-9	15	3	3	-1	.992	-2	1	-1.4
1924	Chi-N	10	14	0	2	0	0	0	0	0	1	.143	.143	.143	-23	-2	-2	0	0	0	0	1.000	-0	1	-0.3
Total	2	63	182	21	44	8	2	2	29	2	13	.242	.258	.341	57	-12	-12	16	3	3	-1	.992	-2	/1	-1.7

■ CARTER ELLIOTT
Elliott, Carter Ward b: 11/29/1893, Atchison, Kan. d: 5/21/59, Palm Springs, Cal. BL/TR, 5'11", 165 lbs. Deb: 9/10/21

YEAR	TM/L	G	AB	R	H	2B	3B	HR	RBI	BB	SO	AVG	OBP	SLG	PRO+	BR	/A	RC	SB	CS	SBR	FA	FR	POS	TPR
1921	Chi-N	12	28	5	7	2	0	0	0	5	3	.250	.364	.321	83	-0	-0	4	0	0	0	.964	4	S	0.4

■ GENE ELLIOTT
Elliott, Eugene Birminghouse b: 2/8/1889, Fayette Co., Pa. d: 1/5/76, Huntingdon, Pa. BL/TR, 5'7", 150 lbs. Deb: 4/13/11

YEAR	TM/L	G	AB	R	H	2B	3B	HR	RBI	BB	SO	AVG	OBP	SLG	PRO+	BR	/A	RC	SB	CS	SBR	FA	FR	POS	TPR
1911	NY-A	5	13	1	1	1	0	0	1	2		.077	.200	.154	-1	-2	-2	0	0			.000	-1	/O3	-0.3

■ ROWDY ELLIOTT
Elliott, Harold B. b: 7/8/1890, Kokomo, Ind. d: 2/12/34, San Francisco, Cal BR/TR, 5'9", 160 lbs. Deb: 9/24/10

YEAR	TM/L	G	AB	R	H	2B	3B	HR	RBI	BB	SO	AVG	OBP	SLG	PRO+	BR	/A	RC	SB	CS	SBR	FA	FR	POS	TPR
1910	Bos-N	3	2	0	0	0	0	0	0	0	0	.000	.000	.000	-96	-1	-1	0	0			1.000	-0	/C	-0.1

YEAR	TM/L	G	AB	R	H	2B	3B	HR	RBI	BB	SO	AVG	OBP	SLG	PRO+	BR	/A	RC	SB	CS	SBR	FA	FR	POS	TPR
1916	Chi-N	23	55	5	14	3	0	0	3	3	5	.255	.293	.309	77	-1	-2	6	1			.969	-1	C	-0.1
1917	Chi-N	85	223	18	56	8	5	0	28	11	11	.251	.292	.332	84	-3	-5	22	4			.969	4	C	0.5
1918	Chi-N	5	10	0	0	0	0	0	0	2	1	.000	.167	.000	-47	-2	-2	0	0			.952	0	/C	-0.1
1920	Bro-N	41	112	13	27	4	0	1	13	3	6	.241	.267	.304	62	-5	-6	9	0	0	0	.964	5	C	0.1
Total	5	157	402	36	97	15	5	1	44	19	23	.241	.281	.311	73	-11	-14	37	5	0		.967	7	C	0.3

■ HARRY ELLIOTT

Elliott, Harry Lewis b: 12/30/23, San Francisco, Cal. BR/TR, 5'9", 175 lbs. Deb: 8/01/53

YEAR	TM/L	G	AB	R	H	2B	3B	HR	RBI	BB	SO	AVG	OBP	SLG	PRO+	BR	/A	RC	SB	CS	SBR	FA	FR	POS	TPR
1953	StL-N	24	59	6	15	6	1	1	6	3	8	.254	.302	.441	91	-1	-1	7	0	0	0	1.000	1	O	-0.1
1955	StL-N	68	117	9	30	4	0	1	12	11	9	.256	.326	.316	71	-5	-5	10	0	2	-1	.978	-2	O	-0.9
Total	2	92	176	15	45	10	1	2	18	14	17	.256	.318	.358	78	-6	-6	17	0	2	-1	.988	-2	/O	-1.0

■ RANDY ELLIOTT

Elliott, Randy Lee b: 6/5/51, Oxnard, Cal. BR/TR, 6'2", 190 lbs. Deb: 9/10/72

YEAR	TM/L	G	AB	R	H	2B	3B	HR	RBI	BB	SO	AVG	OBP	SLG	PRO+	BR	/A	RC	SB	CS	SBR	FA	FR	POS	TPR
1972	SD-N	14	49	5	10	3	1	0	6	2	11	.204	.235	.306	57	-3	-3	3	0	0	0	1.000	0	O	-0.3
1974	SD-N	13	33	5	7	1	0	1	2	7	9	.212	.350	.333	96	-0	0	4	0	1	-1	1.000	-3	O/1	-0.4
1977	SF-N	73	167	17	40	5	1	7	26	8	24	.240	.278	.407	82	-5	-5	17	0	2	-1	.973	1	O	-0.7
1980	Oak-A	14	39	4	5	3	0	0	1	1	13	.128	.150	.205	-4	-6	-5	1	0	0	0	.000	0	D	-0.5
Total	4	114	288	31	62	12	2	8	35	18	57	.215	.264	.354	69	-14	-13	25	0	3	-2	.982	-2	/OD1	-1.9

■ BOB ELLIOTT

Elliott, Robert Irving "Mr. Team" b: 11/26/16, San Francisco, Cal. d: 5/4/66, San Diego, Cal. BR/TR, 6', 185 lbs. Deb: 9/02/39 MC

YEAR	TM/L	G	AB	R	H	2B	3B	HR	RBI	BB	SO	AVG	OBP	SLG	PRO+	BR	/A	RC	SB	CS	SBR	FA	FR	POS	TPR
1939	Pit-N	32	129	18	43	10	3	3	19	9	4	.333	.377	.527	143	7	7	24	0			.978	3	O	0.9
1940	Pit-N	148	551	88	161	34	11	5	64	45	28	.292	.348	.421	112	8	8	81	13			.978	2	*O	0.3
1941	Pit-N★	141	527	74	144	24	10	3	76	64	52	.273	.353	.374	105	4	5	72	6			.970	2	*O	-0.2
1942	Pit-N★	143	560	75	166	26	7	9	89	52	35	.296	.358	.416	123	18	16	84	2			.927	-2	*3/O	1.7
1943	Pit-N	156	581	82	183	30	12	7	101	56	24	.315	.376	.444	132	26	24	96	4			.949	-7	*3/2S	2.1
1944	Pit-N★	143	538	85	160	28	16	10	108	75	42	.297	.383	.465	132	28	25	100	9			.944	-1	*3/S	2.6
1945	Pit-N†	144	541	80	157	36	6	8	108	64	38	.290	.366	.423	115	14	11	84	5			.928	8	3O	1.8
1946	Pit-N	140	486	50	128	25	3	5	68	64	44	.263	.351	.358	99	2	1	62	6			.995	3	O3	0.0
1947	Bos-N†	150	555	93	176	35	5	22	113	87	60	.317	.410	.517	148	37	39	120	3			**.956**	-2	*3	3.6
1948	*Bos-N★	151	540	99	153	24	5	23	100	**131**	57	.283	.423	.474	145	38	39	117	6			.945	-10	*3	2.7
1949	Bos-N	139	482	77	135	29	5	17	76	90	38	.280	.395	.467	138	23	27	92	0			.963	11	*3	3.4
1950	Bos-N	142	531	94	162	28	5	24	107	68	67	.305	.386	.512	143	26	31	103	2			.952	-17	*3	1.1
1951	Bos-N★	136	480	73	137	29	2	15	70	65	56	.285	.371	.448	128	14	18	81	2	0	1	.941	-8	*3	1.0
1952	NY-N	98	272	33	62	6	2	10	35	36	20	.228	.323	.375	92	-3	-3	35	1	0	0	.978	-6	O3	-1.1
1953	StL-A	48	160	19	40	7	1	5	29	30	18	.250	.368	.400	105	2	2	25	0	1	-1	.954	-2	3	-0.1
	Chi-A	67	208	24	54	11	1	4	32	31	21	.260	.358	.380	96	0	-0	31	1	1	-0	.963	-11	3/O	-1.3
	Yr	115	368	43	94	18	2	9	61	61	39	.255	.363	.389	100	3	1	56	1	2	-1	.959	-12	*3/O	-1.4
Total	15	1978	7141	1064	2061	382	94	170	1195	967	604	.289	.375	.440	124	245	250	1206	60	2		.947	-37	*3O/S2	18.5

■ BEN ELLIS

Ellis, Benjamin Franklin b: 7/1870, New York, N.Y. Deb: 7/16/1896

YEAR	TM/L	G	AB	R	H	2B	3B	HR	RBI	BB	SO	AVG	OBP	SLG	PRO+	BR	/A	RC	SB	CS	SBR	FA	FR	POS	TPR
1896	Phi-N	4	16	0	1	0	0	0	0	3	6	.063	.211	.063	-25	-3	-3	0	0			.800	-1	/S3	-0.3

■ RUBE ELLIS

Ellis, George William b: 11/17/1885, Downey, Cal. d: 3/13/38, Rivera, Cal. BL/TL, 6', 170 lbs. Deb: 4/15/09

YEAR	TM/L	G	AB	R	H	2B	3B	HR	RBI	BB	SO	AVG	OBP	SLG	PRO+	BR	/A	RC	SB	CS	SBR	FA	FR	POS	TPR
1909	StL-N	149	575	76	154	10	9	3	46	54		.268	.334	.332	114	5	9	68	16			.955	13	*O	1.8
1910	StL-N	142	550	87	142	18	8	4	54	62	70	.258	.339	.342	102	-1	2	72	25			.942	0	*O	-0.5
1911	StL-N	155	555	69	139	20	11	2	66	66	64	.250	.332	.337	90	-9	-7	66	9			.938	1	*O	-1.4
1912	StL-N	109	305	47	82	18	2	4	33	34	36	.269	.342	.380	100	-1	-0	42	6			.929	0	O	-0.4
Total	4	555	1985	279	517	66	30	13	199	216	170	.260	.336	.344	101	-6	4	248	56			.943	14	O	-0.5

■ JOHN ELLIS

Ellis, John Charles b: 8/21/48, New London, Conn. BR/TR, 6'2.5", 225 lbs. Deb: 5/17/69

YEAR	TM/L	G	AB	R	H	2B	3B	HR	RBI	BB	SO	AVG	OBP	SLG	PRO+	BR	/A	RC	SB	CS	SBR	FA	FR	POS	TPR
1969	NY-A	22	62	2	18	4	0	1	8	1	11	.290	.313	.403	103	-0	-0	7	0	2	-1	.978	1	C	0.0
1970	NY-A	78	226	24	56	12	1	7	29	18	47	.248	.309	.403	100	-2	-1	27	0	1	-1	.992	1	1/3C	-0.5
1971	NY-A	83	238	16	58	12	1	3	34	23	42	.244	.326	.340	95	-3	-1	25	0	0	0	.990	-3	1/C	-1.0
1972	NY-A	52	136	13	40	5	1	5	25	8	22	.294	.333	.456	138	5	5	17	0	0	0	.965	1	C/1	0.8
1973	Cle-A	127	437	59	118	12	2	14	68	46	57	.270	.344	.403	108	6	5	60	0	0	0	.980	-18	CD1	-1.1
1974	Cle-A	128	477	58	136	23	6	10	64	32	53	.285	.331	.421	116	8	9	62	1	2	-1	.992	-8	1CD	-0.3
1975	Cle-A	92	296	22	68	11	1	7	32	14	33	.230	.269	.345	72	-12	-12	24	0	1	-1	.976	-8	C/1D	-1.7
1976	Tex-A	11	31	4	13	2	0	1	8	0	4	.419	.419	.581	187	3	3	7	0	0	0	1.000	-1	/CD	0.2
1977	Tex-A	49	119	7	28	7	0	4	15	8	26	.235	.283	.395	82	-3	-3	13	0	0	0	1.000	-2	CD/1	-0.6
1978	Tex-A	34	94	7	23	4	0	3	17	6	20	.245	.290	.383	88	-2	-2	11	0	1	-1	.958	-2	C/D	-0.5
1979	Tex-A	111	316	33	90	12	0	12	61	15	55	.285	.321	.437	103	0	1	44	2	2	-1	.978	-3	D1/C	-0.4
1980	Tex-A	73	182	12	43	9	1	1	23	14	23	.236	.294	.313	69	-8	-8	17	3	0	1	.992	-2	1D/C	-1.1
1981	Tex-A	23	58	2	8	3	0	1	7	5	10	.138	.219	.241	34	-5	-5	2	0	1	-1	.993	-1	1/D	-0.7
Total	13	883	2672	259	699	116	13	69	391	190	403	.262	.315	.392	99	-14	-9	317	6	10	-4	.989	-45	1CD/3	-6.9

■ ROB ELLIS

Ellis, Robert Walter b: 7/3/50, Grand Rapids, Mich. BR/TR, 5'11", 180 lbs. Deb: 6/18/71

YEAR	TM/L	G	AB	R	H	2B	3B	HR	RBI	BB	SO	AVG	OBP	SLG	PRO+	BR	/A	RC	SB	CS	SBR	FA	FR	POS	TPR
1971	Mil-A	36	111	9	22	2	0	0	6	12	24	.198	.282	.216	43	-8	-8	7	0	2	-1	.923	-7	3O	-1.9
1974	Mil-A	22	48	4	14	2	0	0	4	4	11	.292	.346	.333	97	-0	-0	6	0	0	0	1.000	-1	O/3D	-0.1
1975	Mil-A	6	7	3	2	0	0	0	0	0	0	.286	.286	.286	62	-0	-0	0	0	0	0	1.000	-2	/OD	-0.2
Total	3	64	166	16	38	4	0	0	10	16	35	.229	.301	.253	59	-9	-8	13	0	2	-1	.976	-10	/O3D	-2.2

■ BABE ELLISON

Ellison, Herbert Spencer "Bert" b: 11/15/1895, Rutland, Ark. d: 8/11/55, San Francisco, Cal. BR/TR, 5'11", 170 lbs. Deb: 9/18/16

YEAR	TM/L	G	AB	R	H	2B	3B	HR	RBI	BB	SO	AVG	OBP	SLG	PRO+	BR	/A	RC	SB	CS	SBR	FA	FR	POS	TPR
1916	Det-A	2	7	0	1	0	0	0	1	0	1	.143	.143	.143	-14	-1	-1	0	0			1.000	-1	/3	-0.3
1917	Det-A	9	29	2	5	1	2	1	4	6	3	.172	.333	.448	139	1	1	4	0			.980	-2	/1	-0.1
1918	Det-A	7	23	1	6	1	0	0	2	3	1	.261	.346	.304	100	-0	0	3	1			1.000	-0	/O2	0.0
1919	Det-A	56	134	18	29	4	0	0	11	13	24	.216	.291	.246	53	-8	-8	11	4			.966	-7	2O/S	-1.5
1920	Det-A	61	155	11	34	7	2	0	21	8	26	.219	.258	.290	46	-13	-12	12	4	1	1	.997	2	1/O3	-1.0
Total	5	135	348	32	75	13	4	1	39	30	55	.216	.282	.284	58	-21	-20	30	9	1		.994	-9	/1203S	-2.9

■ VERDO ELMORE

Elmore, Verdo Wilson "Ellie" b: 12/10/1899, Gordo, Ala. d: 8/5/69, Birmingham, Ala. BL/TR, 5'11", 185 lbs. Deb: 9/11/24

YEAR	TM/L	G	AB	R	H	2B	3B	HR	RBI	BB	SO	AVG	OBP	SLG	PRO+	BR	/A	RC	SB	CS	SBR	FA	FR	POS	TPR
1924	StL-A	7	17	2	3	3	0	0	0	1	3	.176	.222	.353	44	-2	-2	1	0	0	0	.000	-2	/O	-0.3

■ ROY ELSH

Elsh, Eugene Reybold b: 3/1/1892, Penns Grove, N.J. d: 11/12/78, Philadelphia, Pa. BR/TR, 5'9", 165 lbs. Deb: 4/19/23

YEAR	TM/L	G	AB	R	H	2B	3B	HR	RBI	BB	SO	AVG	OBP	SLG	PRO+	BR	/A	RC	SB	CS	SBR	FA	FR	POS	TPR
1923	Chi-A	81	209	28	52	7	2	0	24	16	23	.249	.305	.301	61	-12	-12	20	15	8	-0	.957	1	O	-1.4
1924	Chi-A	60	147	21	45	9	1	0	11	10	14	.306	.350	.381	91	-3	-2	20	6	2	1	.953	-6	O/1	-0.9
1925	Chi-A	32	48	6	9	1	0	0	4	5	7	.188	.264	.208	22	-6	-5	3	2	0	1	.964	-1	O/1	-0.6
Total	3	173	404	55	106	17	3	0	39	31	44	.262	.317	.319	67	-21	-19	43	23	10	1	.957	-6	O/1	-2.9

■ KEVIN ELSTER

Elster, Kevin Daniel b: 8/3/64, San Pedro, Cal. BR/TR, 6'2", 180 lbs. Deb: 9/02/86

YEAR	TM/L	G	AB	R	H	2B	3B	HR	RBI	BB	SO	AVG	OBP	SLG	PRO+	BR	/A	RC	SB	CS	SBR	FA	FR	POS	TPR
1986	*NY-N	19	30	3	5	1	0	0	0	3	8	.167	.242	.200	24	-3	-3	2	0	0	0	.962	4	S	0.2
1987	NY-N	5	10	1	4	2	0	0	1	0	1	.400	.400	.600	169	1	1	2	0	0	0	.909	-0	/S	0.1
1988	*NY-N	149	406	41	87	11	1	9	37	35	47	.214	.282	.313	74	-16	-13	37	2	0	1	.977	5	*S	0.3
1989	NY-N	151	458	52	106	25	2	10	55	34	77	.231	.287	.360	88	-10	-8	45	4	3	-1	.976	7	*S	1.0
1990	NY-N	92	314	36	65	20	1	9	45	30	54	.207	.278	.363	75	-11	-11	33	2	0	1	.960	15	S	1.2
1991	NY-N	115	348	33	84	16	2	6	36	40	53	.241	.321	.351	90	-5	-4	40	2	3	-1	.970	11	*S	1.3
1992	NY-N	6	18	0	4	0	0	0	0	0	2	.222	.222	.222	26	-2	-2	1	0	0	0	1.000	-1	/S	-0.2

YEAR	TM/L	G	AB	R	H	2B	3B	HR	RBI	BB	SO	AVG	OBP	SLG	PRO+	BR	/A	RC	SB	CS	SBR	FA	FR	POS	TPR
Total	7	537	1584	166	355	75	6	34	174	142	242	.224	.291	.343	81	-46	-41	159	10	6	-1	.971	42	S	3.9

■ BONES ELY Ely, William Frederick b: 6/7/1863, N.Girard, Pa. d: 1/10/52, Berkeley, Cal. BR/TR, 6'1", 155 lbs. Deb: 6/19/1884

YEAR	TM/L	G	AB	R	H	2B	3B	HR	RBI	BB	SO	AVG	OBP	SLG	PRO+	BR	/A	RC	SB	CS	SBR	FA	FR	POS	TPR
1884	Buf-N	1	4	0	0	0	0	0	0	0	2	.000	.000	.000	-97	-1	-1	0				.000	-1	/OP	-0.1
1886	Lou-a	10	32	5	5	0	0	0		2		.156	.206	.156	14	-3	-3	1	1			1.000	-0	/PO	-0.2
1890	Syr-a	119	496	72	130	16	6	0		31		.262	.308	.319	97	-9	-1	64	44			.915	19	OS/123P	1.6
1891	Bro-N	31	111	9	17	0	1	0	11	7	9	.153	.203	.171	11	-12	-12	5	4			.870	8	S/32	-0.2
1893	StL-N	44	178	25	45	1	6	0	16	17	13	.253	.318	.326	73	-7	-7	20	2			.905	-3	S	-0.7
1894	StL-N	127	510	85	156	20	12	12	89	30	34	.306	.344	.463	95	-7	-7	93	23			.901	1	*S/2P	0.1
1895	StL-N	117	467	68	121	16	2	1	46	19	17	.259	.288	.308	56	-31	-30	52	28			.925	6	*S	-1.5
1896	Pit-N	128	537	85	153	15	9	3	77	33	33	.285	.326	.363	87	-13	-10	74	18			.918	-2	*S	-0.6
1897	Pit-N	133	516	63	146	20	8	2	74	25		.283	.317	.364	83	-17	-13	66	10			.927	3	*S	-0.6
1898	Pit-N	148	519	49	110	14	5	2	44	24		.212	.247	.270	49	-36	-35	38	6			**.943**	8	*S	-1.9
1899	Pit-N	138	522	66	145	18	6	3	72	22		.278	.313	.352	83	-14	-14	65	8			.928	5	*S/2	0.1
1900	*Pit-N	130	475	60	116	6	6	0	51	17		.244	.272	.282	53	-31	-31	40	6			.935	13	*S	-0.8
1901	Pit-N	65	240	18	50	6	3	0	28	6		.208	.234	.258	41	-18	-19	17	5			.916	-9	S/3	-2.2
	Phi-A	45	171	11	37	6	2	0	16	3		.216	.230	.275	38	-14	-15	13	6			.913	1	S	-1.0
1902	Was-A	105	381	39	100	11	2	1	62	21		.262	.303	.310	69	-15	-16	39	3			.923	-9	*S	-1.7
Total	14	1341	5159	655	1331	149	68	24	586	257	108	.258	.295	.327	70	-228	-213	588	164			.923	41	*S/O2P31	-9.7

■ CHESTER EMERSON Emerson, Chester Arthur "Chuck" b: 10/27/1889, Stow, Me. d: 7/2/71, Augusta, Me. BL/TR, 5'8", 165 lbs. Deb: 9/27/11

YEAR	TM/L	G	AB	R	H	2B	3B	HR	RBI	BB	SO	AVG	OBP	SLG	PRO+	BR	/A	RC	SB	CS	SBR	FA	FR	POS	TPR
1911	Phi-A	7	18	2	4	0	0	0	0	6		.222	.417	.222	82	0	0	2	1			1.000	1	/O	0.0
1912	Phi-A	1	1	0	0	0	0	0	0	0		.000	.000	.000	-99	-0	-0	0	0			.000	0	H	0.0
Total	2	8	19	2	4	0	0	0	0	6		.211	.400	.211	74	-0	-0	2	1				1	/O	0.0

■ CAL EMERY Emery, Calvin Wayne b: 6/28/37, Centre Hall, Pa. BL/TL, 6'2", 205 lbs. Deb: 7/15/63 C

YEAR	TM/L	G	AB	R	H	2B	3B	HR	RBI	BB	SO	AVG	OBP	SLG	PRO+	BR	/A	RC	SB	CS	SBR	FA	FR	POS	TPR
1963	Phi-N	16	19	0	3	1	0	0	0	0	2	.158	.158	.211	5	-2	-2	1	0	0	0	1.000	-0	/1	-0.3

■ SPOKE EMERY Emery, Herrick Smith b: 12/10/1898, Bay City, Mich. d: 6/2/75, Cape Canaveral, Fla. BR/TR, 5'9", 165 lbs. Deb: 7/18/24

YEAR	TM/L	G	AB	R	H	2B	3B	HR	RBI	BB	SO	AVG	OBP	SLG	PRO+	BR	/A	RC	SB	CS	SBR	FA	FR	POS	TPR
1924	Phi-N	5	3	3	2	0	0	0	0	0	0	.667	.667	.667	230	1	1	1	0	1	-1	1.000	-0	/O	0.0

■ FRANK EMMER Emmer, Frank William b: 2/17/1896, Crestline, Ohio d: 10/18/63, Homestead, Fla. BR/TR, 5'8", 150 lbs. Deb: 4/25/16

YEAR	TM/L	G	AB	R	H	2B	3B	HR	RBI	BB	SO	AVG	OBP	SLG	PRO+	BR	/A	RC	SB	CS	SBR	FA	FR	POS	TPR
1916	Cin-N	42	89	8	13	3	1	0	2	7	27	.146	.208	.202	27	-8	-7	4	1			.899	5	S/O23	-0.2
1926	Cin-N	80	224	22	44	7	6	0	18	13	30	.196	.244	.281	42	-19	-18	16	1			.918	-7	S	-1.8
Total	2	122	313	30	57	10	7	0	20	20	57	.182	.234	.259	38	-27	-26	20	2			.913	-3	S/O32	-2.0

■ BOB EMMERICH Emmerich, Robert George b: 8/1/1897, New York, N.Y. d: 11/22/48, Bridgeport, Conn. BR/TR, 5'3", 155 lbs. Deb: 9/22/23

YEAR	TM/L	G	AB	R	H	2B	3B	HR	RBI	BB	SO	AVG	OBP	SLG	PRO+	BR	/A	RC	SB	CS	SBR	FA	FR	POS	TPR
1923	Bos-N	13	24	3	2	0	0	0	0	2	3	.083	.154	.083	-37	-5	-5	0	1	1	-0	1.000	-1	/O	-0.6

■ BILL ENDICOTT Endicott, William Franklin b: 9/4/18, Acorn, Mo. BL/TL, 5'11.5", 175 lbs. Deb: 4/21/46

YEAR	TM/L	G	AB	R	H	2B	3B	HR	RBI	BB	SO	AVG	OBP	SLG	PRO+	BR	/A	RC	SB	CS	SBR	FA	FR	POS	TPR
1946	StL-N	20	20	2	4	3	0	0	3	4	4	.200	.333	.350	90	-0	-0	2	0			1.000	-0	/O	0.0

■ CLYDE ENGLE Engle, Arthur Clyde "Hack" b: 3/19/1884, Dayton, Ohio d: 12/26/39, Boston, Mass. BR/TR, 5'10", 190 lbs. Deb: 4/12/09

YEAR	TM/L	G	AB	R	H	2B	3B	HR	RBI	BB	SO	AVG	OBP	SLG	PRO+	BR	/A	RC	SB	CS	SBR	FA	FR	POS	TPR
1909	NY-A	135	492	66	137	20	5	3	71	47		.278	.347	.358	122	13	13	68	18			.946	14	*O	2.4
1910	NY-A	5	13	0	3	0	0	0	0	2		.231	.333	.231	73	-0	-0	1	1			.857	-0	/O	-0.1
	Bos-A	106	363	59	96	18	7	2	38	31		.264	.326	.369	115	7	6	47	12			.915	1	32O/S	0.7
	Yr	111	376	59	99	18	7	2	38	33		.263	.326	.364	113	6	5	49	13			.915	0	32O/S	0.6
1911	Bos-A	146	514	58	139	13	3	2	48	51		.270	.343	.319	86	-9	-8	65	24			.975	-4	132O	-1.2
1912	*Bos-A	58	171	32	40	5	3	0	18	28		.234	.348	.298	81	-2	-3	22	12			.977	-8	123/SO	-1.2
1913	Bos-A	143	498	75	144	17	12	2	50	53	41	.289	.363	.384	116	12	10	76	28			.987	-7	*1/O	0.2
1914	Bos-A	59	134	14	26	2	0	0	9	14	11	.194	.275	.209	46	-8	-8	7	4	9	-4	.976	-4	1/23O	-2.0
	Buf-F	32	110	12	28	4	1	0	12	11	18	.255	.328	.309	80	-2	-3	14	5			.889	-7	3/O	-1.0
1915	Buf-F	141	501	56	131	22	8	3	71	34	43	.261	.312	.355	94	-4	-5	66	24			.969	-3	*O23/1	-1.3
1916	Cle-A	11	26	1	4	0	0	0	1	0	6	.154	.154	.154	-7	-3	-4	1	0			.810	-2	/31O	-0.7
Total	8	836	2822	373	748	101	39	12	318	271	119	.265	.335	.341	99	3	-3	367	128	9		.959	-21	O13/2S	-4.2

■ CHARLIE ENGLE Engle, Charlie August "Cholly" b: 8/27/03, New York, N.Y. d: 10/12/83, San Antonio, Tex. BR/TR, 5'8", 145 lbs. Deb: 9/14/25

YEAR	TM/L	G	AB	R	H	2B	3B	HR	RBI	BB	SO	AVG	OBP	SLG	PRO+	BR	/A	RC	SB	CS	SBR	FA	FR	POS	TPR
1925	Phi-A	1	0	0	0	0	0	0	0	0	0	—	—	—	—	0	0	0	0	0	0	.000	0	/S	0.0
1926	Phi-A	19	19	7	2	0	0	0	0	10	6	.105	.433	.105	43	-1	-1	2	0	0	0	.930	2	S	0.2
1930	Pit-N	67	216	34	57	10	1	0	15	22	20	.264	.335	.319	59	-14	-14	24	1			.975	-1	3S2	-0.9
Total	3	87	235	41	59	10	1	0	15	32	26	.251	.346	.302	59	-14	-15	26	1	0		.937	2	/S32	-0.7

■ DAVE ENGLE Engle, Ralph David b: 11/30/56, San Diego, Cal. BR/TR, 6'3", 216 lbs. Deb: 4/14/81

YEAR	TM/L	G	AB	R	H	2B	3B	HR	RBI	BB	SO	AVG	OBP	SLG	PRO+	BR	/A	RC	SB	CS	SBR	FA	FR	POS	TPR
1981	Min-A	82	248	29	64	14	4	5	32	13	37	.258	.298	.407	95	-0	-2	27	0	1	-1	.980	-0	O/3D	-0.6
1982	Min-A	58	186	20	42	7	2	4	16	10	22	.226	.269	.349	67	-8	-9	16	0	0	0	.985	0	OD	-1.0
1983	Min-A	120	374	46	114	22	4	8	43	28	39	.305	.355	.449	115	10	8	57	2	1	0	.973	-19	CD/O	-0.8
1984	Min-A☆	109	391	56	104	20	1	4	38	26	22	.266	.312	.353	80	-9	-11	39	0	1	-1	.981	-7	CD	-1.5
1985	Min-A	70	172	28	44	8	2	7	25	21	28	.256	.337	.448	106	3	2	26	2	2	-1	.984	-0	DC/O	0.1
1986	Det-A	35	86	6	22	7	0	0	4	7	13	.256	.312	.337	77	-3	-3	9	0	0	0	1.000	-1	1/OCD	-0.5
1987	Mon-N	59	84	7	19	4	0	1	14	6	11	.226	.278	.310	54	-5	-6	6	1	0	0	1.000	0	O/C13	-0.6
1988	Mon-N	34	37	4	8	3	0	0	1	5	5	.216	.310	.297	72	-1	-1	3	0	0	0	1.000	-1	/CO3	-0.2
1989	Mil-A	27	65	5	14	3	0	2	8	4	13	.215	.261	.354	72	-3	-3	6	0	0	0	.973	0	1/CD	-0.4
Total	9	594	1643	201	431	88	13	31	181	120	190	.262	.314	.388	90	-17	-25	189	5	5	-2	.979	-29	COD/13	-5.5

■ CHARLIE ENGLISH English, Charles Dewie b: 4/8/10, Darlington, S.C. BR/TR, 5'9.5", 160 lbs. Deb: 7/23/32

YEAR	TM/L	G	AB	R	H	2B	3B	HR	RBI	BB	SO	AVG	OBP	SLG	PRO+	BR	/A	RC	SB	CS	SBR	FA	FR	POS	TPR
1932	Chi-A	24	63	7	20	3	1	1	8	3	7	.317	.348	.444	111	0	1	10	0	0	0	.821	-2	3/S	-0.1
1933	Chi-A	3	9	2	4	2	0	0	1	1	1	.444	.500	.667	216	1	1	3	0	0	0	.923	-1	/2	0.1
1936	NY-N	6	1	0	0	0	0	0	0	0	0	.000	.000	.000	-99	-0	-0	0	0			.000	0	/2	0.0
1937	Cin-N	17	63	1	15	3	1	0	4	0	2	.238	.238	.317	52	-5	-4	4	0			.958	2	3/2	-0.2
Total	4	50	136	10	39	8	2	1	13	4	10	.287	.307	.397	90	-3	-2	17	0	0		.897	-2	/32S	-0.2

■ WOODY ENGLISH English, Elwood George b: 3/2/07, Fredonia, Ohio BR/TR, 5'10", 155 lbs. Deb: 4/26/27

YEAR	TM/L	G	AB	R	H	2B	3B	HR	RBI	BB	SO	AVG	OBP	SLG	PRO+	BR	/A	RC	SB	CS	SBR	FA	FR	POS	TPR
1927	Chi-N	87	334	46	97	14	4	1	28	16	26	.290	.325	.365	84	-8	-8	39	1			.940	7	S/3	0.7
1928	Chi-N	116	475	68	142	22	4	2	34	30	28	.299	.343	.375	89	-9	-8	60	4			.946	6	*S/3	1.2
1929	*Chi-N	144	608	131	168	29	3	1	52	68	50	.276	.352	.339	72	-25	-25	74	13			.955	15	*S	0.7
1930	Chi-N	156	638	152	214	36	17	14	59	100	72	.335	.430	.511	125	31	30	141	3			.973	-13	3S	2.7
1931	Chi-N	156	634	117	202	38	8	2	53	68	80	.319	.391	.413	114	17	16	108	12			.965	1	*S3	3.1
1932	*Chi-N	127	522	70	142	23	7	3	47	55	73	.272	.344	.360	90	-6	-6	68	5			.957	-2	3S	0.1
1933	Chi-N★	105	398	54	104	19	2	3	41	53	44	.261	.348	.342	98	0	1	51	5			**.973**	-15	*3/S	-0.8
1934	Chi-N	109	421	65	117	26	5	3	31	48	65	.278	.353	.385	99	-1	1	61	6			.971	-10	S3/2	-0.4
1935	Chi-N	34	84	11	17	2	0	2	8	20	4	.202	.368	.298	81	-1	-1	12	1			.868	-5	3S	-0.5
1936	Chi-N	64	182	33	45	9	0	0	20	40	28	.247	.394	.297	86	-0	-1	26	1			.976	1	S3/2	0.3
1937	Bro-N	129	378	45	90	16	2	1	42	65	55	.238	.350	.299	77	-9	-10	42	4			.956	-17	*S2	-1.9
1938	Bro-N	34	72	9	18	2	0	0	7	8	11	.250	.333	.278	68	-3	-3	7	2			.958	1	3/2S	-0.2
Total	12	1261	4746	801	1356	236	52	32	422	571	536	.286	.366	.378	95	-12	-14	690	57			.957	-31	S3/2	5.0

■ **GIL ENGLISH** English, Gilbert Raymond b: 7/2/09, Glenola, N.C. BR/TR, 5'11", 180 lbs. Deb: 9/20/31

YEAR	TM/L	G	AB	R	H	2B	3B	HR	RBI	BB	SO	AVG	OBP	SLG	PRO+	BR	/A	RC	SB	CS	SBR	FA	FR	POS	TPR
1931	NY-N	3	8	0	0	0	0	0	0	1	3	.000	.111	.000	-69	-2	-2	0	0			1.000	-1	/3	-0.3
1932	NY-N	59	204	22	46	7	5	2	19	5	20	.225	.244	.338	56	-13	-13	17	0			.931	4	3S	-0.5
1936	Det-A	1	1	0	0	0	0	0	0	0	1	.000	.000	.000	-99	-0	-0	0	0	0	0	1.000	0	/3	0.0
1937	Det-A	18	65	6	17	1	0	1	6	6	4	.262	.333	.323	65	-3	-3	7	1	1	-0	.962	-8	2/3	-1.0
	Bos-N	79	269	25	78	5	2	2	37	23	27	.290	.348	.346	98	-3	-0	32	3			.958	-7	3	-0.6
1938	Bos-N	53	165	17	41	6	0	2	21	15	16	.248	.315	.321	84	-5	-3	16	1			.956	-4	3/O2S	-0.6
1944	Bro-N	27	79	4	12	3	0	1	7	6	7	.152	.212	.228	24	-8	-8	4	0			.918	-3	S3/2	-1.1
Total	6	240	791	74	194	22	7	8	90	56	78	.245	.298	.321	72	-36	-30	76	5	1		.950	-18	3/S2O	-4.1

■ **DEL ENNIS** Ennis, Delmer b: 6/8/25, Philadelphia, Pa. BR/TR, 6', 195 lbs. Deb: 4/28/46

YEAR	TM/L	G	AB	R	H	2B	3B	HR	RBI	BB	SO	AVG	OBP	SLG	PRO+	BR	/A	RC	SB	CS	SBR	FA	FR	POS	TPR
1946	Phi-N★	141	540	70	169	30	6	17	73	39	65	.313	.364	.485	144	25	27	96	5			.975	14	*O	3.6
1947	Phi-N	139	541	71	149	25	6	12	81	37	51	.275	.325	.410	98	-6	-3	69	9			.979	9	*O	-0.1
1948	Phi-N	152	589	86	171	40	4	30	95	47	58	.290	.345	.525	135	23	25	106	2			.957	5	*O	2.1
1949	Phi-N	154	610	92	184	39	11	25	110	59	61	.302	.367	.525	140	29	32	118	2			.966	6	*O	2.9
1950	*Phi-N	153	595	92	185	34	8	31	**126**	56	59	.311	.372	.551	142	32	33	115	2			.970	-1	*O	2.5
1951	Phi-N★	144	532	76	142	20	5	15	73	68	42	.267	.352	.408	105	4	5	77	4	2	0	.969	-1	*O	-0.2
1952	Phi-N	151	592	90	171	30	10	20	107	47	65	.289	.341	.475	125	17	18	94	6	4	-1	.970	-1	*O	1.0
1953	Phi-N	152	578	79	165	22	3	29	125	57	53	.285	.355	.484	117	13	13	100	1	3	-2	.980	4	*O	0.9
1954	Phi-N	145	556	73	145	23	2	25	119	50	60	.261	.324	.444	98	-3	-3	75	2	1	0	.957	3	*O/1	-0.6
1955	Phi-N★	146	564	82	167	24	7	29	120	46	46	.296	.351	.518	129	20	21	99	4	2	0	.987	6	*O	2.0
1956	Phi-N	153	630	80	164	23	3	26	95	33	62	.260	.300	.430	95	-8	-6	77	7	3	0	.962	0	*O	-1.5
1957	StL-N	136	490	61	140	24	3	24	105	37	50	.286	.337	.494	117	12	11	73	1	3	-2	.943	-15	*O	-1.3
1958	StL-N	106	329	22	86	18	1	3	47	15	35	.261	.296	.350	67	-14	-16	29	0	1	-1	.993	3	O	-1.8
1959	Cin-N	5	12	1	4	0	0	0	1	2	2	.333	.429	.333	103	0	0	2	0	0	0	1.000	-0	/O	0.0
	Chi-A	26	96	10	21	6	0	2	7	4	10	.219	.250	.344	62	-5	-5	8	0	0	0	.909	-3	O	-1.0
Total	14	1903	7254	985	2063	358	69	288	1284	597	719	.284	.341	.472	117	139	151	1137	45	19		.969	28	*O/1	8.5

■ **RUSS ENNIS** Ennis, Russell Elwood "Hack" b: 3/10/1897, Superior, Wis. d: 1/21/49, Superior, Wis. BR/TR, 5'11.5", 160 lbs. Deb: 9/19/26

YEAR	TM/L	G	AB	R	H	2B	3B	HR	RBI	BB	SO	AVG	OBP	SLG	PRO+	BR	/A	RC	SB	CS	SBR	FA	FR	POS	TPR
1926	Was-A	1	0	0	0	0	0	0	0	0	0	—	—	—	—	0	0	0	0	0	0	.000	0	/C	0.0

■ **GEORGE ENRIGHT** Enright, George Albert b: 5/9/54, New Britain, Conn. BR/TR, 5'11", 175 lbs. Deb: 8/08/76

YEAR	TM/L	G	AB	R	H	2B	3B	HR	RBI	BB	SO	AVG	OBP	SLG	PRO+	BR	/A	RC	SB	CS	SBR	FA	FR	POS	TPR
1976	Chi-A	2	1	0	0	0	0	0	0	0	0	.000	.000	.000	-99	-0	-0	0	0	0	0	1.000	1	/C	0.0

■ **MUTZ ENS** Ens, Anton b: 11/8/1884, St.Louis, Mo. d: 6/28/50, St.Louis, Mo. BL/TL, 6'1", 180 lbs. Deb: 9/02/12 F

YEAR	TM/L	G	AB	R	H	2B	3B	HR	RBI	BB	SO	AVG	OBP	SLG	PRO+	BR	/A	RC	SB	CS	SBR	FA	FR	POS	TPR
1912	Chi-A	3	6	0	0	0	0	0	0	0		.000	.000	.000	-99	-2	-2	0	0			.857	-1	/1	-0.2

■ **JEWEL ENS** Ens, Jewel Winklemeyer b: 8/24/1889, St.Louis, Mo. d: 1/17/50, Syracuse, N.Y. BR/TR, 5'10.5", 165 lbs. Deb: 4/29/22 FMC

YEAR	TM/L	G	AB	R	H	2B	3B	HR	RBI	BB	SO	AVG	OBP	SLG	PRO+	BR	/A	RC	SB	CS	SBR	FA	FR	POS	TPR
1922	Pit-N	47	142	18	42	7	3	0	17	7	9	.296	.338	.387	85	-3	-3	19	3	0	1	.951	-16	2/31S	-1.6
1923	Pit-N	12	29	3	8	1	1	0	5	0	3	.276	.276	.379	70	-1	-1	3	2	0	1	.975	-0	/13	-0.1
1924	Pit-N	5	10	2	3	0	0	0	0	0	3	.300	.300	.300	60	-1	-1	1	0	0	0	1.000	-0	/1	-0.1
1925	Pit-N	3	5	2	1	0	0	1	2	0	1	.200	.200	.800	133	0	0	1	0	0	0	1.000	-0	/1	0.0
Total	4	67	186	25	54	8	4	1	24	7	16	.290	.323	.392	83	-5	-5	24	5	0	2	.990	-17	/213S	-1.8

■ **CHARLIE ENWRIGHT** Enwright, Charles Massey b: 10/6/1887, Sacramento, Cal. d: 1/19/17, Sacramento, Cal. BL/TR, 5'10", Deb: 4/19/09

YEAR	TM/L	G	AB	R	H	2B	3B	HR	RBI	BB	SO	AVG	OBP	SLG	PRO+	BR	/A	RC	SB	CS	SBR	FA	FR	POS	TPR
1909	StL-N	3	7	1	1	0	0	0	1	2		.143	.333	.143	51	-0	-0	0	0			.444	-3	/S	-0.4

■ **JACK ENZENROTH** Enzenroth, Clarence Herman b: 11/4/1885, Mineral Point, Wis. d: 2/21/44, Detroit, Mich. BR/TR, 5'10", 164 lbs. Deb: 5/01/14

YEAR	TM/L	G	AB	R	H	2B	3B	HR	RBI	BB	SO	AVG	OBP	SLG	PRO+	BR	/A	RC	SB	CS	SBR	FA	FR	POS	TPR
1914	StL-A	3	6	0	1	0	0	0	0	2	3	.167	.444	.167	88	0	0	0	0	1	-1	.923	-1	/C	-0.2
	KC-F	26	67	7	12	4	1	0	5	5	19	.179	.236	.269	45	-5	-5	4	0			.965	-2	C	-0.5
1915	KC-F	14	19	3	3	0	0	0	3	6	0	.158	.360	.158	57	-1	-1	1	0			.973	2	/C	0.2
Total	2	43	92	10	16	4	1	0	8	13	22	.174	.283	.239	53	-6	-5	6	0	1		.963	-1	/C	-0.5

■ **JIM EPPARD** Eppard, James Gerhard b: 4/27/60, South Bend, Ind. BL/TL, 6'2", 180 lbs. Deb: 9/08/87

YEAR	TM/L	G	AB	R	H	2B	3B	HR	RBI	BB	SO	AVG	OBP	SLG	PRO+	BR	/A	RC	SB	CS	SBR	FA	FR	POS	TPR
1987	Cal-A	8	9	2	3	0	0	0	0	2	0	.333	.455	.333	118	0	0	1	0	0	0	1.000	-0	/O	0.0
1988	Cal-A	56	113	7	32	3	1	0	14	11	15	.283	.347	.327	92	-1	-1	13	0	0	0	.971	-0	OD/1	-0.2
1989	Cal-A	12	12	0	3	0	0	0	2	1	4	.250	.308	.250	60	-1	-1	1	0	0	0	1.000	-0	/1	-0.1
1990	Tor-A	6	5	0	1	0	0	0	0	0	2	.200	.333	.200	52	-0	-0	0	0	0	0	.000	0	/H	0.0
Total	4	82	139	9	39	3	1	0	16	14	21	.281	.351	.317	90	-2	-1	15	0	0	0	.972	-1	/O1D	-0.3

■ **AUBREY EPPS** Epps, Aubrey Lee "Yo-Yo" b: 3/3/12, Memphis, Tenn. d: 11/13/84, Ackerman, Miss. BR/TR, 5'10", 170 lbs. Deb: 9/29/35

YEAR	TM/L	G	AB	R	H	2B	3B	HR	RBI	BB	SO	AVG	OBP	SLG	PRO+	BR	/A	RC	SB	CS	SBR	FA	FR	POS	TPR
1935	Pit-N	1	4	1	3	0	1	0	3	0	0	.750	.750	1.250	414	2	2	4	0			.750	-0	/C	0.1

■ **HAL EPPS** Epps, Harold Franklin b: 3/26/14, Athens, Ga. BL/TL, 6', 175 lbs. Deb: 9/09/38

YEAR	TM/L	G	AB	R	H	2B	3B	HR	RBI	BB	SO	AVG	OBP	SLG	PRO+	BR	/A	RC	SB	CS	SBR	FA	FR	POS	TPR
1938	StL-N	17	50	8	15	0	0	1	3	2	4	.300	.327	.360	84	-1	-1	6	2			.963	-0	O	-0.2
1940	StL-N	11	15	6	3	0	0	0	1	0	3	.200	.200	.200	10	-2	-2	1	0			.800	-1	/O	-0.3
1943	StL-A	8	35	2	10	4	0	0	1	3	4	.286	.342	.400	114	1	1	4	1	1	-0	1.000	-1	/O	-0.1
1944	StL-A	22	62	15	11	1	1	0	3	14	14	.177	.338	.226	59	-2	-3	6	0	1	-1	.962	1	O	-0.4
	Phi-A	67	229	27	60	8	8	0	13	18	18	.262	.316	.367	96	-2	-2	28	2	1	0	.973	-3	O	-0.8
	Yr	89	291	42	71	9	9	0	16	32	32	.244	.321	.337	88	-4	-4	34	2	2	-1	.970	-2	O	-1.2
Total	4	125	391	58	99	13	9	1	21	37	43	.253	.319	.340	86	-6	-7	44	5	3		.968	-4	/O	-1.8

■ **MIKE EPSTEIN** Epstein, Michael Peter "Superjew" b: 4/4/43, Bronx, N.Y. BL/TL, 6'3.5", 230 lbs. Deb: 9/16/66

YEAR	TM/L	G	AB	R	H	2B	3B	HR	RBI	BB	SO	AVG	OBP	SLG	PRO+	BR	/A	RC	SB	CS	SBR	FA	FR	POS	TPR
1966	Bal-A	6	11	1	2	0	1	0	3	1	3	.182	.250	.364	75	-0	-0	1	0	0	0	1.000	0	/1	0.0
1967	Bal-A	9	13	0	2	0	0	0	0	3	5	.154	.313	.154	42	-1	-1	1	0	0	0	1.000	-0	/1	-0.1
	Was-A	96	284	32	65	7	4	9	29	38	74	.229	.332	.377	114	4	5	37	1	4	-2	.987	-2	1	-0.4
	Yr	105	297	32	67	7	4	9	29	41	79	.226	.331	.367	110	3	4	37	1	4	-2	.988	-2	1	-0.5
1968	Was-A	123	385	40	90	8	2	13	33	48	91	.234	.339	.366	117	8	9	48	1	1	-0	.987	1	*1	0.2
1969	Was-A	131	403	73	112	18	1	30	85	85	99	.278	.416	.551	178	40	42	96	2	5	-2	.990	-1	*1	3.2
1970	Was-A	140	430	55	110	15	3	20	56	73	117	.256	.375	.444	131	16	19	76	2	3	-1	.992	-3	*1	0.5
1971	Was-A	24	85	6	21	1	1	1	9	12	31	.247	.366	.318	101	0	1	12	1	0	0	.992	-1	1	-0.2
	*Oak-A	104	329	43	77	13	0	18	51	62	71	.234	.368	.438	130	14	14	57	0	3	-2	.995	-2	1	0.3
	Yr	128	414	49	98	14	1	19	60	74	102	.237	.368	.413	124	14	15	69	1	3	-2	.994	-2	*1	0.1
1972	*Oak-A	138	455	63	123	18	2	26	70	68	68	.270	.378	.490	166	33	36	88	0	1	-1	.990	-2	*1	2.4
1973	Tex-A	27	85	9	16	3	0	1	6	14	19	.188	.324	.259	69	-3	-3	8	0	0	0	.991	-1	1	-0.6
	Cal-A	91	312	30	67	8	2	8	32	34	54	.215	.302	.330	84	-9	-6	31	0	0	0	.993	-0	1	-1.3
	Yr	118	397	39	83	11	2	9	38	48	73	.209	.307	.315	81	-12	-9	40	0	0	0	.993	-1	*1	-1.9
1974	Cal-A	18	62	10	10	2	0	4	6	10	13	.161	.288	.387	98	-1	-0	8	0	0	0	.993	1	1	-0.1
Total	9	907	2854	362	695	93	16	130	380	448	645	.244	.360	.424	130	100	116	461	7	17	-8	.991	-10	1	3.9

■ **JOE ERAUTT** Erautt, Joseph Michael "Stubby" b: 9/1/21, Vibank, Sask., Can. d: 10/6/76, Portland, Ore. BR/TR, 5'9", 175 lbs. Deb: 5/09/50 F

YEAR	TM/L	G	AB	R	H	2B	3B	HR	RBI	BB	SO	AVG	OBP	SLG	PRO+	BR	/A	RC	SB	CS	SBR	FA	FR	POS	TPR
1950	Chi-A	16	18	0	4	0	0	0	1	1	3	.222	.263	.222	26	-2	-2	1	0	0	0	1.000	1	/C	-0.1
1951	Chi-A	16	25	3	4	1	0	0	0	3	2	.160	.276	.200	31	-2	-2	1	0	0	0	.977	3	C	0.1
Total	2	32	43	3	8	1	0	0	1	4	5	.186	.271	.209	29	-4	-4	2	0	0	0	.983	4	/C	0.0

YEAR	TM/L	G	AB	R	H	2B	3B	HR	RBI	BB	SO	AVG	OBP	SLG	PRO+	BR	/A	RC	SB	CS	SBR	FA	FR	POS	TPR

■ HANK ERICKSON
Erickson, Henry Nels "Popeye" b: 11/11/07, Chicago, Ill. d: 12/13/64, Louisville, Ky. BR/TR, 6'1", 185 lbs. Deb: 4/17/35

| 1935 | Cin-N | 37 | 88 | 9 | 23 | 3 | 2 | 1 | 4 | 6 | 4 | .261 | .323 | .375 | 90 | -2 | -1 | 11 | 0 | | | .972 | 2 | C | 0.2 |

■ CAL ERMER
Ermer, Calvin Coolidge b: 11/10/23, Baltimore, Md. BR/TR, 6'0.5", 175 lbs. Deb: 9/26/47 MC

| 1947 | Was-A | 1 | 3 | 0 | 0 | 0 | 0 | 0 | 0 | 0 | 0 | .000 | .000 | .000 | -99 | -1 | -1 | 0 | 0 | 0 | 0 | 1.000 | 1 | /2 | 0.0 |

■ FRANK ERNAGA
Ernaga, Frank John b: 8/22/30, Susanville, Cal. BR/TR, 6'1", 195 lbs. Deb: 5/24/57

1957	Chi-N	20	35	9	11	3	2	2	7	9	14	.314	.455	.686	204	5	5	12	0	0	0	.950	-0	O	0.5
1958	Chi-N	9	8	0	1	0	0	0	0	0	2	.125	.125	.125	-34	-2	-1	0	0	0	0	.000	0	H	-0.2
Total	2	29	43	9	12	3	2	2	7	9	16	.279	.404	.581	163	4	4	12	0	0	0	.955	-0	/O	0.3

■ TEX ERWIN
Erwin, Ross Emil b: 12/22/1885, Forney, Tex. d: 4/5/53, Rochester, N.Y. BL/TR, 6', 185 lbs. Deb: 8/26/07

1907	Det-N	4	5	0	1	0	0	0	1	1		.200	.333	.200	68	-0	-0	0	0			.909	0	/C	0.0
1910	Bro-N	81	202	15	38	3	1	1	10	24	12	.188	.278	.228	49	-13	-12	14	3			.949	-1	C	-0.8
1911	Bro-N	91	218	30	59	13	2	7	34	31	23	.271	.367	.445	132	8	9	37	5			.971	-5	C	1.0
1912	Bro-N	59	133	14	28	3	0	2	14	18	16	.211	.305	.278	62	-7	-6	12	1			.949	-2	C	-0.4
1913	Bro-N	20	31	6	8	1	0	0	3	4	5	.258	.343	.290	80	-1	-1	3	0			.950	-3	C	-0.3
1914	Bro-N	9	11	0	5	0	0	0	1	2	1	.455	.538	.455	192	2	1	3	1			1.000	-1	/C	0.1
	Cin-N	12	35	5	11	3	1	1	7	2	3	.314	.351	.486	144	2	2	6	0			.962	1	C	0.3
	Yr	21	46	5	16	3	1	1	8	4	4	.348	.400	.478	157	3	3	9	1			.966	-0	C	0.4
Total	6	276	635	70	150	23	3	11	70	82	60	.236	.326	.334	90	-10	-7	75	10			.957	-11	C	-0.1

■ NICK ESASKY
Esasky, Nicholas Andrew b: 2/24/60, Hialeah, Fla. BR/TR, 6'3", 205 lbs. Deb: 6/19/83

1983	Cin-N	85	302	41	80	10	5	12	46	27	99	.265	.331	.450	111	5	4	46	6	2	1	.935	-10	3	-0.7
1984	Cin-N	113	322	30	62	10	5	10	45	52	103	.193	.305	.348	79	-7	-9	36	1	2	-1	.910	-8	31	-2.1
1985	Cin-N	125	413	61	108	21	0	21	66	41	102	.262	.334	.465	115	11	8	63	3	4	-2	.946	-6	3O1	-1.1
1986	Cin-N	102	330	35	76	17	2	12	41	47	97	.230	.328	.403	96	-0	-2	44	0	2	1	.991	-3	1O/3	-1.1
1987	Cin-N	100	346	48	94	19	2	22	59	29	76	.272	.328	.529	117	9	8	57	0	0	0	.994	-11	1/3O	-1.1
1988	Cin-N	122	391	40	95	17	2	15	62	48	104	.243	.332	.412	108	6	5	56	7	2	1	.994	-9	*1	-1.3
1989	Bos-A	154	564	79	156	26	2	30	108	66	117	.277	.355	.500	130	28	23	100	1	2	-1	.996	4	*1/O	1.5
1990	Atl-N	9	35	2	6	0	0	0	0	4	14	.171	.256	.171	19	-4	-4	2	0	0	0	.944	-2	/1	-0.7
Total	8	810	2703	336	677	120	21	122	427	314	712	.250	.332	.446	109	49	33	403	18	14	-3	.993	-45	13/O	-5.7

■ NINO ESCALERA
Escalera, Saturnino Cuadrado b: 12/1/29, Santurce, P.R. BL/TR, 5'10", 165 lbs. Deb: 4/17/54

| 1954 | Cin-N | 73 | 69 | 15 | 11 | 1 | 1 | 0 | 3 | 7 | 11 | .159 | .237 | .203 | 15 | -9 | -9 | 4 | 1 | 0 | 0 | .962 | 0 | O/1S | -0.9 |

■ JIM ESCHEN
Eschen, James Godrich b: 8/21/1891, Brooklyn, N.Y. d: 9/27/60, Sloatsburg, N.Y. BR/TR, 5'10.5", 160 lbs. Deb: 7/10/15 F

| 1915 | Cle-A | 15 | 42 | 11 | 10 | 1 | 0 | 0 | 2 | 5 | 9 | .238 | .319 | .262 | 73 | -1 | -1 | 4 | 0 | 1 | -1 | .968 | 1 | O | -0.1 |

■ LARRY ESCHEN
Eschen, Lawrence Edward b: 9/22/20, Suffern, N.Y. BR/TR, 6', 180 lbs. Deb: 6/16/42 F

| 1942 | Phi-A | 12 | 11 | 0 | 0 | 0 | 0 | 0 | 0 | 4 | 6 | .000 | .267 | .000 | -22 | -2 | -2 | 0 | 0 | 0 | 0 | .824 | -1 | /S2 | -0.3 |

■ ANGEL ESCOBAR
Escobar, Angel Rubenque (Rivas) b: 5/12/65, LaSabana, Venez. BB/TR, 6', 160 lbs. Deb: 5/17/88

| 1988 | SF-N | 3 | 3 | 1 | 1 | 0 | 0 | 0 | 0 | 0 | 0 | .333 | .333 | .333 | 96 | -0 | -0 | 0 | 0 | 0 | 0 | 1.000 | 0 | /S3 | 0.0 |

■ JOSE ESCOBAR
Escobar, Jose Elias (Sanchez) b: 10/30/60, Las Flores, Venez. BR/TR, 5'10", 140 lbs. Deb: 4/13/91

| 1991 | Cle-A | 10 | 15 | 0 | 3 | 0 | 0 | 0 | 1 | 1 | 4 | .200 | .250 | .200 | 26 | -1 | -1 | 1 | 0 | 0 | 0 | 1.000 | 2 | /S23 | 0.0 |

■ JIMMY ESMOND
Esmond, James J. b: 10/8/1889, Albany, N.Y. d: 6/26/48, Troy, N.Y. BR/TR, 5'11", 167 lbs. Deb: 4/20/11

1911	Cin-N	73	198	27	54	4	6	1	11	17	30	.273	.330	.369	99	-2	-1	26	7			.918	1	S3/2	0.3
1912	Cin-N	82	231	24	45	5	3	1	40	20	31	.195	.259	.255	42	-19	-18	19	11			.930	-7	S	-2.0
1914	Ind-F	151	542	74	160	23	15	2	49	40	48	.295	.344	.404	101	7	0	88	25			.919	-7	*S	0.6
1915	New-F	155	569	79	147	20	10	5	62	59	54	.258	.324	.359	107	1	5	78	18			.939	6	*S	2.4
Total	4	461	1540	204	406	52	34	9	162	136	163	.264	.324	.359	94	-13	-14	211	61			.929	-8	S/32	1.3

■ JUAN ESPINO
Espino, Juan (Reyes) b: 3/16/56, Bonao, D.R. BR/TR, 6'1", 190 lbs. Deb: 6/25/82

1982	NY-A	3	2	0	0	0	0	0	0	1	.000	.000	.000	-99	-1	-1	0	0	0	0	1.000	0	/C	0.0
1983	NY-A	10	23	1	6	0	0	1	3	1	5	.261	.292	.391	89	-0	-0	3	0	0	0	1.000	-0	C	0.1
1985	NY-A	9	11	0	4	0	0	0	1	0	1	.364	.364	.364	102	-0	-0	1	0	0	0	1.000	1	/C	0.1
1986	NY-A	27	37	1	6	2	0	0	5	2	9	.162	.205	.216	15	-4	-4	2	0	0	0	.987	3	C	-0.1
Total	4	49	73	2	16	2	0	1	8	3	15	.219	.250	.288	48	-5	-5	6	0	0	0	.993	4	/C	0.0

■ ALVARO ESPINOZA
Espinoza, Alvaro Alberto b: 2/19/62, Valencia, Venez. BR/TR, 6', 170 lbs. Deb: 9/14/84

1984	Min-A	1	0	0	0	0	0	0	0	0	0	—	—	—		0	0	0	0	0	0	.000	0	/S	0.0
1985	Min-A	32	57	5	15	2	0	0	9	1	9	.263	.288	.298	58	-3	-3	4	0	1	-1	.949	7	S	0.4
1986	Min-A	37	42	4	9	1	0	0	1	1	10	.214	.233	.238	28	-4	-4	2	0	1	-1	.941	6	2S	0.2
1988	NY-A	3	3	0	0	0	0	0	0	0	0	.000	.000	.000	-99	-1	-1	0	0	0	0	1.000	1	/2S	0.0
1989	NY-A	146	503	51	142	23	1	0	41	14	60	.282	.303	.332	80	-15	-14	48	3	3	-1	.970	17	*S	1.3
1990	NY-A	150	438	31	98	12	2	2	20	16	54	.224	.258	.274	49	-30	-30	29	1	2	-1	.977	21	*S	0.1
1991	NY-A	148	480	51	123	23	2	5	33	16	57	.256	.283	.344	72	-19	-19	45	4	1	1	.969	20	*S/3P	1.3
Total	7	517	1523	142	387	61	5	7	104	48	190	.254	.281	.315	66	-71	-71	129	8	8	-2	.971	71	S/23P	3.3

■ SAMMY ESPOSITO
Esposito, Samuel b: 12/15/31, Chicago, Ill. BR/TR, 5'9", 165 lbs. Deb: 9/28/52

1952	Chi-A	1	4	0	1	0	0	0	0	0	2	.250	.250	.250	39	-0	-0	0	0	1	-1	.500	-1	/S	-0.3
1955	Chi-A	3	4	3	0	0	0	0	0	1	0	.000	.200	.000	-41	-1	-1	0	0	0	0	1.000	-1	/3	-0.2
1956	Chi-A	81	184	30	42	8	2	3	25	41	19	.228	.374	.342	89	-1	-1	26	1	2	-1	.962	4	3S/2	1.3
1957	Chi-A	94	176	26	36	3	0	2	15	38	27	.205	.346	.256	66	-7	-7	19	5	1	1	.960	16	3S/2O	1.3
1958	Chi-A	98	81	16	20	3	0	0	3	12	6	.247	.358	.284	81	-2	-1	9	1	1	-0	.979	11	3S/2O	1.0
1959	*Chi-A	69	66	12	11	1	0	1	5	11	16	.167	.296	.227	43	-5	-5	5	1	0	0	.979	9	3S/2	0.4
1960	Chi-A	57	77	14	14	5	0	0	11	10	20	.182	.276	.286	53	-5	-5	6	0	0	0	.929	3	3S/2	-0.4
1961	Chi-A	63	94	12	16	5	0	1	8	12	21	.170	.264	.255	40	-8	-8	7	0	1	-1	.976	12	3S2	0.5
1962	Chi-A	75	81	14	19	1	0	1	4	17	13	.235	.367	.247	69	-3	-3	8	1	1	-1	.846	3	3S/2	0.2
1963	Chi-A	1	0	0	0	0	0	0	0	0	0	—	—	—		0	0	0	0	0	0	.000	0	R	0.0
	KC-A	18	25	3	5	1	0	0	2	3	3	.200	.286	.240	47	-2	-2	2	0	0	0	1.000	-2	/2S3	-0.3
	Yr	19	25	3	5	1	0	0	2	3	3	.200	.286	.240	47	-2	-2	2	0	0	0	1.000	-2	/2S3	-0.3
Total	10	560	792	130	164	27	2	8	73	145	127	.207	.333	.277	66	-33	-33	81	7	7	-2	.957	51	3S/2O	2.4

■ CECIL ESPY
Espy, Cecil Edward b: 1/20/63, San Diego, Cal. BB/TR, 6'3", 195 lbs. Deb: 9/02/83

1983	LA-N	20	11	4	3	1	0	0	1	1	2	.273	.333	.364	94	-0	-0	1	0	0	0	1.000	1	O	0.1
1987	Tex-A	14	8	1	0	0	0	0	0	1	3	.000	.111	.000	-67	-2	-2	0	2	0	1	1.000	-1	/O	-0.2
1988	Tex-A	123	347	46	86	17	6	2	39	20	83	.248	.291	.349	76	-10	-12	37	33	10	4	.972	-4	OD/SC12	-1.4
1989	Tex-A	142	475	65	122	12	7	3	31	38	99	.257	.315	.331	81	-11	-12	52	45	20	2	.990	-3	*O/D	-1.7
1990	Tex-A	52	71	10	9	1	1	0	1	10	20	.127	.235	.127	4	-9	-9	3	11	5	0	.966	-3	O/2D	-0.7
1991	*Pit-N	43	82	7	20	4	1	0	11	5	17	.244	.287	.329	74	-3	-3	9	4	0	1	.966	-3	O	-0.5
1992	*Pit-N	112	194	21	50	2	1	2	20	15	40	.258	.311	.340	85	-4	-4	21	6	3	0	.955	-20	O	-2.7
Total	7	506	1188	154	290	41	16	7	103	90	264	.244	.299	.323	74	-40	-41	123	101	38	8	.979	-36	O/DS2C1	-8.1

YEAR	TM/L	G	AB	R	H	2B	3B	HR	RBI	BB	SO	AVG	OBP	SLG	PRO+	BR	/A	RC	SB	CS	SBR	FA	FR	POS	TPR

■ CHUCK ESSEGIAN
Essegian, Charles Abraham b: 8/9/31, Boston, Mass. BR/TR, 5'11", 202 lbs. Deb: 4/15/58

1958	Phi-N	39	114	15	28	5	2	5	16	12	34	.246	.317	.456	103	-0	0	17	0	0	0	.952	1	O	-0.1
1959	StL-N	17	39	2	7	2	1	0	5	1	13	.179	.200	.282	25	-4	-4	1	0	0	0	1.000	-1	/O	-0.6
	*LA-N	24	46	6	14	6	0	1	5	4	11	.304	.360	.500	118	2	1	8	0	0	0	1.000	-1	O	-0.1
	Yr	41	85	8	21	8	1	1	10	5	24	.247	.289	.400	76	-3	-3	9	0	0	0	1.000	-2	O	-0.7
1960	LA-N	52	79	8	17	3	0	3	11	8	24	.215	.287	.367	73	-3	-3	9	0	0	0	.968	0	O	-0.4
1961	Bal-A	1	1	0	0	0	0	0	0	0	0	.000	.000	.000	-99	-0	-0	0	0	0	0	.000	0	H	0.0
	KC-A	4	6	1	2	1	0	0	1	1	2	.333	.429	.500	147	0	0	1	0	0	0	1.000	0	/O	0.1
	Cle-A	60	166	25	48	7	1	12	35	10	33	.289	.333	.560	138	7	7	29	0	0	0	.968	-2	O	0.4
	Yr	65	173	26	50	8	1	12	36	11	35	.289	.335	.555	137	7	8	30	0	0	0	.969	-1	O	0.5
1962	Cle-A	106	336	59	92	12	0	21	50	42	68	.274	.366	.497	134	14	16	62	0	0	0	.994	-4	O	0.7
1963	KC-A	101	231	23	52	9	0	5	27	19	48	.225	.287	.329	69	-9	-10	21	0	0	0	.990	-0	O	-1.3
Total	6	404	1018	139	260	45	4	47	150	97	233	.255	.326	.446	106	7	7	148	0	0	0	.981	-7	O	-1.3

■ JIM ESSIAN
Essian, James Sarkis b: 1/2/51, Detroit, Mich. BR/TR, 6'2", 195 lbs. Deb: 9/15/73 M

1973	Phi-N	2	3	0	0	0	0	0	0	0	1	.000	.000	.000	-97	-1	-1	0	0	0	0	.000	0	/C	-0.1
1974	Phi-N	17	20	1	2	0	0	0	0	2	1	.100	.182	.100	-19	-3	-3	0	0	0	0	.976	1	C/13	-0.2
1975	Phi-N	2	1	1	1	0	0	0	1	1	0	1.000	1.000	1.000	439	1	1	1	0	0	0	1.000	0	/C	0.1
1976	Chi-A	78	199	20	49	7	0	0	21	23	28	.246	.327	.281	79	-4	-5	19	2	1	0	.974	3	C/13	0.0
1977	Chi-A	114	322	50	88	18	2	10	44	52	35	.273	.376	.435	120	10	10	53	1	4	-2	.986	5	*C/3	1.6
1978	Oak-A	126	278	21	62	9	1	3	26	44	22	.223	.329	.295	81	-7	-5	28	2	1	0	.981	14	*C/12D	1.1
1979	Oak-A	98	313	34	76	16	0	8	40	25	29	.243	.303	.371	85	-9	-7	33	0	1	-1	.981	10	C3/10D	0.4
1980	Oak-A	87	285	19	66	11	0	5	29	30	18	.232	.305	.323	78	-11	-8	25	1	3	-2	.987	6	CD/1	-0.1
1981	Chi-A	27	52	6	16	3	0	0	5	4	5	.308	.357	.365	111	1	1	6	0	1	-1	.990	5	C/3	0.6
1982	Sea-A	48	153	14	42	8	0	3	20	11	7	.275	.327	.386	92	-1	-2	20	2	0	1	.994	6	C	0.7
1983	Cle-A	48	93	11	19	4	0	2	11	16	8	.204	.321	.312	72	-3	-3	10	0	1	-1	.989	3	C/3	0.1
1984	Oak-A	63	136	17	32	9	0	2	10	23	17	.235	.350	.346	100	-1	1	18	1	1	-0	.985	11	C/3D	1.3
Total	12	710	1855	194	453	85	3	33	207	231	171	.244	.330	.347	90	-28	-21	214	9	13	-5	.984	63	C/3D1O2	5.5

■ BOBBY ESTALELLA
Estalella, Roberto (Ventoza) b: 4/25/11, Cardenas, Cuba d: 1/6/91, Hialeah, Fla. BR/TR, 5'8", 180 lbs. Deb: 9/07/35

1935	Was-A	15	51	7	16	2	0	2	10	17	7	.314	.485	.471	153	5	5	13	1	0	0	.895	2	3	0.7
1936	Was-A	13	9	2	2	0	2	0	0	4	5	.222	.462	.667	186	1	1	3	0	0	0	.000	0	H	0.1
1939	Was-A	82	280	51	77	18	6	8	41	40	27	.275	.368	.468	121	5	8	48	2	3	-1	.964	-3	O	0.2
1941	StL-A	46	83	7	20	6	1	0	14	18	13	.241	.376	.337	87	-1	-1	12	0	0	0	1.000	-4	O	-0.6
1942	Was-A	133	429	68	119	24	5	8	65	85	42	.277	.400	.413	130	20	20	74	5	2	0	.941	-14	3O	0.6
1943	Phi-A	117	367	43	95	14	4	11	63	52	44	.259	.352	.409	123	11	11	52	1	3	-2	.975	-1	O	0.3
1944	Phi-A	140	506	54	151	17	9	7	60	59	60	.298	.374	.409	125	16	17	80	3	3	-1	.988	-2	*O/1	0.8
1945	Phi-A†	126	451	45	135	25	6	8	52	74	46	.299	.399	.435	142	26	26	79	1	6	-3	.988	1	*O	1.8
1949	Phi-A	8	20	2	5	0	0	0	3	1	2	.250	.286	.250	44	-2	-2	0	0	0	0	1.000	0	/O	-0.2
Total	9	680	2196	279	620	106	33	44	308	350	246	.282	.383	.421	127	82	87	361	13	17	-6	.982	-21	O/31	3.7

■ DUDE ESTERBROOK
Esterbrook, Thomas John b: 6/20/1857, Staten Is., N.Y. d: 4/30/01, Middletown, N.Y. BR/TR, 5'11", 167 lbs. Deb: 5/01/1880 M

1880	Buf-N	64	253	20	61	12	1	0	35	0	15	.241	.241	.296	80	-5	-6	19				.939	-3	1O/2SC	-1.2
1882	Cle-N	45	179	13	44	4	3	0	19	5	12	.246	.266	.302	85	-4	-3	15				.893	10	O/1	0.6
1883	NY-a	97	407	55	103	9	7	0		15		.253	.280	.310	86	-5	-7	36				.871	-5	*3	-1.1
1884	*NY-a	112	477	110	150	29	11	1		12		.314	.345	.428	158	27	29	72				.886	9	*3	3.5
1885	NY-N	88	359	48	92	14	5	2	44	4	28	.256	.264	.340	96	-3	-2	33				.885	2	*3/O	0.1
1886	NY-N	123	473	62	125	20	6	3	43	8	43	.264	.277	.351	89	-7	-8	51	13			**.895**	-3	*3	-0.7
1887	NY-a	26	101	11	17	1	0	0		6		.168	.222	.178	14	-11	-11	6	8			.950	-7	/1OS2	-1.5
1888	Ind-N	64	246	21	54	8	0	0	17	2	20	.220	.232	.252	55	-12	-13	17	11			.976	-3	1/3	-2.1
	Lou-a	23	93	9	21	6	0	0	7	3		.226	.265	.290	82	-2	-2	9	5			.962	0	1	-0.3
1889	Lou-a	11	44	8	14	3	0	0	9	5	2	.318	.400	.386	129	2	2	9	6			.931	-1	/1OSM	0.1
1890	NY-N	45	197	29	57	14	1	0	29	10	8	.289	.333	.371	107	1	1	29	12			.984	0	1	-0.1
1891	Bro-N	3	8	1	3	0	0	0	0	0	1	.375	.444	.375	143	0	0	1	0			1.000	-1	/O2	0.0
Total	11	701	2837	387	741	120	34	6	203	70	129	.261	.284	.334	95	-18	-18	297	55			.884	-2	31/O2SC	-2.7

■ FRANK ESTRADA
Estrada, Francisco (Soto) b: 2/12/48, Navojoa, Sonora, Mex. BR/TR, 5'8", 182 lbs. Deb: 9/14/71

1971	NY-N	1	2	0	1	0	0	0	0	0	0	.500	.500	.500	187	0	0	1	0	0	0	1.000	-1	/C	-0.1

■ ANDY ETCHEBARREN
Etchebarren, Andrew Auguste b: 6/20/43, Whittier, Cal. BR/TR, 6'1", 197 lbs. Deb: 9/26/62 C

1962	Bal-A	2	6	0	2	0	0	0	1	0	2	.333	.333	.333	84	-0	-0	1	0	0	0	.875	-1	/C	-0.1
1965	Bal-A	5	6	1	1	0	0	1	4	0	2	.167	.167	.667	123	0	0	1	0	0	0	1.000	3	/C	0.3
1966	*Bal-A☆	121	412	49	91	14	6	11	50	38	106	.221	.295	.364	89	-7	-6	42	0	1	-1	.989	-4	*C	-0.2
1967	Bal-A☆	112	330	29	71	13	0	7	35	38	80	.215	.300	.318	83	-7	-6	31	1	0	0	.989	0	*C	0.0
1968	Bal-A	74	189	20	44	11	2	5	20	19	46	.233	.313	.392	112	3	3	23	0	0	0	.998	9	C	1.7
1969	*Bal-A	73	217	29	54	9	2	3	26	28	42	.249	.353	.350	96	0	-0	25	1	2	-1	.990	2	C	0.5
1970	*Bal-A	78	230	19	56	10	1	4	28	21	41	.243	.315	.348	82	-5	-6	24	4	1	1	.984	2	C	0.0
1971	*Bal-A	70	222	21	60	8	0	9	29	16	40	.270	.322	.428	112	2	3	28	1	4	-2	.986	2	C	0.5
1972	Bal-A	71	188	11	38	6	1	2	21	17	43	.202	.279	.277	64	-8	-8	14	0	2	-1	.992	7	C	-0.1
1973	*Bal-A	54	152	16	39	9	1	2	23	12	21	.257	.319	.368	94	-1	-1	16	1	1	-0	.991	2	C	0.2
1974	*Bal-A	62	180	13	40	8	0	2	15	6	26	.222	.251	.300	60	-10	-9	13	1	0	0	.976	6	C	-0.1
1975	Bal-A	8	20	0	4	1	0	0	3	0	3	.200	.200	.250	28	-2	-2	1	0	0	0	1.000	0	/C	-0.1
	Cal-A	31	100	10	28	0	1	3	17	14	19	.280	.368	.390	123	2	3	15	1	0	0	.981	-4	C	0.1
	Yr	39	120	10	32	1	1	3	20	14	22	.267	.343	.367	108	0	1	15	1	0	0	.983	-3	C	0.0
1976	Cal-A	103	247	15	56	9	1	0	21	24	37	.227	.305	.271	74	-9	-7	20	0	2	-1	.980	6	*C	0.0
1977	Cal-A	80	114	11	29	2	2	0	14	12	19	.254	.325	.307	77	-4	-3	12	3	1	0	.987	1	C	-0.1
1978	Mil-A	4	5	1	2	1	0	0	2	1	2	.400	.500	.600	207	1	1	2	0	0	0	1.000	2	/C	0.3
Total	15	948	2618	245	615	101	17	49	309	246	529	.235	.308	.343	88	-44	-40	268	13	14	-5	.987	32	C	2.9

■ BUCK ETCHISON
Etchison, Clarence Hampton b: 1/27/15, Baltimore, Md. d: 1/24/80, E.New Market, Md. BL/TL, 6'1", 190 lbs. Deb: 9/22/43

1943	Bos-N	10	19	2	6	3	0	0	2	2	2	.316	.381	.474	148	1	1	4	0			.956	-1	/1	0.0
1944	Bos-N	109	308	30	66	16	0	8	33	33	50	.214	.292	.344	76	-9	-11	32	1			.993	-1	1	-1.6
Total	2	119	327	32	72	19	0	8	35	35	52	.220	.298	.352	79	-8	-10	35	1			.991	-2	/1	-1.6

■ BOBBY ETHERIDGE
Etheridge, Bobby Lamar "Luke" b: 11/25/42, Greenville, Miss. BR/TR, 5'9", 170 lbs. Deb: 7/16/67

1967	SF-N	40	115	13	26	7	2	1	15	7	12	.226	.299	.348	86	-2	-2	12	0	0	0	.925	-1	3	-0.4
1969	SF-N	56	131	13	34	9	0	1	10	19	26	.260	.358	.351	101	0	1	15	0	0	0	.899	-2	3/S	-0.2
Total	2	96	246	26	60	16	2	2	25	26	38	.244	.331	.350	94	-2	-1	27	0	0	0	.911	-4	/3S	-0.6

■ NICK ETTEN
Etten, Nicholas Raymond Thomas b: 9/19/13, Spring Grove, Ill. d: 10/18/90, Hinsdale, Ill. BL/TL, 6'2", 198 lbs. Deb: 9/08/38

1938	Phi-A	22	81	6	21	6	2	0	11	9	7	.259	.333	.383	81	-3	-2	11	1	0	0	.987	-2	1	-0.6
1939	Phi-A	43	155	20	39	11	2	3	29	16	11	.252	.322	.406	87	-4	-3	20	0	0	0	.990	-3	1	-1.0
1941	Phi-N	151	540	78	168	27	4	14	79	82	33	.311	.405	.454	147	32	35	104	9			.984	-3	*1	2.1
1942	Phi-N	139	459	37	121	21	3	8	41	67	26	.264	.357	.375	120	10	12	65	3			.985	1	*1	0.5

YEAR	TM/L	G	AB	R	H	2B	3B	HR	RBI	BB	SO	AVG	OBP	SLG	PRO+	BR	/A	RC	SB	CS	SBR	FA	FR	POS	TPR
1943	*NY-A	154	583	78	158	35	5	14	107	76	31	.271	.355	.420	126	19	19	89	3	7	-3	.989	-11	*1	-0.5
1944	NY-A	154	573	88	168	25	4	**22**	91	**97**	29	.293	.399	.466	142	37	35	114	4	2	0	.989	4	*1	3.2
1945	NY-A†	152	565	77	161	24	4	18	**111**	90	23	.285	.387	.437	133	30	27	98	2	3	-1	.989	-9	*1	0.6
1946	NY-A	108	323	37	75	14	1	9	49	38	35	.232	.315	.365	88	-5	-5	39	0	1	-1	.991	-0	1	-1.2
1947	Phi-N	14	41	5	10	4	0	1	8	5	4	.244	.326	.415	99	-0	-0	5	0			.990	1	1	0.1
Total	9	937	3320	426	921	167	25	89	526	480	199	.277	.371	.423	125	116	116	544	22	13		.988	-22	1	3.2

■ FRED EUNICK
Eunick, Fernandas Bowen b: 4/22/1892, Baltimore, Md. d: 12/9/59, Baltimore, Md. BR/TR, 5'6", 148 lbs. Deb: 8/29/17

YEAR	TM/L	G	AB	R	H	2B	3B	HR	RBI	BB	SO	AVG	OBP	SLG	PRO+	BR	/A	RC	SB	CS	SBR	FA	FR	POS	TPR
1917	Cle-A	1	2	0	0	0	0	0	0	0	0	.000	.000	.000	-93	-0	-0	0	0			1.000	-0	/3	-0.1

■ TONY EUSEBIO
Eusebio, Raul Antonio Bare (b: Raul Antontio Bare (Eusebio)) b: 4/27/67, San Jose De Los Llamos, D.R. BR/TR, 6'2", 180 lbs. Deb: 8/08/91

YEAR	TM/L	G	AB	R	H	2B	3B	HR	RBI	BB	SO	AVG	OBP	SLG	PRO+	BR	/A	RC	SB	CS	SBR	FA	FR	POS	TPR
1991	Hou-N	10	19	4	2	1	0	0	0	6	8	.105	.320	.158	41	-1	-1	1	0	0	0	.981	2	/C	0.2

■ FRANK EUSTACE
Eustace, Frank John b: 11/7/1873, New York, N.Y. d: 10/20/32, Pottsville, Pa. 5'9", 160 lbs. Deb: 4/17/1896

YEAR	TM/L	G	AB	R	H	2B	3B	HR	RBI	BB	SO	AVG	OBP	SLG	PRO+	BR	/A	RC	SB	CS	SBR	FA	FR	POS	TPR
1896	Lou-N	25	100	18	17	2	2	1	11	6	14	.170	.217	.260	28	-11	-10	7	4			.841	-5	S/2	-1.2

■ EVANS
Evans Deb: 6/01/1875

YEAR	TM/L	G	AB	R	H	2B	3B	HR	RBI	BB	SO	AVG	OBP	SLG	PRO+	BR	/A	RC	SB	CS	SBR	FA	FR	POS	TPR
1875	NH-n	1	4	1	2	1	0	0		0		.500	.500	.750	374	1	1	2						/O	0.1

■ AL EVANS
Evans, Alfred Hubert b: 9/28/16, Kenly, N.C. d: 4/6/79, Wilson, N.C. BR/TR, 5'11", 190 lbs. Deb: 9/13/39

YEAR	TM/L	G	AB	R	H	2B	3B	HR	RBI	BB	SO	AVG	OBP	SLG	PRO+	BR	/A	RC	SB	CS	SBR	FA	FR	POS	TPR
1939	Was-A	7	21	2	7	0	0	0	1	5	2	.333	.462	.333	115	1	1	4	0	0	0	.964	-1	/C	0.1
1940	Was-A	14	25	1	8	2	0	0	7	6	7	.320	.452	.400	131	1	2	6	1	0	0	1.000	-1	/C	0.2
1941	Was-A	53	159	16	44	8	4	1	19	9	18	.277	.315	.396	91	-3	-2	19	0	3	-2	.969	2	C	0.1
1942	Was-A	74	223	22	51	4	1	0	10	25	36	.229	.309	.256	60	-11	-11	19	3	0	1	.961	-3	C	-0.9
1944	Was-A	14	22	5	2	0	0	0	0	2	6	.091	.167	.091	-27	-4	-3	0	0	0	0	.933	-1	/C	-0.5
1945	Was-A	51	150	19	39	11	2	2	19	17	22	.260	.339	.400	125	3	4	21	2	1	0	.973	-6	C	0.0
1946	Was-A	88	272	30	69	10	4	2	30	30	28	.254	.332	.342	94	-4	-2	32	1	2	-1	.966	-12	C	-1.1
1947	Was-A	99	319	17	77	8	3	2	23	28	25	.241	.303	.304	71	-13	-12	29	2	1	0	.989	-2	C	-0.8
1948	Was-A	93	228	19	59	6	3	2	28	38	20	.259	.367	.338	91	-3	-2	29	1	1	-0	.983	-3	C	0.0
1949	Was-A	109	321	32	87	12	3	2	42	50	19	.271	.369	.346	92	-4	-3	45	4	1	1	**.992**	-16	*C	-1.1
1950	Was-A	90	289	24	68	8	3	2	30	29	21	.235	.309	.304	61	-19	-17	28	0	0	0	.987	-13	C	-2.5
1951	Bos-A	12	24	1	3	1	0	0	2	4	2	.125	.250	.167	13	-3	-3	1	0	0	0	1.000	1	C	-0.2
Total	12	704	2053	188	514	70	23	13	211	243	206	.250	.332	.326	82	-59	-49	234	14	9	-1	.979	-56	C	-6.7

■ BARRY EVANS
Evans, Barry Steven b: 11/30/56, Atlanta, Ga. BR/TR, 6'1", 180 lbs. Deb: 9/04/78

YEAR	TM/L	G	AB	R	H	2B	3B	HR	RBI	BB	SO	AVG	OBP	SLG	PRO+	BR	/A	RC	SB	CS	SBR	FA	FR	POS	TPR
1978	SD-N	24	90	7	24	1	1	0	4	4	10	.267	.298	.300	73	-4	-3	8	0	0	0	.947	1	3	-0.2
1979	SD-N	56	162	9	35	5	0	1	14	5	16	.216	.240	.265	40	-14	-13	10	0	2	-1	.952	11	3/S2	-0.3
1980	SD-N	73	125	11	29	3	2	1	14	17	21	.232	.324	.312	83	-3	-2	14	1	1	-0	.983	-3	32/S1	-0.5
1981	SD-N	54	93	11	30	5	0	0	7	9	9	.323	.382	.376	125	2	3	12	2	2	-1	.969	-4	31/2S	-0.2
1982	NY-A	17	31	2	8	3	0	0	2	6	6	.258	.395	.355	109	1	1	5	0	0	0	1.000	1	/23S	0.2
Total	5	224	501	40	126	17	3	2	41	41	62	.251	.309	.309	77	-18	-15	49	3	5	-2	.960	7	3/2S1	-1.0

■ DARRELL EVANS
Evans, Darrell Wayne b: 5/26/47, Pasadena, Cal. BL/TR, 6'2", 205 lbs. Deb: 4/20/69 C

YEAR	TM/L	G	AB	R	H	2B	3B	HR	RBI	BB	SO	AVG	OBP	SLG	PRO+	BR	/A	RC	SB	CS	SBR	FA	FR	POS	TPR
1969	Atl-N	12	26	3	6	0	0	0	1	1	8	.231	.259	.231	38	-2	-2	2	0	0	0	.917	-2	/3	-0.4
1970	Atl-N	12	44	4	14	1	1	0	9	7	5	.318	.423	.386	112	2	1	7	0	0	0	.941	-1	3	0.0
1971	Atl-N	89	260	42	63	11	1	12	38	39	54	.242	.343	.431	111	6	4	39	2	3	-1	.937	4	3/O	0.7
1972	Atl-N	125	418	67	106	12	0	19	71	90	58	.254	.391	.419	119	20	15	76	4	2	0	.941	9	*3	2.4
1973	Atl-N★	161	595	114	167	25	8	41	104	**124**	104	.281	.407	.556	153	55	49	**143**	6	3	0	.953	8	*31	5.6
1974	Atl-N	160	571	99	137	21	3	25	79	**126**	88	.240	.383	.419	119	23	19	100	4	2	0	.955	16	*3	3.5
1975	Atl-N	156	567	82	138	22	2	22	73	105	106	.243	.364	.406	109	12	10	91	12	3	2	.938	23	*3/1	3.5
1976	Atl-N	44	139	11	24	0	0	1	10	30	33	.173	.320	.194	45	-8	-9	11	3	0	1	.994	0	1/3	-1.1
	SF-N	92	257	42	57	9	1	10	36	42	38	.222	.331	.381	99	1	0	36	6	1	1	.991	9	1/3	0.5
	Yr	136	396	53	81	9	1	11	46	72	71	.205	.327	.316	80	-7	-9	46	9	1	2	.992	9	*13	-0.6
1977	SF-N	144	461	64	117	18	3	17	72	69	50	.254	.355	.416	106	5	5	71	9	6	-1	.937	-6	O13	-0.6
1978	SF-N	159	547	82	133	24	2	20	78	105	64	.243	.365	.404	119	13	16	87	4	5	-2	.952	10	*3	2.3
1979	SF-N	160	562	68	142	23	2	17	70	91	80	.253	.359	.391	112	6	11	83	6	7	-2	.943	**22**	*3	3.0
1980	SF-N	154	556	69	147	23	0	20	78	83	65	.264	.362	.414	119	14	15	87	17	5	2	.946	17	*31	3.3
1981	SF-N	102	357	51	92	13	4	12	48	54	33	.258	.358	.417	122	10	11	56	2	3	-1	.953	7	31	1.5
1982	SF-N	141	465	64	119	20	4	16	61	77	64	.256	.364	.419	119	13	13	74	5	4	-1	.933	-2	31S	0.7
1983	SF-N★	142	523	94	145	29	3	30	82	84	81	.277	.379	.516	151	33	35	104	6	6	-2	.993	1	*13/S	2.9
1984	*Det-A	131	401	60	93	11	1	16	63	77	70	.232	.356	.384	105	5	5	58	2	2	-1	.997	2	D13	0.4
1985	Det-A	151	505	81	125	17	0	**40**	94	85	85	.248	.357	.519	137	25	26	96	0	4	-2	.984	11	*1D/3	2.7
1986	Det-A	151	507	78	122	15	0	29	85	91	105	.241	.357	.442	116	13	13	85	3	2	-0	.998	11	*1D/3	1.5
1987	*Det-A	150	499	90	128	20	0	34	99	100	84	.257	.383	.501	138	25	28	103	6	5	-1	.997	12	*1D/3	3.0
1988	Det-A	144	437	48	91	9	0	22	64	84	89	.208	.337	.380	104	2	4	57	1	4	-2	.993	5	D1	0.1
1989	Atl-N	107	276	31	57	6	1	11	39	41	46	.207	.309	.355	87	-4	-4	33	0	1	-1	.985	6	13	-0.3
Total	21	2687	8973	1344	2223	329	36	414	1354	1605	1410	.248	.364	.431	119	268	266	1499	98	68	-11	.946	161	*31D/OS	35.2

■ DWIGHT EVANS
Evans, Dwight Michael "Dewey" b: 11/3/51, Santa Monica, Cal. BR/TR, 6'2", 205 lbs. Deb: 9/16/72

YEAR	TM/L	G	AB	R	H	2B	3B	HR	RBI	BB	SO	AVG	OBP	SLG	PRO+	BR	/A	RC	SB	CS	SBR	FA	FR	POS	TPR
1972	Bos-A	18	57	2	15	3	1	1	6	7	13	.263	.344	.404	115	2	1	8	0	0	0	1.000	1	O	0.2
1973	Bos-A	119	282	46	63	13	1	10	32	40	52	.223	.322	.383	92	-1	-3	36	5	0	2	.995	-6	*O/D	-1.1
1974	Bos-A	133	463	60	130	19	8	10	70	38	77	.281	.338	.421	110	10	6	65	4	4	-1	.990	11	*O/D	1.1
1975	*Bos-A	128	412	61	113	24	6	13	56	47	60	.274	.354	.456	118	15	10	66	3	4	-2	.987	18	*O/D	2.3
1976	Bos-A	146	501	61	121	34	5	17	62	57	92	.242	.326	.431	107	12	5	69	6	7	-2	**.994**	9	*O/D	0.6
1977	Bos-A	73	230	39	66	9	2	14	36	28	58	.287	.364	.526	125	12	9	45	4	2	0	.992	-2	O/D	0.4
1978	Bos-A★	147	497	75	123	24	2	24	63	65	119	.247	.337	.449	108	12	5	74	8	5	-1	.982	8	*O/D	0.7
1979	Bos-A	152	489	69	134	24	1	21	58	69	76	.274	.365	.456	114	14	11	79	6	9	-4	.988	10	*O	1.1
1980	Bos-A	148	463	72	123	37	5	18	60	64	98	.266	.361	.484	123	19	16	85	3	1	0	.982	2	*O/D	1.3
1981	Bos-A★	108	412	84	122	19	4	**22**	71	**85**	85	.296	.418	.522	160	**40**	**37**	**95**	3	2	-0	.993	14	*O	4.7
1982	Bos-A	162	609	122	178	37	7	32	98	112	125	.292	**.403**	.534	146	48	44	134	3	2	-0	.973	6	*O/D	4.4
1983	Bos-A	126	470	74	112	19	4	22	58	70	97	.238	.339	.436	104	8	3	71	3	0	1	.987	7	OD	0.8
1984	Bos-A	162	630	**121**	186	37	8	32	104	96	115	.295	.392	.532	146	47	43	**132**	3	1	0	.994	2	*O/D	3.9
1985	Bos-A	159	617	110	162	29	1	29	78	**114**	105	.263	.382	.454	123	27	23	112	7	2	1	.990	3	*O/D	2.1
1986	*Bos-A	152	529	86	137	33	2	26	97	97	117	.259	.380	.476	131	25	25	100	3	3	-1	.983	5	*O/D	2.3
1987	Bos-A★	154	541	109	165	37	2	34	123	**106**	98	.305	.422	.569	155	50	47	134	4	6	-2	.982	-7	1O/D	2.8
1988	*Bos-A	149	559	96	164	31	7	21	111	76	99	.293	.379	.487	135	31	28	104	5	1	1	.987	-6	O1/D	1.5
1989	Bos-A	146	520	82	148	27	3	20	100	99	84	.285	.402	.463	135	33	29	100	3	3	-1	.981	2	OD	2.8
1990	*Bos-A	123	445	66	111	18	3	13	63	67	73	.249	.353	.391	103	6	3	60	3	4	-2	.000	0	*D	0.2
1991	Bal-A	101	270	35	73	9	1	6	38	54	54	.270	.396	.378	120	8	10	43	2	3	-1	.984	0	OD	0.7
Total	20	2606	8996	1470	2446	483	73	385	1384	1391	1697	.272	.373	.470	126	418	351	1611	78	59	-12	.987	76	*OD1	32.8

■ JOE EVANS
Evans, Joseph Patton "Doc" b: 5/15/1895, Meridian, Miss. d: 8/9/53, Gulfport, Miss. BR/TR, 5'9", 160 lbs. Deb: 7/03/15

YEAR	TM/L	G	AB	R	H	2B	3B	HR	RBI	BB	SO	AVG	OBP	SLG	PRO+	BR	/A	RC	SB	CS	SBR	FA	FR	POS	TPR
1915	Cle-A	42	109	17	28	4	2	0	11	22	18	.257	.382	.330	111	3	2	17	6	1	1	.885	-0	3/2	0.5
1916	Cle-A	33	82	4	12	1	0	0	1	7	12	.146	.213	.159	11	-9	-9	4	4			.915	4	3	-0.5
1917	Cle-A	132	385	36	73	4	5	2	33	42	44	.190	.271	.242	53	-20	-23	31	12			.939	3	*3	-2.0

YEAR	TM/L	G	AB	R	H	2B	3B	HR	RBI	BB	SO	AVG	OBP	SLG	PRO+	BR	/A	RC	SB	CS	SBR	FA	FR	POS	TPR
1918	Cle-A	79	243	38	64	6	7	1	22	30	29	.263	.344	.358	102	4	1	32	7			.932	4	3	0.7
1919	Cle-A	21	14	9	1	0	0	0	0	2	1	.071	.188	.071	-24	-2	-2	0	1			.923	4	/S	0.1
1920	*Cle-A	56	172	32	60	9	9	0	23	15	3	.349	.404	.506	136	10	9	36	6	2	1	.966	-3	O/S	0.5
1921	Cle-A	57	153	36	51	11	0	0	21	19	5	.333	.410	.405	107	3	3	27	4	1	1	.933	-1	O	0.0
1922	Cle-A	75	145	35	39	6	2	0	22	8	4	.269	.307	.338	67	-7	-7	16	11	2	2	.969	-7	O	-1.4
1923	Was-A	106	372	42	98	15	3	0	38	27	18	.263	.313	.320	70	-18	-15	38	6	5	-1	.982	-4	O3/1	-2.3
1924	StL-A	77	209	30	53	3	3	0	19	24	12	.254	.330	.297	59	-11	-13	21	1	4	-2	.969	2	O	-1.6
1925	StL-A	55	159	27	50	12	0	0	20	16	6	.314	.377	.390	90	-1	-2	25	6	2	1	1.000	4	O	0.0
Total	11	733	2043	306	529	71	31	3	210	212	152	.259	.329	.328	79	-49	-58	247	64	17		.971	5	O3/S12	-6.0

■ STEVE EVANS Evans, Louis Richard b: 2/17/1885, Cleveland, Ohio d: 12/28/43, Cleveland, Ohio BL/TL, 5'10", 175 lbs. Deb: 4/16/08

YEAR	TM/L	G	AB	R	H	2B	3B	HR	RBI	BB	SO	AVG	OBP	SLG	PRO+	BR	/A	RC	SB	CS	SBR	FA	FR	POS	TPR
1908	NY-N	2	2	0	1	0	0	0	0	0		.500	.500	.500	210	0	0	0	0			.000	-1	/O	0.0
1909	StL-N	143	498	67	129	17	6	2	56	66		.259	.362	.329	122	11	15	65	14			.947	-4	*O/1	0.6
1910	StL-N	151	506	73	122	21	8	2	73	78	63	.241	.376	.326	109	8	11	66	10			.968	-6	*O1	-0.2
1911	StL-N	154	547	74	161	24	13	5	71	46	52	.294	.369	.413	122	14	16	88	13			.972	-2	*O	0.6
1912	StL-N	135	491	59	139	23	9	6	72	36	51	.283	.353	.403	109	4	6	73	11			.942	-0	*O	-0.1
1913	StL-N	97	245	18	61	15	6	1	31	20	28	.249	.321	.371	99	-1	-1	29	5			.983	-6	O/1	-1.0
1914	Bro-F	145	514	93	179	41	**15**	12	96	50	49	.348	.416	**.556**	**177**	50	50	130	18			.941	-5	*O1	4.1
1915	Bro-F	63	216	44	64	14	4	3	30	35	22	.296	.411	.440	151	15	15	43	7			.960	-2	O/1	1.1
	Bal-F	88	340	50	107	20	6	1	37	28	34	.315	.379	.418	130	15	13	58	8			.925	-6	O/1	0.4
	Yr	151	556	94	171	**34**	10	4	67	63	56	.308	.392	.426	138	30	29	102	15			.940	-8	*O/1	1.5
Total	8	978	3359	478	963	175	67	32	466	359	299	.287	.374	.407	128	116	126	554	86			.955	-31	O/1	5.5

■ JAKE EVANS Evans, Uriah L. P. "Bloody Jake" b: 9/1856, Baltimore, Md. d: 1/16/07, Baltimore, Md. TR , 5'8", 154 lbs. Deb: 5/01/1879

YEAR	TM/L	G	AB	R	H	2B	3B	HR	RBI	BB	SO	AVG	OBP	SLG	PRO+	BR	/A	RC	SB	CS	SBR	FA	FR	POS	TPR
1879	Tro-N	72	280	30	65	9	5	0	17	5	18	.232	.246	.300	84	-6	-4	21				.884	18	*O	1.0
1880	Tro-N	47	180	31	46	8	1	0	22	7	15	.256	.283	.311	96	0	-1	16				.906	0	O/P	-0.2
1881	Tro-N	83	315	35	76	11	5	0	28	14	30	.241	.274	.308	78	-6	-8	27				.926	14	*O	0.3
1882	Wor-N	80	334	33	71	10	4	0	25	7	22	.213	.229	.266	57	-15	-16	21				.910	20	*OS/32P	0.4
1883	Cle-N	90	332	36	79	13	2	0	31	8	38	.238	.256	.289	66	-13	-13	25				.902	6	*O/S32P	-0.7
1884	Cle-N	80	313	32	81	18	3	1	38	15	49	.259	.293	.345	97	-0	-2	32				**.917**	8	*O/2S	0.4
1885	Bal-a	20	77	18	17	1	1	0		7		.221	.318	.260	88	-1	-0	7				.894	2	O	0.1
Total	7	472	1831	215	435	70	21	1	161	63	172	.238	.264	.300	78	-41	-44	150				.907	67	O/S23P	1.3

■ BILL EVERETT Everett, William L. "Wild Bill" b: 12/13/1868, Ft.Wayne, Ind. d: 1/19/38, Denver, Colo. BL/TR, 6'0.5", 185 lbs. Deb: 4/18/1895

YEAR	TM/L	G	AB	R	H	2B	3B	HR	RBI	BB	SO	AVG	OBP	SLG	PRO+	BR	/A	RC	SB	CS	SBR	FA	FR	POS	TPR
1895	Chi-N	133	550	129	197	16	10	3	88	33	42	.358	.399	.440	111	15	9	119	47			.854	-8	*3/2	0.2
1896	Chi-N	132	575	130	184	16	13	2	46	41	43	.320	.367	.403	101	4	0	105	46			.882	-10	*3O	-0.9
1897	Chi-N	92	379	63	119	14	7	5	39	36		.314	.373	.427	107	6	3	73	26			.864	-5	3/O	0.0
1898	Chi-N	149	596	102	190	15	6	0	69	53		.319	.377	.364	113	11	11	96	28			.974	-2	*1	0.8
1899	Chi-N	136	536	87	166	17	5	1	74	31		.310	.351	.366	99	-3	-1	83	30			.971	8	*1	0.7
1900	Chi-N	23	91	10	24	4	0	0	17	3		.264	.287	.308	67	-5	-4	9	2			.979	-1	1	-0.5
1901	Was-A	33	115	14	22	3	2	0	8	15		.191	.301	.252	55	-7	-6	12	7			.967	-4	1	-1.0
Total	7	698	2842	535	902	85	43	11	341	212	85	.317	.368	.389	103	22	13	497	186			.973	-23	13/O2	-0.7

■ JOHNNY EVERS Evers, John Joseph "Crab" or "Trojan" b: 7/21/1881, Troy, N.Y. d: 3/28/47, Albany, N.Y. BL/TR, 5'9", 125 lbs. Deb: 9/01/02 FMCH

YEAR	TM/L	G	AB	R	H	2B	3B	HR	RBI	BB	SO	AVG	OBP	SLG	PRO+	BR	/A	RC	SB	CS	SBR	FA	FR	POS	TPR
1902	Chi-N	26	90	7	20	0	0	0	2	3		.222	.263	.222	51	-5	-5	6	1			.990	-0	2/S	-0.4
1903	Chi-N	124	464	70	136	27	7	0	52	19		.293	.325	.381	104	-1	1	68	25			.937	-14	*2S/3	-0.8
1904	Chi-N	152	532	49	141	14	7	0	47	28		.265	.307	.318	93	-5	-5	64	26			.943	31	*2	3.2
1905	Chi-N	99	340	44	94	11	2	1	37	27		.276	.333	.329	94	-1	-2	47	19			.937	3	2	0.2
1906	*Chi-N	154	533	65	136	17	6	1	51	36		.255	.305	.315	89	-5	-8	70	49			.947	6	*2/3	-0.1
1907	*Chi-N	151	508	66	127	18	4	2	51	38		.250	.309	.313	89	-3	-7	66	46			.964	**29**	*2	2.4
1908	*Chi-N	126	416	83	125	19	6	0	37	66		.300	.402	.375	143	26	24	79	36			.960	-0	*2/O	2.6
1909	Chi-N	127	463	88	122	19	6	1	24	73		.263	.369	.337	116	13	12	68	28			.942	1	*2	1.2
1910	Chi-N	125	433	87	114	11	7	0	28	108	18	.263	.413	.321	115	15	16	70	28			.950	-4	*2	1.0
1911	Chi-N	46	155	29	35	4	3	0	7	34	10	.226	.372	.290	86	-1	-1	19	6			.975	-6	23	-0.8
1912	Chi-N	143	478	73	163	23	11	1	63	74	18	.341	**.431**	.441	139	29	29	98	16			.959	6	*2	3.1
1913	Chi-N	136	446	81	127	20	5	3	49	50	14	.285	.361	.372	109	7	6	64	11			.960	**30**	*2M	3.5
1914	*Bos-N	139	491	81	137	20	3	1	40	87	26	.279	.390	.338	118	15	15	72	12			**.976**	5	*2	2.1
1915	Bos-N	83	278	38	73	4	1	1	22	50	16	.263	.375	.295	109	4	6	35	7	8	-3	.959	-1	2	0.3
1916	Bos-N	71	241	33	52	4	1	0	15	40	19	.216	.330	.241	80	-5	-3	23	5			.951	-18	2	-2.2
1917	Bos-N	24	83	5	16	0	0	0	0	13	8	.193	.302	.193	56	-4	-3	5	1			.950	-7	2	-1.1
	Phi-N	56	183	20	41	5	1	1	12	30	13	.224	.333	.279	85	-1	-2	19	8			.983	-5	2/3	-0.5
	Yr	80	266	25	57	5	1	1	12	43	21	.214	.324	.252	77	-5	-5	24	9			.973	-12	2/3	-1.6
1922	Chi-A	1	3	0	0	0	0	0	1	2	0	.000	.400	.000	12	-0	-0	0	0	0	0	1.000	-0	/2	0.0
1929	Bos-N	1	0	0	0	0	0	0	0	0	0	—	—	—	—	0	0	0	0			.000	-1	/2	-0.1
Total	18	1784	6137	919	1659	216	70	12	538	778	142	.270	.356	.334	106	80	74	875	324	8		.955	55	*2/3SO	13.6

■ JOE EVERS Evers, Joseph Francis b: 9/10/1891, Troy, N.Y. d: 1/4/49, Albany, N.Y. BR/TR, 5'9", 135 lbs. Deb: 4/24/13 F

YEAR	TM/L	G	AB	R	H	2B	3B	HR	RBI	BB	SO	AVG	OBP	SLG	PRO+	BR	/A	RC	SB	CS	SBR	FA	FR	POS	TPR
1913	NY-N	1	0	0	0	0	0	0	0	0	0	—	—	—	—	0	0	0	0			.000	0	R	0.0

■ TOM EVERS Evers, Thomas Francis b: 3/31/1852, Troy, N.Y. d: 3/23/25, Washington, D.C. TL , Deb: 5/25/1882

YEAR	TM/L	G	AB	R	H	2B	3B	HR	RBI	BB	SO	AVG	OBP	SLG	PRO+	BR	/A	RC	SB	CS	SBR	FA	FR	POS	TPR
1882	Bal-a	1	4	0	0	0	0	0		0		.000	.000	.000	-99	-1	-1	0				.500	-2	/2	-0.3
1884	Was-U	109	427	54	99	6	1	0		7		.232	.244	.251	70	-14	-12	27				.869	11	*2	0.2
Total	2	110	431	54	99	6	1	0		7		.230	.242	.248	68	-15	-13	27				.866	9	2	-0.1

■ HOOT EVERS Evers, Walter Arthur b: 2/8/21, St.Louis, Mo. d: 1/25/91, Houston, Tex. BR/TR, 6'2", 185 lbs. Deb: 9/16/41 C

YEAR	TM/L	G	AB	R	H	2B	3B	HR	RBI	BB	SO	AVG	OBP	SLG	PRO+	BR	/A	RC	SB	CS	SBR	FA	FR	POS	TPR
1941	Det-A	1	4	0	0	0	0	0	0	0	2	.000	.000	.000	-91	-1	-1	0	0	0	0	.000	-0	/O	-0.2
1946	Det-A	81	304	42	81	8	4	4	33	34	43	.266	.344	.359	91	-1	-3	41	7	1	2	.975	0	O	-0.5
1947	Det-A	126	460	67	136	24	5	10	67	45	49	.296	.366	.435	119	13	12	73	8	7	-2	.978	8	*O	1.1
1948	Det-A★	139	538	81	169	33	6	10	103	51	31	.314	.378	.454	117	15	13	92	3	4	-2	.973	2	*O	0.6
1949	Det-A	132	432	68	131	21	6	7	72	70	38	.303	.403	.428	120	14	14	76	6	7	-2	.994	11	*O	1.6
1950	Det-A★	143	526	100	170	35	**11**	21	103	71	40	.323	.408	.551	139	34	31	116	5	9	-4	**.997**	8	*O	2.7
1951	Det-A	116	393	47	88	15	2	11	46	40	47	.224	.297	.356	76	-14	-15	40	5	3	-0	.976	-4	*O	-2.3
1952	Det-A	1	1	0	1	0	0	0	0	0	0	1.000	1.000	1.000	454	0	0	1	0	0	0	.000	0	H	0.0
	Bos-A	106	401	53	105	17	4	14	59	29	55	.262	.318	.429	99	2	-2	54	5	2	0	.974	-5	*O	-1.1
	Yr	107	402	53	106	17	4	14	59	29	55	.264	.320	.430	100	2	-2	55	5	2	0	.974	-5	*O	-1.1
1953	Bos-A	99	300	39	72	10	1	11	31	23	41	.240	.301	.390	81	-7	-9	35	2	1	0	.988	-7	O	-1.9
1954	Bos-A	6	8	1	0	0	0	0	0	0	2	.000	.000	.000	-90	-2	-2	0	0	0	0	1.000	-0	/O	-0.3
	NY-N	12	11	1	1	0	0	1	3	0	6	.091	.091	.364	12	-2	-2	0	0	0	0	1.000	-1	/O	-0.3
	Det-A	30	60	5	11	4	0	0	5	5	8	.183	.258	.250	40	-5	-5	4	1	0	0	1.000	-4	O	-0.9
1955	Bal-A	60	185	21	44	10	1	6	30	19	28	.238	.309	.400	96	-3	-2	21	2	1	0	.991	-4	O	-0.8
	Cle-A	39	66	10	19	7	1	2	9	3	12	.288	.319	.515	117	1	1	10	0	1	-1	1.000	-4	O	-0.4
	Yr	99	251	31	63	17	2	8	39	22	40	.251	.311	.430	101	-2	-1	30	2	2	-1	.993	-8	O	-1.2
1956	Cle-A	3	0	1	0	0	0	0	0	1	0	—	1.000	—	180	0	0	0	0	0	0	.000	0	H	0.0
	Bal-A	48	112	20	27	3	0	1	4	24	18	.241	.375	.295	85	-2	-1	15	1	0	0	.985	-3	O	-0.5

YEAR	TM/L	G	AB	R	H	2B	3B	HR	RBI	BB	SO	AVG	OBP	SLG	PRO+	BR	/A	RC	SB	CS	SBR	FA	FR	POS	TPR
	Yr	51	112	21	27	3	0	1	4	25	18	.241	.380	.295	86	-2	-1	15	1	0	0	.985	-3	O	-0.5
Total	12	1142	3801	556	1055	187	41	98	565	415	420	.278	.353	.426	106	41	29	578	45	36	-8	.983	-4	*O	-3.2

■ GEORGE EWELL
Ewell, George b: Philadelphia, Pa. Deb: 6/26/1871

YEAR	TM/L	G	AB	R	H	2B	3B	HR	RBI	BB	SO	AVG	OBP	SLG	PRO+	BR	/A	RC	SB	CS	SBR	FA	FR	POS	TPR
1871	Cle-n	1	3	0	0	0	0	0	0	0	0	.000	.000	.000	-99	-1	-1	0	0					/O	0.0

■ JOHN EWING
Ewing, John "Long Jong" b: 6/1/1863, Cincinnati, Ohio d: 4/23/1895, Denver, Colo. TR , Deb: 6/18/1883 F

YEAR	TM/L	G	AB	R	H	2B	3B	HR	RBI	BB	SO	AVG	OBP	SLG	PRO+	BR	/A	RC	SB	CS	SBR	FA	FR	POS	TPR
1883	StL-a	1	5	0	0	0	0	0		0		.000	.000	.000	-95	-1	-1	0				.333	-1	/O	-0.2
1884	Cin-U	1	4	0	0	0	0	0		0		.000	.000	.000	-93	-1	-1	0				1.000	-0	/O	-0.1
	Was-U	1	5	1	1	0	1	0		0		.200	.200	.600	166	0	0	1				.500	0	/O	0.0
	Yr	2	9	1	1	0	1	0		0		.111	.111	.333	44	-1	-1	0				.600	0	/O	-0.1
1888	Lou-a	21	79	6	16	1	1	0	5	1		.203	.213	.241	48	-5	-4	6	7			.907	0	P	0.0
1889	Lou-a	41	134	12	23	2	0	0	6	9	30	.172	.234	.187	22	-13	-13	7	5			.953	2	P/1	0.0
1890	NY-P	35	114	18	24	2	1	2	17	5	35	.211	.244	.298	42	-9	-11	9	2			.949	0	P	0.0
1891	NY-N	33	113	10	23	1	0	0	8	3	14	.204	.224	.212	30	-10	-9	6	4			.917	0	P	0.0
Total	6	133	454	47	87	6	3	2	36	18	79	.192	.226	.231	33	-39	-39	29	18			.935	2	P/O1	-0.3

■ REUBEN EWING
Ewing, Reuben (b: Reuben Cohen) b: 11/30/1899, Odessa, Russia d: 10/5/70, W.Hartford, Conn. BR/TR, 5'4.5", 150 lbs. Deb: 6/21/21

YEAR	TM/L	G	AB	R	H	2B	3B	HR	RBI	BB	SO	AVG	OBP	SLG	PRO+	BR	/A	RC	SB	CS	SBR	FA	FR	POS	TPR
1921	StL-N	3	1	0	0	0	0	0	0	0	1	.000	.000	.000	-99	-0	-0	0	0	0	0	1.000	1	/S	0.1

■ SAM EWING
Ewing, Samuel James b: 4/9/49, Lewisburg, Tenn. BL/TL, 6'3", 200 lbs. Deb: 9/11/73

YEAR	TM/L	G	AB	R	H	2B	3B	HR	RBI	BB	SO	AVG	OBP	SLG	PRO+	BR	/A	RC	SB	CS	SBR	FA	FR	POS	TPR
1973	Chi-A	11	20	1	3	1	0	0	2	2	6	.150	.227	.200	20	-2	-2	1	0	0	0	1.000	1	/1	-0.2
1976	Chi-A	19	41	3	9	2	1	0	2	2	8	.220	.256	.317	67	-2	-2	3	0	0	0	1.000	-0	D/1	-0.2
1977	Tor-A	97	244	24	70	8	2	4	34	19	42	.287	.338	.385	95	-1	-1	30	1	1	-0	.957	-5	OD/1	-0.8
1978	Tor-A	40	56	3	10	0	0	2	9	5	9	.179	.246	.286	48	-4	-4	4	0	0	0	1.000	-1	/OD	-0.5
Total	4	167	361	31	92	11	3	6	47	28	65	.255	.308	.352	81	-9	-9	39	1	1	-0	.959	-5	/OD1	-1.7

■ BUCK EWING
Ewing, William b: 10/17/1859, Hoaglands, Ohio d: 10/20/06, Cincinnati, Ohio BR/TR, 5'10", 188 lbs. Deb: 9/09/1880 FMH

YEAR	TM/L	G	AB	R	H	2B	3B	HR	RBI	BB	SO	AVG	OBP	SLG	PRO+	BR	/A	RC	SB	CS	SBR	FA	FR	POS	TPR
1880	Tro-N	13	45	1	8	1	0	0	5	1	3	.178	.196	.200	33	-3	-3	2				.864	-4	C/O	-0.7
1881	Tro-N	67	272	40	68	14	7	0	25	7	8	.250	.269	.353	89	-2	-4	26				.915	**25**	CS/O3	2.2
1882	Tro-N	74	328	67	89	16	11	2	29	10	15	.271	.293	.405	127	7	10	40				.887	14	3C/2O1P	2.3
1883	NY-N	88	376	90	114	11	13	**10**	41	20	14	.303	.338	.481	147	20	21	63				.922	1	CO2/S3	2.3
1884	NY-N	94	382	90	106	15	**20**	3	41	28	22	.277	.327	.445	137	17	16	57				.933	4	*CO/S3P	2.4
1885	NY-N	81	342	81	104	15	12	6	63	13	17	.304	.330	.471	159	20	21	54				.918	9	CO/3S1P	3.2
1886	NY-N	73	275	59	85	11	7	4	31	16	17	.309	.347	.444	138	12	12	50	18			.921	3	CO/1	1.8
1887	NY-N	77	318	83	97	17	13	6	44	30	33	.305	.370	.497	148	17	20	70	26			.863	-1	32/C	1.8
1888	*NY-N	103	415	83	127	18	15	6	58	24	28	.306	.348	.465	162	27	28	88	53			.947	6	C3/SP	3.9
1889	*NY-N	99	407	91	133	23	13	4	87	37	32	.327	.383	.477	141	21	21	89	34			.937	17	*C/PO	4.0
1890	NY-P	83	352	98	119	19	15	8	72	39	12	.338	.406	.545	142	26	20	95	36			**.949**	14	C/2PM	3.2
1891	NY-N	14	49	8	17	2	1	0	18	5	5	.347	.407	.429	152	3	3	11	5			.881	-3	/2C	0.1
1892	NY-N	105	393	58	122	10	15	8	76	38	26	.310	.371	.473	160	26	26	87	42			.974	8	1C/2	3.1
1893	Cle-N	116	500	117	172	28	15	6	122	41	18	.344	.394	.496	130	25	20	119	47			.927	-1	*O/21C	1.1
1894	Cle-N	53	211	32	53	12	4	2	39	24	9	.251	.328	.374	68	-11	-12	33	18			.912	-2	O/2	-1.4
1895	Cin-N	105	434	90	138	24	13	5	94	30	22	.318	.363	.468	111	8	5	88	34			.976	8	*1M	1.3
1896	Cin-N	69	263	41	73	14	4	1	38	29	13	.278	.349	.373	86	-3	-6	50	41			.980	4	1M	0.0
1897	Cin-N	1	1	0	0	0	0	0	0	0		.000	.500	.000	36	0	0	0	0			.800	-0	/1M	0.0
Total	18	1315	5363	1129	1625	250	178	71	883	392	294	.303	.351	.456	131	212	197	1022	354			.931	103	C1O3/2SP	30.6

■ ART EWOLDT
Ewoldt, Arthur Lee "Sheriff" b: 1/8/1894, Paullina, Iowa d: 12/8/77, Des Moines, Iowa BR/TR, 5'10", 165 lbs. Deb: 9/17/19

YEAR	TM/L	G	AB	R	H	2B	3B	HR	RBI	BB	SO	AVG	OBP	SLG	PRO+	BR	/A	RC	SB	CS	SBR	FA	FR	POS	TPR
1919	Phi-A	9	32	2	7	1	0	0	2	1	5	.219	.242	.250	38	-3	-3	2	0			1.000	0	/3	-0.2

■ HOMER EZZELL
Ezzell, Homer Estell b: 2/28/1896, Victoria, Tex. d: 8/3/76, San Antonio, Tex. BR/TR, 5'10", 158 lbs. Deb: 4/22/23

YEAR	TM/L	G	AB	R	H	2B	3B	HR	RBI	BB	SO	AVG	OBP	SLG	PRO+	BR	/A	RC	SB	CS	SBR	FA	FR	POS	TPR
1923	StL-A	88	279	31	68	6	0	0	14	15	20	.244	.287	.265	44	-22	-24	22	4	3	-1	.961	8	3/2	-1.1
1924	Bos-A	90	277	35	75	8	4	0	32	14	21	.271	.311	.329	65	-15	-15	29	12	5	1	.984	9	3S/C	0.1
1925	Bos-A	58	186	40	53	6	4	0	15	19	18	.285	.351	.360	81	-5	-5	24	9	7	-2	.916	-7	3/2	-1.0
Total	3	236	742	106	196	20	8	0	61	48	59	.264	.312	.313	61	-42	-44	75	25	15	-1	.957	10	3/S2C	-2.0

■ JAY FAATZ
Faatz, Jayson S. b: 10/24/1860, Weedsport, N.Y. d: 4/10/23, Syracuse, N.Y. BR/TR, 6'4", Deb: 8/22/1884 M

YEAR	TM/L	G	AB	R	H	2B	3B	HR	RBI	BB	SO	AVG	OBP	SLG	PRO+	BR	/A	RC	SB	CS	SBR	FA	FR	POS	TPR
1884	Pit-a	29	112	18	27	2	3	0		1		.241	.274	.313	92	-1	-1	10				.963	-1	1	-0.5
1888	Cle-a	120	470	73	124	10	2	0	51	12		.264	.312	.294	101	-1	1	65	64			**.989**	2	*1	-0.7
1889	Cle-N	117	442	50	102	12	5	2	38	17	28	.231	.275	.294	61	-24	-22	44	27			.981	6	*1	-2.1
1890	Buf-P	32	111	18	21	0	2	1	16	9	5	.189	.297	.252	53	-8	-6	9	2			.982	-3	1M	-0.8
Total	4	298	1135	159	274	24	12	3	105	39	33	.241	.293	.292	78	-33	-28	128	93			.982	4	1	-4.1

■ BUNNY FABRIQUE
Fabrique, Albert La Verne b: 12/23/1887, Clinton, Mich. d: 1/10/60, Ann Arbor, Mich. BB/TR, 5'8.5", 150 lbs. Deb: 10/04/16

YEAR	TM/L	G	AB	R	H	2B	3B	HR	RBI	BB	SO	AVG	OBP	SLG	PRO+	BR	/A	RC	SB	CS	SBR	FA	FR	POS	TPR
1916	Bro-N	2	2	0	0	0	0	0	0	0	1	.000	.000	.000	-97	-0	-0	0	0			1.000	0	/S	0.0
1917	Bro-N	25	88	8	18	3	0	1	3	8	9	.205	.271	.273	65	-3	-4	6	0			.874	-2	S	-0.6
Total	2	27	90	8	18	3	0	1	3	8	10	.200	.265	.267	62	-4	-4	6	0			.878	-2	/S	-0.6

■ LENNY FAEDO
Faedo, Leonardo Lago b: 5/13/60, Tampa, Fla. BR/TR, 6', 170 lbs. Deb: 9/06/80

YEAR	TM/L	G	AB	R	H	2B	3B	HR	RBI	BB	SO	AVG	OBP	SLG	PRO+	BR	/A	RC	SB	CS	SBR	FA	FR	POS	TPR
1980	Min-A	5	8	1	2	1	0	0	0	0	0	.250	.250	.375	64	-0	-0	1	0	0	0	.818	-1	/S	-0.1
1981	Min-A	12	41	3	8	0	1	0	6	1	5	.195	.214	.244	30	-4	-4	2	0	0	0	.971	2	S	-0.1
1982	Min-A	90	255	16	62	8	0	3	22	16	22	.243	.290	.310	63	-12	-13	22	1	0	0	.967	3	S/D	-0.2
1983	Min-A	51	173	16	48	7	0	1	18	4	19	.277	.294	.335	70	-7	-7	16	0	0	0	.954	-15	S	-1.8
1984	Min-A	16	52	6	13	1	0	1	6	4	3	.250	.304	.327	71	-2	-2	5	0	0	0	.968	-5	S/D	-0.6
Total	5	174	529	42	133	17	1	5	52	25	49	.251	.286	.316	64	-24	-27	46	1	0	0	.961	-16	S/D	-2.8

■ FRED FAGIN
Fagin, Frederick H. b: Cincinnati, Ohio Deb: 6/25/1895

YEAR	TM/L	G	AB	R	H	2B	3B	HR	RBI	BB	SO	AVG	OBP	SLG	PRO+	BR	/A	RC	SB	CS	SBR	FA	FR	POS	TPR
1895	StL-N	1	3	0	1	0	0	0	2	0	0	.333	.333	.333	75	-0	-0	0	0			.636	0	/C	0.0

■ FRANK FAHEY
Fahey, Francis Raymond b: 1/22/1896, Milford, Mass. d: 3/19/54, Boston, Mass. BB/TR, 6'1", 190 lbs. Deb: 4/25/18

YEAR	TM/L	G	AB	R	H	2B	3B	HR	RBI	BB	SO	AVG	OBP	SLG	PRO+	BR	/A	RC	SB	CS	SBR	FA	FR	POS	TPR
1918	Phi-A	10	17	2	3	1	0	0	1	0	3	.176	.176	.235	24	-2	-2	1	0			1.000	-2	/OP	-0.4

■ HOWARD FAHEY
Fahey, Howard Simpson "Cap" or "Kid" b: 6/24/1892, Medford, Mass. d: 10/24/71, Clearwater, Fla. BR/TR, 5'7.5", 145 lbs. Deb: 7/23/12

YEAR	TM/L	G	AB	R	H	2B	3B	HR	RBI	BB	SO	AVG	OBP	SLG	PRO+	BR	/A	RC	SB	CS	SBR	FA	FR	POS	TPR
1912	Phi-A	5	8	0	0	0	0	0	0	0		.000	.000	.000	-99	-2	-2	0	0			1.000	-1	/32S	-0.3

■ BILL FAHEY
Fahey, William Roger b: 6/14/50, Detroit, Mich. BL/TR, 6', 200 lbs. Deb: 9/26/71 C

YEAR	TM/L	G	AB	R	H	2B	3B	HR	RBI	BB	SO	AVG	OBP	SLG	PRO+	BR	/A	RC	SB	CS	SBR	FA	FR	POS	TPR
1971	Was-A	2	8	0	0	0	0	0	0	0	0	.000	.000	.000	-99	-2	-2	0	0	0	0	.909	-0	/C	-0.3
1972	Tex-A	39	119	8	20	2	0	1	10	12	23	.168	.250	.210	40	-9	-8	7	4	0	1	.992	11	C	0.6
1974	Tex-A	6	16	1	4	0	0	0	0	0	1	.250	.250	.250	45	-1	-1	1	0	0	0	1.000	-1	/C	-0.2
1975	Tex-A	21	37	3	11	1	1	0	3	1	10	.297	.316	.378	96	-0	-0	4	0	0	0	.983	-1	C	-0.1
1976	Tex-A	38	80	12	20	2	0	1	9	11	6	.250	.348	.313	92	-0	-0	9	1	0	0	.993	2	C	0.2
1977	Tex-A	37	68	3	15	4	0	0	5	1	8	.221	.232	.279	38	-6	-6	4	0	0	0	1.000	-1	C	-0.6
1979	SD-N	73	209	14	60	8	1	3	19	21	17	.287	.352	.378	106	0	2	28	1	1	-0	.994	-3	C	0.1
1980	SD-N	93	241	18	62	4	0	1	22	21	16	.257	.317	.286	74	-9	-8	23	2	0	1	.977	-4	C	-0.9
1981	Det-A	27	67	5	17	2	0	1	9	2	4	.254	.275	.328	71	-2	-3	6	0	1	-1	.981	3	C	0.1

YEAR	TM/L	G	AB	R	H	2B	3B	HR	RBI	BB	SO	AVG	OBP	SLG	PRO+	BR	/A	RC	SB	CS	SBR	FA	FR	POS	TPR
1982	Det-A	28	67	7	10	2	0	0	4	0	5	.149	.149	.179	-10	-10	-10	2	1	0	0	1.000	5	C	-0.4
1983	Det-A	19	22	4	6	1	0	0	2	5	3	.273	.407	.318	106	0	0	3	0	0	0	1.000	1	C	0.1
Total	11	383	934	75	225	26	2	7	83	74	93	.241	.298	.296	69	-40	-36	87	9	2	2	.989	11	C	-1.4

■ FERRIS FAIN

Fain, Ferris Roy "Burrhead" b: 5/29/21, San Antonio, Tex. BL/TL, 5'11", 186 lbs. Deb: 4/15/47

YEAR	TM/L	G	AB	R	H	2B	3B	HR	RBI	BB	SO	AVG	OBP	SLG	PRO+	BR	/A	RC	SB	CS	SBR	FA	FR	POS	TPR
1947	Phi-A	136	461	70	134	28	6	7	71	95	34	.291	.414	.423	130	25	24	86	4	5	-2	.985	1	*1	1.9
1948	Phi-A	145	520	81	146	27	6	7	88	113	37	.281	.412	.396	115	17	17	93	10	5	0	.989	9	*1	2.3
1949	Phi-A	150	525	81	138	21	5	3	78	136	51	.263	.415	.339	104	8	11	87	8	1	**2**	.984	4	*1	1.4
1950	Phi-A★	151	522	83	147	25	4	10	83	133	26	.282	.430	.402	116	18	20	101	8	5	-1	.987	8	*1	2.2
1951	Phi-A★	117	425	63	146	30	3	6	57	80	20	**.344**	.451	.471	146	34	33	96	0	3	-2	.990	13	*1O	3.7
1952	Phi-A☆	145	538	82	176	**43**	3	2	59	105	26	**.327**	**.438**	.429	133	36	32	107	3	5	-2	.984	16	*1	4.2
1953	Chi-A★	128	446	73	114	18	2	6	52	108	28	.256	.405	.345	101	9	7	72	3	2	-0	.989	10	*1	1.1
1954	Chi-A†	65	235	30	71	10	1	5	51	40	14	.302	.406	.417	121	10	9	44	5	1	1	.987	-4	1	0.3
1955	Det-A	58	140	23	37	8	0	2	23	52	12	.264	.464	.364	128	9	10	28	2	1	0	.988	0	1	0.8
	Cle-A	56	118	9	30	3	0	0	8	42	13	.254	.453	.280	97	4	3	19	3	0	1	.992	3	1	0.5
	Yr	114	258	32	67	11	0	2	31	94	25	.260	.459	.326	113	13	13	48	5	1	1	.990	4	1	1.3
Total	9	1151	3930	595	1139	213	30	48	570	904	261	.290	.425	.396	120	169	163	735	46	28	-3	.987	59	*1/O	18.4

■ GEORGE FAIR

Fair, George T. b: 1/14/1856, Boston, Mass. d: 2/12/39, Roslindale, Mass. 5'7.5", 140 lbs. Deb: 7/29/1876

YEAR	TM/L	G	AB	R	H	2B	3B	HR	RBI	BB	SO	AVG	OBP	SLG	PRO+	BR	/A	RC	SB	CS	SBR	FA	FR	POS	TPR
1876	NY-N	1	4	0	0	0	0	0	0	0	0	.000	.000	.000	-99	-1	-1	0				.750	0	/2	-0.1

■ JIM FAIREY

Fairey, James Burke b: 9/22/44, Orangeburg, S.C. BL/TL, 5'10", 190 lbs. Deb: 4/14/68

YEAR	TM/L	G	AB	R	H	2B	3B	HR	RBI	BB	SO	AVG	OBP	SLG	PRO+	BR	/A	RC	SB	CS	SBR	FA	FR	POS	TPR
1968	LA-N	99	156	17	31	3	3	1	10	9	32	.199	.242	.276	60	-9	-7	10	1	1	-0	.944	1	O	-0.9
1969	Mon-N	20	49	6	14	1	0	1	6	1	7	.286	.300	.367	86	-1	-1	4	0	2	-1	.913	0	O	-0.3
1970	Mon-N	92	211	35	51	9	3	3	25	14	38	.242	.295	.355	74	-8	-8	21	1	3	-2	.978	-2	O	-1.4
1971	Mon-N	92	200	19	49	8	1	1	19	12	23	.245	.288	.310	69	-8	-8	18	3	3	-1	.968	2	O	-1.1
1972	Mon-N	86	141	9	33	7	0	1	15	10	21	.234	.285	.305	66	-6	-6	12	1	3	-2	.932	-4	O	-1.4
1973	LA-N	10	9	0	2	0	0	0	0	1	1	.222	.300	.222	49	-1	-1	1	0	0	0	.000	0	H	-0.1
Total	6	399	766	86	180	28	7	7	75	47	122	.235	.281	.317	69	-33	-32	65	6	12	-5	.957	-3	O	-5.2

■ RON FAIRLY

Fairly, Ronald Ray b: 7/12/38, Macon, Ga. BL/TL, 5'10", 181 lbs. Deb: 9/09/58

YEAR	TM/L	G	AB	R	H	2B	3B	HR	RBI	BB	SO	AVG	OBP	SLG	PRO+	BR	/A	RC	SB	CS	SBR	FA	FR	POS	TPR
1958	LA-N	15	53	6	15	1	0	2	8	6	7	.283	.356	.415	100	0	0	8	0	0	0	.971	-1	O	-0.2
1959	*LA-N	118	244	27	58	12	1	4	23	31	29	.238	.326	.344	73	-7	-9	28	0	4	-2	.963	-10	O	-2.5
1960	LA-N	14	37	6	4	0	3	1	3	7	12	.108	.250	.351	59	-2	-2	3	0	0	0	1.000	-1	O	-0.4
1961	LA-N	111	245	42	79	15	2	10	48	48	22	.322	.435	.522	140	21	18	60	0	0	0	.989	2	O1	1.5
1962	LA-N	147	460	80	128	15	7	14	71	75	59	.278	.383	.433	126	14	18	80	1	1	-0	.989	-12	*1O	-0.3
1963	*LA-N	152	490	62	133	21	0	12	77	58	69	.271	.350	.388	120	9	13	68	5	2	0	**.995**	-8	*1O	-0.1
1964	LA-N	150	454	62	116	19	5	10	74	65	59	.256	.351	.385	116	6	10	66	4	0	1	.987	-1	*1	0.4
1965	*LA-N	158	555	73	152	28	1	9	70	76	72	.274	.364	.377	117	9	14	82	2	0	1	.982	0	*O1	0.8
1966	*LA-N	117	351	53	101	20	0	14	61	52	38	.288	.383	.464	146	18	21	63	3	2	-0	.974	-13	O1	0.3
1967	LA-N	153	486	45	107	19	0	10	55	54	51	.220	.299	.321	85	-14	-9	46	1	4	-2	.986	5	O1	-1.5
1968	LA-N	141	441	32	103	15	1	4	43	41	61	.234	.305	.299	89	-9	-5	40	0	2	-1	.989	0	*O1	-1.6
1969	LA-N	30	64	3	14	3	2	0	8	9	6	.219	.315	.328	86	-2	-1	7	0	0	0	.981	1	1O	-0.2
	Mon-N	70	253	35	73	13	4	12	39	28	22	.289	.359	.514	142	13	13	46	1	0	0	.991	2	1O	1.1
	Yr	100	317	38	87	16	6	12	47	37	28	.274	.350	.476	132	12	13	53	1	0	0	.989	3	1O	0.9
1970	Mon-N	119	385	54	111	19	0	15	61	72	64	.288	.406	.455	130	19	19	76	10	2	2	.995	6	*1/O	1.7
1971	Mon-N	146	447	58	115	23	0	13	71	81	65	.257	.377	.396	119	14	14	71	1	3	-2	.992	7	*1O	0.9
1972	Mon-N	140	446	51	124	15	1	17	68	46	45	.278	.349	.430	118	12	11	66	3	4	-2	.985	5	O1	0.7
1973	Mon-N★	142	413	70	123	13	1	17	49	86	33	.298	.422	.458	139	29	27	85	2	2	-1	.974	-14	*O/1	0.8
1974	Mon-N	101	282	35	69	9	1	12	43	57	28	.245	.374	.411	113	9	7	46	2	1	0	.989	0	1O	0.2
1975	StL-N	107	229	32	69	13	2	7	37	45	22	.301	.422	.467	142	16	15	46	0	1	-1	.980	1	1O	1.3
1976	StL-N	73	110	13	29	4	0	0	21	23	12	.264	.391	.300	97	1	1	14	0	0	0	.995	3	1	0.2
	Oak-A	15	46	9	11	1	0	3	10	9	12	.239	.364	.457	145	2	3	8	0	0	0	1.000	1	1	0.2
1977	Tor-A★	132	458	60	128	24	2	19	64	58	58	.279	.363	.465	122	16	15	75	0	4	-2	.986	3	D1O	1.2
1978	Cal-A	91	235	23	51	5	0	10	40	25	31	.217	.295	.366	88	-5	-4	25	0	1	-1	.998	-2	1/D	-1.0
Total	21	2442	7184	931	1913	307	33	215	1044	1052	877	.266	.363	.408	117	170	187	1107	35	33	-9	.991	-26	*1O/D	3.5

■ ANTON FALCH

Falch, Anton C. b: 12/4/1860, Milwaukee, Wis. d: 3/31/36, Wauwatosa, Wis. 6'6", 220 lbs. Deb: 9/30/1884

YEAR	TM/L	G	AB	R	H	2B	3B	HR	RBI	BB	SO	AVG	OBP	SLG	PRO+	BR	/A	RC	SB	CS	SBR	FA	FR	POS	TPR
1884	Mil-U	5	18	0	2	0	0	0		0		.111	.111	.111	-45	-2	-1	0				.600	-1	/OC	-0.2

■ BIBB FALK

Falk, Bibb August "Jockey" b: 1/27/1899, Austin, Tex. d: 6/8/89, Austin, Tex. BL/TL, 6', 175 lbs. Deb: 9/17/20 FMC

YEAR	TM/L	G	AB	R	H	2B	3B	HR	RBI	BB	SO	AVG	OBP	SLG	PRO+	BR	/A	RC	SB	CS	SBR	FA	FR	POS	TPR
1920	Chi-A	7	17	1	5	1	1	0	2	0	5	.294	.294	.471	100	-0	-0	2	0	0	0	1.000	-1	/O	-0.1
1921	Chi-A	152	585	62	167	31	11	5	82	37	69	.285	.330	.402	87	-14	-13	78	4	4	-1	.958	-14	*O	-3.7
1922	Chi-A	131	483	58	144	27	1	12	79	27	55	.298	.335	.433	99	-2	-2	68	2	6	-3	.963	-9	*O	-2.3
1923	Chi-A	87	274	44	84	18	6	5	38	25	12	.307	.367	.471	121	7	7	47	4	5	-2	.951	-7	O	-0.6
1924	Chi-A	138	526	77	185	37	8	6	99	47	21	.352	.406	.487	134	23	25	103	6	6	-2	.970	10	*O	2.3
1925	Chi-A	154	602	80	181	35	9	4	99	51	25	.301	.357	.409	99	-6	-1	89	4	5	-2	.959	-4	*O	-1.6
1926	Chi-A	155	566	86	195	43	4	8	108	66	22	.345	.415	.477	137	28	31	112	9	10	-3	**.992**	8	*O	2.4
1927	Chi-A	145	535	76	175	35	6	9	83	52	19	.327	.391	.465	125	17	19	93	5	7	-3	.978	18	*O	2.4
1928	Chi-A	98	286	42	83	18	4	1	37	25	16	.290	.347	.392	95	-3	-2	40	5	1	1	.972	2	O	-0.4
1929	Cle-A	125	426	65	133	30	7	13	93	42	14	.312	.374	.507	120	15	12	80	4	4	-1	.943	-4	*O	0.0
1930	Cle-A	82	191	34	62	12	1	4	36	23	8	.325	.397	.461	113	5	4	36	2	0	1	.967	1	O	0.3
1931	Cle-A	79	161	30	49	13	1	2	28	17	13	.304	.371	.435	105	3	1	26	1	1	-0	.949	-3	O	-0.4
Total	12	1353	4652	655	1463	300	59	69	784	412	279	.314	.372	.449	113	71	81	775	46	49	-16	.967	-4	*O	-1.7

■ CHARLIE FALLON

Fallon, Charles Augustus b: 3/7/1881, New York, N.Y. d: 6/10/60, Kings Park, N.Y. BR/TR, 5'6" Deb: 6/30/05

YEAR	TM/L	G	AB	R	H	2B	3B	HR	RBI	BB	SO	AVG	OBP	SLG	PRO+	BR	/A	RC	SB	CS	SBR	FA	FR	POS	TPR
1905	NY-A	1	0	0	0	0	0	0	0	0		—	—	—	—	0	0	0	0			.000	0	R	0.0

■ GEORGE FALLON

Fallon, George Decatur "Flash" b: 7/8/16, Jersey City, N.J. BR/TR, 5'9", 155 lbs. Deb: 9/27/37

YEAR	TM/L	G	AB	R	H	2B	3B	HR	RBI	BB	SO	AVG	OBP	SLG	PRO+	BR	/A	RC	SB	CS	SBR	FA	FR	POS	TPR
1937	Bro-N	4	8	0	2	1	0	0	0	1	0	.250	.333	.375	91	-0	-0	0	0			.895	1	/2	0.1
1943	StL-N	36	78	6	18	1	0	0	5	2	9	.231	.259	.244	44	-5	-6	5	0			.968	15	2	1.1
1944	*StL-N	69	141	16	28	6	0	1	9	16	11	.199	.285	.262	54	-8	-9	11	1			.973	4	2S/3	-0.2
1945	StL-N	24	55	4	13	2	1	0	7	6	6	.236	.311	.309	71	-2	-2	6	1			.948	-2	S/2	-0.3
Total	4	133	282	26	61	10	1	1	21	25	26	.216	.285	.270	56	-16	-17	22	2			.966	18	/2S3	0.7

■ PETE FALSEY

Falsey, Peter James b: 4/24/1891, New Haven, Conn. d: 5/23/76, Los Angeles, Cal. BL/TL, 5'6.5", 132 lbs. Deb: 7/16/14

YEAR	TM/L	G	AB	R	H	2B	3B	HR	RBI	BB	SO	AVG	OBP	SLG	PRO+	BR	/A	RC	SB	CS	SBR	FA	FR	POS	TPR
1914	Pit-N	3	1	0	0	0	0	0	0	0	1	.000	.000	.000	-99	-0	-0	0	0			.000	0	H	0.0

■ JIM FANNING

Fanning, William James b: 9/14/27, Chicago, Ill. BR/TR, 5'11", 180 lbs. Deb: 9/11/54 MC

YEAR	TM/L	G	AB	R	H	2B	3B	HR	RBI	BB	SO	AVG	OBP	SLG	PRO+	BR	/A	RC	SB	CS	SBR	FA	FR	POS	TPR
1954	Chi-N	11	38	2	7	0	0	0	1	1	7	.184	.205	.184	2	-5	-5	1	0	0	0	1.000	-1	C	-0.6
1955	Chi-N	5	10	0	0	0	0	0	0	1	2	.000	.091	.000	-73	-3	-3	0	0	0	0	1.000	3	/C	0.1
1956	Chi-N	1	4	0	1	0	0	0	0	0	0	.250	.250	.250	36	-0	-0	0	0	0	0	.800	1	/C	0.0
1957	Chi-N	47	89	3	16	2	0	0	4	4	17	.180	.223	.202	16	-11	-10	4	0	0	0	.981	2	C	-0.7
Total	4	64	141	5	24	2	0	0	5	6	26	.170	.209	.184	6	-19	-19	4	0	0	0	.979	5	/C	-1.2

YEAR	TM/L	G	AB	R	H	2B	3B	HR	RBI	BB	SO	AVG	OBP	SLG	PRO+	BR	/A	RC	SB	CS	SBR	FA	FR	POS	TPR

■ CARMEN FANZONE
Fanzone, Carmen Ronald   b: 8/30/43, Detroit, Mich.   BR/TR, 6', 200 lbs.   Deb: 7/21/70

1970	Bos-A	10	15	0	3	1	0	0	3	2	2	.200	.333	.267	63	-1	-1	1	0	0	0	.750	0	/3	-0.1
1971	Chi-N	12	43	5	8	2	0	2	5	2	7	.186	.222	.372	57	-2	-3	3	0	0	0	1.000	0	/O31	-0.4
1972	Chi-N	86	222	26	50	11	0	8	42	35	45	.225	.338	.383	95	2	-1	28	2	3	-1	.923	3	312/SO	0.0
1973	Chi-N	64	150	22	41	7	0	6	22	20	38	.273	.359	.440	112	4	3	24	1	2	-1	.922	-3	31/O	-0.3
1974	Chi-N	65	158	13	30	6	0	4	22	15	27	.190	.269	.304	57	-9	-10	13	0	1	-1	.885	-1	32/1O	-1.2
Total	5	237	588	66	132	27	0	20	94	74	119	.224	.317	.372	86	-5	-11	70	3	6	-3	.896	-0	3/12OS	-2.0

■ PAUL FARIES
Faries, Paul Tyrrell   b: 2/20/65, Berkeley, Cal.   BR/TR, 5'10", 165 lbs.   Deb: 9/06/90

1990	SD-N	14	37	4	7	1	0	0	2	4	7	.189	.286	.216	40	-3	-3	3	0	1	-1	1.000	6	/2S3	0.3
1991	SD-N	57	130	13	23	3	1	0	7	14	21	.177	.262	.215	35	-11	-11	8	3	1	0	.988	8	23/S	-0.2
1992	SD-N	10	11	3	5	1	0	0	1	1	2	.455	.500	.545	189	1	1	3	0	0	0	1.000	-2	/23S	0.0
Total	3	81	178	20	35	5	1	0	10	19	30	.197	.281	.236	45	-12	-13	13	3	2	-0	.990	12	/23S	0.1

■ MONTY FARISS
Fariss, Monty Ted   b: 10/13/67, Cordell, Okla.   BR/TR, 6'4", 180 lbs.   Deb: 9/06/91

1991	Tex-A	19	31	6	8	1	0	1	6	7	11	.258	.395	.387	119	1	1	5	0	0	0	1.000	4	/O2D	0.5
1992	Tex-A	67	166	13	36	7	1	3	21	17	51	.217	.297	.325	77	-6	-5	16	0	2	-1	1.000	-15	O2/1D	-2.3
Total	2	86	197	19	44	8	1	4	27	24	62	.223	.314	.335	84	-5	-4	21	0	2	-1	1.000	-11	/O2D1	-1.8

■ BOB FARLEY
Farley, Robert Jacob   b: 11/15/37, Watsontown, Pa.   BL/TL, 6'2", 200 lbs.   Deb: 4/15/61

1961	SF-N	13	20	3	2	0	0	0	1	3	5	.100	.217	.100	-13	-3	-3	1	0	0	0	1.000	-1	/O1	-0.4
1962	Chi-A	35	53	7	10	1	1	1	4	13	13	.189	.348	.302	77	-1	-1	6	0	1	-1	.989	-1	1	-0.4
	Det-A	36	50	9	8	2	0	1	4	14	10	.160	.344	.260	63	-2	-2	6	0	0	0	.857	-4	O/1	-0.7
	Yr	71	103	16	18	3	1	2	8	27	23	.175	.346	.282	70	-3	-4	12	0	1	-1	.974	-5	1O	-1.1
Total	2	84	123	19	20	3	1	2	9	30	28	.163	.327	.252	58	-7	-7	13	0	1	-1	.975	-6	/1O	-1.5

■ TOM FARLEY
Farley, Thomas T.   b: Chicago, Ill.   Deb: 6/24/1884

| 1884 | Was-a | 14 | 52 | 5 | 11 | 4 | 0 | 0 | | 1 | | .212 | .241 | .288 | 84 | -1 | -1 | 4 | | | | .867 | 1 | O | | 0.1 |

■ ALEX FARMER
Farmer, Alexander Johnson   b: 5/9/1880, New York, N.Y.   d: 3/5/20, New York, N.Y.   BR/TR, 6', 175 lbs.   Deb: 9/01/08

| 1908 | Bro-N | 12 | 30 | 1 | 5 | 1 | 0 | 0 | 2 | 1 | | .167 | .194 | .200 | 27 | -3 | -2 | 1 | 0 | | | .966 | -0 | C | -0.2 |

■ JACK FARMER
Farmer, Floyd Haskell   b: 7/14/1892, Granville, Tenn.   d: 5/21/70, Columbia, La.   BR/TR, 6', 180 lbs.   Deb: 7/08/16

1916	Pit-N	55	166	10	45	6	4	0	14	7	24	.271	.309	.355	103	0	0	19	1			.929	-9	2O/S3	-1.0
1918	Cle-A	7	9	1	2	0	0	0	1	0	3	.222	.300	.222	53	-0	-1	1	2			.429	-2	/O	-0.3
Total	2	62	175	11	47	6	4	0	15	7	27	.269	.308	.349	100	-0	-0	20	3			.829	-11	/2OS3	-1.3

■ BILL FARMER
Farmer, William   b: 12/27/1870,   BR/TR, 5'11.5",   Deb: 5/01/1888

1888	Pit-N	2	4	0	0	0	0	0	0	0	1	.000	.000	.000	-99	-1	-1	0	0			.667	0	/CO	0.0
	Phi-a	3	12	0	2	0	0	0	1	0		.167	.167	.167	9	-1	-1	0	0			.960	0	/C	-0.1
Total	1	5	16	0	2	0	0	0	1	0	1	.125	.125	.125	-19	-2	-2	0	0			.903	1	/CO	-0.1

■ SID FARRAR
Farrar, Sidney Douglas   b: 8/10/1859, Paris Hill, Me.   d: 5/7/35, New York, N.Y.   TR, 5'10", 185 lbs.   Deb: 5/01/1883

1883	Phi-N	99	377	41	88	19	8	0	29	4	37	.233	.241	.326	77	-13	-8	30				.965	-0	*1	-1.6
1884	Phi-N	111	428	62	105	16	6	1	45	9	25	.245	.261	.318	85	-10	-7	36				.966	5	*1	-1.3
1885	Phi-N	111	420	49	103	20	3	3	36	28	34	.245	.292	.329	103	0	2	41				.975	2	*1	-0.8
1886	Phi-N	118	439	55	109	19	7	5	50	16	47	.248	.275	.358	90	-6	-6	47	10			**.980**	3	*1	-1.6
1887	Phi-N	116	443	83	125	20	9	4	72	42	29	.282	.358	.395	105	8	3	73	24			.977	3	*1	-0.5
1888	Phi-N	131	508	53	124	24	7	1	53	31	38	.244	.304	.325	98	2	2	58	21			.979	3	*1	-1.0
1889	Phi-N	130	477	70	128	22	2	3	58	52	36	.268	.348	.342	87	-2	-9	68	28			.978	-5	*1	-1.9
1890	Phi-P	127	481	84	122	17	11	1	69	51	23	.254	.331	.341	80	-12	-14	59	9			.973	-2	*1	-1.8
Total	8	943	3573	497	904	157	53	18	412	233	269	.253	.305	.342	91	-32	-41	413	92			.974	8	1	-10.5

■ DUKE FARRELL
Farrell, Charles Andrew   b: 8/31/1866, Oakdale, Mass.   d: 2/15/25, Boston, Mass.   BB/TR, 6'1", 208 lbs.   Deb: 4/21/1888

1888	Chi-N	64	241	34	56	6	3	3	19	4	41	.232	.245	.320	75	-6	-8	21	8			.874	-12	CO/1	-1.7
1889	Chi-N	101	407	66	101	19	7	11	75	41	21	.248	.318	.404	99	1	-2	59	13			.910	3	CO	0.6
1890	Chi-P	117	451	79	131	21	12	2	84	42	28	.290	.352	.404	99	2	-2	69	8			.929	**27**	C1O	2.5
1891	Bos-a	122	473	108	143	19	13	**12**	**110**	59	48	.302	.384	.474	151	29	30	97	21			.918	19	3CO/1	**4.6**
1892	Pit-N	152	605	96	130	10	13	8	77	46	53	.215	.276	.314	80	-16	-16	59	20			.879	-3	*3O	-1.4
1893	Was-N	124	511	84	143	13	13	4	75	47	12	.280	.346	.380	97	-4	-2	73	11			.923	14	C3/1	1.6
1894	*NY-N	114	401	47	114	20	12	4	66	35	15	.284	.346	.424	87	-10	-9	64	9			.926	29	*C/31	2.3
1895	NY-N	90	312	38	90	16	9	1	58	38	18	.288	.371	.407	105	2	3	53	11			.941	4	C3/1	1.1
1896	NY-N	58	191	23	54	7	3	1	37	19	7	.283	.351	.366	94	-2	-1	27	2			.954	-7	CS/3	-0.3
	Was-N	37	130	18	39	7	3	1	30	7	3	.300	.345	.423	104	0	0	21	2			1.000	0	C3	0.2
	Yr	95	321	41	93	14	6	2	67	26	10	.290	.349	.389	98	-2	-1	48	4			.970	-7	C3S	-0.1
1897	Was-N	78	261	41	84	9	6	0	53	17		.322	.366	.402	103	1	1	43	8			.945	10	C/1	1.5
1898	Was-N	99	338	47	106	12	6	1	53	34		.314	.383	.393	123	11	11	57	12			.929	-6	C1	1.0
1899	Was-N	5	12	2	4	1	0	0	1	2		.333	.429	.417	134	1	1	3	1			1.000	-0	/C	0.1
	Bro-N	80	254	40	76	10	7	2	55	35		.299	.399	.417	121	10	9	46	6			.948	11	C	2.3
	Yr	85	266	42	80	11	7	2	56	37		.301	.400	.417	122	10	9	49	7			.949	10	C	2.4
1900	*Bro-N	76	273	33	75	11	5	0	39	11		.275	.308	.352	77	-7	-10	32	3			.944	-4	C	-0.6
1901	Bro-N	80	284	38	84	10	6	1	31	7		.296	.320	.384	101	0	-1	38	7			.979	6	C1	1.1
1902	Bro-N	74	264	14	64	5	2	0	24	12		.242	.286	.277	73	-8	-8	24	6			.976	7	C1	0.4
1903	*Bos-A	17	52	5	21	5	1	0	8	5		.404	.466	.538	190	7	6	14	1			.960	-0	C	0.8
1904	Bos-A	68	198	11	42	9	2	0	15	15		.212	.281	.278	73	-5	-6	17	1			.958	-7	C	-0.8
1905	Bos-A	7	21	2	6	1	0	0	2	1		.286	.318	.333	106	0	0	2	0			1.000	2	/C	0.3
Total	18	1563	5679	826	1563	211	123	51	912	477	246	.275	.337	.383	100	4	-4	818	150			.938	94	*C3O1/S	15.6

■ DOC FARRELL
Farrell, Edward Stephen   b: 12/26/01, Johnson City, N.Y.   d: 12/20/66, Livingston, N.J.   BR/TR, 5'8", 160 lbs.   Deb: 6/23/25

1925	NY-N	27	56	6	12	1	0	0	4	4	6	.214	.267	.232	30	-6	-6	3	0	1	-1	.900	2	S/32	-0.3
1926	NY-N	67	171	19	49	10	1	2	23	12	17	.287	.341	.392	98	-1	-1	22	4			.950	-11	S/2	-0.7
1927	NY-N	42	142	13	55	10	1	3	34	12	11	.387	.442	.535	161	12	12	33	0			.919	-1	S/3	1.5
	Bos-N	110	424	44	124	13	2	1	58	14	21	.292	.315	.340	82	-15	-11	44	4			.931	-4	S23	-0.7
	Yr	152	566	57	179	23	3	4	92	26	32	.316	.348	.389	103	-3	-2	74	4			.926	-4	S23	0.8
1928	Bos-N	134	483	36	104	14	2	3	43	26	26	.215	.263	.271	42	-43	-39	35	3			.933	-17	*S/2	-4.0
1929	Bos-N	5	8	0	1	0	0	0	2	0	1	.125	.125	.125	-39	-2	-2	0	0			.000	-1	/2S	-0.2
	NY-N	63	178	18	38	6	0	0	16	9	17	.213	.251	.247	24	-21	-21	11	2			.925	7	32/S	-1.1
	Yr	68	186	18	39	6	0	0	18	9	18	.210	.246	.242	22	-23	-23	11	2			.925	7	32/S	-1.3
1930	StL-N	23	61	3	13	1	0	0	6	4	2	.213	.262	.262	26	-7	-8	7	1			.944	2	S/21	-0.4
	Chi-N	46	113	21	33	6	0	1	16	9	5	.292	.344	.372	73	-5	-5	14	0			.937	3	S/2	0.2
	Yr	69	174	24	46	7	0	1	22	13	7	.264	.316	.333	56	-12	-12	18	1			.938	5	S/21	-0.4
1932	NY-A	26	63	4	11	1	1	0	4	2	2	.175	.212	.222	13	-8	-8	3	0	0	0	.963	-1	2/S13	-0.4
1933	NY-A	44	93	16	25	0	0	1	6	10	9	.269	.376	.269	78	-3	-2	11	0	0	0	.947	4	S2	-0.4
1935	Bos-A	4	7	1	2	1	0	0	2	1	1	.286	.375	.429	101	0	0	1	0	0	0	.917	-1	/2	0.0
Total	9	591	1799	181	467	63	8	10	213	109	120	.260	.306	.320	66	-98	-89	182	14	1		.934	-24	S2/31	-6.8

YEAR	TM/L	G	AB	R	H	2B	3B	HR	RBI	BB	SO	AVG	OBP	SLG	PRO+	BR	/A	RC	SB	CS	SBR	FA	FR	POS	TPR

■ JACK FARRELL   Farrell, John "Hartford Jack" b: 1/2/1856, Hartford, Conn. d: 11/15/16, Hartford, Conn.   Deb: 10/27/1874

| 1874 | Har-n | 3 | 14 | 3 | 5 | 0 | 0 | 0 | | 0 | | .357 | .357 | .357 | 122 | 0 | 0 | 2 | | | | | | /O | 0.0 |

■ JACK FARRELL   Farrell, John A. "Moose" b: 7/5/1857, Newark, N.J. d: 2/10/14, Overbrook, N.J. BR/TR, 5'9", 165 lbs. Deb: 5/01/1879 M

1879	Syr-N	54	241	40	73	6	2	1	21	3	13	.303	.311	.357	135	5	9	27				.870	-15	2	-0.2
	Pro-N	12	51	5	13	2	0	0	5	0		.255	.255	.294	82	-1	-1	4				.915	7	2	0.6
	Yr	66	292	45	86	8	2	1	26	3	13	.295	.302	.346	125	4	8	31				.879	-7	2	0.4
1880	Pro-N	80	339	46	92	12	5	3	36	10	6	.271	.292	.363	125	7	8	37				.887	-8	*2	0.4
1881	Pro-N	84	345	69	82	16	5	5	36	29	23	.238	.297	.357	106	2	3	37				.881	-5	*2/OM	0.1
1882	Pro-N	84	366	67	93	21	6	2	31	16	23	.254	.285	.361	106	2	2	39				.875	-5	*2	-0.1
1883	Pro-N	95	420	92	128	24	11	3	61	15	21	.305	.329	.436	126	14	13	62				**.924**	**25**	*2	**3.3**
1884	*Pro-N	111	469	70	102	13	6	1	37	35	44	.217	.272	.277	75	-14	-12	36				.922	-4	*2/3	-1.2
1885	Pro-N	68	257	27	53	7	1	0	19	10	25	.206	.236	.253	61	-12	-10	16				.900	-15	2	-2.2
1886	Phi-N	17	60	7	11	0	1	0	3	3	11	.183	.222	.217	34	-5	-5	3	1			.825	-3	2	-0.6
	Was-N	47	171	24	41	11	4	2	18	15	12	.240	.301	.386	114	1	3	24	12			.913	-13	2	-0.7
	Yr	64	231	31	52	11	5	2	21	18	23	.225	.281	.342	92	-3	-2	27	13			.888	-15	2	-1.3
1887	Was-N	87	339	40	75	14	9	0	41	20	12	.221	.267	.316	66	-17	-14	38	31			.876	-8	S2	-1.7
1888	Bal-a	103	398	72	81	19	5	4	36	26		.204	.256	.307	85	-8	-6	40	29			.902	11	S2	0.7
1889	Bal-a	42	157	25	33	3	0	1	26	15	15	.210	.287	.248	54	-9	-9	16	14			.891	-6	S	-1.1
Total	11	884	3613	584	877	148	55	23	370	197	205	.243	.283	.333	95	-32	-19	378	87			.899	-38	2S/3O	-2.7

■ JACK FARRELL   Farrell, John J. b: 6/16/1892, Chicago, Ill. d: 3/24/18, Chicago, Ill. BB/TR, 5'8", 145 lbs. Deb: 4/16/14

1914	Chi-F	156	524	58	123	23	4	0	35	52	65	.235	.307	.294	76	-19	-15	54	12			.954	0	*2/S	-1.6
1915	Chi-F	70	222	27	48	10	1	0	14	25	18	.216	.298	.270	72	-9	-7	22	8			.941	-5	2/S	-1.2
Total	2	226	746	85	171	33	5	0	49	77	83	.229	.305	.287	75	-27	-22	77	20			.950	-4	2/S	-2.8

■ JOHN FARRELL   Farrell, John Sebastian b: 12/4/1876, Covington, Ky. d: 5/13/21, Kansas City, Mo. BR/TR, 5'10", 160 lbs. Deb: 4/26/01

1901	Was-A	135	555	100	151	32	11	3	63	52		.272	.336	.386	101	-0	-1	83	25			.915	17	2O/3	1.4
1902	StL-N	138	565	68	141	13	5	0	25	43		.250	.308	.290	88	-9	-7	56	9			.947	**33**	*2S	3.3
1903	StL-N	130	519	83	141	25	8	1	32	48		.272	.335	.356	100	-2	-0	70	17			.927	**28**	*2O	3.0
1904	StL-N	131	509	72	130	23	3	0	20	46		.255	.320	.312	100	-2	1	58	16			.934	16	*2	2.2
1905	StL-N	7	24	6	4	0	1	0	1	4		.167	.286	.250	62	-1	-1	2	1			.892	-3	/2	-0.4
Total	5	541	2172	329	567	93	28	4	141	193		.261	.324	.335	97	-15	-5	269	68			.932	92	2/OS3	9.5

■ JOE FARRELL   Farrell, Joseph F. b: 1857, Brooklyn, N.Y. d: 4/18/1893, Brooklyn, N.Y. BR, 5'6", 160 lbs. Deb: 5/01/1882

1882	Det-N	69	283	34	70	12	2	1	24	4	20	.247	.258	.314	83	-6	-6	24				.816	-11	32/S	-1.4
1883	Det-N	101	444	58	108	13	5	0	36	5	29	.243	.252	.295	69	-18	-15	34				.845	13	*3	-0.2
1884	Det-N	110	461	59	104	10	5	3	41	14	66	.226	.248	.289	73	-17	-13	34				.842	-7	*3/O	-1.7
1886	Bal-a	73	301	36	63	8	3	1		12		.209	.240	.266	61	-14	-13	21	5			.870	-15	23/O	-2.3
Total	4	353	1489	187	345	43	15	5	101	35	115	.232	.249	.291	71	-55	-46	112	5			.840	-21	3/2SO	-5.6

■ KERBY FARRELL   Farrell, Major Kerby b: 9/3/13, Leapwood, Tenn. d: 12/17/75, Nashville, Tenn. BL/TL, 5'11", 172 lbs. Deb: 4/24/43 MC

1943	Bos-N	85	280	11	75	14	1	0	21	16	15	.268	.307	.325	84	-7	-6	26	1			.996	2	1/P	-0.9
1945	Chi-A	103	396	44	102	11	3	0	34	24	18	.258	.300	.301	76	-13	-12	35	4	9	-4	.989	-0	1	-2.5
Total	2	188	676	55	177	25	4	0	55	40	33	.262	.303	.311	80	-20	-18	61	5	9		.992	1	1/P	-3.4

■ BILL FARRELL   Farrell, William Deb: 5/03/1882

1882	Phi-a	2	7	2	2	1	0	0		1		.286	.375	.429	153	1	0	1				.000	-1	/OC	-0.1
1883	Bal-a	2	7	0	0	0	0	0		1		.000	.125	.000	-55	-1	-1	0				.750	-1	/S	-0.2
Total	2	4	14	2	2	1	0	0		2		.143	.250	.214	51	-1	-1	1				.936	-2	/SOC	-0.3

■ JOHN FARROW   Farrow, John Jacob b: 11/8/1853, Verplanc Point, N.Y d: 12/31/14, Perth Amboy, N.J. BL/TR, Deb: 4/28/1873

1873	Res-n	12	48	2	8	1	0	0		0	3	.167	.167	.188	4	-6	-5	2						/CO1S	-0.3
1874	Atl-n	27	121	16	26	3	0	0		1		.215	.221	.240	53	-7	-4	7						C2	-0.4
1884	Bro-a	16	58	7	11	0	2	0		3		.190	.230	.224	50	-3	-3	3				.915	-1	C	-0.2
Total	2 n	39	169	18	34	4	0	0	3	1	3	.201	.206	.225	38	-12	-9	8						/C2OS1	-0.7

■ BUCK FAUSETT   Fausett, Robert Shaw "Leaky" b: 4/8/08, Sheridan, Ark. BL/TR, 5'10", 170 lbs. Deb: 4/18/44

| 1944 | Cin-N | 13 | 31 | 2 | 3 | 0 | 1 | 0 | 1 | 1 | 2 | .097 | .125 | .161 | -21 | -5 | -5 | 0 | 0 | | | 1.000 | 3 | /3P | -0.1 |

■ JOE FAUTSCH   Fautsch, Joseph Roamon b: 2/28/1887, Minneapolis, Minn. d: 3/16/71, New Hope, Minn. BR/TR, 5'10", 162 lbs. Deb: 4/24/16

| 1916 | Chi-A | 1 | 1 | 0 | 0 | 0 | 0 | 0 | 0 | 0 | | .000 | .000 | .000 | -99 | -0 | -0 | 0 | | | | .000 | 0 | H | 0.0 |

■ ERNIE FAZIO   Fazio, Ernest Joseph b: 1/25/42, Oakland, Cal. BR/TR, 5'7", 165 lbs. Deb: 7/03/62

1962	Hou-N	12	12	3	1	0	0	0	1	2	5	.083	.214	.083	-18	-2	-2	0	0	0	0	.783	0	S	-0.1
1963	Hou-N	102	228	31	42	10	3	2	5	27	70	.184	.273	.281	64	-12	-10	18	4	4	-1	.972	-11	2/S3	-1.8
1966	KC-A	27	34	3	7	0	1	0	2	4	10	.206	.289	.265	62	-2	-2	3	1	0	0	1.000	2	2/S	0.1
Total	3	141	274	37	50	10	4	2	8	33	85	.182	.273	.270	60	-15	-13	22	5	4	-1	.974	-9	/2S3	-1.8

■ AL FEDEROFF   Federoff, Alfred "Whitey" b: 7/11/24, Bairdford, Pa. BR/TR, 5'10.5", 165 lbs. Deb: 9/27/51

1951	Det-A	2	4	0	0	0	0	0	0	0	0	.000	.000	.000	-99	-1	-1	0	0	0	0	.889	1	/2	0.0
1952	Det-A	74	231	14	56	4	2	0	14	16	13	.242	.294	.277	59	-12	-13	20	1	0	0	.976	0	2/S	-0.9
Total	2	76	235	14	56	4	2	0	14	16	13	.238	.290	.272	56	-14	-14	20	1	0	0	.973	1	/2S	-0.9

■ BILL FEHRING   Fehring, William Paul "Dutch" b: 5/31/12, Columbus, Ind. BB/TR, 6', 195 lbs. Deb: 6/25/34

| 1934 | Chi-A | 1 | 1 | 0 | 0 | 0 | 0 | 0 | 0 | 0 | 1 | .000 | .000 | .000 | -97 | -0 | -0 | 0 | 0 | 0 | 0 | 1.000 | 0 | /C | 0.0 |

■ EDDIE FEINBERG   Feinberg, Edward Isadore "Itzzy" b: 9/29/17, Philadelphia, Pa. d: 4/20/86, Hollywood, Fla. BB/TR, 5'9", 165 lbs. Deb: 9/11/38

1938	Phi-N	10	20	0	3	0	0	0	0	1		.150	.150	.150	-18	-3	-3	0	0			.957	3	/SO	0.0
1939	Phi-N	6	18	2	4	1	0	0	0	0		.222	.300	.278	58	-1	-1	2	0			.909	-4	/2S	-0.5
Total	2	16	38	2	7	1	0	0	0	1		.184	.225	.211	20	-4	-4	2	0			.957	-2	/S2O	-0.5

■ MIKE FELDER   Felder, Michael Otis b: 11/18/61, Vallejo, Cal. BB/TR, 5'8", 160 lbs. Deb: 9/11/85

1985	Mil-A	15	56	8	11	1	0	0	0	5	6	.196	.262	.214	33	-5	-5	3	4	1	1	1.000	-0	O	-0.5
1986	Mil-A	44	155	24	37	2	4	1	13	13	16	.239	.298	.323	67	-7	-7	17	16	2	4	1.000	2	O/D	-0.3
1987	Mil-A	108	289	48	77	5	7	2	31	28	23	.266	.331	.353	79	-7	-8	38	34	8	5	.975	-2	O/2D	-0.5
1988	Mil-A	50	81	14	14	1	0	0	5	0	11	.173	.183	.185	3	-10	-10	3	8	2	1	.976	-5	OD/2	-1.5
1989	Mil-A	117	315	50	76	11	3	3	23	23	38	.241	.293	.324	74	-11	-11	33	26	5	5	.985	-1	OD2	-0.9
1990	Mil-A	121	237	38	65	7	2	3	27	22	17	.274	.336	.359	95	-2	-1	31	20	9	1	.972	-12	*O/23D	-1.5
1991	SF-N	132	348	51	92	10	6	0	18	30	31	.264	.325	.328	87	-7	-6	41	21	6	3	.985	-11	*O/32	-1.6
1992	SF-N	145	322	44	92	13	3	4	23	21	29	.286	.333	.382	108	1	3	43	14	4	2	.994	-20	*O/2	-1.9
Total	8	732	1803	277	464	50	25	13	140	142	171	.257	.313	.334	81	-48	-46	208	143	37	21	.984	-47	O/D23	-8.7

■ MARV FELDERMAN   Felderman, Marvin Wilfred "Coonie" b: 12/20/15, Bellevue, Iowa BR/TR, 6'1", 187 lbs. Deb: 4/19/42

| 1942 | Chi-N | 3 | 6 | 0 | 1 | 0 | 0 | 0 | 0 | 1 | 4 | .167 | .286 | .167 | 35 | -0 | -0 | 0 | 0 | | | 1.000 | 1 | /C | 0.0 |

YEAR	TM/L	G	AB	R	H	2B	3B	HR	RBI	BB	SO	AVG	OBP	SLG	PRO+	BR	/A	RC	SB	CS	SBR	FA	FR	POS	TPR
GUS FELIX Felix, August Guenther b: 5/24/1895, Cincinnati, Ohio d: 5/12/60, Montgomery, Ala. BR/TR, 6', 180 lbs. Deb: 4/19/23																									
1923	Bos-N	139	506	64	138	17	2	6	44	51	65	.273	.348	.350	88	-10	-7	62	8	13	-5	.950	0	*O/23	-1.9
1924	Bos-N	59	204	25	43	7	1	1	10	18	16	.211	.275	.270	48	-15	-14	15	0	3	-2	.950	5	O	-1.5
1925	Bos-N	121	459	60	141	25	7	2	66	30	34	.307	.356	.405	103	-4	2	66	5	5	-2	.972	10	*O	0.3
1926	Bro-N	134	432	64	121	21	7	3	53	51	32	.280	.360	.382	101	1	2	60	9			.956	-2	*O	-0.8
1927	Bro-N	130	445	43	118	21	8	0	57	39	47	.265	.327	.348	81	-12	-12	51	6			.947	-3	*O	-2.2
Total	5	583	2046	256	561	91	25	12	230	189	194	.274	.341	.361	89	-40	-29	254	28	21		.957	11	O/23	-6.1
JUNIOR FELIX Felix, Junior Francisco (Sanchez) b: 10/3/67, Laguna Salada, D.R. BB/TR, 6', 170 lbs. Deb: 5/03/89																									
1989	*Tor-A	110	415	62	107	14	8	9	46	33	101	.258	.317	.395	101	-1	0	51	18	12	-2	.966	3	*O/D	-0.1
1990	Tor-A	127	463	73	122	23	7	15	65	45	99	.263	.331	.441	112	8	7	69	13	8	-1	.966	2	*O/D	0.4
1991	Cal-A	66	230	32	65	10	2	2	26	11	55	.283	.324	.370	91	-3	-3	26	7	5	-1	.977	-6	O	-1.1
1992	Cal-A	139	509	63	125	22	5	9	72	33	128	.246	.294	.361	84	-13	-12	52	8	8	-2	.983	7	*O/D	-1.1
Total	4	442	1617	230	419	69	22	35	209	122	383	.259	.315	.394	98	-9	-8	198	46	33	-6	.973	5	O/D	-1.9
JACK FELLER Feller, Jack Leland b: 12/10/36, Adrian, Mich. BR/TR, 5'10.5", 185 lbs. Deb: 9/13/58																									
1958	Det-A	1	0	0	0	0	0	0	0	0	0	—	—	—	—	0	0	0	0	0	0	1.000	-0	/C	0.0
HAPPY FELSCH Felsch, Oscar Emil b: 8/22/1891, Milwaukee, Wis. d: 8/17/64, Milwaukee, Wis. BR/TR, 5'11", 175 lbs. Deb: 4/14/15																									
1915	Chi-A	121	427	65	106	18	11	3	53	51	59	.248	.334	.363	105	4	2	52	16	18	-6	.959	-3	*O	-1.3
1916	Chi-A	146	546	73	164	24	12	7	70	31	67	.300	.341	.427	129	17	16	85	13			**.981**	7	*O	1.7
1917	*Chi-A	152	575	75	177	17	10	6	102	33	52	.308	.352	.403	128	19	17	87	26			.985	19	*O	3.1
1918	Chi-A	53	206	16	52	2	5	1	20	15	13	.252	.306	.325	90	-3	-3	22	6			.957	5	O	-0.1
1919	*Chi-A	135	502	68	138	34	11	7	86	40	35	.275	.336	.428	113	7	7	76	19			.968	21	*O	2.1
1920	Chi-A	142	556	88	188	40	15	14	115	37	25	.338	.384	.540	143	31	31	109	8	13	-5	.981	18	*O	3.2
Total	6	749	2812	385	825	135	64	38	446	207	251	.293	.347	.427	123	75	71	431	88	31		.975	67	O	8.7
JOHN FELSKE Felske, John Frederick b: 5/30/42, Chicago, Ill. BR/TR, 6'3", 195 lbs. Deb: 7/26/68 MC																									
1968	Chi-N	4	2	0	0	0	0	0	0	0	1	.000	.000	.000	-94	-0	-0	0	0	0	0	.833	1	/C	0.0
1972	Mil-A	37	80	6	11	3	0	1	5	8	23	.138	.216	.213	28	-7	-7	4	0	0	0	.972	-2	C/1	-1.0
1973	Mil-A	13	22	1	3	0	1	0	4	1	11	.136	.174	.227	12	-3	-3	1	0	0	0	1.000	0	/C1	-0.3
Total	3	54	104	7	14	3	1	1	9	9	35	.135	.204	.212	23	-10	-10	5	0	0	0	.969	-1	/C1	-1.3
FRANK FENNELLY Fennelly, Francis John b: 2/18/1860, Fall River, Mass. d: 8/4/20, Fall River, Mass. BR/TR, 5'8", 168 lbs. Deb: 5/01/1884																									
1884	Was-a	62	257	52	75	17	7	2		20		.292	.343	.436	176	15	20	39				.863	13	S/2	3.0
	Cin-a	28	122	42	43	5	8	2		11		.352	.415	.574	213	16	15	30				.813	-6	S	0.9
	Yr	90	379	94	118	22	15	4		31		.311	.367	.480	190	32	36	68				.849	7	S/2	3.9
1885	Cin-a	112	454	82	124	14	17	10		38		.273	.333	.445	144	24	23	69				.873	-11	*S	1.2
1886	Cin-a	132	497	113	124	13	17	6		60		.249	.351	.380	127	20	17	80	32			.848	14	*S	2.8
1887	Cin-a	134	526	133	140	15	16	8		82		.266	.369	.401	114	14	12	108	74			.855	-9	*S	0.4
1888	Cin-a	120	448	64	88	8	7	2	56	63		.196	.297	.259	78	-7	-10	48	43			.858	17	*S/2O	0.8
	Phi-a	15	47	13	11	2	2	1	12	9		.234	.357	.426	155	3	3	9	5			.912	-1	S	0.2
	Yr	135	495	77	99	10	9	3	68	72		.200	.303	.275	85	-3	-7	57	48			.863	16	*S/2O	1.0
1889	Phi-a	138	513	70	132	20	5	1	64	65	78	.257	.344	.322	93	-3	-2	64	15			.872	-20	*S	-1.2
1890	Bro-a	45	178	40	44	8	3	2		30		.247	.356	.360	117	4	5	26	6			.858	0	S/3	0.6
Total	7	786	3042	609	781	102	82	34	132	378	78	.257	.345	.378	121	87	83	472	175			.860	-4	S/23O	8.7
BOBBY FENWICK Fenwick, Robert Richard b: 12/10/46, Naha, Okinawa BR/TR, 5'9", 165 lbs. Deb: 4/26/72																									
1972	Hou-N	36	50	7	9	3	0	0	4	3	13	.180	.226	.240	33	-4	-4	2	0	1	-1	.945	3	2/S3	-0.1
1973	StL-N	5	6	0	1	0	0	0	1	0	2	.167	.167	.167	-7	-1	-1	0	0	0	0	.750	-1	/2	-0.2
Total	2	41	56	7	10	3	0	0	5	3	15	.179	.220	.232	29	-5	-5	3	0	1	-1	.932	3	/2S3	-0.3
JOE FERGUSON Ferguson, Joseph Vance b: 9/19/46, San Francisco, Cal. BR/TR, 6'2", 200 lbs. Deb: 9/12/70 C																									
1970	LA-N	5	4	0	1	0	0	0	1	2	2	.250	.500	.250	112	0	0	1	0	0	0	1.000	0	/C	0.0
1971	LA-N	36	102	13	22	3	0	2	7	12	15	.216	.304	.304	77	-3	-3	10	1	0	0	.983	-2	C	-0.3
1972	LA-N	8	24	2	7	3	0	1	5	2	4	.292	.346	.542	152	1	1	4	0	0	0	1.000	2	/CO	0.3
1973	LA-N	136	487	84	128	26	0	25	88	87	81	.263	.376	.470	139	23	26	92	1	1	-0	**.996**	1	*CO	3.2
1974	*LA-N	111	349	54	88	14	1	16	57	75	73	.252	.384	.436	134	16	18	60	2	2	-1	.988	-9	CO	1.1
1975	LA-N	66	202	15	42	2	1	5	23	35	47	.208	.328	.302	79	-6	-5	22	2	1	0	.994	-1	CO	-0.6
1976	LA-N	54	185	24	41	7	0	6	18	25	41	.222	.318	.357	93	-2	-2	22	2	0	1	.966	-3	OC	-0.5
	StL-N	71	189	22	38	8	4	4	21	32	40	.201	.320	.349	89	-2	-2	22	4	2	0	.978	6	CO	0.5
	Yr	125	374	46	79	15	4	10	39	57	81	.211	.319	.353	91	-4	-4	44	6	2	1	.975	4	CO	0.0
1977	Hou-N	132	421	59	108	21	3	16	61	85	79	.257	.381	.435	130	13	19	74	6	2	1	.985	-10	*C/1	1.3
1978	Hou-N	51	150	20	31	5	0	7	22	37	30	.207	.367	.380	118	3	5	22	0	0	0	.994	-6	C	0.0
	*LA-N	67	198	20	47	11	0	7	28	34	41	.237	.352	.399	110	3	3	27	1	2	-1	.984	-9	C/O	-0.6
	Yr	118	348	40	78	16	0	14	50	71	71	.224	.359	.391	113	6	8	49	1	2	-1	.989	-15	*C/O	-0.6
1979	LA-N	122	363	54	95	14	0	20	69	70	68	.262	.384	.466	133	17	18	68	1	0	0	.981	-11	CO	0.8
1980	LA-N	77	172	20	41	3	2	9	29	38	46	.238	.376	.436	128	7	8	27	2	2	-1	.982	-3	C/O	0.6
1981	LA-N	17	14	2	2	1	0	0	1	2	5	.143	.250	.214	34	-1	-1	1	0	0	0	.000	0	/O	-0.1
	Cal-A	12	30	5	7	1	0	1	5	9	8	.233	.410	.367	125	2	2	5	0	0	0	.976	0	/CO	0.2
1982	Cal-A	36	84	10	19	2	0	3	8	12	19	.226	.323	.357	87	-1	-1	9	0	0	0	.993	5	C/O	0.5
1983	Cal-A	12	27	3	2	0	0	0	2	5	8	.074	.219	.074	-15	-4	-4	0	0	0	0	.968	-2	/CO	-0.6
Total	14	1013	3001	407	719	121	11	122	445	562	607	.240	.361	.409	117	66	80	465	22	12	-1	.987	-41	CO/1	5.8
BOB FERGUSON Ferguson, Robert V. b: 1/31/1845, Brooklyn, N.Y. d: 5/3/1894, Brooklyn, N.Y. BB/TR, 5'9.5", 149 lbs. Deb: 5/18/1871 MU																									
1871	Mut-n	33	158	30	38	6	1	0	25	3	2	.241	.255	.291	62	-9	-5	13	4					32/CPM	-0.5
1872	Atl-n	37	166	33	45	6	0	0	19	3	0	.271	.284	.307	70	-3	-9	15						*3M	-0.9
1873	Atl-n	51	228	36	59	5	5	0	24	4	9	.259	.272	.325	83	-7	-2	20						*3/PM	-0.3
1874	Atl-n	56	246	34	63	5	1	0		1		.256	.259	.285	82	-7	-2	19						*3/CPM	-0.1
1875	Har-n	85	366	66	88	12	4	0		2		.240	.245	.295	82	-5	-8	27						*3/PM	-0.7
1876	Har-N	69	310	48	82	8	5	0	32	2	11	.265	.269	.323	89	-1	-5	28				.826	2	*3M	-0.1
1877	Har-N	58	254	40	65	7	2	0	35	3	10	.256	.265	.299	86	-6	-2	21				.841	17	*3/PM	1.4
1878	Chi-N	61	259	44	91	10	2	0	39	10	12	.351	**.375**	.405	147	16	13	40				.881	16	*S/2CM	**2.9**
1879	Tro-N	30	123	18	31	5	2	0	4	4	3	.252	.276	.325	104	-0	1	11				.808	2	3/2M	0.4
1880	Tro-N	82	332	55	87	9	0	0	22	**24**	24	.262	.312	.289	100	3	0	31				.904	-3	*2M	0.1
1881	Tro-N	85	339	56	96	13	5	1	35	29	12	.283	.340	.360	114	9	6	42				.904	-10	*2M	-0.1
1882	Tro-N	81	319	44	82	15	2	0	32	23	21	.257	.307	.317	106	1	3	32				.914	-13	*2/SM	-0.7
1883	Phi-N	86	329	39	85	9	2	0	27	18	21	.258	.297	.298	89	-7	-2	30				.862	-8	*2/PM	-0.8
1884	Pit-a	10	41	2	6	0	0	0		0		.146	.146	.146	-3	-4	-4	1				.714	-3	/O13M	-0.8
Total	5 n	262	1164	199	293	34	11	0	68	13	11	.252	.260	.300	77	-31	-27	94						3/2PC	-2.5
Total	9	562	2306	346	625	76	20	1	226	113	114	.271	.305	.323	102	8	9	236					0	23/SOP1C	2.3
FELIX FERMIN Fermin, Felix Jose (Minaya) b: 10/9/63, Mao Valverde, D.R. BR/TR, 5'11", 179 lbs. Deb: 7/08/87																									
1987	Pit-N	23	68	6	17	0	0	0	4	4	9	.250	.301	.250	48	-5	-5	5	0	0	0	.980	1	S	-0.2
1988	Pit-N	43	87	9	24	0	2	0	2	8	10	.276	.357	.322	98	0	0	10	3	1	0	.955	-5	S	-0.3

YEAR	TM/L	G	AB	R	H	2B	3B	HR	RBI	BB	SO	AVG	OBP	SLG	PRO+	BR	/A	RC	SB	CS	SBR	FA	FR	POS	TPR
1989	Cle-A	156	484	50	115	9	1	0	21	41	27	.238	.302	.260	59	-24	-25	40	6	4	-1	.967	18	*S/2	0.3
1990	Cle-A	148	414	47	106	13	2	1	40	26	22	.256	.300	.304	70	-17	-17	36	3	3	-1	.975	4	*S/2	-0.2
1991	Cle-A	129	424	30	111	13	2	0	31	26	27	.262	.309	.302	69	-17	-17	37	5	4	-1	.980	2	*S	-0.7
1992	Cle-A	79	215	27	58	7	2	0	13	18	10	.270	.329	.321	82	-5	-5	23	0	0	0	.971	-5	S3/21	-0.6
Total	6	578	1692	169	431	42	9	1	111	123	105	.255	.310	.292	69	-68	-69	151	17	12	-2	.972	15	S/321	-1.7

■ ED FERNANDES Fernandes, Edward Paul b: 3/11/18, Oakland, Cal. d: 11/27/68, Hayward, Cal. BB/TR, 5′9″, 185 lbs. Deb: 6/09/40

YEAR	TM/L	G	AB	R	H	2B	3B	HR	RBI	BB	SO	AVG	OBP	SLG	PRO+	BR	/A	RC	SB	CS	SBR	FA	FR	POS	TPR
1940	Pit-N	28	33	1	4	1	0	0	2	7	6	.121	.275	.152	21	-3	-3	2	0			.981	0	C	-0.2
1946	Chi-A	14	32	4	8	2	0	0	4	8	7	.250	.400	.313	105	1	1	5	0	0	0	.922	-1	C	0.0
Total	2	42	65	5	12	3	0	0	6	15	13	.185	.338	.231	61	-3	-3	6	0	0		.952	-0	/C	-0.2

■ FRANK FERNANDEZ Fernandez, Frank b: 4/16/43, Staten Island, N.Y. BR/TR, 6′1″, 192 lbs. Deb: 9/12/67

YEAR	TM/L	G	AB	R	H	2B	3B	HR	RBI	BB	SO	AVG	OBP	SLG	PRO+	BR	/A	RC	SB	CS	SBR	FA	FR	POS	TPR
1967	NY-A	9	28	1	6	2	0	1	4	2	7	.214	.290	.393	104	-0	0	3	1	1	-0	1.000	0	/CO	0.0
1968	NY-A	51	135	15	23	6	1	7	30	35	50	.170	.341	.385	124	4	5	20	1	0	0	.989	6	C/O	1.5
1969	NY-A	89	229	34	51	6	1	12	29	65	68	.223	.401	.415	133	12	13	42	1	3	-2	.994	-8	CO	0.7
1970	Oak-A	94	252	30	54	5	0	15	44	40	76	.214	.327	.413	106	1	2	35	1	0	0	.993	-1	C/O	0.5
1971	Oak-A	2	4	0	0	0	0	0	0	1	2	.000	.200	.000	-40	-1	-1	0	0	0	0	1.000	2	/C	0.1
	Was-A	18	30	0	3	0	0	0	4	4	10	.100	.206	.100	-12	-4	-4	1	0	0	0	1.000	-1	/OC	-0.6
	Oak-A	2	5	1	1	1	0	0	1	0	1	.200	.200	.400	68	-0	-0	0	0	0	0	1.000	-0	/C	-0.1
	Yr	22	39	1	4	1	0	0	5	5	13	.103	.205	.128	-4	-5	-5	1	0	0	0	1.000	0	/OC	-0.6
	Chi-N	17	41	11	7	1	0	4	4	17	15	.171	.414	.488	135	4	3	10	0	0	0	.980	0	C	0.4
1972	Chi-N	3	3	0	0	0	0	0	0	0	2	.000	.000	.000	-90	-1	-1	0	0	0	0	1.000	-0	/C	-0.1
Total	6	285	727	92	145	21	2	39	116	164	231	.199	.351	.395	114	15	17	111	4	4	-1	.992	-2	C/O	2.4

■ NANNY FERNANDEZ Fernandez, Froilan b: 10/25/18, Wilmington, Cal. BR/TR, 5′9″, 170 lbs. Deb: 4/14/42

YEAR	TM/L	G	AB	R	H	2B	3B	HR	RBI	BB	SO	AVG	OBP	SLG	PRO+	BR	/A	RC	SB	CS	SBR	FA	FR	POS	TPR
1942	Bos-N	145	577	63	147	29	3	6	55	38	61	.255	.303	.347	92	-9	-7	58	15			.914	6	3O	-0.3
1946	Bos-N	115	372	37	95	15	2	2	42	30	44	.255	.313	.323	79	-10	-10	37	1			.940	-2	3SO	-1.2
1947	Bos-N	83	209	16	43	4	0	2	21	22	20	.206	.281	.254	44	-17	-16	16	2			.933	-13	S/O3	-2.7
1950	Pit-N	65	198	23	51	11	0	6	27	19	17	.258	.326	.404	88	-3	-4	24	2			.925	-3	3	-0.7
Total	4	408	1356	139	336	59	5	16	145	109	142	.248	.306	.334	80	-38	-38	135	20			.925	-13	3/SO	-4.9

■ CHICO FERNANDEZ Fernandez, Humberto (Perez) b: 3/2/32, Havana, Cuba BR/TR, 6′, 170 lbs. Deb: 7/14/56

YEAR	TM/L	G	AB	R	H	2B	3B	HR	RBI	BB	SO	AVG	OBP	SLG	PRO+	BR	/A	RC	SB	CS	SBR	FA	FR	POS	TPR
1956	Bro-N	34	66	11	15	2	0	1	9	3	10	.227	.261	.303	47	-5	-5	4	2	3	-1	.978	7	S	0.1
1957	Phi-N	149	500	42	131	14	4	5	51	31	64	.262	.306	.336	75	-19	-17	48	18	5	2	.960	-25	*S	-2.7
1958	Phi-N	148	522	38	120	18	5	6	51	37	48	.230	.283	.318	60	-31	-30	45	12	6	0	.975	-12	*S	-3.0
1959	Phi-N	45	123	15	26	5	1	0	3	10	11	.211	.271	.268	43	-10	-10	9	2	1	0	.958	-3	S/2	-1.0
1960	Det-A	133	435	44	105	13	3	4	35	39	50	.241	.305	.313	66	-20	-21	41	13	4	2	.947	-4	*S	-1.5
1961	Det-A	133	435	41	108	15	4	3	40	36	45	.248	.306	.322	66	-20	-21	41	8	5	-1	.958	-8	*S/3	-2.0
1962	Det-A	141	503	64	125	17	2	20	59	42	69	.249	.306	.410	88	-8	-10	62	10	3	1	.960	-27	*S/31	-2.4
1963	Det-A	15	49	3	7	1	0	0	2	6	11	.143	.236	.163	14	-6	-6	1	0	1	-1	.947	2	S	-0.3
	NY-N	58	145	12	29	6	0	1	9	9	30	.200	.247	.262	46	-10	-10	10	3	0	1	.944	-16	S/32	-2.5
Total	8	856	2778	270	666	91	19	40	259	213	338	.240	.295	.329	67	-127	-131	262	68	28	4	.960	-86	S/321	-15.3

■ CHICO FERNANDEZ Fernandez, Lorenzo Marto (Mosquera) b: 4/23/39, Havana, Cuba BR/TR, 5′10″, 160 lbs. Deb: 4/20/68

YEAR	TM/L	G	AB	R	H	2B	3B	HR	RBI	BB	SO	AVG	OBP	SLG	PRO+	BR	/A	RC	SB	CS	SBR	FA	FR	POS	TPR
1968	Bal-A	24	18	0	2	0	0	0	0	1	2	.111	.158	.111	-17	-3	-3	0	0	0	0	.923	3	/S2	0.0

■ TONY FERNANDEZ Fernandez, Octavio Antonio (Castro) (b: Octavio Antonio Fernando (Castro))
b: 8/6/62, San Pedro De Macoris, D.R. BB/TR, 6′2″, 175 lbs. Deb: 9/02/83

YEAR	TM/L	G	AB	R	H	2B	3B	HR	RBI	BB	SO	AVG	OBP	SLG	PRO+	BR	/A	RC	SB	CS	SBR	FA	FR	POS	TPR
1983	Tor-A	15	34	5	9	1	1	0	2	2	2	.265	.324	.353	81	-1	-1	4	0	1	-1	1.000	-3	S/D	-0.4
1984	Tor-A	88	233	29	63	5	3	3	19	17	15	.270	.320	.356	84	-4	-5	25	5	7	-3	.974	3	S3/D	0.1
1985	*Tor-A	161	564	71	163	31	10	2	51	43	41	.289	.342	.390	97	0	-2	75	13	6	0	.962	5	*S	1.9
1986	Tor-A★	163	687	91	213	33	9	10	65	27	52	.310	.340	.428	105	6	4	99	25	12	0	**.983**	3	*S	2.2
1987	Tor-A★	146	578	90	186	29	8	5	67	51	48	.322	.382	.426	112	13	11	94	32	12	2	.979	6	*S	3.0
1988	Tor-A	154	648	76	186	41	4	5	70	45	65	.287	.337	.386	101	2	1	86	15	5	2	.981	10	*S	2.5
1989	*Tor-A★	140	573	64	147	25	9	11	64	29	51	.257	.296	.389	93	-8	-7	66	22	6	3	**.992**	18	*S	2.6
1990	Tor-A	161	635	84	175	27	**17**	4	66	71	70	.276	.355	.391	106	8	7	88	26	13	0	.989	9	*S	2.8
1991	SD-N	145	558	81	152	27	5	4	38	55	74	.272	.338	.360	93	-2	-4	69	23	9	2	.972	3	*S	1.2
1992	SD-N★	155	622	84	171	32	4	4	37	56	62	.275	.339	.359	94	-1	-4	75	20	20	-6	.983	-17	*S	-1.6
Total	10	1328	5132	675	1465	251	70	48	479	396	480	.285	.340	.390	100	13	1	681	181	91	-0	.980	37	*S/3D	14.3

■ AL FERRARA Ferrara, Alfred John "The Bull" b: 12/22/39, Brooklyn, N.Y. BR/TR, 6′1″, 203 lbs. Deb: 7/30/63

YEAR	TM/L	G	AB	R	H	2B	3B	HR	RBI	BB	SO	AVG	OBP	SLG	PRO+	BR	/A	RC	SB	CS	SBR	FA	FR	POS	TPR
1963	LA-N	21	44	2	7	0	0	1	1	6	9	.159	.275	.227	50	-3	-3	3	0	0	0	.950	-0	O	-0.3
1965	LA-N	41	81	5	17	2	1	1	10	9	20	.210	.297	.296	72	-3	-3	8	0	0	0	.927	-1	O	-0.5
1966	*LA-N	63	115	15	31	4	0	5	23	9	35	.270	.339	.435	123	2	3	17	0	0	0	.956	-1	O	0.1
1967	LA-N	122	347	41	96	16	1	16	50	33	73	.277	.345	.467	142	13	16	56	0	1	-1	.978	-10	O	0.2
1968	LA-N	2	7	0	1	0	0	0	0	0	2	.143	.143	.143	-15	-1	-1	0	0	0	0	.500	-1	/O	-0.2
1969	SD-N	138	366	39	95	22	1	14	56	45	69	.260	.352	.440	125	10	12	58	0	0	0	.958	-13	O	-0.6
1970	SD-N	138	372	44	103	15	4	13	51	46	63	.277	.373	.444	123	10	12	64	0	0	0	.968	-16	O	-0.9
1971	SD-N	17	17	0	2	1	0	0	2	5	5	.118	.318	.176	47	-1	-1	1	0	0	0	1.000	-1	/O	-0.2
	Cin-N	32	33	2	6	0	0	1	5	3	10	.182	.270	.273	55	-2	-2	2	0	0	0	1.000	0	/O	-0.2
	Yr	49	50	2	8	1	0	1	7	8	15	.160	.288	.240	53	-3	-3	3	0	0	0	1.000	-0	/O	-0.4
Total	8	574	1382	148	358	60	7	51	198	156	286	.259	.346	.423	120	25	35	209	0	1	-1	.962	-42	O	-2.6

■ MIKE FERRARO Ferraro, Michael Dennis b: 8/18/44, Kingston, N.Y. BR/TR, 5′11″, 175 lbs. Deb: 9/06/66 MC

YEAR	TM/L	G	AB	R	H	2B	3B	HR	RBI	BB	SO	AVG	OBP	SLG	PRO+	BR	/A	RC	SB	CS	SBR	FA	FR	POS	TPR
1966	NY-A	10	28	4	5	0	0	0	0	3	3	.179	.281	.179	37	-2	-2	2	0	0	0	.926	1	3	-0.1
1968	NY-A	23	87	5	14	0	1	0	1	2	17	.161	.180	.184	11	-9	-9	2	0	0	0	.975	4	3	-0.5
1969	Sea-A	5	4	0	0	0	0	0	0	1	0	.000	.200	.000	-41	-1	-1	0	0	0	0	.000	0	H	-0.1
1972	Mil-A	124	381	19	97	18	1	2	29	17	41	.255	.286	.323	83	-10	-9	29	0	5	-3	.950	-16	*3/S	-3.3
Total	4	162	500	28	116	18	2	2	30	23	61	.232	.267	.288	67	-22	-21	33	0	5	-3	.953	-10	3/S	-4.0

■ RICK FERRELL Ferrell, Richard Benjamin b: 10/12/05, Durham, N.C. BR/TR, 5′10″, 160 lbs. Deb: 4/19/29 FCH

YEAR	TM/L	G	AB	R	H	2B	3B	HR	RBI	BB	SO	AVG	OBP	SLG	PRO+	BR	/A	RC	SB	CS	SBR	FA	FR	POS	TPR
1929	StL-A	64	144	21	33	6	1	0	20	32	10	.229	.373	.285	69	-5	-6	18	1	2	-1	.962	0	C	-0.2
1930	StL-A	101	314	43	84	18	4	1	41	46	10	.268	.363	.360	81	-6	-8	43	1	4	-2	.983	-9	*C	-1.0
1931	StL-A	117	386	47	118	30	4	3	57	56	12	.306	.394	.427	112	10	8	67	2	3	-1	.973	4	*C	1.7
1932	StL-A	126	438	67	138	30	5	2	65	66	18	.315	.406	.420	108	12	8	78	5	5	-2	.986	-2	*C	1.1
1933	StL-A	22	72	8	18	2	0	1	5	12	4	.250	.357	.319	76	-2	-2	9	2	0	1	.991	3	C	0.2
	Bos-A	118	421	50	125	19	4	3	72	58	19	.297	.385	.382	105	4	5	66	2	2	-1	.990	5	*C	1.6
	Yr	140	493	58	143	21	4	4	77	70	23	.290	.381	.373	100	3	3	75	4	2	0	.990	8	*C	1.8
1934	Bos-A☆	132	437	50	130	29	4	1	48	66	20	.297	.390	.389	95	3	-2	70	0	0	0	**.990**	3	*C	0.7
1935	Bos-A☆	133	458	54	138	34	4	3	61	65	15	.301	.388	.413	100	7	2	75	5	8	-3	.979	13	*C	1.7
1936	Bos-A★	121	410	59	128	27	5	8	55	65	17	.312	.406	.461	108	10	6	80	0	1	-1	.987	9	*C	1.8
1937	Bos-A	18	65	8	20	2	0	1	4	15	4	.308	.438	.385	105	2	1	12	0	0	0	.990	0	C	0.2
	Was-A	86	279	31	64	6	0	1	32	50	18	.229	.348	.262	59	-17	-15	29	1	1	-0	.987	-6	C	-1.5
	Yr	104	344	39	84	8	0	2	36	65	22	.244	.366	.285	68	-15	-13	41	1	1	-0	.988	-6	*C	-1.3
1938	Was-A☆	135	411	55	120	24	5	1	58	75	17	.292	.401	.382	104	1	6	69	1	0	0	.981	-5	*C	0.7

YEAR	TM/L	G	AB	R	H	2B	3B	HR	RBI	BB	SO	AVG	OBP	SLG	PRO+	BR	/A	RC	SB	CS	SBR	FA	FR	POS	TPR
1939	Was-A	87	274	32	77	13	1	0	31	41	12	.281	.377	.336	90	-5	-2	38	1	1	-0	.976	-6	C	-0.4
1940	Was-A	103	326	35	89	18	2	0	28	47	15	.273	.365	.340	90	-6	-3	44	1	1	-0	.980	-6	C	-0.2
1941	Was-A	21	66	8	18	5	0	0	13	15	4	.273	.407	.348	107	1	1	10	1	0	0	.980	-1	C	0.2
	StL-A	100	321	30	81	14	3	2	23	52	22	.252	.357	.333	81	-6	-8	41	2	1	0	.995	-5	C	-0.4
	Yr	121	387	38	99	19	3	2	36	67	26	.256	.366	.336	85	-5	-6	51	3	1	0	.992	-6	*C	-0.2
1942	StL-A	99	273	20	61	6	1	0	26	33	13	.223	.307	.253	57	-14	-15	23	0	1	-1	.986	9	C	0.0
1943	StL-A	74	209	12	50	7	0	0	20	34	14	.239	.348	.273	81	-3	-4	23	0	0	0	.987	13	C	1.4
1944	Was-A☆	99	339	14	94	11	1	0	25	46	13	.277	.364	.316	99	-0	2	41	2	1	0	.981	3	C	1.2
1945	Was-A†	91	286	33	76	12	1	1	38	43	13	.266	.366	.325	110	2	5	35	2	4	-2	.990	-2	C	0.6
1947	Was-A	37	99	10	30	11	0	0	12	14	7	.303	.389	.414	127	3	4	16	0	0	0	.994	3	C	0.9
Total	18	1884	6028	687	1692	324	45	28	734	931	277	.281	.378	.363	95	-8	-14	888	29	35	-12	.984	20	*C	10.3

■ WES FERRELL Ferrell, Wesley Cheek b: 2/2/08, Greensboro, N.C. d: 12/9/76, Sarasota, Fla. BR/TR, 6'2", 195 lbs. Deb: 9/09/27 F

YEAR	TM/L	G	AB	R	H	2B	3B	HR	RBI	BB	SO	AVG	OBP	SLG	PRO+	BR	/A	RC	SB	CS	SBR	FA	FR	POS	TPR
1927	Cle-A	1	0	0	0	0	0	0	0	0	0	—	—	—	—	0	0	0	0	0	0	.000	-0	/P	0.0
1928	Cle-A	2	4	0	1	0	1	0	0	0	0	.250	.250	.750	152	0	0	1	0	0	0	1.000	0	/P	0.0
1929	Cle-A	47	93	12	22	5	3	1	12	6	28	.237	.283	.387	68	-4	-5	10	1	0	0	.973	3	P	0.0
1930	Cle-A	53	118	19	35	8	3	0	14	12	15	.297	.362	.415	93	-1	-1	18	0	0	0	.967	-3	P	0.0
1931	Cle-A	48	116	24	37	6	1	9	30	10	21	.319	.373	.621	149	9	8	27	0	0	0	.969	5	P	0.0
1932	Cle-A	55	128	14	31	5	2	2	18	6	21	.242	.276	.359	59	-7	-9	13	0	0	0	.986	1	P	0.0
1933	Cle-A☆	61	140	26	38	7	0	7	26	20	22	.271	.363	.471	114	4	3	25	0	0	0	1.000	2	PO	0.1
1934	Bos-A	34	78	12	22	4	0	4	17	7	15	.282	.341	.487	104	1	0	13	1	0	0	.969	-2	P	0.0
1935	Bos-A	75	150	25	52	5	1	7	32	21	16	.347	.427	.533	138	11	9	35	0	0	0	.977	2	P	0.0
1936	Bos-A	61	135	20	36	6	1	5	24	14	10	.267	.336	.437	84	-3	-4	20	0	0	0	.962	-3	P	0.0
1937	Bos-A	18	33	7	12	2	0	1	9	7	3	.364	.475	.515	144	3	3	9	0	0	0	.964	2	P	0.0
	Was-A	53	106	7	27	5	0	0	16	9	18	.255	.313	.302	58	-7	-6	10	0	0	0	.975	-1	P	0.0
	Yr	71	139	14	39	7	0	1	25	16	21	.281	.355	.353	81	-4	-4	18	0	0	0	.971	1	P	0.0
1938	Was-A	26	49	6	11	2	0	1	6	15	7	.224	.406	.327	92	-0	0	8	0	0	0	.976	1	P	0.0
	NY-A	5	12	1	2	1	0	0	1	1	4	.167	.231	.250	20	-2	-2	1	0	0	0	.917	1	/P	0.0
	Yr	31	61	7	13	3	0	1	7	16	11	.213	.377	.311	79	-2	-1	9	0	0	0	.962	2	P	0.0
1939	NY-A	3	8	0	1	1	0	0	1	0	2	.125	.125	.250	-6	-1	-1	0	0	0	0	1.000	0	/P	0.0
1940	Bro-N	2	2	0	0	0	0	0	0	0	2	.000	.000	.000	-94	-1	-1	0	0			1.000	1	/P	0.0
1941	Bos-N	4	4	2	2	0	0	1	2	1	1	.500	.600	1.250	430	2	2	3	0			1.000	-0	/P	0.0
Total	15	548	1176	175	329	57	12	38	208	129	185	.280	.351	.446	99	3	-4	194	2	0		.975	7	P/O	0.1

■ SERGIO FERRER Ferrer, Sergio (Marrero) b: 1/29/51, Santurce, P.R. BB/TR, 5'7", 145 lbs. Deb: 4/05/74

YEAR	TM/L	G	AB	R	H	2B	3B	HR	RBI	BB	SO	AVG	OBP	SLG	PRO+	BR	/A	RC	SB	CS	SBR	FA	FR	POS	TPR
1974	Min-A	24	57	12	16	0	2	0	0	8	6	.281	.379	.351	107	1	1	8	3	2	-0	.855	-12	S/2	-1.0
1975	Min-A	32	81	14	20	3	1	0	2	3	11	.247	.282	.309	66	-4	-4	7	3	4	-2	.924	-1	S2/D	-0.5
1978	NY-N	37	33	8	7	0	1	0	1	4	7	.212	.316	.273	68	-1	-1	3	1	0	0	.971	10	S/23	1.0
1979	NY-N	32	7	7	0	0	0	0	0	2	3	.000	.222	.000	-35	-1	-1	0	0	2	-1	.833	6	3/S2	0.4
Total	4	125	178	41	43	3	4	0	3	17	27	.242	.318	.303	76	-5	-5	18	7	8	-3	.922	3	/S23D	-0.1

■ HOBE FERRIS Ferris, Albert Sayles b: 12/7/1877, Providence, R.I. d: 3/18/38, Detroit, Mich. BR/TR, 5'8", 162 lbs. Deb: 4/26/01

YEAR	TM/L	G	AB	R	H	2B	3B	HR	RBI	BB	SO	AVG	OBP	SLG	PRO+	BR	/A	RC	SB	CS	SBR	FA	FR	POS	TPR
1901	Bos-A	138	523	68	131	16	15	2	63	23		.250	.290	.350	78	-18	-16	60	13			.930	9	*2/S	-0.2
1902	Bos-A	134	499	57	122	16	14	8	63	21		.244	.276	.381	79	-15	-17	58	11			.952	**27**	*2	1.4
1903	*Bos-A	141	525	69	132	19	7	9	66	25		.251	.287	.366	90	-4	-8	61	11			.950	15	*2/S	1.3
1904	Bos-A	156	563	50	120	23	10	3	63	23		.213	.245	.306	70	-18	-21	47	7			.962	2	*2	-1.7
1905	Bos-A	142	523	51	115	24	16	6	59	23		.220	.253	.361	93	-6	-7	53	11			.960	15	*2	1.0
1906	Bos-A	130	495	47	121	25	13	2	44	10		.244	.261	.360	94	-6	-6	51	8			.960	9	*2/3	0.4
1907	Bos-A	150	561	41	135	25	2	4	60	10		.241	.254	.314	82	-14	-14	50	11			.967	15	*2	0.0
1908	StL-A	148	555	54	150	26	7	2	74	14		.270	.291	.353	108	3	3	59	6			**.952**	16	*3	2.7
1909	StL-A	148	556	36	120	18	5	4	58	12		.216	.232	.288	69	-25	-21	39	11			.937	7	*32	-1.2
Total	9	1287	4800	473	1146	192	89	40	550	161		.239	.265	.341	84	-103	-106	477	89			.954	113	*23/S	3.7

■ WILLY FETZER Fetzer, William McKinnon b: 6/24/1884, Concord, N.C. d: 5/3/59, Butner, N.C. BL/TR, 5'10.5", 180 lbs. Deb: 9/04/06

YEAR	TM/L	G	AB	R	H	2B	3B	HR	RBI	BB	SO	AVG	OBP	SLG	PRO+	BR	/A	RC	SB	CS	SBR	FA	FR	POS	TPR
1906	Phi-A	1	1	0	0	0	0	0	0	0		.000	.000	.000	-97	-0	-0	0	0			.000	0	H	0.0

■ CHICK FEWSTER Fewster, Wilson Lloyd b: 11/10/1895, Baltimore, Md. d: 4/16/45, Baltimore, Md. BR/TR, 5'11", 160 lbs. Deb: 9/19/17

YEAR	TM/L	G	AB	R	H	2B	3B	HR	RBI	BB	SO	AVG	OBP	SLG	PRO+	BR	/A	RC	SB	CS	SBR	FA	FR	POS	TPR
1917	NY-A	11	36	2	8	0	0	0	1	5	5	.222	.317	.222	64	-1	-1	3	1			.919	2	2	0.1
1918	NY-A	5	2	1	1	0	0	0	0	0	0	.500	.500	.500	197	0	0	0	0			.000	0	/2	0.0
1919	NY-A	81	244	38	69	9	3	1	15	34	36	.283	.386	.357	108	5	5	36	8			.946	8	OS/23	1.1
1920	NY-A	21	21	8	6	1	0	0	1	7	2	.286	.464	.333	110	1	1	4	0	1	-1	.840	0	/S2	0.1
1921	*NY-A	66	207	44	58	19	0	1	19	28	43	.280	.382	.386	94	-0	-1	32	4	4	-1	.974	-3	O2	-0.7
1922	NY-A	44	132	20	32	4	1	1	9	16	23	.242	.324	.311	65	-6	-7	14	2	4	-2	.975	1	O/2	-1.0
	Bos-A	23	83	8	24	4	1	0	9	6	10	.289	.344	.361	85	-2	-2	11	8	3	1	.959	4	3	0.4
	Yr	67	215	28	56	8	2	1	18	22	33	.260	.332	.330	72	-8	-9	24	10	7	-1	.975	5	O3/2	-0.6
1923	Bos-A	90	284	32	67	10	1	0	15	39	35	.236	.334	.278	62	-14	-14	26	7	14	-6	.938	-10	2S/3	-2.6
1924	Cle-A	101	322	36	86	12	2	0	36	24	36	.267	.324	.317	65	-16	-17	32	12	12	-4	.961	-22	2/3	-4.0
1925	Cle-A	93	294	39	73	16	1	1	38	36	25	.248	.330	.320	65	-15	-15	32	6	9	-4	.939	-9	23/O	-2.5
1926	Bro-N	105	337	53	82	16	3	2	24	45	49	.243	.341	.326	82	-8	-7	39	9			.953	-15	*2	-1.9
1927	Bro-N	4	1	1	0	0	0	0	0	0	0	.000	.000	.000	-99	-0	-0	0	0			.000	0	H	0.0
Total	11	644	1963	282	506	91	12	6	167	240	264	.258	.346	.326	77	-58	-60	230	57	47		.945	-43	2O/S3	-11.0

■ NEIL FIALA Fiala, Neil Stephen b: 8/24/56, St.Louis, Mo. BL/TR, 6'1", 185 lbs. Deb: 9/03/81

YEAR	TM/L	G	AB	R	H	2B	3B	HR	RBI	BB	SO	AVG	OBP	SLG	PRO+	BR	/A	RC	SB	CS	SBR	FA	FR	POS	TPR
1981	StL-N	3	3	0	0	0	0	0	0	0	1	.000	.000	.000	-97	-1	-1	0	0	0	0	.000	0	/H	-0.1
	Cin-N	2	2	1	1	0	0	0	1	0	1	.500	.500	.500	181	0	0	1	0	0	0	.000	0	/H	0.0
	Yr	5	5	1	1	0	0	0	1	0	2	.200	.200	.200	13	-1	-1	0	0	0	0	.000	0		-0.1

■ JIM FIELD Field, James C. b: 4/24/1863, Philadelphia, Pa. d: 5/13/53, Atlantic City, N.J 6'1", 170 lbs. Deb: 6/02/1883

YEAR	TM/L	G	AB	R	H	2B	3B	HR	RBI	BB	SO	AVG	OBP	SLG	PRO+	BR	/A	RC	SB	CS	SBR	FA	FR	POS	TPR
1883	Col-a	76	295	31	75	10	6	1		7		.254	.272	.339	104	-2	2	28				.938	-7	*1	-1.1
1884	Col-a	105	417	74	97	9	7	4		23		.233	.292	.317	110	1	7	40				.958	-4	*1	-0.9
1885	Pit-a	56	209	28	50	9	1	1		13		.239	.306	.306	98	-0	0	20				.965	-0	1	-0.6
	Bal-a	38	144	16	30	3	2	0		13		.208	.278	.257	73	-4	-4	11				.963	1	1	-0.6
	Yr	94	353	44	80	12	3	1		26		.227	.295	.286	88	-4	-3	30				.964	1	1	-1.2
1890	Roc-a	52	188	30	38	7	5	4		21		.202	.309	.356	106	-1	2	24	8			.964	-4	1/P	-0.4
1898	Was-N	5	21	1	2	0	0	0	0	0		.095	.095	.095	-46	-4	-4	0	1			.979	-0	/1	-0.4
Total	5	332	1274	180	292	38	21	10	0	77		.229	.288	.316	98	-9	3	122	9			.956	-15	1/P	-4.0

■ SAM FIELD Field, Samuel Jay b: 10/12/1848, Philadelphia, Pa. d: 10/28/04, Sinking Spring, Pa BR/TR, 5'9.5", 182 lbs. Deb: 5/19/1875

YEAR	TM/L	G	AB	R	H	2B	3B	HR	RBI	BB	SO	AVG	OBP	SLG	PRO+	BR	/A	RC	SB	CS	SBR	FA	FR	POS	TPR
1875	Cen-n	3	11	2	1	0	0	0		0		.091	.091	.091	-40	-1	-1	0						/CO	-0.1
	Was-n	5	17	0	5	0	0	0		0		.294	.294	.294	108	0	0	2						/CO	0.0
	Yr	8	28	2	6	0	0	0		0		.214	.214	.214	51	-1	-1	1						/CO	-0.1
1876	Cin-N	4	14	2	0	0	0	0	0	1	3	.000	.067	.000	-89	-3	-2	0				.667	-3	/C2	-0.5

■ CECIL FIELDER Fielder, Cecil Grant b: 9/21/63, Los Angeles, Cal. BR/TR, 6'3", 230 lbs. Deb: 7/20/85

YEAR	TM/L	G	AB	R	H	2B	3B	HR	RBI	BB	SO	AVG	OBP	SLG	PRO+	BR	/A	RC	SB	CS	SBR	FA	FR	POS	TPR
1985	*Tor-A	30	74	6	23	4	0	4	16	6	16	.311	.363	.527	137	4	4	14	0	0	0	.979	1	1	0.3

YEAR	TM/L	G	AB	R	H	2B	3B	HR	RBI	BB	SO	AVG	OBP	SLG	PRO+	BR	/A	RC	SB	CS	SBR	FA	FR	POS	TPR
1986	Tor-A	34	83	7	13	2	0	4	13	6	27	.157	.222	.325	46	-6	-7	5	0	0	0	1.000	-1	D/13O	-0.8
1987	Tor-A	82	175	30	47	7	1	14	32	20	48	.269	.347	.560	132	8	8	32	0	1	-1	1.000	-1	D1/3	0.6
1988	Tor-A	74	174	24	40	6	1	9	23	14	53	.230	.291	.431	99	-1	-1	20	0	1	-1	.991	0	D1/32	-0.2
1990	Det-A★	159	573	104	159	25	1	**51**	**132**	90	182	.277	.380	**.592**	167	51	51	129	0	1	-1	.989	3	*1D	4.2
1991	Det-A★	162	624	102	163	25	0	**44**	**133**	78	151	.261	.349	.513	133	29	27	110	0	0	0	.993	-3	*1D	1.6
1992	Det-A	155	594	80	145	22	0	35	**124**	73	151	.244	.329	.458	117	13	12	89	0	0	0	.991	2	*1D	0.6
Total	7	696	2297	353	590	91	3	161	473	287	628	.257	.343	.509	132	98	94	399	0	3	-2	.991	2	1D/32O	6.3

■ BRUCE FIELDS Fields, Bruce Alan b: 10/6/60, Cleveland, Ohio BL/TR, 6', 185 lbs. Deb: 9/03/86

YEAR	TM/L	G	AB	R	H	2B	3B	HR	RBI	BB	SO	AVG	OBP	SLG	PRO+	BR	/A	RC	SB	CS	SBR	FA	FR	POS	TPR
1986	Det-A	16	43	4	12	1	1	0	6	1	6	.279	.295	.349	75	-2	-2	4	1	1	-0	.962	-1	O/D	-0.3
1988	Sea-A	39	67	8	18	5	0	1	5	4	11	.269	.310	.388	90	-1	-1	7	0	1	-1	1.000	-5	O/D	-0.7
1989	Sea-A	3	3	2	1	1	0	0	0	0	1	.333	.333	.667	170	0	0	1	0	0	0	.000	-0	/O	0.0
Total	3	58	113	14	31	7	1	1	11	5	18	.274	.305	.381	86	-2	-2	12	1	2	-1	.980	-6	/OD	-1.0

■ GEORGE FIELDS Fields, George W. b: 7/1853, Waterbury, Conn. d: 9/22/33, Waterbury, Conn. Deb: 5/02/1872

YEAR	TM/L	G	AB	R	H	2B	3B	HR	RBI	BB	SO	AVG	OBP	SLG	PRO+	BR	/A	RC	SB	CS	SBR	FA	FR	POS	TPR
1872	Man-n	18	83	14	22	2	2	0	8	0	2	.265	.265	.337	89	-2	-1	8						3/OS	-0.1

■ JOCKO FIELDS Fields, John Joseph b: 10/20/1864, Cork, Ireland d: 10/14/50, Jersey City, N.J. BR/TR, 5'10", 160 lbs. Deb: 5/31/1887

YEAR	TM/L	G	AB	R	H	2B	3B	HR	RBI	BB	SO	AVG	OBP	SLG	PRO+	BR	/A	RC	SB	CS	SBR	FA	FR	POS	TPR
1887	Pit-N	43	164	26	44	9	2	0	17	7	13	.268	.306	.348	88	-4	-2	20	7			.933	1	OC/13P	0.0
1888	Pit-N	45	169	22	33	7	2	1	15	8	19	.195	.232	.278	69	-7	-5	13	9			.887	-5	OC/3	-0.9
1889	Pit-N	75	289	41	90	22	5	2	43	29	30	.311	.376	.443	144	11	16	52	7			.860	-6	OC	0.9
1890	Pit-P	126	526	101	149	18	20	9	86	57	52	.283	.357	.445	126	10	18	94	24			.879	-13	O2C/S	0.4
1891	Pit-N	23	75	10	18	3	0	0	5	10	13	.240	.337	.280	84	-1	-1	8	1			.897	-3	C/S	-0.2
	Phi-N	8	30	4	7	2	1	0	5	4	2	.233	.324	.367	100	0	-0	4	0			.769	-4	/C	-0.3
	Yr	31	105	14	25	5	1	0	10	14	15	.238	.333	.305	89	-1	-1	11	1			.857	-7	C/S	-0.5
1892	NY-N	21	66	8	18	4	2	0	5	9	10	.273	.368	.394	135	3	3	11	2			.917	-1	OC	0.2
Total	6	341	1319	212	359	65	32	12	176	124	139	.272	.338	.397	116	13	29	202	50			.883	-31	O/C2S31P	0.1

■ BIEN FIGUEROA Figueroa, Bienvenido b: 2/7/64, Santo Domingo, D.R. BR/TR, 5'10", 170 lbs. Deb: 5/17/92

YEAR	TM/L	G	AB	R	H	2B	3B	HR	RBI	BB	SO	AVG	OBP	SLG	PRO+	BR	/A	RC	SB	CS	SBR	FA	FR	POS	TPR
1992	StL-N	12	11	1	2	1	0	0	4	1	2	.182	.250	.273	49	-1	-1	1	0	0	0	.938	1	/S2	0.0

■ JESUS FIGUEROA Figueroa, Jesus Maria (Figueroa) b: 2/20/57, Santo Domingo, P.R. BL/TL, 5'10", 160 lbs. Deb: 4/22/80

YEAR	TM/L	G	AB	R	H	2B	3B	HR	RBI	BB	SO	AVG	OBP	SLG	PRO+	BR	/A	RC	SB	CS	SBR	FA	FR	POS	TPR
1980	Chi-N	115	198	20	50	5	0	1	11	14	16	.253	.308	.293	64	-8	-10	18	2	1	0	.979	4	O	-0.7

■ SAM FILE File, Lawrence Samuel b: 5/18/22, Chester, Pa. BR/TR, 5'11", 160 lbs. Deb: 9/10/40

YEAR	TM/L	G	AB	R	H	2B	3B	HR	RBI	BB	SO	AVG	OBP	SLG	PRO+	BR	/A	RC	SB	CS	SBR	FA	FR	POS	TPR
1940	Phi-N	7	13	0	1	0	0	0	1	0	1	.077	.077	.077	-60	-3	-3	0	0			.850	1	/S3	-0.2

■ STEVE FILIPOWICZ Filipowicz, Stephen Charles "Flip" b: 6/28/21, Donora, Pa. d: 2/21/75, Wilkes-Barre, Pa. BR/TR, 5'8", 195 lbs. Deb: 9/03/44

YEAR	TM/L	G	AB	R	H	2B	3B	HR	RBI	BB	SO	AVG	OBP	SLG	PRO+	BR	/A	RC	SB	CS	SBR	FA	FR	POS	TPR
1944	NY-N	15	41	10	8	2	1	0	7	3	7	.195	.250	.293	52	-3	-3	3	0			1.000	-1	O/C	-0.5
1945	NY-N	35	112	14	23	5	0	2	16	4	13	.205	.239	.304	50	-8	-8	8	0			.935	-6	O	-1.6
1948	Cin-N	7	26	0	9	0	1	0	3	2	1	.346	.393	.423	125	1	1	5	0			1.000	-0	/O	0.0
Total	3	57	179	24	40	7	2	2	26	9	21	.223	.265	.318	61	-10	-10	15	0			.961	-8	/OC	-2.1

■ JACK FIMPLE Fimple, John Joseph b: 2/10/59, Darby, Pa. BR/TR, 6'2", 185 lbs. Deb: 7/30/83

YEAR	TM/L	G	AB	R	H	2B	3B	HR	RBI	BB	SO	AVG	OBP	SLG	PRO+	BR	/A	RC	SB	CS	SBR	FA	FR	POS	TPR
1983	•LA-N	54	148	16	37	8	1	2	22	11	39	.250	.302	.358	83	-4	-4	16	1	0	0	.989	12	C	1.1
1984	LA-N	12	26	2	5	1	0	0	3	1	6	.192	.222	.231	28	-3	-2	1	0	0	0	.983	2	C	-0.1
1986	LA-N	13	13	2	1	0	0	0	2	6	6	.077	.368	.077	32	-1	-1	1	0	0	0	1.000	1	/C12	0.0
1987	Cal-A	13	10	1	2	0	0	0	1	1	2	.200	.273	.200	29	-1	-1	1	0	0	0	.913	1	C	0.0
Total	4	92	197	21	45	9	1	2	28	19	53	.228	.296	.315	70	-8	-8	18	1	0	0	.986	15	/C21	1.0

■ JIM FINIGAN Finigan, James Leroy b: 8/19/28, Quincy, Ill. d: 5/16/81, Quincy, Ill. BR/TR, 5'11", 175 lbs. Deb: 4/25/54

YEAR	TM/L	G	AB	R	H	2B	3B	HR	RBI	BB	SO	AVG	OBP	SLG	PRO+	BR	/A	RC	SB	CS	SBR	FA	FR	POS	TPR
1954	Phi-A☆	136	487	57	147	25	6	7	51	64	66	.302	.383	.421	120	14	14	76	2	8	-4	.948	2	*3	1.0
1955	KC-A★	150	545	72	139	30	7	9	68	61	49	.255	.333	.385	92	-6	-7	68	1	3	-2	.975	-7	23	-0.9
1956	KC-A	91	250	29	54	7	2	2	21	30	28	.216	.302	.284	55	-16	-16	23	3	1	0	.969	-1	23	-1.2
1957	Det-A	64	174	20	47	4	2	0	17	23	18	.270	.359	.316	84	-2	-3	21	1	1	-0	.954	4	3/2	0.2
1958	SF-N	23	25	3	5	2	0	0	1	3	5	.200	.310	.280	59	-1	-1	2	0	0	0	.917	-2	/23	-0.3
1959	Bal-A	48	119	14	30	6	0	1	10	9	10	.252	.305	.328	75	-4	-4	11	1	0	0	.959	0	3/2S	-0.3
Total	6	512	1600	195	422	74	17	19	168	190	176	.264	.344	.367	92	-16	-17	200	8	13	-5	.948	-3	32/S	-1.5

■ BOB FINLEY Finley, Robert Edward b: 11/25/15, Ennis, Tex. d: 1/2/86, W.Covina, Cal. BR/TR, 6'1", 200 lbs. Deb: 7/04/43

YEAR	TM/L	G	AB	R	H	2B	3B	HR	RBI	BB	SO	AVG	OBP	SLG	PRO+	BR	/A	RC	SB	CS	SBR	FA	FR	POS	TPR
1943	Phi-N	28	81	9	21	2	0	1	7	4	10	.259	.294	.321	81	-2	-2	7	0			.962	3	C	0.2
1944	Phi-N	94	281	18	70	11	1	1	21	12	25	.249	.292	.306	71	-12	-11	24	1			.967	-2	C	-0.8
Total	2	122	362	27	91	13	1	2	28	16	35	.251	.292	.309	73	-14	-13	31	1			.966	1	/C	-0.6

■ STEVE FINLEY Finley, Steven Allen b: 3/12/65, Union City, Tenn. BL/TL, 6'2", 175 lbs. Deb: 4/03/89

YEAR	TM/L	G	AB	R	H	2B	3B	HR	RBI	BB	SO	AVG	OBP	SLG	PRO+	BR	/A	RC	SB	CS	SBR	FA	FR	POS	TPR
1989	Bal-A	81	217	35	54	5	2	2	25	15	30	.249	.300	.318	77	-7	-6	23	17	3	3	.986	-8	O/D	-1.3
1990	Bal-A	142	464	46	119	16	4	3	37	32	53	.256	.307	.328	80	-14	-12	48	22	9	1	.977	-1	*O/D	-1.5
1991	Hou-N	159	596	84	170	28	10	8	54	42	65	.285	.334	.406	114	5	9	80	34	18	-1	.985	-6	*O	-0.1
1992	Hou-N	162	607	84	177	29	13	5	55	58	63	.292	.356	.407	123	13	17	94	44	9	8	.993	10	*O	3.3
Total	4	544	1884	249	520	78	29	18	171	147	211	.276	.331	.377	104	-3	8	244	117	39	12	.986	-4	O/D	0.4

■ BILL FINLEY Finley, William James b: 10/4/1863, New York, N.Y. d: 10/6/12, Asbury Park, N.J. Deb: 7/12/1886

YEAR	TM/L	G	AB	R	H	2B	3B	HR	RBI	BB	SO	AVG	OBP	SLG	PRO+	BR	/A	RC	SB	CS	SBR	FA	FR	POS	TPR
1886	NY-N	13	44	2	8	0	0	0	5	1	8	.182	.200	.182	17	-4	-4	2	2			.800	-3	/OC	-0.6

■ NEAL FINN Finn, Cornelius Francis "Mickey" b: 1/24/04, Brooklyn, N.Y. d: 7/7/33, Allentown, Pa. BR/TR, 5'11", 168 lbs. Deb: 4/21/30

YEAR	TM/L	G	AB	R	H	2B	3B	HR	RBI	BB	SO	AVG	OBP	SLG	PRO+	BR	/A	RC	SB	CS	SBR	FA	FR	POS	TPR
1930	Bro-N	87	273	42	76	13	0	3	30	26	18	.278	.350	.359	73	-12	-11	35	3			.948	-6	2	-1.2
1931	Bro-N	118	413	46	113	22	2	0	45	21	42	.274	.314	.337	75	-15	-14	45	2			.975	0	*2	-0.7
1932	Bro-N	65	189	22	45	5	2	0	14	11	15	.238	.284	.286	55	-12	-12	16	2			.933	4	3/2S	-0.5
1933	Phi-N	51	169	15	40	4	1	0	13	10	14	.237	.287	.272	54	-8	-11	14	2			.964	-1	2	-1.0
Total	4	321	1044	125	274	44	5	3	102	68	89	.262	.314	.323	67	-47	-48	109	9			.964	-3	2/3S	-3.4

■ HAL FINNEY Finney, Harold Wilson b: 7/30/05, Lafayette, Ala. d: 12/20/91, Lafayette, Ala. BR/TR, 5'11", 170 lbs. Deb: 6/24/31 F

YEAR	TM/L	G	AB	R	H	2B	3B	HR	RBI	BB	SO	AVG	OBP	SLG	PRO+	BR	/A	RC	SB	CS	SBR	FA	FR	POS	TPR
1931	Pit-N	10	26	2	8	1	0	0	2	0	1	.308	.333	.346	84	-1	-1	3	1			1.000	-0	/C	0.0
1932	Pit-N	31	33	14	7	3	0	0	4	3	4	.212	.297	.303	63	-2	-2	3	0			.971	3	C	0.1
1933	Pit-N	56	133	17	31	4	1	1	18	3	19	.233	.250	.301	57	-8	-8	9	0			.993	-2	C	-0.8
1934	Pit-N	5	0	3	0	0	0	0	0	0	0	—	1.000	—	188	0	0	0	0			.000	0	/C	0.0
1936	Pit-N	21	35	3	0	0	0	0	3	0	8	.000	.000	.000	-98	-10	-10	0	0			.956	1	C	-0.8
Total	5	123	227	39	46	8	1	1	27	6	32	.203	.233	.260	37	-19	-19	16	1			.983	1	/C	-1.5

■ LOU FINNEY Finney, Louis Klopsche b: 8/13/10, Buffalo, Ala. d: 4/22/66, Lafayette, Ala. BL/TR, 6', 180 lbs. Deb: 9/12/31 F

YEAR	TM/L	G	AB	R	H	2B	3B	HR	RBI	BB	SO	AVG	OBP	SLG	PRO+	BR	/A	RC	SB	CS	SBR	FA	FR	POS	TPR
1931	Phi-A	9	24	7	9	0	1	0	3	6	1	.375	.516	.458	149	3	2	6	0	0	0	1.000	1	/O	0.3
1933	Phi-A	74	240	26	64	12	2	3	32	13	17	.267	.307	.371	78	-8	-8	27	1	3	-2	.947	2	O	-1.0
1934	Phi-A	92	272	32	76	11	4	1	28	14	17	.279	.315	.360	77	-11	-10	31	4	3	-1	.943	0	O1	-1.3
1935	Phi-A	109	410	45	112	11	6	0	31	18	18	.273	.307	.329	65	-22	-21	42	7	2	1	.943	-2	O1	-2.6
1936	Phi-A	151	653	100	197	26	10	1	41	47	22	.302	.351	.377	81	-21	-19	85	7	9	-3	.990	-4	1O	-3.2
1937	Phi-A	92	379	53	95	14	9	1	20	20	16	.251	.288	.343	59	-25	-24	36	2	5	-2	.989	-4	1O/2	-3.6

YEAR	TM/L	G	AB	R	H	2B	3B	HR	RBI	BB	SO	AVG	OBP	SLG	PRO+	BR	/A	RC	SB	CS	SBR	FA	FR	POS	TPR
1938	Phi-A	122	454	61	125	21	12	10	48	39	25	.275	.333	.441	94	-8	-6	65	5	8	-3	.990	-3	1O	-1.8
1939	Phi-A	9	22	1	3	0	0	0	1	2	0	.136	.208	.136	-10	-4	-4	1	0	0	0	1.000	0	/O	-0.3
	Bos-A	95	249	43	81	18	3	1	46	24	11	.325	.385	.434	105	4	2	41	2	5	-2	.986	-6	1O	-0.9
	Yr	104	271	44	84	18	3	1	47	26	11	.310	.370	.410	96	-0	-1	41	2	5	-2	.986	-6	1O	-1.2
1940	Bos-A★	130	534	73	171	31	15	5	73	33	13	.320	.360	.463	107	8	5	87	5	2	0	.975	2	O1	-0.1
1941	Bos-A	127	497	83	143	24	10	4	53	38	17	.288	.340	.400	93	-4	-6	66	2	5	-2	.945	-3	O1	-1.8
1942	Bos-A	113	397	58	113	16	7	3	61	29	11	.285	.335	.383	98	0	-2	51	3	3	-1	.976	2	O/1	-0.6
1944	Bos-A	68	251	37	72	11	2	0	32	23	7	.287	.347	.347	100	-0	0	31	1	0	0	.987	-5	1/O	-0.8
1945	Bos-A	2	2	0	0	0	0	0	0	0	1	.000	.000	.000	-98	-1	-1	0	0	0	0	.000	0	H	-0.1
	StL-A	57	213	24	59	8	4	2	22	21	6	.277	.345	.380	105	3	1	27	0	0	0	.986	-2	O1/3	-0.4
	Yr	59	215	24	59	8	4	2	22	21	7	.274	.342	.377	103	2	1	27	0	0	0	.986	-2	O1/3	-0.5
1946	StL-A	16	30	0	9	0	0	0	3	2	4	.300	.344	.300	77	-1	-1	3	0	0	0	.938	0	/O	-0.1
1947	Phi-N	4	4	0	0	0	0	0	0	0	0	.000	.000	.000	-99	-1	-1	0	0			.000	0	H	-0.1
Total	15	1270	4631	643	1329	203	85	31	494	329	186	.287	.336	.388	88	-88	-90	599	39	45		.961	-22	O1/32	-18.4

■ MIKE FIORE Fiore, Michael Gary Joseph b: 10/11/44, Brooklyn, N.Y. BL/TL, 6', 185 lbs. Deb: 9/21/68

YEAR	TM/L	G	AB	R	H	2B	3B	HR	RBI	BB	SO	AVG	OBP	SLG	PRO+	BR	/A	RC	SB	CS	SBR	FA	FR	POS	TPR
1968	Bal-A	6	17	2	1	0	0	0	0	4	4	.059	.273	.059	5	-2	-2	1	0	0	0	.943	-0	/1O	-0.3
1969	KC-A	107	339	53	93	14	1	12	35	84	63	.274	.421	.428	137	22	21	66	4	4	-1	.988	10	1O	2.3
1970	KC-A	25	72	6	13	2	0	0	4	13	24	.181	.306	.208	44	-5	-5	5	1	1	-0	.986	1	1	-0.7
	Bos-A	41	50	5	7	0	0	0	4	8	4	.140	.259	.140	12	-6	-6	2	0	0	0	1.000	0	1/O	-0.7
	Yr	66	122	11	20	2	0	0	8	21	28	.164	.287	.180	30	-11	-11	7	1	1	-0	.991	1	1/O	-1.4
1971	Bos-A	51	62	9	11	2	0	1	6	12	14	.177	.311	.258	58	-3	-3	5	0	3	-2	1.000	-0	1	-0.7
1972	StL-N	17	10	0	1	0	0	0	1	2	3	.100	.250	.100	3	-1	-1	0	0	0	0	1.000	-0	/1O	-0.2
	SD-N	7	6	0	0	0	0	0	0	1	3	.000	.143	.000	-61	-1	-1	0	0	0	0	.000	0	H	-0.1
	Yr	24	16	0	1	0	0	0	1	3	6	.063	.211	.063	-20	-2	-2	0	0	0	0	1.000	-0	/1O	-0.3
Total	5	254	556	75	126	18	1	13	50	124	115	.227	.370	.333	97	4	3	79	5	8	-3	.988	10	1/O	-0.4

■ DAN FIROVA Firova, Daniel Michael b: 10/16/56, Refugio, Tex. BR/TR, 6', 185 lbs. Deb: 9/01/81

YEAR	TM/L	G	AB	R	H	2B	3B	HR	RBI	BB	SO	AVG	OBP	SLG	PRO+	BR	/A	RC	SB	CS	SBR	FA	FR	POS	TPR
1981	Sea-A	13	2	0	0	0	0	0	0	0	1	.000	.000	.000	-96	-1	-1	0	0	0	0	1.000	1	C	0.0
1982	Sea-A	3	5	0	0	0	0	0	0	0	0	.000	.000	.000	-97	-1	-1	0	0	0	0	.900	-0	/C	-0.1
1988	Cle-A	1	0	0	0	0	0	0	0	0	0	—	—	—	—	0	0	0	0	0	0	.000	0	/C	0.0
Total	3	17	7	0	0	0	0	0	0	0	1	.000	.000	.000	-97	-2	-2	0	0	0	0	.944	1	/C	-0.1

■ WILLIAM FISCHER Fischer, William Charles b: 3/2/1891, New York, N.Y. d: 9/4/45, Richmond, Va. BL/TR, 6', 174 lbs. Deb: 6/11/13

YEAR	TM/L	G	AB	R	H	2B	3B	HR	RBI	BB	SO	AVG	OBP	SLG	PRO+	BR	/A	RC	SB	CS	SBR	FA	FR	POS	TPR
1913	Bro-N	62	165	16	44	9	4	1	12	10	5	.267	.313	.388	97	-1	-1	19	0			.974	-1	C	0.2
1914	Bro-N	43	105	12	27	1	2	0	8	8	12	.257	.310	.305	81	-2	-2	10	1			.958	3	C	0.3
1915	Chi-F	105	292	30	96	15	4	4	50	24	19	.329	.384	.449	153	16	18	55	5			.972	-6	C	1.9
1916	Chi-N	65	179	15	35	9	2	1	14	11	8	.196	.246	.285	57	-8	-10	14	2			.973	4	C	-0.3
	Pit-N	42	113	11	29	7	1	1	6	10	3	.257	.323	.363	109	1	1	14	1			.974	5	C	1.0
	Yr	107	292	26	64	16	3	2	20	21	11	.219	.276	.315	76	-7	-9	27	3			.973	8	C	0.7
1917	Pit-N	95	245	25	70	9	2	3	25	27	19	.286	.359	.376	121	8	7	35	11			.961	-9	C/1	0.4
Total	5	412	1099	109	301	50	15	10	115	90	66	.274	.332	.374	109	14	12	147	20			.969	-6	C/1	3.5

■ MIKE FISCHLIN Fischlin, Michael Thomas b: 9/13/55, Sacramento, Cal. BR/TR, 6'1", 165 lbs. Deb: 9/03/77

YEAR	TM/L	G	AB	R	H	2B	3B	HR	RBI	BB	SO	AVG	OBP	SLG	PRO+	BR	/A	RC	SB	CS	SBR	FA	FR	POS	TPR
1977	Hou-N	13	15	0	3	0	0	0	0	0	2	.200	.200	.200	8	-2	-2	1	0	0	0	1.000	1	S	0.0
1978	Hou-N	44	86	3	10	1	0	0	0	4	9	.116	.165	.128	-19	-13	-13	2	1	0	0	.928	-4	S	-1.5
1980	Hou-N	1	1	0	0	0	0	0	0	0	1	.000	.000	.000	-99	-0	-0	0	0	0	0	1.000	-0	/S	0.0
1981	Cle-A	22	43	3	10	1	0	0	5	3	6	.233	.283	.256	57	-2	-2	3	3	2	-0	.955	-0	S/2	-0.2
1982	Cle-A	112	276	34	74	12	1	0	21	34	36	.268	.353	.319	86	-4	-4	34	9	5	-0	.970	-7	*S/32C	-0.3
1983	Cle-A	95	225	31	47	5	2	2	23	26	32	.209	.296	.276	56	-12	-13	22	9	2	2	.965	21	2S/3D	1.2
1984	Cle-A	85	133	17	30	4	2	1	14	12	20	.226	.290	.308	64	-6	-6	12	2	2	-1	.981	18	23S	1.3
1985	Cle-A	73	60	12	12	4	1	0	2	5	7	.200	.262	.300	54	-4	-4	5	0	1	-1	.990	27	2S/13D	2.3
1986	NY-A	71	102	9	21	2	0	0	3	8	29	.206	.264	.225	35	-9	-9	6	0	1	-1	.955	7	S2	0.0
1987	Atl-N	1	0	0	0	0	0	0	0	0	0	—	—	—	—	0	0	0	0	0	0	.000	0	/R	0.0
Total	10	517	941	109	207	29	6	3	68	92	142	.220	.293	.273	57	-53	-53	85	24	13	-1	.959	63	S2/31DC	2.8

■ SAM FISHBURN Fishburn, Samuel E. b: 5/15/1893, Haverhill, Mass. d: 4/11/65, Bethlehem, Pa. BR/TR, 5'9", 157 lbs. Deb: 9/30/19

YEAR	TM/L	G	AB	R	H	2B	3B	HR	RBI	BB	SO	AVG	OBP	SLG	PRO+	BR	/A	RC	SB	CS	SBR	FA	FR	POS	TPR
1919	StL-N	9	6	0	2	1	0	0	2	0	0	.333	.333	.500	158	0	0	1	0			1.000	1	/12	0.1

■ JOHN FISHEL Fishel, John Alan b: 11/8/62, Fullerton, Cal. BR/TR, 5'11", 185 lbs. Deb: 7/14/88

YEAR	TM/L	G	AB	R	H	2B	3B	HR	RBI	BB	SO	AVG	OBP	SLG	PRO+	BR	/A	RC	SB	CS	SBR	FA	FR	POS	TPR
1988	Hou-N	19	26	1	6	0	0	1	2	3	6	.231	.310	.346	92	-0	-0	3	0	0	0	1.000	-2	/O	-0.3

■ FISHER Fisher Deb: 6/15/1889

YEAR	TM/L	G	AB	R	H	2B	3B	HR	RBI	BB	SO	AVG	OBP	SLG	PRO+	BR	/A	RC	SB	CS	SBR	FA	FR	POS	TPR
1889	Lou-a	1	2	0	1	0	0	0	0	0	0	.500	.500	.500	192	0	0	1	0			.000	-1	/O	0.0

■ GUS FISHER Fisher, August Harris b: 10/21/1885, Pottsborough, Tex. d: 4/8/72, Portland, Ore. BL/TR, 5'10", 175 lbs. Deb: 4/18/11

YEAR	TM/L	G	AB	R	H	2B	3B	HR	RBI	BB	SO	AVG	OBP	SLG	PRO+	BR	/A	RC	SB	CS	SBR	FA	FR	POS	TPR
1911	Cle-A	70	203	20	53	6	3	0	12	7		.261	.302	.320	73	-8	-8	21	6			.956	8	C/1	0.5
1912	NY-A	4	10	1	1	0	0	0	0	0		.100	.100	.100	-40	-2	-2	0	0			1.000	0	/C	-0.1
Total	2	74	213	21	54	6	3	0	12	7		.254	.293	.310	68	-9	-10	21	6			.958	8	/C1	0.4

■ CHARLES FISHER Fisher, Charles J. b: Philadelphia, Pa. Deb: 6/07/1884

YEAR	TM/L	G	AB	R	H	2B	3B	HR	RBI	BB	SO	AVG	OBP	SLG	PRO+	BR	/A	RC	SB	CS	SBR	FA	FR	POS	TPR
1884	KC-U	10	40	3	8	2	0	0		0		.200	.200	.250	59	-2	-1	2				.711	-0	/3S	-0.1
	CP-U	1	3	1	2	0	0	0		1		.667	.750	.667	385	1	1	2				.500	-1	/3	0.0
	Yr	11	43	4	10	2	0	0		1		.233	.250	.279	89	-1	-0	3				.702	-1	3/S	-0.1

■ SHOWBOAT FISHER Fisher, George Aloys b: 1/16/1899, Jennings, Iowa BL/TR, 5'10", 170 lbs. Deb: 4/24/23

YEAR	TM/L	G	AB	R	H	2B	3B	HR	RBI	BB	SO	AVG	OBP	SLG	PRO+	BR	/A	RC	SB	CS	SBR	FA	FR	POS	TPR
1923	Was-A	13	23	4	6	2	0	0	2	4	3	.261	.370	.348	95	-0	-0	3	0	0	0	.750	0	/O	0.0
1924	Was-A	15	41	7	9	1	0	0	6	6	6	.220	.319	.244	48	-3	-3	4	2	0	1	.933	-2	O	-0.5
1930	*StL-N	92	254	49	95	18	6	8	61	25	21	.374	.432	.587	139	18	17	62	4			.962	-3	O	0.8
1932	StL-A	18	22	2	4	0	0	0	2	2	5	.182	.250	.182	13	-3	-3	1	0	0	0	1.000	-1	/O	-0.4
Total	4	138	340	62	114	21	6	8	71	37	35	.335	.402	.503	119	12	11	71	6	0		.946	-6	/O	-0.1

■ GEORGE FISHER Fisher, George C. b: Wilmington, Del. Deb: 7/17/1884

YEAR	TM/L	G	AB	R	H	2B	3B	HR	RBI	BB	SO	AVG	OBP	SLG	PRO+	BR	/A	RC	SB	CS	SBR	FA	FR	POS	TPR
1884	Phi-U	10	36	7	8	2	0	0		3		.222	.282	.278	97	-0	0	3				.667	-2	/P1	-0.1
	Cle-N	6	24	2	3	0	0	0	0	0	3	.125	.125	.125	-20	-3	-3	0				.897	-3	/2C	-0.6
	Wil-U	8	29	0	2	0	0	0		0		.069	.069	.069	-52	-4	-5	0				.818	-1	/OS	-0.5
1885	Buf-N	1	4	0	0	0	0	0	0	0	0	.000	.000	.000	-97	-1	-1	0				1.000	0	/P	0.0
Total	2	25	93	9	13	2	0	0	0	3	3	.140	.167	.161	9	-9	-9	3				.710	-6	/PO2S1C	-1.2

■ HARRY FISHER Fisher, Harry Devereux b: 1/3/26, Newbury, Ont., Can. d: 9/20/81, Waterloo, Ont., Ca BL/TR, 6', 180 lbs. Deb: 9/16/51

YEAR	TM/L	G	AB	R	H	2B	3B	HR	RBI	BB	SO	AVG	OBP	SLG	PRO+	BR	/A	RC	SB	CS	SBR	FA	FR	POS	TPR
1951	Pit-N	3	3	0	0	0	0	0	0	0	0	.000	.000	.000	-97	-1	-1	0	0	0	0	.000	0	H	-0.1
1952	Pit-N	15	15	0	5	1	0	0	1	0	3	.333	.333	.400	100	-0	-0	2	0	0	0	1.000	-1	/P	0.0
Total	2	18	18	0	5	1	0	0	1	0	3	.278	.278	.333	66	-1	-1	2	0	0	0	.978	-1	/P	-0.1

■ RED FISHER Fisher, John Gus b: 6/22/1887, Pittsburgh, Pa. d: 1/31/40, Louisville, Ky. BL/TR, Deb: 4/25/10

YEAR	TM/L	G	AB	R	H	2B	3B	HR	RBI	BB	SO	AVG	OBP	SLG	PRO+	BR	/A	RC	SB	CS	SBR	FA	FR	POS	TPR
1910	StL-A	23	72	5	9	2	1	0	3	8		.125	.222	.181	28	-6	-5	4	5			.935	-1	O	-0.9

YEAR	TM/L	G	AB	R	H	2B	3B	HR	RBI	BB	SO	AVG	OBP	SLG	PRO+	BR	/A	RC	SB	CS	SBR	FA	FR	POS	TPR
■ **NEWT FISHER**	Fisher, Newton "Ike" b: 6/28/1871, Nashville, Tenn. d: 2/28/47, Norwood Park, Ill. BR/TR, 5'9.5 ", 171 lbs. Deb: 5/17/1898 F																								
1898	Phi-N	9	26	0	3	1	0	0	0	0		.115	.148	.154	-14	-4	-4	1	1			.844	-2	/C3	-0.4
■ **BOB FISHER**	Fisher, Robert Taylor b: 11/3/1886, Nashville, Tenn. d: 8/4/63, Jacksonville, Fla. BR/TR, 5'9.5", 170 lbs. Deb: 6/03/12 F																								
1912	Bro-N	82	257	27	60	10	3	0	26	14	32	.233	.273	.296	58	-16	-15	23	7			.917	-14	S/23	-2.3
1913	Bro-N	132	474	42	124	11	10	4	54	10	43	.262	.278	.352	77	-15	-16	49	16			.923	-19	*S	-2.4
1914	Chi-N	15	50	5	15	2	2	0	5	3	4	.300	.340	.420	126	1	1	8	2			.943	-1	S	0.1
1915	Chi-N	147	568	70	163	22	5	5	53	30	51	.287	.326	.370	110	6	6	69	9	20	-9	.933	-20	*S	-1.4
1916	Cin-N	61	136	9	37	4	3	0	11	8	14	.272	.313	.346	104	0	0	17	7			.905	-12	S/2O	-1.1
1918	StL-N	63	246	36	78	11	3	2	20	15	11	.317	.356	.411	138	9	10	37	7			.979	19	2	3.5
1919	StL-N	3	11	0	3	1	0	0	1	0	2	.273	.273	.364	96	-0	-0	1	0			.900	0	/2	0.1
Total	7	503	1742	189	480	61	26	11	170	80	157	.276	.309	.359	96	-14	-13	203	48	20		.925	-48	S/2O3	-3.5
■ **WILBUR FISHER**	Fisher, Wilbur McCullough b: 7/18/1894, Greenbottom, W.Va d: 10/24/60, Welch, W.Va. BL/TR, 6', 174 lbs. Deb: 6/13/16																								
1916	Pit-N	1	1	0	0	0	0	0	0	0	0	.000	.000	.000	-99	-0	-0	0	0			.000	0	H	0.0
■ **CHEROKEE FISHER**	Fisher, William Charles b: 12/1845, Philadelphia, Pa. d: 9/26/12, New York, N.Y. BR/TR, 5'9", 164 lbs. Deb: 5/06/1871																								
1871	Rok-n	25	123	24	28	3	3	1	22	3	1	.228	.246	.325	65	-6	-5	10	1					*P/S	0.2
1872	Bal-n	46	226	40	52	10	2	1	39	2	5	.230	.237	.305	63	-9	-11	16						P3O	-0.4
1873	Ath-n	51	253	50	66	4	3	1	35	4	5	.261	.272	.312	67	-9	-13	22						*O/P21	-0.5
1874	Har-n	52	242	28	54	8	0	0		0		.223	.223	.256	50	-13	-15	14						PO/3S	0.2
1875	Phi-n	41	177	26	41	2	1	0		1		.232	.236	.254	67	-5	-6	11						P/O	0.4
1876	Cin-N	35	129	12	32	1	0	0	4	0	8	.248	.248	.256	80	-4	-1	8				.793	-5	PO/S1	-0.3
1877	Chi-N	1	4	0	0	0	0	0	0	0	2	.000	.000	.000	-89	-1	-1	0				.667	-0	/3	-0.1
1878	Pro-N	1	3	0	0	0	0	0	0	0	0	.000	.000	.000	-99	-1	-1	0				1.000	0	/P	0.0
Total	5 n	215	1021	168	241	27	9	3	96	10	11	.236	.243	.289	62	-41	-49	74						P/O32S1	-0.1
Total	3	37	136	12	32	1	0	0	4	0	10	.235	.235	.243	68	-6	-3	8				.803	-5	/PO31S	-0.4
■ **CARLTON FISK**	Fisk, Carlton Ernest "Pudge" b: 12/26/47, Bellows Falls, Vt. BR/TR, 6'2", 220 lbs. Deb: 9/18/69																								
1969	Bos-A	2	5	0	0	0	0	0	0	0	2	.000	.000	.000	-95	-1	-1	0	0	0	0	1.000	-1	/C	-0.3
1971	Bos-A	14	48	7	15	2	1	2	6	1	10	.313	.327	.521	128	2	2	8	0	0	0	.975	-1	C	0.1
1972	Bos-A★	131	457	74	134	28	**9**	22	61	52	83	.293	.370	.538	159	37	34	90	5	2	0	.984	1	*C	4.6
1973	Bos-A★	135	508	65	125	21	0	26	71	37	99	.246	.310	.441	103	4	1	69	7	2	1	.983	6	*C/D	1.4
1974	Bos-A†	52	187	36	56	12	1	11	26	24	23	.299	.385	.551	156	16	14	40	5	1	1	.980	2	C/D	2.0
1975	*Bos-A	79	263	47	87	14	4	10	52	27	32	.331	.397	.529	147	20	18	54	4	3	-1	.979	-4	C/D	1.6
1976	Bos-A★	134	487	76	124	17	5	17	58	56	71	.255	.339	.415	107	12	5	70	12	5	1	.984	10	*C/D	2.1
1977	Bos-A★	152	536	106	169	26	3	26	102	75	85	.315	.408	.521	135	40	31	117	7	6	-2	.987	0	*C	3.4
1978	Bos-A★	157	571	94	162	39	5	20	88	71	83	.284	.370	.475	123	28	20	103	7	2	1	.980	11	*C/OD	3.6
1979	Bos-A	91	320	49	87	23	2	10	42	10	38	.272	.307	.450	96	-1	-3	42	3	0	1	.982	-12	DC/O	-1.2
1980	Bos-A★	131	478	73	138	25	3	18	62	36	62	.289	.355	.467	117	15	12	77	11	5	0	.983	-7	*C/O13D	0.9
1981	Chi-A★	96	338	44	89	12	0	7	45	38	37	.263	.358	.361	110	5	6	45	3	2	-0	.990	-2	C/13O	0.7
1982	Chi-A★	135	476	66	127	17	3	14	65	46	60	.267	.339	.403	103	2	2	67	17	2	4	.994	-1	*C/1	1.0
1983	*Chi-A	138	488	85	141	26	4	26	86	46	88	.289	.357	.518	133	24	22	90	9	6	-1	.991	-2	*C/D	2.5
1984	Chi-A	102	359	54	83	20	1	21	43	26	60	.231	.292	.468	102	2	-0	49	6	0	2	.987	-17	C/D	-1.1
1985	Chi-A★	153	543	85	129	23	1	37	107	52	81	.238	.324	.488	114	13	10	85	17	9	-0	.989	-4	*CD	1.2
1986	Chi-A	125	457	42	101	11	0	14	63	22	92	.221	.266	.337	61	-24	-26	39	2	4	-2	.991	2	CO/D	-2.2
1987	Chi-A	135	454	68	116	22	1	23	71	39	72	.256	.325	.460	103	3	1	66	1	4	-2	.990	2	*C/1OD	0.8
1988	Chi-A	76	253	37	70	8	1	19	50	37	40	.277	.380	.542	155	19	19	52	0	0	0	.995	-5	C	1.9
1989	Chi-A	103	375	47	110	25	2	13	68	36	60	.293	.360	.475	137	16	17	61	1	0	0	**.993**	-15	CD	0.8
1990	Chi-A	137	452	65	129	21	0	18	65	61	73	.285	.379	.451	134	20	21	79	7	2	1	.994	5	*CD	3.5
1991	Chi-A★	134	460	42	111	25	0	18	74	32	86	.241	.301	.413	98	-4	-3	52	1	2	-1	.993	-1	*CD1	0.0
1992	Chi-A	62	188	12	43	4	1	3	21	23	38	.229	.316	.309	77	-6	-5	20	3	0	1	.993	-6	C/D	-0.7
Total	23	2474	8703	1274	2346	421	47	375	1326	847	1375	.270	.344	.458	117	241	195	1372	128	57	4	.988	-39	*CD/O13	26.6
■ **WES FISLER**	Fisler, Weston Dickson "Icicle" b: 7/5/1841, Camden, N.J. d: 12/25/22, Philadelphia, Pa. 5'6", 137 lbs. Deb: 5/20/1871																								
1871	Ath-n	28	147	43	41	8	2	0	16	3	2	.279	.293	.361	88	-3	-2	18	6					*1/2	-0.1
1872	Ath-n	47	243	50	84	14	3	0	48	4	4	.346	.356	.428	140	11	11	39						*2	0.6
1873	Ath-n	44	218	44	75	12	4	1	42	2	2	.344	.350	.450	124	9	5	35						*21	0.2
1874	Ath-n	37	179	26	59	12	1	0		0		.330	.330	.408	123	6	4	25						1/2	0.2
1875	Ath-n	58	267	55	74	14	3	0		4		.277	.288	.352	108	5	1	28						1/O2	0.0
1876	Phi-N	59	278	42	80	15	1	1	30	2	4	.288	.293	.360	117	4	5	30				.911	1	O21/S	0.4
Total	5 n	214	1054	218	333	60	13	1	106	13	8	.316	.324	.400	118	29	18	145						1/2OD	0.9
■ **CHARLIE FITZBERGER**	Fitzberger, Charles Casper b: 2/13/04, Baltimore, Md. d: 1/25/65, Baltimore, Md. BL/TL, 6'1.5", 170 lbs. Deb: 9/11/28																								
1928	Bos-N	7	7	0	2	0	0	0	0	0	3	.286	.286	.286	52	-1	-0	1	0			.000	0	H	0.0
■ **DENNIS FITZGERALD**	Fitzgerald, Dennis S. b: 3/1865, England d: 10/16/36, New Haven, Conn. 5'10", 160 lbs. Deb: 4/17/1890																								
1890	Phi-a	2	8	0	2	0	0	0		0		.250	.250	.250	50	-1	-0	1	0			.667	-2	/S	-0.2
■ **ED FITZGERALD**	Fitzgerald, Edward Raymond b: 5/21/24, Santa Ynez, Cal. BR/TR, 6', 180 lbs. Deb: 4/19/48 C																								
1948	Pit-N	102	262	31	70	9	3	1	35	32	37	.267	.349	.336	84	-4	-5	33	3			.961	-2	C	-0.1
1949	Pit-N	75	160	16	42	7	0	2	18	8	27	.262	.302	.344	71	-6	-7	16	1			.974	-5	C	-0.9
1950	Pit-N	6	15	1	1	1	0	0	0	0	3	.067	.067	.133	-47	-3	-3	0	0			.950	-0	/C	-0.4
1951	Pit-N	55	97	8	22	6	0	0	13	7	10	.227	.286	.289	53	-6	-6	7	1	1	-0	.965	-2	C	-0.8
1952	Pit-N	51	73	4	17	1	0	1	7	7	15	.233	.300	.288	62	-3	-4	5	0	2	-1	1.000	-1	C/3	-0.6
1953	Pit-N	6	17	2	2	1	0	0	1	0	2	.118	.118	.176	-25	-3	-3	0	0	0	0	1.000	-1	/C	-0.4
	Was-A	88	288	23	72	13	0	3	39	19	34	.250	.299	.326	70	-13	-12	27	2	1	0	.989	-3	C	-1.1
1954	Was-A	115	360	33	104	13	5	4	40	33	22	.289	.352	.386	108	1	3	48	0	1	-1	.973	-17	*C	-0.9
1955	Was-A	74	236	28	56	3	1	4	19	25	23	.237	.318	.309	73	-10	-8	23	0	1	-1	.982	-7	C	-1.3
1956	Was-A	64	148	15	45	8	0	2	12	20	16	.304	.387	.399	108	2	2	23	0	0	0	.974	2	C	0.6
1957	Was-A	45	125	14	34	8	0	1	13	10	9	.272	.331	.360	90	-2	-2	13	2	0	1	.963	-8	C	-0.8
1958	Was-A	58	114	7	30	3	0	0	11	8	15	.263	.311	.289	68	-5	-5	9	0	0	0	.970	-6	C/1	-1.0
1959	Was-A	19	62	5	12	3	0	0	5	4	8	.194	.242	.242	34	-6	-6	4	0	0	0	1.000	-1	C	-0.5
	Cle-A	49	129	12	35	6	1	1	4	12	14	.271	.343	.357	96	-1	-1	15	0	0	0	.978	1	C	0.2
	Yr	68	191	17	47	9	1	1	9	16	22	.246	.311	.319	76	-7	-6	19	0	0	0	.984	-0	C	-0.3
Total	12	807	2086	199	542	82	10	19	217	185	235	.260	.324	.336	80	-60	-56	223	9	6		.975	-48	C/13	-8.0
■ **HOWIE FITZGERALD**	Fitzgerald, Howard Chumney "Lefty" b: 5/16/02, Eagle Lake, Tex. d: 2/27/59, Matthews, Tex. BL/TL, 5'11.5", 163 lbs. Deb: 9/17/22																								
1922	Chi-N	10	24	3	8	1	0	0	4	3	2	.333	.407	.375	101	0	0	4	1	0	0	.818	-2	/O	-0.1
1924	Chi-N	7	19	1	3	0	0	0	2	0	2	.158	.158	.158	-15	-3	-3	0	0	0	0	1.000	-2	/O	-0.5
1926	Bos-A	31	97	11	25	2	0	0	8	5	7	.258	.294	.278	51	-7	-7	7	1	4	-2	.882	-5	O	-1.5
Total	3	48	140	15	36	3	0	0	14	8	11	.257	.297	.279	52	-10	-10	12	2	4	-2	.878	-8	/O	-2.1
■ **MIKE FITZGERALD**	Fitzgerald, Justin Howard b: 6/22/1890, San Mateo, Cal. d: 1/17/45, San Mateo, Cal. BL/TR, 5'8", 160 lbs. Deb: 6/20/11																								
1911	NY-A	16	37	6	10	1	0	0	6	4		.270	.341	.297	74	-1	-1	5	4			1.000	-2	/O	-0.3

YEAR	TM/L	G	AB	R	H	2B	3B	HR	RBI	BB	SO	AVG	OBP	SLG	PRO+	BR	/A	RC	SB	CS	SBR	FA	FR	POS	TPR
1918	Phi-N	66	133	21	39	8	0	0	6	13	6	.293	.361	.353	110	3	2	18	3			.966	-14	O	-1.5
Total	2	82	170	27	49	9	0	0	12	17	6	.288	.356	.341	102	2	1	23	7			.971	-15	/O	-1.8
■ MATTY FITZGERALD	Fitzgerald, Matthew William b: 8/31/1880, Albany, N.Y. d: 9/22/49, Albany, N.Y. BR/TR, 6', 185 lbs. Deb: 9/15/06																								
1906	NY-N	4	6	2	4	0	0	0	2	0		.667	.667	.667	310	1	1	3	1			1.000	-1	/C	0.1
1907	NY-N	7	15	1	2	1	0	0	1	0		.133	.133	.200	4	-2	-2	0	0			.952	-1	/C	-0.3
Total	2	11	21	3	6	1	0	0	3	0		.286	.286	.333	91	-0	-0	4	1			.967	-2	/C	-0.2
■ MIKE FITZGERALD	Fitzgerald, Michael Patrick b: 3/28/64, Savannah, Ga. BR/TR, 6'1", 196 lbs. Deb: 6/23/88																								
1988	StL-N	13	46	4	9	1	0	0	1	0	9	.196	.213	.217	23	-5	-5	2	0	0	0	.990	-2	1	-0.8
■ MIKE FITZGERALD	Fitzgerald, Michael Roy b: 7/13/60, Long Beach, Cal. BR/TR, 5'11", 190 lbs. Deb: 9/13/83																								
1983	NY-N	8	20	1	2	0	0	1	2	3	6	.100	.217	.250	29	-2	-2	1	0	0	0	.957	2	/C	0.1
1984	NY-N	112	360	20	87	15	1	2	33	24	71	.242	.291	.306	69	-15	-15	29	1	0	0	**.995**	8	*C	-0.2
1985	Mon-N	108	295	25	61	7	1	5	34	38	55	.207	.301	.288	70	-13	-11	26	5	3	-0	.987	-6	*C	-1.3
1986	Mon-N	73	209	20	59	13	1	6	37	27	34	.282	.367	.440	123	6	7	34	3	2	-0	.993	-7	C	0.4
1987	Mon-N	107	287	32	69	11	0	3	36	42	54	.240	.339	.310	71	-10	-11	30	3	4	-2	.981	-1	*C/12	-0.7
1988	Mon-N	63	155	17	42	6	1	5	23	19	22	.271	.351	.419	115	4	3	23	2	2	-1	.979	4	C/O	1.1
1989	Mon-N	100	290	33	69	18	2	7	42	35	61	.238	.324	.386	101	1	1	35	3	4	-2	.984	-6	C/3O	-0.3
1990	Mon-N	111	313	36	76	18	1	9	41	60	60	.243	.368	.393	114	6	8	51	8	1	2	.990	-4	C/O	1.2
1991	Mon-N	71	198	17	40	5	2	4	28	22	35	.202	.282	.308	67	-9	-9	17	4	2	0	.994	2	C/1O	-0.4
1992	Cal-A	95	189	19	40	2	0	6	17	22	34	.212	.294	.317	72	-7	-7	18	2	2	-1	.990	-15	CO/312D	-2.0
Total	10	848	2316	220	545	95	9	48	293	292	432	.235	.323	.346	87	-39	-36	264	31	20	-3		-22	C/O312D	-2.1
■ RAY FITZGERALD	Fitzgerald, Raymond Francis b: 12/5/04, Chicopee, Mass. d: 9/6/77, Westfield, Mass. BR/TR, 5'9", 168 lbs. Deb: 4/18/31																								
1931	Cin-N	1	1	0	0	0	0	0	0	0	0	.000	.000	.000	-99	-0	-0	0	0			.000	0	H	0.0
■ SHAUN FITZMAURICE	Fitzmaurice, Shaun Earle b: 8/25/42, Worcester, Mass. BR/TR, 6', 180 lbs. Deb: 9/09/66																								
1966	NY-N	9	13	2	2	0	0	0	0	2	6	.154	.267	.154	21	-1	-1	1	1	0	0	1.000	1	/O	0.0
■ ED FITZPATRICK	Fitzpatrick, Edward Henry b: 12/9/1889, Lewiston, Pa. d: 10/23/65, Bethlehem, Pa. BR/TR, 5'8", 165 lbs. Deb: 4/17/15																								
1915	Bos-N	105	303	54	67	19	3	0	24	43	36	.221	.344	.304	101	1	3	36	13	8	-1	.967	-6	2O	-0.4
1916	Bos-N	83	216	17	46	8	0	1	18	15	26	.213	.280	.264	70	-8	-7	19	5			.950	-12	2O	-2.2
1917	Bos-N	63	178	20	45	8	4	0	17	12	22	.253	.318	.343	109	1	2	20	4			.929	-13	2O3	-1.2
Total	3	251	697	91	158	35	7	1	59	70	84	.227	.319	.301	94	-6	-2	75	22	8		.956	-31	2/O3	-3.8
■ TOM FITZSIMMONS	Fitzsimmons, Thomas William b: 4/6/1890, Oakland, Cal. d: 12/20/71, Oakland, Cal. BR/TR, 6'1", 190 lbs. Deb: 6/12/19																								
1919	Bro-N	4	4	1	0	0	0	0	0	1	2	.000	.200	.000	-36	-1	-1	0	0			.500	-1	/3	-0.2
■ MAX FLACK	Flack, Max John b: 2/5/1890, Belleville, Ill. d: 7/31/75, Belleville, Ill. BL/TL, 5'7", 148 lbs. Deb: 4/16/14																								
1914	Chi-F	134	502	66	124	15	3	2	39	51	48	.247	.324	.301	83	-13	-9	64	37			.973	-1	*O	-1.6
1915	Chi-F	141	523	88	164	20	14	3	45	40	21	.314	.365	.423	139	19	23	98	37			.969	2	*O	1.9
1916	Chi-N	141	465	65	120	14	3	3	20	42	43	.258	.320	.320	87	-1	-7	53	24	19	-4	**.991**	2	*O	-1.8
1917	Chi-N	131	447	65	111	18	7	0	21	51	34	.248	.325	.320	91	0	-4	50	17			.947	-3	*O	-1.5
1918	*Chi-N	123	478	74	123	17	10	4	41	56	19	.257	.343	.360	112	9	8	63	17			.978	3	*O	0.5
1919	Chi-N	116	469	71	138	20	4	6	35	34	13	.294	.346	.392	121	12	12	67	18			.986	-0	*O	0.4
1920	Chi-N	135	520	85	157	30	6	4	49	52	15	.302	.373	.406	121	17	16	77	13	19	-8	.967	-5	*O	-0.7
1921	Chi-N	133	572	80	172	31	4	6	37	32	15	.301	.342	.400	96	-4	-4	77	17	11	-2	**.989**	4	*O	-1.1
1922	Chi-N	17	54	7	12	1	0	0	6	2	4	.222	.250	.241	27	-6	-6	3	2	1	0	.933	-2	O	-0.9
	StL-N	66	267	46	78	12	1	2	21	31	11	.292	.368	.367	95	-3	-1	37	3	5	-2	.968	-4	O	-1.2
	Yr	83	321	53	90	13	1	2	27	33	15	.280	.349	.346	83	-9	-7	39	5	6	-2	.961	-6	O	-2.1
1923	StL-N	128	505	82	147	16	9	3	28	41	16	.291	.348	.376	93	-6	-5	66	7	8	-3	.951	-6	*O	-2.0
1924	StL-N	67	209	31	55	11	3	2	21	21	5	.263	.330	.373	90	-3	-3	25	3	5	-2	.971	1	O	-0.7
1925	StL-N	79	241	23	60	7	8	0	28	21	9	.249	.309	.344	65	-12	-13	26	5	3	-0	.991	-2	O	-1.8
Total	12	1411	5252	783	1461	212	72	35	391	474	253	.278	.342	.366	100	10	8	706	200	71		.972	-12	*O	-10.5
■ WALLY FLAGER	Flager, Walter Leonard b: 11/3/21, Chicago Heights, Ill. BL/TR, 5'11", 160 lbs. Deb: 4/17/45																								
1945	Cin-N	21	52	5	11	1	0	0	6	8	5	.212	.317	.231	55	-3	-3	4	0			.933	-7	S	-0.9
	Phi-N	49	168	21	42	4	1	2	15	17	15	.250	.323	.321	82	-5	-4	18	1			.946	1	S/2	0.1
	Yr	70	220	26	53	5	1	2	21	25	20	.241	.321	.300	75	-7	-7	23	1			.943	-6	S/2	-0.8
■ IRA FLAGSTEAD	Flagstead, Ira James "Pete" b: 9/22/1893, Montague, Mich. d: 3/13/40, Olympia, Wash. BR/TR, 5'9", 165 lbs. Deb: 7/20/17																								
1917	Det-A	4	4	0	0	0	0	0	0	0	1	.000	.000	.000	-99	-1	-1	0	0			.000	-1	/O	-0.2
1919	Det-A	97	287	43	95	22	3	5	41	35	39	.331	.416	.481	155	21	21	59	6			.951	2	O	1.8
1920	Det-A	110	311	40	73	13	5	3	35	37	27	.235	.318	.338	76	-12	-11	35	3	4	-2	.967	7	O	-1.1
1921	Det-A	85	259	40	79	16	2	0	31	21	21	.305	.371	.382	93	-2	-2	38	7	4	-0	.903	-5	SO/23	-0.3
1922	Det-A	44	91	21	28	5	3	3	8	14	16	.308	.411	.527	148	6	6	20	0	1	-1	.967	-2	O	0.2
1923	Det-A	1	1	0	0	0	0	0	0	0	0	.000	.000	.000	-99	-0	-0	0	0	0	0	.000	0	H	0.0
	Bos-A	109	382	55	119	23	4	8	53	37	26	.312	.380	.455	119	10	10	65	8	10	-4	.965	19	*O/S	1.8
	Yr	110	383	55	119	23	4	8	53	37	26	.311	.379	.454	118	10	10	65	8	10	-4	.965	19	*O/S	1.8
1924	Bos-A	149	560	106	172	35	7	5	43	77	41	.307	.401	.421	112	13	13	97	10	13	-5	.975	-2	*O	-0.3
1925	Bos-A	148	572	84	160	38	2	6	61	63	30	.280	.356	.385	88	-10	-10	81	5	6	-2	.976	**20**	*O	-0.2
1926	Bos-A	98	415	65	124	31	7	3	31	36	22	.299	.363	.429	109	3	5	64	4	6	-2	.982	9	O	0.4
1927	Bos-A	131	466	63	133	26	8	4	69	57	25	.285	.374	.401	103	2	3	71	12	2	2	**.986**	11	*O	0.8
1928	Bos-A	140	510	84	148	41	4	1	39	60	23	.290	.366	.392	101	1	2	75	12	9	-2	.973	5	*O	-0.3
1929	Bos-A	14	36	9	11	2	0	0	3	5	1	.306	.390	.361	97	-0	0	5	1	3	-2	.955	-3	O	-0.5
	Was-A	18	39	5	7	1	0	0	9	4	5	.179	.256	.205	20	-5	-5	3	1	0	0	.971	3	O	-0.2
	Yr	32	75	14	18	3	0	0	12	9	6	.240	.321	.280	57	-5	-5	7	2	3	-1	.965	0	O	-0.7
	Pit-N	26	50	8	14	2	1	0	6	4	2	.280	.333	.360	70	-2	-2	6	1			1.000	0	/O	-0.2
1930	Pit-N	44	156	21	39	7	4	2	21	17	9	.250	.324	.385	70	-8	-8	20	1			.961	-3	O	-1.2
Total	13	1218	4139	644	1202	262	50	40	450	467	288	.290	.370	.407	103	15	22	638	71	58		.974	59	*O/S23	0.5
■ JOHN FLAHERTY	Flaherty, John Timothy b: 10/21/67, New York, N.Y. BR/TR, 6'1", 195 lbs. Deb: 4/12/92																								
1992	Bos-A	35	66	3	13	2	0	0	2	3	7	.197	.232	.227	28	-6	-7	4	0	0	0	.982	-3	C	-0.9
■ MARTIN FLAHERTY	Flaherty, Martin J. b: 9/24/1853, Worcester, Mass d: 6/10/20, Providence, R.I. BL/TL, Deb: 8/18/1881																								
1881	Wor-N	1	2	0	0	0	0	0	0	0	2	.000	.000	.000	-95	-0	-0	0				.000	-1	/O	-0.2
■ PAT FLAHERTY	Flaherty, Patrick Henry b: 1/31/1876, St.Louis, Mo. d: 1/28/46, Chicago, Ill. 5'9", 166 lbs. Deb: 7/11/1894																								
1894	Lou-N	38	145	15	43	5	3	0	15	9	6	.297	.342	.372	79	-6	-4	20	2			.855	-5	3	-0.7
■ PATSY FLAHERTY	Flaherty, Patrick Joseph b: 6/29/1876, Mansfield, Pa. d: 1/23/68, Alexandria, La. BL/TL, 5'8", 165 lbs. Deb: 9/08/1899																								
1899	Lou-N	7	24	3	5	1	1	0	6	3		.208	.296	.333	73	-1	-1	2	0			.692	-1	/PO	0.0
1900	Pit-N	4	9	0	1	0	0	0	0	1		.111	.200	.111	-13	-1	-1	0	0			1.000	1	/P	0.0
1903	Chi-A	40	102	7	14	4	0	0	5	5		.137	.178	.176	7	-11	-11	4	4			.914	3	P	0.0
1904	Chi-A	5	12	1	4	1	0	0	0	4		.333	.500	.417	200	2	2	3	0			.880	1	/P	0.0

YEAR	TM/L	G	AB	R	H	2B	3B	HR	RBI	BB	SO	AVG	OBP	SLG	PRO+	BR	/A	RC	SB	CS	SBR	FA	FR	POS	TPR
	Pit-N	36	104	9	22	3	4	2	19	8		.212	.268	.375	96	-1	-1	11	0			.965	5	P/O	0.0
1905	Pit-N	30	76	7	15	4	2	0	4	3		.197	.228	.303	56	-4	-4	5	0			.894	2	P/O	-0.1
1907	Bos-N	41	115	9	22	3	2	2	11	2		.191	.212	.304	62	-6	-6	8	1			.907	3	P/O	-0.1
1908	Bos-N	32	86	8	12	0	2	0	5	6		.140	.196	.186	22	-8	-7	4	2			.961	2	P	0.0
1910	Phi-N	2	2	0	1	0	0	0	0	0	0	.500	.500	.500	186	-0	-0	0	0			.000	-0	/PO	0.0
1911	Bos-N	38	94	9	27	3	2	2	20	8	11	.287	.343	.426	106	1	0	14	2			.933	-4	O/P	-0.4
Total	9	235	624	53	123	19	13	6	70	40	11	.197	.247	.298	63	-29	-29	52	9			.921	11	P/O	-0.6

■ AL FLAIR
Flair, Albert Dell "Broadway" b: 7/24/16, New Orleans, La. d: 7/25/88, New Orleans, La. BL/TL, 6'4", 195 lbs. Deb: 9/06/41

YEAR	TM/L	G	AB	R	H	2B	3B	HR	RBI	BB	SO	AVG	OBP	SLG	PRO+	BR	/A	RC	SB	CS	SBR	FA	FR	POS	TPR
1941	Bos-A	10	30	3	6	2	1	0	2	1	1	.200	.226	.333	45	-2	-3	2	1	1	-0	1.000	-0	/1	-0.3

■ CHARLIE FLANAGAN
Flanagan, Charles James b: 12/31/1891, Oakland, Cal. d: 1/8/30, San Francisco, Cal. BR/TR, 6', 175 lbs. Deb: 7/09/13

| 1913 | StL-A | 4 | 4 | 0 | 0 | 0 | 0 | 0 | 1 | 0 | | .000 | .250 | .000 | -26 | -0 | -0 | 0 | 0 | | | .000 | -1 | /3O | -0.1 |

■ ED FLANAGAN
Flanagan, Edward J. "Sleepy" b: 9/15/1861, Lowell, Mass. d: 11/10/26, Lowell, Mass. 6'1", 190 lbs. Deb: 4/16/1887

1887	Phi-a	19	80	12	20	5	0	1		3		.250	.286	.350	78	-2	-2	9	3			.948	-1	1	-0.5
1889	Lou-a	23	88	11	22	7	3	0	8	7	11	.250	.305	.398	103	-0	-0	11	1			.953	-1	1	-0.1
Total	2	42	168	23	42	12	3	1	8	10	11	.250	.296	.375	91	-3	-2	20	4			.951	-2	/1	-0.6

■ STEAMER FLANAGAN
Flanagan, James Paul b: 4/20/1881, Kingston, Pa. d: 4/21/47, Wilkes-Barre, Pa. BL/TL, 6'1", 185 lbs. Deb: 9/25/05

| 1905 | Pit-N | 7 | 25 | 7 | 7 | 1 | 1 | 0 | 3 | 1 | | .280 | .308 | .400 | 108 | 0 | 0 | 4 | 3 | | | 1.000 | 1 | /O | 0.1 |

■ JOHN FLANNERY
Flannery, John Michael b: 1/25/57, Long Beach, Cal. BR/TR, 6'3", 173 lbs. Deb: 9/02/77

| 1977 | Chi-A | 7 | 2 | 1 | 0 | 0 | 0 | 0 | 0 | 1 | 1 | .000 | .333 | .000 | 0 | -0 | -0 | 0 | 0 | 0 | 0 | 1.000 | 1 | /S3D | 0.1 |

■ TIM FLANNERY
Flannery, Timothy Earl b: 9/29/57, Tulsa, Okla. BL/TR, 5'11", 175 lbs. Deb: 9/03/79

1979	SD-N	22	65	2	10	0	1	0	4	4	5	.154	.225	.185	14	-8	-7	3	0	0		.991	2	2	-0.4
1980	SD-N	95	292	15	70	12	0	0	25	18	30	.240	.284	.281	62	-16	-14	23	2	2	-1	.988	-4	23	-1.8
1981	SD-N	37	67	4	17	4	1	0	6	2	4	.254	.275	.343	80	-2	-2	6	1	0	0	.967	-1	3/2	-0.3
1982	SD-N	122	379	40	100	11	7	0	30	30	32	.264	.321	.330	87	-9	-6	42	1	0	0	.974	-24	*2/3S	-2.7
1983	SD-N	92	214	24	50	7	3	0	19	20	23	.234	.314	.336	83	-6	-5	23	2	2	-1	.969	10	32/S	0.6
1984	*SD-N	86	128	24	35	3	3	2	10	12	17	.273	.350	.391	108	1	2	19	4	1	1	.944	-6	23S	-0.2
1985	SD-N	126	384	50	108	14	3	1	40	58	39	.281	.388	.341	107	6	7	55	2	5	-2	.977	-19	*2/3	-1.1
1986	SD-N	134	368	48	103	11	2	3	28	54	61	.280	.379	.345	103	3	4	50	3	6	-3	.993	-7	*23/S	-0.2
1987	SD-N	106	276	23	63	5	1	0	20	42	30	.228	.334	.254	61	-15	-14	25	4	2	-2	.986	3	3/2S	-0.9
1988	SD-N	79	170	16	45	5	4	0	19	24	32	.265	.369	.341	107	2	3	23	3	2	-0	.972	-4	3/2S	-0.2
1989	SD-N	73	130	9	30	5	0	0	8	13	20	.231	.301	.269	64	-6	-6	11	2	0	1	.920	2	3/2	-0.4
Total	11	972	2473	255	631	77	25	9	209	277	293	.255	.338	.317	86	-48	-38	279	22	22	-7	.982	-47	23/S	-7.6

■ ROY FLASKAMPER
Flaskamper, Raymond Harold "Flash" b: 10/31/01, St.Louis, Mo. d: 2/3/78, San Antonio, Tex. BB/TR, 5'7", 140 lbs. Deb: 8/16/27

| 1927 | Chi-A | 26 | 95 | 12 | 21 | 5 | 0 | 0 | 6 | 3 | 8 | .221 | .260 | .274 | 40 | -9 | -8 | 7 | 0 | 0 | 0 | .962 | 0 | S | -0.6 |

■ FRANK FLEET
Fleet, Frank H. b: 1848, New York, N.Y. d: 6/13/1900, New York, N.Y. Deb: 10/18/1871

1871	Mut-n	6	1	2	0	0	0	1	0	0		.333	.333	.333	101	-0	-0	1	0					/P	0.0
1872	Eck-n	13	54	10	13	2	0	0	6	0	1	.241	.241	.278	70	-3	-1	4						3/2O	-0.1
1873	Res-n	22	90	11	23	2	0	0	10	1	2	.256	.264	.278	65	-4	-3	6						/2SP31	-0.3
1874	Atl-n	22	95	18	22	1	0	0		2		.232	.247	.242	64	-4	-2	6						C/2O	-0.2
1875	StL-n	4	16	1	1	0	0	0		0		.063	.063	.063	-62	-2	-2	0						/P	-0.0
	Atl-n	26	112	13	25	1	0	0		1		.223	.230	.232	69	-4	-2	6						2C/SP	-0.1
	Yr	30	128	14	26	1	0	0		1		.203	.209	.211	52	-7	-4	6						2C/SP	-0.1
Total	5 n	88	373	54	86	6	0	0		4		.231	.239	.247	62	-18	-10	23						/2CS3P01	-0.7

■ ANGEL FLEITAS
Fleitas, Angel Felix Husta b: 11/10/14, Los Abreus, Cuba BR/TR, 5'9", 160 lbs. Deb: 7/05/48

| 1948 | Was-A | 15 | 13 | 1 | 1 | 0 | 0 | 1 | 3 | 5 | | .077 | .250 | .077 | -11 | -2 | -2 | 0 | 0 | 2 | -1 | .952 | 3 | /S | 0.0 |

■ LES FLEMING
Fleming, Leslie Harvey "Moe" b: 8/7/15, Singleton, Tex. d: 3/5/80, Cleveland, Tex. BL/TL, 5'10", 185 lbs. Deb: 4/22/39

1939	Det-A	8	16	0	0	0	0	0	1	0	4	.000	.000	.000	-93	-5	-5	0	0	0	0	1.000	-0	/O	-0.5
1941	Cle-A	2	8	0	2	1	0	0	2	0		.250	.250	.375	67	-0	-0	1	0	0	0	1.000	-0	/1	-0.1
1942	Cle-A	156	548	71	160	27	4	14	82	106	57	.292	.412	.432	146	32	36	105	6	8	-3	.993	-9	*1	1.5
1945	Cle-A	42	140	18	46	10	2	3	22	11	5	.329	.382	.493	160	9	10	27	0	0	0	.938	-2	O/1	0.6
1946	Cle-A	99	306	40	85	17	5	8	42	50	42	.278	.383	.444	140	14	16	55	1	0	0	.984	3	1/O	1.5
1947	Cle-A	103	281	39	68	14	2	4	43	53	42	.242	.362	.349	101	1	2	40	0	0	0	.989	4	1	0.3
1949	Pit-N	24	31	0	8	0	2	0	7	6	2	.258	.395	.387	108	1	1	5	0			1.000	-1	/1	0.0
Total	7	434	1330	168	369	69	15	29	199	226	152	.277	.386	.417	131	51	59	232	7	8		.990	-6	1/O	3.3

■ TOM FLEMING
Fleming, Thomas Vincent "Sleuth" b: 11/20/1873, Philadelphia, Pa. d: 12/26/57, Boston, Mass. BL/TL, 5'11", 155 lbs. Deb: 9/19/1899

1899	NY-N	22	77	9	16	1	1	0	4	1		.208	.218	.247	28	-8	-7	5	1			.909	-1	O	-0.9
1902	Phi-N	5	16	2	6	0	0	0	2	1		.375	.412	.375	143	1	1	3	0			1.000	-0	O	0.1
1904	Phi-N	3	6	0	0	0	0	0	0	0		.000	.000	.000	-99	-1	-1	0	0			1.000	0	/O	-0.1
Total	3	30	99	11	22	1	1	0	6	2		.222	.238	.253	39	-8	-8	7	1			.920	-0	/O	-0.9

■ ART FLETCHER
Fletcher, Arthur b: 1/5/1885, Collinsville, Ill. d: 2/6/50, Los Angeles, Cal. BR/TR, 5'10.5", 170 lbs. Deb: 4/15/09 MC

1909	NY-N	33	98	7	21	0	1	0	6	1		.214	.238	.235	46	-6	-6	5	0			.893	4	S/23	-0.3
1910	NY-N	51	125	12	28	2	1	0	13	4	9	.224	.248	.256	47	-9	-9	10	9			.895	-5	S23	-1.4
1911	*NY-N	112	326	73	104	17	8	1	37	30	27	.319	.400	.429	128	15	13	64	20			.926	4	S32	2.2
1912	*NY-N	129	419	64	118	17	9	1	57	16	29	.282	.330	.372	89	-6	-7	56	16			.927	16	*S/23	1.9
1913	*NY-N	136	538	76	160	20	9	4	71	24	35	.297	.345	.390	109	6	6	80	32			.932	-3	*S	1.6
1914	NY-N	135	514	62	147	26	8	2	79	22	37	.286	.332	.379	115	6	6	68	15			.922	6	*S	2.7
1915	NY-N	149	562	59	143	17	7	3	74	6	36	.254	.280	.326	88	-13	-10	50	12	18	-7	.936	34	*S	3.2
1916	NY-N	133	500	53	143	23	8	3	66	13	36	.286	.323	.382	122	8	11	68	15			.940	20	*S	4.2
1917	*NY-N	151	557	70	145	24	5	4	56	23	28	.260	.312	.343	104	0	2	60	12			.956	27	*S	4.1
1918	NY-N	124	468	51	123	20	2	0	47	18	26	.263	.311	.314	93	-5	-4	48	12			.959	22	*S	2.6
1919	NY-N	127	488	54	135	20	5	3	54	9	28	.277	.300	.357	98	-3	-3	52	6			.944	24	*S	3.2
1920	NY-N	41	171	21	44	7	2	0	24	1	15	.257	.282	.322	74	-6	-6	15	3	2	-0	.914	-2	S	-0.5
	Phi-N	102	379	36	112	25	7	4	38	15	28	.296	.329	.430	112	7	5	52	4	6	-2	.958	12	*S	2.5
	Yr	143	550	57	156	32	9	4	62	16	43	.284	.315	.396	100	1	-1	66	7	8	-3	.945	10	*S	2.0
1922	Phi-N	110	396	46	111	20	5	7	53	21	14	.280	.325	.409	80	-8	-13	53	3	2	-1	.939	7	*S	0.3
Total	13	1533	5541	684	1534	238	77	32	675	203	348	.277	.319	.365	100	-14	-14	680	159	28		.939	166	*S/32	26.3

■ DARRIN FLETCHER
Fletcher, Darrin Glen b: 10/3/66, Elmhurst, Ill. BL/TR, 6'2", 195 lbs. Deb: 9/10/89 F

1989	LA-N	5	8	1	4	1	0	0	1	0	1	.500	.556	.875	308	2	2	4	0	0	0	1.000	0	/C	0.2
1990	LA-N	2	1	0	0	0	0	0	0	0	1	.000	.000	.000	-99	-0	-0	0	0	0	0	.000	0	/C	0.0
	Phi-N	9	22	3	3	1	0	0	1	0	5	.136	.174	.182	-2	-3	-3	1	0	0	0	1.000	1	/C	-0.2
	Yr	11	23	3	3	1	0	0	1	0	6	.130	.167	.174	-6	-3	-3	1	0	0	0	1.000	1	/C	-0.2
1991	Phi-N	46	136	5	31	7	1	1	12	5	15	.228	.255	.309	59	-8	-8	10	0	1	-1	.992	3	C	-0.3
1992	Mon-N	83	222	13	54	10	2	2	26	14	28	.243	.294	.333	78	-7	-7	20	0	2	-1	.995	-0	C	-0.5

YEAR	TM/L	G	AB	R	H	2B	3B	HR	RBI	BB	SO	AVG	OBP	SLG	PRO+	BR	/A	RC	SB	CS	SBR	FA	FR	POS	TPR
Total	4	145	389	22	92	19	2	4	41	21	49	.237	.279	.326	71	-16	-15	35	0	3	-2	.994	4	C	-0.8

■ ELBIE FLETCHER
Fletcher, Elburt Preston b: 3/18/16, Milton, Mass. BL/TL, 6', 180 lbs. Deb: 9/16/34

YEAR	TM/L	G	AB	R	H	2B	3B	HR	RBI	BB	SO	AVG	OBP	SLG	PRO+	BR	/A	RC	SB	CS	SBR	FA	FR	POS	TPR
1934	Bos-N	8	4	4	2	0	0	0	0	0	2	.500	.500	.500	182	0	0	1	1			.875	-0	/1	0.0
1935	Bos-N	39	148	12	35	7	1	1	9	7	13	.236	.271	.318	63	-9	-7	13	1			.997	2	1	-0.9
1937	Bos-N	148	539	56	133	22	4	1	38	56	64	.247	.321	.308	79	-20	-14	56	3			.993	1	*1	-3.0
1938	Bos-N	147	529	71	144	24	7	6	48	60	40	.272	.351	.378	112	1	8	73	5			.990	10	*1	0.2
1939	Bos-N	35	106	14	26	2	0	0	6	19	5	.245	.365	.264	77	-3	-2	12	1			.986	-5	1	-1.0
	Pit-N	102	370	49	112	23	4	12	71	48	28	.303	.386	.484	134	17	18	69	3			.993	-4	*1	0.3
	Yr	137	476	63	138	25	4	12	77	67	33	.290	.381	.435	122	14	16	81	4			.991	-9	*1	-0.7
1940	Pit-N	147	510	94	139	22	7	16	104	**119**	54	.273	**.418**	.437	137	32	32	103	5			.993	4	*1	2.3
1941	Pit-N	151	521	95	150	29	13	11	74	**118**	54	.288	**.421**	.457	148	38	38	111	5			.991	9	*1	3.7
1942	Pit-N	145	506	86	146	22	5	7	57	105	60	.289	**.417**	.393	134	30	29	94	0			.992	12	*1	3.3
1943	Pit-N★	154	544	91	154	24	5	9	70	95	49	.283	.395	.395	124	24	22	91	1			**.996**	4	*1	1.8
1946	Pit-N	148	532	72	136	25	8	4	66	111	37	.256	.384	.355	108	12	10	82	4			.995	1	*1	0.3
1947	Pit-N	69	157	22	38	9	1	1	22	29	24	.242	.364	.331	83	-2	-3	20	2			.986	-0	1	-0.5
1949	Bos-N	122	413	57	108	19	3	11	51	84	65	.262	.396	.402	121	12	15	72	1			.991	0	*1	1.5
Total	12	1415	4879	723	1323	228	58	79	616	851	495	.271	.384	.390	118	133	148	796	32			.993	33	*1	8.0

■ GEORGE FLETCHER
Fletcher, George H. E. Deb: 6/21/1872

YEAR	TM/L	G	AB	R	H	2B	3B	HR	RBI	BB	SO	AVG	OBP	SLG	PRO+	BR	/A	RC	SB	CS	SBR	FA	FR	POS	TPR
1872	Eck-n	2	8	1	3	0	0	0	1	0	0	.375	.375	.375	155	0	1	1						/O	0.0

■ FRANK FLETCHER
Fletcher, Oliver Frank b: 3/6/1891, Hildreth, Ill. d: 10/7/74, St.Petersburg, Fla. BR/TR, 5'10", 165 lbs. Deb: 7/14/14

YEAR	TM/L	G	AB	R	H	2B	3B	HR	RBI	BB	SO	AVG	OBP	SLG	PRO+	BR	/A	RC	SB	CS	SBR	FA	FR	POS	TPR
1914	Phi-N	1	1	0	0	0	0	0	0	0	1	.000	.000	.000	-94	-0	-0	0	0			.000	0	H	0.0

■ SCOTT FLETCHER
Fletcher, Scott Brian b: 7/30/58, Fort Walton Beach Fla. BR/TR, 5'11", 173 lbs. Deb: 4/25/81

YEAR	TM/L	G	AB	R	H	2B	3B	HR	RBI	BB	SO	AVG	OBP	SLG	PRO+	BR	/A	RC	SB	CS	SBR	FA	FR	POS	TPR
1981	Chi-N	19	46	6	10	4	0	0	1	2	4	.217	.250	.304	54	-3	-3	4	0	0	0	.972	6	2/S3	0.4
1982	Chi-N	11	24	4	4	0	0	0	1	4	5	.167	.286	.167	29	-2	-2	2	1	0	0	1.000	-0	S	-0.2
1983	*Chi-A	114	262	42	62	16	5	3	31	29	22	.237	.317	.370	85	-4	-5	31	5	1	1	.965	18	*S2/3D	2.1
1984	Chi-A	149	456	46	114	13	3	3	35	46	46	.250	.329	.311	75	-12	-15	51	10	4	1	.973	0	*S2/3	-0.1
1985	Chi-A	119	301	38	77	8	1	2	31	35	47	.256	.333	.309	74	-8	-10	31	5	5	-2	.934	-3	3S2/D	-1.1
1986	Tex-A	147	530	82	159	34	5	3	50	47	59	.300	.361	.400	104	6	4	76	12	11	-3	.973	-6	*S32/D	0.8
1987	Tex-A	156	588	82	169	28	4	5	63	61	66	.287	.359	.374	95	-3	-3	78	13	12	-3	.966	5	*S	1.2
1988	Tex-A	140	515	59	142	19	4	0	47	62	34	.276	.367	.328	94	0	-1	66	8	5	-1	.983	1	*S	1.1
1989	Tex-A	83	314	47	75	14	1	0	22	38	41	.239	.325	.290	73	-9	-10	31	1	0	0	.960	-18	S	-2.2
	Chi-A	59	232	30	63	11	1	1	21	26	19	.272	.347	.341	97	-1	-0	29	1	1	-0	1.000	-3	2/SD	-0.1
	Yr	142	546	77	138	25	2	1	43	64	60	.253	.334	.311	83	-10	-10	60	2	1	0	.957	-21	S2/D	-2.3
1990	Chi-A	151	509	54	123	18	3	4	56	45	63	.242	.307	.312	75	-17	-16	50	1	3	-2	.988	-6	*2	-2.1
1991	Chi-A	90	248	14	51	10	1	1	28	17	26	.206	.265	.266	48	-18	-17	18	0	2	-1	.992	-6	2/3	-2.3
1992	Mil-A	123	386	53	106	18	3	3	51	30	33	.275	.338	.360	98	-2	-1	48	17	10	-1	.992	10	*2S/3	1.2
Total	12	1361	4411	557	1155	193	31	25	437	442	465	.262	.336	.337	85	-73	-79	515	74	54	-10	.971	-3	S2/3D	-1.3

■ ELMER FLICK
Flick, Elmer Harrison b: 1/11/1876, Bedford, Ohio d: 1/9/71, Bedford, Ohio BL/TR, 5'9", 168 lbs. Deb: 5/02/1898 H

YEAR	TM/L	G	AB	R	H	2B	3B	HR	RBI	BB	SO	AVG	OBP	SLG	PRO+	BR	/A	RC	SB	CS	SBR	FA	FR	POS	TPR
1898	Phi-N	134	453	84	137	16	13	8	81	86		.302	.430	.448	158	35	38	101	23			.931	7	*O	3.3
1899	Phi-N	127	485	98	166	22	11	2	98	42		.342	.407	.445	139	23	26	104	31			.931	9	*O	2.3
1900	Phi-N	138	545	106	200	32	16	11	**110**	56		.367	.441	.545	173	**54**	**54**	151	35			.914	3	*O	4.3
1901	Phi-N	138	540	112	180	32	17	8	88	52		.333	.398	.500	157	41	39	124	30			.962	15	*O	4.2
1902	Phi-A	11	37	15	11	2	1	0	3	6		.297	.435	.405	128	2	2	9	4			.947	-0	O	0.1
	Cle-A	110	424	70	126	19	11	2	61	47		.297	.371	.408	121	10	12	74	20			.929	-4	*O	0.1
	Yr	121	461	85	137	21	12	2	64	53		.297	.377	.408	121	12	14	83	24			.930	-4	*O	0.2
1903	Cle-A	140	523	81	155	23	16	2	51	51		.296	.368	.413	136	23	24	92	24			.955	1	*O	1.7
1904	Cle-A	150	579	97	177	31	17	6	56	51		.306	.371	.449	160	39	39	115	**38**			.955	10	*O/2	4.5
1905	Cle-A	132	500	72	154	29	**18**	4	64	53		**.308**	.382	**.462**	**165**	**38**	**38**	**105**	35			.938	0	*O/2	3.4
1906	Cle-A	157	624	**98**	194	34	**22**	1	62	54		.311	.372	.441	157	39	40	121	**39**			.981	-11	*O/2	2.3
1907	Cle-A	147	549	78	166	15	**18**	3	58	64		.302	.386	.412	153	36	35	107	41			.956	1	*O	3.3
1908	Cle-A	9	35	4	8	1	1	0	2	3		.229	.289	.314	96	-0	-0	3	0			1.000	-0	/O	-0.1
1909	Cle-A	66	235	28	60	10	2	0	15	22		.255	.322	.315	97	1	-0	26	9			.958	-2	O	-0.6
1910	Cle-A	24	68	5	18	2	1	1	7	10		.265	.359	.368	126	2	2	9	1			.955	-3	O	-0.2
Total	13	1483	5597	948	1752	268	164	48	756	597		.313	.389	.445	149	342	350	1141	330			.947	24	*O/2	28.6

■ LEW FLICK
Flick, Lewis Miller "Noisy" b: 2/18/15, Bristol, Tenn. d: 12/7/90, Weber City, Va. BL/TL, 5'9", 155 lbs. Deb: 9/28/43

YEAR	TM/L	G	AB	R	H	2B	3B	HR	RBI	BB	SO	AVG	OBP	SLG	PRO+	BR	/A	RC	SB	CS	SBR	FA	FR	POS	TPR
1943	Phi-A	1	5	2	3	0	0	0	0	0	0	.600	.600	.600	253	1	1	2	0	0	0	1.000	0	/O	0.1
1944	Phi-A	19	35	1	4	0	0	0	2	1	2	.114	.139	.114	-28	-6	-6	0	1	0	0	1.000	-1	/O	-0.7
Total	2	20	40	3	7	0	0	0	2	1	2	.175	.195	.175	6	-5	-5	2	1	0	0	1.000	-1	/O	-0.6

■ DON FLINN
Flinn, Don Raphael b: 11/17/1892, Bluffdale, Tex. d: 3/9/59, Waco, Tex. BR/TR, 6'1", 185 lbs. Deb: 9/02/17

YEAR	TM/L	G	AB	R	H	2B	3B	HR	RBI	BB	SO	AVG	OBP	SLG	PRO+	BR	/A	RC	SB	CS	SBR	FA	FR	POS	TPR
1917	Pit-N	14	37	1	11	1	1	0	1	1	6	.297	.316	.378	109	0	0	4	1			1.000	0	O	0.0

■ SILVER FLINT
Flint, Frank Sylvester b: 8/3/1855, Philadelphia, Pa. d: 1/14/1892, Chicago, Ill. BR/TR, 6', 180 lbs. Deb: 5/04/1875 M

YEAR	TM/L	G	AB	R	H	2B	3B	HR	RBI	BB	SO	AVG	OBP	SLG	PRO+	BR	/A	RC	SB	CS	SBR	FA	FR	POS	TPR
1875	RS-n	17	61	4	5	0	0	0		1		.082	.097	.082	-42	-8	-7	0						C/3	-0.6
1878	Ind-N	63	254	23	57	7	0	0	18	2	15	.224	.230	.252	67	-11	-6	15				.908	-1	*C/O	-0.6
1879	Chi-N	79	324	46	92	22	6	1	41	6	44	.284	.297	.398	120	9	6	39				.915	3	*C/OM	1.1
1880	Chi-N	74	284	30	46	10	4	0	17	5	32	.162	.176	.225	33	-18	-21	12				**.934**	8	*CO	-1.1
1881	Chi-N	80	306	46	95	18	0	1	34	6	39	.310	.324	.379	115	7	5	38				.938	-8	*C/O1	0.0
1882	Chi-N	81	331	48	83	18	8	4	44	2	50	.251	.255	.390	99	1	-1	34				.935	-3	*CO	-0.1
1883	Chi-N	85	332	57	88	23	4	0	32	3	69	.265	.272	.358	85	-4	-7	33				.877	-8	*CO	-1.0
1884	Chi-N	73	279	35	57	5	2	9	45	7	57	.204	.224	.333	67	-9	-12	21				.884	-2	C	-0.7
1885	*Chi-N	68	249	27	52	8	2	1	17	2	52	.209	.215	.269	49	-12	-17	15				**.927**	14	C/O	0.2
1886	*Chi-N	54	173	30	35	6	2	1	13	12	36	.202	.254	.277	53	-8	-12	13	1			.893	15	C/1	0.7
1887	Chi-N	49	187	22	50	8	6	3	21	4	28	.267	.283	.422	84	-2	-6	25	7			.909	3	C/1	0.1
1888	Chi-N	22	77	6	14	3	0	0	3	1	21	.182	.203	.221	34	-5	-6	4	1			.926	-2	C	-0.6
1889	Chi-N	15	56	6	13	1	0	1	9	3	18	.232	.271	.304	59	-3	-3	5	1			.903	-1	C	-0.3
Total	12	743	2852	376	682	129	34	21	294	53	461	.239	.253	.330	78	-57	-82	254	10			.913	19	C/O1	-2.3

■ CURT FLOOD
Flood, Curtis Charles b: 1/18/38, Houston, Tex. BR/TR, 5'9", 165 lbs. Deb: 9/09/56

YEAR	TM/L	G	AB	R	H	2B	3B	HR	RBI	BB	SO	AVG	OBP	SLG	PRO+	BR	/A	RC	SB	CS	SBR	FA	FR	POS	TPR
1956	Cin-N	5	1	0	0	0	0	0	0	0	1	.000	.000	.000	-94	-0	-0	0	0	0	0	.000	0	H	0.0
1957	Cin-N	3	3	2	1	0	0	1	1	0	0	.333	.333	1.333	299	1	1	1	0	0	0	.000	-1	/32	0.0
1958	StL-N	121	422	50	110	17	2	10	41	31	56	.261	.317	.382	81	-10	-12	44	2	12	-7	.978	19	*O/3	-0.5
1959	StL-N	121	208	24	53	7	3	7	26	16	35	.255	.308	.418	86	-3	-5	26	2	1	0	.967	-19	*O/2	-2.7
1960	StL-N	140	396	37	94	20	1	8	38	35	54	.237	.306	.354	73	-11	-15	41	0	3	-2	**.993**	0	*O/3	-2.3
1961	StL-N	132	335	53	108	15	5	2	21	35	33	.322	.391	.415	104	8	4	56	6	2	1	.984	-3	*O	-0.3
1962	StL-N	151	635	99	188	30	5	12	70	42	57	.296	.349	.416	95	4	-4	92	8	6	-1	.990	9	*O	-0.6
1963	StL-N	158	662	112	200	34	9	5	63	42	57	.302	.346	.403	105	12	6	92	17	12	-2	.988	14	*O	1.0
1964	*StL-N★	162	679	97	**211**	25	3	5	46	43	53	.311	.356	.378	98	7	0	90	8	11	-4	.988	7	*O	-0.5
1965	StL-N	156	617	90	191	30	3	11	83	51	50	.310	.368	.421	111	18	12	97	9	3	1	.986	5	*O	1.1

YEAR	TM/L	G	AB	R	H	2B	3B	HR	RBI	BB	SO	AVG	OBP	SLG	PRO+	BR	/A	RC	SB	CS	SBR	FA	FR	POS	TPR
1966	StL-N★	160	626	64	167	21	5	10	78	26	50	.267	.300	.364	83	-14	-15	67	14	7	0	**1.000**	3	*O	-2.0
1967	*StL-N	134	514	68	172	24	1	5	50	37	46	.335	.382	.414	129	19	20	82	2	2	-1	.988	8	*O	2.2
1968	*StL-N★	150	618	71	186	17	4	5	60	33	58	.301	.341	.366	114	9	10	78	11	6	-0	.983	14	*O	1.8
1969	StL-N	153	606	80	173	31	3	4	57	48	57	.285	.345	.366	99	0	-0	76	9	7	-2	.989	11	*O	0.0
1971	Was-A	13	35	4	7	0	0	0	2	5	2	.200	.300	.200	47	-2	-2	2	0	1	-1	.941	-2	O	-0.6
Total	15	1759	6357	851	1861	271	44	85	636	444	609	.293	.344	.389	99	38	-2	844	88	73	-17	.987	65	*O/32	-3.4

■ TIM FLOOD
Flood, Timothy A. b: 3/13/1877, Montgomery City, Mo. d: 6/15/29, St.Louis, Mo. BR/TR, Deb: 9/24/1899

YEAR	TM/L	G	AB	R	H	2B	3B	HR	RBI	BB	SO	AVG	OBP	SLG	PRO+	BR	/A	RC	SB	CS	SBR	FA	FR	POS	TPR
1899	StL-N	10	31	0	9	0	0	0	3	4		.290	.371	.290	81	-1	-1	4	1			.878	-2	2	-0.1
1902	Bro-N	132	476	43	104	11	4	3	51	23		.218	.262	.277	66	-19	-20	40	8			.942	-16	*2/O	-3.3
1903	Bro-N	89	309	27	77	15	2	0	32	15		.249	.284	.311	72	-13	-12	33	14			.924	-9	2/SO	-1.7
Total	3	231	816	70	190	26	6	3	86	42		.233	.275	.290	69	-33	-32	78	23			.933	-26	2/SO	-5.1

■ KEVIN FLORA
Flora, Kevin Scot b: 6/10/69, Fontana, Cal. BR/TR, 6', 180 lbs. Deb: 9/27/91

YEAR	TM/L	G	AB	R	H	2B	3B	HR	RBI	BB	SO	AVG	OBP	SLG	PRO+	BR	/A	RC	SB	CS	SBR	FA	FR	POS	TPR
1991	Cal-A	3	8	1	1	0	0	0	0	1	5	.125	.222	.125	-1	-1	-1	0	1	0	0	.846	-2	/2	-0.3

■ PAUL FLORENCE
Florence, Paul Robert "Pep" b: 4/22/1900, Chicago, Ill. d: 5/28/86, Gainesville, Fla. BB/TR, 6'1", 185 lbs. Deb: 5/22/26

YEAR	TM/L	G	AB	R	H	2B	3B	HR	RBI	BB	SO	AVG	OBP	SLG	PRO+	BR	/A	RC	SB	CS	SBR	FA	FR	POS	TPR
1926	NY-N	76	188	19	43	4	3	2	14	23	12	.229	.322	.314	73	-7	-7	20	2			.937	-9	C	-1.1

■ GIL FLORES
Flores, Gilberto (Garcia) b: 10/27/52, Ponce, P.R. BR/TR, 6', 185 lbs. Deb: 5/08/77

YEAR	TM/L	G	AB	R	H	2B	3B	HR	RBI	BB	SO	AVG	OBP	SLG	PRO+	BR	/A	RC	SB	CS	SBR	FA	FR	POS	TPR
1977	Cal-A	104	342	41	95	19	4	1	26	23	39	.278	.325	.365	92	-6	-4	36	12	10	-2	.978	-2	O/D	-1.1
1978	NY-N	11	29	8	8	0	1	0	1	3	5	.276	.344	.345	96	-0	-0	4	1	0	0	.944	-0	/O	0.0
1979	NY-N	70	93	9	18	1	1	1	10	8	17	.194	.265	.258	45	-7	-7	7	2	0	1	.976	0	O	-0.7
Total	3	185	464	58	121	20	6	2	37	34	61	.261	.314	.343	82	-13	-11	47	15	10	-2	.976	-2	O/D	-1.8

■ DICKIE FLOWERS
Flowers, Charles Richard b: 1850, Philadelphia, Pa. d: 10/5/1892, Philadelphia, Pa. Deb: 6/03/1871

YEAR	TM/L	G	AB	R	H	2B	3B	HR	RBI	BB	SO	AVG	OBP	SLG	PRO+	BR	/A	RC	SB	CS	SBR	FA	FR	POS	TPR
1871	Tro-n	21	105	39	33	5	4	0	18	4	0	.314	.339	.438	120	3	2	19	8					*S/P2	0.2
1872	Ath-n	3	15	1	4	0	0	0	4	2	2	.267	.353	.267	93	0	0	1						/S	0.0
Total	2 n	24	120	40	37	5	4	0	22	6	2	.308	.341	.417	117	3	2	20						/S2P	0.2

■ JAKE FLOWERS
Flowers, D'Arcy Raymond b: 3/16/02, Cambridge, Md. d: 12/27/62, Clearwater, Fla. BR/TR, 5'11.5", 170 lbs. Deb: 9/07/23 C

YEAR	TM/L	G	AB	R	H	2B	3B	HR	RBI	BB	SO	AVG	OBP	SLG	PRO+	BR	/A	RC	SB	CS	SBR	FA	FR	POS	TPR
1923	StL-N	13	32	0	3	1	0	0	2	2	7	.094	.147	.125	-28	-6	-6	0	1	2	-1	.971	-1	/S23	-0.7
1926	*StL-N	40	74	13	20	1	0	3	9	5	9	.270	.325	.405	92	-1	-1	10	1			.984	1	2/1S	0.0
1927	Bro-N	67	231	26	54	5	5	2	20	21	25	.234	.300	.325	67	-11	-11	23	3			.944	-8	S/2	-1.2
1928	Bro-N	103	339	51	93	11	6	2	44	47	30	.274	.366	.360	92	-3	-3	47	10			.971	-6	2/S	-0.6
1929	Bro-N	46	130	16	26	6	0	1	16	22	6	.200	.316	.269	47	-11	-10	12	9			.962	-5	2	-1.3
1930	Bro-N	89	253	37	81	18	3	2	50	21	18	.320	.372	.439	96	-2	-1	40	5			.949	-8	2/O	-0.5
1931	Bro-N	22	31	3	7	0	0	0	1	7	4	.226	.368	.226	64	-1	-1	3	1			1.000	1	/2S	0.1
	*StL-N	45	137	19	34	11	1	2	19	9	6	.248	.295	.387	79	-4	-5	16	7			.971	3	S2/3	0.1
	Yr	67	168	22	41	11	1	2	20	16	10	.244	.310	.357	77	-5	-6	19	8			.991	4	2S/3	0.2
1932	StL-N	67	247	35	63	11	1	2	18	31	18	.255	.341	.332	79	-5	-6	30	7			.980	-0	3/S2	-0.2
1933	Bro-N	78	210	28	49	11	2	2	22	24	15	.233	.312	.333	88	-4	-3	23	13			.955	-11	S2/3O	-1.1
1934	Cin-N	13	9	1	3	0	0	0	0	1	1	.333	.455	.333	117	0	0	2	1			.000	0	H	0.0
Total	10	583	1693	229	433	75	18	16	201	190	139	.256	.333	.350	80	-47	-46	206	58	2		.967	-34	2S/310	-5.4

■ BUBBA FLOYD
Floyd, Leslie Roe b: 6/23/17, Dallas, Tex. BR/TR, 5'11", 160 lbs. Deb: 6/16/44

YEAR	TM/L	G	AB	R	H	2B	3B	HR	RBI	BB	SO	AVG	OBP	SLG	PRO+	BR	/A	RC	SB	CS	SBR	FA	FR	POS	TPR
1944	Det-A	3	9	1	4	1	0	0	0	1	0	.444	.500	.556	191	1	1	3	0	0	0	1.000	-1	/S	0.0

■ BOBBY FLOYD
Floyd, Robert Nathan b: 10/20/43, Hawthorne, Cal. BR/TR, 6', 181 lbs. Deb: 9/18/68

YEAR	TM/L	G	AB	R	H	2B	3B	HR	RBI	BB	SO	AVG	OBP	SLG	PRO+	BR	/A	RC	SB	CS	SBR	FA	FR	POS	TPR
1968	Bal-A	5	9	0	1	1	0	0	1	0	3	.111	.111	.222	-1	-1	-1	0	0	0	0	1.000	2	/S	0.1
1969	Bal-A	39	84	7	17	4	0	0	1	6	17	.202	.256	.250	41	-7	-7	5	0	0	0	.984	11	2S/3	0.7
1970	Bal-A	3	2	0	0	0	0	0	0	0	2	.000	.000	.000	-99	-1	-1	0	0	0	0	1.000	-1	/S2	-0.1
	KC-A	14	43	5	14	4	0	0	9	4	9	.326	.383	.419	121	1	1	7	0	1	-1	.880	1	/S3	0.3
	Yr	17	45	5	14	4	0	0	9	4	11	.311	.367	.400	111	1	1	7	0	1	-1	.882	1	S/32	0.2
1971	KC-A	31	66	8	10	3	0	0	2	7	21	.152	.233	.197	23	-7	-7	3	0	0	0	.970	5	S/23	0.0
1972	KC-A	61	134	9	24	3	0	0	5	5	29	.179	.209	.201	23	-13	-13	5	1	0	0	.967	-2	3S/2	-1.4
1973	KC-A	51	78	10	26	3	1	0	8	4	14	.333	.366	.397	107	1	1	10	1	1	-0	1.000	9	2S	1.1
1974	KC-A	10	9	1	1	0	0	0	0	2	4	.111	.273	.111	13	-1	-1	0	0	0	0	1.000	2	/23S	0.1
Total	7	214	425	40	93	18	1	0	26	28	99	.219	.267	.266	52	-26	-27	32	2	2	-1	.940	27	/S23	0.8

■ JOHN FLUHRER
Fluhrer, John L. (a.k.a. Wm. G. Morris 1 Game In 1915)
b: 1/3/1894, Adrian, Mich. d: 7/17/46, Columbus, Ohio BR/TR, 5'9", 165 lbs. Deb: 9/05/15

YEAR	TM/L	G	AB	R	H	2B	3B	HR	RBI	BB	SO	AVG	OBP	SLG	PRO+	BR	/A	RC	SB	CS	SBR	FA	FR	POS	TPR
1915	Chi-N	6	6	0	2	0	0	0	0	1	0	.333	.429	.333	132	0	0	1	1			.500	-1	/O	0.0

■ ED FLYNN
Flynn, Edward J. b: 1864, Chicago, Ill. BL , 5'9", 165 lbs. Deb: 5/05/1887

YEAR	TM/L	G	AB	R	H	2B	3B	HR	RBI	BB	SO	AVG	OBP	SLG	PRO+	BR	/A	RC	SB	CS	SBR	FA	FR	POS	TPR
1887	Cle-a	7	27	0	5	1	0	0		1		.185	.214	.222	24	-3	-3	2	3			.786	-0	/3O	-0.2

■ GEORGE FLYNN
Flynn, George A. "Dibby" b: 5/24/1871, Chicago, Ill. d: 12/28/01, Chicago, Ill. Deb: 4/17/1896

YEAR	TM/L	G	AB	R	H	2B	3B	HR	RBI	BB	SO	AVG	OBP	SLG	PRO+	BR	/A	RC	SB	CS	SBR	FA	FR	POS	TPR
1896	Chi-N	29	106	15	27	1	2	0	4	11	9	.255	.336	.302	68	-4	-5	16	12			.878	2	O	-0.4

■ JOCKO FLYNN
Flynn, John A. b: 6/30/1864, Lawrence, Mass. d: 12/30/07, Lawrence, Mass. 5'6.5", 143 lbs. Deb: 5/01/1886

YEAR	TM/L	G	AB	R	H	2B	3B	HR	RBI	BB	SO	AVG	OBP	SLG	PRO+	BR	/A	RC	SB	CS	SBR	FA	FR	POS	TPR
1886	Chi-N	57	205	40	41	6	2	4	19	18	45	.200	.265	.307	64	-6	-11	20	9			.916	-5	PO	-1.0
1887	Chi-N	1	0	0	0	0	0	0	0	0	0	—	—	—	—	0	0	0	0			.000	-1	/O	-0.1
Total	2	58	205	40	41	6	2	4	19	18	45	.200	.265	.307	64	-6	-11	20	9			.850	-6	/PO	-1.1

■ JOHN FLYNN
Flynn, John Anthony b: 9/7/1883, Providence, R.I. d: 3/23/35, Providence, R.I. BR/TR, 6'0.5", 175 lbs. Deb: 4/22/10

YEAR	TM/L	G	AB	R	H	2B	3B	HR	RBI	BB	SO	AVG	OBP	SLG	PRO+	BR	/A	RC	SB	CS	SBR	FA	FR	POS	TPR
1910	Pit-N	96	332	32	91	10	2	6	52	30	47	.274	.336	.370	100	2	-1	44	6			.977	-3	1	-0.4
1911	Pit-N	33	59	5	12	0	1	0	3	9	8	.203	.309	.237	52	-3	-4	4	0			1.000	0	1/O	-0.3
1912	Was-A	20	71	9	12	4	1	0	5	7		.169	.253	.254	45	-5	-5	5	2			.974	1	1	-0.4
Total	3	149	462	46	115	14	4	6	60	46	55	.249	.320	.335	85	-7	-10	53	8			.978	-1	1/O	-1.1

■ JOE FLYNN
Flynn, Joseph b: Philadelphia, Pa. Deb: 4/18/1884

YEAR	TM/L	G	AB	R	H	2B	3B	HR	RBI	BB	SO	AVG	OBP	SLG	PRO+	BR	/A	RC	SB	CS	SBR	FA	FR	POS	TPR
1884	Phi-U	52	209	38	52	9	4	4		11		.249	.286	.388	136	6	8	24				.778	-15	OC/1S	-0.6
	Bos-U	9	31	4	7	2	0	0		2		.226	.273	.290	92	-0	-0	3				.864	4	/CO1	0.4
	Yr	61	240	42	59	11	4	4		13		.246	.285	.375	130	5	8	26				.764	-11	OC/1S	-0.2

■ MIKE FLYNN
Flynn, Michael J. b: Lowell, Mass. Deb: 8/31/1891

YEAR	TM/L	G	AB	R	H	2B	3B	HR	RBI	BB	SO	AVG	OBP	SLG	PRO+	BR	/A	RC	SB	CS	SBR	FA	FR	POS	TPR
1891	Bos-a	1	2	0	0	0	0	0	0	0	1	.000	.000	.000	-99	-1	-0	0	0			1.000	1	/C	0.0

■ DOUG FLYNN
Flynn, Robert Douglas b: 4/18/51, Lexington, Ky. BR/TR, 5'11", 165 lbs. Deb: 4/09/75

YEAR	TM/L	G	AB	R	H	2B	3B	HR	RBI	BB	SO	AVG	OBP	SLG	PRO+	BR	/A	RC	SB	CS	SBR	FA	FR	POS	TPR
1975	Cin-N	89	127	17	34	7	0	1	20	11	13	.268	.326	.346	85	-2	-3	14	3	0	1	.962	10	32S	1.0
1976	*Cin-N	93	219	20	62	5	2	1	20	10	24	.283	.314	.338	83	-4	-5	24	2	0	1	.988	-4	23S	-0.4
1977	Cin-N	36	32	0	8	1	1	0	5	0	6	.250	.250	.344	56	-2	-2	3	0	0	0	1.000	7	3/2S	0.5
	NY-N	90	282	14	54	6	1	0	14	11	23	.191	.222	.220	20	-32	-31	13	1	3	-2	.954	-13	S2/3	-3.8
	Yr	126	314	14	62	7	2	0	19	11	29	.197	.225	.232	24	-34	-33	16	1	3	-2	.956	-6	S23	-3.3
1978	NY-N	156	532	37	126	12	8	0	36	30	50	.237	.279	.289	61	-29	-27	40	3	5	-2	.986	2	*2S	-1.5
1979	NY-N	157	555	35	135	19	5	4	61	17	46	.243	.266	.317	61	-33	-30	42	0	3	-2	.983	1	*2S	-2.1

YEAR	TM/L	G	AB	R	H	2B	3B	HR	RBI	BB	SO	AVG	OBP	SLG	PRO+	BR	/A	RC	SB	CS	SBR	FA	FR	POS	TPR
1980	NY-N	128	443	46	113	9	8	0	24	22	20	.255	.290	.312	70	-19	-18	36	2	2	-1	**.991**	3	*2/S	-0.8
1981	NY-N	105	325	24	72	12	4	1	20	11	19	.222	.247	.292	53	-21	-20	20	1	2	-1	.987	12	*2/S	-0.3
1982	Tex-A	88	270	13	57	6	2	0	19	4	14	.211	.223	.248	31	-26	-24	15	6	2	1	.989	4	2S	-1.5
	Mon-N	58	193	13	47	6	2	0	20	4	23	.244	.259	.295	54	-12	-12	13	0	2	-1	.983	5	2	-0.6
1983	Mon-N	143	452	44	107	18	4	0	26	19	38	.237	.268	.294	56	-28	-27	33	2	1	0	.986	7	*2S	-1.4
1984	Mon-N	124	366	23	89	12	1	0	17	12	41	.243	.267	.281	57	-22	-21	27	0	0	0	.979	-8	2S	-2.5
1985	Mon-N	9	6	0	1	0	0	0	0	0	0	.167	.167	.167	-7	-1	-1	0	0	0	0	1.000	-1	/2S	-0.1
	Det-A	32	51	2	13	2	1	0	2	0	3	.255	.255	.333	60	-3	-3	4	0	0	0	.984	8	2/S3	0.6
Total	11	1308	3853	288	918	115	39	7	284	151	320	.238	.267	.294	57	-234	-224	285	20	20	-6	.986	33	2S/3	-12.9

■ CLIPPER FLYNN Flynn, William b: 4/29/1849, Lansingburgh, N.Y. d: 11/11/1881, Lansingburgh, N.Y. TR , 5'7", 140 lbs. Deb: 5/09/1871

YEAR	TM/L	G	AB	R	H	2B	3B	HR	RBI	BB	SO	AVG	OBP	SLG	PRO+	BR	/A	RC	SB	CS	SBR	FA	FR	POS	TPR
1871	Tro-n	29	142	43	48	6	1	0	27	4	2	.338	.356	.394	114	3	2	22	3					1/O3	0.2
1872	Oly-n	9	40	4	9	1	0	0	2	0	0	.225	.225	.250	48	-2	-2	2						/1	-0.1
Total	2 n	38	182	47	57	7	1	0	29	4	2	.313	.328	.363	101	0	0	24						/1O3	0.1

■ JIM FOGARTY Fogarty, James G. b: 2/12/1864, San Francisco, Cal d: 5/20/1891, Philadelphia, Pa. BR/TR, 5'10.5", 180 lbs. Deb: 5/01/1884 FM

YEAR	TM/L	G	AB	R	H	2B	3B	HR	RBI	BB	SO	AVG	OBP	SLG	PRO+	BR	/A	RC	SB	CS	SBR	FA	FR	POS	TPR
1884	Phi-N	97	378	42	80	12	6	1	37	20	54	.212	.251	.283	71	-14	-11	28				.915	3	*O3/2SP	-0.8
1885	Phi-N	111	427	49	99	13	3	0	39	30	37	.232	.282	.276	83	-8	-7	34				.941	25	*O2/S3	1.5
1886	Phi-N	77	280	54	82	13	5	3	47	42	16	.293	.385	.407	140	15	15	57	30			.953	-3	O2/S3P	1.0
1887	Phi-N	126	495	113	129	26	12	8	50	**82**	44	.261	.376	.410	114	17	11	118	102			.920	32	*O/S32P	3.4
1888	Phi-N	121	454	72	107	14	6	1	35	53	66	.236	.325	.300	97	4	0	65	58			.930	14	*O/3S	1.1
1889	Phi-N	128	499	107	129	15	17	3	54	65	60	.259	.352	.375	96	4	-3	103	**99**			**.961**	19	*O/P	1.1
1890	Phi-P	91	347	71	83	17	6	4	58	59	50	.239	.364	.357	93	-1	-2	60	36			.963	8	O/3M	0.2
Total	7	751	2880	508	709	110	55	20	320	351	327	.246	.335	.343	99	18	4	464	325			.940	98	O/32SP	7.5

■ JOE FOGARTY Fogarty, Joseph J. b: San Francisco, Cal. Deb: 9/18/1885 F

YEAR	TM/L	G	AB	R	H	2B	3B	HR	RBI	BB	SO	AVG	OBP	SLG	PRO+	BR	/A	RC	SB	CS	SBR	FA	FR	POS	TPR
1885	StL-N	2	8	1	1	0	0	0	0	0	1	.125	.125	.125	-20	-1	-1	0				1.000	-0	/O	-0.1

■ LEE FOHL Fohl, Leo Alexander b: 11/28/1876, Lowell, Ohio d: 10/30/65, Cleveland, Ohio BL/TR, 5'10", 175 lbs. Deb: 8/29/02 M

YEAR	TM/L	G	AB	R	H	2B	3B	HR	RBI	BB	SO	AVG	OBP	SLG	PRO+	BR	/A	RC	SB	CS	SBR	FA	FR	POS	TPR
1902	Pit-N	1	3	0	0	0	0	0	1	0		.000	.000	.000	-97	-1	-1	0	0			.875	0	/C	0.0
1903	Cin-N	4	14	3	5	1	1	0	2	0		.357	.400	.571	158	1	1	3	0			.955	-0	/C	0.1
Total	2	5	17	3	5	1	1	0	3	0		.294	.333	.471	120	1	0	3	0			.933	0	/C	0.1

■ HANK FOILES Foiles, Henry Lee b: 6/10/29, Richmond, Va. BR/TR, 6', 195 lbs. Deb: 4/21/53

YEAR	TM/L	G	AB	R	H	2B	3B	HR	RBI	BB	SO	AVG	OBP	SLG	PRO+	BR	/A	RC	SB	CS	SBR	FA	FR	POS	TPR
1953	Cin-N	5	13	1	2	0	0	0	0	1	2	.154	.214	.154	-2	-2	-2	0	0	0	0	.909	-1	/C	-0.2
	Cle-A	7	7	2	1	0	0	0	0	1	1	.143	.250	.143	9	-1	-1	0	0	0	0	.933	1	/C	0.0
1955	Cle-A	62	111	13	29	9	0	1	7	17	18	.261	.359	.369	93	-0	-1	15	0	0	0	.988	14	C	1.4
1956	Cle-A	1	0	0	0	0	0	0	0	0	0	—	—	—	—	0	0	0	0	0	0	.000	0	/C	0.0
	Pit-N	79	222	24	47	10	2	7	25	17	56	.212	.268	.369	71	-10	-10	21	0	1	-1	.988	-2	C	-1.0
1957	Pit-N★	109	281	32	76	10	4	9	36	37	53	.270	.355	.431	113	4	5	43	1	3	-2	.981	-6	*C	0.2
1958	Pit-N	104	264	31	54	10	2	8	30	45	53	.205	.323	.348	80	-8	-7	31	0	1	-1	.990	8	*C	0.6
1959	Pit-N	53	80	10	18	3	0	3	4	7	16	.225	.287	.375	75	-3	-3	8	0	0	0	1.000	9	C	0.7
1960	KC-A	6	7	1	4	0	0	0	1	3	2	.571	.700	.571	246	2	2	3	0	0	0	.900	-0	/C	0.2
	Cle-A	24	68	9	19	1	0	1	6	7	5	.279	.347	.338	89	-1	-1	9	0	0	0	.982	0	C	0.1
	Det-A	26	56	5	14	3	0	0	3	1	8	.250	.263	.304	51	-4	-4	4	1	0	0	1.000	4	C	0.1
	Yr	56	131	15	37	4	0	1	10	11	15	.282	.338	.336	83	-3	-3	16	1	0	0	.987	5	C	0.4
1961	Bal-A	43	124	18	34	6	0	6	19	12	27	.274	.338	.468	115	2	2	18	0	2	-1	.995	3	C	0.5
1962	Cin-N	43	131	17	36	6	1	7	25	13	39	.275	.340	.496	118	4	3	22	0	0	0	.981	1	C	0.6
1963	Cin-N	1	3	0	0	0	0	0	0	1	0	.000	.250	.000	-21	-0	-0	0	1	0	0	1.000	-0	/C	0.0
	LA-A	41	84	8	18	1	1	4	10	8	13	.214	.290	.393	95	-1	-1	9	0	0	0	.974	3	C	0.3
1964	LA-A	4	4	0	1	0	0	0	0	0	2	.250	.250	.250	44	-0	-0	0	0	0	0	.000	0	H	0.0
Total	11	608	1455	171	353	59	10	46	166	170	295	.243	.323	.392	92	-20	-17	185	3	7	-3	.986	35	C	3.5

■ CURRY FOLEY Foley, Charles Joseph b: 1/14/1856, Milltown, Ireland d: 10/20/1898, Boston, Mass. TL , 180 lbs. Deb: 5/13/1879

YEAR	TM/L	G	AB	R	H	2B	3B	HR	RBI	BB	SO	AVG	OBP	SLG	PRO+	BR	/A	RC	SB	CS	SBR	FA	FR	POS	TPR
1879	Bos-N	35	146	16	46	3	1	0	17	3	4	.315	.329	.349	121	4	3	17				.857	-7	PO/1	-0.4
1880	Bos-N	80	332	44	97	13	2	2	31	8	14	.292	.309	.361	130	9	10	38				.953	-3	PO1	0.0
1881	Buf-N	83	375	58	96	20	2	1	25	7	27	.256	.270	.328	88	-6	-5	34				.795	-4	O1P	-1.1
1882	Buf-N	84	341	51	104	16	4	3	49	12	26	.305	.329	.402	131	12	11	46				.833	0	*O/P	1.0
1883	Buf-N	23	111	23	30	5	3	0	6	4	12	.270	.296	.369	98	0	-0	12				.885	-2	O/P	-0.2
Total	5	305	1305	192	373	57	12	6	128	34	83	.286	.304	.362	114	19	19	148				.819	-16	O/P1	-0.7

■ MARV FOLEY Foley, Marvis Edwin b: 8/29/53, Stanford, Ky. BL/TR, 6', 195 lbs. Deb: 9/11/78

YEAR	TM/L	G	AB	R	H	2B	3B	HR	RBI	BB	SO	AVG	OBP	SLG	PRO+	BR	/A	RC	SB	CS	SBR	FA	FR	POS	TPR
1978	Chi-A	11	34	3	12	0	0	0	6	4	6	.353	.421	.353	119	1	1	5	0	1	-1	.938	-3	C	-0.2
1979	Chi-A	34	97	6	24	3	0	2	10	7	5	.247	.298	.340	72	-4	-4	9	0	0	0	.993	-1	C	-0.4
1980	Chi-A	68	137	14	29	5	0	4	15	9	22	.212	.270	.336	65	-7	-7	13	0	0	0	.991	2	C/1	-0.3
1982	Chi-A	27	36	1	4	0	0	0	1	6	4	.111	.238	.111	-0	-5	-5	1	0	0	0	.980	1	C/31D	-0.3
1984	Tex-A	63	115	13	25	2	0	6	19	15	24	.217	.313	.391	91	-1	-2	15	0	0	0	.988	1	C/13D	0.1
Total	5	203	419	37	94	10	0	12	51	41	61	.224	.298	.334	73	-15	-16	44	0	1	-1	.986	0	C/D13	-1.1

■ RAY FOLEY Foley, Raymond Kirwin b: 6/23/06, Naugatuck, Conn. d: 3/22/80, Vero Beach, Fla. BL/TR, 5'11", 173 lbs. Deb: 7/04/28

YEAR	TM/L	G	AB	R	H	2B	3B	HR	RBI	BB	SO	AVG	OBP	SLG	PRO+	BR	/A	RC	SB	CS	SBR	FA	FR	POS	TPR
1928	NY-N	2	1	1	0	0	0	0	0	1	1	.000	.500	.000	41	0	0	0	0			.000	0	H	0.0

■ TOM FOLEY Foley, Thomas J. b: 8/16/1842, Cashel, Ireland d: 11/3/26, Chicago, Ill. 5'9.5", 157 lbs. Deb: 5/08/1871

YEAR	TM/L	G	AB	R	H	2B	3B	HR	RBI	BB	SO	AVG	OBP	SLG	PRO+	BR	/A	RC	SB	CS	SBR	FA	FR	POS	TPR
1871	Chi-n	18	84	18	22	3	1	0	13	3	2	.262	.287	.321	67	-3	-5	8	1					O/C3	-0.3

■ TOM FOLEY Foley, Thomas Michael b: 9/9/59, Columbus, Ga. BL/TR, 6'1", 175 lbs. Deb: 4/09/83

YEAR	TM/L	G	AB	R	H	2B	3B	HR	RBI	BB	SO	AVG	OBP	SLG	PRO+	BR	/A	RC	SB	CS	SBR	FA	FR	POS	TPR
1983	Cin-N	68	98	7	20	4	1	0	9	13	17	.204	.297	.265	55	-5	-6	9	1	0	0	.983	9	S/2	0.6
1984	Cin-N	106	277	26	70	8	3	5	27	24	36	.253	.312	.357	84	-5	-6	32	3	2	-0	.965	1	S2/3	0.1
1985	Cin-N	43	92	7	18	5	1	0	6	6	16	.196	.245	.272	42	-7	-7	7	1	0	0	.983	3	2S/3	-0.3
	Phi-N	46	158	17	42	8	0	3	17	13	18	.266	.322	.373	91	-1	-2	18	1	3	-2	.981	-5	S	-0.4
	Yr	89	250	24	60	13	1	3	23	19	34	.240	.294	.336	73	-8	-9	24	2	3	-1	.978	-3	S2/3	-0.7
1986	Phi-N	39	61	8	18	2	1	0	5	10	11	.295	.394	.361	106	1	1	10	2	0	1	.975	0	S/23	0.3
	Mon-N	64	202	18	52	13	2	1	18	20	26	.257	.324	.356	88	-3	-3	24	8	3	1	.965	-5	S23	-0.5
	Yr	103	263	26	70	15	3	1	23	30	37	.266	.341	.357	92	-2	-2	34	10	3	1	.970	-5	S23	-0.2
1987	Mon-N	106	280	35	82	18	3	5	28	11	40	.293	.322	.432	95	-2	-3	34	6	10	-4	.963	1	S2/3	-0.1
1988	Mon-N	127	377	33	100	21	3	5	43	30	49	.265	.321	.377	95	-0	-2	41	2	7	-4	.972	3	2S/3	0.3
1989	Mon-N	122	375	34	86	19	2	7	39	45	53	.229	.317	.347	88	-5	-5	44	2	3	-1	.988	20	*23S/P	1.8
1990	Mon-N	73	164	11	35	2	1	0	12	12	22	.213	.267	.238	42	-13	-12	10	0	1	-1	.987	3	S2/31	-0.8
1991	Mon-N	86	168	12	35	11	1	0	15	14	30	.208	.273	.286	58	-10	-9	13	2	0	1	.967	-2	S1/32	-1.0
1992	Mon-N	72	115	7	20	3	1	0	5	8	21	.174	.234	.217	29	-11	-11	6	3	0	1	.967	6	S21/3O	-0.2
Total	10	952	2367	215	578	114	19	26	224	206	339	.244	.307	.341	79	-61	-66	246	31	29	-8	.972	35	S2/31OP	-0.2

■ WILL FOLEY Foley, William Brown b: 11/15/1855, Chicago, Ill. d: 11/12/16, Chicago, Ill. BR/TR, 5'9.5", 150 lbs. Deb: 8/23/1875

YEAR	TM/L	G	AB	R	H	2B	3B	HR	RBI	BB	SO	AVG	OBP	SLG	PRO+	BR	/A	RC	SB	CS	SBR	FA	FR	POS	TPR
1875	Chi-n	3	12	0	3	1	0	0		0		.250	.250	.333	99	-0	-0	1						/3	0.0
1876	Cin-N	58	221	19	50	3	2	0	9	0	14	.226	.226	.258	71	-9	-4	13				.804	2	3C	0.0

YEAR	TM/L	G	AB	R	H	2B	3B	HR	RBI	BB	SO	AVG	OBP	SLG	PRO+	BR	/A	RC	SB	CS	SBR	FA	FR	POS	TPR
1877	Cin-N	56	216	23	41	5	1	0	18	4	13	.190	.205	.222	39	-16	-12	10				.836	6	*3	-0.4
1878	Mil-N	56	229	33	62	8	5	0	22	7	14	.271	.292	.349	103	2	0	24				.812	-9	*3/C	-0.6
1879	Cin-N	56	218	22	46	5	1	0	25	2	16	.211	.218	.243	55	-11	-9	12				.820	3	3O/2	-0.7
1881	Det-N	5	15	0	2	0	0	0	1	2	3	.133	.235	.133	18	-1	-1	0				.769	-1	/3	-0.3
1884	CP-U	19	71	15	20	1	1	0		5		.282	.329	.324	122	2	2	8				.804	-3	3	-0.1
Total	6	250	970	112	221	22	10	0	75	20	60	.228	.243	.271	72	-33	-25	67				.817	-2	3/CO2	-2.1

■ TIM FOLI

Foli, Timothy John b: 12/8/50, Culver City, Cal. BR/TR, 6', 179 lbs. Deb: 9/11/70 C

YEAR	TM/L	G	AB	R	H	2B	3B	HR	RBI	BB	SO	AVG	OBP	SLG	PRO+	BR	/A	RC	SB	CS	SBR	FA	FR	POS	TPR
1970	NY-N	5	11	0	4	0	0	0	1	0	2	.364	.364	.364	95	-0	-0	1	0	0	0	1.000	2	/S3	0.2
1971	NY-N	97	288	32	65	12	2	0	24	18	50	.226	.274	.281	58	-16	-16	22	5	0	2	.964	14	23S/O	0.4
1972	Mon-N	149	540	45	130	12	2	2	35	25	43	.241	.282	.281	59	-28	-29	44	11	7	-1	.966	9	*S/2	0.0
1973	Mon-N	126	458	37	110	11	0	2	36	28	40	.240	.285	.277	55	-27	-29	33	6	3	0	.960	9	*S/2O	-0.4
1974	Mon-N	121	441	41	112	10	3	0	39	28	27	.254	.303	.290	63	-19	-22	40	8	2	1	.971	19	*S/3	1.4
1975	Mon-N	152	572	64	136	25	2	1	29	36	49	.238	.285	.294	58	-31	-33	49	13	3	2	.973	6	*S/2	-1.0
1976	Mon-N	149	546	41	144	36	1	6	54	16	33	.264	.285	.366	80	-14	-16	52	6	5	-1	.975	7	*S/3	0.8
1977	Mon-N	13	57	2	10	5	1	0	3	0	4	.175	.175	.298	25	-6	-6	3	0	0	0	1.000	1	S	-0.3
	SF-N	104	368	30	84	17	3	4	27	11	16	.228	.251	.323	53	-25	-25	28	2	4	-2	.974	3	*S/23O	-1.4
	Yr	117	425	32	94	22	4	4	30	11	20	.221	.241	.320	49	-31	-31	30	2	4	-2	.977	4	*S/23O	-1.7
1978	NY-N	113	413	37	106	21	1	1	27	14	30	.257	.284	.320	71	-18	-16	35	2	5	-2	.966	-15	*S	-2.1
1979	NY-N	3	7	0	0	0	0	0	0	0	0	.000	.000	.000	-99	-2	-2	0	0	0	0	1.000	1	/S	-0.1
	*Pit-N	133	525	70	153	23	1	1	65	28	14	.291	.338	.345	83	-9	-12	63	6	5	-1	.978	-1	*S	0.1
	Yr	136	532	70	153	23	1	1	65	28	14	.288	.334	.340	81	-11	-14	62	6	5	-1	.978	-1	*S	0.0
1980	Pit-N	127	495	61	131	22	0	3	38	19	23	.265	.300	.327	74	-17	-18	49	11	7	-1	**.981**	-0	*S	-0.4
1981	Pit-N	86	316	32	78	12	2	0	20	17	10	.247	.287	.297	64	-14	-15	28	7	7	-2	.965	-9	S	-2.0
1982	*Cal-A	150	480	46	121	14	2	3	56	14	22	.252	.276	.308	60	-26	-26	40	2	4	-2	**.985**	8	*S/23	-0.7
1983	Cal-A	88	330	29	83	10	0	2	29	5	18	.252	.265	.300	56	-20	-20	25	2	3	-1	.975	10	S3	-0.4
1984	NY-A	61	163	8	41	11	0	0	16	2	16	.252	.265	.319	63	-9	-8	13	0	0	0	.950	7	S23/1	0.2
1985	Pit-N	19	37	1	7	0	0	0	2	4	2	.189	.268	.189	30	-3	-3	1	0	0	0	.980	3	S	0.1
Total	16	1696	6047	576	1515	241	20	25	501	265	399	.251	.286	.309	64	-284	-297	527	81	55	-9	.973	74	*S/23O1	-5.6

■ DEE FONDY

Fondy, Dee Virgil b: 10/31/24, Slaton, Tex. BL/TL, 6'3", 196 lbs. Deb: 4/17/51

YEAR	TM/L	G	AB	R	H	2B	3B	HR	RBI	BB	SO	AVG	OBP	SLG	PRO+	BR	/A	RC	SB	CS	SBR	FA	FR	POS	TPR
1951	Chi-N	49	170	23	46	7	2	3	20	11	20	.271	.319	.388	88	-3	-3	20	5	6	-2	.976	-3	1	-1.0
1952	Chi-N	145	554	69	166	21	9	10	67	28	60	.300	.334	.424	108	5	4	75	13	11	-3	.990	2	*1	-0.2
1953	Chi-N	150	595	79	184	24	11	18	78	44	106	.309	.358	.477	113	12	11	104	10	7	-1	.987	4	*1	0.7
1954	Chi-N	141	568	77	162	30	4	9	49	35	84	.285	.328	.400	87	-10	-11	75	20	5	**3**	.993	7	*1	-0.8
1955	Chi-N	150	574	69	152	23	8	17	65	35	87	.265	.309	.422	92	-8	-8	71	8	9	-3	.991	1	*1	-1.9
1956	Chi-N	137	543	52	146	22	9	9	46	20	74	.269	.295	.392	84	-14	-13	62	9	7	-2	.985	-3	*1	-2.8
1957	Chi-N	11	51	3	16	3	1	0	2	0	9	.314	.314	.412	94	-1	-1	5	1	2	-1	.991	-1	1	-0.3
	Pit-N	95	323	42	101	13	2	2	35	25	59	.313	.364	.384	104	1	2	46	11	5	0	.982	-3	1	-0.5
	Yr	106	374	45	117	16	3	2	37	25	68	.313	.357	.388	103	1	2	52	12	7	-1	.983	-4	1	-0.8
1958	Cin-N	89	124	23	27	1	1	1	11	5	27	.218	.248	.266	34	-11	-12	9	7	1	2	.987	-1	1O	-1.4
Total	8	967	3502	437	1000	144	47	69	373	203	526	.286	.326	.413	95	-29	-31	467	84	53	-7	.988	3	1/O	-8.2

■ LEW FONSECA

Fonseca, Lewis Albert b: 1/21/1899, Oakland, Cal. d: 11/26/89, Ely, Iowa BR/TR, 5'10.5", 180 lbs. Deb: 4/13/21 M

YEAR	TM/L	G	AB	R	H	2B	3B	HR	RBI	BB	SO	AVG	OBP	SLG	PRO+	BR	/A	RC	SB	CS	SBR	FA	FR	POS	TPR
1921	Cin-N	82	297	38	82	10	3	1	41	8	13	.276	.304	.340	74	-13	-11	30	2	3	-1	.961	-3	21O	-1.5
1922	Cin-N	81	291	55	105	20	3	4	45	14	18	.361	.390	.491	128	11	11	53	7	8	-3	.970	8	2	1.7
1923	Cin-N	65	237	33	66	11	4	3	28	9	16	.278	.310	.397	87	-6	-5	30	4	0	1	.957	8	21	0.4
1924	Cin-N	20	57	5	13	2	1	0	9	4	4	.228	.279	.298	55	-4	-4	5	1	0	0	1.000	-2	2/1	-0.6
1925	Phi-N	126	467	78	149	30	5	7	60	21	42	.319	.352	.450	95	1	-4	74	6	2	1	.956	-8	21	-1.3
1927	Cle-A	112	428	60	133	20	7	2	40	12	17	.311	.333	.404	90	-7	-8	53	12	4	1	.973	-6	21	-0.9
1928	Cle-A	75	263	38	86	19	4	3	36	13	17	.327	.361	.464	114	5	5	44	4	2	0	1.000	5	13/S2	0.5
1929	Cle-A	148	566	97	209	44	15	6	103	50	23	**.369**	.427	.532	140	39	36	128	19	11	-1	.995	6	*1	2.5
1930	Cle-A	40	129	20	36	9	2	0	17	7	7	.279	.316	.380	73	-5	-6	16	1	0	0	.980	2	1/3	-0.5
1931	Cle-A	26	108	21	40	9	1	1	14	8	7	.370	.419	.500	133	6	6	22	3	2	-0	.993	0	1	0.3
	Chi-A	121	465	65	139	26	5	2	71	32	22	.299	.348	.389	99	-4	-1	63	4	4	-1	.974	-17	O2/13	-2.2
	Yr	147	573	86	179	35	6	3	85	40	29	.312	.361	.410	106	2	5	85	7	6	-2	.974	-16	O12/3	-1.9
1932	Chi-A	18	37	0	5	1	0	0	6	1	7	.135	.158	.162	-18	-6	-6	1	0	0	0	1.000	1	/OPM	-0.5
1933	Chi-A	23	59	8	12	2	0	2	15	7	6	.203	.288	.339	68	-3	-3	6	1	0	0	1.000	2	1M	-0.1
Total	12	937	3404	518	1075	203	50	31	485	186	199	.316	.355	.432	103	14	11	524	64	36	-2	.994	-3	12O/3SP	-2.2

■ BARRY FOOTE

Foote, Barry Clifton b: 2/16/52, Smithfield, N.C. BR/TR, 6'3", 210 lbs. Deb: 9/14/73 C

YEAR	TM/L	G	AB	R	H	2B	3B	HR	RBI	BB	SO	AVG	OBP	SLG	PRO+	BR	/A	RC	SB	CS	SBR	FA	FR	POS	TPR
1973	Mon-N	6	6	0	4	0	1	0	1	0	0	.667	.667	1.000	343	2	2	4	0	0	0	.000	0	H	0.2
1974	Mon-N	125	420	44	110	23	4	11	60	35	74	.262	.323	.414	100	2	-1	52	2	1	0	.984	9	*C	1.3
1975	Mon-N	118	387	25	75	16	1	7	30	17	48	.194	.230	.295	43	-30	-32	24	0	1	-1	.985	11	*C	-1.8
1976	Mon-N	105	350	32	82	12	2	7	27	17	32	.234	.272	.340	70	-13	-15	31	2	1	0	.989	7	C/31	-0.5
1977	Mon-N	15	49	4	12	3	1	2	8	4	10	.245	.302	.469	106	0	0	7	0	0	0	.988	0	C	0.1
	Phi-N	18	32	3	7	1	0	1	3	3	6	.219	.286	.344	65	-1	-2	1	0	0	0	.980	-1	C	-0.2
	Yr	33	81	7	19	4	1	3	11	7	16	.235	.295	.420	88	-1	-2	8	0	0	0	.985	-0	C	-0.1
1978	*Phi-N	39	57	4	9	0	0	1	4	1	11	.158	.172	.211	6	-7	-7	2	0	0	0	1.000	2	C	-0.5
1979	Chi-N	132	429	47	109	26	0	16	56	34	49	.254	.316	.427	92	-1	-6	56	5	2	0	.979	-3	*C	-0.4
1980	Chi-N	63	202	16	48	13	1	6	28	13	18	.238	.284	.401	83	-4	-5	21	1	1	-0	.992	1	C	-0.3
1981	Chi-N	9	22	0	0	0	0	0	1	3	7	.000	.120	.000	-61	-5	-5	0	0	0	0	1.000	-1	/C	-0.6
	*NY-A	40	125	12	26	4	0	6	10	8	21	.208	.256	.384	83	-3	-3	10	0	0	0	.996	9	C/1D	0.7
1982	NY-A	17	48	4	7	5	0	0	2	1	11	.146	.163	.250	12	-6	-6	2	0	0	0	.973	-4	C	-0.9
Total	10	687	2127	191	489	103	10	57	230	136	287	.230	.279	.368	75	-67	-80	209	10	6	-1	.985	31	C/D13	-2.9

■ JIM FORAN

Foran, James H. b: 1848, New York 5'6.5", 159 lbs. Deb: 5/04/1871

YEAR	TM/L	G	AB	R	H	2B	3B	HR	RBI	BB	SO	AVG	OBP	SLG	PRO+	BR	/A	RC	SB	CS	SBR	FA	FR	POS	TPR
1871	Kek-n	19	89	21	31	1	3	1	18	2	1	.348	.363	.461	132	4	3	16	1					1/O	0.3

■ DAVY FORCE

Force, David W. "Wee Davy" or "Tom Thumb" b: 7/27/1849, New York, N.Y. d: 6/21/18, Englewood, N.J. BR/TR, 5'4", 130 lbs. Deb: 5/05/1871

YEAR	TM/L	G	AB	R	H	2B	3B	HR	RBI	BB	SO	AVG	OBP	SLG	PRO+	BR	/A	RC	SB	CS	SBR	FA	FR	POS	TPR
1871	Oly-n	32	162	45	45	9	4	0	29	4	0	.278	.295	.383	98	-2	0	21	8					*S/3	0.0
1872	Tro-n	25	133	40	53	7	1	0	16	1	0	.398	.403	.466	164	10	10	25						3/S	0.5
	Bal-n	19	96	29	40	3	2	0	13	1	0	.417	.423	.490	172	9	8	22						3	0.5
	Yr	44	229	69	93	10	3	0	29	2	0	.406	.411	.476	168	19	17	47						3/S	1.0
1873	Bal-n	49	234	77	86	12	3	0	31	9	0	.368	.391	.444	146	13	13	42						3S/P	0.8
1874	Chi-n	59	296	61	93	10	0	0		2		.314	.319	.348	111	4	3	34						3S/PO	0.2
1875	Ath-n	77	384	78	120	21	6	0		8		.313	.327	.398	134	19	12	51						*S	0.8
1876	Phi-N	60	284	48	66	6	0	0	17	5	3	.232	.246	.254	67	-10	-9	18				.898	21	*S/3	1.0
	NY-N	1	3	0	0	0	0	0	0	0	0	.000	.000	.000	-99	-1	-1	0				.833	0	/S	0.0
	Yr	61	287	48	66	6	0	0	17	5	3	.230	.243	.251	66	-10	-10	18				.897	21	S/3	1.0
1877	StL-N	58	225	24	59	5	3	0	22	11	15	.262	.297	.311	97	-2	0	21				**.914**	6	*S/3	0.6
1879	Buf-N	79	316	36	66	5	2	0	8	13	37	.209	.240	.237	57	-14	-15	18				**.929**	2	*S/3	-0.8
1880	Buf-N	81	290	22	49	10	0	0	17	10	35	.169	.197	.203	35	-19	-19	12				.939	31	2S	1.6
1881	Buf-N	75	278	21	50	9	1	0	15	11	29	.180	.211	.219	36	-20	-19	13				.937	24	2S/O3	0.8

YEAR	TM/L	G	AB	R	H	2B	3B	HR	RBI	BB	SO	AVG	OBP	SLG	PRO+	BR	/A	RC	SB	CS	SBR	FA	FR	POS	TPR
1882	Buf-N	73	278	39	67	10	1	1	28	12	17	.241	.272	.295	81	-5	-6	23				**.908**	7	*S3/2	0.4
1883	Buf-N	96	378	40	82	11	3	0	35	12	39	.217	.241	.262	52	-21	-22	24				.884	-6	*S3/2	-2.3
1884	Buf-N	106	403	47	83	13	3	0	36	27	41	.206	.256	.253	59	-17	-20	27				**.898**	-3	*S/2	-1.9
1885	Buf-N	71	253	20	57	6	1	0	15	13	19	.225	.263	.257	66	-8	-10	18				.882	-4	2S/3	-1.1
1886	Was-N	68	242	26	44	5	1	0	16	17	26	.182	.236	.211	39	-18	-16	14	9			.909	17	S/23	0.2
Total	5 n	261	1305	330	437	62	16	0	89	25		.335	.347	.407	132	53	46	195	14					S3/PO	2.8
Total	10	768	2950	323	623	80	15	1	209	131	261	.211	.245	.249	58	-134	-136	189	9			.908	96	S2/3O	-1.5

■ CURT FORD Ford, Curtis Glenn b: 10/11/60, Jackson, Miss. BL/TR, 5'10", 150 lbs. Deb: 6/22/85

YEAR	TM/L	G	AB	R	H	2B	3B	HR	RBI	BB	SO	AVG	OBP	SLG	PRO+	BR	/A	RC	SB	CS	SBR	FA	FR	POS	TPR
1985	StL-N	11	12	2	6	2	0	0	3	4	1	.500	.625	.667	264	3	3	6	1	0	0	.750	-2	/O	0.2
1986	StL-N	85	214	30	53	15	2	2	29	23	29	.248	.321	.364	89	-3	-3	27	13	5	1	.975	1	O	-0.3
1987	*StL-N	89	228	32	65	9	5	3	26	14	32	.285	.329	.408	92	-2	-3	28	11	8	-2	.981	1	O	-0.5
1988	StL-N	91	128	11	25	6	0	1	18	8	26	.195	.243	.266	45	-9	-9	8	6	1	1	.965	-4	O/1	-1.4
1989	Phi-N	108	142	13	31	5	1	1	13	16	33	.218	.302	.289	70	-5	-5	12	5	3	-0	1.000	-8	O/12	-1.6
1990	Phi-N	22	18	0	2	0	0	0	0	1	5	.111	.158	.111	-25	-3	-3	0	0	0	0	1.000	-1	/O	-0.4
Total	6	406	742	88	182	37	8	7	89	66	126	.245	.309	.345	80	-20	-20	82	36	17	1	.977	-12	O/12	-4.0

■ DAN FORD Ford, Darnell Glenn b: 5/19/52, Los Angeles, Cal. BR/TR, 6'1", 185 lbs. Deb: 4/12/75

YEAR	TM/L	G	AB	R	H	2B	3B	HR	RBI	BB	SO	AVG	OBP	SLG	PRO+	BR	/A	RC	SB	CS	SBR	FA	FR	POS	TPR
1975	Min-A	130	440	72	123	21	1	15	59	30	79	.280	.333	.434	113	8	6	60	6	7	-2	.988	-9	*O/D	-0.9
1976	Min-A	145	514	87	137	24	7	20	86	36	118	.267	.327	.457	124	16	14	75	17	6	2	.968	-5	*O/D	0.6
1977	Min-A	144	453	66	121	25	7	11	60	41	79	.267	.341	.426	109	5	6	65	6	4	-1	.964	-10	*O/D	-0.9
1978	Min-A	151	592	78	162	36	10	11	82	48	88	.274	.333	.424	109	8	7	80	7	7	-2	.977	-2	*O/D	-0.4
1979	*Cal-A	142	569	100	165	26	5	21	101	40	86	.290	.340	.464	118	10	13	85	8	5	-1	.977	7	*O	1.2
1980	Cal-A	65	226	22	63	11	0	7	26	19	45	.279	.340	.420	110	2	3	28	0	1	-1	.940	-2	OD	-0.1
1981	Cal-A	97	375	53	104	14	1	15	48	23	71	.277	.328	.440	119	8	8	49	2	2	-1	.960	-2	O	0.2
1982	Bal-A	123	421	46	99	21	3	10	43	23	71	.235	.281	.371	78	-14	-14	43	5	2	0	.975	4	*O/D	-1.2
1983	*Bal-A	103	407	63	114	30	4	9	55	29	55	.280	.333	.440	113	5	6	59	9	2	2	.987	1	*O	0.5
1984	Bal-A	25	91	7	21	4	0	1	5	7	13	.231	.286	.308	66	-4	-4	8	1	0	0	1.000	2	O/D	-0.3
1985	Bal-A	28	75	4	14	2	0	1	1	7	17	.187	.256	.253	41	-6	-6	4	0	1	-1	.000	0	D	-0.6
Total	11	1153	4163	598	1123	214	38	121	566	303	722	.270	.326	.427	108	38	40	556	61	37	-4	.974	-17	*O/D	-1.9

■ ED FORD Ford, Edward L. b: 1862, Richmond, Va. 5'9.5", 160 lbs. Deb: 10/09/1884

YEAR	TM/L	G	AB	R	H	2B	3B	HR	RBI	BB	SO	AVG	OBP	SLG	PRO+	BR	/A	RC	SB	CS	SBR	FA	FR	POS	TPR
1884	Ric-a	2	5	0	0	0	0	0		0		.000	.000	.000	-99	-1	-1	0				.556	1	/S1	0.0

■ HOD FORD Ford, Horace Hills b: 7/23/1897, New Haven, Conn. d: 1/29/77, Winchester, Mass. BR/TR, 5'10", 165 lbs. Deb: 9/08/19

YEAR	TM/L	G	AB	R	H	2B	3B	HR	RBI	BB	SO	AVG	OBP	SLG	PRO+	BR	/A	RC	SB	CS	SBR	FA	FR	POS	TPR
1919	Bos-N	10	28	4	6	0	1	0	3	2	6	.214	.290	.286	77	-1	-1	2	0			.946	3	/S3	0.3
1920	Bos-N	88	257	16	62	12	5	1	30	18	25	.241	.296	.339	86	-6	-5	26	3	3	-1	.972	15	2S/1	1.3
1921	Bos-N	152	555	50	155	29	5	2	61	36	49	.279	.328	.360	87	-14	-10	64	2	11	-6	**.973**	16	*2S	0.6
1922	Bos-N	143	515	58	140	23	9	2	60	30	36	.272	.317	.363	78	-20	-16	61	2	1	0	.953	-4	*S2	-0.7
1923	Bos-N	111	380	27	103	16	7	2	50	31	30	.271	.326	.366	86	-10	-8	46	1	1	-0	.970	-9	2S	-1.4
1924	Phi-N	145	530	58	144	27	5	3	53	27	40	.272	.308	.358	70	-17	-25	56	1	9	-5	.970	12	*2	-1.7
1925	Bro-N	66	216	32	59	11	0	1	15	26	15	.273	.357	.338	81	-6	-5	27	0	3	-2	.966	-0	S	-0.1
1926	Cin-N	57	197	14	55	6	1	0	18	14	12	.279	.336	.320	79	-6	-5	21	1			.963	5	S	0.5
1927	Cin-N	115	409	45	112	16	2	1	46	33	34	.274	.331	.330	80	-12	-11	45	0			.952	-8	*S2	-0.7
1928	Cin-N	149	506	49	122	17	4	0	54	47	31	.241	.308	.291	58	-31	-30	47	1			**.972**	12	*S	0.0
1929	Cin-N	148	529	68	146	14	6	3	50	41	25	.276	.329	.342	70	-27	-23	59	8			.953	8	*S2	0.0
1930	Cin-N	132	424	36	98	16	7	1	34	24	28	.231	.272	.309	42	-42	-38	36	2			.974	2	S2	-2.4
1931	Cin-N	84	175	18	40	8	1	0	13	13	13	.229	.286	.286	57	-11	-10	15	0			.954	1	S/23	-0.4
1932	StL-N	1	2	0	0	0	0	0	0	0	0	.000	.000	.000	-97	-1	-1	0	0			.750	0	/S	0.0
	Bos-N	40	95	9	26	5	2	0	6	6	9	.274	.324	.368	89	-2	-1	12	0			.984	-3	2S/3	-0.2
	Yr	41	97	9	26	5	2	0	6	6	9	.268	.317	.361	85	-2	-2	12	0			.984	-3	2S/3	-0.2
1933	Bos-N	5	15	0	1	0	0	0	1	3	1	.067	.222	.067	-16	-2	-2	0	0			1.000	5	/S	0.4
Total	15	1446	4833	484	1269	200	55	16	494	351	354	.263	.316	.337	72	-207	-191	517	21	28		.960	54	S2/31	-4.5

■ TED FORD Ford, Theodore Henry b: 2/7/47, Vineland, N.J. BR/TR, 5'10", 180 lbs. Deb: 4/07/70

YEAR	TM/L	G	AB	R	H	2B	3B	HR	RBI	BB	SO	AVG	OBP	SLG	PRO+	BR	/A	RC	SB	CS	SBR	FA	FR	POS	TPR
1970	Cle-A	26	46	5	8	1	0	1	1	3	13	.174	.224	.261	32	-4	-5	3	0	0	0	1.000	1	O	-0.4
1971	Cle-A	74	196	15	38	6	0	2	14	9	34	.194	.229	.255	34	-16	-18	10	2	2	-1	1.000	-1	O	-2.4
1972	Tex-A	129	429	43	101	19	1	14	50	37	80	.235	.301	.382	107	0	2	50	4	3	-1	.977	9	*O	0.6
1973	Cle-A	11	40	3	9	0	1	0	3	2	7	.225	.262	.275	50	-3	-3	3	1	0	0	1.000	-4	O	-0.7
Total	4	240	711	66	156	26	2	17	68	51	134	.219	.275	.333	76	-23	-23	66	7	5	-1	.985	6	O	-2.9

■ FRANK FOREMAN Foreman, Francis Isaiah "Monkey" b: 5/1/1863, Baltimore, Md. d: 11/19/57, Baltimore, Md. BL/TL, 6', 160 lbs. Deb: 5/15/1884 F

YEAR	TM/L	G	AB	R	H	2B	3B	HR	RBI	BB	SO	AVG	OBP	SLG	PRO+	BR	/A	RC	SB	CS	SBR	FA	FR	POS	TPR
1884	CP-U	3	11	0	1	0	0	0		0		.091	.091	.091	-39	-2	-2	0				.857	-1	/PO	-0.1
	KC-U	1	3	0	0	0	0	0		0		.000	.000	.000	-99	-1	-1	0				.900	1	/P	0.0
	Yr	4	14	0	1	0	0	0		0		.071	.071	.071	-54	-2	-2	0				.882	0	/PO	-0.1
1885	Bal-a	3	14	4	4	0	1	0		0		.286	.286	.429	128	0	0	2				.800	-1	/PO	0.0
1889	Bal-a	54	181	18	26	2	1	1	11	12	35	.144	.201	.182	11	-21	-21	8	7			.853	-3	P/O	-0.1
1890	Cin-N	25	75	13	10	1	3	1	7	10	13	.133	.253	.267	53	-4	-4	5	0			.867	-3	P/O	0.0
1891	Cin-N	1	4	0	1	1	0	0	0	0	0	.250	.250	.500	117	0	0	1	0			.000	-0	/O	0.0
	Was-a	50	153	26	34	4	5	4	19	23	35	.222	.339	.392	117	2	4	23	6			.952	-1	P/O	0.1
1892	Was-N	11	28	5	13	2	2	1	3	3	3	.464	.516	.786	304	6	6	12	0			.632	-1	P	0.0
	Bal-N	7	23	2	4	1	1	0	1	3	3	.174	.269	.304	73	-1	-1	2	1			.750	-0	/OP	-0.1
	Yr	18	51	7	17	3	3	1	4	6	6	.333	.404	.569	197	6	6	12	1			.731	-1	P/O	-0.1
1893	NY-N	2	3	0	0	0	0	0	0	0	0	.000	.000	.000	-99	-1	-1	0	0			1.000	-0	/P	0.0
1895	Cin-N	32	94	14	29	7	0	2	11	4	14	.309	.350	.447	102	1	-0	16	1			.882	-3	P	0.0
1896	Cin-N	27	74	9	18	2	0	0	8	4	7	.243	.282	.270	45	-6	-6	7	2			.911	-0	P	0.0
1901	Bos-A	1	4	0	0	0	0	0	0	0		.000	.000	.000	-99	-1	-1	0	0			1.000	-0	/P	0.0
	Bal-A	24	80	12	26	2	2	0	10	3		.325	.349	.400	103	1	0	12	1			.887	-3	P	0.0
	Yr	25	84	12	26	2	2	0	10	3		.310	.333	.381	94	-0	-1	11	1			.891	-3	P	0.0
1902	Bal-A	2	7	1	3	1	0	0	1	0		.429	.429	.571	168	1	1	2	0			.818	1	/P	0.0
Total	11	243	754	104	169	23	15	9	71	62	110	.224	.291	.330	75	-25	-26	89	18			.881	-16	P/O	-0.2

■ TOM FORSTER Forster, Thomas W. b: 5/1/1859, New York, N.Y. d: 7/17/46, New York, N.Y. Deb: 8/04/1882

YEAR	TM/L	G	AB	R	H	2B	3B	HR	RBI	BB	SO	AVG	OBP	SLG	PRO+	BR	/A	RC	SB	CS	SBR	FA	FR	POS	TPR
1882	Det-N	21	76	5	7	0	0	0	2	5	12	.092	.148	.092	-21	-10	-10	1				.830	-7	2	-1.5
1884	Pit-a	35	126	10	28	5	0	0		7		.222	.263	.262	73	-3	-4	9				.897	6	S/32	0.3
1885	NY-a	57	213	28	47	7	2	0		17		.221	.281	.272	85	-5	-2	17				.903	-12	2/O	-1.1
1886	NY-a	67	251	33	49	3	2	1		20		.195	.263	.235	61	-12	-10	18	9			.891	-7	2/OS	-1.3
Total	4	180	666	76	131	15	4	1	2	49	12	.197	.256	.236	61	-29	-25	45	9			.885	-19	2/SO3	-3.6

■ ED FORSYTHE Forsythe, Edward James b: 4/30/1887, Kingston, N.Y. d: 6/22/56, Hoboken, N.J. BR/TR, 5'10", 155 lbs. Deb: 10/02/15

YEAR	TM/L	G	AB	R	H	2B	3B	HR	RBI	BB	SO	AVG	OBP	SLG	PRO+	BR	/A	RC	SB	CS	SBR	FA	FR	POS	TPR
1915	Bal-F	1	3	0	0	0	0	0	0	1	0	.000	.250	.000	-23	-0	-0	0	0			.667	-0	/3	-0.1

■ GEORGE FOSS Foss, George Dueward "Deeby" b: 6/13/1897, Register, Va. d: 11/10/69, Brandon, Fla. BR/TR, 5'10.5", 170 lbs. Deb: 4/16/21

YEAR	TM/L	G	AB	R	H	2B	3B	HR	RBI	BB	SO	AVG	OBP	SLG	PRO+	BR	/A	RC	SB	CS	SBR	FA	FR	POS	TPR
1921	Was-A	4	7	0	0	0	0	0	0	0	1	.000	.000	.000	-99	-2	-2	0	0	0	0	.750	0	/3	-0.2

■ RAY FOSSE

Fosse, Raymond Earl b: 4/4/47, Marion, Ill. BR/TR, 6'2", 215 lbs. Deb: 9/08/67

YEAR	TM/L	G	AB	R	H	2B	3B	HR	RBI	BB	SO	AVG	OBP	SLG	PRO+	BR	/A	RC	SB	CS	SBR	FA	FR	POS	TPR
1967	Cle-A	7	16	0	1	0	0	0	0	0	5	.063	.063	.063	-62	-3	-3	0	0	0	0	1.000	5	/C	0.2
1968	Cle-A	1	0	0	0	0	0	0	0	0	0	—	—	—	—	0	0	0	0	0	0	1.000	-0	/C	0.0
1969	Cle-A	37	116	11	20	3	0	2	9	8	29	.172	.232	.250	34	-10	-11	7	1	0	0	.977	3	C	-0.6
1970	Cle-A★	120	450	62	138	17	1	18	61	39	55	.307	.363	.469	122	16	14	74	1	5	-3	.989	6	*C	2.4
1971	Cle-A†	133	486	53	134	21	1	12	62	36	62	.276	.331	.397	97	3	-2	61	4	1	1	.988	-3	*C/1	0.0
1972	Cle-A	134	457	42	110	20	1	10	41	45	46	.241	.313	.354	95	-1	-3	48	5	1	1	.985	6	*C/1	1.0
1973	*Oak-A	143	492	37	126	23	2	7	52	25	62	.256	.293	.354	86	-13	-10	49	2	2	-1	.987	2	*C/D	-0.3
1974	*Oak-A	69	204	20	40	8	3	4	23	11	31	.196	.244	.324	66	-11	-9	15	1	1	-0	.973	-1	C/D	-0.8
1975	*Oak-A	82	136	14	19	3	2	0	12	8	19	.140	.193	.191	9	-16	-16	4	0	1	-1	.981	6	C/12	-0.9
1976	Cle-A	90	276	26	83	9	1	2	30	20	20	.301	.348	.362	109	3	3	33	1	2	-1	.987	1	C/1D	0.6
1977	Cle-A	78	238	25	63	7	1	6	27	7	26	.265	.294	.378	84	-6	-5	24	0	5	-3	.983	9	C/1D	0.2
	Sea-A	11	34	3	12	3	0	0	5	2	2	.353	.389	.441	127	1	1	5	0	1	-1	.968	-3	/CD	-0.2
	Yr	89	272	28	75	10	1	6	32	9	28	.276	.306	.386	90	-5	-4	28	0	6	-4	.982	5	C/D1	0.0
1979	Mil-A	19	52	6	12	3	1	0	2	2	6	.231	.286	.327	65	-3	-3	5	0	0	0	1.000	-1	C/1D	-0.3
Total	12	924	2957	299	758	117	13	61	324	203	363	.256	.308	.367	90	-40	-44	325	15	19	-7	.985	28	C/1D2	1.3

■ POP FOSTER

Foster, Clarence Francis b: 4/8/1878, New Haven, Conn. d: 4/16/44, Princeton, N.J. BR/TR, 5'8.5", Deb: 9/13/1898

YEAR	TM/L	G	AB	R	H	2B	3B	HR	RBI	BB	SO	AVG	OBP	SLG	PRO+	BR	/A	RC	SB	CS	SBR	FA	FR	POS	TPR
1898	NY-N	32	112	10	30	6	1	0	9	0		.268	.268	.339	76	-4	-4	11	0			.967	-5	O3/S	-1.0
1899	NY-N	84	301	48	89	9	7	3	57	20		.296	.348	.402	109	2	3	46	7			.949	-10	O/S3	-1.2
1900	NY-N	31	84	19	22	3	1	0	11	11		.262	.347	.321	89	-1	-1	10	0			1.000	-3	O/S2	-0.3
1901	Was-A	103	392	65	109	16	9	6	54	41		.278	.352	.411	113	6	7	62	10			.925	-1	*O/S	-0.1
	Chi-A	12	35	4	10	2	2	1	6	4		.286	.359	.543	152	2	2	7	0			.909	-1	/O	0.0
	Yr	115	427	69	119	18	11	7	60	45		.279	.353	.422	116	8	9	69	10			.924	-2	*O/S	-0.1
Total	4	262	924	146	260	36	20	10	137	76		.281	.341	.396	107	4	8	135	17			.938	-20	O/S32	-2.6

■ EDDIE FOSTER

Foster, Edward Cunningham "Kid" b: 2/13/1887, Chicago, Ill. d: 1/15/37, Washington, D.C. BR/TR, 5'6.5", 145 lbs. Deb: 4/14/10

YEAR	TM/L	G	AB	R	H	2B	3B	HR	RBI	BB	SO	AVG	OBP	SLG	PRO+	BR	/A	RC	SB	CS	SBR	FA	FR	POS	TPR
1910	NY-A	30	83	5	11	2	0	0	1	8		.133	.217	.157	16	-8	-8	3	2			.909	-2	S	-1.1
1912	Was-A	154	618	98	176	34	9	2	70	53		.285	.345	.379	106	5	4	88	27			.920	12	*3	1.7
1913	Was-A	106	409	56	101	11	5	1	41	36	31	.247	.309	.306	78	-10	-11	42	22			.901	4	*3	-0.6
1914	Was-A	157	616	82	174	16	10	2	50	60	47	.282	.348	.351	106	8	5	79	31	18	-2	.929	-18	*3	-1.0
1915	Was-A	154	618	75	170	25	10	0	52	48	30	.275	.329	.348	101	0	-1	76	20	6	2	.919	-5	32	0.1
1916	Was-A	158	606	75	153	18	9	1	44	68	26	.252	.332	.317	96	-3	-2	66	23	16	-3	.929	-16	32	-1.7
1917	Was-A	143	554	66	130	16	8	0	43	46	23	.235	.293	.292	80	-15	-14	50	11			.935	-6	32	-1.7
1918	Was-A	129	519	70	147	13	3	0	29	41	20	.283	.339	.320	101	-1	0	59	12			.936	2	*3/2	0.6
1919	Was-A	120	478	57	126	12	5	0	26	33	21	.264	.314	.310	76	-16	-15	51	20			.946	7	*3	-0.3
1920	Bos-A	117	386	48	100	17	6	0	41	42	17	.259	.336	.334	82	-11	-9	46	10	4	1	.957	15	32	1.0
1921	Bos-A	120	412	51	117	18	6	0	35	57	15	.284	.371	.357	89	-7	-5	58	13	7	-0	.943	-14	32	-1.1
1922	Bos-A	48	109	11	23	3	0	0	3	9	10	.211	.277	.239	36	-10	-10	8	1	1	-0	.886	-11	3/S	-1.9
	StL-A	37	144	29	44	4	0	0	12	20	8	.306	.394	.333	88	-1	-1	21	3	1	0	.916	-2	3	0.0
	Yr	85	253	40	67	7	0	0	15	29	18	.265	.345	.292	67	-11	-11	28	4	2	0	.905	-12	3/S	-1.9
1923	StL-A	27	100	9	18	2	0	0	4	7	7	.180	.241	.200	16	-12	-13	6	0	0	0	.961	-8	2/3	-2.0
Total	13	1500	5652	732	1490	191	71	6	451	528	255	.264	.329	.326	89	-80	-81	652	195	53		.930	-42	*32/S	-8.0

■ ELMER FOSTER

Foster, Elmer Ellsworth b: 8/15/1861, Minneapolis, Minn. d: 7/22/46, Deephaven, Minn. BR/TL, Deb: 6/18/1884

YEAR	TM/L	G	AB	R	H	2B	3B	HR	RBI	BB	SO	AVG	OBP	SLG	PRO+	BR	/A	RC	SB	CS	SBR	FA	FR	POS	TPR
1884	Phi-a	4	11	4	2	0	0	0		3		.182	.357	.182	79	0	-0	1				.885	-2	/CO	-0.2
	Phi-U	1	3	0	1	0	1	0		0		.333	.333	1.000	362	1	1	1				.625	-1	/C	0.0
1886	NY-a	35	125	16	23	0	1	0		7		.184	.239	.200	41	-8	-8	7	3			.853	-0	2O	-0.6
1888	NY-N	37	136	15	20	3	2	0	10	9	20	.147	.216	.199	35	-10	-9	9	13			.852	-2	O/3	-1.3
1889	NY-N	2	4	2	0	0	0	0	0	3	1	.000	.429	.000	27	-0	-0	1	2			1.000	-0	/O	0.0
1890	Chi-N	27	105	20	26	4	2	5	23	9	21	.248	.325	.467	127	4	3	22	18			.986	2	O	0.3
1891	Chi-N	4	16	3	3	0	0	1	1	1	2	.188	.235	.375	78	-1	-1	2	1			.875	-0	/O	-0.1
Total	6	110	400	60	75	7	6	6	34	32	44	.188	.261	.280	69	-14	-14	42	37			.883	-4	/O2C3	-1.9

■ GEORGE FOSTER

Foster, George Arthur b: 12/1/48, Tuscaloosa, Ala. BR/TR, 6'1", 185 lbs. Deb: 9/10/69

YEAR	TM/L	G	AB	R	H	2B	3B	HR	RBI	BB	SO	AVG	OBP	SLG	PRO+	BR	/A	RC	SB	CS	SBR	FA	FR	POS	TPR
1969	SF-N	9	5	1	2	0	0	0	1	0	1	.400	.400	.400	127	0	0	1	0	0	0	1.000	0	/O	0.0
1970	SF-N	9	19	2	6	1	1	1	4	2	5	.316	.381	.632	168	2	2	4	0	0	0	1.000	0	/O	0.2
1971	SF-N	36	105	11	28	5	0	3	8	6	27	.267	.306	.400	100	-1	-0	11	0	1	-1	.980	-2	O	-0.4
	Cin-N	104	368	39	86	18	4	10	50	23	93	.234	.291	.386	92	-6	-5	36	7	6	-2	.986	7	*O	-0.5
	Yr	140	473	50	114	23	4	13	58	29	120	.241	.295	.389	94	-6	-5	48	7	7	-2	.985	5	*O	-0.9
1972	*Cin-N	59	145	15	29	4	1	2	12	5	44	.200	.232	.283	48	-11	-10	8	2	1	0	.973	-2	O	-1.4
1973	Cin-N	17	39	6	11	3	0	4	9	4	7	.282	.349	.667	185	4	4	8	0	1	-1	1.000	0	O	0.3
1974	Cin-N	106	276	31	73	18	0	7	41	30	52	.264	.345	.406	111	3	4	38	3	2	-0	.989	-4	O	-0.4
1975	*Cin-N	134	463	71	139	24	4	23	78	40	73	.300	.360	.518	139	24	23	82	2	1	0	.990	13	*O/1	3.2
1976	*Cin-N★	144	562	86	172	21	9	29	**121**	52	89	.306	.369	.530	149	37	35	111	17	3	3	**.994**	8	*O/1	4.3
1977	Cin-N★	158	615	**124**	197	31	2	**52**	**149**	61	107	.320	.386	**.631**	165	**56**	**55**	**144**	6	4	-1	.992	13	*O	6.0
1978	Cin-N★	158	604	97	170	26	7	**40**	**120**	70	138	.281	.363	.546	151	39	39	115	4	4	-1	.971	3	*O	3.5
1979	*Cin-N★	121	440	68	133	18	3	30	98	59	105	.302	.388	.561	155	34	33	95	0	2	-1	.982	-2	*O	2.5
1980	Cin-N	144	528	79	144	21	5	25	93	75	99	.273	.364	.473	132	23	23	91	1	0	0	.997	2	*O	2.0
1981	Cin-N★	108	414	64	122	23	2	22	90	51	75	.295	.376	.519	150	28	27	81	4	0	1	.991	4	*O	3.0
1982	NY-N	151	550	64	136	23	2	13	70	50	123	.247	.312	.367	90	-8	-8	62	1	1	-0	.974	8	*O	-0.4
1983	NY-N	157	601	74	145	19	2	28	90	38	111	.241	.291	.419	95	-7	-6	68	1	1	-0	.988	5	*O	-0.7
1984	NY-N	146	553	67	149	22	1	24	86	30	122	.269	.314	.443	112	6	7	73	2	2	-1	.976	11	*O	1.3
1985	NY-N	129	452	57	119	24	1	21	77	46	87	.263	.334	.460	123	11	12	69	0	1	-1	.976	1	*O	0.9
1986	NY-N	72	233	28	53	6	1	13	38	21	53	.227	.291	.429	99	-2	-1	28	1	1	-0	.962	-0	O	-0.4
	Chi-A	15	51	2	11	0	2	1	4	3	8	.216	.259	.353	63	-3	-3	4	0	0	0	1.000	1	O/D	-0.2
Total	18	1977	7023	986	1925	307	47	348	1239	666	1419	.274	.341	.480	127	229	231	1129	51	31	-3	.984	65	*O/D1	22.8

■ LEO FOSTER

Foster, Leonard Norris b: 2/2/51, Covington, Ky. BR/TR, 5'11", 165 lbs. Deb: 7/09/71

YEAR	TM/L	G	AB	R	H	2B	3B	HR	RBI	BB	SO	AVG	OBP	SLG	PRO+	BR	/A	RC	SB	CS	SBR	FA	FR	POS	TPR
1971	Atl-N	9	10	1	0	0	0	0	0	0	1	.000	.000	.000	-94	-3	-3	0	0	0	0	.900	2	/S	-0.1
1973	Atl-N	3	6	1	1	1	0	0	0	0	2	.167	.167	.333	33	-1	-1	0	0	0	0	1.000	-0	/S	-0.1
1974	Atl-N	72	112	16	22	2	0	1	5	9	22	.196	.256	.241	38	-9	-10	7	1	2	-1	.977	-0	S2/3O	-0.8
1976	NY-N	24	59	11	12	2	0	1	15	8	5	.203	.299	.288	71	-2	-2	6	3	0	1	.920	1	/3S2	0.1
1977	NY-N	36	75	6	17	3	0	0	6	5	14	.227	.284	.267	51	-5	-5	6	3	1	0	.968	-4	2/S3	-0.7
Total	5	144	262	35	52	8	0	2	26	22	44	.198	.263	.252	44	-20	-20	19	7	3	0	.964	-2	/S23O	-1.6

■ REDDY FOSTER

Foster, Oscar E. b: 8/1864, Richmond, Va. d: 12/19/08, Richmond, Va. Deb: 6/03/1896

YEAR	TM/L	G	AB	R	H	2B	3B	HR	RBI	BB	SO	AVG	OBP	SLG	PRO+	BR	/A	RC	SB	CS	SBR	FA	FR	POS	TPR
1896	NY-N	1	1	0	0	0	0	0	0	0	0	.000	.000	.000	-99	-0	-0	0	0			.000	0	H	0.0

■ ROY FOSTER

Foster, Roy b: 7/29/45, Bixby, Miss. BR/TR, 6', 185 lbs. Deb: 4/07/70

YEAR	TM/L	G	AB	R	H	2B	3B	HR	RBI	BB	SO	AVG	OBP	SLG	PRO+	BR	/A	RC	SB	CS	SBR	FA	FR	POS	TPR
1970	Cle-A	139	477	66	128	26	0	23	60	54	75	.268	.357	.468	120	17	14	78	3	3	-1	.965	-3	*O	0.3
1971	Cle-A	125	396	51	97	21	1	18	45	35	48	.245	.316	.439	103	5	1	54	6	1	1	.968	-1	*O	-0.4
1972	Cle-A	73	143	19	32	4	0	4	13	21	23	.224	.331	.336	96	0	-0	16	0	2	-1	.966	-6	O	-1.1
Total	3	337	1016	136	257	51	1	45	118	110	146	.253	.338	.438	110	22	14	147	9	6	-1	.967	-11	O	-1.2

■ BOB FOTHERGILL Fothergill, Robert Roy "Fats" b: 8/16/1897, Massillon, Ohio d: 3/20/38, Detroit, Mich. BR/TR, 5'10.5", 230 lbs. Deb: 4/18/22

YEAR	TM/L	G	AB	R	H	2B	3B	HR	RBI	BB	SO	AVG	OBP	SLG	PRO+	BR	/A	RC	SB	CS	SBR	FA	FR	POS	TPR
1922	Det-A	42	152	20	49	12	4	0	29	8	9	.322	.356	.454	113	2	2	22	1	5	-3	.945	-7	O	-0.9
1923	Det-A	101	241	34	76	18	2	1	49	12	19	.315	.358	.419	106	1	2	36	4	4	-1	.977	-8	O	-1.1
1924	Det-A	54	166	28	50	8	3	0	15	5	13	.301	.326	.386	84	-5	-4	20	2	3	-1	.968	-3	O	-1.1
1925	Det-A	71	204	38	72	14	0	2	28	6	3	.353	.377	.451	111	2	3	34	2	2	-1	.977	-2	O	-0.3
1926	Det-A	110	387	63	142	31	7	3	73	33	23	.367	.421	.506	139	23	22	78	4	12	-6	.961	-1	*O	0.9
1927	Det-A	143	527	93	189	38	9	9	114	47	31	.359	.413	.516	138	31	30	102	9	15	-6	.961	-6	*O	0.9
1928	Det-A	111	347	49	110	28	10	3	63	24	19	.317	.366	.481	119	10	9	61	8	3	1	.959	-3	O	0.1
1929	Det-A	115	277	42	98	24	9	6	62	11	11	.354	.378	.570	140	15	15	58	3	1	0	.967	-4	O	0.8
1930	Det-A	55	143	14	37	9	3	2	14	6	10	.259	.289	.406	72	-6	-7	16	1	1	-0	.947	-5	O	-1.3
	Chi-A	52	135	10	40	9	0	0	24	4	8	.296	.326	.363	77	-5	-5	16	0	0	0	.879	-3	O	-0.9
	Yr	107	278	24	77	18	3	2	38	10	18	.277	.307	.385	75	-11	-11	32	1	1	-0	.913	-8	O	-2.2
1931	Chi-A	108	312	25	88	9	4	3	56	17	17	.282	.323	.365	86	-9	-6	37	2	2	-1	.972	1	O	-1.0
1932	Chi-A	116	346	36	102	24	1	7	50	27	10	.295	.348	.431	107	-0	3	51	4	4	-1	.952	-11	O	-1.4
1933	Bos-A	28	32	1	11	1	0	0	5	2	4	.344	.382	.375	102	0	0	5	0	0	0	1.000	-1	/O	-0.1
Total	12	1106	3269	453	1064	225	52	36	582	202	177	.325	.368	.459	115	58	64	537	40	52	-19	.961	-53	O	-5.4

■ JACK FOURNIER Fournier, John Frank b: 9/29/1892, AuSable, Mich. d: 9/5/73, Tacoma, Wash. BL/TR, 6', 195 lbs. Deb: 4/13/12

YEAR	TM/L	G	AB	R	H	2B	3B	HR	RBI	BB	SO	AVG	OBP	SLG	PRO+	BR	/A	RC	SB	CS	SBR	FA	FR	POS	TPR
1912	Chi-A	35	73	6	14	5	2	0	2	4		.192	.262	.315	67	-4	-3	6	1			.988	3	1	-0.1
1913	Chi-A	68	172	20	40	8	5	1	23	21	23	.233	.323	.355	99	-0	-0	21	9			.990	4	1O	0.3
1914	Chi-A	109	379	44	118	14	9	6	44	31	44	.311	.368	.443	146	19	19	61	10	13	-5	.978	5	1/O	1.8
1915	Chi-A	126	422	86	136	20	18	5	77	64	37	.322	.429	**.491**	170	41	39	91	21	16	-3	.986	3	1O	3.6
1916	Chi-A	105	313	36	75	13	9	3	44	36	40	.240	.328	.367	108	3	3	44	19			.976	-3	1/O	-0.4
1917	Chi-A	1	1	0	0	0	0	0	0	0	1	.000	.000	.000	-98	-0	-0	0	0			.000	0	H	0.0
1918	NY-A	27	100	9	35	6	1	0	12	7	7	.350	.393	.430	145	6	5	19	7			.976	-2	1	0.2
1920	StL-N	141	530	77	162	33	14	3	61	42	42	.306	.370	.438	136	22	24	84	26	20	-4	.983	1	*1	1.9
1921	StL-N	149	574	103	197	27	9	16	86	56	48	.343	.409	.505	144	34	36	114	20	22	-7	.987	-4	*1	2.1
1922	StL-N	128	404	64	119	23	9	10	61	40	21	.295	.368	.470	120	8	11	69	6	8	-3	.982	2	*1/P	0.5
1923	Bro-N	133	515	91	181	30	13	22	102	43	28	.351	.411	.588	165	44	46	**125**	11	4	1	.985	4	*1	**4.1**
1924	Bro-N	154	563	93	188	25	4	**27**	116	83	46	.334	.428	.536	162	48	51	133	7	5	-1	.985	7	*1	4.6
1925	Bro-N	145	545	99	191	21	16	22	130	**86**	39	.350	.446	.569	162	50	52	141	4	6	-2	.989	3	*1	4.1
1926	Bro-N	87	243	39	69	9	2	11	48	30	16	.284	.365	.473	126	8	9	42	0			.986	-2	1	0.3
1927	Bos-N	122	374	55	106	18	2	10	53	44	16	.283	.368	.422	121	7	11	59	4			.989	0	*1	0.4
Total	15	1530	5208	822	1631	252	113	136	859	587	408	.313	.392	.483	143	285	302	1010	145	94		.984	20	*1/OP	23.4

■ BILL FOUSER Fouser, William C. b: 10/1855, Philadelphia, Pa. d: 3/1/19, Philadelphia, Pa. Deb: 4/22/1876

YEAR	TM/L	G	AB	R	H	2B	3B	HR	RBI	BB	SO	AVG	OBP	SLG	PRO+	BR	/A	RC	SB	CS	SBR	FA	FR	POS	TPR
1876	Phi-N	21	89	11	12	0	1	0	2	0	0	.135	.135	.157	-3	-9	-9	2				.827	3	2/O1	-0.5

■ DAVE FOUTZ Foutz, David Luther "Scissors" b: 9/7/1856, Carroll Co., Md. d: 3/5/1897, Waverly, Ind. BR/TR, 6'2", 161 lbs. Deb: 7/29/1884 FM

YEAR	TM/L	G	AB	R	H	2B	3B	HR	RBI	BB	SO	AVG	OBP	SLG	PRO+	BR	/A	RC	SB	CS	SBR	FA	FR	POS	TPR
1884	StL-a	33	119	17	27	4	0	0		8		.227	.276	.261	76	-3	-3	9				.940	-3	PO	-0.5
1885	*StL-a	65	238	42	59	6	4	0		11		.248	.281	.307	84	-3	-5	21				.899	6	P1/O	-0.3
1886	*StL-a	102	414	66	116	18	9	3		9		.280	.297	.389	111	6	3	54	17			.949	4	PO1	0.1
1887	*StL-a	102	423	79	151	26	13	4		23		.357	.393	.508	138	28	20	95	22			.899	-4	OP1	0.5
1888	Bro-a	140	563	91	156	20	13	3	99	28		.277	.314	.375	124	13	14	79	35			.895	3	O1P	0.6
1889	*Bro-a	138	553	118	152	19	8	6	113	64	23	.275	.353	.371	108	7	7	90	43			.979	-3	*1P	-0.5
1890	*Bro-N	129	509	106	154	25	13	5	98	52	25	.303	.368	.432	135	22	22	99	42			.978	-1	*1O/P	1.3
1891	Bro-N	130	521	87	134	26	8	2	73	40	25	.257	.313	.349	95	-4	-4	74	48			.976	-3	*1/PS	-1.1
1892	Bro-N	61	220	33	41	5	3	1	26	14	14	.186	.235	.250	50	-14	-13	18	19			.850	-2	OP/1	-1.2
1893	Bro-N	130	557	91	137	20	10	7	67	32	34	.246	.287	.355	75	-25	-20	70	39			.913	-6	O1/PM	-2.6
1894	Bro-N	72	293	40	90	12	9	0	51	14	13	.307	.341	.410	88	-9	-5	48	14			.976	-3	1/PM	-0.5
1895	Bro-N	31	115	14	34	4	1	0	21	4	2	.296	.319	.348	80	-5	-3	14	1			.879	-5	O/1M	-0.7
1896	Bro-N	2	8	0	2	1	0	0	0	1	0	.250	.333	.375	94	-0	-0	1	0			1.000	0	/O1M	0.0
Total	13	1135	4533	784	1253	186	91	31	548	300	136	.276	.323	.378	104	13	11	671	280			.977	-15	1OP/S	-4.9

■ FRANK FOUTZ Foutz, Frank Hayes b: 4/8/1877, Baltimore, Md. d: 12/25/61, Lima, Ohio BR/TR, 5'11", 165 lbs. Deb: 4/26/01 F

YEAR	TM/L	G	AB	R	H	2B	3B	HR	RBI	BB	SO	AVG	OBP	SLG	PRO+	BR	/A	RC	SB	CS	SBR	FA	FR	POS	TPR
1901	Bal-A	20	72	13	17	4	1	2	14	8		.236	.321	.403	96	-0	-1	10	0			.959	-0	1	-0.1

■ BOOB FOWLER Fowler, Joseph Chester "Gink" b: 11/11/1900, Waco, Tex. d: 10/8/88, Dallas, Tex. BL/TR, 5'11.5", 180 lbs. Deb: 5/06/23

YEAR	TM/L	G	AB	R	H	2B	3B	HR	RBI	BB	SO	AVG	OBP	SLG	PRO+	BR	/A	RC	SB	CS	SBR	FA	FR	POS	TPR
1923	Cin-N	11	33	9	11	0	1	1	6	1	3	.333	.353	.485	121	1	1	6	1	0	0	.847	-1	S	0.1
1924	Cin-N	59	129	20	43	6	1	0	9	5	15	.333	.358	.395	103	0	1	18	2	2	-1	.936	-7	S/23	-0.4
1925	Cin-N	6	5	0	2	1	0	0	2	0	1	.400	.400	.600	155	0	0	1	0	0	0	.000	0	H	0.0
1926	Bos-A	2	8	1	1	0	0	0	1	0	0	.125	.125	.125	-36	-2	-2	0	0	0	0	.800	0	/3	-0.1
Total	4	78	175	30	57	7	2	1	18	6	19	.326	.348	.406	102	-0	0	25	3	2	-0	.910	-7	/S32	-0.4

■ CHARLIE FOX Fox, Charles Francis "Irish" b: 10/7/21, New York, N.Y. BR/TR, 5'11", 180 lbs. Deb: 9/24/42 MC

YEAR	TM/L	G	AB	R	H	2B	3B	HR	RBI	BB	SO	AVG	OBP	SLG	PRO+	BR	/A	RC	SB	CS	SBR	FA	FR	POS	TPR
1942	NY-N	3	7	1	3	0	0	0	1	1	2	.429	.500	.429	172	1	1	2	0			1.000	-1	/C	0.0

■ ERIC FOX Fox, Eric Hollis b: 8/15/63, LeMoore, Cal. BB/TL, 5'10", 180 lbs. Deb: 7/08/92

YEAR	TM/L	G	AB	R	H	2B	3B	HR	RBI	BB	SO	AVG	OBP	SLG	PRO+	BR	/A	RC	SB	CS	SBR	FA	FR	POS	TPR
1992	*Oak-A	51	143	24	34	5	2	3	13	13	29	.238	.301	.364	89	-3	-2	16	3	4	-2	.990	-5	O/D	-1.0

■ PETE FOX Fox, Ervin b: 3/8/09, Evansville, Ind. d: 7/5/66, Detroit, Mich. BR/TR, 5'11", 165 lbs. Deb: 4/12/33

YEAR	TM/L	G	AB	R	H	2B	3B	HR	RBI	BB	SO	AVG	OBP	SLG	PRO+	BR	/A	RC	SB	CS	SBR	FA	FR	POS	TPR
1933	Det-A	128	535	82	154	26	13	7	57	23	38	.288	.320	.424	94	-6	-7	71	9	6	-1	.978	1	*O	-1.3
1934	*Det-A	128	516	101	147	31	2	2	45	49	53	.285	.351	.364	85	-11	-11	69	25	10	2	.974	8	*O	-0.6
1935	*Det-A	131	517	116	166	38	8	15	73	45	52	.321	.382	.513	134	21	24	103	14	4	2	.988	-0	*O	1.9
1936	Det-A	73	220	46	67	12	1	4	26	34	23	.305	.405	.423	104	3	3	39	1	3	-2	.968	0	O	-0.1
1937	Det-A	148	628	116	208	39	8	12	82	41	43	.331	.372	.476	110	10	8	109	12	8	-1	.976	-3	*O	-0.1
1938	Det-A	155	634	91	186	35	10	7	96	31	39	.293	.328	.413	80	-17	-22	85	16	7	1	**.994**	-2	*O	-2.6
1939	Det-A	141	519	69	153	24	6	7	66	35	41	.295	.342	.405	84	-8	-14	69	23	12	-0	.970	9	*O	-0.9
1940	*Det-A	93	350	49	101	17	4	5	48	21	30	.289	.329	.403	81	-6	-11	46	7	7	-2	.967	0	O	-1.6
1941	Bos-A	73	268	38	81	12	7	0	31	21	32	.302	.357	.399	98	-0	-1	41	9	2	2	.977	-1	O	-0.4
1942	Bos-A	77	256	42	67	15	5	3	42	20	28	.262	.323	.395	98	-0	-1	31	8	7	-2	.966	-9	O	-1.6
1943	Bos-A	127	489	54	141	24	4	2	44	34	40	.288	.337	.366	104	3	2	62	22	8	2	.961	-3	*O	-0.6
1944	Bos-A☆	121	496	70	156	37	6	1	64	27	34	.315	.354	.419	122	12	12	75	10	5	0	.987	-1	*O	0.5
1945	Bos-A	66	208	21	51	4	1	0	20	11	18	.245	.296	.274	64	-9	-10	18	2	2	-1	.989	-19	O	-3.5
Total	13	1461	5636	895	1678	314	75	65	694	392	471	.298	.347	.415	98	-9	-28	819	158	81	-1	.977	-20	*O	-10.9

■ PADDY FOX Fox, George B. b: 12/1/1868, Pottstown, Pa. d: 5/8/14, Philadelphia, Pa. Deb: 7/13/1891

YEAR	TM/L	G	AB	R	H	2B	3B	HR	RBI	BB	SO	AVG	OBP	SLG	PRO+	BR	/A	RC	SB	CS	SBR	FA	FR	POS	TPR
1891	Lou-a	6	19	1	2	0	1	0	2	2	3	.105	.261	.211	38	-1	-1	1	0			.929	-2	/3	-0.3
1899	Pit-N	13	41	4	10	0	1	1	3	3		.244	.311	.366	86	-1	-1	6	2			.971	2	/1C	0.1
Total	2	19	60	5	12	0	2	1	5	5	3	.200	.294	.317	71	-2	-2	7	2			.956	-1	/13C	-0.2

■ NELLIE FOX Fox, Jacob Nelson b: 12/25/27, St.Thomas, Pa. d: 12/1/75, Baltimore, Md. BL/TR, 5'9", 150 lbs. Deb: 6/08/47 C

YEAR	TM/L	G	AB	R	H	2B	3B	HR	RBI	BB	SO	AVG	OBP	SLG	PRO+	BR	/A	RC	SB	CS	SBR	FA	FR	POS	TPR
1947	Phi-A	7	3	2	0	0	0	0	0	1	0	.000	.250	.000	-26	-0	-0	0	0	0	0	1.000	1	/2	0.1
1948	Phi-A	3	13	0	2	0	0	0	0	1	0	.154	.214	.154	-1	-2	-2	1	1	0	0	.950	-2	/2	-0.3
1949	Phi-A	88	247	42	63	6	2	0	21	32	9	.255	.354	.296	75	-8	-7	28	2	2	-1	.982	-1	2	-0.6

YEAR	TM/L	G	AB	R	H	2B	3B	HR	RBI	BB	SO	AVG	OBP	SLG	PRO+	BR	/A	RC	SB	CS	SBR	FA	FR	POS	TPR
1950	Chi-A	130	457	45	113	12	7	0	30	35	17	.247	.304	.304	58	-31	-29	45	4	3	-1	.974	-0	*2	-2.3
1951	Chi-A★	147	604	93	189	32	12	4	55	43	11	.313	.372	.425	118	13	14	98	9	12	-5	.981	-3	*2	1.4
1952	Chi-A☆	152	648	76	**192**	25	10	0	39	34	14	.296	.334	.366	94	-6	-6	80	5	5	-2	**.985**	7	*2	0.7
1953	Chi-A★	154	624	92	178	31	8	3	72	49	18	.285	.344	.375	91	-5	-7	81	4	5	-2	.983	3	*2	0.2
1954	Chi-A★	155	631	111	**201**	24	8	2	47	51	12	.319	.374	.391	106	9	7	93	16	9	-1	**.989**	-6	*2	1.1
1955	Chi-A★	154	636	100	198	28	7	6	59	38	15	.311	.366	.406	104	7	4	95	7	9	-3	.974	**27**	*2	3.9
1956	Chi-A★	154	649	109	192	20	10	4	52	44	14	.296	.350	.376	90	-8	-9	84	8	4	0	**.986**	3	*2	0.7
1957	Chi-A★	155	619	110	**196**	27	8	6	61	75	13	.317	.404	.415	124	24	24	109	5	6	-2	.986	21	*2	5.6
1958	Chi-A★	155	623	82	**187**	21	6	0	49	47	11	.300	.360	.353	99	-1	1	79	5	6	-2	.985	2	*2	1.2
1959	*Chi-A★	156	624	84	191	34	6	2	70	71	13	.306	.383	.389	114	13	14	97	5	6	-2	**.988**	-3	*2	2.1
1960	Chi-A★	150	605	85	175	24	**10**	2	59	50	13	.289	.353	.372	97	-2	-1	81	2	4	-2	.985	12	*2	2.4
1961	Chi-A★	159	606	67	152	11	5	2	51	59	12	.251	.326	.295	69	-26	-25	60	2	3	-1	.982	-6	*2	-1.4
1962	Chi-A	157	621	79	166	27	7	2	54	38	12	.267	.317	.343	78	-19	-19	67	1	2	-1	**.990**	1	*2	-0.3
1963	Chi-A★	137	539	54	140	19	0	2	42	24	17	.260	.300	.306	72	-21	-20	49	0	2	-1	**.988**	-8	*2	-1.8
1964	Hou-N	133	442	45	117	12	6	0	28	27	13	.265	.322	.319	86	-10	-7	47	0	2	-1	.977	-6	*2	-0.6
1965	Hou-N	21	41	3	11	2	0	0	1	0	2	.268	.286	.317	75	-2	-1	3	0	0	0	1.000	-0	/312	-0.2
Total	19	2367	9232	1279	2663	355	112	35	790	719	216	.288	.349	.363	94	-75	-71	1197	76	80	-25	.984	42	*2/31	11.9

■ JACK FOX

Fox, John Paul b: 5/21/1885, Reading, Pa. d: 6/28/63, Reading, Pa. BR/TR, 5'10", 185 lbs. Deb: 6/02/08

YEAR	TM/L	G	AB	R	H	2B	3B	HR	RBI	BB	SO	AVG	OBP	SLG	PRO+	BR	/A	RC	SB	CS	SBR	FA	FR	POS	TPR
1908	Phi-A	9	30	2	6	0	0	0	0	0		.200	.200	.200	28	-2	-3	2	2			.923	-1	/O	-0.4

■ BILL FOX

Fox, William Henry b: 1/15/1872, Sturbridge, Ma. d: 5/7/46, Minneapolis, Minn. BB/TR, 5'10", 160 lbs. Deb: 8/20/1897

YEAR	TM/L	G	AB	R	H	2B	3B	HR	RBI	BB	SO	AVG	OBP	SLG	PRO+	BR	/A	RC	SB	CS	SBR	FA	FR	POS	TPR
1897	Was-N	4	14	4	4	0	0	0	0	1		.286	.333	.286	64	-1	-1	1	0			.700	0	/S2	0.0
1901	Cin-N	43	159	9	28	2	1	0	7	4		.176	.201	.201	18	-17	-15	9	9			.948	5	2	-0.8
Total	2	47	173	13	32	2	1	0	7	5		.185	.212	.208	23	-17	-16	10	9			.944	5	/2S	-0.8

■ JIMMIE FOXX

Foxx, James Emory "Beast" or "Double X" b: 10/22/07, Sudlersville, Md. d: 7/21/67, Miami, Fla. BR/TR, 6', 195 lbs. Deb: 5/01/25 H

YEAR	TM/L	G	AB	R	H	2B	3B	HR	RBI	BB	SO	AVG	OBP	SLG	PRO+	BR	/A	RC	SB	CS	SBR	FA	FR	POS	TPR
1925	Phi-A	10	9	2	6	1	0	0	0	0	1	.667	.667	.778	249	2	2	4	0	0	0	.000	0	/C	0.2
1926	Phi-A	26	32	8	10	2	1	0	5	1	6	.313	.333	.438	94	-0	-0	5	1	0	0	1.000	2	C/O	0.2
1927	Phi-A	61	130	23	42	6	5	3	20	14	11	.323	.393	.515	127	6	5	25	2	1	0	.975	-2	1/C	0.2
1928	Phi-A	118	400	85	131	29	10	13	79	60	43	.327	.416	.548	147	30	29	91	3	8	-4	.940	-2	31C	2.4
1929	*Phi-A	149	517	123	183	23	9	33	118	103	70	.354	**.463**	.625	171	**63**	60	**154**	9	7	-2	.995	-4	*1/3	3.8
1930	*Phi-A	153	562	127	188	33	13	37	156	93	66	.335	.429	.637	159	57	53	154	7	7	-2	.990	-2	*1	3.0
1931	*Phi-A	139	515	93	150	32	10	30	120	73	84	.291	.380	.567	138	33	28	113	4	3	-1	.993	-3	*13/O	1.4
1932	Phi-A	154	585	**151**	213	33	9	**58**	**169**	116	96	**.364**	.469	**.749**	203	**97**	**93**	**207**	3	7	-3	**.994**	-5	*13	**6.8**
1933	Phi-A☆	149	573	125	204	37	9	**48**	**163**	96	93	**.356**	.449	**.703**	**199**	**83**	**82**	**184**	2	2	-1	.990	6	*1/S	**6.7**
1934	Phi-A★	150	539	120	180	28	6	44	130	**111**	75	.334	.449	.653	188	66	70	165	11	2	2	.993	4	*1/3	5.8
1935	Phi-A★	147	535	118	185	33	7	**36**	115	114	99	.346	.461	**.636**	**182**	**67**	**68**	**163**	6	4	-1	**.997**	6	*1C/3	**5.7**
1936	Bos-A★	155	585	130	198	32	8	41	143	105	119	.338	.440	.631	153	57	51	168	13	4	2	.991	-1	*1O/3	3.3
1937	Bos-A★	150	569	111	162	24	6	36	127	99	96	.285	.392	.538	127	27	24	123	10	8	-2	**.994**	10	*1/C	1.3
1938	Bos-A★	149	565	139	197	33	9	50	**175**	**119**	76	**.349**	**.462**	**.704**	**180**	**78**	**74**	**189**	5	4	-1	.987	6	*1	**5.5**
1939	Bos-A☆	124	467	130	168	31	10	**35**	105	89	72	.360	**.464**	**.694**	185	**66**	**63**	150	4	3	-1	.992	7	*1/P	5.1
1940	Bos-A★	144	515	106	153	30	4	36	119	101	87	.297	.412	.581	148	43	39	124	4	7	-3	.990	-2	1C/3	2.7
1941	Bos-A★	135	487	87	146	27	8	19	105	93	103	.300	.412	.505	138	31	30	102	2	5	-2	.992	7	*1/3O	2.3
1942	Bos-A	30	100	18	27	4	0	5	14	18	15	.270	.392	.460	134	6	5	20	0	0	0	.996	6	1	1.0
	Chi-N	70	205	25	42	8	0	3	19	22	55	.205	.282	.288	69	-9	-8	16	1			.983	-4	1/C	-1.6
1944	Chi-N	15	20	0	1	1	0	0	2	2	5	.050	.136	.100	-33	-4	-4	0	0			1.000	2	/3C	-0.2
1945	Phi-N	89	224	30	60	11	1	7	38	23	39	.268	.336	.420	112	2	3	32	0			.988	-3	13/P	-0.2
Total	20	2317	8134	1751	2646	458	125	534	1922	1452	1311	.325	.428	.609	161	803	768	2189	87	72		.992	30	*13C/OPS	55.4

■ JOE FOY

Foy, Joseph Anthony b: 2/21/43, New York, N.Y. d: 10/12/89, Bronx, N.Y. BR/TR, 6', 215 lbs. Deb: 4/13/66

YEAR	TM/L	G	AB	R	H	2B	3B	HR	RBI	BB	SO	AVG	OBP	SLG	PRO+	BR	/A	RC	SB	CS	SBR	FA	FR	POS	TPR
1966	Bos-A	151	554	97	145	23	8	15	63	91	80	.262	.368	.413	112	20	13	86	2	5	-2	.953	-1	*3S	0.9
1967	*Bos-A	130	446	70	112	22	4	16	49	46	87	.251	.325	.426	111	11	7	59	8	6	-1	.921	-10	*3/O	-0.6
1968	Bos-A	150	515	65	116	18	2	10	60	84	91	.225	.338	.326	96	4	0	64	26	8	3	.935	2	*3/O	0.7
1969	KC-A	145	519	72	136	19	2	11	71	74	75	.262	.360	.370	104	5	5	73	37	15	2	.964	-9	*31O/S2	-0.3
1970	NY-N	99	322	39	76	12	0	6	37	68	58	.236	.376	.329	90	-1	-1	45	22	13	-1	.937	-1	3	-0.4
1971	Was-A	41	128	12	30	8	0	0	11	27	14	.234	.368	.297	96	-0	1	16	4	1	1	.960	4	3/2S	0.5
Total	6	716	2484	355	615	102	16	58	291	390	405	.248	.354	.372	103	38	24	343	99	48	1	.943	-14	3/OS12	0.8

■ JULIO FRANCO

Franco, Julio Cesar (b: Julio Cesar Robles (Franco)) b: 8/23/58, Hato Mayor, D.R. BR/TR, 6', 175 lbs. Deb: 4/23/82

YEAR	TM/L	G	AB	R	H	2B	3B	HR	RBI	BB	SO	AVG	OBP	SLG	PRO+	BR	/A	RC	SB	CS	SBR	FA	FR	POS	TPR
1982	Phi-N	16	29	3	8	1	0	0	3	2	4	.276	.323	.310	76	-1	-1	2	0	2	-1	1.000	-0	S/3	-0.2
1983	Cle-A	149	560	68	153	24	8	8	80	27	50	.273	.309	.387	87	-8	-11	61	32	12	2	.961	-7	*S	-0.1
1984	Cle-A	160	658	82	188	22	5	3	79	43	68	.286	.335	.348	88	-9	-10	73	19	10	-0	.955	-1	*S/D	0.4
1985	Cle-A	160	636	97	183	33	4	6	90	54	74	.288	.347	.381	100	0	1	79	13	9	-2	.949	-22	*S/2D	-0.7
1986	Cle-A	149	599	80	183	30	5	10	74	32	66	.306	.341	.422	108	4	6	76	10	7	-1	.971	-5	*S2/D	1.2
1987	Cle-A	128	495	86	158	24	3	8	52	57	56	.319	.393	.428	117	14	14	82	32	9	4	.963	-24	*S/2D	0.4
1988	Cle-A	152	613	88	186	23	6	10	54	56	72	.303	.364	.409	113	14	12	90	25	11	1	.982	-10	*2/D	0.9
1989	Tex-A★	150	548	80	173	31	5	13	92	66	69	.316	.390	.462	137	30	28	95	21	3	5	.980	-6	*2D	3.1
1990	Tex-A★	157	582	96	172	27	1	11	69	82	83	.296	.384	.402	120	18	18	95	31	10	3	.975	-2	*2/D	2.3
1991	Tex-A☆	146	589	108	201	27	3	15	78	65	78	**.341**	.409	.474	146	36	38	118	36	9	5	.979	-31	*2	1.5
1992	Tex-A	35	107	19	25	7	0	2	8	15	17	.234	.328	.355	94	-1	-1	12	1	1	-0	.906	-6	D/2O	-0.7
Total	11	1402	5416	807	1630	249	40	86	679	499	637	.301	.362	.409	112	99	95	783	220	83	16	.960	-114	S2/DO3	8.1

■ TITO FRANCONA

Francona, John Patsy b: 11/4/33, Aliquippa, Pa. BL/TL, 5'11", 190 lbs. Deb: 4/17/56 F

YEAR	TM/L	G	AB	R	H	2B	3B	HR	RBI	BB	SO	AVG	OBP	SLG	PRO+	BR	/A	RC	SB	CS	SBR	FA	FR	POS	TPR
1956	Bal-A	139	445	62	115	16	4	9	57	51	60	.258	.336	.373	94	-8	-4	58	11	5	0	.977	-8	*O1	-1.8
1957	Bal-A	97	279	35	65	8	3	7	38	29	48	.233	.312	.358	88	-7	-5	31	7	3	0	.992	-10	O/1	-1.9
1958	Chi-A	41	128	10	33	3	2	1	10	14	24	.258	.331	.336	86	-3	-2	13	2	3	-1	1.000	-4	O	-0.9
	Det-A	45	69	11	17	5	0	0	10	15	16	.246	.381	.319	88	0	-0	9	0	0	0	1.000	-3	O/1	-0.5
	Yr	86	197	21	50	8	2	1	20	29	40	.254	.350	.330	86	-2	-3	23	2	3	-1	1.000	-7	O/1	-1.4
1959	Cle-A	122	399	68	145	17	2	20	79	35	42	.363	.419	.566	174	37	**39**	93	2	0	1	.972	-4	O1	2.9
1960	Cle-A	147	544	84	159	**36**	2	17	79	67	67	.292	.375	.460	128	19	21	96	4	1	1	.989	5	*O1	1.9
1961	Cle-A☆	155	592	87	178	30	8	16	85	56	52	.301	.365	.459	122	15	18	100	2	1	0	.987	4	*O1	1.3
1962	Cle-A	158	621	82	169	28	5	14	70	47	74	.272	.330	.401	99	-4	-2	84	3	2	-0	.986	2	*1	-1.1
1963	Cle-A	142	500	57	114	29	0	10	41	47	77	.228	.297	.346	80	-14	-13	52	9	1	2	.986	-2	*O1	-2.1
1964	Cle-A	111	270	35	67	13	2	8	24	44	46	.248	.362	.400	113	6	6	41	1	3	-2	.985	-12	O1	-1.2
1965	StL-N	81	174	15	45	6	2	5	19	17	30	.259	.325	.402	95	1	-1	23	0	0	0	.972	-6	O1	-0.9
1966	StL-N	83	156	14	33	4	1	4	17	7	27	.212	.250	.327	59	-9	-9	13	0	0	0	.987	1	1/O	-1.0
1967	Phi-N	27	73	7	15	1	0	0	3	7	10	.205	.275	.219	43	-5	-5	4	0	1	-1	1.000	1	1/O	-0.6
	Atl-N	82	254	28	63	5	1	6	25	20	34	.248	.305	.346	87	-5	-4	27	1	0	0	.991	0	1/O	-0.8
	Yr	109	327	35	78	6	1	6	28	27	44	.239	.299	.318	77	-10	-9	31	1	1	-0	.993	2	1/O	-1.4
1968	Atl-N	122	346	32	99	13	1	2	47	51	45	.286	.378	.347	118	10	10	47	3	0	1	.978	-10	O1	-0.5
1969	Atl-N	51	88	5	26	1	0	2	22	13	10	.295	.386	.375	114	2	2	13	0	1	-1	.957	-1	O/1	0.0
	Oak-A	32	85	12	29	6	1	3	20	12	11	.341	.423	.541	175	8	8	21	0	0	0	.988	-2	1/O	0.5
1970	Oak-A	32	33	2	8	0	0	1	6	6	6	.242	.375	.333	100	0	0	4	0	0	0	1.000	1	/1O	0.1

YEAR	TM/L	G	AB	R	H	2B	3B	HR	RBI	BB	SO	AVG	OBP	SLG	PRO+	BR	/A	RC	SB	CS	SBR	FA	FR	POS	TPR
	Mil-A	52	65	4	15	3	0	0	4	6	15	.231	.296	.277	58	-4	-4	6	1	0	0	1.000	1	1	-0.3
	Yr	84	98	6	23	3	0	1	10	12	21	.235	.324	.296	73	-3	-3	10	1	0	0	1.000	2	1/O	-0.2
Total	15	1719	5121	650	1395	224	34	125	656	544	694	.272	.346	.403	108	40	55	734	46	21	1	.984	-46	O1	-6.9

■ TERRY FRANCONA Francona, Terry Jon b: 4/22/59, Aberdeen, S.D. BL/TL, 6'1", 190 lbs. Deb: 8/19/81 F

YEAR	TM/L	G	AB	R	H	2B	3B	HR	RBI	BB	SO	AVG	OBP	SLG	PRO+	BR	/A	RC	SB	CS	SBR	FA	FR	POS	TPR
1981	*Mon-N	34	95	11	26	0	1	1	8	5	6	.274	.317	.326	82	-2	-2	11	1	0	0	1.000	0	O/1	-0.3
1982	Mon-N	46	131	14	42	3	0	0	9	8	11	.321	.360	.344	96	-0	-0	16	2	3	-1	.936	-7	O1	-1.0
1983	Mon-N	120	230	21	59	11	1	3	22	6	20	.257	.275	.352	73	-9	-9	20	0	2	-1	.978	-0	O1	-1.3
1984	Mon-N	58	214	18	74	19	2	1	18	5	12	.346	.364	.467	138	8	9	35	0	0	0	.994	6	1/O	1.3
1985	Mon-N	107	281	19	75	15	1	2	31	12	12	.267	.299	.349	86	-8	-6	29	5	5	-2	.988	2	1O/3	-0.9
1986	Chi-N	86	124	13	31	3	0	2	8	6	8	.250	.290	.323	64	-5	-7	11	0	1	-1	1.000	-7	O1	-1.6
1987	Cin-N	102	207	16	47	5	0	3	12	10	12	.227	.266	.295	46	-15	-17	16	2	0	1	.995	3	1/O	-1.6
1988	Cle-A	62	212	24	66	8	0	1	12	5	18	.311	.327	.363	91	-2	-3	24	0	0	0	.977	0	D/1O	-0.3
1989	Mil-A	90	233	26	54	10	1	3	23	8	20	.232	.257	.322	63	-12	-12	18	2	1	0	.989	-2	1DO/P	-1.7
1990	Mil-A	3	4	1	0	0	0	0	0	0	0	.000	.000	.000	-99	-1	-1	0	0	0	0	1.000	-0	/1D	-0.1
Total	10	708	1731	163	474	74	6	16	143	65	119	.274	.302	.351	81	-47	-47	179	12	12	-4	.992	-4	1O/DP3	-7.5

■ CHARLIE FRANK Frank, Charles b: 5/30/1870, Mobile, Ala. d: 5/24/22, Memphis, Tenn. 5'10", 170 lbs. Deb: 8/18/1893

YEAR	TM/L	G	AB	R	H	2B	3B	HR	RBI	BB	SO	AVG	OBP	SLG	PRO+	BR	/A	RC	SB	CS	SBR	FA	FR	POS	TPR
1893	StL-N	40	164	29	55	6	3	1	17	18	8	.335	.408	.427	124	6	6	33	8			.930	3	O	0.6
1894	StL-N	80	319	52	89	12	7	4	42	44	13	.279	.372	.398	87	-6	-6	55	14			.869	-2	O/1P	-1.0
Total	2	120	483	81	144	18	10	5	59	62	21	.298	.384	.408	99	0	-0	88	22			.889	1	O/1P	-0.4

■ FRED FRANK Frank, Frederick b: 3/11/1874, Louisa, Ky. d: 3/27/50, Ashland, Ky. Deb: 9/27/1898

YEAR	TM/L	G	AB	R	H	2B	3B	HR	RBI	BB	SO	AVG	OBP	SLG	PRO+	BR	/A	RC	SB	CS	SBR	FA	FR	POS	TPR
1898	Cle-N	17	53	3	11	1	1	0	3	4		.208	.276	.264	56	-3	-3	4	1			.915	3	O	-0.1

■ FRANKLIN Franklin Deb: 9/27/1884

YEAR	TM/L	G	AB	R	H	2B	3B	HR	RBI	BB	SO	AVG	OBP	SLG	PRO+	BR	/A	RC	SB	CS	SBR	FA	FR	POS	TPR
1884	Was-U	1	3	0	0	0	0	0		0		.000	.000	.000	-99	-1	-1	0				1.000	0	/O	-0.1

■ MOE FRANKLIN Franklin, Murray Asher b: 4/1/14, Chicago, Ill. d: 3/16/78, Harbor City, Cal. BR/TR, 6', 175 lbs. Deb: 8/12/41

YEAR	TM/L	G	AB	R	H	2B	3B	HR	RBI	BB	SO	AVG	OBP	SLG	PRO+	BR	/A	RC	SB	CS	SBR	FA	FR	POS	TPR
1941	Det-A	13	10	1	3	1	0	0	0	2	2	.300	.417	.400	106	0	0	2	0	0	0	.750	-1	/S3	-0.1
1942	Det-A	48	154	24	40	7	0	2	16	7	5	.260	.301	.344	75	-4	-6	16	0	0	0	.967	-6	S/2	-1.0
Total	2	61	164	25	43	8	0	2	16	9	7	.262	.309	.348	77	-4	-6	18	0	0	0	.961	-7	/S23	-1.1

■ HERMAN FRANKS Franks, Herman Louis b: 1/4/14, Price, Utah BL/TR, 5'10.5", 187 lbs. Deb: 4/27/39 MC

YEAR	TM/L	G	AB	R	H	2B	3B	HR	RBI	BB	SO	AVG	OBP	SLG	PRO+	BR	/A	RC	SB	CS	SBR	FA	FR	POS	TPR
1939	StL-N	17	17	1	1	0	0	0	3	3	3	.059	.200	.059	-26	-3	-3	0	0			.973	3	C	0.0
1940	Bro-N	65	131	11	24	4	0	1	14	20	6	.183	.296	.237	46	-9	-10	10	2			.990	9	C	0.2
1941	*Bro-N	57	139	10	28	7	0	1	11	14	13	.201	.275	.273	52	-8	-9	11	0			.986	2	C/O	-0.4
1947	Phi-A	8	15	2	3	0	1	0	1	4	4	.200	.368	.333	94	0	0	2	0	0	0	1.000	-1	/C	-0.1
1948	Phi-A	40	98	10	22	7	1	1	14	16	11	.224	.345	.347	84	-2	-2	12	0	0	0	.977	3	C	0.2
1949	NY-N	1	3	1	2	0	0	0	0	0	0	.667	.667	.667	259	1	1	1	0			1.000	0	/C	0.1
Total	6	188	403	35	80	18	2	3	43	57	37	.199	.302	.275	57	-21	-23	37	2	0		.985	16	C/O	-0.0

■ JOE FRAZIER Frazier, Joseph Filmore b: 10/6/22, Liberty, N.C. BL/TR, 6', 180 lbs. Deb: 8/31/47 M

YEAR	TM/L	G	AB	R	H	2B	3B	HR	RBI	BB	SO	AVG	OBP	SLG	PRO+	BR	/A	RC	SB	CS	SBR	FA	FR	POS	TPR
1947	Cle-A	9	14	1	1	1	0	0	0	1	1	.071	.133	.143	-24	-2	-2	0	0	0	0	.857	-1	/O	-0.4
1954	StL-N	81	88	8	26	5	2	3	18	13	17	.295	.392	.500	129	4	4	18	0	0	0	.938	-1	O/1	0.3
1955	StL-N	58	70	12	14	1	0	4	9	6	12	.200	.273	.386	72	-3	-3	7	0	0	0	1.000	-3	O	-0.6
1956	StL-N	14	19	1	4	2	0	1	4	3	3	.211	.318	.474	109	0	0	3	0	1	-1	.800	-1	/O	-0.1
	Cin-N	10	17	2	4	0	0	1	2	1	7	.235	.278	.412	77	-0	-1	2	0	0	0	.000	-2	/O	-0.2
	Yr	24	36	3	8	2	0	2	6	4	10	.222	.300	.444	94	-0	-0	4	0	1	-1	.800	-2	/O	-0.3
	Bal-A	45	74	7	19	6	0	1	12	11	6	.257	.360	.378	103	-0	1	10	0	0	0	1.000	-0	O	0.0
Total	4	217	282	31	68	15	2	10	45	35	46	.241	.331	.415	97	-2	-1	40	0	1	-1	.961	-7	/O1	-1.0

■ JOHNNY FREDERICK Frederick, John Henry b: 1/26/02, Denver, Colo. d: 6/18/77, Tigard, Ore. BL/TL, 5'11", 165 lbs. Deb: 4/18/29

YEAR	TM/L	G	AB	R	H	2B	3B	HR	RBI	BB	SO	AVG	OBP	SLG	PRO+	BR	/A	RC	SB	CS	SBR	FA	FR	POS	TPR
1929	Bro-N	148	628	127	206	**52**	6	24	75	39	34	.328	.372	.545	126	21	23	122	6			.975	8	*O	1.8
1930	Bro-N	142	616	120	206	44	11	17	76	46	34	.334	.383	.524	118	16	17	120	1			.990	12	*O	1.6
1931	Bro-N	146	611	81	165	34	8	17	71	31	46	.270	.312	.435	99	-3	-3	84	2			.965	2	*O	-1.0
1932	Bro-N	118	384	54	115	28	2	16	56	25	35	.299	.349	.508	130	14	15	69	1			.976	-3	O	0.6
1933	Bro-N	147	556	65	171	22	7	7	64	36	14	.308	.355	.410	123	13	16	84	9			.971	-7	*O	0.2
1934	Bro-N	104	307	51	91	20	1	4	35	33	13	.296	.370	.407	114	4	6	49	4			.957	-3	O/1	0.1
Total	6	805	3102	498	954	200	35	85	377	210	176	.308	.357	.477	118	64	73	527	23			.974	9	O/1	3.3

■ ED FREED Freed, Edwin Charles b: 8/22/19, Centre Valley, Pa. BR/TR, 5'6", 165 lbs. Deb: 9/11/42

YEAR	TM/L	G	AB	R	H	2B	3B	HR	RBI	BB	SO	AVG	OBP	SLG	PRO+	BR	/A	RC	SB	CS	SBR	FA	FR	POS	TPR
1942	Phi-N	13	33	3	10	3	1	0	1	4	3	.303	.378	.455	151	2	2	6	1			1.000	-1	O	0.0

■ ROGER FREED Freed, Roger Vernon b: 6/2/46, Los Angeles, Cal. BR/TR, 6', 190 lbs. Deb: 9/18/70

YEAR	TM/L	G	AB	R	H	2B	3B	HR	RBI	BB	SO	AVG	OBP	SLG	PRO+	BR	/A	RC	SB	CS	SBR	FA	FR	POS	TPR
1970	Bal-A	4	13	0	2	0	0	0	1	3	4	.154	.313	.154	32	-1	-1	1	0	0	0	1.000	0	/1O	-0.1
1971	Phi-N	118	348	23	77	12	1	6	37	44	86	.221	.314	.313	78	-9	-9	35	0	3	-2	.989	-7	*O/C	-2.5
1972	Phi-N	73	129	10	29	4	0	6	18	23	39	.225	.346	.395	108	2	2	18	0	1	-1	.971	2	O	0.2
1974	Cin-N	6	6	1	2	0	0	1	3	1	1	.333	.429	.833	251	1	1	2	0	0	0	1.000	-0	/1	0.1
1976	Mon-N	8	15	0	3	1	0	0	1	0	3	.200	.200	.267	30	-1	-1	1	0	0	0	1.000	-0	/1O	-0.2
1977	StL-N	49	83	10	33	2	1	5	21	11	9	.398	.468	.627	194	11	11	24	0	0	0	1.000	-1	1/O	0.9
1978	StL-N	52	92	3	22	6	0	2	20	8	17	.239	.300	.370	87	-2	-2	10	1	0	0	.992	0	1/O	-0.2
1979	StL-N	34	31	2	8	2	0	2	8	5	7	.258	.361	.516	135	2	2	6	0	0	0	.889	0	/1	0.2
Total	8	344	717	49	176	27	2	22	109	95	166	.245	.337	.381	101	2	2	97	1	4	-2	.982	-6	O/1C	-1.6

■ BILL FREEHAN Freehan, William Ashley b: 11/29/41, Detroit, Mich. BR/TR, 6'2", 205 lbs. Deb: 9/26/61

YEAR	TM/L	G	AB	R	H	2B	3B	HR	RBI	BB	SO	AVG	OBP	SLG	PRO+	BR	/A	RC	SB	CS	SBR	FA	FR	POS	TPR
1961	Det-A	4	10	1	4	0	0	0	4	1	0	.400	.455	.400	127	1	0	2	0	0	0	1.000	1	/C	0.2
1963	Det-A	100	300	37	73	12	2	9	36	39	56	.243	.334	.387	98	1	-0	40	2	0	1	.995	-1	C1	0.2
1964	Det-A☆	144	520	69	156	14	8	18	80	36	68	.300	.355	.462	123	17	16	86	5	1	1	.993	-2	*C/1	2.2
1965	Det-A★	130	431	45	101	15	0	10	43	39	63	.234	.308	.339	83	-9	-10	45	4	2	0	.996	-1	*C	-0.5
1966	Det-A★	136	492	47	115	22	0	12	46	40	72	.234	.295	.352	83	-10	-11	50	5	2	0	**.996**	1	*C/1	-0.2
1967	Det-A★	155	517	66	146	23	1	20	74	73	71	.282	.392	.447	143	34	32	94	1	2	-1	.992	-9	*C1	3.3
1968	*Det-A★	155	540	73	142	24	2	25	84	65	64	.263	.367	.454	143	33	31	94	0	1	-1	.994	6	*C1/O	4.9
1969	Det-A★	143	489	61	128	16	3	16	49	53	55	.262	.344	.405	104	6	3	68	1	2	-1	.992	4	*C1	1.2
1970	Det-A★	117	395	44	95	17	3	16	52	52	48	.241	.335	.420	106	4	3	55	0	3	-2	**.997**	-16	*C	-0.8
1971	Det-A★	148	516	57	143	26	4	21	71	54	48	.277	.356	.465	126	20	18	82	2	7	-4	.996	-12	*C/O	0.9
1972	*Det-A★	111	374	51	98	18	2	10	56	48	51	.262	.355	.401	121	12	11	55	0	1	-1	.989	0	*C/1	1.7
1973	Det-A☆	110	380	33	89	10	1	6	29	40	30	.234	.325	.313	75	-9	-12	39	0	0	0	**.995**	9	C/1D	0.0
1974	Det-A	130	445	58	132	17	5	18	60	42	44	.297	.364	.479	136	23	21	77	2	0	1	.994	-8	1C/D	1.2
1975	Det-A☆	120	427	42	105	17	3	14	47	32	56	.246	.308	.398	94	-2	-4	51	2	0	1	.991	-8	*C/1	-0.8
1976	Det-A	71	237	22	64	10	1	5	27	12	27	.270	.308	.384	98	-0	-1	28	0	0	0	.983	-2	C/1D	-0.1
Total	15	1774	6073	706	1591	241	35	200	758	626	753	.262	.342	.412	111	120	97	867	24	21	-5	.993	-38	*C1/DO	13.4

■ JERRY FREEMAN Freeman, Frank Ellsworth "Buck" b: 12/26/1879, Placerville, Cal. d: 9/30/52, Los Angeles, Cal. BL/TR, 6'2", 220 lbs. Deb: 4/14/08

YEAR	TM/L	G	AB	R	H	2B	3B	HR	RBI	BB	SO	AVG	OBP	SLG	PRO+	BR	/A	RC	SB	CS	SBR	FA	FR	POS	TPR
1908	Was-A	154	531	45	134	15	5	1	45	36		.252	.304	.305	107	-1	3	50	6			.975	-13	*1	-1.4
1909	Was-A	19	48	2	8	0	1	0	3	4		.167	.245	.208	46	-3	-3	3	3			.956	-2	1/O	-0.5

YEAR	TM/L	G	AB	R	H	2B	3B	HR	RBI	BB	SO	AVG	OBP	SLG	PRO+	BR	/A	RC	SB	CS	SBR	FA	FR	POS	TPR
Total	2	173	579	47	142	15	6	1	48	40		.245	.299	.297	101	-4	1	54	9			.974	-14	1/O	-1.9

■ JOHN FREEMAN

Freeman, John Edward b: 1/24/01, Boston, Mass. d: 4/14/58, Washington, D.C. BR/TR, 5'8", 160 lbs. Deb: 6/17/27

YEAR	TM/L	G	AB	R	H	2B	3B	HR	RBI	BB	SO	AVG	OBP	SLG	PRO+	BR	/A	RC	SB	CS	SBR	FA	FR	POS	TPR
1927	Bos-A	4	2	0	0	0	0	0	0	0	0	.000	.000	.000	-99	-1	-1	0	0	0	0	.000	-2	/O	-0.2

■ BUCK FREEMAN

Freeman, John Frank b: 10/30/1871, Catasauqua, Pa. d: 6/25/49, Wilkes-Barre, Pa. BL/TL, 5'9", 169 lbs. Deb: 6/27/1891

YEAR	TM/L	G	AB	R	H	2B	3B	HR	RBI	BB	SO	AVG	OBP	SLG	PRO+	BR	/A	RC	SB	CS	SBR	FA	FR	POS	TPR
1891	Was-a	5	18	1	4	1	0	0	1	2	2	.222	.300	.278	71	-1	-1	2	0			.769	-0	/P	0.0
1898	Was-N	29	107	19	39	2	3	3	21	7		.364	.424	.523	171	10	10	25	2			.978	1	O	0.8
1899	Was-N	155	588	107	187	19	25	**25**	122	23		.318	.361	.563	154	36	37	131	21			.944	-12	*O/P	1.2
1900	Bos-N	117	418	58	126	19	13	6	65	25		.301	.355	.452	109	11	3	73	10			.950	-11	O1	-1.3
1901	Bos-A	129	490	88	166	23	15	12	114	44		.339	.400	.520	157	35	36	112	17			.974	-5	*1/2O	2.7
1902	Bos-A	138	564	75	174	38	19	11	**121**	32		.309	.352	.502	131	23	21	109	17			.944	-1	*O	1.1
1903	*Bos-A	141	567	74	163	39	20	**13**	**104**	30		.287	.328	.496	137	28	25	97	5			.933	-6	*O	1.0
1904	Bos-A	157	597	64	167	20	**19**	7	84	32		.280	.329	.412	127	22	18	87	7			.954	-6	*O	0.4
1905	Bos-A	130	455	59	109	20	8	3	49	46		.240	.315	.338	106	4	4	53	8			.972	-15	1O/3	-1.7
1906	Bos-A	121	392	42	98	18	9	1	30	28		.250	.302	.349	104	1	1	46	5			.989	1	O1/3	-0.2
1907	Bos-A	4	12	1	2	0	0	1	2	3		.167	.333	.417	140	1	1	2	0			1.000	0	/O	0.1
Total	11	1126	4208	588	1235	199	131	82	713	272	2	.293	.346	.462	131	170	155	736	92			.950	-53	O1/P32	4.1

■ LA VEL FREEMAN

Freeman, La Vel Maurice b: 2/18/63, Oakland, Cal. BL/TL, 5'9", 170 lbs. Deb: 4/07/89

YEAR	TM/L	G	AB	R	H	2B	3B	HR	RBI	BB	SO	AVG	OBP	SLG	PRO+	BR	/A	RC	SB	CS	SBR	FA	FR	POS	TPR
1989	Mil-A	2	3	1	0	0	0	0	0	0	2	.000	.000	.000	-99	-1	-1	0	0	0	0	.000	0	/D	-0.1

■ GENE FREESE

Freese, Eugene Lewis "Augie" b: 1/8/34, Wheeling, W.Va. BR/TR, 5'11", 175 lbs. Deb: 4/13/55 F

YEAR	TM/L	G	AB	R	H	2B	3B	HR	RBI	BB	SO	AVG	OBP	SLG	PRO+	BR	/A	RC	SB	CS	SBR	FA	FR	POS	TPR
1955	Pit-N	134	455	69	115	21	8	14	44	34	57	.253	.310	.426	94	-6	-5	60	5	1	1	.943	-2	32	-0.2
1956	Pit-N	65	207	17	43	9	0	3	14	16	45	.208	.274	.295	54	-14	-13	18	2	1	0	.963	-7	32	-1.9
1957	Pit-N	114	346	44	98	18	2	6	31	17	42	.283	.321	.399	95	-4	-3	44	9	4	0	.924	-3	32O	-0.4
1958	Pit-N	17	18	1	3	0	0	1	2	1	2	.167	.211	.333	42	-2	-2	1	0	0	0	.800	1	/3	-0.1
	StL-N	62	191	28	49	11	1	6	16	10	32	.257	.294	.419	83	-4	-5	24	1	1	-0	.924	-25	S2/3	-2.8
	Yr	79	209	29	52	11	1	7	18	11	34	.249	.286	.411	80	-6	-7	24	1	1	-0	.924	-24	S2/3	-2.9
1959	Phi-N	132	400	60	107	14	5	23	70	43	61	.268	.346	.500	120	12	11	69	8	4	0	.916	-24	*3/2	-1.2
1960	Chi-A	127	455	60	124	32	6	17	79	29	65	.273	.318	.481	114	6	6	64	10	6	-1	.946	0	*3	0.5
1961	*Cin-N	152	575	78	159	27	2	26	87	27	78	.277	.309	.466	101	-0	-1	77	8	2	1	.950	-17	*3/2	-1.6
1962	Cin-N	18	42	2	6	1	0	0	1	6	8	.143	.250	.167	14	-5	-5	2	0	0	0	1.000	-2	3	-0.7
1963	Cin-N	66	217	20	53	9	1	6	26	17	42	.244	.305	.378	93	-1	-2	26	4	2	0	.930	-6	3/O	-0.9
1964	Pit-N	99	289	33	65	13	2	9	40	19	45	.225	.273	.377	81	-8	-8	28	1	2	-1	.920	-6	3	-1.6
1965	Pit-N	43	80	6	21	4	0	0	8	6	18	.262	.330	.313	82	-2	-2	7	0	2	-1	.951	-1	3	-0.4
	Chi-A	17	32	2	9	0	1	1	4	5	9	.281	.378	.438	140	1	2	6	0	0	0	.824	-3	/3	-0.1
1966	Chi-A	48	106	8	22	2	0	3	10	8	20	.208	.270	.311	71	-5	-4	9	2	1	0	.894	3	3	-0.2
	Hou-N	21	33	1	3	0	0	0	0	5	11	.091	.211	.091	-13	-5	-5	1	1	0	0	.800	0	/32O	-0.5
Total	12	1115	3446	429	877	161	28	115	432	243	535	.254	.307	.418	94	-37	-36	434	51	26	-0	.934	-90	32/SO	-12.1

■ GEORGE FREESE

Freese, George Walter "Bud" b: 9/12/26, Wheeling, W.Va. BR/TR, 6', 190 lbs. Deb: 4/29/53 F

YEAR	TM/L	G	AB	R	H	2B	3B	HR	RBI	BB	SO	AVG	OBP	SLG	PRO+	BR	/A	RC	SB	CS	SBR	FA	FR	POS	TPR
1953	Det-A	1	1	0	0	0	0	0	0	0	0	.000	.000	.000	-99	-0	-0	0	0	0	0	.000	0	H	0.0
1955	Pit-N	51	179	17	46	8	2	3	22	17	18	.257	.328	.374	87	-3	-3	21	1	1	-0	.936	-8	3	-1.2
1961	Chi-N	9	7	0	2	0	0	0	1	1	4	.286	.375	.286	78	-0	-0	1	0	0	0	.000	0	H	0.0
Total	3	61	187	17	48	8	2	3	23	18	22	.257	.329	.369	86	-4	-4	22	1	1	-0	.933	-8	/3	-1.2

■ JIM FREGOSI

Fregosi, James Louis b: 4/4/42, San Francisco, Cal. BR/TR, 6'1", 190 lbs. Deb: 9/14/61 M

YEAR	TM/L	G	AB	R	H	2B	3B	HR	RBI	BB	SO	AVG	OBP	SLG	PRO+	BR	/A	RC	SB	CS	SBR	FA	FR	POS	TPR
1961	LA-A	11	27	7	6	0	0	0	3	1	4	.222	.250	.222	25	-3	-3	1	0	0	0	.944	-0	S	-0.3
1962	LA-A	58	175	15	51	3	4	3	23	18	27	.291	.358	.406	108	1	2	25	2	1	0	.943	4	S	1.0
1963	LA-A	154	592	83	170	29	12	9	50	36	104	.287	.328	.422	115	6	10	81	2	2	-1	.964	2	*S	2.2
1964	LA-A★	147	505	86	140	22	9	18	72	72	87	.277	.372	.463	145	22	28	89	8	3	1	.966	1	*S	4.1
1965	Cal-A	161	602	66	167	19	7	15	64	54	107	.277	.341	.407	114	9	11	85	13	5	1	.968	6	*S	3.0
1966	Cal-A★	162	611	78	154	32	7	13	67	67	89	.252	.328	.391	109	5	7	80	17	8	0	.959	15	*S/1	3.9
1967	Cal-A★	151	590	75	171	23	6	9	56	49	77	.290	.349	.395	124	14	17	82	9	6	-1	.965	-7	*S	2.6
1968	Cal-A★	159	614	77	150	21	**13**	9	49	60	101	.244	.317	.365	110	4	7	72	9	4	0	.962	-14	*S	1.1
1969	Cal-A★	161	580	78	151	22	6	12	47	93	86	.260	.364	.381	114	9	13	86	9	2	2	.972	-16	*S	1.6
1970	Cal-A★	158	601	95	167	33	5	22	82	69	92	.278	.355	.459	127	18	21	101	0	2	-1	.973	4	*S/1	4.2
1971	Cal-A	107	347	31	81	15	1	5	33	39	61	.233	.320	.326	90	-7	-4	39	2	1	0	.938	-10	S1/O	-0.7
1972	NY-N	101	340	31	79	15	4	5	32	38	71	.232	.311	.344	88	-6	-5	37	0	1	-1	.935	-7	3/S1	-1.3
1973	NY-N	45	124	7	29	4	1	0	11	20	25	.234	.340	.282	75	-4	-3	12	1	2	-1	.906	-5	S3/1O	-0.8
	Tex-A	45	157	25	42	6	2	6	16	12	31	.268	.324	.446	120	3	3	23	0	1	-1	.937	-9	31/S	-0.7
1974	Tex-A	78	230	31	60	5	0	12	34	22	41	.261	.325	.439	121	5	5	29	0	1	-1	1.000	-1	13	0.1
1975	Tex-A	77	191	25	50	5	0	7	33	20	39	.262	.335	.398	107	2	2	24	0	1	-1	.985	2	1D/3	0.1
1976	Tex-A	58	133	17	31	7	0	2	12	23	33	.233	.346	.331	97	1	0	17	2	0	1	.995	-0	1D/3	-0.1
1977	Tex-A	13	28	4	7	1	0	1	5	3	4	.250	.323	.393	93	-0	-0	4	0	0	0	1.000	1	/1D	0.0
	Pit-N	36	56	10	16	1	1	3	16	13	10	.286	.420	.500	142	4	4	13	2	0	1	.981	-1	1/3	0.3
1978	Pit-N	20	20	3	4	1	0	0	1	6	8	.200	.385	.250	77	-0	-0	3	0	0	0	.667	-1	/312	-0.2
Total	18	1902	6523	844	1726	264	78	151	706	715	1097	.265	.340	.398	114	83	113	904	76	40	-1	.963	-40	*S13/DO2	20.1

■ VERN FREIBERGER

Freiberger, Vern Donald b: 12/19/23, Detroit, Mich. BR/TL, 6'1", 170 lbs. Deb: 9/06/41

YEAR	TM/L	G	AB	R	H	2B	3B	HR	RBI	BB	SO	AVG	OBP	SLG	PRO+	BR	/A	RC	SB	CS	SBR	FA	FR	POS	TPR
1941	Cle-A	2	8	0	1	0	0	0	1	0	2	.125	.125	.125	-35	-2	-1	0	0	0	0	.947	1	/1	-0.1

■ HOWARD FREIGAU

Freigau, Howard Earl "Ty" b: 8/1/02, Dayton, Ohio d: 7/18/32, Chattanooga, Tenn BR/TR, 5'10.5", 160 lbs. Deb: 9/13/22

YEAR	TM/L	G	AB	R	H	2B	3B	HR	RBI	BB	SO	AVG	OBP	SLG	PRO+	BR	/A	RC	SB	CS	SBR	FA	FR	POS	TPR
1922	StL-N	3	1	0	0	0	0	0	0	0	0	.000	.000	.000	-99	-0	-0	0	0	0	0	1.000	1	/S3	0.1
1923	StL-N	113	358	30	94	18	1	1	35	25	36	.263	.314	.327	71	-16	-15	37	5	4	-1	.929	2	S2/13O	-0.6
1924	StL-N	98	376	35	101	17	6	2	39	19	24	.269	.306	.362	80	-12	-11	42	10	3	1	.958	3	3/S	0.1
1925	StL-N	9	26	2	4	0	0	0	0	2	1	.154	.214	.154	-4	-4	-4	1	0	0	0	.936	3	/S2	0.0
	Chi-N	117	476	77	146	22	10	8	71	30	31	.307	.349	.445	100	0	-1	73	10	6	-1	.913	-5	3S/1	0.2
	Yr	126	502	79	150	22	10	8	71	32	32	.299	.342	.430	94	-4	-5	73	10	6	-1	.913	-1	3S/12	0.2
1926	Chi-N	140	508	51	137	27	7	3	51	43	42	.270	.327	.368	86	-10	-11	61	6			**.966**	-3	*3/SO	-0.4
1927	Chi-N	30	86	12	20	5	0	0	10	9	10	.233	.313	.291	62	-4	-4	8	0			.883	1	3	-0.3
1928	Bro-N	17	34	6	7	2	0	0	3	1	3	.206	.229	.265	29	-4	-4	2	0			.810	-4	3/S	-0.7
	Bos-N	52	109	11	28	8	1	1	17	9	14	.257	.319	.376	86	-3	-2	13	1			.938	-10	S2	-1.0
	Yr	69	143	17	35	10	1	1	20	10	17	.245	.299	.350	72	-7	-6	15	1			.938	-13	S23	-1.7
Total	7	579	1974	224	537	99	25	15	226	138	161	.272	.322	.370	82	-53	-52	238	32	13		.940	-11	3S/21O	-2.6

■ CHARLIE FRENCH

French, Charles Calvin b: 10/12/1883, Indianapolis, Ind. d: 3/30/62, Indianapolis, Ind. BL/TR, 5'6", 140 lbs. Deb: 5/23/09

YEAR	TM/L	G	AB	R	H	2B	3B	HR	RBI	BB	SO	AVG	OBP	SLG	PRO+	BR	/A	RC	SB	CS	SBR	FA	FR	POS	TPR
1909	Bos-A	51	167	15	42	3	1	0	13	15		.251	.324	.281	90	-1	-1	18	8			.921	-8	2S	-1.1
1910	Bos-A	9	40	4	8	1	0	0	3	1		.200	.220	.225	38	-3	-3	2	0			.889	1	/2	-0.3
	Chi-A	45	170	17	28	1	1	0	4	10		.165	.224	.182	29	-14	-13	8	5			.930	-14	2O	-3.3
	Yr	54	210	21	36	2	1	0	7	11		.171	.223	.190	31	-17	-16	10	5			.919	-14	2O	-3.6
Total	2	105	377	36	78	5	2	0	20	26		.207	.269	.231	58	-18	-18	28	13			.920	-21	/2SO	-4.7

■ PAT FRENCH French, Frank Alexander b: 9/22/1893, Dover, N.H. d: 7/13/69, Bath, Maine BR/TR, 6'1", 180 lbs. Deb: 7/02/17

YEAR	TM/L	G	AB	R	H	2B	3B	HR	RBI	BB	SO	AVG	OBP	SLG	PRO+	BR	/A	RC	SB	CS	SBR	FA	FR	POS	TPR
1917	Phi-A	3	2	0	0	0	0	0	0	0	0	.000	.000	.000	-99	-0	-0	0	0			1.000	-0	/O	-0.1

■ RAY FRENCH French, Raymond Edward b: 1/9/1895, Alameda, Cal. d: 4/3/78, Alameda, Cal. BR/TR, 5'9.5", 158 lbs. Deb: 9/17/20

YEAR	TM/L	G	AB	R	H	2B	3B	HR	RBI	BB	SO	AVG	OBP	SLG	PRO+	BR	/A	RC	SB	CS	SBR	FA	FR	POS	TPR
1920	NY-A	2	2	2	0	0	0	0	1	0	1	.000	.000	.000	-97	-1	-1	0	0	0	0	.500	-0	/S	-0.1
1923	Bro-N	43	73	14	16	2	1	0	7	4	7	.219	.269	.274	45	-6	-6	6	0	0	0	.874	4	S	0.1
1924	Chi-A	37	112	13	20	4	0	0	11	10	13	.179	.246	.214	20	-14	-13	7	3	1	0	.927	-3	S/2	-1.2
Total	3	82	187	29	36	6	1	0	19	14	21	.193	.252	.235	28	-20	-19	12	3	1	0	.897	2	/S2	-1.2

■ JIM FRENCH French, Richard James b: 8/13/41, Warren, Ohio BL/TR, 5'7", 182 lbs. Deb: 9/12/65

YEAR	TM/L	G	AB	R	H	2B	3B	HR	RBI	BB	SO	AVG	OBP	SLG	PRO+	BR	/A	RC	SB	CS	SBR	FA	FR	POS	TPR
1965	Was-A	13	37	4	11	0	0	1	7	9	5	.297	.435	.378	135	2	2	7	1	0	0	.974	-0	C	0.3
1966	Was-A	10	24	0	5	1	0	0	3	4	5	.208	.321	.250	67	-1	-1	2	0	1	-1	.979	-1	C	-0.2
1967	Was-A	6	16	0	1	0	0	0	1	3	4	.063	.211	.063	-16	-2	-2	0	0	0	0	.968	-1	/C	-0.3
1968	Was-A	59	165	9	32	5	0	1	10	19	19	.194	.281	.242	62	-8	-7	13	1	2	-1	.984	2	C	-0.3
1969	Was-A	63	158	14	29	6	3	2	13	41	15	.184	.352	.297	88	-2	-1	20	1	0	0	.989	9	C	1.2
1970	Was-A	69	166	20	35	3	1	1	13	38	23	.211	.358	.259	76	-4	-3	17	0	1	-1	.973	-6	C/O	-0.7
1971	Was-A	14	41	6	6	2	0	0	4	7	7	.146	.271	.195	36	-3	-3	2	0	2	-1	.985	-1	C	-0.5
Total	7	234	607	53	119	17	4	5	51	121	78	.196	.331	.262	74	-18	-15	61	3	6	-3	.982	2	C/O	-0.5

■ WALTER FRENCH French, Walter Edward "Piggy" or "Fitz" b: 7/12/1899, Moorestown, N.J. d: 5/13/84, Mountain Home, Ark BL/TR, 5'7.5", 155 lbs. Deb: 9/15/23

YEAR	TM/L	G	AB	R	H	2B	3B	HR	RBI	BB	SO	AVG	OBP	SLG	PRO+	BR	/A	RC	SB	CS	SBR	FA	FR	POS	TPR
1923	Phi-A	16	39	7	9	3	0	0	2	5	7	.231	.318	.308	64	-2	-2	4	0	1	-1	1.000	-1	O	-0.4
1925	Phi-A	67	100	20	37	9	0	0	14	1	9	.370	.376	.460	104	1	0	16	1	1	-0	.971	0	O	-0.1
1926	Phi-A	112	397	51	121	18	7	1	36	18	24	.305	.340	.393	86	-6	-9	53	2	3	-1	.971	3	O	-1.4
1927	Phi-A	109	326	48	99	10	5	0	41	16	14	.304	.338	.365	78	-9	-11	39	9	1	2	.956	0	O	-1.3
1928	Phi-A	48	74	9	19	4	0	0	7	2	5	.257	.286	.311	55	-5	-5	6	1	1	-0	1.000	-1	O	-0.7
1929	*Phi-A	45	45	7	12	1	0	1	9	2	3	.267	.298	.356	65	-2	-2	5	0	0	0	1.000	-3	O	-0.6
Total	6	397	981	142	297	45	12	2	109	44	62	.303	.336	.379	81	-22	-29	123	13	7	-0	.968	-2	O	-4.5

■ BILL FRENCH French, William b: Baltimore, Md. Deb: 4/14/1873

YEAR	TM/L	G	AB	R	H	2B	3B	HR	RBI	BB	SO	AVG	OBP	SLG	PRO+	BR	/A	RC	SB	CS	SBR	FA	FR	POS	TPR
1873	Mar-n	5	18	3	4	0	0	0	1	0	0	.222	.222	.222	41	-1	-1	1						/1OP3	0.0

■ LONNY FREY Frey, Linus Reinhard "Junior" b: 8/23/10, St.Louis, Mo. BL/TR, 5'10", 160 lbs. Deb: 8/29/33

YEAR	TM/L	G	AB	R	H	2B	3B	HR	RBI	BB	SO	AVG	OBP	SLG	PRO+	BR	/A	RC	SB	CS	SBR	FA	FR	POS	TPR
1933	Bro-N	34	135	25	43	5	3	0	12	13	13	.319	.378	.400	128	4	5	21	4			.896	-14	S	-0.7
1934	Bro-N	125	490	77	139	24	5	8	57	52	54	.284	.358	.402	109	3	7	75	11			.945	13	*S3	2.6
1935	Bro-N	131	515	88	135	35	11	11	77	66	68	.262	.352	.437	113	8	10	82	6			.937	-4	*S/2	1.3
1936	Bro-N	148	524	63	146	29	4	4	60	71	56	.279	.369	.372	99	2	2	77	7			.918	-32	*S2/O	-2.1
1937	Chi-N	78	198	33	55	9	3	1	22	33	15	.278	.381	.369	100	3	1	31	6			.938	-19	S2/3O	-1.4
1938	Cin-N	124	501	76	133	26	6	4	36	49	50	.265	.331	.365	94	-6	-4	66	4			.964	-8	*2/S	-0.4
1939	*Cin-N★	125	484	95	141	27	9	11	55	72	46	.291	.387	.452	124	19	18	91	5			.976	15	*2	4.0
1940	*Cin-N	150	563	102	150	23	6	8	54	80	48	.266	.361	.371	101	4	3	82	**22**			.977	18	*2	3.1
1941	Cin-N★	146	543	78	138	29	5	6	59	72	37	.254	.345	.359	98	0	-0	72	16			**.970**	-2	*2	0.8
1942	Cin-N	141	523	66	139	23	6	2	39	87	38	.266	.373	.344	111	10	11	75	9			.977	5	*2	2.6
1943	Cin-N★	144	586	78	154	20	8	2	43	76	56	.263	.347	.334	99	-0	1	75	7			**.985**	12	*2	2.2
1946	Cin-N	111	333	46	82	10	3	3	24	63	31	.246	.368	.321	100	1	3	44	5			.963	-3	2O	0.3
1947	Chi-N	24	43	4	9	0	0	0	3	4	6	.209	.277	.209	32	-4	-4	3	0			1.000	-2	/2	-0.5
	*NY-A	24	28	10	5	2	0	0	2	10	1	.179	.410	.250	87	0	0	5	3	0	1	.923	3	/2	0.5
1948	NY-A	1	0	1	0	0	0	0	0	0	0	—	—	—	—	0	0	0	0	0	0	.000	0	R	0.0
	NY-N	29	51	6	13	1	0	1	6	4	6	.255	.309	.333	73	-2	-2	6	0			.920	-2	2	-0.3
Total	14	1535	5517	848	1482	263	69	61	549	752	525	.269	.359	.374	104	43	50	803	105	0		.973	-18	2S/O3	12.0

■ PEPE FRIAS Frias, Jesus Maria (Andujar) b: 7/14/48, San De Pedro De Macoris, D.R. BR/TR, 5'10", 159 lbs. Deb: 4/06/73

YEAR	TM/L	G	AB	R	H	2B	3B	HR	RBI	BB	SO	AVG	OBP	SLG	PRO+	BR	/A	RC	SB	CS	SBR	FA	FR	POS	TPR
1973	Mon-N	100	225	19	52	10	1	0	22	10	24	.231	.267	.284	51	-14	-15	16	1	3	-2	.950	17	S2/3O	0.6
1974	Mon-N	75	112	12	24	4	1	0	7	7	10	.214	.261	.268	45	-8	-9	8	1	0	0	.962	17	S32/O	1.2
1975	Mon-N	51	64	4	8	2	0	0	4	3	13	.125	.164	.156	-10	-10	-10	2	0	1	-1	.938	14	S3/2	0.5
1976	Mon-N	76	113	7	28	5	0	0	8	4	14	.248	.274	.292	58	-6	-6	9	1	1	-0	.957	14	2S/3O	1.1
1977	Mon-N	53	70	10	18	1	0	0	5	0	10	.257	.257	.271	43	-6	-5	5	1	0	0	.978	8	2S/3	0.3
1978	Mon-N	73	15	5	4	2	1	0	5	0	3	.267	.267	.533	120	0	0	2	0	0	0	1.000	13	2/S	1.4
1979	Atl-N	140	475	41	123	18	4	1	44	20	36	.259	.292	.320	62	-22	-26	42	3	2	-0	.954	-0	*S	-1.2
1980	Tex-A	116	227	27	55	5	1	0	10	4	23	.242	.259	.273	47	-17	-16	15	5	1	1	.947	-16	*S/32	-2.3
	LA-N	14	9	1	2	1	0	0	0	0	0	.222	.222	.333	54	-1	-1	0	0	0	0	.933	2	S	0.2
1981	LA-N	25	36	6	9	1	0	0	3	1	3	.250	.289	.278	64	-2	-2	3	0	0	0	.906	-5	S/23	-0.6
Total	9	723	1346	132	323	49	8	1	108	49	136	.240	.269	.290	52	-85	-90	102	12	8	-1	.951	64	S2/3O	1.2

■ BERNIE FRIBERG Friberg, Bernard Albert (b: Gustaf Bernhard Friberg)
b: 8/18/1899, Manchester, N.H. d: 12/8/58, Lynn, Mass. BR/TR, 5'11", 178 lbs. Deb: 8/20/19

YEAR	TM/L	G	AB	R	H	2B	3B	HR	RBI	BB	SO	AVG	OBP	SLG	PRO+	BR	/A	RC	SB	CS	SBR	FA	FR	POS	TPR
1919	Chi-N	8	20	0	4	1	0	0	1	0	2	.200	.200	.250	35	-2	-2	1	0			1.000	-1	/O	-0.3
1920	Chi-N	50	114	11	24	5	1	0	7	6	20	.211	.250	.272	49	-7	-8	8	2	2	-1	.963	1	2O	-0.8
1922	Chi-N	97	296	51	92	8	2	0	23	37	37	.311	.391	.351	91	-1	-2	41	8	10	-4	.972	-2	O/132	-1.2
1923	Chi-N	146	547	91	174	27	11	12	88	45	49	.318	.372	.473	122	16	16	91	13	19	-8	.955	7	*3	2.8
1924	Chi-N	142	495	67	138	19	3	5	82	66	53	.279	.369	.360	95	-0	-1	65	19	27	-11	.954	4	*3	0.4
1925	Chi-N	44	152	12	39	5	3	1	16	14	22	.257	.327	.349	72	-6	-6	18	0	1	-1	.889	-5	3O/1S	-1.1
	Phi-N	91	304	41	82	12	1	5	22	39	35	.270	.353	.365	77	-7	-11	41	1	1	-0	.965	4	23/PC	-0.5
	Yr	135	456	53	121	17	4	6	38	53	57	.265	.344	.360	75	-13	-17	59	1	2	-1	.965	-2	23O/1SPC	-1.6
1926	Phi-N	144	478	38	128	21	3	1	51	57	77	.268	.346	.331	79	-10	-13	56	2			.976	22	*2	1.3
1927	Phi-N	111	335	31	78	8	2	1	28	41	49	.233	.322	.278	61	-17	-17	32	3			.959	25	*3/2	1.2
1928	Phi-N	52	94	11	19	3	0	1	7	12	16	.202	.292	.266	45	-7	-8	8	0			.908	1	S/3201	-0.5
1929	Phi-N	128	455	74	137	21	10	7	55	49	54	.301	.370	.437	93	-0	-5	73	1			.923	-26	SO/21	-2.2
1930	Phi-N	105	331	62	113	21	1	4	42	47	35	.341	.425	.447	104	8	4	64	1			.953	-4	2OS/3	0.1
1931	Phi-N	103	353	33	92	19	5	1	26	33	25	.261	.324	.351	75	-9	-13	42	1			.955	6	23/1S	-0.2
1932	Phi-N	61	154	17	37	8	2	0	14	19	23	.240	.324	.318	66	-5	-8	17	0			.957	-1	2	-0.6
1933	Bos-A	17	41	5	13	3	0	0	9	6	1	.317	.404	.390	112	1	1	7	0	0	0	.950	1	/23S	0.3
Total	14	1299	4169	544	1170	181	44	38	471	471	498	.281	.356	.373	87	-46	-71	564	51	60		.953	32	32OS/1CP	-1.3

■ JIM FRIDLEY Fridley, James Riley "Big Jim" b: 9/6/24, Philippi, W.Va. BR/TR, 6'2", 205 lbs. Deb: 4/15/52

YEAR	TM/L	G	AB	R	H	2B	3B	HR	RBI	BB	SO	AVG	OBP	SLG	PRO+	BR	/A	RC	SB	CS	SBR	FA	FR	POS	TPR
1952	Cle-A	62	175	23	44	2	0	4	16	14	40	.251	.311	.331	84	-5	-4	18	3	3	-1	.978	-5	O	-1.2
1954	Bal-A	85	240	25	59	8	5	4	36	21	41	.246	.312	.371	93	-5	-3	25	0	1	-1	.985	-1	O	-0.7
1958	Cin-N	5	9	2	2	2	0	0	1	0	2	.222	.222	.444	67	-0	-0	1	0	0	0	1.000	-1	/O	-0.1
Total	3	152	424	50	105	12	5	8	53	35	83	.248	.310	.356	89	-11	-7	44	3	4	-2	.982	-7	O	-2.0

■ PAT FRIEL Friel, Patrick Henry b: 6/11/1860, Lewsiburg, W.Va. d: 1/15/24, Providence, R.I. BB, 5'11", 170 lbs. Deb: 7/13/1890 F

YEAR	TM/L	G	AB	R	H	2B	3B	HR	RBI	BB	SO	AVG	OBP	SLG	PRO+	BR	/A	RC	SB	CS	SBR	FA	FR	POS	TPR
1890	Syr-a	62	261	51	65	8	2	3		17		.249	.302	.330	99	-4	0	37	34			.913	-6	O	-0.7
1891	Phi-a	2	8	2	2	1	0	0	0	0	0	.250	.250	.375	78	-0	-0	1	0			1.000	-1	/O	-0.1
Total	2	64	269	53	67	9	2	3	0	17	0	.249	.301	.331	98	-5	-0	38	34			.914	-7	/O	-0.8

YEAR	TM/L	G	AB	R	H	2B	3B	HR	RBI	BB	SO	AVG	OBP	SLG	PRO+	BR	/A	RC	SB	CS	SBR	FA	FR	POS	TPR

■ BILL FRIEL   Friel, William Edward   b: 4/1/1876, Renovo, Pa.   d: 12/24/59, St.Louis, Mo.   BL/TR, 5'10", 165 lbs.   Deb: 5/03/01   FU

1901	Mil-A	106	376	51	100	13	7	4	35	23		.266	.310	.370	92	-7	-4	50	15			.866	-9	3O/2S	-1.2
1902	StL-A	80	267	26	64	9	2	2	20	14		.240	.280	.311	64	-13	-13	26	4			.921	-13	O21/3SPC	-2.5
1903	StL-A	97	351	46	80	11	8	0	25	23		.228	.279	.305	77	-10	-9	33	4			.915	-10	23/O	-1.8
Total	3	283	994	123	244	33	17	6	80	60		.245	.291	.331	79	-31	-26	109	23			.924	-32	/2301SCP	-5.5

■ FRANK FRIEND   Friend, Frank B. (b: Frederick Freund)   b: Washington, D.C.   d: 9/5/1897, Atlantic City, N.J   Deb: 8/02/1896

| 1896 | Lou-N | 2 | 5 | 1 | 1 | 0 | 0 | 0 | 1 | 1 | | .200 | .333 | .200 | 46 | -0 | -0 | 0 | 0 | | | 1.000 | -0 | /C | 0.0 |

■ OWEN FRIEND   Friend, Owen Lacey "Red"   b: 3/21/27, Granite City, Ill.   BR/TR, 6'1", 180 lbs.   Deb: 10/02/49   C

1949	StL-A	2	8	1	3	0	0	0	0	0	1	.375	.375	.375	95	-0	-0	1	0	0	0	1.000	1	/2	0.1
1950	StL-A	119	372	48	88	15	2	8	50	40	68	.237	.312	.352	67	-18	-20	41	2	1	0	.961	10	23/S	-0.6
1953	Det-A	31	96	10	17	4	0	3	10	6	9	.177	.233	.313	47	-8	-8	6	0	1	-1	.947	4	2	-0.3
	Cle-A	34	68	7	16	2	0	2	13	5	16	.235	.288	.353	74	-3	-3	7	0	0	0	1.000	6	2/S3	0.4
	Yr	65	164	17	33	6	0	5	23	11	25	.201	.256	.329	58	-11	-10	12	0	1	-1	.964	10	2/S3	0.1
1955	Bos-A	14	42	3	11	3	0	0	2	4	11	.262	.326	.333	71	-1	-2	4	0	0	0	.951	2	S/2	0.1
	Chi-N	6	10	1	1	0	0	0	0	0	3	.100	.100	.100	-47	-2	-2	0	0	0	0	1.000	-1	/3S	-0.3
1956	Chi-N	2	2	0	0	0	0	0	0	0	2	.000	.000	.000	-99	-1	-1	0	0	0	0	.000	0	H	-0.1
Total	5	208	598	69	136	24	2	13	76	55	109	.227	.295	.339	63	-32	-35	59	2	2	-1	.963	23	2/3S	-0.7

■ BUCK FRIERSON   Frierson, Robert Lawrence   b: 7/29/17, Chicota, Tex.   BR/TR, 6'3", 195 lbs.   Deb: 9/09/41

| 1941 | Cle-A | 5 | 11 | 2 | 3 | 1 | 0 | 0 | 2 | 1 | 1 | .273 | .333 | .364 | 89 | -0 | -0 | 1 | 0 | 0 | 0 | 1.000 | -1 | /O | -0.1 |

■ PETE FRIES   Fries, Peter Martin   b: 10/30/1857, Scranton, Pa.   d: 7/30/37, Chicago, Ill.   BL/TL, 5'8", 160 lbs.   Deb: 8/10/1883

1883	Col-a	3	10	1	3	1	0	0			1	.300	.364	.400	158	1	1	1				.857	0	/P	0.0
1884	Ind-a	1	3	0	1	1	0	0				.333	.500	.667	290	1	1	1				.333	0	/O	0.1
Total	2	4	13	1	4	2	0	0			2	.308	.400	.462	191	1	1	3				.966	0	/PO	0.1

■ FRED FRINK   Frink, Fred Ferdinand   b: 8/25/11, Macon, Ga.   BR/TR, 6'1", 180 lbs.   Deb: 7/01/34

| 1934 | Phi-N | 2 | 0 | 0 | 0 | 0 | 0 | 0 | 0 | 0 | 0 | — | — | — | | 0 | 0 | 0 | | | | .000 | -1 | /H | -0.1 |

■ CHARLIE FRISBEE   Frisbee, Charles Augustus "Bunt"   b: 2/2/1874, Dows, Iowa   d: 11/7/54, Alden, Iowa   BB/TR, 5'9", 175 lbs.   Deb: 6/22/1899

1899	Bos-N	42	152	22	50	4	2	0	20	9		.329	.374	.382	98	2	-1	27	10			.875	-2	O	-0.5
1900	NY-N	4	13	2	2	1	0	0	3	2		.154	.267	.231	40	-1	-1	1	0			.400	-2	/O	-0.3
Total	2	46	165	24	52	5	2	0	23	11		.315	.365	.370	94	1	-2	28	10			.849	-4	/O	-0.8

■ FRANKIE FRISCH   Frisch, Frank Francis "The Fordham Flash"   b: 9/9/1898, Bronx, N.Y.   d: 3/12/73, Wilmington, Del.   BB/TR, 5'11", 165 lbs.   Deb: 6/14/19   MCH

1919	NY-N	54	190	21	43	3	2	2	24	4	14	.226	.242	.295	62	-9	-9	16	15			.972	4	23/S	-0.4
1920	NY-N	110	440	57	123	10	10	4	77	20	18	.280	.311	.375	97	-3	-3	52	34	11	4	.967	9	*3/S	1.6
1921	*NY-N	153	618	121	211	31	17	8	100	42	28	.341	.384	.485	128	25	25	118	49	13	7	.936	4	32	4.3
1922	*NY-N	132	514	101	168	16	13	5	51	47	13	.327	.387	.438	111	10	9	87	31	17	-1	.975	13	23/S	2.5
1923	*NY-N	151	641	116	**223**	32	10	12	111	46	12	.348	.395	.485	133	28	29	123	29	12	2	**.973**	4	*23	2.5
1924	*NY-N	145	603	**121**	198	33	15	7	69	56	24	.328	.387	.468	132	24	27	111	22	9	1	.972	25	*2S/3	5.3
1925	NY-N	120	502	89	166	26	6	11	48	32	14	.331	.374	.472	119	11	13	87	21	12	-1	.931	5	32S	2.3
1926	NY-N	135	545	75	171	29	4	5	44	33	16	.314	.353	.409	106	3	4	76	23			.975	11	*2/3	1.8
1927	StL-N	153	617	112	208	31	11	10	78	43	10	.337	.387	.472	125	25	22	109	**48**			**.979**	49	*2/S	**7.3**
1928	*StL-N	141	547	107	164	29	9	10	86	64	17	.300	.374	.441	110	10	9	90	29			**.976**	3	*2	1.5
1929	StL-N	138	527	93	176	40	12	5	74	53	12	.334	.397	.484	116	15	14	99	24			.970	-4	23/S	1.4
1930	StL-N	133	540	121	187	46	9	10	114	55	16	.346	.407	.520	118	20	17	111	15			.969	**28**	*23	4.5
1931	*StL-N	131	518	96	161	24	4	4	82	45	13	.311	.368	.396	101	5	2	78	**28**			.974	16	*2	2.6
1932	StL-N	115	486	59	142	26	3	2	60	25	13	.292	.327	.372	85	-8	-10	60	18			.971	16	23/S	1.3
1933	StL-N★	147	585	74	177	32	6	4	66	48	16	.303	.358	.398	110	13	9	83	18			.982	-3	*2SM	1.6
1934	*StL-N☆	140	550	74	168	30	6	3	75	45	10	.305	.359	.398	96	-3	-2	79	11			.977	5	*23M	1.0
1935	StL-N☆	103	354	52	104	16	2	1	55	33	16	.294	.356	.359	89	-3	-5	48	2			.982	-7	2/3M	-0.5
1936	StL-N	93	303	40	83	10	0	1	26	36	10	.274	.353	.317	82	-6	-6	36	2			.965	-13	23/SM	-1.4
1937	StL-N	17	32	3	7	2	0	0	4	1	0	.219	.242	.281	41	-3	-3	2	0			1.000	-1	/2M	-0.4
Total	19	2311	9112	1532	2880	466	138	105	1244	728	272	.316	.369	.432	110	158	143	1464	419	74		.974	150	*23/S	38.8

■ EMIL FRISK   Frisk, John Emil   b: 10/15/1874, Kalkaska, Mich.   d: 1/27/22, Seattle, Wash.   BL/TR, 6'1", 190 lbs.   Deb: 9/02/1899

1899	Cin-N	9	25	5	7	1	0	0	2	2		.280	.333	.320	78	-1	-1	3	0			.950	-0	/P	0.0
1901	Det-A	20	48	10	15	3	0	1	7	3		.313	.365	.438	117	1	1	8	0			.851	2	P/O	0.0
1905	StL-A	124	429	58	112	11	6	3	36	42		.261	.341	.336	121	9	11	54	7			.923	-8	*O	-0.2
1907	StL-A	5	4	0	1	0	0	0	0	1		.250	.400	.250	109	0	0	0	0			.000	0	H	0.0
Total	4	158	506	73	135	15	6	4	45	48		.267	.343	.344	119	9	12	65	7			.918	-6	O/P	-0.2

■ HARRY FRITZ   Fritz, Harry Koch "Dutchman"   b: 9/30/1890, Philadelphia, Pa.   d: 11/4/74, Columbus, Ohio   BR/TR, 5'8", 170 lbs.   Deb: 9/29/13

1913	Phi-A	5	13	1	0	0	0	0	2	0	4	.000	.188	.000	-45	-2	-2	0	0			.846	-1	/3	-0.4
1914	Chi-F	65	174	16	37	5	1	0	13	18	18	.213	.297	.253	61	-9	-8	15	2			.912	-9	3/S2	-1.6
1915	Chi-F	79	236	27	59	8	4	3	26	13	27	.250	.298	.356	97	-3	-2	28	4			.964	-9	3/2S	-0.8
Total	3	149	423	44	96	13	5	3	39	33	49	.227	.294	.303	77	-15	-12	44	6			.941	-19	3/S2	-2.8

■ LARRY FRITZ   Fritz, Lawrence Joseph   b: 2/14/49, E.Chicago, Ind.   BL/TL, 6'2", 225 lbs.   Deb: 5/30/75

| 1975 | Phi-N | 1 | 1 | 0 | 0 | 0 | 0 | 0 | 0 | 0 | 0 | .000 | .000 | .000 | -96 | -0 | -0 | 0 | 0 | 0 | 0 | .000 | 0 | H | 0.0 |

■ DOUG FROBEL   Frobel, Douglas Steven   b: 6/6/59, Ottawa, Ont., Can.   BL/TL, 6'4", 196 lbs.   Deb: 9/05/82

1982	Pit-N	16	34	5	7	2	0	2	3	1	11	.206	.229	.441	81	-1	-1	3	1	1	-0	1.000	0	O	-0.2
1983	Pit-N	32	60	10	17	4	1	3	11	4	17	.283	.328	.533	132	2	2	9	1	1	-0	.964	-1	O	0.1
1984	Pit-N	126	276	33	56	9	3	12	28	24	84	.203	.272	.388	83	-7	-7	27	7	5	-1	.956	1	*O	-1.0
1985	Pit-N	53	109	14	22	5	0	1	7	19	24	.202	.320	.248	62	-5	-5	9	4	3	-1	.941	-3	O	-1.0
	Mon-N	12	23	3	3	1	0	1	4	2	6	.130	.200	.304	42	-2	-2	1	0	0	0	.923	-0	/O	-0.2
	Yr	65	132	17	25	6	0	1	11	21	30	.189	.301	.258	59	-7	-7	11	4	3	-1	.938	-3	O	-1.2
1987	Cle-A	29	40	5	4	0	0	2	5	5	13	.100	.200	.250	18	-5	-5	2	0	0	0	1.000	-3	O/D	-0.7
Total	5	268	542	70	109	21	4	20	58	55	155	.201	.277	.365	78	-18	-18	52	13	10	-2	.957	-6	O/D	-3.1

■ BEN FROELICH   Froelich, William Palmer   b: 11/12/1887, Pittsburgh, Pa.   d: 9/1/16, Pittsburgh, Pa.   BR/TR,   Deb: 7/02/09

| 1909 | Phi-N | 1 | 1 | 0 | 0 | 0 | 0 | 0 | 0 | 0 | 0 | .000 | .000 | .000 | -99 | -0 | -0 | 0 | 0 | | | .000 | 0 | /C | 0.0 |

■ JERRY FRY   Fry, Jerry Ray   b: 2/29/56, Salinas, Cal.   BR/TR, 6', 185 lbs.   Deb: 9/04/78

| 1978 | Mon-N | 4 | 9 | 0 | 0 | 0 | 0 | 0 | 0 | 1 | 5 | .000 | .100 | .000 | -71 | -2 | -2 | 0 | 0 | 0 | 0 | 1.000 | 1 | /C | -0.1 |

■ JEFF FRYE   Frye, Jeffrey Dustin   b: 8/31/66, Oakland, Cal.   BR/TR, 5'9", 180 lbs.   Deb: 7/09/92

| 1992 | Tex-A | 67 | 199 | 24 | 51 | 9 | 1 | 1 | 12 | 16 | 27 | .256 | .321 | .327 | 85 | -5 | -4 | 22 | 1 | 3 | -2 | .978 | 8 | 2 | 0.4 |

■ TRAVIS FRYMAN   Fryman, David Travis   b: 4/25/69, Lexington, Ky.   BR/TR, 6'1", 180 lbs.   Deb: 7/07/90

| 1990 | Det-A | 66 | 232 | 32 | 69 | 11 | 3 | 9 | 27 | 17 | 51 | .297 | .348 | .470 | 126 | 8 | 7 | 37 | 3 | 3 | -1 | .915 | 5 | 3S/D | 1.3 |
| 1991 | Det-A | 149 | 557 | 65 | 144 | 36 | 3 | 21 | 91 | 40 | 149 | .259 | .312 | .447 | 106 | 4 | 3 | 75 | 12 | 5 | 1 | .946 | -9 | 3S | -0.1 |

YEAR	TM/L	G	AB	R	H	2B	3B	HR	RBI	BB	SO	AVG	OBP	SLG	PRO+	BR	/A	RC	SB	CS	SBR	FA	FR	POS	TPR
1992	Det-A★	161	659	87	175	31	4	20	96	45	144	.266	.318	.416	103	2	1	86	8	4	0	.970	-4	*S3	0.7
Total	3	376	1448	184	388	78	8	50	214	102	344	.268	.321	.436	108	13	11	199	23	12	-0	.967	-9	S3/D	1.9

■ MIKE FUENTES

Fuentes, Michael Jay b: 7/11/58, Miami, Fla. BR/TR, 6'3", 190 lbs. Deb: 9/02/83

YEAR	TM/L	G	AB	R	H	2B	3B	HR	RBI	BB	SO	AVG	OBP	SLG	PRO+	BR	/A	RC	SB	CS	SBR	FA	FR	POS	TPR
1983	Mon-N	6	4	1	1	0	0	0	0	0	2	.250	.250	.250	39	-0	-0	0	0	0	0	.000	0	/H	0.0
1984	Mon-N	3	4	0	1	0	0	0	0	1	2	.250	.400	.250	90	-0	0	1	0	0	0	1.000	0	/O	0.0
Total	2	9	8	1	2	0	0	0	0	1	4	.250	.333	.250	67	-0	-0	1	0	0	0	.967	0	/O	0.0

■ TITO FUENTES

Fuentes, Rigoberto (Peat) b: 1/4/44, Havana, Cuba BB/TR, 5'11", 175 lbs. Deb: 8/18/65

YEAR	TM/L	G	AB	R	H	2B	3B	HR	RBI	BB	SO	AVG	OBP	SLG	PRO+	BR	/A	RC	SB	CS	SBR	FA	FR	POS	TPR
1965	SF-N	26	72	12	15	1	0	0	1	5	14	.208	.269	.222	39	-6	-6	4	0	1	-1	.919	-7	S/23	-1.3
1966	SF-N	133	541	63	141	21	3	9	40	9	57	.261	.277	.360	73	-19	-20	53	6	3	0	.957	-14	S2	-2.4
1967	SF-N	133	344	27	72	12	1	5	29	27	61	.209	.267	.294	61	-18	-17	26	4	3	-1	.980	25	*2/S	1.4
1969	SF-N	67	183	28	54	4	3	1	14	15	25	.295	.352	.366	103	1	1	24	2	4	-2	.925	-6	3S	-0.5
1970	SF-N	123	435	49	116	13	7	2	32	36	52	.267	.327	.343	81	-12	-12	49	4	5	-2	.966	-2	2S3	-0.7
1971	*SF-N	152	630	63	172	28	6	4	52	18	46	.273	.300	.356	86	-14	-13	65	12	2	2	.973	1	*2	0.4
1972	SF-N	152	572	64	151	33	6	7	53	39	56	.264	.314	.379	95	-4	-5	69	16	5	2	.964	-21	*2	-1.6
1973	SF-N	160	656	78	182	25	5	6	63	45	62	.277	.331	.358	87	-8	-11	79	12	6	0	**.993**	-5	*2/3	-0.7
1974	SF-N	108	390	33	97	15	2	0	22	22	32	.249	.294	.297	63	-18	-20	33	7	3	0	.979	-4	*2	-2.0
1975	SD-N	146	565	57	158	21	3	4	43	25	51	.280	.314	.349	89	-13	-9	58	8	8	-2	.970	4	*2	0.0
1976	SD-N	135	520	48	137	18	0	2	36	18	38	.263	.289	.310	76	-21	-16	45	5	3	-0	.971	2	*2	-0.7
1977	Det-A	151	615	83	190	19	10	5	51	38	61	.309	.351	.397	98	3	-1	85	4	4	-1	.970	3	*2/D	1.1
1978	Oak-A	13	43	5	6	1	0	0	2	1	6	.140	.159	.163	-10	-6	-6	1	0	0	0	.944	-12	2	-1.8
Total	13	1499	5566	610	1491	211	46	45	438	298	561	.268	.309	.347	82	-135	-135	593	80	47	-4	.974	-37	*2S/3D	-8.8

■ OLLIE FUHRMAN

Fuhrman, Alfred George b: 7/20/1896, Jordan, Minn. d: 1/11/69, Peoria, Ill. BB/TR, 5'11", 185 lbs. Deb: 4/13/22

YEAR	TM/L	G	AB	R	H	2B	3B	HR	RBI	BB	SO	AVG	OBP	SLG	PRO+	BR	/A	RC	SB	CS	SBR	FA	FR	POS	TPR
1922	Phi-A	6	6	1	2	1	0	0	0	0	0	.333	.333	.500	112	0	0	1	0	0	0	1.000	0	/C	0.0

■ DOT FULGHUM

Fulghum, James Lavoisier b: 7/4/1900, Valdosta, Ga. d: 11/11/67, Miami, Fla. BR/TR, 5'8.5", 165 lbs. Deb: 9/15/21

YEAR	TM/L	G	AB	R	H	2B	3B	HR	RBI	BB	SO	AVG	OBP	SLG	PRO+	BR	/A	RC	SB	CS	SBR	FA	FR	POS	TPR
1921	Phi-A	2	2	0	0	0	0	0	0	1	1	.000	.333	.000	-9	-0	-0	0	0	0	0	.000	0	/S	0.0

■ NIG FULLER

Fuller, Charles F. b: 3/30/1879, Toledo, Ohio d: 11/12/47, Toledo, Ohio BR/TR, Deb: 7/01/02

YEAR	TM/L	G	AB	R	H	2B	3B	HR	RBI	BB	SO	AVG	OBP	SLG	PRO+	BR	/A	RC	SB	CS	SBR	FA	FR	POS	TPR
1902	Bro-N	3	9	0	0	0	0	0	1	0		.000	.000	.000	-99	-2	-2	0	0			1.000	-1	/C	-0.3

■ FRANK FULLER

Fuller, Frank Edward "Rabbit" b: 1/1/1893, Detroit, Mich. d: 10/29/65, Warren, Mich. BB/TR, 5'7", 150 lbs. Deb: 4/14/15

YEAR	TM/L	G	AB	R	H	2B	3B	HR	RBI	BB	SO	AVG	OBP	SLG	PRO+	BR	/A	RC	SB	CS	SBR	FA	FR	POS	TPR
1915	Det-A	14	32	6	5	0	0	0	2	9	7	.156	.341	.156	47	-1	-2	2	2	3	-1	.962	-6	/2S	-0.9
1916	Det-A	20	10	2	1	0	0	0	1	1	4	.100	.182	.100	-15	-1	-1	1	3			.846	3	/2S	0.1
1923	Bos-A	6	21	3	5	0	0	0	0	1	1	.238	.273	.238	35	-2	-2	1	1	1	-0	.952	2	/2	0.0
Total	3	40	63	11	11	0	0	0	3	11	12	.175	.297	.175	35	-5	-5	4	6	4		.938	-1	/2S	-0.8

■ HARRY FULLER

Fuller, Henry W. b: 12/5/1862, Cincinnati, Ohio d: 12/12/1895, Cincinnati, Ohio Deb: 4/08/1891 F

YEAR	TM/L	G	AB	R	H	2B	3B	HR	RBI	BB	SO	AVG	OBP	SLG	PRO+	BR	/A	RC	SB	CS	SBR	FA	FR	POS	TPR
1891	StL-a	1	2	0	0	0	0	0	0	0	1	.000	.000	.000	-87	-1	-1	0	0			.000	-1	/3	-0.1

■ JIM FULLER

Fuller, James Hardy b: 11/28/50, Bethesda, Md. BR/TR, 6'3", 215 lbs. Deb: 9/10/73

YEAR	TM/L	G	AB	R	H	2B	3B	HR	RBI	BB	SO	AVG	OBP	SLG	PRO+	BR	/A	RC	SB	CS	SBR	FA	FR	POS	TPR
1973	Bal-A	9	26	2	3	0	0	2	4	1	17	.115	.148	.346	36	-2	-2	1	0	0	0	1.000	1	/O1D	-0.1
1974	Bal-A	64	189	17	42	11	0	7	28	8	68	.222	.265	.392	90	-4	-3	19	1	0	0	.960	-2	O/1D	-0.8
1977	Hou-N	34	100	5	16	6	0	2	9	10	45	.160	.243	.280	44	-9	-8	7	0	1	-1	.983	3	O/1	-0.7
Total	3	107	315	24	61	17	0	11	41	19	130	.194	.249	.352	70	-15	-13	27	1	1	-0	.969	2	/O1D	-1.6

■ JOHN FULLER

Fuller, John Edward b: 1/29/50, Lynwood, Cal. BL/TL, 6'2", 180 lbs. Deb: 5/09/74

YEAR	TM/L	G	AB	R	H	2B	3B	HR	RBI	BB	SO	AVG	OBP	SLG	PRO+	BR	/A	RC	SB	CS	SBR	FA	FR	POS	TPR
1974	Atl-N	3	3	1	1	0	0	0	0	0	0	.333	.333	.333	83	-0	-0	0	0	0	0	1.000	0	/O	0.0

■ VERN FULLER

Fuller, Vernon Gordon b: 3/1/44, Menomonie, Wis. BR/TR, 6'1", 170 lbs. Deb: 9/05/64

YEAR	TM/L	G	AB	R	H	2B	3B	HR	RBI	BB	SO	AVG	OBP	SLG	PRO+	BR	/A	RC	SB	CS	SBR	FA	FR	POS	TPR
1964	Cle-A	2	1	0	0	0	0	0	0	0	0	.000	.000	.000	-99	-0	-0	0	0	0	0	.000	0	H	0.0
1966	Cle-A	16	47	7	11	2	1	2	2	7	6	.234	.357	.447	129	2	2	8	0	0	0	1.000	-4	2	-0.1
1967	Cle-A	73	206	18	46	10	0	7	21	19	55	.223	.301	.374	98	-1	-1	24	2	3	-1	.986	0	2/S	0.2
1968	Cle-A	97	244	14	59	8	2	0	18	24	49	.242	.320	.291	87	-3	-3	24	2	2	-1	.988	-12	23/S	-1.4
1969	Cle-A	108	254	25	60	11	1	4	22	20	53	.236	.297	.335	74	-8	-9	24	2	1	0	.978	9	*2/3	0.6
1970	Cle-A	29	33	3	6	2	0	1	2	3	9	.182	.250	.333	57	-2	-2	3	0	0	0	.919	3	2/31	0.1
Total	6	325	785	67	182	33	4	14	65	73	172	.232	.307	.338	87	-12	-13	82	6	6	-2	.982	-4	2/3S1	-0.6

■ SHORTY FULLER

Fuller, William Benjamin b: 10/10/1867, Cincinnati, Ohio d: 4/11/04, Cincinnati, Ohio BR/TR, 5'6", 157 lbs. Deb: 7/19/1888 F

YEAR	TM/L	G	AB	R	H	2B	3B	HR	RBI	BB	SO	AVG	OBP	SLG	PRO+	BR	/A	RC	SB	CS	SBR	FA	FR	POS	TPR
1888	Was-N	49	170	11	31	5	2	0	12	10	14	.182	.232	.235	54	-9	-8	11	6			.845	-6	S/2	-1.2
1889	StL-a	140	517	91	117	18	6	0	51	52	56	.226	.303	.284	62	-19	-31	57	38			**.913**	0	*S	-2.0
1890	StL-a	130	526	118	146	9	9	1		73		.278	.377	.335	99	12	-1	91	60			.870	-1	*S	0.5
1891	StL-a	137	586	107	127	15	7	2	63	67	28	.217	.301	.276	59	-23	-38	63	42			.856	-10	*S2	-3.5
1892	NY-N	141	508	74	115	11	4	1	48	52	22	.226	.298	.270	75	-15	-14	53	37			.888	1	*S	-0.7
1893	NY-N	130	474	78	112	14	8	0	51	60	21	.236	.325	.300	68	-21	-21	56	26			.911	11	*S	-0.4
1894	*NY-N	93	368	81	104	14	4	2	46	52	16	.283	.374	.359	80	-11	-10	63	32			.884	-5	*S/O32	-0.8
1895	NY-N	126	458	82	103	11	3	0	32	64	34	.225	.323	.262	55	-29	-27	46	15			.913	34	*S	1.0
1896	NY-N	18	72	10	12	0	0	0	7	14	5	.167	.310	.167	30	-7	-6	5	4			.874	1	S	-0.4
Total	9	964	3679	652	867	97	43	6	310	444	196	.236	.323	.290	69	-122	-156	445	260			.891	26	S/23O	-7.5

■ CHICK FULLIS

Fullis, Charles Philip b: 2/27/04, Girardville, Pa. d: 3/28/46, Ashland, Pa. BR/TR, 5'9", 170 lbs. Deb: 4/13/28

YEAR	TM/L	G	AB	R	H	2B	3B	HR	RBI	BB	SO	AVG	OBP	SLG	PRO+	BR	/A	RC	SB	CS	SBR	FA	FR	POS	TPR
1928	NY-N	11	1	5	0	0	0	0	0	1	1	.000	.500	.000	41	0	0	0	0			.000	0	H	0.0
1929	NY-N	86	274	67	79	11	1	7	29	30	26	.288	.365	.412	92	-3	-3	41	7			.962	-12	O	-1.8
1930	NY-N	13	6	2	0	0	0	0	0	0	1	.000	.000	.000	-99	-2	-2	0	1			.000	-1	/O	-0.3
1931	NY-N	89	302	61	99	15	2	3	28	23	13	.328	.383	.421	119	7	8	50	13			.988	-4	O/2	0.1
1932	NY-N	96	235	35	70	14	3	1	21	11	12	.298	.332	.396	97	-2	-1	31	1			.990	-8	O/2	-1.2
1933	Phi-N	151	647	91	200	31	6	1	45	36	34	.309	.350	.380	96	7	-2	87	18			.977	8	*O/3	-0.2
1934	Phi-N	28	102	8	23	6	0	0	12	10	4	.225	.301	.284	51	-6	-8	10	2			.956	-4	O	-1.3
	*StL-N	69	199	21	52	9	1	0	26	14	11	.261	.310	.317	64	-9	-10	19	4			.969	-3	O	-1.5
	Yr	97	301	29	75	15	1	0	38	24	15	.249	.307	.306	59	-15	-18	29	6			.966	-6	O	-2.8
1936	StL-N	47	89	15	25	6	1	0	6	7	11	.281	.333	.371	90	-1	-1	12	0			1.000	-1	O	-0.3
Total	8	590	1855	305	548	92	14	12	167	132	113	.295	.347	.380	92	-8	-19	250	46			.977	-23	O/23	-6.5

■ CHICK FULMER

Fulmer, Charles John b: 2/12/1851, Philadelphia, Pa. d: 2/15/40, Philadelphia, Pa. BR/TR, 6', 158 lbs. Deb: 8/23/1871 FU

YEAR	TM/L	G	AB	R	H	2B	3B	HR	RBI	BB	SO	AVG	OBP	SLG	PRO+	BR	/A	RC	SB	CS	SBR	FA	FR	POS	TPR
1871	Rok-n	16	63	11	17	1	3	0	3	5	1	.270	.324	.381	106	0	1	8	0					S/1	0.1
1872	Mut-n	36	167	28	51	2	1	1	12	2	3	.305	.314	.347	110	1	3	18						3S	0.0
1873	Phi-n	49	236	42	66	11	3	1	37	2	3	.280	.286	.364	87	-3	-5	26						*S/PC1	-0.4
1874	Phi-n	57	259	49	72	5	3	0		1		.278	.281	.320	88	-3	-4	24						S3	-0.4
1875	Phi-n	69	293	50	65	5	1	0		0		.222	.222	.246	59	-11	-13	16						*S3	-1.3
1876	Lou-N	66	267	28	73	9	5	1	29	1	10	.273	.276	.356	93	2	-5	27				.861	-3	*S	-0.7
1879	Buf-N	76	306	30	82	11	5	0	28	5	34	.268	.280	.337	100	1	-0	30				.905	17	*2	2.0
1880	Buf-N	11	44	3	7	0	0	0	1	2	4	.159	.196	.159	21	-3	-4	1				.882	-2	2	-0.5
1882	Cin-a	79	324	54	91	13	4	0		10		.281	.302	.346	112	6	3	35				**.897**	-13	*S	-0.6
1883	Cin-a	92	361	52	93	13	5	5		13		.258	.283	.363	101	2	-1	38				.863	-2	*S	0.0

YEAR	TM/L	G	AB	R	H	2B	3B	HR	RBI	BB	SO	AVG	OBP	SLG	PRO+	BR	/A	RC	SB	CS	SBR	FA	FR	POS	TPR
1884	Cin-a	31	114	13	20	2	1	0		1		.175	.183	.211	28	-8	-9	4				.786	-10	S/O3	-1.8
	StL-a	1	5	0	0	0	0	0		0		.000	.000	.000	-97	-1	-1	0				.778	-1	/2	-0.2
	Yr	32	119	13	20	2	1	0		1		.168	.175	.202	23	-9	-10	4				.786	-11	S/O32	-2.0
Total	5 n	227	1018	180	271	24	11	2	52	10	7	.266	.273	.317	85	-16	-18	92						S/3P1C	-2.0
Total	6	356	1421	180	366	48	20	6	58	32	48	.258	.274	.332	93	-2	-17	135				.867	-13	S/2O3	-1.8

■ CHRIS FULMER
Fulmer, Christopher b: 7/4/1858, Tamaqua, Pa. d: 11/9/31, Tamaqua, Pa. BR/TR, 5'8", 165 lbs. Deb: 8/04/1884

YEAR	TM/L	G	AB	R	H	2B	3B	HR	RBI	BB	SO	AVG	OBP	SLG	PRO+	BR	/A	RC	SB	CS	SBR	FA	FR	POS	TPR
1884	Was-U	48	181	39	50	9	0	0		11		.276	.318	.326	122	4	5	19				.937	0	CO/1	0.6
1886	Bal-a	80	270	54	66	9	3	1		48		.244	.363	.311	117	7	8	42	29			.949	-4	CO/P	1.0
1887	Bal-a	56	201	52	54	11	4	0		36		.269	.382	.363	118	5	7	42	35			.913	-11	C/O	0.0
1888	Bal-a	52	166	20	31	5	1	0	10	21		.187	.286	.229	70	-5	-4	14	10			.903	-16	C/O	-1.5
1889	Bal-a	16	58	11	15	3	1	0	13	6	12	.259	.338	.345	95	-0	-0	8	2			.938	-5	O/C	-0.5
Total	5	252	876	176	216	37	9	1	23	122	12	.247	.343	.313	108	10	15	125	76			.929	-36	C/O1P	-0.4

■ WASHINGTON FULMER
Fulmer, Washington Fayette b: 6/15/1840, Philadelphia, Pa. d: 12/8/07, Philadelphia, Pa. Deb: 7/19/1875 F

YEAR	TM/L	G	AB	R	H	2B	3B	HR	RBI	BB	SO	AVG	OBP	SLG	PRO+	BR	/A	RC	SB	CS	SBR	FA	FR	POS	TPR
1875	Atl-n	1	4	1	2	0	0	0		0		.500	.500	.500	284	1	1	1						/3	0.1

■ DAVE FULTZ
Fultz, David Lewis b: 5/29/1875, Staunton, Va. d: 10/29/59, DeLand, Fla. BR/TR, 5'11", 170 lbs. Deb: 7/01/1898

YEAR	TM/L	G	AB	R	H	2B	3B	HR	RBI	BB	SO	AVG	OBP	SLG	PRO+	BR	/A	RC	SB	CS	SBR	FA	FR	POS	TPR
1898	Phi-N	19	55	7	10	2	2	0	5	6		.182	.262	.291	61	-3	-3	5	1			.871	-1	O/2S	-0.4
1899	Phi-N	2	5	0	2	0	0	0	0	0		.400	.400	.400	124	0	0	1	1			.750	-1	/2S	-0.1
	Bal-N	57	210	31	62	3	2	0	18	13		.295	.342	.329	80	-4	-6	31	17			.940	-6	O3/21	-1.3
	Yr	59	215	31	64	3	2	0	18	13		.298	.343	.330	81	-4	-6	32	18			.940	-7	O3/2S1	-1.4
1901	Phi-A	132	561	95	164	17	9	0	52	32		.292	.334	.355	87	-7	-11	82	36			.935	-6	*O2/S	-2.1
1902	Phi-A	129	506	**109**	153	20	5	1	49	62		.302	.382	.368	104	8	5	94	44			.961	-5	*O2	-0.7
1903	NY-A	79	295	39	66	12	1	0	25	25		.224	.293	.271	66	-10	-12	34	29			.933	-2	O/3	-1.9
1904	NY-A	97	339	39	93	17	4	2	32	24		.274	.322	.366	112	6	5	49	17			.976	3	O	0.2
1905	NY-A	129	422	49	98	13	3	0	42	39		.232	.306	.277	77	-6	-11	52	44			.966	-6	*O	-2.6
Total	7	644	2393	369	648	84	26	3	223	201		.271	.332	.331	89	-15	-33	348	189			.952	-25	O/23S1	-8.9

■ MARK FUNDERBURK
Funderburk, Mark Clifford b: 5/16/57, Charlotte, N.C. BR/TR, 6'4", 226 lbs. Deb: 9/04/81

YEAR	TM/L	G	AB	R	H	2B	3B	HR	RBI	BB	SO	AVG	OBP	SLG	PRO+	BR	/A	RC	SB	CS	SBR	FA	FR	POS	TPR
1981	Min-A	8	15	2	3	1	0	0	2	2	1	.200	.294	.267	59	-1	-1	1	0	0	0	1.000	-1	/OD	-0.2
1985	Min-A	23	70	7	22	7	1	2	13	5	12	.314	.360	.529	132	4	3	11	0	1	-1	1.000	-1	D/O1	0.1
Total	2	31	85	9	25	8	1	2	15	7	13	.294	.348	.482	120	3	2	13	0	1	-1	1.000	-2	/DO1	-0.1

■ LIZ FUNK
Funk, Elias Calvin b: 10/28/04, LaCygne, Kan. d: 1/16/68, Norman, Okla. BL/TL, 5'8.5", 160 lbs. Deb: 4/26/29

YEAR	TM/L	G	AB	R	H	2B	3B	HR	RBI	BB	SO	AVG	OBP	SLG	PRO+	BR	/A	RC	SB	CS	SBR	FA	FR	POS	TPR
1929	NY-A	1	0	0	0	0	0	0	0	0	0	—	—	—	—	0	0	0	0	0	0	.000	0	R	0.0
1930	Det-A	140	527	74	145	26	11	4	65	29	39	.275	.319	.389	77	-18	-20	66	12	6	0	.965	8	*O	-1.9
1932	Chi-A	122	440	59	114	21	5	2	40	43	19	.259	.325	.343	78	-17	-13	49	17	15	-4	.979	7	*O	-1.6
1933	Chi-A	10	9	1	2	0	0	0	0	1	0	.222	.300	.222	42	-1	-1	1	0	0	0	.000	-1	/O	-0.2
Total	4	273	976	134	261	47	16	6	105	73	58	.267	.322	.367	77	-36	-33	115	29	21	-4	.972	14	O	-3.7

■ CARL FURILLO
Furillo, Carl Anthony "Skoonj" or "The Reading Rifle"
b: 3/8/22, Stony Creek Mills, Pa. d: 1/21/89, Stony Creek Mills, Pa. BR/TR, 6', 190 lbs. Deb: 4/16/46

YEAR	TM/L	G	AB	R	H	2B	3B	HR	RBI	BB	SO	AVG	OBP	SLG	PRO+	BR	/A	RC	SB	CS	SBR	FA	FR	POS	TPR
1946	Bro-N	117	335	29	95	18	6	3	35	31	20	.284	.346	.400	110	4	4	46	6			.984	9	*O	0.9
1947	*Bro-N	124	437	61	129	24	7	8	88	34	24	.295	.347	.437	103	3	1	62	7			.977	2	*O	-0.2
1948	Bro-N	108	364	55	108	20	4	4	44	43	32	.297	.374	.407	108	7	5	57	6			.983	9	*O	0.9
1949	*Bro-N	142	549	95	177	27	10	18	106	37	29	.322	.368	.506	127	23	20	98	4			.965	5	*O	1.8
1950	Bro-N	153	620	99	189	30	6	18	106	41	40	.305	.353	.460	110	9	8	96	8			.971	3	*O	0.4
1951	Bro-N	158	667	93	197	32	4	16	91	43	33	.295	.344	.427	104	5	3	97	8	7	-2	.986	16	*O	1.2
1952	*Bro-N☆	134	425	52	105	18	1	8	59	31	33	.247	.304	.351	80	-11	-12	42	1	4	-2	.988	-1	*O	-2.0
1953	*Bro-N☆	132	479	82	165	38	6	21	92	34	32	**.344**	.393	.580	146	33	32	107	1	1	-0	.988	4	*O	3.0
1954	Bro-N	150	547	56	161	23	1	19	96	49	35	.294	.358	.444	104	6	4	83	2	4	-2	.972	4	*O	0.0
1955	*Bro-N	140	523	83	164	24	3	26	95	43	43	.314	.373	.520	130	25	23	97	4	5	-2	.981	-3	*O	1.1
1956	*Bro-N	149	523	66	151	30	0	21	83	57	41	.289	.360	.467	111	15	10	80	1	1	-0	.984	-9	*O	-0.7
1957	Bro-N	119	395	61	121	17	4	12	66	29	33	.306	.361	.461	108	10	6	62	0	2	-1	.988	-5	*O	-0.7
1958	LA-N	122	411	54	119	19	3	18	83	35	28	.290	.348	.482	113	9	8	64	0	2	-1	.975	-8	*O	-0.7
1959	*LA-N	50	93	8	27	4	0	0	13	7	11	.290	.340	.333	75	-2	-3	10	0	0	0	.920	-5	O	-0.9
1960	LA-N	8	10	1	2	0	1	0	1	0	2	.200	.200	.400	56	-1	-1	1	0	0	0	1.000	-0	/O	-0.1
Total	15	1806	6378	895	1910	324	56	192	1058	514	436	.299	.356	.458	112	136	107	1004	48	26		.979	22	*O	4.0

■ EDDIE FUSSELBACK
Fusselback, Edward L. b: 7/17/1856, Philadelphia, Pa. d: 4/14/26, Philadelphia, Pa. 5'6", 156 lbs. Deb: 5/03/1882

YEAR	TM/L	G	AB	R	H	2B	3B	HR	RBI	BB	SO	AVG	OBP	SLG	PRO+	BR	/A	RC	SB	CS	SBR	FA	FR	POS	TPR
1882	StL-a	35	136	13	31	2	0	0		5		.228	.255	.243	66	-4	-5	9				.853	2	CO/P	-0.1
1884	Bal-U	68	303	60	86	16	3	1		3		.284	.291	.366	109	6	1	33				.912	18	C/3SO	2.1
1885	Phi-a	5	19	2	6	1	0	0		0		.316	.316	.368	112	0	0	2				.911	1	/C	0.1
1888	Lou-a	1	4	0	1	0	0	0	1	0		.250	.250	.250	64	-0	-0	0	0			1.000	0	/O	0.0
Total	4	109	462	75	124	19	3	1	1	8		.268	.281	.329	97	2	-4	44	0			.901	21	/CO3SP	2.1

■ LES FUSSELMAN
Fusselman, Lester Leroy b: 3/7/21, Pryor, Okla. d: 5/21/70, Cleveland, Ohio BR/TR, 6'1", 195 lbs. Deb: 4/16/52

YEAR	TM/L	G	AB	R	H	2B	3B	HR	RBI	BB	SO	AVG	OBP	SLG	PRO+	BR	/A	RC	SB	CS	SBR	FA	FR	POS	TPR
1952	StL-N	32	63	5	10	3	0	1	3	0	9	.159	.159	.254	13	-8	-8	2	0	0	0	.991	3	C	-0.4
1953	StL-N	11	8	1	2	1	0	0	0	0	0	.250	.250	.375	60	-0	-0	0	0	0	0	1.000	2	C	0.1
Total	2	43	71	6	12	4	0	1	3	0	9	.169	.169	.268	18	-8	-8	3	0	0	0	.992	5	/C	-0.3

■ GABE GABLER
Gabler, William Louis b: 8/4/30, St.Louis, Mo. BL/TR, 6'1", 190 lbs. Deb: 9/16/58

YEAR	TM/L	G	AB	R	H	2B	3B	HR	RBI	BB	SO	AVG	OBP	SLG	PRO+	BR	/A	RC	SB	CS	SBR	FA	FR	POS	TPR
1958	Chi-N	3	3	0	0	0	0	0	0	0	3	.000	.000	.000	-99	-1	-1	0	0	0	0	.000	0	H	-0.1

■ LEN GABRIELSON
Gabrielson, Leonard Gary b: 2/14/40, Oakland, Cal. BL/TR, 6'4", 210 lbs. Deb: 9/09/60 F

YEAR	TM/L	G	AB	R	H	2B	3B	HR	RBI	BB	SO	AVG	OBP	SLG	PRO+	BR	/A	RC	SB	CS	SBR	FA	FR	POS	TPR
1960	Mil-N	4	3	1	0	0	0	0	0	1	0	.000	.250	.000	-27	-1	-0	0	0	0	0	.000	-0	/O	-0.1
1963	Mil-N	46	120	14	26	5	0	3	15	8	23	.217	.266	.333	72	-5	-4	11	1	1	-0	1.000	-1	O1/3	-0.8
1964	Mil-N	24	38	0	7	2	0	0	1	1	8	.184	.205	.237	24	-4	-4	2	1	0	0	1.000	-1	1/O	-0.5
	Chi-N	89	272	22	67	11	2	5	23	19	37	.246	.298	.357	80	-6	-7	30	9	4	0	.984	-0	O/1	-1.1
	Yr	113	310	22	74	13	2	5	24	20	45	.239	.287	.342	74	-10	-11	32	10	4	1	.984	-1	O1	-1.6
1965	Chi-N	28	48	4	12	0	0	3	5	7	16	.250	.345	.438	116	1	1	7	0	2	-1	1.000	-1	O/1	-0.2
	SF-N	88	269	36	81	6	5	4	26	26	48	.301	.367	.405	114	7	6	42	4	0	1	.975	-2	O/1	0.2
	Yr	116	317	40	93	6	5	7	31	33	64	.293	.364	.410	114	8	7	49	4	2	0	.977	-3	O/1	0.0
1966	SF-N	94	240	27	52	7	0	4	16	21	51	.217	.280	.296	58	-13	-14	21	0	1	-1	.948	-9	O/1	-2.7
1967	Cal-A	11	12	2	1	0	0	0	2	2	4	.083	.214	.083	-9	-2	-2	0	0	0	0	.000	-0	/O	-0.2
	LA-N	90	238	20	62	10	3	7	29	15	41	.261	.307	.416	114	1	3	30	3	1	0	.980	-1	O	0.0
1968	LA-N	108	304	38	82	16	1	10	35	32	47	.270	.339	.428	140	11	13	44	1	1	-0	.976	-7	O	0.2
1969	LA-N	83	178	13	48	5	1	1	18	12	25	.270	.316	.326	86	-5	-3	18	1	2	-1	.981	-5	O/1	-1.2
1970	LA-N	43	42	1	8	2	0	0	6	1	15	.190	.209	.238	20	-5	-5	2	0	0	0	1.000	0	/O1	-0.4
Total	9	708	1764	178	446	64	12	37	176	145	315	.253	.311	.366	94	-19	-16	206	20	12	-1	.977	-26	O/13	-6.8

■ LEN GABRIELSON
Gabrielson, Leonard Hilbourne b: 9/8/15, Oakland, Cal. BL/TL, 6'3", 210 lbs. Deb: 4/21/39 F

YEAR	TM/L	G	AB	R	H	2B	3B	HR	RBI	BB	SO	AVG	OBP	SLG	PRO+	BR	/A	RC	SB	CS	SBR	FA	FR	POS	TPR
1939	Phi-N	5	18	3	4	0	0	0	1	2	3	.222	.300	.222	43	-1	-1	1	0			.977	2	/1	0.0

YEAR	TM/L	G	AB	R	H	2B	3B	HR	RBI	BB	SO	AVG	OBP	SLG	PRO+	BR	/A	RC	SB	CS	SBR	FA	FR	POS	TPR
■ EDDIE GAEDEL	Gaedel, Edward Carl b: 6/8/25, Chicago, Ill. d: 6/18/61, Chicago, Ill. BR/TL, 3'7", 65 lbs. Deb: 8/19/51																								
1951	StL-A	1	0	0	0	0	0	0	0	1	0	—	1.000	—	182	0	0	0	0	0	0	.000	0	H	0.0
■ GARY GAETTI	Gaetti, Gary Joseph b: 8/19/58, Centralia, Ill. BR/TR, 6', 184 lbs. Deb: 9/20/81																								
1981	Min-A	9	26	4	5	0	0	2	3	0	6	.192	.192	.423	68	-1	-1	2	0	0	0	1.000	1	/3D	0.0
1982	Min-A	145	508	59	117	25	4	25	84	37	107	.230	.286	.443	94	-4	-6	59	0	4	-2	.963	-3	*3/SD	-1.5
1983	Min-A	157	584	81	143	30	3	21	78	54	121	.245	.313	.414	95	-2	-5	74	7	1	2	.967	13	*3/SD	0.7
1984	Min-A	162	588	55	154	29	4	5	65	44	81	.262	.318	.350	81	-12	-15	67	11	5	0	.960	15	*3/OS	-0.2
1985	Min-A	160	560	71	138	31	0	20	63	37	89	.246	.301	.409	87	-7	-11	66	13	5	1	.962	17	*3/O1D	0.4
1986	Min-A	157	596	91	171	34	1	34	108	52	108	.287	.350	.518	129	25	23	99	14	15	-5	.956	19	*3/S2O	3.4
1987	*Min-A	154	584	95	150	36	2	31	109	37	92	.257	.304	.485	101	2	-1	75	10	7	-1	.973	-4	*3/D	-0.8
1988	Min-A★	133	468	66	141	29	2	28	88	36	85	.301	.358	.551	146	30	28	89	7	4	-0	.977	-6	*3/SD	2.2
1989	Min-A★	130	498	63	125	11	4	19	75	25	87	.251	.291	.404	88	-6	-10	56	6	2	1	.973	11	*3/1D	0.2
1990	Min-A	154	577	61	132	27	5	16	85	36	101	.229	.278	.376	76	-16	-21	56	6	1	1	.959	14	*3/1S	-0.5
1991	Cal-A	152	586	58	144	22	1	18	66	33	104	.246	.295	.379	85	-13	-13	63	5	5	-2	.965	**25**	*3	1.1
1992	Cal-A	130	456	41	103	13	2	12	48	21	79	.226	.269	.342	71	-19	-19	41	3	1	0	.927	13	31D	-0.8
Total	12	1643	6031	745	1523	287	28	231	872	412	1060	.253	.306	.424	96	-24	-51	746	82	50	-5	.963	116	*3/1DOS2	4.2
■ FABIAN GAFFKE	Gaffke, Fabian Sebastian b: 8/5/13, Milwaukee, Wis. d: 2/8/92, Milwaukee, Wis. BR/TR, 5'10", 185 lbs. Deb: 9/09/36																								
1936	Bos-A	15	55	5	7	2	0	1	3	4	5	.127	.200	.218	3	-9	-9	3	0	0	0	1.000	-1	O	-1.0
1937	Bos-A	54	184	32	53	10	4	6	34	15	25	.288	.342	.484	102	1	-0	30	1	2	-1	.965	-4	O	-0.7
1938	Bos-A	15	10	2	1	0	0	0	1	3	2	.100	.308	.100	6	-1	-1	1	0	0	0	.000	-1	/OC	-0.2
1939	Bos-A	1	1	0	0	0	0	0	1	0	0	.000	.000	.000	-96	-0	-0	0	0	0	0	.000	0	H	0.0
1941	Cle-A	4	4	0	1	0	0	0	0	2	2	.250	.500	.250	109	0	0	1	0	0	0	1.000	-1	/O	0.0
1942	Cle-A	40	67	4	11	2	0	0	3	6	13	.164	.243	.194	25	-7	-6	3	1	0	0	1.000	-2	O	-0.9
Total	6	129	321	43	73	14	4	7	42	30	47	.227	.297	.361	67	-16	-17	37	2	2	-1	.979	-9	/OC	-2.8
■ PHIL GAGLIANO	Gagliano, Philip Joseph b: 12/27/41, Memphis, Tenn. BR/TR, 6'1", 185 lbs. Deb: 4/16/63 F																								
1963	StL-N	10	5	1	2	0	0	0	1	1	1	.400	.500	.400	149	0	0	1	0	0	0	1.000	2	/23	0.2
1964	StL-N	40	58	5	15	4	0	1	9	3	10	.259	.295	.379	81	-1	-2	6	0	1	-1	.918	1	2/O13	0.0
1965	StL-N	122	363	46	87	14	2	8	53	40	45	.240	.317	.355	81	-5	-9	41	2	1	0	.960	-12	2O3	-1.8
1966	StL-N	90	213	23	54	8	2	2	15	24	29	.254	.332	.338	86	-3	-3	24	2	1	0	.982	-3	3/1O2	-0.9
1967	*StL-N	73	217	20	48	7	0	2	21	19	26	.221	.287	.281	64	-10	-10	17	0	0	0	.972	-13	23/1S	-2.3
1968	*StL-N	53	105	13	24	4	2	0	13	7	12	.229	.283	.305	77	-3	-3	9	0	0	0	.982	-2	23/O	-0.5
1969	StL-N	62	128	7	29	2	0	1	10	14	12	.227	.303	.266	60	-6	-6	10	0	0	0	.989	-2	2/13O	-0.7
1970	StL-N	18	32	0	6	0	0	0	2	1	3	.188	.212	.188	8	-4	-4	1	0	1	-1	1.000	-1	/312	-0.6
	Chi-N	26	40	5	6	0	0	0	5	5	5	.150	.244	.150	7	-5	-6	2	0	0	0	1.000	1	2/13	-0.5
	Yr	44	72	5	12	0	0	0	7	6	8	.167	.231	.167	8	-9	-10	3	0	1	-1	.980	-0	2/31	-1.1
1971	Bos-A	47	68	11	22	5	0	0	13	11	5	.324	.418	.397	123	3	3	12	0	0	0	1.000	-5	O/23	-0.2
1972	Bos-A	52	82	9	21	4	1	0	10	10	13	.256	.337	.329	94	0	-0	10	1	0	0	.962	2	O/321	0.2
1973	*Cin-N	63	69	8	20	2	0	0	7	13	16	.290	.402	.319	108	1	1	10	0	0	0	.824	-2	/321O	0.0
1974	Cin-N	46	31	2	2	0	0	0	0	15	7	.065	.370	.065	27	-2	-2	2	0	0	0	1.000	0	/213	-0.2
Total	12	702	1411	150	336	50	7	14	159	163	184	.238	.319	.313	77	-35	-41	146	5	4	-1	.969	-33	23/O1S	-7.3
■ RALPH GAGLIANO	Gagliano, Ralph Michael b: 10/8/46, Memphis, Tenn. BL/TR, 5'11", 170 lbs. Deb: 9/21/65 F																								
1965	Cle-A	1	0	0	0	0	0	0	0	0	0	—	—	—	—	0	0	0	0	0	0	.000	0	R	0.0
■ GREG GAGNE	Gagne, Gregory Carpenter b: 11/12/61, Fall River, Mass. BR/TR, 5'11", 185 lbs. Deb: 6/05/83																								
1983	Min-A	10	27	2	3	1	0	0	3	0	6	.111	.111	.148	-28	-5	-5	1	0	0	0	.923	-5	S	-1.0
1984	Min-A	2	1	0	0	0	0	0	0	0	0	.000	.000	.000	-96	-0	-0	0	0	0	0	.000	0	/H	0.0
1985	Min-A	114	293	37	66	15	3	2	23	20	57	.225	.282	.317	60	-15	-17	27	10	4	1	.968	4	*S/D	-0.3
1986	Min-A	156	472	63	118	22	6	12	54	30	108	.250	.303	.398	87	-8	-10	57	12	10	-2	.959	-16	*S/2	-1.3
1987	*Min-A	137	437	68	116	28	7	10	40	25	84	.265	.311	.430	91	-5	-7	58	6	6	-2	.970	17	*S/O2D	1.8
1988	Min-A	149	461	70	109	20	6	14	48	27	110	.236	.289	.397	87	-7	-9	50	15	7	0	.970	-15	*S/O23	-1.3
1989	Min-A	149	460	69	125	29	7	9	48	17	80	.272	.301	.424	96	-1	-4	56	11	4	1	.971	-3	*S/O	0.4
1990	Min-A	138	388	38	91	22	3	7	38	24	76	.235	.281	.361	73	-12	-15	38	8	8	-2	.976	2	*S/OD	-0.7
1991	*Min-A	139	408	52	108	23	3	8	42	26	72	.265	.314	.395	90	-4	-6	45	11	9	-2	.984	4	*S/D	0.5
1992	Min-A	146	439	53	108	23	0	7	39	19	83	.246	.280	.346	72	-16	-18	39	6	7	-2	.973	21	*S	1.1
Total	10	1140	3386	452	844	183	35	69	335	188	676	.249	.294	.385	82	-72	-91	371	79	55	-9	.971	8	*S/DO23	-0.8
■ ED GAGNIER	Gagnier, Edward J. b: 4/16/1883, Paris, France d: 9/13/46, Detroit, Mich. BR/TR, 5'9", 170 lbs. Deb: 4/14/14																								
1914	Bro-F	94	337	22	63	12	2	0	25	13	24	.187	.219	.234	29	-32	-31	21	8			.933	-1	S/3	-2.6
1915	Bro-F	20	50	8	13	1	0	0	4	10	5	.260	.393	.280	100	1	1	7	2			.930	2	S/2	0.4
	Buf-F	1	2	0	0	0	0	0	0	0	0	.000	.000	.000	-98	-0	-0	0	0			.800	-0	/2	-0.1
	Yr	21	52	8	13	1	0	0	4	10	5	.250	.381	.269	93	0	0	7	2			.930	2	S/2	0.3
Total	2	115	389	30	76	13	2	0	29	23	29	.195	.244	.239	39	-31	-31	27	10			.933	1	S/23	-2.3
■ CHICK GAGNON	Gagnon, Harold Dennis b: 9/27/1897, Millbury, Mass. d: 4/30/70, Wilmington, Del. BR/TR, 5'7.5", 158 lbs. Deb: 6/27/22																								
1922	Det-A	10	4	2	1	0	0	0	0	0	2	.250	.250	.250	32	-0	-0	0	0	0	0	.000	0	/S3	0.0
1924	Was-A	4	5	1	1	0	0	0	1	0	0	.200	.200	.200	3	-1	-1	0	0	0	0	1.000	1	/S	0.0
Total	2	14	9	3	2	0	0	0	1	0	2	.222	.222	.222	16	-1	-1	0	0	0	0	1.000	1	/S3	0.0
■ DEL GAINER	Gainer, Dellos Clinton "Sheriff" b: 11/10/1886, Montrose, W.Va. d: 1/29/47, Elkins, W.Va. BR/TR, 6', 180 lbs. Deb: 10/02/09																								
1909	Det-A	2	5	0	1	0	0	0	0	0		.200	.200	.200	25	-0	-0	0	0			.929	-0	/1	-0.1
1911	Det-A	70	248	32	75	11	4	2	25	20		.302	.366	.403	109	5	3	40	10			.975	-4	1	-0.1
1912	Det-A	52	179	28	43	5	6	0	20	18		.240	.320	.335	90	-3	-2	24	14			.986	-3	1/O	-0.6
1913	Det-A	105	363	47	97	16	8	2	25	30	45	.267	.333	.372	108	2	3	46	10			.988	-5	*1	-0.3
1914	Det-A	1	0	0	0	0	0	0	0	0	0	—	—	—	—	0	0	0	0			1.000	-0	/1	0.0
	Bos-A	38	84	11	20	9	2	2	13	8	14	.238	.312	.464	133	3	3	12	2	2	-1	.981	-3	12/O	-0.1
	Yr	39	84	11	20	9	2	2	13	8	14	.238	.312	.464	133	3	3	12	2	2	-1	.982	-3	12/O	-0.1
1915	*Bos-A	82	200	30	59	5	8	1	29	21	31	.295	.371	.415	139	8	9	35	7	2	1	.988	0	1/O	1.0
1916	*Bos-A	56	142	14	36	6	0	3	18	10	24	.254	.303	.359	98	-1	-1	18	5			.997	1	1/2	-0.1
1917	Bos-A	52	172	28	53	10	2	2	19	15	21	.308	.374	.424	145	9	9	27	1			.989	-1	1	0.7
1919	Bos-A	47	118	9	28	6	2	0	13	13	15	.237	.318	.322	85	-3	-2	13	5			.978	-3	1O	-0.7
1922	StL-N	43	97	19	26	7	4	2	23	14	6	.268	.360	.485	122	2	3	17	0	2	-1	.979	-1	1O	-0.1
Total	10	548	1608	218	438	75	36	14	185	149	156	.272	.342	.390	113	21	24	232	54	6		.985	-19	1/O2	-0.4
■ JOE GAINES	Gaines, Arnesta Joe b: 11/22/36, Bryan, Tex. BR/TR, 6'1", 190 lbs. Deb: 6/29/60																								
1960	Cin-N	11	15	2	3	0	0	0	1	0	1	.200	.200	.200	10	-2	-2	1	0	0	0	1.000	-1	/O	-0.3
1961	Cin-N	5	3	2	0	0	0	0	0	2	1	.000	.400	.000	18	-0	-0	0	0	0	0	.500	-0	/O	-0.1
1962	Cin-N	64	52	12	12	3	0	1	7	8	16	.231	.333	.346	80	-1	-1	6	0	0	0	1.000	1	O	-0.1
1963	Bal-A	66	126	24	36	4	1	6	20	20	39	.286	.384	.476	142	7	7	23	2	1	0	.945	-6	O	0.0
1964	Bal-A	16	26	2	4	0	0	1	2	3	7	.154	.241	.269	42	-2	-2	2	0	0	0	.846	0	/O	-0.2
	Hou-N	89	307	37	78	9	7	7	34	27	69	.254	.318	.397	106	0	2	39	8	2	1	.957	-3	O	-0.4
1965	Hou-N	100	229	21	52	8	1	6	31	18	59	.227	.292	.349	86	-6	-4	24	4	1	1	.913	-7	O	-1.4

YEAR	TM/L	G	AB	R	H	2B	3B	HR	RBI	BB	SO	AVG	OBP	SLG	PRO+	BR	/A	RC	SB	CS	SBR	FA	FR	POS	TPR
1966	Hou-N	11	13	4	1	1	0	0	0	3	5	.077	.250	.154	17	-1	-1	1	0	0	0	.500	-1	/O	-0.2
Total	7	362	771	104	186	25	9	21	95	81	197	.241	.317	.379	98	-6	-2	96	14	4	2	.934	-17	O	-2.7

■ TY GAINEY Gainey, Telmanch b: 12/25/60, Cheraw, N.C. BL/TR, 6'1", 190 lbs. Deb: 4/24/85

YEAR	TM/L	G	AB	R	H	2B	3B	HR	RBI	BB	SO	AVG	OBP	SLG	PRO+	BR	/A	RC	SB	CS	SBR	FA	FR	POS	TPR
1985	Hou-N	13	37	5	6	0	0	0	0	2	9	.162	.244	.162	16	-4	-4	2	0	0	0	.913	-0	/O	-0.5
1986	Hou-N	26	50	6	15	3	1	1	6	6	19	.300	.375	.460	133	2	2	9	3	1	0	1.000	-3	O	-0.1
1987	Hou-N	18	24	1	3	0	0	0	1	2	9	.125	.192	.125	-14	-4	-4	1	1	0	0	1.000	-0	/O	-0.4
Total	3	57	111	12	24	3	1	1	7	10	37	.216	.293	.288	62	-6	-6	12	4	1	1	.968	-3	/O	-1.0

■ AUGIE GALAN Galan, August John b: 5/25/12, Berkeley, Cal. BB/TR, 6', 175 lbs. Deb: 4/29/34 C

YEAR	TM/L	G	AB	R	H	2B	3B	HR	RBI	BB	SO	AVG	OBP	SLG	PRO+	BR	/A	RC	SB	CS	SBR	FA	FR	POS	TPR
1934	Chi-N	66	192	31	50	6	2	5	22	16	15	.260	.317	.391	90	-3	-3	25	4			.961	-9	2/3S	-0.9
1935	*Chi-N	154	646	**133**	203	41	11	12	79	87	53	.314	.399	.467	131	32	31	133	**22**			.978	7	*O	3.1
1936	Chi-N★	145	575	74	152	26	4	8	81	67	50	.264	.344	.365	89	-6	-8	77	16			.987	5	*O	-0.9
1937	Chi-N	147	611	104	154	24	10	18	78	79	48	.252	.339	.412	99	3	-1	92	**23**			.980	13	*O/2S	0.7
1938	*Chi-N	110	395	52	113	16	9	6	69	49	17	.286	.368	.418	112	9	8	64	8			.987	2	*O	0.7
1939	Chi-N	148	549	104	167	36	8	6	71	75	26	.304	.392	.432	119	18	17	97	8			.970	-2	*O	1.0
1940	Chi-N	68	209	33	48	14	2	3	22	37	23	.230	.346	.359	96	-1	-0	29	9			.984	0	O/2	-0.3
1941	Chi-N	65	120	18	25	3	0	1	13	22	10	.208	.331	.258	70	-4	-4	12	0			.959	-5	O	-1.0
	*Bro-N	17	27	3	7	3	0	0	4	3	1	.259	.333	.370	94	-0	-0	4	0			1.000	-0	/O	-0.1
	Yr	82	147	21	32	6	0	1	17	25	11	.218	.331	.279	74	-4	-4	16	0			.967	-5	O	-1.1
1942	Bro-N	69	209	24	55	16	0	0	22	24	12	.263	.339	.340	97	0	-0	25	2			.990	-5	O/12	-0.8
1943	Bro-N★	139	495	83	142	26	3	9	67	**103**	39	.287	.412	.406	136	28	28	93	6			.981	16	*O1	3.9
1944	Bro-N★	151	547	96	174	43	9	12	93	**101**	23	.318	.426	.495	162	47	48	123	4			.988	-2	*O/2	3.9
1945	Bro-N	152	576	114	177	36	7	9	92	114	27	.307	.423	.441	142	37	37	116	13			.988	-8	1O3	2.3
1946	Bro-N	99	274	53	85	22	5	3	38	68	21	.310	.451	.460	157	25	25	65	8			.935	-10	O31	1.4
1947	Cin-N	124	392	60	123	18	2	6	61	94	19	.314	**.449**	.416	132	24	24	83	0			.988	-4	*O	1.4
1948	Cin-N	54	77	18	22	3	2	2	16	26	4	.286	.471	.455	157	8	8	19	0			.967	-2	O	0.5
1949	NY-N	22	17	0	1	1	0	0	2	5	3	.059	.273	.118	8	-2	-2	1	0			1.000	-1	/1O	-0.3
	Phi-A	12	26	4	8	2	0	0	0	9	2	.308	.486	.385	136	2	2	6	0	0	0	1.000	-1	/O	0.1
Total	16	1742	5937	1004	1706	336	74	100	830	979	393	.287	.390	.419	122	216	211	1064	123	0		.981	-5	*O/132S	14.7

■ ANDRES GALARRAGA Galarraga, Andres Jose (b: Andres Jose Padovani (Galarraga)) b: 6/18/61, Caracas, Venez. BR/TR, 6'3", 235 lbs. Deb: 8/23/85

YEAR	TM/L	G	AB	R	H	2B	3B	HR	RBI	BB	SO	AVG	OBP	SLG	PRO+	BR	/A	RC	SB	CS	SBR	FA	FR	POS	TPR
1985	Mon-N	24	75	9	14	1	0	2	4	3	18	.187	.228	.280	44	-6	-6	5	1	2	-1	.995	4	1	-0.4
1986	Mon-N	105	321	39	87	13	0	10	42	30	79	.271	.339	.405	105	2	2	43	6	5	-1	.995	-8	*1	-1.4
1987	Mon-N	147	551	72	168	40	3	13	90	41	127	.305	.364	.459	113	13	11	88	7	10	-4	.993	0	*1	-0.4
1988	Mon-N★	157	609	99	**184**	**42**	8	29	92	39	153	.302	.354	.540	147	39	36	114	13	4	2	.991	-4	*1	2.2
1989	Mon-N	152	572	76	147	30	1	23	85	48	158	.257	.329	.434	115	11	10	81	12	5	1	.992	-2	*1	-0.3
1990	Mon-N	155	579	65	148	29	0	20	87	40	169	.256	.308	.409	99	-5	-2	72	10	1	2	.993	-5	*1	-1.7
1991	Mon-N	107	375	34	82	13	2	9	33	23	86	.219	.268	.336	70	-16	-16	32	5	6	-2	.991	2	*1	-2.4
1992	StL-N	95	325	38	79	14	2	10	39	11	69	.243	.285	.391	91	-6	-5	34	5	4	-1	.991	-1	1	-1.3
Total	8	942	3407	432	909	182	16	116	472	235	859	.267	.324	.432	108	32	31	467	59	37	-5	.992	-14	1	-5.7

■ MILT GALATZER Galatzer, Milton b: 5/4/07, Chicago, Il.. d: 1/29/76, San Francisco, Cal BL/TL, 5'10", 168 lbs. Deb: 6/25/33

YEAR	TM/L	G	AB	R	H	2B	3B	HR	RBI	BB	SO	AVG	OBP	SLG	PRO+	BR	/A	RC	SB	CS	SBR	FA	FR	POS	TPR
1933	Cle-A	57	160	19	38	2	1	1	17	23	21	.237	.333	.281	61	-8	-9	16	2	3	-1	.975	-0	O/1	-1.2
1934	Cle-A	49	196	29	53	10	2	0	15	21	8	.270	.344	.342	76	-6	-7	24	3	2	-0	.980	3	O	-0.6
1935	Cle-A	93	259	45	78	9	3	0	19	35	8	.301	.389	.359	93	-1	-1	38	4	5	-2	.934	-8	O	-1.3
1936	Cle-A	49	97	12	23	4	1	0	6	13	8	.237	.333	.299	57	-6	-6	10	1	2	-1	.964	-8	O/P1	-1.5
1939	Cin-N	3	5	0	0	0	0	0	0	0	1	.000	.000	.000	-99	-1	-1	0	0			1.000	-0	/1	-0.2
Total	5	251	717	105	192	25	7	1	57	92	46	.268	.354	.326	75	-22	-24	88	10	12		.959	-14	O/1P	-4.8

■ ARCHIE GALBRAITH Galbraith, Archibald Victor b: 9/22/1877, Boxford, Mass. d: 12/25/71, Northampton, Mass Deb: 8/29/02

YEAR	TM/L	G	AB	R	H	2B	3B	HR	RBI	BB	SO	AVG	OBP	SLG	PRO+	BR	/A	RC	SB	CS	SBR	FA	FR	POS	TPR
1902	Chi-N	1	0	0	0	0	0	0	0	0		—	—	—	—	0	0	0	0			.000	0	/3	0.0

■ AL GALLAGHER Gallagher, Alan Mitchell Edward George Patrick Henry b: 10/19/45, San Francisco, Cal. BR/TR, 6', 180 lbs. Deb: 4/07/70

YEAR	TM/L	G	AB	R	H	2B	3B	HR	RBI	BB	SO	AVG	OBP	SLG	PRO+	BR	/A	RC	SB	CS	SBR	FA	FR	POS	TPR
1970	SF-N	109	282	31	75	15	2	4	28	30	37	.266	.337	.376	92	-4	-3	35	2	1	0	.971	1	3	-0.2
1971	*SF-N	136	429	47	119	18	5	5	57	40	57	.277	.342	.378	105	2	3	53	2	1	0	.951	-16	*3	-1.5
1972	SF-N	82	233	19	52	3	1	2	18	33	39	.223	.322	.270	69	-8	-9	21	2	1	0	.974	-4	3	-1.4
1973	SF-N	5	9	1	2	0	0	0	1	0	0	.222	.300	.222	45	-1	-1	0	0	0	0	.833	-1	/3	-0.2
	Cal-A	110	311	16	85	6	1	0	26	35	31	.273	.349	.299	91	-5	-2	32	1	3	-2	.961	4	3/2S	0.0
Total	4	442	1264	114	333	42	9	11	130	138	164	.263	.338	.337	91	-15	-11	142	7	6	-2	.961	-15	3/S2	-3.3

■ SHORTY GALLAGHER Gallagher, Charles William b: 4/30/1872, Detroit, Mich. d: 6/23/24, Detroit, Mich. Deb: 8/13/01

YEAR	TM/L	G	AB	R	H	2B	3B	HR	RBI	BB	SO	AVG	OBP	SLG	PRO+	BR	/A	RC	SB	CS	SBR	FA	FR	POS	TPR
1901	Cle-A	2	4	0	0	0	0	0	0	0		.000	.000	.000	-99	-1	-1	0	0			.667	-1	/O	-0.2

■ DAVE GALLAGHER Gallagher, David Thomas b: 9/20/60, Trenton, N.J. BR/TR, 6' ", 180 lbs. Deb: 4/12/87

YEAR	TM/L	G	AB	R	H	2B	3B	HR	RBI	BB	SO	AVG	OBP	SLG	PRO+	BR	/A	RC	SB	CS	SBR	FA	FR	POS	TPR
1987	Cle-A	15	36	2	4	1	1	0	1	2	5	.111	.158	.194	-7	-6	-6	1	2	0	1	.972	1	O	-0.4
1988	Chi-A	101	347	59	105	15	3	5	31	29	40	.303	.356	.406	113	6	6	49	5	4	-1	1.000	-1	O/D	0.1
1989	Chi-A	161	601	74	160	22	2	1	46	46	79	.266	.320	.314	82	-15	-14	62	5	6	-2	.993	1	*O/D	-1.9
1990	Chi-A	45	75	5	21	3	1	0	5	3	9	.280	.316	.347	87	-2	-1	7	0	1	-1	.981	-6	O/D	-0.9
	Bal-A	23	51	7	11	1	0	0	2	4	3	.216	.273	.235	45	-4	-4	4	1	1	-0	.980	2	O/D	-0.2
	Yr	68	126	12	32	4	1	0	7	7	12	.254	.299	.302	70	-5	-5	11	1	2	-1	.980	-4	O/D	-1.1
1991	Cal-A	90	270	32	79	17	0	1	30	24	43	.293	.355	.367	100	1	1	35	2	4	-2	1.000	1	O/D	-0.2
1992	NY-N	98	175	20	42	11	1	1	21	19	16	.240	.318	.331	85	-3	-3	17	4	5	-2	.982	-8	O	-1.5
Total	6	533	1555	199	422	70	8	8	136	127	195	.271	.329	.342	89	-23	-20	175	19	21	-7	.993	-10	O/D	-5.0

■ JIM GALLAGHER Gallagher, James E. b: Findlay, Ohio d: 3/29/1894, Scranton, Pa. Deb: 9/04/1886

YEAR	TM/L	G	AB	R	H	2B	3B	HR	RBI	BB	SO	AVG	OBP	SLG	PRO+	BR	/A	RC	SB	CS	SBR	FA	FR	POS	TPR
1886	Was-N	1	5	1	1	0	0	0	0	0	2	.200	.200	.200	23	-0	-0	0	0			.875	1	/S	0.0

■ JOHN GALLAGHER Gallagher, John Carroll b: 2/18/1892, Pittsburgh, Pa. d: 3/30/52, Norfolk, Va. BR/TR, 5'10.5", 156 lbs. Deb: 8/20/15

YEAR	TM/L	G	AB	R	H	2B	3B	HR	RBI	BB	SO	AVG	OBP	SLG	PRO+	BR	/A	RC	SB	CS	SBR	FA	FR	POS	TPR
1915	Bal-F	40	126	11	25	4	0	0	4	5	22	.198	.229	.230	34	-10	-11	8	1			.945	-2	2/S3	-1.4

■ JACKIE GALLAGHER Gallagher, John Laurence b: 1/28/02, Providence, R.I. d: 9/10/84, Gladwyn, Pa. BL/TR, 5'10", 175 lbs. Deb: 8/24/23

YEAR	TM/L	G	AB	R	H	2B	3B	HR	RBI	BB	SO	AVG	OBP	SLG	PRO+	BR	/A	RC	SB	CS	SBR	FA	FR	POS	TPR
1923	Cle-A	1	1	0	1	0	0	0	0	0	0	1.000	1.000	1.000	428	0	0	1	0	0	0	.000	-1	/O	0.0

■ JOE GALLAGHER Gallagher, Joseph Emmett "Muscles" b: 3/7/14, Buffalo, N.Y. BR/TR, 6'2", 210 lbs. Deb: 4/20/39

YEAR	TM/L	G	AB	R	H	2B	3B	HR	RBI	BB	SO	AVG	OBP	SLG	PRO+	BR	/A	RC	SB	CS	SBR	FA	FR	POS	TPR
1939	NY-A	14	41	8	10	0	1	2	9	3	8	.244	.311	.439	91	-1	-1	6	1	0	0	1.000	-1	O	-0.2
	StL-A	71	266	41	75	17	2	9	40	17	42	.282	.327	.462	98	-1	-2	38	0	1	-1	.944	2	O	-0.3
	Yr	85	307	49	85	17	3	11	49	20	50	.277	.325	.459	97	-2	-3	44	1	1	-0	.950	1	O	-0.5
1940	StL-A	23	70	14	19	3	1	2	8	4	12	.271	.311	.429	88	-1	-2	9	2	0	1	.966	-1	O	-0.3
	Bro-N	57	110	10	29	6	1	3	16	2	14	.264	.283	.418	86	-2	-3	13	1			.941	-2	O	-0.6
Total	2	165	487	73	133	26	5	16	73	26	76	.273	.314	.446	93	-5	-7	66	4	1		.950	-3	O	-1.4

■ GIL GALLAGHER Gallagher, Lawrence Kirby b: 9/5/1896, Washington, D.C. d: 1/6/57, Washington, D.C. BB/TR, 5'8", 155 lbs. Deb: 9/13/22

YEAR	TM/L	G	AB	R	H	2B	3B	HR	RBI	BB	SO	AVG	OBP	SLG	PRO+	BR	/A	RC	SB	CS	SBR	FA	FR	POS	TPR
1922	Bos-N	7	22	1	1	1	0	0	2	1	7	.045	.087	.091	-57	-5	-5	0	0	0	0	.893	-2	/S	-0.6

YEAR	TM/L	G	AB	R	H	2B	3B	HR	RBI	BB	SO	AVG	OBP	SLG	PRO+	BR	/A	RC	SB	CS	SBR	FA	FR	POS	TPR

■ **BOB GALLAGHER**   Gallagher, Robert Collins   b: 7/7/48, Newton, Mass.   BL/TL, 6′3″, 185 lbs.   Deb: 5/17/72   F

1972	Bos-A	7	5	0	0	0	0	0	0	0	3	.000	.000	.000	-95	-1	-1	0	0	0	0	.000	0	H	-0.1
1973	Hou-N	71	148	16	39	3	1	2	10	3	27	.264	.278	.338	70	-6	-6	13	0	1	-1	1.000	3	O/1	-0.6
1974	Hou-N	102	87	13	15	2	0	0	3	12	23	.172	.280	.195	36	-7	-7	6	1	0	0	.978	2	O/1	-0.6
1975	NY-N	33	15	5	2	1	0	0	0	1	3	.133	.188	.200	8	-2	-2	0	0	0	0	.900	1	O	0.0
Total	4	213	255	34	56	6	1	2	13	16	56	.220	.268	.275	52	-17	-16	20	1	1	-0	.985	6	O/1	-1.3

■ **WILLIAM GALLAGHER**   Gallagher, William H.   b: 2/1874, Lowell, Mass.   d: 3/11/50, Worcester, Mass.   Deb: 8/19/1896

| 1896 | Phi-N | 14 | 49 | 9 | 15 | 2 | 0 | 0 | 6 | 10 | 0 | .306 | .433 | .347 | 111 | 1 | 2 | 8 | 0 | | | .894 | -5 | S | -0.2 |

■ **BILL GALLAGHER**   Gallagher, William John   b: Philadelphia, Pa.   TL,   Deb: 5/02/1883

1883	Bal-a	16	61	9	10	3	1	0			3	.164	.203	.246	43	-4	-4	3				.824	-2	/OPS	-0.3
	Phi-N	2	8	1	0	0	0	0	0	0	4	.000	.000	.000	-99	-2	-2	0				1.000	-0	/O	-0.2
1884	Phi-U	3	11	1	1	0	0	0			0	.091	.091	.091	-41	-2	-1	0				.800	1	/P	0.0
Total	2	21	80	11	11	3	1	0	0	3	4	.138	.169	.200	18	-7	-7	3				.850	-2	/OPS	-0.5

■ **STAN GALLE**   Galle, Stanley Joseph (b: Stanley Joseph Galazewski)   b: 2/7/19, Milwaukee, Wis.   BR/TR, 5′7″, 165 lbs.   Deb: 4/14/42

| 1942 | Was-A | 13 | 18 | 3 | 2 | 0 | 0 | 0 | 1 | 1 | 0 | .111 | .158 | .111 | -24 | -3 | -3 | 0 | 0 | 0 | 0 | .857 | -1 | /3 | -0.4 |

■ **MIKE GALLEGO**   Gallego, Michael Anthon   b: 10/31/60, Whittier, Cal.   BR/TR, 5′8″, 160 lbs.   Deb: 4/11/85

1985	Oak-A	76	77	13	16	5	1	1	9	12	14	.208	.322	.338	87	-2	-1	9	1	1	-0	.991	12	2S3	1.2
1986	Oak-A	20	37	2	10	2	0	0	4	1	6	.270	.289	.324	72	-2	-1	3	0	2	-1	.986	9	2/3S	0.6
1987	Oak-A	72	124	18	31	6	0	2	14	12	21	.250	.321	.347	83	-4	-3	13	0	1	-1	.968	17	23S	1.4
1988	*Oak-A	129	277	38	58	8	0	2	20	34	53	.209	.298	.260	60	-15	-14	23	2	3	-1	.993	4	2S3	-0.7
1989	*Oak-A	133	357	45	90	14	2	3	30	35	43	.252	.329	.328	89	-6	-4	39	7	5	-1	.967	18	2S3/D	-0.3
1990	*Oak-A	140	389	36	80	13	2	3	34	35	50	.206	.278	.272	57	-23	-21	29	5	5	-2	.990	14	2S3/OD	-0.5
1991	Oak-A	159	482	67	119	15	4	12	49	67	84	.247	.345	.369	103	-0	4	63	6	9	-4	.989	-16	*2S	-1.1
1992	NY-A	53	173	24	44	7	1	3	14	20	22	.254	.345	.358	95	-0	-1	22	0	1	-1	.990	1	2S	0.2
Total	8	782	1916	243	448	70	10	26	174	216	293	.234	.318	.322	82	-52	-41	200	21	27	-10	.987	59	2S/3DO	3.1

■ **JIM GALLIGAN**   Galligan, James M.   b: 1862, Easton, Pa.   d: 7/17/01, New York, N.Y.   5′10″, 160 lbs.   Deb: 9/02/1889

| 1889 | Lou-a | 31 | 120 | 6 | 20 | 0 | 2 | 0 | 7 | 6 | 17 | .167 | .213 | .200 | 19 | -13 | -12 | 5 | 1 | | | .915 | 2 | O | -1.0 |

■ **CHICK GALLOWAY**   Galloway, Clarence Edward   b: 8/4/1896, Clinton, S.C.   d: 11/7/69, Clinton, S.C.   BR/TR, 5′8″, 160 lbs.   Deb: 9/09/19

1919	Phi-A	17	63	2	9	0	0	0	4	1	8	.143	.156	.143	-16	-10	-10	1	0			.969	1	S	-0.9
1920	Phi-A	98	298	28	60	9	3	0	18	22	22	.201	.259	.252	35	-28	-28	21	2	2	-1	.928	4	S/23	-1.8
1921	Phi-A	131	465	42	123	28	5	3	47	29	43	.265	.310	.366	72	-21	-21	53	12	7	-1	.922	-22	*S3/2	-3.1
1922	Phi-A	155	571	83	185	26	9	6	69	39	38	.324	.368	.433	105	6	4	92	10	4	1	.952	3	*S	2.3
1923	Phi-A	134	504	64	140	18	9	2	62	37	30	.278	.327	.361	80	-15	-15	59	12	10	-2	.944	2	*S	-0.3
1924	Phi-A	129	464	41	128	16	4	2	48	23	23	.276	.311	.341	67	-23	-23	48	11	12	-4	.952	2	*S	-1.0
1925	Phi-A	149	481	52	116	11	4	3	71	59	28	.241	.324	.299	55	-29	-34	51	16	9	-1	.954	-4	*S	-2.1
1926	Phi-A	133	408	37	98	13	6	0	49	31	20	.240	.295	.301	53	-27	-30	37	8	7	-2	.935	-13	*S	-3.1
1927	Phi-A	77	181	25	48	10	4	0	22	18	9	.265	.332	.365	76	-5	-7	21	1	3	-2	.946	1	S/3	0.1
1928	Det-A	53	148	17	39	5	2	1	17	15	3	.264	.331	.345	77	-5	-5	18	7	2	1	.914	-4	S3/1O	-0.4
Total	10	1076	3583	391	946	136	46	17	407	274	224	.264	.317	.342	69	-155	-170	401	79	56		.943	-26	S/3201	-10.3

■ **JIM GALLOWAY**   Galloway, James Cato "Bad News"   b: 9/16/1887, Iredell, Tex.   d: 5/3/50, Fort Worth, Tex.   BB/TR, 6′3″, 187 lbs.   Deb: 8/24/12

| 1912 | StL-N | 21 | 54 | 4 | 10 | 2 | 0 | 0 | 4 | 5 | 8 | .185 | .254 | .222 | 32 | -5 | -5 | 4 | 2 | | | .971 | 1 | 2/S | -0.4 |

■ **JIM GALVIN**   Galvin, James Joseph   b: 8/11/07, Somerville, Mass.   d: 9/30/69, Marietta, Ga.   BR/TR, 5′11.5″, 180 lbs.   Deb: 9/27/30

| 1930 | Bos-A | 2 | 2 | 0 | 0 | 0 | 0 | 0 | 0 | 0 | 0 | .000 | .000 | .000 | -99 | -1 | -1 | 0 | 0 | 0 | 0 | .000 | 0 | H | -0.1 |

■ **JOHN GALVIN**   Galvin, John S.   b: Brooklyn, N.Y.   d: 4/20/04, Brooklyn, N.Y.   Deb: 5/07/1872

| 1872 | Atl-n | 1 | 4 | 0 | 0 | 0 | 0 | 0 | 0 | 0 | 0 | .000 | .000 | .000 | -85 | -1 | -1 | 0 | | | | | | /2 | -0.1 |

■ **JOHN GAMBLE**   Gamble, John Robert   b: 2/10/48, Reno, Nev.   BR/TR, 5′10″, 165 lbs.   Deb: 9/07/72

1972	Det-A	6	3	0	0	0	0	0	0	0	0	.000	.000	.000	-97	-1	-1	0	0	0	0	1.000	2	/S	0.2
1973	Det-A	7	0	1	0	0	0	0	0	0	0	—	—	—	—	0	0	0	0	0	0	.000	0	R	0.0
Total	2	13	3	1	0	0	0	0	0	0	0	.000	.000	.000	-97	-1	-1	0	0	0	0	.894	2	/S	0.2

■ **LEE GAMBLE**   Gamble, Lee Jesse   b: 6/28/10, Renovo, Pa.   BL/TR, 6′1″, 170 lbs.   Deb: 9/15/35

1935	Cin-N	2	4	2	2	1	0	0	2	1	0	.500	.600	.750	269	1	1	2	1			1.000	-0	/O	0.1
1938	Cin-N	53	75	13	24	3	1	0	5	0	6	.320	.320	.387	96	-1	-1	9	0			1.000	-0	/O	-0.1
1939	*Cin-N	72	221	24	59	7	2	0	14	9	14	.267	.296	.317	64	-11	-11	21	5			.989	-3	O	-1.7
1940	Cin-N	38	42	12	6	1	0	0	0	0	1	.143	.143	.167	-15	-7	-7	1	0			1.000	0	O	-0.7
Total	4	165	342	51	91	12	3	0	21	10	21	.266	.287	.319	64	-17	-17	34	6			.993	-4	/O	-2.4

■ **OSCAR GAMBLE**   Gamble, Oscar Charles   b: 12/20/49, Ramer, Ala.   BL/TR, 5′11″, 165 lbs.   Deb: 8/27/69

1969	Chi-N	24	71	6	16	1	1	1	5	10	12	.225	.321	.310	69	-2	-3	7	0	2	-1	.913	-1	O	-0.6
1970	Phi-N	88	275	31	72	12	4	1	19	27	37	.262	.330	.345	84	-7	-6	30	5	4	-1	.956	1	O	-1.0
1971	Phi-N	92	280	24	62	11	1	6	23	21	35	.221	.278	.332	72	-11	-11	27	5	2	0	.970	-8	O	-2.3
1972	Phi-N	74	135	17	32	5	2	1	13	19	16	.237	.335	.326	86	-2	-2	15	0	1	-1	1.000	1	O/1	-0.5
1973	Cle-A	113	390	56	104	11	3	20	44	34	37	.267	.330	.464	120	10	9	60	3	4	-2	.971	-1	DO	0.5
1974	Cle-A	135	454	74	132	16	4	19	59	48	51	.291	.365	.469	140	22	23	77	5	6	-2	1.000	-1	*DO	2.0
1975	Cle-A	121	348	60	91	16	3	15	45	53	39	.261	.362	.454	130	14	14	58	11	5	0	.987	1	OD	1.3
1976	*NY-A	110	340	43	79	13	1	17	57	38	38	.232	.317	.426	117	6	7	47	5	3	-0	.981	-0	*O/D	0.2
1977	Chi-A	137	408	75	121	22	2	31	83	54	54	.297	.387	.588	162	34	35	96	1	4	-0	.979	-5	DO	2.7
1978	SD-N	126	375	46	103	15	3	7	47	51	45	.275	.370	.387	121	8	11	57	1	2	-1	.979	-4	*O	0.3
1979	Tex-A	64	161	27	54	6	0	8	32	37	15	.335	.462	.522	167	17	17	39	2	1	0	1.000	1	DO	1.7
	NY-A	36	113	21	44	4	1	11	32	13	13	.389	.462	.735	219	18	18	38	0	0	0	.943	1	O/D	1.6
	Yr	100	274	48	98	10	1	19	64	50	28	.358	.458	.609	188	35	35	79	2	1	0	.969	2	OD	3.3
1980	*NY-A	78	194	40	54	10	2	14	50	28	21	.278	.381	.567	159	15	15	44	2	0	1	1.000	-6	OD	0.8
1981	*NY-A	80	189	24	45	8	0	10	27	35	23	.238	.360	.439	131	8	8	31	0	2	-1	1.000	-5	DO	0.4
1982	NY-A	108	316	49	86	21	2	18	57	58	47	.272	.392	.522	151	22	23	69	6	3	0	1.000	5	DO	2.7
1983	NY-A	74	180	26	47	10	2	7	26	25	25	.261	.361	.456	128	6	7	31	0	2	-1	.942	-0	OD	0.6
1984	NY-A	54	125	17	23	2	0	10	27	25	18	.184	.320	.440	112	1	2	19	1	0	0	1.000	-1	DO	0.1
1985	Chi-A	70	148	20	30	5	0	4	20	34	22	.203	.355	.318	83	-2	-2	19	0	0	0			OD/1	-0.2
Total	17	1584	4502	656	1195	188	31	200	666	610	546	.265	.358	.454	127	159	165	766	47	37	-8	.977	-20	OD/1	10.3

■ **DAFF GAMMONS**   Gammons, John Ashley   b: 3/17/1876, New Bedford, Mass.   d: 9/24/63, E.Greenwich, R.I.   BR/TR, 5′11″, 170 lbs.   Deb: 4/23/01

| 1901 | Bos-N | 28 | 93 | 10 | 18 | 0 | 1 | 0 | 10 | 3 | | .194 | .242 | .215 | 31 | -8 | -9 | 7 | 5 | | | .880 | -2 | O/23 | -1.3 |

■ **CHICK GANDIL**   Gandil, Arnold   b: 1/19/1887, St.Paul, Minn.   d: 12/13/70, Calistoga, Cal.   BR/TR, 6′1.5″, 190 lbs.   Deb: 4/14/10

1910	Chi-A	77	275	21	53	7	3	2	21	24		.193	.267	.262	69	-11	-9	22	12			.989	7	1/O	-0.3
1912	Was-A	117	443	59	135	20	15	2	81	27		.305	.350	.431	122	11	11	74	21			.990	3	*1	1.1
1913	Was-A	148	550	61	175	25	8	1	72	36	33	.318	.363	.398	120	14	13	84	22			.990	8	*1	2.1

YEAR	TM/L	G	AB	R	H	2B	3B	HR	RBI	BB	SO	AVG	OBP	SLG	PRO+	BR	/A	RC	SB	CS	SBR	FA	FR	POS	TPR
1914	Was-A	145	526	48	136	24	10	3	75	44	44	.259	.324	.359	101	2	-0	67	30	19	-2	.991	24	*1	2.0
1915	Was-A	136	485	53	141	20	15	2	64	29	33	.291	.340	.406	121	11	10	70	20	13	-2	.986	-1	*1	0.5
1916	Cle-A	146	533	51	138	26	9	0	72	36	48	.259	.312	.341	91	-4	-8	64	13			**.995**	8	*1	-0.5
1917	*Chi-A	149	553	53	151	9	7	0	57	30	36	.273	.316	.315	91	-6	-7	58	16			**.995**	-6	*1	-2.0
1918	Chi-A	114	439	49	119	18	4	0	55	27	19	.271	.319	.330	95	-3	-4	47	9			.992	-3	*1	-1.3
1919	*Chi-A	115	441	54	128	24	7	1	60	20	20	.290	.325	.383	98	-2	-2	57	10			**.997**	-4	*1	-1.1
Total	9	1147	4245	449	1176	173	78	11	557	273	233	.277	.327	.362	103	13	4	544	153	32		.992	36	*1/O	0.5

■ BOB GANDY Gandy, Robert Brinkley "String" b: 8/25/1893, Jacksonville, Fla. d: 6/19/45, Jacksonville, Fla BL/TR, 6'3", 180 lbs. Deb: 10/05/16

YEAR	TM/L	G	AB	R	H	2B	3B	HR	RBI	BB	SO	AVG	OBP	SLG	PRO+	BR	/A	RC	SB	CS	SBR	FA	FR	POS	TPR
1916	Phi-N	1	2	0	0	0	0	0	0	0	1	.000	.000	.000	-97	-0	-0	0	0			1.000	0	/O	0.0

■ BOB GANLEY Ganley, Robert Stephen b: 4/23/1875, Lowell, Mass. d: 10/9/45, Lowell, Mass. BL/TL, 5'7", 156 lbs. Deb: 9/01/05

YEAR	TM/L	G	AB	R	H	2B	3B	HR	RBI	BB	SO	AVG	OBP	SLG	PRO+	BR	/A	RC	SB	CS	SBR	FA	FR	POS	TPR
1905	Pit-N	32	127	12	40	1	2	0	7	8		.315	.356	.354	109	2	1	19	3			1.000	-2	O	-0.3
1906	Pit-N	137	511	63	132	7	6	0	31	41		.258	.316	.295	87	-5	-8	60	19			.965	-2	*O	-1.8
1907	Was-A	154	605	73	167	10	5	1	35	54		.276	.337	.314	117	7	12	83	40			.940	9	*O	1.7
1908	Was-A	150	549	61	131	19	9	1	36	45		.239	.299	.311	107	-1	4	63	30			.964	4	*O	0.2
1909	Was-A	19	63	5	16	3	0	0	5	1		.254	.266	.302	83	-2	-1	6	4			1.000	-3	O	-0.6
	Phi-A	80	274	32	54	4	2	0	9	28		.197	.272	.226	56	-13	-13	24	16			.980	8	O	-1.0
	Yr	99	337	37	70	7	2	0	14	29		.208	.270	.240	61	-14	-15	30	20			.982	4	O	-1.6
Total	5	572	2129	246	540	44	24	2	123	177		.254	.313	.300	97	-12	-4	255	112			.962	13	O	-1.8

■ BILL GANNON Gannon, William G. b: 1876, New Haven, Conn. d: 4/26/27, Fort Worth, Tex. 5'9", 170 lbs. Deb: 9/09/01

YEAR	TM/L	G	AB	R	H	2B	3B	HR	RBI	BB	SO	AVG	OBP	SLG	PRO+	BR	/A	RC	SB	CS	SBR	FA	FR	POS	TPR
1901	Chi-N	15	61	2	9	0	0	0	0	1		.148	.161	.148	-10	-8	-8	2	5			1.000	-1	O	-1.1

■ RON GANT Gant, Ronald Edwin b: 3/2/65, Victoria, Tex. BR/TR, 6' ", 192 lbs. Deb: 9/06/87

YEAR	TM/L	G	AB	R	H	2B	3B	HR	RBI	BB	SO	AVG	OBP	SLG	PRO+	BR	/A	RC	SB	CS	SBR	FA	FR	POS	TPR
1987	Atl-N	21	83	9	22	4	0	2	9	1	11	.265	.274	.386	69	-4	-4	7	4	2	0	.972	-0	2	-0.3
1988	Atl-N	146	563	85	146	28	8	19	60	46	118	.259	.319	.439	110	10	7	78	19	10	-0	.963	-1	*23	1.1
1989	Atl-N	75	260	26	46	8	3	9	25	20	63	.177	.238	.335	61	-14	-14	21	9	6	-1	.887	3	3O	-1.4
1990	Atl-N	152	575	107	174	34	3	32	84	50	86	.303	.359	.539	136	32	28	109	33	16	0	.978	7	*O	3.2
1991	*Atl-N	154	561	101	141	35	3	32	105	71	104	.251	.341	.496	125	23	19	96	34	15	1	.983	8	*O	2.5
1992	*Atl-N★	153	544	74	141	22	6	17	80	45	101	.259	.324	.415	100	5	-0	74	32	10	4	.986	-4	*O	-0.4
Total	6	701	2586	402	670	131	23	111	363	233	483	.259	.324	.456	111	52	35	387	131	59	4	.982	11	O2/3	4.7

■ JOE GANTENBEIN Gantenbein, Joseph Stephen "Sep" b: 8/25/16, San Francisco, Cal BL/TR, 5'9", 168 lbs. Deb: 4/20/39

YEAR	TM/L	G	AB	R	H	2B	3B	HR	RBI	BB	SO	AVG	OBP	SLG	PRO+	BR	/A	RC	SB	CS	SBR	FA	FR	POS	TPR
1939	Phi-A	111	348	47	101	14	4	4	36	32	22	.290	.353	.388	91	-5	-4	48	1	5	-3	.948	-34	23/S	-3.4
1940	Phi-A	75	197	21	47	6	2	4	23	11	21	.239	.282	.350	64	-11	-11	20	1	0	0	.930	-8	3/1SO	-1.7
Total	2	186	545	68	148	20	6	8	59	43	43	.272	.328	.374	82	-17	-15	68	2	5	-2	.934	-42	/23S1O	-5.1

■ JIM GANTNER Gantner, James Elmer b: 1/5/53, Fond Du Lac, Wis. BL/TR, 6', 180 lbs. Deb: 9/03/76

YEAR	TM/L	G	AB	R	H	2B	3B	HR	RBI	BB	SO	AVG	OBP	SLG	PRO+	BR	/A	RC	SB	CS	SBR	FA	FR	POS	TPR
1976	Mil-A	26	69	6	17	1	0	0	7	6	11	.246	.316	.261	71	-2	-2	6	1	0	0	.982	-3	3/D	-0.6
1977	Mil-A	14	47	4	14	1	0	1	2	2	5	.298	.327	.383	93	-1	-1	6	2	1	0	.902	1	3	0.1
1978	Mil-A	43	97	14	21	1	0	1	8	5	10	.216	.269	.258	49	-7	-7	8	2	0	1	.980	5	23/1S	0.0
1979	Mil-A	70	208	29	59	10	3	2	22	16	17	.284	.341	.389	96	-1	-1	27	3	5	-2	.952	4	32/SP	0.2
1980	Mil-A	132	415	47	117	21	3	4	40	30	29	.282	.332	.376	97	-4	-2	50	11	10	-3	.938	-1	32/S	-0.2
1981	*Mil-A	107	352	35	94	14	1	2	33	29	29	.267	.328	.330	95	-4	-2	38	3	6	-3	.984	16	*2	1.8
1982	*Mil-A	132	447	48	132	17	2	4	43	26	36	.295	.337	.369	100	-4	-0	56	6	3	0	.982	9	*2	1.5
1983	Mil-A	161	603	85	170	23	8	11	74	38	46	.282	.331	.401	109	-0	6	79	5	6	-2	.984	10	*2	2.1
1984	Mil-A	153	613	61	173	27	1	3	56	30	51	.282	.319	.344	87	-14	-11	64	6	5	-1	.985	10	*2	0.3
1985	Mil-A	143	523	63	133	15	4	5	44	33	42	.254	.302	.327	73	-20	-19	49	11	8	-2	.988	1	*23/S	-1.5
1986	Mil-A	139	497	58	136	25	1	7	38	26	50	.274	.318	.370	84	-10	-12	56	13	7	-0	.985	-12	*2/3SD	-1.8
1987	Mil-A	81	265	37	72	14	0	4	30	19	22	.272	.332	.370	84	-5	-6	32	6	2	1	.984	5	23/D	0.2
1988	Mil-A	155	539	67	149	28	2	0	47	34	50	.276	.323	.336	84	-11	-11	60	20	8	1	.986	-8	*2/3	-1.2
1989	Mil-A	116	409	51	112	18	3	0	34	21	33	.274	.325	.333	86	-7	-7	45	20	6	2	.987	9	*2/D	0.8
1990	Mil-A	88	323	36	85	8	5	0	25	29	19	.263	.328	.319	82	-7	-7	35	18	3	4	.982	-7	2/3	-0.9
1991	Mil-A	140	526	63	149	27	4	2	47	27	34	.283	.322	.361	91	-8	-7	58	4	6	-2	.976	4	32	-0.4
1992	Mil-A	101	256	22	63	12	1	1	18	12	17	.246	.280	.313	67	-12	-11	21	6	2	1	.994	7	23/1D	-0.3
Total	17	1801	6189	726	1696	262	38	47	568	383	501	.274	.322	.351	88	-115	-99	689	137	78	-6	.985	50	*23/DS1P	0.1

■ CHARLIE GANZEL Ganzel, Charles William b: 6/18/1862, Waterford, Wis. d: 4/7/14, Quincy, Mass. BR/TR, 6', 161 lbs. Deb: 9/27/1884 F

YEAR	TM/L	G	AB	R	H	2B	3B	HR	RBI	BB	SO	AVG	OBP	SLG	PRO+	BR	/A	RC	SB	CS	SBR	FA	FR	POS	TPR
1884	StP-U	7	23	2	5	0	0	0		0		.217	.217	.217	87	-1	0	1				.956	-2	/CO	-0.1
1885	Phi-N	34	125	15	21	3	1	0	6	4	13	.168	.194	.208	31	-10	-9	5				.888	0	C/O	-0.6
1886	Phi-N	1	3	0	0	0	0	0	0	0	1	.000	.000	.000	-99	-1	-1	0	0			.600	-1	/C	-0.1
	Det-N	57	213	28	58	7	2	1	31	7	22	.272	.295	.338	90	-2	-3	23	5			.911	3	C/O1	0.4
	Yr	58	216	28	58	7	2	1	31	7	23	.269	.291	.333	87	-3	-4	23	5			.903	3	C/O1	0.3
1887	*Det-N	57	227	40	59	6	5	0	20	8	2	.260	.288	.330	71	-8	-9	23	3			.913	9	C/O13	0.4
1888	Det-N	95	386	45	96	13	5	1	46	14	15	.249	.277	.316	91	-4	-4	38	12			.900	-1	2C/3OS1	0.0
1889	Bos-N	73	275	30	73	3	5	1	43	15	11	.265	.308	.324	74	-8	-11	32	13			.927	5	CO/1S3	-0.3
1890	Bos-N	38	163	21	44	7	3	0	24	5	6	.270	.300	.350	84	-2	-4	18	1			.958	3	CO/S2	0.1
1891	Bos-N	70	263	33	68	18	5	1	29	12	13	.259	.304	.376	89	-1	-6	33	7			.956	4	CO	0.3
1892	*Bos-N	54	198	25	53	9	3	0	25	18	12	.268	.332	.343	97	2	-1	26	7			.933	-6	C/O1	-0.3
1893	Bos-N	73	281	50	75	10	2	1	48	22	9	.267	.325	.327	70	-10	-14	33	6			.952	-2	CO1	-1.1
1894	Bos-N	70	266	51	74	7	6	3	56	19	6	.278	.326	.383	67	-13	-17	35	1			.897	-5	C/1OS2	-1.3
1895	Bos-N	80	277	38	73	2	5	1	52	24	6	.264	.325	.318	63	-13	-17	30	1			.962	18	C/S1	0.7
1896	Bos-N	47	179	28	47	2	0	1	18	9	5	.263	.305	.291	56	-10	-12	18	2			.989	6	C/1S	-0.1
1897	Bos-N	30	105	15	28	4	3	0	14	4		.267	.300	.362	70	-4	-5	13	2			.942	2	C/1	0.0
Total	14	786	2984	421	774	91	45	10	412	161	121	.259	.301	.330	75	-86	-113	327	60			.934	36	CO/21S3	-2.0

■ BABE GANZEL Ganzel, Foster Pirie b: 5/22/01, Malden, Mass. d: 2/6/78, Jacksonville, Fla. BR/TR, 5'10.5", 172 lbs. Deb: 9/19/27 F

YEAR	TM/L	G	AB	R	H	2B	3B	HR	RBI	BB	SO	AVG	OBP	SLG	PRO+	BR	/A	RC	SB	CS	SBR	FA	FR	POS	TPR
1927	Was-A	13	48	7	21	4	2	1	13	7	3	.438	.509	.667	206	8	8	16	0	0	0	.944	0	O	0.7
1928	Was-A	10	26	2	2	1	0	0	4	1	4	.077	.111	.115	-41	-5	-5	0	0	0	0	1.000	-1	/O	-0.7
Total	2	23	74	9	23	5	2	1	17	8	7	.311	.378	.473	122	2	2	16	0	0	0	.957	-1	/O	0.0

■ JOHN GANZEL Ganzel, John Henry b: 4/7/1874, Kalamazoo, Mich. d: 1/14/59, Orlando, Fla. BR/TR, 6'0.5", 195 lbs. Deb: 4/21/1898 FM

YEAR	TM/L	G	AB	R	H	2B	3B	HR	RBI	BB	SO	AVG	OBP	SLG	PRO+	BR	/A	RC	SB	CS	SBR	FA	FR	POS	TPR
1898	Pit-N	15	45	5	6	0	0	0	2	4		.133	.220	.133	2	-6	-5	1	0			.963	-1	1	-0.6
1900	Chi-N	78	284	29	78	14	4	4	32	10		.275	.316	.394	99	-3	-1	39	5			.980	-4	1	-0.5
1901	NY-N	138	526	42	113	13	3	2	66	20		.215	.255	.262	52	-34	-31	38	6			**.986**	2	*1	-3.0
1903	NY-A	129	476	62	132	25	7	3	71	30		.277	.332	.378	106	8	4	66	9			**.988**	7	*1	0.9
1904	NY-A	130	465	50	121	16	10	6	48	24		.260	.309	.376	111	8	6	60	13			.988	-2	*1/2S	0.1
1907	Cin-N	145	531	61	135	20	**16**	2	64	29		.254	.295	.363	102	1	-1	62	9			.990	1	*1	-0.5
1908	Cin-N	112	388	32	97	16	10	1	53	19		.250	.289	.351	107	0	1	41	6			**.990**	-2	*1M	-0.3
Total	7	747	2715	281	682	104	50	18	336	136		.251	.296	.346	93	-25	-28	308	48			.987	0	1/2S	-3.9

■ JOE GARAGIOLA Garagiola, Joseph Henry b: 2/12/26, St.Louis, Mo. BL/TR, 6', 190 lbs. Deb: 5/26/46

YEAR	TM/L	G	AB	R	H	2B	3B	HR	RBI	BB	SO	AVG	OBP	SLG	PRO+	BR	/A	RC	SB	CS	SBR	FA	FR	POS	TPR
1946	*StL-N	74	211	21	50	4	1	3	22	23	25	.237	.312	.308	73	-6	-7	21	0			.990	-5	C	-1.0
1947	StL-N	77	183	20	47	10	2	5	25	40	14	.257	.398	.415	111	6	5	33	0			.987	1	C	0.9

YEAR	TM/L	G	AB	R	H	2B	3B	HR	RBI	BB	SO	AVG	OBP	SLG	PRO+	BR	/A	RC	SB	CS	SBR	FA	FR	POS	TPR
1948	StL-N	24	56	9	6	1	0	2	7	12	9	.107	.275	.232	36	-5	-5	5	0			.990	2	C	-0.2
1949	StL-N	81	241	25	63	14	0	3	26	31	19	.261	.348	.357	85	-3	-4	31	0			.984	7	C	0.7
1950	StL-N	34	88	8	28	6	1	2	20	10	7	.318	.388	.477	120	3	3	15	0			1.000	-3	C	0.1
1951	StL-N	27	72	9	14	3	2	2	9	9	7	.194	.284	.375	75	-3	-3	7	0	0	0	1.000	-3	C	-0.4
	Pit-N	72	212	24	54	8	2	9	35	32	20	.255	.358	.439	110	4	3	36	4	1	1	.986	-9	C	-0.2
	Yr	99	284	33	68	11	4	11	44	41	27	.239	.339	.423	101	1	1	43	4	1	1	**.989**	-11	C	-0.6
1952	Pit-N	118	344	35	94	15	4	8	54	50	24	.273	.369	.410	113	8	7	55	0	1	-1	.978	-3	*C	0.9
1953	Pit-N	27	73	9	17	5	0	2	14	10	11	.233	.341	.384	89	-1	-1	10	1	0	0	.989	-4	C	-0.3
	Chi-N	74	228	21	62	9	4	1	21	21	23	.272	.336	.360	80	-6	-7	27	0	0	0	.988	0	C	-0.3
	Yr	101	301	30	79	14	4	3	35	31	34	.262	.337	.365	82	-7	-8	38	1	0	0	.988	-4	C	-0.6
1954	Chi-N	63	153	16	43	5	0	5	21	28	12	.281	.405	.412	112	4	4	27	0	0	0	.982	-8	C	-0.1
	NY-N	5	11	1	3	2	0	0	1	1	2	.273	.333	.455	102	0	0	2	0	0	0	1.000	0	/C	0.0
	Yr	68	164	17	46	7	0	5	22	29	14	.280	.401	.415	112	4	4	29	0	0	0	.983	-8	C	-0.1
Total	9	676	1872	198	481	82	16	42	255	267	173	.257	.355	.385	96	2	-5	270	5	2		.986	-23	C	0.1

■ MIKE GARBARK Garbark, Nathaniel Michael (b: Nathaniel Michael Garbach) b: 2/2/16, Houston, Tex. BR/TR, 6', 200 lbs. Deb: 4/18/44 F

YEAR	TM/L	G	AB	R	H	2B	3B	HR	RBI	BB	SO	AVG	OBP	SLG	PRO+	BR	/A	RC	SB	CS	SBR	FA	FR	POS	TPR
1944	NY-A	89	299	23	78	9	4	1	33	25	27	.261	.320	.328	82	-6	-7	30	0	1	-1	.988	8	C	0.6
1945	NY-A	60	176	23	38	5	3	1	26	23	12	.216	.310	.295	73	-5	-6	16	0	1	-1	.972	4	C	0.1
Total	2	149	475	46	116	14	7	2	59	48	39	.244	.316	.316	79	-11	-13	47	0	2	-1	.982	12	C	0.7

■ BOB GARBARK Garbark, Robert Michael (b: Robert Michael Garbach) b: 11/13/09, Houston, Tex. d: 8/15/90, Meadville, Pa. BR/TR, 5'11", 178 lbs. Deb: 9/03/34 F

YEAR	TM/L	G	AB	R	H	2B	3B	HR	RBI	BB	SO	AVG	OBP	SLG	PRO+	BR	/A	RC	SB	CS	SBR	FA	FR	POS	TPR
1934	Cle-A	5	11	1	0	0	0	0	0	1	3	.000	.083	.000	-76	-3	-3	0	0	0	0	1.000	-2	/C	-0.4
1935	Cle-A	6	18	4	6	1	0	0	4	5	1	.333	.478	.389	124	1	1	4	0	0	0	1.000	2	/C	0.3
1937	Chi-N	1	1	0	0	0	0	0	0	0	0	.000	.000	.000	-96	-0	-0	0	0			.000	0	H	0.0
1938	Chi-N	23	54	2	14	0	0	0	5	1	0	.259	.273	.259	46	-4	-4	3	0			1.000	1	C/1	-0.2
1939	Chi-N	24	21	1	3	0	0	0	0	0	3	.143	.143	.143	-23	-4	-4	0	0			1.000	1	C	-0.3
1944	Phi-A	18	23	2	6	2	0	0	2	1	0	.261	.292	.348	83	-1	-1	2	0	0	0	1.000	-0	C	-0.1
1945	Bos-A	68	199	21	52	6	0	0	17	18	10	.261	.329	.291	79	-4	-5	20	0	1	-1	.993	-3	C	-0.6
Total	7	145	327	31	81	9	0	0	28	26	17	.248	.307	.275	64	-15	-15	29	0	1		.996	-2	C/1	-1.3

■ BARBARO GARBEY Garbey, Barbaro (Garbey) b: 12/4/56, Santiago, Cuba BR/TR, 5'10", 170 lbs. Deb: 4/03/84

YEAR	TM/L	G	AB	R	H	2B	3B	HR	RBI	BB	SO	AVG	OBP	SLG	PRO+	BR	/A	RC	SB	CS	SBR	FA	FR	POS	TPR
1984	*Det-A	110	327	45	94	17	1	5	52	17	35	.287	.327	.391	98	-1	-1	38	6	7	-2	.989	-5	13DO/2	-1.2
1985	Det-A	86	237	27	61	9	1	6	29	15	37	.257	.310	.380	88	-4	-4	27	3	2	-0	.991	-2	1OD/3	-0.9
1988	Tex-A	30	62	4	12	2	0	0	5	4	11	.194	.242	.226	31	-6	-6	3	0	0	0	.900	-0	/O13D	-0.7
Total	3	226	626	76	167	28	2	11	86	36	83	.267	.312	.371	88	-11	-11	68	9	9	-3	.990	-8	1/DO32	-2.8

■ ALEX GARBOWSKI Garbowski, Alexander b: 6/25/25, Yonkers, N.Y BR/TR, 6'1", 185 lbs. Deb: 4/16/52

YEAR	TM/L	G	AB	R	H	2B	3B	HR	RBI	BB	SO	AVG	OBP	SLG	PRO+	BR	/A	RC	SB	CS	SBR	FA	FR	POS	TPR
1952	Det-A	2	0	0	0	0	0	0	0	0	0	—	—	—	—	0	0	0	0	0	0	.000	0	R	0.0

■ KIKO GARCIA Garcia, Alfonso Rafael b: 10/14/53, Martinez, Cal. BR/TR, 5'11", 180 lbs. Deb: 9/11/76

YEAR	TM/L	G	AB	R	H	2B	3B	HR	RBI	BB	SO	AVG	OBP	SLG	PRO+	BR	/A	RC	SB	CS	SBR	FA	FR	POS	TPR
1976	Bal-A	11	32	2	7	1	1	1	4	0	4	.219	.219	.406	86	-1	-1	3	2	1	0	1.000	1	S	0.1
1977	Bal-A	65	131	20	29	6	0	2	10	6	31	.221	.255	.313	58	-8	-7	9	2	3	-1	.966	20	S/2	1.5
1978	Bal-A	79	186	17	49	6	4	0	13	7	43	.263	.290	.339	81	-6	-5	18	7	1	2	.945	4	S/2	0.8
1979	*Bal-A	126	417	54	103	15	9	5	24	32	87	.247	.304	.362	82	-13	-11	42	11	9	-2	.955	-18	*S2/3O	-1.8
1980	Bal-A	111	311	27	62	8	0	1	27	24	57	.199	.257	.235	36	-27	-27	18	8	4	0	.974	2	S2/O	-1.5
1981	*Hou-N	48	136	9	37	6	1	0	15	10	16	.272	.327	.331	91	-2	-1	15	2	2	-1	.950	3	S3/2	0.4
1982	Hou-N	34	76	5	16	5	0	1	5	3	15	.211	.241	.316	59	-5	-4	5	1	0	0	.946	5	S/32	0.2
1983	Phi-N	84	118	22	34	7	1	2	9	9	20	.288	.344	.415	111	1	2	15	1	2	-1	.970	19	2S3	2.2
1984	Phi-N	57	60	6	14	2	0	0	5	4	11	.233	.281	.267	54	-4	-4	4	0	0	0	.965	5	S3/2	0.2
1985	Phi-N	4	3	0	0	0	0	0	0	0	1	.000	.000	.000	-97	-1	-1	0	0	0	0	1.000	-1	/S3	-0.2
Total	10	619	1470	162	351	56	16	12	112	95	285	.239	.287	.323	70	-66	-59	128	34	22	-3	.961	39	S2/3O	1.9

■ CARLOS GARCIA Garcia, Carlos Jesus (Guerrero) b: 10/15/67, Tachira, Venez. BR/TR, 6'1", 185 lbs. Deb: 9/20/90

YEAR	TM/L	G	AB	R	H	2B	3B	HR	RBI	BB	SO	AVG	OBP	SLG	PRO+	BR	/A	RC	SB	CS	SBR	FA	FR	POS	TPR
1990	Pit-N	4	4	1	2	0	0	0	0	0	2	.500	.500	.500	183	0	0	1	0	0	0	1.000	1	/S	0.1
1991	Pit-N	12	24	2	6	0	2	0	1	1	8	.250	.280	.417	95	-0	-0	2	0	0	0	.947	2	/S32	0.2
1992	*Pit-N	22	39	4	8	1	0	0	4	0	9	.205	.205	.231	24	-4	-4	2	0	0	0	.977	2	2/S	-0.1
Total	3	38	67	7	16	1	2	0	5	1	19	.239	.250	.313	59	-4	-4	5	0	0	0	.951	5	/S23	0.2

■ DAMASO GARCIA Garcia, Damaso Domingo (Sanchez) b: 2/7/55, Moca, D.R. BR/TR, 6', 170 lbs. Deb: 6/24/78

YEAR	TM/L	G	AB	R	H	2B	3B	HR	RBI	BB	SO	AVG	OBP	SLG	PRO+	BR	/A	RC	SB	CS	SBR	FA	FR	POS	TPR
1978	NY-A	18	41	5	8	0	0	0	1	2	6	.195	.233	.195	22	-4	-4	2	1	0	0	.959	2	2/S	-0.1
1979	NY-A	11	38	3	10	1	0	0	4	0	2	.263	.263	.289	50	-3	-3	3	2	0	1	.902	-6	S/3	-0.6
1980	Tor-A	140	543	50	151	30	7	4	46	12	55	.278	.297	.381	81	-13	-16	54	13	13	-4	.980	16	*2/D	0.5
1981	Tor-A	64	250	24	63	8	1	1	13	9	32	.252	.278	.304	64	-11	-12	21	13	3	2	.972	-15	2/D	-2.2
1982	Tor-A	147	597	89	185	32	3	5	42	21	44	.310	.339	.399	93	1	-6	81	54	20	4	.980	10	*2/D	1.6
1983	Tor-A	131	525	84	161	23	6	3	38	24	34	.307	.339	.390	94	-0	-4	66	31	17	-1	.981	-16	*2	-1.5
1984	Tor-A★	152	633	79	180	32	5	5	46	16	46	.284	.312	.374	86	-10	-13	76	46	12	7	.980	-14	*2/D	-1.6
1985	*Tor-A★	146	600	70	169	25	4	8	65	15	41	.282	.304	.377	83	-13	-15	64	28	15	-1	.981	-34	*2	-4.5
1986	Tor-A	122	424	57	119	22	0	6	46	13	32	.281	.308	.375	83	-9	-11	44	9	6	-1	.985	-7	*2D/1	-1.4
1988	Atl-N	21	60	3	7	1	0	1	4	3	10	.117	.159	.183	-2	-8	-8	1	1	0	0	.984	-4	2	-1.2
1989	Mon-N	80	203	26	55	9	1	3	18	15	20	.271	.321	.369	96	-1	-1	23	5	4	-1	.972	6	2/3	0.6
Total	11	1032	3914	490	1108	183	27	36	323	130	322	.283	.311	.371	84	-72	-94	435	203	90	7	.980	-62	2/DS31	-10.4

■ DANNY GARCIA Garcia, Daniel Raphael b: 4/29/54, Brooklyn, N.Y. BL/TL, 6'1", 182 lbs. Deb: 4/26/81

YEAR	TM/L	G	AB	R	H	2B	3B	HR	RBI	BB	SO	AVG	OBP	SLG	PRO+	BR	/A	RC	SB	CS	SBR	FA	FR	POS	TPR
1981	KC-A	12	14	4	2	0	0	0	0	0	2	.143	.143	.143	-18	-2	-2	0	0	0	0	1.000	-2	/O1	-0.4

■ LEO GARCIA Garcia, Leonardo Antonio (Peralt b: 11/6/62, Santiago, D.R. BL/TL, 5'8", 160 lbs. Deb: 4/06/87

YEAR	TM/L	G	AB	R	H	2B	3B	HR	RBI	BB	SO	AVG	OBP	SLG	PRO+	BR	/A	RC	SB	CS	SBR	FA	FR	POS	TPR
1987	Cin-N	31	30	8	6	0	0	1	2	4	8	.200	.294	.300	55	-2	-2	3	3	1	0	1.000	-2	O	-0.4
1988	Cin-N	23	28	2	4	1	0	0	0	4	5	.143	.250	.179	24	-3	-3	1	0	1	-1	1.000	-1	/O	-0.5
Total	2	54	58	10	10	1	0	1	2	8	13	.172	.273	.241	41	-4	-5	4	3	2	-0	1.000	-4	/O	-0.9

■ PEDRO GARCIA Garcia, Pedro Modesto (Delfi) b: 4/17/50, Guayama, P.R. BR/TR, 5'10", 175 lbs. Deb: 4/06/73

YEAR	TM/L	G	AB	R	H	2B	3B	HR	RBI	BB	SO	AVG	OBP	SLG	PRO+	BR	/A	RC	SB	CS	SBR	FA	FR	POS	TPR
1973	Mil-A	160	580	67	142	**32**	5	15	54	40	119	.245	.299	.395	96	-6	-5	66	11	10	-3	.970	-12	*2	-1.0
1974	Mil-A	141	452	46	90	15	4	12	54	26	67	.199	.251	.330	66	-21	-21	37	8	5	-1	.970	-11	*2	-2.7
1975	Mil-A	98	302	40	68	15	2	6	38	18	59	.225	.273	.348	74	-11	-11	27	12	6	0	.985	19	2/D	1.3
1976	Mil-A	41	106	12	23	7	1	1	9	4	23	.217	.259	.330	73	-4	-4	9	2	2	-1	.971	-3	2	-0.6
	Det-A	77	227	21	45	10	2	3	20	9	40	.198	.242	.300	56	-13	-14	16	2	3	-1	.958	-0	2	-1.1
	Yr	118	333	33	68	17	3	4	29	13	63	.204	.247	.309	61	-17	-17	25	4	5	-2	.962	-3	*2	-1.7
1977	Tor-A	41	130	10	27	10	1	0	9	5	21	.208	.254	.300	50	-9	-9	10	0	0	0	.971	-2	2/D	-0.9
Total	5	558	1797	196	395	89	15	37	184	102	329	.220	.270	.348	75	-64	-64	164	35	26	-5	.971	-8	2/D	-5.0

■ CHICO GARCIA Garcia, Vinicio Uzcanga b: 12/24/24, Verzcruz, Mexico BR/TR, 5'8", 170 lbs. Deb: 4/24/54

YEAR	TM/L	G	AB	R	H	2B	3B	HR	RBI	BB	SO	AVG	OBP	SLG	PRO+	BR	/A	RC	SB	CS	SBR	FA	FR	POS	TPR
1954	Bal-A	39	62	6	7	0	2	0	5	8	3	.113	.214	.177	9	-8	-7	3	0	0	0	.962	8	2	0.1

■ AL GARDELLA Gardella, Alfred Stephan b: 1/11/18, New York, N.Y. BL/TL, 5'10", 172 lbs. Deb: 5/17/45 F

YEAR	TM/L	G	AB	R	H	2B	3B	HR	RBI	BB	SO	AVG	OBP	SLG	PRO+	BR	/A	RC	SB	CS	SBR	FA	FR	POS	TPR
1945	NY-N	16	26	2	2	0	0	0	1	4	3	.077	.226	.077	-14	-4	-4	1	0			.961	-1	/1O	-0.6

YEAR	TM/L	G	AB	R	H	2B	3B	HR	RBI	BB	SO	AVG	OBP	SLG	PRO+	BR	/A	RC	SB	CS	SBR	FA	FR	POS	TPR

■ DANNY GARDELLA Gardella, Daniel Lewis b: 2/26/20, New York, N.Y. BL/TL, 5'7.5", 160 lbs. Deb: 5/14/44 F

1944	NY-N	47	112	20	28	2	2	6	14	11	13	.250	.323	.464	120	2	2	17	0			.912	2	O	0.3
1945	NY-N	121	430	54	117	10	1	18	71	46	55	.272	.349	.426	113	8	7	65	2			.954	-2	O1	-0.1
1950	StL-N	1	1	0	0	0	0	0	0	0	0	.000	.000	.000	-95	-0	-0	0	0			.000	0	H	0.0
Total	3	169	543	74	145	12	3	24	85	57	68	.267	.343	.433	114	10	9	82	2			.943	-0	O/1	0.2

■ RON GARDENHIRE Gardenhire, Ronald Clyde b: 10/24/57, Butzbach, Germany BR/TR, 6', 175 lbs. Deb: 9/01/81 C

1981	NY-N	27	48	2	13	1	0	0	3	5	9	.271	.340	.292	82	-1	-1	5	2	2	-1	.969	4	S/23	0.4
1982	NY-N	141	384	29	92	17	1	3	33	23	55	.240	.283	.313	67	-18	-17	32	5	6	-2	.956	16	*S/23	0.8
1983	NY-N	17	32	1	2	0	0	0	1	1	4	.063	.091	.063	-57	-7	-7	0	0	0	0	1.000	0	S	-0.6
1984	NY-N	74	207	20	51	7	1	1	10	9	43	.246	.278	.304	64	-10	-10	17	6	1	1	.947	-1	S2/3	-0.9
1985	NY-N	26	39	5	7	2	1	0	2	8	11	.179	.319	.282	71	-1	-1	4	0	0	0	.911	-1	S/23	-0.1
Total	5	285	710	57	165	27	3	4	49	46	122	.232	.279	.296	62	-37	-36	57	13	9	-2	.955	16	S/23	-0.4

■ ALEX GARDNER Gardner, Alexander b: 4/28/1861, Toronto, Ont., Can. d: 6/18/26, Danvers, Mass. Deb: 5/10/1884

| 1884 | Was-a | 1 | 3 | 0 | 0 | 0 | 0 | 0 | | 0 | | .000 | .000 | .000 | -99 | -1 | -1 | 0 | | | | .600 | -1 | /C | -0.1 |

■ ART GARDNER Gardner, Arthur Junior b: 9/21/52, Madden, Miss. BL/TL, 5'11", 175 lbs. Deb: 9/02/75

1975	Hou-N	13	31	3	6	0	0	0	2	1	8	.194	.242	.194	24	-3	-3	1	1	0	0	1.000	-0	/O	-0.3
1977	Hou-N	66	65	7	10	0	0	0	3	3	15	.154	.203	.154	-3	-9	-9	2	0	0	0	1.000	4	O	-0.5
1978	SF-N	7	3	2	0	0	0	0	0	0	2	.000	.000	.000	-99	-1	-1	0	0	1	-1	1.000	0	H	-0.1
Total	3	86	99	12	16	0	0	0	5	4	25	.162	.210	.162	2	-13	-12	3	1	1	-0	1.000	4	/O	-0.9

■ EARLE GARDNER Gardner, Earle McClurkin b: 1/24/1884, Sparta, Ill. d: 3/2/43, Sparta, Ill. BR/TR, 5'11", 160 lbs. Deb: 9/18/08

1908	NY-A	20	75	7	16	2	0	0	4	1		.213	.234	.240	53	-4	-4	4	0			.947	4	2	0.0
1909	NY-A	22	85	12	28	4	0	0	15	3		.329	.352	.376	129	3	3	12	4			.945	-8	2	-0.6
1910	NY-A	86	271	36	66	4	2	1	24	21		.244	.303	.284	79	-5	-7	26	9			.936	6	2	-0.2
1911	NY-A	102	357	36	94	13	2	0	39	20		.263	.312	.311	69	-13	-16	39	14			.959	-3	*2	-2.1
1912	NY-A	43	160	14	45	3	1	0	26	5		.281	.303	.313	72	-5	-7	18	11			.922	-5	2	-1.3
Total	5	273	948	105	249	26	5	1	108	50		.263	.305	.304	76	-24	-31	100	38			.944	-6	2	-4.2

■ GID GARDNER Gardner, Frank Washington b: 6/9/1859, Attleboro, Mass. d: 8/1/14, Cambridge, Mass. 165 lbs. Deb: 8/23/1879

1879	Tro-N	2	6	1	1	0	0	0	0	0	0	.167	.167	.167	11	-1	-1	0				.429	-1	/P	0.0
1880	Cle-N	10	32	0	6	1	1	0	4	2	4	.188	.235	.281	76	-1	-1	2				.850	-1	/PO	0.0
1883	Bal-a	42	161	28	44	10	3	1		18		.273	.346	.391	133	7	6	22				.837	-1	O/23P	0.5
1884	Bal-a	41	173	32	37	6	8	2		14		.214	.280	.376	111	3	2	19				.860	4	O/1	0.4
	CP-U	38	149	22	38	10	2	0		10		.255	.302	.349	120	3	3	16				.872	-1	O/3P2	0.1
	Bal-U	1	4	0	1	0	0	0		0		.250	.250	.250	63	-0	-0	0				.714	-0	/S	0.0
	Yr	39	153	22	39	10	2	0		10		.255	.301	.346	119	3	3	16				.872	-1	O/3P2S	0.1
1885	Bal-a	44	170	22	37	5	4	0		12		.218	.269	.294	81	-4	-3	14				.891	3	2/O1P	0.1
1887	Ind-N	18	63	8	11	1	0	1	8	12	11	.175	.307	.238	57	-3	-3	7	7			1.000	-3	O/2	-0.5
1888	Was-N	1	3	0	1	0	0	0	0	1	1	.333	.500	.333	184	0	0	1	0			.750	0	/S	0.1
	Phi-N	1	3	0	2	0	0	0	1	0	0	.667	.667	.667	314	1	1	1	0			1.000	-1	/2	0.0
	Was-N	1	1	0	0	0	0	0	0	0	0	.000	.000	.000	-99	-0	-0	0	0			1.000	-0	/2	-0.1
	Yr	3	7	0	3	0	0	0	1	1	1	.429	.500	.429	206	1	1	2	0			1.000	-1	/2S	0.0
Total	7	199	765	113	178	33	18	4	13	69	16	.233	.298	.339	104	6	5	82	7			.855	0	O/2P31S	0.6

■ JEFF GARDNER Gardner, Jeffrey Scott b: 2/4/64, Newport Beach, Cal. BL/TR, 5'11", 165 lbs. Deb: 9/10/91

1991	NY-N	13	37	3	6	0	0	0	1	4	6	.162	.244	.162	17	-4	-4	2	0	0	0	.818	-2	/S2	-0.6
1992	SD-N	15	19	0	2	0	0	0	0	1	8	.105	.150	.105	-26	-3	-3	0	0	0	0	1.000	3	2	0.0
Total	2	28	56	3	8	0	0	0	1	5	14	.143	.213	.143	2	-7	-7	2	0	0	0	1.000	1	/2S	-0.6

■ RAY GARDNER Gardner, Raymond Vincent b: 10/25/01, Frederick, Md. d: 5/3/68, Frederick, Md. BR/TR, 5'8", 145 lbs. Deb: 4/16/29

1929	Cle-A	82	256	28	67	3	2	1	24	29	16	.262	.337	.301	63	-12	-14	26	10	13	-5	.952	8	S	-0.1
1930	Cle-A	33	13	7	1	0	0	0	1	0	0	.077	.077	.077	-59	-3	-3	0	0	1	0	.861	8	S/23	0.4
Total	2	115	269	35	68	3	2	1	25	29	16	.253	.326	.290	57	-15	-17	26	10	14	-5	.945	16	S/23	0.3

■ BILLY GARDNER Gardner, William Frederick "Shotgun" b: 7/19/27, Waterford, Conn. BR/TR, 6', 180 lbs. Deb: 4/22/54 MC

1954	NY-N	62	108	10	23	5	0	1	7	6	19	.213	.261	.287	42	-9	-9	8	0	1	-1	.987	10	32/S	0.0
1955	NY-N	59	187	26	38	10	1	3	17	13	19	.203	.262	.316	52	-13	-13	16	0	0	0	.940	0	S3/2	-1.0
1956	Bal-A	144	515	53	119	16	2	11	50	29	53	.231	.281	.334	67	-30	-25	45	5	5	-2	.974	-12	*2S/3	-2.6
1957	Bal-A	154	644	79	169	36	3	6	55	53	67	.262	.326	.356	92	-12	-7	75	10	7	-1	.987	6	*2/S	1.0
1958	Bal-A	151	560	32	126	28	2	3	33	34	53	.225	.273	.298	60	-33	-30	45	2	3	-1	.985	-22	*2S	-4.4
1959	Bal-A	140	401	34	87	13	2	6	27	38	61	.217	.286	.304	64	-21	-20	34	2	1	0	.976	31	*2/S3	2.0
1960	Was-A	145	592	71	152	26	5	9	56	43	76	.257	.314	.363	83	-15	-14	66	0	4	-2	.973	-2	*2S	-0.5
1961	Min-A	45	154	13	36	9	0	1	11	10	14	.234	.280	.312	55	-9	-10	12	0	0	0	.973	-4	2/3	-1.0
	*NY-A	41	99	11	21	5	0	1	2	6	18	.212	.278	.293	56	-7	-6	8	0	0	0	.952	3	3/2	-0.3
	Yr	86	253	24	57	14	0	2	13	16	32	.225	.279	.304	56	-16	-16	20	0	0	0	.975	-1	23	-1.3
1962	NY-A	4	1	1	0	0	0	0	0	0	1	.000	.000	.000	-99	-0	-0	0	0	0	0	1.000	1	/23	0.1
	Bos-A	53	199	22	54	9	2	0	12	10	39	.271	.310	.337	72	-7	-8	20	0	1	-1	.963	-8	2/3S	-1.3
	Yr	57	200	23	54	9	2	0	12	10	40	.270	.308	.335	71	-8	-8	20	0	1	-1	.963	-7	2/3S	-1.2
1963	Bos-A	36	84	4	16	2	1	0	1	4	19	.190	.236	.238	32	-7	-8	6	0	0	0	.989	7	2/3	0.0
Total	10	1034	3544	356	841	159	18	41	271	246	439	.237	.293	.327	70	-164	-150	334	19	22	-8	.978	8	2S/3	-8.0

■ LARRY GARDNER Gardner, William Lawrence b: 5/13/1886, Enosburg Falls, Vt d: 3/11/76, St.George, Vt. BL/TR, 5'8", 165 lbs. Deb: 6/25/08

1908	Bos-A	3	10	0	3	1	0	0		0		.300	.300	.400	124	0	0	1	0			.333	-3	/3	-0.3
1909	Bos-A	19	37	7	11	1	2	0	5	4		.297	.381	.432	153	2	2	7	1			.800	-4	/3S	-0.1
1910	Bos-A	113	413	55	117	12	10	2	36	41		.283	.354	.375	125	14	12	58	8			.944	-8	*2	0.3
1911	Bos-A	138	492	80	140	17	8	4	44	64		.285	.373	.376	110	8	8	81	27			.962	24	32	3.0
1912	*Bos-A	143	517	88	163	24	18	3	86	56		.315	.383	.449	131	25	21	98	25			.930	-1	*3	2.2
1913	Bos-A	131	473	64	133	17	10	0	63	47	34	.281	.347	.359	104	4	3	63	18			.943	-16	*3	-1.2
1914	Bos-A	155	553	50	143	23	19	3	68	35	39	.259	.303	.385	107	1	1	61	16	23	-9	.942	0	*3	-0.3
1915	*Bos-A	127	430	51	111	14	6	1	55	39	24	.258	.327	.326	98	-3	-1	49	11	12	-4	.933	-7	*3	-0.7
1916	*Bos-A	148	493	47	152	19	7	2	62	48	27	.308	.372	.387	128	17	17	79	12			.953	-14	*3	0.8
1917	Bos-A	146	501	53	133	23	7	1	61	54	37	.265	.341	.345	110	6	6	66	16			.937	-7	*3	0.3
1918	Phi-A	127	463	50	132	22	6	1	52	43	22	.285	.346	.365	113	7	7	60	9			.964	10	*3	2.2
1919	Cle-A	139	524	67	157	29	7	2	79	39	29	.300	.352	.393	103	6	2	75	7			.946	-6	*3	0.1
1920	*Cle-A	154	597	72	185	31	11	3	118	53	25	.310	.367	.414	103	6	3	86	3	20	-11	.976	-2	*3	-0.2
1921	Cle-A	153	586	101	187	32	14	3	120	65	16	.319	.391	.437	109	11	9	103	3	3	-1	.950	-1	*3	1.7
1922	Cle-A	137	470	74	134	31	3	2	68	49	21	.285	.355	.377	90	-6	-6	64	9	8	-2	.951	-5	*3	-0.4
1923	Cle-A	52	79	4	20	5	1	0	12	12	7	.253	.352	.342	83	-2	-2	10	0	1	-1	.962	3	3	0.1
1924	Cle-A	38	50	3	10	0	0	0	4	5	1	.200	.273	.200	23	-6	-7	3	0	1	0	.875	-4	/32	-0.6
Total	17	1923	6688	866	1931	301	129	27	934	654	282	.289	.355	.384	109	90	77	965	165	68		.948	-39	*32/S	6.6

YEAR	TM/L	G	AB	R	H	2B	3B	HR	RBI	BB	SO	AVG	OBP	SLG	PRO+	BR	/A	RC	SB	CS	SBR	FA	FR	POS	TPR
■ ART GARIBALDI Garibaldi, Arthur Edward b: 8/20/07, San Francisco, Cal d: 10/19/67, Sacramento, Cal. BR/TR, 5'8", 165 lbs. Deb: 6/20/36																									
1936	StL-N	71	232	30	64	12	0	1	20	16	30	.276	.323	.341	79	-7	-7	26	3			.925	-5	32	-0.9
■ DEBS GARMS Garms, Debs C. "Tex" b: 6/26/08, Bangs, Tex. d: 12/16/84, Glen Rose, Tex. BL/TR, 5'8.5", 165 lbs. Deb: 8/10/32																									
1932	StL-A	34	134	20	38	7	1	1	8	17	7	.284	.364	.373	86	-1	-2	19	4	3	-1	.953	-1	O	-0.6
1933	StL-A	78	189	35	60	10	2	4	24	30	21	.317	.416	.455	123	10	8	36	2	5	-2	.960	-2	O	0.1
1934	StL-A	91	232	25	68	14	4	0	31	27	19	.293	.372	.388	89	-1	-4	35	0	0	0	.942	-3	O	-0.8
1935	StL-A	10	15	1	4	0	0	0	0	2	2	.267	.353	.267	59	-1	-1	2	0	0	0	.800	-0	/O	-0.1
1937	Bos-N	125	478	60	124	15	8	2	37	37	33	.259	.317	.337	85	-15	-9	54	2			.977	-8	O3	-1.9
1938	Bos-N	117	428	62	135	19	1	0	47	34	22	.315	.371	.364	114	3	8	60	4			.985	-7	O3/2	0.0
1939	Bos-N	132	513	68	153	24	9	2	37	39	20	.298	.350	.392	107	-1	4	73	2			.964	-4	O3	-0.2
1940	Pit-N	103	358	76	127	23	7	5	57	23	6	.355	.395	.500	147	21	22	72	3			.964	-1	3O	2.2
1941	Pit-N	83	220	25	58	9	3	3	42	22	12	.264	.331	.373	98	-1	-1	28	0			.911	-10	3O	-1.2
1943	*StL-N	90	249	26	64	10	2	0	22	13	8	.257	.299	.313	74	-8	-9	24	1			.980	-5	O3/S	-1.8
1944	*StL-N	73	149	17	30	3	0	0	5	13	8	.201	.265	.221	37	-12	-12	9	0			1.000	-8	O3	-2.2
1945	StL-N	74	146	23	49	7	2	0	18	31	3	.336	.452	.411	137	10	10	30	0			.956	-10	3O	0.0
Total	12	1010	3111	438	910	141	39	17	328	288	161	.293	.355	.379	103	6	14	442	18	8		.966	-58	O3/S2	-6.5
■ PHIL GARNER Garner, Philip Mason b: 4/30/49, Jefferson City, Tenn. BR/TR, 5'10", 177 lbs. Deb: 9/10/73 MC																									
1973	Oak-A	9	5	0	0	0	0	0	0	0	3	.000	.000	.000	-99	-1	-1	0	0	0	0	1.000	1	/3	-0.1
1974	Oak-A	30	28	4	5	1	0	0	1	1	5	.179	.207	.214	23	-3	-3	1	1	1	-0	.955	4	3/S2D	0.1
1975	*Oak-A	160	488	46	120	21	5	6	54	30	65	.246	.296	.346	83	-13	-11	48	4	6	-2	.968	-16	*2/S	-2.2
1976	Oak-A★	159	555	54	145	29	12	8	74	36	71	.261	.309	.400	111	3	5	67	35	13	3	.975	-14	*2	0.5
1977	Pit-N	153	585	99	152	35	10	17	77	55	65	.260	.326	.441	101	2	-0	84	32	9	4	.971	1	*32S	0.7
1978	Pit-N	154	528	66	138	25	9	10	66	66	71	.261	.349	.400	104	7	4	71	27	14	-0	.976	10	23/S	1.9
1979	*Pit-N	150	549	76	161	32	8	11	59	55	74	.293	.361	.441	112	13	10	89	17	8	0	.981	6	23S	2.2
1980	Pit-N★	151	548	62	142	27	6	5	58	46	53	.259	.319	.358	87	-8	-9	64	32	7	5	.976	16	*2/S	2.3
1981	Pit-N★	56	181	22	46	6	2	1	20	21	21	.254	.332	.326	84	-3	-3	19	4	6	-2	.968	-6	2	-1.0
	*Hou-N	31	113	13	27	3	1	0	6	15	11	.239	.328	.283	79	-3	-3	12	6	2	1	.982	0	2	0.0
	Yr	87	294	35	73	9	3	1	26	36	32	.248	.330	.310	82	-6	-6	32	10	8	-2	.973	-6	2	-1.0
1982	Hou-N	155	588	65	161	33	8	13	83	40	92	.274	.323	.423	116	4	9	78	24	13	-1	.980	1	*23	1.7
1983	Hou-N	154	567	76	135	24	2	14	79	63	84	.238	.320	.362	94	-9	-4	68	18	12	-2	.945	4	*3	-0.4
1984	Hou-N	128	374	60	104	17	6	4	45	43	63	.278	.359	.388	118	6	9	53	3	2	-0	.979	23	32	3.3
1985	Hou-N	135	463	65	124	23	10	6	51	34	72	.268	.321	.400	103	-1	1	57	4	4	-1	.932	-9	*32	-1.1
1986	*Hou-N	107	313	43	83	14	3	9	41	30	45	.265	.331	.415	108	2	3	39	12	6	0	.896	1	3/2	0.2
1987	Hou-N	43	112	15	25	5	0	3	15	8	20	.223	.275	.348	66	-6	-5	11	1	0	0	.976	2	3/2	-0.4
	LA-N	70	126	14	24	4	0	2	8	20	24	.190	.301	.270	54	-8	-8	11	5	1	1	.923	6	32/S	-0.1
	Yr	113	238	29	49	9	0	5	23	28	44	.206	.289	.307	60	-14	-13	22	6	1	1	.947	8	32/S	-0.5
1988	SF-N	15	13	0	2	0	0	0	1	1	3	.154	.214	.154	8	-2	-1	0	0	1	-1	.000	0	/3	-0.2
Total	16	1860	6136	780	1594	299	82	109	738	564	842	.260	.326	.389	100	-20	-9	774	225	105	4	.974	30	23/SD	7.4
■ RALPH GARR Garr, Ralph Allen "Road Runner" b: 12/12/45, Monroe, La. BL/TR, 5'11", 197 lbs. Deb: 9/03/68																									
1968	Atl-N	11	7	3	2	0	0	0	0	1	0	.286	.375	.286	100	0	0	1	1	0	0	.000	0	H	0.0
1969	Atl-N	22	27	6	6	1	0	0	2	2	4	.222	.276	.259	50	-2	-2	2	1	1	-0	.857	-0	/O	-0.3
1970	Atl-N	37	96	18	27	3	0	0	8	5	12	.281	.317	.313	65	-4	-5	9	5	2	0	1.000	-0	O	-0.6
1971	Atl-N	154	639	101	219	24	6	9	44	30	68	.343	.374	.441	122	24	20	105	30	14	1	.968	6	*O	1.9
1972	Atl-N	134	554	87	180	22	0	12	53	25	41	.325	.361	.430	113	16	11	86	25	9	2	.962	-1	*O	0.5
1973	Atl-N	148	668	94	200	32	6	11	55	22	64	.299	.324	.415	96	1	-5	87	35	11	4	.968	-1	*O	-0.9
1974	Atl-N★	143	606	87	**214**	24	**17**	11	54	28	52	**.353**	.384	.503	141	35	32	113	26	16	-2	.967	-3	*O	2.2
1975	Atl-N	151	625	74	174	26	**11**	6	31	44	50	.278	.329	.384	94	-3	-6	78	14	9	-1	.966	3	*O	-1.0
1976	Chi-A	136	527	63	158	22	6	4	36	17	41	.300	.324	.387	107	3	3	66	14	5	1	.978	-6	*O/D	-0.8
1977	Chi-A	134	543	78	163	29	7	10	54	27	44	.300	.333	.435	108	4	5	77	12	7	-1	.987	3	*O/D	0.1
1978	Chi-A	118	443	67	122	18	9	3	29	24	41	.275	.314	.377	93	-5	-5	51	7	5	-1	.959	1	*O/D	-1.0
1979	Chi-A	102	307	34	86	10	2	9	39	17	19	.280	.320	.414	96	-2	-2	39	2	4	-2	.951	-8	OD	-1.4
	Cal-A	6	24	0	3	0	0	0	0	0	3	.125	.125	.125	-33	-4	-4	0	0	0	0	.000	0	/D	-0.4
	Yr	108	331	34	89	10	2	9	39	17	22	.269	.307	.393	87	-7	-7	38	2	4	-2	.951	-8	OD/H	-1.8
1980	Cal-A	21	42	5	8	1	0	0	3	4	6	.190	.261	.214	33	-4	-4	2	0	0	0	.750	-0	/OD	-0.4
Total	13	1317	5108	717	1562	212	64	75	408	246	445	.306	.340	.416	106	59	37	716	172	83	2	.968	-8	*O/D	-2.1
■ ADRIAN GARRETT Garrett, Henry Adrian "Pat" b: 1/3/43, Brooksville, Fla. BL/TR, 6'3", 185 lbs. Deb: 4/13/66 FC																									
1966	Atl-N	4	3	0	0	0	0	0	0	0	2	.000	.000	.000	-99	-1	-1	0	0	0	0	.000	0	/O	-0.1
1970	Chi-N	3	3	0	0	0	0	0	0	0	3	.000	.000	.000	-89	-1	-1	0	0	0	0	.000	0	H	-0.1
1971	Oak-A	14	21	1	3	0	0	1	2	5	7	.143	.308	.286	70	-1	-1	2	0	0	0	1.000	-0	/O	-0.1
1972	Oak-A	14	11	0	0	0	0	0	0	1	4	.000	.083	.000	-78	-2	-2	0	0	0	0	1.000	-1	/O	-0.3
1973	Chi-N	36	54	7	12	0	0	3	8	4	18	.222	.276	.389	77	-2	-2	6	1	0	0	1.000	-0	/OC	-0.2
1974	Chi-N	10	8	0	0	0	0	0	0	1	1	.000	.111	.000	-64	-2	-2	0	0	0	0	1.000	1	/C1O	-0.1
1975	Chi-N	16	21	1	2	0	0	1	6	1	8	.095	.136	.238	2	-3	-3	1	0	0	0	1.000	1	/1	-0.2
	Cal-A	37	107	17	28	5	0	6	18	14	28	.262	.347	.477	141	4	5	20	3	0	1	1.000	-0	D1/OC	0.5
1976	Cal-A	29	48	4	6	3	0	0	3	5	16	.125	.208	.188	17	-5	-5	2	0	0	0	.974	-4	C/1D	-0.9
Total	8	163	276	30	51	8	0	11	37	31	87	.185	.267	.333	71	-12	-11	30	4	0	1	.959	-3	/DCO1	-1.5
■ WAYNE GARRETT Garrett, Ronald Wayne b: 12/3/47, Brooksville, Fla. BL/TR, 5'11", 183 lbs. Deb: 4/12/69 F																									
1969	*NY-N	124	400	38	87	11	3	1	39	40	75	.218	.293	.268	57	-22	-23	34	4	2	0	.951	-13	32/S	-3.4
1970	NY-N	114	366	74	93	17	4	12	45	81	60	.254	.392	.421	118	12	12	68	5	1	1	.944	-19	32/S	-0.3
1971	NY-N	56	202	20	43	2	0	1	11	28	31	.213	.312	.238	58	-10	-10	15	1	3	-2	.967	-4	3/2	-1.7
1972	NY-N	111	298	41	69	13	3	2	29	70	58	.232	.378	.315	101	3	4	41	3	2	-0	.960	2	32	0.7
1973	*NY-N	140	504	76	129	20	3	16	58	72	74	.256	.350	.403	110	6	7	74	6	5	-1	.942	11	*3/S2	1.9
1974	NY-N	151	522	55	117	14	3	13	53	89	96	.224	.339	.337	91	-5	-4	64	4	6	-2	.955	14	*3/S	0.7
1975	NY-N	107	274	49	73	8	3	6	34	50	45	.266	.382	.383	118	6	8	44	3	2	-0	.966	11	3/S2	1.9
1976	NY-N	80	251	36	56	8	1	4	26	52	26	.223	.359	.311	97	-1	1	31	7	5	-1	.948	3	32/S	0.4
	Mon-N	59	177	15	43	4	1	2	11	30	20	.243	.353	.311	86	-1	-2	21	2	2	-1	.982	1	2/3	0.2
	Yr	139	428	51	99	12	2	6	37	82	46	.231	.356	.311	92	-2	-1	52	9	7	-2	.949	4	32/S	0.6
1977	Mon-N	68	159	17	43	6	1	2	22	30	18	.270	.389	.358	105	2	3	24	2	2	-1	1.000	2	3/2	0.4
1978	Mon-N	49	69	6	12	0	0	1	2	8	10	.174	.260	.217	35	-6	-6	4	0	0	0	.969	1	3	-0.6
	StL-N	33	63	11	21	4	0	1	10	11	16	.333	.432	.444	148	4	5	12	1	0	0	.927	-2	3	0.3
	Yr	82	132	17	33	4	0	2	12	19	26	.250	.344	.326	89	-2	-1	15	1	0	0	.945	-2	3	-0.3
Total	10	1092	3285	438	786	107	22	61	340	561	529	.239	.352	.341	95	-11	-5	432	38	30	-7	.956	7	32/S	0.5
■ GIL GARRIDO Garrido, Gil Gonzalo b: 6/26/41, Panama City, Pan. BR/TR, 5'8", 160 lbs. Deb: 4/24/64																									
1964	SF-N	14	25	1	2	0	0	0	1	2	7	.080	.148	.080	-33	-4	-4	0	1	0	0	.969	-1	S	-0.5
1968	Atl-N	18	53	5	11	0	0	0	2	2	2	.208	.236	.208	34	-4	-4	3	0	0	0	.987	3	S	0.1
1969	*Atl-N	82	227	18	50	5	1	0	10	16	11	.220	.272	.251	47	-16	-16	14	0	0	0	.973	-11	S	-2.1
1970	Atl-N	101	367	38	97	5	4	1	19	15	16	.264	.293	.308	58	-20	-23	28	0	2	-1	.975	-1	S2	-1.4
1971	Atl-N	79	125	8	27	3	0	0	12	15	12	.216	.300	.240	51	-7	-8	9	0	1	-1	.961	4	S32	-0.1

YEAR	TM/L	G	AB	R	H	2B	3B	HR	RBI	BB	SO	AVG	OBP	SLG	PRO+	BR	/A	RC	SB	CS	SBR	FA	FR	POS	TPR
1972	Atl-N	40	75	11	20	1	0	0	7	11	6	.267	.368	.280	79	-1	-2	8	1	1	-0	.989	1	2S/3	0.0
Total	6	334	872	81	207	14	5	1	51	61	54	.237	.288	.268	53	-52	-57	63	2	4	-2	.974	-4	S/23	-4.0

■ **CECIL GARRIOTT** Garriott, Virgil Cecil b: 8/15/16, Harristown, Ill. d: 2/20/90, Lake Elsinore, Cal BL/TR, 5'8", 165 lbs. Deb: 9/04/46

YEAR	TM/L	G	AB	R	H	2B	3B	HR	RBI	BB	SO	AVG	OBP	SLG	PRO+	BR	/A	RC	SB	CS	SBR	FA	FR	POS	TPR
1946	Chi-N	6	5	1	0	0	0	0	0	0	2	.000	.167	.000	-52	-1	-1	0	0			.000	0	H	-0.1

■ **FORD GARRISON** Garrison, Robert Ford "Rocky" or "Snapper" b: 8/29/15, Greenville, S.C. BR/TR, 5'10.5", 180 lbs. Deb: 4/22/43 C

YEAR	TM/L	G	AB	R	H	2B	3B	HR	RBI	BB	SO	AVG	OBP	SLG	PRO+	BR	/A	RC	SB	CS	SBR	FA	FR	POS	TPR
1943	Bos-A	36	129	13	36	5	1	1	11	5	14	.279	.306	.357	92	-2	-2	13	0	1	-1	.988	-0	O	-0.5
1944	Bos-A	13	49	5	12	3	0	0	2	6	4	.245	.327	.306	82	-1	-1	6	0	0	0	.969	1	O	-0.1
	Phi-A	121	449	58	121	13	2	4	37	22	40	.269	.307	.334	84	-11	-10	47	10	4	1	.987	6	*O	-1.0
	Yr	134	498	63	133	16	2	4	39	28	44	.267	.309	.331	84	-12	-11	52	10	4	1	.985	7	*O	-1.1
1945	Phi-A	6	23	3	7	1	0	1	6	4	3	.304	.407	.478	157	2	2	5	1	0	0	1.000	1	/O	0.2
1946	Phi-A	9	37	1	4	0	0	0	0	0	6	.108	.108	.108	-40	-7	-7	0	0	0	0	1.000	-2	/O	-1.0
Total	4	185	687	80	180	22	3	6	56	37	67	.262	.302	.329	81	-18	-18	71	11	5	0	.986	5	O	-2.4

■ **HANK GARRITY** Garrity, Francis Joseph b: 2/4/08, Boston, Mass. d: 9/1/62, Boston, Mass. BR/TR, 6'1", 185 lbs. Deb: 7/26/31

YEAR	TM/L	G	AB	R	H	2B	3B	HR	RBI	BB	SO	AVG	OBP	SLG	PRO+	BR	/A	RC	SB	CS	SBR	FA	FR	POS	TPR
1931	Chi-A	8	14	0	3	1	0	0	2	1	2	.214	.267	.286	48	-1	-1	1	0	0	0	.941	0	/C	-0.1

■ **STEVE GARVEY** Garvey, Steven Patrick b: 12/22/48, Tampa, Fla. BR/TR, 5'10", 192 lbs. Deb: 9/01/69

YEAR	TM/L	G	AB	R	H	2B	3B	HR	RBI	BB	SO	AVG	OBP	SLG	PRO+	BR	/A	RC	SB	CS	SBR	FA	FR	POS	TPR
1969	LA-N	3	3	0	1	0	0	0	0	0	1	.333	.333	.333	94	-0	-0	0	0	0	0	.000	0	H	0.0
1970	LA-N	34	93	8	25	5	0	1	6	6	17	.269	.313	.355	82	-3	-2	10	1	1	-0	.943	6	3/2	0.3
1971	LA-N	81	225	27	51	12	1	7	26	21	33	.227	.293	.382	95	-4	-2	24	1	2	-1	.939	19	3	1.6
1972	LA-N	96	294	36	79	14	2	9	30	19	36	.269	.315	.422	110	2	3	37	4	2	0	.902	13	3/1	1.6
1973	LA-N	114	349	37	106	17	3	8	50	11	42	.304	.331	.438	116	4	6	47	0	2	-1	.993	-8	1O	-1.0
1974	*LA-N★	156	642	95	200	32	3	21	111	31	66	.312	.346	.469	132	19	22	102	5	4	-1	.995	-13	*1	-0.3
1975	LA-N★	160	659	85	210	38	6	18	95	33	66	.319	.354	.476	135	22	26	106	11	2	2	**.995**	-10	*1	0.7
1976	LA-N★	162	631	85	200	37	4	13	80	50	69	.317	.368	.450	134	25	26	100	19	8	1	**.998**	-16	*1	0.0
1977	*LA-N★	162	646	91	192	25	3	33	115	38	90	.297	.337	.498	121	16	17	103	9	6	-1	**.995**	-16	*1	-1.0
1978	*LA-N★	162	639	89	**202**	36	9	21	113	40	70	.316	.357	.499	138	29	29	108	10	5	0	.994	-9	*1	1.1
1979	LA-N★	162	648	92	204	32	1	28	110	37	59	.315	.354	.497	131	24	25	102	3	6	-3	.995	-2	*1	1.1
1980	LA-N★	163	658	78	**200**	27	1	26	106	36	67	.304	.343	.467	126	19	20	97	6	11	-5	.996	3	*1	0.9
1981	*LA-N★	110	431	63	122	23	1	10	64	25	49	.283	.324	.411	111	3	5	54	3	5	-2	**.999**	-6	*1	-1.1
1982	LA-N	162	625	66	176	35	1	16	86	20	86	.282	.305	.418	103	-2	-0	76	5	3	-0	.995	1	*1	-0.8
1983	SD-N	100	388	76	114	22	0	14	59	29	39	.294	.348	.459	126	10	12	57	4	1	1	.994	-11	*1	-0.4
1984	*SD-N★	161	617	72	175	27	2	8	86	24	64	.284	.312	.373	92	-8	-8	64	1	2	-1	**1.000**	-4	*1	-2.4
1985	SD-N★	162	654	80	184	34	6	17	81	35	67	.281	.321	.430	110	5	6	82	0	0	0	.997	-8	*1	-1.3
1986	SD-N	155	557	58	142	22	0	21	81	23	72	.255	.286	.408	91	-11	-9	59	1	2	-1	.994	-18	*1	-4.0
1987	SD-N	27	76	5	16	2	0	1	9	1	10	.211	.231	.276	35	-7	-7	4	0	0	0	1.000	0	1	-0.8
Total	19	2332	8835	1143	2599	440	43	272	1308	479	1003	.294	.333	.446	117	144	168	1233	83	62	-12	.996	-78	*13/O2	-5.8

■ **ROD GASPAR** Gaspar, Rodney Earl b: 4/3/46, Long Beach, Cal. BB/TR, 5'11", 165 lbs. Deb: 4/08/69

YEAR	TM/L	G	AB	R	H	2B	3B	HR	RBI	BB	SO	AVG	OBP	SLG	PRO+	BR	/A	RC	SB	CS	SBR	FA	FR	POS	TPR
1969	*NY-N	118	215	26	49	6	1	1	14	25	19	.228	.314	.279	66	-9	-9	21	7	3	0	.983	9	O	-0.3
1970	NY-N	11	14	4	0	0	0	0	0	1	4	.000	.067	.000	-80	-4	-4	0	1	0	0	1.000	1	/O	-0.2
1971	SD-N	16	17	1	2	0	0	0	2	3	3	.118	.250	.118	8	-2	-2	1	0	1	-1	1.000	0	/O	-0.3
1974	SD-N	33	14	4	3	0	0	0	1	4	3	.214	.389	.214	75	-0	-0	2	0	0	0	1.000	2	/O1	0.2
Total	4	178	260	35	54	6	1	1	17	33	29	.208	.302	.250	55	-15	-15	24	8	4	0	.986	12	O/1	-0.6

■ **TOM GASTALL** Gastall, Thomas Everett b: 6/13/32, Fall River, Mass. d: 9/20/56, Rivera Beach, Md. BR/TR, 6'2", 187 lbs. Deb: 6/21/55

YEAR	TM/L	G	AB	R	H	2B	3B	HR	RBI	BB	SO	AVG	OBP	SLG	PRO+	BR	/A	RC	SB	CS	SBR	FA	FR	POS	TPR
1955	Bal-A	20	27	4	4	1	0	0	0	3	5	.148	.233	.185	15	-3	-3	1	0	0	0	.967	-1	C	-0.4
1956	Bal-A	32	56	3	11	2	0	0	4	3	8	.196	.250	.232	30	-6	-5	3	0	0	0	1.000	1	C	-0.4
Total	2	52	83	7	15	3	0	0	4	6	13	.181	.244	.217	25	-9	-8	4	0	0	0	.990	0	/C	-0.8

■ **ED GASTFIELD** Gastfield, Edward b: 8/1/1865, Chicago, Ill. d: 12/1/1899, Chicago, Ill. Deb: 8/13/1884

YEAR	TM/L	G	AB	R	H	2B	3B	HR	RBI	BB	SO	AVG	OBP	SLG	PRO+	BR	/A	RC	SB	CS	SBR	FA	FR	POS	TPR
1884	Det-N	23	82	6	6	1	0	0	2	2	34	.073	.095	.085	-45	-13	-12	1				.827	8	C/O1	-0.2
1885	Det-N	1	3	0	0	0	0	0	0	0	2	.000	.000	.000	-99	-1	-1	0				.714	-0	/C	-0.1
	Chi-N	1	3	0	0	0	0	0	0	0	1	.000	.000	.000	-87	-1	-1	0				1.000	1	/C	0.1
	Yr	2	6	0	0	0	0	0	0	0	3	.000	.000	.000	-93	-1	-1	0				.889	1	/C	0.0
Total	2	25	88	6	6	1	0	0	2	2	37	.068	.089	.080	-49	-14	-14	1				.832	9	/C1O	-0.2

■ **ALEX GASTON** Gaston, Alexander Nathaniel b: 3/12/1893, New York, N.Y. d: 2/8/79, Santa Monica, Cal. BR/TR, 5'9", 170 lbs. Deb: 9/26/20 F

YEAR	TM/L	G	AB	R	H	2B	3B	HR	RBI	BB	SO	AVG	OBP	SLG	PRO+	BR	/A	RC	SB	CS	SBR	FA	FR	POS	TPR
1920	NY-N	4	10	2	1	0	0	0	1	1	2	.100	.182	.100	-18	-1	-1	0	0	0	0	.917	-1	/C	-0.3
1921	NY-N	20	22	1	5	1	1	0	3	1	9	.227	.261	.364	63	-1	-1	2	0	0	0	.950	-0	C	-0.1
1922	NY-N	16	26	1	5	0	0	0	1	0	3	.192	.192	.192	-1	-4	-4	1	1	0	0	1.000	0	C	-0.3
1923	NY-N	22	39	3	8	2	0	1	5	0	6	.205	.225	.333	46	-3	-3	3	0	0	0	.957	-0	C	-0.3
1926	Bos-A	98	301	37	67	5	3	0	21	21	28	.223	.282	.259	43	-26	-24	24	3	0	1	.981	-10	C	-2.7
1929	Bos-A	55	116	14	26	5	2	2	9	6	8	.224	.262	.353	58	-8	-8	11	1	0	0	.986	-1	C	-0.5
Total	6	215	514	58	112	13	6	3	40	29	56	.218	.266	.284	45	-43	-42	41	5	0	2	.979	-13	C	-4.2

■ **CITO GASTON** Gaston, Clarence Edwin b: 3/17/44, San Antonio, Tex. BR/TR, 6'4", 210 lbs. Deb: 9/14/67 MC

YEAR	TM/L	G	AB	R	H	2B	3B	HR	RBI	BB	SO	AVG	OBP	SLG	PRO+	BR	/A	RC	SB	CS	SBR	FA	FR	POS	TPR
1967	Atl-N	9	25	1	3	0	1	0	1	0	5	.120	.120	.200	-10	-4	-4	0	1	0	0	.800	-1	/O	-0.5
1969	SD-N	129	391	20	90	11	7	2	28	24	117	.230	.276	.309	67	-19	-17	32	4	4	-1	.959	1	*O	-2.5
1970	SD-N★	146	584	92	186	26	9	29	93	41	142	.318	.365	.543	146	30	33	111	4	1	1	.975	0	*O	2.6
1971	SD-N	141	518	57	118	13	9	17	61	24	121	.228	.265	.386	88	-14	-10	51	1	0	0	.982	-6	*O	-2.5
1972	SD-N	111	379	30	102	14	0	7	44	22	76	.269	.313	.361	98	-5	-2	39	0	2	-1	.977	-3	O	-1.1
1973	SD-N	133	476	51	119	18	4	16	57	20	88	.250	.282	.405	96	-10	-5	52	0	0	0	.947	0	*O	-1.1
1974	SD-N	106	267	19	57	11	0	6	33	16	51	.213	.261	.322	65	-14	-13	22	0	0	0	.992	2	O	-1.4
1975	Atl-N	64	141	17	34	4	0	6	15	17	33	.241	.323	.397	95	-0	-1	18	1	0	0	.974	-0	O/1	-0.2
1976	Atl-N	69	134	15	39	4	0	4	25	13	21	.291	.354	.410	109	3	2	18	1	0	0	.977	-3	O/1	-0.2
1977	Atl-N	56	85	6	23	4	0	3	21	5	19	.271	.311	.424	85	-1	-2	11	1	0	0	1.000	-0	/O1	-0.3
1978	Atl-N	60	118	5	27	1	0	1	9	3	20	.229	.248	.263	38	-9	-11	7	0	0	0	.957	-1	O/1	-1.4
	Pit-N	2	2	1	1	0	0	0	0	0	0	.500	.500	.500	172	0	0	1	0	0	0	.000	0	/O	0.0
	Yr	62	120	6	28	1	0	1	9	3	20	.233	.252	.267	41	-9	-10	7	0	0	0	.957	-1	O/1	-1.4
Total	11	1026	3120	314	799	106	30	91	387	185	693	.256	.300	.397	95	-43	-30	361	13	7	-0	.970	-10	O/1	-8.6

■ **JOE GATES** Gates, Joseph Daniel b: 10/3/54, Gary, Ind. BL/TR, 5'7", 175 lbs. Deb: 9/12/78

YEAR	TM/L	G	AB	R	H	2B	3B	HR	RBI	BB	SO	AVG	OBP	SLG	PRO+	BR	/A	RC	SB	CS	SBR	FA	FR	POS	TPR
1978	Chi-A	8	24	6	6	0	0	0	1	4	6	.250	.379	.250	80	-0	-0	3	1	0	0	.972	-2	/2	-0.2
1979	Chi-A	16	16	5	1	0	1	0	1	2	3	.063	.167	.188	-5	-2	-2	0	1	1	-0	.966	5	/23	0.2
Total	2	24	40	11	7	0	1	0	2	6	9	.175	.298	.225	46	-3	-3	3	2	1	0	.969	2	/23	0.0

■ **MIKE GATES** Gates, Michael Grant b: 9/20/56, Culver City, Cal. BL/TR, 6', 165 lbs. Deb: 5/06/81

YEAR	TM/L	G	AB	R	H	2B	3B	HR	RBI	BB	SO	AVG	OBP	SLG	PRO+	BR	/A	RC	SB	CS	SBR	FA	FR	POS	TPR
1981	Mon-N	1	2	1	1	0	1	0	1	0	1	.500	.500	1.500	445	1	1	2	0	0	0	1.000	-0	/2	0.0
1982	Mon-N	36	121	16	28	2	3	0	8	9	19	.231	.285	.298	62	-6	-6	11	0	0	0	1.000	-9	2	-1.5
Total	2	37	123	17	29	2	4	0	9	9	20	.236	.288	.317	68	-5	-5	12	0	0	0	1.000	-10	/2	-1.5

■ **FRANK GATINS** Gatins, Frank Anthony b: 3/6/1871, Johnstown, Pa. d: 11/8/11, Johnstown, Pa. Deb: 9/21/1898

YEAR	TM/L	G	AB	R	H	2B	3B	HR	RBI	BB	SO	AVG	OBP	SLG	PRO+	BR	/A	RC	SB	CS	SBR	FA	FR	POS	TPR
1898	Was-N	17	58	6	13	2	0	0	5	3		.224	.274	.259	53	-4	-4	5	2			.790	-8	S	-1.1

YEAR	TM/L	G	AB	R	H	2B	3B	HR	RBI	BB	SO	AVG	OBP	SLG	PRO+	BR	/A	RC	SB	CS	SBR	FA	FR	POS	TPR

■ FRANK GATINS   Gatins, Frank Anthony b: 3/6/1871, Johnstown, Pa. d: 11/8/11, Johnstown, Pa. Deb: 9/21/1898

1898	Was-N	17	58	6	13	2	0	0	5	3		.224	.274	.259	53	-4	-4	5	2			.790	-8	S	-1.1
1901	Bro-N	50	197	21	45	7	2	1	21	5		.228	.251	.299	58	-11	-11	17	6			.919	-10	3/S	-2.1
Total	2	67	255	27	58	9	2	1	26	8		.227	.257	.290	57	-14	-15	22	8			.841	-18	/3S	-3.2

■ JIM GAUDET   Gaudet, James Jennings b: 6/3/55, New Orleans, La. BR/TR, 6', 185 lbs. Deb: 9/10/78

1978	KC-A	3	8	0	0	0	0	0	0	0	3	.000	.000	.000	-97	-2	-2	0	0	0	0	.938	1	/C	-0.1
1979	KC-A	3	6	0	1	0	0	0	0	0	0	.167	.167	.167	-10	-1	-1	0	0	0	0	1.000	1	/C	0.0
Total	2	6	14	0	1	0	0	0	0	0	3	.071	.071	.071	-59	-3	-3	0	0	0	0	.966	2	/C	-0.1

■ MIKE GAULE   Gaule, Michael John b: 8/4/1869, Baltimore, Md. d: 1/24/18, Baltimore, Md. BL/TL, 6'2", Deb: 6/15/1889

| 1889 | Lou-a | 1 | 2 | 0 | 0 | 0 | 0 | 0 | 0 | 0 | 1 | .000 | .000 | .000 | -99 | -1 | -1 | 0 | 0 | | | .000 | -1 | /O | -0.1 |

■ DOC GAUTREAU   Gautreau, Walter Paul "Punk" b: 7/26/01, Cambridge, Mass. d: 8/23/70, Salt Lake City, Ut BR/TR, 5'4", 129 lbs. Deb: 6/22/25

1925	Phi-A	4	7	0	0	0	0	0	0	0	3	.000	.000	.000	-94	-2	-2	0	0	0	0	.933	1	/2	-0.1
	Bos-N	68	279	45	73	13	3	0	23	36	13	.262	.346	.330	81	-10	-6	33	11	7	-1	.976	-4	2	-0.9
1926	Bos-N	79	266	36	71	9	4	0	8	35	24	.267	.356	.331	94	-4	-4	33	17			.942	-20	2	-1.8
1927	Bos-N	87	236	38	58	12	2	0	20	25	20	.246	.321	.314	76	-9	-7	24	11			.965	-2	2	-0.7
1928	Bos-N	23	18	3	5	0	1	0	1	4	3	.278	.409	.389	116	0	1	3	1			.750	-1	/2S	0.0
Total	4	261	806	122	207	34	10	0	52	99	63	.257	.341	.324	83	-25	-16	94	40	7		.960	-25	2/S	-3.5

■ SID GAUTREAUX   Gautreaux, Sidney Allen "Pudge" b: 5/4/12, Schriever, La. d: 4/19/80, Morgan City, La. BB/TR, 5'8", 190 lbs. Deb: 4/15/36

1936	Bro-N	75	71	8	19	3	0	0	16	9	7	.268	.358	.310	80	-1	-2	9	0			.963	-1	C	-0.2
1937	Bro-N	11	10	0	1	1	0	0	2	1	1	.100	.182	.200	4	-1	-1	0	0			.000	0	H	-0.1
Total	2	86	81	8	20	4	0	0	18	10	8	.247	.337	.296	71	-3	-3	9	0				-1	/C	-0.3

■ GAVERN   Gavern Deb: 6/15/1874

| 1874 | Atl-n | 1 | 4 | 1 | 0 | 0 | 0 | | 0 | | | .000 | .000 | .000 | -99 | -1 | -1 | 0 | | | | | | /2 | -0.1 |

■ MIKE GAZELLA   Gazella, Michael b: 10/13/1896, Olyphant, Pa. d: 9/11/78, Odessa, Tex. BR/TR, 5'7.5", 165 lbs. Deb: 7/02/23

1923	NY-A	8	13	2	1	0	0	0	1	2	3	.077	.200	.077	-25	-2	-2	0	0	0	0	1.000	-1	/S23	-0.3
1926	*NY-A	66	168	21	39	6	0	0	20	25	24	.232	.335	.268	60	-9	-9	17	2	2	-1	.913	-4	3S	-1.0
1927	NY-A	54	115	17	32	8	4	0	9	23	16	.278	.403	.417	117	3	4	20	4	1	1	.961	-6	3/S	0.0
1928	NY-A	32	56	11	13	0	0	0	2	6	7	.232	.317	.232	48	-4	-4	5	2	1	0	.969	-1	3/2S	-0.4
Total	4	160	352	51	85	14	4	0	32	56	50	.241	.350	.304	73	-13	-12	42	8	4	0	.940	-12	3/S2	-1.7

■ DALE GEAR   Gear, Dale Dudley b: 2/2/1872, Lone Elm, Kan. d: 9/23/51, Topeka, Kan. BR/TR, 5'11", 165 lbs. Deb: 8/15/1896

1896	Cle-N	4	15	5	6	1	1	0	3	1		.400	.438	.600	165	2	1	4	0			.857	-1	/P1	0.0
1897	Cle-N	7	24	3	4	1	0	0	2	3		.167	.286	.208	30	-2	-3	2	2			.750	0	/O	-0.2
1901	Was-A	58	199	17	47	9	2	0	20	4		.236	.251	.302	54	-13	-13	16	2			.944	1	OP	-1.0
Total	3	69	238	25	57	11	3	0	25	8	1	.239	.267	.311	59	-14	-14	22	4			.900	0	/OP1	-1.2

■ GARY GEARHART   Gearhart, Lloyd William b: 8/10/23, New Lebanon, Ohio BR/TL, 5'11", 180 lbs. Deb: 4/18/47

| 1947 | NY-N | 73 | 179 | 26 | 44 | 9 | 0 | 6 | 17 | 17 | 30 | .246 | .315 | .397 | 87 | -4 | -4 | 22 | 1 | | | .961 | -1 | O | -0.7 |

■ HUCK GEARY   Geary, Eugene Francis Joseph b: 1/22/17, Buffalo, N.Y. d: 1/27/81, Cuba, N.Y. BL/TR, 5'10.5", 170 lbs. Deb: 7/17/42

1942	Pit-N	9	22	3	5	0	0	0	2	3	3	.227	.292	.227	52	-1	-1	2	0			.939	0	/S	-0.1
1943	Pit-N	46	166	17	25	4	0	1	13	18	6	.151	.234	.193	23	-16	-17	8	3			.956	-6	S	-2.1
Total	2	55	188	20	30	4	0	1	15	20	9	.160	.240	.197	26	-17	-18	10	3			.954	-5	/S	-2.2

■ ELMER GEDEON   Gedeon, Elmer John b: 4/15/17, Cleveland, Ohio d: 4/20/44, St.Pol, France BR/TR, 6'4", 196 lbs. Deb: 9/18/39

| 1939 | Was-A | 5 | 15 | 1 | 3 | 0 | 0 | 0 | 1 | 2 | 5 | .200 | .294 | .200 | 31 | -2 | -1 | 1 | 0 | 0 | 0 | 1.000 | 1 | /O | -0.1 |

■ JOE GEDEON   Gedeon, Elmer Joseph b: 12/5/1893, Sacramento, Cal. d: 5/19/41, San Francisco, Cal BR/TR, 6', 167 lbs. Deb: 5/13/13

1913	Was-A	29	71	3	13	1	3	0	6	1	6	.183	.205	.282	41	-6	-6	4	3			.929	2	O/32SP	-0.5
1914	Was-A	4	2	0	0	0	0	0	1	0	1	.000	.333	.000	1	0	-0	0	0			.667	1	/O	-0.1
1916	NY-A	122	435	50	92	14	4	0	27	40	61	.211	.282	.262	62	-19	-20	38	14			.955	-10	*2	-3.0
1917	NY-A	33	117	15	28	7	0	0	8	7	13	.239	.288	.299	78	-3	-3	11	4			.983	4	2	0.2
1918	StL-A	123	441	39	94	14	3	1	41	27	29	.213	.271	.265	64	-21	-20	34	7			.977	16	*2	0.4
1919	StL-A	120	437	57	111	13	4	0	27	50	35	.254	.340	.302	79	-9	-11	51	4			.975	-3	*2	-0.8
1920	StL-A	153	606	95	177	33	6	0	61	55	36	.292	.355	.366	89	-7	-9	82	1	3	-2	.964	-26	*2	-3.1
Total	7	584	2109	259	515	82	20	1	171	180	181	.244	.311	.303	75	-65	-69	220	33	3		.969	-18	2/03SP	-6.9

■ RICH GEDMAN   Gedman, Richard Leo b: 9/26/59, Worcester, Mass. BL/TR, 6', 215 lbs. Deb: 9/07/80

1980	Bos-A	9	24	2	5	0	0	0	1	0	5	.208	.208	.208	14	-3	-3	1	0	0	0	.867	-0	/CD	-0.3
1981	Bos-A	62	205	22	59	15	0	5	26	9	31	.288	.321	.434	109	3	2	26	0	0	0	.990	-2	C	0.2
1982	Bos-A	92	289	30	72	17	2	4	26	10	37	.249	.279	.363	71	-10	-13	25	0	1	-1	.977	-7	C	-1.8
1983	Bos-A	81	204	21	60	16	1	2	18	15	37	.294	.345	.412	100	2	0	28	0	1	-1	.980	-3	C	0.0
1984	Bos-A	133	449	54	121	26	4	24	72	29	72	.269	.315	.506	118	12	9	71	0	0	0	.977	-8	*C	0.8
1985	Bos-A★	144	498	66	147	30	5	18	80	50	79	.295	.363	.484	124	20	17	86	2	0	1	.983	4	*C	2.8
1986	*Bos-A★	135	462	49	119	29	0	16	65	37	65	.258	.318	.424	100	-1	-1	59	1	0	0	.994	10	*C	1.8
1987	Bos-A	52	151	11	31	8	0	1	13	10	21	.205	.255	.278	40	-13	-13	11	0	0	0	.976	-4	C	-1.3
1988	*Bos-A	95	299	33	69	14	0	9	39	18	49	.231	.281	.368	77	-9	-10	31	0	0	0	.992	-1	C/D	-0.1
1989	Bos-A	93	260	24	55	9	0	4	16	23	47	.212	.276	.292	57	-14	-16	20	0	1	-1	.981	-0	C	-1.3
1990	Bos-A	10	15	3	3	0	0	0	0	5	6	.200	.429	.200	78	-0	-0	2	0	0	0	.970	0	/C	0.1
	Hou-N	40	104	4	21	7	0	1	10	15	24	.202	.303	.298	68	-5	-4	10	0	0	0	1.000	6	C	0.4
1991	StL-N	46	94	7	10	1	0	3	8	4	15	.106	.143	.213	-1	-13	-13	2	0	1	0	.976	10	C	-0.2
1992	StL-N	41	105	5	23	4	0	1	8	11	22	.219	.293	.286	66	-5	-5	10	0	0	0	.988	11	C	0.9
Total	13	1033	3159	331	795	176	12	88	382	236	509	.252	.307	.399	90	-34	-49	381	3	4	-2	.984	20	C/D	2.0

■ COUNT GEDNEY   Gedney, Alfred W. b: 5/10/1849, Brooklyn, N.Y. d: 3/26/22, Hackensack, N.J. 5'9", 140 lbs. Deb: 4/27/1872

1872	Tro-n	10	51	15	21	2	1	3	18	0		.412	.412	.667	223	7	7	15						/O	0.5
	Eck-n	18	72	4	11	1	0	0	5	0	1	.153	.153	.167	-2	-8	-6	2						O	-0.4
	Yr	28	123	19	32	3	1	3	23	0	1	.260	.260	.374	102	-1	1	13						O	0.1
1873	Mut-n	53	224	41	60	5	5	1	25	7	5	.268	.290	.348	88	-3	-3	23						*O	-0.1
1874	Ath-n	54	222	49	60	6	1	1	7			.270	.293	.320	87	-1	-5	21						*O/1	-0.3
1875	Mut-n	68	266	30	54	12	4	0	2			.203	.209	.278	63	-8	-11	16						*O/P	-0.8
Total	4 n	203	835	139	206	26	11	5		16		.247	.261	.322	82	-14	-17	77						O/1P	-1.1

■ BILLY GEER   Geer, William Henry Harrison (b: George Harrison Geer) b: 8/13/1849, Syracuse, N.Y. TR, 5'8", 160 lbs. Deb: 10/15/1874

1874	Mut-n	2	8	0	2	0	0	0		0		.250	.250	.250	58	-0	-0	1						/O	0.0
1875	NH-N	37	162	20	40	6	1	0		3		.247	.262	.296	102	-2	1	12						O2/S13	0.1
1878	Cin-N	61	237	31	52	13	2	0	20	10	18	.219	.251	.291	86	-5	-2	18				.867	-4	*S/2	-0.3
1880	Wor-N	2	6	0	0	0	0	0	0	0		.000	.000	.000	-92	-1	-1	0				1.000	-1	/OS	-0.2
1884	Phi-U	9	36	7	9	2	1	0		0	4	.250	.325	.361	142	2	2	4				.772	1	/S	0.2
	Bro-a	107	391	68	82	15	7	0		38		.210	.281	.284	87	-4	-4	32				.870	17	*S/P2	1.3

YEAR	TM/L	G	AB	R	H	2B	3B	HR	RBI	BB	SO	AVG	OBP	SLG	PRO+	BR	/A	RC	SB	CS	SBR	FA	FR	POS	TPR
1885	Lou-a	14	51	2	6	2	0	0		2		.118	.167	.157	4	-5	-5	1				.872	2	S	-0.3
Total	2 n	39	170	20	42	6	1	0		1		.247	.251	.294	99	-2	1	13						/O2S31	0.1
Total	4	193	721	108	149	32	10	0	20	54	18	.207	.264	.279	81	-15	-11	55				.864	15	S/2PO	0.7

■ **LOU GEHRIG** Gehrig, Henry Louis "The Iron Horse" b: 6/19/03, New York, N.Y. d: 6/2/41, Riverdale, N.Y. BL/TL, 6', 200 lbs. Deb: 6/15/23 H

YEAR	TM/L	G	AB	R	H	2B	3B	HR	RBI	BB	SO	AVG	OBP	SLG	PRO+	BR	/A	RC	SB	CS	SBR	FA	FR	POS	TPR
1923	NY-A	13	26	6	11	4	1	1	9	2	5	.423	.464	.769	217	4	4	9	0	0	0	.933	-1	/1	0.3
1924	NY-A	10	12	2	6	1	0	0	5	1	3	.500	.538	.583	190	2	2	4	0	0	0	1.000	-0	/1O	0.1
1925	NY-A	126	437	73	129	23	10	20	68	46	49	.295	.365	.531	127	14	15	85	6	3	0	.989	-9	*1/O	-0.1
1926	*NY-A	155	572	135	179	47	**20**	16	112	105	73	.313	.420	.549	154	44	46	137	6	5	-1	.991	-8	*1	2.5
1927	*NY-A	155	584	149	218	**52**	18	47	**175**	109	84	.373	.474	.765	224	**101**	**104**	**203**	10	8	-2	.992	-6	*1	7.8
1928	*NY-A	154	562	139	210	**47**	13	27	**142**	95	69	.374	**.467**	.648	197	76	79	169	4	11	-5	.989	-8	*1	4.9
1929	NY-A	154	553	127	166	32	10	35	126	122	68	.300	.431	.584	170	52	57	146	4	4	-1	.994	-5	*1	3.4
1930	NY-A	154	581	143	220	42	17	41	**174**	101	63	.379	.473	.721	207	88	93	**195**	12	14	-5	.989	1	*1/O	6.5
1931	NY-A	155	619	**163**	**211**	31	15	**46**	**184**	117	56	.341	.446	.662	199	80	85	185	17	12	-2	.991	-10	*1/O	5.3
1932	*NY-A	156	596	138	208	42	9	34	151	108	38	.349	.451	.621	184	69	73	168	4	11	-5	.987	-6	*1	4.5
1933	NY-A★	152	593	**138**	198	41	12	32	139	92	42	.334	.424	.605	181	60	65	151	9	13	-5	.993	-3	*1	3.9
1934	NY-A★	154	579	128	210	40	6	**49**	**165**	109	31	**.363**	**.465**	**.706**	**213**	**86**	**92**	**195**	9	5	-0	.994	1	*1/S	**7.2**
1935	NY-A★	149	535	**125**	176	26	10	30	119	**132**	38	.329	**.466**	.583	180	62	66	154	8	7	-2	.990	0	*1	4.5
1936	*NY-A★	155	579	**167**	205	37	7	**49**	152	**130**	46	.354	**.478**	**.696**	**193**	**82**	**86**	**199**	3	4	-2	.994	1	*1	**6.1**
1937	*NY-A★	157	569	138	200	37	9	37	159	**127**	49	.351	**.473**	.643	**177**	**73**	**73**	**181**	4	3	-1	.989	-6	*1	4.3
1938	*NY-A★	157	576	115	170	32	6	29	114	107	75	.295	.410	.523	133	30	30	131	6	1	1	.991	-1	*1	1.2
1939	NY-A†	8	28	2	4	0	0	0	1	5	1	.143	.273	.143	9	-4	-4	1	0	0	0	.971	-1	/1	-0.5
Total	17	2164	8001	1888	2721	534	163	493	1995	1508	790	.340	.447	.632	182	918	966	2312	102	101	-30	.991	-60	*1/OS	61.9

■ **CHARLIE GEHRINGER** Gehringer, Charles Leonard "The Mechanical Man" b: 5/11/03, Fowlerville, Mich. BL/TR, 5'11", 180 lbs. Deb: 9/22/24 CH

YEAR	TM/L	G	AB	R	H	2B	3B	HR	RBI	BB	SO	AVG	OBP	SLG	PRO+	BR	/A	RC	SB	CS	SBR	FA	FR	POS	TPR
1924	Det-A	5	13	2	6	0	0	0	1	0	2	.462	.462	.462	141	1	1	2	1	1	-0	.967	4	/2	0.4
1925	Det-A	8	18	3	3	0	0	0	0	2	0	.167	.250	.167	7	-3	-2	1	0	1	-1	1.000	4	/2	0.1
1926	Det-A	123	459	62	127	19	17	1	48	30	42	.277	.322	.399	86	-10	-11	59	9	7	-2	.973	-10	*2/3	-1.8
1927	Det-A	133	508	110	161	29	11	4	61	52	31	.317	.383	.441	112	10	9	82	17	8	0	.965	**20**	*2	3.1
1928	Det-A	154	603	108	193	29	16	6	74	69	22	.320	.395	.451	120	21	19	110	15	9	-1	.962	2	*2	2.3
1929	Det-A	155	634	**131**	**215**	**45**	**19**	13	106	64	19	.339	.405	.532	139	37	36	139	**27**	9	**3**	**.975**	-3	*2	3.9
1930	Det-A	154	610	144	201	47	15	16	98	69	17	.330	.404	.534	133	33	32	130	19	15	-3	**.979**	2	*2	3.5
1931	Det-A	101	383	67	119	24	5	4	53	29	15	.311	.359	.431	103	3	2	60	13	4	2	.979	-1	2/1	0.6
1932	Det-A	152	618	112	184	44	11	19	107	68	34	.298	.370	.497	118	19	16	114	9	8	-2	.967	-1	*2	1.9
1933	Det-A★	155	628	103	204	42	6	12	105	68	27	.325	.393	.468	125	25	24	117	5	4	-1	.981	7	*2	3.6
1934	*Det-A★	154	601	**134**	**214**	50	7	11	127	99	25	.356	.450	.517	149	48	48	144	11	8	-2	.981	7	*2	5.7
1935	*Det-A★	150	610	123	201	32	8	19	108	79	16	.330	.409	.502	139	32	35	129	11	4	1	**.985**	3	*2	4.6
1936	Det-A★	154	641	144	227	**60**	12	15	116	83	13	.354	.431	.555	141	43	43	157	4	1	1	**.974**	16	*2	6.1
1937	Det-A★	144	564	133	209	40	1	14	96	90	25	**.371**	.458	.520	143	44	42	140	11	4	1	**.986**	6	*2	5.3
1938	Det-A★	152	568	133	174	32	5	20	107	113	21	.306	.425	.486	121	28	23	128	14	1	**4**	.976	-1	*2	3.1
1939	Det-A	118	406	86	132	29	6	16	86	68	16	.325	.423	.544	135	29	24	97	4	3	-1	**.977**	1	*2	2.8
1940	*Det-A	139	515	108	161	33	3	10	81	101	17	.313	.428	.447	116	26	18	111	10	0	3	.972	-20	*2	1.0
1941	Det-A	127	436	65	96	19	4	3	46	95	26	.220	.363	.303	71	-10	-17	55	1	2	-1	**.982**	-3	*2	-1.2
1942	Det-A	45	45	6	12	0	0	1	7	7	4	.267	.365	.333	90	0	-0	6	0	0	0	1.000	1	/2	0.1
Total	19	2323	8860	1774	2839	574	146	184	1427	1186	372	.320	.404	.480	123	376	339	1781	181	89	1	.976	33	*2/13	45.1

■ **PHIL GEIER** Geier, Philip Louis "Little Phil" b: 11/3/1875, Washington, D.C. d: 9/25/67, Spokane, Wash. BL/TR, 5'7", 145 lbs. Deb: 8/17/1896

YEAR	TM/L	G	AB	R	H	2B	3B	HR	RBI	BB	SO	AVG	OBP	SLG	PRO+	BR	/A	RC	SB	CS	SBR	FA	FR	POS	TPR
1896	Phi-N	17	56	12	13	0	1	0	6	6	7	.232	.317	.268	58	-3	-3	6	3			.813	-3	O/2C	-0.5
1897	Phi-N	92	316	51	88	6	2	1	35	56		.278	.392	.320	91	-2	-0	49	19			.932	-7	O2/S3	-0.7
1900	Cin-N	30	113	18	29	1	4	0	10	7		.257	.306	.336	79	-4	-3	13	3			.941	1	O/3	-0.4
1901	Phi-A	50	211	42	49	5	2	0	23	24		.232	.314	.275	61	-10	-11	21	7			.934	-5	O/S3	-1.8
	Mil-A	11	39	4	7	1	1	0	1	5		.179	.273	.256	50	-3	-2	4	4			1.000	-1	/O3	-0.4
	Yr	61	250	46	56	6	3	0	24	29		.224	.307	.272	60	-12	-13	25	11			.941	-6	O/3S	-2.2
1904	Bos-N	149	580	70	141	17	2	1	27	56		.243	.313	.284	88	-8	-6	60	18			.933	-3	*O/32S	-1.7
Total	5	349	1315	197	327	30	12	2	102	154	7	.249	.332	.294	81	-29	-26	153	54			.932	-17	O/23SC	-5.5

■ **GARY GEIGER** Geiger, Gary Merle b: 4/4/37, Sand Ridge, Ill. BL/TR, 6', 168 lbs. Deb: 4/15/58

YEAR	TM/L	G	AB	R	H	2B	3B	HR	RBI	BB	SO	AVG	OBP	SLG	PRO+	BR	/A	RC	SB	CS	SBR	FA	FR	POS	TPR
1958	Cle-A	91	195	28	45	3	1	1	6	27	43	.231	.333	.272	70	-7	-7	20	2	2	-1	.986	4	O/3P	-0.6
1959	Bos-A	120	335	45	82	10	4	11	48	21	55	.245	.289	.397	83	-7	-9	38	9	3	1	.989	-10	O	-2.3
1960	Bos-A	77	245	32	74	13	3	9	33	23	38	.302	.369	.490	126	10	9	43	2	2	-1	1.000	4	O	0.9
1961	Bos-A	140	499	82	116	21	6	18	64	87	91	.232	.351	.407	99	2	1	78	16	4	2	.988	10	*O	0.5
1962	Bos-A	131	466	67	116	18	4	16	54	67	66	.249	.346	.408	99	2	-0	69	18	11	-1	.987	8	*O	-0.1
1963	Bos-A	121	399	67	105	13	5	16	44	36	63	.263	.329	.441	110	7	5	59	9	4	0	.984	14	O/1	1.5
1964	Bos-A	5	13	3	5	0	1	0	1	2	2	.385	.467	.538	170	1	1	4	0	0	0	1.000	-0	/O	0.1
1965	Bos-A	24	45	5	9	3	0	1	2	13	10	.200	.379	.333	98	1	1	7	3	0	1	.970	0	O	0.1
1966	Atl-N	78	126	23	33	5	3	4	10	21	29	.262	.372	.444	124	5	5	22	0	1	-1	.982	2	O	0.5
1967	Atl-N	69	117	17	19	1	1	1	5	20	35	.162	.285	.214	45	-8	-8	8	1	1	-0	.980	-1	O	-1.1
1969	Hou-N	93	125	19	28	4	1	0	16	24	34	.224	.353	.272	79	-3	-2	14	2	1	0	.968	1	O	-0.3
1970	Hou-N	5	4	0	1	0	0	0	0	0	0	.250	.250	.250	36	-0	-0	0	0	0	0	1.000	0	/O	0.0
Total	12	954	2569	388	633	91	29	77	283	341	466	.246	.339	.394	98	3	-5	363	62	29	1	.986	32	O/13P	-0.8

■ **BILL GEIS** Geis, William J. (b: William J. Geiss) b: 7/15/1858, Chicago, Ill. d: 9/18/24, Chicago, Ill. 5'10", 164 lbs. Deb: 5/01/1884 F

YEAR	TM/L	G	AB	R	H	2B	3B	HR	RBI	BB	SO	AVG	OBP	SLG	PRO+	BR	/A	RC	SB	CS	SBR	FA	FR	POS	TPR
1884	Det-N	75	283	22	50	11	4	2	16	6	60	.177	.194	.265	46	-18	-16	15				.862	-7	2/O1P	-1.9

■ **EMIL GEISS** Geiss, Emil August b: 3/20/1867, Chicago, Ill. d: 10/4/11, Chicago, Ill. BR/TR, Deb: 5/18/1887 F

YEAR	TM/L	G	AB	R	H	2B	3B	HR	RBI	BB	SO	AVG	OBP	SLG	PRO+	BR	/A	RC	SB	CS	SBR	FA	FR	POS	TPR
1887	Chi-N	3	12	0	1	0	0	0	0	0	7	.083	.083	.083	-47	-2	-3	0	0			.571	-1	/21P	-0.3

■ **CHARLIE GELBERT** Gelbert, Charles Magnus b: 1/26/06, Scranton, Pa. d: 1/13/67, Easton, Pa. BR/TR, 5'11", 170 lbs. Deb: 4/16/29

YEAR	TM/L	G	AB	R	H	2B	3B	HR	RBI	BB	SO	AVG	OBP	SLG	PRO+	BR	/A	RC	SB	CS	SBR	FA	FR	POS	TPR
1929	StL-N	146	512	60	134	29	8	3	65	51	46	.262	.329	.367	71	-23	-23	62	8			.948	7	*S	0.1
1930	*StL-N	139	513	92	156	39	11	3	72	43	41	.304	.360	.441	89	-6	-9	80	6			.947	9	*S	1.3
1931	*StL-N	131	447	61	129	29	5	1	62	54	31	.289	.365	.383	97	2	-0	66	7			.959	13	*S	2.5
1932	StL-N	122	455	60	122	28	9	1	45	39	30	.268	.330	.376	87	-6	-8	59	8			.945	0	*S	0.3
1935	StL-N	62	168	24	49	7	2	2	21	17	18	.292	.357	.393	97	1	-0	25	0			.978	5	3S/2	0.6
1936	StL-N	93	280	33	64	15	2	3	27	25	26	.229	.292	.329	67	-13	-13	25	2			.965	8	3S/2	-0.2
1937	Cin-N	43	114	12	22	4	0	1	13	15	12	.193	.287	.254	51	-8	-7	9	1			.968	-2	S/23	-0.7
	Det-A	20	47	4	4	2	0	0	1	4	11	.085	.157	.128	-27	-9	-10	1	0	0	0	.934	-0	S	-0.8
1939	Was-A	68	188	36	48	7	5	3	29	30	11	.255	.361	.394	100	-2	1	28	2	0	1	.970	-4	S3/2	0.0
1940	Was-A	22	54	7	20	7	1	0	7	4	3	.370	.424	.537	157	4	4	13	0	0	0	.920	-5	S/P2	0.0
	Bos-A	30	91	9	18	2	0	0	8	8	16	.198	.263	.220	25	-10	-10	6	0	0	0	.926	5	3/S	-0.5
	Yr	52	145	16	38	9	1	0	15	12	19	.262	.323	.338	72	-6	-6	17	0	0	0	.926	-1	3S/P2	-0.5
Total	9	876	2869	398	766	169	43	17	350	290	245	.267	.336	.374	82	-71	-76	373	34	0		.951	35	S3/2P	2.6

■ **FRANK GENINS** Genins, C. Frank "Frenchy" b: 11/2/1866, St.Louis, Mo. d: 9/30/22, St.Louis, Mo. TR, Deb: 7/05/1892

YEAR	TM/L	G	AB	R	H	2B	3B	HR	RBI	BB	SO	AVG	OBP	SLG	PRO+	BR	/A	RC	SB	CS	SBR	FA	FR	POS	TPR
1892	Cin-N	35	110	12	20	4	0	0	7	12	12	.182	.262	.218	48	-7	-6	8	7			.901	4	SO/3	-0.2
	StL-N	15	51	5	10	1	0	0	4	1	11	.196	.212	.216	32	-4	-4	3	3			.821	-8	S/O	-1.0

YEAR	TM/L	G	AB	R	H	2B	3B	HR	RBI	BB	SO	AVG	OBP	SLG	PRO+	BR	/A	RC	SB	CS	SBR	FA	FR	POS	TPR
	Yr	50	161	17	30	5	0	0	11	13	23	.186	.247	.217	43	-11	-10	11	10			.868	-3	SO/3	-1.2
1895	Pit-N	73	252	43	63	8	0	2	24	22	14	.250	.315	.306	66	-14	-11	34	19			.931	-6	O32/S1	-1.5
1901	Cle-A	26	101	15	23	5	0	0	9	8		.228	.284	.277	59	-6	-5	10	3			.940	1	O	-0.5
Total	3	149	514	75	116	18	0	2	44	43	37	.226	.288	.272	58	-31	-27	55	32			.934	-9	/OS321	-3.2
■ GEORGE GENOVESE Genovese, George Michael b: 2/22/22, Staten Island, N.Y BL/TR, 5′6.5″, 160 lbs. Deb: 4/29/50																									
1950	Was-A	3	1	1	0	0	0	0	0	1	0	.000	.500	.000	39	0	0	0	0	0	0	.000	0	H	0.0
■ JIM GENTILE Gentile, James Edward "Diamond Jim" b: 6/3/34, San Francisco, Cal. BL/TL, 6′4″, 215 lbs. Deb: 9/10/57																									
1957	Bro-N	4	6	1	1	0	0	1	1	1	1	.167	.286	.667	133	0	0	1	0	0	0	1.000	-0	/1	0.0
1958	LA-N	12	30	0	4	1	0	0	4	4	6	.133	.235	.167	9	-4	-4	1	0	0	0	.981	-1	/1	-0.6
1960	Bal-A★	138	384	67	112	17	0	21	98	68	72	.292	.407	.500	146	26	26	82	0	0	0	.993	-6	*1	1.2
1961	Bal-A★	148	486	96	147	25	2	46	141	96	106	.302	.428	.646	187	59	61	138	1	1	-0	.989	2	*1	5.0
1962	Bal-A★	152	545	80	137	21	1	33	87	77	100	.251	.351	.475	126	15	19	92	1	0	0	.988	6	*1	1.5
1963	Bal-A	145	496	65	123	16	1	24	72	76	101	.248	.355	.429	121	14	15	77	1	0	0	**.995**	7	*1	1.7
1964	KC-A	136	439	71	110	10	0	28	71	84	122	.251	.376	.465	128	21	20	81	0	0	0	.988	-0	*1	1.4
1965	KC-A	38	118	14	29	5	0	10	22	9	26	.246	.305	.542	138	5	5	19	0	0	0	.981	-1	1	0.2
	Hou-N	81	227	22	55	11	1	7	31	34	72	.242	.353	.392	118	4	6	33	0	0	0	.993	2	1	0.5
1966	Hou-N	49	144	16	35	6	1	7	18	21	39	.243	.355	.444	129	4	6	24	0	0	0	.989	2	1	0.5
	Cle-A	33	47	2	6	1	0	2	4	5	18	.128	.212	.277	39	-4	-4	3	0	0	0	.944	-0	/1	-0.5
Total	9	936	2922	434	759	113	6	179	549	475	663	.260	.372	.486	136	141	150	550	3	1	0	.990	10	1	10.9
■ SAM GENTILE Gentile, Samuel Christopher b: 10/12/16, Charlestown, Mass. BL/TR, 5′11″, 180 lbs. Deb: 4/24/43																									
1943	Bos-N	8	4	1	1	1	0	0	0	1	0	.250	.400	.500	162	0	0	1	0			.000	0	H	0.0
■ HARVEY GENTRY Gentry, Harvey William b: 5/27/26, Winston-Salem, N.C BL/TR, 6′, 170 lbs. Deb: 4/14/54 F																									
1954	NY-N	5	4	0	1	0	0	0	1	1	0	.250	.400	.250	73	-0	-0	1	0	0	0	.000	0	H	0.0
■ ALEX GEORGE George, Alex Thomas M. b: 9/27/38, Kansas City, Mo. BL/TR, 5′11.5″, 170 lbs. Deb: 9/16/55																									
1955	KC-A	5	10	0	1	0	0	0	0	1	7	.100	.182	.100	-22	-2	-2	0	0	0	0	.917	-1	/S	-0.3
■ GREEK GEORGE George, Charles Peter b: 12/25/12, Waycross, Ga. BR/TR, 6′2″, 200 lbs. Deb: 6/30/35																									
1935	Cle-A	2	0	0	0	0	0	0	0	0	0	—	—	—	—	0	0	0	0	0	0	1.000	1	/C	0.1
1936	Cle-A	23	77	3	15	3	0	0	5	9	16	.195	.279	.234	28	-9	-9	5	0	0	0	.994	16	C	0.7
1938	Bro-N	7	20	0	4	0	1	0	2	0	4	.200	.200	.300	35	-2	-2	1	0			1.000	2	/C	0.0
1941	Chi-N	35	64	4	10	2	0	0	6	2	10	.156	.182	.188	4	-8	-8	2	0			.973	2	C	-0.5
1945	Phi-A	51	138	8	24	4	1	0	11	17	29	.174	.265	.217	41	-10	-10	8	0	0	0	.972	-6	C	-1.5
Total	5	118	299	15	53	9	2	0	24	28	59	.177	.248	.221	29	-29	-29	17	0	0		.983	14	/C	-1.2
■ BILL GEORGE George, William M. b: 1/27/1865, Bellaire, Ohio d: 8/23/16, Wheeling, W.Va. BR/TL, 5′8″, 165 lbs. Deb: 5/11/1887																									
1887	NY-N	13	53	6	9	0	0	0	5	1	6	.170	.185	.170	0	-7	-7	2	2			.854	1	P/O	0.0
1888	*NY-N	9	39	7	9	1	0	1	6	0	2	.231	.231	.333	81	-1	-1	3	1			1.000	-1	/OP	-0.2
1889	NY-N	3	15	1	4	0	0	0	0	0	3	.267	.267	.267	50	-1	-1	1	1			.875	-0	/O	-0.1
	Col-a	5	17	1	4	0	0	0	3	1	1	.235	.278	.235	51	-1	-1	1	1			.667	-1	/OP	-0.2
Total	3	30	124	15	26	1	0	1	14	2	12	.210	.222	.242	37	-10	-9	8	5			.860	-1	/PO	-0.5
■ BEN GERAGHTY Geraghty, Benjamin Raymond b: 7/19/12, Jersey City, N.J. d: 6/18/63, Jacksonville, Fla BR/TR, 5′11″, 175 lbs. Deb: 4/17/36																									
1936	Bro-N	51	129	11	25	4	0	0	9	8	16	.194	.241	.225	26	-13	-13	7	4			.922	-7	S/23	-1.8
1943	Bos-N	8	1	2	0	0	0	0	0	0	0	.000	.000	.000	-99	-0	-0	0	0			1.000	2	/2S3	0.2
1944	Bos-N	11	16	3	4	0	0	0	0	1	2	.250	.294	.250	52	-1	-1	1	0			1.000	0	/23	-0.1
Total	3	70	146	16	29	4	0	0	9	9	18	.199	.245	.226	28	-15	-15	8	4			.922	-5	/S23	-1.7
■ CRAIG GERBER Gerber, Craig Stuart b: 1/8/59, Chicago, Ill. BL/TR, 6′, 175 lbs. Deb: 4/11/85																									
1985	Cal-A	65	91	8	24	1	2	0	6	2	3	.264	.280	.319	64	-5	-5	7	0	3	-2	.970	19	S/32D	1.4
■ WALLY GERBER Gerber, Walter "Spooks" b: 8/18/1891, Columbus, Ohio d: 6/19/51, Columbus, Ohio BR/TR, 5′10″, 152 lbs. Deb: 9/23/14																									
1914	Pit-N	17	54	5	13	1	1	0	5	2	8	.241	.281	.296	75	-2	-2	4	0			.921	1	S	0.1
1915	Pit-N	56	144	8	28	2	0	0	7	9	16	.194	.252	.208	40	-10	-10	9	6	1	1	.930	2	3S/2	-0.4
1917	StL-A	14	39	2	12	1	1	0	2	3	2	.308	.357	.385	131	1	1	6	1			.939	-2	S/2	0.0
1918	StL-A	56	171	10	41	4	0	0	10	19	11	.240	.316	.263	77	-5	-4	15	2			.922	-9	S	-1.2
1919	StL-A	140	462	43	105	14	6	1	37	49	36	.227	.308	.290	67	-19	-20	44	1			.940	-8	*S	-2.1
1920	StL-A	154	584	70	163	26	2	2	60	58	32	.279	.346	.341	80	-13	-16	69	4	13	-7	.939	7	*S	-0.2
1921	StL-A	114	436	55	121	12	9	2	48	34	19	.278	.337	.360	73	-15	-18	53	3	7	-3	.943	-3	*S	-1.3
1922	StL-A	153	604	81	161	22	8	1	51	52	34	.267	.326	.334	70	-24	-27	69	6	4	-1	.944	2	*S	-1.0
1923	StL-A	154	605	85	170	26	3	1	62	54	50	.281	.342	.339	75	-17	-22	72	4	6	-2	.950	6	*S	-0.3
1924	StL-A	148	496	61	135	20	4	0	55	43	34	.272	.341	.329	69	-19	-23	58	4	5	-2	.946	-7	*S	-1.5
1925	StL-A	72	246	29	67	13	1	0	19	26	15	.272	.344	.333	69	-10	-12	29	1	2	-1	.949	5	S	0.0
1926	StL-A	131	411	37	111	8	0	0	42	40	29	.270	.339	.290	62	-20	-22	43	0	2	-1	.944	3	*S	-0.7
1927	StL-A	142	438	44	98	13	9	0	45	35	25	.224	.284	.295	49	-33	-35	36	2	6	-3	.946	9	*S/3	-1.4
1928	StL-A	6	18	1	5	1	0	0	0	1	3	.278	.316	.333	69	-1	-1	2	0	0	0	.783	-2	/S	-0.2
	Bos-A	104	300	21	64	6	1	0	28	32	31	.213	.289	.240	41	-25	-25	24	6	1	1	.955	34	*S	2.0
	Yr	110	318	22	69	7	1	0	28	33	34	.217	.291	.245	43	-26	-25	26	6	1	1	.948	**32**	*S	1.8
1929	Bos-A	61	91	6	15	3	1	0	5	8	12	.165	.232	.220	17	-11	-11	5	1	0	0	.937	14	S2	0.5
Total	15	1522	5099	558	1309	172	46	7	476	465	357	.257	.323	.313	67	-222	-247	538	41	47		.943	54	*S/23	-7.7
■ BOB GEREN Geren, Robert Peter b: 9/22/61, San Diego, Cal. BR/TR, 6′3″, 205 lbs. Deb: 5/17/88																									
1988	NY-A	10	10	0	1	0	0	0	0	2	3	.100	.250	.100	2	-1	-1	0	0	0	0	1.000	1	C	0.0
1989	NY-A	65	205	26	59	5	1	9	27	12	44	.288	.330	.454	120	4	5	28	0	0	0	.991	1	C/D	0.9
1990	NY-A	110	277	21	59	7	0	8	31	13	73	.213	.261	.325	63	-14	-14	23	0	0	0	.993	12	*C/D	0.3
1991	NY-A	64	128	7	28	3	0	2	12	9	31	.219	.270	.289	55	-8	-8	9	0	1	-1	.989	8	C	0.2
Total	4	249	620	54	147	15	1	19	70	36	151	.237	.285	.356	79	-19	-19	60	0	1	-1	.992	22	C/D	1.4
■ JOE GERHARDT Gerhardt, John Joseph "Move Up Joe" b: 2/14/1855, Washington, D.C. d: 3/11/22, Middletown, N.Y. BR/TR, 6′, 160 lbs. Deb: 9/01/1873 M																									
1873	Was-n	13	56	6	12	2	1	0	6	0	5	.214	.214	.286	47	-4	-3	4						S	-0.3
1874	Bal-n	14	61	10	20	1	1	0		0		.328	.328	.377	125	2	2	8						S	0.1
1875	Mut-n	58	251	29	53	8	3	0		0		.211	.211	.267	61	-9	-11	15						32/S	-1.0
1876	Lou-N	65	292	33	76	10	3	2	18	3	5	.260	.268	.336	85	-0	-8	27				.944	5	*1/2SO3	-0.3
1877	Lou-N	59	250	41	76	6	5	1	35	5	8	.304	.318	.380	101	5	-2	31				.888	**20**	*2/OS1	1.8
1878	Cin-N	60	259	46	77	7	2	0	28	7	14	.297	.316	.340	127	4	8	28				.906	5	*2	1.6
1879	Cin-N	79	313	22	62	12	3	1	39	3	19	.198	.206	.265	57	-15	-13	17				.908	7	23/1S	-0.2
1881	Det-N	80	297	35	72	13	6	0	36	7	31	.242	.260	.327	80	-6	-7	26				.908	8	*2/3	0.3
1883	Lou-a	78	319	56	84	11	9	0		14		.263	.294	.354	117	3	6	34				.906	20	*2M	2.4
1884	Lou-a	106	404	39	89	7	8	0		13		.220	.254	.277	79	-10	-8	29				.920	27	*2	2.0
1885	NY-N	112	399	43	62	12	2	0	33	24	47	.155	.203	.195	30	-30	-29	16				.911	11	*2	-1.3
1886	NY-N	123	426	44	81	11	7	0	40	22	63	.190	.230	.249	45	-28	-28	27	8			.924	13	*2	-0.9
1887	NY-N	1	4	0	0	0	0	0	0	0	0	.000	.000	.000	-99	-1	-1	0	0			1.000	0	/3	-0.1

YEAR	TM/L	G	AB	R	H	2B	3B	HR	RBI	BB	SO	AVG	OBP	SLG	PRO+	BR	/A	RC	SB	CS	SBR	FA	FR	POS	TPR
	NY-a	85	307	40	68	13	2	0		24		.221	.280	.277	60	-17	-15	29	15			.896	15	2/3	0.2
1890	Bro-a	99	369	34	75	10	4	2		30		.203	.270	.268	63	-18	-16	30	9			.938	37	*2	2.3
	StL-a	37	125	15	32	0	0	1		9		.256	.321	.280	70	-3	-6	13	5			.955	5	23M	0.1
	Yr	136	494	49	107	10	4	3		39		.217	.283	.271	65	-21	-22	43	14			**.940**	**42**	*23	2.4
1891	Lou-a	2	6	0	0	0	0	0	0	1	0	.000	.143	.000	-58	-1	-1	0	0			.833	-0	/2	-0.1
Total	3 n	85	368	45	85	11	5	0	6	0	5	.231	.231	.288	69	-11	-13	26	0					/3S2	-1.2
Total	12	986	3770	448	854	112	51	7	229	162	187	.227	.261	.289	72	-117	-120	308	37			.913	173	2/13SO	7.8

■ **KEN GERHART** Gerhart, Harold Kenneth b: 5/19/61, Charleston, S.C. BR/TR, 6', 190 lbs. Deb: 9/14/86

YEAR	TM/L	G	AB	R	H	2B	3B	HR	RBI	BB	SO	AVG	OBP	SLG	PRO+	BR	/A	RC	SB	CS	SBR	FA	FR	POS	TPR
1986	Bal-A	20	69	4	16	2	0	1	7	4	18	.232	.274	.304	58	-4	-4	6	0	1	-1	.971	-3	O	-0.8
1987	Bal-A	92	284	41	69	10	2	14	34	17	53	.243	.288	.440	92	-5	-4	35	9	2	2	.973	-6	O	-1.1
1988	Bal-A	103	262	27	51	10	1	9	23	21	57	.195	.260	.344	69	-12	-11	24	7	3	0	.975	-8	O/D	-2.1
Total	3	215	615	72	136	22	3	24	64	42	128	.221	.274	.384	79	-21	-19	64	16	6	1	.974	-16	O/D	-4.0

■ **GEORGE GERKEN** Gerken, George Herbert "Pickles" b: 7/28/03, Chicago, Ill. d: 10/23/77, Arcadia, Cal. BR/TR, 5'11.5", 175 lbs. Deb: 4/19/27

YEAR	TM/L	G	AB	R	H	2B	3B	HR	RBI	BB	SO	AVG	OBP	SLG	PRO+	BR	/A	RC	SB	CS	SBR	FA	FR	POS	TPR
1927	Cle-A	6	14	1	3	0	0	0	2	1	3	.214	.267	.214	26	-2	-2	1	0	0	0	.917	0	/O	-0.2
1928	Cle-A	38	115	16	26	7	2	0	9	12	22	.226	.305	.322	64	-6	-6	12	3	3	-1	.940	-1	O	-1.0
Total	2	44	129	17	29	7	2	0	11	13	25	.225	.301	.310	60	-7	-8	12	3	3	-1	.937	-1	/O	-1.2

■ **JOHNNY GERLACH** Gerlach, John Glenn b: 5/11/17, Shullsburg, Wis. BR/TR, 5'9", 165 lbs. Deb: 9/03/38

YEAR	TM/L	G	AB	R	H	2B	3B	HR	RBI	BB	SO	AVG	OBP	SLG	PRO+	BR	/A	RC	SB	CS	SBR	FA	FR	POS	TPR
1938	Chi-A	9	25	2	7	0	0	0	1	4	2	.280	.379	.280	66	-1	-1	3	0	0	0	.949	1	/S	0.0
1939	Chi-A	3	2	0	2	0	0	0	0	0	0	1.000	1.000	1.000	402	1	1	2	0	0	0	1.000	0	/3	0.1
Total	2	12	27	2	9	0	0	0	1	4	2	.333	.419	.333	89	-0	-0	5	0	0	0	.946	1	/S3	0.1

■ **DICK GERNERT** Gernert, Richard Edward b: 9/28/28, Reading, Pa. BR/TR, 6'3", 210 lbs. Deb: 4/16/52 C

YEAR	TM/L	G	AB	R	H	2B	3B	HR	RBI	BB	SO	AVG	OBP	SLG	PRO+	BR	/A	RC	SB	CS	SBR	FA	FR	POS	TPR
1952	Bos-A	102	367	58	89	20	2	19	67	35	83	.243	.317	.463	107	5	2	56	4	1	1	.987	-1	1	-0.2
1953	Bos-A	139	494	73	125	15	1	21	71	88	82	.253	.371	.415	106	10	7	81	0	7	-4	.986	-3	*1	-0.6
1954	Bos-A	14	23	2	6	2	0	0	1	6	4	.261	.414	.348	99	1	0	3	0	0	0	1.000	-1	/1	-0.1
1955	Bos-A	7	20	6	4	2	0	0	1	1	5	.200	.238	.300	40	-2	-2	1	0	0	0	.974	-0	/1	-0.2
1956	Bos-A	106	306	53	89	11	0	16	68	56	57	.291	.404	.484	119	16	11	63	1	0	0	.985	1	O1	0.7
1957	Bos-A	99	316	45	75	13	3	14	58	39	62	.237	.327	.430	99	2	-1	44	1	1	-0	.989	-2	1O	-0.8
1958	Bos-A	122	431	59	102	19	1	20	69	59	78	.237	.331	.425	100	4	-0	60	2	0	1	.991	8	*1	0.1
1959	Bos-A	117	298	41	78	14	1	11	42	52	49	.262	.371	.426	113	9	7	47	1	2	-1	.995	3	1O	0.4
1960	Chi-N	52	96	8	24	3	0	0	11	10	19	.250	.321	.281	67	-4	-4	8	1	0	0	.987	3	1/O	-0.2
	Det-A	21	50	6	15	4	0	1	5	4	5	.300	.352	.440	110	1	1	8	0	0	0	1.000	-2	1/O	-0.2
1961	Det-A	6	5	1	1	0	0	1	1	1	2	.200	.333	.800	187	1	1	1	0	0	0	.000	0	H	0.1
	*Cin-N	40	63	4	19	1	0	0	7	7	9	.302	.371	.317	84	-1	-1	8	0	0	0	.993	3	1	0.1
1962	Hou-N	10	24	1	5	0	0	0	1	5	7	.208	.345	.208	57	-1	-1	2	0	0	0	1.000	-1	/1	-0.2
Total	11	835	2493	357	632	104	8	103	402	363	462	.254	.352	.426	104	40	19	382	10	11	-4	.990	9	1O	-1.1

■ **CESAR GERONIMO** Geronimo, Cesar Francisco (Zorrilla) b: 3/11/48, ElSeibo, D.R. BL/TL, 6'2", 170 lbs. Deb: 4/16/69

YEAR	TM/L	G	AB	R	H	2B	3B	HR	RBI	BB	SO	AVG	OBP	SLG	PRO+	BR	/A	RC	SB	CS	SBR	FA	FR	POS	TPR
1969	Hou-N	28	8	8	2	1	0	0	0	0	3	.250	.250	.375	74	-0	-0	1	0	0	0	1.000	1	/O	0.1
1970	Hou-N	47	37	5	9	0	0	0	2	2	5	.243	.300	.243	49	-3	-2	3	0	0	0	.920	2	O	-0.1
1971	Hou-N	94	82	13	18	2	2	1	6	5	31	.220	.264	.329	69	-4	-3	7	2	2	-1	.977	3	O	-0.2
1972	*Cin-N	120	255	32	70	9	7	4	29	24	64	.275	.344	.412	121	5	6	34	2	7	-4	.982	-8	*O	-0.9
1973	*Cin-N	139	324	35	68	14	3	4	33	23	74	.210	.269	.309	63	-18	-16	26	5	5	-2	.992	-2	*O	-2.5
1974	Cin-N	150	474	73	133	17	8	7	54	46	96	.281	.347	.395	109	4	5	65	9	5	-0	.987	3	*O	0.2
1975	*Cin-N	148	501	69	129	25	5	6	53	48	97	.257	.327	.363	90	-6	-7	61	13	5	1	.993	8	*O	-0.3
1976	*Cin-N	149	486	59	149	24	11	2	49	56	95	.307	.385	.414	124	19	17	82	22	5	4	.985	-3	*O	1.4
1977	Cin-N	149	492	54	131	22	4	10	52	35	89	.266	.321	.388	88	-8	-9	60	10	4	1	.992	5	*O	-0.9
1978	Cin-N	122	296	28	67	15	1	5	27	43	67	.226	.330	.334	86	-5	-5	35	8	3	1	.981	-5	*O	-1.3
1979	*Cin-N	123	356	38	85	17	4	4	38	37	56	.239	.314	.343	79	-10	-10	38	1	1	-0	.993	1	*O	-1.4
1980	Cin-N	103	145	16	37	5	0	2	9	14	24	.255	.321	.331	82	-3	-3	16	2	1	0	1.000	8	O	0.3
1981	*KC-A	59	118	14	29	0	2	2	13	11	16	.246	.310	.331	85	-2	-2	13	6	1	1	.980	-6	O	-0.9
1982	KC-A	53	119	14	32	6	3	4	23	8	16	.269	.315	.471	112	2	2	16	2	0	1	1.000	-2	O/D	0.0
1983	KC-A	38	87	2	18	4	0	0	4	2	13	.207	.242	.253	36	-8	-8	5	0	1	-1	.986	-2	O	-1.1
Total	15	1522	3780	460	977	161	50	51	392	354	746	.258	.327	.368	93	-37	-36	462	82	40	1	.988	4	*O/D	-7.6

■ **LOU GERTENRICH** Gertenrich, Louis Wilhelm b: 5/4/1875, Chicago, Ill. d: 10/23/33, Chicago, Ill. BR/TR, 5'8", 175 lbs. Deb: 9/15/01

YEAR	TM/L	G	AB	R	H	2B	3B	HR	RBI	BB	SO	AVG	OBP	SLG	PRO+	BR	/A	RC	SB	CS	SBR	FA	FR	POS	TPR
1901	Mil-A	2	3	1	1	0	0	0	0	0		.333	.333	.333	90	-0	-0	0	0			.000	-0	/O	0.0
1903	Pit-N	1	3	0	0	0	0	0	0	0		.000	.000	.000	-97	-1	-1	0	0			1.000	-0	/O	-0.1
Total	2	3	6	1	1	0	0	0	0	0		.167	.167	.167	-6	-1	-1	0	0			1.000	-0	/O	-0.1

■ **DOC GESSLER** Gessler, Harry Homer "Brownie" b: 12/23/1880, Indiana, Pa. d: 12/26/24, Indiana, Pa. BL/TR, 5'10", 180 lbs. Deb: 4/23/03 M

YEAR	TM/L	G	AB	R	H	2B	3B	HR	RBI	BB	SO	AVG	OBP	SLG	PRO+	BR	/A	RC	SB	CS	SBR	FA	FR	POS	TPR
1903	Det-A	29	105	9	25	5	4	0	12	3		.238	.273	.362	92	-2	-1	11	1			.974	-2	O	-0.5
	Bro-N	49	154	20	38	8	3	0	18	17		.247	.359	.338	102	1	2	24	9			.984	-3	O	-0.4
1904	Bro-N	104	341	41	99	18	4	2	28	30		.290	.351	.384	131	11	12	53	13			.920	2	O/12	1.0
1905	Bro-N	126	431	44	125	17	4	3	46	38		.290	.361	.369	127	10	15	69	26			.973	2	*1O	1.3
1906	Bro-N	9	33	3	8	1	2	0	4	3		.242	.324	.394	135	1	1	5	3			.946	1	/1	0.1
	*Chi-N	34	83	8	21	3	0	0	10	12		.253	.354	.289	96	1	0	11	4			1.000	-1	O/1	-0.2
	Yr	43	116	11	29	4	2	0	14	15		.250	.346	.319	105	2	1	16	7			1.000	-1	O1	-0.1
1908	Bos-A	128	435	55	134	13	14	3	63	51		.308	**.394**	.423	161	33	32	80	19			.950	-7	*O	2.2
1909	Bos-A	111	396	57	115	24	1	0	46	31		.290	.354	.356	122	11	10	55	16			.933	-1	*O	0.6
	Was-A	17	54	10	13	2	1	0	8	12		.241	.406	.315	134	3	3	9	4			1.000	-1	O/1	0.2
	Yr	128	450	67	128	26	2	0	54	43		.284	.361	.351	123	14	14	63	20			.940	-2	*O/1	0.8
1910	Was-A	145	487	58	126	17	11	2	50	62		.259	.361	.351	129	16	18	68	18			.953	-3	*O	0.9
1911	Was-A	128	450	65	127	19	5	4	78	74		.282	.406	.373	120	16	17	80	29			.943	-10	*O/1	0.0
Total	8	880	2969	370	831	127	49	14	363	333		.280	.369	.370	128	101	109	464	142			.945	-23	O1/2	5.2

■ **CHARLIE GETTIG** Gettig, Charles Henry b: 12/1870, Baltimore, Md. d: 4/11/35, Baltimore, Md. 5'10", 172 lbs. Deb: 8/05/1896

YEAR	TM/L	G	AB	R	H	2B	3B	HR	RBI	BB	SO	AVG	OBP	SLG	PRO+	BR	/A	RC	SB	CS	SBR	FA	FR	POS	TPR
1896	NY-N	6	9	3	3	1	0	0	0	0	0	.333	.333	.444	109	0	0	1	0			1.000	0	/P	0.0
1897	NY-N	22	75	8	15	6	0	0	12	6		.200	.277	.280	49	-6	-5	7	3			.556	-8	/32OSP	-1.1
1898	NY-N	64	196	30	49	6	2	0	26	15		.250	.310	.301	78	-6	-5	20	5			.833	-10	OP2/S31C	-1.4
1899	NY-N	34	97	7	24	3	0	0	9	7		.247	.305	.278	63	-5	-5	10	4			.833	-3	P/321O	-0.5
Total	4	126	377	48	91	16	2	0	47	28	0	.241	.302	.294	68	-17	-15	39	12			.879	-21	/PO23S1C	-3.0

■ **TOM GETTINGER** Gettinger, Thomas L. b: 1870, Mobile, Ala. BL/TL, 5'10", 180 lbs. Deb: 9/21/1889

YEAR	TM/L	G	AB	R	H	2B	3B	HR	RBI	BB	SO	AVG	OBP	SLG	PRO+	BR	/A	RC	SB	CS	SBR	FA	FR	POS	TPR
1889	StL-a	4	16	2	7	0	0	1	2	2	1	.438	.500	.625	197	3	2	5	0			.750	-1	/O	0.1
1890	StL-a	58	227	31	54	7	5	3		20		.238	.302	.352	83	-2	-7	27	8			.886	-6	O	-1.3
1895	Lou-N	63	260	28	70	11	5	2	32	8	15	.269	.296	.373	78	-11	-8	32	6			.910	-3	O/P	-1.3
Total	3	125	503	61	131	18	10	6	34	30	16	.260	.306	.372	84	-10	-13	64	14			.897	-10	O/P	-2.5

■ **JAKE GETTMAN** Gettman, Jacob John b: 10/25/1876, Frank, Russia d: 10/4/56, Denver, Colo. BB/TL, 5'11", 185 lbs. Deb: 8/20/1897

YEAR	TM/L	G	AB	R	H	2B	3B	HR	RBI	BB	SO	AVG	OBP	SLG	PRO+	BR	/A	RC	SB	CS	SBR	FA	FR	POS	TPR
1897	Was-N	36	143	28	45	7	3	3	29	7		.315	.359	.469	118	3	3	28	8			.981	-3	O	-0.2
1898	Was-N	142	567	75	157	16	5	5	47	29		.277	.319	.349	92	-8	-7	76	32			.926	2	*O/1	-1.5

YEAR	TM/L	G	AB	R	H	2B	3B	HR	RBI	BB	SO	AVG	OBP	SLG	PRO+	BR	/A	RC	SB	CS	SBR	FA	FR	POS	TPR
1899	Was-N	19	62	5	13	1	0	0	2	4		.210	.258	.226	33	-6	-6	5	4			1.000	-1	O/1	-0.7
Total	3	197	772	108	215	24	8	8	78	40		.278	.322	.361	92	-10	-10	109	44			.941	-2	O/1	-2.4

■ GUS GETZ Getz, Gustave "Gee-Gee" b: 8/3/1889, Pittsburgh, Pa. d: 5/28/69, Keansburg, N.J. BR/TR, 5'11", 165 lbs. Deb: 8/15/09

YEAR	TM/L	G	AB	R	H	2B	3B	HR	RBI	BB	SO	AVG	OBP	SLG	PRO+	BR	/A	RC	SB	CS	SBR	FA	FR	POS	TPR
1909	Bos-N	40	148	6	33	2	0	0	9	1		.223	.228	.236	42	-10	-11	8	2			.934	-0	3/2S	-1.1
1910	Bos-N	54	144	14	28	0	1	0	7	6	10	.194	.232	.208	27	-13	-14	7	2			.915	3	32/OS	-1.2
1914	Bro-N	55	210	13	52	8	1	0	20	2	15	.248	.255	.295	62	-10	-11	17	9			.949	12	3	0.4
1915	Bro-N	130	477	39	123	10	5	2	46	8	14	.258	.275	.312	76	-14	-15	41	19	15	-3	.951	8	*3/S	-0.6
1916	*Bro-N	40	96	9	21	1	2	0	8	0	5	.219	.219	.271	49	-6	-6	8	9			.913	-3	3/S1	-0.9
1917	Cin-N	7	14	2	4	0	0	0	3	3	0	.286	.412	.286	121	0	1	2	0			.875	-3	/23	-0.2
1918	Cle-A	6	15	2	2	1	0	0	0	4	1	.133	.350	.200	60	-0	-1	1	0			.941	-0	/3	-0.1
	Pit-N	7	10	0	2	0	0	0	0	0	1	.200	.200	.200	21	-1	-1	0	0			.875	1	/3	0.0
Total	7	339	1114	85	265	22	9	2	93	24	46	.238	.257	.279	60	-54	-57	85	41	15		.942	18	3/2SO1	-3.7

■ CHAPPIE GEYGAN Geygan, James Edward b: 6/3/03, Ironton, Ohio d: 3/15/66, Columbus, Ohio BR/TR, 5'11", 170 lbs. Deb: 7/16/24

YEAR	TM/L	G	AB	R	H	2B	3B	HR	RBI	BB	SO	AVG	OBP	SLG	PRO+	BR	/A	RC	SB	CS	SBR	FA	FR	POS	TPR
1924	Bos-A	33	82	7	21	5	2	0	4	4	16	.256	.307	.366	73	-4	-4	9	0	2	-1	.952	4	S	0.2
1925	Bos-A	3	11	0	2	0	0	0	0	0	2	.182	.182	.182	-8	-2	-2	0	0	0	0	.813	-1	/S	-0.3
1926	Bos-A	4	10	0	3	0	0	0	0	1	1	.300	.364	.300	77	-0	-0	1	0	0	0	.800	-1	/3	-0.1
Total	3	40	103	7	26	5	2	0	4	5	19	.252	.300	.340	65	-6	-6	10	0	2	-1	.938	2	/S3	-0.2

■ PATSY GHARRITY Gharrity, Edward Patrick b: 3/13/1892, Parnell, Iowa d: 10/10/66, Beloit, Wis. BR/TR, 5'10", 170 lbs. Deb: 5/16/16 C

YEAR	TM/L	G	AB	R	H	2B	3B	HR	RBI	BB	SO	AVG	OBP	SLG	PRO+	BR	/A	RC	SB	CS	SBR	FA	FR	POS	TPR
1916	Was-A	39	92	8	21	5	1	0	9	8	18	.228	.297	.304	81	-2	-2	9	2			1.000	-3	C1	-0.5
1917	Was-A	76	176	15	50	5	0	0	18	14	18	.284	.337	.313	99	-0	-0	20	7			.980	1	1/CO	-0.1
1918	Was-A	4	4	0	1	1	0	0	2	0	1	.250	.250	.500	129	0	0	0	0			.000	0	H	0.0
1919	Was-A	111	347	35	94	19	4	2	43	25	39	.271	.325	.366	95	-3	-3	42	4			.969	-5	CO/1	-0.5
1920	Was-A	131	428	51	105	18	3	3	44	37	52	.245	.307	.322	69	-21	-19	44	6	5	-1	.965	-2	*C/1O	-1.4
1921	Was-A	121	387	62	120	19	8	7	55	45	44	.310	.386	.455	120	8	11	70	4	3	-1	.977	-0	*C	1.6
1922	Was-A	96	273	40	70	16	6	5	45	36	30	.256	.351	.414	104	-0	2	41	3	3	-1	.981	3	C	0.7
1923	Was-A	93	251	26	52	9	4	3	33	22	27	.207	.276	.311	57	-17	-16	23	6	2	1	.986	1	C1	-1.4
1929	Was-A	3	2	0	0	0	0	0	0	1	2	.000	.333	.000	-7	-0	-0	0	0	0	0	.000	0	H	0.0
1930	Was-A	2	1	0	0	0	0	0	0	0	0	.000	.000	.000	-99	-0	-0	0	0	0	0	1.000	-0	/1	0.0
Total	10	676	1961	237	513	92	26	20	249	188	231	.262	.331	.366	90	-37	-28	250	32	13		.974	-6	C1/O	-1.6

■ RAY GIANNELLI Giannelli, Raymond John b: 2/5/66, Brooklyn, N.Y. BL/TR, 6', 195 lbs. Deb: 5/04/91

YEAR	TM/L	G	AB	R	H	2B	3B	HR	RBI	BB	SO	AVG	OBP	SLG	PRO+	BR	/A	RC	SB	CS	SBR	FA	FR	POS	TPR
1991	Tor-A	9	24	2	4	1	0	0	0	5	9	.167	.310	.208	45	-2	-2	2	1	0	0	.923	-2	/3	-0.3

■ JOE GIANNINI Giannini, Joseph Francis b: 9/8/1888, San Francisco, Cal d: 9/26/42, San Francisco, Cal. BL/TR, 5'8", 155 lbs. Deb: 8/07/11

YEAR	TM/L	G	AB	R	H	2B	3B	HR	RBI	BB	SO	AVG	OBP	SLG	PRO+	BR	/A	RC	SB	CS	SBR	FA	FR	POS	TPR
1911	Bos-A	1	2	0	1	1	0	0	0	0		.500	.500	1.000	317	1	1	1	0			.500	-0	/S	0.0

■ JOHN GIBBONS Gibbons, John Michael b: 6/8/62, Great Falls, Mont. BR/TR, 5'11", 187 lbs. Deb: 4/11/84

YEAR	TM/L	G	AB	R	H	2B	3B	HR	RBI	BB	SO	AVG	OBP	SLG	PRO+	BR	/A	RC	SB	CS	SBR	FA	FR	POS	TPR
1984	NY-N	10	31	1	2	0	0	0	1	3	11	.065	.171	.065	-32	-5	-5	0	0	0	0	.983	-1	/C	-0.6
1986	NY-N	8	19	4	9	4	0	1	1	3	5	.474	.545	.842	285	5	5	8	0	0	0	1.000	1	/C	0.6
Total	2	18	50	5	11	4	0	1	2	6	16	.220	.316	.360	90	-1	-1	9	0	0	0	.990	-0	/C	0.0

■ JAKE GIBBS Gibbs, Jerry Dean b: 11/7/38, Grenada, Miss. BL/TR, 6', 185 lbs. Deb: 9/11/62

YEAR	TM/L	G	AB	R	H	2B	3B	HR	RBI	BB	SO	AVG	OBP	SLG	PRO+	BR	/A	RC	SB	CS	SBR	FA	FR	POS	TPR
1962	NY-A	2	0	2	0	0	0	0	0	0	0	—	—	—	—	0	0	0	0	0	0	.000	0	/3	0.0
1963	NY-A	4	8	1	2	0	0	0	0	0	1	.250	.250	.250	41	-1	-1	1	0	0	0	1.000	-1	/C	-0.1
1964	NY-A	3	6	1	1	0	0	0	0	0	2	.167	.167	.167	-7	-1	-1	0	0	0	0	1.000	0	/C	-0.1
1965	NY-A	37	68	6	15	1	0	2	7	4	20	.221	.274	.324	70	-3	-3	7	0	0	0	.991	2	C	0.0
1966	NY-A	62	182	19	47	6	0	3	20	19	16	.258	.328	.341	96	-1	-1	20	5	2	0	.988	4	C	0.8
1967	NY-A	116	374	33	87	7	1	4	25	28	57	.233	.293	.289	75	-12	-11	31	7	6	-2	.975	1	C	-0.7
1968	NY-A	124	423	31	90	12	3	3	29	27	68	.213	.270	.277	68	-17	-16	30	9	8	-2	.991	-4	*C	-1.6
1969	NY-A	71	219	18	49	9	2	0	18	23	30	.224	.298	.283	65	-11	-10	18	3	4	-2	.990	8	C	0.1
1970	NY-A	49	153	23	46	9	2	8	26	7	14	.301	.335	.542	146	7	8	27	2	0	1	.987	3	C	1.3
1971	NY-A	70	206	23	45	9	0	5	21	12	23	.218	.271	.335	76	-8	-7	18	2	2	-1	.988	-5	C	-1.1
Total	10	538	1639	157	382	53	8	25	146	120	231	.233	.291	.321	81	-48	-41	152	28	22	-5	.986	8	C/3	-1.4

■ CHARLIE GIBSON Gibson, Charles Ellsworth "Gibby" b: 11/17/1879, Sharon, Pa. d: 11/22/54, Sharon, Pa. BR/TR, 6', 160 lbs. Deb: 9/23/05

YEAR	TM/L	G	AB	R	H	2B	3B	HR	RBI	BB	SO	AVG	OBP	SLG	PRO+	BR	/A	RC	SB	CS	SBR	FA	FR	POS	TPR
1905	StL-A	1	3	0	0	0	0	0	0	0		.000	.000	.000	-99	-1	-1	0	0			1.000	-0	/C	-0.1

■ CHARLIE GIBSON Gibson, Charles Griffin b: 11/21/1899, LaGrange, Ga. d: 12/18/90, LaGrange, Ga. BR/TR, 5'8", 160 lbs. Deb: 5/30/24

YEAR	TM/L	G	AB	R	H	2B	3B	HR	RBI	BB	SO	AVG	OBP	SLG	PRO+	BR	/A	RC	SB	CS	SBR	FA	FR	POS	TPR
1924	Phi-A	12	15	1	2	0	0	0	1	2	0	.133	.235	.133	-3	-2	-2	1	0	0	0	.870	-0	C	-0.2

■ FRANK GIBSON Gibson, Frank Gilbert b: 9/27/1890, Omaha, Neb. d: 4/27/61, Austin, Tex. BB/TR, 6'0.5", 172 lbs. Deb: 4/22/13

YEAR	TM/L	G	AB	R	H	2B	3B	HR	RBI	BB	SO	AVG	OBP	SLG	PRO+	BR	/A	RC	SB	CS	SBR	FA	FR	POS	TPR
1913	Det-A	23	57	8	8	1	0	0	2	3	9	.140	.197	.158	4	-7	-7	2	2			.914	-6	C/O	-1.3
1921	Bos-N	63	125	14	33	5	4	2	13	3	17	.264	.292	.416	90	-3	-2	15	0	0	0	.979	1	C	0.1
1922	Bos-N	66	164	15	49	7	2	3	20	10	27	.299	.339	.421	99	-2	-1	24	4	1	1	.981	-1	C1	0.0
1923	Bos-N	41	50	13	15	1	0	0	5	7	7	.300	.386	.320	92	-0	-0	6	0	2	-1	.923	-2	C	-0.2
1924	Bos-N	90	229	25	71	15	6	1	30	10	23	.310	.342	.441	113	2	3	34	1	1	-0	.972	2	C1/3	0.7
1925	Bos-N	104	316	36	88	23	5	2	50	15	28	.278	.313	.402	89	-10	-6	39	3	3	-1	.968	-2	C/1	-0.4
1926	Bos-N	24	47	3	16	4	0	0	7	4	6	.340	.392	.426	132	1	2	8	0			1.000	2	C	0.4
1927	Bos-N	60	167	7	37	1	2	0	19	3	10	.222	.235	.251	33	-16	-15	9	2			.965	-3	C	-1.5
Total	8	471	1155	121	317	57	19	8	146	55	127	.274	.310	.377	86	-35	-25	137	12	7		.967	-10	C/13O	-2.2

■ GEORGE GIBSON Gibson, George C. "Moon" b: 7/22/1880, London, Ont., Can. d: 1/25/67, London, Ont., Can. BR/TR, 5'11.5", 190 lbs. Deb: 7/02/05 MC

YEAR	TM/L	G	AB	R	H	2B	3B	HR	RBI	BB	SO	AVG	OBP	SLG	PRO+	BR	/A	RC	SB	CS	SBR	FA	FR	POS	TPR
1905	Pit-N	46	135	14	24	2	2	2	14	15		.178	.270	.267	59	-6	-7	11	2			.966	3	C	0.0
1906	Pit-N	81	259	8	46	6	1	0	20	16		.178	.225	.208	34	-19	-21	14	1			.971	-6	C	-2.1
1907	Pit-N	113	382	28	84	8	7	3	35	18		.220	.259	.301	75	-12	-13	32	2			.972	-3	*C/1	-0.6
1908	Pit-N	143	486	37	111	19	4	2	45	19		.228	.260	.296	78	-13	-13	38	4			.973	-14	*C	-1.7
1909	*Pit-N	150	510	42	135	25	9	2	52	44		.265	.326	.361	104	7	2	63	9			**.983**	2	*C	1.9
1910	Pit-N	143	482	53	125	22	6	3	44	47	31	.259	.333	.349	93	-1	-4	58	7			**.984**	3	*C	1.3
1911	Pit-N	100	311	32	65	12	2	0	19	29	16	.209	.281	.260	50	-20	-22	23	3			.979	0	C	-1.2
1912	Pit-N	95	300	23	72	14	3	2	35	20	16	.240	.290	.327	69	-14	-13	28	0			**.990**	-1	C	-0.5
1913	Pit-N	48	118	6	33	4	2	0	12	10	8	.280	.341	.347	101	-0	0	15	2			.986	-7	C	-0.3
1914	Pit-N	102	274	19	78	9	5	0	30	27	27	.285	.359	.354	117	5	6	36	4			.974	-9	*C	0.6
1915	Pit-N	120	351	28	88	15	6	1	30	31	25	.251	.313	.336	98	-1	-1	40	5	2	0	.965	8	*C	1.8
1916	Pit-N	33	84	4	17	2	2	0	4	3	7	.202	.239	.274	57	-4	-4	6	0			.989	7	C	0.5
1917	NY-N	35	82	1	14	3	0	0	5	7	2	.171	.236	.207	38	-6	-6	4	1			.986	1	C	-0.3
1918	NY-N	4	2	0	1	1	0	0	0	0	0	.500	.500	1.000	360	1	1	1	0			1.000	0	/C	0.1
Total	14	1213	3776	295	893	142	49	15	345	286	132	.236	.295	.312	81	-86	-95	367	40	2		.977	-16	*C/1	-0.5

■ RUSS GIBSON Gibson, John Russell b: 5/6/39, Fall River, Mass. BR/TR, 6'1", 195 lbs. Deb: 4/14/67

YEAR	TM/L	G	AB	R	H	2B	3B	HR	RBI	BB	SO	AVG	OBP	SLG	PRO+	BR	/A	RC	SB	CS	SBR	FA	FR	POS	TPR
1967	*Bos-A	49	138	8	28	7	0	1	15	12	31	.203	.267	.275	56	-7	-8	9	0	0	0	1.000	-6	C	-1.3
1968	Bos-A	76	231	15	52	11	1	3	20	8	38	.225	.251	.320	68	-8	-10	17	1	2	-1	.983	1	C/1	-0.6
1969	Bos-A	85	287	21	72	9	1	3	27	15	25	.251	.290	.321	67	-12	-13	24	1	1	-0	.979	-6	C	-1.6
1970	SF-N	24	69	3	16	6	0	0	6	7	12	.232	.303	.319	67	-3	-3	6	0	0	0	.971	2	C	0.0

YEAR	TM/L	G	AB	R	H	2B	3B	HR	RBI	BB	SO	AVG	OBP	SLG	PRO+	BR	/A	RC	SB	CS	SBR	FA	FR	POS	TPR
1971	SF-N	25	57	2	11	1	1	1	7	2	13	.193	.220	.298	46	-4	-4	3	0	0	0	.965	0	C	-0.4
1972	SF-N	5	12	0	2	0	1	0	3	0	4	.167	.167	.333	38	-1	-1	0	0	0	0	1.000	-1	/C	-0.2
Total	6	264	794	49	181	34	4	8	78	44	123	.228	.269	.311	64	-35	-39	60	2	3	-1	.983	-10	C/1	-4.1

■ KIRK GIBSON Gibson, Kirk Harold b: 5/28/57, Pontiac, Mich. BL/TL, 6'3", 215 lbs. Deb: 9/08/79

YEAR	TM/L	G	AB	R	H	2B	3B	HR	RBI	BB	SO	AVG	OBP	SLG	PRO+	BR	/A	RC	SB	CS	SBR	FA	FR	POS	TPR
1979	Det-A	12	38	3	9	3	0	1	4	1	3	.237	.256	.395	70	-2	-2	3	3	3	-1	1.000	-1	O	-0.4
1980	Det-A	51	175	23	46	2	1	9	16	10	45	.263	.306	.440	100	-0	-1	22	4	7	-3	.992	-2	O/D	-0.7
1981	Det-A	83	290	41	95	11	3	9	40	18	64	.328	.371	.479	138	15	14	50	17	5	2	.973	-4	O/D	1.0
1982	Det-A	69	266	34	74	16	2	8	35	25	41	.278	.342	.444	113	5	5	40	9	7	-2	.994	3	O/D	0.5
1983	Det-A	128	401	60	91	12	9	15	51	53	96	.227	.323	.414	104	1	2	59	14	3	2	.975	-1	DO	0.1
1984	*Det-A	149	531	92	150	23	10	27	91	63	103	.282	.367	.516	142	30	30	106	29	9	3	.954	-9	*O/D	2.0
1985	Det-A	154	581	96	167	37	5	29	97	71	137	.287	.370	.518	141	32	33	118	30	4	7	.963	-7	*O/D	2.7
1986	Det-A	119	441	84	118	11	2	28	86	68	107	.268	.374	.492	134	21	22	88	34	6	7	.990	-9	*O/D	1.5
1987	*Det-A	128	487	95	135	25	3	24	79	71	117	.277	.375	.489	132	20	23	95	26	7	4	.974	5	*O/D	2.6
1988	*LA-N	150	542	106	157	28	1	25	76	73	120	.290	.381	.483	151	34	36	107	31	4	7	.964	8	*O	4.9
1989	LA-N	71	253	35	54	8	2	9	28	35	55	.213	.314	.368	96	-2	-1	31	12	3	2	.980	1	O	-0.1
1990	LA-N	89	315	59	82	20	0	8	38	39	65	.260	.347	.400	108	3	4	50	26	2	7	.995	5	O	1.3
1991	KC-A	132	462	81	109	17	6	16	55	69	103	.236	.343	.403	105	4	4	68	18	4	3	.976	-2	OD	0.3
1992	Pit-N	16	56	6	11	0	0	2	5	3	12	.196	.237	.304	53	-4	-4	4	3	1	0	1.000	1	O	-0.3
Total	14	1351	4838	815	1298	213	44	210	701	599	1068	.268	.355	.461	125	157	165	841	256	65	38	.975	-14	*OD	15.4

■ WHITEY GIBSON Gibson, Leighton P. b: 10/6/1868, Lancaster, Pa. d: 10/11/07, Talmadge, Pa. TR , 5'9", 178 lbs. Deb: 5/02/1888

YEAR	TM/L	G	AB	R	H	2B	3B	HR	RBI	BB	SO	AVG	OBP	SLG	PRO+	BR	/A	RC	SB	CS	SBR	FA	FR	POS	TPR
1888	Phi-a	1	3	0	0	0	0	0	0	0		.000	.000	.000	-99	-1	-1	0	0			1.000	1	/C	0.0

■ JOE GIEBEL Giebel, Joseph Henry b: 11/30/1891, Washington, D.C. d: 3/17/81, Silver Spring, Md. BR/TR, 5'10.5", 175 lbs. Deb: 9/30/13

YEAR	TM/L	G	AB	R	H	2B	3B	HR	RBI	BB	SO	AVG	OBP	SLG	PRO+	BR	/A	RC	SB	CS	SBR	FA	FR	POS	TPR
1913	Phi-A	1	3	0	1	0	0	0	0	0	1	.333	.333	.333	97	-0	-0	0	0			1.000	-0	/C	0.0

■ NORM GIGON Gigon, Norman Phillip b: 5/12/38, Teaneck, N.J. BR/TR, 6', 195 lbs. Deb: 4/12/67

YEAR	TM/L	G	AB	R	H	2B	3B	HR	RBI	BB	SO	AVG	OBP	SLG	PRO+	BR	/A	RC	SB	CS	SBR	FA	FR	POS	TPR
1967	Chi-N	34	70	8	12	3	1	1	6	4	14	.171	.237	.286	47	-5	-5	5	0	0	0	.982	-2	2/O3	-0.7

■ GUS GIL Gil, Tomas Gustavo (Guillen) b: 4/19/39, Caracas, Venez. BR/TR, 5'10", 180 lbs. Deb: 4/11/67

YEAR	TM/L	G	AB	R	H	2B	3B	HR	RBI	BB	SO	AVG	OBP	SLG	PRO+	BR	/A	RC	SB	CS	SBR	FA	FR	POS	TPR
1967	Cle-A	51	96	11	11	4	0	0	5	9	18	.115	.198	.156	6	-11	-11	3	0	0	0	1.000	2	2/1	-0.8
1969	Sea-A	92	221	20	49	7	0	0	17	16	28	.222	.274	.253	49	-15	-15	16	2	0	1	.942	1	32S	-1.2
1970	Mil-A	64	119	12	22	4	0	1	12	21	12	.185	.307	.244	53	-7	-7	10	2	0	1	.978	3	23	-0.1
1971	Mil-A	14	32	3	5	1	0	0	3	10	5	.156	.357	.188	59	-1	-1	3	1	0	0	.977	-0	/23	0.0
Total	4	221	468	46	87	16	0	1	37	56	63	.186	.274	.226	43	-34	-34	33	5	0	2	.987	7	2/3S1	-2.1

■ ANDY GILBERT Gilbert, Andrew b: 7/18/14, Bradenville, Pa. d: 8/29/92, Davis, Cal. BR/TR, 6', 203 lbs. Deb: 9/14/42 C

YEAR	TM/L	G	AB	R	H	2B	3B	HR	RBI	BB	SO	AVG	OBP	SLG	PRO+	BR	/A	RC	SB	CS	SBR	FA	FR	POS	TPR
1942	Bos-A	6	11	0	1	0	0	0	1	1	3	.091	.167	.091	-26	-2	-2	0	0	0	0	1.000	-2	/O	-0.4
1946	Bos-A	2	1	1	0	0	0	0	0	0	0	.000	.000	.000	-95	-0	-0	0	0	0	0	.000	-1	/O	-0.1
Total	2	8	12	1	1	0	0	0	1	1	3	.083	.154	.083	-31	-2	-2	0	0	0	0	1.000	-2	/O	-0.5

■ CHARLIE GILBERT Gilbert, Charles Mader b: 7/8/19, New Orleans, La. d: 8/13/83, New Orleans, La. BL/TL, 5'9", 165 lbs. Deb: 4/16/40 F

YEAR	TM/L	G	AB	R	H	2B	3B	HR	RBI	BB	SO	AVG	OBP	SLG	PRO+	BR	/A	RC	SB	CS	SBR	FA	FR	POS	TPR
1940	Bro-N	57	142	23	35	9	1	2	8	8	13	.246	.287	.366	74	-4	-5	16	0			.960	-2	O	-0.9
1941	Chi-N	39	86	11	24	2	1	0	12	11	6	.279	.361	.326	98	-0	0	11	1			1.000	-1	O	-0.2
1942	Chi-N	74	179	18	33	6	3	0	7	25	24	.184	.284	.251	60	-9	-8	14	1			.981	0	O	-1.1
1943	Chi-N	8	20	1	3	0	0	0	0	3	3	.150	.261	.150	20	-2	-2	1	1			1.000	-1	/O	-0.3
1946	Chi-N	15	13	2	1	0	0	0	1	1	4	.077	.143	.077	-38	-2	-2	0	0			1.000	0	/O	-0.3
	Phi-N	88	260	34	63	5	2	1	17	25	18	.242	.314	.288	73	-9	-8	26	3			1.000	6	O	-0.6
	Yr	103	273	36	64	5	2	1	18	26	22	.234	.306	.278	68	-12	-11	25	3			1.000	6	O	-0.9
1947	Phi-N	83	152	20	36	5	2	2	10	13	14	.237	.301	.336	72	-7	-6	15	1			.961	-0	O	-0.8
Total	6	364	852	109	195	27	9	5	55	86	82	.229	.302	.299	70	-34	-33	82	7			.982	3	O	-4.2

■ BUDDY GILBERT Gilbert, Drew Edward b: 7/26/35, Knoxville, Tenn. BL/TR, 6'3", 195 lbs. Deb: 9/09/59

YEAR	TM/L	G	AB	R	H	2B	3B	HR	RBI	BB	SO	AVG	OBP	SLG	PRO+	BR	/A	RC	SB	CS	SBR	FA	FR	POS	TPR
1959	Cin-N	7	20	4	3	0	0	2	2	3	4	.150	.261	.450	82	-1	-1	3	0	0	0	1.000	1	/O	0.0

■ TOOKIE GILBERT Gilbert, Harold Joseph b: 4/4/29, New Orleans, La. d: 6/23/67, New Orleans, La. BL/TR, 6'2.5", 185 lbs. Deb: 5/05/50 F

YEAR	TM/L	G	AB	R	H	2B	3B	HR	RBI	BB	SO	AVG	OBP	SLG	PRO+	BR	/A	RC	SB	CS	SBR	FA	FR	POS	TPR
1950	NY-N	113	322	40	71	12	2	4	32	43	36	.220	.314	.307	64	-16	-16	33	3			.988	1	*1	-1.7
1953	NY-N	70	160	12	27	3	0	3	16	22	21	.169	.269	.244	34	-15	-16	12	1	0	0	.995	1	1	-1.6
Total	2	183	482	52	98	15	2	7	48	65	57	.203	.299	.286	54	-31	-32	45	4	0		.991	2	1	-3.3

■ HARRY GILBERT Gilbert, Harry H. b: 7/7/1868, Pottstown, Pa. d: 12/23/09, Pottstown, Pa. Deb: 6/23/1890 F

YEAR	TM/L	G	AB	R	H	2B	3B	HR	RBI	BB	SO	AVG	OBP	SLG	PRO+	BR	/A	RC	SB	CS	SBR	FA	FR	POS	TPR
1890	Pit-N	2	8	1	2	0	0	0	0	0	3	.250	.250	.250	54	-1	-0	1	0			1.000	-1	/2	-0.1

■ JOHN GILBERT Gilbert, John G. b: 1/8/1864, Pottstown, Pa. d: 11/12/03, Pottstown, Pa. Deb: 6/23/1890 F

YEAR	TM/L	G	AB	R	H	2B	3B	HR	RBI	BB	SO	AVG	OBP	SLG	PRO+	BR	/A	RC	SB	CS	SBR	FA	FR	POS	TPR
1890	Pit-N	2	8	0	0	0	0	0	0	0	2	.000	.000	.000	-99	-2	-2	0	0			1.000	-0	/S	-0.2

■ JACK GILBERT Gilbert, John Robert "Jackrabbit" b: 9/4/1875, Rhinecliff, N.Y. d: 7/7/41, Albany, N.Y. Deb: 9/11/1898

YEAR	TM/L	G	AB	R	H	2B	3B	HR	RBI	BB	SO	AVG	OBP	SLG	PRO+	BR	/A	RC	SB	CS	SBR	FA	FR	POS	TPR
1898	Was-N	2	5	0	1	0	0	0	1	1		.200	.429	.200	82	0	0	1	1			.500	-0	/O	0.0
	NY-N	1	4	0	1	0	0	0	0	0		.250	.250	.250	45	-0	-0	1	1			.500	-0	/O	-0.1
	Yr	3	9	0	2	0	0	0	1	1		.222	.364	.222	70	-0	-0	2	2			.500	-1	/O	-0.1
1904	Pit-N	25	87	13	21	0	0	0	3	12		.241	.347	.241	81	-1	-1	9	3			.857	-6	O	-0.9
Total	2	28	96	13	23	0	0	0	4	13		.240	.348	.240	80	-1	-1	10	5			.821	-6	/O	-1.0

■ LARRY GILBERT Gilbert, Lawrence William b: 12/3/1891, New Orleans, La. d: 2/17/65, New Orleans, La. BL/TL, 5'9", 158 lbs. Deb: 4/14/14 F

YEAR	TM/L	G	AB	R	H	2B	3B	HR	RBI	BB	SO	AVG	OBP	SLG	PRO+	BR	/A	RC	SB	CS	SBR	FA	FR	POS	TPR
1914	*Bos-N	72	224	32	60	6	1	5	25	26	34	.268	.347	.371	114	4	4	30	3			.979	-0	O	0.1
1915	Bos-N	45	106	11	16	4	0	0	4	11	13	.151	.231	.189	29	-9	-9	6	4	1	1	.941	-2	O	-1.3
Total	2	117	330	43	76	10	1	5	29	37	47	.230	.310	.312	88	-5	-4	35	7	1		.969	-3	/O	-1.2

■ MARK GILBERT Gilbert, Mark David b: 8/22/56, Atlanta, Ga. BB/TR, 6', 175 lbs. Deb: 7/21/85

YEAR	TM/L	G	AB	R	H	2B	3B	HR	RBI	BB	SO	AVG	OBP	SLG	PRO+	BR	/A	RC	SB	CS	SBR	FA	FR	POS	TPR
1985	Chi-A	7	22	3	6	1	0	0	3	4	5	.273	.385	.318	92	0	-0	3	0	0	0	1.000	-1	/O	-0.1

■ PETE GILBERT Gilbert, Peter b: 9/6/1867, Baltic, Conn. d: 1/1/12, Springfield, Mass. TR , 5'8", 180 lbs. Deb: 9/06/1890

YEAR	TM/L	G	AB	R	H	2B	3B	HR	RBI	BB	SO	AVG	OBP	SLG	PRO+	BR	/A	RC	SB	CS	SBR	FA	FR	POS	TPR
1890	Bal-a	29	100	25	28	2	1	1		10		.280	.363	.350	108	2	1	17	12			.899	-3	3	0.0
1891	Bal-a	139	513	81	118	15	7	3	72	37	77	.230	.317	.304	79	-12	-13	61	31			.862	2	*3	-0.4
1892	Bal-N	4	15	0	3	0	0	0	0	1	3	.200	.250	.200	37	-1	-1	1	1			.889	1	/3	0.0
1894	Bro-N	6	25	1	2	0	0	0	1	1	3	.080	.148	.080	-46	-6	-6	1	2			.938	1	/23	-0.3
	Lou-N	28	108	13	33	3	1	1	14	5	4	.306	.353	.380	84	-4	-2	16	2			.742	-6	3	-0.6
	Yr	34	133	14	35	3	1	1	15	6	7	.263	.315	.323	60	-10	-8	15	4			.766	-5	3/2	-0.9
Total	4	206	761	120	184	20	9	5	87	54	87	.242	.321	.311	78	-21	-21	96	48			.851	-4	3/2	-1.3

■ WALLY GILBERT Gilbert, Walter John b: 12/19/1900, Oscoda, Mich. d: 9/7/58, Duluth, Minn. BR/TR, 6', 180 lbs. Deb: 8/18/28

YEAR	TM/L	G	AB	R	H	2B	3B	HR	RBI	BB	SO	AVG	OBP	SLG	PRO+	BR	/A	RC	SB	CS	SBR	FA	FR	POS	TPR
1928	Bro-N	39	153	26	31	4	0	0	3	14	8	.203	.274	.229	33	-15	-15	10	2			.965	-1	3	-1.3
1929	Bro-N	143	569	88	173	31	4	3	58	42	29	.304	.359	.388	87	-12	-11	79	7			.956	7	*3	0.2
1930	Bro-N	150	623	92	183	34	5	3	67	47	33	.294	.345	.379	76	-25	-23	80	7			.944	9	*3	-0.5
1931	Bro-N	145	552	60	147	25	6	0	46	39	38	.266	.322	.333	77	-18	-17	62	3			.948	8	*3	0.0

YEAR	TM/L	G	AB	R	H	2B	3B	HR	RBI	BB	SO	AVG	OBP	SLG	PRO+	BR	/A	RC	SB	CS	SBR	FA	FR	POS	TPR
1932	Cin-N	114	420	35	90	18	2	1	40	20	23	.214	.252	.274	43	-35	-33	30	2			.929	-6	*3	-3.2
Total	5	591	2317	301	624	112	17	7	214	162	131	.269	.322	.341	71	-104	-99	261	21			.947	17	3	-4.8

■ BILLY GILBERT
Gilbert, William Oliver b: 6/21/1876, Tullytown, Pa. d: 8/8/27, New York, N.Y. BR/TR, 5'4", 153 lbs. Deb: 4/25/01

YEAR	TM/L	G	AB	R	H	2B	3B	HR	RBI	BB	SO	AVG	OBP	SLG	PRO+	BR	/A	RC	SB	CS	SBR	FA	FR	POS	TPR
1901	Mil-A	127	492	77	133	14	7	0	43	31		.270	.319	.327	83	-13	-10	61	19			.936	-0	*2	-0.4
1902	Bal-A	129	445	74	109	12	3	2	38	45		.245	.325	.299	71	-14	-17	60	38			.907	-5	*S	-1.4
1903	NY-N	128	413	62	104	9	0	1	40	41		.252	.337	.281	74	-10	-13	56	37			.935	11	*2	0.3
1904	NY-N	146	478	57	121	13	3	1	54	46		.253	.326	.299	90	-2	-4	61	33			.946	8	*2	0.8
1905	*NY-N	115	376	45	93	11	3	0	24	41		.247	.329	.293	84	-5	-6	43	11			.947	26	*2	2.2
1906	NY-N	104	307	44	71	6	1	1	27	42		.231	.333	.267	86	-2	-3	38	22			.940	23	2	2.2
1908	StL-N	89	276	12	59	7	0	0	10	20		.214	.274	.239	68	-11	-9	20	6			.952	6	2	-0.4
1909	StL-N	12	29	4	5	0	0	0	1	4		.172	.333	.172	61	-1	-1	2	1			.922	0	2	-0.1
Total	8	850	2816	375	695	72	17	5	237	270		.247	.323	.290	80	-59	-63	340	167			.942	70	2S	3.2

■ ROD GILBREATH
Gilbreath, Rodney Joe b: 9/24/52, Laurel, Miss. BR/TR, 6'2", 185 lbs. Deb: 6/17/72

YEAR	TM/L	G	AB	R	H	2B	3B	HR	RBI	BB	SO	AVG	OBP	SLG	PRO+	BR	/A	RC	SB	CS	SBR	FA	FR	POS	TPR
1972	Atl-N	18	38	2	9	1	0	0	1	2	10	.237	.293	.263	54	-2	-2	3	1	1	-0	1.000	3	/23	0.0
1973	Atl-N	29	74	10	21	2	1	0	2	6	10	.284	.346	.338	84	-1	-1	9	2	1	0	.960	-0	3	-0.2
1974	Atl-N	3	6	2	2	0	0	0	0	2	0	.333	.500	.333	131	1	0	1	0	0	0	1.000	0	/2	0.1
1975	Atl-N	90	202	24	49	3	1	2	16	24	26	.243	.326	.297	71	-7	-8	21	5	5	-2	.980	2	23/S	-0.5
1976	Atl-N	116	383	57	96	11	8	1	32	42	36	.251	.331	.329	83	-5	-8	43	7	7	-2	.975	7	*2/3S	0.3
1977	Atl-N	128	407	47	99	15	2	8	43	45	79	.243	.322	.349	71	-11	-17	44	3	9	-5	.978	3	*2/3	-1.2
1978	Atl-N	116	326	22	80	13	3	3	31	26	51	.245	.301	.331	69	-10	-15	32	7	6	-2	.968	-3	32	-1.9
Total	7	500	1436	164	356	45	15	14	125	147	212	.248	.322	.329	74	-36	-51	152	25	29	-10	.978	11	23/S	-3.4

■ DON GILE
Gile, Donald Loren "Bear" b: 4/19/35, Modesto, Cal. BR/TR, 6'6", 220 lbs. Deb: 9/25/59

YEAR	TM/L	G	AB	R	H	2B	3B	HR	RBI	BB	SO	AVG	OBP	SLG	PRO+	BR	/A	RC	SB	CS	SBR	FA	FR	POS	TPR
1959	Bos-A	3	10	1	2	1	0	0	1	0	2	.200	.273	.300	55	-1	-1	1	0	0	0	1.000	-0	/C	-0.1
1960	Bos-A	29	51	6	9	1	1	1	4	1	13	.176	.192	.294	29	-5	-5	3	0	0	0	1.000	-1	C1	-0.7
1961	Bos-A	8	18	2	5	0	0	1	1	1	5	.278	.316	.444	98	-0	-0	3	0	0	0	.958	-1	/1C	-0.1
1962	Bos-A	18	41	3	2	0	0	1	3	3	15	.049	.133	.122	-30	-8	-8	0	0	0	0	.990	-1	1	-1.0
Total	4	58	120	12	18	2	1	3	9	5	35	.150	.197	.258	21	-14	-14	6	0	0	0	.982	-2	/1C	-1.9

■ BRIAN GILES
Giles, Brian Jeffrey b: 4/27/60, Manhattan, Kan. BR/TR, 6'1", 165 lbs. Deb: 9/12/81

YEAR	TM/L	G	AB	R	H	2B	3B	HR	RBI	BB	SO	AVG	OBP	SLG	PRO+	BR	/A	RC	SB	CS	SBR	FA	FR	POS	TPR
1981	NY-N	9	7	0	0	0	0	0	0	0	3	.000	.000	.000	-99	-2	-2	0	0	0	0	1.000	3	/2S	0.2
1982	NY-N	45	138	14	29	5	0	3	10	12	29	.210	.273	.312	64	-7	-7	13	6	1	1	.992	15	2/S	1.2
1983	NY-N	145	400	39	98	15	0	2	27	36	77	.245	.311	.298	70	-16	-16	37	17	10	-1	.980	15	*2S	0.5
1985	Mil-A	34	58	6	10	1	0	1	1	7	16	.172	.262	.241	39	-5	-5	4	2	1	0	.963	8	S2/D	0.4
1986	Chi-A	9	11	0	3	0	0	0	1	0	2	.273	.273	.273	48	-1	-1	1	0	0	0	1.000	4	/2S	0.3
1990	Sea-A	45	95	15	22	6	0	4	11	15	24	.232	.336	.421	109	1	1	14	2	1	0	.978	6	S/23D	1.0
Total	6	287	709	74	162	27	0	10	50	70	151	.228	.300	.309	70	-29	-28	69	27	13	0	.985	51	2/SD3	3.6

■ GEORGE GILHAM
Gilham, George Louis b: 9/17/1899, Shamokin, Pa. d: 4/25/37, Lansdowne, Pa. BR/TR, 5'11", 164 lbs. Deb: 9/24/20

YEAR	TM/L	G	AB	R	H	2B	3B	HR	RBI	BB	SO	AVG	OBP	SLG	PRO+	BR	/A	RC	SB	CS	SBR	FA	FR	POS	TPR
1920	StL-N	1	3	0	0	0	0	0	0	0	1	.000	.000	.000	-99	-1	-1	0	0	0	0	.750	-1	/C	-0.1
1921	StL-N	1	1	0	0	0	0	0	0	0	0	.000	.000	.000	-99	-0	-0	0	0	0	0	.000	0	H	0.0
Total	2	2	4	0	0	0	0	0	0	0	1	.000	.000	.000	-99	-1	-1	0	0	0	0	.926	-1	/C	-0.1

■ FRANK GILHOOLEY
Gilhooley, Frank Patrick "Flash" b: 6/10/1892, Toledo, Ohio d: 7/11/59, Toledo, Ohio BL/TR, 5'8", 155 lbs. Deb: 9/18/11

YEAR	TM/L	G	AB	R	H	2B	3B	HR	RBI	BB	SO	AVG	OBP	SLG	PRO+	BR	/A	RC	SB	CS	SBR	FA	FR	POS	TPR
1911	StL-N	1	0	0	0	0	0	0	0	0	0	—	—	—	—	0	0	0	0			.000	-0	/O	0.0
1912	StL-N	13	49	5	11	0	0	0	2	3	8	.224	.269	.224	37	-4	-4	3	0			1.000	-2	O	-0.7
1913	NY-A	24	85	10	29	2	1	0	14	4	9	.341	.378	.388	124	2	2	14	6			.977	-1	O	0.1
1914	NY-A	1	3	0	2	0	0	0	0	1	0	.667	.750	.667	327	1	1	2	0			.000	-0	/O	0.1
1915	NY-A	1	4	0	0	0	0	0	0	0	1	.000	.000	.000	-99	-1	-1	0	0			1.000	-0	/O	-0.1
1916	NY-A	58	223	40	62	5	3	1	10	37	17	.278	.383	.341	115	6	6	35	16			.971	3	O	0.6
1917	NY-A	54	165	14	40	6	1	0	8	30	13	.242	.362	.291	99	1	1	19	6			.933	-1	O	-0.2
1918	NY-A	112	427	59	118	13	5	1	23	53	24	.276	.358	.337	107	6	5	53	7			.961	1	*O	-0.1
1919	Bos-A	48	112	14	27	4	0	0	1	12	8	.241	.315	.277	71	-5	-4	10	2			.922	-5	O	-1.2
Total	9	312	1068	142	289	30	10	2	58	140	80	.271	.357	.323	102	8	7	136	37			.957	-7	O	-1.5

■ BERNARD GILKEY
Gilkey, Otis Bernard b: 9/24/66, St.Louis, Mo. BR/TR, 6', 170 lbs. Deb: 9/04/90

YEAR	TM/L	G	AB	R	H	2B	3B	HR	RBI	BB	SO	AVG	OBP	SLG	PRO+	BR	/A	RC	SB	CS	SBR	FA	FR	POS	TPR
1990	StL-N	18	64	11	19	5	2	1	3	8	5	.297	.375	.484	134	3	3	13	6	1	1	.961	3	O	0.7
1991	StL-N	81	268	28	58	7	2	5	20	39	33	.216	.318	.313	78	-7	-7	25	14	8	-1	.994	9	O	-0.1
1992	StL-N	131	384	56	116	19	4	7	43	39	52	.302	.368	.427	126	13	13	60	18	12	-2	.978	7	*O	1.8
Total	3	230	716	95	193	31	8	13	66	86	90	.270	.350	.390	108	9	9	98	38	21	-1	.982	19	O	2.4

■ BOB GILKS
Gilks, Robert James b: 7/2/1864, Cincinnati, Ohio d: 8/21/44, Brunswick, Ga. BR/TR, 5'8", 178 lbs. Deb: 8/25/1887

YEAR	TM/L	G	AB	R	H	2B	3B	HR	RBI	BB	SO	AVG	OBP	SLG	PRO+	BR	/A	RC	SB	CS	SBR	FA	FR	POS	TPR
1887	Cle-a	22	83	12	26	2	0	0		3		.313	.352	.337	98	-0	0	12	5			.881	2	P/1O2	0.0
1888	Cle-a	119	484	59	111	14	4	1	63	7		.229	.245	.281	73	-16	-14	38	16			.899	-1	O3/SP2	-1.5
1889	Cle-N	53	210	17	50	5	2	0	18	7	20	.238	.273	.281	57	-12	-12	18	6			1.000	0	OS1/2	-1.0
1890	Cle-N	130	544	65	116	10	3	0	41	32	38	.213	.265	.243	51	-34	-32	40	17			.941	1	*O/PS2	-3.0
1893	Bal-N	15	64	10	17	2	0	0	7	0	3	.266	.277	.297	53	-4	-4	6	3			.969	3	O	-0.2
Total	5	339	1385	163	320	33	9	1	129	49	61	.231	.265	.270	62	-67	-63	115	47			.937	5	O/3PS12	-5.7

■ JIM GILL
Gill, James C. b: St.Louis, Mo. Deb: 6/27/1889

YEAR	TM/L	G	AB	R	H	2B	3B	HR	RBI	BB	SO	AVG	OBP	SLG	PRO+	BR	/A	RC	SB	CS	SBR	FA	FR	POS	TPR
1889	StL-a	2	8	2	2	1	0	0	1	1	2	.250	.333	.375	92	0	-0	1	1			1.000	-0	/O2	0.0

■ JOHNNY GILL
Gill, John Wesley "Patcheye" b: 3/27/05, Nashville, Tenn. d: 12/26/84, Nashville, Tenn. BL/TR, 6'2", 190 lbs. Deb: 8/28/27

YEAR	TM/L	G	AB	R	H	2B	3B	HR	RBI	BB	SO	AVG	OBP	SLG	PRO+	BR	/A	RC	SB	CS	SBR	FA	FR	POS	TPR
1927	Cle-A	21	60	8	13	3	0	1	4	7	13	.217	.319	.317	65	-3	-3	6	1	1	-0	1.000	-2	O	-0.6
1928	Cle-A	2	2	0	0	0	0	0	0	0	1	.000	.000	.000	-99	-1	-1	0	0	0	0	.000	0	H	-0.1
1931	Was-A	8	30	2	8	2	1	0	5	1	6	.267	.313	.400	86	-1	-1	3	0	1	-1	1.000	3	/O	0.1
1934	Was-A	13	53	7	13	3	0	2	7	2	3	.245	.286	.415	82	-2	-2	6	0	0	0	1.000	-1	O	-0.3
1935	Chi-N	3	3	2	1	1	0	0	1	0	1	.333	.333	.667	161	0	0	1	0			.000	0	H	0.0
1936	Chi-N	71	174	20	44	8	0	7	28	13	19	.253	.309	.420	92	-2	-2	23	0			.938	-3	O	-0.7
Total	6	118	322	39	79	17	1	10	45	23	43	.245	.306	.398	84	-8	-8	40	1	2		.968	-2	/O	-1.6

■ WARREN GILL
Gill, Warren Darst "Doc" b: 12/21/1878, Ladoga, Ind. d: 11/26/52, Laguna Beach, Cal. BR/TR, 6'1", 175 lbs. Deb: 8/26/08

YEAR	TM/L	G	AB	R	H	2B	3B	HR	RBI	BB	SO	AVG	OBP	SLG	PRO+	BR	/A	RC	SB	CS	SBR	FA	FR	POS	TPR
1908	Pit-N	27	76	10	17	0	1	0	14	11		.224	.366	.250	97	1	1	9	3			1.000	-3	1	-0.2

■ SAM GILLEN
Gillen, Samuel (b: Samuel Gilleland) b: 1/1871, Pittsburgh, Pa. d: 5/13/05, Pittsburgh, Pa. Deb: 8/19/1893

YEAR	TM/L	G	AB	R	H	2B	3B	HR	RBI	BB	SO	AVG	OBP	SLG	PRO+	BR	/A	RC	SB	CS	SBR	FA	FR	POS	TPR
1893	Pit-N	3	6	0	0	0	0	0	0	0	1	.000	.000	.000	-99	-2	-2	0	0			.750	-0	/S	-0.2
1897	Phi-N	75	270	32	70	10	3	0	27	35		.259	.353	.319	80	-7	-6	33	2			.896	-28	S/3	-2.8
Total	2	78	276	32	70	10	3	0	27	35	1	.254	.346	.312	76	-9	-8	33	2			.892	-29	/S3	-3.0

■ TOM GILLEN
Gillen, Thomas J. b: 5/18/1862, Philadelphia, Pa. d: 1/26/1889, Philadelphia, Pa. 5'8", 160 lbs. Deb: 4/18/1884

YEAR	TM/L	G	AB	R	H	2B	3B	HR	RBI	BB	SO	AVG	OBP	SLG	PRO+	BR	/A	RC	SB	CS	SBR	FA	FR	POS	TPR
1884	Phi-U	29	116	5	18	2	0	0		1		.155	.162	.172	14	-10	-9	3				.895	-4	C/O	-0.9
1886	Det-N	2	10	2	4	0	0	0	4	0	1	.400	.400	.400	140	0	0	2	0			.889	-2	/C	-0.1
Total	2	31	126	7	22	2	0	0	4	1	1	.175	.181	.190	26	-10	-8	5	0			.895	-6	/CO	-1.0

YEAR	TM/L	G	AB	R	H	2B	3B	HR	RBI	BB	SO	AVG	OBP	SLG	PRO+	BR	/A	RC	SB	CS	SBR	FA	FR	POS	TPR
■ **CARDEN GILLENWATER**	Gillenwater, Carden Edison b: 5/13/18, Riceville, Tenn. BR/TR, 6'1", 178 lbs. Deb: 9/22/40																								
1940	StL-N	7	25	1	4	1	0	0	5	0	2	.160	.160	.200	-1	-3	-4	1	0			1.000	-1	/O	-0.5
1943	Bro-N	8	17	1	3	0	0	0	2	2	3	.176	.263	.176	28	-2	-2	1	0			1.000	-0	/O	-0.2
1945	Bos-N	144	517	74	149	20	2	7	72	73	70	.288	.379	.375	110	10	9	75	13			.979	24	*O	2.5
1946	Bos-N	99	224	30	51	10	1	1	14	39	27	.228	.342	.295	81	-4	-4	25	3			.979	1	O	-0.6
1948	Was-A	77	221	23	54	10	4	3	21	39	36	.244	.358	.367	96	-2	-1	30	4	2	0	.974	-1	O	-0.5
Total	5	335	1004	129	261	41	7	11	114	153	138	.260	.359	.348	96	-1	-1	133	20	2		.979	23	O	0.7
■ **JIM GILLESPIE**	Gillespie, James Wheatfield b: 9/1858, Canada BL/TR, Deb: 10/01/1890																								
1890	Buf-P	1	3	0	0	0	0	0	0	0	2	.000	.000	.000	-99	-1	-1	0	0			.250	-0	/O	-0.1
■ **PAUL GILLESPIE**	Gillespie, Paul Allen b: 9/18/20, Sugar Valley, Ga. d: 8/11/70, Anniston, Ala. BL/TR, 6'3", 195 lbs. Deb: 9/11/42																								
1942	Chi-N	5	16	3	4	0	0	2	4	1	2	.250	.294	.625	172	1	1	3	0			1.000	-1	/C	0.0
1944	Chi-N	9	26	2	7	1	0	1	2	3	3	.269	.345	.423	116	1	1	4	0			.903	-1	/C	0.0
1945	*Chi-N	75	163	12	47	6	0	3	25	18	9	.288	.366	.380	110	2	3	24	2			.989	1	C/O	0.6
Total	3	89	205	17	58	7	0	6	31	22	14	.283	.358	.405	115	4	4	31	2			.978	-1	/CO	0.6
■ **PETE GILLESPIE**	Gillespie, Peter Patrick b: 11/30/1851, Carbondale, Pa. d: 5/5/10, Carbondale, Pa. BL/TR, 6'1.5", 178 lbs. Deb: 5/01/1880																								
1880	Tro-N	82	346	50	84	20	5	2	24	17	35	.243	.278	.347	105	4	2	34				.905	7	*O	0.6
1881	Tro-N	84	348	43	96	14	3	0	41	9	24	.276	.294	.333	92	-1	-4	35				.933	4	*O	-0.2
1882	Tro-N	74	298	46	82	5	4	2	33	9	14	.275	.296	.339	108	1	3	31				.827	-6	*O	-0.3
1883	NY-N	98	411	64	129	23	12	1	62	9	27	.314	.329	.436	131	14	15	60				.897	7	*O	1.8
1884	NY-N	101	413	75	109	7	4	2	44	19	35	.264	.296	.315	90	-4	-5	39				.893	-3	*O	-0.9
1885	NY-N	102	420	67	123	17	6	0	52	15	32	.293	.317	.362	121	8	9	49				**.942**	-4	*O	0.2
1886	NY-N	97	396	65	108	13	8	0	58	16	30	.273	.301	.346	95	-2	-3	48	17			.901	-10	*O	-1.4
1887	NY-N	76	295	40	78	9	3	3	37	12	21	.264	.304	.346	86	-7	-5	43	37			.946	-2	O/3	-0.7
Total	8	714	2927	450	809	108	45	10	351	106	218	.276	.303	.354	104	13	12	340	54			.903	-8	O/3	-0.9
■ **JIM GILLIAM**	Gilliam, James William "Junior" b: 10/17/28, Nashville, Tenn. d: 10/8/78, Inglewood, Cal. BB/TR, 5'10.5", 175 lbs. Deb: 4/14/53 C																								
1953	*Bro-N	151	605	125	168	31	**17**	6	63	100	38	.278	.383	.415	106	10	8	104	21	14	-2	.976	3	*2	1.7
1954	Bro-N	146	607	107	171	28	8	13	52	76	30	.282	.364	.418	100	4	1	95	8	7	-2	.977	-11	*2/O	-0.2
1955	*Bro-N	147	538	110	134	20	8	7	40	70	37	.249	.342	.355	83	-10	-12	67	15	15	-5	.968	-9	2O	-2.0
1956	*Bro-N☆	153	594	102	178	23	8	6	43	95	39	.300	.400	.396	107	17	11	103	21	9	1	.981	18	*2O	3.5
1957	Bro-N	149	617	89	154	26	4	2	37	64	31	.250	.324	.314	66	-22	-30	69	26	10	2	**.986**	3	*2/O	-1.4
1958	LA-N	147	555	81	145	25	5	2	43	78	22	.261	.352	.335	81	-11	-13	71	18	11	-1	.987	8	O32	-0.8
1959	*LA-N★	145	553	91	156	18	4	3	34	**96**	25	.282	.388	.345	91	3	-3	84	23	10	1	.958	2	*3/2O	0.0
1960	LA-N	151	557	96	138	20	2	5	40	96	28	.248	.361	.318	82	-5	-10	72	12	9	-2	.960	9	*32	-0.1
1961	LA-N	144	439	74	107	26	3	4	32	79	34	.244	.359	.344	81	-5	-11	60	8	4	0	.956	2	32O	-0.1
1962	LA-N	160	588	83	159	24	1	4	43	93	35	.270	.372	.335	97	-3	2	81	17	7	1	.981	-13	*23/O	0.1
1963	*LA-N	148	525	77	148	27	4	6	49	60	28	.282	.358	.383	122	10	15	76	19	5	3	.985	-8	*23	2.1
1964	LA-N	116	334	44	76	8	3	2	27	42	21	.228	.319	.287	78	-11	-8	32	4	4	-1	.936	-19	32/O	-2.9
1965	*LA-N	111	372	54	104	19	4	4	39	53	31	.280	.375	.384	123	9	12	58	9	5	-0	.960	-13	3O/2	-0.4
1966	*LA-N	88	235	30	51	9	0	1	16	34	17	.217	.316	.268	70	-10	-8	21	2	1	0	.953	-12	3/12	-2.3
Total	14	1956	7119	1163	1889	304	71	65	558	1036	416	.265	.361	.355	92	-25	-46	992	203	111	-6	.979	-41	*23O/1	-2.8
■ **BARNEY GILLIGAN**	Gilligan, Andrew Bernard b: 1/3/1856, Cambridge, Mass. d: 4/1/34, Lynn, Mass. BR/TR, 5'6.5", 130 lbs. Deb: 9/25/1875																								
1875	Atl-n	2	8	2	2	0	0	0		0		.250	.250	.250	84	-0	-0	1						/CO	0.0
1879	Cle-N	52	205	20	35	6	2	0	11	0	13	.171	.171	.220	28	-15	-15	8				.870	-0	CO/S	-1.5
1880	Cle-N	30	99	9	17	4	3	1	13	6	12	.172	.219	.303	77	-2	-2	7				.969	4	C/OS	0.3
1881	Pro-N	46	183	19	40	7	2	0	20	9	24	.219	.255	.279	69	-6	-6	13				.930	-1	CS/O	-0.5
1882	Pro-N	56	201	32	45	7	6	0	26	4	26	.224	.239	.318	77	-5	-5	16				.932	10	C/S	0.6
1883	Pro-N	74	263	34	52	13	3	0	24	26	32	.198	.270	.270	63	-10	-11	20				.900	10	*C	0.3
1884	*Pro-N	82	294	47	72	13	2	1	38	35	41	.245	.325	.313	104	2	3	31				.928	17	*C/31	2.4
1885	Pro-N	71	252	23	54	7	3	0	12	23	33	.214	.280	.266	80	-6	-4	19				.872	-3	C/SO2	-0.1
1886	Was-N	81	273	23	52	9	2	0	17	39	35	.190	.292	.238	66	-11	-8	21	6			.925	-9	CO/S3	-0.9
1887	Was-N	28	90	7	18	2	0	1	6	5	18	.200	.242	.256	42	-7	-6	6	2			.874	-4	C/SO	-0.7
1888	Det-N	1	5	1	1	0	0	0	0	0	1	.200	.200	.200	29	-0	-0	0	0			.875	-0	/C	0.0
Total	10	521	1865	215	386	68	23	3	167	147	235	.207	.265	.273	71	-62	-56	141	8			.912	24	C/OS321	-0.1
■ **GRANT GILLIS**	Gillis, Grant b: 1/24/01, Grove Hill, Ala. d: 2/4/81, Thomasville, Ala. BR/TR, 5'10", 165 lbs. Deb: 9/19/27																								
1927	Was-A	10	36	8	8	3	1	0	2	2	0	.222	.263	.361	61	-2	-2	3	0	0	0	1.000	-2	S	-0.3
1928	Was-A	24	87	13	22	5	1	0	10	4	5	.253	.309	.333	69	-4	-4	9	0	1	-1	.910	-10	S/23	-1.3
1929	Bos-A	28	73	5	18	4	0	0	11	6	8	.247	.304	.301	58	-5	-4	7	0	1	-1	.956	-4	2	-0.7
Total	3	62	196	26	48	12	2	0	23	12	13	.245	.299	.327	63	-11	-11	19	0	2	-1	.948	-16	/2S3	-2.3
■ **JIM GILMAN**	Gilman, James Deb: 7/10/1893																								
1893	Cle-N	2	7	1	2	0	0	0	1	0	2	.286	.286	.286	50	-0	-1	1	0			.667	-1	/3	-0.1
■ **PIT GILMAN**	Gilman, Pitkin Clark b: 3/14/1864, Laporte, Ohio d: 8/17/50, Elyria, Ohio BL/TL, Deb: 9/18/1884																								
1884	Cle-N	2	10	0	1	0	0	0	0	0	3	.100	.100	.100	-36	-2	-2	0				1.000	0	/O	-0.1
■ **GROVER GILMORE**	Gilmore, Ernest Grover b: 11/1/1888, Chicago, Ill. d: 11/25/19, Sioux City, Iowa BL/TL, 5'9.5", 170 lbs. Deb: 4/18/14																								
1914	KC-F	139	530	91	152	25	5	1	32	37	108	.287	.337	.358	102	-2	1	76	23			.973	3	*O	-0.2
1915	KC-F	119	411	53	117	22	15	1	47	26	50	.285	.347	.418	130	12	14	70	19			.979	7	*O	1.6
Total	2	258	941	144	269	47	20	2	79	63	158	.286	.341	.385	114	10	15	146	42			.976	10	O	1.4
■ **JIM GILMORE**	Gilmore, James b: 5/1853, Baltimore, Md. d: 11/18/28, Baltimore, Md. Deb: 4/26/1875																								
1875	Was-n	3	12	2	3	0	0	0		0		.250	.250	.250	76	-0	-0	1						/C23	0.0
■ **GILROY**	Gilroy Deb: 9/07/1874																								
1874	Chi-n	8	39	4	8	1	0	0		0		.205	.205	.231	38	-3	-3	2						/C	-0.2
1875	Ath-n	2	6	0	1	0	0	0		0		.167	.167	.167	14	-0	-1	0						/CO	0.0
Total	2 n	10	45	4	9	1	0	0		0		.200	.200	.222	35	-3	-3	2						/CO	-0.2
■ **TINSLEY GINN**	Ginn, Tinsley Rucker b: 9/26/1891, Royston, Ga. d: 8/30/31, Atlanta, Ga. BL/TR, 5'9", 180 lbs. Deb: 6/27/14																								
1914	Cle-A	2	1	0	0	0	0	0	0	0	0	.000	.000	.000	-96	-0	-0	0	0			.000	0	/O	0.0
■ **JOE GINSBERG**	Ginsberg, Myron Nathan b: 10/11/26, New York, N.Y. BL/TR, 5'11", 180 lbs. Deb: 9/15/48																								
1948	Det-A	11	36	7	13	0	0	0	1	3	1	.361	.410	.361	103	0	0	5	0	0	0	.943	-2	C	0.0
1950	Det-A	36	95	12	22	6	0	0	12	11	6	.232	.318	.295	56	-6	-6	10	1	0	0	.981	-4	C	-0.8
1951	Det-A	102	304	44	79	10	2	8	37	43	21	.260	.355	.385	100	1	0	43	0	2	-1	.978	-1	C	0.2
1952	Det-A	113	307	29	68	13	2	6	36	51	21	.221	.338	.336	87	-4	-4	37	1	1	-0	.984	-14	*C	-1.4
1953	Det-A	18	53	6	16	2	0	0	3	10	1	.302	.422	.340	109	1	1	9	0	0	0	.988	0	C	0.2
	Cle-A	46	109	10	31	4	0	0	10	14	4	.284	.371	.321	91	-1	-1	14	0	0	0	.966	-5	C	-0.4
	Yr	64	162	16	47	6	0	0	13	24	5	.290	.388	.327	97	0	1	23	0	0	0	.974	-5	C	-0.2

YEAR	TM/L	G	AB	R	H	2B	3B	HR	RBI	BB	SO	AVG	OBP	SLG	PRO+	BR	/A	RC	SB	CS	SBR	FA	FR	POS	TPR
1954	Cle-A	3	2	0	1	0	1	0	1	0	0	.500	.667	1.500	473	1	1	2	0	0	0	1.000	-0	/C	0.1
1956	KC-A	71	195	15	48	8	1	1	12	23	17	.246	.326	.313	69	-8	-8	19	1	1	-0	.989	-2	C	-0.9
	Bal-A	15	28	0	2	0	0	0	2	2	4	.071	.133	.071	-48	-6	-6	0	0	0	0	1.000	-0	/C	-0.6
	Yr	86	223	15	50	8	1	1	14	25	21	.224	.302	.283	56	-14	-14	19	1	1	-0	.990	-3	C	-1.5
1957	Bal-A	85	175	15	48	8	2	1	18	18	19	.274	.349	.360	100	-1	0	23	2	1	0	.986	1	C	0.3
1958	Bal-A	61	109	4	23	1	0	3	16	13	14	.211	.306	.303	72	-5	-4	11	0	0	0	.994	3	C	0.1
1959	Bal-A	65	166	14	30	2	0	1	14	21	13	.181	.273	.211	35	-14	-14	10	1	0	0	.993	3	C	-0.8
1960	Bal-A	14	30	3	8	1	0	0	6	6	1	.267	.389	.300	90	-0	-0	4	0	0	0	.940	0	C	0.1
	Chi-A	28	75	8	19	4	0	0	9	10	8	.253	.349	.307	80	-2	-2	9	1	0	0	.993	4	C	0.4
	Yr	42	105	11	27	5	0	0	15	16	9	.257	.361	.305	83	-2	-2	13	1	0	0	.976	5	C	0.5
1961	Chi-A	6	3	0	0	0	0	0	0	1	2	.000	.250	.000	-27	-1	-1	0	0	0	0	1.000	0	/C	0.0
	Bos-A	19	24	1	6	0	0	0	5	0	2	.250	.250	.250	33	-2	-2	1	0	0	0	1.000	-1	/C	-0.3
	Yr	25	27	1	6	0	0	0	5	1	4	.222	.250	.222	27	-3	-3	1	0	0	0	1.000	-1	/C	-0.3
1962	NY-N	2	5	0	0	0	0	0	0	0	1	.000	.000	.000	-98	-1	-1	0	0	0	0	1.000	1	/C	0.0
Total	13	695	1716	168	414	59	8	20	182	226	135	.241	.334	.320	79	-48	-46	198	7	5	-1	.983	-17	C	-3.8

■ AL GIONFRIDDO

Gionfriddo, Albert Francis b: 3/8/22, Dysart, Pa. BL/TL, 5′6″, 165 lbs. Deb: 9/23/44

YEAR	TM/L	G	AB	R	H	2B	3B	HR	RBI	BB	SO	AVG	OBP	SLG	PRO+	BR	/A	RC	SB	CS	SBR	FA	FR	POS	TPR
1944	Pit-N	4	6	0	1	0	0	0	0	1	1	.167	.286	.167	28	-1	-1	0	0			1.000	0	/O	-0.1
1945	Pit-N	122	409	74	116	18	9	2	42	60	22	.284	.377	.386	108	8	6	64	12			.964	-8	*O	-0.8
1946	Pit-N	64	102	11	26	2	2	0	10	14	5	.255	.345	.314	85	-1	-2	12	1			.944	-5	O	-0.8
1947	Pit-N	1	1	0	0	0	0	0	0	0	0	.000	.000	.000	-97	-0	-0	0	0			.000	0	H	0.0
	*Bro-N	37	62	10	11	2	1	0	6	16	11	.177	.346	.242	57	-3	-3	7	2			.938	-2	O	-0.6
	Yr	38	63	10	11	2	1	0	6	16	11	.175	.342	.238	54	-3	-4	7	2			.938	-2	O	-0.6
Total	4	228	580	95	154	22	12	2	58	91	39	.266	.366	.355	97	3	0	83	15			.959	-15	O	-2.3

■ TOMMY GIORDANO

Giordano, Thomas Arthur "T-Bone" b: 10/9/25, Newark, N.J. BR/TR, 6′, 175 lbs. Deb: 9/11/53

YEAR	TM/L	G	AB	R	H	2B	3B	HR	RBI	BB	SO	AVG	OBP	SLG	PRO+	BR	/A	RC	SB	CS	SBR	FA	FR	POS	TPR
1953	Phi-A	11	40	6	7	2	0	2	5	5	6	.175	.267	.375	69	-2	-2	4	0	1	-1	.984	1	2	-0.1

■ JOE GIRARDI

Girardi, Joseph Elliott b: 10/14/64, Peoria, Ill. BR/TR, 5′11″, 195 lbs. Deb: 4/04/89

YEAR	TM/L	G	AB	R	H	2B	3B	HR	RBI	BB	SO	AVG	OBP	SLG	PRO+	BR	/A	RC	SB	CS	SBR	FA	FR	POS	TPR
1989	*Chi-N	59	157	15	39	10	0	1	14	11	26	.248	.306	.331	76	-4	-5	15	2	1	0	.981	13	C	1.1
1990	Chi-N	133	419	36	113	24	2	1	38	17	50	.270	.303	.344	72	-13	-17	40	8	3	1	.985	-9	*C	-1.8
1991	Chi-N	21	47	3	9	2	0	0	6	6	6	.191	.283	.234	45	-3	-3	4	0	0	0	.972	4	C	0.1
1992	Chi-N	91	270	19	73	3	1	1	12	19	38	.270	.321	.300	75	-8	-9	25	0	2	-1	.991	-4	C	-1.1
Total	4	304	893	73	234	39	3	3	70	53	120	.262	.308	.323	72	-28	-34	84	10	6	-1	.985	4	C	-1.7

■ TONY GIULIANI

Giuliani, Angelo John b: 11/24/12, St.Paul, Minn. BR/TR, 5′11″, 175 lbs. Deb: 4/18/36

YEAR	TM/L	G	AB	R	H	2B	3B	HR	RBI	BB	SO	AVG	OBP	SLG	PRO+	BR	/A	RC	SB	CS	SBR	FA	FR	POS	TPR
1936	StL-A	71	198	17	43	3	0	0	13	11	13	.217	.258	.232	21	-24	-25	12	0	0	0	.966	5	C	-1.6
1937	StL-A	19	53	6	16	1	0	0	3	3	3	.302	.339	.321	67	-3	-3	6	0	0	0	.986	-0	C	-0.2
1938	Was-A	46	115	10	25	4	0	0	15	8	3	.217	.268	.252	33	-12	-11	8	1	0	0	1.000	-1	C	-0.9
1939	Was-A	54	172	20	43	6	2	0	18	4	7	.250	.267	.308	50	-14	-12	13	0	1	-1	.979	1	C	-0.8
1940	Bro-N	1	1	0	0	0	0	0	0	0	1	.000	.000	.000	-94	-0	-0	0	0			1.000	-0	/C	0.0
1941	Bro-N	3	2	0	0	0	0	0	0	0	0	.000	.000	.000	-96	-1	-1	0	0			1.000	1	/C	0.0
1943	Was-A	49	133	5	30	4	1	0	20	12	14	.226	.290	.271	67	-6	-5	11	0	1	-1	.962	-1	C	-0.4
Total	7	243	674	58	157	18	3	0	69	38	41	.233	.274	.269	42	-60	-57	50	1	2		.976	6	C	-3.9

■ JIM GLADD

Gladd, James Walter b: 10/2/22, Ft.Gibson, Okla. d: 11/8/77, Long Beach, Cal. BR/TR, 6′2″, 190 lbs. Deb: 9/09/46

YEAR	TM/L	G	AB	R	H	2B	3B	HR	RBI	BB	SO	AVG	OBP	SLG	PRO+	BR	/A	RC	SB	CS	SBR	FA	FR	POS	TPR
1946	NY-N	4	11	0	1	0	0	0	0	1	4	.091	.167	.091	-26	-2	-2	0	0			1.000	4	/C	0.2

■ DAN GLADDEN

Gladden, Clinton Daniel b: 7/7/57, San Jose, Cal. BR/TR, 5′11″, 180 lbs. Deb: 9/05/83

YEAR	TM/L	G	AB	R	H	2B	3B	HR	RBI	BB	SO	AVG	OBP	SLG	PRO+	BR	/A	RC	SB	CS	SBR	FA	FR	POS	TPR
1983	SF-N	18	63	6	14	2	0	1	9	5	11	.222	.279	.302	63	-3	-3	4	4	3	-1	1.000	2	O	-0.2
1984	SF-N	86	342	71	120	17	2	4	31	33	37	.351	.411	.447	146	20	21	64	31	16	-0	.988	9	O	2.8
1985	SF-N	142	502	64	122	15	8	7	41	40	78	.243	.308	.347	87	-12	-9	54	32	15	1	.975	1	*O	-1.2
1986	SF-N	102	351	55	97	16	1	4	29	39	59	.276	.357	.362	104	1	3	49	27	10	2	.987	12	O	1.4
1987	*Min-A	121	438	69	109	21	2	8	38	38	72	.249	.313	.361	75	-14	-16	50	25	9	2	.987	6	*O/D	-1.1
1988	Min-A	141	576	91	155	32	6	11	62	46	74	.269	.327	.403	100	2	-0	78	28	8	4	.991	16	*O/23P	1.6
1989	Min-A	121	461	69	136	23	3	8	46	23	53	.295	.335	.410	102	5	1	64	23	7	3	.966	5	*O/PD	0.6
1990	Min-A	136	534	64	147	27	6	5	40	26	67	.275	.316	.376	87	-6	-10	60	25	9	2	.980	12	*O/D	0.0
1991	*Min-A	126	461	65	114	14	9	6	52	36	60	.247	.309	.356	80	-11	-13	49	15	9	-1	.988	1	*O	-1.6
1992	Det-A	113	417	57	106	20	1	7	42	30	64	.254	.307	.357	85	-8	-9	45	4	2	0	.987	0	*O/D	-1.2
Total	10	1106	4145	611	1120	187	38	61	390	316	575	.270	.328	.378	94	-27	-36	518	214	88	11	.984	65	*O/DP32	1.1

■ BUCK GLADMAN

Gladman, John H. b: 1864, Washington, D.C. Deb: 7/07/1883

YEAR	TM/L	G	AB	R	H	2B	3B	HR	RBI	BB	SO	AVG	OBP	SLG	PRO+	BR	/A	RC	SB	CS	SBR	FA	FR	POS	TPR
1883	Phi-N	1	4	1	0	0	0	0	0	0	2	.000	.000	.000	-99	-1	-1	0				1.000	-1	/3	-0.1
1884	Was-a	56	224	17	35	5	3	1		3		.156	.178	.219	35	-16	-13	9				.796	-3	3/OS	-1.4
1886	Was-N	44	152	17	21	5	3	1	15	12	30	.138	.201	.230	33	-13	-11	8	5			.830	-6	3	-1.5
Total	3	101	380	35	56	10	6	2	15	15	32	.147	.186	.221	32	-30	-25	17	5			.812	-10	/3OS	-3.0

■ ROLAND GLADU

Gladu, Roland Edouard b: 5/10/13, Montreal, Que., Can BL/TR, 5′8.5″, 185 lbs. Deb: 4/18/44

YEAR	TM/L	G	AB	R	H	2B	3B	HR	RBI	BB	SO	AVG	OBP	SLG	PRO+	BR	/A	RC	SB	CS	SBR	FA	FR	POS	TPR
1944	Bos-N	21	66	5	16	2	1	1	7	3	8	.242	.275	.348	72	-2	-3	6	0			.891	-5	3/O	-0.8

■ JACK GLASSCOCK

Glasscock, John Wesley "Pebbly Jack" b: 7/22/1859, Wheeling, W.Va. d: 2/24/47, Wheeling, W.Va. BR/TR, 5′8″, 160 lbs. Deb: 5/01/1879 M

YEAR	TM/L	G	AB	R	H	2B	3B	HR	RBI	BB	SO	AVG	OBP	SLG	PRO+	BR	/A	RC	SB	CS	SBR	FA	FR	POS	TPR
1879	Cle-N	80	325	31	68	9	3	0	29	6	24	.209	.224	.255	58	-14	-14	19				.919	-6	*23	-1.4
1880	Cle-N	77	296	37	72	13	3	0	27	2	21	.243	.248	.307	89	-4	-3	23				.891	7	*S	0.8
1881	Cle-N	85	335	49	86	9	5	0	33	15	8	.257	.289	.313	94	-4	-1	31				**.911**	9	*S/2	1.2
1882	Cle-N	84	358	66	104	27	9	4	46	13	9	.291	.315	.450	147	16	18	52				.900	**24**	*S/3	**4.1**
1883	Cle-N	96	383	67	110	19	6	0	46	13	23	.287	.311	.368	107	2	3	45				**.922**	17	*S/2	1.9
1884	Cle-N	72	281	45	70	4	4	1	22	25	16	.249	.310	.302	91	-1	-3	27				.893	27	S/2P	2.2
	Cin-U	38	172	48	72	9	5	2		8		.419	.444	.564	221	24	22	44				.889	1	S/2	2.0
1885	StL-N	111	446	66	125	18	3	1	40	29	10	.280	.324	.341	123	8	12	51				**.917**	19	*S/2	3.1
1886	StL-N	121	486	96	158	29	7	3	40	38	13	.325	.374	.432	154	26	31	95	38			**.906**	14	*S/O	4.1
1887	Ind-N	122	483	91	142	18	7	0	40	41	8	.294	.361	.360	107	4	7	87	62			.906	**35**	*S/P	3.6
1888	Ind-N	113	442	63	119	17	3	1	45	14	17	.269	.302	.328	101	1	0	60	48			**.901**	11	*S/2P	1.4
1889	Ind-N	134	582	128	**205**	40	3	7	85	31	10	.352	.390	.467	138	30	28	132	57			**.915**	**36**	*S/2PM	**6.0**
1890	NY-N	124	512	91	**172**	32	9	1	66	41	8	**.336**	.395	.439	145	29	29	113	54			.910	22	*S	**5.1**
1891	NY-N	97	369	46	89	12	6	0	55	36	11	.241	.317	.306	87	-7	-5	46	29			.913	-2	*S	-0.2
1892	StL-N	139	566	83	151	27	5	3	72	44	19	.267	.327	.348	112	4	8	75	26			.916	6	*SM	1.8
1893	StL-N	48	195	32	56	8	1	1	26	25	3	.287	.382	.354	98	1	1	35	20			.907	-7	S	-0.3
	Pit-N	66	293	49	100	7	11	1	74	17	4	.341	.385	.451	126	9	10	58	16			.934	12	S	2.0
	Yr	114	488	81	156	15	12	2	100	42	7	.320	.384	.412	115	10	11	93	36			.923	6	*S	1.7
1894	Pit-N	86	332	46	93	10	7	1	63	31	4	.280	.349	.361	74	-14	-13	51	18			.933	8	S	-0.1
1895	Lou-N	18	74	9	25	3	1	1	6	3	1	.338	.387	.446	124	2	3	14	1			.900	2	S/1	0.5
	Was-N	25	100	20	23	2	0	0	10	7	3	.230	.300	.250	45	-8	-8	9	3			.895	6	S	0.0
	Yr	43	174	29	48	5	1	1	16	10	4	.276	.337	.333	78	-6	-5	22	4			.897	9	S/1	0.5
Total	17	1736	7030	1163	2040	313	98	27	825	439	212	.290	.337	.374	114	103	124	1067	372			.910	242	*S/231PO	37.8

■ TOMMY GLAVIANO Glaviano, Thomas Giatano "Rabbit" b: 10/26/23, Sacramento, Cal. BR/TR, 5'9", 175 lbs. Deb: 4/19/49

YEAR	TM/L	G	AB	R	H	2B	3B	HR	RBI	BB	SO	AVG	OBP	SLG	PRO+	BR	/A	RC	SB	CS	SBR	FA	FR	POS	TPR
1949	StL-N	87	258	32	69	16	1	6	36	41	35	.267	.380	.407	106	5	4	42	0			.929	14	3/2	1.6
1950	StL-N	115	410	92	117	29	2	11	44	90	74	.285	.421	.446	122	21	18	85	6			.935	6	*3/2S	2.2
1951	StL-N	54	104	20	19	4	0	1	4	26	18	.183	.356	.250	66	-4	-4	12	3	0	1	.972	-3	O/2	-0.6
1952	StL-N	80	162	30	39	5	1	3	19	27	26	.241	.366	.340	97	0	0	21	0	0	0	.934	4	3/2	0.4
1953	Phi-N	53	74	17	15	1	2	3	5	24	20	.203	.410	.392	111	2	2	14	2	0	1	.892	-2	32/S	0.1
Total	5	389	1008	191	259	55	6	24	108	208	173	.257	.395	.395	108	26	21	174	11	0		.931	18	3/2OS	3.7

■ HARRY GLEASON Gleason, Harry Gilbert b: 3/28/1875, Camden, N.J. d: 10/21/61, Camden, N.J. BR/TR, 5'6", 160 lbs. Deb: 9/27/01 F

YEAR	TM/L	G	AB	R	H	2B	3B	HR	RBI	BB	SO	AVG	OBP	SLG	PRO+	BR	/A	RC	SB	CS	SBR	FA	FR	POS	TPR
1901	Bos-A	1	1	0	1	0	0	0	0	0		1.000	1.000	1.000	464	0	0	2	1			.667	1	/3	0.1
1902	Bos-A	71	240	30	54	5	5	2	25	10		.225	.265	.313	58	-14	-15	23	6			.930	-0	3O/2	-1.5
1903	Bos-A	6	13	3	2	1	0	0	2	0		.154	.154	.231	13	-1	-1	0	0			.750	-1	/3	-0.3
1904	StL-A	46	155	10	33	7	1	0	6	4		.213	.247	.271	68	-6	-5	11	1			.908	-3	S3/2O	-0.8
1905	StL-A	150	535	45	116	11	5	1	57	34		.217	.269	.262	72	-19	-16	47	23			.911	-15	*3/2	-2.8
Total	5	274	944	88	206	24	11	3	90	48		.218	.263	.276	67	-40	-37	84	31			.914	-19	3/OS2	-5.3

■ JACK GLEASON Gleason, John Day b: 7/14/1854, St.Louis, Mo. d: 9/4/44, St.Louis, Mo. BR/TR, 170 lbs. Deb: 10/02/1877 F

YEAR	TM/L	G	AB	R	H	2B	3B	HR	RBI	BB	SO	AVG	OBP	SLG	PRO+	BR	/A	RC	SB	CS	SBR	FA	FR	POS	TPR
1877	StL-N	1	4	0	1	0	0	0	0	0	1	.250	.250	.250	61	-0	-0	0				.000	-0	/O	-0.1
1882	StL-a	78	331	53	84	10	1	2		**27**		.254	.310	.308	105	4	2	32				.768	2	*3/O2	0.5
1883	StL-a	9	34	2	8	0	0	0		4		.235	.316	.235	76	-1	-1	3				.833	0	/O3	0.0
	Lou-a	84	355	69	105	11	4	2		25		.296	.342	.366	138	12	16	46				.795	-33	*3/S	-1.6
	Yr	93	389	71	113	11	4	2		29		.290	.340	.355	132	11	15	48				.798	-33	3/OS	-1.6
1884	StL-U	92	395	90	128	30	2	4		23		.324	.361	.441	164	28	26	64				.768	-6	*3	1.8
1885	StL-N	2	7	0	1	0	0	0	0	0	1	.143	.143	.143	-8	-1	-1	0				.857	-0	/3	-0.1
1886	Phi-a	77	299	39	56	8	7	1		16		.187	.255	.271	65	-11	-12	23	8			.797	-6	3	-1.4
Total	6	343	1425	253	383	59	14	9	0	95	2	.269	.319	.349	119	31	30	169	8			.781	-43	3/OS2	-0.9

■ ROY GLEASON Gleason, Roy William b: 4/9/43, Melrose Park, Ill. BB/TR, 6'5.5", 220 lbs. Deb: 9/03/63

YEAR	TM/L	G	AB	R	H	2B	3B	HR	RBI	BB	SO	AVG	OBP	SLG	PRO+	BR	/A	RC	SB	CS	SBR	FA	FR	POS	TPR
1963	LA-N	8	1	3	1	1	0	0	0	0	0	1.000	1.000	2.000	795	1	1	2	0	0	0	.000	0	H	0.1

■ BILL GLEASON Gleason, William G. "Will" b: 11/12/1858, St.Louis, Mo. d: 7/21/32, St.Louis, Mo. BR/TR, 5'8", 170 lbs. Deb: 5/02/1882 FU

YEAR	TM/L	G	AB	R	H	2B	3B	HR	RBI	BB	SO	AVG	OBP	SLG	PRO+	BR	/A	RC	SB	CS	SBR	FA	FR	POS	TPR
1882	StL-a	79	347	63	100	11	6	1		6		.288	.300	.363	118	8	6	39				.833	9	*S	1.7
1883	StL-a	98	425	81	122	21	9	2		16		.287	.313	.393	119	12	8	54				.871	-2	*S	0.8
1884	StL-a	110	472	97	127	21	7	1		28		.269	.326	.350	119	13	10	55				.867	-17	*S/3	-0.5
1885	*StL-a	112	472	79	119	9	5	3		29		.252	.316	.311	97	2	-1	48				.869	-42	*S	-3.7
1886	*StL-a	125	524	97	141	18	5	0		43		.269	.333	.323	103	6	2	64	19			.853	-29	*S	-2.4
1887	*StL-a	135	598	135	172	19	1	0		41		.288	.342	.323	79	-8	-20	76	23			.875	-10	*S	-2.3
1888	Phi-a	123	499	55	112	10	2	0	61	12		.224	.256	.253	66	-19	-18	40	27			.858	-14	*S/31	-2.7
1889	Lou-a	16	58	6	14	2	0	0	5	4	1	.241	.302	.276	68	-2	-2	5	1			.822	-3	S	-0.4
Total	8	798	3395	613	907	111	35	7	66	179	1	.267	.314	.327	97	11	-16	380	70				-106	S/31	-9.5

■ KID GLEASON Gleason, William J. b: 10/26/1866, Camden, N.J. d: 1/2/33, Philadelphia, Pa. BB/TR, 5'7", 158 lbs. Deb: 4/20/1888 FMC

YEAR	TM/L	G	AB	R	H	2B	3B	HR	RBI	BB	SO	AVG	OBP	SLG	PRO+	BR	/A	RC	SB	CS	SBR	FA	FR	POS	TPR
1888	Phi-N	24	83	4	17	2	0	0	5	3	16	.205	.233	.229	47	-5	-5	5	3			.841	-3	P/O	0.0
1889	Phi-N	30	99	11	25	5	0	0	8	8	12	.253	.308	.303	67	-4	-5	11	4			.862	-1	P/O2	-0.1
1890	Phi-N	63	224	22	47	3	0	0	17	12	21	.210	.250	.223	39	-17	-18	15	10			.937	-1	P/2	-0.1
1891	Phi-N	65	214	31	53	5	2	0	17	20	17	.248	.318	.290	77	-5	-6	22	6			.896	-6	P/OS	-0.4
1892	StL-N	66	233	35	50	4	2	3	25	34	23	.215	.315	.288	88	-4	-2	24	7			.934	3	PO/21	-0.2
1893	StL-N	59	199	25	51	6	4	0	20	19	8	.256	.327	.327	75	-7	-7	22	2			.907	-0	PO/S	-0.3
1894	StL-N	9	28	3	7	0	1	0	1	2	1	.250	.300	.321	51	-2	-2	3	0			.885	1	/P1	0.0
	*Bal-N	26	86	22	30	5	1	0	17	7	2	.349	.398	.430	97	0	-0	16	1			.900	-2	P/1	0.0
	Yr	35	114	25	37	5	2	0	18	9	3	.325	.374	.404	86	-2	-3	19	1			.894	-0	P/1	0.0
1895	*Bal-N	112	421	90	130	14	12	0	74	33	18	.309	.366	.399	96	-0	-2	71	19			.899	-19	23/PO	-1.3
1896	NY-N	133	541	79	162	17	5	4	89	42	13	.299	.352	.372	95	-5	-3	90	46			.938	3	*2/3O	0.7
1897	NY-N	131	540	85	172	16	4	1	106	26		.319	.353	.369	93	-7	-5	88	43			.930	1	*2/S	0.2
1898	NY-N	150	570	78	126	8	5	0	62	39		.221	.278	.253	54	-35	-32	48	21			.938	19	*2/S	-0.3
1899	NY-N	146	576	72	152	14	4	0	59	24		.264	.293	.302	66	-30	-27	62	29			.946	26	*2	0.6
1900	NY-N	111	420	60	104	11	3	1	29	17		.248	.279	.295	61	-24	-21	43	23			.931	14	*2/S	-0.2
1901	Det-A	135	547	82	150	16	12	3	75	41		.274	.327	.364	87	-7	-10	79	32			.925	6	*2	0.1
1902	Det-A	118	441	42	109	11	4	1	38	25		.247	.292	.297	62	-22	-23	46	17			.941	6	*2	-1.2
1903	Phi-N	106	412	65	117	19	6	1	49	23		.284	.326	.367	101	-2	-0	57	12			.959	-4	*2/O	-0.1
1904	Phi-N	153	587	61	161	23	6	0	42	37		.274	.321	.334	106	2	4	74	17			.942	1	*2/3	1.0
1905	Phi-N	155	608	95	150	17	7	1	50	45		.247	.301	.303	83	-15	-12	67	16			.947	-8	*2	-1.9
1906	Phi-N	135	494	47	112	17	2	0	34	36		.227	.281	.269	72	-16	-16	47	17			.947	-29	*2	-5.1
1907	Phi-N	36	126	11	18	3	0	0	6	7		.143	.194	.167	13	-13	-12	6	3			.979	-2	2/1SO	-1.7
1908	Phi-N	2	1	0	0	0	0	0	0	0		.000	.000	.000	-97	-0	-0	0	0			1.000	0	/2O	0.0
1912	Chi-A	1	2	0	1	0	0	0	0	0		.500	.500	.500	192	0	0	0	0			1.000	-0	/2	0.0
Total	22	1966	7452	1020	1944	216	80	15	823	500	131	.261	.310	.317	79	-216	-205	897	328			.938	6	*2P/OS31	-10.3

■ BILLY GLEASON Gleason, William Patrick b: 9/6/1894, Chicago, Ill. d: 1/9/57, Holyoke, Mass. BR/TR, 5'6.5", 157 lbs. Deb: 9/25/16

YEAR	TM/L	G	AB	R	H	2B	3B	HR	RBI	BB	SO	AVG	OBP	SLG	PRO+	BR	/A	RC	SB	CS	SBR	FA	FR	POS	TPR
1916	Pit-N	1	2	0	0	0	0	0	0	0	0	.000	.000	.000	-99	-0	-0	0	0			1.000	-0	/2	-0.1
1917	Pit-N	13	42	3	7	1	0	0	0	5	5	.167	.255	.190	36	-3	-3	2	1			.978	-5	2	-0.9
1921	StL-A	26	74	6	19	0	1	0	8	6	6	.257	.329	.284	54	-4	-5	7	0	1	-1	.960	-5	2	-1.0
Total	3	40	118	9	26	1	1	0	8	11	11	.220	.298	.246	47	-8	-9	9	1	1		.966	-10	/2	-2.0

■ JIM GLEESON Gleeson, James Joseph "Gee Gee" b: 3/5/12, Kansas City, Mo. BB/TR, 6'1", 191 lbs. Deb: 4/25/36 C

YEAR	TM/L	G	AB	R	H	2B	3B	HR	RBI	BB	SO	AVG	OBP	SLG	PRO+	BR	/A	RC	SB	CS	SBR	FA	FR	POS	TPR
1936	Cle-A	41	139	26	36	9	2	4	12	18	17	.259	.344	.439	91	-2	-2	22	2	1	0	.958	-2	O	-0.5
1939	Chi-N	111	332	43	74	19	6	4	45	39	46	.223	.308	.352	76	-11	-12	38	7			.957	-4	O	-1.9
1940	Chi-N	129	485	76	152	39	11	5	61	54	52	.313	.389	.470	139	24	26	91	4			.983	3	*O	2.2
1941	Cin-N	102	301	47	70	10	0	3	34	45	30	.233	.340	.296	80	-6	-6	33	7			.981	-8	O	-2.0
1942	Cin-N	9	20	3	4	0	0	0	2	2	2	.200	.304	.200	49	-1	-1	2	0			.889	-0	/O	-0.2
Total	5	392	1277	195	336	77	19	16	154	158	147	.263	.350	.391	101	4	4	185	20	1		.972	-11	O	-2.4

■ FRANK GLEICH Gleich, Frank Elmer "Inch" b: 3/7/1894, Columbus, Ohio d: 3/27/49, Columbus, Ohio BL/TR, 5'11", 175 lbs. Deb: 9/17/19

YEAR	TM/L	G	AB	R	H	2B	3B	HR	RBI	BB	SO	AVG	OBP	SLG	PRO+	BR	/A	RC	SB	CS	SBR	FA	FR	POS	TPR
1919	NY-A	5	4	0	1	0	0	0	1	1	0	.250	.400	.250	84	-0	-0	0	0			.000	-2	/O	-0.2
1920	NY-A	24	41	6	5	0	0	0	3	6	10	.122	.234	.122	-4	-6	-6	2	0	0	0	.864	-4	O	-1.1
Total	2	29	45	6	6	0	0	0	4	7	10	.133	.250	.133	4	-6	-6	2	0	0		.826	-7	/O	-1.3

■ BOB GLENALVIN Glenalvin, Robert J. (b: Robert J. Dowling) b: 1/17/1867, Indianapolis, Ind. d: 3/24/44, Detroit, Mich. TR , 5'9", 160 lbs. Deb: 7/12/1890

YEAR	TM/L	G	AB	R	H	2B	3B	HR	RBI	BB	SO	AVG	OBP	SLG	PRO+	BR	/A	RC	SB	CS	SBR	FA	FR	POS	TPR
1890	Chi-N	66	250	43	67	10	3	4	26	19	31	.268	.337	.380	107	3	2	43	30			.928	-14	2	-0.8
1893	Chi-N	16	61	11	21	3	1	0	12	7	3	.344	.412	.426	127	2	3	14	7			.928	-5	2	-0.2
Total	2	82	311	54	88	13	4	4	38	26	34	.283	.352	.389	111	6	4	57	37			.928	-19	/2	-1.0

■ ED GLENN Glenn, Edward C. "Mouse" b: 9/19/1860, Richmond, Va. d: 2/10/1892, Richmond, Va. BR/TR, 5'10", 160 lbs. Deb: 8/05/1884

YEAR	TM/L	G	AB	R	H	2B	3B	HR	RBI	BB	SO	AVG	OBP	SLG	PRO+	BR	/A	RC	SB	CS	SBR	FA	FR	POS	TPR
1884	Ric-a	43	175	26	43	2	4	1		5		.246	.271	.320	96	-1	-1	16				.833	5	O	0.3
1886	Pit-a	71	277	32	53	6	5	0		17		.191	.241	.249	55	-14	-14	22	19			.865	0	O	-1.3

YEAR	TM/L	G	AB	R	H	2B	3B	HR	RBI	BB	SO	AVG	OBP	SLG	PRO+	BR	/A	RC	SB	CS	SBR	FA	FR	POS	TPR
1888	KC-a	3	8	0	0	0	0	0	0	0		.000	.200	.000	-30	-1	-1	0	1			.857	-0	/O	-0.1
	Bos-N	20	65	8	10	0	2	0	3	2	8	.154	.203	.215	34	-5	-5	3	0			.957	2	O/3	-0.3
Total	3	137	525	66	106	8	11	1	3	24	8	.202	.245	.265	64	-21	-21	40	20			.867	7	O/3	-1.4

■ ED GLENN

Glenn, Edward D. b: 10/1875, Ohio d: 12/6/11, Ludlow, Ky. BR/TR, Deb: 9/07/1898

YEAR	TM/L	G	AB	R	H	2B	3B	HR	RBI	BB	SO	AVG	OBP	SLG	PRO+	BR	/A	RC	SB	CS	SBR	FA	FR	POS	TPR
1898	Was-N	1	4	0	0	0	0	0	0	0		.000	.000	.000	-99	-1	-1	0	0			1.000	-1	/S	-0.2
	NY-N	2	4	1	1	0	0	0	0	3		.250	.571	.250	142	1	1	2	1			.750	-2	/S	-0.2
	Yr	3	8	1	1	0	0	0	0	3		.125	.364	.125	42	-0	-0	1	1			.857	-3	/S	-0.4
1902	Chi-N	2	7	0	0	0	0	0	0	1		.000	.125	.000	-63	-1	-1	0	0			1.000	-1	/S	-0.3
Total	2	5	15	1	1	0	0	0	0	4		.067	.263	.067	-2	-2	-2	2	1			.923	-4	/S	-0.7

■ HARRY GLENN

Glenn, Harry Melville "Husky" b: 6/9/1890, Shelburn, Ind. d: 10/12/18, St.Paul, Minn. BR/TR, 6'1", 200 lbs. Deb: 4/14/15

YEAR	TM/L	G	AB	R	H	2B	3B	HR	RBI	BB	SO	AVG	OBP	SLG	PRO+	BR	/A	RC	SB	CS	SBR	FA	FR	POS	TPR
1915	StL-N	6	16	1	5	0	0	0	1	3	0	.313	.421	.313	123	1	1	2	0			.929	-1	/C	0.0

■ JOHN GLENN

Glenn, John b: 7/10/28, Moultrie, Ga. BR/TR, 6'3", 180 lbs. Deb: 6/16/60

YEAR	TM/L	G	AB	R	H	2B	3B	HR	RBI	BB	SO	AVG	OBP	SLG	PRO+	BR	/A	RC	SB	CS	SBR	FA	FR	POS	TPR
1960	StL-N	32	31	4	8	0	1	0	5	0	9	.258	.258	.323	53	-2	-2	3	0	0	0	1.000	-7	O	-1.0

■ JOHN GLENN

Glenn, John W. b: 1849, Rochester, N.Y. d: 11/10/1888, Sandy Hill, N.Y. BR/TR, 5'8.5", 169 lbs. Deb: 5/13/1871

YEAR	TM/L	G	AB	R	H	2B	3B	HR	RBI	BB	SO	AVG	OBP	SLG	PRO+	BR	/A	RC	SB	CS	SBR	FA	FR	POS	TPR
1871	Oly-n	26	120	25	37	3	2	0	21	3	1	.308	.325	.367	104	-0	1	15	1					*O	0.2
1872	Oly-n	9	40	5	6	2	0	0	3	1	0	.150	.171	.200	14	-4	-3	1						/O	-0.3
	Nat-n	1	4	0	2	0	0	0	0	0	0	.500	.500	.500	179	0	0	1						/O	0.0
	Yr	10	44	5	8	2	0	0	3	1	0	.182	.200	.227	32	-3	-3	2						O	-0.3
1873	Was-n	39	185	39	49	9	2	1	18	3	0	.265	.277	.351	86	-4	-3	19						*1	0.0
1874	Chi-n	55	235	33	66	8	0	0		6		.281	.299	.315	95	-1	-1	23						1O	-0.1
1875	Chi-n	69	303	46	75	9	0	0		5		.248	.260	.277	85	-4	-5	22						O1	-0.4
1876	Chi-N	66	276	55	84	9	2	0	32	12	6	.304	.333	.351	115	8	3	33				.881	-2	*O1	0.1
1877	Chi-N	50	202	31	46	6	1	0	20	8	16	.228	.257	.267	58	-8	-11	14				.948	0	O1	-1.1
Total	5 n	199	887	148	235	31	4	1	42	18	1	.265	.280	.312	88	-12	-10	81						1/O	-0.6
Total	2	116	478	86	130	15	3	0	52	20	22	.272	.301	.316	90	1	-8	47				.920	-2	/O1	-1.0

■ JOE GLENN

Glenn, Joseph Charles "Gabby" (b: Joseph Charles Gurzensky)
b: 11/19/08, Dickson City, Pa. d: 5/6/85, Tunkhannock, Pa. BR/TR, 5'11", 175 lbs. Deb: 9/15/32

YEAR	TM/L	G	AB	R	H	2B	3B	HR	RBI	BB	SO	AVG	OBP	SLG	PRO+	BR	/A	RC	SB	CS	SBR	FA	FR	POS	TPR
1932	NY-A	6	16	0	2	0	0	0	0	1	5	.125	.222	.125	-8	-3	-2	1	0	0	0	1.000	-2	/C	-0.4
1933	NY-A	5	21	1	3	0	0	0	1	0	3	.143	.143	.143	-26	-4	-4	0	0	0	0	1.000	-2	/C	-0.5
1935	NY-A	17	43	7	10	4	0	0	6	4	1	.233	.298	.326	65	-3	-2	4	0	0	0	.984	0	C	-0.1
1936	NY-A	44	129	21	35	7	0	1	20	20	10	.271	.373	.349	82	-4	-3	18	1	1	-0	.970	3	C	0.1
1937	NY-A	25	53	6	15	2	2	0	4	10	11	.283	.397	.396	100	0	0	9	0	0	0	.978	4	C	0.4
1938	NY-A	41	123	10	32	7	2	0	25	10	14	.260	.316	.350	67	-7	-6	14	1	0	0	.974	0	C	-0.4
1939	StL-A	88	286	29	78	13	1	4	29	31	40	.273	.344	.367	80	-8	-8	36	4	4	-1	.968	-13	C	-1.7
1940	Bos-A	22	47	3	6	1	0	0	4	5	7	.128	.212	.149	-5	-7	-8	1	0	0	0	.961	-0	C	-0.7
Total	8	248	718	77	181	34	5	5	89	81	91	.252	.330	.334	69	-33	-33	84	6	5	-1	.972	-10	C	-3.3

■ NORM GLOCKSON

Glockson, Norman Stanley b: 6/15/1894, Blue Island, Ill. d: 8/5/55, Maywood, Ill. BR/TR, 6'2", 200 lbs. Deb: 9/16/14

YEAR	TM/L	G	AB	R	H	2B	3B	HR	RBI	BB	SO	AVG	OBP	SLG	PRO+	BR	/A	RC	SB	CS	SBR	FA	FR	POS	TPR
1914	Cin-N	7	12	0	0	0	0	0	0	1	6	.000	.077	.000	-74	-3	-3	0	0			.923	-1	/C	-0.3

■ AL GLOSSOP

Glossop, Alban b: 7/23/15, Christopher, Ill. d: 7/2/91, Walnut Creek, Cal. BB/TR, 6', 170 lbs. Deb: 9/23/39

YEAR	TM/L	G	AB	R	H	2B	3B	HR	RBI	BB	SO	AVG	OBP	SLG	PRO+	BR	/A	RC	SB	CS	SBR	FA	FR	POS	TPR
1939	NY-N	10	32	3	6	0	0	1	3	4	2	.188	.278	.281	50	-2	-2	3	0			.980	0	2	-0.1
1940	NY-N	27	91	16	19	3	0	4	8	10	16	.209	.294	.374	82	-2	-2	10	1			.952	0	2	0.0
	Bos-N	60	148	17	35	2	1	3	14	17	22	.236	.315	.324	81	-4	-3	16	1			.938	6	23/S	0.4
	Yr	87	239	33	54	5	1	7	22	27	38	.226	.307	.343	82	-7	-6	26	2			.947	7	23/S	0.4
1942	Phi-N	121	454	33	102	15	1	4	40	29	35	.225	.273	.289	68	-21	-19	36	3			.961	7	*2/3	-0.5
1943	Bro-N	87	217	28	37	9	0	3	21	28	27	.171	.268	.253	51	-13	-14	17	0			.927	-7	S23/O	-1.9
1946	Chi-N	4	10	2	0	0	0	0	0	1	3	.000	.231	.000	-32	-2	-2	0	0			1.000	-2	/2S	-0.3
Total	5	309	952	99	199	29	2	15	86	89	105	.209	.280	.291	66	-45	-42	83	5			.954	6	2/S3O	-2.4

■ BILL GLYNN

Glynn, William Vincent b: 7/30/25, Sussex, N.J. BL/TL, 6', 190 lbs. Deb: 9/16/49

YEAR	TM/L	G	AB	R	H	2B	3B	HR	RBI	BB	SO	AVG	OBP	SLG	PRO+	BR	/A	RC	SB	CS	SBR	FA	FR	POS	TPR
1949	Phi-N	8	10	0	2	0	0	0	1	0	3	.200	.200	.200	8	-1	-1	0	0			1.000	0	/1	-0.1
1952	Cle-A	44	92	15	25	5	0	2	7	5	16	.272	.309	.391	101	-1	-0	11	1	0	0	.973	0	1	-0.1
1953	Cle-A	147	411	60	100	14	2	3	30	44	65	.243	.324	.309	74	-16	-14	45	1	3	-2	**.993**	6	*1/O	-1.4
1954	*Cle-A	111	171	19	43	3	2	5	18	12	21	.251	.301	.380	84	-4	-4	19	3	2	-0	.987	3	1/O	-0.4
Total	4	310	684	94	170	22	4	10	56	61	105	.249	.315	.336	79	-22	-20	75	5	5		.989	9	1/O	-2.0

■ JOHN GOCHNAUER

Gochnauer, John Peter b: 9/12/1875, Altoona, Pa. d: 9/27/29, Altoona, Pa. BR/TR, 5'9", 160 lbs. Deb: 9/29/01

YEAR	TM/L	G	AB	R	H	2B	3B	HR	RBI	BB	SO	AVG	OBP	SLG	PRO+	BR	/A	RC	SB	CS	SBR	FA	FR	POS	TPR
1901	Bro-N	3	11	1	4	0	0	0	2	1		.364	.417	.364	124	0	0	2	1			1.000	-1	/S	0.0
1902	Cle-A	127	459	45	85	16	4	0	37	38		.185	.247	.237	36	-40	-38	31	7			.933	-3	*S	-3.2
1903	Cle-A	134	438	48	81	16	4	0	48	48		.185	.265	.240	53	-24	-23	35	10			.867	-22	*S	-4.2
Total	3	264	908	94	170	32	8	0	87	87		.187	.258	.240	45	-64	-61	67	18			.901	-26	S	-7.4

■ JOHN GODAR

Godar, John Michael b: 10/25/1864, Cincinnati, Ohio d: 6/23/49, Park Ridge, Ill. BR/TR, 5'9", 170 lbs. Deb: 7/08/1892

YEAR	TM/L	G	AB	R	H	2B	3B	HR	RBI	BB	SO	AVG	OBP	SLG	PRO+	BR	/A	RC	SB	CS	SBR	FA	FR	POS	TPR
1892	Bal-N	5	14	2	3	0	0	0	1	2	1	.214	.353	.214	72	-0	-0	1	1			1.000	-0	/O	-0.1

■ DANNY GODBY

Godby, Danny Ray b: 11/4/46, Logan, W.Va. BR/TR, 6', 185 lbs. Deb: 8/10/74

YEAR	TM/L	G	AB	R	H	2B	3B	HR	RBI	BB	SO	AVG	OBP	SLG	PRO+	BR	/A	RC	SB	CS	SBR	FA	FR	POS	TPR
1974	StL-N	13	13	2	2	0	0	0	1	3	4	.154	.313	.154	34	-1	-1	1	0	0	0	1.000	2	/O	0.0

■ JOE GODDARD

Goddard, Joseph Harold b: 7/23/50, Beckley, W.Va. BR/TR, 5'11", 181 lbs. Deb: 7/31/72

YEAR	TM/L	G	AB	R	H	2B	3B	HR	RBI	BB	SO	AVG	OBP	SLG	PRO+	BR	/A	RC	SB	CS	SBR	FA	FR	POS	TPR
1972	SD-N	12	35	0	7	2	0	0	2	5	9	.200	.300	.257	64	-2	-1	3	0	0	0	.973	-2	C	-0.4

■ JOHN GODWIN

Godwin, John Henry "Bunny" b: 3/10/1877, E.Liverpool, Ohio d: 5/5/56, E.Liverpool, Ohio BR/TR, 6', 190 lbs. Deb: 8/14/05

YEAR	TM/L	G	AB	R	H	2B	3B	HR	RBI	BB	SO	AVG	OBP	SLG	PRO+	BR	/A	RC	SB	CS	SBR	FA	FR	POS	TPR
1905	Bos-A	15	43	4	14	1	0	0	10	3		.326	.408	.349	139	2	2	8	3			.950	1	/O2	0.3
1906	Bos-A	66	193	11	36	2	1	0	15	6		.187	.215	.207	33	-15	-15	11	6			.907	2	3SO/21	-1.4
Total	2	81	236	15	50	3	1	0	25	9		.212	.253	.233	53	-13	-13	19	9			.935	3	/3OS21	-1.1

■ ED GOEBEL

Goebel, Edwin b: 9/1/1899, Brooklyn, N.Y. d: 8/12/59, Brooklyn, N.Y. BR/TR, 5'11", 170 lbs. Deb: 5/13/22

YEAR	TM/L	G	AB	R	H	2B	3B	HR	RBI	BB	SO	AVG	OBP	SLG	PRO+	BR	/A	RC	SB	CS	SBR	FA	FR	POS	TPR
1922	Was-A	37	59	13	16	1	0	1	3	8	16	.271	.358	.339	87	-1	-1	7	1	1	-0	1.000	-1	O	-0.2

■ BILLY GOECKEL

Goeckel, William John b: 9/3/1871, Wilkes-Barre, Pa. d: 11/1/22, Philadelphia, Pa. BR/TL, Deb: 8/10/1899

YEAR	TM/L	G	AB	R	H	2B	3B	HR	RBI	BB	SO	AVG	OBP	SLG	PRO+	BR	/A	RC	SB	CS	SBR	FA	FR	POS	TPR
1899	Phi-N	37	141	17	37	3	1	0	16	1		.262	.283	.298	61	-8	-7	15	6			.978	-3	1	-0.9

■ JERRY GOFF

Goff, Jerry Leroy b: 4/12/64, San Rafael, Cal. BL/TR, 6'3", 205 lbs. Deb: 5/15/90

YEAR	TM/L	G	AB	R	H	2B	3B	HR	RBI	BB	SO	AVG	OBP	SLG	PRO+	BR	/A	RC	SB	CS	SBR	FA	FR	POS	TPR
1990	Mon-N	52	119	14	27	1	0	3	7	21	36	.227	.343	.311	84	-2	-2	14	0	2	-1	.963	-1	C/13	-0.2
1992	Mon-N	3	3	0	0	0	0	0	0	0	3	.000	.000	.000	-99	-1	-1	0	0	0	0	.000	0	/H	-0.1
Total	2	55	122	14	27	1	0	3	7	21	39	.221	.336	.303	80	-3	-3	14	0	2	-1	.958	-1	/C31	-0.3

■ CHUCK GOGGIN

Goggin, Charles Francis b: 7/7/45, Pompano Beach, Fla. BB/TR, 5'11", 175 lbs. Deb: 9/08/72

YEAR	TM/L	G	AB	R	H	2B	3B	HR	RBI	BB	SO	AVG	OBP	SLG	PRO+	BR	/A	RC	SB	CS	SBR	FA	FR	POS	TPR
1972	Pit-N	5	7	0	2	0	0	0	0	1	1	.286	.375	.286	92	-0	-0	1	0	0	0	1.000	0	/2	0.0
1973	Pit-N	1	1	1	1	0	0	0	0	0	0	1.000	1.000	1.000	468	0	0	1	0	0	0	1.000	-0	/C	0.0
	Atl-N	64	90	18	26	5	0	0	7	9	19	.289	.354	.344	88	-0	-1	11	0	1	-1	.938	-8	2/OSC	-0.9

YEAR	TM/L	G	AB	R	H	2B	3B	HR	RBI	BB	SO	AVG	OBP	SLG	PRO+	BR	/A	RC	SB	CS	SBR	FA	FR	POS	TPR
	Yr	65	91	19	27	5	0	0	7	9	19	.297	.360	.352	91	-0	-1	11	0	1	-1	.938	-8	2/OSC	-0.9
1974	Bos-A	2	1	0	0	0	0	0	0	0	1	.000	.000	.000	-93	-0	-0	0	0	0	0	.667	1	/2	0.0
Total	3	72	99	19	29	5	0	0	7	10	21	.293	.358	.343	90	-0	-1	13	0	1	-1	.927	-7	/2OSC	-0.9
■ MIKE GOLDEN	Golden, Michael Henry b: 9/11/1851, Shirley, Mass. d: 1/11/29, Rockford, Ill. BR/TR, 5'8", 168 lbs. Deb: 5/05/1875																								
1875	Wes-n	13	46	5	6	0	0	0		0		.130	.130	.130	-9	-5	-5	1						P	0.0
	Chi-n	39	155	16	40	3	0	0		2		.258	.268	.277	88	-2	-2	12						OP/1	0.0
	Yr	52	201	21	46	3	0	0		2		.229	.236	.244	65	-7	-7	12						PO/1	0.0
1878	Mil-N	55	214	16	44	6	3	0	20	3	35	.206	.217	.262	53	-10	-12	12				.831	-3	OP/1	-1.3
■ JONAH GOLDMAN	Goldman, Jonah John b: 8/29/06, New York, N.Y. d: 8/17/80, Palm Beach, Fla. BR/TR, 5'7", 170 lbs. Deb: 9/22/28																								
1928	Cle-A	7	21	1	5	1	0	0	2	3	0	.238	.333	.286	63	-1	-1	2	0	0	0	.878	0	/S	0.0
1930	Cle-A	111	306	32	74	18	0	1	44	28	25	.242	.312	.310	56	-19	-21	31	3	5	-2	.945	21	S3	0.6
1931	Cle-A	30	62	0	8	1	0	0	3	4	6	.129	.182	.145	-12	-10	-11	2	1	1	-0	.947	14	S	0.4
Total	3	148	389	33	87	20	0	1	49	35	31	.224	.293	.283	46	-30	-33	35	4	6	-2	.941	35	S/3	1.0
■ GORDON GOLDSBERRY	Goldsberry, Gordon Frederick b: 8/30/27, Sacramento, Cal. BL/TL, 6', 170 lbs. Deb: 4/20/49																								
1949	Chi-A	39	145	25	36	3	2	1	13	18	9	.248	.331	.317	74	-6	-5	17	2	0	1	.990	-1	1	-0.6
1950	Chi-A	82	127	19	34	8	2	2	25	26	18	.268	.392	.409	108	2	2	22	0	2	-1	.989	3	1/O	0.3
1951	Chi-A	10	11	4	1	0	0	0	1	2	2	.091	.231	.091	-11	-2	-2	0	0	0	0	1.000	1	/1	0.0
1952	StL-A	86	227	30	52	9	3	3	17	34	37	.229	.330	.335	83	-4	-5	27	0	2	-1	.983	-3	1/O	-1.1
Total	4	217	510	78	123	20	7	6	56	80	66	.241	.344	.343	85	-10	-9	66	2	4	-2	.987	1	1/O	-1.4
■ WALT GOLDSBY	Goldsby, Walton Hugh b: 12/31/1861, Louisiana d: 1/11/14, Dallas, Tex. BL , Deb: 5/28/1884																								
1884	StL-a	5	20	2	4	0	0	0		0		.200	.200	.200	32	-1	-2	1				.800	-1	/O	-0.2
	Was-a	6	24	4	9	0	0	0		1		.375	.400	.375	179	1	2	4				.909	1	/O	0.2
	Ric-a	11	40	4	9	1	0	0		1		.225	.262	.250	71	-1	-1	3				.737	-1	O	-0.2
	Yr	22	84	10	22	1	0	0		2		.262	.287	.274	89	-1	-1	7				.800	-1	O	-0.2
1886	Was-N	6	18	0	4	1	0	0	1	2	3	.222	.300	.278	81	-0	-0	2	0			.818	-1	/O	-0.1
1888	Bal-a	45	165	13	39	1	1	0	14	8		.236	.288	.255	79	-4	-3	17	17			.903	-6	O	-0.9
Total	3	73	267	23	65	3	1	0	15	12	3	.243	.289	.262	83	-5	-4	26	17			.858	-8	/O	-1.2
■ FRED GOLDSMITH	Goldsmith, Fred Ernest b: 5/15/1856, New Haven, Conn. d: 3/28/39, Berkley, Mich. BR/TR, 6'1", 195 lbs. Deb: 10/23/1875 U																								
1875	NH-n	1	4	0	2	0	0	0		0		.500	.500	.500	283	1	1	1						/2	0.1
1879	Tro-N	9	38	6	9	1	0	0	2	1	3	.237	.256	.263	77	-1	-1	3				.833	0	/PO1	0.0
1880	Chi-N	35	142	24	37	4	2	0	15	2	15	.261	.271	.317	93	-0	-1	12				.968	1	PO/1	-0.2
1881	Chi-N	42	158	24	38	3	4	0	16	6	17	.241	.268	.310	78	-3	-4	13				.863	5	P/O	0.0
1882	Chi-N	45	183	23	42	11	1	0	19	4	29	.230	.246	.301	71	-5	-6	14				.939	-2	P/1	0.0
1883	Chi-N	60	235	38	52	12	3	1	16	4	35	.221	.234	.311	60	-10	-12	18				.865	1	PO/1	-0.3
1884	Chi-N	22	81	11	11	2	0	2	6	7	26	.136	.205	.235	35	-6	-7	4				.774	-3	P/O	0.0
	Bal-a	4	14	2	2	0	0	0		2		.143	.250	.143	32	-1	-1	1				.889	1	/P1	0.0
Total	6	217	851	128	191	33	10	3	74	26	125	.224	.247	.297	69	-27	-33	64				.882	4	P/O1	-0.5
■ WALLY GOLDSMITH	Goldsmith, Wallace b: 1849, Baltimore, Md. 5'7", 146 lbs. Deb: 5/04/1871																								
1871	Kek-n	19	88	8	18	1	0	0	12	4	2	.205	.239	.216	31	-7	-8	5	0					S/3C2	-0.5
1872	Oly-n	9	40	4	10	0	0	0	5	0	0	.250	.250	.250	57	-2	-2	3						/S2	-0.1
1873	Mar-n	1	4	0	0	0	0	0	0	0	0	.000	.000	.000	-99	-1	-1	0						/2	-0.1
1875	Wes-n	13	51	3	6	0	0	0		0		.118	.118	.118	-17	-6	-6	1						3	-0.5
Total	4 n	42	183	15	34	1	0	0		4		.186	.203	.191	21	-16	-17	8						/3S2C	-1.2
■ LONNIE GOLDSTEIN	Goldstein, Leslie Elmer b: 5/13/18, Austin, Tex. BL/TL, 6'2.5", 190 lbs. Deb: 9/11/43																								
1943	Cin-N	5	5	1	1	0	0	0	0	2	1	.200	.429	.200	85	0	0	0	0			1.000	-0	/1	0.0
1946	Cin-N	6	5	1	0	0	0	0	0	1	1	.000	.167	.000	-53	-1	-1	0	0			.000	0	H	-0.1
Total	2	11	10	2	1	0	0	0	0	3	2	.100	.308	.100	20	-1	-1	0	0			.985	-0	/1	-0.1
■ PURNAL GOLDY	Goldy, Purnal William b: 11/28/37, Camden, N.J. BR/TR, 6'5", 200 lbs. Deb: 4/12/62																								
1962	Det-A	20	70	8	16	1	1	3	12	0	12	.229	.239	.400	66	-3	-4	6	0	0	0	.964	-0	O	-0.5
1963	Det-A	9	8	1	2	0	0	0	0	0	4	.250	.250	.250	39	-1	-1	1	0	0	0	.000	0	H	-0.1
Total	2	29	78	9	18	1	1	3	12	0	16	.231	.241	.385	64	-4	-4	6	0	0	0		-0	/O	-0.6
■ STAN GOLETZ	Goletz, Stanley "Stash" b: 5/21/18, Crescent, Ohio BL/TL, 6'3", 200 lbs. Deb: 9/09/41																								
1941	Chi-A	5	5	0	3	0	0	0	0	0	2	.600	.600	.600	221	1	1	2	0	0	0	.000	0	H	0.1
■ MIKE GOLIAT	Goliat, Mike Mitchel b: 11/5/25, Yatesboro, Pa. BR/TR, 6', 180 lbs. Deb: 8/03/49																								
1949	Phi-N	55	189	24	40	6	3	3	19	20	32	.212	.290	.323	66	-10	-9	17	0			.969	-2	2/1	-0.9
1950	*Phi-N	145	483	49	113	13	6	13	64	53	75	.234	.314	.366	80	-16	-15	53	3			.972	-18	*2	-2.6
1951	Phi-N	41	138	14	31	2	1	4	15	9	18	.225	.277	.341	66	-7	-7	13	0	1	-1	.968	-7	2/3	-1.3
	StL-A	5	11	0	2	0	0	0	1	0	1	.182	.182	.182	-1	-2	-2	0	0	0	0	1.000	0	/2	-0.1
1952	StL-A	3	4	0	0	0	0	0	0	1	1	.000	.200	.000	-40	-1	-1	0	0	0	0	1.000	1	/2	0.0
Total	4	249	825	87	186	21	10	20	99	83	127	.225	.300	.348	73	-35	-33	84	3	1		.971	-26	2/13	-4.9
■ WALT GOLVIN	Golvin, Walter George b: 2/1/1894, Hershey, Neb. d: 6/11/73, Gardena, Cal. BL/TL, 6', 165 lbs. Deb: 4/15/22																								
1922	Chi-N	2	2	0	0	0	0	0	1	0	0	.000	.000	.000	-98	-1	-1	0	0	0	0	1.000	-0	/1	-0.1
■ CHILE GOMEZ	Gomez, Jose Luis (Rodriguez) b: 5/23/09, Villaunion, Mex. BR/TR, 5'10", 165 lbs. Deb: 7/27/35																								
1935	Phi-N	67	222	24	51	3	0	0	16	17	34	.230	.285	.243	39	-17	-20	15	2			.948	12	S2	-0.4
1936	Phi-N	108	332	24	77	4	1	0	28	14	32	.232	.265	.250	36	-28	-32	22	0			.948	18	2S	-0.7
1942	Was-A	25	73	8	14	2	2	0	6	9	7	.192	.280	.274	57	-4	-4	6	1	0	0	.973	-1	2/3	-0.4
Total	3	200	627	56	142	9	3	0	50	40	73	.226	.274	.250	39	-49	-57	43	3	0		.954	29	2/S3	-1.5
■ LEO GOMEZ	Gomez, Leonardo (Velez) b: 3/2/66, Canovanas, P.R. BR/TR, 6', 180 lbs. Deb: 9/17/90																								
1990	Bal-A	12	39	3	9	0	0	0	1	8	7	.231	.362	.231	71	-1	-1	4	0	0	0	.886	-2	3	-0.3
1991	Bal-A	118	391	40	91	17	2	16	45	40	82	.233	.307	.409	100	-3	-1	48	1	1	-0	.972	-13	*3D/1	-1.4
1992	Bal-A	137	468	62	124	24	0	17	64	63	78	.265	.362	.425	120	13	14	72	2	3	-1	.951	-13	*3	0.0
Total	3	267	898	105	224	41	2	33	110	111	167	.249	.339	.410	110	9	12	124	3	4	-2	.956	-28	3/D1	-1.7
■ LUIS GOMEZ	Gomez, Luis (Sanchez) b: 8/19/51, Guadalajara, Mex. BR/TR, 5'9", 150 lbs. Deb: 4/28/74																								
1974	Min-A	82	168	18	35	1	0	0	3	12	16	.208	.261	.214	37	-13	-14	10	2	3	-1	.960	20	S/2D	1.2
1975	Min-A	89	72	7	10	0	0	0	5	4	12	.139	.184	.139	-7	-10	-10	2	0	2	-1	.975	20	S/2D	1.0
1976	Min-A	38	57	5	11	1	0	0	3	3	3	.193	.233	.211	30	-5	-5	3	1	0	0	.988	7	S/23OD	0.4
1977	Min-A	32	65	6	16	4	2	0	11	4	9	.246	.290	.369	79	-2	-2	7	0	2	-1	.983	4	2/S3OD	0.2
1978	Tor-A	153	413	39	92	7	3	0	32	34	41	.223	.282	.254	51	-26	-27	28	2	10	-5	.976	-10	*S	-2.5
1979	Tor-A	59	163	11	39	7	0	0	11	6	17	.239	.266	.282	48	-12	-12	11	1	0	0	1.000	4	32S	-0.6
1980	Atl-N	121	278	18	53	6	0	0	24	17	27	.191	.240	.212	26	-27	-28	13	0	4	-2	.968	12	*S	-0.9
1981	Atl-N	35	35	4	7	0	0	0	1	6	4	.200	.317	.200	48	-2	-2	3	0	1	-1	.895	-3	S/32P	-0.5
Total	8	609	1251	108	263	26	5	0	90	86	129	.210	.262	.239	40	-97	-100	76	6	22	-11	.970	53	S/23DOP	-1.7

YEAR	TM/L	G	AB	R	H	2B	3B	HR	RBI	BB	SO	AVG	OBP	SLG	PRO+	BR	/A	RC	SB	CS	SBR	FA	FR	POS	TPR

■ PRESTON GOMEZ   Gomez, Pedro (Martinez)   b: 4/20/23, Preston, Cuba   BR/TR, 5'11", 170 lbs.   Deb: 5/05/44   MC

| 1944 | Was-A | 8 | 7 | 2 | 2 | 1 | 0 | 0 | 2 | 0 | 4 | .286 | .286 | .429 | 107 | -0 | 0 | 1 | 0 | 0 | 0 | 1.000 | -1 | /2S | -0.1 |

■ RANDY GOMEZ   Gomez, Randell Scott   b: 2/4/57, San Mateo, Cal.   BR/TR, 5'10", 185 lbs.   Deb: 8/21/84

| 1984 | SF-N | 14 | 30 | 0 | 5 | 1 | 0 | 0 | 0 | 8 | 3 | .167 | .342 | .200 | 57 | -1 | -1 | 2 | 0 | 0 | 0 | .951 | 3 | C | 0.3 |

■ JESSE GONDER   Gonder, Jesse Lemar   b: 1/20/36, Monticello, Ark.   BL/TR, 5'10", 190 lbs.   Deb: 9/23/60

1960	NY-A	7	7	1	2	0	0	1	3	1	1	.286	.375	.714	199	0	1	2	0	0	0	1.000	1	/C	0.2
1961	NY-A	15	12	2	4	1	0	0	3	3	1	.333	.467	.417	146	1	1	2	0	0	0	.000	0	H	0.1
1962	Cin-N	4	4	0	0	0	0	0	0	0	3	.000	.000	.000	-97	-1	-1	0	0	0	0	.000	0	H	-0.1
1963	Cin-N	31	32	5	10	2	0	3	5	2	12	.313	.333	.656	172	3	3	7	0	0	0	1.000	1	/C	0.4
	NY-N	42	126	12	38	4	0	3	15	6	25	.302	.333	.405	110	2	1	16	1	2	-1	.978	-14	C	-1.4
	Yr	73	158	17	48	6	0	6	20	7	37	.304	.333	.456	122	5	4	23	1	2	-1	.981	-13	C	-1.0
1964	NY-N	131	341	28	92	11	1	7	35	29	65	.270	.331	.370	99	-1	-0	38	0	0	0	.979	-1	C	0.3
1965	NY-N	53	105	6	25	4	0	4	9	11	20	.238	.310	.390	100	-1	-0	11	0	0	0	.992	-5	C	-0.4
	Mil-N	31	53	2	8	2	0	1	5	4	9	.151	.211	.245	28	-5	-5	2	0	0	0	.989	5	C	0.0
	Yr	84	158	8	33	6	0	5	14	15	29	.209	.277	.342	75	-6	-5	13	0	0	0	.991	-0	C	-0.4
1966	Pit-N	59	160	13	36	3	1	7	16	12	39	.225	.287	.387	85	-3	-3	16	0	0	0	.978	-2	C	-0.2
1967	Pit-N	22	36	4	5	1	0	0	3	5	9	.139	.279	.167	30	-3	-3	2	0	0	0	.971	-0	C	-0.3
Total	8	395	876	73	220	28	2	26	94	72	184	.251	.312	.377	94	-8	-7	97	1	2	-1	.981	-15	C	-1.4

■ DAN GONZALES   Gonzales, Daniel David   b: 9/30/53, Whittier, Cal.   BL/TR, 6'1", 195 lbs.   Deb: 4/07/79

1979	Det-A	7	18	1	4	1	0	0	2	0	2	.222	.222	.278	33	-2	-2	1	1	0	0	1.000	-1	/O	-0.2
1980	Det-A	2	7	1	1	0	0	0	0	0	1	.143	.143	.143	-21	-1	-1	0	0	0	0	.750	0	/OD	-0.1
Total	2	9	25	2	5	1	0	0	2	0	3	.200	.200	.240	18	-3	-3	1	1	0	0	.857	-1	/OD	-0.3

■ RENE GONZALES   Gonzales, Rene Adrian   b: 9/3/60, Austin, Tex.   BR/TR, 6'3", 191 lbs.   Deb: 7/27/84

1984	Mon-N	29	30	5	7	1	0	0	2	2	5	.233	.303	.267	64	-1	-1	3	0	0	0	.957	1	S	0.0
1986	Mon-N	11	26	1	3	0	0	0	0	2	7	.115	.179	.115	-17	-4	-4	0	0	2	-1	1.000	2	/S3	-0.4
1987	Bal-A	37	60	14	16	2	1	1	7	3	11	.267	.302	.383	82	-2	-2	7	1	0	0	.963	6	3/2S	0.4
1988	Bal-A	92	237	13	51	6	0	2	15	13	32	.215	.265	.266	50	-16	-15	17	2	0	1	.966	15	32/S10	0.0
1989	Bal-A	71	166	16	36	4	0	1	11	12	30	.217	.270	.259	51	-11	-10	11	5	3	-0	.978	-1	23/S	-1.0
1990	Bal-A	67	103	13	22	3	1	1	12	11	14	.214	.296	.291	67	-5	-4	9	1	2	-1	.994	9	23/SO	0.5
1991	*Tor-A	71	118	16	23	3	0	1	6	12	22	.195	.291	.246	48	-8	-8	9	1	1	-0	.973	10	S32/1	0.3
1992	Cal-A	104	329	47	91	17	1	7	38	41	46	.277	.364	.398	115	7	7	45	7	4	-0	.954	5	321/S	1.3
Total	8	482	1069	125	249	36	3	13	91	97	167	.233	.304	.309	72	-40	-38	101	16	11	-2	.956	46	32/S10	1.1

■ TONY GONZALEZ   Gonzalez, Andres Antonio (Gonzalez)   b: 8/28/36, Central Cunagua, Cuba   BL/TR, 5'9", 170 lbs.   Deb: 4/12/60

1960	Cin-N	39	99	10	21	5	1	3	14	4	27	.212	.250	.374	67	-5	-5	9	1	0	0	.957	-4	O	-1.0
	Phi-N	78	241	27	72	17	5	6	33	11	47	.299	.337	.485	122	7	8	38	2	2	-1	.981	-1	O	0.3
	Yr	117	340	37	93	22	6	9	47	15	74	.274	.312	.453	106	2	2	47	3	2	-0	.975	-4	O	-0.7
1961	Phi-N	126	426	58	118	16	8	12	58	49	66	.277	.360	.437	112	7	8	68	15	5	2	.984	-8	*O	-0.5
1962	Phi-N	118	437	76	132	16	4	20	63	40	82	.302	.372	.494	134	19	20	80	17	8	0	1.000	1	*O	1.5
1963	Phi-N	155	555	78	170	36	12	4	66	31	68	.306	.375	.436	134	24	25	91	13	8	-1	.986	-9	*O	0.9
1964	Phi-N	131	421	55	117	25	3	4	40	44	74	.278	.355	.380	108	5	6	56	0	5	-3	.996	-3	*O	-0.6
1965	Phi-N	108	370	48	109	19	1	13	41	31	52	.295	.354	.457	129	13	13	54	9	3	1	.983	-11	*O	-0.3
1966	Phi-N	132	384	53	110	20	4	6	40	26	60	.286	.337	.406	105	3	3	51	2	6	-3	.986	0	*O	-0.5
1967	Phi-N	149	508	74	172	23	9	6	59	47	58	.339	.400	.472	147	33	32	94	10	9	-2	.993	4	*O	2.9
1968	Phi-N	121	416	45	110	13	4	3	38	40	42	.264	.339	.337	103	3	3	47	6	5	-1	.979	-7	*O	-1.3
1969	SD-N	53	182	17	41	4	0	2	8	19	24	.225	.309	.280	69	-8	-7	16	1	0	0	.975	2	O	-0.8
	*Atl-N	89	320	51	94	15	2	10	50	27	22	.294	.358	.447	124	10	10	51	3	1	0	.989	3	O	0.9
	Yr	142	502	68	135	19	2	12	58	46	46	.269	.340	.386	104	2	3	66	4	1	1	.983	4	*O	0.1
1970	Atl-N	123	430	57	114	18	2	7	55	46	45	.265	.347	.365	86	-5	-8	54	3	5	-2	.987	-6	*O	-2.2
	Cal-A	26	92	9	28	2	0	1	12	0	11	.304	.326	.359	92	-2	-1	10	3	2	-0	.960	-1	O	-0.4
1971	Cal-A	111	314	32	77	9	2	3	38	28	28	.245	.313	.315	84	-9	-6	30	0	1	-1	.987	-6	O	-1.8
Total	12	1559	5195	690	1485	238	57	103	615	467	706	.286	.353	.413	114	95	100	749	79	61	-13	.987	-46	*O	-2.9

■ DENNY GONZALEZ   Gonzalez, Denio Mariano (Manzueta)   b: 7/22/63, Sabana Grande Boya, D.R.   BR/TR, 5'11", 185 lbs.   Deb: 8/06/84

1984	Pit-N	26	82	9	15	3	1	0	4	7	21	.183	.247	.244	38	-7	-7	4	1	1	-0	1.000	1	3S/O	-0.5
1985	Pit-N	35	124	11	28	4	0	4	12	13	27	.226	.299	.355	83	-3	-3	13	2	4	-2	.894	-4	3O/2	-1.0
1987	Pit-N	5	7	1	0	0	0	0	0	0	2	.000	.125	.000	-63	-2	-2	0	0	0	0	1.000	-1	/S	-0.3
1988	Pit-N	24	32	5	6	1	0	0	1	6	10	.188	.316	.219	57	-2	-2	3	0	0	0	1.000	0	S/23	-0.1
1989	Cle-N	8	17	3	5	1	0	0	1	1	4	.294	.333	.353	92	-0	-0	2	0	0	0	.000	0	/3D	-0.1
Total	5	98	262	29	54	9	1	4	18	27	64	.206	.283	.294	62	-13	-13	22	3	5	-2	.925	-4	/3SO2D	-2.0

■ EUSEBIO GONZALEZ   Gonzalez, Eusebio Miguel (Lopez) "Papo"   b: 7/13/1892, Havana, Cuba   d: 2/14/76, Havana, Cuba   BR/TR, 5'10", 165 lbs.   Deb: 7/26/18

| 1918 | Bos-A | 3 | 5 | 2 | 2 | 0 | 1 | 0 | 1 | 0 | 1 | .400 | .571 | .800 | 319 | 1 | 1 | 2 | 0 | | | 1.000 | -1 | /S3 | 0.1 |

■ FERNANDO GONZALEZ   Gonzalez, Jose Fernando (Quinones)   b: 6/19/50, Arecibo, P.R.   BR/TR, 5'10", 170 lbs.   Deb: 9/15/72

1972	Pit-N	3	2	0	0	0	0	0	0	0	2	.000	.000	.000	-99	-1	-1	0	0	0	0	.500	0	/3	-0.1
1973	Pit-N	37	49	5	11	0	1	1	5	1	11	.224	.255	.327	62	-3	-3	4	0	0	0	.923	-1	/3	-0.4
1974	KC-A	9	21	1	3	1	0	0	2	0	4	.143	.143	.190	-5	-3	-3	1	0	0	0	1.000	-0	/3D	-0.3
	NY-A	51	121	11	26	5	1	1	7	7	7	.215	.258	.298	61	-6	-6	9	0	0	0	.982	2	2/3S	-0.2
	Yr	60	142	12	29	6	1	1	9	7	11	.204	.242	.282	51	-9	-9	9	0	0	0	.982	2	23/SD	-0.5
1977	Pit-N	80	181	17	50	10	4	4	27	13	21	.276	.325	.398	90	-2	-3	20	3	3	-1	.972	6	3O/2S	-1.0
1978	Pit-N	9	21	0	4	1	0	0	0	1	3	.190	.227	.238	29	-2	-2	1	0	0	0	.923	-4	/23	-0.7
	SD-N	101	320	27	80	10	2	2	29	18	32	.250	.290	.313	74	-14	-11	29	4	4	-1	.982	0	2	-0.6
	Yr	110	341	29	84	11	2	2	29	19	35	.246	.286	.308	71	-16	-13	30	4	4	-1	.981	-4	2/3	-0.6
1979	SD-N	114	332	27	72	13	3	9	34	18	34	.217	.258	.359	71	-16	-14	27	1	0	0	.976	-14	*2/3	-2.2
Total	6	404	1038	85	244	40	7	17	104	58	114	.235	.276	.336	71	-46	-42	92	8	7	-2	.979	-23	2/3OSD	-5.5

■ JOSE GONZALEZ   Gonzalez, Jose Rafael (Gutierrez)   b: 11/23/64, Puerto Plata, D.R.   BR/TR, 6'2", 196 lbs.   Deb: 9/02/85

1985	LA-N	23	11	6	3	2	0	0	1	1	3	.273	.333	.455	122	0	0	1	1	1	-0	1.000	-6	O	-0.6
1986	LA-N	57	93	15	20	5	1	2	6	7	29	.215	.270	.355	76	-4	-4	9	4	3	-1	.924	-10	O	-1.6
1987	LA-N	19	16	2	3	0	0	1	1	2	5	.188	.235	.313	45	-1	-1	2	5	0	2	1.000	-1	O	-0.1
1988	*LA-N	37	24	7	2	1	0	0	0	2	10	.083	.154	.125	-20	-4	-4	0	3	0	1	.938	-8	O	-1.2
1989	LA-N	95	261	31	70	11	3	3	18	23	53	.268	.327	.360	98	-1	-0	32	9	3	1	.968	-0	O	-0.2
1990	LA-N	106	99	15	23	5	3	2	8	6	27	.232	.283	.404	89	-2	-2	11	3	5	-1	1.000	-22	O	-2.5
1991	LA-N	42	28	3	0	0	0	0	0	4	9	.000	.067	.000	-82	-7	-7	0	0	0	0	1.000	-7	O	-1.4
	Pit-N	16	20	2	2	0	0	0	3	0	6	.100	.100	.250	-5	-3	-3	1	0	0	0	1.000	-1	O	-0.5
	Yr	58	48	5	2	0	0	0	3	4	15	.042	.080	.104	-50	-9	-9	1	0	0	0	1.000	-8	O	-1.9
	Cle-A	33	69	10	11	2	0	1	5	5	14	.159	.284	.261	51	-4	-4	7	0	0	0	.981	-3	O	-0.9
1992	Cal-A	33	55	4	10	2	0	0	2	7	20	.182	.274	.218	40	-4	-4	3	1	0	1	1.000	-4	O	-0.9
Total	8	461	676	95	144	30	7	9	42	60	186	.213	.279	.318	69	-30	-28	66	33	9	5	.972	-62	O	-9.6

YEAR	TM/L	G	AB	R	H	2B	3B	HR	RBI	BB	SO	AVG	OBP	SLG	PRO+	BR	/A	RC	SB	CS	SBR	FA	FR	POS	TPR

■ **JUAN GONZALEZ** Gonzalez, Juan Alberto (Vazquez) b: 10/20/69, Arecibo, P.R. BR/TR, 6'3", 175 lbs. Deb: 9/01/89

1989	Tex-A	24	60	6	9	3	0	1	7	6	17	.150	.227	.250	34	-5	-5	3	0	0	0	.964	-2	O	-0.8
1990	Tex-A	25	90	11	26	7	1	4	12	2	18	.289	.319	.522	131	3	3	14	0	1	-1	1.000	-1	O/D	0.1
1991	Tex-A	142	545	78	144	34	1	27	102	42	118	.264	.323	.479	121	12	13	82	4	4	-1	.981	-19	*O/D	-1.1
1992	Tex-A	155	584	77	152	24	2	**43**	109	35	143	.260	.308	.529	135	19	22	90	0	1	-1	.975	5	*O/D	2.2
Total	4	346	1279	172	331	68	4	75	230	85	296	.259	.311	.494	124	29	32	188	4	6	-2	.978	-17	O/D	0.4

■ **JULIO GONZALEZ** Gonzalez, Julio Cesar (Hernandez) b: 12/25/52, Caguas, P.R. BR/TR, 5'11", 165 lbs. Deb: 4/08/77

1977	Hou-N	110	383	34	94	18	3	1	27	19	45	.245	.288	.316	68	-21	-16	34	3	3	-1	.921	-26	S2	-3.4
1978	Hou-N	78	223	24	52	3	1	1	16	8	31	.233	.263	.269	53	-15	-13	15	6	1	1	.983	-20	2S/3	-3.0
1979	Hou-N	68	181	16	45	5	2	0	10	5	14	.249	.280	.298	62	-11	-9	15	2	1	0	.987	1	2S/3	-0.4
1980	Hou-N	40	52	5	6	1	0	0	1	1	8	.115	.132	.135	-28	-9	-8	1	1	0	0	1.000	3	S3/2	-0.4
1981	StL-N	20	22	2	7	1	0	1	3	1	3	.318	.348	.500	135	1	1	3	0	0	0	1.000	1	/S23	0.2
1982	StL-N	42	87	9	21	3	2	1	7	1	24	.241	.258	.356	70	-4	-4	7	1	1	-0	.907	-1	3/2S	-0.6
1983	Det-A	12	21	0	3	1	0	0	2	1	7	.143	.182	.190	3	-3	-3	1	0	0	0	.889	3	/S23	0.1
Total	7	370	969	90	228	32	8	4	66	36	132	.235	.269	.297	59	-61	-53	76	13	6	0	.976	-39	2S/3	-7.5

■ **LUIS GONZALEZ** Gonzalez, Luis Emilio b: 9/3/67, Tampa, Fla. BL/TR, 6'2", 180 lbs. Deb: 9/04/90

1990	Hou-N	12	21	1	4	2	0	0	0	2	5	.190	.261	.286	52	-1	-1	2	0	0	0	1.000	2	/31	0.1
1991	Hou-N	137	473	51	120	28	9	13	69	40	101	.254	.322	.433	117	6	9	65	10	7	-1	.984	14	*O	1.9
1992	Hou-N	122	387	40	94	19	3	10	55	24	52	.243	.291	.385	95	-6	-4	41	7	7	-2	.993	15	*O	0.8
Total	3	271	881	92	218	49	12	23	124	66	158	.247	.307	.409	106	-2	4	108	17	14	-3	.988	31	O/31	2.8

■ **MIKE GONZALEZ** Gonzalez, Miguel Angel (Cordero) b: 9/24/1890, Havana, Cuba d: 2/19/77, Havana, Cuba BR/TR, 6'1", 200 lbs. Deb: 9/28/12 MC

1912	Bos-N	1	2	0	0	0	0	0	1	0	1	.000	.333	.000	-5	-0	-0	0				.875	1	/C	0.1
1914	Cin-N	95	176	19	41	6	0	0	10	13	16	.233	.293	.267	65	-7	-8	14	2			.954	10	C	0.8
1915	StL-N	51	97	12	22	2	0	0	10	8	9	.227	.306	.289	80	-2	-2	9	4	2	0	.992	4	C/1	0.3
1916	StL-N	118	331	33	79	15	4	0	29	28	18	.239	.304	.308	89	-4	-4	34	5			.981	7	C1	1.0
1917	StL-N	106	290	28	76	8	1	1	28	22	24	.262	.316	.307	94	-3	-2	31	12			.977	0	C1/O	0.3
1918	StL-N	117	349	33	88	13	4	3	20	39	30	.252	.327	.338	107	2	3	41	14			.978	-1	*C/O1	1.1
1919	NY-N	58	158	18	30	6	0	0	8	20	9	.190	.293	.228	58	-7	-7	11	3			.962	-3	C/1	-0.7
1920	NY-N	11	13	1	3	0	0	0	0	3	1	.231	.375	.231	77	-0	-0	1	0	0	0	1.000	-1	/C	-0.0
1921	NY-N	13	24	3	9	1	0	0	1	0	0	.375	.400	.417	116	1	1	4	0	0	0	.981	0	/1C	0.0
1924	StL-N	120	402	34	119	27	1	3	53	24	22	.296	.337	.391	96	-3	-2	52	1	5	-3	.986	-7	*C	-0.4
1925	StL-N	22	71	9	22	3	0	0	4	6	2	.310	.380	.352	86	-1	-1	9	1	2	-1	.982	4	C	0.3
	Chi-N	70	197	26	52	13	1	3	18	13	15	.264	.316	.386	77	-7	-7	24	2	1	0	.989	1	C/1	-0.4
	Yr	92	268	35	74	16	1	3	22	19	17	.276	.333	.377	80	-8	-8	34	3	3	-1	.987	5	C/1	-0.1
1926	Chi-N	80	253	24	63	13	3	0	23	13	17	.249	.288	.336	67	-12	-12	24	3			**.989**	6	C	-0.1
1927	Chi-N	39	108	15	26	4	1	0	15	10	8	.241	.311	.324	70	-4	-5	11	1			.994	9	C	0.6
1928	Chi-N	49	158	12	43	9	2	1	21	12	7	.272	.324	.373	83	-4	-4	19	2			.983	8	C	0.8
1929	*Chi-N	60	167	15	40	3	0	0	18	18	14	.240	.317	.257	44	-14	-14	14	1			.992	6	C	-0.3
1931	StL-N	15	19	1	2	0	0	0	3	0	3	.105	.105	.105	-42	-4	-4	0	0			1.000	-0	C	-0.4
1932	StL-N	17	14	0	2	0	0	0	3	0	2	.143	.143	.143	-22	-2	-2	0	0			1.000	2	/C	-0.1
Total	17	1042	2829	283	717	123	19	13	263	231	198	.253	.314	.324	81	-73	-71	300	52	10		.980	45	C/1O	2.9

■ **ORLANDO GONZALEZ** Gonzalez, Orlando Eugene b: 11/15/51, Havana, Cuba BL/TL, 6'2", 180 lbs. Deb: 6/07/76

1976	Cle-A	28	68	5	17	2	0	0	4	5	7	.250	.301	.279	72	-2	-2	5	1	2	-1	.992	-2	1/OD	-0.7
1978	*Phi-N	26	26	1	5	0	0	0	0	1	1	.192	.222	.192	17	-3	-3	1	0	0	0	1.000	1	O/1	-0.2
1980	Oak-A	25	70	10	17	0	0	0	1	9	8	.243	.329	.243	64	-4	-3	6	0	2	-1	.990	1	1/OD	-0.4
Total	3	79	164	16	39	2	0	0	5	15	16	.238	.302	.250	59	-9	-8	12	1	4	-2	.991	-0	/1OD	-1.3

■ **PEDRO GONZALEZ** Gonzalez, Pedro (Olivares) b: 12/12/37, San Pedro De Macoris, D.R. BR/TR, 6', 176 lbs. Deb: 4/11/63

1963	NY-A	14	26	3	5	1	0	0	1	0	5	.192	.192	.231	18	-3	-3	1	0	1	-1	.963	-1	/2	-0.4
1964	*NY-A	80	112	18	31	8	1	0	5	7	22	.277	.331	.366	92	-1	-1	13	3	4	-2	.992	1	1O/32	-0.2
1965	NY-A	7	5	0	2	1	0	0	0	0	2	.400	.400	.600	181	0	0	1	0	0	0	.000	0	H	0.1
	Cle-A	116	400	38	101	14	3	5	39	18	57	.253	.290	.340	78	-12	-12	38	7	4	-0	.980	8	*2/O3	0.5
	Yr	123	405	38	103	15	3	5	39	18	59	.254	.291	.343	79	-11	-12	39	7	4	-0	.980	8	*2/O3	0.6
1966	Cle-A	110	352	21	82	9	2	5	17	15	54	.233	.268	.287	60	-18	-18	27	8	5	-1	.984	11	*2/3O	-0.1
1967	Cle-A	80	189	19	43	6	0	1	8	12	36	.228	.277	.275	63	-8	-9	13	4	6	-2	.971	-5	2/13S	-1.4
Total	5	407	1084	99	264	39	6	8	70	52	176	.244	.283	.313	70	-42	-43	93	22	20	-5	.980	14	2/103S	-1.5

■ **CHARLIE GOOCH** Gooch, Charles Furman b: 6/5/02, Smyrna, Tenn. d: 5/30/82, Lanham, Md. BR/TR, 5'9", 170 lbs. Deb: 4/18/29

| 1929 | Was-A | 39 | 57 | 6 | 16 | 2 | 1 | 0 | 5 | 7 | 8 | .281 | .359 | .351 | 83 | -1 | -1 | 7 | 0 | 1 | -1 | .970 | -2 | /13S | -0.3 |

■ **JOHNNY GOOCH** Gooch, John Beverley b: 11/9/1897, Smyrna, Tenn. d: 5/15/75, Nashville, Tenn. BB/TR, 5'11", 175 lbs. Deb: 9/09/21 C

1921	Pit-N	13	38	2	9	0	0	0	3	3	3	.237	.293	.237	41	-3	-3	3	1	0	-0	.985	3	C	0.0
1922	Pit-N	105	353	45	116	15	3	1	42	39	15	.329	.403	.397	106	6	5	59	1	1	-0	.970	-2	*C	0.8
1923	Pit-N	66	202	16	56	10	2	1	20	17	13	.277	.336	.361	82	-4	-5	25	2	1	0	.975	5	C	0.2
1924	Pit-N	70	224	26	65	6	5	0	25	16	12	.290	.343	.362	88	-3	-4	27	1	3	-2	.988	-6	C	-0.7
1925	*Pit-N	79	215	24	64	8	4	0	30	20	16	.298	.357	.372	81	-4	-6	30	0			.968	-5	C	-0.7
1926	Pit-N	86	218	19	59	15	1	0	42	20	14	.271	.340	.362	85	-3	-5	27	1			.980	-5	C	-0.5
1927	*Pit-N	101	291	22	75	17	2	2	48	19	21	.258	.305	.351	70	-11	-13	31	0			.974	-5	C	-0.5
1928	Pit-N	31	80	7	19	2	1	0	5	3	6	.237	.265	.287	43	-7	-7	6	0			.957	4	C	-0.1
	Bro-N	42	101	9	32	1	2	0	12	7	9	.317	.361	.366	92	-1	-1	13	0			.969	-2	C	-0.1
	Yr	73	181	16	51	3	3	0	17	10	15	.282	.319	.331	70	-8	-8	19	0			.964	2	C	-0.1
1929	Bro-N	1	1	0	0	0	0	0	0	0	0	.000	.000	.000	-99	-0	-0	0	0			.000	0	H	0.0
	Cin-N	92	287	22	86	13	5	0	34	24	10	.300	.356	.380	86	-8	-6	38	4			.975	5	C	0.6
	Yr	93	288	22	86	13	5	0	34	24	10	.299	.355	.378	86	-8	-6	38	4			.975	5	C	0.6
1930	Cin-N	82	276	29	67	10	3	2	30	27	15	.243	.315	.322	57	-20	-18	28	0			.955	-5	C	-1.5
1933	Bos-N	37	77	6	14	1	0	0	2	11	7	.182	.284	.221	36	-7	-7	5	0	0	0	.991	4	C	-0.1
Total	11	805	2363	227	662	98	29	7	293	206	141	.280	.342	.355	79	-65	-69	292	11	5		.973	-1	C	-2.5

■ **LEE GOOCH** Gooch, Lee Currin b: 2/23/1890, Oxford, N.C. d: 5/18/66, Raleigh, N.C. BR/TR, 6', 190 lbs. Deb: 8/17/15

1915	Cle-A	2	2	0	1	0	0	0	0	0	0	.500	.500	.500	196	0	0	1	0			.000	0	H	0.0
1917	Phi-A	17	59	4	17	2	0	1	8	4	10	.288	.333	.373	117	1	1	7	0			.893	-2	O	-0.2
Total	2	19	61	4	18	2	0	1	8	4	10	.295	.338	.377	120	1	1	8	0				-2	/O	-0.2

■ **GENE GOOD** Good, Eugene J. b: 12/13/1882, Roxbury, Mass. d: 8/6/47, Boston, Mass. BL/TL, 5'6", 130 lbs. Deb: 4/12/06

| 1906 | Bos-N | 34 | 119 | 4 | 18 | 0 | 0 | 0 | 0 | 13 | | .151 | .246 | .151 | 25 | -10 | -10 | 5 | 2 | | | .873 | -2 | O | -1.5 |

■ **WILBUR GOOD** Good, Wilbur David "Lefty" b: 9/28/1885, Punxsutawney, Pa. d: 12/30/63, Brooksville, Fla. BL/TL, 5'6", 165 lbs. Deb: 8/18/05

1905	NY-A	5	8	2	3	0	0	0	0	0		.375	.375	.375	124	0	0	1	0			.889	0	/P	0.0
1908	Cle-A	46	154	23	43	1	3	1	14	13		.279	.351	.344	126	5	5	21	7			.845	-8	O	-0.6
1909	Cle-A	94	318	33	68	6	5	0	17	28		.214	.296	.264	74	-7	-9	28	13			.953	2	O	-1.2
1910	Bos-N	23	86	15	29	5	4	0	11	6	13	.337	.394	.488	150	6	6	18	5			.969	5	O	0.9

YEAR	TM/L	G	AB	R	H	2B	3B	HR	RBI	BB	SO	AVG	OBP	SLG	PRO+	BR	/A	RC	SB	CS	SBR	FA	FR	POS	TPR
1911	Bos-N	43	165	21	44	9	3	0	15	12	22	.267	.316	.358	82	-3	-5	19	3			.945	8	O	0.1
	Chi-N	58	145	27	39	5	4	2	21	11	17	.269	.329	.400	103	0	0	22	10			.928	-5	O	-0.7
	Yr	101	310	48	83	14	7	2	36	23	39	.268	.322	.377	92	-3	-4	41	13			.938	3	O	-0.6
1912	Chi-N	39	35	7	5	0	0	0	1	3	7	.143	.211	.143	-2	-5	-5	2	3			1.000	-3	O	-0.8
1913	Chi-N	49	91	11	23	3	2	1	12	11	16	.253	.340	.363	100	0	0	12	5			.974	-3	O	-0.4
1914	Chi-N	154	580	70	158	24	7	2	43	53	74	.272	.341	.348	105	4	4	77	31			.930	-1	*O	-0.4
1915	Chi-N	128	498	66	126	18	9	2	27	34	65	.253	.307	.337	95	-3	-4	52	19	17	-5	.936	-2	*O	-1.8
1916	Phi-N	75	136	25	34	4	3	1	15	8	13	.250	.306	.346	96	-0	-1	17	7			.983	-5	O	-0.8
1918	Chi-A	35	148	24	37	9	4	0	11	11	16	.250	.315	.365	104	0	0	16	1			.982	4	O	0.3
Total	11	749	2364	324	609	84	44	9	187	190	243	.258	.322	.342	98	-3	-8	286	104	17		.942	-8	O/P	-5.4

■ BILL GOODENOUGH

Goodenough, William B. b: 1863, St.Louis, Mo. d: 5/24/05, St.Louis, Mo. 6'1", 170 lbs. Deb: 8/31/1893

YEAR	TM/L	G	AB	R	H	2B	3B	HR	RBI	BB	SO	AVG	OBP	SLG	PRO+	BR	/A	RC	SB	CS	SBR	FA	FR	POS	TPR
1893	StL-N	10	31	4	5	1	0	0	2	3	4	.161	.297	.194	33	-3	-3	2	2			.880	-1	O	-0.4

■ MIKE GOODFELLOW

Goodfellow, Michael J. b: 10/3/1866, Port Jervis, N.Y. d: 2/12/20, Newark, N.J. BR/TR, 6', 180 lbs. Deb: 6/13/1887

YEAR	TM/L	G	AB	R	H	2B	3B	HR	RBI	BB	SO	AVG	OBP	SLG	PRO+	BR	/A	RC	SB	CS	SBR	FA	FR	POS	TPR
1887	StL-a	1	4	0	0	0	0	0		0		.000	.000	.000	-90	-1	-1	0	0			.800	-0	/C	-0.1
1888	Cle-a	68	269	24	66	7	0	0	29	11		.245	.283	.271	83	-6	-4	23	7			.863	-3	O/C1S	-0.8
Total	2	69	273	24	66	7	0	0	29	11		.242	.279	.267	80	-7	-6	23	7			.909	-3	/OC1S	-0.9

■ IVAL GOODMAN

Goodman, Ival Richard "Goodie" b: 7/23/08, Northview, Mo. d: 11/25/84, Cincinnati, Ohio BL/TR, 5'11", 170 lbs. Deb: 4/16/35

YEAR	TM/L	G	AB	R	H	2B	3B	HR	RBI	BB	SO	AVG	OBP	SLG	PRO+	BR	/A	RC	SB	CS	SBR	FA	FR	POS	TPR
1935	Cin-N	148	592	86	159	23	**18**	12	72	35	50	.269	.314	.429	101	-4	-1	83	14			.960	8	*O	0.1
1936	Cin-N	136	489	81	139	15	**14**	17	71	38	53	.284	.347	.476	128	12	16	82	6			.972	3	*O	1.4
1937	Cin-N	147	549	86	150	25	12	12	55	55	58	.273	.347	.428	115	7	11	85	10			.974	6	*O	1.1
1938	Cin-N★	145	568	103	166	27	10	30	92	53	51	.292	.368	.533	149	33	35	116	3			.988	5	*O	3.6
1939	*Cin-N★	124	470	85	152	37	16	7	84	54	32	.323	.401	.515	144	30	30	101	2			.981	7	*O	3.1
1940	*Cin-N	136	519	78	134	20	6	12	63	60	54	.258	.335	.389	98	-0	-1	72	9			.970	-5	*O	-1.4
1941	Cin-N	42	149	14	40	5	2	1	12	16	15	.268	.343	.349	95	-1	-1	18	1			.966	1	O	-0.3
1942	Cin-N	87	226	21	55	18	1	0	15	24	32	.243	.319	.332	91	-3	-3	24	0			.991	1	O	-0.5
1943	Chi-N	80	225	31	72	10	5	3	45	24	20	.320	.390	.449	144	12	13	40	4			.968	-7	O	0.3
1944	Chi-N	62	141	24	37	8	1	1	16	23	15	.262	.377	.355	107	2	2	20	0			1.000	-6	O	-0.5
Total	10	1107	3928	609	1104	188	85	95	525	382	380	.281	.352	.445	120	90	101	641	49			.975	12	O	6.9

■ JAKE GOODMAN

Goodman, Jacob b: 9/14/1853, Lancaster, Pa. d: 3/9/1890, Reading, Pa. Deb: 5/02/1878

YEAR	TM/L	G	AB	R	H	2B	3B	HR	RBI	BB	SO	AVG	OBP	SLG	PRO+	BR	/A	RC	SB	CS	SBR	FA	FR	POS	TPR
1878	Mil-N	60	252	28	62	4	3	1	27	7	33	.246	.266	.298	80	-4	-6	20				.944	-4	*1	-1.2
1882	Pit-a	10	41	5	13	2	2	0		2		.317	.349	.463	180	3	3	7				.962	1	1	0.3
Total	2	70	293	33	75	6	5	1	27	9	33	.256	.278	.321	92	-1	-3	27				.946	-3	/1	-0.9

■ BILLY GOODMAN

Goodman, William Dale b: 3/22/26, Concord, N.C. d: 10/1/84, Sarasota, Fla. BL/TR, 5'11", 165 lbs. Deb: 4/19/47 C

YEAR	TM/L	G	AB	R	H	2B	3B	HR	RBI	BB	SO	AVG	OBP	SLG	PRO+	BR	/A	RC	SB	CS	SBR	FA	FR	POS	TPR
1947	Bos-A	12	11	1	2	0	0	0	1	1	2	.182	.250	.182	20	-1	-1	1	0	0	0	1.000	0	/O	-0.1
1948	Bos-A	127	445	65	138	27	2	1	66	74	44	.310	.414	.387	108	12	9	75	5	3	-0	.993	-4	*1/23	0.5
1949	Bos-A★	122	443	54	132	23	3	0	56	58	21	.298	.382	.363	91	0	-4	65	2	0	1	**.992**	-1	*1	-0.6
1950	Bos-A	110	424	91	150	25	3	4	68	52	25	**.354**	.427	.455	115	18	12	86	2	4	-2	.991	-2	O31/2S	0.5
1951	Bos-A	141	546	92	162	34	4	0	50	79	37	.297	.388	.374	97	8	1	85	7	4	-0	.995	-2	12O/3	-0.4
1952	Bos-A	138	513	79	157	27	3	4	56	48	23	.306	.370	.394	104	9	4	80	8	2	1	.975	**20**	*21/3O	3.1
1953	Bos-A★	128	514	73	161	33	5	2	41	57	11	.313	.384	.409	108	11	8	87	1	4	-2	.974	-11	*21	0.0
1954	Bos-A	127	489	71	148	25	4	1	36	51	15	.303	.371	.376	95	4	-2	70	3	3	-1	.979	1	21O3	0.0
1955	Bos-A	149	599	100	176	31	2	0	52	99	44	.294	.397	.352	94	7	-0	90	5	5	-2	.969	-18	*2/1O	-0.9
1956	Bos-A	105	399	61	117	22	8	2	38	40	22	.293	.358	.404	90	0	-6	59	0	3	-2	.966	-11	2	-1.0
1957	Bos-A	18	16	1	1	1	0	0	0	2	1	.063	.167	.125	-18	-3	-3	0	0	0	0	.000	0	H	-0.3
	Bal-A	73	263	36	81	10	3	3	33	21	18	.308	.366	.403	117	4	6	36	0	2	-1	.961	-10	3/O12S	-0.4
	Yr	91	279	37	82	11	3	3	33	23	19	.294	.354	.387	106	1	3	36	0	2	-1	.961	-10	3/O12S	-0.7
1958	Chi-A	116	425	41	127	15	5	0	40	37	21	.299	.358	.358	100	-0	1	55	1	0	1	.954	-18	*3/12S	-1.7
1959	*Chi-A	104	268	21	67	14	1	1	28	19	20	.250	.304	.321	73	-10	-10	27	3	0	1	.950	-2	3/2	-1.1
1960	Chi-A	30	77	5	18	4	0	0	6	12	8	.234	.337	.286	71	-3	-3	8	0	0	0	.982	3	3/2	0.1
1961	Chi-A	41	51	4	13	4	0	1	10	7	6	.255	.345	.392	98	-0	-0	7	0	0	0	.944	-0	/312	0.0
1962	Hou-N	82	161	12	41	4	1	0	10	12	11	.255	.306	.292	66	-8	-7	14	0	0	0	.972	-9	23/1	-1.4
Total	16	1623	5644	807	1691	299	44	19	591	669	329	.300	.377	.378	98	49	4	844	37	30	-7	.972	-63	213O/S	-3.7

■ ED GOODSON

Goodson, James Edward b: 1/25/48, Pulaski, Va. BL/TR, 6'3", 185 lbs. Deb: 9/05/70

YEAR	TM/L	G	AB	R	H	2B	3B	HR	RBI	BB	SO	AVG	OBP	SLG	PRO+	BR	/A	RC	SB	CS	SBR	FA	FR	POS	TPR
1970	SF-N	7	11	1	3	0	0	0	0	0	2	.273	.273	.273	47	-1	-1	1	0	0	0	.941	0	/1	-0.1
1971	SF-N	20	42	4	8	1	0	0	1	2	4	.190	.227	.214	26	-4	-4	2	0	0	0	1.000	1	1	-0.5
1972	SF-N	58	150	15	42	1	1	6	30	8	12	.280	.321	.420	107	1	1	18	0	0	0	.991	2	1	0.0
1973	SF-N	102	384	37	116	20	1	12	53	15	44	.302	.332	.453	111	6	5	54	0	1	-1	.911	-14	3	-1.1
1974	SF-N	98	298	25	81	15	0	6	48	18	22	.272	.320	.383	91	-2	-4	35	1	0	0	.997	-4	1/3	-1.2
1975	SF-N	39	121	10	25	7	0	1	8	7	14	.207	.250	.289	47	-9	-9	8	0	1	-1	.993	2	13	-0.9
	Atl-N	47	76	5	16	2	0	1	8	2	8	.211	.231	.276	39	-6	-7	4	0	0	0	.990	0	1/3	-0.8
	Yr	86	197	15	41	9	0	2	16	9	22	.208	.243	.284	44	-15	-16	11	0	1	-1	.992	2	13	-1.7
1976	LA-N	83	118	8	27	4	0	3	17	8	19	.229	.278	.339	76	-4	-4	9	0	0	0	.833	-4	3/1O2	-0.9
1977	*LA-N	61	66	3	11	1	0	1	5	3	10	.167	.203	.227	15	-8	-8	2	0	1	-1	1.000	1	1/3	-0.8
Total	8	515	1266	108	329	51	2	30	170	63	135	.260	.298	.374	84	-27	-31	133	1	3	-2	.994	-16	13/O2	-6.3

■ PEP GOODWIN

Goodwin, Claire Vernon b: 12/19/1891, Pocatello, Idaho d: 2/15/72, Oakland, Cal. BL/TR, 5'10.5", 160 lbs. Deb: 4/16/14

YEAR	TM/L	G	AB	R	H	2B	3B	HR	RBI	BB	SO	AVG	OBP	SLG	PRO+	BR	/A	RC	SB	CS	SBR	FA	FR	POS	TPR
1914	KC-F	112	374	38	88	15	6	1	32	27	23	.235	.290	.316	75	-14	-12	37	4			.907	-13	S3/1	-1.9
1915	KC-F	81	229	22	54	5	1	0	16	15	23	.236	.291	.266	67	-10	-9	22	6			.906	-8	S2	-1.5
Total	2	193	603	60	142	20	7	1	48	42	46	.235	.291	.297	72	-24	-21	59	10			.907	-21	S/321	-3.4

■ DANNY GOODWIN

Goodwin, Danny Kay b: 9/2/53, St.Louis, Mo. BL/TR, 6'1", 195 lbs. Deb: 9/03/75

YEAR	TM/L	G	AB	R	H	2B	3B	HR	RBI	BB	SO	AVG	OBP	SLG	PRO+	BR	/A	RC	SB	CS	SBR	FA	FR	POS	TPR
1975	Cal-A	4	10	0	1	0	0	0	0	0	5	.100	.100	.100	-47	-2	-2	-0	0	0	0	.000	0	/D	-0.2
1977	Cal-A	35	91	5	19	6	1	1	8	5	19	.209	.250	.330	59	-6	-5	7	0	0	0	.000	0	D	-0.5
1978	Cal-A	24	58	9	16	5	0	2	10	10	13	.276	.382	.466	143	3	3	11	0	0	0	.000	0	D	0.3
1979	Min-A	58	159	22	46	8	5	5	27	11	23	.289	.335	.497	117	4	3	25	0	0	0	1.000	-0	D/1	0.3
1980	Min-A	55	115	12	23	5	0	1	11	17	32	.200	.303	.270	54	-6	-7	10	0	0	0	1.000	0	D1	-0.8
1981	Min-A	59	151	18	34	6	1	2	17	16	32	.225	.299	.318	73	-4	-5	15	3	1	0	.992	-2	1/OD	-1.0
1982	Oak-A	17	52	6	11	2	1	2	8	2	13	.212	.241	.404	77	-2	-2	4	0	0	0	.000	0	D	-0.2
Total	7	252	636	72	150	32	8	13	81	61	137	.236	.303	.373	84	-13	-15	72	3	1	0	.994	-2	D/1O	-2.1

■ TOM GOODWIN

Goodwin, Thomas Jones b: 7/27/68, Fresno, Cal. BL/TR, 6'1", 165 lbs. Deb: 9/01/91

YEAR	TM/L	G	AB	R	H	2B	3B	HR	RBI	BB	SO	AVG	OBP	SLG	PRO+	BR	/A	RC	SB	CS	SBR	FA	FR	POS	TPR
1991	LA-N	16	7	3	1	0	0	0	0	0	0	.143	.143	.143	-20	-1	-1	0	1	1	-0	1.000	-1	/O	-0.2
1992	LA-N	57	73	15	17	1	1	0	3	6	10	.233	.291	.274	62	-4	-4	6	7	3	0	1.000	-9	O	-1.4
Total	2	73	80	18	18	1	1	0	3	6	10	.225	.279	.262	55	-5	-5	6	8	4	0	1.000	-10	/O	-1.6

■ RAY GOOLSBY

Goolsby, Raymond Daniel "Ox" b: 9/5/19, Florala, Ala. BR/TR, 6'1", 185 lbs. Deb: 4/18/46

YEAR	TM/L	G	AB	R	H	2B	3B	HR	RBI	BB	SO	AVG	OBP	SLG	PRO+	BR	/A	RC	SB	CS	SBR	FA	FR	POS	TPR
1946	Was-A	3	4	0	0	0	0	0	0	1	1	.000	.200	.000	-43	-1	-1	0	0	0	0	1.000	-0	/O	-0.1

■ GREG GOOSSEN
Goossen, Gregory Bryant b: 12/14/45, Los Angeles, Cal. BR/TR, 6'1.5", 210 lbs. Deb: 9/03/65

YEAR	TM/L	G	AB	R	H	2B	3B	HR	RBI	BB	SO	AVG	OBP	SLG	PRO+	BR	/A	RC	SB	CS	SBR	FA	FR	POS	TPR
1965	NY-N	11	31	2	9	0	0	1	2	1	5	.290	.313	.387	99	-0	-0	4	0	0	0	.979	-1	/C	-0.1
1966	NY-N	13	32	1	6	2	0	1	5	1	11	.188	.235	.344	60	-2	-2	2	0	0	0	1.000	-4	C	-0.6
1967	NY-N	37	69	2	11	1	0	0	3	4	26	.159	.216	.174	13	-8	-8	3	0	0	0	.973	-1	C	-0.8
1968	NY-N	38	106	4	22	7	0	0	6	10	21	.208	.288	.274	69	-4	-4	8	0	0	0	.992	4	1/C	-0.2
1969	Sea-A	52	139	19	43	8	1	10	24	14	29	.309	.385	.597	174	13	13	30	1	1	-0	.993	2	1/O	1.2
1970	Mil-A	21	47	3	12	3	0	1	3	10	12	.255	.407	.383	118	2	2	8	0	0	0	.990	-1	1	-0.1
	Was-A	21	36	2	8	3	0	0	1	2	8	.222	.263	.306	59	-2	-2	3	0	0	0	1.000	-0	/O1	-0.3
	Yr	42	83	5	20	6	0	1	4	12	20	.241	.351	.349	96	-0	-0	11	0	0	0	.992	-2	1/O	-0.4
Total	6	193	460	33	111	24	1	13	44	42	112	.241	.317	.383	99	-1	-1	58	1	1	-0	.992	-2	/1CO	-0.9

■ GLEN GORBOUS
Gorbous, Glen Edward b: 7/8/30, Drumheller, Alberta, Canada d: 6/12/90, Calgary, Alberta, Canada BL/TR, 6'2", 175 lbs. Deb: 4/11/55

YEAR	TM/L	G	AB	R	H	2B	3B	HR	RBI	BB	SO	AVG	OBP	SLG	PRO+	BR	/A	RC	SB	CS	SBR	FA	FR	POS	TPR
1955	Cin-N	8	18	2	6	3	0	0	4	3	1	.333	.429	.500	137	1	1	4	0	0	0	.857	-0	/O	0.1
	Phi-N	91	224	25	53	9	1	4	23	21	17	.237	.302	.339	71	-10	-9	22	0	3	-2	.984	6	O	-0.7
	Yr	99	242	27	59	12	1	4	27	24	18	.244	.312	.351	77	-8	-8	25	0	3	-2	.971	6	O	-0.6
1956	Phi-N	15	33	1	6	0	0	0	1	0	1	.182	.182	.182	-2	-5	-5	1	0	0	0	1.000	-2	/O	-0.7
1957	Phi-N	3	2	1	1	1	0	0	1	1	0	.500	.667	1.000	351	1	1	2	0	0	0	.000	0	H	0.1
Total	3	117	277	29	66	13	1	4	29	25	19	.238	.301	.336	70	-12	-12	28	0	3	-2	.973	4	/O	-1.2

■ JOE GORDON
Gordon, Joseph Lowell "Flash" b: 2/18/15, Los Angeles, Cal. d: 4/14/78, Sacramento, Cal. BR/TR, 5'10", 180 lbs. Deb: 4/18/38 MC

YEAR	TM/L	G	AB	R	H	2B	3B	HR	RBI	BB	SO	AVG	OBP	SLG	PRO+	BR	/A	RC	SB	CS	SBR	FA	FR	POS	TPR
1938	*NY-A	127	458	83	117	24	7	25	97	56	72	.255	.340	.502	109	3	3	81	11	3	2	.960	**24**	*2	3.2
1939	*NY-A★	151	567	92	161	32	5	28	111	75	57	.284	.370	.506	124	17	18	103	11	10	-3	.967	6	*2	2.7
1940	NY-A★	155	616	112	173	32	10	30	103	52	57	.281	.340	.511	122	13	16	107	18	8	1	.975	14	*2	3.8
1941	*NY-A★	156	588	104	162	26	7	24	87	72	80	.276	.358	.466	118	13	14	98	10	9	-2	.958	6	*21	2.4
1942	*NY-A★	147	538	88	173	29	4	18	103	79	95	.322	.409	.491	156	39	40	108	12	6	0	.966	4	*2	5.3
1943	*NY-A☆	152	543	82	135	28	5	17	69	98	75	.249	.365	.413	126	21	20	84	4	7	-3	.969	26	*2	5.5
1946	NY-A★	112	376	35	79	15	0	11	47	49	72	.210	.308	.338	79	-10	-11	38	2	5	-2	.974	22	*2	1.6
1947	Cle-A★	155	562	89	153	27	6	29	93	62	49	.272	.346	.496	136	21	23	96	7	3	0	.978	-4	*2	3.1
1948	*Cle-A★	144	550	96	154	21	4	32	124	77	68	.280	.371	.507	136	23	25	106	5	2	0	.971	-7	*2/S	2.6
1949	Cle-A★	148	541	74	136	18	3	20	84	83	33	.251	.355	.407	103	0	2	79	5	6	-2	.980	-18	*2	-1.1
1950	Cle-A	119	368	59	87	12	1	19	57	56	44	.236	.340	.429	99	-3	-2	56	4	1	1	.969	-18	*2	-1.4
Total	11	1566	5707	914	1530	264	52	253	975	759	702	.268	.357	.466	121	137	150	959	89	60	-9	.970	54	*2/1S	27.7

■ MIKE GORDON
Gordon, Michael William b: 9/11/53, Leominster, Mass. BB/TR, 6'3", 215 lbs. Deb: 4/07/77

YEAR	TM/L	G	AB	R	H	2B	3B	HR	RBI	BB	SO	AVG	OBP	SLG	PRO+	BR	/A	RC	SB	CS	SBR	FA	FR	POS	TPR
1977	Chi-N	8	23	0	1	0	0	0	2	2	8	.043	.120	.043	-49	-5	-5	0	0	0	0	.970	-3	/C	-0.9
1978	Chi-N	4	5	0	1	0	0	0	0	3	2	.200	.556	.200	106	1	1	1	0	0	0	1.000	-0	/C	0.0
Total	2	12	28	0	2	0	0	0	2	5	10	.071	.235	.071	-11	-4	-5	1	0	0	0	.979	-3	/C	-0.9

■ SID GORDON
Gordon, Sidney b: 8/13/17, Brooklyn, N.Y. d: 6/17/75, New York, N.Y. BR/TR, 5'10", 185 lbs. Deb: 9/11/41

YEAR	TM/L	G	AB	R	H	2B	3B	HR	RBI	BB	SO	AVG	OBP	SLG	PRO+	BR	/A	RC	SB	CS	SBR	FA	FR	POS	TPR
1941	NY-N	9	31	4	8	1	1	0	4	6	1	.258	.378	.355	105	1	0	5	0			1.000	-1	/O	-0.1
1942	NY-N	6	19	4	6	0	1	0	2	3	2	.316	.409	.421	142	1	1	3	0			.913	1	/3	0.3
1943	NY-N	131	474	50	119	9	11	9	63	43	32	.251	.315	.373	98	-2	-2	50	2			.941	3	31O/2	-0.2
1946	NY-N	135	450	64	132	15	4	5	45	60	27	.293	.380	.378	115	11	11	66	1			.995	1	*O3	0.8
1947	NY-N	130	437	57	119	19	8	13	57	50	21	.272	.347	.442	107	4	4	67	2			.971	1	*O/3	-0.2
1948	NY-N☆	142	521	100	156	26	4	30	107	74	39	.299	.390	.537	148	35	35	108	8			**.948**	-5	*3O	2.7
1949	NY-N★	141	489	87	139	26	2	26	90	95	37	.284	.404	.505	142	32	32	99	1			.958	-23	*3O/1	0.6
1950	Bos-N	134	481	78	146	33	4	27	103	78	31	.304	.403	.557	160	35	40	109	2			.990	6	*O3	3.8
1951	Bos-N	150	550	96	158	28	1	29	109	80	32	.287	.383	.500	146	28	33	103	2	0	1	.984	-4	*O3	2.5
1952	Bos-N	144	522	69	151	22	2	25	75	77	49	.289	.384	.483	144	28	31	101	0	4	-2	**.996**	2	*O/3	2.5
1953	Mil-N	140	464	67	127	22	4	19	75	71	40	.274	.372	.461	123	12	16	82	1	1	-0	.977	-1	*O	0.9
1954	Pit-N	131	363	38	111	12	0	12	49	67	24	.306	.414	.438	124	15	15	70	0	0	0	.977	-6	O3	0.5
1955	Pit-N	16	47	2	8	1	0	0	1	2	6	.170	.204	.191	6	-6	-6	1	0	0	0	1.000	2	/3O	-0.5
	NY-N	66	144	19	35	6	1	7	25	25	15	.243	.355	.444	110	2	2	25	0	0	0	1.000	6	3O	0.7
	Yr	82	191	21	43	7	1	7	26	27	21	.225	.321	.382	86	-4	-4	25	0	0	0	1.000	7	3O	0.2
Total	13	1475	4992	735	1415	220	43	202	805	731	356	.283	.377	.466	130	196	211	889	19	5		.985	-19	O3/12	14.3

■ GEORGE GORE
Gore, George F. "Piano Legs" b: 5/3/1857, Saccarappa, Me. d: 9/16/33, Utica, N.Y. BL/TR, 5'11", 195 lbs. Deb: 5/01/1879 M

YEAR	TM/L	G	AB	R	H	2B	3B	HR	RBI	BB	SO	AVG	OBP	SLG	PRO+	BR	/A	RC	SB	CS	SBR	FA	FR	POS	TPR
1879	Chi-N	63	266	43	70	17	4	0	32	8	30	.263	.285	.357	104	3	1	28				.872	-2	O/1	-0.4
1880	Chi-N	77	322	70	116	23	2	2	47	21	10	**.360**	**.399**	**.463**	**180**	**30**	**28**	**61**				.879	6	*O/1	3.0
1881	Chi-N	73	309	**86**	92	18	9	1	44	27	23	.298	.354	.424	137	16	14	48				.874	2	*O/31	1.3
1882	Chi-N	84	367	**99**	117	15	7	3	51	**29**	19	.319	.369	.422	146	22	20	59				.842	6	*O	2.2
1883	Chi-N	92	392	105	131	30	9	2	52	27	13	.334	.377	.472	148	26	23	72				.867	11	*O	2.8
1884	Chi-N	103	422	104	134	18	4	5	34	**61**	26	.318	.404	.415	146	31	25	72				.868	2	*O	2.3
1885	*Chi-N	109	441	115	138	21	13	5	57	68	25	.313	.405	.454	154	41	30	83				.884	-3	*O	2.3
1886	*Chi-N	118	444	150	135	20	12	6	63	**102**	30	.304	.434	.444	145	43	31	98	23			.876	-3	*O	2.2
1887	NY-N	111	459	95	133	16	5	1	49	42	18	.290	.358	.353	105	2	6	74	39			.889	1	*O	0.4
1888	*NY-N	64	254	37	56	4	4	2	17	30	31	.220	.308	.291	95	-1	-0	27	11			.836	-9	O	-1.1
1889	*NY-N	120	488	132	149	21	7	7	54	84	28	.305	.416	.420	135	27	27	99	28			.864	-8	*O	1.4
1890	NY-P	93	399	132	127	26	8	10	55	77	23	.318	.432	.499	138	31	24	101	28			.877	-12	O	0.7
1891	NY-N	130	528	103	150	22	7	2	48	74	34	.284	.379	.364	124	16	19	82	19			.909	-6	*O	0.8
1892	NY-N	53	193	47	49	11	2	0	11	49	16	.254	.412	.332	130	10	11	35	20			.932	1	O	0.9
	StL-N	20	73	9	15	0	1	0	4	18	6	.205	.363	.233	87	-0	0	7	2			.844	-2	OM	-0.2
	Yr	73	266	56	64	11	3	0	15	67	22	.241	.399	.305	119	10	11	42	22			.908	-0	O	0.7
Total	14	1310	5357	1327	1612	262	94	46	618	717	332	.301	.386	.411	136	297	258	945	170			.876	-15	*O/13	18.6

■ BOB GORINSKI
Gorinski, Robert John b: 1/7/52, Latrobe, Pa. BR/TR, 6'3", 215 lbs. Deb: 4/10/77

YEAR	TM/L	G	AB	R	H	2B	3B	HR	RBI	BB	SO	AVG	OBP	SLG	PRO+	BR	/A	RC	SB	CS	SBR	FA	FR	POS	TPR
1977	Min-A	54	118	14	23	4	1	3	22	5	29	.195	.228	.322	49	-9	-9	9	1	0	0	.936	-7	O/D	-1.6

■ HERB GORMAN
Gorman, Herbert Allen b: 12/18/24, San Francisco, Cal d: 4/5/53, San Diego, Cal. BL/TL, 5'11", 180 lbs. Deb: 4/19/52

YEAR	TM/L	G	AB	R	H	2B	3B	HR	RBI	BB	SO	AVG	OBP	SLG	PRO+	BR	/A	RC	SB	CS	SBR	FA	FR	POS	TPR
1952	StL-N	1	1	0	0	0	0	0	0	0	0	.000	.000	.000	-99	-0	-0	0	0	0	0	.000	0	H	0.0

■ HOWIE GORMAN
Gorman, Howard Paul "Lefty" b: 5/14/13, Pittsburgh, Pa. d: 4/29/84, Harrisburg, Pa. BL/TL, 6'2", 160 lbs. Deb: 8/07/37

YEAR	TM/L	G	AB	R	H	2B	3B	HR	RBI	BB	SO	AVG	OBP	SLG	PRO+	BR	/A	RC	SB	CS	SBR	FA	FR	POS	TPR
1937	Phi-N	13	19	3	4	1	0	0	1	1	1	.211	.250	.263	37	-2	-2	1	1			.500	-3	/O	-0.5
1938	Phi-N	1	1	0	0	0	0	0	0	0	0	.000	.000	.000	-99	-0	-0	0	0			.000	0	H	0.0
Total	2	14	20	3	4	1	0	0	1	1	1	.200	.238	.250	30	-2	-2	1	1			.980	-3	/O	-0.5

■ JACK GORMAN
Gorman, John F. "Stooping Jack" b: 1859, St.Louis, Mo. d: 9/9/1889, St.Louis, Mo. Deb: 7/01/1883

YEAR	TM/L	G	AB	R	H	2B	3B	HR	RBI	BB	SO	AVG	OBP	SLG	PRO+	BR	/A	RC	SB	CS	SBR	FA	FR	POS	TPR
1883	StL-a	1	4	0	0	0	0	0		0		.000	.000	.000	-95	-1	-1	0				.667	0	/O	0.0
1884	KC-U	33	137	25	38	5	2	0		4		.277	.298	.343	133	2	5	14				.954	-2	1/O3	0.0
	Pit-a	8	27	3	4	0	1	0		1		.148	.179	.222	31	-2	-2	1				.750	-2	/PO3	-0.3
Total	2	42	168	28	42	5	3	0		5		.250	.272	.315	108	-1	2	15				.944	-4	/1O3P	-0.3

■ JOHNNY GORYL
Goryl, John Albert b: 10/21/33, Cumberland, R.I. BR/TR, 5'10", 175 lbs. Deb: 9/20/57 MC

YEAR	TM/L	G	AB	R	H	2B	3B	HR	RBI	BB	SO	AVG	OBP	SLG	PRO+	BR	/A	RC	SB	CS	SBR	FA	FR	POS	TPR
1957	Chi-N	9	38	7	8	2	0	0	1	5	9	.211	.318	.263	59	-2	-2	3	0	1	-1	.952	-1	/3	-0.4
1958	Chi-N	83	219	27	53	9	3	4	14	27	34	.242	.331	.365	85	-5	-4	24	0	1	-1	.931	11	32	0.8

YEAR	TM/L	G	AB	R	H	2B	3B	HR	RBI	BB	SO	AVG	OBP	SLG	PRO+	BR	/A	RC	SB	CS	SBR	FA	FR	POS	TPR
1959	Chi-N	25	48	1	9	3	1	1	6	5	3	.188	.264	.354	63	-3	-3	4	1	1	-0	.973	0	2/3	-0.2
1962	Min-A	37	26	6	5	0	1	2	2	2	6	.192	.250	.500	93	-0	-0	3	0	0	0	.923	8	/2S	0.7
1963	Min-A	64	150	29	43	5	3	9	24	15	29	.287	.355	.540	144	9	9	28	0	0	0	.958	-9	23/S	0.3
1964	Min-A	58	114	9	16	0	2	0	1	10	25	.140	.216	.175	10	-14	-14	5	1	0	0	.975	2	23	-1.0
Total	6	276	595	79	134	19	10	16	48	64	106	.225	.306	.371	83	-15	-14	66	2	3	-1	.960	11	2/3S	0.2

■ JIM GOSGER Gosger, James Charles b: 11/6/42, Port Huron, Mich. BL/TL, 5′11″, 185 lbs. Deb: 5/04/63

1963	Bos-A	19	16	3	1	0	0	0	0	3	5	.063	.211	.063	-19	-3	-3	0	0	0	0	.818	-0	/O	-0.3
1965	Bos-A	81	324	45	83	15	4	9	35	29	61	.256	.321	.410	100	2	0	43	3	1	0	.975	9	O	0.6
1966	Bos-A	40	126	16	32	4	0	5	17	15	20	.254	.333	.405	101	2	0	18	0	1	-1	.985	-1	O	-0.3
	KC-A	88	272	34	61	14	1	5	27	37	53	.224	.322	.338	93	-3	-2	32	5	3	-0	.994	1	O	-0.5
	Yr	128	398	50	93	18	1	10	44	52	73	.234	.325	.359	96	-1	-1	50	5	4	-1	.991	0	*O	-0.8
1967	KC-A	134	356	31	86	14	5	5	36	53	69	.242	.340	.351	108	3	5	44	5	7	-3	.981	-1	*O	-0.4
1968	Oak-A	88	150	7	27	1	1	0	5	17	21	.180	.263	.200	44	-10	-9	8	4	0	1	1.000	-2	O	-1.4
1969	Sea-A	39	55	4	6	2	1	1	1	6	11	.109	.197	.236	21	-6	-6	3	2	1	0	1.000	-3	O	-1.0
	NY-N	10	15	0	2	2	0	0	1	1	6	.133	.188	.267	25	-2	-2	1	0	0	0	1.000	-0	/O	-0.2
1970	Mon-N	91	274	38	72	11	2	5	37	35	35	.263	.348	.372	93	-2	-2	37	5	3	-0	1.000	-1	O1	-0.8
1971	Mon-N	51	102	7	16	2	2	0	8	9	17	.157	.232	.216	27	-10	-10	5	1	1	-0	.952	0	O/1	-1.2
1973	NY-N	38	92	9	22	2	0	0	10	9	16	.239	.307	.261	60	-5	-5	7	0	1	-1	1.000	-2	O	-0.9
1974	NY-N	26	33	3	3	0	0	0	0	3	2	.091	.167	.091	-27	-6	-5	0	0	0	0	1.000	-1	O	-0.7
Total	10	705	1815	197	411	67	16	30	177	217	316	.226	.311	.331	83	-38	-38	199	25	18	-3	.985	-1	O/1	-7.1

■ GOOSE GOSLIN Goslin, Leon Allen b: 10/16/1900, Salem, N.J. d: 5/15/71, Bridgeton, N.J. BL/TR, 5′11.5″, 185 lbs. Deb: 9/16/21 H

1921	Was-A	14	50	8	13	1	1	1	6	6	5	.260	.351	.380	91	-1	-1	7	0	0	0	1.000	0	O	-0.1
1922	Was-A	101	358	44	116	19	7	3	53	25	26	.324	.373	.441	117	6	8	58	4	4	-1	.932	-3	O	-0.3
1923	Was-A	150	600	86	180	29	**18**	9	99	40	53	.300	.347	.453	115	5	10	95	7	2	1	.957	7	*O	0.7
1924	*Was-A	154	579	100	199	30	17	12	**129**	68	29	.344	.421	.516	145	36	38	126	16	14	-4	.960	5	*O	2.8
1925	*Was-A	150	601	116	201	34	**20**	18	113	53	50	.334	.394	.547	140	31	33	131	26	8	**3**	.971	14	*O	3.6
1926	Was-A	147	568	105	201	26	15	17	108	63	38	.354	.425	.542	155	42	44	131	8	8	-2	.964	19	*O	4.8
1927	Was-A	148	581	96	194	37	15	13	120	50	28	.334	.392	.516	136	28	29	111	21	6	3	.955	2	*O	2.2
1928	Was-A	135	456	80	173	36	10	17	102	48	19	**.379**	.442	.614	176	49	49	125	16	3	**3**	.962	3	*O	4.5
1929	Was-A	145	553	82	159	28	7	18	91	66	33	.288	.366	.461	111	9	8	97	10	3	1	.968	-4	*O	-0.4
1930	Was-A	47	188	34	51	11	5	7	38	19	19	.271	.344	.495	110	2	2	32	3	2	-0	.937	-5	O	-0.6
	StL-A	101	396	81	129	25	7	30	100	48	35	.326	.400	.652	156	35	33	101	14	9	-1	.973	12	*O	3.3
	Yr	148	584	115	180	36	12	37	138	67	54	.308	.382	.601	142	37	35	132	17	11	-2	.964	7	*O	2.7
1931	StL-A	151	591	114	194	42	10	24	105	80	41	.328	.412	.555	147	45	42	137	9	6	-1	.960	5	*O	3.2
1932	StL-A	150	572	88	171	28	9	17	104	92	35	.299	.398	.469	117	22	17	110	12	9	-2	.951	8	*O/3	1.3
1933	*Was-A	132	549	97	163	35	10	10	64	42	32	.297	.348	.452	112	7	7	87	5	2	0	.965	8	*O	0.8
1934	*Det-A	151	614	106	187	38	7	13	100	65	38	.305	.373	.453	112	11	10	105	5	4	-1	.953	2	*O	0.5
1935	*Det-A	147	590	88	172	34	6	9	109	56	31	.292	.355	.415	102	-2	1	88	5	4	-1	.965	0	*O	-0.4
1936	Det-A★	147	572	122	180	33	8	24	125	85	50	.315	.403	.526	127	25	25	126	14	4	2	.955	-5	*O	1.4
1937	Det-A	79	181	30	43	11	1	4	35	35	18	.238	.367	.376	86	-3	-3	27	0	1	-1	.954	-2	O/1	-0.7
1938	Was-A	38	57	6	9	3	0	2	8	8	5	.158	.262	.316	47	-5	-5	5	0	0	0	1.000	-1	O	-0.6
Total	18	2287	8656	1483	2735	500	173	248	1609	949	585	.316	.387	.500	128	341	348	1700	175	89	-1	.960	63	*O/13	26.0

■ HOWIE GOSS Goss, Howard Wayne b: 11/1/34, Wewoka, Okla. BR/TR, 6′4″, 204 lbs. Deb: 4/10/62

1962	Pit-N	89	111	19	27	6	0	2	10	9	36	.243	.306	.351	76	-4	-4	12	5	2	0	.985	4	O	-0.1
1963	Hou-N	133	411	37	86	18	2	9	44	31	128	.209	.265	.328	74	-16	-14	36	4	6	-2	.993	2	*O	-2.1
Total	2	222	522	56	113	24	2	11	54	40	164	.216	.274	.333	75	-20	-17	48	9	8	-2	.991	6	O	-2.2

■ DICK GOSSETT Gossett, John Star b: 8/21/1891, Dennison, Ohio d: 10/6/62, Massillon, Ohio BR/TR, 5′11″, 185 lbs. Deb: 4/30/13

1913	NY-A	39	105	9	17	2	0	0	9	10	22	.162	.254	.181	28	-9	-9	5	1			.972	-5	C	-1.2
1914	NY-A	10	21	3	3	0	0	0	1	5	5	.143	.333	.143	44	-1	-1	1	0			.977	-1	C	-0.2
Total	2	49	126	12	20	2	0	0	10	15	27	.159	.269	.175	31	-10	-10	6	1			.973	-6	/C	-1.4

■ JULIO GOTAY Gotay, Julio Enrique (Sanchez) b: 6/9/39, Fajardo, P.R. BR/TR, 6′, 180 lbs. Deb: 8/06/60

1960	StL-N	3	8	1	3	0	0	0	0	0	2	.375	.375	.375	98	0	-0	1	1	0	0	.750	-2	/S3	-0.1
1961	StL-N	10	45	5	11	4	0	0	5	3	5	.244	.292	.333	59	-2	-3	4	0	0	0	.804	-4	S	-0.7
1962	StL-N	127	369	47	94	12	1	2	27	27	47	.255	.316	.309	62	-16	-20	34	7	3	0	.956	6	*S/2O3	-0.5
1963	Pit-N	4	2	0	1	0	0	0	0	0	0	.500	.500	.500	188	0	0	1	0	0	0	.667	1	/2	0.1
1964	Pit-N	3	2	1	1	0	0	0	0	1	0	.500	.667	.500	235	1	1	1	0	0	0	.000	0	H	0.1
1965	Cal-A	40	77	6	19	4	0	1	3	4	9	.247	.284	.338	78	-3	-2	7	0	0	0	.961	3	2/3S	0.2
1966	Hou-N	4	5	0	0	0	0	0	0	0	0	.000	.000	.000	-99	-1	-1	0	0	0	0	1.000	0	/3	-0.1
1967	Hou-N	77	234	30	66	10	2	2	15	15	30	.282	.331	.368	103	-0	1	28	1	1	-0	.971	-4	2S/3	0.1
1968	Hou-N	75	165	9	41	3	0	1	11	4	21	.248	.271	.285	68	-7	-6	11	1	2	-1	.982	10	2/3	0.6
1969	Hou-N	46	81	7	21	5	0	0	9	7	13	.259	.318	.321	81	-2	-2	7	2	1	0	.987	6	2/3	0.5
Total	10	389	988	106	257	38	3	6	70	61	127	.260	.309	.323	75	-30	-34	94	12	7	-1	.944	16	S2/3O	0.2

■ CHARLIE GOULD Gould, Charles Harvey b: 8/21/1847, Cincinnati, Ohio d: 4/10/17, Flushing, N.Y. BR/TR, 6′, 172 lbs. Deb: 5/05/1871 M

1871	Bos-n	31	151	38	43	9	2	2	32	3	1	.285	.299	.411	98	0	-1	21	6					*1/O	0.0
1872	Bos-n	45	214	39	57	7	**8**	0	33	2	3	.266	.273	.374	92	-1	-3	22						*1/O	-0.1
1874	Bal-n	33	142	20	31	6	0	0		3		.218	.234	.261	58	-6	-6	9						1/C	-0.5
1875	NH-n	27	109	9	29	2	1	0		1		.266	.273	.303	113	-0	2	9						1/OM	0.2
1876	Cin-N	61	258	27	65	7	0	0	11	6	11	.252	.269	.279	97	-4	1	20				.939	1	*1/PM	0.1
1877	Cin-N	24	91	5	25	2	1	0	13	5	5	.275	.313	.319	112	0	2	9				.922	-1	1/O	0.1
Total	4 n	136	616	106	160	24	11	2	65	9	4	.260	.270	.344	89	-7	-9	61						1/OC	-0.4
Total	2	85	349	32	90	9	1	0	24	11	16	.258	.281	.289	101	-4	3	29				.934	0	/1PO	0.2

■ NICK GOULISH Goulish, Nicholas Edward b: 11/13/17, Punxsutawney, Pa. d: 5/15/84, Youngstown, Ohio BL/TL, 6′1″, 179 lbs. Deb: 4/19/44

1944	Phi-N	1	1	0	0	0	0	0	0	0	0	.000	.000	.000	-99	-0	-0	0	0			.000	0	H	0.0
1945	Phi-N	13	11	4	3	0	0	0	2	1	3	.273	.333	.273	72	-0	-0	1	0			1.000	-1	/O	-0.1
Total	2	14	12	4	3	0	0	0	2	1	3	.250	.308	.250	58	-1	-1	1	0			.981	-1	/O	-0.1

■ CLAUDE GOUZZIE Gouzzie, Claude b: 1873, France d: 9/21/07, Denver, Colo. BR/TR, 5′9″, 170 lbs. Deb: 7/22/03

1903	StL-A	1	1	0	0	0	0	0	0	0		.000	.000	.000	-99	-0	-0	0	0			1.000	0	/2	0.0

■ HANK GOWDY Gowdy, Henry Morgan b: 8/24/1889, Columbus, Ohio d: 8/1/66, Columbus, Ohio BR/TR, 6′2″, 182 lbs. Deb: 9/13/10 MC

1910	NY-N	7	14	1	3	1	0	0	2	2	3	.214	.313	.286	75	-0	-0	2	1			.943	0	/1	0.0
1911	NY-N	4	4	1	1	1	0	0	0	2	0	.250	.500	.500	175	1	1	1	0			1.000	-0	/1	0.0
	Bos-N	29	97	9	28	4	2	0	16	4	19	.289	.324	.371	87	-1	-2	12	2			.966	-1	1/C	-0.3
	Yr	33	101	10	29	5	2	0	16	6	19	.287	.333	.376	92	-0	-1	13	2			.969	-1	1/C	-0.3
1912	Bos-N	44	96	16	26	6	1	3	10	16	13	.271	.386	.448	126	4	4	18	3			.926	-2	C/1	0.3
1913	Bos-N	3	5	0	3	1	0	0	2	3	2	.600	.750	.800	336	2	2	3	0			1.000	-1	/C	0.1
1914	*Bos-N	128	366	42	89	17	6	3	46	48	40	.243	.337	.347	104	3	3	46	14			.968	-5	*C/1	0.7
1915	Bos-N	118	316	27	78	15	3	2	30	41	34	.247	.339	.332	108	3	4	38	10	4	1	.974	0	*C	1.5

YEAR	TM/L	G	AB	R	H	2B	3B	HR	RBI	BB	SO	AVG	OBP	SLG	PRO+	BR	/A	RC	SB	CS	SBR	FA	FR	POS	TPR
1916	Bos-N	118	349	32	88	14	1	1	34	24	33	.252	.311	.307	94	-4	-2	38	8			.980	3	*C	1.1
1917	Bos-N	49	154	12	33	7	0	0	14	15	13	.214	.288	.260	73	-5	-4	12	2			.969	-1	C	-0.2
1919	Bos-N	78	219	18	61	8	1	1	22	19	16	.279	.339	.338	108	1	2	26	5			.977	5	C/1	1.4
1920	Bos-N	80	214	14	52	11	2	0	18	20	15	.243	.314	.313	84	-5	-4	23	6	1	1	.980	11	C	1.3
1921	Bos-N	64	164	17	49	7	2	2	17	16	11	.299	.368	.402	110	1	3	26	2	0	1	.981	-1	C	0.4
1922	Bos-N	92	221	23	70	11	1	1	27	24	13	.317	.391	.389	107	2	3	35	2	1	0	.971	1	C/1	0.7
1923	Bos-N	23	48	5	6	1	1	0	5	15	5	.125	.354	.188	48	-3	-3	5	1	1	-0	.982	-2	C	-0.4
	*NY-N	53	122	13	40	6	3	1	18	21	9	.328	.427	.451	133	7	7	25	2	0	1	.986	-7	C	0.2
	Yr	76	170	18	46	7	4	1	23	36	14	.271	.404	.376	109	4	4	29	3	1	0	.985	-10	C	-0.2
1924	*NY-N	87	191	25	62	9	1	4	37	26	11	.325	.411	.445	133	9	10	37	1	0	0	.982	5	C	1.9
1925	NY-N	47	114	14	37	4	3	3	19	12	7	.325	.389	.491	128	4	5	22	0	0	0	1.000	2	C	0.8
1929	Bos-N	10	16	1	7	0	0	0	3	0	2	.438	.438	.438	122	0	1	3	0			1.000	-0	/C	0.0
1930	Bos-N	16	25	0	5	1	0	0	2	3	1	.200	.310	.240	37	-3	-2	2	0			.972	1	C	-0.1
Total	17	1050	2735	270	738	124	27	21	322	311	247	.270	.351	.358	105	15	25	372	59	7		.975	5	C/1	9.4

■ **BILLY GRABARKEWITZ** Grabarkewitz, Billy Cordell b: 1/18/46, Lockhart, Tex. BR/TR, 5'10", 170 lbs. Deb: 4/22/69

YEAR	TM/L	G	AB	R	H	2B	3B	HR	RBI	BB	SO	AVG	OBP	SLG	PRO+	BR	/A	RC	SB	CS	SBR	FA	FR	POS	TPR
1969	LA-N	34	65	4	6	1	1	0	5	4	19	.092	.145	.138	-22	-10	-10	1	1	0	0	.954	-2	S/32	-1.1
1970	LA-N★	156	529	92	153	20	8	17	84	95	149	.289	.403	.454	135	25	29	103	19	9	0	.959	-1	3S2	3.2
1971	LA-N	44	71	9	16	5	0	0	6	19	16	.225	.389	.296	102	1	1	9	1	2	-1	1.000	4	23/S	0.6
1972	LA-N	53	144	17	24	4	0	4	16	18	53	.167	.268	.278	57	-8	-8	12	3	0	1	.902	-4	32/S	-1.1
1973	Cal-A	61	129	27	21	6	1	3	9	28	27	.163	.316	.295	79	-4	-3	13	2	2	-1	.965	-6	23/SOD	-0.9
	Phi-N	25	66	12	19	2	0	2	7	12	18	.288	.397	.409	121	3	2	12	3	1	0	.960	0	2/3O	0.4
1974	Phi-N	34	30	7	4	0	0	1	2	5	10	.133	.257	.233	36	-2	-3	2	3	1	0	1.000	1	/O3	-0.2
	Chi-N	53	125	21	31	3	2	1	12	21	28	.248	.361	.328	90	-0	-1	16	1	2	-1	.954	2	2/S3	0.2
	Yr	87	155	28	35	3	2	2	14	26	38	.226	.341	.310	80	-3	-4	18	4	3	-1	.954	3	2/3SO	0.0
1975	Oak-A	6	2	0	0	0	0	0	0	0	1	.000	.000	.000	-99	-1	-1	0	0	0	0	.833	0	/2D	0.0
Total	7	466	1161	189	274	41	12	28	141	202	321	.236	.354	.364	101	3	8	169	33	17	-0	.952	-6	32/SOD	1.1

■ **ROD GRABER** Graber, Rodney Blaine b: 6/20/31, Marshallville, O. BL/TL, 5'11", 175 lbs. Deb: 9/09/58

YEAR	TM/L	G	AB	R	H	2B	3B	HR	RBI	BB	SO	AVG	OBP	SLG	PRO+	BR	/A	RC	SB	CS	SBR	FA	FR	POS	TPR
1958	Cle-A	4	8	0	1	0	0	0	0	1	2	.125	.222	.125	-2	-1	-1	0	0	0	0	1.000	-0	/O	-0.1

■ **JOHNNY GRABOWSKI** Grabowski, John Patrick "Nig b: 1/7/1900, Ware, Mass. d: 5/23/46, Albany, N.Y. BR/TR, 5'10", 185 lbs. Deb: 7/11/24

YEAR	TM/L	G	AB	R	H	2B	3B	HR	RBI	BB	SO	AVG	OBP	SLG	PRO+	BR	/A	RC	SB	CS	SBR	FA	FR	POS	TPR
1924	Chi-A	20	56	10	14	3	0	0	3	2	4	.250	.276	.304	51	-4	-4	5	0	0	0	.972	1	C	-0.2
1925	Chi-A	21	46	5	14	4	1	0	10	2	4	.304	.333	.435	99	-1	-0	6	0	1	-1	.983	0	C	0.0
1926	Chi-A	48	122	6	32	1	1	1	11	4	15	.262	.286	.311	58	-8	-8	11	0	1	-1	.973	-2	C/1	-0.8
1927	*NY-A	70	195	29	54	2	4	0	25	20	15	.277	.350	.328	79	-6	-5	23	0	0	0	.984	0	C	-0.1
1928	NY-A	75	202	21	48	7	1	1	21	10	21	.238	.274	.297	51	-15	-14	17	0	0	0	.987	2	C	-0.7
1929	NY-A	22	59	4	12	1	0	0	2	3	6	.203	.242	.220	21	-7	-6	3	1	0	0	.943	-0	C	-0.5
1931	Det-A	40	136	9	32	7	1	1	14	6	19	.235	.268	.324	53	-9	-10	12	0	0	0	.984	2	C	-0.5
Total	7	296	816	84	206	25	8	3	86	47	84	.252	.295	.314	60	-50	-48	76	1	2	-1	.979	4	C/1	-2.8

■ **JOE GRACE** Grace, Joseph Laverne b: 1/5/14, Gorham, Ill. d: 9/18/69, Murphysboro, Ill. BL/TR, 6'1", 180 lbs. Deb: 9/24/38

YEAR	TM/L	G	AB	R	H	2B	3B	HR	RBI	BB	SO	AVG	OBP	SLG	PRO+	BR	/A	RC	SB	CS	SBR	FA	FR	POS	TPR
1938	StL-A	12	47	7	16	1	0	0	4	2	3	.340	.367	.362	83	-1	-1	6	0	1	-1	.933	-2	O	-0.4
1939	StL-A	74	207	35	63	11	2	3	22	19	24	.304	.363	.420	98	-0	-1	33	3	2	-0	.968	-4	O	-0.6
1940	StL-A	80	229	45	59	14	2	5	25	26	23	.258	.336	.402	88	-3	-4	32	2	2	-1	.958	-5	OC	-1.1
1941	StL-A	115	362	53	112	17	4	6	60	57	31	.309	.410	.428	118	14	12	69	1	3	-2	.983	-2	O/C	0.4
1946	StL-A	48	161	21	37	7	2	1	13	16	20	.230	.307	.317	71	-5	-6	16	1	3	-2	.967	1	O	-0.9
	Was-A	77	321	39	97	17	4	2	31	24	19	.302	.358	.399	118	5	7	46	1	4	-2	.959	4	O	0.5
	Yr	125	482	60	134	24	6	3	44	40	39	.278	.341	.371	101	-1	0	61	2	7	-4	.962	5	*O	-0.4
1947	Was-A	78	234	25	58	9	4	3	17	35	15	.248	.348	.359	99	-0	0	31	1	2	-1	.976	2	O	-0.2
Total	6	484	1561	225	442	76	18	20	172	179	135	.283	.362	.393	102	8	7	231	9	17	-8	.969	-6	O/C	-2.3

■ **MARK GRACE** Grace, Mark Eugene b: 6/28/64, Winston-Salem, N.C BL/TL, 6'2", 190 lbs. Deb: 5/02/88

YEAR	TM/L	G	AB	R	H	2B	3B	HR	RBI	BB	SO	AVG	OBP	SLG	PRO+	BR	/A	RC	SB	CS	SBR	FA	FR	POS	TPR
1988	Chi-N	134	486	65	144	23	4	7	57	60	43	.296	.374	.403	118	16	13	74	3	3	-1	.987	-4	*1	-0.2
1989	*Chi-N	142	510	74	160	28	3	13	79	80	42	.314	.407	.457	136	34	29	96	14	7	0	.996	13	*1	3.3
1990	Chi-N	157	589	72	182	32	1	9	82	59	54	.309	.377	.413	109	15	10	94	15	6	1	.992	27	*1	2.6
1991	Chi-N	160	619	87	169	28	5	8	58	70	53	.273	.350	.373	99	4	1	84	3	4	-2	.995	20	*1	0.9
1992	Chi-N	158	603	72	185	37	5	9	79	72	36	.307	.384	.430	127	26	24	102	6	1	1	.998	9	*1	2.5
Total	5	751	2807	370	840	148	18	46	355	341	228	.299	.378	.414	117	94	77	450	41	21	-0	.994	65	1	9.1

■ **MIKE GRACE** Grace, Michael Lee b: 6/14/56, Pontiac, Mich. BR/TR, 6', 175 lbs. Deb: 4/18/78

YEAR	TM/L	G	AB	R	H	2B	3B	HR	RBI	BB	SO	AVG	OBP	SLG	PRO+	BR	/A	RC	SB	CS	SBR	FA	FR	POS	TPR
1978	Cin-N	5	3	0	0	0	0	0	0	0	2	.000	.000	.000	-99	-1	-1	0	0	0	0	1.000	1	/3	0.0

■ **EARL GRACE** Grace, Robert Earl b: 2/24/07, Barlow, Ky. d: 12/22/80, Phoenix, Ariz. BL/TR, 6', 175 lbs. Deb: 4/23/29

YEAR	TM/L	G	AB	R	H	2B	3B	HR	RBI	BB	SO	AVG	OBP	SLG	PRO+	BR	/A	RC	SB	CS	SBR	FA	FR	POS	TPR
1929	Chi-N	27	80	7	20	1	0	2	17	9	7	.250	.333	.338	67	-4	-4	9	0			1.000	3	C	0.1
1931	Chi-N	7	9	2	1	0	0	0	1	4	1	.111	.385	.111	39	-1	-1	1	0			1.000	-0	/C	0.0
	Pit-N	47	150	8	42	6	1	1	20	13	5	.280	.337	.353	87	-3	-3	19	0			.974	-1	C	0.0
	Yr	54	159	10	43	6	1	1	21	17	6	.270	.341	.340	84	-3	-3	20	0			.976	-1	C	0.0
1932	Pit-N	115	390	41	107	17	5	8	55	14	23	.274	.305	.405	91	-7	-6	48	0			**.998**	-7	*C	-0.6
1933	Pit-N	93	291	22	84	13	1	3	44	26	23	.289	.349	.371	106	3	3	40	0			.980	1	C	0.9
1934	Pit-N	95	289	27	78	17	1	4	24	20	19	.270	.317	.377	83	-6	-7	35	0			.982	-9	C/1	-1.2
1935	Pit-N	77	224	19	59	8	1	3	29	32	17	.263	.355	.348	87	-2	-3	27	1			.990	3	C	0.3
1936	Phi-N	86	221	24	55	11	0	4	32	34	20	.249	.352	.353	82	-2	-5	30	0			.976	-4	C	-0.7
1937	Phi-N	80	223	19	47	10	1	6	29	33	15	.211	.313	.345	73	-6	-9	25	0			.990	-2	C	-0.8
Total	8	627	1877	169	493	83	10	31	251	185	130	.263	.331	.367	86	-29	-35	235	1			.987	-17	C/1	-2.0

■ **JOHN GRADY** Grady, John J. b: 6/18/1860, Lowell, Mass. d: 7/15/1893, Lowell, Mass. 5'7", 150 lbs. Deb: 5/10/1884

YEAR	TM/L	G	AB	R	H	2B	3B	HR	RBI	BB	SO	AVG	OBP	SLG	PRO+	BR	/A	RC	SB	CS	SBR	FA	FR	POS	TPR
1884	Alt-U	9	36	5	11	3	0	0		2		.306	.342	.389	145	2	2	5				.909	-1	/1O	-0.1

■ **MIKE GRADY** Grady, Michael William b: 12/23/1869, Kennett Square, Pa d: 12/3/43, Kennett Square, Pa. BR/TR, 5'11", 190 lbs. Deb: 4/24/1894

YEAR	TM/L	G	AB	R	H	2B	3B	HR	RBI	BB	SO	AVG	OBP	SLG	PRO+	BR	/A	RC	SB	CS	SBR	FA	FR	POS	TPR
1894	Phi-N	60	190	45	69	13	8	0	40	14	13	.363	.427	.516	132	9	10	44	3			.878	-13	C1/O	0.0
1895	Phi-N	46	123	21	40	3	1	1	23	14	8	.325	.407	.390	108	2	2	23	5			.926	-10	C/O31	-0.5
1896	Phi-N	71	242	49	77	20	7	1	44	16	19	.318	.382	.471	128	9	9	49	10			.942	-8	C/3	0.7
1897	Phi-N	4	13	1	2	0	0	0	0	1		.154	.214	.154	-2	-2	-2	0	0			1.000	1	/C	-0.1
	StL-N	83	322	48	90	11	3	7	45	26		.280	.352	.398	100	-1	-0	49	7			.974	-1	1/O	-0.1
	Yr	87	335	49	92	11	3	7	45	27		.275	.347	.388	96	-3	-2	49	7			.974	-0	1/CO	-0.2
1898	NY-N	93	287	64	85	19	5	3	49	38		.296	.399	.429	142	15	17	59	20			.944	-4	CO/1S	1.4
1899	NY-N	86	311	47	104	18	8	2	54	29		.334	.403	.463	142	16	18	68	20			.939	-13	C3/O1	0.8
1900	NY-N	83	251	36	55	8	4	0	27	34		.219	.331	.283	74	-9	-7	28	9			.932	-13	C1S/3O2	-1.4
1901	Was-A	94	347	57	99	17	10	9	56	27		.285	.351	.470	128	11	12	64	14			.975	6	1C/O	1.8
1904	StL-N	101	323	44	101	15	11	5	43	31		.313	.376	.474	170	23	25	62	6			.955	-19	C1/23	1.5
1905	StL-N	100	311	41	89	20	7	4	41	33		.286	.358	.434	140	13	15	56	15			.956	-11	C1	1.1
1906	StL-N	97	280	33	70	11	3	3	27	48		.250	.366	.343	127	9	10	39	5			.983	-11	C1	0.4
Total	11	918	3000	486	881	155	67	35	449	311	40	.294	.373	.425	127	96	109	540	114			.946	-95	C1/3OS2	5.6

■ FRED GRAFF Graff, Frederick Gottleib b: 8/25/1889, Canton, Ohio d: 10/4/79, Chattanooga, Tenn. BR/TR, 5'10.5", 164 lbs. Deb: 5/14/13

YEAR	TM/L	G	AB	R	H	2B	3B	HR	RBI	BB	SO	AVG	OBP	SLG	PRO+	BR	/A	RC	SB	CS	SBR	FA	FR	POS	TPR
1913	StL-A	4	5	1	2	1	0	0	2	3	3	.400	.625	.600	266	1	1	2	0			1.000	-1	/3	0.1

■ LOUIS GRAFF Graff, Louis George "Chappie" b: 7/25/1866, Philadelphia, Pa. d: 4/16/55, Bryn Mawr, Pa. TR , Deb: 6/23/1890

YEAR	TM/L	G	AB	R	H	2B	3B	HR	RBI	BB	SO	AVG	OBP	SLG	PRO+	BR	/A	RC	SB	CS	SBR	FA	FR	POS	TPR
1890	Syr-a	1	5	0	2	1	0	0		0		.400	.400	.600	220	1	1	1	0			.333	-2	/C	-0.1

■ MILT GRAFF Graff, Milton Edward b: 12/30/30, Jefferson Center, Pa. BL/TR, 5'7.5", 158 lbs. Deb: 4/16/57 C

YEAR	TM/L	G	AB	R	H	2B	3B	HR	RBI	BB	SO	AVG	OBP	SLG	PRO+	BR	/A	RC	SB	CS	SBR	FA	FR	POS	TPR
1957	KC-A	56	155	16	28	4	3	0	10	15	10	.181	.262	.245	39	-13	-13	10	2	5	-2	.988	1	2	-1.1
1958	KC-A	5	1	0	0	0	0	0	0	0	0	.000	.000	.000	-98	-0	-0	0	0	0	0	1.000	1	/2	0.1
Total	2	61	156	16	28	4	3	0	10	15	10	.179	.260	.244	38	-13	-14	10	2	5	-2	.988	3	/2	-1.0

■ MOONLIGHT GRAHAM Graham, Archibald Wright b: 11/9/1876, Fayetteville, N.C. d: 8/25/65, Chisolm, Minn. BL/TR, 5'10.5", 170 lbs. Deb: 6/29/05

YEAR	TM/L	G	AB	R	H	2B	3B	HR	RBI	BB	SO	AVG	OBP	SLG	PRO+	BR	/A	RC	SB	CS	SBR	FA	FR	POS	TPR
1905	NY-N	1	0	0	0	0	0	0	0	0		—	—	—	—	0	0	0	0			.000	-0	/O	0.0

■ SKINNY GRAHAM Graham, Arthur William b: 8/12/09, Somerville, Mass. d: 7/10/67, Cambridge, Mass. BL/TR, 5'7", 162 lbs. Deb: 9/14/34

YEAR	TM/L	G	AB	R	H	2B	3B	HR	RBI	BB	SO	AVG	OBP	SLG	PRO+	BR	/A	RC	SB	CS	SBR	FA	FR	POS	TPR
1934	Bos-A	13	47	7	11	2	1	0	3	6	13	.234	.321	.319	61	-2	-3	5	2	2	-1	1.000	-1	O	-0.5
1935	Bos-A	8	10	1	3	0	0	0	1	1	3	.300	.364	.300	69	-0	-0	1	1	0	0	1.000	-1	/O	-0.1
Total	2	21	57	8	14	2	1	0	4	7	16	.246	.328	.316	62	-3	-3	6	3	2	-0	1.000	-2	/O	-0.6

■ BARNEY GRAHAM Graham, Barney b: Philadelphia, Pa. d: 12/31/1896, Mobile, Ala. Deb: 9/04/1889

YEAR	TM/L	G	AB	R	H	2B	3B	HR	RBI	BB	SO	AVG	OBP	SLG	PRO+	BR	/A	RC	SB	CS	SBR	FA	FR	POS	TPR
1889	Phi-a	4	18	0	3	0	0	0	0	0	0	.167	.167	.167	-4	-2	-2	1	0			.933	1	/3	-0.1

■ BERNIE GRAHAM Graham, Bernard W. b: 1860, Beloit, Wis. d: 10/30/1886, Mobile, Ala. Deb: 7/11/1884

YEAR	TM/L	G	AB	R	H	2B	3B	HR	RBI	BB	SO	AVG	OBP	SLG	PRO+	BR	/A	RC	SB	CS	SBR	FA	FR	POS	TPR
1884	CP-U	1	5	2	1	0	0	0		0		.200	.200	.200	36	-0	-0	0				1.000	-0	/O	0.0
	Bal-U	41	167	21	45	11	0	0		2		.269	.278	.335	96	1	-2	16				.814	1	O/1	-0.1
	Yr	42	172	23	46	11	0	0		2		.267	.276	.331	95	1	-2	16				.816	1	O/1	-0.1

■ BERT GRAHAM Graham, Bert "B.G." b: 4/3/1886, Tilton, Ill. d: 6/19/71, Cottonwood, Ariz. BB/TR, 5'11.5", 187 lbs. Deb: 9/09/10

YEAR	TM/L	G	AB	R	H	2B	3B	HR	RBI	BB	SO	AVG	OBP	SLG	PRO+	BR	/A	RC	SB	CS	SBR	FA	FR	POS	TPR
1910	StL-A	8	26	1	3	2	1	0	5	1		.115	.148	.269	32	-2	-2	1	0			.964	1	/12	-0.1

■ CHARLIE GRAHAM Graham, Charles Henry b: 4/25/1878, Santa Clara, Cal. d: 8/29/48, San Francisco, Cal BR/TR, 5'11", 180 lbs. Deb: 4/16/06

YEAR	TM/L	G	AB	R	H	2B	3B	HR	RBI	BB	SO	AVG	OBP	SLG	PRO+	BR	/A	RC	SB	CS	SBR	FA	FR	POS	TPR
1906	Bos-A	30	90	10	21	1	0	1	12	10		.233	.330	.278	91	-0	-0	9	1			.963	7	C	1.0

■ DAN GRAHAM Graham, Daniel Jay b: 7/19/54, Ray, Ariz. BL/TR, 6'1", 205 lbs. Deb: 6/08/79

YEAR	TM/L	G	AB	R	H	2B	3B	HR	RBI	BB	SO	AVG	OBP	SLG	PRO+	BR	/A	RC	SB	CS	SBR	FA	FR	POS	TPR
1979	Min-A	2	4	0	0	0	0	0	0	0	0	.000	.000	.000	-96	-1	-1	0	0	0	0	.000	0	/H	-0.1
1980	Bal-A	86	266	32	74	7	1	15	54	14	40	.278	.314	.481	116	4	4	40	0	0	0	.981	0	C/3OD	0.7
1981	Bal-A	55	142	7	25	3	0	2	11	13	32	.176	.245	.239	40	-11	-11	8	0	0	0	.975	-4	C/3D	-1.5
Total	3	143	412	39	99	10	1	17	65	27	72	.240	.287	.393	88	-8	-8	48	0	0	0	.979	-4	C/3DO	-0.9

■ TINY GRAHAM Graham, Dawson Francis b: 9/9/1892, Nashville, Tenn. d: 12/29/62, Nashville, Tenn. BR/TR, 6'2", 185 lbs. Deb: 8/30/14

YEAR	TM/L	G	AB	R	H	2B	3B	HR	RBI	BB	SO	AVG	OBP	SLG	PRO+	BR	/A	RC	SB	CS	SBR	FA	FR	POS	TPR
1914	Cin-N	25	61	5	14	1	0	0	3	3	10	.230	.266	.246	51	-4	-4	4	1			.961	-2	1	-0.6

■ PEACHES GRAHAM Graham, George Frederick b: 3/23/1877, Aledo, Ill. d: 7/25/39, Long Beach, Cal. BR/TR, 5'9", 180 lbs. Deb: 9/14/02 F

YEAR	TM/L	G	AB	R	H	2B	3B	HR	RBI	BB	SO	AVG	OBP	SLG	PRO+	BR	/A	RC	SB	CS	SBR	FA	FR	POS	TPR
1902	Cle-A	2	6	0	2	0	0	0	1	1		.333	.429	.333	118	0	0	1	0			1.000	0	/2	0.0
1903	Chi-N	1	2	0	0	0	0	0	0	0		.000	.000	.000	-99	-1	-1	0	0			1.000	0	/P	0.0
1908	Bos-N	75	215	22	59	5	0	0	22	23		.274	.361	.298	113	4	4	25	4			.955	-3	C/2	0.8
1909	Bos-N	92	267	27	64	6	3	0	17	24		.240	.302	.285	79	-5	-7	26	7			.948	-4	C/OS3	-0.4
1910	Bos-N	110	291	31	82	13	2	0	21	33	15	.282	.359	.340	100	2	1	38	5			.966	-8	C/31O	0.1
1911	Bos-N	33	88	7	24	6	1	0	12	14	5	.273	.373	.364	98	1	0	13	2			.912	-5	C	-0.2
	Chi-N	36	71	6	17	3	0	0	8	11	8	.239	.365	.282	82	-1	-1	8	2			.972	-5	C	-0.4
	Yr	69	159	13	41	9	1	0	20	25	13	.258	.369	.327	92	0	-1	21	4			.937	-10	C	-0.6
1912	Phi-N	24	59	6	17	1	0	1	4	8	5	.288	.373	.356	94	0	-0	8	1			.944	-2	C	0.0
Total	7	373	999	99	265	34	6	1	85	114	33	.265	.347	.314	95	1	-3	118	21			.953	-25	C/O231SP	-0.1

■ JACK GRAHAM Graham, John Bernard b: 12/24/16, Minneapolis, Minn. BL/TL, 6'2", 200 lbs. Deb: 4/16/46 F

YEAR	TM/L	G	AB	R	H	2B	3B	HR	RBI	BB	SO	AVG	OBP	SLG	PRO+	BR	/A	RC	SB	CS	SBR	FA	FR	POS	TPR
1946	Bro-N	2	5	0	1	0	0	0	0	0	0	.200	.200	.200	14	-1	-1	0	0			1.000	0	/1	-0.1
	NY-N	100	270	34	59	6	4	14	47	23	37	.219	.282	.426	99	-2	-2	32	1			.949	-1	O/1	-0.7
	Yr	102	275	34	60	6	4	14	47	23	37	.218	.281	.422	97	-3	-3	32	1			.949	-1	O/1	-0.8
1949	StL-A	137	500	71	119	22	1	24	79	61	62	.238	.326	.430	95	-4	-7	72	0	1	-1	.984	-6	*1	-1.4
Total	2	239	775	105	179	28	5	38	126	84	99	.231	.310	.427	96	-7	-10	104	1	1		.985	-7	1/O	-2.2

■ LEE GRAHAM Graham, Lee Willard b: 9/22/59, Summerfield, Fla. BL/TL, 5'10", 170 lbs. Deb: 9/03/83

YEAR	TM/L	G	AB	R	H	2B	3B	HR	RBI	BB	SO	AVG	OBP	SLG	PRO+	BR	/A	RC	SB	CS	SBR	FA	FR	POS	TPR
1983	Bos-A	5	6	2	0	0	0	0	1	0	0	.000	.000	.000	-93	-2	-2	-0	0	1	-1	1.000	1	/O	-0.2

■ ROY GRAHAM Graham, Roy Vincent b: 2/22/1895, San Francisco, Cal d: 4/26/33, Manila, Phillipines BR/TR, 5'10.5", 175 lbs. Deb: 5/28/22

YEAR	TM/L	G	AB	R	H	2B	3B	HR	RBI	BB	SO	AVG	OBP	SLG	PRO+	BR	/A	RC	SB	CS	SBR	FA	FR	POS	TPR
1922	Chi-A	5	3	0	0	0	0	0	0	0	0	.000	.400	.000	12	-0	-0	0	0	0	0	1.000	-0	/C	0.0
1923	Chi-A	36	82	3	16	2	0	0	6	9	6	.195	.290	.220	36	-7	-7	6	0	0	0	.949	-7	C	-1.3
Total	2	41	85	3	16	2	0	0	6	9	6	.188	.296	.212	35	-8	-8	6	0	0	0	.950	-7	/C	-1.3

■ WAYNE GRAHAM Graham, Wayne Leon b: 4/6/37, Yoakum, Tex. BR/TR, 6', 200 lbs. Deb: 4/10/63

YEAR	TM/L	G	AB	R	H	2B	3B	HR	RBI	BB	SO	AVG	OBP	SLG	PRO+	BR	/A	RC	SB	CS	SBR	FA	FR	POS	TPR
1963	Phi-N	10	22	1	4	0	0	0	0	3	1	.182	.280	.182	36	-2	-2	1	0	0	0	.857	-1	/O	-0.3
1964	NY-N	20	33	1	3	1	0	0	0	0	5	.091	.091	.121	-42	-6	-6	0	0	0	0	1.000	-2	3	-0.9
Total	2	30	55	2	7	1	0	0	0	3	6	.127	.172	.145	-9	-8	-8	2	0	0	0	.960	-3	/3O	-1.2

■ ALEX GRAMMAS Grammas, Alexander Peter b: 4/3/26, Birmingham, Ala. BR/TR, 6', 178 lbs. Deb: 4/13/54 MC

YEAR	TM/L	G	AB	R	H	2B	3B	HR	RBI	BB	SO	AVG	OBP	SLG	PRO+	BR	/A	RC	SB	CS	SBR	FA	FR	POS	TPR
1954	StL-N	142	401	57	106	17	4	2	29	40	29	.264	.339	.342	77	-12	-13	47	6	1	1	.966	30	*S/3	2.8
1955	StL-N	128	366	32	88	19	2	3	25	33	36	.240	.308	.328	69	-16	-16	37	4	1	1	.968	7	*S	0.1
1956	StL-N	6	12	1	3	0	0	0	1	1	1	.250	.308	.250	52	-1	-1	1	0	0	0	1.000	0	/S	-0.1
	Cin-N	77	140	17	34	11	0	0	16	16	18	.243	.325	.321	70	-5	-6	16	0	1	-1	.968	4	3S/2	-0.2
	Yr	83	152	18	37	11	0	0	17	17	19	.243	.324	.316	69	-5	-7	17	0	1	-1	.968	4	3S/2	-0.3
1957	Cin-N	73	99	14	30	4	0	0	8	10	6	.303	.367	.343	86	-1	-2	11	1	3	-2	.966	2	S2/3	0.1
1958	Cin-N	105	216	25	47	8	0	0	12	34	24	.218	.329	.255	54	-12	-14	20	2	2	-1	.993	-2	S32	-1.3
1959	StL-N	131	368	43	99	14	2	3	30	38	26	.269	.339	.342	77	-8	-12	43	3	3	-1	.964	12	*S	1.0
1960	StL-N	102	196	20	48	4	1	4	17	12	15	.245	.292	.337	66	-8	-10	17	0	1	-1	.972	20	S23	1.3
1961	StL-N	89	170	23	36	10	1	0	21	19	21	.212	.295	.282	49	-11	-13	15	0	1	-1	.960	17	S2/3	0.7
1962	StL-N	21	18	0	2	0	0	0	1	1	6	.111	.158	.111	-24	-3	-3	0	0	0	0	.933	1	S/2	-0.2
	Chi-N	23	60	3	14	3	0	0	3	2	7	.233	.270	.283	47	-4	-5	4	1	1	-0	1.000	1	S/23	-0.2
	Yr	44	78	3	16	3	0	0	4	3	13	.205	.244	.244	29	-8	-8	4	1	1	-0	.978	3	S/23	-0.4
1963	Chi-N	16	27	1	5	0	0	0	0	0	3	.185	.185	.185	7	-3	-3	1	0	0	0	.955	-3	S	-0.7
Total	10	913	2073	236	512	90	10	12	163	206	192	.247	.320	.317	67	-84	-96	212	17	14	-3	.968	88	S32	3.3

■ JACK GRANEY Graney, John Gladstone b: 6/10/1886, St.Thomas, Ont., Can. d: 4/20/78, Louisiana, Mo. BL/TL, 5'9", 180 lbs. Deb: 4/30/08

YEAR	TM/L	G	AB	R	H	2B	3B	HR	RBI	BB	SO	AVG	OBP	SLG	PRO+	BR	/A	RC	SB	CS	SBR	FA	FR	POS	TPR
1908	Cle-A	2	0	0	0	0	0	0	0	0		—	—	—	—	0	0	0	0			.000	-0	/P	0.0
1910	Cle-A	116	454	62	107	13	9	1	31	37		.236	.293	.311	88	-6	-7	46	18			.949	1	*O	-1.3
1911	Cle-A	146	527	84	142	25	5	1	45	66		.269	.363	.342	96	0	-1	73	21			.927	2	*O	-0.7
1912	Cle-A	78	264	44	64	13	2	0	20	50		.242	.367	.307	90	0	-1	33	9			.958	4	O	-0.1

YEAR	TM/L	G	AB	R	H	2B	3B	HR	RBI	BB	SO	AVG	OBP	SLG	PRO+	BR	/A	RC	SB	CS	SBR	FA	FR	POS	TPR
1913	Cle-A	148	517	56	138	18	12	3	68	48	55	.267	.335	.366	102	3	1	69	27			.970	2	*O	-0.4
1914	Cle-A	130	460	63	122	17	10	1	39	67	46	.265	.362	.352	111	10	8	60	20	18	-5	.935	5	*O	0.3
1915	Cle-A	116	404	42	105	20	7	1	56	59	29	.260	.357	.351	110	7	6	51	12	15	-5	.972	5	*O	0.1
1916	Cle-A	155	589	106	142	**41**	14	5	54	102	72	.241	.355	.384	115	17	13	85	10			.959	3	*O	0.8
1917	Cle-A	146	535	87	122	29	7	3	35	**94**	49	.228	.348	.325	98	6	2	65	16			.959	-8	*O	-1.5
1918	Cle-A	70	177	27	42	7	4	0	9	28	13	.237	.351	.322	94	2	-0	20	3			.975	-6	O	-0.9
1919	Cle-A	128	461	79	108	22	8	1	30	**105**	39	.234	.380	.323	93	4	0	60	7			.961	6	*O	-0.3
1920	*Cle-A	62	152	31	45	11	1	0	13	27	21	.296	.412	.382	108	4	3	27	4	2	0	.941	-6	O	-0.5
1921	Cle-A	68	107	19	32	3	0	2	18	20	9	.299	.414	.383	103	2	2	19	1	1	-0	.933	-9	O	-0.9
1922	Cle-A	37	58	6	9	0	0	0	2	9	12	.155	.279	.155	16	-7	-7	3	0	0	0	.862	-1	O	-0.9
Total	14	1402	4705	706	1178	219	79	18	420	712	345	.250	.354	.342	100	42	18	610	148	36		.953	-3	*O/P	-6.3

■ EDDIE GRANT Grant, Edward Leslie "Harvard Eddie" b: 5/21/1883, Franklin, Mass. d: 10/5/18, Argonne Forest, France BL/TR, 5'11.5", 168 lbs. Deb: 8/04/05

YEAR	TM/L	G	AB	R	H	2B	3B	HR	RBI	BB	SO	AVG	OBP	SLG	PRO+	BR	/A	RC	SB	CS	SBR	FA	FR	POS	TPR
1905	Cle-A	2	8	1	3	0	0	0	0	0		.375	.375	.375	136	0	0	1	0			.833	-2	/2	-0.2
1907	Phi-N	74	268	26	65	4	3	0	19	10		.243	.272	.280	74	-9	-8	24	10			.916	-2	3	-1.0
1908	Phi-N	147	598	69	146	13	8	0	32	35		.244	.289	.293	83	-10	-12	58	27			.930	2	*3S	-0.6
1909	Phi-N	154	631	75	170	18	4	1	37	35		.269	.311	.315	94	-5	-6	71	28			.957	1	*3	0.0
1910	Phi-N	152	579	70	155	15	5	1	67	39	54	.268	.315	.316	81	-12	-15	67	25			.935	-10	*3	-2.2
1911	Cin-N	136	458	49	102	12	7	1	53	51	47	.223	.301	.286	67	-22	-19	49	28			.953	-7	*3S	-2.4
1912	Cin-N	96	255	37	61	6	1	2	20	18	27	.239	.292	.294	62	-14	-13	25	11			.948	0	S3	-0.8
1913	Cin-N	27	94	12	20	1	0	0	9	11	10	.213	.295	.223	49	-6	-6	8	7			.929	-5	3	-1.1
	*NY-N	27	20	8	4	1	0	0	1	2	2	.200	.273	.250	49	-1	-1	1	1			1.000	6	/32S	0.5
	Yr	54	114	20	24	2	0	0	10	13	12	.211	.291	.228	49	-7	-7	9	8			.940	2	3/2S	-0.6
1914	NY-N	88	282	34	78	7	1	0	29	23	21	.277	.333	.309	94	-3	-1	32	11			.948	-7	3S2	-0.6
1915	NY-N	87	192	18	40	2	1	0	10	9	20	.208	.248	.229	47	-13	-12	11	5	6	-2	.970	-5	3/21S	-1.9
Total	10	990	3385	399	844	79	30	5	277	233	181	.249	.300	.295	78	-94	-93	347	153	6		.942	-28	3S/21	-10.3

■ JIMMY GRANT Grant, James Charles b: 10/6/18, Racine, Wis. d: 7/8/70, Rochester, Minn. BL/TR, 5'8", 166 lbs. Deb: 9/08/42

YEAR	TM/L	G	AB	R	H	2B	3B	HR	RBI	BB	SO	AVG	OBP	SLG	PRO+	BR	/A	RC	SB	CS	SBR	FA	FR	POS	TPR
1942	Chi-A	12	36	0	6	1	1	0	1	5	6	.167	.268	.250	47	-3	-2	3	0	0	0	.944	1	3	-0.2
1943	Chi-A	58	197	23	51	9	2	4	22	18	34	.259	.321	.386	106	1	1	23	4	3	-1	.893	1	3	0.2
	Cle-A	15	22	3	3	2	0	0	1	4	7	.136	.269	.227	49	-1	-1	2	0	0	0	.941	2	/3	0.1
	Yr	73	219	26	54	11	2	4	23	22	41	.247	.315	.370	101	-0	-0	24	4	3	-1	.897	3	3	0.3
1944	Cle-A	61	99	12	27	4	3	1	12	11	20	.273	.357	.404	122	2	3	16	1	0	0	.926	-4	2/3	0.0
Total	3	146	354	38	87	16	6	5	36	38	67	.246	.322	.367	101	-1	0	43	5	3	-0	.907	-0	/32	0.1

■ TOM GRANT Grant, Thomas Raymond b: 5/28/57, Worcester, Mass. BL/TR, 6'2", 190 lbs. Deb: 6/17/83

YEAR	TM/L	G	AB	R	H	2B	3B	HR	RBI	BB	SO	AVG	OBP	SLG	PRO+	BR	/A	RC	SB	CS	SBR	FA	FR	POS	TPR
1983	Chi-N	16	20	2	3	1	0	0	2	3	4	.150	.261	.200	28	-2	-2	1	0	0	0	1.000	0	O	-0.2

■ GEORGE GRANTHAM Grantham, George Farley "Boots" b: 5/20/1900, Galena, Kan. d: 3/16/54, Kingman, Ariz. BL/TR, 5'10", 170 lbs. Deb: 9/20/22

YEAR	TM/L	G	AB	R	H	2B	3B	HR	RBI	BB	SO	AVG	OBP	SLG	PRO+	BR	/A	RC	SB	CS	SBR	FA	FR	POS	TPR
1922	Chi-N	7	23	3	4	1	1	0	3	1	3	.174	.208	.304	30	-2	-3	2	2	0	1	1.000	-3	/3	-0.4
1923	Chi-N	152	570	81	160	36	8	8	70	71	92	.281	.360	.414	104	4	4	85	43	28	-4	.942	1	*2	0.3
1924	Chi-N	127	469	85	148	19	6	12	60	55	63	.316	.390	.458	125	19	18	81	21	21	-6	.941	1	*2/3	1.4
1925	*Pit-N	114	359	74	117	24	6	8	52	50	29	.326	.413	.493	122	18	14	77	14	4	2	.989	-4	*1	0.6
1926	Pit-N	141	449	66	143	27	13	8	70	60	42	.318	.400	.490	131	25	22	88	6			.990	-2	*1	1.2
1927	*Pit-N	151	531	96	162	33	11	8	66	74	39	.305	.396	.454	119	22	17	97	9			.953	-24	*21	-0.4
1928	Pit-N	124	440	93	142	24	9	10	85	59	37	.323	.408	.486	128	22	20	87	9			.986	1	*1/23	1.1
1929	Pit-N	110	349	85	107	23	10	12	90	93	38	.307	.454	.533	140	28	27	89	10			.967	-5	2O1	2.2
1930	Pit-N	146	552	120	179	34	14	18	99	81	66	.324	.413	.534	126	25	25	121	5			.958	-13	*2/1	1.6
1931	Pit-N	127	465	91	142	26	6	10	46	71	50	.305	.400	.452	130	21	22	89	5			.985	-22	12	-0.4
1932	Cin-N	126	493	81	144	29	6	6	39	56	40	.292	.364	.412	112	7	9	77	4			.959	-29	*21	-1.5
1933	Cin-N	87	260	32	53	14	3	4	28	38	21	.204	.310	.327	83	-5	-5	29	4			.948	-11	21	-1.4
1934	NY-N	32	29	5	7	2	0	1	4	8	6	.241	.405	.414	123	1	1	6	0			1.000	0	/13	0.1
Total	13	1444	4989	912	1508	292	93	105	712	717	526	.302	.392	.461	121	185	171	927	132	53		.949	-109	21/O3	4.4

■ MICKEY GRASSO Grasso, Newton Michael b: 5/10/20, Newark, N.J. d: 10/15/75, Miami, Fla. BR/TR, 6', 195 lbs. Deb: 9/18/46

YEAR	TM/L	G	AB	R	H	2B	3B	HR	RBI	BB	SO	AVG	OBP	SLG	PRO+	BR	/A	RC	SB	CS	SBR	FA	FR	POS	TPR
1946	NY-N	7	22	1	3	0	0	0	1	0	3	.136	.136	.136	-22	-4	-4	0	0			.967	0	/C	-0.3
1950	Was-A	75	195	25	56	4	1	1	22	25	31	.287	.374	.333	86	-4	-3	26	1	1	-0	.942	6	C	0.5
1951	Was-A	52	175	16	36	3	0	1	14	14	17	.206	.268	.240	39	-15	-15	10	0	0	0	.967	-2	C	-1.5
1952	Was-A	115	361	22	78	9	0	0	27	29	36	.216	.276	.241	46	-27	-25	24	1	0	0	.970	6	*C	-1.4
1953	Was-A	61	196	13	41	7	0	2	22	9	20	.209	.251	.276	43	-16	-16	12	0	0	0	.984	1	C	-1.3
1954	*Cle-A	4	6	1	2	0	0	1	1	1	1	.333	.500	.833	256	1	1	3	0	0	0	.833	-1	/C	0.1
1955	NY-N	8	2	0	0	0	0	0	0	3	0	.000	.600	.000	77	0	0	0	0	0	0	.900	-0	/C	0.0
Total	7	322	957	78	216	23	1	5	87	81	108	.226	.291	.268	53	-64	-60	76	2	1		.964	9	C	-3.9

■ LEW GRAULICH Graulich, Lewis b: Camden, N.J. Deb: 9/17/1891

YEAR	TM/L	G	AB	R	H	2B	3B	HR	RBI	BB	SO	AVG	OBP	SLG	PRO+	BR	/A	RC	SB	CS	SBR	FA	FR	POS	TPR
1891	Phi-N	7	26	2	8	0	0	0	3	1	2	.308	.333	.308	87	-0	-0	3	0			.640	-3	/C1	-0.3

■ FRANK GRAVES Graves, Frank M. b: 11/2/1860, Cincinnati, Ohio 6', 163 lbs. Deb: 5/10/1886

YEAR	TM/L	G	AB	R	H	2B	3B	HR	RBI	BB	SO	AVG	OBP	SLG	PRO+	BR	/A	RC	SB	CS	SBR	FA	FR	POS	TPR
1886	StL-N	43	138	7	21	2	0	0	9	7	48	.152	.193	.167	11	-15	-13	7	11			.885	4	C/OP	-0.4

■ JOE GRAVES Graves, Joseph Ebenezer b: 2/27/06, Marblehead, Mass. d: 12/22/80, Salem, Mass. BR/TR, 5'10", 160 lbs. Deb: 9/26/26 F

YEAR	TM/L	G	AB	R	H	2B	3B	HR	RBI	BB	SO	AVG	OBP	SLG	PRO+	BR	/A	RC	SB	CS	SBR	FA	FR	POS	TPR
1926	Chi-N	2	5	0	0	0	0	0	0	0	1	.000	.000	.000	-99	-1	-1	0	0			.250	-1	/3	-0.3

■ SID GRAVES Graves, Samuel Sidney "Whitey" b: 11/30/01, Marblehead, Mass. d: 12/26/83, Biddeford, Maine BR/TR, 6', 170 lbs. Deb: 7/23/27 F

YEAR	TM/L	G	AB	R	H	2B	3B	HR	RBI	BB	SO	AVG	OBP	SLG	PRO+	BR	/A	RC	SB	CS	SBR	FA	FR	POS	TPR
1927	Bos-N	7	20	5	5	1	1	0	2	0	1	.250	.250	.400	78	-1	-1	2	1			.857	0	/O	-0.1

■ GARY GRAY Gray, Gary George b: 9/21/52, New Orleans, La. BR/TR, 6', 203 lbs. Deb: 6/23/77

YEAR	TM/L	G	AB	R	H	2B	3B	HR	RBI	BB	SO	AVG	OBP	SLG	PRO+	BR	/A	RC	SB	CS	SBR	FA	FR	POS	TPR
1977	Tex-A	1	2	0	0	0	0	0	0	0	1	.000	.000	.000	-99	-1	-1	0	0	0	0	.000	-0	/O	-0.1
1978	Tex-A	17	50	4	12	1	0	2	6	1	12	.240	.255	.380	76	-2	-2	5	1	0	0	.000	0	D	-0.2
1979	Tex-A	16	42	4	10	0	0	0	1	2	8	.238	.273	.238	40	-4	-3	2	1	1	-0	.000	0	D	-0.4
1980	Cle-A	28	54	4	8	1	0	2	4	3	13	.148	.193	.278	27	-6	-6	2	0	0	0	1.000	-2	/1OD	-0.8
1981	Sea-A	69	208	27	51	7	1	13	31	4	44	.245	.259	.476	104	1	-0	22	2	0	1	.993	-2	1D/O	-0.4
1982	Sea-A	80	269	26	69	14	2	7	29	24	59	.257	.322	.401	95	-1	-2	35	1	1	-0	.984	-3	1D	-0.8
Total	6	211	625	65	150	23	3	24	71	34	137	.240	.281	.402	86	-12	-14	66	5	2	0	.988	-7	1/DO	-2.7

■ REDDY GRAY Gray, James D. TR, Deb: 6/17/1890

YEAR	TM/L	G	AB	R	H	2B	3B	HR	RBI	BB	SO	AVG	OBP	SLG	PRO+	BR	/A	RC	SB	CS	SBR	FA	FR	POS	TPR
1890	Pit-P	2	9	3	2	0	0	1	3	0	2	.222	.222	.556	115	-0	0	1	0			.813	-1	/2	-0.1
	Pit-N	1	3	0	0	0	0	0	0	0	1	.000	.000	.000	-99	-1	-1	0	0			.571	-1	/S	-0.1
1893	Pit-N	2	9	0	4	1	0	0	2	0	1	.444	.444	.556	171	1	1	2	0			.800	-3	/S	-0.2
Total	2	5	21	3	6	1	0	1	5	0	4	.286	.286	.476	112	-0	0	3	0			.667	-4	/S2	-0.4

■ JIM GRAY Gray, James W. b: 8/7/1862, Pittsburgh, Pa. d: 1/31/38, Allegheny, Pa. TR, Deb: 10/09/1884

YEAR	TM/L	G	AB	R	H	2B	3B	HR	RBI	BB	SO	AVG	OBP	SLG	PRO+	BR	/A	RC	SB	CS	SBR	FA	FR	POS	TPR
1884	Pit-a	1	2	0	1	0	0	0		0		.500	.500	.500	228	0	0	1				.500	-0	/3	0.0

■ LORENZO GRAY Gray, Lorenzo b: 3/4/58, Mound Bayou, Miss. BR/TR, 6'1", 180 lbs. Deb: 7/08/82

YEAR	TM/L	G	AB	R	H	2B	3B	HR	RBI	BB	SO	AVG	OBP	SLG	PRO+	BR	/A	RC	SB	CS	SBR	FA	FR	POS	TPR
1982	Chi-A	17	28	4	8	1	0	0	0	2	4	.286	.333	.321	81	-1	-1	3	1	0	0	.864	-3	3	-0.4

YEAR	TM/L	G	AB	R	H	2B	3B	HR	RBI	BB	SO	AVG	OBP	SLG	PRO+	BR	/A	RC	SB	CS	SBR	FA	FR	POS	TPR
1983	Chi-A	41	78	18	14	3	0	1	4	8	16	.179	.256	.256	40	-6	-7	5	1	0	0	.940	2	3/D	-0.5
Total	2	58	106	22	22	4	0	1	4	10	20	.208	.276	.274	50	-7	-7	8	2	0	1	.921	-1	/3D	-0.9

■ MILT GRAY Gray, Milton Marshall b: 2/21/14, Louisville, Ky. d: 6/30/69, Quincy, Fla. BR/TR, 6'1", 170 lbs. Deb: 5/27/37

YEAR	TM/L	G	AB	R	H	2B	3B	HR	RBI	BB	SO	AVG	OBP	SLG	PRO+	BR	/A	RC	SB	CS	SBR	FA	FR	POS	TPR
1937	Was-A	2	6	0	0	0	0	0	0	0	1	.000	.000	.000	-99	-2	-2	0	0	0	0	1.000	0	/C	-0.1

■ PETE GRAY Gray, Peter J. (b: Peter Wyshner) b: 3/6/15, Nanticoke, Pa. BL/TL, 6'1", 169 lbs. Deb: 4/17/45

YEAR	TM/L	G	AB	R	H	2B	3B	HR	RBI	BB	SO	AVG	OBP	SLG	PRO+	BR	/A	RC	SB	CS	SBR	FA	FR	POS	TPR
1945	StL-A	77	234	26	51	6	2	0	13	13	11	.218	.259	.261	49	-15	-16	16	5	6	-2	.959	1	O	-2.2

■ DICK GRAY Gray, Richard Benjamin b: 7/11/31, Jefferson, Pa. BR/TR, 5'11", 165 lbs. Deb: 4/15/58

YEAR	TM/L	G	AB	R	H	2B	3B	HR	RBI	BB	SO	AVG	OBP	SLG	PRO+	BR	/A	RC	SB	CS	SBR	FA	FR	POS	TPR
1958	LA-N	58	197	25	49	5	6	9	30	19	30	.249	.327	.472	105	2	1	29	1	1	-0	.929	14	3	1.5
1959	LA-N	21	52	8	8	1	0	2	4	6	12	.154	.241	.288	38	-5	-5	4	0	0	0	1.000	-0	3	-0.6
	StL-N	36	51	9	16	1	0	1	6	6	8	.314	.386	.392	101	1	0	9	3	0	1	.958	-9	S/32O	-0.7
	Yr	57	103	17	24	2	0	3	10	12	20	.233	.313	.340	69	-4	-5	12	3	0	1	.935	-9	3S/2O	-1.3
1960	StL-N	9	5	1	0	0	0	0	1	2	2	.000	.286	.000	-13	-1	-1	0	0	0	0	1.000	1	/23	0.1
Total	3	124	305	43	73	7	6	12	41	33	52	.239	.322	.420	91	-3	-4	42	4	1	1	.930	6	/3S2O	0.3

■ STAN GRAY Gray, Stanley Oscar "Dolly" b: 12/10/1888, Ladonia, Tex. d: 10/11/64, Snyder, Tex. BR/TR, 6'0.5", 184 lbs. Deb: 9/17/12

YEAR	TM/L	G	AB	R	H	2B	3B	HR	RBI	BB	SO	AVG	OBP	SLG	PRO+	BR	/A	RC	SB	CS	SBR	FA	FR	POS	TPR
1912	Pit-N	6	20	4	5	0	1	0	2	0	3	.250	.250	.350	64	-1	-1	2	0			1.000	-1	/1	-0.2

■ CRAIG GREBECK Grebeck, Craig Allen b: 12/29/64, Johnstown, Pa. BR/TR, 5'8", 160 lbs. Deb: 4/13/90

YEAR	TM/L	G	AB	R	H	2B	3B	HR	RBI	BB	SO	AVG	OBP	SLG	PRO+	BR	/A	RC	SB	CS	SBR	FA	FR	POS	TPR
1990	Chi-A	59	119	7	20	3	1	1	9	8	24	.168	.233	.235	32	-11	-11	7	0	0	0	.987	7	3S/2D	-0.2
1991	Chi-A	107	224	37	63	16	3	6	31	38	40	.281	.388	.460	137	11	12	42	1	3	-2	.933	-1	32S	1.2
1992	Chi-A	88	287	24	77	21	2	3	35	30	34	.268	.344	.387	107	2	3	39	0	3	-2	.980	-4	S/3O	0.3
Total	3	254	630	68	160	40	6	10	75	76	98	.254	.340	.384	104	2	4	87	1	6	-3	.972	2	S/32OD	1.3

■ DAVID GREEN Green, David Alejandro (Casaya) b: 12/4/60, Managua, Nicaragua BR/TR, 6'3", 170 lbs. Deb: 9/04/81

YEAR	TM/L	G	AB	R	H	2B	3B	HR	RBI	BB	SO	AVG	OBP	SLG	PRO+	BR	/A	RC	SB	CS	SBR	FA	FR	POS	TPR
1981	StL-N	21	34	6	5	1	0	0	2	6	5	.147	.275	.176	29	-3	-3	2	0	1	-1	.970	2	O	-0.2
1982	*StL-N	76	166	21	47	7	1	2	23	8	29	.283	.320	.373	92	-2	-2	20	11	3	2	.991	5	O	0.4
1983	StL-N	146	422	52	120	14	10	8	69	26	76	.284	.327	.422	106	2	2	53	34	16	1	.970	-11	*O	-1.1
1984	StL-N	126	452	49	121	14	4	15	65	20	105	.268	.300	.416	102	-2	-1	53	17	9	-0	.991	-5	*1O	-1.3
1985	SF-N	106	294	36	73	10	2	5	20	22	58	.248	.303	.347	85	-8	-6	28	6	5	-1	.987	-3	1O	-1.5
1987	StL-N	14	30	4	8	2	1	1	1	2	5	.267	.313	.500	109	0	0	4	0	1	-1	.882	-1	O/1	-0.2
Total	6	489	1398	168	374	48	18	31	180	84	278	.268	.311	.394	97	-12	-9	161	68	35	-1	.972	-12	O1	-3.9

■ DANNY GREEN Green, Edward b: 11/6/1876, Burlington, N.J. d: 11/9/14, Camden, N.J. BL/TR, Deb: 8/17/1898

YEAR	TM/L	G	AB	R	H	2B	3B	HR	RBI	BB	SO	AVG	OBP	SLG	PRO+	BR	/A	RC	SB	CS	SBR	FA	FR	POS	TPR
1898	Chi-N	47	188	26	59	4	3	4	27	7		.314	.342	.431	121	4	4	33	12			.970	5	O	0.5
1899	Chi-N	117	475	90	140	12	11	6	56	35		.295	.352	.404	110	4	6	77	18			.947	1	*O	-0.1
1900	Chi-N	103	389	63	116	21	5	5	49	17		.298	.339	.416	112	3	5	67	28			.938	0	*O	-0.2
1901	Chi-N	133	537	82	168	16	12	6	61	40		.313	.364	.421	132	18	21	96	31			.932	8	*O	1.8
1902	Chi-A	129	481	77	150	16	11	0	62	53		.312	.389	.391	122	13	16	92	35			.942	-3	*O	0.4
1903	Chi-A	135	499	75	154	26	7	6	62	47		.309	.375	.425	146	25	28	94	29			.933	2	*O	2.2
1904	Chi-A	147	536	83	142	16	10	2	62	63		.265	.352	.343	125	15	18	78	28			.964	1	*O	1.1
1905	Chi-A	112	379	56	92	13	6	0	44	53		.243	.345	.309	113	6	8	48	11			.914	-11	*O	-0.9
Total	8	923	3484	552	1021	124	65	29	423	315		.293	.360	.391	124	88	105	585	192			.941	3	O	4.8

■ PUMPSIE GREEN Green, Elijah Jerry b: 10/27/33, Oakland, Cal. BB/TR, 6', 175 lbs. Deb: 7/21/59

YEAR	TM/L	G	AB	R	H	2B	3B	HR	RBI	BB	SO	AVG	OBP	SLG	PRO+	BR	/A	RC	SB	CS	SBR	FA	FR	POS	TPR
1959	Bos-A	50	172	30	40	6	3	1	10	29	22	.233	.350	.320	81	-3	-4	22	4	2	0	.972	4	2/S	0.4
1960	Bos-A	133	260	36	63	10	3	3	21	44	47	.242	.354	.338	85	-3	-4	32	3	4	-2	.982	-13	2S	-1.3
1961	Bos-A	88	219	33	57	12	3	6	27	42	32	.260	.379	.425	112	6	5	38	4	2	0	.940	-5	S/2	0.5
1962	Bos-A	56	91	12	21	2	1	2	11	11	18	.231	.314	.341	74	-3	-3	11	1	0	0	.953	-9	2/S	-1.1
1963	NY-N	17	54	8	15	1	2	1	5	12	13	.278	.409	.426	139	3	3	9	0	2	-1	.857	-1	3	0.2
Total	5	344	796	119	196	31	12	13	74	138	132	.246	.360	.364	94	1	-3	112	12	10	-2	.975	-24	2S/3	-1.3

■ GARY GREEN Green, Gary Allan b: 1/14/62, Pittsburgh, Pa. BR/TR, 6'3", 175 lbs. Deb: 9/14/86 F

YEAR	TM/L	G	AB	R	H	2B	3B	HR	RBI	BB	SO	AVG	OBP	SLG	PRO+	BR	/A	RC	SB	CS	SBR	FA	FR	POS	TPR
1986	SD-N	13	33	2	7	1	0	0	2	1	11	.212	.235	.242	33	-3	-3	2	0	0	0	1.000	5	S	0.3
1989	SD-N	15	27	4	7	3	0	0	0	1	1	.259	.286	.370	86	-1	-1	3	0	1	-1	.921	4	S/3	0.3
1990	Tex-A	62	88	10	19	3	0	0	8	6	18	.216	.266	.250	45	-6	-6	6	1	1	-0	.972	21	S	1.6
1991	Tex-A	8	20	0	3	1	0	0	1	1	6	.150	.190	.200	8	-2	-2	1	0	0	0	.968	1	/S	-0.2
1992	Cin-N	8	12	3	4	1	0	0	0	0	2	.333	.333	.417	106	0	0	2	0	0	0	1.000	-1	/S3	-0.1
Total	5	106	180	19	40	9	0	0	11	9	38	.222	.259	.272	49	-12	-12	13	1	2	-1	.970	29	/S3	1.9

■ GENE GREEN Green, Gene Leroy b: 6/26/33, Los Angeles, Cal. d: 5/23/81, St.Louis, Mo. BR/TR, 6'2", 205 lbs. Deb: 9/10/57

YEAR	TM/L	G	AB	R	H	2B	3B	HR	RBI	BB	SO	AVG	OBP	SLG	PRO+	BR	/A	RC	SB	CS	SBR	FA	FR	POS	TPR
1957	StL-N	6	15	0	3	1	0	0	2	0	3	.200	.200	.267	23	-2	-2	1	0	0	0	1.000	-1	/O	-0.3
1958	StL-N	137	442	47	124	18	3	13	55	37	48	.281	.338	.423	96	-0	-3	56	2	1	0	.956	9	OC	0.5
1959	StL-N	30	74	8	14	6	0	1	3	5	18	.189	.241	.311	43	-6	-6	5	0	0	0	.944	4	OC	-0.3
1960	Bal-A	1	4	0	1	0	0	0	0	0	0	.250	.250	.250	36	-0	-0	0	0	0	0	1.000	0	/O	0.0
1961	Was-A	110	364	52	102	16	3	18	62	35	65	.280	.345	.489	122	9	10	51	0	2	-1	.986	-22	CO	-0.9
1962	Cle-A	66	143	16	40	4	1	11	28	8	21	.280	.318	.552	133	5	5	23	0	0	0	.964	-2	O/1	0.2
1963	Cle-A	43	78	4	16	3	0	2	7	4	22	.205	.262	.321	63	-4	-4	6	0	0	0	1.000	-3	O	-0.8
	Cin-N	15	31	3	7	1	0	1	3	0	8	.226	.250	.355	70	-1	-1	2	0	0	0	.932	-2	/C	-0.3
Total	7	408	1151	130	307	49	7	46	160	89	185	.267	.322	.441	101	1	-1	145	2	3	-1	.963	-16	OC/1	-1.9

■ JIM GREEN Green, James R. b: Cleveland, Ohio Deb: 7/19/1884

YEAR	TM/L	G	AB	R	H	2B	3B	HR	RBI	BB	SO	AVG	OBP	SLG	PRO+	BR	/A	RC	SB	CS	SBR	FA	FR	POS	TPR
1884	Was-U	10	36	4	5	1	0	0		0		.139	.139	.167	3	-4	-3	1				.818	-0	/3O	-0.3

■ JOE GREEN Green, Joseph Henry (a.k.a. Joseph Henry Greene) b: 9/17/1897, Philadelphia, Pa. d: 2/4/72, Bryn Mawr, Pa. BR/TR, 6'2", 170 lbs. Deb: 7/02/24

YEAR	TM/L	G	AB	R	H	2B	3B	HR	RBI	BB	SO	AVG	OBP	SLG	PRO+	BR	/A	RC	SB	CS	SBR	FA	FR	POS	TPR
1924	Phi-A	1	1	0	0	0	0	0	0	0	0	.000	.000	.000	-99	-0	-0	0	0	0	0	.000	0	H	0.0

■ LENNY GREEN Green, Leonard Charles b: 1/6/33, Detroit, Mich. BL/TL, 5'11", 170 lbs. Deb: 8/25/57

YEAR	TM/L	G	AB	R	H	2B	3B	HR	RBI	BB	SO	AVG	OBP	SLG	PRO+	BR	/A	RC	SB	CS	SBR	FA	FR	POS	TPR
1957	Bal-A	19	33	2	6	1	1	1	5	1	4	.182	.206	.364	56	-2	-2	2	0	1	-1	.950	-4	O	-0.8
1958	Bal-A	69	91	10	21	4	0	0	4	9	10	.231	.300	.275	63	-5	-4	8	0	2	-1	.965	-11	O	-1.8
1959	Bal-A	27	24	3	7	0	0	1	2	1	3	.292	.346	.417	111	0	0	4	0	0	0	1.000	-6	O	-0.7
	Was-A	88	190	29	46	6	1	2	15	20	15	.242	.314	.316	74	-7	-7	20	9	5	-0	.979	-4	O	-1.4
	Yr	115	214	32	53	6	1	3	17	21	18	.248	.318	.327	78	-6	-6	24	9	5	-0	.981	-11	O	-2.1
1960	Was-A	127	330	62	97	16	7	5	33	43	25	.294	.385	.430	121	11	11	58	21	8	2	.991	-6	*O	0.3
1961	Min-A	156	600	92	171	28	7	9	50	81	50	.285	.376	.400	102	9	4	96	17	11	-2	.978	-15	*O	-2.1
1962	Min-A	158	619	97	168	33	3	14	63	88	36	.271	.369	.402	104	9	6	98	8	4	0	.995	-17	*O	-2.1
1963	Min-A	145	280	41	67	10	1	4	27	31	21	.239	.319	.325	80	-6	-7	32	11	5	0	.988	-25	*O	-3.8
1964	Min-A	26	15	3	0	0	0	0	0	4	6	.000	.211	.000	-35	-3	-3	0	0	1	-1	1.000	-2	/O	-0.6
	LA-A	39	92	13	23	2	0	2	4	10	8	.250	.330	.337	96	-2	-0	11	2	0	1	.977	-1	O	-0.2
	Bal-A	14	21	0	4	0	0	0	1	7	3	.190	.393	.190	69	-0	-0	2	1	0	0	1.000	1	/O	0.1
	Yr	79	128	16	27	2	0	2	5	21	17	.211	.327	.273	72	-5	-4	13	3	1	0	.985	-2	O	-0.7
1965	Bos-A	119	373	69	103	24	6	7	24	48	43	.276	.363	.429	117	13	10	60	8	2	1	.980	2	O	0.9
1966	Bos-A	85	133	18	32	6	0	1	12	15	19	.241	.327	.308	76	-2	-4	13	0	1	-1	.978	-1	O	-0.7
1967	Det-A	58	151	22	42	8	1	1	13	9	17	.278	.319	.364	99	0	-0	17	1	1	-0	.983	-4	O	-0.7

YEAR	TM/L	G	AB	R	H	2B	3B	HR	RBI	BB	SO	AVG	OBP	SLG	PRO+	BR	/A	RC	SB	CS	SBR	FA	FR	POS	TPR
1968	Det-A	6	4	0	1	0	0	0	0	1	0	.250	.400	.250	97	0	0	0	0	0	0	.000	-1	/O	-0.1
Total	12	1136	2956	461	788	138	27	47	253	368	260	.267	.353	.379	99	14	3	421	78	41	-1	.984	-95	O	-13.7
■ DICK GREEN	Green, Richard Larry b: 4/21/41, Sioux City, Iowa BR/TR, 5'10", 180 lbs. Deb: 9/09/63																								
1963	KC-A	13	37	5	10	2	0	1	4	2	10	.270	.325	.405	99	0	-0	5	0	0	0	.941	2	/S2	0.3
1964	KC-A	130	435	48	115	14	5	11	37	27	87	.264	.312	.395	92	-3	-5	52	3	3	-1	.990	17	*2	2.1
1965	KC-A	133	474	64	110	15	1	15	55	50	110	.232	.309	.363	92	-6	-5	53	0	2	-1	.980	-7	*2	-0.2
1966	KC-A	140	507	58	127	24	3	9	62	27	101	.250	.298	.363	92	-8	-6	54	6	1	1	.979	-1	*2/3	0.5
1967	KC-A	122	349	26	69	12	4	5	37	30	68	.198	.261	.298	67	-16	-14	28	6	3	0	.946	-2	32/1S	-1.5
1968	Oak-A	76	202	19	47	6	0	6	18	21	41	.233	.308	.351	104	-0	1	23	3	1	0	.974	13	2/C3	1.9
1969	Oak-A	136	483	61	133	25	6	12	64	53	94	.275	.357	.427	123	12	14	72	2	3	-1	**.986**	10	*2	3.4
1970	Oak-A	135	384	34	73	7	0	4	29	38	73	.190	.268	.240	43	-30	-29	25	3	0	1	.978	0	*2/3C	-1.9
1971	*Oak-A	144	475	58	116	14	1	12	49	51	83	.244	.321	.354	93	-5	-4	53	1	1	-0	.986	8	*2/S	1.6
1972	*Oak-A	26	42	1	12	1	1	0	3	3	5	.286	.348	.357	116	1	1	5	0	1	-1	.964	2	2	0.3
1973	*Oak-A	133	332	33	87	17	0	3	42	21	63	.262	.310	.340	88	-8	-6	33	0	2	-1	.988	-9	*2/S3	-0.9
1974	*Oak-A	100	287	20	61	8	2	2	22	22	50	.213	.269	.275	61	-16	-14	20	2	3	-1	.983	-5	*2	-1.6
Total	12	1288	4007	427	960	145	23	80	422	345	785	.240	.305	.347	87	-80	-67	424	26	20	-4	.983	28	*2/3SC1	4.0
■ HANK GREENBERG	Greenberg, Henry Benjamin "Hammerin' Hank" b: 1/1/11, New York, N.Y. d: 9/4/86, Beverly Hills, Cal BR/TR, 6'3.5", 210 lbs. Deb: 9/14/30 H																								
1930	Det-A	1	1	0	0	0	0	0	0	0	0	.000	.000	.000	-98	-0	-0	0	0	0	0	.000	0	H	0.0
1933	Det-A	117	449	59	135	33	3	12	87	46	78	.301	.367	.468	118	12	11	79	6	2	1	.988	1	*1	0.1
1934	*Det-A	153	593	118	201	**63**	7	26	139	63	93	.339	.404	.600	156	47	47	144	9	5	-0	.990	1	*1	3.2
1935	*Det-A	152	619	121	203	46	16	**36**	**170**	87	91	.328	.411	.628	171	57	61	161	4	3	-1	.992	6	*1	4.5
1936	Det-A	12	46	10	16	6	2	1	16	9	6	.348	.455	.630	165	5	5	14	1	0	0	.992	1	1	0.4
1937	Det-A☆	154	594	137	200	49	14	40	**183**	102	101	.337	.436	.668	171	67	65	178	8	3	1	.992	5	*1	4.8
1938	Det-A†	155	556	**144**	175	23	4	**58**	146	**119**	92	.315	.438	.683	167	66	61	172	7	5	-1	.991	7	*1	4.3
1939	Det-A★	138	500	112	156	42	7	33	112	91	95	.312	.420	.622	152	47	41	136	8	3	1	**.993**	-1	*1	2.4
1940	*Det-A★	148	573	129	195	**50**	8	**41**	**150**	93	75	.340	.433	**.670**	166	**69**	**61**	**171**	6	3	0	.954	1	*O	**5.0**
1941	Det-A	19	67	12	18	5	1	2	12	16	12	.269	.410	.463	118	3	2	14	1	0	0	.914	-3	O	-0.1
1945	*Det-A	78	270	47	84	20	2	13	60	42	40	.311	.404	.544	164	25	23	61	3	1	0	1.000	-6	O	1.4
1946	Det-A	142	523	91	145	29	5	**44**	**127**	80	88	.277	.373	.604	160	46	42	119	5	1	1	.989	2	*1	3.8
1947	Pit-N	125	402	71	100	13	2	25	74	**104**	73	.249	.408	.478	131	23	22	83	0			.992	2	*1	1.9
Total	13	1394	5193	1051	1628	379	71	331	1276	852	844	.313	.412	.605	157	468	440	1331	58	26		.991	15	*1O	31.7
■ AL GREENE	Greene, Altar Alphonse b: 11/9/54, Detroit, Mich. BL/TR, 5'11", 190 lbs. Deb: 7/23/79																								
1979	Det-A	29	59	9	8	1	0	3	6	10	15	.136	.261	.305	50	-4	-4	5	0	1	-1	1.000	0	D/O	-0.5
■ JUNE GREENE	Greene, Julius Foust b: 6/25/1899, Ramseur, N.C. d: 3/19/74, Glendora, Cal. BL/TR, 6'2.5", 185 lbs. Deb: 4/20/28																								
1928	Phi-N	11	6	0	3	0	0	0	0	3	1	.500	.667	.500	202	1	1	2	0			1.000	0	/P	0.0
1929	Phi-N	21	19	1	4	1	0	0	0	2	4	.211	.286	.263	35	-2	-2	1	0			1.000	0	/P	0.0
Total	2	32	25	1	7	1	0	0	0	5	5	.280	.400	.320	79	-0	-1	4	0			1.000	1	/P	0.0
■ PADDY GREENE	Greene, Patrick Joseph "Patsy" (a.k.a. Patrick Foley In 1902) b: 3/20/1875, Providence, R.I. d: 10/20/34, Providence, R.I. BR/TR, 5'8", 150 lbs. Deb: 9/10/02																								
1902	Phi-N	19	65	6	11	1	0	0	1	2		.169	.206	.185	21	-6	-6	3	2			.912	1	3	-0.6
1903	NY-A	4	13	1	4	1	0	0	0	0		.308	.308	.385	100	0	-0	2	0			1.000	1	/3S	0.1
	Det-A	1	3	0	0	0	0	0	0	0		.000	.000	.000	-99	-1	-1	0	0			.750	-0	/3	-0.1
	Yr	5	16	1	4	1	0	0	0	0		.250	.250	.313	65	-1	-1	1	0			.933	1	/3S	0.0
Total	2	24	81	7	15	2	0	0	1	2		.185	.214	.210	30	-7	-7	5	2			.916	2	/3S	-0.6
■ WILLIE GREENE	Greene, Willie Louis b: 9/23/71, Milledgeville, Ga. BL/TR, 5'11", 180 lbs. Deb: 9/01/92																								
1992	Cin-N	29	93	10	25	5	2	2	13	10	23	.269	.340	.430	111	2	1	13	0	2	-1	.949	-1	3	0.0
■ JIM GREENGRASS	Greengrass, James Raymond b: 10/24/27, Addison, N.Y. BR/TR, 6'1", 200 lbs. Deb: 9/09/52																								
1952	Cin-N	18	68	10	21	2	1	5	24	7	12	.309	.373	.588	163	5	5	15	0	0	0	.965	2	O	0.6
1953	Cin-N	154	606	86	173	22	7	20	100	47	83	.285	.340	.444	102	1	1	89	6	4	-1	.983	8	*O	0.2
1954	Cin-N	139	542	79	152	27	4	27	95	41	81	.280	.331	.494	109	7	5	82	0	3	-2	.968	5	*O	0.2
1955	Cin-N	13	39	1	4	2	0	0	1	9	9	.103	.271	.154	16	-5	-5	2	0	0	0	1.000	2	O	-0.3
	Phi-N	94	323	43	88	20	2	12	37	33	43	.272	.342	.458	112	4	5	48	0	2	-1	.988	2	O/3	0.2
	Yr	107	362	44	92	22	2	12	38	42	52	.254	.333	.425	100	-0	0	50	0	2	-1	.990	4	O/3	-0.1
1956	Phi-N	86	215	24	44	9	2	5	25	28	43	.205	.296	.335	71	-9	-9	20	0	0	0	.991	-2	O	-1.4
Total	5	504	1793	243	482	82	16	69	282	165	271	.269	.332	.448	102	4	2	257	6	9	-4	.980	17	O/3	-0.5
■ MIKE GREENWELL	Greenwell, Michael Lewis b: 7/18/63, Louisville, Ky. BL/TR, 6', 200 lbs. Deb: 9/05/85																								
1985	Bos-A	17	31	7	10	1	0	4	8	3	4	.323	.382	.742	191	4	4	9	1	0	0	1.000	-5	O	-0.1
1986	*Bos-A	31	35	4	11	2	0	0	4	5	7	.314	.400	.371	111	1	1	5	0	0	0	1.000	-1	O/D	-0.1
1987	Bos-A	125	412	71	135	31	6	19	89	35	40	.328	.389	.570	146	29	27	90	5	4	-1	.971	1	OD/C	2.4
1988	*Bos-A★	158	590	86	192	39	8	22	119	87	38	.325	.420	.531	158	53	50	134	16	8	0	.981	7	*OD	5.2
1989	Bos-A★	145	578	87	178	36	0	14	95	56	44	.308	.372	.443	121	22	18	91	13	5	1	.967	-4	*O/D	1.1
1990	*Bos-A	159	610	71	181	30	6	14	73	65	43	.297	.368	.434	118	20	16	94	8	7	-2	.977	4	*O	1.5
1991	Bos-A	147	544	76	163	26	6	9	83	43	35	.300	.354	.419	108	10	6	81	15	5	2	.989	6	*O/D	1.0
1992	Bos-A	49	180	16	42	2	0	2	18	18	19	.233	.310	.278	63	-8	-9	14	2	3	-1	1.000	1	O/D	-1.1
Total	8	831	2980	418	912	167	26	84	489	312	230	.306	.377	.464	126	131	114	519	60	32	-1	.980	8	O/DC	9.9
■ BILL GREENWOOD	Greenwood, William F. b: 1857, Philadelphia, Pa. d: 5/2/02, Philadelphia, Pa. BB/TL, 5'7.5", 180 lbs. Deb: 9/16/1882																								
1882	Phi-a	7	30	8	9	1	0	0		1		.300	.323	.333	109	1	0	3				.909	-1	/O2	-0.1
1884	Bro-a	92	385	52	83	8	3	3		10		.216	.237	.275	69	-13	-13	26				.900	-8	*2/S	-1.7
1887	Bal-a	118	495	114	130	16	6	0		54		.263	.336	.319	91	-8	-3	79	71			**.928**	7	*2/O	0.6
1888	Bal-a	115	409	69	78	13	1	0	29	30		.191	.256	.227	60	-18	-16	36	46			.913	-22	2S/O	-3.2
1889	Col-a	118	414	62	93	7	10	3	49	58	71	.225	.327	.312	89	-7	-3	56	37			.914	-3	*2	0.0
1890	Roc-a	124	437	76	97	11	6	2		48		.222	.310	.288	85	-11	-5	53	40			.921	2	*2/S	0.4
Total	6	574	2170	381	490	56	26	8	78	201	71	.226	.298	.287	80	-55	-40	253	194			.916	-26	2/SO	-4.0
■ BRIAN GREER	Greer, Brian Keith b: 5/14/59, Lynwood, Cal. BR/TR, 6'3", 210 lbs. Deb: 9/13/77																								
1977	SD-N	1	1	0	0	0	0	0	0	0	1	.000	.000	.000	-99	-0	-0	0	0	0	0	.000	0	H	0.0
1979	SD-N	4	3	0	0	0	0	0	0	0	1	.000	.000	.000	-99	-1	-1	0	0	0	0	1.000	1	/O	0.0
Total	2	5	4	0	0	0	0	0	0	0	2	.000	.000	.000	-99	-1	-1	0	0	0	0		1	/O	0.0
■ ED GREER	Greer, Edward C. b: 1865, Philadelphia, Pa. d: 2/4/1890, Philadelphia, Pa. BR , Deb: 6/24/1885																								
1885	Bal-a	56	211	32	42	7	0	0		8		.199	.235	.232	51	-11	-11	12				.908	-0	OC	-1.1
1886	Bal-a	11	38	2	5	1	0	0		2		.132	.175	.158	6	-4	-4	2	4			.875	-2	/OC	-0.5
	Phi-a	71	264	33	51	5	3	1		8		.193	.223	.246	48	-16	-16	18	12			.921	6	O/C	-1.1
	Yr	82	302	35	56	6	3	1		10		.185	.217	.235	42	-20	-20	19	16			.919	4	O/C	-1.6
1887	Phi-a	3	11	1	2	0	0	0		0		.182	.182	.182	3	-1	-1	1	2			.857	0	/O	-0.1
	Bro-a	91	327	49	83	13	2	2		25		.254	.318	.324	80	-8	-8	45	33			.921	3	OC	-0.4

YEAR	TM/L	G	AB	R	H	2B	3B	HR	RBI	BB	SO	AVG	OBP	SLG	PRO+	BR	/A	RC	SB	CS	SBR	FA	FR	POS	TPR
	Yr	94	338	50	85	13	2	2		25		.251	.314	.320	78	-9	-10	46	35			.918	3	OC	-0.5
Total	3	232	851	117	183	26	5	3		43		.215	.261	.268	60	-40	-41	77	51			.916	6	O/C	-3.2

■ TOMMY GREGG Gregg, William Thomas b: 7/29/63, Boone, N.C. BL/TL, 6'1", 190 lbs. Deb: 9/14/87

YEAR	TM/L	G	AB	R	H	2B	3B	HR	RBI	BB	SO	AVG	OBP	SLG	PRO+	BR	/A	RC	SB	CS	SBR	FA	FR	POS	TPR
1987	Pit-N	10	8	3	2	1	0	0	0	0	2	.250	.250	.375	62	-0	-0	0	0	0	0	1.000	-2	/O	-0.2
1988	Pit-N	14	15	4	3	1	0	1	3	1	4	.200	.250	.467	103	-0	-0	1	0	1	-1	1.000	-2	/O	-0.3
	Atl-N	11	29	1	10	3	0	0	4	2	2	.345	.387	.448	132	1	1	5	0	0	0	1.000	2	/O	0.3
	Yr	25	44	5	13	4	0	1	7	3	6	.295	.340	.455	125	1	1	6	0	1	-1	1.000	0	O	0.0
1989	Atl-N	102	276	24	67	8	0	6	23	18	45	.243	.289	.337	76	-8	-9	26	3	4	-2	.967	-10	O1	-2.5
1990	Atl-N	124	239	18	63	13	1	5	32	20	39	.264	.323	.389	90	-2	-3	31	4	3	-1	.987	-2	1O	-0.9
1991	*Atl-N	72	107	13	20	8	1	1	4	12	24	.187	.275	.308	60	-5	-6	9	2	2	-1	1.000	-2	O1	-1.0
1992	Atl-N	18	19	1	5	0	0	1	1	1	7	.263	.300	.421	94	-0	-0	2	1	0	0	1.000	-1	/O	-0.1
Total	6	351	693	64	170	34	2	14	67	54	123	.245	.302	.361	82	-14	-18	74	10	10	-3	.979	-16	O1	-4.7

■ ED GREMMINGER Gremminger, Lorenzo Edward "Battleship" b: 3/30/1874, Canton, Ohio d: 5/26/42, Canton, Ohio BR/TR, 6'1", 200 lbs. Deb: 4/21/1895

YEAR	TM/L	G	AB	R	H	2B	3B	HR	RBI	BB	SO	AVG	OBP	SLG	PRO+	BR	/A	RC	SB	CS	SBR	FA	FR	POS	TPR
1895	Cle-N	20	78	10	21	1	0	0	15	5	13	.269	.313	.282	53	-5	-6	7	0			.873	-2	3	-0.6
1902	Bos-N	140	522	55	134	20	12	1	65	39		.257	.314	.347	103	2	1	61	7			**.951**	3	*3	0.6
1903	Bos-N	140	511	57	135	24	9	5	56	31		.264	.313	.376	100	-4	-1	66	12			.935	16	*3	1.6
1904	Det-A	83	309	18	66	13	3	1	28	14		.214	.257	.285	74	-10	-9	25	3			.950	-16	3	-2.6
Total	4	383	1420	140	356	58	24	7	164	89	13	.251	.301	.340	93	-18	-15	160	22			.940	1	3	-1.0

■ BUDDY GREMP Gremp, Lewis Edward b: 8/5/19, Denver, Col. BR/TR, 6'1", 175 lbs. Deb: 9/13/40

YEAR	TM/L	G	AB	R	H	2B	3B	HR	RBI	BB	SO	AVG	OBP	SLG	PRO+	BR	/A	RC	SB	CS	SBR	FA	FR	POS	TPR
1940	Bos-N	4	9	0	2	0	0	0	2	0	0	.222	.222	.222	24	-1	-1	0	0			1.000	-0	/1	-0.1
1941	Bos-N	37	75	7	18	3	0	0	10	5	3	.240	.287	.280	63	-4	-4	5	0			.977	-3	1/2C	-0.8
1942	Bos-N	72	207	12	45	11	0	3	19	13	21	.217	.267	.314	71	-8	-8	17	1			.991	1	1/3	-1.1
Total	3	113	291	19	65	14	0	3	31	18	24	.223	.271	.302	67	-13	-12	22	1			.988	-3	/12C3	-2.0

■ REDDY GREY Grey, Romer Carl (b: Romer Carl Gray) b: 4/8/1875, Zanesville, Ohio d: 11/9/34, Altadena, Cal. TL , 5'11", 175 lbs. Deb: 5/28/03

YEAR	TM/L	G	AB	R	H	2B	3B	HR	RBI	BB	SO	AVG	OBP	SLG	PRO+	BR	/A	RC	SB	CS	SBR	FA	FR	POS	TPR
1903	Pit-N	1	3	1	1	0	0	0	1	1		.333	.500	.333	135	0	0	1	0			1.000	-0	/O	0.0

■ BILL GREY Grey, William Tobin b: 4/15/1871, Philadelphia, Pa. d: 12/8/32, Philadelphia, Pa. 5'11", 175 lbs. Deb: 5/14/1890

YEAR	TM/L	G	AB	R	H	2B	3B	HR	RBI	BB	SO	AVG	OBP	SLG	PRO+	BR	/A	RC	SB	CS	SBR	FA	FR	POS	TPR
1890	Phi-N	34	128	20	31	8	4	0	21	6	3	.242	.287	.367	90	-2	-2	15	5			1.000	-10	O/32C1	-1.0
1891	Phi-N	23	75	11	18	0	0	0	7	3	10	.240	.296	.240	57	-4	-4	6	3			.804	-6	CO/S3	-0.8
1895	Cin-N	52	181	24	55	17	4	1	29	15	8	.304	.364	.459	109	3	2	33	4			.906	-5	32/SCO	-0.1
1896	Cin-N	46	121	15	25	2	1	0	17	19	11	.207	.314	.240	46	-8	-10	12	6			.927	2	2C/SO13	-0.5
1898	Pit-N	137	528	56	121	17	5	0	67	28		.229	.283	.280	63	-27	-25	47	5			.879	-20	*3	-4.2
Total	5	292	1033	126	250	44	14	1	141	71	32	.242	.303	.315	72	-37	-39	113	23			.879	-38	3/2COS1	-6.6

■ BOBBY GRICH Grich, Robert Anthony b: 1/15/49, Muskegon, Mich. BR/TR, 6'2", 190 lbs. Deb: 6/29/70

YEAR	TM/L	G	AB	R	H	2B	3B	HR	RBI	BB	SO	AVG	OBP	SLG	PRO+	BR	/A	RC	SB	CS	SBR	FA	FR	POS	TPR
1970	Bal-A	30	95	11	20	1	3	0	8	9	21	.211	.279	.284	55	-6	-6	7	1	1	-0	.915	2	S/23	-0.1
1971	Bal-A	7	30	7	9	0	0	1	6	5	8	.300	.400	.400	128	1	1	6	1	0	0	1.000	3	/S2	0.5
1972	Bal-A★	133	460	66	128	21	3	12	50	53	96	.278	.362	.415	127	18	17	71	13	6	0	.950	-25	S21/3	0.5
1973	*Bal-A	162	581	82	146	29	7	12	50	107	91	.251	.374	.387	116	15	16	92	17	9	-0	**.995**	21	*2	4.6
1974	*Bal-A★	160	582	92	153	29	6	19	82	90	117	.263	.380	.431	137	28	30	99	17	11	-2	.979	9	*2	4.7
1975	Bal-A	150	524	81	136	26	4	13	57	107	88	.260	.393	.399	133	22	26	90	14	10	-2	.977	24	*2	5.7
1976	Bal-A★	144	518	93	138	31	4	13	54	86	99	.266	.374	.417	140	23	27	87	14	6	1	.985	-1	*2/3D	3.7
1977	Cal-A	52	181	24	44	6	0	7	23	37	40	.243	.374	.392	114	4	5	27	6	6	-2	.983	-3	S	0.5
1978	Cal-A	144	487	68	122	16	2	6	42	75	83	.251	.359	.329	98	-1	2	64	4	3	-1	.983	0	*2	1.2
1979	*Cal-A★	153	534	78	157	30	5	30	101	59	84	.294	.366	.537	145	29	32	103	1	0	0	.984	2	*2	4.2
1980	Cal-A★	150	498	60	135	22	2	14	62	84	108	.271	.381	.408	119	14	16	78	3	7	-3	.989	3	*2/1	2.4
1981	Cal-A	100	352	56	107	14	2	**22**	61	40	71	.304	.381	**.543**	**164**	28	28	73	2	4	-2	.983	11	*2	4.5
1982	*Cal-A★	145	506	74	132	28	5	19	65	82	109	.261	.372	.449	124	19	19	87	3	3	-1	.986	11	*2/D	3.6
1983	Cal-A	120	387	65	113	17	0	16	62	76	62	.292	.417	.460	142	26	26	77	2	4	-2	.969	16	*2/S	4.5
1984	Cal-A	116	363	60	93	15	1	18	58	57	70	.256	.360	.452	124	12	13	58	2	5	-2	.982	3	213	1.5
1985	Cal-A	144	479	74	116	17	3	13	53	81	77	.242	.355	.372	100	2	2	63	3	5	-2	**.997**	15	*213/D	1.8
1986	*Cal-A	98	313	42	84	18	0	9	30	39	54	.268	.355	.412	109	4	5	45	1	3	-2	.980	-10	21/3	-0.5
Total	17	2008	6890	1033	1833	320	47	224	864	1087	1278	.266	.373	.424	125	239	259	1129	104	83	-19	.984	80	*2S/13D	43.3

■ TIM GRIESENBECK Griesenbeck, Carlos Phillipe Timothy b: 12/10/1897, San Antonio, Tex. d: 3/25/53, San Antonio, Tex. BR/TR, 5'10.5", 190 lbs. Deb: 9/11/20

YEAR	TM/L	G	AB	R	H	2B	3B	HR	RBI	BB	SO	AVG	OBP	SLG	PRO+	BR	/A	RC	SB	CS	SBR	FA	FR	POS	TPR
1920	StL-N	5	3	1	1	0	0	0	0	0	0	.333	.333	.333	95	-0	-0	0	0	0	0	1.000	0	/C	0.0

■ TOM GRIEVE Grieve, Thomas Alan b: 3/4/48, Pittsfield, Mass. BR/TR, 6'2", 190 lbs. Deb: 7/05/70

YEAR	TM/L	G	AB	R	H	2B	3B	HR	RBI	BB	SO	AVG	OBP	SLG	PRO+	BR	/A	RC	SB	CS	SBR	FA	FR	POS	TPR
1970	Was-A	47	116	12	23	5	1	3	10	14	38	.198	.290	.336	76	-5	-4	12	0	0	0	.939	-3	O	-0.8
1972	Tex-A	64	142	12	29	2	1	3	11	11	39	.204	.271	.296	72	-6	-5	11	1	3	-2	.985	-4	O	-1.3
1973	Tex-A	66	123	22	38	6	0	7	21	7	25	.309	.351	.528	151	7	7	22	1	0	0	1.000	-12	O/D	-0.6
1974	Tex-A	84	259	30	66	10	4	9	32	20	48	.255	.313	.429	114	3	4	33	0	0	0	1.000	2	DO/1	0.4
1975	Tex-A	118	369	46	102	17	1	14	61	22	74	.276	.317	.442	113	4	5	48	0	2	-1	.990	-7	OD	-0.5
1976	Tex-A	149	546	57	139	23	3	20	81	35	119	.255	.304	.418	108	5	3	65	4	1	1	.983	2	DO	0.4
1977	Tex-A	79	236	24	53	9	0	7	30	13	57	.225	.274	.352	68	-11	-11	23	1	0	0	.976	-6	OD	-1.8
1978	NY-N	54	101	5	21	3	0	2	8	9	23	.208	.273	.297	61	-6	-5	8	0	1	-1	.979	2	O/1	-0.5
1979	StL-N	9	15	1	3	1	0	0	0	4	1	.200	.368	.267	76	-0	-0	2	0	0	0	.875	-1	/O	-0.1
Total	9	670	1907	209	474	76	10	65	254	135	424	.249	.303	.401	100	-8	-6	224	7	7	-2	.982	-25	OD/1	-4.8

■ KEN GRIFFEY Griffey, George Kenneth Jr. b: 11/21/69, Donora, Pa. BL/TL, 6'3", 195 lbs. Deb: 4/03/89 F

YEAR	TM/L	G	AB	R	H	2B	3B	HR	RBI	BB	SO	AVG	OBP	SLG	PRO+	BR	/A	RC	SB	CS	SBR	FA	FR	POS	TPR
1989	Sea-A	127	455	61	120	23	0	16	61	44	83	.264	.331	.420	107	6	4	65	16	7	1	.969	5	*O	0.7
1990	Sea-A★	155	597	91	179	28	7	22	80	63	81	.300	.369	.481	134	28	27	103	16	11	-2	.980	1	*O/D	2.2
1991	Sea-A★	154	548	76	179	42	1	22	100	71	82	.327	.405	.527	156	42	42	118	18	6	2	.989	9	*O/D	4.9
1992	Sea-A★	142	565	83	174	39	4	27	103	44	67	.308	.363	.535	147	34	34	104	10	5	0	.997	6	*O/D	3.7
Total	4	578	2165	311	652	132	12	87	344	222	313	.301	.369	.494	137	110	107	391	60	29	1	.984	21	O/D	11.5

■ KEN GRIFFEY Griffey, George Kenneth Sr. b: 4/10/50, Donora, Pa. BL/TL, 6', 200 lbs. Deb: 8/25/73 F

YEAR	TM/L	G	AB	R	H	2B	3B	HR	RBI	BB	SO	AVG	OBP	SLG	PRO+	BR	/A	RC	SB	CS	SBR	FA	FR	POS	TPR
1973	*Cin-N	25	86	19	33	5	1	3	14	6	10	.384	.424	.570	182	8	9	21	4	2	0	1.000	-5	O	0.3
1974	Cin-N	88	227	24	57	9	5	2	19	27	43	.251	.333	.361	96	-2	-1	29	9	4	0	1.000	0	O	-0.3
1975	*Cin-N	132	463	95	141	15	9	4	46	67	67	.305	.394	.402	119	16	14	77	16	7	1	.967	-9	*O	0.2
1976	*Cin-N★	148	562	111	189	28	9	6	74	62	65	.336	.403	.450	139	32	30	109	34	11	4	.979	-3	*O	2.6
1977	Cin-N☆	154	585	117	186	35	8	12	57	69	84	.318	.390	.467	126	25	24	108	17	8	0	.990	6	*O	2.3
1978	Cin-N	158	614	90	177	33	8	10	63	54	70	.288	.346	.417	112	9	9	93	23	5	4	.969	2	*O	0.9
1979	Cin-N	95	380	62	120	27	4	8	32	36	39	.316	.376	.471	129	16	15	68	12	5	1	.984	1	O	1.3
1980	Cin-N★	146	544	89	160	28	10	13	85	62	77	.294	.367	.454	128	21	21	99	23	1	6	.978	-4	*O	1.8
1981	Cin-N	101	396	65	123	21	6	2	34	39	42	.311	.374	.409	120	12	11	61	12	4	1	.989	6	O	1.5
1982	NY-A	127	484	70	134	23	2	12	54	39	58	.277	.331	.407	103	1	2	65	10	4	1	.983	7	*O	0.6
1983	NY-A	118	458	60	140	21	3	11	46	34	45	.306	.356	.437	121	10	13	74	6	1	1	.992	-2	*1/OD	0.6
1984	NY-A	120	399	44	109	20	1	7	56	29	32	.273	.324	.381	98	-3	-1	49	2	2	-1	.974	-0	O1/D	-0.6
1985	NY-A	127	438	68	120	28	4	10	69	41	51	.274	.336	.425	109	4	5	63	7	7	-2	.970	5	*O/1D	0.4

YEAR	TM/L	G	AB	R	H	2B	3B	HR	RBI	BB	SO	AVG	OBP	SLG	PRO+	BR	/A	RC	SB	CS	SBR	FA	FR	POS	TPR
1986	NY-A	59	198	33	60	7	0	9	26	15	24	.303	.355	.475	125	6	6	31	2	2	-1	.971	1	O/D	0.5
	Atl-N	80	292	36	90	15	3	12	32	20	43	.308	.353	.503	126	12	10	51	12	7	-1	.986	1	O/1	0.8
1987	Atl-N	122	399	65	114	24	1	14	64	46	54	.286	.361	.456	109	9	6	62	4	7	-3	.995	1	*O/1	0.0
1988	Atl-N	69	193	21	48	5	0	2	19	17	26	.249	.310	.306	74	-5	-7	17	1	3	-2	.969	-4	O1	-1.5
	Cin-N	25	50	5	14	1	0	2	4	2	5	.280	.308	.420	103	0	0	7	0	0	0	.986	-0	1	-0.1
	Yr	94	243	26	62	6	0	4	23	19	31	.255	.309	.329	80	-5	-6	24	1	3	-2	.969	-4	O1	-1.6
1989	Cin-N	106	236	26	62	8	3	8	30	29	42	.263	.346	.424	115	6	5	36	4	2	0	.987	-8	O/1	-0.5
1990	Cin-N	46	63	6	13	2	0	1	8	2	5	.206	.242	.286	43	-5	-5	5	2	1	0	.979	0	/1O	-0.6
	Sea-A	21	77	13	29	2	0	3	18	10	3	.377	.448	.519	168	8	7	19	0	0	0	.963	-2	O	0.5
1991	Sea-A	30	85	10	24	7	0	1	9	13	13	.282	.384	.400	117	2	2	14	0	0	0	1.000	-4	O/D	-0.2
Total	19	2097	7229	1129	2143	364	77	152	859	719	898	.296	.361	.431	118	181	177	1156	200	83	10	.981	-13	*O1/D	10.5

■ ALFREDO GRIFFIN Griffin, Alfredo Claudino (b: Alfredo Claudino Baptist (Griffin)) b: 10/6/57, Santo Domingo, D.R. BB/TR, 5'11", 165 lbs. Deb: 9/04/76

YEAR	TM/L	G	AB	R	H	2B	3B	HR	RBI	BB	SO	AVG	OBP	SLG	PRO+	BR	/A	RC	SB	CS	SBR	FA	FR	POS	TPR
1976	Cle-A	12	4	0	1	0	0	0	0	0	2	.250	.250	.250	47	-0	-0	0	0	1	-1	.750	0	/SD	0.0
1977	Cle-A	14	41	5	6	1	0	0	3	3	5	.146	.205	.171	4	-5	-5	1	2	2	-1	.940	-1	S/D	-0.6
1978	Cle-A	5	4	1	2	1	0	0	0	2	1	.500	.667	.750	301	1	1	2	0	0	0	.917	3	/S	0.4
1979	Tor-A	153	624	81	179	22	10	2	31	40	59	.287	.335	.364	87	-10	-11	75	21	16	-3	.956	6	*S	0.9
1980	Tor-A	155	653	63	166	26	**15**	2	41	24	58	.254	.285	.349	70	-25	-29	59	18	23	-8	.955	2	*S	-1.8
1981	Tor-A	101	388	30	81	19	6	0	21	17	38	.209	.244	.289	50	-24	-27	24	8	12	-5	.937	-19	S/32	-4.4
1982	Tor-A	162	539	57	130	20	8	1	48	22	48	.241	.271	.314	55	-30	-36	45	10	8	-2	.968	6	*S	-1.7
1983	Tor-A	162	528	62	132	22	9	4	47	27	44	.250	.290	.348	71	-19	-23	52	8	11	-4	.965	-4	*S/2D	-1.6
1984	Tor-A★	140	419	53	101	8	2	4	30	4	33	.241	.250	.298	49	-28	-30	31	11	3	2	.962	-5	*S2/D	-2.3
1985	Oak-A	162	614	75	166	18	7	2	64	20	50	.270	.293	.332	77	-25	-19	60	24	9	2	.960	-15	*S	-1.6
1986	Oak-A	162	594	74	169	23	6	4	51	35	52	.285	.326	.364	95	-10	-4	71	33	16	0	.966	-11	*S	0.0
1987	Oak-A	144	494	69	130	23	5	3	60	28	41	.263	.308	.348	79	-19	-14	52	26	13	0	.963	0	*S/2	-0.2
1988	*LA-N	95	316	39	63	8	3	1	27	24	30	.199	.260	.253	49	-21	-20	22	7	5	-1	.965	2	S	-1.2
1989	LA-N	136	506	49	125	27	2	0	29	29	57	.247	.288	.308	72	-20	-19	45	10	7	-1	.975	-8	*S	-1.8
1990	LA-N	141	461	38	97	11	3	1	35	29	65	.210	.260	.254	43	-36	-35	31	6	3	0	.959	10	*S	-1.5
1991	LA-N	109	350	27	85	6	2	0	27	22	49	.243	.290	.271	60	-19	-18	28	5	4	-1	.961	19	*S	0.8
1992	*Tor-A	63	150	21	35	7	0	0	10	9	19	.233	.277	.280	54	-9	-10	12	3	1	0	.981	-0	S2	-0.7
Total	17	1916	6685	744	1668	242	78	24	524	335	651	.250	.288	.320	67	-298	-298	611	192	134	-23	.961	-14	*S/2D3	-17.3

■ DOUG GRIFFIN Griffin, Douglas Lee b: 6/4/47, South Gate, Cal. BR/TR, 6', 170 lbs. Deb: 9/11/70

YEAR	TM/L	G	AB	R	H	2B	3B	HR	RBI	BB	SO	AVG	OBP	SLG	PRO+	BR	/A	RC	SB	CS	SBR	FA	FR	POS	TPR
1970	Cal-A	18	55	2	7	1	0	0	4	6	5	.127	.213	.145	1	-7	-7	2	0	0	0	.964	1	2/3	-0.5
1971	Bos-A	125	483	51	118	23	2	3	27	31	45	.244	.293	.319	68	-17	-21	44	11	5	0	.986	7	*2	-0.4
1972	Bos-A	129	470	43	122	12	1	2	35	45	48	.260	.327	.302	83	-6	-9	50	9	2	2	.978	2	*2	0.3
1973	Bos-A	113	396	43	101	14	5	1	33	21	42	.255	.298	.323	71	-13	-16	36	7	5	-1	.990	-14	*2	-2.6
1974	Bos-A	93	312	35	83	12	4	0	33	28	21	.266	.330	.330	85	-3	-6	32	2	8	-4	.979	-13	2/S	-2.0
1975	*Bos-A	100	287	21	69	6	0	1	29	18	29	.240	.290	.272	55	-15	-18	22	2	2	-1	.967	-10	2/S	-2.5
1976	Bos-A	49	127	14	24	2	0	0	4	9	14	.189	.248	.205	30	-10	-12	7	2	1	0	.989	-1	2/D	-1.2
1977	Bos-A	5	6	0	0	0	0	0	0	0	0	.000	.000	.000	-90	-2	-2	0	0	0	0	1.000	0	/2	-0.1
Total	8	632	2136	209	524	70	12	7	165	158	204	.245	.301	.299	68	-75	-91	193	33	23	-4	.981	-28	2/3DS	-9.0

■ PUG GRIFFIN Griffin, Francis Arthur b: 4/24/1896, Lincoln, Neb. d: 10/12/51, Colorado Springs, Colo. BR/TR, 5'11.5", 187 lbs. Deb: 7/27/17

YEAR	TM/L	G	AB	R	H	2B	3B	HR	RBI	BB	SO	AVG	OBP	SLG	PRO+	BR	/A	RC	SB	CS	SBR	FA	FR	POS	TPR
1917	Phi-A	18	25	4	5	1	0	1	3	1	9	.200	.231	.360	81	-1	-1	2	1			1.000	1	/1	0.0
1920	NY-N	5	4	0	1	0	0	0	0	1	2	.250	.400	.250	90	0	0	0	0	0	0	1.000	-1	/O	-0.1
Total	2	23	29	4	6	1	0	1	3	2	11	.207	.258	.345	83	-1	-1	3	1	0			-0	/1O	-0.1

■ IVY GRIFFIN Griffin, Ivy Moore b: 11/16/1896, Thomasville, Ala. d: 8/25/57, Gainesville, Fla. BL/TR, 5'11", 180 lbs. Deb: 9/09/19

YEAR	TM/L	G	AB	R	H	2B	3B	HR	RBI	BB	SO	AVG	OBP	SLG	PRO+	BR	/A	RC	SB	CS	SBR	FA	FR	POS	TPR
1919	Phi-A	17	68	5	20	2	2	0	6	3	10	.294	.333	.382	99	-0	-0	8	0			.989	4	1	0.3
1920	Phi-A	129	467	46	111	15	1	0	20	17	49	.238	.281	.274	47	-35	-36	37	3	3	-1	.990	5	*1/2	-3.4
1921	Phi-A	39	103	14	33	4	2	0	13	5	6	.320	.369	.398	95	-1	-1	15	1	2	-1	.973	-2	1	-0.4
Total	3	185	638	65	164	21	5	0	39	25	65	.257	.301	.306	60	-36	-37	60	4	5		.988	7	1/2	-3.5

■ MIKE GRIFFIN Griffin, Michael Joseph b: 3/20/1865, Utica, N.Y. d: 4/10/08, Utica, N.Y. BL/TR, 5'7", 160 lbs. Deb: 4/16/1887 M

YEAR	TM/L	G	AB	R	H	2B	3B	HR	RBI	BB	SO	AVG	OBP	SLG	PRO+	BR	/A	RC	SB	CS	SBR	FA	FR	POS	TPR
1887	Bal-a	136	532	142	160	32	13	3		55		.301	.375	.427	133	19	25	123	94			.924	-12	*O	0.9
1888	Bal-a	137	542	103	139	21	11	0	46	55		.256	.331	.336	120	12	14	77	46			.938	7	*O	1.6
1889	Bal-a	137	531	**152**	148	21	14	4	48	91	29	.279	.387	.394	123	21	19	98	39			.910	-10	*OS/2	0.6
1890	Phi-P	115	489	127	140	29	6	6	54	64	19	.286	.377	.407	109	9	7	88	30			**.954**	18	*O	1.6
1891	Bro-N	134	521	106	139	**36**	9	3	65	57	31	.267	.340	.388	115	9	9	93	65			**.960**	26	*O	2.7
1892	Bro-N	129	452	103	125	17	11	3	66	68	36	.277	.376	.383	137	19	22	86	49			**.986**	13	*O/S	2.7
1893	Bro-N	95	362	85	103	21	7	6	59	59	23	.285	.396	.431	128	13	16	76	30			**.965**	9	*O/2	1.6
1894	Bro-N	107	402	122	144	28	4	5	75	78	14	.358	.467	.485	142	26	32	113	39			.969	7	*O	2.4
1895	Bro-N	131	519	140	173	38	7	4	65	93	29	.333	.444	.457	147	32	41	121	27			**.969**	14	*O/S	3.5
1896	Bro-N	122	493	101	152	27	9	4	51	48	25	.308	.380	.424	121	10	15	91	23			.961	3	*O	0.7
1897	Bro-N	134	534	136	169	25	11	2	56	81		.316	.416	.416	127	19	25	103	16			.956	5	*O	1.7
1898	Bro-N	134	537	88	161	18	6	2	40	60		.300	.379	.367	114	12	12	83	15			**.974**	10	*OM	1.1
Total	12	1511	5914	1405	1753	313	108	42	625	809	206	.296	.388	.407	126	201	236	1153	473			.956	88	*O/S2	21.1

■ THOMAS GRIFFIN Griffin, Thomas William b: 1/1857, Titusville, Pa. d: 4/17/33, Rockford, Ill. Deb: 9/27/1884

YEAR	TM/L	G	AB	R	H	2B	3B	HR	RBI	BB	SO	AVG	OBP	SLG	PRO+	BR	/A	RC	SB	CS	SBR	FA	FR	POS	TPR
1884	Mil-U	11	41	5	9	2	0	0		3		.220	.273	.268	154	-1	2	3				.918	-2	1	0.0

■ SANDY GRIFFIN Griffin, Tobias Charles b: 7/19/1858, Fayetteville, N.Y d: 6/5/26, Fayetteville, N.Y. BR/TR, 5'10", 160 lbs. Deb: 5/26/1884 M

YEAR	TM/L	G	AB	R	H	2B	3B	HR	RBI	BB	SO	AVG	OBP	SLG	PRO+	BR	/A	RC	SB	CS	SBR	FA	FR	POS	TPR
1884	NY-N	16	62	7	11	2	0	0	6	1	19	.177	.190	.210	25	-5	-5	3				.842	-3	O	-0.8
1890	Roc-a	107	407	85	125	28	4	5		50		.307	.388	.432	156	23	28	78	21			.856	-19	*O/2	0.5
1891	Was-a	20	69	15	19	4	2	0	10	10	3	.275	.398	.391	135	3	4	12	2			.939	-3	OM	0.0
1893	StL-N	23	92	9	18	1	1	0	9	16	2	.196	.315	.228	47	-6	-6	7	2			.906	-2	O	-0.8
Total	4	166	630	116	173	35	7	5	25	77	24	.275	.361	.376	123	14	20	100	25			.873	-27	O/2	-1.1

■ BERT GRIFFITH Griffith, Bartholomew Joseph "Buck" b: 3/30/1896, St.Louis, Mo. d: 5/5/73, Bishop, Cal. BR/TR, 5'11", 185 lbs. Deb: 4/13/22

YEAR	TM/L	G	AB	R	H	2B	3B	HR	RBI	BB	SO	AVG	OBP	SLG	PRO+	BR	/A	RC	SB	CS	SBR	FA	FR	POS	TPR
1922	Bro-N	106	325	45	100	22	8	2	35	5	11	.308	.322	.443	96	-4	-3	43	5	7	-3	.981	-1	O/1	-1.2
1923	Bro-N	79	248	23	73	8	4	2	37	13	16	.294	.332	.383	91	-4	-4	31	1	2	-1	.949	-8	O	-1.5
1924	Was-A	6	8	1	1	0	0	0	0	0	1	.125	.125	.125	-37	-2	-2	0	0	0	0	1.000	0	/O	-0.1
Total	3	191	581	69	174	30	12	4	72	18	28	.299	.324	.413	92	-10	-8	74	6	9	-4	.968	-9	O/1	-2.8

■ CLARK GRIFFITH Griffith, Clark Calvin "The Old Fox" b: 11/20/1869, Clear Creek, Mo. d: 10/27/55, Washington, D.C. BR/TR, 5'6.5", 156 lbs. Deb: 4/11/1891 MH

YEAR	TM/L	G	AB	R	H	2B	3B	HR	RBI	BB	SO	AVG	OBP	SLG	PRO+	BR	/A	RC	SB	CS	SBR	FA	FR	POS	TPR
1891	StL-a	27	77	11	12	1	0	1	8	8	15	.156	.253	.208	30	-6	-8	5	2			.930	0	P	0.0
	Bos-a	10	23	6	4	1	1	1	3	6	5	.174	.367	.435	134	1	1	4	1			.778	-1	/PO	0.0
	Yr	37	100	17	16	2	1	2	11	14	20	.160	.282	.260	52	-5	-7	8	3			.909	-1	P/O	0.0
1893	Chi-N	4	11	1	2	0	0	0	2	0	1	.182	.182	.182	-2	-2	-2	0	0			1.000	1	/P	0.0
1894	Chi-N	46	142	27	33	5	4	0	15	23	9	.232	.339	.324	59	-8	-10	18	6			.942	-3	P/OS	-0.4
1895	Chi-N	43	144	20	46	3	0	1	27	16	9	.319	.391	.361	91	0	-2	22	2			.923	1	P/O	0.0
1896	Chi-N	38	135	22	36	5	2	1	16	9	7	.267	.313	.356	75	-5	-5	17	3			.917	1	P	0.0

YEAR	TM/L	G	AB	R	H	2B	3B	HR	RBI	BB	SO	AVG	OBP	SLG	PRO+	BR	/A	RC	SB	CS	SBR	FA	FR	POS	TPR
1897	Chi-N	46	162	27	38	8	4	0	21	18		.235	.311	.333	67	-7	-8	18	2			.947	2	P/OS31	-0.1
1898	Chi-N	38	122	15	20	2	3	0	15	13		.164	.244	.230	36	-10	-10	8	1			.952	1	P	0.0
1899	Chi-N	39	120	15	31	5	0	0	14	14		.258	.346	.300	80	-3	-3	14	2			.933	6	P/S	-0.1
1900	Chi-N	30	95	16	24	4	1	1	7	8		.253	.311	.347	85	-3	-2	11	2			.917	-1	P	0.0
1901	Chi-A	35	89	21	27	3	1	2	14	23		.303	.446	.427	147	7	7	18	0			.946	0	PM	0.0
1902	Chi-A	35	92	11	20	3	0	0	8	7		.217	.273	.250	48	-7	-6	7	0			1.000	-2	P/OM	-0.1
1903	NY-A	25	69	5	11	4	0	1	7	11		.159	.284	.261	61	-3	-3	6	1			.983	-3	PM	0.0
1904	NY-A	16	42	2	6	2	0	0	1	4		.143	.217	.190	28	-3	-3	2	0			.946	-1	PM	0.0
1905	NY-A	26	32	2	7	1	1	0	5	3		.219	.286	.313	81	-0	-1	3	0			.960	-3	P/OM	0.0
1906	NY-A	17	18	0	2	0	0	0	1	3		.111	.238	.111	10	-2	-2	1	0			1.000	1	PM	0.0
1907	NY-A	5	2	0	0	0	0	0	0	0		.000	.000	.000	-93	-0	-0	0	0			.800	0	/PM	0.0
1909	Cin-N	1	2	0	0	0	0	0	0	0		.000	.000	.000	-99	-0	-0	0	0			1.000	1	/PM	0.0
1910	Cin-N	1	0	1	0	0	0	0	0	0	0	—	—	—	—	0	0	0	0			.000	0	RM	0.0
1912	Was-A	1	1	0	0	0	0	0	0	0		.000	.000	.000	-99	-0	-0	0	0			.000	1	/P2M	0.0
1913	Was-A	1	1	0	1	1	0	0	1	0	0	1.000	1.000	2.000	758	1	1	2	0			.000	-0	/POM	0.0
1914	Was-A	1	1	0	1	1	0	0	1	0	0	1.000	1.000	2.000	769	1	1	0	0	1	-1	.000	-0	/PM	0.0
Total	21	485	1380	202	321	49	17	8	166	166	46	.233	.318	.310	70	-50	-57	155	22	1		.942	1	P/OS213	-0.7

■ **DERRELL GRIFFITH** Griffith, Robert Derrell b: 12/12/43, Anadarko, Okla. BL/TR, 6', 168 lbs. Deb: 9/26/63

YEAR	TM/L	G	AB	R	H	2B	3B	HR	RBI	BB	SO	AVG	OBP	SLG	PRO+	BR	/A	RC	SB	CS	SBR	FA	FR	POS	TPR
1963	LA-N	1	2	0	0	0	0	0	0	0	0	.000	.000	.000	-99	-1	-0	0	0	0	0	.000	0	/2	-0.1
1964	LA-N	78	238	27	69	16	2	4	23	5	21	.290	.307	.424	112	0	2	29	5	1	1	.769	-12	3O	-1.1
1965	LA-N	22	41	3	7	0	0	1	2	0	9	.171	.171	.244	16	-5	-4	1	0	0	0	1.000	0	O	-0.5
1966	LA-N	23	15	3	1	0	0	0	2	2	3	.067	.176	.067	-32	-3	-2	0	0	0	0	1.000	1	/O	-0.2
Total	4	124	296	33	77	16	2	5	27	7	33	.260	.280	.378	90	-7	-5	31	5	1	1	.970	-11	/O32	-1.9

■ **TOMMY GRIFFITH** Griffith, Thomas Herman b: 10/26/1889, Prospect, Ohio d: 4/13/67, Cincinnati, Ohio BL/TR, 5'10", 175 lbs. Deb: 8/28/13

YEAR	TM/L	G	AB	R	H	2B	3B	HR	RBI	BB	SO	AVG	OBP	SLG	PRO+	BR	/A	RC	SB	CS	SBR	FA	FR	POS	TPR
1913	Bos-N	37	127	16	32	4	1	1	12	9	8	.252	.301	.323	77	-4	-4	12	1			.886	1	O	-0.5
1914	Bos-N	16	48	3	5	0	0	0	1	2	6	.104	.140	.104	-27	-7	-7	1	0			.931	3	O	-0.6
1915	Cin-N	160	583	59	179	31	16	4	85	41	34	.307	.355	.436	136	25	24	85	6	24	-13	.952	-13	*O	-1.0
1916	Cin-N	155	595	50	158	28	7	2	61	36	37	.266	.310	.346	104	0	2	69	16			.967	6	*O	0.0
1917	Cin-N	115	363	45	98	18	7	1	45	19	23	.270	.308	.366	111	2	3	41	5			.974	6	*O	0.5
1918	Cin-N	118	427	47	113	10	4	2	48	39	30	.265	.326	.321	99	-1	0	47	10			.969	2	*O	-0.5
1919	Bro-N	125	484	65	136	18	4	6	57	23	32	.281	.315	.372	104	2	1	57	8			.954	-1	*O	-0.9
1920	*Bro-N	93	334	41	87	9	4	2	30	15	18	.260	.292	.329	76	-10	-11	32	3	3	-1	.972	-11	O	-3.2
1921	Bro-N	129	455	66	142	21	6	12	71	36	13	.312	.364	.464	113	11	9	77	3	3	-1	.972	7	*O	0.6
1922	Bro-N	99	329	44	104	17	8	4	49	23	10	.316	.361	.453	110	4	4	55	7	1	2	.952	4	O	0.4
1923	Bro-N	131	481	70	141	21	9	8	66	50	19	.293	.361	.424	109	5	7	76	8	2	1	.927	-7	*O	-0.7
1924	Bro-N	140	482	43	121	19	5	3	67	34	19	.251	.300	.330	71	-21	-19	48	0	5	-3	.965	-11	*O	-4.2
1925	Bro-N	7	4	2	0	0	0	0	0	3	2	.000	.429	.000	20	-0	-0	1	1	0	0	1.000	-1	/O	-0.1
	Chi-N	76	235	38	67	12	1	7	27	21	11	.285	.346	.434	97	-1	-1	35	2	4	-2	.937	-4	O	-1.0
	Yr	83	239	40	67	12	1	7	27	24	13	.280	.348	.427	96	-1	-2	35	3	4	-2	.938	-4	O	-1.1
Total	13	1401	4947	589	1383	208	72	52	619	351	262	.280	.328	.382	102	5	7	634	70	42		.956	-19	*O	-11.2

■ **ART GRIGGS** Griggs, Arthur Carle b: 12/10/1883, Topeka, Kan. d: 12/19/38, Los Angeles, Cal. BR/TR, 5'11", 185 lbs. Deb: 5/02/09

YEAR	TM/L	G	AB	R	H	2B	3B	HR	RBI	BB	SO	AVG	OBP	SLG	PRO+	BR	/A	RC	SB	CS	SBR	FA	FR	POS	TPR
1909	StL-A	108	364	38	102	17	5	0	43	24		.280	.330	.354	125	6	9	46	11			.982	-6	1O/2S	0.1
1910	StL-A	123	416	28	98	22	5	2	30	25		.236	.281	.327	96	-6	-3	40	11			.878	-11	O21/S3	-1.9
1911	Cle-A	27	68	7	17	3	2	1	7	5		.250	.301	.397	93	-1	-1	8	1			.949	-2	2/O31	-0.3
1912	Cle-A	89	273	29	83	16	7	0	39	33		.304	.381	.414	123	10	9	47	10			.986	1	1	0.9
1914	Bro-F	40	112	10	32	6	1	1	15	5	11	.286	.328	.384	103	0	0	15	1			.980	-3	1/O	-0.4
1915	Bro-F	27	38	4	11	1	0	1	2	3	7	.289	.372	.395	126	1	1	6	0			1.000	1	/1O	0.2
1918	Det-A	28	99	11	36	8	0	0	16	10	5	.364	.422	.444	168	7	8	19	2			.986	-3	1	0.4
Total	7	442	1370	127	379	73	20	5	152	105	23	.277	.332	.370	116	18	23	181	36			.983	-23	1/O23S	-1.0

■ **DENVER GRIGSBY** Grigsby, Denver Clarence b: 3/25/01, Jackson, Ky. d: 11/10/73, Sapulpa, Okla. BL/TR, 5'9", 155 lbs. Deb: 9/01/23

YEAR	TM/L	G	AB	R	H	2B	3B	HR	RBI	BB	SO	AVG	OBP	SLG	PRO+	BR	/A	RC	SB	CS	SBR	FA	FR	POS	TPR
1923	Chi-N	24	72	8	21	5	2	0	5	7	5	.292	.363	.417	105	1	1	10	1	3	-2	1.000	-2	O	-0.4
1924	Chi-N	124	411	58	123	18	2	3	48	31	47	.299	.357	.375	95	-1	-2	51	10	19	-8	.974	3	*O	-1.5
1925	Chi-N	51	137	20	35	5	0	0	20	19	12	.255	.346	.292	64	-7	-7	16	1	1	-0	.966	-1	O	-1.0
Total	3	199	620	86	179	28	4	3	73	57	64	.289	.355	.361	89	-7	-8	77	12	23	-10	.975	0	O	-2.9

■ **JOHN GRIM** Grim, John Helm b: 8/9/1867, Lebanon, Ky. d: 7/28/61, Indianapolis, Ind BR/TR, 6'2", 175 lbs. Deb: 9/29/1888

YEAR	TM/L	G	AB	R	H	2B	3B	HR	RBI	BB	SO	AVG	OBP	SLG	PRO+	BR	/A	RC	SB	CS	SBR	FA	FR	POS	TPR
1888	Phi-N	2	7	0	1	0	0	0	0	0	0	.143	.143	.143	-7	-1	-1	0	0			.000	-1	/O2	-0.1
1890	Roc-a	50	192	30	51	6	9	2		7		.266	.299	.422	124	2	4	29	14			.851	-7	SC/32O1P	0.0
1891	Mil-a	29	119	14	28	5	1	1	14	2	5	.235	.248	.319	53	-6	-10	10	1			.926	3	C3/2	-0.4
1892	Lou-N	97	370	40	90	16	4	1	36	13	24	.243	.280	.316	89	-9	-5	39	18			.940	-10	C12/OS3	-0.9
1893	Lou-N	99	415	68	111	19	8	3	54	12	10	.267	.303	.373	88	-13	-8	53	15			.952	-4	*C/12OS	-0.3
1894	Lou-N	108	410	66	122	27	7	7	70	16	15	.298	.339	.449	97	-8	-3	70	14			.931	10	C2/13	1.2
1895	Bro-N	93	329	54	92	17	5	0	44	13	9	.280	.321	.362	84	-11	-7	43	9			.947	-0	*C/O1	0.2
1896	Bro-N	81	281	32	75	13	1	2	35	12	14	.267	.311	.342	78	-11	-8	34	7			.939	-0	C/1	0.0
1897	Bro-N	80	290	26	72	10	1	0	25	1		.248	.259	.290	47	-24	-21	24	3			.947	5	C	-0.7
1898	Bro-N	52	178	17	50	5	1	0	11	8		.281	.323	.320	85	-4	-4	20	1			.950	-4	C	-0.3
1899	Bro-N	15	47	3	13	1	0	0	7	1		.277	.320	.298	68	-2	-2	5	0			.966	2	C	0.0
Total	11	706	2638	350	705	119	37	16	296	85	77	.267	.302	.359	83	-87	-63	325	82			.943	-6	C/21S3OP	-1.3

■ **ED GRIMES** Grimes, Edward Adelbert b: 9/8/05, Chicago, Ill. d: 10/5/74, Chicago, Ill. BR/TR, 5'10", 165 lbs. Deb: 4/19/31

YEAR	TM/L	G	AB	R	H	2B	3B	HR	RBI	BB	SO	AVG	OBP	SLG	PRO+	BR	/A	RC	SB	CS	SBR	FA	FR	POS	TPR
1931	StL-A	43	57	9	15	1	2	0	5	9	3	.263	.364	.351	86	-1	-1	8	1	0	0	.892	-2	3/2S	-0.2
1932	StL-A	31	68	7	16	0	1	0	13	6	12	.235	.297	.265	44	-5	-6	5	0	1	-1	.891	2	3/2S	-0.3
Total	2	74	125	16	31	1	3	0	18	15	15	.248	.329	.304	63	-6	-7	14	1	1	-0	.891	0	/32S	-0.5

■ **ROY GRIMES** Grimes, Austin Roy "Bummer" b: 9/11/1893, Bergholz, Ohio d: 9/13/54, Gilford Lake, O. BR/TR, 6'1", 176 lbs. Deb: 7/31/20 F

YEAR	TM/L	G	AB	R	H	2B	3B	HR	RBI	BB	SO	AVG	OBP	SLG	PRO+	BR	/A	RC	SB	CS	SBR	FA	FR	POS	TPR
1920	NY-N	26	57	5	9	1	0	0	3	3	8	.158	.200	.175	8	-7	-7	2	1	1	-0	.948	-1	2	-0.9

■ **OSCAR GRIMES** Grimes, Oscar Ray Jr. b: 4/13/15, Minerva, Ohio BR/TR, 5'11", 178 lbs. Deb: 9/28/38 F

YEAR	TM/L	G	AB	R	H	2B	3B	HR	RBI	BB	SO	AVG	OBP	SLG	PRO+	BR	/A	RC	SB	CS	SBR	FA	FR	POS	TPR
1938	Cle-A	4	10	2	2	0	1	0	2	2	0	.200	.333	.400	85	-0	-0	1	0	0	0	1.000	-1	/21	-0.1
1939	Cle-A	119	364	51	98	20	5	4	56	56	61	.269	.368	.385	96	-3	-1	55	8	3	1	.968	-11	21S/3	-1.0
1940	Cle-A	11	13	3	0	0	0	0	0	0	5	.000	.000	.000	-99	-4	-4	0	0	0	0	.958	2	/13	-0.2
1941	Cle-A	77	244	28	58	9	3	4	24	39	47	.238	.345	.348	88	-5	-3	34	4	0	1	.995	-5	12/3	-1.1
1942	Cle-A	51	84	10	15	2	0	0	2	13	17	.179	.289	.202	42	-6	-6	6	3	2	-0	.944	-3	2/31S	-0.9
1943	NY-A	9	20	4	3	0	0	0	1	3	7	.150	.261	.150	21	-2	-2	1	0	0	0	1.000	-1	/S1	-0.3
1944	NY-A	116	387	44	108	17	8	5	46	59	57	.279	.377	.403	119	13	12	67	6	0	2	.945	-10	3S	0.6
1945	NY-A	142	480	64	127	19	7	4	45	97	73	.265	.395	.358	114	17	14	77	7	6	-2	.937	3	*3/1	2.0
1946	NY-A	14	39	1	8	1	0	0	4	1	7	.205	.225	.231	27	-4	-4	2	0	1	-1	.895	0	/S2	-0.4
	Phi-A	59	191	28	50	5	0	1	20	27	29	.262	.356	.304	86	-3	-2	23	2	0	1	.958	-12	2/3S	-1.1
	Yr	73	230	29	58	6	0	1	24	28	36	.252	.336	.291	76	-6	-6	24	2	1	0	.957	-12	2S/3	-1.5
Total	9	602	1832	235	469	73	24	18	200	297	303	.256	.363	.352	98	3	3	266	30	12	2	.940	-39	321/S	-2.5

■ RAY GRIMES Grimes, Oscar Ray Sr. b: 9/11/1893, Bergholz, Ohio d: 5/25/53, Minerva, Ohio BR/TR, 5'11", 168 lbs. Deb: 9/24/20 F

YEAR	TM/L	G	AB	R	H	2B	3B	HR	RBI	BB	SO	AVG	OBP	SLG	PRO+	BR	/A	RC	SB	CS	SBR	FA	FR	POS	TPR
1920	Bos-A	1	4	1	1	0	0	0	0	1	0	.250	.400	.250	78	-0	-0	0	0	0	0	1.000	-0	/1	0.0
1921	Chi-N	147	530	91	170	38	6	6	79	70	55	.321	.406	.449	126	23	23	99	5	8	-3	.993	-5	*1	1.1
1922	Chi-N	138	509	99	180	45	12	14	99	75	33	.354	.442	.572	157	47	46	130	7	7	-2	.987	-2	*1	3.4
1923	Chi-N	64	216	32	71	7	2	2	36	24	17	.329	.401	.407	114	5	5	38	5	0	2	.991	-1	1	0.3
1924	Chi-N	51	177	33	53	6	5	5	34	28	15	.299	.401	.475	132	9	9	35	4	2	0	.982	-7	1	-0.1
1926	Phi-N	32	101	13	30	5	0	0	15	6	13	.297	.343	.347	82	-2	-3	12	0			.981	0	1	-0.4
Total	6	433	1537	269	505	101	25	27	263	204	133	.329	.413	.480	132	82	80	314	21	17		.989	-14	1	4.3

■ CHARLIE GRIMM Grimm, Charles John "Jolly Cholly" b: 8/28/1898, St.Louis, Mo. d: 11/15/83, Scottsdale, Ariz. BL/TL, 5'11.5", 173 lbs. Deb: 7/30/16 MC

YEAR	TM/L	G	AB	R	H	2B	3B	HR	RBI	BB	SO	AVG	OBP	SLG	PRO+	BR	/A	RC	SB	CS	SBR	FA	FR	POS	TPR
1916	Phi-A	12	22	0	2	0	0	0	0	2	4	.091	.167	.091	-24	-3	-3	0	0			.875	-2	/O	-0.6
1918	StL-N	50	141	11	31	7	0	0	12	6	15	.220	.262	.270	64	-6	-6	10	2			.971	-3	1/O3	-1.2
1919	Pit-N	14	44	6	14	1	3	0	6	2	4	.318	.348	.477	141	2	2	7	1			.968	-3	1	-0.1
1920	Pit-N	148	533	38	121	13	7	2	54	30	40	.227	.273	.289	60	-26	-28	42	7	8	-3	**.995**	4	*1	-3.3
1921	Pit-N	151	562	62	154	21	17	7	71	31	38	.274	.314	.409	88	-9	-11	70	6	8	-3	.994	-6	*1	-2.4
1922	Pit-N	154	593	64	173	28	13	0	76	43	15	.292	.343	.383	86	-12	-13	76	6	10	-4	.994	-3	*1	-2.5
1923	Pit-N	152	563	78	194	29	13	7	99	41	43	.345	.389	.480	125	22	20	102	6	9	-4	**.995**	2	*1	1.1
1924	Pit-N	151	542	53	156	25	12	2	63	37	22	.288	.336	.389	92	-5	-6	70	3	6	-3	**.995**	-3	*1	-2.2
1925	Chi-N	141	519	73	159	29	5	10	76	38	25	.306	.354	.439	100	0	-1	80	4	3	-1	.989	0	*1	-0.8
1926	Chi-N	147	524	58	145	30	6	8	82	49	25	.277	.342	.403	99	-0	-1	72	3			.988	-6	*1	-1.6
1927	Chi-N	147	543	68	169	29	6	2	74	45	21	.311	.367	.398	105	4	4	79	3			.990	3	*1	-0.3
1928	Chi-N	147	547	67	161	25	5	5	62	39	20	.294	.342	.386	91	-8	-7	71	7			**.993**	-2	*1	-2.2
1929	*Chi-N	120	463	66	138	28	3	10	91	42	25	.298	.358	.436	95	-4	-4	71	3			.992	0	*1	-1.4
1930	Chi-N	114	429	58	124	27	2	6	66	41	26	.289	.359	.403	83	-11	-11	62	1			**.995**	1	*1	-1.9
1931	Chi-N	146	531	65	176	33	11	4	66	53	29	.331	.393	.458	126	22	21	99	1			**.993**	2	*1	0.9
1932	*Chi-N	149	570	66	175	42	2	7	80	35	22	.307	.349	.425	108	5	6	86	2			.993	10	*1M	0.4
1933	Chi-N	107	384	38	95	15	2	3	37	23	15	.247	.290	.320	74	-13	-13	33	1			**.996**	9	*1M	-1.4
1934	Chi-N	75	267	24	79	8	1	5	47	16	12	.296	.338	.390	96	-2	-1	34	1			.995	1	1M	-0.6
1935	Chi-N	2	8	0	0	0	0	0	0	0	1	.000	.000	.000	-99	-2	-2	0	0			1.000	-0	/1M	-0.3
1936	Chi-N	39	132	13	33	4	0	1	16	5	8	.250	.277	.303	55	-8	-9	10	0			1.000	5	1M	-0.6
Total	20	2166	7917	908	2299	394	108	79	1078	578	410	.290	.341	.397	95	-54	-63	1077	57	44		.993	10	*1/O3	-21.0

■ MOOSE GRIMSHAW Grimshaw, Myron Frederick b: 11/30/1875, St.Johnsville, N.Y d: 12/11/36, Canajoharie, N.Y. BB/TR, 6'1", 173 lbs. Deb: 4/25/05

YEAR	TM/L	G	AB	R	H	2B	3B	HR	RBI	BB	SO	AVG	OBP	SLG	PRO+	BR	/A	RC	SB	CS	SBR	FA	FR	POS	TPR
1905	Bos-A	85	285	39	68	8	2	4	35	21		.239	.293	.323	94	-2	-2	30	4			.980	-5	1	-1.0
1906	Bos-A	110	428	46	124	16	12	0	48	23		.290	.332	.383	124	11	11	58	5			.987	-1	*1	0.7
1907	Bos-A	64	181	19	37	7	2	0	33	16		.204	.273	.265	72	-6	-5	16	6			.966	-7	O1/S	-1.5
Total	3	259	894	104	229	31	16	4	116	60		.256	.307	.340	104	4	4	104	15			.984	-13	1/OS	-1.8

■ MARQUIS GRISSOM Grissom, Marquis Deon b: 4/17/67, Atlanta, Ga. BR/TR, 5'11", 190 lbs. Deb: 8/22/89

YEAR	TM/L	G	AB	R	H	2B	3B	HR	RBI	BB	SO	AVG	OBP	SLG	PRO+	BR	/A	RC	SB	CS	SBR	FA	FR	POS	TPR
1989	Mon-N	26	74	16	19	2	0	1	2	12	21	.257	.360	.324	96	0	0	10	1	0	0	.943	-4	O	-0.5
1990	Mon-N	98	288	42	74	14	2	3	29	27	40	.257	.321	.351	88	-6	-5	36	22	2	5	.988	-4	O	-0.5
1991	Mon-N	148	558	73	149	23	9	6	39	34	89	.267	.310	.373	93	-7	-6	69	**76**	17	**13**	.984	20	*O	2.4
1992	Mon-N	159	653	99	180	39	6	14	66	42	81	.276	.324	.418	109	6	6	94	**78**	13	**16**	.983	7	*O	2.7
Total	4	431	1573	230	422	78	17	24	136	115	231	.268	.321	.385	99	-7	-4	209	177	32	34	.983	19	O	4.1

■ DICK GROAT Groat, Richard Morrow b: 11/4/30, Wilkinsburg, Pa. BR/TR, 5'11.5", 180 lbs. Deb: 6/19/52

YEAR	TM/L	G	AB	R	H	2B	3B	HR	RBI	BB	SO	AVG	OBP	SLG	PRO+	BR	/A	RC	SB	CS	SBR	FA	FR	POS	TPR
1952	Pit-N	95	384	38	109	6	1	1	29	19	27	.284	.319	.313	74	-12	-14	35	2	4	-2	.952	1	S	-0.7
1955	Pit-N	151	521	45	139	28	2	4	51	38	26	.267	.318	.351	78	-17	-16	54	0	2	-1	.961	15	*S	1.1
1956	Pit-N	142	520	40	142	19	3	0	37	35	25	.273	.319	.321	74	-19	-18	52	0	3	-2	.954	0	*S/3	-0.8
1957	Pit-N	125	501	58	158	30	5	7	54	27	28	.315	.354	.437	114	7	9	74	0	1	-1	.968	-1	*S/3	2.0
1958	Pit-N	151	584	67	175	36	9	3	66	23	32	.300	.331	.408	97	-6	-4	72	2	2	-1	.975	3	*S	1.2
1959	Pit-N★	147	593	74	163	22	7	5	51	32	35	.275	.314	.361	80	-18	-17	62	0	2	-1	.964	3	*S	-0.3
1960	*Pit-N★	138	573	85	186	26	4	2	50	39	35	**.325**	.372	.394	109	9	8	85	0	2	-1	.966	11	*S	2.9
1961	Pit-N	148	596	71	164	25	6	6	55	40	44	.275	.322	.367	82	-15	-15	65	0	4	-2	.957	9	*S/3	0.4
1962	Pit-N★	161	678	76	199	34	3	2	61	31	61	.294	.327	.361	85	-15	-15	78	2	1	0	.956	14	*S	1.4
1963	StL-N★	158	631	85	201	**43**	11	6	73	56	58	.319	.380	.450	126	31	25	106	3	1	0	.964	-13	*S	2.5
1964	*StL-N★	161	636	70	186	35	6	1	70	44	42	.292	.338	.371	92	0	-6	78	2	3	-1	.949	-12	*S	-0.9
1965	StL-N	153	587	55	149	26	5	0	52	56	50	.254	.320	.315	73	-15	-21	61	1	1	-0	.962	-8	*S/3	-2.1
1966	Phi-N	155	584	58	152	21	4	2	53	40	38	.260	.313	.320	77	-18	-18	56	2	1	0	.974	11	*S3/1	0.6
1967	Phi-N	10	26	3	3	0	0	0	1	4	4	.115	.233	.115	3	-3	-3	1	0	0	0	.947	2	/S	0.0
	SF-N	34	70	4	12	1	1	0	4	6	7	.171	.237	.214	30	-6	-6	3	0	0	0	.912	-8	S/2	-1.3
	Yr	44	96	7	15	1	1	0	5	10	11	.156	.236	.188	23	-9	-9	4	0	0	0	.925	-5	S/2	-1.3
Total	14	1929	7484	829	2138	352	67	39	707	490	512	.286	.332	.366	89	-95	-110	882	14	27	-12	.961	28	*S/321	6.0

■ HEINIE GROH Groh, Henry Knight b: 9/18/1889, Rochester, N.Y. d: 8/22/68, Cincinnati, Ohio BR/TR, 5'8", 158 lbs. Deb: 4/12/12 FM

YEAR	TM/L	G	AB	R	H	2B	3B	HR	RBI	BB	SO	AVG	OBP	SLG	PRO+	BR	/A	RC	SB	CS	SBR	FA	FR	POS	TPR
1912	NY-N	27	48	8	13	2	1	0	3	8	7	.271	.375	.354	97	0	0	8	6			.887	3	2/S3	0.3
1913	NY-N	4	2	0	0	0	0	0	0	0	1	.000	.000	.000	-99	-1	-1	0	0			1.000	1	/3S	0.0
	Cin-N	117	397	51	112	19	5	3	48	38	36	.282	.351	.378	109	5	5	59	24			.963	10	*2/S	1.3
	Yr	121	399	51	112	19	5	3	48	38	37	.281	.349	.376	107	4	4	59	24			.963	10	*2/S3	1.3
1914	Cin-N	139	455	59	131	18	4	2	32	64	28	.288	.391	.358	120	17	15	72	24			.936	-7	*2/S	0.7
1915	Cin-N	160	587	72	170	32	9	3	50	50	33	.290	.354	.390	123	18	17	83	12	17	-7	.969	11	*32	3.0
1916	Cin-N	149	553	85	149	24	14	2	28	**84**	34	.269	.370	.374	132	22	24	83	13			.957	19	*32/S	**5.3**
1917	Cin-N	156	599	91	**182**	**39**	11	1	53	71	30	.304	**.385**	.411	150	33	36	96	15			**.966**	8	*3/2	5.2
1918	Cin-N	126	493	**86**	158	**28**	3	1	37	54	24	.320	**.395**	.396	144	**26**	**27**	79	11			**.969**	2	*3M	**3.5**
1919	*Cin-N	122	448	79	139	17	11	5	63	56	26	.310	.392	.431	151	27	29	81	21			.971	-2	*3	3.4
1920	Cin-N	145	550	86	164	28	12	0	49	60	29	.298	.375	.393	122	17	18	81	16	19	-7	.969	-6	*3/S	1.3
1921	Cin-N	97	357	54	118	19	6	0	48	36	17	.331	.398	.417	122	10	12	60	22	14	-2	.950	1	3	1.7
1922	*NY-N	115	426	63	113	21	3	3	51	53	21	.265	.353	.350	81	-10	-11	55	5	6	-2	**.965**	1	*3	-0.3
1923	*NY-N	123	465	91	135	22	5	4	48	60	22	.290	.379	.385	103	3	4	71	3	4	-2	**.975**	4	*3	1.6
1924	*NY-N	145	559	82	157	32	3	2	46	52	29	.281	.354	.360	94	-5	-3	74	8	6	-1	**.983**	3	*3	1.0
1925	NY-N	25	65	7	15	4	0	0	4	6	3	.231	.296	.292	53	-5	-4	6	0	0	0	.909	-5	3/2	-0.8
1926	NY-N	12	35	2	8	2	0	0	3	2	3	.229	.270	.286	50	-2	-2	3	0			.950	-1	/3	-0.3
1927	*Pit-N	14	35	2	10	1	0	0	3	2	2	.286	.324	.314	67	-1	-2	3	0			.958	-1	3	-0.2
Total	16	1676	6074	918	1774	308	87	26	566	696	345	.292	.373	.384	119	155	164	915	180	66		.967	39	*32/S	26.7

■ LEW GROH Groh, Lewis Carl "Silver" b: 10/16/1883, Rochester, N.Y. d: 10/20/60, Rochester, N.Y. BR/TR, Deb: 8/02/19 F

YEAR	TM/L	G	AB	R	H	2B	3B	HR	RBI	BB	SO	AVG	OBP	SLG	PRO+	BR	/A	RC	SB	CS	SBR	FA	FR	POS	TPR
1919	Phi-A	2	4	0	0	0	0	0	0	0	2	.000	.000	.000	-99	-1	-1	0	0			1.000	-0	/3	-0.1

■ HOWDIE GROSKLOSS Groskloss, Howard Hoffman b: 4/9/07, Pittsburgh, Pa. BR/TR, 5'9", 176 lbs. Deb: 6/23/30

YEAR	TM/L	G	AB	R	H	2B	3B	HR	RBI	BB	SO	AVG	OBP	SLG	PRO+	BR	/A	RC	SB	CS	SBR	FA	FR	POS	TPR
1930	Pit-N	2	3	0	1	0	0	0	1	0	0	.333	.333	.333	62	-0	-0	0	0			.000	-1	/S	-0.1
1931	Pit-N	53	161	13	45	7	2	0	20	11	16	.280	.326	.348	82	-4	-4	19	1			.981	-1	2/S	-0.3
1932	Pit-N	17	20	1	2	0	0	0	0	0	3	.100	.100	.100	-47	-4	-4	0	0			.800	-1	/S	-0.5
Total	3	72	184	14	48	7	2	0	21	11	19	.261	.303	.321	68	-8	-8	19	1			.700	-3	/2S	-0.9

YEAR	TM/L	G	AB	R	H	2B	3B	HR	RBI	BB	SO	AVG	OBP	SLG	PRO+	BR	/A	RC	SB	CS	SBR	FA	FR	POS	TPR
■ EMIL GROSS	Gross, Emil Michael b: 3/3/1858, Chicago, Ill. d: 8/24/21, Eagle River, Wis. BR/TR, 6', 190 lbs. Deb: 8/13/1879																								
1879	Pro-N	30	132	31	46	9	5	0	24	4	8	.348	.368	.492	183	11	11	24				.897	-5	C	0.7
1880	Pro-N	87	347	43	90	18	3	1	34	16	15	.259	.292	.337	116	5	6	35				.866	-14	*C	-0.6
1881	Pro-N	51	182	15	50	9	4	1	24	13	11	.275	.323	.385	124	5	5	23				.893	-4	C/O	0.3
1883	Phi-N	57	231	39	71	25	7	1	25	12	18	.307	.342	.489	163	13	16	40				.789	-24	C/O	-0.4
1884	CP-U	23	95	13	34	6	2	4		6		.358	.396	.589	231	13	13	23				.860	-2	C/O	1.0
Total	5	248	987	141	291	67	21	7	107	51	52	.295	.329	.427	149	46	52	145				.859	-49	C/O	1.0
■ TURKEY GROSS	Gross, Ewell b: 2/21/1896, Mesquite, Tex. d: 1/11/36, Dallas, Tex. BR/TR, 6', 165 lbs. Deb: 4/14/25																								
1925	Bos-A	9	32	2	3	0	1	0	2	2	2	.094	.171	.156	-16	-6	-6	1	0	0	0	.976	-1	/S	-0.5
■ GREG GROSS	Gross, Gregory Eugene b: 8/1/52, York, Pa. BL/TL, 5'11", 175 lbs. Deb: 9/05/73																								
1973	Hou-N	14	39	5	9	2	1	0	1	4	4	.231	.302	.333	76	-1	-1	4	2	1	0	1.000	0	/O	-0.2
1974	Hou-N	156	589	78	185	21	8	0	36	76	39	.314	.393	.377	121	16	19	86	12	20	-8	.994	8	*O	1.2
1975	Hou-N	132	483	67	142	14	10	0	41	63	37	.294	.375	.364	114	6	10	69	2	2	-1	.958	2	*O	0.7
1976	Hou-N	128	426	52	122	12	3	0	27	64	39	.286	.380	.329	112	4	9	56	2	6	-3	.978	2	*O	0.3
1977	Chi-N	115	239	43	77	10	4	5	32	33	19	.322	.404	.460	118	12	8	45	0	1	-1	.991	-6	O	-0.1
1978	Chi-N	124	347	34	92	12	7	1	39	33	19	.265	.329	.349	80	-5	-10	41	3	1	0	.979	-18	*O	-3.4
1979	Phi-N	111	174	21	58	6	3	0	15	29	5	.333	.429	.402	124	8	8	32	5	2	0	.978	1	O	0.7
1980	*Phi-N	127	154	19	37	7	2	0	12	24	7	.240	.346	.312	80	-2	-3	18	1	1	-0	.973	1	O/1	-0.4
1981	*Phi-N	83	102	14	23	6	1	0	7	15	5	.225	.325	.304	76	-2	-3	10	2	2	-1	.982	5	O	0.1
1982	Phi-N	119	134	14	40	4	0	0	10	19	8	.299	.386	.328	99	1	1	17	4	3	-1	.983	2	O	0.1
1983	*Phi-N	136	245	25	74	12	3	0	29	34	16	.302	.389	.376	114	6	6	36	3	5	-2	.991	-6	*O/1	-0.4
1984	Phi-N	112	202	19	65	9	1	0	16	24	11	.322	.396	.376	116	6	6	31	1	0	0	.986	-4	O1	0.1
1985	Phi-N	93	169	21	44	5	2	0	14	32	9	.260	.378	.314	93	1	-0	22	1	0	0	1.000	-7	O/1	-0.8
1986	Phi-N	87	101	11	25	5	0	0	8	21	11	.248	.382	.297	87	-0	-1	12	1	0	0	1.000	-3	O/1P	-0.4
1987	Phi-N	114	133	14	38	4	1	1	12	25	12	.286	.403	.353	99	2	1	21	0	0	0	1.000	-12	O1	-1.2
1988	Phi-N	98	133	10	27	1	0	0	5	16	3	.203	.293	.211	46	-9	-9	9	0	0	0	1.000	-11	O1	-2.4
1989	Hou-N	60	75	2	15	0	0	0	4	11	6	.200	.310	.200	51	-5	-4	5	0	0	0	.929	-3	O/1P	-0.8
Total	17	1809	3745	449	1073	130	46	7	308	523	250	.287	.375	.351	103	38	37	511	39	44	-15	.982	-49	*O/1P	-6.9
■ WAYNE GROSS	Gross, Wayne Dale b: 1/14/52, Riverside, Cal. BL/TR, 6'2", 210 lbs. Deb: 8/21/76																								
1976	Oak-A	10	18	0	4	0	0	0	1	2	1	.222	.300	.222	57	-1	-1	1	0	0	0	.966	-1	/1OD	-0.2
1977	Oak-A☆	146	485	66	113	21	1	22	63	86	84	.233	.354	.416	111	8	9	76	5	4	-1	.932	-23	*3/1	-1.7
1978	Oak-A	118	285	18	57	10	2	7	23	40	63	.200	.309	.323	82	-8	-6	31	0	2	-1	.917	-8	*31	-1.7
1979	Oak-A	138	442	54	99	19	1	14	50	72	62	.224	.334	.367	94	-6	-2	57	4	3	-1	.943	-10	*31/O	-1.5
1980	Oak-A	113	366	45	103	20	3	14	61	44	39	.281	.360	.467	134	13	16	64	5	3	-0	.948	-28	31/D	-1.4
1981	*Oak-A	82	243	29	50	7	1	10	31	34	28	.206	.308	.366	98	-2	-0	28	2	1	0	.946	-9	3/1D	-1.2
1982	Oak-A	129	386	43	97	14	0	9	41	53	50	.251	.345	.358	98	-2	0	52	3	1	0	.970	-7	*31/D	-1.0
1983	Oak-A	137	339	34	79	18	0	12	44	36	52	.233	.312	.392	98	-4	-1	41	3	5	-2	.996	-5	13/PD	-1.2
1984	Bal-A	127	342	53	74	9	1	22	64	68	69	.216	.348	.442	119	9	10	55	1	2	-1	.937	-5	*3/1D	0.2
1985	Bal-A	103	217	31	51	8	0	11	18	46	48	.235	.369	.424	120	6	7	37	1	1	-0	.933	-0	3D/1	0.5
1986	Oak-A	3	2	0	0	0	0	0	0	1	0	.000	.333	.000	0	-0	-0	0	0	0	0	.000	-0	/3	-0.1
Total	11	1106	3125	373	727	126	9	121	396	482	496	.233	.339	.395	106	13	31	443	24	22	-6	.941	-96	31/DOP	-9.3
■ GEORGE GROSSART	Grossart, George Albert b: 4/11/1880, Meadville, Pa. d: 4/18/02, Pittsburgh, Pa. Deb: 6/07/01																								
1901	Bos-N	7	26	4	3	0	0	0	1	0		.115	.115	.115	-30	-4	-5	0	0			1.000	0	/O	-0.5
■ JERRY GROTE	Grote, Gerald Wayne b: 10/6/42, San Antonio, Tex. BR/TR, 5'10", 190 lbs. Deb: 9/21/63																								
1963	Hou-N	3	5	0	1	0	0	0	1	1	3	.200	.333	.200	61	-0	-0	1	0	0	0	1.000	-1	/C	-0.1
1964	Hou-N	100	298	26	54	9	3	3	24	20	75	.181	.242	.262	44	-23	-21	18	0	2	-1	.985	2	C	-1.7
1966	NY-N	120	317	26	75	12	2	3	31	40	81	.237	.328	.315	82	-7	-7	33	4	3	-1	.981	0	*C/3	-0.1
1967	NY-N	120	344	25	67	8	0	4	23	14	65	.195	.228	.253	38	-28	-27	19	2	2	-1	.990	2	*C	-2.2
1968	NY-N★	124	404	29	114	18	0	3	31	44	81	.282	.357	.349	112	8	7	50	1	5	-3	.994	8	*C	2.3
1969	*NY-N	113	365	38	92	12	3	6	40	32	59	.252	.314	.351	84	-7	-8	39	2	1	0	.991	19	*C	1.8
1970	NY-N	126	415	38	106	14	1	2	34	36	39	.255	.316	.308	68	-18	-18	39	2	1	0	.991	10	*C	-0.2
1971	NY-N	125	403	35	109	25	0	2	35	40	47	.270	.339	.347	96	-2	-1	44	1	4	-2	.990	5	*C	0.7
1972	NY-N	64	205	15	43	5	1	3	21	26	27	.210	.308	.288	72	-7	-7	19	1	0	0	.998	3	C/3O	-0.1
1973	*NY-N	84	285	17	73	10	2	1	32	13	23	.256	.291	.316	69	-12	-12	24	0	0	0	.995	9	C/3	0.0
1974	NY-N★	97	319	25	82	8	1	5	36	33	33	.257	.331	.335	88	-5	-5	35	0	1	-1	.988	-3	C	-0.5
1975	NY-N	119	386	28	114	14	5	2	39	38	23	.295	.360	.373	109	3	5	51	0	1	-1	**.995**	6	*C	1.6
1976	NY-N	101	323	30	88	14	2	4	28	38	19	.272	.351	.365	110	2	4	39	1	2	-1	.993	12	C/O	1.9
1977	NY-N	42	115	8	31	3	1	0	7	9	12	.270	.333	.313	78	-4	-3	11	0	0	0	1.000	-2	C3	-0.4
	*LA-N	18	27	3	7	0	0	0	4	2	5	.259	.310	.259	55	-2	-2	2	0	1	-1	1.000	4	C/3	0.2
	Yr	60	142	11	38	3	1	0	11	11	17	.268	.329	.303	73	-5	-5	13	0	1	-1	1.000	2	C3	-0.2
1978	*LA-N	41	70	5	19	5	0	0	9	10	5	.271	.363	.343	98	0	0	10	0	0	0	.985	8	C/3	0.9
1981	KC-A	22	56	4	17	3	1	1	9	3	2	.304	.350	.446	129	2	2	9	1	0	0	1.000	4	C	0.7
	LA-N	2	2	0	0	0	0	0	0	0	1	.000	.000	.000	-99	-1	-1	0	0	0	0	1.000	0	/C	0.0
Total	16	1421	4339	352	1092	160	22	39	404	399	600	.252	.318	.326	83	-102	-92	443	15	23	-9	.991	86	*C/3O	4.8
■ JEFF GROTEWOLD	Grotewold, Jeffrey Scott b: 12/8/65, Madera, Cal. BL/TR, 6', 215 lbs. Deb: 4/12/92																								
1992	Phi-N	72	65	7	13	2	0	3	5	9	16	.200	.307	.369	91	-1	-1	7	0	0	0	1.000	-1	/CO1	-0.2
■ JOHNNY GROTH	Groth, John Thomas b: 7/23/26, Chicago, Ill. BR/TR, 6', 182 lbs. Deb: 9/05/46																								
1946	Det-A	4	9	1	0	0	0	0	0	0	3	.000	.000	.000	-94	-2	-2	0	0	0	0	1.000	-1	/O	-0.4
1947	Det-A	2	4	1	1	0	0	0	0	2	1	.250	.500	.250	109	0	0	0	0	0	0	1.000	1	/O	0.1
1948	Det-A	6	17	3	8	3	0	1	5	1	1	.471	.500	.824	242	3	3	7	0	0	0	.900	0	/O	0.3
1949	Det-A	103	348	60	102	19	5	11	73	65	27	.293	.407	.471	132	17	17	66	3	7	-3	.966	1	O	0.9
1950	Det-A	157	566	95	173	30	8	12	85	95	27	.306	.407	.451	116	19	16	106	1	5	-3	.985	-12	*O	-0.5
1951	Det-A	118	428	41	128	29	1	3	49	31	32	.299	.349	.393	100	-0	-1	57	1	1	-0	**.993**	-1	*O	-0.5
1952	Det-A	141	524	56	149	22	2	4	51	51	39	.284	.348	.357	96	-2	-3	64	2	10	-5	.986	0	*O	-1.4
1953	StL-A	141	557	65	141	27	4	10	57	42	53	.253	.308	.370	81	-15	-16	62	5	6	-2	.991	17	*O	-0.7
1954	Chi-A	125	422	41	116	20	0	7	60	42	37	.275	.343	.372	93	-2	-4	49	3	9	-5	.988	-1	*O	-1.5
1955	Chi-A	32	77	13	26	7	0	2	11	6	13	.338	.386	.506	135	4	4	15	1	0	0	1.000	-0	O	0.3
	Was-A	63	183	22	40	4	5	2	17	18	18	.219	.289	.328	69	-9	-8	18	2	0	1	.984	-1	O	-1.0
	Yr	95	260	35	66	11	5	4	28	24	31	.254	.317	.381	89	-5	-5	32	3	0	1	.989	-1	O	-0.7
1956	KC-A	95	244	22	63	13	3	5	37	30	31	.258	.339	.398	94	-2	-2	32	1	2	-1	1.000	-7	O	-1.4
1957	KC-A	55	59	10	15	0	0	0	2	7	6	.254	.333	.254	62	-3	-3	5	0	0	0	.974	-13	O	-1.7
	Det-A	38	103	11	30	10	0	0	16	6	7	.291	.336	.388	95	-0	-1	14	0	0	0	1.000	-3	O	-0.5
	Yr	93	162	21	45	10	0	0	18	13	13	.278	.335	.340	83	-3	-4	19	0	0	0	.991	-16	O	-2.2
1958	Det-A	88	146	24	41	5	2	2	11	13	19	.281	.340	.384	92	-0	-2	18	0	1	-1	.990	-11	O	-1.6
1959	Det-A	55	102	12	24	7	1	1	10	7	14	.235	.284	.353	70	-4	-5	11	0	0	0	.983	-6	O	-1.2
1960	Det-A	25	19	3	7	1	0	0	2	3	1	.368	.455	.421	135	1	1	4	0	1	-1	1.000	-3	/O	-0.2
Total	15	1248	3808	480	1064	197	31	60	486	419	329	.279	.353	.395	99	4	-5	528	19	42	-20	.987	-40	*O	-11.0

YEAR	TM/L	G	AB	R	H	2B	3B	HR	RBI	BB	SO	AVG	OBP	SLG	PRO+	BR	/A	RC	SB	CS	SBR	FA	FR	POS	TPR

■ ROY GROVER Grover, Roy Arthur b: 1/17/1892, Snohomish, Wash. d: 2/7/78, Milwaukie, Ore. BR/TR, 5'8", 150 lbs. Deb: 9/13/16

1916	Phi-A	20	77	8	21	1	2	0	7	6	10	.273	.325	.338	104	-0	0	11	5			.952	-7	2	-0.7
1917	Phi-A	141	482	45	108	15	7	0	34	43	53	.224	.292	.284	77	-14	-13	46	12			.960	5	*2	-0.2
1919	Phi-A	22	56	8	13	1	0	0	2	5	6	.232	.295	.250	53	-3	-3	5	0			.915	-6	2/3	-0.9
	Was-A	24	75	6	14	0	0	0	7	6	10	.187	.256	.187	25	-7	-7	4	2			.947	-4	2	-1.0
	Yr	46	131	14	27	1	0	0	9	11	16	.206	.273	.214	37	-11	-11	9	2			.936	-10	2/3	-1.9
Total	3	207	690	67	156	17	9	0	50	60	79	.226	.292	.277	72	-25	-24	66	19			.956	-12	2/3	-2.8

■ HARVEY GRUBB Grubb, Harvey Harrison b: 9/18/1890, Lexington, N.C. d: 1/25/70, Corpus Christi, Tex. BR/TR, 6', 165 lbs. Deb: 9/27/12

| 1912 | Cle-A | 1 | 0 | 0 | 0 | 0 | 0 | 0 | 0 | 0 | 0 | — | 1.000 | — | 187 | 0 | 0 | 0 | 0 | | | 1.000 | -0 | /O | 0.0 |

■ JOHNNY GRUBB Grubb, John Maywood b: 8/4/48, Richmond, Va. BL/TR, 6'3", 188 lbs. Deb: 9/10/72

1972	SD-N	7	21	4	7	1	1	0	1	1	3	.333	.364	.476	147	1	1	3	0	1	-1	1.000	1	/O	0.1
1973	SD-N	113	389	52	121	22	3	8	37	37	50	.311	.374	.445	137	14	18	66	9	3	1	.988	3	*O/3	1.8
1974	SD-N★	140	444	53	127	20	4	8	42	46	47	.286	.358	.403	118	8	10	68	4	0	1	.976	3	*O/3	1.0
1975	SD-N	144	553	72	149	36	2	4	38	59	59	.269	.345	.363	103	-2	3	71	2	7	-4	.991	-9	*O	-1.6
1976	SD-N	109	384	54	109	22	1	5	27	65	53	.284	.393	.385	132	14	18	62	1	2	-1	.974	-8	O/13	0.5
1977	Cle-A	34	93	8	28	3	3	2	14	19	18	.301	.425	.462	146	6	7	18	0	3	-2	1.000	-0	O/D	0.4
1978	Cle-A	113	378	54	100	16	6	14	61	59	60	.265	.367	.450	130	15	16	66	5	1	1	.973	5	*O	1.8
	Tex-A	21	33	8	13	3	0	1	6	11	5	.394	.545	.576	215	6	6	12	1	1	-0	1.000	-1	O/D	0.5
	Yr	134	411	62	113	19	6	15	67	70	65	.275	.383	.460	137	21	22	78	6	2	1	.974	5	*O/D	2.3
1979	Tex-A	102	289	42	79	14	0	10	37	34	44	.273	.352	.426	110	4	4	43	2	4	-2	.986	-8	O	-0.8
1980	Tex-A	110	274	40	76	12	1	9	32	42	35	.277	.377	.427	124	9	10	43	2	3	-1	.952	-7	O/D	-0.1
1981	Tex-A	67	199	26	46	9	1	3	26	23	25	.231	.317	.332	92	-3	-2	20	0	3	-2	.990	-4	O	-0.9
1982	Tex-A	103	308	35	86	13	3	3	26	39	37	.279	.371	.370	110	3	6	44	0	3	-2	.965	-6	OD	-0.4
1983	Det-A	57	134	20	34	5	2	4	22	28	17	.254	.390	.410	124	5	6	23	0	0	0	1.000	-3	OD	0.2
1984	*Det-A	86	176	25	47	5	0	8	17	36	36	.267	.397	.432	130	9	9	33	1	0	0	1.000	-6	OD	0.3
1985	Det-A	78	155	19	38	7	1	5	25	24	25	.245	.350	.400	106	2	2	22	0	1	-1	1.000	-3	DO	-0.2
1986	Det-A	81	210	32	70	13	1	13	51	28	28	.333	.417	.590	171	21	21	54	0	1	-1	1.000	-2	DO	1.7
1987	*Det-A	59	114	9	23	6	0	2	13	15	16	.202	.295	.307	63	-7	-6	10	0	0	0	1.000	-4	OD/3	-0.9
Total	16	1424	4154	553	1153	207	29	99	475	566	558	.278	.369	.413	121	105	127	658	27	33	-12	.981	-46	*OD/13	3.4

■ FRANK GRUBE Grube, Franklin Thomas "Hans" b: 1/7/05, Easton, Pa. d: 7/2/45, New York, N.Y. BR/TR, 5'9", 190 lbs. Deb: 5/12/31

1931	Chi-A	88	265	29	58	13	2	1	24	22	22	.219	.284	.294	55	-19	-16	23	2	2	-1	.977	-10	C	-2.1
1932	Chi-A	93	277	36	78	16	2	0	31	33	13	.282	.362	.354	92	-5	-2	38	6	1	1	.957	-2	C	0.2
1933	Chi-A	85	256	23	59	13	0	0	23	38	20	.230	.334	.281	67	-12	-10	27	1	1	-0	.984	-7	C	-1.3
1934	StL-A	65	170	22	49	10	0	0	11	24	11	.288	.379	.347	82	-2	-4	24	2	1	0	.963	-0	C	-0.2
1935	StL-A	3	6	3	2	1	0	0	0	0	1	.333	.333	.500	108	0	0	1	0	0	0	1.000	0	/C	0.0
	Chi-A	9	19	1	7	2	0	0	6	3	2	.368	.455	.474	137	1	1	4	0	0	0	.944	3	/C	0.4
	Yr	12	25	4	9	3	0	0	6	3	3	.360	.429	.480	131	1	1	5	0	0	0	.955	3	C	0.4
1936	Chi-A	33	93	6	15	2	1	0	11	9	15	.161	.235	.204	9	-14	-14	5	1	0	0	.991	2	C	-1.0
1941	StL-A	18	39	1	6	2	0	0	1	2	4	.154	.195	.205	6	-5	-6	2	0	0	0	.951	3	C	-0.2
Total	7	394	1125	121	274	59	5	1	107	131	88	.244	.326	.308	67	-54	-51	124	12	5	1	.970	-13	C	-4.2

■ KELLY GRUBER Gruber, Kelly Wayne b: 2/26/62, Houston, Tex. BR/TR, 6', 185 lbs. Deb: 4/20/84

1984	Tor-A	15	16	1	1	0	0	1	2	0	5	.063	.063	.250	-18	-3	-3	0	0	0	0	.933	1	3/OS	-0.1
1985	Tor-A	5	13	0	3	0	0	1	0	3	.231	.231	.231	26	-1	-1	1	0	0	0	1.000	-1	/32	-0.2
1986	Tor-A	87	143	20	28	4	1	5	15	5	27	.196	.223	.343	50	-10	-11	8	2	5	-2	.940	7	32D/OS	-0.6
1987	Tor-A	138	341	50	80	14	3	12	36	17	70	.235	.285	.399	77	-11	-12	37	12	2	2	.948	8	*3S/2OD	-0.2
1988	Tor-A	158	569	75	158	33	5	16	81	38	92	.278	.331	.438	113	9	9	79	23	5	4	.971	25	*3/2OSD	3.7
1989	*Tor-A★	135	545	83	158	24	4	18	73	30	60	.290	.330	.448	120	11	12	77	10	5	0	.945	19	*3O/SD	3.2
1990	Tor-A★	150	592	92	162	36	6	31	118	48	94	.274	.336	.512	132	24	23	101	14	2	3	.955	-3	*3/OD	2.4
1991	*Tor-A	113	429	58	108	18	2	20	65	31	70	.252	.311	.443	102	2	0	58	12	7	-1	.962	4	*3/D	0.4
1992	*Tor-A	120	446	42	102	16	3	11	43	26	72	.229	.277	.352	72	-16	-18	39	7	7	-2	.949	-4	*3	-2.5
Total	9	921	3094	421	800	145	24	114	434	195	493	.259	.310	.431	102	5	-1	401	80	33	4	.955	57	3/O2SD	6.1

■ SIG GRYSKA Gryska, Sigmund Stanley b: 11/4/15, Chicago, Ill. BR/TR, 5'11.5", 173 lbs. Deb: 9/28/38

1938	StL-A	7	21	3	10	2	1	0	4	3	3	.476	.542	.667	202	3	3	8	0	0	0	.912	1	/S	0.4
1939	StL-A	18	49	4	13	2	0	0	8	6	10	.265	.345	.306	66	-2	-2	6	3	1	0	.873	-4	S	-0.5
Total	2	25	70	7	23	4	1	0	12	9	13	.329	.405	.414	107	1	1	13	3	1	0	.887	-4	/S	-0.1

■ MARV GUDAT Gudat, Marvin John b: 8/27/05, Goliad, Tex. d: 3/1/54, Los Angeles, Cal. BL/TL, 5'11", 162 lbs. Deb: 5/21/29

1929	Cin-N	9	10	0	2	0	0	0	0	0	0	.200	.200	.200	-1	-2	-1	0	0			.800	-1	/P	0.0
1932	*Chi-N	60	94	15	24	4	1	1	15	16	10	.255	.369	.351	96	0	0	13	0			.933	-6	O/1P	-0.7
Total	2	69	104	15	26	4	1	1	15	16	10	.250	.355	.337	87	-2	-1	14	0			.800	-6	/O1P	-0.7

■ MIKE GUERRA Guerra, Fermin (Romero) b: 10/11/12, Havana, Cuba BR/TR, 5'9", 162 lbs. Deb: 9/19/37

1937	Was-A	1	3	0	0	0	0	0	0	0	2	.000	.000	.000	-99	-1	-1	0	0	0	0	.750	-1	/C	-0.1
1944	Was-A	75	210	29	59	7	2	1	29	13	14	.281	.323	.348	96	-3	-1	25	8	2	1	.960	-5	C/O	-0.2
1945	Was-A	56	138	11	29	1	1	1	15	10	12	.210	.268	.254	57	-9	-7	9	4	1	1	.990	5	C	0.0
1946	Was-A	41	83	3	21	2	1	0	4	5	6	.253	.295	.301	71	-4	-3	7	1	0	0	.938	-2	C	-0.4
1947	Phi-A	72	209	20	45	2	2	0	18	10	15	.215	.251	.244	37	-18	-18	13	1	2	-1	.964	3	C	-1.3
1948	Phi-A	53	142	18	30	4	2	1	23	18	13	.211	.300	.289	57	-9	-9	12	2	3	-1	.973	-0	C	-0.7
1949	Phi-A	98	298	41	79	14	1	3	31	37	26	.265	.346	.349	87	-7	-5	37	3	0	1	.982	-3	C	-0.2
1950	Phi-A	87	252	25	71	10	4	2	26	16	12	.282	.325	.377	81	-9	-8	31	1	0	0	.990	-6	C	-1.0
1951	Bos-A	10	32	1	5	0	0	0	2	3	4	.156	.289	.156	21	-3	-4	2	1	0	0	1.000	-1	C	-0.4
	Was-A	72	214	20	43	2	1	1	20	16	18	.201	.257	.234	34	-20	-20	13	4	4	-1	.977	-11	C	-2.9
	Yr	82	246	21	48	2	1	1	22	22	23	.195	.261	.224	32	-23	-23	14	5	4	-1	.982	-11	C	-3.3
Total	9	565	1581	168	382	42	14	9	168	131	123	.242	.300	.303	65	-81	-76	148	25	12	0	.975	-20	C/O	-7.2

■ JUAN GUERRERO Guerrero, Juan Antonio b: 2/1/67, Los Llanos, D.R. BR/TR, 5'11", 160 lbs. Deb: 4/09/92

| 1992 | Hou-N | 79 | 125 | 8 | 25 | 4 | 2 | 1 | 14 | 10 | 32 | .200 | .265 | .288 | 60 | -7 | -6 | 10 | 1 | 0 | 0 | .980 | -7 | S3/O2 | -1.3 |

■ MARIO GUERRERO Guerrero, Mario Miguel (Abud) b: 9/28/49, Santo Domingo, D.R. BR/TR, 5'10", 155 lbs. Deb: 4/08/73

1973	Bos-A	66	219	19	51	5	2	0	11	10	21	.233	.273	.274	51	-13	-15	16	2	2	-1	.974	1	S2	-0.9
1974	Bos-A	93	284	18	70	6	2	0	23	13	22	.246	.284	.282	59	-13	-16	21	3	1	0	.969	-0	S	-0.5
1975	StL-N	64	184	17	44	9	0	0	11	10	7	.239	.286	.288	57	-10	-11	14	0	0	0	.955	6	S	0.1
1976	Cal-A	83	268	24	76	12	0	1	18	7	12	.284	.309	.340	96	-4	-2	27	0	0	0	.973	-12	2S/D	-0.9
1977	Cal-A	86	244	17	69	8	2	1	28	4	16	.283	.294	.344	76	-9	-8	24	0	0	0	.985	-2	SD2	-0.6
1978	Oak-A	143	505	27	139	18	4	3	38	15	35	.275	.304	.345	87	-13	-9	49	0	5	-3	.958	-40	*S	-3.6
1979	Oak-A	46	166	12	38	5	0	0	18	6	7	.229	.256	.259	42	-14	-13	10	0	1	-1	.952	-4	S	-1.2
1980	Oak-A	116	381	32	91	16	2	2	23	9	32	.239	.277	.307	64	-21	-18	29	3	3	-1	.962	-42	*S/2D	-4.8
Total	8	697	2251	166	578	79	12	7	170	84	152	.257	.288	.312	69	-98	-91	190	8	13	-6	.961	-94	S/2D	-12.4

PEDRO GUERRERO
Guerrero, Pedro b: 6/29/56, San Pedro De Macoris, D.R. BR/TR, 6', 195 lbs. Deb: 9/22/78

YEAR	TM/L	G	AB	R	H	2B	3B	HR	RBI	BB	SO	AVG	OBP	SLG	PRO+	BR	/A	RC	SB	CS	SBR	FA	FR	POS	TPR
1978	LA-N	5	8	3	5	0	1	0	1	0	0	.625	.625	.875	316	2	2	4	0	0	0	1.000	0	/1	0.2
1979	LA-N	25	62	7	15	2	0	2	9	1	14	.242	.254	.371	69	-3	-3	6	2	0	1	1.000	-1	O/13	-0.4
1980	LA-N	75	183	27	59	9	1	7	31	12	31	.322	.364	.497	141	9	9	33	2	1	0	.987	2	O2/31	1.1
1981	*LA-N★	98	347	46	104	17	2	12	48	34	57	.300	.366	.464	139	15	17	54	5	9	-4	.974	0	O3/1	1.1
1982	LA-N	150	575	87	175	27	5	32	100	65	89	.304	.380	.536	157	40	42	120	22	5	4	.976	6	*O3	4.9
1983	*LA-N★	160	584	87	174	28	6	32	103	72	110	.298	.377	.531	150	38	38	118	23	7	3	.934	6	*3/1	4.6
1984	LA-N	144	535	85	162	29	4	16	72	49	105	.303	.362	.462	132	21	21	89	9	8	-2	.917	-8	3O1	0.8
1985	*LA-N†	137	487	99	156	22	2	33	87	83	68	.320	**.425**	**.577**	**183**	**53**	**55**	121	12	4	1	.974	8	O31	6.2
1986	LA-N	31	61	7	15	3	0	5	10	2	19	.246	.281	.541	131	1	2	9	0	0	0	1.000	-2	O/1	-0.1
1987	LA-N★	152	545	89	184	25	2	27	89	74	85	.338	.421	.539	156	43	45	121	9	7	-2	.971	1	*O1	3.7
1988	LA-N	59	215	24	64	7	1	5	35	25	33	.298	.379	.409	130	8	9	35	2	1	0	.895	-13	31/O	-0.6
	StL-N	44	149	16	40	7	1	5	30	21	26	.268	.366	.430	126	6	6	24	2	0	1	1.000	-2	1/O	0.1
	Yr	103	364	40	104	14	2	10	65	46	59	.286	.373	.418	128	14	14	60	4	1	1	.998	-15	13/O	-0.5
1989	StL-N★	162	570	60	177	**42**	1	17	117	79	84	.311	.398	.477	145	38	36	109	2	0	1	.990	-14	*1	1.1
1990	StL-N	136	498	42	140	31	1	13	80	44	70	.281	.341	.426	109	6	6	69	1	1	-0	.989	-10	*1	-1.5
1991	StL-N	115	427	41	116	12	1	8	70	37	46	.272	.331	.361	94	-3	-3	50	4	2	0	.985	-8	*1	-1.9
1992	StL-N	43	146	10	32	6	1	1	16	11	25	.219	.274	.295	62	-8	-7	11	2	2	-1	.988	-7	1O	-1.9
Total	15	1536	5392	730	1618	267	29	215	898	609	862	.300	.374	.480	138	266	273	974	97	47	1	.988	-42	1O3/2	17.4

OZZIE GUILLEN
Guillen, Oswaldo Jose (Barrios) b: 1/20/64, Oculare Del Tuy, Venezuela BL/TR, 5'11", 150 lbs. Deb: 4/09/85

YEAR	TM/L	G	AB	R	H	2B	3B	HR	RBI	BB	SO	AVG	OBP	SLG	PRO+	BR	/A	RC	SB	CS	SBR	FA	FR	POS	TPR
1985	Chi-A	150	491	71	134	21	9	1	33	12	36	.273	.292	.358	74	-16	-19	50	7	4	-0	**.980**	12	*S	0.6
1986	Chi-A	159	547	58	137	19	4	2	47	12	52	.250	.268	.311	55	-33	-35	43	8	4	0	.970	14	*S/D	-0.6
1987	Chi-A	149	560	64	156	22	7	2	51	22	52	.279	.307	.354	73	-21	-22	61	25	8	3	.975	13	*S	0.6
1988	Chi-A†	156	566	58	148	16	7	0	39	25	40	.261	.295	.314	71	-22	-22	50	25	13	-0	.977	**43**	*S	3.3
1989	Chi-A	155	597	63	151	20	8	1	54	15	48	.253	.271	.318	67	-28	-26	49	36	17	1	.973	14	*S	0.1
1990	Chi-A★	160	516	61	144	21	4	1	58	26	37	.279	.315	.341	85	-12	-10	52	13	17	-6	.977	3	*S	-0.1
1991	Chi-A★	154	524	52	143	20	3	3	49	11	38	.273	.288	.340	75	-20	-18	48	21	15	-3	.970	-3	*S	-1.3
1992	Chi-A	12	40	5	8	4	0	0	7	1	5	.200	.220	.300	45	-3	-3	3	1	0	0	1.000	1	S	-0.1
Total	8	1095	3841	432	1021	143	42	10	338	124	308	.266	.290	.333	71	-155	-156	355	136	78	-6	.975	97	*S/D	2.5

BOBBY GUINDON
Guindon, Robert Joseph b: 9/4/43, Brookline, Mass. BL/TL, 6'2", 185 lbs. Deb: 9/19/64

YEAR	TM/L	G	AB	R	H	2B	3B	HR	RBI	BB	SO	AVG	OBP	SLG	PRO+	BR	/A	RC	SB	CS	SBR	FA	FR	POS	TPR
1964	Bos-A	5	8	0	1	1	0	0	0	1	4	.125	.222	.250	30	-1	-1	1	0	0	0	1.000	-0	/1O	-0.1

BEN GUINEY
Guiney, Benjamin Franklin b: 11/16/1858, Detroit, Mich. d: 12/5/30, Detroit, Mich. BB/TR, 6', 170 lbs. Deb: 9/04/1883

YEAR	TM/L	G	AB	R	H	2B	3B	HR	RBI	BB	SO	AVG	OBP	SLG	PRO+	BR	/A	RC	SB	CS	SBR	FA	FR	POS	TPR
1883	Det-N	1	5	1	1	0	0	0	0	0	1	.200	.200	.200	23	-0	-0	0				.000	-1	/O	-0.1
1884	Det-N	2	7	0	0	0	0	0	0	0	3	.000	.000	.000	-99	-2	-1	0				.750	-2	/C	-0.3
Total	2	3	12	1	1	0	0	0	0	0	4	.083	.083	.083	-51	-2	-2	0					-2	/CO	-0.4

BEN GUINTINI
Guintini, Benjamin John b: 1/13/20, Los Banos, Cal. BR/TR, 6'1.5", 190 lbs. Deb: 4/21/46

YEAR	TM/L	G	AB	R	H	2B	3B	HR	RBI	BB	SO	AVG	OBP	SLG	PRO+	BR	/A	RC	SB	CS	SBR	FA	FR	POS	TPR
1946	Pit-N	2	3	0	0	0	0	0	0	0	0	.000	.000	.000	-98	-1	-1	0	0			1.000	-0	/O	-0.1
1950	Phi-A	3	4	0	0	0	0	0	0	0	1	.000	.000	.000	-99	-1	-1	0	0	0	0	1.000	0	/O	-0.1
Total	2	5	7	0	0	0	0	0	0	0	1	.000	.000	.000	-99	-2	-2	0	0	0		1.000	0	/O	-0.2

LOU GUISTO
Guisto, Louis Joseph b: 1/16/1895, Napa, Cal. d: 10/15/89, Napa, Cal. BR/TR, 5'11", 193 lbs. Deb: 9/10/16

YEAR	TM/L	G	AB	R	H	2B	3B	HR	RBI	BB	SO	AVG	OBP	SLG	PRO+	BR	/A	RC	SB	CS	SBR	FA	FR	POS	TPR
1916	Cle-A	6	19	2	3	0	0	0	2	4	3	.158	.304	.158	37	-1	-1	1	1			1.000	0	/1	-0.2
1917	Cle-A	73	200	9	37	4	2	0	29	25	18	.185	.282	.225	51	-10	-12	14	3			.989	-1	1	-1.7
1921	Cle-A	2	2	0	1	0	0	0	1	0	1	.500	.500	.500	153	0	0	0	0	0	0	1.000	0	/1	0.0
1922	Cle-A	35	84	7	21	10	1	0	9	2	7	.250	.276	.393	72	-4	-4	9	0	0	0	.995	1	1	-0.4
1923	Cle-A	40	144	17	26	5	0	0	18	15	15	.181	.262	.215	27	-15	-15	9	1	1	-0	.988	1	1	-1.6
Total	5	156	449	35	88	19	3	0	59	46	44	.196	.277	.252	47	-30	-32	33	5	1		.990	1	1	-3.9

BRAD GULDEN
Gulden, Bradley Lee b: 6/10/56, New Ulm, Minn. BL/TR, 5'11", 180 lbs. Deb: 9/22/78

YEAR	TM/L	G	AB	R	H	2B	3B	HR	RBI	BB	SO	AVG	OBP	SLG	PRO+	BR	/A	RC	SB	CS	SBR	FA	FR	POS	TPR
1978	LA-N	3	4	0	0	0	0	0	0	0	2	.000	.000	.000	-99	-1	-1	0	0	0	0	1.000	1	/C	0.0
1979	NY-A	40	92	10	15	4	0	0	6	9	16	.163	.238	.207	21	-10	-10	4	0	1	-1	.995	11	C	0.2
1980	NY-A	2	3	1	1	0	0	1	2	0	0	.333	.333	1.333	340	1	1	1	0	0	0	1.000	-1	/C	0.0
1981	Sea-A	8	16	0	3	2	0	0	1	0	2	.188	.188	.313	40	-1	-1	1	0	0	0	1.000	2	/C	0.0
1982	Mon-N	5	6	1	0	0	0	0	0	1	1	.000	.143	.000	-56	-1	-1	0	0	0	0	1.000	1	/C	-0.1
1984	Cin-N	107	292	31	66	8	2	4	33	33	35	.226	.309	.308	71	-10	-11	28	2	2	-1	.975	-4	*C	-1.3
1986	SF-N	17	22	2	2	0	0	0	1	2	5	.091	.167	.091	-28	-4	-4	0	0	0	0	1.000	-1	C	-0.4
Total	7	182	435	45	87	14	2	5	43	45	61	.200	.278	.276	53	-26	-28	35	2	3	-1	.982	9	C	-1.6

TOM GULLEY
Gulley, Thomas Jefferson b: 12/25/1899, Garner, N.C. d: 11/24/66, St.Charles, Ark. BL/TR, 5'11", 178 lbs. Deb: 8/24/23

YEAR	TM/L	G	AB	R	H	2B	3B	HR	RBI	BB	SO	AVG	OBP	SLG	PRO+	BR	/A	RC	SB	CS	SBR	FA	FR	POS	TPR
1923	Cle-A	2	3	1	1	1	0	0	0	0	0	.333	.333	.667	159	0	0	1	0	0	0	1.000	-0	/O	0.0
1924	Cle-A	8	20	4	3	0	1	0	1	3	2	.150	.261	.250	32	-2	-2	1	0	0	0	.933	0	/O	-0.2
1926	Chi-A	16	35	5	8	3	1	0	8	5	2	.229	.325	.371	84	-1	-1	5	0	0	0	1.000	-2	O	-0.3
Total	3	26	58	10	12	4	2	0	9	8	4	.207	.303	.345	69	-3	-3	7	0	0	0	.971	-2	/O	-0.5

TED GULLIC
Gullic, Theodore Jasper b: 1/2/07, Koshkonong, Mo. BR/TR, 6'2", 175 lbs. Deb: 4/15/30

YEAR	TM/L	G	AB	R	H	2B	3B	HR	RBI	BB	SO	AVG	OBP	SLG	PRO+	BR	/A	RC	SB	CS	SBR	FA	FR	POS	TPR
1930	StL-A	92	308	39	77	7	5	4	44	27	43	.250	.310	.344	64	-16	-18	35	4	0	1	.967	3	O/1	-1.8
1933	StL-A	104	304	34	74	18	3	5	35	15	38	.243	.281	.372	67	-14	-16	32	3	1	0	.988	10	O31	-0.7
Total	2	196	612	73	151	25	8	9	79	42	81	.247	.296	.358	65	-30	-34	67	7	1	2	.975	12	O/31	-2.5

GLENN GULLIVER
Gulliver, Glenn James b: 10/15/54, Detroit, Mich. BL/TR, 5'11", 175 lbs. Deb: 7/17/82

YEAR	TM/L	G	AB	R	H	2B	3B	HR	RBI	BB	SO	AVG	OBP	SLG	PRO+	BR	/A	RC	SB	CS	SBR	FA	FR	POS	TPR
1982	Bal-A	50	145	24	29	7	0	1	5	37	18	.200	.363	.269	77	-3	-3	17	0	0	0	.970	-4	3	-0.8
1983	Bal-A	23	47	5	10	3	0	0	2	9	5	.213	.339	.277	73	-1	-1	5	0	1	-1	1.000	0	3	-0.2
Total	2	73	192	29	39	10	0	1	7	46	23	.203	.357	.271	76	-4	-4	22	0	1	-1	.978	-4	/3	-1.0

FRED GUNKLE
Gunkle, Frederick W. b: Dubuque, Iowa Deb: 5/17/1879

YEAR	TM/L	G	AB	R	H	2B	3B	HR	RBI	BB	SO	AVG	OBP	SLG	PRO+	BR	/A	RC	SB	CS	SBR	FA	FR	POS	TPR
1879	Cle-N	1	3	1	0	0	0	0	0	0	1	.000	.000	.000	-99	-1	-1	0				1.000	-2	/OC	-0.3

HY GUNNING
Gunning, Hyland b: 8/6/1888, Maplewood, N.J. d: 3/28/75, Togus, Me. BL/TR, 6'1.5", 189 lbs. Deb: 8/08/11

YEAR	TM/L	G	AB	R	H	2B	3B	HR	RBI	BB	SO	AVG	OBP	SLG	PRO+	BR	/A	RC	SB	CS	SBR	FA	FR	POS	TPR
1911	Bos-A	4	9	0	1	0	0	0	2	2		.111	.273	.111	9	-1	-1	0	0			1.000	-1	/1	-0.2

TOM GUNNING
Gunning, Thomas Francis b: 3/4/1862, Newmarket, N.H. d: 3/17/31, Fall River, Mass. BR/TR, 5'10", 160 lbs. Deb: 7/26/1884 U

YEAR	TM/L	G	AB	R	H	2B	3B	HR	RBI	BB	SO	AVG	OBP	SLG	PRO+	BR	/A	RC	SB	CS	SBR	FA	FR	POS	TPR
1884	Bos-N	12	45	4	5	1	1	0	2	1	12	.111	.130	.178	-4	-5	-5	1				.914	-5	C	-0.9
1885	Bos-N	48	174	17	32	3	0	0	15	5	29	.184	.207	.201	34	-13	-12	7				.877	-7	C	-1.4
1886	Bos-N	27	98	15	22	2	1	0	7	3	19	.224	.248	.265	58	-5	-5	7	3			.892	-5	C	-0.6
1887	Phi-N	28	104	22	27	6	1	1	16	5	6	.260	.306	.365	83	-2	-3	18	18			.895	6	C	0.5
1888	Phi-a	23	92	18	18	0	0	0	5	2		.196	.237	.196	42	-6	-6	8	14			.894	-1	C	-0.4
1889	Phi-a	8	24	3	6	0	1	1	1	0	4	.250	.250	.458	103	-0	-0	4	3			.838	-2	/C	-0.1
Total	6	146	537	79	110	12	4	2	46	16	70	.205	.235	.253	51	-31	-30	45	38			.887	-15	C	-2.9

JOE GUNSON
Gunson, Joseph Brook b: 3/23/1863, Philadelphia, Pa. d: 11/15/42, Philadelphia, Pa. BR/TR, 5'6", 160 lbs. Deb: 6/14/1884

YEAR	TM/L	G	AB	R	H	2B	3B	HR	RBI	BB	SO	AVG	OBP	SLG	PRO+	BR	/A	RC	SB	CS	SBR	FA	FR	POS	TPR
1884	Was-U	45	166	15	23	2	0	0		3		.139	.154	.151	3	-16	-15	4				.915	10	CO	-0.3

YEAR	TM/L	G	AB	R	H	2B	3B	HR	RBI	BB	SO	AVG	OBP	SLG	PRO+	BR	/A	RC	SB	CS	SBR	FA	FR	POS	TPR
1889	KC-a	34	122	15	24	3	1	0	12	3	17	.197	.228	.238	32	-10	-12	7	2			.862	-6	C/O3	-1.3
1892	Bal-N	89	314	35	67	10	5	0	32	16	17	.213	.267	.277	64	-13	-14	24	2			.921	-1	CO/12	-1.0
1893	StL-N	40	151	20	41	5	0	0	15	6	6	.272	.321	.305	68	-7	-7	15	0			.927	3	C/O	-0.1
	Cle-N	21	73	11	19	1	0	0	9	6	0	.260	.316	.274	56	-4	-5	6	0			.942	2	C	-0.1
	Yr	61	224	31	60	6	0	0	24	12	6	.268	.320	.295	64	-11	-12	22	0			.932	5	C/O	-0.2
Total	4	229	826	96	174	21	6	0	68	34	40	.211	.254	.251	49	-50	-53	57	4			.912	8	C/O123	-2.8

■ ERNIE GUST

Gust, Ernest Herman Frank "Red" b: 1/24/1888, Bay City, Mich. d: 10/26/45, Maupin, Ore. BR/TR, 6', 170 lbs. Deb: 8/17/11

YEAR	TM/L	G	AB	R	H	2B	3B	HR	RBI	BB	SO	AVG	OBP	SLG	PRO+	BR	/A	RC	SB	CS	SBR	FA	FR	POS	TPR
1911	StL-A	3	12	0	0	0	0	0	0	0		.000	.000	.000	-99	-3	-3	0	0			.974	-0	/1	-0.3

■ FRANKIE GUSTINE

Gustine, Frank William b: 2/20/20, Hoopeston, Ill. d: 4/1/91, Davenport, Iowa BR/TR, 6', 180 lbs. Deb: 9/13/39

YEAR	TM/L	G	AB	R	H	2B	3B	HR	RBI	BB	SO	AVG	OBP	SLG	PRO+	BR	/A	RC	SB	CS	SBR	FA	FR	POS	TPR
1939	Pit-N	22	70	5	13	3	0	0	3	9	4	.186	.278	.229	38	-6	-6	5	0			.896	4	3	-0.2
1940	Pit-N	133	524	59	147	32	7	1	55	35	39	.281	.328	.374	94	-5	-5	63	7			.941	-8	*2	-0.4
1941	Pit-N	121	463	46	125	24	7	1	46	28	38	.270	.313	.359	89	-8	-8	51	5			.954	-1	*23	-0.1
1942	Pit-N	115	388	34	89	11	4	2	35	29	27	.229	.286	.294	68	-15	-16	31	5			.954	-10	*2/S3C	-2.1
1943	Pit-N	112	414	40	120	21	3	0	43	32	36	.290	.341	.355	98	0	-1	51	12			.938	-5	S2/1	0.1
1944	Pit-N	127	405	42	93	18	3	2	42	33	41	.230	.288	.304	64	-18	-20	34	8			.938	-27	*S2/3	-4.0
1945	Pit-N	128	478	67	134	27	5	2	66	37	33	.280	.335	.370	92	-3	-6	58	8			.930	-19	*S2/C	-1.5
1946	Pit-N★	131	495	60	128	23	6	8	52	40	52	.259	.318	.378	95	-3	-5	59	2			.967	8	*2S/3	1.2
1947	Pit-N★	156	616	102	183	30	6	9	67	63	65	.297	.364	.409	102	5	3	92	5			.944	15	*3	1.8
1948	Pit-N★	131	449	68	120	19	2	9	42	42	62	.267	.333	.379	90	-5	-6	56	5			.947	9	*3	0.1
1949	Chi-N	76	261	29	59	13	4	4	27	18	22	.226	.279	.352	70	-12	-12	24	3			.931	1	32	-1.1
1950	StL-A	9	19	1	3	1	0	0	2	3	8	.158	.273	.211	24	-2	-2	1	0	1	-1	.857	-0	/3	-0.3
Total	12	1261	4582	553	1214	222	47	38	480	369	427	.265	.322	.359	87	-73	-83	525	60	1		.955	-33	23S/C1	-6.5

■ BUCKY GUTH

Guth, Charles Henry b: 8/18/47, Baltimore, Md. BR/TR, 6'1", 180 lbs. Deb: 9/12/72

YEAR	TM/L	G	AB	R	H	2B	3B	HR	RBI	BB	SO	AVG	OBP	SLG	PRO+	BR	/A	RC	SB	CS	SBR	FA	FR	POS	TPR
1972	Min-A	3	3	1	0	0	0	0	0	0	0	.000	.000	.000	-95	-1	-1	0	0	0	0	1.000	1	/S	0.0

■ CESAR GUTIERREZ

Gutierrez, Cesar Dario "Coca" b: 1/26/43, Coro, Venez. BR/TR, 5'9", 155 lbs. Deb: 4/16/67

YEAR	TM/L	G	AB	R	H	2B	3B	HR	RBI	BB	SO	AVG	OBP	SLG	PRO+	BR	/A	RC	SB	CS	SBR	FA	FR	POS	TPR
1967	SF-N	18	21	4	3	0	0	0	0	1	4	.143	.217	.143	5	-3	-3	1	1	0	0	.946	3	S/2	0.1
1969	SF-N	15	23	4	5	1	0	0	0	6	2	.217	.379	.261	84	-0	-0	3	1	0	0	.882	-0	/3S	0.0
	Det-A	17	49	5	12	1	0	0	0	5	3	.245	.315	.265	61	-2	-3	4	1	2	-1	.946	1	S	-0.1
1970	Det-A	135	415	40	101	11	6	0	22	18	39	.243	.276	.299	58	-24	-24	33	4	3	-1	.957	-18	*S	-3.0
1971	Det-A	38	37	8	7	0	0	0	4	0	3	.189	.211	.189	13	-4	-4	2	0	0	0	.971	5	S/32	0.1
Total	4	223	545	61	128	13	6	0	26	30	51	.235	.279	.281	55	-33	-33	43	7	5	-1	.955	-9	S/32	-2.9

■ JACKIE GUTIERREZ

Gutierrez, Joaquin Fernando b: 6/27/60, Cartagena, Colombia BR/TR, 5'11", 175 lbs. Deb: 9/06/83

YEAR	TM/L	G	AB	R	H	2B	3B	HR	RBI	BB	SO	AVG	OBP	SLG	PRO+	BR	/A	RC	SB	CS	SBR	FA	FR	POS	TPR
1983	Bos-A	5	10	2	3	0	0	0	0	1	1	.300	.364	.300	79	-0	-0	1	0	1	-1	.938	-0	/S	-0.1
1984	Bos-A	151	449	55	118	12	3	2	29	15	49	.263	.287	.316	64	-20	-23	37	12	5	1	.949	-33	*S	-4.3
1985	Bos-A	103	275	33	60	5	2	2	21	12	37	.218	.251	.273	42	-21	-23	18	10	2	2	.943	5	S	-0.8
1986	Bal-A	61	145	8	27	3	0	0	4	3	27	.186	.208	.207	14	-17	-17	6	3	1	0	.990	7	2/3D	-0.8
1987	Bal-A	3	1	0	0	0	0	0	0	0	0	.000	.000	.000	-99	-0	-0	0	0	0	0	.000	0	/23	0.0
1988	Phi-N	33	77	8	19	4	0	0	9	2	9	.247	.266	.299	61	-4	-4	6	0	0	0	.919	-2	S3	-0.6
Total	6	356	957	106	227	24	5	4	63	33	123	.237	.263	.285	50	-63	-67	67	25	9	2	.945	-23	S/23D	-6.6

■ DON GUTTERIDGE

Gutteridge, Donald Joseph b: 6/19/12, Pittsburg, Kan. BR/TR, 5'10.5", 165 lbs. Deb: 9/07/36 MC

YEAR	TM/L	G	AB	R	H	2B	3B	HR	RBI	BB	SO	AVG	OBP	SLG	PRO+	BR	/A	RC	SB	CS	SBR	FA	FR	POS	TPR
1936	StL-N	23	91	13	29	3	4	3	16	1	14	.319	.326	.538	130	3	3	16	3			.967	0	3	0.4
1937	StL-N	119	447	66	121	26	10	7	61	25	66	.271	.311	.421	95	-3	-5	59	12			.978	2	*3/S	0.0
1938	StL-N	142	552	61	141	21	15	9	64	29	49	.255	.293	.397	83	-11	-15	64	14			.945	0	3S	-0.8
1939	StL-N	148	524	71	141	27	4	7	54	27	70	.269	.309	.376	78	-14	-18	61	5			.934	-18	*3/S	-3.5
1940	StL-N	69	108	19	29	5	0	3	14	5	15	.269	.301	.398	86	-2	-2	13	3			.877	-2	3	-0.4
1942	StL-A	147	616	90	157	27	11	1	50	59	54	.255	.320	.339	84	-12	-13	69	16	13	-3	.973	3	*2/3	-0.5
1943	StL-A	132	538	77	147	35	6	1	36	50	46	.273	.335	.366	103	3	2	68	10	9	-2	.958	-31	*2	-2.6
1944	*StL-A	148	603	89	148	27	11	3	36	51	63	.245	.304	.342	80	-13	-17	67	20	8	1	.957	-8	*2	-1.7
1945	StL-A	143	543	72	129	24	3	2	49	43	46	.238	.295	.304	70	-19	-22	51	9	6	-1	.970	-20	*2O	-3.8
1946	*Bos-A	22	47	8	11	3	0	1	6	2	7	.234	.265	.362	70	-2	-2	5	0	0	0	1.000	-1	/23	-0.3
1947	Bos-A	54	131	20	22	2	0	2	5	17	13	.168	.264	.229	35	-11	-12	9	3	1	0	.938	-1	23	-1.3
1948	Pit-N	4	2	0	0	0	0	0	0	0	1	.000	.000	.000	-98	-1	-1	0	0			.000	0	H	-0.1
Total	12	1151	4202	586	1075	200	64	39	391	309	444	.256	.308	.362	84	-81	-102	484	95	37		.964	-76	23/SO	-14.6

■ DOUG GWOSDZ

Gwosdz, Douglas Wayne b: 6/20/60, Houston, Tex. BR/TR, 5'11", 185 lbs. Deb: 8/17/81

YEAR	TM/L	G	AB	R	H	2B	3B	HR	RBI	BB	SO	AVG	OBP	SLG	PRO+	BR	/A	RC	SB	CS	SBR	FA	FR	POS	TPR
1981	SD-N	16	24	1	4	2	0	0	3	3	6	.167	.259	.250	48	-2	-1	2	0	0	0	1.000	2	C	0.1
1982	SD-N	7	17	1	3	0	0	0	0	2	7	.176	.263	.176	27	-2	-2	1	0	0	0	1.000	2	/C	0.0
1983	SD-N	39	55	7	6	1	0	1	4	7	19	.109	.210	.182	10	-7	-7	2	0	0	0	.971	2	C	-0.4
1984	SD-N	7	8	0	2	0	0	0	1	2	5	.250	.400	.250	86	-0	-0	1	0	0	0	.963	2	/C	0.2
Total	4	69	104	9	15	3	0	1	8	14	37	.144	.246	.202	27	-10	-10	6	0	0	0	.981	8	/C	-0.1

■ TONY GWYNN

Gwynn, Anthony Keith b: 5/9/60, Los Angeles, Cal. BL/TL, 5'11", 200 lbs. Deb: 7/19/82 F

YEAR	TM/L	G	AB	R	H	2B	3B	HR	RBI	BB	SO	AVG	OBP	SLG	PRO+	BR	/A	RC	SB	CS	SBR	FA	FR	POS	TPR
1982	SD-N	54	190	33	55	12	2	1	17	14	16	.289	.338	.389	109	1	2	25	8	3	1	.991	-1	O	0.0
1983	SD-N	86	304	34	94	12	2	1	37	23	21	.309	.358	.372	106	1	3	39	7	4	-0	.994	2	O	0.2
1984	*SD-N★	158	606	88	**213**	21	10	5	71	59	23	**.351**	.411	.444	140	34	34	108	33	18	-1	.989	16	*O	4.5
1985	SD-N★	154	622	90	197	29	5	6	46	45	33	.317	.365	.408	118	13	14	88	14	11	-2	.989	17	*O	2.5
1986	SD-N★	160	642	**107**	**211**	33	7	14	59	52	35	.329	.382	.467	136	28	30	113	37	9	6	.989	20	*O	5.2
1987	SD-N★	157	589	119	**218**	36	13	7	54	82	35	**.370**	.450	.511	160	50	52	143	56	12	10	.981	9	*O	6.4
1988	SD-N	133	521	64	163	22	5	7	70	51	40	**.313**	.374	.415	128	18	19	81	26	11	1	.982	3	*O	2.1
1989	SD-N★	158	604	82	**203**	27	7	4	62	56	30	**.336**	.393	.424	133	27	27	101	40	16	2	.984	11	*O	3.9
1990	SD-N★	141	573	79	177	29	10	4	72	44	23	.309	.359	.415	112	10	9	83	17	8	0	.985	15	*O	2.2
1991	SD-N★	134	530	69	168	27	11	4	62	34	19	.317	.358	.432	118	14	12	78	8	8	-2	.990	11	*O	1.9
1992	SD-N★	128	520	77	165	27	3	6	41	46	16	.317	.373	.415	119	16	14	77	3	6	-3	.982	12	*O	2.1
Total	11	1463	5701	842	1864	275	75	59	591	506	291	.327	.383	.433	128	213	218	935	249	106	11	.986	115	*O	31.0

■ CHRIS GWYNN

Gwynn, Christopher Karlton b: 10/13/64, Los Angeles, Cal. BL/TL, 6' ", 200 lbs. Deb: 8/14/87 F

YEAR	TM/L	G	AB	R	H	2B	3B	HR	RBI	BB	SO	AVG	OBP	SLG	PRO+	BR	/A	RC	SB	CS	SBR	FA	FR	POS	TPR
1987	LA-N	17	32	2	7	1	0	0	2	1	7	.219	.242	.250	32	-3	-3	2	0	0	0	1.000	-1	O	-0.4
1988	LA-N	12	11	1	2	0	0	0	0	1	2	.182	.250	.182	27	-1	-1	1	0	0	0	.000	-2	/O	-0.3
1989	LA-N	32	68	8	16	4	1	0	7	2	9	.235	.257	.324	66	-3	-3	6	1	0	0	1.000	-2	O	-0.6
1990	LA-N	101	141	19	40	2	1	5	22	7	28	.284	.318	.418	104	-0	0	18	0	1	-1	1.000	-9	O	-1.1
1991	LA-N	94	139	18	35	5	1	5	22	10	23	.252	.307	.410	102	-0	-0	17	1	0	0	1.000	-9	O	-1.0
1992	KC-A	34	84	10	24	3	2	1	7	3	10	.286	.310	.405	98	-0	-1	10	0	0	0	1.000	-2	O/D	-0.2
Total	6	290	475	58	124	15	5	11	60	24	79	.261	.298	.383	90	-8	-7	53	2	1	0	1.000	-25	O/D	-3.6

■ DICK GYSELMAN

Gyselman, Richard Renald b: 4/6/08, San Francisco, Cal. d: 9/20/90, Seattle, Wash. BR/TR, 6'2", 170 lbs. Deb: 4/20/33

YEAR	TM/L	G	AB	R	H	2B	3B	HR	RBI	BB	SO	AVG	OBP	SLG	PRO+	BR	/A	RC	SB	CS	SBR	FA	FR	POS	TPR
1933	Bos-N	58	155	10	37	6	2	0	12	7	21	.239	.272	.303	70	-7	-6	12	0			.926	6	3/2S	0.3
1934	Bos-N	24	36	7	6	1	1	0	4	2	11	.167	.211	.250	25	-4	-4	2	0			.739	-2	3/2	-0.5
Total	2	82	191	17	43	7	3	0	16	9	32	.225	.260	.293	61	-11	-10	14	0			.901	4	/32S	-0.2

YEAR	TM/L	G	AB	R	H	2B	3B	HR	RBI	BB	SO	AVG	OBP	SLG	PRO+	BR	/A	RC	SB	CS	SBR	FA	FR	POS	TPR

■ BERT HAAS Haas, Berthold John b: 2/8/14, Naperville, Ill. BR/TR, 5'11", 180 lbs. Deb: 9/09/37

1937	Bro-N	16	25	2	10	3	0	0	2	1	1	.400	.423	.520	152	2	2	5	0			1.000	-1	/O1	0.1
1938	Bro-N	1	0	0	0	0	0	0	0	0	0	—	—	—	—	0	0	0	0			.000	0	H	0.0
1942	Cin-N	154	585	59	140	21	6	6	54	59	54	.239	.310	.326	86	-10	-10	61	6			.925	-10	*3/1O	-2.0
1943	Cin-N	101	332	39	87	17	6	4	44	22	26	.262	.308	.386	101	-1	-1	38	6			.993	9	13O	0.5
1946	Cin-N	140	535	57	141	24	7	3	50	33	42	.264	.310	.351	91	-10	-8	58	22			.994	0	*1/3	-1.7
1947	Cin-N★	135	482	58	138	17	7	3	67	42	27	.286	.346	.369	91	-7	-6	63	9			.956	-4	O1	-1.6
1948	Phi-N	95	333	35	94	9	2	4	34	36	25	.282	.354	.357	95	-2	-2	42	8			.892	-8	31	-1.1
1949	Phi-N	2	1	0	0	0	0	0	0	1	1	.000	.500	.000	47	0	0	0	0			.000	0	H	0.0
	NY-N	54	104	12	27	2	3	1	10	5	8	.260	.294	.365	76	-4	-4	11				.983	-1	13	-0.5
	Yr	56	105	12	27	2	3	1	10	6	9	.257	.297	.362	76	-4	-4	11	0			.983	-1	13	-0.5
1951	Chi-A	23	43	1	7	0	1	1	2	5	4	.163	.250	.279	44	-4	-3	3	0	0	0	1.000	-1	/1O3	-0.5
Total	9	721	2440	263	644	93	32	22	263	204	188	.264	.323	.355	91	-36	-32	283	51	0		.991	-17	13/O	-6.8

■ BRUNO HAAS Haas, Bruno Philip "Boon" b: 5/5/1891, Worcester, Mass. d: 6/5/52, Sarasota, Fla. BB/TL, 5'10", 180 lbs. Deb: 6/23/15

| 1915 | Phi-A | 12 | 18 | 1 | 1 | 0 | 0 | 0 | 1 | 7 | | .056 | .105 | .056 | -54 | -3 | -3 | 0 | 0 | | | .875 | 1 | /PO | -0.2 |

■ EDDIE HAAS Haas, George Edwin b: 5/26/35, Paducah, Ky. BL/TR, 5'11", 178 lbs. Deb: 9/08/57 MC

1957	Chi-N	14	24	1	5	1	0	0	4	1	5	.208	.240	.250	32	-2	-2	2	0	0	0	1.000	-1	/O	-0.3
1958	Mil-N	9	14	2	5	0	0	0	1	2	1	.357	.438	.357	124	0	1	2	0	0	0	1.000	-0	/O	0.0
1960	Mil-N	32	32	4	7	2	0	1	5	5	14	.219	.324	.375	98	-0	-0	4	0	0	0	1.000	-1	/O	-0.1
Total	3	55	70	7	17	3	0	1	10	8	20	.243	.321	.329	80	-2	-2	8	0	0	0	1.000	-2	/O	-0.4

■ MULE HAAS Haas, George William b: 10/15/03, Montclair, N.J. d: 6/30/74, New Orleans, La. BL/TR, 6'1", 175 lbs. Deb: 8/15/25 C

1925	Pit-N	4	3	1	0	0	0	0	0	0	1	.000	.000	.000	-94	-1	-1	0	0			1.000	-1	/O	-0.2
1928	Phi-A	91	332	41	93	21	4	6	39	23	20	.280	.331	.422	94	-3	-4	46	2	3	-1	.974	-3	O	-1.3
1929	*Phi-A	139	578	115	181	41	9	16	82	34	38	.313	.356	.498	113	13	10	100	0	4	-2	.982	3	*O	0.0
1930	*Phi-A	132	532	91	159	33	7	2	68	43	33	.299	.352	.398	86	-8	-11	76	2	4	-2	.976	12	*O	-0.8
1931	*Phi-A	102	440	82	142	29	7	8	56	30	29	.323	.366	.475	113	11	7	77	0	0	0	.989	4	*O	0.4
1932	Phi-A	143	558	91	170	28	5	6	65	62	49	.305	.381	.405	99	3	0	89	1	0	0	.987	7	*O	-0.2
1933	Chi-A	146	585	97	168	33	4	1	51	65	41	.287	.360	.362	96	-5	-2	79	0	5	-3	.983	-5	*O	-1.6
1934	Chi-A	106	351	54	94	16	3	2	22	47	22	.268	.354	.348	79	-9	-10	47	1	0	0	.991	-2	O	-1.5
1935	Chi-A	92	327	44	95	22	1	2	40	37	15	.291	.363	.382	90	-3	-4	48	4	1	1	.989	-1	O	-0.8
1936	Chi-A	119	408	75	116	26	2	0	46	64	29	.284	.383	.358	81	-8	-11	61	1	1	-0	.989	-6	O/1	-1.9
1937	Chi-A	54	111	16	23	3	3	0	15	16	10	.207	.313	.288	52	-8	-8	11	1	0	0	.975	1	1/O	-1.0
1938	Phi-A	40	78	7	16	2	0	0	12	12	10	.205	.311	.231	39	-7	-7	7	0	0	0	1.000	-2	O/1	-1.0
Total	12	1168	4303	706	1257	254	45	43	496	433	299	.292	.359	.402	93	-24	-41	642	12	16	-6	.984	5	*O/1	-9.9

■ EMIL HABERER Haberer, Emil Karl b: 2/2/1878, Cincinnati, Ohio d: 10/19/51, Louisville, Ky. BR/TR, 6'1", 204 lbs. Deb: 7/09/01

1901	Cin-N	6	18	2	3	0	1	0	1		3	.167	.286	.278	68	-1	-1	1	0			.545	-2	/31	-0.2
1903	Cin-N	5	13	1	1	0	0	0	0		2	.077	.200	.077	-18	-2	-2	0	0			.933	-2	/C	-0.4
1909	Cin-N	5	16	1	3	1	0	0	2		0	.188	.188	.250	36	-1	-1	1	0			.895	-2	/C	-0.3
Total	3	16	47	4	7	1	1	0	3		5	.149	.231	.213	31	-4	-4	2	0			.912	-6	/C31	-0.9

■ IRV HACH Hach, Irvin William "Major" b: 6/6/1873, Louisville, Ky. d: 8/13/36, Louisville, Ky. BR/TR, Deb: 7/01/1897

| 1897 | Lou-N | 16 | 51 | 5 | 11 | 2 | 0 | 0 | 3 | 5 | | .216 | .322 | .255 | 55 | -3 | -3 | 5 | 1 | | | .889 | -1 | /23 | -0.3 |

■ STAN HACK Hack, Stanley Camfield "Smiling Stan" b: 12/6/09, Sacramento, Cal d: 12/15/79, Dixon, Ill. BL/TR, 6', 170 lbs. Deb: 4/12/32 MC

1932	*Chi-N	72	178	32	42	5	6	2	19	17	16	.236	.306	.365	80	-5	-5	21	5			.913	-5	3	-0.7
1933	Chi-N	20	60	10	21	3	1	1	2	8	3	.350	.451	.483	167	6	6	15	4			.983	6	3	1.3
1934	Chi-N	111	402	54	116	16	6	1	21	45	42	.289	.363	.366	98	-1	-0	57	11			.949	0	*3	0.5
1935	*Chi-N	124	427	75	133	23	9	4	64	65	17	.311	.406	.436	125	19	18	83	14			.942	11	*3/1	3.1
1936	Chi-N	149	561	102	167	27	4	6	78	89	39	.298	.396	.392	110	14	12	94	17			.950	-12	*31	0.4
1937	Chi-N	154	582	106	173	27	6	2	63	83	42	.297	.388	.375	104	10	7	94	16			.968	-9	*3/1	0.2
1938	*Chi-N★	152	609	109	195	34	11	4	67	94	39	.320	.411	.432	128	31	28	119	**16**			.954	7	*3	3.7
1939	Chi-N★	156	641	112	191	28	6	8	56	65	35	.298	.364	.398	103	5	4	97	**17**			.956	-7	*3	-0.1
1940	Chi-N	149	603	101	**191**	38	6	8	40	75	24	**.317**	.395	.439	132	27	28	112	21			.954	14	*3/1	4.4
1941	Chi-N★	151	586	111	**186**	33	5	7	45	99	40	.317	.417	.427	143	34	37	114	10			.954	-16	*3/1	2.5
1942	Chi-N	140	553	91	166	36	3	6	39	94	40	.300	.402	.409	143	30	32	100	9			**.965**	-10	*3	2.6
1943	Chi-N	144	533	78	154	24	4	3	35	82	27	.289	.384	.366	119	15	16	83	5			.960	-7	*3	1.1
1944	Chi-N	98	383	65	108	16	1	3	32	53	21	.282	.369	.352	104	4	4	53	5			.939	2	31	0.6
1945	*Chi-N	150	597	110	193	29	7	2	43	99	30	.323	.420	.405	133	29	31	111	12			**.975**	18	*3/1	5.2
1946	Chi-N	92	323	55	92	13	4	0	26	83	32	.285	.431	.350	125	16	16	56	3			.968	-3	3	1.6
1947	Chi-N	76	240	28	65	11	2	0	12	41	19	.271	.377	.333	94	-2	-0	33	0			.962	7	3	0.7
Total	16	1938	7278	1239	2193	363	81	57	642	1092	466	.301	.394	.397	120	231	235	1241	165			.957	-4	*3/1	27.1

■ RICH HACKER Hacker, Richard Warren b: 10/6/47, Belleville, Ill. BB/TR, 6', 160 lbs. Deb: 7/02/71 C

| 1971 | Mon-N | 16 | 33 | 2 | 4 | 1 | 0 | 0 | 2 | 3 | 12 | .121 | .194 | .152 | -1 | -4 | -4 | 1 | 0 | 0 | 0 | .984 | 5 | S | 0.2 |

■ JIM HACKETT Hackett, James Joseph "Sunny Jim" b: 10/1/1877, Jacksonville, Ill. d: 3/28/61, Douglas, Mich. BR/TR, 6'2", 185 lbs. Deb: 9/14/02

1902	StL-N	6	21	2	6	1	0	0	4	2		.286	.348	.333	115	0	0	3	1			.833	-1	/PO	0.0
1903	StL-N	99	351	24	80	13	8	0	36	19		.228	.272	.311	68	-16	-15	31	2			.972	-6	1/P	-2.1
Total	2	105	372	26	86	14	8	0	40	21		.231	.276	.312	71	-16	-15	34	3			.893	-7	/1PO	-2.1

■ MERT HACKETT Hackett, Mortimer Martin b: 11/11/1859, Cambridge, Mass. d: 2/22/38, Cambridge, Mass. BR/TR, 5'10.5", 175 lbs. Deb: 5/02/1883 F

1883	Bos-N	46	179	20	42	8	6	2	24	1	48	.235	.239	.380	82	-3	-4	17				.909	-6	C/O	-0.7
1884	Bos-N	72	268	28	55	13	2	1	20	2	66	.205	.211	.280	53	-14	-14	16				.928	12	C/3	0.3
1885	Bos-N	34	115	9	21	7	1	0	4	2	28	.183	.197	.261	49	-7	-6	6				.901	5	C	0.2
1886	KC-N	62	230	18	50	8	3	3	25	4	59	.217	.231	.317	61	-10	-12	18	1			.926	-17	CO	-2.2
1887	Ind-N	42	147	12	35	6	3	2	10	7	24	.238	.282	.361	82	-4	-3	16	4			.938	-9	C/O1	-0.7
Total	5	256	939	87	203	42	15	8	83	16	225	.216	.231	.318	65	-39	-40	73	5			.921	-15	C/O13	-3.1

■ WALTER HACKETT Hackett, Walter Henry b: 8/15/1857, Cambridge, Mass. d: 10/2/20, Cambridge, Mass. Deb: 4/17/1884 F

1884	Bos-U	103	415	71	101	19	0	1		7		.243	.256	.296	88	-6	-5	32				**.855**	12	*S	0.7
1885	Bos-N	35	125	8	23	3	0	0	9	3		.184	.203	.208	34	-9	-8	5				.893	-12	2S	-1.9
Total	2	138	540	79	124	22	0	1	9	10	22	.230	.244	.276	75	-15	-14	38				.852	1	S/2	-1.2

■ KENT HADLEY Hadley, Kent William b: 12/17/34, Pocatello, Idaho BL/TL, 6'3", 190 lbs. Deb: 9/14/58

1958	KC-A	3	11	1	2	0	0	0	0	0	4	.182	.182	.182	0	-1	-1	0	0	0	0	1.000	-1	/1	-0.2
1959	KC-A	113	288	40	73	11	1	10	39	24	74	.253	.313	.403	93	-3	-3	36	1	2	-1	.989	-2	1	-1.1
1960	NY-A	55	64	8	13	2	0	4	11	6	19	.203	.271	.422	90	-2	-2	7	1	0	0	.991	-0	1	-0.2
Total	3	171	363	49	88	13	1	14	50	30	97	.242	.302	.399	90	-6	-6	43	2	2	-1	.989	-3	1	-1.5

■ BILL HAEFFNER Haeffner, William Bernhard b: 7/8/1894, Philadelphia, Pa. d: 1/27/82, Springfield, Pa. BR/TR, 5'9", 165 lbs. Deb: 6/29/15

| 1915 | Phi-A | 3 | 4 | 0 | 1 | 0 | 0 | 0 | 0 | 0 | 1 | .250 | .250 | .250 | 51 | -0 | -0 | 0 | | | | 1.000 | -1 | /C | -0.2 |

YEAR	TM/L	G	AB	R	H	2B	3B	HR	RBI	BB	SO	AVG	OBP	SLG	PRO+	BR	/A	RC	SB	CS	SBR	FA	FR	POS	TPR
1920	Pit-N	54	175	8	34	4	1	0	14	8	14	.194	.230	.229	31	-15	-16	9	1	1	-0	.972	-3	C	-1.7
1928	NY-N	2	1	0	0	0	0	0	0	0	0	.000	.000	.000	-99	-0	-0	0	0			.750	0	/C	0.0
Total	3	59	180	8	35	4	1	0	14	8	15	.194	.229	.228	30	-16	-16	10	1	1		.968	-5	/C	-1.9
■ **CHICK HAFEY** Hafey, Charles James b: 2/12/03, Berkeley, Cal. d: 7/2/73, Calistoga, Cal. BR/TR, 6', 185 lbs. Deb: 8/28/24 H																									
1924	StL-N	24	91	10	23	5	2	2	22	4	8	.253	.292	.418	90	-2	-2	11	1	0	0	.927	-1	O	-0.3
1925	StL-N	93	358	36	108	25	2	5	57	10	29	.302	.321	.425	87	-7	-8	45	3	7	-3	.955	-1	O	-1.7
1926	*StL-N	78	225	30	61	19	2	4	38	11	36	.271	.311	.427	93	-2	-3	29	2			.974	-6	O	-1.2
1927	StL-N	103	346	62	114	26	5	18	63	36	41	.329	.401	.590	157	29	28	80	12			.980	5	O	2.7
1928	*StL-N	138	520	101	175	46	6	27	111	40	53	.337	.386	.604	152	39	37	116	8			.965	3	*O	3.0
1929	StL-N	134	517	101	175	47	9	29	125	45	42	.338	.394	.632	148	37	36	124	7			.966	3	*O	2.8
1930	*StL-N	120	446	108	150	39	12	26	107	46	51	.336	.407	.652	146	35	33	114	12			.976	-3	*O	1.9
1931	*StL-N	122	450	94	157	35	8	16	95	39	43	**.349**	**.404**	.569	153	36	34	105	11			.983	-4	*O	2.2
1932	Cin-N	83	253	34	87	19	3	2	36	22	20	.344	.403	.466	137	12	13	49	4			.965	-3	O	0.7
1933	Cin-N★	144	568	77	172	34	6	7	62	40	44	.303	.351	.421	121	14	15	85	3			.987	8	*O	1.6
1934	Cin-N	140	535	75	157	29	6	18	67	52	63	.293	.359	.471	123	15	17	93	4			.967	4	*O	1.5
1935	Cin-N	15	59	10	20	6	1	1	9	4	5	.339	.400	.525	151	4	4	13	1			.912	-3	O	0.1
1937	Cin-N	89	257	39	67	11	5	9	41	23	42	.261	.324	.447	113	2	4	38	2			.971	-2	O	-0.1
Total	13	1283	4625	777	1466	341	67	164	833	372	477	.317	.372	.526	133	212	208	902	70	7		.971	1	*O	13.2
■ **BUD HAFEY** Hafey, Daniel Albert b: 8/6/12, Berkeley, Cal. d: 7/27/86, Sacramento, Cal. BR/TR, 6', 185 lbs. Deb: 4/21/35 F																									
1935	Chi-A	2	0	1	0	0	0	0	0	0	0	—	—	—	—	0	0	0	0	0	0	.000	0	R	0.0
	Pit-N	58	184	29	42	11	2	6	16	16	48	.228	.290	.408	83	-4	-5	22	0			.970	4	O	-0.3
1936	Pit-N	39	118	19	25	6	1	4	13	10	27	.212	.273	.381	73	-5	-5	12	0			.932	0	O	-0.6
1939	Cin-N	6	13	1	2	1	0	0	1	1	4	.154	.214	.231	19	-1	-2	1	1			1.000	-0	/O	-0.2
	Phi-N	18	51	3	9	1	0	0	3	3	12	.176	.222	.196	14	-6	-6	2	1			1.000	1	O/P	-0.6
	Yr	24	64	4	11	2	0	0	4	4	16	.172	.221	.203	15	-8	-8	3	2			1.000	1	O/P	-0.8
Total	3	123	366	53	78	19	3	10	33	30	91	.213	.273	.363	68	-17	-18	36	2	0		.963	4	/OP	-1.7
■ **TOM HAFEY** Hafey, Thomas Francis "Heave-O" or "The Arm" b: 7/12/13, Berkeley, Cal. BR/TR, 6'1", 180 lbs. Deb: 7/21/39 F																									
1939	NY-N	70	256	37	62	10	1	6	26	10	44	.242	.271	.359	67	-12	-13	24	1			.960	-0	3	-1.2
1944	StL-A	8	14	1	5	2	0	0	2	1	4	.357	.400	.500	148	1	1	3	0	0	0	1.000	-0	/O1	0.1
Total	2	78	270	38	67	12	1	6	28	11	48	.248	.278	.367	72	-11	-12	27	1	0			-0	/3O1	-1.1
■ **JOE HAGUE** Hague, Joe Clarence b: 4/25/44, Huntington, W.Va. BL/TL, 6', 198 lbs. Deb: 9/19/68																									
1968	StL-N	7	17	2	4	0	0	1	1	2	2	.235	.316	.412	119	0	0	2	0	0	0	.800	-1	/O1	0.0
1969	StL-N	40	100	8	17	2	1	2	8	12	23	.170	.259	.270	48	-7	-7	7	0	2	-1	.939	-0	O/1	-1.1
1970	StL-N	139	451	58	122	16	4	14	68	63	87	.271	.361	.417	106	6	5	69	2	1	0	.994	-3	1O	-0.7
1971	StL-N	129	380	46	86	9	3	16	54	58	69	.226	.332	.392	100	3	1	51	0	3	-2	.996	-1	1O	-1.1
1972	StL-N	27	76	8	18	5	1	3	11	17	18	.237	.376	.447	135	4	4	13	0	1	-1	1.000	0	1/O	0.2
	*Cin-N	69	138	17	34	7	1	4	20	20	18	.246	.342	.399	116	2	3	18	1	1	-0	1.000	-0	1O	0.0
	Yr	96	214	25	52	12	2	7	31	37	36	.243	.355	.416	124	6	7	32	1	2	-1	1.000	0	1O	0.2
1973	Cin-N	19	33	2	5	2	0	0	1	5	5	.152	.263	.212	35	-3	-3	2	1	0	0	1.000	-1	/O1	-0.4
Total	6	430	1195	141	286	41	10	40	163	177	222	.239	.339	.391	101	5	3	163	4	8	-4	.996	-6	1O	-3.1
■ **BILL HAGUE** Hague, William L. (b: William L. Haug) b: 1852, Philadelphia, Pa. BR/TR, 5'9", 164 lbs. Deb: 5/04/1875																									
1875	StL-n	62	260	24	56	2	0	0		2		.215	.221	.223	60	-12	-8	13						*3/1	-0.7
1876	Lou-N	67	294	31	78	8	0	1	22	2	10	.265	.270	.303	77	-3	-11	25				.754	-26	*3/S	-3.2
1877	Lou-N	59	263	38	70	7	1	1	24	7	18	.266	.285	.312	75	-3	-10	24				.843	-19	*3	-2.5
1878	Pro-N	62	250	21	51	3	0	0	25	5	34	.204	.220	.216	44	-15	-15	12				**.925**	19	*3	0.7
1879	Pro-N	51	209	20	47	3	1	0	21	3	19	.225	.236	.249	61	-9	-8	13				.822	5	3	-0.2
Total	4	239	1016	110	246	21	2	2	92	17	81	.242	.255	.273	66	-30	-44	73				.843	-22	3/S	-5.2
■ **DON HAHN** Hahn, Donald Antone b: 11/16/48, San Francisco, Cal. BR/TR, 6'1", 185 lbs. Deb: 4/08/69																									
1969	Mon-N	4	9	0	1	0	0	0	2	0	5	.111	.111	.111	-37	-2	-2	0	0	0	0	1.000	1	/O	-0.1
1970	Mon-N	82	149	22	38	8	0	0	8	27	27	.255	.376	.309	86	-2	-2	21	4	2	0	.986	0	O	-0.3
1971	NY-N	98	178	16	42	5	1	1	11	21	32	.236	.320	.292	76	-5	-5	17	2	3	-1	.973	10	O	0.2
1972	NY-N	17	37	0	6	0	0	0	1	4	12	.162	.244	.162	18	-4	-4	2	0	0	0	1.000	-2	O	-0.7
1973	*NY-N	93	262	22	60	10	0	2	21	22	43	.229	.289	.290	62	-14	-13	22	2	1	0	.989	-6	O	-2.4
1974	NY-N	110	323	34	81	14	1	4	28	37	34	.251	.330	.337	88	-5	-5	36	2	0	1	.987	-8	*O	-1.7
1975	Phi-N	9	5	0	0	0	0	0	0	0	2	.000	.000	.000	-96	-1	-1	0	0	0	0	1.000	1	/O	0.0
	StL-N	7	8	3	1	0	0	0	0	1	1	.125	.222	.125	-2	-1	-1	0	0	0	0	1.000	0	/O	-0.1
	SD-N	34	26	7	6	1	2	0	3	10	2	.231	.444	.423	151	2	2	5	1	0	0	1.000	2	O	0.5
	Yr	50	39	10	7	1	2	0	3	11	5	.179	.360	.308	89	-0	-0	5	1	0	0	1.000	4	O	0.4
Total	7	454	997	104	235	38	4	7	74	122	158	.236	.321	.303	75	-32	-30	103	11	6	-0	.985	-2	O	-4.6
■ **DICK HAHN** Hahn, Richard Frederick b: 7/24/16, Canton, Ohio BR/TR, 5'11", 176 lbs. Deb: 9/07/40																									
1940	Was-A	1	3	0	0	0	0	0	0	0	0	.000	.000	.000	-99	-1	-1	0	0	0	0	1.000	0	/C	-0.1
■ **ED HAHN** Hahn, William Edgar b: 8/27/1875, Nevada, Ohio d: 11/29/41, Des Moines, Iowa BL/TR, 160 lbs. Deb: 8/31/05																									
1905	NY-A	43	160	32	51	5	0	0	11	25		.319	.423	.350	131	10	8	25	1			.957	2	O	0.9
1906	NY-A	11	22	2	2	1	0	0	1	3		.091	.231	.136	15	-2	-2	1	2			1.000	-1	/O	-0.4
	*Chi-A	130	484	80	110	7	5	0	27	69		.227	.335	.262	90	-3	-1	52	19			.949	-6	*O	-1.5
	Yr	141	506	82	112	8	5	0	28	72		.221	.330	.257	86	-5	-4	54	21			.952	-6	*O	-1.9
1907	Chi-A	156	592	87	151	9	7	0	45	84		.255	.359	.294	113	11	13	72	17			**.990**	-5	*O	0.2
1908	Chi-A	122	447	58	112	12	8	0	21	39		.251	.329	.313	111	6	7	50	11			.965	-11	*O	-1.1
1909	Chi-A	76	287	30	52	6	0	1	16	31		.181	.268	.213	54	-15	-13	19	9			.990	-7	O	-2.7
1910	Chi-A	15	53	2	6	2	0	0	1	7		.113	.217	.151	16	-5	-5	2	0			.933	-3	O	-1.0
Total	6	553	2045	291	484	42	20	1	122	258		.237	.334	.278	97	3	6	222	59			.970	-30	O	-5.6
■ **ED HAIGH** Haigh, Edward E. b: 2/7/1867, Philadelphia, Pa. d: 2/13/53, Atlantic City, N.J Deb: 8/14/1892																									
1892	StL-N	1	4	0	1	0	0	0	0	0	2	.250	.250	.250	55	-0	-0	0	0			1.000	1	/O	0.0
■ **HINKEY HAINES** Haines, Henry Luther b: 12/23/1898, Red Lion, Pa. d: 1/9/79, Sharon Hill, Pa. BR/TR, 5'10", 170 lbs. Deb: 4/20/23																									
1923	*NY-A	28	25	9	4	2	0	0	3	4	5	.160	.276	.240	36	-2	-2	2	3	1	0	1.000	-3	O	-0.5
■ **JERRY HAIRSTON** Hairston, Jerry Wayne b: 2/16/52, Birmingham, Ala. BB/TR, 5'10", 180 lbs. Deb: 7/26/73 F																									
1973	Chi-A	60	210	25	57	11	1	0	23	33	30	.271	.373	.333	97	2	1	29	0	0	0	.944	2	O1/D	-0.1
1974	Chi-A	45	109	8	25	7	0	0	8	13	18	.229	.311	.294	73	-3	-4	10	0	2	-1	.926	-4	OD	-1.0
1975	Chi-A	69	219	26	62	8	0	0	23	46	23	.283	.410	.320	107	6	5	33	1	0	0	.951	1	O/D	0.4
1976	Chi-A	44	119	20	27	2	2	0	10	24	19	.227	.357	.277	87	-1	-1	14	1	1	-0	.973	-3	O	-0.6
1977	Chi-A	13	26	3	8	2	0	0	4	5	7	.308	.419	.385	121	1	1	4	0	0	0	1.000	-2	O	-0.1
	Pit-N	51	52	5	10	2	0	2	6	6	10	.192	.276	.346	64	-3	-3	5	0	0	0	.923	-1	O/2	-0.4
1981	Chi-A	9	25	5	7	1	0	1	6	2	4	.280	.357	.440	131	1	1	4	0	0	0	.933	-1	/O	0.0
1982	Chi-A	85	90	11	21	5	0	5	18	9	15	.233	.303	.456	105	0	0	12	0	0	0	1.000	-8	O/D	-0.8

YEAR	TM/L	G	AB	R	H	2B	3B	HR	RBI	BB	SO	AVG	OBP	SLG	PRO+	BR	/A	RC	SB	CS	SBR	FA	FR	POS	TPR
1983	*Chi-A	101	126	17	37	9	1	5	22	23	16	.294	.403	.500	141	9	8	26	0	1	-1	.968	-9	O/D	-0.2
1984	Chi-A	115	227	41	59	13	2	5	19	41	29	.260	.375	.401	110	6	5	37	2	1	0	.967	-5	OD	-0.1
1985	Chi-A	95	140	9	34	8	0	2	20	29	18	.243	.380	.343	96	1	1	20	0	0	0	1.000	-1	D/O	0.0
1986	Chi-A	101	225	32	61	15	0	5	26	26	26	.271	.349	.404	101	2	1	31	0	0	0	1.000	-3	D1O	-0.3
1987	Chi-A	66	126	14	29	8	0	5	20	25	25	.230	.362	.413	102	1	1	20	0	0	0	1.000	-0	OD/1	0.0
1988	Chi-A	2	2	0	0	0	0	0	0	0	0	.000	.000	.000	-99	-1	-1	0	0	0	0	.000	0	/H	-0.1
1989	Chi-A	3	3	0	1	0	0	0	0	0	0	.333	.333	.333	91	-0	-0	0	0	0	0	.000	0	/D	0.0
Total	14	859	1699	216	438	91	6	30	205	282	240	.258	.366	.371	103	21	15	245	4	5	-2	.963	-32	OD/12	-3.3

■ **JOHNNY HAIRSTON** Hairston, John Louis b: 8/29/45, Birmingham, Ala. BR/TR, 6'2", 200 lbs. Deb: 9/06/69 F

YEAR	TM/L	G	AB	R	H	2B	3B	HR	RBI	BB	SO	AVG	OBP	SLG	PRO+	BR	/A	RC	SB	CS	SBR	FA	FR	POS	TPR
1969	Chi-N	3	4	0	1	0	0	0	0	0	2	.250	.250	.250	36	-0	-0	0	0	0	0	1.000	-0	/CO	-0.1

■ **SAMMY HAIRSTON** Hairston, Samuel b: 1/28/20, Crawford, Miss. BR/TR, 5'10.5", 187 lbs. Deb: 7/21/51 FC

YEAR	TM/L	G	AB	R	H	2B	3B	HR	RBI	BB	SO	AVG	OBP	SLG	PRO+	BR	/A	RC	SB	CS	SBR	FA	FR	POS	TPR
1951	Chi-A	4	5	1	2	1	0	0	1	2	0	.400	.571	.600	222	1	1	2	0	0	0	1.000	-1	/C	0.0

■ **CHET HAJDUK** Hajduk, Chester b: 7/21/18, Chicago, Ill. BR/TR, 6', 195 lbs. Deb: 4/16/41

YEAR	TM/L	G	AB	R	H	2B	3B	HR	RBI	BB	SO	AVG	OBP	SLG	PRO+	BR	/A	RC	SB	CS	SBR	FA	FR	POS	TPR
1941	Chi-A	1	1	0	0	0	0	0	0	0	0	.000	.000	.000	-99	-0	-0	0	0	0	0	.000	0	H	0.0

■ **GEORGE HALAS** Halas, George Stanley b: 2/2/1895, Chicago, Ill. d: 10/31/83, Chicago, Ill. BB/TR, 6', 164 lbs. Deb: 5/06/19

YEAR	TM/L	G	AB	R	H	2B	3B	HR	RBI	BB	SO	AVG	OBP	SLG	PRO+	BR	/A	RC	SB	CS	SBR	FA	FR	POS	TPR
1919	NY-A	12	22	0	2	0	0	0	0	0	8	.091	.091	.091	-49	-4	-4	0	0			1.000	-1	/O	-0.6

■ **JOHN HALDEMAN** Haldeman, John Avery b: 12/2/1855, Pee Wee Valley, Ky. d: 9/17/1899, Louisville, Ky. BL/TR, 5'10", 175 lbs. Deb: 7/03/1877

YEAR	TM/L	G	AB	R	H	2B	3B	HR	RBI	BB	SO	AVG	OBP	SLG	PRO+	BR	/A	RC	SB	CS	SBR	FA	FR	POS	TPR
1877	Lou-N	1	4	0	0	0	0	0	0	0	0	.000	.000	.000	-85	-1	-1	0				.571	-1	/2	-0.2

■ **ODELL HALE** Hale, Arvel Odell "Bad News" b: 8/10/08, Hosston, La. d: 6/9/80, ElDorado, Ark. BR/TR, 5'10", 175 lbs. Deb: 8/01/31

YEAR	TM/L	G	AB	R	H	2B	3B	HR	RBI	BB	SO	AVG	OBP	SLG	PRO+	BR	/A	RC	SB	CS	SBR	FA	FR	POS	TPR
1931	Cle-A	25	92	14	26	2	4	1	5	8	8	.283	.340	.424	94	-0	-1	14	2	0	1	.918	-4	32/S	-0.3
1933	Cle-A	98	351	49	97	19	8	10	64	30	37	.276	.333	.462	104	3	1	53	2	3	-1	.954	3	23	0.8
1934	Cle-A	143	563	82	170	44	6	13	101	48	50	.302	.357	.471	110	8	7	91	8	12	-5	.956	**26**	*2/3	3.3
1935	Cle-A	150	589	80	179	37	11	16	101	52	55	.304	.361	.486	115	13	11	101	15	13	-3	.938	7	*3/2	1.9
1936	Cle-A	153	620	126	196	50	13	14	87	64	43	.316	.380	.506	116	15	14	120	8	5	-1	.946	17	*3/2	3.1
1937	Cle-A	154	561	74	150	32	4	6	82	56	41	.267	.335	.371	77	-19	-20	71	9	6	-1	.964	26	32	1.1
1938	Cle-A	130	496	69	138	32	2	8	69	44	39	.278	.338	.399	86	-13	-12	70	8	1	2	.963	-13	*2	-1.4
1939	Cle-A	108	253	36	79	16	2	4	48	25	18	.312	.374	.439	111	3	4	39	4	5	-2	.966	-16	2/3	-0.9
1940	Cle-A	48	50	3	11	3	1	0	6	5	7	.220	.291	.320	60	-3	-3	5	0	0	0	.700	-1	/3	-0.3
1941	Bos-A	12	24	5	5	2	0	1	1	3	4	.208	.296	.417	85	-1	-1	3	0	0	0	.857	-3	/32	-0.4
	NY-N	41	102	13	20	3	0	0	9	18	13	.196	.317	.225	53	-5	-6	9	1			.964	1	2	-0.3
Total	10	1062	3701	551	1071	240	51	73	573	353	315	.289	.352	.441	100	-1	-5	576	57	45		.959	42	23/S	6.6

■ **GEORGE HALE** Hale, George Wagner "Ducky" b: 8/3/1894, Dexter, Kan. d: 11/1/45, Wichita, Kan. BR/TR, 5'10", 160 lbs. Deb: 8/24/14

YEAR	TM/L	G	AB	R	H	2B	3B	HR	RBI	BB	SO	AVG	OBP	SLG	PRO+	BR	/A	RC	SB	CS	SBR	FA	FR	POS	TPR
1914	StL-A	6	11	1	2	0	0	0	0	0	3	.182	.182	.182	10	-1	-1	0	0			.895	-0	/C	-0.1
1916	StL-A	4	1	0	0	0	0	0	0	0	1	.000	.500	.000	54	0	0	0	0			1.000	0	/C	0.0
1917	StL-A	38	61	4	12	2	1	0	8	10	12	.197	.310	.262	78	-2	-1	5	0			.927	3	C	0.3
1918	StL-A	12	30	0	4	1	0	0	1	1	5	.133	.161	.167	-1	-4	-4	1	0			.981	2	C	-0.1
Total	4	60	103	5	18	3	1	0	9	11	21	.175	.261	.223	49	-6	-6	6	0			.940	5	/C	0.1

■ **JOHN HALE** Hale, John Steven b: 8/5/53, Fresno, Cal. BL/TR, 6'2", 195 lbs. Deb: 9/08/74

YEAR	TM/L	G	AB	R	H	2B	3B	HR	RBI	BB	SO	AVG	OBP	SLG	PRO+	BR	/A	RC	SB	CS	SBR	FA	FR	POS	TPR
1974	LA-N	4	4	2	4	1	0	0	2	0	0	1.000	1.000	1.250	549	2	2	5	0	0	0	.000	0	/O	0.2
1975	LA-N	71	204	20	43	7	0	6	22	26	51	.211	.306	.333	81	-6	-5	22	1	2	-1	.977	1	O	-0.8
1976	LA-N	44	91	4	14	2	1	0	8	16	14	.154	.294	.198	42	-6	-6	7	4	1	1	.983	0	O	-0.7
1977	LA-N	79	108	10	26	4	1	2	11	15	28	.241	.333	.352	84	-2	-2	14	2	1	0	.986	1	O	-0.3
1978	Sea-A	107	211	24	36	8	0	4	22	34	64	.171	.286	.265	56	-12	-12	18	3	4	-2	.988	-13	O/D	-3.0
1979	Sea-A	54	63	6	14	3	0	2	7	12	26	.222	.347	.365	91	-0	-1	8	0	0	0	1.000	-11	O	-1.2
Total	6	359	681	66	137	25	2	14	72	103	183	.201	.310	.305	72	-25	-24	74	10	8	-2	.985	-22	O/D	-5.8

■ **BOB HALE** Hale, Robert Houston b: 11/7/33, Sarasota, Fla. BL/TL, 5'10", 195 lbs. Deb: 7/04/55

YEAR	TM/L	G	AB	R	H	2B	3B	HR	RBI	BB	SO	AVG	OBP	SLG	PRO+	BR	/A	RC	SB	CS	SBR	FA	FR	POS	TPR
1955	Bal-A	67	182	13	65	7	1	0	29	5	19	.357	.378	.407	119	3	4	25	0	2	-1	.974	2	1	0.3
1956	Bal-A	85	207	18	49	10	1	1	24	11	10	.237	.279	.309	60	-14	-12	16	0	2	-1	.975	-0	1	-1.6
1957	Bal-A	42	44	2	11	0	0	0	7	2	2	.250	.283	.250	50	-3	-3	2	0	0	0	1.000	-0	/1	-0.3
1958	Bal-A	19	20	2	7	2	0	0	3	2	1	.350	.409	.450	144	1	1	3	0	0	0	1.000	1	/1	0.2
1959	Bal-A	40	54	2	10	3	0	0	7	2	6	.185	.214	.241	25	-6	-5	3	0	0	0	1.000	-1	/1	-0.6
1960	Cle-A	70	70	2	21	7	0	0	12	3	6	.300	.329	.400	99	-1	-0	10	0	0	0	.944	0	/1	0.0
1961	Cle-A	42	36	0	6	0	0	0	6	1	7	.167	.211	.167	2	-5	-5	2	0	0	0	.000	0	H	-0.5
	NY-A	11	13	2	2	0	0	1	1	0	0	.154	.154	.385	41	-1	-1	0	0	0	0	1.000	-0	/1	-0.1
	Yr	53	49	2	8	0	0	1	7	1	7	.163	.196	.224	12	-6	-6	2	0	0	0	1.000	-0	/1	-0.6
Total	7	376	626	41	171	29	2	2	89	26	51	.273	.305	.335	76	-26	-21	61	0	4	-2	.977	2	1	-2.6

■ **SAMMY HALE** Hale, Samuel Douglas b: 9/10/1896, Glen Rose, Tex. d: 9/6/74, Wheeler, Tex. BR/TR, 5'8.5", 160 lbs. Deb: 4/20/20

YEAR	TM/L	G	AB	R	H	2B	3B	HR	RBI	BB	SO	AVG	OBP	SLG	PRO+	BR	/A	RC	SB	CS	SBR	FA	FR	POS	TPR
1920	Det-A	76	116	13	34	3	3	1	14	5	15	.293	.322	.397	92	-2	-2	15	2	0	1	.886	-3	3/O2	-0.3
1921	Det-A	9	2	2	0	0	0	0	0	0	1	.000	.000	.000	-99	-1	-1	0	0	1	-1	.000	0	H	-0.1
1923	Phi-A	115	434	68	125	22	8	3	51	17	31	.288	.327	.396	89	-8	-9	57	8	3	1	.916	-19	*3	-1.7
1924	Phi-A	80	261	41	83	14	2	2	17	17	19	.318	.367	.410	99	-0	-1	39	3	2	-0	.948	-8	3/OS	-0.4
1925	Phi-A	110	391	62	135	30	11	8	63	17	27	.345	.376	.540	122	15	11	77	7	4	-0	.919	-4	3/2	1.2
1926	Phi-A	111	327	49	92	22	9	4	43	13	36	.281	.311	.440	89	-5	-7	43	1	4	-2	.947	-2	3/O	-0.7
1927	Phi-A	131	501	77	157	24	8	5	81	32	32	.313	.358	.423	97	1	-3	73	11	3	2	.961	1	*3	0.5
1928	Phi-A	88	314	38	97	20	9	4	58	9	21	.309	.334	.468	106	2	1	49	2	0	1	.932	12	3	1.7
1929	Phi-A	101	379	51	105	14	3	1	40	12	18	.277	.303	.338	62	-20	-22	40	6	2	1	.956	-7	3/2	-2.4
1930	StL-A	62	190	21	52	8	1	2	25	8	18	.274	.303	.358	65	-10	-11	20	1	1	-0	.947	-3	3	-1.0
Total	10	883	2915	422	880	157	54	30	392	130	218	.302	.336	.424	93	-27	-42	412	41	20	0	.939	-33	3/O2S	-3.2

■ **CHIP HALE** Hale, Walter William b: 12/2/64, San Jose, Cal. BL/TR, 5'11", 180 lbs. Deb: 8/27/89

YEAR	TM/L	G	AB	R	H	2B	3B	HR	RBI	BB	SO	AVG	OBP	SLG	PRO+	BR	/A	RC	SB	CS	SBR	FA	FR	POS	TPR
1989	Min-A	28	67	6	14	3	0	0	4	1	6	.209	.221	.254	31	-6	-6	4	0	0	0	.980	-3	2/3D	-1.0
1990	Min-A	1	2	0	0	0	0	0	2	0	1	.000	.000	.000	-94	-1	-1	0	0	0	0	1.000	1	/2	0.1
Total	2	29	69	6	14	3	0	0	6	1	7	.203	.214	.246	28	-6	-7	4	0	0	0	.983	-2	/23D	-0.9

■ **FRED HALEY** Haley, Fred b: Wheeling, W.Va. TR , Deb: 6/22/1880

YEAR	TM/L	G	AB	R	H	2B	3B	HR	RBI	BB	SO	AVG	OBP	SLG	PRO+	BR	/A	RC	SB	CS	SBR	FA	FR	POS	TPR
1880	Tro-N	2	7	0	0	0	0	0	0	1	2	.000	.125	.000	-51	-1	-1	0				.750	-2	/C	-0.3

■ **RAY HALEY** Haley, Raymond Timothy "Pat" b: 1/23/1891, Danbury, Iowa d: 10/8/73, Bradenton, Fla. BR/TR, 5'11", 180 lbs. Deb: 4/21/15

YEAR	TM/L	G	AB	R	H	2B	3B	HR	RBI	BB	SO	AVG	OBP	SLG	PRO+	BR	/A	RC	SB	CS	SBR	FA	FR	POS	TPR
1915	Bos-A	5	7	2	1	1	0	0	0	1	0	.143	.250	.286	62	-0	-0	1	0			1.000	0	/C	0.0
1916	Bos-A	1	1	0	0	0	0	0	0	0	1	.000	.000	.000	-99	-0	-0	0	0			.000	0	H	0.0
	Phi-A	34	108	8	25	5	0	0	4	6	19	.231	.278	.278	70	-5	-4	8	0			.982	6	C	0.5
	Yr	35	109	8	25	5	0	0	4	6	20	.229	.276	.275	69	-5	-4	8	0			.982	6	C	0.5
1917	Phi-A	41	98	7	27	2	1	0	11	4	12	.276	.311	.316	93	-1	-1	10	2			.947	-6	C	-0.6
Total	3	81	214	17	53	8	1	0	15	11	32	.248	.291	.294	80	-6	-6	19	2			.970	1	/C	-0.1

■ ALBERT HALL Hall, Albert b: 3/7/58, Birmingham, Ala. BB/TR, 5'11", 155 lbs. Deb: 9/12/81

YEAR	TM/L	G	AB	R	H	2B	3B	HR	RBI	BB	SO	AVG	OBP	SLG	PRO+	BR	/A	RC	SB	CS	SBR	FA	FR	POS	TPR
1981	Atl-N	6	2	1	0	0	0	0	0	1	1	.000	.333	.000	1	-0	-0	0	0	0	0	.000	0	/O	0.0
1982	Atl-N	5	0	1	0	0	0	0	0	0	0	—	—	—	—	0	0	0	0	0	0	.000	0	/R	0.0
1983	Atl-N	10	8	2	0	0	0	0	0	2	2	.000	.200	.000	-37	-2	-2	0	1	1	-0	.750	0	/O	-0.2
1984	Atl-N	87	142	25	37	6	1	1	9	10	18	.261	.309	.338	76	-3	-5	15	6	4	-1	.932	-10	O	-1.7
1985	Atl-N	54	47	5	7	0	1	0	3	9	12	.149	.286	.191	34	-4	-4	3	1	1	-0	.900	-4	O	-0.9
1986	Atl-N	16	50	6	12	2	0	0	1	5	6	.240	.309	.280	60	-2	-3	5	8	3	1	.900	0	O	-0.3
1987	Atl-N	92	292	54	83	20	4	3	24	38	36	.284	.370	.411	102	4	2	48	33	10	4	.981	3	O	0.6
1988	Atl-N	85	231	27	57	7	1	1	15	21	35	.247	.315	.299	73	-6	-8	22	15	10	-2	.973	2	O	-1.0
1989	Pit-N	20	33	4	6	2	1	0	1	3	5	.182	.250	.303	59	-2	-2	3	3	0	1	.909	-3	O	-0.4
Total	9	375	805	125	202	37	8	5	53	89	115	.251	.329	.335	80	-16	-21	95	67	29	3	.958	-12	O	-3.9

■ AL HALL Hall, Archibald W. b: Worcester, Mass. d: 2/10/1885, Warren, Pa. Deb: 5/01/1879

YEAR	TM/L	G	AB	R	H	2B	3B	HR	RBI	BB	SO	AVG	OBP	SLG	PRO+	BR	/A	RC	SB	CS	SBR	FA	FR	POS	TPR
1879	Tro-N	67	306	30	79	7	3	0	14	3	13	.258	.265	.301	92	-5	-2	25				.842	5	*O	0.0
1880	Cle-N	3	8	1	1	0	0	0	0	0	0	.125	.125	.125	-15	-1	-1	0				1.000	-1	/O	-0.2
Total	2	70	314	31	80	7	3	0	14	3	13	.255	.262	.296	90	-5	-3	25				.843	4	/O	-0.2

■ CHARLIE HALL Hall, Charles Walter "Doc" b: 8/24/1863, Toulon, Ill. d: 6/24/21, Tacoma, Wash. Deb: 5/03/1887

YEAR	TM/L	G	AB	R	H	2B	3B	HR	RBI	BB	SO	AVG	OBP	SLG	PRO+	BR	/A	RC	SB	CS	SBR	FA	FR	POS	TPR
1887	NY-a	3	12	1	1	0	0	0		2		.083	.214	.083	-15	-2	-2	0	1			1.000	0	/O	-0.1

■ GEORGE HALL Hall, George William b: 3/29/1849, Stepney, England d: 6/11/23, Ridgewood, N.J. BL , 5'7", 142 lbs. Deb: 5/05/1871

YEAR	TM/L	G	AB	R	H	2B	3B	HR	RBI	BB	SO	AVG	OBP	SLG	PRO+	BR	/A	RC	SB	CS	SBR	FA	FR	POS	TPR
1871	Oly-n	32	136	31	40	3	3	2	17	8	0	.294	.333	.404	117	2	4	19	2					*O	0.3
1872	Bal-n	53	252	69	82	14	**8**	1	40	3	1	.325	.333	.456	135	11	9	41						*O/1	0.8
1873	Bal-n	35	168	44	58	8	4	1	30	2	0	.345	.353	.458	137	7	8	28						O	0.6
1874	Bos-n	47	222	58	64	11	7	1		2		.288	.295	.414	117	5	3	28						*O	0.3
1875	Ath-n	77	360	71	107	12	**13**	5		1		.297	.299	.444	138	19	12	49						*O	1.1
1876	Phi-N	60	268	51	98	7	13	**5**	45	8	4	.366	.384	.545	208	29	29	57				.801	-2	*O	2.4
1877	Lou-N	61	269	53	87	15	8	0	26	12	19	.323	.352	.439	125	14	7	43				**.900**	-6	*O	-0.1
Total	5 n	244	1138	273	351	48	35	10	87	16	1	.308	.318	.438	130	45	36	165						O/1	3.1
Total	2	121	537	104	185	22	21	5	71	20	23	.345	.368	.492	162	43	37	100				.837	-7	O	2.3

■ IRV HALL Hall, Irvin Gladstone b: 10/7/18, Alberton, Md. BR/TR, 5'10.5", 160 lbs. Deb: 4/20/43

YEAR	TM/L	G	AB	R	H	2B	3B	HR	RBI	BB	SO	AVG	OBP	SLG	PRO+	BR	/A	RC	SB	CS	SBR	FA	FR	POS	TPR
1943	Phi-A	151	544	37	139	15	4	0	54	22	42	.256	.292	.298	73	-20	-19	47	10	7	-1	.948	-11	*S/23	-2.2
1944	Phi-A	143	559	60	150	20	8	0	45	31	46	.268	.309	.333	85	-13	-12	56	2	5	-2	.980	-5	2S/1	-1.2
1945	Phi-A	151	616	62	161	17	5	0	50	35	42	.261	.307	.305	78	-18	-17	58	3	10	-5	.978	**26**	*2	1.4
1946	Phi-A	63	185	19	46	6	2	0	19	9	18	.249	.287	.303	65	-9	-9	16	1	1	-0	.973	-4	2/S	-1.1
Total	4	508	1904	178	496	58	19	0	168	97	148	.261	.302	.311	77	-59	-57	176	16	23	-9	.977	6	2S/13	-3.1

■ JIM HALL Hall, James d: 1/30/1886, Brooklyn, N.Y. Deb: 5/20/1872

YEAR	TM/L	G	AB	R	H	2B	3B	HR	RBI	BB	SO	AVG	OBP	SLG	PRO+	BR	/A	RC	SB	CS	SBR	FA	FR	POS	TPR
1872	Atl-n	13	56	9	16	1	1	0	6	1	0	.286	.298	.339	82	-0	-2	6						2/O	-0.2
1874	Atl-n	2	9	0	1	0	0	0		0		.111	.111	.111	-33	-1	-1	0						/2	-0.1
1875	Wes-n	1	3	0	1	0	1	0		0		.333	.333	1.000	325	1	1	1						/O	0.1
Total	3 n	16	68	9	18	1	2	0		1		.265	.275	.338	79	-1	-3	7						/2O	-0.2

■ JIMMIE HALL Hall, Jimmie Randolph b: 3/17/38, Mt.Holly, N.C. BL/TR, 6', 175 lbs. Deb: 4/09/63

YEAR	TM/L	G	AB	R	H	2B	3B	HR	RBI	BB	SO	AVG	OBP	SLG	PRO+	BR	/A	RC	SB	CS	SBR	FA	FR	POS	TPR
1963	Min-A	156	497	88	129	21	5	33	80	63	101	.260	.343	.521	136	24	23	89	3	3	-1	.982	-10	*O	0.6
1964	Min-A★	149	510	61	144	20	3	25	75	44	112	.282	.341	.480	125	16	16	83	5	2	0	.985	13	*O	2.5
1965	*Min-A★	148	522	81	149	25	4	20	86	51	79	.285	.350	.464	124	19	17	86	14	7	0	.976	-2	*O	0.9
1966	Min-A	120	356	52	85	7	4	20	47	33	66	.239	.303	.449	106	5	2	44	1	2	-1	.978	-1	*O	-0.4
1967	Cal-A	129	401	54	100	8	3	16	55	42	65	.249	.321	.404	117	6	8	52	4	1	1	.990	-2	*O	0.1
1968	Cal-A	46	126	15	27	3	0	1	8	16	19	.214	.303	.262	75	-4	-3	10	1	0	0	.981	-4	O	-1.0
	Cle-A	53	111	4	22	4	0	1	8	10	19	.198	.264	.261	61	-5	-5	8	1	0	0	.983	2	O	-0.5
	Yr	99	237	19	49	7	0	2	16	26	38	.207	.285	.262	68	-9	-8	18	2	0	1	.982	-2	O	-1.5
1969	Cle-A	4	10	1	0	0	0	0	0	2	3	.000	.167	.000	-48	-2	-2	0	1	0	0	1.000	-0	/O	-0.2
	NY-A	80	212	21	50	8	5	3	26	19	34	.236	.299	.363	88	-5	-4	24	8	3	1	.963	-5	O/1	-1.2
	Yr	84	222	22	50	8	5	3	26	21	37	.225	.292	.347	81	-7	-6	24	9	3	1	.966	-5	O/1	-1.4
	Chi-N	11	24	1	5	1	0	0	1	1	5	.208	.240	.250	33	-2	-2	2	0	0	0	1.000	-1	/O	-0.4
1970	Chi-N	28	32	2	3	1	0	0	1	4	12	.094	.194	.125	-11	-5	-6	1	0	0	0	1.000	0	/O	-0.6
	Atl-N	39	47	7	10	2	0	2	4	2	14	.213	.245	.383	62	-3	-3	4	0	0	0	1.000	0	O	-0.3
	Yr	67	79	9	13	3	0	2	5	6	26	.165	.224	.278	31	-8	-9	5	0	0	0	1.000	1	O	-0.9
Total	8	963	2848	387	724	100	24	121	391	287	529	.254	.323	.434	112	46	41	402	38	18	1	.982	-9	O/1	-0.5

■ MEL HALL Hall, Melvin b: 9/16/60, Lyons, N.Y. BL/TL, 6'1", 205 lbs. Deb: 9/03/81

YEAR	TM/L	G	AB	R	H	2B	3B	HR	RBI	BB	SO	AVG	OBP	SLG	PRO+	BR	/A	RC	SB	CS	SBR	FA	FR	POS	TPR
1981	Chi-N	10	11	1	1	0	0	1	2	1	4	.091	.167	.364	45	-1	-1	1	0	0	0	.000	0	/O	-0.1
1982	Chi-N	24	80	6	21	3	2	0	4	5	17	.262	.322	.350	86	-1	-2	9	0	1	-1	.939	1	O	-0.2
1983	Chi-N	112	410	60	116	23	5	17	56	42	101	.283	.354	.488	125	16	14	71	6	6	-2	.988	-6	*O	0.3
1984	Chi-N	48	150	25	42	11	3	4	22	12	23	.280	.333	.473	114	4	3	23	2	1	0	.961	-2	O	0.0
	Cle-A	83	257	43	66	13	1	7	30	35	55	.257	.350	.397	104	3	2	38	1	1	-0	.993	0	O/D	0.0
1985	Cle-A	23	66	7	21	6	0	0	12	8	12	.318	.392	.409	121	2	2	10	0	1	-1	1.000	-3	O/D	-0.2
1986	Cle-A	140	442	68	131	29	2	18	77	33	65	.296	.348	.493	128	15	16	75	6	2	1	.972	-7	*O/D	0.6
1987	Cle-A	142	485	57	136	21	1	18	76	20	68	.280	.310	.439	95	-4	-5	63	5	4	-1	.989	6	*OD	-0.3
1988	Cle-A	150	515	69	144	32	4	6	71	28	50	.280	.317	.392	95	-3	-4	63	7	3	0	.967	-3	*O/D	-1.1
1989	NY-A	113	361	54	94	9	0	17	58	21	37	.260	.301	.427	104	-0	1	44	0	0	0	.993	-2	OD	-0.3
1990	NY-A	113	360	41	93	23	2	12	46	6	46	.258	.274	.433	95	-4	-5	40	0	0	0	.973	-6	DO	-1.1
1991	NY-A	141	492	67	140	23	2	19	80	26	40	.285	.324	.455	113	7	7	72	0	1	-1	.987	-0	*OD	0.3
1992	NY-A	152	583	67	163	36	3	15	81	29	53	.280	.315	.429	104	3	1	75	4	2	0	.990	6	*OD	0.4
Total	12	1251	4212	565	1168	229	25	134	615	266	571	.277	.323	.439	107	37	30	584	31	22	-4	.981	-16	*OD	-1.7

■ DICK HALL Hall, Richard Wallace b: 9/27/30, St.Louis, Mo. BR/TR, 6'6", 200 lbs. Deb: 4/15/52

YEAR	TM/L	G	AB	R	H	2B	3B	HR	RBI	BB	SO	AVG	OBP	SLG	PRO+	BR	/A	RC	SB	CS	SBR	FA	FR	POS	TPR
1952	Pit-N	26	80	6	11	1	0	0	2	2	17	.138	.159	.150	-14	-12	-13	2	0	1	-1	.972	0	O/3	-1.4
1953	Pit-N	7	24	2	4	0	0	0	1	1	3	.167	.200	.167	-3	-4	-4	1	1	1	-0	.978	11	/2	0.6
1954	Pit-N	112	310	38	74	8	4	2	27	33	46	.239	.312	.310	64	-17	-16	29	3	0	1	.956	-2	*O	-2.0
1955	Pit-N	21	40	3	7	1	0	1	3	6	5	.175	.283	.275	50	-3	-3	3	0	0	0	1.000	-3	P/O	-0.2
1956	Pit-N	33	29	5	10	0	0	0	1	5	7	.345	.441	.345	118	1	1	5	0	0	0	1.000	-1	P/1	0.0
1957	Pit-N	10	1	0	0	0	0	0	0	0	1	.000	.000	.000	-99	-0	-0	0	0	0	0	.000	-0	/P	0.0
1959	Pit-N	2	2	0	0	0	0	0	0	0	0	.000	.000	.000	-99	-1	-1	0	0	0	0	1.000	-0	/P	0.0
1960	KC-A	32	56	5	6	0	0	0	4	4	15	.107	.167	.107	-24	-10	-10	2	1	0	0	.925	-1	P	0.0
1961	Bal-A	30	36	4	5	0	0	0	1	3	13	.139	.205	.139	-6	-5	-5	1	0	0	0	.970	1	P	0.0
1962	Bal-A	44	24	3	4	1	0	0	1	4	9	.167	.286	.208	37	-2	-2	2	0	0	0	1.000	-0	P	0.0
1963	Bal-A	48	28	7	13	1	0	1	4	0	8	.464	.464	.607	202	3	4	8	0	0	0	1.000	1	P	0.0
1964	Bal-A	45	16	1	2	0	0	0	3	1	3	.125	.176	.125	-14	-2	-2	0	0	0	0	1.000	-0	P	0.0
1965	Bal-A	49	15	1	5	2	0	0	4	1	4	.333	.412	.467	146	1	1	3	0	0	0	.923	-1	P	0.0
1966	Bal-A	32	12	0	2	0	0	0	2	0	5	.167	.231	.167	17	-1	-1	1	0	0	0	1.000	-0	P	0.0
1967	Phi-N	48	14	1	1	0	0	0	0	0	5	.071	.071	.071	-58	-3	-3	0	0	0	0	1.000	1	P	0.0

YEAR	TM/L	G	AB	R	H	2B	3B	HR	RBI	BB	SO	AVG	OBP	SLG	PRO+	BR	/A	RC	SB	CS	SBR	FA	FR	POS	TPR
1968	Phi-N	32	3	0	1	0	0	0	0	0	1	.333	.333	.333	101	-0	-0	0	0	0	0	1.000	-0	P	0.0
1969	*Bal-A	39	7	1	2	0	0	0	2	1	1	.286	.375	.286	86	-0	-0	1	1	0	0	1.000	-1	P	0.0
1970	*Bal-A	32	12	2	1	0	0	0	1	0	3	.083	.083	.083	-53	-2	-2	0	0	0	0	1.000	-1	P	0.0
1971	Bal-A	27	5	0	2	1	0	0	0	0	1	.400	.400	.600	182	0	0	1	0	0	0	.800	-1	P	0.0
Total	19	669	714	79	150	15	4	4	56	61	147	.210	.274	.259	44	-57	-56	59	6	2	1	.976	2	PO/231	-3.0
■ BOB HALL	Hall, Robert Prill b: 12/20/1878, Baltimore, Md. d: 12/1/50, Wellesley, Mass. TR , 5'10", 158 lbs. Deb: 4/18/04																								
1904	Phi-N	46	163	11	26	4	0	0	17	14		.160	.226	.184	28	-14	-13	8	5			.843	-10	3S1	-2.4
1905	NY-N	1	3	1	1	0	0	0	0	0		.333	.333	.333	97	-0	-0	0	0			.000	-0	/O	0.0
	Bro-N	56	203	21	48	4	1	2	15	11		.236	.279	.296	77	-7	-5	20	8			.939	6	O/21	-0.2
	Yr	57	206	22	49	4	1	2	15	11		.238	.280	.296	78	-7	-6	20	8			.939	5	O/21	-0.2
Total	2	103	369	33	75	8	1	2	32	25		.203	.256	.247	56	-21	-18	29	13			.877	-5	/O3S12	-2.6
■ RUSS HALL	Hall, Robert Russell b: 9/29/1871, Shelbyville, Ky. d: 7/1/37, Los Angeles, Cal. TL , Deb: 4/15/1898																								
1898	StL-N	39	143	13	35	2	1	0	10	7		.245	.285	.273	59	-7	-8	12	1			.835	-14	S/3O	-1.9
1901	Cle-A	1	4	2	2	0	0	0	0	0		.500	.500	.500	185	0	0	1	0			.500	-1	/S	-0.1
Total	2	40	147	15	37	2	1	0	10	7		.252	.290	.279	62	-7	-8	13	1			.824	-15	/S3O	-2.0
■ BILL HALL	Hall, William Lemuel b: 7/30/28, Moultrie, Ga. d: 1/1/86, Moultrie, Ga. BL/TR, 5'11", 165 lbs. Deb: 4/18/54																								
1954	Pit-N	5	7	0	0	0	0	0	0	0	0	.000	.000	.000	-99	-2	-2	0	0	0	0	1.000	-0	/C	-0.2
1956	Pit-N	1	3	0	0	0	0	0	0	0	1	.000	.000	.000	-99	-1	-1	0	0	0	0	1.000	1	/C	0.0
1958	Pit-N	51	116	15	33	6	0	1	15	15	13	.284	.366	.362	96	-1	-0	15	0	0	0	.982	7	C	0.9
Total	3	57	126	15	33	6	0	1	15	15	14	.262	.340	.333	81	-3	-3	15	0	0	0		8	/C	0.7
■ TOM HALLER	Haller, Thomas Frank b: 6/23/37, Lockport, Ill. BL/TR, 6'4", 195 lbs. Deb: 4/11/61 C																								
1961	SF-N	30	62	5	9	1	0	2	8	9	23	.145	.264	.258	41	-5	-5	4	0	1	-1	1.000	2	C	-0.3
1962	*SF-N	99	272	53	71	13	1	18	55	51	59	.261	.385	.515	142	16	17	56	1	4	-2	.992	-2	C	1.5
1963	SF-N	98	298	32	76	8	1	14	44	34	45	.255	.335	.430	120	7	8	41	4	6	-2	.994	-4	C/O	0.5
1964	SF-N	117	388	43	98	14	3	16	48	55	51	.253	.348	.428	115	10	9	58	4	2	0	.989	-0	*C/O	1.4
1965	SF-N	134	422	40	106	4	3	16	49	47	67	.251	.338	.389	101	3	2	56	0	0	0	.987	-5	*C	0.4
1966	SF-N☆	142	471	74	113	19	2	27	67	53	74	.240	.325	.461	112	9	8	69	1	3	-2	.991	-7	*C/1	0.8
1967	SF-N★	141	455	54	114	23	5	14	49	62	61	.251	.345	.415	118	11	12	68	0	4	-2	.997	-0	*C/O	1.7
1968	LA-N★	144	474	37	135	27	5	4	53	46	76	.285	.351	.388	132	13	17	66	1	4	-2	.994	3	*C	3.0
1969	LA-N	134	445	46	117	18	3	6	39	48	58	.263	.337	.357	102	-2	1	55	0	3	-2	.992	-9	*C	-0.2
1970	LA-N	112	325	47	93	16	6	10	47	32	35	.286	.354	.465	123	7	9	54	3	0	1	.993	-8	*C	0.7
1971	LA-N	84	202	23	54	5	0	5	32	25	30	.267	.354	.366	111	2	3	26	0	2	-1	.978	4	C	0.9
1972	*Det-A	59	121	7	25	5	2	2	13	15	14	.207	.294	.331	83	-2	-3	12	0	1	-1	1.000	8	C	0.7
Total	12	1294	3935	461	1011	153	31	134	504	477	593	.257	.342	.414	114	68	77	567	14	30	-14	.992	-18	*C/O1	11.1
■ NEWT HALLIDAY	Halliday, Newton Reese b: 6/18/1896, Chicago, Ill. d: 4/6/18, Great Lakes, Ill. BR/TR, 6'1", 175 lbs. Deb: 8/19/16																								
1916	Pit-N	1	1	0	0	0	0	0	0	0	1	.000	.000	.000	-99	-0	-0	0	0			1.000	0	/1	0.0
■ JOCKO HALLIGAN	Halligan, William E. b: 12/8/1868, Avon, N.Y. d: 2/13/45, Buffalo, N.Y. 5'9", 166 lbs. Deb: 5/13/1890																								
1890	Buf-P	57	211	28	53	9	2	3	33	20	19	.251	.319	.355	89	-6	-2	27	7			.824	-5	OC	-0.6
1891	Cin-N	61	247	43	77	13	6	3	44	24	25	.312	.375	.449	141	13	12	45	5			.856	-3	O	0.7
1892	Cin-N	26	101	14	29	4	0	2	12	12	9	.287	.363	.386	130	4	4	16	3			.875	-1	O	0.2
	Bal-N	46	178	38	47	4	7	2	43	30	24	.264	.376	.399	133	9	8	30	8			.861	-7	O1/C	-0.1
	Yr	72	279	52	76	8	7	4	55	42	33	.272	.372	.394	132	12	12	46	11			.869	-8	O1/C	0.1
Total	3	190	737	123	206	30	15	10	132	86	77	.280	.358	.402	122	19	22	117	23			.848	-16	O/C1	0.2
■ ED HALLINAN	Hallinan, Edward S. b: 8/23/1888, San Francisco, Cal d: 8/24/40, San Francisco, Cal BR/TR, 5'9", 168 lbs. Deb: 5/13/11																								
1911	StL-A	52	169	13	35	3	1	0	14	14		.207	.268	.237	43	-13	-12	11	4			.902	-6	S2/3	-1.6
1912	StL-A	29	86	11	19	2	0	0	1	5		.221	.272	.244	50	-6	-5	7	3			.866	-7	S	-1.0
Total	2	81	255	24	54	5	1	0	15	19		.212	.269	.239	45	-19	-18	18	7			.887	-12	/S23	-2.6
■ JIMMY HALLINAN	Hallinan, James H. b: 5/27/1849, Ireland d: 10/28/1879, Chicago, Ill. BL/TL, 5'9", 172 lbs. Deb: 7/26/1871																								
1871	Kek-n	5	25	7	5	0	0	0	2	2	0	.200	.259	.200	34	-2	-2	2	1					/S	-0.1
1875	Wes-n	13	51	12	14	1	1	0		0		.275	.275	.333	104	0	-0	5						S	0.0
	Mut-n	44	202	29	58	7	3	3		1		.287	.291	.396	128	7	5	24						S/3	0.3
	Yr	57	253	41	72	8	4	3		1		.285	.287	.383	123	7	5	29						S/3	0.3
1876	NY-N	54	240	45	67	7	6	2	36	2	4	.279	.285	.383	139	5	10	27				.764	-14	*S/2O	-0.4
1877	Cin-N	16	73	18	27	1	1	0	7	1	1	.370	.378	.411	167	4	5	12				.854	-6	2	0.0
	Chi-N	19	89	17	25	4	1	0	11	4	2	.281	.312	.348	96	1	-1	10				.800	-2	O	-0.3
	Yr	35	162	35	52	5	2	0	18	5	3	.321	.341	.377	124	5	4	21				.800	-8	O2	-0.3
1878	Chi-N	16	67	14	19	3	0	0	2	5	6	.284	.333	.328	111	1	1	8				.789	-4	O/2	-0.3
	Ind-N	3	12	0	3	2	0	0	1	0	2	.250	.250	.417	134	0	0	1				.667	-1	/O	-0.1
	Yr	19	79	14	22	5	0	0	3	5	8	.278	.321	.342	114	2	1	9				.760	-5	O/2	-0.4
Total	2 n	62	278	48	77	8	4	3	2	3		.277	.285	.367	114	5	3	30						/S3	0.2
Total	3	108	481	94	141	17	8	2	57	12	15	.293	.310	.374	129	11	15	57				.783	-27	/SO2	-1.1
■ BILL HALLMAN	Hallman, William Harry b: 3/15/1876, Philadelphia, Pa. d: 4/23/50, Philadelphia, Pa. BL/TL, Deb: 4/25/01																								
1901	Mil-A	139	549	70	135	27	6	2	47	41		.246	.301	.328	78	-19	-15	61	12			.905	-2	*O	-2.6
1903	Chi-A	63	207	29	43	7	4	0	18	31		.208	.320	.280	85	-3	-2	23	11			.953	2	O	-0.4
1906	Pit-N	23	89	12	24	3	1	1	6	15		.270	.375	.360	124	4	3	14	3			.935	-1	O	0.2
1907	Pit-N	94	302	39	67	6	2	0	15	33		.222	.303	.255	74	-8	-8	32	21			.966	-6	O	-2.0
Total	4	319	1147	150	269	43	13	3	86	120		.235	.311	.303	82	-27	-22	129	47			.933	-7	O	-4.8
■ BILL HALLMAN	Hallman, William Wilson b: 3/31/1867, Pittsburgh, Pa. d: 9/11/20, Philadelphia, Pa. BR/TR, 5'8", 160 lbs. Deb: 4/23/1888 M																								
1888	Phi-N	18	63	5	13	4	1	0	6	1	12	.206	.219	.302	63	-2	-3	4	1			.898	-7	C/2OS3	-0.9
1889	Phi-N	119	462	67	117	21	8	2	60	36	54	.253	.313	.346	79	-9	-16	58	20			.895	8	*S2/C	-0.2
1890	Phi-P	84	356	59	95	16	7	1	37	33	24	.267	.338	.360	86	-6	-8	46	6			.885	-8	OC23/S	-1.0
1891	Phi-a	141	587	112	166	21	13	6	69	38	56	.283	.332	.394	107	5	3	85	18			.930	-5	*2	0.3
1892	Phi-N	138	586	106	171	27	10	2	84	32	52	.292	.335	.382	119	11	12	83	19			.936	-24	*2	-0.9
1893	Phi-N	132	596	119	183	28	7	5	76	51	27	.307	.367	.403	107	5	5	98	22			.950	-15	*21	-0.6
1894	Phi-N	119	505	107	156	19	7	0	66	36	15	.309	.360	.374	81	-17	-14	85	36			.930	-20	*2	-2.2
1895	Phi-N	124	539	94	169	26	5	1	91	34	20	.314	.359	.386	94	-5	-5	84	16			.943	5	*2/S	0.5
1896	Phi-N	120	469	82	150	21	3	2	83	45	23	.320	.382	.390	107	5	6	80	16			.945	3	*2/P	1.4
1897	Phi-N	31	126	16	33	3	0	0	15	8		.262	.326	.286	64	-7	-6	13	1			.958	-10	2	-1.2
	StL-N	79	298	31	66	6	2	0	26	24		.221	.288	.255	45	-24	-23	27	12			.939	3	2/1M	-1.4
	Yr	110	424	47	99	9	2	0	41	32		.233	.300	.264	51	-30	-29	40	13			.944	-7	*2/1	-2.6
1898	Bro-N	134	509	57	124	10	7	2	63	29		.244	.291	.303	70	-20	-20	50	9			.944	-3	*23	-1.4
1901	Cle-A	5	19	2	4	0	0	0	3	2		.211	.286	.211	41	-1	-1	1	0			.815	-3	/S	-0.4
	Phi-N	123	445	46	82	13	5	0	38	26		.184	.236	.236	36	-36	-37	32	13			.971	-5	23	-3.7
1902	Phi-N	73	254	14	63	8	4	0	35	14		.248	.287	.311	84	-5	-5	27	9			.932	-6	3	-1.1
1903	Phi-N	63	198	20	42	11	2	0	17	16		.212	.271	.288	62	-11	-10	18	2			.932	-3	23/1OS	-1.2

YEAR	TM/L	G	AB	R	H	2B	3B	HR	RBI	BB	SO	AVG	OBP	SLG	PRO+	BR	/A	RC	SB	CS	SBR	FA	FR	POS	TPR
Total	14	1503	6012	937	1634	234	81	21	769	425	283	.272	.325	.348	86	-116	-122	793	200			.940	-89	*23S/OC1P	-14.0

■ JIM HALPIN Halpin, James Nathaniel b: 10/4/1863, England d: 1/4/1893, Boston, Mass. Deb: 6/15/1882

YEAR	TM/L	G	AB	R	H	2B	3B	HR	RBI	BB	SO	AVG	OBP	SLG	PRO+	BR	/A	RC	SB	CS	SBR	FA	FR	POS	TPR
1882	Wor-N	2	8	0	0	0	0	0	0	0	2	.000	.000	.000	-98	-2	-2	0				.625	-1	/3	-0.3
1884	Was-U	46	168	24	31	3	0	0		2		.185	.194	.202	35	-11	-10	7				.809	-7	S/3	-1.5
1885	Det-N	15	54	3	7	2	0	0	1	1	12	.130	.145	.167	1	-6	-6	1				.846	1	S	-0.5
Total	3	63	230	27	38	5	0	0	1	3	14	.165	.176	.187	22	-19	-18	8				.821	-8	/S3	-2.3

■ AL HALT Halt, Alva William b: 11/23/1890, Sandusky, Ohio d: 1/22/73, Sandusky, Ohio BR/TR, 6', 180 lbs. Deb: 5/29/14

YEAR	TM/L	G	AB	R	H	2B	3B	HR	RBI	BB	SO	AVG	OBP	SLG	PRO+	BR	/A	RC	SB	CS	SBR	FA	FR	POS	TPR
1914	Bro-F	80	261	26	61	6	2	3	25	13	39	.234	.270	.307	64	-13	-13	26	11			.890	-11	S/2O	-1.9
1915	Bro-F	151	524	41	131	22	7	3	64	39	79	.250	.307	.336	90	-8	-8	63	20			.930	2	*3S	0.3
1918	Cle-A	26	69	9	12	2	0	0	1	9	12	.174	.269	.203	39	-5	-5	4	4			.971	-1	3/2S1	-0.7
Total	3	257	854	76	204	30	9	6	90	61	130	.239	.293	.316	77	-26	-26	93	35			.933	-9	3S/21O	-2.3

■ RALPH HAM Ham, Ralph A. b: 3/1853, Troy, N.Y. d: 2/13/05, Troy, N.Y. 5'8", 158 lbs. Deb: 5/06/1871

YEAR	TM/L	G	AB	R	H	2B	3B	HR	RBI	BB	SO	AVG	OBP	SLG	PRO+	BR	/A	RC	SB	CS	SBR	FA	FR	POS	TPR
1871	Rok-n	25	113	25	28	4	0	0	12	1	7	.248	.254	.283	57	-6	-5	10	6					O/2S	-0.3
1872	Man-n	1	5	0	2	0	0	0	1	0	0	.400	.400	.400	156	0	0	1						/S	0.0
Total	2 n	26	118	25	30	4	0	0	13	1	7	.254	.261	.288	61	-6	-5	11						/O2S	-0.3

■ CHARLIE HAMBURG Hamburg, Charles M. (b: Charles M. Hambrick) b: 11/22/1863, Louisville, Ky. d: 5/18/31, Union, N.J. 6', 175 lbs. Deb: 4/18/1890

YEAR	TM/L	G	AB	R	H	2B	3B	HR	RBI	BB	SO	AVG	OBP	SLG	PRO+	BR	/A	RC	SB	CS	SBR	FA	FR	POS	TPR
1890	*Lou-a	133	485	93	132	22	2	3		69		.272	.370	.344	116	11	12	81	46			.946	-2	*O	0.6

■ JIM HAMBY Hamby, James Sanford "Cracker" b: 7/29/1897, Wilkesboro, N.C. d: 10/21/91, Springfield, Ill. BR/TR, 6', 170 lbs. Deb: 9/20/26

YEAR	TM/L	G	AB	R	H	2B	3B	HR	RBI	BB	SO	AVG	OBP	SLG	PRO+	BR	/A	RC	SB	CS	SBR	FA	FR	POS	TPR
1926	NY-N	1	3	0	0	0	0	0	0	0	0	.000	.000	.000	-99	-1	-1	0	0			.600	-1	/C	-0.2
1927	NY-N	21	52	6	10	0	1	0	5	7	7	.192	.288	.231	40	-4	-4	4	1			.904	-0	C	-0.3
Total	2	22	55	6	10	0	1	0	5	7	7	.182	.274	.218	33	-5	-5	4	1			.885	-1	/C	-0.5

■ DARRYL HAMILTON Hamilton, Darryl Quinn b: 12/3/64, Baton Rouge, La. BL/TR, 6'1", 180 lbs. Deb: 6/03/88

YEAR	TM/L	G	AB	R	H	2B	3B	HR	RBI	BB	SO	AVG	OBP	SLG	PRO+	BR	/A	RC	SB	CS	SBR	FA	FR	POS	TPR
1988	Mil-A	44	103	14	19	4	0	1	11	12	9	.184	.276	.252	49	-7	-7	8	7	3	0	1.000	-1	O/D	-0.8
1990	Mil-A	89	156	27	46	5	0	1	18	9	12	.295	.333	.346	91	-2	-2	19	10	3	1	.992	-6	O/D	-0.8
1991	Mil-A	122	405	64	126	15	6	1	57	33	38	.311	.363	.385	110	4	6	57	16	6	1	.996	-10	*O	-0.5
1992	Mil-A	128	470	67	140	19	7	5	62	45	42	.298	.360	.400	115	8	10	70	41	14	4	**1.000**	1	*O	1.2
Total	4	383	1134	172	331	43	13	8	148	99	101	.292	.350	.374	104	4	7	153	74	26	7	.997	-16	O/D	-0.9

■ JEFF HAMILTON Hamilton, Jeffrey Robert b: 3/19/64, Flint, Mich. BR/TR, 6'3", 207 lbs. Deb: 6/28/86

YEAR	TM/L	G	AB	R	H	2B	3B	HR	RBI	BB	SO	AVG	OBP	SLG	PRO+	BR	/A	RC	SB	CS	SBR	FA	FR	POS	TPR
1986	LA-N	71	147	22	33	5	0	5	19	2	43	.224	.235	.361	66	-8	-7	12	0	0	0	.968	11	3/S	0.3
1987	LA-N	35	83	5	18	3	0	0	1	7	22	.217	.286	.253	45	-7	-6	6	0	1	-1	.935	9	3/S	0.2
1988	*LA-N	111	309	34	73	14	2	6	33	10	51	.236	.269	.353	80	-10	-9	27	0	2	-1	.941	-0	*3/S1	-1.1
1989	LA-N	151	548	45	134	35	1	12	56	20	71	.245	.275	.378	86	-13	-12	55	0	0	0	.951	-6	*3/P2S	-1.8
1990	LA-N	7	24	1	3	0	0	0	1	0	3	.125	.125	.125	-32	-4	-4	0	0	0	0	1.000	1	/3	-0.3
1991	LA-N	41	94	4	21	4	0	1	14	4	21	.223	.255	.298	56	-6	-5	7	0	0	0	.928	0	3/S	-0.5
Total	6	416	1205	111	282	61	3	24	124	43	211	.234	.265	.349	74	-47	-43	107	0	3	-2	.948	15	3/S2P1	-3.2

■ TOM HAMILTON Hamilton, Thomas Ball "Ham" b: 9/29/25, Altoona, Kan. d: 11/29/73, Tyler, Tex. BL/TR, 6'4", 213 lbs. Deb: 9/04/52

YEAR	TM/L	G	AB	R	H	2B	3B	HR	RBI	BB	SO	AVG	OBP	SLG	PRO+	BR	/A	RC	SB	CS	SBR	FA	FR	POS	TPR
1952	Phi-A	9	10	1	2	1	0	0	1	1	1	.200	.273	.300	56	-1	-1	1	0	0	0	1.000	-0	/1	-0.1
1953	Phi-A	58	56	8	11	2	0	0	5	7	11	.196	.286	.232	40	-4	-5	4	0	0	0	1.000	-1	/1O	-0.6
Total	2	67	66	9	13	3	0	0	6	8	12	.197	.284	.242	42	-5	-5	5	0	0	0	1.000	-1	/1O	-0.7

■ BILLY HAMILTON Hamilton, William Robert "Sliding Billy" b: 2/16/1866, Newark, N.J. d: 12/16/40, Worcester, Mass. BL/TR, 5'6", 165 lbs. Deb: 7/31/1888 H

YEAR	TM/L	G	AB	R	H	2B	3B	HR	RBI	BB	SO	AVG	OBP	SLG	PRO+	BR	/A	RC	SB	CS	SBR	FA	FR	POS	TPR
1888	KC-a	35	129	21	34	4	4	0	11	4		.264	.307	.357	108	2	1	20	19			.961	-2	O	-0.2
1889	KC-a	137	534	144	161	17	12	3	77	87	41	.301	.413	.395	126	28	22	136	**111**			.857	-7	*O	1.0
1890	Phi-N	123	496	133	161	13	9	2	49	83	37	.325	.430	.399	141	33	31	**132**	**102**			.882	4	*O	2.8
1891	Phi-N	133	527	**141**	**179**	23	7	2	60	**102**	28	**.340**	**.453**	.421	154	**46**	**43**	**155**	**111**			.907	5	*O	3.9
1892	Phi-N	139	554	132	183	21	7	3	53	81	29	.330	.423	.410	155	40	41	123	57			.919	14	*O	4.4
1893	Phi-N	82	355	110	135	22	7	5	44	63	7	**.380**	**.490**	.524	**172**	41	41	115	43			.937	4	O	3.3
1894	Phi-N	129	544	**192**	220	25	15	4	87	**126**	17	.404	**.523**	.528	160	61	65	207	**98**			.964	5	*O	4.6
1895	Phi-N	123	517	**166**	201	22	6	7	74	**96**	30	.389	.490	.495	157	51	51	**178**	**97**			.913	-1	*O	3.2
1896	Bos-N	131	523	152	191	24	9	3	52	**110**	29	.365	**.477**	.463	142	47	41	160	83			.934	-11	*O	1.6
1897	*Bos-N	127	507	**152**	174	17	5	3	61	**105**		.343	.461	.414	124	32	26	131	66			.962	-3	*O	1.1
1898	Bos-N	110	417	110	154	16	5	3	50	87		.369	**.480**	.453	**159**	43	40	120	54			.904	-15	*O	1.6
1899	Bos-N	84	297	63	92	7	1	1	33	72		.310	.446	.350	109	14	9	57	19			.952	-2	O	0.0
1900	Bos-N	136	520	103	173	20	5	1	47	107		.333	.449	.396	120	32	22	110	32			.947	2	*O	1.2
1901	Bos-N	102	348	71	100	11	2	3	38	64		.287	.402	.356	111	13	9	61	20			.945	1	O	0.2
Total	14	1591	6268	1690	2158	242	94	40	736	1187	218	.344	.455	.432	141	484	441	1705	912			.926	-5	*O	28.7

■ KEN HAMLIN Hamlin, Kenneth Lee b: 5/18/35, Detroit, Mich. BR/TR, 5'10", 170 lbs. Deb: 6/17/57

YEAR	TM/L	G	AB	R	H	2B	3B	HR	RBI	BB	SO	AVG	OBP	SLG	PRO+	BR	/A	RC	SB	CS	SBR	FA	FR	POS	TPR
1957	Pit-N	2	1	0	0	0	0	0	0	0	0	.000	.000	.000	-99	-0	-0	0	0	0	0	1.000	0	/S	0.0
1959	Pit-N	3	8	1	1	0	0	0	0	2	1	.125	,300	.125	19	-1	-1	0	0	0	0	1.000	-1	/S	-0.2
1960	KC-A	140	428	51	96	10	2	2	24	44	48	.224	.298	.271	55	-26	-26	35	1	1	-0	.955	-41	*S	-5.9
1961	LA-A	42	91	4	19	3	0	1	5	11	9	.209	.301	.275	49	-6	-7	7	0	1	-1	.963	13	S	0.7
1962	Was-A	98	292	29	74	12	0	3	22	22	22	.253	.306	.325	70	-12	-12	28	7	7	-2	.963	-11	S/2	-1.9
1965	Was-A	117	362	45	99	21	1	4	22	33	45	.273	.336	.370	102	0	1	47	8	2	1	.976	-29	2S/3	-2.0
1966	Was-A	66	158	13	34	7	1	1	16	13	21	.215	.275	.291	63	-8	-7	12	1	0	0	.963	6	2/3	0.2
Total	7	468	1340	143	323	53	4	11	89	125	146	.241	.307	.311	71	-52	-53	129	17	11	-2	.959	-63	S2/3	-9.1

■ STEVE HAMMOND Hammond, Steven Benjamin b: 5/9/57, Atlanta, Ga. BL/TR, 6'2", 190 lbs. Deb: 6/28/82 F

YEAR	TM/L	G	AB	R	H	2B	3B	HR	RBI	BB	SO	AVG	OBP	SLG	PRO+	BR	/A	RC	SB	CS	SBR	FA	FR	POS	TPR
1982	KC-A	46	126	14	29	5	1	1	11	4	18	.230	.254	.310	54	-8	-8	8	0	1	-1	1.000	3	O/D	-0.7

■ JACK HAMMOND Hammond, Walter Charles "Wobby" b: 2/26/1891, Amsterdam, N.Y. d: 3/4/42, Kenosha, Wis. BR/TR, 5'11", 170 lbs. Deb: 4/15/15

YEAR	TM/L	G	AB	R	H	2B	3B	HR	RBI	BB	SO	AVG	OBP	SLG	PRO+	BR	/A	RC	SB	CS	SBR	FA	FR	POS	TPR
1915	Cle-A	35	84	9	18	2	1	0	4	1	19	.214	.224	.262	44	-6	-6	5	0	1	-1	.957	-8	2	-1.6
1922	Cle-A	1	4	1	1	0	0	0	0	0	0	.250	.250	.250	30	-0	-0	0	0	0	0	.333	-1	/2	-0.2
	Pit-N	9	11	3	3	0	0	0	0	1	0	.273	.333	.273	57	-1	-1	1	0	0	0	1.000	2	/2	0.1
Total	2	45	99	13	22	2	1	0	4	2	19	.222	.238	.263	45	-7	-7	7	0	1	-1	.943	-7	/2	-1.7

■ GRANNY HAMNER Hamner, Granville Wilbur b: 4/26/27, Richmond, Va. BR/TR, 5'10", 163 lbs. Deb: 9/14/44 F

YEAR	TM/L	G	AB	R	H	2B	3B	HR	RBI	BB	SO	AVG	OBP	SLG	PRO+	BR	/A	RC	SB	CS	SBR	FA	FR	POS	TPR
1944	Phi-N	21	77	6	19	1	0	0	5	3	7	.247	.275	.260	53	-5	-5	6	0			.933	6	S	0.3
1945	Phi-N	14	41	3	7	2	0	0	6	1	3	.171	.190	.220	14	-5	-5	2	0			.861	3	S	-0.1
1946	Phi-N	2	7	0	1	0	0	0	0	0	3	.143	.143	.143	-19	-1	-1	0	0			.857	-1	/S	-0.2
1947	Phi-N	2	7	1	2	0	0	0	0	1	0	.286	.375	.286	81	-0	-0	1	0			1.000	0	/S	0.0
1948	Phi-N	129	446	42	116	21	5	3	48	22	39	.260	.298	.350	76	-17	-16	45	2			.967	-8	2S/3	-1.7
1949	Phi-N	154	662	83	174	32	5	6	53	25	47	.263	.290	.353	74	-28	-26	63	6			.961	-0	*S	-1.5
1950	*Phi-N	157	637	78	172	27	5	11	82	39	35	.270	.314	.380	83	-18	-17	74	2			.944	-5	*S	-0.9
1951	Phi-N	150	589	61	150	23	7	9	72	29	32	.255	.290	.363	76	-22	-21	58	10	5	0	.958	-2	*S	-1.2
1952	Phi-N★	151	596	74	164	30	5	17	87	27	51	.275	.307	.428	103	-1	-0	75	7	3	0	.951	-4	*S	0.7
1953	Phi-N★	154	609	90	168	30	8	21	92	32	28	.276	.313	.455	98	-5	-4	84	2	1	0	.970	-8	2S	-0.3
1954	Phi-N★	152	596	83	178	39	11	13	89	53	44	.299	.356	.466	112	10	10	98	1	2	-1	.978	-23	*2/S	-0.3

YEAR	TM/L	G	AB	R	H	2B	3B	HR	RBI	BB	SO	AVG	OBP	SLG	PRO+	BR	/A	RC	SB	CS	SBR	FA	FR	POS	TPR
1955	Phi-N	104	405	57	104	12	4	5	43	41	30	.257	.327	.343	79	-12	-11	46	0	1	-1	.960	-36	2S	-3.9
1956	Phi-N	122	401	42	90	24	3	4	42	30	42	.224	.278	.329	64	-21	-20	35	2	0	1	.937	-13	*S2/P	-2.4
1957	Phi-N	133	502	59	114	19	5	10	62	34	42	.227	.276	.345	68	-25	-23	43	3	1	0	.963	-39	*2/SP	-5.4
1958	Phi-N	35	133	18	40	7	3	2	18	8	16	.301	.340	.444	107	1	1	17	0	0	0	.984	-3	32/S	-0.1
1959	Phi-N	21	64	10	19	4	0	2	6	5	5	.297	.348	.453	109	1	1	9	0	1	-1	.947	-7	S/3	-0.6
	Cle-A	27	67	4	11	1	1	1	3	1	8	.164	.176	.254	17	-8	-7	3	0	0	0	.960	-2	S/23	-0.9
1962	KC-A	3	0	0	0	0	0	0	0	0	0	—	—	—	—	0	0	0	0	0	0	1.000	0	/P	0.0
Total	17	1531	5839	711	1529	272	62	104	708	351	432	.262	.304	.383	84	-157	-145	657	35	14		.946	-139	S2/3P	-18.5

■ GARVIN HAMNER Hamner, Wesley Garvin b: 3/18/24, Richmond, Va. BR/TR, 5'11", 172 lbs. Deb: 4/17/45 F

YEAR	TM/L	G	AB	R	H	2B	3B	HR	RBI	BB	SO	AVG	OBP	SLG	PRO+	BR	/A	RC	SB	CS	SBR	FA	FR	POS	TPR
1945	Phi-N	32	101	12	20	3	0	0	5	7	9	.198	.250	.228	34	-9	-9	6	2			.962	-4	2/S3	-1.1

■ IKE HAMPTON Hampton, Isaac Bernard b: 8/22/51, Camden, S.C. BB/TR, 6'1", 185 lbs. Deb: 9/12/74

YEAR	TM/L	G	AB	R	H	2B	3B	HR	RBI	BB	SO	AVG	OBP	SLG	PRO+	BR	/A	RC	SB	CS	SBR	FA	FR	POS	TPR
1974	NY-N	4	4	0	0	0	0	0	1	0	1	.000	.000	.000	-99	-1	-1	0	0	0	0	1.000	-0	/C	-0.1
1975	Cal-A	31	66	8	10	3	0	0	4	7	19	.152	.243	.197	28	-6	-6	4	0	0	0	.947	-5	C/S3	-1.0
1976	Cal-A	3	2	0	0	0	0	0	0	0	0	.000	.000	.000	-99	-0	-0	0	0	0	0	1.000	1	/CS	0.0
1977	Cal-A	52	44	5	13	1	0	3	9	2	10	.295	.340	.523	137	2	2	7	0	0	0	.968	1	C/D	0.3
1978	Cal-A	19	14	2	3	0	1	1	4	2	7	.214	.313	.571	149	1	1	3	1	0	0	.905	1	C/1D	0.2
1979	Cal-A	4	5	0	2	0	0	0	0	0	1	.400	.400	.400	121	0	0	1	0	0	0	1.000	1	/1	0.1
Total	6	113	135	15	28	4	1	4	18	11	38	.207	.277	.341	75	-5	-4	14	1	0	0	.953	-2	/CD1S3	-0.5

■ BERT HAMRIC Hamric, Odbert Herman b: 3/1/28, Clarksburg, W.Va. d: 8/8/84, Springboro, Ohio BL/TR, 6', 165 lbs. Deb: 4/24/55

YEAR	TM/L	G	AB	R	H	2B	3B	HR	RBI	BB	SO	AVG	OBP	SLG	PRO+	BR	/A	RC	SB	CS	SBR	FA	FR	POS	TPR
1955	Bro-N	2	1	0	0	0	0	0	0	0	1	.000	.000	.000	-97	-0	-0	0	0	0	0	.000	0	H	0.0
1958	Bal-A	8	8	0	1	0	0	0	0	0	6	.125	.125	.125	-33	-1	-1	0	0	0	0	.000	0	H	-0.1
Total	2	10	9	0	1	0	0	0	0	0	7	.111	.111	.111	-41	-2	-2	0	0	0	0		0		-0.1

■ RAY HAMRICK Hamrick, Raymond Bernard b: 8/1/21, Nashville, Tenn. BR/TR, 5'11.5", 160 lbs. Deb: 8/14/43

YEAR	TM/L	G	AB	R	H	2B	3B	HR	RBI	BB	SO	AVG	OBP	SLG	PRO+	BR	/A	RC	SB	CS	SBR	FA	FR	POS	TPR
1943	Phi-N	44	160	12	32	3	1	0	9	8	28	.200	.238	.231	37	-13	-13	9	0			.960	-11	2S	-2.3
1944	Phi-N	74	292	22	60	10	1	1	23	23	34	.205	.268	.257	50	-20	-19	20	1			.948	20	S	0.8
Total	2	118	452	34	92	13	2	1	32	31	62	.204	.258	.248	46	-33	-31	29	1			.946	9	/S2	-1.5

■ BUDDY HANCKEN Hancken, Morris Medlock b: 8/30/14, Birmingham, Ala. BR/TR, 6'1", 175 lbs. Deb: 5/14/40 C

YEAR	TM/L	G	AB	R	H	2B	3B	HR	RBI	BB	SO	AVG	OBP	SLG	PRO+	BR	/A	RC	SB	CS	SBR	FA	FR	POS	TPR
1940	Phi-A	1	0	0	0	0	0	0	0	0	0	—	—	—	—	0	0	0	0	0	0	1.000	-0	/C	0.0

■ FRED HANCOCK Hancock, Fred James b: 3/28/20, Allenport, Pa. d: 3/12/86, Clearwater, Fla. BR/TR, 5'8", 170 lbs. Deb: 4/26/49

YEAR	TM/L	G	AB	R	H	2B	3B	HR	RBI	BB	SO	AVG	OBP	SLG	PRO+	BR	/A	RC	SB	CS	SBR	FA	FR	POS	TPR
1949	Chi-A	39	52	7	7	2	1	0	9	8	9	.135	.262	.212	27	-6	-5	3	0	1	-1	.978	-3	S/3O	-0.8

■ GARRY HANCOCK Hancock, Ronald Garry b: 1/23/54, Tampa, Fla. BL/TL, 6', 175 lbs. Deb: 7/16/78

YEAR	TM/L	G	AB	R	H	2B	3B	HR	RBI	BB	SO	AVG	OBP	SLG	PRO+	BR	/A	RC	SB	CS	SBR	FA	FR	POS	TPR
1978	Bos-A	38	80	10	18	3	0	0	4	1	12	.225	.235	.262	36	-6	-7	5	0	0	0	1.000	-0	OD	-0.9
1980	Bos-A	46	115	9	33	6	0	4	19	3	11	.287	.305	.443	97	-0	-1	14	0	3	-2	.963	-2	OD	-0.6
1981	Bos-A	26	45	4	7	3	0	0	3	2	4	.156	.191	.222	18	-5	-5	2	0	0	0	1.000	-0	/OD	-0.6
1982	Bos-A	11	14	3	0	0	0	0	0	1	1	.000	.067	.000	-75	-3	-4	0	0	0	0	1.000	-2	/O	-0.6
1983	Oak-A	101	256	29	70	7	3	8	30	5	13	.273	.290	.418	98	-4	-2	30	2	0	1	.981	-9	O1/D	-1.3
1984	Oak-A	51	60	2	13	2	0	0	8	0	1	.217	.217	.250	31	-6	-5	2	0	0	0	1.000	-5	O/1PD	-1.1
Total	6	273	570	57	141	21	3	12	64	12	42	.247	.264	.358	71	-24	-24	53	2	3	-1	.982	-19	O/D1P	-5.1

■ MIKE HANDIBOE Handiboe, Aloysius James "Coalyard Mike" b: 7/21/1887, Washington, D.C. d: 1/31/53, Savannah, Ga. BL/TL, 5'10", 155 lbs. Deb: 9/08/11

YEAR	TM/L	G	AB	R	H	2B	3B	HR	RBI	BB	SO	AVG	OBP	SLG	PRO+	BR	/A	RC	SB	CS	SBR	FA	FR	POS	TPR
1911	NY-A	5	15	0	1	0	0	0	0	2		.067	.176	.067	-29	-3	-3	0	0			1.000	-0	/O	-0.3

■ GENE HANDLEY Handley, Eugene Louis b: 11/25/14, Kennett, Mo. BR/TR, 5'10.5", 165 lbs. Deb: 4/16/46 F

YEAR	TM/L	G	AB	R	H	2B	3B	HR	RBI	BB	SO	AVG	OBP	SLG	PRO+	BR	/A	RC	SB	CS	SBR	FA	FR	POS	TPR
1946	Phi-A	89	251	31	63	8	5	0	21	22	25	.251	.311	.323	78	-8	-7	26	8	3	1	.947	-17	2/3S	-2.1
1947	Phi-A	36	90	10	23	2	1	0	8	10	2	.256	.330	.300	74	-3	-3	9	1	0	0	.973	-5	23/S	-0.7
Total	2	125	341	41	86	10	6	0	29	32	27	.252	.316	.317	77	-10	-10	35	9	3	1	.952	-23	/23S	-2.8

■ LEE HANDLEY Handley, Lee Elmer "Jeep" b: 7/31/13, Clarion, Iowa d: 4/8/70, Pittsburgh, Pa. BR/TR, 5'7", 160 lbs. Deb: 4/15/36 F

YEAR	TM/L	G	AB	R	H	2B	3B	HR	RBI	BB	SO	AVG	OBP	SLG	PRO+	BR	/A	RC	SB	CS	SBR	FA	FR	POS	TPR
1936	Cin-N	24	78	10	24	1	0	2	8	7	16	.308	.365	.397	112	1	1	12	3			.926	-0	2/3	0.2
1937	Pit-N	127	480	59	120	21	12	3	37	37	40	.250	.305	.363	81	-14	-14	55	5			.950	-14	*2/3	-1.9
1938	Pit-N	139	570	91	153	25	8	6	51	53	31	.268	.332	.372	93	-5	-6	72	7			.948	9	*3	0.5
1939	Pit-N	101	376	43	107	14	5	1	42	32	20	.285	.341	.356	89	-6	-5	45	**17**			.936	-10	*3	-1.5
1940	Pit-N	98	302	50	85	7	4	1	19	27	16	.281	.340	.341	89	-4	-4	37	7			.925	1	3/2	-0.2
1941	Pit-N	124	459	59	132	18	4	0	33	35	22	.288	.338	.344	93	-4	-4	53	16			.947	-1	*3	-0.2
1944	Pit-N	40	86	7	19	2	0	0	5	3	5	.221	.247	.244	37	-7	-7	4	1			.947	2	23/S	-0.4
1945	Pit-N	98	312	39	93	16	2	1	32	20	16	.298	.340	.372	94	-1	-3	40	7			.947	15	3	1.4
1946	Pit-N	116	416	43	99	8	7	1	28	29	20	.238	.289	.298	65	-19	-20	36	4			.958	13	*3/2	-0.5
1947	Phi-N	101	277	17	70	10	3	0	42	24	18	.253	.312	.310	68	-13	-12	26	1			.975	2	3/2S	-0.9
Total	10	968	3356	418	902	122	45	15	297	267	204	.269	.323	.345	84	-73	-73	380	68			.949	16	32/S	-3.5

■ HARRY HANEBRINK Hanebrink, Harry Aloysius b: 11/12/27, St.Louis, Mo. BL/TR, 6', 165 lbs. Deb: 5/03/53

YEAR	TM/L	G	AB	R	H	2B	3B	HR	RBI	BB	SO	AVG	OBP	SLG	PRO+	BR	/A	RC	SB	CS	SBR	FA	FR	POS	TPR
1953	Mil-N	51	80	8	19	1	1	1	8	6	8	.237	.291	.313	61	-5	-4	8	1	0	0	.979	4	2/3	0.0
1957	Mil-N	6	7	0	2	0	0	0	0	1	2	.286	.375	.286	87	-0	-0	1	0	0	0	1.000	1	/3	0.1
1958	*Mil-N	63	133	14	25	3	0	4	10	13	9	.188	.270	.301	56	-10	-8	10	0	1	-1	.982	-0	O/3	-1.0
1959	Phi-N	57	97	10	25	3	1	1	7	2	12	.258	.273	.340	61	-5	-6	8	0	0	0	.889	-6	2/3O	-1.1
Total	4	177	317	32	71	7	2	6	25	22	31	.224	.279	.315	60	-20	-18	27	1	1	-0	.959	-2	/2O3	-2.0

■ FRED HANEY Haney, Fred Girard "Pudge" b: 4/25/1898, Albuquerque, N.Mex d: 11/9/77, Beverly Hills, Cal. BR/TR, 5'6", 170 lbs. Deb: 4/18/22 MC

YEAR	TM/L	G	AB	R	H	2B	3B	HR	RBI	BB	SO	AVG	OBP	SLG	PRO+	BR	/A	RC	SB	CS	SBR	FA	FR	POS	TPR
1922	Det-A	81	213	41	75	7	4	0	25	32	14	.352	.439	.423	129	10	11	40	3	7	-3	.937	2	31/S	1.2
1923	Det-A	142	503	85	142	13	4	4	67	45	23	.282	.347	.348	85	-12	-10	64	12	5	1	.955	-2	23S	-0.5
1924	Det-A	86	256	54	79	11	1	1	30	39	13	.309	.400	.371	101	2	2	41	7	4	-0	.933	4	3/S2	1.0
1925	Det-A	114	398	84	111	15	3	0	40	66	29	.279	.384	.332	84	-7	-6	58	11	1	3	.953	-2	*3	0.2
1926	Bos-A	138	462	47	102	15	7	0	52	74	28	.221	.330	.284	63	-25	-23	50	13	6	0	.957	6	*3	-0.7
1927	Bos-A	47	116	23	32	4	1	3	12	25	14	.276	.404	.405	113	3	3	20	4	1	1	.936	-2	3/O	0.3
	Chi-N	4	3	0	0	0	0	0	0	0	0	.000	.000	.000	-99	-1	-1	0	0			.000	0	H	-0.1
1929	StL-N	10	26	4	3	1	1	0	2	1	2	.115	.179	.231	1	-4	-4	1	0			.958	3	/3	-0.1
Total	7	622	1977	338	544	66	21	8	228	282	123	.275	.368	.342	87	-35	-28	274	50	24		.949	9	3/2S1O	1.3

■ TODD HANEY Haney, Todd Michael b: 7/30/65, Waco, Texas BR/TR, 5'9", 165 lbs. Deb: 9/09/92

YEAR	TM/L	G	AB	R	H	2B	3B	HR	RBI	BB	SO	AVG	OBP	SLG	PRO+	BR	/A	RC	SB	CS	SBR	FA	FR	POS	TPR
1992	Mon-N	7	10	0	3	1	0	0	1	0	0	.300	.300	.400	97	-0	-0	1	0	0	0	1.000	-0	/2	-0.1

■ LARRY HANEY Haney, Wallace Larry b: 11/19/42, Charlottesville, Va BR/TR, 6'2", 195 lbs. Deb: 7/27/66 FC

YEAR	TM/L	G	AB	R	H	2B	3B	HR	RBI	BB	SO	AVG	OBP	SLG	PRO+	BR	/A	RC	SB	CS	SBR	FA	FR	POS	TPR
1966	Bal-A	20	56	3	9	1	0	1	3	1	15	.161	.190	.232	21	-6	-6	3	0	0	0	.985	3	C	-0.2
1967	Bal-A	58	164	13	44	11	0	3	20	6	28	.268	.294	.390	101	-0	-0	18	1	0	0	.991	2	C	0.5
1968	Bal-A	38	89	5	21	3	1	1	5	0	19	.236	.236	.326	69	-4	-4	6	0	0	0	.994	4	C	0.2
1969	Sea-A	22	59	3	15	3	0	2	7	6	12	.254	.323	.407	105	0	0	7	1	1	-0	.956	-2	C	-0.1
	Oak-A	53	86	8	13	4	0	2	12	7	19	.151	.223	.267	38	-8	-7	4	0	0	0	.994	-0	C	-0.6
	Yr	75	145	11	28	7	0	4	19	13	31	.193	.264	.324	66	-7	-7	11	1	1	-0	.979	-2	C	-0.7
1970	Oak-A	2	2	2	0	0	0	0	0	2	1	.000	.500	.000	51	0	0	0	0	0	0	1.000	0	/C	0.0

YEAR	TM/L	G	AB	R	H	2B	3B	HR	RBI	BB	SO	AVG	OBP	SLG	PRO+	BR	/A	RC	SB	CS	SBR	FA	FR	POS	TPR
1972	Oak-A	5	4	0	0	0	0	0	0	0	1	.000	.000	.000	-99	-1	-1	0	0	0	0	.800	-1	/C2	-0.3
1973	Oak-A	2	2	0	1	0	0	0	0	0	0	.500	.500	.500	192	0	0	0	0	0	0	1.000	-0	/C	0.0
	StL-N	2	1	0	0	0	0	0	0	0	1	.000	.000	.000	-99	-0	-0	0	0	0	0	1.000	0	/C	0.0
1974	*Oak-A	76	121	12	20	4	0	2	3	3	18	.165	.185	.248	25	-12	-11	5	1	0	0	.992	10	C/31	0.1
1975	Oak-A	47	26	3	5	0	0	1	2	1	4	.192	.222	.308	50	-2	-2	2	0	0	0	1.000	7	C/3	0.6
1976	Oak-A	88	177	12	40	2	0	0	10	13	26	.226	.283	.237	56	-10	-9	12	0	1	-1	.974	9	C	0.1
1977	Mil-A	63	127	7	29	2	0	0	10	5	30	.228	.258	.244	38	-11	-11	8	0	0	0	.985	8	C	-0.1
1978	Mil-A	4	5	0	1	0	0	0	1	0	1	.200	.200	.200	13	-1	-1	0	0	0	0	1.000	-0	/C	-0.1
Total	12	480	919	68	198	30	1	12	73	44	175	.215	.254	.289	57	-54	-51	66	3	2	-0	.985	40	C/312	0.1

■ CHARLIE HANFORD
Hanford, Charles Joseph b: 6/3/1881, Tunstall, England d: 7/19/63, Trenton, N.J. BR/TR, 5'6.5", 145 lbs. Deb: 4/13/14

YEAR	TM/L	G	AB	R	H	2B	3B	HR	RBI	BB	SO	AVG	OBP	SLG	PRO+	BR	/A	RC	SB	CS	SBR	FA	FR	POS	TPR
1914	Buf-F	155	597	83	174	28	13	13	90	32	81	.291	.332	.447	118	13	11	104	37			.973	10	*O	1.5
1915	Chi-F	77	179	27	43	4	5	0	22	12	28	.240	.295	.318	85	-5	-3	21	10			.971	-4	O	-1.0
Total	2	232	776	110	217	32	18	13	112	44	109	.280	.323	.418	111	8	8	125	47			.972	6	O	0.5

■ JAY HANKINS
Hankins, Jay Nelson b: 11/7/35, St.Louis Co., Mo. BL/TR, 5'7", 170 lbs. Deb: 4/15/61

YEAR	TM/L	G	AB	R	H	2B	3B	HR	RBI	BB	SO	AVG	OBP	SLG	PRO+	BR	/A	RC	SB	CS	SBR	FA	FR	POS	TPR
1961	KC-A	76	173	23	32	0	3	3	6	8	17	.185	.225	.272	32	-17	-17	11	2	0	1	.970	-10	O	-2.9
1963	KC-A	10	34	2	6	0	1	1	4	0	3	.176	.176	.324	35	-3	-3	2	0	1	-1	.952	1	/O	-0.4
Total	2	86	207	25	38	0	4	4	10	8	20	.184	.218	.280	33	-20	-20	13	2	1	0	.967	-10	/O	-3.3

■ FRANK HANKINSON
Hankinson, Frank Edward b: 4/29/1856, New York, N.Y. d: 4/5/11, Palisades Park, N.J BR/TR, 5'11", 168 lbs. Deb: 5/01/1878

YEAR	TM/L	G	AB	R	H	2B	3B	HR	RBI	BB	SO	AVG	OBP	SLG	PRO+	BR	/A	RC	SB	CS	SBR	FA	FR	POS	TPR
1878	Chi-N	58	240	38	64	8	3	1	27	5	36	.267	.282	.338	96	1	-2	23				.875	8	*3/P	0.8
1879	Chi-N	44	171	14	31	4	0	0	8	2	14	.181	.191	.205	29	-12	-14	7				.933	6	PO/3	-0.4
1880	Cle-N	69	263	32	55	7	4	1	19	1	23	.209	.212	.278	66	-10	-9	16				.844	-12	*3O/P	-2.0
1881	Tro-N	85	321	34	62	15	0	1	19	10	41	.193	.218	.249	44	-19	-22	18				.907	7	*3/S	-1.2
1883	NY-N	94	337	40	74	13	6	2	30	19	38	.220	.261	.312	74	-10	-10	28				.870	-4	*3/O	-1.3
1884	NY-N	105	389	44	90	16	7	2	43	23	59	.231	.274	.324	85	-5	-7	35				.871	-1	*3/O	-0.6
1885	NY-a	94	362	43	81	12	2	2		12		.224	.251	.285	77	-12	-7	26				**.906**	18	*3/P	1.1
1886	NY-a	136	522	66	126	14	5	2		49		.241	.306	.299	96	-4	-0	52	10			.873	25	*3	2.4
1887	NY-a	127	512	79	137	29	11	1		38		.268	.318	.373	99	-4	-0	68	19			.864	8	*3	0.8
1888	KC-a	37	155	20	27	4	1	1	20	11		.174	.229	.232	47	-8	-10	9	2			.947	-5	2/SO31	-1.3
Total	10	849	3272	410	747	122	39	13	166	170	211	.228	.267	.301	78	-85	-80	283	31			.875	50	3/OP2S1	-1.7

■ NED HANLON
Hanlon, Edward Hugh b: 8/22/1857, Montville, Conn. d: 4/14/37, Baltimore, Md. BL/TR, 5'9.5", 170 lbs. Deb: 5/01/1880 M

YEAR	TM/L	G	AB	R	H	2B	3B	HR	RBI	BB	SO	AVG	OBP	SLG	PRO+	BR	/A	RC	SB	CS	SBR	FA	FR	POS	TPR
1880	Cle-N	73	280	30	69	10	3	0	32	11	30	.246	.275	.304	98	-1	-0	24				.804	-3	*O/S	-0.4
1881	Det-N	76	305	63	85	14	8	2	28	22	11	.279	.327	.397	122	10	8	41				.897	-5	*O/S	0.1
1882	Det-N	82	347	68	80	18	6	5	38	26	25	.231	.284	.360	105	2	3	36				.887	14	*O/2	1.4
1883	Det-N	100	413	65	100	13	2	1	40	34	44	.242	.300	.291	84	-8	-5	37				.884	2	*O2	-0.4
1884	Det-N	114	450	86	119	18	6	5	39	40	52	.264	.324	.364	124	9	13	55				.874	13	*O	2.2
1885	Det-N	105	424	93	128	18	8	1	29	47	18	.302	.372	.389	146	23	23	63				.863	4	*O	2.2
1886	Det-N	126	494	105	116	6	6	4	60	57	39	.235	.314	.296	84	-6	-9	63	50			.929	-4	*O/2	-1.4
1887	*Det-N	118	471	79	129	13	7	4	69	30	24	.274	.320	.357	87	-6	-9	78	69			.904	3	*O	-0.7
1888	Det-N	109	459	64	122	6	8	5	39	15	32	.266	.295	.346	106	3	3	60	38			.919	-6	*O	-0.6
1889	Pit-N	116	461	81	110	14	10	2	37	58	25	.239	.326	.325	93	-9	-1	68	53			.919	-3	*OM	-0.6
1890	Pit-P	118	472	106	131	16	6	1	44	80	24	.278	.389	.343	107	3	11	90	65			.911	-2	*OM	0.4
1891	Pit-N	119	455	87	121	12	8	0	60	48	30	.266	.341	.327	100	-0	1	71	54			.881	0	*O/SM	-0.2
1892	Bal-N	11	43	3	7	1	1	0	2	3	3	.163	.217	.233	36	-3	-3	2	0			.786	-0	OM	-0.4
Total	13	1267	5074	930	1317	159	79	30	517	471	357	.260	.325	.340	103	15	33	687	329			.891	14	*O/2S	1.6

■ BILL HANLON
Hanlon, William Joseph "Big Bill" b: 6/24/1876, Los Angeles, Cal. d: 11/23/05, Los Angeles, Cal. 6', Deb: 4/16/03

YEAR	TM/L	G	AB	R	H	2B	3B	HR	RBI	BB	SO	AVG	OBP	SLG	PRO+	BR	/A	RC	SB	CS	SBR	FA	FR	POS	TPR
1903	Chi-N	8	21	4	2	0	0	0	2	6		.095	.296	.095	14	-2	-2	1	1			.980	-0	/1	-0.2

■ JOHN HANNA
Hanna, John b: 11/3/1863, Philadelphia, Pa. d: 11/7/30, Philadelphia, Pa. Deb: 5/23/1884

YEAR	TM/L	G	AB	R	H	2B	3B	HR	RBI	BB	SO	AVG	OBP	SLG	PRO+	BR	/A	RC	SB	CS	SBR	FA	FR	POS	TPR
1884	Was-a	23	76	8	5	0	0	0		6		.066	.134	.066	-36	-10	-9	1				.874	0	C/O	-0.7
	Ric-a	22	67	6	13	2	1	0		0		.194	.206	.254	52	-3	-3	4				.924	4	C/S	0.3
	Yr	45	143	14	18	2	1	0		6		.126	.167	.154	7	-14	-12	4				.900	4	C/OS	-0.4

■ TRUCK HANNAH
Hannah, James Harrison b: 6/5/1889, Larimore, N.D. d: 4/27/82, Fountain Valley, Cal. BR/TR, 6'1", 190 lbs. Deb: 4/15/18

YEAR	TM/L	G	AB	R	H	2B	3B	HR	RBI	BB	SO	AVG	OBP	SLG	PRO+	BR	/A	RC	SB	CS	SBR	FA	FR	POS	TPR
1918	NY-A	90	250	24	55	6	0	2	21	51	25	.220	.361	.268	88	-0	-1	26	5			.974	3	C	1.0
1919	NY-A	75	227	14	54	8	3	1	20	22	19	.238	.313	.313	76	-7	-7	22	0			**.984**	-9	C/1	-1.0
1920	NY-A	79	259	24	64	11	1	2	25	24	35	.247	.313	.320	66	-12	-13	28	2	0	1	.961	-5	C	-1.2
Total	3	244	736	62	173	25	4	5	66	97	79	.235	.331	.300	76	-19	-21	76	7	0		.973	-11	C/1	-1.2

■ JACK HANNIFIN
Hannifin, John Joseph b: 2/25/1883, Holyoke, Mass. d: 10/27/45, Northampton, Mass. BR/TR, 5'11", 167 lbs. Deb: 4/19/06

YEAR	TM/L	G	AB	R	H	2B	3B	HR	RBI	BB	SO	AVG	OBP	SLG	PRO+	BR	/A	RC	SB	CS	SBR	FA	FR	POS	TPR
1906	Phi-A	1	1	0	1	0	0	0	0	0		1.000	1.000	1.000	512	0	0	1	0			.000	0	H	0.0
	NY-N	10	30	4	6	0	1	0	3	2		.200	.250	.267	60	-1	-1	2	1			.903	-1	/S32	-0.2
1907	NY-N	56	149	16	34	7	3	1	15	15		.228	.303	.336	97	-0	-1	18	6			.996	-4	13/SO	-0.5
1908	NY-N	1	2	0	0	0	0	0	0	0		.000	.000	.000	-95	-0	-0	0	0			.000	-0	/O	-0.1
	Bos-N	90	257	30	53	6	2	2	22	28		.206	.284	.268	78	-6	-6	22	7			.930	5	32S/O	0.0
	Yr	91	259	30	53	6	2	2	22	28		.205	.282	.266	77	-7	-6	22	7			.930	5	32S/O	-0.1
Total	3	158	439	50	94	13	6	3	40	45		.214	.289	.292	84	-8	-8	43	14			.937	0	/3S12O	-0.8

■ PAT HANNIFIN
Hannifin, Patrick James b: 1868, Nova Scotia, Canada d: 11/5/08, Springfield, Mass. Deb: 4/29/1897

YEAR	TM/L	G	AB	R	H	2B	3B	HR	RBI	BB	SO	AVG	OBP	SLG	PRO+	BR	/A	RC	SB	CS	SBR	FA	FR	POS	TPR
1897	Bro-N	10	20	4	5	0	0	0	2	1		.250	.375	.250	71	-1	-1	4	4			.867	2	/O2	0.1

■ DAVE HANSEN
Hansen, David Andrew b: 11/24/68, Long Beach, Cal. BL/TR, 6', 180 lbs. Deb: 9/16/90

YEAR	TM/L	G	AB	R	H	2B	3B	HR	RBI	BB	SO	AVG	OBP	SLG	PRO+	BR	/A	RC	SB	CS	SBR	FA	FR	POS	TPR
1990	LA-N	5	7	0	1	0	0	0	1	0	3	.143	.143	.143	-22	-1	-1	0	0	0	0	.500	-1	/3	-0.2
1991	LA-N	53	56	3	15	4	0	1	5	2	12	.268	.293	.393	93	-1	-1	6	1	0	0	1.000	2	3/S	0.1
1992	LA-N	132	341	30	73	11	0	6	22	34	49	.214	.287	.299	67	-15	-14	29	0	2	-1	**.968**	7	*3	-0.9
Total	3	190	404	33	89	15	0	7	28	36	64	.220	.286	.309	69	-17	-16	35	1	2	-1	.967	8	3/S	-1.0

■ DOUG HANSEN
Hansen, Douglas William b: 12/16/28, Los Angeles, Cal. BR/TR, 6', 180 lbs. Deb: 9/04/51

YEAR	TM/L	G	AB	R	H	2B	3B	HR	RBI	BB	SO	AVG	OBP	SLG	PRO+	BR	/A	RC	SB	CS	SBR	FA	FR	POS	TPR
1951	Cle-A	3	0	2	0	0	0	0	0	0	0	—	—	—	—	0	0	0	0	0	0	.000	0	R	0.0

■ BOB HANSEN
Hansen, Robert Joseph b: 5/26/48, Boston, Mass. BL/TL, 6', 195 lbs. Deb: 5/10/74

YEAR	TM/L	G	AB	R	H	2B	3B	HR	RBI	BB	SO	AVG	OBP	SLG	PRO+	BR	/A	RC	SB	CS	SBR	FA	FR	POS	TPR
1974	Mil-A	58	88	8	26	4	1	2	9	3	16	.295	.319	.432	115	1	1	12	2	1	0	1.000	-0	D/1	0.1
1976	Mil-A	24	61	4	10	1	0	0	4	6	8	.164	.239	.180	24	-6	-6	3	0	0	0	.000	-0	D/1	-0.6
Total	2	82	149	12	36	5	1	2	13	9	24	.242	.285	.329	78	-4	-4	15	2	1	0	1.000	-0	/D1	-0.5

■ RON HANSEN
Hansen, Ronald Lavern b: 4/5/38, Oxford, Neb. BR/TR, 6'3", 200 lbs. Deb: 4/15/58 C

YEAR	TM/L	G	AB	R	H	2B	3B	HR	RBI	BB	SO	AVG	OBP	SLG	PRO+	BR	/A	RC	SB	CS	SBR	FA	FR	POS	TPR
1958	Bal-A	12	19	1	0	0	0	0	1	0	7	.000	.050	.000	-90	-5	-5	0	0	0	0	.943	-0	S	-0.5
1959	Bal-A	2	4	0	0	0	0	0	0	1	1	.000	.200	.000	-41	-1	-1	0	0	0	0	.889	1	/S	0.0
1960	Bal-A★	153	530	72	135	22	5	22	86	69	94	.255	.343	.440	111	7	8	78	3	3	-1	.964	6	*S	2.5
1961	Bal-A	155	533	51	132	13	2	12	51	66	96	.248	.332	.347	83	-13	-12	60	1	3	-2	.959	12	*S/2	1.2
1962	Bal-A	71	196	12	34	7	0	3	17	30	36	.173	.289	.255	50	-14	-13	14	0	1	-1	.965	4	S	-0.4
1963	Chi-A	144	482	55	109	17	2	13	67	78	74	.226	.334	.351	94	-3	-2	57	1	1	-0	.983	**27**	*S	3.6

YEAR	TM/L	G	AB	R	H	2B	3B	HR	RBI	BB	SO	AVG	OBP	SLG	PRO+	BR	/A	RC	SB	CS	SBR	FA	FR	POS	TPR
1964	Chi-A	158	575	85	150	25	3	20	68	73	73	.261	.350	.419	116	11	13	86	1	0	0	.975	16	*S	4.2
1965	Chi-A	162	587	61	138	23	4	11	66	60	73	.235	.308	.344	91	-11	-7	60	1	1	-0	.969	17	*S/2	2.2
1966	Chi-A	23	74	3	13	1	0	0	4	15	10	.176	.322	.189	55	-4	-3	6	0	1	-1	.946	3	S	0.1
1967	Chi-A	157	498	35	116	20	0	8	51	64	51	.233	.320	.321	94	-5	-3	53	0	3	-2	.964	2	*S	1.4
1968	Was-A	86	275	28	51	12	0	8	28	35	49	.185	.282	.316	84	-6	-5	23	0	0	0	.963	2	S/3	0.6
	Chi-A	40	87	7	20	3	0	1	4	11	12	.230	.316	.299	86	-1	-1	8	0	0	0	.959	6	3/S2	0.6
	Yr	126	362	35	71	15	0	9	32	46	61	.196	.290	.312	84	-7	-6	31	0	0	0	.963	7	S3/2	1.2
1969	Chi-A	85	185	15	48	6	1	2	22	18	25	.259	.328	.335	82	-3	-4	20	2	0	1	.967	-1	21/S3	-0.4
1970	NY-A	59	91	13	27	4	0	4	14	19	9	.297	.423	.473	155	7	7	20	0	1	-1	.983	-3	S3/2	0.6
1971	NY-A	61	145	6	30	3	0	2	20	9	27	.207	.253	.269	51	-10	-9	9	0	0	0	.918	-3	3/2S	-1.2
1972	KC-A	16	30	2	4	0	0	0	2	3	6	.133	.212	.133	4	-3	-3	1	0	0	0	.944	3	/S32	0.0
Total	15	1384	4311	446	1007	156	17	106	501	551	643	.234	.323	.351	92	-55	-40	494	9	14	-6	.968	90	*S/321	14.5

■ DON HANSKI Hanski, Donald Thomas (b: Donald Thomas Hanyzewski) b: 2/27/16, Laporte, Ind. d: 9/2/57, Worth, Ill. BL/TL, 5'11", 180 lbs. Deb: 5/06/43

YEAR	TM/L	G	AB	R	H	2B	3B	HR	RBI	BB	SO	AVG	OBP	SLG	PRO+	BR	/A	RC	SB	CS	SBR	FA	FR	POS	TPR
1943	Chi-A	9	21	1	5	1	0	0	2	0	5	.238	.238	.286	53	-1	-1	1	0	1	-1	.952	-0	/1P	-0.3
1944	Chi-A	2	1	0	0	0	0	0	0	0	0	.000	.000	.000	-99	-0	-0	0	0	0	0	.000	-0	/P	0.0
Total	2	11	22	1	5	1	0	0	2	0	5	.227	.227	.273	46	-2	-2	1	0	1	-1	—	-1	/1P	-0.3

■ HARRY HANSON Hanson, Harry Francis b: 1/17/1896, Elgin, Ill. d: 10/5/66, Savannah, Ga. BR/TR, 5'11", Deb: 7/14/13

YEAR	TM/L	G	AB	R	H	2B	3B	HR	RBI	BB	SO	AVG	OBP	SLG	PRO+	BR	/A	RC	SB	CS	SBR	FA	FR	POS	TPR
1913	NY-A	1	2	0	0	0	0	0	0	0	0	.000	.000	.000	-99	-0	-0	0	0			1.000	-0	/C	-0.1

■ JOHN HAPPENNY Happenny, John Clifford "Cliff" b: 5/18/01, Waltham, Mass. d: 12/29/88, Coral Springs, Fla BR/TR, 5'11", 165 lbs. Deb: 7/02/23

YEAR	TM/L	G	AB	R	H	2B	3B	HR	RBI	BB	SO	AVG	OBP	SLG	PRO+	BR	/A	RC	SB	CS	SBR	FA	FR	POS	TPR
1923	Chi-A	32	86	7	19	5	0	0	10	3	13	.221	.256	.279	41	-8	-7	6	0	0	0	.947	0	2/S3	-0.6

■ BILL HARBIDGE Harbidge, William Arthur "Yaller Bill" b: 3/29/1855, Philadelphia, Pa. d: 3/17/24, Philadelphia, Pa. BL/TL, 162 lbs. Deb: 5/15/1875

YEAR	TM/L	G	AB	R	H	2B	3B	HR	RBI	BB	SO	AVG	OBP	SLG	PRO+	BR	/A	RC	SB	CS	SBR	FA	FR	POS	TPR
1875	Har-n	53	205	32	50	3	3	0		**12**		.244	.286	.288	94	0	-1	17						CO2/1	0.0
1876	Har-N	30	106	11	23	2	1	0	6	3	2	.217	.239	.255	59	-4	-5	7				.799	1	C/O1	-0.3
1877	Har-N	41	167	18	37	5	2	0	8	3	6	.222	.235	.275	68	-7	-5	11				.881	-4	C/O23	-0.7
1878	Chi-N	54	240	32	71	12	0	0	37	6	13	.296	.313	.346	109	4	2	27				.878	-8	*C/O	-0.5
1879	Chi-N	4	18	2	2	0	0	0	1	0	5	.111	.111	.111	-25	-2	-2	0				.571	-1	/O	-0.4
1880	Tro-N	9	27	3	10	0	1	0	2	0	3	.370	.370	.444	166	2	2	5				.887	0	/CO	0.2
1882	Tro-N	32	123	11	23	1	1	0	13	10	17	.187	.248	.211	52	-7	-6	7				.836	-4	O/1C	-0.9
1883	Phi-N	73	280	32	62	12	3	0	21	24	20	.221	.283	.286	81	-8	-4	23				.796	-11	OS/2C3	-1.3
1884	Cin-U	82	341	59	95	12	5	2		25		.279	.328	.361	123	12	8	41				.906	5	*O/S1	0.9
Total	8	325	1302	168	323	44	13	2	88	71	66	.248	.287	.306	92	-10	-11	120				.849	-21	OC/S213	-3.0

■ SCOTT HARDESTY Hardesty, Scott Durbin b: 1/26/1870, Bellville, Ohio d: 10/29/44, Fostoria, Ohio Deb: 8/17/1899

YEAR	TM/L	G	AB	R	H	2B	3B	HR	RBI	BB	SO	AVG	OBP	SLG	PRO+	BR	/A	RC	SB	CS	SBR	FA	FR	POS	TPR
1899	NY-N	22	72	4	16	0	0	0	4	1		.222	.243	.222	29	-7	-7	5	2			.895	2	S/1	-0.3

■ PAT HARDGROVE Hardgrove, William Henry b: 5/10/1895, Palmyra, Kan. d: 1/26/73, Jackson, Miss. BR/TR, 5'10", 158 lbs. Deb: 6/08/18

YEAR	TM/L	G	AB	R	H	2B	3B	HR	RBI	BB	SO	AVG	OBP	SLG	PRO+	BR	/A	RC	SB	CS	SBR	FA	FR	POS	TPR
1918	Chi-A	2	2	0	0	0	0	0	0	0	0	.000	.000	.000	-99	-0	-0	0	0			.000	0	H	-0.1

■ LOU HARDIE Hardie, Louis W. b: 8/24/1864, New York, N.Y. d: 3/5/29, Oakland, Cal. 5'11", 180 lbs. Deb: 5/22/1884

YEAR	TM/L	G	AB	R	H	2B	3B	HR	RBI	BB	SO	AVG	OBP	SLG	PRO+	BR	/A	RC	SB	CS	SBR	FA	FR	POS	TPR
1884	Phi-N	3	8	0	3	2	0	0	0	0	2	.375	.375	.625	219	1	1	2				.857	-3	/C	-0.1
1886	Chi-N	16	51	4	9	0	0	0	3	4	10	.176	.236	.176	24	-4	-5	2	1			.964	-0	C/O3	-0.4
1890	Bos-N	47	185	17	42	8	0	3	17	18	36	.227	.296	.319	75	-5	-7	19	4			.886	-0	CO/3S1	-0.5
1891	Bal-a	15	56	7	13	0	3	0	1	8	8	.232	.328	.339	93	-0	-0	7	3			1.000	1	O	0.0
Total	4	81	300	28	67	10	3	3	21	30	56	.223	.294	.307	72	-8	-12	31	8			.910	-2	/CO31S	-1.0

■ BUD HARDIN Hardin, William Edgar b: 6/14/22, Shelby, N.C. BR/TR, 5'10", 165 lbs. Deb: 4/15/52

YEAR	TM/L	G	AB	R	H	2B	3B	HR	RBI	BB	SO	AVG	OBP	SLG	PRO+	BR	/A	RC	SB	CS	SBR	FA	FR	POS	TPR
1952	Chi-N	3	7	1	1	0	0	0	0	0	0	.143	.143	.143	-20	-1	-1	0	0	0	0	1.000	0	/S2	-0.1

■ LOU HARDING Harding, Louis Edward "Jumbo" b: San Francisco, Cal. 5'9.5", 213 lbs. Deb: 10/05/1886

YEAR	TM/L	G	AB	R	H	2B	3B	HR	RBI	BB	SO	AVG	OBP	SLG	PRO+	BR	/A	RC	SB	CS	SBR	FA	FR	POS	TPR
1886	StL-a	1	3	0	1	1	0	0		0		.333	.333	.667	203	0	0	1	0			.889	1	/C	0.1

■ CARROLL HARDY Hardy, Carroll William b: 5/18/33, Sturgis, S.Dak. BR/TR, 6', 185 lbs. Deb: 4/15/58

YEAR	TM/L	G	AB	R	H	2B	3B	HR	RBI	BB	SO	AVG	OBP	SLG	PRO+	BR	/A	RC	SB	CS	SBR	FA	FR	POS	TPR
1958	Cle-A	27	49	10	10	3	0	1	6	6	14	.204	.304	.327	75	-2	-2	5	1	2	-1	1.000	1	O	-0.2
1959	Cle-A	32	53	12	11	1	0	0	2	3	7	.208	.250	.226	33	-5	-5	3	1	1	-0	1.000	1	O	-0.5
1960	Cle-A	29	18	7	2	1	0	0	1	2	2	.111	.200	.167	0	-3	-2	1	0	0	0	1.000	-4	O	-0.7
	Bos-A	73	145	26	34	5	2	2	15	17	40	.234	.315	.338	74	-5	-5	14	3	2	-0	.968	-6	O	-1.4
	Yr	102	163	33	36	6	2	2	16	19	42	.221	.302	.319	67	-7	-8	15	3	2	-0	.973	-11	O	-2.1
1961	Bos-A	85	281	46	74	20	2	3	36	26	53	.263	.330	.381	87	-4	-5	36	4	2	0	.961	-1	O	-1.0
1962	Bos-A	115	362	52	78	13	5	8	36	54	68	.215	.321	.345	77	-10	-12	40	3	7	-3	.991	1	*O	-2.0
1963	Hou-N	15	44	5	10	3	0	0	3	3	7	.227	.277	.295	69	-2	-2	4	1	0	0	.947	-0	O	-0.3
1964	Hou-N	46	157	13	29	1	1	2	12	8	30	.185	.234	.242	36	-14	-13	8	0	0	0	.990	5	O	-1.0
1967	Min-A	11	8	1	3	0	0	1	2	1	1	.375	.444	.750	229	1	1	3	0	0	0	.000	-1	/O	0.0
Total	8	433	1117	172	251	47	10	17	113	120	222	.225	.304	.330	72	-42	-44	114	13	14	-5	.981	-5	O	-7.1

■ JACK HARDY Hardy, John Doolittle b: 6/23/1877, Cleveland, Ohio d: 10/20/21, Cleveland, Ohio BR/TR, 6', 185 lbs. Deb: 8/29/03

YEAR	TM/L	G	AB	R	H	2B	3B	HR	RBI	BB	SO	AVG	OBP	SLG	PRO+	BR	/A	RC	SB	CS	SBR	FA	FR	POS	TPR
1903	Cle-A	5	19	1	3	1	0	0	1	1		.158	.200	.211	24	-2	-2	1	1			1.000	-1	/O	-0.3
1907	Chi-N	1	4	0	1	0	0	0	0	0		.250	.250	.250	53	-0	-0	0	0			.909	0	/C	0.0
1909	Was-A	10	24	3	4	0	0	0	4	1		.167	.200	.167	17	-2	-2	1	0			.974	-2	/C2	-0.4
1910	Was-A	7	8	1	2	0	0	0	0	0		.250	.250	.250	59	-0	-0	0	0			.933	1	/CO	0.0
Total	4	23	55	5	10	1	0	0	5	2		.182	.211	.200	28	-5	-4	2	1			.953	-2	/CO2	-0.7

■ SHAWN HARE Hare, Shawn Robert b: 3/26/67, St.Louis, Mo. BL/TL, 6'2", 190 lbs. Deb: 9/06/91

YEAR	TM/L	G	AB	R	H	2B	3B	HR	RBI	BB	SO	AVG	OBP	SLG	PRO+	BR	/A	RC	SB	CS	SBR	FA	FR	POS	TPR
1991	Det-A	9	19	0	1	1	0	0	0	2	1	.053	.143	.105	-30	-3	-3	0	0	0	0	1.000	0	/OD	-0.4
1992	Det-A	15	26	0	3	1	0	0	5	2	4	.115	.179	.154	-6	-4	-4	1	0	0	0	1.000	-2	/O1	-0.6
Total	2	24	45	0	4	2	0	0	5	4	5	.089	.163	.133	-16	-7	-7	1	0	0	0	1.000	-2	/O1D	-1.0

■ GARY HARGIS Hargis, Gary Lynn b: 11/2/56, Minneapolis, Minn. BR/TR, 5'11", 165 lbs. Deb: 9/29/79

YEAR	TM/L	G	AB	R	H	2B	3B	HR	RBI	BB	SO	AVG	OBP	SLG	PRO+	BR	/A	RC	SB	CS	SBR	FA	FR	POS	TPR
1979	Pit-N	1	0	0	0	0	0	0	0	0	0	—	—	—	—	0	0	0	0	0	0	.000	0	/R	0.0

■ BUBBLES HARGRAVE Hargrave, Eugene Franklin b: 7/15/1892, New Haven, Ind. d: 2/23/69, Cincinnati, Ohio BR/TR, 5'10.5", 174 lbs. Deb: 9/18/13 F

YEAR	TM/L	G	AB	R	H	2B	3B	HR	RBI	BB	SO	AVG	OBP	SLG	PRO+	BR	/A	RC	SB	CS	SBR	FA	FR	POS	TPR
1913	Chi-N	3	3	0	1	0	0	0	1	0	0	.333	.333	.333	90	-0	-0	0	0			1.000	0	/C	0.0
1914	Chi-N	23	36	3	8	2	0	0	2	0	4	.222	.222	.278	48	-2	-2	2	2			.930	-4	C	-0.6
1915	Chi-N	15	19	2	3	0	1	0	2	1	5	.158	.200	.263	40	-1	-1	1	0			1.000	-1	/C	-0.2
1921	Cin-N	93	263	28	76	17	8	1	38	12	15	.289	.327	.426	102	-1	0	36	4	2	0	.973	-7	C	-0.3
1922	Cin-N	98	320	49	101	22	10	7	57	26	18	.316	.371	.512	128	11	12	60	7	4	-0	.982	-9	C	0.7
1923	Cin-N	118	378	54	126	23	9	10	78	44	22	.333	.419	.521	150	27	28	84	4	5	-2	.988	3	*C	3.2
1924	Cin-N	98	312	42	94	19	10	3	33	30	20	.301	.370	.455	122	9	10	53	2	2	-1	.983	-1	C	1.4
1925	Cin-N	87	273	28	82	13	6	2	33	25	23	.300	.361	.414	100	-1	0	41	4	3	-1	.979	-6	C	-0.2
1926	Cin-N	105	326	42	115	22	8	6	62	25	17	.353	.406	.525	153	22	23	67	2			.988	-12	C	1.7
1927	Cin-N	102	305	36	94	18	3	0	35	31	18	.308	.376	.387	108	3	4	45	0			**.988**	-10	C	0.1
1928	Cin-N	65	190	19	56	12	3	0	23	13	14	.295	.353	.389	95	-2	-1	26	4			.991	2	C	0.5
1930	NY-A	45	108	11	30	7	0	0	12	10	9	.278	.339	.343	77	-4	-3	13	0	0	0	.992	-5	C	-0.5

YEAR	TM/L	G	AB	R	H	2B	3B	HR	RBI	BB	SO	AVG	OBP	SLG	PRO+	BR	/A	RC	SB	CS	SBR	FA	FR	POS	TPR
Total	12	852	2533	314	786	155	58	29	376	217	165	.310	.372	.452	119	60	68	429	29	16		.983	-50	C	5.8

■ PINKY HARGRAVE

Hargrave, William McKinley b: 1/31/1896, New Haven, Ind. d: 10/3/42, Ft.Wayne, Ind. BB/TR, 5'8.5", 180 lbs. Deb: 5/18/23 F

YEAR	TM/L	G	AB	R	H	2B	3B	HR	RBI	BB	SO	AVG	OBP	SLG	PRO+	BR	/A	RC	SB	CS	SBR	FA	FR	POS	TPR
1923	Was-A	33	59	4	17	2	0	0	8	2	6	.288	.311	.322	70	-3	-2	6	0	0	0	.917	-4	/3CO	-0.6
1924	Was-A	24	33	3	5	1	1	0	5	1	4	.152	.176	.242	8	-5	-5	1	0	0	0	1.000	-1	/C	-0.5
1925	Was-A	5	6	0	3	0	0	0	0	1	2	.500	.571	.500	177	1	1	2	0	0	0	1.000	1	/C	0.2
	StL-A	67	225	34	64	15	2	8	43	13	13	.284	.326	.476	97	-1	-3	35	2	0	1	.981	-6	C	-0.5
	Yr	72	231	34	67	15	2	8	43	14	15	.290	.333	.476	99	-0	-2	37	2	0	1	.981	-5	C	-0.3
1926	StL-A	92	235	20	66	16	3	7	37	10	38	.281	.319	.464	98	-1	-2	35	3	0	1	.977	-2	C	0.0
1928	Det-A	121	320	38	88	13	5	10	63	32	28	.275	.343	.441	103	1	1	50	4	1	1	.977	-14	C	-0.5
1929	Det-A	76	185	26	61	12	0	3	26	20	24	.330	.401	.443	117	5	5	33	2	2	-1	.973	-1	C	0.7
1930	Det-A	55	137	18	39	8	0	5	18	20	12	.285	.380	.453	108	2	2	25	2	0	1	.984	-4	C	0.2
	Was-A	10	31	3	6	2	2	1	7	3	1	.194	.265	.484	85	-1	-1	4	1	0	0	1.000	1	/C	0.1
	Yr	65	168	21	45	10	2	6	25	23	13	.268	.359	.458	104	1	1	29	3	0	1	.987	-3	C	0.3
1931	Was-A	40	80	6	26	8	0	1	19	9	12	.325	.393	.463	124	3	3	15	1	0	0	.978	-2	C	0.2
1932	Bos-N	82	217	20	57	14	3	4	33	24	18	.263	.336	.410	103	-0	1	31	1			.968	-4	C	0.1
1933	Bos-N	45	73	5	13	0	0	0	6	5	7	.178	.241	.178	23	-7	-7	3	1			.957	1	C	-0.5
Total	10	650	1601	177	445	91	16	39	265	140	165	.278	.339	.428	98	-5	-7	241	17	3		.976	-35	C/3O	-1.1

■ CHARLIE HARGREAVES

Hargreaves, Charles Russell b: 12/14/1896, Trenton, N.J. d: 5/9/79, Neptune, N.J. BR/TR, 6', 170 lbs. Deb: 7/15/23

YEAR	TM/L	G	AB	R	H	2B	3B	HR	RBI	BB	SO	AVG	OBP	SLG	PRO+	BR	/A	RC	SB	CS	SBR	FA	FR	POS	TPR
1923	Bro-N	20	57	5	16	0	0	0	4	1	2	.281	.293	.281	54	-4	-4	5	0	0	0	.921	-4	C	-0.6
1924	Bro-N	15	27	4	11	2	0	0	5	1	1	.407	.429	.481	148	2	2	5	0	1	-1	1.000	-1	/C	0.0
1925	Bro-N	45	83	9	23	3	1	0	13	6	1	.277	.326	.337	72	-4	-3	9	1	1	-0	.986	2	C/1	-0.1
1926	Bro-N	85	208	14	52	13	2	2	23	19	10	.250	.316	.361	83	-6	-5	24	1			.986	4	C	0.2
1927	Bro-N	46	133	9	38	3	1	0	11	14	7	.286	.362	.323	85	-2	-2	16	1			.985	-1	C	0.0
1928	Bro-N	20	61	3	12	2	0	0	5	6	6	.197	.269	.230	32	-6	-6	4	1			.979	2	C	-0.2
	Pit-N	79	260	15	74	8	2	1	32	12	9	.285	.319	.342	70	-10	-12	28	1			.962	-5	C	-1.0
	Yr	99	321	18	86	10	2	1	37	18	15	.268	.309	.321	63	-16	-18	31	2			.966	-3	C	-1.2
1929	Pit-N	102	328	33	88	12	5	1	44	16	12	.268	.306	.345	60	-20	-21	34	1			.981	2	*C	-1.0
1930	Pit-N	11	31	4	7	1	0	0	2	2	1	.226	.273	.258	29	-4	-4	2	0			1.000	6	C	0.3
Total	8	423	1188	96	321	44	11	4	139	77	49	.270	.318	.336	69	-54	-55	126	6	2		.977	4	C/1	-2.4

■ MIKE HARGROVE

Hargrove, Dudley Michael b: 10/26/49, Perryton, Tex. BL/TL, 6', 195 lbs. Deb: 4/07/74 MC

YEAR	TM/L	G	AB	R	H	2B	3B	HR	RBI	BB	SO	AVG	OBP	SLG	PRO+	BR	/A	RC	SB	CS	SBR	FA	FR	POS	TPR
1974	Tex-A	131	415	57	134	18	6	4	66	49	42	.323	.400	.424	141	21	23	71	0	0	0	.987	9	1D/O	2.7
1975	Tex-A★	145	519	82	157	22	2	11	62	79	66	.303	.399	.416	132	24	25	88	4	3	-1	.964	3	O1D	2.1
1976	Tex-A	151	541	80	155	30	1	7	58	**97**	64	.287	.401	.384	128	26	25	91	2	3	-1	.984	1	*1/D	1.5
1977	Tex-A	153	525	98	160	28	4	18	69	103	59	.305	.424	.476	143	38	37	110	2	5	-2	.993	-0	*1	2.5
1978	Tex-A	146	494	63	124	24	1	7	40	**107**	47	.251	.391	.346	109	12	12	73	2	5	-2	.987	7	*1/D	0.8
1979	SD-N	52	125	15	24	5	0	0	8	25	15	.192	.327	.232	59	-7	-6	11	0	2	-1	.986	-2	1	-1.2
	Cle-A	100	338	60	110	21	4	10	56	63	40	.325	.438	.500	152	28	28	76	2	3	-1	.993	0	O1/D	2.2
1980	Cle-A	160	589	86	179	22	2	11	85	111	36	.304	.421	.404	127	29	28	105	4	2	0	.993	-5	*1	1.3
1981	Cle-A	94	322	43	102	21	0	2	49	60	16	.317	**.432**	.401	143	21	22	57	5	4	-1	.989	6	1/D	2.2
1982	Cle-A	160	591	67	160	26	1	4	65	101	58	.271	.380	.338	100	4	4	79	2	2	-1	.996	11	*1/D	0.7
1983	Cle-A	134	469	57	134	21	4	3	57	78	40	.286	.393	.367	107	11	8	71	0	6	-4	.994	12	*1/D	0.9
1984	Cle-A	133	352	44	94	14	2	2	44	53	38	.267	.363	.335	93	-1	-1	43	0	2	-1	.991	6	*1	-0.3
1985	Cle-A	107	284	31	81	14	1	1	27	39	29	.285	.372	.352	100	1	2	38	1	0	0	.991	5	1	0.2
Total	12	1666	5564	783	1614	266	28	80	686	965	550	.290	.400	.391	121	208	206	914	24	37	-15	.991	53	*1O/D	15.6

■ TIM HARKNESS

Harkness, Thomas William b: 12/23/37, Lachine, Que., Can. BL/TL, 6'2", 182 lbs. Deb: 9/12/61

YEAR	TM/L	G	AB	R	H	2B	3B	HR	RBI	BB	SO	AVG	OBP	SLG	PRO+	BR	/A	RC	SB	CS	SBR	FA	FR	POS	TPR
1961	LA-N	5	8	4	4	2	0	0	0	3	1	.500	.636	.750	245	2	2	5	1	0	0	1.000	-0	/1	0.2
1962	LA-N	92	62	9	16	2	0	2	7	10	20	.258	.370	.387	110	1	1	10	1	0	0	1.000	1	1	0.2
1963	NY-N	123	375	35	79	12	3	10	41	36	79	.211	.292	.339	80	-9	-10	38	4	3	-1	.986	16	*1	0.2
1964	NY-N	39	117	11	33	2	1	2	13	9	18	.282	.339	.368	101	-0	0	13	1	1	-0	.993	3	1	0.2
Total	4	259	562	59	132	18	4	14	61	58	118	.235	.316	.356	90	-6	-6	66	7	4	-0	.989	21	1	0.8

■ DICK HARLEY

Harley, Richard Joseph b: 9/25/1872, Philadelphia, Pa. d: 4/3/52, Philadelphia, Pa. BL/TR, 5'10.5", 165 lbs. Deb: 6/02/1897

YEAR	TM/L	G	AB	R	H	2B	3B	HR	RBI	BB	SO	AVG	OBP	SLG	PRO+	BR	/A	RC	SB	CS	SBR	FA	FR	POS	TPR
1897	StL-N	89	330	43	96	6	4	3	35	36		.291	.379	.361	98	-0	1	56	23			.899	1	*O	-0.4
1898	StL-N	142	549	74	135	6	5	0	42	34		.246	.315	.275	68	-21	-22	54	13			.926	9	*O	-2.2
1899	Cle-N	142	567	70	142	15	7	1	50	40		.250	.315	.307	76	-22	-16	61	15			.924	5	*O	-2.1
1900	Cin-N	5	21	2	9	1	0	0	5	1		.429	.455	.476	161	2	2	7	4			1.000	-1	/O	0.0
1901	Cin-N	133	535	69	146	13	2	4	27	31		.273	.322	.327	95	-7	-3	72	37			.898	-5	*O	-1.7
1902	Det-A	125	491	59	138	9	8	2	44	36		.281	.343	.344	89	-5	-7	68	20			.930	-2	*O	-1.6
1903	Chi-N	104	386	72	89	9	1	0	33	45		.231	.328	.259	70	-14	-12	45	27			.923	3	*O	-1.5
Total	7	740	2879	389	755	59	27	10	236	223		.262	.331	.312	83	-68	-57	363	139				10	O	-9.5

■ LARRY HARLOW

Harlow, Larry Duane b: 11/13/51, Colorado Springs, Colo. BL/TL, 6'2", 185 lbs. Deb: 9/20/75

YEAR	TM/L	G	AB	R	H	2B	3B	HR	RBI	BB	SO	AVG	OBP	SLG	PRO+	BR	/A	RC	SB	CS	SBR	FA	FR	POS	TPR
1975	Bal-A	4	3	1	1	0	0	0	0	0	1	.333	.333	.333	95	-0	-0	0	0	0	0	1.000	-2	/O	-0.2
1977	Bal-A	46	48	4	10	0	1	0	0	5	8	.208	.283	.250	50	-3	-3	4	6	1	1	.887	-12	O	-1.4
1978	Bal-A	147	460	67	112	25	1	8	26	55	72	.243	.326	.354	97	-5	-1	53	14	11	-2	.979	-5	*O/P	-1.5
1979	Bal-A	38	41	5	11	1	0	0	1	7	4	.268	.375	.293	86	-1	-0	4	1	3	-2	.970	-10	O	-1.2
	*Cal-A	62	159	22	37	8	2	0	14	25	34	.233	.344	.308	80	-4	-3	18	1	3	-2	.975	-2	O	-0.9
	Yr	100	200	27	48	9	2	0	15	32	38	.240	.350	.305	81	-5	-4	22	2	6	-3	.974	-12	O	-2.1
1980	Cal-A	109	301	47	83	13	4	4	27	48	61	.276	.377	.385	112	6	7	45	3	2	-0	.976	12	O/1D	1.5
1981	Cal-A	43	82	13	17	1	0	0	4	16	25	.207	.337	.220	63	-3	-3	7	1	1	-0	.981	-8	O	-1.3
Total	6	449	1094	159	271	48	8	12	72	156	205	.248	.344	.339	94	-11	-5	132	26	21	-5	.971	-26	O/D1P	-5.0

■ BILL HARMAN

Harman, William Bell b: 1/2/19, Bridgewater, Va. BR/TR, 6'4", 200 lbs. Deb: 6/17/41

YEAR	TM/L	G	AB	R	H	2B	3B	HR	RBI	BB	SO	AVG	OBP	SLG	PRO+	BR	/A	RC	SB	CS	SBR	FA	FR	POS	TPR
1941	Phi-N	15	14	1	1	0	0	0	0	0	3	.071	.071	.071	-62	-3	-3	0	0			1.000	-1	/PC	-0.2

■ CHUCK HARMON

Harmon, Charles Byron b: 4/23/26, Washington, Ind. BR/TR, 6'2", 175 lbs. Deb: 4/17/54

YEAR	TM/L	G	AB	R	H	2B	3B	HR	RBI	BB	SO	AVG	OBP	SLG	PRO+	BR	/A	RC	SB	CS	SBR	FA	FR	POS	TPR
1954	Cin-N	94	286	39	68	7	3	2	25	17	27	.238	.283	.304	52	-20	-21	26	7	3	0	.961	4	3/1	-1.8
1955	Cin-N	96	198	31	50	6	3	5	28	26	24	.253	.348	.389	90	-1	-2	27	9	9	-3	.935	4	3O/1	-0.3
1956	Cin-N	13	4	2	0	0	0	0	0	0	0	.000	.000	.000	-94	-1	-1	0	1	0	0	1.000	-2	/O1	-0.3
	StL-N	20	15	2	0	0	0	0	0	2	2	.000	.118	.000	-65	-4	-4	0	0	0	0	1.000	-4	O/13	-0.8
	Yr	33	19	4	0	0	0	0	0	2	2	.000	.095	.000	-70	-5	-5	0	1	0	0	1.000	-6	O/13	-1.1
1957	StL-N	9	3	2	1	0	1	0	1	0	0	.333	.333	1.000	236	1	1	1	1	0	0	1.000	-3	/O	-0.2
	Phi-N	57	86	14	22	2	1	0	5	1	4	.256	.264	.302	53	-6	-6	6	7	2	1	1.000	-2	O/31	-0.7
	Yr	66	89	16	23	2	2	0	6	1	4	.258	.267	.326	60	-5	-5	7	8	2	1	1.000	-5	O/31	-0.9
Total	4	289	592	90	141	15	8	7	59	46	57	.238	.298	.326	62	-31	-33	60	25	14	-1	.952	-3	3/O1	-4.1

■ TERRY HARMON

Harmon, Terry Walter b: 4/12/44, Toledo, Ohio BR/TR, 6'2", 180 lbs. Deb: 7/23/67

YEAR	TM/L	G	AB	R	H	2B	3B	HR	RBI	BB	SO	AVG	OBP	SLG	PRO+	BR	/A	RC	SB	CS	SBR	FA	FR	POS	TPR
1967	Phi-N	2	0	0	0	0	0	0	0	0	0	—	—	—	—	0	0	0	0	0	0	.000	0	R	0.0
1969	Phi-N	87	201	25	48	8	1	0	16	22	31	.239	.323	.289	74	-7	-6	20	1	2	-1	.968	8	S2/3	0.7
1970	Phi-N	71	129	16	32	2	4	0	7	12	22	.248	.317	.326	75	-5	-4	14	6	3	0	.989	-3	S2/3	-0.4
1971	Phi-N	79	221	27	45	4	2	0	12	20	45	.204	.282	.240	49	-14	-14	17	3	2	-0	.986	8	2/S31	-0.1

YEAR	TM/L	G	AB	R	H	2B	3B	HR	RBI	BB	SO	AVG	OBP	SLG	PRO+	BR	/A	RC	SB	CS	SBR	FA	FR	POS	TPR
1972	Phi-N	73	218	35	62	8	2	2	13	29	28	.284	.373	.367	108	4	4	32	3	2	-0	.996	-1	2S/3	0.6
1973	Phi-N	72	148	17	31	3	0	0	8	13	14	.209	.278	.230	41	-11	-12	10	1	0	0	.988	2	2S/3	-0.7
1974	Phi-N	27	15	5	2	0	0	0	0	3	3	.133	.278	.133	17	-2	-2	1	0	0	0	1.000	3	/S2	0.1
1975	Phi-N	48	72	14	13	1	2	0	5	9	13	.181	.280	.250	46	-5	-5	5	0	0	0	.989	1	S/23	-0.2
1976	*Phi-N	42	61	12	18	4	1	0	6	3	10	.295	.328	.393	101	0	-0	8	3	0	1	.960	3	S2/3	0.6
1977	Phi-N	46	60	13	11	1	0	2	5	6	9	.183	.269	.300	50	-4	-4	4	0	2	-1	.982	8	2S/3	0.4
Total	10	547	1125	164	262	31	12	4	72	117	175	.233	.312	.292	69	-43	-44	112	17	11	-2	.989	29	2S/31	1.0

■ BRIAN HARPER Harper, Brian David b: 10/16/59, Los Angeles, Cal. BR/TR, 6'2", 195 lbs. Deb: 9/29/79

YEAR	TM/L	G	AB	R	H	2B	3B	HR	RBI	BB	SO	AVG	OBP	SLG	PRO+	BR	/A	RC	SB	CS	SBR	FA	FR	POS	TPR
1979	Cal-A	1	2	0	0	0	0	0	0	0	1	.000	.000	.000	-99	-1	-1	0	0	0	0	.000	0	/H	-0.1
1981	Cal-A	4	11	1	3	0	0	0	1	0	0	.273	.273	.273	58	-1	-1	1	1	0	0	.833	-0	/OD	0.0
1982	Pit-N	20	29	4	8	1	0	2	4	1	4	.276	.300	.517	121	1	1	4	0	0	0	1.000	-0	/O	0.0
1983	Pit-N	61	131	16	29	4	1	7	20	2	15	.221	.239	.427	79	-4	-5	12	0	0	0	1.000	-4	O/1	-1.0
1984	Pit-N	46	112	4	29	4	0	2	11	5	11	.259	.303	.348	82	-3	-3	11	0	0	0	.981	-2	O/C	-0.6
1985	*StL-N	43	52	5	13	4	0	0	8	2	3	.250	.278	.327	69	-2	-2	4	0	0	0	1.000	-4	O/3C1	-0.7
1986	Det-A	19	36	2	5	1	0	0	3	3	3	.139	.205	.167	3	-5	-5	1	0	0	0	.929	-2	O/C1D	-0.7
1987	Oak-A	11	17	1	4	1	0	0	3	0	4	.235	.235	.294	42	-1	-1	1	0	0	0	.000	-0	/OD	-0.2
1988	Min-A	60	166	15	49	11	1	3	20	10	12	.295	.346	.428	112	3	3	20	0	3	-2	.991	-7	C/3D	-0.3
1989	Min-A	126	385	43	125	24	0	8	57	13	16	.325	.356	.449	118	12	9	57	2	4	-2	.978	-14	*CD/013	-0.1
1990	Min-A	134	479	61	141	42	3	6	54	19	27	.294	.331	.432	105	6	2	62	3	2	-0	.985	2	*CD/31	1.2
1991	*Min-A	123	441	54	137	28	1	10	69	14	22	.311	.341	.447	111	8	6	62	1	2	-1	.988	-5	*C/1OD	0.7
1992	Min-A	140	502	58	154	25	0	9	73	26	22	.307	.350	.410	109	8	5	68	0	1	-1	.984	-7	*C/D	0.6
Total	13	788	2363	264	697	145	6	47	323	95	140	.295	.331	.421	104	21	9	304	7	12	-5	.985	-44	CO/D31	-1.2

■ GEORGE HARPER Harper, George Washington b: 6/24/1892, Arlington, Ky. d: 8/18/78, Magnolia, Ark. BL/TR, 5'8", 167 lbs. Deb: 4/15/16

YEAR	TM/L	G	AB	R	H	2B	3B	HR	RBI	BB	SO	AVG	OBP	SLG	PRO+	BR	/A	RC	SB	CS	SBR	FA	FR	POS	TPR
1916	Det-A	44	56	4	9	1	0	0	3	5	8	.161	.230	.179	22	-5	-5	2	0			.938	-4	O	-1.1
1917	Det-A	47	117	6	24	3	0	0	12	11	15	.205	.290	.231	59	-5	-5	9	2			.980	-3	O	-1.1
1918	Det-A	69	227	19	55	5	2	0	16	18	14	.242	.301	.282	79	-7	-6	21	3			.956	-1	O	-1.2
1922	Cin-N	128	430	67	146	22	8	2	68	35	22	.340	.397	.442	118	11	12	75	11	10	-3	.955	1	*O	0.2
1923	Cin-N	61	125	14	32	4	2	3	16	11	9	.256	.316	.392	88	-3	-2	15	0	2	-1	.967	-2	O	-0.7
1924	Cin-N	28	74	7	20	3	0	0	3	13	5	.270	.393	.311	92	-0	0	10	1	3	-2	.964	1	O	-0.2
	Phi-N	109	411	68	121	26	6	16	55	38	23	.294	.361	.504	115	16	9	72	10	11	-4	.991	3	*O	0.2
	Yr	137	485	75	141	29	6	16	58	51	28	.291	.366	.474	113	16	10	82	11	14	-5	.986	4	*O	0.0
1925	Phi-N	132	495	86	173	35	7	18	97	28	32	.349	.391	.558	128	28	21	105	10	8	-2	.971	6	*O	1.7
1926	Phi-N	56	194	32	61	6	5	7	38	16	7	.314	.367	.505	126	8	7	35	6			.942	-6	O	-0.3
1927	NY-N	145	483	85	160	19	6	16	87	84	27	.331	.435	.495	149	37	37	106	7			.975	-2	*O	2.7
1928	NY-N	19	57	11	13	1	0	2	7	10	4	.228	.353	.351	84	-1	-1	8	1			.957	2	O	0.0
	*StL-N	99	272	41	83	8	2	17	58	51	15	.305	.418	.537	145	20	20	62	2			.988	1	O	1.5
	Yr	118	329	52	96	9	2	19	65	61	19	.292	.407	.505	135	19	18	69	3			.982	3	*O	1.5
1929	Bos-N	136	457	65	133	25	5	10	68	69	27	.291	.389	.433	108	4	7	79	5			.972	-1	*O	-0.3
Total	11	1073	3398	505	1030	158	43	91	528	389	208	.303	.380	.455	118	103	94	597	58	34		.957	-5	O	1.4

■ TERRY HARPER Harper, Terry Joe b: 8/19/55, Douglasville, Ga. BR/TR, 6'4", 195 lbs. Deb: 9/12/80

YEAR	TM/L	G	AB	R	H	2B	3B	HR	RBI	BB	SO	AVG	OBP	SLG	PRO+	BR	/A	RC	SB	CS	SBR	FA	FR	POS	TPR
1980	Atl-N	21	54	3	10	2	1	0	3	6	5	.185	.279	.259	49	-3	-4	4	2	1	0	.968	-1	O	-0.6
1981	Atl-N	40	73	9	19	1	0	2	8	11	17	.260	.357	.356	100	1	0	10	5	1	1	.976	1	O	0.1
1982	*Atl-N	48	150	16	43	3	0	2	16	14	28	.287	.352	.347	92	-0	-1	19	7	4	-0	.987	-0	O	-0.3
1983	Atl-N	80	201	19	53	13	1	3	26	20	43	.264	.333	.383	91	-1	-2	24	6	5	-1	.952	-0	O	-0.6
1984	Atl-N	40	102	4	16	3	1	0	8	4	21	.157	.196	.206	12	-12	-13	3	4	1	1	1.000	4	O	-0.9
1985	Atl-N	138	492	58	130	15	2	17	72	44	76	.264	.328	.407	98	2	-1	62	9	9	-3	.978	1	*O	-0.7
1986	Atl-N	106	265	26	68	12	0	8	30	29	39	.257	.332	.392	94	-0	-2	30	3	6	-3	.970	-11	O	-1.9
1987	Det-A	31	64	4	13	3	0	3	10	9	8	.203	.301	.391	85	-2	-1	8	1	0	0	.952	-2	DO	-0.3
	Pit-N	36	66	8	19	3	0	1	7	7	11	.288	.356	.379	94	-0	-0	7	0	1	-1	1.000	-3	O	-0.4
Total	8	540	1467	147	371	55	5	36	180	144	248	.253	.323	.371	88	-16	-24	167	37	28	-6	.976	-13	O/D	-5.6

■ TOMMY HARPER Harper, Tommy b: 10/14/40, Oak Grove, La. BR/TR, 5'10", 168 lbs. Deb: 4/09/62 C

YEAR	TM/L	G	AB	R	H	2B	3B	HR	RBI	BB	SO	AVG	OBP	SLG	PRO+	BR	/A	RC	SB	CS	SBR	FA	FR	POS	TPR
1962	Cin-N	6	23	1	4	0	0	0	1	2	6	.174	.240	.174	13	-3	-3	1	1	0	0	.929	-1	/3	-0.4
1963	Cin-N	129	408	67	106	12	3	10	37	44	72	.260	.336	.377	102	3	2	54	12	1	3	.983	5	*O/3	0.5
1964	Cin-N	102	317	42	77	5	2	4	22	39	56	.243	.328	.309	78	-7	-8	37	24	3	5	.994	-0	O/3	-0.8
1965	Cin-N	159	646	**126**	166	28	3	18	64	78	127	.257	.342	.393	99	7	1	94	35	6	7	.983	-2	*O/32	-0.1
1966	Cin-N	149	553	85	154	22	5	5	31	57	85	.278	.349	.363	91	0	-5	74	29	10	3	.996	2	*O	-0.9
1967	Cin-N	103	365	55	82	17	3	7	22	43	51	.225	.306	.345	77	-6	-11	42	23	8	2	.995	8	*O	-0.7
1968	Cle-A	130	235	26	51	15	2	6	26	26	56	.217	.298	.374	104	1	1	26	11	7	-1	.984	-16	*O/2	-2.3
1969	Sea-A	148	537	78	126	10	2	9	41	95	90	.235	.351	.311	88	-7	-5	71	**73**	18	11	.959	-15	23O	-0.6
1970	Mil-A★	154	604	104	179	35	4	31	82	77	107	.296	.380	.522	145	37	37	122	38	16	2	.943	-3	*32O	3.6
1971	Mil-A	152	585	79	151	26	3	14	52	65	92	.258	.333	.385	104	2	3	82	25	3	6	.975	-19	O3/2	-1.6
1972	Bos-A	144	556	92	141	29	2	14	49	67	104	.254	.343	.388	111	13	10	81	25	7	3	.985	1	*O	0.8
1973	Bos-A	147	566	92	159	23	3	17	71	61	93	.281	.352	.422	111	13	9	91	**54**	14	**8**	.985	3	*O/D	1.3
1974	Bos-A	118	443	66	105	15	3	5	24	46	65	.237	.313	.318	77	-10	-13	47	28	12	1	.982	-3	OD	-1.8
1975	Cal-A	89	285	40	68	10	1	3	31	38	51	.239	.332	.312	89	-5	-3	32	19	8	1	.992	-2	D1/O	-0.5
	*Oak-A	34	69	11	22	4	0	2	7	5	9	.319	.373	.464	139	3	3	12	7	0	2	.963	-3	1/O3D	0.1
	Yr	123	354	51	90	14	1	5	38	43	60	.254	.340	.342	99	-2	0	44	26	8	3	.978	-5	D1O/3	-0.4
1976	Bal-A	46	77	8	18	5	0	1	7	10	16	.234	.322	.338	99	-1	0	9	4	3	-1	1.000	-1	D/1O	-0.1
Total	15	1810	6269	972	1609	256	36	146	567	753	1080	.257	.340	.379	100	41	16	876	408	116	53	.986	-47	*O3D/21	-3.5

■ TOBY HARRAH Harrah, Colbert Dale b: 10/26/48, Sissonville, W.Va. BR/TR, 6', 180 lbs. Deb: 9/05/69 MC

YEAR	TM/L	G	AB	R	H	2B	3B	HR	RBI	BB	SO	AVG	OBP	SLG	PRO+	BR	/A	RC	SB	CS	SBR	FA	FR	POS	TPR
1969	Was-A	8	1	4	0	0	0	0	0	0	0	.000	.000	.000	-99	-0	-0	0	0	0	0	.000	0	/S	0.0
1971	Was-A	127	383	45	88	11	3	2	22	40	48	.230	.303	.290	73	-15	-13	33	10	9	-2	.955	-7	*S/3	-0.9
1972	Tex-A†	116	374	47	97	14	3	1	31	34	31	.259	.321	.321	95	-4	-2	41	16	7	1	.960	-9	*S	0.5
1973	Tex-A	118	461	64	120	16	1	10	50	46	49	.260	.330	.364	100	-3	-0	56	10	3	1	.951	-13	S3	-0.2
1974	Tex-A	161	573	79	149	23	2	21	74	50	65	.260	.322	.417	114	7	9	72	15	14	-4	.963	-2	*S/3	2.4
1975	Tex-A☆	151	522	81	153	24	1	20	93	98	71	.293	.406	.458	145	34	34	105	23	9	2	.963	14	*S32	**6.2**
1976	Tex-A★	155	584	64	152	21	1	15	67	91	59	.260	.363	.377	114	15	14	82	8	5	-1	.955	-0	*S/3D	3.2
1977	Tex-A	159	539	90	142	25	5	27	87	**109**	73	.263	.397	.479	136	32	31	112	27	5	5	.963	-24	*3/S	1.0
1978	Tex-A	139	450	56	103	17	3	12	59	83	66	.229	.351	.360	100	3	3	65	31	8	5	.965	-8	3S	0.4
1979	Cle-A	149	527	99	147	25	1	20	77	89	60	.279	.391	.444	124	21	21	98	20	9	1	.940	-48	*3S/D	-2.5
1980	Cle-A	160	561	100	150	22	4	11	72	98	60	.267	.383	.380	109	12	11	89	17	2	4	.971	2	*3/SD	1.5
1981	Cle-A	103	361	64	105	12	4	5	44	57	44	.291	.389	.388	126	14	14	60	12	1	3	.949	-12	*3/SD	0.4
1982	Cle-A☆	162	602	100	183	29	4	25	78	84	52	.304	.400	.490	144	38	38	123	17	3	3	.971	-19	*3/2S	1.9
1983	Cle-A	138	526	81	140	23	1	9	53	75	49	.266	.365	.365	98	4	1	73	16	10	-1	**.971**	-11	*3/2D	-1.3
1984	NY-A	88	253	40	55	9	4	1	26	42	28	.217	.333	.296	79	-7	-6	27	3	0	1	.968	3	3/2OD	-0.2
1985	Tex-A	126	396	65	107	18	1	9	44	113	60	.270	.437	.389	127	23	22	80	11	4	1	.989	-14	*2/SD	1.4
1986	Tex-A	95	289	36	63	18	2	7	41	44	53	.218	.325	.367	86	-4	-5	35	2	5	-2	.982	-20	2	-2.4
Total	17	2155	7402	1115	1954	307	40	195	918	1153	868	.264	.368	.395	114	169	173	1152	238	94	15	.963	-166	*3S2/DO	11.4

YEAR	TM/L	G	AB	R	H	2B	3B	HR	RBI	BB	SO	AVG	OBP	SLG	PRO+	BR	/A	RC	SB	CS	SBR	FA	FR	POS	TPR
■ **JOHN HARRELL**	Harrell, John Robert b: 11/27/47, Long Beach, Cal. BR/TR, 6'2", 190 lbs. Deb: 10/01/69																								
1969	SF-N	2	6	0	3	0	0	0	2	2	1	.500	.625	.500	223	1	1	2	0	0	0	1.000	-0	/C	0.1
■ **BILLY HARRELL**	Harrell, William b: 7/18/28, Norristown, Pa. BR/TR, 6'1.5", 180 lbs. Deb: 9/02/55																								
1955	Cle-A	13	19	2	8	0	0	0	1	3	3	.421	.500	.421	144	2	2	5	1	0	0	.926	-0	S	0.2
1957	Cle-A	22	57	6	15	1	1	1	5	4	7	.263	.311	.368	86	-1	-1	7	3	1	0	.893	-4	S/32	-0.4
1958	Cle-A	101	229	36	50	4	0	7	19	15	36	.218	.272	.328	66	-12	-11	22	12	2	2	.986	-7	3S/2O	-1.2
1961	Bos-A	37	37	10	6	2	0	0	1	1	8	.162	.184	.216	6	-5	-5	1	1	0	0	1.000	7	3/S1	0.2
Total	4	173	342	54	79	7	1	8	26	23	54	.231	.283	.327	68	-16	-16	35	17	3	3	.933	-5	/S321O	-1.2
■ **BUD HARRELSON**	Harrelson, Derrel McKinley b: 6/6/44, Niles, Cal. BB/TR, 5'11", 160 lbs. Deb: 9/02/65 MC																								
1965	NY-N	19	37	3	4	1	1	0	0	2	11	.108	.154	.189	-4	-5	-5	1	0	0	0	.955	4	S	-0.1
1966	NY-N	33	99	20	22	2	4	0	4	13	23	.222	.313	.323	79	-3	-3	11	7	3	0	.993	5	S	0.5
1967	NY-N	151	540	59	137	16	4	1	28	48	64	.254	.319	.304	80	-13	-12	54	12	13	-4	.958	7	*S	0.5
1968	NY-N	111	402	38	88	7	3	0	14	29	68	.219	.273	.251	58	-20	-20	28	4	5	-2	.972	-5	*S	-1.8
1969	*NY-N	123	395	42	98	11	6	0	24	54	54	.248	.341	.306	81	-7	-8	44	1	3	-2	.969	-5	*S	-0.2
1970	NY-N★	157	564	72	137	18	8	1	42	95	74	.243	.355	.309	79	-13	-13	72	23	4	5	.971	-28	*S	-1.8
1971	NY-N★	142	547	55	138	16	6	0	32	53	59	.252	.321	.303	79	-15	-14	59	28	7	4	.978	11	*S	2.0
1972	NY-N	115	418	54	90	10	4	1	24	58	57	.215	.315	.266	68	-17	-15	40	12	4	1	.970	-12	*S	-1.0
1973	*NY-N	106	356	35	92	12	3	0	20	48	49	.258	.348	.309	85	-6	-6	42	5	1	1	.979	-3	*S	0.6
1974	NY-N	106	331	48	75	10	0	1	13	71	39	.227	.366	.266	80	-6	-5	39	9	4	0	.968	16	S	2.4
1975	NY-N	34	73	5	16	2	0	0	3	12	13	.219	.329	.247	65	-3	-3	7	0	0	0	.941	1	S	0.1
1976	NY-N	118	359	34	84	12	4	1	26	63	56	.234	.351	.298	91	-4	-1	44	9	3	1	.962	-5	*S	0.9
1977	NY-N	107	269	25	48	6	2	1	12	27	28	.178	.256	.227	32	-26	-25	17	5	4	-1	.984	-2	S	-1.8
1978	Phi-N	71	103	16	22	1	0	0	9	18	21	.214	.331	.223	57	-5	-5	10	5	2	0	.972	15	2S	1.3
1979	Phi-N	53	71	7	20	6	0	0	7	13	14	.282	.400	.366	107	2	1	11	3	3	-1	.990	6	2S/3O	0.8
1980	Tex-A	87	180	26	49	6	0	1	9	29	23	.272	.373	.322	95	-1	0	24	4	4	-1	.952	11	S/2	1.7
Total	16	1533	4744	539	1120	136	45	7	267	633	653	.236	.329	.288	75	-142	-133	502	127	60	2	.969	16	*S/23O	4.1
■ **KEN HARRELSON**	Harrelson, Kenneth Smith "Hawk" b: 9/4/41, Woodruff, S.C. BR/TR, 6'2", 190 lbs. Deb: 6/09/63																								
1963	KC-A	79	226	16	52	10	1	6	23	23	58	.230	.301	.363	82	-5	-6	23	1	1	-0	.980	-5	1O	-1.4
1964	KC-A	49	139	15	27	5	0	7	12	13	34	.194	.263	.381	74	-5	-5	12	0	1	-1	.977	3	O1	-0.5
1965	KC-A	150	483	61	115	17	3	23	66	66	112	.238	.331	.429	116	9	10	65	9	7	-2	.992	-4	*1/O	-0.2
1966	KC-A	63	210	24	47	5	0	5	22	27	59	.224	.312	.319	85	-4	-4	23	9	2	2	.985	2	1/O	-0.4
	Was-A	71	250	25	62	8	1	7	28	26	53	.248	.321	.372	100	-0	-0	30	4	1	1	.991	-4	1	-0.9
	Yr	134	460	49	109	13	1	12	50	53	112	.237	.317	.348	93	-5	-4	53	13	3	2	.989	-2	*1/O	-1.3
1967	Was-A	26	79	10	16	0	0	3	10	7	15	.203	.267	.316	75	-3	-2	6	1	0	0	.996	0	1	-0.3
	KC-A	61	174	23	53	11	0	6	30	17	17	.305	.366	.471	151	10	10	31	8	2	1	.992	-1	1	0.9
	*Bos-A	23	80	9	16	4	1	3	14	5	12	.200	.247	.387	79	-2	-3	7	1	1	-0	.929	-3	O/1	-0.8
	Yr	110	333	42	85	15	1	12	54	29	44	.255	.315	.414	115	5	5	43	10	3	1	.993	-4	1O	-0.2
1968	Bos-A★	150	535	79	147	17	4	35	**109**	69	90	.275	.360	.518	153	40	36	94	2	6	-3	**1.000**	8	*O1	3.8
1969	Bos-A	10	46	6	10	1	0	3	8	4	6	.217	.280	.435	92	-0	-1	5	0	1	-1	.991	2	1	-0.1
	Cle-A	149	519	83	115	13	4	27	84	95	96	.222	.344	.418	109	9	7	76	17	8	0	.985	5	*O1	0.4
	Yr	159	565	89	125	14	4	30	92	99	102	.221	.339	.419	107	9	6	81	17	9	-0	.985	6	*O1	0.3
1970	Cle-A	17	39	3	11	1	0	1	1	6	4	.282	.378	.385	106	1	1	6	0	0	0	1.000	1	1	0.0
1971	Cle-A	52	161	20	32	2	0	5	14	24	21	.199	.303	.304	66	-6	-7	16	1	0	0	.988	-1	1/O	-1.3
Total	9	900	2941	374	703	94	14	131	421	382	577	.239	.328	.414	109	44	37	393	53	30	-2	.990	2	1O	-0.8
■ **ANDY HARRINGTON**	Harrington, Andrew Matthew b: 2/12/03, Mountain View, Cal d: 1/26/79, Boise, Idaho BR/TR, 5'11", 170 lbs. Deb: 4/18/25																								
1925	Det-A	1	1	0	0	0	0	0	0	0	0	.000	.000	.000	-99	-0	-0	0	0	0	0	.000	0	H	0.0
■ **MICKEY HARRINGTON**	Harrington, Charles Michael b: 10/8/34, Hattiesburg, Miss. BR/TR, 6'4", 205 lbs. Deb: 7/10/63																								
1963	Phi-N	1	0	0	0	0	0	0	0	0	0	—	—	—	—	0	0	0	0	0	0	.000	0	R	0.0
■ **JERRY HARRINGTON**	Harrington, Jeremiah Peter b: 8/12/1869, Keokuk, Iowa d: 4/16/13, Keokuk, Iowa BR/TR, 5'11", 220 lbs. Deb: 4/30/1890																								
1890	Cin-N	65	236	25	58	7	1	1	23	15	29	.246	.299	.297	76	-7	-7	23	4			.957	5	C	0.3
1891	Cin-N	92	333	25	76	10	5	2	41	19	34	.228	.272	.306	69	-13	-14	30	4			.908	-3	C/3	-0.8
1892	Cin-N	22	61	6	13	1	0	0	3	6	1	.213	.284	.230	58	-3	-3	4	0			.989	1	C/1	-0.1
1893	Lou-N	10	36	4	4	1	0	0	6	3	9	.111	.179	.139	-15	-6	-5	1	0			.853	-4	C	-0.7
Total	4	189	666	60	151	19	6	3	73	43	73	.227	.278	.287	66	-29	-29	57	8			.932	-1	C/13	-1.3
■ **JOE HARRINGTON**	Harrington, Joseph C. b: 12/21/1869, Fall River, Mass. d: 9/13/33, Fall River, Mass. 5'8.5", 162 lbs. Deb: 9/10/1895																								
1895	Bos-N	18	65	21	18	0	2	2	13	7	5	.277	.356	.431	97	0	-1	12	3			.912	0	2	0.1
1896	Bos-N	54	198	25	39	5	3	1	25	19	17	.197	.271	.268	41	-16	-18	16	2			.816	-10	3/S2	-2.3
Total	2	72	263	46	57	5	5	3	38	26	22	.217	.292	.308	55	-16	-19	27	5			.901	-10	/32S	-2.2
■ **CANDY HARRIS**	Harris, Alonzo b: 9/17/47, Selma, Ala. BB/TR, 6', 160 lbs. Deb: 4/13/67																								
1967	Hou-N	6	1	0	0	0	0	0	0	0	1	.000	.000	.000	-99	-0	-0	0	0	0	0	.000	0	H	0.0
■ **SPENCER HARRIS**	Harris, Anthony Spencer b: 8/12/1900, Duluth, Minn. d: 7/3/82, Minneapolis, Minn. BL/TL, 5'9", 145 lbs. Deb: 4/14/25																								
1925	Chi-A	56	92	12	26	2	0	1	13	14	13	.283	.383	.337	89	-2	-1	12	1	3	-2	.957	-5	O	-0.8
1926	Chi-A	80	222	36	56	11	3	2	27	20	15	.252	.317	.356	78	-8	-7	26	8	3	1	.949	-6	O	-1.6
1929	Was-A	6	14	1	3	1	0	0	1	0	3	.214	.214	.286	27	-2	-2	1	1	0	0	1.000	-1	/O	-0.2
1930	Phi-A	22	49	4	9	1	0	0	5	5	2	.184	.259	.204	18	-6	-6	3	0	0	0	.958	0	O	-0.6
Total	4	164	377	53	94	15	3	3	46	39	33	.249	.323	.329	70	-18	-16	43	10	6	-1	.954	-11	O	-3.2
■ **GAIL HARRIS**	Harris, Boyd Gail b: 10/15/31, Abingdon, Va. BL/TL, 6', 195 lbs. Deb: 6/03/55																								
1955	NY-N	79	263	27	61	9	0	12	36	20	46	.232	.291	.403	82	-8	-8	30	0	0	0	.982	0	1	-1.1
1956	NY-N	12	38	2	5	0	1	1	1	3	10	.132	.233	.263	33	-4	-4	3	0	0	0	.975	0	1	-0.4
1957	NY-N	90	225	28	54	7	3	9	31	16	28	.240	.308	.418	93	-3	-3	29	1	0	0	.985	-2	1	-0.8
1958	Det-A	134	451	63	123	18	8	20	83	36	60	.273	.332	.481	113	11	7	70	1	2	-1	.986	3	*1	0.2
1959	Det-A	114	349	39	77	4	3	9	39	29	49	.221	.292	.327	66	-15	-17	33	0	1	-1	.992	3	1	-2.2
1960	Det-A	8	5	0	0	0	0	0	0	2	1	.000	.286	.000	-15	-1	-1	0	0	0	0	1.000	0	/1	-0.1
Total	6	437	1331	159	320	38	15	51	190	106	194	.240	.306	.406	88	-18	-25	165	2	3	-1	.986	4	1	-4.4
■ **CHARLIE HARRIS**	Harris, Charles Jenkins b: 10/21/1877, Macon, Ga. d: 3/14/63, Gainesville, Fla. BR/TR, 5'8", 200 lbs. Deb: 5/25/1899																								
1899	Bal-N	30	68	16	19	3	0	0	1	3		.279	.319	.324	73	-2	-3	9	4			.872	-5	3/O2S	-0.7
■ **DAVE HARRIS**	Harris, David Stanley "Sheriff" b: 7/14/1900, Summerfield, N.C. d: 9/18/73, Atlanta, Ga. BR/TR, 5'11", 170 lbs. Deb: 4/14/25																								
1925	Bos-N	92	340	49	90	8	7	5	36	27	44	.265	.321	.374	84	-12	-8	41	6	4	-1	.962	8	O	-0.6
1928	Bos-N	7	17	2	2	1	0	0	0	2	6	.118	.211	.176	2	-2	-2	1	0			.833	-1	/O	-0.4
1930	Chi-A	33	86	16	21	2	1	5	13	7	22	.244	.309	.465	96	-1	-1	13	0	0	0	1.000	-0	O/2	-0.2
	Was-A	73	205	40	65	19	8	4	44	28	35	.317	.399	.546	137	12	11	45	6	3	0	.983	1	O	0.8
	Yr	106	291	56	86	21	9	9	57	35	57	.296	.373	.522	125	10	11	57	6	3	0	.988	1	O/2	0.6
1931	Was-A	77	231	49	72	14	8	5	50	49	38	.312	.434	.506	146	18	17	53	7	6	-2	.950	-2	O	0.9

YEAR	TM/L	G	AB	R	H	2B	3B	HR	RBI	BB	SO	AVG	OBP	SLG	PRO+	BR	/A	RC	SB	CS	SBR	FA	FR	POS	TPR
1932	Was-A	81	156	26	51	7	4	6	29	19	34	.327	.400	.538	143	9	10	33	4	4	-1	.932	-2	O	0.4
1933	*Was-A	82	177	33	46	9	2	5	38	25	26	.260	.358	.418	106	1	2	28	3	1	0	.964	-7	O/13	-0.7
1934	Was-A	97	235	28	59	14	3	2	37	39	40	.251	.358	.362	89	-4	-3	32	2	3	-1	.973	-4	O/3	-0.9
Total	7	542	1447	243	406	74	33	32	247	196	245	.281	.368	.444	112	20	26	246	28	21		.963	-8	O/312	-0.7
■ DONALD HARRIS	Harris, Donald b: 11/12/67, Waco, Tex. BR/TR, 6'1", 185 lbs. Deb: 9/04/91																								
1991	Tex-A	18	8	4	3	0	0	1	2	1	3	.375	.444	.750	228	1	1	3	1	0	0	1.000	-5	O/D	-0.3
1992	Tex-A	24	33	3	6	1	0	0	1	0	15	.182	.182	.212	10	-4	-4	1	1	0	0	.974	-4	O	-0.8
Total	2	42	41	7	9	1	0	1	3	1	18	.220	.238	.317	55	-3	-2	4	2	0	1	.978	-9	/OD	-1.1
■ FRANK HARRIS	Harris, Frank W. b: 11/2/1858, Pittsburgh, Pa. d: 11/26/39, E.Moline, Ill. BR/TR, Deb: 4/17/1884																								
1884	Alt-U	24	95	10	25	2	1	0		3		.263	.286	.305	98	-0	-0	8				.941	-1	1/O	-0.2
■ BILLY HARRIS	Harris, James William b: 11/24/43, Hamlet, N.C. BL/TR, 6', 175 lbs. Deb: 6/16/68																								
1968	Cle-A	38	94	10	20	5	1	0	3	8	22	.213	.275	.287	71	-3	-3	7	2	0	1	.970	-1	23/S	-0.2
1969	KC-A	5	7	1	2	1	0	0	0	0	1	.286	.286	.429	97	-0	-0	1	0	0	0	1.000	-0	/2	0.0
Total	2	43	101	11	22	6	1	0	3	8	23	.218	.275	.297	73	-3	-3	8	2	0	1	.971	-1	/23S	-0.2
■ JOHN HARRIS	Harris, John Thomas b: 9/13/54, Portland, Ore. BL/TL, 6'3", 205 lbs. Deb: 9/26/79																								
1979	Cal-A	1	2	0	0	0	0	0	0	0	0	.000	.000	.000	-99	-1	-1	0	0	0	0	1.000	-0	/1	-0.1
1980	Cal-A	19	41	8	12	5	0	2	7	7	4	.293	.396	.561	163	3	4	8	0	1	-1	1.000	-0	1/O	0.2
1981	Cal-A	36	77	5	19	3	0	3	9	3	11	.247	.275	.403	93	-1	-1	7	0	0	0	.976	-4	1O/D	-0.6
Total	3	56	120	13	31	8	0	5	16	10	15	.258	.315	.450	115	2	2	15	0	1	-1	.987	-4	/1OD	-0.5
■ JOE HARRIS	Harris, Joseph "Moon" b: 5/30/1891, Coulters, Pa. d: 12/10/59, Renton, Pa. BR/TR, 5'9", 170 lbs. Deb: 6/09/14																								
1914	NY-A	2	1	0	0	0	0	0	0	3	1	.000	.800	.000	143	1	1	1	0			1.000	-1	/1O	0.0
1917	Cle-A	112	369	40	112	22	4	0	65	55	32	.304	.398	.385	129	19	16	59	11			.985	10	1/O3	2.5
1919	Cle-A	62	184	30	69	16	1	1	46	33	21	.375	.472	.489	160	19	18	43	2			.988	2	1/S	1.9
1922	Bos-A	119	408	53	129	30	9	6	54	30	15	.316	.364	.478	119	9	10	69	2	6	-3	.953	7	O1	0.7
1923	Bos-A	142	483	82	162	28	11	13	76	52	27	.335	.406	.520	142	29	29	104	7	3	0	.968	-2	*O/1	1.8
1924	Bos-A	133	491	82	148	36	9	3	77	81	25	.301	.406	.430	115	14	14	92	6	1	1	.993	6	*1/O	1.2
1925	Bos-A	8	19	4	3	0	1	1	2	5	5	.158	.333	.421	90	-0	-0	3	0	0	0	1.000	-1	/1	-0.1
	*Was-A	100	300	60	97	21	9	12	59	51	28	.323	.430	.573	156	25	26	76	5	3	-0	.989	-0	1O	1.8
	Yr	108	319	64	100	21	10	13	61	56	33	.313	.424	.564	152	24	25	79	5	3	-0	.990	-1	1O	1.7
1926	Was-A	92	257	43	79	13	9	5	55	37	9	.307	.405	.486	135	12	13	52	2	3	-1	.994	-3	1O	0.5
1927	*Pit-N	129	411	57	134	27	9	5	73	48	19	.326	.402	.472	125	20	16	78	0			.990	2	*1/O	1.0
1928	Pit-N	16	23	2	9	2	1	0	2	4	2	.391	.500	.565	171	3	3	7	0			1.000	1	/1	0.4
	Bro-N	55	89	8	21	6	1	1	8	14	4	.236	.340	.360	84	-2	-2	11	0			.958	-2	O	-0.4
	Yr	71	112	10	30	8	2	1	10	18	6	.268	.374	.402	103	1	1	17	0			.958	-0	O/1	0.0
Total	10	970	3035	461	963	201	64	47	517	413	188	.317	.404	.472	131	150	143	595	35	16		.989	20	1O/S3	11.3
■ LENNY HARRIS	Harris, Leonard Anthony b: 10/28/64, Miami, Fla. BL/TR, 5'10", 195 lbs. Deb: 9/07/88																								
1988	Cin-N	16	43	7	16	1	0	0	8	5	4	.372	.438	.395	135	3	2	9	4	1	1	1.000	1	3/2	0.4
1989	Cin-N	61	188	17	42	4	0	2	11	9	20	.223	.263	.277	52	-11	-12	12	10	6	-1	.980	1	2S3	-1.0
	LA-N	54	147	19	37	6	1	1	15	11	13	.252	.308	.327	83	-3	-3	12	4	3	-1	1.000	-7	O2/3S	-1.1
	Yr	115	335	36	79	10	1	3	26	20	33	.236	.283	.299	66	-15	-15	25	14	9	-1	.975	-5	23OS	-2.1
1990	LA-N	137	431	61	131	16	4	2	29	29	31	.304	.349	.374	102	-0	1	55	15	10	-2	.959	-8	32/OS	-0.7
1991	LA-N	145	429	59	123	16	1	3	38	37	32	.287	.350	.350	100	-0	1	52	12	3	2	.943	-1	*32S/O	0.3
1992	LA-N	135	347	28	94	11	0	0	30	24	24	.271	.320	.303	78	-10	-9	33	19	7	2	.963	17	23OS	1.1
Total	5	548	1585	191	443	54	6	8	131	115	124	.279	.332	.336	89	-23	-20	174	64	30	1	.948	4	32/SO	-1.0
■ NED HARRIS	Harris, Robert Ned b: 7/9/16, Ames, Iowa d: 12/18/76, W.Palm Beach, Fla. BL/TL, 5'11", 175 lbs. Deb: 4/20/41																								
1941	Det-A	26	61	11	13	3	1	1	4	6	13	.213	.284	.344	59	-3	-4	7	1	0	0	1.000	-2	O	-0.7
1942	Det-A	121	398	53	108	16	10	9	45	49	35	.271	.351	.430	110	9	5	63	5	4	-1	.944	-10	*O	-1.1
1943	Det-A	114	354	43	90	14	3	6	32	47	29	.254	.343	.362	99	3	0	46	6	8	-3	.961	-3	O	-1.1
1946	Det-A	1	1	0	0	0	0	0	0	0	0	.000	.000	.000	-94	-0	-0	0	0	0	0	.000	0	H	0.0
Total	4	262	814	107	211	33	14	16	81	102	77	.259	.342	.393	101	9	1	115	12	12	-4	.955	-15	O	-2.9
■ BUCKY HARRIS	Harris, Stanley Raymond b: 11/8/1896, Port Jervis, N.Y. d: 11/8/77, Bethesda, Md. BR/TR, 5'9.5", 156 lbs. Deb: 8/28/19 M																								
1919	Was-A	8	28	0	6	2	0	0	4	1	3	.214	.267	.286	56	-2	-2	2	0			.925	2	/2	0.1
1920	Was-A	136	506	76	152	26	6	1	68	41	36	.300	.377	.381	104	3	5	73	16	17	-5	.958	-10	*2	-0.6
1921	Was-A	154	584	82	169	22	8	0	54	54	39	.289	.367	.354	89	-11	-7	83	29	9	3	.959	12	*2	1.2
1922	Was-A	154	602	95	162	24	8	2	40	52	38	.269	.341	.346	84	-17	-13	75	25	11	1	.970	**26**	*2	1.8
1923	Was-A	145	532	60	150	21	13	2	70	50	29	.282	.358	.382	100	-4	0	74	23	16	-3	.961	20	*2/S	1.8
1924	*Was-A	143	544	88	146	28	9	1	58	56	41	.268	.344	.358	84	-15	-12	72	19	10	-0	.968	-13	*2M	-2.3
1925	*Was-A	144	551	91	158	30	3	1	66	64	21	.287	.370	.358	87	-10	-9	77	14	12	-3	.970	3	*2M	-0.5
1926	Was-A	141	537	94	152	39	9	1	63	58	41	.283	.363	.395	100	-2	0	80	16	11	-2	.963	-11	*2M	-0.8
1927	Was-A	128	475	98	127	20	3	1	55	66	33	.267	.363	.328	81	-11	-11	59	18	3	4	**.972**	1	*2M	-0.1
1928	Was-A	99	358	34	73	11	5	0	28	27	26	.204	.264	.263	39	-32	-32	26	5	2	0	.970	11	2/3OM	-1.8
1929	Det-A	7	11	3	1	0	0	0	0	2	2	.091	.231	.091	-14	-2	-2	1	1	0	0	.900	0	/2SM	-0.1
1931	Det-A	4	8	1	1	1	0	0	0	1	1	.125	.222	.250	23	-1	-1	0	0	0	0	1.000	0	/2M	-0.1
Total	12	1263	4736	722	1297	224	64	9	506	472	310	.274	.352	.354	86	-104	-82	623	166	91		.965	43	*2/SO3	-1.4
■ VIC HARRIS	Harris, Victor Lanier b: 3/27/50, Los Angeles, Cal. BB/TR, 6', 170 lbs. Deb: 7/21/72																								
1972	Tex-A	61	186	8	26	5	1	0	10	12	39	.140	.192	.177	11	-20	-20	7	7	3	0	.960	0	2/S	-1.9
1973	Tex-A	152	555	71	138	14	7	8	44	55	81	.249	.319	.342	90	-10	-7	58	13	12	-3	.977	2	*O32	-1.3
1974	Chi-N	62	200	18	39	6	3	0	11	29	26	.195	.297	.255	53	-11	-12	18	9	3	1	.943	-17	2	-2.7
1975	Chi-N	51	56	6	10	0	0	0	5	6	7	.179	.258	.179	22	-6	-6	3	0	0	0	.900	1	O/32	-0.6
1976	StL-N	97	259	21	59	12	3	1	19	16	55	.228	.275	.309	65	-12	-12	21	1	2	-1	.945	-5	2O3/S	-1.9
1977	SF-N	69	165	28	43	12	0	2	14	19	36	.261	.337	.370	90	-2	-2	22	2	1	0	.973	-8	2S/3O	-0.8
1978	SF-N	53	100	8	15	4	0	1	11	11	24	.150	.234	.220	29	-10	-9	6	0	0	0	.934	-6	S2/O	-1.4
1980	Mil-A	34	89	8	19	4	1	1	7	12	13	.213	.307	.315	73	-3	-3	10	4	1	1	.967	-2	O/32	-0.5
Total	8	579	1610	168	349	57	15	13	121	160	281	.217	.289	.295	65	-75	-72	145	36	22	-2	.954	-35	2O/3S	-11.1
■ CHUCK HARRISON	Harrison, Charles William b: 4/25/41, Abilene, Tex. BR/TR, 5'10", 190 lbs. Deb: 9/15/65																								
1965	Hou-N	15	45	2	9	4	0	1	9	8	9	.200	.321	.356	97	-0	-0	6	0	0	0	.983	0	1	-0.1
1966	Hou-N	119	434	52	111	23	2	9	52	37	69	.256	.317	.380	100	-4	-1	51	2	0	1	.992	4	*1	-0.4
1967	Hou-N	70	177	13	43	7	3	2	26	13	30	.243	.295	.350	87	-4	-3	18	0	0	0	.987	-0	1	-0.7
1969	KC-A	75	213	18	47	5	1	3	18	16	20	.221	.278	.296	60	-11	-12	17	1	2	-1	.993	2	1	-1.6
1971	KC-A	49	143	9	31	4	0	2	21	11	19	.217	.273	.287	59	-8	-8	12	0	0	0	.992	0	1	-1.2
Total	5	328	1012	94	241	43	6	17	126	85	147	.238	.299	.343	83	-28	-23	104	3	2	-0	.991	5	1	-4.0
■ BEN HARRISON	Harrison, Leo J. BR , Deb: 9/27/01																								
1901	Was-A	1	2	0	0	0	0	0	0	1		.000	.333	.000	-2	-0	-0	0	0			.000	-0	/O	-0.1

YEAR	TM/L	G	AB	R	H	2B	3B	HR	RBI	BB	SO	AVG	OBP	SLG	PRO+	BR	/A	RC	SB	CS	SBR	FA	FR	POS	TPR
■ **TOM HARRISON**	Harrison, Thomas James b: 1/18/45, Trail, B.C., Canada BR/TR, 6'3", 200 lbs. Deb: 5/07/65																								
1965	KC-A	2	0	0	0	0	0	0	0	0	0	—	—	—	—	0	0	0	0	0	0	.000	-0	/P	0.0
■ **RIT HARRISON**	Harrison, Washington Ritter b: 9/16/1849, Waterbury, Conn. d: 11/7/1888, Bridgeport, Conn. Deb: 5/20/1875																								
1875	NH-n	1	4	0	2	1	0	0		0		.500	.500	.750	374	1	1	2						/C	0.1
■ **SAM HARSHANY**	Harshany, Samuel b: 5/1/10, Madison, Ill. BR/TR, 6', 180 lbs. Deb: 9/28/37																								
1937	StL-A	5	11	0	1	1	0	0	0	3	0	.091	.286	.182	20	-1	-1	1	0	0	0	.905	1	/C	-0.1
1938	StL-A	11	24	2	7	0	0	0	0	3	2	.292	.370	.292	68	-1	-1	3	0	0	0	.975	-0	C	-0.1
1939	StL-A	42	145	15	35	2	0	0	15	9	8	.241	.290	.255	40	-13	-13	10	0	1	-1	.994	-2	C	-1.3
1940	StL-A	3	1	0	0	0	0	0	0	1	0	.000	.500	.000	41	0	0	0	0	0	0	.000	0	/C	0.0
Total	4	61	181	17	43	3	0	0	15	16	10	.238	.303	.254	43	-15	-16	14	0	1	-1	.983	-2	/C	-1.5
■ **JACK HARSHMAN**	Harshman, John Elvin b: 7/12/27, San Diego, Cal. BL/TL, 6'2", 185 lbs. Deb: 9/16/48																								
1948	NY-N	5	8	0	2	0	0	0	1	1	3	.250	.333	.250	60	-0	-0	1	0			1.000	0	/1	0.0
1950	NY-N	9	32	3	4	0	0	2	4	3	6	.125	.200	.313	32	-3	-3	2	0			.989	0	/1	-0.3
1952	NY-N	3	2	0	0	0	0	0	0	0	0	.000	.000	.000	-99	-1	-1	0	0	0	0	1.000	0	/P	0.0
1954	Chi-A	36	56	6	8	1	0	2	5	12	21	.143	.294	.268	53	-3	-4	5	0	0	0	.967	-1	P/1	0.0
1955	Chi-A	32	60	6	11	1	0	2	8	9	17	.183	.290	.300	57	-4	-4	6	0	0	0	.970	-0	P	0.0
1956	Chi-A	36	71	8	12	1	0	6	19	11	21	.169	.280	.437	86	-2	-2	10	0	0	0	.886	-2	P	0.0
1957	Chi-A	30	45	5	10	1	0	2	5	10	17	.222	.364	.378	102	0	0	7	0	0	0	.947	-3	P	0.0
1958	Bal-A	47	82	11	16	1	0	6	14	17	22	.195	.333	.427	114	1	2	12	0	0	0	.980	0	P/O	0.0
1959	Bal-A	15	10	3	2	0	0	1	1	2	2	.200	.333	.500	128	0	0	2	0	0	0	1.000	1	P	0.0
	Bos-A	9	7	1	1	0	0	0	2	2	2	.143	.333	.143	34	-1	-1	1	0	0	0	1.000	-1	/P	0.0
	Cle-A	21	34	3	7	1	0	0	5	5	4	.206	.308	.235	53	-2	-2	3	0	0	0	1.000	-0	P	0.0
	Yr	45	51	7	10	1	0	1	8	9	8	.196	.317	.275	65	-2	-2	5	0	0	0	1.000	1	P	0.0
1960	Cle-A	15	17	0	3	1	0	0	1	0	4	.176	.176	.235	11	-2	-2	1	0	0	0	1.000	-1	P	0.0
Total	10	258	424	46	76	7	0	21	65	72	119	.179	.298	.344	74	-16	-16	49	0	0		.962	-5	P/1O	-0.3
■ **BURT HART**	Hart, James Burton b: 6/28/1870, Brown Co., Minn. d: 1/29/21, Sacramento, Cal. BB, 6'3", 200 lbs. Deb: 6/06/01																								
1901	Bal-A	58	206	33	64	3	5	0	23	20		.311	.383	.374	106	4	2	33	7			.976	-8	1	-0.6
■ **HUB HART**	Hart, James Henry b: 2/2/1878, Everett, Mass. d: 10/10/60, Fort Wayne, Ind. BL/TR, 5'11", 170 lbs. Deb: 7/16/05																								
1905	Chi-A	11	20	3	2	0	0	0	4	3		.100	.217	.100	2	-2	-2	0	0			1.000	-2	/C	-0.4
1906	Chi-A	17	37	1	6	0	0	0	0	2		.162	.205	.162	16	-4	-3	1	0			.935	-4	C	-0.7
1907	Chi-A	29	70	6	19	1	0	0	7	5		.271	.329	.286	100	-0	0	8	1			.956	-5	C	-0.3
Total	3	57	127	10	27	1	0	0	11	10		.213	.275	.220	60	-6	-5	9	1			.957	-11	/C	-1.4
■ **MIKE HART**	Hart, James Michael b: 12/20/51, Kalamazoo, Mich. BB/TR, 6'3", 185 lbs. Deb: 6/12/80																								
1980	Tex-A	5	4	1	1	0	0	0	0	1	1	.250	.400	.250	85	-0	-0	1	0	0	0	1.000	-1	/O	-0.1
■ **JIM RAY HART**	Hart, James Ray b: 10/30/41, Hookerton, N.C. BR/TR, 5'11", 185 lbs. Deb: 7/07/63																								
1963	SF-N	7	20	1	4	1	0	0	2	3	6	.200	.360	.250	80	-0	-0	2	0	0	0	1.000	0	/3	0.0
1964	SF-N	153	566	71	162	15	6	31	81	47	94	.286	.345	.498	132	25	23	95	5	2	0	.937	5	*3/O	2.8
1965	SF-N	160	591	91	177	30	6	23	96	47	75	.299	.353	.487	130	25	24	98	6	4	-1	.919	-12	*3O	0.8
1966	SF-N★	156	578	88	165	23	4	33	93	48	75	.285	.344	.510	130	25	23	92	2	5	-2	.941	-7	*3O	1.1
1967	SF-N	158	578	98	167	26	7	29	99	77	100	.289	.376	.509	153	39	40	111	1	1	-0	.937	-14	3O	2.4
1968	SF-N	136	480	67	124	14	3	23	78	46	74	.258	.327	.444	130	17	17	66	3	1	0	.925	-16	3O	-0.2
1969	SF-N	95	236	27	60	9	0	3	26	28	49	.254	.346	.331	92	-2	-2	27	0	0	0	.943	-8	O/3	-1.3
1970	SF-N	76	255	30	72	12	1	8	37	30	29	.282	.365	.431	114	5	5	38	0	0	0	.908	-17	3O	-1.3
1971	*SF-N	31	39	5	10	0	0	2	5	6	8	.256	.356	.410	118	1	1	5	0	1	-1	.833	-1	/3O	-0.1
1972	SF-N	24	79	10	24	5	0	5	8	6	10	.304	.360	.557	155	6	5	14	0	1	-1	.886	-9	3	-0.4
1973	SF-N	5	3	0	0	0	0	0	1	3	1	.000	.500	.000	48	0	0	1	0	0	0	.600	0	/3	0.0
	NY-A	114	339	29	86	13	2	13	52	36	45	.254	.325	.419	112	3	5	42	0	2	-1	.000	0	*D	0.3
1974	NY-A	10	19	1	1	0	0	0	0	3	7	.053	.182	.053	-31	-3	-3	0	0	0	0	.000	0	/D	-0.3
Total	12	1125	3783	518	1052	148	29	170	578	380	573	.278	.348	.467	128	139	138	592	17	17	-5	.929	-76	3OD	3.8
■ **MIKE HART**	Hart, Michael Lawrence b: 2/17/58, Milwaukee, Wis. BL/TL, 5'11", 185 lbs. Deb: 5/08/84																								
1984	Min-A	13	29	0	5	0	0	0	5	1	2	.172	.200	.172	4	-4	-4	1	0	1	-1	1.000	1	O	-0.4
1987	Bal-A	34	76	7	12	2	0	4	12	6	19	.158	.220	.342	47	-6	-6	5	1	4	-2	1.000	-2	O	-1.0
Total	2	47	105	7	17	2	0	4	17	7	21	.162	.214	.295	35	-10	-10	5	1	5	-3	1.000	-1	/O	-1.4
■ **TOM HART**	Hart, Thomas Henry "Bushy" b: 6/15/1869, Canaan, N.Y. d: 9/17/39, Gardner, Mass. Deb: 4/15/1891																								
1891	Was-a	8	24	1	3	0	0	0	2	2	1	.125	.192	.125	-8	-3	-3	1	1			1.000	1	/CO	-0.2
■ **BILL HART**	Hart, William Woodrow b: 3/4/13, Wiconisco, Pa. d: 7/29/68, Lykins, Pa. BR/TR, 6', 175 lbs. Deb: 9/18/43																								
1943	Bro-N	8	19	0	3	0	0	0	1	1	2	.158	.200	.158	4	-2	-2	0	0			1.000	4	/3S	0.2
1944	Bro-N	29	90	8	16	4	2	0	4	9	7	.178	.253	.267	47	-7	-6	7	1			.941	-8	S/3	-1.3
1945	Bro-N	58	161	27	37	6	2	3	27	14	21	.230	.291	.348	78	-5	-5	17	7			.913	-2	3/S	-0.6
Total	3	95	270	35	56	10	4	3	32	24	30	.207	.272	.307	63	-14	-14	24	8			.923	-6	/3S	-1.7
■ **CHUCK HARTENSTEIN**	Hartenstein, Charles Oscar "Twiggy" b: 5/26/42, Seguin, Tex. BR/TR, 5'11", 165 lbs. Deb: 9/11/65 C																								
1965	Chi-N	1	0	0	0	0	0	0	0	0	0	—	—	—	—	0	0	0	0	0	0	.000	0	R	0.0
1966	Chi-N	5	0	0	0	0	0	0	0	0	0	—	—	—	—	0	0	0	0	0	0	1.000	0	/P	0.0
1967	Chi-N	45	16	0	1	0	0	0	1	0	9	.063	.063	.063	-61	-3	-3	0	0	0	0	.950	-0	P	0.0
1968	Chi-N	28	2	0	0	0	0	0	0	0	0	.000	.000	.000	-94	-0	-0	0	0	0	0	.818	-0	P	0.0
1969	Pit-N	56	14	0	1	0	0	0	0	1	8	.071	.133	.071	-42	-3	-3	0	0	0	0	1.000	1	P	0.0
1970	Pit-N	17	1	1	0	0	0	0	0	0	0	.000	.000	.000	-99	-0	-0	0	0	0	0	.900	1	P	0.0
	StL-N	6	2	0	0	0	0	0	0	1	2	.000	.333	.000	-3	-0	-0	0	0	0	0	1.000	0	/P	0.0
	Yr	23	3	1	0	0	0	0	0	1	2	.000	.250	.000	-27	-1	-1	0	0	0	0	.923	1	P	0.0
	Bos-A	17	2	0	0	0	0	0	0	1	2	.000	.333	.000	-0	-0	-0	0	0	0	0	1.000	-1	P	0.0
1977	Tor-A	13	0	0	0	0	0	0	0	0	0	—	—	—	—	0	0	0	0	0	0	1.000	-0	P	0.0
Total	7	188	37	1	2	0	0	0	1	3	21	.054	.125	.054	-47	-7	-7	0	0	0	0	.952	2	P	0.0
■ **BRUCE HARTFORD**	Hartford, Bruce Daniel b: 5/14/1892, Chicago, Ill. d: 5/25/75, Los Angeles, Cal. BR/TR, 6'0.5", 190 lbs. Deb: 6/03/14																								
1914	Cle-A	8	22	5	4	1	0	0	0	4	9	.182	.308	.227	59	-1	-1	2	0			.913	-3	/S	-0.4
■ **CHRIS HARTJE**	Hartje, Christian Henry b: 3/25/15, San Francisco, Cal d: 6/26/46, Seattle, Wash. BR/TR, 5'10.5", 165 lbs. Deb: 9/09/39																								
1939	Bro-N	9	16	2	5	1	0	0	5	1	0	.313	.353	.375	92	-0	-0	2	0			.909	-2	/C	-0.2
■ **GROVER HARTLEY**	Hartley, Grover Allen "Slick" b: 7/2/1888, Osgood, Ind. d: 10/19/64, Daytona Beach, Fla BR/TR, 5'11", 175 lbs. Deb: 5/13/11 C																								
1911	NY-N	11	18	1	4	2	0	0	1	1	1	.222	.263	.333	64	-1	-1	2	1			.962	3	C	0.2
1912	NY-N	25	34	3	8	2	1	0	7	0	4	.235	.257	.353	64	-2	-2	3	2			.960	2	C	0.1
1913	NY-N	23	19	4	6	0	0	0	0	1	2	.316	.350	.316	90	-0	-0	3	4			.978	3	C/1	0.3
1914	StL-F	86	212	24	61	13	2	1	25	12	26	.288	.329	.382	97	0	-1	30	4			.956	-9	C2/13O	-0.8
1915	StL-F	120	394	47	108	21	6	1	50	42	21	.274	.356	.365	107	7	4	58	10			.972	-7	*C/1	0.7

YEAR	TM/L	G	AB	R	H	2B	3B	HR	RBI	BB	SO	AVG	OBP	SLG	PRO+	BR	/A	RC	SB	CS	SBR	FA	FR	POS	TPR
1916	StL-A	89	222	19	50	8	0	0	12	30	24	.225	.325	.261	80	-5	-4	21	4			.968	1	C	0.2
1917	StL-A	19	13	2	3	0	0	0	0	2	1	.231	.333	.231	75	-0	-0	1	0			.875	1	/CS3	0.1
1924	NY-N	4	7	1	2	1	0	0	1	1	0	.286	.375	.429	118	0	0	1	1	0	0	1.000	-0	/C	0.1
1925	NY-N	46	95	9	30	1	1	0	8	8	3	.316	.375	.347	89	-2	-1	13	2	0	1	.974	4	C/1	0.5
1926	NY-N	13	21	0	1	0	0	0	0	5	0	.048	.231	.048	-22	-4	-3	0	0			1.000	0	C	-0.3
1927	Bos-A	103	244	23	67	11	0	1	31	22	14	.275	.337	.332	76	-9	-8	28	1	0	0	.967	-13	C	-1.5
1929	Cle-A	24	33	2	9	0	1	0	8	2	1	.273	.314	.333	64	-2	-2	3	0	0	0	1.000	-3	C	-0.4
1930	Cle-A	1	4	0	3	0	0	0	1	0	0	.750	.750	.750	271	1	1	2	0	0	0	.750	-0	/C	0.1
1934	StL-A	5	3	0	1	1	0	0	0	1	0	.333	.500	.667	183	0	0	1	0	0	0	1.000	0	/C	0.1
Total	14	569	1319	135	353	60	11	3	144	127	97	.268	.339	.337	89	-15	-17	167	29	0		.968	-18	C/123OS	-0.6

■ CHICK HARTLEY Hartley, Walter Scott b: 8/22/1880, Philadelphia, Pa. d: 7/18/48, Philadelphia, Pa. BR/TR, 5'8", 180 lbs. Deb: 6/04/02

YEAR	TM/L	G	AB	R	H	2B	3B	HR	RBI	BB	SO	AVG	OBP	SLG	PRO+	BR	/A	RC	SB	CS	SBR	FA	FR	POS	TPR
1902	NY-N	1	4	0	0	0	0	0	0	0		.000	.000	.000	-99	-1	-1	0	0			1.000	-0	/O	-0.1

■ FRED HARTMAN Hartman, Frederick Orrin "Dutch" b: 4/25/1868, Allegheny, Pa. d: 11/11/38, McKeesport, Pa. BR/TR, 5'8", 170 lbs. Deb: 7/26/1894

YEAR	TM/L	G	AB	R	H	2B	3B	HR	RBI	BB	SO	AVG	OBP	SLG	PRO+	BR	/A	RC	SB	CS	SBR	FA	FR	POS	TPR
1894	Pit-N	49	182	41	58	4	7	2	20	16	11	.319	.389	.451	105	1	2	38	12			.876	-4	3	-0.2
1897	StL-N	124	516	67	158	21	8	2	67	26		.306	.350	.390	97	-4	-3	79	18			.867	-4	*3	-0.3
1898	NY-N	123	475	57	129	16	11	2	88	25		.272	.312	.364	97	-6	-4	59	11			.882	9	*3	0.6
1899	NY-N	50	174	25	41	3	5	1	16	12		.236	.307	.328	77	-6	-5	19	2			.886	-4	3	-0.8
1901	Chi-A	120	473	77	146	23	13	3	89	25		.309	.355	.431	120	10	12	86	31			.894	-5	*3	0.7
1902	StL-N	114	416	30	90	10	3	0	52	14		.216	.249	.255	58	-22	-20	32	14			.908	-4	*3/S1	-2.5
Total	6	580	2236	297	622	77	47	10	332	118	11	.278	.325	.368	95	-27	-18	313	88			.886	-12	3/S1	-2.5

■ J C HARTMAN Hartman, J C b: 4/15/34, Cottonton, Ala. BR/TR, 6', 175 lbs. Deb: 7/21/62

YEAR	TM/L	G	AB	R	H	2B	3B	HR	RBI	BB	SO	AVG	OBP	SLG	PRO+	BR	/A	RC	SB	CS	SBR	FA	FR	POS	TPR
1962	Hou-N	51	148	11	33	5	0	0	5	4	16	.223	.248	.257	39	-13	-12	9	1	1	-0	.972	7	S	-0.2
1963	Hou-N	39	90	2	11	1	0	0	3	2	13	.122	.151	.133	-19	-13	-13	2	1	0	0	.950	0	S	-1.2
Total	2	90	238	13	44	6	0	0	8	6	29	.185	.211	.210	18	-27	-25	10	2	1	0	.964	7	/S	-1.4

■ GABBY HARTNETT Hartnett, Charles Leo b: 12/20/1900, Woonsocket, R.I. d: 12/20/72, Park Ridge, Ill. BR/TR, 6'1", 195 lbs. Deb: 4/12/22 MCH

YEAR	TM/L	G	AB	R	H	2B	3B	HR	RBI	BB	SO	AVG	OBP	SLG	PRO+	BR	/A	RC	SB	CS	SBR	FA	FR	POS	TPR
1922	Chi-N	31	72	4	14	1	1	0	4	6	8	.194	.256	.236	27	-8	-8	5	1	0	0	.982	6	C	-0.1
1923	Chi-N	85	231	28	62	12	2	8	39	25	22	.268	.347	.442	107	2	2	37	4	0	1	.994	4	C1	0.7
1924	Chi-N	111	354	56	106	17	7	16	67	39	37	.299	.377	.523	137	19	18	72	10	2	2	.963	-4	*C	2.3
1925	Chi-N	117	398	61	115	28	3	24	67	36	77	.289	.351	.555	126	14	13	75	1	5	-3	.958	10	*C	2.5
1926	Chi-N	93	284	35	78	25	3	8	41	32	37	.275	.352	.468	118	7	7	46	0			.978	5	C	1.7
1927	Chi-N	127	449	56	132	32	5	10	80	44	42	.294	.361	.454	117	10	10	73	2			.973	4	*C	2.3
1928	Chi-N	120	388	61	117	26	9	14	57	65	32	.302	.404	.523	143	24	25	83	3			**.989**	9	*C	4.2
1929	*Chi-N	25	22	2	6	2	1	1	9	5	5	.273	.407	.591	144	2	2	5	1			1.000	-0	/C	0.1
1930	Chi-N	141	508	84	172	31	3	37	122	55	62	.339	.404	.630	144	35	35	125	0			**.989**	3	*C	4.4
1931	Chi-N	116	380	53	107	32	1	8	70	52	48	.282	.370	.434	113	9	8	64	3			.981	2	*C	1.7
1932	*Chi-N	121	406	52	110	25	3	12	52	51	59	.271	.354	.436	112	7	7	66	0			.982	6	*C/1	1.9
1933	Chi-N★	140	490	55	135	21	4	16	88	37	51	.276	.326	.433	115	9	9	67	1			.989	7	*C	2.6
1934	Chi-N★	130	438	58	131	21	1	22	90	37	46	.299	.358	.502	130	16	17	77	0			**.996**	14	*C	3.5
1935	*Chi-N★	116	413	67	142	32	6	13	91	41	46	.344	.404	.545	152	30	30	91	1			.984	15	*C	4.8
1936	Chi-N★	121	424	49	130	25	6	7	64	30	36	.307	.361	.443	113	9	8	68	0			**.991**	9	*C	2.1
1937	Chi-N★	110	356	47	126	21	6	12	82	43	19	.354	.424	.548	156	31	29	85	0			**.996**	1	*C	3.4
1938	*Chi-N☆	88	299	40	82	19	1	10	59	48	17	.274	.380	.445	123	12	11	53	1			**.995**	-4	CM	1.1
1939	Chi-N	97	306	36	85	18	2	12	59	37	32	.278	.358	.467	118	8	8	50	0			.992	-8	CM	0.4
1940	Chi-N	37	64	3	17	3	0	1	12	8	7	.266	.347	.359	97	-0	-0	8	0			.951	1	C/1M	0.2
1941	NY-N	64	150	20	45	5	0	5	26	12	14	.300	.356	.433	119	4	4	22	0			.994	-3	C	0.3
Total	20	1990	6432	867	1912	396	64	236	1179	703	697	.297	.370	.489	126	241	234	1173	28	7		.984	74	*C/1	40.1

■ PAT HARTNETT Hartnett, Patrick J. "Happy" b: 10/20/1863, Boston, Mass. d: 4/10/35, Boston, Mass. 6'1", 175 lbs. Deb: 4/18/1890

YEAR	TM/L	G	AB	R	H	2B	3B	HR	RBI	BB	SO	AVG	OBP	SLG	PRO+	BR	/A	RC	SB	CS	SBR	FA	FR	POS	TPR
1890	StL-a	14	53	6	10	2	1	0		6		.189	.283	.264	56	-2	-4	4	1			.954	-1	1	-0.4

■ GREG HARTS Harts, Gregory Rudolph b: 4/21/50, Atlanta, Ga. BL/TL, 6', 168 lbs. Deb: 9/15/73

YEAR	TM/L	G	AB	R	H	2B	3B	HR	RBI	BB	SO	AVG	OBP	SLG	PRO+	BR	/A	RC	SB	CS	SBR	FA	FR	POS	TPR
1973	NY-N	3	2	0	1	0	0	0	0	0	0	.500	.500	.500	181	0	0	1	0	0	0	.000	0	H	0.0

■ TOPSY HARTSEL Hartsel, Tully Frederick b: 6/26/1874, Polk, Ohio d: 10/14/44, Toledo, Ohio BL/TL, 5'5", 155 lbs. Deb: 9/14/1898

YEAR	TM/L	G	AB	R	H	2B	3B	HR	RBI	BB	SO	AVG	OBP	SLG	PRO+	BR	/A	RC	SB	CS	SBR	FA	FR	POS	TPR
1898	Lou-N	22	71	11	23	0	0	0	9	11		.324	.422	.324	116	2	2	11	2			.931	-2	O	-0.1
1899	Lou-N	30	75	8	18	1	1	1	7	11		.240	.345	.320	83	-1	-1	9	1			.927	-2	O	-0.4
1900	Cin-N	18	64	10	21	2	1	2	5	8		.328	.403	.484	148	4	4	16	7			.957	-5	O	-0.2
1901	Chi-N	140	558	111	187	25	16	7	54	74		.335	.414	.475	164	43	46	130	41			.951	-1	*O	3.3
1902	Phi-A	137	545	**109**	154	20	12	5	58	**87**		.283	.384	.391	110	14	11	103	**47**			.955	-1	*O	0.1
1903	Phi-A	98	373	65	116	19	14	5	26	49		.311	.391	.477	152	28	26	77	13			.968	-6	O	1.5
1904	Phi-A	147	534	79	135	17	12	2	25	75		.253	.347	.341	113	14	11	73	19			.959	-4	*O	-0.2
1905	*Phi-A	150	538	88	148	22	8	0	28	**121**		.275	**.408**	.346	138	33	32	96	37			.939	-7	*O	1.9
1906	Phi-A	144	533	96	136	21	9	1	30	**88**		.255	.362	.334	115	15	14	79	31			.969	0	*O	0.7
1907	Phi-A	143	507	93	142	23	6	3	29	**106**		.280	**.405**	.367	143	33	32	87	20			.967	-11	*O	1.6
1908	Phi-A	129	460	73	112	16	6	4	29	**93**		.243	.371	.330	120	19	16	62	15			.960	-5	*O	0.6
1909	Phi-A	83	267	30	72	4	4	1	18	48		.270	.381	.326	121	10	9	35	3			.966	-4	O	0.3
1910	*Phi-A	90	285	45	63	10	3	0	22	58		.221	.353	.277	99	2	3	32	11			.945	-6	O	-0.8
1911	Phi-A	25	38	8	9	2	0	0	1	8		.237	.396	.289	94	0	0	5	0			.941	1	/O	0.1
Total	14	1356	4848	826	1336	182	92	31	341	837		.276	.383	.370	128	217	203	815	247			.956	-53	*O	8.4

■ ROY HARTSFIELD Hartsfield, Roy Thomas "Spec" b: 10/25/25, Chattahoochee, Ga. BR/TR, 5'9", 165 lbs. Deb: 4/28/50 MC

YEAR	TM/L	G	AB	R	H	2B	3B	HR	RBI	BB	SO	AVG	OBP	SLG	PRO+	BR	/A	RC	SB	CS	SBR	FA	FR	POS	TPR
1950	Bos-N	107	419	62	116	15	2	7	24	27	61	.277	.322	.372	88	-11	-8	52	7			.949	-24	2	-2.7
1951	Bos-N	120	450	63	122	11	2	6	31	41	73	.271	.333	.344	89	-10	-6	56	7	2	1	.969	-5	*2	-0.5
1952	Bos-N	38	107	13	28	4	3	0	4	5	12	.262	.295	.355	82	-3	-3	11	0	0	0	.950	-6	2	-0.7
Total	3	265	976	138	266	30	7	13	59	73	146	.273	.324	.358	88	-25	-17	119	14	2		.959	-34	2	-3.9

■ CLINT HARTUNG Hartung, Clinton Clarence "Floppy" or "The Hondo Hurricane" b: 8/10/22, Hondo, Tex. BR/TR, 6'4", 215 lbs. Deb: 4/15/47

YEAR	TM/L	G	AB	R	H	2B	3B	HR	RBI	BB	SO	AVG	OBP	SLG	PRO+	BR	/A	RC	SB	CS	SBR	FA	FR	POS	TPR
1947	NY-N	34	94	13	29	4	3	4	13	3	21	.309	.330	.543	127	3	3	16	0			1.000	-2	P/O	-0.1
1948	NY-N	43	56	5	10	1	1	0	3	7	24	.179	.270	.232	37	-5	-5	4	0			1.000	-0	P	0.0
1949	NY-N	38	63	7	12	0	0	4	7	4	21	.190	.239	.381	64	-4	-4	6	0			.957	2	P	0.0
1950	NY-N	32	43	7	13	2	1	3	10	1	13	.302	.318	.605	136	2	2	8	0			.939	3	P/O1	0.0
1951	*NY-N	21	44	4	9	1	0	0	2	1	9	.205	.222	.227	21	-5	-5	2	0	0	0	1.000	-2	O	-0.8
1952	NY-N	28	78	6	17	2	1	3	8	9	24	.218	.299	.385	88	-1	-1	10	0	0	0	.932	-1	O	-0.3
Total	6	196	378	42	90	10	6	14	43	25	112	.238	.285	.407	84	-10	-10	46	0	0		.972	-2	P/O1	-1.2

■ ROY HARTZELL Hartzell, Roy Allen b: 7/6/1881, Golden, Colo. d: 11/6/61, Golden, Colo. BL/TR, 5'8.5", 155 lbs. Deb: 4/17/06

YEAR	TM/L	G	AB	R	H	2B	3B	HR	RBI	BB	SO	AVG	OBP	SLG	PRO+	BR	/A	RC	SB	CS	SBR	FA	FR	POS	TPR
1906	StL-A	113	404	43	86	7	0	0	24	19		.213	.266	.230	58	-20	-18	32	21			.889	-2	*3/S2	-1.8
1907	StL-A	60	220	20	52	3	5	0	13	11		.236	.285	.295	86	-4	-4	22	7			.911	-0	32/SO	-0.3
1908	StL-A	115	422	41	112	5	6	2	32	19		.265	.302	.320	102	0	-0	48	24			.943	-6	OS/32	-1.0
1909	StL-A	152	595	64	161	12	5	0	32	29		.271	.312	.308	103	-3	1	61	14			.940	4	OS/2	0.3
1910	StL-A	151	542	52	118	13	5	2	30	49		.218	.290	.271	81	-15	-11	48	18			.929	1	3SO	-0.8

YEAR	TM/L	G	AB	R	H	2B	3B	HR	RBI	BB	SO	AVG	OBP	SLG	PRO+	BR	/A	RC	SB	CS	SBR	FA	FR	POS	TPR
1911	NY-A	144	527	67	156	17	11	3	91	63		.296	.375	.387	106	10	5	86	22			.936	-12	*3S/O	-0.5
1912	NY-A	125	416	50	113	10	11	1	38	64		.272	.370	.356	102	6	3	63	20			.906	-7	3OS/2	-0.6
1913	NY-A	141	490	60	127	18	1	0	38	67	40	.259	.353	.300	91	-3	-3	60	26			.942	-0	2O3/S	-0.5
1914	NY-A	137	481	55	112	15	9	1	32	68	38	.233	.335	.308	94	-2	-2	52	22	25	-8	.973	0	*O/2	-1.8
1915	NY-A	119	387	39	97	11	2	3	60	57	37	.251	.351	.313	99	1	1	42	7	19	-9	.963	-3	*O/23	-1.7
1916	NY-A	33	64	12	12	1	0	0	7	9	3	.188	.297	.203	49	-3	-4	5	1			1.000	-6	O	-1.2
Total	11	1290	4548	503	1146	112	55	12	397	455	118	.252	.327	.309	93	-32	-30	518	182	44		.959	-32	O3S2	-9.9

■ **LUTHER HARVEL** Harvel, Luther Raymond "Red" b: 9/30/05, Cambria, Ill. d: 4/10/86, Kansas City, Mo. BR/TR, 5'11", 180 lbs. Deb: 7/31/28

YEAR	TM/L	G	AB	R	H	2B	3B	HR	RBI	BB	SO	AVG	OBP	SLG	PRO+	BR	/A	RC	SB	CS	SBR	FA	FR	POS	TPR
1928	Cle-A	40	136	12	30	6	1	0	12	4	17	.221	.264	.279	42	-11	-12	10	1	1	-0	.948	-2	O	-1.5

■ **ERWIN HARVEY** Harvey, Ervin King "Zaza" b: 1/5/1879, Saratoga, Cal. d: 6/3/54, Santa Monica, Cal. BL/TL, 6', 190 lbs. Deb: 5/03/00

YEAR	TM/L	G	AB	R	H	2B	3B	HR	RBI	BB	SO	AVG	OBP	SLG	PRO+	BR	/A	RC	SB	CS	SBR	FA	FR	POS	TPR
1900	Chi-N	2	3	0	0	0	0	0	0	0		.000	.000	.000	-99	-1	-1	0	0			1.000	-0	/P	0.0
1901	Chi-A	17	40	11	10	3	1	0	3	2		.250	.302	.375	89	-1	-1	5	1			.930	2	P	0.0
	Cle-A	45	170	21	60	5	5	1	24	9		.353	.392	.459	141	8	9	37	15			.890	2	O	0.7
	Yr	62	210	32	70	8	6	1	27	11		.333	.375	.443	131	7	8	42	16			.890	3	OP	0.7
1902	Cle-A	12	46	5	16	2	0	0	5	3		.348	.388	.391	121	1	1	8	1			1.000	0	O	0.1
Total	3	76	259	37	86	10	6	1	32	14		.332	.373	.429	127	7	9	50	17			.907	4	/OP	0.8

■ **ZIGGY HASBROOK** Hasbrook, Robert Lyndon "Ziggy" b: 11/21/1893, Grundy Center, Ia. d: 2/9/76, Garland, Tex. BR/TR, 6'1", 180 lbs. Deb: 9/06/16

YEAR	TM/L	G	AB	R	H	2B	3B	HR	RBI	BB	SO	AVG	OBP	SLG	PRO+	BR	/A	RC	SB	CS	SBR	FA	FR	POS	TPR
1916	Chi-A	9	8	1	1	0	0	0	0	1	2	.125	.222	.125	4	-1	-1	0	0			1.000	1	/1	0.0
1917	Chi-A	2	1	1	0	0	0	0	0	0	0	.000	.000	.000	-98	-0	-0	0	0			1.000	1	/2	0.0
Total	2	11	9	2	1	0	0	0	0	1	2	.111	.200	.111	-6	-1	-1	0	0				1	/12	0.0

■ **BILL HASELMAN** Haselman, William Joseph b: 5/25/66, Long Branch, N.J. BR/TR, 6'3", 205 lbs. Deb: 9/03/90

YEAR	TM/L	G	AB	R	H	2B	3B	HR	RBI	BB	SO	AVG	OBP	SLG	PRO+	BR	/A	RC	SB	CS	SBR	FA	FR	POS	TPR
1990	Tex-A	7	13	0	2	0	0	0	3	1	5	.154	.214	.154	5	-2	-2	0	0	0	0	1.000	0	/CD	-0.1
1992	Sea-A	8	19	1	5	0	0	0	0	0	7	.263	.263	.263	47	-1	-1	1	0	0	0	1.000	-1	/CO	-0.2
Total	2	15	32	1	7	0	0	0	3	1	12	.219	.242	.219	30	-3	-3	2	0	0	0	1.000	-1	/CDO	-0.3

■ **DON HASENMAYER** Hasenmayer, Donald Irvin b: 4/4/27, Roslyn, Pa. BR/TR, 5'10.5", 180 lbs. Deb: 5/02/45

YEAR	TM/L	G	AB	R	H	2B	3B	HR	RBI	BB	SO	AVG	OBP	SLG	PRO+	BR	/A	RC	SB	CS	SBR	FA	FR	POS	TPR
1945	Phi-N	5	18	1	2	0	0	0	1	2	1	.111	.200	.111	-13	-3	-3	1	0			.920	3	/23	0.0
1946	Phi-N	6	12	0	1	1	0	0	0	0	2	.083	.083	.167	-31	-2	-2	0	0			1.000	2	/3	0.0
Total	2	11	30	1	3	1	0	0	1	2	3	.100	.156	.133	-19	-5	-5	1	0			1.000	5	/32	0.0

■ **MICKEY HASLIN** Haslin, Michael Joseph b: 10/31/10, Wilkes-Barre, Pa. BR/TR, 5'8", 165 lbs. Deb: 9/07/33

YEAR	TM/L	G	AB	R	H	2B	3B	HR	RBI	BB	SO	AVG	OBP	SLG	PRO+	BR	/A	RC	SB	CS	SBR	FA	FR	POS	TPR
1933	Phi-N	26	89	3	21	2	0	0	9	3	5	.236	.261	.258	43	-6	-7	6	1			.956	-4	2	-1.1
1934	Phi-N	72	166	28	44	8	2	1	11	16	13	.265	.330	.355	74	-4	-7	19	1			.941	-3	32/S	-0.7
1935	Phi-N	110	407	53	108	17	3	3	52	19	25	.265	.300	.344	66	-16	-21	42	5			.931	-3	S3/2	-1.8
1936	Phi-N	16	64	6	22	1	1	0	6	3	5	.344	.373	.391	96	1	-0	9	0			.938	-5	2/3	-0.4
	Bos-N	36	104	14	29	1	2	2	11	5	9	.279	.312	.385	93	-2	-1	11	0			.892	-5	3/2	-0.5
	Yr	52	168	20	51	2	3	2	17	8	14	.304	.335	.387	95	-2	-1	20	0			.854	-10	32	-0.9
1937	NY-N	27	42	8	8	1	0	0	5	9	3	.190	.333	.214	51	-2	-3	3	1			.920	6	/S23	0.4
1938	NY-N	31	102	13	33	3	0	3	15	4	4	.324	.361	.441	119	3	2	16	0			.902	-2	32	0.1
Total	6	318	974	125	265	33	8	9	109	59	64	.272	.316	.350	74	-27	-37	108	8			.927	-15	S/23	-4.0

■ **PETE HASNEY** Hasney, Peter James b: 5/26/1865, England d: 5/24/08, Philadelphia, Pa. Deb: 9/13/1890

YEAR	TM/L	G	AB	R	H	2B	3B	HR	RBI	BB	SO	AVG	OBP	SLG	PRO+	BR	/A	RC	SB	CS	SBR	FA	FR	POS	TPR
1890	Phi-a	2	7	1	1	0	0	0		1		.143	.250	.143	18	-1	-1	0	0			.000	-1	/O	-0.2

■ **BILL HASSAMAER** Hassamaer, William Louis "Roaring Bill" b: 7/26/1864, St.Louis, Mo. d: 5/29/10, St.Louis, Mo. 6', 180 lbs. Deb: 4/19/1894

YEAR	TM/L	G	AB	R	H	2B	3B	HR	RBI	BB	SO	AVG	OBP	SLG	PRO+	BR	/A	RC	SB	CS	SBR	FA	FR	POS	TPR
1894	Was-N	118	494	106	159	33	17	4	90	41	20	.322	.375	.482	110	4	7	99	16			.916	4	O32/S	0.6
1895	Was-N	85	358	42	100	18	4	1	60	26	13	.279	.328	.360	80	-11	-10	47	8			.964	-7	O/1S3	-1.9
	Lou-N	23	96	7	20	2	2	0	14	3	4	.208	.232	.271	33	-10	-9	6	0			.980	3	1/2S	-0.4
	Yr	108	454	49	120	20	6	1	74	29	17	.264	.308	.341	71	-21	-19	53	8			.964	-4	O1/S32	-2.3
1896	Lou-N	30	106	8	26	5	0	2	14	14	7	.245	.333	.349	85	-3	-2	13	1			.976	6	1	0.4
Total	3	256	1054	163	305	58	23	7	178	84	44	.289	.342	.408	92	-20	-14	165	25			.938	6	O/132S	-1.3

■ **BUDDY HASSETT** Hassett, John Aloysius b: 9/5/11, New York, N.Y. BL/TL, 5'11", 180 lbs. Deb: 4/14/36

YEAR	TM/L	G	AB	R	H	2B	3B	HR	RBI	BB	SO	AVG	OBP	SLG	PRO+	BR	/A	RC	SB	CS	SBR	FA	FR	POS	TPR
1936	Bro-N	156	635	79	197	29	11	3	82	35	17	.310	.350	.405	102	2	1	92	5			.983	5	*1	-0.9
1937	Bro-N	137	556	71	169	31	6	1	53	20	19	.304	.334	.387	94	-4	-5	71	13			.984	9	*1/O	-1.2
1938	Bro-N	115	335	49	98	11	6	0	40	32	19	.293	.356	.361	95	-0	-1	44	3			.945	-2	O/1	-0.7
1939	Bos-N	147	590	72	182	15	3	2	60	29	14	.308	.342	.354	94	-10	-5	72	13			.985	9	*1O	-1.0
1940	Bos-N	124	458	59	107	19	4	0	27	25	16	.234	.273	.293	59	-28	-24	34	4			.979	7	1O	-2.8
1941	Bos-N	118	405	59	120	9	4	1	33	36	15	.296	.354	.346	102	-1	1	51	10			.991	7	1	0.1
1942	*NY-A	132	538	80	153	16	6	5	48	32	16	.284	.325	.364	95	-6	-4	65	5	5	-2	.991	11	*1	-0.3
Total	7	929	3517	469	1026	130	40	12	343	209	116	.292	.333	.362	92	-47	-38	431	53	5		.985	45	1O	-6.8

■ **RON HASSEY** Hassey, Ronald William b: 2/27/53, Tucson, Ariz. BL/TR, 6'2", 200 lbs. Deb: 4/23/78

YEAR	TM/L	G	AB	R	H	2B	3B	HR	RBI	BB	SO	AVG	OBP	SLG	PRO+	BR	/A	RC	SB	CS	SBR	FA	FR	POS	TPR
1978	Cle-A	25	74	5	15	0	0	2	9	5	7	.203	.262	.284	54	-5	-4	6	2	0	1	.993	5	C	0.2
1979	Cle-A	75	223	20	64	14	0	4	32	19	19	.287	.343	.404	100	0	0	30	1	0	0	.992	6	C/1	0.9
1980	Cle-A	130	390	43	124	18	4	8	65	49	51	.318	.395	.446	130	18	17	68	0	2	-1	.993	-7	*C/1D	1.3
1981	Cle-A	61	190	8	44	4	0	1	25	17	11	.232	.301	.268	66	-8	-8	16	0	1	-1	.991	8	C/1D	0.2
1982	Cle-A	113	323	33	81	18	0	5	34	53	32	.251	.358	.353	97	0	0	42	3	2	-0	.993	8	*C/1D	1.2
1983	Cle-A	117	341	48	92	21	0	6	42	38	35	.270	.346	.384	97	1	-1	45	2	2	-1	.995	-3	*C/D	0.0
1984	Cle-A	48	149	11	38	5	1	0	19	15	26	.255	.323	.302	73	-5	-5	15	1	0	0	1.000	-1	C/1D	-0.4
	Chi-N	19	33	5	11	0	0	2	5	4	6	.333	.405	.515	144	3	2	6	0	1	-1	1.000	-0	/C1	0.2
1985	NY-A	92	267	31	79	16	1	13	42	28	21	.296	.369	.509	141	14	15	49	0	0	0	.984	-2	C/1D	1.6
1986	NY-A	64	191	23	57	14	0	6	29	24	16	.298	.382	.466	131	8	9	33	1	1	-0	.985	-13	C/D	-0.2
	Chi-A	49	150	22	53	11	1	3	20	22	11	.353	.439	.500	150	12	12	32	0	0	0	1.000	1	DC	1.3
	Yr	113	341	45	110	25	1	9	49	46	27	.323	.408	.481	140	21	20	65	1	1	-0	.988	-12	CD	1.1
1987	Chi-A	49	145	15	31	9	0	3	12	17	11	.214	.305	.338	69	-6	-7	13	0	0	0	1.000	1	CD	-0.4
1988	*Oak-A	107	323	32	83	15	0	7	45	30	42	.257	.328	.368	98	-2	-1	39	2	0	1	.994	-1	C/D	0.5
1989	*Oak-A	97	268	29	61	12	0	5	23	24	45	.228	.294	.328	78	-9	-8	25	1	0	0	.991	7	C/1D	0.3
1990	*Oak-A	94	254	18	54	7	0	5	22	27	29	.213	.291	.299	68	-12	-10	23	0	0	0	.997	3	CD/1	-0.4
1991	Mon-N	52	119	5	27	8	0	1	14	13	16	.227	.303	.319	76	-4	-4	11	1	1	-0	.989	-4	C	-0.7
Total	14	1192	3440	348	914	172	7	71	438	385	378	.266	.343	.382	100	6	8	453	14	10	-2	.993	9	C/D1	5.6

■ **JOE HASSLER** Hassler, Joseph Frederick b: 4/7/05, Ft.Smith, Ark. d: 9/4/71, Duncan, Okla. BR/TR, 6', 165 lbs. Deb: 5/26/28

YEAR	TM/L	G	AB	R	H	2B	3B	HR	RBI	BB	SO	AVG	OBP	SLG	PRO+	BR	/A	RC	SB	CS	SBR	FA	FR	POS	TPR
1928	Phi-A	28	34	5	9	2	0	0	3	2	4	.265	.306	.324	64	-2	-2	3	0	1	-1	.879	1	S	0.0
1929	Phi-A	4	4	1	0	0	0	0	0	0	2	.000	.000	.000	-97	-1	-1	0	0	0	0	.600	-0	/S	-0.1
1930	StL-A	5	8	3	2	0	0	0	1	0	1	.250	.250	.250	26	-1	-1	0	0	0	0	1.000	1	/S	0.0
Total	3	37	46	9	11	2	0	0	4	2	7	.239	.271	.283	43	-4	-4	4	0	1	-1	.875	2	/S	-0.1

■ **GENE HASSON** Hasson, Charles Eugene b: 7/20/15, Connellsville, Pa BL/TL, 6', 197 lbs. Deb: 9/09/37

YEAR	TM/L	G	AB	R	H	2B	3B	HR	RBI	BB	SO	AVG	OBP	SLG	PRO+	BR	/A	RC	SB	CS	SBR	FA	FR	POS	TPR
1937	Phi-A	28	98	12	30	6	3	3	14	13	14	.306	.387	.520	129	4	4	20	0	0	0	1.000	-2	1	-0.1
1938	Phi-A	19	69	10	19	6	2	1	12	12	7	.275	.383	.464	114	1	2	13	0	0	0	.958	-4	1	-0.4
Total	2	47	167	22	49	12	5	4	26	25	21	.293	.385	.497	123	5	6	33	0	0	0	.985	-6	/1	-0.5

YEAR	TM/L	G	AB	R	H	2B	3B	HR	RBI	BB	SO	AVG	OBP	SLG	PRO+	BR	/A	RC	SB	CS	SBR	FA	FR	POS	TPR
■ SCOTT HASTINGS	Hastings, Winfield Scott b: 8/10/1847, Hillsboro, Ohio d: 8/14/07, Sawtelle, Cal. BR/TR, 5'8", 161 lbs. Deb: 5/06/1871 M																								
1871	Rok-n	25	118	27	30	6	4	0	20	2	4	.254	.267	.373	85	-3	-2	15	11					*C/2OM	-0.1
1872	Cle-n	22	117	34	45	6	0	0	16	3	2	.385	.400	.436	166	8	9	22						C/O2M	0.7
	Bal-n	13	61	16	19	3	1	0	4	1	2	.311	.323	.393	114	1	1	8						/C2	0.0
	Yr	35	178	50	64	9	1	0	20	4	4	.360	.374	.421	147	9	10	30						C/O2	0.7
1873	Bal-n	30	146	41	41	5	0	0	12	4	1	.281	.300	.315	82	-3	-3	15						CO/2	-0.2
1874	Har-n	52	248	60	80	13	1	0		4		.323	.333	.383	121	7	5	32						CO/2	0.5
1875	Chi-n	65	284	43	73	9	0	0		9		.257	.280	.289	96	-1	-1	24						CO/2	0.1
1876	Lou-N	67	283	36	73	6	1	0	21	5	11	.258	.271	.286	73	-4	-12	22				.872	-7	*O/C	-1.8
1877	Cin-N	20	71	7	10	1	0	0	3	3	6	.141	.176	.155	6	-7	-6	2				.791	-9	C/O	-1.4
Total	5 n	207	974	221	288	42	6	0	52	23	9	.296	.312	.351	108	10	9	116						C/O2	1.0
Total	2	87	354	43	83	7	1	0	24	8	17	.234	.251	.260	61	-11	-18	24				.872	-17	/OC	-3.2
■ MICKEY HATCHER	Hatcher, Michael Vaughn b: 3/15/55, Cleveland, Ohio BR/TR, 6'2", 200 lbs. Deb: 8/03/79																								
1979	LA-N	33	93	9	25	4	1	1	5	7	12	.269	.327	.366	90	-1	-1	9	1	3	-2	.974	1	O3	-0.3
1980	LA-N	57	84	4	19	2	0	1	5	2	12	.226	.244	.286	48	-6	-6	4	0	2	-1	1.000	1	O3	-0.6
1981	Min-A	99	377	36	96	23	2	3	37	15	29	.255	.287	.350	77	-9	-12	36	3	1	0	.992	4	O/13D	-1.2
1982	Min-A	84	277	23	69	13	2	3	26	8	27	.249	.270	.343	65	-13	-14	21	0	2	-1	.988	0	OD/3	-1.6
1983	Min-A	106	375	50	119	15	3	9	47	14	19	.317	.344	.445	111	7	5	54	2	0	1	.979	6	OD/13	1.0
1984	Min-A	152	576	61	174	35	5	5	69	37	34	.302	.346	.406	103	6	2	78	0	1	-1	.974	13	*OD1/3	1.1
1985	Min-A	116	444	46	125	28	0	3	49	16	23	.282	.310	.365	79	-10	-13	46	0	0	0	.991	8	OD/1	-0.9
1986	Min-A	115	317	40	88	13	3	3	32	19	26	.278	.318	.366	84	-6	-7	36	2	1	0	.971	-3	OD1/3	-1.3
1987	LA-N	101	287	27	81	19	1	7	42	20	19	.282	.331	.429	102	-1	0	39	2	3	-1	.929	0	31/O	-0.4
1988	*LA-N	88	191	22	56	8	0	1	25	7	7	.293	.325	.351	97	-2	-1	20	0	0	0	1.000	-2	O1/3	-0.6
1989	LA-N	94	224	18	66	9	2	2	25	13	16	.295	.336	.379	106	1	1	27	1	2	-1	.961	-3	O3/1P	-0.4
1990	LA-N	85	132	12	28	3	1	0	13	6	22	.212	.252	.250	40	-11	-11	9	0	0	0	1.000	-4	13O	-1.6
Total	12	1130	3377	348	946	172	20	38	375	164	246	.280	.316	.377	89	-46	-56	378	11	15	-6	.983	21	O1D3/P	-6.8
■ BILLY HATCHER	Hatcher, William Augustus b: 10/4/60, Williams, Ariz. BR/TR, 5'9", 175 lbs. Deb: 9/10/84																								
1984	Chi-N	8	9	1	1	0	0	0	0	1	0	.111	.200	.111	-10	-1	-1	0	2	0	1	1.000	-0	/O	-0.1
1985	Chi-N	53	163	24	40	12	1	2	10	8	12	.245	.293	.368	75	-4	-6	14	2	4	-2	.988	-3	O	-1.3
1986	*Hou-N	127	419	55	108	15	4	6	36	22	52	.258	.303	.356	83	-11	-10	47	38	14	3	.983	-5	*O	-1.6
1987	Hou-N	141	564	96	167	28	3	11	63	42	70	.296	.354	.415	107	3	6	89	53	9	11	.986	10	*O	2.1
1988	Hou-N	145	530	79	142	25	4	7	52	37	56	.268	.325	.370	103	-1	2	66	32	13	2	.983	2	*O	0.1
1989	Hou-N	108	395	49	90	15	3	3	44	30	53	.228	.284	.304	71	-16	-15	37	22	6	3	.991	2	*O	-1.3
	Pit-N	27	86	10	21	4	0	1	7	0	9	.244	.253	.326	67	-4	-4	7	2	1	0	1.000	-4	O	-0.9
	Yr	135	481	59	111	19	3	4	51	30	62	.231	.279	.308	70	-21	-19	44	24	7	3	.992	-2	*O	-2.2
1990	*Cin-N	139	504	68	139	28	5	5	25	33	42	.276	.328	.381	91	-4	-7	65	30	10	3	**.997**	8	*O	0.1
1991	Cin-N	138	442	45	116	25	3	4	41	26	55	.262	.314	.360	86	-7	-9	48	11	9	-2	.981	-2	*O	-1.6
1992	Cin-N	43	94	10	27	3	0	2	10	5	11	.287	.323	.383	95	-0	-1	11	0	2	-1	.967	-3	O	-0.5
	Bos-A	75	315	37	75	16	2	1	23	17	41	.238	.284	.311	63	-14	-16	25	4	6	-2	.968	-1	O	-2.3
Total	9	1004	3521	474	926	171	25	42	311	221	401	.263	.314	.362	87	-61	-61	409	196	74	14	.985	4	O	-7.3
■ FRED HATFIELD	Hatfield, Fred James b: 3/18/25, Lanett, Ala. BL/TR, 6'1", 171 lbs. Deb: 8/31/50 C																								
1950	Bos-A	10	12	3	3	0	0	0	2	3	1	.250	.400	.250	63	-0	-1	2	0	0	0	1.000	3	/3	0.2
1951	Bos-A	80	163	23	28	4	2	2	14	22	27	.172	.274	.258	40	-13	-15	13	1	0	0	.959	21	3	0.5
1952	Bos-A	19	25	6	8	1	1	1	3	4	2	.320	.433	.560	162	3	2	4	0	3	-2	1.000	4	3	0.4
	Det-A	112	441	42	104	12	2	2	25	35	52	.236	.301	.286	63	-21	-22	38	2	2	-1	.968	14	*3/S	-1.0
	Yr	131	466	48	112	13	3	3	28	39	54	.240	.309	.300	69	-19	-20	43	2	5	-2	**.971**	18	*3/S	-0.6
1953	Det-A	109	311	41	79	11	1	3	19	40	34	.254	.341	.325	81	-8	-7	36	3	5	-2	.978	9	32/S	0.0
1954	Det-A	81	218	31	64	12	0	2	25	28	24	.294	.386	.376	112	4	5	33	4	2	0	.972	-7	23	0.0
1955	Det-A	122	413	51	96	15	3	8	33	61	49	.232	.338	.341	85	-9	-8	51	3	2	-0	.975	-6	23S	-0.6
1956	Det-A	8	12	2	3	0	0	0	2	2	1	.250	.400	.250	75	-0	-0	2	0	0	0	1.000	-1	/2	-0.1
	Chi-A	106	321	46	84	9	1	7	33	37	36	.262	.352	.361	88	-4	-5	43	1	0	0	.961	5	*3/S	0.1
	Yr	114	333	48	87	9	1	7	35	39	37	.261	.354	.357	87	-5	-5	44	1	0	0	.961	4	*3/2S	0.0
1957	Chi-A	69	114	14	23	3	0	0	8	15	20	.202	.321	.228	52	-7	-7	10	1	0	0	.951	2	3	-0.4
1958	Cle-A	3	8	0	1	0	0	0	1	1	1	.125	.222	.125	-2	-1	-1	0	0	0	0	1.000	1	/3	0.0
	Cin-N	3	1	0	0	0	0	0	0	0	0	.000	.000	.000	-95	-0	-0	0	0	0	0	.000	0	/23	0.0
Total	9	722	2039	259	493	67	10	25	165	248	247	.242	.334	.321	78	-57	-58	233	15	14	-4	.962	43	32/S	-0.9
■ GIL HATFIELD	Hatfield, Gilbert "Colonel" b: 1/27/1855, Hoboken, N.J. d: 5/27/21, Hoboken, N.J. TR , 5'9.5", 168 lbs. Deb: 9/24/1885 F																								
1885	Buf-N	11	30	1	4	0	1	0	0	0	11	.133	.133	.200	6	-3	-3	1				.913	-0	/32	-0.3
1887	NY-N	2	7	2	3	1	0	0	3	0	1	.429	.429	.571	186	1	1	2	0			1.000	0	/3	0.1
1888	*NY-N	28	105	7	19	1	0	0	9	2	18	.181	.211	.190	31	-8	-8	6	8			.813	-1	3S/O2	-0.8
1889	NY-N	32	125	21	23	2	0	1	12	9	15	.184	.250	.224	34	-11	-11	9	9			.858	1	S/P3	-0.6
1890	NY-P	71	287	32	80	13	6	2	37	17	19	.279	.328	.387	85	-4	-8	41	12			.842	-19	3S/PO	-1.9
1891	Was-a	134	500	83	128	11	8	1	48	50	39	.256	.335	.316	93	-6	-2	69	43			.869	9	*S3/PO	1.2
1893	Bro-N	34	120	24	35	3	3	2	19	17	5	.292	.388	.417	122	3	4	23	9			.875	-7	3	-0.2
1895	Lou-N	5	16	3	3	0	0	0	1	1	1	.188	.278	.188	24	-2	-2	1	0			.889	-1	/3S	-0.2
Total	8	317	1190	173	295	31	18	6	129	96	109	.248	.315	.319	81	-30	-29	153	81			.850	-17	S3/PO2	-2.7
■ JOHN HATFIELD	Hatfield, John Van Buskirk b: 7/20/1847, New Jersey d: 2/20/09, Long Island City, N.Y. 5'10", 165 lbs. Deb: 5/18/1871 FM																								
1871	Mut-n	33	168	41	43	3	2	0	22	4	0	.256	.273	.298	70	-8	-4	17	10					*O/23	-0.2
1872	Mut-n	56	287	75	91	12	2	1	45	9	5	.317	.338	.383	130	7	11	40						*2M	0.5
1873	Mut-n	52	255	54	78	6	7	2	45	3	2	.306	.314	.408	111	3	3	34						*32/OM	0.1
1874	Mut-n	63	289	46	68	12	2	0		8		.235	.256	.291	71	-8	-10	22						*O/3P1	-0.6
1875	Mut-n	2	9	2	3	1	0	0		0		.333	.333	.444	158	1	0	1						/O	0.0
1876	NY-N	1	4	0	1	0	0	0	1	0	0	.250	.250	.250	77	-0	-0	0				.833	-0	/2	0.0
Total	5 n	206	1008	218	283	34	13	3	112	24	7	.281	.297	.349	98	-5	2	114						/O23P1	-0.2
■ GRADY HATTON	Hatton, Grady Edgebert b: 10/7/22, Beaumont, Tex. BL/TR, 5'9", 175 lbs. Deb: 4/16/46 MC																								
1946	Cin-N	116	436	56	118	18	3	14	69	66	53	.271	.369	.422	129	15	17	73	6			.941	-19	*3/O	-0.1
1947	Cin-N	146	524	91	147	24	8	16	77	81	50	.281	.377	.448	119	15	15	92	7			.938	-8	*3	0.7
1948	Cin-N	133	458	58	110	17	2	9	44	72	50	.240	.343	.345	90	-7	-5	59	7			.932	4	*3/2SO	-0.2
1949	Cin-N	137	537	71	141	38	5	11	69	62	48	.263	.342	.413	101	1	0	79	4			**.975**	-1	*3	-0.3
1950	Cin-N	130	438	67	114	17	1	11	54	70	39	.260	.366	.379	96	-0	-1	67	6			.954	-3	*3/2S	-0.5
1951	Cin-N	96	331	41	84	9	3	4	37	33	32	.254	.321	.335	76	-10	-11	38	4	2	0	.972	3	3/O	-0.9
1952	Cin-N☆	128	433	48	92	14	1	9	57	66	60	.212	.319	.312	76	-13	-13	48	5	4	-1	**.990**	-17	*2	-2.6
1953	Cin-N	83	159	22	37	3	1	7	22	29	24	.233	.351	.396	94	-1	-1	24	0	1	-1	.991	-11	21/3	-1.1
1954	Cin-N	1	1	0	0	0	0	0	0	0	0	.000	.000	.000	-97	-0	-0	0	0	0	0	.000	0	H	0.0
	Chi-A	13	30	3	5	1	0	0	3	5	3	.167	.286	.200	34	-3	-3	2	1	0	0	1.000	-1	3/1	-0.4
	Bos-A	99	302	40	85	12	3	5	33	58	25	.281	.401	.391	106	10	5	51	1	1	-0	.966	6	3/1S	1.0
	Yr	112	332	43	90	13	3	5	36	63	28	.271	.390	.373	100	7	3	53	2	1	0	**.969**	5	*3/1S	0.6
1955	Bos-A	126	380	48	93	11	4	4	49	76	28	.245	.371	.326	81	-3	-8	51	0	1	-1	.976	-2	*3/2	-1.1

YEAR	TM/L	G	AB	R	H	2B	3B	HR	RBI	BB	SO	AVG	OBP	SLG	PRO+	BR	/A	RC	SB	CS	SBR	FA	FR	POS	TPR
1956	Bos-A	5	5	0	2	0	0	0	2	0	0	.400	.400	.400	100	0	0	1	0	0	0	.000	0	H	0.0
	StL-N	44	73	10	18	1	2	0	7	13	7	.247	.360	.315	84	-1	-1	9	1	0	0	.951	-4	2/3	-0.4
	Bal-A	27	61	4	9	1	0	1	3	13	6	.148	.297	.213	40	-5	-5	5	0	0	0	1.000	-5	23	-0.8
1960	Chi-N	28	38	3	13	0	0	0	7	2	5	.342	.390	.342	104	0	0	5	0	0	0	.931	-2	/2	-0.1
Total	12	1312	4206	562	1068	166	33	91	533	646	430	.254	.355	.374	96	-4	-10	604	42	9		.956	-60	32/1OS	-6.8
■ ARTHUR HAUGER Hauger, John Arthur b: 11/18/1893, Delhi, Ohio d: 8/2/44, Redwood City, Cal BL/TR, 5'11", 168 lbs. Deb: 7/17/12																									
1912	Cle-A	15	18	0	1	0	0	0	0	1		.056	.105	.056	-52	-4	-4	0	0			1.000	-2	/O	-0.5
■ ARNOLD HAUSER Hauser, Arnold George "Peewee" or "Stub" b: 9/25/1888, Chicago, Ill. d: 5/22/66, Aurora, Ill. BR/TR, 5'6", 145 lbs. Deb: 4/21/10																									
1910	StL-N	119	375	37	77	7	2	2	36	49	39	.205	.312	.251	67	-15	-13	34	15			.931	-8	*S/3	-1.8
1911	StL-N	136	515	61	124	11	8	3	46	26	67	.241	.286	.311	69	-24	-22	53	24			.918	-15	*S/3	-2.9
1912	StL-N	133	479	73	124	14	7	1	42	39	69	.259	.319	.324	78	-16	-14	58	26			.934	10	*S	0.7
1913	StL-N	22	45	3	13	0	3	0	9	2	2	.289	.347	.422	121	1	1	7	1			.848	-3	/S2	-0.2
1915	Chi-F	23	54	6	11	1	0	0	4	5	7	.204	.283	.222	52	-3	-3	4	2			.851	-3	S/3	-0.5
Total	5	433	1468	180	349	33	20	6	137	121	184	.238	.305	.300	73	-57	-52	157	68			.924	-19	S/32	-4.7
■ JOE HAUSER Hauser, Joseph John "Unser Choe" b: 1/12/1899, Milwaukee, Wis. BL/TL, 5'10.5", 175 lbs. Deb: 4/18/22																									
1922	Phi-A	111	368	61	119	21	5	9	43	30	37	.323	.378	.481	119	11	10	65	1	5	-3	.986	-3	1	0.0
1923	Phi-A	146	537	93	165	21	9	17	94	69	52	.307	.398	.475	127	23	22	104	6	6	-2	.990	-3	*1	0.9
1924	Phi-A	149	562	97	162	31	8	27	115	56	52	.288	.358	.516	123	16	15	104	7	5	-1	.993	-3	*1	0.2
1926	Phi-A	91	229	31	44	10	0	8	36	39	34	.192	.312	.341	66	-10	-12	26	1	2	-1	.996	0	1	-1.6
1928	Phi-A	95	300	61	78	19	5	16	59	52	45	.260	.369	.517	127	13	12	60	4	2	0	.986	-6	1	-0.2
1929	Cle-A	37	48	8	12	1	1	3	9	4	8	.250	.321	.500	104	0	0	8	0	0	0	.986	1	/1	0.0
Total	6	629	2044	351	580	103	28	80	356	250	228	.284	.368	.479	117	53	47	367	19	20	-6	.990	-14	1	-0.7
■ GEORGE HAUSMANN Hausmann, George John b: 2/11/16, St.Louis, Mo. BR/TR, 5'5", 145 lbs. Deb: 4/18/44																									
1944	NY-N	131	466	70	124	20	4	1	30	40	25	.266	.324	.333	85	-9	-9	52	3			.960	-7	*2	-0.9
1945	NY-N	154	623	98	174	15	8	2	45	73	46	.279	.356	.339	92	-3	-5	81	7			.968	5	*2	1.0
1949	NY-N	16	47	5	6	0	1	0	3	7	6	.128	.241	.170	12	-6	-6	3	0			.984	-0	2	-0.6
Total	3	301	1136	173	304	35	13	3	78	120	77	.268	.338	.329	86	-18	-19	135	10			.965	-3	2	-0.5
■ CHARLIE HAUTZ Hautz, Charles A. b: 2/5/1852, St.Louis, Mo. d: 1/24/29, St.Louis, Mo. 5'7", 150 lbs. Deb: 5/04/1875																									
1875	RS-n	19	83	5	25	2	0	0		1		.301	.310	.325	133	2	3	9						1	0.2
1884	Pit-a	7	24	0	5	0	0	0		3		.208	.296	.208	69	-1	-1	2				.980	0	/1O	-0.1
■ ROY HAWES Hawes, Roy Lee b: 7/5/26, Shiloh, Ill. BL/TL, 6'2", 190 lbs. Deb: 9/23/51																									
1951	Was-A	3	6	0	1	0	0	0	0	0	1	.167	.167	.167	-10	-1	-1	0	0	0	0	1.000	-0	/1	-0.1
■ BILL HAWES Hawes, William Hildreth b: 11/17/1853, Nashua, N.H. d: 6/16/40, Lowell, Mass. BR/TR, 5'10", 155 lbs. Deb: 5/01/1879																									
1879	Bos-N	38	155	19	31	3	3	0	9	2	13	.200	.210	.258	52	-8	-8	9				.828	-3	O/C	-1.2
1884	Cin-U	79	349	80	97	7	4	4		5		.278	.288	.355	108	5	1	37				.827	-7	O1	-0.8
Total	2	117	504	99	128	10	7	4	9	7	13	.254	.264	.325	91	-2	-7	45				.827	-10	/O1C	-2.0
■ THORNY HAWKES Hawkes, Thorndike Proctor b: 10/15/1852, Danvers, Mass. d: 2/3/29, Danvers, Mass. BR/TR, 5'8", 135 lbs. Deb: 5/01/1879																									
1879	Tro-N	64	250	24	52	6	1	0	20	4	14	.208	.220	.240	55	-13	-10	14				.896	16	*2	0.9
1884	Was-a	38	151	16	42	4	2	0		4		.278	.297	.331	121	1	4	15				.917	3	2/O	0.7
Total	2	102	401	40	94	10	3	0	20	8	14	.234	.249	.274	80	-12	-7	29				.903	19	2/O	1.6
■ CHICKEN HAWKS Hawks, Nelson Louis b: 2/3/1896, San Francisco, Cal. d: 5/26/73, San Rafael, Cal. BL/TL, 5'11", 167 lbs. Deb: 4/14/21																									
1921	NY-A	41	73	16	21	2	3	2	15	5	12	.288	.333	.479	103	0	-0	11	0	1	-1	.970	-2	O	-0.3
1925	Phi-N	105	320	52	103	15	5	5	45	32	33	.322	.387	.447	103	7	2	55	3	6	-3	.986	-0	1	-0.5
Total	2	146	393	68	124	17	8	7	60	37	45	.316	.377	.453	103	7	2	66	3	7	-3		-2	/1O	-0.8
■ HOWIE HAWORTH Haworth, Homer Howard "Cully" b: 8/27/1893, Newberg, Ore. d: 1/28/53, Troutdale, Ore. BL/TR, 5'10.5", 165 lbs. Deb: 8/14/15																									
1915	Cle-A	7	7	0	1	0	0	0	1	2	2	.143	.333	.143	42	-0	-0	0	0			.917	-1	/C	-0.1
■ JACK HAYDEN Hayden, John Francis b: 10/21/1880, Bryn Mawr, Pa. d: 8/3/42, Haverford, Pa. BL/TL, 5'9", Deb: 4/26/01																									
1901	Phi-A	51	211	35	56	6	4	0	17	18		.265	.323	.332	78	-5	-6	25	4			.841	-4	O	-1.3
1906	Bos-A	85	322	22	80	6	4	1	14	17		.248	.292	.301	86	-5	-5	32	6			.973	-1	O	-1.2
1908	Chi-N	11	45	3	9	2	0	0	2	1		.200	.217	.244	46	-3	-3	3	1			1.000	-1	O	-0.5
Total	3	147	578	60	145	14	8	1	33	36		.251	.298	.308	80	-13	-15	60	11			.929	-5	O	-3.0
■ CHARLIE HAYES Hayes, Charles Dewayne b: 5/29/65, Hattiesburg, Miss. BR/TR, 6', 190 lbs. Deb: 9/11/88																									
1988	SF-N	7	11	0	1	0	0	0	0	0	3	.091	.091	.091	-50	-2	-2	0	0	0	0	1.000	-1	/O3	-0.3
1989	SF-N	3	5	0	1	0	0	0	0	0	1	.200	.200	.200	15	-1	-1	0	0	0	0	1.000	-0	/3	-0.1
	Phi-N	84	299	26	77	15	1	8	43	11	49	.258	.284	.395	92	-4	-4	32	3	1	0	.910	10	3	0.7
	Yr	87	304	26	78	15	1	8	43	11	50	.257	.283	.391	91	-5	-5	32	3	1	0	.911	10	3	0.6
1990	Phi-N	152	561	56	145	20	0	10	57	28	91	.258	.296	.348	77	-19	-19	55	4	4	-1	.957	24	*3/12	0.5
1991	Phi-N	142	460	34	106	23	1	12	53	16	75	.230	.258	.363	74	-18	-18	39	3	3	-1	.958	7	*3/S	-1.1
1992	NY-A	142	509	52	131	19	2	18	66	28	100	.257	.300	.409	95	-4	-5	59	3	5	-2	.963	-11	*3/1	-1.9
Total	5	530	1845	168	461	77	4	48	219	83	319	.250	.284	.374	83	-48	-48	185	13	13	-4	.951	29	3/1OS2	-2.2
■ FRANKIE HAYES Hayes, Frank Witman "Blimp" b: 10/13/14, Jamesburg, N.J. d: 6/22/55, Point Pleasant, N.J. BR/TR, 6', 185 lbs. Deb: 9/21/33																									
1933	Phi-A	3	5	0	0	0	0	0	0	0	2	.000	.000	.000	-99	-1	-1	0	0	0	0	.889	0	/C	-0.1
1934	Phi-A	92	248	24	56	10	0	6	30	20	44	.226	.286	.339	63	-15	-14	25	2	1	0	.955	-11	C	-2.0
1936	Phi-A	144	505	59	137	25	2	10	67	46	58	.271	.335	.388	79	-19	-17	66	3	5	-2	.972	-22	*C	-3.0
1937	Phi-A	60	188	24	49	11	1	10	38	29	34	.261	.359	.489	114	3	3	34	0	0	0	.971	-4	C	0.2
1938	Phi-A	99	316	56	92	19	3	11	55	54	51	.291	.396	.475	120	9	10	62	2	3	-1	.975	-16	C	-0.2
1939	Phi-A☆	124	431	66	122	28	5	20	83	40	55	.283	.348	.510	119	9	10	76	4	1	1	.978	-12	*C	0.4
1940	Phi-A★	136	465	73	143	23	4	16	70	61	59	.308	.389	.477	126	17	18	89	9	3	1	.971	-13	*C/1	1.5
1941	Phi-A★	126	439	66	123	27	4	12	63	62	56	.280	.369	.442	117	9	10	70	2	0	1	.983	-11	*C	1.0
1942	Phi-A	21	63	8	15	4	0	0	5	9	8	.238	.333	.302	80	-2	-1	6	1	1	-0	1.000	-4	C	-0.5
	StL-A	56	159	14	40	6	0	2	17	28	39	.252	.364	.327	94	-0	-0	22	0	0	0	.971	-8	C	-0.4
	Yr	77	222	22	55	10	0	2	22	37	47	.248	.355	.320	90	-2	-2	28	1	1	-0	.979	-12	C	-0.9
1943	StL-A	88	250	16	47	7	0	5	30	37	36	.188	.295	.276	66	-10	-10	22	1	0	0	.983	-9	C/1	-1.5
1944	Phi-A★	155	581	62	144	18	6	13	78	57	59	.248	.315	.367	96	-5	-4	68	2	1	0	.982	3	*C/1	0.9
1945	Phi-A	32	110	12	25	2	1	3	14	18	14	.227	.336	.345	98	-0	0	14	1	0	0	.994	2	C	0.4
	Cle-A	119	385	39	91	15	6	6	43	53	52	.236	.335	.353	104	0	2	49	1	1	-0	.988	2	*C	1.2
	Yr	151	495	51	116	17	7	9	57	71	66	.234	.335	.352	103	0	3	63	2	1	0	.989	3	*C	1.6
1946	Cle-A★	51	156	11	40	12	0	3	18	21	26	.256	.345	.391	112	1	2	20	1	3	-2	.981	-1	C	0.3
	Chi-A	53	179	15	38	6	0	2	16	29	33	.212	.322	.279	72	-7	-6	17	1	1	-0	.979	-3	C	-0.7
	Yr	104	335	26	78	18	0	5	34	50	59	.233	.332	.331	90	-5	-3	37	2	4	-2	.980	-4	*C	-0.4
1947	Bos-A	5	13	0	2	0	0	0	1	0	1	.154	.154	.154	-13	-2	-2	0	0	0	0	.917	1	/C	-0.1
Total	14	1364	4493	545	1164	213	32	119	628	564	627	.259	.343	.400	100	-13	1	640	30	20	-3	.977	-106	*C/1	-2.6

■ **JACKIE HAYES** Hayes, John J. b: 6/27/1861, Brooklyn, N.Y. TR , Deb: 5/02/1882

YEAR	TM/L	G	AB	R	H	2B	3B	HR	RBI	BB	SO	AVG	OBP	SLG	PRO+	BR	/A	RC	SB	CS	SBR	FA	FR	POS	TPR
1882	Wor-N	78	326	27	88	22	4	4	54	6	26	.270	.283	.399	113	5	4	38				.855	-10	*OC/3S	-0.5
1883	Pit-a	85	351	41	92	23	5	3		15		.262	.292	.382	121	6	8	40				.911	-18	CO/S12	-0.5
1884	Pit-a	33	124	11	28	6	1	0		4		.226	.256	.290	79	-3	-3	9				.912	-1	C/1O2	-0.2
	Bro-a	16	51	4	12	3	0	0		3		.235	.278	.294	89	-1	-1	4				.946	6	C/O	0.6
	Yr	49	175	15	40	9	1	0		7		.229	.262	.291	82	-3	-3	14				.925	6	C/1O2	0.4
1885	Bro-a	42	137	10	18	3	0	0		5		.131	.179	.153	7	-14	-14	4				.900	-2	C	-1.2
1886	Was-N	26	89	8	17	3	0	3	9	4	23	.191	.226	.326	70	-4	-3	7	0			.926	-4	CO/2	-0.6
1887	Bal-a	8	28	2	4	3	0	0		0		.143	.143	.250	10	-3	-3	1	0			.250	-4	/O3C	-0.6
1890	Bro-P	12	42	3	8	0	0	0	5	2	4	.190	.227	.190	13	-5	-6	2	0			.867	-3	/OSC2	-0.7
Total	7	300	1148	106	267	63	10	10	68	39	53	.233	.260	.331	87	-18	-17	105	0			.906	-36	CO/1S32	-3.7

■ **MIKE HAYES** Hayes, Michael b: 1853, Cleveland, Ohio 5'7.5", 170 lbs. Deb: 9/09/1876

YEAR	TM/L	G	AB	R	H	2B	3B	HR	RBI	BB	SO	AVG	OBP	SLG	PRO+	BR	/A	RC	SB	CS	SBR	FA	FR	POS	TPR
1876	NY-N	5	21	1	3	0	2	0	2	0	0	.143	.143	.333	63	-1	-1	1				.882	0	/O	0.0

■ **JACKIE HAYES** Hayes, Minter Carney b: 7/19/06, Clanton, Ala. d: 2/9/83, Birmingham, Ala. BR/TR, 5'10.5", 165 lbs. Deb: 8/05/27

YEAR	TM/L	G	AB	R	H	2B	3B	HR	RBI	BB	SO	AVG	OBP	SLG	PRO+	BR	/A	RC	SB	CS	SBR	FA	FR	POS	TPR
1927	Was-A	10	29	2	7	0	0	0	2	1	2	.241	.267	.241	33	-3	-3	2	0	0	0	.969	-1	/S3	-0.3
1928	Was-A	60	210	30	54	7	3	0	22	5	10	.257	.274	.319	56	-14	-14	19	3	0	1	.974	8	2S/3	-0.2
1929	Was-A	123	424	52	117	20	3	2	57	24	29	.276	.316	.351	71	-18	-19	47	4	5	-2	.945	3	32/S	-1.2
1930	Was-A	51	166	25	47	7	2	1	20	7	8	.283	.312	.367	71	-7	-7	18	2	3	-1	.981	8	2/31	0.1
1931	Was-A	38	108	11	24	2	1	0	8	6	4	.222	.263	.259	38	-10	-10	8	2	0	1	.962	-4	2/3S	-1.1
1932	Chi-A	117	475	53	122	20	5	2	54	30	28	.257	.302	.333	69	-25	-21	48	7	4	-0	.967	1	2S3	-1.3
1933	Chi-A	138	535	65	138	23	5	2	47	55	36	.258	.331	.331	79	-18	-15	61	2	3	-1	.981	10	*2	0.2
1934	Chi-A	62	226	19	58	9	1	1	31	23	20	.257	.325	.319	65	-11	-12	25	3	2	-0	.980	-9	2	-1.6
1935	Chi-A	89	329	45	88	14	0	4	45	29	15	.267	.327	.347	72	-13	-14	39	3	1	0	.966	-6	2	-1.2
1936	Chi-A	108	417	53	130	34	3	5	84	35	25	.312	.366	.444	96	-1	-4	69	4	2	0	.979	**17**	2S/3	1.8
1937	Chi-A	143	573	63	131	27	4	2	79	41	37	.229	.282	.300	47	-47	-47	49	1	6	-3	.984	21	*2	-1.9
1938	Chi-A	62	238	40	78	21	2	1	20	24	6	.328	.389	.445	106	3	3	42	3	2	-0	.976	-3	2	0.2
1939	Chi-A	72	269	34	67	12	3	0	23	27	10	.249	.320	.316	62	-15	-16	28	0	3	-2	.974	5	2	-0.8
1940	Chi-A	18	41	2	8	0	1	0	1	2	11	.195	.233	.244	23	-5	-5	3	0	0	0	.981	-0	2	-0.4
Total	14	1091	4040	494	1069	196	33	20	493	309	241	.265	.318	.344	70	-184	-183	456	34	31	-8	.976	52	2/3S1	-7.7

■ **VON HAYES** Hayes, Von Francis b: 8/31/58, Stockton, Cal. BL/TR, 6'5", 185 lbs. Deb: 4/14/81

YEAR	TM/L	G	AB	R	H	2B	3B	HR	RBI	BB	SO	AVG	OBP	SLG	PRO+	BR	/A	RC	SB	CS	SBR	FA	FR	POS	TPR
1981	Cle-A	43	109	21	28	8	2	1	17	14	10	.257	.352	.394	116	2	3	17	8	1	2	.939	1	DO/3	0.5
1982	Cle-A	150	527	65	132	25	3	14	82	42	63	.250	.311	.389	91	-7	-7	63	32	13	2	.981	6	*O/31	-0.3
1983	*Phi-N	124	351	45	93	9	5	6	32	36	55	.265	.338	.370	97	-1	-1	42	20	12	-1	.972	-3	*O	-0.8
1984	Phi-N	152	561	85	164	27	6	16	67	59	84	.292	.360	.447	124	19	18	94	48	13	7	.988	-8	*O	1.3
1985	Phi-N	152	570	76	150	30	4	13	70	61	99	.263	.334	.398	101	3	1	79	21	8	2	.984	-6	*O	-0.8
1986	Phi-N	158	610	**107**	186	**46**	2	19	98	74	77	.305	.381	.480	131	30	28	111	24	12	0	.990	2	*1O	2.0
1987	Phi-N	158	556	84	154	36	5	21	84	121	77	.277	.406	.473	128	30	27	113	16	7	1	.990	-13	*1O	0.4
1988	Phi-N	104	367	43	100	28	2	6	45	49	59	.272	.360	.409	118	11	10	57	20	9	1	.990	-1	1O/3	0.1
1989	Phi-N★	154	540	93	140	27	2	26	78	101	103	.259	.380	.461	139	30	30	103	28	7	4	.980	3	*O13	3.4
1990	Phi-N	129	467	70	122	14	3	17	73	87	81	.261	.382	.413	119	15	15	78	16	7	1	.979	5	*O	1.8
1991	Phi-N	77	284	43	64	15	1	0	21	31	42	.225	.308	.285	69	-11	-11	27	9	2	2	.990	11	O	0.0
1992	Cal-A	94	307	35	69	17	1	4	29	37	54	.225	.308	.326	79	-9	-8	31	11	6	-0	.983	-1	O/1D	-1.2
Total	12	1495	5249	767	1402	282	36	143	696	712	804	.267	.357	.416	113	111	105	814	253	97	18	.983	-4	*O1/D3	6.4

■ **BILL HAYES** Hayes, William Ernest b: 10/24/57, Cheverly, Md. BR/TR, 6', 195 lbs. Deb: 9/30/80

YEAR	TM/L	G	AB	R	H	2B	3B	HR	RBI	BB	SO	AVG	OBP	SLG	PRO+	BR	/A	RC	SB	CS	SBR	FA	FR	POS	TPR
1980	Chi-N	4	9	0	2	1	0	0	0	0	3	.222	.222	.333	49	-1	-1	1	0	0	0	1.000	-0	/C	-0.1
1981	Chi-N	1	0	0	0	0	0	0	0	0	0	—	—	—	—	0	0	0	0	0	0	.000	0	/C	0.0
Total	2	5	9	0	2	1	0	0	0	0	3	.222	.222	.333	49	-1	-1	1	0	0	0	1.000	-0	/C	-0.1

■ **RED HAYWORTH** Hayworth, Myron Claude b: 5/14/15, High Point, N.C. BR/TR, 6'1.5", 200 lbs. Deb: 4/21/44 F

YEAR	TM/L	G	AB	R	H	2B	3B	HR	RBI	BB	SO	AVG	OBP	SLG	PRO+	BR	/A	RC	SB	CS	SBR	FA	FR	POS	TPR
1944	*StL-A	90	270	20	60	11	1	1	25	10	13	.222	.253	.281	50	-17	-19	20	0	0	0	.967	1	C	-1.5
1945	StL-A	56	160	7	31	4	0	0	17	7	6	.194	.228	.219	28	-14	-15	7	0	2	-1	.992	4	C	-1.1
Total	2	146	430	27	91	15	1	1	42	17	19	.212	.243	.258	42	-32	-34	28	0	2	-1	.976	4	C	-2.6

■ **RAY HAYWORTH** Hayworth, Raymond Hall b: 1/29/04, High Point, N.C. BR/TR, 6', 180 lbs. Deb: 6/27/26 FC

YEAR	TM/L	G	AB	R	H	2B	3B	HR	RBI	BB	SO	AVG	OBP	SLG	PRO+	BR	/A	RC	SB	CS	SBR	FA	FR	POS	TPR
1926	Det-A	12	11	1	3	0	0	0	5	1	1	.273	.333	.273	59	-1	-1	1	0	0	0	1.000	-1	/C	-0.1
1929	Det-A	14	43	5	11	0	0	0	4	3	8	.256	.304	.256	45	-3	-3	4	0	0	0	.951	0	C	-0.2
1930	Det-A	77	227	24	63	15	4	0	22	20	19	.278	.336	.379	79	-7	-7	29	0	2	-1	.977	-13	C	-1.3
1931	Det-A	88	273	28	70	10	3	0	25	19	27	.256	.307	.315	62	-14	-16	27	0	1	-1	.973	4	C	-0.6
1932	Det-A	109	338	41	99	20	2	2	44	31	22	.293	.354	.382	87	-4	-6	47	1	1	-0	.991	3	*C	0.2
1933	Det-A	134	425	37	104	14	3	1	45	35	28	.245	.302	.299	59	-24	-26	40	0	0	0	.994	2	*C	-1.6
1934	*Det-A	54	167	20	49	5	2	0	27	16	22	.293	.355	.347	82	-4	-4	21	0	2	-1	.984	7	C	0.3
1935	Det-A	51	175	22	54	14	2	0	22	9	14	.309	.342	.411	98	-2	-1	25	0	0	0	.996	11	C	1.2
1936	Det-A	81	250	31	60	10	0	1	30	39	18	.240	.347	.292	59	-15	-15	28	0	0	0	**.988**	-4	C	-1.4
1937	Det-A	30	78	9	21	2	0	1	8	14	15	.269	.394	.333	83	-1	-1	12	0	0	0	.992	6	C	0.5
1938	Det-A	8	19	1	4	0	0	0	5	3	4	.211	.318	.211	33	-2	-2	2	1	0	0	.971	2	/C	0.1
	Bro-N	5	4	0	0	0	0	0	0	1	1	.000	.200	.000	-40	-1	-1	0	0			1.000	0	/C	-0.1
1939	Bro-N	21	26	0	4	2	0	0	1	4	7	.154	.267	.231	34	-2	-3	2	0			1.000	1	C	-0.1
	NY-N	5	13	1	3	0	0	0	0	0	1	.231	.231	.231	24	-1	-1	1	0			1.000	1	/C	0.0
	Yr	26	39	1	7	2	0	0	1	4	8	.179	.256	.231	31	-4	-4	2	0			1.000	2	C	-0.1
1942	StL-A	1	1	0	1	0	0	0	0	0	0	1.000	1.000	1.000	456	0	0	1	0	0	0	.000	0	H	0.0
1944	Bro-N	7	10	0	0	0	0	0	0	2	1	.000	.167	.000	-51	-2	-2	0	0			1.000	2	/C	0.0
1945	Bro-N	2	2	0	0	0	0	0	0	1	0	.000	.333	.000	-3	-0	-0	0	0			1.000	0	/C	0.0
Total	15	699	2062	220	546	92	16	5	238	198	188	.265	.331	.332	71	-84	-89	237	2	6		.987	20	C	-3.1

■ **DRUNGO HAZEWOOD** Hazewood, Drungo La Rue b: 9/2/59, Mobile, Ala. BR/TR, 6'3", 210 lbs. Deb: 9/19/80

YEAR	TM/L	G	AB	R	H	2B	3B	HR	RBI	BB	SO	AVG	OBP	SLG	PRO+	BR	/A	RC	SB	CS	SBR	FA	FR	POS	TPR
1980	Bal-A	6	5	1	0	0	0	0	0	0	4	.000	.000	.000	-99	-1	-1	0	0	0	0	1.000	-1	/O	-0.2

■ **BOB HAZLE** Hazle, Robert Sidney "Hurricane" b: 12/9/30, Laurens, S.C. d: 4/25/92, Columbia, S.C. BL/TR, 6', 190 lbs. Deb: 9/08/55

YEAR	TM/L	G	AB	R	H	2B	3B	HR	RBI	BB	SO	AVG	OBP	SLG	PRO+	BR	/A	RC	SB	CS	SBR	FA	FR	POS	TPR
1955	Cin-N	6	13	0	3	0	0	0	0	0	3	.231	.231	.231	22	-1	-2	1	0	0	0	1.000	2	/O	0.0
1957	*Mil-N	41	134	26	54	12	0	7	27	18	15	.403	.477	.649	214	19	21	41	1	3	-2	.906	-5	O	1.2
1958	Mil-N	20	56	6	10	0	0	0	5	9	4	.179	.303	.179	34	-5	-5	4	0	0	0	1.000	-1	O	-0.7
	Det-A	43	58	5	14	2	0	2	5	5	13	.241	.302	.379	80	-1	-2	7	0	0	0	1.000	-2	O	-0.4
Total	3	110	261	37	81	14	0	9	37	32	35	.310	.390	.467	135	12	13	53	1	3	-2	.951	-7	/O	0.1

■ **DOC HAZLETON** Hazleton, Willard Carpenter b: 8/28/1876, Strafford, Vt. d: 3/17/41, Burlington, Vt. Deb: 4/17/02

YEAR	TM/L	G	AB	R	H	2B	3B	HR	RBI	BB	SO	AVG	OBP	SLG	PRO+	BR	/A	RC	SB	CS	SBR	FA	FR	POS	TPR
1902	StL-N	7	23	0	3	0	0	0	0	2		.130	.231	.130	12	-2	-2	1	0			.973	0	/1	-0.2

■ **FRAN HEALY** Healy, Francis Xavier b: 9/6/46, Holyoke, Mass. BR/TR, 6'5", 220 lbs. Deb: 9/03/69

YEAR	TM/L	G	AB	R	H	2B	3B	HR	RBI	BB	SO	AVG	OBP	SLG	PRO+	BR	/A	RC	SB	CS	SBR	FA	FR	POS	TPR
1969	KC-A	6	10	0	4	1	0	0	0	0	5	.400	.400	.500	149	1	1	2	0	0	0	1.000	0	/C	0.1
1971	SF-N	47	93	10	26	3	0	2	11	15	24	.280	.380	.376	117	2	3	14	1	0	0	.966	-2	C	0.2
1972	SF-N	45	99	12	15	4	0	1	8	13	24	.152	.257	.222	37	-8	-8	6	0	1	-1	.995	7	C	-0.1

YEAR	TM/L	G	AB	R	H	2B	3B	HR	RBI	BB	SO	AVG	OBP	SLG	PRO+	BR	/A	RC	SB	CS	SBR	FA	FR	POS	TPR
1973	KC-A	95	279	25	77	15	2	6	34	31	56	.276	.348	.409	104	5	2	40	3	4	-2	.979	-3	C/D	0.1
1974	KC-A	139	445	59	112	24	2	9	53	62	73	.252	.344	.375	101	5	2	59	16	8	0	.977	-7	*C	0.1
1975	KC-A	56	188	16	48	5	2	2	18	14	19	.255	.307	.335	79	-5	-5	18	4	3	-1	.982	-7	C/D	-1.1
1976	KC-A	8	24	2	3	0	0	0	1	4	10	.125	.250	.125	12	-3	-3	1	2	0	1	1.000	0	/CD	-0.2
	NY-A	46	120	10	32	3	0	0	9	9	17	.267	.318	.292	80	-3	-3	11	3	1	0	.983	3	C/D	0.1
	Yr	54	144	12	35	3	0	0	10	13	27	.243	.306	.264	68	-5	-5	12	5	1	1	.987	3	CD	-0.1
1977	NY-A	27	67	10	15	5	0	0	7	6	13	.224	.288	.299	61	-4	-4	6	1	0	0	.971	-0	C	-0.3
1978	NY-A	1	1	0	0	0	0	0	0	0	1	.000	.000	.000	-99	-0	-0	0	0	0	0	.000	0	/C	0.0
Total	9	470	1326	144	332	60	6	20	141	154	242	.250	.329	.350	90	-9	-16	158	30	17	-1	.980	-8	C/D	-1.1

■ FRANCIS HEALY

Healy, Francis Xavier Paul b: 6/29/10, Holyoke, Mass. BR/TR, 5'9.5", 175 lbs. Deb: 4/29/30

YEAR	TM/L	G	AB	R	H	2B	3B	HR	RBI	BB	SO	AVG	OBP	SLG	PRO+	BR	/A	RC	SB	CS	SBR	FA	FR	POS	TPR
1930	NY-N	7	2	2	0	0	0	0	0	0	0	.000	.000	.000	-99	-1	-1	0	0			.000	0	/C	-0.1
1931	NY-N	6	7	1	1	0	0	0	0	0	0	.143	.143	.143	-24	-1	-1	0	0			1.000	0	/C	-0.1
1932	NY-N	14	32	5	8	2	0	0	4	2	8	.250	.294	.313	65	-2	-2	3	0			.960	2	C	0.1
1934	StL-N	15	13	1	4	1	0	0	1	0	2	.308	.308	.385	79	-0	-0	1	0			1.000	1	/C3O	0.0
Total	4	42	54	9	13	3	0	0	5	2	10	.241	.268	.296	51	-4	-4	4	0			.969	3	/CO3	-0.1

■ THOMAS HEALY

Healy, Thomas Fitzgerald b: 10/30/1895, Altoona, Pa. d: 1/15/74, Cleveland, Ohio BR/TR, 6', 172 lbs. Deb: 7/13/15

YEAR	TM/L	G	AB	R	H	2B	3B	HR	RBI	BB	SO	AVG	OBP	SLG	PRO+	BR	/A	RC	SB	CS	SBR	FA	FR	POS	TPR
1915	Phi-A	23	77	11	17	1	0	0	5	6	4	.221	.310	.234	65	-3	-3	5	0	4	-2	.933	5	3/S	0.1
1916	Phi-A	6	23	4	6	1	1	0	2	1	2	.261	.320	.391	119	0	0	3	1			.947	-1	/3	0.0
Total	2	29	100	15	23	2	1	0	7	7	6	.230	.313	.270	77	-3	-2	8	1	4		.936	4	/3S	0.1

■ CHARLIE HEARD

Heard, Charles b: 1/30/1872, Philadelphia, Pa. d: 2/20/45, Philadelphia, Pa. BR/TR, 6'2", 190 lbs. Deb: 7/14/1890

YEAR	TM/L	G	AB	R	H	2B	3B	HR	RBI	BB	SO	AVG	OBP	SLG	PRO+	BR	/A	RC	SB	CS	SBR	FA	FR	POS	TPR
1890	Pit-N	12	43	2	8	2	0	0	0	1	15	.186	.205	.233	32	-4	-3	2	0			.600	-3	/OP	-0.4

■ ED HEARN

Hearn, Edmund b: 9/17/1888, Ventura, Cal. d: 9/8/52, Sawtelle, Cal. BR/TR, 5'9", 160 lbs. Deb: 6/09/10

YEAR	TM/L	G	AB	R	H	2B	3B	HR	RBI	BB	SO	AVG	OBP	SLG	PRO+	BR	/A	RC	SB	CS	SBR	FA	FR	POS	TPR
1910	Bos-A	2	2	0	0	0	0	0	0	0		.000	.000	.000	-98	-0	-0	0	0			1.000	2	/S	0.1

■ ED HEARN

Hearn, Edward John b: 8/23/60, Stuart, Fla. BR/TR, 6'3", 215 lbs. Deb: 5/17/86

YEAR	TM/L	G	AB	R	H	2B	3B	HR	RBI	BB	SO	AVG	OBP	SLG	PRO+	BR	/A	RC	SB	CS	SBR	FA	FR	POS	TPR
1986	NY-N	49	136	16	36	5	0	4	10	12	19	.265	.324	.390	99	-1	-0	16	0	1	-1	.987	-6	C	-0.5
1987	KC-A	6	17	2	5	2	0	0	3	4	2	.294	.429	.412	121	1	1	3	0	0	0	1.000	-2	/C	-0.1
1988	KC-A	7	18	1	4	2	0	0	1	0	1	.222	.222	.333	53	-1	-1	1	0	0	0	1.000	-0	/CD	-0.1
Total	3	62	171	19	45	9	0	4	14	16	22	.263	.326	.386	97	-1	-1	20	0	1	-1		-8	/CD	-0.7

■ HUGHIE HEARNE

Hearne, Hugh Joseph b: 4/18/1873, Troy, N.Y. d: 9/22/32, Troy, N.Y. BR/TR, 5'8", 182 lbs. Deb: 8/29/01

YEAR	TM/L	G	AB	R	H	2B	3B	HR	RBI	BB	SO	AVG	OBP	SLG	PRO+	BR	/A	RC	SB	CS	SBR	FA	FR	POS	TPR
1901	Bro-N	2	5	1	2	0	0	0	3	0		.400	.400	.400	129	0	0	1	0			1.000	0	/C	0.0
1902	Bro-N	66	231	22	65	10	0	0	28	16		.281	.339	.325	104	2	1	28	3			.966	-9	C	-0.1
1903	Bro-N	26	57	8	16	3	2	0	4	3		.281	.317	.404	108	0	0	8	2			.960	3	C/1	0.5
Total	3	94	293	31	83	13	2	0	35	19		.283	.335	.341	105	2	2	37	5			.965	-6	/C1	0.4

■ JEFF HEARRON

Hearron, Jeffrey Vernon b: 11/19/61, Long Beach, Cal. BR/TR, 6'1", 195 lbs. Deb: 8/25/85

YEAR	TM/L	G	AB	R	H	2B	3B	HR	RBI	BB	SO	AVG	OBP	SLG	PRO+	BR	/A	RC	SB	CS	SBR	FA	FR	POS	TPR
1985	*Tor-A	4	7	0	1	0	0	0	0	0	2	.143	.143	.143	-21	-1	-1	0	0	0	0	1.000	2	/C	0.0
1986	Tor-A	12	23	2	5	1	0	0	4	3	7	.217	.308	.261	55	-1	-1	2	0	0	0	.980	1	C	0.0
Total	2	16	30	2	6	1	0	0	4	3	9	.200	.273	.233	39	-2	-3	2	0	0	0	.985	2	/C	0.0

■ JEFF HEATH

Heath, John Geoffrey b: 4/1/15, Ft.William, Ont., Canada d: 12/9/75, Seattle, Wash. BL/TR, 5'11.5", 200 lbs. Deb: 9/13/36

YEAR	TM/L	G	AB	R	H	2B	3B	HR	RBI	BB	SO	AVG	OBP	SLG	PRO+	BR	/A	RC	SB	CS	SBR	FA	FR	POS	TPR
1936	Cle-A	12	41	6	14	3	3	1	8	3	4	.341	.386	.634	147	3	3	10	1	0	0	1.000	-3	O	0.0
1937	Cle-A	20	61	8	14	1	4	0	8	0	9	.230	.230	.377	50	-5	-5	5	0	1	-1	1.000	-1	O	-0.6
1938	Cle-A	126	502	104	172	31	**18**	21	112	33	55	.343	.383	.602	146	29	31	114	3	1	0	.974	1	*O	2.5
1939	Cle-A	121	431	64	126	31	7	14	69	41	64	.292	.354	.494	119	8	10	75	8	4	0	.964	6	*O	1.1
1940	Cle-A	100	356	55	78	16	3	14	50	40	62	.219	.298	.399	81	-12	-11	45	5	3	-0	.971	2	O	-1.4
1941	Cle-A★	151	585	89	199	32	**20**	24	123	50	69	.340	.396	.586	165	45	49	138	18	12	-2	.949	-4	*O	3.2
1942	Cle-A	147	568	82	158	37	13	10	76	62	66	.278	.350	.442	130	15	19	89	9	9	-3	.980	2	*O	1.1
1943	Cle-A★	118	424	58	116	22	6	18	79	63	58	.274	.369	.481	157	25	28	79	5	8	-3	.968	-4	*O	1.6
1944	Cle-A	60	151	20	50	5	2	5	33	18	12	.331	.402	.490	160	11	11	31	0	1	-1	.952	-1	O	0.9
1945	Cle-A	102	370	60	113	16	7	15	61	56	39	.305	.398	.508	169	29	31	80	3	1	0	.973	-4	*O	2.4
1946	Was-A	48	166	23	47	12	3	4	27	36	36	.283	.411	.464	153	11	12	34	0	4	-2	.969	-2	O	0.6
	StL-A	86	316	46	87	20	4	12	57	37	37	.275	.353	.478	124	12	10	56	0	2	-1	.962	-6	O	-0.2
	Yr	134	482	69	134	32	7	16	84	73	73	.278	.374	.473	134	23	23	91	0	6	-4	.965	-9	*O	0.4
1947	StL-A	141	491	81	123	20	7	27	85	88	87	.251	.366	.485	133	23	22	91	2	1	0	.987	-3	*O	1.2
1948	Bos-N	115	364	64	116	26	5	20	76	51	46	.319	.404	.582	167	32	33	89	2			**.991**	-2	*O	2.6
1949	Bos-N	36	111	17	34	7	0	9	23	15	26	.306	.389	.613	174	10	10	27	0			.983	-2	O	0.7
Total	14	1383	4937	777	1447	279	102	194	887	593	670	.293	.370	.509	140	235	254	964	56	47		.972	-20	*O	15.7

■ KELLY HEATH

Heath, Kelly Mark b: 9/4/57, Plattsburg, N.Y. BR/TR, 5'7", 155 lbs. Deb: 4/20/82

YEAR	TM/L	G	AB	R	H	2B	3B	HR	RBI	BB	SO	AVG	OBP	SLG	PRO+	BR	/A	RC	SB	CS	SBR	FA	FR	POS	TPR
1982	KC-A	1	1	0	0	0	0	0	0	0	0	.000	.000	.000	-99	-0	-0	0	0	0	0	1.000	1	/2	0.1

■ MIKE HEATH

Heath, Michael Thomas b: 2/5/55, Tampa, Fla. BR/TR, 5'11", 190 lbs. Deb: 6/03/78

YEAR	TM/L	G	AB	R	H	2B	3B	HR	RBI	BB	SO	AVG	OBP	SLG	PRO+	BR	/A	RC	SB	CS	SBR	FA	FR	POS	TPR
1978	*NY-A	33	92	6	21	3	1	0	8	4	9	.228	.268	.283	56	-6	-5	7	0	0	0	.970	3	C	-0.2
1979	Oak-A	74	258	19	66	8	0	3	27	17	18	.256	.309	.322	75	-10	-9	23	1	0	0	.978	-1	OC/3D	-1.1
1980	Oak-A	92	305	27	74	10	2	1	33	16	28	.243	.280	.298	63	-17	-15	24	3	3	-1	.986	8	CD/O	-0.6
1981	*Oak-A	84	301	26	71	7	1	8	30	13	36	.236	.270	.346	80	-10	-8	25	3	3	-1	.978	4	C/O	-0.2
1982	Oak-A	101	318	43	77	18	4	3	39	27	36	.242	.301	.352	82	-9	-8	35	8	3	1	.973	-8	CO/3	-1.2
1983	Oak-A	96	345	45	97	17	0	6	33	18	59	.281	.319	.383	98	-4	-2	39	3	4	-2	.973	-10	CO/3D	-1.0
1984	Oak-A	140	475	49	118	21	5	13	64	26	72	.248	.289	.396	94	-9	-5	50	7	4	-0	.986	-19	*CO/3S	-2.1
1985	Oak-A	138	436	71	109	18	6	13	55	41	63	.250	.316	.408	104	-3	2	53	7	7	-2	.981	-13	*CO3	-0.9
1986	StL-N	65	190	19	39	8	1	4	25	23	36	.205	.294	.321	70	-8	-8	17	2	3	-1	.967	-7	C/O	-1.2
	Det-A	30	98	11	26	3	0	4	11	4	17	.265	.294	.418	92	-1	-1	12	4	1	1	.987	-2	C/3	-0.1
1987	*Det-A	93	270	34	76	16	0	8	33	21	42	.281	.340	.430	107	1	2	38	1	5	-3	.989	2	CO/13S2	0.5
1988	Det-A	86	219	24	54	7	2	5	18	18	32	.247	.307	.365	91	-4	-3	24	1	0	0	.984	-1	C/O	0.2
1989	Det-A	122	396	38	104	16	2	10	43	24	71	.263	.311	.389	98	-3	-2	44	7	1	2	.986	0	*C/3OD	0.6
1990	Det-A	122	370	46	100	18	2	7	38	19	71	.270	.313	.386	94	-3	-4	41	7	6	-2	.980	-2	*C/OSD	0.0
1991	Atl-N	49	139	4	29	3	1	1	12	7	26	.209	.252	.266	43	-10	-11	9	0	0	0	.991	-1	C	-1.0
Total	14	1325	4212	462	1061	173	27	86	469	278	616	.252	.302	.367	87	-97	-75	443	54	40	-8	.981	-46	*CO/D31S2	-8.3

■ MICKEY HEATH

Heath, Minor Wilson b: 10/30/03, Toledo, Ohio d: 7/30/86, Dallas, Tex. BL/TL, 6', 175 lbs. Deb: 4/18/31

YEAR	TM/L	G	AB	R	H	2B	3B	HR	RBI	BB	SO	AVG	OBP	SLG	PRO+	BR	/A	RC	SB	CS	SBR	FA	FR	POS	TPR
1931	Cin-N	7	26	2	7	0	0	0	3	2	5	.269	.321	.269	64	-1	-1	2	0			1.000	-0	/1	-0.2
1932	Cin-N	39	134	14	27	1	3	0	15	20	23	.201	.310	.254	55	-8	-8	12	0			.991	2	1	-0.9
Total	2	46	160	16	34	1	3	0	18	22	28	.213	.311	.256	57	-10	-9	15	0			.992	2	/1	-1.1

■ TOMMY HEATH

Heath, Thomas George b: 8/18/13, Akron, Col. d: 2/26/67, Los Gatos, Cal. BR/TR, 5'10", 185 lbs. Deb: 4/23/35

YEAR	TM/L	G	AB	R	H	2B	3B	HR	RBI	BB	SO	AVG	OBP	SLG	PRO+	BR	/A	RC	SB	CS	SBR	FA	FR	POS	TPR
1935	StL-A	47	93	10	22	3	0	0	9	20	13	.237	.372	.269	65	-3	-4	11	0	0	0	.982	-2	C	-0.4
1937	StL-A	17	43	4	10	0	2	1	3	10	3	.233	.377	.395	94	-0	-0	7	0	0	0	1.000	-0	C	0.0
1938	StL-A	70	194	22	44	13	0	2	22	35	24	.227	.345	.325	69	-9	-9	24	0	1	-1	.986	7	C	0.0
Total	3	134	330	36	76	16	2	3	34	65	40	.230	.357	.318	71	-12	-13	42	0	1	-1	.987	5	C	-0.4

■ BILL HEATH Heath, William Chris b: 3/10/39, Yuba City, Cal. BL/TR, 5'8", 175 lbs. Deb: 10/03/65

YEAR	TM/L	G	AB	R	H	2B	3B	HR	RBI	BB	SO	AVG	OBP	SLG	PRO+	BR	/A	RC	SB	CS	SBR	FA	FR	POS	TPR
1965	Chi-A	1	1	0	0	0	0	0	0	0	0	.000	.000	.000	-99	-0	-0	0	0	0	0	.000	0	H	0.0
1966	Hou-N	55	123	12	37	6	0	0	8	9	11	.301	.353	.350	103	-0	1	15	1	0	0	.995	-1	C	0.2
1967	Hou-N	9	11	0	1	0	0	0	0	4	3	.091	.333	.091	28	-1	-1	1	0	0	0	1.000	1	/C	0.0
	Det-A	20	32	0	4	0	0	0	4	1	4	.125	.152	.125	-17	-5	-5	1	0	0	0	1.000	1	/C	-0.4
1969	Chi-N	27	32	1	5	0	1	0	1	12	4	.156	.386	.219	65	-0	-1	4	0	0	0	.979	0	/C	-0.1
Total	4	112	199	13	47	6	1	0	13	26	22	.236	.327	.276	73	-6	-6	20	1	0	0	.993	1	/C	-0.3

■ CLIFF HEATHCOTE Heathcote, Clifton Earl b: 1/24/1898, Glen Rock, Pa. d: 1/19/39, York, Pa. BL/TL, 5'10.5", 160 lbs. Deb: 6/04/18

YEAR	TM/L	G	AB	R	H	2B	3B	HR	RBI	BB	SO	AVG	OBP	SLG	PRO+	BR	/A	RC	SB	CS	SBR	FA	FR	POS	TPR
1918	StL-N	88	348	37	90	12	3	4	32	20	40	.259	.301	.345	100	-2	-1	38	12			.934	-4	O	-1.1
1919	StL-N	114	401	53	112	13	4	1	29	20	41	.279	.315	.339	103	-2	1	49	27			.967	-3	*O/1	-1.0
1920	StL-N	133	489	55	139	18	8	3	56	25	31	.284	.320	.372	102	-2	0	57	21	14	-2	.964	10	*O	-0.1
1921	StL-N	62	156	18	38	6	2	0	9	10	9	.244	.293	.308	61	-9	-9	14	7	5	-1	.926	-8	O	-2.1
1922	StL-N	34	98	11	24	5	2	0	14	9	4	.245	.315	.337	71	-5	-4	10	0	2	-1	.950	2	O	-0.5
	Chi-N	76	243	37	68	8	7	1	34	18	15	.280	.330	.383	82	-6	-7	31	5	2	0	.986	-2	O	-1.2
	Yr	110	341	48	92	13	9	1	48	27	19	.270	.325	.370	79	-11	-11	41	5	4	-1	.971	0	O	-1.7
1923	Chi-N	117	393	48	98	14	3	1	27	25	22	.249	.298	.308	60	-23	-23	36	32	17	-1	.980	4	*O	-2.5
1924	Chi-N	113	392	66	121	19	7	0	30	28	28	.309	.356	.393	100	1	0	51	26	24	-7	.979	-2	*O	-1.6
1925	Chi-N	109	380	57	100	14	5	5	39	39	26	.263	.343	.366	80	-10	-11	49	15	11	-2	.970	14	O	-0.5
1926	Chi-N	139	510	98	141	33	3	10	53	58	30	.276	.353	.412	104	4	3	74	18			**.985**	13	*O	0.7
1927	Chi-N	83	228	28	67	12	4	2	25	20	16	.294	.359	.408	105	2	2	33	6			.987	8	O	0.7
1928	Chi-N	67	137	26	39	8	0	3	18	17	12	.285	.364	.409	103	1	1	21	6			.973	-2	O	-0.4
1929	*Chi-N	82	224	45	70	17	0	2	31	25	17	.313	.384	.415	98	-0	-0	36	9			.985	3	O	-0.1
1930	Chi-N	70	150	30	39	10	1	9	18	18	15	.260	.343	.520	104	0	0	26	4			.986	-2	O	-0.3
1931	Cin-N	90	252	34	65	15	6	0	28	32	16	.258	.342	.365	96	-3	-1	33	3			.989	12	O	0.7
1932	Cin-N	8	3	3	0	0	0	0	0	0	0	.000	.000	.000	-99	-1	-1	0	0			.000	0	H	-0.1
	Phi-N	30	39	7	11	2	0	1	5	3	3	.282	.333	.410	88	-0	-1	6	0			.962	-0	/1	-0.1
	Yr	38	42	10	11	2	0	1	5	3	3	.262	.311	.381	78	-1	-1	5	0			.962	-0	/1	-0.2
Total	15	1415	4443	653	1222	206	55	42	448	367	325	.275	.333	.375	92	-55	-50	563	191	75		.971	43	*O/1	-9.5

■ RICHIE HEBNER Hebner, Richard Joseph b: 11/26/47, Boston, Mass. BL/TR, 6'1", 197 lbs. Deb: 9/23/68 C

YEAR	TM/L	G	AB	R	H	2B	3B	HR	RBI	BB	SO	AVG	OBP	SLG	PRO+	BR	/A	RC	SB	CS	SBR	FA	FR	POS	TPR
1968	Pit-N	2	1	0	0	0	0	0	0	0	0	.000	.000	.000	-99	-0	-0	0	0	0	0	.000	0	H	0.0
1969	Pit-N	129	459	72	138	23	4	8	47	53	53	.301	.383	.420	127	17	18	77	4	1	1	.944	3	*3/1	2.3
1970	*Pit-N	120	420	60	122	24	8	11	46	42	48	.290	.365	.464	123	12	13	71	2	3	-1	.940	1	*3	1.2
1971	*Pit-N	112	388	50	105	17	8	17	67	32	68	.271	.331	.487	130	13	13	62	2	2	-1	.949	-8	*3	0.4
1972	*Pit-N	124	427	63	128	24	4	19	72	52	54	.300	.384	.508	155	29	30	85	0	0	0	.969	-15	*3	1.5
1973	Pit-N	144	509	73	138	28	1	25	74	56	60	.271	.348	.477	130	17	19	85	0	1	-1	.939	-14	*3	0.4
1974	*Pit-N	146	550	97	160	21	6	18	68	60	53	.291	.367	.449	132	20	22	90	0	3	-2	.937	-6	*3	1.4
1975	*Pit-N	128	472	65	116	16	4	15	57	43	48	.246	.322	.392	98	-2	-2	61	0	1	-1	.946	-15	*3	-1.9
1976	Pit-N	132	434	60	108	21	3	8	51	47	39	.249	.328	.366	96	-2	-2	54	1	3	-2	.953	-10	*3	-1.5
1977	*Phi-N	118	397	67	113	17	4	18	62	61	46	.285	.384	.484	125	18	16	74	7	8	-3	.991	2	*13/2	1.0
1978	*Phi-N	137	435	61	123	22	3	17	71	53	58	.283	.372	.464	131	19	19	74	4	7	-3	.994	-2	*13/2	0.8
1979	NY-N	136	473	54	127	25	2	10	79	59	59	.268	.359	.393	109	5	7	71	3	1	0	.940	-7	*3/1	-0.1
1980	Det-A	104	341	48	99	10	7	12	82	38	45	.290	.365	.466	123	12	11	57	0	3	-2	.998	-5	13/D	0.1
1981	Det-A	78	226	19	51	8	2	5	28	27	28	.226	.314	.345	87	-3	-4	24	1	2	-1	.995	-3	1D	-1.1
1982	Det-A	68	179	25	49	6	0	8	18	25	21	.274	.363	.441	119	5	5	30	1	1	-0	.990	2	1D	0.5
	Pit-N	25	70	6	21	2	0	2	12	5	3	.300	.347	.414	109	1	1	11	4	0	1	.964	-1	O/13	0.0
1983	Pit-N	78	162	23	43	4	1	5	26	17	28	.265	.339	.395	100	1	0	22	8	3	1	.967	-5	3/1O	-0.6
1984	*Chi-N	44	81	12	27	3	0	2	8	10	15	.333	.407	.444	127	4	4	15	1	0	0	.963	-2	3/1O	0.2
1985	Chi-N	83	120	10	26	2	0	3	22	7	15	.217	.266	.308	54	-7	-8	9	0	1	-1	.991	-0	1/3O	-1.0
Total	18	1908	6144	865	1694	273	57	203	890	687	741	.276	.356	.438	120	161	163	972	38	40	-13	.946	-83	*31/DO2	3.6

■ MIKE HECHINGER Hechinger, Michael Vincent b: 2/14/1890, Chicago, Ill. d: 8/13/67, Chicago, Ill. BR/TR, 6', 175 lbs. Deb: 9/27/12

YEAR	TM/L	G	AB	R	H	2B	3B	HR	RBI	BB	SO	AVG	OBP	SLG	PRO+	BR	/A	RC	SB	CS	SBR	FA	FR	POS	TPR
1912	Chi-N	2	3	0	0	0	0	0	0	2	0	.000	.400	.000	14	-0	-0	0	0			1.000	0	/C	0.0
1913	Chi-N	2	2	0	0	0	0	0	0	0	0	.000	.000	.000	-99	-1	-1	0	0			.000	0	H	-0.1
	Bro-N	9	11	1	2	1	0	0	0	0	2	.182	.182	.273	28	-1	-1	0	0			1.000	-1	/C	-0.2
	Yr	11	13	1	2	1	0	0	0	0	2	.154	.154	.231	9	-2	-2	0	0			1.000	-1	/C	-0.3
Total	2	13	16	1	2	1	0	0	0	2	2	.125	.222	.188	16	-2	-2	0	0			1.000	-1	/C	-0.3

■ GUY HECKER Hecker, Guy Jackson b: 4/3/1856, Youngsville, Pa. d: 12/3/38, Wooster, Ohio BR/TR, 6', 190 lbs. Deb: 5/02/1882 MU

YEAR	TM/L	G	AB	R	H	2B	3B	HR	RBI	BB	SO	AVG	OBP	SLG	PRO+	BR	/A	RC	SB	CS	SBR	FA	FR	POS	TPR
1882	Lou-a	78	340	62	94	14	4	3		5		.276	.287	.368	126	6	9	37				.958	5	*1P/O	0.1
1883	Lou-a	79	322	56	88	6	6	1		10		.273	.295	.339	112	1	5	33				.936	3	PO1	0.0
1884	Lou-a	78	316	53	94	14	8	4		10		.297	.323	.430	154	15	17	45				.951	6	*P/O	0.0
1885	Lou-a	70	297	48	81	9	2	2		5		.273	.287	.337	99	-1	-1	29				.927	3	P1/O	-0.3
1886	Lou-a	84	343	76	117	14	5	4		32		.341	.402	.446	159	27	24	73	25			.875	-6	P1O	0.1
1887	Lou-a	91	370	89	118	21	6	4		31		.319	.381	.441	128	15	14	82	48			.954	-4	1PO	-0.3
1888	Lou-a	56	211	32	48	9	2	0	29	11		.227	.285	.289	89	-3	-2	24	20			.936	-4	1P/O	-0.8
1889	Lou-a	81	327	42	93	17	5	1	36	18	27	.284	.333	.376	106	1	2	48	17			.969	-0	1P/O	-0.2
1890	Pit-N	86	340	43	77	13	9	0	38	19	17	.226	.285	.318	88	-10	-4	35	13			.962	1	1P/OM	-0.4
Total	9	703	2866	501	810	117	47	19	103	141	44	.283	.324	.376	120	52	64	407	123			.935	4	P1/O	-1.8

■ DANNY HEEP Heep, Daniel William b: 7/3/57, San Antonio, Tex. BL/TL, 5'11", 185 lbs. Deb: 8/31/79

YEAR	TM/L	G	AB	R	H	2B	3B	HR	RBI	BB	SO	AVG	OBP	SLG	PRO+	BR	/A	RC	SB	CS	SBR	FA	FR	POS	TPR
1979	Hou-N	14	14	0	2	0	0	0	2	1	4	.143	.200	.143	-5	-2	-2	1	0	0	0	1.000	1	/O	-0.1
1980	*Hou-N	33	87	6	24	8	0	0	6	8	9	.276	.344	.368	107	-0	1	12	0	0	0	.990	-2	1	-0.2
1981	Hou-N	33	96	6	24	3	0	0	11	10	11	.250	.321	.281	76	-3	-3	9	0	0	0	.990	-3	1/O	-0.7
1982	Hou-N	85	198	16	47	14	1	4	22	21	31	.237	.314	.379	100	-2	-0	23	0	2	-1	1.000	-4	O1	-0.7
1983	NY-N	115	253	30	64	12	0	8	21	29	40	.253	.332	.395	102	0	1	33	3	3	-1	1.000	-4	O1	-0.6
1984	NY-N	99	199	36	46	9	2	1	12	27	22	.231	.326	.312	81	-5	-4	20	3	1	0	.967	1	O1	-0.5
1985	NY-N	95	271	26	76	17	0	7	42	27	27	.280	.348	.421	117	5	6	37	2	2	-1	.977	-5	O/1	-0.3
1986	*NY-N	86	195	24	55	8	2	5	33	30	31	.282	.381	.421	124	6	7	31	1	4	-2	.988	-2	O	0.1
1987	LA-N	60	98	7	16	4	0	0	9	8	10	.163	.226	.204	16	-12	-12	4	1	0	0	.962	-1	O/1	-1.4
1988	*LA-N	95	149	14	36	2	0	0	11	22	13	.242	.343	.255	76	-4	-3	14	2	0	1	1.000	-2	O1/P	-0.7
1989	Bos-A	113	320	36	96	17	0	5	49	29	26	.300	.360	.400	107	6	4	43	0	1	-1	.989	-12	O1/D	-1.2
1990	*Bos-A	41	69	3	12	1	1	0	8	7	14	.174	.260	.217	33	-6	-6	5	0	0	0	1.000	-0	O/1PD	-0.7
1991	Atl-N	14	12	4	5	1	0	0	3	1	4	.417	.462	.500	161	1	1	2	0	1	-1	1.000	-0	/1O	0.0
Total	13	883	1961	208	503	96	6	30	229	220	242	.257	.334	.357	95	-15	-11	233	12	14	-5	.986	-33	O1/DP	-7.0

■ BERT HEFFERNAN Heffernan, Bertram Alexander b: 3/3/65, Centereach, N.Y. BL/TR, 5'10", 185 lbs. Deb: 5/13/92

YEAR	TM/L	G	AB	R	H	2B	3B	HR	RBI	BB	SO	AVG	OBP	SLG	PRO+	BR	/A	RC	SB	CS	SBR	FA	FR	POS	TPR
1992	Sea-A	8	11	0	1	1	0	0	1	0	1	.091	.091	.182	-25	-2	-2	0	0	0	0	1.000	1	/C	-0.1

■ DON HEFFNER Heffner, Donald Henry "Jeep" b: 2/8/11, Rouzerville, Pa. d: 8/1/89, Pasadena, Cal. BR/TR, 5'10", 155 lbs. Deb: 4/17/34 MC

YEAR	TM/L	G	AB	R	H	2B	3B	HR	RBI	BB	SO	AVG	OBP	SLG	PRO+	BR	/A	RC	SB	CS	SBR	FA	FR	POS	TPR
1934	NY-A	72	241	29	63	8	3	0	25	25	18	.261	.331	.320	73	-11	-9	27	1	1	-0	.971	-8	2	-1.3
1935	NY-A	10	36	3	11	3	1	0	8	4	1	.306	.375	.444	118	1	1	6	0	0	0	.980	-1	2	0.1
1936	NY-A	19	48	7	11	2	1	0	6	6	5	.229	.315	.313	57	-3	-3	5	0	0	0	.971	4	/32S	0.1

YEAR	TM/L	G	AB	R	H	2B	3B	HR	RBI	BB	SO	AVG	OBP	SLG	PRO+	BR	/A	RC	SB	CS	SBR	FA	FR	POS	TPR
1937	NY-A	60	201	23	50	6	5	0	21	19	19	.249	.314	.328	62	-12	-12	20	1	4	-2	.980	-8	2S/310	-1.7
1938	StL-A	141	473	47	116	23	3	2	69	65	53	.245	.341	.319	67	-23	-23	56	1	1	-0	.971	-9	*2	-2.2
1939	StL-A	110	375	45	100	10	2	1	35	48	39	.267	.350	.312	69	-15	-16	41	1	7	-4	.944	-4	S2	-1.5
1940	StL-A	126	487	52	115	23	2	3	53	39	37	.236	.295	.310	56	-31	-32	45	5	5	-2	**.977**	**19**	*2	-0.6
1941	StL-A	110	399	48	93	14	2	0	17	38	27	.233	.303	.278	53	-26	-27	36	5	6	-2	.974	3	*2	-2.0
1942	StL-A	19	36	2	6	2	0	0	3	1	4	.167	.189	.222	15	-4	-4	1	1	0	0	.906	1	/21	-0.2
1943	StL-A	18	33	2	4	1	0	0	2	2	2	.121	.171	.152	-5	-4	-4	1	0	0	0	.974	-0	2/1	-0.5
	Phi-A	52	178	17	37	6	0	0	8	18	12	.208	.284	.242	55	-10	-10	13	3	2	-0	.978	-10	2/1	-1.9
	Yr	70	211	19	41	7	0	0	10	20	14	.194	.267	.227	45	-14	-14	14	3	2	-0	.978	-10	2/1	-2.4
1944	Det-A	6	19	0	4	1	0	0	1	5	1	.211	.375	.263	80	-0	-0	2	0	0	0	.962	-1	/2	-0.1
Total	11	743	2526	275	610	99	19	6	248	270	218	.241	.317	.303	61	-139	-141	254	18	26	-10	.973	-13	2/S310	-11.8

■ JIM HEGAN Hegan, James Edward b: 8/3/20, Lynn, Mass. d: 6/17/84, Swampscott, Mass. BR/TR, 6′2″, 195 lbs. Deb: 9/09/41 FC

YEAR	TM/L	G	AB	R	H	2B	3B	HR	RBI	BB	SO	AVG	OBP	SLG	PRO+	BR	/A	RC	SB	CS	SBR	FA	FR	POS	TPR
1941	Cle-A	16	47	4	15	2	0	1	5	4	7	.319	.373	.426	116	1	1	8	0	0	0	.973	-0	C	0.2
1942	Cle-A	68	170	10	33	5	0	0	11	11	31	.194	.243	.224	34	-15	-14	9	1	3	-2	.977	8	C	-0.4
1946	Cle-A	88	271	29	64	11	5	0	17	17	44	.236	.284	.314	71	-12	-10	23	1	4	-2	.991	9	C	0.1
1947	Cle-A☆	135	378	38	94	14	5	4	42	41	49	.249	.324	.344	88	-7	-6	44	3	1	0	.989	7	*C	0.9
1948	*Cle-A	144	472	60	117	21	6	14	61	48	74	.248	.317	.407	94	-8	-6	62	6	3	0	.990	21	*C	2.3
1949	Cle-A☆	152	468	54	105	19	5	8	55	49	89	.224	.298	.338	69	-24	-22	49	1	0	0	.990	10	*C	-0.3
1950	Cle-A★	131	415	53	91	16	5	14	58	42	52	.219	.291	.383	74	-20	-18	47	1	0	0	.993	24	*C	1.1
1951	Cle-A★	133	416	60	99	17	5	6	43	38	72	.238	.302	.346	79	-16	-13	45	0	3	-2	.991	11	*C	0.2
1952	Cle-A☆	112	333	39	75	17	2	4	41	29	47	.225	.287	.324	75	-14	-12	32	0	2	-1	.987	7	*C	-0.1
1953	Cle-A	112	299	37	65	10	1	9	37	25	41	.217	.280	.348	71	-14	-13	29	1	2	-1	.976	3	*C	-0.7
1954	*Cle-A	139	423	56	99	12	7	11	40	34	48	.234	.291	.374	80	-13	-14	43	0	1	-1	**.994**	13	*C	0.5
1955	Cle-A	116	304	30	67	5	2	9	40	34	33	.220	.299	.339	69	-13	-14	31	0	1	-1	**.997**	7	*C	-0.5
1956	Cle-A	122	315	42	70	15	2	6	34	49	54	.222	.327	.340	75	-11	-12	36	1	1	-0	.985	16	*C	0.8
1957	Cle-A	58	148	14	32	7	0	4	15	16	23	.216	.293	.345	74	-6	-5	15	0	1	-1	1.000	3	C	-0.2
1958	Det-A	45	130	14	25	6	0	1	7	10	32	.192	.250	.262	38	-11	-12	8	0	0	0	.996	1	C	-0.9
	Phi-N	25	59	5	13	6	0	0	6	4	16	.220	.270	.322	57	-4	-4	5	0	0	0	.991	4	C	0.1
1959	Phi-N	25	51	1	10	1	0	0	8	3	10	.196	.241	.216	22	-6	-6	3	0	1	-1	.990	1	C	-0.5
	SF-N	21	30	0	4	1	0	0	0	1	10	.133	.161	.167	-13	-5	-5	1	0	1	-1	.975	5	C	0.0
	Yr	46	81	1	14	2	0	0	8	4	20	.173	.212	.198	10	-10	-10	3	0	2	-1	.983	5	C	-0.5
1960	Chi-N	24	43	4	9	2	1	1	5	1	10	.209	.244	.372	67	-2	-2	3	0	0	0	.977	2	C	0.1
Total	17	1666	4772	550	1087	187	46	92	525	456	742	.228	.296	.344	74	-199	-187	491	15	24	-10	.990	149	*C	2.7

■ MIKE HEGAN Hegan, James Michael b: 7/21/42, Cleveland, Ohio BL/TL, 6′1″, 190 lbs. Deb: 9/13/64 F

YEAR	TM/L	G	AB	R	H	2B	3B	HR	RBI	BB	SO	AVG	OBP	SLG	PRO+	BR	/A	RC	SB	CS	SBR	FA	FR	POS	TPR
1964	*NY-A	5	5	0	0	0	0	0	0	1	2	.000	.167	.000	-48	-1	-1	0	0	0	0	1.000	1	/1	0.0
1966	NY-A	13	39	7	8	0	1	0	2	7	11	.205	.326	.256	73	-1	-1	3	1	1	-0	.991	-0	1	-0.3
1967	NY-A	68	118	12	16	4	1	1	3	20	40	.136	.266	.212	44	-8	-7	9	7	1	2	1.000	1	1O	-0.8
1969	Sea-A†	95	267	54	78	9	6	8	37	62	61	.292	.427	.461	151	20	21	58	6	5	-1	.955	2	O1	1.8
1970	Mil-A	148	476	70	116	21	2	11	52	67	116	.244	.338	.366	93	-3	-3	61	9	7	-2	.994	11	*1/O	-0.6
1971	Mil-A	46	122	19	27	4	1	4	11	26	19	.221	.358	.369	107	2	2	18	1	1	-0	1.000	4	1	0.3
	*Oak-A	65	55	5	13	3	0	0	3	5	13	.236	.300	.291	69	-2	-2	5	1	0	0	1.000	2	1/O	-0.1
	Yr	111	177	24	40	7	1	4	14	31	32	.226	.341	.345	96	-0	-0	23	2	1	0	1.000	6	1/O	0.2
1972	*Oak-A	98	79	13	26	3	1	1	5	7	20	.329	.384	.430	150	4	5	14	1	0	0	1.000	2	1/O	0.6
1973	Oak-A	75	71	8	13	2	0	1	5	5	17	.183	.237	.254	40	-6	-5	4	0	0	0	.988	-3	1/OD	-0.9
	NY-A	37	131	12	36	3	2	6	14	7	34	.275	.312	.466	121	2	3	19	0	0	0	.992	2	1	0.1
	Yr	112	202	20	49	5	2	7	19	12	51	.243	.285	.391	93	-4	-3	22	0	0	0	.991	-1	1/OD	-0.8
1974	NY-A	18	53	3	12	2	0	2	9	5	9	.226	.317	.377	102	-0	0	6	1	1	-0	1.000	-0	1	-0.1
	Mil-A	89	190	21	45	7	1	7	32	33	34	.237	.350	.395	114	4	4	27	0	4	-2	.991	-2	D1O	-0.1
	Yr	107	243	24	57	9	1	9	41	38	43	.235	.343	.391	112	4	4	33	1	5	-3	.996	-2	D1O	-0.2
1975	Mil-A	93	203	19	51	11	0	5	22	31	42	.251	.350	.379	106	2	2	28	1	1	-0	.984	-4	O1/D	-0.4
1976	Mil-A	80	218	30	54	4	3	5	31	25	54	.248	.328	.362	104	1	1	27	0	0	0	1.000	-3	DO1	-0.3
1977	Mil-A	35	53	8	9	0	0	2	3	10	17	.170	.313	.283	64	-2	-2	6	0	0	0	1.000	-3	/O1D	-0.6
Total	12	965	2080	281	504	73	18	53	229	311	489	.242	.343	.371	103	12	15	285	28	21	-4	.995	11	1O/D	-1.4

■ BOB HEGMAN Hegman, Robert Hilmer b: 2/26/58, Springfield, Minn. BR/TR, 6′1″, 180 lbs. Deb: 8/08/85

YEAR	TM/L	G	AB	R	H	2B	3B	HR	RBI	BB	SO	AVG	OBP	SLG	PRO+	BR	/A	RC	SB	CS	SBR	FA	FR	POS	TPR
1985	KC-A	1	0	0	0	0	0	0	0	0	0	—	—	—	—	0	0	0	0	0	0	.000	0	/2	0.0

■ JACK HEIDEMANN Heidemann, Jack Seale b: 7/11/49, Brenham, Tex. BR/TR, 6′, 178 lbs. Deb: 5/02/69

YEAR	TM/L	G	AB	R	H	2B	3B	HR	RBI	BB	SO	AVG	OBP	SLG	PRO+	BR	/A	RC	SB	CS	SBR	FA	FR	POS	TPR
1969	Cle-A	3	3	0	0	0	0	0	0	0	2	.000	.250	.000	-24	-0	-0	0	0	0	0	1.000	1	/S	0.0
1970	Cle-A	133	445	44	94	14	2	6	37	34	88	.211	.270	.292	52	-28	-30	35	2	4	-2	.961	-2	*S	-2.0
1971	Cle-A	81	240	16	50	7	0	0	9	12	46	.208	.252	.237	36	-19	-22	14	1	3	-2	.977	-9	S	-2.5
1972	Cle-A	10	20	0	3	0	0	0	0	2	3	.150	.261	.150	24	-2	-2	1	0	0	0	.964	-1	S	-0.3
1974	Cle-A	12	11	2	1	0	0	0	0	0	2	.091	.091	.091	-48	-2	-2	0	0	0	0	1.000	-1	/3S12	-0.3
	StL-N	47	70	8	19	1	0	0	3	5	10	.271	.320	.286	71	-3	-3	7	0	0	0	.967	-10	S/3	-1.0
1975	NY-N	61	145	12	31	4	2	1	16	17	28	.214	.296	.290	66	-7	-6	13	1	0	0	.951	-12	S/32	-1.5
1976	NY-N	5	12	0	1	0	0	0	0	0	0	.083	.083	.083	-56	-2	-2	0	0	0	0	1.000	0	/S2	-0.2
	Mil-A	69	146	11	32	1	0	2	10	7	24	.219	.255	.267	54	-9	-8	10	1	3	-2	.962	-7	32/D	-1.7
1977	Mil-A	5	1	1	0	0	0	0	0	1	0	.000	.500	.000	50	0	0	0	0	0	0	1.000	1	/2D	0.1
Total	8	426	1093	94	231	27	4	9	75	78	203	.211	.268	.268	49	-72	-76	80	5	10	-5	.965	-42	S/32D1	-9.4

■ EMMETT HEIDRICK Heidrick, John Emmett "Snags" b: 7/9/1876, Queenstown, Pa. d: 1/20/16, Clarion, Pa. BL/TR, 6′, 185 lbs. Deb: 9/14/1898

YEAR	TM/L	G	AB	R	H	2B	3B	HR	RBI	BB	SO	AVG	OBP	SLG	PRO+	BR	/A	RC	SB	CS	SBR	FA	FR	POS	TPR
1898	Cle-N	19	76	10	23	2	2	0	8	3		.303	.329	.382	105	0	0	11	3			.850	-1	O	-0.2
1899	StL-N	146	591	109	194	21	14	2	82	34		.328	.368	.421	114	12	10	116	55			.925	4	*O	0.2
1900	StL-N	85	339	51	102	6	8	2	45	18		.301	.338	.383	100	-1	-1	53	22			.959	15	O	0.7
1901	StL-N	118	502	94	170	24	12	6	67	21		.339	.366	.470	149	24	28	102	32			.945	1	*O	1.9
1902	StL-A	110	447	75	129	19	10	3	56	34		.289	.339	.396	105	1	2	70	17			.940	2	*O/PS3	-0.3
1903	StL-A	120	461	55	129	20	15	1	42	19		.280	.310	.395	113	5	6	66	19			.954	2	*O/C	0.1
1904	StL-A	133	538	66	147	14	10	1	36	16		.273	.294	.342	108	-1	3	68	35			.963	11	*O	0.7
1908	StL-A	26	93	8	20	2	2	1	6	1		.215	.223	.312	73	-3	-3	7	3			.957	-1	O	-0.6
Total	8	757	3047	468	914	108	73	16	342	146		.300	.333	.399	114	37	45	493	186			.946	33	O/C3SP	2.5

■ FRANK HEIFER Heifer, Franklin "Heck" b: 1/18/1854, Reading, Pa. d: 8/29/1893, Reading, Pa. 5′10.5″, 175 lbs. Deb: 6/04/1875

YEAR	TM/L	G	AB	R	H	2B	3B	HR	RBI	BB	SO	AVG	OBP	SLG	PRO+	BR	/A	RC	SB	CS	SBR	FA	FR	POS	TPR
1875	Bos-n	11	51	11	14	0	3	0		0		.275	.275	.392	123	1	1	6						/1OP	0.1

■ CHINK HEILEMAN Heileman, John George b: 8/10/1872, Cincinnati, Ohio d: 7/19/40, Cincinnati, Ohio BR/TR, 5′8″, 155 lbs. Deb: 7/08/01

YEAR	TM/L	G	AB	R	H	2B	3B	HR	RBI	BB	SO	AVG	OBP	SLG	PRO+	BR	/A	RC	SB	CS	SBR	FA	FR	POS	TPR
1901	Cin-N	5	15	1	2	1	0	0	1	0		.133	.133	.200	-4	-2	-2	0	0			.667	-1	/32	-0.3

■ HARRY HEILMANN Heilmann, Harry Edwin "Slug" b: 8/3/1894, San Francisco, Cal. d: 7/9/51, Southfield, Mich. BR/TR, 6′1″, 195 lbs. Deb: 5/16/14 CH

YEAR	TM/L	G	AB	R	H	2B	3B	HR	RBI	BB	SO	AVG	OBP	SLG	PRO+	BR	/A	RC	SB	CS	SBR	FA	FR	POS	TPR
1914	Det-A	69	182	25	41	8	1	2	18	22	29	.225	.316	.313	86	-2	-3	18	1	8	-5	.870	-6	O1/2	-1.6
1916	Det-A	136	451	57	127	30	11	2	73	42	40	.282	.349	.410	124	14	12	70	9			.952	-10	O1/2	-0.2
1917	Det-A	150	556	57	156	22	11	5	86	41	54	.281	.333	.387	120	11	11	73	11			.960	-2	*O1	0.2
1918	Det-A	79	286	34	79	10	6	5	39	35	10	.276	.359	.406	136	10	12	45	13			.957	-4	O1/2	0.4
1919	Det-A	140	537	74	172	30	15	8	93	37	41	.320	.366	.477	139	23	25	93	7			.979	-10	*1	1.1

YEAR	TM/L	G	AB	R	H	2B	3B	HR	RBI	BB	SO	AVG	OBP	SLG	PRO+	BR	/A	RC	SB	CS	SBR	FA	FR	POS	TPR
1920	Det-A	145	543	66	168	28	5	9	89	39	32	.309	.358	.429	111	5	7	82	3	7	-3	.985	-1	*1O	-0.1
1921	Det-A	149	602	114	**237**	43	14	19	139	53	37	**.394**	.444	.606	167	58	59	159	2	6	-3	.962	-11	*O/1	3.2
1922	Det-A	118	455	92	162	27	10	21	92	58	28	.356	.432	.598	172	44	46	119	8	4	0	.948	-10	*O/1	2.6
1923	Det-A	144	524	121	211	44	11	18	115	74	40	**.403**	.481	.632	195	71	72	159	8	7	-2	.960	2	*O1	6.0
1924	Det-A	153	570	107	197	**45**	16	10	114	78	41	.346	.428	.533	149	40	42	134	13	5	1	.970	9	*O/1	3.9
1925	Det-A	150	573	97	225	40	11	13	134	67	27	**.393**	.457	.569	161	**52**	**54**	149	6	6	-2	.970	-3	*O	3.6
1926	Det-A	141	502	90	184	41	8	9	103	67	19	.367	.445	.534	152	42	41	120	6	7	-2	.972	-2	*O	2.7
1927	Det-A	141	505	106	201	50	9	14	120	72	16	**.398**	.475	.616	179	62	61	142	11	5	0	.966	-8	*O	4.2
1928	Det-A	151	558	83	183	38	10	14	107	57	45	.328	.390	.507	132	27	26	112	7	3	0	.971	1	*O1	1.6
1929	Det-A	125	453	86	156	41	7	15	120	50	39	.344	.412	.565	148	33	32	104	5	6	-2	.966	-6	*O/1	1.6
1930	Cin-N	142	459	79	153	43	6	19	91	64	50	.333	.416	.577	144	28	32	109	2			.955	12	*O1	3.0
1932	Cin-N	15	31	3	8	2	0	0	6	0	2	.258	.258	.323	57	-2	-2	3	0			.981	-0	/1	-0.3
Total	17	2148	7787	1291	2660	542	151	183	1539	856	550	.342	.410	.520	148	517	527	1690	112	64		.962	-48	*O1/2	31.9

■ VAL HEIM Heim, Val Raymond b: 11/4/20, Plymouth, Wis. BL/TR, 5'11", 170 lbs. Deb: 8/31/42

YEAR	TM/L	G	AB	R	H	2B	3B	HR	RBI	BB	SO	AVG	OBP	SLG	PRO+	BR	/A	RC	SB	CS	SBR	FA	FR	POS	TPR
1942	Chi-A	13	45	6	9	1	1	0	7	5	3	.200	.294	.267	60	-2	-2	4	1	0	0	.958	-1	O	-0.4

■ BUD HEINE Heine, William Henry b: 9/22/1900, Elmira, N.Y. d: 9/2/76, Ft.Lauderdale, Fla BL/TR, 5'8", 145 lbs. Deb: 10/01/21

YEAR	TM/L	G	AB	R	H	2B	3B	HR	RBI	BB	SO	AVG	OBP	SLG	PRO+	BR	/A	RC	SB	CS	SBR	FA	FR	POS	TPR
1921	NY-N	1	2	0	0	0	0	0	0	0	0	.000	.000	.000	-99	-1	-1	0	0	0	0	1.000	-0	/2	-0.1

■ TOM HEINTZELMAN Heintzelman, Thomas Kenneth b: 11/3/46, St.Charles, Mo. BR/TR, 6'1", 180 lbs. Deb: 8/12/73 F

YEAR	TM/L	G	AB	R	H	2B	3B	HR	RBI	BB	SO	AVG	OBP	SLG	PRO+	BR	/A	RC	SB	CS	SBR	FA	FR	POS	TPR
1973	StL-N	23	29	5	9	0	0	0	0	3	3	.310	.375	.310	92	-0	-0	3	0	0	0	1.000	1	/2	0.1
1974	StL-N	38	74	10	17	4	0	1	6	9	14	.230	.313	.324	79	-2	-2	8	0	0	0	.978	0	2/3S	-0.1
1977	SF-N	2	2	0	0	0	0	0	0	0	0	.000	.000	.000	-99	-1	-1	0	0	0	0	.000	0	H	-0.1
1978	SF-N	27	35	2	8	1	0	2	6	2	5	.229	.270	.429	96	-1	-0	4	0	0	0	1.000	2	/231	0.2
Total	4	90	140	17	34	5	0	3	12	14	22	.243	.312	.343	84	-3	-3	16	0	0	0	.984	4	/231S	0.1

■ JACK HEINZMAN Heinzman, John Peter b: 9/27/1863, New Albany, Ind. d: 11/10/14, Louisville, Ky. BR/TR, Deb: 10/02/1886

YEAR	TM/L	G	AB	R	H	2B	3B	HR	RBI	BB	SO	AVG	OBP	SLG	PRO+	BR	/A	RC	SB	CS	SBR	FA	FR	POS	TPR
1886	Lou-a	1	5	1	0	0	0	0		0		.000	.000	.000	-95	-1	-1	0	0			1.000	-0	/1	-0.1

■ BOB HEISE Heise, Robert Lowell b: 5/12/47, San Antonio, Tex. BR/TR, 6', 175 lbs. Deb: 9/12/67

YEAR	TM/L	G	AB	R	H	2B	3B	HR	RBI	BB	SO	AVG	OBP	SLG	PRO+	BR	/A	RC	SB	CS	SBR	FA	FR	POS	TPR
1967	NY-N	16	62	7	20	4	0	0	3	3	1	.323	.354	.387	114	1	1	8	0	1	-1	.973	2	2/S3	0.3
1968	NY-N	6	23	3	5	0	0	0	1	1	1	.217	.250	.217	41	-2	-2	1	0	0	0	.929	-5	/S2	-0.8
1969	NY-N	4	10	1	3	1	0	0	0	3	2	.300	.462	.400	140	1	1	2	0	0	0	1.000	-3	/S	-0.1
1970	SF-N	67	154	15	36	5	1	1	22	5	13	.234	.258	.299	49	-11	-11	11	0	1	-1	.915	-1	S2/3	-0.9
1971	SF-N	13	11	2	0	0	0	0	0	0	1	.000	.000	.000	-99	-3	-3	0	0	0	0	.833	0	/S32	-0.3
	Mil-A	68	189	10	48	7	0	0	7	7	15	.254	.281	.291	63	-10	-9	14	1	1	-0	.961	7	S3/2O	0.3
1972	Mil-A	95	271	23	72	10	1	0	12	12	14	.266	.302	.310	84	-6	-6	25	1	1	-0	.990	-3	23/S	-0.7
1973	Mil-A	49	98	8	20	2	0	0	4	4	4	.204	.235	.224	31	-9	-9	5	1	0	0	.956	-1	S/312D	-0.7
1974	StL-N	3	7	0	1	0	0	0	0	0	0	.143	.143	.143	-20	-1	-1	0	0	0	0	1.000	2	/2	0.1
	Cal-A	29	75	7	20	7	0	0	6	5	10	.267	.313	.360	99	-1	-0	8	0	1	-1	1.000	2	2/3S	0.2
1975	Bos-A	63	126	12	27	3	0	0	21	4	6	.214	.250	.238	35	-10	-11	8	0	0	0	.940	11	32/S1	0.0
1976	Bos-A	32	56	5	15	2	0	0	5	1	2	.268	.293	.304	67	-2	-3	5	0	1	-1	.968	2	3/S2	0.0
1977	KC-A	54	62	11	16	2	1	0	5	2	8	.258	.292	.323	67	-3	-3	6	0	1	-1	1.000	10	2S3/1	0.8
Total	11	499	1144	104	283	43	3	1	86	47	77	.247	.281	.293	63	-55	-56	92	3	7	-3	.945	23	S23/1DO	-1.8

■ AL HEIST Heist, Alfred Michael b: 10/5/27, Brooklyn, N.Y. BR/TR, 6'2", 185 lbs. Deb: 7/17/60 C

YEAR	TM/L	G	AB	R	H	2B	3B	HR	RBI	BB	SO	AVG	OBP	SLG	PRO+	BR	/A	RC	SB	CS	SBR	FA	FR	POS	TPR
1960	Chi-N	41	102	11	28	5	3	1	6	10	12	.275	.339	.412	106	1	1	14	3	1	0	.985	-2	O	-0.2
1961	Chi-N	109	321	48	82	14	3	7	37	39	51	.255	.338	.383	90	-4	-4	42	3	3	-1	.978	-4	O	-1.4
1962	Hou-N	27	72	4	16	1	0	0	3	3	9	.222	.263	.236	38	-6	-6	4	0	0	0	.974	1	O	-0.6
Total	3	177	495	63	126	20	6	8	46	52	72	.255	.328	.368	86	-10	-9	60	6	4	-1	.979	-5	O	-2.2

■ HEINIE HEITMULLER Heitmuller, William Frederick b: 5/25/1883, San Francisco, Cal d: 10/8/12, Los Angeles, Cal. BR/TR, 6'2", 215 lbs. Deb: 4/26/09

YEAR	TM/L	G	AB	R	H	2B	3B	HR	RBI	BB	SO	AVG	OBP	SLG	PRO+	BR	/A	RC	SB	CS	SBR	FA	FR	POS	TPR
1909	Phi-A	64	210	36	60	9	8	0	15	18		.286	.351	.405	136	9	8	32	7			.927	-2	O	0.5
1910	Phi-A	31	111	11	27	2	2	0	7	7		.243	.288	.297	84	-2	-2	11	6			.981	-0	O	-0.4
Total	2	95	321	47	87	11	10	0	22	25		.271	.330	.368	118	7	6	43	13			.943	-2	/O	0.1

■ WOODIE HELD Held, Woodson George b: 3/25/32, Sacramento, Cal. BR/TR, 5'11", 180 lbs. Deb: 9/05/54

YEAR	TM/L	G	AB	R	H	2B	3B	HR	RBI	BB	SO	AVG	OBP	SLG	PRO+	BR	/A	RC	SB	CS	SBR	FA	FR	POS	TPR
1954	NY-A	4	3	2	0	0	0	0	0	2	1	.000	.400	.000	17	-0	-0	0	0	0	0	1.000	-1	/S3	-0.1
1957	NY-A	1	1	0	0	0	0	0	0	0	0	.000	.000	.000	-99	-0	-0	0	0	0	0	.000	0	H	0.0
	KC-A	92	326	48	78	14	3	20	50	37	81	.239	.322	.485	116	7	6	52	4	0	1	.996	17	O	1.8
	Yr	93	327	48	78	14	3	20	50	37	81	.239	.322	.483	115	6	6	52	4	0	1	.996	17	O	1.8
1958	KC-A	47	131	13	28	2	0	4	16	10	28	.214	.280	.321	64	-6	-7	11	0	1	-1	1.000	-3	O/3S	-1.3
	Cle-A	67	144	12	28	4	1	3	17	15	36	.194	.288	.299	63	-7	-7	12	1	2	-1	.966	-0	OS/3	-0.9
	Yr	114	275	25	56	6	1	7	33	25	64	.204	.284	.309	64	-14	-14	23	1	3	-2	.982	-4	OS/3	-2.2
1959	Cle-A	143	525	82	132	19	3	29	71	46	118	.251	.314	.465	115	6	8	74	1	2	-1	.962	-9	*S3/O2	0.7
1960	Cle-A	109	376	45	97	15	1	21	67	44	73	.258	.344	.471	122	9	10	62	0	1	-1	.967	9	*S	2.7
1961	Cle-A	146	509	67	136	23	5	23	78	69	111	.267	.358	.468	122	13	15	85	0	0	0	.960	-14	*S	1.3
1962	Cle-A	139	466	55	116	12	2	19	58	73	107	.249	.364	.406	110	6	8	72	5	1	1	.956	-14	*S/3O	0.7
1963	Cle-A	133	416	61	103	19	4	17	61	61	96	.248	.355	.435	121	12	13	66	2	2	-1	.982	-3	2O/S3	1.7
1964	Cle-A	118	364	50	86	13	0	18	49	43	88	.236	.329	.420	107	3	4	51	1	0	0	.966	0	2O3	0.6
1965	Was-A	122	332	46	82	16	2	16	54	49	74	.247	.349	.452	128	12	12	53	0	0	0	.963	-19	*O/32S	-1.1
1966	Bal-A	56	82	6	17	3	1	1	7	12	30	.207	.309	.305	78	-2	-2	9	0	0	0	1.000	-4	O/2S3	-0.6
1967	Bal-A	26	41	4	6	3	0	1	6	6	12	.146	.286	.293	72	-1	-1	4	0	0	0	.974	1	/23O	0.0
	Cal-A	58	141	15	31	3	0	4	17	18	41	.220	.317	.326	94	-1	-1	14	0	2	-1	.979	-4	3OS/2	-0.6
	Yr	84	182	19	37	6	0	5	23	24	53	.203	.310	.319	88	-3	-2	18	0	2	-1	.962	-3	3OS2	-0.6
1968	Cal-A	33	45	4	5	1	0	0	0	5	15	.111	.231	.133	13	-5	-4	2	0	0	0	1.000	-3	/2S3O	-0.8
	Chi-A	40	54	5	9	1	0	0	2	5	14	.167	.250	.185	33	-4	-4	3	0	0	0	1.000	-6	O/32	-1.2
	Yr	73	99	9	14	2	0	0	2	10	29	.141	.241	.162	24	-9	-9	5	0	0	0	1.000	-9	O3/2S	-2.0
1969	Chi-A	56	63	9	9	2	0	3	6	13	19	.143	.299	.317	69	-2	-3	7	0	0	0	1.000	-3	O/S32	-0.6
Total	14	1390	4019	524	963	150	22	179	559	508	944	.240	.333	.421	109	38	47	578	14	11	-2	.960	-56	SO23	2.3

■ HANK HELF Helf, Henry Hartz b: 8/26/13, Austin, Tex. d: 10/27/84, Austin, Tex. BR/TR, 6'1", 196 lbs. Deb: 5/05/38

YEAR	TM/L	G	AB	R	H	2B	3B	HR	RBI	BB	SO	AVG	OBP	SLG	PRO+	BR	/A	RC	SB	CS	SBR	FA	FR	POS	TPR
1938	Cle-A	6	13	1	1	0	0	0	1	1	1	.077	.143	.077	-44	-3	-3	0	0	0	0	.947	0	/C	-0.2
1940	Cle-A	1	1	0	0	0	0	0	0	0	0	.000	.000	.000	-99	-0	-0	0	0	0	0	1.000	-0	/C	0.0
1946	StL-A	71	182	17	35	11	0	6	21	9	40	.192	.234	.352	59	-10	-11	14	0	1	-1	.965	12	C	0.3
Total	3	78	196	18	36	11	0	6	22	10	41	.184	.227	.332	51	-14	-14	14	0	1	-1	.964	12	/C	0.1

■ TY HELFRICH Helfrich, Emory Wilbur b: 10/9/1890, Pleasantville, N.J. d: 3/18/55, Pleasantville, N.J BR/TR, 5'10", 178 lbs. Deb: 6/30/15

YEAR	TM/L	G	AB	R	H	2B	3B	HR	RBI	BB	SO	AVG	OBP	SLG	PRO+	BR	/A	RC	SB	CS	SBR	FA	FR	POS	TPR
1915	Bro-F	43	104	12	25	6	0	0	5	15	21	.240	.336	.298	88	-1	-1	12	2			.912	-4	2/O	-0.5

■ HELLINGS Hellings b: Philadelphia, Pa. Deb: 7/19/1875

YEAR	TM/L	G	AB	R	H	2B	3B	HR	RBI	BB	SO	AVG	OBP	SLG	PRO+	BR	/A	RC	SB	CS	SBR	FA	FR	POS	TPR
1875	Atl-n	1	4	0	1	0	0	0		0		.250	.250	.250	84	-0	-0	0						/2	0.0

■ TONY HELLMAN Hellman, Anthony J. b: 1861, Cincinnati, Ohio d: 3/29/1898, Cincinnati, Ohio Deb: 10/10/1886

YEAR	TM/L	G	AB	R	H	2B	3B	HR	RBI	BB	SO	AVG	OBP	SLG	PRO+	BR	/A	RC	SB	CS	SBR	FA	FR	POS	TPR
1886	Bal-a	1	3	0	0	0	0	0		0		.000	.000	.000	-99	-1	-1	0	0			1.000	1	/C	0.0

■ TOMMY HELMS Helms, Tommy Vann b: 5/5/41, Charlotte, N.C. BR/TR, 5'10", 175 lbs. Deb: 9/23/64 MC

YEAR	TM/L	G	AB	R	H	2B	3B	HR	RBI	BB	SO	AVG	OBP	SLG	PRO+	BR	/A	RC	SB	CS	SBR	FA	FR	POS	TPR
1964	Cin-N	2	1	0	0	0	0	0	0	0	1	.000	.000	.000	-97	-0	-0	0	0	0	0	.000	0	H	0.0
1965	Cin-N	21	42	4	16	2	2	0	6	3	7	.381	.435	.524	158	4	4	10	1	0	0	.973	-2	/S32	0.3
1966	Cin-N	138	542	72	154	23	1	9	49	24	31	.284	.317	.380	85	-6	-11	61	3	4	-2	.961	-13	*32	-2.8
1967	Cin-N★	137	497	40	136	27	4	2	35	24	41	.274	.307	.356	80	-7	-14	49	5	10	-5	.978	-9	2S	-1.9
1968	Cin-N★	127	507	35	146	28	2	2	47	12	27	.288	.307	.363	94	-1	-4	53	5	6	-2	.979	8	*2/S3	1.1
1969	Cin-N	126	480	38	129	18	1	1	40	18	33	.269	.297	.317	68	-18	-21	39	4	6	-2	.975	-3	*2/S	-1.7
1970	*Cin-N	150	575	42	136	21	1	1	45	21	33	.237	.263	.282	46	-44	-44	39	2	2	-1	**.983**	1	*2S	-3.2
1971	Cin-N	150	547	40	141	26	1	3	52	26	33	.258	.293	.325	76	-19	-17	48	3	4	-2	**.990**	14	*2	0.9
1972	Hou-N	139	518	45	134	20	5	5	60	24	27	.259	.297	.346	84	-13	-12	52	4	3	-1	.979	**27**	*2	2.4
1973	Hou-N	146	543	44	156	28	2	4	61	32	21	.287	.327	.368	93	-6	-6	63	1	1	-0	.988	-1	*2	0.1
1974	Hou-N	137	452	32	126	21	1	5	50	23	27	.279	.315	.363	93	-7	-5	48	5	4	-1	**.985**	-11	*2	-1.2
1975	Hou-N	64	135	7	28	2	0	0	14	10	8	.207	.267	.222	40	-11	-10	8	0	0	0	.988	-0	2/3S	-0.9
1976	Pit-N	62	87	10	24	5	1	1	13	10	5	.276	.357	.391	111	2	1	13	0	0	0	.921	2	32/S	0.4
1977	Pit-N	15	12	0	0	0	0	0	0	0	3	.000	.000	.000	-97	-3	-3	0	0	0	0	.000	0	H	-0.3
	Bos-A	21	59	5	16	2	0	1	5	4	4	.271	.328	.356	77	-1	-2	7	0	0	0	1.000	-2	D/32	-0.3
Total	14	1435	4997	414	1342	223	21	34	477	231	301	.269	.303	.342	79	-132	-145	491	33	40	-14	.983	11	*23/SD	-7.1

■ HEINIE HELTZEL Heltzel, William Wade b: 12/21/13, York, Pa. BR/TR, 5'10", 150 lbs. Deb: 7/27/43

YEAR	TM/L	G	AB	R	H	2B	3B	HR	RBI	BB	SO	AVG	OBP	SLG	PRO+	BR	/A	RC	SB	CS	SBR	FA	FR	POS	TPR
1943	Bos-N	29	86	6	13	3	0	0	5	7	13	.151	.215	.186	17	-9	-9	4	0			.880	-3	3	-1.2
1944	Phi-N	11	22	1	4	1	0	0	0	2	3	.182	.280	.227	45	-2	-1	1	0			.919	-2	S	-0.3
Total	2	40	108	7	17	4	0	0	5	9	16	.157	.229	.194	23	-11	-11	5	0				-5	/3S	-1.5

■ ED HEMINGWAY Hemingway, Edson Marshall b: 5/8/1893, Sheridan, Mich. d: 7/5/69, Grand Rapids, Mich BB/TR, 5'11.5", 165 lbs. Deb: 9/17/14

YEAR	TM/L	G	AB	R	H	2B	3B	HR	RBI	BB	SO	AVG	OBP	SLG	PRO+	BR	/A	RC	SB	CS	SBR	FA	FR	POS	TPR
1914	StL-A	3	5	0	0	0	0	0	0	1	1	.000	.167	.000	-51	-1	-1	0	1			1.000	0	/3	-0.1
1917	NY-N	7	25	3	8	1	1	0	1	2	1	.320	.370	.440	153	1	1	4	2			.958	1	/3	0.3
1918	Phi-N	33	108	7	23	4	1	0	12	7	9	.213	.267	.269	59	-5	-6	9	4			.955	2	2/31	-0.2
Total	3	43	138	10	31	5	2	0	13	10	11	.225	.282	.290	71	-4	-5	14	7			.952	3	/231	0.0

■ SCOTT HEMOND Hemond, Scott Mathew b: 11/18/65, Taunton, Mass. BR/TR, 6', 205 lbs. Deb: 9/09/89

YEAR	TM/L	G	AB	R	H	2B	3B	HR	RBI	BB	SO	AVG	OBP	SLG	PRO+	BR	/A	RC	SB	CS	SBR	FA	FR	POS	TPR
1989	Oak-A	4	0	2	0	0	0	0	0	0	0	—	—	—	—	0	0	0	0	0	0	.000	0	R	0.0
1990	Oak-A	7	13	0	2	0	0	0	1	0	5	.154	.154	.154	-14	-2	-2	0	0	0	0	1.000	-1	/32	-0.3
1991	Oak-A	23	23	4	5	0	0	0	0	1	7	.217	.250	.217	32	-2	-2	1	1	2	-1	.947	5	/C23SD	0.2
1992	Oak-A	17	27	7	6	1	0	0	1	3	7	.222	.300	.259	60	-1	-1	2	1	0	0	1.000	-0	/CS3OD	-0.1
	Chi-A	8	13	1	3	1	0	0	1	1	6	.231	.286	.308	68	-1	-1	1	0	0	0	1.000	-0	/OC3D	-0.1
	Yr	25	40	8	9	2	0	0	2	4	13	.225	.295	.275	63	-2	-2	3	1	0	0	1.000	-1	/CDOS3	-0.2
Total	4	59	76	14	16	2	0	0	3	5	25	.211	.259	.237	41	-6	-6	4	2	2	-1	.981	4	/C3D2OS	-0.3

■ DUCKY HEMP Hemp, William H. b: 12/27/1867, St.Louis, Mo. d: 3/6/23, St.Louis, Mo. Deb: 10/06/1887

YEAR	TM/L	G	AB	R	H	2B	3B	HR	RBI	BB	SO	AVG	OBP	SLG	PRO+	BR	/A	RC	SB	CS	SBR	FA	FR	POS	TPR
1887	Lou-a	1	3	1	1	1	0	0		1		.333	.500	.667	222	1	1	1	0			.000	-1	/O	0.0
1890	Pit-N	21	81	9	19	0	2	0	4	8	12	.235	.311	.284	86	-2	-1	8	3			.867	0	O	-0.1
	Syr-a	9	33	1	5	1	0	0		0		.152	.176	.182	8	-4	-3	1	1			.947	2	/O	-0.1
Total	2	31	117	11	25	2	2	0	4	9	12	.214	.281	.265	69	-6	-4	11	4			.877	2	/O	-0.2

■ CHARLIE HEMPHILL Hemphill, Charles Judson "Eagle Eye" b: 4/20/1876, Greenville, Mich. d: 6/22/53, Detroit, Mich. BL/TL, 5'9", 160 lbs. Deb: 6/27/1899 F

YEAR	TM/L	G	AB	R	H	2B	3B	HR	RBI	BB	SO	AVG	OBP	SLG	PRO+	BR	/A	RC	SB	CS	SBR	FA	FR	POS	TPR
1899	StL-N	11	37	4	9	0	0	1	3	6		.243	.364	.324	87	-0	-0	5	0			.750	-2	O	-0.3
	Cle-N	55	202	23	56	3	5	2	23	6		.277	.298	.371	90	-6	-4	24	3			.859	-8	O	-1.4
	Yr	66	239	27	65	3	5	3	26	12		.272	.310	.364	90	-6	-4	29	3			.837	-10	O	-1.7
1901	Bos-A	136	545	71	142	10	10	3	62	39		.261	.312	.332	80	-16	-14	63	11			.925	-4	*O	-2.5
1902	Cle-A	25	94	14	25	2	0	0	11	5		.266	.303	.287	67	-4	-4	10	4			.860	-1	O	-0.6
	StL-A	103	416	67	132	14	11	6	58	44		.317	.383	.447	131	17	18	82	23			.952	-3	*O/2	0.8
	Yr	128	510	81	157	16	11	6	69	49		.308	.369	.418	120	12	14	91	27			.935	-3	*O/2	0.2
1903	StL-A	105	383	36	94	6	3	3	29	23		.245	.292	.300	80	-10	-9	40	16			.961	2	*O	-1.3
1904	StL-A	114	438	47	112	13	2	2	45	35		.256	.311	.308	103	-1	2	52	23			.926	-2	*O/2	-0.7
1906	StL-A	154	585	90	169	19	12	4	62	43		.289	.338	.383	131	16	19	91	33			.961	1	*O	1.4
1907	StL-A	153	603	66	156	20	9	0	38	51		.259	.319	.322	105	3	4	70	14			.957	-2	*O	-0.5
1908	NY-A	142	505	62	150	12	9	0	44	59		.297	.373	.356	136	23	22	82	42			.937	-2	*O	1.7
1909	NY-A	73	181	23	44	5	1	0	10	32		.243	.357	.282	101	2	2	22	10			.976	-1	O	-0.1
1910	NY-A	102	351	45	84	9	4	0	21	55		.239	.350	.288	95	3	0	42	19			.971	-2	O	-0.7
1911	NY-A	69	201	32	57	4	2	1	15	37		.284	.397	.338	99	4	2	31	9			.952	-7	O	-0.8
Total	11	1242	4541	580	1230	117	68	22	421	435		.271	.337	.341	106	31	38	613	207			.944	-29	*O/2	-5.0

■ FRANK HEMPHILL Hemphill, Frank Vernon b: 5/13/1878, Greenville, Mich. d: 11/16/50, Chicago, Ill. BR/TR, 5'11", 165 lbs. Deb: 4/17/06 F

YEAR	TM/L	G	AB	R	H	2B	3B	HR	RBI	BB	SO	AVG	OBP	SLG	PRO+	BR	/A	RC	SB	CS	SBR	FA	FR	POS	TPR
1906	Chi-A	13	40	0	3	0	0	0	2	9		.075	.275	.075	12	-3	-3	1	1			.970	1	O	-0.3
1909	Was-A	1	3	0	0	0	0	0	0	0		.000	.000	.000	-99	-1	-1	0	0			1.000	0	/O	-0.1
Total	2	14	43	0	3	0	0	0	2	9		.070	.259	.070	5	-4	-4	1	1			.971	1	/O	-0.4

■ ROLLIE HEMSLEY Hemsley, Ralston Burdett b: 6/24/07, Syracuse, Ohio d: 7/31/72, Washington, D.C. BR/TR, 5'10", 170 lbs. Deb: 4/13/28 C

YEAR	TM/L	G	AB	R	H	2B	3B	HR	RBI	BB	SO	AVG	OBP	SLG	PRO+	BR	/A	RC	SB	CS	SBR	FA	FR	POS	TPR
1928	Pit-N	50	133	14	36	2	3	0	18	4	10	.271	.292	.331	60	-7	-8	12	1			.962	1	C	-0.4
1929	Pit-N	88	235	31	68	13	7	0	37	11	22	.289	.321	.404	77	-8	-9	29	1			.954	8	C	0.4
1930	Pit-N	104	324	45	82	19	6	2	45	22	21	.253	.301	.367	60	-21	-22	35	3			.979	3	C	-0.9
1931	Pit-N	10	35	3	6	3	0	0	1	3	3	.171	.237	.257	33	-3	-3	2	0			1.000	1	/C	-0.2
	Chi-N	66	204	28	63	17	4	3	31	17	30	.309	.362	.475	121	6	6	36	4			.975	5	C	1.5
	Yr	76	239	31	69	20	4	3	32	20	33	.289	.344	.444	109	3	3	37	4			.978	6	C	1.3
1932	*Chi-N	60	151	27	36	10	3	4	20	10	16	.238	.286	.424	89	-3	-3	19	2			.974	2	C/O	0.1
1933	Cin-N	49	116	9	22	8	0	0	7	6	8	.190	.230	.259	40	-9	-9	6	0			.970	5	C	-0.2
	StL-A	32	95	7	23	2	1	1	15	11	12	.242	.321	.316	65	-4	-5	10	0	0	0	.965	-3	C	-0.6
1934	StL-A	123	431	47	133	31	7	2	52	29	37	.309	.355	.427	93	-0	-5	66	6	2	1	.973	23	*C/O	2.2
1935	StL-A★	144	504	57	146	32	7	0	48	44	41	.290	.349	.381	85	-8	-12	69	3	2	-0	.979	10	*C	0.5
1936	StL-A☆	116	377	43	99	24	2	2	39	46	30	.263	.343	.353	70	-16	-18	47	2	3	-1	.969	-11	*C	-2.2
1937	StL-A	100	334	30	74	12	3	3	28	25	29	.222	.276	.302	45	-29	-29	29	0	0	0	.969	-5	C/1	-2.7
1938	Cle-A	66	203	27	60	11	3	2	28	23	14	.296	.367	.409	96	-2	-1	31	1	1	-0	.980	15	C	1.4
1939	Cle-A☆	107	395	58	104	17	4	2	36	26	26	.263	.309	.342	69	-21	-19	41	2	4	-2	.984	6	*C	-0.8
1940	Cle-A★	119	416	46	111	20	5	4	42	22	25	.267	.304	.368	75	-17	-16	45	1	3	-2	**.994**	9	*C	0.1
1941	Cle-A	98	288	29	69	10	5	2	24	18	19	.240	.284	.330	65	-16	-15	27	2	0	1	.980	-2	C	-0.8
1942	Cin-N	36	115	7	13	1	2	0	7	4	11	.113	.143	.157	-12	-16	-16	3	0			.982	11	C	-0.3
	NY-A	31	85	12	25	3	1	0	15	5	9	.294	.333	.353	95	-1	-1	10	1	0	0	.991	1	C	0.3
1943	NY-A	62	180	12	43	6	3	2	24	13	9	.239	.290	.339	83	-4	-4	18	0	1	-1	.981	2	C	0.0
1944	NY-A★	81	284	23	76	12	5	2	26	9	13	.268	.290	.366	84	-6	-7	25	0	2	-1	.983	-2	C	-0.6
1946	Phi-N	49	139	7	31	4	1	0	11	9	10	.223	.270	.266	54	-9	-8	10	0			.977	11	C	0.5
1947	Phi-N	2	3	0	1	0	0	0	1	0	0	.333	.333	.333	80	-0	-0	0	0			1.000	-0	/C	0.0
Total	19	1593	5047	562	1321	257	72	31	555	357	395	.262	.311	.360	74	-196	-204	571	29	18		.978	90	*C/O1	-2.7

YEAR	TM/L	G	AB	R	H	2B	3B	HR	RBI	BB	SO	AVG	OBP	SLG	PRO+	BR	/A	RC	SB	CS	SBR	FA	FR	POS	TPR
■ SOLLY HEMUS	Hemus, Solomon Joseph b: 4/17/23, Phoenix, Ariz. BL/TR, 5'9", 175 lbs. Deb: 4/27/49 MC																								
1949	StL-N	20	33	8	11	1	0	0	2	7	3	.333	.450	.364	115	2	1	6	0			.981	2	2	0.4
1950	StL-N	11	15	1	2	1	0	0	0	2	4	.133	.235	.200	15	-2	-2	1	0			1.000	1	/3	-0.1
1951	StL-N	120	420	68	118	18	9	2	32	75	31	.281	.395	.381	109	9	9	70	7	7	-2	.965	13	*S2	2.8
1952	StL-N	151	570	**105**	153	28	8	15	52	96	55	.268	.392	.425	126	25	24	103	1	5	-3	.960	4	*S/3	3.8
1953	StL-N	154	585	110	163	32	11	14	61	86	40	.279	.382	.443	114	15	15	107	2	1	0	.964	7	*S/2	3.1
1954	StL-N	124	214	43	65	15	3	2	27	55	27	.304	.456	.430	131	14	14	50	5	1	1	.944	-20	S32	-0.1
1955	StL-N	96	206	36	50	10	2	5	21	27	22	.243	.336	.383	91	-3	-2	28	1	1	-0	.956	-4	32/S	-0.6
1956	StL-N	8	5	1	1	0	0	0	2	1	1	.200	.429	.200	77	-0	-0	1	0	0	0	.000	0	H	0.0
	Phi-N	78	187	24	54	10	4	5	24	28	21	.289	.401	.465	134	10	10	36	1	1	-0	.974	-25	2/3	-1.1
	Yr	86	192	25	55	10	4	5	26	29	22	.286	.402	.458	133	10	10	36	1	1	-0	.974	-25	2/3	-1.1
1957	Phi-N	70	108	8	20	6	1	0	5	20	8	.185	.323	.259	61	-6	-5	8	1	1	-0	.980	-3	2	-0.7
1958	Phi-N	105	334	53	95	14	3	8	36	51	34	.284	.392	.416	116	9	10	59	3	1	0	.969	-14	2/3	0.2
1959	StL-N	24	17	2	4	2	0	0	1	8	2	.235	.500	.353	124	2	1	4	0	0	0	1.000	1	/23M	0.2
Total	11	961	2694	459	736	137	41	51	263	456	248	.273	.390	.411	115	74	75	472	21	18		.962	-38	S2/3	7.9
■ DAVE HENDERSON	Henderson, David Lee b: 7/21/58, Merced, Cal. BR/TR, 6'2", 220 lbs. Deb: 4/09/81																								
1981	Sea-A	59	126	17	21	3	0	6	13	16	24	.167	.266	.333	69	-5	-5	11	2	1	0	1.000	-7	O	-1.5
1982	Sea-A	104	324	47	82	17	1	14	48	36	67	.253	.328	.441	106	4	2	46	2	5	-2	.985	7	*O	0.5
1983	Sea-A	137	484	50	130	24	5	17	55	28	93	.269	.310	.444	101	2	-1	67	9	3	1	.982	12	*O/D	0.8
1984	Sea-A	112	350	42	98	23	0	14	43	19	56	.280	.321	.466	116	6	6	51	5	5	-2	.988	8	OD	1.0
1985	Sea-A	139	502	70	121	28	2	14	68	48	104	.241	.311	.388	90	-7	-7	61	6	1	1	.986	-4	*O	-1.5
1986	Sea-A	103	337	51	93	19	4	14	44	37	95	.276	.351	.481	123	11	10	57	1	3	-2	.979	5	OD	1.1
	*Bos-A	36	51	8	10	3	0	1	3	2	15	.196	.226	.314	45	-4	-4	4	1	0	0	.981	-5	O	-0.9
	Yr	139	388	59	103	22	4	15	47	39	110	.265	.336	.459	113	7	6	60	2	3	-1	.980	0	*OD	0.2
1987	Bos-A	75	184	30	43	10	0	8	25	22	48	.234	.316	.418	90	-2	-3	25	1	1	-0	.958	-5	O/D	-1.0
	SF-N	15	21	2	5	2	0	0	1	8	5	.238	.448	.333	117	1	1	5	2	0	1	1.000	-1	/O	0.0
1988	*Oak-A	146	507	100	154	38	1	24	94	47	92	.304	.367	.525	152	31	33	94	2	4	-2	.982	5	*O	3.2
1989	*Oak-A	152	579	77	145	24	3	15	80	54	131	.250	.318	.380	99	-4	-1	69	8	5	-1	.977	5	*O/D	-0.1
1990	*Oak-A	127	450	65	122	28	0	20	63	40	105	.271	.332	.467	126	11	14	71	3	1	0	.988	9	*O/D	2.0
1991	Oak-A★	150	572	86	158	33	0	25	85	58	113	.276	.347	.465	130	17	21	92	6	6	-2	.997	11	*O/2D	2.6
1992	Oak-A	20	63	1	9	1	0	0	2	2	16	.143	.169	.159	-8	-9	-9	2	0	0	0	.950	-3	O/D	-1.2
Total	12	1375	4550	646	1191	253	16	172	624	417	964	.262	.327	.438	111	51	57	653	48	35	-7	.984	36	*O/D2	5.0
■ KEN HENDERSON	Henderson, Kenneth Joseph b: 6/15/46, Carroll, Iowa BB/TR, 6'2", 180 lbs. Deb: 4/23/65																								
1965	SF-N	63	73	10	14	1	1	0	7	9	19	.192	.280	.233	45	-5	-5	4	1	1	-0	.980	5	O	-0.2
1966	SF-N	11	29	4	9	1	1	1	1	2	3	.310	.375	.517	141	2	2	6	0	0	0	.917	-1	O	0.0
1967	SF-N	65	179	15	34	3	0	4	14	19	52	.190	.275	.274	58	-10	-9	14	0	1	-1	.947	-1	O	-1.5
1968	SF-N	3	3	1	1	0	0	0	0	2	1	.333	.600	.333	186	1	1	1	0	0	0	1.000	0	/O	0.1
1969	SF-N	113	374	42	84	14	4	6	44	42	64	.225	.311	.332	82	-10	-9	39	6	4	-1	.969	-3	*O/3	-1.8
1970	SF-N	148	554	104	163	35	3	17	88	87	78	.294	.395	.460	130	25	25	106	20	3	4	.966	5	*O	2.7
1971	*SF-N	141	504	80	133	26	6	15	65	84	76	.264	.372	.429	128	19	20	86	18	3	4	.966	-4	*O/1	1.4
1972	SF-N	130	439	60	113	21	2	18	51	38	66	.257	.319	.437	112	6	6	61	14	7	0	.974	8	*O	0.9
1973	Chi-A	73	262	32	68	13	0	6	32	27	49	.260	.331	.378	96	-0	-1	30	3	4	-2	.972	-1	OD	-0.6
1974	Chi-A	162	602	76	176	35	5	20	95	66	112	.292	.364	.467	134	29	27	100	12	7	-1	.987	9	*O	2.9
1975	Chi-A	140	513	65	129	20	3	9	53	74	65	.251	.350	.355	98	2	1	64	5	3	-0	.990	13	*O/D	0.8
1976	Atl-N	133	435	52	114	19	0	13	61	62	68	.262	.355	.395	106	8	5	60	5	7	-3	.987	-7	*O	-1.0
1977	Tex-A	75	244	23	63	14	0	5	23	18	37	.258	.317	.377	87	-4	-4	28	2	1	0	.983	-6	O/D	-1.3
1978	NY-N	7	22	2	5	2	0	1	4	4	4	.227	.346	.455	127	1	1	3	0	1	-1	1.000	0	/O	0.0
	Cin-N	64	144	10	24	6	1	3	19	23	32	.167	.281	.285	59	-8	-8	11	0	0	0	1.000	-1	O	-1.1
	Yr	71	166	12	29	8	1	4	23	27	36	.175	.290	.307	67	-7	-7	14	0	1	-1	1.000	-1	O	-1.1
1979	Cin-N	10	13	1	3	1	0	0	2	0	2	.231	.231	.308	45	-1	-1	1	0	0	0	1.000	-0	/O	-0.1
	Chi-N	62	81	11	19	2	0	2	8	15	16	.235	.361	.333	83	-0	-1	11	0	0	0	.950	-3	O	-0.5
	Yr	72	94	12	22	3	0	2	10	15	18	.234	.345	.330	79	-1	-2	12	0	0	0	.955	-3	O	-0.6
1980	Chi-N	44	82	7	16	3	0	2	9	17	19	.195	.333	.305	74	-2	-3	9	0	0	0	.944	-0	O	-0.4
Total	16	1444	4553	595	1168	216	26	122	576	589	763	.257	.346	.396	106	53	45	634	86	42	1	.977	11	*O/D31	0.3
■ RICKEY HENDERSON	Henderson, Rickey Henley b: 12/25/58, Chicago, Ill. BR/TL, 5'10", 195 lbs. Deb: 6/24/79																								
1979	Oak-A	89	351	49	96	13	3	1	26	34	39	.274	.341	.336	88	-7	-5	44	33	11	3	.973	3	O	-0.2
1980	Oak-A★	158	591	111	179	22	4	9	53	117	54	.303	.422	.399	136	29	34	120	**100**	26	14	.984	23	*O/D	6.4
1981	*Oak-A	108	423	**89**	**135**	18	7	6	35	64	68	.319	.411	.437	152	27	29	81	**56**	22	4	.979	20	*O	**5.0**
1982	Oak-A★	149	536	119	143	24	4	10	51	**116**	94	.267	.399	.382	121	17	21	99	**130**	42	**14**	.977	14	*O/D	4.3
1983	Oak-A★	145	513	105	150	25	7	9	48	**103**	80	.292	.415	.421	139	27	31	109	**108**	19	**21**	.992	9	*O/D	5.5
1984	Oak-A★	142	502	113	147	27	4	16	58	86	81	.293	.401	.458	147	29	33	103	**66**	18	9	.969	8	*O	4.5
1985	NY-A★	143	547	**146**	172	28	5	24	72	99	65	.314	.422	.516	159	45	47	138	**80**	10	**18**	.980	16	*O/D	**7.3**
1986	NY-A★	153	608	**130**	160	31	5	28	74	89	81	.263	.359	.469	125	20	21	112	**87**	18	**15**	.986	12	*O/D	4.2
1987	NY-A★	95	358	78	104	17	3	17	37	80	52	.291	.423	.497	144	26	26	84	41	8	8	.980	7	OD	3.6
1988	NY-A★	140	554	118	169	30	2	6	50	82	54	.305	.397	.399	125	21	22	107	**93**	13	**20**	.965	10	*O/D	4.7
1989	NY-A	65	235	41	58	13	1	3	22	56	29	.247	.394	.349	112	6	7	40	25	8	3	.993	4	O	1.2
	*Oak-A	85	306	72	90	13	2	9	35	70	39	.294	.429	.438	150	22	24	70	52	6	12	.985	7	O/D	4.0
	Yr	150	541	**113**	148	26	3	12	57	**126**	68	.274	.413	.399	133	29	31	110	**77**	14	**15**	.988	11	*O/D	**5.2**
1990	*Oak-A★	136	489	**119**	159	33	3	28	61	97	60	.325	**.441**	.577	**190**	**58**	**60**	**137**	**65**	10	**14**	.983	11	*OD	**8.1**
1991	Oak-A★	134	470	105	126	17	1	18	57	98	73	.268	.402	.423	136	23	27	91	**58**	18	7	.970	10	*OD	4.0
1992	*Oak-A	117	396	77	112	18	3	15	46	95	56	.283	.429	.457	154	31	33	92	48	11	8	.984	6	*O/D	4.4
Total	14	1859	6879	1472	2000	329	54	199	725	1286	925	.291	.406	.441	139	374	412	1428	1042	240	169	.980	157	*O/D	67.0
■ STEVE HENDERSON	Henderson, Stephen Curtis b: 11/18/52, Houston, Tex. BR/TR, 6'2", 190 lbs. Deb: 6/16/77																								
1977	NY-N	99	350	67	104	16	6	12	65	43	79	.297	.376	.480	134	14	16	61	6	3	0	.980	0	O	1.2
1978	NY-N	157	587	83	156	30	9	10	65	60	109	.266	.336	.399	108	3	6	74	13	7	-0	.968	7	*O	0.6
1979	NY-N	98	350	42	107	16	8	5	39	38	58	.306	.380	.440	128	12	13	59	13	5	1	.990	4	O	1.5
1980	NY-N	143	513	75	149	17	8	8	58	62	90	.290	.370	.402	119	12	14	75	23	12	-0	.981	5	*O	1.4
1981	Chi-N	82	287	32	84	9	5	5	35	42	61	.293	.387	.411	121	11	10	45	5	7	-3	.951	-11	O	-0.7
1982	Chi-N	92	257	23	60	12	4	2	29	22	64	.233	.294	.335	73	-9	-9	25	6	5	-1	.956	-3	O	-1.6
1983	Sea-A	121	436	50	128	32	3	10	54	44	82	.294	.358	.450	116	12	10	66	10	14	-5	.970	1	*O/D	0.2
1984	Sea-A	109	325	42	85	12	3	10	35	38	62	.262	.341	.409	108	3	4	45	2	4	-2	.936	-2	OD	-0.2
1985	Oak-A	85	193	25	58	8	3	3	31	18	34	.301	.360	.420	122	4	5	27	0	0	0	.953	-7	O/D	-0.3
1986	Oak-A	11	26	2	2	1	0	0	3	0	5	.077	.077	.115	-52	-5	-5	-0	0	0	0	.800	-2	/OD	-0.7
1987	Oak-A	46	114	14	33	7	0	3	9	12	19	.289	.357	.430	115	1	2	16	0	0	0	.943	-7	O/D	-0.5
1988	Hou-N	42	46	4	10	2	0	0	5	7	14	.217	.321	.261	72	-2	-1	4	1	1	-0	1.000	0	/O1	-0.2
Total	12	1085	3484	459	976	162	49	68	428	386	677	.280	.354	.413	113	58	65	497	79	58	-11	.968	-14	O/D1	0.7
■ GEORGE HENDRICK	Hendrick, George Andrew b: 10/18/49, Los Angeles, Cal. BR/TR, 6'3", 195 lbs. Deb: 6/04/71																								
1971	Oak-A	42	114	8	27	4	1	0	8	3	20	.237	.256	.289	55	-7	-7	7	0	1	-1	.981	-7	O	-1.8
1972	*Oak-A	58	121	10	22	1	1	4	15	3	22	.182	.208	.306	54	-8	-7	7	3	2	-0	1.000	-7	O	-1.8

YEAR	TM/L	G	AB	R	H	2B	3B	HR	RBI	BB	SO	AVG	OBP	SLG	PRO+	BR	/A	RC	SB	CS	SBR	FA	FR	POS	TPR
1973	Cle-A	113	440	64	118	18	0	21	61	25	71	.268	.310	.452	111	5	4	58	7	6	-2	.988	-3	*O	-0.6
1974	Cle-A★	139	495	65	138	23	1	19	67	33	73	.279	.325	.444	121	11	11	66	6	4	-1	.989	3	*O/D	0.8
1975	Cle-A★	145	561	82	145	21	2	24	86	40	78	.258	.308	.431	107	3	3	65	6	7	-2	.983	1	*O	-0.5
1976	Cle-A	149	551	72	146	20	3	25	81	51	82	.265	.327	.448	127	16	17	77	4	4	-1	.987	3	*O/D	1.3
1977	SD-N	152	541	75	168	25	2	23	81	61	74	.311	.382	.492	148	25	32	102	11	6	-0	.983	8	*O	3.4
1978	SD-N	36	111	9	27	4	0	3	8	12	16	.243	.317	.360	96	-2	-1	13	1	1	-0	.986	2	O	-0.1
	StL-N	102	382	55	110	27	1	17	67	28	44	.288	.340	.497	133	14	15	63	1	0	0	.996	1	*O	1.2
	Yr	138	493	64	137	31	1	20	75	40	60	.278	.335	.467	126	13	14	76	2	1	0	.994	2	*O	1.1
1979	StL-N	140	493	67	148	27	1	16	75	49	62	.300	.363	.456	121	15	14	78	2	3	-1	.993	7	*O	1.5
1980	StL-N★	150	572	73	173	33	2	25	109	32	67	.302	.344	.498	128	22	20	94	6	1	1	.994	4	*O	2.0
1981	StL-N	101	394	67	112	19	3	18	61	41	44	.284	.358	.485	134	18	17	67	4	2	0	.983	-12	*O	0.2
1982	*StL-N	136	515	65	145	20	5	19	104	37	80	.282	.331	.450	115	10	9	74	3	2	-0	.980	-8	*O	-0.3
1983	StL-N☆	144	529	73	168	33	3	18	97	51	76	.318	.380	.493	140	28	28	96	3	4	-2	.992	-1	1O	2.0
1984	StL-N	120	441	57	122	28	1	9	69	32	75	.277	.327	.406	108	2	3	55	0	2	-1	.990	-1	*O/1	-0.2
1985	Pit-N	69	256	23	59	15	0	2	25	18	42	.230	.281	.313	66	-12	-12	21	1	0	0	.971	3	O	-1.1
	Cal-A	16	41	5	5	1	0	2	6	4	8	.122	.200	.293	33	-4	-4	1	0	0	0	1.000	-1	O/D	-0.5
1986	*Cal-A	102	283	45	77	13	1	14	47	26	41	.272	.335	.473	119	6	7	42	1	1	-0	.968	-6	O/1D	-0.2
1987	Cal-A	65	162	14	39	10	0	5	25	14	18	.241	.301	.395	85	-4	-4	17	0	0	0	.967	-8	O/1D	-1.3
1988	Cal-A	69	127	12	31	1	0	3	19	7	20	.244	.289	.323	73	-5	-5	12	0	1	-1	.933	-1	O1/D	-0.8
Total	18	2048	7129	941	1980	343	27	267	1111	567	1013	.278	.333	.446	117	134	143	1015	59	47	-11	.985	-25	*O1/D	3.2

■ HARVEY HENDRICK

Hendrick, Harvey "Gink" b: 11/9/1897, Mason, Tenn. d: 10/29/41, Covington, Tenn. BL/TR, 6'2", 190 lbs. Deb: 4/20/23

YEAR	TM/L	G	AB	R	H	2B	3B	HR	RBI	BB	SO	AVG	OBP	SLG	PRO+	BR	/A	RC	SB	CS	SBR	FA	FR	POS	TPR
1923	*NY-A	37	66	9	18	3	1	3	12	2	8	.273	.294	.485	101	-0	-1	10	3	0	1	.947	-2	O	-0.2
1924	NY-A	40	76	7	20	0	0	1	11	2	7	.263	.291	.303	53	-5	-5	7	1	0	0	.975	0	O	-0.6
1925	Cle-A	25	28	2	8	1	2	0	9	3	5	.286	.355	.464	106	0	0	5	0	0	0	1.000	0	/1	0.0
1927	Bro-N	128	458	55	142	18	11	4	50	24	40	.310	.350	.424	106	3	3	66	29			.969	-16	O1/2	-2.0
1928	Bro-N	126	425	83	135	15	10	11	59	54	34	.318	.397	.478	129	18	19	80	16			.913	3	3O	2.5
1929	Bro-N	110	384	69	136	25	6	14	82	31	20	.354	.404	.560	139	21	22	84	14			.975	0	O1/3S	1.5
1930	Bro-N	68	167	29	43	10	1	5	28	20	19	.257	.344	.419	84	-5	-4	24	2			.947	-3	O/1	-0.9
1931	Bro-N	1	1	0	0	0	0	0	0	0	0	.000	.000	.000	-99	-0	-0	0	0			.000	0	H	0.0
	Cin-N	137	530	74	167	32	9	1	75	53	40	.315	.379	.415	121	11	15	87	3			.987	-5	*1	-0.3
	Yr	138	531	74	167	32	9	1	75	53	40	.315	.379	.414	120	11	15	87	3			.987	-5	*1	-0.3
1932	StL-N	28	72	8	18	2	0	1	5	5	9	.250	.299	.319	64	-3	-4	7	0			.862	-3	3/O	-0.6
	Cin-N	94	398	56	120	30	3	4	40	23	29	.302	.341	.422	107	2	4	58	3			.986	-4	1	-0.8
	Yr	122	470	64	138	32	3	5	45	28	38	.294	.335	.406	100	-1	-0	65	3			.986	-7	13/O	-1.4
1933	Chi-N	69	189	30	55	13	3	4	23	13	17	.291	.346	.455	128	6	6	31	4			.983	-1	1/O3	0.2
1934	Phi-N	59	116	12	34	8	0	0	19	9	15	.293	.344	.362	79	-2	-4	15	0			.962	-3	O/13	-0.7
Total	11	922	2910	434	896	157	46	48	413	239	243	.308	.364	.443	113	46	52	473	75	0		.986	-32	103/S2	-1.9

■ ELLIE HENDRICKS

Hendricks, Elrod Jerome b: 12/22/40, Charlotte Amalie, V.I. BL/TR, 6'1", 175 lbs. Deb: 4/13/68 C

YEAR	TM/L	G	AB	R	H	2B	3B	HR	RBI	BB	SO	AVG	OBP	SLG	PRO+	BR	/A	RC	SB	CS	SBR	FA	FR	POS	TPR
1968	Bal-A	79	183	19	37	8	1	7	23	19	51	.202	.281	.372	96	-1	-1	19	0	0	0	.991	-5	C	-0.3
1969	*Bal-A	105	295	36	72	5	0	12	38	39	44	.244	.336	.383	100	1	0	40	0	1	-1	**.998**	5	C/1	1.0
1970	*Bal-A	106	322	32	78	9	0	12	41	33	44	.242	.320	.382	92	-3	-4	41	1	0	0	.986	-8	C	-0.7
1971	*Bal-A	101	316	33	79	14	1	9	42	39	38	.250	.336	.386	105	2	2	41	0	0	0	.985	-8	C/1	-0.2
1972	Bal-A	33	84	6	13	4	0	0	4	12	19	.155	.260	.202	38	-6	-6	5	0	1	-1	.986	2	C	-0.5
	Chi-N	17	43	7	5	1	0	2	6	13	8	.116	.321	.279	65	-1	-2	4	0	1	-1	.978	1	C	-0.1
1973	Bal-A	41	101	9	18	5	1	3	15	10	22	.178	.259	.337	67	-5	-5	9	0	0	0	.994	4	C/D	0.1
1974	*Bal-A	66	159	18	33	8	2	3	8	17	25	.208	.288	.340	83	-4	-4	16	0	0	0	1.000	-4	C/1D	-0.6
1975	Bal-A	85	223	32	48	8	2	8	38	34	40	.215	.322	.377	103	-1	1	28	0	1	-1	**.995**	-1	C	0.3
1976	Bal-A	28	79	2	11	1	0	1	4	7	13	.139	.209	.190	19	-8	-8	3	0	1	-1	.971	-5	C	-1.3
	*NY-A	26	53	6	12	1	0	3	5	3	10	.226	.268	.415	99	-0	-0	6	0	0	0	1.000	1	C	0.1
	Yr	54	132	8	23	2	0	4	9	10	23	.174	.232	.280	52	-9	-8	9	0	1	-1	.982	-4	C	-1.2
1977	NY-A	10	11	1	3	1	0	1	5	0	2	.273	.273	.636	140	0	0	2	0	0	0	1.000	0	/C	0.1
1978	Bal-A	13	18	4	6	1	0	1	1	3	3	.333	.429	.556	186	2	2	4	0	0	0	.955	0	/CPD	0.2
1979	Bal-A	1	1	0	0	0	0	0	0	0	0	.000	.000	.000	-99	-0	-0	0	0	0	0	.500	-1	/C	-0.1
Total	12	711	1888	205	415	66	7	62	230	229	319	.220	.308	.361	90	-26	-24	218	1	5	-3	.990	-17	C/1DP	-2.0

■ JACK HENDRICKS

Hendricks, John Charles b: 4/9/1875, Joliet, Ill. d: 5/13/43, Chicago, Ill. BL/TL, 5'11.5", 160 lbs. Deb: 6/12/02 M

YEAR	TM/L	G	AB	R	H	2B	3B	HR	RBI	BB	SO	AVG	OBP	SLG	PRO+	BR	/A	RC	SB	CS	SBR	FA	FR	POS	TPR
1902	NY-N	8	26	1	6	2	0	0	0	2		.231	.286	.308	84	-1	-1	3	2			.929	0	/O	-0.1
	Chi-N	2	7	0	4	0	1	0	0	0		.571	.571	.857	350	2	2	3	0			1.000	0	/O	0.2
	Yr	10	33	1	10	2	1	0	0	2		.303	.343	.424	138	1	1	6	2			.950	1	/O	0.1
1903	Was-A	32	112	10	20	1	3	0	4	13		.179	.264	.241	51	-6	-6	9	3			.891	-4	O	-1.3
Total	2	42	145	11	30	3	4	0	4	15		.207	.281	.283	70	-5	-5	16	5			.909	-3	/O	-1.2

■ TIM HENDRYX

Hendryx, Timothy Green b: 1/31/1891, Leroy, Ill d: 8/14/57, Corpus Christi, Tex. BR/TR, 5'9", 170 lbs. Deb: 9/04/11

YEAR	TM/L	G	AB	R	H	2B	3B	HR	RBI	BB	SO	AVG	OBP	SLG	PRO+	BR	/A	RC	SB	CS	SBR	FA	FR	POS	TPR
1911	Cle-A	4	7	0	2	0	0	0	0	0		.286	.286	.286	59	-0	-0	1	0			1.000	-1	/3	-0.1
1912	Cle-A	23	70	9	17	2	4	1	14	8		.243	.329	.429	112	1	1	11	3			1.000	-2	O	-0.2
1915	NY-A	13	40	4	8	2	0	0	1	4	2	.200	.289	.250	61	-2	-2	2	0	3	-2	.968	1	O	-0.4
1916	NY-A	15	62	10	18	7	1	0	5	8	6	.290	.380	.435	142	3	3	12	4			1.000	-2	O	0.1
1917	NY-A	125	393	43	98	14	7	5	44	62	45	.249	.359	.359	118	11	10	53	6			.955	5	*O	1.0
1918	StL-A	88	219	22	61	14	3	0	33	37	35	.279	.388	.370	133	9	10	34	5			.982	-9	O	-0.2
1920	Bos-A	99	363	54	119	21	5	0	73	42	27	.328	.400	.413	121	10	12	60	7	9	-3	.964	-10	O	-0.8
1921	Bos-A	49	137	10	33	8	2	0	22	24	13	.241	.362	.328	79	-4	-3	18	1	1	-0	.958	-4	O	-1.0
Total	8	416	1291	152	356	68	22	6	192	185	128	.276	.372	.376	115	28	31	191	26	13		.966	-21	O/3	-1.6

■ DAVE HENGEL

Hengel, David Lee b: 12/18/61, Oakland, Cal. BR/TR, 6', 185 lbs. Deb: 9/03/86

YEAR	TM/L	G	AB	R	H	2B	3B	HR	RBI	BB	SO	AVG	OBP	SLG	PRO+	BR	/A	RC	SB	CS	SBR	FA	FR	POS	TPR
1986	Sea-A	21	63	3	12	1	0	1	6	1	13	.190	.215	.254	27	-6	-6	3	0	0	0	1.000	-1	D/O	-0.7
1987	Sea-A	10	19	2	6	0	0	1	4	0	4	.316	.316	.474	100	0	-0	2	0	0	0	.875	-2	/OD	-0.2
1988	Sea-A	26	60	3	10	1	0	2	7	1	15	.167	.180	.283	27	-6	-6	3	0	0	0	.952	-1	OD	-0.8
1989	Cle-A	12	25	2	3	1	0	0	1	2	4	.120	.185	.160	-2	-3	-3	1	0	0	0	1.000	-1	/OD	-0.4
Total	4	69	167	10	31	3	0	4	18	4	36	.186	.209	.275	31	-16	-16	9	0	0	0	.962	-5	/OD	-2.1

■ MOXIE HENGLE

Hengle, Emery J. b: 10/7/1857, Chicago, Ill. d: 12/11/24, Forest River, Ill. BR , 5'8", 144 lbs. Deb: 4/20/1884

YEAR	TM/L	G	AB	R	H	2B	3B	HR	RBI	BB	SO	AVG	OBP	SLG	PRO+	BR	/A	RC	SB	CS	SBR	FA	FR	POS	TPR
1884	CP-U	19	74	9	15	2	1	0		3		.203	.234	.257	66	-3	-2	5				.840	-7	2	-0.8
	StP-U	9	33	2	5	1	1	0		0		.152	.152	.242	58	-2	0	1				.923	1	/2	0.1
	Yr	28	107	11	20	3	2	0		3		.187	.209	.252	65	-5	-2	6				.870	-6	2	-0.7
1885	Buf-N	7	26	2	4	0	0	0	0	1	2	.154	.185	.154	10	-2	-3	1				.864	-3	/2O	-0.5
Total	2	35	133	13	24	3	2	0	0	4	2	.180	.204	.233	52	-7	-5	7				.869	-9	/2O	-1.2

■ GAIL HENLEY

Henley, Gail Curtice b: 10/15/28, Wichita, Kan. BL/TR, 5'9", 180 lbs. Deb: 4/13/54

YEAR	TM/L	G	AB	R	H	2B	3B	HR	RBI	BB	SO	AVG	OBP	SLG	PRO+	BR	/A	RC	SB	CS	SBR	FA	FR	POS	TPR
1954	Pit-N	14	30	7	9	1	0	1	2	4	4	.300	.382	.433	114	1	1	5	0	0	0	1.000	-0	/O	0.0

■ BUTCH HENLINE

Henline, Walter John b: 12/20/1894, Ft.Wayne, Ind. d: 10/9/57, Sarasota, Fla. BR/TR, 5'10", 175 lbs. Deb: 4/13/21 U

YEAR	TM/L	G	AB	R	H	2B	3B	HR	RBI	BB	SO	AVG	OBP	SLG	PRO+	BR	/A	RC	SB	CS	SBR	FA	FR	POS	TPR
1921	NY-N	1	1	0	0	0	0	0	0	0	1	.000	.000	.000	-99	-0	-0	0	0	0	0	.000	0	H	0.0
	Phi-N	33	111	8	34	2	0	0	8	2	6	.306	.319	.324	65	-5	-6	11	1	0	0	.987	9	C	0.5

YEAR	TM/L	G	AB	R	H	2B	3B	HR	RBI	BB	SO	AVG	OBP	SLG	PRO+	BR	/A	RC	SB	CS	SBR	FA	FR	POS	TPR
	Yr	34	112	8	34	2	0	0	8	2	7	.304	.316	.321	64	-5	-6	11	1	0	0	.987	9	C	0.5
1922	Phi-N	125	430	57	136	20	4	14	64	36	33	.316	.380	.479	110	13	7	79	2	2	-1	**.983**	2	*C	1.3
1923	Phi-N	111	330	45	107	14	3	7	46	37	33	.324	.407	.448	112	14	8	62	7	5	-1	.978	-16	C/O	-0.4
1924	Phi-N	115	289	41	82	18	4	5	35	27	15	.284	.361	.426	98	4	-0	45	1	2	-1	.973	-1	C/O	0.2
1925	Phi-N	93	263	43	80	12	5	8	48	24	16	.304	.380	.479	108	7	4	49	3	1	0	.956	-2	C/O	0.5
1926	Phi-N	99	283	32	80	14	1	2	30	21	18	.283	.339	.360	84	-4	-6	35	1			.970	-10	C/1O	-1.2
1927	Bro-N	67	177	12	47	10	3	1	18	17	10	.266	.337	.373	90	-2	-3	22	1			.947	1	C	0.2
1928	Bro-N	55	132	12	28	3	1	2	8	17	8	.212	.302	.295	58	-8	-8	12	2			.976	-4	C	-0.8
1929	Bro-N	27	62	5	15	2	0	1	7	9	9	.242	.338	.323	66	-3	-3	7	0			.967	1	C	-0.1
1930	Chi-A	3	8	1	1	0	0	0	2	0	3	.125	.125	.125	-38	-2	-2	0	0	0	0	1.000	0	/C	-0.1
1931	Chi-A	11	15	2	1	1	0	0	2	2	4	.067	.176	.133	-19	-3	-2	0	0	0	0	.889	0	/C	-0.2
Total	11	740	2101	258	611	96	21	40	268	192	156	.291	.361	.414	96	10	-12	324	18	10		.971	-20	C/O1	-0.1
■ LES HENNESSEY Hennessey, Lester Baker b: 12/12/1893, Lynn, Mass. d: 11/20/76, New York, N.Y. BR/TR, 6', 190 lbs. Deb: 6/04/13																									
1913	Det-A	14	22	2	3	0	0	0	0	3	6	.136	.240	.136	11	-2	-2	1	2			.880	-2	2	-0.5
■ FRITZ HENRICH Henrich, Frank Wilde b: 5/8/1899, Cincinnati, Ohio d: 5/1/59, Philadelphia, Pa. BL/TL, 5'10", 160 lbs. Deb: 4/21/24																									
1924	Phi-N	36	90	4	19	4	0	0	4	2	12	.211	.228	.256	26	-9	-10	5	0	0	0	.978	-9	O	-2.1
■ BOBBY HENRICH Henrich, Robert Edward b: 12/24/38, Lawrence, Kan. BR/TR, 6'1", 185 lbs. Deb: 5/03/57																									
1957	Cin-N	29	10	8	2	0	0	0	1	1	4	.200	.273	.200	28	-1	-1	1	0	0	0	.875	0	/SO32	-0.1
1958	Cin-N	5	3	2	0	0	0	0	0	0	2	.000	.000	.000	-95	-1	-1	0	0	0	0	1.000	1	/S	0.0
1959	Cin-N	14	3	3	0	0	0	0	0	0	1	.000	.000	.000	-97	-1	-1	0	0	0	0	1.000	3	/S3	0.2
Total	3	48	16	13	2	0	0	0	1	1	7	.125	.176	.125	-17	-3	-3	1	0	0	0	.929	4	/SO32	0.1
■ TOMMY HENRICH Henrich, Thomas David "The Clutch" or "Old Reliable" b: 2/20/13, Massillon, Ohio BL/TL, 6', 180 lbs. Deb: 5/11/37 C																									
1937	NY-A	67	206	39	66	14	5	8	42	35	17	.320	.419	.553	142	14	14	50	4	0	1	.970	-4	O	0.8
1938	*NY-A	131	471	109	127	24	7	22	91	92	32	.270	.391	.490	120	15	15	96	6	2	1	.984	-1	*O	1.0
1939	NY-A	99	347	64	96	18	4	9	57	51	23	.277	.371	.429	106	3	3	60	7	0	2	.991	2	O/1	0.4
1940	NY-A	90	293	57	90	28	5	10	53	48	30	.307	.408	.539	149	20	21	68	1	2	-1	.969	-1	O/1	1.4
1941	*NY-A	144	538	106	149	27	5	31	85	81	40	.277	.377	.519	137	26	27	113	3	1	0	.980	-1	*O	1.7
1942	NY-A★	127	483	77	129	30	5	13	67	58	42	.267	.352	.431	122	12	13	79	4	4	-1	.987	-1	*O/1	0.4
1946	NY-A	150	565	92	142	25	4	19	83	87	63	.251	.358	.411	113	12	11	92	5	2	0	.992	2	*O1	0.6
1947	*NY-A★	142	550	109	158	35	**13**	16	98	71	54	.287	.372	.485	139	26	27	104	3	2	-0	.983	6	*O/1	2.6
1948	NY-A★	146	588	**138**	181	42	**14**	25	100	76	42	.308	.391	.554	151	39	40	130	2	3	-1	.978	-0	*O1	3.1
1949	*NY-A☆	115	411	90	118	20	3	24	85	86	34	.287	.416	.526	148	30	30	98	2	2	-1	.958	-4	O1	2.1
1950	NY-A★	73	151	20	41	6	8	6	34	27	6	.272	.382	.536	137	7	8	30	0	1	-1	.987	-5	1	0.1
Total	11	1284	4603	901	1297	269	73	183	795	712	383	.282	.382	.491	132	203	209	922	37	19	-0	.981	-7	*O1	14.2
■ OLAF HENRIKSEN Henriksen, Olaf "Swede" b: 4/26/1888, Kirkerup, Denmark d: 10/17/62, Norwood, Mass. BL/TL, 5'7.5", 158 lbs. Deb: 8/11/11																									
1911	Bos-A	27	93	17	34	2	1	0	8	14		.366	.449	.409	141	6	6	19	4			.953	-0	O	0.4
1912	*Bos-A	44	56	20	18	3	1	0	8	14		.321	.457	.411	142	5	4	11	0			.909	-2	O	0.1
1913	Bos-A	31	40	8	15	1	0	0	2	7	5	.375	.468	.400	151	3	3	8	3			1.000	-1	/O	0.2
1914	Bos-A	63	95	16	25	2	1	1	5	22	12	.263	.407	.337	124	4	4	14	5	4	-1	.947	-5	O	-0.3
1915	*Bos-A	73	92	9	18	2	2	0	13	18	7	.196	.333	.261	80	-2	-1	8	1	5	-3	.967	-4	O	-0.9
1916	*Bos-A	68	99	13	20	2	2	0	11	19	15	.202	.331	.263	78	-2	-2	10	2			1.000	-4	O	-0.8
1917	Bos-A	15	12	1	1	0	0	0	1	3	4	.083	.267	.083	7	-1	-1	0	0			.000	0	H	-0.1
Total	7	321	487	84	131	12	7	1	48	97	43	.269	.392	.329	112	13	13	70	15	9		.966	-17	O	-1.4
■ SNAKE HENRY Henry, Frederick Marshall b: 7/19/1895, Waynesville, N.C. d: 10/12/87, Wendell, N.C. BL/TL, 6', 170 lbs. Deb: 9/15/22																									
1922	Bos-N	18	66	5	13	4	1	0	5	2	8	.197	.221	.288	32	-7	-7	4	2	2	-1	.995	1	1	-0.6
1923	Bos-N	11	9	1	1	0	0	0	2	1	1	.111	.200	.111	-17	-2	-1	0	0	0	0	.000	0	H	-0.1
Total	2	29	75	6	14	4	1	0	7	3	9	.187	.218	.267	26	-9	-8	4	2	2	-1		1	/1	-0.7
■ GEORGE HENRY Henry, George Washington b: 8/10/1863, Philadelphia, Pa. d: 12/30/34, Lynn, Mass. BR/TR, 5'9", 180 lbs. Deb: 4/27/1893																									
1893	Cin-N	21	83	11	23	3	0	0	13	11	12	.277	.375	.313	84	-1	-1	11	2			.965	5	O	0.2
■ JOHN HENRY Henry, John Michael b: 9/2/1863, Springfield, Mass. d: 6/11/39, Hartford, Conn. TL , Deb: 8/13/1884																									
1884	Cle-N	9	26	2	4	0	0	0	0	0	12	.154	.154	.154	-3	-3	-3	1				1.000	0	/PO	-0.1
1885	Bal-a	10	34	4	9	3	0	0		1		.265	.286	.353	105	0	0	4				.931	2	/PO	0.0
1886	Was-N	4	14	3	5	0	0	0	0	0	3	.357	.357	.357	125	0	0	2	0			.833	-0	/P	0.0
1890	NY-N	37	144	19	35	6	0	0	16	7	12	.243	.283	.285	67	-6	-6	15	12			.870	-3	O	-0.9
Total	4	60	218	28	53	9	0	0	16	8	27	.243	.273	.284	68	-9	-9	21	12			.867	-1	/OP	-1.0
■ JOHN HENRY Henry, John Park "Bull" b: 12/26/1889, Amherst, Mass. d: 11/24/41, Fort Huachuca, Ariz. BR/TR, 6', 180 lbs. Deb: 7/08/10																									
1910	Was-A	29	87	2	13	1	1	0	5	2		.149	.169	.184	11	-9	-9	3	2			.989	2	C1	-0.6
1911	Was-A	85	261	24	53	5	0	0	21	25		.203	.273	.222	39	-21	-20	18	8			.969	9	C1	-0.7
1912	Was-A	66	191	23	37	4	1	0	9	31		.194	.309	.225	53	-10	-11	16	10			.977	8	C	0.4
1913	Was-A	96	273	26	61	8	4	1	26	30	43	.223	.309	.293	75	-8	-8	26	5			**.982**	3	C	0.3
1914	Was-A	92	261	22	44	7	4	0	20	37	47	.169	.274	.226	49	-15	-16	19	7	3	0	.980	6	C	-0.3
1915	Was-A	95	277	20	61	9	2	1	22	36	28	.220	.323	.278	78	-6	-7	29	10	2	2	.972	4	C	0.7
1916	Was-A	117	305	28	76	12	3	0	46	49	40	.249	.364	.308	103	3	4	40	12			.981	-4	*C	0.8
1917	Was-A	65	163	10	31	6	0	0	18	24	16	.190	.302	.227	62	-7	-6	12	1			.988	1	C	-0.1
1918	Bos-N	43	102	6	21	2	0	0	4	10	15	.206	.283	.225	58	-5	-5	6	0			.964	1	C	-0.1
Total	9	688	1920	161	397	54	15	2	171	244	189	.207	.303	.254	65	-78	-78	169	55	5		.978	31	C/1	0.4
■ RON HENRY Henry, Ronald Baxter b: 8/7/36, Chester, Pa. BR/TR, 6'1", 180 lbs. Deb: 4/15/61																									
1961	Min-A	20	28	1	4	0	0	0	3	2	7	.143	.200	.143	-6	-4	-4	0	0	0	0	1.000	-1	/C1	-0.5
1964	Min-A	22	41	4	5	1	1	2	5	2	17	.122	.163	.341	36	-4	-4	2	0	0	0	.984	-0	C	-0.4
Total	2	42	69	5	9	1	1	2	8	4	24	.130	.178	.261	18	-8	-8	3	0	0	0	.988	-1	/C1	-0.9
■ BABE HERMAN Herman, Floyd Caves b: 6/26/03, Buffalo, N.Y. d: 11/27/87, Glendale, Cal. BL/TL, 6'4", 190 lbs. Deb: 4/14/26 C																									
1926	Bro-N	137	496	64	158	35	11	11	81	44	53	.319	.375	.500	136	22	23	91	8			.986	0	*1O	1.5
1927	Bro-N	130	412	65	112	26	9	14	73	39	41	.272	.336	.481	116	8	8	65	4			.980	0	*1/O	0.1
1928	Bro-N	134	486	64	165	37	6	12	91	38	36	.340	.390	.514	136	23	24	94	1			.937	-7	*O	0.9
1929	Bro-N	146	569	105	217	42	13	21	113	55	45	.381	.436	.612	160	50	51	146	21			.941	-17	*O/1	2.2
1930	Bro-N	153	614	143	241	48	11	35	130	66	56	.393	.455	.678	171	69	70	183	18			.978	-20	*O	3.3
1931	Bro-N	151	610	93	191	43	16	18	97	50	65	.313	.365	.525	137	29	30	118	17			.960	-1	*O	1.8
1932	Cin-N	148	577	87	188	38	**19**	16	87	60	45	.326	.389	.541	152	38	40	124	7			.969	16	*O	4.6
1933	Chi-N	137	508	77	147	36	12	16	93	50	57	.289	.353	.502	142	26	26	90	6			.957	-5	*O	1.5
1934	Chi-N	125	467	65	142	34	5	14	84	35	71	.304	.353	.488	125	14	15	81	1			.971	-10	*O/1	0.0
1935	Pit-N	26	81	8	19	8	1	0	7	3	10	.235	.271	.358	65	-4	-4	7	0			.958	-3	O/1	-0.8
	Cin-N	92	349	44	117	23	5	10	58	35	25	.335	.396	.516	147	21	23	75	5			.976	-1	O1	1.7
	Yr	118	430	52	136	31	6	10	65	38	35	.316	.373	.486	131	17	18	80	5			.974	-4	O1	0.9
1936	Cin-N	119	380	59	106	25	2	13	71	39	36	.279	.348	.458	123	7	11	61	4			.967	-7	O/1	0.0

YEAR	TM/L	G	AB	R	H	2B	3B	HR	RBI	BB	SO	AVG	OBP	SLG	PRO+	BR	/A	RC	SB	CS	SBR	FA	FR	POS	TPR
1937	Det-A	17	20	2	6	3	0	0	3	1	6	.300	.364	.450	102	0	0	4	2	0	1	1.000	-0	/O	0.0
1945	Bro-N	37	34	6	9	1	0	1	9	5	7	.265	.359	.382	107	0	0	5	0			.000	-1	/O	-0.1
Total	13	1552	5603	882	1818	399	110	181	997	520	553	.324	.383	.532	141	304	318	1143	94	0		.961	-55	*O1	16.7

■ BILLY HERMAN Herman, William Jennings Bryan b: 7/7/09, New Albany, Ind. d: 9/5/92, W.Palm Beach, Fla. BR/TR, 5'11", 180 lbs. Deb: 8/29/31 MCH

YEAR	TM/L	G	AB	R	H	2B	3B	HR	RBI	BB	SO	AVG	OBP	SLG	PRO+	BR	/A	RC	SB	CS	SBR	FA	FR	POS	TPR
1931	Chi-N	25	98	14	32	7	0	0	16	13	6	.327	.405	.398	115	3	3	17	2			.939	3	2	0.7
1932	*Chi-N	154	656	102	206	42	7	1	51	40	33	.314	.358	.404	105	5	6	97	14			.961	17	*2	3.0
1933	Chi-N	153	619	82	173	35	2	0	44	45	34	.279	.332	.342	93	-5	-5	70	5			.956	29	*2	3.5
1934	Chi-N★	113	456	79	138	21	6	3	42	34	31	.303	.355	.395	102	1	2	66	6			.975	16	*2	2.3
1935	*Chi-N★	154	666	113	**227**	**57**	6	7	83	42	29	.341	.383	.476	128	27	26	121	6			**.964**	19	*2	5.4
1936	Chi-N★	153	632	101	211	57	7	5	93	59	30	.334	.392	.470	128	28	26	118	5			**.975**	15	*2	5.0
1937	Chi-N★	138	564	106	189	35	11	8	65	56	22	.335	.396	.479	131	29	26	112	2			.954	19	*2	5.3
1938	*Chi-N★	152	624	86	173	34	7	1	56	59	31	.277	.342	.359	90	-5	-7	76	3			**.981**	25	*2	2.6
1939	Chi-N★	156	623	111	191	34	**18**	7	70	66	31	.307	.378	.453	120	20	18	104	9			.967	-3	*2	2.3
1940	Chi-N★	135	558	77	163	24	4	5	57	47	30	.292	.347	.376	101	0	1	72	1			.974	19	*2	2.9
1941	Chi-N	11	36	4	7	0	1	0	0	9	5	.194	.356	.250	75	-1	-1	4	0			.898	-5	2	-0.5
	*Bro-N	133	536	77	156	30	4	3	41	58	38	.291	.361	.379	104	7	4	75	1			.970	-27	*2	-1.4
	Yr	144	572	81	163	30	5	3	41	67	43	.285	.361	.371	103	6	4	79	1			.964	-32	*2	-1.9
1942	Bro-N★	155	571	76	146	34	2	2	65	72	52	.256	.339	.333	95	-1	-2	68	6			.973	-11	*2/1	-0.4
1943	Bro-N★	153	585	76	193	41	2	2	100	66	26	.330	.398	.417	135	28	28	97	4			.971	-17	*23	2.0
1946	Bro-N	47	184	24	53	8	4	0	28	26	10	.288	.376	.375	112	4	4	26	2			.945	-2	32	0.4
	Bos-N	75	252	32	77	23	1	3	22	43	13	.306	.409	.440	139	15	15	47	1			.956	-16	21/3	0.1
	Yr	122	436	56	130	31	5	3	50	69	23	.298	.395	.413	128	19	18	73	3			.968	-18	231	0.5
1947	Pit-N	15	47	3	10	4	0	0	6	2	7	.213	.245	.298	42	-4	-4	3	0			1.000	-9	2/1M	-1.2
Total	15	1922	7707	1163	2345	486	82	47	839	737	428	.304	.367	.407	112	151	141	1173	67			.967	71	*2/31	32.0

■ AL HERMANN Hermann, Albert Bartel b: 3/28/1899, Milltown, N.J. d: 8/20/80, Lewes, Del. BR/TR, 6', 180 lbs. Deb: 7/17/23

YEAR	TM/L	G	AB	R	H	2B	3B	HR	RBI	BB	SO	AVG	OBP	SLG	PRO+	BR	/A	RC	SB	CS	SBR	FA	FR	POS	TPR
1923	Bos-N	31	93	2	22	4	0	0	11	0	7	.237	.237	.280	37	-9	-8	6	3	2	-0	.957	-6	2/31	-1.4
1924	Bos-N	1	1	0	0	0	0	0	0	0	1	.000	.000	.000	-99	-0	-0	0	0	0	0	.000	0	H	0.0
Total	2	32	94	2	22	4	0	0	11	0	8	.234	.234	.277	36	-9	-8	6	3	2	-0		-6	/231	-1.4

■ GENE HERMANSKI Hermanski, Eugene Victor b: 5/11/20, Pittsfield, Mass. BL/TR, 5'11.5", 185 lbs. Deb: 8/15/43

YEAR	TM/L	G	AB	R	H	2B	3B	HR	RBI	BB	SO	AVG	OBP	SLG	PRO+	BR	/A	RC	SB	CS	SBR	FA	FR	POS	TPR
1943	Bro-N	18	60	6	18	2	1	0	12	11	7	.300	.417	.367	127	3	3	10	1			.976	3	O	0.5
1946	Bro-N	64	110	15	22	2	2	0	8	17	10	.200	.313	.255	61	-5	-5	9	2			.938	-7	O	-1.4
1947	*Bro-N	79	189	36	52	7	1	7	39	28	7	.275	.377	.434	111	5	4	33	5			.982	-7	O	-0.5
1948	Bro-N	133	400	63	116	22	7	15	60	64	46	.290	.391	.493	133	22	20	81	15			.971	4	*O	1.8
1949	*Bro-N	87	224	48	67	12	3	8	42	47	21	.299	.431	.487	140	17	15	50	12			.980	-4	O	0.9
1950	Bro-N	94	289	36	86	17	3	7	34	36	26	.298	.381	.450	115	8	7	50	2			.989	3	O	0.7
1951	Bro-N	31	80	8	20	4	0	1	5	10	12	.250	.333	.338	79	-2	-2	9	0	2	-1	.977	1	O	-0.3
	Chi-N	75	231	28	65	12	1	3	20	35	30	.281	.385	.381	105	4	3	37	3	0	1	.966	5	O	0.6
	Yr	106	311	36	85	16	1	4	25	45	42	.273	.372	.370	98	2	1	46	3	2	-0	.969	6	O	0.3
1952	Chi-N	99	275	28	70	6	0	4	34	29	32	.255	.330	.320	80	-6	-7	32	2	0	1	.981	2	O	-0.7
1953	Chi-N	18	40	1	6	1	0	0	1	4	7	.150	.227	.175	7	-5	-6	2	1	0	0	1.000	-2	O	-0.7
	Pit-N	41	62	7	11	0	0	1	4	8	14	.177	.282	.226	35	-6	-6	4	0	0	0	1.000	-0	O	-0.6
	Yr	59	102	8	17	1	0	1	5	12	21	.167	.261	.206	24	-11	-11	6	1	0	0	1.000	-2	O	-1.3
Total	9	739	1960	276	533	85	18	46	259	289	212	.272	.372	.404	107	33	27	316	43	2		.977	-1	O	0.3

■ REMY HERMOSO Hermoso, Angel Remigio b: 10/1/46, Carabobo, Venezuela BR/TR, 5'8", 155 lbs. Deb: 9/14/67

YEAR	TM/L	G	AB	R	H	2B	3B	HR	RBI	BB	SO	AVG	OBP	SLG	PRO+	BR	/A	RC	SB	CS	SBR	FA	FR	POS	TPR
1967	Atl-N	11	26	3	8	0	0	0	0	2	4	.308	.357	.308	93	-0	-0	3	1	0	0	.952	1	/S2	0.2
1969	Mon-N	28	74	6	12	0	0	0	3	5	10	.162	.225	.162	10	-9	-9	3	3	1	0	.968	4	2/S	-0.3
1970	Mon-N	4	1	1	0	0	0	0	0	0	0	.000	.000	.000	-99	-0	-0	0	0	0	0	1.000	0	/23	0.0
1974	Cle-A	48	122	15	27	3	1	0	5	7	7	.221	.264	.262	52	-8	-7	9	2	2	-1	.967	7	2	0.1
Total	4	91	223	25	47	3	1	0	8	14	21	.211	.261	.233	42	-17	-17	15	6	3	0	.968	12	/2S3	-0.0

■ CARLOS HERNANDEZ Hernandez, Carlos Alberto (Almeida) b: 5/24/67, San Felix, Venez. BR/TR, 5'11", 185 lbs. Deb: 4/20/90

YEAR	TM/L	G	AB	R	H	2B	3B	HR	RBI	BB	SO	AVG	OBP	SLG	PRO+	BR	/A	RC	SB	CS	SBR	FA	FR	POS	TPR
1990	LA-N	10	20	2	4	1	0	0	1	0	2	.200	.200	.250	24	-2	-2	1	0	0	0	1.000	1	C	-0.1
1991	LA-N	15	14	1	3	1	0	0	1	0	5	.214	.267	.286	57	-1	-1	1	1	0	0	.966	1	C/3	0.0
1992	LA-N	69	173	11	45	4	0	3	17	11	21	.260	.319	.335	87	-3	-3	17	0	1	-1	.979	2	C	0.2
Total	3	94	207	14	52	6	0	3	19	11	28	.251	.305	.324	79	-6	-6	18	1	1	-0	.980	3	/C3	0.1

■ CESAR HERNANDEZ Hernandez, Cesar Dario (Perez) b: 9/28/66, Yamasa, D.R. BR/TR, 6', 160 lbs. Deb: 7/19/92

YEAR	TM/L	G	AB	R	H	2B	3B	HR	RBI	BB	SO	AVG	OBP	SLG	PRO+	BR	/A	RC	SB	CS	SBR	FA	FR	POS	TPR
1992	Cin-N	34	51	6	14	4	0	0	4	0	10	.275	.275	.353	73	-2	-2	5	3	1	0	.952	-2	O	-0.5

■ ENZO HERNANDEZ Hernandez, Enzo Octavio b: 2/12/49, Valle De Guanape, Venez. BR/TR, 5'8", 155 lbs. Deb: 4/17/71

YEAR	TM/L	G	AB	R	H	2B	3B	HR	RBI	BB	SO	AVG	OBP	SLG	PRO+	BR	/A	RC	SB	CS	SBR	FA	FR	POS	TPR
1971	SD-N	143	549	58	122	9	3	0	12	54	34	.222	.295	.250	60	-31	-26	46	21	5	3	.955	-11	*S	-1.6
1972	SD-N	114	329	33	64	11	2	1	15	22	25	.195	.245	.249	44	-26	-23	23	24	3	5	.963	6	*S/O	0.2
1973	SD-N	70	247	26	55	2	1	0	9	17	14	.223	.273	.239	47	-19	-16	17	15	4	2	.977	-1	S	-0.7
1974	SD-N	147	512	55	119	19	2	0	34	38	36	.232	.285	.277	60	-29	-26	45	37	10	5	.966	-8	*S	-1.0
1975	SD-N	116	344	37	75	12	2	0	19	26	25	.218	.277	.265	54	-23	-20	28	20	4	4	.965	8	*S	0.2
1976	SD-N	113	340	31	87	13	3	1	24	32	16	.256	.320	.321	89	-8	-4	36	12	7	-1	.964	4	*S	1.1
1977	SD-N	7	3	1	0	0	0	0	0	0	0	.000	.000	.000	-99	-1	-1	0	0	0	0	1.000	2	/S	0.1
1978	LA-N	4	3	0	0	0	0	0	0	0	1	.000	.000	.000	-99	-1	-1	0	0	0	0	.000	0	/S	-0.1
Total	8	714	2327	241	522	66	13	2	113	189	151	.224	.284	.266	59	-136	-118	196	129	33	19	.964	-0	S/O	-1.8

■ JACKIE HERNANDEZ Hernandez, Jacinto (Zulueta) b: 9/11/40, Central Tinguaro, Cuba BR/TR, 6', 175 lbs. Deb: 9/14/65

YEAR	TM/L	G	AB	R	H	2B	3B	HR	RBI	BB	SO	AVG	OBP	SLG	PRO+	BR	/A	RC	SB	CS	SBR	FA	FR	POS	TPR
1965	Cal-A	6	6	2	2	1	0	0	1	0	1	.333	.333	.500	137	0	0	1	1	0	0	1.000	-0	/S3	0.0
1966	Cal-A	58	23	19	1	0	0	0	2	1	4	.043	.083	.043	-64	-5	-5	0	1	1	-0	.857	15	3/2SO	1.1
1967	Min-A	29	28	1	4	0	0	0	3	0	6	.143	.143	.143	-14	-4	-4	1	0	0	0	.974	6	S3	0.2
1968	Min-A	83	199	13	35	3	0	2	17	9	52	.176	.219	.221	32	-16	-17	10	5	2	0	.927	9	S/1	-0.2
1969	KC-A	145	504	54	112	14	2	4	40	38	111	.222	.279	.282	57	-29	-29	42	17	7	1	.954	-15	*S	-3.0
1970	KC-A	83	238	14	55	4	1	2	10	15	50	.231	.282	.282	56	-14	-14	18	1	3	-2	.951	-5	S	-1.4
1971	*Pit-N	88	233	30	48	7	3	3	26	17	45	.206	.260	.300	59	-13	-13	18	0	2	-1	.950	12	S/3	0.6
1972	Pit-N	72	176	12	33	7	1	1	14	9	43	.188	.227	.256	38	-15	-14	10	0	0	0	.929	17	S/3	0.9
1973	Pit-N	54	73	8	18	1	2	0	8	4	12	.247	.286	.315	68	-3	-3	6	0	0	0	.940	17	S	1.6
Total	9	618	1480	153	308	37	9	12	121	93	324	.208	.258	.270	49	-99	-99	106	25	15	-1	.945	55	S/3201	-0.2

■ JOSE HERNANDEZ Hernandez, Jose Antonio (Figueroa) b: 7/14/69, Rio Piedras, P.R. BR/TR, 6'1", 180 lbs. Deb: 8/09/91

YEAR	TM/L	G	AB	R	H	2B	3B	HR	RBI	BB	SO	AVG	OBP	SLG	PRO+	BR	/A	RC	SB	CS	SBR	FA	FR	POS	TPR
1991	Tex-A	45	98	8	18	2	1	0	4	3	31	.184	.208	.224	20	-11	-10	4	0	1	-1	.975	9	S/3	0.0
1992	Cle-A	3	4	0	0	0	0	0	0	0	2	.000	.000	.000	-99	-1	-1	0	0	0	0	.857	-0	/S	-0.1
Total	2	48	102	8	18	2	1	0	4	3	33	.176	.200	.216	15	-12	-12	4	0	1	-1	.970	9	/S3	-0.1

■ KEITH HERNANDEZ Hernandez, Keith b: 10/20/53, San Francisco, Cal. BL/TL, 6', 195 lbs. Deb: 8/30/74

YEAR	TM/L	G	AB	R	H	2B	3B	HR	RBI	BB	SO	AVG	OBP	SLG	PRO+	BR	/A	RC	SB	CS	SBR	FA	FR	POS	TPR
1974	StL-N	14	34	3	10	1	2	0	2	7	8	.294	.415	.441	141	2	2	7	0	0	0	.973	-2	/1	-0.1
1975	StL-N	64	188	20	47	8	2	3	20	17	26	.250	.312	.362	84	-4	-4	20	0	1	-1	.996	3	1	-0.5
1976	StL-N	129	374	54	108	21	5	7	46	49	53	.289	.376	.428	126	14	14	61	4	2	0	.990	16	*1	2.4

YEAR	TM/L	G	AB	R	H	2B	3B	HR	RBI	BB	SO	AVG	OBP	SLG	PRO+	BR	/A	RC	SB	CS	SBR	FA	FR	POS	TPR
1977	StL-N	161	560	90	163	41	4	15	91	79	88	.291	.380	.459	126	20	22	95	7	7	-2	.992	5	*1	1.5
1978	StL-N	159	542	90	138	32	4	11	64	82	68	.255	.355	.389	109	7	8	78	13	5	1	.994	3	*1	0.3
1979	StL-N★	161	610	**116**	210	**48**	11	11	105	80	78	**.344**	**.421**	.513	152	47	46	**135**	11	6	-0	.995	19	*1	5.6
1980	StL-N★	159	595	**111**	191	39	8	16	99	86	73	.321	**.410**	.494	147	43	41	122	14	8	-1	.995	5	*1	3.7
1981	StL-N	103	376	65	115	27	4	8	48	61	45	.306	.405	.463	142	25	23	73	12	5	1	.997	6	1/O	2.6
1982	*StL-N	160	579	79	173	33	6	7	94	100	67	.299	.404	.413	128	27	26	101	19	11	-1	.994	7	*1/O	2.5
1983	StL-N	55	218	34	62	15	4	3	26	24	30	.284	.355	.431	117	5	5	34	1	1	-0	.991	3	1	0.5
	NY-N	95	320	43	98	8	3	9	37	64	42	.306	.425	.434	140	20	21	64	8	4	0	.993	11	1	2.6
	Yr	150	538	77	160	23	7	12	63	88	72	.297	.398	.433	131	25	26	98	9	5	-0	.992	14	*1	3.1
1984	NY-N★	154	550	83	171	31	0	15	94	97	89	.311	.415	.449	145	35	37	108	2	3	-1	.994	18	*1	4.5
1985	NY-N	158	593	87	183	34	4	10	91	77	59	.309	.390	.430	132	25	27	100	3	3	-1	**.997**	16	*1	3.3
1986	*NY-N★	149	551	94	171	34	1	13	83	**94**	69	.310	.414	.446	141	32	34	106	2	1	0	**.996**	18	*1	4.3
1987	NY-N★	154	587	87	170	28	2	18	89	81	104	.290	.379	.436	122	15	19	98	0	2	-1	.993	18	*1	2.4
1988	*NY-N	95	348	43	96	16	0	11	55	31	57	.276	.337	.417	121	7	8	47	2	1	0	.998	8	1	0.9
1989	NY-N	75	215	18	50	8	0	4	19	27	39	.233	.324	.326	90	-3	-2	23	0	3	-2	.991	-2	1	-1.0
1990	Cle-A	43	130	7	26	2	0	1	8	14	17	.200	.283	.238	47	-9	-9	9	0	0	0	.994	-2	1	-1.4
Total	17	2088	7370	1124	2182	426	60	162	1071	1070	1012	.296	.388	.436	129	310	319	1282	98	63	-8	.994	149	*1/O	34.1

■ LEO HERNANDEZ
Hernandez, Leonardo Jesus b: 11/6/59, Santa Lucia, Venz. BR/TR, 5'11", 170 lbs. Deb: 9/19/82

YEAR	TM/L	G	AB	R	H	2B	3B	HR	RBI	BB	SO	AVG	OBP	SLG	PRO+	BR	/A	RC	SB	CS	SBR	FA	FR	POS	TPR
1982	Bal-A	2	2	0	0	0	0	0	0	0	2	.000	.000	.000	-99	-1	-1	0	0	0	0	.000	0	/H	-0.1
1983	Bal-A	64	203	21	50	6	1	6	26	12	19	.246	.288	.374	82	-6	-5	21	1	0	0	.922	-12	3	-1.7
1985	Bal-A	12	21	0	1	0	0	0	0	0	4	.048	.048	.048	-76	-5	-5	-0	0	0	0	1.000	-1	/1OD	-0.5
1986	NY-A	7	22	2	5	2	0	1	4	1	8	.227	.261	.455	91	-0	-0	3	0	0	0	1.000	-1	/32	-0.1
Total	4	85	248	23	56	8	1	7	30	13	33	.226	.264	.351	69	-12	-11	24	1	0	0	.927	-13	/3D2O1	-2.4

■ PEDRO HERNANDEZ
Hernandez, Pedro Julio (b: Pedro Julio Montas (Hernandez)) b: 4/4/59, LaRomana, D.R. BR/TR, 6'1", 160 lbs. Deb: 9/08/79

YEAR	TM/L	G	AB	R	H	2B	3B	HR	RBI	BB	SO	AVG	OBP	SLG	PRO+	BR	/A	RC	SB	CS	SBR	FA	FR	POS	TPR
1979	Tor-A	3	0	1	0	0	0	0	0	0	0	—	—	—	—	0	0	0	0	0	0	.000	0	/R	0.0
1982	Tor-A	8	9	1	0	0	0	0	0	0	3	.000	.000	.000	-92	-2	-3	0	0	0	0	.000	-1	/3OD	-0.3
Total	2	11	9	2	0	0	0	0	0	0	3	.000	.000	.000	-92	-2	-3	0	0	0	0		-1	/D3O	-0.3

■ TOBY HERNANDEZ
Hernandez, Rafael Tobias (Alvarado) b: 11/30/58, Calabozo, Venz. BR/TR, 6'1", 160 lbs. Deb: 6/22/84

YEAR	TM/L	G	AB	R	H	2B	3B	HR	RBI	BB	SO	AVG	OBP	SLG	PRO+	BR	/A	RC	SB	CS	SBR	FA	FR	POS	TPR
1984	Tor-A	3	2	1	1	0	0	0	0	0	0	.500	.500	.500	171	0	0	1	0	0	0	1.000	-1	/C	0.0

■ RUDY HERNANDEZ
Hernandez, Rodolfo (Acosta) b: 10/18/51, Enpalme, Mexico BR/TR, 5'9", 150 lbs. Deb: 9/06/72

YEAR	TM/L	G	AB	R	H	2B	3B	HR	RBI	BB	SO	AVG	OBP	SLG	PRO+	BR	/A	RC	SB	CS	SBR	FA	FR	POS	TPR
1972	Chi-A	8	21	0	4	0	0	0	1	0	3	.190	.190	.190	13	-2	-2	1	0	0	0	1.000	1	/S	-0.1

■ CHICO HERNANDEZ
Hernandez, Salvador Jose (Ramos) b: 1/3/16, Havana, Cuba d: 1/3/86, Havana, Cuba BR/TR, 6', 195 lbs. Deb: 4/16/42

YEAR	TM/L	G	AB	R	H	2B	3B	HR	RBI	BB	SO	AVG	OBP	SLG	PRO+	BR	/A	RC	SB	CS	SBR	FA	FR	POS	TPR
1942	Chi-N	47	118	6	27	5	0	0	7	11	13	.229	.295	.271	69	-5	-4	10	0			.975	-2	C	-0.4
1943	Chi-N	43	126	10	34	4	0	0	9	9	9	.270	.324	.302	82	-3	-3	12	0			.981	-2	C	-0.2
Total	2	90	244	16	61	9	0	0	16	20	22	.250	.309	.287	76	-8	-7	22	0			.978	-4	/C	-0.6

■ LARRY HERNDON
Herndon, Larry Darnell b: 11/3/53, Sunflower, Miss. BR/TR, 6'3", 195 lbs. Deb: 9/04/74 C

YEAR	TM/L	G	AB	R	H	2B	3B	HR	RBI	BB	SO	AVG	OBP	SLG	PRO+	BR	/A	RC	SB	CS	SBR	FA	FR	POS	TPR
1974	StL-N	12	1	3	1	0	0	0	0	0	0	1.000	1.000	1.000	465	0	0	1	0	0	0	1.000	1	/O	0.2
1976	SF-N	115	337	42	97	11	3	2	23	23	45	.288	.337	.356	94	-1	-3	40	12	10	-2	.967	-11	*O	-2.1
1977	SF-N	49	109	13	26	4	3	1	5	5	20	.239	.278	.358	69	-5	-5	10	4	2	0	.957	6	O	0.0
1978	SF-N	151	471	52	122	15	9	1	32	35	71	.259	.312	.335	84	-12	-10	48	13	8	-1	.974	-3	*O	-2.1
1979	SF-N	132	354	35	91	14	5	7	36	29	70	.257	.315	.384	96	-5	-2	43	8	6	-1	.963	-5	*O	-1.3
1980	SF-N	139	493	54	127	17	11	8	49	19	91	.258	.287	.385	88	-11	-10	50	8	8	-2	.959	-1	*O	-1.8
1981	SF-N	96	364	48	105	15	8	5	41	20	55	.288	.327	.415	111	3	4	46	15	6	1	.977	5	O	0.7
1982	Det-A	157	614	92	179	21	13	23	88	38	92	.292	.334	.480	120	15	15	90	12	9	-2	.983	6	*O/D	1.5
1983	Det-A	153	603	88	182	28	9	20	92	46	95	.302	.354	.478	130	21	23	97	9	3	1	.951	1	*OD	2.0
1984	*Det-A	125	407	52	114	18	5	7	43	32	63	.280	.336	.400	103	1	2	55	6	2	1	.986	-5	*O/D	-0.5
1985	Det-A	137	442	45	108	12	7	12	37	33	79	.244	.298	.385	86	-10	-9	50	2	1	0	.976	5	*O	-0.8
1986	Det-A	106	283	33	70	13	1	8	37	27	40	.247	.315	.385	90	-4	-4	36	2	1	0	.988	-1	OD	-0.8
1987	*Det-A	89	225	32	73	13	2	9	47	23	35	.324	.387	.520	144	12	14	42	1	0	0	.989	-4	OD	0.8
1988	Det-A	76	174	16	39	5	0	4	20	23	37	.224	.318	.322	83	-4	-3	17	0	1	-1	1.000	-2	DO	-0.6
Total	14	1537	4877	605	1334	186	76	107	550	353	793	.274	.325	.409	103	1	12	624	92	57	-7	.972	-8	*OD	-4.8

■ TOM HERNON
Hernon, Thomas H. b: 11/4/1866, E.Bridgewater, Mass d: 2/4/02, New Bedford, Mass. BR/TR, Deb: 9/13/1897

YEAR	TM/L	G	AB	R	H	2B	3B	HR	RBI	BB	SO	AVG	OBP	SLG	PRO+	BR	/A	RC	SB	CS	SBR	FA	FR	POS	TPR
1897	Chi-N	4	16	2	1	0	0	0	2	0		.063	.063	.063	-65	-4	-4	0	1			1.000	0	/O	-0.4

■ ED HERR
Herr, Edward Joseph b: 5/18/1862, St.Louis, Mo. d: 7/18/43, St.Louis, Mo. BR/TR, 5'9.5", 179 lbs. Deb: 4/16/1887

YEAR	TM/L	G	AB	R	H	2B	3B	HR	RBI	BB	SO	AVG	OBP	SLG	PRO+	BR	/A	RC	SB	CS	SBR	FA	FR	POS	TPR
1887	Cle-a	11	44	6	12	2	0	0		6		.273	.360	.318	95	-0	0	6	2			.729	-3	3	-0.2
1888	*StL-a	43	172	21	46	7	1	3	43	11		.267	.323	.372	113	5	2	24	9			.872	-9	SO/3	-0.6
1890	StL-a	12	41	5	9	2	1	0		5		.220	.347	.317	86	0	-1	5	2			.793	-7	/2O3	-0.6
Total	3	66	257	32	67	11	2	3	43	22		.261	.333	.354	105	5	1	35	13			.762	-18	/S3O2	-1.4

■ TOM HERR
Herr, Thomas Mitchell b: 4/4/56, Lancaster, Pa. BB/TR, 6', 185 lbs. Deb: 8/13/79

YEAR	TM/L	G	AB	R	H	2B	3B	HR	RBI	BB	SO	AVG	OBP	SLG	PRO+	BR	/A	RC	SB	CS	SBR	FA	FR	POS	TPR
1979	StL-N	14	10	4	2	0	0	0	1	2	2	.200	.333	.200	49	-1	-1	1	1	0	0	1.000	6	/2	0.5
1980	StL-N	76	222	29	55	12	5	0	15	16	21	.248	.301	.347	78	-6	-7	22	9	2	2	.984	2	2S	0.1
1981	StL-N	103	411	50	110	14	9	0	46	39	30	.268	.333	.345	90	-4	-5	49	23	7	3	**.992**	4	*2	0.9
1982	*StL-N	135	493	83	131	19	4	0	36	57	56	.266	.344	.320	86	-7	-7	59	25	12	0	.987	4	*2	0.3
1983	StL-N	89	313	43	101	14	4	2	31	43	27	.323	.406	.412	127	13	13	53	6	8	-3	.986	-19	2	-0.4
1984	StL-N	145	558	67	154	23	2	4	49	49	56	.276	.337	.346	94	-5	-3	66	13	7	-0	.992	-1	*2	0.1
1985	*StL-N★	159	596	97	180	38	3	8	110	80	55	.302	.386	.416	126	22	23	107	31	3	8	.985	-31	*2	0.5
1986	StL-N	152	559	48	141	30	4	2	61	73	75	.252	.344	.331	88	-8	-7	69	22	8	2	.988	-22	*2	-2.2
1987	*StL-N	141	510	73	134	29	0	2	83	68	62	.263	.353	.331	81	-11	-12	65	19	4	3	.989	-17	*2	-1.9
1988	StL-N	15	50	4	13	0	0	1	3	11	4	.260	.393	.320	106	1	1	8	3	0	1	.984	-6	2	-0.4
	Min-A	86	304	42	80	16	0	1	21	40	47	.263	.349	.326	88	-3	-4	36	10	3	1	.988	-8	2/SD	-0.8
1989	Phi-N	151	561	65	161	25	6	2	37	54	63	.287	.353	.364	105	5	5	73	10	7	-1	.990	2	*2	1.1
1990	Phi-N	119	447	39	118	21	3	4	50	36	47	.264	.322	.351	85	-9	-9	51	7	1	2	.991	-3	*2	-0.8
	NY-N	27	100	9	25	5	0	1	10	14	11	.250	.342	.330	86	-2	-2	12	0	0	0	.979	-5	2	-0.6
	Yr	146	547	48	143	26	3	5	60	50	58	.261	.326	.347	85	-11	-10	64	7	1	2	.989	-8	*2	-1.4
1991	NY-N	70	155	17	30	7	0	1	14	32	21	.194	.332	.258	68	-5	-5	16	7	2	1	1.000	7	2/O	0.3
	SF-N	32	60	6	15	1	1	0	7	13	7	.250	.384	.300	98	0	1	8	2	0	1	1.000	-6	2/3	-0.5
	Yr	102	215	23	45	8	1	1	21	45	28	.209	.346	.270	77	-5	-5	24	9	2	2	1.000	1	2/3O	-0.2
Total	13	1514	5349	676	1450	254	41	28	574	627	584	.271	.350	.350	95	-17	-19	694	188	64	18	.989	-94	*2/S3DO	-3.8

■ JOSE HERRERA
Herrera, Jose Concepcion (Ontiveros) "Loco" b: 4/8/42, San Lorenzo, Venez. BR/TR, 5'8", 165 lbs. Deb: 6/03/67

YEAR	TM/L	G	AB	R	H	2B	3B	HR	RBI	BB	SO	AVG	OBP	SLG	PRO+	BR	/A	RC	SB	CS	SBR	FA	FR	POS	TPR
1967	Hou-N	5	4	0	1	0	0	0	1	0	1	.250	.250	.250	45	-0	-0	0	0	0	0	.000	0	H	0.0
1968	Hou-N	27	100	9	24	5	0	0	7	4	12	.240	.269	.290	69	-4	-4	7	0	2	-1	.958	-3	O/2	-1.0
1969	Mon-N	47	126	7	36	5	0	2	12	3	14	.286	.302	.373	88	-2	-2	13	1	2	-1	.980	-1	O/23	-0.6
1970	Mon-N	1	1	0	0	0	0	0	0	0	1	.000	.000	.000	-99	-0	-0	0	0	0	0	.000	0	H	0.0
Total	4	80	231	16	61	10	0	2	20	7	28	.264	.286	.333	79	-7	-7	21	1	4	-2	.973	-4	/O23	-1.6

YEAR	TM/L	G	AB	R	H	2B	3B	HR	RBI	BB	SO	AVG	OBP	SLG	PRO+	BR	/A	RC	SB	CS	SBR	FA	FR	POS	TPR
■ **PANCHO HERRERA** Herrera, Juan Francisco (Willavicencio) b: 6/16/34, Santiago, Cuba BR/TR, 6'3", 220 lbs. Deb: 4/15/58																									
1958	Phi-N	29	63	5	17	3	0	1	6	7	15	.270	.352	.365	92	-1	-1	8	1	2	-1	.980	2	31	0.0
1960	Phi-N	145	512	61	144	26	6	17	71	51	136	.281	.352	.455	119	13	13	78	2	3	-1	.988	10	*12	1.4
1961	Phi-N	126	400	56	103	17	2	13	51	55	120	.257	.353	.408	102	2	2	58	5	1	1	.993	6	*1	0.0
Total	3	300	975	122	264	46	8	31	128	113	271	.271	.352	.430	110	14	15	145	8	6	-1	.990	18	1/23	1.4
■ **MIKE HERRERA** Herrera, Ramon b: 12/19/1897, Havana, Cuba d: 2/3/78, Havana, Cuba BR/TR, 5'6", 147 lbs. Deb: 9/22/25																									
1925	Bos-A	10	39	2	15	0	0	0	8	2	2	.385	.415	.385	104	0	0	6	1	0	0	.958	3	2	0.4
1926	Bos-A	74	237	20	61	14	1	0	19	15	13	.257	.304	.325	66	-13	-12	23	0	5	-3	.962	5	23/S	-0.7
Total	2	84	276	22	76	14	1	0	27	17	15	.275	.320	.333	72	-12	-11	29	1	5	-3	.961	8	/23S	-0.3
■ **LEFTY HERRING** Herring, Silas Clarke b: 3/4/1880, Philadelphia, Pa. d: 2/11/65, Massapequa, N.Y. BL/TL, 5'11", 160 lbs. Deb: 5/16/1899																									
1899	Was-N	2	1	1	1	0	0	0	0	1		1.000	1.000	1.000	454	1	1	1	0			1.000	0	/P	0.0
1904	Was-A	15	46	3	8	1	0	0	2	7		.174	.283	.196	54	-2	-2	3	0			.991	1	1/O	-0.2
Total	2	17	47	4	9	1	0	0	2	8		.191	.309	.213	67	-1	-1	4	0				1	/1OP	-0.2
■ **ED HERRMANN** Herrmann, Edward Martin b: 8/27/46, San Diego, Cal. BL/TR, 6'1", 210 lbs. Deb: 9/01/67 F																									
1967	Chi-A	2	3	1	2	1	0	0	1	1	0	.667	.750	1.000	429	1	1	2	0	0	0	1.000	1	/C	0.3
1969	Chi-A	102	290	31	67	8	0	8	31	30	35	.231	.320	.341	81	-6	-7	32	0	2	-1	.983	-3	C	-0.8
1970	Chi-A	96	297	42	84	9	0	19	52	31	41	.283	.356	.505	130	13	12	54	0	1	-1	.988	5	C	2.1
1971	Chi-A	101	294	32	63	6	0	11	35	44	48	.214	.321	.347	86	-4	-5	33	2	0	1	.995	9	C	0.9
1972	Chi-A	116	354	23	88	9	0	10	40	43	37	.249	.337	.359	105	4	3	41	0	0	0	.989	0	*C	0.9
1973	Chi-A	119	379	42	85	17	1	10	39	31	55	.224	.295	.354	79	-10	-11	37	2	4	-2	.984	5	*C/D	-0.4
1974	Chi-A†	107	367	32	95	13	1	10	39	16	49	.259	.290	.381	90	-5	-6	37	1	0	0	.987	3	*C	0.2
1975	NY-A	80	200	16	51	9	2	6	30	16	23	.255	.310	.410	105	-0	1	24	0	0	0	.979	7	DC	0.9
1976	Cal-A	29	46	5	8	3	0	2	8	7	8	.174	.283	.370	96	-1	-0	5	0	0	0	.954	-6	C	-0.6
	Hou-N	79	265	14	54	8	0	3	25	22	40	.204	.275	.268	60	-16	-13	20	0	0	0	.987	0	C	-1.1
1977	Hou-N	56	158	7	46	7	0	1	17	15	18	.291	.356	.354	100	-1	0	20	1	1	-0	.990	9	C	1.0
1978	Hou-N	16	36	1	4	1	0	0	0	3	3	.111	.179	.139	-11	-5	-5	1	0	0	0	1.000	-1	C	-0.6
	Mon-N	19	40	1	7	1	0	0	3	1	4	.175	.195	.200	11	-5	-5	1	0	0	0	.977	-1	C	-0.6
	Yr	35	76	2	11	2	0	0	3	4	7	.145	.188	.171	1	-10	-10	2	0	0	0	.991	-2	C	-1.2
Total	11	922	2729	247	654	92	4	80	320	260	361	.240	.312	.364	91	-33	-35	308	6	8	-3	.987	29	C/D	2.2
■ **RICK HERRSCHER** Herrscher, Richard Franklin b: 11/3/36, St.Louis, Mo. BR/TR, 6'2.5", 187 lbs. Deb: 8/01/62																									
1962	NY-N	35	50	5	11	3	0	1	6	5	11	.220	.291	.340	68	-2	-2	5	0	0	0	1.000	3	1/3OS	0.1
■ **JOHN HERRNSTEIN** Herrnstein, John Ellett b: 5/31/38, Hampton, Va. BL/TL, 6'3", 215 lbs. Deb: 9/15/62																									
1962	Phi-N	6	5	0	1	0	0	0	1	1	3	.200	.333	.200	48	-0	-0	0	0	0	0	.000	0	/O	0.0
1963	Phi-N	15	12	1	2	0	0	1	1	1	5	.167	.231	.417	83	-0	-0	1	0	0	0	1.000	0	/O1	0.0
1964	Phi-N	125	303	38	71	12	4	6	25	22	67	.234	.291	.360	83	-7	-7	31	1	2	-1	.977	-7	O1	-2.0
1965	Phi-N	63	85	8	17	2	0	1	5	2	18	.200	.227	.259	37	-7	-7	4	0	0	0	.984	1	1O	-0.7
1966	Phi-N	4	10	0	1	0	0	0	1	0	7	.100	.100	.100	-44	-2	-2	0	0	0	0	1.000	-0	/O	-0.2
	Chi-N	9	17	3	3	0	0	0	0	3	8	.176	.300	.176	36	-1	-1	1	0	0	0	.975	-1	/1O	-0.3
	Atl-N	17	18	2	4	0	0	0	1	0	7	.222	.222	.222	24	-2	-2	1	0	0	0	1.000	0	/O	-0.2
	Yr	30	45	5	8	0	0	0	2	3	22	.178	.229	.178	15	-5	-5	2	0	0	0	1.000	-1	/O1	-0.7
Total	5	239	450	52	99	14	4	8	34	29	115	.220	.272	.322	67	-20	-20	39	1	2	-1	.983	-7	/O1	-3.4
■ **EARL HERSH** Hersh, Earl Walter b: 5/21/32, Ebbvale, Md. BL/TL, 6', 205 lbs. Deb: 9/04/56																									
1956	Mil-N	7	13	0	3	3	0	0	0	0	5	.231	.231	.462	85	-0	-0	1	0	0	0	.000	-1	/O	-0.1
■ **MIKE HERSHBERGER** Hershberger, Norman Michael b: 10/9/39, Massillon, Ohio BR/TR, 5'10", 175 lbs. Deb: 9/05/61																									
1961	Chi-A	15	55	9	17	3	0	0	5	2	2	.309	.333	.364	88	-1	-1	6	1	1	-0	1.000	2	O	-0.1
1962	Chi-A	148	427	54	112	14	2	4	46	37	36	.262	.325	.333	78	-13	-13	43	10	6	-1	.984	-7	*O	-2.7
1963	Chi-A	135	476	64	133	26	2	3	45	39	39	.279	.339	.361	98	-2	-1	60	9	3	1	.976	-5	*O	-1.2
1964	Chi-A	141	452	55	104	15	3	2	31	48	47	.230	.310	.290	70	-18	-17	42	8	6	-1	.984	-8	*O	-3.3
1965	KC-A	150	494	43	114	15	5	5	48	37	42	.231	.291	.312	72	-18	-18	42	7	3	0	.988	4	*O	-2.0
1966	KC-A	146	538	55	136	27	7	2	57	47	37	.253	.316	.340	92	-7	-5	58	13	5	1	.977	12	*O	0.1
1967	KC-A	142	480	55	122	25	1	1	49	38	40	.254	.318	.317	91	-6	-5	49	10	3	1	.982	7	*O	-0.3
1968	Oak-A	99	246	23	67	9	2	5	32	21	22	.272	.332	.386	123	5	6	32	8	3	1	.978	-7	O	-0.4
1969	Oak-A	51	129	11	26	2	0	1	10	10	15	.202	.259	.240	42	-10	-10	8	1	2	-1	.980	-5	O	-1.9
1970	Mil-A	49	98	7	23	5	0	1	6	10	8	.235	.306	.316	71	-4	-4	9	1	2	-1	.946	-6	O	-1.2
1971	Chi-A	74	177	22	46	9	0	2	15	30	23	.260	.379	.345	103	3	2	25	6	2	1	.960	-8	O	-0.8
Total	11	1150	3572	398	900	150	22	26	344	319	311	.252	.319	.328	85	-72	-64	374	74	36	1	.980	-21	*O	-13.8
■ **WILLARD HERSHBERGER** Hershberger, Willard McKee "Bill" b: 5/28/10, Lemon Cove, Cal. d: 8/3/40, Boston, Mass. BR/TR, 5'10.5", 167 lbs. Deb: 4/19/38																									
1938	Cin-N	49	105	12	29	3	1	0	12	5	6	.276	.315	.324	78	-3	-3	11	1			.960	-1	C/2	-0.2
1939	*Cin-N	63	174	23	60	9	2	0	32	9	4	.345	.384	.420	115	4	4	27	1			.987	-2	C	0.5
1940	Cin-N	48	123	6	38	4	2	0	26	6	6	.309	.351	.374	99	0	-0	15	0			.985	-2	C	0.0
Total	3	160	402	41	127	16	5	0	70	20	16	.316	.356	.381	101	1	1	53	2			.980	-5	C/2	0.3
■ **NEAL HERTWECK** Hertweck, Neal Charles b: 11/22/31, St.Louis, Mo. BL/TL, 6'1.5", 175 lbs. Deb: 9/27/52																									
1952	StL-N	2	6	0	0	0	0	0	0	1	1	.000	.143	.000	-57	-1	-1	0	0	0	0	1.000	-0	/1	-0.2
■ **STEVE HERTZ** Hertz, Stephen Allan b: 2/26/45, Farfield, Ohio BR/TR, 6'1", 195 lbs. Deb: 4/21/64																									
1964	Hou-N	5	4	2	0	0	0	0	0	0	3	.000	.000	.000	-99	-1	-1	0	0	0	0	1.000	0	/3	-0.1
■ **BUCK HERZOG** Herzog, Charles Lincoln b: 7/9/1885, Baltimore, Md. d: 9/4/53, Baltimore, Md. BR/TR, 5'11", 160 lbs. Deb: 4/17/08 M																									
1908	NY-N	64	160	38	48	6	2	0	11	36		.300	.448	.363	152	14	13	34	16			.921	1	2S/3O	1.6
1909	NY-N	42	130	16	24	2	0	0	8	13		.185	.264	.200	43	-8	-8	7	2			.914	-2	O/23S	-1.3
1910	Bos-N	106	380	51	95	20	3	3	32	30	34	.250	.329	.342	92	-2	-4	48	13			.915	4	*3	0.3
1911	Bos-N	79	294	53	91	19	5	5	41	33	21	.310	.398	.459	129	16	12	65	26			.934	8	S/3	2.5
	*NY-N	69	247	37	66	14	4	1	26	14	19	.267	.325	.368	91	-3	-4	36	22			.926	10	3/2S	0.7
	Yr	148	541	90	157	33	9	6	67	47	40	.290	.365	.418	112	13	9	100	48			.935	18	S3/2	3.2
1912	*NY-N	140	482	72	127	20	9	2	47	57	34	.263	.350	.355	90	-4	-6	73	37			.942	19	*3	1.4
1913	*NY-N	96	290	46	83	15	3	3	31	22	12	.286	.349	.390	110	4	4	45	23			.947	3	3/2	0.8
1914	Cin-N	138	498	54	140	14	8	1	40	42	27	.281	.348	.347	104	5	3	72	46			.939	31	*S/1M	4.8
1915	Cin-N	155	579	61	153	14	10	1	42	34	21	.264	.314	.328	93	-4	-5	66	35	16	1	.945	31	*S/1M	4.2
1916	Cin-N	79	281	30	75	14	2	1	24	21	12	.267	.329	.342	109	2	3	33	15	12	-3	.931	-2	S3/OM	0.5
	NY-N	77	280	40	73	10	4	0	25	22	24	.261	.326	.325	106	0	2	31	19	16	-4	.978	14	23/S	2.1
	Yr	156	561	70	148	24	6	1	49	43	36	.264	.327	.333	107	3	5	64	34	28	-7	.926	12	S23/O	2.6
1917	*NY-N	114	417	69	98	10	8	2	31	31	36	.235	.308	.312	93	-4	-3	43	12			.948	-9	*2	-0.6
1918	Bos-N	118	473	57	108	12	6	0	26	29	28	.228	.280	.279	74	-16	-14	39	10			.961	4	21/S	-0.5
1919	Bos-N	73	275	27	77	8	5	1	25	13	11	.280	.327	.356	110	2	3	36	16			.953	-14	2/1	-0.9
	Chi-N	52	193	15	53	4	4	0	17	10	7	.275	.336	.337	102	1	1	25	12			.987	-11	2	-0.8
	Yr	125	468	42	130	12	9	1	42	23	18	.278	.331	.348	106	3	4	61	28			.967	-25	*2/1	-1.7

YEAR	TM/L	G	AB	R	H	2B	3B	HR	RBI	BB	SO	AVG	OBP	SLG	PRO+	BR	/A	RC	SB	CS	SBR	FA	FR	POS	TPR
1920	Chi-N	91	305	39	59	9	2	0	19	20	21	.193	.261	.236	43	-22	-22	20	8	9	-3	.938	-6	23/1	-3.1
Total	13	1493	5284	705	1370	191	75	20	445	427	307	.259	.329	.335	96	-18	-25	674	312	53		.954	79	23S/01	11.7

■ WHITEY HERZOG
Herzog, Dorrel Norman Elvert b: 11/9/31, New Athens, Ill. BL/TL, 5'11", 182 lbs. Deb: 4/17/56 MC

YEAR	TM/L	G	AB	R	H	2B	3B	HR	RBI	BB	SO	AVG	OBP	SLG	PRO+	BR	/A	RC	SB	CS	SBR	FA	FR	POS	TPR
1956	Was-A	117	421	49	103	13	7	4	35	35	74	.245	.303	.337	69	-20	-20	44	8	5	-1	.980	1	*O/1	-2.4
1957	Was-A	36	78	7	13	3	0	0	4	13	12	.167	.301	.205	41	-6	-6	6	1	2	-1	.981	-3	O	-1.2
1958	Was-A	8	5	0	0	0	0	0	0	1	5	.000	.167	.000	-51	-1	-1	0	0	0	0	1.000	-2	/O	-0.3
	KC-A	88	96	11	23	1	2	0	9	16	21	.240	.348	.292	77	-2	-2	10	0	3	-2	.968	-10	O1	-1.6
	Yr	96	101	11	23	1	2	0	9	17	26	.228	.339	.277	71	-3	-3	10	0	3	-2	.972	-12	O1	-1.9
1959	KC-A	38	123	25	36	7	1	1	9	34	23	.293	.446	.390	129	8	7	25	1	0	0	.963	2	O/1	0.8
1960	KC-A	83	252	43	67	10	2	8	38	40	32	.266	.366	.417	111	5	5	39	0	1	-1	.985	1	O/1	0.1
1961	Bal-A	113	323	39	94	11	6	5	35	50	41	.291	.388	.409	115	8	9	53	1	4	-2	1.000	-11	O	-0.9
1962	Bal-A	99	263	34	70	13	1	7	35	41	36	.266	.371	.403	114	4	6	41	2	3	-1	.978	0	O	0.1
1963	Det-A	52	53	5	8	2	1	0	7	11	17	.151	.308	.226	51	-3	-3	5	0	0	0	.976	-2	/1O	-0.6
Total	8	634	1614	213	414	60	20	25	172	241	261	.257	.356	.365	95	-8	-6	222	13	18	-7	.982	-23	O/1	-6.0

■ OTTO HESS
Hess, Otto C. b: 10/10/1878, Berne, Switzerland d: 2/25/26, Tucson, Ariz. BL/TL, 6'1", 170 lbs. Deb: 8/03/02

YEAR	TM/L	G	AB	R	H	2B	3B	HR	RBI	BB	SO	AVG	OBP	SLG	PRO+	BR	/A	RC	SB	CS	SBR	FA	FR	POS	TPR
1902	Cle-A	7	14	2	1	0	0	0	1	2		.071	.188	.071	-27	-2	-2	0	0			.870	1	/P	0.0
1904	Cle-A	34	100	4	12	2	1	0	5	3		.120	.146	.160	-3	-12	-12	2	0			.951	-1	PO	-0.5
1905	Cle-A	54	173	15	44	8	1	2	13	7		.254	.291	.347	101	-0	-0	19	2			.950	3	OP	0.1
1906	Cle-A	53	154	13	31	5	2	0	11	2		.201	.212	.260	48	-10	-9	9	1			.949	-3	P/O	-0.2
1907	Cle-A	19	30	4	4	0	0	0	0	4		.133	.278	.133	32	-2	-2	2	1			.941	-1	P/O	-0.1
1908	Cle-A	9	14	0	0	0	0	0	0	1		.000	.067	.000	-78	-3	-3	0	0			1.000	-1	/PO	-0.4
1912	Bos-N	33	94	10	23	4	4	0	10	0	26	.245	.245	.372	66	-5	-5	9	0			.951	-4	P	0.0
1913	Bos-N	35	83	9	26	0	1	2	11	7	15	.313	.367	.410	119	2	2	12	0			.945	1	P	0.0
1914	Bos-N	31	47	5	11	1	0	1	6	1	11	.234	.250	.319	69	-2	-2	4	0			.947	1	P/1	-0.1
1915	Bos-N	5	5	1	2	1	0	0	1	0	2	.400	.400	.600	210	1	1	1	0			.800	-0	/P1	0.0
Total	10	280	714	63	154	21	9	5	58	27	54	.216	.248	.291	64	-32	-33	58	4			.941	-3	P/O1	-1.2

■ TOM HESS
Hess, Thomas (b: Thomas Heslin) b: 8/15/1875, Brooklyn, N.Y. d: 12/15/45, Albany, N.Y. Deb: 6/06/1892

YEAR	TM/L	G	AB	R	H	2B	3B	HR	RBI	BB	SO	AVG	OBP	SLG	PRO+	BR	/A	RC	SB	CS	SBR	FA	FR	POS	TPR
1892	Bal-N	1	2	0	0	0	0	0	0	0	0	.000	.000	.000	-97	-0	-0	0	0			.000	0	/C	0.0

■ GUS HETLING
Hetling, August Julius b: 11/21/1885, St.Louis, Mo. d: 10/13/62, Wichita, Kan. BR/TR, 5'10", 165 lbs. Deb: 10/06/06

YEAR	TM/L	G	AB	R	H	2B	3B	HR	RBI	BB	SO	AVG	OBP	SLG	PRO+	BR	/A	RC	SB	CS	SBR	FA	FR	POS	TPR
1906	Det-A	2	7	0	1	0	0	0	0	0		.143	.143	.143	-10	-1	-1	0	0			1.000	-0	/3	-0.1

■ GEORGE HEUBEL
Heubel, George A. b: 1849, Paterson, N.J. d: 1/22/1896, Philadelphia, Pa. 5'11.5", 178 lbs. Deb: 5/20/1871 U

YEAR	TM/L	G	AB	R	H	2B	3B	HR	RBI	BB	SO	AVG	OBP	SLG	PRO+	BR	/A	RC	SB	CS	SBR	FA	FR	POS	TPR
1871	Ath-n	17	75	18	23	4	2	0	13	2	0	.307	.325	.413	111	1	1	11	1					O/1	0.1
1872	Oly-n	5	23	2	3	1	0	0	1	0	0	.130	.130	.174	-8	-3	-3	1						/O	-0.2
1876	NY-N	1	4	0	0	0	0	0	0	0	0	.000	.000	.000	-99	-1	-1	0				.750	-0	/1	-0.1
Total	2 n	22	98	20	26	5	2	0	14	2		.265	.280	.357	86	-2	-1	11						/O1	-0.1

■ JOHNNIE HEVING
Heving, John Aloysius b: 4/29/1896, Covington, Ky. d: 12/24/68, Salisbury, N.C. BR/TR, 6', 175 lbs. Deb: 9/24/20 F

YEAR	TM/L	G	AB	R	H	2B	3B	HR	RBI	BB	SO	AVG	OBP	SLG	PRO+	BR	/A	RC	SB	CS	SBR	FA	FR	POS	TPR
1920	StL-A	1	1	0	0	0	0	0	0	0	0	.000	.000	.000	-97	-0	-0	0	0	0	0	.000	0	H	0.0
1924	Bos-A	45	109	15	31	5	1	0	11	10	7	.284	.345	.349	79	-3	-3	14	0	0	0	.969	4	C	0.2
1925	Bos-A	45	119	14	20	7	0	0	6	12	7	.168	.244	.227	20	-15	-15	7	0	1	-1	.958	3	C	-1.0
1928	Bos-A	82	158	11	41	7	2	0	11	11	10	.259	.308	.329	69	-8	-7	16	1	1	-0	.967	-4	C	-0.7
1929	Bos-A	76	188	26	60	4	3	0	23	8	7	.319	.354	.372	89	-3	-3	24	1	2	-1	.988	5	C	0.6
1930	Bos-A	75	220	15	61	5	3	0	17	11	14	.277	.312	.327	65	-12	-11	23	2	0	1	.987	-4	C	-0.8
1931	*Phi-A	42	113	8	27	3	2	1	12	6	8	.239	.277	.327	55	-7	-8	10	0	0	0	.993	2	C	-0.3
1932	Phi-A	33	77	14	21	6	1	0	10	7	6	.273	.333	.377	81	-2	-2	10	0	0	0	1.000	-1	C	-0.2
Total	8	399	985	103	261	37	12	1	90	65	59	.265	.312	.330	66	-51	-50	104	4	4	-1	.981	4	C	-2.2

■ MIKE HEYDON
Heydon, Michael Edward "Ed" b: 7/15/1874, Missouri d: 10/13/13, Indianapolis, Ind. BL/TR, 6', Deb: 10/12/1898

YEAR	TM/L	G	AB	R	H	2B	3B	HR	RBI	BB	SO	AVG	OBP	SLG	PRO+	BR	/A	RC	SB	CS	SBR	FA	FR	POS	TPR
1898	Bal-N	3	9	2	1	0	0	0	1	2		.111	.333	.111	28	-1	-1	0	0			.917	-1	/C	-0.1
1899	Was-N	3	3	0	0	0	0	0	0	2		.000	.400	.000	14	-0	-0	0	0			.833	-0	/C	0.0
1901	StL-N	16	43	2	9	1	1	1	6	5		.209	.292	.349	90	-1	-1	5	2			.941	-3	C/O	-0.2
1904	Chi-A	4	10	0	1	1	0	0	1	1		.100	.250	.200	45	-1	-1	1	0			1.000	1	/C	0.1
1905	Was-A	77	245	20	47	7	4	1	26	21		.192	.261	.265	70	-9	-8	19	5			.955	11	C	1.3
1906	Was-A	49	145	14	23	7	1	0	10	14		.159	.237	.221	46	-9	-8	8	2			.937	-2	C	-0.6
1907	Was-A	62	164	14	30	3	0	0	9	25		.183	.298	.201	65	-6	-5	11	3			.961	-8	C	-0.8
Total	7	214	619	52	111	19	6	2	53	70		.179	.270	.239	64	-26	-23	45	12			.952	-1	C/O	-0.3

■ JACK HIATT
Hiatt, Jack E b: 7/27/42, Bakersfield, Cal. BR/TR, 6'2", 190 lbs. Deb: 9/07/64 C

YEAR	TM/L	G	AB	R	H	2B	3B	HR	RBI	BB	SO	AVG	OBP	SLG	PRO+	BR	/A	RC	SB	CS	SBR	FA	FR	POS	TPR
1964	LA-A	9	16	2	6	0	0	0	2	2	3	.375	.444	.375	145	1	1	3	0	0	0	.889	-1	/C1	0.0
1965	SF-N	40	67	5	19	4	0	1	7	12	14	.284	.392	.388	118	2	2	10	0	0	0	.987	-2	C/1	0.0
1966	SF-N	18	23	2	7	2	0	0	1	4	5	.304	.407	.391	120	1	1	4	0	0	0	.982	1	/1	0.2
1967	SF-N	73	153	24	42	6	0	6	26	27	37	.275	.387	.431	136	8	8	27	0	0	0	.990	-2	1/CO	0.4
1968	SF-N	90	224	14	52	10	2	4	34	41	61	.232	.353	.348	111	5	5	29	0	0	0	.994	-1	C1	0.8
1969	SF-N	69	194	18	38	4	0	7	34	48	58	.196	.355	.325	93	-0	0	25	0	0	0	.992	0	C/1	0.3
1970	Mon-N	17	43	4	14	2	0	0	7	14	14	.326	.491	.372	135	3	3	9	0	0	0	.961	-4	C/1	0.1
	Chi-N	66	178	19	43	12	1	2	22	31	48	.242	.354	.354	81	-2	-5	23	0	0	0	.990	5	C/1	0.3
	Yr	83	221	23	57	14	1	2	29	45	62	.258	.383	.357	91	2	-1	33	0	0	0	.986	2	C/1	0.4
1971	Hou-N	69	174	16	48	8	1	1	16	35	39	.276	.403	.351	118	6	6	28	0	1	-1	.991	-1	C/1	0.7
1972	Hou-N	10	25	2	5	3	0	0	0	5	5	.200	.333	.320	88	-0	-0	3	0	0	0	1.000	-3	C	-0.3
	Cal-A	22	45	4	13	0	1	1	5	5	11	.289	.360	.400	133	1	2	7	0	0	0	1.000	-8	C	-0.7
Total	9	483	1142	110	287	51	5	22	154	224	295	.251	.376	.363	109	25	23	168	0	1	-1	.990	-16	C/1O	1.8

■ JIM HIBBS
Hibbs, James Kerr b: 9/10/44, Klamath Falls, Ore. BR/TR, 6', 190 lbs. Deb: 4/12/67

YEAR	TM/L	G	AB	R	H	2B	3B	HR	RBI	BB	SO	AVG	OBP	SLG	PRO+	BR	/A	RC	SB	CS	SBR	FA	FR	POS	TPR
1967	Cal-A	3	3	0	0	0	0	0	0	0	2	.000	.000	.000	-99	-1	-1	0	0	0	0	.000	0	H	-0.1

■ EDDIE HICKEY
Hickey, Edward A. b: 8/18/1872, Cleveland, Ohio d: 3/25/41, Tacoma, Wash. Deb: 9/03/01

YEAR	TM/L	G	AB	R	H	2B	3B	HR	RBI	BB	SO	AVG	OBP	SLG	PRO+	BR	/A	RC	SB	CS	SBR	FA	FR	POS	TPR
1901	Chi-N	10	37	4	6	0	0	0	3	2		.162	.225	.162	14	-4	-4	2	1			.743	-2	3	-0.5

■ MIKE HICKEY
Hickey, Michael Francis b: 12/25/1871, Chicopee, Mass. d: 6/11/18, Springfield, Mass BR/TR, 5'10.5", 150 lbs. Deb: 9/14/1899

YEAR	TM/L	G	AB	R	H	2B	3B	HR	RBI	BB	SO	AVG	OBP	SLG	PRO+	BR	/A	RC	SB	CS	SBR	FA	FR	POS	TPR
1899	Bos-N	1	3	0	1	0	0	0	0	0		.333	.333	.333	76	-0	-0	0	0			.889	1	/2	0.1

■ CHARLIE HICKMAN
Hickman, Charles Taylor "Cheerful Charlie" or "Piano Legs"
b: 3/4/1876, Taylortown, Dunkard Township, Pa. d: 4/19/34, Morgantown, W.Va. BR/TR, 5'11.5", 215 lbs. Deb: 9/08/1897

YEAR	TM/L	G	AB	R	H	2B	3B	HR	RBI	BB	SO	AVG	OBP	SLG	PRO+	BR	/A	RC	SB	CS	SBR	FA	FR	POS	TPR
1897	*Bos-N	2	3	1	2	0	0	1	2	0		.667	.667	1.667	475	2	2	3	0			1.000	0	/P	0.0
1898	Bos-N	19	58	4	15	2	0	0	7	1		.259	.283	.293	62	-3	-3	5	0			1.000	-1	/O1P	-0.3
1899	Bos-N	19	63	15	25	2	7	0	15	2		.397	.433	.651	178	8	7	19	1			.941	-2	P/O1	0.1
1900	NY-N	127	473	65	148	19	17	9	91	17		.313	.359	.482	137	18	21	88	10			.842	-5	*3/O	1.5
1901	NY-N	112	406	44	113	20	6	4	62	15		.278	.315	.387	107	0	2	52	5			.904	-7	OS3/P21	-0.6
1902	Bos-A	28	108	13	32	5	2	3	16	3		.296	.339	.463	117	3	2	18	1			.939	1	O	0.1
	Cle-A	102	426	61	161	31	11	8	94	12		.378	.399	.559	170	34	36	101	8			.966	-7	1/2P	2.6
	Yr	130	534	74	**193**	36	13	11	110	15		.361	.387	.539	159	36	38	118	9			.966	-6	1O/2P	2.7

YEAR	TM/L	G	AB	R	H	2B	3B	HR	RBI	BB	SO	AVG	OBP	SLG	PRO+	BR	/A	RC	SB	CS	SBR	FA	FR	POS	TPR
1903	Cle-A	131	522	64	154	31	11	12	97	17		.295	.325	.466	137	20	21	86	14			.972	-7	*1/2	1.3
1904	Cle-A	86	337	34	97	22	10	4	45	13		.288	.318	.448	142	14	14	53	9			.943	-1	21/O	1.5
	Det-A	42	144	18	35	6	6	2	22	11		.243	.297	.410	126	3	4	19	3			.970	-2	1	0.1
	Yr	128	481	52	132	28	16	6	67	24		.274	.312	.437	137	17	18	72	12			.969	-3	12/O	1.6
1905	Det-A	59	213	21	47	12	3	2	20	12		.221	.275	.333	92	-2	-2	22	3			.940	3	O1	-0.3
	Was-A	88	360	48	112	25	9	2	46	9		.311	.332	.447	153	16	18	57	3			.922	7	2/1	2.8
	Yr	147	573	69	159	37	12	4	66	21		.277	.310	.405	129	14	16	77	6			.922	9	2O1	2.5
1906	Was-A	120	451	53	128	25	5	9	57	14		.284	.308	.421	134	12	14	64	9			.955	-1	O1/32	0.9
1907	Was-A	60	198	20	55	9	4	1	23	14		.278	.335	.379	139	6	8	27	4			.965	-4	1O/2P	0.2
	Chi-A	21	23	1	6	2	0	0	1	4		.261	.370	.348	134	1	1	3	0			.667	-1	/O	0.0
	Yr	81	221	21	61	11	4	1	24	18		.276	.339	.376	137	7	9	30	4			.965	-5	1O/2P	0.2
1908	Cle-A	65	197	16	46	6	1	2	16	9		.234	.271	.305	87	-3	-3	16	2			.907	-0	O1/2	-0.6
Total	12	1081	3982	478	1176	217	92	59	614	153		.295	.330	.440	134	128	141	633	72			.968	-27	1O23/PS	9.3

■ JIM HICKMAN

Hickman, David James b: 5/19/1894, Johnson City, Tenn d: 12/30/58, Brooklyn, N.Y. BR/TR, 5′7.5″, 170 lbs. Deb: 9/17/15

YEAR	TM/L	G	AB	R	H	2B	3B	HR	RBI	BB	SO	AVG	OBP	SLG	PRO+	BR	/A	RC	SB	CS	SBR	FA	FR	POS	TPR
1915	Bal-F	20	81	7	17	4	1	1	7	4	14	.210	.256	.321	67	-3	-4	8	5			.963	4	O	0.0
1916	Bro-N	9	5	3	1	0	0	0	0	2	0	.200	.429	.200	94	0	0	1	1			1.000	-1	/O	-0.1
1917	Bro-N	114	370	46	81	15	4	6	36	17	66	.219	.253	.330	76	-11	-12	33	14			.942	7	*O	-1.1
1918	Bro-N	53	167	14	39	4	7	1	16	8	31	.234	.281	.359	95	-2	-2	17	5			.914	-3	O	-0.8
1919	Bro-N	57	104	14	20	3	1	0	11	6	17	.192	.236	.240	43	-7	-7	6	2			.962	-4	O	-1.4
Total	5	253	727	84	158	26	13	8	70	37	128	.217	.259	.322	75	-23	-24	65	27			.941	4	O	-3.4

■ JIM HICKMAN

Hickman, James Lucius b: 5/10/37, Henning, Tenn. BR/TR, 6′4″, 205 lbs. Deb: 4/14/62

YEAR	TM/L	G	AB	R	H	2B	3B	HR	RBI	BB	SO	AVG	OBP	SLG	PRO+	BR	/A	RC	SB	CS	SBR	FA	FR	POS	TPR
1962	NY-N	140	392	54	96	18	2	13	46	47	96	.245	.330	.401	94	-3	-4	52	4	4	-1	.971	-9	*O	-2.0
1963	NY-N	146	494	53	113	21	6	17	51	44	120	.229	.293	.399	96	-3	-4	56	0	5	-3	.963	-6	O3	-1.9
1964	NY-N	139	409	48	105	14	1	11	57	36	90	.257	.320	.377	98	-2	-1	48	0	1	-1	.976	-4	*O/3	-1.2
1965	NY-N	141	369	32	87	18	0	15	40	27	76	.236	.291	.407	98	-4	-2	42	3	1	0	.965	-1	O13	-0.7
1966	NY-N	58	160	15	38	7	0	4	16	13	34	.237	.299	.356	83	-4	-4	17	2	1	0	.986	5	O1	-0.1
1967	LA-N	65	98	7	16	6	1	0	10	14	28	.163	.268	.245	52	-6	-6	6	1	1	-0	1.000	3	O/13P	-0.4
1968	Chi-N	75	188	22	42	6	3	5	23	18	38	.223	.295	.367	91	-1	-2	20	1	1	-0	.975	-1	O	-0.7
1969	Chi-N	134	338	38	80	11	2	21	54	47	74	.237	.330	.467	107	9	3	52	2	1	0	.981	-13	*O	-1.6
1970	Chi-N★	149	514	102	162	33	4	32	115	93	99	.315	.421	.582	148	50	41	129	0	1	-1	.974	3	O1	3.3
1971	Chi-N	117	383	50	98	13	2	19	60	50	61	.256	.346	.449	108	12	5	58	0	1	-1	.982	-5	O1	-0.8
1972	Chi-N	115	368	65	100	15	2	17	64	52	64	.272	.365	.462	121	17	12	64	3	1	0	.992	7	1O	1.3
1973	Chi-N	92	201	27	49	1	2	3	20	42	42	.244	.374	.313	86	-0	-2	25	1	1	-0	.988	0	1O	-0.6
1974	StL-N	50	60	5	16	0	0	2	4	8	10	.267	.353	.367	102	0	0	7	0	0	0	.986	1	1/3	0.1
Total	13	1421	3974	518	1002	163	25	159	560	491	832	.252	.337	.426	106	64	38	578	17	19	-6	.976	-20	O1/3P	-5.3

■ BUDDY HICKS

Hicks, Clarence Walter b: 2/15/27, Belvedere, Cal. BB/TR, 5′10″, 170 lbs. Deb: 4/17/56

YEAR	TM/L	G	AB	R	H	2B	3B	HR	RBI	BB	SO	AVG	OBP	SLG	PRO+	BR	/A	RC	SB	CS	SBR	FA	FR	POS	TPR
1956	Det-A	26	47	5	10	2	0	0	5	3	2	.213	.260	.255	36	-4	-4	3	0	1	-1	1.000	-1	S/23	-0.5

■ JIM HICKS

Hicks, James Edward b: 5/18/40, East Chicago, Ind. BR/TR, 6′3″, 205 lbs. Deb: 10/02/64

YEAR	TM/L	G	AB	R	H	2B	3B	HR	RBI	BB	SO	AVG	OBP	SLG	PRO+	BR	/A	RC	SB	CS	SBR	FA	FR	POS	TPR
1964	Chi-A	2	0	0	0	0	0	0	0	0	0	—	—	—	—	0	0	0	0	0	0	.000	0	R	0.0
1965	Chi-A	13	19	2	5	1	0	1	2	0	9	.263	.263	.474	112	-0	0	2	0	0	0	.750	-2	/O	-0.2
1966	Chi-A	18	26	3	5	0	1	0	1	1	5	.192	.222	.269	43	-2	-2	1	0	0	0	1.000	-1	O/1	-0.4
1969	StL-N	19	44	5	8	0	2	1	3	4	14	.182	.250	.341	64	-2	-2	4	0	0	0	1.000	2	O	-0.1
	Cal-A	37	48	6	4	0	0	3	8	13	18	.083	.279	.271	57	-3	-3	4	0	1	-1	1.000	-3	O/1	-0.8
1970	Cal-A	4	4	0	1	0	0	0	0	0	2	.250	.250	.250	40	-0	-0	0	0	0	0	.000	0	H	0.0
Total	5	93	141	16	23	1	3	5	14	18	48	.163	.258	.319	64	-8	-7	12	0	1	-1	.981	-4	/O1	-1.5

■ NAT HICKS

Hicks, Nathaniel Woodhull b: 4/19/1845, Hempstead, N.Y. d: 4/21/07, Hoboken, N.J. BR/TR, 6′1″, 186 lbs. Deb: 4/22/1872 M

YEAR	TM/L	G	AB	R	H	2B	3B	HR	RBI	BB	SO	AVG	OBP	SLG	PRO+	BR	/A	RC	SB	CS	SBR	FA	FR	POS	TPR
1872	Mut-n	56	266	55	81	12	2	0	35	5	3	.305	.317	.365	117	3	7	33						*C/O	0.4
1873	Mut-n	28	121	12	29	2	2	1	14	7	0	.240	.281	.314	75	-4	-3	12						C	-0.2
1874	Phi-n	58	264	50	74	8	2	0		5		.280	.294	.326	94	-1	-2	26						*C/O	-0.1
1875	Mut-n	62	269	32	67	11	2	0		2		.249	.255	.305	88	-2	-4	21						*C/OM	-0.2
1876	NY-N	45	188	20	44	4	1	0	15	3	4	.234	.246	.266	81	-6	-2	13				.741	-6	C	-0.5
1877	Cin-N	8	32	3	6	0	0	0	3	1	2	.188	.212	.188	30	-3	-2	1				.868	0	/C	-0.1
Total	4 n	204	920	149	251	33	8	1	49	19	3	.273	.288	.329	96	-3	-3	91						C/O	-0.1
Total	2	53	220	23	50	4	1	0	18	4	6	.227	.241	.255	73	-8	-4	14				.757	-5	/C	-0.6

■ JOE HICKS

Hicks, William Joseph b: 4/7/33, Ivy, Va. BL/TR, 6′, 180 lbs. Deb: 9/18/59

YEAR	TM/L	G	AB	R	H	2B	3B	HR	RBI	BB	SO	AVG	OBP	SLG	PRO+	BR	/A	RC	SB	CS	SBR	FA	FR	POS	TPR
1959	Chi-A	6	7	0	3	0	0	0	0	1	1	.429	.500	.429	160	1	1	1	0	1	-1	1.000	-0	/O	0.0
1960	Chi-A	36	47	3	9	1	0	0	2	6	3	.191	.296	.213	40	-4	-4	3	0	1	-1	1.000	-4	O	-0.9
1961	Was-A	12	29	2	5	0	0	1	1	0	4	.172	.172	.276	18	-3	-3	1	0	1	-1	1.000	1	/O	-0.4
1962	Was-A	102	174	20	39	4	2	6	14	15	34	.224	.286	.374	76	-6	-6	19	3	1	0	.962	-3	O	-1.1
1963	NY-N	56	159	16	36	6	1	5	22	7	31	.226	.272	.371	82	-4	-4	16	0	2	-1	.966	1	O	-0.7
Total	5	212	416	41	92	11	3	12	39	29	73	.221	.278	.349	72	-17	-17	40	3	6	-3	.970	-6	O	-3.1

■ MAHLON HIGBEE

Higbee, Mahlon Jesse b: 8/16/01, Louisville, Ky. d: 4/7/68, DePauw, Ind. BR/TR, 5′11″, 165 lbs. Deb: 9/27/22

YEAR	TM/L	G	AB	R	H	2B	3B	HR	RBI	BB	SO	AVG	OBP	SLG	PRO+	BR	/A	RC	SB	CS	SBR	FA	FR	POS	TPR
1922	NY-N	3	10	2	4	0	0	1	5	0	2	.400	.400	.700	177	1	1	3	0	0	0	1.000	-1	/O	0.0

■ HIGBY

Higby Deb: 9/18/1872

YEAR	TM/L	G	AB	R	H	2B	3B	HR	RBI	BB	SO	AVG	OBP	SLG	PRO+	BR	/A	RC	SB	CS	SBR	FA	FR	POS	TPR
1872	Atl-n	1	4	0	0	0	0	0	0	0	0	.000	.000	.000	-85	-1	-1	0						/O	-0.1

■ BILL HIGDON

Higdon, William Travis b: 4/27/24, Camp Hill, Ala. d: 8/30/86, Pascagoula, Miss. BL/TR, 6′1″, 193 lbs. Deb: 9/10/49

YEAR	TM/L	G	AB	R	H	2B	3B	HR	RBI	BB	SO	AVG	OBP	SLG	PRO+	BR	/A	RC	SB	CS	SBR	FA	FR	POS	TPR
1949	Chi-A	11	23	3	7	3	0	0	1	6	3	.304	.448	.435	139	1	2	6	1	0	0	1.000	-1	/O	0.1

■ MARK HIGGINS

Higgins, Mark Douglas b: 7/9/63, Miami, Fla. BR/TR, 6′2″, 210 lbs. Deb: 9/07/89

YEAR	TM/L	G	AB	R	H	2B	3B	HR	RBI	BB	SO	AVG	OBP	SLG	PRO+	BR	/A	RC	SB	CS	SBR	FA	FR	POS	TPR
1989	Cle-A	6	10	1	1	0	0	0	0	1	6	.100	.182	.100	-18	-2	-2	0	0	0	0	1.000	1	/1	-0.1

■ PINKY HIGGINS

Higgins, Michael Franklin "Mike" b: 5/27/09, Red Oak, Tex. d: 3/21/69, Dallas, Tex. BR/TR, 6′1″, 185 lbs. Deb: 6/25/30 M

YEAR	TM/L	G	AB	R	H	2B	3B	HR	RBI	BB	SO	AVG	OBP	SLG	PRO+	BR	/A	RC	SB	CS	SBR	FA	FR	POS	TPR
1930	Phi-A	14	24	1	6	2	0	0	0	4	5	.250	.357	.333	73	-1	-1	3	0	0	0	1.000	-2	/32S	-0.3
1933	Phi-A	152	567	85	178	35	11	13	99	61	53	.314	.383	.483	127	22	22	104	2	7	-4	.947	-6	*3	2.0
1934	Phi-A☆	144	543	89	179	37	6	16	90	56	70	.330	.392	.508	136	24	27	110	9	2	2	.914	-19	*3	1.5
1935	Phi-A	133	524	69	155	32	4	23	94	42	62	.296	.350	.504	120	12	12	93	6	2	1	.947	-14	*3	0.4
1936	Phi-A★	146	550	89	159	32	2	12	80	67	61	.289	.366	.420	96	-6	-4	87	7	4	-0	.941	-14	*3	-1.2
1937	Bos-A	153	570	88	172	33	5	9	106	76	51	.302	.385	.425	100	5	1	95	2	6	-3	.935	-17	*3	-1.3
1938	Bos-A	139	524	77	159	29	5	5	106	71	55	.303	.388	.406	95	1	-3	85	10	9	-2	.914	-10	*3	-1.2
1939	Det-A	132	489	57	135	23	2	8	76	56	41	.276	.353	.380	81	-9	-14	66	7	4	-0	.914	-11	*3	-2.2
1940	*Det-A	131	480	70	130	24	3	13	76	61	31	.271	.357	.415	91	-0	-7	73	4	2	0	.928	-11	*3	-1.4
1941	Det-A	147	540	79	161	28	3	11	73	67	45	.298	.378	.422	101	10	2	86	5	4	-1	.946	1	*3	0.6
1942	Det-A	143	499	65	133	34	2	11	79	72	21	.267	.362	.409	108	12	7	72	3	7	-3	.926	-14	*3	-0.8
1943	Det-A	138	523	62	145	20	1	10	84	57	31	.277	.349	.377	104	8	4	68	2	5	-2	.940	-7	*3	-0.4
1944	Det-A★	148	543	79	161	32	4	7	76	81	34	.297	.392	.409	122	23	19	91	4	4	-1	.954	-7	*3	1.3
1946	Det-A	18	60	2	13	3	1	0	8	5	6	.217	.277	.300	58	-3	-4	5	0	1	-1	.949	-2	3	-0.6

YEAR	TM/L	G	AB	R	H	2B	3B	HR	RBI	BB	SO	AVG	OBP	SLG	PRO+	BR	/A	RC	SB	CS	SBR	FA	FR	POS	TPR
	*Bos-A	64	200	18	55	11	1	2	28	24	24	.275	.356	.370	97	1	-0	26	0	2	-1	.947	0	3	0.0
	Yr	82	260	20	68	14	2	2	36	29	30	.262	.338	.354	88	-2	-4	30	0	3	-2	.947	-2	3	-0.6
Total	14	1802	6636	930	1941	375	50	140	1075	800	590	.292	.370	.427	105	100	62	1065	61	59	-17	.935	-131	*3/2S	-3.6

■ BOB HIGGINS
Higgins, Robert Stone b: 9/23/1886, Fayetteville, Tenn. d: 5/25/41, Chattanooga, Tenn. BR/TR, 5'8", 176 lbs. Deb: 9/13/09

YEAR	TM/L	G	AB	R	H	2B	3B	HR	RBI	BB	SO	AVG	OBP	SLG	PRO+	BR	/A	RC	SB	CS	SBR	FA	FR	POS	TPR
1909	Cle-A	8	23	0	2	0	0	0	0	0		.087	.087	.087	-43	-4	-4	0	0			1.000	3	/C	0.0
1911	Bro-N	4	10	1	3	0	0	0	2	1	0	.300	.364	.300	90	-0	-0	1	1			.933	0	/C3	0.0
1912	Bro-N	1	2	0	0	0	0	0	0	0	1	.000	.000	.000	-99	-1	-1	0	0			.750	-0	/C	-0.1
Total	3	13	35	1	5	0	0	0	2	1	1	.143	.167	.143	-6	-4	-4	2	1			.970	3	/C3	-0.1

■ BILL HIGGINS
Higgins, William Edward b: 9/8/1861, Wilmington, Del. d: 4/25/19, Wilmington, Del. TR , Deb: 8/09/1888

YEAR	TM/L	G	AB	R	H	2B	3B	HR	RBI	BB	SO	AVG	OBP	SLG	PRO+	BR	/A	RC	SB	CS	SBR	FA	FR	POS	TPR
1888	Bos-N	14	54	5	10	1	0	0	4	1	3	.185	.200	.204	30	-4	-4	2	1			.906	5	2	0.2
1890	StL-a	67	258	39	65	6	2	0		24		.252	.316	.291	71	-6	-12	27	7			.951	13	2	0.5
	Syr-a	1	4	1	1	1	0	0		0		.250	.250	.500	137	0	0	1	0			1.000	1	/2	0.1
	Yr	68	262	40	66	7	2	0		24		.252	.315	.294	72	-6	-11	27	7			.952	14	2	0.6
Total	2	82	316	45	76	8	2	0	4	25	3	.241	.296	.278	66	-10	-16	29	8			.943	20	/2	0.8

■ ANDY HIGH
High, Andrew Aird "Handy Andy" b: 11/21/1897, Ava, Ill. d: 2/22/81, Toledo, Ohio BL/TR, 5'6", 155 lbs. Deb: 4/12/22 FC

YEAR	TM/L	G	AB	R	H	2B	3B	HR	RBI	BB	SO	AVG	OBP	SLG	PRO+	BR	/A	RC	SB	CS	SBR	FA	FR	POS	TPR
1922	Bro-N	153	579	82	164	27	10	6	65	59	26	.283	.354	.396	94	-6	-5	80	3	12	-6	.958	-5	*3S/2	-0.4
1923	Bro-N	123	426	51	115	23	9	3	37	47	13	.270	.344	.387	95	-4	-3	60	4	1	1	.969	-9	3S/2	0.1
1924	Bro-N	144	582	98	191	26	13	6	61	57	16	.328	.390	.448	128	21	23	102	3	6	-3	.964	-10	*2S/3	1.3
1925	Bro-N	44	115	11	23	4	1	0	6	14	5	.200	.287	.252	40	-10	-10	9	0	1	-1	.938	-5	23/S	-1.4
	Bos-N	60	219	31	63	11	1	4	28	24	2	.288	.361	.402	104	-1	1	32	3	5	-2	.979	-9	3/2	-0.6
	Yr	104	334	42	86	15	2	4	34	38	7	.257	.335	.350	80	-12	-9	40	3	6	-3	.963	-14	32/S	-2.0
1926	Bos-N	130	476	55	141	17	10	2	66	39	9	.296	.351	.387	108	-1	5	64	4			.962	-6	32	0.5
1927	Bos-N	113	384	59	116	15	9	4	46	26	11	.302	.350	.419	114	2	6	55	4			.915	-20	3/2S	-1.0
1928	*StL-N	111	368	58	105	14	3	6	37	37	10	.285	.355	.389	93	-3	-3	51	2			.935	-19	32	-1.8
1929	StL-N	146	603	95	178	32	4	10	63	38	18	.295	.340	.411	84	-15	-16	82	7			**.967**	-19	*32	-2.6
1930	*StL-N	72	215	34	60	12	2	2	29	23	6	.279	.349	.381	74	-8	-9	29	1			.990	-7	3/2	-1.2
1931	*StL-N	63	131	20	35	6	1	0	19	24	4	.267	.389	.328	91	0	-0	19	0			1.000	-5	32	-0.3
1932	Cin-N	84	191	16	36	4	2	0	12	23	6	.188	.276	.230	39	-16	-15	14	1			.950	-10	32	-2.2
1933	Cin-N	24	43	4	9	2	0	1	6	5	1	.209	.292	.326	77	-1	-1	4	0			.966	1	3/2	0.0
1934	Phi-N	47	68	4	14	2	0	0	7	9	3	.206	.299	.235	40	-5	-6	4	1			.906	-2	3/2	-0.8
Total	13	1314	4400	618	1250	195	65	44	482	425	130	.284	.350	.388	94	-47	-33	603	33	25		.956	-125	32/S	-10.4

■ CHARLIE HIGH
High, Charles Edwin b: 12/1/1898, Ava, Ill. d: 9/11/60, Oak Grove, Ore. BL/TR, 5'9", 170 lbs. Deb: 9/05/19 F

YEAR	TM/L	G	AB	R	H	2B	3B	HR	RBI	BB	SO	AVG	OBP	SLG	PRO+	BR	/A	RC	SB	CS	SBR	FA	FR	POS	TPR
1919	Phi-A	11	29	2	2	0	0	0	1	3	4	.069	.182	.069	-28	-5	-5	1	2			.944	-0	/O	-0.6
1920	Phi-A	17	65	7	20	2	1	1	6	3	6	.308	.375	.415	108	1	1	10	0	2	-1	.882	-1	O	-0.2
Total	2	28	94	9	22	2	1	1	7	6	10	.234	.314	.309	68	-4	-4	11	2	2		.904	-1	/O	-0.8

■ HUGH HIGH
High, Hugh Jenken "Bunny" b: 10/24/1887, Pottstown, Pa. d: 11/16/62, St.Louis, Mo. BL/TL, 5'7.5", 155 lbs. Deb: 4/11/13 F

YEAR	TM/L	G	AB	R	H	2B	3B	HR	RBI	BB	SO	AVG	OBP	SLG	PRO+	BR	/A	RC	SB	CS	SBR	FA	FR	POS	TPR
1913	Det-A	87	183	18	42	6	1	0	16	28	24	.230	.335	.273	80	-4	-4	18	6			.982	1	O	-0.5
1914	Det-A	84	184	25	49	5	3	0	17	26	21	.266	.363	.326	104	3	2	24	7	6	-2	.959	-7	O	-1.0
1915	NY-A	119	427	51	110	19	7	1	43	62	47	.258	.356	.342	109	6	6	56	22	13	-1	**.981**	-1	*O	-0.2
1916	NY-A	116	377	44	99	13	4	1	28	47	44	.263	.349	.326	101	2	1	51	13			.950	-1	*O	-0.6
1917	NY-A	103	365	37	86	11	6	1	19	48	31	.236	.329	.307	93	-1	-2	39	8			.986	0	*O	-0.8
1918	NY-A	7	10	1	0	0	0	0	0	1	1	.000	.091	.000	-71	-2	-2	0	0			1.000	0	/O	-0.2
Total	6	516	1546	176	386	54	21	3	123	212	168	.250	.345	.318	98	4	2	189	56	19		.972	-8	O	-3.3

■ DICK HIGHAM
Higham, Richard b: 1852, England d: 3/18/05, Chicago, Ill. BL/TR, 5'8.5", 171 lbs. Deb: 6/01/1871 MU

YEAR	TM/L	G	AB	R	H	2B	3B	HR	RBI	BB	SO	AVG	OBP	SLG	PRO+	BR	/A	RC	SB	CS	SBR	FA	FR	POS	TPR
1871	Mut-n	21	94	21	34	3	1	0	9	2	0	.362	.375	.415	139	3	5	16	3					2/OC3	0.3
1872	Bal-n	50	244	72	85	9	2	2	40	2	3	.348	.354	.426	133	11	8	37						CO/21	0.5
1873	Mut-n	49	245	57	77	6	7	0	34	2	1	.314	.320	.396	110	3	3	31						O2C	0.1
1874	Mut-n	65	331	58	87	13	4	1		4		.263	.272	.335	89	-3	-5	31						*CO/2M	-0.3
1875	Chi-n	42	204	44	49	3	3	0		0		.240	.240	.284	80	-4	-4	14						C2/O	-0.3
	Mut-n	15	64	12	25	5	0	0		0		.391	.391	.469	186	6	5	12						/C2O1	0.5
	Yr	57	268	56	74	8	3	0		0		.276	.276	.328	106	2	1	25						C2/O1	0.2
1876	Har-N	67	312	59	102	**21**	2	0	35	2	7	.327	.331	.407	134	14	10	43				.869	-2	*OC/S2	0.7
1878	Pro-N	62	281	**60**	90	**22**	1	1	29	5	16	.320	.332	.416	145	13	13	40				.811	3	*O/C	1.2
1880	Tro-N	1	5	1	1	0	0	0	0	0	0	.200	.200	.200	34	-0	-0	0				.000	-2	/OC	-0.3
Total	5 n	242	1182	264	357	39	17	3	83	10	4	.302	.308	.371	111	16	13	142						C/O213	0.8
Total	3	130	598	120	193	43	3	1	64	7	23	.323	.331	.410	138	26	23	83				.834	-2	O/C2S	1.6

■ JOHN HILAND
Hiland, John William b: 9/1860, Rhode Island d: 4/10/01, Philadelphia, Pa. BL/TL, Deb: 8/20/1885

YEAR	TM/L	G	AB	R	H	2B	3B	HR	RBI	BB	SO	AVG	OBP	SLG	PRO+	BR	/A	RC	SB	CS	SBR	FA	FR	POS	TPR
1885	Phi-N	3	9	0	0	0	0	0	0	0	4	.000	.000	.000	-99	-2	-2	0				.833	-2	/2	-0.4

■ GEORGE HILDEBRAND
Hildebrand, George Albert b: 9/6/1878, San Francisco, Cal d: 5/30/60, Woodland Hills, Cal. BR/TR, 5'8", 170 lbs. Deb: 4/17/02 U

YEAR	TM/L	G	AB	R	H	2B	3B	HR	RBI	BB	SO	AVG	OBP	SLG	PRO+	BR	/A	RC	SB	CS	SBR	FA	FR	POS	TPR
1902	Bro-N	11	41	3	9	1	0	0	5	3		.220	.289	.244	64	-2	-2	3	0			1.000	2	O	0.0

■ PALMER HILDEBRAND
Hildebrand, Palmer Marion "Pete" b: 12/23/1884, Shauck, Ohio d: 1/25/60, N.Canton, Ohio BR/TR, 5'10", 170 lbs. Deb: 5/14/13

YEAR	TM/L	G	AB	R	H	2B	3B	HR	RBI	BB	SO	AVG	OBP	SLG	PRO+	BR	/A	RC	SB	CS	SBR	FA	FR	POS	TPR
1913	StL-N	26	55	3	9	2	0	0	1	1	10	.164	.207	.200	17	-6	-6	2	1			.968	1	C/O	-0.4

■ R. E. HILDEBRAND
Hildebrand, R. E. Deb: 8/29/02

YEAR	TM/L	G	AB	R	H	2B	3B	HR	RBI	BB	SO	AVG	OBP	SLG	PRO+	BR	/A	RC	SB	CS	SBR	FA	FR	POS	TPR
1902	Chi-N	1	4	1	0	0	0	0	0	1		.000	.200	.000	-39	-1	-1	0	0			1.000	-0	/O	-0.1

■ BELDEN HILL
Hill, Belden L. b: 8/24/1864, Kewanee, Ill. d: 10/22/34, Cedar Rapids, Iowa BR/TR, 6', Deb: 8/27/1890

YEAR	TM/L	G	AB	R	H	2B	3B	HR	RBI	BB	SO	AVG	OBP	SLG	PRO+	BR	/A	RC	SB	CS	SBR	FA	FR	POS	TPR
1890	Bal-a	9	30	3	5	2	0	0		3		.167	.306	.233	58	-1	-1	4	6			.857	1	/3	0.0

■ DONNIE HILL
Hill, Donald Earl b: 11/12/60, Pomona, Cal. BB/TR, 5'10", 160 lbs. Deb: 7/25/83

YEAR	TM/L	G	AB	R	H	2B	3B	HR	RBI	BB	SO	AVG	OBP	SLG	PRO+	BR	/A	RC	SB	CS	SBR	FA	FR	POS	TPR
1983	Oak-A	53	158	20	42	7	0	2	15	4	21	.266	.284	.348	77	-6	-5	15	1	1	-0	.961	0	S	-0.1
1984	Oak-A	73	174	21	40	6	0	2	16	5	12	.230	.251	.299	55	-12	-10	13	1	1	-0	.949	-12	S/23D	-1.7
1985	Oak-A	123	393	45	112	13	2	3	48	23	33	.285	.325	.351	92	-8	-4	45	9	4	0	.973	-41	*2	-4.0
1986	Oak-A	108	339	37	96	16	2	4	29	23	38	.283	.329	.378	99	-4	-1	41	5	2	0	.984	-12	23/SD	-1.1
1987	Chi-A	111	410	57	98	14	6	9	46	30	35	.239	.293	.368	72	-16	-17	43	1	0	0	.987	-29	23/D	-4.1
1988	Chi-A	83	221	17	48	6	1	2	20	26	32	.217	.300	.281	64	-10	-10	20	3	1	0	.975	-11	23/D	-1.9
1990	Cal-A	103	352	36	93	18	2	3	32	29	27	.264	.322	.352	90	-5	-4	39	1	2	-1	.990	3	2S3/1PD	0.0
1991	Cal-A	77	209	36	50	8	1	1	20	30	21	.239	.335	.301	77	-6	-5	24	1	0	0	.971	-2	2S/1	-0.5
1992	Min-A	25	51	7	15	3	0	0	2	5	6	.294	.368	.353	100	0	0	7	0	0	0	.944	-3	S/23O	-0.2
Total	9	756	2307	276	594	91	14	26	228	175	225	.257	.311	.343	81	-66	-57	247	22	11	0	.980	-106	2S3/D1OP	-13.6

■ GLENALLEN HILL
Hill, Glenallen b: 3/22/65, Santa Cruz, Cal. BR/TR, 6'3", 210 lbs. Deb: 9/01/89

YEAR	TM/L	G	AB	R	H	2B	3B	HR	RBI	BB	SO	AVG	OBP	SLG	PRO+	BR	/A	RC	SB	CS	SBR	FA	FR	POS	TPR
1989	Tor-A	19	52	4	15	0	0	1	7	3	12	.288	.327	.346	92	-1	-1	6	2	1	0	.964	-2	O/D	-0.3
1990	Tor-A	84	260	47	60	11	3	12	32	18	62	.231	.281	.435	95	-2	-3	31	8	3	1	.983	0	OD	-0.3
1991	Tor-A	35	99	14	25	5	2	3	11	7	24	.253	.302	.434	97	-0	-1	12	2	2	-1	.967	1	DO	-0.1
	Cle-A	37	122	15	32	3	0	5	14	16	30	.262	.348	.410	108	2	2	17	4	2	0	.978	-1	O/D	0.0
	Yr	72	221	29	57	8	2	8	25	23	54	.258	.328	.421	103	1	1	29	6	4	-1	.975	-0	OD	-0.1

YEAR	TM/L	G	AB	R	H	2B	3B	HR	RBI	BB	SO	AVG	OBP	SLG	PRO+	BR	/A	RC	SB	CS	SBR	FA	FR	POS	TPR
1992	Cle-A	102	369	38	89	16	1	18	49	20	73	.241	.288	.436	99	-2	-2	42	9	6	-1	.956	2	OD	-0.2
Total	4	277	902	118	221	35	6	39	113	64	201	.245	.298	.427	99	-3	-5	108	25	14	-1	.971	0	O/D	-0.9

■ HERMAN HILL Hill, Herman Alexander b: 10/12/45, Tuskegee, Ala. d: 12/14/70, Valencia, Venez. BL/TR, 6'2", 190 lbs. Deb: 9/02/69

YEAR	TM/L	G	AB	R	H	2B	3B	HR	RBI	BB	SO	AVG	OBP	SLG	PRO+	BR	/A	RC	SB	CS	SBR	FA	FR	POS	TPR
1969	Min-A	16	2	4	0	0	0	0	0	0	1	.000	.000	.000	-98	-1	-1	-1	1	2	-1	.000	-1	/O	-0.2
1970	Min-A	27	22	8	2	0	0	0	0	0	6	.091	.091	.091	-49	-4	-4	0	0	0	0	1.000	-2	O	-0.7
Total	2	43	24	12	2	0	0	0	0	0	7	.083	.083	.083	-53	-5	-5	-0	1	2	-1	1.000	-3	/O	-0.9

■ HUGH HILL Hill, Hugh Ellis b: 7/21/1879, Ringgold, Ga. d: 9/6/58, Cincinnati, Ohio BL/TR, 5'11.5", 168 lbs. Deb: 5/01/03 F

YEAR	TM/L	G	AB	R	H	2B	3B	HR	RBI	BB	SO	AVG	OBP	SLG	PRO+	BR	/A	RC	SB	CS	SBR	FA	FR	POS	TPR
1903	Cle-A	1	1	0	0	0	0	0	0	0		.000	.000	.000	-99	-0	-0	0	0			.000	0	H	0.0
1904	StL-N	23	93	13	21	2	1	3	4	2		.226	.242	.366	91	-2	-1	9	3			1.000	0	O	-0.3
Total	2	24	94	13	21	2	1	3	4	2		.223	.240	.362	89	-2	-2	9	3				0	/O	-0.3

■ HUNTER HILL Hill, Hunter Benjamin b: 6/21/1879, Austin, Tex. d: 2/22/59, Austin, Tex. BR/TR, Deb: 7/01/03

YEAR	TM/L	G	AB	R	H	2B	3B	HR	RBI	BB	SO	AVG	OBP	SLG	PRO+	BR	/A	RC	SB	CS	SBR	FA	FR	POS	TPR
1903	StL-A	86	317	30	77	11	3	0	25	8		.243	.264	.297	70	-13	-12	28	2			.923	-1	3	-1.2
1904	StL-A	58	219	19	47	3	0	0	14	6		.215	.246	.228	54	-12	-11	16	4			.826	-16	3/O	-2.9
	Was-A	77	290	18	57	6	1	0	17	11		.197	.228	.224	44	-18	-18	18	10			.895	-6	3/O	-2.5
	Yr	135	509	37	104	9	1	0	31	17		.204	.236	.226	48	-31	-29	34	14			.864	-22	*3/O	-5.4
1905	Was-A	104	374	37	78	12	1	1	24	32		.209	.278	.254	72	-12	-11	34	10			.908	-1	*3	-0.8
Total	3	325	1200	104	259	32	5	1	80	57		.216	.257	.253	62	-55	-51	96	26			.895	-24	3/O	-7.4

■ JESSE HILL Hill, Jesse Terrill b: 1/20/07, Yates, Mo. BR/TR, 5'9", 165 lbs. Deb: 4/17/35

YEAR	TM/L	G	AB	R	H	2B	3B	HR	RBI	BB	SO	AVG	OBP	SLG	PRO+	BR	/A	RC	SB	CS	SBR	FA	FR	POS	TPR
1935	NY-A	107	392	69	115	20	3	4	33	42	32	.293	.362	.390	100	-3	0	58	14	4	2	.951	2	O	0.1
1936	Was-A	85	233	50	71	19	5	0	34	29	23	.305	.384	.429	106	1	3	42	11	0	3	.967	-8	O	-0.3
1937	Was-A	33	92	24	20	2	1	1	4	13	16	.217	.314	.293	57	-6	-6	9	2	1	0	.986	2	O	-0.4
	Phi-A	70	242	32	71	12	3	1	37	31	20	.293	.374	.380	92	-3	-2	38	16	3	3	.954	-5	O	-0.6
	Yr	103	334	56	91	14	4	2	41	44	36	.272	.357	.356	82	-9	-8	47	18	4	3	.964	-3	O	-1.0
Total	3	295	959	175	277	53	12	6	108	115	91	.289	.366	.388	95	-11	-5	147	43	8	8	.959	-8	O	-1.2

■ MARC HILL Hill, Marc Kevin b: 2/18/52, Elsberry, Mo. BR/TR, 6'3", 210 lbs. Deb: 9/28/73 C

YEAR	TM/L	G	AB	R	H	2B	3B	HR	RBI	BB	SO	AVG	OBP	SLG	PRO+	BR	/A	RC	SB	CS	SBR	FA	FR	POS	TPR
1973	StL-N	1	3	0	0	0	0	0	0	0	1	.000	.000	.000	-99	-1	-1	0	0	0	0	1.000	0	/C	-0.1
1974	StL-N	10	21	2	5	1	0	0	2	4	5	.238	.360	.286	83	-0	-0	2	0	0	0	1.000	3	/C	0.3
1975	SF-N	72	182	14	39	4	0	5	23	25	27	.214	.309	.319	71	-6	-7	18	0	0	0	.994	1	C/3	-0.4
1976	SF-N	54	131	11	24	5	0	3	15	10	19	.183	.246	.290	50	-9	-9	9	0	1	-1	.995	1	C/1	-0.8
1977	SF-N	108	320	28	80	10	0	9	50	34	34	.250	.322	.366	84	-7	-7	36	0	1	-1	.989	-3	*C	-0.7
1978	SF-N	117	358	20	87	15	1	3	36	45	39	.243	.329	.316	84	-8	-6	36	1	2	-1	.986	0	*C/1	-0.5
1979	SF-N	63	169	20	35	3	0	3	15	26	25	.207	.313	.278	67	-8	-7	15	0	1	-1	.991	-6	C/1	-1.1
1980	SF-N	17	41	1	7	2	0	0	0	1	7	.171	.190	.220	14	-5	-5	2	0	0	0	.972	2	C	-0.2
	Sea-A	29	70	8	16	2	1	2	9	3	10	.229	.260	.371	70	-3	-3	6	0	0	0	.991	-0	C	-0.3
1981	Chi-A	16	6	0	0	0	0	0	0	0	1	.000	.000	.000	-99	-2	-1	0	0	0	0	1.000	0	C/13	-0.1
1982	Chi-A	53	88	9	23	2	0	3	13	6	13	.261	.316	.386	92	-1	-1	10	0	0	0	.993	6	C/13	0.5
1983	Chi-A	58	133	11	30	6	0	1	11	9	24	.226	.275	.293	54	-8	-9	10	0	1	-1	.991	5	C/1D	-0.2
1984	Chi-A	77	193	15	45	10	1	5	20	9	26	.233	.275	.373	74	-6	-7	16	0	1	-1	.991	4	C/1	-0.1
1985	Chi-A	40	75	5	10	2	0	0	4	12	9	.133	.253	.160	16	-8	-9	4	0	0	0	.985	9	C/3	0.1
1986	Chi-A	22	19	2	3	0	0	0	0	1	3	.158	.238	.158	10	-2	-2	1	0	0	0	1.000	7	C	0.5
Total	14	737	1809	146	404	62	3	34	198	185	243	.223	.298	.317	69	-75	-75	165	1	7	-4	.990	30	C/13D	-3.1

■ OLIVER HILL Hill, Oliver Clinton b: 10/16/12, Powder Springs, Ga d: 9/20/70, Decatur, Ga. BL/TR, 5'11", 178 lbs. Deb: 4/19/39

YEAR	TM/L	G	AB	R	H	2B	3B	HR	RBI	BB	SO	AVG	OBP	SLG	PRO+	BR	/A	RC	SB	CS	SBR	FA	FR	POS	TPR
1939	Bos-N	2	2	1	1	1	0	0	0	0	0	.500	.500	1.000	317	1	1	1	0			.000	0	H	0.1

■ HOMER HILLEBRAND Hillebrand, Homer Hiller Henry "Doc" b: 10/10/1879, Freeport, Ill. d: 1/20/74, Elsinore, Cal. BR/TL, 5'8", 165 lbs. Deb: 4/24/05

YEAR	TM/L	G	AB	R	H	2B	3B	HR	RBI	BB	SO	AVG	OBP	SLG	PRO+	BR	/A	RC	SB	CS	SBR	FA	FR	POS	TPR
1905	Pit-N	39	110	9	26	3	2	0	7	6		.236	.282	.300	72	-4	-4	10	1			.978	-3	1P/OC	-0.6
1906	Pit-N	7	21	1	5	1	0	0	3	1		.238	.273	.286	71	-1	-1	2	0			1.000	1	/P	0.0
1908	Pit-N	1	0	0	0	0	0	0	0	0		—	—	—	—	0	0	0	0			.000	-0	/P	0.0
Total	3	47	131	10	31	4	2	0	10	7		.237	.281	.298	72	-4	-5	12	1			1.000	-1	/P1OC	-0.6

■ CHUCK HILLER Hiller, Charles Joseph b: 10/1/34, Johnsburg, Ill. BL/TR, 5'11", 170 lbs. Deb: 4/11/61 C

YEAR	TM/L	G	AB	R	H	2B	3B	HR	RBI	BB	SO	AVG	OBP	SLG	PRO+	BR	/A	RC	SB	CS	SBR	FA	FR	POS	TPR
1961	SF-N	70	240	38	57	12	1	2	12	32	30	.237	.330	.321	76	-8	-7	28	4	4	-1	.973	-14	2	-1.6
1962	*SF-N	161	602	94	166	22	2	3	48	55	49	.276	.344	.334	84	-13	-11	71	5	4	-1	.964	-18	*2	-1.4
1963	SF-N	111	417	44	93	10	2	6	33	20	23	.223	.262	.300	62	-21	-20	31	3	2	-0	.963	-15	*2	-2.9
1964	SF-N	80	205	21	37	8	1	1	17	17	23	.180	.247	.244	38	-16	-17	13	1	1	-0	.977	2	2/3	-1.2
1965	SF-N	7	7	1	1	0	0	1	1	0	1	.143	.143	.571	88	-0	-0	0	0	0	0	1.000	-1	/2	-0.1
	NY-N	100	286	24	68	11	1	5	21	14	24	.238	.276	.336	74	-11	-10	25	1	1	-0	.959	-12	2/O3	-1.7
	Yr	107	293	25	69	11	1	6	22	14	25	.235	.273	.341	74	-11	-10	26	1	1	-0	.959	-12	2/O3	-1.8
1966	NY-N	108	254	25	71	8	2	2	14	15	22	.280	.332	.350	92	-3	-2	31	0	0	0	.981	10	23/O	1.0
1967	NY-N	25	54	0	5	3	0	0	3	2	11	.093	.125	.148	-22	-9	-8	1	0	0	0	.968	2	2	-0.6
	Phi-N	31	43	4	13	1	0	0	2	2	4	.302	.333	.326	88	-1	-1	4	0	2	-1	.947	-3	/2	-0.4
	Yr	56	97	4	18	4	0	0	5	4	15	.186	.218	.227	27	-9	-9	4	0	2	-1	.963	-0	2	-1.0
1968	Pit-N	11	13	2	5	1	0	0	1	0	0	.385	.385	.462	155	1	1	2	0	0	0	.857	-0	/2	0.1
Total	8	704	2121	253	516	76	9	20	152	157	187	.243	.301	.316	72	-81	-77	206	14	14	-4	.967	-49	2/3O	-8.8

■ HOB HILLER Hiller, Harvey Max b: 5/12/1893, E.Mauch Chunk, Pa. d: 12/27/56, Leighton, Pa. BR/TR, 5'8", 162 lbs. Deb: 4/22/20

YEAR	TM/L	G	AB	R	H	2B	3B	HR	RBI	BB	SO	AVG	OBP	SLG	PRO+	BR	/A	RC	SB	CS	SBR	FA	FR	POS	TPR
1920	Bos-A	17	29	4	5	1	1	0	2	2	5	.172	.226	.276	34	-3	-3	1	0	3	-2	.905	1	/3S2O	-0.3
1921	Bos-A	1	1	0	0	0	0	0	0	0	0	.000	.000	.000	-99	-0	-0	0	0	0	0	.000	0	H	0.0
Total	2	18	30	4	5	1	1	0	2	2	5	.167	.219	.267	29	-3	-3	1	0	3	-2		1	/3S2O	-0.3

■ ED HILLEY Hilley, Edward Garfield "Whitey" b: 6/17/1879, Cleveland, Ohio d: 11/14/56, Cleveland, Ohio BR/TR, 5'10.5", 170 lbs. Deb: 9/29/03

YEAR	TM/L	G	AB	R	H	2B	3B	HR	RBI	BB	SO	AVG	OBP	SLG	PRO+	BR	/A	RC	SB	CS	SBR	FA	FR	POS	TPR
1903	Phi-A	1	3	1	1	0	0	0	0	1		.333	.500	.333	147	0	0	1	0			.800	-0	/3	0.0

■ MACK HILLIS Hillis, Malcolm David b: 7/23/01, Cambridge, Mass. d: 6/16/61, Cambridge, Mass. BR/TR, 5'10", 165 lbs. Deb: 9/13/24

YEAR	TM/L	G	AB	R	H	2B	3B	HR	RBI	BB	SO	AVG	OBP	SLG	PRO+	BR	/A	RC	SB	CS	SBR	FA	FR	POS	TPR
1924	NY-A	1	1	1	0	0	0	0	0	0	0	.000	.000	.000	-99	-0	-0	0	0	0	0	.000	0	/2	0.0
1928	Pit-N	11	36	6	9	2	3	1	7	0	6	.250	.250	.556	101	-0	-0	5	1			.973	-1	/23	-0.1
Total	2	12	37	7	9	2	3	1	7	0	6	.243	.243	.541	96	-0	-1	5	1	0		.973	-1	/23	-0.1

■ PAT HILLY Hilly, William Edward (b: William Edward Hilgerink) b: 2/24/1887, Fostoria, Ohio d: 7/25/53, Eureka, Mo. BR/TR, 5'11", 180 lbs. Deb: 5/07/14

YEAR	TM/L	G	AB	R	H	2B	3B	HR	RBI	BB	SO	AVG	OBP	SLG	PRO+	BR	/A	RC	SB	CS	SBR	FA	FR	POS	TPR
1914	Phi-N	8	10	2	3	0	0	0	1	1	5	.300	.364	.300	92	0	-0	1	0			1.000	-1	/O	-0.1

■ CHARLIE HILSEY Hilsey, Charles T. b: 3/23/1864, Philadelphia, Pa. d: 10/31/18, Philadelphia, Pa. 5'7", 180 lbs. Deb: 9/27/1883

YEAR	TM/L	G	AB	R	H	2B	3B	HR	RBI	BB	SO	AVG	OBP	SLG	PRO+	BR	/A	RC	SB	CS	SBR	FA	FR	POS	TPR
1883	Phi-N	3	10	0	1	0	0	0	1	0	4	.100	.100	.100	-43	-2	-1	0				.714	-0	/P	0.0
1884	Phi-a	6	24	5	5	1	1	0		0		.208	.208	.333	71	-1	-1	2				.250	-0	/OP	-0.1
Total	2	9	34	5	6	1	1	0	1	0	4	.176	.176	.265	39	-2	-2	2				.824	-1	/PO	-0.1

■ DAVE HILTON Hilton, John David b: 9/15/50, Uvalde, Tex. BR/TR, 5'11", 191 lbs. Deb: 9/10/72 C

YEAR	TM/L	G	AB	R	H	2B	3B	HR	RBI	BB	SO	AVG	OBP	SLG	PRO+	BR	/A	RC	SB	CS	SBR	FA	FR	POS	TPR
1972	SD-N	13	47	2	10	2	1	0	5	3	6	.213	.260	.298	63	-3	-2	4	1	0	0	.939	-3	3	-0.5
1973	SD-N	70	234	21	46	9	0	5	16	19	35	.197	.260	.299	59	-15	-13	18	2	1	0	.970	-4	32	-1.7
1974	SD-N	74	217	17	52	8	2	1	12	13	28	.240	.283	.309	68	-10	-9	17	3	5	-2	.948	-5	32	-1.7

YEAR	TM/L	G	AB	R	H	2B	3B	HR	RBI	BB	SO	AVG	OBP	SLG	PRO+	BR	/A	RC	SB	CS	SBR	FA	FR	POS	TPR
1975	SD-N	4	8	0	0	0	0	0	0	0	0	.000	.000	.000	-99	-2	-2	0	0	0	0	.900	1	/3	-0.1
Total	4	161	506	40	108	19	3	6	33	35	69	.213	.266	.298	61	-30	-26	40	6	6	-2	.954	-11	3/2	-4.0
■ JACK HIMES Himes, John Herb b: 9/22/1878, Bryan, Ohio d: 12/16/49, Joliet, Ill. BL/TR, 6'2", 180 lbs. Deb: 9/18/05																									
1905	StL-N	12	41	3	6	0	0	0	0	1		.146	.167	.146	-7	-5	-5	1	0			1.000	-1	O	-0.7
1906	StL-N	40	155	10	42	5	2	0	14	7		.271	.307	.329	103	-1	-0	18	4			.977	5	O	0.3
Total	2	52	196	13	48	5	2	0	14	8		.245	.278	.291	79	-6	-5	19	4			.981	4	/O	-0.4
■ HARRY HINCHMAN Hinchman, Harry Sibley b: 8/4/1878, Philadelphia, Pa. d: 1/19/33, Toledo, Ohio BB/TR, 5'11", 165 lbs. Deb: 7/29/07 F																									
1907	Cle-A	15	51	3	11	3	1	0	9	5		.216	.286	.314	91	-1	-1	6	2			.904	4	2	0.4
■ BILL HINCHMAN Hinchman, William White b: 4/4/1883, Philadelphia, Pa. d: 2/21/63, Columbus, Ohio BR/TR, 5'11", 190 lbs. Deb: 9/24/05 FC																									
1905	Cin-N	17	51	10	13	4	1	0	10	13		.255	.415	.373	122	3	2	10	4			.905	-3	O/31	-0.1
1906	Cin-N	18	54	7	11	1	1	0	1	8		.204	.306	.259	74	-1	-1	5	2			.963	1	O	-0.2
1907	Cle-A	152	514	62	117	19	9	1	50	47		.228	.311	.305	96	-0	-1	57	15			.958	-5	*O/12	-1.3
1908	Cle-A	137	464	55	107	23	8	6	59	38		.231	.301	.353	112	6	6	52	9			.975	-6	OS/1	-0.2
1909	Cle-A	139	457	57	118	20	13	2	53	41		.258	.331	.372	117	11	9	64	22			.918	1	*O/S	0.6
1915	Pit-N	156	577	72	177	33	14	5	77	48	75	.307	.368	.438	146	30	31	94	17	17	-5	.969	4	*O	2.4
1916	Pit-N	152	555	64	175	18	**16**	4	76	54	61	.315	.378	.427	146	31	31	96	10			.962	-4	*O1	2.2
1917	Pit-N	69	244	27	46	5	5	2	29	33	27	.189	.288	.275	70	-7	-8	20	5			.945	-1	O1	-1.5
1918	Pit-N	50	111	10	26	5	2	0	13	15	8	.234	.336	.315	96	0	-0	12	1			1.000	-4	O/1	-0.6
1920	Pit-N	18	16	0	3	0	0	0	1	1	3	.188	.278	.188	34	-1	-1	1	0	0	0	.000	0	H	-0.1
Total	10	908	3043	364	793	128	69	20	369	298	174	.261	.336	.368	118	72	67	410	85	17		.954	-17	O/1S32	1.2
■ HUNKEY HINES Hines, Henry Fred b: 9/29/1867, Elgin, Ill. d: 1/2/28, Rockford, Ill. BR/TR, 5'7", 165 lbs. Deb: 5/16/1895																									
1895	Bro-N	2	8	3	2	0	0	0	1	2	0	.250	.400	.250	78	-0	-0	1	0			1.000	0	/O	0.0
■ MIKE HINES Hines, Michael P. b: 9/1862, Ireland d: 3/14/10, New Bedford, Mass. BR/TL, 5'10", 176 lbs. Deb: 5/01/1883																									
1883	Bos-N	63	231	38	52	13	1	0	16	7	36	.225	.248	.290	61	-10	-11	17				.887	8	C/O	0.0
1884	Bos-N	35	132	16	23	3	0	0	3	3	24	.174	.193	.197	23	-11	-11	5				.919	6	C	-0.2
1885	Bos-N	14	56	11	13	4	0	0	4	4	5	.232	.283	.304	93	-1	-0	5				.857	-3	O	-0.4
	Bro-a	3	13	1	1	0	1	0		0		.077	.077	.231	-5	-1	-2	0				1.000	-1	/C	-0.2
	Pro-N	1	3	0	0	0	0	0	0	0	2	.000	.000	.000	-99	-1	-1	0				.636	-0	/C	-0.1
1888	Bos-N	4	16	3	2	0	1	0	2	2	0	.125	.222	.250	51	-1	-1	1	0			1.000	-0	/OC	-0.1
Total	4	120	451	69	91	20	3	0	25	16	67	.202	.229	.259	51	-25	-25	28	0			.896	9	/CO	-1.0
■ PAUL HINES Hines, Paul A. b: 3/1/1852, Washington, D.C. d: 7/10/35, Hyattsville, Md. BR/TR, 5'9.5", 173 lbs. Deb: 4/20/1872																									
1872	Nat-n	11	50	10	12	1	1	0	4	0	0	.240	.240	.300	56	-2	-4	4						1/3	-0.2
1873	Was-n	39	181	33	60	11	2	2	26	1	1	.331	.335	.448	132	6	7	27						*O/2C	0.5
1874	Chi-n	59	270	47	81	12	1	0		4		.300	.310	.352	109	3	3	30						*O2/S	0.2
1875	Chi-n	69	308	45	97	13	4	0		1		.315	.317	.383	140	12	12	38						O2	1.0
1876	Chi-N	64	305	62	101	**21**	3	2	59	1	3	.331	.333	.439	139	17	11	46				**.923**	5	*O/2	1.3
1877	Chi-N	60	261	44	73	11	7	0	23	1	8	.280	.282	.375	94	1	-3	28				.806	-10	*O2	-1.3
1878	Pro-N	62	257	42	92	13	4	**4**	**50**	2	10	**.358**	.363	**.486**	178	**20**	20	**47**				.849	3	*O/S	1.8
1879	Pro-N	85	409	81	**146**	25	10	2	52	8	16	**.357**	.369	.482	181	33	**34**	**75**				.867	7	*O	3.3
1880	Pro-N	85	374	64	115	20	2	3	35	13	17	.307	.331	.396	150	17	19	50				**.927**	8	*O/21	2.4
1881	Pro-N	80	361	65	103	**27**	5	2	31	13	12	.285	.310	.404	125	9	10	46				.897	-1	*O/21	0.6
1882	Pro-N	84	379	73	117	28	10	4	34	10	14	.309	.326	.467	151	21	21	59				.861	1	*O/1	1.9
1883	Pro-N	97	442	94	132	32	4	4	45	18	23	.299	.326	.416	120	12	10	61				.905	7	*O/1	1.4
1884	*Pro-N	114	490	94	148	**36**	10	3	41	44	28	.302	.360	.435	152	28	30	78				.895	2	*O/1P	2.5
1885	Pro-N	98	411	63	111	20	4	1	35	19	18	.270	.302	.345	114	4	6	44				.865	4	*O/1S32	0.7
1886	Was-N	121	487	80	152	30	8	9	56	35	21	.312	.358	.462	157	27	31	90	21			.899	3	*O31/S2	2.9
1887	Was-N	123	478	83	147	32	5	10	72	48	24	.308	.380	.458	141	23	27	103	46			.886	-14	*O/12S	0.9
1888	Ind-N	133	513	84	144	26	3	4	58	41	45	.281	.343	.366	126	18	16	77	31			.912	-7	*O/1S	0.5
1889	Ind-N	121	486	77	148	27	1	6	72	49	22	.305	.374	.401	116	13	11	88	34			.964	4	*1O	0.7
1890	Pit-N	31	121	11	22	1	0	0	9	11	7	.182	.256	.190	36	-10	-8	8	6			.973	2	1O	-0.6
	Bos-N	69	273	41	72	12	3	2	48	32	20	.264	.350	.352	99	3	-1	38	9			.881	-12	O/1	-1.3
	Yr	100	394	52	94	13	3	2	57	43	27	.239	.321	.302	82	-7	-8	44	15			.871	-10	O1	-1.9
1891	Was-a	54	206	25	58	7	5	0	31	21	16	.282	.376	.364	120	5	6	31	6			.856	-3	O/1	0.1
Total	4 n	178	809	135	250	37	8	2	30	6	1	.309	.314	.382	121	19	18	100	0					O/21SC3	1.5
Total	16	1481	6253	1083	1881	368	84	56	751	366	304	.301	.343	.413	134	239	241	970	153			.887	-3	*O1/23SP	17.8
■ GORDIE HINKLE Hinkle, Daniel Gordon b: 4/3/05, Toronto, Ohio d: 3/19/72, Houston, Tex. BR/TR, 6', 185 lbs. Deb: 4/19/34																									
1934	Bos-A	27	75	7	13	6	1	0	9	7	23	.173	.244	.280	33	-8	-8	5	0	0	0	.992	4	C	-0.3
■ GEORGE HINSHAW Hinshaw, George Addison b: 10/23/59, Los Angeles, Cal. BR/TR, 6', 185 lbs. Deb: 9/19/82																									
1982	SD-N	6	15	1	4	0	0	0	1	3	5	.267	.389	.267	91	-0	0	2	0	0	0	1.000	1	/O	0.0
1983	SD-N	7	16	1	7	1	0	0	4	0	4	.438	.438	.500	165	1	1	4	1	0	0	1.000	-0	/3	0.1
Total	2	13	31	2	11	1	0	0	5	3	9	.355	.412	.387	129	1	1	5	1	0	0		0	/O3	0.1
■ PAUL HINSON Hinson, James Paul b: 5/9/04, Van Leer, Tenn. d: 9/23/60, Muskogee, Okla. BR/TR, 5'10", 150 lbs. Deb: 4/19/28																									
1928	Bos-A	3	0	1	0	0	0	0	0	0	0	—	—	—	—	0	0	0	0	0	0	.000	0	R	0.0
■ CHUCK HINTON Hinton, Charles Edward b: 5/3/34, Rocky Mount, N.C. BR/TR, 6'1", 197 lbs. Deb: 5/14/61																									
1961	Was-A	106	339	51	88	13	5	6	34	40	81	.260	.339	.381	93	-4	-3	47	22	5	4	.963	0	O	-0.4
1962	Was-A	151	542	73	168	25	6	17	75	47	66	.310	.365	.472	124	17	18	92	28	10	2	.988	-10	*O2/S	0.4
1963	Was-A	150	566	80	152	20	12	15	55	64	79	.269	.344	.426	115	11	11	84	25	9	2	.989	-1	*O3/1S	0.6
1964	Was-A★	138	514	71	141	25	7	11	53	57	77	.274	.348	.414	112	8	8	71	17	6	2	.985	10	*O/3	1.4
1965	Cle-A	133	431	59	110	17	6	18	54	53	65	.255	.338	.448	120	12	11	68	17	3	3	.966	-9	O12/3	0.3
1966	Cle-A	123	348	46	89	9	3	12	50	35	66	.256	.326	.402	108	3	3	45	10	6	-1	.973	-8	*O/12	-1.0
1967	Cle-A	147	498	55	122	19	3	10	37	43	100	.245	.306	.355	94	-3	-4	53	6	8	-3	.976	-13	*O/2	-2.8
1968	Cal-A	116	267	28	52	10	3	7	23	24	61	.195	.261	.333	82	-7	-6	22	3	1	0	.987	-6	1O3/2	-1.8
1969	Cle-A	94	121	18	31	3	2	3	19	8	22	.256	.308	.388	91	-1	-2	15	2	0	1	.941	-10	O3	-1.2
1970	Cle-A	107	195	24	62	4	0	9	29	25	34	.318	.395	.477	133	11	10	37	0	2	-1	.994	-6	1O/C23	0.0
1971	Cle-A	88	147	13	33	7	0	5	14	20	34	.224	.317	.374	87	-1	-2	18	0	0	0	1.000	-7	1O/C	-1.2
Total	11	1353	3968	518	1048	152	47	113	443	416	685	.264	.335	.412	108	46	45	553	130	50	9	.979	-59	O1/23CS	-5.7
■ JOHN HINTON Hinton, John Robert "Red" b: 6/20/1876, Pittsburgh, Pa. d: 7/19/20, Braddock, Pa. BR/TR, 6', 200 lbs. Deb: 6/03/01																									
1901	Bos-N	4	13	0	1	0	0	0	0	2		.077	.200	.077	-16	-2	-2	0	0			.750	-2	/3	-0.4
■ TOMMY HINZO Hinzo, Thomas Lee b: 6/18/64, San Diego, Cal. BB/TR, 5'10", 170 lbs. Deb: 7/16/87																									
1987	Cle-A	67	257	31	68	9	3	3	21	10	47	.265	.297	.358	72	-10	-10	26	9	4	0	.973	-4	2	-1.0
1989	Cle-A	18	17	4	0	0	0	0	0	2	6	.000	.105	.000	-67	-4	-4	0	1	2	-1	.867	0	/2SD	-0.4
Total	2	85	274	35	68	9	3	3	21	12	53	.248	.285	.336	64	-14	-14	26	10	6	-1	.968	-4	/2DS	-1.4

■ GENE HISER
Hiser, Gene Taylor b: 12/11/48, Baltimore, Md. BL/TL, 5'11", 175 lbs. Deb: 8/20/71

YEAR	TM/L	G	AB	R	H	2B	3B	HR	RBI	BB	SO	AVG	OBP	SLG	PRO+	BR	/A	RC	SB	CS	SBR	FA	FR	POS	TPR
1971	Chi-N	17	29	4	6	0	0	0	1	4	8	.207	.303	.207	41	-2	-2	2	1	0	0	1.000	1	/O	-0.2
1972	Chi-N	32	46	2	9	0	0	0	4	6	8	.196	.288	.196	36	-3	-4	3	1	0	0	1.000	2	O	-0.2
1973	Chi-N	100	109	15	19	3	0	1	6	11	17	.174	.256	.229	33	-9	-10	7	4	5	-2	.980	-1	O	-1.5
1974	Chi-N	12	17	2	4	1	0	0	1	0	3	.235	.235	.294	46	-1	-1	1	0	0	0	1.000	0	/O	-0.1
1975	Chi-N	45	62	11	15	3	0	0	6	11	7	.242	.356	.290	77	-1	-1	7	0	1	-1	1.000	-0	O/1	-0.3
Total	5	206	263	34	53	7	0	1	18	32	43	.202	.291	.240	46	-17	-20	20	6	6	-2	.992	2	O/1	-2.3

■ LARRY HISLE
Hisle, Larry Eugene b: 5/5/47, Portsmouth, Ohio BR/TR, 6'2", 195 lbs. Deb: 4/10/68 C

YEAR	TM/L	G	AB	R	H	2B	3B	HR	RBI	BB	SO	AVG	OBP	SLG	PRO+	BR	/A	RC	SB	CS	SBR	FA	FR	POS	TPR
1968	Phi-N	7	11	1	4	1	0	0	1	1	4	.364	.417	.455	161	1	1	2	0	0	0	1.000	1	/O	0.1
1969	Phi-N	145	482	75	128	23	5	20	56	48	152	.266	.338	.459	125	13	14	75	18	8	1	.977	6	*O	1.3
1970	Phi-N	126	405	52	83	22	4	10	44	53	139	.205	.302	.353	77	-15	-13	44	5	5	-2	.978	0	*O	-2.1
1971	Phi-N	36	76	7	15	3	0	0	3	6	22	.197	.256	.237	40	-6	-6	4	1	0	0	.962	2	O	-0.4
1973	Min-A	143	545	88	148	25	6	15	64	64	128	.272	.352	.422	113	13	10	82	11	4	1	.975	6	*O	1.1
1974	Min-A	143	510	68	146	20	7	19	79	48	112	.286	.357	.465	130	22	20	83	12	6	0	.979	-8	*O	0.6
1975	Min-A	80	255	37	80	9	2	11	51	27	39	.314	.382	.494	143	15	15	50	17	3	3	.976	-7	OD	0.8
1976	Min-A	155	581	81	158	19	5	14	96	56	93	.272	.340	.394	111	11	9	77	31	18	-2	.984	14	*O	1.5
1977	Min-A★	141	546	95	165	36	3	28	**119**	56	106	.302	.373	.533	146	32	33	107	21	10	0	.974	1	*O/D	2.8
1978	Mil-A★	142	520	96	151	24	0	34	115	67	90	.290	.377	.533	153	36	36	103	10	6	-1	.978	-2	OD	3.1
1979	Mil-A	26	96	18	27	7	0	3	14	11	19	.281	.355	.448	115	2	2	15	1	0	0	1.000	1	DO	0.3
1980	Mil-A	17	60	16	17	0	0	6	16	14	7	.283	.427	.583	180	7	7	16	1	1	-0	.000	0	D	0.6
1981	Mil-A	27	87	11	20	4	0	4	11	6	17	.230	.295	.414	108	-0	1	11	0	0	0	.000	0	D	0.1
1982	Mil-A	9	31	7	4	0	0	2	5	5	13	.129	.250	.323	60	-2	-2	2	0	0	0	.000	0	/D	-0.2
Total	14	1197	4205	652	1146	193	32	166	674	462	941	.273	.350	.452	123	129	126	671	128	61	2	.978	13	*OD	9.6

■ JIM HITCHCOCK
Hitchcock, James Franklin b: 6/28/11, Inverness, Ala. d: 6/23/59, Montgomery, Ala. BR/TR, 5'11", 175 lbs. Deb: 8/24/38 F

YEAR	TM/L	G	AB	R	H	2B	3B	HR	RBI	BB	SO	AVG	OBP	SLG	PRO+	BR	/A	RC	SB	CS	SBR	FA	FR	POS	TPR
1938	Bos-N	28	76	2	13	0	0	0	7	2	11	.171	.192	.171	1	-10	-9	2	1			.881	-2	S/3	-1.0

■ BILLY HITCHCOCK
Hitchcock, William Clyde b: 7/31/16, Inverness, Ala. BR/TR, 6'1.5", 185 lbs. Deb: 4/14/42 FMC

YEAR	TM/L	G	AB	R	H	2B	3B	HR	RBI	BB	SO	AVG	OBP	SLG	PRO+	BR	/A	RC	SB	CS	SBR	FA	FR	POS	TPR
1942	Det-A	85	280	27	59	8	1	0	29	26	21	.211	.280	.246	45	-19	-22	20	2	2	-1	.944	-3	S/3	-2.1
1946	Det-A	3	3	0	0	0	0	0	0	1	0	.000	.250	.000	-25	-0	-1	0	0	0	0	1.000	0	/2	0.0
	Was-A	98	354	27	75	8	3	0	25	26	52	.212	.268	.251	48	-26	-23	23	2	4	-2	.966	-4	S3	-2.7
	Yr	101	357	27	75	8	3	0	25	27	52	.210	.268	.249	48	-26	-24	23	2	4	-2	.966	-3	S3/2	-2.7
1947	StL-A	80	275	25	61	2	2	1	28	21	34	.222	.277	.255	47	-19	-20	20	3	0	1	.977	11	23/S1	-0.5
1948	Bos-A	49	124	15	37	3	2	1	20	7	9	.298	.341	.379	87	-2	-3	16	0	0	0	.951	6	23	0.3
1949	Bos-A	55	147	22	30	6	1	0	9	17	11	.204	.291	.259	43	-12	-13	11	2	3	-1	.993	-8	1/2	-2.2
1950	Phi-A	115	399	35	109	22	5	1	54	45	32	.273	.347	.361	83	-11	-10	45	3	1	0	.967	-3	*2/S	-0.7
1951	Phi-A	77	222	27	68	10	4	1	36	21	23	.306	.371	.401	107	3	2	36	2	0	1	.929	7	32/1	1.0
1952	Phi-A	119	407	45	100	8	4	1	56	39	45	.246	.318	.292	66	-15	-19	40	1	1	-0	.942	-1	*31	-2.3
1953	Det-A	22	38	8	8	0	0	0	0	3	3	.211	.268	.211	31	-4	-4	2	0	0	0	.929	0	3/2S	-0.4
Total	9	703	2249	231	547	67	22	5	257	206	230	.243	.310	.299	65	-105	-110	212	15	11	-2	.938	7	32S/1	-9.6

■ MYRIL HOAG
Hoag, Myril Oliver b: 3/9/08, Davis, Cal. d: 7/28/71, High Springs, Fla BR/TR, 5'11", 180 lbs. Deb: 4/15/31

YEAR	TM/L	G	AB	R	H	2B	3B	HR	RBI	BB	SO	AVG	OBP	SLG	PRO+	BR	/A	RC	SB	CS	SBR	FA	FR	POS	TPR
1931	NY-A	44	28	6	4	2	0	0	3	1	8	.143	.172	.214	1	-4	-4	1	0	0	0	1.000	-7	O/3	-1.0
1932	*NY-A	46	54	18	20	5	0	1	7	7	13	.370	.443	.519	156	4	4	12	1	1	-0	.962	-10	O/1	-0.6
1934	NY-A	97	251	45	67	8	2	3	34	21	21	.267	.324	.351	79	-10	-8	28	1	3	-2	.974	-9	O	-1.9
1935	NY-A	48	110	13	28	4	1	1	13	12	19	.255	.328	.336	76	-4	-4	13	4	2	0	.986	-2	O/3	-0.6
1936	NY-A	45	156	23	47	9	4	3	34	7	16	.301	.343	.468	102	-1	-0	25	3	1	0	.955	-4	O	-0.5
1937	*NY-A	106	362	48	109	19	8	3	46	33	33	.301	.364	.423	97	-1	-2	55	4	7	-3	.955	-6	O	-1.3
1938	*NY-A	85	267	28	74	14	3	0	48	25	31	.277	.344	.352	75	-10	-10	33	4	3	-1	.965	-4	O	-1.6
1939	StL-A★	129	482	58	142	23	4	10	75	24	35	.295	.329	.421	89	-8	-10	62	9	5	-0	.971	-8	*O/P	-2.0
1940	StL-A	76	191	20	50	11	0	3	26	13	30	.262	.309	.366	73	-8	-8	22	2	0	1	.971	-6	O	-1.5
1941	StL-A	1	1	0	0	0	0	0	0	0	0	.000	.000	.000	-97	-0	-0	0	0	0	0	.000	0	H	0.0
	Chi-A	106	380	30	97	13	3	1	44	27	29	.255	.306	.313	65	-20	-19	34	6	10	-4	.957	-6	O	-3.4
	Yr	107	381	30	97	13	3	1	44	27	29	.255	.306	.312	65	-20	-19	34	6	10	-4	.957	-6	O	-3.4
1942	Chi-A	113	412	47	99	18	2	2	37	36	21	.240	.301	.308	73	-16	-15	38	17	8	0	.972	-4	*O	-2.5
1944	Chi-A	17	48	5	11	1	0	0	4	10	1	.229	.362	.250	77	-1	-1	5	1	3	-2	.969	-1	O	-0.4
	Cle-A	67	277	33	79	9	3	1	27	25	23	.285	.347	.350	103	0	1	35	6	4	-1	.947	-1	O	-0.4
	Yr	84	325	38	90	10	3	1	31	35	24	.277	.349	.335	99	-1	0	39	7	7	-2	.950	-2	O	-0.8
1945	Cle-A	40	128	10	27	5	3	0	3	11	18	.211	.279	.297	70	-6	-5	11	1	2	-1	.987	0	O/P	-0.8
Total	13	1020	3147	384	854	141	33	28	401	252	298	.271	.328	.364	83	-85	-79	374	59	49	-12	.965	-67	O/P31	-18.5

■ DON HOAK
Hoak, Donald Albert "Tiger" b: 2/5/28, Roulette, Pa. d: 10/9/69, Pittsburgh, Pa. BR/TR, 6', 175 lbs. Deb: 4/18/54 C

YEAR	TM/L	G	AB	R	H	2B	3B	HR	RBI	BB	SO	AVG	OBP	SLG	PRO+	BR	/A	RC	SB	CS	SBR	FA	FR	POS	TPR
1954	Bro-N	88	261	41	64	9	5	7	26	25	39	.245	.321	.398	83	-6	-7	33	8	3	1	.950	4	3	-0.4
1955	*Bro-N	94	279	50	67	13	3	5	19	46	50	.240	.350	.362	87	-3	-4	36	9	5	-0	.960	17	3	1.2
1956	Chi-N	121	424	51	91	18	4	5	37	41	46	.215	.285	.311	61	-24	-23	40	8	3	1	.949	-18	*3	-4.0
1957	Cin-N★	149	529	78	155	**39**	2	19	89	74	54	.293	.384	.482	122	24	20	94	8	15	-7	**.971**	-0	*3/2	1.6
1958	Cin-N	114	417	51	109	30	0	6	50	43	36	.261	.333	.376	83	-7	-10	50	6	8	-3	.964	4	*3/S	-0.8
1959	Pit-N	155	564	60	166	29	3	8	65	71	75	.294	.377	.399	108	8	9	86	9	2	2	.961	9	*3	2.0
1960	*Pit-N	155	553	97	156	24	9	16	79	74	74	.282	.368	.445	120	17	17	90	3	2	-0	.948	4	*3	2.1
1961	Pit-N	145	503	72	150	27	7	12	61	73	53	.298	.390	.451	122	18	18	90	4	2	0	.953	-3	*3	1.6
1962	Pit-N	121	411	63	99	14	8	5	48	49	49	.241	.323	.350	81	-11	-11	44	4	2	0	**.969**	-3	*3	-1.2
1963	Phi-N	115	377	35	87	11	3	6	24	27	52	.231	.284	.324	75	-12	-12	32	5	5	-2	.958	6	*3	-0.8
1964	Phi-N	6	4	0	0	0	0	0	0	0	2	.000	.000	.000	-99	-1	-1	0	0	0	0	.000	0	H	-0.1
Total	11	1263	4322	598	1144	214	44	89	498	523	530	.265	.347	.396	98	4	-4	597	64	47	-9	.959	20	*3/S2	1.2

■ BILL HOBBS
Hobbs, William Lee "Smokey" b: 5/7/1893, Grant's Lick, Ky. d: 1/5/45, Hamilton, Ohio BR/TR, 5'9.5", 155 lbs. Deb: 8/09/13

YEAR	TM/L	G	AB	R	H	2B	3B	HR	RBI	BB	SO	AVG	OBP	SLG	PRO+	BR	/A	RC	SB	CS	SBR	FA	FR	POS	TPR
1913	Cin-N	4	4	0	0	0	0	0	0	0	3	.000	.000	.000	-99	-1	-1	0	0			1.000	1	/23	0.0
1916	Cin-N	6	11	1	2	1	0	0	1	2	0	.182	.308	.273	81	-0	-0	1	1			.947	6	/S	0.6
Total	2	10	15	1	2	1	0	0	1	2	3	.133	.235	.200	32	-1	-1	1	1				6	/S32	0.6

■ DICK HOBLITZEL
Hoblitzel, Richard Carleton "Doc" (b: Richard Carleton Hoblitzell)
b: 10/26/1888, Waverly, W.Va. d: 11/14/62, Parkersburg, W.Va. BL/TL, 6', 172 lbs. Deb: 9/05/08

YEAR	TM/L	G	AB	R	H	2B	3B	HR	RBI	BB	SO	AVG	OBP	SLG	PRO+	BR	/A	RC	SB	CS	SBR	FA	FR	POS	TPR
1908	Cin-N	32	114	8	29	3	2	0	8	7		.254	.309	.316	103	-0	0	12	2			.985	2	1	0.1
1909	Cin-N	142	517	59	159	23	11	4	67	44		.308	.364	.418	144	24	25	86	17			.982	-3	*1	2.3
1910	Cin-N	155	611	85	170	24	13	4	70	47	32	.278	.332	.380	112	4	7	85	28			.984	-8	*1/2	-0.1
1911	Cin-N	158	622	81	180	19	13	11	91	42	44	.289	.342	.415	116	7	10	98	32			.990	2	*1	1.2
1912	Cin-N	148	558	73	164	32	12	2	85	48	28	.294	.352	.405	110	4	7	88	23			.985	2	*1	0.6
1913	Cin-N	137	502	59	143	23	7	3	62	35	26	.285	.334	.376	103	1	1	67	18			.988	-5	*1	-0.6
1914	Cin-N	78	248	31	52	8	7	0	26	26	26	.210	.287	.298	72	-8	-9	24	7			.988	-4	1	-1.6
	Bos-A	69	229	31	73	10	3	0	33	19	21	.319	.386	.389	133	9	9	35	12	12	-4	.979	-5	1	-0.1
1915	*Bos-A	124	399	54	113	15	12	2	61	38	26	.283	.351	.396	128	11	12	57	9	14	-6	.987	-1	*1	0.3
1916	*Bos-A	130	417	57	108	17	1	0	39	47	28	.259	.338	.305	93	-2	-3	50	10			.989	-1	*1	-0.9
1917	Bos-A	120	420	49	108	19	7	1	47	46	22	.257	.336	.343	108	4	4	53	12			.990	-8	*1	-0.9

YEAR	TM/L	G	AB	R	H	2B	3B	HR	RBI	BB	SO	AVG	OBP	SLG	PRO+	BR	/A	RC	SB	CS	SBR	FA	FR	POS	TPR
1918	Bos-A	25	69	4	11	1	0	0	4	8	3	.159	.266	.174	33	-5	-5	4	3			.996	1	1	-0.5
Total	11	1318	4706	591	1310	194	88	27	593	407	256	.278	.341	.374	111	49	60	659	173	26		.987	-29	*1/2	-0.2

■ BUTCH HOBSON

Hobson, Clell Lavern b: 8/17/51, Tuscaloosa, Ala. BR/TR, 6'1", 193 lbs. Deb: 9/07/75 M

YEAR	TM/L	G	AB	R	H	2B	3B	HR	RBI	BB	SO	AVG	OBP	SLG	PRO+	BR	/A	RC	SB	CS	SBR	FA	FR	POS	TPR
1975	Bos-A	2	4	0	1	0	0	0	0	0	2	.250	.250	.250	38	-0	-0	0	0	0	0	1.000	1	/3	0.0
1976	Bos-A	76	269	34	63	7	5	8	34	15	62	.234	.275	.387	82	-4	-8	26	0	1	-1	.936	-7	3	-1.7
1977	Bos-A	159	593	77	157	33	5	30	112	27	162	.265	.301	.489	100	6	-3	80	5	4	-1	.946	-28	*3	-3.3
1978	Bos-A	147	512	65	128	26	2	17	80	50	122	.250	.317	.408	92	1	-6	65	1	0	0	.899	-14	*3D	-2.2
1979	Bos-A	146	528	74	138	26	7	28	93	30	78	.261	.301	.496	105	5	1	70	3	2	-0	.935	-21	*3/2	-2.1
1980	Bos-A	93	324	35	74	6	0	11	39	25	69	.228	.284	.349	69	-13	-15	30	1	1	-0	.910	-9	3D	-2.5
1981	Cal-A	85	268	27	63	7	4	4	36	35	60	.235	.326	.336	91	-2	-2	31	1	1	-0	.929	-11	3/D	-1.7
1982	NY-A	30	58	2	10	2	0	0	3	1	14	.172	.186	.207	8	-7	-7	2	0	0	0	.951	-1	D1	-0.8
Total	8	738	2556	314	634	107	23	98	397	183	569	.248	.300	.423	91	-15	-40	305	11	9	-2	.926	-90	3/D12	-14.3

■ ED HOCK

Hock, Edward Francis b: 3/27/1899, Franklin Furnace, Ohio d: 11/21/63, Portsmouth, Ohio BL/TL, 5'10.5", 165 lbs. Deb: 7/08/20

YEAR	TM/L	G	AB	R	H	2B	3B	HR	RBI	BB	SO	AVG	OBP	SLG	PRO+	BR	/A	RC	SB	CS	SBR	FA	FR	POS	TPR
1920	StL-N	1	0	0	0	0	0	0	0	0	0	—	—	—	—	0	0	0	0	0	0	.000	-1	/O	-0.1
1923	Cin-N	2	0	0	0	0	0	0	0	0	0	—	—	—	—	0	0	0	0	0	0	.000	0	R	0.0
1924	Cin-N	16	10	7	1	0	0	0	0	0	2	.100	.182	.100	-23	-2	-2	0	0	0	0	1.000	-0	/O	-0.2
Total	3	19	10	7	1	0	0	0	0	0	2	.100	.182	.100	-23	-2	-2	0	0	0	0	1.000	-1	/O	-0.3

■ ORIS HOCKETT

Hockett, Oris Leon "Brown" b: 9/29/09, Amboy, Ind. d: 3/23/69, Torrance, Cal. BL/TR, 5'9", 182 lbs. Deb: 9/04/38

YEAR	TM/L	G	AB	R	H	2B	3B	HR	RBI	BB	SO	AVG	OBP	SLG	PRO+	BR	/A	RC	SB	CS	SBR	FA	FR	POS	TPR
1938	Bro-N	21	70	8	23	5	1	1	8	4	9	.329	.365	.471	126	3	2	13	0			.893	-4	O	-0.2
1939	Bro-N	9	13	3	3	0	0	0	1	1	1	.231	.286	.231	39	-1	-1	1	0			1.000	1	/O	-0.1
1941	Cle-A	2	6	0	2	0	0	0	1	2	0	.333	.500	.333	131	0	0	1	0	0	0	1.000	-1	/O	0.0
1942	Cle-A	148	601	85	150	22	7	7	48	45	45	.250	.305	.344	88	-15	-11	63	12	12	-4	.980	-2	*O	-2.5
1943	Cle-A	141	601	70	166	33	4	2	51	45	45	.276	.331	.354	107	-0	4	69	13	18	-7	.960	1	*O	-1.0
1944	Cle-A☆	124	457	47	132	29	5	1	50	35	27	.289	.339	.381	110	3	5	59	8	9	-3	.986	-4	*O	-0.8
1945	Chi-A	106	417	46	122	23	4	2	55	27	30	.293	.340	.381	112	4	5	52	10	9	-2	.982	1	*O	-0.2
Total	7	551	2165	259	598	112	21	13	214	159	157	.276	.329	.365	103	-7	4	258	43	48		.974	-6	O	-4.8

■ JOHNNY HODAPP

Hodapp, Urban John b: 9/26/05, Cincinnati, Ohio d: 6/14/80, Cincinnati, Ohio BR/TR, 6', 185 lbs. Deb: 8/19/25

YEAR	TM/L	G	AB	R	H	2B	3B	HR	RBI	BB	SO	AVG	OBP	SLG	PRO+	BR	/A	RC	SB	CS	SBR	FA	FR	POS	TPR
1925	Cle-A	37	130	12	31	5	1	0	14	11	7	.238	.298	.292	50	-10	-10	11	2	3	-1	.960	3	3	-0.5
1926	Cle-A	3	5	0	1	0	0	0	0	0	1	.200	.200	.200	4	-1	-1	0	0	0	0	.750	-1	/3	-0.1
1927	Cle-A	79	240	25	73	15	3	5	40	14	23	.304	.343	.454	105	1	1	35	2	2	-1	.935	1	3/1	0.3
1928	Cle-A	116	449	51	145	31	6	2	73	20	20	.323	.352	.432	104	2	2	68	2	1	0	.944	-2	*31	0.4
1929	Cle-A	90	294	30	96	12	7	4	51	15	14	.327	.361	.456	105	3	2	47	3	3	-1	.977	5	2	0.8
1930	Cle-A	154	635	111	**225**	**51**	8	9	121	32	29	.354	.386	.502	119	21	18	120	6	5	-1	.970	12	*2	3.3
1931	Cle-A	122	468	71	138	19	4	2	56	27	23	.295	.336	.365	80	-11	-14	56	1	5	-3	.969	16	*2	0.6
1932	Cle-A	7	16	2	2	1	0	0	0	0	2	.125	.125	.188	-19	-3	-3	0	0	0	0	1.000	-2	/2	-0.5
	Chi-A	68	176	21	40	8	0	3	20	11	3	.227	.273	.324	58	-12	-11	16	1	0	0	.967	-5	O/23	-1.6
	Yr	75	192	23	42	9	0	3	20	11	5	.219	.261	.313	51	-15	-14	16	1	0	0	.967	-7	O2/3	-2.1
1933	Bos-A	115	413	55	129	27	5	3	54	33	14	.312	.365	.424	109	5	5	64	1	1	-0	.960	3	*21	1.2
Total	9	791	2826	378	880	169	34	28	429	163	136	.311	.350	.425	98	-4	-12	419	18	20	-7	.967	30	23/O1	3.9

■ MEL HODERLEIN

Hoderlein, Melvin Anthony b: 6/24/23, Mt.Carmel, Ohio BB/TR, 5'10", 185 lbs. Deb: 8/16/51

YEAR	TM/L	G	AB	R	H	2B	3B	HR	RBI	BB	SO	AVG	OBP	SLG	PRO+	BR	/A	RC	SB	CS	SBR	FA	FR	POS	TPR
1951	Bos-A	9	14	1	5	1	1	0	1	6	2	.357	.550	.571	185	3	2	4	0	1	-1	1.000	1	/23	0.3
1952	Was-A	72	208	16	56	8	2	0	17	18	22	.269	.333	.327	87	-4	-3	20	2	0	1	.978	-2	2	-0.1
1953	Was-A	23	47	5	9	0	0	0	5	6	9	.191	.283	.191	31	-4	-4	3	0	0	0	.953	-3	2/S	-0.7
1954	Was-A	14	25	0	4	1	0	0	1	1	4	.160	.192	.200	8	-3	-3	1	0	0	0	.939	1	/S2	-0.1
Total	4	118	294	22	74	10	3	0	24	31	37	.252	.327	.306	78	-9	-8	28	2	1	0	.973	-3	/2S3	-0.6

■ CHARLIE HODES

Hodes, Charles b: 1848, New York, N.Y. d: 2/14/1875, Brooklyn, N.Y. TR, 5'11.5", 175 lbs. Deb: 5/08/1871

YEAR	TM/L	G	AB	R	H	2B	3B	HR	RBI	BB	SO	AVG	OBP	SLG	PRO+	BR	/A	RC	SB	CS	SBR	FA	FR	POS	TPR
1871	Chi-n	28	130	32	36	4	1	2	25	7	0	.277	.314	.369	86	-1	-4	16	3					C/3OS	-0.3
1872	Tro-n	13	65	17	15	5	0	0	12	1	0	.231	.242	.308	67	-2	-3	5						/SOC3	-0.2
1874	Atl-n	22	82	8	13	2	1	0		0		.159	.159	.207	17	-7	-6	3						O/2	-0.4
Total	3 n	63	277	57	64	11	2	2		8		.231	.253	.307	66	-10	-12	24						/OC3S2	-0.9

■ BERT HODGE

Hodge, Edward Burton b: 5/25/17, Knoxville, Tenn. BL/TR, 5'11", 170 lbs. Deb: 4/14/42

YEAR	TM/L	G	AB	R	H	2B	3B	HR	RBI	BB	SO	AVG	OBP	SLG	PRO+	BR	/A	RC	SB	CS	SBR	FA	FR	POS	TPR
1942	Phi-N	8	11	0	2	0	0	0	0	1	0	.182	.250	.182	29	-1	-1	0	0			1.000	-1	/3	-0.2

■ GOMER HODGE

Hodge, Harold Morris b: 4/3/44, Rutherfordton, N.C. BB/TR, 6'2", 185 lbs. Deb: 4/06/71

YEAR	TM/L	G	AB	R	H	2B	3B	HR	RBI	BB	SO	AVG	OBP	SLG	PRO+	BR	/A	RC	SB	CS	SBR	FA	FR	POS	TPR
1971	Cle-A	80	83	3	17	3	0	1	9	4	19	.205	.258	.277	47	-5	-6	6	0	0	0	1.000	-2	/132	-0.9

■ GIL HODGES

Hodges, Gilbert Raymond (b: Gilbert Ray Hodge)
b: 4/4/24, Princeton, Ind. d: 4/2/72, West Palm Beach, Fla BR/TR, 6'1.5", 200 lbs. Deb: 10/03/43 M

YEAR	TM/L	G	AB	R	H	2B	3B	HR	RBI	BB	SO	AVG	OBP	SLG	PRO+	BR	/A	RC	SB	CS	SBR	FA	FR	POS	TPR
1943	Bro-N	1	2	0	0	0	0	0	0	1	2	.000	.333	.000	0	-0	-0	0	1			.600	0	/3	0.0
1947	*Bro-N	28	77	9	12	3	1	1	7	14	19	.156	.286	.260	44	-6	-6	6	0			.958	-2	C	-0.7
1948	Bro-N	134	481	48	120	18	5	11	70	43	61	.249	.311	.376	82	-11	-13	56	7			.986	-1	1C	-1.2
1949	*Bro-N★	156	596	94	170	23	4	23	115	66	64	.285	.360	.453	112	14	11	99	10			**.995**	-4	*1	0.5
1950	Bro-N☆	153	561	98	159	26	2	32	113	73	73	.283	.367	.508	125	22	20	105	6			**.994**	1	*1	1.6
1951	Bro-N★	158	582	118	156	25	3	40	103	93	99	.268	.374	.527	137	32	31	119	9	7	-2	.992	7	*1	2.9
1952	*Bro-N☆	153	508	87	129	27	1	32	102	107	90	.254	.386	.500	142	32	32	106	2	4	-2	.992	5	*1	3.0
1953	*Bro-N★	141	520	101	157	22	7	31	122	75	84	.302	.393	.550	139	33	31	119	1	4	-2	.993	8	*1O	3.0
1954	Bro-N★	154	579	106	176	23	5	42	130	74	84	.304	.384	.579	142	38	36	128	3	3	-1	.995	9	*1	3.5
1955	*Bro-N★	150	546	75	158	24	5	27	102	80	91	.289	.383	.500	128	26	24	105	2	1	0	.991	1	*1O	1.6
1956	*Bro-N	153	550	86	146	29	4	32	87	76	91	.265	.355	.507	119	22	16	97	3	3	-1	.992	1	*1O/C	0.7
1957	Bro-N★	150	579	94	173	28	7	27	98	63	91	.299	.370	.511	122	27	20	109	5	3	-0	.990	2	*1/32	1.2
1958	LA-N	141	475	68	123	15	1	22	64	52	87	.259	.332	.434	98	0	-2	67	8	2	1	.992	1	*13/OC	-0.7
1959	*LA-N	124	413	57	114	19	2	25	80	58	92	.276	.369	.513	123	19	15	77	3	2	-0	**.992**	0	*1/3	0.8
1960	LA-N	101	197	22	39	8	1	8	30	26	37	.198	.295	.371	76	-5	-7	22	0	1	-1	.995	1	13	-1.1
1961	LA-N	109	215	25	52	4	0	8	31	24	43	.242	.318	.372	76	-5	-8	26	3	1	0	.998	0	*1	-1.2
1962	NY-N	54	127	15	32	1	0	9	17	15	27	.252	.331	.472	111	2	2	19	0	0	0	.986	3	1	0.3
1963	NY-N	11	22	2	5	0	0	0	3	3	2	.227	.320	.227	60	-1	-1	2	0	0	0	1.000	2	1	0.0
Total	18	2071	7030	1105	1921	295	48	370	1274	943	1137	.273	.361	.487	119	238	200	1261	63	31		.992	34	*1/OC32	14.2

■ RON HODGES

Hodges, Ronald Wray b: 6/22/49, Rocky Mount, Va. BL/TR, 6'1", 185 lbs. Deb: 6/13/73

YEAR	TM/L	G	AB	R	H	2B	3B	HR	RBI	BB	SO	AVG	OBP	SLG	PRO+	BR	/A	RC	SB	CS	SBR	FA	FR	POS	TPR
1973	*NY-N	45	127	5	33	2	0	1	18	11	19	.260	.319	.299	73	-5	-4	11	0	1	-1	.992	2	C	-0.1
1974	NY-N	59	136	16	30	4	0	4	14	19	11	.221	.316	.338	84	-3	-3	15	0	0	0	.953	-2	C	-0.3
1975	NY-N	9	34	3	7	1	0	2	4	1	6	.206	.229	.412	79	-1	-1	3	0	0	0	1.000	0	/C	-0.1
1976	NY-N	56	155	21	35	6	0	4	24	27	16	.226	.341	.342	100	-1	1	19	2	0	1	.976	-9	C	-0.7
1977	NY-N	66	117	6	31	4	0	1	5	9	17	.265	.317	.325	76	-4	-4	12	0	2	-1	.992	-0	C	-0.4
1978	NY-N	47	102	4	26	4	1	0	7	10	11	.255	.327	.314	83	-3	-2	10	1	2	-1	.982	6	C	0.4
1979	NY-N	59	86	4	14	4	0	0	5	19	16	.163	.314	.209	47	-6	-5	7	0	0	0	.980	1	C	-0.3
1980	NY-N	36	42	4	10	2	0	0	5	10	13	.238	.385	.286	92	0	0	5	1	1	-0	.982	4	/C	0.4
1981	NY-N	35	43	5	13	2	0	1	6	5	8	.302	.375	.419	127	1	2	7	1	0	0	1.000	-1	/C	0.1

YEAR	TM/L	G	AB	R	H	2B	3B	HR	RBI	BB	SO	AVG	OBP	SLG	PRO+	BR	/A	RC	SB	CS	SBR	FA	FR	POS	TPR
1982	NY-N	80	228	26	56	12	1	5	27	41	40	.246	.361	.373	106	3	3	32	4	3	-1	.980	-0	C	0.5
1983	NY-N	110	250	20	65	12	0	0	21	49	42	.260	.385	.308	95	1	1	31	0	3	-2	.971	-10	C	-0.7
1984	NY-N	64	106	5	22	3	0	1	11	23	18	.208	.354	.264	77	-2	-2	11	1	1	-0	.979	-1	C	-0.2
Total	12	666	1426	119	342	56	2	19	147	224	217	.240	.345	.322	88	-19	-15	165	10	13	-5	.978	-9	C	-1.4

■ RALPH HODGIN Hodgin, Elmer Ralph b: 2/10/16, Greensboro, N.C. BL/TR, 5'10", 170 lbs. Deb: 4/19/39

YEAR	TM/L	G	AB	R	H	2B	3B	HR	RBI	BB	SO	AVG	OBP	SLG	PRO+	BR	/A	RC	SB	CS	SBR	FA	FR	POS	TPR
1939	Bos-N	32	48	4	10	1	0	0	4	3	4	.208	.255	.229	33	-5	-4	2	0			1.000	-1	/O	-0.6
1943	Chi-A	117	407	52	128	22	8	1	50	20	24	.314	.356	.415	125	12	12	59	3	5	-2	.945	-7	3O	0.2
1944	Chi-A	121	465	56	137	25	7	1	51	21	14	.295	.333	.385	106	2	2	60	3	1	0	.942	12	3O	1.5
1946	Chi-A	87	258	32	65	10	1	0	25	19	6	.252	.308	.298	73	-10	-9	23	0	1	-1	.983	-2	O	-1.6
1947	Chi-A	59	180	26	53	10	3	1	24	13	4	.294	.352	.400	113	2	3	25	1	0	0	.990	1	O	0.2
1948	Chi-A	114	331	28	88	11	5	1	34	21	11	.266	.310	.338	75	-14	-12	33	0	3	-2	.970	5	O	-1.4
Total	6	530	1689	198	481	79	24	4	188	97	63	.285	.330	.367	98	-13	-9	203	7	10		.985	7	O3	-1.7

■ PAUL HODGSON Hodgson, Paul Joseph Denis b: 4/14/60, Montreal, Que., Can. BR/TR, 6'2", 190 lbs. Deb: 8/31/80

YEAR	TM/L	G	AB	R	H	2B	3B	HR	RBI	BB	SO	AVG	OBP	SLG	PRO+	BR	/A	RC	SB	CS	SBR	FA	FR	POS	TPR
1980	Tor-A	20	41	5	9	0	1	1	5	3	12	.220	.273	.341	64	-2	-2	3	0	1	-1	1.000	-0	O/D	-0.3

■ ART HOELSKOETTER Hoelskoetter, Arthur "Holley" or "Hoss" (a.k.a. Arthur H. Hostetter)
b: 9/30/1882, St.Louis, Mo. d: 8/3/54, St.Louis, Mo. BR/TR, 6'2", Deb: 9/10/05

YEAR	TM/L	G	AB	R	H	2B	3B	HR	RBI	BB	SO	AVG	OBP	SLG	PRO+	BR	/A	RC	SB	CS	SBR	FA	FR	POS	TPR
1905	StL-N	24	83	7	20	2	1	0	5	3		.241	.267	.289	68	-4	-3	7	1			.972	1	3/2P	-0.2
1906	StL-N	94	317	21	71	6	3	0	14	4		.224	.238	.262	59	-17	-16	22	2			.943	-6	3SPO/2	-2.0
1907	StL-N	119	397	21	98	6	3	2	28	27		.247	.298	.292	88	-7	-6	38	5			.927	10	21/COP3	0.5
1908	StL-N	62	155	10	36	7	1	0	6	6		.232	.265	.290	81	-4	-3	13	1			.948	0	C/312	0.0
Total	4	299	952	59	225	21	8	2	53	40		.236	.271	.282	76	-32	-28	79	9			.924	6	/23C1OSP	-1.7

■ JACK HOEY Hoey, John Bernard b: 11/10/1881, Watertown, Mass. d: 11/14/47, Waterbury, Conn. BL/TL, 5'9", 185 lbs. Deb: 6/27/06

YEAR	TM/L	G	AB	R	H	2B	3B	HR	RBI	BB	SO	AVG	OBP	SLG	PRO+	BR	/A	RC	SB	CS	SBR	FA	FR	POS	TPR
1906	Bos-A	94	361	27	88	8	4	0	24	14		.244	.274	.288	76	-10	-10	34	10			.915	-8	O	-2.5
1907	Bos-A	39	96	7	21	2	1	0	8	1		.219	.227	.260	56	-5	-5	6	2			.857	-5	O	-1.2
1908	Bos-A	13	43	5	7	0	0	0	3	0		.163	.163	.163	6	-4	-5	1	1			1.000	-0	O	-0.6
Total	3	146	500	39	116	10	5	0	35	15		.232	.256	.272	67	-20	-20	41	13			.913	-13	O	-4.3

■ STEW HOFFERTH Hofferth, Stewart Edward b: 1/27/13, Logansport, Ind. BR/TR, 6'2", 195 lbs. Deb: 4/19/44

YEAR	TM/L	G	AB	R	H	2B	3B	HR	RBI	BB	SO	AVG	OBP	SLG	PRO+	BR	/A	RC	SB	CS	SBR	FA	FR	POS	TPR
1944	Bos-N	66	180	14	36	8	0	1	26	11	5	.200	.246	.261	41	-14	-15	10	0			.984	0	C	-1.2
1945	Bos-N	50	170	13	40	2	0	3	15	14	11	.235	.297	.300	66	-8	-8	15	1			.980	6	C	0.1
1946	Bos-N	20	58	3	12	1	1	0	10	3	6	.207	.246	.259	43	-4	-5	4	0			1.000	-1	C	-0.5
Total	3	136	408	30	88	11	1	4	51	28	22	.216	.268	.277	52	-26	-27	30	1			.985	6	C	-1.6

■ DUTCH HOFFMAN Hoffman, Clarence Casper "Red" b: 1/28/04, Freeburg, Ill. d: 12/6/62, Belleville, Ill. BR/TR, 6', 175 lbs. Deb: 4/23/29

YEAR	TM/L	G	AB	R	H	2B	3B	HR	RBI	BB	SO	AVG	OBP	SLG	PRO+	BR	/A	RC	SB	CS	SBR	FA	FR	POS	TPR
1929	Chi-A	107	337	27	87	16	5	3	37	24	28	.258	.307	.362	73	-15	-14	38	6	3	0	.984	-1	O	-2.0

■ DANNY HOFFMAN Hoffman, Daniel John b: 3/2/1880, Canaan, Conn. d: 3/14/22, Manchester, Conn. BL/TL, 5'9", 175 lbs. Deb: 4/20/03

YEAR	TM/L	G	AB	R	H	2B	3B	HR	RBI	BB	SO	AVG	OBP	SLG	PRO+	BR	/A	RC	SB	CS	SBR	FA	FR	POS	TPR
1903	Phi-A	74	248	29	61	5	7	2	22	6		.246	.267	.347	79	-6	-7	26	7			.950	0	O/P	-1.1
1904	Phi-A	53	204	31	61	7	5	3	24	5		.299	.325	.426	130	8	7	32	9			.936	0	O	0.5
1905	*Phi-A	120	459	66	120	10	10	1	35	33		.261	.312	.333	103	2	1	66	**46**			.942	-2	*O	-0.7
1906	Phi-A	7	22	4	5	0	0	0	0	3		.227	.320	.227	70	-1	-1	3	1			1.000	1	/O	0.0
	NY-A	100	320	34	82	10	6	0	23	27		.256	.318	.325	92	1	-3	45	32			.938	-9	O	-1.8
	Yr	107	342	38	87	10	6	0	23	30		.254	.318	.319	91	0	-3	48	33			.943	-8	*O	-1.8
1907	NY-A	136	517	81	131	10	3	5	46	42		.253	.322	.313	95	3	-2	65	30			.953	8	*O	0.0
1908	StL-A	99	363	41	91	9	7	1	25	23		.251	.304	.322	103	1	1	40	17			.962	11	O	0.9
1909	StL-A	110	387	44	104	6	7	2	26	41		.269	.349	.336	125	9	12	53	24			.968	2	*O	1.1
1910	StL-A	106	380	20	90	11	5	0	27	34		.237	.306	.292	93	-5	-2	38	16			.960	1	*O	-0.8
1911	StL-A	24	81	11	17	3	2	0	7	12		.210	.326	.296	77	-3	-2	9	3			.908	3	O	0.0
Total	9	829	2981	361	762	71	52	14	235	226		.256	.316	.328	101	9	4	377	185			.951	14	O/P	-1.9

■ TEX HOFFMAN Hoffman, Edward Adolph b: 11/30/1893, San Antonio, Tex. d: 5/19/47, New Orleans, La. BL/TR, 5'9", 195 lbs. Deb: 7/11/15

YEAR	TM/L	G	AB	R	H	2B	3B	HR	RBI	BB	SO	AVG	OBP	SLG	PRO+	BR	/A	RC	SB	CS	SBR	FA	FR	POS	TPR
1915	Cle-A	9	13	1	2	0	0	0	2	1	5	.154	.214	.154	10	-1	-1	1	0			.750	-2	/3	-0.3

■ GLENN HOFFMAN Hoffman, Glenn Edward b: 7/7/58, Orange, Cal. BR/TR, 6'2", 190 lbs. Deb: 4/12/80

YEAR	TM/L	G	AB	R	H	2B	3B	HR	RBI	BB	SO	AVG	OBP	SLG	PRO+	BR	/A	RC	SB	CS	SBR	FA	FR	POS	TPR
1980	Bos-A	114	312	37	89	15	4	4	42	19	41	.285	.330	.397	94	-1	-3	39	2	4	-2	.946	-0	*3/S2	-0.6
1981	Bos-A	78	242	28	56	10	0	1	20	12	25	.231	.271	.285	57	-12	-14	18	0	1	-1	.960	5	S/3	-0.2
1982	Bos-A	150	469	53	98	23	2	7	49	30	69	.209	.264	.311	54	-28	-31	35	0	4	-2	.972	13	*S	-0.8
1983	Bos-A	143	473	56	123	24	1	4	41	30	76	.260	.307	.340	73	-14	-19	51	1	1	-0	.962	-6	*S	-1.1
1984	Bos-A	64	74	8	14	4	0	0	4	5	10	.189	.241	.243	33	-7	-7	4	0	1	-1	.957	5	S/32	0.0
1985	Bos-A	96	279	40	77	17	2	6	34	25	40	.276	.346	.416	103	3	2	40	2	2	-1	.975	-1	S/23	0.8
1986	Bos-A	12	23	1	5	2	0	0	1	2	3	.217	.280	.304	59	-1	-1	2	0	0	0	.923	-2	S/3	-0.3
1987	Bos-A	21	55	5	11	3	0	0	6	3	9	.200	.267	.255	38	-5	-5	4	0	0	0	.984	2	S/32	-0.1
	LA-N	40	132	10	29	5	0	0	10	7	23	.220	.270	.258	42	-11	-11	9	0	1	-1	.966	1	S	-0.7
1989	Cal-A	48	104	9	22	3	0	1	3	3	13	.212	.241	.269	44	-8	-8	6	0	2	-1	.982	3	S3/21D	-0.5
Total	9	766	2163	247	524	106	9	23	210	136	309	.242	.293	.331	68	-84	-97	207	5	16	-8	.966	21	S3/2D1	-3.5

■ IZZY HOFFMAN Hoffman, Harry C. b: 1/5/1875, Bridgeport, N.J. d: 11/13/42, Philadelphia, Pa. BL/TL, Deb: 4/14/04

YEAR	TM/L	G	AB	R	H	2B	3B	HR	RBI	BB	SO	AVG	OBP	SLG	PRO+	BR	/A	RC	SB	CS	SBR	FA	FR	POS	TPR
1904	Was-A	10	30	1	3	1	0	0	1	2		.100	.156	.133	-8	-4	-4	1	0			1.000	1	/O	-0.4
1907	Bos-N	19	86	17	24	3	1	0	3	6		.279	.326	.337	108	1	1	10	2			.897	-2	O	-0.2
Total	2	29	116	18	27	4	1	0	4	8		.233	.282	.284	79	-3	-3	11	2			.939	-1	/O	-0.6

■ JOHN HOFFMAN Hoffman, John Edward "Pork Chop" b: 10/31/43, Aberdeen, S.D. BL/TR, 6', 190 lbs. Deb: 7/30/64

YEAR	TM/L	G	AB	R	H	2B	3B	HR	RBI	BB	SO	AVG	OBP	SLG	PRO+	BR	/A	RC	SB	CS	SBR	FA	FR	POS	TPR
1964	Hou-N	6	15	1	1	0	0	0	0	1	7	.067	.125	.067	-47	-3	-3	0	0	0	0	1.000	-2	/C	-0.5
1965	Hou-N	2	6	1	2	0	0	0	1	0	3	.333	.333	.333	95	-0	-0	1	0	0	0	1.000	-1	/C	-0.1
Total	2	8	21	2	3	0	0	0	1	1	10	.143	.182	.143	-8	-3	-3	1	0	0	0	1.000	-2	/C	-0.6

■ LARRY HOFFMAN Hoffman, Lawrence Charles b: 7/18/1878, Chicago, Ill. d: 12/29/48, Chicago, Ill. BR/TR, Deb: 7/09/01

YEAR	TM/L	G	AB	R	H	2B	3B	HR	RBI	BB	SO	AVG	OBP	SLG	PRO+	BR	/A	RC	SB	CS	SBR	FA	FR	POS	TPR
1901	Chi-N	6	22	2	7	1	0	0	6	0		.318	.348	.364	111	0	0	3	1			.800	-2	/32	-0.1

■ HICKEY HOFFMAN Hoffman, Otto Charles b: 10/27/1856, Cleveland, Ohio d: 10/27/15, Peoria, Ill. Deb: 5/10/1879

YEAR	TM/L	G	AB	R	H	2B	3B	HR	RBI	BB	SO	AVG	OBP	SLG	PRO+	BR	/A	RC	SB	CS	SBR	FA	FR	POS	TPR
1879	Cle-N	2	6	0	0	0	0	0	0	0	3	.000	.000	.000	-99	-1	-1	0				.857	0	/CO	-0.1

■ RAY HOFFMAN Hoffman, Raymond Lamont b: 6/14/17, Detroit, Mich. BL/TR, 6'0.5", 175 lbs. Deb: 8/30/42

YEAR	TM/L	G	AB	R	H	2B	3B	HR	RBI	BB	SO	AVG	OBP	SLG	PRO+	BR	/A	RC	SB	CS	SBR	FA	FR	POS	TPR
1942	Was-A	7	19	2	1	0	0	0	2	1	1	.053	.100	.053	-57	-4	-4	0	0	0	0	.815	2	/3	-0.2

■ JESSE HOFFMEISTER Hoffmeister, Jesse H. b: Toledo, Ohio Deb: 7/24/1897

YEAR	TM/L	G	AB	R	H	2B	3B	HR	RBI	BB	SO	AVG	OBP	SLG	PRO+	BR	/A	RC	SB	CS	SBR	FA	FR	POS	TPR
1897	Pit-N	48	188	33	58	6	9	3	36	8		.309	.337	.484	120	3	4	34	6			.792	-13	3	-0.7

■ SOLLY HOFMAN Hofman, Arthur Frederick "Circus Solly" b: 10/29/1882, St.Louis, Mo. d: 3/10/56, St.Louis, Mo. BR/TR, 6', 160 lbs. Deb: 7/28/03

YEAR	TM/L	G	AB	R	H	2B	3B	HR	RBI	BB	SO	AVG	OBP	SLG	PRO+	BR	/A	RC	SB	CS	SBR	FA	FR	POS	TPR
1903	Pit-N	3	2	1	0	0	0	0	0	0		.000	.000	.000	-97	-1	-1	0	0			.000	-1	/O	-0.1
1904	Chi-N	7	26	7	7	0	0	1	4	1		.269	.296	.385	110	0	0	4	2			1.000	0	/OS	0.0
1905	Chi-N	86	287	43	68	14	4	1	38	20		.237	.289	.324	80	-7	-8	33	15			.955	4	2/1S3O	-0.4
1906	*Chi-N	64	195	30	50	2	3	2	20	20		.256	.326	.328	99	1	-0	26	13			.976	-1	O1/S23	-0.3

YEAR	TM/L	G	AB	R	H	2B	3B	HR	RBI	BB	SO	AVG	OBP	SLG	PRO+	BR	/A	RC	SB	CS	SBR	FA	FR	POS	TPR
1907	Chi-N	134	470	67	126	11	3	1	36	41		.268	.328	.311	94	1	-3	62	29			.938	4	OS1/32	0.0
1908	*Chi-N	120	411	55	100	15	5	2	42	33		.243	.307	.319	96	0	-2	46	15			.955	5	O12/3	0.1
1909	Chi-N	153	527	60	150	21	4	2	58	53		.285	.351	.351	115	11	10	74	20			.965	5	*O	1.0
1910	*Chi-N	136	477	83	155	24	16	3	86	65	34	.325	.406	.461	154	32	33	102	29			.975	5	*O1/3	3.4
1911	Chi-N	143	512	66	129	17	2	2	70	66	40	.252	.341	.305	81	-11	-11	65	30			.968	-6	*O1	-2.4
1912	Chi-N	36	125	28	34	11	0	0	18	22	13	.272	.385	.360	105	2	2	19	5			.987	4	O/1	0.4
	Pit-N	17	53	7	15	4	1	0	2	5	6	.283	.345	.396	104	0	0	7	0			1.000	2	O	0.2
	Yr	53	178	35	49	15	1	0	20	27	19	.275	.374	.371	105	2	2	26	5			.991	6	O/1	0.6
1913	Pit-N	28	83	11	19	5	2	0	7	8	6	.229	.297	.337	84	-2	-2	9	3			.964	-1	O	-0.4
1914	Bro-F	147	515	65	148	25	12	5	83	54	41	.287	.357	.412	119	12	13	91	34			.951	5	*21O/S	1.6
1915	Buf-F	109	346	29	81	10	6	0	27	30	28	.234	.295	.298	73	-11	-12	36	12			.961	1	O1/32S	-1.6
1916	NY-A	6	27	0	8	1	1	0	2	1	1	.296	.321	.407	116	0	0	4	1			1.000	2	/O	0.2
	Chi-N	5	16	2	5	2	1	0	2	2	2	.313	.389	.563	172	2	1	4	0			1.000	0	/O	0.2
Total	14	1194	4072	554	1095	162	60	19	495	421	171	.269	.339	.352	104	30	21	582	208			.967	28	O21/S3	1.9

■ BOBBY HOFMAN Hofman, Robert George b: 10/5/25, St.Louis, Mo. BR/TR, 5'11", 175 lbs. Deb: 4/19/49 C

YEAR	TM/L	G	AB	R	H	2B	3B	HR	RBI	BB	SO	AVG	OBP	SLG	PRO+	BR	/A	RC	SB	CS	SBR	FA	FR	POS	TPR
1949	NY-N	19	48	4	10	0	0	0	3	5	6	.208	.296	.208	38	-4	-4	3	0			.939	-0	2	-0.4
1952	NY-N	32	63	11	18	2	2	2	4	8	10	.286	.375	.476	134	3	3	11	0	0	0	.964	3	2/31	0.7
1953	NY-N	74	169	21	45	7	2	12	34	12	23	.266	.315	.544	117	4	3	27	1	1	-0	.918	2	32	0.5
1954	NY-N	71	125	12	28	5	0	8	30	17	15	.224	.322	.456	99	-0	-1	19	0	0	0	.994	-4	12/3	-0.5
1955	NY-N	96	207	32	55	7	2	10	28	22	31	.266	.339	.464	110	3	3	30	0	2	-1	1.000	-5	1C2/3	-0.4
1956	NY-N	47	56	1	10	1	0	0	2	6	8	.179	.270	.196	28	-6	-5	3	0	0	0	1.000	1	/C312	-0.4
1957	NY-N	2	2	0	0	0	0	0	0	0	1	.000	.000	.000	-99	-1	-1	0	0	0	0	.000	0	H	-0.1
Total	7	341	670	81	166	22	6	32	101	70	94	.248	.323	.442	100	-1	-2	93	1	3		.969	-3	/213C	-0.6

■ FRED HOFMANN Hofmann, Fred "Bootnose" b: 6/10/1894, St.Louis, Mo. d: 11/19/64, St.Helena, Cal. BR/TR, 5'11.5", 175 lbs. Deb: 9/26/19 C

YEAR	TM/L	G	AB	R	H	2B	3B	HR	RBI	BB	SO	AVG	OBP	SLG	PRO+	BR	/A	RC	SB	CS	SBR	FA	FR	POS	TPR
1919	NY-A	1	1	0	0	0	0	0	0	0	0	.000	.000	.000	-99	-0	-0	0	0			1.000	0	/C	0.0
1920	NY-A	15	24	3	7	0	0	0	1	1	2	.292	.346	.292	68	-1	-1	2	0	0	0	.905	-4	C	-0.4
1921	NY-A	23	62	7	11	1	1	1	5	5	13	.177	.250	.274	33	-6	-7	4	0	0	0	.952	-0	C/1	-0.6
1922	NY-A	37	91	13	27	5	3	2	10	9	12	.297	.360	.484	116	2	2	16	0	0	0	.962	-4	C	-0.1
1923	*NY-A	72	238	24	69	10	4	3	26	18	27	.290	.350	.403	96	-1	-2	34	2	1	0	.979	-3	C	-0.2
1924	NY-A	62	166	17	29	6	1	1	11	12	15	.175	.239	.241	24	-19	-19	10	2	1	0	.991	2	C	-1.4
1925	NY-A	3	2	0	0	0	0	0	0	0	0	.000	.000	.000	-99	-1	-1	0	0	0	0	1.000	0	/C	0.0
1927	Bos-A	87	217	20	59	19	1	0	24	21	26	.272	.342	.369	86	-5	-4	28	2	0	1	.943	-2	C	-0.1
1928	Bos-A	78	199	14	45	8	1	0	16	11	25	.226	.270	.276	45	-16	-16	15	0	1	-1	.982	4	C	-0.7
Total	9	378	1000	98	247	49	11	7	93	77	120	.247	.308	.339	68	-48	-48	110	6	3		.969	-7	C/1	-3.5

■ HARRY HOGAN Hogan, Harry S. b: 11/1/1875, Syracuse, N.Y. d: 1/24/34, Syracuse, N.Y. Deb: 8/13/01

YEAR	TM/L	G	AB	R	H	2B	3B	HR	RBI	BB	SO	AVG	OBP	SLG	PRO+	BR	/A	RC	SB	CS	SBR	FA	FR	POS	TPR
1901	Cle-A	1	4	0	0	0	0	0	0	0		.000	.000	.000	-99	-1	-1	0	0			.000	-0	/O	-0.1

■ SHANTY HOGAN Hogan, James Francis b: 3/21/06, Somerville, Mass. d: 4/7/67, Boston, Mass. BR/TR, 6'1", 240 lbs. Deb: 6/23/25

YEAR	TM/L	G	AB	R	H	2B	3B	HR	RBI	BB	SO	AVG	OBP	SLG	PRO+	BR	/A	RC	SB	CS	SBR	FA	FR	POS	TPR
1925	Bos-N	9	21	2	6	1	1	0	3	1	3	.286	.318	.429	97	-0	-0	3	0	0	0	1.000	-1	/O	-0.1
1926	Bos-N	4	14	1	4	1	1	0	5	0	0	.286	.286	.500	119	0	0	2	0			.852	1	/C	0.1
1927	Bos-N	71	229	24	66	17	1	3	32	9	23	.288	.324	.410	104	-2	0	29	2			.985	2	C	0.6
1928	NY-N	131	411	48	137	25	2	10	71	42	25	.333	.406	.477	129	19	19	79	0			.978	-10	*C	1.9
1929	NY-N	102	317	19	95	13	0	5	45	25	22	.300	.362	.388	86	-6	-6	44	1			.979	-4	C	-0.2
1930	NY-N	122	389	60	132	26	2	13	75	21	24	.339	.378	.517	116	8	9	73	2			.982	-3	C	1.3
1931	NY-N	123	396	42	119	17	1	12	65	29	29	.301	.354	.439	115	6	8	63	1			**.996**	-0	*C	1.5
1932	NY-N	140	502	36	144	18	2	8	77	26	22	.287	.323	.378	90	-9	-7	62	0			.983	-8	*C	-0.7
1933	Bos-N	96	328	15	83	7	0	3	30	13	9	.253	.288	.302	75	-13	-10	25	0			**.997**	-1	C	-0.6
1934	Bos-N	92	279	20	73	5	2	4	34	16	13	.262	.316	.337	81	-10	-7	27	0			.986	-2	C	-0.5
1935	Bos-N	59	163	9	49	8	0	2	25	21	8	.301	.394	.387	120	4	5	27	0			.990	-4	C	0.4
1936	Was-A	19	65	8	21	4	0	1	7	11	2	.323	.421	.431	117	2	2	12	0	1	-1	.989	2	C	0.4
1937	Was-A	21	66	4	10	4	0	0	5	6	8	.152	.222	.212	10	-9	-9	3	0	1	-1	.979	2	C	-0.6
Total	13	989	3180	288	939	146	12	61	474	220	188	.295	.348	.406	101	-12	3	449	6	2		.985	-26	C/O	3.5

■ KENNY HOGAN Hogan, Kenneth Sylvester b: 10/9/02, Cleveland, Ohio d: 1/2/80, Cleveland, Ohio BL/TR, 5'9", 145 lbs. Deb: 10/02/21

YEAR	TM/L	G	AB	R	H	2B	3B	HR	RBI	BB	SO	AVG	OBP	SLG	PRO+	BR	/A	RC	SB	CS	SBR	FA	FR	POS	TPR
1921	Cin-N	1	2	0	0	0	0	0	0	0	1	.000	.000	.000	-99	-1	-1	0	0	0	0	.000	-1	/O	-0.1
1923	Cle-A	1	0	0	0	0	0	0	0	0	0	—	—	—	—	0	0	0	0	0	0	.000	0	R	0.0
1924	Cle-A	2	1	0	0	0	0	0	0	0	0	.000	.000	.000	-99	-0	-0	0	0	0	0	.000	0	H	0.0
Total	3	4	3	0	0	0	0	0	0	0	1	.000	.000	.000	-99	-1	-1	0	0	0	0		-1	/O	-0.1

■ MARTY HOGAN Hogan, Martin F. b: 10/15/1869, Wensbury, England d: 8/15/23, Youngstown, Ohio 5'8", 145 lbs. Deb: 8/06/1894

YEAR	TM/L	G	AB	R	H	2B	3B	HR	RBI	BB	SO	AVG	OBP	SLG	PRO+	BR	/A	RC	SB	CS	SBR	FA	FR	POS	TPR
1894	Cin-N	6	23	4	3	0	0	0	3	1	4	.130	.167	.130	-26	-5	-5	1	2			.846	-0	/O	-0.4
	StL-N	29	100	11	28	3	4	0	13	3	13	.280	.308	.390	69	-5	-5	15	7			.887	-1	O	-0.7
	Yr	35	123	15	31	3	4	0	16	4	17	.252	.281	.341	50	-10	-10	15	9			.879	-2	O	-1.1
1895	StL-N	5	18	2	3	1	0	0	2	3	0	.167	.286	.222	34	-2	-2	2	2			.833	1	/O	-0.1
Total	2	40	141	17	34	4	4	0	18	7	17	.241	.282	.326	49	-12	-12	18	11			.869	-1	/O	-1.2

■ EDDIE HOGAN Hogan, Robert Edward b: 4/1860, St.Louis, Mo. BR , 5'7", 153 lbs. Deb: 7/05/1882

YEAR	TM/L	G	AB	R	H	2B	3B	HR	RBI	BB	SO	AVG	OBP	SLG	PRO+	BR	/A	RC	SB	CS	SBR	FA	FR	POS	TPR
1882	StL-a	1	3	1	1	0	0	0		0		.333	.333	.333	121	0	0	0				.333	-1	/P	0.0
1884	Mil-U	11	37	6	3	1	0	0		7		.081	.227	.108	31	-3	0	1				.806	7	O	0.6
1887	NY-a	32	120	22	24	6	1	0		30		.200	.373	.267	86	-1	0	17	12			.750	-7	O/S3	-0.6
1888	Cle-a	78	269	60	61	16	6	0	24	50		.227	.368	.331	132	12	13	45	30			.896	-5	O	0.6
Total	4	122	429	89	89	23	7	0	24	87		.207	.357	.294	113	8	14	63	42			.844	-6	O/S3P	0.6

■ WILLIE HOGAN Hogan, William Henry "Happy" b: 9/14/1884, N.San Juan, Cal. d: 9/28/74, San Jose, Cal. BR/TR, 5'10", 175 lbs. Deb: 4/12/11 F

YEAR	TM/L	G	AB	R	H	2B	3B	HR	RBI	BB	SO	AVG	OBP	SLG	PRO+	BR	/A	RC	SB	CS	SBR	FA	FR	POS	TPR
1911	Phi-A	7	19	1	2	1	0	0	2	0		.105	.105	.158	-28	-3	-3	0	0			.900	0	/O	-0.3
	StL-A	123	443	53	115	17	8	2	62	43		.260	.328	.348	92	-7	-5	57	18			.929	13	*O/1	0.2
	Yr	130	462	54	117	18	8	2	64	43		.253	.320	.340	87	-10	-8	56	18			.928	13	*O/1	-0.1
1912	StL-A	108	360	32	77	10	2	1	36	34		.214	.284	.261	58	-20	-19	32	17			.972	11	*O	-1.3
Total	2	238	822	86	194	28	10	3	100	77		.236	.304	.305	75	-31	-26	89	35			.947	24	O/1	-1.4

■ BERT HOGG Hogg, Wilbert George "Sonny" b: 4/21/13, Detroit, Mich. d: 11/5/73, Detroit, Mich. BR/TR, 5'11.5", 162 lbs. Deb: 6/01/34

YEAR	TM/L	G	AB	R	H	2B	3B	HR	RBI	BB	SO	AVG	OBP	SLG	PRO+	BR	/A	RC	SB	CS	SBR	FA	FR	POS	TPR
1934	Bro-N	2	1	0	0	0	0	0	0	0	0	.000	.000	.000	-99	-0	-0	0	0			.000	0	/3	0.0

■ GEORGE HOGRIEVER Hogriever, George C. b: 3/17/1869, Cincinnati, Ohio d: 1/26/61, Appleton, Wis. BR/TR, 5'8", 160 lbs. Deb: 4/24/1895

YEAR	TM/L	G	AB	R	H	2B	3B	HR	RBI	BB	SO	AVG	OBP	SLG	PRO+	BR	/A	RC	SB	CS	SBR	FA	FR	POS	TPR
1895	Cin-N	69	239	61	65	8	7	2	34	36	17	.272	.374	.389	95	1	-1	52	41			.934	2	O/2	-0.3
1901	Mil-A	54	221	25	52	10	2	0	16	30		.235	.329	.299	79	-7	-5	25	7			.901	2	O	-0.6
Total	2	123	460	86	117	18	9	2	50	66	17	.254	.353	.346	88	-6	-6	77	48			.920	4	O/2	-0.9

■ BILL HOHMAN Hohman, William Henry b: 11/27/03, Brooklyn, Md. d: 10/29/68, Baltimore, Md. BR/TR, 6', 178 lbs. Deb: 8/24/27

YEAR	TM/L	G	AB	R	H	2B	3B	HR	RBI	BB	SO	AVG	OBP	SLG	PRO+	BR	/A	RC	SB	CS	SBR	FA	FR	POS	TPR
1927	Phi-N	7	18	1	5	0	0	0	0	2	3	.278	.350	.278	69	-1	-1	2	0			.917	-0	/O	-0.1

■ EDDIE HOHNHORST Hohnhorst, Edward Hicks b: 1/31/1885, Kentucky d: 3/28/16, Covington, Ky. BL/TL, 6'1", 175 lbs. Deb: 9/10/10

YEAR	TM/L	G	AB	R	H	2B	3B	HR	RBI	BB	SO	AVG	OBP	SLG	PRO+	BR	/A	RC	SB	CS	SBR	FA	FR	POS	TPR
1910	Cle-A	18	63	8	20	3	1	0	6	4		.317	.358	.397	135	2	2	10	3			.972	-1	1	0.1

YEAR	TM/L	G	AB	R	H	2B	3B	HR	RBI	BB	SO	AVG	OBP	SLG	PRO+	BR	/A	RC	SB	CS	SBR	FA	FR	POS	TPR
1912	Cle-A	15	54	5	11	1	0	0	2	2		.204	.232	.222	29	-5	-5	4	5			.963	-1	1	-0.6
Total	2	33	117	13	31	4	1	0	8	6		.265	.301	.316	83	-3	-3	14	8			.968	-2	/1	-0.5

■ CHRIS HOILES
Hoiles, Christopher Allen b: 3/20/65, Bowling Green, O. BR/TR, 6', 195 lbs. Deb: 4/25/89

YEAR	TM/L	G	AB	R	H	2B	3B	HR	RBI	BB	SO	AVG	OBP	SLG	PRO+	BR	/A	RC	SB	CS	SBR	FA	FR	POS	TPR
1989	Bal-A	6	9	0	1	1	0	0	1	1	3	.111	.200	.222	19	-1	-1	0	0	0	0	1.000	1	/CD	0.0
1990	Bal-A	23	63	7	12	3	0	1	6	5	12	.190	.250	.286	51	-4	-4	5	0	0	0	1.000	-1	/C1D	-0.5
1991	Bal-A	107	341	36	83	15	0	11	31	29	61	.243	.305	.384	93	-6	-4	37	0	2	-1	**.998**	-14	CD/1	-1.4
1992	Bal-A	96	310	49	85	10	1	20	40	55	60	.274	.387	.506	149	21	21	62	0	2	-1	.994	-11	C/D	1.5
Total	4	232	723	92	181	29	1	32	78	90	136	.250	.336	.426	113	10	12	104	0	4	-2	.996	-25	C/D1	-0.4

■ BILL HOLBERT
Holbert, William Henry b: 3/14/1855, Baltimore, Md. d: 3/20/35, Laurel, Md. BR/TR, Deb: 9/05/1876 MU

YEAR	TM/L	G	AB	R	H	2B	3B	HR	RBI	BB	SO	AVG	OBP	SLG	PRO+	BR	/A	RC	SB	CS	SBR	FA	FR	POS	TPR
1876	Lou-N	12	43	3	11	0	0	0	5	0	3	.256	.256	.256	60	-1	-2	3				.843	7	C	0.4
1878	Mil-N	45	173	10	32	2	0	0	12	3	14	.185	.199	.197	28	-13	-14	7				.818	7	OC	-0.8
1879	Syr-N	59	229	11	46	0	0	0	21	1	20	.201	.204	.201	39	-16	-12	10				.897	-1	*C/OM	-1.0
	Tro-N	4	15	1	4	0	0	0	2	0	1	.267	.267	.267	82	-0	-0	1				.893	1	/C	0.0
	Yr	63	244	12	50	0	0	0	23	1	21	.205	.208	.205	41	-16	-12	11				.897	0	C/O	-1.0
1880	Tro-N	60	212	18	40	5	1	0	8	9	18	.189	.222	.222	48	-10	-12	11				.911	12	*C/O	0.1
1881	Tro-N	46	180	16	49	3	0	0	14	3	13	.272	.284	.289	77	-4	-5	15				.918	7	C/O	0.3
1882	Tro-N	71	251	24	46	5	0	0	23	11	22	.183	.218	.203	38	-17	-16	11				.892	16	*C3/O	0.2
1883	NY-a	73	299	26	71	9	1	0		1		.237	.240	.274	63	-11	-13	20				.920	**35**	*C/O2	2.3
1884	*NY-a	65	255	28	53	5	0	0		7		.208	.235	.227	55	-12	-11	14				.920	21	C/OS	1.4
1885	NY-a	56	202	13	35	3	0	0		8		.173	.205	.188	29	-16	-14	8				.900	12	CO/3	0.2
1886	NY-a	48	171	8	35	4	2	0		6		.205	.232	.251	55	-9	-8	11	4			.922	19	C/OS	1.4
1887	NY-a	69	255	20	58	4	3	0		7		.227	.248	.267	47	-19	-17	20	12			.894	2	C/1S2	-0.8
1888	Bro-a	15	50	4	6	1	0	0	1	2		.120	.170	.140	1	-5	-5	1	0			.926	2	C	-0.2
Total	12	623	2335	182	486	41	7	0	86	58	91	.208	.228	.232	48	-135	-130	133	16			.907	140	C/O31S2	3.5

■ SAMMY HOLBROOK
Holbrook, James Marbury b: 7/17/10, Meridian, Miss. d: 4/10/91, Jackson, Miss. BR/TR, 5'11", 189 lbs. Deb: 4/25/35

YEAR	TM/L	G	AB	R	H	2B	3B	HR	RBI	BB	SO	AVG	OBP	SLG	PRO+	BR	/A	RC	SB	CS	SBR	FA	FR	POS	TPR
1935	Was-A	52	135	20	35	2	2	2	25	30	16	.259	.408	.348	101	1	2	22	0	0	0	.952	-11	C	-0.7

■ JOE HOLDEN
Holden, Joseph Francis "Socks" b: 6/4/13, St.Clair, Pa. BL/TR, 5'8", 175 lbs. Deb: 6/14/34

YEAR	TM/L	G	AB	R	H	2B	3B	HR	RBI	BB	SO	AVG	OBP	SLG	PRO+	BR	/A	RC	SB	CS	SBR	FA	FR	POS	TPR
1934	Phi-N	10	14	1	1	0	0	0	0	0	2	.071	.071	.071	-54	-3	-3	0	0			1.000	2	/C	-0.1
1935	Phi-N	6	9	0	1	0	0	0	0	0	3	.111	.111	.111	-36	-2	-2	-0	1			1.000	-1	/C	-0.2
1936	Phi-N	1	1	0	0	0	0	0	0	0	0	.000	.000	.000	-91	-0	-0	0	0			.000	0	H	0.0
Total	3	17	24	1	2	0	0	0	0	0	5	.083	.083	.083	-49	-5	-6	-0	1			1.000	2	/C	-0.3

■ BILL HOLDEN
Holden, William Paul b: 9/7/1889, Birmingham, Ala. d: 9/14/71, Pensacola, Fla. BR/TR, 6', 170 lbs. Deb: 9/11/13

YEAR	TM/L	G	AB	R	H	2B	3B	HR	RBI	BB	SO	AVG	OBP	SLG	PRO+	BR	/A	RC	SB	CS	SBR	FA	FR	POS	TPR
1913	NY-A	18	53	6	16	3	1	0	8	8	5	.302	.393	.396	131	2	2	9	0			.977	3	O	0.5
1914	NY-A	50	165	12	30	3	2	0	12	16	26	.182	.254	.224	44	-11	-11	9	2	4	-2	.981	-1	O	-1.8
	Cin-N	11	28	2	6	0	0	0	1	3	5	.214	.290	.214	49	-2	-2	2	0			1.000	-2	O	-0.4
Total	2	79	246	20	52	6	3	0	21	27	36	.211	.289	.260	64	-11	-11	20	2	4		.981	0	/O	-1.7

■ JIM HOLDSWORTH
Holdsworth, James "Long Jim" b: 7/14/1850, New York, N.Y. d: 3/22/18, New York, N.Y. BR/TR, Deb: 5/14/1872

YEAR	TM/L	G	AB	R	H	2B	3B	HR	RBI	BB	SO	AVG	OBP	SLG	PRO+	BR	/A	RC	SB	CS	SBR	FA	FR	POS	TPR
1872	Cle-n	22	111	19	33	5	1	0	11	1	2	.297	.304	.360	110	0	2	13						*S	0.1
	Eck-n	2	7	1	2	0	0	0	0	0	0	.286	.286	.286	90	-0	0	1						/S	0.0
	Yr	24	118	20	35	5	1	0	11	1	2	.297	.303	.356	109	0	2	13						S	0.1
1873	Mut-n	53	233	46	75	6	8	0	27	0	3	.322	.322	.416	116	4	4	32						*S	0.2
1874	Phi-n	57	286	60	97	8	9	0		1		.339	.341	.430	139	13	12	43						3S/O	0.8
1875	Mut-n	71	325	45	91	11	1	0		1		.280	.282	.320	102	2	-0	30						OS	-0.1
1876	NY-N	52	241	23	64	3	2	0	19	1	2	.266	.269	.295	101	-3	2	20				.902	1	*O/2	0.1
1877	Har-N	55	260	26	66	5	2	0	20	2	8	.254	.260	.288	81	-8	-4	20				.833	-3	*O	-0.8
1882	Tro-N	1	3	0	0	0	0	0	0	0	1	.000	.000	.000	-99	-1	-1	0				1.000	1	/O	0.0
1884	Ind-a	5	18	1	2	0	0	0		2		.111	.200	.111	6	-2	-2	0				.929	1	/O	0.0
Total	4 n	205	962	171	298	30	19	0	38	3	5	.310	.312	.380	118	20	17	119						S/O3	1.0
Total	4	113	522	50	132	8	4	0	39	5	11	.253	.260	.284	86	-14	-5	40				.875	0	O/2	-0.7

■ WALTER HOLKE
Holke, Walter Henry "Union Man" b: 12/25/1892, St.Louis, Mo. d: 10/12/54, St.Louis, Mo. BB/TL, 6'1.5", 185 lbs. Deb: 10/06/14 C

YEAR	TM/L	G	AB	R	H	2B	3B	HR	RBI	BB	SO	AVG	OBP	SLG	PRO+	BR	/A	RC	SB	CS	SBR	FA	FR	POS	TPR
1914	NY-N	2	6	0	2	0	0	0	0	0	0	.333	.333	.333	102	-0	-0	1	0			.950	0	/1	0.0
1916	NY-N	34	111	16	39	4	2	0	13	6	16	.351	.390	.423	158	6	7	22	10			.997	-0	1	0.6
1917	*NY-N	153	527	55	146	12	7	2	55	34	54	.277	.327	.338	107	3	4	61	13			.989	-5	*1	-0.8
1918	NY-N	88	326	38	82	17	4	1	27	10	26	.252	.276	.337	88	-6	-6	32	10			.990	5	1	-0.5
1919	Bos-N	137	518	48	151	14	6	0	48	21	25	.292	.325	.342	105	0	2	63	19			.993	6	*1	0.4
1920	Bos-N	144	551	53	162	15	11	3	64	28	31	.294	.329	.377	107	1	4	66	4	11	-5	.991	-3	*1	-0.8
1921	Bos-N	150	579	60	151	15	10	3	63	17	41	.261	.284	.337	67	-31	-27	53	8	11	-4	**.997**	3	*1	-3.2
1922	Bos-N	105	395	35	115	9	4	0	46	14	23	.291	.317	.334	71	-19	-16	40	6	8	-3	.993	-4	*1	-2.6
1923	Phi-N	147	562	64	175	31	4	7	70	16	37	.311	.330	.418	86	-5	-13	74	7	9	-3	.991	-1	*1/P	-2.5
1924	Phi-N	148	563	60	169	23	6	6	64	25	33	.300	.330	.394	83	-6	-15	70	3	8	-4	.993	4	*1	-2.4
1925	Phi-N	39	86	11	21	5	0	1	17	3	6	.244	.270	.337	50	-6	-7	8	0	0	0	.994	1	1	-0.7
	Cin-N	65	232	24	65	8	4	1	20	17	12	.280	.329	.362	78	-8	-7	28	1	3	-2	.997	1	1	-1.1
	Yr	104	318	35	86	13	4	2	37	20	18	.270	.314	.355	69	-14	-15	35	1	3	-2	.996	2	1	-1.8
Total	11	1212	4456	464	1278	153	58	24	487	191	304	.287	.318	.363	89	-71	-74	517	81	50		.993	7	*1/P	-13.6

■ BILL HOLLAHAN
Hollahan, William James "Happy" b: 11/22/1896, New York, N.Y. d: 11/27/65, New York, N.Y. BR/TR, 5'8", 165 lbs. Deb: 9/27/20

YEAR	TM/L	G	AB	R	H	2B	3B	HR	RBI	BB	SO	AVG	OBP	SLG	PRO+	BR	/A	RC	SB	CS	SBR	FA	FR	POS	TPR
1920	Was-A	3	4	0	1	0	0	0	1	1	2	.250	.400	.250	77	-0	-0	1	1	0	0	1.000	0	/3	0.1

■ DUTCH HOLLAND
Holland, Robert Clyde b: 10/12/03, Middlesex, N.C. d: 6/16/67, Lumberton, N.C. BR/TR, 6'1", 190 lbs. Deb: 8/16/32

YEAR	TM/L	G	AB	R	H	2B	3B	HR	RBI	BB	SO	AVG	OBP	SLG	PRO+	BR	/A	RC	SB	CS	SBR	FA	FR	POS	TPR
1932	Bos-N	39	156	15	46	11	1	1	18	12	20	.295	.345	.397	103	-0	1	22	0			.990	2	O	0.0
1933	Bos-N	13	31	3	8	3	0	0	3	3	8	.258	.324	.355	102	-0	0	4	1			.867	-1	/O	-0.2
1934	Cle-A	50	128	19	32	12	1	2	13	13	11	.250	.319	.406	85	-3	-3	17	0	0	0	.957	-4	O	-0.8
Total	3	102	315	37	86	26	2	3	34	28	39	.273	.332	.397	95	-3	-3	43	1	0		.969	-3	/O	-1.0

■ WILL HOLLAND
Holland, Willard A. b: Georgetown, Del. d: 7/19/30, Philadelphia, Pa. 5'10", 180 lbs. Deb: 7/10/1889

YEAR	TM/L	G	AB	R	H	2B	3B	HR	RBI	BB	SO	AVG	OBP	SLG	PRO+	BR	/A	RC	SB	CS	SBR	FA	FR	POS	TPR
1889	Bal-a	40	143	13	27	1	2	0	16	9	28	.189	.247	.224	35	-12	-12	9	4			.853	-15	S/O	-2.2

■ GARY HOLLE
Holle, Gary Charles b: 8/11/54, Albany, N.Y. BR/TL, 6'6", 210 lbs. Deb: 6/02/79

YEAR	TM/L	G	AB	R	H	2B	3B	HR	RBI	BB	SO	AVG	OBP	SLG	PRO+	BR	/A	RC	SB	CS	SBR	FA	FR	POS	TPR
1979	Tex-A	5	6	0	1	1	0	0	0	1	0	.167	.286	.333	67	-0	-0	1	0	0	0	1.000	-0	/1	-0.1

■ BUG HOLLIDAY
Holliday, James Wear b: 2/8/1867, St.Louis, Mo. d: 2/15/10, Cincinnati, Ohio BR/TR, 5'11", 151 lbs. Deb: 4/17/1889 U

YEAR	TM/L	G	AB	R	H	2B	3B	HR	RBI	BB	SO	AVG	OBP	SLG	PRO+	BR	/A	RC	SB	CS	SBR	FA	FR	POS	TPR
1889	Cin-a	135	563	107	181	28	7	**19**	104	43	59	.321	.372	.497	144	33	30	124	46			.923	-7	*O	1.7
1890	Cin-N	131	518	93	140	18	14	4	75	49	36	.270	.341	.382	114	8	9	87	50			.948	-2	*O	0.2
1891	Cin-N	111	442	74	141	21	10	9	84	37	28	.319	.376	.473	148	26	25	92	30			.939	-8	*O	1.2
1892	Cin-N	152	602	114	176	23	16	**13**	91	57	39	.292	.355	.449	147	30	31	114	43			.933	-4	*O/P	2.0
1893	Cin-N	126	500	108	155	24	10	5	89	73	22	.310	.401	.428	119	18	16	101	32			.944	-10	*O/1	-0.1
1894	Cin-N	121	511	119	190	24	7	13	119	40	20	.372	.420	.523	123	23	19	128	29			.914	0	*O/1	0.8
1895	Cin-N	32	127	25	38	9	2	0	20	10	3	.299	.350	.402	92	-1	-2	21	6			.940	-4	O	-0.7
1896	Cin-N	29	84	17	27	4	0	0	8	9	4	.321	.394	.369	97	1	-0	13	1			.925	-2	O/1SP	-0.3

YEAR	TM/L	G	AB	R	H	2B	3B	HR	RBI	BB	SO	AVG	OBP	SLG	PRO+	BR	/A	RC	SB	CS	SBR	FA	FR	POS	TPR
1897	Cin-N	61	195	50	61	9	4	2	20	27		.313	.399	.431	112	6	4	37	6			.940	-7	O/S21	-0.5
1898	Cin-N	30	106	21	25	2	1	0	7	14		.236	.325	.274	67	-3	-5	12	5			.969	-2	O	-0.8
Total	10	928	3648	728	1134	162	71	65	617	359	211	.311	.376	.448	127	140	127	728	248			.935	-45	O/1S2P	3.5
■ HOLLY HOLLINGSHEAD	Hollingshead, John Samuel (a.k.a. Samuel John Holly) b: 1/17/1853, Washington, D.C. d: 10/6/26, Washington, D.C. Deb: 4/20/1872 M																								
1872	Nat-n	9	46	12	15	0	1	0	5	1	0	.326	.340	.370	102	1	-1	6						/2	-0.1
1873	Was-n	30	136	25	35	1	3	0	19	0	6	.257	.257	.309	68	-6	-5	11						O/2	-0.3
1875	Was-n	19	81	7	20	0	2	0		0		.247	.247	.296	90	-1	-1	6						OM	0.0
Total	3 n	58	263	44	70	1	6	0		1		.266	.269	.316	81	-6	-6	23						/O2	-0.4
■ DAVE HOLLINS	Hollins, David Michaels b: 5/25/66, Buffalo, N.Y. BB/TR, 6'1", 195 lbs. Deb: 4/12/90																								
1990	Phi-N	72	114	14	21	0	0	5	15	10	28	.184	.256	.316	57	-7	-7	10	0	0	0	.932	-1	3/1	-0.9
1991	Phi-N	56	151	18	45	10	2	6	21	17	26	.298	.380	.510	150	10	10	30	1	1	-0	.922	-3	3/1	0.6
1992	Phi-N	156	586	104	158	28	4	27	93	76	110	.270	.372	.469	138	30	30	107	9	6	-1	.954	-20	*3/1	1.1
Total	3	284	851	136	224	38	6	38	129	103	164	.263	.358	.456	129	32	33	146	10	7	-1	.946	-24	3/1	0.8
■ STAN HOLLMIG	Hollmig, Stanley Ernest "Hondo" b: 1/2/26, Fredericksburg, Tex d: 12/4/81, San Antonio, Tex. BR/TR, 6'2.5", 190 lbs. Deb: 4/19/49																								
1949	Phi-N	81	251	28	64	11	6	2	26	20	43	.255	.315	.371	85	-6	-5	28	1			.958	-6	O	-1.4
1950	Phi-N	11	12	1	3	2	0	0	1	0	3	.250	.250	.417	73	-1	-1	1	0			1.000	-1	/O	-0.1
1951	Phi-N	2	2	0	0	0	0	0	0	0	0	.000	.000	.000	-99	-1	-1	0	0	0	0	.000	0	H	-0.1
Total	3	94	265	29	67	13	6	2	27	20	46	.253	.310	.370	84	-7	-6	29	1	0		.959	-6	/O	-1.6
■ CHARLIE HOLLOCHER	Hollocher, Charles Jacob b: 6/11/1896, St.Louis, Mo. d: 8/14/40, Frontenac, Mo. BL/TR, 5'7", 154 lbs. Deb: 4/16/18																								
1918	*Chi-N	131	509	72	**161**	23	6	2	38	47	30	.316	.379	.397	133	23	22	**85**	26			.929	-19	*S	0.9
1919	Chi-N	115	430	51	116	14	5	3	26	44	19	.270	.347	.347	108	6	6	57	16			.941	6	*S	2.0
1920	Chi-N	80	301	53	96	17	2	0	22	41	15	.319	.406	.389	126	13	13	49	20	14	-2	.954	9	S	2.7
1921	Chi-N	140	558	71	161	28	8	3	37	43	13	.289	.342	.384	91	-6	-6	70	5	16	-8	**.963**	3	*S	0.2
1922	Chi-N	152	592	90	201	37	8	3	69	58	5	.340	.403	.444	116	18	16	100	19	29	-12	**.965**	-5	*S	1.4
1923	Chi-N	66	260	46	89	14	2	1	28	26	5	.342	.410	.423	120	9	9	44	9	10	-3	.963	-9	S	0.3
1924	Chi-N	76	286	28	70	12	4	2	21	18	7	.245	.292	.336	67	-13	-14	26	4	11	-5	.969	4	S	-0.8
Total	7	760	2936	411	894	145	35	14	241	277	94	.304	.370	.392	110	50	45	432	99	80		.954	-13	S	6.7
■ ED HOLLY	Holly, Edward William (b: Edward William Ruthlavy) b: 7/6/1879, Chicago, Ill. d: 11/27/73, Williamsport, Pa. BR/TR, 5'10", 165 lbs. Deb: 7/18/06																								
1906	StL-N	10	34	1	2	0	0	0	7	5		.059	.179	.059	-26	-5	-5	0	0			.939	-3	S	-0.8
1907	StL-N	150	545	55	125	18	3	1	40	36		.229	.283	.279	79	-15	-13	51	16			.927	13	*S/2	0.4
1914	Pit-F	100	350	28	86	9	4	0	26	17	52	.246	.281	.294	64	-17	-17	35	14			.942	-2	S/O2	-1.2
1915	Pit-F	16	42	8	11	2	0	0	5	5	6	.262	.354	.310	97	0	0	6	3			.865	-4	S/3	-0.4
Total	4	276	971	92	224	29	7	1	78	63	58	.231	.282	.278	71	-37	-34	93	33			.931	4	S/23O	-2.0
■ WATTIE HOLM	Holm, Roscoe Albert b: 12/28/01, Peterson, Iowa d: 5/19/50, Everly, Iowa BR/TR, 5'9.5", 160 lbs. Deb: 4/15/24																								
1924	StL-N	81	293	40	86	10	4	0	23	8	16	.294	.317	.355	81	-9	-8	32	1	4	-2	.988	2	O/C3	-1.3
1925	StL-N	13	58	10	12	1	1	0	2	3	1	.207	.246	.259	28	-6	-6	4	1	0	0	.976	2	O	-0.5
1926	*StL-N	55	144	18	41	5	1	0	21	18	14	.285	.364	.333	85	-2	-2	18	3			.962	-3	O	-0.8
1927	StL-N	110	419	55	120	27	8	3	66	24	29	.286	.327	.411	93	-3	-5	54	4			.967	-8	O/3	-1.9
1928	*StL-N	102	386	61	107	24	6	3	47	32	17	.277	.334	.394	88	-6	-7	50	1			.918	-10	3/O	-1.3
1929	StL-N	64	176	21	41	5	6	0	14	12	8	.233	.282	.330	50	-14	-14	16	1			.944	3	O/3	-1.3
1932	StL-N	11	17	2	3	1	0	0	1	3	1	.176	.333	.235	55	-1	-1	2	0			1.000	0	/O	-0.1
Total	7	436	1493	207	410	73	26	6	174	100	86	.275	.322	.370	81	-41	-44	176	11	4		.970	-15	O/3C	-7.2
■ BILLY HOLM	Holm, William Frederick Henry b: 7/21/12, Chicago, Ill. d: 7/27/77, East Chicago, Ind BR/TR, 5'10.5", 168 lbs. Deb: 9/24/43																								
1943	Chi-N	7	15	0	1	0	0	0	0	2	4	.067	.176	.067	-29	-2	-2	0	0			1.000	1	/C	-0.1
1944	Chi-N	54	132	10	18	2	0	0	6	16	19	.136	.235	.152	10	-15	-15	6	1			.979	-2	C	-1.6
1945	Bos-A	58	135	12	25	2	1	0	9	23	17	.185	.317	.215	54	-7	-7	11	1	1	-0	.980	-4	C	-0.9
Total	3	119	282	22	44	4	1	0	15	41	40	.156	.272	.177	30	-24	-25	17	2	1		.981	-4	C	-2.6
■ GARY HOLMAN	Holman, Gary Richard b: 1/25/44, Long Beach, Cal. BL/TL, 6'1", 200 lbs. Deb: 6/26/68																								
1968	Was-A	75	85	10	25	5	1	0	7	13	15	.294	.388	.376	137	4	4	13	0	0	0	1.000	2	1O	0.6
1969	Was-A	41	31	1	5	1	0	0	2	4	7	.161	.257	.194	29	-3	-3	2	0	0	0	1.000	-1	1/O	-0.4
Total	2	116	116	11	30	6	1	0	9	17	22	.259	.353	.328	107	1	1	15	0	0	0	1.000	1	/1O	0.2
■ FRED HOLMES	Holmes, Frederick C. b: 7/1/1878, Chicago, Ill. d: 2/13/56, Norwood Park, Ill. BR/TR, Deb: 8/23/03																								
1903	NY-A	1	0	0	0	0	0	0	0	1		—	1.000	—	208	0	0	0	0			.833	-0	/1	0.0
1904	Chi-N	1	3	1	1	1	0	0	0	0		.333	.333	.667	207	0	0	1	0			1.000	0	/C	0.0
Total	2	2	3	1	1	1	0	0	0	1		.333	.500	.667	256	1	1	1	0				-0	/C1	0.0
■ DUCKY HOLMES	Holmes, Howard Elbert b: 7/8/1883, Dayton, Ohio d: 9/18/45, Dayton, Ohio BR/TR, 5'10", 160 lbs. Deb: 4/18/06																								
1906	StL-N	9	27	2	5	0	0	0	2	2		.185	.267	.185	43	-2	-2	1	0			.979	-1	/C	-0.1
■ DUCKY HOLMES	Holmes, James William b: 1/28/1869, Des Moines, Iowa d: 8/6/32, Truro, Iowa BL/TR, 5'6", 170 lbs. Deb: 8/08/1895																								
1895	Lou-N	40	161	33	60	10	2	3	20	12	9	.373	.426	.516	154	11	12	40	9			.780	-11	O/S3P	0.0
1896	Lou-N	47	141	22	38	3	2	0	18	13	5	.270	.360	.319	85	-3	-2	20	8			.790	-7	O/PS2	-1.0
1897	Lou-N	2	4	0	0	0	0	0	0	1		.000	.200	.000	-46	-1	-1	0	0			1.000	1	/S	0.0
	NY-N	79	306	51	82	8	6	1	44	18		.268	.317	.343	76	-12	-10	44	30			.904	-7	O/S	-2.0
	Yr	81	310	51	82	8	6	1	44	19		.265	.315	.339	75	-13	-11	44	30			.904	-6	O/S	-2.0
1898	StL-N	23	101	9	24	1	1	0	0	2		.238	.260	.267	50	-7	-7	8	4			.900	2	O	-0.6
	Bal-N	113	442	54	126	10	9	1	64	23		.285	.333	.355	96	-2	-3	63	25			.935	4	*O	-0.7
	Yr	136	543	63	150	11	10	1	64	25		.276	.320	.339	87	-9	-10	71	29			.930	6	*O	-1.3
1899	Bal-N	138	553	80	177	31	7	4	66	39		.320	.381	.423	114	15	11	112	50			.927	6	*O	0.6
1901	Det-A	131	537	90	158	28	10	4	62	37		.294	.347	.406	103	5	2	91	35			.907	-2	*O	-0.9
1902	Det-A	92	362	50	93	15	4	2	33	28		.257	.321	.337	81	-8	-9	46	16			.950	6	O	-0.9
1903	Was-A	21	71	13	16	3	1	1	8	5		.225	.286	.338	85	-1	-1	10	10			.912	1	O/32	-0.1
	Chi-A	86	344	53	96	7	5	0	18	25		.279	.335	.328	104	1	3	49	25			.965	2	O/3	0.0
	Yr	107	415	66	112	10	6	1	26	30		.270	.327	.330	101	-0	1	60	35			.956	3	O/32	-0.1
1904	Chi-A	68	251	42	78	11	9	1	19	14		.311	.354	.438	156	14	15	46	13			.975	2	O	1.4
1905	Chi-A	92	328	42	66	15	2	0	22	19		.201	.258	.259	67	-13	-12	29	11			.936	-1	O	-1.9
Total	10	932	3601	539	1014	142	58	17	374	236	14	.282	.337	.367	100	-1	-3	560	236				-5	O/3SP2	-6.1
■ TOMMY HOLMES	Holmes, Thomas Francis "Kelly" b: 3/29/17, Brooklyn, N.Y. BL/TL, 5'10", 180 lbs. Deb: 4/14/42 M																								
1942	Bos-N	141	558	56	155	24	4	4	41	64	10	.278	.353	.357	110	7	8	76	2			.990	15	*O	1.6
1943	Bos-N	152	629	75	170	33	10	5	41	58	20	.270	.334	.378	107	4	5	82	7			.993	8	*O	0.5
1944	Bos-N	155	631	93	195	42	6	13	73	61	11	.309	.372	.456	127	26	23	110	4			.991	6	*O	2.1
1945	Bos-N†	154	636	125	**224**	**47**	6	**28**	117	70	9	.352	.420	**.577**	**175**	**63**	**62**	**156**	15			.983	1	*O	**5.4**
1946	Bos-N	149	568	80	176	35	6	6	79	58	14	.310	.377	.424	126	20	19	91	7			.987	8	*O	2.1
1947	Bos-N	150	618	90	**191**	33	3	9	53	44	16	.309	.360	.416	108	4	6	91	3			.989	10	*O	0.8
1948	*Bos-N★	139	585	85	190	35	7	6	61	46	20	.325	.375	.439	122	16	17	94	1			.983	3	*O	1.2
1949	Bos-N	117	380	47	101	20	4	8	59	39	6	.266	.337	.403	103	-2	1	51	1			.987	5	*O	0.1

YEAR	TM/L	G	AB	R	H	2B	3B	HR	RBI	BB	SO	AVG	OBP	SLG	PRO+	BR	/A	RC	SB	CS	SBR	FA	FR	POS	TPR
1950	Bos-N	105	322	44	96	20	1	9	51	33	8	.298	.370	.450	122	7	10	53	0			1.000	-0	O	0.6
1951	Bos-N	27	29	1	5	2	0	0	5	3	4	.172	.250	.241	35	-3	-2	2	0	0	0	1.000	-1	/OM	-0.4
1952	*Bro-N	31	36	2	4	1	0	0	1	4	4	.111	.200	.139	-4	-5	-5	1	0	0	0	1.000	-1	/O	-0.6
Total	11	1320	4992	698	1507	292	47	88	581	480	122	.302	.366	.432	122	138	145	809	40	0		.989	53	*O	13.4

■ **RED HOLT** Holt, James Emmett Madison b: 7/25/1894, Dayton, Tenn. d: 2/2/61, Birmingham, Ala. BL/TL, 5'11", 175 lbs. Deb: 9/05/25

YEAR	TM/L	G	AB	R	H	2B	3B	HR	RBI	BB	SO	AVG	OBP	SLG	PRO+	BR	/A	RC	SB	CS	SBR	FA	FR	POS	TPR
1925	Phi-A	27	88	13	24	7	0	1	8	12	9	.273	.360	.386	84	-1	-2	13	0	0	0	.986	0	1	-0.3

■ **JIM HOLT** Holt, James William b: 5/27/44, Graham, N.C. BL/TR, 6', 195 lbs. Deb: 4/17/68

YEAR	TM/L	G	AB	R	H	2B	3B	HR	RBI	BB	SO	AVG	OBP	SLG	PRO+	BR	/A	RC	SB	CS	SBR	FA	FR	POS	TPR
1968	Min-A	70	106	9	22	2	1	0	8	4	20	.208	.236	.245	44	-7	-7	5	0	1	-1	.973	-5	O/1	-1.7
1969	Min-A	12	14	3	5	0	0	1	2	0	4	.357	.357	.571	153	1	1	3	0	0	0	1.000	-2	/O1	-0.1
1970	*Min-A	142	319	37	85	9	3	3	40	17	32	.266	.304	.342	77	-10	-11	32	3	1	0	.995	-11	*O/1	-2.7
1971	Min-A	126	340	35	88	11	3	1	29	16	28	.259	.294	.318	71	-12	-13	30	5	1	1	.986	-5	*O/1	-2.3
1972	Min-A	10	27	6	12	1	0	1	6	0	1	.444	.444	.593	197	3	3	6	0	0	0	.917	0	/O1	0.3
1973	Min-A	132	441	52	131	25	3	11	58	29	43	.297	.343	.442	115	10	8	63	0	3	-2	.990	5	*O1	0.5
1974	Min-A	79	197	24	50	11	0	0	16	14	16	.254	.307	.310	75	-6	-6	18	0	0	0	.996	5	1/O	-0.5
	*Oak-A	30	42	1	6	0	0	0	0	1	9	.143	.182	.143	-6	-6	-5	1	0	0	0	1.000	1	1/D	-0.5
	Yr	109	239	25	56	11	0	0	16	15	25	.234	.285	.280	62	-11	-11	19	0	0	0	.996	6	1/OD	-1.0
1975	*Oak-A	102	123	7	27	3	0	2	16	11	11	.220	.294	.293	68	-5	-5	10	0	0	0	.991	1	1/OCD	-0.6
1976	Oak-A	4	7	0	2	2	0	0	2	1	2	.286	.375	.571	182	1	1	2	0	0	0	.000	0	/D	0.1
Total	9	707	1616	174	428	64	10	19	177	93	166	.265	.308	.352	84	-31	-35	170	8	6	-1	.988	-11	O1/DC	-7.5

■ **ROGER HOLT** Holt, Roger Boyd b: 4/8/56, Daytona Beach, Fla. BB/TR, 5'11", 165 lbs. Deb: 10/04/80

YEAR	TM/L	G	AB	R	H	2B	3B	HR	RBI	BB	SO	AVG	OBP	SLG	PRO+	BR	/A	RC	SB	CS	SBR	FA	FR	POS	TPR
1980	NY-A	2	6	0	1	0	0	0	1	1	2	.167	.286	.167	28	-1	-1	0	0	0	0	1.000	1	/2	0.0

■ **MARTY HONAN** Honan, Martin Weldon b: 1870, Chicago, Ill. d: 8/20/08, Chicago, Ill. Deb: 10/03/1890

YEAR	TM/L	G	AB	R	H	2B	3B	HR	RBI	BB	SO	AVG	OBP	SLG	PRO+	BR	/A	RC	SB	CS	SBR	FA	FR	POS	TPR
1890	Chi-N	1	3	0	0	0	0	0	1	0	2	.000	.000	.000	-96	-1	-1	0	0			.857	-0	/C	-0.1
1891	Chi-N	5	12	1	2	0	1	0	3	1	3	.167	.231	.333	65	-1	-1	1	0			.963	2	/C	0.1
Total	2	6	15	1	2	0	1	0	4	1	5	.133	.188	.267	33	-1	-1	1	0			.941	1	/C	0.0

■ **ABIE HOOD** Hood, Albie Larrison b: 1/31/03, Sanford, N.C. d: 10/14/88, Chesapeake, Va. BL/TR, 5'7", 152 lbs. Deb: 7/15/25

YEAR	TM/L	G	AB	R	H	2B	3B	HR	RBI	BB	SO	AVG	OBP	SLG	PRO+	BR	/A	RC	SB	CS	SBR	FA	FR	POS	TPR
1925	Bos-N	5	21	2	6	2	0	1	2	1	0	.286	.318	.524	122	0	0	3	0	0	0	.920	-4	/2	-0.3

■ **WALLY HOOD** Hood, Wallace James Sr. b: 2/9/1895, Whittier, Cal. d: 5/2/65, Hollywood, Cal. BR/TR, 5'11.5", 160 lbs. Deb: 4/15/20 F

YEAR	TM/L	G	AB	R	H	2B	3B	HR	RBI	BB	SO	AVG	OBP	SLG	PRO+	BR	/A	RC	SB	CS	SBR	FA	FR	POS	TPR
1920	Bro-N	7	14	4	2	1	0	0	1	4	4	.143	.333	.214	58	-1	-1	2	2	0	1	.944	1	/O	0.1
	Pit-N	2	1	1	0	0	0	0	0	1	0	.000	.500	.000	50	0	0	0	1	0	0	.000	0	H	0.0
	Yr	9	15	5	2	1	0	0	1	5	4	.133	.350	.200	59	-0	-1	2	3	0	1	.944	1	/O	0.1
1921	Bro-N	56	65	16	17	1	2	1	4	9	14	.262	.360	.385	94	-0	-0	9	2	2	-1	.957	-6	O	-0.7
1922	Bro-N	2	0	2	0	0	0	0	0	0	0	—	—	—	—	0	0	0	0	0	0	.000	0	R	0.0
Total	3	67	80	23	19	2	2	1	5	14	18	.237	.358	.350	88	-1	-1	11	5	2	0		-4	/O	-0.6

■ **ALEX HOOKS** Hooks, Alexander Marcus b: 8/29/06, Edgewood, Tex. BL/TL, 6'1", 183 lbs. Deb: 4/17/35

YEAR	TM/L	G	AB	R	H	2B	3B	HR	RBI	BB	SO	AVG	OBP	SLG	PRO+	BR	/A	RC	SB	CS	SBR	FA	FR	POS	TPR
1935	Phi-A	15	44	4	10	3	0	0	4	3	10	.227	.277	.295	48	-3	-3	4	0	0	0	1.000	0	1	-0.4

■ **HARRY HOOPER** Hooper, Harry Bartholomew b: 8/24/1887, Bell Station, Cal. d: 12/18/74, Santa Cruz, Cal. BL/TR, 5'10", 168 lbs. Deb: 4/16/09 H

YEAR	TM/L	G	AB	R	H	2B	3B	HR	RBI	BB	SO	AVG	OBP	SLG	PRO+	BR	/A	RC	SB	CS	SBR	FA	FR	POS	TPR
1909	Bos-A	81	255	29	72	3	4	0	12	16		.282	.337	.325	107	3	2	33	15			.952	4	O	0.4
1910	Bos-A	155	584	81	156	9	10	2	27	62		.267	.346	.327	108	9	7	82	40			.938	11	*O	1.1
1911	Bos-A	130	524	93	163	20	6	4	45	73		.311	.399	.395	123	18	19	98	38			.954	6	*O	1.7
1912	*Bos-A	147	590	98	143	20	12	2	53	66		.242	.326	.327	83	-10	-14	73	29			.964	2	*O	-1.9
1913	Bos-A	148	586	100	169	29	12	4	40	60	51	.288	.359	.399	119	16	14	89	26			.968	9	*O/P	1.8
1914	Bos-A	142	530	85	137	23	15	1	41	58	47	.258	.336	.364	110	6	6	66	19	14	-3	.973	11	*O	0.9
1915	*Bos-A	149	566	90	133	20	13	2	51	89	36	.235	.342	.327	103	2	4	66	22	20	-5	.972	11	*O	0.3
1916	*Bos-A	151	575	75	156	20	11	1	37	80	35	.271	.361	.350	113	11	11	80	27	11	2	.966	8	*O	1.4
1917	Bos-A	151	559	89	143	21	11	3	45	80	40	.256	.355	.349	116	12	13	76	21			.971	-1	*O	0.4
1918	*Bos-A	126	474	81	137	26	13	1	44	75	25	.289	.391	.405	143	25	26	82	24			.963	-0	*O	2.1
1919	Bos-A	128	491	76	131	25	6	3	49	79	28	.267	.374	.360	113	7	11	72	23			.979	10	*O	1.2
1920	Bos-A	139	536	91	167	30	17	7	53	88	27	.312	.411	.470	139	28	31	104	16	18	-6	.963	7	*O	2.1
1921	Chi-A	108	419	74	137	26	5	8	58	55	21	.327	.406	.470	125	16	16	82	13	7	-0	.975	-3	*O	0.5
1922	Chi-A	152	602	111	183	35	8	11	80	68	33	.304	.379	.444	114	13	13	102	16	12	-2	.962	7	*O	0.7
1923	Chi-A	145	576	87	166	32	4	10	65	68	22	.288	.370	.410	106	5	6	88	18	18	-5	.960	-4	*O	-1.3
1924	Chi-A	130	476	107	156	27	8	10	62	65	26	.328	.413	.481	134	22	25	95	16	13	-3	.986	11	*O	2.2
1925	Chi-A	127	442	62	117	23	5	6	55	54	21	.265	.351	.380	90	-10	-6	62	12	8	-1	.976	4	*O	-1.0
Total	17	2309	8785	1429	2466	389	160	75	817	1136	412	.281	.368	.387	114	174	185	1349	375	121		.966	91	*O/P	12.6

■ **MIKE HOOPER** Hooper, Michael H. b: 2/7/1850, Baltimore, Md. d: 12/1/17, Baltimore, Md. 5'6", 165 lbs. Deb: 6/27/1873

YEAR	TM/L	G	AB	R	H	2B	3B	HR	RBI	BB	SO	AVG	OBP	SLG	PRO+	BR	/A	RC	SB	CS	SBR	FA	FR	POS	TPR
1873	Mar-n	3	14	3	3	0	0	0	0	0	0	.214	.214	.214	35	-1	-1	1						/OC	0.0

■ **CHARLIE HOOVER** Hoover, Charles E. b: 9/21/1865, Mound City, Ill. BL/TR, Deb: 10/09/1888

YEAR	TM/L	G	AB	R	H	2B	3B	HR	RBI	BB	SO	AVG	OBP	SLG	PRO+	BR	/A	RC	SB	CS	SBR	FA	FR	POS	TPR
1888	KC-a	3	10	0	3	0	0	0	1	0		.300	.300	.300	90	-0	-0	1	0			.857	0	/C	0.0
1889	KC-a	71	258	44	64	2	5	1	25	29	38	.248	.329	.306	79	-5	-7	30	9			.916	-4	C/3O	-0.5
Total	2	74	268	44	67	2	5	1	26	29	38	.250	.328	.306	79	-5	-8	31	9			.913	-4	/C3O	-0.5

■ **JOE HOOVER** Hoover, Robert Joseph b: 4/15/15, Brawley, Tex. d: 9/2/65, Los Angeles, Cal. BR/TR, 5'11", 175 lbs. Deb: 4/21/43

YEAR	TM/L	G	AB	R	H	2B	3B	HR	RBI	BB	SO	AVG	OBP	SLG	PRO+	BR	/A	RC	SB	CS	SBR	FA	FR	POS	TPR
1943	Det-A	144	575	78	140	15	8	4	38	36	101	.243	.289	.318	72	-18	-23	54	6	5	-1	.944	-6	*S	-2.1
1944	Det-A	120	441	67	104	20	2	0	29	35	66	.236	.301	.290	66	-17	-20	40	7	10	-4	.932	15	*S/2	0.1
1945	*Det-A	74	222	33	57	10	5	1	17	21	35	.257	.324	.360	92	-1	-2	28	6	2	1	.944	-7	S	-0.5
Total	3	338	1238	178	301	45	15	5	84	92	202	.243	.300	.316	73	-36	-45	122	19	17	-5	.939	3	S/2	-2.5

■ **BUSTER HOOVER** Hoover, William J. b: 1863, Philadelphia, Pa. BR/TR, 6'1", 178 lbs. Deb: 4/17/1884

YEAR	TM/L	G	AB	R	H	2B	3B	HR	RBI	BB	SO	AVG	OBP	SLG	PRO+	BR	/A	RC	SB	CS	SBR	FA	FR	POS	TPR
1884	Phi-U	63	275	76	100	20	8	0		12		.364	.390	.495	213	27	30	54				.780	-1	OS/123	2.4
	Phi-N	10	42	6	8	1	0	1	4	4	9	.190	.261	.286	75	-1	-1	3				.929	-1	O	-0.2
1886	Bal-a	40	157	25	34	2	6	0		16		.217	.297	.306	93	-1	-1	19	15			.839	-1	O	-0.3
1892	Cin-N	14	51	7	9	0	0	0	2	5	4	.176	.250	.176	31	-4	-4	3	1			.966	1	O	-0.3
Total	3	127	525	114	151	23	14	1	6	37	13	.288	.337	.390	143	20	25	79	16			.840	-3	O/S213	1.6

■ **DON HOPKINS** Hopkins, Donald b: 1/9/52, West Point, Miss. BL/TR, 6', 175 lbs. Deb: 4/08/75

YEAR	TM/L	G	AB	R	H	2B	3B	HR	RBI	BB	SO	AVG	OBP	SLG	PRO+	BR	/A	RC	SB	CS	SBR	FA	FR	POS	TPR
1975	*Oak-A	82	6	25	1	0	0	0	0	2	0	.167	.375	.167	59	-0	-0	-9	21	9	1	1.000	-2	D/OR	-0.1
1976	Oak-A	3	0	0	0	0	0	0	0	0	0	—	—	—	—	0	0	0	0	1	-1	.000	0	R	-0.1
Total	2	85	6	25	1	0	0	0	0	2	0	.167	.375	.167	59	-0	-0	-9	21	10	0		-2	/DO	-0.2

■ **GAIL HOPKINS** Hopkins, Gail Eason b: 2/19/43, Tulsa, Okla. BL/TR, 5'10", 200 lbs. Deb: 6/29/68

YEAR	TM/L	G	AB	R	H	2B	3B	HR	RBI	BB	SO	AVG	OBP	SLG	PRO+	BR	/A	RC	SB	CS	SBR	FA	FR	POS	TPR
1968	Chi-A	29	37	4	8	2	0	0	2	6	3	.216	.326	.270	81	-1	-1	4	0	0	0	1.000	-1	/1	-0.2
1969	Chi-A	124	373	52	99	13	3	8	46	50	28	.265	.354	.381	100	4	1	51	2	1	0	.994	-3	*1	-1.0
1970	Chi-A	116	287	32	82	8	1	6	29	28	19	.286	.351	.383	99	1	-0	39	0	0	0	.987	-2	1/C	-0.8
1971	KC-A	103	295	35	82	16	1	9	47	37	13	.278	.366	.431	126	10	10	47	3	1	0	.990	3	1	0.6
1972	KC-A	53	71	1	15	2	0	0	5	7	4	.211	.282	.239	56	-4	-4	5	0	0	0	.990	-2	1/3	-0.7

YEAR	TM/L	G	AB	R	H	2B	3B	HR	RBI	BB	SO	AVG	OBP	SLG	PRO+	BR	/A	RC	SB	CS	SBR	FA	FR	POS	TPR
1973	KC-A	74	138	17	34	6	1	2	16	29	15	.246	.385	.348	100	3	1	18	1	2	-1	1.000	0	D1	0.1
1974	LA-N	15	18	1	4	0	0	0	0	3	1	.222	.333	.222	60	-1	-1	1	0	0	0	1.000	1	/C1	0.0
Total	7	514	1219	142	324	47	6	25	145	160	83	.266	.355	.376	103	13	8	165	6	4	-1	.991	-4	1/DC3	-2.0
■ **BUCK HOPKINS**	Hopkins, John Winton "Sis" b: 1/3/1883, Grafton, Va. d: 10/2/29, Phoebus, Va. BR/TR, 5'10", 165 lbs. Deb: 7/22/07																								
1907	StL-N	15	44	7	6	3	0	0	3	10		.136	.333	.205	71	-1	-1	4	2			.875	-4	O	-0.6
■ **MARTY HOPKINS**	Hopkins, Meredith Hilliard b: 2/22/07, Wolfe City, Tex. d: 11/20/63, Dallas, Tex. BR/TR, 5'11", 175 lbs. Deb: 4/17/34																								
1934	Phi-N	10	25	6	3	2	0	0	3	7	5	.120	.313	.200	36	-2	-2	2	0			1.000	-1	/3	-0.3
	Chi-A	67	210	22	45	7	0	2	28	42	26	.214	.348	.276	61	-10	-11	23	0	3	-2	.957	4	3	-0.6
1935	Chi-A	59	144	20	32	3	0	2	17	36	23	.222	.378	.285	72	-4	-5	19	1	0	0	.960	-7	3/2	-0.9
Total	2	136	379	48	80	12	0	4	48	85	54	.211	.357	.274	63	-16	-18	44	1	3		.960	-4	3/2	-1.8
■ **MIKE HOPKINS**	Hopkins, Michael Joseph "Skinner" b: 11/1/1872, Glasgow, Scotland d: 2/5/52, Pittsburgh, Pa. BR/TR, 5'8", 160 lbs. Deb: 8/24/02																								
1902	Pit-N	1	2	0	2	1	0	0	0	0		1.000	1.000	1.500	647	1	1	3	0			1.000	0	/C	0.1
■ **JOHNNY HOPP**	Hopp, John Leonard "Hippity" b: 7/18/16, Hastings, Neb. BL/TL, 5'10", 175 lbs. Deb: 9/18/39 C																								
1939	StL-N	6	4	1	2	1	0	0	2	1	1	.500	.600	.750	246	1	1	2	0			1.000	0	/1	0.1
1940	StL-N	80	152	24	41	7	4	1	14	9	21	.270	.315	.388	88	-2	-3	18	3			.967	-2	O1	-0.6
1941	StL-N	134	445	83	135	25	11	4	50	50	63	.303	.378	.436	121	17	14	77	15			.982	1	O1	0.8
1942	*StL-N	95	314	41	81	16	7	3	37	36	40	.258	.334	.382	102	4	1	43	14			.983	-4	1	-0.8
1943	*StL-N	91	241	33	54	10	2	2	25	24	22	.224	.297	.307	71	-8	-9	24	8			.950	-2	O1	-1.5
1944	*StL-N	139	527	106	177	35	9	11	72	58	47	.336	.404	.499	150	37	36	110	15			**.997**	-10	*O/1	2.0
1945	StL-N	124	446	67	129	22	8	3	44	49	24	.289	.363	.395	108	7	6	68	14			.980	-7	*O1	-0.7
1946	Bos-N★	129	445	71	148	23	8	3	48	34	34	.333	.386	.440	133	20	19	77	21			.981	-1	1O	1.3
1947	Bos-N	134	430	74	124	20	2	2	32	58	30	.288	.376	.358	98	-0	1	62	13			.980	-6	*O	-1.1
1948	Pit-N	120	392	64	109	15	12	1	31	40	25	.278	.345	.385	95	-1	-2	53	5			1.000	1	O1	-0.6
1949	Pit-N	20	55	5	12	3	1	0	3	7	3	.218	.306	.309	64	-3	-3	5	0			.929	-1	/O1	-0.4
	Bro-N	8	14	0	0	0	0	0	0	0	3	.000	.000	.000	-96	-4	-4	0	0			1.000	1	/O1	-0.4
	Pit-N	85	316	50	106	11	4	5	36	30	26	.335	.393	.443	121	11	10	56	9			.994	-0	1/O	0.8
	Yr	113	385	55	118	14	5	5	39	37	32	.306	.367	.408	105	5	3	59	9			.990	-0	1O	0.0
1950	Pit-N	106	318	51	108	24	5	8	47	43	17	.340	.420	.522	141	22	21	71	7			.990	-6	1/O	1.3
	*NY-A	19	27	9	9	2	1	1	8	8	1	.333	.486	.593	180	3	4	8	0	1	-1	1.000	-1	1/O	0.2
1951	*NY-A	46	63	10	13	1	0	2	4	9	11	.206	.306	.317	71	-3	-2	7	2	0	1	.992	-1	1	-0.4
1952	NY-A	15	25	4	4	0	0	0	2	2	3	.160	.250	.160	17	-3	-3	1	2	0	1	1.000	1	1	-0.2
	Det-A	42	46	5	10	1	0	0	3	6	7	.217	.308	.239	53	-3	-3	4	0	0	0	1.000	-1	/O1	-0.4
	Yr	57	71	9	14	1	0	0	5	8	10	.197	.287	.211	41	-5	-5	5	2	0	1	1.000	-0	1/O	-0.6
Total	14	1393	4260	698	1262	216	74	46	458	464	378	.296	.368	.414	113	96	82	685	128	1		.985	-36	O1	-0.6
■ **SHAGS HORAN**	Horan, Joseph Patrick b: 9/6/1895, St.Louis, Mo. d: 2/13/69, Torrance, Cal. BR/TR, 5'10", 170 lbs. Deb: 7/14/24																								
1924	NY-A	22	31	4	9	1	0	0	7	1	5	.290	.313	.323	64	-2	-2	3	0	0	0	1.000	-4	O	-0.6
■ **SAM HORN**	Horn, Samuel Lee b: 11/2/63, Dallas, Tex. BL/TL, 6'5", 250 lbs. Deb: 7/25/87																								
1987	Bos-A	46	158	31	44	7	0	14	34	17	55	.278	.356	.589	141	10	9	32	0	1	-1	.000	0	D	0.8
1988	Bos-A	24	61	4	9	0	0	2	8	11	20	.148	.278	.246	46	-4	-4	5	0	0	0	.000	0	D	-0.5
1989	Bos-A	33	54	1	8	2	0	0	4	8	16	.148	.258	.185	25	-5	-6	2	0	0	0	1.000	-0	D/1	-0.6
1990	Bal-A	79	246	30	61	13	0	14	45	32	62	.248	.335	.472	127	7	8	38	0	0	0	.970	-0	D1	0.7
1991	Bal-A	121	317	45	74	16	0	23	61	41	99	.233	.327	.502	131	10	12	51	0	0	0	.000	0	*D	1.2
1992	Bal-A	63	162	13	38	10	1	5	19	21	60	.235	.326	.401	103	1	1	20	0	0	0	.000	0	D	0.1
Total	6	366	998	124	234	48	1	58	171	130	312	.234	.326	.459	116	18	20	147	0	1	-1	.972	-0	D/1	1.7
■ **BOB HORNER**	Horner, James Robert b: 8/6/57, Junction City, Kan. BR/TR, 6'1", 210 lbs. Deb: 6/16/78																								
1978	Atl-N	89	323	50	86	17	1	23	63	24	42	.266	.321	.539	123	13	9	54	0	0	0	.956	6	3	1.5
1979	Atl-N	121	487	66	153	15	1	33	98	22	74	.314	.348	.552	132	25	21	89	0	2	-1	.930	-7	31	1.0
1980	Atl-N	124	463	81	124	14	1	35	89	27	50	.268	.310	.529	126	15	14	70	3	1	0	.935	5	*3/1	1.8
1981	Atl-N	79	300	42	83	10	0	15	42	32	39	.277	.348	.460	125	10	9	47	2	3	-1	.938	-15	3	-0.9
1982	*Atl-N★	140	499	85	130	24	0	32	97	66	75	.261	.351	.501	131	23	21	86	3	5	-2	.970	-17	*3	-0.2
1983	Atl-N	104	386	75	117	25	1	20	68	50	63	.303	.384	.528	140	26	23	76	4	2	0	.958	-13	*3/1	0.9
1984	Atl-N	32	113	15	31	8	0	3	19	14	17	.274	.354	.425	110	3	2	17	0	0	0	.965	-1	3	0.1
1985	Atl-N	130	483	61	129	25	3	27	89	50	57	.267	.337	.499	123	18	15	77	1	1	-0	1.000	-10	13	-0.2
1986	Atl-N	141	517	70	141	22	0	27	87	52	72	.273	.342	.472	116	14	11	79	1	4	-2	.995	2	*1	0.1
1988	StL-N	60	206	15	53	9	1	3	33	32	23	.257	.360	.354	105	3	2	26	0	0	0	.990	-1	1	-0.3
Total	10	1020	3777	560	1047	169	8	218	685	369	512	.277	.344	.499	125	151	126	621	14	18	-7	.946	-50	31	3.8
■ **ROGERS HORNSBY**	Hornsby, Rogers "Rajah" b: 4/27/1896, Winters, Tex. d: 1/5/63, Chicago, Ill. BR/TR, 5'11", 175 lbs. Deb: 9/10/15 MCH																								
1915	StL-N	18	57	5	14	2	0	0	4	2	6	.246	.271	.281	67	-2	-2	4	0	2	-1	.922	1	S	-0.2
1916	StL-N	139	495	63	155	17	15	6	65	40	63	.313	.369	.444	150	28	28	88	17			.928	-2	3S1/2	3.5
1917	StL-N	145	523	86	171	24	**17**	8	66	45	34	.327	.385	**.484**	**170**	**40**	**41**	100	17			.939	21	*S	**7.6**
1918	StL-N	115	416	51	117	19	11	5	60	40	43	.281	.349	.416	138	16	17	60	8			.933	10	*S/O	3.5
1919	StL-N	138	512	68	163	15	9	8	71	48	41	.318	.384	.430	**154**	29	**32**	87	17			.933	2	3S2/1	4.3
1920	StL-N	149	589	96	**218**	**44**	20	9	**94**	60	50	**.370**	**.431**	**.559**	**190**	**63**	**65**	**138**	12	15	-5	.962	11	*2	**7.9**
1921	StL-N	154	592	**131**	**235**	**44**	**18**	21	**126**	60	48	**.397**	**.458**	**.639**	**191**	**74**	**76**	**169**	13	13	-4	.969	-3	*2/OS31	7.0
1922	StL-N	154	623	**141**	**250**	**46**	14	**42**	**152**	65	50	**.401**	**.459**	**.722**	**210**	**90**	**94**	**200**	17	12	-2	**.967**	-7	*2	**8.1**
1923	StL-N	107	424	89	163	32	10	17	83	55	29	**.384**	**.459**	**.627**	**188**	**52**	**53**	120	3	7	-3	.962	-17	21	3.2
1924	StL-N	143	536	**121**	**227**	**43**	14	25	94	**89**	32	**.424**	**.507**	**.696**	**223**	**94**	**95**	**186**	5	12	-6	.965	-4	*2	**8.4**
1925	StL-N	138	504	133	203	41	10	**39**	**143**	83	39	**.403**	**.489**	**.756**	**208**	**87**	**85**	**187**	5	3	-0	.954	-20	*2M	**6.2**
1926	*StL-N	134	527	96	167	34	5	11	93	61	39	.317	.388	.463	123	21	19	94	3			.962	-29	*2M	-0.7
1927	NY-N	155	568	**133**	205	32	9	26	125	**86**	38	.361	**.448**	**.586**	**176**	**63**	**63**	**148**	9			.972	3	*2M	6.9
1928	Bos-N	140	486	99	188	42	7	21	94	**107**	41	**.387**	**.498**	**.632**	**204**	**72**	**76**	**154**	5			.973	-24	*2M	**5.4**
1929	*Chi-N	156	602	**156**	229	47	8	39	149	87	65	.380	.459	**.679**	**178**	**74**	**74**	**183**	2			.973	1	*2	**7.2**
1930	Chi-N	42	104	15	32	5	1	2	18	12	12	.308	.385	.433	96	-0	-0	17	0			.916	-3	2M	-0.2
1931	Chi-N	100	357	64	118	37	1	16	90	56	23	.331	.421	.574	162	34	33	90	1			.951	-15	23M	2.3
1932	Chi-N	19	58	10	13	2	0	1	7	10	4	.224	.357	.310	82	-1	-1	7	0			1.000	-4	O/3M	-0.5
1933	StL-N	46	83	9	27	6	0	2	21	12	6	.325	.423	.470	147	7	6	17	1			.967	-7	2	0.0
	StL-A	11	9	2	3	1	0	1	2	2	1	.333	.455	.778	208	2	1	3	0	0	0	.000	0	HM	0.1
1934	StL-A	24	23	2	7	2	0	1	11	7	4	.304	.484	.522	147	3	2	7	0	0	0	1.000	0	/3OM	0.2
1935	StL-A	10	24	1	5	3	0	0	3	3	6	.208	.296	.333	60	-1	-2	2	0	0	0	1.000	0	/123M	-0.2
1936	StL-A	2	5	1	2	0	0	0	2	1	0	.400	.500	.400	121	0	0	1	0	0	0	1.000	-0	/1M	0.0
1937	StL-A	20	56	7	18	3	0	1	11	7	5	.321	.397	.429	107	1	1	10	0	0	0	.947	-5	2M	-0.2
Total	23	2259	8173	1579	2930	541	169	301	1584	1038	679	.358	.434	.577	176	844	859	2074	135	64		.965	-91	*2S3/1O	79.8
■ **JOE HORNUNG**	Hornung, Michael Joseph "Ubbo Ubbo" b: 6/12/1857, Carthage, N.Y. d: 10/30/31, Howard Beach, N.Y. BR/TR, 5'8.5", 164 lbs. Deb: 5/01/1879 U																								
1879	Buf-N	78	319	46	85	18	7	0	38	2	27	.266	.271	.367	105	2	1	33				.844	-2	*O/1	-0.4
1880	Buf-N	85	342	47	91	8	11	1	42	8	29	.266	.283	.363	115	6	5	36				.874	-0	*O1/2P	0.1
1881	Bos-N	83	324	40	78	12	8	2	25	5	25	.241	.252	.346	90	-5	-3	29				**.948**	12	*O	0.6

YEAR	TM/L	G	AB	R	H	2B	3B	HR	RBI	BB	SO	AVG	OBP	SLG	PRO+	BR	/A	RC	SB	CS	SBR	FA	FR	POS	TPR
1882	Bos-N	85	388	67	117	14	11	1	50	2	25	.302	.305	.402	124	10	10	49				**.932**	11	*O/1	1.8
1883	Bos-N	98	446	**107**	124	25	13	8	66	8	54	.278	.291	.446	117	10	8	59				**.936**	7	*O/3	1.3
1884	Bos-N	115	518	119	139	27	10	7	51	17	80	.268	.292	.400	116	8	8	62				.916	3	*O/1	0.8
1885	Bos-N	25	109	14	22	4	1	1	7	1	20	.202	.209	.284	61	-5	-5	7				.919	-3	O	-0.7
1886	Bos-N	94	424	67	109	12	2	2	40	10	62	.257	.274	.309	80	-12	-10	41	16			**.948**	7	*O	-0.5
1887	Bos-N	98	437	85	118	10	6	5	49	17	28	.270	.302	.355	83	-10	-10	61	41			**.935**	13	*O	0.1
1888	Bos-N	107	431	61	103	11	7	3	53	16	39	.239	.269	.318	87	-6	-7	46	29			.947	-8	*O	-1.7
1889	Bal-a	135	533	73	122	13	9	1	78	22	72	.229	.269	.293	60	-27	-29	52	34			.913	11	*O/3	-1.8
1890	NY-N	120	513	62	122	18	5	0	65	12	37	.238	.258	.292	62	-26	-26	50	39			.931	-3	O1/3S	-2.9
Total	12	1123	4784	788	1230	172	90	31	564	120	498	.257	.277	.350	92	-56	-57	524	159			.922	49	*O/132SP	-3.3

■ TONY HORTON

Horton, Anthony Darrin b: 12/6/44, Santa Monica, Cal. BR/TR, 6'3", 210 lbs. Deb: 7/31/64

YEAR	TM/L	G	AB	R	H	2B	3B	HR	RBI	BB	SO	AVG	OBP	SLG	PRO+	BR	/A	RC	SB	CS	SBR	FA	FR	POS	TPR
1964	Bos-A	36	126	9	28	5	0	1	8	3	20	.222	.240	.286	44	-9	-10	7	0	0	0	1.000	1	O/1	-1.1
1965	Bos-A	60	163	23	48	8	1	7	23	18	36	.294	.365	.485	131	8	7	29	0	2	-1	.980	-1	1	0.3
1966	Bos-A	6	22	0	3	0	0	0	2	0	5	.136	.136	.136	-19	-3	-4	0	0	0	0	1.000	1	/1	-0.4
1967	Bos-A	21	39	2	12	3	0	0	9	0	5	.308	.308	.385	96	0	-0	4	0	0	0	.929	-1	/1	-0.2
	Cle-A	106	363	35	102	13	4	10	44	18	52	.281	.322	.421	117	7	7	48	3	0	1	.991	-6	1	-0.4
	Yr	127	402	37	114	16	4	10	53	18	57	.284	.321	.418	114	7	6	52	3	0	1	.987	-6	*1	-0.6
1968	Cle-A	133	477	57	119	29	3	14	59	34	56	.249	.304	.411	117	7	8	59	3	1	0	.992	-4	*1	-0.6
1969	Cle-A	159	625	77	174	25	4	27	93	37	91	.278	.321	.461	113	10	8	85	3	3	-1	.989	-0	*1	-0.6
1970	Cle-A	115	413	48	111	19	3	17	59	30	54	.269	.324	.453	107	5	3	55	3	2	-0	.994	3	*1	-0.4
Total	7	636	2228	251	597	102	15	76	297	140	319	.268	.315	.430	109	26	19	287	12	8	-1	.990	-7	1/O	-3.4

■ WILLIE HORTON

Horton, Willie Watterson b: 10/18/42, Arno, Va. BR/TR, 5'11", 209 lbs. Deb: 9/10/63 C

YEAR	TM/L	G	AB	R	H	2B	3B	HR	RBI	BB	SO	AVG	OBP	SLG	PRO+	BR	/A	RC	SB	CS	SBR	FA	FR	POS	TPR
1963	Det-A	15	43	6	14	2	1	1	4	0	8	.326	.326	.488	120	1	1	7	2	0	1	1.000	-1	/O	0.0
1964	Det-A	25	80	6	13	1	3	1	10	11	20	.162	.272	.287	55	-5	-5	7	0	0	0	.943	-2	O	-0.8
1965	Det-A★	143	512	69	140	20	2	29	104	48	101	.273	.343	.490	132	22	21	81	5	9	-4	.988	5	*O/3	1.6
1966	Det-A	146	526	72	138	22	6	27	100	44	103	.262	.323	.481	125	17	16	80	1	1	-0	.979	-4	*O	0.6
1967	Det-A	122	401	47	110	20	3	19	67	36	80	.274	.340	.481	137	19	18	64	0	0	0	.971	-0	*O	1.4
1968	*Det-A★	143	512	68	146	20	2	36	85	49	110	.285	.357	.543	165	41	40	95	0	3	-2	.973	0	*O	3.5
1969	Det-A	141	508	66	133	17	1	28	91	52	93	.262	.334	.465	116	13	10	78	3	3	-1	.972	9	*O	1.1
1970	Det-A★	96	371	53	113	18	2	17	69	28	43	.305	.357	.501	133	16	16	65	0	1	-1	.982	5	O	1.6
1971	Det-A	119	450	64	130	25	1	22	72	37	75	.289	.352	.496	133	21	19	73	1	5	-3	.963	-10	*O	0.0
1972	*Det-A	108	333	44	77	9	5	11	36	27	47	.231	.295	.387	99	-0	-1	37	0	0	0	1.000	-10	O	-1.8
1973	Det-A★	111	411	42	130	19	3	17	53	23	57	.316	.363	.501	132	21	18	69	1	4	-2	.942	-10	*O/D	0.1
1974	Det-A	72	238	32	71	8	1	15	47	21	36	.298	.363	.529	149	16	15	44	0	1	-1	.947	-4	O/D	0.8
1975	Det-A	159	615	62	169	13	1	25	92	44	109	.275	.323	.421	104	5	2	79	1	2	-1	.000	0	*D	0.1
1976	Det-A	114	401	40	105	17	0	14	56	49	63	.262	.345	.409	116	10	9	55	0	0	0	.000	0	*D	0.9
1977	Det-A	1	4	0	1	0	0	0	0	0	0	.250	.250	.250	35	-0	-0	0	0	0	0	1.000	-0	/O	-0.1
	Tex-A	139	519	55	150	23	3	15	75	42	117	.289	.342	.432	108	6	6	73	2	3	-1	.938	-1	*DO	0.3
	Yr	140	523	55	151	23	3	15	75	42	117	.289	.342	.430	108	6	5	73	2	3	-1	.941	-2	*DO	0.2
1978	Cle-A	50	169	15	42	7	0	5	22	15	25	.249	.314	.379	95	-2	-1	19	3	0	1	.000	0	D	0.0
	Oak-A	32	102	11	32	8	0	3	19	9	15	.314	.369	.480	145	5	6	18	0	1	-1	.333	-1	D/O	0.4
	Tor-A	33	122	12	25	6	0	3	19	4	29	.205	.230	.328	54	-8	-8	8	0	0	0	.000	0	D	-0.8
	Yr	115	393	38	99	21	0	11	60	28	69	.252	.303	.389	95	-4	-4	44	3	1	0	.333	-1	*D/O	-0.4
1979	Sea-A	162	646	77	180	19	5	29	106	42	112	.279	.327	.458	107	6	5	91	1	1	-0	.000	0	*D	0.4
1980	Sea-A	97	335	32	74	10	1	8	36	39	70	.221	.310	.328	74	-11	-12	35	0	4	-2	.000	0	D	-1.4
Total	18	2028	7298	873	1993	284	40	325	1163	620	1313	.273	.335	.457	119	194	171	1077	20	38	-17	.972	-23	*OD/3	7.9

■ STEVE HOSEY

Hosey, Steven Bernard b: 4/2/69, Oakland, Cal. BR/TR, 6'3", 215 lbs. Deb: 8/29/92

YEAR	TM/L	G	AB	R	H	2B	3B	HR	RBI	BB	SO	AVG	OBP	SLG	PRO+	BR	/A	RC	SB	CS	SBR	FA	FR	POS	TPR
1992	SF-N	21	56	6	14	1	0	1	6	0	15	.250	.250	.321	64	-3	-3	4	1	1	-0	.960	-2	O	-0.6

■ TIM HOSLEY

Hosley, Timothy Kenneth b: 5/10/47, Spartanburg, S.C. BR/TR, 5'10", 195 lbs. Deb: 9/08/70

YEAR	TM/L	G	AB	R	H	2B	3B	HR	RBI	BB	SO	AVG	OBP	SLG	PRO+	BR	/A	RC	SB	CS	SBR	FA	FR	POS	TPR
1970	Det-A	7	12	1	2	0	0	1	2	0	6	.167	.167	.417	55	-1	-1	1	0	0	0	1.000	2	/C	0.1
1971	Det-A	7	16	2	3	0	0	2	6	0	1	.188	.188	.563	102	-0	-0	1	0	0	0	1.000	-0	/C1	0.0
1973	Oak-A	13	14	3	3	0	0	0	2	2	3	.214	.313	.214	53	-1	-1	1	0	0	0	.952	-1	C	-0.2
1974	Oak-A	11	7	3	2	0	0	0	1	1	2	.286	.375	.286	99	-0	0	1	0	0	0	1.000	0	/C1	0.0
1975	Chi-N	62	141	22	36	7	0	6	20	27	25	.255	.382	.433	120	6	5	24	1	1	-0	.968	-2	C	0.5
1976	Oak-A	37	55	4	9	2	0	1	4	8	12	.164	.270	.255	56	-3	-3	4	0	0	0	.968	-1	C	-0.3
	Chi-N	1	1	0	0	0	0	0	0	0	0	.000	.000	.000	-92	-0	-0	0	0	0	0	.000	0	H	0.0
1977	Oak-A	39	78	5	15	0	0	1	10	16	13	.192	.337	.231	59	-4	-4	7	0	0	0	.955	3	CD/1	-0.1
1978	Oak-A	13	23	1	7	2	0	0	3	1	6	.304	.360	.391	117	0	1	3	0	0	0	.962	0	/CD	0.1
1981	Oak-A	18	21	2	2	0	0	1	5	2	5	.095	.174	.238	19	-2	-2	1	0	0	0	.750	-0	/1D	-0.3
Total	9	208	368	43	79	11	0	12	53	57	73	.215	.326	.342	87	-5	-5	44	1	1	-0	.968	0	C/D1	-0.2

■ CHUCK HOSTETLER

Hostetler, Charles Cloyd b: 9/22/03, McClellandtown, Pa. d: 2/18/71, Fort Collins, Colo BL/TR, 6', 175 lbs. Deb: 4/18/44

YEAR	TM/L	G	AB	R	H	2B	3B	HR	RBI	BB	SO	AVG	OBP	SLG	PRO+	BR	/A	RC	SB	CS	SBR	FA	FR	POS	TPR
1944	Det-A	90	265	42	79	9	2	0	20	21	31	.298	.350	.347	94	0	-2	33	4	4	-1	.985	0	O	-0.6
1945	*Det-A	42	44	3	7	3	0	0	2	7	8	.159	.275	.227	43	-3	-3	3	0	0	0	.889	-3	/O	-0.6
Total	2	132	309	45	86	12	2	0	22	28	39	.278	.338	.330	87	-3	-5	36	4	4	-1	.979	-2	/O	-1.2

■ DAVE HOSTETLER

Hostetler, David Alan b: 3/27/56, Pasadena, Cal. BR/TR, 6'4", 215 lbs. Deb: 9/15/81

YEAR	TM/L	G	AB	R	H	2B	3B	HR	RBI	BB	SO	AVG	OBP	SLG	PRO+	BR	/A	RC	SB	CS	SBR	FA	FR	POS	TPR
1981	Mon-N	5	6	1	3	0	0	1	1	0	2	.500	.500	1.000	314	2	2	3	0	0	0	1.000	-0	/1	0.1
1982	Tex-A	113	418	53	97	12	3	22	67	42	113	.232	.304	.433	105	-1	1	52	2	2	-1	.990	-11	*1/D	-1.6
1983	Tex-A	94	304	31	67	9	2	11	46	42	103	.220	.325	.372	93	-3	-2	36	0	2	-1	1.000	-0	D/1	-0.4
1984	Tex-A	37	82	7	18	2	1	3	10	13	27	.220	.326	.378	91	-0	-1	9	0	0	0	1.000	1	1D	-0.1
1988	Pit-N	6	8	0	2	0	0	0	0	0	3	.250	.250	.250	45	-1	-1	1	0	0	0	.944	-0	/1C	-0.1
Total	5	255	818	92	187	23	6	37	124	97	248	.229	.315	.407	100	-4	-1	101	2	4	-2	.990	-11	1D/C	-2.1

■ PETE HOTALING

Hotaling, Peter James "Monkey" b: 12/16/1856, Mohawk, N.Y. d: 7/3/28, Cleveland, Ohio BL/TR, 5'8", 166 lbs. Deb: 5/01/1879

YEAR	TM/L	G	AB	R	H	2B	3B	HR	RBI	BB	SO	AVG	OBP	SLG	PRO+	BR	/A	RC	SB	CS	SBR	FA	FR	POS	TPR
1879	Cin-N	81	369	64	103	20	9	1	27	12	17	.279	.302	.390	133	10	13	45				.843	-0	*O/C23	0.9
1880	Cle-N	78	325	40	78	17	8	0	41	10	30	.240	.263	.342	105	1	2	30				.896	-2	*O/C	-0.3
1881	Wor-N	77	317	51	98	15	3	1	35	18	12	.309	.346	.385	123	11	8	43				.862	-3	*O/C	0.3
1882	Bos-N	84	378	64	98	16	5	0	28	16	21	.259	.289	.328	97	-1	-1	37				.865	2	*O	0.1
1883	Cle-N	100	417	54	108	20	8	0	30	12	31	.259	.280	.345	90	-6	-5	41				.829	1	*O	-0.4
1884	Cle-N	102	408	69	99	16	6	3	27	28	50	.243	.291	.333	93	-2	-4	41				.849	-1	*O/2	-0.6
1885	Bro-a	94	370	73	95	9	5	1		49		.257	.350	.316	114	9	8	42				.893	0	*O	0.6
1887	Cle-a	126	505	108	151	28	13	3		53		.299	.373	.424	128	17	20	98	43			.903	1	*O	1.5
1888	Cle-a	98	403	67	101	7	6	0	55	26		.251	.307	.298	100	-0	1	49	35			.878	-9	*O	-1.0
Total	9	840	3492	590	931	148	63	9	243	224	161	.267	.314	.353	110	39	43	426	78			.869	-11	O/C23	1.1

■ KEN HOTTMAN

Hottman, Kenneth Roger b: 5/7/48, Stockton, Cal. BR/TR, 5'11", 190 lbs. Deb: 9/11/71

YEAR	TM/L	G	AB	R	H	2B	3B	HR	RBI	BB	SO	AVG	OBP	SLG	PRO+	BR	/A	RC	SB	CS	SBR	FA	FR	POS	TPR
1971	Chi-A	6	16	1	2	0	0	0	0	1	2	.125	.176	.125	-13	-2	-2	0	0	0	0	1.000	-1	/O	-0.4

■ SADIE HOUCK

Houck, Sargent Perry b: 1856, Washington, D.C. d: 5/26/19, Washington, D.C. BR/TR, 5'7", 151 lbs. Deb: 5/01/1879

YEAR	TM/L	G	AB	R	H	2B	3B	HR	RBI	BB	SO	AVG	OBP	SLG	PRO+	BR	/A	RC	SB	CS	SBR	FA	FR	POS	TPR
1879	Bos-N	80	356	69	95	24	9	2	49	4	11	.267	.275	.402	117	7	6	40				.814	-8	OS	-0.2

YEAR	TM/L	G	AB	R	H	2B	3B	HR	RBI	BB	SO	AVG	OBP	SLG	PRO+	BR	/A	RC	SB	CS	SBR	FA	FR	POS	TPR
1880	Bos-N	12	47	2	7	0	0	0	2	0	6	.149	.149	.149	1	-5	-4	1				.786	-1	O	-0.6
	Pro-N	49	184	27	37	7	7	1	22	3	6	.201	.214	.332	85	-3	-3	13				.873	-1	O	-0.5
	Yr	61	231	29	44	7	7	1	24	3	12	.190	.201	.294	68	-8	-7	14				.855	-3	O	-1.1
1881	Det-N	75	308	43	86	16	6	1	36	6	6	.279	.293	.380	106	3	1	35				.868	1	*S	0.6
1883	Det-N	101	416	52	105	18	12	0	40	9	18	.252	.268	.353	91	-7	-4	40				.852	5	*S	0.3
1884	Phi-a	108	472	93	140	19	14	0		7		.297	.318	.396	126	17	12	61				**.893**	23	*S/2	3.3
1885	Phi-a	93	388	74	99	10	9	0		10		.255	.286	.327	91	-2	-5	37				.863	22	*S	1.6
1886	Bal-a	61	260	29	50	8	1	0		4		.192	.216	.231	42	-17	-16	19	25			.849	-5	S/2O	-1.9
	Was-N	52	195	14	42	3	0	0	14	2	28	.215	.223	.231	41	-14	-13	11	4			.858	0	S/2	-1.1
1887	NY-a	10	33	3	5	1	0	0		3		.152	.243	.182	22	-3	-3	2	2			.831	4	S/2	0.1
Total	8	641	2659	406	666	106	58	4	163	48	75	.250	.269	.338	92	-25	-29	261	31			.863	39	SO/2	1.6

■ RALPH HOUK

Houk, Ralph George "Major" b: 8/9/19, Lawrence, Kan. BR/TR, 5'11", 193 lbs. Deb: 4/26/47 MC

YEAR	TM/L	G	AB	R	H	2B	3B	HR	RBI	BB	SO	AVG	OBP	SLG	PRO+	BR	/A	RC	SB	CS	SBR	FA	FR	POS	TPR
1947	*NY-A	41	92	7	25	3	1	0	12	11	5	.272	.356	.326	91	-1	-1	11	0	0	0	.987	2	C	0.3
1948	NY-A	14	29	3	8	2	0	0	3	0	0	.276	.276	.345	65	-2	-2	3	0	0	0	1.000	5	C	0.3
1949	NY-A	5	7	0	4	0	0	0	1	0	1	.571	.571	.571	203	1	1	2	0	0	0	.889	-1	/C	0.1
1950	NY-A	10	9	0	1	1	0	0	1	0	2	.111	.111	.222	-17	-2	-2	0	0	0	0	.929	1	/C	-0.1
1951	NY-A	3	5	0	1	0	0	0	2	0	1	.200	.200	.200	9	-1	-1	0	0	0	0	1.000	-1	/C	-0.1
1952	*NY-A	9	6	0	2	0	0	0	0	1	0	.333	.429	.333	121	0	0	1	0	0	0	.917	1	/C	0.1
1953	NY-A	8	9	2	2	0	0	0	1	0	1	.222	.222	.222	21	-1	-1	0	0	0	0	1.000	-0	/C	-0.1
1954	NY-A	1	1	0	0	0	0	0	0	0	0	.000	.000	.000	-99	-0	-0	0	0	0	0	.000	0	H	0.0
Total	8	91	158	12	43	6	1	0	20	12	10	.272	.327	.323	79	-5	-4	18	0	0	0	.981	6	/C	0.5

■ FRANK HOUSE

House, Henry Franklin "Pig" b: 2/18/30, Bessemer, Ala. BL/TR, 6'1.5", 190 lbs. Deb: 7/21/50

YEAR	TM/L	G	AB	R	H	2B	3B	HR	RBI	BB	SO	AVG	OBP	SLG	PRO+	BR	/A	RC	SB	CS	SBR	FA	FR	POS	TPR
1950	Det-A	5	5	1	2	1	0	0	0	0	1	.400	.400	.600	148	0	0	1	0	0	0	1.000	0	/C	0.0
1951	Det-A	18	41	3	9	2	0	1	4	6	2	.220	.319	.341	78	-1	-1	4	1	1	-0	.957	1	C	0.0
1954	Det-A	114	352	35	88	12	1	9	38	31	34	.250	.313	.366	87	-8	-7	41	2	1	0	.992	-1	*C	-0.3
1955	Det-A	102	328	37	85	11	1	15	53	22	25	.259	.312	.436	102	-2	-1	45	0	0	0	.987	2	C	0.4
1956	Det-A	94	321	44	77	6	2	10	44	21	19	.240	.293	.364	72	-14	-14	31	1	1	-0	.986	-6	C	-1.7
1957	Det-A	106	348	31	90	9	0	7	36	35	26	.259	.328	.345	82	-7	-8	38	1	1	-0	.997	9	C	0.4
1958	KC-A	76	202	16	51	6	3	4	24	12	13	.252	.298	.371	81	-5	-6	20	1	0	0	.992	-7	C	-1.0
1959	KC-A	98	347	32	82	14	3	1	30	20	23	.236	.282	.303	59	-19	-20	27	0	3	-2	.982	-8	C	-2.5
1960	Cin-N	23	28	0	5	2	0	0	3	0	2	.179	.179	.250	16	-3	-3	1	0	0	0	1.000	1	/C	-0.2
1961	Det-A	17	22	3	5	1	1	0	3	4	2	.227	.346	.364	87	-0	-0	3	0	0	0	.974	-1	C	-0.1
Total	10	653	1994	202	494	64	11	47	235	151	147	.248	.304	.362	80	-59	-60	210	6	7	-2	.988	-10	C	-5.0

■ CHARLIE HOUSEHOLDER

Householder, Charles F. b: 1856, Harrisburg, Pa. BR/TR, 5'7", 150 lbs. Deb: 4/20/1884

YEAR	TM/L	G	AB	R	H	2B	3B	HR	RBI	BB	SO	AVG	OBP	SLG	PRO+	BR	/A	RC	SB	CS	SBR	FA	FR	POS	TPR
1884	CP-U	83	310	32	74	12	5	1		12		.239	.267	.319	98	-1	-0	27				.796	-6	3O/SP	-0.6

■ CHARLIE HOUSEHOLDER

Householder, Charles W. b: 1856, Harrisburg, Pa. d: 12/26/08, Harrisburg, Pa. BL/TL, 5'11", 158 lbs. Deb: 5/02/1882

YEAR	TM/L	G	AB	R	H	2B	3B	HR	RBI	BB	SO	AVG	OBP	SLG	PRO+	BR	/A	RC	SB	CS	SBR	FA	FR	POS	TPR
1882	Bal-a	74	307	42	78	10	7	1		4		.254	.264	.342	111	0	4	28				.971	3	*1/C	-0.2
1884	Bro-a	76	273	28	66	15	3	3		12		.242	.279	.352	106	2	2	27				.959	-5	1C/O2	-0.4
Total	2	150	580	70	144	25	10	4		16		.248	.271	.347	109	3	6	56					-2	1/CO2	-0.6

■ ED HOUSEHOLDER

Householder, Edward H. b: 10/12/1869, Pittsburgh, Pa. d: 7/3/24, Los Angeles, Cal. Deb: 4/17/03

YEAR	TM/L	G	AB	R	H	2B	3B	HR	RBI	BB	SO	AVG	OBP	SLG	PRO+	BR	/A	RC	SB	CS	SBR	FA	FR	POS	TPR
1903	Bro-N	12	43	5	9	0	0	0	9	2		.209	.244	.209	31	-4	-4	3	3			.967	1	O	-0.4

■ PAUL HOUSEHOLDER

Householder, Paul Wesley b: 9/4/58, Columbus, Ohio BB/TR, 6', 180 lbs. Deb: 8/26/80

YEAR	TM/L	G	AB	R	H	2B	3B	HR	RBI	BB	SO	AVG	OBP	SLG	PRO+	BR	/A	RC	SB	CS	SBR	FA	FR	POS	TPR
1980	Cin-N	20	45	3	11	1	1	0	7	1	13	.244	.261	.311	59	-3	-3	4	1	0	0	1.000	0	O	-0.2
1981	Cin-N	23	69	12	19	4	0	2	9	10	16	.275	.367	.420	121	2	2	11	3	1	0	1.000	-1	O	0.1
1982	Cin-N	138	417	40	88	11	5	9	34	30	77	.211	.267	.326	64	-20	-21	35	17	11	-2	.992	3	*O	-2.4
1983	Cin-N	123	380	40	97	24	4	6	43	44	60	.255	.336	.387	96	0	-2	48	12	12	-4	**.991**	2	*O	-0.7
1984	Cin-N	14	12	3	1	1	0	0	0	3	3	.083	.267	.167	23	-1	-1	1	1	1	-0	1.000	-2	O	-0.4
	StL-N	13	14	1	2	0	0	0	0	0	3	.143	.143	.143	-20	-2	-2	0	0	0	0	1.000	-3	/O	-0.6
	Yr	27	26	4	3	1	0	0	0	3	6	.115	.207	.154	3	-3	-3	1	1	1	-0	1.000	-5	O	-1.0
1985	Mil-A	95	299	41	77	15	0	11	34	27	60	.258	.321	.418	101	-0	0	40	1	2	-1	.986	-1	O/D	-0.5
1986	Mil-A	26	78	4	17	3	1	1	16	7	16	.218	.291	.321	64	-4	-4	7	1	2	-1	1.000	-3	O/D	-0.8
1987	Hou-N	14	12	2	1	1	0	0	1	4	2	.083	.313	.167	33	-1	-1	1	0	0	0	1.000	-2	/O	-0.3
Total	8	466	1326	146	313	60	11	29	144	126	250	.236	.305	.363	83	-29	-31	146	36	29	-7	.991	-7	O/D	-5.8

■ JOHN HOUSEMAN

Houseman, John Franklin b: 1/10/1870, Holland d: 11/4/22, Chicago, Ill. 160 lbs. Deb: 9/11/1894

YEAR	TM/L	G	AB	R	H	2B	3B	HR	RBI	BB	SO	AVG	OBP	SLG	PRO+	BR	/A	RC	SB	CS	SBR	FA	FR	POS	TPR
1894	Chi-N	4	15	5	6	3	1	0	4	5	3	.400	.571	.733	204	3	3	8	2			.950	-0	/S2	0.2
1897	StL-N	80	278	34	68	6	6	0	21	28		.245	.329	.309	70	-12	-11	35	16			.918	-4	2O/S3	-1.2
Total	2	84	293	39	74	9	7	0	25	33	3	.253	.344	.331	79	-9	-8	43	18			.916	-4	/2OS3	-1.0

■ BEN HOUSER

Houser, Benjamin Franklin b: 11/30/1883, Shenandoah, Pa. d: 1/15/52, Augusta, Maine BL/TL, 6'1", 185 lbs. Deb: 5/02/10

YEAR	TM/L	G	AB	R	H	2B	3B	HR	RBI	BB	SO	AVG	OBP	SLG	PRO+	BR	/A	RC	SB	CS	SBR	FA	FR	POS	TPR
1910	Phi-A	34	69	9	13	3	2	0	7	7		.188	.263	.290	74	-2	-2	5	0			1.000	-0	1	-0.3
1911	Bos-N	20	71	11	18	1	0	1	9	8	6	.254	.329	.310	73	-2	-3	8	2			.988	0	1	-0.2
1912	Bos-N	108	332	38	95	17	3	8	52	22	29	.286	.332	.428	105	2	1	47	1			.986	-3	1	-0.3
Total	3	162	472	58	126	21	5	9	68	37	35	.267	.322	.390	96	-2	-4	60	3			.989	-3	1	-0.8

■ WAYNE HOUSIE

Housie, Wayne Tyrone b: 5/20/65, Hampton, Va. BB/TR, 5'9", 165 lbs. Deb: 9/17/91

YEAR	TM/L	G	AB	R	H	2B	3B	HR	RBI	BB	SO	AVG	OBP	SLG	PRO+	BR	/A	RC	SB	CS	SBR	FA	FR	POS	TPR
1991	Bos-A	11	8	2	2	1	0	0	0	1	3	.250	.333	.375	91	-0	-0	1	1	0	0	1.000	-1	/OD	-0.1

■ LEFTY HOUTZ

Houtz, Fred Fritz b: 9/4/1875, Connersville, Ind. d: 2/15/59, Wapakoneta, Ohio BL/TL, 5'10", 170 lbs. Deb: 7/23/1899

YEAR	TM/L	G	AB	R	H	2B	3B	HR	RBI	BB	SO	AVG	OBP	SLG	PRO+	BR	/A	RC	SB	CS	SBR	FA	FR	POS	TPR
1899	Cin-N	5	17	1	4	0	1	0	0	4		.235	.381	.353	100	0	0	3	1			1.000	4	/O	0.4

■ STEVE HOVLEY

Hovley, Stephen Eugene b: 12/18/44, Ventura, Cal. BL/TL, 5'10", 188 lbs. Deb: 6/26/69

YEAR	TM/L	G	AB	R	H	2B	3B	HR	RBI	BB	SO	AVG	OBP	SLG	PRO+	BR	/A	RC	SB	CS	SBR	FA	FR	POS	TPR
1969	Sea-A	91	329	41	91	14	3	3	20	30	34	.277	.339	.365	98	-1	-1	43	10	4	1	.989	7	O	0.2
1970	Mil-A	40	135	17	38	9	0	0	16	17	11	.281	.366	.348	97	0	0	18	5	1	1	.958	-2	O	-0.3
	Oak-A	72	100	8	19	1	0	0	1	5	11	.190	.229	.200	20	-11	-11	5	3	0	1	1.000	-6	O	-1.7
	Yr	112	235	25	57	10	0	0	17	22	22	.243	.310	.285	67	-11	-10	22	8	1	2	.977	-8	O	-2.0
1971	Oak-A	24	27	3	3	2	0	0	3	7	9	.111	.314	.185	45	-2	-2	3	2	0	1	1.000	-1	O	-0.2
1972	KC-A	105	196	24	53	5	1	3	24	24	29	.270	.353	.352	111	3	3	26	3	3	-1	.982	-5	O	-0.5
1973	KC-A	104	232	29	59	8	1	2	24	33	34	.254	.347	.323	83	-2	-4	28	6	4	-1	.975	-10	OD	-1.8
Total	5	436	1019	122	263	39	5	8	88	116	128	.258	.336	.330	88	-13	-14	122	29	12	2	.982	-16	O/D	-4.3

■ CHRIS HOWARD

Howard, Christopher Hugh b: 2/27/66, San Diego, Cal. BR/TR, 6'2", 200 lbs. Deb: 9/15/91

YEAR	TM/L	G	AB	R	H	2B	3B	HR	RBI	BB	SO	AVG	OBP	SLG	PRO+	BR	/A	RC	SB	CS	SBR	FA	FR	POS	TPR
1991	Sea-A	9	6	1	1	1	0	0	0	1	2	.167	.286	.333	71	-0	-0	1	0	0	0	1.000	1	/C	0.1

■ DAVE HOWARD

Howard, David Austin "Del" b: 5/1/1889, Washington, D.C. d: 1/26/56, Dallas, Tex. BR/TR, 5'11", 165 lbs. Deb: 5/08/12

YEAR	TM/L	G	AB	R	H	2B	3B	HR	RBI	BB	SO	AVG	OBP	SLG	PRO+	BR	/A	RC	SB	CS	SBR	FA	FR	POS	TPR
1912	Was-A	1	0	1	0	0	0	0	0	0		—	—	—	—	0	0	0	0			.000	-0	R	0.0
1915	Bro-F	24	36	5	8	1	0	0	1	1	8	.222	.243	.250	45	-3	-2	2	0			.925	3	2/OS3	0.0
Total	2	25	36	6	8	1	0	0	1	1	8	.222	.243	.250	45	-3	-2	2	0				3	/2O3S	0.0

YEAR	TM/L	G	AB	R	H	2B	3B	HR	RBI	BB	SO	AVG	OBP	SLG	PRO+	BR	/A	RC	SB	CS	SBR	FA	FR	POS	TPR

■ DAVID HOWARD Howard, David Wayne b: 2/26/67, Sarasota, Fla. BB/TR, 6', 165 lbs. Deb: 4/14/91 F

1991	KC-A	94	236	20	51	7	0	1	17	16	45	.216	.269	.258	46	-17	-17	18	3	2	-0	.962	19	S2/3OD	0.6
1992	KC-A	74	219	19	49	6	2	1	18	15	43	.224	.274	.283	56	-13	-13	17	3	4	-2	.976	-3	S/O	-1.2
Total	2	168	455	39	100	13	2	2	35	31	88	.220	.271	.270	51	-30	-30	35	6	6	-2	.970	16	S/20D3	-0.6

■ DOUG HOWARD Howard, Douglas Lynn b: 2/6/48, Salt Lake City, Utah BR/TR, 6'3", 185 lbs. Deb: 9/06/72

1972	Cal-A	11	38	4	10	1	0	0	2	1	3	.263	.300	.289	81	-1	-1	3	0	0	0	1.000	-1	/O13	-0.2
1973	Cal-A	8	21	2	2	0	0	0	1	1	6	.095	.136	.095	-37	-4	-3	0	0	0	0	1.000	-1	/O13	-0.5
1974	Cal-A	22	39	5	9	0	1	0	5	2	1	.231	.268	.282	62	-2	-2	2	1	0	0	1.000	-2	/O1D	-0.4
1975	StL-N	17	29	1	6	0	0	1	1	0	7	.207	.207	.310	41	-2	-2	2	0	0	0	1.000	1	/1	-0.2
1976	Cle-N	39	90	7	19	4	0	0	13	3	13	.211	.245	.256	47	-6	-6	5	1	1	-0	.991	1	1/OD	-0.7
Total	5	97	217	19	46	5	1	1	22	7	30	.212	.243	.258	46	-15	-15	13	2	1	-0	.994	-1	/1OD3	-2.0

■ ELSTON HOWARD Howard, Elston Gene b: 2/23/29, St.Louis, Mo. d: 12/14/80, New York, N.Y. BR/TR, 6'2", 200 lbs. Deb: 4/14/55 C

1955	*NY-A	97	279	33	81	8	7	10	43	20	36	.290	.340	.477	120	5	6	45	0	0	0	.978	2	O/C	0.5
1956	*NY-A	98	290	35	76	8	3	5	34	21	30	.262	.314	.362	81	-10	-8	30	0	1	-1	.990	-5	OC	-1.5
1957	*NY-A☆	110	356	33	90	13	4	8	44	16	43	.253	.285	.379	81	-11	-10	31	2	5	-2	.961	-12	OC/1	-2.8
1958	*NY-A☆	103	376	45	118	19	5	11	66	22	60	.314	.352	.479	131	12	14	60	1	1	-0	.997	2	CO/1	1.8
1959	NY-A☆	125	443	59	121	24	6	18	73	20	57	.273	.309	.476	116	5	7	61	0	1	-1	.985	-2	1CO	0.2
1960	*NY-A★	107	323	29	79	11	3	6	39	28	43	.245	.305	.353	82	-11	-8	35	3	0	1	.987	2	C/1	-0.1
1961	*NY-A★	129	446	64	155	17	5	21	77	28	65	.348	.390	.549	156	29	32	94	0	3	-2	.993	7	*C/1	4.1
1962	*NY-A★	136	494	63	138	23	5	21	91	31	76	.279	.323	.474	115	6	8	69	1	1	-0	.995	-1	*C	1.2
1963	*NY-A★	135	487	75	140	21	6	28	85	35	68	.287	.343	.528	141	24	25	83	0	0	0	.994	-3	*C	2.7
1964	*NY-A★	150	550	63	172	27	3	15	84	48	73	.313	.373	.455	127	22	21	93	1	1	-0	.998	11	*C	3.9
1965	NY-A☆	110	391	38	91	15	1	9	45	24	65	.233	.279	.345	77	-13	-12	34	0	0	0	.991	-5	C/1O	-1.3
1966	NY-A	126	410	38	105	19	2	6	35	37	65	.256	.319	.356	97	-3	-1	45	0	0	0	.985	-4	*C1	0.1
1967	NY-A	66	199	13	39	6	0	3	17	12	36	.196	.249	.271	56	-12	-11	13	0	0	0	.984	-1	C/1	-1.0
	*Bos-A	42	116	9	17	3	0	1	11	9	24	.147	.214	.198	21	-11	-12	5	0	0	0	.996	2	C	-0.9
	Yr	108	315	22	56	9	0	4	28	21	60	.178	.236	.244	42	-23	-23	17	0	0	0	.990	1	C/1	-1.9
1968	Bos-A	71	203	22	49	4	0	5	18	22	45	.241	.319	.335	92	-0	-2	21	1	1	-0	.995	-3	C	-0.1
Total	14	1605	5363	619	1471	218	50	167	762	373	786	.274	.322	.427	108	34	47	718	9	14	-6	.993	-9	*CO/1	6.8

■ FRANK HOWARD Howard, Frank Oliver "Hondo" or "The Capital Punisher" b: 8/8/36, Columbus, Ohio BR/TR, 6'7", 255 lbs. Deb: 9/10/58 MC

1958	LA-N	8	29	3	7	1	0	1	2	1	11	.241	.267	.379	66	-1	-1	3	0	0	0	1.000	0	/O	-0.2
1959	LA-N	9	21	2	3	0	1	1	6	2	9	.143	.217	.381	52	-1	-2	2	0	0	0	1.000	-0	/O	-0.2
1960	LA-N	117	448	54	120	15	2	23	77	32	108	.268	.321	.464	105	6	3	66	0	1	-1	.984	-2	*O/1	-0.6
1961	LA-N	92	267	36	79	10	2	15	45	21	50	.296	.349	.517	116	9	6	44	0	1	-1	.934	-5	O/1	-0.3
1962	LA-N	141	493	80	146	25	6	31	119	39	108	.296	.349	.560	148	25	29	90	1	0	0	.972	3	*O	2.5
1963	*LA-N	123	417	58	114	16	1	28	64	33	116	.273	.333	.518	151	21	24	70	1	2	-1	.960	-2	*O	1.6
1964	LA-N	134	433	60	98	13	2	24	69	51	113	.226	.308	.432	114	3	7	56	1	0	0	.979	-8	*O	-0.8
1965	Was-A	149	516	53	149	22	6	21	84	55	112	.289	.360	.477	138	24	25	90	0	0	0	.981	-8	*O	1.2
1966	Was-A	146	493	52	137	19	4	18	71	53	104	.278	.349	.442	127	16	17	74	1	1	-0	.982	-2	*O	0.9
1967	Was-A	149	519	71	133	20	2	36	89	60	155	.256	.339	.511	154	30	32	88	0	1	-1	.986	-7	*O/1	1.9
1968	Was-A★	158	598	79	164	28	3	44	106	54	141	.274	.340	.552	172	45	47	110	0	0	0	.955	2	*O1	4.5
1969	Was-A★	161	592	111	175	17	2	48	111	102	96	.296	.403	.574	180	57	61	132	1	0	0	.974	-18	*O1	3.4
1970	Was-A★	161	566	90	160	15	1	44	126	132	125	.283	.420	.546	173	54	58	130	1	2	-1	.973	-9	*O1	3.9
1971	Was-A★	153	549	60	153	25	2	26	83	77	121	.279	.369	.474	146	27	31	89	1	0	0	.993	3	*O1	2.6
1972	Tex-A	95	287	28	70	9	0	9	31	42	55	.244	.342	.369	117	5	6	34	1	0	0	.981	-6	1O	-0.6
	Det-A	14	33	1	8	1	0	1	7	4	8	.242	.324	.364	101	0	0	4	0	0	0	.952	-1	1/O	-0.1
	Yr	109	320	29	78	10	0	10	38	46	63	.244	.341	.369	115	5	6	39	1	0	0	.978	-7	1O	-0.7
1973	Det-A	85	227	26	58	9	1	12	29	24	28	.256	.327	.463	113	5	3	30	0	1	-1	.923	-1	D/1	0.2
Total	16	1895	6488	864	1774	245	35	382	1119	782	1460	.273	.355	.499	143	324	344	1110	8	9	-3	.975	-60	*O1/D	19.9

■ DEL HOWARD Howard, George Elmer b: 12/24/1877, Kenney, Ill. d: 12/24/56, Seattle, Wash. BL/TR, 6', 180 lbs. Deb: 4/15/05 F

1905	Pit-N	123	435	56	127	18	5	2	63	27		.292	.345	.370	110	7	5	65	19			.978	-7	1O/P	-0.5
1906	Bos-N	147	545	46	142	19	8	1	54	26		.261	.306	.330	102	-2	-0	63	17			.911	-12	O2S/1	-1.7
1907	Bos-N	50	187	20	51	4	2	1	13	11		.273	.330	.332	108	2	2	25	11			.969	-3	O/2	-0.3
	*Chi-N	51	148	10	34	2	2	0	13	6		.230	.269	.270	65	-5	-6	12	3			.972	-4	1/O	-1.3
	Yr	101	335	30	85	6	4	1	26	17		.254	.304	.304	88	-4	-5	36	14			.961	-6	O1/2	-1.6
1908	*Chi-N	96	315	42	88	7	3	1	26	23		.279	.338	.330	109	5	4	39	11			.965	-5	O/1	-0.6
1909	Chi-N	69	203	25	40	4	2	1	24	18		.197	.282	.251	64	-8	-8	17	6			.980	0	1	-1.0
Total	5	536	1833	199	482	54	22	6	193	111		.263	.318	.326	98	-2	-4	221	67			.946	-30	O1/2SP	-5.4

■ IVON HOWARD Howard, Ivon Chester b: 10/12/1882, Kenney, Ill. d: 3/30/67, Medford, Ore. BB/TR, 5'10", 170 lbs. Deb: 4/25/14 F

1914	StL-A	81	209	21	51	6	2	0	20	28	42	.244	.342	.292	94	-1	-0	23	14	10	-2	.936	-7	31/OS	-1.0
1915	StL-A	113	324	43	90	10	7	2	43	43	48	.278	.368	.370	126	9	11	50	29	12	2	.992	5	130/2S	1.7
1916	Cle-A	81	246	20	46	11	5	0	23	30	34	.187	.298	.272	68	-8	-10	24	9			.970	7	2/1	-0.1
1917	Cle-A	27	39	7	4	0	0	0	0	3	5	.103	.167	.103	-17	-5	-6	1	1			.833	2	/32O	-0.4
Total	4	302	818	91	191	27	14	2	86	104	129	.233	.331	.308	92	-6	-5	98	53	22		.990	6	/1230S	0.2

■ LARRY HOWARD Howard, Lawrence Rayford b: 6/6/45, Columbus, Ohio BR/TR, 6'3", 200 lbs. Deb: 8/09/70

1970	Hou-N	31	88	11	27	6	0	2	16	10	23	.307	.378	.443	124	2	3	15	0	0	0	.993	-5	C/1O	-0.1
1971	Hou-N	24	64	6	15	3	0	2	14	3	17	.234	.269	.375	83	-2	-2	6	0	1	-1	.992	2	C	0.1
1972	Hou-N	54	157	16	35	7	0	2	13	17	30	.223	.299	.306	74	-6	-5	14	0	0	0	.980	0	C/O	-0.3
1973	Hou-N	20	48	3	8	3	0	0	4	5	12	.167	.245	.229	32	-4	-4	3	0	0	0	.989	-1	C	-0.5
	Atl-N	4	8	0	1	0	0	0	0	2	3	.125	.300	.125	20	-1	-1	0	0	0	0	1.000	-0	/C	-0.1
	Yr	24	56	3	9	3	0	0	4	7	15	.161	.254	.214	31	-5	-5	3	0	0	0	.990	-1	C	-0.6
Total	4	133	365	36	86	19	0	6	47	37	85	.236	.306	.337	81	-10	-9	37	0	1	-1	.986	-4	C/O1	-0.9

■ MIKE HOWARD Howard, Michael Fredric b: 4/2/58, Seattle, Wash. BB/TR, 6'2", 185 lbs. Deb: 9/12/81

1981	NY-N	14	24	4	4	1	0	0	3	6	4	.167	.286	.208	43	-2	-2	2	2	0	1	.952	2	O	0.0
1982	NY-N	33	39	5	7	0	0	1	3	6	7	.179	.304	.256	59	-2	-2	4	2	0	1	1.000	4	O/2	0.2
1983	NY-N	1	3	0	1	0	0	0	1	0	1	.333	.333	.333	86	-0	-0	0	0	0	0	.000	0	/O	0.0
Total	3	48	66	9	12	1	0	1	7	10	14	.182	.299	.242	54	-4	-4	6	4	0	1	.980	5	/O2	0.2

■ PAUL HOWARD Howard, Paul Joseph "Del" b: 5/20/1884, Boston, Mass. d: 8/29/68, Miami, Fla. BR/TR, 5'8", 170 lbs. Deb: 9/16/09

| 1909 | Bos-A | 6 | 15 | 2 | 3 | 1 | 0 | 0 | 2 | 3 | | .200 | .368 | .267 | 99 | 0 | 0 | 2 | 0 | 0 | 0 | 1.000 | -1 | /O | -0.1 |

■ STEVE HOWARD Howard, Steven Bernard b: 12/7/63, Oakland, Cal. BR/TR, 6'2", 205 lbs. Deb: 6/16/90

| 1990 | Oak-A | 21 | 52 | 5 | 12 | 4 | 0 | 1 | 4 | 17 | | .231 | .286 | .308 | 69 | -2 | -2 | 5 | 0 | 0 | 0 | .933 | -4 | O/D | -0.6 |

YEAR	TM/L	G	AB	R	H	2B	3B	HR	RBI	BB	SO	AVG	OBP	SLG	PRO+	BR	/A	RC	SB	CS	SBR	FA	FR	POS	TPR
■ THOMAS HOWARD Howard, Thomas Sylvester b: 12/11/64, Middletown, Ohio BB/TR, 6'2", 200 lbs. Deb: 7/03/90																									
1990	SD-N	20	44	4	12	2	0	0	0	0	11	.273	.273	.318	61	-2	-2	3	0	1	-1	.950	-2	O	-0.5
1991	SD-N	106	281	30	70	12	3	4	22	24	57	.249	.310	.356	84	-5	-6	31	10	7	-1	.995	3	O	-0.6
1992	SD-N	5	3	1	1	0	0	0	0	0	0	.333	.333	.333	86	-0	-0	0	0	0	0	.000	0	/H	0.0
	Cle-A	117	358	36	99	15	2	2	32	17	60	.277	.309	.346	82	-8	-9	38	15	8	-0	.990	-6	O/D	-1.8
Total	3	248	686	71	182	29	5	6	54	41	128	.265	.308	.348	82	-16	-17	72	25	16	-2	.990	-5	O/D	-2.9
■ WILBUR HOWARD Howard, Wilbur Leon b: 1/8/49, Lowell, N.C. BB/TR, 6'2", 175 lbs. Deb: 9/04/73																									
1973	Mil-A	16	39	3	8	0	0	0	1	2	10	.205	.244	.205	28	-4	-4	2	0	1	-1	.969	2	O/D	-0.2
1974	Hou-N	64	111	19	24	4	0	2	5	5	18	.216	.250	.306	57	-7	-6	7	4	5	-2	1.000	4	O	-0.6
1975	Hou-N	121	392	62	111	16	8	0	21	21	67	.283	.325	.365	98	-5	-2	49	32	11	3	.995	4	O	0.2
1976	Hou-N	94	191	26	42	7	2	1	18	7	28	.220	.247	.293	58	-12	-10	12	7	5	-1	.961	1	O/2	-1.2
1977	Hou-N	87	187	22	48	6	0	2	13	5	30	.257	.276	.321	65	-11	-9	17	11	1	3	.990	2	O/2	-0.6
1978	Hou-N	84	148	17	34	4	1	1	13	5	22	.230	.269	.291	61	-9	-7	12	6	2	1	1.000	1	O/C2	-0.7
Total	6	466	1068	149	267	37	11	6	71	45	175	.250	.284	.322	73	-48	-39	98	60	25	3	.987	14	O/2CD	-3.1
■ JIM HOWARTH Howarth, James Eugene b: 3/7/47, Biloxi, Miss. BL/TL, 5'11", 175 lbs. Deb: 9/05/71																									
1971	SF-N	7	13	3	3	1	0	0	2	3	3	.231	.375	.308	97	0	0	2	0	0	0	1.000	0	/O	0.0
1972	SF-N	74	119	16	28	4	0	1	7	16	18	.235	.326	.294	76	-3	-3	12	3	2	-0	1.000	-1	O/1	-0.6
1973	SF-N	65	90	8	18	1	1	0	7	7	8	.200	.258	.233	36	-8	-8	6	0	0	0	1.000	2	O/1	-0.7
1974	SF-N	6	4	0	0	0	0	0	0	0	0	.000	.000	.000	-96	-1	-1	0	0	0	0	.000	0	/O	-0.1
Total	4	152	226	27	49	6	1	1	16	26	29	.217	.298	.265	58	-12	-12	19	3	2	-0	1.000	1	/O1	-1.4
■ ART HOWE Howe, Arthur Henry b: 12/15/46, Pittsburgh, Pa. BR/TR, 6'2", 190 lbs. Deb: 7/10/74 MC																									
1974	*Pit-N	29	74	10	18	4	1	1	5	9	13	.243	.325	.365	96	-1	-0	9	0	0	0	.937	4	3/S	0.3
1975	Pit-N	63	146	13	25	9	0	1	10	15	15	.171	.248	.253	40	-12	-12	9	1	0	0	.938	3	3/S	-0.9
1976	Hou-N	21	29	0	4	1	0	0	0	6	6	.138	.286	.172	35	-2	-2	2	0	0	0	.938	2	/32	0.0
1977	Hou-N	125	413	44	109	23	7	8	58	41	60	.264	.338	.412	110	-0	5	57	0	1	-1	.985	6	23S	1.7
1978	Hou-N	119	420	46	123	33	3	7	55	34	41	.293	.347	.436	127	9	13	60	2	3	-1	.977	-4	*23/1	1.6
1979	Hou-N	118	355	32	88	15	2	6	33	36	37	.248	.319	.352	88	-8	-6	41	3	1	0	.991	6	23/1	0.4
1980	*Hou-N	110	321	34	91	12	5	10	46	34	29	.283	.354	.445	132	9	12	50	1	0	0	.986	1	13/S2	1.0
1981	*Hou-N	103	361	43	107	22	4	3	36	41	23	.296	.368	.404	125	10	12	53	1	3	-2	.966	5	3/1	1.4
1982	Hou-N	110	365	29	87	15	1	5	38	41	45	.238	.317	.326	87	-9	-6	38	2	0	1	.972	8	31	-0.1
1984	StL-N	89	139	17	30	5	0	2	12	18	18	.216	.306	.295	71	-5	-5	12	0	2	-1	.979	8	31/2S	0.1
1985	StL-N	4	3	0	0	0	0	0	0	0	0	.000	.000	.000	-99	-1	-1	0	0	0	0	1.000	0	/13	-0.1
Total	11	891	2626	268	682	139	23	43	293	275	287	.260	.332	.379	103	-11	10	330	10	10	-3	.965	38	321/S	5.4
■ SHORTY HOWE Howe, John b: New York, N.Y. Deb: 6/17/1890																									
1890	NY-N	19	64	4	11	0	0	0	4	3	2	.172	.221	.172	16	-7	-7	3	3			.887	3	2/3	-0.2
1893	NY-N	1	5	1	3	0	0	0	2	0	0	.600	.600	.600	222	1	1	2	1			.400	-1	/3	0.0
Total	2	20	69	5	14	0	0	0	6	3	2	.203	.247	.203	32	-6	-6	6	4			.400	2	/23	-0.2
■ HARRY HOWELL Howell, Henry Harry b: 11/14/1876, New Jersey d: 5/22/56, Spokane, Wash. BR/TR, 5'9", Deb: 10/10/1898 U																									
1898	Bro-N	2	8	1	2	0	0	0	1	1		.250	.333	.250	68	-0	-0	1	0			1.000	0	/P	0.0
1899	Bal-N	28	82	4	12	2	2	0	3	3		.146	.195	.220	13	-10	-11	4	0			.940	1	P	0.0
1900	*Bro-N	22	42	6	12	2	0	1	6	6		.286	.388	.405	112	1	1	7	1			.949	1	P	0.0
1901	Bal-A	53	188	26	41	10	5	2	26	5		.218	.242	.356	62	-10	-11	18	6			.905	-4	P/OS12	-0.5
1902	Bal-A	96	347	42	93	16	11	2	42	18		.268	.310	.395	90	-4	-6	47	7			.951	-9	P2O3S/1	-1.7
1903	NY-A	40	106	14	23	3	2	1	12	5		.217	.259	.311	66	-4	-5	9	1			1.000	1	P/3S12	-0.4
1904	StL-A	36	113	9	25	5	2	1	6	4		.221	.261	.327	91	-2	-1	10	0			.971	9	P	0.0
1905	StL-A	42	135	9	26	6	2	1	10	3		.193	.216	.289	63	-7	-6	9	0			.966	18	P/O	0.0
1906	StL-A	35	103	5	13	3	1	0	6	6		.126	.174	.175	10	-11	-10	4	2			.934	7	P	0.0
1907	StL-A	44	114	12	27	5	0	2	7	7		.237	.281	.333	96	-1	-1	12	2			.982	9	P/O	0.1
1908	StL-A	41	120	10	22	7	0	1	9	4		.183	.210	.267	54	-6	-6	6	0			.961	0	P	0.0
1909	StL-A	18	34	5	6	1	0	0	3	2		.176	.222	.206	38	-3	-2	2	0			.938	1	P/3O	0.0
1910	StL-A	1	2	0	0	0	0	0	0	0		.000	.000	.000	-99	-0	-0	0	0			1.000	0	/P	0.0
Total	13	458	1394	143	302	60	25	11	131	64		.217	.257	.319	69	-56	-59	130	19			.958	35	P/O32S1	-2.5
■ DIXIE HOWELL Howell, Homer Elliott b: 4/24/20, Louisville, Ky. d: 10/5/90, Binghamton, N.Y. BR/TR, 5'11", 195 lbs. Deb: 5/06/47																									
1947	Pit-N	76	214	23	59	11	0	4	25	27	34	.276	.357	.383	94	-1	-1	31	1			.974	-3	C	0.0
1949	Cin-N	64	172	17	42	6	1	2	18	8	21	.244	.286	.326	63	-9	-9	15	0			.987	5	C	-0.1
1950	Cin-N	82	224	30	50	9	1	2	22	32	31	.223	.326	.299	65	-11	-11	23	0			.986	-4	C	-1.1
1951	Cin-N	77	207	22	52	6	1	2	18	15	34	.251	.302	.319	66	-10	-10	20	0	2	-1	.987	4	C	-0.5
1952	Cin-N	17	37	4	7	1	1	2	4	3	9	.189	.250	.432	86	-1	-1	3	0	0	0	.981	1	C	0.0
1953	Bro-N	1	1	0	0	0	0	0	0	0	1	.000	.000	.000	-98	-0	-0	0	0	0	0	.000	0	H	0.0
1955	Bro-N	16	42	2	11	4	0	0	5	1	7	.262	.279	.357	66	-2	-2	4	0	0	0	.981	-2	C	-0.3
1956	Bro-N	7	13	0	3	2	0	0	1	1	3	.231	.286	.385	72	-0	-1	2	0	0	0	1.000	-0	/C	-0.1
Total	8	340	910	98	224	39	4	12	93	87	140	.246	.315	.337	73	-34	-35	98	1	2		.984	2	C	-2.1
■ JACK HOWELL Howell, Jack Robert b: 8/18/61, Tucson, Ariz. BL/TR, 6', 185 lbs. Deb: 5/20/85																									
1985	Cal-A	43	137	19	27	4	0	5	18	16	33	.197	.281	.336	68	-6	-6	14	1	1	-0	.931	-1	3	-0.8
1986	*Cal-A	63	151	26	41	14	2	4	21	19	28	.272	.353	.470	123	5	5	27	2	0	1	.977	-1	3/OD	0.4
1987	Cal-A	138	449	64	110	18	5	23	64	57	118	.245	.333	.461	111	4	7	70	4	3	-1	.987	-8	O32	-0.5
1988	Cal-A	154	500	59	127	32	2	16	63	46	130	.254	.324	.422	110	4	6	67	2	6	-3	.953	-20	*3/O	-1.8
1989	Cal-A	144	474	56	108	19	4	20	52	52	125	.228	.308	.411	103	-0	1	60	0	3	-2	**.974**	23	*3/O	2.3
1990	Cal-A	105	316	35	72	19	1	8	33	46	61	.228	.328	.370	97	-2	-1	42	3	0	1	.939	7	*3/1S	0.8
1991	Cal-A	32	81	11	17	2	0	2	7	11	11	.210	.304	.309	70	-3	-3	8	1	1	-0	.968	2	2/3O1D	-0.2
	SD-N	58	160	24	33	3	1	6	16	18	33	.206	.287	.350	76	-5	-5	17	0	0	0	.985	6	3	0.1
Total	7	737	2268	294	535	111	15	84	274	265	539	.236	.319	.409	101	-3	3	304	13	14	-5	.961	8	3O/21DS	0.3
■ RED HOWELL Howell, Murray Donald "Porky" b: 1/29/09, Atlanta, Ga. d: 10/1/50, Travelers Rest, S.C BR/TR, 6', 215 lbs. Deb: 4/24/41																									
1941	Cle-A	11	7	0	2	0	0	0	2	4	2	.286	.545	.286	132	1	1	2	0	0	0	.000	0	H	0.1
■ PAT HOWELL Howell, Patrick O'Neal b: 8/31/68, Mobile, Ala. BB/TR, 5'11", 155 lbs. Deb: 7/10/92																									
1992	NY-N	31	75	9	14	1	0	0	1	2	15	.187	.218	.200	19	-8	-8	3	4	2	0	1.000	-0	O	-1.0
■ ROY HOWELL Howell, Roy Lee b: 12/18/53, Lompoc, Cal. BL/TR, 6'1", 190 lbs. Deb: 9/09/74																									
1974	Tex-A	13	44	2	11	1	0	1	3	2	10	.250	.283	.341	81	-1	-1	4	0	0	0	.906	-2	3	-0.3
1975	Tex-A	125	383	43	96	15	2	10	51	39	79	.251	.325	.379	99	-1	-1	48	2	2	-1	.933	-7	*3/D	-0.8
1976	Tex-A	140	491	55	124	28	2	8	53	30	106	.253	.297	.367	92	-5	-6	51	1	0	0	.926	-8	*3/D	-1.6
1977	Tex-A	7	17	0	0	0	0	0	0	2	4	.000	.105	.000	-68	-4	-4	0	0	0	0	1.000	-0	/O13D	-0.4
	Tor-A	96	364	41	115	17	1	10	44	42	76	.316	.388	.451	126	15	14	61	4	1	1	.953	-7	3/D	0.7
	Yr	103	381	41	115	17	1	10	44	44	80	.302	.376	.430	117	11	10	60	4	1	1	.954	-7	3D/O1	0.3
1978	Tor-A★	140	551	67	149	28	3	8	61	44	78	.270	.326	.376	95	-3	-4	67	0	1	-1	.950	11	*3/OD	0.4
1979	Tor-A	138	511	60	126	28	4	15	72	42	91	.247	.311	.405	90	-7	-8	62	1	4	-2	.952	-1	*3/D	-1.2

YEAR	TM/L	G	AB	R	H	2B	3B	HR	RBI	BB	SO	AVG	OBP	SLG	PRO+	BR	/A	RC	SB	CS	SBR	FA	FR	POS	TPR
1980	Tor-A	142	528	51	142	28	9	10	57	50	92	.269	.338	.413	100	3	0	74	0	0	0	.958	-18	*3/D	-2.0
1981	*Mil-A	76	244	37	58	13	1	6	33	23	39	.238	.309	.373	101	-2	-0	28	0	0	0	.958	-6	3D/1O	-0.7
1982	*Mil-A	98	300	31	78	11	2	4	38	21	39	.260	.308	.350	86	-8	-6	33	0	2	-1	.933	-1	D/1O	-0.8
1983	Mil-A	69	194	23	54	9	6	4	25	15	29	.278	.330	.448	121	3	5	27	1	3	-2	.960	1	D/1	0.4
1984	Mil-A	68	164	12	38	5	1	4	17	8	32	.232	.284	.348	77	-6	-5	14	0	1	-1	.907	1	3/1D	-0.5
Total	11	1112	3791	422	991	183	31	80	454	318	675	.261	.322	.389	97	-16	-16	470	9	14	-6	.944	-35	3D/1O	-6.8

■ BILL HOWERTON
Howerton, William Ray "Hopalong" b: 12/12/21, Lompoc, Cal. BL/TR, 5'11", 185 lbs. Deb: 9/11/49

YEAR	TM/L	G	AB	R	H	2B	3B	HR	RBI	BB	SO	AVG	OBP	SLG	PRO+	BR	/A	RC	SB	CS	SBR	FA	FR	POS	TPR
1949	StL-N	9	13	1	4	1	0	0	1	0	2	.308	.308	.385	81	-0	-0	2	0			.900	-1	/O	-0.2
1950	StL-N	110	313	50	88	20	8	10	59	47	60	.281	.375	.492	120	12	10	61	0			.969	-11	O	-0.4
1951	StL-N	24	65	10	17	4	1	1	4	10	12	.262	.360	.400	104	1	1	9	0	1	-1	.949	1	O	0.0
	Pit-N	80	219	29	60	12	2	11	37	26	44	.274	.351	.498	122	7	7	37	1	0	0	.950	-8	O/3	-0.3
	Yr	104	284	39	77	16	3	12	41	36	56	.271	.353	.475	118	8	7	47	1	1	-0	.950	-8	O/3	-0.3
1952	Pit-N	13	25	3	8	1	1	0	4	6	5	.320	.452	.440	144	2	2	5	0	0	0	.900	-2	/O3	0.0
	NY-N	11	15	2	1	1	0	0	1	3	2	.067	.222	.133	1	-2	-2	1	0	0	0	1.000	-0	/O	-0.2
	Yr	24	40	5	9	2	1	0	5	9	7	.225	.367	.325	92	0	-0	5	0	0	0	.938	-2	/O3	-0.2
Total	4	247	650	95	178	39	12	22	106	92	125	.274	.364	.472	117	20	16	115	1	1		.958	-22	O/3	-1.1

■ DANN HOWITT
Howitt, Dann Paul John b: 2/13/64, Battle Creek, Mich. BL/TR, 6'5", 205 lbs. Deb: 9/15/89

YEAR	TM/L	G	AB	R	H	2B	3B	HR	RBI	BB	SO	AVG	OBP	SLG	PRO+	BR	/A	RC	SB	CS	SBR	FA	FR	POS	TPR
1989	Oak-A	3	3	0	0	0	0	0	0	0	2	.000	.000	.000	-99	-1	-1	0	0	0	0	1.000	-1	/1O	-0.1
1990	Oak-A	14	22	3	3	0	1	0	1	3	12	.136	.240	.227	33	-2	-2	1	0	0	0	1.000	-2	O/13	-0.4
1991	Oak-A	21	42	5	7	1	0	1	3	1	12	.167	.186	.262	24	-4	-4	2	0	0	0	1.000	-4	O/1	-0.9
1992	Oak-A	22	48	1	6	0	0	1	2	5	4	.125	.208	.188	12	-6	-5	1	0	0	0	.951	1	O/1	-0.5
	Sea-A	13	37	6	10	4	1	1	8	3	5	.270	.325	.514	130	1	1	5	1	1	-0	1.000	1	O/D	0.2
	Yr	35	85	7	16	4	1	2	10	8	9	.188	.258	.329	65	-4	-4	6	1	1	-0	.970	2	O/1D	-0.3
Total	4	73	152	15	26	5	2	3	14	12	35	.171	.232	.289	46	-12	-11	10	1	1	-0	.982	-5	/O1D3	-1.7

■ DAN HOWLEY
Howley, Daniel Philip "Howling Dan" or "Dapper Dan" b: 10/16/1885, Weymouth, Mass. d: 3/10/44, Weymouth, Mass. BR/TR, 6', 187 lbs. Deb: 5/15/13 MC

YEAR	TM/L	G	AB	R	H	2B	3B	HR	RBI	BB	SO	AVG	OBP	SLG	PRO+	BR	/A	RC	SB	CS	SBR	FA	FR	POS	TPR
1913	Phi-N	26	32	5	4	2	0	0	2	4	4	.125	.222	.188	17	-3	-4	2	3			.954	1	C	-0.2

■ DICK HOWSER
Howser, Richard Dalton b: 5/14/36, Miami, Fla. d: 6/17/87, Kansas City, Mo. BR/TR, 5'8", 155 lbs. Deb: 4/11/61 MC

YEAR	TM/L	G	AB	R	H	2B	3B	HR	RBI	BB	SO	AVG	OBP	SLG	PRO+	BR	/A	RC	SB	CS	SBR	FA	FR	POS	TPR
1961	KC-A★	158	611	108	171	29	6	3	45	92	38	.280	.379	.362	99	3	3	95	37	9	6	.950	-17	*S	0.5
1962	KC-A	83	286	53	68	8	3	6	34	38	8	.238	.329	.350	80	-6	-8	37	19	2	5	.962	-8	S	-0.5
1963	KC-A	15	41	4	8	0	0	0	1	7	3	.195	.313	.195	44	-3	-3	3	0	0	0	.957	-4	S	-0.6
	Cle-A	49	162	25	40	5	0	1	10	22	18	.247	.337	.296	80	-4	-4	17	9	3	1	.950	-17	S	-1.7
	Yr	64	203	29	48	5	0	1	11	29	21	.236	.332	.276	72	-6	-6	21	9	3	1	.951	-20	S	-2.3
1964	Cle-A	162	637	101	163	23	4	3	52	76	39	.256	.337	.319	84	-12	-11	74	20	7	2	.974	3	*S	0.6
1965	Cle-A	107	307	47	72	8	2	1	6	57	25	.235	.356	.283	83	-4	-4	38	17	4	3	.977	-6	S2	-0.1
1966	Cle-A	67	140	18	32	9	1	2	4	15	23	.229	.303	.350	87	-2	-2	14	2	4	-2	.986	-7	2S	-0.8
1967	NY-A	63	149	18	40	6	0	0	10	25	15	.268	.381	.309	110	3	3	19	1	4	-2	.990	-6	23/S	-0.4
1968	NY-A	85	150	24	23	2	1	0	3	35	17	.153	.321	.180	57	-6	-6	11	0	1	-1	.982	5	2/3S	0.0
Total	8	789	2483	398	617	90	17	16	165	367	186	.248	.348	.318	87	-32	-32	308	105	34	11	.963	-56	S/23	-3.0

■ DUMMY HOY
Hoy, William Ellsworth b: 5/23/1862, Houckstown, Ohio d: 12/15/61, Cincinnati, Ohio BL/TR, 5'4", 148 lbs. Deb: 4/20/1888

YEAR	TM/L	G	AB	R	H	2B	3B	HR	RBI	BB	SO	AVG	OBP	SLG	PRO+	BR	/A	RC	SB	CS	SBR	FA	FR	POS	TPR
1888	Was-N	136	503	77	138	10	8	2	29	69	48	.274	.374	.338	139	21	26	97	**82**			.897	7	*O	2.8
1889	Was-N	127	507	98	139	11	6	0	39	75	30	.274	.374	.320	103	2	7	76	35			.890	-4	*O	0.0
1890	Buf-P	122	493	107	147	17	8	1	53	94	36	.298	.418	.371	124	16	24	95	39			.912	6	*O/2	2.0
1891	StL-a	141	567	136	165	14	5	5	66	**119**	25	.291	.424	.360	111	29	13	114	59			.909	-1	*O	0.7
1892	Was-N	152	593	108	166	19	8	3	75	86	23	.280	.375	.354	126	20	22	104	60			.884	-12	*O	0.3
1893	Was-N	130	564	106	138	12	6	0	45	66	9	.245	.337	.287	70	-23	-20	73	48			.892	-1	*O	-2.3
1894	Cin-N	126	495	114	148	22	13	5	70	87	18	.299	.416	.426	101	8	4	103	27			.896	3	*O	-0.2
1895	Cin-N	107	429	93	119	21	12	3	55	52	8	.277	.363	.403	96	0	-3	83	50			.883	-3	*O	-1.2
1896	Cin-N	121	443	120	132	23	7	4	57	65	13	.298	.403	.409	109	14	8	99	50			.946	5	*O	0.3
1897	Cin-N	128	497	87	145	24	6	2	42	54		.292	.375	.376	92	1	-5	89	37			.934	7	*O	-0.6
1898	Lou-N	148	582	104	177	15	16	6	66	49		.304	.367	.416	126	18	19	107	37			.946	6	*O	1.3
1899	Lou-N	154	633	116	194	17	13	5	49	61		.306	.374	.398	112	11	11	111	32			.927	-6	*O	-0.6
1901	Chi-A	132	527	112	155	28	11	2	60	**86**		.294	.407	.400	128	22	25	101	27			.958	2	*O	1.5
1902	Cin-N	72	279	48	81	15	2	2	20	41		.290	.389	.380	125	14	11	48	11			.933	-5	O	0.1
Total	14	1796	7112	1426	2044	248	121	40	726	1004	210	.287	.385	.373	111	151	140	1300	594			.915	2	*O/2	4.1

■ KENT HRBEK
Hrbek, Kent Alan b: 5/21/60, Minneapolis, Minn. BL/TR, 6'4", 235 lbs. Deb: 8/24/81

YEAR	TM/L	G	AB	R	H	2B	3B	HR	RBI	BB	SO	AVG	OBP	SLG	PRO+	BR	/A	RC	SB	CS	SBR	FA	FR	POS	TPR
1981	Min-A	24	67	5	16	5	0	1	7	5	9	.239	.301	.358	84	-1	-2	8	0	0	0	1.000	-2	1/D	-0.4
1982	Min-A★	140	532	82	160	21	4	23	92	54	80	.301	.365	.485	128	22	21	91	3	1	0	.993	-0	*1/D	1.3
1983	Min-A	141	515	75	153	41	5	16	84	57	71	.297	.370	.489	130	24	22	91	4	6	-2	.990	-2	*1/D	0.9
1984	Min-A	149	559	80	174	31	3	27	107	65	87	.311	.387	.522	142	37	34	110	1	1	-0	.990	-6	*1/D	1.8
1985	Min-A	158	593	78	165	31	2	21	93	67	87	.278	.353	.444	110	14	9	93	1	1	-0	.995	1	*1/D	0.1
1986	Min-A	149	550	85	147	27	1	29	91	71	81	.267	.357	.478	122	19	17	93	2	2	-1	.992	-2	*1/D	0.4
1987	*Min-A	143	477	85	136	20	1	34	90	84	60	.285	.392	.545	140	32	30	103	5	2	0	.996	-10	*1/D	1.0
1988	Min-A	143	510	75	159	31	0	25	76	67	54	.312	.392	.520	149	37	35	104	0	3	-2	.997	-6	*1D	1.8
1989	Min-A	109	375	59	102	17	0	25	84	53	35	.272	.364	.517	136	22	19	73	3	0	1	.995	1	1D	1.4
1990	Min-A	143	492	61	141	26	0	22	79	69	45	.287	.382	.474	129	26	22	89	5	2	0	**.997**	1	*1D/3	1.4
1991	*Min-A	132	462	72	131	20	1	20	89	67	48	.284	.374	.461	124	20	17	78	4	4	-1	.994	4	*1	1.1
1992	Min-A	112	394	52	96	20	0	15	58	71	56	.244	.359	.409	111	9	7	59	5	2	0	.997	-1	*1/D	0.0
Total	12	1543	5526	809	1580	290	17	258	950	730	713	.286	.372	.485	129	262	231	992	33	24	-5	.994	-22	*1D/3	10.8

■ WALT HRINIAK
Hriniak, Walter John b: 5/22/43, Natick, Mass. BL/TR, 5'11", 180 lbs. Deb: 9/10/68 C

YEAR	TM/L	G	AB	R	H	2B	3B	HR	RBI	BB	SO	AVG	OBP	SLG	PRO+	BR	/A	RC	SB	CS	SBR	FA	FR	POS	TPR
1968	Atl-N	9	26	0	9	0	0	0	3	0	3	.346	.346	.346	108	0	0	3	0	0	0	.967	3	/C	0.4
1969	Atl-N	7	7	0	1	0	0	0	0	2	1	.143	.333	.143	38	-0	-0	0	0	0	0	1.000	-1	/C	-0.1
	SD-N	31	66	4	15	0	0	0	1	8	11	.227	.329	.227	61	-3	-3	5	0	0	0	.981	-2	C	-0.4
	Yr	38	73	4	16	0	0	0	1	10	12	.219	.329	.219	58	-4	-3	6	0	0	0	.982	-3	C	-0.5
Total	2	47	99	4	25	0	0	0	4	10	15	.253	.333	.253	71	-4	-3	9	0	0	0	.977	-0	/C	-0.1

■ AL HUBBARD
Hubbard, Allen (Played Under Name Of Al West For 1 Game In 1883) b: 12/9/1860, Westfield, Mass. d: 12/14/30, Newton, Mass. Deb: 9/13/1883

YEAR	TM/L	G	AB	R	H	2B	3B	HR	RBI	BB	SO	AVG	OBP	SLG	PRO+	BR	/A	RC	SB	CS	SBR	FA	FR	POS	TPR
1883	Phi-a	2	6	2	2	0	0	0		1		.333	.429	.333	137	0	0	1				.750	-0	/SC	0.0

■ GLENN HUBBARD
Hubbard, Glenn Dee b: 9/25/57, Hahn Air Force Base, Germany BR/TR, 5'7", 180 lbs. Deb: 7/14/78

YEAR	TM/L	G	AB	R	H	2B	3B	HR	RBI	BB	SO	AVG	OBP	SLG	PRO+	BR	/A	RC	SB	CS	SBR	FA	FR	POS	TPR
1978	Atl-N	44	163	15	42	4	0	2	13	10	20	.258	.309	.319	68	-5	-7	17	2	1	0	.979	3	2	-0.1
1979	Atl-N	97	325	34	75	12	0	3	29	27	43	.231	.292	.295	56	-17	-20	28	0	6	-4	.968	5	2	-1.4
1980	Atl-N	117	431	55	107	21	3	9	43	49	69	.248	.325	.374	91	-3	-5	53	7	5	-1	.978	19	*2	2.2
1981	Atl-N	99	361	39	85	13	5	6	33	33	59	.235	.303	.349	82	-8	-9	39	4	2	0	.991	-4	2	-0.7
1982	*Atl-N	145	532	75	132	25	1	9	59	59	62	.248	.327	.350	86	-7	-10	65	4	3	-1	.983	20	*2	1.8
1983	Atl-N★	148	517	65	136	24	6	12	70	55	71	.263	.339	.402	97	3	-2	69	3	8	-4	.985	22	*2	2.4
1984	Atl-N	120	397	53	93	27	2	9	43	55	61	.234	.333	.380	93	1	-3	53	4	1	1	.988	20	*2	2.2
1985	Atl-N	142	439	51	102	21	0	5	39	56	54	.232	.325	.314	75	-11	-14	47	4	3	-1	.989	**62**	*2	5.3
1986	Atl-N	143	408	42	94	16	1	4	36	66	74	.230	.343	.304	76	-9	-12	47	3	2	-0	.976	**41**	*2	3.5

YEAR	TM/L	G	AB	R	H	2B	3B	HR	RBI	BB	SO	AVG	OBP	SLG	PRO+	BR	/A	RC	SB	CS	SBR	FA	FR	POS	TPR
1987	Atl-N	141	443	69	117	33	2	5	38	77	57	.264	.380	.381	98	5	2	67	1	1	-0	.986	**28**	*2	3.6
1988	*Oak-A	105	294	35	75	12	2	3	33	33	50	.255	.336	.340	93	-3	-2	34	1	3	-2	.987	4	*2/D	0.4
1989	Oak-A	53	131	12	26	6	0	3	12	19	20	.198	.300	.313	76	-4	-4	13	2	0	1	.968	10	2/D	0.8
Total	12	1354	4441	545	1084	214	22	70	448	539	640	.244	.330	.349	85	-59	-85	530	35	35	-11	.983	229	*2/D	20.0

■ KEN HUBBS Hubbs, Kenneth Douglas b: 12/23/41, Riverside, Cal. d: 2/13/64, Provo, Utah BR/TR, 6'2", 175 lbs. Deb: 9/10/61

YEAR	TM/L	G	AB	R	H	2B	3B	HR	RBI	BB	SO	AVG	OBP	SLG	PRO+	BR	/A	RC	SB	CS	SBR	FA	FR	POS	TPR
1961	Chi-N	10	28	4	5	1	1	1	2	0	8	.179	.179	.393	46	-2	-2	2	0	0	0	1.000	-2	/2	-0.3
1962	Chi-N	160	661	90	172	24	9	5	49	35	129	.260	.300	.346	71	-26	-29	64	3	7	-3	.983	4	*2	-1.1
1963	Chi-N	154	566	54	133	19	3	8	47	39	93	.235	.287	.322	71	-18	-22	48	8	9	-3	.974	20	*2	1.0
Total	3	324	1255	148	310	44	13	14	98	74	230	.247	.292	.336	70	-46	-53	114	11	16	-6	.979	23	2	-0.4

■ CLARENCE HUBER Huber, Clarence Bill "Gilly" b: 10/27/1896, Tyler, Tex. d: 2/22/65, Laredo, Tex. BR/TR, 5'10", 165 lbs. Deb: 9/17/20

YEAR	TM/L	G	AB	R	H	2B	3B	HR	RBI	BB	SO	AVG	OBP	SLG	PRO+	BR	/A	RC	SB	CS	SBR	FA	FR	POS	TPR
1920	Det-A	11	42	4	9	2	1	0	5	0	5	.214	.214	.310	39	-4	-4	3	0	0	0	.907	2	3	-0.1
1921	Det-A	1	0	0	0	0	0	0	0	0	0	—	—	—	—	0	0	0	0	0	0	1.000	-0	/3	0.0
1925	Phi-N	124	436	46	124	28	5	5	54	17	33	.284	.311	.406	75	-13	-18	53	3	5	-2	.947	-9	*3	-2.0
1926	Phi-N	118	376	45	92	17	7	1	34	42	29	.245	.324	.335	74	-11	-14	42	9			.956	8	*3	0.0
Total	4	254	854	95	225	47	13	6	93	59	67	.263	.313	.370	73	-28	-36	97	12	5		.948	1	3	-2.1

■ OTTO HUBER Huber, Otto b: 3/12/14, Garfield, N.J. d: 4/9/89, Passaic, N.J. BR/TR, 5'10", 165 lbs. Deb: 6/10/39

YEAR	TM/L	G	AB	R	H	2B	3B	HR	RBI	BB	SO	AVG	OBP	SLG	PRO+	BR	/A	RC	SB	CS	SBR	FA	FR	POS	TPR
1939	Bos-N	11	22	2	6	1	0	0	3	0	1	.273	.273	.318	63	-1	-1	2	0			1.000	-0	/23	-0.1

■ DAVE HUDGENS Hudgens, David Mark b: 12/5/56, Oroville, Cal. BL/TL, 6'2", 210 lbs. Deb: 9/04/83

YEAR	TM/L	G	AB	R	H	2B	3B	HR	RBI	BB	SO	AVG	OBP	SLG	PRO+	BR	/A	RC	SB	CS	SBR	FA	FR	POS	TPR
1983	Oak-A	6	7	0	1	0	0	0	0	0	3	.143	.143	.143	-22	-1	-1	0	0	0	0	1.000	-0	/1D	-0.1

■ JIMMY HUDGENS Hudgens, James Price b: 8/24/02, Newburg, Mo. d: 8/26/55, St.Louis, Mo. BL/TR, 6', 180 lbs. Deb: 9/14/23

YEAR	TM/L	G	AB	R	H	2B	3B	HR	RBI	BB	SO	AVG	OBP	SLG	PRO+	BR	/A	RC	SB	CS	SBR	FA	FR	POS	TPR
1923	StL-N	6	12	2	3	1	0	0	0	3	3	.250	.400	.333	97	0	0	2	0	0	0	1.000	1	/12	0.1
1925	Cin-N	3	7	0	3	1	1	0	0	1	1	.429	.500	.857	245	1	1	3	0	0	0	1.000	0	/1	0.1
1926	Cin-N	17	20	2	5	1	0	0	1	1	0	.250	.286	.300	59	-1	-1	2	0			1.000	0	/1	-0.1
Total	3	26	39	4	11	3	1	0	1	5	4	.282	.364	.410	107	0	0	7	0	0		1.000	1	/12	0.1

■ REX HUDLER Hudler, Rex Allen b: 9/2/60, Tempe, Ariz. BR/TR, 6'1", 180 lbs. Deb: 9/09/84

YEAR	TM/L	G	AB	R	H	2B	3B	HR	RBI	BB	SO	AVG	OBP	SLG	PRO+	BR	/A	RC	SB	CS	SBR	FA	FR	POS	TPR
1984	NY-A	9	7	2	1	1	0	0	0	1	5	.143	.333	.286	76	-0	-0	1	0	0	0	1.000	0	/2	0.0
1985	NY-A	20	51	4	8	0	1	0	1	1	9	.157	.173	.196	1	-7	-7	2	0	1	-1	.977	7	2/1S	0.0
1986	Bal-A	14	1	1	0	0	0	0	0	0	0	.000	.000	.000	-99	-0	-0	0	1	0	0	.800	1	2/3	0.1
1988	Mon-N	77	216	38	59	14	2	4	14	10	34	.273	.305	.412	100	0	-1	28	29	7	5	.978	-1	2S/O	0.6
1989	Mon-N	92	155	21	38	7	0	6	13	6	23	.245	.278	.406	92	-2	-2	17	15	4	2	.958	-14	2OS	-1.4
1990	Mon-N	4	3	1	1	0	0	0	0	0	1	.333	.333	.333	87	-0	-0	0	0	0	0	.000	0	/H	0.0
	StL-N	89	217	30	61	11	2	7	22	12	31	.281	.325	.447	110	2	2	29	18	10	-1	.979	0	O2/13S	0.1
	Yr	93	220	31	62	11	2	7	22	12	32	.282	.325	.445	109	2	2	30	18	10	-1	.979	0	O2/13S	0.1
1991	StL-N	101	207	21	47	10	2	1	15	10	29	.227	.263	.309	60	-11	-11	16	12	8	-1	.981	-3	O1/2	-1.8
1992	StL-N	61	98	17	24	4	0	3	5	2	23	.245	.267	.378	82	-3	-3	8	2	6	-3	.957	-8	2O/1	-1.4
Total	8	467	955	135	239	47	7	21	70	42	155	.250	.285	.380	85	-21	-22	102	77	36	2	.968	-18	2O/S13	-3.8

■ JOHNNY HUDSON Hudson, John Wilson "Mr. Chips" b: 6/30/12, Bryan, Tex. d: 11/7/70, Bryan, Tex. BR/TR, 5'10", 160 lbs. Deb: 6/20/36

YEAR	TM/L	G	AB	R	H	2B	3B	HR	RBI	BB	SO	AVG	OBP	SLG	PRO+	BR	/A	RC	SB	CS	SBR	FA	FR	POS	TPR
1936	Bro-N	6	12	1	2	0	0	0	0	2	1	.167	.286	.167	24	-1	-1	1	0			.889	-1	/S2	-0.2
1937	Bro-N	13	27	3	5	4	0	0	2	3	9	.185	.267	.333	61	-1	-2	2	0			.867	-4	S/2	-0.5
1938	Bro-N	135	498	59	130	21	5	2	37	39	76	.261	.315	.335	77	-14	-16	51	7			.963	-4	*2/S	-1.2
1939	Bro-N	109	343	46	87	17	3	2	32	30	36	.254	.317	.338	74	-11	-13	36	5			.959	-18	S2/3	-2.5
1940	Bro-N	85	179	13	39	4	3	0	19	9	26	.218	.255	.274	43	-13	-15	12	2			.921	0	S2/3	-1.1
1941	Chi-N	50	99	8	20	4	0	0	6	3	15	.202	.225	.242	33	-9	-9	5	3			.907	-1	S23	-0.8
1945	NY-N	28	11	8	0	0	0	0	0	1	1	.000	.083	.000	-75	-3	-3	0	0			.875	5	/32	0.2
Total	7	426	1169	138	283	50	11	4	96	87	164	.242	.296	.314	65	-53	-57	107	17			.962	-22	2S/3	-6.1

■ FRANK HUELSMAN Huelsman, Frank Elmer b: 6/5/1874, St.Louis, Mo. d: 6/9/59, Affton, Mo. BR/TR, 6'2", 210 lbs. Deb: 10/03/1897

YEAR	TM/L	G	AB	R	H	2B	3B	HR	RBI	BB	SO	AVG	OBP	SLG	PRO+	BR	/A	RC	SB	CS	SBR	FA	FR	POS	TPR
1897	StL-N	2	7	0	2	1	0	0	0	0		.286	.286	.429	89	-0	-0	1	0			.000	-1	/O	-0.1
1904	Chi-A	3	6	0	1	1	0	0	0	0		.167	.167	.333	58	-0	-0	0	0			.000	-1	/O	-0.1
	Det-A	4	18	1	6	1	0	0	4	1		.333	.368	.389	144	1	1	3	1			1.000	-1	/O	0.0
	Chi-A	1	1	0	0	0	0	0	0	0		.000	.000	.000	-99	-0	-0	0	0			.000	0	H	0.0
	StL-A	20	68	6	15	2	1	0	1	6		.221	.303	.279	90	-1	-0	6	0			1.000	-3	O	-0.5
	Was-A	84	303	21	75	19	4	2	30	24		.248	.313	.356	113	4	5	37	6			.960	-3	O	-0.4
	Yr	112	396	28	97	23	5	2	35	31		.245	.311	.343	110	3	5	46	7			.960	-8	*O	-1.0
1905	Was-A	121	421	48	114	28	8	3	62	31		.271	.333	.397	137	14	16	61	11			.929	-9	*O	0.2
Total	3	235	824	76	213	52	13	5	97	62		.258	.322	.371	123	18	20	109	18			.941	-18	O	-0.9

■ MIKE HUFF Huff, Michael Kale b: 8/11/63, Honolulu, Hawaii BR/TR, 6'1", 180 lbs. Deb: 8/07/89

YEAR	TM/L	G	AB	R	H	2B	3B	HR	RBI	BB	SO	AVG	OBP	SLG	PRO+	BR	/A	RC	SB	CS	SBR	FA	FR	POS	TPR
1989	LA-N	12	25	4	5	1	0	1	2	3	6	.200	.310	.360	93	-0	-0	3	0	1	-1	1.000	-0	/O	-0.1
1991	Cle-A	51	146	28	35	6	1	2	10	25	30	.240	.366	.336	95	0	0	22	11	2	2	.990	-3	O/2	-0.2
	Chi-A	51	97	14	26	4	1	1	15	12	18	.268	.360	.361	103	0	1	12	3	2	-0	.986	-11	O/2D	-1.1
	Yr	102	243	42	61	10	2	3	25	37	48	.251	.364	.346	98	1	1	34	14	4	2	.988	-14	O/2D	-1.3
1992	Chi-A	60	115	13	24	5	0	0	8	10	24	.209	.278	.252	51	-8	-7	8	1	2	-1	1.000	-10	O/D	-2.0
Total	3	174	383	59	90	16	2	4	35	50	78	.235	.336	.319	84	-7	-7	45	15	7	0	.992	-25	O/2D	-3.4

■ BEN HUFFMAN Huffman, Benjamin Franklin b: 6/26/14, Rileyville, Va. BL/TR, 5'11.5", 175 lbs. Deb: 4/23/37

YEAR	TM/L	G	AB	R	H	2B	3B	HR	RBI	BB	SO	AVG	OBP	SLG	PRO+	BR	/A	RC	SB	CS	SBR	FA	FR	POS	TPR
1937	StL-A	76	176	18	48	9	0	1	24	10	7	.273	.323	.341	67	-9	-9	20	1	0	0	.970	-8	C	-1.3

■ ED HUG Hug, Edward Ambrose b: 7/14/1880, Fayetteville, O. d: 5/11/53, Cincinnati, Ohio BR/TR, Deb: 7/06/03

YEAR	TM/L	G	AB	R	H	2B	3B	HR	RBI	BB	SO	AVG	OBP	SLG	PRO+	BR	/A	RC	SB	CS	SBR	FA	FR	POS	TPR
1903	Bro-N	1	0	0	0	0	0	0	0	1		—	1.000	—	200	0	0	0	0			.000	0	/C	0.0

■ MILLER HUGGINS Huggins, Miller James "Hug" or "Mighty Mite"
b: 3/27/1879, Cincinnati, Ohio d: 9/25/29, New York, N.Y. BB/TR, 5'6.5", 140 lbs. Deb: 4/15/04 MH

YEAR	TM/L	G	AB	R	H	2B	3B	HR	RBI	BB	SO	AVG	OBP	SLG	PRO+	BR	/A	RC	SB	CS	SBR	FA	FR	POS	TPR
1904	Cin-N	140	491	96	129	12	7	2	30	88		.263	.376	.328	109	15	10	69	13			.945	1	*2	1.6
1905	Cin-N	149	564	117	154	11	8	1	38	**103**		.273	.390	.326	103	16	8	86	27			.945	**36**	*2	4.7
1906	Cin-N	146	545	81	159	11	7	0	26	71		.292	.374	.338	117	17	14	89	41			.948	22	*2	4.0
1907	Cin-N	156	561	64	139	12	4	1	31	**83**		.248	.346	.289	95	3	0	71	28			.961	0	*2	-0.1
1908	Cin-N	135	498	65	119	14	5	0	23	58		.239	.321	.287	97	-1	0	57	30			.959	4	*2	0.3
1909	Cin-N	57	159	18	34	3	1	0	6	28		.214	.335	.245	81	-2	-2	17	11			.933	4	23	0.1
1910	StL-N	151	547	101	145	15	6	1	36	**116**	46	.265	.399	.320	114	14	17	85	34			.963	3	*2	1.8
1911	StL-N	138	509	106	133	19	2	1	24	96	52	.261	.385	.312	99	3	5	76	37			.961	11	*2	1.3
1912	StL-N	120	431	82	131	15	4	0	29	87	31	.304	.422	.357	117	14	16	80	35			.943	-7	*2	0.6
1913	StL-N	121	382	74	109	12	0	0	27	92	49	.285	**.432**	.317	117	16	17	62	23			**.977**	0	*2M	1.5
1914	StL-N	148	509	85	134	17	4	1	24	**105**	63	.263	.396	.318	115	15	16	75	32			.964	-5	*2M	1.1
1915	StL-N	107	353	57	85	5	2	2	24	74	68	.241	.377	.283	101	5	5	40	13	12	-3	.957	4	*2M	0.7
1916	StL-N	18	9	2	3	0	0	0	0	2	3	.333	.500	.333	159	1	1	2	0			1.000	4	/2M	0.6
Total	13	1586	5558	948	1474	146	50	9	318	1003	312	.265	.381	.314	107	117	107	811	324	12		.956	77	*2/3	18.2

YEAR	TM/L	G	AB	R	H	2B	3B	HR	RBI	BB	SO	AVG	OBP	SLG	PRO+	BR	/A	RC	SB	CS	SBR	FA	FR	POS	TPR

■ ED HUGHES   Hughes, Edward J.   b: 10/5/1880, Chicago, Ill.   d: 10/11/27, McHenry, Ill.   BR/TR, 6'1", 180 lbs.   Deb: 8/29/02   F

1902	Chi-A	1	4	0	1	0	0	0	0	0		.250	.250	.250	41	-0	-0	0	0			.778	0	/C	0.0
1905	Bos-A	6	14	2	3	0	0	0	2	0		.214	.214	.214	36	-1	-1	1	0			.500	-2	/P	0.0
1906	Bos-A	2	3	0	0	0	0	0	0	0		.000	.000	.000	-99	-1	-1	0	0			.750	-0	/P	0.0
Total	3	9	21	2	4	0	0	0	2	0		.190	.190	.190	18	-2	-2	1	0			.571	-2	/PC	0.0

■ JOE HUGHES   Hughes, Joseph Thompson   b: 2/21/1880, Pardo, Pa.   d: 3/13/51, Cleveland, Ohio   BR/TR, 5'10", 165 lbs.   Deb: 8/30/02

| 1902 | Chi-N | 1 | 3 | 0 | 0 | 0 | 0 | 0 | 0 | 0 | | .000 | .000 | .000 | -99 | -1 | -1 | 0 | 0 | | | .000 | -0 | /O | -0.1 |

■ KEITH HUGHES   Hughes, Keith Wills   b: 9/12/63, Bryn Mawr, Pa.   BL/TL, 6'3", 210 lbs.   Deb: 5/19/87

1987	NY-A	4	4	0	0	0	0	0	0	0	2	.000	.000	.000	-99	-1	-1	0	0	0	0	.000	0	/H	-0.1
	Phi-N	37	76	8	20	2	0	0	10	7	11	.263	.333	.289	65	-3	-4	8	0	0	0	.963	-2	O	-0.6
1988	Bal-A	41	108	10	21	4	2	2	14	16	27	.194	.298	.324	76	-4	-3	11	1	0	0	.969	2	O/D	-0.2
1990	NY-N	8	9	0	0	0	0	0	0	0	4	.000	.000	.000	-99	-2	-2	0	0	0	0	1.000	-1	O	-0.4
Total	3	90	197	18	41	6	2	2	24	23	44	.208	.294	.289	60	-10	-10	19	1	0	0	.969	-2	/OD	-1.3

■ ROY HUGHES   Hughes, Roy John "Jeep" or "Sage"   b: 1/11/11, Cincinnati, Ohio   BR/TR, 5'10.5", 167 lbs.   Deb: 4/16/35

1935	Cle-A	82	266	40	78	15	3	0	14	18	17	.293	.340	.372	83	-6	-7	35	13	3	2	.987	-1	2S/3	-0.1
1936	Cle-A	152	638	112	188	35	9	0	63	57	40	.295	.356	.378	81	-18	-19	88	20	9	1	.973	5	*2	-0.2
1937	Cle-A	104	346	57	96	12	6	1	40	40	22	.277	.352	.355	78	-11	-11	45	11	6	0	.939	12	32	0.4
1938	StL-A	58	96	16	27	3	0	2	13	12	11	.281	.361	.375	85	-2	-2	14	5	4	0	.957	4	2/3S	0.4
1939	StL-A	17	23	6	2	0	0	0	1	4	4	.087	.222	.087	-18	-4	-4	1	0	0	0	1.000	1	/2S	-0.3
	Phi-N	65	237	22	54	5	1	1	16	21	18	.228	.291	.270	53	-16	-15	18	4			.984	2	2	-1.1
1940	Phi-N	1	0	0	0	0	0	0	0	0	0	—	—	—			0	0	0			1.000	-0	/2	0.0
1944	Chi-N	126	478	86	137	16	6	0	28	35	30	.287	.337	.351	94	-4	-3	58	16			.951	11	3S	1.3
1945	*Chi-N	69	222	34	58	8	1	0	8	16	18	.261	.311	.306	73	-8	-8	22	6			.931	2	S2/31	-1.1
1946	Phi-N	89	276	23	65	11	1	0	22	19	15	.236	.287	.283	64	-14	-13	23	7			.942	-12	S3/2	-2.4
Total	9	763	2582	396	705	105	27	5	205	222	175	.273	.332	.340	78	-83	-82	305	80	18		.980	12	23S/1	-3.1

■ TERRY HUGHES   Hughes, Terry Wayne   b: 5/13/49, Spartanburg, S.C.   BR/TR, 6'1", 185 lbs.   Deb: 9/02/70

1970	Chi-N	2	3	0	1	0	0	0	0	0	0	.333	.333	.333	71	-0	-0	0	0	0	0	.000	0	/3O	0.0
1973	StL-N	11	14	1	3	1	0	0	1	1	4	.214	.267	.286	53	-1	-1	1	0	0	0	1.000	0	/31	-0.1
1974	Bos-A	41	69	5	14	2	0	1	6	6	18	.203	.286	.275	58	-3	-4	6	0	0	0	.958	4	3/D	-0.1
Total	3	54	86	6	18	3	0	1	7	7	22	.209	.284	.279	58	-4	-5	7	0	0	0	.961	4	/3D1O	-0.1

■ TOM HUGHES   Hughes, Thomas Franklin   b: 8/6/07, Emmet, Ark.   BL/TR, 6'1", 190 lbs.   Deb: 9/09/30

| 1930 | Det-A | 17 | 59 | 8 | 22 | 2 | 3 | 0 | 5 | 4 | 8 | .373 | .413 | .508 | 130 | 3 | 3 | 12 | 0 | 1 | -1 | .897 | -3 | O | -0.2 |

■ BILL HUGHES   Hughes, William R.   b: 11/25/1866, Bladensville, Ill.   d: 8/25/43, Santa Ana, Cal.   BL/TL,   Deb: 9/28/1884

1884	Was-U	14	49	5	6	0	0	0			2	.122	.157	.122	-5	-5	-5	1				.955	0	/1O	-0.5
1885	Phi-a	4	16	3	3	1	1	0				.188	.278	.375	101	0	0	2				1.000	-0	/OP	0.0
Total	2	18	65	8	9	1	1	0			3	.138	.188	.185	25	-5	-5	3				.—0	/1OP	-0.5

■ EMIL HUHN   Huhn, Emil Hugo "Hap"   b: 3/10/1892, North Vernon, Ind.   d: 9/5/25, Camden, S.C.   BR/TR, 6', 180 lbs.   Deb: 4/10/15

1915	New-F	124	415	34	94	18	1	1	41	28	40	.227	.279	.282	69	-19	-16	39	13			.985	-2	*1C	-2.1
1916	Cin-N	37	94	4	24	3	2	0	3	2	11	.255	.271	.330	86	-2	-2	8	0			.989	1	C1/O	0.0
1917	Cin-N	23	51	2	10	1	2	0	3	2	5	.196	.226	.294	62	-3	-2	3	1			.969	-2	C/1	-0.4
Total	3	184	560	40	128	22	5	1	47	32	56	.229	.273	.291	71	-23	-20	51	14			.986	-3	1/CO	-2.5

■ TIM HULETT   Hulett, Timothy Craig   b: 1/12/60, Springfield, Ill.   BR/TR, 6', 185 lbs.   Deb: 9/15/83

1983	Chi-A	6	5	0	1	0	0	0	0	0	0	.200	.200	.200	10	-1	-1	0	1	0	0	.875	2	/2	0.1
1984	Chi-A	8	7	1	0	0	0	0	0	1	4	.000	.125	.000	-59	-2	-2	0	1	0	0	1.000	4	/32	0.3
1985	Chi-A	141	395	52	106	19	4	5	37	30	81	.268	.326	.375	88	-5	-7	48	6	4	-1	.924	8	*32/O	0.0
1986	Chi-A	150	520	53	120	16	5	17	44	21	91	.231	.262	.379	70	-22	-24	49	4	1	1	.951	-6	32	-2.8
1987	Chi-A	68	240	20	52	10	0	7	28	10	41	.217	.248	.346	54	-16	-17	19	0	2	-1	.953	-3	3/2	-2.0
1989	Bal-A	33	97	12	27	5	0	3	18	10	17	.278	.346	.423	119	2	2	14	0	0	0	.976	-5	23	-0.2
1990	Bal-A	53	153	16	39	7	1	3	16	15	41	.255	.321	.373	97	-1	-1	19	1	0	0	.961	6	32/D	0.6
1991	Bal-A	79	206	29	42	9	0	7	18	13	49	.204	.255	.350	68	-10	-9	18	0	1	-1	.976	-8	32D/S	-1.7
1992	Bal-A	57	142	11	41	7	2	2	21	10	31	.289	.340	.408	109	1	2	17	0	1	-1	.935	10	3D2/S	1.1
Total	9	595	1765	194	428	73	12	44	182	110	355	.242	.290	.372	79	-53	-55	185	13	9	-2	.945	9	32/DSO	-4.6

■ BILLY HULEN   Hulen, William Franklin   b: 3/12/1870, Dixon, Cal.   d: 10/2/47, Santa Rosa, Cal.   BL/TL, 5'8", 148 lbs.   Deb: 5/02/1896

1896	Phi-N	88	339	87	90	18	7	0	38	55	20	.265	.368	.360	95	-1	-0	56	23			.874	-21	SO/2	-1.6
1899	Was-N	19	68	10	10	1	0	0	3	10		.147	.256	.162	16	-8	-8	4	5			.902	-4	S	-1.0
Total	2	107	407	97	100	19	7	0	41	65	20	.246	.350	.327	83	-9	-8	60	28			.880	-25	/SO2	-2.6

■ DAVID HULSE   Hulse, David Lindsey   b: 2/25/68, San Angelo, Tex.   BL/TL, 5'11", 170 lbs.   Deb: 8/11/92

| 1992 | Tex-A | 32 | 92 | 14 | 28 | 4 | 0 | 2 | 3 | 18 | | .304 | .326 | .348 | 92 | -1 | -1 | 11 | 3 | 1 | 0 | .984 | -4 | O | -0.5 |

■ RUDY HULSWITT   Hulswitt, Rudolph Edward   b: 2/23/1877, Newport, Ky.   d: 1/16/50, Louisville, Ky.   BR/TR, 5'8.5", 165 lbs.   Deb: 6/16/1899   C

1899	Lou-N	1	0	0	0	0	0	0	0	0		—	—	—		0	0	0	0			.333	-1	/S	-0.1
1902	Phi-N	128	497	59	135	11	7	0	38	30		.272	.314	.322	96	-3	-3	56	12			.917	8	*S/3	1.3
1903	Phi-N	138	519	56	128	22	9	1	58	28		.247	.288	.329	79	-18	-15	55	10			.906	-3	*S	-1.2
1904	Phi-N	113	406	36	99	11	4	1	36	16		.244	.276	.298	80	-11	-10	38	8			.912	-13	*S	-2.0
1908	Cin-N	119	386	27	88	5	7	1	28	30		.228	.285	.285	85	-8	-7	33	7			.936	-6	*S/2	-1.2
1909	StL-N	82	289	21	81	8	3	0	29	19		.280	.329	.329	111	1	3	33	7			.930	-6	S2	-0.2
1910	StL-N	63	133	9	33	7	2	0	14	13	10	.248	.320	.331	93	-2	-1	15	5			.854	-13	S/23	-1.3
Total	7	644	2230	208	564	64	32	3	203	136	10	.253	.299	.314	89	-40	-32	231	49			.915	-32	S/23	-4.7

■ JOHN HUMMEL   Hummel, John Edwin "Silent John"   b: 4/4/1883, Bloomsburg, Pa.   d: 5/18/59, Springfield, Mass.   BR/TR, 5'11", 160 lbs.   Deb: 9/12/05

1905	Bro-N	30	109	19	29	3	4	0	7	9		.266	.322	.367	114	1	2	16	6			.962	0	2	0.2
1906	Bro-N	97	286	20	57	6	4	1	21	36		.199	.289	.259	77	-9	-6	25	10			.953	1	2O1	-0.7
1907	Bro-N	107	342	41	80	12	3	3	31	26		.234	.290	.313	97	-5	-2	36	8			.951	13	2O1/S	1.0
1908	Bro-N	154	594	51	143	11	12	6	41	34		.241	.284	.320	97	-6	-4	58	20			.973	9	O2/S1	0.0
1909	Bro-N	146	542	54	152	15	9	4	52	22		.280	.311	.363	113	3	5	67	16			.987	-17	12SO	-1.4
1910	Bro-N	153	578	67	141	21	13	5	74	57	81	.244	.314	.351	97	-6	-4	69	21			.965	-14	*2	-2.2
1911	Bro-N	137	477	54	129	21	11	5	58	67	66	.270	.360	.392	115	7	10	73	16			.972	-5	*2/1S	0.2
1912	Bro-N	122	411	55	116	21	7	5	54	49	55	.282	.359	.404	113	5	7	62	7			.969	-15	2O1	-1.2
1913	Bro-N	67	198	20	48	7	7	2	24	13	23	.242	.292	.379	88	-3	-4	22	4			.938	-1	OS/12	-0.4
1914	Bro-N	73	208	25	55	8	9	0	20	16	25	.264	.331	.389	107	2	1	26	5			.982	-2	1O/2S	-0.2
1915	Bro-N	53	100	6	23	2	1	0	8	6	11	.230	.274	.310	75	-3	-3	9	1	1	-0	1.000	0	O1/S	-0.9
1918	NY-A	22	61	9	18	1	2	0	4	11	8	.295	.411	.377	135	3	3	10	3			.960	-3	O/12	-0.1
Total	12	1161	3906	421	991	128	84	29	394	346	269	.254	.316	.352	103	-11	6	473	117	1		.963	-39	2O1/S	-5.7

YEAR	TM/L	G	AB	R	H	2B	3B	HR	RBI	BB	SO	AVG	OBP	SLG	PRO+	BR	/A	RC	SB	CS	SBR	FA	FR	POS	TPR

■ AL HUMPHREY
Humphrey, Albert b: 2/28/1886, Ashtabula, Ohio d: 5/13/61, Ashtabula, Ohio BL/TR, 5'11", 180 lbs. Deb: 9/01/11

| 1911 | Bro-N | 8 | 27 | 4 | 5 | 0 | 0 | 0 | 3 | 7 | .185 | .267 | .185 | 29 | -3 | -2 | 2 | | | | .923 | -2 | /O | -0.5 |

■ TERRY HUMPHREY
Humphrey, Terryal Gene b: 8/4/49, Chickasha, Okla. BR/TR, 6'3", 190 lbs. Deb: 9/05/71

1971	Mon-N	9	26	1	5	1	0	0	1	0	4	.192	.192	.231	19	-3	-3	1	0	0	0	.981	2	/C	0.0
1972	Mon-N	69	215	13	40	8	0	1	9	16	38	.186	.249	.237	38	-17	-18	12	4	1	1	.986	-3	C	-1.9
1973	Mon-N	43	90	5	15	2	0	1	9	5	16	.167	.211	.222	19	-10	-10	4	0	1	-1	1.000	5	C	-0.5
1974	Mon-N	20	52	3	10	3	0	0	3	4	9	.192	.250	.250	38	-4	-5	4	0	0	0	.990	6	C	0.2
1975	Det-A	18	41	0	10	0	0	0	1	2	6	.244	.279	.244	47	-3	-3	3	0	0	0	1.000	1	C	-0.1
1976	Cal-A	71	196	17	48	10	0	1	19	13	30	.245	.308	.311	87	-4	-3	18	0	1	-1	.980	1	C	-0.1
1977	Cal-A	123	304	17	69	11	0	2	34	21	58	.227	.286	.283	58	-18	-17	24	1	1	-0	.989	-0	*C	-1.4
1978	Cal-A	53	114	11	25	4	1	1	9	6	12	.219	.270	.298	62	-6	-6	9	0	1	-1	.978	11	C/23	0.5
1979	Cal-A	9	17	2	1	0	0	0	1	0	2	.059	.111	.059	-55	-4	-4	0	0	0	0	.983	6	/C	0.3
Total	9	415	1055	69	223	39	1	6	85	68	175	.211	.268	.267	51	-69	-67	75	5	5	-2	.986	28	C/32	-3.0

■ MIKE HUMPHREYS
Humphreys, Michael Butler b: 4/10/67, Dallas, Tex. BR/TR, 6', 185 lbs. Deb: 7/29/91

1991	NY-A	25	40	9	8	0	0	0	3	9	7	.200	.347	.200	55	-2	-2	4	2	0	1	1.000	-2	/O3D	-0.3
1992	NY-A	4	10	0	1	0	0	0	0	0	1	.100	.100	.100	-43	-2	-2	-0	0	0	0	1.000	1	/OD	-0.1
Total	2	29	50	9	9	0	0	0	3	9	8	.180	.305	.180	38	-4	-4	4	2	0	1	1.000	-1	/OD3	-0.4

■ JOHN HUMPHRIES
Humphries, John Henry b: 11/12/1861, N.Gower, Ont., Can. d: 11/29/33, Salinas, Cal. BL/TL, 6', 185 lbs. Deb: 7/07/1883

1883	NY-N	29	107	5	12	1	0	0	4	1	22	.112	.120	.121	-26	-16	-15	2				.815	-5	CO	-1.8
1884	Was-a	49	193	23	34	2	0	0			9	.176	.217	.187	39	-13	-10	8				.890	-6	CO/1	-1.2
	NY-N	20	64	6	6	0	0	0	2	9	19	.094	.205	.094	-2	-7	-7	1				.896	11	C	0.4
Total	2	98	364	34	52	3	0	0	6	19	41	.143	.188	.151	10	-36	-33	11				.876	-0	/CO1	-2.6

■ RANDY HUNDLEY
Hundley, Cecil Randolph b: 6/1/42, Martinsville, Va. BR/TR, 6', 175 lbs. Deb: 9/27/64 FC

1964	SF-N	2	1	1	0	0	0	0	0	0	1	.000	.000	.000	-98	-0	-0	0	0	0	0	.000	0	/C	0.0
1965	SF-N	6	15	0	1	0	0	0	0	0	4	.067	.067	.067	-61	-3	-3	0	0	0	0	1.000	4	/C	0.1
1966	Chi-N	149	526	50	124	22	3	19	63	35	113	.236	.287	.397	87	-10	-10	58	1	3	-2	.986	-11	*C	-1.4
1967	Chi-N	152	539	68	144	25	3	14	60	44	75	.267	.325	.403	102	4	2	68	2	4	-2	.996	-12	*C	-0.4
1968	Chi-N	160	553	41	125	18	4	7	65	39	69	.226	.282	.311	73	-15	-19	46	1	0	0	.995	-14	*C	-2.4
1969	Chi-N★	151	522	67	133	15	1	18	64	61	90	.255	.336	.391	91	2	-6	69	2	3	-1	.992	12	*C	1.4
1970	Chi-N	73	250	13	61	5	0	7	36	16	52	.244	.289	.348	62	-11	-15	25	0	1	-1	.990	-1	C	-1.2
1971	Chi-N	9	21	1	7	1	0	0	2	0	2	.333	.333	.381	89	-0	-0	3	0	0	0	.979	3	/C	0.3
1972	Chi-N	114	357	23	78	12	0	5	30	22	62	.218	.264	.294	53	-20	-24	25	1	0	0	.995	7	*C	-1.3
1973	Chi-N	124	368	35	83	11	1	10	43	30	51	.226	.284	.342	68	-14	-17	33	5	6	-2	.993	11	*C	-0.4
1974	Min-A	32	88	2	17	2	0	0	3	4	12	.193	.228	.216	27	-8	-8	4	0	0	0	.965	1	C	-0.7
1975	SD-N	74	180	7	37	5	1	2	14	19	29	.206	.285	.278	60	-10	-9	14	0	0	0	.970	1	C	-0.7
1976	Chi-N	13	18	3	3	2	0	0	1	1	4	.167	.211	.278	35	-2	-2	1	0	0	0	.923	-0	/C	-0.2
1977	Chi-N	2	4	0	0	0	0	0	0	0	1	.000	.000	.000	-90	-1	-1	0	0	0	0	1.000	0	/C	-0.1
Total	14	1061	3442	311	813	118	13	82	381	271	565	.236	.294	.350	76	-87	-114	346	12	17	-7	.990	1	*C	-7.0

■ TODD HUNDLEY
Hundley, Todd Randolph b: 5/27/69, Martinsville, Va. BB/TR, 5'11", 170 lbs. Deb: 5/18/90 F

1990	NY-N	36	67	8	14	6	0	0	2	6	18	.209	.274	.299	58	-4	-4	6	0	0	0	.988	2	C	-0.1
1991	NY-N	21	60	5	8	0	1	1	7	6	14	.133	.224	.217	25	-6	-6	3	0	0	0	1.000	-6	C	-1.1
1992	NY-N	123	358	32	75	17	0	7	32	19	76	.209	.257	.316	62	-19	-19	29	3	0	1	.996	3	*C	-1.0
Total	3	180	485	45	97	23	1	8	41	31	108	.200	.255	.301	57	-29	-28	37	3	0	1	.995	-1	C	-2.2

■ BERNIE HUNGLING
Hungling, Bernard Herman "Bud" b: 3/5/1896, Dayton, Ohio d: 3/30/68, Dayton, Ohio BR/TR, 6'2", 180 lbs. Deb: 4/14/22

1922	Bro-N	39	102	9	23	1	2	1	13	6	20	.225	.269	.304	48	-8	-8	9	2	0	1	.968	1	C	-0.4
1923	Bro-N	2	4	0	0	0	0	0	0	0	2	.000	.000	.000	-99	-1	-1	0	0	1	-1	.667	-1	/C	-0.2
1930	StL-A	10	31	4	10	2	0	0	2	5	3	.323	.417	.387	102	1	0	5	0	1	-1	1.000	-4	/C	-0.3
Total	3	51	137	13	33	3	2	1	15	11	25	.241	.297	.314	57	-9	-9	14	2	2	-1	.968	-3	/C	-0.9

■ BILL HUNNEFIELD
Hunnefield, William Fenton "Wild Bill" b: 1/5/1899, Dedham, Mass. d: 8/28/76, Nantucket, Mass. BB/TR, 5'10", 165 lbs. Deb: 4/17/26

1926	Chi-A	131	470	81	129	26	4	3	48	37	28	.274	.329	.366	84	-14	-11	59	24	9	2	.931	-8	S32	-0.7
1927	Chi-A	112	365	45	104	25	1	2	36	25	24	.285	.332	.375	85	-9	-8	40	13	13	-4	.933	-20	S2/3	-2.3
1928	Chi-A	94	333	42	98	8	3	2	24	26	24	.294	.351	.354	87	-6	-6	43	16	6	1	.967	-12	2/S3	-1.3
1929	Chi-A	47	127	13	23	5	0	0	9	7	3	.181	.224	.220	15	-16	-16	7	5	2	0	.969	-4	2/3S	-1.8
1930	Chi-A	31	81	11	22	2	0	1	5	4	10	.272	.314	.333	67	-4	-4	9	1	1	-0	.932	-11	S/1	-1.2
1931	Cle-A	21	71	13	17	4	1	0	4	9	4	.239	.325	.324	67	-3	-3	8	3	1	0	.853	-10	S/2	-1.0
	Bos-N	11	21	2	6	0	0	0	1	0	2	.286	.286	.286	56	-1	-1	2	0			.864	1	/32	0.1
	NY-N	64	196	23	53	5	0	1	17	9	16	.270	.302	.311	67	-9	-9	19	3			.951	-5	2/S	-1.0
	Yr	75	217	25	59	5	0	1	18	9	18	.272	.301	.309	66	-11	-10	20	3			.951	-3	2/3S	-0.9
Total	6	511	1664	230	482	75	9	9	144	117	111	.272	.322	.344	76	-64	-59	187	65	32		.925	-67	S2/31	-9.2

■ RANDY HUNT
Hunt, James Randall b: 1/3/60, Prattville, Ala. BR/TR, 6', 185 lbs. Deb: 6/04/85

1985	StL-N	14	19	1	3	0	0	0	1	0	5	.158	.158	.158	-12	-3	-3	0	0	1	-1	1.000	1	C	-0.2
1986	Mon-N	21	48	4	10	0	0	2	5	5	16	.208	.283	.333	70	-2	-2	4	0	0	0	.960	6	C	0.5
Total	2	35	67	5	13	0	0	2	6	5	21	.194	.250	.284	48	-5	-5	4	0	1	-1	.967	7	/C	0.3

■ KEN HUNT
Hunt, Kenneth Lawrence b: 7/13/34, Grand Forks, N.Dak BR/TR, 6'1", 205 lbs. Deb: 9/10/59

1959	NY-A	6	12	2	4	1	0	0	1	0	3	.333	.333	.417	108	0	0	2	0	0	0	1.000	0	/O	0.0
1960	NY-A	25	22	4	6	2	0	0	1	4	4	.273	.407	.364	117	1	1	4	0	0	0	.957	-6	O	-0.6
1961	LA-A	149	479	70	122	29	3	25	84	49	120	.255	.329	.484	103	8	1	76	8	2	1	.950	-6	*O/2	-1.1
1962	LA-A	13	11	4	2	0	0	1	1	1	5	.182	.250	.455	88	-0	-0	1	1	0	0	.867	-1	/1	-0.1
1963	LA-A	59	142	17	26	6	1	5	16	15	46	.183	.261	.345	72	-6	-5	12	0	1	-1	.972	-6	O	-1.5
	Was-A	7	20	1	4	0	0	1	4	2	9	.200	.273	.350	73	-1	-1	1	0	0	0	1.000	-0	O	-0.1
	Yr	66	162	18	30	6	1	6	20	17	55	.185	.263	.346	73	-7	-6	14	0	1	-1	.976	-6	O	-1.6
1964	Was-A	51	96	9	13	4	0	1	4	14	35	.135	.245	.208	28	-9	-9	5	0	1	-1	1.000	-2	/O	-1.4
Total	6	310	782	107	177	42	4	33	111	85	222	.226	.306	.417	89	-8	-14	101	9	4	0	.964	-21	O/12	-4.8

■ JOEL HUNT
Hunt, Oliver Joel "Jodie" b: 10/11/05, Texico, N.Mex. d: 7/24/78, Teague, Tex. BR/TR, 5'10", 165 lbs. Deb: 4/27/31

1931	StL-N	4	1	2	0	0	0	0	0	0	1	.000	.000	.000	-96	-0	-0	0	0			.000	-1	/O	-0.1
1932	StL-N	12	21	0	4	1	0	0	3	4	3	.190	.320	.238	51	-1	-1	2	0			1.000	0	/O	-0.1
Total	2	16	22	2	4	1	0	0	3	4	4	.182	.308	.227	45	-2	-2	2	0			1.000	-0	/O	-0.2

■ DICK HUNT
Hunt, Richard M. b: 1847, New York d: 11/20/1895, Brooklyn, N.Y. 5'9", 145 lbs. Deb: 5/07/1872

| 1872 | Eck-n | 11 | 48 | 11 | 15 | 4 | 0 | 0 | 5 | 1 | 0 | .313 | .327 | .396 | 143 | 1 | 3 | 6 | | | | | | /O2 | 0.2 |

■ RON HUNT
Hunt, Ronald Kenneth b: 2/23/41, St.Louis, Mo. BR/TR, 6', 186 lbs. Deb: 4/16/63

1963	NY-N	143	533	64	145	28	4	10	42	40	50	.272	.338	.396	109	8	7	71	5	4	-1	.967	2	*2/3	2.3
1964	NY-N★	127	475	59	144	19	6	6	42	29	30	.303	.357	.406	117	10	11	66	6	2	1	.979	-8	*23	1.4
1965	NY-N	57	196	21	47	12	1	1	10	14	19	.240	.310	.327	82	-5	-4	18	2	7	-4	.979	-5	2/3	-0.9

YEAR	TM/L	G	AB	R	H	2B	3B	HR	RBI	BB	SO	AVG	OBP	SLG	PRO+	BR	/A	RC	SB	CS	SBR	FA	FR	POS	TPR
1966	NY-N★	132	479	63	138	19	2	3	33	41	34	.288	.358	.355	101	1	2	61	8	10	-4	.970	7	*2/S3	1.5
1967	LA-N	110	388	44	102	17	3	3	33	39	24	.263	.346	.345	107	1	4	48	2	1	0	.980	-16	2/3	-0.6
1968	SF-N	148	529	79	132	19	0	2	28	78	41	.250	.372	.297	103	7	7	66	6	6	-2	.972	-17	*2	-0.3
1969	SF-N	128	478	72	125	23	3	3	41	51	47	.262	.363	.341	100	2	3	66	9	2	2	.979	-9	*2/3	0.6
1970	SF-N	117	367	70	103	17	1	6	41	44	29	.281	.396	.381	111	8	9	59	1	2	-1	.968	-28	23	-1.4
1971	Mon-N	152	520	89	145	20	3	5	38	58	41	.279	.403	.358	116	18	17	85	5	7	-3	.979	-9	*23	1.7
1972	Mon-N	129	443	56	112	20	0	0	18	51	29	.253	.363	.298	88	-2	-3	55	9	2	2	.982	-7	*2/3	-0.2
1973	Mon-N	113	401	61	124	14	0	0	18	52	19	.309	.419	.344	110	12	11	63	10	7	-1	.982	-21	*23	-0.6
1974	Mon-N	115	403	66	108	15	0	0	26	55	17	.268	.375	.305	87	-1	-4	51	2	5	-2	.941	-14	32/S	-2.0
	StL-N	12	23	1	4	0	0	0	0	3	2	.174	.321	.174	42	-2	-2	2	0	0	0	1.000	-1	/2	-0.3
	Yr	127	426	67	112	15	0	0	26	58	19	.263	.372	.298	85	-3	-5	53	2	5	-2	.941	-16	32/S	-2.3
Total	12	1483	5235	745	1429	223	23	39	370	555	382	.273	.369	.347	104	56	58	711	65	55	-14	.976	-126	*23/S	1.2

■ **BRIAN HUNTER** Hunter, Brian Ronald b: 3/4/68, Toorance, Cal. BR/TL, 6', 195 lbs. Deb: 5/31/91

YEAR	TM/L	G	AB	R	H	2B	3B	HR	RBI	BB	SO	AVG	OBP	SLG	PRO+	BR	/A	RC	SB	CS	SBR	FA	FR	POS	TPR
1991	*Atl-N	97	271	32	68	16	1	12	50	17	48	.251	.298	.450	101	1	-0	34	0	2	-1	.988	-4	1/O	-1.1
1992	*Atl-N	102	238	34	57	13	2	14	41	21	50	.239	.301	.487	111	5	3	35	1	2	-1	.997	3	1/O	0.1
Total	2	199	509	66	125	29	3	26	91	38	98	.246	.299	.468	106	6	2	69	1	4	-2	.992	-1	1/O	-1.0

■ **EDDIE HUNTER** Hunter, Edison Franklin b: 2/6/05, Bellevue, Ky. d: 3/14/67, Collrain Turnpike Ohio BR/TR, 5'7.5", 150 lbs. Deb: 8/05/33

YEAR	TM/L	G	AB	R	H	2B	3B	HR	RBI	BB	SO	AVG	OBP	SLG	PRO+	BR	/A	RC	SB	CS	SBR	FA	FR	POS	TPR
1933	Cin-N	1	0	0	0	0	0	0	0	0	0	—	—	—	—	0	0	0	0			.000	0	/3	0.0

■ **NEWT HUNTER** Hunter, Frederick Creighton b: 1/5/1880, Chillicothe, Ohio d: 10/26/63, Columbus, Ohio BR/TR, 6', 180 lbs. Deb: 4/12/11 C

YEAR	TM/L	G	AB	R	H	2B	3B	HR	RBI	BB	SO	AVG	OBP	SLG	PRO+	BR	/A	RC	SB	CS	SBR	FA	FR	POS	TPR
1911	Pit-N	65	209	35	53	10	6	2	24	25	43	.254	.345	.388	101	1	0	31	9			.989	-2	1	-0.2

■ **GEORGE HUNTER** Hunter, George Henry b: 7/8/1887, Buffalo, N.Y. d: 1/11/68, Harrisburg, Pa. BB/TL, 5'8.5", 165 lbs. Deb: 5/04/09 F

YEAR	TM/L	G	AB	R	H	2B	3B	HR	RBI	BB	SO	AVG	OBP	SLG	PRO+	BR	/A	RC	SB	CS	SBR	FA	FR	POS	TPR
1909	Bro-N	44	123	8	28	7	0	0	8	9		.228	.286	.285	80	-3	-3	10	1			.871	-4	OP	-0.8
1910	Bro-N	1	0	0	0	0	0	0	0	0	0	—	—	—	—	0	0	0	0			.000	-0	/O	0.0
Total	2	45	123	8	28	7	0	0	8	9	0	.228	.286	.285	80	-3	-3	10	1			.871	-5	/OP	-0.8

■ **BILLY HUNTER** Hunter, Gordon William b: 6/4/28, Punxsutawney, Pa. BR/TR, 6', 180 lbs. Deb: 4/14/53 MC

YEAR	TM/L	G	AB	R	H	2B	3B	HR	RBI	BB	SO	AVG	OBP	SLG	PRO+	BR	/A	RC	SB	CS	SBR	FA	FR	POS	TPR
1953	StL-A★	154	567	50	124	18	1	1	37	24	45	.219	.253	.259	38	-49	-50	37	3	1	0	.970	15	*S	-2.5
1954	Bal-A	125	411	28	100	9	5	2	27	21	38	.243	.283	.304	66	-23	-19	33	5	4	-1	.948	1	*S	-1.0
1955	NY-A	98	255	14	58	7	1	3	20	15	18	.227	.270	.298	54	-17	-17	20	9	2	2	.958	1	S	-0.8
1956	NY-A	39	75	8	21	3	4	0	11	2	4	.280	.299	.427	93	-2	-1	8	0	1	-1	1.000	10	S/3	0.9
1957	KC-A	116	319	39	61	10	4	8	29	27	43	.191	.261	.323	58	-19	-20	27	1	2	-1	.974	-5	2S3	-2.0
1958	KC-A	22	58	6	9	1	1	2	11	5	7	.155	.222	.310	44	-5	-5	4	1	1	-0	.933	-3	S/23	-0.7
	Cle-A	76	190	21	37	10	2	0	9	17	37	.195	.264	.268	48	-14	-13	14	4	1	1	.948	1	S/3	-0.6
	Yr	98	248	27	46	11	3	2	20	22	44	.185	.255	.278	47	-18	-18	18	5	2	0	.946	-1	S/23	-1.3
Total	6	630	1875	166	410	58	18	16	144	111	192	.219	.265	.294	53	-128	-125	144	23	12	-0	.958	19	S/23	-6.7

■ **BUDDY HUNTER** Hunter, Harold James b: 8/9/47, Omaha, Neb. BR/TR, 5'10", 170 lbs. Deb: 7/01/71

YEAR	TM/L	G	AB	R	H	2B	3B	HR	RBI	BB	SO	AVG	OBP	SLG	PRO+	BR	/A	RC	SB	CS	SBR	FA	FR	POS	TPR
1971	Bos-A	8	9	2	2	1	0	0	0	2	1	.222	.364	.333	92	0	-0	1	0	0	0	1.000	1	/2	0.1
1973	Bos-A	13	7	3	3	1	0	0	2	3	1	.429	.636	.571	229	2	2	3	0	0	0	1.000	3	/32D	0.5
1975	Bos-A	1	1	0	0	0	0	0	0	0	0	.000	.000	.000	-92	-0	-0	0	0	0	0	.750	0	/2	0.0
Total	3	22	17	5	5	2	0	0	2	5	2	.294	.478	.412	144	2	2	5	0	0	0	.968	5	/23D	0.6

■ **HERB HUNTER** Hunter, Herbert Harrison b: 12/25/1896, Boston, Mass. d: 7/25/70, Orlando, Fla. BL/TR, 6'0.5", 165 lbs. Deb: 4/29/16

YEAR	TM/L	G	AB	R	H	2B	3B	HR	RBI	BB	SO	AVG	OBP	SLG	PRO+	BR	/A	RC	SB	CS	SBR	FA	FR	POS	TPR
1916	NY-N	21	28	3	7	0	0	1	4	0	5	.250	.250	.357	90	-1	-0	3	0			1.000	0	/31	0.0
	Chi-N	2	4	0	0	0	0	0	0	0	0	.000	.000	.000	-90	-1	-1	0	0			.750	0	/3	-0.1
	Yr	23	32	3	7	0	0	1	4	0	5	.219	.219	.313	65	-2	-1	2	0			.941	1	/31	-0.1
1917	Chi-N	3	3	0	0	0	0	0	0	0	0	.000	.000	.000	-93	-1	-1	0	0			1.000	0	/23	0.0
1920	Bos-A	4	12	2	1	0	0	0	0	1	1	.083	.154	.083	-38	-2	-2	0	0	0	0	.857	-1	/O	-0.3
1921	StL-N	9	2	3	0	0	0	0	0	1	0	.000	.333	.000	-4	-0	-0	-0	0	3	-2	1.000	0	/1	-0.2
Total	4	39	49	8	8	0	0	1	4	2	6	.163	.196	.224	24	-5	-5	3	0	3		.905	1	/3O12	-0.6

■ **LEM HUNTER** Hunter, Robert Lemuel b: 1/16/1863, Warren, Ohio d: 11/9/56, W.Lafayette, Ohio Deb: 9/01/1883

YEAR	TM/L	G	AB	R	H	2B	3B	HR	RBI	BB	SO	AVG	OBP	SLG	PRO+	BR	/A	RC	SB	CS	SBR	FA	FR	POS	TPR
1883	Cle-N	1	4	1	1	0	0	0	0	0	2	.250	.250	.250	53	-0	-0	0				.000	-1	/OP	0.0

■ **BILL HUNTER** Hunter, William Ellsworth b: 7/8/1887, Buffalo, N.Y. d: 4/10/34, Buffalo, N.Y. BL/TL, 5'7.5", 155 lbs. Deb: 8/06/12 F

YEAR	TM/L	G	AB	R	H	2B	3B	HR	RBI	BB	SO	AVG	OBP	SLG	PRO+	BR	/A	RC	SB	CS	SBR	FA	FR	POS	TPR
1912	Cle-A	21	55	6	9	2	0	0	2	10		.164	.303	.200	43	-4	-4	4	0			1.000	-0	O	-0.5

■ **BILL HUNTER** Hunter, William Robert b: St.Thomas, Ont., Can. 5'7.5", 160 lbs. Deb: 5/02/1884

YEAR	TM/L	G	AB	R	H	2B	3B	HR	RBI	BB	SO	AVG	OBP	SLG	PRO+	BR	/A	RC	SB	CS	SBR	FA	FR	POS	TPR
1884	Lou-a	2	7	1	1	0	0	0		0		.143	.143	.143	-5	-1	-1	0				.667	-2	/C	-0.3

■ **STEVE HUNTZ** Huntz, Stephen Michael b: 12/3/45, Cleveland, Ohio BB/TR, 6'1", 204 lbs. Deb: 9/19/67

YEAR	TM/L	G	AB	R	H	2B	3B	HR	RBI	BB	SO	AVG	OBP	SLG	PRO+	BR	/A	RC	SB	CS	SBR	FA	FR	POS	TPR
1967	StL-N	3	6	1	1	0	0	0	0	1	2	.167	.286	.167	33	-0	-0	0	0	0	0	1.000	-1	/2	-0.2
1969	StL-N	71	139	13	27	4	0	3	13	27	34	.194	.325	.288	73	-4	-4	13	0	0	0	.945	-6	S2/3	-0.6
1970	SD-N	106	352	54	77	8	0	11	37	66	69	.219	.344	.335	86	-7	-5	44	0	3	-2	.958	-12	S3	-1.3
1971	Chi-A	35	86	10	18	3	1	2	6	7	9	.209	.269	.337	69	-4	-4	8	1	0	0	1.000	-1	2/S3	-0.3
1975	SD-N	22	53	3	8	4	0	0	4	7	8	.151	.250	.226	35	-5	-4	3	0	0	0	.939	1	3/2	-0.3
Total	5	237	636	81	131	19	1	16	60	108	122	.206	.322	.314	76	-20	-18	70	1	3	-2	.955	-18	S/32	-2.7

■ **DAVE HUPPERT** Huppert, David Blain b: 4/1/57, Southgate, Cal. BR/TR, 6'1", 190 lbs. Deb: 9/15/83

YEAR	TM/L	G	AB	R	H	2B	3B	HR	RBI	BB	SO	AVG	OBP	SLG	PRO+	BR	/A	RC	SB	CS	SBR	FA	FR	POS	TPR
1983	Bal-A	2	0	0	0	0	0	0	0	0	0	—	—	—	—	0	0	0	0	0	0	1.000	0	/C	0.0
1985	Mil-A	15	21	1	1	0	0	0	0	2	7	.048	.130	.048	-49	-4	-4	0	0	0	0	.960	2	C	-0.2
Total	2	17	21	1	1	0	0	0	0	2	7	.048	.130	.048	-49	-4	-4	0	0	0	0	.962	3	/C	-0.2

■ **CLINT HURDLE** Hurdle, Clinton Merrick b: 7/30/57, Big Rapids, Mich. BL/TR, 6'3", 195 lbs. Deb: 9/18/77

YEAR	TM/L	G	AB	R	H	2B	3B	HR	RBI	BB	SO	AVG	OBP	SLG	PRO+	BR	/A	RC	SB	CS	SBR	FA	FR	POS	TPR
1977	KC-A	9	26	5	8	0	0	2	7	2	7	.308	.357	.538	139	1	1	5	0	0	0	1.000	-0	/O	0.1
1978	*KC-A	133	417	48	110	25	5	7	56	56	84	.264	.352	.398	108	7	5	61	1	3	-2	.958	-11	O1/3D	-1.3
1979	KC-A	59	171	16	41	10	3	3	30	28	24	.240	.350	.386	96	0	-0	24	0	1	-1	.968	-3	O/3D	-0.6
1980	*KC-A	130	395	50	116	31	2	10	60	34	61	.294	.353	.458	119	11	10	62	0	0	0	.960	-3	*O	0.3
1981	*KC-A	28	76	12	25	3	1	4	15	13	10	.329	.427	.553	182	8	8	18	0	0	0	1.000	1	O	0.8
1982	Cin-N	19	34	2	7	1	0	0	1	2	6	.206	.270	.235	42	-3	-3	2	0	1	-1	.950	1	O	-0.3
1983	NY-N	13	33	3	6	2	0	0	2	2	10	.182	.229	.242	31	-3	-3	2	0	0	0	.800	-1	/3O	-0.5
1985	NY-N	43	82	7	16	4	0	3	7	13	20	.195	.313	.354	88	-1	-1	9	0	1	-1	1.000	-2	CO	-0.3
1986	StL-N	78	154	18	30	5	1	3	15	26	38	.195	.315	.299	71	-6	-6	16	0	0	0	.994	-2	1O/C3	-1.0
1987	NY-N	3	3	1	1	0	0	0	0	0	1	.333	.333	.333	82	-0	-0	0	0	0	0	1.000	-0	/1	0.0
Total	10	515	1391	162	360	81	12	32	193	176	261	.259	.345	.403	106	14	12	199	1	6	-3	.965	-20	O/1C3D	-2.8

■ **JERRY HURLEY** Hurley, Jeremiah b: 4/1875, New York, N.Y. d: 12/27/19, New York, N.Y. BR/TR, Deb: 9/23/01

YEAR	TM/L	G	AB	R	H	2B	3B	HR	RBI	BB	SO	AVG	OBP	SLG	PRO+	BR	/A	RC	SB	CS	SBR	FA	FR	POS	TPR
1901	Cin-N	9	21	1	1	0	0	0	0	1		.048	.130	.048	-51	-4	-4	0	1			.938	1	/C	-0.2
1907	Bro-N	1	2	0	0	0	0	0	0	1		.000	.333	.000	6	-0	-0	0	0			1.000	-0	/C	0.0
Total	2	10	23	1	1	0	0	0	0	2		.043	.154	.043	-44	-4	-4	0	1			.943	1	/C	-0.2

YEAR	TM/L	G	AB	R	H	2B	3B	HR	RBI	BB	SO	AVG	OBP	SLG	PRO+	BR	/A	RC	SB	CS	SBR	FA	FR	POS	TPR

■ JERRY HURLEY   Hurley, Jeremiah Joseph   b: 6/15/1863, Boston, Mass.   d: 9/17/50, Boston, Mass.   BR/TR, 6′, 190 lbs.   Deb: 5/01/1889

1889	Bos-N	1	4	0	0	0	0	0	0	0	0	.000	.000	.000	-94	-1	-1	0	0			.000	-1	/OC	-0.2
1890	Pit-P	8	22	5	6	1	0	0	2	2	5	.273	.333	.318	83	-1	-0	2	0			.906	-0	/CO	0.0
1891	Cin-a	24	66	10	14	3	2	0	6	12	13	.212	.333	.318	82	-1	-2	8	2			.862	-3	C/O1	-0.3
Total	3	33	92	15	20	4	2	0	8	14	18	.217	.321	.304	75	-2	-3	10	2			.870	-5	/CO1	-0.5

■ DICK HURLEY   Hurley, William H.   b: 1847, Honesdale, Pa.   5′7″, 160 lbs.   Deb: 4/18/1872

| 1872 | Oly-n | 2 | 7 | 0 | 0 | 0 | 0 | 0 | 0 | | | .000 | .000 | .000 | -99 | -2 | -2 | 0 | | | | | | /O | -0.1 |

■ DON HURST   Hurst, Frank O'Donnell   b: 8/12/05, Maysville, Ky.   d: 12/6/52, Los Angeles, Cal.   BL/TL, 6′, 215 lbs.   Deb: 5/13/28

1928	Phi-N	107	396	73	113	23	4	19	64	68	40	.285	.391	.508	129	20	18	80	3			.989	4	*1	1.2
1929	Phi-N	154	589	100	179	29	4	31	125	80	36	.304	.390	.525	117	22	16	120	10			.985	5	*1	0.5
1930	Phi-N	119	391	78	128	19	3	17	78	46	22	.327	.401	.522	113	14	9	81	6			.984	-3	1/O	-0.3
1931	Phi-N	137	489	63	149	37	5	11	91	64	28	.305	.386	.468	119	21	15	93	8			.986	11	*1	1.4
1932	Phi-N	150	579	109	196	41	4	24	**143**	65	27	.339	.412	.547	139	46	37	134	10			**.993**	-3	*1	2.2
1933	Phi-N	147	550	58	147	27	8	8	76	48	32	.267	.327	.389	92	3	-6	72	3			.985	7	*1	-1.3
1934	Phi-N	40	130	16	34	9	0	2	21	12	7	.262	.324	.377	77	-2	-5	17	1			.994	-1	1	-0.8
	Chi-N	51	151	13	30	5	0	3	12	8	18	.199	.239	.291	42	-13	-12	10	0			.986	-2	1	-1.8
	Yr	91	281	29	64	14	0	5	33	20	25	.228	.279	.331	60	-15	-17	27	1			.990	-3	1	-2.6
Total	7	905	3275	510	976	190	28	115	610	391	210	.298	.375	.478	113	110	72	606	41			.987	19	1/O	1.1

■ JEFF HUSON   Huson, Jeffrey Kent   b: 8/15/64, Scottsdale, Ariz.   BL/TR, 6′3″, 180 lbs.   Deb: 9/02/88

1988	Mon-N	20	42	7	13	2	0	0	3	4	3	.310	.370	.357	105	1	0	5	2	1	0	.932	1	S/23O	0.2
1989	Mon-N	32	74	1	12	5	0	0	2	6	6	.162	.225	.230	30	-7	-7	3	3	0	1	.886	4	S/23	-0.1
1990	Tex-A	145	396	57	95	12	2	0	28	46	54	.240	.322	.280	70	-15	-15	39	12	4	1	.960	-12	*S32	-1.8
1991	Tex-A	119	268	36	57	8	3	2	26	39	32	.213	.313	.287	68	-11	-10	26	8	3	1	.965	0	*S/23	-0.3
1992	Tex-A	123	318	49	83	14	3	4	24	41	43	.261	.347	.362	102	0	2	43	18	6	2	.968	-9	S2/O	-0.2
Total	5	439	1098	150	260	41	8	6	83	136	138	.237	.323	.305	77	-31	-30	116	43	14	5	.958	-16	S/23O	-2.0

■ CARL HUSTA   Husta, Carl Lawrence "Sox"   b: 4/8/02, Egg Harbor, N.J.   d: 11/6/51, Kingston, N.Y.   BR/TR, 5′11″, 176 lbs.   Deb: 9/24/25

| 1925 | Phi-A | 6 | 22 | 2 | 3 | 0 | 0 | 0 | 2 | 2 | 3 | .136 | .208 | .136 | -11 | -4 | -4 | 1 | 0 | 0 | 0 | .976 | 2 | /S | -0.1 |

■ HARRY HUSTON   Huston, Harry Emanuel Kress   b: 10/14/1883, Bellefontaine, O.   d: 10/13/69, Blackwell, Okla.   BR/TR, 5′9″, 168 lbs.   Deb: 9/03/06

| 1906 | Phi-N | 2 | 4 | 0 | 0 | 0 | 0 | 0 | 0 | 1 | | .000 | .200 | .000 | -37 | -1 | -1 | 0 | | | | 1.000 | -0 | /C | -0.1 |

■ WARREN HUSTON   Huston, Warren Llewellyn   b: 10/31/13, Newtonville, Mass.   BR/TR, 6′, 170 lbs.   Deb: 6/24/37

1937	Phi-A	38	54	5	7	3	0	0	3	2	9	.130	.161	.185	-13	-10	-9	1	0	1	-1	.918	8	2S/3	-0.1
1944	Bos-N	33	55	7	11	1	0	0	1	8	5	.200	.313	.218	49	-3	-3	4	0		1	.979	3	3/2S	0.0
Total	2	71	109	12	18	4	0	0	4	10	14	.165	.242	.202	19	-13	-13	5	0	1		.964	11	/32S	-0.1

■ JOE HUTCHESON   Hutcheson, Joseph Johnson "Slug" or "Poodles"   b: 2/5/05, Springtown, Tex.   BL/TR, 6′2″, 200 lbs.   Deb: 7/08/33

| 1933 | Bro-N | 55 | 184 | 19 | 43 | 4 | 1 | 6 | 21 | 15 | 13 | .234 | .295 | .364 | 91 | -3 | -2 | 20 | 1 | | | .989 | 1 | O | -0.4 |

■ ED HUTCHINSON   Hutchinson, Edwin Forrest   b: 5/19/1867, Pittsburgh, Pa.   d: 7/19/34, Colfax, Cal.   BL/TR, 5′11″, 175 lbs.   Deb: 6/17/1890

| 1890 | Chi-N | 4 | 17 | 0 | 1 | 1 | 0 | 0 | 0 | 0 | 0 | .059 | .059 | .118 | -47 | -3 | -3 | 0 | 0 | | | 1.000 | 6 | /2 | 0.2 |

■ FRED HUTCHINSON   Hutchinson, Frederick Charles   b: 8/12/19, Seattle, Wash.   d: 11/12/64, Bradenton, Fla.   BL/TR, 6′2″, 200 lbs.   Deb: 5/02/39   M

1939	Det-A	13	34	5	13	1	0	0	6	2	0	.382	.417	.412	105	1	0	5	0	0	0	1.000	-0	P	0.0
1940	*Det-A	17	30	1	8	1	0	0	2	0	2	.267	.267	.300	43	-2	-3	2	0	0	0	.900	0	P	0.0
1941	Det-A	2	2	0	0	0	0	0	0	0	2	.000	.000	.000	-91	-1	-1	0	0	0	0	.000	0	H	-0.1
1946	Det-A	40	89	11	28	4	0	0	13	6	1	.315	.358	.360	95	0	-0	12	0	0	0	.983	3	P	0.0
1947	Det-A	56	106	8	32	5	2	2	15	6	6	.302	.339	.443	113	2	1	15	2	0	1	.982	3	P	0.0
1948	Det-A	76	112	11	23	1	0	1	12	22	9	.205	.341	.241	55	-6	-7	11	3	0	1	1.000	3	P	0.0
1949	Det-A	38	73	12	18	2	1	0	7	6	7	.247	.329	.301	67	-3	-3	7	1	0	0	.983	2	P	0.0
1950	Det-A	44	95	15	31	7	0	0	20	12	3	.326	.407	.400	104	2	1	17	0	0	0	.944	2	P	0.0
1951	Det-A★	47	85	7	16	2	0	0	7	7	4	.188	.250	.212	26	-9	-9	5	0	1	-1	.939	2	P	0.0
1952	Det-A	17	18	0	1	0	0	0	0	3	0	.056	.190	.056	-29	-3	-3	0	0	0	0	1.000	2	PM	0.0
1953	Det-A	4	6	1	1	0	0	1	0	0	0	.167	.167	.667	118	0	0	1	0	0	0	1.000	-0	/P1M	0.0
Total	11	354	650	71	171	23	3	4	83	66	30	.263	.334	.326	75	-20	-23	76	6	1	1	.970	15	P/1	-0.1

■ ROY HUTSON   Hutson, Roy Lee   b: 2/27/02, Luray, Mo.   d: 5/20/57, LaMesa, Cal.   BL/TR, 5′9″, 165 lbs.   Deb: 9/20/25

| 1925 | Bro-N | 7 | 8 | 1 | 4 | 0 | 0 | 0 | 1 | 1 | 1 | .500 | .556 | .500 | 177 | 1 | 1 | 2 | 0 | 0 | 0 | 1.000 | -1 | /O | 0.0 |

■ JIM HUTTO   Hutto, James Neamon   b: 10/17/47, Norfolk, Va.   BR/TR, 5′11″, 195 lbs.   Deb: 4/17/70

1970	Phi-N	57	92	7	17	2	0	3	12	5	20	.185	.227	.304	42	-8	-8	6	0	0	0	1.000	-1	O1/C3	-1.0
1975	Bal-A	4	5	0	0	0	0	0	0	0	2	.000	.000	.000	-99	-1	-1	0	0	0	0	1.000	-0	/C	-0.1
Total	2	61	97	7	17	2	0	3	12	5	22	.175	.216	.289	35	-9	-9	6	0	0	0	1.000	-2	/O1C3	-1.1

■ TOM HUTTON   Hutton, Thomas George   b: 4/20/46, Los Angeles, Cal.   BL/TL, 5′11″, 180 lbs.   Deb: 9/16/66

1966	LA-N	3	2	0	0	0	0	0	0	0	0	.000	.000	.000	-99	-1	-1	0	0	0	0	1.000	-0	/1	-0.1
1969	LA-N	16	48	2	13	0	0	0	4	5	7	.271	.340	.271	78	-2	-1	5	0	0	0	.993	4	1	0.2
1972	Phi-N	134	381	40	99	16	2	4	38	56	24	.260	.355	.344	97	1	0	47	5	8	-3	.992	0	1O	-1.1
1973	Phi-N	106	247	31	65	11	0	5	29	32	31	.263	.348	.368	96	0	-1	31	3	1	0	.998	4	1	0.0
1974	Phi-N	96	208	32	50	6	3	4	30	30	13	.240	.336	.356	90	-1	-2	25	2	2	-1	.996	-2	1O	-0.9
1975	Phi-N	113	165	24	41	6	0	3	24	27	10	.248	.354	.339	90	-1	-2	19	2	5	-2	.994	5	1O	-0.1
1976	*Phi-N	95	124	15	25	5	1	0	13	27	11	.202	.344	.282	77	-2	-3	13	1	2	-1	1.000	4	1/O	-0.2
1977	*Phi-N	107	81	12	25	3	0	2	11	12	10	.309	.398	.420	114	3	2	13	1	1	0	.993	3	1/O	0.0
1978	Tor-A	64	173	19	44	9	0	2	9	19	11	.254	.328	.341	87	-2	-3	19	1	2	-1	1.000	-5	O/1	-1.1
	Mon-N	39	59	4	12	3	0	0	5	10	5	.203	.319	.254	63	-3	-3	5	0	0	0	1.000	-2	1/O	-0.5
1979	Mon-N	86	83	14	21	2	1	1	13	10	7	.253	.333	.337	84	-2	-2	9	0	0	0	1.000	1	1/O	0.1
1980	Mon-N	62	55	2	12	0	0	2	9	5	4	.218	.271	.255	47	-4	-4	4	0	0	0	1.000	-0	/1OP	-0.4
1981	Mon-N	31	29	1	3	0	0	0	2	1	1	.103	.161	.103	-23	-5	-5	1	0	0	0	1.000	0	/1O	-0.5
Total	12	952	1655	196	410	63	7	22	186	234	140	.248	.341	.334	87	-18	-22	190	15	21	-8	.995	16	1O/P	-4.2

■ HAM HYATT   Hyatt, Robert Hamilton   b: 11/1/1884, Buncombe Co., N.C.   d: 9/11/63, Liberty Lake, Wash.   BL/TR, 6′1″, 185 lbs.   Deb: 4/15/09

1909	*Pit-N	49	67	9	20	3	4	0	7	3		.299	.329	.463	134	3	2	10	1			.933	3	/O1	0.6
1910	Pit-N	74	175	19	46	5	6	1	30	8	14	.263	.306	.377	94	-1	-2	20	3			.986	-2	1/O	-0.4
1912	Pit-N	46	97	13	28	3	1	0	22	6	8	.289	.330	.340	85	-2	-2	11	2			.955	-2	O/1	-0.5
1913	Pit-N	63	81	8	27	6	2	4	16	3	8	.333	.372	.605	184	7	8	18	0			1.000	-2	/10	0.6
1914	Pit-N	74	79	2	17	6	1	0	15	7	14	.215	.295	.316	86	-2	-1	7	1			.980	-2	/1C	-0.4
1915	StL-N	106	295	23	79	8	5	2	46	28	24	.268	.337	.376	116	6	6	38	3	3	-1	.991	-6	1O	-0.4
1918	NY-A	53	131	11	30	5	2	0	10	8	8	.229	.273	.336	82	-3	-4	12	1			1.000	-1	O/1	-0.7
Total	7	465	925	85	247	36	23	10	146	63	76	.267	.321	.388	108	7	6	117	3	3		.989	-11	1/OC	-1.1

■ JIM HYNDMAN   Hyndman, James William   b: 7/1865, Ontario   Deb: 7/23/1886

| 1886 | Phi-a | 1 | 4 | 0 | 0 | 0 | 0 | 0 | 0 | 0 | | .000 | .000 | .000 | -99 | -1 | -1 | 0 | 0 | | | 1.000 | 0 | /OP | -0.1 |

YEAR	TM/L	G	AB	R	H	2B	3B	HR	RBI	BB	SO	AVG	OBP	SLG	PRO+	BR	/A	RC	SB	CS	SBR	FA	FR	POS	TPR

■ PAT HYNES   Hynes, Patrick J.   b: 3/12/1884, St.Louis, Mo.   d: 3/12/07, St.Louis, Mo.   TL ,   Deb: 9/27/03

1903	StL-N	1	3	0	0	0	0	0	0	0	0	.000	.000	.000	-99	-1	-1	0	0			.500	-1	/P	0.0
1904	StL-A	66	254	23	60	7	3	0	15	15	3	.236	.248	.287	74	-9	-8	20	3			.901	-12	O/P	-2.4
Total	2	67	257	23	60	7	3	0	15	15	3	.233	.245	.284	71	-10	-9	20	3			.857	-12	/OP	-2.4

■ PETE INCAVIGLIA   Incaviglia, Peter Joseph   b: 4/2/64, Pebble Beach, Cal.   BR/TR, 6'1", 225 lbs.   Deb: 4/08/86

1986	Tex-A	153	540	82	135	21	2	30	88	55	185	.250	.324	.463	108	7	5	82	3	2	-0	.921	-11	*OD	-1.0
1987	Tex-A	139	509	85	138	26	4	27	80	48	168	.271	.335	.497	116	11	11	85	9	3	1	.945	-3	*O/D	0.4
1988	Tex-A	116	418	59	104	19	3	22	54	39	153	.249	.323	.467	116	9	8	63	6	4	-1	.989	6	OD	1.0
1989	Tex-A	133	453	48	107	27	4	21	81	32	136	.236	.295	.453	106	3	2	56	5	7	-3	.973	-3	*O/D	-0.7
1990	Tex-A	153	529	59	123	27	0	24	85	45	146	.233	.304	.420	100	-1	-1	63	3	4	-2	.974	-0	*O/D	-0.7
1991	Det-A	97	337	38	72	12	1	11	38	36	92	.214	.291	.353	76	-11	-11	35	1	3	-2	.973	-3	OD	-1.2
1992	Hou-N	113	349	31	93	22	1	11	44	25	99	.266	.321	.430	118	4	6	47	2	2	-1	.970	4	O	0.8
Total	7	904	3135	402	772	154	15	146	470	280	979	.246	.314	.445	106	22	19	431	29	25	-6	.964	-7	OD	-1.4

■ ALEXIS INFANTE   Infante, Fermin Alexis (Carpio)   b: 12/4/61, Barquisimeto, Venez.   BR/TR, 5'10", 175 lbs.   Deb: 9/27/87

1987	Tor-A	1	0	0	0	0	0	0	0	0	0	—	—	—		0	0	0	0	0	0	.000	0	/R	0.0
1988	Tor-A	19	15	7	3	0	0	0	0	2	4	.200	.294	.200	41	-1	-1	1	0	0	0	.909	1	/3SD	0.0
1989	Tor-A	20	12	1	2	0	0	0	0	0	1	.167	.167	.167	-6	-2	-2	0	1	0	0	1.000	4	/S32D	0.3
1990	Atl-N	20	28	3	1	1	0	0	0	0	7	.036	.069	.071	-58	-6	-6	0	0	0	0	.964	4	2/3S	-0.2
Total	4	60	55	11	6	1	0	0	0	2	12	.109	.155	.127	-20	-9	-9	1	1	0	0	.933	9	/3S2D	0.1

■ SCOTTY INGERTON   Ingerton, William John   b: 4/19/1886, Peninsula, Ohio   d: 6/15/56, Cleveland, Ohio   BR/TR, 6'1", 172 lbs.   Deb: 4/12/11

| 1911 | Bos-N | 136 | 521 | 63 | 130 | 24 | 4 | 5 | 61 | 39 | 68 | .250 | .304 | .340 | 74 | -15 | -21 | 55 | 6 | | | .942 | 18 | 3012/S | -0.4 |

■ CHARLIE INGRAHAM   Ingraham, Charles W.   b: 4/8/1860, Illinois   d: 2/18/06, Chicago, Ill.   5'11", 170 lbs.   Deb: 7/04/1883

| 1883 | Bal-a | 1 | 4 | 0 | 1 | 0 | 0 | 0 | 0 | 0 | 0 | .250 | .250 | .250 | 60 | -0 | -0 | 0 | | | | .833 | -1 | /C | -0.1 |

■ MEL INGRAM   Ingram, Melvin David   b: 7/4/04, Asheville, N.C.   d: 10/28/79, Medford, Ore.   BR/TR, 5'11.5", 175 lbs.   Deb: 7/24/29

| 1929 | Pit-N | 3 | 0 | 1 | 0 | 0 | 0 | 0 | 0 | 0 | 0 | — | — | — | | 0 | 0 | 0 | 0 | | | .000 | 0 | R | 0.0 |

■ DANE IORG   Iorg, Dane Charles   b: 5/11/50, Eureka, Cal.   BL/TR, 6', 180 lbs.   Deb: 4/09/77   F

1977	Phi-N	12	30	3	5	1	0	0	2	1	3	.167	.194	.200	6	-4	-4	1	0	0	0	.986	-0	/1	-0.5
	StL-N	30	32	2	10	1	0	0	4	5	4	.313	.405	.344	105	0	1	4	0	1	-1	.875	-1	/O	-0.1
	Yr	42	62	5	15	2	0	0	6	6	7	.242	.309	.274	58	-4	-4	5	0	1	-1	.986	-1	/1O	-0.6
1978	StL-N	35	85	6	23	4	1	0	4	4	10	.271	.303	.341	81	-2	-2	8	0	0	0	1.000	1	O	-0.2
1979	StL-N	79	179	12	52	11	1	1	21	12	28	.291	.339	.380	95	-1	-1	22	1	2	1	.964	-4	O1	-0.8
1980	StL-N	105	251	33	76	23	1	3	36	20	34	.303	.354	.438	116	6	6	38	1	1	-0	.991	-6	O/13	-0.3
1981	StL-N	75	217	23	71	11	2	2	39	7	9	.327	.348	.424	115	4	4	30	2	0	1	.963	-9	O/13	-0.7
1982	*StL-N	102	238	17	70	14	1	0	34	23	23	.294	.356	.361	100	1	1	28	0	1	0	.971	-3	O13	-0.5
1983	StL-N	58	116	6	31	9	1	0	11	10	11	.267	.331	.362	92	-1	-1	13	1	0	0	.974	-2	O1	-0.4
1984	StL-N	15	28	3	4	2	0	0	3	2	6	.143	.200	.214	17	-3	-3	1	0	0	0	1.000	-1	/1O	-0.4
	*KC-A	78	235	27	60	16	2	5	30	13	15	.255	.294	.404	90	-3	-4	26	0	1	-1	.995	-4	1O/3D	-1.2
1985	*KC-A	64	130	7	29	9	1	1	21	8	16	.223	.268	.331	63	-7	-7	10	0	1	-1	1.000	-5	O/13D	-1.3
1986	SD-N	90	106	10	24	2	1	2	11	2	21	.226	.241	.321	55	-7	-7	8	0	0	0	1.000	-2	1/3OP	-0.9
Total	10	743	1647	149	455	103	11	14	216	107	180	.276	.321	.378	92	-17	-19	190	5	7	-3	.977	-33	O1/3DP	-7.3

■ GARTH IORG   Iorg, Garth Ray   b: 10/12/54, Arcata, Cal.   BR/TR, 5'11", 170 lbs.   Deb: 4/09/78   F

1978	Tor-A	19	49	3	8	0	0	0	3	3	4	.163	.226	.163	1	-6	-6	2	0	0	0	.966	4	2	-0.1
1980	Tor-A	80	222	24	55	10	1	2	14	12	39	.248	.286	.329	65	-10	-11	20	2	1	0	.988	8	2301/SD	-0.2
1981	Tor-A	70	215	17	52	11	0	0	10	7	31	.242	.269	.293	58	-11	-12	16	2	3	-1	.963	-0	23/S1D	-1.2
1982	Tor-A	129	417	45	119	20	5	1	36	12	38	.285	.312	.365	78	-9	-14	47	3	2	-0	.946	-3	*32/D	-1.9
1983	Tor-A	122	375	40	103	22	5	2	39	13	45	.275	.301	.376	80	-8	-11	41	7	0	2	.976	-3	32/S	-1.2
1984	Tor-A	121	247	24	56	10	3	1	25	5	16	.227	.245	.304	49	-17	-18	16	1	3	-2	.945	1	*3/2SD	-1.9
1985	*Tor-A	131	288	33	90	22	1	7	37	21	26	.313	.359	.469	122	9	8	45	3	6	-3	.951	11	*32	1.6
1986	Tor-A	137	327	30	85	19	1	3	44	20	47	.260	.305	.352	76	-10	-11	35	3	0	1	.955	-15	32/S	-2.4
1987	Tor-A	122	310	35	65	11	0	4	30	21	52	.210	.264	.284	45	-24	-25	23	2	2	-1	.982	-13	23/D	-3.4
Total	9	931	2450	251	633	125	16	20	238	114	298	.258	.294	.347	72	-85	-100	244	23	17	-3	.955	-12	32/O1DS	-10.7

■ HAPPY IOTT   Iott, Frederick "Happy Jack" or "Biddo" (b: Frederick Hoyot)   b: 7/7/1876, Houlton, Me.   d: 2/17/41, Island Falls, Me.   BR/TR, 5'10", 175 lbs.   Deb: 9/16/03

| 1903 | Cle-A | 3 | 10 | 1 | 2 | 0 | 0 | 0 | 2 | | | .200 | .333 | .200 | 64 | -0 | -0 | 1 | 1 | | | .875 | -0 | /O | -0.1 |

■ HAL IRELAN   Irelan, Harold "Grump"   b: 8/5/1890, Burnettsville, Ind.   d: 7/16/44, Carmel, Ind.   BB/TR, 5'7", 165 lbs.   Deb: 4/23/14

| 1914 | Phi-N | 67 | 165 | 16 | 39 | 8 | 0 | 1 | 16 | 21 | 22 | .236 | .326 | .303 | 82 | -2 | -3 | 17 | 3 | | | .909 | 11 | 2/S13 | 0.8 |

■ TIM IRELAND   Ireland, Timothy Neal   b: 3/14/53, Oakland, Cal.   BR/TR, 6', 180 lbs.   Deb: 9/20/81

1981	KC-A	4	0	1	0	0	0	0	0	0	0	—	—	—		0	0	0	0	1	-1	1.000	-0	/1	-0.1
1982	KC-A	7	7	2	1	0	0	0	0	0	1	.143	.250	.143	11	-1	-1	0	0	0	0	1.000	0	/2O3	-0.1
Total	2	11	7	3	1	0	0	0	0	1	1	.143	.250	.143	11	-1	-1	0	0	1	-1		0	/21O3	-0.2

■ MONTE IRVIN   Irvin, Monford   b: 2/25/19, Columbia, Ala.   BR/TR, 6'1", 195 lbs.   Deb: 7/08/49   H

1949	NY-N	36	76	7	17	3	2	0	7	17	11	.224	.366	.316	84	-1	-1	10	0			1.000	0	O/13	-0.1
1950	NY-N	110	374	61	112	19	5	15	66	52	41	.299	.392	.497	131	18	18	76	3			.979	5	1O/3	1.9
1951	*NY-N	151	558	94	174	19	11	24	121	89	44	.312	.415	.514	147	41	40	127	12	2	2	.996	11	*O1	4.6
1952	NY-N†	46	126	10	39	2	1	4	21	10	11	.310	.365	.437	120	4	3	20	0	1	-1	1.000	-2	O	0.0
1953	NY-N	124	444	72	146	21	5	21	97	55	34	.329	.406	.541	142	29	28	96	2	0	1	.973	8	*O	3.1
1954	*NY-N	135	432	62	113	13	3	19	64	70	23	.262	.367	.438	108	6	6	69	7	4	-0	.976	4	*O/13	0.5
1955	NY-N	51	150	16	38	7	1	1	17	17	15	.253	.341	.333	80	-4	-4	18	3	0	1	.961	1	O	-0.4
1956	Chi-N	111	339	44	92	13	3	15	50	41	41	.271	.350	.460	118	7	7	53	1	0	0	.991	11	O	1.5
Total	8	764	2499	366	731	97	31	99	443	351	220	.293	.385	.475	126	101	99	468	28	7		.983	38	O1/3	11.1

■ ED IRVIN   Irvin, William Edward   b: 1882, Philadelphia, Pa.   d: 2/18/16, Philadelphia, Pa.   TR ,   Deb: 5/18/12

| 1912 | Det-A | 1 | 3 | 0 | 2 | 0 | 0 | 0 | 0 | 0 | 0 | .667 | .667 | 2.000 | 675 | 2 | 2 | 4 | 0 | | | .500 | -1 | /3 | 0.1 |

■ ARTHUR IRWIN   Irwin, Arthur Albert "Doc" or "Sandy"   b: 2/14/1858, Toronto, Ont., Can.   d: 7/16/21, Atlantic Ocean   BL/TR, 5'8.5", 158 lbs.   Deb: 5/01/1880   FMU

1880	Wor-N	85	352	53	91	19	4	1	35	11	27	.259	.281	.344	102	4	-0	35				.895	31	*S/3C	3.4
1881	Wor-N	50	206	27	55	8	2	0	24	7	4	.267	.291	.325	88	-1	-3	20				.851	-8	S	-0.7
1882	Wor-N	84	333	30	73	12	4	0	30	14	34	.219	.251	.279	68	-11	-12	24				.837	21	3S	1.0
1883	Pro-N	98	406	67	116	22	7	0	44	12	38	.286	.306	.374	103	2	1	48				.856	-7	*S/2	-0.3
1884	*Pro-N	102	404	73	97	14	3	2	44	28	52	.240	.289	.304	89	-6	-4	36				.881	-6	*S/P	-0.7
1885	Pro-N	59	218	16	39	2	1	0	14	14	29	.179	.228	.197	40	-14	-13	10				.875	4	S/32	-0.7
1886	Phi-N	101	373	51	87	6	6	0	34	35	39	.233	.299	.282	77	-9	-10	40	24			.891	4	*S/3	-0.5
1887	Phi-N	100	374	65	95	14	8	2	56	48	26	.254	.344	.350	90	-1	-5	53	19			.892	-10	*S	-1.1
1888	Phi-N	125	448	51	98	12	4	0	28	33	56	.219	.277	.263	71	-11	-15	39	19			.900	12	*S/2	1.0
1889	Phi-N	18	73	9	16	5	0	0	10	6	6	.219	.278	.288	55	-4	-5	8	6			.845	-6	S	-0.9

YEAR	TM/L	G	AB	R	H	2B	3B	HR	RBI	BB	SO	AVG	OBP	SLG	PRO+	BR	/A	RC	SB	CS	SBR	FA	FR	POS	TPR
	Was-N	85	313	49	73	10	5	0	32	42	37	.233	.326	.297	81	-9	-6	34	9			.895	12	S/P2M	0.9
	Yr	103	386	58	89	15	5	0	42	48	43	.231	.317	.295	76	-13	-10	42	15			.888	6	*S/P2	0.0
1890	Bos-P	96	354	60	92	17	1	0	45	57	29	.260	.364	.314	78	-6	-11	47	16			.878	3	*S	-0.2
1891	Bos-a	6	17	1	2	0	0	0	0	2	1	.118	.286	.118	19	-2	-2	1	0			.778	-1	/SM	-0.2
1894	Phi-N	1	0	0	0	0	0	0	0	0	0	—	—	—	—	0	0	0	0			.000	0	/SM	0.0
Total	13	1010	3871	552	934	141	45	5	396	309	378	.241	.299	.305	82	-68	-83	394	93			.881	49	S/32PC	-0.0

■ CHARLIE IRWIN Irwin, Charles Edwin b: 2/15/1869, Clinton, Ill. d: 9/21/25, Chicago, Ill. BL/TR, 5'10", 160 lbs. Deb: 9/03/1893

YEAR	TM/L	G	AB	R	H	2B	3B	HR	RBI	BB	SO	AVG	OBP	SLG	PRO+	BR	/A	RC	SB	CS	SBR	FA	FR	POS	TPR
1893	Chi-N	21	82	14	25	6	2	0	13	10	1	.305	.394	.427	122	3	3	16	4			.910	-1	S	0.2
1894	Chi-N	128	498	84	144	24	9	8	95	63	23	.289	.379	.422	90	-4	-9	96	35			.822	-11	3S	-1.3
1895	Chi-N	3	10	4	2	0	0	0	0	2	1	.200	.333	.200	39	-1	-1	1	0			.900	-2	/S	-0.2
1896	Cin-N	127	476	77	141	16	6	1	67	26	17	.296	.338	.361	81	-9	-15	71	31			**.931**	7	*3	-0.5
1897	Cin-N	134	505	89	146	26	6	0	74	47		.289	.359	.364	85	-6	-11	79	27			.940	-6	*3	-1.2
1898	Cin-N	136	501	77	120	14	5	3	55	31		.240	.294	.305	67	-19	-24	53	18			.940	13	*3	-0.9
1899	Cin-N	90	314	42	73	4	8	1	52	26		.232	.295	.306	64	-15	-16	38	26			.909	-13	3/S21	-2.6
1900	Cin-N	87	333	59	91	15	6	1	44	14		.273	.314	.363	89	-7	-6	43	9			.931	-11	3S/O2	-1.4
1901	Cin-N	67	260	25	62	12	2	0	25	14		.238	.285	.300	75	-10	-8	27	13			.893	4	3	-0.3
	Bro-N	65	242	25	52	13	2	0	20	14		.215	.269	.285	59	-12	-13	21	4			.956	-2	3	-1.4
	Yr	132	502	50	114	25	4	0	45	28		.227	.277	.293	67	-22	-21	48	17			.921	3	*3	-1.7
1902	Bro-N	131	458	59	125	14	0	2	43	39		.273	.341	.317	102	3	2	57	13			.927	-10	*3/S	-0.7
Total	10	989	3679	555	981	144	46	16	488	286	42	.267	.329	.344	82	-77	-97	501	180			.921	-32	3S/O21	-10.3

■ JOHN IRWIN Irwin, John b: 7/21/1861, Toronto, Ont., Can d: 2/28/34, Boston, Mass. BL/TR, 5'10", 168 lbs. Deb: 5/31/1882 F

YEAR	TM/L	G	AB	R	H	2B	3B	HR	RBI	BB	SO	AVG	OBP	SLG	PRO+	BR	/A	RC	SB	CS	SBR	FA	FR	POS	TPR
1882	Wor-N	1	4	0	0	0	0	0	0	0	2	.000	.000	.000	-98	-1	-1	0				.636	-1	/1	-0.2
1884	Bos-U	105	432	81	101	22	6	1		15		.234	.260	.319	96	-2	-1	37				.780	4	*3	0.3
1886	Phi-a	3	13	4	3	1	0	0		0		.231	.231	.308	69	-0	-1	1	0			.714	-1	/S3	-0.2
1887	Was-N	8	31	6	11	2	0	2	3	3	6	.355	.429	.613	198	4	4	11	6			.875	-2	/S3	0.1
1888	Was-N	37	126	14	28	5	2	0	8	5	18	.222	.263	.294	84	-3	-2	14	15			.860	-1	S3	-0.3
1889	Was-N	58	228	42	66	11	4	0	25	25	14	.289	.370	.373	116	4	6	36	10			.868	0	3	0.7
1890	Buf-P	77	308	62	72	11	4	0	34	43	19	.234	.335	.295	77	-11	-6	37	18			.883	4	31/2	0.0
1891	Bos-a	19	72	6	16	2	2	0	15	6	9	.222	.282	.306	71	-3	-3	8	6			.882	0	O/3S	-0.2
	Lou-a	14	55	7	15	1	1	0	7	5	6	.273	.344	.327	96	-0	-0	7	1			.795	-7	3	-0.5
	Yr	33	127	13	31	3	3	0	22	11	15	.244	.309	.315	82	-3	-3	15	7			.882	-6	O3/S	-0.7
Total	8	322	1269	222	312	55	19	3	92	102	74	.246	.308	.326	94	-14	-4	151	56			.829	-4	3/SO12	-0.3

■ TOMMY IRWIN Irwin, Thomas Andrew b: 12/20/12, Altoona, Pa. BR/TR, 5'11", 165 lbs. Deb: 10/01/38

YEAR	TM/L	G	AB	R	H	2B	3B	HR	RBI	BB	SO	AVG	OBP	SLG	PRO+	BR	/A	RC	SB	CS	SBR	FA	FR	POS	TPR
1938	Cle-A	3	9	1	1	0	0	0	0	3	1	.111	.333	.111	16	-1	-1	1	0	0	0	1.000	0	/S	-0.1

■ WALT IRWIN Irwin, Walter Kingsley b: 9/23/1897, Henrietta, Pa. d: 8/18/76, Spring Lake, Mich. BR/TR, 5'10.5", 170 lbs. Deb: 4/24/21

YEAR	TM/L	G	AB	R	H	2B	3B	HR	RBI	BB	SO	AVG	OBP	SLG	PRO+	BR	/A	RC	SB	CS	SBR	FA	FR	POS	TPR
1921	StL-N	4	1	1	0	0	0	0	0	0	1	.000	.000	.000	-99	-0	-0	0	0	0	0	.000	0	H	0.0

■ ORLANDO ISALES Isales, Orlando (Pizarro) b: 12/22/59, Santurce, P.R. BR/TR, 5'9", 175 lbs. Deb: 9/11/80

YEAR	TM/L	G	AB	R	H	2B	3B	HR	RBI	BB	SO	AVG	OBP	SLG	PRO+	BR	/A	RC	SB	CS	SBR	FA	FR	POS	TPR
1980	Phi-N	3	5	1	2	0	1	0	3	1	0	.400	.500	.800	244	1	1	2	0	0	0	1.000	0	/O	0.1

■ FRANK ISBELL Isbell, William Frank "Bald Eagle" b: 8/21/1875, Delevan, N.Y. d: 7/15/41, Wichita, Kan. BL/TR, 5'11", 190 lbs. Deb: 5/01/1898

YEAR	TM/L	G	AB	R	H	2B	3B	HR	RBI	BB	SO	AVG	OBP	SLG	PRO+	BR	/A	RC	SB	CS	SBR	FA	FR	POS	TPR
1898	Chi-N	45	159	17	37	4	0	0	8	3		.233	.252	.258	46	-11	-11	12	3			.956	-7	OP/32S	-1.6
1901	Chi-A	137	556	93	143	15	8	3	70	36		.257	.311	.329	80	-17	-15	76	**52**			.980	14	*1/2PS3	-0.2
1902	Chi-A	137	515	62	130	14	4	4	59	14		.252	.276	.318	67	-26	-22	59	38			.986	10	*1/SPC	-1.4
1903	Chi-A	138	546	52	132	25	9	2	59	12		.242	.266	.332	82	-15	-12	59	26			.984	7	*13/2SO	-0.7
1904	Chi-A	96	314	27	66	10	3	1	34	16		.210	.255	.271	69	-12	-11	29	19			.986	0	12/OS	-1.2
1905	Chi-A	94	341	55	101	21	11	2	45	15		.296	.335	.440	152	16	17	59	15			.964	-2	2O/1S	1.5
1906	*Chi-A	143	549	71	153	18	11	0	57	30		.279	.324	.352	115	7	9	80	37			.949	-22	*2O/PC	-1.4
1907	Chi-A	125	486	60	118	19	7	0	41	22		.243	.280	.311	92	-7	-5	52	22			.957	9	*2/OPS	0.2
1908	Chi-A	84	320	31	79	15	3	1	49	19		.247	.297	.322	103	0	1	36	18			.990	2	12	0.1
1909	Chi-A	120	433	33	97	17	6	0	33	23		.224	.265	.291	79	-13	-11	40	23			.994	1	*1/O2	-1.3
Total	10	1119	4219	501	1056	158	62	13	455	190		.250	.289	.326	89	-78	-61	502	253			.986	12	12O/3PSC	-6.0

■ MIKE IVIE Ivie, Michael Wilson b: 8/8/52, Atlanta, Ga. BR/TR, 6'3", 205 lbs. Deb: 9/04/71

YEAR	TM/L	G	AB	R	H	2B	3B	HR	RBI	BB	SO	AVG	OBP	SLG	PRO+	BR	/A	RC	SB	CS	SBR	FA	FR	POS	TPR
1971	SD-N	6	17	0	8	0	0	0	3	1	1	.471	.526	.471	198	2	2	3	0	0	0	1.000	-2	/C	0.1
1974	SD-N	12	34	1	3	0	0	1	3	2	8	.088	.139	.176	-13	-5	-5	1	0	0	0	.986	-0	1	-0.6
1975	SD-N	111	377	36	94	16	2	8	46	20	63	.249	.294	.366	88	-10	-7	37	4	4	-1	.989	-5	13/C	-1.8
1976	SD-N	140	405	51	118	19	5	7	70	30	41	.291	.348	.415	126	8	12	56	6	6	-2	.995	1	*1/C3	0.4
1977	SD-N	134	489	66	133	29	2	9	66	39	57	.272	.328	.395	104	-5	1	64	3	2	-0	.992	-5	*13	-1.0
1978	SF-N	117	318	34	98	14	3	11	55	27	45	.308	.366	.475	139	14	15	55	3	0	1	.995	-9	1O	0.3
1979	SF-N	133	402	58	115	18	3	27	89	47	80	.286	.362	.547	155	24	27	79	5	1	1	.995	-4	1O/32	1.9
1980	SF-N	79	286	21	69	16	1	4	25	19	40	.241	.289	.346	78	-9	-9	27	1	2	-1	.993	-6	1	-2.2
1981	SF-N	7	17	1	5	2	0	0	3	0	1	.294	.294	.412	100	-0	-0	2	0	0	0	1.000	1	/1	0.0
	Hou-N	19	42	2	10	3	0	0	6	2	11	.238	.273	.310	68	-2	-2	3	0	1	-1	.989	2	1	-0.1
	Yr	26	59	3	15	5	0	0	9	2	12	.254	.279	.339	78	-2	-2	5	0	1	-1	.992	3	1	-0.1
1982	Hou-N	7	6	0	2	0	0	0	0	1	0	.333	.429	.333	125	0	0	1	0	0	0	.000	0	/H	0.0
	Det-A	80	259	35	60	12	1	14	38	24	51	.232	.302	.448	102	0	0	35	0	0	0	.000	0	D	0.0
1983	Det-A	12	42	4	9	4	0	0	7	2	4	.214	.250	.310	54	-3	-3	3	0	0	0	1.000	-0	1	-0.4
Total	11	857	2694	309	724	133	17	81	411	214	402	.269	.326	.421	112	13	32	366	22	16	-3	.993	-27	1/3DOC2	-3.4

■ HANK IZQUIERDO Izquierdo, Enrique Roberto (Valdes) b: 3/20/31, Matanzas, Cuba BR/TR, 5'11", 175 lbs. Deb: 8/09/67

YEAR	TM/L	G	AB	R	H	2B	3B	HR	RBI	BB	SO	AVG	OBP	SLG	PRO+	BR	/A	RC	SB	CS	SBR	FA	FR	POS	TPR
1967	Min-A	16	26	4	7	2	0	0	2	1	2	.269	.296	.346	83	-0	-1	3	0	0	0	.986	3	C	0.3

■ RAY JABLONSKI Jablonski, Raymond Leo "Jabbo" b: 12/17/26, Chicago, Ill. d: 11/25/85, Chicago, Ill. BR/TR, 5'10", 183 lbs. Deb: 4/14/53

YEAR	TM/L	G	AB	R	H	2B	3B	HR	RBI	BB	SO	AVG	OBP	SLG	PRO+	BR	/A	RC	SB	CS	SBR	FA	FR	POS	TPR
1953	StL-N	157	604	64	162	23	5	21	112	34	61	.268	.308	.427	89	-11	-11	77	2	2	-1	.932	-16	*3	-3.0
1954	StL-N★	152	611	80	181	33	3	12	104	49	42	.296	.350	.419	99	-1	-1	88	9	4	0	.925	-7	*3/1	-1.1
1955	Cin-N	74	221	28	53	9	0	9	28	13	35	.240	.291	.403	77	-6	-8	25	0	1	-1	.872	-10	3O	-2.0
1956	Cin-N	130	407	42	104	25	1	15	66	37	57	.256	.328	.432	96	1	-2	54	2	4	-2	.970	-25	*3/2	-2.9
1957	NY-N	107	305	37	88	15	1	9	57	31	47	.289	.354	.433	110	5	5	46	0	2	-1	.941	-3	3/1O	0.2
1958	SF-N	82	230	28	53	15	1	12	46	17	50	.230	.289	.461	97	-3	-2	27	2	0	1	.946	-8	3	-0.9
1959	StL-N	60	87	11	22	4	0	3	14	8	19	.253	.316	.402	84	-1	-2	11	1	0	0	.900	-3	3/S	-0.5
	KC-A	25	65	4	17	1	0	2	8	3	11	.262	.294	.369	79	-2	-2	7	0	0	0	.947	-3	3	-0.5
1960	KC-A	21	32	3	7	1	0	0	3	4	8	.219	.306	.250	52	-2	-2	3	0	0	0	.944	0	/3	-0.2
Total	8	808	2562	297	687	126	11	83	438	196	330	.268	.324	.423	94	-21	-26	338	16	13	-3	.936	-75	3/O1S2	-10.9

■ FRED JACKLITSCH Jacklitsch, Frederick Lawrence b: 5/24/1876, Brooklyn, N.Y. d: 7/18/37, Brooklyn, N.Y. BR/TR, 5'9", 180 lbs. Deb: 6/06/00

YEAR	TM/L	G	AB	R	H	2B	3B	HR	RBI	BB	SO	AVG	OBP	SLG	PRO+	BR	/A	RC	SB	CS	SBR	FA	FR	POS	TPR
1900	Phi-N	5	11	0	2	1	0	0	3	0		.182	.182	.273	25	-1	-1	1	0			1.000	-2	/C	-0.2
1901	Phi-N	33	120	14	30	4	3	0	24	12		.250	.328	.333	90	-1	-1	14	2			.971	-1	C/3	0.1
1902	Phi-N	38	114	8	23	4	0	0	8	9		.202	.278	.237	59	-5	-5	8	2			.927	-8	C/O	-1.1
1903	Bro-N	60	176	31	47	8	3	1	21	33		.267	.386	.364	118	5	6	27	4			.975	-9	C/2O	0.2
1904	Bro-N	26	77	8	18	3	1	0	8	7		.234	.298	.299	87	-1	-1	9	7			.957	-7	1/2C	-0.8

YEAR	TM/L	G	AB	R	H	2B	3B	HR	RBI	BB	SO	AVG	OBP	SLG	PRO+	BR	/A	RC	SB	CS	SBR	FA	FR	POS	TPR
1905	NY-A	1	3	1	0	0	0	0	1	1		.000	.250	.000	-17	-0	-0	0	0			1.000	-0	/C	0.0
1907	Phi-N	73	202	19	43	7	0	0	17	27		.213	.309	.248	76	-5	-5	18	7			.984	11	C/1O	1.3
1908	Phi-N	37	86	6	19	3	0	0	7	14		.221	.337	.256	87	-0	-1	9	3			.976	3	C	0.6
1909	Phi-N	20	32	6	10	1	1	0	1	10		.313	.476	.406	173	4	4	7	1			.964	-2	C/2	0.3
1910	Phi-N	25	51	7	10	3	0	0	2	5	9	.196	.268	.255	51	-3	-3	3	0			.989	5	C/123	0.3
1914	Bal-F	122	337	40	93	21	4	2	48	52	66	.276	.376	.380	112	8	7	53	7			**.988**	2	*C	2.0
1915	Bal-F	49	135	20	32	9	0	2	13	31	25	.237	.387	.348	113	5	4	20	2			.992	-7	C/S	0.1
1917	Bos-N	1	0	0	0	0	0	0	0	0	0	—	—	—	—	0	0	0	0			1.000	-0	/C	0.0
Total	13	490	1344	160	327	64	12	5	153	201	100	.243	.347	.320	97	4	3	169	35			.978	-13	C/1203S	2.8

■ CHARLIE JACKSON

Jackson, Charles Herbert "Lefty" b: 2/7/1894, Granite City, Ill. d: 5/27/68, Radford, Va. BL/TL, 5'9", 150 lbs. Deb: 8/20/15

YEAR	TM/L	G	AB	R	H	2B	3B	HR	RBI	BB	SO	AVG	OBP	SLG	PRO+	BR	/A	RC	SB	CS	SBR	FA	FR	POS	TPR
1915	Chi-A	1	1	0	0	0	0	0	0	0	1	.000	.000	.000	-97	-0	-0	0	0			.000	0	H	0.0
1917	Pit-N	41	121	7	29	3	2	0	1	10	22	.240	.303	.298	82	-2	-2	12	4			.986	0	O	-0.4
Total	2	42	122	7	29	3	2	0	1	10	23	.238	.301	.295	80	-2	-3	12	4				0	/O	-0.4

■ CHUCK JACKSON

Jackson, Charles Leo b: 3/19/63, Seattle, Wash. BR/TR, 6' ", 185 lbs. Deb: 5/26/87

YEAR	TM/L	G	AB	R	H	2B	3B	HR	RBI	BB	SO	AVG	OBP	SLG	PRO+	BR	/A	RC	SB	CS	SBR	FA	FR	POS	TPR
1987	Hou-N	35	71	3	15	3	0	1	6	7	19	.211	.282	.296	55	-5	-4	6	1	1	-0	.957	-1	3O/S	-0.6
1988	Hou-N	46	83	7	19	5	1	1	8	7	16	.229	.289	.349	86	-2	-2	8	1	1	-0	.908	1	3/SO	-0.1
Total	2	81	154	10	34	8	1	2	14	14	35	.221	.286	.325	71	-7	-6	14	2	2	-1	.928	1	/3OS	-0.7

■ DARRIN JACKSON

Jackson, Darrin Jay b: 8/22/62, Los Angeles, Cal. BR/TR, 6'1", 170 lbs. Deb: 6/17/85

YEAR	TM/L	G	AB	R	H	2B	3B	HR	RBI	BB	SO	AVG	OBP	SLG	PRO+	BR	/A	RC	SB	CS	SBR	FA	FR	POS	TPR
1985	Chi-N	5	11	0	1	0	0	0	0	0	3	.091	.091	.091	-44	-2	-2	0	0	0	0	1.000	-1	/O	-0.3
1987	Chi-N	7	5	2	4	1	0	0	0	0	0	.800	.800	1.000	359	2	2	4	0	0	0	1.000	-2	/O	0.0
1988	Chi-N	100	188	29	50	11	3	6	20	5	28	.266	.289	.452	105	1	0	24	4	1	1	.983	-10	O	-1.1
1989	Chi-N	45	83	7	19	4	0	1	8	6	17	.229	.281	.313	65	-3	-4	7	1	2	-1	.970	-1	O	-0.7
	SD-N	25	87	10	18	3	0	3	12	7	17	.207	.266	.345	73	-3	-3	7	0	2	-1	.954	2	O	-0.3
	Yr	70	170	17	37	7	0	4	20	13	34	.218	.273	.329	68	-7	-7	14	1	4	-2	.962	1	O	-1.0
1990	SD-N	58	113	10	29	3	0	3	9	5	24	.257	.288	.363	77	-4	-4	12	3	0	1	.985	-5	O	-0.9
1991	SD-N	122	359	51	94	12	1	21	49	27	66	.262	.317	.476	117	8	7	54	5	3	-0	.992	7	O/P	1.2
1992	SD-N	155	587	72	146	23	5	17	70	26	106	.249	.285	.392	87	-10	-12	60	14	3	2	.996	24	*O	1.2
Total	7	517	1433	181	361	57	9	51	168	76	261	.252	.293	.411	94	-11	-16	168	27	11	2	.988	14	O/P	-0.9

■ GEORGE JACKSON

Jackson, George Christopher "Hickory" b: 10/14/1882, Springfield, Mo. d: 11/25/72, Cleburne, Tex. BR/TR, 6'0.5", 180 lbs. Deb: 8/02/11

YEAR	TM/L	G	AB	R	H	2B	3B	HR	RBI	BB	SO	AVG	OBP	SLG	PRO+	BR	/A	RC	SB	CS	SBR	FA	FR	POS	TPR
1911	Bos-N	39	147	28	51	11	2	0	25	12	21	.347	.404	.449	128	8	6	31	12			.929	-2	O	0.2
1912	Bos-N	110	397	55	104	13	5	4	48	38	72	.262	.342	.350	88	-5	-6	55	22			.943	2	*O	-1.0
1913	Bos-N	3	10	2	3	0	0	0	0	0	2	.300	.300	.300	70	-0	-0	1	0			.875	0	/O	0.0
Total	3	152	554	85	158	24	7	4	73	50	95	.285	.357	.375	98	2	-1	87	34			.938	-0	O	-0.8

■ HENRY JACKSON

Jackson, Henry Everett b: 6/23/1861, Union City, Ind. d: 9/14/32, Chicago, Ill. BR/TR, 6'2", 185 lbs. Deb: 9/13/1887

YEAR	TM/L	G	AB	R	H	2B	3B	HR	RBI	BB	SO	AVG	OBP	SLG	PRO+	BR	/A	RC	SB	CS	SBR	FA	FR	POS	TPR
1887	Ind-N	10	38	1	10	1	0	0	3	0	12	.263	.263	.289	57	-2	-2	4	2			.933	-1	1	-0.4

■ JIM JACKSON

Jackson, James Benner b: 11/28/1877, Philadelphia, Pa. d: 10/9/55, Philadelphia, Pa. BR/TR, Deb: 4/26/01

YEAR	TM/L	G	AB	R	H	2B	3B	HR	RBI	BB	SO	AVG	OBP	SLG	PRO+	BR	/A	RC	SB	CS	SBR	FA	FR	POS	TPR
1901	Bal-A	99	364	42	91	17	3	2	50	20		.250	.291	.330	69	-14	-17	41	11			**.971**	3	O	-1.9
1902	NY-N	35	110	14	20	5	1	0	13	15		.182	.280	.245	63	-5	-4	10	6			.897	-2	O	-1.0
1905	Cle-A	109	426	59	109	12	4	2	31	34		.256	.317	.317	100	1	0	49	15			.950	4	*O/3	0.0
1906	Cle-A	105	374	44	80	13	2	0	38	38		.214	.290	.259	74	-11	-10	38	25			.975	-6	*O	-2.3
Total	4	348	1274	159	300	47	10	4	132	107		.235	.298	.297	80	-29	-31	138	57			.959	-1	O/3	-5.2

■ JOE JACKSON

Jackson, Joseph Jefferson "Shoeless Joe" b: 7/16/1889, Pickens Co., S.C. d: 12/5/51, Greenville, S.C. BL/TR, 6'1", 200 lbs. Deb: 8/25/08

YEAR	TM/L	G	AB	R	H	2B	3B	HR	RBI	BB	SO	AVG	OBP	SLG	PRO+	BR	/A	RC	SB	CS	SBR	FA	FR	POS	TPR
1908	Phi-A	5	23	0	3	0	0	0	3	0		.130	.130	.130	-14	-3	-3	0	0			.875	-1	/O	-0.4
1909	Phi-A	5	17	3	3	0	0	0	3	1		.176	.222	.176	26	-1	-1	1	0			.833	-0	/O	-0.2
1910	Cle-A	20	75	15	29	2	5	1	11	8		.387	.446	.587	220	10	10	21	4			.977	0	O	1.0
1911	Cle-A	147	571	126	233	45	19	7	83	56		.408	**.468**	.590	192	72	71	175	41			.958	8	*O	6.8
1912	Cle-A	154	572	121	**226**	44	**26**	3	90	54		.395	.458	.579	190	70	68	166	35			.950	13	*O	7.1
1913	Cle-A	148	528	109	**197**	**39**	17	7	71	80	26	.373	.460	**.551**	190	**66**	**64**	**140**	26			.930	2	*O	6.2
1914	Cle-A	122	453	61	153	22	13	3	53	41	34	.338	.399	.464	153	32	30	86	22	15	-2	.967	2	*O	2.6
1915	Cle-A	83	303	42	99	16	9	3	45	28	11	.327	.389	.469	154	20	19	54	10	10	-3	.961	-3	O1	1.0
	Chi-A	45	158	21	43	4	5	2	36	24	12	.272	.378	.399	129	7	6	23	6	10	-4	.947	-2	O	-0.2
	Yr	128	461	63	142	20	14	5	81	52	23	.308	.385	.445	145	27	25	77	16	20	-7	.953	-5	O1	0.8
1916	Chi-A	155	592	91	202	40	**21**	3	78	46	25	.341	.393	.495	165	45	44	119	24	14	-1	.975	-1	*O	3.7
1917	*Chi-A	146	538	91	162	20	17	5	75	57	25	.301	.375	.429	142	29	27	89	13			.984	9	*O	3.2
1918	Chi-A	17	65	9	23	2	2	1	20	8	1	.354	.425	.492	175	6	6	15	3			1.000	-0	O	0.5
1919	*Chi-A	139	516	79	181	31	14	7	96	60	10	.351	.422	.506	159	42	41	111	9			.967	-4	*O	2.9
1920	Chi-A	146	570	105	218	42	**20**	12	121	56	14	.382	.444	.589	172	58	58	145	9	12	-5	.965	-1	*O	4.0
Total	13	1332	4981	873	1772	307	168	54	785	519	158	.356	.423	.517	169	452	440	1146	202	61		.962	22	*O/1	38.2

■ KEN JACKSON

Jackson, Kenneth Bernard b: 8/21/63, Shreveport, La. BR/TR, 5'9", 170 lbs. Deb: 9/12/87

YEAR	TM/L	G	AB	R	H	2B	3B	HR	RBI	BB	SO	AVG	OBP	SLG	PRO+	BR	/A	RC	SB	CS	SBR	FA	FR	POS	TPR
1987	Phi-N	8	16	1	4	2	0	0	2	1	4	.250	.333	.375	85	-0	-0	2	0	0	0	.955	-1	/S	-0.1

■ LOU JACKSON

Jackson, Louis Clarence b: 7/26/35, Riverton, La. d: 5/27/69, Tokyo, Japan BL/TR, 5'10", 168 lbs. Deb: 7/23/58

YEAR	TM/L	G	AB	R	H	2B	3B	HR	RBI	BB	SO	AVG	OBP	SLG	PRO+	BR	/A	RC	SB	CS	SBR	FA	FR	POS	TPR
1958	Chi-N	24	35	5	6	2	1	1	6	1	9	.171	.194	.371	46	-3	-3	2	0	1	-1	1.000	-4	O	-0.8
1959	Chi-N	6	4	2	1	0	0	0	1	0	2	.250	.250	.250	34	-0	-0	0	0	0	0	.000	0	H	0.0
1964	Bal-A	4	8	0	3	0	0	0	0	0	2	.375	.375	.375	110	0	0	1	0	0	0	1.000	1	/O	0.1
Total	3	34	47	7	10	2	1	1	7	1	13	.213	.229	.362	55	-3	-3	3	0	1	-1	1.000	-4	/O	-0.7

■ RANDY JACKSON

Jackson, Ransom Joseph "Handsome Ransom" b: 2/10/26, Little Rock, Ark. BR/TR, 6'1.5", 180 lbs. Deb: 5/02/50

YEAR	TM/L	G	AB	R	H	2B	3B	HR	RBI	BB	SO	AVG	OBP	SLG	PRO+	BR	/A	RC	SB	CS	SBR	FA	FR	POS	TPR
1950	Chi-N	34	111	13	25	4	3	3	6	7	25	.225	.271	.396	74	-5	-5	11	4			.911	-4	3	-0.9
1951	Chi-N	145	557	78	153	24	6	16	76	47	44	.275	.332	.425	101	1	-1	77	14	3	2	.956	8	*3	0.8
1952	Chi-N	116	379	44	88	8	5	9	34	27	42	.232	.285	.351	75	-13	-14	36	6	5	-1	.958	-3	*3/O	-2.1
1953	Chi-N	139	498	61	142	22	8	19	66	42	61	.285	.341	.476	108	6	5	77	8	4	0	.949	3	*3	0.5
1954	Chi-N★	126	484	77	132	17	6	19	67	44	55	.273	.336	.450	102	1	0	74	2	1	0	.955	-1	*3	-0.3
1955	Chi-N★	138	499	73	132	13	7	21	70	58	58	.265	.342	.445	107	5	5	75	0	2	-1	.949	-13	*3	-1.0
1956	*Bro-N	101	307	37	84	15	7	8	53	28	38	.274	.338	.446	101	4	0	43	2	1	0	.993	21	3	2.3
1957	Bro-N	48	131	7	26	1	0	2	16	9	20	.198	.250	.252	32	-12	-13	8	0	0	0	.976	-2	3	-1.6
1958	LA-N	35	65	8	12	3	0	1	4	5	10	.185	.243	.277	36	-6	-6	4	0	0	0	.964	7	3	0.1
	Cle-A	29	91	7	22	3	1	4	13	3	18	.242	.266	.429	90	-2	-2	9	0	0	0	.901	5	3	0.4
1959	Cle-A	3	7	0	1	0	0	0	0	0	1	.143	.143	.143	-22	-1	-1	0	0	0	0	1.000	-1	/3	-0.2
	Chi-N	41	74	7	18	5	1	1	10	11	10	.243	.341	.378	92	-1	-1	9	0	0	0	.941	-3	3/O	-0.3
Total	10	955	3203	412	835	115	44	103	415	281	382	.261	.322	.421	94	-24	-32	422	36	16		.955	18	3/O	-2.3

■ REGGIE JACKSON

Jackson, Reginald Martinez b: 5/18/46, Wyncote, Pa. BL/TL, 6', 200 lbs. Deb: 6/09/67

YEAR	TM/L	G	AB	R	H	2B	3B	HR	RBI	BB	SO	AVG	OBP	SLG	PRO+	BR	/A	RC	SB	CS	SBR	FA	FR	POS	TPR
1967	KC-A	35	118	13	21	4	4	1	6	10	46	.178	.271	.305	72	-4	-4	10	1	1	-0	.933	-2	O	-0.9
1968	Oak-A	154	553	82	138	13	6	29	74	50	171	.250	.317	.452	138	19	22	83	14	4	2	.959	8	*O	2.7
1969	Oak-A★	152	549	**123**	151	36	3	47	118	114	142	.275	.410	**.608**	**190**	62	**65**	144	13	5	1	.964	5	*O	6.3
1970	Oak-A	149	426	57	101	21	2	23	66	75	135	.237	.361	.458	129	15	17	70	26	17	-2	.956	-11	*O	-0.3

YEAR	TM/L	G	AB	R	H	2B	3B	HR	RBI	BB	SO	AVG	OBP	SLG	PRO+	BR	/A	RC	SB	CS	SBR	FA	FR	POS	TPR
1971	*Oak-A★	150	567	87	157	29	3	32	80	63	161	.277	.355	.508	145	30	31	103	16	10	-1	.977	9	*O	3.3
1972	*Oak-A★	135	499	72	132	25	2	25	75	59	125	.265	.352	.473	152	26	29	84	9	8	-2	.971	2	*O	2.5
1973	*Oak-A★	151	539	**99**	158	28	2	**32**	**117**	76	111	.293	.387	**.531**	**165**	41	**44**	112	22	8	2	.971	4	*O/D	4.4
1974	*Oak-A★	148	506	90	146	25	1	29	93	86	105	.289	.396	.514	**171**	41	45	109	25	5	**5**	.968	9	*OD	5.4
1975	*Oak-A★	157	593	91	150	39	3	**36**	104	67	133	.253	.332	.511	138	25	27	100	17	8	0	.965	9	*O/D	3.0
1976	Bal-A	134	498	84	138	27	2	27	91	54	108	.277	.353	**.502**	**158**	29	32	86	28	7	4	.964	2	*OD	3.5
1977	*NY-A★	146	525	93	150	39	2	32	110	74	129	.286	.377	.550	151	36	36	116	17	3	3	.949	-1	*OD	3.3
1978	*NY-A†	139	511	82	140	13	5	27	97	58	133	.274	.358	.477	136	22	24	87	14	11	-2	.986	3	*OD	2.0
1979	NY-A★	131	465	78	138	24	2	29	89	65	107	.297	.385	.544	151	31	33	93	9	8	-2	.986	7	*O/D	3.0
1980	*NY-A★	143	514	94	154	22	4	**41**	111	83	122	.300	.399	.597	172	49	50	125	1	2	-1	.962	-2	OD	4.3
1981	*NY-A★	94	334	33	79	17	1	15	54	46	82	.237	.331	.428	119	7	8	47	0	3	-2	.974	0	OD	0.4
1982	*Cal-A★	153	530	92	146	17	1	**39**	101	85	156	.275	.378	.532	147	35	35	107	4	5	-2	.972	-18	*O/D	1.2
1983	Cal-A†	116	397	43	77	14	1	14	49	52	140	.194	.294	.340	74	-14	-14	42	0	2	-1	.986	-5	DO	-2.1
1984	Cal-A★	143	525	67	117	17	2	25	81	55	141	.223	.300	.406	94	-6	-5	64	8	4	0	1.000	0	*D/O	-0.5
1985	Cal-A	143	460	64	116	27	0	27	85	78	138	.252	.362	.487	130	20	20	79	1	2	-1	.944	-9	OD	0.8
1986	*Cal-A	132	419	65	101	12	2	18	58	92	115	.241	.381	.408	116	12	13	68	1	1	-0	.833	-0	*D/O	1.2
1987	Oak-A	115	336	42	74	14	1	15	43	33	97	.220	.298	.402	89	-9	-6	42	2	1	0	1.000	-2	DO	-0.8
Total	21	2820	9864	1551	2584	463	49	563	1702	1375	2597	.262	.358	.490	140	466	503	1772	228	115	-1	.967	8	*OD	42.7

■ **SONNY JACKSON** Jackson, Roland Thomas b: 7/9/44, Washington, D.C. BL/TR, 5'9", 155 lbs. Deb: 9/27/63 C

YEAR	TM/L	G	AB	R	H	2B	3B	HR	RBI	BB	SO	AVG	OBP	SLG	PRO+	BR	/A	RC	SB	CS	SBR	FA	FR	POS	TPR
1963	Hou-N	1	3	0	0	0	0	0	0	0	1	.000	.000	.000	-99	-1	-1	0	0	0	0	.833	1	/S	0.0
1964	Hou-N	9	23	3	8	1	0	0	1	2	3	.348	.400	.391	131	1	1	4	1	0	0	.870	-4	/S	-0.2
1965	Hou-N	10	23	1	3	0	0	0	0	1	1	.130	.167	.130	-16	-3	-3	0	1	1	-0	.969	-1	/S3	-0.4
1966	Hou-N	150	596	80	174	6	5	3	25	42	53	.292	.342	.334	95	-8	-3	74	49	14	6	.951	-13	*S	0.5
1967	Hou-N	129	520	67	123	18	3	0	25	36	45	.237	.286	.283	66	-24	-22	42	22	9	1	.943	-8	*S	-1.8
1968	Atl-N	105	358	37	81	8	2	1	19	25	35	.226	.282	.268	66	-14	-14	27	16	6	1	.952	-17	S	-2.4
1969	*Atl-N	98	318	41	76	3	5	1	27	35	33	.239	.318	.289	71	-11	-11	32	12	7	-1	.961	-23	S	-2.6
1970	Atl-N	103	328	60	85	14	3	0	20	45	27	.259	.350	.320	76	-7	-10	41	11	4	1	.933	-23	S	-2.2
1971	Atl-N	149	547	58	141	20	5	2	25	35	45	.258	.304	.324	73	-16	-20	54	7	6	-2	.980	-3	*O	-3.5
1972	Atl-N	60	126	20	30	6	3	0	8	7	9	.238	.278	.333	67	-5	-6	11	1	0	0	.976	-3	SO/3	-0.7
1973	Atl-N	117	206	29	43	5	2	0	12	22	13	.209	.288	.252	47	-13	-15	17	6	3	0	.981	-1	OS	-1.5
1974	Atl-N	5	7	0	3	0	0	0	0	0	0	.429	.429	.429	134	0	0	1	0	1	-1	1.000	0	/O	0.0
Total	12	936	3055	396	767	81	28	7	162	250	265	.251	.310	.303	73	-102	-105	301	126	51	7	.949	-94	SO/3	-14.8

■ **RON JACKSON** Jackson, Ronald Harris b: 10/22/33, Kalamazoo, Mich. BR/TR, 6'7", 225 lbs. Deb: 6/15/54

YEAR	TM/L	G	AB	R	H	2B	3B	HR	RBI	BB	SO	AVG	OBP	SLG	PRO+	BR	/A	RC	SB	CS	SBR	FA	FR	POS	TPR
1954	Chi-A	40	93	10	26	4	0	4	10	6	20	.280	.337	.452	111	1	1	14	2	1	0	.988	-3	1	-0.3
1955	Chi-A	40	74	10	15	1	1	2	7	8	22	.203	.280	.324	61	-4	-4	7	1	0	0	.988	-1	1	-0.6
1956	Chi-A	22	56	7	12	3	0	1	4	10	13	.214	.333	.321	73	-2	-2	6	1	0	0	1.000	1	1	-0.2
1957	Chi-A	13	60	4	19	3	0	2	8	1	12	.317	.328	.467	114	1	1	9	0	0	0	.992	-1	1	-0.1
1958	Chi-A	61	146	19	34	4	0	7	21	18	46	.233	.325	.404	101	-0	0	20	2	0	1	.997	-2	1	-0.3
1959	Chi-A	10	14	3	3	1	0	1	2	1	0	.214	.313	.500	121	0	0	2	0	0	0	1.000	-0	/1	0.0
1960	Bos-A	10	31	1	7	2	0	0	0	1	6	.226	.250	.290	44	-2	-3	2	0	0	0	.973	-0	/1	-0.3
Total	7	196	474	54	116	18	1	17	52	45	119	.245	.317	.395	92	-6	-7	60	6	1	1	.992	-6	1	-1.8

■ **RON JACKSON** Jackson, Ronnie Damien b: 5/9/53, Birmingham, Ala. BR/TR, 6', 205 lbs. Deb: 9/12/75

YEAR	TM/L	G	AB	R	H	2B	3B	HR	RBI	BB	SO	AVG	OBP	SLG	PRO+	BR	/A	RC	SB	CS	SBR	FA	FR	POS	TPR
1975	Cal-A	13	39	2	9	2	0	0	2	2	10	.231	.268	.282	60	-2	-2	3	1	1	-0	.947	-0	/O3D	-0.3
1976	Cal-A	127	410	44	93	18	3	8	40	30	58	.227	.291	.344	91	-8	-5	40	5	4	-1	.950	1	*3/2OD	-0.6
1977	Cal-A	106	292	38	71	15	2	8	28	24	42	.243	.303	.390	91	-6	-4	34	3	2	-0	.990	2	13D/OS	-0.5
1978	Cal-A	105	387	49	115	18	6	6	57	16	31	.297	.340	.421	117	6	8	53	2	3	-1	.994	-3	13/OD	-0.1
1979	Min-A	159	583	85	158	40	5	14	68	51	59	.271	.339	.429	102	4	1	84	3	1	0	.994	11	*1/S3O	0.3
1980	Min-A	131	396	48	105	29	3	5	42	28	41	.265	.319	.391	87	-4	-8	43	1	8	-5	.991	-1	*1O/3D	-1.9
1981	Min-A	54	175	17	46	9	0	4	28	10	15	.263	.306	.383	91	-1	-2	20	2	2	-1	.988	1	1/O3D	-0.4
	Det-A	31	95	12	27	8	1	1	12	8	11	.284	.340	.421	114	2	2	15	4	1	1	1.000	-1	1	0.0
	Yr	85	270	29	73	17	1	5	40	18	26	.270	.318	.396	99	1	-1	34	6	3	0	.993	1	1/OD3	-0.4
1982	*Cal-A	53	142	15	47	6	0	2	19	10	12	.331	.383	.415	119	4	4	22	0	1	-1	.994	0	1/3	0.2
1983	Cal-A	102	348	41	80	16	1	8	39	27	33	.230	.291	.351	76	-12	-11	34	2	2	-1	.957	2	31DO	-1.3
1984	Cal-A	33	91	5	15	2	1	0	5	7	13	.165	.224	.209	21	-10	-10	4	0	0	0	.990	-0	1/3O	-1.1
	Bal-A	12	28	0	8	2	0	0	2	0	4	.286	.286	.357	78	-1	-1	2	0	2	-1	.960	2	3	-0.1
	Yr	45	119	5	23	4	1	0	7	7	17	.193	.238	.244	34	-11	-11	6	0	2	-1	.990	1	13/O	-1.2
Total	10	926	2986	356	774	165	22	56	342	213	329	.259	.316	.385	94	-27	-29	355	23	27	-9	.993	14	13/OD2S	-5.8

■ **SAM JACKSON** Jackson, Samuel b: 3/24/1849, Ripon, England d: 8/4/1893, Chilton Springs, N.Y. BR/TR, 5'5.5", 160 lbs. Deb: 5/16/1871

YEAR	TM/L	G	AB	R	H	2B	3B	HR	RBI	BB	SO	AVG	OBP	SLG	PRO+	BR	/A	RC	SB	CS	SBR	FA	FR	POS	TPR
1871	Bos-n	16	76	17	17	5	3	0	11	1	4	.224	.234	.368	67	-3	-4	7	0					2/O	-0.3
1872	Atl-n	3	12	0	2	1	0	0	0	0	0	.167	.167	.250	23	-1	-1	1						/O	-0.1
Total	2 n	19	88	17	19	6	3	0	11	1	4	.216	.225	.352	61	-4	-5	7						/2O	-0.4

■ **TRAVIS JACKSON** Jackson, Travis Calvin "Stonewall" b: 11/2/03, Waldo, Ark. d: 7/27/87, Waldo, Ark. BR/TR, 5'10.5", 160 lbs. Deb: 9/27/22 CH

YEAR	TM/L	G	AB	R	H	2B	3B	HR	RBI	BB	SO	AVG	OBP	SLG	PRO+	BR	/A	RC	SB	CS	SBR	FA	FR	POS	TPR
1922	NY-N	3	8	1	0	0	0	0	0	0	2	.000	.000	.000	-99	-2	-2	0	0	0	0	.909	0	/S	-0.2
1923	*NY-N	96	327	45	90	12	7	4	37	22	40	.275	.321	.391	88	-7	-6	41	3	3	-1	.943	-3	S3/2	-0.3
1924	*NY-N	151	596	81	180	26	8	11	76	21	56	.302	.326	.428	103	-1	1	80	6	7	-2	.937	-0	*S	1.5
1925	NY-N	112	411	51	117	15	2	9	59	24	43	.285	.327	.397	87	-10	-8	54	8	3	1	.941	5	*S	0.8
1926	NY-N	111	385	64	126	24	8	8	51	20	26	.327	.362	.494	130	14	14	66	2			.962	1	*S/O	2.5
1927	NY-N	127	469	67	149	29	4	14	98	32	30	.318	.363	.486	126	15	15	80	8			.952	28	*S/3	5.4
1928	NY-N	150	537	73	145	35	6	14	77	56	46	.270	.339	.436	101	-0	-1	79	8			.952	28	*S	4.3
1929	NY-N	149	551	92	162	21	12	21	94	64	56	.294	.367	.490	111	8	8	98	10			**.969**	19	*S	4.1
1930	NY-N	116	431	70	146	27	8	13	82	32	25	.339	.386	.529	121	12	14	85	6			.956	11	*S	3.3
1931	NY-N	145	555	65	172	26	10	5	71	36	23	.310	.353	.420	110	5	7	83	13			**.970**	10	*S	3.0
1932	NY-N	52	195	23	50	17	1	4	38	13	16	.256	.310	.415	95	-2	-2	26	1			.925	-5	S	-0.2
1933	*NY-N	53	122	11	30	5	0	0	12	8	11	.246	.292	.287	67	-5	-5	10	2			.890	7	S3	0.4
1934	NY-N★	137	523	75	140	26	7	16	101	37	71	.268	.316	.436	102	-2	-0	71	1			.945	12	*S/3	1.9
1935	NY-N	128	511	74	154	20	12	9	80	29	64	.301	.340	.440	110	5	6	76	3			.947	-7	*3	0.4
1936	*NY-N	126	465	41	107	8	1	7	53	18	56	.230	.260	.297	50	-33	-33	36	0			.952	-1	*3/S	-2.9
Total	15	1656	6086	833	1768	291	86	135	929	412	565	.291	.337	.433	102	-5	8	883	71	13		.952	104	*S3/O2	24.0

■ **BO JACKSON** Jackson, Vincent Edward b: 11/30/62, Bessemer, Ala. BR/TR, 6'1", 225 lbs. Deb: 9/02/86

YEAR	TM/L	G	AB	R	H	2B	3B	HR	RBI	BB	SO	AVG	OBP	SLG	PRO+	BR	/A	RC	SB	CS	SBR	FA	FR	POS	TPR
1986	KC-A	25	82	9	17	2	1	2	9	7	34	.207	.286	.329	66	-4	-4	8	3	1	0	.886	-3	O/D	-0.7
1987	KC-A	116	396	46	93	17	2	22	53	30	158	.235	.297	.455	93	-4	-5	55	10	4	1	.955	-7	*O/D	-1.5
1988	KC-A	124	439	63	108	16	4	25	68	25	146	.246	.288	.472	108	3	2	59	27	6	5	.973	6	*O/D	1.0
1989	KC-A★	135	515	86	132	15	6	32	105	39	172	.256	.312	.495	125	14	14	77	26	9	2	.967	7	*OD	2.1
1990	KC-A	111	405	74	110	16	1	28	78	44	128	.272	.346	.523	142	20	21	70	15	9	-1	.952	8	OD	2.6
1991	Chi-A	23	71	8	16	4	0	3	14	12	25	.225	.337	.408	108	1	1	9	0	1	-1	.000	0	D	0.0
Total	6	534	1908	286	476	70	14	112	327	157	663	.249	.311	.477	114	30	29	279	81	30	6	.960	11	O/D	3.5

YEAR	TM/L	G	AB	R	H	2B	3B	HR	RBI	BB	SO	AVG	OBP	SLG	PRO+	BR	/A	RC	SB	CS	SBR	FA	FR	POS	TPR
■ **BILL JACKSON** Jackson, William Riley b: 4/4/1881, Pittsburgh, Pa. d: 9/24/58, Peoria, Ill. BL/TL, 5'11.5", 160 lbs. Deb: 4/30/14																									
1914	Chi-F	26	25	2	1	0	0	0	1	3	5	.040	.143	.040	-50	-5	-5	0	0			.917	0	/O1	-0.5
1915	Chi-F	50	98	15	16	1	0	1	12	14	15	.163	.268	.204	42	-7	-6	7	3			.983	0	1/O	-0.8
Total	2	76	123	17	17	1	0	1	13	17	20	.138	.243	.171	23	-12	-11	7	3			.984	0	/1O	-1.3
■ **SPOOK JACOBS** Jacobs, Forrest Vandergrift b: 11/4/25, Cheswold, Del. BR/TR, 5'8.5", 155 lbs. Deb: 4/13/54																									
1954	Phi-A	132	508	63	131	11	1	0	26	60	22	.258	.336	.283	71	-18	-18	55	17	3	3	.974	-19	*2	-2.7
1955	KC-A	13	23	7	6	0	0	0	1	3	0	.261	.370	.261	71	-1	-1	2	1	2	-1	1.000	-3	/2	-0.4
1956	KC-A	32	97	13	21	3	0	0	5	15	5	.216	.321	.247	52	-6	-6	8	4	1	1	.968	-4	2	-0.7
	Pit-N	11	37	4	6	2	0	0	1	2	5	.162	.225	.216	20	-4	-4	2	0	2	-1	.926	-4	2	-0.9
Total	3	188	665	87	164	16	1	0	33	80	32	.247	.329	.274	65	-29	-30	67	22	8	2	.971	-29	2	-4.7
■ **JAKE JACOBS** Jacobs, Lamar Gary b: 6/9/37, Youngstown, Ohio BR/TR, 6', 175 lbs. Deb: 9/13/60																									
1960	Was-A	6	2	0	0	0	0	0	0	0	0	.000	.000	.000	-99	-1	-1	0	0	0	0	.000	0	H	-0.1
1961	Min-A	4	8	0	2	0	0	0	0	0	2	.250	.250	.250	32	-1	-1	1	0	0	0	1.000	-1	/O	-0.2
Total	2	10	10	0	2	0	0	0	0	0	2	.200	.200	.200	7	-1	-1	1	0	0	0		-1	/O	-0.3
■ **MIKE JACOBS** Jacobs, Morris Elmore b: 1877, d: 3/21/49, Louisville, Ky. Deb: 7/16/02																									
1902	Chi-N	5	19	1	4	0	0	0	2	0		.211	.211	.211	31	-2	-2	1	0			.880	-2	/S	-0.3
■ **OTTO JACOBS** Jacobs, Otto Albert b: 4/19/1889, Chicago, Ill. d: 11/19/55, Chicago, Ill. BR/TR, 5'9", 180 lbs. Deb: 6/13/18																									
1918	Chi-A	29	73	4	15	3	1	0	3	5	8	.205	.256	.274	59	-4	-4	5	0			.955	-4	C	-0.7
■ **RAY JACOBS** Jacobs, Raymond F. b: 1/2/02, Salt Lake City, Utah d: 4/5/52, Los Angeles, Cal. BR/TR, 6', 160 lbs. Deb: 4/20/28																									
1928	Chi-N	2	2	0	0	0	0	0	0	0	1	.000	.000	.000	-99	-1	-1	0	0			.000	0	H	-0.1
■ **MERWIN JACOBSON** Jacobson, Merwin John William "Jake" b: 3/7/1894, New Britain, Conn. d: 1/13/78, Baltimore, Md. BL/TL, 5'11.5", 165 lbs. Deb: 9/08/15																									
1915	NY-N	8	24	0	2	0	0	0	0	1	5	.083	.120	.083	-40	-4	-4	0	0			.909	0	/O	-0.4
1916	Chi-N	4	13	2	3	0	0	0	0	1	4	.231	.286	.231	54	-1	-1	1	2			1.000	0	/O	-0.1
1926	Bro-N	110	288	41	71	9	2	0	23	36	24	.247	.330	.292	70	-12	-11	29	5			.975	-3	O	-1.9
1927	Bro-N	11	6	4	0	0	0	0	1	0	1	.000	.000	.000	-99	-2	-2	0	0			1.000	-1	/O	-0.3
Total	4	133	331	47	76	9	2	0	24	38	34	.230	.309	.269	59	-18	-17	31	7			.973	-4	/O	-2.7
■ **BABY DOLL JACOBSON** Jacobson, William Chester b: 8/16/1890, Cable, Ill. d: 1/16/77, Orion, Ill. BR/TR, 6'3", 215 lbs. Deb: 4/14/15																									
1915	Det-A	37	65	5	14	6	2	0	4	5	14	.215	.282	.369	90	-1	-1	6	0	2	-1	.983	-2	1/O	-0.6
	StL-A	34	115	13	24	6	1	1	9	10	26	.209	.295	.304	82	-3	-3	10	3	3	-1	.981	-1	O	-0.7
	Yr	71	180	18	38	12	3	1	13	15	40	.211	.290	.328	84	-4	-4	17	3	5	-2	.984	-4	O1	-1.3
1917	StL-A	148	529	53	131	23	7	4	55	31	67	.248	.294	.340	97	-6	-4	53	10			.975	6	*O1	-0.6
1919	StL-A	120	455	70	147	31	8	4	51	24	47	.323	.362	.453	125	15	14	75	9			.949	1	*O/1	0.7
1920	StL-A	154	609	97	216	34	14	9	122	46	37	.355	.402	.501	134	32	30	121	11	7	-1	.979	11	*O/1	2.7
1921	StL-A	151	599	90	211	38	14	5	90	42	30	.352	.398	.487	118	22	17	114	8	8	-2	.982	5	*O1	0.8
1922	StL-A	145	555	88	176	22	16	9	102	46	36	.317	.379	.463	114	15	12	100	19	6	2	.969	4	*O/1	0.8
1923	StL-A	147	592	76	183	29	6	8	81	29	27	.309	.343	.419	95	-2	-6	84	6	6	-2	.974	8	*O	-1.0
1924	StL-A	152	579	103	184	41	12	19	97	35	45	.318	.361	.528	120	19	14	107	6	8	-3	.986	16	*O	1.6
1925	StL-A	142	540	103	184	30	9	15	76	45	26	.341	.392	.513	122	21	17	105	8	11	-4	.965	1	*O	0.5
1926	StL-A	50	182	18	52	15	1	2	21	9	14	.286	.319	.412	86	-4	-5	23	1	2	-1	.964	-6	O	-1.5
	Bos-A	98	394	44	120	36	1	6	69	22	22	.305	.344	.447	109	1	3	61	4	1	1	.980	-8	O	-1.1
	Yr	148	576	62	172	51	2	8	90	31	36	.299	.337	.436	101	-2	-2	84	5	3	-0	.975	-15	*O	-2.6
1927	Bos-A	45	155	11	38	9	3	0	24	5	12	.245	.278	.342	61	-10	-9	14	1	0	0	.979	1	O	-1.0
	Cle-A	32	103	13	26	5	0	0	13	6	4	.252	.300	.301	56	-7	-7	9	0	0	0	.932	-1	O	-0.9
	Phi-A	17	35	3	8	3	0	1	5	0	3	.229	.229	.400	57	-2	-3	3	0	0	0	1.000	-5	O	-0.8
	Yr	94	293	27	72	17	3	1	42	11	19	.246	.280	.334	59	-19	-19	27	1	0	0	.959	-5	O	-2.7
Total	11	1472	5507	787	1714	328	94	83	819	355	410	.311	.357	.450	111	91	69	886	86	54		.973	28	*O/1	-1.1
■ **BROOK JACOBY** Jacoby, Brook Wallace b: 11/23/59, Philadelphia, Pa. BR/TR, 5'11", 195 lbs. Deb: 9/13/81																									
1981	Atl-N	11	10	0	2	0	0	0	1	0	3	.200	.200	.200	13	-1	-1	0	0	0	0	1.000	2	/3	0.1
1983	Atl-N	4	8	0	0	0	0	0	0	0	1	.000	.000	.000	-93	-2	-2	0	0	0	0	1.000	-1	/3	-0.3
1984	Cle-A	126	439	64	116	19	3	7	40	32	73	.264	.319	.369	88	-6	-7	50	3	2	-0	.951	-20	*3/S	-2.9
1985	Cle-A	161	606	72	166	26	3	20	87	48	120	.274	.327	.426	105	3	3	81	2	3	-1	.958	-7	*3/2	-0.7
1986	Cle-A★	158	583	83	168	30	4	17	80	56	137	.288	.351	.441	116	11	12	88	2	1	0	.941	-13	*3	-0.3
1987	Cle-A	155	540	73	162	26	4	32	69	75	73	.300	.388	.541	142	34	33	110	2	3	-1	.946	-7	*3/1D	2.2
1988	Cle-A	152	552	59	133	25	0	9	49	48	101	.241	.303	.335	76	-16	-18	55	2	3	-1	.975	1	*3	-1.9
1989	Cle-A	147	519	49	141	26	5	13	64	62	90	.272	.353	.416	114	12	10	75	2	5	-2	.955	-10	*3/D	-0.1
1990	Cle-A★	155	553	77	162	24	4	14	75	63	58	.293	.367	.427	122	17	17	83	1	4	-2	.981	-12	31	-0.2
1991	Cle-A	66	231	14	54	9	1	4	24	16	32	.234	.289	.333	71	-9	-9	21	0	1	-1	.988	-0	13	-1.3
	Oak-A	56	188	14	40	12	0	0	20	11	22	.213	.260	.277	51	-13	-12	13	2	0	1	.982	-8	3/1	-2.0
	Yr	122	419	28	94	21	1	4	44	27	54	.224	.276	.308	63	-22	-21	34	2	1	0	.987	-8	31	-3.3
1992	Cle-A	120	291	30	76	7	0	4	36	28	54	.261	.328	.326	83	-6	-6	29	0	3	-2	.957	3	*31	-0.5
Total	11	1311	4520	535	1220	204	24	120	545	439	764	.270	.337	.405	103	23	21	605	16	25	-10	.958	-71	*31/D2S	-7.9
■ **HARRY JACOBY** Jacoby, Harry b: Philadelphia, Pa. Deb: 5/02/1882																									
1882	Bal-a	31	121	17	21	1	1	1		7		.174	.219	.223	53	-6	-5	6				.776	8	3O	0.3
1885	Bal-a	11	43	4	6	2	0	0		2		.140	.178	.186	17	-4	-4	1				.896	-8	2	-1.1
Total	2	42	164	21	27	3	1	1		9		.165	.208	.213	43	-10	-9	8					-0	/3O2	-0.8
■ **JOHN JAHA** Jaha, John Emile b: 5/27/66, Portland, Ore. BR/TR, 6'1", 195 lbs. Deb: 7/09/92																									
1992	Mil-A	47	133	17	30	3	1	2	10	12	30	.226	.299	.308	72	-5	-5	15	10	0	3	1.000	-0	1/OD	-0.4
■ **ART JAHN** Jahn, Arthur Charles b: 12/2/1895, Struble, Iowa d: 1/9/48, Little Rock, Ark. BR/TR, 6', 180 lbs. Deb: 7/02/25																									
1925	Chi-N	58	226	30	68	10	8	0	37	11	20	.301	.336	.416	90	-3	-4	31	2	2	-1	.985	2	O	-0.6
1928	NY-N	10	29	7	8	1	0	1	7	2	5	.276	.323	.414	91	-0	-0	4	0			1.000	1	/O	0.0
	Phi-N	36	94	8	21	4	0	0	11	4	11	.223	.270	.266	39	-8	-9	7	0			.978	-4	O	-1.4
	Yr	46	123	15	29	5	0	1	18	6	16	.236	.282	.301	51	-9	-9	10	0			.985	-3	O	-1.4
Total	2	104	349	45	97	15	8	1	55	17	36	.278	.317	.375	76	-12	-13	41	2	2		.985	-1	/O	-2.0
■ **ART JAMES** James, Arthur b: 8/2/52, Detroit, Mich. BL/TL, 6', 170 lbs. Deb: 4/10/75																									
1975	Det-A	11	40	2	9	2	0	0	1	1	3	.225	.244	.275	44	-3	-3	2	1	2	-1	1.000	2	O	-0.3
■ **BERT JAMES** James, Berton Hulon "Jesse" b: 7/7/1886, Coopertown, Tenn. d: 1/2/59, Adairville, Ky. BL/TR, 5'11", 175 lbs. Deb: 9/18/09																									
1909	StL-N	6	21	1	6	0	0	0	0	4		.286	.400	.286	120	1	1	3	1			.909	0	/O	0.1
■ **CHARLIE JAMES** James, Charles Wesley b: 12/22/37, St.Louis, Mo. BR/TR, 6'1", 195 lbs. Deb: 8/02/60																									
1960	StL-N	43	50	5	9	1	0	2	5	1	12	.180	.196	.320	35	-4	-5	3	0	0	0	.917	-10	O	-1.6
1961	StL-N	108	349	43	89	19	2	4	44	15	59	.255	.292	.355	64	-15	-19	34	2	2	-1	.962	-5	O	-3.0
1962	StL-N	129	388	50	107	13	4	8	59	10	58	.276	.301	.392	77	-9	-14	42	3	4	-2	.988	-9	*O	-3.0
1963	StL-N	116	347	34	93	14	2	10	45	10	64	.268	.292	.406	91	-2	-5	37	2	1	0	.994	-3	*O	-1.3

YEAR	TM/L	G	AB	R	H	2B	3B	HR	RBI	BB	SO	AVG	OBP	SLG	PRO+	BR	/A	RC	SB	CS	SBR	FA	FR	POS	TPR
1964	*StL-N	88	233	24	52	9	1	5	17	11	58	.223	.261	.335	61	-11	-13	19	0	0	0	.963	-5	O	-2.2
1965	Cin-N	26	39	2	8	0	0	0	2	1	9	.205	.225	.205	21	-4	-4	1	0	0	0	.909	-0	/O	-0.5
Total	6	510	1406	158	358	56	9	29	172	48	260	.255	.284	.369	71	-45	-60	137	7	7	-2	.976	-32	O	-11.6
■ CLEO JAMES	James, Cleo Joel b: 8/31/40, Clarksdale, Miss. BR/TR, 5'10", 176 lbs. Deb: 4/15/68																								
1968	LA-N	10	10	2	2	1	0	0	0	0	6	.200	.200	.300	52	-1	-1	1	0	0	0	1.000	0	/O	0.0
1970	Chi-N	100	176	33	37	7	2	3	14	17	24	.210	.298	.324	59	-8	-11	18	5	0	2	1.000	7	O	-0.5
1971	Chi-N	54	150	25	43	7	0	2	13	10	16	.287	.355	.373	93	2	-1	21	6	2	1	.979	2	O/3	-0.1
1973	Chi-N	44	45	9	5	0	0	0	0	1	6	.111	.130	.111	-30	-8	-8	1	5	0	2	.960	2	O	-0.5
Total	4	208	381	69	87	15	2	5	27	28	52	.228	.300	.318	63	-15	-21	40	16	2	4	.988	12	O/3	-1.1
■ DION JAMES	James, Dion b: 11/9/62, Philadelphia, Pa. BL/TL, 6'1", 170 lbs. Deb: 9/16/83																								
1983	Mil-A	11	20	1	2	0	0	0	1	2	2	.100	.182	.100	-22	-3	-3	1	1	0	0	1.000	-3	/OD	-0.7
1984	Mil-A	128	387	52	114	19	5	1	30	32	41	.295	.353	.377	106	2	4	50	10	10	-3	.989	-1	*O	-0.4
1985	Mil-A	18	49	5	11	1	0	0	3	6	6	.224	.309	.245	54	-3	-3	4	0	0	0	1.000	-2	O/D	-0.5
1987	Atl-N	134	494	80	154	37	6	10	61	70	63	.312	.399	.472	124	23	20	95	10	8	-2	**.996**	1	*O	1.4
1988	Atl-N	132	386	46	99	17	5	3	30	58	59	.256	.355	.350	98	3	1	48	9	9	-3	.987	-12	*O	-1.9
1989	Atl-N	63	170	15	44	7	0	1	11	25	23	.259	.357	.318	92	-0	-1	20	1	3	-2	1.000	-0	O/1	-0.4
	Cle-A	71	245	26	75	11	0	4	29	24	26	.306	.368	.400	114	6	5	35	1	4	-2	.976	0	OD/1	0.2
1990	Cle-A	87	248	28	68	15	2	1	22	27	23	.274	.348	.363	99	0	0	31	5	3	-0	.996	-5	1OD	-0.8
1992	NY-A	67	145	24	38	8	0	3	17	22	15	.262	.363	.379	106	2	2	21	1	0	0	1.000	-8	O/D	-0.7
Total	8	711	2144	277	605	115	18	23	204	266	258	.282	.364	.385	106	30	25	305	38	37	-11	.989	-31	O/D1	-3.8
■ CHRIS JAMES	James, Donald Chris b: 10/4/62, Rusk, Tex. BR/TR, 6'1", 195 lbs. Deb: 4/23/86																								
1986	Phi-N	16	46	5	13	3	0	1	5	1	13	.283	.298	.413	91	-1	-1	5	0	0	0	1.000	-1	O	-0.2
1987	Phi-N	115	358	48	105	20	6	17	54	27	67	.293	.346	.525	123	12	11	66	3	1	0	.990	-2	*O	0.7
1988	Phi-N	150	566	57	137	24	1	19	66	31	73	.242	.285	.389	90	-8	-9	59	7	4	-0	.989	-4	*O/3	-1.8
1989	Phi-N	45	179	14	37	4	0	2	19	4	23	.207	.224	.263	39	-14	-14	8	3	1	0	.985	-1	O3	-1.8
	SD-N	87	303	41	80	13	2	11	46	22	45	.264	.316	.429	111	3	3	38	2	1	0	.987	-0	O/3	0.1
	Yr	132	482	55	117	17	2	13	65	26	68	.243	.283	.367	84	-11	-11	45	5	2	0	.986	-1	*O3	-1.7
1990	Cle-A	140	528	62	158	32	4	12	70	31	71	.299	.343	.443	119	12	12	78	4	3	-1	1.000	0	*DO	1.1
1991	Cle-A	115	437	31	104	16	2	5	41	18	61	.238	.275	.318	63	-22	-22	36	3	4	-2	1.000	0	DO1	-2.6
1992	SF-N	111	248	25	60	10	4	5	32	14	45	.242	.288	.375	91	-5	-4	26	2	3	-1	.974	1	O	-0.6
Total	7	779	2665	283	694	122	19	72	333	148	398	.260	.303	.402	95	-22	-24	317	24	17	-3	.988	-7	OD/31	-5.1
■ SKIP JAMES	James, Philip Robert b: 10/21/49, Elmhurst, Ill. BL/TL, 6', 185 lbs. Deb: 9/12/77																								
1977	SF-N	10	15	3	4	1	0	0	3	2	3	.267	.353	.333	86	-0	-0	2	0	0	0	1.000	1	/1	0.0
1978	SF-N	41	21	5	2	1	0	0	3	4	5	.095	.240	.143	10	-3	-2	1	1	0	0	1.000	2	1	-0.1
Total	2	51	36	8	6	2	0	0	6	6	8	.167	.286	.222	42	-3	-3	2	1	0	0	1.000	3	/1	-0.1
■ BERNIE JAMES	James, Robert Byrne b: 9/2/05, Angleton, Tex. BB/TR, 5'9.5", 150 lbs. Deb: 5/06/29																								
1929	Bos-N	46	101	12	31	3	2	0	9	9	13	.307	.369	.376	89	-2	-1	14	3			.940	-9	2/O	-0.9
1930	Bos-N	8	11	1	2	1	0	0	1	0	1	.182	.182	.273	8	-2	-2	1	0			.941	0	/2	-0.1
1933	NY-N	60	125	22	28	2	1	1	10	8	12	.224	.271	.280	58	-7	-7	10	5			.948	2	2/S3	-0.3
Total	3	114	237	35	61	6	3	1	20	17	26	.257	.310	.321	70	-11	-10	25	8			.944	-7	/2S3O	-1.3
■ CHARLIE JAMIESON	Jamieson, Charles Devine "Cuckoo" b: 2/7/1893, Paterson, N.J. d: 10/27/69, Paterson, N.J. BL/TL, 5'8.5", 165 lbs. Deb: 9/20/15																								
1915	Was-A	17	68	9	19	3	2	0	7	6	9	.279	.338	.382	113	1	1	9	0			1.000	4	O	0.4
1916	Was-A	64	145	16	36	4	0	0	13	18	18	.248	.331	.276	83	-3	-2	16	5			.913	-4	O/1P	-0.9
1917	Was-A	20	35	4	6	2	0	0	2	6	5	.171	.293	.229	60	-2	-1	2	0			.875	-2	/OP	-0.4
	Phi-A	85	345	41	92	6	2	0	27	37	36	.267	.341	.296	96	-1	-1	36	8			.937	-2	O	-0.8
	Yr	105	380	45	98	8	2	0	29	43	41	.258	.336	.289	92	-3	-2	38	8			.930	-4	O/P	-1.2
1918	Phi-A	110	416	50	84	11	2	0	11	54	30	.202	.297	.238	61	-18	-19	30	11			.970	-0	*O/P	-2.7
1919	Cle-A	26	17	3	6	2	1	0	2	0	2	.353	.353	.588	153	1	1	4	2			.750	-1	/PO	0.0
1920	*Cle-A	108	370	69	118	17	7	1	40	41	26	.319	.388	.411	108	7	6	58	2	9	-5	.966	-2	O/1	-0.8
1921	Cle-A	140	536	94	166	33	10	1	46	67	27	.310	.387	.414	103	5	4	89	8	4	0	.974	-6	*O	-1.1
1922	Cle-A	145	567	87	183	29	11	3	57	54	22	.323	.388	.429	112	11	11	96	15	8	-0	.978	-2	*O/P	-0.1
1923	Cle-A	152	644	130	**222**	36	12	2	51	80	37	.345	.422	.447	129	30	30	125	19	12	-2	.974	8	*O	2.5
1924	Cle-A	143	594	98	213	34	8	3	54	47	15	.359	.407	.458	121	20	19	111	21	11	-0	.974	4	*O	1.3
1925	Cle-A	138	557	109	165	24	5	4	42	72	26	.296	.380	.379	92	-4	-5	81	14	18	-7	.955	7	*O	-1.3
1926	Cle-A	143	555	89	166	33	7	2	45	53	22	.299	.361	.395	96	-2	-3	80	9	8	-2	.960	-0	*O	-1.5
1927	Cle-A	127	489	73	151	23	6	0	36	64	14	.309	.394	.380	101	4	4	72	7	9	-3	.969	5	*O	-0.3
1928	Cle-A	112	433	63	133	18	4	1	37	56	20	.307	.388	.374	100	3	2	63	3	12	-6	.984	20	*O	0.8
1929	Cle-A	102	364	56	106	22	1	0	26	50	12	.291	.378	.357	87	-3	-5	48	2	13	-7	.980	-2	O	-2.0
1930	Cle-A	103	366	64	110	22	1	1	52	36	20	.301	.368	.374	85	-5	-7	53	5	2	0	.955	-5	O	-1.7
1931	Cle-A	28	43	7	13	2	1	0	4	5	1	.302	.375	.395	97	0	-0	6	1	1	-0	.833	-2	/O	-0.2
1932	Cle-A	16	16	0	1	1	0	0	0	2	3	.063	.211	.125	-10	-3	-3	1	0	0	0	1.000	1	/O	-0.2
Total	18	1779	6560	1062	1990	322	80	18	552	748	345	.303	.378	.385	101	43	32	980	132	107		.967	19	*O/P1	-9.0
■ VIC JANOWICZ	Janowicz, Victor Felix b: 2/26/30, Elyria, Ohio BR/TR, 5'9", 185 lbs. Deb: 5/31/53																								
1953	Pit-N	42	123	10	31	3	1	2	8	5	31	.252	.287	.341	63	-7	-7	11	0	1	-1	.937	-12	C	-1.7
1954	Pit-N	41	73	10	11	3	0	0	2	7	23	.151	.235	.192	13	-9	-9	4	0	0	0	.904	1	3/O	-0.9
Total	2	83	196	20	42	6	1	2	10	12	54	.214	.267	.286	44	-16	-16	15	0	1	-1		-11	/C3O	-2.6
■ RAY JANSEN	Jansen, Raymond William b: 1/16/1889, St.Louis, Mo. d: 3/19/34, St.Louis, Mo. BR/TR, 5'11", 155 lbs. Deb: 9/30/10																								
1910	StL-A	1	5	0	4	0	0	0	0	0		.800	.800	.800	428	2	2	3	0			.700	0	/3	0.2
■ HEINIE JANTZEN	Jantzen, Walter C. b: 4/9/1890, Chicago, Ill. d: 4/1/48, Hines, Ill. BR/TR, 5'11.5", 170 lbs. Deb: 6/29/12																								
1912	StL-A	31	119	10	22	0	1	1	8	4		.185	.218	.227	28	-11	-11	6	3			1.000	3	O	-1.0
■ HAL JANVRIN	Janvrin, Harold Chandler "Childe Harold" b: 8/27/1892, Haverhill, Mass. d: 3/1/62, Boston, Mass. BR/TR, 5'11.5", 168 lbs. Deb: 7/09/11																								
1911	Bos-A	9	27	2	4	1	0	0	1	3		.148	.258	.185	25	-3	-3	1	0			.733	-2	/31	-0.5
1913	Bos-A	87	276	18	57	5	1	3	25	23	27	.207	.272	.264	56	-15	-16	24	17			.923	-10	S3/21	-2.4
1914	Bos-A	145	492	65	117	18	6	1	51	38	50	.238	.296	.305	81	-12	-12	48	29	20	-3	.919	-22	21S/3	-4.2
1915	*Bos-A	99	316	41	85	9	1	0	37	14	27	.269	.317	.304	88	-6	-5	31	8	14	-6	.917	-20	S3/2	-2.7
1916	*Bos-A	117	310	32	69	11	4	0	26	32	32	.223	.299	.284	75	-9	-9	31	6			.921	-19	S2/13	-2.7
1917	Bos-A	55	127	21	25	3	0	0	8	11	13	.197	.266	.220	49	-8	-7	9	2			.940	1	2S/1	-0.5
1919	Was-A	61	208	17	37	4	1	1	13	19	17	.178	.253	.221	34	-18	-18	13	8			.927	-27	2/S	-4.6
	StL-N	7	14	1	3	1	0	0	1	2	2	.214	.313	.286	86	-0	-0	1	0			1.000	-2	/2S3	-0.2
1920	StL-N	87	270	33	74	8	4	1	28	17	19	.274	.317	.344	93	-4	-2	29	5	6	-2	.926	-2	S1O/2	-0.8
1921	StL-N	18	32	5	9	1	0	0	5	1	0	.281	.303	.313	65	-2	-2	3	1	0	0	.968	0	/12	-0.1
	Bro-N	44	92	8	18	4	0	0	14	7	6	.196	.253	.239	30	-9	-10	6	3	1	0	.922	-4	S2/13O	-1.2
	Yr	62	124	13	27	5	0	0	19	8	6	.218	.265	.258	38	-11	-11	9	4	1	1	.922	-3	1S2/3O	-1.3
1922	Bro-N	30	57	7	17	3	1	0	1	4	4	.298	.344	.386	89	-1	-1	8	0	0	0	.889	-4	2/S31O	-0.4
Total	10	759	2221	250	515	68	18	6	210	171	197	.232	.292	.287	70	-87	-85	205	79	41		.907	-110	S21/3O	-20.3

YEAR	TM/L	G	AB	R	H	2B	3B	HR	RBI	BB	SO	AVG	OBP	SLG	PRO+	BR	/A	RC	SB	CS	SBR	FA	FR	POS	TPR

■ ROY JARVIS　Jarvis, Leroy Gilbert　b: 6/27/26, Shawnee, Okla.　d: 1/13/90, Oklahoma City, Okla.　BR/TR, 5'9", 160 lbs.　Deb: 4/30/44

1944	Bro-N	1	1	0	0	0	0	0	0	0	1	.000	.000	.000	-99	-0	-0	0	0			1.000	-0	/C	0.0
1946	Pit-N	2	4	0	1	0	0	0	0	1	1	.250	.400	.250	84	0	-0	1	0			.800	-0	/C	0.0
1947	Pit-N	18	45	4	7	1	0	1	4	6	5	.156	.255	.244	32	-4	-5	3	0			.967	-0	C	-0.4
Total	3	21	50	4	8	1	0	1	4	7	7	.160	.263	.240	34	-5	-5	3	0			.955	-1	/C	-0.4

■ PAUL JATA　Jata, Paul　b: 9/4/49, Astoria, N.Y.　BR/TR, 6'1", 190 lbs.　Deb: 4/19/72

| 1972 | Det-A | 32 | 74 | 8 | 17 | 2 | 0 | 0 | 3 | 7 | 14 | .230 | .296 | .257 | 64 | -3 | -3 | 6 | 0 | 1 | -1 | .991 | -1 | 1O/C | -0.7 |

■ AL JAVIER　Javier, Ignacio Alfred (b: Ignacio Alfredo Wilkes (Javier))　b: 2/4/54, San Pedro De Macoris, D.R.　BR/TR, 5'11", 170 lbs.　Deb: 9/09/76

| 1976 | Hou-N | 8 | 24 | 1 | 5 | 0 | 0 | 0 | 0 | 2 | 5 | .208 | .269 | .208 | 41 | -2 | -2 | 1 | 0 | 0 | 0 | 1.000 | -2 | /O | -0.4 |

■ JULIAN JAVIER　Javier, Manuel Julian (Liranzo)　b: 8/9/36, San Francisco De Macoris, D.R.　BR/TR, 6'1", 175 lbs.　Deb: 5/28/60　F

1960	StL-N	119	451	55	107	19	8	4	21	21	72	.237	.273	.341	62	-21	-26	43	19	4	3	.962	5	*2	-0.6
1961	StL-N	113	445	58	124	14	3	2	41	30	51	.279	.327	.337	70	-14	-20	51	11	4	1	.966	-0	*2	-0.8
1962	StL-N	155	598	97	157	25	5	7	39	47	73	.263	.317	.356	73	-16	-24	70	26	9	2	.977	1	*2/S	-0.6
1963	StL-N★	161	609	82	160	27	9	9	46	24	86	.263	.297	.381	68	-6	-12	68	18	10	-1	.969	-14	*2	-1.2
1964	*StL-N	155	535	66	129	19	5	12	65	30	82	.241	.283	.363	74	-15	-20	52	9	7	-2	.966	-7	*2	-1.7
1965	StL-N	77	229	34	52	6	4	2	23	8	44	.227	.262	.314	56	-12	-14	17	5	5	-2	.975	-6	2	-1.7
1966	StL-N	147	460	52	105	13	5	7	31	26	63	.228	.271	.324	64	-22	-22	40	11	5	0	.981	2	*2	-1.2
1967	*StL-N	140	520	68	146	16	3	14	64	25	92	.281	.315	.404	106	2	2	63	6	7	-2	.965	-19	*2	-1.1
1968	*StL-N★	139	519	54	135	25	4	4	52	24	61	.260	.294	.347	93	-6	-5	52	10	3	1	.976	-24	*2	-2.3
1969	StL-N	143	493	59	139	28	2	10	42	40	74	.282	.337	.408	107	4	4	67	8	4	0	.967	-18	*2	-0.2
1970	StL-N	139	513	62	129	16	3	2	42	24	70	.251	.286	.306	58	-30	-31	42	6	4	-1	.980	13	*2	-0.8
1971	StL-N	90	259	32	67	6	4	3	28	9	33	.259	.289	.347	76	-8	-9	25	5	1	1	.978	2	2/3	-0.1
1972	*Cin-N	44	91	3	19	2	0	2	12	6	11	.209	.258	.297	61	-5	-7	7	1	0	0	.896	-3	3/21	-0.8
Total	13	1622	5722	722	1469	216	55	78	506	314	812	.257	.298	.355	78	-149	-182	597	135	63	3	.972	-68	*2/3S1	-13.1

■ STAN JAVIER　Javier, Stanley Julian Antonio (De Javier)　b: 1/9/64, San Francisco De Macoris, D.R.　BB/TR, 6', 185 lbs.　Deb: 4/15/84　F

1984	NY-A	7	7	1	1	0	0	0	0	0	1	.143	.143	.143	-22	-1	-1	0	0	0	0	1.000	-2	/O	-0.3
1986	Oak-A	59	114	13	23	8	0	0	8	16	27	.202	.305	.272	63	-6	-5	11	8	0	2	1.000	-1	O/D	-0.5
1987	Oak-A	81	151	22	28	3	1	2	9	19	33	.185	.276	.258	46	-12	-11	12	3	2	-0	.983	-9	O/1D	-2.1
1988	*Oak-A	125	397	49	102	13	3	2	35	32	63	.257	.316	.320	81	-11	-9	42	20	1	5	.980	-13	*O/1D	-2.0
1989	*Oak-A	112	310	42	77	12	3	1	28	31	45	.248	.319	.316	82	-8	-6	33	12	2	2	.991	-8	*O/12	-1.4
1990	Oak-A	19	33	4	8	0	2	0	3	3	6	.242	.306	.364	90	-1	-0	4	0	0	0	1.000	-2	O/D	-0.3
	LA-N	104	276	56	84	9	4	3	24	37	44	.304	.387	.399	120	7	8	44	15	7	0	1.000	2	O	0.9
1991	LA-N	121	176	21	36	5	3	1	11	16	36	.205	.271	.284	57	-10	-10	14	7	1	2	.986	-14	O/1	-2.4
1992	LA-N	56	58	6	11	3	0	1	5	6	11	.190	.277	.293	62	-3	-3	5	1	2	-1	1.000	-7	O	-1.2
	Phi-N	74	276	36	72	14	1	0	24	31	43	.261	.340	.319	88	-4	-3	34	17	1	5	.986	13	O	1.3
	Yr	130	334	42	83	17	1	1	29	37	54	.249	.329	.314	84	-6	-6	39	18	3	4	.987	6	*O	0.1
Total	8	758	1798	250	442	67	17	10	147	191	309	.246	.321	.319	81	-48	-40	200	83	16	15	.990	-41	O/1D2	-8.0

■ TEX JEANES　Jeanes, Ernest Lee　b: 12/19/1900, Maypearl, Tex.　d: 4/5/73, Longview, Tex.　BR/TR, 6', 176 lbs.　Deb: 4/20/21

1921	Cle-A	5	3	2	2	1	0	0	4	1	0	.667	.750	1.000	338	1	1	2	0	0	0	1.000	-1	/O	0.0
1922	Cle-A	1	1	0	0	0	0	0	0	1	0	.000	.500	.000	39	0	0	0	0	0	0	.000	-1	/PO	0.0
1925	Was-A	15	19	2	5	1	0	1	4	3	2	.263	.364	.474	113	0	0	4	1	0	0	1.000	-5	O	-0.5
1926	Was-A	21	30	6	7	2	0	0	3	0	3	.233	.233	.300	39	-3	-3	2	0	0	0	1.000	-3	O	-0.6
1927	NY-N	11	20	5	6	0	0	0	0	2	2	.300	.364	.300	79	-0	-0	2	0			1.000	1	/OP	0.0
Total	5	53	73	15	20	4	0	1	14	7	7	.274	.338	.370	85	-2	-2	10	1	0		1.000	-9	/OP	-1.1

■ HAL JEFFCOAT　Jeffcoat, Harold Bentley　b: 9/6/24, W.Columbia, S.C.　BR/TR, 5'10.5", 185 lbs.　Deb: 4/20/48　F

1948	Chi-N	134	473	53	132	16	4	4	42	24	68	.279	.315	.355	85	-13	-11	54	8			.976	9	*O	-0.9
1949	Chi-N	108	363	43	89	18	6	2	26	20	48	.245	.286	.344	70	-17	-16	36	12			.963	7	*O	-1.4
1950	Chi-N	66	179	21	42	13	1	2	18	6	23	.235	.259	.352	60	-11	-11	13	7			.967	-3	O	-1.6
1951	Chi-N	113	278	44	76	20	2	4	27	16	23	.273	.315	.403	90	-4	-5	35	8	4	0	.989	-2	O	-0.8
1952	Chi-N	102	297	29	65	17	2	4	30	15	40	.219	.259	.330	61	-16	-16	22	7	2	1	.996	3	O	-1.6
1953	Chi-N	106	183	22	43	3	1	4	22	21	26	.235	.314	.328	66	-9	-9	20	5	0	2	.973	-17	*O	-2.6
1954	Chi-N	56	31	13	8	2	1	1	6	1	7	.258	.281	.484	94	-0	-0	4	2	0	1	.889	-1	P/O	-0.1
1955	Chi-N	52	23	3	4	0	0	1	1	2	9	.174	.240	.304	43	-2	-2	1	0	0	0	.903	1	P	0.0
1956	Cin-N	49	54	5	8	2	0	0	5	3	20	.148	.193	.185	2	-7	-8	2	0	1	-1	.969	3	P	0.0
1957	Cin-N	53	69	13	14	3	1	4	11	5	20	.203	.267	.449	82	-2	-2	8	0	0	0	.958	-1	P	0.0
1958	Cin-N	50	9	2	5	0	0	0	1	2	2	.556	.600	.556	198	2	1	3	0	0	0	1.000	2	P/O	0.0
1959	Cin-N	17	1	1	1	1	0	0	0	0	0	1.000	1.000	2.000	655	1	1	2	0	0	0	1.000	0	P	0.0
	StL-N	12	3	0	0	0	0	0	0	0	3	.000	.000	.000	-94	-1	-1	0	0	0	0	1.000	0	P	0.0
	Yr	29	4	1	1	1	0	0	0	0	3	.250	.250	.500	90	-0	-0	1	0	0	0	1.000	0	P	0.0
Total	12	918	1963	249	487	95	18	26	188	114	289	.248	.291	.355	73	-79	-78	200	49	7		.978	0	OP	-9.0

■ GREGG JEFFERIES　Jefferies, Gregory Scott　b: 8/1/67, Burlingame, Cal.　BB/TR, 5'11", 175 lbs.　Deb: 9/06/87

1987	NY-N	6	6	0	3	1	0	0	2	0	0	.500	.500	.667	217	1	1	2	0	0	0	.000	0	/H	0.1
1988	*NY-N	29	109	19	35	8	2	6	17	8	10	.321	.368	.596	181	10	10	24	5	1	1	.979	-3	32	0.8
1989	NY-N	141	508	72	131	28	2	12	56	39	46	.258	.317	.392	107	0	3	61	21	6	3	.975	-31	*23	-2.3
1990	NY-N	153	604	96	171	**40**	3	15	68	46	40	.283	.339	.434	111	8	8	89	11	2	2	.976	-9	*23	0.4
1991	NY-N	136	486	59	132	19	2	9	62	47	38	.272	.338	.374	101	1	1	64	26	5	5	.982	-16	23	-0.9
1992	KC-A	152	604	66	172	36	3	10	75	43	29	.285	.333	.404	105	4	3	75	19	9	0	.939	-2	*3/2D	0.2
Total	6	617	2317	312	644	132	12	52	280	183	163	.278	.334	.413	110	23	26	315	82	23	11	.977	-61	23/D	-1.7

■ REGGIE JEFFERSON　Jefferson, Reginald Jirod　b: 9/25/68, Tallahassee, Fla.　BB/TL, 6'4", 210 lbs.　Deb: 5/18/91

1991	Cin-N	5	7	1	1	0	0	1	1	1	2	.143	.250	.571	120	0	0	1	0	0	0	1.000	0	/1	0.0
	Cle-A	26	101	10	20	3	0	2	12	3	22	.198	.221	.287	39	-8	-9	6	0	0	0	.993	1	1/D	-0.8
1992	Cle-A	24	89	8	30	6	2	1	6	1	17	.337	.352	.483	130	3	3	14	0	0	0	.993	1	1/D	0.3
Total	2	55	197	19	51	9	2	4	19	5	41	.259	.281	.386	83	-5	-5	22	0	0	0	.993	3	/1D	-0.5

■ STAN JEFFERSON　Jefferson, Stanley　b: 12/4/62, New York, N.Y.　BB/TR, 5'11", 175 lbs.　Deb: 9/07/86

1986	NY-N	14	24	6	5	1	0	1	3	2	8	.208	.296	.375	86	-1	-0	3	0	0	0	1.000	-1	/O	-0.1
1987	SD-N	116	422	59	97	8	7	8	29	39	92	.230	.298	.339	71	-19	-17	45	34	11	4	.987	-10	*O	-2.8
1988	SD-N	49	111	16	16	1	2	1	4	9	22	.144	.215	.216	25	-11	-11	6	5	1	1	1.000	-4	O	-1.6
1989	NY-A	10	12	1	1	0	0	0	1	0	4	.083	.083	.083	-54	-2	-2	0	1	1	-0	1.000	-3	/OD	-0.6
	Bal-A	35	127	19	33	7	0	4	20	4	22	.260	.288	.409	97	-1	-1	15	9	3	1	.988	2	O/D	0.1
	Yr	45	139	20	34	7	0	4	21	4	26	.245	.271	.381	84	-4	-3	14	10	4	1	.988	-2	O/D	-0.5
1990	Bal-A	10	19	1	0	0	0	0	2	8	12	.000	.095	.000	-74	-4	-4	0	0	0	0	1.000	-2	/OD	-0.6
	Cle-A	49	98	21	27	8	0	2	10	8	18	.276	.343	.418	112	1	2	14	8	4	0	.985	0	O/D	0.1
	Yr	59	117	22	27	8	0	2	12	16	30	.231	.302	.350	83	-3	-3	13	8	4	0	.987	-2	/OD	-0.5
1991	Cin-N	13	19	2	1	0	0	0	0	1	4	.053	.100	.053	-54	-4	-4	0	2	0	1	1.000	-2	/O	-0.5
Total	6	296	832	125	180	25	9	16	67	65	177	.216	.279	.326	66	-41	-39	82	60	20	6	.990	-20	O/D	-6.0

YEAR	TM/L	G	AB	R	H	2B	3B	HR	RBI	BB	SO	AVG	OBP	SLG	PRO+	BR	/A	RC	SB	CS	SBR	FA	FR	POS	TPR
■ IRV JEFFRIES Jeffries, Irvine Franklin b: 9/10/05, Louisville, Ky. d: 6/8/82, Louisville, Ky. BR/TR, 5'10", 175 lbs. Deb: 4/30/30																									
1930	Chi-A	40	97	14	23	3	0	2	11	3	2	.237	.275	.330	54	-7	-7	9	1	2	-1	.976	-3	3S	-0.8
1931	Chi-A	79	223	29	50	10	0	2	16	14	9	.224	.270	.296	52	-17	-15	19	3	0	1	.949	2	3/2SO	-0.8
1934	Phi-N	56	175	28	43	6	0	4	19	15	10	.246	.305	.349	66	-6	-9	18	2			.962	4	2/3	-0.3
Total	3	175	495	71	116	19	0	8	46	32	21	.234	.284	.321	58	-30	-31	46	6	2		.955	3	/32SO	-1.9
■ CHRIS JELIC Jelic, Christopher John b: 12/16/63, Bethlehem, Pa. BR/TR, 5'11", 180 lbs. Deb: 9/30/90																									
1990	NY-N	4	11	2	1	0	0	1	1	0	3	.091	.091	.364	19	-1	-1	0	0	0	0	1.000	-1	/O	-0.3
■ FRANK JELINICH Jelinich, Frank Anthony "Jelly" b: 9/3/19, San Jose, Cal. BR/TR, 6'2", 198 lbs. Deb: 9/06/41																									
1941	Chi-N	4	8	0	1	0	0	0	2	1	2	.125	.222	.125	-1	-1	-1	0	0			1.000	-1	/O	-0.2
■ GREG JELKS Jelks, Gregory Dion b: 8/16/61, Cherokee, Ala. BR/TR, 6'2", 190 lbs. Deb: 8/20/87																									
1987	Phi-N	10	11	2	1	1	0	0	0	3	4	.091	.286	.182	26	-1	-1	1	0	0	0	.750	0	/31O	-0.1
■ STEVE JELTZ Jeltz, Larry Steven b: 5/28/59, Paris, France BB/TR, 5'11", 180 lbs. Deb: 7/17/83																									
1983	Phi-N	13	8	0	1	0	1	0	1	1	2	.125	.222	.375	63	-0	-0	0	0	0	0	1.000	1	/2S3	0.0
1984	Phi-N	28	68	7	14	0	1	1	7	7	11	.206	.280	.279	57	-4	-4	5	2	1	0	.992	11	S/3	1.0
1985	Phi-N	89	196	17	37	4	1	0	12	26	55	.189	.284	.219	41	-14	-15	13	1	1	-0	.958	6	S	-0.3
1986	Phi-N	145	439	44	96	11	4	0	36	65	97	.219	.321	.262	60	-20	-22	40	6	3	0	.967	-2	*S	-1.2
1987	Phi-N	114	293	37	68	9	6	0	12	39	54	.232	.324	.304	66	-13	-14	28	1	2	-1	.971	3	*S/O	-0.4
1988	Phi-N	148	379	39	71	11	4	0	27	59	58	.187	.297	.237	54	-20	-21	29	3	0	1	.976	-1	*S	-1.2
1989	Phi-N	116	263	28	64	7	3	4	25	45	44	.243	.356	.338	99	1	1	34	4	2	0	.985	1	S32/O	0.7
1990	KC-A	74	103	11	16	4	0	0	10	6	21	.155	.202	.194	11	-12	-12	4	1	1	-0	.977	9	2SO/3D	-0.2
Total	8	727	1749	183	367	46	20	5	130	248	342	.210	.309	.268	61	-83	-88	153	18	10	-1	.971	28	S/23OD	-1.6
■ JOHN JENKINS Jenkins, John Robert b: 7/7/1896, Bosworth, Mo. d: 8/3/68, Columbia, Mo. BR/TR, 5'8", 160 lbs. Deb: 8/05/22																									
1922	Chi-A	5	3	0	0	0	0	0	1	0	2	.000	.000	.000	-99	-1	-1	0	0	0	0	.000	-0	/2S	-0.1
■ JOE JENKINS Jenkins, Joseph Daniel b: 10/12/1890, Shelbyville, Tenn. d: 6/21/74, Fresno, Cal. BR/TR, 5'11", 170 lbs. Deb: 4/30/14																									
1914	StL-A	19	32	0	4	1	1	0	0	1	11	.125	.152	.219	12	-4	-3	1	2			.931	-4	/C	-0.8
1917	Chi-A	10	9	0	1	0	0	0	2	0	5	.111	.111	.111	-32	-1	-1	0	0			.000	0	/C	-0.2
1919	Chi-A	11	19	0	3	1	0	0	1	1	1	.158	.200	.211	15	-2	-2	1	1			.824	-2	/C	-0.4
Total	3	40	60	0	8	2	1	0	3	2	17	.133	.161	.200	6	-7	-7	2	3			.891	-6	/C	-1.4
■ TOM JENKINS Jenkins, Thomas Griffith "Tut" b: 4/10/1898, Camden, Ala. d: 5/3/79, Weymouth, Mass. BL/TR, 6'1.5", 174 lbs. Deb: 9/15/25																									
1925	Bos-A	15	64	9	19	2	1	0	5	3	4	.297	.338	.359	77	-2	-2	8	0	0	0	.938	-2	O	-0.5
1926	Bos-A	21	50	3	9	1	1	0	6	3	7	.180	.226	.240	22	-6	-6	3	0	0	0	1.000	-1	O	-0.8
	Phi-A	6	23	3	4	2	0	0	0	0	2	.174	.174	.261	12	-3	-3	1	0	0	0	1.000	0	/O	-0.4
	Yr	27	73	6	13	3	1	0	6	3	9	.178	.211	.247	19	-9	-9	4	0	0	0	1.000	-1	O	-1.2
1929	StL-A	21	22	1	4	0	1	0	0	4	8	.182	.308	.273	49	-2	-2	2	0	0	0	1.000	-1	/O	-0.3
1930	StL-A	2	8	1	2	1	1	0	3	0	1	.250	.250	.625	110	0	0	1	0	0	0	1.000	-0	/O	0.0
1931	StL-A	81	230	20	61	7	2	3	25	17	25	.265	.316	.352	73	-8	-10	25	1	3	-2	.952	-4	O	-1.7
1932	StL-A	25	62	5	20	1	0	0	5	1	6	.323	.333	.339	70	-2	-3	7	0	0	0	.939	2	O	-0.2
Total	6	171	459	42	119	14	6	3	44	28	53	.259	.303	.336	64	-23	-25	47	1	3	-2	.958	-6	O	-3.9
■ ALAMAZOO JENNINGS Jennings, Alfred Gorden b: 11/30/1850, Newport, Ky. d: 11/2/1894, Cincinnati, Ohio Deb: 8/15/1878 U																									
1878	Mil-N	1	2	0	0	0	0	0	0	1	0	.000	.333	.000	16	-0	-0	0				.429	-2	/C	-0.2
■ HUGHIE JENNINGS Jennings, Hugh Ambrose "Ee-Yah" b: 4/2/1869, Pittston, Pa. d: 2/1/28, Scranton, Pa. BR/TR, 5'8.5", 165 lbs. Deb: 6/01/1891 MCH																									
1891	Lou-a	90	360	53	105	10	8	1	58	17	36	.292	.339	.372	108	2	3	51	12			.894	7	S1/3	1.1
1892	Lou-N	152	594	65	132	16	4	2	61	30	30	.222	.270	.273	71	-25	-18	53	28			.907	15	*S	0.3
1893	Lou-N	23	88	6	12	3	0	0	9	3	3	.136	.174	.170	-8	-14	-12	3	0			.899	6	S	-0.5
	Bal-N	16	55	6	14	0	0	1	6	4	3	.255	.339	.309	73	-2	-2	6	0			.886	-2	S/O	-0.3
	Yr	39	143	12	26	3	0	1	15	7	6	.182	.240	.224	26	-15	-14	8	0			.895	4	S/O	-0.8
1894	*Bal-N	128	501	134	168	28	16	4	109	37	17	.335	.411	.479	111	14	9	118	37			**.928**	**33**	*S	3.7
1895	*Bal-N	131	529	159	204	41	7	4	125	24	17	.386	.444	.512	145	39	36	150	53			**.940**	**36**	*S	**6.2**
1896	*Bal-N	130	521	125	209	27	9	0	121	19	11	.401	.472	.488	154	46	44	158	70			**.928**	34	*S	**6.9**
1897	*Bal-N	117	439	133	156	26	9	2	79	42		.355	.463	.469	146	35	35	128	60			**.933**	27	*S	**5.4**
1898	Bal-N	143	534	135	175	25	11	1	87	78		.328	.454	.421	149	44	43	119	28			.929	-0	*S2/O	4.6
1899	Bro-N	16	41	7	7	0	2	0	6	9		.171	.346	.268	68	-1	-1	6	4			.825	-6	S/1	-0.6
	Bal-N	2	8	2	3	0	2	0	2	0		.375	.375	.875	227	1	1	3	0			1.000	-1	/2	0.0
	Bro-N	51	175	35	57	3	8	0	34	13		.326	.424	.434	133	10	9	40	14			.987	-0	1/2S	0.8
	Yr	69	224	44	67	3	12	0	42	22		.299	.408	.420	124	10	9	48	18			.985	-7	1S/2	0.2
1900	*Bro-N	115	441	61	120	18	6	1	69	31		.272	.348	.347	87	-4	-8	67	31			.982	6	*1/2	-0.2
1901	Phi-N	82	302	38	79	21	2	1	39	25		.262	.342	.354	100	2	1	43	13			.979	-3	1/2S	-0.3
1902	Phi-N	78	290	32	79	13	4	1	32	14		.272	.328	.355	111	3	3	38	8			.983	1	1/S2	0.4
1903	Bro-N	6	17	2	4	0	0	0	1	1		.235	.316	.235	60	-1	-1	2	1			1.000	-0	/O	-0.1
1907	Det-A	1	4	0	1	1	0	0	0	0		.250	.250	.500	134	0	0	1	0			.750	-1	/2SM	-0.1
1909	Det-A	2	4	1	2	0	0	0	2	0		.500	.500	.500	207	0	0	1	0			1.000	0	/1M	0.1
1912	Det-A	1	1	0	0	0	0	0	0	0		.000	.000	.000	-99	-0	-0	0	0			.000	0	HM	0.0
1918	Det-A	1	0	0	0	0	0	0	0	0	0	—	—	—	—	0	0	0	0			1.000	-0	/1M	0.0
Total	17	1285	4904	994	1527	232	88	18	840	347	117	.311	.390	.406	119	150	143	985	359			.922	151	S1/2O3	27.4
■ DOUG JENNINGS Jennings, James Douglas b: 9/30/64, Atlanta, Ga. BL/TL, 5'10", 175 lbs. Deb: 4/08/88																									
1988	Oak-A	71	101	9	21	6	0	1	15	21	28	.208	.355	.297	88	-1	-1	12	0	1	-1	1.000	-3	O1/D	-0.5
1989	Oak-A	4	4	0	0	0	0	0	0	0	2	.000	.000	.000	-99	-1	-1	0	0	0	0	1.000	-1	/O	-0.2
1990	*Oak-A	64	156	19	30	7	2	2	14	17	48	.192	.280	.301	65	-8	-7	14	0	3	-2	.984	-8	O/1D	-1.9
1991	Oak-A	8	9	0	1	0	0	0	0	2	2	.111	.273	.111	11	-1	-1	0	0	1	-1	1.000	-1	/O	-0.2
Total	4	147	270	28	52	13	2	3	29	40	80	.193	.306	.289	70	-11	-10	26	0	5	-3	.991	-13	/O1D	-2.8
■ BILL JENNINGS Jennings, William Lee b: 9/28/25, St.Louis, Mo. BR/TR, 6'2", 175 lbs. Deb: 7/19/51																									
1951	StL-A	64	195	20	35	10	2	0	13	26	42	.179	.276	.251	42	-15	-16	15	1	0	0	.953	-5	S	-1.7
■ WOODY JENSEN Jensen, Forrest Docenus b: 8/11/07, Bremerton, Wash. BL/TL, 5'10.5", 160 lbs. Deb: 4/20/31																									
1931	Pit-N	73	267	43	65	5	4	3	17	10	18	.243	.276	.326	62	-15	-15	25	4			.974	5	O	-1.4
1932	Pit-N	7	5	2	0	0	0	0	0	0	2	.000	.000	.000	-99	-1	-1	0	0			.000	-1	/O	-0.2
1933	Pit-N	70	196	29	58	7	3	0	15	8	2	.296	.330	.362	98	-1	-1	25	1			.980	-0	O	-0.3
1934	Pit-N	88	283	34	82	13	4	0	27	4	13	.290	.304	.364	76	-9	-10	30	2			.993	-3	O	-1.5
1935	Pit-N	143	627	97	203	28	7	8	62	15	14	.324	.344	.429	103	4	2	90	9			.977	-4	*O	-0.7
1936	Pit-N	153	696	98	197	34	10	10	58	16	19	.283	.305	.404	87	-13	-15	84	2			.975	1	*O	-2.0
1937	Pit-N	124	509	77	142	23	9	5	45	15	29	.279	.301	.389	86	-11	-11	58	2			.963	-0	*O	-1.6
1938	Pit-N	68	125	12	25	4	0	0	10	1	3	.200	.213	.232	22	-13	-13	6	0			.900	-11	O	-2.6
1939	Pit-N	12	12	0	2	0	0	0	1	0	0	.167	.167	.167	-10	-2	-2	0	0			1.000	-1	/O	-0.3
Total	9	738	2720	392	774	114	37	26	235	69	100	.285	.307	.382	84	-61	-66	318	20			.972	-13	O	-10.6

■ JACKIE JENSEN Jensen, Jack Eugene b: 3/9/27, San Francisco, Cal. d: 7/14/82, Charlottesville, Va. BR/TR, 5'11", 190 lbs. Deb: 4/18/50

YEAR	TM/L	G	AB	R	H	2B	3B	HR	RBI	BB	SO	AVG	OBP	SLG	PRO+	BR	/A	RC	SB	CS	SBR	FA	FR	POS	TPR
1950	*NY-A	45	70	13	12	2	2	1	5	7	8	.171	.247	.300	41	-7	-7	5	4	0	1	.947	-4	O	-0.9
1951	NY-A	56	168	30	50	8	1	8	25	18	18	.298	.369	.500	138	7	8	34	8	2	1	.974	1	O	0.8
1952	NY-A	7	19	3	2	1	1	0	2	4	4	.105	.261	.263	49	-1	-1	1	1	0	0	1.000	-1	/O	-0.2
	Was-A	144	570	80	163	29	5	10	80	63	40	.286	.360	.407	117	10	13	86	17	6	2	.977	6	*O	1.5
	Yr	151	589	83	165	30	6	10	82	67	44	.280	.357	.402	115	9	11	88	18	6	**2**	.978	5	*O	1.3
1953	Was-A	147	552	87	147	32	8	10	84	73	51	.266	.357	.408	109	5	7	82	18	8	1	.983	-4	*O	-0.2
1954	Bos-A	152	580	92	160	25	7	25	117	79	52	.276	.365	.472	115	21	13	94	**22**	7	2	.986	-7	*O	0.3
1955	Bos-A★	152	574	95	158	27	6	26	**116**	89	63	.275	.375	.479	118	23	16	102	16	7	1	.977	1	*O	1.1
1956	Bos-A	151	578	80	182	23	**11**	20	97	89	43	.315	.407	.497	123	33	23	116	11	3	2	.962	2	*O	1.7
1957	Bos-A	145	544	82	153	29	2	23	103	75	66	.281	.370	.469	121	21	17	91	8	5	-1	.960	4	*O	1.3
1958	Bos-A★	154	548	83	157	31	0	35	**122**	99	65	.286	.398	.535	144	43	38	120	9	4	0	.981	3	*O	3.4
1959	Bos-A	148	535	101	148	31	0	28	**112**	88	67	.277	.379	.492	131	28	25	100	20	5	3	.982	15	*O	3.5
1961	Bos-A	137	498	64	131	21	2	13	66	66	69	.263	.353	.392	96	0	-2	68	9	8	-2	.986	11	*O	0.0
Total	11	1438	5236	810	1463	259	45	199	929	750	546	.279	.372	.460	119	184	151	900	143	55	10	.977	28	*O	12.3

■ DAN JESSEE Jessee, Daniel Edward b: 2/22/01, Olive Hill, Ky. d: 4/30/70, Venice, Fla. BL/TR, 5'10", 165 lbs. Deb: 8/14/29

YEAR	TM/L	G	AB	R	H	2B	3B	HR	RBI	BB	SO	AVG	OBP	SLG	PRO+	BR	/A	RC	SB	CS	SBR	FA	FR	POS	TPR
1929	Cle-A	1	0	0	0	0	0	0	0	0	0	—	—	—	—	0	0	0	0	0	0	.000	0	R	0.0

■ GARRY JESTADT Jestadt, Garry Arthur b: 3/19/47, Chicago, Ill. BR/TR, 6'2", 188 lbs. Deb: 9/17/69

YEAR	TM/L	G	AB	R	H	2B	3B	HR	RBI	BB	SO	AVG	OBP	SLG	PRO+	BR	/A	RC	SB	CS	SBR	FA	FR	POS	TPR
1969	Mon-N	6	6	1	0	0	0	0	1	0	0	.000	.000	.000	-99	-2	-2	0	0	0	0	.667	-0	/S	-0.2
1971	Chi-N	3	3	0	0	0	0	0	0	0	0	.000	.000	.000	-87	-1	-1	0	0	0	0	.000	0	/3	-0.1
	SD-N	75	189	17	55	13	0	0	13	11	24	.291	.330	.360	102	-1	0	19	1	3	-2	.935	11	32/S	1.1
	Yr	78	192	17	55	13	0	0	13	11	24	.286	.325	.354	98	-2	-1	19	1	3	-2	.935	11	32/S	1.0
1972	SD-N	92	256	15	63	5	1	6	22	13	21	.246	.283	.344	83	-8	-6	24	0	0	0	.944	-17	23/S	-2.3
Total	3	176	454	33	118	18	1	6	36	24	45	.260	.297	.344	87	-12	-8	44	1	3	-2	.942	-7	/32S	-1.5

■ JOHNNY JETER Jeter, John b: 10/24/44, Shreveport, La. BR/TR, 6'1", 180 lbs. Deb: 6/14/69 F

YEAR	TM/L	G	AB	R	H	2B	3B	HR	RBI	BB	SO	AVG	OBP	SLG	PRO+	BR	/A	RC	SB	CS	SBR	FA	FR	POS	TPR
1969	Pit-N	28	29	7	9	1	1	1	6	3	15	.310	.375	.517	151	2	2	6	1	1	-0	1.000	1	O	0.2
1970	*Pit-N	85	126	27	30	3	2	2	12	13	34	.238	.314	.341	77	-4	-4	13	9	5	-0	1.000	1	O	-0.5
1971	SD-N	18	75	8	24	4	0	1	3	2	16	.320	.338	.413	120	1	1	11	2	0	1	.967	4	O	0.6
1972	SD-N	110	326	25	72	4	3	7	21	18	92	.221	.266	.316	70	-16	-13	25	11	5	0	.987	-3	O	-2.1
1973	Chi-A	89	300	38	72	14	4	7	26	9	74	.240	.262	.383	77	-9	-11	28	4	3	-1	.955	-3	O/D	-1.8
1974	Cle-A	6	17	3	6	1	0	0	1	1	6	.353	.389	.412	132	1	1	2	1	2	-1	.833	-2	/O	-0.2
Total	6	336	873	108	213	27	10	18	69	46	237	.244	.284	.360	82	-26	-24	85	28	16	-1	.975	-2	O/D	-3.8

■ SHAWN JETER Jeter, Shawn Darrell b: 6/28/66, Shreveport, La. BL/TR, 6'2", 185 lbs. Deb: 6/13/92 F

YEAR	TM/L	G	AB	R	H	2B	3B	HR	RBI	BB	SO	AVG	OBP	SLG	PRO+	BR	/A	RC	SB	CS	SBR	FA	FR	POS	TPR
1992	Chi-A	13	18	1	2	0	0	0	0	0	7	.111	.111	.111	-39	-3	-3	0	0	0	0	.909	-2	/OD	-0.5

■ SAM JETHROE Jethroe, Samuel "Jet" b: 1/20/22, E.St.Louis, Ill. BB/TR, 6'1", 178 lbs. Deb: 4/18/50

YEAR	TM/L	G	AB	R	H	2B	3B	HR	RBI	BB	SO	AVG	OBP	SLG	PRO+	BR	/A	RC	SB	CS	SBR	FA	FR	POS	TPR
1950	Bos-N	141	582	100	159	28	8	18	58	52	93	.273	.338	.442	110	2	7	89	**35**			.969	8	*O	0.9
1951	Bos-N	148	572	101	160	29	10	18	65	57	88	.280	.356	.460	127	14	19	103	**35**	5	**8**	.974	7	*O	2.8
1952	Bos-N	151	608	79	141	23	7	13	58	68	112	.232	.318	.357	90	-11	-8	76	28	9	3	.970	4	*O	-0.7
1954	Pit-N	2	1	0	0	0	0	0	0	0	0	.000	.000	.000	-99	-0	-0	0	0	0	0	1.000	-0	/O	-0.1
Total	4	442	1763	280	460	80	25	49	181	177	293	.261	.337	.418	108	5	18	267	98	14		.971	19	O	2.9

■ NAT JEWETT Jewett, Nathan W. b: 12/25/1842, New York, N.Y. d: 2/23/14, Bronx, N.Y. 5'6", 137 lbs. Deb: 7/04/1872

YEAR	TM/L	G	AB	R	H	2B	3B	HR	RBI	BB	SO	AVG	OBP	SLG	PRO+	BR	/A	RC	SB	CS	SBR	FA	FR	POS	TPR
1872	Eck-n	2	8	1	1	0	0	0	0	0	0	.125	.125	.125	-27	-1	-1	0						/C	-0.1

■ HOUSTON JIMENEZ Jimenez, Alfonso (Gonzalez) b: 10/30/57, Navojoa, Sonora, Mex BR/TR, 5'8", 144 lbs. Deb: 6/13/83

YEAR	TM/L	G	AB	R	H	2B	3B	HR	RBI	BB	SO	AVG	OBP	SLG	PRO+	BR	/A	RC	SB	CS	SBR	FA	FR	POS	TPR
1983	Min-A	36	86	5	15	5	1	0	9	4	11	.174	.211	.256	27	-9	-9	5	0	1	-1	.969	4	S	-0.3
1984	Min-A	108	298	28	60	11	1	0	19	15	34	.201	.240	.245	33	-26	-28	17	0	1	-1	.959	-5	*S	-2.5
1987	Pit-N	5	6	0	0	0	0	0	0	1	2	.000	.143	.000	-58	-1	-1	0	0	0	0	1.000	1	/2S	0.0
1988	Cle-A	9	21	1	1	0	0	0	1	0	2	.048	.048	.048	-71	-5	-5	0	0	0	0	.973	6	/2S	0.1
Total	4	158	411	34	76	16	2	0	29	20	49	.185	.223	.234	25	-41	-43	21	0	2	-1	.962	7	S/2	-2.7

■ ELVIO JIMENEZ Jimenez, Felix Elvio (Rivera) b: 1/6/40, San Pedro De Macoris, D.R. BR/TR, 5'9", 170 lbs. Deb: 10/04/64 F

YEAR	TM/L	G	AB	R	H	2B	3B	HR	RBI	BB	SO	AVG	OBP	SLG	PRO+	BR	/A	RC	SB	CS	SBR	FA	FR	POS	TPR
1964	NY-A	1	6	0	2	0	0	0	0	0	0	.333	.333	.333	85	-0	-0	1	0	0	0	1.000	0	/O	0.0

■ MANNY JIMENEZ Jimenez, Manuel Emilio (Rivera) b: 11/19/38, San Pedro De Macoris, D.R. BL/TR, 6'1", 195 lbs. Deb: 4/11/62 F

YEAR	TM/L	G	AB	R	H	2B	3B	HR	RBI	BB	SO	AVG	OBP	SLG	PRO+	BR	/A	RC	SB	CS	SBR	FA	FR	POS	TPR
1962	KC-A	139	479	48	144	24	2	11	69	31	34	.301	.357	.428	107	7	5	72	0	1	-1	.985	-5	*O	-0.8
1963	KC-A	60	157	12	44	9	0	0	15	16	14	.280	.365	.338	95	0	-0	19	0	1	-1	.960	1	O	-0.2
1964	KC-A	95	204	19	46	7	0	12	38	15	24	.225	.295	.436	97	-1	-1	21	0	0	0	.939	-4	O	-0.7
1966	KC-A	13	35	1	4	0	1	0	1	6	4	.114	.244	.171	22	-3	-3	2	0	0	0	.909	-2	O	-0.6
1967	Pit-N	50	56	3	14	2	0	2	10	1	4	.250	.276	.393	89	-1	-1	5	0	0	0	1.000	-1	/O	-0.2
1968	Pit-N	66	66	7	20	1	1	1	11	6	15	.303	.403	.394	142	4	4	11	0	0	0	.857	-1	/O	0.3
1969	Chi-N	6	6	0	1	0	0	0	0	0	2	.167	.167	.167	-6	-1	-1	0	0	0	0	.000	0	H	-0.1
Total	7	429	1003	90	273	43	4	26	144	75	97	.272	.339	.401	101	5	2	130	0	2	-1	.966	-10	O	-2.3

■ TOMMY JOHNS Johns, Thomas Pearce b: 9/7/1851, Baltimore, Md. d: 4/13/27, Baltimore, Md. Deb: 5/14/1873

YEAR	TM/L	G	AB	R	H	2B	3B	HR	RBI	BB	SO	AVG	OBP	SLG	PRO+	BR	/A	RC	SB	CS	SBR	FA	FR	POS	TPR
1873	Mar-n	1	4	0	0	0	0	0	0	0	0	.000	.000	.000	-99	-1	-1	0						/O	-0.1

■ PETE JOHNS Johns, William R. b: 1/17/1889, Cleveland, Ohio d: 8/9/64, Cleveland, Ohio BR/TR, 5'10", 165 lbs. Deb: 8/25/15

YEAR	TM/L	G	AB	R	H	2B	3B	HR	RBI	BB	SO	AVG	OBP	SLG	PRO+	BR	/A	RC	SB	CS	SBR	FA	FR	POS	TPR
1915	Chi-A	28	100	7	21	2	1	0	11	8	11	.210	.275	.250	56	-5	-6	6	2	7	-4	.943	4	3	-0.5
1918	StL-A	46	89	5	16	1	1	0	11	4	6	.180	.215	.213	30	-8	-8	4	0			.990	-1	1/S3O2	-1.0
Total	2	74	189	12	37	3	2	0	22	12	17	.196	.248	.233	44	-13	-13	10	2	7		.929	2	/31OS2	-1.5

■ ABBIE JOHNSON Johnson, Albert J. b: 7/26/1872, Sweden d: 5/2/24, Oak Forest, Ill. Deb: 9/01/1896

YEAR	TM/L	G	AB	R	H	2B	3B	HR	RBI	BB	SO	AVG	OBP	SLG	PRO+	BR	/A	RC	SB	CS	SBR	FA	FR	POS	TPR
1896	Lou-N	25	87	10	20	2	1	0	14	4	6	.230	.264	.276	46	-7	-6	7	0			.937	-4	2	-0.8
1897	Lou-N	48	161	16	39	6	1	0	23	13		.242	.303	.292	59	-10	-9	15	2			.879	-10	2S	-1.5
Total	2	73	248	26	59	8	2	0	37	17	6	.238	.289	.286	55	-17	-15	22	2			.903	-14	/2S	-2.3

■ ALEX JOHNSON Johnson, Alexander b: 12/7/42, Helena, Ark. BR/TR, 6', 205 lbs. Deb: 7/25/64

YEAR	TM/L	G	AB	R	H	2B	3B	HR	RBI	BB	SO	AVG	OBP	SLG	PRO+	BR	/A	RC	SB	CS	SBR	FA	FR	POS	TPR
1964	Phi-N	43	109	18	33	7	1	4	18	6	26	.303	.345	.495	135	5	5	18	1	2	-1	.980	-0	O	0.2
1965	Phi-N	97	262	27	77	9	3	8	28	15	60	.294	.337	.443	120	6	6	37	4	4	-1	.966	-2	O	0.0
1966	StL-N	25	86	7	16	0	1	2	6	5	18	.186	.231	.279	41	-7	-7	4	1	1	-0	.962	-3	O	-1.2
1967	StL-N	81	175	20	39	9	2	1	12	9	26	.223	.273	.314	68	-7	-7	15	6	3	0	.970	7	O	-0.2
1968	Cin-N	149	603	79	188	32	6	2	58	26	71	.312	.343	.395	114	14	11	77	16	6	1	.947	-5	*O	-0.1
1969	Cin-N	139	523	86	165	18	4	17	88	25	69	.315	.357	.463	122	18	15	82	11	8	-2	.927	-9	*O	-0.3
1970	Cal-A★	156	614	85	202	26	6	14	86	35	68	**.329**	.372	.459	133	22	25	99	17	2	4	.959	5	*O	2.6
1971	Cal-A	65	242	19	63	8	0	2	21	15	34	.260	.309	.318	84	-7	-5	22	5	2	0	.926	-6	O	-1.5
1972	Cle-A	108	356	31	85	10	1	8	37	22	40	.239	.285	.340	83	-7	-8	30	6	8	-3	.955	-5	O	-2.4
1973	Tex-A	158	624	62	179	26	3	8	68	32	82	.287	.324	.377	101	-4	-1	72	10	5	0	.987	1	*DO	-0.1
1974	Tex-A	114	453	57	132	14	3	4	41	28	59	.291	.338	.362	104	1	2	52	20	9	1	.956	6	OD	0.5
	NY-A	10	28	3	6	1	0	1	2	0	3	.214	.214	.357	64	-1	-1	2	0	0	0	.000	-0	/OD	-0.2

YEAR	TM/L	G	AB	R	H	2B	3B	HR	RBI	BB	SO	AVG	OBP	SLG	PRO+	BR	/A	RC	SB	CS	SBR	FA	FR	POS	TPR
	Yr	124	481	60	138	15	3	5	43	28	62	.287	.331	.362	102	-1	1	54	20	9	1	.956	5	OD	0.3
1975	NY-A	52	119	15	31	5	1	1	15	7	21	.261	.302	.345	85	-3	-3	11	2	3	-1	1.000	-1	D/O	-0.5
1976	Det-A	125	429	41	115	15	2	6	45	19	49	.268	.302	.354	88	-5	-7	41	14	10	-2	.954	-3	OD	-1.7
Total	13	1322	4623	550	1331	180	33	78	525	244	626	.288	.329	.392	105	23	24	563	113	63	-4	.953	-16	OD	-4.9

■ TONY JOHNSON
Johnson, Anthony Clair b: 6/23/56, Memphis, Tenn. BR/TR, 6'3", 145 lbs. Deb: 9/28/81

YEAR	TM/L	G	AB	R	H	2B	3B	HR	RBI	BB	SO	AVG	OBP	SLG	PRO+	BR	/A	RC	SB	CS	SBR	FA	FR	POS	TPR
1981	Mon-N	2	1	0	0	0	0	0	0	0	0	.000	.000	.000	-99	-0	-0	0	0	0	0	.000	0	/O	0.0
1982	Tor-A	70	98	17	23	2	1	3	14	11	26	.235	.312	.367	79	-2	-3	7	3	13	-7	.979	-2	OD	-1.3
Total	2	72	99	17	23	2	1	3	14	11	26	.232	.309	.364	77	-2	-3	7	3	13	-7	.979	-2	/OD	-1.3

■ BOB JOHNSON
Johnson, Bobby Earl b: 7/31/59, Dallas, Tex. BR/TR, 6'3", 195 lbs. Deb: 9/01/81

YEAR	TM/L	G	AB	R	H	2B	3B	HR	RBI	BB	SO	AVG	OBP	SLG	PRO+	BR	/A	RC	SB	CS	SBR	FA	FR	POS	TPR
1981	Tex-A	6	18	2	5	0	0	2	4	1	3	.278	.316	.611	171	1	1	3	0	0	0	1.000	-1	/C1	0.1
1982	Tex-A	20	56	4	7	2	0	2	7	3	22	.125	.183	.268	23	-6	-6	2	0	1	-1	1.000	0	C/1	-0.6
1983	Tex-A	72	175	18	37	6	1	5	16	16	55	.211	.281	.343	72	-7	-7	16	3	0	1	1.000	3	C1	-0.1
Total	3	98	249	24	49	8	1	9	27	20	80	.197	.262	.345	68	-12	-11	21	3	1	0	1.000	3	/C1	-0.6

■ CALEB JOHNSON
Johnson, Caleb Clark b: 5/23/1844, Fulton, Ill. d: 3/7/25, Sterling, Ill. Deb: 5/24/1871

YEAR	TM/L	G	AB	R	H	2B	3B	HR	RBI	BB	SO	AVG	OBP	SLG	PRO+	BR	/A	RC	SB	CS	SBR	FA	FR	POS	TPR
1871	Cle-n	16	67	10	15	1	0	0	7	0	1	.224	.224	.239	35	-6	-5	4	1					/2OS	-0.3

■ CHARLIE JOHNSON
Johnson, Charles Cleveland "Home Run" b: 3/12/1885, Slatington, Pa. d: 8/28/40, Marcus Hook, Pa. BL/TL, 5'9", 150 lbs. Deb: 9/21/08

YEAR	TM/L	G	AB	R	H	2B	3B	HR	RBI	BB	SO	AVG	OBP	SLG	PRO+	BR	/A	RC	SB	CS	SBR	FA	FR	POS	TPR
1908	Phi-N	6	16	2	4	0	1	0	2	1		.250	.333	.375	122	0	0	2	0			1.000	-0	/O	0.0

■ CLIFF JOHNSON
Johnson, Clifford b: 7/22/47, San Antonio, Tex. BR/TR, 6'4", 225 lbs. Deb: 9/13/72

YEAR	TM/L	G	AB	R	H	2B	3B	HR	RBI	BB	SO	AVG	OBP	SLG	PRO+	BR	/A	RC	SB	CS	SBR	FA	FR	POS	TPR
1972	Hou-N	5	4	0	1	0	0	0	0	2	0	.250	.500	.250	121	0	0	1	0	0	0	1.000	1	/C	0.1
1973	Hou-N	7	20	6	6	2	0	2	6	1	7	.300	.364	.700	189	2	2	5	0	0	0	1.000	-0	/1	0.2
1974	Hou-N	83	171	26	39	4	1	10	29	33	45	.228	.362	.439	129	6	7	28	0	1	-1	.978	-4	C1	0.3
1975	Hou-N	122	340	52	94	16	1	20	65	46	64	.276	.371	.506	152	19	22	65	1	0	0	.991	-13	1C/O	0.8
1976	Hou-N	108	318	36	72	21	2	10	49	62	59	.226	.359	.399	126	8	12	48	0	0	0	.977	-13	CO1	-0.1
1977	Hou-N	51	144	22	43	8	0	10	23	23	30	.299	.409	.563	173	12	14	35	0	1	-1	.946	-1	O1	1.1
	NY-A	56	142	24	42	8	0	12	31	20	23	.296	.405	.606	173	14	15	36	0	1	-1	1.000	3	DC1	1.6
1978	NY-A	76	174	20	32	9	1	6	19	30	32	.184	.307	.351	87	-3	-3	19	0	0	0	.975	0	DC/1	-0.2
1979	NY-A	28	64	11	17	6	0	2	6	10	7	.266	.365	.453	122	2	2	11	0	0	0	1.000	0	D/C	0.2
	Cle-A	72	240	37	65	10	0	18	61	24	39	.271	.349	.538	135	11	11	45	2	0	1	.000	-0	D/C	1.1
	Yr	100	304	48	82	16	0	20	67	34	46	.270	.353	.520	132	13	13	57	2	0	1	1.000	-0	D/C	1.3
1980	Cle-A	54	174	25	40	3	1	6	28	25	30	.230	.327	.362	88	-2	-3	19	0	1	-1	.000	0	D	-0.3
	Chi-N	68	196	28	46	8	0	10	34	29	35	.235	.336	.429	104	3	1	29	0	0	0	.992	-6	1/OC	-0.7
1981	Oak-A	84	273	40	71	8	0	17	59	28	60	.260	.336	.476	138	10	12	44	5	3	-0	1.000	-1	D/1	1.1
1982	Oak-A	73	214	19	51	10	0	7	31	26	41	.238	.326	.383	98	-2	-0	27	1	2	-1	.987	1	D1	-0.1
1983	Tor-A	142	407	59	108	23	1	22	76	67	69	.265	.376	.489	128	21	18	76	0	1	-1	1.000	0	*D/1	1.7
1984	Tor-A	127	359	51	109	23	1	16	61	50	62	.304	.393	.507	142	24	22	72	0	1	-1	1.000	-1	*D/1	2.1
1985	Tex-A	82	296	31	76	17	1	12	56	31	44	.257	.333	.443	109	4	3	45	0	0	0	.000	0	D	0.3
	Tor-A	24	73	4	20	0	0	1	10	9	15	.274	.354	.315	83	-1	-1	9	0	0	0	.947	-1	D/1	-0.2
	Yr	106	369	35	96	17	1	13	66	40	59	.260	.337	.417	104	3	2	54	0	0	0	.947	-1	*D/1	0.1
1986	Tor-A	107	336	48	84	12	1	15	55	52	57	.250	.357	.426	109	7	5	52	0	1	-1	1.000	0	D/1	0.5
Total	15	1369	3945	539	1016	188	10	196	699	568	719	.258	.358	.459	125	135	139	667	9	12	-5	.993	-34	D1C/O	9.5

■ DARRELL JOHNSON
Johnson, Darrell Dean b: 8/25/28, Horace, Neb. BR/TR, 6'1", 180 lbs. Deb: 4/20/52 MC

YEAR	TM/L	G	AB	R	H	2B	3B	HR	RBI	BB	SO	AVG	OBP	SLG	PRO+	BR	/A	RC	SB	CS	SBR	FA	FR	POS	TPR
1952	StL-A	29	78	9	22	2	1	0	9	11	4	.282	.371	.333	94	0	-0	10	0	0	0	.990	1	C	0.2
	Chi-A	22	37	3	4	0	0	0	1	5	9	.108	.214	.108	-8	-5	-5	1	1	0	0	.955	5	C	0.0
	Yr	51	115	12	26	2	1	0	10	16	13	.226	.321	.261	62	-5	-6	11	1	0	0	.974	6	C	0.2
1957	NY-A	21	46	4	10	1	0	1	8	3	10	.217	.280	.304	61	-3	-3	4	0	0	0	1.000	4	C	0.2
1958	NY-A	5	16	1	4	0	0	0	0	0	2	.250	.250	.250	39	-1	-1	1	0	0	0	1.000	1	/C	0.0
1960	StL-N	8	2	0	0	0	0	0	0	1	0	.000	.333	.000	1	-0	-0	0	0	0	0	1.000	1	/C	0.1
1961	Phi-N	21	61	4	14	1	0	0	3	3	8	.230	.277	.246	41	-5	-5	4	0	0	0	.982	2	C	-0.2
	*Cin-N	20	54	3	17	2	0	1	6	1	2	.315	.327	.407	92	-1	-1	7	0	0	0	1.000	4	C	0.4
	Yr	41	115	7	31	3	0	1	9	4	10	.270	.300	.322	65	-6	-6	11	0	0	0	.991	6	C	0.2
1962	Cin-N	2	4	0	0	0	0	0	0	2	0	.000	.333	.000	-2	-0	-1	0	0	0	0	1.000	2	/C	0.1
	Bal-A	6	22	0	4	0	0	0	1	0	4	.182	.182	.182	-2	-3	-3	1	0	0	0	1.000	-1	/C	-0.4
Total	6	134	320	24	75	6	1	2	28	26	39	.234	.296	.278	57	-19	-19	28	1	0	0	.988	20	C	0.4

■ DAVEY JOHNSON
Johnson, David Allen b: 1/30/43, Orlando, Fla. BR/TR, 6'1", 180 lbs. Deb: 4/13/65 M

YEAR	TM/L	G	AB	R	H	2B	3B	HR	RBI	BB	SO	AVG	OBP	SLG	PRO+	BR	/A	RC	SB	CS	SBR	FA	FR	POS	TPR
1965	Bal-A	20	47	5	8	3	0	0	1	5	6	.170	.250	.234	38	-4	-4	3	3	0	1	.929	3	/32S	0.0
1966	*Bal-A	131	501	47	129	20	3	7	56	31	64	.257	.302	.351	88	-9	-8	52	3	4	-2	.971	2	*2/S	0.2
1967	Bal-A	148	510	62	126	30	3	10	64	59	82	.247	.330	.376	109	6	6	63	4	5	-2	.981	0	*2/3	1.6
1968	Bal-A★	145	504	50	122	24	4	9	56	44	80	.242	.309	.359	102	1	1	53	7	3	0	.978	4	*2S	1.6
1969	*Bal-A†	142	511	52	143	34	1	7	57	57	52	.280	.356	.391	108	7	6	70	3	4	-2	.984	-3	*2/S	1.3
1970	*Bal-A★	149	530	68	149	27	1	10	53	66	68	.281	.361	.392	106	7	6	77	2	1	0	.990	1	*2/S	1.9
1971	*Bal-A	142	510	67	144	26	1	18	72	51	55	.282	.353	.443	125	16	16	79	3	1	0	.984	-1	*2	2.9
1972	Bal-A	118	376	31	83	22	3	5	32	52	68	.221	.322	.335	93	-1	-2	41	1	1	-0	**.990**	10	*2	1.6
1973	Atl-N★	157	559	84	151	25	0	43	99	81	93	.270	.371	.546	140	38	33	116	5	3	-0	.966	-3	*2	4.0
1974	Atl-N	136	454	56	114	18	0	15	62	75	59	.251	.361	.390	105	8	5	64	1	2	-1	.993	7	12	1.0
1975	Atl-N	1	1	0	1	1	0	0	1	0	0	1.000	1.000	2.000	691	1	1	2	0	0	0	.000	0	H	0.1
1977	*Phi-N	78	156	23	50	9	1	8	36	23	20	.321	.414	.545	148	13	12	35	1	1	-0	1.000	-2	1/23	0.8
1978	Phi-N	44	89	14	17	2	0	2	14	10	19	.191	.287	.281	59	-5	-5	8	0	0	0	.930	-6	2/31	-1.1
	Chi-N	24	49	5	15	1	1	2	6	5	9	.306	.393	.490	130	3	2	10	0	0	0	.839	-3	3	-0.1
	Yr	68	138	19	32	3	1	4	20	15	28	.232	.325	.355	86	-2	-2	17	0	0	0	.844	-9	32/1	-1.2
Total	13	1435	4797	564	1252	242	18	136	609	559	675	.261	.343	.404	110	80	70	673	33	25	-5	.980	10	*21/S3	15.8

■ DERON JOHNSON
Johnson, Deron Roger b: 7/17/38, San Diego, Cal. d: 4/23/92, Poway, Cal. BR/TR, 6'2", 209 lbs. Deb: 9/20/60 C

YEAR	TM/L	G	AB	R	H	2B	3B	HR	RBI	BB	SO	AVG	OBP	SLG	PRO+	BR	/A	RC	SB	CS	SBR	FA	FR	POS	TPR
1960	NY-A	6	4	0	2	1	0	0	0	0	0	.500	.500	.750	247	1	1	2	0	0	0	.750	0	/3	0.1
1961	NY-A	13	19	1	2	0	0	0	2	2	5	.105	.190	.105	-20	-3	-3	0	0	0	0	1.000	2	/3	-0.1
	KC-A	83	283	31	61	11	3	8	42	14	44	.216	.255	.360	62	-16	-16	24	0	1	-1	.948	3	O3/1	-1.7
	Yr	96	302	32	63	11	3	8	44	16	49	.209	.251	.344	58	-19	-19	23	0	1	-1	.948	5	O3/1	-1.8
1962	KC-A	17	19	1	2	1	0	0	0	3	8	.105	.227	.158	6	-3	-3	1	0	0	0	1.000	-1	/13O	-0.4
1964	Cin-N	140	477	63	130	24	4	21	79	37	98	.273	.328	.472	118	13	11	71	4	3	-1	.990	3	*1O/3	0.8
1965	Cin-N	159	616	92	177	30	7	32	**130**	52	97	.287	.345	.515	129	30	25	105	0	4	-2	.948	-12	*3	0.7
1966	Cin-N	142	505	75	130	25	3	24	81	39	87	.257	.313	.461	103	7	2	70	1	2	-1	.980	-13	*O13	-1.9
1967	Cin-N	108	361	39	81	18	1	13	53	22	104	.224	.273	.388	78	-7	-12	36	0	1	-1	.997	-4	13	-2.3
1968	Atl-N	127	342	29	71	11	1	8	33	35	79	.208	.287	.316	81	-8	-8	31	0	1	-1	.996	-1	13	-1.8
1969	Phi-N	138	475	51	121	19	4	17	80	60	111	.255	.338	.419	114	7	8	66	4	2	0	1.000	-15	O31	-1.2
1970	Phi-N	159	574	66	147	28	3	27	93	72	132	.256	.339	.456	114	8	10	89	0	0	0	.995	-11	*1/3	-1.4
1971	Phi-N	158	582	74	154	29	0	34	95	72	146	.265	.348	.490	135	26	26	96	0	1	-1	.995	-4	*13	0.9
1972	Phi-N	96	230	19	49	4	1	9	31	26	69	.213	.301	.357	84	-4	-5	24	0	1	-1	.982	-4	1	-1.6
1973	Phi-N	12	36	3	6	2	0	1	5	5	10	.167	.286	.306	62	-2	-2	3	0	0	0	.976	-0	1	-0.3
	*Oak-A	131	464	61	114	14	2	19	81	59	116	.246	.332	.407	113	4	7	63	0	1	-1	.994	-3	*D1	0.2

YEAR	TM/L	G	AB	R	H	2B	3B	HR	RBI	BB	SO	AVG	OBP	SLG	PRO+	BR	/A	RC	SB	CS	SBR	FA	FR	POS	TPR
1974	Oak-A	50	174	16	34	1	2	7	23	11	37	.195	.243	.345	72	-8	-7	13	1	0	0	.991	-2	1D	-1.1
	Mil-A	49	152	14	23	3	0	6	18	21	41	.151	.254	.289	56	-9	-9	11	1	0	0	.833	-0	D/1	-0.9
	Bos-A	11	25	0	3	0	0	0	2	0	6	.120	.120	.120	-29	-4	-4	0	0	0	0	.000	0	/D	-0.5
	Yr	110	351	30	60	4	2	13	43	32	84	.171	.240	.305	57	-21	-20	25	2	0	1	.983	-3	D1/H	-2.5
1975	Chi-A	148	555	66	129	25	1	18	72	48	117	.232	.295	.378	88	-9	-10	58	0	1	-1	.994	-4	D1	-1.9
	Bos-A	3	10	2	6	0	0	1	3	2	0	.600	.667	.900	313	3	3	6	0	0	0	1.000	-1	/1D	0.3
	Yr	151	565	68	135	25	1	19	75	50	117	.239	.302	.388	92	-6	-7	63	0	1	-1	.994	-5	D1	-1.6
1976	Bos-A	15	38	3	5	1	1	0	0	5	11	.132	.233	.211	27	-3	-4	2	0	0	0	1.000	-0	/1D	-0.5
Total	16	1765	5941	706	1447	247	33	245	923	585	1318	.244	.313	.420	103	22	10	772	11	18	-8	.993	-68	13DO	-14.6

■ DON JOHNSON

Johnson, Donald Spore "Pep" b: 12/7/11, Chicago, Ill. BR/TR, 6', 170 lbs. Deb: 9/26/43 F

YEAR	TM/L	G	AB	R	H	2B	3B	HR	RBI	BB	SO	AVG	OBP	SLG	PRO+	BR	/A	RC	SB	CS	SBR	FA	FR	POS	TPR
1943	Chi-N	10	42	5	8	2	0	0	1	2	4	.190	.227	.238	35	-4	-4	2	0			.957	3	2	0.0
1944	Chi-N☆	154	608	50	169	37	1	2	71	28	48	.278	.311	.352	87	-12	-12	65	8			.947	1	*2	-0.3
1945	*Chi-N†	138	557	94	168	23	2	2	58	32	34	.302	.343	.361	98	-4	-2	70	9			.975	10	*2	1.7
1946	Chi-N	83	314	37	76	10	1	1	19	26	39	.242	.306	.290	71	-12	-12	29	6			.981	-10	2	-1.7
1947	Chi-N	120	402	33	104	17	2	3	26	24	45	.259	.302	.333	71	-18	-16	41	2			.970	-4	*2/3	-1.3
1948	Chi-N	6	12	0	3	0	0	0	0	0	1	.250	.250	.250	37	-1	-1	1	1			1.000	-2	/23	-0.3
Total	6	511	1935	219	528	89	6	8	175	112	171	.273	.315	.337	83	-51	-46	208	26			.947	-2	2/3	-1.9

■ ED JOHNSON

Johnson, Edwin Cyril b: 3/31/1899, Morganfield, Ky. d: 7/3/75, Morganfield, Ky. BL/TR, 5'9", 160 lbs. Deb: 9/26/20

YEAR	TM/L	G	AB	R	H	2B	3B	HR	RBI	BB	SO	AVG	OBP	SLG	PRO+	BR	/A	RC	SB	CS	SBR	FA	FR	POS	TPR
1920	Was-A	4	13	1	3	0	0	0	2	3	2	.231	.375	.231	65	-1	-0	1	0	0	0	.625	-1	/O	-0.1

■ ELMER JOHNSON

Johnson, Elmer Ellsworth "Hickory" b: 6/12/1884, Beard, Ind. d: 10/31/66, Hollywood, Fla. BR/TR, 5'9", 185 lbs. Deb: 4/24/14

YEAR	TM/L	G	AB	R	H	2B	3B	HR	RBI	BB	SO	AVG	OBP	SLG	PRO+	BR	/A	RC	SB	CS	SBR	FA	FR	POS	TPR
1914	NY-N	11	12	0	2	1	0	0	0	1	3	.167	.231	.250	44	-1	-1	1	0			.947	-1	C	-0.2

■ ERNIE JOHNSON

Johnson, Ernest Rudolph b: 4/29/1888, Chicago, Ill. d: 5/1/52, Monrovia, Cal. BL/TR, 5'9", 151 lbs. Deb: 8/05/12 F

YEAR	TM/L	G	AB	R	H	2B	3B	HR	RBI	BB	SO	AVG	OBP	SLG	PRO+	BR	/A	RC	SB	CS	SBR	FA	FR	POS	TPR
1912	Chi-A	21	42	7	11	0	1	0	5	1		.262	.279	.310	70	-2	-2	4	0			.984	3	S	0.2
1915	StL-F	152	512	58	123	18	10	7	67	46	35	.240	.305	.355	89	-5	-8	69	32			.942	18	*S	2.3
1916	StL-A	74	236	29	54	9	3	0	19	30	23	.229	.323	.292	89	-4	-2	27	13			.936	-8	S3	-0.7
1917	StL-A	80	199	28	49	6	2	2	20	12	16	.246	.296	.327	93	-3	-2	23	13			.924	11	S23	1.2
1918	StL-A	29	34	7	9	1	0	0	0	0	2	.265	.286	.294	77	-1	-1	4	4			.821	-2	S/3	-0.3
1921	Chi-A	142	613	93	181	28	7	1	51	29	24	.295	.328	.369	78	-21	-20	73	22	13	-1	.947	18	*S	0.9
1922	Chi-A	144	603	85	153	17	3	0	56	40	30	.254	.304	.292	56	-38	-38	54	21	18	-5	.952	3	*S	-2.4
1923	Chi-A	12	53	5	10	2	0	0	1	3	5	.189	.246	.226	25	-6	-6	3	2	1	0	.922	-0	S	-0.5
	*NY-A	19	38	6	17	1	1	1	8	1	1	.447	.462	.605	176	4	4	10	0	0	0	.977	-1	S/3	0.4
	Yr	31	91	11	27	3	1	1	9	4	6	.297	.333	.385	88	-2	-2	12	2	1	0	.944	-1	S/3	-0.1
1924	NY-A	64	119	24	42	4	8	3	12	11	7	.353	.412	.597	158	10	10	26	1	6	-3	.955	-1	2/S3	0.5
1925	NY-A	76	170	30	48	5	1	5	17	8	10	.282	.315	.412	85	-5	-5	22	6	3	0	.955	-10	2S/3	-1.2
Total	10	813	2619	372	697	91	36	19	256	181	153	.266	.317	.350	82	-72	-70	315	114	41		.944	31	S/23	0.4

■ FRANK JOHNSON

Johnson, Frank Herbert b: 7/22/42, ElPaso, Tex. BR/TR, 6'1", 155 lbs. Deb: 9/07/66

YEAR	TM/L	G	AB	R	H	2B	3B	HR	RBI	BB	SO	AVG	OBP	SLG	PRO+	BR	/A	RC	SB	CS	SBR	FA	FR	POS	TPR
1966	SF-N	15	32	2	7	0	0	0	0	2	7	.219	.265	.219	35	-3	-3	2	0	1	-1	1.000	-1	O	-0.5
1967	SF-N	8	10	3	3	0	0	0	0	1	2	.300	.364	.300	93	-0	-0	1	0	0	0	.889	1	/O	0.1
1968	SF-N	67	174	11	33	2	0	1	7	12	23	.190	.246	.218	40	-12	-12	10	1	0	0	.944	4	3/OS2	-1.0
1969	SF-N	7	10	2	1	0	0	0	0	0	1	.100	.100	.100	-45	-2	-2	0	0	0	0	1.000	0	/O	-0.2
1970	SF-N	67	161	25	44	1	2	3	31	19	18	.273	.357	.360	94	-1	-1	18	1	1	-0	.979	-0	O1	-0.4
1971	SF-N	32	49	4	4	1	0	0	5	3	9	.082	.135	.102	-33	-8	-8	1	0	0	0	.975	-2	/1O	-1.2
Total	6	196	436	47	92	4	2	4	43	37	60	.211	.277	.257	52	-27	-26	31	2	2	-1	.979	2	/O13S2	-3.2

■ HOWARD JOHNSON

Johnson, Howard Michael b: 11/29/60, Clearwater, Fla. BB/TR, 5'11", 178 lbs. Deb: 4/14/82

YEAR	TM/L	G	AB	R	H	2B	3B	HR	RBI	BB	SO	AVG	OBP	SLG	PRO+	BR	/A	RC	SB	CS	SBR	FA	FR	POS	TPR
1982	Det-A	54	155	23	49	5	0	4	14	16	30	.316	.384	.426	122	5	5	25	7	4	-0	.901	-9	3D/O	-0.5
1983	Det-A	27	66	11	14	0	0	3	5	7	10	.212	.297	.348	79	-2	-2	7	0	0	0	.851	-6	3/D	-0.8
1984	*Det-A	116	355	43	88	14	1	12	50	40	67	.248	.326	.394	99	-1	-0	46	10	6	-1	.944	-18	*3/S1OD	-2.0
1985	NY-N	126	389	38	94	18	4	11	46	34	78	.242	.303	.393	96	-4	-3	45	6	4	-1	.941	-13	*3/SO	-1.8
1986	*NY-N	88	220	30	54	14	0	10	39	31	64	.245	.341	.445	119	4	5	36	8	1	2	.903	-2	3S/O	0.7
1987	NY-N	157	554	93	147	22	1	36	99	83	113	.265	.366	.504	135	22	26	106	32	10	4	.938	-18	*3S/O	1.2
1988	*NY-N	148	495	85	114	21	1	24	68	86	104	.230	.348	.422	126	14	17	78	23	7	3	.951	-14	*3/S	0.9
1989	NY-N★	153	571	**104**	164	41	3	36	101	77	126	.287	.373	.559	171	46	49	127	41	8	8	.910	-33	*3S	2.8
1990	NY-N	154	590	89	144	37	3	23	90	69	100	.244	.323	.434	107	4	4	87	34	8	5	.913	-5	3S	1.1
1991	NY-N★	156	564	108	146	34	4	**38**	**117**	78	120	.259	.350	.535	147	33	33	107	30	16	-1	.927	-4	*3OS	3.1
1992	NY-N	100	350	48	78	19	0	7	43	55	79	.223	.332	.337	90	-3	-3	43	22	5	4	.981	-4	O	-0.6
Total	11	1279	4309	672	1092	225	17	204	672	576	891	.253	.344	.456	124	118	132	708	213	69	23	.928	-124	3SO/D1	4.1

■ SPUD JOHNSON

Johnson, John Ralph b: 1860, Canada BL/TL, 5'9", 175 lbs. Deb: 4/18/1889

YEAR	TM/L	G	AB	R	H	2B	3B	HR	RBI	BB	SO	AVG	OBP	SLG	PRO+	BR	/A	RC	SB	CS	SBR	FA	FR	POS	TPR
1889	Col-a	116	459	91	130	14	10	2	79	39	47	.283	.355	.370	114	6	10	74	34			.879	-11	O3/1S	-0.1
1890	Col-a	135	538	106	186	23	18	1		48		.346	.409	.461	171	39	45	122	43			.926	-16	*O	2.2
1891	Cle-N	80	327	49	84	8	3	1	46	22	23	.257	.319	.309	82	-6	-8	38	16			.872	-5	O/1	-1.4
Total	3	331	1324	246	400	45	31	4	125	109	70	.302	.368	.392	128	40	48	235	93			.899	-32	O/31S	0.7

■ LANCE JOHNSON

Johnson, Kenneth Lance b: 7/6/63, Cincinnati, Ohio BL/TL, 5'10", 160 lbs. Deb: 7/10/87

YEAR	TM/L	G	AB	R	H	2B	3B	HR	RBI	BB	SO	AVG	OBP	SLG	PRO+	BR	/A	RC	SB	CS	SBR	FA	FR	POS	TPR
1987	*StL-N	33	59	4	13	2	1	0	7	4	6	.220	.270	.288	47	-4	-5	5	6	1	1	.931	-6	O	-1.0
1988	Chi-A	33	124	11	23	4	1	0	6	6	11	.185	.223	.234	28	-12	-12	7	6	2	1	.970	-4	O/D	-1.6
1989	Chi-A	50	180	28	54	8	2	0	16	17	24	.300	.360	.367	108	2	2	27	16	3	3	.983	0	O/D	0.4
1990	Chi-A	151	541	76	154	18	9	1	51	33	45	.285	.327	.357	93	-7	-5	59	36	22	-2	.973	-2	*O/D	-1.3
1991	Chi-A	159	588	72	161	14	**13**	0	49	26	58	.274	.306	.342	81	-17	-16	59	26	11	1	.995	13	*O	-0.5
1992	Chi-A	157	567	67	158	15	**12**	3	47	34	33	.279	.321	.363	93	-7	-6	62	41	14	4	.987	8	*O	0.3
Total	6	583	2059	258	563	61	38	4	176	120	177	.273	.314	.346	86	-46	-40	219	131	53	8	.984	11	O/D	-3.7

■ LAMAR JOHNSON

Johnson, Lamar b: 9/2/50, Bessemer, Ala. BR/TR, 6'2", 225 lbs. Deb: 5/18/74

YEAR	TM/L	G	AB	R	H	2B	3B	HR	RBI	BB	SO	AVG	OBP	SLG	PRO+	BR	/A	RC	SB	CS	SBR	FA	FR	POS	TPR
1974	Chi-A	10	29	1	10	0	0	0	2	0	3	.345	.345	.345	97	-0	-0	2	0	0	0	1.000	-0	/1D	-0.1
1975	Chi-A	8	30	2	6	3	0	1	1	1	5	.200	.226	.400	73	-1	-1	3	0	0	0	.960	-1	/1D	-0.3
1976	Chi-A	82	222	29	71	11	1	4	33	19	37	.320	.379	.432	136	10	10	34	2	1	0	.983	-1	D1/O	0.8
1977	Chi-A	118	374	52	113	12	5	18	65	24	53	.302	.344	.505	128	13	13	59	1	1	-0	.990	1	D1	1.2
1978	Chi-A	148	498	52	136	23	2	8	72	43	46	.273	.333	.376	98	-1	-1	59	6	5	-1	.992	2	*1D	-0.7
1979	Chi-A	133	479	60	148	29	1	12	74	41	56	.309	.366	.449	118	12	12	73	8	2	1	.987	-1	1D	0.7
1980	Chi-A	147	541	51	150	26	3	13	81	47	53	.277	.335	.409	103	2	2	71	2	3	-1	.990	2	1D	-0.1
1981	Chi-A	41	134	10	37	7	0	1	15	5	14	.276	.302	.351	89	-2	-2	12	0	2	-1	.989	-2	1/D	-0.8
1982	Tex-A	105	324	37	84	11	0	7	38	31	40	.259	.326	.358	92	-5	-3	35	3	5	-2	.982	-2	D1	-0.7
Total	9	792	2631	294	755	122	12	64	381	211	307	.287	.342	.415	109	28	30	349	22	19	-5	.989	-1	1D/O	0.0

■ LARRY JOHNSON

Johnson, Larry Doby b: 8/17/50, Cleveland, Ohio BR/TR, 6', 185 lbs. Deb: 10/03/72

YEAR	TM/L	G	AB	R	H	2B	3B	HR	RBI	BB	SO	AVG	OBP	SLG	PRO+	BR	/A	RC	SB	CS	SBR	FA	FR	POS	TPR
1972	Cle-A	1	2	0	1	0	0	0	0	0	1	.500	.500	.500	192	0	0	1	0	0	0	1.000	0	/C	0.1
1974	Cle-A	1	0	1	0	0	0	0	0	0	0	—	—	—	—	0	0	0	0	0	0	.000	0	R	0.0
1975	Mon-N	1	3	0	1	1	0	0	1	1	1	.333	.500	.667	212	1	1	1	0	0	0	1.000	-0	/C	0.1
1976	Mon-N	6	13	0	2	1	0	0	0	0	2	.154	.154	.231	8	-2	-2	1	0	0	0	1.000	1	/C	-0.1

YEAR	TM/L	G	AB	R	H	2B	3B	HR	RBI	BB	SO	AVG	OBP	SLG	PRO+	BR	/A	RC	SB	CS	SBR	FA	FR	POS	TPR
1978	Chi-A	3	8	0	1	0	0	0	0	1	4	.125	.222	.125	0	-1	-1	0	0	0	0	.857	-0	/CD	-0.2
Total	5	12	26	1	5	2	0	0	1	2	8	.192	.250	.269	46	-2	-2	2	0	0	0	.975	1	/CD	-0.1

■ **LOU JOHNSON** Johnson, Louis Brown "Slick" b: 9/22/34, Lexington, Ky. BR/TR, 5'11", 175 lbs. Deb: 4/17/60

YEAR	TM/L	G	AB	R	H	2B	3B	HR	RBI	BB	SO	AVG	OBP	SLG	PRO+	BR	/A	RC	SB	CS	SBR	FA	FR	POS	TPR
1960	Chi-N	34	68	6	14	2	1	0	1	5	19	.206	.270	.265	48	-5	-5	5	3	1	0	1.000	1	O	-0.4
1961	LA-A	1	0	0	0	0	0	0	0	0	0	—	—	—	—	0	0	0	0	0	0	.000	-0	/O	0.0
1962	Mil-N	61	117	22	33	4	5	2	13	11	27	.282	.349	.453	116	2	3	20	6	1	1	1.000	0	O	0.2
1965	*LA-N	131	468	57	121	24	1	12	58	24	81	.259	.317	.391	105	-1	2	58	15	6	1	.985	-7	*O	-1.0
1966	*LA-N	152	526	71	143	20	2	17	73	21	75	.272	.317	.414	110	0	5	63	8	10	-4	.985	2	*O	-0.3
1967	LA-N	104	330	39	89	14	1	11	41	24	52	.270	.332	.418	124	6	9	44	4	3	-1	.976	-1	O	0.3
1968	Chi-N	62	205	14	50	14	3	1	14	6	23	.244	.289	.356	87	-2	-4	20	3	1	0	.970	-6	O	-1.4
	Cle-A	65	202	25	52	11	1	5	23	9	24	.257	.302	.396	112	2	2	24	6	1	1	.989	1	O	0.2
1969	Cal-A	67	133	10	27	8	0	0	9	10	19	.203	.274	.263	53	-9	-8	10	5	1	1	.935	-5	O	-1.5
Total	8	677	2049	244	529	97	14	48	232	110	320	.258	.313	.389	103	-7	4	244	50	24	1	.981	-14	O	-3.9

■ **OTIS JOHNSON** Johnson, Otis L. b: 11/5/1883, Fowler, Ind. d: 11/9/15, Johnson City, N.Y. BB/TR, 5'9", 185 lbs. Deb: 4/12/11

YEAR	TM/L	G	AB	R	H	2B	3B	HR	RBI	BB	SO	AVG	OBP	SLG	PRO+	BR	/A	RC	SB	CS	SBR	FA	FR	POS	TPR
1911	NY-A	71	209	21	49	9	6	3	36	39		.234	.363	.378	100	3	1	34	12			.907	-9	S2/3	-0.6

■ **PAUL JOHNSON** Johnson, Paul Oscar b: 9/2/1896, N.Grosvenordale, Conn. d: 2/14/73, McAllen, Tex. BR/TR, 5'8", 160 lbs. Deb: 9/13/20

YEAR	TM/L	G	AB	R	H	2B	3B	HR	RBI	BB	SO	AVG	OBP	SLG	PRO+	BR	/A	RC	SB	CS	SBR	FA	FR	POS	TPR
1920	Phi-A	18	72	6	15	0	0	0	5	4	8	.208	.250	.208	22	-8	-8	4	1	1	-0	.933	-3	O	-1.2
1921	Phi-A	48	127	17	40	6	2	1	10	9	17	.315	.360	.417	97	-1	-1	18	0	2	-1	.969	-5	O	-0.8
Total	2	66	199	23	55	6	2	1	15	13	25	.276	.321	.342	71	-8	-9	22	1	3	-2	.958	-7	/O	-2.0

■ **RANDY JOHNSON** Johnson, Randall Glenn b: 6/10/56, Escondido, Cal. BR/TR, 6'1", 190 lbs. Deb: 4/27/82

YEAR	TM/L	G	AB	R	H	2B	3B	HR	RBI	BB	SO	AVG	OBP	SLG	PRO+	BR	/A	RC	SB	CS	SBR	FA	FR	POS	TPR
1982	Atl-N	27	46	5	11	5	0	0	6	6	4	.239	.352	.348	93	0	-0	6	0	1	-1	.955	5	2/3	0.5
1983	Atl-N	86	144	22	36	3	0	1	17	20	27	.250	.345	.292	73	-3	-5	15	1	3	-2	.991	10	3/2	0.3
1984	Atl-N	91	294	28	82	13	0	5	30	21	21	.279	.329	.374	91	-1	-4	35	4	7	-3	.939	5	3	-0.3
Total	3	204	484	55	129	21	0	6	53	47	52	.267	.336	.347	85	-5	-9	56	5	11	-5	.842	20	3/2	0.5

■ **RANDY JOHNSON** Johnson, Randall Stuart b: 8/15/58, Miami, Fla. BL/TL, 6'2", 195 lbs. Deb: 7/05/80

YEAR	TM/L	G	AB	R	H	2B	3B	HR	RBI	BB	SO	AVG	OBP	SLG	PRO+	BR	/A	RC	SB	CS	SBR	FA	FR	POS	TPR
1980	Chi-A	12	20	0	4	0	0	0	3	2	4	.200	.304	.200	41	-2	-1	2	0	0	0	.000	-0	/1OD	-0.2
1982	Min-A	89	234	26	58	10	0	10	33	30	46	.248	.333	.419	102	2	1	34	0	0	0	1.000	-0	D/O	0.0
Total	2	101	254	26	62	10	0	10	36	32	50	.244	.331	.402	98	0	-1	36	0	0	0	.956	-1	/DO1	-0.2

■ **FOOTER JOHNSON** Johnson, Richard Allan "Treads" b: 2/15/32, Dayton, Ohio BL/TL, 5'11", 175 lbs. Deb: 6/22/58

YEAR	TM/L	G	AB	R	H	2B	3B	HR	RBI	BB	SO	AVG	OBP	SLG	PRO+	BR	/A	RC	SB	CS	SBR	FA	FR	POS	TPR
1958	Chi-N	8	5	1	0	0	0	0	0	0	1	.000	.000	.000	-99	-1	-1	0	0	0	0	.000	0	H	-0.1

■ **BOB JOHNSON** Johnson, Robert Lee "Indian Bob" b: 11/26/06, Pryor, Okla. d: 7/6/82, Tacoma, Wash. BR/TR, 6', 180 lbs. Deb: 4/12/33 F

YEAR	TM/L	G	AB	R	H	2B	3B	HR	RBI	BB	SO	AVG	OBP	SLG	PRO+	BR	/A	RC	SB	CS	SBR	FA	FR	POS	TPR
1933	Phi-A	142	535	103	155	44	4	21	93	85	74	.290	.387	.505	133	27	26	109	8	3	1	.952	2	*O	2.0
1934	Phi-A	141	547	111	168	26	6	34	92	58	60	.307	.375	.563	144	29	31	114	12	8	-1	.967	10	*O	3.2
1935	Phi-A★	147	582	103	174	29	5	28	109	78	76	.299	.384	.510	130	25	25	116	2	4	-2	.946	4	*O	2.0
1936	Phi-A	153	566	91	165	29	14	25	121	88	71	.292	.389	.525	126	20	22	118	6	6	-2	.962	3	*O2/1	1.6
1937	Phi-A	138	477	91	146	32	6	25	108	98	65	.306	.425	.556	148	35	36	117	9	7	-2	.976	9	*O/2	3.6
1938	Phi-A★	152	563	114	176	27	9	30	113	87	73	.313	.406	.552	142	33	35	128	9	8	-2	.963	10	*O/23	3.5
1939	Phi-A☆	150	544	115	184	30	9	23	114	99	59	.338	.440	.553	156	46	48	138	15	5	2	.967	7	*O/2	4.6
1940	Phi-A☆	138	512	93	137	25	4	31	103	83	64	.268	.374	.514	130	21	22	100	8	2	1	.962	5	*O	2.1
1941	Phi-A	149	552	98	152	30	8	22	107	95	75	.275	.385	.478	130	22	24	106	6	4	-1	.990	7	*O1	2.0
1942	Phi-A★	149	550	78	160	35	7	13	80	82	61	.291	.384	.451	135	26	26	99	3	2	-0	.963	5	*O	2.4
1943	Was-A★	117	438	65	116	22	8	7	63	64	50	.265	.362	.400	127	14	15	67	11	5	0	.996	9	O31	2.1
1944	Bos-A★	144	525	106	170	40	8	17	106	95	67	.324	**.431**	.528	**175**	**53**	**54**	124	2	7	-4	.977	4	*O	4.8
1945	Bos-A†	143	529	71	148	27	7	12	74	63	56	.280	.358	.425	124	17	16	83	5	3	-0	.975	3	*O	1.2
Total	13	1863	6920	1239	2051	396	95	288	1283	1075	851	.296	.393	.506	139	366	381	1418	96	64	-10	.952	79	*O/123	35.1

■ **BOB JOHNSON** Johnson, Robert Wallace b: 3/4/36, Omaha, Neb. BR/TR, 5'10", 175 lbs. Deb: 4/19/60

YEAR	TM/L	G	AB	R	H	2B	3B	HR	RBI	BB	SO	AVG	OBP	SLG	PRO+	BR	/A	RC	SB	CS	SBR	FA	FR	POS	TPR
1960	KC-A	76	146	12	30	4	0	1	9	19	23	.205	.301	.253	51	-9	-10	11	2	0	1	.947	12	S23	0.6
1961	Was-A	61	224	27	66	13	1	6	28	19	26	.295	.352	.442	113	3	4	32	4	2	0	.956	-2	S/23	0.6
1962	Was-A	135	466	58	134	20	2	12	43	32	50	.288	.335	.416	102	-0	0	59	9	6	-1	.944	-4	3S/2O	0.1
1963	Bal-A	82	254	34	75	10	0	8	32	18	35	.295	.347	.429	119	5	6	39	5	1	1	.987	-2	2/1S3	1.0
1964	Bal-A	93	210	18	52	8	2	3	29	9	37	.248	.282	.348	74	-8	-8	19	0	0	0	.964	-12	S12/3O	-1.9
1965	Bal-A	87	273	36	66	13	2	5	27	15	34	.242	.284	.359	80	-7	-8	26	1	0	0	.996	-11	1S3/2	-2.0
1966	Bal-A	71	157	13	34	5	0	1	10	12	24	.217	.276	.268	58	-9	-8	11	0	1	-1	.966	0	21/3	-0.9
1967	Bal-A	4	3	1	1	0	0	0	0	1	1	.333	.500	.333	152	0	0	1	0	0	0	.000	0	H	0.0
	NY-N	90	230	26	80	8	3	5	27	12	29	.348	.380	.474	145	12	13	39	1	1	-0	.987	-7	21S/3	0.7
1968	Cin-N	16	15	2	4	0	0	0	1	1	2	.267	.313	.267	71	-0	-1	1	0	0	0	.500	-1	/S1	-0.1
	Atl-N	59	187	15	49	5	1	0	11	10	20	.262	.299	.299	80	-4	-5	16	0	0	0	.948	1	3/2	-0.3
	Yr	75	202	17	53	5	1	0	12	11	22	.262	.300	.297	79	-5	-5	17	0	0	0	.948	1	3/2S1	-0.4
1969	StL-N	19	29	1	6	0	0	1	2	2	4	.207	.258	.310	58	-2	-2	2	0	0	0	.833	-1	/31	-0.3
	Oak-A	51	67	5	23	1	0	1	9	3	4	.343	.380	.403	125	2	2	11	0	0	0	1.000	0	/12	0.2
1970	Oak-A	30	46	6	8	1	0	1	2	3	2	.174	.240	.261	39	-4	-4	3	2	1	0	.952	1	/31	-0.3
Total	11	874	2307	254	628	88	11	44	230	156	291	.272	.321	.377	95	-21	-19	269	24	12	0	.968	-26	S231/O	-2.6

■ **RON JOHNSON** Johnson, Ronald David b: 3/23/56, Long Beach, Cal. BR/TR, 6'3", 215 lbs. Deb: 9/12/82

YEAR	TM/L	G	AB	R	H	2B	3B	HR	RBI	BB	SO	AVG	OBP	SLG	PRO+	BR	/A	RC	SB	CS	SBR	FA	FR	POS	TPR
1982	KC-A	8	14	2	4	2	0	0	0	4	3	.286	.444	.429	141	1	1	3	0	0	0	.976	-0	/1	0.0
1983	KC-A	9	27	2	7	0	0	0	1	3	1	.259	.333	.259	66	-1	-1	3	0	0	0	.971	-1	/1C	-0.3
1984	Mon-N	5	5	0	1	0	0	0	1	0	2	.200	.200	.200	13	-1	-1	0	0	0	0	1.000	-1	/1O	-0.1
Total	3	22	46	4	12	2	0	0	2	7	6	.261	.358	.304	85	-1	-1	6	0	0	0	.974	-2	/1CO	-0.4

■ **RONDIN JOHNSON** Johnson, Rondin Allen b: 12/16/58, Bremerton, Wash. BB/TR, 5'10", 160 lbs. Deb: 9/03/86

YEAR	TM/L	G	AB	R	H	2B	3B	HR	RBI	BB	SO	AVG	OBP	SLG	PRO+	BR	/A	RC	SB	CS	SBR	FA	FR	POS	TPR
1986	KC-A	11	31	1	8	0	1	0	2	0	3	.258	.258	.323	56	-2	-2	3	0	0	0	1.000	4	2	0.2

■ **ROY JOHNSON** Johnson, Roy Cleveland b: 2/23/03, Pryor, Okla. d: 9/10/73, Tacoma, Wash. BL/TR, 5'9", 175 lbs. Deb: 4/18/29 F

YEAR	TM/L	G	AB	R	H	2B	3B	HR	RBI	BB	SO	AVG	OBP	SLG	PRO+	BR	/A	RC	SB	CS	SBR	FA	FR	POS	TPR
1929	Det-A	148	640	128	201	**45**	14	10	69	67	60	.314	.379	.475	118	17	17	114	20	15	-3	.928	14	*O	1.7
1930	Det-A	125	462	84	127	30	13	2	35	40	46	.275	.333	.409	85	-10	-11	63	17	10	-1	.936	4	*O	-1.4
1931	Det-A	151	621	107	173	37	**19**	8	55	72	51	.279	.355	.438	104	6	3	96	33	21	-3	.960	15	*O	0.5
1932	Det-A	49	195	33	49	14	2	3	22	20	26	.251	.324	.390	81	-5	-6	26	7	2	1	.929	0	O	-0.7
	Bos-A	94	349	70	104	24	4	11	47	44	41	.298	.378	.484	125	11	13	66	13	4	2	.930	-6	O	0.3
	Yr	143	544	103	153	38	6	14	69	64	67	.281	.359	.450	109	6	7	91	20	6	2	.930	-5	*O	-0.4
1933	Bos-A	133	483	88	151	30	7	10	95	55	36	.313	.387	.466	126	18	19	88	13	10	-2	.922	4	*O	1.3
1934	Bos-A	143	569	85	182	43	10	7	119	54	36	.320	.379	.467	109	14	8	102	11	5	0	.948	-3	*O	-0.1
1935	Bos-A	145	553	70	174	33	9	3	66	74	34	.315	.398	.423	105	13	7	95	11	12	-4	.944	-2	*O	-0.3
1936	*NY-A	63	147	21	39	8	2	1	19	21	14	.265	.361	.367	83	-4	-3	21	3	1	0	.944	0	O	-0.4
1937	NY-A	12	51	5	15	3	0	0	6	3	2	.294	.333	.353	73	-2	-2	6	1	0	0	.840	-2	O	-0.4
	Bos-N	85	260	24	72	8	3	3	22	38	29	.277	.369	.365	110	1	5	37	5			.965	-1	O/3	0.2
1938	Bos-N	7	29	2	5	0	0	0	1	1	5	.172	.200	.172	4	-4	-3	1	1			.769	-2	/O	-0.6
Total	10	1155	4359	717	1292	275	83	58	556	489	380	.296	.369	.437	107	55	45	715	135	80		.938	22	*O/3	0.1

YEAR	TM/L	G	AB	R	H	2B	3B	HR	RBI	BB	SO	AVG	OBP	SLG	PRO+	BR	/A	RC	SB	CS	SBR	FA	FR	POS	TPR

■ ROY JOHNSON Johnson, Roy Edward b: 6/27/59, Parkin, Ark. BL/TL, 6'4", 205 lbs. Deb: 7/03/82

1982	Mon-N	17	32	2	7	2	0	0	2	1	6	.219	.242	.281	45	-2	-2	2	0	0	0	1.000	1	O	-0.2
1984	Mon-N	16	33	2	5	2	0	1	2	7	10	.152	.300	.303	73	-1	-1	4	1	0	0	.938	-1	O	-0.2
1985	Mon-N	3	5	0	0	0	0	0	0	0	3	.000	.000	.000	-99	-1	-1	0	0	0	0	.000	-1	O	-0.3
Total	3	36	70	4	12	4	0	1	4	8	19	.171	.256	.271	49	-5	-5	6	1	0	0	.971	-2	/O	-0.7

■ STAN JOHNSON Johnson, Stanley Lucius b: 2/12/37, Dallas, Tex. BL/TL, 5'10", 180 lbs. Deb: 9/18/60

1960	Chi-A	5	6	1	1	0	0	1	1	0	1	.167	.167	.667	116	0	0	0	0	1	-1	1.000	-1	/O	-0.1
1961	KC-A	3	3	1	0	0	0	0	0	2	1	.000	.400	.000	17	-0	-0	0	0	0	0	.000	-1	/O	-0.1
Total	2	8	9	2	1	0	0	1	1	2	2	.111	.273	.444	90	-0	-0	0	0	1	-1	1.000	-2	/O	-0.2

■ TIM JOHNSON Johnson, Timothy Evald b: 7/22/49, Grand Forks, N.D. BL/TR, 6'1", 170 lbs. Deb: 4/24/73

1973	Mil-A	136	465	39	99	10	2	0	32	29	93	.213	.261	.243	44	-35	-34	30	6	3	0	.962	-18	*S	-3.6
1974	Mil-A	93	245	25	60	7	7	0	25	11	48	.245	.280	.331	76	-8	-8	23	4	3	-1	.970	-2	S2/3OD	-0.3
1975	Mil-A	38	85	6	12	1	0	0	2	6	17	.141	.198	.153	0	-11	-11	3	3	0	1	1.000	1	23S/1D	-0.8
1976	Mil-A	105	273	25	75	4	3	0	14	19	32	.275	.327	.311	89	-4	-3	28	4	1	1	.980	-18	*23/1S	-1.7
1977	Mil-A	30	33	5	2	1	0	0	2	5	10	.061	.184	.091	-22	-6	-6	1	1	0	0	.929	3	2/S3OD	-0.2
1978	Mil-A	3	3	1	0	0	0	0	0	2	0	.000	.400	.000	22	-0	-0	0	0	0	0	1.000	-1	/S	-0.1
	Tor-A	68	79	9	19	2	0	0	3	8	16	.241	.318	.266	65	-3	-3	7	0	1	-1	.975	5	S2	0.4
	Yr	71	82	10	19	2	0	0	3	10	16	.232	.323	.256	63	-3	-4	8	0	1	-1	.975	4	S2	0.3
1979	Tor-A	43	86	6	16	2	1	0	6	8	15	.186	.255	.233	32	-8	-8	5	0	1	-1	.958	6	2/31	-0.2
Total	7	516	1269	116	283	27	13	0	84	88	231	.223	.276	.265	55	-76	-74	98	18	9	0	.965	-25	S2/31DO	-6.5

■ WALLACE JOHNSON Johnson, Wallace Darnell b: 12/25/56, Gary, Ind. BB/TR, 5'11", 185 lbs. Deb: 9/08/81

1981	*Mon-N	11	9	1	2	0	1	0	3	1	1	.222	.300	.444	108	0	0	0	1	1	-0	1.000	1	/2	0.1
1982	Mon-N	36	57	5	11	0	2	0	2	5	5	.193	.258	.263	45	-4	-4	4	4	1	1	.952	-6	2	-0.9
1983	Mon-N	3	2	1	1	0	0	0	0	1	0	.500	.667	.500	229	1	1	1	1	0	0	.000	0	/H	0.1
	SF-N	7	8	0	1	0	0	0	1	0	0	.125	.125	.125	-32	-1	-1	0	0	0	0	1.000	1	/2	-0.1
	Yr	10	10	1	2	0	0	0	1	1	0	.200	.273	.200	34	-1	-1	1	1	0	0	1.000	1	/2	0.0
1984	Mon-N	17	24	3	5	0	0	0	4	5	4	.208	.345	.208	61	-1	-1	2	0	0	0	.968	0	/1	-0.1
1986	Mon-N	61	127	13	36	3	1	1	10	7	9	.283	.321	.346	85	-3	-3	14	6	3	0	.991	-0	1	-0.5
1987	Mon-N	75	85	7	21	5	0	1	14	7	6	.247	.304	.341	69	-4	-4	10	5	0	2	.972	-1	/1	-0.4
1988	Mon-N	86	94	7	29	5	1	0	3	12	15	.309	.387	.383	116	3	3	14	0	2	-1	.989	1	1/2	0.2
1989	Mon-N	85	114	9	31	3	1	2	17	7	12	.272	.314	.368	93	-1	-1	13	1	0	0	.972	-1	/1	-0.4
1990	Mon-N	47	49	6	8	1	0	1	5	7	6	.163	.281	.245	48	-4	-3	4	1	0	0	1.000	-1	/1	-0.5
Total	9	428	569	52	145	17	6	5	59	52	58	.255	.318	.332	81	-14	-14	63	19	7	2	.983	-7	/12	-2.5

■ WALTER JOHNSON Johnson, Walter Perry "Barney" or "The Big Train"
b: 11/6/1887, Humboldt, Kan. d: 12/10/46, Washington, D.C. BR/TR, 6'1", 200 lbs. Deb: 8/02/07 MH

1907	Was-A	14	36	3	4	0	1	0	1	1		.111	.135	.167	-4	-4	-4	1	0			.893	-2	P	0.0
1908	Was-A	36	79	7	13	3	2	0	5	6		.165	.250	.253	69	-3	-2	5	0			.938	-4	P	0.0
1909	Was-A	40	101	6	13	3	0	1	6	1		.129	.137	.188	3	-11	-11	2	0			.926	-2	P	0.0
1910	Was-A	45	137	14	24	6	1	2	12	4		.175	.199	.277	51	-9	-8	7	2			.950	-1	P	0.0
1911	Was-A	42	128	18	30	5	3	1	15	0		.234	.234	.344	62	-8	-7	10	1			.965	4	P	0.0
1912	Was-A	55	144	16	38	6	4	2	20	7		.264	.298	.403	99	-1	-1	18	2			.964	1	P	0.0
1913	Was-A	54	134	12	35	5	6	2	14	5	14	.261	.293	.433	109	1	0	16	2			1.000	-0	P/O	0.0
1914	Was-A	55	136	23	30	4	1	3	16	10	27	.221	.274	.331	79	-4	-4	13	2	1	0	.964	2	P/O	-0.1
1915	Was-A	64	147	14	34	7	4	2	17	8	34	.231	.276	.374	93	-2	-3	15	0	2	-1	.951	0	P/O	-0.2
1916	Was-A	58	142	13	32	2	4	1	7	11	28	.225	.286	.317	82	-4	-4	13	0			.937	-5	P	0.0
1917	Was-A	57	130	15	33	12	1	0	15	9	30	.254	.312	.362	107	0	1	14	1			1.000	-1	P	0.0
1918	Was-A	65	150	10	40	4	4	1	18	9	18	.267	.321	.367	109	1	1	18	2			.988	-3	P/O	0.0
1919	Was-A	56	125	13	24	1	3	1	8	12	17	.192	.263	.272	51	-8	-8	9	1			.988	-0	P/O	-0.1
1920	Was-A	33	64	6	17	1	3	1	7	3	10	.266	.299	.422	92	-1	-1	8	0	0	0	.971	-1	P	0.0
1921	Was-A	38	111	10	30	7	0	0	10	6	14	.270	.308	.333	67	-6	-5	11	0	0	0	.982	-3	P	0.0
1922	Was-A	43	108	8	22	3	0	1	15	2	12	.204	.218	.259	25	-12	-12	6	0	0	0	1.000	1	P	0.0
1923	Was-A	42	93	11	18	3	3	0	13	4	15	.194	.227	.290	37	-9	-8	6	0	0	0	.970	-2	P	0.0
1924	*Was-A	39	113	18	32	9	0	1	14	3	11	.283	.308	.389	82	-4	-4	13	0	0	0	1.000	-1	P	0.0
1925	*Was-A	36	97	12	42	6	1	2	20	3	6	.433	.455	.577	164	9	9	24	0	1	-1	1.000	-4	P	0.0
1926	Was-A	35	103	6	20	5	0	1	12	3	11	.194	.217	.272	28	-11	-11	6	0	0	0	.980	-5	P	0.0
1927	Was-A	26	46	6	16	2	0	2	10	3	4	.348	.388	.522	136	2	2	9	0	0	0	1.000	0	P	0.0
Total	21	933	2324	241	547	94	41	24	255	110	251	.235	.274	.342	76	-86	-80	228	13	4		.969	-25	P/O	-0.4

■ BILL JOHNSON Johnson, William F. "Sleepy Bill" b: 9/1862, New Jersey d: 7/17/42, Chester,Pa. BL/TL, 140 lbs. Deb: 6/27/1884

1884	Phi-U	1	4	0	0	0	0	0		0		.000	.000	.000	-99	-1	-1	0				.000	-0	/O	-0.1
1887	Ind-N	11	42	3	8	0	0	0	3	0	6	.190	.209	.190	13	-5	-5	3	5			.765	-2	O	-0.6
1890	Bal-a	24	95	15	28	2	3	0		7		.295	.350	.379	112	2	1	16	8			.865	2	O	0.2
1891	Bal-a	129	480	101	130	13	14	2	79	89	55	.271	.389	.369	119	16	15	83	32			.877	6	*O	1.4
1892	Bal-N	4	15	2	2	0	0	0	2	2	0	.133	.235	.133	13	-1	-2	0	0			.667	-1	/O	-0.3
Total	5	169	636	121	168	15	17	2	84	98	61	.264	.368	.351	108	11	10	102	45			1.000	5	O	0.6

■ BILL JOHNSON Johnson, William Lawrence b: 10/18/1892, Chicago, Ill. d: 11/3/50, Los Angeles, Cal. BL/TR, 5'11", 170 lbs. Deb: 9/22/16

1916	Phi-A	4	15	1	4	1	0	0	1	0	4	.267	.267	.333	84	-0	-0	1	0			1.000	-1	/O	-0.2
1917	Phi-A	48	109	7	19	2	2	1	8	8	14	.174	.237	.257	51	-7	-7	8	4			.900	-3	O	-1.2
Total	2	52	124	8	23	3	2	1	9	8	18	.185	.241	.266	55	-7	-7	9	4			.867	-4	/O	-1.4

■ BILLY JOHNSON Johnson, William Russell "Bull" b: 8/30/18, Montclair, N.J. BR/TR, 5'10", 180 lbs. Deb: 4/22/43

1943	*NY-A	155	592	70	166	24	6	5	94	53	30	.280	.344	.367	107	6	5	71	3	5	-2	.966	12	*3	1.8
1946	NY-A	85	296	51	77	14	5	4	35	31	42	.260	.334	.382	98	-0	-1	40	1	0	0	.955	7	3	0.8
1947	*NY-A★	132	494	67	141	19	8	10	95	44	42	.285	.351	.417	114	8	8	69	1	2	-1	.952	-17	*3	-0.9
1948	NY-A	127	446	59	131	20	6	12	64	41	30	.294	.358	.446	114	7	7	68	0	2	0	.947	6	*3	1.2
1949	*NY-A	113	329	48	82	11	3	8	56	48	44	.249	.348	.374	91	-4	-4	43	1	0	0	.951	-2	31/2	-0.8
1950	*NY-A	108	327	44	85	16	2	6	40	42	30	.260	.346	.376	87	-8	-6	43	1	0	0	.958	-1	*3/1	-0.8
1951	NY-A	15	40	5	12	3	0	0	4	7	0	.300	.404	.375	116	1	1	6	0	1	-1	.960	-3	3	-0.2
	StL-N	124	442	52	116	23	1	14	64	46	49	.262	.340	.414	101	1	1	63	5	3	-0	.976	11	*3	1.0
1952	StL-N	94	282	23	71	10	2	2	34	34	21	.252	.339	.323	84	-5	-5	32	1	0	0	.951	2	3	-0.5
1953	StL-N	11	5	0	1	1	0	0	1	1	1	.200	.333	.400	90	-0	-0	1	0	0	0	1.000	2	3	0.2
Total	9	964	3253	419	882	141	33	61	487	347	290	.271	.346	.391	102	5	6	437	13	11	-3	.959	18	3/12	1.8

■ GREGORY JOHNSTON Johnston, Gregory Bernard b: 2/12/55, Los Angeles, Cal. BL/TL, 6', 175 lbs. Deb: 7/27/79

1979	SF-N	42	74	5	15	2	1	1	7	2	17	.203	.224	.270	37	-7	-6	4	0	0	0	.966	0	O	-0.7
1980	Min-A	14	27	3	5	3	0	0	1	2	4	.185	.241	.296	43	-2	-2	1	0	0	0	1.000	-3	O	-0.5
1981	Min-A	7	16	2	2	0	0	0	2	5	5	.125	.222	.125	-2	-2	-2	0	0	0	0	1.000	0	/O	-0.2
Total	3	63	117	10	22	5	1	1	8	6	26	.188	.256	.256	33	-11	-11	6	0	0	0	.985	-2	/O	-1.4

YEAR	TM/L	G	AB	R	H	2B	3B	HR	RBI	BB	SO	AVG	OBP	SLG	PRO+	BR	/A	RC	SB	CS	SBR	FA	FR	POS	TPR
■ JIMMY JOHNSTON Johnston, James Harle b: 12/10/1889, Cleveland, Tenn. d: 2/14/67, Chattanooga, Tenn. BR/TR, 5'10", 160 lbs. Deb: 5/03/11 FC																									
1911	Chi-A	1	2	0	0	0	0	0	2	0		.000	.000	.000	-99	-1	-1	0	0			1.000	-0	/O	-0.1
1914	Chi-N	50	101	9	23	3	2	1	8	4	9	.228	.264	.327	76	-3	-3	9	3			.929	4	O/2	0.0
1916	*Bro-N	118	425	58	107	13	8	1	26	35	38	.252	.313	.327	94	-1	-3	44	22	19	-5	.964	7	*O	-0.7
1917	Bro-N	103	330	33	89	10	4	0	25	23	28	.270	.321	.324	96	-1	-2	39	16			.958	4	O1/S23	-0.2
1918	Bro-N	123	484	54	136	16	8	0	27	33	31	.281	.328	.347	106	3	3	59	22			.956	8	O1/32	0.5
1919	Bro-N	117	405	56	114	11	4	1	23	29	26	.281	.334	.336	100	1	0	48	11			.960	-6	2O/1S	-0.2
1920	*Bro-N	155	635	87	185	17	12	1	52	43	23	.291	.338	.361	98	1	-2	77	19	15	-3	.934	-6	*3/OS	-0.4
1921	Bro-N	152	624	104	203	41	14	5	56	45	26	.325	.372	.460	115	16	14	105	28	16	-1	.935	8	*3/S	3.0
1922	Bro-N	138	567	110	181	20	7	4	49	38	17	.319	.364	.400	98	-2	-1	83	18	9	0	.947	7	2S3	1.3
1923	Bro-N	151	625	111	203	29	11	4	60	53	15	.325	.378	.426	115	11	13	100	16	13	-3	.948	19	2S3	3.5
1924	Bro-N	86	315	51	94	11	2	2	29	27	10	.298	.356	.365	97	-2	-1	41	5	6	-2	.939	-4	S3/1O	0.1
1925	Bro-N	123	431	63	128	13	3	2	43	45	15	.297	.369	.355	88	-7	-6	59	7	5	-1	.886	-23	3O/1S	-2.4
1926	Bos-N	23	57	7	14	1	0	1	5	10	3	.246	.358	.316	91	-1	-0	7	2			.865	-4	3/2O	-0.3
	NY-N	37	69	11	16	0	0	0	5	6	5	.232	.293	.232	43	-5	-5	5	0			1.000	-5	O	-1.1
	Yr	60	126	18	30	1	0	1	10	16	8	.238	.324	.270	64	-6	-6	11	2			1.000	-8	O3/2	-1.4
Total	13	1377	5070	754	1493	185	75	22	410	391	246	.294	.347	.374	100	9	8	676	169	83		.926	10	3O2S/1	3.0
■ JOHNNY JOHNSTON Johnston, John Thomas b: 3/28/1890, Longview, Tex. d: 3/7/40, San Diego, Cal. BL/TR, 5'11", 172 lbs. Deb: 4/10/13																									
1913	StL-A	111	380	37	85	14	4	2	27	42	51	.224	.308	.297	79	-11	-9	38	11			.965	12	*O	-0.2
■ REX JOHNSTON Johnston, Rex David b: 11/8/37, Colton, Cal. BB/TR, 6'1.5", 202 lbs. Deb: 4/15/64																									
1964	Pit-N	14	7	1	0	0	0	0	0	3	0	.000	.300	.000	-7	-1	-1	0	0	0	0	1.000	0	/O	-0.1
■ DICK JOHNSTON Johnston, Richard Frederick b: 4/6/1863, Kingston, N.Y. d: 4/4/34, Detroit, Mich. BR/TR, 5'8", 155 lbs. Deb: 8/12/1884																									
1884	Ric-a	39	146	23	41	5	5	2		2		.281	.291	.425	135	5	5	18				.865	9	O/S	1.2
1885	Bos-N	26	111	17	26	6	3	1	23	0	15	.234	.234	.369	96	-1	-1	10				.842	1	O	0.0
1886	Bos-N	109	413	48	99	18	9	1	57	3	70	.240	.245	.334	78	-13	-11	37	11			.892	17	*O	0.3
1887	Bos-N	127	507	87	131	13	20	5	77	16	35	.258	.281	.393	86	-10	-10	72	52			.933	25	*O	1.1
1888	Bos-N	135	585	102	173	31	**18**	12	68	15	33	.296	.314	.472	148	30	29	100	35			.898	7	*O	3.1
1889	Bos-N	132	539	80	123	16	4	5	67	41	60	.228	.285	.301	61	-25	-31	57	34			.917	-7	*O	-3.6
1890	Bos-P	2	9	0	1	0	0	0	0	0	1	.111	.111	.111	-37	-2	-2	0	0			.800	0	/O	-0.2
	NY-P	77	306	37	74	9	7	1	43	18	25	.242	.288	.327	60	-16	-20	32	7			.897	3	O/S	-1.6
	Yr	79	315	37	75	9	7	1	43	18	26	.238	.284	.321	58	-17	-22	31	7			.894	3	O/S	-1.8
1891	Cin-a	99	376	59	83	11	2	6	51	38	44	.221	.301	.309	71	-11	-17	39	12			.895	-1	*O	-1.8
Total	8	746	2992	453	751	109	68	33	386	133	283	.251	.285	.366	88	-44	-58	367	151			.903	54	O/S	-1.5
■ DOC JOHNSTON Johnston, Wheeler Roger b: 9/9/1887, Cleveland, Tenn. d: 2/17/61, Chattanooga, Tenn. BL/TL, 6', 170 lbs. Deb: 10/03/09 F																									
1909	Cin-N	3	10	1	0	0	0	0	1	0		.000	.000	.000	-99	-2	-2	-0	0			1.000	0	/1	-0.2
1912	Cle-A	43	164	22	46	7	4	1	11	11		.280	.326	.390	101	0	-0	23	8			.991	-2	1	-0.3
1913	Cle-A	133	530	74	135	19	12	2	39	35	65	.255	.309	.347	89	-7	-9	60	19			.989	-1	*1	-1.2
1914	Cle-A	103	340	43	83	15	1	0	23	28	46	.244	.311	.294	79	-7	-9	34	14	9	-1	.987	-7	1/O	-2.1
1915	Pit-N	147	543	71	144	19	12	5	64	38	40	.265	.328	.372	113	7	8	72	26	17	-2	.991	-12	*1	-1.1
1916	Pit-N	114	404	33	86	10	10	0	39	20	42	.213	.262	.287	68	-15	-16	37	17			.987	-2	*1	-2.5
1918	Cle-A	74	273	30	62	12	2	0	25	26	19	.227	.301	.286	70	-8	-10	27	12			.989	-3	1	-1.8
1919	Cle-A	102	331	42	101	17	3	1	33	25	18	.305	.359	.384	102	4	1	53	21			.984	-3	1	-0.5
1920	*Cle-A	147	535	68	156	24	10	2	71	28	32	.292	.333	.385	87	-9	-11	69	13	6	0	.992	-1	*1	-1.5
1921	Cle-A	118	384	53	114	20	7	2	46	29	15	.297	.353	.401	90	-5	-6	53	2	9	-5	.988	-1	*1	-1.3
1922	Phi-A	71	260	41	65	11	7	1	29	24	15	.250	.316	.358	73	-10	-11	30	7	6	-2	.990	-5	1	-2.0
Total	11	1055	3774	478	992	154	68	14	381	264	292	.263	.319	.351	88	-51	-65	457	139	47		.989	-37	*1/O	-14.5
■ FRED JOHNSTON Johnston, Wilfred Ivy b: 7/9/1899, Charlotte, N.C. d: 7/14/59, Tyler, Tex. BR/TR, 5'11.5", 170 lbs. Deb: 6/29/24																									
1924	Bro-N	4	4	1	1	0	0	0	0	0	1	.250	.250	.250	35	-0	-0	0	0	0	0	.667	0	/23	0.0
■ JAY JOHNSTONE Johnstone, John William b: 11/20/45, Manchester, Conn. BL/TR, 6'1", 175 lbs. Deb: 7/30/66																									
1966	Cal-A	61	254	35	67	12	4	3	17	11	36	.264	.297	.378	95	-3	-2	28	3	3	-1	.975	-2	O	-0.8
1967	Cal-A	79	230	18	48	7	1	2	10	5	37	.209	.226	.274	49	-16	-15	13	3	2	-0	.973	2	O	-1.7
1968	Cal-A	41	115	11	30	4	1	0	3	7	15	.261	.303	.313	90	-2	-1	12	2	1	0	.984	2	O	-0.1
1969	Cal-A	148	540	64	146	20	5	10	59	38	75	.270	.324	.381	102	-3	0	65	3	9	-5	.983	12	*O	0.0
1970	Cal-A	119	320	34	76	10	5	11	39	24	53	.237	.293	.403	93	-5	-4	37	1	0	0	.981	-1	*O	-0.9
1971	Chi-A	124	388	53	101	14	1	16	40	38	50	.260	.331	.425	109	6	4	56	10	5	0	.968	-3	*O	-0.4
1972	Chi-A	113	261	27	49	9	0	4	17	25	42	.188	.259	.268	56	-14	-14	19	2	1	0	.988	-12	O	-3.4
1973	Oak-A	23	28	1	3	1	0	0	3	2	4	.107	.167	.143	-13	-4	-4	1	0	1	-1	1.000	-2	/O2D	-0.7
1974	Phi-N	64	200	30	59	10	4	6	30	24	28	.295	.371	.475	130	9	8	35	5	5	-2	.968	-5	O	-0.1
1975	Phi-N	122	350	50	115	19	2	7	54	42	39	.329	.401	.454	132	18	16	64	7	3	0	.976	-4	*O	0.9
1976	*Phi-N	129	440	62	140	38	4	5	53	41	39	.318	.379	.457	132	21	19	75	5	5	-2	.982	6	*O/1	2.0
1977	*Phi-N	112	363	64	103	18	4	15	59	38	38	.284	.355	.479	116	11	8	59	3	7	-3	1.000	-0	O1	0.1
1978	Phi-N	35	56	3	10	2	0	0	4	6	9	.179	.258	.214	33	-5	-5	3	0	2	-1	.988	1	/1O	-0.6
	*NY-A	36	65	6	17	0	0	1	6	4	10	.262	.333	.308	83	-1	-1	7	0	1	-1	1.000	-3	O/D	-0.5
1979	NY-A	23	48	7	10	1	0	1	7	2	7	.208	.240	.292	44	-4	-4	4	1	0	0	1.000	-2	O	-0.6
	SD-N	75	201	10	59	8	2	0	32	18	21	.294	.352	.353	99	-2	-0	24	1	3	-2	.985	-1	O1	-0.5
1980	LA-N	109	251	31	77	15	2	2	20	24	29	.307	.372	.406	119	6	7	39	3	2	-0	.965	-0	O	0.5
1981	*LA-N	61	83	8	17	3	0	3	6	7	13	.205	.267	.349	76	-3	-3	7	0	1	-1	.957	1	O/1	-0.3
1982	LA-N	21	13	1	1	1	0	0	2	5	2	.077	.333	.154	41	-1	-1	1	0	0	0	.000	0	H	-0.1
	Chi-N	98	269	39	67	13	1	10	43	40	41	.249	.346	.416	109	5	4	40	0	2	-1	.982	1	O	0.2
	Yr	119	282	40	68	14	1	10	45	45	43	.241	.346	.404	107	4	3	41	0	2	-1	.982	1	O	0.1
1983	Chi-N	86	140	16	36	7	0	6	22	20	24	.257	.362	.436	115	4	3	22	1	1	-0	.935	-1	O	0.1
1984	Chi-N	52	73	8	21	2	2	0	3	7	18	.288	.350	.370	94	0	-0	9	0	0	0	1.000	-4	O	-0.5
1985	*LA-N	17	15	0	2	1	0	0	2	1	2	.133	.188	.200	9	-2	-2	0	0	0	0	.000	0	H	-0.2
Total	20	1748	4703	578	1254	215	38	102	531	429	632	.267	.331	.394	103	15	14	618	50	54	-17	.979	-14	*O/1D2	-7.6
■ STAN JOK Jok, Stanley Edward "Tucker" b: 5/3/26, Buffalo, N.Y. d: 3/6/72, Buffalo, N.Y. BR/TR, 6', 190 lbs. Deb: 4/13/54																									
1954	Phi-N	3	3	0	0	0	0	0	0	0	2	.000	.000	.000	-99	-1	-1	0	0	0	0	.000	0	H	-0.1
	Chi-A	3	12	1	2	0	0	0	2	1	2	.167	.231	.167	10	-1	-2	0	0	0	0	1.000	-0	/3	-0.2
1955	Chi-A	6	4	3	1	0	0	1	2	1	1	.250	.400	1.000	260	1	1	2	0	0	0	.857	1	/3O	0.1
Total	2	12	19	4	3	0	0	1	4	2	5	.158	.238	.316	47	-1	-2	2	0	0	0	.941	0	/3O	-0.2
■ SMEAD JOLLEY Jolley, Smead Powell "Guinea" or "Smudge" b: 1/14/02, Wesson, Ark. d: 11/17/91, Almeda, Cal. BL/TR, 6'3.5", 210 lbs. Deb: 4/17/30																									
1930	Chi-A	152	616	76	193	38	12	16	114	28	52	.313	.346	.492	114	7	10	103	3	1	0	.950	-3	*O	-0.3
1931	Chi-A	54	110	5	33	11	0	3	28	7	4	.300	.353	.482	125	2	3	19	0	0	0	.857	-5	O	-0.3
1932	Chi-A	12	42	3	15	3	0	0	7	3	0	.357	.413	.429	127	1	2	8	1	0	0	.923	-2	O	-0.1
	Bos-A	137	531	57	164	27	5	18	99	27	29	.309	.345	.480	115	7	9	85	0	5	-3	.943	-5	*O/C	-0.6
	Yr	149	573	60	179	30	5	18	106	30	29	.312	.350	.476	116	8	10	93	1	5	-3	.942	-8	*O/C	-0.7
1933	Bos-A	118	411	47	116	32	4	9	65	24	20	.282	.325	.445	103	-1	0	59	1	1	-0	.955	-4	*O	-0.9

YEAR	TM/L	G	AB	R	H	2B	3B	HR	RBI	BB	SO	AVG	OBP	SLG	PRO+	BR	/A	RC	SB	CS	SBR	FA	FR	POS	TPR
Total	4	473	1710	188	521	111	21	46	313	89	105	.305	.343	.475	112	17	24	274	5	7	-3	.944	-19	O/C	-2.2
■ JONES Jones Deb: 5/14/1873																									
1873	Mar-n	1	4	0	3	1	0	0	0	0	0	.750	.750	1.000	535	1	2	3						/O	0.1
1874	Bal-n	2	7	0	1	0	0	0		0		.143	.143	.143	-9	-1	-1	0						/CO	-0.1
Total	2 n	3	11	0	4	1	0	0		0		.364	.364	.455	166	1	1	3						/OC	0.0
■ JONES Jones b: Johnstown, Pa. Deb: 7/14/1884																									
1884	Was-a	4	17	2	5	0	0	0		1		.294	.333	.294	124	0	0	2				1.000	-0	/O	0.0
■ CHARLIE JONES Jones, Charles C. "Casey" b: 6/2/1876, Butler, Pa. d: 4/2/47, Two Harbors, Minn. BR/TR, 6'1", Deb: 5/03/01																									
1901	Bos-A	10	41	6	6	2	0	0	6	1		.146	.167	.195	0	-6	-5	2	2			.929	-2	O	-0.8
1904	Chi-A	5	17	2	4	0	1	0	1	1		.235	.278	.353	103	-0	0	2	0			1.000	1	/O	0.1
1905	Was-A	142	544	68	113	18	4	2	41	31		.208	.254	.267	68	-22	-19	45	24			.971	16	*O	-1.1
1906	Was-A	131	497	56	120	11	11	3	42	24		.241	.279	.326	94	-7	-5	58	34			.961	8	*O/2	-0.3
1907	Was-A	121	437	48	116	14	10	0	37	22		.265	.301	.343	114	1	5	56	26			.967	-1	*O/21S	0.0
1908	StL-A	74	263	37	61	11	2	0	17	14		.232	.279	.289	84	-5	-5	25	14			.963	-1	O	-1.0
Total	6	483	1799	217	420	56	28	5	144	93		.233	.274	.304	87	-38	-29	187	100			.966	20	O/21S	-3.1
■ CHARLIE JONES Jones, Charles F. b: New York, N.Y. Deb: 6/28/1884																									
1884	Bro-a	25	90	10	16	1	0	0		5		.178	.221	.189	37	-6	-6	4				.871	-7	23/O	-1.2
1885	NY-a	1	4	0	1	0	0	0		0		.250	.250	.250	66	-0	-0	0				1.000	1	/3	0.1
Total	2	26	94	10	17	1	0	0		5		.181	.222	.191	38	-6	-6	4				.879	-6	/23O	-1.1
■ CHARLEY JONES Jones, Charles Wesley "Baby" (b: Benjamin Wesley Rippay) b: 4/30/1850, Alamance Co., N.C. BR/TR, 5'11.5", 202 lbs. Deb: 5/04/1875 U																									
1875	Wes-n	12	47	5	13	2	4	0		0		.277	.277	.489	151	3	2	7						O	0.2
	Har-n	1	4	1	0	0	0	0		0		.000	.000	.000	-95	-1	-1	0						/O	-0.1
	Yr	13	51	6	13	2	4	0		0		.255	.255	.451	132	2	1	6						O	0.1
1876	Cin-N	64	276	40	79	17	4	4	38	7	17	.286	.304	.420	162	11	17	36				.857	3	*O	1.7
1877	Cin-N	17	69	16	21	3	3	1	10	4	8	.304	.342	.478	175	4	6	12				.920	1	1/O	0.5
	Chi-N	2	8	1	3	1	0	0	2	1	0	.375	.444	.500	176	1	1	2				1.000	1	/O	0.1
	Cin-N	38	163	36	51	8	7	1	26	10	17	.313	.353	.466	175	10	13	27				.838	10	O	1.9
	Yr	57	240	53	75	12	10	2	38	15	25	.313	.353	.471	175	16	19	41				.845	12	O1	**2.5**
1878	Cin-N	61	261	50	81	11	7	3	39	4	17	.310	.321	.441	163	13	16	38				.896	6	*O	1.7
1879	Bos-N	83	355	**85**	112	22	10	**9**	**62**	**29**	38	.315	.367	.510	182	**33**	32	68				**.933**	12	*O	3.6
1880	Bos-N	66	280	44	84	15	3	5	37	11	27	.300	.326	.429	159	15	16	40				.826	-4	*O	1.0
1883	Cin-a	90	391	84	115	15	12	10		20		.294	.328	.471	146	23	19	62				.876	2	*O	1.8
1884	Cin-a	112	472	117	148	19	17	7		37		.314	**.376**	.470	170	40	37	85				.887	3	*O	3.4
1885	Cin-a	112	487	108	157	19	17	5		21		.322	.362	.462	159	33	32	83				.891	12	*O	3.6
1886	Cin-a	127	500	87	135	22	10	6		61		.270	.356	.390	132	22	19	72	3			.879	3	*O	1.7
1887	Cin-a	41	153	28	48	7	4	2		19		.314	.400	.451	136	9	8	31	7			.900	-0	O	0.6
	NY-a	62	247	30	63	11	3	3		12		.255	.306	.360	91	-5	-3	30	8			.917	4	O/P1	0.0
	Yr	103	400	58	111	18	7	5		31		.278	.343	.395	110	4	5	61	15			.910	4	*O/P1	0.6
1888	KC-a	6	25	2	4	0	1	0	5	1		.160	.192	.240	38	-2	-2	1	1			.750	-1	/O	-0.2
Total	11	881	3687	728	1101	170	98	56	219	237	124	.299	.347	.443	152	208	212	589	19			.882	51	O/1P	21.4
■ CHRIS JONES Jones, Christopher Carlos b: 12/16/65, Utica, N.Y. BR/TR, 6'2", 205 lbs. Deb: 4/21/91																									
1991	Cin-N	52	89	14	26	1	2	2	6	2	31	.292	.308	.416	98	-0	-1	11	2	1	0	1.000	-5	O	-0.6
1992	Hou-N	54	63	7	12	2	1	1	4	7	21	.190	.271	.302	66	-3	-3	6	3	0	1	.929	-14	O	-1.7
Total	2	106	152	21	38	3	3	3	10	9	52	.250	.292	.368	85	-3	-3	17	5	1	1	.964	-19	/O	-2.3
■ CHRIS JONES Jones, Christopher Dale b: 7/13/57, Los Angeles, Cal. BL/TL, 6', 183 lbs. Deb: 6/08/85																									
1985	Hou-N	31	25	0	5	0	0	0	1	3	7	.200	.286	.200	39	-2	-2	2	0	0	0	1.000	-3	O	-0.6
1986	SF-N	3	1	0	0	0	0	0	0	0	0	.000	.000	.000	-99	-0	-0	0	1	0	0	.000	0	/H	0.0
Total	2	34	26	0	5	0	0	0	1	3	7	.192	.276	.192	34	-2	-2	2	1	0	0		-3	/O	-0.6
■ CLARENCE JONES Jones, Clarence Woodrow b: 11/7/41, Zanesville, Ohio BL/TL, 6'2", 185 lbs. Deb: 4/20/67 C																									
1967	Chi-N	53	135	13	34	7	0	2	16	14	33	.252	.322	.348	88	-1	-2	16	0	0	0	.978	-4	O1	-0.8
1968	Chi-N	5	2	0	0	0	0	0	0	2	1	.000	.500	.000	56	0	0	0	0	0	0	1.000	-0	/1	0.0
Total	2	58	137	13	34	7	0	2	16	16	34	.248	.327	.343	88	-1	-2	16	0	0	0	.979	-4	/O1	-0.8
■ CLEON JONES Jones, Cleon Joseph b: 8/4/42, Plateau, Ala. BR/TL, 6', 200 lbs. Deb: 9/14/63																									
1963	NY-N	6	15	1	2	0	0	0	1	0	4	.133	.133	.133	-23	-2	-2	0	0	0	0	1.000	-0	/O	-0.3
1965	NY-N	30	74	2	11	1	0	1	9	2	23	.149	.171	.203	5	-9	-9	3	1	0	0	1.000	1	O	-0.9
1966	NY-N	139	495	74	136	16	4	8	57	30	62	.275	.320	.372	94	-6	-4	57	16	8	0	.979	-3	*O	-1.4
1967	NY-N	129	411	46	101	10	5	5	30	19	57	.246	.286	.331	77	-13	-12	39	12	2	2	.977	-6	*O	-2.4
1968	NY-N	147	509	63	151	29	4	14	55	31	98	.297	.343	.452	136	22	21	77	23	12	-0	.963	-7	*O	0.8
1969	*NY-N★	137	483	92	164	25	4	12	75	64	60	.340	.424	.482	150	37	36	100	16	8	0	.991	-0	*O1	2.9
1970	NY-N	134	506	71	140	25	8	10	63	57	87	.277	.356	.417	106	5	5	71	12	3	2	.981	5	*O	0.5
1971	NY-N	136	505	63	161	24	6	14	69	53	87	.319	.386	.473	144	28	29	92	6	5	-1	.981	-1	*O	2.2
1972	NY-N	106	375	39	92	15	1	5	52	30	83	.245	.308	.331	84	-9	-8	36	1	6	-3	.986	0	O1	-1.8
1973	*NY-N	92	339	48	88	13	0	11	48	28	51	.260	.322	.395	99	-2	-1	41	1	1	-0	.967	-1	O	-0.7
1974	NY-N	124	461	62	130	23	1	13	60	38	79	.282	.345	.421	115	7	8	66	3	3	-1	.970	0	*O	0.2
1975	NY-N	21	50	2	12	1	0	0	2	3	6	.240	.283	.260	54	-3	-3	4	0	0	0	1.000	-3	O	-0.7
1976	Chi-A	12	40	2	8	1	0	0	3	5	5	.200	.304	.225	56	-2	-2	3	0	0	0	1.000	-2	/OD	-0.5
Total	13	1213	4263	565	1196	183	33	93	524	360	702	.281	.342	.404	111	53	57	589	91	48	-2	.978	-17	*O/1D	-2.1
■ COBE JONES Jones, Coburn Dyas b: 8/21/07, Denver, Colo. d: 6/3/69, Denver, Colo. BB/TR, 5'7", 155 lbs. Deb: 9/27/28																									
1928	Pit-N	1	2	0	1	0	0	0	0	0	0	.500	.500	.500	156	0	0	0	0			1.000	-0	/S	0.0
1929	Pit-N	25	63	6	16	5	1	0	4	1	5	.254	.266	.365	53	-5	-5	6	1			.919	-8	S	-1.0
Total	2	26	65	6	17	5	1	0	4	1	5	.262	.273	.369	56	-5	-5	6	1			.921	-8	/S	-1.0
■ DARRYL JONES Jones, Darryl Lee b: 6/5/51, Meadville, Pa. BR/TR, 5'10", 175 lbs. Deb: 6/06/79 F																									
1979	NY-A	18	47	6	12	5	1	0	6	2	7	.255	.286	.404	86	-1	-1	5	0	0	0	1.000	-1	D/O	-0.2
■ DAVY JONES Jones, David Jefferson "Kangaroo" b: 6/30/1880, Cambria, Wis. d: 3/31/72, Mankato, Minn. BL/TR, 5'10", 165 lbs. Deb: 9/15/01																									
1901	Mil-A	14	52	12	9	0	0	3	5	11		.173	.328	.346	92	-1	-0	7	4			.911	1	O	0.0
1902	StL-A	15	49	4	11	1	1	0	3	6		.224	.321	.286	70	-2	-2	6	5			.973	5	O	0.2
	Chi-N	64	243	41	74	12	3	0	14	38		.305	.399	.379	144	13	14	44	12			.955	-1	O	0.9
1903	Chi-N	130	497	64	140	18	3	1	62	53		.282	.352	.336	100	-1	1	67	15			.970	0	*O	-0.6
1904	Chi-N	98	336	44	82	11	5	3	39	41		.244	.330	.333	105	3	3	43	14			.932	-10	O	-1.3
1906	Det-A	84	323	41	84	12	2	0	24	41		.260	.347	.310	104	4	3	43	21			.981	4	O	0.4
1907	*Det-A	126	491	101	134	10	6	0	27	60		.273	.357	.318	112	11	9	70	30			.971	13	*O	1.9
1908	*Det-A	56	121	17	25	2	1	0	10	13		.207	.284	.240	68	-4	-4	11	11			.960	2	O	-0.3
1909	*Det-A	69	204	44	57	2	2	0	10	28		.279	.369	.309	110	5	4	28	12			.982	-2	O	0.0
1910	Det-A	113	377	77	100	6	6	0	24	51		.265	.362	.313	105	7	4	52	25			.956	1	*O	0.1

YEAR	TM/L	G	AB	R	H	2B	3B	HR	RBI	BB	SO	AVG	OBP	SLG	PRO+	BR	/A	RC	SB	CS	SBR	FA	FR	POS	TPR
1911	Det-A	98	341	78	93	10	0	0	19	41		.273	.354	.302	80	-6	-8	45	25			.950	-1	O	-1.4
1912	Det-A	99	316	54	93	5	2	0	24	38		.294	.370	.323	102	1	2	44	16			.962	-1	O	-0.2
1913	Chi-A	12	21	2	6	0	0	0	0	9	0	.286	.500	.286	132	2	2	4	1			.867	-1	/O	0.1
1914	Pit-F	97	352	58	96	9	8	2	24	42	16	.273	.355	.361	105	3	3	54	15			.970	8	O	0.7
1915	Pit-F	14	49	6	16	0	1	0	4	6	0	.327	.400	.367	127	2	2	8	1			.926	-1	O	0.1
Total	14	1089	3772	643	1020	98	40	9	289	478	16	.270	.356	.325	103	39	34	526	207			.962	18	*O	0.6

■ FIELDER JONES Jones, Fielder Allison b: 8/13/1871, Shinglehouse, Pa. d: 3/13/34, Portland, Ore. BL/TR, 5'11", 180 lbs. Deb: 4/18/1896 M

1896	Bro-N	104	395	82	140	10	8	3	46	48	15	.354	.427	.443	140	20	24	85	18			.928	-4	*O	1.0
1897	Bro-N	135	548	134	172	15	10	1	49	61		.314	.392	.383	111	6	12	105	48			.941	4	*O	0.5
1898	Bro-N	146	596	89	181	15	9	1	69	46		.304	.362	.364	108	7	7	96	36			.946	-7	*O/S	-1.0
1899	Bro-N	102	365	75	104	8	2	2	38	54		.285	.390	.334	97	3	2	56	18			.946	-3	O	-0.8
1900	*Bro-N	136	552	106	171	26	4	4	54	57		.310	.382	.393	108	12	7	99	33			.957	0	*O	-0.3
1901	Chi-A	133	521	120	162	16	3	2	65	84		.311	.412	.365	120	17	20	99	38			.937	1	*O	1.0
1902	Chi-A	135	532	98	171	16	5	0	54	57		.321	.394	.370	118	12	16	96	33			.972	13	*O	1.8
1903	Chi-A	136	530	71	152	18	5	0	45	47		.287	.348	.340	112	6	9	75	21			**.985**	0	*O	0.1
1904	Chi-A	149	547	72	133	14	5	3	42	53		.243	.316	.303	100	-1	2	66	25			.977	5	*OM	-0.3
1905	Chi-A	153	568	91	139	17	12	2	38	73		.245	.335	.327	115	9	12	73	20			.970	7	*OM	1.3
1906	*Chi-A	144	496	77	114	22	4	2	34	83		.230	.346	.302	107	6	8	67	26			**.988**	8	*OM	1.0
1907	Chi-A	154	559	72	146	18	1	0	47	67		.261	.345	.297	109	7	9	70	17			.973	2	*OM	0.5
1908	Chi-A	149	529	92	134	11	7	1	50	86		.253	.366	.306	121	16	17	71	26			.968	-2	*OM	1.1
1914	StL-F	5	3	0	1	0	0	0	0	1	0	.333	.500	.333	132	0	0	1	0			.000	0	HM	0.0
1915	StL-F	7	6	1	0	0	0	0	0	0	0	.000	.000	.000	-95	-1	-2	0	0			1.000	-1	/OM	-0.3
Total	15	1788	6747	1180	1920	206	75	21	631	817	15	.285	.368	.347	112	120	142	1059	359			.964	24	*O/S	5.6

■ FRANK JONES Jones, Frank M. b: 8/25/1858, Princeton, Ill. d: 2/4/36, Marietta, Ohio Deb: 7/02/1884

1884	Det-N	2	8	0	1	0	0	0	0	0	1	.125	.125	.125	-22	-1	-1	0				.667	-1	/SO	-0.2

■ DEACON JONES Jones, Grover William b: 4/18/34, White Plains, N.Y. BL/TR, 5'10", 185 lbs. Deb: 9/08/62 C

1962	Chi-A	18	28	3	9	2	0	0	8	4	6	.321	.406	.393	117	1	1	5	0	0	0	.962	-0	/1	0.0
1963	Chi-A	17	16	4	3	0	1	1	2	2	2	.188	.316	.500	127	0	1	2	0	0	0	1.000	0	/1	0.1
1966	Chi-A	5	5	0	2	0	0	0	0	0	0	.400	.400	.400	140	0	0	1	0	0	0	.000	0	H	0.0
Total	3	40	49	7	14	2	1	1	10	6	8	.286	.375	.429	122	2	2	8	0	0	0	.966	-0	/1	0.1

■ HAL JONES Jones, Harold Marion b: 4/9/36, Louisiana, Mo. BR/TR, 6'2", 194 lbs. Deb: 4/25/61

1961	Cle-A	12	35	2	6	0	0	2	4	2	12	.171	.216	.343	48	-3	-3	2	0	0	0	.974	-2	1	-0.5
1962	Cle-A	5	16	2	5	1	0	0	1	0	4	.313	.353	.375	99	-0	-0	2	0	0	0	.969	0	/1	0.0
Total	2	17	51	4	11	1	0	2	5	2	16	.216	.259	.353	64	-3	-3	5	0	0	0	.973	-2	/1	-0.5

■ HENRY JONES Jones, Henry M. "Baldy" b: Cadillac, Mich. Deb: 8/20/1884

1884	Det-N	34	127	24	28	3	1	0	3	16	18	.220	.308	.260	86	-2	-1	10				.897	-2	2O/S	-0.3
1890	Pit-N	5	9	0	2	0	0	0	0	0	0	.222	.222	.222	35	-1	-1	1	1			1.000	-1	/P	0.0
Total	2	39	136	24	30	3	1	0	3	16	18	.221	.303	.257	82	-3	-2	11	1				-3	/2OSP	-0.3

■ HOWIE JONES Jones, Howard "Cotton" (b: Howard Painter) b: 3/1/1897, Irwin, Pa. d: 7/15/72, Jeanette, Pa. BL/TL, 5'11", 165 lbs. Deb: 9/05/21

1921	StL-N	3	2	0	0	0	0	0	0	0	1	.000	.000	.000	-99	-1	-1	0	0	0	0	.000	-1	/O	-0.1

■ DALTON JONES Jones, James Dalton b: 12/10/43, McComb, Miss. BL/TR, 6'1", 180 lbs. Deb: 4/17/64

1964	Bos-A	118	374	37	86	16	4	6	39	22	38	.230	.275	.342	67	-15	-18	36	6	3	0	.959	-8	2/S3	-2.0
1965	Bos-A	112	367	41	99	13	5	5	37	28	45	.270	.325	.373	92	-1	-4	46	8	1	2	.930	-3	3/2	-0.7
1966	Bos-A	115	252	26	59	11	5	4	23	22	27	.234	.303	.365	83	-3	-6	27	1	2	-1	.962	-15	2/3	-1.9
1967	*Bos-A	89	159	18	46	6	2	3	25	11	23	.289	.335	.409	110	3	2	21	0	1	-1	.912	-4	32/1	-0.3
1968	Bos-A	111	354	38	83	13	0	5	29	17	53	.234	.272	.314	72	-10	-13	28	1	1	-0	.996	-6	12/3	-2.6
1969	Bos-A	111	336	50	74	18	3	3	33	39	36	.220	.305	.318	71	-11	-13	34	1	1	-0	.992	-1	1/32	-2.2
1970	Det-A	89	191	29	42	7	0	6	21	33	33	.220	.338	.351	90	-2	-2	24	1	1	-0	.985	-3	231	-0.4
1971	Det-A	83	138	15	35	5	0	5	11	9	21	.254	.304	.399	94	-1	-1	15	1	3	-2	1.000	-7	O3/12	-1.1
1972	Det-A	7	7	0	0	0	0	0	0	0	2	.000	.000	.000	-97	-2	-2	0	0	0	0	.000	0	H	-0.2
	Tex-A	72	151	14	24	2	0	4	19	10	31	.159	.211	.252	39	-12	-11	8	1	0	0	.979	-7	32/1O	-2.1
	Yr	79	158	14	24	2	0	4	19	10	33	.152	.202	.241	33	-14	-13	8	1	0	0	.979	-7	32/1O	-2.3
Total	9	907	2329	268	548	91	19	41	237	191	309	.235	.296	.343	79	-54	-68	240	20	13	-2	.967	-54	231/OS	-13.5

■ JAKE JONES Jones, James Murrell b: 11/23/20, Epps, La. BR/TR, 6'3", 197 lbs. Deb: 9/20/41

1941	Chi-A	3	11	0	0	0	0	0	0	0	4	.000	.000	.000	-99	-3	-3	0	0	0	0	1.000	-1	/1	-0.4
1942	Chi-A	7	20	2	3	1	0	0	0	2	2	.150	.227	.200	21	-2	-2	1	1	0	0	.961	-1	/1	-0.3
1946	Chi-A	24	79	10	21	5	1	3	13	2	13	.266	.284	.468	112	0	0	10	0	0	0	.986	-3	1	-0.4
1947	Chi-A	45	171	15	41	7	1	3	20	13	25	.240	.297	.345	81	-5	-5	18	1	0	0	.988	-1	1	-0.7
	Bos-A	109	404	50	95	14	3	16	76	41	60	.235	.310	.403	91	-3	-7	52	5	4	-1	.991	-2	*1	-1.4
	Yr	154	575	65	136	21	4	19	96	54	85	.237	.306	.386	88	-9	-11	70	6	4	-1	.990	-3	*1	-2.1
1948	Bos-A	36	105	3	21	4	0	1	8	11	26	.200	.276	.267	43	-8	-9	8	1	0	0	.993	2	1	-0.7
Total	5	224	790	80	181	31	5	23	117	69	130	.229	.294	.368	80	-22	-25	88	8	4	0	.989	-6	1	-3.9

■ JIM JONES Jones, James Tilford "Sheriff" b: 12/25/1876, London, Ky. d: 5/6/53, London, Ky. BR/TR, 5'10", 162 lbs. Deb: 6/29/1897

1897	Lou-N	2	4	2	1	1	0	0	0	1		.250	.400	.500	141	0	0	1	0			.000	-0	/P	0.0
1901	NY-N	21	91	10	19	4	3	0	5	4		.209	.250	.319	67	-4	-4	8	2			.900	1	O/P	-0.4
1902	NY-N	67	249	16	59	11	1	0	19	13		.237	.275	.289	75	-8	-8	23	7			.897	-1	O	-1.4
Total	3	90	344	28	79	16	4	0	24	18		.230	.270	.299	74	-12	-11	31	9			.898	-0	/OP	-1.8

■ JEFF JONES Jones, Jeffrey Raymond b: 10/22/57, Philadelphia, Pa. BR/TR, 6'2", 200 lbs. Deb: 4/04/83

1983	Cin-N	16	44	6	10	3	0	0	5	11	13	.227	.393	.295	90	0	0	7	2	0	1	1.000	0	O/1	0.0

■ BINKY JONES Jones, John Joseph b: 7/11/1899, St.Louis, Mo. d: 5/13/61, St.Louis, Mo. BR/TR, 5'9", 154 lbs. Deb: 4/15/24

1924	Bro-N	10	37	0	4	1	0	0	2	0	3	.108	.108	.135	-36	-7	-7	1	0	0	0	.898	-1	S	-0.7

■ JOHN JONES Jones, John William "Skins" b: 5/13/01, Coatesville, Pa. d: 11/3/56, Baltimore, Md. BL/TL, 5'11", 185 lbs. Deb: 9/26/23

1923	Phi-A	1	4	0	1	0	0	0	1	0	1	.250	.250	.250	31	-0	-0	0	0	0	0	1.000	0	/O	0.0
1932	Phi-A	4	6	0	1	0	0	0	0	0	3	.167	.167	.167	-13	-1	-1	0	0	0	0	1.000	-0	/O	-0.1
Total	2	5	10	0	2	0	0	0	1	0	4	.200	.200	.200	4	-1	-1	0	0	0	0	1.000	0	/O	-0.1

■ LYNN JONES Jones, Lynn Morris b: 1/1/53, Meadville, Pa. BR/TR, 5'9", 175 lbs. Deb: 4/13/79 FC

1979	Det-A	95	213	33	63	8	0	4	26	17	22	.296	.351	.390	96	0	-1	28	9	6	-1	.980	-10	O	-1.4
1980	Det-A	30	55	9	14	2	2	0	6	10	5	.255	.369	.364	99	0	0	8	1	0	0	1.000	-2	O/D	-0.1
1981	Det-A	71	174	19	45	5	0	2	19	18	10	.259	.332	.322	86	-2	-3	18	1	2	-1	.989	-4	O/D	-1.0
1982	Det-A	58	139	15	31	3	1	0	14	7	14	.223	.260	.259	43	-11	-11	9	0	2	-1	1.000	-5	O/D	-1.8
1983	Det-A	49	64	9	17	1	2	0	6	3	6	.266	.299	.344	78	-2	-2	7	1	0	0	.968	-7	O/D	-0.8
1984	*KC-A	47	103	11	31	6	0	1	10	4	9	.301	.333	.388	98	-0	-0	11	1	3	-2	.962	-12	O	-1.5
1985	*KC-A	110	152	12	32	7	0	0	9	8	15	.211	.264	.257	43	-12	-12	10	0	1	-1	.983	-24	*O/D	-3.8

YEAR	TM/L	G	AB	R	H	2B	3B	HR	RBI	BB	SO	AVG	OBP	SLG	PRO+	BR	/A	RC	SB	CS	SBR	FA	FR	POS	TPR
1986	KC-A	67	47	1	6	2	0	0	1	6	5	.128	.226	.170	10	-6	-6	2	0	0	0	.971	-21	O/2D	-2.7
Total	8	527	947	109	239	34	5	7	91	73	86	.252	.310	.321	73	-32	-34	92	13	14	-5	.983	-84	O/D2	-13.1

■ MACK JONES Jones, Mack "Mack The Knife" b: 11/6/38, Alanta, Ga. BL/TR, 6'1", 180 lbs. Deb: 7/13/61

YEAR	TM/L	G	AB	R	H	2B	3B	HR	RBI	BB	SO	AVG	OBP	SLG	PRO+	BR	/A	RC	SB	CS	SBR	FA	FR	POS	TPR
1961	Mil-N	28	104	13	24	3	2	0	12	12	28	.231	.322	.298	70	-5	-4	10	4	4	-1	1.000	-2	O	-0.9
1962	Mil-N	91	333	51	85	17	4	10	36	44	100	.255	.354	.420	110	4	5	52	5	1	1	.973	-6	O	-0.6
1963	Mil-N	93	228	36	50	11	4	3	22	26	59	.219	.318	.342	91	-2	-2	26	8	4	0	.978	-11	O	-1.8
1965	Mil-N	143	504	78	132	18	7	31	75	29	122	.262	.314	.510	127	16	16	81	8	2	1	.980	-11	*O	0.0
1966	Atl-N	118	417	60	110	14	1	23	66	39	85	.264	.338	.468	120	12	11	65	16	10	-1	.981	-6	*O/1	-0.1
1967	Atl-N	140	454	72	115	23	4	17	50	64	108	.253	.357	.434	127	16	17	73	10	6	-1	.985	-3	*O	0.7
1968	Cin-N	103	234	40	59	9	1	10	34	28	46	.252	.345	.427	123	9	8	34	2	3	-1	.988	-5	O	-0.2
1969	Mon-N	135	455	73	123	23	5	22	79	67	110	.270	.382	.488	142	27	27	85	6	7	-2	.959	-1	*O	1.7
1970	Mon-N	108	271	51	65	11	3	14	32	59	74	.240	.399	.458	129	14	14	56	5	3	-0	.968	-7	O	0.3
1971	Mon-N	43	91	11	15	3	0	3	9	15	24	.165	.296	.297	68	-4	-4	9	1	0	0	.952	-2	O	-0.7
Total	10	1002	3091	485	778	132	31	133	415	383	756	.252	.349	.444	120	87	87	492	65	40	-5	.976	-56	O/1	-1.6

■ RED JONES Jones, Maurice Morris b: 11/2/14, Timpson, Tex. d: 6/30/75, Lincoln, Cal. BL/TR, 6'3", 190 lbs. Deb: 4/16/40

YEAR	TM/L	G	AB	R	H	2B	3B	HR	RBI	BB	SO	AVG	OBP	SLG	PRO+	BR	/A	RC	SB	CS	SBR	FA	FR	POS	TPR
1940	StL-N	12	11	0	1	0	0	0	1	1	2	.091	.167	.091	-26	-2	-2	0	0			1.000	-0	/O	-0.2

■ RICKY JONES Jones, Ricky Miron b: 6/4/58, Tupelo, Miss. BR/TR, 6'3", 186 lbs. Deb: 9/03/86

YEAR	TM/L	G	AB	R	H	2B	3B	HR	RBI	BB	SO	AVG	OBP	SLG	PRO+	BR	/A	RC	SB	CS	SBR	FA	FR	POS	TPR
1986	Bal-A	16	33	2	6	2	0	0	4	6	8	.182	.308	.242	53	-2	-2	3	0	0	0	1.000	7	2/3	0.5

■ BOB JONES Jones, Robert Oliver b: 10/11/49, Elkton, Md. BL/TL, 6'2", 195 lbs. Deb: 10/01/74

YEAR	TM/L	G	AB	R	H	2B	3B	HR	RBI	BB	SO	AVG	OBP	SLG	PRO+	BR	/A	RC	SB	CS	SBR	FA	FR	POS	TPR
1974	Tex-A	2	5	0	0	0	0	0	0	0	1	.000	.000	.000	-99	-1	-1	0	0	0	0	1.000	0	/O	-0.1
1975	Tex-A	9	11	2	1	0	0	0	0	3	3	.091	.286	.091	11	-1	-1	1	0	0	0	1.000	-1	/OD	-0.2
1976	Cal-A	78	166	22	35	6	0	6	17	14	30	.211	.276	.355	90	-4	-3	16	3	0	1	.990	-5	O/D	-0.8
1977	Cal-A	14	17	3	3	0	0	1	3	4	5	.176	.333	.353	91	-0	-0	2	0	0	0	.000	0	/D	0.0
1981	Tex-A	10	34	4	9	1	0	3	7	1	7	.265	.286	.559	146	1	2	5	0	1	-1	1.000	3	O	0.4
1983	Tex-A	41	72	5	16	4	0	1	11	5	17	.222	.291	.319	69	-3	-3	6	0	2	-1	1.000	0	OD/1	-0.4
1984	Tex-A	64	143	14	37	4	0	4	22	10	19	.259	.312	.371	85	-2	-3	17	1	1	-0	1.000	-0	O1/D	-0.5
1985	Tex-A	83	134	14	30	2	0	5	23	11	30	.224	.288	.351	73	-5	-5	14	1	0	0	1.000	-7	OD/1	-1.2
1986	Tex-A	13	21	1	2	0	0	0	3	2	5	.095	.174	.095	-24	-4	-4	0	0	0	0	.909	-2	/O1	-0.6
Total	9	314	603	65	133	17	0	20	86	50	117	.221	.286	.348	78	-19	-18	62	5	4	-1	.992	-11	O/D1	-3.4

■ BOB JONES Jones, Robert Walter "Ducky" b: 12/2/1889, Clayton, Cal. d: 8/30/64, San Diego, Cal. BL/TR, 6', 170 lbs. Deb: 4/11/17

YEAR	TM/L	G	AB	R	H	2B	3B	HR	RBI	BB	SO	AVG	OBP	SLG	PRO+	BR	/A	RC	SB	CS	SBR	FA	FR	POS	TPR
1917	Det-A	46	77	16	12	1	2	0	2	4	8	.156	.198	.221	28	-7	-7	4	3			.938	-1	2/3	-0.8
1918	Det-A	74	287	43	79	14	4	0	21	17	16	.275	.320	.352	107	-0	1	34	7			.947	-8	3/1O	-0.7
1919	Det-A	127	439	37	114	18	6	1	57	34	39	.260	.314	.335	84	-11	-9	50	11			.944	-24	*3	-3.0
1920	Det-A	81	265	35	66	6	3	1	18	22	13	.249	.309	.306	65	-14	-13	26	3	4	-2	.942	-5	3/2S	-1.6
1921	Det-A	141	554	82	168	23	9	1	72	37	24	.303	.348	.383	87	-12	-11	73	8	9	-3	.950	10	*3	0.6
1922	Det-A	124	455	65	117	10	6	3	44	36	18	.257	.314	.325	69	-22	-20	48	8	6	-1	**.962**	11	*3	-0.2
1923	Det-A	100	372	51	93	15	4	1	40	29	13	.250	.306	.320	66	-19	-18	38	7	6	-2	.954	5	3	-0.6
1924	Det-A	110	393	52	107	27	4	0	47	20	20	.272	.308	.361	73	-18	-17	43	1	5	-3	.956	-2	*3	-1.3
1925	Det-A	50	148	18	35	6	0	0	15	9	5	.236	.280	.277	42	-13	-13	12	1	1	-0	.985	9	3	-0.2
Total	9	853	2990	399	791	120	38	7	316	208	156	.265	.314	.337	75	-115	-107	327	49	31		.953	-5	3/21SO	-7.8

■ RON JONES Jones, Ronald Glen b: 6/11/64, Seguin, Tex. BL/TR, 5'10", 195 lbs. Deb: 8/26/88

YEAR	TM/L	G	AB	R	H	2B	3B	HR	RBI	BB	SO	AVG	OBP	SLG	PRO+	BR	/A	RC	SB	CS	SBR	FA	FR	POS	TPR
1988	Phi-N	33	124	15	36	6	1	8	26	2	14	.290	.302	.548	136	5	5	20	0	0	0	1.000	2	O	0.7
1989	Phi-N	12	31	7	9	0	0	2	4	9	1	.290	.450	.484	167	3	3	7	1	0	0	1.000	2	O	0.5
1990	Phi-N	24	58	5	16	2	0	3	7	9	9	.276	.373	.466	130	2	2	10	0	1	-1	1.000	-1	O	0.1
1991	Phi-N	28	26	0	4	2	0	0	3	2	9	.154	.214	.231	25	-3	-3	1	0	0	0	.000	0	H	-0.3
Total	4	97	239	27	65	10	1	13	40	22	33	.272	.333	.485	128	8	8	38	1	1	-0	1.000	3	/O	1.0

■ ROSS JONES Jones, Ross A. b: 1/14/60, Miami, Fla. BR/TR, 6'2", 185 lbs. Deb: 4/02/84

YEAR	TM/L	G	AB	R	H	2B	3B	HR	RBI	BB	SO	AVG	OBP	SLG	PRO+	BR	/A	RC	SB	CS	SBR	FA	FR	POS	TPR
1984	NY-N	17	10	2	1	1	0	0	1	3	4	.100	.308	.200	46	-1	-1	1	0	0	0	.833	1	/S23	0.1
1986	Sea-A	11	21	0	2	0	0	0	0	0	4	.095	.095	.095	-48	-4	-4	0	0	1	-1	1.000	1	/S23D	-0.4
1987	KC-A	39	114	10	29	4	2	0	10	5	15	.254	.292	.325	62	-6	-6	10	1	0	0	.974	1	S/2	-0.2
Total	3	67	145	12	32	5	2	0	11	8	23	.221	.266	.283	46	-11	-11	11	1	1	-0	.971	3	/S23D	-0.5

■ RUPPERT JONES Jones, Ruppert Sanderson b: 3/12/55, Dallas, Tex. BL/TL, 5'10", 175 lbs. Deb: 8/01/76

YEAR	TM/L	G	AB	R	H	2B	3B	HR	RBI	BB	SO	AVG	OBP	SLG	PRO+	BR	/A	RC	SB	CS	SBR	FA	FR	POS	TPR
1976	KC-A	28	51	9	11	1	1	1	7	3	16	.216	.259	.333	72	-2	-2	4	0	2	-1	1.000	-5	O/D	-0.9
1977	Sea-A★	160	597	85	157	26	8	24	76	55	120	.263	.327	.454	111	7	8	89	13	9	-2	.981	22	*O/D	2.2
1978	Sea-A	129	472	48	111	24	3	6	46	55	85	.235	.315	.337	84	-10	-10	51	22	6	3	.985	16	*O	0.4
1979	Sea-A	162	622	109	166	29	9	21	78	85	78	.267	.358	.444	113	14	12	99	33	12	3	.989	14	*O	2.2
1980	NY-A	83	328	38	73	11	3	9	42	34	50	.223	.301	.357	81	-9	-9	36	18	8	1	.988	8	O	-0.3
1981	SD-N	105	397	53	99	34	1	4	39	43	66	.249	.323	.370	104	-2	1	47	7	9	-3	.993	6	*O	0.0
1982	SD-N★	116	424	69	120	20	2	12	61	62	90	.283	.376	.425	130	15	18	69	18	15	-4	.984	2	*O	1.4
1983	SD-N	133	335	42	78	12	3	12	49	35	58	.233	.305	.394	96	-4	-3	37	11	11	-3	.981	-8	*O/1	-1.8
1984	*Det-A	79	215	26	61	12	1	12	37	21	47	.284	.347	.516	136	10	10	36	2	4	-2	1.000	-5	O/D	0.2
1985	Cal-A	125	389	66	90	17	2	21	67	57	82	.231	.330	.447	111	5	6	60	7	4	-0	.995	10	OD	1.3
1986	*Cal-A	126	393	73	90	21	3	17	49	64	87	.229	.341	.427	109	5	5	60	10	3	1	.981	-12	*O	-0.9
1987	Cal-A	85	192	25	47	8	2	8	28	20	38	.245	.316	.432	99	-1	-1	26	2	1	0	.965	-15	O/D	-1.6
Total	12	1331	4415	643	1103	215	38	147	579	534	817	.250	.332	.416	106	27	37	614	143	84	-8	.986	34	*O/D1	2.2

■ JACK JONES Jones, Ryerson L. "Ri" or "Angel Sleeves" b: Cincinnati, Ohio TR , Deb: 8/13/1883

YEAR	TM/L	G	AB	R	H	2B	3B	HR	RBI	BB	SO	AVG	OBP	SLG	PRO+	BR	/A	RC	SB	CS	SBR	FA	FR	POS	TPR
1883	Lou-a	2	7	1	0	0	0	0		0		.000	.000	.000	-99	-1	-1	0				.500	-1	/OS	-0.2
1884	Cin-U	69	272	36	71	5	1	2		12		.261	.292	.309	96	1	-2	25				.858	2	S23	0.0
Total	2	71	279	37	71	5	1	2		12		.254	.285	.301	91	-0	-4	25				.857	1	/S23O	-0.2

■ TOM JONES Jones, Thomas b: 1/22/1877, Honesdale, Pa. d: 6/21/23, Danville, Pa. BR/TR, 6'1", 195 lbs. Deb: 8/25/02

YEAR	TM/L	G	AB	R	H	2B	3B	HR	RBI	BB	SO	AVG	OBP	SLG	PRO+	BR	/A	RC	SB	CS	SBR	FA	FR	POS	TPR
1902	Bal-A	37	159	22	45	8	4	0	14	2		.283	.292	.384	82	-4	-5	19	1			.955	-2	1/2	-0.7
1904	StL-A	156	625	53	152	15	10	2	68	15		.243	.270	.309	88	-13	-9	59	16			.988	0	*12/O	-1.3
1905	StL-A	135	504	44	122	16	2	0	48	30		.242	.289	.282	86	-11	-8	46	5			.985	7	*1	-0.5
1906	StL-A	144	539	51	136	22	6	0	30	24		.252	.290	.315	94	-7	-4	63	27			.985	11	*1	0.2
1907	StL-A	155	549	53	137	17	3	0	34	34		.250	.298	.291	89	-7	-7	60	24			.983	2	*1	-1.1
1908	StL-A	155	549	43	135	14	2	1	50	30		.246	.290	.284	86	-8	-8	52	18			.986	-2	*1	-1.5
1909	StL-A	97	337	30	84	9	3	0	29	18		.249	.299	.294	94	-5	-2	34	13			.989	7	1/3	0.5
	*Det-A	44	153	13	43	9	0	0	18	5		.281	.317	.340	103	1	0	20	9			.984	2	1	0.2
	Yr	141	490	43	127	18	3	0	47	23		.259	.305	.308	97	-4	-2	54	22			.988	9	*1/3	0.7
1910	Det-A	135	432	32	110	12	4	1	45	35		.255	.325	.308	92	-0	-4	53	22			.985	-4	*1	-0.8
Total	8	1058	3847	341	964	122	34	4	336	193		.251	.294	.303	90	-54	-47	406	135			.984	22	*1/2O3	-5.0

■ TRACY JONES Jones, Tracy Donald b: 3/31/61, Hawthorne, Cal. BR/TR, 6'3", 220 lbs. Deb: 4/07/86

YEAR	TM/L	G	AB	R	H	2B	3B	HR	RBI	BB	SO	AVG	OBP	SLG	PRO+	BR	/A	RC	SB	CS	SBR	FA	FR	POS	TPR
1986	Cin-N	46	86	16	30	3	0	2	10	9	5	.349	.411	.453	132	5	4	17	7	1	2	1.000	-0	O/1	0.5
1987	Cin-N	117	359	53	104	17	3	10	44	23	40	.290	.338	.437	99	1	-1	52	31	8	5	.990	-3	O	-0.2

YEAR	TM/L	G	AB	R	H	2B	3B	HR	RBI	BB	SO	AVG	OBP	SLG	PRO+	BR	/A	RC	SB	CS	SBR	FA	FR	POS	TPR
1988	Cin-N	37	83	9	19	1	0	1	9	8	6	.229	.304	.277	65	-3	-4	8	9	0	3	.955	-2	O	-0.4
	Mon-N	53	141	20	47	5	1	2	15	12	12	.333	.390	.426	128	6	6	23	9	6	-1	1.000	-8	O	-0.5
	Yr	90	224	29	66	6	1	3	24	20	18	.295	.358	.371	105	3	2	31	18	6	2	.980	-10	O	-0.9
1989	SF-N	40	97	5	18	4	0	0	12	5	14	.186	.233	.227	33	-9	-8	4	2	1	0	1.000	-8	O	-1.8
	Det-A	46	158	17	41	10	0	3	26	16	16	.259	.331	.380	102	0	1	21	1	1	-0	.986	-1	O/D	-0.2
1990	Det-A	50	118	15	27	4	1	4	9	6	13	.229	.283	.381	84	-3	-3	12	1	1	-0	.952	-2	OD	-0.5
	Sea-A	25	86	8	26	4	0	2	15	3	12	.302	.341	.419	110	1	1	11	0	1	-1	1.000	-1	O/D	-0.1
	Yr	75	204	23	53	8	1	6	24	9	25	.260	.307	.397	95	-2	-2	23	1	2	-1	.973	-3	OD	-0.6
1991	Sea-A	79	175	30	44	8	1	3	24	18	22	.251	.325	.360	89	-2	-2	20	2	0	1	1.000	-5	DO	-0.7
Total	6	493	1303	173	356	56	6	27	164	100	140	.273	.331	.388	96	-4	-7	168	62	19	7	.988	-31	O/D1	-3.9

■ NIPPY JONES
Jones, Vernal Leroy b: 6/29/25, Los Angeles, Cal. BR/TR, 6'1", 185 lbs. Deb: 6/08/46

YEAR	TM/L	G	AB	R	H	2B	3B	HR	RBI	BB	SO	AVG	OBP	SLG	PRO+	BR	/A	RC	SB	CS	SBR	FA	FR	POS	TPR
1946	*StL-N	16	12	3	4	0	0	0	1	2	2	.333	.429	.333	113	0	0	1	0			.800	1	/2	0.1
1947	StL-N	23	73	6	18	4	0	1	5	2	10	.247	.267	.342	58	-4	-5	6	0			.935	-2	2/O	-0.5
1948	StL-N	132	481	58	122	21	9	10	81	36	45	.254	.307	.397	84	-9	-12	52	2			.986	-9	*1	-2.2
1949	StL-N	110	380	51	114	20	2	8	62	16	20	.300	.330	.426	97	-0	-3	50	1			.984	-8	1	-1.1
1950	StL-N	13	26	0	6	1	0	0	6	3	1	.231	.310	.269	52	-2	-2	2	0			.983	-1	/1	-0.2
1951	StL-N	80	300	20	79	12	0	3	41	9	13	.263	.287	.333	66	-15	-15	25	1	2	-1	.991	-1	1	-2.0
1952	Phi-N	8	30	3	5	0	0	1	5	0	4	.167	.167	.267	19	-3	-3	1	0	0	0	.976	0	/1	-0.3
1957	*Mil-N	30	79	5	21	2	1	2	8	3	7	.266	.293	.392	88	-2	-1	9	0	0	0	.994	-0	1/O	-0.3
Total	8	412	1381	146	369	60	12	25	209	71	102	.267	.304	.382	81	-35	-41	147	4	2		.987	-19	1/2O	-6.5

■ BILL JONES
Jones, William b: Syracuse, N.Y. Deb: 5/17/1882

YEAR	TM/L	G	AB	R	H	2B	3B	HR	RBI	BB	SO	AVG	OBP	SLG	PRO+	BR	/A	RC	SB	CS	SBR	FA	FR	POS	TPR
1882	Bal-a	4	15	1	1	0	0	0		0		.067	.067	.067	-59	-2	-2	0				1.000	0	/OC	-0.2
1884	Phi-U	4	14	2	2	0	0	0		1		.143	.200	.143	19	-1	-1	0				.862	0	/CO	0.0
Total	2	8	29	3	3	0	0	0		1		.103	.133	.103	-21	-3	-3	0				.857	1	/CO	-0.2

■ BILL JONES
Jones, William Dennis "Midget" b: 4/8/1887, Hartland, N.B., Can. d: 10/10/46, Boston, Mass. BL/TR, 5'6.5", 157 lbs. Deb: 6/20/11

YEAR	TM/L	G	AB	R	H	2B	3B	HR	RBI	BB	SO	AVG	OBP	SLG	PRO+	BR	/A	RC	SB	CS	SBR	FA	FR	POS	TPR
1911	Bos-N	24	51	6	11	2	1	0	3	15	7	.216	.394	.294	87	0	-0	6	1			.867	-1	O	-0.2
1912	Bos-N	3	2	0	1	0	0	0	2	0	1	.500	.500	.500	171	0	0	0	0			.000	0	H	0.0
Total	2	27	53	6	12	2	1	0	5	15	8	.226	.397	.302	89	1	-0	7	1				-1	/O	-0.2

■ TEX JONES
Jones, William Roderick b: 8/4/1885, Marion, Kan. d: 2/26/38, Wichita, Kan. BR/TR, 6', 192 lbs. Deb: 4/13/11

YEAR	TM/L	G	AB	R	H	2B	3B	HR	RBI	BB	SO	AVG	OBP	SLG	PRO+	BR	/A	RC	SB	CS	SBR	FA	FR	POS	TPR
1911	Chi-A	9	31	4	6	1	0	0	4	3		.194	.265	.226	39	-3	-2	2	1			1.000	3	/1	0.1

■ TIM JONES
Jones, William Timothy b: 12/1/62, Sumter, S.C. BL/TR, 5'10", 172 lbs. Deb: 7/26/88

YEAR	TM/L	G	AB	R	H	2B	3B	HR	RBI	BB	SO	AVG	OBP	SLG	PRO+	BR	/A	RC	SB	CS	SBR	FA	FR	POS	TPR
1988	StL-N	31	52	2	14	0	0	0	3	4	10	.269	.321	.269	70	-2	-2	5	4	1	1	.955	5	/S23	0.4
1989	StL-N	42	75	11	22	6	0	0	7	7	8	.293	.361	.373	107	1	1	10	1	0	0	1.000	-2	2S/3CO	0.0
1990	StL-N	67	128	9	28	7	1	1	12	12	20	.219	.291	.313	66	-6	-6	12	3	4	-2	.944	2	S2/3P	-0.4
1991	StL-N	16	24	1	4	2	0	0	2	2	6	.167	.231	.250	35	-2	-2	1	0	1	-1	1.000	-2	S/2	-0.5
1992	StL-N	67	145	9	29	4	0	0	3	11	29	.200	.256	.228	39	-12	-11	9	5	2	0	.972	2	S2/3O	-0.7
Total	5	223	424	32	97	19	1	1	27	36	73	.229	.292	.285	63	-20	-20	37	13	8	-1	.961	5	/S23OPC	-1.2

■ WILLIE JONES
Jones, Willie Edward "Puddin' Head" b: 8/16/25, Dillon, S.C. d: 10/18/83, Cincinnati, Ohio BR/TR, 6'1", 192 lbs. Deb: 9/10/47

YEAR	TM/L	G	AB	R	H	2B	3B	HR	RBI	BB	SO	AVG	OBP	SLG	PRO+	BR	/A	RC	SB	CS	SBR	FA	FR	POS	TPR
1947	Phi-N	18	62	5	14	0	1	0	10	7	0	.226	.304	.258	53	-4	-4	5	2			.909	2	3	-0.1
1948	Phi-N	17	60	9	20	2	0	2	9	3	5	.333	.365	.467	126	2	2	9	0			.926	2	3	0.4
1949	Phi-N	149	532	71	130	35	1	19	77	65	66	.244	.328	.421	102	-1	1	71	3			.948	-4	*3	-0.6
1950	*Phi-N★	157	610	100	163	28	6	25	88	61	40	.267	.337	.456	108	4	5	93	5			.954	-6	*3	-0.3
1951	Phi-N★	148	564	79	161	28	5	22	81	60	47	.285	.358	.470	123	16	17	100	6	2	1	.966	-9	*3	0.7
1952	Phi-N	147	541	60	135	12	3	18	72	53	36	.250	.323	.383	96	-4	-3	68	5	3	-0	**.969**	4	*3	-0.3
1953	Phi-N	149	481	61	108	16	2	19	70	85	45	.225	.342	.385	90	-7	-6	69	1	1	-0	**.975**	-3	*3	-1.2
1954	Phi-N	142	535	64	145	28	3	12	56	61	54	.271	.346	.402	94	-4	-4	77	4	1	1	**.968**	-2	*3	-0.9
1955	Phi-N	146	516	65	133	20	3	16	81	77	51	.258	.357	.401	103	2	4	77	6	2	1	**.960**	-13	*3	-0.9
1956	Phi-N	149	520	88	144	20	4	17	78	92	49	.277	.387	.429	121	17	18	89	5	4	-1	**.973**	1	*3	2.1
1957	Phi-N	133	440	58	96	19	2	9	47	61	41	.218	.313	.332	76	-16	-14	47	1	0	0	.966	-7	*3	-1.9
1958	Phi-N	118	398	52	108	15	1	14	60	49	45	.271	.354	.420	105	3	3	60	1	2	-1	**.967**	-13	*3/1	-1.0
1959	Phi-N	47	160	23	43	9	1	7	24	19	14	.269	.346	.469	113	3	3	26	0	0	0	.975	-3	3	0.0
	Cle-A	11	18	1	4	1	0	0	1	1	3	.222	.263	.278	51	-1	-1	1	0	0	0	.929	2	/3	0.1
	Cin-N	72	233	33	58	12	1	7	31	28	26	.249	.332	.399	91	-2	-3	30	0	2	-1	.966	-3	3	-0.7
1960	Cin-N	79	149	16	40	7	0	3	27	31	16	.268	.394	.376	110	4	4	25	1	0	0	.962	-3	3/2	0.0
1961	Cin-N	9	7	1	0	0	0	0	0	2	3	.000	.222	.000	-34	-1	-1	0	0	0	0	.000	-0	/3	-0.2
Total	15	1691	5826	786	1502	252	33	190	812	755	541	.258	.345	.410	102	10	20	845	40	17		.963	-55	*3/21	-4.8

■ BUBBER JONNARD
Jonnard, Clarence James b: 11/23/1897, Nashville, Tenn. d: 8/23/77, New York, N.Y. BR/TR, 6'1", 185 lbs. Deb: 10/01/20 FC

YEAR	TM/L	G	AB	R	H	2B	3B	HR	RBI	BB	SO	AVG	OBP	SLG	PRO+	BR	/A	RC	SB	CS	SBR	FA	FR	POS	TPR
1920	Chi-A	2	5	0	0	0	0	0	0	0	1	.000	.000	.000	-99	-1	-1	0	0	0	0	.857	0	/C	-0.1
1922	Pit-N	10	21	4	5	0	1	0	2	2	4	.238	.304	.333	64	-1	-1	2	0	0	0	.974	2	C	0.1
1926	Phi-N	19	34	3	4	1	0	0	2	3	4	.118	.189	.147	-8	-5	-5	1	0			.949	0	C	-0.5
1927	Phi-N	53	143	18	42	6	0	0	14	7	7	.294	.327	.336	77	-4	-5	15	0			.967	-9	C	-1.1
1929	StL-N	18	31	1	3	0	0	0	2	0	6	.097	.097	.097	-51	-7	-7	0	0			.957	1	C	-0.5
1935	Phi-N	1	1	0	0	0	0	0	0	0	1	.000	.000	.000	-91	-0	-0	0	0			1.000	-0	/C	0.0
Total	6	103	235	26	54	7	1	0	20	12	23	.230	.267	.268	41	-20	-20	19	0	0		.960	-5	/C	-2.1

■ EDDIE JOOST
Joost, Edwin David b: 6/5/16, San Francisco, Cal BR/TR, 6', 175 lbs. Deb: 9/11/36 M

YEAR	TM/L	G	AB	R	H	2B	3B	HR	RBI	BB	SO	AVG	OBP	SLG	PRO+	BR	/A	RC	SB	CS	SBR	FA	FR	POS	TPR
1936	Cin-N	13	26	1	4	1	0	0	1	2	5	.154	.214	.192	11	-3	-3	1	0			.947	-1	/S2	-0.4
1937	Cin-N	6	12	0	1	0	0	0	0	0	0	.083	.083	.083	-57	-3	-2	0	0			.875	0	/2	-0.2
1939	Cin-N	42	143	23	36	6	3	0	14	12	15	.252	.310	.336	73	-5	-5	15	1			.957	-3	2/S	-0.6
1940	*Cin-N	88	278	24	60	7	2	1	24	32	40	.216	.301	.266	57	-15	-16	24	4			.960	-1	S/23	-1.0
1941	Cin-N	152	537	67	136	25	4	4	40	69	59	.253	.340	.337	91	-5	-5	66	9			.942	-6	*S/213	0.0
1942	Cin-N	142	562	65	126	30	3	6	41	62	57	.224	.307	.320	84	-11	-11	59	9			.933	-10	*S2	-1.4
1943	Bos-N	124	421	34	78	16	3	2	20	68	80	.185	.299	.252	61	-20	-19	35	5			.945	13	32/S	-0.3
1945	Bos-N	35	141	16	35	7	1	0	9	13	7	.248	.312	.312	73	-5	-5	14	0			.945	-7	23	-1.1
1947	Phi-A	151	540	76	111	22	3	13	64	114	110	.206	.348	.330	87	-5	-6	73	6	6	-2	.956	-3	*S	-0.3
1948	Phi-A	135	509	99	127	22	2	16	55	119	87	.250	.393	.395	110	11	11	91	2	4	-2	.973	5	*S	2.1
1949	Phi-A★	144	525	128	138	25	3	23	81	149	80	.263	.429	.453	138	32	35	119	2	1	0	.969	8	*S	5.1
1950	Phi-A	131	476	79	111	12	3	18	58	103	68	.233	.373	.384	96	-2	-1	77	5	1	1	.956	-7	*S	0.3
1951	Phi-A	140	553	107	160	28	5	19	78	106	70	.289	.409	.461	132	30	29	115	10	8	-2	.974	4	*S	3.9
1952	Phi-A☆	146	540	94	132	26	3	20	75	122	94	.244	.388	.415	116	21	17	98	5	8	-3	.962	-7	*S	1.8
1953	Phi-A	51	177	39	44	6	0	6	15	45	24	.249	.401	.384	109	5	4	32	3	2	-0	.958	-6	S	0.1
1954	Phi-A	19	47	7	17	3	0	1	9	10	10	.362	.474	.489	163	5	5	10	0	1	-1	.963	-3	/S32M	0.2
1955	Bos-A	55	119	15	23	2	0	5	17	17	21	.193	.299	.336	65	-5	-7	13	0	0	0	.932	5	S2/3	0.1
Total	17	1574	5606	874	1339	238	35	134	601	1043	827	.239	.361	.366	99	25	19	842	61	31		.958	-20	*S2/31	8.3

■ DUTCH JORDAN
Jordan, Adolf Otto b: 1/5/1880, Pittsburgh, Pa. d: 12/23/72, W.Allegheny, Pa. BR/TR, 5'10", 185 lbs. Deb: 4/25/03

YEAR	TM/L	G	AB	R	H	2B	3B	HR	RBI	BB	SO	AVG	OBP	SLG	PRO+	BR	/A	RC	SB	CS	SBR	FA	FR	POS	TPR
1903	Bro-N	78	267	27	63	11	1	0	21	19		.236	.287	.285	65	-13	-12	26	9			.928	-14	23/O1	-2.3
1904	Bro-N	87	252	21	45	10	2	0	19	13		.179	.225	.234	43	-17	-16	17	7			.958	-17	23/1	-3.4

YEAR	TM/L	G	AB	R	H	2B	3B	HR	RBI	BB	SO	AVG	OBP	SLG	PRO+	BR	/A	RC	SB	CS	SBR	FA	FR	POS	TPR
Total	2	165	519	48	108	21	3	0	40	32		.208	.257	.260	55	-30	-28	43	16			.945	-31	2/31O	-5.7

■ BUCK JORDAN
Jordan, Baxter Byerly b: 1/16/07, Cooleemee, N.C. BL/TR, 6', 170 lbs. Deb: 9/15/27

YEAR	TM/L	G	AB	R	H	2B	3B	HR	RBI	BB	SO	AVG	OBP	SLG	PRO+	BR	/A	RC	SB	CS	SBR	FA	FR	POS	TPR
1927	NY-N	5	5	0	1	0	0	0	0	0	3	.200	.200	.200	7	-1	-1	0	0			.000	0	H	-0.1
1929	NY-N	2	2	1	1	1	0	0	0	0	0	.500	.500	1.000	262	0	0	1	0			1.000	-0	/1	0.0
1931	Was-A	9	18	3	4	2	0	0	1	1	3	.222	.263	.333	56	-1	-1	2	0	0	0	.978	-1	/1	-0.2
1932	Bos-N	49	212	27	68	12	3	2	29	4	5	.321	.333	.434	109	1	2	30	1			.991	-1	1	-0.4
1933	Bos-N	152	588	77	168	29	9	4	46	34	22	.286	.327	.386	112	2	7	74	4			.991	-3	*1	-1.1
1934	Bos-N	124	489	68	152	26	9	2	58	35	19	.311	.358	.413	114	4	9	74	3			.989	-3	*1	-0.4
1935	Bos-N	130	470	62	131	24	5	5	35	19	17	.279	.307	.383	91	-11	-6	54	3			.983	1	1/3O	-1.5
1936	Bos-N	138	555	81	179	27	5	3	66	45	22	.323	.375	.405	118	9	14	83	2			.993	1	*1	0.2
1937	Bos-N	8	8	1	2	0	0	0	0	0	0	.250	.250	.250	40	-1	-1	0	0			.000	0	H	-0.1
	Cin-N	98	316	45	89	14	3	1	28	25	14	.282	.334	.354	92	-5	-3	39	6			.989	-2	1	-1.4
	Yr	106	324	46	91	14	3	1	28	25	14	.281	.332	.352	91	-6	-4	39	6			.989	-2	1	-1.5
1938	Cin-N	9	7	0	2	0	0	0	0	2	0	.286	.444	.286	107	0	0	1	0			.000	0	H	0.0
	Phi-N	87	310	31	93	18	1	0	18	17	4	.300	.336	.365	95	-3	-2	38	1			.973	-4	31	-0.7
	Yr	96	317	31	95	18	1	0	18	19	4	.300	.339	.363	96	-3	-2	39	1			.973	-4	31	-0.7
Total	10	811	2980	396	890	153	35	17	281	182	109	.299	.340	.391	106	-6	18	397	20	0		.990	-12	1/3O	-5.7

■ BRIAN JORDAN
Jordan, Brian O'Neal b: 3/29/67, Baltimore, Md. BR/TR, 6'1", 205 lbs. Deb: 4/08/92

YEAR	TM/L	G	AB	R	H	2B	3B	HR	RBI	BB	SO	AVG	OBP	SLG	PRO+	BR	/A	RC	SB	CS	SBR	FA	FR	POS	TPR
1992	StL-N	55	193	17	40	9	4	5	22	10	48	.207	.250	.373	75	-7	-7	16	7	2	1	.991	-1	O	-0.8

■ SLATS JORDAN
Jordan, Clarence Veasey b: 9/26/1879, Baltimore, Md. d: 12/7/53, Catonsville, Md. BL/TL, 6'1", 190 lbs. Deb: 9/28/01

YEAR	TM/L	G	AB	R	H	2B	3B	HR	RBI	BB	SO	AVG	OBP	SLG	PRO+	BR	/A	RC	SB	CS	SBR	FA	FR	POS	TPR
1901	Bal-A	1	3	0	0	0	0	0	0	0		.000	.000	.000	-96	-1	-1	0	0			.867	-1	/1	-0.1
1902	Bal-A	1	4	0	0	0	0	0	0	0		.000	.000	.000	-96	-1	-1	0	0			.000	-0	/O	-0.2
Total	2	2	7	0	0	0	0	0	0	0		.000	.000	.000	-96	-2	-2	0	0				-1	/O1	-0.3

■ JIMMY JORDAN
Jordan, James William "Lord" b: 1/13/08, Tucapau, S.C. d: 12/4/57, Gastonia, N.C. BR/TR, 5'9", 157 lbs. Deb: 4/20/33

YEAR	TM/L	G	AB	R	H	2B	3B	HR	RBI	BB	SO	AVG	OBP	SLG	PRO+	BR	/A	RC	SB	CS	SBR	FA	FR	POS	TPR
1933	Bro-N	70	211	16	54	12	1	0	17	4	6	.256	.270	.322	71	-9	-8	18	3			.969	12	S2	0.8
1934	Bro-N	97	369	34	98	17	2	0	43	9	32	.266	.285	.322	66	-20	-17	33	1			.956	-13	S2/3	-2.5
1935	Bro-N	94	295	26	82	7	0	0	30	9	17	.278	.302	.302	64	-15	-14	27	3			.983	27	2S/3	1.6
1936	Bro-N	115	398	26	93	15	1	2	28	15	21	.234	.262	.291	48	-29	-29	31	1			.970	-17	2/S3	-3.9
Total	4	376	1273	102	327	51	4	2	118	37	76	.257	.279	.308	60	-73	-69	108	8			.969	8	2S/3	-4.0

■ MIKE JORDAN
Jordan, Michael Henry "Mitty" b: 2/7/1863, Lawrence, Mass. d: 9/25/40, Lawrence, Mass. Deb: 8/21/1890

YEAR	TM/L	G	AB	R	H	2B	3B	HR	RBI	BB	SO	AVG	OBP	SLG	PRO+	BR	/A	RC	SB	CS	SBR	FA	FR	POS	TPR
1890	Pit-N	37	125	8	12	1	0	0	6	15	19	.096	.210	.104	-7	-16	-14	4	5			.947	2	O	-1.2

■ RICKY JORDAN
Jordan, Paul Scott b: 5/26/65, Richmond, Cal. BR/TR, 6'5", 210 lbs. Deb: 7/17/88

YEAR	TM/L	G	AB	R	H	2B	3B	HR	RBI	BB	SO	AVG	OBP	SLG	PRO+	BR	/A	RC	SB	CS	SBR	FA	FR	POS	TPR
1988	Phi-N	69	273	41	84	15	1	11	43	7	39	.308	.325	.491	128	9	9	41	1	1	-0	.992	-5	1	-0.2
1989	Phi-N	144	523	63	149	22	3	12	75	23	62	.285	.321	.407	107	3	3	62	4	3	-1	.993	-11	*1	-2.1
1990	Phi-N	92	324	32	78	21	0	5	44	13	39	.241	.281	.352	73	-13	-13	30	2	0	1	.995	-8	1	-2.7
1991	Phi-N	101	301	38	82	21	3	9	49	14	49	.272	.309	.452	113	3	4	38	0	2	-1	.987	-6	1	-0.8
1992	Phi-N	94	276	33	84	19	0	4	34	5	44	.304	.317	.417	107	1	1	34	3	0	1	.995	-6	1O	-0.8
Total	5	500	1697	207	477	98	7	41	245	62	233	.281	.311	.420	105	4	5	206	10	6	-1	.992	-36	1/O	-6.6

■ SCOTT JORDAN
Jordan, Scott Allan b: 5/27/63, Waco, Tex. BR/TR, 6', 175 lbs. Deb: 9/02/88

YEAR	TM/L	G	AB	R	H	2B	3B	HR	RBI	BB	SO	AVG	OBP	SLG	PRO+	BR	/A	RC	SB	CS	SBR	FA	FR	POS	TPR
1988	Cle-A	7	9	0	1	0	0	0	1	0	3	.111	.111	.111	-37	-2	-2	0	0	0	0	1.000	-1	/O	-0.3

■ TOM JORDAN
Jordan, Thomas Jefferson b: 9/5/19, Lawton, Okla. BR/TR, 6'1.5", 195 lbs. Deb: 9/04/44

YEAR	TM/L	G	AB	R	H	2B	3B	HR	RBI	BB	SO	AVG	OBP	SLG	PRO+	BR	/A	RC	SB	CS	SBR	FA	FR	POS	TPR
1944	Chi-A	14	45	2	12	1	1	0	3	1	0	.267	.283	.333	77	-2	-2	4	0	0	0	.947	-1	C	-0.2
1946	Chi-A	10	15	1	4	2	1	0	0	0	1	.267	.267	.533	124	0	0	1	0	0	0	1.000	1	/C	0.1
	Cle-A	14	35	2	7	1	0	1	3	3	1	.200	.263	.314	65	-2	-2	2	1	1	-0	.974	-6	C	-0.8
	Yr	24	50	3	11	3	1	1	3	3	2	.220	.264	.380	83	-2	-1	3	1	1	-0	.980	-5	C	-0.7
1948	StL-A	1	1	0	0	0	0	0	0	0	0	.000	.000	.000	-97	-0	-0	0	0	0	0	.000	0	H	0.0
Total	3	39	96	5	23	4	2	1	6	4	2	.240	.270	.354	78	-4	-3	7	1	1	-0	.963	-6	/C	-0.9

■ TIM JORDAN
Jordan, Timothy Joseph b: 2/14/1879, New York, N.Y. d: 9/13/49, Bronx, N.Y. BL/TL, 6'1", 170 lbs. Deb: 8/10/01

YEAR	TM/L	G	AB	R	H	2B	3B	HR	RBI	BB	SO	AVG	OBP	SLG	PRO+	BR	/A	RC	SB	CS	SBR	FA	FR	POS	TPR
1901	Was-A	6	20	2	4	1	0	0	2	3		.200	.304	.250	56	-1	-1	2	0			.941	-1	/1	-0.2
1903	NY-A	2	8	2	1	0	0	0	0	0		.125	.125	.125	-23	-1	-1	0	0			.889	-1	/1	-0.2
1906	Bro-N	129	450	67	118	20	8	**12**	78	59		.262	.350	.422	153	21	25	75	16			.978	-9	*1	1.3
1907	Bro-N	147	485	43	133	15	8	4	53	74		.274	.371	.363	142	19	24	73	10			.980	-6	*1	1.6
1908	Bro-N	148	515	58	127	18	5	**12**	60	59		.247	.326	.371	128	13	15	65	9			.982	-15	*1	-0.3
1909	Bro-N	103	330	47	90	20	3	3	36	59		.273	.386	.379	142	17	18	54	13			.983	-9	1	0.9
1910	Bro-N	5	5	1	1	0	0	1	3	0	2	.200	.200	.800	195	0	0	1	0			.000	0	H	0.0
Total	7	540	1813	220	474	74	24	32	232	254	2	.261	.354	.382	139	69	81	269	48			.980	-40	1	3.1

■ ART JORGENS
Jorgens, Arndt Ludwig b: 5/18/05, Modum, Norway d: 3/1/80, Wilmette, Ill. BR/TR, 5'9", 160 lbs. Deb: 4/26/29 F

YEAR	TM/L	G	AB	R	H	2B	3B	HR	RBI	BB	SO	AVG	OBP	SLG	PRO+	BR	/A	RC	SB	CS	SBR	FA	FR	POS	TPR
1929	NY-A	18	34	6	11	3	0	0	4	6	7	.324	.425	.412	125	1	2	6	0	2	-1	.979	-0	C	0.1
1930	NY-A	16	30	7	11	3	0	0	1	2	4	.367	.406	.467	126	1	1	6	0	0	0	.960	-0	C	0.2
1931	NY-A	46	100	12	27	1	2	0	14	9	3	.270	.330	.320	76	-4	-3	11	0	1	-1	.962	-1	C	-0.3
1932	NY-A	56	151	13	33	7	1	2	19	14	11	.219	.285	.318	59	-10	-9	14	0	0	0	.967	0	C	-0.6
1933	NY-A	21	50	9	11	3	0	2	13	12	3	.220	.371	.400	111	1	1	8	1	0	0	.982	2	C	0.4
1934	NY-A	58	183	14	38	6	1	0	20	23	24	.208	.296	.251	45	-15	-14	15	2	0	1	.984	6	C	-0.4
1935	NY-A	36	84	6	20	2	0	0	8	12	10	.238	.333	.262	59	-5	-4	8	0	0	0	1.000	6	C	0.2
1936	NY-A	31	66	5	18	3	1	0	5	2	3	.273	.294	.348	60	-5	-4	7	0	0	0	.990	3	C	0.0
1937	NY-A	13	23	3	3	1	0	0	3	2	5	.130	.200	.174	-5	-4	-4	1	0	0	0	1.000	0	C	-0.3
1938	NY-A	9	17	3	4	2	0	0	2	3	3	.235	.350	.353	77	-1	-1	2	0	0	0	.923	1	/C	0.0
1939	NY-A	3	0	1	0	0	0	0	0	0	0	—	—	—	—	0	0	0	0	0	0	1.000	1	/C	0.1
Total	11	307	738	79	176	31	5	4	89	85	73	.238	.317	.310	66	-41	-35	78	3	3	-1	.978	18	C	-0.6

■ PINKY JORGENSEN
Jorgensen, Carl b: 11/21/14, Laton, Cal. BR/TR, 6'1", 195 lbs. Deb: 9/14/37

YEAR	TM/L	G	AB	R	H	2B	3B	HR	RBI	BB	SO	AVG	OBP	SLG	PRO+	BR	/A	RC	SB	CS	SBR	FA	FR	POS	TPR
1937	Cin-N	6	14	1	4	0	0	0	1	1	2	.286	.333	.286	73	-1	-0	2	0			.875	0	/O	0.0

■ SPIDER JORGENSEN
Jorgensen, John Donald b: 11/3/19, Folsom, Cal. BL/TR, 5'9", 155 lbs. Deb: 4/15/47

YEAR	TM/L	G	AB	R	H	2B	3B	HR	RBI	BB	SO	AVG	OBP	SLG	PRO+	BR	/A	RC	SB	CS	SBR	FA	FR	POS	TPR
1947	*Bro-N	129	441	57	121	29	8	5	67	58	45	.274	.360	.410	100	3	1	69	4			.949	-5	*3	-0.3
1948	Bro-N	31	90	15	27	6	2	1	13	16	13	.300	.411	.444	127	5	4	18	1			.887	-6	3	-0.2
1949	*Bro-N	53	134	15	36	5	1	1	14	23	13	.269	.376	.343	90	-0	-1	19	0			.946	-5	3	-0.6
1950	Bro-N	2	2	0	0	0	0	0	1	1	0	.000	.333	.000	-4	-0	-0	0	0			1.000	-0	/3	0.0
	NY-N	24	37	5	5	0	0	0	4	5	2	.135	.238	.135	1	-5	-5	2	0			.913	1	/3	-0.4
	Yr	26	39	5	5	0	0	0	5	6	2	.128	.244	.128	1	-6	-6	2	0			.917	1	/3	-0.4
1951	NY-N	28	51	5	12	0	0	2	8	3	2	.235	.291	.353	72	-2	-2	6	0	0	0	1.000	-2	O/3	-0.5
Total	5	267	755	97	201	40	11	9	107	106	75	.266	.359	.384	95	-0	-4	114	5	0		.940	-17	3/O	-2.0

■ MIKE JORGENSEN
Jorgensen, Michael b: 8/16/48, Passaic, N.J. BL/TL, 6', 195 lbs. Deb: 9/10/68

YEAR	TM/L	G	AB	R	H	2B	3B	HR	RBI	BB	SO	AVG	OBP	SLG	PRO+	BR	/A	RC	SB	CS	SBR	FA	FR	POS	TPR
1968	NY-N	8	14	0	2	1	0	0	0	0	4	.143	.143	.214	6	-2	-2	0	0	0	0	1.000	-0	/1	-0.2
1970	NY-N	76	87	15	17	3	1	3	4	10	23	.195	.278	.356	69	-4	-4	9	2	2	-1	.992	4	1O	-0.2

YEAR	TM/L	G	AB	R	H	2B	3B	HR	RBI	BB	SO	AVG	OBP	SLG	PRO+	BR	/A	RC	SB	CS	SBR	FA	FR	POS	TPR
1971	NY-N	45	118	16	26	1	1	5	11	11	24	.220	.303	.373	92	-2	-1	12	1	2	-1	.951	-0	O/1	-0.4
1972	Mon-N	113	372	48	86	12	3	13	47	53	75	.231	.333	.384	102	2	2	47	12	13	-4	.995	3	1O	-0.9
1973	Mon-N	138	413	49	95	16	2	9	47	64	49	.230	.338	.344	86	-5	-7	52	16	7	1	**.995**	6	*1O	-0.9
1974	Mon-N	131	287	45	89	16	1	11	59	70	39	.310	.448	.488	153	28	26	68	3	5	-2	.998	7	1O	2.6
1975	Mon-N	144	445	58	116	18	0	18	67	79	75	.261	.380	.422	117	16	13	76	3	3	-1	.994	5	*1/O	1.0
1976	Mon-N	125	343	36	87	13	0	6	23	52	48	.254	.352	.344	94	1	-1	45	7	1	2	.989	4	1O	-0.2
1977	Mon-N	19	20	3	4	1	0	0	0	3	4	.200	.304	.250	52	-1	-1	2	0	0	0	1.000	1	/1	0.0
	Oak-A	66	203	18	50	4	1	8	32	25	44	.246	.335	.394	99	-0	0	28	3	2	-0	.989	1	1O/D	-0.3
1978	Tex-A	96	97	20	19	3	0	1	9	18	10	.196	.322	.258	65	-4	-4	9	3	1	0	.994	6	1/OD	0.1
1979	Tex-A	90	157	21	35	7	0	6	16	14	29	.223	.295	.382	82	-4	-4	17	0	2	-1	.988	2	1O	-0.6
1980	NY-N	119	321	43	82	11	0	7	43	46	55	.255	.349	.355	100	-0	1	39	0	3	-2	.995	0	1O	-0.6
1981	NY-N	86	122	8	25	5	2	3	15	12	24	.205	.276	.352	79	-4	-4	13	4	0	1	.991	1	1O	-0.3
1982	NY-N	120	114	16	29	6	0	2	14	21	24	.254	.370	.360	106	2	2	17	2	0	1	.991	-1	1O	0.0
1983	NY-N	38	24	5	6	3	0	1	3	2	4	.250	.333	.500	129	1	1	3	0	1	-1	1.000	1	1	0.1
	Atl-N	57	48	5	12	1	0	1	8	8	8	.250	.357	.333	86	-0	-1	6	0	0	0	1.000	1	1/O	0.0
	Yr	95	72	10	18	4	0	2	11	10	12	.250	.349	.389	100	1	0	10	0	1	-1	1.000	1	1/O	0.1
1984	Atl-N	31	26	4	7	1	0	0	5	3	6	.269	.345	.308	79	-0	-1	3	0	1	-1	1.000	-1	/1O	-0.3
	StL-N	59	98	5	24	4	2	1	12	10	17	.245	.315	.357	91	-2	-1	11	0	0	0	.991	2	1	-0.1
	Yr	90	124	9	31	5	2	1	17	13	23	.250	.321	.347	87	-2	-2	14	0	1	-1	.992	0	1/O	-0.4
1985	*StL-N	72	112	14	22	6	0	0	11	31	27	.196	.375	.250	79	-1	-1	13	2	1	0	.994	-2	1/O	-0.6
Total	17	1633	3421	429	833	132	13	95	426	532	589	.243	.349	.373	100	19	12	470	58	44	-9	.994	36	*1O/D	-1.8

■ TERRY JORGENSEN

Jorgensen, Terry Allen b: 9/2/66, Kewaunee, Wis. BR/TR, 6'4", 208 lbs. Deb: 9/10/89

YEAR	TM/L	G	AB	R	H	2B	3B	HR	RBI	BB	SO	AVG	OBP	SLG	PRO+	BR	/A	RC	SB	CS	SBR	FA	FR	POS	TPR
1989	Min-A	10	23	1	4	1	0	0	2	4	5	.174	.296	.217	44	-2	-2	2	0	0	0	.958	3	/3	0.1
1992	Min-A	22	58	5	18	1	0	0	5	3	11	.310	.355	.328	89	-0	-1	5	1	2	-1	1.000	2	1/3S	0.0
Total	2	32	81	6	22	2	0	0	7	7	16	.272	.337	.296	76	-2	-2	7	1	2	-1	.955	5	/31S	0.1

■ FELIX JOSE

Jose, Domingo Felix Andujar (b: Domingo Felix Andujar (Jose)) b: 5/2/65, Santo Domingo, D.R. BB/TR, 6'1", 190 lbs. Deb: 9/02/88

YEAR	TM/L	G	AB	R	H	2B	3B	HR	RBI	BB	SO	AVG	OBP	SLG	PRO+	BR	/A	RC	SB	CS	SBR	FA	FR	POS	TPR
1988	Oak-A	8	6	2	2	1	0	0	1	0	1	.333	.333	.500	135	0	0	1	1	0	0	1.000	-1	/O	0.0
1989	Oak-A	20	57	3	11	2	0	0	5	4	13	.193	.246	.228	36	-5	-5	3	0	1	-1	.974	-0	O	-0.6
1990	Oak-A	101	341	42	90	12	0	8	39	16	65	.264	.307	.370	92	-6	-4	38	8	2	1	.977	0	O/D	-0.5
	StL-N	25	85	12	23	4	1	3	13	8	16	.271	.333	.447	112	1	1	12	4	4	-1	1.000	-2	O	-0.2
1991	StL-N★	154	568	69	173	40	6	8	77	50	113	.305	.363	.438	123	18	18	88	20	12	-1	.990	4	*O	1.8
1992	StL-N	131	509	62	150	22	3	14	75	40	100	.295	.347	.432	121	12	13	75	28	12	1	.979	11	*O	2.4
Total	5	439	1566	190	449	81	10	33	210	118	308	.287	.340	.414	112	21	23	217	61	31	-0	.983	12	O/D	2.9

■ RICK JOSEPH

Joseph, Ricardo Emelindo (Harrigan) b: 8/24/39, San Pedro De Macoris, D.R. d: 9/8/79, Santiago, D.R. BR/TR, 6'1", 195 lbs. Deb: 6/18/64

YEAR	TM/L	G	AB	R	H	2B	3B	HR	RBI	BB	SO	AVG	OBP	SLG	PRO+	BR	/A	RC	SB	CS	SBR	FA	FR	POS	TPR
1964	KC-A	17	54	3	12	2	0	0	1	3	11	.222	.263	.259	45	-4	-4	3	0	1	-1	.981	-1	1/3	-0.7
1967	Phi-N	17	41	4	9	2	0	1	5	4	10	.220	.289	.341	79	-1	-1	4	0	0	0	1.000	1	1	0.0
1968	Phi-N	66	155	20	34	5	0	3	12	16	35	.219	.297	.310	82	-3	-3	14	0	1	-1	.992	1	13/O	-0.6
1969	Phi-N	99	264	35	72	15	0	6	37	22	57	.273	.331	.398	106	1	2	34	2	1	0	.956	7	31/2	0.8
1970	Phi-N	71	119	7	27	2	1	3	10	6	28	.227	.264	.336	61	-7	-7	9	0	0	0	.917	-4	O1/3	-1.2
Total	5	270	633	69	154	26	1	13	65	51	141	.243	.302	.349	85	-14	-13	66	2	3	-1	.933	3	/31O2	-1.7

■ DUANE JOSEPHSON

Josephson, Duane Charles b: 6/3/42, New Hampton, Iowa BR/TR, 6', 195 lbs. Deb: 9/15/65

YEAR	TM/L	G	AB	R	H	2B	3B	HR	RBI	BB	SO	AVG	OBP	SLG	PRO+	BR	/A	RC	SB	CS	SBR	FA	FR	POS	TPR
1965	Chi-A	4	9	2	1	0	0	0	0	2	4	.111	.273	.111	14	-1	-1	0	0	0	0	1.000	1	/C	0.0
1966	Chi-A	11	38	3	9	1	0	0	3	3	3	.237	.293	.263	65	-2	-2	3	0	0	0	.974	3	C	0.2
1967	Chi-A	62	189	11	45	5	1	1	9	6	24	.238	.262	.291	65	-9	-8	13	0	3	-2	1.000	-6	C	-1.4
1968	Chi-A★	128	434	35	107	16	6	6	45	18	52	.247	.286	.353	92	-5	-5	41	2	4	-2	.990	12	*C	1.5
1969	Chi-A	52	162	19	39	6	2	1	20	13	17	.241	.301	.321	71	-6	-7	16	0	0	0	.984	-1	C	-0.5
1970	Chi-A	96	285	28	90	12	1	4	41	24	28	.316	.375	.407	111	6	5	42	0	1	-1	.985	-11	C	-0.2
1971	Bos-A	91	306	38	75	14	1	10	39	22	35	.245	.296	.395	88	-3	-6	31	2	0	1	.989	-4	C	-0.7
1972	Bos-A	26	82	11	22	4	1	1	7	4	11	.268	.310	.378	99	0	-0	7	0	2	-1	.980	-1	1/C	-0.4
Total	8	470	1505	147	388	58	12	23	164	92	174	.258	.305	.358	89	-19	-23	153	4	10	-5	.989	-7	C/1	-1.5

■ VON JOSHUA

Joshua, Von Everett b: 5/1/48, Oakland, Cal. BL/TL, 5'10", 170 lbs. Deb: 9/02/69

YEAR	TM/L	G	AB	R	H	2B	3B	HR	RBI	BB	SO	AVG	OBP	SLG	PRO+	BR	/A	RC	SB	CS	SBR	FA	FR	POS	TPR
1969	LA-N	14	8	2	2	0	0	0	0	0	2	.250	.250	.250	43	-1	-1	1	1	0	0	.800	0	/O	0.0
1970	LA-N	72	109	23	29	1	3	1	8	6	24	.266	.304	.358	80	-4	-3	12	2	2	-1	.941	1	O	-0.4
1971	LA-N	11	7	2	0	0	0	0	0	0	1	.000	.000	.000	-99	-2	-2	0	0	0	0	1.000	1	/O	-0.1
1973	LA-N	75	159	19	40	4	1	2	17	8	29	.252	.292	.327	74	-6	-6	16	7	2	1	.984	-2	O	-0.9
1974	*LA-N	81	124	11	29	5	1	1	16	7	17	.234	.280	.315	69	-6	-5	10	3	2	-0	.943	-3	O	-1.0
1975	SF-N	129	507	75	161	25	10	7	43	32	75	.318	.359	.448	118	14	12	81	20	10	0	**.993**	3	*O	1.0
1976	SF-N	42	156	13	41	5	2	0	2	4	20	.263	.281	.321	68	-6	-7	13	1	3	-2	.948	-2	O	-1.3
	Mil-A	107	423	44	113	13	5	5	28	18	58	.267	.297	.357	93	-6	-5	42	8	10	-4	.982	6	*O/D	-0.8
1977	Mil-A	144	536	58	140	25	7	9	49	21	74	.261	.289	.384	82	-15	-15	53	12	9	-2	.970	-6	*O	-2.8
1979	LA-N	94	142	22	40	7	1	3	14	7	23	.282	.315	.408	97	-1	-1	17	1	1	-0	.967	0	O	-0.2
1980	SD-N	53	63	8	15	2	1	2	7	5	15	.238	.294	.397	97	-1	-1	7	0	1	-1	1.000	1	O/1	-0.1
Total	10	822	2234	277	610	87	31	30	184	108	338	.273	.307	.380	91	-33	-33	250	55	40	-8	.975	-2	O/1D	-6.6

■ TED JOURDAN

Jourdan, Theodore Charles b: 9/5/1895, New Orleans, La. d: 9/23/61, New Orleans, La. BL/TL, 6', 175 lbs. Deb: 9/18/16

YEAR	TM/L	G	AB	R	H	2B	3B	HR	RBI	BB	SO	AVG	OBP	SLG	PRO+	BR	/A	RC	SB	CS	SBR	FA	FR	POS	TPR
1916	Chi-A	3	2	0	0	0	0	0	0	1	1	.000	.333	.000	1	-0	-0	1	2			.000	0	H	0.0
1917	Chi-A	17	34	2	5	0	1	0	2	1	3	.147	.171	.206	15	-4	-4	1	0			.973	-0	1	-0.5
1918	Chi-A	7	10	1	1	0	0	0	1	0	0	.100	.100	.100	-39	-2	-2	0	0			1.000	-0	/1	-0.2
1920	Chi-A	48	150	16	36	5	2	0	8	17	17	.240	.337	.300	70	-6	-6	17	3	2	-0	.982	-4	1	-1.1
Total	4	75	196	19	42	5	3	0	11	19	21	.214	.300	.270	56	-11	-11	18	5	2		.981	-4	/1	-1.8

■ POP JOY

Joy, Aloysius C. b: 6/11/1860, Washington, D.C. d: 6/28/37, Washington, D.C. Deb: 6/03/1884

YEAR	TM/L	G	AB	R	H	2B	3B	HR	RBI	BB	SO	AVG	OBP	SLG	PRO+	BR	/A	RC	SB	CS	SBR	FA	FR	POS	TPR
1884	Was-U	36	130	12	28	0	0	0		2		.215	.227	.215	52	-7	-6	7				.966	0	1	-0.9

■ JOYCE

Joyce Deb: 8/14/1886

YEAR	TM/L	G	AB	R	H	2B	3B	HR	RBI	BB	SO	AVG	OBP	SLG	PRO+	BR	/A	RC	SB	CS	SBR	FA	FR	POS	TPR
1886	Was-N	1	0	0	0	0	0	0	0	0	0	—	—	—	—	0	0	0	0			.000	-0	/O	0.0

■ BILL JOYCE

Joyce, William Michael "Scrappy Bill" b: 9/21/1865, St.Louis, Mo. d: 5/8/41, St.Louis, Mo. BL/TR, 5'11", 185 lbs. Deb: 4/19/1890 M

YEAR	TM/L	G	AB	R	H	2B	3B	HR	RBI	BB	SO	AVG	OBP	SLG	PRO+	BR	/A	RC	SB	CS	SBR	FA	FR	POS	TPR
1890	Bro-P	133	489	121	123	18	18	1	78	**123**	77	.252	.413	.368	105	15	9	95	43			.811	-11	*3	0.2
1891	Bos-a	65	243	76	75	9	15	3	51	63	27	.309	.460	.506	183	29	30	75	36			.849	-1	3/1	2.7
1892	Bro-N	97	372	89	91	15	12	6	45	82	55	.245	.392	.398	147	23	25	69	23			.862	-19	3/O	0.9
1894	Was-N	99	355	103	126	25	14	17	89	87	33	.355	.496	.648	**182**	48	51	128	21			.866	-3	*3	3.6
1895	Was-N	126	474	110	148	25	13	17	95	**96**	54	.312	.442	.527	154	40	42	127	29			.844	-9	*3	2.8
1896	Was-N	81	310	85	97	16	10	8	51	67	20	.313	.454	.506	155	29	29	88	32			.888	-7	32	2.1
	NY-N	49	165	36	61	9	2	5	43	34	14	.370	.500	.539	182	21	22	53	13			.883	0	3M	2.0
	Yr	130	475	121	158	25	12	**13**	94	101	34	.333	.470	.518	165	50	51	140	45			.885	-6	32	4.1
1897	NY-N	109	388	109	118	15	13	3	64	78		.304	.441	.433	135	23	25	92	33			.852	-1	*3/1M	2.3
1898	NY-N	145	508	91	131	20	9	10	91	88		.258	.385	.392	127	19	21	93	34			.966	8	*13/2M	2.7
Total	8	904	3304	820	970	152	106	70	607	718	280	.294	.435	.467	146	247	253	818	264			.851	-41	31/2O	19.3

YEAR	TM/L	G	AB	R	H	2B	3B	HR	RBI	BB	SO	AVG	OBP	SLG	PRO+	BR	/A	RC	SB	CS	SBR	FA	FR	POS	TPR
■ **WALLY JOYNER** Joyner, Wallace Keith b: 6/16/62, Atlanta, Ga. BL/TL, 6'2", 190 lbs. Deb: 4/08/86																									
1986	*Cal-A★	154	593	82	172	27	3	22	100	57	58	.290	.354	.457	120	15	16	96	5	2	0	.989	9	*1	1.4
1987	Cal-A	149	564	100	161	33	1	34	117	72	64	.285	.371	.528	140	28	31	111	8	2	1	.993	-7	*1	1.4
1988	Cal-A	158	597	81	176	31	2	13	85	55	51	.295	.359	.419	120	14	16	89	8	2	1	.995	12	*1	1.6
1989	Cal-A	159	593	78	167	30	2	16	79	46	58	.282	.340	.420	115	9	11	82	3	2	-0	**.997**	-4	*1	-0.6
1990	Cal-A	83	310	35	83	15	0	8	41	41	34	.268	.355	.394	111	5	5	43	2	1	0	.995	2	1	0.1
1991	Cal-A	143	551	79	166	34	3	21	96	52	66	.301	.363	.488	133	24	24	98	2	0	1	.994	1	*1	1.6
1992	KC-A	149	572	66	154	36	2	9	66	55	50	.269	.338	.386	101	2	1	72	11	5	0	.993	14	*1/D	0.6
Total	7	995	3780	521	1079	206	13	123	584	378	381	.285	.354	.444	121	97	105	591	39	14	3	.994	27	1/D	6.1
■ **FRANK JUDE** Jude, Frank b: 1884, Libby, Minn. d: 5/4/61, Brownsville, Tex. BR/TR, 5'7", 150 lbs. Deb: 7/09/06																									
1906	Cin-N	80	308	31	64	6	4	1	31	16		.208	.252	.263	58	-15	-16	23	7			.965	-3	O	-2.5
■ **JOE JUDGE** Judge, Joseph Ignatius b: 5/25/1894, Brooklyn, N.Y. d: 3/11/63, Washington, D.C. BL/TL, 5'8.5", 155 lbs. Deb: 9/20/15 C																									
1915	Was-A	12	41	7	17	2	0	0	9	4	6	.415	.500	.463	185	5	5	10	2	3	-1	.990	-1	1/O	0.3
1916	Was-A	103	336	42	74	10	8	0	28	54	44	.220	.333	.298	91	-3	-2	40	18			.986	4	*1	-0.2
1917	Was-A	102	393	62	112	15	15	2	30	50	40	.285	.369	.415	141	18	19	63	17			.988	-1	*1	1.6
1918	Was-A	130	502	56	131	23	7	1	46	49	32	.261	.332	.341	105	1	2	63	20			.985	2	*1	-0.1
1919	Was-A	135	521	83	150	33	12	2	31	81	35	.288	.386	.409	124	18	19	87	23			.988	-4	*1	1.1
1920	Was-A	126	493	103	164	19	15	5	51	65	34	.333	.416	.462	136	25	27	96	12	12	-4	.992	-8	*1	1.2
1921	Was-A	153	622	87	187	26	11	7	72	68	35	.301	.372	.412	105	1	5	100	21	6	3	.996	-3	*1	0.1
1922	Was-A	148	591	84	174	32	15	10	81	50	20	.294	.355	.450	114	6	10	91	5	15	-8	.996	3	*1	-0.1
1923	Was-A	113	405	56	127	24	6	2	63	58	20	.314	.406	.417	123	12	15	72	11	7	-1	**.993**	8	*1	1.5
1924	*Was-A	140	516	71	167	38	9	3	79	53	21	.324	.393	.450	121	13	16	93	13	8	-1	.994	-2	*1	0.4
1925	*Was-A	112	376	65	118	31	5	8	66	55	21	.314	.406	.487	128	15	16	73	7	12	-5	**.993**	3	*1	0.8
1926	Was-A	134	453	70	132	25	11	7	92	53	25	.291	.367	.442	113	6	8	75	7	5	-1	.994	10	*1	0.9
1927	Was-A	137	522	68	161	29	11	2	71	45	22	.308	.366	.418	104	2	3	77	10	5	0	**.996**	-6	*1	-1.1
1928	Was-A	153	542	78	166	31	10	3	93	80	19	.306	.396	.417	115	14	14	96	16	4	2	.996	1	*1	0.4
1929	Was-A	143	543	83	171	35	8	6	71	73	33	.315	.397	.442	115	15	14	100	12	5	1	**.996**	3	*1	0.3
1930	Was-A	126	442	83	144	29	11	10	80	60	29	.326	.410	.509	131	22	22	95	13	6	0	**.998**	2	*1	1.2
1931	Was-A	35	74	11	21	3	0	0	9	8	8	.284	.354	.324	79	-2	-2	9	0	0	0	.994	1	1	-0.2
1932	Was-A	82	291	45	75	16	3	3	29	37	19	.258	.343	.364	84	-7	-6	38	3	3	-1	.997	1	1	-1.1
1933	Bro-N	42	112	7	24	2	1	0	9	7	10	.214	.261	.250	48	-8	-7	7	1			.989	0	1	-1.0
	Bos-A	35	108	20	32	8	1	0	22	13	4	.296	.372	.389	103	1	1	16	2	1	0	1.000	-0	1	-0.2
1934	Bos-A	10	15	3	5	2	0	0	2	2	1	.333	.412	.467	118	1	0	3	0	0	0	1.000	0	/1	0.0
Total	20	2171	7898	1184	2352	433	159	71	1034	965	478	.298	.378	.420	115	157	179	1304	213	92		.993	13	*1/O	5.8
■ **WALLY JUDNICH** Judnich, Walter Franklin b: 1/24/17, San Francisco, Cal d: 7/12/71, Glendale, Cal. BL/TL, 6'1", 205 lbs. Deb: 4/16/40																									
1940	StL-A	137	519	97	157	27	7	24	89	54	71	.303	.368	.520	125	20	18	102	8	5	-1	**.989**	-1	*O	1.0
1941	StL-A	146	546	90	155	40	6	14	83	80	45	.284	.377	.456	116	16	13	98	5	5	-2	.980	3	*O	0.6
1942	StL-A	132	457	78	143	22	6	17	82	74	41	.313	.413	.499	153	35	34	101	3	2	-0	**.991**	-2	*O	2.6
1946	StL-A	142	511	60	134	23	4	15	72	60	54	.262	.340	.411	104	6	3	74	0	4	-2	**.995**	11	*O	0.5
1947	StL-A	144	500	58	129	24	3	18	64	60	62	.258	.338	.426	109	6	5	75	2	5	-2	.989	-6	*1O	-0.9
1948	*Cle-A	79	218	36	56	13	3	2	29	56	23	.257	.411	.372	112	6	6	38	2	3	-1	.970	-8	O1	-0.5
1949	Pit-N	10	35	5	8	1	0	0	1	1	2	.229	.250	.257	35	-3	-3	2	0			1.000	1	/O	-0.3
Total	7	790	2786	424	782	150	29	90	420	385	298	.281	.369	.452	119	85	77	491	20	24		.988	-2	O1	3.0
■ **LYLE JUDY** Judy, Lyle Leroy "Punch" b: 11/15/13, Lawrenceville, Ill d: 1/15/91, Ormond Beach, Fla. BR/TR, 5'10", 150 lbs. Deb: 9/17/35																									
1935	StL-N	8	11	2	0	0	0	0	0	2	2	.000	.154	.000	-53	-2	-2	0	2			1.000	1	/2	-0.2
■ **RED JUELICH** Juelich, John Samuel b: 9/20/16, St.Louis, Mo. d: 12/25/70, St.Louis, Mo. BR/TR, 5'11.5", 170 lbs. Deb: 5/30/39																									
1939	Pit-N	17	46	5	11	0	2	0	4	2	4	.239	.271	.326	61	-3	-3	3	0			.935	-5	2/3	-0.7
■ **GEORGE JUMONVILLE** Jumonville, George Benedict b: 5/16/17, Mobile, Ala. BR/TR, 6', 175 lbs. Deb: 9/13/40																									
1940	Phi-N	11	34	0	3	0	0	0	0	1	6	.088	.139	.088	-38	-6	-6	0	0			.952	-4	S/3	-1.0
1941	Phi-N	6	7	1	3	0	0	1	2	0	0	.429	.429	.857	266	1	1	3	0			1.000	1	/2S	0.2
Total	2	17	41	1	6	0	0	1	2	1	6	.146	.186	.220	12	-5	-5	3	0			.953	-4	/S23	-0.8
■ **ED JURAK** Jurak, Edward James b: 10/24/57, Los Angeles, Cal. BR/TR, 6'2", 185 lbs. Deb: 6/30/82																									
1982	Bos-A	12	21	3	7	0	0	0	7	2	4	.333	.391	.333	96	0	-0	3	0	0	0	.923	2	3/O	0.1
1983	Bos-A	75	159	19	44	8	4	0	18	18	25	.277	.354	.377	95	1	-1	21	1	2	-1	.943	9	S13/2D	0.8
1984	Bos-A	47	66	6	16	3	1	1	7	12	12	.242	.359	.364	96	0	0	9	0	2	-1	1.000	5	12/3S	0.3
1985	Bos-A	26	13	4	3	0	0	0	0	1	3	.231	.286	.231	42	-1	-1	1	0	0	0	.833	4	/3S1OD	0.2
1988	Oak-A	3	1	1	0	0	0	0	0	0	0	.000	.000	.000	-99	-0	-0	0	0	0	0	.000	-0	/3D	0.0
1989	SF-N	30	42	2	10	0	0	0	1	5	5	.238	.319	.238	63	-2	-2	3	0	0	0	.875	-2	/S32O1	-0.4
Total	6	193	302	35	80	11	5	1	33	38	49	.265	.349	.344	88	-2	-4	37	1	4	-2	.941	17	/S312DO	1.0
■ **BILLY JURGES** Jurges, William Frederick b: 5/9/08, Bronx, N.Y. BR/TR, 5'11", 175 lbs. Deb: 5/04/31 MC																									
1931	Chi-N	88	293	34	59	15	5	0	23	25	41	.201	.264	.287	47	-22	-22	24	2			.963	11	32/S	-0.6
1932	*Chi-N	115	396	40	100	24	4	2	52	19	26	.253	.288	.348	71	-17	-16	41	1			**.964**	**32**	*S/3	2.4
1933	Chi-N	143	487	49	131	17	6	5	50	26	39	.269	.313	.359	92	-6	-6	52	3			.958	20	*S	2.6
1934	Chi-N	100	358	43	88	15	2	8	33	19	34	.246	.289	.366	76	-14	-13	37	1			.966	14	S	0.7
1935	*Chi-N	146	519	69	125	33	1	1	59	42	39	.241	.304	.314	66	-24	-24	50	3			**.964**	**30**	*S	1.3
1936	Chi-N	118	429	51	120	25	1	1	42	23	25	.280	.321	.350	79	-12	-13	46	4			.960	17	*S	1.1
1937	Chi-N☆	129	450	53	134	18	10	1	65	42	41	.298	.365	.389	101	4	2	66	2			**.975**	-7	*S	0.3
1938	*Chi-N	137	465	53	114	18	3	1	47	58	53	.245	.335	.303	75	-13	-15	48	3			.953	-0	*S	-0.4
1939	NY-N☆	138	543	84	155	21	11	6	63	47	34	.285	.349	.398	99	0	-0	71	3			**.965**	15	*S	2.7
1940	NY-N†	63	214	23	54	3	3	2	36	25	14	.252	.347	.322	85	-3	-3	23	2			.967	-1	S	0.1
1941	NY-N	134	471	50	138	25	2	5	61	47	36	.293	.361	.386	108	7	6	66	0			.957	7	*S	2.4
1942	NY-N	127	464	45	119	7	1	2	30	43	42	.256	.324	.289	79	-11	-11	42	1			.978	7	*S	0.4
1943	NY-N	136	481	46	110	8	2	4	29	53	38	.229	.310	.279	70	-17	-17	44	2			.955	1	S3	-1.0
1944	NY-N	85	246	28	52	2	1	1	23	23	20	.211	.279	.240	47	-17	-17	17	4			.961	-1	3S/2	-1.7
1945	NY-N	61	176	22	57	3	1	3	24	24	11	.324	.405	.403	123	7	7	30	2			.937	2	3/S	1.0
1946	Chi-N	82	221	26	49	9	2	0	17	43	28	.222	.351	.281	82	-4	-3	24	3			.976	-3	S/32	-0.3
1947	Chi-N	14	40	5	8	2	0	1	2	9	9	.200	.347	.325	83	-1	-1	5	0			.925	-4	S	-0.4
Total	17	1816	6253	721	1613	245	55	43	656	568	530	.258	.325	.335	82	-140	-147	686	36			.964	140	*S3/2	10.6
■ **JOE JUST** Just, Joseph Erwin (b: Joseph Erwin Juszczak) b: 1/8/16, Milwaukee, Wis. BR/TR, 5'11", 185 lbs. Deb: 5/13/44																									
1944	Cin-N	11	11	0	2	0	0	0	0	0	2	.182	.250	.182	24	-1	-1	0	0			.923	0	C	-0.1
1945	Cin-N	14	34	2	5	0	0	0	2	4	7	.147	.237	.147	8	-4	-4	1	0			.947	-2	C	-0.5
Total	2	25	45	2	7	0	0	0	2	4	9	.156	.240	.156	12	-5	-5	2	0			.941	-1	/C	-0.6
■ **DAVID JUSTICE** Justice, David Christopher b: 4/14/66, Cincinnati, Ohio BL/TL, 6'3", 195 lbs. Deb: 5/24/89																									
1989	Atl-N	16	51	7	12	3	0	1	3	3	9	.235	.291	.353	81	-1	-1	5	2	1	0	1.000	-1	O	-0.3
1990	Atl-N	127	439	76	124	23	2	28	78	64	92	.282	.374	.535	139	28	25	92	11	6	-0	.981	-2	1O	1.6

YEAR	TM/L	G	AB	R	H	2B	3B	HR	RBI	BB	SO	AVG	OBP	SLG	PRO+	BR	/A	RC	SB	CS	SBR	FA	FR	POS	TPR
1991	*Atl-N	109	396	67	109	25	1	21	87	65	81	.275	.381	.503	138	25	22	78	8	8	-2	.968	5	*O	2.4
1992	*Atl-N	144	484	78	124	19	5	21	72	79	85	.256	.363	.446	118	19	14	84	2	4	-2	.976	14	*O	2.5
Total	4	396	1370	228	369	70	8	71	240	211	267	.269	.369	.488	129	71	60	258	23	19	-5	.973	15	O/1	6.2

■ SKIP JUTZE Jutze, Alfred Henry b: 5/28/46, Queens, N.Y. BR/TR, 5'11", 195 lbs. Deb: 9/01/72

YEAR	TM/L	G	AB	R	H	2B	3B	HR	RBI	BB	SO	AVG	OBP	SLG	PRO+	BR	/A	RC	SB	CS	SBR	FA	FR	POS	TPR
1972	StL-N	21	71	1	17	2	0	0	5	1	16	.239	.250	.268	48	-5	-5	4	0	1	-1	.964	0	C	-0.5
1973	Hou-N	90	278	18	62	6	0	0	18	19	37	.223	.275	.245	45	-20	-20	17	0	1	-1	.984	-6	C	-2.5
1974	Hou-N	8	13	0	3	0	0	0	1	1	1	.231	.286	.231	48	-1	-1	1	0	0	0	1.000	-0	/C	-0.1
1975	Hou-N	51	93	9	21	2	0	0	6	2	4	.226	.242	.247	39	-8	-7	6	1	0	0	.988	3	C	-0.3
1976	Hou-N	42	92	7	14	2	3	0	6	4	16	.152	.188	.239	22	-10	-9	4	0	0	0	.986	2	C	-0.7
1977	Sea-A	42	109	10	24	2	0	3	15	7	12	.220	.267	.321	60	-6	-6	8	0	4	-2	.984	-2	C	-0.9
Total	6	254	656	45	141	14	3	3	51	34	86	.215	.255	.259	44	-50	-48	39	1	6	-3	.983	-3	C	-5.0

■ HERB JUUL Juul, Herbert Victor b: 2/2/1886, Chicago, Ill. d: 11/14/28, Chicago, Ill. BL/TL, 5'11", 150 lbs. Deb: 7/11/11

YEAR	TM/L	G	AB	R	H	2B	3B	HR	RBI	BB	SO	AVG	OBP	SLG	PRO+	BR	/A	RC	SB	CS	SBR	FA	FR	POS	TPR
1911	Cin-N	2	2	0	0	0	0	0	0	0	0	.000	.000	.000	-99	-1	-1	0	0			.000	-0	/P	0.0

■ JIM KAAT Kaat, James Lee b: 11/7/38, Zeeland, Mich. BL/TL, 6'4", 217 lbs. Deb: 8/02/59 C

YEAR	TM/L	G	AB	R	H	2B	3B	HR	RBI	BB	SO	AVG	OBP	SLG	PRO+	BR	/A	RC	SB	CS	SBR	FA	FR	POS	TPR
1959	Was-A	3	1	0	0	0	0	0	0	0	1	.000	.000	.000	-99	-0	-0	0	0	0	0	1.000	0	/P	0.0
1960	Was-A	13	14	0	2	0	0	0	0	0	6	.143	.143	.143	-23	-2	-2	0	0	0	0	1.000	0	P	0.0
1961	Min-A	47	63	10	15	3	1	0	1	4	13	.238	.294	.317	60	-3	-4	6	0	0	0	.968	3	P	0.0
1962	Min-A☆	48	100	9	18	3	1	1	10	8	40	.180	.241	.260	33	-9	-10	7	0	0	0	.967	6	P	0.0
1963	Min-A	36	61	2	8	1	0	1	8	2	19	.131	.185	.197	7	-8	-8	2	0	0	0	.984	4	P	0.0
1964	Min-A	46	83	11	14	1	0	3	11	11	31	.169	.266	.289	54	-5	-5	7	0	0	0	.928	3	P	0.0
1965	*Min-A	56	93	6	23	4	0	1	9	3	29	.247	.271	.323	65	-4	-5	9	2	0	1	.929	3	P	0.0
1966	Min-A★	47	118	12	23	2	1	2	13	5	41	.195	.228	.280	42	-8	-9	8	0	0	0	.956	0	P	0.0
1967	Min-A	45	99	7	17	3	1	1	4	7	26	.172	.226	.253	38	-7	-8	6	0	0	0	.952	1	P	0.0
1968	Min-A	36	77	7	12	3	0	0	5	2	18	.156	.177	.195	12	-8	-8	2	0	0	0	.976	-0	P	0.0
1969	Min-A	43	87	8	18	8	0	2	10	4	20	.207	.250	.368	69	-4	-4	8	0	0	0	.826	-3	P	0.0
1970	*Min-A	56	76	17	15	1	0	1	8	6	20	.197	.265	.250	42	-6	-6	5	0	0	0	.935	2	P	0.0
1971	Min-A	54	93	6	15	3	0	0	5	2	16	.161	.179	.194	5	-12	-12	4	2	0	1	.982	-0	P	0.0
1972	Min-A	24	45	3	13	3	0	2	4	1	16	.289	.304	.489	127	1	1	6	0	1	-1	.923	-0	P	0.0
1973	Min-A	31	0	1	0	0	0	0	0	0	0	—	—	—	—	0	0	0	0	0	0	.969	-1	P	0.0
	Chi-A	7	0	0	0	0	0	0	0	0	0	—	—	—	—	0	0	0	0	0	0	1.000	-0	/P	0.0
	Yr	38	0	1	0	0	0	0	0	0	0	—	—	—	—	0	0	0	0	0	0	.973	-2	P	0.0
1974	Chi-A	42	1	0	0	0	0	0	0	0	0	.000	.000	.000	-98	-0	-0	0	0	0	0	.959	-2	P	0.0
1975	Chi-A★	43	0	0	0	0	0	0	0	0	0	—	—	—	—	0	0	0	0	0	0	.982	-2	P	0.0
1976	*Phi-N	42	79	4	14	3	1	1	8	2	24	.177	.198	.278	33	-7	-7	5	0	0	0	.949	-3	P	0.0
1977	Phi-N	36	53	4	10	3	0	0	2	2	12	.189	.218	.245	23	-6	-6	3	0	0	0	.897	-2	P	0.0
1978	Phi-N	26	48	4	7	1	0	0	4	0	15	.146	.163	.167	-8	-7	-7	1	0	0	0	1.000	-2	P	0.0
1979	Phi-N	3	1	0	0	0	0	0	0	0	1	.000	.500	.000	47	0	0	0	0	0	0	1.000	-0	/P	0.0
	NY-A	40	0	0	0	0	0	0	0	0	0	—	—	—	—	0	0	0	0	0	0	.909	-1	P	0.0
1980	NY-A	4	0	0	0	0	0	0	0	0	0	—	—	—	—	0	0	0	0	0	0	.800	1	/P	0.0
	StL-N	49	35	4	5	1	0	1	2	2	13	.143	.189	.257	23	-4	-4	2	1	0	0	.952	-2	P	0.0
1981	StL-N	41	8	2	3	1	0	0	2	1	0	.375	.444	.500	163	1	1	2	0	0	0	.895	1	P	0.0
1982	*StL-N	62	12	0	0	0	0	0	0	1	4	.000	.077	.000	-76	-3	-3	0	0	0	0	.917	1	P	0.0
1983	StL-N	24	4	0	0	0	0	0	0	0	2	.000	.000	.000	-99	-1	-1	0	0	0	0	.889	0	P	0.0
Total	25	1004	1251	117	232	44	5	16	106	63	367	.185	.229	.267	38	-102	-108	83	5	1	1	.947	6	P	0.0

■ JACK KADING Kading, John Frederick b: 11/17/1884, Waukesha, Wis. d: 6/2/64, Chicago, Ill. BR/TR, 6'3", 190 lbs. Deb: 9/12/10

YEAR	TM/L	G	AB	R	H	2B	3B	HR	RBI	BB	SO	AVG	OBP	SLG	PRO+	BR	/A	RC	SB	CS	SBR	FA	FR	POS	TPR
1910	Pit-N	8	23	5	7	2	1	0	4	4	5	.304	.407	.478	149	2	2	5	0			1.000	1	/1	0.3
1914	Chi-F	3	3	0	0	0	0	0	0	0	0	.000	.000	.000	-99	-1	-1	0	0			.000	0	H	-0.1
Total	2	11	26	5	7	2	1	0	4	4	5	.269	.367	.423	124	1	1	5	0			.983	1	/1	0.2

■ JAKE KAFORA Kafora, Frank Jacob "Tomatoes" b: 10/16/1888, Chicago, Ill. d: 3/23/28, Chicago, Ill. BR/TR, 6', 180 lbs. Deb: 10/05/13

YEAR	TM/L	G	AB	R	H	2B	3B	HR	RBI	BB	SO	AVG	OBP	SLG	PRO+	BR	/A	RC	SB	CS	SBR	FA	FR	POS	TPR
1913	Pit-N	1	1	1	0	0	0	0	0	0	1	.000	.500	.000	52	0	0	0	0			1.000	-1	/C	-0.1
1914	Pit-N	21	23	2	3	0	0	0	0	0	6	.130	.200	.130	-1	-3	-3	1	0			1.000	-1	C	-0.4
Total	2	22	24	3	3	0	0	0	0	0	7	.125	.222	.125	4	-3	-3	1	0			1.000	-2	/C	-0.5

■ IKE KAHDOT Kahdot, Isaac Leonard "Chief" b: 10/22/01, Georgetown, Okla. BR/TR, 5'5.5", 145 lbs. Deb: 9/05/22

YEAR	TM/L	G	AB	R	H	2B	3B	HR	RBI	BB	SO	AVG	OBP	SLG	PRO+	BR	/A	RC	SB	CS	SBR	FA	FR	POS	TPR
1922	Cle-A	4	2	0	0	0	0	0	0	0	1	.000	.000	.000	-99	-1	-1	0	0	0	0	1.000	1	/3	0.0

■ NICK KAHL Kahl, Nicholas Alexander b: 4/10/1879, Coulterville, Ill. d: 7/13/59, Sparta, Ill. BR/TR, 5'9", 185 lbs. Deb: 5/02/05

YEAR	TM/L	G	AB	R	H	2B	3B	HR	RBI	BB	SO	AVG	OBP	SLG	PRO+	BR	/A	RC	SB	CS	SBR	FA	FR	POS	TPR
1905	Cle-A	40	135	16	29	4	1	0	21	4		.215	.248	.259	60	-6	-6	9	1			.948	0	2/SO	-0.6

■ BOB KAHLE Kahle, Robert Wayne b: 11/23/15, Newcastle, Ind. d: 12/16/88, Inglewood, Cal. BR/TR, 6', 170 lbs. Deb: 4/21/38

YEAR	TM/L	G	AB	R	H	2B	3B	HR	RBI	BB	SO	AVG	OBP	SLG	PRO+	BR	/A	RC	SB	CS	SBR	FA	FR	POS	TPR
1938	Bos-N	8	3	2	1	0	0	0	0	0	0	.333	.333	.333	93	-0	-0	0	0			.000	0	H	0.0

■ OWEN KAHN Kahn, Owen Earle "Jack" b: 6/5/05, Richmond, Va. d: 1/17/81, Richmond, Va. BR/TR, 5'11", 160 lbs. Deb: 5/24/30

YEAR	TM/L	G	AB	R	H	2B	3B	HR	RBI	BB	SO	AVG	OBP	SLG	PRO+	BR	/A	RC	SB	CS	SBR	FA	FR	POS	TPR
1930	Bos-N	1	0	1	0	0	0	0	0	0	0	—	—	—	—	0	0	0	0			.000	0	R	0.0

■ MIKE KAHOE Kahoe, Michael Joseph b: 9/3/1873, Yellow Springs, O d: 5/14/49, Akron, Ohio BR/TR, 6', 185 lbs. Deb: 9/22/1895

YEAR	TM/L	G	AB	R	H	2B	3B	HR	RBI	BB	SO	AVG	OBP	SLG	PRO+	BR	/A	RC	SB	CS	SBR	FA	FR	POS	TPR
1895	Cin-N	3	4	0	0	0	0	0	0	0	0	.000	.000	.000	-96	-1	-1	0	0			1.000	-1	/C	-0.1
1899	Cin-N	14	42	2	7	1	1	0	4	0		.167	.167	.238	10	-5	-5	2	1			.957	4	C	0.0
1900	Cin-N	52	175	18	33	3	3	1	9	4		.189	.215	.257	31	-17	-16	11	3			.963	6	C/S	-0.6
1901	Cin-N	4	13	0	4	0	0	0	0	1		.308	.357	.308	100	-0	0	1	0			1.000	-2	/C	-0.2
	Chi-N	67	237	21	53	12	2	1	21	8		.224	.249	.304	62	-13	-11	20	5			.974	11	C/1	0.5
	Yr	71	250	21	57	12	2	1	21	9		.228	.255	.304	64	-13	-11	22	5			.974	9	C/1	0.3
1902	Chi-N	7	18	0	4	1	0	0	2	0		.222	.222	.278	56	-1	-1	1	0			.875	-1	/C3S	-0.1
	StL-A	55	197	21	48	9	2	2	28	6		.244	.270	.340	69	-9	-9	20	4			.967	-1	C	-0.3
1903	StL-A	77	244	26	46	7	5	0	23	11		.189	.227	.258	46	-16	-15	16	1			.971	-3	C/O	-1.2
1904	StL-A	72	236	9	51	6	1	0	12	8		.216	.242	.250	59	-12	-10	17	4			.968	1	C	-0.2
1905	Phi-N	16	51	2	13	2	0	0	4	1		.255	.269	.294	71	-2	-2	5	1			.975	0	C	0.0
1907	Chi-N	5	10	0	4	0	0	0	1	0		.400	.400	.400	142	1	0	2	0			1.000	-1	/C1	-0.1
	Was-A	17	47	3	9	1	0	0	1	0		.191	.191	.213	31	-4	-3	2	0			.976	1	C	-0.2
1908	Was-A	17	27	1	5	1	0	0	0	0		.185	.185	.222	35	-2	-2	1	0			.983	4	C	0.3
1909	Was-A	4	8	0	1	0	0	0	0	0		.125	.125	.125	-22	-1	-1	0	2			.867	-0	/C	-0.1
Total	11	410	1309	103	278	43	14	4	105	39	0	.212	.237	.276	52	-83	-78	98	21			.968	17	C/103S	-2.3

■ AL KAISER Kaiser, Alfred Edward "Deerfoot" b: 8/3/1886, Cincinnati, Ohio d: 4/11/69, Cincinnati, Ohio BR/TR, 5'9", 165 lbs. Deb: 4/18/11

YEAR	TM/L	G	AB	R	H	2B	3B	HR	RBI	BB	SO	AVG	OBP	SLG	PRO+	BR	/A	RC	SB	CS	SBR	FA	FR	POS	TPR
1911	Chi-N	26	84	16	21	0	5	0	7	7	12	.250	.308	.369	89	-2	-2	11	6			.905	-3	O	-0.6
	Bos-N	66	197	20	40	5	2	2	15	10	26	.203	.249	.279	44	-14	-17	15	4			.922	-6	O	-2.5
	Yr	92	281	36	61	5	7	2	22	17	38	.217	.267	.306	57	-16	-18	26	10			.918	-9	O	-3.1
1912	Bos-N	4	13	0	0	0	0	0	0	0	3	.000	.000	.000	-98	-4	-4	-0	0			.900	0	/O	-0.4
1914	Ind-F	59	187	22	43	10	0	1	16	17	41	.230	.301	.299	64	-7	-10	20	6			.918	-3	O/1	-1.5
Total	3	155	481	58	104	15	7	3	38	34	82	.216	.274	.295	56	-27	-31	46	16			.917	-12	O/1	-5.0

YEAR	TM/L	G	AB	R	H	2B	3B	HR	RBI	BB	SO	AVG	OBP	SLG	PRO+	BR	/A	RC	SB	CS	SBR	FA	FR	POS	TPR

■ JOHN KALAHAN
Kalahan, John Joseph b: 9/30/1878, Philadelphia, Pa. d: 6/20/52, Philadelphia, Pa. BR/TR, 6', 165 lbs. Deb: 9/29/03

| 1903 | Phi-A | 1 | 5 | 0 | 0 | 0 | 0 | 0 | 0 | 0 | 0 | .000 | .000 | .000 | -96 | -1 | -1 | 0 | 0 | | | 1.000 | -1 | /C | -0.2 |

■ CHARLIE KALBFUS
Kalbfus, Charles Henry "Skinny" b: 12/28/1864, Washington, D.C. d: 11/18/41, Washington, D.C. BR/TR, 5'11", 145 lbs. Deb: 4/18/1884

| 1884 | Was-U | 1 | 5 | 1 | 1 | 0 | 0 | 0 | | 0 | | .200 | .200 | .200 | 37 | -0 | -0 | 0 | | | | .000 | -0 | /O | -0.1 |

■ FRANK KALIN
Kalin, Frank Bruno "Fats" (b: Frank Bruno Kalinkiewicz) b: 10/3/17, Steubenville, Ohio d: 1/12/75, Weirton, W.Va. BR/TR, 6', 200 lbs. Deb: 9/25/40

1940	Pit-N	3	3	0	0	0	0	0	1	2	0	.000	.400	.000	19	-0	-0	0	0			.667	-1	/O	-0.1
1943	Chi-A	4	4	0	0	0	0	0	0	0	0	.000	.000	.000	-99	-1	-1	0	0	0	0	.000	0	H	-0.1
Total	2	7	7	0	0	0	0	0	1	2	0	.000	.222	.000	-34	-1	-1	0	0	0		.929	-1	/O	-0.2

■ AL KALINE
Kaline, Albert William b: 12/19/34, Baltimore, Md. BR/TR, 6'2", 180 lbs. Deb: 6/25/53 H

1953	Det-A	30	28	9	7	0	0	1	2	1	5	.250	.300	.357	78	-1	-1	3	1	0	0	1.000	-7	O	-0.8
1954	Det-A	138	504	42	139	18	3	4	43	22	45	.276	.305	.347	80	-16	-15	48	9	5	-0	.971	11	*O	-1.0
1955	Det-A★	152	588	121	**200**	24	8	27	102	82	57	**.340**	.425	.546	163	50	52	135	6	8	-3	.979	7	*O	4.9
1956	Det-A★	153	617	96	194	32	10	27	128	70	55	.314	.385	.530	139	33	33	129	7	1	2	.984	17	*O	4.2
1957	Det-A★	149	577	83	170	29	4	23	90	43	38	.295	.347	.478	120	17	15	92	11	9	-2	.985	7	*O	1.1
1958	Det-A★	146	543	84	170	34	7	16	85	54	47	.313	.377	.490	127	27	22	96	7	4	-0	.994	23	*O	3.8
1959	Det-A★	136	511	86	167	19	2	27	94	72	42	.327	.414	**.530**	149	42	38	114	10	4	1	.989	11	*O	4.2
1960	Det-A★	147	551	77	153	29	4	15	68	65	47	.278	.357	.426	108	9	7	84	19	4	3	.987	9	*O	1.2
1961	Det-A★	153	586	116	190	41	7	19	82	66	42	.324	.396	.515	138	35	33	121	14	1	4	.990	12	*O/3	3.9
1962	Det-A★	100	398	78	121	16	6	29	94	47	39	.304	.379	.593	152	31	29	85	4	0	1	.983	12	*O	3.5
1963	Det-A★	145	551	89	172	24	3	27	101	54	48	.312	.378	.514	142	34	32	105	6	4	-1	.992	-2	*O	2.3
1964	Det-A†	146	525	77	154	31	5	17	68	75	51	.293	.385	.469	134	27	26	97	4	1	1	.990	11	*O	3.2
1965	Det-A★	125	399	72	112	18	2	18	72	72	49	.281	.391	.471	142	25	24	77	6	0	2	.985	-4	*O/3	1.9
1966	Det-A★	142	479	85	138	29	1	29	88	81	66	.288	.396	.534	161	42	41	105	5	5	-2	**.993**	5	*O	4.0
1967	Det-A†	131	458	94	141	28	2	25	78	83	47	.308	.415	.541	176	48	47	104	8	2	1	.983	8	*O	5.3
1968	*Det-A	102	327	49	94	14	1	10	53	55	39	.287	.395	.428	145	22	21	59	6	4	-1	.978	-1	O1	1.6
1969	Det-A	131	456	74	124	17	0	21	69	54	61	.272	.350	.447	117	13	10	71	1	2	-1	.966	1	*O/1	0.3
1970	Det-A	131	467	64	130	24	4	16	71	77	49	.278	.382	.450	127	20	19	79	2	2	-1	.988	1	O1	1.2
1971	Det-A★	133	405	69	119	19	2	15	54	82	57	.294	.421	.462	144	31	29	81	4	6	-2	**1.000**	-6	*O/1	1.5
1972	*Det-A	106	278	46	87	11	2	10	32	28	33	.313	.380	.475	148	18	17	48	1	0	0	.991	-6	O1	0.9
1973	Det-A	91	310	40	79	13	0	10	45	29	28	.255	.325	.394	95	0	-2	39	4	1	1	1.000	-5	O1	-1.2
1974	Det-A★	147	558	71	146	28	2	13	64	65	75	.262	.340	.389	105	7	5	75	2	2	-1	.000	0	*D	0.4
Total	22	2834	10116	1622	3007	498	75	399	1583	1277	1020	.297	.379	.480	134	513	481	1846	137	65	2	.986	103	*OD1/3	46.4

■ WILLIE KAMM
Kamm, William Edward b: 2/2/1900, San Francisco, Cal. d: 12/21/88, Belmont, Cal. BR/TR, 5'10.5", 170 lbs. Deb: 4/18/23

1923	Chi-A	149	544	57	159	39	9	6	87	62	82	.292	.366	.430	110	7	8	86	17	13	-3	.960	8	*3	2.5
1924	Chi-A	147	528	58	134	28	6	6	93	64	59	.254	.337	.364	83	-16	-13	68	9	8	-2	**.971**	8	*3	0.4
1925	Chi-A	152	509	82	142	32	4	6	83	**90**	36	.279	.391	.393	105	2	7	83	11	13	-5	**.957**	-0	*3	1.2
1926	Chi-A	143	480	63	141	24	10	0	62	77	24	.294	.396	.385	108	6	9	80	14	4	2	**.978**	14	*3	3.2
1927	Chi-A	148	540	85	146	32	13	0	59	70	18	.270	.354	.378	92	-7	-5	71	7	9	-3	**.972**	1	*3	-0.1
1928	Chi-A	155	552	70	170	30	12	1	84	73	22	.308	.391	.411	112	11	12	93	17	9	-0	**.977**	-3	*3	1.7
1929	Chi-A	147	523	72	140	33	6	3	63	75	23	.268	.363	.371	90	-7	-6	76	12	5	1	**.978**	4	*3	0.4
1930	Chi-A	112	331	49	89	21	6	3	47	51	20	.269	.368	.396	97	-2	-0	51	5	4	-1	.939	15	*3	1.7
1931	Chi-A	18	59	9	15	4	1	0	9	7	6	.254	.333	.356	86	-2	-1	7	1	1	-0	.938	2	*3	0.1
	Cle-A	114	410	68	121	31	4	0	66	64	13	.295	.392	.390	100	6	3	66	13	9	-2	.947	1	*3	0.8
	Yr	132	469	77	136	35	5	0	75	71	19	.290	.384	.386	99	5	2	73	14	10	-2	.945	3	*3	0.9
1932	Cle-A	148	524	76	150	34	9	3	83	75	36	.286	.379	.403	96	4	-1	85	6	3	0	.967	7	*3	1.4
1933	Cle-A	133	447	59	126	17	2	1	47	54	27	.282	.359	.336	81	-8	-11	58	6	3	0	**.984**	1	*3	-0.2
1934	Cle-A	121	386	52	104	23	3	0	42	62	38	.269	.372	.345	84	-6	-7	55	7	1	2	**.978**	11	*3	1.0
1935	Cle-A	6	18	2	6	0	0	0	1	0	1	.333	.333	.333	72	-1	-1	2	0	1	-1	.875	-2	/3	-0.3
Total	13	1693	5851	802	1643	348	85	29	826	824	405	.281	.372	.384	97	-12	-7	881	125	83	-12	.967	65	*3	13.8

■ ALEX KAMPOURIS
Kampouris, Alexis William b: 11/13/12, Sacramento, Cal. BR/TR, 5'8", 155 lbs. Deb: 7/31/34

1934	Cin-N	19	66	6	13	1	0	0	3	3	18	.197	.254	.212	27	-7	-7	4	2			.946	-1	2	-0.7
1935	Cin-N	148	499	46	123	26	5	7	62	32	84	.246	.295	.361	77	-18	-16	55	8			.957	-1	*2/S	-0.6
1936	Cin-N	122	355	43	85	10	4	5	46	24	46	.239	.289	.332	72	-17	-14	35	3			.969	28	*2/O	2.0
1937	Cin-N	146	458	62	114	21	4	17	71	60	65	.249	.342	.424	112	4	8	67	2			.961	3	*2	2.0
1938	Cin-N	21	74	13	19	1	0	2	7	10	13	.257	.353	.351	97	-0	-0	9	0			.973	0	2	0.1
	NY-N	82	268	35	66	9	1	5	37	27	50	.246	.318	.343	81	-7	-7	30	0			.972	13	2	1.1
	Yr	103	342	48	85	10	1	7	44	37	63	.249	.325	.345	84	-7	-7	39	0			.972	14	*2	1.2
1939	NY-N	74	201	23	50	12	2	5	29	30	41	.249	.349	.403	101	1	1	29	0			.973	10	23	1.3
1941	Bro-N	16	51	8	16	4	2	1	9	11	8	.314	.444	.588	181	6	6	15	0			.987	0	2	0.8
1942	Bro-N	10	21	3	5	2	1	0	3	0	4	.238	.238	.429	92	-0	-0	2	0			.970	2	/2	0.2
1943	Bro-N	19	44	9	10	4	1	0	4	17	6	.227	.452	.364	136	4	4	9	0			.946	-1	2	0.3
	Was-A	51	145	24	30	4	0	2	13	30	25	.207	.361	.276	91	-1	0	19	7	1	2	.936	-3	32/O	-0.1
Total	9	708	2182	272	531	94	20	45	284	244	360	.243	.325	.367	91	-34	-26	272	22	1		.964	50	2/3SO	6.4

■ FRANK KANE
Kane, Francis Thomas "Sugar" b: 3/9/1895, Whitman, Mass. d: 12/2/62, Brockton, Mass. BL/TR, 5'11.5", 175 lbs. Deb: 9/13/15

1915	Bro-F	3	10	2	2	1	0	0	2	0	0	.200	.200	.400	75	-0	-0	1	0			1.000	1	/O	0.0
1919	NY-A	1	1	0	0	0	0	0	0	0	0	.000	.000	.000	-99	-0	-0	0	0			.000	0	H	0.0
Total	2	4	11	2	2	1	0	0	2	0	0	.182	.182	.364	58	-1	-1	1	0			.966	1	/O	0.0

■ JIM KANE
Kane, James Joseph "Shamus" b: 11/27/1881, Scranton, Pa. d: 10/2/47, Omaha, Neb. BL/TL, 6'2", 225 lbs. Deb: 4/21/08

| 1908 | Pit-N | 55 | 145 | 16 | 35 | 3 | 3 | 0 | 22 | 12 | | .241 | .299 | .303 | 93 | -1 | -1 | 15 | 5 | | | .966 | -2 | 1 | -0.4 |

■ JOHN KANE
Kane, John Francis b: 9/24/1882, Chicago, Ill. d: 1/28/34, St.Anthony, Idaho BR/TR, 5'6", 138 lbs. Deb: 4/11/07

1907	Cin-N	79	262	40	65	9	4	3	19	22		.248	.325	.347	107	3	2	39	20			.959	-1	O3/S2	0.1
1908	Cin-N	130	455	61	97	11	7	3	23	43		.213	.298	.288	90	-5	-4	49	30			**.981**	4	*O/2	-0.6
1909	Chi-N	20	45	6	4	1	0	0	5	2		.089	.146	.111	-20	-6	-6	1	1			.917	3	/OS32	-0.4
1910	*Chi-N	32	62	11	15	0	0	1	12	9	10	.242	.338	.290	84	-1	-1	7	2			1.000	-7	O/23S	-0.8
Total	4	261	824	118	181	21	11	7	59	76	10	.220	.302	.297	89	-9	-9	96	53			.975	-0	O/32S	-1.7

■ JOHN KANE
Kane, John Francis b: 2/19/1900, Chicago, Ill. d: 7/25/56, Chicago, Ill. BB/TR, 5'10.5", 162 lbs. Deb: 9/03/25

| 1925 | Chi-A | 14 | 56 | 6 | 10 | 1 | 0 | 0 | 3 | 0 | 3 | .179 | .193 | .196 | -1 | -9 | -8 | 2 | 0 | 0 | 0 | .935 | 1 | /S2 | -0.6 |

■ TOM KANE
Kane, Thomas Joseph "Sugar" b: 12/15/06, Chicago, Ill. d: 11/26/73, Chicago, Ill. BR/TR, 5'10.5", 160 lbs. Deb: 8/03/38

| 1938 | Bos-N | 2 | 2 | 0 | 0 | 0 | 0 | 0 | 0 | 2 | 0 | .000 | .500 | .000 | 53 | 0 | 0 | 0 | 0 | | | 1.000 | -1 | /2 | -0.1 |

■ JERRY KANE
Kane, William b: 1867, Collinsville, Ill. BR/TR, 6', 175 lbs. Deb: 5/02/1890

| 1890 | StL-a | 8 | 25 | 3 | 5 | 0 | 0 | 0 | | .200 | .259 | .200 | 33 | -2 | -2 | 1 | 0 | | | .907 | -1 | /1C | -0.3 |

■ ROD KANEHL Kanehl, Roderick Edwin "Hot Rod" b: 4/1/34, Wichita, Kan. BR/TR, 6'1", 180 lbs. Deb: 4/15/62

YEAR	TM/L	G	AB	R	H	2B	3B	HR	RBI	BB	SO	AVG	OBP	SLG	PRO+	BR	/A	RC	SB	CS	SBR	FA	FR	POS	TPR
1962	NY-N	133	351	52	87	10	2	4	27	23	36	.248	.296	.322	65	-17	-18	32	8	6	-1	.944	18	23O/1S	0.5
1963	NY-N	109	191	26	46	6	0	1	9	5	26	.241	.268	.288	59	-10	-10	13	6	3	0	.974	4	O32/1	-0.8
1964	NY-N	98	254	25	59	7	1	1	11	7	18	.232	.256	.280	52	-17	-16	19	3	1	0	.988	21	2O3/1	0.6
Total	3	340	796	103	192	23	3	6	47	35	80	.241	.277	.300	60	-43	-44	64	17	10	-1	.950	43	2O/31S	0.3

■ HEINIE KAPPEL Kappel, Henry b: 9/1863, Philadelphia, Pa. d: 8/27/05, Philadelphia, Pa. BR/TR, 5'8", 160 lbs. Deb: 5/22/1887 F

YEAR	TM/L	G	AB	R	H	2B	3B	HR	RBI	BB	SO	AVG	OBP	SLG	PRO+	BR	/A	RC	SB	CS	SBR	FA	FR	POS	TPR
1887	Cin-a	23	78	11	22	3	2	0		2		.282	.309	.372	89	-1	-1	10	3			.667	-3	/3O2S	-0.3
1888	Cin-a	36	143	18	37	4	4	1	15	2		.259	.274	.364	101	0	-1	20	20			.790	-12	S2/3	-1.1
1889	Col-a	46	173	25	47	7	5	3	21	21	28	.272	.354	.422	129	5	7	30	10			.791	-2	S3	0.6
Total	3	105	394	54	106	14	11	4	36	25	28	.269	.318	.391	111	4	5	60	33			.796	-17	/S32O	-0.8

■ JOE KAPPEL Kappel, Joseph b: 4/27/1857, Philadelphia, Pa. d: 7/8/29, Philadelphia, Pa. BR , 5'11", 175 lbs. Deb: 5/26/1884 F

YEAR	TM/L	G	AB	R	H	2B	3B	HR	RBI	BB	SO	AVG	OBP	SLG	PRO+	BR	/A	RC	SB	CS	SBR	FA	FR	POS	TPR
1884	Phi-N	4	15	1	1	0	0	0	0	0	2	.067	.067	.067	-61	-3	-3	0				.727	-3	/C	-0.5
1890	Phi-a	56	208	29	50	8	1	1		20		.240	.310	.303	85	-4	-4	24	12			.851	-5	OS3/C2	-0.7
Total	2	60	223	30	51	8	1	1	0	20	2	.229	.295	.287	76	-7	-6	24	12			.773	-8	/OS3C2	-1.2

■ RON KARKOVICE Karkovice, Ronald Joseph b: 8/8/63, Union, N.J. BR/TR, 6'1", 215 lbs. Deb: 8/17/86

YEAR	TM/L	G	AB	R	H	2B	3B	HR	RBI	BB	SO	AVG	OBP	SLG	PRO+	BR	/A	RC	SB	CS	SBR	FA	FR	POS	TPR
1986	Chi-A	37	97	13	24	7	0	4	13	9	37	.247	.318	.443	101	0	-0	13	1	0	0	.996	14	C	1.6
1987	Chi-A	39	85	7	6	0	0	2	7	7	40	.071	.160	.141	-19	-15	-15	2	3	0	1	.982	10	C/D	-0.2
1988	Chi-A	46	115	10	20	4	0	3	9	7	30	.174	.228	.287	43	-9	-9	8	4	2	0	.995	9	C	0.2
1989	Chi-A	71	182	21	48	9	2	3	24	10	56	.264	.309	.385	97	-2	-1	23	0	0	0	.986	17	C/D	1.9
1990	Chi-A	68	183	30	45	10	0	6	20	16	52	.246	.310	.399	99	-1	-1	24	2	0	1	.994	6	C/D	0.9
1991	Chi-A	75	167	25	41	13	0	5	22	15	42	.246	.311	.413	101	-1	-0	22	0	0	0	.988	12	C/O	1.4
1992	Chi-A	123	342	39	81	12	1	13	50	30	89	.237	.304	.392	96	-4	-3	42	10	4	1	.990	4	*C/O	0.8
Total	7	459	1171	145	265	55	3	36	145	94	346	.226	.290	.371	83	-31	-29	135	20	6	2	.990	72	C/DO	6.6

■ BILL KARLON Karlon, William John "Hank" b: 1/21/09, Palmer, Mass. d: 12/7/64, Ware, Mass. BR/TR, 6'1", 190 lbs. Deb: 4/28/30

YEAR	TM/L	G	AB	R	H	2B	3B	HR	RBI	BB	SO	AVG	OBP	SLG	PRO+	BR	/A	RC	SB	CS	SBR	FA	FR	POS	TPR
1930	NY-A	2	5	0	0	0	0	0	0	0	1	.000	.000	.000	-99	-2	-1	0	0	0	0	1.000	-0	/O	-0.2

■ MARTY KAROW Karow, Martin Gregory (b: Martin Gregory Karowsky) b: 7/18/04, Braddock, Pa. d: 4/27/86, Bryan, Texas BR/TR, 5'10.5", 170 lbs. Deb: 6/21/27

YEAR	TM/L	G	AB	R	H	2B	3B	HR	RBI	BB	SO	AVG	OBP	SLG	PRO+	BR	/A	RC	SB	CS	SBR	FA	FR	POS	TPR
1927	Bos-A	6	10	0	2	1	0	0	0	0	2	.200	.200	.300	29	-1	-1	1	0	0	0	1.000	0	/S3	-0.1

■ ERIC KARROS Karros, Eric Peter b: 11/4/67, Hackensack, N.J. BR/TR, 6'4", 205 lbs. Deb: 9/01/91

YEAR	TM/L	G	AB	R	H	2B	3B	HR	RBI	BB	SO	AVG	OBP	SLG	PRO+	BR	/A	RC	SB	CS	SBR	FA	FR	POS	TPR
1991	LA-N	14	14	0	1	1	0	0	1	1	6	.071	.133	.143	-23	-2	-2	0	0	0	0	1.000	0	1	-0.2
1992	LA-N	149	545	63	140	30	1	20	88	37	103	.257	.307	.426	107	2	3	67	2	4	-2	.993	11	*1	0.3
Total	2	163	559	63	141	31	1	20	89	38	109	.252	.302	.419	104	-0	1	67	2	4	-2	.993	11	1	0.1

■ JOHN KARST Karst, John Gottlieb "King" b: 10/15/1893, Philadelphia, Pa. d: 5/21/76, Cape May Court House, N.J. BL/TR, 5'11.5", 175 lbs. Deb: 10/06/15

YEAR	TM/L	G	AB	R	H	2B	3B	HR	RBI	BB	SO	AVG	OBP	SLG	PRO+	BR	/A	RC	SB	CS	SBR	FA	FR	POS	TPR
1915	Bro-N	1	0	0	0	0	0	0	0	0	0	—	—	—	—	0	0	0	0			1.000	0	/3	0.0

■ EDDIE KASKO Kasko, Edward Michael b: 6/27/32, Linden, N.J. BR/TR, 6', 180 lbs. Deb: 4/18/57 M

YEAR	TM/L	G	AB	R	H	2B	3B	HR	RBI	BB	SO	AVG	OBP	SLG	PRO+	BR	/A	RC	SB	CS	SBR	FA	FR	POS	TPR
1957	StL-N	134	479	59	131	16	5	1	35	33	53	.273	.320	.334	75	-16	-17	52	6	1	1	.961	-7	*3S/2	-2.0
1958	StL-N	104	259	20	57	8	1	2	22	21	25	.220	.279	.282	47	-19	-20	19	1	2	-1	.961	6	S2/3	-0.9
1959	Cin-N	118	329	39	93	14	1	2	31	14	38	.283	.312	.350	74	-11	-13	35	2	2	-1	.976	12	S3/2	0.6
1960	Cin-N	126	479	56	140	21	1	6	51	46	37	.292	.362	.378	101	3	2	66	9	9	-3	.966	0	32S	0.3
1961	*Cin-N★	126	469	64	127	22	1	2	27	32	36	.271	.323	.335	74	-16	-17	52	4	3	-1	.964	-18	*S3/2	-2.7
1962	Cin-N	134	533	74	148	26	2	4	41	35	44	.278	.328	.356	81	-12	-14	59	3	3	-1	.941	-8	*3S	-2.0
1963	Cin-N	76	199	25	48	9	0	3	10	21	29	.241	.314	.332	83	-3	-4	21	0	2	-1	.959	-1	3S/2	-0.5
1964	Hou-N	133	448	45	109	16	1	0	22	37	52	.243	.302	.283	70	-19	-16	38	4	6	-2	**.978**	10	*S/3	0.0
1965	Hou-N	68	215	18	53	7	1	1	10	11	20	.247	.296	.302	74	-9	-7	17	1	3	-2	.976	-10	S/3	-1.6
1966	Bos-A	58	136	11	29	7	0	1	12	15	19	.213	.291	.287	61	-6	-7	11	1	0	0	.976	8	S3/2	0.2
Total	10	1077	3546	411	935	146	13	22	261	265	353	.264	.318	.331	76	-108	-113	370	31	31	-9	.971	-9	S3/2	-8.6

■ RAY KATT Katt, Raymond Frederick b: 5/9/27, New Braunfels, Tex. BR/TR, 6'2", 200 lbs. Deb: 9/16/52 C

YEAR	TM/L	G	AB	R	H	2B	3B	HR	RBI	BB	SO	AVG	OBP	SLG	PRO+	BR	/A	RC	SB	CS	SBR	FA	FR	POS	TPR
1952	NY-N	9	27	4	6	0	0	0	1	1	5	.222	.250	.222	32	-2	-2	1	0	0	0	1.000	1	/C	-0.1
1953	NY-N	8	29	2	5	1	0	0	1	1	3	.172	.200	.207	6	-4	-4	1	0	0	0	.975	-1	/C	-0.4
1954	NY-N	86	200	26	51	7	1	9	33	19	29	.255	.320	.435	94	-2	-2	28	1	0	0	.973	-7	C	-0.6
1955	NY-N	124	326	27	70	7	2	7	28	22	38	.215	.269	.313	54	-22	-22	25	0	0	0	.987	-8	*C	-2.6
1956	NY-N	37	101	10	23	4	0	7	14	6	16	.228	.278	.475	98	-1	-1	13	0	1	-1	.978	0	C	0.0
	StL-N	47	158	11	41	4	0	6	20	6	24	.259	.291	.399	83	-4	-4	18	0	1	-1	.984	-2	C	-0.5
	Yr	84	259	21	64	8	0	13	34	12	40	.247	.286	.429	89	-5	-5	31	0	2	-1	.982	-1	C	-0.5
1957	NY-N	72	165	11	38	3	1	2	17	15	35	.230	.302	.297	62	-9	-9	15	1	0	0	.981	-6	C	-1.3
1958	StL-N	19	41	1	7	1	0	1	4	4	6	.171	.244	.268	34	-4	-4	2	0	0	0	.971	0	C	-0.4
1959	StL-N	15	24	0	7	2	0	0	2	0	8	.292	.292	.375	71	-1	-1	2	0	0	0	.976	-0	C	-0.1
Total	8	417	1071	92	248	29	4	32	120	74	164	.232	.285	.356	69	-49	-49	105	2	2	-1	.981	-22	C	-6.0

■ BENNY KAUFF Kauff, Benjamin Michael b: 1/5/1890, Pomeroy, Ohio d: 11/17/61, Columbus, Ohio BL/TL, 5'8", 157 lbs. Deb: 4/20/12

YEAR	TM/L	G	AB	R	H	2B	3B	HR	RBI	BB	SO	AVG	OBP	SLG	PRO+	BR	/A	RC	SB	CS	SBR	FA	FR	POS	TPR
1912	NY-A	5	11	4	3	0	0	0	2	3		.273	.429	.273	96	0	0	2	1			1.000	-1	/O	-0.1
1914	Ind-F	154	571	**120**	**211**	**44**	13	8	95	72	55	**.370**	**.447**	.534	161	**60**	**52**	**175**	**75**			.953	16	*O	**6.2**
1915	Bro-F	136	483	92	165	23	11	12	83	85	50	**.342**	**.446**	**.509**	**182**	**52**	**53**	**138**	**55**			.959	15	*O	**6.4**
1916	NY-N	154	552	71	146	22	15	9	74	68	65	.264	.348	.408	139	21	25	81	40	26	-4	.962	2	*O	1.7
1917	*NY-N	153	559	89	172	22	4	5	68	59	54	.308	.379	.388	140	25	27	91	30			.976	-4	*O	1.6
1918	NY-N	67	270	41	85	19	4	2	39	16	30	.315	.355	.437	144	12	13	43	9			.952	-1	O	0.9
1919	NY-N	135	491	73	136	27	7	10	67	39	45	.277	.334	.422	128	15	15	72	21			.950	-3	*O	0.4
1920	NY-N	55	157	31	43	12	3	3	26	25	14	.274	.380	.446	138	8	8	26	3	7	-3	.960	-1	O	0.1
Total	8	859	3094	521	961	169	57	49	454	367	313	.311	.389	.450	149	195	194	628	234	33		.960	23	O	17.2

■ DICK KAUFFMAN Kauffman, Howard Richard b: 6/22/1888, E.Lewisburg, Pa. d: 4/16/48, Mifflinburg, Pa. BB/TR, 6'3", 190 lbs. Deb: 9/17/14

YEAR	TM/L	G	AB	R	H	2B	3B	HR	RBI	BB	SO	AVG	OBP	SLG	PRO+	BR	/A	RC	SB	CS	SBR	FA	FR	POS	TPR
1914	StL-A	7	15	1	4	1	0	0	2	0	3	.267	.267	.333	83	-0	-0	1	0			.967	-1	/1	-0.2
1915	StL-A	37	124	9	32	8	2	0	14	5	27	.258	.298	.355	99	-1	-1	12	0	3	-2	.984	-1	1/O	-0.5
Total	2	44	139	10	36	9	2	0	16	5	30	.259	.295	.353	97	-2	-1	14	0	3		.982	-2	/1O	-0.7

■ TONY KAUFMANN Kaufmann, Anthony Charles b: 12/16/1900, Chicago, Ill. d: 6/4/82, Elgin, Ill. BR/TR, 5'11", 165 lbs. Deb: 9/23/21 C

YEAR	TM/L	G	AB	R	H	2B	3B	HR	RBI	BB	SO	AVG	OBP	SLG	PRO+	BR	/A	RC	SB	CS	SBR	FA	FR	POS	TPR
1921	Chi-N	2	5	0	2	1	0	0	0	0	1	.400	.400	.600	161	0	0	1	0	0	0	1.000	-1	/P	0.0
1922	Chi-N	38	45	4	9	2	1	1	4	2	14	.200	.234	.356	49	-4	-4	4	0	0	0	.933	-1	P	0.0
1923	Chi-N	33	74	10	16	2	0	2	10	7	17	.216	.284	.324	60	-4	-4	7	0	0	0	.962	-1	P	0.0
1924	Chi-N	35	76	6	24	5	0	1	14	3	10	.316	.342	.421	102	0	0	11	0	0	0	.981	-1	P	0.0
1925	Chi-N	31	78	8	15	7	0	2	13	2	17	.192	.213	.359	42	-7	-7	6	0	0	0	.981	-0	P	0.0
1926	Chi-N	30	60	9	15	2	0	1	7	2	10	.250	.274	.333	62	-3	-3	5	1			1.000	-2	P	0.0
1927	Chi-N	9	16	2	5	0	0	1	6	4	4	.313	.450	.500	154	1	1	4	0			1.000	2	/P	0.0
	Phi-N	8	7	1	1	0	0	1	2	0	1	.143	.143	.571	83	-0	-0	1	0			1.000	-1	/PO	0.0
	StL-N	1	0	0	0	0	0	0	0	0	0	—	—	—	—	0	0	0	0			.000	0	/P	0.0
	Yr	18	23	3	6	0	0	2	8	4	5	.261	.370	.522	136	1	1	4	0			1.000	1	P/O	0.0
1928	StL-N	5	0	0	0	0	0	0	0	0	0	—	—	—	—	0	0	0	0			1.000	-0	/P	0.0

YEAR	TM/L	G	AB	R	H	2B	3B	HR	RBI	BB	SO	AVG	OBP	SLG	PRO+	BR	/A	RC	SB	CS	SBR	FA	FR	POS	TPR
1929	NY-N	39	32	18	1	0	0	0	1	6	4	.031	.184	.031	-43	-7	-7	1	3			.964	-4	O	-1.0
1930	StL-N	2	3	1	1	0	0	0	0	1	1	.333	.500	.333	103	0	0	1	0			1.000	-0	/P	0.0
1931	StL-N	20	18	1	2	0	0	0	0	1	3	.111	.158	.111	-26	-3	-3	0	0			.929	-1	P/O	-0.1
1935	StL-N	7	0	2	0	0	0	0	0	0	0	—	—	—	—	0	0	0	0			1.000	0	/P	0.0
Total	12	260	414	62	91	19	1	9	57	28	82	.220	.269	.336	57	-27	-28	40	4	0		.972	-9	P/O	-1.1

■ CHARLIE KAVANAGH Kavanagh, Charles Hugh "Silk" b: 6/9/1893, Chicago, Ill. d: 9/6/73, Reedsburg, Wis. BR/TR, 5'9", 165 lbs. Deb: 6/11/14

1914	Chi-A	6	5	0	1	0	0	0	0	0	2	.200	.333	.200	62	-0	-0	0	0			.000	0	H	0.0

■ LEO KAVANAGH Kavanagh, Leo Daniel b: 8/9/1894, Chicago, Ill. d: 8/10/50, Chicago, Ill. BR/TR, 5'9", 180 lbs. Deb: 4/22/14

1914	Chi-F	5	11	0	3	0	0	0	1	1	0	.273	.333	.273	78	-0	-0	1	0			1.000	-1	/S	-0.1

■ MARTY KAVANAGH Kavanagh, Martin Joseph b: 6/13/1891, Harrison, N.J. d: 7/28/60, Eloise, Mich. BR/TR, 6', 187 lbs. Deb: 4/18/14

1914	Det-A	128	439	60	109	21	6	4	35	41	42	.248	.318	.351	98	-0	-2	51	16	14	-4	.929	-7	*2/1	-1.5
1915	Det-A	113	332	55	98	14	13	4	49	42	44	.295	.378	.452	141	19	17	57	8	8	-2	.987	-15	12/SO3	-0.1
1916	Det-A	58	78	6	11	4	0	0	5	9	15	.141	.239	.192	29	-7	-7	4	0			1.000	0	O/23	-0.8
	Cle-A	19	44	4	11	2	1	1	10	2	5	.250	.283	.409	102	0	-0	5	0			.894	-0	/213	0.0
	Yr	77	122	10	22	6	1	1	15	11	20	.180	.254	.270	55	-7	-7	9	0			1.000	-0	O2/31	-0.8
1917	Cle-A	14	14	1	0	0	0	0	0	3	2	.000	.176	.000	-43	-2	-2	0	0			1.000	0	/O	-0.3
1918	Cle-A	13	38	4	8	2	0	0	6	7	7	.211	.348	.263	77	-0	-1	4	1			.967	-1	1	-0.3
	StL-N	12	44	6	8	1	0	1	8	3	1	.182	.234	.273	56	-2	-2	3	1			1.000	-2	/O2	-0.5
	Det-A	13	44	2	12	3	0	0	9	11	6	.273	.418	.341	135	2	3	6	0			.964	-1	1	0.1
Total	5	370	1033	138	257	47	20	10	122	118	122	.249	.330	.362	104	9	5	130	26	22		.926	-26	2/1O3S	-3.4

■ KAVANAUGH Kavanaugh Deb: 9/11/1872

1872	Eck-n	5	22	3	6	1	0	0	2	0	0	.273	.273	.318	96	-0	0	2						/1O	0.0

■ BILL KAY Kay, Walter Brocton "King Bill" b: 2/14/1878, New Castle, Va. d: 12/3/45, Roanoke, Va. BL/TR, 6'2", 180 lbs. Deb: 8/12/07

1907	Was-A	25	60	8	20	1	1	0	7	0		.333	.333	.383	140	2	2	8	0			1.000	-0	O	0.2

■ EDDIE KAZAK Kazak, Edward Terrance (b: Edward Terrance Tkaczuk) b: 7/18/20, Steubenville, O. BR/TR, 6', 175 lbs. Deb: 9/29/48

1948	StL-N	6	22	1	6	3	0	0	2	0	2	.273	.273	.409	78	-1	-1	2	0			.900	1	/3	0.0
1949	StL-N★	92	326	43	99	15	3	6	42	29	17	.304	.362	.423	105	5	3	49	0			.926	-4	3/2	-0.2
1950	StL-N	93	207	21	53	2	2	5	23	18	19	.256	.319	.357	74	-7	-8	23	0			.936	1	3	-0.7
1951	StL-N	11	33	2	6	2	0	0	4	5	5	.182	.289	.242	44	-2	-3	3	0	0	0	.933	-1	3	-0.4
1952	StL-N	3	2	1	0	0	0	0	0	0	0	.000	.000	.000	-99	-1	-1	0	0	0	0	1.000	0	/3	0.0
	Cin-N	13	15	1	1	0	1	0	0	0	2	.067	.067	.200	-29	-3	-3	0	0	0	0	.667	-1	/31	-0.3
	Yr	16	17	2	1	0	1	0	0	0	2	.059	.059	.176	-37	-3	-3	0	0	0	0	.750	-0	/31	-0.3
Total	5	218	605	69	165	22	6	11	71	52	45	.273	.332	.383	87	-9	-12	77	0	0		.927	-3	3/21	-1.6

■ TED KAZANSKI Kazanski, Theodore Stanley b: 1/25/34, Hamtramck, Mich. BR/TR, 6'1", 175 lbs. Deb: 6/25/53

1953	Phi-N	95	360	39	78	17	5	2	27	26	53	.217	.275	.308	52	-26	-25	31	1	1	-0	.949	-19	S	-3.7
1954	Phi-N	39	104	7	14	2	0	1	8	4	14	.135	.167	.183	-9	-17	-17	2	0	1	-1	.945	-7	S	-2.2
1955	Phi-N	9	12	1	1	0	0	1	1	1	1	.083	.154	.333	25	-1	-1	1	0	0	0	1.000	1	/S3	-0.1
1956	Phi-N	117	379	35	80	11	1	4	34	20	41	.211	.253	.277	43	-31	-30	25	0	2	-1	.979	-10	*2/S	-3.4
1957	Phi-N	62	185	15	49	7	1	3	11	17	20	.265	.327	.362	88	-4	-3	21	1	1	-0	.968	-3	32/S	-0.4
1958	Phi-N	95	289	21	66	12	2	3	35	22	34	.228	.292	.315	62	-16	-16	25	2	3	-1	.988	-13	2S3	-2.6
Total	6	417	1329	118	288	49	9	14	116	90	163	.217	.270	.299	51	-95	-92	105	4	8	-4	.981	-51	2S/3	-12.4

■ BOB KEARNEY Kearney, Robert Henry b: 10/3/56, San Antonio, Tex. BR/TR, 6', 190 lbs. Deb: 9/25/79

1979	SF-N	2	0	0	0	0	0	0	0	1	0	—	1.000	—	211	0	0	0	0	0	0	.000	0	/C	0.0
1981	Oak-A	1	0	0	0	0	0	0	0	0	0	—	—	—	—	0	0	0	0	0	0	.000	0	/C	0.0
1982	Oak-A	22	71	7	12	3	0	0	5	3	10	.169	.224	.211	21	-8	-7	4	0	0	0	.970	5	C	-0.2
1983	Oak-A	108	298	33	76	11	0	8	32	21	50	.255	.313	.372	93	-5	-3	32	1	4	-2	.982	5	*C/D	0.4
1984	Sea-A	133	431	39	97	24	1	7	43	18	72	.225	.259	.334	64	-22	-22	36	7	5	-1	.988	5	*C	-1.2
1985	Sea-A	108	305	24	74	14	1	6	27	11	59	.243	.278	.354	71	-12	-13	29	1	1	-0	**.995**	6	*C	-0.2
1986	Sea-A	81	204	23	49	10	0	6	25	12	35	.240	.282	.377	77	-7	-7	20	0	2	-1	.989	14	C	1.0
1987	Sea-A	24	47	5	8	4	1	0	1	1	9	.170	.188	.298	25	-5	-5	3	0	0	0	.981	6	C	0.1
Total	8	479	1356	131	316	66	3	27	133	67	235	.233	.275	.346	70	-59	-56	123	9	12	-5	.987	41	C/D	-0.1

■ TEDDY KEARNS Kearns, Edward Joseph b: 1/1/1900, Trenton, N.J. d: 12/21/49, Trenton, N.J. BR/TR, 5'11", 180 lbs. Deb: 10/01/20

1920	Phi-A	1	1	0	0	0	0	0	0	0	0	.000	.000	.000	-99	-0	-0	0	0	0	0	.000	0	H	0.0
1924	Chi-N	4	16	0	4	0	1	0	1	1	1	.250	.294	.375	77	-1	-1	2	0	0	0	1.000	-0	/1	-0.1
1925	Chi-N	3	2	0	1	0	0	0	0	0	0	.500	.500	.500	154	0	0	0	0	0	0	1.000	-0	/1	0.0
Total	3	8	19	0	5	0	1	0	1	1	1	.263	.300	.368	76	-1	-1	2	0	0	0	1.000	-0	/1	-0.1

■ TOM KEARNS Kearns, Thomas J. "Dasher" b: 11/9/1859, Rochester, N.Y. d: 12/7/38, Buffalo, N.Y. TR , 5'7", 160 lbs. Deb: 8/26/1880

1880	Buf-N	2	7	0	0	0	0	0	0	0	0	.000	.000	.000	-98	-1	-1	0				.667	-1	/C	-0.3
1882	Det-N	4	13	2	4	2	0	0	1	0	4	.308	.308	.462	143	1	1	2				.733	-3	/2	-0.2
1884	Det-N	21	79	9	16	0	1	0	7	2	10	.203	.222	.228	45	-5	-4	4				.810	-10	2	-1.3
Total	3	27	99	11	20	2	1	0	8	2	14	.202	.218	.242	48	-6	-5	6				.801	-14	/2C	-1.8

■ EDDIE KEARSE Kearse, Edward Paul "Truck" b: 2/23/16, San Francisco, Cal d: 7/15/68, Eureka, Cal. BR/TR, 6'1", 195 lbs. Deb: 6/13/42

1942	NY-A	11	26	2	5	0	0	0	2	3	1	.192	.276	.192	34	-2	-2	2	1	0	0	1.000	3	C	0.2

■ CHICK KEATING Keating, Walter Francis b: 8/8/1891, Philadelphia, Pa. d: 7/13/59, Philadelphia, Pa. BR/TR, 5'9.5", 155 lbs. Deb: 9/26/13

1913	Chi-N	2	5	0	1	1	0	0	0	0	1	.200	.200	.400	69	-0	-0	0	0			1.000	-1	/S	-0.1
1914	Chi-N	20	30	3	3	0	1	0	0	6	9	.100	.250	.167	25	-3	-3	1	0			.951	0	S	-0.2
1915	Chi-N	4	8	1	0	0	0	0	0	0	3	.000	.000	.000	-99	-2	-2	0	1			.750	-0	/S	-0.2
1926	Phi-N	4	2	0	0	0	0	0	0	0	0	.000	.000	.000	-95	-1	-1	0	0			1.000	-0	/2S3	-0.1
Total	4	30	45	4	4	1	1	0	0	6	13	.089	.196	.156	4	-5	-5	2	1			.903	-1	/S23	-0.6

■ GREG KEATLEY Keatley, Gregory Steven b: 9/12/53, Princeton, W.Va. BR/TR, 6'2", 200 lbs. Deb: 9/27/81

1981	KC-A	2	0	0	0	0	0	0	0	0	0	—	—	—	—	0	0	0	0	0	0	1.000	-0	/C	0.0

■ PAT KEEDY Keedy, Charles Patrick b: 1/10/58, Birmingham, Ala. BR/TR, 6'4", 205 lbs. Deb: 9/10/85

1985	Cal-A	3	4	1	2	1	0	1	1	0	0	.500	.500	1.500	424	2	2	2	0	1	-1	.000	-0	/3O	0.1
1987	Chi-A	17	41	6	7	1	0	2	2	2	14	.171	.209	.341	42	-4	-4	3	1	0	0	.943	4	3/12SOD	0.1
1989	Cle-A	9	14	3	3	2	0	0	1	2	5	.214	.313	.357	87	-0	-0	2	0	0	0	1.000	-0	/O31SD	0.0
Total	3	29	59	10	12	4	0	3	4	4	19	.203	.254	.424	77	-2	-2	6	1	1	-0	.929	3	/3O1DS2	0.2

■ WILLIE KEELER Keeler, William Henry "Wee Willie" b: 3/3/1872, Brooklyn, N.Y. d: 1/1/23, Brooklyn, N.Y. BL/TL, 5'4.5", 140 lbs. Deb: 9/30/1892 H

1892	NY-N	14	53	7	17	3	0	0	6	3	3	.321	.368	.377	130	2	2	9	5			.878	-3	3	-0.1
1893	NY-N	7	24	5	8	2	1	1	7	5	1	.333	.448	.625	186	3	3	8	3			.667	-5	/O2S	-0.2
	Bro-N	20	80	14	25	1	1	1	9	4	4	.313	.353	.387	103	-0	0	12	2			.833	-1	3/O	0.0
	Yr	27	104	19	33	3	2	2	16	9	5	.317	.377	.442	123	3	3	20	5			.833	-6	3O/2S	-0.2

YEAR	TM/L	G	AB	R	H	2B	3B	HR	RBI	BB	SO	AVG	OBP	SLG	PRO+	BR	/A	RC	SB	CS	SBR	FA	FR	POS	TPR
1894	*Bal-N	129	590	165	219	27	22	5	94	40	6	.371	.427	.517	123	28	23	149	32			.938	3	*O/2	1.3
1895	*Bal-N	131	565	162	213	24	15	4	78	37	12	.377	.429	.494	136	34	31	145	47			.946	0	*O	1.6
1896	*Bal-N	126	544	153	210	22	13	4	82	37	9	.386	.432	.496	145	37	35	150	67			.969	6	*O	2.6
1897	*Bal-N	129	564	145	**239**	27	19	0	74	35		**.424**	.464	.539	164	**52**	**52**	**176**	64			.970	-2	*O	3.4
1898	Bal-N	129	561	126	**216**	7	2	1	44	31		**.385**	.420	.410	136	28	27	112	28			.961	0	*O/3	1.6
1899	Bro-N	141	570	**140**	216	12	13	1	61	37		.379	.425	.451	137	32	30	133	45			.979	-2	*O	1.6
1900	*Bro-N	136	563	106	**204**	13	12	4	68	30		.362	.402	.449	127	26	21	123	41			.940	5	*O/2	1.5
1901	Bro-N	136	595	123	202	18	12	2	43	21		.339	.368	.420	125	20	18	105	23			**.985**	-6	*O3/2	0.3
1902	Bro-N	133	559	86	186	20	5	0	38	21		.333	.365	.386	131	19	19	91	19			**.978**	2	*O	1.3
1903	NY-A	132	512	95	160	14	7	0	32	32		.313	.366	.367	113	14	10	83	24			.935	-9	*O/3	-0.8
1904	NY-A	143	543	78	186	14	8	2	40	35		.343	.388	.409	145	32	29	100	21			.935	-3	*O	2.0
1905	NY-A	149	560	81	169	14	4	4	38	43		.302	.356	.363	115	18	11	86	19			.968	-4	*O2/3	0.1
1906	NY-A	152	592	96	180	8	3	2	33	40		.304	.351	.338	106	12	5	85	23			.987	-2	*O	-0.5
1907	NY-A	107	423	50	99	5	2	0	17	15		.234	.265	.255	61	-16	-20	34	7			.969	-3	*O	-3.0
1908	NY-A	91	323	38	85	3	1	1	14	31		.263	.331	.288	101	2	1	37	14			.936	-1	O	-0.4
1909	NY-A	99	360	44	95	7	5	1	32	24		.264	.327	.319	104	2	2	44	10			.968	-5	O	-0.8
1910	NY-N	19	10	5	3	0	0	0	0	3	1	.300	.462	.300	123	1	1	2	1			1.000	-1	/O	0.0
Total	19	2123	8591	1719	2932	241	145	33	810	524	36	.341	.387	.415	126	345	300	1685	495			.960	-30	*O/32S	11.5

■ BOB KEELY Keely, Robert William b: 8/22/09, St.Louis, Mo. BR/TR, 6', 175 lbs. Deb: 7/25/44 C

YEAR	TM/L	G	AB	R	H	2B	3B	HR	RBI	BB	SO	AVG	OBP	SLG	PRO+	BR	/A	RC	SB	CS	SBR	FA	FR	POS	TPR
1944	StL-N	1	0	0	0	0	0	0	0	0	0	—	—	—	—	0	0	0	0			1.000	-0	/C	0.0
1945	StL-N	1	1	0	0	0	0	0	0	0	0	.000	.000	.000	-98	-0	-0	0	0			1.000	-0	/C	0.0
Total	2	2	1	0	0	0	0	0	0	0	0	.000	.000	.000	-98	-0	-0	0	0			1.000	-0	/C	0.0

■ BILL KEEN Keen, William Brown "Buster" b: 8/16/1892, Oglethorpe, Ga. d: 7/16/47, South Point, Ohio BR/TR, 6', 181 lbs. Deb: 8/08/11

YEAR	TM/L	G	AB	R	H	2B	3B	HR	RBI	BB	SO	AVG	OBP	SLG	PRO+	BR	/A	RC	SB	CS	SBR	FA	FR	POS	TPR
1911	Pit-N	6	7	0	0	0	0	0	0	1	4	.000	.125	.000	-62	-2	-2	0	0			1.000	-0	/1	-0.2

■ JIM KEENAN Keenan, James W. b: 2/10/1858, New Haven, Conn. d: 9/21/26, Cincinnati, Ohio BR/TR, 5'10", 186 lbs. Deb: 5/17/1875

YEAR	TM/L	G	AB	R	H	2B	3B	HR	RBI	BB	SO	AVG	OBP	SLG	PRO+	BR	/A	RC	SB	CS	SBR	FA	FR	POS	TPR
1875	NH-n	4	13	1	1	0	0	0		0		.077	.077	.077	-53	-2	-2	0						/3C	-0.1
1880	Buf-N	2	7	1	1	0	0	0	0	1	1	.143	.250	.143	36	-0	-0	0				.947	3	/C	0.2
1882	Pit-a	25	96	10	21	7	0	1		1		.219	.227	.323	87	-2	-1	7				.906	1	C/OS	0.1
1884	Ind-a	68	249	36	73	14	4	3		16		.293	.343	.418	154	14	15	37				.923	-2	C/1OSP	1.6
1885	Cin-a	36	132	16	35	2	2	1		8		.265	.307	.333	103	1	0	14				.926	-1	C/1P	0.2
1886	Cin-a	44	148	31	40	4	3	3		18		.270	.357	.399	134	7	6	22	0			.915	0	C/O31P	0.8
1887	Cin-a	47	174	19	44	4	1	0		11		.253	.301	.287	65	-8	-8	18	7			.934	9	C1	0.2
1888	Cin-a	85	313	38	73	9	8	1	40	22		.233	.294	.323	95	0	-2	33	9			.946	3	C1	0.6
1889	Cin-a	87	300	52	86	10	11	6	60	48	35	.287	.395	.453	140	18	17	62	18			.962	1	C1/3	1.9
1890	Cin-N	54	202	21	28	4	2	3	19	19	36	.139	.216	.223	30	-18	-18	11	5			.950	4	C/1O3	-0.9
1891	Cin-N	75	252	30	51	7	5	4	33	33	39	.202	.302	.317	82	-5	-6	25	2			.974	-4	1C/3	-0.7
Total	10	523	1873	254	452	61	36	22	152	177	111	.241	.314	.348	101	7	3	229	41			.935	14	C1/O3PS	4.0

■ GEORGE KEERL Keerl, George Henry b: 4/10/1847, Baltimore, Md. d: 9/13/23, Menominee, Mich. BR/TR, 5'7", 145 lbs. Deb: 5/05/1875

YEAR	TM/L	G	AB	R	H	2B	3B	HR	RBI	BB	SO	AVG	OBP	SLG	PRO+	BR	/A	RC	SB	CS	SBR	FA	FR	POS	TPR
1875	Chi-n	6	23	2	3	0	0	0		0		.130	.130	.130	-9	-2	-2	0						/2	-0.2

■ JIM KEESEY Keesey, James Ward b: 10/27/02, Perryville, Md. d: 9/5/51, Boise, Idaho BR/TR, 6'0.5", 170 lbs. Deb: 9/06/25

YEAR	TM/L	G	AB	R	H	2B	3B	HR	RBI	BB	SO	AVG	OBP	SLG	PRO+	BR	/A	RC	SB	CS	SBR	FA	FR	POS	TPR
1925	Phi-A	5	5	1	2	0	0	0	1	0	2	.400	.400	.400	97	0	-0	1	0	0	0	1.000	-0	/1	0.0
1930	Phi-A	11	12	2	3	1	0	0	2	1	2	.250	.308	.333	60	-1	-1	1	0	0	0	.909	-0	/1	-0.1
Total	2	16	17	3	5	1	0	0	3	1	4	.294	.333	.353	71	-1	-1	2	0	0	0	.923	-1	/1	-0.1

■ BILL KEISTER Keister, William Hoffman "Wagon Tongue" b: 8/17/1874, Baltimore, Md. d: 8/19/24, Baltimore, Md. BL/TR, 5'5.5", 168 lbs. Deb: 5/20/1896

YEAR	TM/L	G	AB	R	H	2B	3B	HR	RBI	BB	SO	AVG	OBP	SLG	PRO+	BR	/A	RC	SB	CS	SBR	FA	FR	POS	TPR
1896	Bal-N	15	58	8	14	3	0	0	5	3	5	.241	.302	.293	58	-3	-4	6	4			.923	-5	/23	-0.7
1898	Bos-N	10	30	5	5	2	0	0	4	0		.167	.167	.233	14	-3	-4	1	0			1.000	1	/S2O	-0.3
1899	Bal-N	136	523	96	172	22	16	3	73	16		.329	.368	.449	117	15	11	102	33			.895	-30	S2/O	-0.9
1900	StL-N	126	497	78	149	26	10	1	72	25		.300	.347	.398	106	3	3	82	32			.927	-24	*2/S3	-1.4
1901	Bal-A	115	442	78	145	20	**21**	2	93	18		.328	.365	.482	128	18	15	89	24			.851	-23	*S	0.1
1902	Was-A	119	483	82	145	33	9	9	90	14		.300	.329	.462	117	9	8	85	27			.912	-4	O23/S	0.2
1903	Phi-N	100	400	53	128	27	7	3	63	14		.320	.351	.445	131	12	14	69	11			.940	3	*O	1.0
Total	7	621	2433	400	758	133	63	18	400	90	5	.312	.349	.440	116	50	44	435	131			.870	-81	S2O/3	-2.0

■ MICKEY KELIHER Keliher, Maurice Michael b: 1/11/1890, Washington, D.C. d: 9/7/30, Washington, D.C. BL/TL, 6', 175 lbs. Deb: 9/09/11

YEAR	TM/L	G	AB	R	H	2B	3B	HR	RBI	BB	SO	AVG	OBP	SLG	PRO+	BR	/A	RC	SB	CS	SBR	FA	FR	POS	TPR
1911	Pit-N	3	7	0	0	0	0	0	0	0	5	.000	.000	.000	-96	-2	-2	0	0			.875	-0	/1	-0.2
1912	Pit-N	2	0	1	0	0	0	0	0	0	0	—	—	—	—	0	0	0	0			.000	0	R	0.0
Total	2	5	7	1	0	0	0	0	0	0	5	.000	.000	.000	-96	-2	-2	0	0			.941	-0	/1	-0.2

■ SKEETER KELL Kell, Everett Lee b: 10/11/29, Swifton, Ark. BR/TR, 5'9", 160 lbs. Deb: 4/19/52 F

YEAR	TM/L	G	AB	R	H	2B	3B	HR	RBI	BB	SO	AVG	OBP	SLG	PRO+	BR	/A	RC	SB	CS	SBR	FA	FR	POS	TPR
1952	Phi-A	75	213	24	47	8	3	0	17	14	18	.221	.275	.286	53	-13	-14	18	5	1	1	.963	-5	2	-1.6

■ GEORGE KELL Kell, George Clyde b: 8/23/22, Swifton, Ark. BR/TR, 5'9", 175 lbs. Deb: 9/28/43 FH

YEAR	TM/L	G	AB	R	H	2B	3B	HR	RBI	BB	SO	AVG	OBP	SLG	PRO+	BR	/A	RC	SB	CS	SBR	FA	FR	POS	TPR
1943	Phi-A	1	5	1	1	0	1	0	1	0	0	.200	.200	.600	131	0	0	1	0	0	0	1.000	0	/3	0.0
1944	Phi-A	139	514	51	138	15	3	0	44	22	23	.268	.300	.309	75	-18	-17	43	5	2	0	.958	-5	*3	-2.1
1945	Phi-A	147	567	50	154	30	3	4	56	27	15	.272	.306	.356	92	-8	-8	61	2	0	1	**.964**	22	*3	2.0
1946	Phi-A	26	87	3	26	6	1	0	11	10	6	.299	.378	.391	116	2	2	14	0	0	0	.979	3	3	0.6
	Det-A	105	434	67	142	19	9	4	41	30	14	.327	.371	.440	119	14	11	71	3	2	-0	.984	5	*3/1	1.8
	Yr	131	521	70	168	25	10	4	52	40	20	.322	.372	.432	118	16	13	85	3	2	-0	**.983**	8	*3/1	2.4
1947	Det-A★	152	588	75	188	29	5	5	93	61	16	.320	.387	.412	118	18	16	95	9	11	-4	.962	18	*3	3.1
1948	Det-A☆	92	368	47	112	24	3	2	44	33	15	.304	.369	.402	102	3	1	56	2	2	-1	.969	-8	3	-0.8
1949	Det-A★	134	522	97	179	38	9	3	59	71	13	**.343**	.424	.467	136	28	28	106	7	5	-1	.975	1	*3	2.5
1950	Det-A★	157	641	114	**218**	**56**	6	8	101	66	18	.340	.403	.484	122	25	22	123	3	3	-1	**.982**	-3	*3	1.5
1951	Det-A★	147	598	92	**191**	**36**	3	2	59	61	18	.319	.386	.400	112	12	12	97	10	3	1	**.960**	9	*3	2.0
1952	Det-A	39	152	11	45	8	0	1	17	15	13	.296	.359	.368	102	1	1	21	0	1	-1	.959	-2	3	-0.3
	Bos-A	75	276	41	88	15	2	6	40	31	10	.319	.390	.453	124	13	10	48	0	1	-1	.959	-7	3	0.2
	Yr	114	428	52	133	23	2	7	57	46	23	.311	.379	.423	117	13	11	69	0	2	-1	.959	-9	*3	-0.1
1953	Bos-A★	134	460	68	141	41	2	12	73	52	22	.307	.383	.483	126	21	18	88	5	2	0	**.972**	-14	*3/O	0.1
1954	Bos-A	26	93	15	24	3	0	0	10	15	3	.258	.361	.290	72	-2	-3	11	0	0	0	.920	-3	3	-0.7
	Chi-A	71	233	25	66	10	0	5	48	18	12	.283	.335	.391	95	-1	-2	30	1	1	-0	.996	-11	13/O	-1.7
	Yr	97	326	40	90	13	0	5	58	33	15	.276	.343	.362	88	-3	-5	41	1	1	-0	.936	-14	31/O	-2.4
1955	Chi-A	128	429	44	134	24	1	8	81	51	36	.312	.393	.429	118	14	12	75	2	2	-1	**.976**	-19	*31/O	-0.8
1956	Chi-A	21	80	7	25	5	0	1	11	8	6	.313	.375	.412	106	1	1	12	0	0	0	1.000	-4	3/1	-0.3
	Bal-A	102	345	45	90	17	2	8	37	25	31	.261	.316	.391	93	-8	-4	42	0	1	-1	.974	-7	3/12	-1.0
	Yr	123	425	52	115	22	2	9	48	33	37	.271	.328	.395	96	-7	-4	54	0	1	-1	**.978**	-11	*3/12	-1.3
1957	Bal-A★	99	310	28	92	9	0	9	44	25	16	.297	.353	.413	116	4	6	44	2	0	1	.979	-4	31	0.3
Total	15	1795	6702	881	2054	385	50	78	870	621	287	.306	.368	.414	111	118	106	1038	51	36	-6	.969	-29	*3/1O2	6.4

■ DUKE KELLEHER Kelleher, Albert Aloysius b: 9/30/1893, New York, N.Y. d: 9/28/47, Staten Island, N.Y. TR , Deb: 8/18/16

YEAR	TM/L	G	AB	R	H	2B	3B	HR	RBI	BB	SO	AVG	OBP	SLG	PRO+	BR	/A	RC	SB	CS	SBR	FA	FR	POS	TPR
1916	NY-N	1	0	0	0	0	0	0	0	0	0	—	—	—	—	0	0	0	0			.000	0	/C	0.0

■ FRANKIE KELLEHER
Kelleher, Francis Eugene b: 8/22/16, San Francisco, Cal d: 4/13/79, Stockton, Cal. BR/TR, 6'1", 195 lbs. Deb: 7/18/42

YEAR	TM/L	G	AB	R	H	2B	3B	HR	RBI	BB	SO	AVG	OBP	SLG	PRO+	BR	/A	RC	SB	CS	SBR	FA	FR	POS	TPR
1942	Cin-N	38	110	13	20	3	1	3	12	16	20	.182	.286	.309	74	-4	-4	10	0			.986	0	O	-0.5
1943	Cin-N	9	10	1	0	0	0	0	0	2	0	.000	.167	.000	-51	-2	-2	0	0			1.000	-0	/O	-0.2
Total	2	47	120	14	20	3	1	3	12	18	20	.167	.275	.283	64	-6	-5	10	0			.986	0	/O	-0.7

■ JOHN KELLEHER
Kelleher, John Patrick b: 9/13/1893, Brookline, Mass. d: 8/21/60, Brighton, Mass. BR/TR, 5'11", 150 lbs. Deb: 7/31/12

YEAR	TM/L	G	AB	R	H	2B	3B	HR	RBI	BB	SO	AVG	OBP	SLG	PRO+	BR	/A	RC	SB	CS	SBR	FA	FR	POS	TPR
1912	StL-N	8	12	0	4	1	0	0	1	0	2	.333	.333	.417	107	0	0	2	0			1.000	1	/3	0.1
1916	Bro-N	2	3	0	0	0	0	0	0	0	0	.000	.000	.000	-97	-1	-1	0	0			1.000	-1	/S3	-0.2
1921	Chi-N	95	301	31	93	11	7	4	47	16	16	.309	.346	.432	104	2	2	44	2	5	-2	.947	3	321S/O	0.6
1922	Chi-N	63	193	23	50	7	1	0	20	15	14	.259	.316	.306	60	-11	-11	18	5	7	-3	.932	4	3/S1	-0.7
1923	Chi-N	66	193	27	59	10	0	6	21	14	9	.306	.353	.451	110	3	2	29	2	4	-2	.975	-7	1S3/2	-0.5
1924	Bos-N	1	1	0	0	0	0	0	0	0	1	.000	.000	.000	-99	-0	-0	0	0	0	0	.000	0	H	0.0
Total	6	235	703	81	206	29	8	10	89	45	42	.293	.337	.400	92	-8	-8	93	9	16		.924	-0	/312SO	-0.7

■ MICK KELLEHER
Kelleher, Michael Dennis b: 7/25/47, Seattle, Wash. BR/TR, 5'9", 176 lbs. Deb: 9/01/72 C

YEAR	TM/L	G	AB	R	H	2B	3B	HR	RBI	BB	SO	AVG	OBP	SLG	PRO+	BR	/A	RC	SB	CS	SBR	FA	FR	POS	TPR
1972	StL-N	23	63	5	10	2	1	0	1	6	15	.159	.232	.222	30	-6	-6	4	0	0	0	.984	5	S	0.3
1973	StL-N	43	38	4	7	2	0	0	2	4	11	.184	.279	.237	44	-3	-3	3	0	0	0	.955	9	S	0.8
1974	Hou-N	19	57	4	9	0	0	0	2	5	10	.158	.226	.158	9	-7	-7	2	1	1	-0	.944	4	S	-0.1
1975	StL-N	7	4	0	0	0	0	0	0	0	1	.000	.000	.000	-97	-1	-1	0	0	0	0	.909	2	/S	0.1
1976	Chi-N	124	337	28	77	12	1	0	22	15	32	.228	.266	.270	48	-21	-25	22	0	4	-2	.980	12	*S3/2	-0.5
1977	Chi-N	63	122	14	28	5	2	0	11	9	12	.230	.288	.303	53	-7	-9	10	0	0	0	.976	18	2S/3	1.2
1978	Chi-N	68	95	8	24	1	0	0	6	7	11	.253	.304	.263	53	-5	-6	7	4	1	1	1.000	18	32S	1.3
1979	Chi-N	73	142	14	36	4	1	0	10	7	9	.254	.298	.296	57	-7	-9	13	2	0	1	.966	22	32S	1.5
1980	Chi-N	105	96	12	14	1	1	0	4	9	17	.146	.219	.177	11	-11	-12	3	1	3	-2	.974	25	23S	1.4
1981	Det-A	61	77	10	17	4	0	0	6	7	10	.221	.286	.273	59	-4	-4	6	0	0	0	.930	6	32/S	0.3
1982	Det-A	2	1	0	0	0	0	0	0	0	0	.000	.000	.000	-99	-0	-0	0	0	0	0	1.000	-0	/23	-0.1
	Cal-A	34	49	9	8	1	0	0	1	5	5	.163	.255	.184	23	-5	-5	2	1	1	-0	.965	7	S/3	0.3
	Yr	36	50	9	8	1	0	0	1	5	5	.160	.250	.180	20	-5	-5	2	1	1	-0	.965	7	S/32	0.2
Total	11	622	1081	108	230	32	6	0	65	74	133	.213	.268	.253	43	-77	-86	72	9	10	-3	.976	128	S32	6.5

■ CHARLIE KELLER
Keller, Charles Ernest "King Kong" b: 9/12/16, Middletown, Md. d: 5/23/90, Frederick, Md. BL/TR, 5'10", 190 lbs. Deb: 4/22/39 F

YEAR	TM/L	G	AB	R	H	2B	3B	HR	RBI	BB	SO	AVG	OBP	SLG	PRO+	BR	/A	RC	SB	CS	SBR	FA	FR	POS	TPR
1939	*NY-A	111	398	87	133	21	6	11	83	81	49	.334	.447	.500	144	29	30	97	6	3	0	.969	-3	*O	2.1
1940	NY-A★	138	500	102	143	18	15	21	93	**106**	65	.286	.411	.508	142	30	33	114	8	2	1	.967	2	*O	2.7
1941	*NY-A★	140	507	102	151	24	10	33	122	102	65	.298	.416	.580	163	46	47	134	6	4	-1	.980	4	*O	4.0
1942	*NY-A	152	544	106	159	24	9	26	108	114	61	.292	.417	.513	164	47	48	131	14	2	3	.985	-0	*O	4.3
1943	*NY-A†	141	512	97	139	15	11	31	86	**106**	60	.271	.396	.525	**167**	**46**	**45**	**116**	7	5	-1	.994	4	*O	4.3
1945	NY-A	44	163	26	49	7	4	10	34	31	21	.301	.412	.577	178	18	17	41	0	2	-1	1.000	4	O	1.8
1946	NY-A★	150	538	98	148	29	10	30	101	113	101	.275	.405	.533	158	46	45	127	1	4	-2	.979	-1	*O	3.6
1947	NY-A†	45	151	36	36	6	1	13	36	41	18	.238	.404	.550	165	14	14	37	0	0	0	.967	-2	O	1.0
1948	NY-A	83	247	41	66	15	2	6	44	41	25	.267	.372	.417	111	4	4	40	1	1	-0	.977	-5	O	-0.5
1949	NY-A	60	116	17	29	4	1	3	16	25	15	.250	.392	.379	104	2	2	20	2	0	1	.976	-6	O	-0.5
1950	Det-A	50	51	7	16	1	3	2	16	13	6	.314	.453	.569	155	5	5	15	0	0	0	1.000	-1	/O	0.4
1951	Det-A	54	62	6	16	2	0	3	21	11	12	.258	.370	.435	117	2	2	11	0	0	0	1.000	1	/O	0.2
1952	NY-A	2	1	0	0	0	0	0	0	0	1	.000	.000	.000	-99	-0	-0	0	0	0	0	.000	-0	/O	-0.1
Total	13	1170	3790	725	1085	166	72	189	760	784	499	.286	.410	.518	152	287	291	883	45	23	-0	.980	-4	*O	23.3

■ HAL KELLER
Keller, Harold Kefauver b: 7/7/27, Middletown, Md. BL/TR, 6'1", 200 lbs. Deb: 9/13/49 F

YEAR	TM/L	G	AB	R	H	2B	3B	HR	RBI	BB	SO	AVG	OBP	SLG	PRO+	BR	/A	RC	SB	CS	SBR	FA	FR	POS	TPR
1949	Was-A	3	3	1	1	0	0	0	0	0	0	.333	.333	.333	78	-0	-0	0	0	0	0	.000	0	H	0.0
1950	Was-A	11	28	1	6	3	0	1	5	2	2	.214	.267	.429	79	-1	-1	3	0	0	0	1.000	-2	/C	-0.2
1952	Was-A	11	23	2	4	2	0	0	0	1	1	.174	.208	.261	31	-2	-2	1	0	0	0	.967	-0	/C	-0.2
Total	3	25	54	4	11	5	0	1	5	3	3	.204	.246	.352	60	-4	-3	5	0	0	0	.982	-2	/C	-0.4

■ FRANK KELLERT
Kellert, Frank William b: 7/6/24, Oklahoma City, Okla. d: 11/19/76, Oklahoma City, Okla. BR/TR, 6'2.5", 185 lbs. Deb: 4/18/53

YEAR	TM/L	G	AB	R	H	2B	3B	HR	RBI	BB	SO	AVG	OBP	SLG	PRO+	BR	/A	RC	SB	CS	SBR	FA	FR	POS	TPR
1953	StL-A	2	4	0	0	0	0	0	0	0	0	.000	.000	.000	-98	-1	-1	0	0	0	0	1.000	-0	/1	-0.1
1954	Bal-A	10	34	3	7	2	0	0	1	5	4	.206	.308	.265	62	-2	-2	3	0	0	0	1.000	-1	/1	-0.3
1955	*Bro-N	39	80	12	26	4	2	4	19	9	10	.325	.393	.575	149	6	6	18	0	1	-1	.983	-0	1	0.4
1956	Chi-N	71	129	10	24	3	1	4	17	12	22	.186	.255	.318	54	-9	-8	9	0	0	0	.991	3	1	-0.8
Total	4	122	247	25	57	9	3	8	37	26	36	.231	.304	.389	85	-6	-5	30	0	1	-1	.990	1	/1	-0.8

■ RED KELLETT
Kellett, Donald Stafford b: 7/15/09, Brooklyn, N.Y. d: 11/3/70, Ft.Lauderdale, Fla. BR/TR, 6', 185 lbs. Deb: 7/02/34

YEAR	TM/L	G	AB	R	H	2B	3B	HR	RBI	BB	SO	AVG	OBP	SLG	PRO+	BR	/A	RC	SB	CS	SBR	FA	FR	POS	TPR
1934	Bos-A	9	9	0	0	0	0	0	0	1	5	.000	.100	.000	-68	-2	-2	0	0	0	0	.778	1	/S23	-0.1

■ JOE KELLEY
Kelley, Joseph James b: 12/9/1871, Cambridge, Mass. d: 8/14/43, Baltimore, Md. BR/TR, 5'11", 190 lbs. Deb: 7/27/1891 MCH

YEAR	TM/L	G	AB	R	H	2B	3B	HR	RBI	BB	SO	AVG	OBP	SLG	PRO+	BR	/A	RC	SB	CS	SBR	FA	FR	POS	TPR
1891	Bos-N	12	45	7	11	1	1	0	3	2	7	.244	.277	.311	65	-2	-2	4	0			.852	-1	O	-0.3
1892	Pit-N	56	205	26	49	7	7	0	28	17	21	.239	.297	.341	94	-2	-2	24	8			.919	2	O	-0.2
	Bal-N	10	33	3	7	0	0	0	4	4	7	.212	.316	.212	60	-1	-1	3	2			.824	-3	O	-0.4
	Yr	66	238	29	56	7	7	0	32	21	28	.235	.300	.324	90	-3	-3	27	10			.908	-1	O	-0.6
1893	Bal-N	125	502	120	153	27	16	9	76	77	44	.305	.401	.476	133	26	24	112	33			.940	7	*O	2.0
1894	*Bal-N	129	507	165	199	48	20	6	111	107	36	.393	.502	.602	160	62	57	182	46			.951	2	*O	3.8
1895	*Bal-N	131	518	148	189	26	19	10	134	77	29	.365	.456	.546	156	49	46	159	54			.964	11	*O	3.8
1896	*Bal-N	131	519	148	189	31	19	8	100	91	19	.364	.469	.543	167	56	55	**178**	**87**			.958	4	*O	4.0
1897	*Bal-N	131	505	113	183	31	9	5	118	70		.362	.447	.489	147	37	37	134	44			.959	-2	*O/S3	2.2
1898	Bal-N	124	464	71	149	18	15	2	110	56		.321	.398	.438	137	24	23	93	24			.969	1	*O/3	1.4
1899	Bro-N	143	538	108	175	21	14	6	93	70		.325	.410	.450	133	28	26	116	31			.977	8	*O	2.1
1900	*Bro-N	121	454	90	145	23	17	6	91	53		.319	.399	.485	135	27	23	101	26			.959	0	O13	1.6
1901	Bro-N	120	492	77	151	22	12	4	65	40		.307	.361	.425	124	17	15	85	18			.975	6	*1/3	2.0
1902	Bal-A	60	222	50	69	17	7	1	34	34		.311	.402	.464	134	13	11	48	12			.973	-0	O/31	0.7
	Cin-N	40	156	24	50	9	2	1	12	15		.321	.380	.423	135	9	7	27	3			.971	3	O2/3SM	1.0
1903	Cin-N	105	383	85	121	22	4	3	45	51		.316	.402	.418	121	19	12	74	18			.947	-7	OS2/31M	0.3
1904	Cin-N	123	449	75	126	21	13	0	63	49		.281	.355	.385	119	16	11	70	15			.988	0	*1/O2M	0.9
1905	Cin-N	90	321	43	89	7	6	1	37	27		.277	.339	.346	94	2	-2	43	8			.974	-3	O/1M	-1.0
1906	Cin-N	129	465	43	106	19	11	1	53	44		.228	.300	.323	91	-3	-6	52	9			.966	-5	*O/1S3	-1.9
1908	Bos-N	73	228	25	59	8	2	2	17	27		.259	.342	.338	119	5	6	28	5			.938	-4	O1M	-0.1
Total	17	1853	7006	1421	2220	358	194	65	1194	911	163	.317	.401	.451	133	382	340	1533	443			.955	20	*O1/32S	21.9

■ MIKE KELLEY
Kelley, Michael Joseph b: 12/2/1875, Templeton, Mass. d: 6/6/55, Minneapolis, Minn. BR/TR, 6', 210 lbs. Deb: 7/15/1899

YEAR	TM/L	G	AB	R	H	2B	3B	HR	RBI	BB	SO	AVG	OBP	SLG	PRO+	BR	/A	RC	SB	CS	SBR	FA	FR	POS	TPR
1899	Lou-N	76	282	48	68	11	2	3	33	21		.241	.305	.326	73	-11	-11	33	10			.974	-0	1	-1.0

■ FRANK KELLIHER
Kelliher, Francis Mortimer "Yucka" b: 5/23/1899, Somerville, Mass. d: 3/4/56, Somerville, Mass. BL/TL, 5'9.5", 175 lbs. Deb: 9/19/19

YEAR	TM/L	G	AB	R	H	2B	3B	HR	RBI	BB	SO	AVG	OBP	SLG	PRO+	BR	/A	RC	SB	CS	SBR	FA	FR	POS	TPR
1919	Was-A	1	1	0	0	0	0	0	0	0	0	.000	.000	.000	-99	-0	-0	0	0			.000	0	H	0.0

■ NATE KELLOGG
Kellogg, Nathaniel Monroe b: 9/28/1858, Rochester, Iowa d: 15, 5'9", 175 lbs. Deb: 8/27/1885

YEAR	TM/L	G	AB	R	H	2B	3B	HR	RBI	BB	SO	AVG	OBP	SLG	PRO+	BR	/A	RC	SB	CS	SBR	FA	FR	POS	TPR
1885	Det-N	5	17	4	2	1	0	0	0	1	5	.118	.167	.176	11	-2	-2	1				.783	-2	/S	-0.3

YEAR	TM/L	G	AB	R	H	2B	3B	HR	RBI	BB	SO	AVG	OBP	SLG	PRO+	BR	/A	RC	SB	CS	SBR	FA	FR	POS	TPR

■ BILL KELLOGG   Kellogg, William Dearstyne   b: 5/25/1884, Albany, N.Y.   d: 12/12/71, Baltimore, Md.   BR/TR, 5'10", 153 lbs.   Deb: 4/14/14

| 1914 | Cin-N | 71 | 126 | 14 | 22 | 0 | 1 | 0 | 7 | 14 | 28 | .175 | .262 | .190 | 34 | -10 | -10 | 8 | | 7 | | .988 | -1 | 12/O3 | -1.2 |

■ RED KELLY   Kelly, Albert Michael   b: 11/15/1884, Union, Ill.   d: 2/4/61, Zephyr Hills, Fla.   BR/TR, 5'11.5", 165 lbs.   Deb: 6/18/10

| 1910 | Chi-A | 14 | 45 | 6 | 7 | 0 | 1 | 0 | 1 | 7 | | .156 | .296 | .200 | 58 | -2 | -2 | 3 | | 0 | | 1.000 | -1 | O | -0.3 |

■ CHARLIE KELLY   Kelly, Charles H.   Deb: 6/14/1883

1883	Phi-N	2	7	1	1	0	1	0	0	0	3	.143	.143	.429	71	-0	-0	0				.700	0	/3	0.0
1886	Phi-a	1	3	0	0	0	0	0	0			.000	.000	.000	-99	-1	-1	0		0		.333	-1	/S	-0.2
Total	2	3	10	1	1	0	1	0	0	0	3	.100	.100	.300	19	-1	-1	0		0		.857	-1	/3S	-0.2

■ PAT KELLY   Kelly, Dale Patrick   b: 8/27/55, Santa Maria, Cal.   BR/TR, 6'3", 210 lbs.   Deb: 5/28/80

| 1980 | Tor-A | 3 | 7 | 0 | 2 | 0 | 0 | 0 | 0 | 0 | 4 | .286 | .286 | .286 | 55 | -0 | -0 | 1 | 0 | 0 | 0 | 1.000 | 1 | /C | 0.1 |

■ GEORGE KELLY   Kelly, George Lange "Highpockets"   b: 9/10/1895, San Francisco, Cal.   d: 10/13/84, Burlingame, Cal.   BR/TR, 6'4", 190 lbs.   Deb: 8/18/15   FCH

1915	NY-N	17	38	2	6	0	0	1	4	1	9	.158	.179	.237	27	-3	-3	1	0	1	-1	.983	-0	/1O	-0.5
1916	NY-N	49	76	4	12	2	1	0	3	6	24	.158	.220	.211	34	-6	-6	4	1			.981	-3	1O/3	-1.1
1917	NY-N	11	7	0	0	0	0	0	0	0	3	.000	.000	.000	-99	-2	-2	0	0			1.000	-1	/1	-0.2
	Pit-N	8	23	2	2	0	1	0	0	1	9	.087	.125	.174	-9	-3	-3	0	0			.971	-1	/1OP12	-0.5
	Yr	19	30	2	2	0	1	0	0	1	12	.067	.097	.133	-30	-5	-5	0	0			.972	-1	/1OP2	-0.7
1919	NY-N	32	107	12	31	6	2	1	14	3	15	.290	.315	.411	119	2	2	14	1			.994	-3	1	-0.2
1920	NY-N	155	590	69	157	22	11	11	**94**	41	92	.266	.320	.397	106	3	4	71	6	16	-8	.994	4	*1	-0.4
1921	*NY-N	149	587	95	181	42	9	**23**	122	40	73	.308	.356	.528	131	23	23	104	4	12	-6	.990	12	*1	2.5
1922	*NY-N	151	592	96	194	33	8	17	107	30	65	.328	.363	.497	119	15	14	106	12	3	2	.993	-6	*1	1.8
1923	*NY-N	145	560	82	172	23	5	16	103	47	64	.307	.362	.452	115	10	11	92	14	7	0	.993	-6	*1	-0.3
1924	*NY-N	144	571	91	185	37	9	21	**136**	38	52	.324	.371	.531	143	29	31	112	7	2	1	.993	-1	*1O/23	2.3
1925	NY-N	147	586	87	181	29	3	20	99	35	54	.309	.350	.471	112	5	8	96	5	2	0	.981	18	*21O	2.4
1926	NY-N	136	499	70	151	24	4	13	80	36	52	.303	.352	.445	115	8	9	76	4			**.993**	8	*12	1.0
1927	Cin-N	61	222	27	60	16	4	5	21	11	23	.270	.308	.446	103	-1	-0	29	1			.992	-3	12/O	-0.6
1928	Cin-N	116	402	46	119	33	7	3	58	28	35	.296	.345	.435	104	1	2	59	2			.991	9	1O	0.2
1929	Cin-N	147	577	73	169	45	9	5	103	33	61	.293	.332	.428	91	-13	-9	79	7			.993	-9	*1	-1.8
1930	Cin-N	51	188	18	54	10	1	5	35	7	20	.287	.313	.431	81	-7	-6	24	1			.993	2	1	-0.8
	Chi-N	39	166	22	55	6	1	3	19	7	16	.331	.362	.434	91	-2	-2	25	0			.998	4	1	-0.2
	Yr	90	354	40	109	16	2	8	54	14	36	.308	.336	.432	86	-10	-8	49	1			.995	5	1	-1.0
1932	Bro-N	64	202	23	49	9	1	4	22	22	27	.243	.317	.356	82	-5	-5	24	0			.984	-2	1/O	-1.1
Total	16	1622	5993	819	1778	337	76	148	1020	386	694	.297	.342	.452	110	53	68	918	65	<u>43</u>		.992	51	*12/O3P	2.5

■ PAT KELLY   Kelly, Harold Patrick   b: 7/30/44, Philadelphia, Pa.   BL/TL, 6'1", 185 lbs.   Deb: 9/06/67

1967	Min-A	8	1	1	0	0	0	0	0	0	1	.000	.000	.000	-93	-0	-0	0	0	0	0	.000	0	H	0.0
1968	Min-A	12	35	2	4	2	0	1	2	3	10	.114	.205	.257	37	-3	-3	1	0	2	-1	.955	0	O	-0.5
1969	KC-A	112	417	61	110	20	4	8	32	49	70	.264	.348	.388	105	4	3	61	40	13	4	.980	12	*O	1.4
1970	KC-A	136	452	56	106	16	1	6	38	76	105	.235	.347	.314	84	-8	-8	55	34	16	1	.963	11	*O	-0.2
1971	Chi-A	67	213	32	62	6	3	3	22	36	29	.291	.396	.390	119	8	7	34	14	9	-1	.991	1	O	0.5
1972	Chi-A	119	402	57	105	14	7	5	24	55	69	.261	.356	.368	113	9	8	59	32	9	4	.968	-2	*O	0.6
1973	Chi-A★	144	550	77	154	24	5	1	44	65	91	.280	.358	.347	96	2	-1	67	22	15	-2	.978	2	*O/D	-0.8
1974	Chi-A	122	424	60	119	16	3	4	21	46	58	.281	.354	.361	103	4	3	54	18	11	-1	.976	-5	DO	-0.5
1975	Chi-A	133	471	73	129	21	7	9	45	58	69	.274	.356	.406	113	10	9	67	18	10	-1	**.991**	-3	*OD	0.1
1976	Chi-A	107	311	42	79	20	3	5	34	45	45	.254	.354	.386	116	7	7	44	15	7	0	.950	-4	DO	0.3
1977	Bal-A	120	360	50	92	13	0	10	49	64	75	.256	.357	.375	106	1	5	53	25	7	3	.984	-14	*O/D	-1.0
1978	Bal-A	100	274	38	75	12	1	11	40	34	58	.274	.358	.441	133	9	11	41	10	8	-2	.969	-6	OD	0.0
1979	*Bal-A	68	153	25	44	11	0	9	25	20	25	.288	.374	.536	147	9	10	30	4	5	-2	1.000	-3	OD	0.4
1980	Bal-A	89	200	38	52	10	1	3	26	34	54	.260	.368	.365	102	2	2	31	16	2	4	1.000	-3	OD	0.2
1981	Cle-A	48	75	8	16	4	0	1	16	14	9	.213	.337	.307	88	-1	-1	7	2	4	-2	1.000	-2	D/O	-0.5
Total	15	1385	4338	620	1147	189	35	76	418	588	768	.264	.356	.377	107	54	54	604	250	118	4	.978	-15	OD	0.0

■ JIM KELLY   Kelly, James Robert (Also Played Under Real Name Of Robert John Taggert In 1918)   b: 2/1/1884, Bloomfield, N.J.   d: 4/10/61, Kingsport, Tenn.   BL/TR, 5'10.5", 180 lbs.   Deb: 4/26/14

1914	Pit-N	32	44	4	10	2	1	0	3	2	3	.227	.261	.318	75	-2	-1	4	0			1.000	0	/O	-0.2
1915	Pit-F	148	524	68	154	12	17	4	50	35	46	.294	.340	.405	120	11	11	89	38			.952	14	*O	1.9
1918	Bos-N	35	146	19	48	1	4	0	4	9	9	.329	.376	.390	140	6	7	22	4			.955	1	O	0.6
Total	3	215	714	91	212	15	22	4	57	46	58	.297	.343	.396	121	15	16	115	42			.954	15	O	2.3

■ TOM KELLY   Kelly, Jay Thomas   b: 8/15/50, Graceville, Minn.   BL/TL, 5'11", 188 lbs.   Deb: 5/11/75   M

| 1975 | Min-A | 49 | 127 | 11 | 23 | 5 | 1 | 1 | 11 | 15 | 22 | .181 | .268 | .244 | 44 | -9 | -9 | 9 | 0 | 0 | 0 | .985 | 1 | 1/O | -1.1 |

■ JOHN KELLY   Kelly, John B.   b: 3/13/1879, Clifton Heights, Pa.   d: 3/19/44, Baltimore, Md.   5'9", 165 lbs.   Deb: 4/11/07

| 1907 | StL-N | 53 | 197 | 12 | 37 | 5 | 0 | 0 | 6 | 13 | | .188 | .245 | .213 | 45 | -13 | -12 | 13 | 7 | | | .968 | -1 | O | -1.7 |

■ JOHN KELLY   Kelly, John Francis "Honest John" or "Father"   b: 3/3/1859, Paterson, N.J.   d: 4/13/08, Paterson, N.J.   BR/TR, 6', 185 lbs.   Deb: 5/01/1882

1882	Cle-N	30	104	6	14	2	0	0	5	0	24	.135	.143	.154	-5	-12	-11	2				.800	-14	C	-2.3
1883	Bal-a	48	202	18	46	9	2	0		3		.228	.239	.292	68	-7	-8	14				.803	-17	CO	-2.0
	Phi-N	1	3	0	0	0	0	0	0	0	2	.000	.000	.000	-99	-1	-1	0				1.000	1	/O	0.0
1884	Cin-U	38	142	23	40	5	1	1		6		.282	.311	.352	115	3	2	16				.865	-1	C/O	0.3
	Was-U	4	14	1	5	1	0	0		0		.357	.357	.429	170	1	1	2				.967	1	/CO	0.1
	Yr	42	156	24	45	6	1	1		6		.288	.315	.359	119	4	3	18				.874	-1	C/O	0.4
Total	3	121	465	48	105	17	3	1	5	10	26	.226	.242	.282	69	-15	-17	35				.857	-31	C/O	-3.9

■ KICK KELLY   Kelly, John O. "Diamond John"   b: 10/31/1856, New York, N.Y.   d: 3/27/26, Malba, N.Y.   6'0.5", 185 lbs.   Deb: 5/01/1879   MU

1879	Syr-N	10	36	4	4	1	0	0	2	0	6	.111	.111	.139	-20	-4	-4	1				.827	-1	/C1	-0.5
	Tro-N	6	22	1	5	0	0	0	0	0	1	.227	.227	.227	54	-1	-1	1				.789	-3	/CO3	-0.3
	Yr	16	58	5	9	1	0	0	2	0	7	.155	.155	.172	9	-6	-5	2				.817	-4	C/1O3	-0.8

■ JOE KELLY   Kelly, Joseph Henry   b: 9/23/1886, Weir City, Kan.   d: 8/16/77, St.Joseph, Mo.   BR/TR, 5'10", 175 lbs.   Deb: 4/14/14

1914	Pit-N	141	508	47	113	19	9	1	48	39	59	.222	.283	.301	77	-17	-14	48	21			.946	4	*O	-1.9
1916	Chi-N	54	169	18	43	7	1	2	15	9	16	.254	.296	.343	87	-1	-3	20	10			.953	-1	O	-0.7
1917	Bos-N	116	445	41	99	9	8	3	36	26	45	.222	.268	.299	78	-14	-12	40	21			.946	14	*O	-0.5
1918	Bos-N	47	155	20	36	2	4	0	15	6	12	.232	.265	.297	74	-6	-5	14	12			.933	-0	O	-0.8
1919	Bos-N	18	64	3	9	1	0	0	3	0	11	.141	.154	.156	-7	-8	-8	2	2			.943	0	O	-1.0
Total	5	376	1341	129	300	38	22	6	117	80	143	.224	.272	.298	75	-46	-42	123	66			.945	16	O	-4.9

■ JOE KELLY   Kelly, Joseph James   b: 4/23/1900, New York, N.Y.   d: 11/24/67, Lynbrook, N.Y.   BL/TL, 6', 180 lbs.   Deb: 4/13/26

1926	Chi-N	65	176	16	59	15	3	0	32	7	11	.335	.361	.455	117	4	4	27	0			.953	-5	O	-0.3
1928	Chi-N	32	52	3	11	1	0	1	7	1	3	.212	.255	.288	42	-5	-4	4	0			.974	0	1	-0.5
Total	2	97	228	19	70	16	3	1	39	8	14	.307	.336	.417	100	-1	-1	31	0			.993	-4	/O1	-0.8

■ **KING KELLY** Kelly, Michael Joseph b: 12/31/1857, Troy, N.Y. d: 11/8/1894, Boston, Mass. BR/TR, 5'10", 170 lbs. Deb: 5/01/1878 MH

YEAR	TM/L	G	AB	R	H	2B	3B	HR	RBI	BB	SO	AVG	OBP	SLG	PRO+	BR	/A	RC	SB	CS	SBR	FA	FR	POS	TPR
1878	Cin-N	60	237	29	67	7	1	0	27	7	7	.283	.303	.321	116	1	4	24				.765	11	*OC/3	1.3
1879	Cin-N	77	345	78	120	20	12	2	47	8	14	.348	.363	.493	**188**	28	31	63				.832	12	3OC/2	**3.8**
1880	Chi-N	84	344	72	100	17	9	1	60	12	22	.291	.315	.401	133	14	11	45				.779	-3	*OC3/S2P	0.8
1881	Chi-N	82	353	84	114	**27**	3	2	55	16	14	.323	.352	.433	139	18	16	55				.841	-0	*OC/3	1.3
1882	Chi-N	84	377	81	115	**37**	4	1	55	10	27	.305	.323	.432	134	16	13	54				.810	-1	SOC/31	1.3
1883	Chi-N	98	428	92	109	28	10	3	61	16	35	.255	.282	.388	95	0	-4	48				.813	3	*OC/23P	0.0
1884	Chi-N	108	452	**120**	160	28	5	13	95	46	24	**.354**	**.414**	.524	178	**49**	**43**	**100**				.794	-5	OCS3/1P	3.5
1885	*Chi-N	107	438	**124**	126	24	7	9	75	46	24	.288	.355	.436	135	27	18	70				.867	4	OC/231	2.1
1886	*Chi-N	118	451	**155**	175	32	11	4	79	83	33	**.388**	**.483**	.534	182	64	53	**146**	53			.811	3	OC/132S	5.3
1887	Bos-N	116	484	120	156	34	11	8	63	55	40	.322	.393	.488	145	30	30	129	84			.856	-11	O2C/PS3M	1.8
1888	Bos-N	107	440	85	140	22	11	9	71	31	39	.318	.368	.480	168	34	33	101	56			.905	-3	CO	3.6
1889	Bos-N	125	507	120	149	**41**	5	9	78	65	40	.294	.376	.448	124	22	16	114	68			.848	-9	*OC	0.5
1890	Bos-P	89	340	83	111	18	6	4	66	52	22	.326	.419	.450	126	18	14	88	51			.915	-3	CS/O13PM	1.3
1891	Cin-a	82	283	56	84	15	7	1	53	51	28	.297	.408	.410	126	16	11	58	22			.904	14	C/3O21PS	2.5
	Bos-a	4	15	2	4	0	0	1	4	0	2	.267	.267	.467	113	0	0	2	1			.950	-1	/C	0.0
	Yr	86	298	58	88	15	7	2	57	51	30	.295	.402	.413	126	16	11	60	23			.906	13	C/3O21PS	2.5
	Bos-N	16	52	7	12	1	0	0	5	6	10	.231	.322	.250	62	-2	-3	6	6			.844	-5	C/O	-0.6
1892	*Bos-N	78	281	40	53	7	0	2	41	39	31	.189	.287	.235	55	-12	-16	27	24			.912	0	C/O31P	-1.0
1893	NY-N	20	67	9	18	1	0	0	15	6	5	.269	.329	.284	65	-3	-3	7	3			.895	-4	C/O	-0.5
Total	16	1455	5894	1357	1813	359	102	69	950	549	417	.308	.368	.438	137	321	268	1135	368			.820	1	OC/3S21P	27.0

■ **PAT KELLY** Kelly, Patrick Franklin b: 10/14/67, Philadelphia, Pa. BR/TR, 6', 180 lbs. Deb: 5/20/91

YEAR	TM/L	G	AB	R	H	2B	3B	HR	RBI	BB	SO	AVG	OBP	SLG	PRO+	BR	/A	RC	SB	CS	SBR	FA	FR	POS	TPR
1991	NY-A	96	298	35	72	12	4	3	23	15	52	.242	.289	.339	73	-11	-11	31	12	1	3	.926	7	32	-0.1
1992	NY-A	106	318	38	72	22	2	7	27	25	72	.226	.303	.374	87	-5	-6	36	8	5	-1	.978	6	*2/D	0.2
Total	2	202	616	73	144	34	6	10	50	40	124	.234	.297	.357	80	-16	-17	67	20	6	2	.978	13	2/3D	0.1

■ **SPEED KELLY** Kelly, R B b: 8/12/1884, Brian, Ohio d: 5/6/49, Goshen, Ind. BR/TR, 6'2", 185 lbs. Deb: 7/13/09

YEAR	TM/L	G	AB	R	H	2B	3B	HR	RBI	BB	SO	AVG	OBP	SLG	PRO+	BR	/A	RC	SB	CS	SBR	FA	FR	POS	TPR
1909	Was-A	17	42	3	6	2	1	0	1	3		.143	.200	.238	40	-3	-3	2	1			.852	-1	3/2O	-0.5

■ **ROBERTO KELLY** Kelly, Roberto Conrado (Gray) b: 10/1/64, Panama City, Pan. BR/TR, 6'4", 185 lbs. Deb: 7/29/87

YEAR	TM/L	G	AB	R	H	2B	3B	HR	RBI	BB	SO	AVG	OBP	SLG	PRO+	BR	/A	RC	SB	CS	SBR	FA	FR	POS	TPR
1987	NY-A	23	52	12	14	3	0	1	7	5	15	.269	.333	.385	91	-1	-1	7	9	3	1	.955	-0	O/D	0.0
1988	NY-A	38	77	9	19	4	1	1	7	3	15	.247	.275	.364	78	-3	-2	8	5	2	0	.986	-2	O/D	-0.4
1989	NY-A	137	441	65	133	18	3	9	48	41	89	.302	.369	.417	123	13	14	70	35	12	3	.984	7	*O	2.1
1990	NY-A	162	641	85	183	32	4	15	61	33	148	.285	.324	.418	106	4	3	87	42	17	2	.988	8	*O/D	1.0
1991	NY-A	126	486	68	130	22	2	20	69	45	77	.267	.336	.444	114	8	8	72	32	9	4	.986	3	*O	1.3
1992	NY-A★	152	580	81	158	31	2	10	66	41	96	.272	.325	.384	96	-2	-4	71	28	5	5	.983	10	*O	0.8
Total	6	638	2277	320	637	110	12	56	258	168	440	.280	.334	.412	107	19	18	315	151	48	17	.984	26	O/D	4.8

■ **VAN KELLY** Kelly, Van Howard b: 3/18/46, Charlotte, N.C. BL/TR, 5'11", 180 lbs. Deb: 6/13/69

YEAR	TM/L	G	AB	R	H	2B	3B	HR	RBI	BB	SO	AVG	OBP	SLG	PRO+	BR	/A	RC	SB	CS	SBR	FA	FR	POS	TPR
1969	SD-N	73	209	16	51	7	1	3	15	12	24	.244	.285	.330	75	-8	-7	19	0	1	-1	.971	-3	32	-1.1
1970	SD-N	38	89	9	15	3	0	1	9	15	21	.169	.288	.236	44	-7	-7	7	0	1	-1	.971	1	3/2	-0.7
Total	2	111	298	25	66	10	1	4	24	27	45	.221	.286	.302	65	-15	-14	26	0	2	-1	.971	-3	/32	-1.8

■ **BILL KELLY** Kelly, William Henry "Big Bill" b: 12/28/1898, Syracuse, N.Y. d: 4/8/90, Syracuse, N.Y. BR/TR, 6', 190 lbs. Deb: 9/06/20

YEAR	TM/L	G	AB	R	H	2B	3B	HR	RBI	BB	SO	AVG	OBP	SLG	PRO+	BR	/A	RC	SB	CS	SBR	FA	FR	POS	TPR
1920	Phi-A	9	13	0	3	1	0	0	0	0	2	.231	.231	.308	41	-1	-1	1	0	0	0	1.000	0	/1	-0.1
1928	Phi-N	23	71	6	12	1	1	0	5	7	20	.169	.244	.211	19	-8	-9	4	0			.991	1	1	-0.9
Total	2	32	84	6	15	2	1	0	5	7	22	.179	.242	.226	22	-9	-10	5	0	0		.992	2	/1	-1.0

■ **BILL KELLY** Kelly, William J. b: New York, N.Y. Deb: 5/04/1871

YEAR	TM/L	G	AB	R	H	2B	3B	HR	RBI	BB	SO	AVG	OBP	SLG	PRO+	BR	/A	RC	SB	CS	SBR	FA	FR	POS	TPR
1871	Kek-n	18	67	16	15	1	1	0	7	6	1	.224	.288	.269	60	-3	-3	5	0					O/1	-0.2

■ **BILLY KELLY** Kelly, William Joseph b: 5/1/1886, Baltimore, Md. d: 6/3/40, Detroit, Mich. BR/TR, 6'0.5", 183 lbs. Deb: 5/02/10

YEAR	TM/L	G	AB	R	H	2B	3B	HR	RBI	BB	SO	AVG	OBP	SLG	PRO+	BR	/A	RC	SB	CS	SBR	FA	FR	POS	TPR
1910	StL-N	2	2	1	0	0	0	0	0	1	0	.000	.333	.000	-1	-0	-0	0	0			.000	0	/C	0.0
1911	Pit-N	6	8	0	1	0	0	0	0	0	2	.125	.125	.125	-29	-1	-1	0	0			1.000	1	/C	0.0
1912	Pit-N	48	132	20	42	3	2	1	11	2	16	.318	.328	.394	99	-1	-1	20	8			.990	-9	C	-0.6
1913	Pit-N	48	82	11	22	2	2	0	9	2	12	.268	.302	.341	87	-2	-1	8	1			.960	5	C	0.5
Total	4	104	224	32	65	5	4	1	20	5	30	.290	.312	.362	89	-5	-4	28	9			.977	-4	/C	-0.1

■ **BILLY KELSEY** Kelsey, George William b: 8/24/1881, Covington, Ohio d: 4/25/68, Springfield, Ohio BR/TR, 5'10", 150 lbs. Deb: 10/04/07

YEAR	TM/L	G	AB	R	H	2B	3B	HR	RBI	BB	SO	AVG	OBP	SLG	PRO+	BR	/A	RC	SB	CS	SBR	FA	FR	POS	TPR
1907	Pit-N	2	5	1	2	0	0	0	0	0		.400	.400	.400	149	0	0	1	0			1.000	-1	/C	0.0

■ **KEN KELTNER** Keltner, Kenneth Frederick "Butch" b: 10/31/16, Milwaukee, Wis. d: 12/12/91, New Berlin, Wis. BR/TR, 6', 190 lbs. Deb: 10/02/37

YEAR	TM/L	G	AB	R	H	2B	3B	HR	RBI	BB	SO	AVG	OBP	SLG	PRO+	BR	/A	RC	SB	CS	SBR	FA	FR	POS	TPR
1937	Cle-A	1	1	0	0	0	0	0	1	0	0	.000	.000	.000	-99	-0	-0	0	0	0	0	1.000	0	/3	0.0
1938	Cle-A	149	576	86	159	31	9	26	113	33	75	.276	.319	.497	103	-4	-2	90	4	3	-1	.956	-10	*3	-0.9
1939	Cle-A	154	587	84	191	35	11	13	97	51	41	.325	.379	.489	125	17	20	105	6	6	-2	**.974**	6	*3	2.3
1940	Cle-A★	149	543	67	138	24	10	15	77	51	56	.254	.322	.418	93	-9	-7	75	10	5	0	.953	-6	*3	-0.9
1941	Cle-A★	149	581	83	156	31	13	23	84	51	56	.269	.330	.485	119	8	11	95	2	2	-1	**.971**	23	*3	3.5
1942	Cle-A★	152	624	72	179	34	4	6	78	20	36	.287	.312	.383	101	-7	-3	72	4	3	-1	**.945**	16	*3	1.5
1943	Cle-A★	110	427	47	111	31	3	4	39	36	20	.260	.317	.375	109	-0	3	50	2	2	-1	.969	6	*3	1.0
1944	Cle-A★	149	573	74	169	41	9	13	91	53	29	.295	.355	.466	139	23	25	91	4	3	-1	.968	15	*3	4.3
1946	Cle-A★	116	398	47	96	17	1	13	45	30	38	.241	.294	.387	95	-7	-4	42	0	3	-2	.965	-2	*3	-0.7
1947	Cle-A	151	541	49	139	29	3	11	76	59	45	.257	.331	.383	101	-2	-0	72	5	4	-1	.972	-9	*3	-1.0
1948	*Cle-A★	153	558	91	166	24	4	31	119	89	52	.297	.395	.522	146	33	35	116	2	1	0	.969	0	*3	3.2
1949	Cle-A	80	246	35	57	9	2	8	30	38	26	.232	.335	.382	91	-4	-4	32	0	1	-1	.980	-1	3	-0.7
1950	Bos-A	13	28	2	9	2	0	0	2	3	6	.321	.387	.393	91	0	-0	4	0	0	0	.947	-2	/31	-0.2
Total	13	1526	5683	737	1570	308	69	163	852	514	480	.276	.338	.441	113	46	74	843	39	33	-8	.965	36	*3/1	11.4

■ **JOHN KELTY** Kelty, John James "Chief" b: 1867, Jersey City, N.J. 5'10", 175 lbs. Deb: 4/19/1890

YEAR	TM/L	G	AB	R	H	2B	3B	HR	RBI	BB	SO	AVG	OBP	SLG	PRO+	BR	/A	RC	SB	CS	SBR	FA	FR	POS	TPR
1890	Pit-N	59	207	24	49	10	2	1	27	22	42	.237	.322	.319	101	-2	1	25	10			.898	-3	O	-0.3

■ **BILL KEMMER** Kemmer, William Edward (b: William Edward Kemmerer) b: 11/15/1873, Pennsylvania d: 6/8/45, Washingtonm, D.C. BR/TR, 6'2", Deb: 6/03/1895

YEAR	TM/L	G	AB	R	H	2B	3B	HR	RBI	BB	SO	AVG	OBP	SLG	PRO+	BR	/A	RC	SB	CS	SBR	FA	FR	POS	TPR
1895	Lou-N	11	38	5	7	0	0	1	3	2	4	.184	.225	.263	29	-4	-4	2	0			.809	3	/31	-0.1

■ **RUDY KEMMLER** Kemmler, Rudolph (b: Rudolph Kemler) b: 1860, Chicago, Ill. d: 6/20/09, Chicago, Ill. BR/TR, Deb: 7/26/1879

YEAR	TM/L	G	AB	R	H	2B	3B	HR	RBI	BB	SO	AVG	OBP	SLG	PRO+	BR	/A	RC	SB	CS	SBR	FA	FR	POS	TPR
1879	Pro-N	2	7	0	1	0	0	0	0	0	1	.143	.143	.143	-6	-1	-1	0				.833	2	/C	0.1
1881	Cle-N	1	3	0	0	0	0	0	0	0	1	.000	.000	.000	-99	-1	-1	0				1.000	1	/C	0.0
1882	Cin-a	3	11	0	1	1	0	0		0		.091	.091	.182	-10	-1	-1	0				.909	-1	/CO	-0.2
	Pit-a	24	99	7	25	4	0	0		1		.253	.260	.293	90	-1	-1	8				.920	2	C/O	0.2
	Yr	27	110	7	26	5	0	0		1		.236	.243	.282	79	-3	-2	8				.919	1	C/O	0.0
1883	Col-a	84	318	27	66	6	2	0		13		.208	.239	.239	59	-16	-12	19				.872	-9	*C/O	-1.4
1884	Col-a	61	211	28	42	3	3	0		15		.199	.252	.242	70	-8	-5	13				.906	-19	C/1O	-1.8
1885	Pit-a	18	64	2	13	2	1	0		2		.203	.239	.266	62	-3	-3	4				.870	-3	C	-0.3
1886	StL-a	35	123	13	17	2	0	0		8		.138	.197	.154	11	-12	-13	4	0			.914	4	C/1	-0.5
1889	Col-a	8	26	2	3	0	0	0	0	3	3	.115	.207	.115	-6	-3	-3	1	0			.930	1	/C	-0.1

YEAR	TM/L	G	AB	R	H	2B	3B	HR	RBI	BB	SO	AVG	OBP	SLG	PRO+	BR	/A	RC	SB	CS	SBR	FA	FR	POS	TPR
Total	8	236	862	79	168	18	6	0	0	42	5	.195	.234	.230	53	-46	-39	48	0			.894	-22	C/1O	-4.0
STEVE KEMP Kemp, Steven F b: 8/7/54, San Angelo, Tex. BL/TL, 6', 195 lbs. Deb: 4/07/77																									
1977	Det-A	151	552	75	142	29	4	18	88	71	93	.257	.347	.422	103	7	3	83	3	3	-1	.981	-3	*O	-0.7
1978	Det-A	159	582	75	161	18	4	15	79	97	87	.277	.381	.399	116	18	16	94	2	3	-1	.977	8	*O	1.6
1979	Det-A★	134	490	88	156	26	3	26	105	68	70	.318	.404	.543	148	37	35	106	5	6	-2	.976	6	*OD	3.2
1980	Det-A	135	508	88	149	23	3	21	101	69	64	.293	.382	.474	130	24	23	89	5	1	1	.995	6	OD	2.6
1981	Det-A	105	372	52	103	18	4	9	49	70	48	.277	.393	.419	129	19	17	64	9	3	1	.986	3	OD	1.8
1982	Chi-A	160	580	91	166	23	1	19	98	89	83	.286	.384	.428	123	21	21	99	7	7	-2	.976	-7	*O/D	0.8
1983	NY-A	109	373	53	90	17	3	12	49	41	37	.241	.320	.399	100	-2	-0	45	1	0	0	.987	1	*O/D	-0.2
1984	NY-A	94	313	37	91	12	1	7	41	40	54	.291	.373	.403	119	7	9	47	4	1	1	.972	-2	OD	0.5
1985	Pit-N	92	236	19	59	13	2	2	21	25	54	.250	.322	.347	88	-4	-4	27	1	0	0	1.000	-1	O	-0.6
1986	Pit-N	13	16	1	3	0	0	1	1	4	6	.188	.350	.375	98	0	0	2	1	0	0	1.000	0	/O	0.1
1988	Tex-A	16	36	2	8	0	0	0	2	2	9	.222	.263	.222	36	-3	-3	2	1	0	0	1.000	-2	/O1D	-0.4
Total	11	1168	4058	581	1128	179	25	130	634	576	605	.278	.370	.431	119	126	118	658	39	24	-3	.982	10	*O/D1	8.7
FRED KENDALL Kendall, Fred Lyn b: 1/31/49, Torrance, Cal. BR/TR, 6'1", 190 lbs. Deb: 9/08/69																									
1969	SD-N	10	26	2	4	0	0	0	0	2	5	.154	.214	.154	5	-3	-3	1	0	0	0	1.000	-1	/C	-0.4
1970	SD-N	4	9	0	0	0	0	0	1	0	0	.000	.000	.000	-99	-3	-2	0	0	0	0	1.000	-1	/C1O	-0.4
1971	SD-N	49	111	2	19	1	0	1	7	7	16	.171	.220	.207	23	-11	-11	5	1	0	0	1.000	1	C/13	-0.9
1972	SD-N	91	273	18	59	3	4	6	18	11	42	.216	.249	.322	66	-15	-12	21	0	0	0	.995	2	C/1	-0.7
1973	SD-N	145	507	39	143	22	3	10	59	30	35	.282	.323	.396	107	-2	3	61	3	1	0	.984	-17	*C	-0.8
1974	SD-N	141	424	32	98	15	2	8	45	49	33	.231	.311	.333	84	-11	-9	43	0	1	-1	.983	-23	*C	-2.9
1975	SD-N	103	286	16	57	12	1	0	24	26	28	.199	.266	.248	46	-22	-20	18	0	1	-1	.977	-8	C	-2.6
1976	SD-N	146	456	30	112	17	0	2	39	36	42	.246	.305	.296	77	-17	-13	39	1	1	-0	.994	-19	*C	-3.0
1977	Cle-A	103	317	18	79	13	1	3	39	16	27	.249	.287	.325	69	-15	-13	29	0	1	-1	.991	-13	*C/D	-2.5
1978	Bos-A	20	41	3	8	1	0	0	4	1	2	.195	.214	.220	20	-4	-5	2	0	0	0	1.000	3	1/CD	-0.2
1979	SD-N	46	102	8	17	2	0	1	6	11	7	.167	.248	.216	29	-10	-9	5	0	0	0	.977	5	C/1	-0.4
1980	SD-N	19	24	2	7	0	0	0	2	0	3	.292	.292	.292	67	-1	-1	2	0	0	0	.938	0	C/1	-0.1
Total	12	877	2576	170	603	86	11	31	244	189	240	.234	.288	.312	72	-114	-96	225	5	5	-2	.987	-71	C/1D3O	-14.9
AL KENDERS Kenders, Albert Daniel George b: 4/4/37, Barrington, N.J. BR/TR, 6', 185 lbs. Deb: 8/14/61																									
1961	Phi-N	10	23	0	4	1	0	0	1	1	0	.174	.208	.217	13	-3	-3	1	0	0	0	1.000	-2	C	-0.4
EDDIE KENNA Kenna, Edward Aloysius "Scrap Iron" b: 9/30/1897, San Francisco, Cal. d: 8/21/72, San Francisco, Cal BR/TR, 5'7.5", 150 lbs. Deb: 6/02/28																									
1928	Was-A	41	118	14	35	4	2	1	20	14	8	.297	.376	.390	102	1	1	16	1	5	-3	.942	-3	C	-0.2
ED KENNEDY Kennedy, Edward b: 4/1/1856, Carbondale, Pa. d: 5/20/05, New York, N.Y. Deb: 5/02/1883																									
1883	NY-a	94	356	57	78	6	7	2		17		.219	.255	.292	73	-9	-11	27				.884	-7	*O	-1.7
1884	*NY-a	103	378	49	72	6	2	1		16		.190	.225	.225	51	-20	-18	20				.915	6	*O/S2C	-1.2
1885	NY-a	96	349	35	71	8	4	2		12		.203	.238	.266	67	-15	-11	23				.841	2	*O	-1.0
1886	Bro-a	6	22	1	4	0	0	0		2		.182	.250	.182	37	-1	-2	1	1			.909	-1	/O	-0.2
Total	4	299	1105	142	225	20	13	5		47		.204	.239	.259	63	-45	-42	71	1			.878	-0	O/C2S	-4.1
JIM KENNEDY Kennedy, James Earl b: 11/1/46, Tulsa, Okla. BL/TR, 5'9", 160 lbs. Deb: 6/14/70 F																									
1970	StL-N	12	24	1	3	0	0	0	0	0	0	.125	.125	.125	-32	-4	-5	0	0	0	0	.909	1	/S2	-0.3
JOHN KENNEDY Kennedy, John Edward b: 5/29/41, Chicago, Ill. BR/TR, 6', 185 lbs. Deb: 9/05/62																									
1962	Was-A	14	42	6	11	0	1	1	2	2	7	.262	.295	.381	81	-1	-1	5	0	1	-1	.974	0	/S3	-0.1
1963	Was-A	36	62	3	11	1	1	0	4	6	22	.177	.261	.226	38	-5	-5	4	2	0	1	.954	6	3/S	0.2
1964	Was-A	148	482	55	111	16	4	7	35	29	119	.230	.281	.324	68	-21	-21	41	3	3	-1	.941	9	*3S/2	-1.2
1965	*LA-N	104	105	12	18	3	0	1	5	8	33	.171	.243	.229	36	-9	-8	6	1	0	0	.971	11	3/S	0.3
1966	*LA-N	125	274	15	55	9	2	3	24	10	64	.201	.242	.281	49	-20	-18	18	1	2	-1	.965	13	3S2	-0.5
1967	NY-A	78	179	22	35	4	0	1	17	17	35	.196	.269	.235	52	-11	-10	12	2	1	0	.915	7	S3/2	0.0
1969	Sea-A	61	128	18	30	3	1	4	14	14	25	.234	.315	.367	92	-2	-2	16	4	0	1	.916	-4	S3	-0.2
1970	Mil-A	25	55	8	14	2	0	2	6	5	9	.255	.317	.400	96	-0	-0	6	0	1	-1	.921	-1	2/3S1	-0.1
	Bos-A	43	129	15	33	7	1	4	17	6	14	.256	.294	.419	88	-2	-3	16	0	0	0	.960	3	3/2	0.0
	Yr	68	184	23	47	9	1	6	23	11	23	.255	.301	.413	91	-2	-3	22	0	1	-1	.962	1	32/S1	-0.1
1971	Bos-A	74	272	41	75	12	5	5	22	14	42	.276	.321	.412	99	1	-1	36	1	1	-0	.974	-18	2S/3	-1.3
1972	Bos-A	71	212	22	52	11	1	2	22	18	40	.245	.313	.335	88	-2	-3	23	0	1	-1	.962	-6	2S3	-0.6
1973	Bos-A	67	155	17	28	9	1	1	16	12	45	.181	.249	.271	44	-11	-12	11	0	0	0	.980	7	23/D	-0.4
1974	Bos-A	10	15	3	2	0	0	1	1	1	6	.133	.188	.333	44	-1	-1	0	0	0	0	.778	-1	/23	-0.2
Total	12	856	2110	237	475	77	17	32	185	142	461	.225	.282	.323	70	-84	-85	193	14	10	-2	.953	26	3S2/D1	-4.1
JOHN KENNEDY Kennedy, John Irvin b: 11/23/34, Sumter, S.C. BR/TR, 5'10", 175 lbs. Deb: 4/22/57																									
1957	Phi-N	5	2	1	0	0	0	0	0	0	1	.000	.000	.000	-99	-1	-1	0	0	0	0	.500	1	/3	0.0
JUNIOR KENNEDY Kennedy, Junior Raymond b: 8/9/50, Fort Gibson, Okla. BR/TR, 6', 185 lbs. Deb: 8/09/74 F																									
1974	Cin-N	22	19	2	3	0	0	0	0	6	4	.158	.360	.158	49	-1	-1	1	0	0	0	.909	-1	2/3	-0.2
1978	Cin-N	89	157	22	40	2	2	0	11	31	28	.255	.381	.293	91	-0	-0	20	4	1	1	.979	13	2/3	1.7
1979	Cin-N	83	220	29	60	7	0	1	17	28	31	.273	.355	.318	85	-3	-4	26	4	3	-1	.980	-1	2/S3	-0.1
1980	Cin-N	104	337	31	88	16	3	1	34	36	34	.261	.332	.335	87	-5	-5	39	3	1	0	.988	2	*2	0.3
1981	Cin-N	27	44	5	11	1	0	0	5	1	5	.250	.267	.273	52	-3	-3	3	0	0	0	.980	2	2/3	0.0
1982	Chi-N	105	242	22	53	3	1	2	25	21	34	.219	.281	.264	52	-15	-16	17	1	4	-2	.978	13	2S/3	0.0
1983	Chi-N	17	22	3	3	0	0	0	3	1	6	.136	.174	.136	-12	-3	-3	0	0	0	0	1.000	2	/23S	-0.1
Total	7	447	1041	114	258	29	6	4	95	124	142	.248	.328	.299	75	-31	-32	107	12	9	-2	.982	30	2/S3	1.6
DOC KENNEDY Kennedy, Michael Joseph b: 8/11/1853, Brooklyn, N.Y. d: 5/23/20, Grove, N.Y. BR/TR, 5'9.5", 185 lbs. Deb: 5/01/1879																									
1879	Cle-N	49	193	19	56	8	2	1	18	2	10	.290	.297	.368	119	3	4	22				.891	3	C/1	0.8
1880	Cle-N	66	250	26	50	10	1	0	18	5	12	.200	.216	.248	58	-11	-10	14				.899	-1	*C/O	-1.0
1881	Cle-N	39	150	19	47	7	1	0	15	5	13	.313	.335	.373	129	4	5	19				.920	5	C/O3	1.0
1882	Cle-N	1	3	0	1	0	0	0	0	1	0	.333	.500	.333	180	0	0	1				.857	3	/C	0.3
1883	Buf-N	5	19	3	6	0	0	0	2	2	2	.316	.381	.316	113	0	0	2				.583	-2	/O1	-0.1
Total	5	160	615	67	160	25	4	1	53	15	37	.260	.278	.319	98	-3	-1	57				.901	9	C/O13	1.0
RAY KENNEDY Kennedy, Raymond Lincoln b: 5/19/1895, Pittsburgh, Pa. d: 1/18/69, Casselberry, Fla. BR/TR, 5'9", 165 lbs. Deb: 9/08/16																									
1916	StL-A	1	1	0	0	0	0	0	0	0	0	.000	.000	.000	-99	-0	-0	0	0			.000	0	H	0.0
BOB KENNEDY Kennedy, Robert Daniel b: 8/18/20, Chicago, Ill. BR/TR, 6'2", 193 lbs. Deb: 9/14/39 FMC																									
1939	Chi-A	3	8	0	2	0	0	0	1	0	0	.250	.250	.250	27	-1	-1	0	0	0	0	.750	-1	/3	-0.2
1940	Chi-A	154	606	74	153	23	3	3	52	42	58	.252	.301	.315	59	-36	-37	55	3	7	-3	.938	-3	*3	-3.8
1941	Chi-A	76	257	16	53	9	3	1	29	17	23	.206	.255	.276	41	-22	-22	19	5	3	-0	.934	3	3	-1.7
1942	Chi-A	113	412	37	95	18	5	0	38	22	41	.231	.270	.299	61	-23	-22	31	11	7	-1	.956	4	3O	-1.8
1946	Chi-A	113	411	43	106	13	5	5	34	24	42	.258	.300	.350	85	-11	-9	40	6	8	-3	.965	4	O3	-1.2
1947	Chi-A	115	428	47	112	19	3	6	48	18	38	.262	.291	.362	84	-13	-11	42	3	4	-2	.968	-3	*O/3	-2.2
1948	Chi-A	30	113	4	28	8	1	0	14	4	17	.248	.274	.336	64	-7	-6	9	0	2	-1	.970	-0	O	-0.9

YEAR	TM/L	G	AB	R	H	2B	3B	HR	RBI	BB	SO	AVG	OBP	SLG	PRO+	BR	/A	RC	SB	CS	SBR	FA	FR	POS	TPR
	*Cle-A	66	73	10	22	3	2	0	5	4	6	.301	.338	.397	98	-1	-1	10	0	0	0	1.000	-13	O/21	-1.4
	Yr	96	186	14	50	11	3	0	19	8	23	.269	.299	.360	77	-7	-7	18	0	2	-1	.981	-13	O/21	-2.3
1949	Cle-A	121	424	49	117	23	5	9	57	37	40	.276	.334	.417	100	-3	-2	57	5	5	-2	.990	3	O3	-0.6
1950	Cle-A	146	540	79	157	27	5	9	54	53	31	.291	.355	.409	99	-5	-2	79	3	4	-2	.987	1	*O	-0.8
1951	Cle-A	108	321	30	79	15	4	7	29	34	33	.246	.320	.383	95	-5	-3	38	4	2	0	.968	-1	*O	-0.7
1952	Cle-A	22	40	6	12	3	1	0	12	9	5	.300	.429	.425	148	3	3	9	1	0	0	1.000	0	O/3	0.3
1953	Cle-A	100	161	22	38	5	0	3	22	19	11	.236	.320	.323	76	-6	-5	16	0	2	-1	1.000	-21	O	-3.0
1954	Cle-A	1	0	0	0	0	0	0	0	0	0	—	—	—	—	0	0	0	0	0	0	.000	-0	/O	0.0
	Bal-A	106	323	37	81	13	2	6	45	28	43	.251	.311	.359	90	-8	-5	33	2	1	0	.938	-6	3O	-1.4
	Yr	107	323	37	81	13	2	6	45	28	43	.251	.311	.359	90	-8	-5	33	2	1	0	.938	-7	3O	-1.4
1955	Bal-A	26	70	10	10	1	0	0	5	10	10	.143	.250	.157	12	-9	-8	3	0	1	-1	1.000	-1	O/13	-1.0
	Chi-A	83	214	28	65	10	2	9	43	16	16	.304	.352	.495	122	7	6	35	0	2	-1	.938	-13	3O/1	-0.9
	Yr	109	284	38	75	11	2	9	48	26	26	.264	.326	.412	97	-2	-2	35	0	3	-2	.938	-13	3O/1	-1.9
1956	Chi-A	8	13	0	1	0	0	0	0	2	4	.077	.200	.077	-24	-2	-2	0	0	0	0	1.000	-1	/3	-0.3
	Det-A	69	177	17	41	5	0	4	22	24	19	.232	.330	.328	74	-6	-6	18	2	2	-1	.931	-3	O3	-1.0
	Yr	77	190	17	42	5	0	4	22	26	23	.221	.321	.311	67	-9	-9	18	2	2	-1	.909	-4	3O	-1.3
1957	Chi-A	4	2	0	0	0	0	0	0	0	1	.000	.000	.000	-99	-1	-1	0	0	0	0	.000	0	H	-0.1
	Bro-N	19	31	5	4	1	0	1	4	1	5	.129	.156	.258	8	-4	-4	1	0	0	0	1.000	-4	/O3	-0.9
Total	16	1483	4624	514	1176	196	41	63	514	364	443	.254	.310	.355	80	-153	-139	495	45	50	-17	.978	-55	O3/12	-23.6

■ SNAPPER KENNEDY Kennedy, Sherman Montgomery b: 11/1/1878, Conneaut, Ohio d: 8/15/45, Pasadena, Tex. BB/TR, 5′10″, 165 lbs. Deb: 5/01/02

YEAR	TM/L	G	AB	R	H	2B	3B	HR	RBI	BB	SO	AVG	OBP	SLG	PRO+	BR	/A	RC	SB	CS	SBR	FA	FR	POS	TPR
1902	Chi-N	1	5	0	0	0	0	0	0	0		.000	.000	.000	-99	-1	-1	0	0			1.000	1	/O	-0.1

■ TERRY KENNEDY Kennedy, Terrence Edward b: 6/4/56, Euclid, Ohio BL/TR, 6′3″, 220 lbs. Deb: 9/04/78 F

YEAR	TM/L	G	AB	R	H	2B	3B	HR	RBI	BB	SO	AVG	OBP	SLG	PRO+	BR	/A	RC	SB	CS	SBR	FA	FR	POS	TPR
1978	StL-N	10	29	0	5	0	0	0	2	4	3	.172	.273	.172	27	-3	-3	1	0	0	0	.980	0	C	-0.3
1979	StL-N	33	109	11	31	7	0	2	17	6	20	.284	.322	.404	96	-1	-1	14	0	0	0	.993	-4	C	-0.4
1980	StL-N	84	248	28	63	12	3	4	34	28	34	.254	.330	.375	93	-1	-2	30	0	0	0	.967	-3	CO	-0.5
1981	SD-N★	101	382	32	115	24	1	2	41	22	53	.301	.342	.385	114	3	6	49	0	2	-1	.964	-8	*C	0.0
1982	SD-N	153	562	75	166	42	1	21	97	26	91	.295	.332	.486	133	17	20	90	1	0	0	.990	-18	*C1	0.7
1983	SD-N☆	149	549	47	156	27	2	17	98	51	89	.284	.347	.434	119	11	13	81	1	3	-2	.986	-8	*C/1	1.0
1984	*SD-N	148	530	54	127	16	1	14	57	33	99	.240	.287	.353	79	-16	-16	50	1	2	-1	.982	-14	*C	-2.6
1985	SD-N★	143	532	54	139	27	1	10	74	31	102	.261	.302	.372	89	-10	-9	55	0	0	0	.986	0	*C/1	-0.2
1986	SD-N	141	432	46	114	22	1	12	57	37	74	.264	.325	.403	102	-1	0	54	0	3	-2	.990	-0	*C	0.6
1987	Bal-A★	143	512	51	128	13	1	18	62	35	112	.250	.299	.385	82	-16	-14	57	1	0	0	.993	-16	*C	-1.9
1988	Bal-A	85	265	20	60	10	0	3	16	15	53	.226	.270	.298	61	-15	-14	19	0	0	0	.994	-8	C	-1.7
1989	*SF-N	125	355	19	85	15	0	5	34	35	56	.239	.308	.324	83	-9	-7	35	1	3	-2	.986	-3	*C/1	-0.6
1990	SF-N	107	303	25	84	22	0	2	26	31	38	.277	.344	.370	100	-1	0	38	1	2	-1	.991	-12	*C	-0.8
1991	SF-N	69	171	12	40	7	1	3	13	11	31	.234	.284	.339	77	-6	-5	16	0	0	0	.978	-3	C/1	-0.6
Total	14	1491	4979	474	1313	244	12	113	628	365	855	.264	.316	.386	97	-47	-31	588	6	15	-7	.985	-99	*C/O1	-7.3

■ ED KENNEDY Kennedy, William Edward b: 4/5/1861, Bellevue, Ky. d: 12/22/12, Cheyenne, Wyoming BR/TR, 5′7″, 160 lbs. Deb: 5/17/1884

YEAR	TM/L	G	AB	R	H	2B	3B	HR	RBI	BB	SO	AVG	OBP	SLG	PRO+	BR	/A	RC	SB	CS	SBR	FA	FR	POS	TPR
1884	Cin-U	13	48	6	10	1	1	0		1		.208	.224	.271	62	-2	-2	3				.857	0	/3SO	-0.2

■ JERRY KENNEY Kenney, Gerald T b: 6/30/45, St.Louis, Mo. BL/TR, 6′1″, 170 lbs. Deb: 9/05/67

YEAR	TM/L	G	AB	R	H	2B	3B	HR	RBI	BB	SO	AVG	OBP	SLG	PRO+	BR	/A	RC	SB	CS	SBR	FA	FR	POS	TPR
1967	NY-A	20	58	4	18	2	0	1	5	10	8	.310	.412	.397	145	3	4	11	2	1	0	.952	-4	S	0.2
1969	NY-A	130	447	49	115	14	2	2	34	48	36	.257	.331	.311	83	-11	-9	47	25	14	-1	.975	11	3OS	0.1
1970	NY-A	140	404	46	78	10	7	4	35	52	44	.193	.285	.282	60	-23	-21	34	20	6	2	.960	15	*3/2	-0.5
1971	NY-A	120	325	50	85	10	3	0	20	56	38	.262	.372	.311	101	1	3	40	9	8	-2	.953	11	*3/S1	1.2
1972	NY-A	50	119	16	25	2	0	0	7	16	13	.210	.304	.227	62	-5	-5	8	3	0	1	.969	5	S/3	0.6
1973	Cle-A	5	16	0	4	0	1	0	2	2	0	.250	.333	.375	97	-0	-0	2	0	0	0	1.000	-2	/2	-0.1
Total	6	465	1369	165	325	38	13	7	103	184	139	.237	.329	.299	82	-36	-28	142	59	29	0	.962	36	3/SO21	1.5

■ JOHN KENNEY Kenney, John Deb: 5/02/1872

YEAR	TM/L	G	AB	R	H	2B	3B	HR	RBI	BB	SO	AVG	OBP	SLG	PRO+	BR	/A	RC	SB	CS	SBR	FA	FR	POS	TPR
1872	Atl-n	5	19	0	0	0	0	0	1	0	1	.000	.000	.000	-85	-4	-5	0						/2O	-0.4

■ JEFF KENT Kent, Jeffrey Franklin b: 3/7/68, Bellflower, Cal. BR/TR, 6′1″, 185 lbs. Deb: 4/12/92

YEAR	TM/L	G	AB	R	H	2B	3B	HR	RBI	BB	SO	AVG	OBP	SLG	PRO+	BR	/A	RC	SB	CS	SBR	FA	FR	POS	TPR
1992	Tor-A	65	192	36	46	13	1	8	35	20	47	.240	.330	.443	110	4	2	29	2	1	0	.915	-3	32/1	0.0
	NY-N	37	113	16	27	8	1	3	15	7	29	.239	.289	.407	96	-1	-1	12	0	2	-1	.980	8	2/3S	0.7
Total	1	102	305	52	73	21	2	11	50	27	76	.239	.316	.430	105	2	1	41	2	3	-1	.981	5	/231S	0.7

■ DICK KENWORTHY Kenworthy, Richard Lee b: 4/1/41, Red Oak, Iowa BR/TR, 5′9″, 170 lbs. Deb: 9/08/62

YEAR	TM/L	G	AB	R	H	2B	3B	HR	RBI	BB	SO	AVG	OBP	SLG	PRO+	BR	/A	RC	SB	CS	SBR	FA	FR	POS	TPR
1962	Chi-A	3	4	0	0	0	0	0	0	0	3	.000	.000	.000	-99	-1	-1	0	0	0	0	1.000	1	/2	0.0
1964	Chi-A	2	2	0	0	0	0	0	0	0	1	.000	.000	.000	-99	-1	-1	0	0	0	0	.000	0	H	-0.1
1965	Chi-A	3	1	0	0	0	0	0	0	1	0	.000	.667	.000	113	0	0	0	0	0	0	.000	0	H	0.0
1966	Chi-A	9	25	1	5	0	0	0	0	0	0	.200	.200	.200	16	-3	-3	1	0	0	0	.875	-3	/3	-0.6
1967	Chi-A	50	97	9	22	4	1	4	11	4	17	.227	.265	.412	101	-1	-0	9	0	2	-1	.971	1	3	-0.1
1968	Chi-A	58	122	2	27	2	0	0	2	5	21	.221	.252	.238	49	-7	-8	7	0	1	-1	.938	4	3	-0.4
Total	6	125	251	12	54	6	1	4	13	10	42	.215	.251	.295	63	-12	-12	18	0	3	-2	.948	4	/32	-1.2

■ DUKE KENWORTHY Kenworthy, William Jennings "Iron Duke" b: 7/4/1886, Cambridge, Ohio d: 9/21/50, Eureka, Cal. BB/TR, 5′7″, 165 lbs. Deb: 8/28/12

YEAR	TM/L	G	AB	R	H	2B	3B	HR	RBI	BB	SO	AVG	OBP	SLG	PRO+	BR	/A	RC	SB	CS	SBR	FA	FR	POS	TPR
1912	Was-A	12	38	6	9	1	0	0	2	2		.237	.293	.263	59	-2	-2	4	3			1.000	-0	O	-0.3
1914	KC-F	146	545	93	173	40	14	15	91	36	44	.317	.372	.525	160	35	38	124	37			.952	21	*2	5.9
1915	KC-F	122	396	59	118	30	7	3	52	28	32	.298	.355	.432	136	14	16	71	20			.936	-7	*2/O	1.1
1917	StL-A	5	10	1	1	0	0	0	1	1	1	.100	.182	.100	-14	-1	-1	0	1			.889	1	/2	0.0
Total	4	285	989	159	301	71	21	18	146	67	77	.304	.360	.473	145	46	51	200	61			.945	14	2/O	6.7

■ JOE KEOUGH Keough, Joseph William b: 1/7/46, Pomona, Cal. BL/TL, 6′, 185 lbs. Deb: 8/07/68 F

YEAR	TM/L	G	AB	R	H	2B	3B	HR	RBI	BB	SO	AVG	OBP	SLG	PRO+	BR	/A	RC	SB	CS	SBR	FA	FR	POS	TPR
1968	Oak-A	34	98	7	21	2	1	2	18	8	11	.214	.274	.316	82	-3	-2	9	1	0	0	.962	1	O/1	-0.3
1969	KC-A	70	166	17	31	2	0	0	7	13	13	.187	.254	.199	28	-16	-16	10	5	2	0	1.000	-3	O/1	-2.2
1970	KC-A	57	183	28	59	6	2	4	21	23	18	.322	.398	.443	132	8	8	32	1	1	-0	.985	2	O1	0.7
1971	KC-A	110	351	34	87	14	2	3	30	35	26	.248	.318	.325	83	-8	-7	34	0	6	-4	.982	-6	*O	-2.4
1972	KC-A	56	64	8	14	2	0	0	5	8	7	.219	.324	.250	73	-2	-2	6	2	0	1	1.000	-3	O	-0.5
1973	Chi-A	5	1	1	0	0	0	0	0	0	0	.000	.000	.000	-97	-0	-0	0	0	0	0	.000	0	H	0.0
Total	6	332	863	95	212	26	5	9	81	87	75	.246	.318	.319	82	-20	-19	90	9	9	-3	.984	-9	O/1	-4.7

■ MARTY KEOUGH Keough, Richard Martin b: 4/14/35, Oakland, Cal. BL/TL, 6′, 180 lbs. Deb: 4/21/56 F

YEAR	TM/L	G	AB	R	H	2B	3B	HR	RBI	BB	SO	AVG	OBP	SLG	PRO+	BR	/A	RC	SB	CS	SBR	FA	FR	POS	TPR
1956	Bos-A	3	2	1	0	0	0	0	1	1	0	.000	.333	.000	-5	-0	-0	0	0	0	0	.000	0	H	0.0
1957	Bos-A	9	17	1	1	0	0	0	0	4	3	.059	.238	.059	-14	-3	-3	0	0	0	0	1.000	0	/O	-0.3
1958	Bos-A	68	118	21	26	3	3	1	9	7	29	.220	.264	.322	57	-7	-8	10	1	1	-0	.974	-5	O/1	-1.4
1959	Bos-A	96	251	40	61	13	5	7	27	26	40	.243	.321	.418	97	0	-1	35	3	1	0	.993	-1	O/1	-0.6
1960	Bos-A	38	105	15	26	6	1	1	9	8	8	.248	.301	.352	73	-4	-4	11	2	2	-1	1.000	1	O	-0.6
	Cle-A	65	149	19	37	5	0	3	11	9	23	.248	.296	.342	74	-6	-5	15	2	3	-1	.986	-4	O	-1.3
	Yr	103	254	34	63	11	1	4	20	17	31	.248	.298	.346	74	-10	-9	26	4	5	-2	.992	-3	O	-1.9
1961	Was-A	135	390	57	97	18	9	9	34	32	60	.249	.309	.410	92	-6	-6	50	12	5	1	.978	2	*O1	-0.9
1962	Cin-N	111	230	34	64	8	2	7	27	21	31	.278	.349	.422	102	2	1	35	3	1	0	.968	4	O1	0.1

YEAR	TM/L	G	AB	R	H	2B	3B	HR	RBI	BB	SO	AVG	OBP	SLG	PRO+	BR	/A	RC	SB	CS	SBR	FA	FR	POS	TPR
1963	Cin-N	95	172	21	39	8	2	6	21	25	37	.227	.338	.401	109	3	3	24	1	4	-2	.992	1	1O	0.0
1964	Cin-N	109	276	29	71	9	1	9	28	22	58	.257	.314	.395	95	-1	-2	35	1	2	-1	.991	-1	O/1	-0.8
1965	Cin-N	62	43	14	5	0	0	0	3	3	14	.116	.191	.116	-10	-6	-7	1	0	0	0	.988	1	1/O	-0.7
1966	Atl-N	17	17	1	1	0	0	0	1	1	6	.059	.111	.059	-50	-3	-3	0	0	0	0	1.000	-1	/1O	-0.5
	Chi-N	33	26	3	6	1	0	0	5	5	9	.231	.375	.269	82	-0	-0	3	1	0	0	1.000	0	/O	0.0
	Yr	50	43	4	7	1	0	0	6	6	15	.163	.280	.186	32	-4	-4	3	1	0	0	.667	-1	/O1	-0.5
Total	11	841	1796	256	434	71	23	43	176	164	318	.242	.311	.379	86	-31	-36	220	26	19	-4	.984	-3	O1	-7.0

■ **JOHN KERINS** Kerins, John Nelson b: 7/15/1858, Indianapolis, Ind d: 9/8/19, Louisville, Ky. BR/TR, 5'10", 177 lbs. Deb: 5/01/1884 MU

YEAR	TM/L	G	AB	R	H	2B	3B	HR	RBI	BB	SO	AVG	OBP	SLG	PRO+	BR	/A	RC	SB	CS	SBR	FA	FR	POS	TPR
1884	Ind-a	94	364	58	78	10	3	6		6		.214	.229	.308	78	-9	-8	26				**.972**	6	*1/CO3	-1.1
1885	Lou-a	112	456	65	111	9	16	3		20		.243	.281	.353	102	1	1	46				.947	3	*1C/O3	-0.5
1886	Lou-a	120	487	113	131	19	9	4		66		.269	.360	.370	124	19	15	76	26			.933	**39**	C1/OS	**4.8**
1887	Lou-a	112	476	101	140	18	**19**	5		38		.294	.349	.443	120	13	11	93	49			.970	25	1C/O	2.6
1888	Lou-a	83	319	38	75	11	4	2	41	25		.235	.297	.313	101	-0	1	35	16			.844	2	OC/132M	0.4
1889	Lou-a	2	9	2	3	1	0	0	3	0	1	.333	.333	.444	125	0	0	1	0			.500	-1	/OC	-0.1
	Bal-a	16	53	7	15	2	0	0	12	2	4	.283	.321	.321	84	-1	-1	6	2			.981	-2	/1COS	-0.2
	Yr	18	62	9	18	3	0	0	15	2	5	.290	.323	.339	89	-1	-1	8	2			.981	-2	/1COS	-0.3
1890	StL-a	18	63	8	8	2	0	0		8		.127	.225	.159	13	-6	-8	3	2			.968	1	1/CM	-0.7
Total	7	557	2227	392	561	72	51	20	56	165	5	.252	.308	.357	104	16	10	287	95			.963	73	1C/O3S2	5.2

■ **ORIE KERLIN** Kerlin, Orie Milton "Cy" b: 1/23/1891, Summerfield, La. d: 10/29/74, Shreveport, La. BL/TR, 5'7", 149 lbs. Deb: 6/06/15

YEAR	TM/L	G	AB	R	H	2B	3B	HR	RBI	BB	SO	AVG	OBP	SLG	PRO+	BR	/A	RC	SB	CS	SBR	FA	FR	POS	TPR
1915	Pit-F	3	1	0	0	0	0	0	0	0	0	.000	.000	.000	-99	-0	-0	0	0			.000	-0	/C	0.0

■ **BILL KERN** Kern, William George b: 2/28/33, Coplay, Pa. BR/TR, 6'2", 184 lbs. Deb: 9/19/62

YEAR	TM/L	G	AB	R	H	2B	3B	HR	RBI	BB	SO	AVG	OBP	SLG	PRO+	BR	/A	RC	SB	CS	SBR	FA	FR	POS	TPR
1962	KC-A	8	16	1	4	0	0	1	1	0	3	.250	.250	.438	78	-1	-1	2	0	0	0	1.000	1	/O	0.0

■ **JOE KERNAN** Kernan, Joseph b: Baltimore, Md. Deb: 4/14/1873

YEAR	TM/L	G	AB	R	H	2B	3B	HR	RBI	BB	SO	AVG	OBP	SLG	PRO+	BR	/A	RC	SB	CS	SBR	FA	FR	POS	TPR
1873	Mar-n	2	8	1	3	0	0	0	1	0	0	.375	.375	.375	158	0	1	1						/2O	0.0

■ **GEORGE KERNEK** Kernek, George Boyd b: 1/12/40, Holdenville, Okla. BL/TL, 6'3", 170 lbs. Deb: 9/05/65

YEAR	TM/L	G	AB	R	H	2B	3B	HR	RBI	BB	SO	AVG	OBP	SLG	PRO+	BR	/A	RC	SB	CS	SBR	FA	FR	POS	TPR
1965	StL-N	10	31	6	9	3	1	0	3	2	4	.290	.333	.452	109	1	0	5	0	0	0	.972	-0	/1	0.0
1966	StL-N	20	50	5	12	0	1	0	3	4	9	.240	.309	.280	65	-2	-2	5	1	0	0	.984	-0	1	-0.3
Total	2	30	81	11	21	3	2	0	6	6	13	.259	.318	.346	82	-2	-2	9	1	0	0	.980	-0	/1	-0.3

■ **RUSS KERNS** Kerns, Russell Eldon b: 11/10/20, Fremont, Ohio BL/TR, 6', 188 lbs. Deb: 8/18/45

YEAR	TM/L	G	AB	R	H	2B	3B	HR	RBI	BB	SO	AVG	OBP	SLG	PRO+	BR	/A	RC	SB	CS	SBR	FA	FR	POS	TPR
1945	Det-A	1	1	0	0	0	0	0	0	0	0	.000	.000	.000	-94	-0	-0	0	0	0	0	.000	0	H	0.0

■ **JOHN KERR** Kerr, John Francis b: 11/26/1898, San Francisco, Cal BR/TR, 5'8", 158 lbs. Deb: 5/01/23

YEAR	TM/L	G	AB	R	H	2B	3B	HR	RBI	BB	SO	AVG	OBP	SLG	PRO+	BR	/A	RC	SB	CS	SBR	FA	FR	POS	TPR
1923	Det-A	19	42	4	9	1	0	0	1	4	5	.214	.283	.238	39	-4	-4	3	0	0	0	.877	4	S	0.2
1924	Det-A	17	11	3	3	0	0	0	1	0	0	.273	.273	.273	42	-1	-1	1	0	0	0	.000	-0	/3O	-0.1
1929	Chi-A	127	419	50	108	20	4	1	39	31	24	.258	.310	.332	66	-22	-21	44	9	8	-2	.971	24	*2/S	0.6
1930	Chi-A	70	266	37	77	11	6	3	27	21	23	.289	.351	.410	95	-3	-2	39	4	2	0	.980	0	2S	0.3
1931	Chi-A	128	444	51	119	17	2	2	50	35	22	.268	.324	.329	77	-18	-14	50	9	3	1	.968	8	*2/3S	0.2
1932	Was-A	51	132	14	36	6	1	0	15	13	3	.273	.338	.333	75	-5	-4	15	3	2	-0	.954	-1	2S/3	-0.3
1933	*Was-A	28	40	5	8	0	0	0	0	3	2	.200	.256	.200	22	-4	-4	2	0	0	0	.966	3	2/3	-0.1
1934	Was-A	31	103	8	28	4	0	0	12	8	13	.272	.324	.311	67	-5	-5	11	1	1	-0	.971	10	32	0.5
Total	8	471	1457	172	388	59	13	6	145	115	92	.266	.323	.337	73	-62	-55	165	26	16	-2	.970	48	2/S3O	1.3

■ **DOC KERR** Kerr, John Jonas b: 1/17/1882, Del Roy, Ohio d: 6/9/37, Baltimore, Md. BB/TR, 5'10.5", 190 lbs. Deb: 4/22/14

YEAR	TM/L	G	AB	R	H	2B	3B	HR	RBI	BB	SO	AVG	OBP	SLG	PRO+	BR	/A	RC	SB	CS	SBR	FA	FR	POS	TPR
1914	Pit-F	42	71	3	17	4	2	1	7	10	13	.239	.333	.394	107	1	1	10	0			.970	1	C	0.3
	Bal-F	14	34	4	9	1	1	0	1	1	6	.265	.286	.353	79	-1	-1	4	1			.979	5	C/1	0.4
	Yr	56	105	7	26	5	3	1	8	11	19	.248	.319	.381	98	-0	-0	14	1			.974	5	C/1	0.7
1915	Bal-F	3	6	1	2	0	0	0	0	1	0	.333	.429	.333	121	0	0	1	0			1.000	-1	/C1	-0.1
Total	2	59	111	8	28	5	3	1	8	12	19	.252	.325	.378	100	-0	-0	14	1			.975	4	/C1	0.6

■ **BUDDY KERR** Kerr, John Joseph b: 11/6/22, Astoria, N.Y. BR/TR, 6'2", 180 lbs. Deb: 9/08/43

YEAR	TM/L	G	AB	R	H	2B	3B	HR	RBI	BB	SO	AVG	OBP	SLG	PRO+	BR	/A	RC	SB	CS	SBR	FA	FR	POS	TPR
1943	NY-N	27	98	14	28	3	0	2	12	8	5	.286	.352	.378	110	1	1	13	1			.955	5	S	0.8
1944	NY-N	150	548	68	146	31	4	9	63	37	32	.266	.316	.387	97	-3	-3	65	14			.954	**17**	*S	2.6
1945	NY-N	149	546	53	136	20	3	4	40	41	34	.249	.304	.319	72	-20	-21	54	5			.964	**28**	*S	1.9
1946	NY-N	145	497	50	124	20	3	6	40	53	31	.249	.324	.338	87	-8	-8	57	7			**.982**	6	*S3	0.6
1947	NY-N	138	547	73	157	23	5	7	49	36	49	.287	.331	.386	89	-9	-9	69	2			.977	12	*S	1.0
1948	NY-N★	144	496	41	119	16	4	0	46	56	36	.240	.317	.288	64	-23	-24	48	9			.967	3	*S	-1.2
1949	NY-N	90	220	16	46	4	0	0	19	21	23	.209	.284	.227	39	-19	-18	16	0			.959	6	S	-0.8
1950	Bos-N	155	507	45	115	24	6	2	46	50	50	.227	.296	.310	64	-30	-25	45	0			.965	2	*S	-1.1
1951	Bos-N	69	172	18	32	4	0	1	18	22	20	.186	.282	.227	41	-14	-13	13	0	0	0	.969	13	S/2	0.4
Total	9	1067	3631	378	903	145	25	31	333	324	280	.249	.312	.328	76	-124	-120	380	38	0		.967	92	*S/32	4.2

■ **MEL KERR** Kerr, John Melville b: 5/22/03, Souris, Man., Can. d: 8/9/80, Vero Beach, Fla. BL/TL, 5'11.5", 155 lbs. Deb: 9/16/25 C

YEAR	TM/L	G	AB	R	H	2B	3B	HR	RBI	BB	SO	AVG	OBP	SLG	PRO+	BR	/A	RC	SB	CS	SBR	FA	FR	POS	TPR
1925	Chi-N	1	0	1	0	0	0	0	0	0	0	—	—	—	—	0	0	0	0	0	0	.000	0	R	0.0

■ **DAN KERWIN** Kerwin, Daniel Patrick (b: Daniel Patrick Kervin) b: 7/9/1879, Philadelphia, Pa. d: 7/13/60, Philadelphia, Pa. BL/TL, 5'9", 164 lbs. Deb: 9/27/03

YEAR	TM/L	G	AB	R	H	2B	3B	HR	RBI	BB	SO	AVG	OBP	SLG	PRO+	BR	/A	RC	SB	CS	SBR	FA	FR	POS	TPR
1903	Cin-N	2	6	1	4	1	0	0	1	2		.667	.778	.833	324	3	2	4	0			.500	-1	/O	0.1

■ **DON KESSINGER** Kessinger, Donald Eulon b: 7/17/42, Forrest City, Ark. BB/TR, 6'1", 175 lbs. Deb: 9/07/64 M

YEAR	TM/L	G	AB	R	H	2B	3B	HR	RBI	BB	SO	AVG	OBP	SLG	PRO+	BR	/A	RC	SB	CS	SBR	FA	FR	POS	TPR
1964	Chi-N	4	12	1	2	0	0	0	0	0	1	.167	.167	.167	-6	-2	-2	0	0	0	0	1.000	-1	/S	-0.3
1965	Chi-N	106	309	19	62	4	3	0	14	20	44	.201	.254	.233	37	-25	-26	18	1	2	-1	.948	21	*S	0.1
1966	Chi-N	150	533	50	146	8	2	1	43	26	46	.274	.308	.302	70	-21	-21	49	13	7	-0	.951	-10	*S	-2.0
1967	Chi-N	145	580	61	134	10	7	0	42	33	80	.231	.277	.272	55	-31	-34	43	6	13	-6	.973	-3	*S	-3.3
1968	Chi-N★	160	655	63	157	14	7	1	32	38	86	.240	.283	.287	67	-22	-27	54	9	9	-3	.962	18	*S	0.6
1969	Chi-N★	158	664	109	181	38	6	4	53	61	70	.273	.335	.366	85	-3	-13	84	11	8	-2	**.976**	25	*S	2.8
1970	Chi-N★	154	631	100	168	21	14	1	39	66	59	.266	.338	.349	75	-13	-23	76	12	6	0	.972	9	*S	0.4
1971	Chi-N★	155	617	77	159	18	6	2	38	52	54	.258	.318	.316	70	-15	-25	63	15	8	-0	.966	4	*S	-0.2
1972	Chi-N★	149	577	77	158	20	6	1	39	67	44	.274	.351	.334	87	-1	-8	70	8	7	-2	.965	8	*S	2.0
1973	Chi-N	160	577	52	151	22	3	0	43	57	44	.262	.328	.310	72	-16	-21	57	6	6	-2	.964	17	*S	1.5
1974	Chi-N★	153	599	83	155	20	7	1	42	62	54	.259	.332	.321	80	-12	-15	64	7	7	-2	.958	2	*S	0.4
1975	Chi-N	154	601	77	146	26	10	0	46	68	47	.243	.321	.319	75	-17	-20	66	4	7	-3	.967	-2	*S3	-1.1
1976	StL-N	145	502	55	120	22	6	1	40	61	51	.239	.323	.313	80	-11	-12	53	3	0	1	.969	-4	*S2/3	0.0
1977	StL-N	59	134	14	32	4	0	0	7	14	26	.239	.311	.269	58	-8	-7	12	0	0	0	.978	2	S2/3	-0.2
	Chi-A	39	119	12	28	3	2	0	11	13	7	.235	.311	.294	66	-5	-5	11	2	1	0	.959	-4	S2/3	-0.7
1978	Chi-A	131	431	35	110	18	1	1	31	36	34	.255	.313	.309	75	-14	-14	41	2	4	-2	.974	-19	*S/2	-2.0
1979	Chi-A	56	110	14	22	6	0	1	7	10	12	.200	.267	.282	48	-8	-8	8	1	0	0	.988	-1	S/12	-0.4
Total	16	2078	7651	899	1931	254	80	14	527	684	759	.252	.316	.312	72	-225	-283	769	100	85	-21	.966	61	*S/231	-2.4

■ **HENRY KESSLER** Kessler, Henry "Lucky" b: 1847, Brooklyn, N.Y. d: 1/9/1900, Franklin, Pa. BR/TR, 5'10", 144 lbs. Deb: 8/04/1873

YEAR	TM/L	G	AB	R	H	2B	3B	HR	RBI	BB	SO	AVG	OBP	SLG	PRO+	BR	/A	RC	SB	CS	SBR	FA	FR	POS	TPR
1873	Atl-n	1	5	0	1	0	0	0	1	0	0	.200	.200	.200	20	-0	-0	0						/1	0.0
1874	Atl-n	14	57	8	16	2	0	0		0		.281	.281	.316	101	-1	1	5						/C2O3	0.0

YEAR	TM/L	G	AB	R	H	2B	3B	HR	RBI	BB	SO	AVG	OBP	SLG	PRO+	BR	/A	RC	SB	CS	SBR	FA	FR	POS	TPR
1875	Atl-n	25	104	17	26	2	0	0		1		.250	.257	.269	94	-2	0	7						S/OC2	0.0
1876	Cin-N	59	248	26	64	5	0	0	11	7	10	.258	.278	.278	100	-3	2	20				.788	-8	SO	-0.6
1877	Cin-N	6	20	0	2	0	0	0	0	2	1	.100	.182	.100	-10	-2	-2	0				.500	-5	/C1	-0.7
Total	3 n	40	166	25	43	4	0	0	1	1		.259	.263	.283	94	-3	0	13						/SCO231	0.0
Total	2	65	268	26	66	5	0	0	11	9	11	.246	.271	.265	91	-6	0	20				.953	-14	/SOC1	-1.3

■ **FRED KETCHUM** Ketchum, Frederick L. b: 7/27/1875, Elmira, N.Y. d: 3/12/08, Cortland, N.Y. BL/TR, 5'8", 157 lbs. Deb: 9/12/1899

YEAR	TM/L	G	AB	R	H	2B	3B	HR	RBI	BB	SO	AVG	OBP	SLG	PRO+	BR	/A	RC	SB	CS	SBR	FA	FR	POS	TPR
1899	Lou-N	15	61	13	18	1	0	0	5	0		.295	.306	.311	70	-3	-3	7	2			1.000	-4	O	-0.7
1901	Phi-A	5	22	5	5	0	0	0	2	0		.227	.227	.227	25	-2	-2	1	0			.875	-1	/O	-0.4
Total	2	20	83	18	23	1	0	0	7	0		.277	.286	.289	58	-5	-5	8	2			.960	-5	/O	-1.1

■ **PHIL KETTER** Ketter, Philip (b: Philip Ketterer) b: 4/13/1884, St.Louis, Mo. d: 4/9/65, St.Louis, Mo. TR , Deb: 5/23/12

YEAR	TM/L	G	AB	R	H	2B	3B	HR	RBI	BB	SO	AVG	OBP	SLG	PRO+	BR	/A	RC	SB	CS	SBR	FA	FR	POS	TPR
1912	StL-A	2	6	1	2	0	0	0	0	0		.333	.333	.333	94	-0	-0	1	0			1.000	-1	/C	-0.1

■ **SAM KHALIFA** Khalifa, Sam b: 12/5/63, Fontana, Cal. BR/TR, 5'11", 170 lbs. Deb: 6/25/85

YEAR	TM/L	G	AB	R	H	2B	3B	HR	RBI	BB	SO	AVG	OBP	SLG	PRO+	BR	/A	RC	SB	CS	SBR	FA	FR	POS	TPR
1985	Pit-N	95	320	30	76	14	3	2	31	34	56	.237	.311	.319	77	-10	-9	32	5	2	0	.967	13	S	1.3
1986	Pit-N	64	151	8	28	6	0	0	4	19	28	.185	.276	.225	39	-12	-12	9	0	2	-1	.961	14	S/2	0.4
1987	Pit-N	5	17	1	3	0	0	0	2	0	2	.176	.176	.176	-6	-3	-3	1	0	0	0	.917	-5	/S	-0.7
Total	3	164	488	39	107	20	3	2	37	53	86	.219	.296	.285	62	-24	-24	41	5	4	-1	.964	22	S/2	1.0

■ **HOD KIBBIE** Kibbie, Horace Kent b: 7/18/03, Ft.Worth, Tex. d: 10/19/75, Ft.Worth, Tex. BR/TR, 5'10", 150 lbs. Deb: 6/13/25

YEAR	TM/L	G	AB	R	H	2B	3B	HR	RBI	BB	SO	AVG	OBP	SLG	PRO+	BR	/A	RC	SB	CS	SBR	FA	FR	POS	TPR
1925	Bos-N	11	41	5	11	2	0	0	2	5	6	.268	.348	.317	78	-2	-1	5	0	0	0	.904	-0	/2S	-0.1

■ **JACK KIBBLE** Kibble, John Westly "Happy" b: 1/2/1892, Seatonville, Ill. d: 12/13/69, Roundup, Mont. BB/TR, 5'9.5", 154 lbs. Deb: 9/10/12

YEAR	TM/L	G	AB	R	H	2B	3B	HR	RBI	BB	SO	AVG	OBP	SLG	PRO+	BR	/A	RC	SB	CS	SBR	FA	FR	POS	TPR
1912	Cle-A	5	8	1	0	0	0	0	0	0		.000	.111	.000	-65	-2	-2	0	0			1.000	4	/32	0.2

■ **STEVE KIEFER** Kiefer, Steven George b: 10/18/60, Chicago, Ill. BR/TR, 6'1", 180 lbs. Deb: 9/03/84

YEAR	TM/L	G	AB	R	H	2B	3B	HR	RBI	BB	SO	AVG	OBP	SLG	PRO+	BR	/A	RC	SB	CS	SBR	FA	FR	POS	TPR
1984	Oak-A	23	40	7	7	1	2	0	2	2	10	.175	.214	.300	43	-3	-3	3	2	1	0	.904	1	S/3D	-0.2
1985	Oak-A	40	66	8	13	1	1	1	10	1	18	.197	.209	.288	37	-6	-5	4	0	0	0	.881	3	3/D	-0.3
1986	Mil-A	2	6	0	0	0	0	0	0	0	4	.000	.000	.000	-97	-2	-2	0	0	0	0	1.000	3	/S	0.1
1987	Mil-A	28	99	17	20	4	0	5	17	7	28	.202	.262	.394	69	-5	-5	10	0	0	0	.966	-3	3/2	-0.8
1988	Mil-A	7	10	2	3	1	0	1	1	2	3	.300	.462	.700	219	2	2	4	0	0	0	1.000	-1	/23	0.1
1989	NY-A	5	8	0	1	0	0	0	0	0	5	.125	.125	.125	-30	-1	-1	0	0	0	0	1.000	-1	/3	-0.3
Total	6	105	229	34	44	7	3	7	30	12	68	.192	.239	.341	56	-15	-15	20	2	1	0	.920	1	/3S2D	-1.4

■ **BILL KIENZLE** Kienzle, William H. b: Philadelphia, Pa. BL/TL, Deb: 9/15/1882

YEAR	TM/L	G	AB	R	H	2B	3B	HR	RBI	BB	SO	AVG	OBP	SLG	PRO+	BR	/A	RC	SB	CS	SBR	FA	FR	POS	TPR
1882	Phi-a	9	33	8	11	3	2	0		5		.333	.421	.545	200	4	4	8				.842	-1	/O	0.3
1884	Phi-U	67	299	76	76	13	8	0		21		.254	.303	.351	130	7	10	33				.772	-2	O	0.6
Total	2	76	332	84	87	16	10	0		26		.262	.316	.370	139	11	14	40				.781	-3	/O	0.9

■ **PETE KILDUFF** Kilduff, Peter John b: 4/4/1893, Weir City, Kan. d: 2/14/30, Pittsburg, Kan. BR/TR, 5'7", 155 lbs. Deb: 4/18/17

YEAR	TM/L	G	AB	R	H	2B	3B	HR	RBI	BB	SO	AVG	OBP	SLG	PRO+	BR	/A	RC	SB	CS	SBR	FA	FR	POS	TPR
1917	NY-N	31	78	12	16	3	0	1	12	4	11	.205	.253	.282	66	-3	-3	6	2			.954	-2	2/S3	-0.5
	Chi-N	56	202	23	56	9	5	0	15	12	19	.277	.324	.371	105	3	1	27	11			.920	-14	S/2	-1.2
	Yr	87	280	35	72	12	5	1	27	16	30	.257	.304	.346	96	-1	-2	32	13			.917	-16	S2/3	-1.7
1918	Chi-N	30	93	7	19	2	2	0	13	7	7	.204	.267	.269	62	-4	-4	8	1			.935	-3	2	-0.6
1919	Chi-N	31	88	5	24	4	2	0	8	10	5	.273	.360	.364	117	2	2	12	1			.974	-4	3/2S	-0.1
	Bro-N	32	73	9	22	3	1	0	8	12	11	.301	.407	.370	132	4	4	13	5			.862	-4	3/2	0.1
	Yr	63	161	14	46	7	3	0	16	22	16	.286	.382	.366	124	6	6	24	6			.903	-8	3/2S	0.0
1920	*Bro-N	141	478	62	130	26	8	0	58	58	43	.272	.351	.360	101	4	2	61	2	9	-5	.967	8	*2/3	1.1
1921	Bro-N	107	372	45	107	15	10	3	45	31	36	.288	.344	.406	94	-1	-3	52	6	6	-2	.963	13	*2/3	1.0
Total	5	428	1384	163	374	62	28	4	159	134	132	.270	.338	.364	98	4	-1	178	28	15		.963	-7	2/S3	-0.2

■ **JOHN KILEY** Kiley, John Frederick b: 7/1/1859, S.Dedham, Mass. d: 12/18/40, Norwood, Mass. BL/TL, 5'7", 147 lbs. Deb: 5/01/1884

YEAR	TM/L	G	AB	R	H	2B	3B	HR	RBI	BB	SO	AVG	OBP	SLG	PRO+	BR	/A	RC	SB	CS	SBR	FA	FR	POS	TPR
1884	Was-a	14	56	9	12	2	2	0		3		.214	.267	.321	106	-0	1	5				.571	-4	O	-0.3
1891	Bos-N	1	2	0	0	0	0	0	0	1	1	.000	.500	.000	47	0	0	0	0			1.000	0	/P	0.0
Total	2	15	58	9	12	2	2	0	0	4	1	.207	.281	.310	105	-0	1	5	0			1.000	-4	/OP	-0.3

■ **PAT KILHULLEN** Kilhullen, Joseph Isadore b: 8/10/1890, Carbondale, Pa. d: 11/2/22, Oakland, Cal. BR/TR, 5'9", 175 lbs. Deb: 6/10/14

YEAR	TM/L	G	AB	R	H	2B	3B	HR	RBI	BB	SO	AVG	OBP	SLG	PRO+	BR	/A	RC	SB	CS	SBR	FA	FR	POS	TPR
1914	Pit-N	1	1	0	0	0	0	0	0	0	0	.000	.000	.000	-99	-0	-0	0	0			.000	0	/C	0.0

■ **HARMON KILLEBREW** Killebrew, Harmon Clayton "Killer" b: 6/29/36, Payette, Idaho BR/TR, 5'11", 213 lbs. Deb: 6/23/54 H

YEAR	TM/L	G	AB	R	H	2B	3B	HR	RBI	BB	SO	AVG	OBP	SLG	PRO+	BR	/A	RC	SB	CS	SBR	FA	FR	POS	TPR
1954	Was-A	9	13	1	4	1	0	0	3	2	3	.308	.400	.385	122	0	0	2	0	0	0	1.000	-2	/2	-0.2
1955	Was-A	38	80	12	16	1	0	4	7	9	31	.200	.281	.363	76	-4	-3	8	0	0	0	.935	5	3/2	0.2
1956	Was-A	44	99	10	22	2	0	5	13	10	39	.222	.294	.394	80	-3	-3	11	0	0	0	.951	-0	3/2	-0.3
1957	Was-A	9	31	4	9	2	0	2	5	2	8	.290	.333	.548	139	1	1	6	0	0	0	.947	-1	/32	0.1
1958	Was-A	13	31	2	6	0	0	0	2	0	12	.194	.219	.194	15	-4	-4	1	0	0	0	1.000	0	/3	-0.3
1959	Was-A★	153	546	98	132	20	2	**42**	105	90	116	.242	.356	.516	137	27	27	103	3	2	-0	.938	-8	*3/O	2.0
1960	Was-A	124	442	84	122	19	1	31	80	71	106	.276	.377	.534	145	27	27	91	1	0	0	.987	-9	13	1.3
1961	Min-A★	150	541	94	156	20	7	46	122	107	109	.288	.409	.606	159	53	49	138	1	2	-1	.987	-10	*13/O	2.8
1962	Min-A	155	552	85	134	21	1	**48**	**126**	106	142	.243	.369	.545	137	33	30	113	1	2	-1	.967	-10	*O/1	1.1
1963	Min-A★	142	515	88	133	18	0	**45**	96	72	105	.258	.353	**.555**	147	33	32	99	0	0	0	.987	-3	*O	2.2
1964	Min-A★	158	577	95	156	11	1	**49**	111	93	135	.270	.379	.548	153	43	43	122	0	0	0	.971	-7	*O	3.0
1965	*Min-A★	113	401	78	108	16	1	25	75	72	69	.269	.386	.501	144	28	26	79	0	0	0	.988	-9	13/O	1.3
1966	Min-A★	162	569	89	160	27	1	39	110	**103**	98	.281	.393	.538	155	50	45	122	0	2	-1	.951	-17	*31O	2.3
1967	Min-A★	163	547	105	147	24	1	**44**	113	**131**	111	.269	.413	.558	170	62	57	131	1	0	0	.992	-8	*1/3	4.3
1968	Min-A★	100	295	40	62	7	2	17	40	70	70	.210	.365	.420	131	16	14	46	0	0	0	.994	3	13	1.3
1969	*Min-A★	162	555	106	153	20	2	**49**	**140**	**145**	84	.276	**.430**	.584	177	**66**	64	**146**	8	2	1	.929	-21	*31	4.0
1970	*Min-A★	157	527	96	143	20	1	41	113	128	84	.271	.416	.546	161	50	49	116	0	3	-2	.948	-29	*31	1.5
1971	Min-A★	147	500	61	127	19	1	28	**119**	**114**	96	.254	.393	.464	137	31	29	92	3	2	-0	.997	-15	13	0.5
1972	Min-A	139	433	53	100	13	2	26	74	94	91	.231	.369	.450	136	26	23	73	0	1	-1	.992	11	*1	2.6
1973	Min-A	69	248	29	60	9	1	5	32	41	59	.242	.352	.347	94	0	-1	31	0	0	0	.998	4	1/D	-0.1
1974	Min-A	122	333	28	74	7	0	13	54	45	61	.222	.315	.360	90	-2	-4	37	0	0	0	.992	2	D1	-0.4
1975	KC-A	106	312	25	62	13	0	14	44	54	70	.199	.319	.375	93	-2	-3	39	1	2	-1	1.000	-1	D/1	-0.5
Total	22	2435	8147	1283	2086	290	24	573	1584	1559	1699	.256	.379	.509	142	532	500	1609	19	18	-5	.992	-123	13OD/2	28.7

■ **RED KILLEFER** Killefer, Wade Hampton b: 4/13/1884, Bloomingdale, Mich d: 9/4/58, Los Angeles, Cal. BR/TR, 5'9", 175 lbs. Deb: 9/16/07 F

YEAR	TM/L	G	AB	R	H	2B	3B	HR	RBI	BB	SO	AVG	OBP	SLG	PRO+	BR	/A	RC	SB	CS	SBR	FA	FR	POS	TPR
1907	Det-A	1	4	0	0	0	0	0	0	0		.000	.000	.000	-97	-1	-1	0	0			1.000	0	/O	-0.1
1908	Det-A	28	75	9	16	1	0	0	11	3		.213	.253	.227	54	-4	-4	6	4			.956	-5	2/S3	-1.1
1909	Det-A	23	61	6	17	2	2	1	4	3		.279	.343	.426	137	3	3	9	2			.912	-1	2/O	0.1
	Was-A	40	121	11	21	1	0	0	5	13		.174	.265	.182	43	-8	-7	7	4			.957	-3	O/3C2S	-1.2
	Yr	63	182	17	38	3	2	1	9	16		.209	.291	.264	76	-5	-4	16	6			.957	-4	O2/3CS	-1.1
1910	Was-A	106	345	35	79	17	1	0	24	29		.229	.318	.284	93	-3	-1	39	17			.940	-4	2O	-0.8
1914	Cin-N	42	141	16	39	6	1	0	12	20	18	.277	.386	.333	111	4	3	22	11			.968	-4	O/23	-0.3
1915	Cin-N	155	555	75	151	25	11	1	41	38	33	.272	.340	.362	110	9	8	69	12	18	-7	.970	5	*O/1	-0.2
1916	Cin-N	70	234	29	57	9	1	1	18	21	8	.244	.327	.303	96	-1	-0	26	7			.966	-2	O	-0.6
	NY-N	2	1	0	1	0	0	0	1	1	0	1.000	1.000	1.000	544	1	1	1	0			.000	0	H	0.1

YEAR	TM/L	G	AB	R	H	2B	3B	HR	RBI	BB	SO	AVG	OBP	SLG	PRO+	BR	/A	RC	SB	CS	SBR	FA	FR	POS	TPR
	Yr	72	235	29	58	9	1	1	19	22	8	.247	.332	.306	99	0	1	27	7			.966	-2	O	-0.5
Total	7	467	1537	181	381	61	16	3	116	128	59	.248	.328	.314	98	0	1	179	57	18		.965	-15	O2/3SC1	-4.1

■ BILL KILLEFER

Killefer, William Lavier " b: 10/10/1887, Bloomingdale, Mich d: 7/3/60, Elsmere, Del. BR/TR, 5'10.5", 200 lbs. Deb: 9/13/09 FMC

YEAR	TM/L	G	AB	R	H	2B	3B	HR	RBI	BB	SO	AVG	OBP	SLG	PRO+	BR	/A	RC	SB	CS	SBR	FA	FR	POS	TPR
1909	StL-A	11	29	0	4	0	0	0	1	0		.138	.138	.138	-14	-4	-4	1	2			.905	2	C	-0.1
1910	StL-A	74	193	14	24	2	2	0	7	12		.124	.184	.155	7	-21	-19	6	0			.938	13	C	-0.1
1911	Phi-N	6	16	3	3	0	0	0	2	0	2	.188	.188	.188	5	-2	-2	1	0			.975	2	/C	0.0
1912	Phi-N	85	268	18	60	6	3	1	21	4	14	.224	.241	.280	40	-22	-24	20	6			.973	17	C	0.1
1913	Phi-N	120	360	25	88	14	3	0	24	4	17	.244	.255	.300	56	-20	-22	27	2			.988	18	*C/1	0.6
1914	Phi-N	98	299	27	70	10	1	0	27	8	17	.234	.261	.274	56	-16	-18	22	3			.978	18	C	0.8
1915	*Phi-N	105	320	26	76	9	2	0	24	18	14	.237	.287	.278	70	-11	-11	26	5	3	-0	.972	14	*C	1.1
1916	Phi-N	97	286	22	62	5	4	3	27	8	14	.217	.246	.294	63	-12	-13	22	2			**.985**	-1	C	-0.8
1917	Phi-N	125	409	28	112	12	0	0	31	15	21	.274	.306	.303	84	-6	-8	38	4			**.984**	10	*C/O	1.3
1918	*Chi-N	104	331	30	77	10	3	0	22	17	10	.233	.276	.281	68	-12	-13	27	5			.982	9	*C	0.5
1919	Chi-N	103	315	17	90	10	2	0	22	15	8	.286	.322	.330	96	-1	-2	35	5			**.987**	17	*C	2.6
1920	Chi-N	62	191	16	42	7	1	0	16	8	5	.220	.280	.267	56	-10	-11	15	2	2	-1	.977	18	C	1.2
1921	Chi-N	45	133	11	43	1	0	0	16	4	4	.323	.357	.331	83	-3	-3	15	3	3	-1	.964	-1	CM	-0.3
Total	13	1035	3150	237	751	86	21	4	240	113	126	.238	.273	.283	63	-141	-150	255	39	8		.976	137	*C/O1	6.9

■ GENE KIMBALL

Kimball, Eugene Boynton b: 8/31/1850, Rochester, N.Y. d: 8/2/1882, Rochester, N.Y. 5'10", 160 lbs. Deb: 5/04/1871

YEAR	TM/L	G	AB	R	H	2B	3B	HR	RBI	BB	SO	AVG	OBP	SLG	PRO+	BR	/A	RC	SB	CS	SBR	FA	FR	POS	TPR
1871	Cle-n	29	131	18	25	1	0	0	9	3	2	.191	.209	.198	19	-13	-12	7	5					2/SO	-0.8

■ DICK KIMBLE

Kimble, Richard Lewis b: 7/27/15, Buchtel, Ohio BL/TR, 5'9", 160 lbs. Deb: 8/20/45

YEAR	TM/L	G	AB	R	H	2B	3B	HR	RBI	BB	SO	AVG	OBP	SLG	PRO+	BR	/A	RC	SB	CS	SBR	FA	FR	POS	TPR
1945	Was-A	20	49	5	12	1	1	0	1	5	2	.245	.315	.306	88	-1	-1	5	0	0	0	.950	-3	S	-0.3

■ BRUCE KIMM

Kimm, Bruce Edward b: 6/29/51, Cedar Rapids, Iowa BR/TR, 5'11", 175 lbs. Deb: 5/04/76 C

YEAR	TM/L	G	AB	R	H	2B	3B	HR	RBI	BB	SO	AVG	OBP	SLG	PRO+	BR	/A	RC	SB	CS	SBR	FA	FR	POS	TPR
1976	Det-A	63	152	13	40	8	0	1	6	15	20	.263	.329	.336	91	-1	-1	17	4	3	-1	.970	4	C/D	0.4
1977	Det-A	14	25	2	2	1	0	0	1	0	4	.080	.115	.120	-34	-5	-5	0	0	1	-1	.958	3	C/D	-0.2
1979	Chi-N	9	11	0	1	0	0	0	0	0	0	.091	.091	.091	-46	-2	-2	0	0	1	-1	.969	2	/C	-0.1
1980	Chi-A	100	251	20	61	10	1	0	19	17	26	.243	.291	.291	60	-14	-13	19	1	3	-2	.985	-1	C	-1.3
Total	4	186	439	35	104	19	1	1	26	32	50	.237	.290	.292	62	-21	-22	37	5	8	-3	.977	8	C/D	-1.2

■ WALLY KIMMICK

Kimmick, Walter Lyons b: 5/30/1897, Turtle Creek, Pa. d: 7/24/89, Boswell, Pa. BR/TR, 5'11", 174 lbs. Deb: 9/13/19

YEAR	TM/L	G	AB	R	H	2B	3B	HR	RBI	BB	SO	AVG	OBP	SLG	PRO+	BR	/A	RC	SB	CS	SBR	FA	FR	POS	TPR
1919	StL-N	2	1	1	0	0	0	0	0	1	0	.000	.500	.000	61	0	0	0	1			1.000	0	/S	0.0
1921	Cin-N	3	6	0	1	0	0	0	1	0	1	.167	.167	.167	-12	-1	-1	0	0	0	0	.667	-0	/3	-0.1
1922	Cin-N	39	89	11	22	2	1	0	12	3	12	.247	.272	.292	46	-7	-7	7	0	0	0	.965	2	S/23	-0.3
1923	Cin-N	29	80	11	18	2	1	0	6	5	15	.225	.271	.275	45	-6	-6	7	3	0	1	.972	8	2/3S	0.3
1925	Phi-N	70	141	16	43	3	2	1	10	22	26	.305	.399	.376	91	1	-1	21	0	3	-2	.904	-3	S32	-0.3
1926	Phi-N	20	28	0	6	2	1	0	2	3	7	.214	.290	.357	70	-1	-1	3	0			1.000	-2	/1S32	-0.3
Total	6	163	345	39	90	9	5	1	31	34	61	.261	.327	.325	67	-15	-16	39	4	3		.933	4	/S231	-0.7

■ JERRY KINDALL

Kindall, Gerald Donald "Slim" b: 5/27/35, St.Paul, Minn. BR/TR, 6'2.5", 175 lbs. Deb: 7/01/56

YEAR	TM/L	G	AB	R	H	2B	3B	HR	RBI	BB	SO	AVG	OBP	SLG	PRO+	BR	/A	RC	SB	CS	SBR	FA	FR	POS	TPR
1956	Chi-N	32	55	7	9	1	1	0	0	6	17	.164	.246	.218	27	-6	-6	3	1	0	0	.956	2	S	-0.2
1957	Chi-N	72	181	18	29	3	0	6	12	8	48	.160	.196	.276	25	-19	-19	9	1	0	0	.920	-4	23/S	-2.1
1958	Chi-N	3	6	0	1	1	0	0	0	0	3	.167	.167	.333	29	-1	-1	0	0	0	0	1.000	1	/2	0.1
1960	Chi-N	89	246	17	59	16	2	2	23	5	52	.240	.255	.346	63	-13	-13	19	4	3	-1	.966	14	2/S	0.7
1961	Chi-N	96	310	37	75	22	3	9	44	18	89	.242	.288	.419	84	-8	-8	36	2	2	-1	.950	7	2S	0.6
1962	Cle-A	154	530	51	123	21	1	13	55	45	107	.232	.292	.349	74	-22	-20	53	4	3	-1	.978	21	*2	1.7
1963	Cle-A	86	234	27	48	4	1	5	20	18	71	.205	.268	.295	58	-13	-13	19	3	1	0	.958	3	S2/1	-0.5
1964	Cle-A	23	25	5	9	1	0	2	2	2	7	.360	.407	.640	188	3	3	6	0	0	0	.989	3	1	0.6
	Min-A	62	128	8	19	2	0	1	6	7	44	.148	.199	.188	8	-16	-16	5	0	0	0	.969	5	2/S1	-0.9
	Yr	85	153	13	28	3	0	3	8	9	51	.183	.233	.261	37	-13	-13	9	0	0	0	.969	8	21/S	-0.3
1965	Min-A	125	342	41	67	12	1	6	36	36	97	.196	.278	.289	59	-17	-19	29	2	2	-1	.963	-1	*23/S	-1.2
Total	9	742	2057	211	439	83	9	44	198	145	535	.213	.268	.327	62	-112	-111	180	17	11	-2	.967	50	2S/31	-1.2

■ RALPH KINER

Kiner, Ralph McPherran b: 10/27/22, Santa Rita, N.Mex. BR/TR, 6'2", 195 lbs. Deb: 4/16/46 H

YEAR	TM/L	G	AB	R	H	2B	3B	HR	RBI	BB	SO	AVG	OBP	SLG	PRO+	BR	/A	RC	SB	CS	SBR	FA	FR	POS	TPR
1946	Pit-N	144	502	63	124	17	3	**23**	81	74	109	.247	.345	.430	116	12	11	75	3			.969	1	*O	0.5
1947	Pit-N	152	565	118	177	23	4	**51**	127	98	81	.313	.417	**.639**	**172**	**61**	**59**	**154**	1			.983	13	*O	**6.2**
1948	Pit-N★	156	555	104	147	19	5	**40**	123	112	61	.265	.391	.533	145	39	37	120	1			.975	7	*O	3.5
1949	Pit-N★	152	549	116	170	19	5	**54**	**127**	**117**	61	.310	.432	**.658**	**183**	70	68	163	6			.979	-1	*O	**5.8**
1950	Pit-N★	150	547	112	149	21	6	**47**	118	122	79	.272	.408	.590	154	49	46	133	2			.965	-3	*O	3.5
1951	Pit-N★	151	531	**124**	164	31	6	**42**	109	**137**	57	.309	**.452**	**.627**	182	**71**	69	165	2	1	0	.967	-5	O1	5.6
1952	Pit-N☆	149	516	90	126	17	2	**37**	87	**110**	77	.244	.384	.500	140	33	31	111	3	0	1	.970	-6	*O	2.0
1953	Pit-N	41	148	27	40	6	1	7	29	25	21	.270	.383	.466	121	5	5	30	1	0	0	1.000	1	O	0.4
	Chi-N	117	414	73	117	14	2	28	87	75	67	.283	.394	.529	135	24	23	91	1	1	-0	.964	-4	*O	1.4
	Yr	158	562	100	157	20	3	35	116	100	88	.279	.391	.512	131	29	28	120	2	1	0	.973	-3	*O	1.8
1954	Chi-N	147	557	88	159	36	5	22	73	76	90	.285	.373	.487	121	18	17	101	2	0	1	.971	-0	*O	1.1
1955	Cle-A	113	321	56	78	13	0	18	54	65	46	.243	.370	.452	116	10	8	57	0	0	0	.986	-5	O	-0.1
Total	10	1472	5205	971	1451	216	39	369	1015	1011	749	.279	.398	.548	148	391	373	1201	22	2		.974	-2	*O/1	29.9

■ CHICK KING

King, Charles Gilbert b: 11/10/30, Paris, Tenn. BR/TR, 6'2", 190 lbs. Deb: 8/27/54

YEAR	TM/L	G	AB	R	H	2B	3B	HR	RBI	BB	SO	AVG	OBP	SLG	PRO+	BR	/A	RC	SB	CS	SBR	FA	FR	POS	TPR
1954	Det-A	11	28	4	6	0	1	0	3	3	8	.214	.290	.286	59	-2	-2	2	0	0	0	.958	1	/O	-0.1
1955	Det-A	7	21	3	5	0	0	0	0	1	2	.238	.273	.238	39	-2	-2	1	0	0	0	.923	-0	/O	-0.2
1956	Det-A	7	9	0	2	0	0	0	0	1	4	.222	.300	.222	40	-1	-1	1	0	0	0	.800	-1	/O	-0.2
1958	Chi-N	8	8	1	2	0	0	0	1	3	1	.250	.455	.250	95	0	0	1	0	0	0	1.000	-2	/O	-0.2
1959	Chi-N	7	3	3	0	0	0	0	0	0	1	.000	.000	.000	-99	-1	-1	0	0	0	0	1.000	-0	/O	-0.1
	StL-N	5	7	0	3	0	0	0	1	0	2	.429	.429	.429	121	0	0	1	0	0	0	1.000	-0	/O	0.0
	Yr	12	10	3	3	0	0	0	1	0	3	.300	.300	.300	59	-1	-1	1	0	0	0	1.000	-0	/O	-0.1
Total	5	45	76	11	18	0	1	0	5	8	18	.237	.310	.263	56	-5	-4	7	0	0	0	.947	-3	/O	-0.8

■ LEE KING

King, Edward Lee b: 3/28/1894, Waltham, Mass. d: 9/7/38, Newton Centre, Mass. BR/TR, 5'10", 160 lbs. Deb: 6/24/16

YEAR	TM/L	G	AB	R	H	2B	3B	HR	RBI	BB	SO	AVG	OBP	SLG	PRO+	BR	/A	RC	SB	CS	SBR	FA	FR	POS	TPR
1916	Phi-A	42	144	13	27	1	2	0	8	7	15	.188	.230	.222	38	-11	-11	9	4			1.000	-10	OS/32	-2.4
1919	Bos-N	2	1	0	0	0	0	0	0	0	0	.000	.000	.000	-99	-0	-0	0	0			.000	0	H	0.0
Total	2	44	145	13	27	1	2	0	8	7	15	.186	.229	.221	37	-12	-11	9	4			.980	-10	/OS32	-2.4

■ HAL KING

King, Harold b: 2/1/44, Oviedo, Fla. BL/TR, 6'1", 200 lbs. Deb: 9/06/67

YEAR	TM/L	G	AB	R	H	2B	3B	HR	RBI	BB	SO	AVG	OBP	SLG	PRO+	BR	/A	RC	SB	CS	SBR	FA	FR	POS	TPR
1967	Hou-N	15	44	2	11	1	2	0	6	2	9	.250	.283	.364	87	-1	-1	5	0	0	0	1.000	-2	C	-0.3
1968	Hou-N	27	55	4	8	2	1	0	2	7	16	.145	.242	.218	40	-4	-4	3	0	0	0	.968	-4	C	-0.8
1970	Atl-N	89	204	29	53	8	0	11	30	32	41	.260	.366	.461	113	6	4	35	1	0	0	.985	-11	C	-0.4
1971	Atl-N	86	198	14	41	9	0	5	19	29	43	.207	.320	.328	79	-4	-5	20	0	0	0	.983	-2	C	-0.5
1972	Tex-A	50	122	12	22	5	0	4	12	25	35	.180	.333	.320	99	0	1	14	0	0	0	.970	-7	C	-0.6
1973	*Cin-N	35	43	5	8	0	0	4	10	6	10	.186	.286	.465	110	0	0	6	0	0	0	1.000	-1	/C	0.0
1974	Cin-N	20	17	1	3	1	0	0	3	3	4	.176	.300	.235	52	-1	-1	1	0	0	0	1.000	0	/C	-0.1
Total	7	322	683	67	146	26	3	24	82	104	158	.214	.325	.366	93	-3	-5	85	1	0	0	.982	-27	C	-2.7

YEAR	TM/L	G	AB	R	H	2B	3B	HR	RBI	BB	SO	AVG	OBP	SLG	PRO+	BR	/A	RC	SB	CS	SBR	FA	FR	POS	TPR
■ **JIM KING**	King, James Hubert b: 8/27/32, Elkins, Ark. BL/TR, 6′, 185 lbs. Deb: 4/17/55																								
1955	Chi-N	113	301	43	77	12	3	11	45	24	39	.256	.315	.425	95	-3	-3	41	2	1	0	.990	5	O	-0.1
1956	Chi-N	118	317	32	79	13	2	15	54	30	40	.249	.316	.445	103	0	1	44	1	2	-1	.990	14	O	1.0
1957	StL-N	22	35	1	11	0	0	0	2	4	2	.314	.385	.314	89	-0	-0	4	0	0	0	1.000	-2	/O	-0.3
1958	SF-N	34	56	8	12	2	1	2	8	10	8	.214	.343	.393	96	-0	-0	8	0	1	-1	1.000	-2	O	-0.3
1961	Was-A	110	263	43	71	12	1	11	46	38	45	.270	.366	.449	118	7	7	46	4	0	1	.980	-6	O/C	-0.2
1962	Was-A	132	333	39	81	15	0	11	35	55	37	.243	.355	.387	101	1	2	49	4	2	0	.979	3	*O	-0.1
1963	Was-A	136	459	61	106	16	5	24	62	45	43	.231	.301	.444	106	2	2	60	3	0	1	.987	1	*O	-0.2
1964	Was-A	134	415	46	100	15	1	18	56	55	65	.241	.337	.412	108	4	5	60	3	1	0	.973	8	*O	0.8
1965	Was-A	120	258	46	55	10	2	14	49	44	50	.213	.339	.430	119	6	7	38	1	0	0	.993	-2	O	0.2
1966	Was-A	117	310	41	77	14	2	10	30	38	41	.248	.330	.403	111	4	4	41	4	0	1	.987	0	O	0.3
1967	Was-A	47	100	10	21	2	2	1	12	15	13	.210	.331	.300	91	-1	-1	11	1	1	-0	.962	-3	O/C	-0.5
	Chi-A	23	50	2	6	1	0	0	2	4	16	.120	.185	.140	-3	-6	-6	1	0	0	0	1.000	-2	O	-1.0
	Cle-A	19	21	2	3	0	0	0	0	1	2	.143	.182	.143	-3	-3	-3	1	0	0	0	1.000	-0	/O	-0.3
	Yr	89	171	14	30	3	2	1	14	20	31	.175	.273	.234	53	-10	-9	12	1	1	-0	.971	-5	O/C	-1.8
Total	11	1125	2918	374	699	112	19	117	401	363	401	.240	.328	.411	104	11	15	406	23	8	2	.984	13	O/C	-0.7
■ **JEFF KING**	King, Jeffrey Wayne b: 12/26/64, Marion, Ind. BR/TR, 6′1″, 175 lbs. Deb: 6/02/89																								
1989	Pit-N	75	215	31	42	13	3	5	19	20	34	.195	.270	.353	80	-7	-6	21	4	2	0	.995	-2	13/2S	-1.2
1990	*Pit-N	127	371	46	91	17	1	14	53	21	50	.245	.288	.410	93	-7	-5	40	3	3	-1	.938	16	*3/1	1.1
1991	Pit-N	33	109	16	26	1	1	4	18	14	15	.239	.331	.376	100	-0	0	14	3	1	0	.975	1	3	0.1
1992	*Pit-N	130	480	56	111	21	2	14	65	27	56	.231	.275	.371	82	-13	-13	47	4	6	-2	.953	-4	312/SO	-2.1
Total	4	365	1175	149	270	52	7	37	155	82	155	.230	.283	.380	87	-27	-23	121	14	12	-3	.948	12	3/12SO	-2.1
■ **LEE KING**	King, Lee b: 12/26/1892, Hundred, W.Va. d: 9/16/67, Shinnstown, W.Va. BR/TR, 5′8″, 160 lbs. Deb: 9/20/16																								
1916	Pit-N	8	18	0	2	0	0	0	1	0	7	.111	.111	.111	-31	-3	-3	0	0			.714	-1	/O	-0.5
1917	Pit-N	111	381	32	95	14	5	1	35	15	58	.249	.281	.320	81	-8	-9	35	8			.968	9	*O	-0.6
1918	Pit-N	36	112	9	26	3	2	1	11	11	15	.232	.301	.321	87	-1	-2	11	3			.909	-8	O	-1.3
1919	NY-N	21	20	5	2	1	0	0	1	1	6	.100	.143	.150	-12	-3	-3	0	0			.667	-3	/O	-0.6
1920	NY-N	93	261	32	72	11	4	7	42	21	38	.276	.335	.429	120	6	6	36	3	7	-3	.951	-11	O	-1.4
1921	NY-N	39	94	17	21	4	2	0	7	13	6	.223	.324	.309	68	-4	-4	10	0	2	-1	.921	-5	O/1	-1.2
	Phi-N	64	216	25	58	19	4	4	32	8	37	.269	.298	.449	88	-3	-5	27	1	4	-2	.911	-2	O	-1.3
	Yr	103	310	42	79	23	6	4	39	21	43	.255	.306	.406	83	-7	-9	37	1	6	-3	.914	-7	O/1	-2.5
1922	Phi-N	19	53	8	12	5	1	2	13	8	6	.226	.328	.472	95	0	-1	9	0	0	0	.946	-0	O	-0.2
	NY-N	20	34	6	6	3	0	0	2	5	2	.176	.282	.265	41	-3	-3	3	1	0	0	1.000	0	/1O	-0.3
	Yr	39	87	14	18	8	1	2	15	13	8	.207	.310	.391	76	-3	-4	11	1	0	0	.961	-0	O/1	-0.5
Total	7	411	1189	134	294	60	18	15	144	82	175	.247	.299	.366	87	-19	-23	131	16	13		.940	-21	O/1	-7.4
■ **LYNN KING**	King, Lynn Paul "Dig" b: 11/28/07, Villisca, Iowa d: 5/11/72, Atlantic, Iowa BL/TR, 5′9″, 165 lbs. Deb: 9/21/35																								
1935	StL-N	8	22	6	4	0	0	0	0	4	1	.182	.308	.182	34	-2	-2	1	2			1.000	2	/O	0.0
1936	StL-N	78	100	12	19	2	1	0	10	9	14	.190	.257	.230	32	-9	-9	6	2			.984	-4	O	-1.4
1939	StL-N	89	85	10	20	2	0	0	11	15	3	.235	.350	.259	62	-3	-4	9	2			.982	-10	O	-1.4
Total	3	175	207	28	43	4	1	0	21	28	18	.208	.302	.237	45	-15	-16	16	6			.986	-12	/O	-2.8
■ **MART KING**	King, Marshal Ney b: 12/1849, Troy, N.Y. d: 10/19/11, Troy, N.Y. TR, 5′9.5″, 176 lbs. Deb: 5/08/1871																								
1871	Chi-n	20	101	23	21	1	0	2	16	8	1	.208	.266	.277	51	-5	-8	9	5					O/CS	-0.5
1872	Tro-n	3	11	0	0	0	0	0	1	0	1	.000	.000	.000	-99	-2	-3	0						O	-0.2
Total	2 n	23	112	23	21	1	0	2	17	8	2	.188	.242	.250	39	-8	-11	9						/OCS	-0.7
■ **SAM KING**	King, Samuel Warren b: 5/17/1852, Peabody, Mass. d: 8/11/22, Peabody, Mass. TL, 6′, Deb: 5/01/1884																								
1884	Was-a	12	45	3	8	2	0	0		1		.178	.213	.222	50	-3	-2	2				.912	-1	1	-0.4
■ **STEVE KING**	King, Stephen F. b: 1844, Troy, N.Y. d: 7/8/1895, Troy, N.Y. 5′9″, 175 lbs. Deb: 5/09/1871																								
1871	Tro-n	29	144	45	57	10	6	0	34	1	1	.396	.400	.549	167	12	12	34	3					*O	0.8
1872	Tro-n	25	129	33	40	9	1	0	21	1	2	.310	.315	.395	116	2	2	16						O	0.2
Total	2 n	54	273	78	97	19	7	0	55	2	3	.355	.360	.476	144	15	14	50						/O	1.0
■ **WES KINGDON**	Kingdon, Westcott William b: 7/4/1900, Los Angeles, Cal. d: 4/19/75, Capistrano, Cal. BR/TR, 5′8″, 148 lbs. Deb: 6/12/32																								
1932	Was-A	18	34	10	11	3	1	0	3	5	2	.324	.410	.471	129	2	2	7	0	0	0	.929	-2	/3S	0.0
■ **MIKE KINGERY**	Kingery, Michael Scott b: 3/29/61, St.James, Minn. BL/TL, 6′, 180 lbs. Deb: 7/07/86																								
1986	KC-A	62	209	25	54	8	5	3	14	12	30	.258	.299	.388	83	-5	-5	23	7	3	0	.973	-3	O	-1.0
1987	Sea-A	120	354	38	99	25	4	9	52	27	43	.280	.334	.449	100	2	-0	51	7	9	-3	.992	10	*O/D	0.3
1988	Sea-A	57	123	21	25	6	0	1	9	19	23	.203	.315	.276	64	-5	-6	12	3	1	0	.989	-1	O1	-0.8
1989	Sea-A	31	76	14	17	3	0	2	6	7	14	.224	.289	.342	75	-2	-3	7	1	1	-0	1.000	3	O	-0.1
1990	SF-N	105	207	24	61	7	1	0	24	12	19	.295	.336	.338	89	-4	-3	25	6	1	1	.978	-12	O	-1.5
1991	SF-N	91	110	13	20	2	2	0	8	15	21	.182	.280	.236	48	-8	-7	8	1	0	0	.975	-7	O/1	-1.5
1992	Oak-A	12	28	3	3	0	0	0	1	1	3	.107	.138	.107	-32	-5	-5	0	0	0	0	1.000	-2	O	-0.7
Total	7	478	1107	138	279	51	12	15	114	93	153	.252	.312	.360	82	-26	-28	128	25	15	-1	.986	-13	O/1D	-5.3
■ **DAVE KINGMAN**	Kingman, David Arthur b: 12/21/48, Pendleton, Ore. BR/TR, 6′6″, 210 lbs. Deb: 7/30/71																								
1971	*SF-N	41	115	17	32	10	2	6	24	9	35	.278	.336	.557	151	7	7	22	5	0	2	.981	-3	1O	0.4
1972	SF-N	135	472	65	106	17	4	29	83	51	140	.225	.306	.462	114	8	7	67	16	6	1	.932	2	31O	0.6
1973	SF-N	112	305	54	62	10	1	24	55	41	122	.203	.302	.479	109	4	2	42	8	5	-1	.910	3	31/P	0.3
1974	SF-N	121	350	41	78	18	2	18	55	37	125	.223	.303	.440	101	1	-1	44	8	8	-2	.983	2	13/O	-0.7
1975	NY-N	134	502	65	116	22	1	36	88	34	153	.231	.285	.494	119	4	7	66	7	5	-1	.958	2	O13	0.3
1976	NY-N★	123	474	70	113	14	1	37	86	28	135	.238	.288	.506	130	10	13	65	7	4	-0	.959	2	*O1	0.9
1977	NY-N	58	211	22	44	7	0	9	28	13	66	.209	.264	.370	71	-10	-9	20	3	2	-0	.974	-4	O1	-1.6
	SD-N	56	168	16	40	9	0	11	39	12	48	.238	.297	.488	119	1	3	23	2	3	-1	.964	0	O1/3	0.0
	Yr	114	379	38	84	16	0	20	67	25	114	.222	.279	.422	92	-10	-6	43	5	5	-2	.970	-3	O1/3	-1.6
	Cal-A	10	36	4	7	2	0	2	4	1	16	.194	.237	.417	77	-1	-1	4	0	0	0	.974	-1	/1O	-0.2
	NY-A	8	24	5	6	2	0	4	7	2	13	.250	.333	.833	208	3	3	6	0	1	-1	.000	0	/D	0.3
	Yr	18	60	9	13	4	0	6	11	3	29	.217	.277	.583	131	2	2	9	0	1	-1	.974	-1	/1HO	0.1
1978	Chi-N	119	395	65	105	17	4	28	79	39	111	.266	.341	.542	128	21	15	73	3	4	-2	.978	-6	*O/1	0.4
1979	Chi-N†	145	532	97	153	19	5	**48**	115	45	131	.288	.348	**.613**	143	38	32	112	4	2	0	.954	-3	*O	2.4
1980	Chi-N★	81	255	31	71	8	0	18	57	21	44	.278	.333	.522	126	11	8	40	2	2	-1	.941	-1	O/1	0.5
1981	NY-N	100	353	40	78	11	3	22	59	55	105	.221	.328	.456	122	9	10	54	6	0	2	.974	-7	1O	0.0
1982	NY-N	149	535	80	109	9	1	**37**	99	59	156	.204	.288	.432	99	-3	-3	67	4	0	1	.986	-14	*1	-2.4
1983	NY-N	100	248	25	49	7	0	13	29	22	57	.198	.266	.383	79	-9	-8	26	2	1	0	.994	-5	1/O	-1.7
1984	Oak-A	147	549	68	147	23	1	35	118	44	119	.268	.329	.505	136	18	23	91	2	1	0	1.000	-2	*D/1	2.0
1985	Oak-A	158	592	66	141	16	0	30	91	62	114	.238	.313	.417	105	-3	3	75	3	2	-0	1.000	-1	*D/1	0.1
1986	Oak-A	144	561	70	118	19	0	35	94	33	126	.210	.258	.431	90	-16	-10	57	3	3	-1	.895	-1	*D/1	-1.2
Total	16	1941	6677	901	1575	240	25	442	1210	608	1816	.236	.305	.478	115	91	100	955	85	49	-4	.957	-34	O1D3/P	0.4

YEAR	TM/L	G	AB	R	H	2B	3B	HR	RBI	BB	SO	AVG	OBP	SLG	PRO+	BR	/A	RC	SB	CS	SBR	FA	FR	POS	TPR

■ HARRY KINGMAN Kingman, Henry Lees b: 4/3/1892, Tientsin, China d: 12/27/82, Oakland, Cal. BL/TL, 6'1.5", 165 lbs. Deb: 7/01/14

| 1914 | NY-A | 4 | 3 | 0 | 0 | 0 | 0 | 0 | 0 | 1 | 2 | .000 | .250 | .000 | -24 | -0 | -0 | 0 | 0 | | | 1.000 | -0 | /1 | -0.1 |

■ WALT KINLOCK Kinlock, Walter b: 1878, St.Joseph, Mo. Deb: 8/01/1895

| 1895 | StL-N | 1 | 3 | 0 | 1 | 0 | 0 | 0 | 0 | 0 | 2 | .333 | .333 | .333 | 75 | -0 | -0 | 0 | 0 | | | 1.000 | 1 | /3 | 0.0 |

■ BOB KINSELLA Kinsella, Robert Francis "Red" b: 1/5/1899, Springfield, Ill. d: 12/30/51, Los Angeles, Cal. BL/TR, 5'9.5", 165 lbs. Deb: 9/20/19

1919	NY-N	3	9	1	2	0	0	0	0	0	3	.222	.222	.222	34	-1	-1	1	1			.500	-2	/O	-0.3
1920	NY-N	1	3	0	1	0	0	0	1	0	2	.333	.333	.333	93	-0	-0	0	0	0	0	.500	-1	/O	-0.1
Total	2	4	12	1	3	0	0	0	1	0	5	.250	.250	.250	49	-1	-1	1	1	0		.500	-2	/O	-0.4

■ KINSLER Kinsler b: Staten Island, N.Y. Deb: 6/08/1893

| 1893 | NY-N | 1 | 3 | 1 | 0 | 0 | 0 | 0 | 0 | 0 | 1 | .000 | .250 | .000 | -30 | -1 | -1 | 0 | 0 | | | 1.000 | -0 | /1 | -0.1 |

■ TOM KINSLOW Kinslow, Thomas F. b: 1/12/1866, Washington, D.C. d: 2/22/01, Washington, D.C. BR/TR, 5'10", 160 lbs. Deb: 6/04/1886

1886	Was-N	3	8	1	2	0	0	0	1	0	1	.250	.250	.250	56	-0	-0	1	0			1.000	-0	/C	0.0
1887	NY-a	2	6	0	0	0	0	0	0	0		.000	.000	.000	-99	-2	-2	0	0			1.000	-0	/C	-0.1
1890	Bro-P	64	242	30	64	11	6	4	46	10	22	.264	.299	.409	85	-5	-8	31	2			.909	11	C	0.7
1891	Bro-N	61	228	22	54	6	0	0	33	9	22	.237	.266	.263	56	-13	-13	17	3			.922	-9	C	-1.5
1892	Bro-N	66	246	37	75	6	11	2	40	13	16	.305	.342	.443	144	10	11	40	4			.933	5	C	1.9
1893	Bro-N	78	312	38	76	8	4	4	45	11	13	.244	.272	.333	65	-18	-16	30	4			.932	-2	C/O	-0.9
1894	Bro-N	62	223	39	68	5	6	2	41	20	11	.305	.362	.408	94	-5	-2	36	4			.907	-9	C/1	-0.4
1895	Pit-N	19	62	10	14	2	0	0	5	2	2	.226	.250	.258	34	-6	-6	5	1			.962	-2	C	-0.5
1896	Lou-N	8	25	4	7	0	1	0	7	1	5	.280	.308	.360	80	-1	-1	3	0			.810	-2	C1	-0.1
1898	Was-N	3	9	0	1	0	0	0	0	0	1	.111	.111	.111	-36	-2	-2	0	0			.800	-1	/C1	-0.2
	StL-N	14	53	5	15	2	1	0	4	1		.283	.309	.358	89	-1	-1	6	0			.925	1	C	0.1
	Yr	17	62	5	16	2	1	0	4	1		.258	.281	.323	72	-2	-3	6	0			.909	0	C/1	-0.1
Total	10	380	1414	186	376	40	29	12	222	67	92	.266	.301	.361	83	-42	-37	168	18			.923	-7	C/1O	-1.0

■ WALT KINZIE Kinzie, Walter Harris b: 3/1858, Kansas d: 11/5/09, BR, 5'10.5", 161 lbs. Deb: 7/17/1882

1882	Det-N	13	53	5	5	0	1	0	2	0	8	.094	.094	.132	-28	-7	-7	1				.852	-4	S	-1.0
1884	Chi-N	19	82	4	13	3	0	2	8	0	13	.159	.159	.268	29	-6	-7	4				.831	-3	S/3	-0.9
	StL-a	2	9	0	1	0	0	0		0		.111	.111	.111	-25	-1	-1	0				.727	-3	/2	-0.4
Total	2	34	144	9	19	3	1	2	10	0	21	.132	.132	.208	6	-15	-16	4				.840	-9	/S23	-2.3

■ ED KIPPERT Kippert, Edward August "Kickapoo" b: 1/3/1880, Detroit, Mich. d: 6/3/60, Detroit, Mich. BR/TR, 5'10.5", 180 lbs. Deb: 4/14/14

| 1914 | Cin-N | 2 | 2 | 0 | 0 | 0 | 0 | 0 | 0 | 0 | 0 | .000 | .000 | .000 | -97 | -0 | -0 | 0 | 0 | | | 1.000 | -1 | /O | -0.1 |

■ JIM KIRBY Kirby, James Herschel b: 5/5/23, Nashville, Tenn. BR/TR, 5'11", 175 lbs. Deb: 5/01/49

| 1949 | Chi-N | 3 | 2 | 0 | 1 | 0 | 0 | 0 | 0 | 0 | 0 | .500 | .500 | .500 | 174 | 0 | 0 | 1 | 0 | | | .000 | 0 | H | 0.0 |

■ LA RUE KIRBY Kirby, La Rue b: 12/30/1889, Eureka, Mich. d: 6/10/61, Lansing, Mich. BB/TR, 6', 185 lbs. Deb: 8/07/12

1912	NY-N	3	5	1	1	1	0	0	0	0	0	.200	.200	.400	60	-0	-0	0	0			1.000	0	/P	0.0
1914	StL-F	52	195	21	48	6	3	2	18	14	30	.246	.303	.338	78	-5	-6	22	5			.973	2	O	-0.7
1915	StL-F	61	178	15	38	7	2	0	16	17	31	.213	.282	.275	61	-8	-9	16	3			.969	-3	O/P	-1.5
Total	3	116	378	37	87	14	5	2	34	31	61	.230	.292	.310	70	-13	-15	39	8			.971	-1	O/P	-2.2

■ WAYNE KIRBY Kirby, Wayne Leonard b: 1/22/64, Williamsburg, Va. BL/TR, 5'10", 185 lbs. Deb: 9/12/91

1991	Cle-A	21	43	4	9	2	0	0	5	2	6	.209	.244	.256	38	-4	-4	2	1	2	-1	1.000	-1	O	-0.6
1992	Cle-A	21	18	9	3	1	0	1	1	3	2	.167	.286	.389	86	-0	-0	1	0	3	-2	1.000	-0	/OD	-0.3
Total	2	42	61	13	12	3	0	1	6	5	8	.197	.258	.295	53	-4	-4	3	1	5	-3	1.000	-1	/OD	-0.9

■ TOM KIRK Kirk, Thomas Daniel b: 9/27/27, Philadelphia, Pa. d: 8/1/74, Philadelphia, Pa. BL/TL, 5'10.5", 182 lbs. Deb: 6/24/47

| 1947 | Phi-A | 1 | 1 | 0 | 0 | 0 | 0 | 0 | 0 | 0 | 0 | .000 | .000 | .000 | -98 | -0 | -0 | 0 | 0 | 0 | 0 | .000 | 0 | H | 0.0 |

■ JAY KIRKE Kirke, Judson Fabian b: 6/16/1888, Fleischmann's, N.Y d: 8/31/68, New Orleans, La. BL/TR, 6', 195 lbs. Deb: 9/28/10

1910	Det-A	8	25	3	5	1	0	0	3	1		.200	.231	.240	44	-2	-2	2	1			.917	-3	/2O	-0.5
1911	Bos-N	20	89	9	32	5	5	0	12	6	2	.360	.380	.528	142	6	5	19	3			.929	-1	0/12S3	0.3
1912	Bos-N	103	359	53	115	11	4	4	62	9	46	.320	.339	.407	102	0	/-1	51	7			.903	-2	O3/S1	-0.5
1913	Bos-N	18	38	3	9	2	0	0	3	1	6	.237	.293	.289	65	-2	-2	3	0			.923	2	O	0.0
1914	Cle-A	67	242	18	66	10	2	1	25	7	30	.273	.296	.343	89	-4	-5	23	5	10	-5	.974	0	O1	-1.2
1915	Cle-A	87	339	35	105	19	2	2	40	14	21	.310	.346	.395	120	7	7	47	5	6	-2	.986	-1	1	0.2
1918	NY-N	17	56	1	14	1	0	0	3	1	3	.250	.263	.268	63	-3	-2	4	0			.978	1	1	-0.3
Total	7	320	1148	122	346	49	13	7	148	35	112	.301	.328	.385	103	4	0	149	21	16		.927	-3	O1/32S	-2.0

■ WILLIE KIRKLAND Kirkland, Willie Charles b: 2/17/34, Siluria, Ala. BL/TR, 6'1", 206 lbs. Deb: 4/15/58

1958	SF-N	122	418	48	108	25	6	14	56	43	69	.258	.335	.447	107	2	4	64	3	2	-0	.961	-0	*O	-0.3
1959	SF-N	126	463	64	126	22	3	22	68	42	84	.272	.337	.475	116	8	9	75	5	3	-0	.969	1	*O	0.4
1960	SF-N	146	515	59	130	21	10	21	65	44	86	.252	.316	.454	115	4	8	74	12	7	-1	.978	4	*O	0.4
1961	Cle-A	146	525	84	136	22	5	27	95	48	77	.259	.322	.474	113	5	7	84	7	0	2	.974	8	*O	1.0
1962	Cle-A	137	419	56	84	9	1	21	72	43	62	.200	.275	.377	76	-17	-15	44	9	1	2	.972	0	*O	-1.9
1963	Cle-A	127	427	51	98	13	2	15	47	45	99	.230	.304	.375	90	-6	-6	50	8	2	1	.984	7	*O	-0.4
1964	Bal-A	66	150	14	30	5	0	3	22	17	26	.200	.286	.342	62	-8	-8	14	3	2	-0	.989	0	O	-1.0
	Was-A	32	102	8	22	6	0	5	13	6	30	.216	.259	.422	86	-2	-2	11	0	0	-0	.907	-3	O	-0.7
	Yr	98	252	22	52	11	0	8	35	23	56	.206	.275	.345	72	-10	-10	25	3	2	-0	.964	-3	O	-1.7
1965	Was-A	123	312	38	72	9	1	14	54	19	65	.231	.275	.401	91	-5	-5	33	3	2	-0	.987	-6	O	-1.6
1966	Was-A	124	163	21	31	2	1	6	17	16	50	.190	.263	.325	68	-7	-7	14	2	0	1	.983	-12	O	-2.1
Total	9	1149	3494	443	837	134	29	148	509	323	648	.240	.307	.422	99	-26	-15	463	52	19	4	.974	-2	O	-6.2

■ ED KIRKPATRICK Kirkpatrick, Edgar Leon b: 10/8/44, Spokane, Wash. BL/TR, 5'11.5", 195 lbs. Deb: 9/13/62

1962	LA-A	3	6	0	0	0	0	0	0	0	2	.000	.000	.000	-99	-2	-2	0	0	0	0	1.000	1	/C	-0.1
1963	LA-A	34	77	4	15	5	0	2	7	6	19	.195	.262	.338	71	-4	-3	7	1	0	0	.986	-0	CO	-0.3
1964	LA-A	75	219	20	53	13	3	2	22	23	30	.242	.320	.356	97	-3	-1	24	2	1	-1	.969	-2	O	-0.6
1965	Cal-A	19	73	8	19	5	0	3	8	3	9	.260	.289	.452	110	0	1	8	1	2	-1	.969	1	O	-0.1
1966	Cal-A	117	312	31	60	7	4	9	44	51	67	.192	.315	.327	87	-5	-4	35	7	4	-0	.994	-6	*O/1	-1.6
1967	Cal-A	3	8	0	0	0	0	0	0	0	2	.000	.000	.000	-99	-2	-2	0	0	0	0	1.000	-2	/CO	-0.5
1968	Cal-A	89	161	23	37	4	0	1	25	25	24	.230	.337	.273	90	-2	-1	16	1	3	-2	.982	-5	O/C1	1.2
1969	KC-A	120	315	40	81	11	4	14	49	43	42	.257	.352	.451	122	10	9	52	3	5	-2	.995	8	O/C132	1.2
1970	KC-A	134	424	59	97	17	2	18	62	55	65	.229	.319	.406	98	-1	-1	54	4	4	-1	.978	-8	CO1	-0.9
1971	KC-A	120	365	46	80	12	1	9	46	48	60	.219	.313	.332	83	-8	-7	37	3	4	-2	.992	-1	OC	-1.1
1972	KC-A	113	364	43	100	15	1	9	43	51	50	.275	.368	.396	128	14	14	55	3	5	-2	.991	-5	*C/1	1.3
1973	KC-A	126	429	61	113	24	3	6	45	46	48	.263	.336	.375	93	0	-0	52	3	7	-3	.990	-5	*OC/D	-1.7
1974	*Pit-N	116	271	32	67	9	0	6	38	51	30	.247	.370	.347	105	3	4	37	3	4	-2	.993	-3	1O/C	-0.4
1975	*Pit-N	89	144	15	34	14	0	1	15	16	22	.236	.321	.375	93	-2	-1	13	0	0	0	1.000	-1	1O	-0.4
1976	Pit-N	83	146	14	34	7	0	0	16	14	15	.233	.300	.295	69	-6	-6	13	0	0	0	.990	0	1/O3	-0.7

YEAR	TM/L	G	AB	R	H	2B	3B	HR	RBI	BB	SO	AVG	OBP	SLG	PRO+	BR	/A	RC	SB	CS	SBR	FA	FR	POS	TPR
1977	Pit-N	21	28	5	4	2	0	1	4	8	6	.143	.333	.321	75	-1	-1	3	1	0	0	.972	-0	1/O3	-0.1
	Tex-A	20	48	2	9	1	0	0	3	4	11	.188	.250	.208	26	-5	-5	3	2	0	1	1.000	1	/O1CD	-0.4
	Mil-A	29	77	8	21	4	0	0	6	10	8	.273	.364	.325	89	-1	-1	10	0	1	-1	.973	-2	O/3D	-0.4
	Yr	49	125	10	30	5	0	0	9	14	19	.240	.321	.280	65	-5	-6	12	2	1	0	.980	-2	O/D1C3	-0.8
Total	16	1311	3467	411	824	143	18	85	424	456	518	.238	.330	.363	97	-13	-11	424	34	39	-13	.989	-30	OC1/D32	-7.8

■ ENOS KIRKPATRICK

Kirkpatrick, Enos Claire b: 12/8/1885, Pittsburgh, Pa. d: 4/14/64, Pittsburgh, Pa. BR/TR, 5'10", 175 lbs. Deb: 8/24/12

YEAR	TM/L	G	AB	R	H	2B	3B	HR	RBI	BB	SO	AVG	OBP	SLG	PRO+	BR	/A	RC	SB	CS	SBR	FA	FR	POS	TPR
1912	Bro-N	32	94	13	18	1	1	0	6	9	15	.191	.269	.223	37	-8	-8	7	5			.968	6	3/S	-0.2
1913	Bro-N	48	89	13	22	4	1	1	5	3	18	.247	.287	.348	79	-2	-3	10	5			.897	-1	S/123	-0.4
1914	Bal-F	55	174	22	44	7	2	2	16	18	30	.253	.330	.351	91	-1	-2	24	10			.932	-5	3S/O1	-0.5
1915	Bal-F	68	171	22	41	8	2	0	19	24	15	.240	.337	.310	88	-1	-2	23	12			.911	-3	32/1S	-0.4
Total	4	203	528	70	125	20	6	3	46	54	78	.237	.315	.314	78	-13	-15	65	32			.936	-2	/3S21O	-1.5

■ JOE KIRRENE

Kirrene, Joseph John b: 10/4/31, San Francisco, Cal. BR/TR, 6'2", 195 lbs. Deb: 10/01/50

YEAR	TM/L	G	AB	R	H	2B	3B	HR	RBI	BB	SO	AVG	OBP	SLG	PRO+	BR	/A	RC	SB	CS	SBR	FA	FR	POS	TPR
1950	Chi-A	1	4	0	1	0	0	0	0	0	1	.250	.250	.250	29	-0	-0	0	0	0	0	1.000	-1	/3	-0.1
1954	Chi-A	9	23	4	7	1	0	0	4	5	2	.304	.448	.348	116	1	1	4	1	0	0	.947	-2	/3	-0.1
Total	2	10	27	4	8	1	0	0	4	5	3	.296	.424	.333	105	1	1	4	1	0	0	.952	-3	/3	-0.2

■ ERNIE KISH

Kish, Ernest Alexander b: 2/6/18, Washington, D.C. BL/TR, 5'9.5", 170 lbs. Deb: 7/29/45

YEAR	TM/L	G	AB	R	H	2B	3B	HR	RBI	BB	SO	AVG	OBP	SLG	PRO+	BR	/A	RC	SB	CS	SBR	FA	FR	POS	TPR
1945	Phi-A	43	110	10	27	5	1	0	10	9	9	.245	.320	.309	83	-2	-2	11	0	3	-2	.932	-4	O	-1.0

■ BILL KISSINGER

Kissinger, William Francis "Shang" b: 8/15/1871, Dayton, Ky. d: 4/20/29, Cincinnati, Ohio BR/TR, 185 lbs. Deb: 5/30/1895

YEAR	TM/L	G	AB	R	H	2B	3B	HR	RBI	BB	SO	AVG	OBP	SLG	PRO+	BR	/A	RC	SB	CS	SBR	FA	FR	POS	TPR
1895	Bal-N	2	5	1	1	0	0	0	0	0	1	.200	.200	.200	4	-1	-1	0	0			1.000	-0	/P	0.0
	StL-N	33	97	8	24	6	1	0	8	0	11	.247	.247	.330	50	-8	-7	8	1			.975	-4	P/SO3	-0.5
	Yr	35	102	9	25	6	1	0	8	0	12	.245	.245	.324	48	-8	-8	9	1			.976	-4	P/SO3	-0.5
1896	StL-N	23	73	8	22	4	0	0	12	0	4	.301	.301	.356	78	-3	-2	8	0			.906	0	P/O3	-0.2
1897	StL-N	14	39	7	13	3	2	0	6	3		.333	.381	.513	137	2	2	8	0			.786	-2	/OP	-0.1
Total	3	72	214	24	60	13	3	0	26	3	16	.280	.290	.369	74	-9	-9	25	1			.935	-6	/POS3	-0.8

■ CHRIS KITSOS

Kitsos, Christopher Anestos b: 2/11/28, New York, N.Y. BB/TR, 5'9", 165 lbs. Deb: 4/21/54

YEAR	TM/L	G	AB	R	H	2B	3B	HR	RBI	BB	SO	AVG	OBP	SLG	PRO+	BR	/A	RC	SB	CS	SBR	FA	FR	POS	TPR
1954	Chi-N	1	0	0	0	0	0	0	0	0	0	—	—	—	—	0	0	0	0	0	0	1.000	0	/S	0.0

■ RON KITTLE

Kittle, Ronald Dale b: 1/5/58, Gary, Indiana BR/TR, 6'4", 220 lbs. Deb: 9/02/82

YEAR	TM/L	G	AB	R	H	2B	3B	HR	RBI	BB	SO	AVG	OBP	SLG	PRO+	BR	/A	RC	SB	CS	SBR	FA	FR	POS	TPR
1982	Chi-A	20	29	3	7	2	0	1	7	3	12	.241	.313	.414	97	-0	-0	4	0	0	0	1.000	-2	/OD	-0.2
1983	*Chi-A★	145	520	75	132	19	3	35	100	39	150	.254	.316	.504	117	13	11	81	8	3	1	.964	-9	*O/D	-0.2
1984	Chi-A	139	466	67	100	15	0	32	74	49	137	.215	.298	.453	100	1	-2	62	3	6	-3	.972	3	*O/D	-0.5
1985	Chi-A	116	379	51	87	12	0	26	58	31	92	.230	.296	.467	101	1	-1	48	1	4	-2	.989	-3	OD	-0.7
1986	Chi-A	86	296	34	63	11	0	17	48	28	87	.213	.287	.422	87	-5	-6	34	2	1	0	1.000	2	DO	-0.5
	NY-A	30	80	8	19	2	0	4	12	7	23	.237	.299	.412	92	-1	-1	11	2	0	1	1.000	0	D/O	0.0
	Yr	116	376	42	82	13	0	21	60	35	110	.218	.290	.420	89	-6	-7	45	4	1	1	1.000	2	DO	-0.5
1987	NY-A	59	159	21	44	5	0	12	28	10	36	.277	.324	.535	123	4	5	26	0	1	-1	1.000	1	D/O	0.5
1988	Cle-A	75	225	31	58	8	0	18	43	16	65	.258	.329	.533	134	10	9	42	0	0	0	.000	0	D	1.0
1989	Chi-A	51	169	26	51	10	0	11	37	22	42	.302	.385	.556	166	14	14	37	0	1	-1	.982	-3	1D/O	0.8
1990	Chi-A	83	277	29	68	14	0	16	43	24	77	.245	.313	.469	118	5	5	41	0	0	0	.987	-4	D1	0.0
	Bal-A	22	61	4	10	2	0	2	3	2	14	.164	.203	.295	39	-5	-5	3	0	0	0	1.000	-1	D/1	-0.6
	Yr	105	338	33	78	16	0	18	46	26	91	.231	.293	.438	104	-1	0	43	0	0	0	.989	-5	D1	-0.6
1991	Chi-A	17	47	7	9	0	0	2	7	5	9	.191	.296	.319	72	-2	-2	4	0	0	0	.982	-1	1	-0.4
Total	10	843	2708	356	648	100	3	176	460	236	744	.239	.309	.473	110	35	28	392	16	16	-5	.974	-17	OD/1	-0.8

■ MALACHI KITTRIDGE

Kittridge, Malachi Jedediah "Jedediah" b: 10/12/1869, Clinton, Mass. d: 6/23/28, Gary, Ind. BR/TR, 5'7", 170 lbs. Deb: 4/19/1890 M

YEAR	TM/L	G	AB	R	H	2B	3B	HR	RBI	BB	SO	AVG	OBP	SLG	PRO+	BR	/A	RC	SB	CS	SBR	FA	FR	POS	TPR
1890	Chi-N	96	333	46	67	8	3	3	35	39	53	.201	.287	.270	62	-14	-17	29	7			.944	2	*C	-0.6
1891	Chi-N	79	296	26	62	8	5	2	27	17	28	.209	.252	.291	59	-16	-16	23	4			.940	-0	C	-0.8
1892	Chi-N	69	229	19	41	5	0	0	10	11	27	.179	.217	.201	27	-20	-20	11	2			.946	14	C	-0.1
1893	Chi-N	70	255	32	59	9	5	2	30	17	15	.231	.279	.329	64	-14	-14	25	3			.939	6	C	-0.2
1894	Chi-N	51	168	36	53	8	2	0	23	26	20	.315	.407	.387	89	-0	-2	29	2			.925	2	C	0.3
1895	Chi-N	60	212	30	48	6	3	3	29	16	9	.226	.284	.325	55	-13	-16	23	6			.976	-1	C	-0.9
1896	Chi-N	65	215	17	48	4	1	1	19	14	14	.223	.274	.265	42	-17	-19	18	6			.962	1	C/P	-0.8
1897	Chi-N	79	262	25	53	5	5	1	30	22		.202	.264	.271	40	-23	-24	22	9			.952	3	C	-1.1
1898	Lou-N	86	287	27	70	8	5	1	31	15		.244	.281	.317	73	-12	-11	30	9			.944	-11	C	-1.2
1899	Lou-N	45	129	11	26	2	1	0	12	26		.202	.340	.233	58	-6	-6	14	3			.974	8	C	0.5
	Was-N	44	133	14	20	3	0	0	11	10		.150	.215	.173	7	-17	-17	6	2			.949	5	C	-0.8
	Yr	89	262	25	46	5	1	0	23	36		.176	.280	.202	33	-23	-23	19	5			.961	13	C	-0.3
1901	Bos-N	114	381	24	96	14	0	2	40	32		.252	.312	.304	73	-10	-14	39	2			**.984**	12	*C	0.9
1902	Bos-N	80	255	18	60	7	0	2	30	24		.235	.304	.286	81	-5	-5	25	4			.981	4	C	0.7
1903	Bos-N	32	99	10	21	2	0	0	6	11		.212	.291	.232	52	-6	-6	8	1			.981	5	C	0.2
	Was-A	60	192	8	41	4	1	0	16	10		.214	.252	.245	49	-12	-12	13	1			.978	-3	C	-0.9
1904	Was-A	81	265	11	64	7	0	0	24	8		.242	.266	.268	70	-9	-9	21	2			.982	1	CM	0.0
1905	Was-A	77	238	16	39	8	0	0	14	15		.164	.213	.197	32	-19	-17	12	1			.978	4	C	-0.6
1906	Was-A	22	68	5	13	0	0	0	3	1		.191	.203	.191	25	-6	-6	3	0			.946	-2	C	-0.7
	Cle-A	5	10	0	1	0	0	0	0	0		.100	.100	.100	-38	-2	-2	0	0			.938	-1	/C	-0.2
	Yr	27	78	5	14	0	0	0	3	1		.179	.190	.179	17	-7	-7	3	0			.945	-3	C	-0.9
Total	16	1215	4027	375	882	108	31	17	390	314	166	.219	.277	.274	57	-220	-231	350	64			.961	49	*C/P	-6.3

■ BOBBY KLAUS

Klaus, Robert Francis b: 12/27/37, Spring Grove, Ill. BR/TR, 5'10", 170 lbs. Deb: 4/21/64 F

YEAR	TM/L	G	AB	R	H	2B	3B	HR	RBI	BB	SO	AVG	OBP	SLG	PRO+	BR	/A	RC	SB	CS	SBR	FA	FR	POS	TPR
1964	Cin-N	40	93	10	17	5	1	2	6	4	13	.183	.216	.323	48	-6	-7	7	1	0	0	.972	4	23/S	-0.2
	NY-N	56	209	25	51	8	3	2	11	25	30	.244	.325	.340	90	-3	-2	24	3	4	-2	.986	-3	23/S	-0.5
	Yr	96	302	35	68	13	4	4	17	29	43	.225	.293	.334	76	-9	-9	30	4	4	-1	.981	1	23/S	-0.7
1965	NY-N	119	288	30	55	12	0	2	12	45	49	.191	.302	.253	61	-15	-13	24	1	6	-3	.968	15	2S3	0.4
Total	2	215	590	65	123	25	4	6	29	74	92	.208	.298	.295	69	-24	-23	54	5	10	-5	.973	16	2/3S	-0.3

■ BILLY KLAUS

Klaus, William Joseph b: 12/9/28, Fox Lake, Ill. BL/TR, 5'10", 165 lbs. Deb: 4/16/52 F

YEAR	TM/L	G	AB	R	H	2B	3B	HR	RBI	BB	SO	AVG	OBP	SLG	PRO+	BR	/A	RC	SB	CS	SBR	FA	FR	POS	TPR
1952	Bos-N	7	4	3	0	0	0	0	0	1	1	.000	.200	.000	-42	-1	-1	0	0	0	0	.500	-1	/S	-0.2
1953	Mil-N	2	2	1	0	0	0	0	1	0	0	.000	.000	.000	-99	-1	-1	0	0	0	0	.000	0	H	-0.1
1955	Bos-A	135	541	83	153	26	2	7	60	60	44	.283	.354	.377	89	-2	-8	78	6	0	2	.955	-7	*S/3	-0.3
1956	Bos-A	135	520	91	141	29	5	7	59	90	43	.271	.380	.387	92	5	-4	83	1	0	0	.945	-4	*3S	-0.4
1957	Bos-A	127	477	76	120	18	4	10	42	55	53	.252	.329	.369	85	-6	-10	59	2	0	1	.961	11	*S	1.4
1958	Bos-A	61	88	5	14	4	0	1	7	5	16	.159	.204	.239	20	-10	-10	4	0	0	0	.883	-6	S	-1.6
1959	Bal-A	104	321	33	80	11	0	3	25	51	38	.249	.352	.312	86	-5	-4	37	2	4	-2	.970	-12	S3/2	-1.4
1960	Bal-A	46	43	8	9	2	0	1	6	9	9	.209	.346	.326	84	-1	-1	5	0	0	0	.960	8	2S/3	0.8
1961	Was-A	91	251	26	57	8	2	7	30	30	34	.227	.314	.359	81	-7	-7	30	2	2	-1	.961	-5	3S/2O	-1.0
1962	Phi-N	102	248	30	51	8	2	4	20	29	43	.206	.291	.302	61	-14	-13	23	1	1	-0	.983	-6	3S2	-1.6
1963	Phi-N	11	18	1	1	0	0	0	0	1	4	.056	.105	.056	-53	-3	-3	0	0	0	0	1.000	-2	/S3	-0.6
Total	11	821	2513	357	626	106	15	40	250	331	285	.249	.337	.351	82	-45	-62	320	14	7	0	.955	-24	S3/2O	-5.0

■ OLLIE KLEE

Klee, Ollie Chester "Babe" b: 5/20/1900, Piqua, Ohio d: 2/9/77, Toledo, Ohio BL/TL, 5'9.5", 160 lbs. Deb: 8/10/25

YEAR	TM/L	G	AB	R	H	2B	3B	HR	RBI	BB	SO	AVG	OBP	SLG	PRO+	BR	/A	RC	SB	CS	SBR	FA	FR	POS	TPR
1925	Cin-N	3	1	0	0	0	0	0	0	0	1	.000	.000	.000	-99	-0	-0	0	0	0	0	.000	-1	/O	-0.1

■ CHUCK KLEIN

Klein, Charles Herbert b: 10/7/04, Indianapolis, Ind. d: 3/28/58, Indianapolis, Ind. BL/TR, 6', 185 lbs. Deb: 7/30/28 CH

YEAR	TM/L	G	AB	R	H	2B	3B	HR	RBI	BB	SO	AVG	OBP	SLG	PRO+	BR	/A	RC	SB	CS	SBR	FA	FR	POS	TPR
1928	Phi-N	64	253	41	91	14	4	11	34	14	22	.360	.396	.577	146	18	16	55	0			.978	1	O	1.3
1929	Phi-N	149	616	126	219	45	6	**43**	145	54	61	.356	.407	.657	149	53	47	158	5			.966	-2	*O	3.2
1930	Phi-N	156	648	**158**	250	**59**	8	40	170	54	50	.386	.436	.687	155	67	60	186	4			.960	23	*O	**6.2**
1931	Phi-N	148	594	**121**	200	34	10	**31**	**121**	59	49	.337	.398	**.584**	149	**49**	**43**	**140**	7			.971	-5	*O	2.8
1932	Phi-N	154	650	**152**	**226**	50	15	**38**	137	60	49	.348	.404	**.646**	158	**68**	58	**171**	**20**			.960	9	*O	**5.6**
1933	Phi-N★	152	606	101	**223**	**44**	7	**28**	**120**	56	36	**.368**	**.422**	**.602**	168	**69**	**60**	**162**	15			.986	9	*O	**6.2**
1934	Chi-N★	115	435	78	131	27	2	20	80	47	38	.301	.372	.510	136	20	22	86	3			.962	-3	*O	1.4
1935	*Chi-N	119	434	71	127	14	4	21	73	41	42	.293	.355	.488	123	14	14	76	4			.958	-1	*O	0.9
1936	Chi-N	29	109	19	32	5	0	5	18	16	14	.294	.384	.477	128	5	5	21	0			.917	1	O	0.4
	Phi-N	117	492	83	152	30	7	20	86	33	45	.309	.352	.520	120	20	13	92	6			.930	-4	*O	0.4
	Yr	146	601	102	184	35	7	25	104	49	59	.306	.358	.512	122	25	18	114	6			.927	-4	*O	0.8
1937	Phi-N	115	406	74	132	20	2	15	57	39	21	.325	.386	.495	127	21	17	81	3			.949	-4	*O	0.9
1938	Phi-N	129	458	53	113	22	2	8	61	38	30	.247	.304	.356	83	-12	-11	52	7			.960	-3	*O	-1.7
1939	Phi-N	25	47	8	9	2	1	1	9	10	4	.191	.333	.340	84	-1	-1	6	1			1.000	-0	O/1	-0.1
	Pit-N	85	270	37	81	16	4	11	47	26	17	.300	.361	.511	134	11	12	50	1			.951	-2	O	0.8
	Yr	110	317	45	90	18	5	12	56	36	21	.284	.357	.486	127	10	11	57	2			.958	-2	O/1	0.7
1940	Phi-N	116	354	39	77	16	2	7	37	44	30	.218	.304	.333	79	-12	-10	37	2			.984	-3	O	-1.8
1941	Phi-N	50	73	6	9	0	0	1	3	10	6	.123	.229	.164	12	-8	-8	3	0			.958	-1	O	-1.0
1942	Phi-N	14	14	0	1	0	0	0	0	0	2	.071	.071	.071	-61	-3	-3	0	0			.000	0	H	-0.3
1943	Phi-N	12	20	0	2	0	0	0	3	0	3	.100	.100	.100	-44	-4	-4	0	1			.000	-1	/O	-0.5
1944	Phi-N	4	7	1	1	0	0	0	0	0	2	.143	.143	.143	-20	-1	-1	0	0			1.000	1	/O	-0.1
Total	17	1753	6486	1168	2076	398	74	300	1201	601	521	.320	.379	.543	135	375	330	1378	79			.962	16	*O/1	24.6

■ LOU KLEIN

Klein, Louis Frank b: 10/22/18, New Orleans, La. d: 6/20/76, Metaire, La. BR/TR, 5'11", 170 lbs. Deb: 4/21/43 MC

YEAR	TM/L	G	AB	R	H	2B	3B	HR	RBI	BB	SO	AVG	OBP	SLG	PRO+	BR	/A	RC	SB	CS	SBR	FA	FR	POS	TPR
1943	*StL-N	154	627	91	180	28	14	7	62	50	70	.287	.342	.410	112	12	9	91	9			.973	-19	*2S	0.0
1945	StL-N	19	57	12	13	4	1	1	6	14	9	.228	.389	.386	113	2	2	10	0			.929	-0	/SO32	0.2
1946	StL-N	23	93	12	18	3	0	1	4	9	7	.194	.265	.258	47	-6	-7	7	1			.975	-3	2	-0.9
1949	StL-N	58	114	25	25	6	0	2	12	22	20	.219	.355	.325	80	-2	-3	15	0			.890	-4	S/23	-0.6
1951	Cle-A	2	2	0	0	0	0	0	0	0	1	.000	.000	.000	-99	-1	-1	0	0	0	0	.000	0	H	-0.1
	Phi-A	49	144	22	33	7	0	5	17	10	12	.229	.279	.382	76	-5	-6	15	0	0	0	.975	-4	2	-0.8
	Yr	51	146	22	33	7	0	5	17	10	13	.226	.276	.377	74	-6	-6	15	0	0	0	.975	-4	2	-0.9
Total	5	305	1037	162	269	48	15	16	101	105	119	.259	.330	.381	97	-1	-5	139	10	0		.975	-30	2/S3O	-2.2

■ RED KLEINOW

Kleinow, John Peter b: 7/20/1879, Milwaukee, Wis. d: 10/9/29, New York, N.Y. BR/TR, 5'10", 165 lbs. Deb: 5/03/04

YEAR	TM/L	G	AB	R	H	2B	3B	HR	RBI	BB	SO	AVG	OBP	SLG	PRO+	BR	/A	RC	SB	CS	SBR	FA	FR	POS	TPR
1904	NY-A	68	209	12	43	8	4	0	16	15		.206	.259	.282	68	-7	-8	17	4			.966	-6	C/3O	-0.9
1905	NY-A	88	253	23	56	6	3	1	24	20		.221	.278	.281	70	-6	-10	23	7			.978	-8	C/1	-1.0
1906	NY-A	96	268	30	59	9	3	0	31	24		.220	.287	.276	70	-7	-10	26	8			.972	-1	C/1	-0.3
1907	NY-A	90	269	30	71	6	4	0	26	24		.264	.327	.316	97	2	-0	31	5			.967	-13	C/1	-0.6
1908	NY-A	96	279	16	47	3	2	1	13	22		.168	.232	.204	42	-17	-18	14	5			.973	-4	C/2	-1.7
1909	NY-A	78	206	24	47	11	4	0	15	25		.228	.315	.320	100	1	0	23	7			.966	-3	C	0.4
1910	NY-A	6	12	2	5	0	0	0	2	1		.417	.462	.417	166	1	1	3	2			1.000	0	/C	0.2
	Bos-A	50	147	9	22	1	0	1	8	20		.150	.251	.177	34	-11	-11	7	3			.968	5	C	-0.2
	Yr	56	159	11	27	1	0	1	10	21		.170	.267	.195	44	-9	-10	9	5			.970	5	C	0.0
1911	Bos-A	8	14	0	3	0	0	0	0	2		.214	.313	.214	48	-1	-1	1	1			1.000	0	/C	0.0
	Phi-N	4	8	0	1	1	0	0	0	0	1	.125	.125	.250	4	-1	-1	0	0			1.000	-0	/C	-0.1
Total	8	584	1665	146	354	45	20	3	135	153	1	.213	.280	.269	70	-46	-57	147	42			.971	-30	C/123O	-4.2

■ RYAN KLESKO

Klesko, Ryan Anthony b: 6/12/71, Westminster, Cal. BL/TL, 6'3", 220 lbs. Deb: 9/12/92

YEAR	TM/L	G	AB	R	H	2B	3B	HR	RBI	BB	SO	AVG	OBP	SLG	PRO+	BR	/A	RC	SB	CS	SBR	FA	FR	POS	TPR
1992	Atl-N	13	14	0	0	0	0	0	1	0	5	.000	.067	.000	-74	-3	-3	0	0	0	0	1.000	-1	/1	-0.4

■ JAY KLEVEN

Kleven, Jay Allen b: 12/2/49, Oakland, Cal. BR/TR, 6'2", 190 lbs. Deb: 6/20/76

YEAR	TM/L	G	AB	R	H	2B	3B	HR	RBI	BB	SO	AVG	OBP	SLG	PRO+	BR	/A	RC	SB	CS	SBR	FA	FR	POS	TPR
1976	NY-N	2	5	0	1	0	0	0	2	0	1	.200	.200	.200	15	-1	-1	0	0	0	0	1.000	0	/C	0.0

■ LOU KLIMCHOCK

Klimchock, Louis Stephen b: 10/15/39, Hostetter, Pa. BL/TR, 5'11", 180 lbs. Deb: 9/27/58

YEAR	TM/L	G	AB	R	H	2B	3B	HR	RBI	BB	SO	AVG	OBP	SLG	PRO+	BR	/A	RC	SB	CS	SBR	FA	FR	POS	TPR
1958	KC-A	2	10	2	2	0	0	1	1	0	1	.200	.200	.500	84	-0	-0	1	0	0	0	1.000	-1	/2	-0.1
1959	KC-A	17	66	10	18	1	0	4	13	1	6	.273	.284	.470	101	-0	-0	8	0	0	0	.949	-4	2	-0.3
1960	KC-A	10	10	0	3	0	0	0	0	0	0	.300	.300	.300	62	-1	-1	1	0	0	0	.000	0	/2	-0.1
1961	KC-A	57	121	8	26	4	1	1	16	5	13	.215	.246	.289	42	-10	-10	9	0	0	0	.976	-5	1/O32	-1.7
1962	Mil-N	8	8	0	0	0	0	0	0	0	2	.000	.000	.000	-99	-2	-2	0	0	0	0	.000	0	H	-0.2
1963	Was-A	9	14	1	2	0	0	0	2	0	1	.143	.143	.143	-20	-2	-2	0	0	0	0	1.000	1	/2	-0.1
	Mil-N	24	46	6	9	1	0	0	1	0	12	.196	.196	.217	19	-5	-5	2	0	1	-1	.988	0	1	-0.6
1964	Mil-N	10	21	3	7	2	0	0	2	1	2	.333	.364	.429	121	1	1	3	0	0	0	1.000	-3	/32	-0.2
1965	Mil-N	34	39	3	3	0	0	0	3	2	8	.077	.122	.077	-42	-7	-7	0	0	0	0	.923	1	/1	-0.7
1966	NY-N	5	5	0	0	0	0	0	0	0	3	.000	.000	.000	-99	-1	-1	0	0	0	0	.000	0	H	-0.1
1968	Cle-A	11	15	0	2	0	0	0	3	1	0	.133	.188	.133	-2	-2	-2	0	0	0	0	.500	-3	/312	-0.5
1969	Cle-A	90	258	26	74	13	2	6	26	18	14	.287	.333	.422	107	3	2	36	0	0	0	.934	-16	32/C	-1.3
1970	Cle-A	41	56	5	9	0	0	1	2	3	9	.161	.217	.214	18	-6	-7	3	0	0	0	1.000	-1	/12	-0.8
Total	12	318	669	64	155	21	3	13	69	31	71	.232	.267	.330	63	-33	-35	63	0	1	-1	.906	-30	/3210C	-6.7

■ BOBBY KLINE

Kline, John Robert b: 1/27/29, St.Petersburg, Fla BR/TR, 6', 179 lbs. Deb: 4/11/55

YEAR	TM/L	G	AB	R	H	2B	3B	HR	RBI	BB	SO	AVG	OBP	SLG	PRO+	BR	/A	RC	SB	CS	SBR	FA	FR	POS	TPR
1955	Was-A	77	140	12	31	5	0	0	9	11	27	.221	.288	.257	50	-10	-9	11	0	0	0	.943	13	S/23P	0.7

■ JOHNNY KLING

Kling, John "Noisy" b: 2/25/1875, Kansas City, Mo. d: 1/31/47, Kansas City, Mo. BR/TR, 5'9.5", 160 lbs. Deb: 9/11/00 FM

YEAR	TM/L	G	AB	R	H	2B	3B	HR	RBI	BB	SO	AVG	OBP	SLG	PRO+	BR	/A	RC	SB	CS	SBR	FA	FR	POS	TPR
1900	Chi-N	15	51	8	15	3	1	0	7	2		.294	.321	.392	100	-0	-0	7	0			.901	-3	C	-0.1
1901	Chi-N	74	256	26	70	6	3	0	21	9		.273	.301	.320	83	-7	-5	28	8			.952	-11	C/1O	-0.9
1902	Chi-N	114	431	49	123	19	3	0	57	29		.285	.330	.343	111	4	5	60	24			.974	5	*C/S	2.4
1903	Chi-N	132	491	67	146	29	13	3	68	22		.297	.330	.428	119	7	9	80	23			.969	2	*C	2.4
1904	Chi-N	123	452	41	110	18	0	2	46	16		.243	.269	.296	75	-14	-14	41	7			.974	-11	*CO/1	-1.5
1905	Chi-N	111	380	26	83	8	6	1	52	28		.218	.272	.279	62	-17	-19	35	13			.966	0	*C/O1	-0.8
1906	*Chi-N	107	343	45	107	15	8	2	46	23		.312	.357	.420	135	16	13	59	14			**.982**	5	C/O	3.0
1907	*Chi-N	104	334	44	95	15	8	1	43	27		.284	.342	.386	121	10	8	49	9			**.987**	7	C/1	2.7
1908	*Chi-N	126	424	51	117	23	5	4	59	21		.276	.315	.382	117	9	7	55	16			.979	2	*C/O1	2.2
1910	*Chi-N	91	297	31	80	17	2	2	32	37	27	.269	.354	.360	109	4	4	39	3			.979	-5	C	0.8
1911	Chi-N	27	80	8	14	3	2	1	5	8	14	.175	.250	.300	53	-5	-5	6	1			.969	5	C	0.2
	Bos-N	75	241	32	54	8	1	2	24	30	29	.224	.310	.290	63	-10	-13	22	0			.951	-5	C/3	-1.1
	Yr	102	321	40	68	11	3	3	29	38	43	.212	.295	.293	61	-15	-18	28	1			.956	-0	C/3	-0.9
1912	Bos-N	81	252	26	80	10	3	2	30	15	30	.317	.356	.405	106	2	2	37	3			.958	5	CM	1.3
1913	Cin-N	80	209	20	57	7	6	0	23	14	14	.273	.318	.364	95	-2	-2	24	2			.975	9	C	1.3
Total	13	1260	4241	474	1151	181	61	20	513	281	114	.271	.318	.357	100	-4	-10	540	123			.971	4	*C/O13S	11.9

YEAR	TM/L	G	AB	R	H	2B	3B	HR	RBI	BB	SO	AVG	OBP	SLG	PRO+	BR	/A	RC	SB	CS	SBR	FA	FR	POS	TPR

■ RUDY KLING
Kling, Rudolph A.　b: 3/23/1870, St.Louis, Mo.　d: 3/14/37, St.Louis, Mo.　BR/TR, 5'10", 178 lbs.　Deb: 9/21/02

| 1902 | StL-N | 4 | 10 | 1 | 2 | 0 | 0 | 0 | 0 | 4 | | .200 | .429 | .200 | 99 | 0 | 0 | 2 | 1 | | | .842 | -2 | /S | -0.1 |

■ JOE KLINGER
Klinger, Joseph John　b: 8/2/02, Canonsburg, Pa.　d: 7/31/60, Little Rock, Ark.　BR/TR, 6', 190 lbs.　Deb: 9/13/27

1927	NY-N	3	5	0	2	0	0	0	0	0	2	.400	.400	.400	115	0	0	1	0			1.000	0	/O	0.0
1930	Chi-A	4	8	0	3	0	0	0	1	0	0	.375	.375	.375	94	-0	-0	1	0	0	0	1.000	-1	/C1	-0.1
Total	2	7	13	0	5	0	0	0	1	0	2	.385	.385	.385	102	0	0	2	0	0		.845	-1	/1CO	-0.1

■ NAP KLOZA
Kloza, John Clarence　b: 9/7/03, Poland　d: 6/11/62, Milwaukee, Wis.　BR/TR, 5'11", 180 lbs.　Deb: 8/16/31

1931	StL-A	3	7	1	1	0	0	0	1	4		.143	.250	.143	5	-1	-1	0	0	0	0	1.000	-0	/O	-0.1
1932	StL-A	19	13	4	2	0	1	0	2	4		.154	.353	.308	69	-0	-1	2	0	0	0	1.000	-1	/O	-0.2
Total	2	22	20	5	3	0	1	0	2	5		.150	.320	.250	48	-1	-2	2	0	0	0	1.000	-2	/O	-0.3

■ JOE KLUGMANN
Klugmann, Joe　b: 3/26/1895, St.Louis, Mo.　d: 7/18/51, Moberly, Mo.　BR/TR, 5'11", 175 lbs.　Deb: 9/23/21

1921	Chi-N	6	21	3	6	0	0	0	2	1	2	.286	.348	.286	69	-1	-1	2	0	1	-1	.969	0	/2	-0.1
1922	Chi-N	2	2	0	0	0	0	0	0	0	0	.000	.000	.000	-98	-1	-1	0	0	0	0	1.000	1	/2	0.0
1924	Bro-N	31	79	7	13	2	1	0	3	2	9	.165	.185	.215	7	-10	-10	3	0	0	0	.929	-1	2/S	-1.1
1925	Cle-A	38	85	12	28	9	2	0	12	8	4	.329	.387	.482	119	2	2	16	3	1	0	.959	-3	2/13	-0.0
Total	4	77	187	22	47	11	3	0	17	11	15	.251	.296	.342	67	-9	-9	21	3	2	-0	.947	-3	/213S	-1.2

■ ELMER KLUMPP
Klumpp, Elmer Edward　b: 8/26/06, St.Louis, Mo.　BR/TR, 6', 184 lbs.　Deb: 4/17/34

1934	Was-A	12	15	2	2	0	0	0	0	0	1	.133	.188	.133	-17	-3	-3	0	0	0	0	.889	-1	C	-0.3
1937	Bro-N	5	11	0	1	0	0	0	2	1	4	.091	.167	.091	-28	-2	-2	0	0	0		1.000	1	/C	-0.1
Total	2	17	26	2	3	0	0	0	2	1	5	.115	.179	.115	-21	-5	-4	1	0	0		.943	-0	/C	-0.4

■ BILLY KLUSMAN
Klusman, William F.　b: 3/24/1865, Cincinnati, Ohio　d: 6/24/07, Cincinnati, Ohio　BR/TR, 5'10.5", 185 lbs.　Deb: 6/21/1888

1888	Bos-N	28	107	9	18	4	0	2	11	5	13	.168	.205	.262	49	-6	-6	7	3			.914	-9	2	-1.4
1890	StL-a	15	65	9	18	4	1	1		1		.277	.288	.415	96	0	-1	8	1			.896	-3	2	-0.3
Total	2	43	172	18	36	8	1	3	11	6	13	.209	.236	.320	68	-6	-7	15	4			.908	-12	/2	-1.7

■ TED KLUSZEWSKI
Kluszewski, Theodore Bernard "Big Klu"　b: 9/10/24, Argo, Ill.　d: 3/29/88, Cincinnati, Ohio　BL/TL, 6'2", 225 lbs.　Deb: 4/18/47　C

1947	Cin-N	9	10	1	1	0	0	0	2	1	2	.100	.182	.100	-23	-2	-2	0	0			1.000	-0	/1	-0.2
1948	Cin-N	113	379	49	104	23	4	12	57	18	32	.274	.307	.451	107	-1	1	48	1			.990	1	1	0.2
1949	Cin-N	136	531	63	164	26	2	8	68	19	24	.309	.333	.411	97	-3	-3	70	3			.989	-7	*1	-1.1
1950	Cin-N	134	538	76	165	37	5	25	111	33	28	.307	.348	.515	123	16	16	89	3			.987	-11	*1	0.1
1951	Cin-N	154	607	74	157	35	2	13	77	35	33	.259	.301	.387	83	-15	-17	69	6	2	1	.997	-6	*1	-3.0
1952	Cin-N	135	497	62	159	24	11	16	86	47	29	.320	.383	.509	146	30	30	97	3	3	-1	.993	-10	*1	1.5
1953	Cin-N★	149	570	97	180	25	0	40	108	55	34	.316	.380	.570	142	35	34	126	2	0	1	.995	-18	*1	1.1
1954	Cin-N★	149	573	104	187	28	3	49	141	78	35	.326	.410	.642	165	57	55	151	0	2	-1	.996	-4	*1	4.2
1955	Cin-N★	153	612	116	192	25	0	47	113	66	40	.314	.384	.585	144	45	40	136	1	1	-0	.995	-9	*1	2.2
1956	Cin-N★	138	517	91	156	14	1	35	102	49	31	.302	.366	.536	130	27	23	99	1	0		.990	-5	*1	1.0
1957	Cin-N	69	127	12	34	7	0	6	21	5	5	.268	.301	.465	95	-0	-1	17	0	1		.989	0	1	-0.3
1958	Pit-N	100	301	29	88	13	4	4	37	26	16	.292	.351	.402	101	-1	-1	41	0	0	0	.994	-5	1	-0.9
1959	Pit-N	60	122	11	32	10	1	2	17	5	14	.262	.291	.410	85	-3	-3	14	0	0	0	1.000	-1	1	-0.5
	*Chi-A	31	101	11	30	2	1	2	10	9	10	.297	.355	.396	107	1	1	13	0	1	-1	1.000	-2	1	-0.4
1960	Chi-A	81	181	20	53	9	0	5	39	22	10	.293	.369	.425	116	4	4	29	0	1	-1	.997	-2	1	-0.1
1961	LA-A	107	263	32	64	12	0	15	39	24	23	.243	.307	.460	91	-1	-4	37	0	1	-1	.989	-5	1	-1.4
Total	15	1718	5929	848	1766	290	29	279	1028	492	365	.298	.354	.498	122	190	175	1036	20	10		.993	-82	*1	2.4

■ MICKEY KLUTTS
Klutts, Gene Ellis　b: 9/20/54, Montebello, Cal.　BR/TR, 5'11", 189 lbs.　Deb: 7/07/76

1976	NY-A	2	3	0	0	0	0	0	0	0	1	.000	.000	.000	-99	-1	-1	0	0	0	0	.875	0	/S	0.0
1977	NY-A	5	15	3	4	1	0	1	4	2	1	.267	.389	.533	150	1	1	3	0	1	-1	1.000	2	/3S	0.3
1978	NY-A	1	2	1	2	1	0	0	0	0	0	1.000	1.000	1.500	608	2	2	3	0	0	0	.750	-2	/3	0.2
1979	Oak-A	24	73	3	14	2	1	1	4	7	20	.192	.262	.288	51	-5	-5	5	0	1	-1	.882	-4	S/23	-0.8
1980	Oak-A	75	197	20	53	14	0	4	21	13	41	.269	.314	.401	102	-2	-0	22	1	4	-2	.947	-6	3/S2D	-0.8
1981	*Oak-A	15	46	9	17	0	0	5	11	2	9	.370	.396	.696	220	6	6	13	0	0	0	.957	-5	3	0.1
1982	Oak-A	55	157	10	28	8	0	0	14	9	18	.178	.223	.229	26	-16	-15	8	0	0	0	.946	-3	3	-1.9
1983	Tor-A	22	43	3	11	0	0	3	5	1	11	.256	.289	.465	98	-0	-0	5	0	0	0	1.000	-3	3/D	-0.4
Total	8	199	536	49	129	26	1	14	59	34	101	.241	.290	.371	84	-16	-12	60	1	7	-4	.948	-18	3/S2D	-3.3

■ CLYDE KLUTTZ
Kluttz, Clyde Franklin　b: 12/12/17, Rockwell, N.C.　d: 5/12/79, Salisbury, N.C.　BR/TR, 6', 198 lbs.　Deb: 4/20/42

1942	Bos-N	72	210	21	56	10	1	1	31	7	13	.267	.294	.338	86	-5	-4	20	0			.979	0	C	0.0
1943	Bos-N	66	207	13	51	7	0	0	20	15	9	.246	.297	.280	68	-9	-8	17	0			.973	2	C	-0.2
1944	Bos-N	81	229	20	64	12	2	2	19	13	14	.279	.318	.376	91	-2	-3	28	0			.980	4	C	0.4
1945	Bos-N	25	81	9	24	4	1	0	10	2	6	.296	.313	.370	89	-1	-1	8	0			.987	-0	C	-0.1
	NY-N	73	222	25	62	14	0	4	21	15	10	.279	.331	.396	100	-0	-1	29	1			.978	-6	C	-0.3
	Yr	98	303	34	86	18	1	4	31	17	16	.284	.326	.389	97	-2	-2	37	1			.981	-6	C	-0.4
1946	NY-N	5	8	0	3	0	0	0	1	0	1	.375	.375	.375	112	0	0	1	0			.857	-1	/C	0.0
	StL-N	52	136	8	36	7	0	0	14	10	10	.265	.315	.316	76	-4	-4	14	0			.980	2	C	0.2
	Yr	57	144	8	39	7	0	0	15	10	11	.271	.318	.319	78	-4	-4	15	0			.976	1	C	0.0
1947	Pit-N	73	232	26	70	9	2	6	42	17	16	.302	.355	.435	106	3	2	37	1			.987	3	C	0.9
1948	Pit-N	94	271	26	60	12	2	4	20	20	19	.221	.275	.325	61	-15	-16	25	3			.978	0	C	-1.0
1951	StL-A	4	4	2	2	1	0	0	1	0		.500	.600	.750	256	1	1	2	0	0	0	1.000	1	/C	0.2
	Was-A	53	159	15	49	9	1	0	22	20	8	.308	.389	.384	111	3	3	26	0	0	0	.968	-7	C	-0.2
	Yr	57	163	17	51	10	1	0	23	21	8	.313	.395	.393	115	4	4	27	0	0	0	.968	-6	C	-0.1
1952	Was-A	58	144	7	33	5	0	1	11	12	11	.229	.293	.285	63	-8	-7	11	0	0	0	.979	-1	C	-0.6
Total	9	656	1903	172	510	90	8	19	212	132	119	.268	.318	.354	86	-37	-39	218	5	0		.978	-3	C	-0.9

■ OTTO KNABE
Knabe, Franz Otto "Dutch"　b: 6/12/1884, Carrick, Pa.　d: 5/17/61, Philadelphia, Pa.　BR/TR, 5'8", 175 lbs.　Deb: 10/03/05　M

1905	Pit-N	3	10	0	3	1	0	0	2	3		.300	.462	.400	154	1	1	2	0			.786	0	/3	0.1
1907	Phi-N	129	444	67	113	16	9	1	34	52		.255	.339	.338	114	7	8	64	18			.960	1	*2/O	0.9
1908	Phi-N	151	555	63	121	26	8	0	27	49		.218	.290	.294	84	-8	-10	57	27			.969	11	*2	-0.1
1909	Phi-N	113	402	40	94	13	3	0	34	35		.234	.308	.281	82	-7	-8	39	9			.938	7	*2/O	-0.3
1910	Phi-N	137	510	73	133	18	6	1	44	47	42	.261	.327	.325	87	-6	-8	62	15			.954	14	*2	0.3
1911	Phi-N	142	528	99	125	15	6	1	42	94	35	.237	.352	.294	80	-10	-11	64	23			.950	4	*2	-1.0
1912	Phi-N	126	426	56	120	11	4	0	46	55	20	.282	.366	.326	85	-4	-7	57	16			.952	1	*2	-0.9
1913	Phi-N	148	571	70	150	25	7	2	53	45	26	.263	.320	.342	85	-8	-11	68	14			.959	12	*2	-0.2
1914	Bal-F	147	469	45	106	26	2	2	42	53	28	.226	.307	.303	72	-15	-17	51	10			.956	1	*2M	-1.8
1915	Bal-F	103	308	38	81	16	2	1	25	37	16	.263	.334	.325	91	-2	-3	40	7			.975	7	2/OM	0.6
1916	Pit-N	28	89	4	17	3	0	0	2	9	7	.191	.258	.247	55	-5	-5	7	1			.962	-0	2	-0.5
	Chi-N	51	145	17	40	8	0	0	7	9	18	.276	.327	.331	92	0	-1	17	3			.939	6	2/S3O	0.6
	Yr	79	234	21	57	11	0	0	16	15	24	.244	.300	.299	79	-4	-6	24	4			.948	5	2/S3O	0.1
Total	11	1278	4469	572	1103	178	48	6	365	485	191	.247	.320	.313	86	-56	-73	529	143			.957	64	*2/O3S	-2.3

YEAR	TM/L	G	AB	R	H	2B	3B	HR	RBI	BB	SO	AVG	OBP	SLG	PRO+	BR	/A	RC	SB	CS	SBR	FA	FR	POS	TPR

■ COTTON KNAUPP
Knaupp, Henry Antone　b: 8/13/1889, San Antonio, Tex.　d: 7/6/67, New Orleans, La.　BR/TR, 5'9", 165 lbs.　Deb: 8/30/10

1910	Cle-A	18	59	3	14	3	1	0	11	8		.237	.338	.322	105	1	1	1	1			.884	-8	S	-0.8
1911	Cle-A	13	39	2	4	1	0	0	0	0		.103	.103	.128	-35	-7	-7	1	3			.964	2	S	-0.5
Total	2	31	98	5	18	4	1	0	11	8		.184	.252	.245	48	-6	-7	8	4			.913	-6	/S	-1.3

■ ALAN KNICELY
Knicely, Alan Lee　b: 5/19/55, Harrisonburg, Va.　BR/TR, 6'0.5", 194 lbs.　Deb: 8/12/79

1979	Hou-N	7	6	0	0	0	0	0	0	2	3	.000	.250	.000	-27	-1	-1	0	0	0	0	1.000	-2	/C3	-0.3
1980	Hou-N	1	1	0	0	0	0	0	0	0	1	.000	.000	.000	-99	-0	-0	0	0	0	0	.000	0	/H	0.0
1981	Hou-N	3	7	2	4	0	0	2	2	0	1	.571	.571	1.429	477	3	3	6	0	0	0	1.000	1	/CO	0.4
1982	Hou-N	59	133	10	25	2	0	2	12	14	30	.188	.270	.248	50	-9	-8	9	0	1	-1	.977	-7	CO/3	-1.6
1983	Cin-N	59	98	11	22	3	0	2	10	16	28	.224	.333	.316	78	-2	-3	9	0	2	-1	1.000	-1	C/O1	-0.5
1984	Cin-N	10	29	0	4	0	0	0	5	3	6	.138	.219	.138	2	-4	-4	1	0	0	0	.984	-1	/1C	-0.5
1985	Cin-N	48	158	17	40	9	0	5	26	16	34	.253	.326	.405	98	1	-0	20	0	0	0	.968	-14	C	-1.2
	Phi-N	7	7	0	0	0	0	0	0	0	4	.000	.000	.000	-97	-2	-2	0	0	0	0	1.000	-0	/1	-0.2
	Yr	55	165	17	40	9	0	5	26	16	38	.242	.313	.388	91	-1	-2	19	0	0	0	.968	-14	C/1	-1.4
1986	StL-N	34	82	8	16	3	0	1	6	17	21	.195	.333	.268	68	-3	-3	9	1	1	-0	.995	-1	1/C	-0.6
Total	8	228	521	48	111	17	0	12	61	68	128	.213	.306	.315	73	-18	-18	53	1	4	-2	.979	-24	C/1O3	-4.5

■ AUSTIN KNICKERBOCKER
Knickerbocker, Austin Jay　b: 10/15/18, Bangall, N.Y.　BR/TR, 5'11", 185 lbs.　Deb: 4/19/47

| 1947 | Phi-A | 21 | 48 | 8 | 12 | 3 | 2 | 0 | 2 | 3 | 4 | .250 | .294 | .396 | 89 | -1 | -1 | 5 | 0 | 1 | -1 | .943 | 0 | O | -0.2 |

■ BILL KNICKERBOCKER
Knickerbocker, William Hart　b: 12/29/11, Los Angeles, Cal.　d: 9/8/63, Sebastopol, Cal.　BR/TR, 5'11", 170 lbs.　Deb: 4/12/33

1933	Cle-A	80	279	20	63	16	3	2	32	11	30	.226	.255	.326	51	-20	-21	22	1	4	-2	.939	2	S	-1.6
1934	Cle-A	146	593	82	188	32	5	4	67	25	40	.317	.347	.408	93	-6	-8	82	6	6	-2	.962	-7	*S	-0.7
1935	Cle-A	132	540	77	161	34	5	0	55	27	31	.298	.332	.380	82	-14	-15	64	2	12	-7	.956	9	*S	-0.5
1936	Cle-A	155	618	81	182	35	3	8	73	56	30	.294	.354	.400	85	-14	-15	85	5	14	-7	.952	-1	*S	-1.1
1937	StL-A	121	491	53	128	29	5	4	61	30	32	.261	.303	.365	67	-26	-26	55	3	2	-0	.958	-13	*S/2	-2.9
1938	NY-A	46	128	15	32	8	3	1	21	11	10	.250	.309	.383	73	-6	-6	16	0	0	0	.982	2	2/S	-0.5
1939	NY-A	6	13	2	2	1	0	0	1	0	0	.154	.154	.231	-3	-2	-2	0	0	0	0	1.000	2	/2S	0.0
1940	NY-A	45	124	19	30	8	1	1	10	14	8	.242	.333	.347	80	-4	-3	15	1	1	-0	.985	-3	S3	-0.4
1941	Chi-A	89	343	51	84	23	2	7	29	41	27	.245	.329	.385	89	-6	-6	46	6	5	-1	.970	-17	2	-1.7
1942	Phi-A	87	289	25	73	12	0	1	19	29	30	.253	.323	.304	77	-8	-8	28	1	2	-1	.964	-12	2/S	-1.7
Total	10	907	3418	423	943	198	27	28	368	244	238	.276	.326	.374	79	-107	-110	413	25	46	-20	.955	-42	S2/3	-11.1

■ LON KNIGHT
Knight, Alonzo P.　b: 6/16/1853, Philadelphia, Pa.　d: 4/23/32, Philadelphia, Pa.　BR/TR, 5'11.5", 165 lbs.　Deb: 9/04/1875　MU

1875	Ath-n	13	47	4	6	2	0	0			0	.128	.128	.170	2	-4	-5	1						P	0.0
1876	Phi-N	55	240	32	60	9	3	0	24	2	2	.250	.256	.313	89	-3	-3	20				.804	-7	P1/O2	-0.6
1880	Wor-N	49	201	31	48	11	3	0	21	5	8	.239	.257	.323	88	-1	-3	17				.863	5	O	0.0
1881	Det-N	83	340	67	92	16	3	1	52	23	21	.271	.317	.344	104	4	2	38				.890	1	*O/21	0.1
1882	Det-N	86	347	39	72	12	6	0	24	16	21	.207	.242	.277	66	-13	-13	24				.867	1	*O/1	-0.3
1883	Phi-a	97	429	98	108	23	9	1		21		.252	.287	.354	97	3	-3	45				.858	0	*O/32M	-0.1
1884	Phi-a	108	484	94	131	18	12	1		10		.271	.287	.364	106	6	2	52				.911	11	*O/P1M	0.9
1885	Phi-a	29	119	17	25	1	1	0		9		.210	.271	.235	60	-4	-6	8				.921	4	O/P	-0.2
	Pro-N	25	81	8	13	1	0	0	8	11	17	.160	.261	.173	44	-5	-4	4				.957	1	O/P	-0.3
Total	7	532	2241	386	549	91	37	3	129	97	69	.245	.277	.323	90	-13	-28	207				.887	17	O/P123	-1.5

■ RAY KNIGHT
Knight, Charles Ray　b: 12/28/52, Albany, Ga.　BR/TR, 6'2", 190 lbs.　Deb: 9/10/74

1974	Cin-N	14	11	1	2	1	0	0	2	1	2	.182	.250	.273	47	-1	-1	1	0	0	0	1.000	1	3	0.0
1977	Cin-N	80	92	8	24	5	1	1	13	9	16	.261	.327	.370	85	-2	-2	12	1	1	-0	.941	5	32/OS	0.3
1978	Cin-N	83	65	7	13	3	0	1	4	3	13	.200	.235	.292	47	-5	-5	3	0	0	0	.868	6	3/201S	0.1
1979	*Cin-N	150	551	64	175	37	4	10	79	38	57	.318	.365	.454	121	16	16	85	4	4	-1	.962	-16	*3	-0.3
1980	Cin-N★	162	618	71	163	39	7	14	78	36	62	.264	.309	.417	101	-1	-1	72	1	2	-1	.969	-15	*3	-2.1
1981	Cin-N	106	386	43	100	23	1	6	34	33	51	.259	.324	.370	95	-2	-3	42	2	4	-2	.957	-13	*3	-2.2
1982	Hou-N★	158	609	72	179	36	6	6	70	48	58	.294	.350	.402	119	8	14	83	2	5	-2	.990	-2	13	0.2
1983	Hou-N	145	507	43	154	36	4	9	70	42	62	.304	.362	.444	130	15	19	77	0	3	-2	.993	-11	*1	-0.2
1984	Hou-N	88	278	15	62	10	0	2	29	14	30	.223	.263	.281	57	-18	-15	20	0	1	-0	.946	-2	31	-2.2
	NY-N	27	93	13	26	4	0	1	6	7	13	.280	.337	.355	96	-1	-0	11	0	0	0	.962	-4	3/1	-0.5
	Yr	115	371	28	88	14	0	3	35	21	43	.237	.282	.299	67	-18	-16	31	0	1	-0	.951	-6	31	-2.7
1985	NY-N	90	271	22	59	12	0	6	36	13	32	.218	.256	.328	64	-14	-13	18	1	1	-0	.958	-11	3/21	-2.7
1986	*NY-N	137	486	51	145	24	2	11	76	40	63	.298	.357	.424	118	9	11	70	2	0	0	.948	-11	*3/1	-0.3
1987	Bal-A	150	563	46	144	24	0	14	65	39	90	.256	.311	.373	82	-16	-14	63	0	0	0	.956	10	*3D/1	-0.6
1988	Det-A	105	299	34	65	12	2	3	33	20	30	.217	.273	.301	63	-16	-14	23	1	1	-0	.991	-3	1D3/O	-2.3
Total	13	1495	4829	490	1311	266	27	84	595	343	579	.271	.325	.390	99	-26	-10	579	14	25	-11	.957	-67	*31/D2OS	-12.8

■ JOHN KNIGHT
Knight, John Wesley "Schoolboy"　b: 10/6/1885, Philadelphia, Pa.　d: 12/19/65, Walnut Creek, Cal.　BR/TR, 6'2.5", 180 lbs.　Deb: 4/14/05

1905	Phi-A	88	325	28	66	12	1	3	29	9		.203	.227	.274	58	-16	-17	23	4			.895	-28	S/3	-4.8
1906	Phi-A	74	253	29	49	7	2	3	20	19		.194	.250	.273	62	-11	-11	20	6			.922	1	3/2	-1.0
1907	Phi-A	40	139	6	29	7	1	0	12	10		.209	.272	.273	72	-4	-4	11	1			.862	3	3/2	-0.4
	Bos-A	98	360	31	78	9	3	2	29	19		.217	.256	.275	70	-13	-12	28	8			.924	8	3/2	-0.2
	Yr	138	499	37	107	16	4	2	41	29		.214	.260	.275	71	-17	-17	40	9			.906	8	*3/2	-0.6
1909	NY-A	116	360	46	85	8	5	0	40	37		.236	.311	.286	88	-4	-4	38	15			.901	1	S12	-0.3
1910	NY-A	117	414	58	129	25	4	3	45	34		.312	.372	.413	138	21	19	72	23			.929	-1	S1/230	2.3
1911	NY-A	132	470	69	126	16	7	3	62	42		.268	.342	.351	88	-4	-8	63	18			.907	3	S12/3	-0.2
1912	Was-A	32	93	10	15	2	1	0	9	16		.161	.284	.204	40	-7	-7	7	4			.926	-1	2/1	-1.2
1913	NY-A	70	250	24	59	10	0	2	24	25	27	.236	.310	.276	72	-8	-9	23	7			.980	8	12	-0.2
Total	8	767	2664	301	636	96	24	14	270	211	27	.239	.300	.309	84	-45	-54	285	86			.909	-14	S312/O	-5.8

■ JOE KNIGHT
Knight, Jonas William "Quiet Joe"　b: 9/28/1859, Point Stanley, Ont., Canada　d: 10/18/38, St.Thomas, Ont., Can.　BL/TL, 5'11", 185 lbs.　Deb: 5/16/1884

1884	Phi-N	6	24	2	6	3	0	0	2	0	2	.250	.250	.375	98	-0	-0	2				.789	-0	/P	0.0
1890	Cin-N	127	481	67	150	26	8	4	67	38	31	.312	.367	.424	133	19	19	83	17			.925	-6	*O	0.8
Total	2	133	505	69	156	29	8	4	69	38	33	.309	.362	.422	132	19	19	85	17			.977	-6	O/P	0.8

■ PETE KNISELY
Knisely, Peter Cole　b: 8/11/1887, Waynesburg, Pa.　d: 7/1/48, Brownsville, Pa.　BR/TR, 5'9", 185 lbs.　Deb: 9/04/12

1912	Cin-N	21	67	10	22	7	3	0	7	4	5	.328	.375	.522	148	4	4	14	3			.939	-2	O/2S	0.1
1913	Chi-N	2	2	0	0	0	0	0	0	0	1	.000	.000	.000	-99	-1	-1	0	0			.000	0	H	-0.1
1914	Chi-N	37	69	5	9	0	1	0	5	5	6	.130	.200	.159	7	-8	-8	2	0			.975	0	O2	-0.7
1915	Chi-N	64	134	12	33	9	0	0	17	15	18	.246	.331	.313	95	-0	-0	14	1	2	-1	.940	-7	O/2	-1.1
Total	4	124	272	27	64	16	4	0	29	24	30	.235	.307	.324	86	-5	-5	30	4	2		.951	-7	/O2S	-1.8

■ CHUCK KNOBLAUCH
Knoblauch, Edward Charles　b: 7/7/68, Houston, Tex.　BR/TR, 5'9", 175 lbs.　Deb: 4/09/91

1991	*Min-A	151	565	78	159	24	6	1	50	59	40	.281	.354	.350	91	-2	-5	76	25	5	5	.975	-1	*2/S	0.1
1992	Min-A★	155	600	104	178	19	6	2	56	88	60	.297	.391	.358	108	13	11	93	34	13	2	.992	-16	*2/SD	0.1
Total	2	306	1165	182	337	43	12	3	106	147	100	.289	.373	.355	100	12	6	169	59	18	7	.984	-17	2/SD	0.2

YEAR	TM/L	G	AB	R	H	2B	3B	HR	RBI	BB	SO	AVG	OBP	SLG	PRO+	BR	/A	RC	SB	CS	SBR	FA	FR	POS	TPR

■ MIKE KNODE   Knode, Kenneth Thomson b: 11/8/1895, Westminster, Md. d: 12/20/80, South Bend, Ind. BR/TR, 5'10", 160 lbs. Deb: 6/28/20 F

| 1920 | StL-N | 42 | 65 | 11 | 15 | 1 | 1 | 0 | 12 | 5 | 6 | .231 | .306 | .277 | 71 | -2 | -2 | 6 | 0 | 1 | -1 | .824 | -0 | /O2S3 | -0.4 |

■ RAY KNODE   Knode, Robert Troxell "Bob" b: 1/28/01, Westminster, Md. d: 4/13/82, Battle Creek, Mich BL/TL, 5'10", 160 lbs. Deb: 6/30/23 F

1923	Cle-A	22	38	7	11	0	0	2	4	2	4	.289	.325	.447	102	-0	-0	6	1	0	0	.992	0	1	0.0
1924	Cle-A	11	37	6	9	1	0	0	4	3	0	.243	.300	.270	47	-3	-3	3	2	1	0	.992	1	1	-0.2
1925	Cle-A	45	108	13	27	5	0	0	11	10	4	.250	.314	.296	55	-7	-7	10	3	3	-1	.990	1	1	-0.9
1926	Cle-A	31	24	6	8	1	1	0	4	3	4	.333	.407	.458	124	1	1	5	0	0	0	.984	1	1	0.1
Total	4	109	207	32	55	7	1	2	23	18	12	.266	.324	.338	70	-9	-9	24	6	4	-1	.990	2	/1	-1.0

■ PUNCH KNOLL   Knoll, Charles Elmer b: 10/7/1881, Evansville, Ind. d: 2/8/60, Evansville, Ind. BR/TR, 5'7.5", 170 lbs. Deb: 4/27/05

| 1905 | Was-A | 79 | 244 | 24 | 52 | 10 | 5 | 0 | 29 | 9 | | .213 | .247 | .295 | 75 | -8 | -7 | 20 | 3 | | | .937 | 2 | O/C1 | -0.9 |

■ BOBBY KNOOP   Knoop, Robert Frank b: 10/18/38, Sioux City, Iowa BR/TR, 6'1", 170 lbs. Deb: 4/13/64 C

1964	LA-A	162	486	42	105	8	1	7	38	46	109	.216	.291	.280	66	-26	-20	39	3	2	-0	.978	37	*2	3.1
1965	Cal-A	142	465	47	125	24	4	7	43	31	101	.269	.315	.383	99	-2	-1	56	3	2	-0	.971	13	*2	2.5
1966	Cal-A★	161	590	54	137	18	11	17	72	43	144	.232	.285	.386	94	-8	-6	61	1	5	-3	.981	17	*2	2.0
1967	Cal-A	159	511	51	125	18	5	9	38	44	136	.245	.306	.352	98	-4	-2	54	2	2	-1	.986	1	*2	1.0
1968	Cal-A	152	494	48	123	20	4	3	39	35	128	.249	.303	.324	93	-6	-4	47	3	2	-0	.981	16	*2	2.3
1969	Cal-A	27	71	5	14	1	0	1	6	13	16	.197	.321	.254	66	-3	-3	6	1	3	-2	.977	2	2	-0.1
	Chi-A	104	345	34	79	14	1	6	41	35	68	.229	.304	.328	73	-11	-13	34	2	0	1	.985	23	*2	2.0
	Yr	131	416	39	93	15	1	7	47	48	84	.224	.307	.315	72	-14	-16	40	3	3	-1	.984	25	*2	1.9
1970	Chi-A	130	402	34	92	13	2	5	36	34	79	.229	.292	.308	63	-19	-21	37	0	1	-1	.984	35	*2	2.4
1971	KC-A	72	161	14	33	8	1	1	11	15	36	.205	.273	.286	59	-9	-9	12	1	0	0	.968	-1	2/3	-0.6
1972	KC-A	44	97	8	23	5	0	0	7	9	16	.237	.302	.289	77	-3	-3	8	0	0	0	.972	3	2/3	0.7
Total	9	1153	3622	337	856	129	29	56	331	305	833	.236	.298	.334	83	-91	-81	353	16	17	-5	.980	150	*2/3	15.3

■ RANDY KNORR   Knorr, Randy Duane b: 11/12/68, San Gabriel, Cal. BR/TR, 6'2", 205 lbs. Deb: 9/05/91

1991	Tor-A	3	1	0	0	0	0	0	0	1	1	.000	.500	.000	49	0	0	0	0	0	0	1.000	1	/C	0.1
1992	Tor-A	8	19	1	5	0	0	1	2	1	5	.263	.300	.421	96	-0	-0	2	0	0	0	1.000	1	/C	0.1
Total	2	11	20	1	5	0	0	1	2	2	6	.250	.318	.400	96	-0	-0	3	0	0	0	1.000	1	/C	0.2

■ GEORGE KNOTHE   Knothe, George Bertram b: 1/12/1898, Bayonne, N.J. d: 7/3/81, Dover, N.J. BR/TR, 5'10", 165 lbs. Deb: 4/25/32 F

| 1932 | Phi-N | 6 | 12 | 2 | 1 | 1 | 0 | 0 | 0 | 0 | 0 | .083 | .083 | .167 | -31 | -2 | -2 | 0 | 0 | | | .923 | -1 | /2 | -0.3 |

■ FRITZ KNOTHE   Knothe, Wilfred Edgar b: 5/1/03, Passaic, N.J. d: 3/27/63, Passaic, N.J. BR/TR, 5'10.5", 180 lbs. Deb: 4/12/32 F

1932	Bos-N	89	344	45	82	19	1	1	36	39	37	.238	.318	.308	72	-14	-12	36	5			.947	-3	3	-0.9
1933	Bos-N	44	158	15	36	5	2	1	6	13	25	.228	.291	.304	76	-6	-5	15	1			.978	-7	3/S	-0.9
	Phi-N	41	113	10	17	2	0	0	11	6	19	.150	.193	.168	3	-14	-16	2	2			.949	15	3/2	0.1
	Yr	85	271	25	53	7	2	1	17	19	44	.196	.251	.247	42	-20	-21	17	3			.961	8	3/S2	-0.8
Total	2	174	615	70	135	26	3	2	53	58	81	.220	.289	.281	59	-34	-32	55	8			.953	5	3/S2	-1.7

■ JOE KNOTTS   Knotts, Joseph Steven b: 3/3/1884, Greensboro, Pa. d: 9/15/50, Philadelphia, Pa. BR/TR, Deb: 9/18/07

| 1907 | Bos-N | 3 | 8 | 0 | 0 | 0 | 0 | 0 | 0 | 0 | | .000 | .111 | .000 | -65 | -1 | -1 | 0 | | | | 1.000 | -0 | /C | -0.2 |

■ ED KNOUFF   Knouff, Edward "Fred" b: 6/1868, Philadelphia, Pa. d: 9/14/1900, Philadelphia, Pa. BR/TR, 210 lbs. Deb: 7/01/1885

1885	Phi-a	14	48	5	9	0	0	0			2	.188	.220	.188	30	-4	-4	2				.867	1	P/O	0.0
1886	Bal-a	1	3	0	0	0	0	0				.000	.250	.000	-18	-0	-0	0	0			1.000	1	/P	0.0
1887	Bal-a	9	31	4	9	0	0	0			1	.290	.313	.290	75	-1	-1	3	1			.889	1	/PO	-0.1
	StL-a	15	56	4	10	1	2	0			1	.179	.207	.268	30	-5	-6	3	1			.800	-2	/OP	-0.5
	Yr	24	87	8	19	1	2	0			2	.218	.244	.276	44	-6	-7	7	2			.897	-3	PO	-0.6
1888	StL-a	9	31	1	3	0	0	0	1	3		.097	.200	.097	-2	-3	-4	1	1			.842	-2	/P	0.0
	Cle-a	2	6	0	1	1	0	0	0	1		.167	.286	.333	104	0	0	1	0			1.000	1	P/2	0.0
	Yr	11	37	1	4	1	0	0	1	4		.108	.214	.135	14	-3	-4	1	1			.880	-1	P/2	0.0
1889	Phi-a	3	12	2	3	1	0	0	2	1	1	.250	.308	.333	85	-0	-0	1	1			1.000	-1	/P	0.0
Total	5	53	187	16	35	3	2	0	3	9	1	.187	.236	.225	37	-14	-15	12	4			.891	-3	/PO2	-0.6

■ JAKE KNOWDELL   Knowdell, Jacob Augustus b: 7/27/1840, Brooklyn, N.Y. 5'7.5", 148 lbs. Deb: 6/20/1874

1874	Atl-n	23	84	8	12	1	1	0			2	.143	.163	.179	10	-8	-6	3						C/O	-0.5
1875	Atl-n	43	161	17	32	3	0	0			2	.199	.209	.217	55	-8	-5	7						C/SO	-0.3
1878	Mil-N	4	14	2	3	1	0	0	2	0	3	.214	.214	.286	59	-1	-1	1				.875	-2	/COS	-0.3
Total	2 n	66	245	25	44	4	1	0				.180	.193	.204	38	-16	-11	10						/CSO	-0.8

■ JIMMY KNOWLES   Knowles, James "Darby" b: 1859, Toronto, Ont., Canada 5'9", 160 lbs. Deb: 5/02/1884

1884	Pit-a	46	182	19	42	5	7	0			16	.231	.259	.335	93	-1	-1	16				.961	-0	1	-0.6
	Bro-a	41	153	19	36	5	1	1			3	.235	.255	.301	82	-3	-3	12				.953	1	13	-0.5
	Yr	87	335	38	78	10	8	1			8	.233	.257	.319	88	-4	-4	28				.958	1	13	-1.1
1886	Was-N	115	443	43	94	16	11	3	35	14	73	.212	.238	.318	72	-18	-14	39	20			.899	28	23	1.6
1887	NY-a	16	60	12	15	1	1	0			1	.250	.262	.300	61	-3	-3	6	6			.934	-3	2/3	-0.5
1890	Roc-a	123	491	83	138	12	8	5		59		.281	.359	.369	127	11	17	87	55			.881	7	*3	2.5
1892	NY-N	16	59	9	9	1	0	0	7	6	8	.153	.231	.169	23	-5	-5	3	2			.792	-5	3/S	-0.9
Total	5	357	1388	185	334	40	28	9	42	89	81	.241	.288	.329	93	-19	-9	164	83			.861	28	3/21S	1.6

■ ANDY KNOX   Knox, Andrew Jackson "Dasher" b: 1/6/1864, Philadelphia, Pa. d: 9/14/40, Philadelphia, Pa. BR/TR, Deb: 9/19/1890

| 1890 | Phi-a | 21 | 75 | 6 | 19 | 3 | 0 | 0 | 9 | | | .253 | .333 | .293 | 89 | -1 | -1 | 9 | 5 | | | .963 | -2 | 1 | -0.3 |

■ CLIFF KNOX   Knox, Clifford Hiram "Bud" b: 1/7/02, Coalville, Iowa d: 9/24/65, Oskaloosa, Iowa BB/TR, 5'11.5", 178 lbs. Deb: 7/01/24

| 1924 | Pit-N | 6 | 18 | 1 | 4 | 0 | 0 | 0 | 2 | 2 | 0 | .222 | .300 | .222 | 41 | -1 | -1 | 1 | 0 | 0 | 0 | .917 | 2 | /C | 0.1 |

■ JOHN KNOX   Knox, John Clinton b: 7/26/48, Newark, N.J. BL/TR, 6', 170 lbs. Deb: 8/01/72

1972	*Det-A	14	13	1	1	1	0	0	1	0	2	.077	.143	.154	-11	-2	-2	0	0	0	0	1.000	4	/2	0.2
1973	Det-A	12	32	1	9	1	0	0	3	3	3	.281	.343	.313	80	-1	-1	4	1	1	-0	1.000	-3	/2	-0.3
1974	Det-A	55	88	11	27	1	0	0	6	6	13	.307	.351	.341	96	-0	-0	9	5	4	-1	.956	8	2/3D	0.7
1975	Det-A	43	86	8	23	1	0	0	2	10	9	.267	.344	.279	74	-2	-3	8	1	2	-1	.980	-1	2/3D	-0.4
Total	4	124	219	21	60	4	1	0	11	20	27	.274	.335	.301	79	-4	-5	21	7	7	-2	.973	8	/2D3	0.2

■ NICK KOBACK   Koback, Nicholas Nicholie b: 7/19/35, Hartford, Conn. BR/TR, 6', 187 lbs. Deb: 7/29/53

1953	Pit-N	7	16	1	2	0	0	0	1	0	4	.125	.176	.250	10	-2	-2	0	0	0	0	1.000	-3	/C	-0.5
1954	Pit-N	4	10	0	0	0	0	0	0	0	8	.000	.000	.000	-99	-3	-3	0	0	0	0	1.000	0	/C	-0.3
1955	Pit-N	5	7	0	2	0	0	0	0	1	1	.286	.286	.286	53	-0	0	1	0	0	0	1.000	0	/C	0.0
Total	3	16	33	1	4	0	0	0	1	1	13	.121	.147	.182	-15	-6	-6	1	0	0	0	1.000	-3	/C	-0.8

■ BARNEY KOCH   Koch, Barnett b: 3/23/23, Campbell, Neb. d: 6/6/87, Tacoma, Wash. BR/TR, 5'8", 140 lbs. Deb: 7/23/44

| 1944 | Bro-N | 33 | 96 | 11 | 21 | 2 | 0 | 1 | 3 | 9 | | .219 | .242 | .240 | 37 | -8 | -8 | 6 | 0 | | | .956 | -6 | 2/S | -1.3 |

YEAR	TM/L	G	AB	R	H	2B	3B	HR	RBI	BB	SO	AVG	OBP	SLG	PRO+	BR	/A	RC	SB	CS	SBR	FA	FR	POS	TPR

■ BRAD KOCHER Kocher, Bradley Wilson b: 1/16/1888, White Haven, Pa. d: 1/13/65, White Haven, Pa. BR/TR, 5'11", 188 lbs. Deb: 4/24/12

1912	Det-A	29	63	5	13	3	1	0	9	2		.206	.231	.286	49	-5	-4	4	0			.904	-3	C	-0.6
1915	NY-N	4	11	3	5	0	1	0	2	0	1	.455	.455	.636	243	2	2	3	0			1.000	-1	/C	0.1
1916	NY-N	34	65	1	7	2	0	0	1	2	10	.108	.134	.138	-17	-9	-9	1	0			.978	-7	C	-1.6
Total	3	67	139	9	25	5	2	0	12	4	11	.180	.203	.245	34	-12	-11	9	0			.943	-11	/C	-2.1

■ PETE KOEGEL Koegel, Peter John b: 7/31/47, Mineola, N.Y. BR/TR, 6'6.5", 230 lbs. Deb: 9/01/70

1970	Mil-A	7	8	2	2	0	0	1	1	1	3	.250	.333	.625	157	1	1	2	0	0	0	1.000	-0	/O	0.0
1971	Mil-A	2	3	0	0	0	0	0	0	2	2	.000	.400	.000	22	-0	-0	0	0	0	0	1.000	-0	/1	0.0
	Phi-N	12	26	1	6	1	0	0	3	2	7	.231	.286	.269	58	-1	-1	2	0	0	0	1.000	-1	/CO	-0.2
1972	Phi-N	41	49	3	7	2	0	0	1	6	16	.143	.236	.184	20	-5	-5	0	0	0	0	1.000	-2	/1C3O	-0.8
Total	3	62	86	6	15	3	0	1	5	11	28	.174	.268	.244	45	-6	-6	6	0	0	0	.971	-3	/C13O	-1.0

■ BEN KOEHLER Koehler, Benard James b: 1/26/1877, Schoerndorn, Germany d: 5/21/61, South Bend, Ind. BR/TR, 5'10.5", 175 lbs. Deb: 4/23/05

1905	StL-A	142	536	55	127	14	6	3	47	32		.237	.284	.297	89	-10	-7	54	22			.969	6	*O1/2	-0.8
1906	StL-A	66	186	27	41	1	1	0	15	24		.220	.319	.232	78	-4	-3	18	9			.957	-4	O/2S3	-1.0
Total	2	208	722	82	168	15	7	2	62	56		.233	.293	.281	86	-14	-10	72	31			.966	1	O/213S	-1.8

■ PIP KOEHLER Koehler, Horace Levering b: 1/16/02, Gilbert, Pa. d: 12/8/86, Tacoma, Wash. BR/TR, 5'10", 165 lbs. Deb: 4/22/25

| 1925 | NY-N | 12 | 2 | 1 | 0 | 0 | 0 | 0 | 0 | 0 | 1 | .000 | .000 | .000 | -99 | -1 | -1 | 0 | 0 | 0 | 0 | 1.000 | -1 | /O | -0.1 |

■ LEN KOENECKE Koenecke, Leonard George b: 1/18/04, Baraboo, Wis. d: 9/17/35, Toronto, Ont., Can BL/TR, 5'11", 180 lbs. Deb: 4/12/32

1932	NY-N	42	137	33	35	5	0	4	14	11	13	.255	.320	.380	89	-2	-2	17	3			.924	-5	O	-0.9
1934	Bro-N	123	460	79	147	31	7	14	73	70	38	.320	.411	.509	152	31	34	103	8			.994	2	*O	3.0
1935	Bro-N	100	325	43	92	13	2	4	27	43	45	.283	.369	.372	102	1	2	49	0			.966	-4	O	-0.5
Total	3	265	922	155	274	49	9	22	114	124	96	.297	.383	.441	125	30	34	169	11			.976	-7	O	1.6

■ MARK KOENIG Koenig, Mark Anthony b: 7/19/02, San Francisco, Cal. BB/TR, 6', 180 lbs. Deb: 9/08/25

1925	NY-A	28	110	14	23	6	1	0	4	5	4	.209	.243	.282	34	-12	-11	7	0	1	-1	.944	-3	S	-1.1
1926	*NY-A	147	617	93	167	26	8	5	62	43	37	.271	.319	.363	79	-22	-20	72	4	3	-1	.931	-0	*S	-0.6
1927	*NY-A	123	526	99	150	20	11	3	62	25	21	.285	.320	.382	84	-16	-13	62	3	2	-0	.936	14	*S	1.2
1928	*NY-A	132	533	89	170	19	10	4	63	32	19	.319	.360	.415	106	2	4	78	3	5	-2	.923	-20	*S	-0.7
1929	NY-A	116	373	44	109	27	5	3	41	23	17	.292	.335	.416	99	-5	-2	52	1	1	-0	.911	-13	S3/2	-0.7
1930	NY-A	21	74	9	17	5	0	0	9	6	5	.230	.296	.297	53	-5	-5	7	0	0	0	.905	2	S	-0.1
	Det-A	76	267	37	64	9	2	1	16	20	15	.240	.295	.300	50	-20	-21	25	2	0	1	.922	-14	S/P3O	-2.4
	Yr	97	341	46	81	14	2	1	25	26	20	.238	.295	.299	51	-25	-25	32	2	0	1	.918	-13	S/P3O	-2.5
1931	Det-A	106	364	33	92	24	4	1	39	14	12	.253	.282	.349	63	-19	-21	36	8	2	1	.955	-23	2S/P	-3.4
1932	*Chi-N	33	102	15	36	5	1	3	11	3	5	.353	.377	.510	137	5	5	19	0			.932	10	S	1.7
1933	Chi-N	80	218	32	62	12	1	3	25	15	9	.284	.330	.390	105	1	1	28	5			.922	5	3S/2	1.0
1934	Cin-N	151	633	60	172	26	6	1	67	15	24	.272	.289	.336	68	-30	-28	59	5			.930	6	3S2/1	-1.5
1935	NY-N	107	396	40	112	12	0	3	37	13	18	.283	.306	.336	74	-15	-15	39	0			.968	-11	2S3	-1.8
1936	*NY-N	42	58	7	16	4	0	0	7	8	4	.276	.373	.397	109	1	1	10	0			.905	-1	S/23	0.0
Total	12	1162	4271	572	1190	195	49	28	443	222	190	.279	.316	.367	81	-135	-125	495	31	14		.927	-50	S32/P1O	-8.0

■ HENRY KOHLER Kohler, Henry C. b: 5/5/1852, Baltimore, Md. d: 8/27/34, Baltimore, Md. Deb: 7/12/1871

1871	Kek-n	3	12	0	2	1	0	0	1	0	0	.167	.167	.250	17	-1	-1	1	0					/13	-0.1
1873	Mar-n	6	25	2	3	3	0	0	0	0	0	.120	.120	.240	4	-3	-2	1						/3C1	-0.1
1874	Bal-n	2	4	0	0	0	0	0	0	0		.000	.000	.000	-99	-1	-1	0						/1	-0.1
Total	3 n	11	41	2	5	4	0	0	1	0	0	.122	.122	.220	-2	-5	-4	1						/31C	-0.3

■ DICK KOKOS Kokos, Richard Jerome (b: Richard Jerome Kokoszka) b: 2/28/28, Chicago, Ill. d: 4/9/86, Chicago, Ill. BL/TL, 5'8.5", 170 lbs. Deb: 7/08/48

1948	StL-A	71	258	40	77	15	3	4	40	28	32	.298	.374	.426	110	4	4	44	4	3	-1	.964	-1	O	-0.1
1949	StL-A	143	501	80	131	28	1	23	77	66	91	.261	.351	.459	109	7	4	86	3	5	-2	.981	8	*O	0.4
1950	StL-A	143	490	77	128	27	5	18	67	88	73	.261	.375	.447	106	7	4	87	8	8	-2	.970	9	*O	0.5
1953	StL-A	107	299	41	72	12	0	13	38	56	53	.241	.361	.411	106	4	3	47	0	5	-3	.963	-1	O	-0.4
1954	Bal-A	11	10	1	2	0	0	1	1	4	3	.200	.429	.500	166	1	1	2	0			1.000	-0	/O	0.1
Total	5	475	1558	239	410	82	9	59	223	242	252	.263	.365	.441	108	24	17	266	15	21	-8	.971	16	O	0.5

■ GARY KOLB Kolb, Gary Alan b: 3/13/40, Rock Falls, Ill. BL/TR, 6', 195 lbs. Deb: 9/07/60

1960	StL-N	9	3	1	0	0	0	0	0	0	0	.000	.000	.000	-92	-1	-1	0	0	0	0	1.000	-0	/O	-0.1
1962	StL-N	6	14	1	5	0	0	0	1	3		.357	.400	.357	96	-0	-0	2	0	0	0	1.000	0	/O	0.0
1963	StL-N	75	96	23	26	1	5	3	10	22	26	.271	.407	.479	141	8	7	21	2	1	0	.981	0	O/C3	0.6
1964	Mil-N	36	64	7	12	1	0	0	2	6	10	.188	.257	.203	31	-6	-6	4	3	2	-0	1.000	-3	O/32C	-0.9
1965	Mil-N	24	27	3	7	0	0	0	1	1	6	.259	.286	.259	54	-2	-2	2	0	0	0	1.000	1	O	-0.1
	NY-N	40	90	8	15	2	0	1	7	3	28	.167	.194	.222	17	-10	-10	4	3	0	1	.976	2	O/13	-0.9
	Yr	64	117	11	22	2	0	1	8	4	34	.188	.215	.231	26	-11	-11	5	3	0	1	.981	3	O/13	-1.0
1968	Pit-N	74	119	16	26	4	1	2	6	11	17	.218	.285	.319	82	-3	-3	11	2	1	0	.900	0	OC/32	-0.3
1969	Pit-N	29	37	4	3	1	0	0	3	2	14	.081	.128	.108	-34	-7	-6	1	0	0	0	1.000	0	/C	-0.7
Total	7	293	450	63	94	9	6	6	29	46	104	.209	.282	.296	65	-19	-20	43	10	4	1	.965	0	O/C321	-2.4

■ DON KOLLOWAY Kolloway, Donald Martin "Butch" or "Cab" b: 8/4/18, Posen, Ill. BR/TR, 6'3", 200 lbs. Deb: 9/16/40

1940	Chi-A	10	40	5	9	1	0	3	0	3	0	.225	.225	.250	23	-5	-5	2	1	0	0	.922	-2	2	-0.5
1941	Chi-A	71	280	33	76	8	3	3	24	6	12	.271	.292	.354	71	-13	-12	27	11	4	1	.955	-7	2/1	-1.5
1942	Chi-A	147	601	72	164	40	4	3	60	30	39	.273	.311	.368	92	-10	-8	66	16	14	-4	.966	-9	*21	-1.6
1943	Chi-A	85	348	29	75	14	4	1	33	9	30	.216	.235	.287	53	-22	-22	22	11	7	-1	.968	-1	2	-2.1
1946	Chi-A	123	482	45	135	23	4	3	53	9	29	.280	.293	.363	86	-13	-11	52	14	6	1	.972	5	23	0.2
1947	Chi-A	124	485	49	135	25	4	2	35	17	34	.278	.303	.359	87	-13	-10	48	11	4	1	.962	5	21/3	0.2
1948	Chi-A	119	417	60	114	14	4	6	38	18	18	.273	.303	.369	81	-15	-13	44	2	4	-2	.966	11	23	0.1
1949	Chi-A	4	4	0	0	0	0	0	0	0	1	.000	.000	.000	-99	-1	-1	0	0	0	0	.000	0	/3	-0.1
	Det-A	126	483	71	142	19	3	2	47	49	25	.294	.361	.358	91	-6	-6	62	7	7	-2	.956	-21	21/3	-2.6
	Yr	130	487	71	142	19	3	2	47	49	26	.292	.359	.355	89	-7	-7	61	7	7	-2	.956	-21	21/3	-2.7
1950	Det-A	125	467	55	135	20	4	6	62	29	28	.289	.331	.388	81	-13	-15	57	1	3	-2	.989	3	*1/2	-1.6
1951	Det-A	78	212	28	54	7	0	1	17	15	12	.255	.307	.302	65	-10	-10	19	2	3	-1	.992	6	1	-0.8
1952	Det-A	65	173	19	42	9	0	2	21	7	19	.243	.280	.329	69	-8	-8	15	0	2	-0	.979	-4	1/2	-1.1
1953	Phi-A	2	1	0	0	0	0	0	0	0	0	.000	.000	.000	-96	-0	-0	0	0	0	0	.000	0	/3	0.0
Total	12	1079	3993	466	1081	180	30	29	393	189	251	.271	.305	.353	80	-128	-122	413	76	54	-10	.964	-13	21/3	-11.6

■ KARL KOLSETH Kolseth, Karl Dickey "Koley" b: 12/25/1892, Cambridge, Mass. d: 5/3/56, Cumberland, Md. BL/TR, 6', 182 lbs. Deb: 9/30/15

| 1915 | Bal-F | 6 | 23 | 1 | 6 | 1 | 1 | 0 | 1 | 0 | | .261 | .292 | .391 | 97 | -0 | -0 | 3 | 0 | | | .915 | -2 | /1 | -0.2 |

■ FRED KOMMERS Kommers, Frederick Raymond "Bugs" b: 3/31/1886, Chicago, Ill. d: 6/14/43, Chicago, Ill. BL/TR, 6', 175 lbs. Deb: 6/25/13

1913	Pit-N	40	155	14	36	5	4	0	22	10	29	.232	.279	.316	73	-6	-6	13	1			.979	-2	O	-1.0
1914	StL-F	76	244	33	75	9	8	3	41	24	36	.307	.376	.447	127	11	9	46	7			.908	-2	O	0.4
	Bal-F	16	42	5	9	1	0	1	1	7	7	.214	.340	.310	83	-1	-1	5	0			.938	-2	O	-0.4
	Yr	92	286	38	84	10	8	4	42	31	43	.294	.371	.427	121	10	8	50	7			.911	-4	O	0.0

YEAR	TM/L	G	AB	R	H	2B	3B	HR	RBI	BB	SO	AVG	OBP	SLG	PRO+	BR	/A	RC	SB	CS	SBR	FA	FR	POS	TPR
Total	2	132	441	52	120	15	12	4	64	41	72	.272	.340	.388	105	4	3	64	8			.938	-6	O	-1.0

■ **BRAD KOMMINSK** Komminsk, Brad Lynn b: 4/4/61, Lima, Ohio BR/TR, 6'2", 205 lbs. Deb: 9/28/83

YEAR	TM/L	G	AB	R	H	2B	3B	HR	RBI	BB	SO	AVG	OBP	SLG	PRO+	BR	/A	RC	SB	CS	SBR	FA	FR	POS	TPR
1983	Atl-N	19	36	2	8	2	0	0	4	5	7	.222	.317	.278	62	-2	-2	3	0	0	0	.944	0	O	-0.2
1984	Atl-N	90	301	37	61	10	0	8	36	29	77	.203	.277	.316	62	-14	-16	27	18	8	1	.993	-2	O	-2.2
1985	Atl-N	106	300	52	68	12	3	4	21	38	71	.227	.316	.327	75	-8	-10	32	10	8	-2	.959	-4	O	-1.9
1986	Atl-N	5	5	1	2	0	0	0	1	0	1	.400	.400	.400	115	0	0	0	0	1	-1	1.000	-0	/3O	-0.1
1987	Mil-A	7	15	0	1	0	0	0	0	1	7	.067	.125	.067	-46	-3	-3	0	1	0	0	1.000	0	/OD	-0.3
1989	Cle-A	71	198	27	47	8	2	8	33	24	55	.237	.323	.419	106	2	1	28	8	2	1	.995	3	O	0.4
1990	SF-N	8	5	2	1	0	0	0	0	1	2	.200	.333	.200	52	-0	-0	0	0	0	0	1.000	-3	/O	-0.3
	Bal-A	46	101	18	24	4	0	3	8	14	29	.238	.342	.366	101	0	0	13	1	1	-0	1.000	-5	O/D	-0.5
1991	Oak-A	24	25	1	3	1	0	0	2	2	9	.120	.185	.160	-4	-4	-3	1	1	0	0	1.000	-6	O	-0.9
Total	8	376	986	140	215	37	5	23	105	114	258	.218	.303	.336	75	-28	-33	105	39	20	-0	.984	-16	O/D3	-6.0

■ **ED KONETCHY** Konetchy, Edward Joseph "Big Ed" b: 9/3/1885, Lacrosse, Wis. d: 5/27/47, Ft.Worth, Tex. BR/TR, 6'2.5", 195 lbs. Deb: 6/29/07

YEAR	TM/L	G	AB	R	H	2B	3B	HR	RBI	BB	SO	AVG	OBP	SLG	PRO+	BR	/A	RC	SB	CS	SBR	FA	FR	POS	TPR
1907	StL-N	91	331	34	83	11	8	3	30	26		.251	.317	.360	116	4	5	44	13			.975	4	1	0.8
1908	StL-N	154	545	46	135	19	12	5	50	38		.248	.309	.354	117	6	9	65	16			.986	11	*1	1.9
1909	StL-N	152	576	88	165	23	14	4	80	65		.286	.366	.396	145	25	29	92	25			.985	5	*1	3.5
1910	StL-N	144	520	87	157	23	16	3	78	78	59	.302	.397	.425	145	28	31	94	18			**.991**	8	*1/P	**4.0**
1911	StL-N	158	571	90	165	**38**	13	6	88	81	63	.289	.384	.433	132	23	25	105	27			**.991**	-6	*1	1.8
1912	StL-N	143	538	81	169	26	13	8	82	62	66	.314	.389	.455	134	23	25	105	25			.991	6	*1/O	2.7
1913	StL-N	140	504	75	139	18	17	8	68	53	41	.276	.353	.427	124	14	15	82	27			**.995**	7	*1/P	2.2
1914	Pit-N	154	563	56	140	23	9	4	51	32	48	.249	.291	.343	92	-10	-7	61	20			**.995**	5	*1	-0.6
1915	Pit-F	152	576	79	181	31	18	10	93	41	52	.314	.363	.483	149	31	32	115	27			**.994**	-0	*1	3.0
1916	Bos-N	158	566	76	147	29	13	3	70	43	46	.260	.320	.373	117	8	10	74	13			.990	9	*1	1.5
1917	Bos-N	130	474	56	129	19	13	2	54	36	40	.272	.330	.380	125	9	12	62	16			**.994**	2	*1	1.1
1918	Bos-N	119	437	33	103	15	5	2	56	32	35	.236	.291	.307	86	-9	-7	40	5			**.992**	-2	*1/OP	-1.5
1919	Bro-N	132	486	46	145	24	9	1	47	29	39	.298	.342	.391	117	11	10	68	14			**.994**	7	*1	1.3
1920	*Bro-N	131	497	62	153	22	12	5	63	33	18	.308	.352	.431	120	14	13	75	3	2	-0	.990	1	*1	1.0
1921	Bro-N	55	197	25	53	6	5	3	23	19	21	.269	.336	.396	90	-2	-3	26	3	3	-1	.987	-1	1	-0.6
	Phi-N	72	268	38	86	17	4	8	59	21	17	.321	.379	.504	122	12	9	52	3	0	1	.986	6	1	1.3
	Yr	127	465	63	139	23	9	11	82	40	38	.299	.361	.458	109	10	6	78	6	3	0	.986	4	*1	0.7
Total	15	2085	7649	972	2150	344	181	75	992	689	545	.281	.346	.403	123	187	207	1161	255	5		.990	59	*1/OP	23.4

■ **MIKE KONNICK** Konnick, Michael Aloysius b: 1/13/1889, Glen Lyon, Pa. d: 7/9/71, Wilkes-Barre, Pa. BR/TR, 5'9", 180 lbs. Deb: 10/03/09

YEAR	TM/L	G	AB	R	H	2B	3B	HR	RBI	BB	SO	AVG	OBP	SLG	PRO+	BR	/A	RC	SB	CS	SBR	FA	FR	POS	TPR
1909	Cin-N	2	5	0	2	1	0	0	1	0		.400	.400	.600	211	1	1	1	0			1.000	-1	/C	0.0
1910	Cin-N	1	3	0	0	0	0	0	0	1	0	.000	.250	.000	-27	-0	-0	0	0			1.000	-1	/S	-0.1
Total	2	3	8	0	2	1	0	0	1	1	0	.250	.333	.375	117	0	0	1	0			.914	-1	/CS	-0.1

■ **BRUCE KONOPKA** Konopka, Bruno Bruce b: 9/16/19, Hammond, Ind. BL/TL, 6'2", 190 lbs. Deb: 6/07/42

YEAR	TM/L	G	AB	R	H	2B	3B	HR	RBI	BB	SO	AVG	OBP	SLG	PRO+	BR	/A	RC	SB	CS	SBR	FA	FR	POS	TPR
1942	Phi-A	5	10	2	3	0	0	0	1	1	0	.300	.364	.300	88	-0	-0	1	0	0	0	1.000	-0	/1	0.0
1943	Phi-A	2	2	0	0	0	0	0	0	0	1	.000	.000	.000	-99	-0	-0	0	0	0	0	.000	0	H	-0.1
1946	Phi-A	38	93	7	22	4	1	0	9	4	8	.237	.268	.301	59	-5	-5	7	0	0	0	.994	1	1/O	-0.5
Total	3	45	105	9	25	4	1	0	10	5	9	.238	.273	.295	59	-6	-6	8	0	0	0	.995	1	/1O	-0.6

■ **HARRY KOONS** Koons, Henry M. b: 1863, Philadelphia, Pa. BR/TR, 5'8", 174 lbs. Deb: 4/17/1884

YEAR	TM/L	G	AB	R	H	2B	3B	HR	RBI	BB	SO	AVG	OBP	SLG	PRO+	BR	/A	RC	SB	CS	SBR	FA	FR	POS	TPR
1884	Alt-U	21	78	8	18	2	1	0		2		.231	.250	.282	78	-2	-2	6				.866	5	3/C	0.3
	CP-U	1	3	0	0	0	0	0		0		.000	.000	.000	-99	-1	-1	0				.000	0	/3	-0.1
	Yr	22	81	8	18	2	1	0		2		.222	.241	.272	72	-2	-2	5				.866	5	3/C	0.2

■ **GEORGE KOPACZ** Kopacz, George Felix "Sonny" b: 2/26/41, Chicago, Ill. BL/TL, 6'1", 195 lbs. Deb: 9/18/66

YEAR	TM/L	G	AB	R	H	2B	3B	HR	RBI	BB	SO	AVG	OBP	SLG	PRO+	BR	/A	RC	SB	CS	SBR	FA	FR	POS	TPR
1966	Atl-N	6	9	1	0	0	0	0	0	1	5	.000	.100	.000	-68	-2	-2	0	0	0	0	.909	-1	/1	-0.3
1970	Pit-N	10	16	1	3	0	0	0	0	0	5	.188	.188	.188	1	-2	-2	1	0	0	0	1.000	-1	/1	-0.3
Total	2	16	25	2	3	0	0	0	0	1	10	.120	.154	.120	-25	-4	-4	1	0	0	0	.964	-1	/1	-0.6

■ **WALLY KOPF** Kopf, Walter Henry b: 7/10/1899, Stonington, Conn. d: 4/30/79, Hamilton Co., Ohio BB/TR, 5'11", 168 lbs. Deb: 10/01/21 F

YEAR	TM/L	G	AB	R	H	2B	3B	HR	RBI	BB	SO	AVG	OBP	SLG	PRO+	BR	/A	RC	SB	CS	SBR	FA	FR	POS	TPR
1921	NY-N	2	3	0	1	0	0	0	0	1	1	.333	.500	.333	125	0	0	1	0	0	0	1.000	2	/3	0.2

■ **LARRY KOPF** Kopf, William Lorenz (a.k.a. Fred Brady In 1913) b: 11/3/1890, Bristol, Conn. d: 10/15/86, Anderson Twp., O. BB/TR, 5'9", 160 lbs. Deb: 9/02/13 F

YEAR	TM/L	G	AB	R	H	2B	3B	HR	RBI	BB	SO	AVG	OBP	SLG	PRO+	BR	/A	RC	SB	CS	SBR	FA	FR	POS	TPR
1913	Cle-A	6	10	2	3	1	0	0	1	0	0	.300	.300	.400	101	-0	-0	1	0			.923	2	/23	0.2
1914	Phi-A	37	69	8	13	2	2	0	12	8	14	.188	.300	.275	76	-2	-2	8	6			.899	1	S/32	0.3
1915	Phi-A	118	386	39	87	10	2	1	33	41	45	.225	.314	.269	77	-11	-9	33	5	9	-4	.920	-8	S3/2	-1.5
1916	Cin-N	11	40	2	11	2	0	0	5	1	8	.275	.293	.325	92	-1	-1	4	1			.942	-2	S	-0.3
1917	Cin-N	148	573	81	146	19	8	2	26	28	48	.255	.297	.326	95	-7	-4	59	17			.916	-11	*S	-1.0
1919	*Cin-N	135	503	51	136	18	5	0	58	28	27	.270	.313	.326	95	-5	-3	54	18			.943	-34	*S	-3.3
1920	Cin-N	126	458	56	112	15	6	0	59	35	24	.245	.305	.303	76	-14	-13	43	14	13	-4	.929	-33	*S/23O	-4.2
1921	Cin-N	107	367	36	80	8	3	1	25	43	20	.218	.310	.264	56	-23	-21	30	3	14	-8	.947	-15	S/23O	-3.4
1922	Bos-N	126	466	59	124	6	3	1	37	45	22	.266	.332	.298	67	-24	-21	48	8	9	-3	.944	-14	2S3	-3.0
1923	Bos-N	39	138	15	38	3	1	0	10	13	6	.275	.338	.312	75	-5	-4	15	0	3	-2	.905	-8	S/2	-1.0
Total	10	853	3010	349	750	84	30	5	266	242	214	.249	.312	.302	78	-91	-78	295	72	48		.928	-122	S/23O	-17.2

■ **MERLIN KOPP** Kopp, Merlin Henry "Manny" b: 1/2/1892, Toledo, Ohio d: 5/6/60, Sacramento, Cal. BB/TR, 5'8", 158 lbs. Deb: 8/02/15

YEAR	TM/L	G	AB	R	H	2B	3B	HR	RBI	BB	SO	AVG	OBP	SLG	PRO+	BR	/A	RC	SB	CS	SBR	FA	FR	POS	TPR
1915	Was-A	16	32	2	8	0	0	0	0	5	7	.250	.351	.250	79	-1	-1	3	1			.933	-1	/O	-0.2
1918	Phi-A	96	363	60	85	7	7	0	18	42	55	.234	.320	.292	84	-6	-6	40	22			.972	12	O	0.0
1919	Phi-A	75	235	34	53	2	4	1	12	42	43	.226	.348	.281	77	-5	-6	27	16			.924	-2	O	-1.3
Total	3	187	630	96	146	9	11	1	30	89	105	.232	.332	.286	81	-12	-13	70	39			.953	8	O	-1.5

■ **JOE KOPPE** Koppe, Joseph (b: Joseph Kopchia) b: 10/19/30, Detroit, Mich. BR/TR, 5'10", 165 lbs. Deb: 8/09/58

YEAR	TM/L	G	AB	R	H	2B	3B	HR	RBI	BB	SO	AVG	OBP	SLG	PRO+	BR	/A	RC	SB	CS	SBR	FA	FR	POS	TPR
1958	Mil-N	16	9	3	4	0	0	0	0	1	1	.444	.500	.444	167	1	1	2	0	0	0	.833	6	/S	0.7
1959	Phi-N	126	422	68	110	18	7	7	28	41	80	.261	.329	.386	88	-6	-7	54	7	7	-2	.954	5	*S2	0.6
1960	Phi-N	58	170	13	29	6	1	1	13	23	47	.171	.273	.235	41	-14	-14	12	3	2	-0	.956	-12	S/3	-2.3
1961	Phi-N	6	3	1	0	0	0	0	0	0	0	.000	.000	.000	-99	-1	-1	0	0	0	0	.800	0	/S	-0.1
	LA-A	91	338	46	85	12	2	5	40	45	77	.251	.341	.343	75	-7	-12	42	3	3	-1	.947	-6	S/23	-1.1
1962	LA-A	128	375	47	85	16	0	4	40	73	84	.227	.356	.301	81	-8	-7	45	2	1	0	.957	4	*S/23	0.8
1963	LA-A	76	143	11	30	4	1	1	12	9	30	.210	.261	.273	53	-10	-9	10	0	0	0	.962	8	S32/O	0.1
1964	LA-A	54	113	10	29	4	1	0	6	14	16	.257	.339	.310	91	-2	-1	13	0	0	0	.945	15	S2/3	1.7
1965	Cal-A	23	33	3	7	1	0	1	2	3	10	.212	.278	.333	75	-1	-1	3	1	0	0	.979	9	2/S3	0.9
Total	8	578	1606	202	379	61	12	19	141	209	345	.236	.327	.324	76	-48	-50	181	16	13	-3	.952	30	S/23O	1.3

■ **GEORGE KOPSHAW** Kopshaw, George Karl b: 7/5/1895, Passaic, N.J. d: 12/26/34, Lynchburg, Va. BR/TR, 5'11.5", 176 lbs. Deb: 8/04/23

YEAR	TM/L	G	AB	R	H	2B	3B	HR	RBI	BB	SO	AVG	OBP	SLG	PRO+	BR	/A	RC	SB	CS	SBR	FA	FR	POS	TPR
1923	StL-N	2	5	1	1	1	0	0	0	0	1	.200	.200	.400	56	-0	-0	0	0	0	0	1.000	-1	/C	-0.1

■ **STEVE KORCHECK** Korcheck, Stephen Joseph "Hoss" b: 8/11/32, McClellandtown, Pa. BR/TR, 6'1", 205 lbs. Deb: 9/06/54

YEAR	TM/L	G	AB	R	H	2B	3B	HR	RBI	BB	SO	AVG	OBP	SLG	PRO+	BR	/A	RC	SB	CS	SBR	FA	FR	POS	TPR
1954	Was-A	2	7	0	1	0	0	0	0	0	2	.143	.143	.143	-23	-1	-1	0	0	0	0	.857	-1	/C	-0.2
1955	Was-A	13	36	3	10	2	0	0	2	0	5	.278	.297	.333	73	-2	-1	4	0	0	0	1.000	1	C	0.0
1958	Was-A	21	51	6	4	2	1	0	1	1	16	.078	.096	.157	-32	-9	-9	1	0	0	0	.975	0	C	-0.8

YEAR	TM/L	G	AB	R	H	2B	3B	HR	RBI	BB	SO	AVG	OBP	SLG	PRO+	BR	/A	RC	SB	CS	SBR	FA	FR	POS	TPR
1959	Was-A	22	51	3	8	2	0	0	4	5	13	.157	.232	.196	19	-6	-6	3	0	0	0	.974	6	C	0.1
Total	4	58	145	12	23	6	1	0	7	6	36	.159	.197	.214	13	-18	-17	7	0	0	0	.976	7	/C	-0.9

■ ART KORES Kores, Arthur Emil "Dutch" b: 7/22/1886, Milwaukee, Wis. d: 3/26/74, Milwaukee, Wis. BR/TR, 5'9", 167 lbs. Deb: 7/24/15

YEAR	TM/L	G	AB	R	H	2B	3B	HR	RBI	BB	SO	AVG	OBP	SLG	PRO+	BR	/A	RC	SB	CS	SBR	FA	FR	POS	TPR
1915	StL-F	60	201	18	47	9	2	1	22	21	13	.234	.306	.313	78	-4	-6	24	6			.960	19	3	1.7

■ ANDY KOSCO Kosco, Andrew John b: 10/5/41, Youngstown, Ohio BR/TR, 6'3", 207 lbs. Deb: 8/13/65

YEAR	TM/L	G	AB	R	H	2B	3B	HR	RBI	BB	SO	AVG	OBP	SLG	PRO+	BR	/A	RC	SB	CS	SBR	FA	FR	POS	TPR
1965	Min-A	23	55	3	13	4	0	1	6	1	15	.236	.250	.364	69	-2	-2	5	0	0	0	1.000	0	O/1	-0.3
1966	Min-A	57	158	11	35	5	0	2	13	7	31	.222	.255	.291	53	-9	-10	11	0	1	-1	.986	-1	O/1	-1.5
1967	Min-A	9	28	4	4	1	0	0	4	2	4	.143	.200	.179	12	-3	-3	1	0	0	0	.923	-0	/O	-0.4
1968	NY-A	131	466	47	112	19	1	15	59	16	71	.240	.270	.382	99	-4	-3	45	2	2	-1	.960	3	O1	-0.9
1969	LA-N	120	424	51	105	13	2	19	74	21	66	.248	.285	.422	103	-5	-1	46	0	1	-1	.981	-8	*O/1	-1.6
1970	LA-N	74	224	21	51	12	0	8	27	1	40	.228	.231	.388	66	-13	-12	17	1	1	-0	.981	-1	O/1	-1.6
1971	Mil-A	98	264	27	60	6	2	10	39	24	57	.227	.292	.379	90	-5	-4	28	1	3	-2	.988	-3	O13	-1.3
1972	Cal-A	49	142	15	34	4	2	6	13	5	23	.239	.270	.423	110	-0	1	15	1	0	0	.985	0	O	0.0
	Bos-A	17	47	5	10	2	1	3	6	2	9	.213	.260	.489	113	1	0	4	0	0	0	1.000	0	O	0.0
	Yr	66	189	20	44	6	3	9	19	7	32	.233	.268	.439	111	1	1	19	1	0	0	.988	1	O	0.0
1973	*Cin-N	47	118	17	33	7	0	9	21	13	26	.280	.351	.568	159	7	8	22	0	0	0	1.000	-4	O/1	0.3
1974	Cin-N	33	37	3	7	2	0	0	5	7	8	.189	.318	.243	59	-2	-2	3	0	0	0	.846	-2	/3O	-0.4
Total	10	658	1963	204	464	75	8	73	267	99	350	.236	.275	.394	92	-34	-28	197	5	8	-3	.979	-15	O/13	-7.7

■ CLEM KOSHOREK Koshorek, Clement John "Scooter" b: 6/20/25, Royal Oak, Mich. d: 9/8/91, Royal Oak, Mich. BR/TR, 5'4.5", 165 lbs. Deb: 4/15/52

YEAR	TM/L	G	AB	R	H	2B	3B	HR	RBI	BB	SO	AVG	OBP	SLG	PRO+	BR	/A	RC	SB	CS	SBR	FA	FR	POS	TPR
1952	Pit-N	98	322	27	84	17	0	0	15	26	39	.261	.320	.314	74	-10	-11	33	4	7	-3	.949	1	S23	-1.0
1953	Pit-N	1	1	0	0	0	0	0	0	0	1	.000	.000	.000	-99	-0	-0	0	0	0	0	.000	0	H	0.0
Total	2	99	323	27	84	17	0	0	15	26	40	.260	.319	.313	74	-10	-11	33	4	7	-3	.985	1	/S23	-1.0

■ KEVIN KOSLOFSKI Koslofski, Kevin Craig b: 9/24/66, Decatur, Ill. BL/TR, 5'8", 165 lbs. Deb: 6/28/92

YEAR	TM/L	G	AB	R	H	2B	3B	HR	RBI	BB	SO	AVG	OBP	SLG	PRO+	BR	/A	RC	SB	CS	SBR	FA	FR	POS	TPR
1992	KC-A	55	133	20	33	0	2	3	13	12	23	.248	.315	.346	84	-3	-3	15	2	1	0	.991	-1	O	-0.5

■ MIKE KOSMAN Kosman, Michael Thomas b: 12/10/17, Hamtramck, Mich. BR/TR, 5'9", 160 lbs. Deb: 4/20/44

YEAR	TM/L	G	AB	R	H	2B	3B	HR	RBI	BB	SO	AVG	OBP	SLG	PRO+	BR	/A	RC	SB	CS	SBR	FA	FR	POS	TPR
1944	Cin-N	1	0	0	0	0	0	0	0	0	0	—	—	—	—	0	0	0	0			.000	0	R	0.0

■ FRED KOSTER Koster, Frederick Charles "Fritz" b: 12/21/05, Louisville, Ky. d: 4/24/79, St.Matthews, Ky. BL/TL, 5'10.5", 165 lbs. Deb: 4/27/31

YEAR	TM/L	G	AB	R	H	2B	3B	HR	RBI	BB	SO	AVG	OBP	SLG	PRO+	BR	/A	RC	SB	CS	SBR	FA	FR	POS	TPR
1931	Phi-N	76	151	21	34	2	2	0	8	14	21	.225	.291	.265	47	-10	-12	13	4			.923	-4	O	-1.8

■ FRANK KOSTRO Kostro, Frank Jerry b: 8/4/37, Windber, Pa. BR/TR, 6'2", 190 lbs. Deb: 9/02/62

YEAR	TM/L	G	AB	R	H	2B	3B	HR	RBI	BB	SO	AVG	OBP	SLG	PRO+	BR	/A	RC	SB	CS	SBR	FA	FR	POS	TPR
1962	Det-A	16	41	5	11	3	0	0	3	1	6	.268	.286	.341	66	-2	-2	4	0	0	0	.967	1	3	-0.1
1963	Det-A	31	52	4	12	1	0	0	0	9	13	.231	.344	.250	67	-2	-2	5	0	0	0	.929	-1	/31O	-0.3
	LA-A	43	99	6	22	2	1	2	10	6	17	.222	.267	.323	68	-5	-4	8	0	0	0	.960	-2	3/1O	-0.7
	Yr	74	151	10	34	3	1	2	10	15	30	.225	.295	.298	68	-6	-6	13	0	0	0	.953	-3	3/1O	-1.0
1964	Min-A	59	103	10	28	5	0	3	12	4	21	.272	.306	.408	96	-1	-1	12	0	0	0	.912	-3	3/2O1	-0.4
1965	Min-A	20	31	2	5	2	0	0	1	4	5	.161	.257	.226	37	-2	-3	2	0	0	0	.923	-1	/23O	-0.3
1967	Min-A	32	31	4	10	0	0	0	2	3	2	.323	.382	.323	102	1	0	3	0	0	0	1.000	-1	/O3	-0.1
1968	Min-A	63	108	9	26	4	1	0	9	6	20	.241	.281	.296	71	-3	-4	9	0	0	0	1.000	-1	O/1	-0.7
1969	Min-A	2	2	0	0	0	0	0	0	0	1	.000	.000	.000	-98	-1	-1	0	0	0	0	.000	0	H	-0.1
Total	7	266	467	40	114	17	2	5	37	33	85	.244	.295	.321	74	-15	-16	44	0	0	0	.926	-8	/3O21	-2.7

■ ERNIE KOY Koy, Ernest Anyz "Chief" b: 9/17/09, Sealy, Tex. BR/TR, 6', 200 lbs. Deb: 4/19/38

YEAR	TM/L	G	AB	R	H	2B	3B	HR	RBI	BB	SO	AVG	OBP	SLG	PRO+	BR	/A	RC	SB	CS	SBR	FA	FR	POS	TPR
1938	Bro-N	142	521	78	156	29	13	11	76	38	76	.299	.352	.468	121	15	14	87	15			.984	-1	*O/3	0.9
1939	Bro-N	125	425	57	118	37	5	8	67	39	64	.278	.338	.445	105	4	2	63	11			.962	-0	*O	-0.2
1940	Bro-N	24	48	9	11	2	1	1	8	3	3	.229	.275	.375	73	-2	-2	5	1			1.000	-4	O	-0.6
	StL-N	93	348	44	108	19	5	8	52	28	59	.310	.368	.463	121	13	10	60	12			.970	-3	O	0.3
	Yr	117	396	53	119	21	6	9	60	31	62	.301	.357	.452	115	11	8	65	13			.973	-6	*O	-0.3
1941	StL-N	13	40	5	8	1	0	2	4	1	8	.200	.220	.375	61	-2	-2	3	0			1.000	-2	O	-0.5
	Cin-N	67	204	24	51	11	2	2	27	14	22	.250	.301	.353	84	-5	-5	22	1			.990	-1	O	-1.0
	Yr	80	244	29	59	12	2	4	31	15	30	.242	.288	.357	80	-7	-7	25	1			.991	-3	O	-1.5
1942	Cin-N	3	2	0	0	0	0	0	0	0	2	.000	.000	.000	-99	-0	-0	0	0			.000	0	H	-0.1
	Phi-N	91	258	21	63	9	3	4	26	14	50	.244	.283	.349	89	-6	-5	25	0			.981	-9	O	-1.8
	Yr	94	260	21	63	9	3	4	26	14	52	.242	.281	.346	87	-7	-5	25	0			.981	-9	O	-1.9
Total	5	558	1846	238	515	108	29	36	260	137	284	.279	.332	.427	107	18	12	266	40			.977	-20	O/3	-3.0

■ AL KOZAR Kozar, Albert Kenneth b: 7/5/22, McKees Rocks, Pa. BR/TR, 5'9.5", 173 lbs. Deb: 4/19/48

YEAR	TM/L	G	AB	R	H	2B	3B	HR	RBI	BB	SO	AVG	OBP	SLG	PRO+	BR	/A	RC	SB	CS	SBR	FA	FR	POS	TPR
1948	Was-A	150	577	61	144	25	8	1	58	66	52	.250	.327	.326	76	-22	-19	63	4	2	0	.967	-21	*2	-3.1
1949	Was-A	105	350	46	94	15	2	4	31	25	23	.269	.321	.357	81	-12	-11	41	2	1	0	.977	-7	*2	-1.4
1950	Was-A	20	55	7	11	1	0	0	3	5	8	.200	.267	.218	27	-6	-6	3	0	0	0	.962	-0	2	-0.5
	Chi-A	10	10	4	3	0	0	1	2	0	3	.300	.300	.600	129	0	0	1	0	0	0	1.000	3	/23	0.3
	Yr	30	65	11	14	1	0	1	5	5	11	.215	.271	.277	42	-6	-6	5	0	0	0	.968	2	2/3	-0.2
Total	3	285	992	118	252	41	10	6	94	96	86	.254	.321	.334	76	-39	-35	108	6	3	0	.971	-26	2/3	-4.7

■ JOE KRACHER Kracher, Joseph Peter "Jug" b: 11/4/15, Philadelphia, Pa. d: 12/24/81, San Angelo, Tex. BR/TR, 5'11", 185 lbs. Deb: 9/17/39

YEAR	TM/L	G	AB	R	H	2B	3B	HR	RBI	BB	SO	AVG	OBP	SLG	PRO+	BR	/A	RC	SB	CS	SBR	FA	FR	POS	TPR
1939	Phi-N	5	5	1	1	0	0	0	0	2	1	.200	.429	.200	76	-0	0	1	0			1.000	-1	/C	-0.1

■ CLARENCE KRAFT Kraft, Clarence Otto "Big Boy" b: 6/9/1887, Evansville, Ind. d: 3/26/58, Fort Worth, Tex. BR/TR, 6', 190 lbs. Deb: 5/01/14

YEAR	TM/L	G	AB	R	H	2B	3B	HR	RBI	BB	SO	AVG	OBP	SLG	PRO+	BR	/A	RC	SB	CS	SBR	FA	FR	POS	TPR
1914	Bos-N	3	3	0	1	0	0	0	0	0	1	.333	.333	.333	99	-0	-0	0	0			1.000	0	/1	0.0

■ ED KRANEPOOL Kranepool, Edward Emil b: 11/8/44, New York, N.Y. BL/TL, 6'3", 215 lbs. Deb: 9/22/62

YEAR	TM/L	G	AB	R	H	2B	3B	HR	RBI	BB	SO	AVG	OBP	SLG	PRO+	BR	/A	RC	SB	CS	SBR	FA	FR	POS	TPR
1962	NY-N	3	6	0	1	1	0	0	0	0	1	.167	.167	.333	30	-1	-1	0	0	0	0	1.000	1	/1	0.0
1963	NY-N	86	273	22	57	12	2	2	14	18	50	.209	.258	.289	56	-15	-16	19	4	2	0	.954	-2	O1	-2.3
1964	NY-N	119	420	47	108	19	4	10	45	32	50	.257	.313	.393	100	-2	-1	51	0	1	-1	.991	3	*1/O	-0.3
1965	NY-N☆	153	525	44	133	24	4	10	53	39	71	.253	.307	.371	94	-7	-5	57	1	4	-2	.992	-2	*1	-1.7
1966	NY-N	146	464	51	118	15	2	16	57	41	66	.254	.319	.399	100	-1	-0	60	1	1	-0	.992	4	*1O	-0.5
1967	NY-N	141	469	37	126	17	1	10	54	37	51	.269	.323	.373	100	-1	0	53	0	4	-2	.992	4	*1	-0.7
1968	NY-N	127	373	29	86	13	1	3	20	19	39	.231	.272	.295	70	-14	-14	29	0	3	-2	.994	4	*1/O	-2.3
1969	*NY-N	112	353	36	84	9	2	11	49	37	32	.238	.310	.368	88	-5	-6	39	3	2	-0	.993	3	*1/O	-1.2
1970	NY-N	43	47	2	8	0	0	0	3	5	2	.170	.250	.170	15	-6	-6	2	0	0	0	1.000	0	/1	-0.6
1971	NY-N	122	421	61	118	20	4	14	58	38	33	.280	.341	.447	123	11	12	63	0	4	-2	**.998**	-1	*1O	-0.1
1972	NY-N	122	327	28	88	15	1	8	34	34	35	.269	.340	.394	111	4	5	42	1	0	0	.996	-0	*1/O	-0.3
1973	*NY-N	100	284	28	68	12	2	1	35	30	28	.239	.312	.306	73	-10	-10	28	1	0	0	.998	-0	1O	-1.5
1974	NY-N	94	217	20	65	11	1	4	24	18	14	.300	.353	.415	116	4	4	32	1	0	0	.977	-6	O1	-0.4
1975	NY-N	106	325	42	105	16	0	4	43	27	21	.323	.375	.409	123	8	10	47	1	1	-0	.997	0	1/O	0.4
1976	NY-N	123	415	47	121	17	1	10	49	35	38	.292	.347	.410	121	7	10	58	1	0	0	.996	-6	1O	-0.2
1977	NY-N	108	281	28	79	17	0	10	40	23	20	.281	.336	.448	113	3	4	38	1	4	-2	.984	2	O1	0.1
1978	NY-N	66	81	7	17	2	0	3	19	8	12	.210	.289	.346	79	-3	-2	7	0	0	0	1.000	0	O/1	-0.3
1979	NY-N	82	155	7	36	5	0	2	17	13	18	.232	.296	.303	66	-8	-7	13	0	1	-1	1.000	1	1/O	-0.8
Total	18	1853	5436	536	1418	225	25	118	614	454	581	.261	.319	.377	97	-36	-22	638	15	27	-12	.994	7	*1O	-12.7

YEAR	TM/L	G	AB	R	H	2B	3B	HR	RBI	BB	SO	AVG	OBP	SLG	PRO+	BR	/A	RC	SB	CS	SBR	FA	FR	POS	TPR

■ CHARLIE KRAUSE
Krause, Charles b: 10/2/1873, Detroit, Mich. d: 3/30/48, Eloise, Mich. TR, Deb: 7/27/01

| 1901 | Cin-N | 1 | 4 | 0 | 1 | 0 | 0 | 0 | 0 | 0 | 0 | .250 | .250 | .250 | 49 | -0 | -0 | 0 | 0 | | | .000 | 0 | /2 | 0.0 |

■ DANNY KRAVITZ
Kravitz, Daniel "Dusty" or "Beak" b: 12/21/30, Lopez, Pa. BL/TR, 5'11", 195 lbs. Deb: 4/17/56

1956	Pit-N	32	68	6	18	2	2	2	10	5	9	.265	.315	.441	103	-0	-0	9	1	1	-0	.944	0	C/3	0.1
1957	Pit-N	19	41	2	6	1	0	0	4	2	10	.146	.186	.171	-3	-6	-6	1	0	0	0	1.000	0	C	-0.5
1958	Pit-N	45	100	9	24	3	2	1	5	11	10	.240	.315	.340	76	-4	-3	10	0	0	0	.967	-6	C	-0.8
1959	Pit-N	52	162	18	41	9	1	3	21	5	14	.253	.275	.377	72	-7	-7	16	0	1	-1	.986	-1	C	-0.6
1960	Pit-N	8	6	0	0	0	0	0	0	1	2	.000	.143	.000	-57	-1	-0	0	0	0	0	1.000	-0	/C	-0.1
	KC-A	59	175	17	41	7	2	4	14	11	19	.234	.280	.366	73	-7	-7	16	0	0	0	.971	-4	C	-0.8
Total	5	215	552	52	130	22	7	10	54	35	64	.236	.281	.355	70	-25	-24	53	1	2	-1	.973	-10	C/3	-2.7

■ MIKE KREEVICH
Kreevich, Michael Andreas b: 6/10/08, Mt.Olive, Ill. BR/TR, 5'7.5", 168 lbs. Deb: 9/07/31

1931	Chi-N	5	12	0	2	0	0	0	0	0	6	.167	.167	.167	-10	-2	-2	0	1			1.000	-0	/O	-0.2
1935	Chi-A	6	23	3	10	2	0	0	2	1	0	.435	.458	.522	149	2	2	5	1	1	-0	1.000	-2	/3	-0.1
1936	Chi-A	137	550	99	169	32	11	5	69	61	46	.307	.378	.433	96	0	-3	93	10	5	0	.964	-2	*O	-0.9
1937	Chi-A	144	583	94	176	29	16	12	73	43	45	.302	.350	.468	104	2	2	97	10	1	2	.988	7	*O	0.6
1938	Chi-A★	129	489	73	145	26	12	6	73	55	23	.297	.371	.436	99	1	-1	82	13	5	1	.975	4	*O	0.0
1939	Chi-A	145	541	85	175	30	8	5	77	59	40	.323	.390	.436	108	10	8	93	23	10	1	.975	16	*O/3	1.8
1940	Chi-A	144	582	86	154	27	10	8	55	34	49	.265	.305	.387	77	-20	-21	66	15	7	0	.982	12	*O	-1.6
1941	Chi-A	121	436	44	101	16	8	0	37	35	26	.232	.289	.305	58	-27	-27	40	17	5	2	.994	0	*O	-3.1
1942	Phi-A	116	444	57	113	19	1	1	30	47	31	.255	.326	.309	79	-12	-11	46	7	9	-3	.981	4	*O	-1.6
1943	StL-A	60	161	24	41	6	0	0	10	26	13	.255	.358	.292	89	-1	-1	20	4	1	1	.993	5	O	0.2
1944	*StL-A	105	402	55	121	15	6	5	44	27	24	.301	.348	.405	108	7	4	56	3	3	-1	.986	-1	*O	-0.3
1945	StL-A	84	295	34	70	11	1	2	21	37	27	.237	.322	.302	78	-6	-8	31	4	1	1	.991	4	O	-0.9
	Was-A	45	158	22	44	8	2	1	23	21	9	.278	.363	.373	124	3	5	22	7	5	-1	.971	-2	O	0.0
	Yr	129	453	56	114	19	3	3	44	58	36	.252	.337	.327	92	-3	-3	53	11	6	-0	.985	2	*O	-0.9
Total	12	1241	4676	676	1321	221	75	45	514	446	339	.283	.346	.391	92	-43	-54	651	115	53		.982	46	*O/3	-6.1

■ CHARLIE KREHMEYER
Krehmeyer, Charles L. b: 7/5/1863, St.Louis, Mo. d: 2/10/26, St.Louis, Mo. BL/TL, Deb: 7/08/1884

1884	StL-a	21	70	3	16	0	1	0			2	.229	.250	.257	66	-2	-3	5				.619	-5	O/C1	-0.7
1885	Lou-a	7	31	4	7	1	1	0			1	.226	.250	.323	82	-1	-1	3				.909	-1	/CO1	-0.1
	StL-N	1	3	0	0	0	0	0	0	0	2	.000	.000	.000	-99	-1	-1	0				.429	-2	/C	-0.2
Total	2	29	104	7	23	1	2	0	0	3	2	.221	.243	.269	66	-4	-4	7				.571	-7	/OC1	-1.0

■ MICKEY KREITNER
Kreitner, Albert Joseph b: 10/10/22, Nashville, Tenn. BR/TR, 6'3", 190 lbs. Deb: 9/28/43

1943	Chi-N	3	8	0	3	0	0	0	2	1	2	.375	.444	.375	140	-0	-0	1	0			1.000	-0	/C	0.0
1944	Chi-N	39	85	3	13	2	0	0	1	8	16	.153	.234	.176	17	-9	-9	4	0			.992	-1	C	-0.9
Total	2	42	93	3	16	2	0	0	3	9	18	.172	.252	.194	27	-9	-9	6	0			.992	-1	/C	-0.9

■ RALPH KREITZ
Kreitz, Ralph Wesley "Red" b: 11/13/1885, Plum Creek, Neb. d: 7/20/41, Portland, Ore. BR/TR, 5'9.5", 175 lbs. Deb: 8/01/11

| 1911 | Chi-A | 7 | 17 | 0 | 4 | 1 | 0 | 0 | | | 2 | .235 | .316 | .294 | 73 | -1 | -1 | 2 | 0 | | | 1.000 | -3 | /C | -0.3 |

■ JIMMY KREMERS
Kremers, James Edward b: 10/8/65, Little Rock, Ark. BL/TR, 6'3", 205 lbs. Deb: 6/05/90

| 1990 | Atl-N | 29 | 73 | 7 | 8 | 1 | 1 | 1 | 2 | 6 | 27 | .110 | .177 | .192 | 1 | -10 | -10 | 3 | 0 | 0 | 0 | .992 | -3 | C | -1.3 |

■ WAYNE KRENCHICKI
Krenchicki, Wayne Richard b: 9/17/54, Trenton, N.J. BL/TR, 6'1", 180 lbs. Deb: 6/15/79

1979	Bal-A	16	21	1	4	1	0	0	4	1	1	.190	.190	.238	15	-2	-2	1	0	0	0	.875	1	/32	-0.1
1980	Bal-A	9	14	1	2	0	0	0	0	1	3	.143	.200	.143	-4	-2	-2	0	0	0	0	1.000	0	/S2D	-0.2
1981	Bal-A	33	56	7	12	4	0	0	6	4	9	.214	.267	.286	59	-3	-3	4	0	0	0	.964	4	S/23D	0.3
1982	Cin-N	94	187	19	53	6	1	2	21	13	23	.283	.330	.358	91	-2	-2	22	5	3	-0	.955	7	3/2	0.4
1983	Cin-N	51	77	6	21	2	0	0	11	8	4	.273	.349	.299	78	-2	-2	8	0	0	0	.980	1	3/2	-0.2
	Det-A	59	133	18	37	7	0	1	16	11	17	.278	.338	.353	93	-1	-1	17	0	0	0	.934	-8	3/2S1	-0.9
1984	Cin-N	97	181	18	54	9	2	6	22	19	23	.298	.365	.470	127	8	7	30	0	1	-1	.967	3	3/12	0.9
1985	Cin-N	90	173	16	47	9	4	4	25	28	20	.272	.373	.393	109	4	3	27	0	0	0	.967	4	3/2	0.7
1986	Mon-N	101	221	21	53	6	2	2	23	22	32	.240	.309	.312	72	-8	-8	22	2	4	-2	.991	3	13/2O	-1.2
Total	8	550	1063	107	283	44	5	15	124	106	141	.266	.334	.359	92	-9	-11	131	7	8	-3	.955	14	3/12SDO	-1.2

■ CHUCK KRESS
Kress, Charles Steven b: 12/9/21, Philadelphia, Pa. BL/TL, 6', 190 lbs. Deb: 4/16/47

1947	Cin-N	11	27	4	4	0	0	0	6	4	4	.148	.303	.148	23	-3	-3	2	0			.983	1	/1	-0.2
1949	Cin-N	27	29	3	6	3	0	0	3	3	5	.207	.281	.310	58	-2	-2	2	0			.974	0	1	-0.2
	Chi-A	97	353	45	98	17	6	1	44	39	44	.278	.349	.368	93	-5	-4	47	6	7	-2	.994	-0	1	-0.7
1950	Chi-A	3	8	0	0	0	0	0	0	0	2	.000	.000	.000	-99	-2	-2	-0	0	0	0	1.000	0	/1	-0.2
1954	Det-A	24	37	4	7	0	1	0	3	1	4	.189	.211	.243	24	-4	-4	2	0	1	-1	.971	-0	/1O	-0.5
	Bro-N	13	12	1	1	0	0	0	2	0	0	.083	.083	.083	-55	-3	-3	-0	0	0	0	.500	-0	/1	-0.3
Total	4	175	466	57	116	20	7	1	52	49	59	.249	.320	.328	74	-19	-17	53	6	8		.990	0	1/O	-2.1

■ RED KRESS
Kress, Ralph b: 1/2/07, Columbia, Cal. d: 11/29/62, Los Angeles, Cal. BR/TR, 5'11.5", 165 lbs. Deb: 9/24/27 C

1927	StL-A	7	23	3	7	2	1	1	3	3	3	.304	.385	.609	150	2	2	5	0			.974	1	/S	0.3
1928	StL-A	150	560	78	153	26	10	3	81	48	70	.273	.332	.371	82	-13	-15	71	5	4	-1	.929	-17	*S	-1.4
1929	StL-A	147	557	82	170	38	4	9	107	52	54	.305	.366	.436	102	4	1	88	5	8	-3	.946	-2	*S	1.3
1930	StL-A	154	614	94	192	43	8	16	112	50	56	.313	.366	.487	110	12	9	105	3	12	-6	.938	-12	*S3	0.6
1931	StL-A	150	605	87	188	46	8	16	114	46	48	.311	.360	.493	118	17	14	101	3	16	-3	.936	-11	3OS1	-0.2
1932	StL-A	14	52	2	9	0	1	2	9	4	6	.173	.232	.327	41	-5	-5	4	1	1	-0	.909	2	3	-0.2
	Chi-A	135	515	83	147	42	4	9	57	47	36	.285	.346	.435	108	-0	5	79	6	3	0	.956	11	OS3/1	1.6
	Yr	149	567	85	156	42	5	11	66	51	42	.275	.336	.425	101	-5	-0	82	7	4	-0	.956	13	OS3/1	1.4
1933	Chi-A	129	467	47	116	20	5	10	78	37	40	.248	.304	.377	83	-15	-12	54	4	4	-1	.978	-4	*1/O	-2.7
1934	Chi-A	8	14	3	4	0	0	0	1	3	3	.286	.412	.286	80	-0	-0	2	0	0	0	1.000	-4	/2	-0.4
	Was-A	56	171	18	39	4	3	4	24	17	19	.228	.298	.357	71	-9	-8	19	3	0	1	.993	-2	10/2S3	-1.0
	Yr	64	185	21	43	4	3	4	25	20	22	.232	.307	.351	72	-9	-8	21	3	0	1	.993	-6	10/2S3	-1.4
1935	Was-A	84	252	32	75	13	4	2	42	25	16	.298	.361	.405	101	-1	-0	37	3	3	-1	.964	17	S/1PO2	1.7
1936	Was-A	109	391	51	111	20	6	8	51	39	25	.284	.349	.427	96	-7	-3	60	6	2	0	.927	3	S2/1	1.2
1938	StL-A	150	566	74	171	33	3	7	79	69	47	.302	.378	.408	97	-2	-1	90	5	4	-2	.965	-15	*S	-0.5
1939	StL-A	13	43	5	12	1	0	0	8	6	2	.279	.367	.302	72	-1	-2	4	1	0	0	.933	-3	S	-0.3
	Det-A	51	157	19	38	7	0	1	22	17	16	.242	.316	.306	55	-9	-11	15	2	1	0	.959	2	S2/3	-0.6
	Yr	64	200	24	50	8	0	1	30	23	18	.250	.327	.305	59	-11	-13	19	3	1	0	.951	-1	S2/3	-0.9
1940	Det-A	33	99	13	22	3	1	1	11	10	12	.222	.294	.303	50	-7	-8	8	0	0	0	.924	9	3S	0.2
1946	NY-N	1	1	0	0	0	0	0	0	1	0	.000	.500	.000	48	0	0	0	0			1.000	1	/P	0.0
Total	14	1391	5087	691	1454	298	58	89	799	474	453	.286	.347	.420	96	-32	-35	742	47	56		.944	-16	S310/2P	-0.4

■ CHAD KREUTER
Kreuter, Chadden Michael b: 8/26/64, Greenbrae, Cal. BB/TR, 6'2", 190 lbs. Deb: 9/14/88

1988	Tex-A	16	51	3	14	2	1	5	7	13	.275	.362	.412	113	1	1	8	0	0	0	.990	2	C	0.4
1989	Tex-A	87	158	16	24	3	0	5	9	27	40	.152	.276	.266	52	-10	-10	13	0	1	-1	.992	12	C	0.4
1990	Tex-A	22	22	2	1	1	0	0	8	8	9	.045	.300	.091	14	-2	-2	1	0	0	0	.977	-2	C/D	-0.4
1991	Tex-A	3	4	0	0	0	0	0	0	0	1	.000	.000	.000	-99	-1	-1	0	0	0	0	1.000	0	/C	-0.1

YEAR	TM/L	G	AB	R	H	2B	3B	HR	RBI	BB	SO	AVG	OBP	SLG	PRO+	BR	/A	RC	SB	CS	SBR	FA	FR	POS	TPR
1992	Det-A	67	190	22	48	9	0	2	16	20	38	.253	.324	.332	83	-4	-4	19	0	1	-1	.983	5	C/D	0.3
Total	5	195	425	43	87	15	1	8	32	62	101	.205	.306	.301	70	-15	-16	41	0	2	-1	.988	16	C/D	0.6

■ PAUL KRICHELL Krichell, Paul Bernard b: 12/19/1882, New York, N.Y. d: 6/4/57, New York, N.Y. BR/TR, 5'7", 150 lbs. Deb: 5/12/11

YEAR	TM/L	G	AB	R	H	2B	3B	HR	RBI	BB	SO	AVG	OBP	SLG	PRO+	BR	/A	RC	SB	CS	SBR	FA	FR	POS	TPR
1911	StL-A	28	82	6	19	3	0	0	8	4		.232	.276	.268	54	-5	-5	7	2			.943	-2	C	-0.4
1912	StL-A	59	161	19	35	6	0	0	8	19		.217	.304	.255	62	-8	-7	13	2			.959	-1	C	-0.3
Total	2	87	243	25	54	9	0	0	16	23		.222	.295	.259	60	-13	-12	20	4			.955	-3	/C	-0.7

■ BILL KRIEG Krieg, William Frederick b: 1/29/1859, Petersburg, Ill. d: 3/25/30, Chillicothe, Ill. BR/TR, 5'8", 180 lbs. Deb: 4/20/1884

YEAR	TM/L	G	AB	R	H	2B	3B	HR	RBI	BB	SO	AVG	OBP	SLG	PRO+	BR	/A	RC	SB	CS	SBR	FA	FR	POS	TPR
1884	CP-U	71	279	35	69	15	4	0		11		.247	.276	.330	105	1	1	26				.932	17	CO/S1	2.0
1885	Chi-N	1	3	0	0	0	0	0	0	0	2	.000	.000	.000	-87	-1	-1	0				.800	2	/O	0.1
	Bro-a	17	60	7	9	4	0	1		2		.150	.177	.267	40	-4	-4	3				.910	-4	C/1	-0.7
1886	Was-N	27	98	11	25	6	3	1	15	3	12	.255	.277	.408	113	0	1	12	2			.975	-1	1	-0.3
1887	Was-N	25	95	9	24	4	1	2	17	7	5	.253	.311	.379	97	-1	-0	12	2			.973	-3	1/O	-0.4
Total	4	141	535	62	127	29	8	4	32	23	19	.237	.270	.344	96	-4	-2	53	4			.929	12	/C1OS	0.7

■ KRIEGER Krieger Deb: 7/28/1884

YEAR	TM/L	G	AB	R	H	2B	3B	HR	RBI	BB	SO	AVG	OBP	SLG	PRO+	BR	/A	RC	SB	CS	SBR	FA	FR	POS	TPR
1884	KC-U	1	3	0	0	0	0	0		0		.000	.000	.000	-99	-1	-1	0				.000	-1	/OP	0.0

■ JOHN KRONER Kroner, John Harold b: 11/13/08, St.Louis, Mo. d: 8/26/68, St.Louis, Mo. BR/TR, 6', 185 lbs. Deb: 9/29/35

YEAR	TM/L	G	AB	R	H	2B	3B	HR	RBI	BB	SO	AVG	OBP	SLG	PRO+	BR	/A	RC	SB	CS	SBR	FA	FR	POS	TPR
1935	Bos-A	2	4	1	1	0	0	0	0	1	1	.250	.400	.250	67	-0	-0	1	0	0	0	1.000	-1	/3	-0.1
1936	Bos-A	84	298	40	87	17	8	4	62	26	24	.292	.349	.443	89	-4	-6	46	2	3	-1	.964	-2	23S/O	-0.4
1937	Cle-A	86	283	29	67	14	1	2	26	22	25	.237	.292	.314	52	-21	-21	27	1	1	-0	.969	-3	23	-1.9
1938	Cle-A	51	117	13	29	16	0	1	17	19	6	.248	.353	.410	92	-2	-1	18	0	1	-1	.974	12	2/13S	1.0
Total	4	223	702	83	184	47	9	7	105	68	56	.262	.327	.385	75	-26	-29	91	3	5	-2	.968	6	2/3S10	-1.4

■ MIKE KRSNICH Krsnich, Michael b: 9/24/31, W.Allis, Wis. BR/TR, 6'1", 190 lbs. Deb: 4/23/60 F

YEAR	TM/L	G	AB	R	H	2B	3B	HR	RBI	BB	SO	AVG	OBP	SLG	PRO+	BR	/A	RC	SB	CS	SBR	FA	FR	POS	TPR
1960	Mil-N	4	9	0	3	1	0	0	2	0	0	.333	.333	.444	120	0	0	1	0	0	0	1.000	-0	/O	0.0
1962	Mil-N	11	12	0	1	1	0	0	2	0	4	.083	.083	.167	-36	-2	-2	0	0	0	0	1.000	0	/O13	-0.2
Total	2	15	21	0	4	2	0	0	4	0	4	.190	.190	.286	28	-2	-2	1	0	0	0	1.000	0	/O31	-0.2

■ ROCKY KRSNICH Krsnich, Rocco Peter b: 8/5/27, W.Allis, Wis. BR/TR, 6'1", 174 lbs. Deb: 9/13/49 F

YEAR	TM/L	G	AB	R	H	2B	3B	HR	RBI	BB	SO	AVG	OBP	SLG	PRO+	BR	/A	RC	SB	CS	SBR	FA	FR	POS	TPR
1949	Chi-A	16	55	7	12	3	1	1	9	6	4	.218	.295	.364	76	-2	-2	6	0	1	-1	.935	4	3	0.0
1952	Chi-A	40	91	11	21	7	2	1	15	12	9	.231	.327	.385	97	-0	-0	11	0	0	0	.959	10	3	0.9
1953	Chi-A	64	129	9	26	8	0	1	14	12	11	.202	.270	.287	49	-9	-10	10	0	2	-1	.929	9	3	-0.3
Total	3	120	275	27	59	18	3	3	38	30	24	.215	.294	.335	70	-12	-12	27	0	3	-2	.942	23	3	0.6

■ OTTO KRUEGER Krueger, Arthur William "Oom Paul" b: 9/17/1876, Chicago, Ill. d: 2/20/61, St.Louis, Mo. BR/TR, 5'7", 165 lbs. Deb: 9/16/1899

YEAR	TM/L	G	AB	R	H	2B	3B	HR	RBI	BB	SO	AVG	OBP	SLG	PRO+	BR	/A	RC	SB	CS	SBR	FA	FR	POS	TPR
1899	Cle-N	13	44	4	10	1	0	0	2	8		.227	.358	.250	74	-1	-1	4	1			.763	-2	/3S2	-0.3
1900	StL-N	12	35	8	14	3	2	1	3	10		.400	.543	.686	240	7	7	14	0			.852	-4	2	0.3
1901	StL-N	142	520	77	143	16	12	2	79	50		.275	.353	.363	114	7	11	77	19			.881	-9	*3	0.3
1902	StL-N	128	467	55	124	7	8	0	46	29		.266	.314	.315	98	-3	-1	53	14			.897	1	*S3	0.7
1903	Pit-N	80	256	42	63	6	8	1	28	21		.246	.323	.344	88	-3	-4	32	5			.884	-5	SO3/2	-0.9
1904	Pit-N	86	268	34	52	6	2	1	26	29		.194	.278	.243	60	-11	-12	22	8			.905	-5	OS3	-1.9
1905	Phi-N	46	114	10	21	1	1	0	12	13		.184	.273	.211	47	-7	-7	8	1			.930	-9	S/O3	-1.7
Total	7	507	1704	230	427	40	33	5	196	160		.251	.326	.322	94	-12	-7	210	48			.879	-34	S3/O2	-3.5

■ ERNIE KRUEGER Krueger, Ernest George b: 12/27/1890, Chicago, Ill. d: 4/22/76, Waukegan, Ill. BR/TR, 5'10.5", 185 lbs. Deb: 8/04/13

YEAR	TM/L	G	AB	R	H	2B	3B	HR	RBI	BB	SO	AVG	OBP	SLG	PRO+	BR	/A	RC	SB	CS	SBR	FA	FR	POS	TPR
1913	Cle-A	5	6	0	0	0	0	0	0	0	2	.000	.000	.000	-97	-1	-2	0	0			1.000	-0	/C	-0.2
1915	NY-A	10	29	3	5	1	0	0	0	0	5	.172	.200	.207	22	-3	-3	1	0	1	-1	.905	-4	/C	-0.7
1917	NY-N	8	10	0	0	0	0	0	0	0	4	.000	.000	.000	-99	-2	-2	0	0			.857	-2	/C	-0.5
	Bro-N	31	81	10	22	2	2	1	6	5	7	.272	.330	.383	115	2	1	10	1			.979	1	C	0.5
	Yr	39	91	10	22	2	2	1	6	5	11	.242	.296	.341	94	-1	-1	9	1			.973	-1	C	0.0
1918	Bro-N	30	87	4	25	4	2	0	7	4	9	.287	.319	.379	113	1	1	10	2			.986	6	C	0.9
1919	Bro-N	80	226	24	56	7	4	5	36	19	25	.248	.312	.381	105	2	1	27	4			.963	5	C	1.4
1920	*Bro-N	52	146	21	42	4	2	1	17	16	13	.288	.358	.363	104	2	1	20	2	0	1	.959	-4	C	0.1
1921	Bro-N	65	163	18	43	11	4	3	20	14	12	.264	.322	.436	95	-1	-2	23	2	2	-1	.969	-2	C	-0.1
1925	Cin-N	37	88	7	27	4	0	1	7	6	8	.307	.351	.386	90	-1	-1	11	1	2	-1	.946	-4	C	-0.4
Total	8	318	836	87	220	33	14	11	93	64	85	.263	.319	.376	97	-3	-4	102	12	5		.964	-3	C	1.0

■ CHRIS KRUG Krug, Everett Ben b: 12/25/39, Los Angeles, Cal. BR/TR, 6'4", 200 lbs. Deb: 5/30/65

YEAR	TM/L	G	AB	R	H	2B	3B	HR	RBI	BB	SO	AVG	OBP	SLG	PRO+	BR	/A	RC	SB	CS	SBR	FA	FR	POS	TPR
1965	Chi-N	60	169	16	34	5	0	5	24	13	52	.201	.262	.320	61	-8	-9	12	0	1	-1	.980	1	C	-0.7
1966	Chi-N	11	28	1	6	1	0	0	1	1	8	.214	.241	.250	36	-2	-2	2	0	0	0	1.000	3	C	0.1
1969	SD-N	8	17	0	1	0	0	0	0	1	6	.059	.111	.059	-53	-3	-3	0	0	0	0	.938	-1	/C	-0.4
Total	3	79	214	17	41	6	0	5	25	15	66	.192	.248	.290	50	-14	-15	14	0	1	-1	.980	3	/C	-1.0

■ GENE KRUG Krug, Gary Eugene b: 2/12/55, Garden City, Kan. BL/TL, 6'4", 225 lbs. Deb: 4/29/81

YEAR	TM/L	G	AB	R	H	2B	3B	HR	RBI	BB	SO	AVG	OBP	SLG	PRO+	BR	/A	RC	SB	CS	SBR	FA	FR	POS	TPR
1981	Chi-N	7	5	0	2	0	0	0	0	1	1	.400	.500	.400	151	0	0	1	0	0	0	.000	0	/H	0.0

■ HENRY KRUG Krug, Henry Charles b: 12/4/1876, San Francisco, Cal. d: 1/14/08, San Francisco, Cal BR/TR, Deb: 7/26/02

YEAR	TM/L	G	AB	R	H	2B	3B	HR	RBI	BB	SO	AVG	OBP	SLG	PRO+	BR	/A	RC	SB	CS	SBR	FA	FR	POS	TPR
1902	Phi-N	53	198	20	45	3	3	0	14	7		.227	.264	.273	66	-8	-8	16	2			.947	-6	O2/S3	-1.6

■ MARTY KRUG Krug, Martin John b: 9/10/1888, Coblenz, Germany d: 6/27/66, Glendale, Cal. BR/TR, 5'9", 165 lbs. Deb: 5/29/12

YEAR	TM/L	G	AB	R	H	2B	3B	HR	RBI	BB	SO	AVG	OBP	SLG	PRO+	BR	/A	RC	SB	CS	SBR	FA	FR	POS	TPR
1912	Bos-A	24	39	6	12	2	1	0	7	5		.308	.386	.410	122	1	1	7	2			.895	-2	/S2	0.0
1922	Chi-N	127	450	67	124	23	4	4	60	43	43	.276	.343	.371	82	-10	-12	58	7	9	-3	.937	-6	*32/S	-1.1
Total	2	151	489	73	136	25	5	4	67	48	43	.278	.346	.374	85	-9	-10	65	9	9		.910	-8	3/2S	-1.1

■ ART KRUGER Kruger, Arthur T. b: 3/16/1881, San Antonio, Tex. d: 11/28/49, Hondo, Cal. BR/TR, 6', 185 lbs. Deb: 4/11/07

YEAR	TM/L	G	AB	R	H	2B	3B	HR	RBI	BB	SO	AVG	OBP	SLG	PRO+	BR	/A	RC	SB	CS	SBR	FA	FR	POS	TPR
1907	Cin-N	100	317	25	74	10	9	0	28	18		.233	.285	.322	87	-4	-6	34	10			.972	0	O	-1.0
1910	Cle-A	47	168	14	26	4	2	0	10	15		.155	.237	.202	37	-12	-12	11	10			.947	2	O	-1.4
	Bos-N	1	1	0	0	0	0	0	0	0	0	.000	.000	.000	-96	-0	-0	0	0			.000	0	H	0.0
	Cle-A	15	55	5	12	2	1	0	4	5		.218	.295	.291	82	-1	-1	5	2			.974	2	O	0.0
1914	KC-F	122	441	45	114	24	7	4	47	23	59	.259	.297	.372	93	-8	-6	55	11			.963	-7	*O	-1.8
1915	KC-F	80	240	24	57	9	2	2	26	12	29	.237	.277	.317	77	-8	-7	24	5			.984	0	O	-1.1
Total	4	365	1222	113	283	49	21	6	115	73	88	.232	.281	.321	80	-34	-32	129	38			.968	-2	O	-5.3

■ JOHN KRUK Kruk, John Martin b: 2/9/61, Charleston, W.Va. BL/TL, 5'10", 200 lbs. Deb: 4/07/86

YEAR	TM/L	G	AB	R	H	2B	3B	HR	RBI	BB	SO	AVG	OBP	SLG	PRO+	BR	/A	RC	SB	CS	SBR	FA	FR	POS	TPR
1986	SD-N	122	278	33	86	16	2	4	38	45	58	.309	.406	.424	132	13	14	47	2	4	-2	.981	-5	O/1	0.5
1987	SD-N	138	447	72	140	14	2	20	91	73	93	.313	.410	.488	142	26	28	92	18	10	-1	.996	3	*1O	2.3
1988	SD-N	120	378	54	91	17	1	9	44	80	68	.241	.373	.362	114	9	10	56	5	3	-0	.995	-2	1O	0.1
1989	SD-N	31	76	7	14	0	0	3	6	17	14	.184	.333	.303	83	-1	-1	8	0	0	0	.962	1	O	0.0
	Phi-N	81	281	46	93	13	6	5	38	27	39	.331	.390	.473	146	17	17	53	3	0	1	.983	-4	O/1	1.2
	Yr	112	357	53	107	13	6	8	44	44	53	.300	.377	.437	132	15	15	59	3	0	1	.977	-3	O/1	1.2
1990	Phi-N	142	443	52	129	25	8	7	67	69	70	.291	.387	.431	125	17	17	75	10	5	0	.986	-5	O1	0.7
1991	Phi-N☆	152	538	84	158	27	6	21	92	67	100	.294	.373	.483	141	28	29	99	7	0	2	.997	-1	*1O	2.3
1992	Phi-N★	144	507	86	164	30	4	10	70	92	88	.323	.428	.458	152	39	39	103	3	5	-2	.993	-12	*1O	1.8

YEAR	TM/L	G	AB	R	H	2B	3B	HR	RBI	BB	SO	AVG	OBP	SLG	PRO+	BR	/A	RC	SB	CS	SBR	FA	FR	POS	TPR
Total	7	930	2948	434	875	142	29	79	446	470	530	.297	.394	.445	135	147	152	532	48	27	-2	.995	-25	1O	8.9

■ **DICK KRYHOSKI** Kryhoski, Richard David b: 3/24/25, Leonia, N.J. BL/TL, 6'2", 200 lbs. Deb: 4/19/49

YEAR	TM/L	G	AB	R	H	2B	3B	HR	RBI	BB	SO	AVG	OBP	SLG	PRO+	BR	/A	RC	SB	CS	SBR	FA	FR	POS	TPR
1949	NY-A	54	177	18	52	10	3	1	27	9	17	.294	.335	.401	94	-2	-2	22	2	4	-2	.983	-1	1	-0.5
1950	Det-A	53	169	20	37	10	0	4	19	8	11	.219	.258	.349	53	-13	-13	15	0	1	-1	.991	-0	1	-1.4
1951	Det-A	119	421	58	121	19	4	12	57	28	29	.287	.335	.437	107	3	2	60	1	2	-1	.991	3	*1	-0.1
1952	StL-A	111	342	38	83	13	1	11	42	23	42	.243	.296	.383	86	-7	-8	39	2	0	1	.989	-5	1	-1.6
1953	StL-A	104	338	35	94	18	4	16	50	26	33	.278	.333	.497	119	8	7	52	0	5	-3	.992	5	1	0.6
1954	Bal-A	100	300	32	78	13	2	1	34	19	24	.260	.308	.327	80	-11	-8	29	0	0	0	.992	3	1	-0.9
1955	KC-A	28	47	2	10	2	0	0	2	6	7	.213	.302	.255	50	-3	-3	4	0	1	-1	.988	0	1	-0.4
Total	7	569	1794	203	475	85	14	45	231	119	163	.265	.315	.403	93	-25	-25	221	5	13	-6	.990	5	1	-4.3

■ **TONY KUBEK** Kubek, Anthony Christopher b: 10/12/36, Milwaukee, Wis. BL/TR, 6'3", 191 lbs. Deb: 4/20/57

YEAR	TM/L	G	AB	R	H	2B	3B	HR	RBI	BB	SO	AVG	OBP	SLG	PRO+	BR	/A	RC	SB	CS	SBR	FA	FR	POS	TPR
1957	*NY-A	127	431	56	128	21	3	3	39	24	48	.297	.338	.381	98	-3	-2	56	6	6	-2	.938	1	OS3/2	-0.2
1958	*NY-A☆	138	559	66	148	21	1	2	48	25	57	.265	.297	.317	72	-24	-21	52	5	4	-1	.961	20	*S/O12	1.0
1959	NY-A★	132	512	67	143	25	7	6	51	24	46	.279	.314	.391	95	-6	-4	60	3	3	-1	.968	-1	SO3/2	-0.2
1960	*NY-A	147	568	77	155	25	3	14	62	31	42	.273	.314	.401	98	-8	-4	70	3	0	1	.968	-4	*SO	0.3
1961	*NY-A★	153	617	84	170	38	6	8	46	27	60	.276	.307	.395	91	-14	-10	74	1	3	-2	.959	13	*S	1.4
1962	*NY-A	45	169	28	53	6	1	4	17	12	17	.314	.359	.432	115	3	3	26	2	1	0	.954	5	S/O	1.2
1963	*NY-A	135	557	72	143	21	3	7	44	28	68	.257	.295	.343	79	-17	-16	57	4	2	0	.980	10	*S/O	0.3
1964	NY-A	106	415	46	95	16	3	8	31	26	55	.229	.276	.340	69	-17	-18	39	4	1	1	.978	4	S	-0.6
1965	NY-A	109	339	26	74	5	3	5	35	20	48	.218	.262	.295	58	-19	-19	25	1	3	-2	.964	-10	S/O1	-2.6
Total	9	1092	4167	522	1109	178	30	57	373	217	441	.266	.305	.364	85	-104	-90	459	29	23	-5	.967	39	SO/321	0.6

■ **TED KUBIAK** Kubiak, Theodore Rodger b: 5/12/42, New Brunswick, N.J. BB/TR, 6', 175 lbs. Deb: 4/14/67

YEAR	TM/L	G	AB	R	H	2B	3B	HR	RBI	BB	SO	AVG	OBP	SLG	PRO+	BR	/A	RC	SB	CS	SBR	FA	FR	POS	TPR
1967	KC-A	53	102	6	16	2	1	0	5	12	20	.157	.246	.196	33	-8	-8	5	0	0	0	.984	-3	S2/3	-1.0
1968	Oak-A	48	120	10	30	5	2	0	8	8	18	.250	.308	.325	96	-1	-1	12	1	1	-0	.929	-3	2S	-0.2
1969	Oak-A	92	305	38	76	9	1	2	27	25	35	.249	.308	.305	75	-11	-10	29	2	0	1	.976	-0	S2	-0.2
1970	Mil-A	158	540	63	136	9	6	4	41	72	51	.252	.340	.313	81	-12	-12	56	4	9	-4	.989	-17	2S	-1.9
1971	Mil-A	89	260	26	59	6	5	3	17	41	31	.227	.332	.323	87	-4	-3	28	0	5	-3	.971	-3	2S	-0.1
	StL-N	32	72	8	18	3	2	1	10	11	12	.250	.349	.389	105	1	1	11	1	0	0	.959	-4	S2	-0.1
1972	Tex-A	46	116	5	26	3	0	0	7	12	12	.224	.302	.250	69	-5	-4	8	0	1	-1	.990	-3	2S/3	-0.5
	*Oak-A	51	94	14	17	4	1	0	8	9	11	.181	.252	.245	51	-6	-5	6	0	0	0	.988	2	2/3	-0.2
	Yr	97	210	19	43	7	1	0	15	21	23	.205	.280	.248	61	-10	-9	15	0	1	-1	.989	-1	2S/3	-0.7
1973	*Oak-A	106	182	15	40	6	1	3	17	12	19	.220	.268	.313	67	-9	-8	15	1	1	-0	.973	6	2S/3	0.2
1974	Oak-A	99	220	22	46	3	0	0	18	18	15	.209	.269	.223	46	-16	-14	12	1	1	-0	.995	-9	2S3/D	-2.1
1975	Oak-A	20	28	2	7	1	0	0	4	2	2	.250	.300	.286	68	-1	-1	2	0	0	0	1.000	2	/S32	0.2
	SD-N	87	196	13	44	5	0	0	14	24	18	.224	.309	.250	60	-11	-9	16	3	1	0	.954	1	32/1	-0.8
1976	SD-N	96	212	16	50	5	2	0	26	25	28	.236	.316	.278	76	-8	-6	18	0	3	-2	.971	-9	32/S1	-1.7
Total	10	977	2447	238	565	61	21	13	202	271	272	.231	.309	.289	73	-91	-81	219	13	22	-9	.981	-39	2S3/1D	-8.4

■ **JACK KUBISZYN** Kubiszyn, John Henry b: 12/19/36, Buffalo, N.Y. BR/TR, 5'11", 170 lbs. Deb: 4/23/61

YEAR	TM/L	G	AB	R	H	2B	3B	HR	RBI	BB	SO	AVG	OBP	SLG	PRO+	BR	/A	RC	SB	CS	SBR	FA	FR	POS	TPR
1961	Cle-A	25	42	4	9	0	0	0	0	2	5	.214	.250	.214	26	-4	-4	2	0	0	0	1.000	3	/3S2	-0.1
1962	Cle-A	25	59	3	10	2	0	1	2	5	7	.169	.234	.254	32	-6	-6	4	0	0	0	.964	2	S/3	-0.2
Total	2	50	101	7	19	2	0	1	2	7	12	.188	.241	.238	30	-10	-10	6	0	0	0	.969	5	/S32	-0.3

■ **GIL KUBSKI** Kubski, Gilbert Thomas b: 10/12/54, Longview, Tex. BL/TR, 6'3", 185 lbs. Deb: 9/02/80

YEAR	TM/L	G	AB	R	H	2B	3B	HR	RBI	BB	SO	AVG	OBP	SLG	PRO+	BR	/A	RC	SB	CS	SBR	FA	FR	POS	TPR
1980	Cal-A	22	63	11	16	3	0	0	6	6	10	.254	.319	.302	73	-2	-2	6	1	1	-0	1.000	1	O	-0.3

■ **STEVE KUCZEK** Kuczek, Stanislaw Leo b: 12/28/24, Amsterdam, N.Y. BR/TR, 6', 160 lbs. Deb: 9/29/49

YEAR	TM/L	G	AB	R	H	2B	3B	HR	RBI	BB	SO	AVG	OBP	SLG	PRO+	BR	/A	RC	SB	CS	SBR	FA	FR	POS	TPR
1949	Bos-N	1	1	0	1	1	0	0	0	0	0	1.000	1.000	2.000	723	1	1	2	0			.000	0	H	0.1

■ **BILL KUEHNE** Kuehne, William J. (b: William J. Knelme) b: 10/24/1858, Leipzig, Germany d: 10/27/21, Sulphur Springs, O BR/TR, 185 lbs. Deb: 5/01/1883

YEAR	TM/L	G	AB	R	H	2B	3B	HR	RBI	BB	SO	AVG	OBP	SLG	PRO+	BR	/A	RC	SB	CS	SBR	FA	FR	POS	TPR
1883	Col-a	95	374	38	85	8	14	1		2		.227	.231	.332	86	-9	-4	29				.833	-5	*32/SO	-0.8
1884	Col-a	110	415	48	98	13	16	5		9		.236	.254	.381	116	3	7	41				.881	11	*3	1.8
1885	Pit-a	104	411	54	93	9	19	0		15		.226	.257	.341	91	-5	-4	37				.865	-1	*3/S	-0.3
1886	Pit-a	117	481	73	98	16	17	1		19		.204	.237	.314	74	-16	-16	43	26			.899	-1	O31	-1.7
1887	Pit-N	102	402	68	120	18	15	1	41	14	39	.299	.324	.425	115	3	7	62	17			.883	-13	*S/31O	-0.4
1888	Pit-N	138	524	60	123	22	11	3	62	9	68	.235	.250	.336	95	-8	-3	54	34			.910	0	3S	0.0
1889	Pit-N	97	390	43	96	20	5	5	57	9	36	.246	.263	.362	83	-15	-9	42	15			.885	-1	3O/2S1	-0.7
1890	Pit-P	126	528	66	126	21	12	5	73	28	37	.239	.277	.352	75	-25	-18	59	21			.850	6	*3	-0.5
1891	Col-a	68	261	32	56	9	0	2	22	10	22	.215	.244	.272	52	-18	-15	23	21			.885	-2	3	-1.2
	Lou-a	41	159	28	44	3	1	1	18	8	13	.277	.315	.327	88	-3	-3	20	10			.904	3	3	0.1
	Yr	109	420	60	100	12	1	3	40	18	35	.238	.271	.293	66	-21	-18	43	31			.893	0	*3	-1.1
1892	Lou-N	76	287	22	48	4	5	0	36	13	36	.167	.203	.216	30	-25	-22	14	6			.874	-3	3	-2.1
	StL-N	6	24	1	4	1	0	0	0	0	3	.167	.200	.208	26	-2	-2	1	1			.895	0	/3S	-0.1
	Cin-N	6	24	3	5	1	0	1	4	1	5	.208	.240	.375	88	-1	-1	2	0			.941	2	/32	0.1
	StL-N	1	4	0	0	0	0	0	0	0	1	.000	.000	.000	-99	-1	-1	0	0			1.000	1	/3	0.0
	Yr	89	339	26	57	6	5	1	40	14	45	.168	.203	.224	33	-29	-25	17	7			.880	-0	3/2S	-2.1
Total	10	1087	4284	536	996	145	115	25	313	137	260	.232	.258	.338	84	-122	-83	428	151			.876	-4	3S/O21	-5.8

■ **HARVEY KUENN** Kuenn, Harvey Edward b: 12/4/30, W.Allis, Wis. d: 2/28/88, Peoria, Ariz. BR/TR, 6'2", 190 lbs. Deb: 9/06/52 MC

YEAR	TM/L	G	AB	R	H	2B	3B	HR	RBI	BB	SO	AVG	OBP	SLG	PRO+	BR	/A	RC	SB	CS	SBR	FA	FR	POS	TPR
1952	Det-A	19	80	2	26	2	2	0	8	2	1	.325	.349	.400	107	1	1	10	2	1	0	.962	2	S	0.4
1953	Det-A★	155	679	94	**209**	33	7	2	48	50	31	.308	.356	.386	101	0	1	96	6	5	-1	.973	-21	*S	-0.9
1954	Det-A☆	155	656	81	**201**	28	6	5	48	29	13	.306	.337	.390	100	-3	-1	80	9	9	-3	.966	3	*S	1.2
1955	Det-A★	145	620	101	190	**38**	5	8	62	40	27	.306	.349	.423	109	4	6	92	8	3	1	.956	-28	*S	-0.9
1956	Det-A★	146	591	96	**196**	32	7	12	88	55	34	.332	.391	.470	126	23	22	109	9	5	-0	**.968**	-20	*S/O	1.4
1957	Det-A★	151	624	74	173	30	6	9	44	47	28	.277	.328	.388	92	-5	-7	75	5	8	-3	.955	-49	*S3/1	-4.8
1958	Det-A☆	139	561	73	179	**39**	3	8	54	51	34	.319	.376	.442	116	19	14	89	5	10	-5	.984	15	*O	1.7
1959	Det-A★	139	561	99	**198**	**42**	7	9	71	48	37	**.353**	.405	.501	140	36	32	117	7	2	1	.988	1	*O	2.7
1960	Cle-A★	126	474	65	146	24	0	9	54	55	25	.308	.381	.416	119	11	13	77	3	0	1	.966	1	*O/3	1.0
1961	SF-N	131	471	60	125	22	4	5	46	47	34	.265	.333	.361	87	-10	-8	55	5	4	-1	.988	-8	O3/S	-2.2
1962	*SF-N	130	487	73	148	23	5	10	68	49	37	.304	.369	.433	116	10	12	77	3	6	-3	.970	-14	*O3	-1.1
1963	SF-N	120	417	61	121	13	2	6	31	44	38	.290	.361	.374	113	8	8	57	2	1	0	.975	-28	O3	-2.5
1964	SF-N	111	351	42	92	16	2	4	22	35	32	.262	.331	.353	91	-3	-4	42	0	1	-1	.952	-13	O1/3	-2.3
1965	SF-N	23	59	4	14	0	0	0	6	10	3	.237	.357	.237	69	-2	-2	6	3	1	0	1.000	-1	O/1	-0.4
	Chi-N	54	120	11	26	5	0	0	6	22	13	.217	.338	.258	69	-4	-4	12	1	0	0	.975	-3	O/1	-0.9
	Yr	77	179	15	40	5	0	0	12	32	16	.223	.344	.251	69	-5	-6	18	4	1	1	.981	-4	O/1	-1.3
1966	Chi-N	3	3	0	1	0	0	0	0	0	1	.333	.333	.333	85	-0	-0	0	0	0	0	.000	0	/O	0.0
	Phi-N	86	159	15	47	9	0	0	15	10	16	.296	.337	.352	92	-2	-2	18	0	0	0	1.000	-4	O1/3	-0.8
	Yr	89	162	15	48	9	0	0	15	10	17	.296	.337	.352	92	-2	-2	19	0	0	0	1.000	-4	O1/3	-0.8
Total	15	1833	6913	951	2092	356	56	87	671	594	404	.303	.359	.408	108	85	82	1013	68	56	-13	.978	-166	OS3/1	-8.4

■ **JOE KUHEL** Kuhel, Joseph Anthony b: 6/25/06, Cleveland, Ohio d: 2/26/84, Kansas City, Kan. BL/TL, 6', 180 lbs. Deb: 7/31/30 M

YEAR	TM/L	G	AB	R	H	2B	3B	HR	RBI	BB	SO	AVG	OBP	SLG	PRO+	BR	/A	RC	SB	CS	SBR	FA	FR	POS	TPR
1930	Was-A	18	63	9	18	3	3	0	17	5	6	.286	.348	.429	95	-0	-1	10	1	0	0	.981	-1	1	-0.2

YEAR	TM/L	G	AB	R	H	2B	3B	HR	RBI	BB	SO	AVG	OBP	SLG	PRO+	BR	/A	RC	SB	CS	SBR	FA	FR	POS	TPR
1931	Was-A	139	524	70	141	34	8	8	85	47	45	.269	.335	.410	94	-5	-5	73	7	5	-1	.991	-7	*1	-2.4
1932	Was-A	101	347	52	101	21	5	4	52	32	19	.291	.353	.415	99	-1	-0	52	5	2	0	.994	-2	1	-0.8
1933	*Was-A	153	602	89	194	34	10	11	107	59	48	.322	.385	.467	126	21	22	110	17	8	0	**.996**	-7	*1	0.1
1934	Was-A	63	263	49	76	12	3	3	25	30	14	.289	.364	.392	99	-2	-0	37	2	7	-4	.994	-4	1	-1.3
1935	Was-A	151	633	99	165	25	9	2	74	78	44	.261	.345	.338	80	-20	-17	78	5	4	-1	.991	0	*1	-3.2
1936	Was-A	149	588	107	189	42	8	16	118	64	30	.321	.392	.502	126	17	22	117	15	7	0	.993	-2	*1	0.5
1937	Was-A	136	547	73	155	24	11	6	61	63	39	.283	.357	.400	95	-8	-4	81	6	3	0	.993	3	*1	-1.5
1938	Chi-A	117	412	67	110	27	4	8	51	72	35	.267	.376	.410	95	-1	-2	67	9	7	-2	.988	-7	*1	-2.2
1939	Chi-A	139	546	107	164	24	9	15	56	64	51	.300	.376	.460	110	10	8	99	18	5	2	.992	-4	*1	-0.7
1940	Chi-A	155	603	111	169	28	8	27	94	87	59	.280	.374	.488	120	19	18	116	12	5	1	.988	-5	*1	-0.1
1941	Chi-A	153	600	99	150	39	5	12	63	70	55	.250	.331	.392	92	-9	-8	81	20	5	3	.994	-1	*1	-1.6
1942	Chi-A	115	413	60	103	14	4	4	52	60	22	.249	.347	.332	94	-3	-2	54	22	9	1	.991	-4	*1	-1.2
1943	Chi-A	153	531	55	113	21	1	5	46	76	45	.213	.319	.284	77	-13	-13	54	14	8	-1	.995	1	*1	-2.4
1944	Was-A	139	518	90	144	26	7	4	51	68	40	.278	.364	.378	117	10	13	75	11	6	-0	.987	-2	*1	0.3
1945	Was-A	142	533	73	152	29	13	2	75	79	31	.285	.378	.400	137	19	25	88	10	5	0	.989	-6	*1	1.0
1946	Was-A	14	20	2	3	0	0	0	2	5	2	.150	.320	.150	36	-2	-1	1	0	0	0	1.000	0	/1	-0.1
	Chi-A	64	238	24	65	9	3	4	20	21	24	.273	.335	.387	105	0	1	30	4	4	-1	.994	-2	1	-0.6
	Yr	78	258	26	68	9	3	4	22	26	26	.264	.333	.368	100	-1	-0	32	4	4	-1	.994	-2	1	-0.7
1947	Chi-A	3	3	0	0	0	0	0	0	0	3	.000	.000	.000	-99	-1	-1	0	0	0	0	.000	0	H	-0.1
Total	18	2104	7984	1236	2212	412	111	131	1049	980	612	.277	.359	.406	104	33	54	1223	178	90	-1	.992	-48	*1	-16.5

■ **KENNY KUHN** Kuhn, Kenneth Harold b: 3/20/37, Louisville, Ky. BL/TR, 5'10.5", 175 lbs. Deb: 7/07/55

YEAR	TM/L	G	AB	R	H	2B	3B	HR	RBI	BB	SO	AVG	OBP	SLG	PRO+	BR	/A	RC	SB	CS	SBR	FA	FR	POS	TPR
1955	Cle-A	4	6	0	2	0	0	0	0	1	0	.333	.429	.333	103	0	0	1	1	0	0	1.000	-2	/S	-0.1
1956	Cle-A	27	22	7	6	1	0	0	2	0	4	.273	.273	.318	54	-1	-2	2	0	1	-1	1.000	2	S/2	0.0
1957	Cle-A	40	53	5	9	0	0	0	5	4	9	.170	.228	.170	10	-6	-6	2	0	0	0	.974	-3	2/3S	-0.9
Total	3	71	81	12	17	1	0	0	7	5	13	.210	.256	.222	30	-8	-8	5	1	1	-0	.963	-3	/S23	-1.0

■ **WALT KUHN** Kuhn, Walter Charles "Red" b: 2/2/1884, Fresno, Cal. d: 6/14/35, Fresno, Cal. BR/TR, 5'7", 162 lbs. Deb: 4/18/12

YEAR	TM/L	G	AB	R	H	2B	3B	HR	RBI	BB	SO	AVG	OBP	SLG	PRO+	BR	/A	RC	SB	CS	SBR	FA	FR	POS	TPR
1912	Chi-A	76	178	16	36	7	0	0	10	20		.202	.286	.242	53	-11	-10	14	5			.966	9	C/2	0.4
1913	Chi-A	26	50	5	8	1	0	0	5	13	8	.160	.333	.180	52	-2	-2	3	1			.980	-2	C	-0.3
1914	Chi-A	17	40	4	11	1	0	0	0	8	11	.275	.396	.300	111	1	1	5	2	3	-1	.987	-1	C	0.0
Total	3	119	268	25	55	9	0	0	15	41	19	.205	.313	.239	62	-12	-11	22	8	3		.971	6	C/2	0.1

■ **CHARLIE KUHNS** Kuhns, Charles B. b: 10/27/1877, Freeport, Pa. d: 7/15/22, Pittsbugh, Pa. 5'9", 160 lbs. Deb: 6/04/1897

YEAR	TM/L	G	AB	R	H	2B	3B	HR	RBI	BB	SO	AVG	OBP	SLG	PRO+	BR	/A	RC	SB	CS	SBR	FA	FR	POS	TPR
1897	Pit-N	1	3	0	0	0	0	0	0	1		.000	.250	.000	-32	-1	-1	0	0			.667	0	/3	0.0
1899	Bos-N	7	18	2	5	0	0	0	3	2		.278	.350	.278	67	-1	-1	2	0			.813	-1	/S3	-0.2
Total	2	8	21	2	5	0	0	0	3	3		.238	.333	.238	53	-1	-1	2	0			.733	-1	/3S	-0.2

■ **DUANE KUIPER** Kuiper, Duane Eugene b: 6/19/50, Racine, Wis. BL/TR, 6', 175 lbs. Deb: 9/09/74

YEAR	TM/L	G	AB	R	H	2B	3B	HR	RBI	BB	SO	AVG	OBP	SLG	PRO+	BR	/A	RC	SB	CS	SBR	FA	FR	POS	TPR
1974	Cle-A	10	22	7	11	2	0	0	4	2	2	.500	.542	.591	228	4	4	6	1	1	-0	1.000	1	/2	0.5
1975	Cle-A	90	346	42	101	11	1	0	25	30	26	.292	.362	.329	97	-0	-0	39	19	18	-5	.972	-14	2/D	-1.5
1976	Cle-A	135	506	47	133	13	6	0	37	30	42	.263	.305	.312	82	-12	-12	43	10	17	-7	**.987**	20	*2/1D	0.9
1977	Cle-A	148	610	62	169	15	8	1	50	37	55	.277	.326	.333	83	-16	-14	66	11	11	-3	.985	2	*2	-0.4
1978	Cle-A	149	547	52	155	18	6	0	43	19	35	.283	.312	.338	84	-13	-12	54	4	9	-4	.979	-19	*2	-2.5
1979	Cle-A	140	479	46	122	9	5	0	39	37	27	.255	.313	.294	65	-23	-23	41	4	9	-4	**.988**	-4	*2	-2.1
1980	Cle-A	42	149	10	42	5	0	0	9	13	8	.282	.340	.315	80	-4	-4	17	0	1	-1	.995	-8	2	-0.9
1981	Cle-A	72	206	15	53	6	0	0	14	8	13	.257	.285	.286	66	-9	-9	17	1	1	-0	.983	-5	2	-1.1
1982	SF-N	107	218	26	61	9	1	0	17	32	24	.280	.377	.330	100	1	1	28	2	2	-1	.978	-7	2	-0.4
1983	SF-N	72	176	14	44	2	2	0	14	27	13	.250	.356	.284	82	-4	-3	18	0	1	-1	.988	-9	2	-1.0
1984	SF-N	83	115	8	23	1	0	0	11	12	10	.200	.276	.209	39	-9	-9	7	0	1	-1	.969	6	2/1	-0.3
1985	SF-N	9	5	0	3	0	0	0	0	1	0	.600	.667	.600	270	1	1	2	0	0	0	.000	0	/H	0.1
Total	12	1057	3379	329	917	91	29	1	263	248	255	.271	.326	.316	81	-83	-78	340	52	71	-27	.983	-36	2/1D	-8.7

■ **JEFF KUNKEL** Kunkel, Jeffrey William b: 3/25/62, W.Palm Beach, Fla. BR/TR, 6'2", 180 lbs. Deb: 7/23/84 F

YEAR	TM/L	G	AB	R	H	2B	3B	HR	RBI	BB	SO	AVG	OBP	SLG	PRO+	BR	/A	RC	SB	CS	SBR	FA	FR	POS	TPR
1984	Tex-A	50	142	13	29	2	3	3	7	2	35	.204	.221	.324	47	-10	-11	9	4	3	-1	.922	-1	S/D	-0.9
1985	Tex-A	2	4	1	1	0	0	0	0	0	3	.250	.250	.250	37	-0	-0	0	0	0	0	1.000	1	/S	0.1
1986	Tex-A	8	13	3	3	0	0	1	2	0	2	.231	.231	.462	81	-0	-0	1	0	0	0	.769	-0	/SD	-0.1
1987	Tex-A	15	32	1	7	0	0	1	2	0	10	.219	.242	.313	46	-3	-3	2	0	1	-1	.955	2	2/3O1SD	-0.1
1988	Tex-A	55	154	14	35	8	3	2	15	4	35	.227	.252	.357	67	-7	-7	12	0	1	-1	.949	6	2S3/OPD	0.0
1989	Tex-A	108	293	39	79	21	2	8	29	20	75	.270	.323	.437	110	4	3	41	3	2	-0	.936	2	SO/23PD	0.8
1990	Tex-A	99	200	17	34	11	1	3	17	11	66	.170	.221	.280	39	-17	-17	11	2	1	0	.958	9	S32/OD	-0.5
1992	Chi-N	20	29	0	4	2	0	0	1	0	8	.138	.138	.207	-4	-4	-4	1	0	0	0	1.000	4	/S2O	0.0
Total	8	357	867	88	192	44	9	18	73	37	234	.221	.260	.355	69	-37	-39	78	9	8	-2	.940	21	S/2O3DP1	-0.7

■ **RUSTY KUNTZ** Kuntz, Russell Jay b: 2/4/55, Orange, Cal. BR/TR, 6'3", 190 lbs. Deb: 9/01/79 C

YEAR	TM/L	G	AB	R	H	2B	3B	HR	RBI	BB	SO	AVG	OBP	SLG	PRO+	BR	/A	RC	SB	CS	SBR	FA	FR	POS	TPR
1979	Chi-A	5	11	0	1	0	0	0	0	2	6	.091	.231	.091	-9	-2	-2	0	0	0	0	1.000	1	/O	-0.1
1980	Chi-A	36	62	5	14	4	0	0	3	5	13	.226	.284	.290	58	-4	-4	5	1	0	0	.979	-5	O	-0.9
1981	Chi-A	67	55	15	14	2	0	0	4	6	8	.255	.339	.291	85	-1	-1	6	1	0	0	1.000	-13	O/D	-1.5
1982	Chi-A	21	26	4	5	1	0	0	3	2	8	.192	.250	.231	33	-2	-2	1	0	0	0	1.000	-7	O	-1.0
1983	Chi-A	28	42	6	11	1	0	0	1	6	13	.262	.354	.286	76	-1	-1	5	1	0	0	.976	-6	O/D	-0.7
	Min-A	31	100	13	19	3	0	3	5	12	28	.190	.277	.310	59	-5	-6	8	0	0	0	.986	0	O	-0.7
	Yr	59	142	19	30	4	0	3	6	18	41	.211	.300	.303	64	-6	-7	13	1	0	0	.982	-6	O/D	-1.4
1984	*Det-A	84	140	32	40	12	0	2	22	25	28	.286	.398	.414	126	6	6	25	2	2	-1	.987	-16	OD	-1.2
1985	Det-A	5	5	0	0	0	0	0	0	2	2	.000	.286	.000	-13	-1	-1	0	0	1	-1	.000	-0	/1D	-0.2
Total	7	277	441	75	104	23	0	5	38	60	106	.236	.330	.322	81	-10	-10	50	5	3	-0	.988	-46	O/D1	-6.3

■ **WHITEY KUROWSKI** Kurowski, George John b: 4/19/18, Reading, Pa. BR/TR, 5'11", 193 lbs. Deb: 9/23/41

YEAR	TM/L	G	AB	R	H	2B	3B	HR	RBI	BB	SO	AVG	OBP	SLG	PRO+	BR	/A	RC	SB	CS	SBR	FA	FR	POS	TPR
1941	StL-N	5	9	1	3	2	0	0	2	0	2	.333	.400	.556	157	1	1	2	0			1.000	-1	/3	0.0
1942	*StL-N	115	366	51	93	17	3	9	42	33	60	.254	.326	.391	102	4	0	48	7			.944	9	*3/SO	1.1
1943	*StL-N☆	139	522	69	150	24	8	13	70	31	54	.287	.330	.439	116	11	9	74	3			.952	1	*3/S	1.3
1944	*StL-N★	149	555	95	150	25	7	20	87	58	40	.270	.341	.449	119	14	13	85	2			**.965**	4	*3/2S	1.9
1945	StL-N†	133	511	84	165	27	3	21	102	45	45	.323	.383	.511	144	31	29	100	1			.964	2	*3/S	3.4
1946	*StL-N★	142	519	76	156	32	5	14	89	72	47	.301	.391	.462	136	29	26	97	2			**.966**	0	*3	3.0
1947	StL-N★	146	513	108	159	27	6	27	104	87	56	.310	.420	.544	148	42	39	118	4			.954	-14	*3	2.4
1948	StL-N	77	220	34	47	8	0	2	33	42	28	.214	.352	.277	68	-7	-8	25	0			.939	-11	3	-2.0
1949	StL-N	10	14	0	2	0	0	0	0	1	0	.143	.200	.143	-6	-2	-2	0	0			1.000	-0	/3	-0.3
Total	9	916	3229	518	925	162	32	106	529	369	332	.286	.366	.455	124	123	106	551	19			.957	-10	3/S2O	10.8

■ **CRAIG KUSICK** Kusick, Craig Robert b: 9/30/48, Milwaukee, Wis. BR/TR, 6'3", 232 lbs. Deb: 9/08/73

YEAR	TM/L	G	AB	R	H	2B	3B	HR	RBI	BB	SO	AVG	OBP	SLG	PRO+	BR	/A	RC	SB	CS	SBR	FA	FR	POS	TPR
1973	Min-A	15	48	4	12	2	0	0	4	7	9	.250	.357	.292	81	-1	-1	6	0	0	0	.989	-1	1/OD	-0.3
1974	Min-A	76	201	36	48	7	1	8	26	35	36	.239	.354	.403	113	5	4	30	0	0	0	.996	4	1	0.4
1975	Min-A	57	156	14	37	8	0	6	27	21	23	.237	.346	.404	109	3	2	23	0	0	0	.990	1	1	0.0
1976	Min-A	109	266	33	69	13	0	11	36	35	44	.259	.348	.432	124	9	8	43	5	1	1	.977	3	D1	1.2
1977	Min-A	115	268	34	68	12	0	12	45	49	60	.254	.375	.433	121	9	9	43	3	1	0	.972	-2	D1	0.7
1978	Min-A	77	191	23	33	3	2	4	20	37	38	.173	.310	.272	64	-8	-8	17	3	2	-0	.987	2	D1/O	-0.9

YEAR	TM/L	G	AB	R	H	2B	3B	HR	RBI	BB	SO	AVG	OBP	SLG	PRO+	BR	/A	RC	SB	CS	SBR	FA	FR	POS	TPR
1979	Min-A	24	54	8	13	4	0	3	6	3	11	.241	.281	.481	97	-0	-1	7	0	0	0	1.000	0	D/1	-0.1
	Tor-A	24	54	3	11	1	0	2	7	7	7	.204	.306	.333	72	-2	-2	6	0	0	0	.978	1	1/PD	-0.2
	Yr	48	108	11	24	5	0	5	13	10	18	.222	.294	.407	85	-2	-3	13	0	0	0	.983	1	1D/P	-0.3
Total	7	497	1238	155	291	50	3	46	171	194	228	.235	.345	.392	105	15	12	174	11	4	1	.988	9	1D/OP	0.8
■ ART KUSNYER Kusnyer, Arthur William b: 12/19/45, Akron, Ohio BR/TR, 6'2", 198 lbs. Deb: 9/21/70 C																									
1970	Chi-A	4	10	0	1	0	0	0	0	0	4	.100	.100	.100	-43	-2	-2	0	0	0	0	.941	1	/C	-0.1
1971	Cal-A	6	13	0	2	0	0	0	0	0	3	.154	.154	.154	-14	-2	-2	0	0	0	0	.958	1	/C	-0.1
1972	Cal-A	64	179	13	37	2	1	2	13	16	33	.207	.276	.263	64	-9	-7	14	0	0	0	.975	-3	C	-0.9
1973	Cal-A	41	64	5	8	2	0	0	3	2	12	.125	.152	.156	-14	-10	-9	1	0	1	-1	.979	1	C	-0.8
1976	Mil-A	15	34	2	4	1	0	0	3	1	5	.118	.167	.147	-8	-5	-5	1	1	0	0	.938	-1	C	-0.5
1978	KC-A	9	13	1	3	1	0	1	2	2	4	.231	.333	.538	138	1	1	3	0	0	0	.946	3	/C	0.4
Total	6	139	313	21	55	6	1	3	21	21	61	.176	.232	.230	37	-26	-24	19	1	1	-0	.970	2	C	-2.0
■ JUL KUSTUS Kustus, Joseph J. "Joe" or "Kul" b: 9/5/1882, Detroit, Mich. d: 4/27/16, Eloise, Mich. BR/TR, 5'10", Deb: 4/17/09																									
1909	Bro-N	53	173	12	25	5	0	1	11	11		.145	.204	.191	23	-16	-15	9	9			.951	0	O	-1.9
■ RANDY KUTCHER Kutcher, Randy Scott b: 4/20/60, Anchorage, Alaska BR/TR, 5'11", 175 lbs. Deb: 6/19/86																									
1986	SF-N	71	186	28	44	9	1	7	16	11	41	.237	.279	.409	92	-4	-3	20	6	5	-1	.990	-1	OS/32	-0.6
1987	SF-N	14	16	7	3	1	1	0	1	1	5	.188	.235	.375	61	-1	-1	2	1	0	0	1.000	1	/O23S	0.0
1988	Bos-A	19	12	2	2	1	0	0	0	0	2	.167	.167	.250	14	-1	-1	0	0	1	-1	1.000	0	/O3D	-0.2
1989	Bos-A	77	160	28	36	10	3	2	18	11	46	.225	.275	.363	74	-5	-6	15	3	0	1	.982	-3	O/3CD	-0.9
1990	*Bos-A	63	74	18	17	4	1	1	5	13	18	.230	.345	.351	91	-0	-1	9	3	3	-1	1.000	-0	O3/2D	-0.2
Total	5	244	448	83	102	25	6	10	40	36	112	.228	.285	.377	82	-12	-12	46	13	9	-2	.989	-3	O/3DS2C	-1.9
■ JOE KUTINA Kutina, Joseph Peter b: 1/16/1885, Chicago, Ill. d: 4/13/45, Chicago, Ill. BR/TR, 6'2", 205 lbs. Deb: 9/06/11																									
1911	StL-A	26	101	12	26	6	2	3	15	2		.257	.279	.446	105	-1	-0	13	2			.981	-1	1	-0.1
1912	StL-A	69	205	18	42	9	3	1	18	13		.205	.262	.293	61	-12	-11	16	0			.985	-3	1/O	-1.4
Total	2	95	306	30	68	15	5	4	33	15		.222	.268	.343	76	-12	-11	28	2			.984	-4	/1O	-1.5
■ AL KVASNAK Kvasnak, Alexander b: 1/11/21, Sagamore, Pa. BR/TR, 6'1", 170 lbs. Deb: 4/15/42																									
1942	Was-A	5	11	3	2	0	0	0	0	2	1	.182	.308	.182	40	-1	-1	1	0	0	0	1.000	-0	/O	-0.1
■ ANDY KYLE Kyle, Andrew Ewing b: 10/29/1889, Toronto, Ont., Can. d: 9/6/71, Toronto, Ont., Can. BL/TL, 5'8", 160 lbs. Deb: 9/07/12																									
1912	Cin-N	9	21	3	7	1	0	0	4	4	2	.333	.440	.381	129	1	1	4	0			1.000	0	/O	0.1
■ CHET LAABS Laabs, Chester Peter b: 4/30/12, Milwaukee, Wis. d: 1/26/83, Warren, Mich. BR/TR, 5'8", 175 lbs. Deb: 5/05/37																									
1937	Det-A	72	242	31	58	13	5	8	37	24	66	.240	.308	.434	83	-7	-8	33	6	2	1	.971	-7	O	-1.5
1938	Det-A	64	211	26	50	7	3	7	37	15	52	.237	.288	.398	66	-11	-13	24	3	2	-0	.971	-1	O	-1.4
1939	Det-A	5	16	1	5	1	1	0	2	2	0	.313	.389	.500	117	1	0	3	0	0	0	.933	1	/O	0.1
	StL-A	95	317	52	95	20	5	10	62	33	62	.300	.368	.489	115	7	6	57	4	1	1	.972	-0	O	0.4
	Yr	100	333	53	100	21	6	10	64	35	62	.300	.369	.489	115	8	7	60	4	1	1	.969	1	O	0.5
1940	StL-A	105	218	32	59	11	5	10	40	34	59	.271	.372	.505	122	8	7	43	3	3	-1	.969	-7	O	-0.3
1941	StL-A	118	392	64	109	23	6	15	59	51	59	.278	.361	.482	117	11	9	71	5	2	0	.982	-2	*O	0.2
1942	StL-A	144	520	90	143	21	7	27	99	88	88	.275	.380	.498	144	32	31	103	0	3	-2	.970	-4	*O	1.8
1943	StL-A★	151	580	83	145	27	7	17	85	73	105	.250	.338	.409	115	12	11	82	5	7	-3	.976	2	*O	0.3
1944	*StL-A	66	201	28	47	10	2	5	23	29	33	.234	.330	.378	96	1	-1	27	3	1	0	1.000	-2	O	-0.5
1945	StL-A	35	109	15	26	4	3	1	8	16	17	.239	.352	.358	101	1	1	15	0	0	0	.986	-4	O	-0.5
1946	StL-A	80	264	40	69	13	0	16	52	20	50	.261	.316	.492	117	6	5	38	3	1	0	.987	1	O	0.4
1947	Phi-A	15	32	5	7	1	0	1	5	4	4	.219	.306	.344	79	-1	-1	4	0	0	0	1.000	1	/O	-0.1
Total	11	950	3102	467	813	151	44	117	509	389	595	.262	.346	.452	113	60	48	501	32	22	-4	.977	-21	O	-1.1
■ COCO LABOY Laboy, Jose Alberto b: 7/3/39, Ponce, P.R. BR/TR, 5'10", 170 lbs. Deb: 4/08/69																									
1969	Mon-N	157	562	53	145	29	1	18	83	40	96	.258	.312	.409	100	-1	-1	70	0	2	-1	.944	4	*3	0.1
1970	Mon-N	137	432	37	86	26	1	5	53	31	81	.199	.256	.299	48	-33	-32	31	0	2	-1	.946	-4	*3/2	-3.9
1971	Mon-N	76	151	10	38	4	0	1	14	11	19	.252	.302	.298	70	-6	-6	13	0	1	-1	.937	1	3/2	-0.6
1972	Mon-N	28	69	6	18	2	0	3	14	10	16	.261	.354	.420	117	2	2	11	0	0	0	.980	-2	3/2S	0.0
1973	Mon-N	22	33	2	4	1	0	1	2	5	8	.121	.237	.242	32	-3	-3	2	0	0	0	.889	1	3/2	-0.2
Total	5	420	1247	108	291	62	2	28	166	97	220	.233	.292	.354	77	-41	-41	127	0	5	-3	.944	-0	3/2S	-4.6
■ CANDY LaCHANCE LaChance, George Joseph b: 2/15/1870, Waterbury, Conn. d: 8/18/32, Waterville, Conn. BB/TR, 6'1", 183 lbs. Deb: 8/15/1893																									
1893	Bro-N	11	35	1	6	1	0	0	6	2	12	.171	.237	.200	19	-4	-4	2	0			.654	-6	/CO	-0.8
1894	Bro-N	68	257	48	83	13	8	5	52	16	32	.323	.365	.494	115	2	5	55	20			.979	-8	1C/O	-0.2
1895	Bro-N	127	536	99	167	22	8	8	108	29	48	.312	.356	.427	112	2	9	97	37			.983	-6	*1/O	0.5
1896	Bro-N	89	348	60	99	10	13	7	58	23	32	.284	.331	.448	112	1	5	59	17			.986	-3	*1	0.2
1897	Bro-N	126	520	86	160	28	16	4	90	15		.308	.333	.446	111	0	5	89	26			.978	-4	*1	0.1
1898	Bro-N	136	526	62	130	23	7	5	65	31		.247	.299	.346	85	-12	-12	64	23			.988	-20	1SO	-2.9
1899	Bal-N	125	472	65	145	23	10	1	75	21		.307	.350	.405	101	3	-1	80	31			.984	-7	*1	-0.6
1901	Cle-A	133	548	81	166	22	9	1	75	7		.303	.314	.381	96	-7	-4	72	11			.979	-3	*1	-0.8
1902	Bos-A	138	541	60	151	13	4	6	56	18		.279	.309	.351	80	-14	-16	64	8			.983	-11	*1	-2.8
1903	*Bos-A	141	522	60	134	22	6	1	53	28		.257	.303	.328	85	-7	-10	60	12			.984	-11	*1	-2.4
1904	Bos-A	157	573	55	130	19	5	1	47	23		.227	.265	.283	70	-17	-21	49	7			**.992**	-14	*1	-4.3
1905	Bos-A	12	41	1	6	1	0	0	5	6		.146	.255	.171	36	-3	-3	2	0			.988	-0	1	-0.4
Total	12	1263	4919	678	1377	197	86	39	690	219	124	.280	.318	.379	94	-56	-45	693	192			.984	-93	*1/SOC	-14.4
■ RENE LACHEMANN Lachemann, Rene George b: 5/4/45, Los Angeles, Cal. BR/TR, 6', 198 lbs. Deb: 5/04/65 FMC																									
1965	KC-A	92	216	20	49	7	1	9	29	12	57	.227	.268	.394	87	-5	-5	22	0	0	0	.980	2	C	0.1
1966	KC-A	7	5	0	1	1	0	0	0	0	1	.200	.200	.400	70	-0	-0	0	0	0	0	1.000	1	/C	0.1
1968	Oak-A	19	60	3	9	1	0	0	4	1	11	.150	.177	.167	5	-7	-7	2	0	0	0	.967	-6	C	-1.4
Total	3	118	281	23	59	9	1	9	33	13	69	.210	.247	.345	70	-12	-11	24	0	0	0	.978	-3	/C	-1.2
■ PETE LaCOCK LaCock, Ralph Pierre b: 1/17/52, Burbank, Cal. BL/TL, 6'3", 210 lbs. Deb: 9/06/72																									
1972	Chi-N	5	6	3	3	0	0	0	4	0	1	.500	.500	.500	167	1	1	2	1	0	0	1.000	-0	/O	0.1
1973	Chi-N	11	16	1	4	1	0	0	3	1	2	.250	.294	.313	63	-1	-1	2	0	0	0	1.000	1	/O	0.0
1974	Chi-N	35	110	9	20	4	1	1	8	12	16	.182	.268	.264	47	-7	-8	8	0	0	0	.974	2	O1	-0.8
1975	Chi-N	106	249	30	57	8	1	6	30	37	27	.229	.329	.341	82	-4	-6	27	0	2	-1	.988	5	1O	-0.5
1976	Chi-N	106	244	34	54	9	2	8	28	42	37	.221	.338	.373	93	1	-2	31	1	4	-2	.975	-2	1O	-1.0
1977	*KC-A	88	218	25	66	12	1	3	29	15	25	.303	.350	.408	105	2	2	31	2	1	0	.990	1	1DO	0.1
1978	*KC-A	118	322	44	95	21	2	5	48	21	27	.295	.338	.419	109	4	3	44	1	0	0	.993	-6	*1	-0.7
1979	KC-A	132	408	54	113	25	4	3	56	37	26	.277	.339	.380	92	-3	-5	50	2	1	0	**.997**	1	*1D	-0.9
1980	*KC-A	114	156	14	32	6	0	1	18	17	10	.205	.287	.263	51	-10	-10	11	1	0	0	.997	-3	1O	-1.5
Total	9	715	1729	214	444	86	11	27	224	182	171	.257	.329	.366	89	-18	-25	206	8	8	-2	.991	-0	1O/D	-5.2
■ LEE LACY Lacy, Leondaus b: 4/10/48, Longview, Tex. BR/TR, 6'1", 175 lbs. Deb: 6/30/72																									
1972	LA-N	60	243	34	63	7	3	0	12	19	37	.259	.313	.313	80	-7	-6	24	5	3	-0	.973	-8	2	-1.2
1973	LA-N	57	135	14	28	2	0	0	8	15	34	.207	.287	.222	45	-10	-9	9	2	3	-1	.965	-1	2	-1.0

YEAR	TM/L	G	AB	R	H	2B	3B	HR	RBI	BB	SO	AVG	OBP	SLG	PRO+	BR	/A	RC	SB	CS	SBR	FA	FR	POS	TPR
1974	*LA-N	48	78	13	22	6	0	0	8	2	14	.282	.300	.359	87	-2	-2	9	2	0	1	.968	2	2/3	0.2
1975	LA-N	101	306	44	96	11	5	7	40	22	29	.314	.360	.451	129	9	11	44	5	9	-4	.935	-6	2O/S	0.0
1976	Atl-N	50	180	25	49	4	2	3	20	6	12	.272	.299	.367	83	-3	-5	18	2	2	-1	.969	-9	2/O3	-1.3
	LA-N	53	158	17	42	7	1	0	14	16	13	.266	.333	.323	88	-2	-2	16	1	2	-1	.979	1	O/32	-0.4
	Yr	103	338	42	91	11	3	3	34	22	25	.269	.316	.346	86	-6	-6	34	3	4	-2	.970	-9	2O/3	-1.7
1977	*LA-N	75	169	28	45	7	0	6	21	10	21	.266	.307	.414	92	-2	-2	22	4	0	1	1.000	-5	O23	-0.5
1978	*LA-N	103	245	29	64	16	4	13	40	27	30	.261	.337	.518	136	11	11	42	7	4	-0	.971	-5	O2/3S	0.6
1979	Pit-N	84	182	17	45	9	3	5	15	22	36	.247	.332	.412	97	0	-1	27	6	1	1	.973	-6	O/2	-0.7
1980	Pit-N	109	278	45	93	20	4	7	33	28	33	.335	.399	.511	150	20	19	57	18	9	0	.984	5	O/3	2.2
1981	Pit-N	78	213	31	57	11	4	2	10	11	29	.268	.307	.385	92	-2	-3	28	24	3	5	.977	0	O/3	0.2
1982	Pit-N	121	359	66	112	16	3	5	31	32	57	.312	.370	.415	116	10	8	56	40	15	3	.965	-5	*O/3	0.4
1983	Pit-N	108	288	40	87	12	3	4	13	22	36	.302	.352	.406	107	4	3	42	31	13	2	1.000	-4	O	-0.2
1984	Pit-N	138	474	66	152	26	3	12	70	32	61	.321	.364	.464	131	18	18	77	21	11	-0	**.996**	4	*O/2	2.0
1985	Bal-A	121	492	69	144	22	4	9	48	39	95	.293	.347	.409	109	4	6	70	10	3	1	.984	4	*O/D	0.7
1986	Bal-A	130	491	77	141	18	0	11	47	37	71	.287	.337	.391	99	-2	-1	62	4	6	-2	.992	6	*O/D	-0.1
1987	Bal-A	87	258	35	63	13	3	7	28	32	49	.244	.328	.399	94	-3	-2	34	3	2	-0	.973	2	O/D	-0.2
Total	16	1523	4549	650	1303	207	42	91	458	372	657	.286	.342	.410	108	42	44	637	185	86	4	.983	-23	*O2/3DS	0.7

■ GUY LACY
Lacy, Osceola Guy b: 6/12/1897, Cleveland, Tenn. d: 11/19/53, Cleveland, Tenn. BR/TR, 5'11.5", 170 lbs. Deb: 5/07/26

YEAR	TM/L	G	AB	R	H	2B	3B	HR	RBI	BB	SO	AVG	OBP	SLG	PRO+	BR	/A	RC	SB	CS	SBR	FA	FR	POS	TPR
1926	Cle-A	13	24	2	4	0	0	1	2	2	2	.167	.259	.292	43	-2	-2	2	0	0	0	.976	1	2/3	-0.1

■ HI LADD
Ladd, Arthur Clifford b: 2/9/1870, Willimantic, Conn. d: 5/7/48, Cranston, R.I. BL/TR, 6'4", 180 lbs. Deb: 7/12/1898

YEAR	TM/L	G	AB	R	H	2B	3B	HR	RBI	BB	SO	AVG	OBP	SLG	PRO+	BR	/A	RC	SB	CS	SBR	FA	FR	POS	TPR
1898	Pit-N	1	1	0	0	0	0	0	0	0		.000	.000	.000	-99	-0	-0	0	0			.000	0	H	0.0
	Bos-N	1	4	1	1	0	0	0	0	0		.250	.250	.250	41	-0	-0	0	0			1.000	-0	/O	0.0
	Yr	2	5	1	1	0	0	0	0	0		.200	.200	.200	14	-1	-1	0	0			1.000	-0	/O	0.0

■ STEVE LADEW
Ladew, Stephen b: St.Louis, Mo. Deb: 9/27/1889

YEAR	TM/L	G	AB	R	H	2B	3B	HR	RBI	BB	SO	AVG	OBP	SLG	PRO+	BR	/A	RC	SB	CS	SBR	FA	FR	POS	TPR
1889	KC-a	2	4	0	0	0	0	0	0	0	3	.000	.000	.000	-95	-1	-1	0	0			1.000	-0	/OP	-0.1

■ JOE LAFATA
Lafata, Joseph Joseph b: 8/3/21, Detroit, Mich. BL/TL, 6', 163 lbs. Deb: 4/17/47

YEAR	TM/L	G	AB	R	H	2B	3B	HR	RBI	BB	SO	AVG	OBP	SLG	PRO+	BR	/A	RC	SB	CS	SBR	FA	FR	POS	TPR
1947	NY-N	62	95	13	21	1	0	2	18	15	18	.221	.333	.295	68	-4	-4	10	1			.974	-1	O/1	-0.6
1948	NY-N	1	1	0	0	0	0	0	0	0	1	.000	.000	.000	-99	-0	-0	0	0			.000	0	H	0.0
1949	NY-N	64	140	18	33	2	2	3	16	9	23	.236	.282	.343	67	-7	-7	14	1			.984	-4	1	-1.1
Total	3	127	236	31	54	3	2	5	34	24	42	.229	.303	.322	67	-11	-11	24	2			.985	-5	/1O	-1.7

■ FLIP LAFFERTY
Lafferty, Frank Bernard b: 5/4/1854, Scranton, Pa. d: 2/8/10, Wilmington, Del. TR , Deb: 9/15/1876

YEAR	TM/L	G	AB	R	H	2B	3B	HR	RBI	BB	SO	AVG	OBP	SLG	PRO+	BR	/A	RC	SB	CS	SBR	FA	FR	POS	TPR
1876	Phi-N	1	3	0	0	0	0	0	0	0	0	.000	.000	.000	-99	-1	-1	0				.750	0	/P	0.0
1877	Lou-N	4	17	2	1	1	0	0	0	0	4	.059	.059	.118	-39	-3	-3	0				.750	-1	/O	-0.4
Total	2	5	20	2	1	1	0	0	0	0	4	.050	.050	.100	-46	-3	-4	0				.973	-1	/OP	-0.4

■ TY LaFOREST
LaForest, Byron Joseph b: 4/18/17, Edmunston, N.B., Canada d: 5/5/47, Arlington, Mass. BR/TR, 5'9", 165 lbs. Deb: 8/04/45

YEAR	TM/L	G	AB	R	H	2B	3B	HR	RBI	BB	SO	AVG	OBP	SLG	PRO+	BR	/A	RC	SB	CS	SBR	FA	FR	POS	TPR
1945	Bos-A	52	204	25	51	7	4	2	16	10	35	.250	.285	.353	83	-5	-5	19	4	4	-1	.966	1	3/O	-0.5

■ ROGER LaFRANCOIS
LaFrancois, Roger Victor b: 8/2/54, Norwich, Conn. BL/TR, 6'2", 215 lbs. Deb: 5/27/82

YEAR	TM/L	G	AB	R	H	2B	3B	HR	RBI	BB	SO	AVG	OBP	SLG	PRO+	BR	/A	RC	SB	CS	SBR	FA	FR	POS	TPR
1982	Bos-A	8	10	1	4	1	0	0	1	0	0	.400	.400	.500	137	1	1	2	0	0	0	1.000	-0	/C	0.0

■ MIKE LAGA
Laga, Michael Russell b: 6/14/60, Ridgewood, N.J. BL/TL, 6'2", 210 lbs. Deb: 9/01/82

YEAR	TM/L	G	AB	R	H	2B	3B	HR	RBI	BB	SO	AVG	OBP	SLG	PRO+	BR	/A	RC	SB	CS	SBR	FA	FR	POS	TPR
1982	Det-A	27	88	6	23	9	0	3	11	4	23	.261	.293	.466	104	0	0	12	1	0	0	.994	-2	1/D	-0.3
1983	Det-A	12	21	2	4	0	0	0	2	1	9	.190	.227	.190	17	-2	-2	1	0	0	0	1.000	0	/1D	-0.2
1984	Det-A	9	11	1	6	0	0	0	1	1	2	.545	.583	.545	216	2	2	4	0	0	0	1.000	0	/1D	0.2
1985	Det-A	9	36	3	6	1	0	2	6	0	9	.167	.167	.361	40	-3	-3	2	0	0	0	.974	1	/1D	-0.3
1986	Det-A	15	45	6	9	1	0	3	8	5	13	.200	.280	.422	88	-1	-1	6	0	0	0	1.000	-0	1/D	-0.2
	StL-N	18	46	7	10	4	0	3	8	5	18	.217	.308	.500	120	1	1	7	0	0	0	1.000	2	1	0.2
1987	StL-N	17	29	4	4	1	0	1	4	2	7	.138	.194	.276	22	-3	-3	1	0	0	0	.973	1	1	-0.3
1988	StL-N	41	100	5	13	0	0	1	4	2	21	.130	.147	.160	-12	-14	-14	2	0	0	0	1.000	1	1	-1.8
1989	SF-N	17	20	1	4	1	0	1	7	1	6	.200	.238	.400	82	-1	-1	2	0	0	0	1.000	-0	/1	-0.1
1990	SF-N	23	27	4	5	1	0	2	4	1	7	.185	.241	.444	88	-1	-1	3	0	0	0	1.000	1	1	0.0
Total	9	188	423	39	84	18	0	16	55	22	115	.199	.242	.355	63	-23	-22	39	1	0	0	.996	2	1/D	-2.8

■ JOE LAHOUD
Lahoud, Joseph Michael b: 4/14/47, Danbury, Conn. BL/TL, 6', 202 lbs. Deb: 4/10/68

YEAR	TM/L	G	AB	R	H	2B	3B	HR	RBI	BB	SO	AVG	OBP	SLG	PRO+	BR	/A	RC	SB	CS	SBR	FA	FR	POS	TPR
1968	Bos-A	29	78	5	15	1	0	1	6	16	16	.192	.330	.244	71	-2	-2	7	0	2	-1	.926	-3	O	-0.9
1969	Bos-A	101	218	32	41	5	0	9	21	40	43	.188	.317	.335	78	-5	-6	26	2	1	0	.979	-7	O/1	-1.7
1970	Bos-A	17	49	6	12	1	0	2	5	7	6	.245	.339	.388	93	0	-0	7	0	0	0	.963	2	O	0.1
1971	Bos-A	107	256	39	55	9	3	14	32	40	45	.215	.330	.438	108	5	3	38	2	2	-1	.993	3	O	0.3
1972	Mil-A	111	316	35	75	9	3	12	34	45	54	.237	.332	.399	119	7	7	41	3	4	-2	.974	-2	O	0.0
1973	Mil-A	96	225	29	46	9	0	5	26	27	36	.204	.304	.311	75	-8	-7	20	5	5	-2	1.000	2	DO	-0.8
1974	Cal-A	127	325	46	88	16	3	13	44	47	57	.271	.368	.458	145	16	18	55	4	5	-2	.976	-6	*OD	0.7
1975	Cal-A	76	192	21	41	6	2	6	33	48	33	.214	.373	.359	116	4	6	30	2	1	0	1.000	-3	DO	0.2
1976	Cal-A	42	96	8	17	4	0	0	4	18	16	.177	.319	.219	63	-4	-3	8	0	0	0	.962	-2	O/D	-0.7
	Tex-A	38	89	10	20	3	1	1	5	10	16	.225	.303	.315	79	-2	-2	8	1	0	0	1.000	-2	D/O	-0.4
	Yr	80	185	18	37	7	1	1	9	28	32	.200	.312	.265	72	-6	-6	16	1	0	0	.964	-4	OD	-1.1
1977	*KC-A	34	65	8	17	5	0	2	8	11	16	.262	.368	.431	116	2	2	11	1	0	0	.952	-1	O/D	0.1
1978	KC-A	13	16	0	2	0	0	0	0	0	1	.125	.125	.125	-29	-3	-3	0	0	0	0	.000	-0	/OD	-0.3
Total	11	791	1925	239	429	68	12	65	218	309	339	.223	.335	.372	103	11	12	252	20	20	-6	.979	-19	OD/1	-3.4

■ DICK LAJESKIE
Lajeskie, Richard Edward b: 1/8/26, Passaic, N.J. d: 8/15/76, Ramsey, N.J. BR/TR, 5'11", 175 lbs. Deb: 9/10/46

YEAR	TM/L	G	AB	R	H	2B	3B	HR	RBI	BB	SO	AVG	OBP	SLG	PRO+	BR	/A	RC	SB	CS	SBR	FA	FR	POS	TPR
1946	NY-N	6	10	3	2	0	0	0	0	3	2	.200	.429	.200	81	0	0	1	0			.964	5	/2	0.5

■ NAP LAJOIE
Lajoie, Napoleon "Larry" b: 9/5/1874, Woonsocket, R.I. d: 2/7/59, Daytona Beach, Fla. BR/TR, 6'1", 195 lbs. Deb: 8/12/1896 MH

YEAR	TM/L	G	AB	R	H	2B	3B	HR	RBI	BB	SO	AVG	OBP	SLG	PRO+	BR	/A	RC	SB	CS	SBR	FA	FR	POS	TPR
1896	Phi-N	39	175	36	57	12	7	4	42	1	11	.326	.330	.543	131	6	6	35	7			.995	-3	1	0.3
1897	Phi-N	127	545	107	197	40	23	9	127	15		.361	.392	**.569**	156	36	38	133	20			.984	-6	*1O/3	2.7
1898	Phi-N	147	608	113	197	**43**	11	6	**127**	21		.324	.354	.461	139	22	25	111	25			.949	-1	*2/1	3.1
1899	Phi-N	77	312	70	118	19	9	6	70	12		.378	.419	.554	172	27	28	80	13			.954	23	2/O	4.8
1900	Phi-N	102	451	95	152	33	12	7	92	10		.337	.362	.510	141	21	21	94	22			**.954**	30	*2/3	**5.0**
1901	Phi-A	131	544	**145**	**232**	**48**	14	**14**	**125**	24		**.426**	**.463**	**.643**	**196**	**74**	**71**	**179**	27			**.960**	**29**	*2S	**9.2**
1902	Phi-A	1	4	0	1	0	0	0	1	0		.250	.250	.250	37	-0	-0	1	1			1.000	-0	/2	-0.1
	Cle-A	86	348	81	132	35	5	7	64	19		.379	.421	.569	180	33	35	94	19			.974	30	2	6.2
	Yr	87	352	81	133	35	5	7	65	19		.378	.419	.565	178	32	34	95	20			.974	29	2	**6.1**
1903	Cle-A	125	485	90	167	41	11	7	93	24		**.344**	.379	**.518**	**170**	**38**	**39**	107	21			.955	**40**	*2/13	**8.3**
1904	Cle-A	140	553	92	**208**	**49**	15	6	**102**	27		**.376**	**.413**	**.552**	**205**	**63**	**63**	**142**	29			.962	-0	2S/1	**7.2**
1905	Cle-A	65	249	29	82	12	2	2	41	17		.329	.377	.418	150	14	14	45	11			.991	9	2/1M	2.5
1906	Cle-A	152	602	88	**214**	**48**	9	0	91	30		.355	.392	.465	170	45	46	122	20			**.973**	32	*23/SM	**8.5**
1907	Cle-A	137	509	53	152	30	6	2	63	30		.299	.345	.393	134	19	19	81	24			**.969**	**45**	*2/1M	**6.7**
1908	Cle-A	157	581	77	168	32	6	2	74	47		.289	.352	.375	136	23	23	83	15			**.964**	**49**	*2/1M	**7.8**
1909	Cle-A	128	469	56	152	33	7	1	47	35		.324	.378	.431	149	29	27	81	13			.959	19	*2/1M	4.8

YEAR	TM/L	G	AB	R	H	2B	3B	HR	RBI	BB	SO	AVG	OBP	SLG	PRO+	BR	/A	RC	SB	CS	SBR	FA	FR	POS	TPR
1910	Cle-A	159	591	94	**227**	**51**	7	4	76	60		**.384**	.445	.514	198	**68**	**67**	147	26			.966	17	*21	**8.7**
1911	Cle-A	90	315	36	115	20	1	2	60	26		.365	.420	.454	142	19	18	65	13			.990	-7	12	1.0
1912	Cle-A	117	448	66	165	34	4	0	90	28		.368	.414	.462	146	29	27	93	18			.959	5	21	2.8
1913	Cle-A	137	465	66	156	25	2	1	68	33	17	.335	.398	.404	131	21	19	79	17			**.970**	9	*2	2.8
1914	Cle-A	121	419	37	108	14	3	0	50	32	15	.258	.313	.305	83	-7	-9	41	14	15	-5	.959	6	21	-1.0
1915	Phi-A	129	490	40	137	24	5	1	61	11	16	.280	.301	.355	100	-5	-3	55	10	6	-1	.962	14	*2S/13	1.3
1916	Phi-A	113	426	33	105	14	4	2	35	14	26	.246	.272	.312	79	-15	-12	42	15			.973	30	*2/1O	2.3
Total	21	2480	9589	1504	3242	657	163	83	1599	516	85	.338	.380	.467	150	558	561	1907	380	21		.963	369	*21/SO3	94.9

■ EDDIE LAKE Lake, Edward Erving "Sparky" b: 3/18/16, Antioch, Cal. BR/TR, 5'7", 160 lbs. Deb: 9/26/39

YEAR	TM/L	G	AB	R	H	2B	3B	HR	RBI	BB	SO	AVG	OBP	SLG	PRO+	BR	/A	RC	SB	CS	SBR	FA	FR	POS	TPR
1939	StL-N	2	4	0	1	0	0	0	0	1	0	.250	.400	.250	74	-0	-0	1	0			.857	-1	/S	-0.1
1940	StL-N	32	66	12	14	3	0	2	7	12	17	.212	.342	.348	86	-1	-1	8	1			.957	-7	2/S	-0.7
1941	StL-N	45	76	9	8	2	0	0	0	15	22	.105	.253	.132	10	-9	-9	3	3			.903	6	S3/2	-0.3
1943	Bos-A	75	216	26	43	10	0	3	16	47	35	.199	.345	.287	84	-2	-2	24	3	6	-3	.961	3	S	0.3
1944	Bos-A	57	126	21	26	5	0	0	8	23	22	.206	.329	.246	66	-5	-4	13	5	2	0	.927	-5	S/P23	-0.7
1945	Bos-A	133	473	81	132	27	1	11	51	106	37	.279	**.412**	.410	136	29	27	89	9	7	-2	.948	19	*S/2	5.8
1946	Det-A	155	587	105	149	24	1	8	31	103	69	.254	.369	.339	93	3	-2	83	15	9	-1	.947	-21	*S	-1.6
1947	Det-A	158	602	96	127	19	6	12	46	120	54	.211	.343	.322	83	-9	-11	74	11	10	-3	.943	-29	*S	-3.6
1948	Det-A	64	198	51	52	6	0	2	18	57	20	.263	.427	.323	99	4	3	33	3	3	-1	.972	-3	23	0.2
1949	Det-A	94	240	38	47	9	1	1	15	61	33	.196	.359	.254	63	-10	-10	26	2	8	-4	.959	-10	S23	-2.1
1950	Det-A	20	7	3	0	0	0	0	1	1	3	.000	.125	.000	-64	-2	-2	0	0	0	0	.000	0	/S3	-0.2
Total	11	835	2595	442	599	105	9	39	193	546	312	.231	.366	.323	91	-1	-11	354	52	45		.947	-48	S/23P	-3.0

■ FRED LAKE Lake, Frederick Lovett b: 10/16/1866, Nova Scotia, Can. d: 11/24/31, Boston, Mass. BR/TR, 5'10", 170 lbs. Deb: 5/07/1891 M

YEAR	TM/L	G	AB	R	H	2B	3B	HR	RBI	BB	SO	AVG	OBP	SLG	PRO+	BR	/A	RC	SB	CS	SBR	FA	FR	POS	TPR
1891	Bos-N	5	7	1	1	0	0	0	0	2	4	.143	.333	.143	38	-0	-1	0	0			1.000	-0	/CO	-0.1
1894	Lou-N	16	42	8	12	2	0	1	10	11	6	.286	.474	.405	124	2	3	9	2			.864	-3	/2SC	0.0
1897	*Bos-N	19	62	2	15	4	0	0	5	1		.242	.254	.306	45	-5	-6	6	2			.970	-1	C	-0.4
1898	Pit-N	5	13	1	1	0	0	0	1	2		.077	.200	.077	-20	-2	-2	0	0			1.000	-0	/1	-0.2
1910	Bos-N	3	1	0	0	0	0	0	0	1	0	.000	.500	.000	46	0	0	0	0			.000	0	HM	0.0
Total	5	48	125	12	29	6	0	1	16	17	10	.232	.342	.304	68	-5	-5	16	4			.930	-5	/C2S1O	-0.7

■ STEVE LAKE Lake, Steven Michael b: 3/14/57, Inglewood, Cal. BR/TR, 6'1", 190 lbs. Deb: 4/09/83

YEAR	TM/L	G	AB	R	H	2B	3B	HR	RBI	BB	SO	AVG	OBP	SLG	PRO+	BR	/A	RC	SB	CS	SBR	FA	FR	POS	TPR
1983	Chi-N	38	85	9	22	4	1	1	7	2	6	.259	.284	.365	75	-3	-3	7	0	0	0	1.000	4	C	0.2
1984	*Chi-N	25	54	4	12	4	0	2	7	0	7	.222	.236	.407	71	-2	-2	5	0	0	0	.955	0	C	-0.2
1985	Chi-N	58	119	5	18	2	0	1	11	3	21	.151	.179	.193	4	-15	-17	4	1	0	0	.995	6	C	-1.0
1986	Chi-N	10	19	4	8	1	0	0	4	1	2	.421	.450	.474	144	1	1	4	0	0	0	1.000	-0	C	0.2
	StL-N	26	49	4	12	1	0	2	10	2	5	.245	.275	.388	81	-1	-1	5	0	0	0	.976	1	C	0.0
	Yr	36	68	8	20	2	0	2	14	3	7	.294	.324	.412	100	-0	-0	8	0	0	0	.983	1	C	0.2
1987	*StL-N	74	179	19	45	7	2	2	19	10	18	.251	.291	.346	67	-8	-9	18	0	0	0	.996	-2	C	-0.7
1988	StL-N	36	54	5	15	3	0	1	4	3	15	.278	.339	.389	107	1	1	8	0	0	0	.983	-1	C	0.1
1989	Phi-N	58	155	9	39	5	1	2	14	12	20	.252	.305	.335	83	-3	-3	15	0	0	0	.990	3	C	0.2
1990	Phi-N	29	80	4	20	2	0	0	6	3	12	.250	.286	.275	55	-5	-5	6	0	0	0	.993	4	C	0.0
1991	Phi-N	58	158	12	36	4	1	1	11	2	26	.228	.237	.285	47	-11	-11	10	0	0	0	.993	2	C	-0.7
1992	Phi-N	20	53	3	13	2	0	1	2	1	8	.245	.259	.340	69	-2	-2	4	0	0	0	.975	0	C	-0.2
Total	10	432	1005	78	240	35	5	13	95	39	140	.239	.271	.322	63	-50	-53	86	1	0	0	.990	17	C	-2.1

■ AL LAKEMAN Lakeman, Albert Wesley "Moose" b: 12/31/18, Cincinnati, Ohio d: 5/25/76, Spartanburg, S.C. BR/TR, 6'2", 195 lbs. Deb: 4/19/42 C

YEAR	TM/L	G	AB	R	H	2B	3B	HR	RBI	BB	SO	AVG	OBP	SLG	PRO+	BR	/A	RC	SB	CS	SBR	FA	FR	POS	TPR
1942	Cin-N	20	38	0	6	1	0	0	2	3	10	.158	.238	.184	24	-4	-4	2	0			.970	3	C	0.0
1943	Cin-N	22	55	5	14	2	1	0	6	3	11	.255	.293	.327	80	-2	-2	5	0			1.000	-2	C	-0.2
1944	Cin-N	1	1	0	0	0	0	0	0	0	1	.000	.000	.000	-99	-0	-0	0	0			.000	0	H	0.0
1945	Cin-N	76	258	22	66	9	4	8	31	17	45	.256	.304	.415	101	-2	-1	31	0			.963	-11	C	-0.7
1946	Cin-N	23	30	0	4	0	0	0	4	2	7	.133	.188	.133	-9	-4	-4	1	0			1.000	-0	/C	-0.5
1947	Cin-N	2	2	0	0	0	0	0	0	0	1	.000	.000	.000	-99	-1	-1	0	0			.000	0	H	-0.1
	Phi-N	55	182	11	29	3	0	6	19	5	39	.159	.186	.275	22	-21	-20	9	0			.995	-5	1C	-2.5
	Yr	57	184	11	29	3	0	6	19	5	40	.158	.184	.272	20	-22	-21	9	0			.995	-5	1C	-2.6
1948	Phi-N	32	68	2	11	2	0	1	4	5	22	.162	.219	.235	23	-7	-7	4	0			1.000	-2	C/P	-0.8
1949	Bos-N	3	6	0	1	0	0	0	0	1	0	.167	.286	.167	26	-1	-1	0	0			1.000	1	/1	0.0
1954	Det-A	5	6	0	0	0	0	0	0	0	1	.000	.000	.000	-99	-2	-2	0	0	0	0	1.000	1	/C	-0.1
Total	9	239	646	40	131	17	5	15	66	36	137	.203	.248	.314	55	-43	-41	51	0	0		.974	-16	C/1P	-4.9

■ TIM LAKER Laker, Timothy John b: 11/27/69, Encino, Cal. BR/TR, 6'3", 195 lbs. Deb: 8/18/92

YEAR	TM/L	G	AB	R	H	2B	3B	HR	RBI	BB	SO	AVG	OBP	SLG	PRO+	BR	/A	RC	SB	CS	SBR	FA	FR	POS	TPR
1992	Mon-N	28	46	8	10	3	0	0	4	2	14	.217	.250	.283	51	-3	-3	3	1	1	-0	.991	5	C	0.3

■ DAN LALLY Lally, Daniel J. b: 8/12/1867, Jersey City, N.J. d: 4/14/36, Milwaukee, Wis. BR/TR, 5'11.5", 210 lbs. Deb: 8/19/1891

YEAR	TM/L	G	AB	R	H	2B	3B	HR	RBI	BB	SO	AVG	OBP	SLG	PRO+	BR	/A	RC	SB	CS	SBR	FA	FR	POS	TPR
1891	Pit-N	41	143	24	32	6	2	1	17	16	20	.224	.319	.315	89	-2	-1	15	0			.839	-7	O	-0.8
1897	StL-N	87	355	56	99	15	5	2	42	9		.279	.310	.366	80	-12	-11	46	12			.897	2	O/1	-1.3
Total	2	128	498	80	131	21	7	3	59	25	20	.263	.313	.351	82	-14	-13	60	12			.886	-4	O/1	-2.1

■ RAY LAMANNO Lamanno, Raymond Simond b: 11/17/19, Oakland, Cal. BR/TR, 6', 185 lbs. Deb: 9/11/41

YEAR	TM/L	G	AB	R	H	2B	3B	HR	RBI	BB	SO	AVG	OBP	SLG	PRO+	BR	/A	RC	SB	CS	SBR	FA	FR	POS	TPR
1941	Cin-N	1	0	0	0	0	0	0	0	0	0	—	1.000	—	197	0	0	0	0			1.000	-0	/C	0.0
1942	Cin-N	111	371	40	98	12	2	12	43	31	54	.264	.324	.404	113	5	5	46	0			.978	-11	*C	0.2
1946	Cin-N★	85	239	18	58	12	0	1	30	11	26	.243	.285	.305	70	-11	-10	20	0			.974	2	C	-0.5
1947	Cin-N	118	413	33	106	21	3	5	50	28	39	.257	.307	.358	77	-15	-14	46	0			.986	9	*C	0.2
1948	Cin-N	127	385	31	93	12	0	0	27	48	32	.242	.329	.273	67	-18	-16	35	2			.978	-11	*C	-1.9
Total	5	442	1408	122	355	57	5	18	150	118	151	.252	.314	.338	82	-38	-35	147	2			.980	-11	C	-2.0

■ BILL LAMAR Lamar, William Harmong "Good Time Bill" b: 3/21/1897, Rockville, Md. d: 5/24/70, Rockport, Mass. BL/TR, 6'1", 185 lbs. Deb: 9/19/17

YEAR	TM/L	G	AB	R	H	2B	3B	HR	RBI	BB	SO	AVG	OBP	SLG	PRO+	BR	/A	RC	SB	CS	SBR	FA	FR	POS	TPR
1917	NY-A	11	41	2	10	0	0	0	3	0	2	.244	.244	.244	48	-3	-3	3	1			1.000	0	O	-0.3
1918	NY-A	28	110	12	25	3	0	0	2	6	2	.227	.267	.255	56	-6	-6	8	2			.884	-2	O	-1.1
1919	NY-A	11	16	1	3	1	0	0	0	2	1	.188	.278	.250	48	-1	-1	1	1			1.000	-1	/O1	-0.2
	Bos-A	48	148	18	43	5	1	0	14	5	9	.291	.314	.338	88	-4	-3	16	3			.922	-2	O	-0.8
	Yr	59	164	19	46	6	1	0	14	7	10	.280	.310	.329	83	-5	-4	18	4			.926	-3	O/1	-1.0
1920	*Bro-N	24	44	5	12	4	0	0	4	0	1	.273	.273	.364	79	-1	-1	4	0	0	0	1.000	-3	O	-0.5
1921	Bro-N	3	3	2	1	0	0	0	0	0	0	.333	.333	.333	74	-0	-0	0	0	0	0	.000	-1	/O	-0.1
1924	Phi-A	87	367	68	121	22	5	7	48	18	21	.330	.361	.474	113	6	5	60	8	8	-2	.971	4	O	0.1
1925	Phi-A	138	568	85	202	39	8	3	77	21	17	.356	.379	.468	107	10	5	97	2	6	-3	.953	4	*O	-0.3
1926	Phi-A	116	419	62	119	17	6	5	50	18	15	.284	.315	.389	78	-12	-15	50	4	5	-2	.954	-3	*O	-2.7
1927	Phi-A	84	324	48	97	23	3	4	47	16	10	.299	.334	.426	91	-3	-6	41	4	8	-4	.952	-3	O	-1.6
Total	9	550	2040	303	633	114	23	19	245	86	78	.310	.339	.417	94	-14	-24	280	25	27		.952	-6	O/1	-7.5

■ LYMAN LAMB Lamb, Lyman Raymond b: 3/17/1895, Lincoln, Neb. d: 10/5/55, Fayetteville, Ark. BR/TR, 5'7", 150 lbs. Deb: 9/14/20

YEAR	TM/L	G	AB	R	H	2B	3B	HR	RBI	BB	SO	AVG	OBP	SLG	PRO+	BR	/A	RC	SB	CS	SBR	FA	FR	POS	TPR
1920	StL-A	9	24	4	9	2	0	0	4	0	7	.375	.375	.458	116	1	0	4	2	0	1	1.000	-2	/O	-0.1
1921	StL-A	45	134	18	34	9	2	1	17	4	12	.254	.281	.373	62	-8	-9	14	0	0	0	.942	-9	3/2O	-1.5
Total	2	54	158	22	43	11	2	1	21	4	19	.272	.294	.386	70	-7	-8	19	2	0	1	1.000	-11	/3O2	-1.6

YEAR	TM/L	G	AB	R	H	2B	3B	HR	RBI	BB	SO	AVG	OBP	SLG	PRO+	BR	/A	RC	SB	CS	SBR	FA	FR	POS	TPR

■ PETE LAMER   Lamer, Pierre b: 12/1873, New York, N.Y. d: 10/24/31, Brooklyn, N.Y. TR , 5'10", 170 lbs. Deb: 9/10/02

	1902	Chi-N	2	9	2	2	0	0	0	0	0	0	.222	.222	.222	38	-1	-1	0	0			.857	-0	/C	-0.1
1907	Cin-N	1	2	0	0	0	0	0	0	0	0	.000	.000	.000	-96	-0	-0	0	0			1.000	-0	/C	-0.1
Total	2	3	11	2	2	0	0	0	0	0	0	.182	.182	.182	13	-1	-1	0	0			.867	-1	/C	-0.2

■ GENE LAMONT   Lamont, Gene William b: 12/25/46, Rockford, Ill. BL/TR, 6'1", 195 lbs. Deb: 9/02/70 MC

1970	Det-A	15	44	3	13	3	1	1	4	2	9	.295	.340	.477	122	1	1	7	0	0	0	1.000	1	C	0.3
1971	Det-A	7	15	2	1	0	0	0	1	0	5	.067	.067	.067	-60	-3	-3	0	0	0	0	.952	2	/C	-0.1
1972	Det-A	1	0	0	0	0	0	0	0	0	0	—	—	—	—	0	0	0	0	0	0	1.000	-0	/C	0.0
1974	Det-A	60	92	9	20	4	0	3	8	7	19	.217	.273	.359	78	-3	-3	6	0	0	0	.974	8	C	0.7
1975	Det-A	4	8	1	3	1	0	0	1	0	2	.375	.375	.500	139	0	0	2	1	0	0	.944	1	/C	0.2
Total	5	87	159	15	37	8	1	4	14	9	35	.233	.278	.371	80	-4	-5	18	1	0		.977	12	/C	1.1

■ BOBBY LaMOTTE   LaMotte, Robert Eugene b: 2/15/1898, Savannah, Ga. d: 11/2/70, Chatham, Ga. BR/TR, 5'11", 160 lbs. Deb: 9/01/20

1920	Was-A	4	3	0	0	0	0	0	0	0	1	.000	.250	.000	-31	-1	-1	0	0	0	0	.750	0	/S3	0.0
1921	Was-A	16	41	5	8	0	0	0	2	5	0	.195	.283	.195	25	-5	-4	3	0	0	0	.940	2	S	-0.2
1922	Was-A	68	214	22	54	10	2	1	23	15	21	.252	.307	.332	70	-11	-9	23	6	1	1	.954	8	3/S	0.5
1925	StL-A	97	356	61	97	20	4	2	51	34	22	.272	.338	.368	75	-12	-14	45	5	5	-2	.926	3	S/3	-0.4
1926	StL-A	36	79	11	16	4	3	0	9	11	6	.203	.300	.329	61	-4	-5	9	0	0	0	.919	-2	S/3	-0.4
Total	5	221	693	99	175	34	9	3	85	66	50	.253	.320	.341	69	-32	-33	80	11	6	-0	.927	10	S/3	-0.5

■ KEITH LAMPARD   Lampard, Christopher Keith b: 12/20/45, Warrington, England BL/TR, 6'2", 197 lbs. Deb: 9/15/69

1969	Hou-N	9	12	2	3	0	0	1	2	0	3	.250	.250	.500	108	-0	0	2	0	0	0	1.000	1	/O	0.1
1970	Hou-N	53	72	8	17	8	1	0	5	5	24	.236	.295	.375	82	-2	-2	7	0	0	0	1.000	1	O/1	-0.1
Total	2	62	84	10	20	8	1	1	7	5	27	.238	.289	.393	85	-2	-2	9	0	0	0	1.000	2	/O1	0.0

■ TOM LAMPKIN   Lampkin, Thomas Michael b: 3/4/64, Cincinnati, Ohio BL/TR, 5'11", 180 lbs. Deb: 9/10/88

1988	Cle-A	4	4	0	0	0	0	0	0	0	0	.000	.200	.000	-38	-1	-1	0	0	0	0	1.000	-1	/C	-0.2
1990	SD-N	26	63	4	14	0	1	1	4	4	9	.222	.269	.302	56	-4	-4	4	0	1	-1	.971	1	C	-0.3
1991	SD-N	38	58	4	11	3	1	0	3	3	9	.190	.230	.276	40	-5	-5	4	0	0	0	1.000	0	C	-0.4
1992	SD-N	9	17	3	4	0	0	0	0	6	1	.235	.458	.235	98	1	1	3	2	0	1	1.000	-2	/CO	0.0
Total	4	77	142	11	29	3	2	1	7	14	19	.204	.280	.275	54	-8	-9	11	2	1	0	.985	-1	/CO	-0.9

■ RICK LANCELLOTTI   Lancellotti, Richard Anthony b: 7/5/56, Providence, R.I. BL/TL, 6'3", 195 lbs. Deb: 8/27/82

1982	SD-N	17	39	2	7	2	0	0	4	2	8	.179	.220	.231	28	-4	-4	2	0	0	0	1.000	-1	/1O	-0.6
1986	SF-N	15	18	2	4	0	0	2	6	0	7	.222	.222	.556	113	-0	0	2	0	0	0	1.000	0	/1O	0.1
1990	Bos-A	4	8	0	0	0	0	0	1	0	3	.000	.000	.000	-96	-2	-2	0	0	0	0	1.000	0	/1	-0.2
Total	3	36	65	4	11	2	0	2	11	2	18	.169	.194	.292	35	-6	-6	4	0	0	0	1.000	-0	/1O	-0.7

■ GROVER LAND   Land, Grover Cleveland b: 9/22/1884, Frankfort, Ky. d: 7/22/58, Phoenix, Ariz. BR/TR, 6', 190 lbs. Deb: 9/02/08 C

1908	Cle-A	8	16	1	3	0	0	0	2	0		.188	.188	.188	22	-1	-1	1	0			.955	-1	/C	-0.3
1909	Cle-A	1	4	0	2	0	0	0	1	0		.500	.500	.500	207	0	0	1	0			1.000	0	/C	0.1
1910	Cle-A	34	111	4	23	0	0	0	7	2		.207	.228	.207	36	-8	-8	6	1			.982	5	C	0.0
1911	Cle-A	35	107	5	15	1	2	0	10	3		.140	.164	.187	-2	-15	-15	3	2			.961	1	C/1	-1.2
1913	Cle-A	17	47	3	11	1	0	0	9	4	1	.234	.321	.255	67	-2	-2	4	1			.924	1	C	0.0
1914	Bro-F	102	335	24	92	6	2	0	29	12	23	.275	.306	.304	74	-12	-11	35	7			.970	-1	C	-0.3
1915	Bro-F	96	290	25	75	13	2	0	22	6	20	.259	.279	.317	75	-10	-10	28	3			.960	-6	C	-1.0
Total	7	293	910	62	221	21	6	0	80	27	44	.243	.271	.279	60	-47	-47	78	14			.964	-1	C/1	-2.7

■ DOC LAND   Land, William Gilbert (b: Doc Burrell Land) b: 5/14/03, Bennsville, Miss. d: 4/14/86, Livingston, Ala. BL/TL, 5'11", 165 lbs. Deb: 10/06/29

| 1929 | Was-A | 1 | 3 | 0 | 0 | 0 | 0 | 0 | 1 | 0 | .000 | .250 | .000 | -30 | -1 | -1 | 0 | 0 | 0 | 0 | 1.000 | -0 | /O | -0.1 |

■ KEN LANDENBERGER   Landenberger, Kenneth Henry "Red" b: 7/29/28, Lyndhurst, Ohio d: 7/28/60, Cleveland, Ohio BL/TR, 6'3", 200 lbs. Deb: 9/20/52

| 1952 | Chi-A | 2 | 5 | 0 | 1 | 0 | 0 | 0 | 0 | 0 | 2 | .200 | .200 | .200 | 11 | -1 | -1 | 0 | 0 | 0 | 0 | 1.000 | 0 | /1 | 0.0 |

■ RAFAEL LANDESTOY   Landestoy, Rafael Silvialdo (Santana) b: 5/28/53, Bani, D.R. BB/TR, 5'10", 165 lbs. Deb: 8/27/77 C

1977	*LA-N	15	18	6	5	0	0	0	3	2	.278	.381	.278	80	-0	-2	2	2	0	1	1.000	3	/2S	0.3
1978	Hou-N	59	218	18	58	5	1	0	9	8	23	.266	.292	.298	70	-10	-8	19	7	4	-0	.980	-13	S/O2	-1.6
1979	Hou-N	129	282	33	76	9	6	0	30	29	24	.270	.340	.344	92	-4	-2	36	13	4	2	.971	-2	*2/S	0.3
1980	*Hou-N	149	393	42	97	13	8	1	27	31	37	.247	.307	.328	84	-12	-11	41	23	12	-0	.991	-6	2S/3	-0.6
1981	Hou-N	35	74	6	11	1	1	0	4	16	9	.149	.300	.189	43	-5	-5	5	4	1	1	.966	-4	2	-0.7
	Cin-N	12	11	2	2	0	0	0	1	1	0	.182	.250	.182	24	-1	-0	1	0	0	0	1.000	0	/2	-0.1
	Yr	47	85	8	13	1	1	0	5	17	9	.153	.294	.188	40	-6	-6	5	5	1	1	.967	-5	2	-0.8
1982	Cin-N	73	111	11	21	3	0	1	9	8	14	.189	.250	.243	38	-9	-9	7	0	0	0	1.000	5	32/OS	-0.4
1983	Cin-N	7	5	0	0	0	0	0	0	0	0	.000	.000	.000	-97	-1	-1	0	0	0	0	1.000	0	/13O	-0.2
	*LA-N	64	64	6	11	1	1	0	1	3	8	.172	.209	.266	31	-6	-6	3	0	2	-1	1.000	5	23O/S	-0.2
	Yr	71	69	6	11	1	1	0	1	3	8	.159	.194	.246	21	-7	-7	3	0	2	-1	1.000	4	23O/1S	-0.4
1984	LA-N	53	54	10	10	0	0	1	2	1	6	.185	.200	.241	24	-6	-5	2	2	1	0	.886	1	23/O	-0.4
Total	8	596	1230	134	291	32	17	4	83	100	123	.237	.297	.300	70	-55	-47	115	54	24	2	.976	-13	2S/3O1	-3.6

■ JIM LANDIS   Landis, James Henry b: 3/9/34, Fresno, Cal. BR/TR, 6'1", 180 lbs. Deb: 4/16/57

1957	Chi-A	96	274	38	58	11	6	3	16	45	61	.212	.329	.296	72	-9	-10	31	14	4	2	.985	4	O	-0.9
1958	Chi-A	142	523	72	145	23	7	15	64	52	80	.277	.352	.434	117	11	12	82	19	7	2	.986	6	*O	1.2
1959	*Chi-A	149	515	78	140	26	7	5	60	78	68	.272	.376	.379	109	8	9	81	20	9	1	.993	16	*O	1.8
1960	Chi-A	148	494	89	125	25	6	10	49	80	84	.253	.367	.389	106	5	6	78	23	6	3	.985	13	*O	1.5
1961	Chi-A	140	534	87	151	18	8	22	85	65	71	.283	.365	.470	123	16	17	95	19	5	3	.988	19	*O	3.1
1962	Chi-A★	149	534	82	122	21	6	15	61	80	105	.228	.339	.375	92	-5	-5	73	19	7	2	.995	10	*O	-0.2
1963	Chi-A	133	396	56	89	6	6	13	45	47	75	.225	.316	.369	93	-4	-3	48	8	6	-1	.993	1	*O	-1.0
1964	Chi-A	106	298	30	62	8	4	1	18	36	64	.208	.306	.272	64	-14	-13	28	5	0	2	.995	-4	*O	-2.1
1965	KC-A	118	364	46	87	15	1	3	36	57	84	.239	.347	.310	90	-4	-3	42	8	3	1	.985	6	*O	-0.2
1966	Cle-A	85	158	23	35	5	1	3	14	20	25	.222	.317	.323	84	-3	-3	17	2	1	0	1.000	-11	O	-1.7
1967	Det-A	25	48	4	10	0	0	2	4	7	12	.208	.309	.333	87	-1	-1	5	0	2	-1	.952	0	O	-0.2
	Bos-A	5	7	1	1	0	0	0	1	1	3	.143	.250	.571	126	0	0	1	0	0	0	1.000	-1	/O	-0.1
	Yr	30	55	5	11	0	0	2	5	8	15	.200	.302	.364	92	-0	-0	6	0	2	-1	.964	-1	O	-0.3
	Hou-N	50	143	16	36	11	1	1	14	20	35	.252	.348	.364	107	1	2	20	2	1	0	1.000	-1	/O	-0.1
Total	11	1346	4288	625	1061	169	50	93	467	588	767	.247	.346	.375	100	3	10	602	139	51	11	.989	57	*O	1.1

■ KEN LANDREAUX   Landreaux, Kenneth Francis b: 12/22/54, Los Angeles, Cal. BL/TR, 5'10", 165 lbs. Deb: 9/11/77

1977	Cal-A	23	76	6	19	5	1	0	5	5	15	.250	.296	.342	76	-3	-2	8	1	1	-0	.970	5	O	0.2
1978	Cal-A	93	260	37	58	7	5	5	23	20	20	.223	.284	.346	79	-9	-7	25	7	3	0	.986	-7	O/D	-1.7
1979	Min-A	151	564	81	172	27	5	15	83	37	57	.305	.352	.450	110	11	8	88	10	8	-1	.981	-8	*O/D	-1.7
1980	Min-A★	129	484	56	136	23	11	7	62	39	42	.281	.337	.417	98	3	-1	65	8	6	-1	.976	-9	*O/D	-1.7
1981	*LA-N	99	390	48	98	16	4	4	41	25	42	.251	.298	.367	91	-7	-6	44	18	4	3	1.000	-8	O	-1.5
1982	LA-N	129	461	71	131	23	4	10	50	39	54	.284	.345	.410	113	8	4	68	31	10	3	.986	-4	*O	0.5
1983	*LA-N	141	481	63	135	25	3	17	66	34	52	.281	.331	.451	115	8	4	70	30	11	2	.990	-8	*O	-0.1

YEAR	TM/L	G	AB	R	H	2B	3B	HR	RBI	BB	SO	AVG	OBP	SLG	PRO+	BR	/A	RC	SB	CS	SBR	FA	FR	POS	TPR
1984	LA-N	134	438	39	110	11	5	11	47	29	35	.251	.299	.374	89	-8	-7	47	10	9	-2	.986	-16	*O	-3.1
1985	*LA-N	147	482	70	129	26	2	12	50	33	37	.268	.316	.405	103	-1	1	61	15	5	2	.975	-7	*O	-1.0
1986	LA-N	103	283	34	74	13	2	4	29	22	39	.261	.317	.364	94	-5	-3	32	10	5	0	.955	-5	O	-1.0
1987	LA-N	115	182	17	37	4	0	6	23	16	28	.203	.271	.324	58	-12	-11	16	5	3	-0	.951	-6	O	-1.9
Total	11	1264	4101	522	1099	180	45	91	479	299	421	.268	.321	.400	99	-16	-13	524	145	60	8	.981	-73	*O/D	-11.8

■ HOBIE LANDRITH

Landrith, Hobert Neal b: 3/16/30, Decatur, Ill. BL/TR, 5'10", 170 lbs. Deb: 7/30/50 C

YEAR	TM/L	G	AB	R	H	2B	3B	HR	RBI	BB	SO	AVG	OBP	SLG	PRO+	BR	/A	RC	SB	CS	SBR	FA	FR	POS	TPR
1950	Cin-N	4	14	1	3	0	0	0	1	2	1	.214	.313	.214	41	-1	-1	1	0			1.000	-1	/C	-0.2
1951	Cin-N	4	13	3	5	1	0	0	0	1	1	.385	.429	.462	137	1	1	3	0	0	0	1.000	1	/C	0.2
1952	Cin-N	15	50	1	13	4	0	0	4	0	4	.260	.260	.340	65	-2	-2	4	0	1	-1	1.000	0	C	-0.2
1953	Cin-N	52	154	15	37	3	1	3	16	12	8	.240	.299	.331	64	-8	-8	16	2	0	1	.985	0	C	-0.5
1954	Cin-N	48	81	12	16	0	0	5	14	18	9	.198	.343	.383	86	-1	-1	12	1	0	0	.986	4	C	0.4
1955	Cin-N	43	87	9	22	3	0	4	7	10	14	.253	.330	.425	93	-0	-1	12	0	1	-1	1.000	4	C	0.3
1956	Chi-N	111	312	22	69	10	3	4	32	39	38	.221	.310	.311	69	-14	-13	32	0	2	-1	.975	-3	C	-1.3
1957	StL-N	75	214	18	52	6	0	3	26	25	27	.243	.322	.313	70	-8	-9	22	1	2	-1	.987	5	C	-0.2
1958	StL-N	70	144	9	31	4	0	3	13	26	21	.215	.335	.306	68	-5	-6	16	0	1	-1	.992	2	C	-0.2
1959	SF-N	109	283	30	71	14	0	3	29	43	23	.251	.350	.332	85	-6	-5	34	0	4	-2	.992	7	*C	0.5
1960	SF-N	71	190	18	46	10	0	1	20	23	11	.242	.324	.311	79	-6	-5	20	1	1	-0	.966	-5	C	-0.7
1961	SF-N	43	71	11	17	4	0	2	10	12	7	.239	.349	.380	97	-0	-0	9	0	0	0	.985	2	C	0.2
1962	NY-N	23	45	6	13	3	0	1	7	8	3	.289	.396	.422	118	2	1	8	0	0	0	.968	-1	C	0.1
	Bal-A	60	167	18	37	4	1	4	17	19	9	.222	.305	.329	74	-7	-6	17	0	0	0	.982	5	C	0.1
1963	Bal-A	2	1	0	0	0	0	0	0	0	0	.000	.000	.000	-99	-0	-0	0	0	0	0	1.000	-0	/C	0.0
	Was-A	42	103	6	18	3	0	1	7	15	12	.175	.280	.233	46	-7	-7	7	0	0	0	.978	2	C	-0.5
	Yr	44	104	6	18	3	0	1	7	15	12	.173	.277	.231	44	-7	-7	7	0	0	0	.978	2	C	-0.5
Total	14	772	1929	179	450	69	5	34	203	253	188	.233	.323	.327	75	-64	-62	213	5	12		.983	22	C	-2.0

■ CED LANDRUM

Landrum, Cedric Bernard b: 9/3/63, Butler, Ala. BL/TR, 5'7", 167 lbs. Deb: 5/28/91

YEAR	TM/L	G	AB	R	H	2B	3B	HR	RBI	BB	SO	AVG	OBP	SLG	PRO+	BR	/A	RC	SB	CS	SBR	FA	FR	POS	TPR
1991	Chi-N	56	86	28	20	2	1	0	6	10	18	.233	.313	.279	65	-3	-4	10	27	5	5	.968	-9	O	-0.9

■ DON LANDRUM

Landrum, Donald Leroy b: 2/16/36, Santa Rosa, Cal. BL/TR, 6', 180 lbs. Deb: 9/28/57

YEAR	TM/L	G	AB	R	H	2B	3B	HR	RBI	BB	SO	AVG	OBP	SLG	PRO+	BR	/A	RC	SB	CS	SBR	FA	FR	POS	TPR
1957	Phi-N	2	7	1	1	1	0	0	0	2	1	.143	.333	.286	71	-0	-0	1	0	0	0	1.000	1	/O	0.0
1960	StL-N	13	49	7	12	0	1	2	3	4	6	.245	.315	.408	88	-0	-1	7	3	0	1	1.000	-0	O	-0.1
1961	StL-N	28	66	5	11	2	0	1	3	5	14	.167	.225	.242	22	-7	-8	4	1	0	0	1.000	3	O/2	-0.6
1962	StL-N	32	35	11	11	0	0	0	3	4	2	.314	.385	.314	82	-0	-1	5	2	0	1	1.000	-0	O	-0.1
	Chi-N	83	238	29	67	5	2	1	15	30	31	.282	.369	.332	87	-2	-3	33	9	2	2	.969	1	O	-0.5
	Yr	115	273	40	78	5	2	1	18	34	33	.286	.371	.330	85	-2	-4	38	11	2	2	.973	0	O	-0.6
1963	Chi-N	84	227	27	55	4	1	1	10	13	42	.242	.295	.282	64	-9	-11	19	6	3	0	.972	-1	O	-1.6
1964	Chi-N	11	11	2	0	0	0	0	0	1	2	.000	.083	.000	-71	-3	-3	0	0	0	0	1.000	1	/O	-0.2
1965	Chi-N	131	425	60	96	20	4	6	34	36	84	.226	.301	.334	77	-12	-13	45	14	8	-1	.988	-4	*O	-2.4
1966	SF-N	72	102	9	19	4	0	1	7	9	18	.186	.259	.255	42	-8	-8	7	1	1	-0	.968	5	O	-0.4
Total	8	456	1160	151	272	36	8	12	75	104	200	.234	.308	.310	69	-41	-47	121	36	14	2	.982	4	O/2	-5.9

■ JESSE LANDRUM

Landrum, Jesse Glenn b: 7/31/12, Crockett, Tex. d: 6/27/83, Beaumont, Tex. BR/TR, 5'11.5", 175 lbs. Deb: 4/26/38

YEAR	TM/L	G	AB	R	H	2B	3B	HR	RBI	BB	SO	AVG	OBP	SLG	PRO+	BR	/A	RC	SB	CS	SBR	FA	FR	POS	TPR
1938	Chi-A	4	6	0	0	0	0	0	1	0	2	.000	.000	.000	-98	-2	-2	0	0	0	0	1.000	-1	/2	-0.3

■ TITO LANDRUM

Landrum, Terry Lee b: 10/25/54, Joplin, Mo. BR/TR, 5'11", 175 lbs. Deb: 7/23/80

YEAR	TM/L	G	AB	R	H	2B	3B	HR	RBI	BB	SO	AVG	OBP	SLG	PRO+	BR	/A	RC	SB	CS	SBR	FA	FR	POS	TPR
1980	StL-N	35	77	6	19	2	2	0	7	6	17	.247	.310	.325	75	-2	-3	7	3	2	-0	.976	-1	O	-0.5
1981	StL-N	81	119	13	31	5	4	0	10	6	14	.261	.302	.370	87	-2	-2	13	4	2	0	1.000	4	O	0.1
1982	StL-N	79	72	12	20	3	0	2	14	8	18	.278	.358	.403	111	1	1	11	0	1	-1	1.000	5	O	0.5
1983	StL-N	6	5	0	1	0	1	0	0	1	2	.200	.333	.600	154	0	0	1	1	0	0	1.000	-0	/O	0.0
	*Bal-A	26	42	8	13	2	0	1	4	1	11	.310	.326	.429	108	0	0	5	0	2	-1	1.000	-6	O	-0.7
1984	StL-N	105	173	21	47	9	1	3	26	10	27	.272	.311	.387	98	-1	-1	18	3	4	-2	.979	-21	O	-2.7
1985	*StL-N	85	161	21	45	8	2	4	21	19	30	.280	.356	.429	119	4	4	24	1	4	-2	1.000	-11	O	-1.0
1986	StL-N	96	205	24	43	7	1	2	17	20	41	.210	.283	.283	57	-12	-12	17	3	1	0	.993	-4	O	-1.8
1987	StL-N	30	50	5	10	1	0	0	6	7	14	.200	.298	.220	39	-4	-4	3	1	1	-0	1.000	-2	O/1	-0.7
	LA-N	51	67	8	16	3	0	1	4	3	16	.239	.282	.328	63	-4	-4	6	1	1	-0	.971	-5	O	-0.9
	Yr	81	117	13	26	4	0	1	10	10	30	.222	.289	.282	53	-8	-8	10	2	2	-1	.987	-7	O/1	-1.6
1988	Bal-A	13	24	2	3	0	1	0	2	4	6	.125	.250	.208	31	-2	-2	2	0	0	0	1.000	-3	O/D	-0.5
Total	9	607	995	120	248	40	12	13	111	85	196	.249	.312	.353	84	-22	-21	106	17	18	-6	.992	-43	O/D1	-8.2

■ CHAPPY LANE

Lane, George M. b: Pittsburgh, Pa. Deb: 5/16/1882

YEAR	TM/L	G	AB	R	H	2B	3B	HR	RBI	BB	SO	AVG	OBP	SLG	PRO+	BR	/A	RC	SB	CS	SBR	FA	FR	POS	TPR
1882	Pit-a	57	214	26	38	8	2	3		5		.178	.196	.276	60	-9	-8	12				.974	5	1O/C	-0.6
1884	Tol-a	57	215	26	49	9	5	1		2		.228	.242	.330	84	-3	-4	18				.948	4	1/O3C	-0.5
Total	2	114	429	52	87	17	7	4		7		.203	.219	.303	73	-12	-12	29				.961	9	/1OC3	-1.1

■ HUNTER LANE

Lane, James Hunter "Dodo" b: 7/20/1900, Pulaski, Tenn. BR/TR, 5'11", 165 lbs. Deb: 5/13/24

YEAR	TM/L	G	AB	R	H	2B	3B	HR	RBI	BB	SO	AVG	OBP	SLG	PRO+	BR	/A	RC	SB	CS	SBR	FA	FR	POS	TPR
1924	Bos-N	7	15	0	1	0	0	0	0	1	1	.067	.125	.067	-49	-3	-3	0	0	0	0	.909	-1	/32	-0.4

■ MARVIN LANE

Lane, Marvin b: 1/18/50, Sandersville, Ga. BR/TR, 5'11", 180 lbs. Deb: 9/04/71

YEAR	TM/L	G	AB	R	H	2B	3B	HR	RBI	BB	SO	AVG	OBP	SLG	PRO+	BR	/A	RC	SB	CS	SBR	FA	FR	POS	TPR
1971	Det-A	8	14	0	2	0	0	0	1	1	3	.143	.200	.143	-1	-2	-2	0	0	0	0	1.000	-1	/O	-0.3
1972	Det-A	8	6	2	0	0	0	0	0	0	2	.000	.000	.000	-97	-1	-1	0	0	0	0	1.000	-1	/O	-0.2
1973	Det-A	6	8	2	2	0	0	1	2	2	2	.250	.400	.625	173	1	1	2	0	0	0	1.000	-1	/O	0.0
1974	Det-A	50	103	16	24	4	1	2	9	19	24	.233	.352	.350	99	1	0	14	2	0	1	.986	-3	O/D	-0.3
1976	Det-A	18	48	3	9	1	0	0	5	6	11	.188	.278	.208	42	-3	-3	3	0	0	0	.960	-2	O	-0.6
Total	5	90	179	23	37	5	1	3	17	28	42	.207	.314	.296	74	-5	-5	19	2	0	1	.983	-8	/OD	-1.4

■ DICK LANE

Lane, Richard Harrison b: 6/28/27, Highland Park, Mich. BR/TR, 5'11", 178 lbs. Deb: 6/20/49

YEAR	TM/L	G	AB	R	H	2B	3B	HR	RBI	BB	SO	AVG	OBP	SLG	PRO+	BR	/A	RC	SB	CS	SBR	FA	FR	POS	TPR
1949	Chi-A	12	42	4	5	0	0	0	4	5	3	.119	.213	.119	-11	-7	-7	1	0	1	-1	1.000	1	O	-0.6

■ DON LANG

Lang, Donald Charles b: 3/15/15, Selma, Cal. BR/TR, 6', 175 lbs. Deb: 7/04/38

YEAR	TM/L	G	AB	R	H	2B	3B	HR	RBI	BB	SO	AVG	OBP	SLG	PRO+	BR	/A	RC	SB	CS	SBR	FA	FR	POS	TPR
1938	Cin-N	21	50	5	13	3	1	1	11	2	7	.260	.288	.420	95	-1	-1	5	0			.976	2	3/2S	0.1
1948	StL-N	117	323	30	87	14	1	4	31	47	38	.269	.364	.356	90	-1	-3	46	2			.964	9	3/2	0.5
Total	2	138	373	35	100	17	2	5	42	49	45	.268	.355	.365	91	-1	-4	51	2			.966	10	3/2S	0.6

■ BILL LANGE

Lange, William Alexander "Little Eva" b: 6/6/1871, San Francisco, Cal d: 7/23/50, San Francisco, Cal. BR/TR, 6'1.5", 190 lbs. Deb: 4/27/1893

YEAR	TM/L	G	AB	R	H	2B	3B	HR	RBI	BB	SO	AVG	OBP	SLG	PRO+	BR	/A	RC	SB	CS	SBR	FA	FR	POS	TPR
1893	Chi-N	117	469	92	132	8	7	8	88	52	20	.281	.358	.380	99	-1	0	83	47			.888	2	2O/3SC	0.2
1894	Chi-N	111	442	84	145	16	9	6	90	56	18	.328	.405	.446	101	6	1	109	65			.910	4	*O/S3	-0.2
1895	Chi-N	123	478	120	186	27	16	10	98	55	24	.389	.456	.575	157	48	42	160	67			.924	10	*O	3.4
1896	Chi-N	122	469	114	153	21	16	4	92	65	24	.326	.414	.465	129	24	21	129	84			.932	10	*O/C	1.8
1897	Chi-N	118	479	119	163	24	14	5	83	48		.340	.406	.480	128	23	20	127	**73**			.946	2	*O	1.2
1898	Chi-N	113	442	79	141	16	11	5	69	36		.319	.377	.439	134	18	18	84	22			.970	10	*O/1	1.9
1899	Chi-N	107	416	81	135	21	7	1	58	38		.325	.382	.416	122	11	13	85	41			.976	12	O1	1.5
Total	7	811	3195	689	1055	133	80	39	578	350	86	.330	.401	.459	125	130	116	776	399			.942	50	O/21S3C	9.8

■ SAM LANGFORD

Langford, Elton b: 5/21/1900, Briggs, Tex. BL/TR, 6', 180 lbs. Deb: 4/13/26

YEAR	TM/L	G	AB	R	H	2B	3B	HR	RBI	BB	SO	AVG	OBP	SLG	PRO+	BR	/A	RC	SB	CS	SBR	FA	FR	POS	TPR
1926	Bos-A	1	1	1	0	0	0	0	0	0	0	.000	.000	.000	-99	-0	-0	0	0	0	0	.000	0	H	0.0

YEAR	TM/L	G	AB	R	H	2B	3B	HR	RBI	BB	SO	AVG	OBP	SLG	PRO+	BR	/A	RC	SB	CS	SBR	FA	FR	POS	TPR
1927	Cle-A	20	67	10	18	5	0	1	7	5	7	.269	.347	.388	90	-1	-1	9	0	1	-1	1.000	-2	O	-0.5
1928	Cle-A	110	427	50	118	17	8	4	50	21	35	.276	.312	.382	81	-13	-13	49	3	7	-3	.972	-8	*O	-3.1
Total	3	131	495	61	136	22	8	5	57	26	42	.275	.316	.382	81	-14	-14	58	3	8	-4	.976	-11	O	-3.6

■ BOB LANGSFORD Langsford, Robert William (b: Robert Hugo Lankswert) b: 8/5/1865, Louisville, Ky. d: 1/10/07, Louisville, Ky. BR/TR, Deb: 6/18/1899

YEAR	TM/L	G	AB	R	H	2B	3B	HR	RBI	BB	SO	AVG	OBP	SLG	PRO+	BR	/A	RC	SB	CS	SBR	FA	FR	POS	TPR
1899	Lou-N	1	4	0	0	0	0	0	0	0		.000	.000	.000	-99	-1	-1	0	0			1.000	-0	/S	-0.1

■ HAL LANIER Lanier, Harold Clifton b: 7/4/42, Denton, N.C. BR/TR, 6'2", 180 lbs. Deb: 6/18/64 FMC

YEAR	TM/L	G	AB	R	H	2B	3B	HR	RBI	BB	SO	AVG	OBP	SLG	PRO+	BR	/A	RC	SB	CS	SBR	FA	FR	POS	TPR
1964	SF-N	98	383	40	105	16	3	2	28	5	44	.274	.284	.347	75	-12	-13	34	2	1	0	.979	10	2/S	0.5
1965	SF-N	159	522	41	118	15	9	0	39	21	67	.226	.256	.289	52	-33	-34	34	2	1	0	.976	-5	*2/S	-2.7
1966	SF-N	149	459	37	106	14	2	3	37	16	49	.231	.257	.290	50	-30	-31	30	1	0	0	.991	28	*2S	0.7
1967	SF-N	151	525	37	112	16	3	0	42	16	61	.213	.239	.255	42	-40	-39	29	2	2	-1	.974	29	*S2	0.3
1968	SF-N	151	486	37	100	14	1	0	27	12	57	.206	.225	.239	39	-36	-36	23	2	2	-1	**.979**	14	*S	-0.8
1969	SF-N	150	495	37	113	9	1	0	35	25	68	.228	.265	.251	46	-36	-35	31	0	1	-1	.969	**29**	*S	0.9
1970	SF-N	134	438	33	101	13	1	2	41	21	41	.231	.266	.279	47	-34	-33	28	1	2	-1	.967	13	*S/21	-0.7
1971	*SF-N	109	206	21	48	8	0	1	13	15	26	.233	.285	.286	63	-10	-10	16	0	0	0	.957	5	32/S1	-0.4
1972	NY-A	60	103	5	22	3	0	0	6	2	13	.214	.236	.243	44	-7	-7	5	1	2	-1	.973	9	3/S2	0.1
1973	NY-A	35	86	9	18	3	0	0	5	3	10	.209	.244	.244	39	-7	-7	5	0	0	0	.960	1	S/23	-0.3
Total	10	1196	3703	297	843	111	20	8	273	136	436	.228	.256	.275	50	-244	-245	236	11	11	-3	.971	132	S23/1	-2.4

■ RIMP LANIER Lanier, Lorenzo b: 10/19/48, Tuskegee, Ala. BL/TR, 5'8", 150 lbs. Deb: 9/11/71

YEAR	TM/L	G	AB	R	H	2B	3B	HR	RBI	BB	SO	AVG	OBP	SLG	PRO+	BR	/A	RC	SB	CS	SBR	FA	FR	POS	TPR
1971	Pit-N	6	4	0	0	0	0	0	0	0	1	.000	.200	.000	-39	-1	-1	0	0	0	0	.000	0	H	-0.1

■ RAY LANKFORD Lankford, Raymond Lewis b: 6/5/67, Modesto, Cal. BL/TL, 5'11", 180 lbs. Deb: 8/21/90

YEAR	TM/L	G	AB	R	H	2B	3B	HR	RBI	BB	SO	AVG	OBP	SLG	PRO+	BR	/A	RC	SB	CS	SBR	FA	FR	POS	TPR
1990	StL-N	39	126	12	36	10	1	3	12	13	27	.286	.353	.452	119	3	3	21	8	2	1	.989	2	O	0.6
1991	StL-N	151	566	83	142	23	**15**	9	69	41	114	.251	.303	.392	93	-6	-6	67	44	20	1	.984	11	*O	0.3
1992	StL-N	153	598	87	175	40	6	20	86	72	147	.293	.373	.480	142	32	33	108	42	24	-2	.996	10	*O	4.0
Total	3	343	1290	182	353	73	22	32	167	126	288	.274	.341	.439	118	29	30	197	94	46	1	.990	24	O	4.9

■ RED LANNING Lanning, Lester Alfred b: 5/13/1895, Harvard, Ill. d: 6/13/62, Bristol, Conn. BL/TL, 5'9", 165 lbs. Deb: 6/20/16

YEAR	TM/L	G	AB	R	H	2B	3B	HR	RBI	BB	SO	AVG	OBP	SLG	PRO+	BR	/A	RC	SB	CS	SBR	FA	FR	POS	TPR
1916	Phi-A	19	33	5	6	2	0	0	1	10	9	.182	.372	.242	89	0	0	3	0			.909	-4	/OP	-0.4

■ CARNEY LANSFORD Lansford, Carney Ray b: 2/7/57, San Jose, Cal. BR/TR, 6'2", 195 lbs. Deb: 4/08/78 F

YEAR	TM/L	G	AB	R	H	2B	3B	HR	RBI	BB	SO	AVG	OBP	SLG	PRO+	BR	/A	RC	SB	CS	SBR	FA	FR	POS	TPR
1978	Cal-A	121	453	63	133	23	2	8	52	31	67	.294	.344	.406	115	6	8	65	20	9	1	.942	-26	*3/SD	-1.9
1979	*Cal-A	157	654	114	188	30	5	19	79	39	115	.287	.330	.436	108	3	6	91	20	8	1	**.983**	-24	*3	-1.8
1980	Cal-A	151	602	87	157	27	3	15	80	50	93	.261	.317	.390	95	-7	-5	75	14	5	1	.955	-24	*3	-3.0
1981	Bos-A	102	399	61	134	23	3	4	52	34	28	**.336**	.391	.439	131	20	17	68	15	10	-2	.951	-0	3D	1.4
1982	Bos-A	128	482	65	145	28	4	11	63	46	48	.301	.364	.444	114	14	10	76	9	4	0	.968	-13	*3D	-0.5
1983	Oak-A	80	299	43	92	16	2	10	45	22	33	.308	.361	.475	136	11	13	47	3	8	-4	.957	-5	3/S	0.3
1984	Oak-A	151	597	70	179	31	5	14	74	40	62	.300	.347	.439	124	12	17	90	9	3	1	.957	-8	*3	0.9
1985	Oak-A	98	401	51	111	18	2	13	46	18	27	.277	.314	.429	109	-0	4	53	2	3	-1	.976	-32	3	-3.1
1986	Oak-A	151	591	80	168	16	4	19	72	39	51	.284	.334	.421	112	3	8	80	16	7	1	.982	-18	*31/2D	-1.5
1987	Oak-A	151	554	89	160	27	4	19	76	60	44	.289	.368	.455	125	14	19	96	27	8	3	**.980**	-3	*31/D	1.6
1988	*Oak-A★	150	556	80	155	20	2	7	57	35	35	.279	.329	.360	96	-5	-3	65	29	8	4	**.979**	-12	*3/12D	-1.2
1989	*Oak-A	148	551	81	185	28	2	2	52	51	25	.336	.401	.405	132	22	25	88	37	15	2	.957	-26	*31/D	0.1
1990	*Oak-A	134	507	58	136	15	1	3	50	45	50	.268	.335	.320	88	-10	-7	54	16	14	-4	**.970**	-21	*3/1D	-3.2
1991	Oak-A	5	16	0	1	0	0	0	1	0	2	.063	.063	.063	-69	-4	-3	0	0	0	0	1.000	-1	/3D	-0.5
1992	*Oak-A	135	496	65	130	30	1	7	75	43	39	.262	.330	.369	99	-3	-0	61	7	2	1	.965	-23	*31/SD	-2.3
Total	15	1862	7158	1007	2074	332	40	151	874	553	719	.290	.346	.411	112	77	110	1007	224	104	5	.966	-235	*31/DS2	-14.7

■ JODY LANSFORD Lansford, Joseph Dale b: 1/15/61, San Jose, Cal. BR/TR, 6'5", 225 lbs. Deb: 7/31/82 F

YEAR	TM/L	G	AB	R	H	2B	3B	HR	RBI	BB	SO	AVG	OBP	SLG	PRO+	BR	/A	RC	SB	CS	SBR	FA	FR	POS	TPR
1982	SD-N	13	22	6	4	0	0	0	3	6	4	.182	.357	.182	58	-1	-1	2	0	1	-1	.986	-1	/1	-0.3
1983	SD-N	12	8	1	2	0	0	1	2	0	3	.250	.250	.625	140	0	0	1	0	0	0	1.000	0	/1	0.0
Total	2	25	30	7	6	0	0	1	5	6	7	.200	.333	.300	82	-1	-1	3	0	1	-1	.988	-1	/1	-0.3

■ PETE LAPAN Lapan, Peter Nelson b: 6/25/1891, Easthampton, Mass d: 1/5/53, Norwalk, Cal. BR/TR, 5'7", 165 lbs. Deb: 9/16/22

YEAR	TM/L	G	AB	R	H	2B	3B	HR	RBI	BB	SO	AVG	OBP	SLG	PRO+	BR	/A	RC	SB	CS	SBR	FA	FR	POS	TPR
1922	Was-A	11	34	7	11	1	0	1	6	3	4	.324	.378	.441	119	1	1	6	1	0	0	.958	-0	C	0.2
1923	Was-A	2	2	0	0	0	0	0	0	0	0	.000	.000	.000	-99	-1	-1	0	0	0	0	.000	0	H	-0.1
Total	2	13	36	7	11	1	0	1	6	3	4	.306	.359	.417	107	0	0	6	1	0	0	.907	-0	/C	0.1

■ RALPH LaPOINTE LaPointe, Ralph Robert b: 1/8/22, Winooski, Vt. d: 9/13/67, Burlington, Vt. BR/TR, 5'11", 185 lbs. Deb: 4/15/47

YEAR	TM/L	G	AB	R	H	2B	3B	HR	RBI	BB	SO	AVG	OBP	SLG	PRO+	BR	/A	RC	SB	CS	SBR	FA	FR	POS	TPR
1947	Phi-N	56	211	33	65	7	0	1	15	17	15	.308	.362	.355	95	-2	-1	29	8			.956	-10	S	-0.8
1948	StL-N	87	222	27	50	3	0	0	15	18	19	.225	.283	.239	40	-17	-19	16	1			.965	8	2S/3	-0.8
Total	2	143	433	60	115	10	0	1	30	35	34	.266	.322	.296	66	-19	-20	45	9			.955	-2	/S23	-1.6

■ FRANK LaPORTE LaPorte, Frank Breyfogle "Pot" b: 2/6/1880, Uhrichsville, Ohio d: 9/25/39, Newcomerstown, O. BR/TR, 5'8", 175 lbs. Deb: 9/29/05

YEAR	TM/L	G	AB	R	H	2B	3B	HR	RBI	BB	SO	AVG	OBP	SLG	PRO+	BR	/A	RC	SB	CS	SBR	FA	FR	POS	TPR
1905	NY-A	11	40	4	16	1	0	1	12	1		.400	.415	.500	170	4	3	9	1			.918	-3	2	0.1
1906	NY-A	123	454	60	120	23	9	2	54	22		.264	.298	.368	98	3	-2	55	10			.904	-5	*3/2O	-0.4
1907	NY-A	130	470	56	127	20	11	0	48	27		.270	.317	.360	107	7	3	59	10			.896	-10	3O/1	-0.8
1908	Bos-A	62	156	14	37	1	3	0	15	12		.237	.296	.282	86	-2	-2	14	3			.950	10	23/O	0.8
	NY-A	39	145	7	38	3	4	1	15	8		.262	.301	.359	113	2	2	16	3			.934	-3	2O	-0.3
	Yr	101	301	21	75	4	7	1	30	20		.249	.298	.319	99	-0	-1	30	6			.942	6	2O3	0.5
1909	NY-A	89	309	35	92	19	3	0	31	18		.298	.340	.379	126	9	8	41	5			.938	-15	2	-1.0
1910	NY-A	124	432	43	114	14	6	2	67	33		.264	.321	.338	100	3	-0	52	16			.959	-10	2O3	-1.4
1911	StL-A	136	507	71	159	37	12	2	82	34		.314	.361	.446	130	15	18	83	4			.950	-6	*2/3	0.9
1912	StL-A	80	266	32	83	11	4	1	38	20		.312	.367	.395	122	6	7	41	7			.944	-3	2O	0.2
	Was-A	40	136	13	42	9	1	0	17	12		.309	.365	.390	115	3	3	20	3			.939	3	2	0.4
	Yr	120	402	45	125	20	5	1	55	32		.311	.366	.393	120	9	10	62	10			.941	-0	2O	0.6
1913	Was-A	79	242	25	61	5	4	0	18	17	16	.252	.309	.306	78	-6	-7	25	10			.952	3	32O	-0.5
1914	Ind-F	133	505	86	157	27	12	4	**107**	36	36	.311	.361	.436	114	16	9	89	15			.956	6	*2	1.5
1915	New-F	148	550	55	139	28	10	2	56	48	33	.253	.314	.351	101	-4	-0	69	14			.960	5	*2	0.7
Total	11	1194	4212	501	1185	198	79	15	560	288	85	.281	.331	.377	109	54	41	573	101			.952	-29	23O/1	0.2

■ JACK LAPP Lapp, John Walker b: 9/10/1884, Frazer, Pa. d: 2/6/20, Philadelphia, Pa. BL/TR, 5'8", Deb: 9/11/08

YEAR	TM/L	G	AB	R	H	2B	3B	HR	RBI	BB	SO	AVG	OBP	SLG	PRO+	BR	/A	RC	SB	CS	SBR	FA	FR	POS	TPR
1908	Phi-A	13	35	4	5	0	1	0	1	5		.143	.268	.200	49	-2	-2	2	0			.947	-3	C	-0.4
1909	Phi-A	21	56	8	19	3	1	0	10	3		.339	.373	.429	150	3	3	9	1			.938	1	C	0.6
1910	*Phi-A	71	192	18	45	4	3	0	17	20		.234	.310	.286	88	-3	-2	17	0			.980	7	C	1.2
1911	*Phi-A	68	167	35	59	10	3	1	26	24		.353	.435	.467	154	12	13	36	4			.972	-6	C/1	1.1
1912	Phi-A	91	281	26	82	15	6	1	35	19		.292	.337	.399	114	3	4	38	3			.958	-14	C	-0.2
1913	*Phi-A	82	238	23	54	4	4	1	20	37	26	.227	.336	.290	85	-4	-3	23	1			.968	-14	C/1	-1.1
1914	*Phi-A	69	199	22	46	7	2	0	19	31	14	.231	.338	.286	91	-2	-1	20	1	4	-2	.977	-7	C	-0.4
1915	Phi-A	112	312	26	85	16	5	2	31	30	29	.272	.340	.375	118	5	6	43	5	2	0	.967	-4	C1	0.9
1916	Chi-A	40	101	6	21	0	1	0	7	8	10	.208	.266	.228	48	-6	-6	7	1			.989	-0	C	-0.5
Total	9	567	1581	168	416	59	26	5	166	177	79	.263	.340	.343	105	7	11	194	16	6		.969	-38	C/1	1.2

■ NORM LARKER
Larker, Norman Howard John b: 12/27/30, Beaver Meadows, Pa. BL/TL, 6', 200 lbs. Deb: 4/15/58

YEAR	TM/L	G	AB	R	H	2B	3B	HR	RBI	BB	SO	AVG	OBP	SLG	PRO+	BR	/A	RC	SB	CS	SBR	FA	FR	POS	TPR
1958	LA-N	99	253	32	70	16	5	4	29	29	21	.277	.358	.427	103	3	2	38	1	1	-0	.985	-2	O1	-0.4
1959	*LA-N	108	311	37	90	14	1	8	49	26	25	.289	.348	.418	96	1	-2	43	0	1	-1	.990	4	1O	-0.3
1960	LA-N★	133	440	56	142	26	3	5	78	36	24	.323	.375	.430	112	12	9	71	1	0	0	.993	4	*1/O	0.4
1961	LA-N	97	282	29	76	16	1	5	38	24	22	.270	.329	.387	82	-4	-8	34	0	0	0	.995	2	1/O	-1.2
1962	Hou-N	147	506	58	133	19	5	9	63	70	47	.263	.360	.374	105	0	5	71	1	1	-0	.991	6	*1/O	0.2
1963	Mil-N	64	147	15	26	6	0	1	14	24	24	.177	.301	.238	58	-7	-7	12	0	2	-1	.992	4	1	-0.6
	SF-N	19	14	0	1	0	0	0	0	2	2	.071	.188	.071	-22	-2	-2	0	0	0	0	.929	-0	1	-0.3
	Yr	83	161	15	27	6	0	1	14	26	26	.168	.291	.224	51	-10	-9	12	0	2	-1	.987	4	1	-0.9
Total	6	667	1953	227	538	97	15	32	271	211	165	.275	.351	.390	97	3	-3	269	3	5	-2	.991	18	1/O	-2.2

■ BARRY LARKIN
Larkin, Barry Louis b: 4/28/64, Cincinnati, Ohio BR/TR, 6', 185 lbs. Deb: 8/13/86

YEAR	TM/L	G	AB	R	H	2B	3B	HR	RBI	BB	SO	AVG	OBP	SLG	PRO+	BR	/A	RC	SB	CS	SBR	FA	FR	POS	TPR
1986	Cin-N	41	159	27	45	4	3	3	19	9	21	.283	.321	.403	94	-1	-1	22	8	0	2	.976	-0	S/2	0.4
1987	Cin-N	125	439	64	107	16	2	12	43	36	52	.244	.308	.371	76	-14	-16	52	21	6	3	.965	-0	*S	-0.4
1988	Cin-N★	151	588	91	174	32	5	12	56	41	24	.296	.350	.429	118	16	14	94	40	7	8	.960	10	*S	4.6
1989	Cin-N☆	97	325	47	111	14	4	4	36	20	23	.342	.383	.446	132	15	14	54	10	5	0	.976	16	S	3.8
1990	*Cin-N★	158	614	85	185	25	6	7	67	49	49	.301	.360	.396	103	7	4	91	30	5	6	.977	20	*S	4.3
1991	Cin-N★	123	464	88	140	27	4	20	69	55	64	.302	.379	.506	141	29	27	93	24	6	4	.976	18	*S	5.9
1992	Cin-N	140	533	76	162	32	6	12	78	63	58	.304	.382	.454	129	26	23	94	15	4	2	.983	8	*S	4.7
Total	7	835	3122	478	924	150	30	70	368	273	291	.296	.358	.430	114	79	64	499	148	33	25	.973	72	S/2	23.3

■ ED LARKIN
Larkin, Edward Francis b: 7/1/1885, Wyalusing, Pa. d: 3/28/34, Wyalusing, Pa. BR/TR, 5'8", Deb: 10/02/09

YEAR	TM/L	G	AB	R	H	2B	3B	HR	RBI	BB	SO	AVG	OBP	SLG	PRO+	BR	/A	RC	SB	CS	SBR	FA	FR	POS	TPR
1909	Phi-A	2	6	0	1	0	0	0	1	1		.167	.286	.167	42	-0	-0	0	0			.769	-2	/C	-0.2

■ GENE LARKIN
Larkin, Eugene Thomas b: 10/24/62, Flushing, N.Y. BB/TR, 6'3", 212 lbs. Deb: 5/21/87

YEAR	TM/L	G	AB	R	H	2B	3B	HR	RBI	BB	SO	AVG	OBP	SLG	PRO+	BR	/A	RC	SB	CS	SBR	FA	FR	POS	TPR
1987	*Min-A	85	233	23	62	11	2	4	28	25	31	.266	.342	.382	89	-2	-4	30	1	4	-2	.989	-2	D1	-0.9
1988	Min-A	149	505	56	135	30	2	8	70	68	55	.267	.371	.382	108	10	8	75	3	2	-0	.994	-5	D1	-0.2
1989	Min-A	136	446	61	119	25	1	6	46	54	57	.267	.358	.368	98	5	1	60	5	2	0	.992	-7	1DO	-1.2
1990	Min-A	119	401	46	108	26	4	5	42	42	55	.269	.346	.392	99	4	0	56	5	3	-0	1.000	-2	OD1	-0.6
1991	*Min-A	98	255	34	73	14	1	2	19	30	21	.286	.364	.373	99	2	1	33	2	3	-1	.968	-10	O1/23D	-1.4
1992	Min-A	115	337	38	83	18	1	6	42	28	43	.246	.312	.359	85	-6	-7	38	7	2	1	.992	-6	1O/D	-1.7
Total	6	702	2177	258	580	124	11	31	247	247	262	.266	.351	.376	98	13	-1	292	23	16	-3	.993	-32	1DO/32	-6.0

■ TERRY LARKIN
Larkin, Frank S. d: 9/16/1894, Brooklyn, N.Y. BR/TR, Deb: 5/20/1876

YEAR	TM/L	G	AB	R	H	2B	3B	HR	RBI	BB	SO	AVG	OBP	SLG	PRO+	BR	/A	RC	SB	CS	SBR	FA	FR	POS	TPR
1876	NY-N	1	4	0	0	0	0	0	0	0	0	.000	.000	.000	-99	-1	-1	0				.500	-0	/P	0.0
1877	Har-N	58	228	28	52	6	5	1	18	5	23	.228	.245	.311	83	-7	-3	18				.885	-1	*P/32	0.0
1878	Chi-N	58	226	33	65	9	4	0	32	**17**	17	.288	.337	.363	122	8	6	28				.858	-4	*P/O3	0.1
1879	Chi-N	60	228	26	50	12	2	0	18	8	24	.219	.246	.289	71	-6	-8	17				.918	-7	*P/O	-0.1
1880	Tro-N	6	20	1	3	1	0	0	1	3	4	.150	.261	.200	56	-1	-1	1				1.000	-0	/POS	-0.1
1884	Was-U	17	70	11	17	0	0	0		4		.243	.284	.243	82	-1	-1	5				.726	-4	3	-0.4
	Ric-a	40	139	17	28	1	4	0		9		.201	.265	.266	77	-3	-3	10				.907	0	2	-0.2
Total	6	240	915	116	215	29	15	1	69	46	68	.235	.274	.303	88	-10	-10	79				.884	-16	P/23OS	-0.7

■ HENRY LARKIN
Larkin, Henry E. "Ted" b: 1/12/1860, Reading, Pa. d: 1/31/42, Reading, Pa. BR/TR, 5'10", 175 lbs. Deb: 5/01/1884 M

YEAR	TM/L	G	AB	R	H	2B	3B	HR	RBI	BB	SO	AVG	OBP	SLG	PRO+	BR	/A	RC	SB	CS	SBR	FA	FR	POS	TPR
1884	Phi-a	85	326	59	90	21	9	3		15		.276	.324	.423	136	16	12	46				.856	-7	*O/2	0.4
1885	Phi-a	108	453	114	149	**37**	14	8		26		.329	.372	.525	174	42	37	91				.882	12	*O	4.1
1886	Phi-a	139	565	133	180	**36**	16	2		59		.319	**.390**	.450	163	43	42	114	32			.866	5	*O	3.8
1887	Phi-a	126	497	105	154	22	12	3		48		.310	.380	.421	125	18	18	96	37			.895	3	O12	1.4
1888	Phi-a	135	546	92	147	28	12	7	101	33		.269	.326	.403	137	21	22	80	20			.967	-8	*12	0.3
1889	Phi-a	133	516	105	164	23	12	3	74	83	41	.318	.428	.426	148	36	37	101	11			.973	-4	*1/32	2.1
1890	Cle-P	125	506	93	168	32	15	5	112	65	18	.332	.420	.484	156	33	41	108	5			.978	-8	*1/OM	2.1
1891	Phi-a	133	526	94	147	27	14	10	93	66	56	.279	.376	.441	133	25	22	90	2			.974	-5	*1O	1.0
1892	Was-N	119	464	76	130	13	7	8	96	39	21	.280	.346	.390	128	13	15	72	21			.969	1	*1/O	1.0
1893	Was-N	81	319	54	101	20	3	4	73	50	5	.317	.422	.436	134	16	18	61	1			.963	-9	1	0.6
Total	10	1184	4718	925	1430	259	114	53	549	484	141	.303	.380	.440	144	262	264	858	129			.971	-21	1O/23	16.8

■ BOB LARMORE
Larmore, Robert McKahan "Red" b: 12/6/1896, Anderson, Ind. d: 1/15/64, St.Louis, Mo. BR/TR, 5'10.5", 185 lbs. Deb: 5/14/18

YEAR	TM/L	G	AB	R	H	2B	3B	HR	RBI	BB	SO	AVG	OBP	SLG	PRO+	BR	/A	RC	SB	CS	SBR	FA	FR	POS	TPR
1918	StL-N	4	7	0	2	0	0	0	1	0	2	.286	.286	.286	77	-0	-0	1	0			.778	-1	/S	-0.1

■ SAM LaROQUE
LaRoque, Samuel H. J. b: 2/26/1864, St.Mathias, Que., Canada TR, 5'11", 190 lbs. Deb: 7/30/1888

YEAR	TM/L	G	AB	R	H	2B	3B	HR	RBI	BB	SO	AVG	OBP	SLG	PRO+	BR	/A	RC	SB	CS	SBR	FA	FR	POS	TPR
1888	Det-N	2	9	1	4	0	0	0	2	1	1	.444	.500	.444	207	1	1	2	0			.789	0	/2	0.1
1890	Pit-N	111	434	59	105	20	4	1	40	35	29	.242	.316	.313	97	-7	1	53	27			.925	-10	2S/1O	-0.3
1891	Pit-N	1	4	0	0	0	0	0	0	0	1	.000	.000	.000	-99	-1	-1	0	0			.714	0	/3	-0.1
	Lou-a	10	35	6	11	2	1	1	8	5	8	.314	.429	.514	175	3	4	8	1			.875	-3	2/1	0.1
Total	3	124	482	66	120	22	5	2	50	41	39	.249	.326	.328	104	-4	4	63	28			.916	-13	/2S13O	-0.2

■ VIC LaROSE
LaRose, Victor Raymond b: 12/23/44, Los Angeles, Cal. BR/TR, 5'11", 180 lbs. Deb: 9/13/68

YEAR	TM/L	G	AB	R	H	2B	3B	HR	RBI	BB	SO	AVG	OBP	SLG	PRO+	BR	/A	RC	SB	CS	SBR	FA	FR	POS	TPR
1968	Chi-N	4	2	0	0	0	0	0	0	0	1	.000	.333	.000	6	-0	-0	0	0	0	0	1.000	1	/2S	0.1

■ HARRY LaROSS
LaRoss, Harry Raymond "Spike" b: 1/2/1888, Easton, Pa. d: 3/22/54, Chicago, Ill. BR/TR, 5'11.5", 170 lbs. Deb: 6/24/14

YEAR	TM/L	G	AB	R	H	2B	3B	HR	RBI	BB	SO	AVG	OBP	SLG	PRO+	BR	/A	RC	SB	CS	SBR	FA	FR	POS	TPR
1914	Cin-N	22	48	7	11	1	0	0	5	2	10	.229	.260	.250	50	-3	-3	4	4			.739	-6	O	-1.0

■ SWEDE LARSEN
Larsen, Erling Adeli b: 11/15/13, Jersey City, N.J. BR/TR, 5'11", 170 lbs. Deb: 6/17/36

YEAR	TM/L	G	AB	R	H	2B	3B	HR	RBI	BB	SO	AVG	OBP	SLG	PRO+	BR	/A	RC	SB	CS	SBR	FA	FR	POS	TPR
1936	Bos-N	3	1	0	0	0	0	0	0	0	0	.000	.000	.000	-99	-0	-0	0	0			1.000	-0	/2	0.0

■ TONY LaRUSSA
LaRussa, Anthony b: 10/4/44, Tampa, Fla. BR/TR, 6'1", 190 lbs. Deb: 5/10/63 MC

YEAR	TM/L	G	AB	R	H	2B	3B	HR	RBI	BB	SO	AVG	OBP	SLG	PRO+	BR	/A	RC	SB	CS	SBR	FA	FR	POS	TPR
1963	KC-A	34	44	4	11	1	1	0	1	7	12	.250	.353	.318	86	-0	-1	6	0	0	0	.957	2	S/2	0.2
1968	Oak-A	5	3	0	1	0	0	0	0	0	0	.333	.333	.333	108	-0	0	0	0	0	0	.000	0	H	0.0
1969	Oak-A	8	8	0	0	0	0	0	0	0	1	.000	.000	.000	-99	-2	-2	0	0	0	0	.000	0	H	-0.2
1970	Oak-A	52	106	6	21	4	1	0	6	15	19	.198	.303	.255	57	-6	-6	9	0	0	0	.969	-1	2	-0.4
1971	Oak-A	23	8	3	0	0	0	0	0	0	4	.000	.000	.000	-99	-2	-2	0	0	0	0	.833	5	/2S3	0.3
	Atl-N	9	7	1	2	0	0	0	0	1	1	.286	.375	.286	84	-0	-0	0	0	0	0	.933	0	/2	0.1
1973	Chi-N	1	0	1	0	0	0	0	0	0	0	—	—	—	—	0	0	0	0	0	0	.000	0	R	0.0
Total	6	132	176	15	35	5	2	0	7	23	37	.199	.295	.250	54	-11	-10	16	0	0	0	.963	7	/2S3	0.0

■ AL LARY
Lary, Alfred Allen b: 9/26/29, Northport, Ala. BR/TR, 6'3", 185 lbs. Deb: 9/06/54 F

YEAR	TM/L	G	AB	R	H	2B	3B	HR	RBI	BB	SO	AVG	OBP	SLG	PRO+	BR	/A	RC	SB	CS	SBR	FA	FR	POS	TPR
1954	Chi-N	2	2	0	1	0	0	0	0	0	1	.500	.500	.500	160	0	0	1	0	0	0	1.000	0	/P	0.0
1955	Chi-N	4	0	1	0	0	0	0	0	0	0	—	—	—	—	0	0	0	0	0	0	.000	0	R	0.0
1962	Chi-N	23	6	1	1	0	0	0	0	2	1	.167	.375	.167	49	-0	-0	1	0	0	0	.857	-0	P	0.0
Total	3	29	8	2	2	0	0	0	0	2	2	.250	.400	.250	75	-0	-0	1	0	0	0	.889	-0	/P	0.0

■ LYN LARY
Lary, Lynford Hobart "Broadway" b: 1/28/06, Armona, Cal. d: 1/9/73, Downey, Cal. BR/TR, 6', 165 lbs. Deb: 5/11/29

YEAR	TM/L	G	AB	R	H	2B	3B	HR	RBI	BB	SO	AVG	OBP	SLG	PRO+	BR	/A	RC	SB	CS	SBR	FA	FR	POS	TPR
1929	NY-A	80	236	48	73	9	2	5	26	24	15	.309	.380	.428	115	3	5	40	4	1	1	.943	5	3S/2	1.3
1930	NY-A	117	464	93	134	20	8	3	52	45	40	.289	.357	.386	92	-7	-4	68	14	2	**3**	.940	-8	*S	0.3
1931	NY-A	155	610	100	171	35	9	10	107	88	54	.280	.376	.416	115	9	14	99	13	10	-2	.946	9	*S	3.4

YEAR	TM/L	G	AB	R	H	2B	3B	HR	RBI	BB	SO	AVG	OBP	SLG	PRO+	BR	/A	RC	SB	CS	SBR	FA	FR	POS	TPR
1932	NY-A	91	280	56	65	14	4	3	39	52	28	.232	.358	.343	87	-6	-4	39	9	3	1	.941	2	S/123O	0.5
1933	NY-A	52	127	25	28	3	3	0	13	28	17	.220	.361	.291	79	-4	-2	16	2	1	0	.938	2	3S/1O	0.1
1934	NY-A	1	0	0	0	0	0	0	0	1	0	—	1.000	—	189	0	0	0	0	0	0	.800	-0	/1	0.0
	Bos-A	129	419	58	101	20	4	2	54	66	51	.241	.344	.322	68	-16	-20	52	12	5	1	**.965**	-5	*S	-1.6
	Yr	130	419	58	101	20	4	2	54	67	51	.241	.346	.322	68	-15	-20	52	12	5	1	.965	-5	*S/1	-1.6
1935	Was-A	39	103	8	20	4	0	0	7	12	10	.194	.278	.233	35	-10	-10	8	3	0	1	.953	-4	S	-1.0
	StL-A	93	371	78	107	25	7	2	35	64	43	.288	.396	.410	104	7	4	68	25	4	5	.962	13	S	2.5
	Yr	132	474	86	127	29	7	2	42	76	53	.268	.371	.371	90	-3	-5	74	28	4	**6**	.960	9	*S	1.5
1936	StL-A	155	619	112	179	30	6	2	52	117	54	.289	.404	.367	89	-3	-6	105	**37**	9	**6**	.956	-4	*S	0.5
1937	Cle-A	156	644	110	187	46	7	8	77	88	64	.290	.378	.421	100	2	2	107	18	8	1	.963	6	*S	1.7
1938	Cle-A	141	568	94	152	36	4	3	51	88	65	.268	.366	.361	84	-13	-12	82	23	6	3	.964	-0	*S	0.2
1939	Cle-A	3	2	0	0	0	0	0	0	0	1	.000	.000	.000	-99	-1	-1	0	0	0	0	.000	-1	/S	-0.1
	Bro-N	29	31	7	5	1	1	0	1	12	6	.161	.409	.258	80	0	-0	5	1			.947	1	S/3	0.2
	StL-N	34	75	11	14	3	0	0	9	16	15	.187	.330	.227	49	-4	-5	6	1			.961	-6	S/3	-0.9
	Yr	63	106	18	19	4	1	0	10	28	21	.179	.356	.236	59	-4	-5	11	2			.958	-4	S3	-0.7
1940	StL-A	27	54	5	3	1	1	0	3	4	7	.056	.136	.111	-35	-11	-11	1	0	0	0	.952	1	S/2	-0.9
Total	12	1302	4603	805	1239	247	56	38	526	705	470	.269	.369	.372	90	-53	-48	696	162	49		.956	11	*S/312O	6.2

■ **DON LASSETTER** Lassetter, Donald O'Neal b: 3/27/33, Newnan, Ga. BR/TR, 6'3", 200 lbs. Deb: 9/21/57

YEAR	TM/L	G	AB	R	H	2B	3B	HR	RBI	BB	SO	AVG	OBP	SLG	PRO+	BR	/A	RC	SB	CS	SBR	FA	FR	POS	TPR
1957	StL-N	4	13	2	2	0	1	0	0	1	3	.154	.214	.308	37	-1	-1	0	0	0	0	1.000	1	/O	-0.1

■ **JUICE LATHAM** Latham, George Warren "Jumbo" b: 9/6/1852, Utica, N.Y. d: 5/26/14, Utica, N.Y. BR/TR, 5'8", 164 lbs. Deb: 4/19/1875 M

YEAR	TM/L	G	AB	R	H	2B	3B	HR	RBI	BB	SO	AVG	OBP	SLG	PRO+	BR	/A	RC	SB	CS	SBR	FA	FR	POS	TPR
1875	Bos-n	16	77	23	21	4	1	0		0		.273	.273	.351	110	1	1	8						1	0.0
	NH-n	20	76	6	15	1	0	0		0		.197	.197	.211	47	-4	-3	3						1/S3M	-0.3
	Yr	36	153	29	36	5	1	0		0		.235	.235	.281	82	-3	-2	10						1/S3	-0.3
1877	Lou-N	59	278	42	81	10	6	0	22	5	6	.291	.304	.371	94	3	-4	32				.950	2	*1	-0.2
1882	Phi-a	74	323	47	92	10	2	0		10		.285	.306	.328	102	5	-1	33				**.972**	-0	*1M	-0.9
1883	Lou-a	88	368	60	92	7	6	0		12		.250	.274	.302	92	-6	-2	31				.956	-3	*12/S	-0.9
1884	Lou-a	77	308	31	52	3	3	0		8		.169	.197	.198	33	-22	-20	12				.961	3	*1/3	-2.4
Total	4	298	1277	180	317	30	17	0	22	35	6	.248	.270	.298	82	-20	-27	109				.960	1	1/2S3	-4.4

■ **ARLIE LATHAM** Latham, Walter Arlington "The Freshest Man On Earth"
b: 3/15/1860, W.Lebanon, N.H. d: 11/29/52, Garden City, N.Y. BR/TR, 5'8", 150 lbs. Deb: 7/05/1880 MUC

YEAR	TM/L	G	AB	R	H	2B	3B	HR	RBI	BB	SO	AVG	OBP	SLG	PRO+	BR	/A	RC	SB	CS	SBR	FA	FR	POS	TPR
1880	Buf-N	22	79	9	10	3	1	0	3	1	8	.127	.138	.190	10	-7	-7	2				.887	-2	SO/C	-0.9
1883	StL-a	98	406	86	96	12	7	0		18		.236	.269	.300	79	-7	-11	34				.866	22	*3/C	0.9
1884	StL-a	110	474	115	130	17	12	1		19		.274	.311	.367	119	12	9	55				.864	**40**	*3/C	4.5
1885	*StL-a	110	485	84	100	15	3	1		18		.206	.242	.256	57	-21	-25	31				.875	1	*3/C	-2.0
1886	*StL-a	134	578	**152**	174	23	8	1		55		.301	.368	.374	129	24	20	104	60			.827	0	*3/2	2.0
1887	*StL-a	136	627	163	198	35	10	2		45		.316	.366	.413	108	16	4	146	129			.877	2	*3/2C	0.7
1888	*StL-a	133	570	119	151	19	5	2	31	43		.265	.325	.326	101	9	-1	98	**109**			.882	3	*3/S	0.4
1889	StL-a	118	512	110	126	13	3	4	49	42	30	.246	.317	.307	71	-12	-24	73	69			.883	9	*3/2	-0.9
1890	Chi-P	52	214	47	49	7	2	1	20	22	22	.229	.310	.294	61	-11	-12	30	32			.880	3	3	-0.6
	Cin-N	41	164	35	41	6	2	0	15	23	18	.250	.346	.311	94	-0	-0	25	20			.853	5	3/O	0.6
1891	Cin-N	135	533	119	145	20	10	7	53	74	35	.272	.372	.386	122	18	17	112	87			.879	20	*3/C	3.9
1892	Cin-N	152	622	111	148	20	4	0	44	60	54	.238	.310	.283	82	-13	-11	77	66			.883	-5	*3/2O	-1.0
1893	Cin-N	127	531	101	150	18	6	2	49	62	20	.282	.368	.350	91	-3	-5	92	57			.892	-11	*3	-1.2
1894	Cin-N	129	524	129	164	23	6	4	60	60	24	.313	.393	.403	90	-3	-7	110	59			.860	-10	*3/2	-1.3
1895	Cin-N	112	460	93	143	14	6	2	69	42	25	.311	.375	.380	93	-1	-4	86	48			.861	-15	*3/12	-1.4
1896	StL-N	8	35	3	7	0	0	0	5	4	3	.200	.282	.200	31	-3	-3	3	2			.744	-1	/3M	-0.4
1899	Was-N	6	6	1	1	0	0	0	0	1		.167	.286	.167	26	-1	-1	0	0			1.000	-0	/O2	-0.1
1909	NY-N	4	2	1	0	0	0	0	0	0		.000	.000	.000	-99	-0	-0	-0	1			1.000	1	/2	0.0
Total	17	1627	6822	1478	1833	245	85	27	398	589	239	.269	.334	.341	93	-5	-63	1078	739			.870	61	*3/2OSC1	3.2

■ **CHICK LATHERS** Lathers, Charles Ten Eyck b: 10/22/1888, Detroit, Mich. d: 7/26/71, Petoskey, Mich. BL/TR, 6', 180 lbs. Deb: 5/01/10

YEAR	TM/L	G	AB	R	H	2B	3B	HR	RBI	BB	SO	AVG	OBP	SLG	PRO+	BR	/A	RC	SB	CS	SBR	FA	FR	POS	TPR
1910	Det-A	41	82	4	19	2	0	0	3	8		.232	.300	.256	70	-2	-3	6	0			.926	5	3/2S	0.2
1911	Det-A	29	45	5	10	1	0	0	4	5		.222	.314	.244	54	-2	-3	4	0			.867	-3	/23S1	-0.5
Total	2	70	127	9	29	3	0	0	7	13		.228	.305	.252	64	-5	-6	10	0			.933	2	/32S1	-0.3

■ **TACKS LATIMER** Latimer, Clifford Wesley b: 11/30/1877, Loveland, Ohio d: 4/24/36, Loveland, Ohio BR/TR, 6', 160 lbs. Deb: 10/01/1898

YEAR	TM/L	G	AB	R	H	2B	3B	HR	RBI	BB	SO	AVG	OBP	SLG	PRO+	BR	/A	RC	SB	CS	SBR	FA	FR	POS	TPR
1898	NY-N	5	17	1	5	1	0	0	1	0		.294	.294	.353	88	-0	-0	2	0			.889	-1	/CO	-0.1
1899	Lou-N	9	29	3	8	1	0	0	4	2		.276	.323	.310	74	-1	-1	3	1			.980	2	/C1	0.2
1900	Pit-N	4	12	1	4	1	0	0	2	0		.333	.333	.417	106	0	0	2	0			.947	-0	/C	0.0
1901	Bal-A	1	4	0	1	0	0	0	0	0		.250	.250	.250	37	-0	-0	0	0			1.000	-0	/C	-0.1
1902	Bro-N	8	24	0	1	0	0	0	0	0		.042	.042	.042	-74	-5	-5	0	0			.947	-0	/C	-0.5
Total	5	27	86	5	19	3	0	0	7	2		.221	.239	.256	41	-7	-7	7	1			.949	1	/CO1	-0.5

■ **CHARLIE LAU** Lau, Charles Richard b: 4/12/33, Romulus, Mich. d: 3/18/84, Key Colony Beach, Fla. BL/TR, 6', 190 lbs. Deb: 9/12/56 C

YEAR	TM/L	G	AB	R	H	2B	3B	HR	RBI	BB	SO	AVG	OBP	SLG	PRO+	BR	/A	RC	SB	CS	SBR	FA	FR	POS	TPR
1956	Det-A	3	9	1	2	0	0	0	0	0	1	.222	.222	.222	18	-1	-1	0	0	0	0	1.000	1	/C	0.0
1958	Det-A	30	68	8	10	1	2	0	6	12	15	.147	.293	.221	41	-5	-6	5	0	0	0	.985	1	C	-0.4
1959	Det-A	2	6	0	1	0	0	0	0	0	2	.167	.167	.167	-8	-1	-1	0	0	0	0	1.000	1	/C	0.0
1960	Mil-N	21	53	4	10	2	0	0	2	6	10	.189	.271	.226	41	-4	-4	4	0	0	0	1.000	5	C	0.2
1961	Mil-N	28	82	3	17	5	0	0	5	14	11	.207	.330	.268	65	-4	-3	8	1	1	-0	.968	-3	C	-0.5
	Bal-A	17	47	3	8	0	0	1	4	1	3	.170	.188	.234	12	-6	-6	2	0	0	0	.990	5	C	-0.1
1962	Bal-A	81	197	21	58	11	2	6	37	7	11	.294	.322	.462	114	1	3	29	1	0	0	.996	-5	C	0.0
1963	Bal-A	29	48	4	9	2	0	0	6	1	5	.188	.204	.229	22	-5	-5	2	0	0	0	.964	1	/C	-0.4
	KC-A	62	187	15	55	11	0	3	26	14	17	.294	.343	.401	104	2	1	24	1	0	0	.982	-11	C	-0.8
	Yr	91	235	19	64	13	0	3	32	15	22	.272	.316	.366	89	-3	-4	25	1	0	0	.979	-9	C	-1.2
1964	KC-A	43	118	11	32	7	1	2	9	10	18	.271	.328	.398	98	0	-0	16	0	0	0	.990	-6	C	-0.5
	Bal-A	62	158	16	41	15	1	1	14	17	27	.259	.335	.386	100	0	0	20	0	0	0	.992	-3	C	-0.1
	Yr	105	276	27	73	22	2	3	23	27	45	.264	.332	.391	99	0	-0	36	0	0	0	.991	-9	C	-0.6
1965	Bal-A	68	132	15	39	5	2	2	18	17	18	.295	.376	.409	120	4	4	20	0	0	0	.989	-6	C	0.0
1966	Bal-A	18	12	1	6	2	1	0	5	4	1	.500	.625	.833	320	4	4	7	0	0	0	.000	0	H	0.4
1967	Bal-A	11	8	0	1	1	0	0	3	2	2	.125	.300	.250	65	-0	-0	1	0	0	0	.000	0	H	0.0
	Atl-N	52	45	3	9	1	0	1	5	4	9	.200	.265	.289	59	-2	-2	3	0	0	0	.000	0	H	-0.3
Total	11	527	1170	105	298	63	9	16	140	109	150	.255	.321	.365	89	-17	-17	141	3	1	0	.988	-21	C	-2.5

■ **BILLY LAUDER** Lauder, William b: 2/23/1874, New York, N.Y. d: 5/20/33, Norwalk, Conn. BR/TR, 5'10", 160 lbs. Deb: 6/25/1898 C

YEAR	TM/L	G	AB	R	H	2B	3B	HR	RBI	BB	SO	AVG	OBP	SLG	PRO+	BR	/A	RC	SB	CS	SBR	FA	FR	POS	TPR
1898	Phi-N	97	361	42	95	14	7	2	67	19		.263	.300	.357	92	-7	-5	43	6			.866	-16	3	-1.9
1899	Phi-N	151	583	74	156	17	6	3	90	34		.268	.310	.333	79	-20	-17	67	15			.893	-14	*3	-2.7
1901	Phi-A	2	8	1	1	0	0	0	0	0		.125	.125	.125	-29	-1	-1	0	0			.833	1	/3	-0.1
1902	NY-N	125	482	41	114	20	1	1	44	10		.237	.252	.288	67	-20	-20	41	19			.907	3	*3/O	-1.7
1903	NY-N	108	395	52	111	13	0	0	53	14		.281	.307	.314	75	-12	-14	47	19			.908	-7	*3	-1.8
Total	5	483	1829	210	477	64	14	6	254	77		.261	.292	.321	77	-61	-57	199	59			.894	-33	3/O	-8.2

■ TIM LAUDNER
Laudner, Timothy Jon b: 6/7/58, Mason City, Iowa BR/TR, 6'3", 212 lbs. Deb: 8/28/81

YEAR	TM/L	G	AB	R	H	2B	3B	HR	RBI	BB	SO	AVG	OBP	SLG	PRO+	BR	/A	RC	SB	CS	SBR	FA	FR	POS	TPR
1981	Min-A	14	43	4	7	2	0	2	5	3	17	.163	.234	.349	62	-2	-2	4	0	0	0	1.000	-1	C/D	-0.3
1982	Min-A	93	306	37	78	19	1	7	33	34	74	.255	.329	.392	95	-1	-2	39	0	2	-1	.976	-15	C	-1.4
1983	Min-A	62	168	20	31	9	0	6	18	15	49	.185	.251	.345	60	-9	-10	15	0	0	0	.986	6	C/D	-0.2
1984	Min-A	87	262	31	54	16	1	10	35	18	78	.206	.260	.389	73	-9	-11	26	0	0	0	.978	9	C/D	0.2
1985	Min-A	72	164	16	39	5	0	7	19	12	45	.238	.294	.396	82	-3	-5	19	0	1	-1	.969	-4	C/1	-0.7
1986	Min-A	76	193	21	47	10	0	10	29	24	56	.244	.336	.451	109	3	2	30	1	0	0	.984	-15	C	-0.8
1987	*Min-A	113	288	30	55	7	1	16	43	23	80	.191	.253	.389	65	-15	-16	29	1	0	0	.987	-8	*C/1D	-1.7
1988	Min-A★	117	375	38	94	18	1	13	54	36	89	.251	.318	.408	99	0	-1	46	0	0	0	.992	0	*C/1D	0.7
1989	Min-A	100	239	24	53	11	1	6	27	25	65	.222	.295	.351	76	-6	-8	25	1	0	0	.991	0	CD1	-0.4
Total	9	734	2038	221	458	97	5	77	263	190	553	.225	.293	.391	83	-42	-52	233	3	3	-1	.984	-27	C/D1	-4.6

■ CHUCK LAUER
Lauer, John Charles b: 1865, Pittsburgh, Pa. TR , Deb: 7/17/1884

YEAR	TM/L	G	AB	R	H	2B	3B	HR	RBI	BB	SO	AVG	OBP	SLG	PRO+	BR	/A	RC	SB	CS	SBR	FA	FR	POS	TPR
1884	Pit-a	13	44	5	5	0	0	0		0		.114	.114	.114	-24	-6	-6	1				.938	-1	O/P1	-0.5
1889	Pit-N	4	16	2	3	0	0	0	1	0	5	.188	.188	.188	6	-2	-2	1	0			.815	1	/CO	0.0
1890	Chi-N	2	8	1	2	1	0	0	2	0	0	.250	.250	.375	80	-0	-0	1	0			.833	0	/C	0.0
Total	3	19	68	8	10	1	0	0	3	0	5	.147	.147	.162	-3	-8	-8	2	0			.944	-0	/OCP1	-0.5

■ BEN LAUGHLIN
Laughlin, Benjamin Deb: 4/28/1873

YEAR	TM/L	G	AB	R	H	2B	3B	HR	RBI	BB	SO	AVG	OBP	SLG	PRO+	BR	/A	RC	SB	CS	SBR	FA	FR	POS	TPR
1873	Res-n	12	50	3	12	1	0	0	6	0	0	.240	.240	.260	51	-3	-2	3						2	-0.2

■ BILL LAUTERBORN
Lauterborn, William Bernard b: 6/9/1879, Hornell, N.Y. d: 4/19/65, Andover, N.Y. BR/TR, 5'6", 140 lbs. Deb: 9/20/04

YEAR	TM/L	G	AB	R	H	2B	3B	HR	RBI	BB	SO	AVG	OBP	SLG	PRO+	BR	/A	RC	SB	CS	SBR	FA	FR	POS	TPR
1904	Bos-N	20	69	7	19	2	0	0	2	1		.275	.286	.304	86	-2	-1	7	1			.943	-3	2	-0.4
1905	Bos-N	67	200	11	37	1	1	0	9	12		.185	.238	.200	32	-17	-16	11	1			.843	-7	32/SO	-2.3
Total	2	87	269	18	56	3	1	0	11	13		.208	.250	.227	45	-18	-17	17	2			.929	-10	/23SO	-2.7

■ COOKIE LAVAGETTO
Lavagetto, Harry Arthur b: 12/1/12, Oakland, Cal. d: 8/10/90, Orinda, Cal. BR/TR, 6', 170 lbs. Deb: 4/17/34 MC

YEAR	TM/L	G	AB	R	H	2B	3B	HR	RBI	BB	SO	AVG	OBP	SLG	PRO+	BR	/A	RC	SB	CS	SBR	FA	FR	POS	TPR
1934	Pit-N	87	304	41	67	16	3	3	46	32	39	.220	.295	.322	64	-15	-16	31	6			.961	-14	2	-2.4
1935	Pit-N	78	231	27	67	9	4	0	19	18	15	.290	.341	.364	87	-3	-4	29	1			.951	-11	23	-1.2
1936	Pit-N	60	197	21	48	15	2	2	26	15	13	.244	.300	.371	78	-6	-7	22	0			.951	-1	23/S	-0.5
1937	Bro-N	149	503	64	142	26	6	8	70	74	41	.282	.375	.406	110	11	9	79	13			.949	-7	*23	1.0
1938	Bro-N☆	137	487	68	133	34	6	6	79	68	31	.273	.364	.405	109	9	7	76	15			.929	-11	*3/2	-0.2
1939	Bro-N☆	153	587	93	176	28	5	10	87	78	30	.300	.387	.416	112	15	12	95	14			.948	-5	*3	0.9
1940	Bro-N★	118	448	56	115	21	3	4	43	70	32	.257	.361	.344	90	-0	-4	59	4			.932	-14	*3	-1.5
1941	*Bro-N★	132	441	75	122	24	7	1	78	80	21	.277	.388	.370	109	12	9	69	7			.938	-20	*3	-0.9
1946	Bro-N	88	242	36	57	9	1	3	27	38	17	.236	.339	.318	86	-3	-3	28	3			.927	-5	3	-0.8
1947	*Bro-N	41	69	6	18	1	0	3	11	12	5	.261	.370	.406	102	1	0	11	0			.961	3	3/1	0.3
Total	10	1043	3509	487	945	183	37	40	486	485	244	.269	.360	.377	98	20	5	500	63			.936	-85	32/1S	-5.3

■ MIKE LaVALLIERE
LaValliere, Michael Eugene b: 8/18/60, Charlotte, N.C. BL/TR, 5'9", 190 lbs. Deb: 9/09/84

YEAR	TM/L	G	AB	R	H	2B	3B	HR	RBI	BB	SO	AVG	OBP	SLG	PRO+	BR	/A	RC	SB	CS	SBR	FA	FR	POS	TPR
1984	Phi-N	6	7	0	0	0	0	0	0	2	2	.000	.222	.000	-32	-1	-1	0	0	0	0	1.000	2	/C	0.1
1985	StL-N	12	34	2	5	1	0	0	6	7	3	.147	.293	.176	34	-3	-3	2	0	0	0	1.000	-2	C	-0.4
1986	StL-N	110	303	18	71	10	2	3	30	36	37	.234	.318	.310	74	-10	-10	31	0	1	-1	.988	2	*C	-0.2
1987	Pit-N	121	340	33	102	19	0	1	36	43	32	.300	.380	.365	98	1	1	50	0	0	0	.992	8	*C	1.5
1988	Pit-N	120	352	24	92	18	0	2	47	50	34	.261	.356	.330	99	1	2	43	3	2	-0	.987	-0	*C	1.0
1989	Pit-N	68	190	15	60	10	0	2	23	29	24	.316	.406	.400	136	9	10	31	0	2	-1	.991	-7	C	0.5
1990	*Pit-N	96	279	27	72	15	0	3	31	44	20	.258	.363	.344	99	-0	1	36	0	3	-2	.990	2	C	0.7
1991	*Pit-N	108	336	25	97	11	2	3	41	33	27	.289	.356	.360	103	2	2	43	2	1	0	**.998**	2	*C	1.1
1992	*Pit-N	95	293	22	75	13	1	2	29	44	21	.256	.355	.328	96	-0	-0	34	0	3	-2	.994	-1	C/3	0.2
Total	9	736	2134	166	574	97	5	16	243	288	200	.269	.358	.342	97	-2	2	269	5	12	-6	.992	5	C/3	4.5

■ DOC LAVAN
Lavan, John Leonard (b: John Leonard Laven) b: 10/28/1890, Grand Rapids, Mich d: 5/29/52, Detroit, Mich. BR/TR, 5'8.5", 151 lbs. Deb: 6/22/13

YEAR	TM/L	G	AB	R	H	2B	3B	HR	RBI	BB	SO	AVG	OBP	SLG	PRO+	BR	/A	RC	SB	CS	SBR	FA	FR	POS	TPR
1913	StL-A	46	149	8	21	2	1	0	4	10	46	.141	.210	.168	11	-17	-16	6	3			.899	-5	S	-1.8
	Phi-A	5	14	1	1	0	1	0	1	0	0	.071	.071	.214	-17	-2	-2	0	0			1.000	0	/S	-0.2
	Yr	51	163	9	22	2	2	0	5	10	46	.135	.199	.172	9	-19	-18	6	3			.906	-5	S	-2.0
1914	StL-A	75	239	21	63	7	4	1	21	17	39	.264	.318	.339	101	-1	-0	24	6	12	-5	.916	-12	S	-1.3
1915	StL-A	157	514	44	112	17	7	1	48	42	83	.218	.281	.284	72	-21	-18	42	13	19	-8	.913	5	*S	-0.9
1916	StL-A	110	343	32	81	13	1	0	19	32	38	.236	.305	.280	80	-10	-8	32	7			.950	**34**	*S	3.4
1917	StL-A	118	355	19	85	8	5	0	30	19	34	.239	.284	.290	78	-11	-10	30	5			.923	12	*S/2	0.8
1918	Was-A	117	464	44	129	17	2	0	45	14	21	.278	.302	.323	90	-8	-7	47	12			.917	-10	*S/O	-1.4
1919	StL-N	100	356	25	86	12	2	1	25	11	30	.242	.264	.295	72	-14	-12	28	4			.929	9	S	0.3
1920	StL-N	142	516	52	149	21	10	1	63	19	38	.289	.318	.374	102	-2	-0	58	11	14	-5	.942	16	*S	2.4
1921	StL-N	150	560	58	145	23	11	2	82	23	30	.259	.291	.350	70	-26	-24	56	7	7	-2	.950	**19**	*S	0.6
1922	StL-N	89	264	24	60	8	1	0	27	13	10	.227	.271	.265	41	-24	-22	20	3	1	0	.937	15	S/3	0.0
1923	StL-N	50	111	10	22	6	0	1	12	9	7	.198	.264	.279	44	-9	-9	8	0	3	-2	.924	1	S/312	-0.7
1924	StL-N	4	6	0	0	0	0	0	0	0	0	.000	.000	.000	-99	-2	-2	0	0	0	0	1.000	2	/2S	0.0
Total	12	1163	3891	338	954	134	45	7	377	209	376	.245	.288	.308	75	-147	-131	351	71	56		.930	85	*S/2310	1.2

■ ART LaVIGNE
LaVigne, Arthur David b: 1/26/1885, Worcester, Mass. d: 7/18/50, Worcester, Mass. BR/TR, 5'10", 162 lbs. Deb: 4/24/14

YEAR	TM/L	G	AB	R	H	2B	3B	HR	RBI	BB	SO	AVG	OBP	SLG	PRO+	BR	/A	RC	SB	CS	SBR	FA	FR	POS	TPR
1914	Buf-F	51	90	10	14	2	0	0	4	7	25	.156	.216	.178	12	-10	-10	4	0			.967	6	C/1	-0.2

■ JOHNNY LAVIN
Lavin, John b: Bay City, Mich. 5'11", 175 lbs. Deb: 9/10/1884

YEAR	TM/L	G	AB	R	H	2B	3B	HR	RBI	BB	SO	AVG	OBP	SLG	PRO+	BR	/A	RC	SB	CS	SBR	FA	FR	POS	TPR
1884	StL-a	16	52	9	11	2	0	0		3		.212	.268	.250	70	-1	-2	4				.750	-3	O	-0.5

■ RUDY LAW
Law, Rudy Karl b: 10/7/56, Waco, Tex. BL/TL, 6'1", 165 lbs. Deb: 9/12/78

YEAR	TM/L	G	AB	R	H	2B	3B	HR	RBI	BB	SO	AVG	OBP	SLG	PRO+	BR	/A	RC	SB	CS	SBR	FA	FR	POS	TPR
1978	LA-N	11	12	2	3	0	0	0	1	1	2	.250	.308	.250	58	-1	-1	1	3	1	0	1.000	-0	/O	-0.1
1980	LA-N	128	388	55	101	5	4	1	23	23	27	.260	.307	.302	72	-15	-14	39	40	13	4	.988	-8	*O	-2.3
1982	Chi-A	121	336	55	107	15	8	3	32	23	41	.318	.362	.438	118	8	8	55	36	10	5	.973	-5	O/D	0.6
1983	*Chi-A	141	501	95	142	20	7	3	34	42	36	.283	.341	.369	92	-2	-5	74	77	12	16	**.994**	-4	*O/D	0.4
1984	Chi-A	136	487	68	122	14	7	6	37	39	42	.251	.310	.345	77	-12	-15	50	29	17	-2	.985	-2	*O	-2.3
1985	Chi-A	125	390	62	101	21	6	4	36	27	40	.259	.312	.374	84	-7	-9	49	29	6	5	.987	-5	*O/D	-1.3
1986	KC-A	87	307	42	80	26	5	1	36	29	22	.261	.328	.388	92	-2	-3	40	14	6	1	.987	-8	O/D	-1.3
Total	7	749	2421	379	656	101	37	18	199	184	210	.271	.326	.366	88	-32	-39	308	228	65	29	.986	-32	O/D	-6.3

■ VANCE LAW
Law, Vance Aaron b: 10/1/56, Boise, Idaho BR/TR, 6'2", 190 lbs. Deb: 6/01/80 F

YEAR	TM/L	G	AB	R	H	2B	3B	HR	RBI	BB	SO	AVG	OBP	SLG	PRO+	BR	/A	RC	SB	CS	SBR	FA	FR	POS	TPR
1980	Pit-N	25	74	11	17	2	2	0	3	3	7	.230	.260	.311	58	-4	-4	6	2	0	1	.964	-3	2/S3	-0.6
1981	Pit-N	30	67	1	9	0	1	0	3	2	15	.134	.159	.164	-8	-9	-10	1	1	1	-0	1.000	5	2/S3	-0.5
1982	Chi-A	114	359	40	101	20	1	5	54	26	46	.281	.332	.384	96	-2	-2	45	4	2	0	.953	-3	S32/O	0.1
1983	*Chi-A	145	408	55	99	21	5	4	42	51	56	.243	.328	.348	83	-7	-9	49	3	1	0	.966	5	*3/2SOD	-0.5
1984	Chi-A	151	481	60	121	18	2	17	59	41	75	.252	.312	.403	92	-3	-6	59	4	1	1	.955	-12	*32/OS	-1.9
1985	Mon-N	147	519	75	138	30	6	10	52	86	96	.266	.372	.405	124	14	18	82	6	5	-1	.985	-1	*213/O	2.1
1986	Mon-N	112	360	37	81	17	2	5	44	37	66	.225	.299	.325	73	-14	-13	34	3	5	-2	.993	17	213/PO	0.5
1987	Mon-N	133	436	52	119	27	1	12	56	51	62	.273	.349	.422	100	2	0	65	8	5	-1	.980	-9	*231/P	-0.6
1988	Chi-N★	151	556	73	163	29	2	11	78	55	79	.293	.360	.412	116	16	13	80	1	4	-2	.953	-12	*3/O	-0.2
1989	*Chi-N	130	408	38	96	22	3	7	42	38	73	.235	.300	.355	81	-7	-11	43	2	2	-1	.949	-18	*3/O	-3.2

YEAR	TM/L	G	AB	R	H	2B	3B	HR	RBI	BB	SO	AVG	OBP	SLG	PRO+	BR	/A	RC	SB	CS	SBR	FA	FR	POS	TPR
1991	Oak-A	74	134	11	28	7	1	0	9	18	27	.209	.303	.276	65	-7	-6	12	0	0	0	.951	-6	3/SO1P	-1.1
Total	11	1212	3802	453	972	193	26	71	442	408	602	.256	.329	.376	94	-21	-29	476	34	26	-5	.956	-37	32S/1OPD	-5.9

■ GARLAND LAWING Lawing, Garland Frederick "Knobby" "Knobby" b: 8/29/19, Gastonia, N.C. BR/TR, 6'1", 180 lbs. Deb: 5/29/46

YEAR	TM/L	G	AB	R	H	2B	3B	HR	RBI	BB	SO	AVG	OBP	SLG	PRO+	BR	/A	RC	SB	CS	SBR	FA	FR	POS	TPR
1946	Cin-N	2	3	0	0	0	0	0	0	0	2	.000	.000	.000	-99	-1	-1	0	0			.000	-1	/O	-0.1
	NY-N	8	12	2	2	0	0	0	0	0	3	.167	.167	.167	-5	-2	-2	0	0			1.000	-1	/O	-0.3
	Yr	10	15	2	2	0	0	0	0	0	5	.133	.133	.133	-24	-2	-2	0	0			1.000	-1	/O	-0.4

■ TOM LAWLESS Lawless, Thomas James b: 12/19/56, Erie, Pa. BR/TR, 5'11", 170 lbs. Deb: 7/15/82

YEAR	TM/L	G	AB	R	H	2B	3B	HR	RBI	BB	SO	AVG	OBP	SLG	PRO+	BR	/A	RC	SB	CS	SBR	FA	FR	POS	TPR
1982	Cin-N	49	165	19	35	6	0	0	4	9	30	.212	.253	.248	40	-13	-13	10	16	5	2	.978	7	2	-0.3
1984	Cin-N	43	80	10	20	2	0	1	2	8	12	.250	.318	.313	74	-2	-3	8	6	3	0	1.000	-3	2/3	-0.5
	Mon-N	11	17	1	3	1	0	0	0	0	4	.176	.176	.235	15	-2	-2	0	1	0	0	1.000	0	/2	-0.1
	Yr	54	97	11	23	3	0	1	2	8	16	.237	.295	.299	66	-4	-4	8	7	3	0	1.000	-3	2/3	-0.6
1985	*StL-N	47	58	8	12	3	1	0	8	5	4	.207	.270	.293	58	-3	-3	5	2	1	0	.971	9	32	0.6
1986	StL-N	46	39	5	11	1	0	0	3	2	8	.282	.317	.308	74	-1	-1	5	8	1	2	.875	3	3/2O	0.3
1987	*StL-N	19	25	5	2	1	0	0	0	3	5	.080	.179	.120	-19	-4	-4	1	2	0	1	1.000	-1	/23O	-0.5
1988	StL-N	54	65	9	10	2	1	1	3	7	9	.154	.236	.262	42	-5	-5	5	6	0	2	1.000	2	3/O21	-0.2
1989	Tor-A	59	70	20	16	1	0	0	3	7	12	.229	.299	.243	55	-4	-4	7	12	1	3	1.000	1	O3D/2C	0.0
1990	Tor-A	15	12	1	1	0	0	0	1	0	1	.083	.083	.083	-52	-2	-2	-0	0	2	-1	.800	2	/3O2D	-0.2
Total	8	343	531	78	110	17	2	2	24	41	85	.207	.264	.258	46	-38	-38	41	53	13	8	.988	20	2/3ODC1	-0.9

■ MIKE LAWLOR Lawlor, Michael H. b: 3/11/1854, Troy, N.Y. d: 8/3/18, Troy, N.Y. TR , 6', 180 lbs. Deb: 5/27/1880

YEAR	TM/L	G	AB	R	H	2B	3B	HR	RBI	BB	SO	AVG	OBP	SLG	PRO+	BR	/A	RC	SB	CS	SBR	FA	FR	POS	TPR
1880	Tro-N	4	9	1	1	0	0	0	0	1	1	.111	.200	.111	8	-1	-1	0				.867	1	/C	0.0
1884	Was-U	2	7	0	0	0	0	0		0		.000	.000	.000	-99	-1	-1	0				1.000	1	/C	0.0
Total	2	6	16	1	1	0	0	0	0	1	1	.063	.118	.063	-37	-2	-2	0				.920	2	/C	0.0

■ JIM LAWRENCE Lawrence, James Ross b: 2/12/39, Hamilton, Ont., Can. BL/TR, 6'1", 185 lbs. Deb: 5/30/63

YEAR	TM/L	G	AB	R	H	2B	3B	HR	RBI	BB	SO	AVG	OBP	SLG	PRO+	BR	/A	RC	SB	CS	SBR	FA	FR	POS	TPR
1963	Cle-A	2	0	0	0	0	0	0	0	0	0	—	—	—	—	0	0	0	0	0	0	.750	0	/C	0.0

■ BILL LAWRENCE Lawrence, William Henry b: 3/11/06, San Mateo, Cal. BR/TR, 6'4", 194 lbs. Deb: 4/13/32

YEAR	TM/L	G	AB	R	H	2B	3B	HR	RBI	BB	SO	AVG	OBP	SLG	PRO+	BR	/A	RC	SB	CS	SBR	FA	FR	POS	TPR
1932	Det-A	25	46	10	10	1	0	0	3	5	5	.217	.294	.239	38	-4	-4	3	0	2	-1	1.000	2	O	-0.4

■ OTIS LAWRY Lawry, Otis Carroll "Rabbit" b: 11/1/1893, Fairfield, Me. d: 10/23/65, China, Maine BL/TR, 5'8", 133 lbs. Deb: 6/28/16

YEAR	TM/L	G	AB	R	H	2B	3B	HR	RBI	BB	SO	AVG	OBP	SLG	PRO+	BR	/A	RC	SB	CS	SBR	FA	FR	POS	TPR
1916	Phi-A	41	123	10	25	0	0	0	4	9	21	.203	.263	.203	42	-9	-8	8	4			.905	-10	2/O	-2.0
1917	Phi-A	30	55	7	9	1	0	0	1	2	9	.164	.193	.182	15	-6	-6	2	1			.921	-3	2/O	-0.9
Total	2	71	178	17	34	1	0	0	5	11	30	.191	.242	.197	34	-14	-14	10	5			.911	-13	/2O	-2.9

■ MARCUS LAWTON Lawton, Marcus Dwayne b: 8/18/65, Gulfport, Miss. BB/TR, 6'1", 160 lbs. Deb: 8/11/89

YEAR	TM/L	G	AB	R	H	2B	3B	HR	RBI	BB	SO	AVG	OBP	SLG	PRO+	BR	/A	RC	SB	CS	SBR	FA	FR	POS	TPR
1989	NY-A	10	14	1	3	0	0	0	0	0	3	.214	.214	.214	21	-1	-1	1	1	0	0	.818	-2	/OD	-0.3

■ GENE LAYDEN Layden, Eugene Francis b: 3/14/1894, Pittsburgh, Pa. d: 12/12/84, Pittsburgh, Pa. BL/TL, 5'10", 160 lbs. Deb: 7/29/15

YEAR	TM/L	G	AB	R	H	2B	3B	HR	RBI	BB	SO	AVG	OBP	SLG	PRO+	BR	/A	RC	SB	CS	SBR	FA	FR	POS	TPR
1915	NY-A	3	7	2	2	0	0	0	0	0	1	.286	.286	.286	71	-0	-0	0	0	1	-1	.750	-1	/O	-0.2

■ PETE LAYDON Laydon, Peter John b: 12/30/19, Dallas, Tex. d: 7/18/82, Edna, Tex. BR/TR, 5'11", 185 lbs. Deb: 4/28/48

YEAR	TM/L	G	AB	R	H	2B	3B	HR	RBI	BB	SO	AVG	OBP	SLG	PRO+	BR	/A	RC	SB	CS	SBR	FA	FR	POS	TPR
1948	StL-A	41	104	11	26	2	1	0	4	6	10	.250	.297	.288	55	-7	-7	9	4	2	0	.973	-1	O	-0.9

■ HERMAN LAYNE Layne, Herman b: 2/13/01, New Haven, W.Va. d: 8/27/73, Gallipolis, Ohio BR/TR, 5'11", 165 lbs. Deb: 4/16/27

YEAR	TM/L	G	AB	R	H	2B	3B	HR	RBI	BB	SO	AVG	OBP	SLG	PRO+	BR	/A	RC	SB	CS	SBR	FA	FR	POS	TPR
1927	Pit-N	11	6	3	0	0	0	0	0	1	0	.000	.143	.000	-55	-1	-1	0	0			.000	-1	/O	-0.3

■ HILLIS LAYNE Layne, Ivoria Hillis "Tony" b: 2/23/18, Whitwell, Tenn. BL/TR, 6', 170 lbs. Deb: 9/16/41

YEAR	TM/L	G	AB	R	H	2B	3B	HR	RBI	BB	SO	AVG	OBP	SLG	PRO+	BR	/A	RC	SB	CS	SBR	FA	FR	POS	TPR
1941	Was-A	13	50	8	14	2	0	0	6	4	5	.280	.333	.320	77	-2	-2	5	1	1	-0	.953	0	3	-0.1
1944	Was-A	33	87	6	17	2	0	0	8	6	10	.195	.263	.218	40	-7	-6	6	2	0	1	.949	1	3/2	-0.4
1945	Was-A	61	147	23	44	5	4	1	14	10	7	.299	.352	.408	132	3	5	20	0	1	-1	.956	-5	3	0.0
Total	3	107	284	37	75	9	4	1	28	20	22	.264	.321	.335	92	-5	-3	30	3	2	-0	.953	-3	/32	-0.5

■ LES LAYTON Layton, Lester Lee b: 11/18/21, Nardin, Okla. BR/TR, 6', 165 lbs. Deb: 4/24/48

YEAR	TM/L	G	AB	R	H	2B	3B	HR	RBI	BB	SO	AVG	OBP	SLG	PRO+	BR	/A	RC	SB	CS	SBR	FA	FR	POS	TPR
1948	NY-N	63	91	14	21	4	4	2	12	6	21	.231	.286	.429	90	-2	-2	11	1			.951	-1	O	-0.3

■ JOHNNY LAZOR Lazor, John Paul b: 9/9/12, Taylor, Wash. BL/TR, 5'9.5", 180 lbs. Deb: 4/22/43

YEAR	TM/L	G	AB	R	H	2B	3B	HR	RBI	BB	SO	AVG	OBP	SLG	PRO+	BR	/A	RC	SB	CS	SBR	FA	FR	POS	TPR
1943	Bos-A	83	208	21	47	10	2	0	13	21	25	.226	.297	.293	72	-7	-7	18	5	6	-2	.979	-3	O	-1.6
1944	Bos-A	16	24	0	2	1	0	0	0	1	0	.083	.120	.125	-30	-4	-4	0	0	0	0	1.000	0	/OC	-0.4
1945	Bos-A	101	335	35	104	19	2	5	45	18	17	.310	.346	.424	120	8	7	50	3	2	-0	.961	-8	O	-0.6
1946	Bos-A	23	29	1	4	0	0	1	4	2	11	.138	.194	.241	20	-3	-3	1	0	0	0	1.000	-2	/O	-0.6
Total	4	223	596	57	157	30	4	6	62	42	53	.263	.312	.357	92	-6	-8	70	8	8	-2	.971	-13	O/C	-3.2

■ TONY LAZZERI Lazzeri, Anthony Michael "Poosh 'Em Up Tony"
b: 12/6/03, San Francisco, Cal. d: 8/6/46, San Francisco, Cal. BR/TR, 5'11.5", 170 lbs. Deb: 4/13/26 CH

YEAR	TM/L	G	AB	R	H	2B	3B	HR	RBI	BB	SO	AVG	OBP	SLG	PRO+	BR	/A	RC	SB	CS	SBR	FA	FR	POS	TPR
1926	*NY-A	155	589	79	162	28	14	18	114	54	96	.275	.338	.462	109	3	4	93	16	7	1	.961	-20	*2/S3	-1.0
1927	*NY-A	153	570	92	176	29	8	18	102	69	82	.309	.383	.482	127	19	22	98	22	14	-2	.971	5	*2S/3	3.0
1928	*NY-A	116	404	62	134	30	11	10	82	43	50	.332	.397	.535	148	24	26	87	15	5	2	.956	-11	*2	1.9
1929	NY-A	147	545	101	193	37	11	18	106	68	45	.354	.429	.561	164	44	49	130	9	10	-3	.969	-4	*2	4.5
1930	NY-A	143	571	109	173	34	15	9	121	60	62	.303	.372	.462	115	9	13	100	4	4	-1	.971	6	23/S1O	2.3
1931	NY-A	135	484	67	129	27	7	8	83	79	80	.267	.371	.401	109	4	8	76	18	9	0	.958	-3	23	1.1
1932	*NY-A	142	510	79	153	28	16	15	113	82	64	.300	.399	.506	140	26	30	104	11	11	-3	.978	6	*2/3	3.6
1933	NY-A☆	139	523	94	154	22	12	18	104	73	62	.294	.383	.486	137	22	26	100	15	7	0	.968	-14	*2	2.0
1934	NY-A	123	438	59	117	24	6	14	67	71	64	.267	.369	.445	117	6	11	77	11	1	3	.976	-13	23	0.7
1935	NY-A	130	477	72	130	18	6	13	83	63	75	.273	.361	.417	107	1	5	75	11	5	0	.970	-21	*2/S	-0.6
1936	*NY-A	150	537	82	154	29	6	14	109	97	65	.287	.397	.441	110	8	11	100	8	5	-1	.968	-32	*2/S	-0.9
1937	*NY-A	126	446	56	109	21	3	14	70	71	76	.244	.348	.399	87	-8	-9	67	7	1	2	.966	-8	*2	-0.6
1938	*Chi-N	54	120	21	32	5	0	5	23	22	30	.267	.380	.433	120	4	4	20	0			.946	-8	S/32O	-0.2
1939	Bro-N	14	39	6	11	2	0	3	6	10	7	.282	.451	.564	165	5	4	11	1			.914	0	2/3	0.5
	NY-N	13	44	7	13	0	0	1	8	7	6	.295	.392	.364	103	1	1	6	0			.889	-2	3	-0.2
	Yr	27	83	13	24	2	0	4	14	17	13	.289	.422	.458	133	5	5	17	1			.897	-2	32	0.3
Total	14	1740	6297	986	1840	334	115	178	1191	869	864	.292	.380	.467	122	166	205	1146	148	79		.967	-119	*23/SO1	16.1

■ FREDDY LEACH Leach, Frederick b: 11/23/1897, Springfield, Mo. d: 12/10/81, Hagerman, Idaho BL/TR, 5'11", 183 lbs. Deb: 5/24/23

YEAR	TM/L	G	AB	R	H	2B	3B	HR	RBI	BB	SO	AVG	OBP	SLG	PRO+	BR	/A	RC	SB	CS	SBR	FA	FR	POS	TPR
1923	Phi-N	52	104	5	27	4	0	1	16	3	14	.260	.280	.327	54	-6	-8	9	1	2	-1	.950	-6	O	-1.6
1924	Phi-N	8	28	6	13	2	1	2	7	2	1	.464	.500	.821	221	6	5	11	0	0	0	1.000	-1	/O	0.4
1925	Phi-N	65	292	47	91	15	4	5	28	5	21	.312	.323	.442	86	-4	-7	40	1	2	-1	.952	-2	O	-1.4
1926	Phi-N	129	492	73	162	29	7	11	71	16	33	.329	.352	.484	117	13	10	79	6			.979	1	*O	0.3
1927	Phi-N	140	536	69	164	30	4	12	83	21	32	.306	.342	.444	108	5	4	78	2			.981	14	*O	0.9
1928	Phi-N	145	588	83	179	36	11	13	96	30	30	.304	.342	.469	107	6	4	91	4			.978	11	*O1	0.4
1929	NY-N	113	411	74	119	22	6	8	47	17	14	.290	.324	.431	85	-11	-11	55	10			.974	-12	O	-2.7
1930	NY-N	126	544	90	178	19	13	13	71	22	25	.327	.361	.482	104	0	2	91	3			.978	-3	*O	-0.8
1931	NY-N	129	515	75	159	30	5	6	61	29	9	.309	.348	.421	109	4	5	76	4			.976	-4	*O	-0.7
1932	Bos-N	84	223	21	55	9	2	1	29	18	10	.247	.306	.318	71	-10	-9	23	1			.977	-2	O	-1.4

YEAR	TM/L	G	AB	R	H	2B	3B	HR	RBI	BB	SO	AVG	OBP	SLG	PRO+	BR	/A	RC	SB	CS	SBR	FA	FR	POS	TPR
Total	10	991	3733	543	1147	196	53	72	509	163	189	.307	.341	.446	101	4	-3	553	32	4		.975	-5	O/1	-6.6

■ RICK LEACH Leach, Richard Max b: 5/4/57, Ann Arbor, Mich. BL/TL, 6', 195 lbs. Deb: 4/30/81

YEAR	TM/L	G	AB	R	H	2B	3B	HR	RBI	BB	SO	AVG	OBP	SLG	PRO+	BR	/A	RC	SB	CS	SBR	FA	FR	POS	TPR
1981	Det-A	54	83	9	16	3	1	1	11	16	15	.193	.323	.289	75	-2	-2	7	0	1	-1	1.000	-1	1O/D	-0.6
1982	Det-A	82	218	23	52	7	2	3	12	21	29	.239	.305	.330	74	-7	-8	24	4	0	1	.995	-1	1O/D	-1.0
1983	Det-A	99	242	22	60	17	0	3	26	19	21	.248	.305	.355	83	-6	-5	25	2	2	-1	.994	3	1O/D	-0.6
1984	Tor-A	65	88	11	23	6	2	0	7	8	14	.261	.323	.375	89	-1	-1	10	0	0	0	1.000	-1	O1/PD	-0.3
1985	Tor-A	16	35	2	7	0	1	0	1	3	9	.200	.263	.257	42	-3	-3	3	0	0	0	.987	-0	1/O	-0.4
1986	Tor-A	110	246	35	76	14	1	5	39	13	24	.309	.344	.435	108	3	2	35	0	0	0	.978	-8	DO/1	-0.7
1987	Tor-A	98	195	26	55	13	1	3	25	25	25	.282	.372	.405	104	2	2	30	0	1	-1	.981	-6	OD/1	-0.6
1988	Tor-A	87	199	21	55	13	1	0	23	18	27	.276	.336	.352	93	-2	-2	22	0	1	-1	1.000	-4	OD/1	-0.8
1989	Tex-A	110	239	32	65	14	1	1	23	32	33	.272	.360	.351	100	1	1	31	2	1	0	.951	-4	DO/1	-0.4
1990	SF-N	78	174	24	51	13	0	2	16	21	20	.293	.372	.402	117	4	4	27	0	2	-1	.989	-3	O/1	-0.1
Total	10	799	1719	205	460	100	10	18	183	176	217	.268	.338	.369	94	-10	-11	214	8	8	-2	.983	-26	O1D/P	-5.5

■ TOMMY LEACH Leach, Thomas William b: 11/4/1877, French Creek, N.Y. d: 9/29/69, Haines City, Fla. BR/TR, 5'6.5", 150 lbs. Deb: 9/28/1898

YEAR	TM/L	G	AB	R	H	2B	3B	HR	RBI	BB	SO	AVG	OBP	SLG	PRO+	BR	/A	RC	SB	CS	SBR	FA	FR	POS	TPR
1898	Lou-N	3	10	0	1	0	0	0	0	0		.100	.100	.100	-43	-2	-2	0	0			.727	-0	/32	-0.2
1899	Lou-N	106	406	75	117	10	6	5	57	37		.288	.349	.379	100	-0	-0	63	19			.908	1	3S/2	0.3
1900	*Pit-N	51	160	20	34	1	2	1	16	21		.213	.304	.262	57	-9	-9	16	8			.864	1	3/S2O	-0.7
1901	Pit-N	98	374	64	114	12	13	2	44	20		.305	.347	.422	119	10	8	63	16			.903	9	3/S	1.8
1902	Pit-N	135	514	97	143	14	**22**	**6**	85	45		.278	.341	.426	132	20	18	87	25			.926	13	*3	3.3
1903	*Pit-N	127	507	97	151	16	17	7	87	40		.298	.352	.438	121	15	12	89	22			.879	7	*3	2.0
1904	Pit-N	146	579	92	149	15	12	2	56	45		.257	.315	.335	99	1	-1	71	23			.907	**36**	*3	4.1
1905	Pit-N	131	499	71	128	10	14	2	53	37		.257	.309	.345	93	-4	-5	62	17			.988	11	O3/2S	0.5
1906	Pit-N	133	476	66	136	10	7	1	39	33		.286	.333	.342	106	5	3	65	21			.929	2	3O/S	0.5
1907	Pit-N	149	547	102	166	19	12	4	43	40		.303	.352	.404	135	22	21	98	43			.980	11	*O3/S2	3.2
1908	Pit-N	152	583	93	151	24	16	5	41	54		.259	.324	.381	125	15	15	80	24			.937	-4	*3/O	1.9
1909	*Pit-N	151	587	**126**	153	29	8	6	43	66		.261	.337	.368	110	13	7	83	27			.969	3	*O3	0.5
1910	Pit-N	135	529	83	143	24	5	4	52	38	62	.270	.319	.357	92	-4	-7	66	18			.966	9	*O/S2	-0.5
1911	Pit-N	108	386	60	92	12	6	3	43	46	50	.238	.323	.324	78	-10	-12	46	19			.987	2	OS/3	-1.4
1912	Pit-N	28	97	24	29	4	2	0	19	12	9	.299	.376	.381	109	1	1	16	6			.986	4	O	0.4
	Chi-N	82	265	50	64	10	3	2	32	55	20	.242	.378	.325	93	0	0	38	14			.975	5	O/3	0.2
	Yr	110	362	74	93	14	5	2	51	67	29	.257	.377	.340	97	1	2	54	20			.978	9	O/3	0.6
1913	Chi-N	131	456	**99**	131	23	10	6	32	77	44	.287	.391	.421	132	21	21	80	21			**.990**	3	*O/3	1.9
1914	Chi-N	153	577	80	152	24	9	7	46	79	50	.263	.353	.373	116	13	13	80	16			.968	9	*O3	1.8
1915	Cin-N	107	335	42	75	7	5	0	17	56	38	.224	.338	.275	85	-3	-4	34	20	14	-2	.959	-4	O	-1.6
1918	Pit-N	30	72	14	14	2	3	0	5	19	5	.194	.363	.306	101	1	1	9	2			.952	-2	O/S	-0.2
Total	19	2156	7959	1355	2143	266	172	63	810	820	278	.269	.340	.370	108	107	82	1144	361	14		.975	113	*O3/S2	17.8

■ DAN LEAHY Leahy, Daniel C. b: 8/8/1870, Knoxville, Tenn. d: 12/30/03, Knoxville, Tenn. Deb: 9/02/1896

YEAR	TM/L	G	AB	R	H	2B	3B	HR	RBI	BB	SO	AVG	OBP	SLG	PRO+	BR	/A	RC	SB	CS	SBR	FA	FR	POS	TPR
1896	Phi-N	2	6	0	2	1	0	0	1	1	2	.333	.429	.500	148	0	0	1	0			.857	1	/S	0.1

■ TOM LEAHY Leahy, Thomas Joseph b: 6/2/1869, New Haven, Conn. d: 6/11/51, New Haven, Conn. TR, 168 lbs. Deb: 5/18/1897

YEAR	TM/L	G	AB	R	H	2B	3B	HR	RBI	BB	SO	AVG	OBP	SLG	PRO+	BR	/A	RC	SB	CS	SBR	FA	FR	POS	TPR
1897	Pit-N	24	92	10	24	3	3	0	12	7		.261	.320	.359	82	-3	-2	12	3			.935	-3	O/C3	-0.5
	Was-N	19	52	12	20	2	1	0	7	9		.385	.529	.462	164	6	6	16	6			.727	-4	O/32C	0.2
	Yr	43	144	22	44	5	4	0	19	16		.306	.405	.396	114	3	4	28	9			.881	-7	O3/C2	-0.3
1898	Was-N	15	55	10	10	2	0	0	5	8		.182	.297	.218	48	-3	-3	5	6			.913	-0	3/2	-0.3
1901	Mil-A	33	99	18	24	6	2	0	10	11		.242	.348	.343	97	-1	0	13	3			.941	-4	C/O2	-0.1
	Phi-A	5	15	1	5	1	0	0	1	1		.333	.375	.400	110	0	0	2	0			1.000	-1	/OCS	0.0
	Yr	38	114	19	29	7	2	0	11	12		.254	.351	.351	99	-0	0	16	3			.944	-5	C/O2S	-0.1
1905	StL-N	35	97	3	22	1	3	0	7	8		.227	.286	.299	77	-3	-3	9	0			.946	-9	C	-0.9
Total	4	131	410	54	105	15	9	0	42	44		.256	.348	.337	93	-3	-2	58	18			.942	-20	/CO32S	-1.6

■ FRED LEAR Lear, Frederick Francis "King" b: 4/7/1894, New York, N.Y. d: 10/13/55, E.Orange, N.J. BR/TR, 6'0.5", 180 lbs. Deb: 6/07/15

YEAR	TM/L	G	AB	R	H	2B	3B	HR	RBI	BB	SO	AVG	OBP	SLG	PRO+	BR	/A	RC	SB	CS	SBR	FA	FR	POS	TPR
1915	Phi-A	2	2	0	0	0	0	0	0	0	2	.000	.000	.000	-99	-0	-0	0	0			.600	-0	/3	-0.1
1918	Chi-N	2	1	0	0	0	0	0	0	1	0	.000	.500	.000	56	0	0	0	0			.000	0	H	0.0
1919	Chi-N	40	76	8	17	3	1	1	11	8	11	.224	.306	.329	90	-1	-1	8	2			.990	-2	/12S	-0.3
1920	NY-N	31	87	12	22	0	1	1	7	8	15	.253	.323	.310	83	-2	-2	9	0	2	-1	.951	-3	3/2	-0.5
Total	4	75	166	20	39	3	2	2	18	17	28	.235	.314	.313	85	-3	-3	17	2	2		.924	-5	/321S	-0.9

■ BILL LEARD Leard, William Wallace "Wild Bill" b: 10/14/1885, Oneida, N.Y. d: 1/15/70, San Francisco, Cal BR/TR, 5'10", 155 lbs. Deb: 7/21/17

YEAR	TM/L	G	AB	R	H	2B	3B	HR	RBI	BB	SO	AVG	OBP	SLG	PRO+	BR	/A	RC	SB	CS	SBR	FA	FR	POS	TPR
1917	Bro-N	3	3	0	0	0	0	0	0	0	1	.000	.000	.000	-97	-1	-1	0	0			.000	0	/2	-0.1

■ JACK LEARY Leary, John J. b: 1858, New Haven, Conn. TL, 5'11", 186 lbs. Deb: 8/21/1880

YEAR	TM/L	G	AB	R	H	2B	3B	HR	RBI	BB	SO	AVG	OBP	SLG	PRO+	BR	/A	RC	SB	CS	SBR	FA	FR	POS	TPR
1880	Bos-N	1	3	1	0	0	0	0	0	1	0	.000	.250	.000	-7	-0	-0	0				1.000	1	/OP	0.0
1881	Det-N	3	11	2	3	1	1	0	4	1	1	.273	.333	.545	165	1	1	2				.833	0	/OP	0.1
1882	Pit-a	60	257	32	75	7	3	1		5		.292	.305	.354	128	5	7	28				.759	-14	3O/P12	-0.6
	Bal-a	4	18	3	4	1	0	0		0		.222	.222	.278	73	-1	-0	1				.900	-0	/PO	0.0
	Yr	64	275	35	79	8	3	1		5		.287	.300	.349	124	5	7	30				.759	-14	3O/P12	-0.6
1883	Lou-a	40	165	16	31	1	3	3		2		.188	.198	.285	58	-8	-7	10				.816	-1	S	-0.6
	Bal-a	3	11	1	2	0	2	0		0		.182	.182	.545	122	0	0	1				.727	-1	/2	-0.1
	Yr	43	176	17	33	1	5	3		2		.188	.197	.301	62	-8	-6	11				.816	-2	S/2	-0.7
1884	Alt-U	8	33	1	3	0	0	0		1		.091	.118	.091	-28	-4	-4	0				.692	-2	/OP3	-0.4
	CP-U	10	40	0	7	1	0	0		0		.175	.175	.200	27	-3	-3	1				.840	1	/23OP	-0.2
	Yr	18	73	1	10	1	0	0		1		.137	.149	.151	1	-7	-7	2				.625	-1	/OP32	-0.6
Total	5	129	538	56	125	11	9	4	4	10	1	.232	.246	.309	87	-10	-6	44				.725	-17	/SO3P21	-1.8

■ JOHN LEARY Leary, John Louis "Jack" b: 5/2/1891, Waltham, Mass. d: 8/18/61, Waltham, Mass. BR/TR, 5'11.5", 180 lbs. Deb: 4/14/14

YEAR	TM/L	G	AB	R	H	2B	3B	HR	RBI	BB	SO	AVG	OBP	SLG	PRO+	BR	/A	RC	SB	CS	SBR	FA	FR	POS	TPR
1914	StL-A	144	533	35	141	28	7	0	45	10	71	.265	.282	.343	91	-11	-9	49	9	15	-6	.987	-4	*1C	-2.3
1915	StL-A	75	227	19	55	10	0	0	15	5	36	.242	.268	.286	68	-10	-9	17	2	4	-2	.985	-2	1C	-1.5
Total	2	219	760	54	196	38	7	0	60	15	107	.258	.278	.326	85	-21	-18	66	11	19	-8	.987	-7	1/C	-3.8

■ HAL LEATHERS Leathers, Harold Langford "Chuck" b: 12/2/1898, Selma, Cal. d: 4/12/77, Modesto, Cal. BL/TR, 5'8", 152 lbs. Deb: 9/13/20

YEAR	TM/L	G	AB	R	H	2B	3B	HR	RBI	BB	SO	AVG	OBP	SLG	PRO+	BR	/A	RC	SB	CS	SBR	FA	FR	POS	TPR
1920	Chi-N	9	23	3	7	1	0	1	1	1	1	.304	.333	.478	129	1	1	4	1	0	0	.825	-1	/S2	0.1

■ EMIL LEBER Leber, Emil Bohmiel b: 5/15/1881, Cleveland, Ohio d: 11/6/24, Cleveland, Ohio BR/TR, 5'11", 170 lbs. Deb: 9/02/05

YEAR	TM/L	G	AB	R	H	2B	3B	HR	RBI	BB	SO	AVG	OBP	SLG	PRO+	BR	/A	RC	SB	CS	SBR	FA	FR	POS	TPR
1905	Cle-A	2	6	1	0	0	0	0	0	1		.000	.143	.000	-53	-1	-1	0	0			1.000	-0	/3	-0.1

■ BEVO LeBOURVEAU LeBourveau, De Witt Wiley b: 8/24/1894, Dana, Cal. d: 12/9/47, Nevada City, Cal. BL/TR, 5'11", 175 lbs. Deb: 9/09/19

YEAR	TM/L	G	AB	R	H	2B	3B	HR	RBI	BB	SO	AVG	OBP	SLG	PRO+	BR	/A	RC	SB	CS	SBR	FA	FR	POS	TPR
1919	Phi-N	17	63	4	17	0	0	0	0	10	8	.270	.370	.270	88	0	-0	7	2			1.000	2	O	0.1
1920	Phi-N	84	261	29	67	7	2	3	12	11	36	.257	.295	.333	76	-7	-8	26	9	6	-1	.949	3	O	-1.2
1921	Phi-N	93	281	42	83	12	5	6	35	29	51	.295	.361	.438	102	4	1	44	4	5	-2	.911	-8	O	-1.4
1922	Phi-N	74	167	24	45	8	3	2	20	24	29	.269	.368	.389	87	-1	-3	24	0	3	-2	.920	-3	O	-1.0
1929	Phi-A	12	16	1	5	0	1	0	2	5	1	.313	.476	.438	132	1	1	3	0	1	-1	1.000	0	/O	0.0
Total	5	280	788	100	217	27	11	11	69	79	125	.275	.345	.379	91	-2	-9	104	15	15		.935	-7	O	-3.5

YEAR	TM/L	G	AB	R	H	2B	3B	HR	RBI	BB	SO	AVG	OBP	SLG	PRO+	BR	/A	RC	SB	CS	SBR	FA	FR	POS	TPR

■ MIKE LEDWITH   Ledwith, Michael   b: Brooklyn, N.Y.   d: 1/2/29, Bronx, N.Y.   Deb: 8/19/1874

| 1874 | Atl-n | 1 | 4 | 1 | 1 | 0 | 0 | 0 | | 0 | | .250 | .250 | .250 | 68 | -0 | -0 | 0 | | | | | | /C | 0.0 |

■ CLIFF LEE   Lee, Clifford Walker   b: 8/4/1896, Lexington, Neb.   d: 8/25/80, Denver, Colo.   BR/TR, 6'1", 175 lbs.   Deb: 5/15/19

1919	Pit-N	42	112	5	22	2	4	0	2	6	8	.196	.237	.286	55	-6	-7	8	2			.962	-11	C/O	-1.8
1920	Pit-N	37	76	9	18	2	2	0	8	4	14	.237	.275	.316	67	-3	-3	6	0	1	-1	.974	0	C/O	-0.3
1921	Phi-N	88	286	31	88	14	4	4	29	13	34	.308	.338	.427	94	-0	-3	41	5	2	0	.987	-7	1O/C	0.0
1922	Phi-N	122	422	65	136	29	6	17	77	32	43	.322	.371	.540	121	18	13	83	2	3	-1	.967	-5	O1/3	0.0
1923	Phi-N	107	355	54	114	20	4	11	47	20	39	.321	.357	.493	110	10	4	61	3	3	-1	.959	-11	O1	-1.2
1924	Phi-N	21	56	4	14	3	2	1	7	2	5	.250	.276	.429	77	-1	-2	6	0	1	-1	1.000	-1	O/1	-0.4
	Cin-N	6	6	1	2	1	0	0	2	0	2	.333	.333	.500	122	0	0	1	0	0		.000	-0	/O	0.0
	Yr	27	62	5	16	4	2	1	9	2	7	.258	.281	.435	82	-1	-2	7	0	1	-1	1.000	-1	O/1	-0.4
1925	Cle-A	77	230	43	74	15	6	4	42	21	33	.322	.378	.491	118	6	6	43	2	1	0	.951	-3	O	-0.1
1926	Cle-A	21	40	4	7	1	0	1	2	6	8	.175	.283	.275	45	-3	-3	3	0	0	0	1.000	0	/OC	-0.4
Total	8	521	1583	216	475	87	28	38	216	104	186	.300	.344	.462	103	20	5	252	14	11		.960	-36	O/1C3	-5.4

■ DUD LEE   Lee, Ernest Dudley (a.k.a. Ernest Dudley In 1920-21)   b: 8/22/1899, Denver, Colo.   d: 1/7/71, Denver, Colo.   BL/TR, 5'9", 150 lbs.   Deb: 10/03/20

1920	StL-A	1	2	2	2	0	0	0	0	0	0	1.000	1.000	1.000	418	1	1	2	1	0	0	.333	-1	/S	0.0
1921	StL-A	72	180	18	30	4	2	0	11	14	34	.167	.235	.211	14	-24	-25	10	1	1	-0	.922	5	S2/3	-1.6
1924	Bos-A	94	288	36	73	9	4	0	29	40	17	.253	.350	.313	72	-11	-11	35	8	4	0	.937	-8	S	-0.9
1925	Bos-A	84	255	22	57	7	3	0	19	34	19	.224	.315	.275	51	-19	-19	24	2	3	-1	.924	17	S	0.4
1926	Bos-A	2	7	2	1	0	0	0	0	0	0	.143	.250	.143	4	-1	-1	0	0	0	0	1.000	-1	/S	-0.2
Total	5	253	732	80	163	20	9	0	60	88	70	.223	.311	.275	50	-53	-55	71	12	8	-1	.928	12	S/23	-2.3

■ HAL LEE   Lee, Harold Burnham "Sheriff"   b: 2/15/05, Ludlow, Miss.   d: 9/4/89, Pascagoula, Miss.   BR/TR, 5'11", 180 lbs.   Deb: 4/19/30

1930	Bro-N	22	37	5	6	0	0	1	4	4	5	.162	.244	.243	19	-5	-5	2	0			1.000	-1	O	-0.6
1931	Phi-N	44	131	13	29	10	0	2	12	10	18	.221	.282	.344	62	-6	-8	13	0			.967	-1	O	-1.1
1932	Phi-N	149	595	76	180	42	10	18	85	36	45	.303	.343	.497	110	17	8	102	6			.965	11	*O	1.0
1933	Phi-N	46	167	25	48	12	2	0	12	18	13	.287	.360	.383	100	3	1	24	1			.981	1	O	-0.1
	Bos-N	88	312	32	69	15	9	1	28	18	26	.221	.266	.337	77	-92MZ		29	1			.977	2	O	-1.2
	Yr	134	479	57	117	27	11	1	40	36	39	.244	.300	.353	87	-9	-9	53	2			.978	3	*O	-1.3
1934	Bos-N	139	521	70	152	23	6	8	79	47	43	.292	.353	.405	111	2	7	76	3			.985	5	*O/2	0.7
1935	Bos-N	112	422	49	128	18	6	0	39	18	25	.303	.333	.374	98	-6	-2	51	0			.962	-6	*O	0.0
1936	Bos-N	152	565	46	143	24	7	3	64	52	50	.253	.318	.336	82	-18	-13	59	4			.973	-6	*O	-2.5
Total	7	752	2750	316	755	144	40	33	323	203	225	.275	.326	.392	95	-25	-21	357	15			.973	16	O/2	-3.8

■ LEONIDAS LEE   Lee, Leonidas Pyrrhus (b: Leonidas Pyrrhus Funkhouser)   b: 12/13/1860, St.Louis, Mo.   d: 6/11/12, Hendersonville, N.C.   Deb: 7/17/1877

| 1877 | StL-N | 4 | 18 | 0 | 5 | 1 | 0 | 0 | 0 | 0 | 1 | .278 | .278 | .333 | 97 | -0 | -0 | 2 | | | | .667 | -2 | /OS | -0.2 |

■ LERON LEE   Lee, Leron   b: 3/4/48, Bakersfield, Cal.   BL/TR, 6', 196 lbs.   Deb: 9/05/69

1969	StL-N	7	23	3	5	1	0	0	0	3	8	.217	.308	.261	60	-1	-1	2	0	0	0	1.000	-0	/O	-0.2
1970	StL-N	121	264	28	60	13	1	6	23	24	66	.227	.294	.352	71	-11	-11	28	5	1	1	.969	-6	O	-2.0
1971	StL-N	25	28	3	5	1	0	1	2	4	12	.179	.281	.321	68	-1	-1	2	0	1	-1	.800	-1	O	-0.3
	SD-N	79	256	29	70	20	2	4	21	18	45	.273	.321	.414	115	2	4	32	4	5	-2	.920	-9	O	-1.1
	Yr	104	284	32	75	21	2	5	23	22	57	.264	.317	.405	108	1	2	34	4	6	-2	.914	-10	O	-1.4
1972	SD-N	101	370	50	111	23	7	12	47	29	58	.300	.356	.497	151	18	21	62	2	5	-2	.975	2	O	1.8
1973	SD-N	118	333	36	79	7	2	3	30	33	61	.237	.308	.297	74	-14	-10	31	4	2	0	.970	-2	O	-1.6
1974	Cle-A	79	232	18	54	13	0	5	25	15	42	.233	.279	.353	82	-6	-6	21	3	2	-0	.958	4	O/D	-0.6
1975	Cle-A	13	23	3	3	1	0	0	0	2	5	.130	.231	.174	16	-3	-3	1	1	0	0	1.000	0	/OD	-0.3
	LA-N	48	43	2	11	4	0	0	2	3	9	.256	.304	.349	85	-1	-1	5	0	0	0	1.000	-0	/O	-0.1
1976	LA-N	23	45	1	6	0	1	0	2	2	9	.133	.170	.178	-1	-6	-6	1	0	0	0	1.000	-2	O	-0.9
Total	8	614	1617	173	404	83	13	31	152	133	315	.250	.309	.375	95	-23	-15	185	19	14	-3	.962	-16	O/D	-5.3

■ MANUEL LEE   Lee, Manuel Lora "Manny" (b: Manuel Lora (Lee))   b: 6/17/65, San Pedro De Macoris, D.R.   BB/TR, 5'9", 151 lbs.   Deb: 4/10/85

1985	*Tor-A	64	40	9	8	0	0	0	0	2	9	.200	.238	.200	21	-4	-4	1	1	4	-2	.971	19	2/S3D	1.2
1986	Tor-A	35	78	8	16	0	1	1	7	4	10	.205	.244	.269	39	-7	-7	4	0	1	-1	.990	4	2/S/3	-0.3
1987	Tor-A	56	121	14	31	2	3	1	11	6	13	.256	.291	.347	67	-6	-6	13	2	0	1	.966	12	2S/D	0.8
1988	Tor-A	116	381	38	111	16	3	2	38	26	64	.291	.337	.365	96	-2	-2	44	3	3	-1	.988	10	2S/3D	1.1
1989	*Tor-A	99	300	27	78	9	2	3	34	20	60	.260	.306	.333	82	-8	-7	30	4	2	0	.985	-2	2S3D/O	-0.6
1990	Tor-A	117	391	45	95	12	4	6	41	26	90	.243	.290	.340	74	-13	-14	38	3	1	0	.993	-10	*2/S	-2.1
1991	*Tor-A	138	445	41	104	18	3	0	29	24	107	.234	.276	.288	54	-26	-29	35	7	2	1	.967	-28	*S	-4.6
1992	*Tor-A	128	396	49	104	10	1	3	39	50	73	.263	.345	.316	83	-6	-8	46	6	2	1	.987	-17	*S	-1.5
Total	8	753	2152	231	547	67	17	16	199	158	426	.254	.306	.323	74	-71	-77	210	26	15	-1	.974	-12	S2/3DO	-6.0

■ TERRY LEE   Lee, Terry James   b: 3/13/62, San Francisco, Cal.   BR/TR, 6'5", 215 lbs.   Deb: 9/03/90

1990	Cin-N	12	19	1	4	1	0	0	3	2	2	.211	.286	.263	50	-1	-1	1	0	0	0	1.000	0	/1	-0.2
1991	Cin-N	3	6	0	0	0	0	0	0	0	2	.000	.000	.000	-96	-2	-2	0	0	0	0	1.000	1	/1	0.0
Total	2	15	25	1	4	1	0	0	3	2	4	.160	.222	.200	17	-3	-3	1	0	0	0	1.000	0	/1	-0.2

■ BILLY LEE   Lee, William Joseph   b: 1/9/1892, Bayonne, N.J.   d: 1/6/84, West Hazelton, Pa.   BR/TR, 5'9", 165 lbs.   Deb: 4/15/15

1915	StL-A	18	59	2	11	1	0	0	4	6	5	.186	.262	.203	41	-4	-4	3	1	1	-0	1.000	2	O/3	-0.3
1916	StL-A	7	11	1	2	0	0	0	0	1	1	.182	.250	.182	31	-1	-1	1	0			1.000	-1	/O	-0.2
Total	2	25	70	3	13	1	0	0	4	7	6	.186	.260	.200	39	-5	-5	4	1	1	1	1.000	2	/O3	-0.5

■ WATTY LEE   Lee, Wyatt Arnold   b: 8/12/1879, Lynch's Station, Va.   d: 3/6/36, Washington, D.C.   BL/TL, 5'10.5", 171 lbs.   Deb: 4/30/01

1901	Was-A	43	129	15	33	6	3	0	12	7		.256	.304	.349	82	-4	-3	14	0			.948	0	P/O	-0.2
1902	Was-A	109	391	61	100	21	5	4	45	33		.256	.320	.366	89	-6	-6	50	8			.916	0	OP	-1.2
1903	Was-A	75	231	17	48	8	4	0	13	18		.208	.265	.277	62	-10	-11	19	5			.930	7	OP	-0.6
1904	Pit-N	8	12	1	4	0	1	0	0	0		.333	.333	.500	152	1	1	2	0			.889	0	/P	0.0
Total	4	235	763	94	185	35	13	4	70	58		.242	.301	.338	81	-19	-19	86	13			.917	8	O/P	-2.0

■ GENE LEEK   Leek, Eugene Harold   b: 7/15/36, San Diego, Cal.   BR/TR, 6', 185 lbs.   Deb: 4/22/59

1959	Cle-A	13	36	7	8	3	0	1	5	2	7	.222	.263	.389	80	-1	-1	4	0	0	0	.955	-2	3/S	-0.3
1961	LA-A	57	199	16	45	9	1	5	20	7	54	.226	.260	.357	57	-11	-14	16	0	1	-1	.958	18	3/SO	0.4
1962	LA-A	7	14	0	2	0	0	0	0	0	6	.143	.143	.143	-24	-2	-2	0	0	0	0	1.000	0	/3	-0.2
Total	3	77	249	23	55	12	1	6	25	9	67	.221	.254	.349	55	-15	-17	20	0	1	-1	.959	16	/3SO	-0.1

■ DAVE LEEPER   Leeper, David Dale   b: 10/30/59, Santa Ana, Cal.   BL/TL, 5'11", 170 lbs.   Deb: 9/10/84

1984	KC-A	4	6	1	0	0	0	0	0	0	1	.000	.000	.000	-99	-2	-2	0	0	0	0	1.000	-0	/OD	-0.2
1985	KC-A	15	34	1	3	0	0	0	4	1	3	.088	.114	.088	-43	-7	-7	0	0	0	0	.929	-1	O/D	-0.8
Total	2	19	40	2	3	0	0	0	4	1	4	.075	.098	.075	-52	-8	-8	0	0	0	0	.944	-1	OD	-1.0

■ GEORGE LEES   Lees, George Edward   b: 2/2/1895, Bethlehem, Pa.   d: 1/2/80, Harrisburg, Pa.   BR/TR, 5'9", 150 lbs.   Deb: 5/07/21

| 1921 | Chi-A | 20 | 42 | 3 | 9 | 2 | 0 | 0 | 4 | 0 | 3 | .214 | .214 | .262 | 21 | -5 | -5 | 2 | 1 | 0 | -1 | .951 | -2 | C | -0.7 |

YEAR	TM/L	G	AB	R	H	2B	3B	HR	RBI	BB	SO	AVG	OBP	SLG	PRO+	BR	/A	RC	SB	CS	SBR	FA	FR	POS	TPR
■ JIM LEFEBVRE	Lefebvre, James Kenneth b: 1/7/42, Inglewood, Cal. BB/TR, 6', 185 lbs. Deb: 4/12/65 MC																								
1965	*LA-N	157	544	57	136	21	4	12	69	71	92	.250	.339	.369	106	1	5	71	3	5	-2	.970	-12	*2	0.5
1966	*LA-N★	152	544	69	149	23	3	24	74	48	72	.274	.336	.460	129	13	18	84	1	1	-0	.980	-11	*23	1.6
1967	LA-N	136	494	51	129	18	5	8	50	44	64	.261	.325	.366	106	-1	3	57	1	5	-3	.955	6	32/1	0.8
1968	LA-N	84	286	23	69	12	1	5	31	26	55	.241	.307	.343	102	-2	0	31	0	0	0	.978	-10	23/O1	-0.8
1969	LA-N	95	275	29	65	15	2	4	44	48	37	.236	.352	.349	104	0	3	35	2	1	0	.985	1	32/1	0.7
1970	LA-N	109	314	33	79	15	1	4	44	29	42	.252	.317	.344	81	-10	-8	34	1	1	-0	.988	-4	23/1	-0.8
1971	LA-N	119	388	40	95	14	2	12	68	39	55	.245	.317	.384	104	-1	1	44	0	2	-1	.988	-17	*2/3	-0.8
1972	LA-N	70	169	11	34	8	0	5	24	17	30	.201	.274	.337	75	-6	-6	16	0	0	0	.987	-1	23	-0.6
Total	8	922	3014	313	756	126	18	74	404	322	447	.251	.326	.378	105	-7	17	372	8	15	-7	.979	-48	23/1O	0.6
■ JOE LEFEBVRE	Lefebvre, Joseph Henry b: 2/22/56, Concord, N.H. BL/TR, 5'10", 175 lbs. Deb: 5/22/80																								
1980	*NY-A	74	150	26	34	1	1	8	21	27	30	.227	.345	.407	107	1	2	21	0	0	0	.975	-14	O	-1.4
1981	SD-N	86	246	31	63	13	4	8	31	35	33	.256	.353	.439	133	8	10	35	6	4	-1	.994	-1	O	0.7
1982	SD-N	102	239	25	57	9	0	4	21	18	50	.238	.295	.326	78	-9	-7	24	0	0	0	.972	-2	3O/C	-1.1
1983	SD-N	18	20	1	5	0	0	0	1	2	3	.250	.318	.250	61	-1	-1	2	0	0	0	1.000	0	/O3C	-0.1
	*Phi-N	101	258	34	80	20	8	8	38	31	46	.310	.390	.543	158	19	20	53	5	3	-0	.990	-7	O/3C	1.1
	Yr	119	278	35	85	20	8	8	39	33	49	.306	.385	.522	151	18	19	54	5	3	-0	.990	-6	O3/C	1.0
1984	Phi-N	52	160	22	40	9	0	3	18	23	37	.250	.351	.363	99	1	1	20	0	2	-1	.966	0	O/3	-0.2
1986	Phi-N	14	18	0	2	0	0	0	0	3	5	.111	.238	.111	-1	-2	-2	0	0	0	0	1.000	-0	/O	-0.3
Total	6	447	1091	139	281	52	13	31	130	139	204	.258	.346	.414	115	18	22	155	11	9	-2	.986	-23	O/3C	-1.3
■ BILL LeFEBVRE	LeFebvre, Wilfrid Henry "Lefty" b: 11/11/15, Natick, R.I. BL/TL, 5'11.5", 180 lbs. Deb: 6/10/38																								
1938	Bos-A	1	1	1	1	0	0	1	1	0	0	1.000	1.000	4.000	1048	1	1	4	0	0	0	.000	-0	/P	0.0
1939	Bos-A	7	10	3	3	0	0	0	1	2	2	.300	.417	.300	83	-0	-0	1	0	0	0	1.000	-1	/P	0.0
1943	Was-A	7	14	0	4	3	0	0	1	1	0	.286	.333	.500	148	1	1	2	0	0	0	1.000	-0	/P	0.0
1944	Was-A	60	62	4	16	2	2	0	8	12	9	.258	.378	.355	115	1	2	9	0	0	0	.933	-0	P/1	0.0
Total	4	75	87	8	24	5	2	1	11	15	11	.276	.382	.414	129	3	4	17	0	0	0	.960	-1	/P1	0.0
■ AL LEFEVRE	Lefevre, Alfredo Modesto b: 9/16/1898, New York, N.Y. d: 1/21/82, Glen Cove, N.Y. BR/TR, 5'10.5", 160 lbs. Deb: 6/28/20																								
1920	NY-N	17	27	5	4	0	1	0	0	0	13	.148	.148	.222	5	-3	-3	1	0	0	0	1.000	3	/S23	0.0
■ WADE LEFLER	Lefler, Wade Hampton b: 6/5/1896, Cooleemee, N.C. d: 3/6/81, Hickory, N.C. BL/TR, 5'11", 162 lbs. Deb: 4/16/24																								
1924	Bos-N	1	1	0	0	0	0	0	0	0	1	.000	.000	.000	-99	-0	-0	0	0	0	0	.000	0	H	0.0
	Was-A	5	8	0	5	3	0	0	4	0	0	.625	.625	1.000	325	2	2	5	0	0	0	1.000	-0	/O	0.2
Total	1	6	9	0	5	3	0	0	4	0	1	.556	.556	.889	279	2	2	5	0	0	0	.950	-0	/O	0.2
■ RON LeFLORE	LeFlore, Ronald b: 6/16/48, Detroit, Mich. BR/TR, 6', 200 lbs. Deb: 8/01/74																								
1974	Det-A	59	254	37	66	8	1	2	13	13	58	.260	.304	.323	78	-7	-8	26	23	9	2	.935	3	O	-0.6
1975	Det-A	136	550	66	142	13	6	8	37	33	139	.258	.303	.347	80	-13	-16	57	28	20	-4	.973	6	*O	-2.0
1976	Det-A★	135	544	93	172	23	8	4	39	51	111	.316	.377	.410	125	21	19	86	58	20	5	.973	16	*O/D	3.6
1977	Det-A	154	652	100	212	30	10	16	57	37	121	.325	.365	.475	121	23	19	110	39	19	0	.972	2	*O	1.4
1978	Det-A	155	666	**126**	198	30	3	12	62	65	104	.297	.363	.405	113	15	13	105	**68**	16	11	.976	9	*O	2.6
1979	Det-A	148	600	110	180	22	10	9	57	52	95	.300	.356	.415	104	6	4	94	78	14	15	.990	4	*OD	1.7
1980	Mon-N	139	521	95	134	21	11	4	39	62	99	.257	.337	.363	95	-2	-2	76	**97**	19	**18**	.957	-2	*O	0.9
1981	Chi-A	82	337	46	83	10	4	0	24	28	70	.246	.306	.300	77	-10	-10	32	36	11	4	.960	-1	O	-0.9
1982	Chi-A	91	334	58	96	15	4	4	25	22	91	.287	.331	.392	98	-1	-1	42	28	14	0	.939	-4	O/D	-0.7
Total	9	1099	4458	731	1283	172	57	59	353	363	888	.288	.344	.392	103	33	18	628	455	142	51	.968	33	*O/D	6.0
■ LOU LEGETT	Legett, Louis Alfred "Doc" b: 6/1/01, New Orleans, La. d: 3/6/88, New Orleans, La. BR/TR, 5'10", 166 lbs. Deb: 5/08/29																								
1929	Bos-N	39	81	7	13	2	0	0	6	3	18	.160	.190	.185	-7	-14	-13	3	2			.914	-1	C	-1.2
1933	Bos-A	8	5	1	1	1	0	0	1	0	0	.200	.200	.400	56	-0	-0	0	0	0	0	1.000	1	/C	0.1
1934	Bos-A	19	38	4	11	0	0	0	1	2	4	.289	.325	.289	56	-2	-3	4	0	0	0	.977	-0	C	-0.2
1935	Bos-A	2	0	1	0	0	0	0	0	0	0	—	—	—	—	0	0	0	0	0	0	.000	0	R	0.0
Total	4	68	124	13	25	3	0	0	8	5	22	.202	.233	.226	16	-16	-16	7	2	0		.938	-0	/C	-1.3
■ GREG LEGG	Legg, Gregory Lynn b: 4/21/60, San Jose, Cal. BR/TR, 6'1", 185 lbs. Deb: 4/18/86																								
1986	Phi-N	11	20	2	9	1	0	0	1	0	3	.450	.450	.500	156	2	2	5	0	0	0	.941	2	/2S	0.4
1987	Phi-N	3	2	1	0	0	0	0	0	0	0	.000	.000	.000	-97	-1	-1	0	0	0	0	1.000	-0	/2S3	-0.1
Total	2	14	22	3	9	1	0	0	1	0	3	.409	.409	.455	132	1	1	5	0	0	0	.952	2	/2S3	0.3
■ MIKE LEHANE	Lehane, Michael Patrick b: 4/15/1865, New York, N.Y. BR , 6'1.5", 180 lbs. Deb: 4/26/1884																								
1884	Was-U	3	12	1	4	2	0	0		0		.333	.333	.500	184	1	1	2				.688	-1	/SO3	0.0
1890	Col-a	140	512	54	108	19	5	0		43		.211	.276	.268	67	-24	-18	42	13			**.982**	10	*1	-1.3
1891	Col-a	137	511	59	110	12	7	1	52	34	77	.215	.268	.272	60	-29	-24	43	16			**.981**	7	*1	-2.0
Total	3	280	1035	114	222	33	12	1	52	77	77	.214	.273	.272	65	-52	-42	87	29			.982	16	1/S3O	-3.3
■ PAUL LEHNER	Lehner, Paul Eugene "Peanuts" or "Gulliver" b: 7/1/20, Dolomite, Ala. d: 12/27/67, Birmingham, Ala. BL/TL, 5'9", 165 lbs. Deb: 9/10/46																								
1946	StL-A	16	45	6	10	1	2	0	5	1	5	.222	.239	.333	56	-3	-3	4	0	0	0	.941	-3	O	-0.7
1947	StL-A	135	483	59	120	25	9	7	48	28	29	.248	.294	.381	85	-11	-12	50	5	5	-2	.980	-6	*O	-2.7
1948	StL-A	103	333	23	92	15	4	2	46	30	19	.276	.336	.363	84	-7	-8	40	0	2	-1	.974	-6	O/1	-2.0
1949	StL-A	104	297	25	68	13	0	3	37	16	20	.229	.271	.303	50	-22	-23	22	0	2	-1	.987	2	O1	-2.6
1950	Phi-A	114	427	48	132	17	5	9	52	32	33	.309	.357	.436	104	0	1	66	1	1	-0	.981	6	*O	0.3
1951	Phi-A	9	28	1	4	1	0	0	1	1	1	.143	.172	.179	-5	-4	-4	0	0	0	0	1.000	1	/O	-0.3
	Chi-A	23	72	9	15	3	1	0	3	10	4	.208	.305	.278	60	-4	-4	7	0	0	0	.980	-4	O	-0.8
	StL-A	21	67	2	9	5	0	1	2	6	5	.134	.205	.254	23	-8	-8	3	0	1	-1	1.000	-1	O	-1.0
	Cle-A	12	13	2	3	0	0	0	1	1	2	.231	.286	.231	43	-1	-1	1	0	0	0	1.000	-0	/O	-0.1
	Yr	65	180	14	31	9	1	1	7	18	12	.172	.247	.250	35	-17	-17	11	0	1	-1	.991	-4	O	-2.2
1952	Bos-A	3	3	0	2	0	0	0	2	2	0	.667	.800	.667	288	1	1	2	0	0	0	1.000	-0	/O	0.1
Total	7	540	1768	175	455	80	21	22	197	127	118	.257	.309	.364	78	-58	-61	196	6	11	-5	.981	-11	O/1	-9.8
■ CLARENCE LEHR	Lehr, Clarence Emanuel "King" b: 5/16/1886, Escanaba, Mich. d: 1/31/48, Detroit, Mich. BR/TR, 5'11", 165 lbs. Deb: 5/18/11																								
1911	Phi-N	23	27	2	4	0	0	0	2	0	7	.148	.148	.148	-17	-4	-4	1	0			1.000	-1	/O2S	-0.5
■ HANK LEIBER	Leiber, Henry Edward b: 1/17/11, Phoenix, Ariz. BR/TR, 6'1.5", 205 lbs. Deb: 4/16/33																								
1933	NY-N	6	10	1	2	0	0	0	0	0	2	.200	.200	.200	15	-1	-1	0	0			1.000	1	/O	0.0
1934	NY-N	63	187	17	45	5	3	2	25	4	13	.241	.257	.332	58	-12	-11	15	1			.971	-6	O	-1.9
1935	NY-N	154	613	110	203	37	4	22	107	48	29	.331	.389	.512	143	34	36	121	0			.965	-15	*O	1.5
1936	*NY-N	101	337	44	94	19	7	9	67	37	41	.279	.352	.457	118	7	8	57	1			.961	-7	O/1	-0.3
1937	*NY-N	51	184	24	54	7	3	4	32	15	27	.293	.347	.429	108	2	2	26	1			.988	-7	O	-0.6
1938	NY-N★	98	360	50	97	18	4	12	65	31	45	.269	.327	.442	109	4	3	54	0			.974	-9	O	-0.8
1939	Chi-N	112	365	65	113	16	1	24	88	59	42	.310	.411	.556	155	30	30	83	1			.977	4	O	2.9
1940	Chi-N†	117	440	68	133	24	2	17	86	45	68	.302	.371	.482	136	20	21	80	1			.985	-6	*O1	0.9
1941	Chi-N†	53	162	20	35	5	0	7	25	16	25	.216	.291	.377	90	-3	-3	18	0			.964	-4	O1	-1.0
1942	NY-N	58	147	11	32	6	0	4	23	19	27	.218	.315	.340	91	-1	-1	15	0			.990	-0	O/P	-0.4

YEAR	TM/L	G	AB	R	H	2B	3B	HR	RBI	BB	SO	AVG	OBP	SLG	PRO+	BR	/A	RC	SB	CS	SBR	FA	FR	POS	TPR
Total	10	813	2805	410	808	137	24	101	518	274	319	.288	.356	.462	122	80	83	469	5			.973	-49	O/1P	0.3

■ NEMO LEIBOLD Leibold, Harry Loran b: 2/17/1892, Butler, Ind. d: 2/4/77, Detroit, Mich. BL/TR, 6'6.5", 157 lbs. Deb: 4/12/13

YEAR	TM/L	G	AB	R	H	2B	3B	HR	RBI	BB	SO	AVG	OBP	SLG	PRO+	BR	/A	RC	SB	CS	SBR	FA	FR	POS	TPR
1913	Cle-A	93	286	37	74	11	6	0	12	21	43	.259	.309	.339	87	-4	-5	33	16			.945	-0	O	-1.0
1914	Cle-A	115	402	46	106	13	3	0	32	54	56	.264	.354	.311	96	2	0	45	12	14	-5	.931	9	*O	-0.1
1915	Cle-A	57	207	28	53	5	4	0	4	24	16	.256	.339	.319	95	-0	-1	24	5	3	-0	.969	9	O	0.6
	Chi-A	36	74	10	17	1	0	0	11	15	11	.230	.360	.243	78	-1	-1	8	1	3	-2	1.000	5	O	0.1
	Yr	93	281	38	70	6	4	0	15	39	27	.249	.345	.299	91	-1	-2	31	6	6	-2	.978	14	O	0.7
1916	Chi-A	45	82	5	20	1	2	0	13	7	7	.244	.303	.305	82	-2	-2	10	7			1.000	-5	O	-0.8
1917	*Chi-A	125	428	59	101	12	6	0	29	74	34	.236	.350	.292	94	1	0	50	27			.961	-1	*O	-0.8
1918	Chi-A	116	440	57	110	14	7	0	31	63	32	.250	.344	.314	97	1	0	50	13			.979	8	*O	0.2
1919	*Chi-A	122	434	81	131	18	2	0	26	72	30	.302	.404	.353	113	12	12	67	17			.928	7	*O	1.1
1920	Chi-A	108	413	61	91	16	3	1	28	55	30	.220	.316	.281	59	-23	-23	37	7	15	-7	.977	6	*O	-3.2
1921	Bos-A	123	467	88	143	26	6	0	31	41	27	.306	.363	.388	94	-5	-4	67	13	7	-0	.949	4	*O	-0.8
1922	Bos-A	81	271	42	70	8	1	1	18	41	14	.258	.360	.306	76	-8	-8	31	1	6	-3	.966	6	O	-1.0
1923	Bos-A	12	18	1	2	0	0	0	0	1	2	.111	.158	.111	-28	-3	-3	0	0	1	-1	.909	-3	O	-0.7
	Was-A	95	315	68	96	13	4	1	22	53	16	.305	.408	.381	114	7	9	53	7	5	-1	.980	1	O	0.4
	Yr	107	333	69	98	13	4	1	22	54	18	.294	.396	.366	106	3	5	52	7	6	-2	.977	-2	O	-0.3
1924	*Was-A	84	246	41	72	6	4	0	20	42	10	.293	.398	.350	97	-0	1	37	6	5	-1	.994	-3	O	-0.7
1925	*Was-A	56	84	14	23	1	1	0	7	8	7	.274	.337	.310	66	-4	-4	9	1	0	0	.972	-6	O/3	-1.0
Total	13	1268	4167	638	1109	145	49	3	284	571	335	.266	.357	.327	91	-30	-30	523	133	59		.961	38	*O/3	-7.7

■ ELMER LEIFER Leifer, Elmer Edwin b: 5/23/1893, Clarington, Ohio d: 9/26/48, Everett, Wash. BL/TR, 5'9.5", 170 lbs. Deb: 9/07/21

YEAR	TM/L	G	AB	R	H	2B	3B	HR	RBI	BB	SO	AVG	OBP	SLG	PRO+	BR	/A	RC	SB	CS	SBR	FA	FR	POS	TPR
1921	Chi-A	9	10	0	3	0	0	0	1	0	4	.300	.300	.300	54	-1	-1	1	0	0	0	1.000	-1	/3O	-0.1

■ JOHN LEIGHTON Leighton, John Atkinson b: 10/4/1861, Peabody, Mass. d: 10/31/56, Lynn, Mass. 5'11", 170 lbs. Deb: 7/12/1890

YEAR	TM/L	G	AB	R	H	2B	3B	HR	RBI	BB	SO	AVG	OBP	SLG	PRO+	BR	/A	RC	SB	CS	SBR	FA	FR	POS	TPR
1890	Syr-a	7	27	6	8	2	0	0		3		.296	.367	.370	134	1	1	5	2			.938	-0	/O	0.0

■ BILL LEINHAUSER Leinhauser, William Charles b: 11/4/1893, Philadelphia, Pa. d: 4/14/78, Elkins Park, Pa. BR/TR, 5'10", 150 lbs. Deb: 5/18/12

YEAR	TM/L	G	AB	R	H	2B	3B	HR	RBI	BB	SO	AVG	OBP	SLG	PRO+	BR	/A	RC	SB	CS	SBR	FA	FR	POS	TPR
1912	Det-A	1	4	0	0	0	0	0	0	0		.000	.000	.000	-99	-1	-1	0	0			1.000	0	/O	-0.1

■ ED LEIP Leip, Edgar Ellsworth b: 11/29/10, Trenton, N.J. d: 11/24/83, Zephyrhills, Fla. BR/TR, 5'9", 160 lbs. Deb: 9/16/39

YEAR	TM/L	G	AB	R	H	2B	3B	HR	RBI	BB	SO	AVG	OBP	SLG	PRO+	BR	/A	RC	SB	CS	SBR	FA	FR	POS	TPR
1939	Was-A	9	32	4	11	1	0	0	2	2	4	.344	.382	.375	102	-0	0	4	0	1	-1	.951	-1	/2	-0.1
1940	Pit-N	3	5	2	1	0	0	0	0	0	0	.200	.200	.200	11	-1	-1	0	0			1.000	-0	/2	-0.1
1941	Pit-N	15	25	1	5	0	2	0	3	1	2	.200	.231	.360	65	-1	-1	1	1			.889	2	/23	0.1
1942	Pit-N	3	0	0	0	0	0	0	0	0	0	—	—	—	—	0	0	0	0			.000	0	R	0.0
Total	4	30	62	7	17	1	2	0	5	3	6	.274	.308	.355	80	-2	-2	6	1	1		.931	0	/23	-0.1

■ SCOTT LEIUS Leius, Scott Thomas b: 9/24/65, Yonkers, N.Y. BR/TR, 6'3", 180 lbs. Deb: 9/03/90

YEAR	TM/L	G	AB	R	H	2B	3B	HR	RBI	BB	SO	AVG	OBP	SLG	PRO+	BR	/A	RC	SB	CS	SBR	FA	FR	POS	TPR
1990	Min-A	14	25	4	6	1	0	1	4	2	2	.240	.296	.400	87	-0	-1	2	0	0	0	1.000	3	S/3	0.3
1991	*Min-A	109	199	35	57	7	2	5	20	30	35	.286	.380	.417	115	6	5	32	5	5	-2	.953	-2	3S/O	0.3
1992	Min-A	129	409	50	102	18	2	2	35	34	61	.249	.309	.318	73	-13	-15	39	6	5	-1	.955	4	*3S	-1.1
Total	3	252	633	89	165	26	4	8	59	66	98	.261	.331	.352	87	-7	-10	74	11	10	-3	.954	6	3/SO	-0.5

■ FRANK LEJA Leja, Frank John b: 2/7/36, Holyoke, Mass. d: 5/3/91, Boston, Mass. BL/TL, 6'4", 205 lbs. Deb: 5/01/54

YEAR	TM/L	G	AB	R	H	2B	3B	HR	RBI	BB	SO	AVG	OBP	SLG	PRO+	BR	/A	RC	SB	CS	SBR	FA	FR	POS	TPR
1954	NY-A	12	5	2	1	0	0	0	0	0	1	.200	.200	.200	10	-1	-1	0	0	0	0	1.000	0	/1	-0.1
1955	NY-A	7	2	1	0	0	0	0	0	0	1	.000	.000	.000	-99	-1	-1	0	0	0	0	1.000	0	/1	0.0
1962	LA-A	7	16	0	0	0	0	0	0	1	6	.000	.059	.000	-85	-4	-4	0	0	0	0	.953	-0	/1	-0.5
Total	3	26	23	3	1	0	0	0	0	1	8	.043	.083	.043	-67	-5	-5	0	0	0	0	.958	0	/1	-0.6

■ LARRY LeJEUNE LeJeune, Sheldon Aldenbert b: 7/22/1885, Chicago, Ill. d: 4/21/52, Eloise, Mich. BR/TR, 6', 185 lbs. Deb: 5/10/11

YEAR	TM/L	G	AB	R	H	2B	3B	HR	RBI	BB	SO	AVG	OBP	SLG	PRO+	BR	/A	RC	SB	CS	SBR	FA	FR	POS	TPR
1911	Bro-N	6	19	2	3	0	0	0	2	2	8	.158	.238	.158	12	-2	-2	1	2			.818	-2	/O	-0.4
1915	Pit-N	18	65	4	11	0	1	0	2	2	7	.169	.206	.200	23	-6	-6	3	4	3	-1	.940	2	O	-0.6
Total	2	24	84	6	14	0	1	0	4	4	15	.167	.213	.190	21	-8	-8	4	6	3		.918	1	/O	-1.0

■ DON LeJOHN LeJohn, Donald Everett b: 5/13/34, Daisytown, Pa. BR/TR, 5'10", 175 lbs. Deb: 6/30/65

YEAR	TM/L	G	AB	R	H	2B	3B	HR	RBI	BB	SO	AVG	OBP	SLG	PRO+	BR	/A	RC	SB	CS	SBR	FA	FR	POS	TPR
1965	*LA-N	34	78	2	20	2	0	0	7	5	13	.256	.301	.282	70	-3	-3	6	0	1	-1	.959	1	3	-0.3

■ JACK LELIVELT Lelivelt, John Frank b: 11/14/1885, Chicago, Ill. d: 1/20/41, Seattle, Wash. BL/TL, 5'11", 175 lbs. Deb: 6/24/09 F

YEAR	TM/L	G	AB	R	H	2B	3B	HR	RBI	BB	SO	AVG	OBP	SLG	PRO+	BR	/A	RC	SB	CS	SBR	FA	FR	POS	TPR
1909	Was-A	91	318	25	93	8	6	0	24	19		.292	.334	.355	124	6	7	40	8			.970	8	O	1.3
1910	Was-A	110	347	40	92	10	3	0	33	40		.265	.343	.311	110	3	5	45	20			.964	4	O/1	0.6
1911	Was-A	72	225	29	72	12	4	0	22	22		.320	.386	.409	124	7	7	38	7			.939	4	O/1	0.8
1912	NY-A	36	149	12	54	6	7	2	23	4		.362	.383	.537	153	11	9	32	7			.963	-1	O	0.7
1913	NY-A	18	28	2	6	0	1	0	4	2	2	.214	.267	.286	61	-1	-1	2	1			1.000	1	/O	-0.1
	Cle-A	23	23	0	9	2	0	0	7	0	3	.391	.391	.478	150	1	1	4	1			.000	-1	/O	0.1
	Yr	41	51	2	15	2	1	0	11	2	5	.294	.321	.373	101	-0	-0	6	2			1.000	1	/O	0.0
1914	Cle-A	34	64	6	21	5	1	0	13	2	10	.328	.348	.438	131	2	2	9	2	3	-1	.933	-3	O/1	-0.2
Total	6	384	1154	114	347	43	22	2	126	89	15	.301	.353	.381	124	29	31	171	46	3		.962	13	O/1	3.2

■ JOHNNIE LeMASTER LeMaster, Johnnie Lee b: 6/19/54, Portsmouth, Ohio BR/TR, 6'2", 167 lbs. Deb: 9/02/75

YEAR	TM/L	G	AB	R	H	2B	3B	HR	RBI	BB	SO	AVG	OBP	SLG	PRO+	BR	/A	RC	SB	CS	SBR	FA	FR	POS	TPR
1975	SF-N	22	74	4	14	4	0	2	9	4	15	.189	.241	.324	53	-5	-5	6	2	1	0	.967	-1	S	-0.4
1976	SF-N	33	100	9	21	3	2	0	9	2	21	.210	.225	.280	42	-8	-8	6	2	0	1	.937	11	S	0.6
1977	SF-N	68	134	13	20	5	1	0	8	13	27	.149	.224	.201	15	-16	-16	7	2	1	0	.934	7	S/3	-0.5
1978	SF-N	101	272	23	64	18	3	1	14	21	45	.235	.293	.335	78	-9	-8	26	6	6	-2	.966	2	S/2	0.2
1979	SF-N	108	343	42	87	11	2	3	29	23	55	.254	.304	.324	77	-13	-11	34	9	5	-0	.959	-0	*S	-0.1
1980	SF-N	135	405	33	87	16	6	3	31	25	57	.215	.260	.306	59	-24	-22	32	0	1	-1	.957	-14	*S	-2.4
1981	SF-N	104	324	27	82	9	1	0	28	24	46	.253	.307	.287	70	-13	-12	26	3	7	-3	.964	-8	*S	-1.4
1982	SF-N	130	436	34	94	14	1	2	30	31	78	.216	.268	.266	50	-29	-29	30	13	4	2	.963	-8	*S	-2.5
1983	SF-N	141	534	81	128	16	1	6	30	60	96	.240	.319	.307	77	-17	-15	57	39	19	0	.964	-22	*S	-2.5
1984	SF-N	132	451	46	98	13	2	4	32	31	97	.217	.268	.282	56	-27	-26	36	17	5	2	.964	4	*S	-0.8
1985	SF-N	12	16	1	0	0	0	0	0	1	5	.000	.059	.000	-86	-4	-4	0	0	0	0	.955	-1	S	-0.4
	Cle-A	11	20	0	3	0	0	0	2	0	6	.150	.150	.150	-18	-3	-3	0	0	1	-1	.949	3	S	0.0
	Pit-N	22	58	4	9	0	0	1	6	5	12	.155	.222	.207	21	-6	-6	3	1	0	0	.983	13	S	0.9
1987	Oak-A	20	24	3	2	0	0	0	1	1	4	.083	.120	.083	-48	-5	-5	0	0	1	-1	1.000	5	/3S2D	0.0
Total	12	1039	3191	320	709	109	19	22	229	241	564	.222	.278	.289	60	-180	-170	263	94	51	-2	.961	-9	S/32D	-9.3

■ STEVE LEMBO Lembo, Stephen Neal b: 11/13/26, Brooklyn, N.Y. d: 12/4/89, Flushing, N.Y. BR/TR, 6'1", 185 lbs. Deb: 9/16/50

YEAR	TM/L	G	AB	R	H	2B	3B	HR	RBI	BB	SO	AVG	OBP	SLG	PRO+	BR	/A	RC	SB	CS	SBR	FA	FR	POS	TPR
1950	Bro-N	5	6	0	1	0	0	0	0	1	0	.167	.286	.167	22	-1	-1	0	0			1.000	2	/C	0.2
1952	Bro-N	2	5	0	1	0	0	0	1	0	1	.200	.200	.200	11	-1	-1	0	0	0	0	1.000	0	/C	0.0
Total	2	7	11	0	2	0	0	0	1	1	1	.182	.250	.182	18	-1	-1	0	0	0		1.000	3	/C	0.2

■ MARK LEMKE Lemke, Mark Alan b: 8/13/65, Utica, N.Y. BB/TR, 5'10", 167 lbs. Deb: 9/17/88

YEAR	TM/L	G	AB	R	H	2B	3B	HR	RBI	BB	SO	AVG	OBP	SLG	PRO+	BR	/A	RC	SB	CS	SBR	FA	FR	POS	TPR
1988	Atl-N	16	58	8	13	4	0	0	2	4	5	.224	.274	.293	60	-3	-3	4	0	2	-1	.970	4	2	0.1
1989	Atl-N	14	55	4	10	2	1	2	10	5	7	.182	.250	.364	72	-2	-2	5	0	1	-1	1.000	-2	2	-0.4
1990	Atl-N	102	239	22	54	13	0	0	21	21	22	.226	.288	.280	54	-14	-15	19	0	1	-1	.989	23	32/S	0.8
1991	*Atl-N	136	269	36	63	11	2	2	23	29	27	.234	.309	.312	71	-9	-11	25	1	2	-1	.978	13	*23	0.3

YEAR	TM/L	G	AB	R	H	2B	3B	HR	RBI	BB	SO	AVG	OBP	SLG	PRO+	BR	/A	RC	SB	CS	SBR	FA	FR	POS	TPR
1992	*Atl-N	155	427	38	97	7	4	6	26	50	39	.227	.308	.304	68	-14	-18	41	0	3	-2	.984	-10	*23	-2.9
Total	5	423	1048	108	237	37	7	10	82	109	100	.226	.299	.303	65	-41	-49	94	1	9	-5	.982	29	2/3S	-2.1
■ CHET LEMON Lemon, Chester Earl b: 2/12/55, Jackson, Miss. BR/TR, 6′, 195 lbs. Deb: 9/09/75																									
1975	Chi-A	9	35	2	9	2	0	0	1	2	6	.257	.297	.314	72	-1	-1	4	1	0	0	.923	-4	/3OD	-0.5
1976	Chi-A	132	451	46	111	15	5	4	38	28	65	.246	.300	.328	83	-9	-10	44	13	7	-0	.992	11	*O	-0.4
1977	Chi-A	150	553	99	151	38	4	19	67	52	88	.273	.347	.459	118	13	13	89	8	7	-2	.978	**35**	*O	4.0
1978	Chi-A★	105	357	51	107	24	6	13	55	39	46	.300	.381	.510	147	23	23	65	5	9	-4	.983	14	OD	2.8
1979	Chi-A★	148	556	79	177	**44**	2	17	86	56	68	.318	.394	.496	138	31	31	104	7	11	-5	.977	9	*O	2.8
1980	Chi-A	147	514	76	150	32	6	11	51	71	56	.292	.390	.442	128	22	22	90	6	6	-2	.981	2	*O/2D	1.6
1981	Chi-A	94	328	50	99	23	6	9	50	33	48	.302	.388	.491	155	22	23	60	5	8	-3	.984	2	O	1.9
1982	Det-A	125	436	75	116	20	1	19	52	56	69	.266	.369	.447	122	15	15	72	1	4	-2	.984	1	*O/D	1.0
1983	Det-A	145	491	78	125	21	5	24	69	54	70	.255	.352	.464	126	16	17	79	0	7	-4	.988	11	*O	1.9
1984	*Det-A★	141	509	77	146	34	6	20	76	51	83	.287	.360	.495	135	23	23	86	5	5	-2	.995	16	*O/D	3.3
1985	Det-A	145	517	69	137	28	4	18	68	45	93	.265	.336	.439	111	7	7	78	0	2	-1	.990	11	*O	1.2
1986	Det-A	126	403	45	101	21	3	12	53	39	53	.251	.329	.407	99	-1	-0	52	2	1	0	.985	3	*O	-0.1
1987	*Det-A	146	470	75	130	30	3	20	75	70	82	.277	.380	.481	132	19	22	86	0	0	0	.992	3	*O	1.9
1988	Det-A	144	512	67	135	29	4	17	64	59	65	.264	.348	.436	123	13	15	75	1	2	-1	.974	4	*O	1.4
1989	Det-A	127	414	45	98	19	2	7	47	46	71	.237	.325	.343	90	-6	-4	47	1	5	-3	.985	-6	*OD	-1.6
1990	Det-A	104	322	39	83	16	4	5	32	48	61	.258	.361	.379	106	4	4	46	3	2	-0	.973	6	O/D	0.8
Total	16	1988	6868	973	1875	396	61	215	884	749	1024	.273	.357	.442	121	191	201	1078	58	76	-28	.984	116	*O/D32	22.0
■ JIM LEMON Lemon, James Robert b: 3/23/28, Covington, Va. BR/TR, 6′4″, 200 lbs. Deb: 8/20/50 MC																									
1950	Cle-A	12	34	4	6	1	0	1	1	3	12	.176	.243	.294	38	-3	-3	2	0	0	0	.824	-2	O	-0.5
1953	Cle-A	16	46	5	8	1	0	1	5	3	15	.174	.224	.261	32	-5	-4	3	0	0	0	.913	-1	O/1	-0.6
1954	Was-A	37	128	12	30	2	3	2	13	9	34	.234	.285	.344	76	-5	-5	12	0	0	0	.951	-3	O	-0.9
1955	Was-A	10	25	3	5	2	0	1	3	3	4	.200	.286	.400	88	-1	-1	3	0	0	0	.923	-0	/O	-0.1
1956	Was-A	146	538	77	146	21	**11**	27	96	65	138	.271	.352	.502	123	16	16	94	2	4	-2	.963	8	*O	1.4
1957	Was-A	137	518	58	147	23	6	17	64	49	94	.284	.349	.450	118	11	12	77	1	7	-4	.971	-3	*O/1	-0.3
1958	Was-A	142	501	65	123	15	9	26	75	50	120	.246	.315	.467	114	7	8	71	2	4	-2	.978	0	*O	-0.1
1959	Was-A	147	531	73	148	18	3	33	100	46	99	.279	.337	.510	130	19	19	91	5	2	0	.969	3	*O	1.5
1960	Was-A★	148	528	81	142	10	1	38	100	67	114	.269	.359	.508	133	22	23	99	2	0	1	.960	-1	*O	1.6
1961	Min-A	129	423	57	109	26	1	14	52	44	98	.258	.333	.423	95	-0	-3	59	1	1	-0	.940	-6	*O	-1.6
1962	Min-A	12	17	1	3	0	0	1	5	3	4	.176	.300	.353	72	-1	-1	2	0	0	0	1.000	-1	/O	-0.2
1963	Min-A	7	17	0	2	0	0	0	1	1	5	.118	.167	.118	-18	-3	-3	0	0	0	0	.800	-1	/O	-0.4
	Phi-N	31	59	6	16	2	0	2	6	8	18	.271	.358	.407	121	2	2	9	0	0	0	.963	-0	O	0.1
	Chi-A	36	80	4	16	0	1	1	8	12	32	.200	.304	.262	62	-4	-4	7	0	0	0	.979	-3	1	-0.8
Total	12	1010	3445	446	901	121	35	164	529	363	787	.262	.335	.460	114	55	57	530	13	18	-7	.961	-10	O/1	-0.9
■ BOB LEMON Lemon, Robert Granville b: 9/22/20, San Bernardino, Cal. BL/TR, 6′, 185 lbs. Deb: 9/09/41 MCH																									
1941	Cle-A	5	4	0	1	0	0	0	0	0	1	.250	.250	.250	34	-0	-0	0	0	0	0	1.000	0	/3	0.0
1942	Cle-A	5	5	0	0	0	0	0	0	0	3	.000	.000	.000	-99	-1	-1	0	0	0	0	.500	0	/3	-0.1
1946	Cle-A	55	89	9	16	3	0	1	4	7	18	.180	.240	.247	39	-8	-7	6	0	1	-1	.976	6	PO	-0.3
1947	Cle-A	47	56	11	18	4	3	2	5	6	9	.321	.387	.607	179	5	5	14	0	0	0	.983	4	P/O	-0.1
1948	*Cle-A☆	52	119	20	34	9	0	5	21	8	23	.286	.331	.487	119	2	2	20	0	0	0	.965	8	P	0.0
1949	Cle-A☆	46	108	17	29	6	2	7	19	10	20	.269	.331	.556	135	4	4	21	0	0	0	.963	6	P	0.0
1950	Cle-A★	72	136	21	37	9	1	6	26	13	25	.272	.340	.485	113	1	2	24	0	0	0	.957	5	P	0.0
1951	Cle-A★	56	102	11	21	4	1	3	13	9	22	.206	.270	.353	72	-5	-4	10	0	0	0	.976	4	P	0.0
1952	Cle-A★	54	124	14	28	5	0	2	9	4	21	.226	.250	.315	60	-8	-7	10	0	0	0	.982	7	P	0.0
1953	Cle-A☆	51	112	12	26	9	1	2	17	7	20	.232	.277	.384	79	-4	-4	13	2	0	1	.972	8	P	0.0
1954	*Cle-A★	40	98	11	21	4	1	2	10	6	24	.214	.260	.337	61	-5	-6	9	0	0	0	.963	4	P	0.0
1955	Cle-A	49	78	11	19	0	0	1	9	13	16	.244	.352	.282	69	-3	-3	9	0	0	0	.983	2	P	0.0
1956	Cle-A	43	93	8	18	0	0	5	12	9	21	.194	.272	.355	63	-5	-6	10	0	0	0	.934	4	P	0.0
1957	Cle-A	25	46	2	3	1	0	1	1	0	14	.065	.065	.152	-43	-9	-9	0	0	0	0	1.000	3	P	0.0
1958	Cle-A	15	13	1	3	0	0	0	1	1	4	.231	.286	.231	45	-1	-1	1	0	0	0	1.000	1	P	0.0
Total	15	615	1183	148	274	54	9	37	147	93	241	.232	.289	.386	82	-38	-35	147	2	1	0	.969	62	P/O3	-0.5
■ DON LENHARDT Lenhardt, Donald Eugene "Footsie" b: 10/4/22, Alton, Ill. BR/TR, 6′3″, 190 lbs. Deb: 4/18/50 C																									
1950	StL-A	139	480	75	131	22	6	22	81	90	94	.273	.390	.481	118	16	14	98	3	2	-0	.988	-12	1O3	-0.2
1951	StL-A	31	103	9	27	3	0	5	18	6	13	.262	.303	.437	95	-1	-1	14	1	0	0	.982	-2	O/1	-0.4
	Chi-A	64	199	23	53	9	1	10	45	24	25	.266	.351	.472	124	5	6	35	1	1	-0	.983	-2	O/1	0.2
	Yr	95	302	32	80	12	1	15	63	30	38	.265	.335	.460	114	4	4	49	2	1	0	.983	-4	O/1	-0.2
1952	Bos-A	30	105	18	31	4	0	7	24	15	18	.295	.383	.533	142	7	6	21	0	1	-1	.981	-2	O	0.3
	Det-A	45	144	18	27	2	1	3	13	28	18	.188	.320	.278	67	-6	-6	14	0	1	-1	.989	3	O	-0.5
	StL-A	18	48	5	13	4	1	1	5	4	8	.271	.327	.458	114	1	1	7	0	0	0	1.000	0	O/1	0.1
	Yr	93	297	41	71	10	2	11	42	47	44	.239	.343	.397	102	2	1	42	0	2	-1	.988	2	O/1	-0.1
1953	StL-A	97	303	37	96	15	0	10	35	41	41	.317	.400	.465	131	15	14	58	1	2	-1	.969	2	O/3	1.2
1954	Bal-A	13	33	2	5	1	0	0	1	3	9	.152	.222	.182	12	-4	-4	1	0	0	0	1.000	-1	/O1	-0.5
	Bos-A	44	66	5	18	4	0	3	17	3	9	.273	.314	.470	101	1	-0	9	0	0	0	1.000	-3	O/3	-0.4
	Yr	57	99	7	23	5	0	3	18	6	18	.232	.283	.374	74	-3	-4	10	0	0	0	1.000	-4	O/13	-0.9
Total	5	481	1481	192	401	64	9	61	239	214	235	.271	.365	.450	114	34	29	258	6	7	-2	.980	-15	O/13	-0.2
■ PATRICK LENNON Lennon, Patrick Orlando b: 4/27/68, Whiteville, N.C. BR/TR, 6′2″, 200 lbs. Deb: 9/15/91																									
1991	Sea-A	9	8	2	1	1	0	0	1	3	1	.125	.364	.250	73	-0	-0	1	0	0	0	1.000	0	/OD	0.0
1992	Sea-A	1	2	0	0	0	0	0	0	0	0	.000	.000	.000	-99	-1	-1	0	0	0	0	1.000	-0	/1	-0.1
Total	2	10	10	2	1	1	0	0	1	3	1	.100	.308	.200	44	-1	-1	1	0	0	0	.961	-0	/D1O	-0.1
■ BOB LENNON Lennon, Robert Albert "Arch" b: 9/15/28, Brooklyn, N.Y. BL/TL, 6′, 200 lbs. Deb: 9/09/54																									
1954	NY-N	3	3	0	0	0	0	0	0	0	0	.000	.000	.000	-99	-1	-1	0	0	0	0	.000	0	H	-0.1
1956	NY-N	26	55	3	10	1	0	0	1	4	17	.182	.237	.200	19	-6	-6	3	0	0	0	.885	-4	O	-1.2
1957	Chi-N	9	21	2	3	1	0	1	3	1	9	.143	.182	.333	35	-2	-2	1	0	0	0	1.000	-1	/O	-0.4
Total	3	38	79	5	13	2	0	1	4	5	26	.165	.214	.228	19	-9	-9	4	0	0	0	.900	-6	/O	-1.7
■ BILL LENNON Lennon, William F. b: 1848, Brooklyn, N.Y. 5′7″, 145 lbs. Deb: 5/04/1871 MU																									
1871	Kek-n	12	48	5	11	3	0	0	5	1	0	.229	.245	.292	52	-3	-3	4	1					CM	-0.2
1872	Nat-n	11	55	11	12	2	0	0	5	0	0	.218	.218	.255	39	-3	-5	3						C	-0.4
1873	Mar-n	5	19	2	4	1	0	0	0	0	0	.211	.211	.263	50	-1	-0	1						/1C3	0.0
Total	3 n	28	122	18	27	6	0	0	10	1		.221	.228	.270	45	-8	-9	8						/C13	-0.6
■ ED LENNOX Lennox, James Edgar "Eggie" b: 11/3/1885, Camden, N.J. d: 10/26/39, Camden, N.J. BR/TR, 5′10″, 174 lbs. Deb: 8/08/06																									
1906	Phi-A	6	17	1	1	1	0	0	0	1		.059	.111	.118	-27	-3	-3	0	0			.909	5	/3	0.3
1909	Bro-N	126	435	33	114	18	9	2	44	47		.262	.337	.359	120	8	10	56	11			**.959**	-5	*3	1.0
1910	Bro-N	110	367	19	95	19	4	3	32	36	39	.259	.333	.357	104	0	2	46	7			.950	-16	*3	-1.2
1912	Chi-N	27	81	13	19	4	1	1	16	12	10	.235	.347	.346	90	-1	-1	11	1			.934	-5	3	-0.6
1914	Pit-F	124	430	71	134	25	10	11	84	71	38	.312	.414	.493	159	34	35	100	19			.954	-15	*3	2.4

YEAR	TM/L	G	AB	R	H	2B	3B	HR	RBI	BB	SO	AVG	OBP	SLG	PRO+	BR	/A	RC	SB	CS	SBR	FA	FR	POS	TPR
1915	Pit-F	55	53	1	16	3	1	1	9	7	12	.302	.383	.453	147	3	3	10	0			1.000	2	/3	0.6
Total	6	448	1383	138	379	70	25	18	185	174	99	.274	.361	.400	126	42	46	222	38			.953	-33	3	2.5
■ **JIM LENTINE** Lentine, James Matthew b: 7/16/54, Los Angeles, Cal. BR/TR, 6', 175 lbs. Deb: 9/03/78																									
1978	StL-N	8	11	1	2	0	0	0	1	0	0	.182	.250	.182	23	-1	-1	1	1	0	0	1.000	0	/O	-0.1
1979	StL-N	11	23	2	9	1	0	0	1	3	6	.391	.462	.435	145	2	2	5	0	1	-1	1.000	1	/O	0.2
1980	StL-N	9	10	1	1	0	0	0	1	0	2	.100	.100	.100	-43	-2	-2	0	0	0	0	1.000	-0	/O	-0.2
	Det-A	67	161	19	42	8	1	1	17	28	30	.261	.377	.342	96	1	0	23	2	1	0	.963	-3	O/D	-0.4
Total	3	95	205	23	54	9	1	1	20	31	38	.263	.368	.332	92	-0	-1	28	3	2	-0	.969	-2	/OD	-0.5
■ **EDDIE LEON** Leon, Eduardo Antonio b: 8/11/46, Tucson, Ariz. BR/TR, 6', 175 lbs. Deb: 9/09/68																									
1968	Cle-A	6	1	0	0	0	0	0	0	0	1	.000	.000	.000	-99	-0	-0	0	0	0	0	1.000	3	/S	0.3
1969	Cle-A	64	213	20	51	6	0	3	19	19	37	.239	.302	.310	69	-8	-9	20	2	2	-1	.952	9	S	0.6
1970	Cle-A	152	549	58	136	20	4	10	56	47	89	.248	.309	.353	78	-14	-17	61	1	2	-1	.982	8	*2S/3	0.4
1971	Cle-A	131	429	35	112	12	2	4	35	34	69	.261	.317	.326	76	-10	-14	41	3	5	-2	.983	0	*2S	-0.5
1972	Cle-A	89	225	14	45	2	1	4	16	20	47	.200	.268	.271	59	-11	-12	15	0	2	-1	.993	-1	2S	-0.9
1973	Chi-A	127	399	37	91	10	3	3	30	34	103	.228	.294	.291	63	-18	-20	34	1	5	-3	.972	-2	*S/2	-0.9
1974	Chi-A	31	46	1	5	1	0	0	3	2	12	.109	.146	.130	-20	-7	-7	1	0	0	0	.962	8	S/23D	0.2
1975	NY-A	1	0	0	0	0	0	0	0	0	0	—	—	—	—	0	0	0	0	0	0	.000	0	/S	0.0
Total	8	601	1862	165	440	51	10	24	159	156	358	.236	.298	.313	69	-68	-79	171	7	16	-8	.963	25	S2/3D	-0.8
■ **LEONARD** Leonard Deb: 9/12/1892																									
1892	StL-N	1	0	0	0	0	0	0	0	1	0	—	1.000	—	225	0	0	1	1			.000	0	/O	0.0
■ **ANDY LEONARD** Leonard, Andrew Jackson b: 6/1/1846, County Cavan, Ireland d: 8/21/03, Boston, Mass. BR/TR, 5'7", 168 lbs. Deb: 5/05/1871																									
1871	Oly-n	31	148	33	43	8	3	0	30	3	1	.291	.305	.385	102	-1	1	22	14					*2O/S	0.0
1872	Bos-n	46	243	59	84	8	2	2	44	0	2	.346	.346	.420	128	9	6	37						*O/32	0.5
1873	Bos-n	58	302	81	95	12	6	0	58	4	0	.315	.324	.394	102	4	-2	39						*O2/13	-0.2
1874	Bos-n	71	340	68	109	18	4	0		2		.321	.325	.397	122	10	7	45						*OS/2	0.6
1875	Bos-n	80	394	87	127	14	6	1		1		.322	.324	.396	143	18	16	52						*O/S32	1.4
1876	Bos-N	64	303	53	85	10	2	0	27	4	6	.281	.290	.327	103	1	1	29				.925	-1	O2	0.0
1877	Bos-N	58	272	46	78	5	0	0	27	5	5	.287	.300	.305	88	-3	-4	25				.875	-4	OS	-0.8
1878	Bos-N	60	262	41	68	8	5	0	16	3	19	.260	.268	.328	88	-2	-4	24				.777	-7	*O	-1.3
1880	Cin-N	33	133	15	28	3	0	1	17	8	11	.211	.255	.256	75	-3	-3	9				.833	-12	S3	-1.3
Total	5 n	286	1427	328	458	60	21	3	132	10	3	.321	.326	.399	121	40	28	194						O/2S31	2.3
Total	4	215	970	155	259	26	7	1	87	20	41	.267	.282	.311	91	-6	-11	87				.856	-23	O/S23	-3.4
■ **JEFFREY LEONARD** Leonard, Jeffrey b: 9/22/55, Philadelphia, Pa. BR/TR, 6'2", 200 lbs. Deb: 9/02/77																									
1977	LA-N	11	10	1	3	0	1	0	2	1	4	.300	.364	.500	130	0	0	1	0	0	0	1.000	0	O	0.1
1978	Hou-N	8	26	2	10	2	0	0	4	1	2	.385	.407	.462	154	1	2	5	0	1	-1	1.000	1	/O	0.2
1979	Hou-N	134	411	47	119	15	5	0	47	46	68	.290	.364	.350	102	-1	2	53	23	10	1	.959	-4	*O	-0.5
1980	*Hou-N	88	216	29	46	7	5	3	20	19	46	.213	.277	.333	75	-9	-7	19	4	1	1	.979	-0	O1	-0.9
1981	Hou-N	7	18	1	3	1	1	0	3	0	4	.167	.167	.333	41	-2	-1	1	1	0	0	1.000	-0	/1O	-0.2
	SF-N	37	127	20	39	11	3	4	26	12	21	.307	.371	.535	158	9	9	23	4	2	0	1.000	3	O/1	1.1
	Yr	44	145	21	42	12	4	4	29	12	25	.290	.348	.510	145	7	8	24	5	2	0	1.000	3	O/1	0.9
1982	SF-N	80	278	32	72	16	1	9	49	19	65	.259	.311	.421	103	0	0	34	18	5	2	.958	-5	O/1	-0.4
1983	SF-N	139	516	74	144	17	7	21	87	35	116	.279	.326	.461	120	9	11	77	26	7	4	.975	6	*O	1.7
1984	SF-N	136	514	76	155	27	2	21	86	47	123	.302	.360	.484	140	23	25	87	17	7	1	.970	6	*O	2.9
1985	SF-N	133	507	49	122	20	3	17	62	21	107	.241	.272	.393	88	-13	-10	47	11	6	-0	.977	3	*O	-1.3
1986	SF-N	89	341	48	95	11	3	6	42	20	62	.279	.324	.381	99	-3	-1	44	16	3	3	.970	3	O	0.2
1987	*SF-N★	131	503	70	141	29	4	19	63	21	68	.280	.312	.467	108	0	3	66	16	7	1	.966	-4	*O	-0.4
1988	SF-N	44	160	12	41	8	1	2	20	9	24	.256	.296	.356	90	-3	-2	15	7	5	-1	.987	-3	O	-0.8
	Mil-A	94	374	45	88	19	0	8	44	16	68	.235	.272	.350	72	-14	-15	34	10	4	1	.985	3	O/D	-1.4
1989	Sea-A★	150	566	69	144	20	1	24	93	38	125	.254	.307	.420	100	1	-2	72	6	1	1	.982	2	*DO	0.0
1990	Sea-A	134	478	39	120	20	0	10	75	37	97	.251	.309	.356	84	-10	-10	49	4	2	0	.983	-8	OD	-2.0
Total	14	1415	5045	614	1342	223	37	144	723	342	1000	.266	.316	.411	103	-11	4	627	163	61	12	.974	4	*OD/1	-1.7
■ **JOE LEONARD** Leonard, Joseph Howard b: 11/15/1894, W.Chicago, Ill. d: 5/1/20, Washington, D.C. BL/TR, 5'7.5", 156 lbs. Deb: 5/07/14																									
1914	Pit-N	53	126	17	25	2	2	0	4	12	21	.198	.268	.246	56	-7	-7	10	4			.909	-8	3/S	-1.5
1916	Cle-A	3	2	1	0	0	0	0	0	0	1	.000	.000	.000	-94	-0	-0	0	0			1.000	0	/2	0.0
	Was-A	42	168	20	46	7	0	0	14	22	23	.274	.358	.315	103	1	1	20	4			.952	-8	3	-0.5
	Yr	45	170	21	46	7	0	0	14	22	24	.271	.354	.312	101	1	1	20	4			.952	-7	3/2	-0.5
1917	Was-A	99	297	30	57	6	7	0	23	45	40	.192	.302	.259	72	-9	-9	25	6			.925	-2	31/SO	-1.2
1919	Was-A	71	198	26	51	8	3	2	20	20	28	.258	.329	.359	94	-2	-2	23	3			.944	-9	23/1O	-1.0
1920	Was-A	1	0	0	0	0	0	0	0	0	0	—	—	—	—	0	0	0	0	0	0	.000	0	R	0.0
Total	5	269	791	94	179	23	12	2	61	99	113	.226	.315	.293	82	-17	-16	78	17	0		.937	-27	3/21OS	-4.2
■ **MARK LEONARD** Leonard, Mark David b: 8/14/64, Mountain View, Cal. BL/TR, 6'1", 195 lbs. Deb: 7/21/90																									
1990	SF-N	11	17	3	3	1	0	1	2	3	8	.176	.300	.412	97	-0	-0	2	0	0	0	1.000	-1	/O	-0.1
1991	SF-N	64	129	14	31	7	1	2	14	12	25	.240	.310	.357	90	-2	-2	14	0	1	-1	1.000	-6	O	-0.9
1992	SF-N	55	128	13	30	7	0	4	16	16	31	.234	.333	.383	108	1	1	17	0	1	-1	.984	0	O	0.0
Total	3	130	274	30	64	15	1	7	32	31	64	.234	.320	.372	99	-2	-0	33	0	2	-1	.991	-7	/O	-1.0
■ **JOHN LEOVICH** Leovich, John Joseph b: 5/5/18, Portland, Ore. BR/TR, 6'0.5", 200 lbs. Deb: 5/01/41																									
1941	Phi-A	1	2	0	1	1	0	0	0	0	0	.500	.500	1.000	296	0	1	0	0	0	0	.000	-0	/C	0.0
■ **TED LEPCIO** Lepcio, Thaddeus Stanley b: 7/28/30, Utica, N.Y. BR/TR, 5'10", 177 lbs. Deb: 4/15/52																									
1952	Bos-A	84	274	34	72	17	2	5	26	24	41	.263	.329	.394	93	-0	-3	37	3	3	-1	.972	8	23/S	0.6
1953	Bos-A	66	161	17	38	4	2	4	11	17	24	.236	.313	.360	77	-4	-6	18	0	0	0	.981	17	2S3	1.3
1954	Bos-A	116	398	42	102	19	4	8	45	42	62	.256	.332	.384	86	-3	-8	51	3	4	-2	.971	16	23S	1.2
1955	Bos-A	51	134	19	31	9	0	6	15	12	36	.231	.313	.433	91	-1	-2	18	1	1	-0	.943	6	3	0.3
1956	Bos-A	83	284	34	74	10	0	15	51	30	77	.261	.338	.454	96	2	-3	44	1	3	-2	.966	7	23	0.8
1957	Bos-A	79	232	24	56	10	2	9	37	29	61	.241	.328	.418	97	1	-1	32	0	0	0	.976	9	2	1.3
1958	Bos-A	50	136	10	27	3	0	6	14	12	47	.199	.268	.353	65	-6	-7	13	0	1	-1	.980	-3	2	-0.8
1959	Bos-A	3	3	1	1	1	0	0	1	0	2	.333	.333	.667	160	0	0	1	0	0	0	1.000	0	/2	0.0
	Det-A	76	215	25	60	8	0	7	24	17	49	.279	.332	.414	98	1	-1	28	2	0	1	.951	-6	S23	-0.2
	Yr	79	218	26	61	9	0	7	25	17	51	.280	.332	.417	99	1	-1	29	2	0	1	.951	-6	S23	-0.2
1960	Phi-N	69	141	16	32	7	0	2	8	17	41	.227	.319	.319	75	-4	-4	14	0	3	-2	.942	-5	3S/2	-1.1
1961	Chi-A	5	2	0	0	0	0	0	0	1	0	.000	.333	.000	-2	-0	-0	0	0	0	0	.000	0	/3	0.0
	Min-A	47	112	11	19	3	1	7	19	8	31	.170	.231	.402	62	-6	-7	10	1	0	0	.919	2	32/S	-0.3
	Yr	52	114	11	19	3	1	7	19	9	31	.167	.234	.395	62	-7	-7	10	1	0	0	.895	2	32/S	-0.3
Total	10	729	2092	233	512	91	11	69	251	209	471	.245	.319	.398	87	-22	-42	266	11	15	-6	.972	52	23/S	3.1
■ **PETE LePINE** LePine, Louis Joseph b: 9/5/1876, Montreal, Que., Can d: 12/3/49, Woonsocket, R.I. BL/TL, Deb: 7/21/02																									
1902	Det-A	30	96	8	20	3	2	1	19	8		.208	.276	.313	62	-5	-5	9	1			1.000	-2	O/1	-0.8

YEAR	TM/L	G	AB	R	H	2B	3B	HR	RBI	BB	SO	AVG	OBP	SLG	PRO+	BR	/A	RC	SB	CS	SBR	FA	FR	POS	TPR

■ DON LEPPERT — Leppert, Don Eugene "Tiger" b: 11/20/30, Memphis, Tenn. BL/TR, 5'8", 175 lbs. Deb: 4/11/55

| 1955 | Bal-A | 40 | 70 | 6 | 8 | 0 | 1 | 0 | 2 | 9 | 10 | .114 | .215 | .143 | -2 | -10 | -9 | 2 | 1 | 1 | -0 | .937 | -7 | 2 | -1.6 |

■ DON LEPPERT — Leppert, Donald George b: 10/19/31, Indianapolis, Ind. BR/TR, 6'2", 220 lbs. Deb: 6/18/61 C

1961	Pit-N	22	60	6	16	2	1	3	5	1	11	.267	.279	.483	97	-1	-1	5	0	0	0	.968	1	C	0.1
1962	Pit-N	45	139	14	37	6	1	3	18	12	21	.266	.329	.388	92	-2	-2	16	0	1	-1	.989	4	C	0.3
1963	Was-A☆	73	211	20	50	11	0	6	24	20	29	.237	.306	.374	90	-3	-3	23	0	0	0	.984	-8	C	-0.9
1964	Was-A	50	122	6	19	3	0	3	12	11	32	.156	.226	.254	33	-11	-11	7	0	0	0	.990	1	C	-0.9
Total	4	190	532	46	122	22	2	15	59	44	93	.229	.291	.363	78	-16	-16	51	0	1	-1	.969	-2	C	-1.4

■ DUTCH LERCHEN — Lerchen, Bertram Roe b: 4/4/1889, Detroit, Mich. d: 1/7/62, Detroit, Mich. BR/TR, 5'8", 160 lbs. Deb: 8/14/10 F

| 1910 | Bos-A | 6 | 15 | 1 | 0 | 0 | 0 | 0 | 0 | 1 | | .000 | .063 | .000 | -78 | -3 | -3 | 0 | 0 | | | .929 | -3 | /S | -0.8 |

■ GEORGE LERCHEN — Lerchen, George Edward b: 12/1/22, Detroit, Mich. BB/TR, 5'11", 175 lbs. Deb: 4/15/52 F

1952	Det-A	14	32	1	5	1	0	1	3	7	10	.156	.308	.281	64	-1	-1	3	1	0	0	1.000	-0	/O	-0.2
1953	Cin-N	22	17	2	5	1	0	0	2	5	6	.294	.455	.353	113	1	1	3	0	0	0	1.000	-0	/O	0.0
Total	2	36	49	3	10	2	0	1	5	12	16	.204	.361	.306	82	-1	-1	7	1	0	0	1.000	-1	/O	-0.2

■ WALT LERIAN — Lerian, Walter Irvin "Peck" b: 2/10/03, Baltimore, Md. d: 10/22/29, Baltimore, Md. BR/TR, 5'11", 170 lbs. Deb: 4/16/28

1928	Phi-N	96	239	28	65	16	2	2	25	41	29	.272	.385	.381	97	2	1	37	1			.977	-3	C	0.4
1929	Phi-N	105	273	28	61	13	2	6	25	53	37	.223	.354	.352	71	-10	-13	36	0			.986	1	*C	-0.3
Total	2	201	512	56	126	29	4	8	50	94	66	.246	.368	.365	83	-8	-12	73	1			.982	-1	C	0.1

■ ROY LESLIE — Leslie, Roy Reid b: 8/23/1894, Bailey, Tex. d: 4/9/72, Sherman, Tex. BR/TR, 6'1", 175 lbs. Deb: 9/06/17

1917	Chi-N	7	19	1	4	0	0	0	1	1	5	.211	.250	.211	39	-1	-1	1	1			.969	-0	/1	-0.2
1919	StL-N	12	24	2	5	1	0	0	4	4	3	.208	.321	.250	78	-1	-0	2	0			.957	-0	/1	-0.1
1922	Phi-N	141	513	44	139	23	2	6	50	37	49	.271	.320	.359	68	-20	-26	58	3	7	-3	.990	-4	*1	-3.8
Total	3	160	556	47	148	24	2	6	55	42	57	.266	.318	.349	68	-21	-28	61	4	7		.988	-4	1	-4.1

■ SAM LESLIE — Leslie, Samuel Andrew "Sambo" b: 7/26/05, Moss Point, Miss. d: 1/21/79, Pascagoula, Miss. BL/TL, 6', 192 lbs. Deb: 10/06/29

1929	NY-N	1	1	0	0	0	0	0	1	0	0	.000	.000	.000	-99	-0	-0	0	0			1.000	-0	/O	-0.1
1930	NY-N	2	2	0	1	0	0	0	0	0	1	.500	.500	.500	146	0	-0	0	0			.000	0	H	0.0
1931	NY-N	53	53	11	16	4	0	3	5	1	2	.302	.315	.547	131	2	2	9	3			1.000	-0	/1	0.2
1932	NY-N	77	75	5	22	4	0	1	15	2	5	.293	.329	.387	94	-1	-1	10	1			1.000	-0	/1	-0.1
1933	NY-N	40	137	21	44	12	3	3	27	12	9	.321	.380	.518	157	9	10	27	0			.990	-1	1	0.7
	Bro-N	96	364	41	104	11	4	5	46	23	14	.286	.340	.379	110	3	4	45	1			.982	-6	1	-1.2
	Yr	136	501	62	148	23	7	8	73	35	23	.295	.351	.417	123	12	14	71	1			.984	-6	*1	-0.5
1934	Bro-N	146	546	75	181	29	6	9	102	69	34	.332	.409	.456	138	27	31	108	5			.993	5	*1	2.3
1935	Bro-N	142	520	72	160	30	7	5	93	55	19	.308	.379	.421	117	12	14	87	4			.989	-0	*1	-0.1
1936	*NY-N	117	417	49	123	19	5	6	54	23	16	.295	.335	.408	100	-1	-1	55	0			.991	0	1	-1.0
1937	*NY-N	72	191	25	59	7	2	3	30	20	12	.309	.380	.414	114	5	4	30	1			.990	3	1	0.2
1938	NY-N	76	154	12	39	7	1	1	16	11	6	.253	.307	.331	75	-5	-5	16	0			.988	-3	1	-1.1
Total	10	822	2460	311	749	123	28	36	389	216	118	.304	.366	.421	117	50	58	385	14			.989	-2	1/O	-0.2

■ CHARLIE LETCHAS — Letchas, Charlie b: 10/3/15, Thomasville, Ga. BR/TR, 5'10", 150 lbs. Deb: 9/16/39

1939	Phi-N	12	44	2	10	2	0	1	3	1	2	.227	.244	.341	57	-3	-3	3	0			.933	-1	2	-0.3
1941	Was-A	2	8	0	1	0	0	0	1	1	1	.125	.222	.125	-6	-1	-1	0	0	0	0	.800	-1	/2	-0.2
1944	Phi-N	116	396	29	94	8	0	0	33	30	27	.237	.298	.258	59	-22	-20	30	0			.968	6	23S	-0.9
1946	Phi-N	6	13	1	3	0	0	0	0	1	1	.231	.286	.231	49	-1	-1	1	0			1.000	1	/2	0.0
Total	4	136	461	32	108	10	0	1	37	35	31	.234	.291	.262	58	-27	-25	35	0	0		.959	5	/23S	-1.4

■ TOM LETCHER — Letcher, Thomas F. b: 1868, Grand Rapids, Mich. Deb: 9/27/1891

| 1891 | Mil-a | 6 | 21 | 3 | 4 | 1 | 0 | 0 | 0 | 2 | 0 | .190 | .190 | .238 | 20 | -2 | -3 | 1 | 1 | | | .857 | 0 | /O | -0.2 |

■ LEUTZ — Leutz Deb: 5/07/1872

| 1872 | Eck-n | 4 | 13 | 2 | 1 | 0 | 0 | 0 | 0 | 0 | 0 | .077 | .077 | .077 | -62 | -2 | -2 | 0 | | | | | | /C | -0.1 |

■ JESSE LEVAN — Levan, Jesse Roy b: 7/15/26, Reading, Pa. BL/TR, 6', 172 lbs. Deb: 9/27/47

1947	Phi-N	2	9	3	4	0	0	0	1	0	0	.444	.444	.444	142	0	1	2	0			1.000	-1	/O	0.0
1954	Was-A	7	10	1	3	0	0	0	0	0	0	.300	.300	.300	68	-0	-0	1	0	0	0	.000	-0	/31	-0.1
1955	Was-A	16	16	1	3	0	0	1	4	0	2	.188	.188	.375	51	-1	-1	1	0	0	0	.000	0	H	-0.1
Total	3	25	35	5	10	0	0	1	5	0	2	.286	.286	.371	80	-1	-1	3	0	0		.917	-1	/3O1	-0.2

■ JIM LEVEY — Levey, James Julius b: 9/13/06, Pittsburgh, Pa. d: 3/14/70, Dallas, Tex. BB/TR, 5'10.5", 154 lbs. Deb: 9/17/30

1930	StL-A	8	37	7	9	2	0	0	3	3	2	.243	.300	.297	50	-3	-3	3	0	0	0	.958	2	/S	0.0
1931	StL-A	139	498	53	104	19	2	5	38	35	83	.209	.264	.285	43	-41	-44	38	13	8	-1	.920	-10	*S	-3.9
1932	StL-A	152	568	59	159	30	8	4	63	21	48	.280	.310	.382	74	-19	-24	66	6	4	-1	.939	-18	*S	-2.8
1933	StL-A	141	529	43	103	10	4	2	36	26	68	.195	.237	.240	25	-56	-61	30	4	6	-2	.945	-6	*S	-5.7
Total	4	440	1632	162	375	61	14	11	140	85	201	.230	.272	.305	48	-119	-131	138	23	18	-4	.936	-33	S	-12.4

■ CHARLIE LEVIS — Levis, Charles H. b: 6/21/1860, St.Louis, Mo. d: 10/16/26, St.Louis, Mo. Deb: 4/17/1884

1884	Bal-U	87	373	59	85	11	4	6			3	.228	.234	.327	80	-5	-11	29				.955	-0	*1	-1.9
	Was-U	1	3	0	0	0	0	0			0	.000	.000	.000	-99	-1	-1	0				1.000	0	/1	-0.1
	Yr	88	376	59	85	11	4	6			3	.226	.232	.324	78	-6	-12	29				.955	-0	1	-2.0
	Ind-a	3	10	0	2	0	0	0			0	.200	.200	.200	34	-1	-1	0				1.000	-0	/1	-0.1
1885	Bal-a	1	4	2	1	0	0	0			0	.250	.400	.250	114	0	0	0				.889	-0	/1	0.0
Total	2	92	390	61	88	11	4	6			3	.226	.234	.321	78	-6	-12	30				.956	-0	1	-2.1

■ JESSE LEVIS — Levis, Jesse b: 4/14/68, Philadelphia, Pa. BL/TR, 5'9", 180 lbs. Deb: 4/24/92

| 1992 | Cle-A | 28 | 43 | 2 | 12 | 4 | 0 | 1 | 3 | 0 | 5 | .279 | .279 | .442 | 98 | -0 | -0 | 5 | 0 | 0 | 0 | .985 | 1 | C/D | 0.1 |

■ ED LEVY — Levy, Edward Clarence (b: Edward Clarence Whitner) b: 10/28/16, Birmingham, Ala. BR/TR, 6'5.5", 190 lbs. Deb: 4/16/40

1940	Phi-N	1	1	0	0	0	0	0	0	0	0	.000	.000	.000	-99	-0	-0	0				.000	0	H	0.0
1942	NY-A	13	41	5	5	0	0	0	3	4	5	.122	.200	.122	-9	-6	-6	1	1	0	0	.992	2	1	-0.5
1944	NY-A	40	153	12	37	11	2	4	29	6	19	.242	.270	.418	92	-2	-3	17	1	1	-0	.962	-1	O	-0.6
Total	3	54	195	17	42	11	2	4	32	10	24	.215	.254	.354	70	-8	-9	18	2	1		.951	0	/O1	-1.1

■ LEWIS — Lewis b: Brooklyn, N.Y. Deb: 7/12/1890

| 1890 | Buf-P | 1 | 5 | 1 | 1 | 0 | 0 | 0 | 0 | 0 | 0 | .200 | .200 | .200 | 9 | -1 | -1 | 0 | 0 | | | .000 | 0 | /OP | -0.1 |

■ ALLAN LEWIS — Lewis, Allan Sydney "The Panamanian Express" b: 12/12/41, Colon, Panama BB/TR, 6', 170 lbs. Deb: 4/11/67

1967	KC-A	34	6	7	1	0	0	0	0	0	3	.167	.167	.167	-1	-1	-1	-6	14	5	1	.000	0	H	0.1
1968	Oak-A	26	4	9	1	0	0	0	0	1	0	.250	.400	.250	105	-0	-0	0	13	1	1	.000	-0	/O	0.0
1969	Oak-A	12	1	2	0	0	0	0	0	0	0	.000	.000	.000	-99	-0	-0	0	0	0	0	.000	0	H	0.0
1970	Oak-A	25	8	8	2	0	0	0	0	0	1	.250	.250	.625	139	-0	0	1	7	1	2	1.000	-0	/O	0.2
1972	*Oak-A	24	10	5	2	1	0	0	2	0	1	.200	.200	.300	50	-1	-1	-1	8	3	1	.900	-1	/O	-0.1

YEAR	TM/L	G	AB	R	H	2B	3B	HR	RBI	BB	SO	AVG	OBP	SLG	PRO+	BR	/A	RC	SB	CS	SBR	FA	FR	POS	TPR
1973	*Oak-A	35	0	16	0	0	0	0	0	0	0	—	—	—	—	0	0	0	7	4	-0	1.000	-0	/OD	0.0
Total	6	156	29	47	6	1	0	1	3	1	4	.207	.233	.345	69	-1	-1	-7	44	17	3	.923	-2	/OD	0.2

■ DARREN LEWIS Lewis, Darren Joel b: 8/28/67, Berkeley, Cal. BR/TR, 6', 180 lbs. Deb: 8/21/90

1990	Oak-A	25	35	4	8	0	0	0	1	7	4	.229	.372	.229	75	-1	-1	4	2	0	1	1.000	-5	O/D	-0.5
1991	SF-N	72	222	41	55	5	3	1	15	36	30	.248	.358	.311	93	-2	-1	28	13	7	-0	1.000	3	O	0.1
1992	SF-N	100	320	38	74	8	1	1	18	29	46	.231	.297	.272	66	-15	-13	30	28	8	4	1.000	0	O	-1.3
Total	3	197	577	83	137	13	4	2	34	72	80	.237	.326	.284	77	-18	-15	62	43	15	4	1.000	-1	O/D	-1.7

■ FRED LEWIS Lewis, Frederick Miller b: 10/13/1858, Buffalo, N.Y. d: 6/5/45, Utica, N.Y. BB/TR, 5'10.5", 194 lbs. Deb: 7/02/1881

1881	Bos-N	27	114	17	25	6	0	0	9	7	5	.219	.264	.272	72	-4	-3	8				.837	-2	O	-0.5
1883	Phi-N	38	160	21	40	7	0	0	18	4	13	.250	.268	.294	78	-5	-3	13				.814	1	O	-0.2
	StL-a	49	209	37	63	8	4	1		1		.301	.305	.392	116	5	3	26				.848	-0	O	0.2
1884	StL-a	73	300	59	97	25	3	0		16		.323	.366	.427	156	20	18	48				.853	3	O	1.7
	StL-U	8	30	6	9	1	0	0		3		.300	.364	.333	132	1	1	4				.909	-2	/O	0.0
1885	StL-N	45	181	12	53	9	0	1	27	9	10	.293	.326	.359	130	4	6	22				.957	7	O	1.1
1886	Cin-a	77	324	72	103	14	6	2		20		.318	.365	.417	142	17	15	53	8			.884	-2	O/3	1.0
Total	5	317	1318	224	390	70	13	4	54	60	28	.296	.330	.378	126	37	37	174	8			.866	4	O/3	3.3

■ DUFFY LEWIS Lewis, George Edward b: 4/18/1888, San Francisco, Cal d: 6/17/79, Salem, N.H. BL/TL, 5'10.5", 165 lbs. Deb: 4/16/10 C

1910	Bos-A	151	541	64	153	29	7	8	68	32		.283	.328	.407	127	16	14	76	10			.944	10	*O	1.9
1911	Bos-A	130	469	64	144	32	4	7	86	25		.307	.355	.437	122	11	12	77	11			.939	5	*O	1.0
1912	*Bos-A	154	581	85	165	36	9	6	109	52		.284	.346	.408	110	10	6	86	9			.947	7	*O	0.5
1913	Bos-A	149	551	54	164	31	12	0	90	30	55	.298	.336	.397	112	8	6	77	12			.960	11	*O/P3	1.2
1914	Bos-A	146	510	53	142	37	9	2	79	57	41	.278	.357	.398	127	16	16	70	22	31	-12	.952	-2	*O	-0.4
1915	*Bos-A	152	557	69	162	31	7	2	76	45	63	.291	.348	.382	122	11	13	80	14	7	0	.952	-7	*O	-0.1
1916	*Bos-A	152	563	56	151	29	5	1	56	33	56	.268	.313	.343	97	-4	-4	68	16			.970	-1	*O	-1.4
1917	Bos-A	150	553	55	167	29	9	1	65	29	54	.302	.342	.392	125	14	14	77	8			.972	4	*O	1.1
1919	NY-A	141	559	67	152	23	4	7	89	17	42	.272	.293	.365	84	-14	-15	61	8			.985	-6	*O	-3.2
1920	NY-A	107	365	34	99	8	1	4	61	24	32	.271	.320	.332	70	-14	-16	38	2	8	-4	.961	-2	O	-2.9
1921	Was-A	27	102	11	19	4	1	0	14	8	10	.186	.252	.245	29	-11	-11	7	1	1	-0	.980	-2	O	-1.5
Total	11	1459	5351	612	1518	289	68	38	793	352	353	.284	.333	.384	108	42	36	716	113	47		.959	16	*O/3P	-3.8

■ JACK LEWIS Lewis, John David b: 2/12/1884, Pittsburgh, Pa. d: 2/25/56, Steubenville, Ohio BR/TR, 5'8", 158 lbs. Deb: 9/16/11

1911	Bos-A	18	59	7	16	0	0	0	6	7		.271	.368	.271	80	-1	-1	7	2			.931	-2	2	-0.3
1914	Pit-F	117	394	32	92	14	5	1	48	17	46	.234	.276	.302	65	-19	-19	39	9			.949	9	*2/S	-1.0
1915	Pit-F	82	231	24	61	6	5	0	26	8	31	.264	.292	.333	84	-5	-5	26	7			.962	-2	2S/O13	-0.7
Total	3	217	684	63	169	20	10	1	80	32	77	.247	.290	.310	73	-26	-25	72	18			.951	5	2/SO13	-2.0

■ BUDDY LEWIS Lewis, John Kelly b: 8/10/16, Gastonia, N.C. BL/TR, 6'1", 175 lbs. Deb: 9/16/35

1935	Was-A	8	28	0	3	0	0	0	2	0	5	.107	.107	.107	-46	-6	-6	0	0	0	0	.941	-0	/3	-0.6
1936	Was-A	143	601	100	175	21	13	6	67	47	46	.291	.347	.399	89	-16	-11	83	6	6	-2	.933	5	*3	-0.2
1937	Was-A	156	668	107	210	32	6	10	79	52	44	.314	.367	.425	104	-1	3	105	11	5	0	.938	-19	*3	-1.0
1938	Was-A★	151	656	122	194	35	9	12	91	58	35	.296	.354	.431	103	-6	1	101	17	9	-0	.912	-0	*3	0.3
1939	Was-A	140	536	87	171	23	**16**	10	75	72	27	.319	.402	.478	134	20	27	106	10	9	-2	.933	14	*3	3.6
1940	Was-A	148	600	101	190	38	10	6	63	74	36	.317	.393	.443	124	16	22	109	15	10	-2	.960	-1	*O3	1.4
1941	Was-A	149	569	97	169	29	11	9	72	82	30	.297	.386	.434	122	15	19	99	10	7	-1	.972	3	O3	1.5
1945	Was-A	69	258	42	86	14	7	2	37	37	15	.333	.423	.465	172	20	23	54	1	2	-1	.981	4	O	2.3
1946	Was-A	150	582	82	170	28	13	7	45	59	26	.292	.359	.421	125	13	17	92	5	3	-0	.970	4	*O	1.5
1947	Was-A★	140	506	67	132	15	4	6	48	51	27	.261	.330	.342	89	-9	-7	56	6	6	-2	.968	1	*O	-1.5
1949	Was-A	95	257	25	63	14	4	3	28	41	12	.245	.355	.366	93	-3	-2	36	2	2	-1	.979	-0	O	-0.6
Total	11	1349	5261	830	1563	249	93	71	607	573	303	.297	.368	.420	112	44	85	841	83	59	-11	.927	11	3O	6.7

■ JOHNNY LEWIS Lewis, Johnny Joe b: 8/10/39, Greenville, Ala. BL/TR, 6'1", 189 lbs. Deb: 4/14/64 C

1964	StL-N	40	94	10	22	2	2	2	7	13	23	.234	.327	.362	86	-1	-2	11	2	2	-1	.966	2	O	-0.1
1965	NY-N	148	477	64	117	15	3	15	45	59	117	.245	.332	.384	105	1	3	61	4	7	-3	.975	-6	*O	-1.2
1966	NY-N	65	166	21	32	6	1	5	20	21	43	.193	.283	.331	72	-7	-6	17	2	0	1	.988	-2	O	-1.0
1967	NY-N	13	34	2	4	1	0	0	2	2	11	.118	.167	.147	-10	-5	-5	1	0	0	0	1.000	0	O	-0.5
Total	4	266	771	97	175	24	6	22	74	95	194	.227	.314	.359	90	-11	-9	91	8	9	-3	.977	-5	O	-2.8

■ MARK LEWIS Lewis, Mark David b: 11/30/69, Hamilton, Ohio BR/TR, 6'1", 190 lbs. Deb: 4/26/91

1991	Cle-A	84	314	29	83	15	1	0	30	15	45	.264	.298	.318	70	-13	-13	27	2	2	-1	.966	-14	2S	-2.4
1992	Cle-A	122	413	44	109	21	0	5	30	25	69	.264	.311	.351	84	-9	-9	42	4	5	-2	.954	-10	*S/3	-1.2
Total	2	206	727	73	192	36	1	5	60	40	114	.264	.305	.337	78	-21	-22	69	6	7	-2	.962	-24	S/23	-3.6

■ PHIL LEWIS Lewis, Philip b: 10/7/1883, Pittsburgh, Pa. d: 8/8/59, Port Wentworth, Ga. BR/TR, 6', 195 lbs. Deb: 4/14/05

1905	Bro-N	118	433	32	110	9	2	3	33	16		.254	.282	.305	81	-14	-10	44	16			.904	-6	*S	-1.5
1906	Bro-N	136	452	40	110	8	4	0	37	43		.243	.309	.279	91	-8	-4	47	14			.922	-22	*S	-2.5
1907	Bro-N	136	475	52	118	11	1	0	30	23		.248	.286	.276	83	-14	-9	45	16			.938	-20	*S	-3.0
1908	Bro-N	118	415	22	91	5	6	1	30	13		.219	.243	.267	66	-18	-17	29	9			.943	-7	*S	-2.5
Total	4	508	1775	146	429	33	13	4	130	95		.242	.281	.282	81	-54	-40	166	55			.926	-55	S	-9.5

■ BILL LEWIS Lewis, William Henry "Buddy" b: 10/15/04, Ripley, Tenn. d: 10/24/77, Memphis, Tenn. BR/TR, 5'9", 165 lbs. Deb: 6/03/33

1933	StL-N	15	35	8	14	1	0	1	8	2	3	.400	.432	.514	161	3	3	8	0			1.000	1	/C	0.4
1935	Bos-N	6	4	1	0	0	0	0	0	1	1	.000	.200	.000	-45	-1	-1	0	0			.000	0	/C	-0.1
1936	Bos-N	29	62	11	19	2	0	0	3	12	7	.306	.419	.339	113	1	2	10	0			.967	-4	C	-0.1
Total	3	50	101	20	33	3	0	1	11	15	11	.327	.414	.386	124	4	4	19	0			.981	-3	/C	0.2

■ JIM LEYRITZ Leyritz, James Joseph b: 12/27/63, Lakewood, Ohio BR/TR, 6', 190 lbs. Deb: 6/08/90

1990	NY-A	92	303	28	78	13	1	5	25	27	51	.257	.332	.356	92	-3	-3	34	2	3	-1	.929	-19	3OC	-2.3
1991	NY-A	32	77	8	14	3	0	0	4	13	15	.182	.300	.221	46	-5	-5	6	0	1	-1	.909	-8	3/C1D	-1.4
1992	NY-A	63	144	17	37	6	0	7	26	14	22	.257	.348	.444	118	4	4	23	0	1	-1	.990	3	DC/1302	0.7
Total	3	187	524	53	129	22	1	12	55	54	88	.246	.332	.361	93	-4	-4	63	2	5	-2	.927	-24	/3CD012	-3.0

■ CARLOS LEZCANO Lezcano, Carlos Manuel (Rubio) b: 9/30/55, Arecibo, P.R. BR/TR, 6'2", 185 lbs. Deb: 4/10/80

1980	Chi-N	42	88	15	18	4	1	3	12	11	29	.205	.300	.375	81	-2	-2	9	1	2	-1	.948	4	O	0.0
1981	Chi-N	7	14	1	1	0	0	0	2	0	4	.071	.071	.071	-57	-3	-3	0	0	0	0	1.000	0	/O	-0.3
Total	2	49	102	16	19	4	1	3	14	11	33	.186	.272	.333	64	-4	-5	9	1	2	-1	.952	4	/O	-0.3

■ SIXTO LEZCANO Lezcano, Sixto Joaquin (Curras) b: 11/28/53, Arecibo, P.R. BR/TR, 5'11", 175 lbs. Deb: 9/10/74

1974	Mil-A	15	54	5	13	2	0	2	9	4	9	.241	.293	.389	95	-1	-0	6	1	1	-0	.972	2	O	0.1
1975	Mil-A	134	429	55	106	19	3	11	43	46	93	.247	.326	.382	99	-0	-1	51	5	5	-2	.977	-3	*O/D	-1.0
1976	Mil-A	145	513	53	146	19	5	7	56	51	112	.285	.352	.382	117	10	11	70	14	10	-2	.973	8	*O/D	1.2
1977	Mil-A	109	400	50	109	21	4	21	49	52	78	.273	.359	.503	132	17	18	72	6	5	-1	.988	13	*O	2.4
1978	Mil-A	132	442	62	129	21	4	15	61	64	83	.292	.383	.459	135	22	22	81	3	3	-1	.979	10	*O/D	2.6
1979	Mil-A	138	473	84	152	29	3	28	101	77	74	.321	.420	.573	165	45	45	115	4	3	-1	.986	4	*O	4.0

YEAR	TM/L	G	AB	R	H	2B	3B	HR	RBI	BB	SO	AVG	OBP	SLG	PRO+	BR	/A	RC	SB	CS	SBR	FA	FR	POS	TPR
1980	Mil-A	112	411	51	94	19	3	18	55	39	75	.229	.300	.421	98	-4	-2	53	1	1	-0	.983	6	*O/D	-0.1
1981	StL-N	72	214	26	57	8	2	5	28	40	40	.266	.382	.393	117	7	6	33	0	1	-1	.973	-7	O	-0.4
1982	SD-N	138	470	73	136	26	6	16	84	78	69	.289	.393	.472	149	28	31	90	2	1	0	.990	10	*O	3.9
1983	SD-N	97	317	41	74	11	2	8	49	47	66	.233	.334	.356	95	-3	-2	39	0	0	0	.968	1	O	-0.4
	*Phi-N	18	39	8	11	1	0	0	7	5	9	.282	.364	.308	89	-0	-0	5	1	0	0	1.000	1	O	0.0
	Yr	115	356	49	85	12	2	8	56	52	75	.239	.337	.351	94	-3	-2	45	1	0	0	.971	2	*O	-0.4
1984	Phi-N	109	256	36	71	6	2	14	40	38	43	.277	.371	.480	135	13	13	44	0	1	-1	.981	-1	O	0.9
1985	Pit-N	72	116	16	24	2	0	3	9	35	17	.207	.395	.302	98	2	2	16	0	0	0	.967	-2	O	-0.1
Total	12	1291	4134	560	1122	184	34	148	591	576	768	.271	.363	.440	125	136	142	675	37	31	-8	.980	40	*O/D	13.1

■ STEVE LIBBY Libby, Stephen Augustus b: 12/8/1853, Scarborough, Me. d: 3/31/35, Milford, Conn. 6′1.5″, 168 lbs. Deb: 5/10/1879

1879	Buf-N	1	2	0	0	0	0	0	0	0	1	.000	.000	.000	-98	-0	-0	0				1.000	0	/1	0.0

■ AL LIBKE Libke, Albert Walter b: 9/12/18, Tacoma, Wash. BL/TR, 6′4″, 215 lbs. Deb: 4/19/45

1945	Cin-N	130	449	41	127	23	5	4	53	34	62	.283	.336	.383	102	-1	0	59	6			.963	2	*O/P1	-0.4
1946	Cin-N	124	431	32	109	22	1	5	42	43	50	.253	.322	.343	92	-7	-5	46	0			.972	-5	*O/P	-1.6
Total	2	254	880	73	236	45	6	9	95	77	112	.268	.329	.364	97	-7	-4	105	6			.967	-3	O/P1	-2.0

■ FRANKIE LIBRAN Libran, Francisco (Rosas) b: 5/6/48, Mayaguez, P.R. BR/TR, 6′, 168 lbs. Deb: 9/03/69

1969	SD-N	10	10	1	1	1	0	0	1	1	2	.100	.182	.200	7	-1	-1	0	0	0	0	1.000	1	/S	0.0

■ JOHN LICKERT Lickert, John Wilbur b: 4/4/60, Pittsburgh, Pa. BR/TR, 5′11″, 175 lbs. Deb: 9/19/81

1981	Bos-A	1	0	0	0	0	0	0	0	0	0	—	—	—	—	0	0	0	0	0	0	1.000	-0	/C	0.0

■ DAVE LIDDELL Liddell, David Alexander (b: b: 6/15/66, Los Angeles, Cal. BR/TR, 6′, 190 lbs. Deb: 6/03/90

1990	NY-N	1	1	1	1	0	0	0	0	0	0	1.000	1.000	1.000	453	0	0	1	0	0	0	1.000	-0	/C	0.0

■ FRED LIESE Liese, Frederick Richard b: 10/7/1885, Wisconsin d: 6/30/67, Los Angeles, Cal. BL/TL, 5′8″, 150 lbs. Deb: 4/14/10

1910	Bos-N	5	4	0	0	0	0	0	0	1	2	.000	.200	.000	-39	-1	-1	0	0			.000	0	H	-0.1

■ GENE LILLARD Lillard, Robert Eugene b: 11/12/13, Santa Barbara, Cal d: 4/12/91, Goleta, Cal. BR/TR, 5′10.5″, 178 lbs. Deb: 5/08/36 F

1936	Chi-N	19	34	6	7	1	0	0	2	3	8	.206	.270	.235	36	-3	-3	2	0			.947	-1	/S3	-0.3
1939	Chi-N	23	10	3	1	0	0	0	0	6	3	.100	.438	.100	51	-0	-0	1	0			1.000	0	P	0.0
1940	StL-N	2	0	0	0	0	0	0	0	0	0	—	—	—	—	0	0	0	0			1.000	0	/P	0.0
Total	3	44	44	9	8	1	0	0	2	9	11	.182	.321	.205	43	-3	-3	3	0			1.000	-1	/PS3	-0.3

■ BILL LILLARD Lillard, William Beverly b: 1/10/18, Goleta, Cal. BR/TR, 5′10″, 170 lbs. Deb: 9/11/39 F

1939	Phi-A	7	19	4	6	1	0	0	1	3	1	.316	.409	.368	102	0	0	3	0	0	0	.974	2	/S	0.3
1940	Phi-A	73	206	26	49	8	2	1	21	28	28	.238	.332	.311	69	-9	-9	23	0	1	-1	.921	-18	S/2	-2.1
Total	2	80	225	30	55	9	2	1	22	31	29	.244	.339	.316	72	-9	-8	27	0	1	-1	.927	-16	/S2	-1.8

■ JIM LILLIE Lillie, James J. "Grasshopper" (b: James J. Lilly) b: 7/27/1861, New Haven, Conn. d: 11/9/1890, Kansas City, Mo. Deb: 5/17/1883

1883	Buf-N	50	201	25	47	7	3	1	29	1	31	.234	.238	.313	64	-8	-9	15				.835	-7	O/PCS32	-1.4
1884	Buf-N	114	471	68	105	12	5	3	53	5	71	.223	.231	.289	60	-20	-23	32				.852	16	*O/P	-0.8
1885	Buf-N	112	430	49	107	13	3	2	30	6	39	.249	.259	.307	80	-9	-11	35				.862	0	*O/S1	-1.3
1886	KC-N	114	416	37	73	9	0	0	22	11	80	.175	.197	.197	19	-39	-43	19	13			.884	11	*O/P	-3.2
Total	4	390	1518	179	332	41	11	6	134	23	221	.219	.230	.272	54	-77	-86	102	13			.863	21	O/PSC123	-6.7

■ BOB LILLIS Lillis, Robert Perry b: 6/2/30, Altadena, Cal. BR/TR, 5′11″, 160 lbs. Deb: 8/30/58 MC

1958	LA-N	20	69	10	27	3	1	1	5	4	2	.391	.432	.507	143	5	5	14	1	2	-1	.964	-3	S	0.2
1959	LA-N	30	48	7	11	2	0	0	2	3	4	.229	.275	.271	43	-4	-4	4	0	0	0	.919	8	S	0.5
1960	LA-N	48	60	6	16	4	0	0	6	2	6	.267	.290	.333	66	-3	-3	6	2	0	1	.982	15	S3/2	1.3
1961	LA-N	19	9	0	1	0	0	0	1	1	1	.111	.200	.111	-13	-1	-2	0	0	0	0	1.000	1	3/2S	0.0
	StL-N	86	230	24	50	4	0	0	21	7	13	.217	.247	.235	26	-23	-26	12	3	3	-1	.928	2	S2	-2.0
	Yr	105	239	24	51	4	0	0	22	8	14	.213	.245	.230	25	-25	-28	12	3	3	-1	.924	3	S23	-2.0
1962	Hou-N	129	457	38	114	12	4	1	30	28	23	.249	.293	.300	64	-26	-22	40	7	3	0	.972	9	S2/3	-0.1
1963	Hou-N	147	469	31	93	13	1	1	19	15	35	.198	.230	.237	37	-39	-36	24	3	4	-2	.957	-5	*S2/3	-3.7
1964	Hou-N	109	332	31	89	11	2	0	17	11	10	.268	.292	.313	75	-13	-11	27	4	9	-4	.995	1	2S3	-0.9
1965	Hou-N	124	408	34	90	12	1	0	20	20	10	.221	.267	.255	51	-28	-24	27	2	2	-1	.968	-12	*S/32	-3.3
1966	Hou-N	68	164	14	38	6	0	0	11	7	4	.232	.263	.268	52	-11	-10	10	1	1	-0	.951	-9	2S/3	-1.7
1967	Hou-N	37	82	3	20	1	0	0	5	1	8	.244	.253	.256	48	-6	-5	4	0	1	-1	.947	3	S/23	-0.1
Total	10	817	2328	198	549	68	9	3	137	99	116	.236	.271	.277	54	-149	-139	167	23	25	-8	.959	8	S2/3	-9.8

■ LOU LIMMER Limmer, Louis b: 3/10/25, New York, N.Y. BL/TL, 6′2″, 190 lbs. Deb: 4/22/51

1951	Phi-A	94	214	25	34	9	1	5	30	28	40	.159	.256	.280	44	-17	-18	17	1	0	0	.988	2	1	-1.8
1954	Phi-A	115	316	41	73	10	3	14	32	35	37	.231	.308	.415	96	-3	-3	40	2	3	-1	.988	2	1	-0.6
Total	2	209	530	66	107	19	4	19	62	63	77	.202	.287	.360	75	-20	-21	57	3	3	-1	.988	4	1	-2.4

■ RUFINO LINARES Linares, Rufino (b: Rufino De La Cruz (Linares)) b: 2/28/51, San Pedro De Macoris, D.R. BR/TR, 6′, 170 lbs. Deb: 4/10/81

1981	Atl-N	78	253	27	67	9	2	5	25	9	28	.265	.290	.375	85	-5	-6	23	8	4	0	.963	1	O	-0.7
1982	Atl-N	77	191	28	57	7	1	2	17	7	29	.298	.327	.377	92	-1	-2	20	5	2	0	1.000	2	O	-0.1
1984	Atl-N	34	58	4	12	3	0	1	10	6	12	.207	.281	.310	62	-3	-3	5	0	0	0	.958	1	O	-0.3
1985	Cal-A	18	43	7	11	2	0	3	11	2	5	.256	.289	.512	114	1	1	6	2	0	1	1.000	-1	D/O	0.1
Total	4	207	545	66	147	21	3	11	63	24	74	.270	.302	.380	88	-8	-10	55	15	6	1	.977	3	O/D	-1.0

■ CARL LIND Lind, Henry Carl "Hooks" b: 9/19/03, New Orleans, La. d: 8/2/46, New York, N.Y. BR/TR, 6′, 160 lbs. Deb: 9/14/27

1927	Cle-A	12	37	2	5	0	0	0	1	5	7	.135	.256	.135	4	-5	-5	2	1	0	0	.969	2	2/S	-0.3
1928	Cle-A	154	650	102	191	42	4	1	54	36	48	.294	.331	.375	84	-15	-15	81	8	5	-1	.960	4	*2	-0.8
1929	Cle-A	66	225	19	54	8	1	0	13	13	17	.240	.282	.284	44	-18	-19	18	0	2	-1	.957	16	2/3	-0.2
1930	Cle-A	24	69	8	17	3	0	0	6	3	7	.246	.278	.290	43	-6	-6	5	0	1	-1	.940	11	S/2	0.5
Total	4	256	981	131	267	53	5	1	74	57	79	.272	.313	.339	69	-44	-46	106	9	8	-2	.960	33	2/S3	-0.8

■ JACK LIND Lind, Jackson Hugh b: 6/8/46, Denver, Col. BB/TR, 6′, 170 lbs. Deb: 9/10/74

1974	Mil-A	9	17	4	4	2	0	0	1	3	2	.235	.350	.353	103	0	0	2	0	0	0	1.000	-0	/S2	0.1
1975	Mil-A	17	20	1	1	0	0	0	0	2	12	.050	.136	.050	-45	-4	-4	0	1	0	0	.919	5	/S31	0.2
Total	2	26	37	5	5	2	0	0	1	5	14	.135	.238	.189	23	-4	-4	2	1	0	0	.943	5	/S321	0.3

■ JOSE LIND Lind, Jose (Salgado) b: 5/1/64, Toabaja, P.R. BR/TR, 5′11″, 170 lbs. Deb: 8/28/87

1987	Pit-N	35	143	21	46	8	4	0	11	8	12	.322	.358	.434	108	2	2	21	2	1	0	.995	6	2	0.9
1988	Pit-N	154	611	82	160	24	4	2	49	42	75	.262	.309	.324	83	-14	-13	63	15	4	2	.987	3	*2	-0.2
1989	Pit-N	153	578	52	134	21	3	2	48	39	64	.232	.283	.289	66	-27	-25	49	15	1	4	.976	-14	*2	-3.2
1990	*Pit-N	152	514	46	134	28	5	1	48	35	52	.261	.309	.340	82	-15	-13	51	8	0	2	.991	17	*2	1.0
1991	*Pit-N	150	502	53	133	16	6	3	54	30	56	.265	.309	.339	83	-12	-11	48	7	4	-0	.989	23	*2	1.5
1992	*Pit-N	135	468	38	110	14	1	0	39	26	29	.235	.277	.269	56	-27	-27	33	3	1	0	**.992**	11	*2	-1.3
Total	6	779	2816	292	717	111	23	8	249	180	288	.255	.301	.319	76	-94	-87	264	50	11	8	.987	46	2	-1.3

YEAR	TM/L	G	AB	R	H	2B	3B	HR	RBI	BB	SO	AVG	OBP	SLG	PRO+	BR	/A	RC	SB	CS	SBR	FA	FR	POS	TPR
■ EM LINDBECK Lindbeck, Emerit Desmond b: 8/27/35, Kewanee, Ill. BL/TR, 6', 185 lbs. Deb: 4/22/60																									
1960	Det-A	2	1	0	0	0	0	0	0	1	0	.000	.500	.000	46	0	0	0	0	0	0	.000	0	H	0.0
■ JOHNNY LINDELL Lindell, John Harlan b: 8/30/16, Greeley, Colo. d: 8/27/85, Newport Beach, Cal. BR/TR, 6'4.5", 217 lbs. Deb: 4/18/41																									
1941	NY-A	1	1	0	0	0	0	0	0	0	0	.000	.000	.000	-99	-0	-0	0	0	0	0	.000	0	H	0.0
1942	NY-A	27	24	1	6	1	0	0	4	0	5	.250	.250	.292	53	-2	-2	2	0	0	0	.923	-0	P	0.0
1943	*NY-A☆	122	441	53	108	17	**12**	4	51	51	55	.245	.329	.365	102	1	1	53	2	5	-2	.966	-2	*O	-1.0
1944	NY-A	149	594	91	178	33	**16**	18	103	44	56	.300	.351	.500	137	29	26	102	5	4	-1	.986	9	*O	2.7
1945	NY-A	41	159	26	45	6	3	1	20	17	10	.283	.363	.377	110	3	2	23	2	1	0	.982	0	O	0.0
1946	NY-A	102	332	41	86	10	5	10	40	32	47	.259	.328	.410	104	1	1	44	4	1	1	.982	-0	O1	-0.3
1947	*NY-A	127	476	66	131	18	7	11	67	32	70	.275	.322	.412	104	-0	0	61	1	2	-1	.978	7	*O	0.1
1948	NY-A	88	309	58	98	17	2	13	55	35	50	.317	.387	.511	139	15	16	62	0	0	0	.994	2	O	1.3
1949	*NY-A	78	211	33	51	10	0	6	27	35	27	.242	.350	.374	92	-3	-3	29	3	0	1	.983	-6	O	-1.0
1950	NY-A	7	21	2	4	0	0	0	2	4	2	.190	.320	.190	34	-2	-2	1	0	0	0	.857	-2	/O	-0.4
	StL-N	36	113	16	21	5	2	5	16	15	24	.186	.287	.398	74	-4	-5	12	0			.984	-2	O	-0.8
1953	Pit-N	58	91	11	26	6	1	4	15	16	15	.286	.404	.505	136	5	5	18	0	0	0	.962	2	P/1	0.0
	Phi-N	11	18	3	7	1	0	0	2	6	2	.389	.542	.444	162	2	2	5	0	0	0	1.000	-1	/PO	0.0
	Yr	69	109	14	33	7	1	4	17	22	17	.303	.429	.495	141	7	8	24	0	0	0	.964	1	P/1O	0.0
1954	Phi-N	7	5	0	1	0	0	0	2	2	3	.200	.429	.200	70	-0	-0	1	0	0	0	.000	0	H	0.0
Total	12	854	2795	401	762	124	48	72	404	289	366	.273	.344	.429	113	47	44	412	17	13		.980	7	O/P1	0.6
■ JIM LINDEMAN Lindeman, James William b: 1/10/62, Evanston, Ill. BR/TR, 6'1", 200 lbs. Deb: 9/03/86																									
1986	StL-N	19	55	7	14	1	0	1	6	2	10	.255	.281	.327	68	-3	-2	4	1	1	-0	.992	-1	1/3O	-0.5
1987	*StL-N	75	207	20	43	13	0	8	28	11	56	.208	.258	.386	67	-10	-11	20	3	1	0	.976	-1	O1	-1.4
1988	StL-N	17	43	3	9	1	0	2	7	2	9	.209	.244	.372	74	-2	-2	4	0	0	0	.941	-2	O/1	-0.4
1989	StL-N	73	45	8	5	1	0	0	2	3	18	.111	.167	.133	-13	-7	-7	1	0	0	0	.989	0	1/O	-0.8
1990	Det-A	12	32	5	7	1	0	2	8	2	13	.219	.265	.438	92	-0	-1	4	0	0	0	1.000	-1	D/1O	-0.1
1991	Phi-N	65	95	13	32	5	0	0	12	13	14	.337	.417	.389	129	4	4	16	0	1	-1	1.000	-5	O/1	-0.2
1992	Phi-N	29	39	6	10	1	0	1	6	3	11	.256	.310	.359	89	-1	-1	4	0	0	0	1.000	-3	/O	-0.4
Total	7	290	516	62	120	23	0	14	69	36	131	.233	.286	.359	75	-18	-18	53	4	3	-1	.979	-12	O/1D3	-3.8
■ BOB LINDEMANN Lindemann, John Frederick Mann b: 6/5/1881, Philadelphia, Pa. d: 12/19/51, Williamsport, Pa. BB/TR, 6', 175 lbs. Deb: 8/28/01																									
1901	Phi-A	3	9	0	1	0	0	0	0	0		.111	.111	.111	-37	-2	-2	0	0			.600	-0	/O	-0.2
■ WALT LINDEN Linden, Walter Charles b: 3/27/24, Chicago, Ill. BR/TR, 6'1", 190 lbs. Deb: 4/30/50																									
1950	Bos-N	3	5	0	2	1	0	0	0	1	0	.400	.500	.600	201	1	1	2	0			1.000	-1	/C	0.0
■ CHRIS LINDSAY Lindsay, Christian Haller "Pinky" or "The Crab" b: 7/24/1878, Baker's Yard, Moon Township, Beaver County, Pa d: 1/25/41, Cleveland, Ohio BR/TR, 6', 190 lbs. Deb: 7/06/05																									
1905	Det-A	88	329	38	88	14	1	0	31	18		.267	.315	.316	100	0	-0	38	10			.978	-0	1	-0.3
1906	Det-A	141	499	59	112	16	2	0	33	45		.224	.293	.265	73	-13	-15	48	18			.977	-8	*12/3	-2.9
Total	2	229	828	97	200	30	3	0	64	63		.242	.301	.285	83	-13	-15	86	28			.978	-8	1/23	-3.2
■ BILL LINDSAY Lindsay, William Gibbons b: 2/24/1881, Madison, N.C. d: 7/14/63, Greensboro, N.C. BL/TR, 5'10.5", 165 lbs. Deb: 6/21/11																									
1911	Cle-A	19	66	6	16	2	0	0	5	1		.242	.265	.273	49	-5	-5	5	2			.883	2	3/2	-0.2
■ DOUG LINDSEY Lindsey, Michael Douglas b: 9/22/67, Austin, Tex. BR/TR, 6'2", 200 lbs. Deb: 10/06/91																									
1991	Phi-N	1	3	0	0	0	0	0	0	0	3	.000	.000	.000	-99	-1	-1	0	0	0	0	1.000	0	/C	0.0
■ BILL LINDSEY Lindsey, William Donald b: 4/12/60, Staten Island, N.Y. BR/TR, 6'3", 195 lbs. Deb: 7/18/87																									
1987	Chi-A	9	16	2	3	0	0	0	1	0	3	.188	.188	.188	-0	-2	-2	0	0	0	0	1.000	2	/C	0.0
■ CHUCK LINDSTROM Lindstrom, Charles William b: 9/7/36, Chicago, Ill. BR/TR, 5'11", 175 lbs. Deb: 9/28/58 F																									
1958	Chi-A	1	1	1	1	0	1	0	1	1	0	1.000	1.000	3.000	975	1	1	3	0	0	0	1.000	-0	/C	0.1
■ FREDDY LINDSTROM Lindstrom, Frederick Charles (b: Frederick Anthony Lindstrom) b: 11/21/05, Chicago, Ill. d: 10/4/81, Chicago, Ill. BR/TR, 5'11", 170 lbs. Deb: 4/15/24 FH																									
1924	NY-N	52	79	19	20	3	1	0	4	6	10	.253	.314	.316	71	-3	-3	8	3	1	0	.911	7	23	0.5
1925	NY-N	104	356	43	102	15	12	4	33	22	20	.287	.332	.430	97	-5	-3	48	5	9	-4	.957	-1	3/2S	-0.1
1926	NY-N	140	543	90	164	19	9	9	76	39	21	.302	.351	.420	108	4	5	78	11			.962	-3	*3/O	1.1
1927	NY-N	138	562	107	172	36	8	7	58	40	40	.306	.354	.436	111	8	8	85	10			.968	1	3O	1.0
1928	NY-N	153	646	99	**231**	39	9	14	107	25	21	.358	.383	.511	131	28	27	120	15			**.958**	15	*3	4.8
1929	NY-N	130	549	99	175	23	6	15	91	30	28	.319	.354	.464	101	-1	-0	87	10			.966	7	*3	1.1
1930	NY-N	148	609	127	231	39	7	22	106	48	33	.379	.425	.575	142	38	40	143	15			.953	6	*3	4.8
1931	NY-N	78	303	38	91	12	6	5	36	26	12	.300	.356	.429	113	4	5	47	5			.975	-7	O/2	-0.6
1932	NY-N	144	595	83	161	26	5	15	92	27	28	.271	.303	.407	91	-10	-9	74	6			.982	0	*O3	-1.6
1933	Pit-N	138	538	70	167	39	10	5	55	33	22	.310	.350	.448	127	17	17	86	1			.988	11	*O	2.3
1934	Pit-N	97	383	59	111	24	4	4	49	23	21	.290	.333	.405	94	-2	-3	51	1			.990	1	O	-0.6
1935	Chi-N	90	342	49	94	22	4	3	62	10	13	.275	.297	.389	82	-9	-9	37	1			.979	-2	O3	-1.2
1936	Bro-N	26	106	12	28	4	0	0	10	5	7	.264	.297	.302	61	-6	-6	9	1			.982	1	O	-0.5
Total	13	1438	5611	895	1747	301	81	103	779	334	276	.311	.351	.449	110	64	70	873	84	10		.959	37	3O/2S	11.0
■ CARL LINHART Linhart, Carl James b: 12/14/29, Zborov, Czech. BL/TR, 5'11", 184 lbs. Deb: 8/02/52																									
1952	Det-A	3	2	0	0	0	0	0	0	0	0	.000	.000	.000	-99	-1	-1	0	0	0	0	.000	0	H	-0.1
■ BOB LINTON Linton, Claud Clarence b: 4/18/03, Emerson, Ark. d: 4/3/80, Destin, Fla. BL/TR, 6', 185 lbs. Deb: 4/26/29																									
1929	Pit-N	17	18	0	2	0	0	0	1	1	2	.111	.158	.111	-31	-4	-4	0	0			1.000	0	/C	-0.3
■ LARRY LINTZ Lintz, Larry b: 10/10/49, Martinez, Cal. BB/TR, 5'9", 150 lbs. Deb: 7/14/73																									
1973	Mon-N	52	116	20	29	1	0	0	3	17	18	.250	.351	.259	69	-4	-4	14	12	4	1	.945	2	2S	0.2
1974	Mon-N	113	319	60	76	10	1	0	20	44	50	.238	.334	.276	68	-10	-13	40	50	7	11	.961	-13	2S/3	-0.8
1975	Mon-N	46	132	18	26	0	0	0	3	23	18	.197	.316	.197	43	-9	-10	10	17	9	-0	.970	-6	2/S	-1.4
	StL-N	27	18	6	5	1	0	0	1	3	2	.278	.381	.333	96	0	0	3	4	0	1	.889	9	/2S	1.0
	Yr	73	150	24	31	1	0	0	4	26	20	.207	.324	.213	49	-9	-10	13	21	9	1	.963	3	2/S	-0.4
1976	Oak-A	68	1	21	0	0	0	0	0	2	0	.000	.667	.000	111	0	0	-39	31	11	3	1.000	1	D/2O	0.4
1977	Oak-A	41	30	11	4	1	0	0	0	8	13	.133	.333	.167	42	-2	-2	3	13	5	1	1.000	11	2/S3D	1.0
1978	Cle-A	3	0	1	0	0	0	0	0	0	0	—	—	—	—	0	0	0	1	2	-1	.000	0	R	-0.1
Total	6	350	616	137	140	13	1	0	27	97	101	.227	.336	.252	63	-24	-28	32	128	38	16	.962	4	2/SD03	0.3
■ PHIL LINZ Linz, Philip Francis b: 6/4/39, Baltimore, Md. BR/TR, 6'1", 180 lbs. Deb: 4/13/62																									
1962	NY-A	71	129	28	37	8	0	1	14	6	17	.287	.319	.372	88	-3	-2	15	6	2	1	.937	-3	S/32O	-0.3
1963	*NY-A	72	186	22	50	9	0	2	12	15	18	.269	.330	.349	91	-2	-2	19	1	6	-3	.963	1	S3O/2	-0.3
1964	*NY-A	112	368	63	92	21	3	5	25	43	61	.250	.332	.364	92	-3	-3	45	3	4	-2	.952	11	S3/2O	1.0
1965	NY-A	99	285	37	59	12	1	2	16	30	33	.207	.283	.277	60	-15	-15	24	2	1	0	.954	11	S/3O2	0.1
1966	Phi-N	40	70	4	14	3	0	0	6	2	14	.200	.222	.243	29	-7	-7	3	0	0	0	.971	1	3/S2	-0.6
1967	Phi-N	23	18	4	4	2	0	1	5	2	1	.222	.300	.500	124	0	0	2	0	0	0	.833	-1	/S3	-0.1

YEAR	TM/L	G	AB	R	H	2B	3B	HR	RBI	BB	SO	AVG	OBP	SLG	PRO+	BR	/A	RC	SB	CS	SBR	FA	FR	POS	TPR
	NY-N	24	58	8	12	2	0	0	1	4	10	.207	.270	.241	48	-4	-4	4	0	0	0	.964	-2	2/S3O	-0.5
	Yr	47	76	12	16	4	0	1	6	6	11	.211	.277	.303	66	-3	-3	6	0	0	0	.963	-4	S2/3O	-0.6
1968	NY-N	78	258	19	54	7	0	0	17	10	41	.209	.244	.236	45	-17	-17	14	1	0	0	.968	-12	2	-2.9
Total	7	519	1372	185	322	64	4	11	96	112	195	.235	.296	.311	72	-49	-49	126	13	13	-4	.952	6	S2/3O	-3.6
■ JOHNNY LIPON	Lipon, John Joseph "Skids" b: 11/10/22, Martin's Ferry, O. BR/TR, 6', 175 lbs. Deb: 8/16/42 MC																								
1942	Det-A	34	131	5	25	2	0	0	9	7	7	.191	.232	.206	22	-13	-15	6	1	3	-2	.945	7	S	-0.7
1946	Det-A	14	20	4	6	0	0	0	1	5	3	.300	.440	.300	103	1	1	3	0	0	0	.933	3	/S3	0.4
1948	Det-A	121	458	65	133	18	8	5	52	68	22	.290	.384	.397	105	7	5	75	4	4	-1	.970	-12	*S/23	-0.1
1949	Det-A	127	439	57	110	14	6	3	59	75	24	.251	.362	.330	84	-8	-8	55	2	4	-2	.965	4	*S	0.2
1950	Det-A	147	601	104	176	27	6	2	63	81	26	.293	.378	.368	89	-5	-8	87	9	6	-1	.958	9	*S	1.0
1951	Det-A	129	487	56	129	15	1	0	38	49	27	.265	.335	.300	72	-17	-18	52	7	6	-2	.949	-13	*S	-2.3
1952	Det-A	39	136	17	30	4	2	0	12	16	6	.221	.303	.279	62	-7	-7	12	3	1	0	.978	-3	S	-0.6
	Bos-A	79	234	25	48	8	1	0	18	32	20	.205	.301	.248	50	-14	-16	20	1	1	-0	.982	14	S/3	0.3
	Yr	118	370	42	78	12	3	0	30	48	26	.211	.301	.259	54	-21	-23	33	4	2	0	**.981**	12	*S/3	-0.3
1953	Bos-A	60	145	18	31	7	0	0	13	14	16	.214	.283	.262	46	-10	-11	11	1	0	0	.951	4	S	-0.4
	StL-A	7	9	0	2	0	0	0	1	0	1	.222	.222	.222	20	-1	-1	0	0	0	0	1.000	-1	/32	-0.2
	Yr	67	154	18	33	7	0	0	14	14	17	.214	.280	.260	44	-11	-12	12	1	0	0	.951	3	S/32	-0.6
1954	Cin-N	1	1	0	0	0	0	0	0	0	0	.000	.000	.000	-97	-0	-0	0	0	0	0	.000	0	H	0.0
Total	9	758	2661	351	690	95	24	10	266	347	152	.259	.346	.324	77	-69	-79	323	28	25	-7	.961	13	S/32	-2.4
■ NIG LIPSCOMB	Lipscomb, Gerard b: 2/24/11, Rutherfordton, N.C d: 2/27/78, Huntersville, N.C. BR/TR, 6', 175 lbs. Deb: 4/23/37																								
1937	StL-A	36	96	11	31	9	1	0	8	11	10	.323	.398	.438	110	2	2	17	0	0	0	.963	2	2/P3	0.6
■ BOB LIPSKI	Lipski, Robert Peter b: 7/7/38, Scranton, Pa. BL/TR, 6'1", 180 lbs. Deb: 4/28/63																								
1963	Cle-A	2	1	0	0	0	0	0	0	0	1	.000	.000	.000	-99	-0	-0	0	0	0	0	1.000	0	/C	0.0
■ NELSON LIRIANO	Liriano, Nelson Arturo (Bonilla) b: 6/3/64, Santo Domingo, D.R. BB/TR, 5'10", 172 lbs. Deb: 8/25/87																								
1987	Tor-A	37	158	29	38	6	2	2	10	16	22	.241	.310	.342	71	-6	-7	18	13	2	3	.995	3	2	0.1
1988	Tor-A	99	276	36	73	6	2	3	23	11	40	.264	.298	.333	76	-9	-9	27	12	5	1	.961	-13	2D/3	-1.9
1989	*Tor-A	132	418	51	110	26	3	5	53	43	51	.263	.335	.376	102	0	1	53	16	7	1	.980	-18	*2/D	-1.2
1990	Tor-A	50	170	16	36	7	2	1	15	16	20	.212	.283	.294	61	-9	-9	13	3	5	-2	.983	-12	2	-2.3
	Min-A	53	185	30	47	5	7	0	13	22	24	.254	.333	.357	87	-1	-3	23	5	2	0	.968	-15	2/SD	-1.8
	Yr	103	355	46	83	12	9	1	28	38	44	.234	.310	.327	75	-10	-12	36	8	7	-2	.975	-28	2/DS	-4.1
1991	KC-A	10	22	5	9	0	0	0	1	0	2	.409	.409	.409	127	1	1	3	0	1	-1	1.000	1	2	0.1
Total	5	381	1229	167	313	50	16	11	115	108	159	.255	.317	.348	84	-24	-25	138	49	22	2	.977	-56	2/DS3	-7.0
■ JOE LIS	Lis, Joseph Anthony b: 8/15/46, Somerville, N.J. BR/TR, 6', 195 lbs. Deb: 9/05/70																								
1970	Phi-N	13	37	1	7	2	0	1	4	5	11	.189	.286	.324	65	-2	-2	4	0	0	0	.947	-1	/O	-0.3
1971	Phi-N	59	123	16	26	6	0	6	10	16	43	.211	.312	.407	102	0	0	16	0	1	-1	.978	-4	O	-0.6
1972	Phi-N	62	140	13	34	6	0	6	18	30	34	.243	.380	.414	122	6	5	24	0	1	-1	.996	1	1O	0.3
1973	Min-A	103	253	37	62	11	1	9	25	28	66	.245	.327	.403	101	1	0	31	0	1	-1	.987	2	1/D	-0.4
1974	Min-A	24	41	5	8	0	0	0	3	5	12	.195	.298	.195	42	-3	-3	3	0	0	0	.992	0	1	-0.4
	Cle-A	57	109	15	22	3	0	6	16	14	30	.202	.293	.394	97	-1	-1	12	1	0	0	1.000	-0	1/3OD	-0.2
	Yr	81	150	20	30	3	0	6	19	19	42	.200	.294	.340	82	-3	-4	14	1	0	0	.997	-0	1/3DO	-0.6
1975	Cle-A	9	13	4	4	2	0	2	8	3	3	.308	.471	.923	286	3	3	6	0	0	0	1.000	-0	/1D	0.3
1976	Cle-A	20	51	4	16	1	0	2	7	8	8	.314	.407	.451	153	4	4	10	0	0	0	1.000	-0	1/D	0.3
1977	Sea-A	9	13	1	3	0	0	0	1	1	2	.231	.286	.231	43	-1	-1	0	0	0	0	1.000	-1	/1C	-0.2
Total	8	356	780	96	182	31	1	32	92	110	209	.233	.334	.399	105	8	6	106	1	3	-2	.992	-3	1/OD3C	-1.2
■ RICK LISI	Lisi, Riccardo Patrick Emilio b: 3/17/56, Halifax, N.S., Can. BR/TR, 6', 175 lbs. Deb: 5/09/81																								
1981	Tex-A	9	16	6	5	0	0	0	1	4	0	.313	.450	.313	130	1	1	2	0	1	-1	1.000	-2	/O	-0.2
■ PAT LISTACH	Listach, Patrick Alan b: 9/12/67, Natchitoches, La. BR/TR, 5'9", 170 lbs. Deb: 4/08/92																								
1992	Mil-A	149	579	93	168	19	6	1	47	55	124	.290	.353	.349	99	-1	1	79	54	18	5	.966	-7	*S/2O	1.1
■ PETE LISTER	Lister, Morris Elmer b: 7/21/1881, Savanna, Ill. d: 3/27/47, St.Petersburg, Fla BR/TR, Deb: 9/14/07																								
1907	Cle-A	22	65	5	18	2	0	0	4	3		.277	.319	.308	99	0	-0	7	2			.974	-1	1	-0.2
■ SCOTT LITTLE	Little, Dennis Scott b: 1/19/63, E.St.Louis, Ill. BR/TR, 6', 198 lbs. Deb: 7/27/89																								
1989	Pit-N	3	4	0	1	0	0	0	0	0	1	.250	.250	.250	45	-0	-0	0	0	0	0	1.000	1	/O	0.1
■ HARRY LITTLE	Little, Harry A. b: St.Louis, Mo. TR, Deb: 7/16/1877																								
1877	StL-N	3	12	2	2	0	0	0	0	1	6	.167	.231	.167	29	-1	-1	0				1.000	-0	/O	-0.1
	Lou-N	1	3	0	0	0	0	0	0	1	1	.000	.250	.000	-13	-0	-0	0				.857	0	/2	0.0
	Yr	4	15	2	2	0	0	0	0	2	7	.133	.235	.133	19	-1	-1	0				1.000	0	/O2	-0.1
■ BRYAN LITTLE	Little, Richard Bryan "Twig" b: 10/8/59, Houston, Tex. BB/TR, 5'10", 160 lbs. Deb: 7/29/82																								
1982	Mon-N	29	42	6	9	0	0	0	3	4	6	.214	.283	.214	40	-3	-3	3	2	1	0	1.000	-2	2S	-0.5
1983	Mon-N	106	350	48	91	15	3	1	36	50	22	.260	.356	.329	91	-3	-2	42	4	5	-2	.968	-32	S2	-3.0
1984	Mon-N	85	266	31	65	11	1	0	9	34	19	.244	.332	.293	81	-7	-6	28	2	3	-1	.982	-22	2/S	-2.7
1985	Chi-A	73	188	35	47	9	1	2	27	26	21	.250	.350	.340	87	-2	-3	24	0	1	-1	.989	-6	2/3S	-0.7
1986	Chi-A	20	35	3	6	1	0	0	2	4	4	.171	.256	.200	25	-4	-4	2	0	0	0	1.000	0	2/S3	-0.3
	NY-A	14	41	3	8	1	0	0	0	2	7	.195	.233	.220	24	-4	-4	2	0	0	0	.975	5	2	0.1
	Yr	34	76	6	14	2	0	0	2	6	11	.184	.244	.211	25	-8	-8	4	0	0	0	.983	6	2/S3	-0.2
Total	5	327	922	126	226	37	5	3	77	120	79	.245	.336	.306	80	-22	-22	100	8	10	-4	.987	-56	2/S3	-7.1
■ JACK LITTLE	Little, William Arthur b: 3/12/1891, Mart, Tex. d: 7/27/61, Dallas, Tex. BR/TR, 5'11", 175 lbs. Deb: 7/02/12																								
1912	NY-A	3	12	2	3	0	0	0	0	1		.250	.357	.250	70	-0	-0	2	2			1.000	0	/O	0.0
■ DENNIS LITTLEJOHN	Littlejohn, Dennis Gerald b: 10/4/54, Santa Monica, Cal. BR/TR, 6'2", 200 lbs. Deb: 7/09/78																								
1978	SF-N	2	0	0	0	0	0	0	0	0	0	—	—	—	—	0	0	0	0	0	0	.000	0	/C	0.0
1979	SF-N	63	193	15	38	6	1	1	13	21	46	.197	.276	.254	49	-14	-13	14	0	0	0	.986	5	C	-0.5
1980	SF-N	13	29	2	7	1	0	0	2	7	7	.241	.389	.276	91	-0	0	4	0	0	0	.983	2	C	0.2
Total	3	78	222	17	45	7	1	1	15	28	53	.203	.292	.257	55	-14	-13	18	0	0	0	.985	7	/C	-0.3
■ LARRY LITTLETON	Littleton, Larry Marvin b: 4/3/54, Charlotte, N.C. BR/TR, 6'1", 185 lbs. Deb: 4/12/81																								
1981	Cle-A	26	23	2	0	0	0	0	1	3	6	.000	.115	.000	-65	-5	-5	0	0	0	0	1.000	-10	O	-1.6
■ GREG LITTON	Litton, Jon Gregory b: 7/13/64, New Orleans, La. BR/TR, 6', 175 lbs. Deb: 5/02/89																								
1989	*SF-N	71	143	12	36	5	3	4	17	7	29	.252	.291	.413	102	-1	-0	16	0	2	-1	.953	-5	32/SOC	-0.6
1990	SF-N	93	204	17	50	9	1	1	24	11	45	.245	.287	.314	68	-10	-9	18	1	0	0	.985	-11	O2/S3	-2.1
1991	SF-N	59	127	13	23	7	1	1	15	11	25	.181	.252	.276	50	-9	-8	9	0	2	-1	.989	-2	123/SOCP	-1.2
1992	SF-N	68	140	9	32	5	0	4	15	11	33	.229	.285	.350	83	-4	-3	14	0	1	-1	.992	-3	23/1SO	-0.6
Total	4	291	614	51	141	26	5	10	71	40	132	.230	.280	.337	75	-23	-21	57	1	5	-3	.996	-20	/2O3S1CP	-4.5

■ **JACK LITTRELL** Littrell, Jack Napier b: 1/22/29, Louisville, Ky. BR/TR, 6', 179 lbs. Deb: 4/19/52

YEAR	TM/L	G	AB	R	H	2B	3B	HR	RBI	BB	SO	AVG	OBP	SLG	PRO+	BR	/A	RC	SB	CS	SBR	FA	FR	POS	TPR
1952	Phi-A	4	2	0	0	0	0	0	0	1	2	.000	.333	.000	-2	-0	-0	0	0	0	0	1.000	0	/S3	0.0
1954	Phi-A	9	30	7	9	2	0	1	3	6	3	.300	.417	.467	141	2	2	6	1	0	0	.976	-1	/S	0.2
1955	KC-A	37	70	7	14	0	1	0	1	4	12	.200	.243	.229	27	-7	-7	4	0	0	0	.947	0	S/12	-0.6
1957	Chi-N	61	153	8	29	4	2	1	13	9	43	.190	.235	.261	34	-15	-14	10	0	0	0	.944	1	S/23	-0.9
Total	4	111	255	22	52	6	3	2	17	20	60	.204	.262	.275	45	-20	-20	20	1	0	0	.949	0	/S213	-1.3

■ **DANNY LITWHILER** Litwhiler, Daniel Webster b: 8/31/16, Ringtown, Pa. BR/TR, 5'10.5", 198 lbs. Deb: 4/25/40 C

YEAR	TM/L	G	AB	R	H	2B	3B	HR	RBI	BB	SO	AVG	OBP	SLG	PRO+	BR	/A	RC	SB	CS	SBR	FA	FR	POS	TPR
1940	Phi-N	36	142	10	49	2	2	5	17	3	13	.345	.363	.493	139	6	7	25	1			.986	1	O	0.6
1941	Phi-N	151	590	72	180	29	6	18	66	39	43	.305	.350	.466	134	20	22	93	1			.964	17	*O	3.1
1942	Phi-N★	151	591	59	160	25	9	9	56	27	42	.271	.310	.389	109	1	4	68	2			**1.000**	-2	*O	-0.6
1943	Phi-N	36	139	23	36	6	0	5	17	11	14	.259	.313	.410	113	1	1	18	1			.989	5	O	0.5
	*StL-N	80	258	40	72	14	3	7	31	19	31	.279	.333	.438	117	6	5	38	1			1.000	1	O	0.3
	Yr	116	397	63	108	20	3	12	48	30	45	.272	.326	.428	115	7	6	56	2			.996	6	*O	0.8
1944	*StL-N	140	492	53	130	25	5	15	82	37	56	.264	.328	.427	109	6	5	69	2			.974	-1	*O	-0.2
1946	StL-N	6	5	0	0	0	0	0	0	1	1	.000	.167	.000	-49	-1	-1	0	0			.000	0	H	-0.1
	Bos-N	79	247	29	72	12	2	8	38	19	23	.291	.347	.453	125	7	7	39	1			.985	-3	O/3	0.1
	Yr	85	252	29	72	12	2	8	38	20	24	.286	.343	.444	121	6	6	39	1			.985	-3	O/3	0.0
1947	Bos-N	91	226	38	59	5	2	7	31	25	43	.261	.337	.394	96	-2	-1	30	1			.976	-6	O	-1.0
1948	Bos-N	13	33	0	9	2	0	0	6	4	2	.273	.385	.333	97	0	0	5	0			1.000	2	/O	0.1
	Cin-N	106	338	51	93	19	2	14	44	48	41	.275	.365	.467	128	11	13	56	1			.988	2	O3	1.1
	Yr	119	371	51	102	21	2	14	50	52	43	.275	.367	.456	125	11	13	61	1			.990	4	O3	1.2
1949	Cin-N	102	292	35	85	18	1	11	48	44	42	.291	.384	.473	127	12	12	56	0			.987	-5	O/3	0.3
1950	Cin-N	54	112	15	29	4	0	6	12	20	21	.259	.371	.455	116	3	3	19	0			.958	-3	O	-0.1
1951	Cin-N	12	29	3	8	1	0	2	3	2	5	.276	.323	.517	120	1	1	5	0	0	0	.933	-1	/O	0.0
Total	11	1057	3494	428	982	162	32	107	451	299	377	.281	.342	.438	119	71	77	521	11	0		.982	9	O/3	4.1

■ **PADDY LIVINGSTON** Livingston, Patrick Joseph b: 1/14/1880, Cleveland, Ohio d: 9/19/77, Cleveland, Ohio BR/TR, 5'8", 197 lbs. Deb: 9/02/01

YEAR	TM/L	G	AB	R	H	2B	3B	HR	RBI	BB	SO	AVG	OBP	SLG	PRO+	BR	/A	RC	SB	CS	SBR	FA	FR	POS	TPR
1901	Cle-A	1	2	0	0	0	0	0	0	0		.000	.333	.000	-2	-0	-0	0	0			1.000	-0	/C	0.0
1906	Cin-N	50	139	8	22	1	4	0	8	12		.158	.250	.223	46	-8	-9	9	0			.960	3	C	-0.2
1909	Phi-A	64	175	15	41	6	4	0	15	15		.234	.323	.314	99	1	0	20	4			.969	9	C	1.7
1910	Phi-A	37	120	11	25	4	3	0	9	6		.208	.264	.292	75	-4	-4	10	2			.968	4	C	0.5
1911	Phi-A	27	71	9	17	4	0	0	8	7		.239	.316	.296	72	-3	-2	7	1			.977	5	C	0.4
1912	Cle-A	20	47	5	11	2	1	0	3	1		.234	.280	.319	69	-2	-2	4	0			.976	0	C	-0.1
1917	StL-N	7	20	0	4	0	0	0	2	0	1	.200	.200	.200	23	-2	-2	1	2			1.000	1	/C	-0.1
Total	7	206	574	48	120	17	12	0	45	41	1	.209	.285	.280	72	-18	-19	50	9			.969	22	C	2.2

■ **MICKEY LIVINGSTON** Livingston, Thompson Orville b: 11/15/14, Newberry, S.C. d: 4/3/83, Newberry, S.C. BR/TR, 6'1.5", 185 lbs. Deb: 9/17/38

YEAR	TM/L	G	AB	R	H	2B	3B	HR	RBI	BB	SO	AVG	OBP	SLG	PRO+	BR	/A	RC	SB	CS	SBR	FA	FR	POS	TPR
1938	Was-A	2	4	0	3	2	0	0	1	0	1	.750	.750	1.250	421	2	2	4	0	0	0	.667	-1	/C	0.1
1941	Phi-N	95	207	16	42	6	1	0	18	20	38	.203	.276	.242	49	-14	-13	13	2			.974	-1	C/1	-0.9
1942	Phi-N	89	239	20	49	6	1	2	22	25	20	.205	.283	.264	64	-12	-10	19	0			.987	-6	C/1	-1.2
1943	Phi-N	84	265	25	66	9	2	3	18	19	18	.249	.304	.332	87	-6	-5	27	1			.988	-2	C/1	-0.1
	Chi-N	36	111	11	29	5	1	4	16	12	8	.261	.333	.432	122	3	3	14	1			1.000	-5	C/1	0.0
	Yr	120	376	36	95	14	3	7	34	31	26	.253	.313	.362	98	-3	-2	41	2			**.991**	-7	*C/1	-0.1
1945	*Chi-N	71	224	19	57	4	2	2	23	19	6	.254	.324	.317	80	-6	-6	23	2			.990	-1	C/1	-0.2
1946	Chi-N	66	176	14	45	14	0	2	20	20	19	.256	.338	.369	103	0	1	23	0			.981	2	C	0.5
1947	Chi-N	19	33	2	7	2	0	0	3	1	5	.212	.235	.273	36	-3	-3	2	0			1.000	-0	/C	-0.3
	NY-N	5	6	0	1	0	0	0	0	1	2	.167	.286	.167	23	-1	-1	0	0			.800	0	/C	0.0
	Yr	24	39	2	8	2	0	0	3	2	7	.205	.244	.256	34	-4	-4	3	0			.970	-0	/C	-0.3
1948	NY-N	45	99	9	21	4	1	2	12	21	11	.212	.350	.333	85	-1	-1	13	1			.980	-1	C	0.0
1949	NY-N	19	57	6	17	2	0	4	12	2	8	.298	.333	.544	132	2	2	10	0			.985	-1	C	0.2
	Bos-N	28	64	6	15	2	1	0	6	3	5	.234	.290	.297	61	-4	-3	6	0			.977	1	C	-0.2
	Yr	47	121	12	32	4	1	4	18	5	13	.264	.310	.413	95	-2	-1	15	0			.980	-1	C	0.0
1951	Bro-N	2	5	0	2	0	0	0	2	1	0	.400	.500	.400	142	0	0	1	0	0	0	1.000	-0	/C	0.0
Total	10	561	1490	128	354	56	9	19	153	144	141	.238	.310	.326	82	-40	-35	154	7	0		.984	-15	C/1	-2.1

■ **SCOTT LIVINGSTONE** Livingstone, Scott Louis b: 7/15/65, Dallas, Tex. BL/TR, 6', 190 lbs. Deb: 7/19/91

YEAR	TM/L	G	AB	R	H	2B	3B	HR	RBI	BB	SO	AVG	OBP	SLG	PRO+	BR	/A	RC	SB	CS	SBR	FA	FR	POS	TPR
1991	Det-A	44	127	19	37	5	0	2	11	10	25	.291	.343	.378	98	-0	-0	17	2	1	0	.980	1	3	0.0
1992	Det-A	117	354	43	100	21	0	4	46	21	36	.282	.323	.376	94	-3	-3	41	1	3	-2	.962	-6	*3	-1.0
Total	2	161	481	62	137	26	0	6	57	31	61	.285	.328	.376	95	-3	-4	58	3	4	-2	.967	-5	3	-1.0

■ **ABEL LIZOTTE** Lizotte, Abel b: 4/13/1870, Lewiston, Me. d: 12/4/26, Wilkes-Barre, Pa. 5'8", 174 lbs. Deb: 9/17/1896

YEAR	TM/L	G	AB	R	H	2B	3B	HR	RBI	BB	SO	AVG	OBP	SLG	PRO+	BR	/A	RC	SB	CS	SBR	FA	FR	POS	TPR
1896	Pit-N	7	29	3	3	0	0	0	3	2	2	.103	.161	.103	-30	-5	-5	1	1			.952	1	/1	-0.4

■ **WINSTON LLENAS** Llenas, Winston Enriquillo (Davila) b: 9/23/43, Santiago, D.R. BR/TR, 5'10", 165 lbs. Deb: 8/15/68 C

YEAR	TM/L	G	AB	R	H	2B	3B	HR	RBI	BB	SO	AVG	OBP	SLG	PRO+	BR	/A	RC	SB	CS	SBR	FA	FR	POS	TPR
1968	Cal-A	16	39	5	5	1	0	0	1	2	5	.128	.190	.154	6	-4	-4	1	0	0	0	.800	-3	/3	-0.9
1969	Cal-A	34	47	4	8	2	0	0	0	2	10	.170	.204	.213	18	-5	-5	2	0	0	0	.929	-2	/3	-0.7
1972	Cal-A	44	64	3	17	3	0	0	7	3	8	.266	.299	.313	87	-1	-1	5	0	0	0	.950	-1	3/2O	-0.3
1973	Cal-A	78	130	16	35	1	0	1	25	10	16	.269	.326	.300	84	-4	-2	13	0	0	0	1.000	-4	23/OD	-0.6
1974	Cal-A	72	138	16	36	6	0	2	17	11	19	.261	.315	.348	96	-2	-1	15	0	0	0	1.000	-8	O2D/3	-1.0
1975	Cal-A	56	113	6	21	4	0	0	11	10	11	.186	.252	.221	37	-10	-9	6	0	1	-1	1.000	4	2O/13D	-0.5
Total	6	300	531	50	122	17	0	3	61	38	69	.230	.284	.279	66	-26	-22	42	0	1	-1	1.000	-13	/2O3D1	-4.0

■ **MIKE LOAN** Loan, William Joseph b: 9/27/1894, Philadelphia, Pa. d: 11/21/66, Springfield, Pa. BR/TR, 5'11", 185 lbs. Deb: 9/18/12

YEAR	TM/L	G	AB	R	H	2B	3B	HR	RBI	BB	SO	AVG	OBP	SLG	PRO+	BR	/A	RC	SB	CS	SBR	FA	FR	POS	TPR
1912	Phi-N	1	2	1	1	0	0	0	0	0	0	.500	.500	.500	163	0	0	0	0			1.000	-1	/C	0.0

■ **BOB LOANE** Loane, Robert Kenneth b: 8/6/14, Berkeley, Cal. BR/TR, 6', 190 lbs. Deb: 7/29/39

YEAR	TM/L	G	AB	R	H	2B	3B	HR	RBI	BB	SO	AVG	OBP	SLG	PRO+	BR	/A	RC	SB	CS	SBR	FA	FR	POS	TPR
1939	Was-A	3	9	2	0	0	0	0	1	4	4	.000	.308	.000	-16	-1	-1	0	0	0	0	.909	2	/O	0.0
1940	Bos-N	13	22	4	5	3	0	0	1	2	5	.227	.292	.364	84	-1	-0	3	2			1.000	0	O	0.0
Total	2	16	31	6	5	3	0	0	2	6	9	.161	.297	.258	54	-2	-2	3	2	0		.969	2	/O	0.0

■ **FRANK LOBERT** Lobert, Frank John b: 11/26/1883, Williamsport, Pa. d: 5/29/32, Pittsburgh, Pa. BR/TR, 6', 180 lbs. Deb: 6/06/14 F

YEAR	TM/L	G	AB	R	H	2B	3B	HR	RBI	BB	SO	AVG	OBP	SLG	PRO+	BR	/A	RC	SB	CS	SBR	FA	FR	POS	TPR
1914	Bal-F	11	30	3	6	0	1	0	2	0	0	.200	.200	.267	31	-3	-3	2	0			.870	-2	/32	-0.4

■ **HANS LOBERT** Lobert, John Bernard "Honus" b: 10/18/1881, Wilmington, Del. d: 9/14/68, Philadelphia, Pa. BR/TR, 5'9", 170 lbs. Deb: 9/21/03 FMC

YEAR	TM/L	G	AB	R	H	2B	3B	HR	RBI	BB	SO	AVG	OBP	SLG	PRO+	BR	/A	RC	SB	CS	SBR	FA	FR	POS	TPR
1903	Pit-N	5	13	1	1	1	0	0	0	1		.077	.143	.154	-15	-2	-2	1	1			.778	-1	/32S	-0.3
1905	Chi-N	14	46	7	9	2	0	0	1	3		.196	.260	.239	47	-3	-3	5	4			.918	0	3/O	-0.3
1906	Cin-N	79	268	39	83	5	5	0	19	19		.310	.364	.366	123	9	7	46	20			.959	-11	3S2/O	-0.2
1907	Cin-N	148	537	61	132	9	12	1	41	37		.246	.299	.313	88	-6	-8	64	30			.941	-18	*S/3	-2.5
1908	Cin-N	155	570	71	167	17	18	4	63	46		.293	.348	.407	145	25	27	97	47			.921	-26	3SO	0.5
1909	Cin-N	122	425	50	90	13	5	4	52	48		.212	.304	.294	86	-7	-6	47	30			.921	-15	*3	-1.9
1910	Cin-N	93	314	43	97	6	6	3	40	30	9	.309	.369	.395	128	9	11	61	41			.932	-2	3	1.2
1911	Phi-N	147	541	94	154	20	9	9	72	66	31	.285	.368	.405	115	12	11	97	40			.954	-17	*3	-0.4
1912	Phi-N	65	257	37	84	12	5	2	33	19	13	.327	.373	.436	113	7	5	46	13			.976	-13	3	-0.8
1913	Phi-N	150	573	98	172	28	11	7	55	42	34	.300	.353	.424	117	15	12	96	41			**.974**	-17	*3/S2	-0.3

YEAR	TM/L	G	AB	R	H	2B	3B	HR	RBI	BB	SO	AVG	OBP	SLG	PRO+	BR	/A	RC	SB	CS	SBR	FA	FR	POS	TPR
1914	Phi-N	135	505	83	139	24	5	1	52	49	32	.275	.343	.349	99	4	0	69	31			**.943**	-26	*3/S	-2.3
1915	NY-N	106	386	46	97	18	4	0	38	25	24	.251	.304	.319	94	-6	-3	38	14	15	-5	.950	-5	*3	-1.0
1916	NY-N	48	76	6	17	3	2	0	11	5	8	.224	.272	.316	84	-2	-1	8	2			.961	2	3	0.1
1917	NY-N	50	52	4	10	1	0	1	5	5	5	.192	.276	.269	70	-2	-2	4	2			.906	2	3	0.0
Total	14	1317	4563	640	1252	159	82	32	482	395	156	.274	.337	.366	109	54	47	679	316	15		.944	-146	3S/O2	-8.2
■ HARRY LOCHHEAD Lochhead, Robert Henry b: 3/29/1876, Stockton, Cal. d: 8/22/09, Stockton, Cal. TR, Deb: 4/16/1899																									
1899	Cle-N	148	541	52	129	7	1	1	43	21		.238	.280	.261	52	-38	-32	48	23			.909	2	*S/2P	-1.7
1901	Det-A	1	4	2	2	0	0	0	0	0		.500	.600	.500	198	1	1	1	0			.857	0	/S	0.1
	Phi-A	9	34	3	3	0	0	0	2	3		.088	.162	.088	-28	-6	-6	0	0			.757	-8	/S	-1.3
	Yr	10	38	5	5	0	0	0	2	3		.132	.214	.132	-2	-5	-5	1	0			.773	-8	S	-1.2
Total	2	158	579	57	134	7	1	1	45	24		.231	.275	.252	48	-43	-38	50	23			.903	-6	S/P2	-2.9
■ DON LOCK Lock, Don Wilson b: 7/27/36, Wichita, Kan. BR/TR, 6'2", 202 lbs. Deb: 7/17/62																									
1962	Was-A	71	225	30	57	6	2	12	37	30	63	.253	.341	.458	114	4	4	33	4	5	-2	.973	3	O	0.1
1963	Was-A	149	531	71	134	20	1	27	82	70	151	.252	.342	.446	119	14	14	83	7	3	0	.980	15	*O	2.2
1964	Was-A	152	512	73	127	17	4	28	80	79	137	.248	.350	.461	124	17	17	84	4	2	0	.987	13	*O	2.4
1965	Was-A	143	418	52	90	15	1	16	39	57	115	.215	.317	.371	96	-2	-2	48	1	3	-2	.969	2	*O	-0.7
1966	Was-A	138	386	52	90	13	1	16	48	57	126	.233	.335	.396	110	5	6	51	2	6	-3	.977	7	*O	0.5
1967	Phi-N	112	313	46	79	13	1	14	51	43	98	.252	.352	.435	123	10	10	50	9	5	-0	.973	5	O	1.1
1968	Phi-N	99	248	27	52	7	2	8	34	26	64	.210	.285	.351	90	-3	-3	24	3	4	-2	.955	3	O	-0.6
1969	Phi-N	4	4	0	0	0	0	0	0	0	1	.000	.000	.000	-99	-1	-1	0	0	0	0	.000	0	/O	-0.1
	Bos-A	53	58	8	13	1	0	1	2	11	21	.224	.348	.293	77	-1	-1	6	0	1	-1	1.000	-6	O/1	-0.9
Total	8	921	2695	359	642	92	12	122	373	373	776	.238	.334	.417	111	42	43	379	30	29	-8	.976	41	O/1	4.0
■ MARSHALL LOCKE Locke, Marshall b: Indianapolis, Ind. Deb: 7/05/1884																									
1884	Ind-a	7	29	5	7	0	1	0		0		.241	.241	.310	83	-1	-1	2				.800	-1	/O	-0.2
■ GENE LOCKLEAR Locklear, Gene b: 7/19/49, Lumberton, N.C. BL/TR, 5'10", 165 lbs. Deb: 4/05/73																									
1973	Cin-N	29	26	6	5	0	0	0	0	2	5	.192	.276	.192	34	-2	-2	1	0	0	0	1.000	0	/O	-0.2
	SD-N	67	154	20	37	6	1	3	25	21	22	.240	.331	.351	97	-2	-0	19	9	4	0	.952	-0	O	-0.2
	Yr	96	180	26	42	6	1	3	25	23	27	.233	.324	.328	87	-4	-3	20	9	4	0	.954	-0	O	-0.4
1974	SD-N	39	74	7	20	3	2	1	3	4	12	.270	.308	.405	103	-0	-0	9	0	1	-1	1.000	-1	O	-0.2
1975	SD-N	100	237	31	76	11	1	5	27	22	26	.321	.381	.439	135	9	10	40	4	2	0	.970	-4	O	0.5
1976	SD-N	43	67	9	15	3	0	0	8	4	15	.224	.268	.269	57	-4	-4	5	0	0	0	.952	-1	O	-0.6
	NY-A	13	32	2	7	1	0	0	1	2	7	.219	.265	.250	52	-2	-2	2	0	0	0	1.000	-1	/OD	-0.3
1977	NY-A	1	5	1	3	0	0	0	2	0	0	.600	.600	.600	231	1	1	2	0	0	0	.667	-0	/O	0.1
Total	5	292	595	76	163	24	4	9	66	55	87	.274	.337	.373	105	-1	3	78	13	7	-0	.962	-6	O/D	-0.9
■ STU LOCKLIN Locklin, Stuart Carlton b: 7/22/28, Appleton, Wis. BL/TL, 6'1.5", 190 lbs. Deb: 6/23/55																									
1955	Cle-A	16	18	4	3	1	0	0	0	3	4	.167	.286	.222	37	-2	-2	1	0	0	0	1.000	-3	/O	-0.4
1956	Cle-A	9	6	0	1	0	0	0	0	0	1	.167	.167	.167	-12	-1	-1	0	0	0	0	1.000	-0	/O	-0.1
Total	2	25	24	4	4	1	0	0	0	3	5	.167	.259	.208	26	-2	-3	1	0	0	0	1.000	-3	/O	-0.5
■ WHITEY LOCKMAN Lockman, Carroll Walter b: 7/25/26, Lowell, N.C. BL/TR, 6'1", 175 lbs. Deb: 7/05/45 MC																									
1945	NY-N	32	129	16	44	9	0	3	18	13	10	.341	.410	.481	145	8	8	27	1			.961	-4	O	0.3
1947	NY-N	2	2	0	1	0	0	0	1	0	0	.500	.500	.500	165	0	0	1	0			.000	0	H	0.0
1948	NY-N	146	584	117	167	24	10	18	59	68	63	.286	.361	.454	119	15	15	101	8			.987	7	*O	1.4
1949	NY-N	151	617	97	186	32	7	11	65	62	31	.301	.368	.429	113	12	12	101	12			.973	4	*O	0.9
1950	NY-N	129	532	72	157	28	5	6	52	42	29	.295	.349	.400	96	-3	-3	76	1			.978	9	*O	0.1
1951	*NY-N	153	614	85	173	27	7	12	73	50	32	.282	.339	.407	99	-1	-1	83	4	5	-2	.986	4	*1O	-0.6
1952	NY-N★	154	606	99	176	17	4	13	58	67	52	.290	.363	.396	110	10	9	92	2	4	-2	.992	2	*1	0.4
1953	NY-N	150	607	85	179	22	4	9	61	52	36	.295	.351	.389	91	-6	-7	87	3	4	-2	.989	7	*1O	-0.8
1954	*NY-N	148	570	73	143	17	3	16	60	59	31	.251	.321	.375	80	-16	-17	73	2	2	-1	.987	-8	*1/O	-3.2
1955	NY-N	147	576	76	157	19	0	15	49	39	34	.273	.322	.384	86	-12	-12	72	3	3	-1	.983	-4	O1	-2.4
1956	NY-N	48	169	13	46	7	1	1	10	16	17	.272	.335	.343	83	-4	-4	20	0	2	-1	.960	-1	O/1	-0.8
	StL-N	70	193	14	48	0	2	0	10	18	8	.249	.313	.269	59	-11	-11	17	2	2	-1	.955	-8	O/1	-2.3
	Yr	118	362	27	94	7	3	1	20	34	25	.260	.323	.304	70	-14	-14	37	2	4	-2	.957	-8	O/1	-3.1
1957	NY-N	133	456	51	113	9	4	7	30	39	19	.248	.310	.331	73	-17	-17	48	5	5	-2	.991	-6	*1O	-3.3
1958	SF-N	92	122	15	29	5	0	2	7	13	8	.238	.311	.328	71	-5	-5	14	0	0	0	1.000	-11	O2/1	-1.6
1959	Bal-A	38	69	7	15	1	1	0	2	8	4	.217	.299	.261	56	-4	-4	6	0	0	0	.992	-4	1/2O	-0.8
	Cin-N	52	84	10	22	5	1	0	7	4	6	.262	.295	.345	68	-4	-4	9	0	0	0	.971	0	1/23O	-0.4
1960	Cin-N	21	10	6	2	0	0	1	1	2	3	.200	.385	.500	138	1	1	2	0	0	0	1.000	0	/1	0.1
Total	15	1666	5940	836	1658	222	49	114	563	552	383	.279	.342	.391	95	-36	-40	826	43	27		.989	-9	1O/23	-13.0
■ SKIP LOCKWOOD Lockwood, Claude Edward b: 8/17/46, Boston, Mass. BR/TR, 6', 190 lbs. Deb: 4/23/65																									
1965	KC-A	42	33	4	4	0	0	0	0	7	11	.121	.293	.121	23	-3	-3	2	0	0	0	1.000	2	/3	-0.1
1969	Sea-A	6	7	0	0	0	0	0	0	0	2	.000	.000	.000	-99	-2	-2	0	0	0	0	1.000	0	/P	0.0
1970	Mil-A	27	53	2	12	1	0	1	2	1	11	.226	.241	.302	48	-4	-4	4	0	0	0	.970	-1	P	0.0
1971	Mil-A	36	62	2	5	1	0	1	4	5	20	.081	.149	.145	-17	-10	-9	2	0	0	0	1.000	-3	P	0.0
1972	Mil-A	31	53	3	7	0	0	0	0	3	12	.132	.193	.132	-2	-7	-6	1	0	1	-1	.958	-3	P	0.0
1973	Mil-A	37	0	0	0	0	0	0	0	0	0	—	—	—	—	0	0	0	0	0	0	.944	0	P	0.0
1974	Cal-A	37	0	0	0	0	0	0	0	0	0	—	—	—	—	0	0	0	0	0	0	1.000	-0	P	0.0
1975	NY-N	24	6	0	1	0	0	0	1	0	0	.167	.167	.167	-8	-1	-1	0	0	0	0	.800	-1	P	0.0
1976	NY-N	56	18	2	6	1	0	0	2	2	3	.333	.400	.389	132	1	1	3	0	1	-1	.867	-0	P	0.0
1977	NY-N	63	15	1	3	0	0	0	1	0	1	.200	.200	.200	8	-2	-2	1	0	0	0	.875	-2	P	0.0
1978	NY-N	57	11	1	2	1	0	1	1	0	5	.182	.182	.545	100	-0	-0	1	0	0	0	.900	-2	P	0.0
1979	NY-N	28	2	0	0	0	0	0	0	0	1	.000	.000	.000	-99	-1	-1	0	0	0	0	.800	-1	P	0.0
1980	Bos-A	24	0	0	0	0	0	0	0	0	0	—	—	—	—	0	0	0	0	0	0	1.000	-1	P	0.0
Total	13	468	260	15	40	4	0	3	11	18	66	.154	.214	.204	19	-28	-27	14	0	2	-1	.947	-11	P/3	-0.1
■ MILO LOCKWOOD Lockwood, Milo Hathaway b: 4/7/1858, Solon, Ohio d: 10/9/1897, Economy, Pa. 5'10", 160 lbs. Deb: 4/17/1884																									
1884	Was-U	20	67	9	14	1	0	0		8		.209	.293	.224	80	-1	-1	5				.773	2	OP/3	0.0
■ DARIO LODIGIANI Lodigiani, Dario Antonio b: 6/6/16, San Francisco, Cal BR/TR, 5'8", 150 lbs. Deb: 4/18/38 C																									
1938	Phi-A	93	325	36	91	15	1	6	44	34	25	.280	.361	.388	90	-6	-5	48	3	0	1	.953	-6	23	-0.5
1939	Phi-A	121	393	46	102	22	4	6	44	42	18	.260	.337	.382	85	-10	-9	52	2	0	1	.944	2	32	-0.4
1940	Phi-A	1	1	0	0	0	0	0	0	0	0	.000	.000	.000	-99	-0	-0	0	0	0	0	.000	0	H	0.0
1941	Chi-A	87	322	39	77	19	2	4	40	31	19	.239	.316	.348	76	-12	-11	34	0	4	-2	.962	6	3	-0.5
1942	Chi-A	59	168	9	47	7	0	0	15	18	10	.280	.353	.321	92	-2	-1	19	3	4	-2	.944	6	3/2	0.4
1946	Chi-A	44	155	12	38	8	0	0	13	16	14	.245	.324	.297	77	-5	-4	17	4	0	1	.935	-5	3	-0.7
Total	6	405	1364	142	355	71	7	16	156	141	86	.260	.338	.358	84	-34	-30	170	12	8	-1	.947	3	32	-1.7
■ GEORGE LOEPP Loepp, George Herbert b: 9/11/01, Detroit, Mich. d: 9/4/67, Los Angeles, Cal. BR/TR, 5'11", 170 lbs. Deb: 8/29/28																									
1928	Bos-A	15	51	6	9	3	1	0	3	5	12	.176	.250	.275	38	-5	-5	4	0	0	0	.949	-0	O	-0.6

YEAR	TM/L	G	AB	R	H	2B	3B	HR	RBI	BB	SO	AVG	OBP	SLG	PRO+	BR	/A	RC	SB	CS	SBR	FA	FR	POS	TPR
1930	Was-A	50	134	23	37	7	1	0	14	20	9	.276	.382	.343	85	-2	-2	18	0	4	-2	.958	-5	O	-1.1
Total	2	65	185	29	46	10	2	0	17	25	21	.249	.347	.324	73	-7	-7	22	0	4	-2	.956	-6	/O	-1.7
■ **KENNY LOFTON**	Lofton, Kenneth b: 5/31/67, E.Chicago, Ind. BL/TL, 6', 180 lbs. Deb: 9/14/91																								
1991	Hou-N	20	74	9	15	1	0	0	0	5	19	.203	.253	.216	35	-6	-6	4	2	1	0	.977	0	O	-0.7
1992	Cle-A	148	576	96	164	15	8	5	42	68	54	.285	.362	.365	103	5	4	87	**66**	12	**13**	.982	17	*O	3.0
Total	2	168	650	105	179	16	8	5	42	73	73	.275	.350	.348	96	-1	-2	92	68	13	13	.981	17	O	2.3
■ **DICK LOFTUS**	Loftus, Richard Joseph b: 3/7/01, Concord, Mass. d: 1/21/72, Concord, Mass. BL/TR, 6', 155 lbs. Deb: 4/20/24																								
1924	Bro-N	46	81	18	22	6	0	0	8	7	2	.272	.330	.346	84	-2	-2	10	1	0	0	1.000	-3	O/1	-0.6
1925	Bro-N	51	131	16	31	6	0	0	13	5	5	.237	.275	.282	44	-11	-11	11	2	0	1	.977	1	O	-1.1
Total	2	97	212	34	53	12	0	0	21	12	7	.250	.296	.307	59	-13	-12	20	3	0	1	.985	-3	/O1	-1.7
■ **TOM LOFTUS**	Loftus, Thomas Joseph b: 11/15/1856, St.Louis, Mo. d: 4/16/10, Dubuque, Iowa BR , 168 lbs. Deb: 8/17/1877 M																								
1877	StL-N	3	11	2	2	0	0	0	0	0	1	.182	.182	.182	16	-1	-1	0				.778	2	/O	0.1
1883	StL-a	6	22	1	4	0	0	0		2		.182	.250	.182	39	-1	-2	1				.882	0	/O	-0.1
Total	2	9	33	3	6	0	0	0	0	2	1	.182	.229	.182	32	-2	-2	1				.846	2	/O	0.0
■ **JOHNNY LOGAN**	Logan, John "Yatcha" b: 3/23/27, Endicott, N.Y. BR/TR, 5'11", 175 lbs. Deb: 4/17/51																								
1951	Bos-N	62	169	14	37	7	1	0	16	18	13	.219	.298	.272	59	-11	-9	14	0	0	0	.958	4	S	-0.1
1952	Bos-N	117	456	56	129	21	3	4	42	31	33	.283	.334	.368	98	-3	-1	57	1	2	-1	**.972**	18	*S	2.4
1953	Mil-N	150	611	100	167	27	8	11	73	41	33	.273	.326	.398	93	-12	-6	80	2	2	-1	**.975**	21	*S	2.4
1954	Mil-N	154	560	66	154	17	7	8	66	51	51	.275	.342	.373	92	-11	-6	73	2	0	1	**.969**	14	*S	2.2
1955	Mil-N★	154	595	95	177	**37**	5	13	83	58	58	.297	.364	.442	118	11	15	96	3	3	-1	.963	8	*S	3.5
1956	Mil-N	148	545	69	153	27	5	15	46	46	49	.281	.342	.431	113	5	9	81	3	0	1	.968	3	*S	2.5
1957	*Mil-N☆	129	494	59	135	19	7	10	49	31	49	.273	.321	.401	100	-6	-1	62	5	0	2	.960	24	*S	3.7
1958	*Mil-N★	145	530	54	120	20	0	11	53	40	57	.226	.287	.326	68	-29	-24	51	1	2	-1	.959	10	*S	-0.1
1959	Mil-N☆	138	470	59	137	17	0	13	50	57	45	.291	.372	.411	118	7	12	71	1	3	-2	.975	-3	*S	2.0
1960	Mil-N	136	482	52	118	14	4	7	42	43	40	.245	.309	.334	82	-16	-11	50	1	1	-0	.956	2	*S	0.1
1961	Mil-N	18	19	0	2	1	0	0	1	1	3	.105	.150	.158	-19	-3	-3	0	0	0	0	1.000	-0	/S	-0.3
	Pit-N	27	52	5	12	4	0	0	5	4	8	.231	.286	.308	57	-3	-3	4	0	0	0	1.000	0	/3S	-0.2
	Yr	45	71	5	14	5	0	0	6	5	11	.197	.250	.268	38	-6	-6	4	0	0	0	.964	0	/S3	-0.5
1962	Pit-N	44	80	7	24	3	0	1	12	7	6	.300	.356	.375	96	-0	-0	10	0	0	0	.980	2	3	0.2
1963	Pit-N	81	181	15	42	2	1	0	9	23	27	.232	.325	.254	69	-6	-6	15	0	0	0	.920	2	S/3	-0.2
Total	13	1503	5244	651	1407	216	41	93	547	451	472	.268	.331	.378	95	-77	-35	665	19	13	-2	.965	105	*S/3	18.1
■ **PETE LOHMAN**	Lohman, George F. b: 10/21/1864, Lake Elmo, Minn. d: 11/21/28, Los Angeles, Cal. Deb: 5/11/1891																								
1891	Was-a	32	109	18	21	1	4	1	11	16	17	.193	.302	.303	79	-3	-2	11	1			.914	-3	C/O3S2	-0.3
■ **HOWARD LOHR**	Lohr, Howard Sylvester b: 6/3/1892, Philadelphia, Pa. d: 6/9/77, Philadelphia, Pa. BR/TR, 6', 165 lbs. Deb: 6/17/14																								
1914	Cin-N	18	47	6	10	1	1	0	7	0	8	.213	.213	.277	44	-3	-3	3	2			.926	-3	O	-0.8
1916	Cle-A	3	7	0	1	0	0	0	1	0	1	.143	.143	.143	-13	-1	-1	0	1			1.000	-1	/O	-0.2
Total	2	21	54	6	11	1	1	0	8	0	9	.204	.204	.259	36	-4	-5	3	3			.933	-4	/O	-1.0
■ **JACK LOHRKE**	Lohrke, Jack Wayne "Lucky" b: 2/25/24, Los Angeles, Cal. BR/TR, 6', 180 lbs. Deb: 4/18/47																								
1947	NY-N	112	329	44	79	12	4	11	35	46	29	.240	.337	.401	95	-2	-3	45	3			.939	-2	*3	-0.4
1948	NY-N	97	280	35	70	15	1	5	31	30	30	.250	.323	.364	85	-6	-6	33	3			.898	-2	32	-0.6
1949	NY-N	55	180	32	48	11	4	5	22	16	12	.267	.333	.456	110	2	2	27	3			.969	4	23S	0.7
1950	NY-N	30	43	4	8	0	0	0	4	4	8	.186	.255	.186	18	-5	-5	2	0			.958	0	3/2	-0.5
1951	*NY-N	23	40	3	8	0	0	1	3	10	2	.200	.360	.275	73	-1	-1	4	0	0	0	.943	-1	3/S	-0.2
1952	Phi-N	25	29	4	6	0	0	0	1	4	3	.207	.303	.207	44	-2	-2	2	0	0	0	1.000	1	/S32	-0.1
1953	Phi-N	12	13	3	2	0	0	0	0	1	2	.154	.214	.154	-2	-2	-2	0	0	0	0	.750	1	/2S3	-0.1
Total	7	354	914	125	221	38	9	22	96	111	86	.242	.327	.375	87	-16	-17	114	9	0		.928	2	3/2S	-1.2
■ **ALBERTO LOIS**	Lois, Alberto (b: Alberto Louis (Pie)) b: 5/6/56, Hato Mayor, D.R. BR/TR, 5'9", 175 lbs. Deb: 9/08/78																								
1978	Pit-N	3	4	0	1	0	1	0	0	0	1	.250	.250	.750	163	0	0	1	0	0	0	1.000	1	/O	0.1
1979	Pit-N	11	0	6	0	0	0	0	0	0	0	—	—	—	—	0	0	0	1	1	-0	.000	0	/R	0.0
Total	2	14	4	6	1	0	1	0	0	0	1	.250	.250	.750	163	0	0	1	1	1	-0	.959	1	/O	0.1
■ **RON LOLICH**	Lolich, Ronald John b: 9/19/46, Portland, Ore. BR/TR, 6'1", 185 lbs. Deb: 7/18/71																								
1971	Chi-A	2	8	0	1	1	0	0	0	0	2	.125	.125	.250	4	-1	-1	0	0	0	0	1.000	-1	/O	-0.2
1972	Cle-A	24	80	4	15	1	0	2	8	4	20	.188	.226	.275	47	-5	-5	5	0	0	0	1.000	-1	O	-0.8
1973	Cle-A	61	140	16	32	7	0	2	15	7	27	.229	.265	.321	63	-7	-7	11	0	2	-1	.909	-4	OD	-1.4
Total	3	87	228	20	48	9	0	4	23	11	49	.211	.247	.303	56	-13	-14	16	0	2	-1	.953	-5	/OD	-2.4
■ **SHERM LOLLAR**	Lollar, John Sherman b: 8/23/24, Durham, Ark. d: 9/24/77, Springfield, Mo. BR/TR, 6'1", 185 lbs. Deb: 4/20/46 C																								
1946	Cle-A	28	62	7	15	6	0	1	9	5	9	.242	.299	.387	97	-1	-1	7	0	1	-1	.990	-3	C	-0.4
1947	*NY-A	11	32	4	7	0	1	1	6	1	5	.219	.242	.375	71	-2	-1	2	0	1	-1	1.000	1	/C	-0.1
1948	NY-A	22	38	0	8	0	0	0	4	1	6	.211	.231	.211	18	-4	-4	1	0	0	0	.976	1	C	-0.2
1949	StL-A	109	284	28	74	9	1	8	49	32	22	.261	.340	.384	88	-4	-6	38	0	1	-1	.988	-3	C	-0.5
1950	StL-A☆	126	396	55	111	22	3	13	65	64	25	.280	.391	.449	110	10	7	74	2	0	1	.981	-5	*C	0.8
1951	StL-A	98	310	44	78	21	0	8	44	43	26	.252	.350	.397	99	1	-0	41	1	0	0	**.995**	-2	C/3	0.2
1952	Chi-A	132	375	35	90	15	0	13	50	54	34	.240	.354	.384	104	4	3	53	1	0	0	.989	-2	*C	0.7
1953	Chi-A	113	334	46	96	19	0	8	54	47	29	.287	.388	.416	114	10	8	59	1	0	0	**.994**	-2	*C/1	1.1
1954	Chi-A☆	107	316	31	77	13	0	7	34	37	28	.244	.336	.351	85	-5	-6	39	0	1	-1	.993	-3	C	-0.5
1955	Chi-A☆	138	426	67	111	13	1	16	61	68	34	.261	.375	.408	108	8	6	68	2	2	-1	.995	10	*C	2.0
1956	Chi-A★	136	450	55	132	28	2	11	75	53	34	.293	.387	.438	116	13	12	76	2	0	1	**.993**	4	*C	2.0
1957	Chi-A	101	351	33	90	11	2	11	70	35	24	.256	.346	.393	101	1	1	50	2	0	1	.998	-2	C	0.4
1958	Chi-A☆	127	421	53	115	16	0	20	84	57	37	.273	.370	.454	128	16	17	72	2	1	0	.987	2	*C	2.6
1959	*Chi-A★	140	505	63	134	22	3	22	84	55	49	.265	.348	.451	119	12	13	73	4	3	-1	.993	10	*C1	2.8
1960	Chi-A★	129	421	43	106	23	0	7	46	42	39	.252	.331	.356	87	-8	-7	47	2	0	1	**.995**	-2	*C	-0.2
1961	Chi-A	116	337	38	95	10	1	7	41	37	22	.282	.363	.380	100	0	1	48	0	0	0	**.998**	-10	*C	-0.3
1962	Chi-A	84	220	17	59	12	0	2	26	32	23	.268	.369	.350	95	-0	-0	29	1	0	0	.991	-8	C	-0.6
1963	Chi-A	35	73	4	17	4	0	0	6	8	7	.233	.317	.288	72	-3	-2	7	0	0	0	.981	-2	C/1	-0.4
Total	18	1752	5351	623	1415	244	14	155	808	671	453	.264	.359	.402	104	47	40	782	20	10	0	.992	-16	*C/13	9.4
■ **DOUG LOMAN**	Loman, Douglas Edward b: 5/9/58, Bakersfield, Cal. BL/TL, 5'11", 185 lbs. Deb: 9/03/84																								
1984	Mil-A	23	76	13	21	4	0	2	12	15	7	.276	.402	.408	130	3	4	13	0	2	-1	.967	3	O	0.5
1985	Mil-A	24	66	10	14	3	2	0	7	1	12	.212	.224	.318	47	-5	-5	5	0	0	0	1.000	1	O	-0.4
Total	2	47	142	23	35	7	2	2	19	16	19	.246	.327	.366	93	-2	-1	18	0	2	-1	.981	4	/O	0.1
■ **ERNIE LOMBARDI**	Lombardi, Ernesto Natali "Schnozz" or "Bocci" b: 4/6/08, Oakland, Cal. d: 9/26/77, Santa Cruz, Cal. BR/TR, 6'3", 230 lbs. Deb: 4/15/31 H																								
1931	Bro-N	73	182	20	54	7	1	4	23	12	12	.297	.340	.412	102	0	0	26	1			.984	3	C	0.6
1932	Cin-N	118	413	43	125	22	9	11	68	41	19	.303	.371	.479	131	16	18	76	0			.963	-11	*C	1.3
1933	Cin-N	107	350	30	99	21	1	4	47	16	17	.283	.322	.383	102	-0	0	36	2			.972	-16	C	-1.0
1934	Cin-N	132	417	42	127	19	4	9	62	16	22	.305	.335	.434	107	2	3	53	0			.989	-3	*C	0.5

YEAR	TM/L	G	AB	R	H	2B	3B	HR	RBI	BB	SO	AVG	OBP	SLG	PRO+	BR	/A	RC	SB	CS	SBR	FA	FR	POS	TPR
1935	Cin-N	120	332	36	114	23	3	12	64	16	6	.343	.379	.539	148	19	21	65	0			.983	-6	C	1.8
1936	Cin-N☆	121	387	42	129	23	2	12	68	19	16	.333	.375	.496	142	17	20	69	1			.962	-13	*C	1.1
1937	Cin-N☆	120	368	41	123	22	1	9	59	14	17	.334	.362	.473	132	12	14	60	1			.973	-18	C	0.1
1938	Cin-N★	129	489	60	167	30	1	19	95	40	14	**.342**	.391	.524	154	32	34	91	0			.985	-3	*C	3.7
1939	*Cin-N★	130	450	43	129	26	2	20	85	35	19	.287	.342	.487	120	11	11	67	0			.984	4	*C	2.1
1940	*Cin-N★	109	376	50	120	22	0	14	74	31	14	.319	.382	.489	137	20	19	66	0			.989	-4	*C	2.3
1941	Cin-N	117	398	33	105	12	1	10	60	36	14	.264	.325	.374	96	-2	-2	45	1			.983	-1	*C	0.6
1942	Bos-N★	105	309	32	102	14	0	11	46	37	12	.330	.403	.482	162	23	24	56	1			.980	-16	C	1.5
1943	NY-N★	104	295	19	90	7	0	10	51	16	11	.305	.347	.431	123	8	8	38	1			.971	-14	C	-0.1
1944	NY-N	117	373	37	95	13	0	10	58	33	25	.255	.317	.370	93	-4	-4	38	0			.968	-15	*C	-1.3
1945	NY-N†	115	368	46	113	7	1	19	70	43	11	.307	.387	.486	140	21	20	69	0			.983	2	C	2.8
1946	NY-N	88	238	19	69	4	1	12	39	18	24	.290	.347	.466	129	8	8	37	0			.978	1	C	1.3
1947	NY-N	48	110	8	31	5	0	4	21	7	9	.282	.325	.436	100	-0	-0	15	0			.980	-3	C	-0.2
Total	17	1853	5855	601	1792	277	27	190	990	430	262	.306	.358	.460	126	180	191	907	8			.979	-113	*C	17.1

■ PHIL LOMBARDI
Lombardi, Phillip Andrew b: 2/20/63, Abilene, Tex. BR/TR, 6'2", 200 lbs. Deb: 4/26/86

YEAR	TM/L	G	AB	R	H	2B	3B	HR	RBI	BB	SO	AVG	OBP	SLG	PRO+	BR	/A	RC	SB	CS	SBR	FA	FR	POS	TPR
1986	NY-A	20	36	6	10	3	0	2	6	4	7	.278	.366	.528	141	2	2	6	0	0	0	.867	-1	/OC	0.1
1987	NY-A	5	8	0	1	0	0	0	0	0	2	.125	.125	.125	-34	-2	-1	0	0	0	0	1.000	-0	/C	-0.2
1989	NY-N	18	48	4	11	1	0	1	3	5	8	.229	.302	.313	80	-1	-1	4	0	0	0	.980	-1	C/1	-0.2
Total	3	43	92	10	22	4	0	3	9	9	17	.239	.314	.380	95	-1	-1	11	0	0	0	.975	-2	/CO1	-0.3

■ STEVE LOMBARDOZZI
Lombardozzi, Stephen Paul b: 4/26/60, Malden, Mass. BR/TR, 6', 175 lbs. Deb: 7/12/85

YEAR	TM/L	G	AB	R	H	2B	3B	HR	RBI	BB	SO	AVG	OBP	SLG	PRO+	BR	/A	RC	SB	CS	SBR	FA	FR	POS	TPR
1985	Min-A	28	54	10	20	4	1	0	6	6	6	.370	.433	.481	142	4	4	12	3	2	-0	.982	11	2	1.5
1986	Min-A	156	453	53	103	20	5	8	33	52	76	.227	.308	.347	76	-14	-15	50	3	1	0	**.991**	-3	*2	-1.2
1987	*Min-A	136	432	51	103	19	3	8	38	33	66	.238	.299	.352	69	-18	-20	46	5	1	1	.977	-1	*2	-1.3
1988	Min-A	103	287	34	60	15	2	3	27	35	48	.209	.299	.307	68	-11	-12	28	2	5	-2	.986	-7	2S/3	-1.8
1989	Hou-N	21	37	5	8	3	1	1	3	4	9	.216	.293	.432	109	0	0	5	0	0	0	.922	0	2/3	0.1
1990	Hou-N	2	1	0	0	0	0	0	0	1	1	.000	.500	.000	52	0	0	0	0	0	0	.000	0	/H	0.0
Total	6	446	1264	153	294	61	12	20	107	131	206	.233	.308	.347	76	-38	-43	141	13	9	-2	.983	1	2/S3	-2.7

■ WALTER LONERGAN
Lonergan, Walter E. b: 9/22/1885, Boston, Mass. d: 1/23/58, Lexington, Mass. BR/TR, 5'7", 156 lbs. Deb: 8/17/11

YEAR	TM/L	G	AB	R	H	2B	3B	HR	RBI	BB	SO	AVG	OBP	SLG	PRO+	BR	/A	RC	SB	CS	SBR	FA	FR	POS	TPR
1911	Bos-A	10	26	2	7	0	0	0	1	1		.269	.296	.269	59	-1	-1	3	1			.935	-1	/2S3	-0.2

■ DAN LONG
Long, Daniel W. b: 8/27/1867, Boston, Mass. d: 4/30/29, Sausalito, Cal. Deb: 8/29/1888

YEAR	TM/L	G	AB	R	H	2B	3B	HR	RBI	BB	SO	AVG	OBP	SLG	PRO+	BR	/A	RC	SB	CS	SBR	FA	FR	POS	TPR
1888	Lou-a	1	2	0	0	0	0	0	0	1		.000	.333	.000	14	-0	-0	0	0			.000	-0	/O	0.0
1890	Bal-a	21	77	19	12	0	0	0		14		.156	.301	.156	35	-5	-6	9	16			.939	-1	O	-0.6
Total	2	22	79	19	12	0	0	0	0	15		.152	.302	.152	35	-5	-6	9	16			.939	-1	/O	-0.6

■ HERMAN LONG
Long, Herman C. "Germany" or "Flying Dutchman" b: 4/13/1866, Chicago, Ill. d: 9/17/09, Denver, Colo. BL/TR, 5'8.5", 160 lbs. Deb: 4/17/1889

YEAR	TM/L	G	AB	R	H	2B	3B	HR	RBI	BB	SO	AVG	OBP	SLG	PRO+	BR	/A	RC	SB	CS	SBR	FA	FR	POS	TPR
1889	KC-a	136	574	137	158	32	6	3	60	64	63	.275	.358	.368	103	8	2	110	89			.874	32	*S/2O	3.5
1890	Bos-N	101	431	95	108	15	3	8	52	40	34	.251	.320	.355	91	-1	-7	66	49			.898	11	*S	0.9
1891	Bos-N	139	577	129	163	21	11	10	76	80	51	.282	.377	.409	117	25	14	115	60			.902	15	*S	3.2
1892	*Bos-N	151	646	115	181	33	6	6	78	44	36	.280	.334	.378	107	12	3	103	57			.889	14	*SO/3	2.1
1893	Bos-N	128	552	**149**	159	22	6	6	58	73	32	.288	.376	.382	96	5	-3	96	38			.883	16	*S/2	1.5
1894	Bos-N	104	475	136	154	28	11	12	79	35	17	.324	.375	.505	104	8	0	102	24			.885	4	*S/O2	0.7
1895	Bos-N	124	535	109	169	23	10	9	75	31	12	.316	.357	.447	100	5	-3	102	35			.891	-7	*S/2	-0.3
1896	Bos-N	120	501	105	172	26	8	6	100	26	16	.343	.382	.463	117	16	11	106	36			.897	10	*S	2.2
1897	*Bos-N	107	450	89	145	32	7	3	69	23		.322	.358	.444	105	5	1	83	22			.905	-2	*S/O	0.1
1898	Bos-N	144	589	99	156	21	10	6	99	39		.265	.311	.365	89	-7	-12	77	20			.923	2	*S/2	-0.3
1899	Bos-N	145	578	91	153	30	8	6	100	45		.265	.321	.375	83	-9	-18	81	20			.929	-10	*S/1	-1.5
1900	Bos-N	125	486	80	127	19	4	**12**	66	44		.261	.325	.391	87	-3	-12	74	26			.937	-6	*S	-0.8
1901	Bos-N	138	518	54	112	14	6	3	68	25		.216	.254	.284	51	-30	-36	45	20			**.946**	-3	*S	-2.7
1902	Bos-N	120	439	40	101	11	0	2	44	31		.230	.281	.269	69	-16	-16	42	24			**.946**	23	*S2	1.4
1903	NY-A	22	80	6	15	3	0	0	8	2		.188	.207	.225	28	-7	-7	5	3			.889	-4	S	-1.1
	Det-A	69	239	21	53	12	0	0	23	10		.222	.256	.272	60	-12	-11	21	11			.879	2	S2	-0.7
	Yr	91	319	27	68	15	0	0	31	12		.213	.244	.260	52	-19	-19	26	14			.883	-2	S2	-1.8
1904	Phi-N	1	4	0	1	0	0	0	0	0		.250	.250	.250	57	-0	-0	0	0			.889	1	/2	0.1
Total	16	1874	7674	1455	2127	342	96	92	1055	612	261	.277	.335	.383	94	-1	-93	1228	534			.906	97	*S/2013	8.3

■ JIMMIE LONG
Long, James Albert b: 6/29/1898, Ft.Dodge, Iowa d: 9/14/70, Ft.Dodge, Iowa BR/TR, 5'11", 160 lbs. Deb: 9/12/22

YEAR	TM/L	G	AB	R	H	2B	3B	HR	RBI	BB	SO	AVG	OBP	SLG	PRO+	BR	/A	RC	SB	CS	SBR	FA	FR	POS	TPR
1922	Chi-A	3	3	0	0	0	0	0	0	1	0	.000	.250	.000	-30	-1	-1	0	0	0	0	1.000	-1	/C	-0.1

■ JIM LONG
Long, James M. b: 11/15/1862, Louisville, Ky. d: 12/12/32, Louisville, Ky. Deb: 8/09/1891

YEAR	TM/L	G	AB	R	H	2B	3B	HR	RBI	BB	SO	AVG	OBP	SLG	PRO+	BR	/A	RC	SB	CS	SBR	FA	FR	POS	TPR
1891	Lou-a	6	25	5	6	0	0	0	4	3	6	.240	.367	.240	78	-0	-0	3	1			.857	1	/O	0.0
1893	Bal-N	55	226	31	48	8	1	2	25	16	27	.212	.276	.283	49	-16	-17	25	23			.893	-1	O	-1.7
Total	2	61	251	36	54	8	1	2	29	19	33	.215	.286	.279	52	-17	-17	27	24			.890	-0	/O	-1.7

■ JEOFF LONG
Long, Jeoffrey Keith b: 10/9/41, Covington, Ky. BR/TR, 6'1", 200 lbs. Deb: 7/31/63

YEAR	TM/L	G	AB	R	H	2B	3B	HR	RBI	BB	SO	AVG	OBP	SLG	PRO+	BR	/A	RC	SB	CS	SBR	FA	FR	POS	TPR
1963	StL-N	5	5	0	1	0	0	0	0	0	1	.200	.200	.200	14	-1	-1	0	0	0	0	.000	0	H	-0.1
1964	StL-N	28	43	5	10	1	0	1	4	6	18	.233	.340	.326	81	-0	-1	5	0	0	0	.833	-2	/O1	-0.3
	Chi-A	23	35	0	5	0	0	0	5	4	15	.143	.231	.143	7	-4	-4	1	0	0	0	1.000	-1	/1O	-0.5
Total	2	56	83	5	16	1	0	1	9	10	34	.193	.287	.241	48	-5	-6	7	0	0	0	.750	-2	/O1	-0.9

■ DALE LONG
Long, Richard Dale b: 2/6/26, Springfield, Mo. d: 1/27/91, Palm Coast, Fla. BL/TL, 6'4", 210 lbs. Deb: 4/21/51 C

YEAR	TM/L	G	AB	R	H	2B	3B	HR	RBI	BB	SO	AVG	OBP	SLG	PRO+	BR	/A	RC	SB	CS	SBR	FA	FR	POS	TPR
1951	Pit-N	10	12	1	2	0	0	1	1	0	3	.167	.167	.417	50	-1	-1	1	0	0	0	1.000	-0	/1	-0.1
	StL-A	34	105	11	25	5	1	2	11	10	22	.238	.310	.362	79	-3	-3	13	0	0	0	.988	-1	1/O	-0.5
1955	Pit-N	131	419	59	122	19	**13**	16	79	48	72	.291	.365	.513	132	18	18	76	0	1	-1	.988	6	*1	1.7
1956	Pit-N★	148	517	64	136	20	7	27	91	54	85	.263	.333	.485	119	11	12	83	1	0	0	.982	-3	*1	0.1
1957	Pit-N	7	22	0	4	1	0	0	5	4	10	.182	.308	.227	48	-2	-1	2	0	0	0	1.000	0	/1	-0.2
	Chi-N	123	397	55	121	19	0	21	62	52	63	.305	.387	.511	141	22	23	79	1	1	-0	.995	-1	*1	1.5
	Yr	130	419	55	125	20	0	21	67	56	73	.298	.382	.496	136	21	22	80	1	1	-0	.995	-1	*1	1.3
1958	Chi-N	142	480	68	130	26	4	20	75	66	64	.271	.361	.467	119	12	13	80	2	0	1	.992	-2	*1/C	0.4
1959	Chi-N	110	296	34	70	10	3	14	37	31	53	.236	.309	.432	96	-3	-3	39	0	0	0	.985	-2	1	-0.9
1960	SF-N	37	54	4	9	0	0	3	6	7	7	.167	.262	.333	66	-3	-3	4	0	0	0	1.000	0	1	-0.3
	*NY-A	26	41	6	15	3	1	3	10	5	6	.366	.435	.707	216	6	6	12	0	0	0	.988	-1	1	0.5
1961	Was-A	123	377	52	94	20	4	17	49	39	41	.249	.321	.459	107	2	3	56	0	0	0	.983	-5	1	-1.0
1962	Was-A	67	191	17	46	8	0	4	24	18	22	.241	.310	.346	77	-6	-6	20	5	1	1	.996	-0	1	-0.9
	*NY-A	41	94	12	28	4	0	4	17	18	9	.298	.411	.468	140	5	6	19	1	0	0	.992	1	1	0.6
	Yr	108	285	29	74	12	0	8	41	36	31	.260	.345	.386	98	-1	-0	39	6	1	1	.995	1	1	-0.3
1963	NY-A	14	15	1	3	0	0	0	0	1	3	.200	.250	.200	28	-1	-1	1	0	0	0	.917	-1	/1	-0.2
Total	10	1013	3020	384	805	135	33	132	467	353	460	.267	.345	.464	116	57	63	485	10	3	1	.988	-7	1/CO	0.7

■ TOM LONG
Long, Thomas Augustus b: 6/1/1890, Mitchum, Ala. d: 6/15/72, Mobile, Ala. BR/TR, 5'10.5", 165 lbs. Deb: 9/11/11

YEAR	TM/L	G	AB	R	H	2B	3B	HR	RBI	BB	SO	AVG	OBP	SLG	PRO+	BR	/A	RC	SB	CS	SBR	FA	FR	POS	TPR
1911	Was-A	14	48	1	11	3	0	0	5	1		.229	.245	.292	50	-3	-3	4	4			.875	-2	O	-0.6
1912	Was-A	1	1	0	0	0	0	0	0	0		.000	.000	.000	-99	-0	-0	0	0			.000	0	H	0.0

YEAR	TM/L	G	AB	R	H	2B	3B	HR	RBI	BB	SO	AVG	OBP	SLG	PRO+	BR	/A	RC	SB	CS	SBR	FA	FR	POS	TPR
1915	StL-N	140	507	61	149	21	**25**	2	61	31	50	.294	.339	.446	137	20	20	77	19	15	-3	.927	-4	*O	0.8
1916	StL-N	119	403	37	118	11	10	1	33	10	43	.293	.312	.377	112	4	4	48	21	14	-2	.945	-8	*O	-1.3
1917	StL-N	144	530	49	123	12	14	3	41	37	44	.232	.285	.325	89	-9	-7	52	21			.919	-19	*O	-3.9
Total	5	418	1489	148	401	47	49	6	140	79	137	.269	.309	.379	110	11	13	182	65	29		.928	-33	O	-5.0
■ **JOE LONNETT**	Lonnett, Joseph Paul b: 2/7/27, Beaver Falls, Pa. BR/TR, 5'10", 180 lbs. Deb: 4/22/56 C																								
1956	Phi-N	16	22	2	4	0	0	0	0	2	7	.182	.250	.182	19	-2	-2	1	0	0	0	1.000	0	/C	-0.2
1957	Phi-N	67	160	12	27	5	0	5	15	22	39	.169	.273	.294	54	-11	-10	14	0	0	0	.997	5	C	-0.3
1958	Phi-N	17	50	0	7	2	0	0	2	2	11	.140	.173	.180	-6	-8	-8	2	0	0	0	.988	2	C	-0.5
1959	Phi-N	43	93	8	16	1	0	1	10	14	17	.172	.287	.215	36	-8	-8	6	0	1	-1	.983	-6	C	-1.4
Total	4	143	325	22	54	8	0	6	27	40	74	.166	.262	.246	37	-29	-29	22	0	1	-1	.992	1	C	-2.4
■ **BRUCE LOOK**	Look, Bruce Michael b: 6/9/43, Lansing, Mich. BL/TR, 5'11", 183 lbs. Deb: 4/17/68 F																								
1968	Min-A	59	118	7	29	4	0	0	9	20	24	.246	.355	.280	90	0	-1	12	0	1	-1	.996	2	C	0.3
■ **DEAN LOOK**	Look, Dean Zachary b: 7/23/37, Lansing, Mich. BR/TR, 5'11", 185 lbs. Deb: 9/22/61 F																								
1961	Chi-A	3	6	0	0	0	0	0	0	0	1	.000	.000	.000	-99	-2	-2	0	0	0	0	1.000	-0	/O	-0.2
■ **STAN LOPATA**	Lopata, Stanley Edward "Stash" b: 9/12/25, Delray, Mich. BR/TR, 6'2", 210 lbs. Deb: 9/19/48																								
1948	Phi-N	6	15	2	2	1	0	0	2	0	4	.133	.133	.200	-11	-2	-2	0	0			1.000	0	/C	-0.2
1949	Phi-N	83	240	31	65	9	2	8	27	21	44	.271	.330	.425	104	-0	1	33	1			.973	-3	C	0.1
1950	*Phi-N	58	129	10	27	2	2	1	11	22	25	.209	.325	.279	61	-7	-7	12	1			.974	1	C	-0.4
1951	Phi-N	3	5	0	0	0	0	0	0	0	0	.000	.000	.000	-99	-1	-1	0	0	0	0	1.000	0	/C	-0.1
1952	Phi-N	57	179	25	49	9	1	4	27	36	33	.274	.395	.402	123	7	7	31	1	1	-0	.987	6	C	1.6
1953	Phi-N	81	234	34	56	12	3	8	31	28	39	.239	.321	.419	91	-3	-3	35	3	1	0	.987	4	C	0.5
1954	Phi-N	86	259	42	75	14	5	14	42	33	37	.290	.372	.544	136	13	13	50	1	3	-2	.989	9	C/1	2.3
1955	Phi-N★	99	303	49	82	9	3	22	58	58	62	.271	.391	.538	146	20	21	64	4	1	1	.995	4	C1	2.6
1956	Phi-N☆	146	535	96	143	33	7	32	95	75	93	.267	.358	.535	138	27	28	100	5	2	0	.982	-18	*C1	1.3
1957	Phi-N	116	388	50	92	18	2	18	67	56	81	.237	.335	.433	108	3	4	56	2	2	-1	.988	-9	*C	-0.1
1958	Phi-N	86	258	36	64	9	0	9	33	60	63	.248	.394	.388	109	6	6	39	0	1	-1	.987	-9	C	0.1
1959	Mil-N	25	48	0	5	0	0	0	4	3	13	.104	.157	.104	-31	-9	-8	1	0	0	0	1.000	-3	C/1	-1.1
1960	Mil-N	7	8	0	1	0	0	0	0	1	3	.125	.222	.125	-2	-1	-1	0	0	0	0	.944	1	/C	0.0
Total	13	853	2601	375	661	116	25	116	397	393	497	.254	.354	.452	115	50	56	422	18	11		.986	-15	C/1	6.6
■ **DAVEY LOPES**	Lopes, David Earl b: 5/3/45, E.Providence, R.I. BR/TR, 5'9", 170 lbs. Deb: 9/22/72 C																								
1972	LA-N	11	42	6	9	4	0	0	1	7	6	.214	.327	.310	84	-1	-1	5	4	0	1	.964	-2	2	-0.1
1973	LA-N	142	535	77	147	13	5	6	37	62	77	.275	.355	.351	101	-1	2	69	36	16	1	.984	-12	*2/OS3	-0.1
1974	*LA-N	145	530	95	141	26	3	10	35	66	71	.266	.352	.383	110	5	7	77	59	18	7	.965	-22	*2	-0.1
1975	LA-N	155	618	108	162	24	6	8	41	91	93	.262	.359	.359	104	2	5	97	**77**	12	**16**	.979	-21	*2OS	0.7
1976	LA-N	117	427	72	103	17	7	4	20	56	49	.241	.335	.342	94	-3	-2	58	**63**	10	**13**	.964	-19	*2O	-0.3
1977	*LA-N	134	502	85	142	19	5	11	53	73	69	.283	.376	.406	110	9	9	87	47	12	7	.979	8	*2	3.4
1978	*LA-N★	151	587	93	163	25	4	17	58	71	70	.278	.356	.421	117	13	13	97	45	4	**11**	.974	3	*2/O	4.0
1979	LA-N★	153	582	109	154	20	6	28	73	97	88	.265	.373	.464	129	23	25	113	44	4	**11**	.981	-34	*2	1.2
1980	LA-N★	141	553	79	139	15	3	10	49	58	71	.251	.324	.344	88	-9	-8	65	23	7	3	.980	-16	*2	-1.3
1981	*LA-N★	58	214	35	44	2	0	5	17	22	35	.206	.289	.285	66	-10	-9	20	20	2	5	.993	-4	2	-0.5
1982	Oak-A	128	450	58	109	19	3	11	42	40	51	.242	.305	.371	89	-10	-7	49	28	12	1	.977	-19	*2/O	-1.9
1983	Oak-A	147	494	64	137	13	4	17	67	51	61	.277	.347	.423	118	8	11	76	22	4	4	.983	-38	*2D/O3	-1.7
1984	Oak-A	72	230	32	59	11	1	9	36	31	36	.257	.347	.430	122	5	7	36	12	0	4	.965	-8	O2/3D	0.2
	*Chi-N	16	17	5	4	1	0	0	0	6	5	.235	.435	.294	99	1	0	4	3	0	1	1.000	-2	/O2	-0.1
1985	Chi-N	99	275	52	78	11	0	11	44	46	37	.284	.386	.444	118	13	9	52	47	4	12	.991	-12	O/32	0.7
1986	Chi-N	59	157	38	47	8	2	6	22	31	16	.299	.421	.490	140	12	11	34	17	6	2	.902	-4	3O	0.7
	*Hou-N	37	98	11	23	2	1	1	13	12	9	.235	.318	.306	75	-3	-3	10	8	2	1	1.000	5	O/3	0.2
	Yr	96	255	49	70	10	3	7	35	43	25	.275	.383	.420	117	9	8	43	25	8	3	1.000	1	O3	0.9
1987	Hou-N	47	43	4	10	2	0	1	6	13	8	.233	.411	.349	108	1	1	7	2	1	0	.857	-1	/O	0.0
Total	16	1812	6354	1023	1671	232	50	155	614	833	852	.263	.351	.388	107	54	71	955	557	114	99	.977	-197	*2O/3DS	5.0
■ **AL LOPEZ**	Lopez, Alfonso Ramon b: 8/20/08, Tampa, Fla. BR/TR, 5'11", 165 lbs. Deb: 9/27/28 MH																								
1928	Bro-N	3	12	0	0	0	0	0	0	0	0	.000	.000	.000	-99	-3	-3	0	0			1.000	-2	/C	-0.5
1930	Bro-N	128	421	60	130	20	4	6	57	33	35	.309	.362	.418	89	-8	-7	62	3			.983	5	*C	0.7
1931	Bro-N	111	360	38	97	13	4	0	40	28	33	.269	.324	.328	76	-12	-12	40	1			.977	-8	*C	-1.2
1932	Bro-N	126	404	44	111	18	6	1	43	34	35	.275	.331	.356	87	-8	-7	50	3			.976	-2	*C	-0.2
1933	Bro-N	126	372	39	112	11	4	3	41	21	39	.301	.338	.376	108	2	4	47	10			.991	18	*C/2	3.0
1934	Bro-N★	140	439	58	120	23	2	7	54	49	44	.273	.349	.383	101	-2	1	60	2			.982	-7	*C/23	0.1
1935	Bro-N	128	379	50	95	12	4	3	39	35	36	.251	.316	.327	75	-14	-13	41	2			.980	6	*C	-0.1
1936	Bos-N	128	426	46	103	12	5	7	50	41	41	.242	.311	.343	81	-14	-11	45	1			.975	10	*C/1	0.5
1937	Bos-N	105	334	31	68	11	1	3	38	35	57	.204	.281	.269	55	-23	-19	25	3			.984	8	*C	-0.5
1938	Bos-N	71	236	19	63	6	1	1	14	11	24	.267	.305	.314	78	-9	-7	22	5			.989	3	C	0.0
1939	Bos-N	131	412	32	104	22	1	8	49	40	45	.252	.319	.369	91	-9	-6	49	1			.986	3	*C	0.4
1940	Bos-N	36	119	20	35	3	1	2	17	6	8	.294	.328	.387	102	-1	0	15	1			.987	2	C	0.4
	Pit-N	59	174	15	45	6	2	1	24	13	13	.259	.310	.333	78	-5	-5	17	5			.992	4	C	0.2
	Yr	95	293	35	80	9	3	3	41	19	21	.273	.317	.355	87	-6	-5	31	6			**.990**	6	C	0.6
1941	Pit-N★	114	317	33	84	9	1	5	43	31	23	.265	.330	.347	91	-4	-3	36	0			.980	-0	*C	0.5
1942	Pit-N	103	289	17	74	8	2	1	26	34	17	.256	.338	.308	88	-3	-4	31	0			**.995**	6	C	0.9
1943	Pit-N	118	372	40	98	9	4	1	39	44	25	.263	.341	.317	88	-3	-5	43	2			**.991**	9	*C/3	1.3
1944	Pit-N	115	331	27	76	12	1	1	34	34	24	.230	.303	.281	62	-15	-16	29	4			**.984**	4	*C	-0.7
1945	Pit-N	91	243	22	53	8	0	0	18	35	12	.218	.317	.251	57	-12	-14	21	1			.992	8	C	-0.1
1946	Pit-N	56	150	13	46	2	0	1	12	23	14	.307	.399	.340	108	3	3	21	1			.985	1	C	0.7
1947	Cle-A	61	126	9	33	1	0	0	14	9	13	.262	.311	.270	64	-6	-6	11	1	1	-0	1.000	0	C	-0.4
Total	19	1950	5916	613	1547	206	43	51	652	556	538	.261	.326	.337	83	-147	-128	664	46	1		.985	67	*C/321	5.0
■ **ART LOPEZ**	Lopez, Arturo (Rodriguez) b: 6/8/37, Mayaguez, P.R. BL/TL, 5'9", 170 lbs. Deb: 4/12/65																								
1965	NY-A	38	49	5	7	0	0	0	0	1	6	.143	.160	.143	-13	-7	-7	1	0	0	0	.958	-2	O	-1.0
■ **CARLOS LOPEZ**	Lopez, Carlos Antonio (Morales) b: 9/27/50, Mazatlan, Mexico BR/TR, 6', 190 lbs. Deb: 9/17/76																								
1976	Cal-A	9	10	1	0	0	0	0	0	2	3	.000	.167	.000	-52	-2	-2	0	2	0	1	1.000	-1	/OD	-0.3
1977	Sea-A	99	297	39	84	18	1	8	34	14	61	.283	.322	.431	104	1	1	44	16	4	2	.972	3	O/D	0.3
1978	Bal-A	129	193	21	46	6	0	4	20	9	34	.238	.276	.332	75	-8	-7	15	5	7	-3	.988	-25	*O/D	-3.8
Total	3	237	500	61	130	24	1	12	54	25	98	.260	.301	.384	90	-9	-7	59	23	11	0	.979	-23	O/D	-3.8
■ **HECTOR LOPEZ**	Lopez, Hector Headley (Swainson) b: 7/9/29, Colon, Panama BR/TR, 5'11", 182 lbs. Deb: 5/12/55																								
1955	KC-A	128	483	50	140	15	2	15	68	33	58	.290	.339	.422	103	1	0	65	1	4	-2	.936	15	32	1.6
1956	KC-A	151	561	91	153	27	3	18	69	63	73	.273	.349	.428	104	3	2	83	4	5	-2	.940	1	*3O/2S	0.3
1957	KC-A	121	391	51	115	19	4	11	35	41	66	.294	.361	.448	118	10	10	61	1	6	-3	.937	4	*3/2O	1.3
1958	KC-A	151	564	84	147	28	4	17	73	49	61	.261	.322	.415	99	-0	-1	70	2	2	-1	.974	6	23/SO	1.2
1959	KC-A	35	135	22	38	10	3	6	24	8	23	.281	.326	.533	129	5	5	24	1	0	0	.933	-12	2	-0.4

YEAR	TM/L	G	AB	R	H	2B	3B	HR	RBI	BB	SO	AVG	OBP	SLG	PRO+	BR	/A	RC	SB	CS	SBR	FA	FR	POS	TPR
	NY-A	112	406	60	115	16	2	16	69	28	54	.283	.339	.451	119	7	9	61	3	1	0	.926	-5	3O	0.2
	Yr	147	541	82	153	26	5	22	93	36	77	.283	.336	.471	122	12	14	85	4	1	1	.926	-17	3O2	-0.2
1960	*NY-A	131	408	66	116	14	6	9	42	46	64	.284	.362	.414	116	6	9	63	1	1	-0	.976	-0	*O/23	0.3
1961	*NY-A	93	243	27	54	7	2	3	22	24	38	.222	.295	.305	64	-14	-12	22	1	0	0	.977	1	O	-1.4
1962	*NY-A	106	335	45	92	19	1	6	48	33	53	.275	.340	.391	99	-2	-0	41	0	1	-1	.984	3	O/23	-0.2
1963	*NY-A	130	433	54	108	13	4	14	52	35	71	.249	.306	.395	95	-4	-3	50	1	2	-1	.957	-3	*O/2	-1.4
1964	*NY-A	127	285	34	74	9	3	10	34	24	54	.260	.319	.418	101	1	0	37	1	1	-0	.971	-13	*O/3	-1.7
1965	NY-A	111	283	25	74	12	2	7	39	26	61	.261	.326	.392	104	1	1	34	0	0	0	.942	-8	O/1	-1.0
1966	NY-A	54	117	14	25	4	1	4	16	8	20	.214	.270	.368	84	-3	-3	11	0	0	0	.936	-2	O	-0.7
Total	12	1450	4644	623	1251	193	37	136	591	418	696	.269	.333	.415	104	12	17	622	16	23	-9	.967	-13	O32/S1	-1.9

■ JAVY LOPEZ
Lopez, Javier Torres b: 11/5/70, Ponce, P.R. BR/TR, 6'3", 185 lbs. Deb: 9/18/92

YEAR	TM/L	G	AB	R	H	2B	3B	HR	RBI	BB	SO	AVG	OBP	SLG	PRO+	BR	/A	RC	SB	CS	SBR	FA	FR	POS	TPR
1992	*Atl-N	9	16	3	6	2	0	0	2	0	1	.375	.375	.500	135	1	1	3	0	0	0	1.000	1	/C	0.2

■ LUIS LOPEZ
Lopez, Luis Antonio b: 9/1/64, Brooklyn, N.Y. BR/TR, 6'1", 190 lbs. Deb: 9/14/90

YEAR	TM/L	G	AB	R	H	2B	3B	HR	RBI	BB	SO	AVG	OBP	SLG	PRO+	BR	/A	RC	SB	CS	SBR	FA	FR	POS	TPR
1990	LA-N	6	6	0	0	0	0	0	0	0	2	.000	.000	.000	-99	-2	-2	0	0	0	0	1.000	-0	/1	-0.2
1991	Cle-A	35	82	7	18	4	1	0	7	4	7	.220	.264	.293	54	-5	-5	7	0	0	0	1.000	-2	C1/3OD	-0.8
Total	2	41	88	7	18	4	1	0	7	4	9	.205	.247	.273	43	-7	-7	7	0	0	0	.977	-2	/C1DO3	-1.0

■ BRIS LORD
Lord, Bristol Robotham "The Human Eyeball" b: 9/21/1883, Upland, Pa. d: 11/13/64, Annapolis, Md. BR/TR, 5'9", 185 lbs. Deb: 4/21/05

YEAR	TM/L	G	AB	R	H	2B	3B	HR	RBI	BB	SO	AVG	OBP	SLG	PRO+	BR	/A	RC	SB	CS	SBR	FA	FR	POS	TPR
1905	*Phi-A	66	238	38	57	14	0	0	13	14		.239	.285	.298	84	-4	-5	23	3			.963	0	O	-0.8
1906	Phi-A	118	434	50	101	13	7	1	44	27		.233	.279	.302	80	-9	-11	44	12			.941	-2	*O	-2.0
1907	Phi-A	57	170	12	31	3	0	1	11	14		.182	.249	.218	48	-9	-10	11	2			.951	-2	O/P	-1.5
1909	Cle-A	69	249	26	67	7	3	1	25	8		.269	.295	.333	94	-1	-2	27	10			.992	6	O	0.1
1910	Cle-A	58	210	23	46	8	7	0	17	12		.219	.268	.324	84	-4	-5	19	4			.958	4	O	-0.4
	*Phi-A	70	279	53	78	13	11	1	20	23		.280	.337	.416	137	10	11	41	6			.980	4	O	1.2
	Yr	128	489	76	124	21	18	1	37	35		.254	.307	.376	114	6	6	60	10			.972	8	*O	0.8
1911	*Phi-A	134	574	92	178	37	11	3	55	35		.310	.355	.429	120	12	13	92	15			.963	8	*O	1.4
1912	Phi-A	97	378	63	90	12	9	0	25	34		.238	.309	.317	82	-10	-8	42	15			.942	-0	O	-1.4
1913	Bos-N	73	235	22	59	12	1	6	26	8	22	.251	.276	.387	86	-5	-5	25	7			.914	-10	O	-1.9
Total	8	742	2767	379	707	119	49	13	236	175	22	.256	.304	.348	95	-22	-22	325	74			.957	8	O/P	-5.3

■ HARRY LORD
Lord, Harry Donald b: 3/8/1882, Porter, Me. d: 8/9/48, Westbrook, Maine BL/TR, 5'10.5", 165 lbs. Deb: 9/25/07 M

YEAR	TM/L	G	AB	R	H	2B	3B	HR	RBI	BB	SO	AVG	OBP	SLG	PRO+	BR	/A	RC	SB	CS	SBR	FA	FR	POS	TPR
1907	Bos-A	10	38	4	6	1	0	0	3	1		.158	.179	.184	16	-4	-4	2	1			.919	0	3	-0.3
1908	Bos-A	145	560	61	145	15	6	2	37	22		.259	.297	.318	97	-1	-3	61	23			.902	-10	*3	-0.8
1909	Bos-A	136	534	86	166	12	7	0	31	20		.311	.345	.360	120	13	11	79	36			.929	-7	*3	1.0
1910	Bos-A	77	288	25	72	5	5	1	32	14		.250	.294	.313	88	-4	-5	32	17			.927	-5	3/S	-0.9
	Chi-A	44	165	26	49	6	3	0	10	14		.297	.352	.370	132	5	6	27	17			.952	-11	3	-0.4
	Yr	121	453	51	121	11	8	1	42	28		.267	.315	.333	103	1	1	59	34			.935	-16	*3/S	-1.3
1911	Chi-A	141	561	103	180	18	18	3	61	32		.321	.364	.433	126	15	17	104	43			.941	-17	*3	0.2
1912	Chi-A	151	570	81	152	19	12	5	54	52		.267	.333	.368	104	-0	2	80	28			.895	-27	*3O	-2.6
1913	Chi-A	150	547	62	144	18	12	1	42	45	39	.263	.327	.346	98	-3	-2	68	24			.924	-31	*3	-3.4
1914	Chi-A	21	69	8	13	1	1	1	3	5	3	.188	.243	.275	57	-4	-4	5	2	2	-1	.933	-6	3/O	-1.1
1915	Buf-F	97	359	50	97	12	6	1	21	21	15	.270	.311	.345	91	-4	-5	45	15			.946	-14	3/OM	-1.6
Total	9	972	3691	506	1024	107	70	14	294	226	57	.277	.326	.356	105	12	14	503	206	2		.924	-126	3/OS	-9.9

■ CARLTON LORD
Lord, William Carlton b: 1/7/1900, Philadelphia, Pa. d: 8/15/47, Chester, Pa. BR/TR, 5'11", 170 lbs. Deb: 7/12/23

YEAR	TM/L	G	AB	R	H	2B	3B	HR	RBI	BB	SO	AVG	OBP	SLG	PRO+	BR	/A	RC	SB	CS	SBR	FA	FR	POS	TPR
1923	Phi-N	17	47	3	11	2	0	0	2	2	3	.234	.265	.277	39	-4	-5	3	0	1	-1	.833	-1	3	-0.5

■ SCOTT LOUCKS
Loucks, Scott Gregory b: 11/11/56, Anchorage, Alaska BR/TR, 6', 178 lbs. Deb: 9/01/80

YEAR	TM/L	G	AB	R	H	2B	3B	HR	RBI	BB	SO	AVG	OBP	SLG	PRO+	BR	/A	RC	SB	CS	SBR	FA	FR	POS	TPR
1980	Hou-N	8	3	4	1	0	0	0	0	0	2	.333	.333	.333	94	-0	-0	0	0	0	0	1.000	0	/O	0.0
1981	Hou-N	10	7	2	4	0	0	0	0	1	3	.571	.625	.571	254	1	1	3	1	0	0	1.000	1	/O	0.3
1982	Hou-N	44	49	6	11	2	0	0	3	3	17	.224	.269	.265	54	-3	-3	4	4	1	1	.978	5	O	0.3
1983	Hou-N	7	14	2	3	0	0	0	0	1	4	.214	.267	.214	37	-1	-1	1	2	2	-1	1.000	2	/O	0.0
1985	Pit-N	4	7	1	2	2	0	0	1	2	2	.286	.444	.571	184	1	1	2	0	0	0	1.000	-1	/O	0.0
Total	5	73	80	15	21	4	0	0	4	7	28	.262	.322	.313	83	-2	-2	10	7	3	0	.985	7	/O	0.6

■ BALDY LOUDEN
Louden, William P. b: 8/27/1885, Piedmont, W.Va. d: 12/8/35, Piedmont, W.Va. BR/TR, 5'11", 175 lbs. Deb: 9/13/07

YEAR	TM/L	G	AB	R	H	2B	3B	HR	RBI	BB	SO	AVG	OBP	SLG	PRO+	BR	/A	RC	SB	CS	SBR	FA	FR	POS	TPR
1907	NY-A	4	9	4	1	0	0	0	0	2		.111	.273	.111	22	-1	-1	1	1			.750	1	/3	0.0
1912	Det-A	122	403	57	97	12	4	1	36	58		.241	.352	.298	89	-5	-3	53	28			.951	23	23/S	1.8
1913	Det-A	76	191	28	46	4	5	0	23	24	22	.241	.344	.314	94	-1	-1	23	6			.906	0	23/SO	0.0
1914	Buf-F	126	431	73	135	11	4	6	63	52	41	.313	.391	.399	122	16	15	85	35			.931	-18	*S	0.7
1915	Buf-F	141	469	67	132	18	5	4	48	64	45	.281	.372	.367	115	12	11	80	30			.978	13	2S3	3.0
1916	Cin-N	134	439	38	96	16	4	1	32	54	54	.219	.313	.280	85	-7	-6	42	12			**.968**	17	*2S	1.8
Total	6	603	1942	267	507	61	22	12	202	254	162	.261	.355	.334	103	15	16	284	112			.961	37	2S/3O	7.3

■ CHARLIE LOUDENSLAGER
Loudenslager, Charles Edward b: 5/21/1881, Baltimore, Md. d: 10/31/33, Baltimore, Md. TR, 5'9", 186 lbs. Deb: 4/15/04

YEAR	TM/L	G	AB	R	H	2B	3B	HR	RBI	BB	SO	AVG	OBP	SLG	PRO+	BR	/A	RC	SB	CS	SBR	FA	FR	POS	TPR
1904	Bro-N	1	2	0	0	0	0	0	0	0		.000	.000	.000	-99	-0	-0	0	0			1.000	-1	/2	-0.1

■ BILL LOUGHLIN
Loughlin, William H. b: Baltimore, Md. Deb: 5/09/1883

YEAR	TM/L	G	AB	R	H	2B	3B	HR	RBI	BB	SO	AVG	OBP	SLG	PRO+	BR	/A	RC	SB	CS	SBR	FA	FR	POS	TPR
1883	Bal-a	1	5	0	2	0	0	0		0		.400	.400	.400	154	0	0	1				.000	-0	/O	0.0

■ LOUGHRAN
Loughran b: New York, N.Y. Deb: 6/06/1884

YEAR	TM/L	G	AB	R	H	2B	3B	HR	RBI	BB	SO	AVG	OBP	SLG	PRO+	BR	/A	RC	SB	CS	SBR	FA	FR	POS	TPR
1884	NY-N	9	29	4	3	1	1	0	3	7	11	.103	.278	.207	54	-1	-1	2				.857	-3	/CO	-0.3

■ TOM LOVELACE
Lovelace, Thomas Rivers b: 10/19/1897, Wolfe City, Tex. d: 7/12/79, Dallas, Tex. BR/TR, 5'11", 170 lbs. Deb: 9/23/22

YEAR	TM/L	G	AB	R	H	2B	3B	HR	RBI	BB	SO	AVG	OBP	SLG	PRO+	BR	/A	RC	SB	CS	SBR	FA	FR	POS	TPR
1922	Pit-N	1	1	0	0	0	0	0	0	0	0	.000	.000	.000	-99	-0	-0	0	0	0	0	.000	0	H	0.0

■ LEN LOVETT
Lovett, Leonard Walker b: 7/17/1852, Lancaster Co., Pa d: 11/18/22, Newark, Del. BR/TR, Deb: 8/04/1873

YEAR	TM/L	G	AB	R	H	2B	3B	HR	RBI	BB	SO	AVG	OBP	SLG	PRO+	BR	/A	RC	SB	CS	SBR	FA	FR	POS	TPR
1873	Res-n	1	5	1	2	0	0	0	1	0	0	.400	.400	.400	148	0	0	1						/P	0.0
1875	Cen-n	6	21	2	5	1	0	0		1		.238	.273	.286	102	-0	0	2						/O	0.0
Total	2 n	7	26	3	7	1	0	0		1		.269	.296	.308	112	0	0	2						/OP	0.0

■ MEM LOVETT
Lovett, Merritt Marwood b: 6/15/12, Chicago, Ill. BR/TR, 5'9.5", 165 lbs. Deb: 9/04/33

YEAR	TM/L	G	AB	R	H	2B	3B	HR	RBI	BB	SO	AVG	OBP	SLG	PRO+	BR	/A	RC	SB	CS	SBR	FA	FR	POS	TPR
1933	Chi-A	1	1	0	0	0	0	0	0	0	0	.000	.000	.000	-99	-0	-0	0	0	0	0	.000	0	H	0.0

■ JAY LOVIGLIO
Loviglio, John Paul b: 5/30/56, Freeport, N.Y. BR/TR, 5'9", 160 lbs. Deb: 9/02/80

YEAR	TM/L	G	AB	R	H	2B	3B	HR	RBI	BB	SO	AVG	OBP	SLG	PRO+	BR	/A	RC	SB	CS	SBR	FA	FR	POS	TPR
1980	Phi-N	16	5	7	0	0	0	0	0	1	0	.000	.167	.000	-47	-1	-1	-0	1	2	-1	1.000	7	/2	0.5
1981	Chi-A	14	15	5	4	0	0	0	2	1	1	.267	.313	.267	70	-1	-1	0	2	2	-1	.786	3	/32D	0.2
1982	Chi-A	15	31	5	6	0	0	0	2	1	4	.194	.219	.194	14	-4	-4	1	2	1	0	.964	4	2/D	0.1
1983	Chi-N	1	1	0	0	0	0	0	0	0	1	.000	.000	.000	-95	-0	-0	0	0	0	0	.000	0	/H	0.0
Total	4	46	52	17	10	0	0	0	4	3	6	.192	.236	.192	21	-5	-5	2	5	5	-2	.971	14	/2D3	0.8

■ JOE LOVITTO
Lovitto, Joseph b: 1/6/51, San Pedro, Cal. BB/TR, 6', 185 lbs. Deb: 4/15/72

YEAR	TM/L	G	AB	R	H	2B	3B	HR	RBI	BB	SO	AVG	OBP	SLG	PRO+	BR	/A	RC	SB	CS	SBR	FA	FR	POS	TPR
1972	Tex-A	117	330	23	74	9	1	1	19	37	54	.224	.306	.267	75	-11	-9	27	13	11	-3	.976	4	*O	-1.4
1973	Tex-A	26	44	3	6	1	0	0	0	5	7	.136	.224	.159	10	-5	-5	2	1	0	0	.898	1	3/O	-0.4

YEAR	TM/L	G	AB	R	H	2B	3B	HR	RBI	BB	SO	AVG	OBP	SLG	PRO+	BR	/A	RC	SB	CS	SBR	FA	FR	POS	TPR
1974	Tex-A	113	283	27	63	9	3	2	26	25	36	.223	.286	.297	69	-12	-11	21	6	8	-3	.972	-12	*O/1	-3.1
1975	Tex-A	50	106	17	22	3	0	1	8	13	16	.208	.294	.264	59	-6	-5	9	2	2	-1	.985	-6	O/1CD	-1.4
Total	4	306	763	70	165	22	4	4	53	80	113	.216	.292	.271	67	-33	-30	59	22	21	-6	.975	-14	O/31DC	-6.3

■ TOREY LOVULLO Lovullo, Salvatore Anthony b: 7/25/65, Santa Monica, Cal. BB/TR, 6'1", 185 lbs. Deb: 9/10/88

YEAR	TM/L	G	AB	R	H	2B	3B	HR	RBI	BB	SO	AVG	OBP	SLG	PRO+	BR	/A	RC	SB	CS	SBR	FA	FR	POS	TPR
1988	Det-A	12	21	2	8	1	1	1	2	1	2	.381	.409	.667	204	3	3	5	0	0	0	1.000	-0	/23	0.3
1989	Det-A	29	87	8	10	2	0	1	4	14	20	.115	.238	.172	18	-9	-9	4	0	0	0	1.000	-3	13	-1.4
1991	NY-A	22	51	0	9	2	0	0	2	5	7	.176	.250	.216	30	-5	-5	3	0	0	0	.940	0	3	-0.5
Total	3	63	159	10	27	5	1	2	8	20	29	.170	.263	.252	45	-12	-11	12	0	0	0	.949	-3	/312	-1.6

■ FLETCHER LOW Low, Fletcher b: 4/7/1893, Essex, Mass. d: 6/6/73, Hanover, N.H. BR/TR, 5'10.5", 175 lbs. Deb: 10/07/15

YEAR	TM/L	G	AB	R	H	2B	3B	HR	RBI	BB	SO	AVG	OBP	SLG	PRO+	BR	/A	RC	SB	CS	SBR	FA	FR	POS	TPR
1915	Bos-N	1	4	1	1	0	1	0	1	0	0	.250	.250	.750	207	0	0	1	0			1.000	-0	/3	0.0

■ CHARLIE LOWE Lowe, Charles b: Baltimore, Md. Deb: 9/28/1872

YEAR	TM/L	G	AB	R	H	2B	3B	HR	RBI	BB	SO	AVG	OBP	SLG	PRO+	BR	/A	RC	SB	CS	SBR	FA	FR	POS	TPR
1872	Atl-n	7	32	1	5	0	0	0	2	0	2	.156	.156	.156	-3	-4	-5	1						/2	-0.4

■ DICK LOWE Lowe, Richard Alvern b: 1/28/1854, Evansville, Wis. d: 6/28/22, Janesville, Wis. Deb: 6/26/1884

YEAR	TM/L	G	AB	R	H	2B	3B	HR	RBI	BB	SO	AVG	OBP	SLG	PRO+	BR	/A	RC	SB	CS	SBR	FA	FR	POS	TPR
1884	Det-N	1	3	0	1	0	0	0	0	0	1	.333	.333	.333	117	0	0	0				.125	-3	/C	-0.2

■ BOBBY LOWE Lowe, Robert Lincoln "Link" b: 7/10/1868, Pittsburgh, Pa. d: 12/8/51, Detroit, Mich. BR/TR, 5'10", 150 lbs. Deb: 4/19/1890 M

YEAR	TM/L	G	AB	R	H	2B	3B	HR	RBI	BB	SO	AVG	OBP	SLG	PRO+	BR	/A	RC	SB	CS	SBR	FA	FR	POS	TPR
1890	Bos-N	52	207	35	58	13	2	2	21	26	32	.280	.366	.391	114	6	4	36	15			.951	-9	SO3	-0.3
1891	Bos-N	125	497	92	129	19	5	6	74	53	54	.260	.342	.354	94	4	-5	77	43			.927	-6	*O2/S3P	-1.3
1892	*Bos-N	124	475	79	115	16	7	3	57	37	46	.242	.308	.324	85	-4	-10	60	36			.928	13	O3S2	0.0
1893	Bos-N	126	526	130	157	19	5	14	89	55	29	.298	.369	.433	106	10	3	95	22			.936	1	*2/S	0.6
1894	Bos-N	133	613	158	212	34	11	17	115	50	25	.346	.401	.520	113	21	11	141	23			.927	-6	*2/S3	0.8
1895	Bos-N	99	412	101	122	12	7	7	62	40	16	.296	.370	.410	95	2	-4	75	24			.954	15	*2	1.3
1896	Bos-N	73	305	59	98	11	4	2	48	20	11	.321	.371	.403	100	3	-0	53	15			.965	24	2	2.4
1897	*Bos-N	123	499	87	154	24	8	5	106	32		.309	.355	.419	98	2	-4	83	16			.952	-4	*2	-0.1
1898	Bos-N	147	559	65	152	11	7	4	94	29		.272	.311	.338	82	-11	-16	67	12			.958	17	*2/S	1.0
1899	Bos-N	152	559	81	152	5	9	4	88	35		.272	.316	.335	72	-17	-25	68	17			.954	3	*2/S	-1.3
1900	Bos-N	127	474	65	132	11	5	3	71	26		.278	.323	.342	74	-11	-20	60	15			.951	-7	*2	-1.9
1901	Bos-N	129	491	47	125	11	1	3	47	17		.255	.284	.299	63	-20	-25	50	22			.912	-5	*32	-2.9
1902	Chi-N	119	472	41	116	13	3	0	31	11		.246	.270	.286	74	-17	-15	43	16			.957	26	*2/3	1.6
1903	Chi-N	32	105	14	28	5	3	0	15	4		.267	.319	.371	99	-1	-0	15	5			.948	4	2/13	0.4
1904	Pit-N	1	1	0	0	0	0	0	0	0		.000	.000	.000	-97	-0	-0	0	0			.000	0	H	0.0
	Det-A	140	506	47	105	14	6	0	40	17		.208	.236	.259	58	-25	-24	37	15			.964	-0	*2M	-2.2
1905	Det-A	58	181	17	35	7	2	0	9	13		.193	.255	.254	61	-8	-8	14	3			.980	-1	O3/2S1	-1.0
1906	Det-A	41	145	11	30	3	0	1	12	4		.207	.233	.248	50	-8	-9	10	3			.915	8	S2/3	0.0
1907	Det-A	17	37	2	9	2	0	0	5	4		.243	.317	.297	93	-0	-0	4	0			.870	-4	3/OS	-0.5
Total	18	1818	7064	1131	1929	230	85	71	984	473	213	.273	.325	.360	87	-74	-148	987	302			.950	68	*2O3/S1P	-3.4

■ JOHN LOWENSTEIN Lowenstein, John Lee b: 1/27/47, Wolf Point, Mont. BL/TR, 6', 175 lbs. Deb: 9/02/70

YEAR	TM/L	G	AB	R	H	2B	3B	HR	RBI	BB	SO	AVG	OBP	SLG	PRO+	BR	/A	RC	SB	CS	SBR	FA	FR	POS	TPR
1970	Cle-A	17	43	5	11	3	1	1	6	1	9	.256	.273	.442	89	-1	-1	5	1	0	0	1.000	4	2/3OS	0.4
1971	Cle-A	58	140	15	26	5	0	4	9	16	28	.186	.269	.307	58	-7	-8	11	1	5	-3	.986	-6	2O/S	-1.6
1972	Cle-A	68	151	16	32	8	1	6	21	20	43	.212	.304	.397	104	1	1	18	2	4	-2	1.000	-2	O/1	-0.6
1973	Cle-A	98	305	42	89	16	1	6	40	23	41	.292	.341	.410	109	4	3	41	5	3	-0	.931	-10	O2/31D	-0.7
1974	Cle-A	140	508	65	123	14	2	8	48	53	85	.242	.316	.325	85	-9	-9	55	36	17	1	.986	-1	*O31/2	-1.5
1975	Cle-A	91	265	37	64	5	1	12	33	28	28	.242	.314	.404	102	0	0	32	15	10	-2	.983	-5	OD/32	-0.8
1976	Cle-A	93	229	33	47	8	2	2	14	25	35	.205	.283	.284	67	-9	-9	18	11	8	-2	.972	-5	OD/1	-1.9
1977	Cle-A	81	149	24	36	6	1	4	12	21	29	.242	.335	.376	97	-1	-0	16	1	8	-5	1.000	-3	OD/1	-0.9
1978	Tex-A	77	176	28	39	8	3	5	21	37	29	.222	.363	.386	110	4	4	29	16	3	3	.926	-9	3DO	-0.3
1979	*Bal-A	97	197	33	50	8	2	11	34	30	37	.254	.355	.482	128	7	8	36	16	4	2	.992	-8	O/13D	0.0
1980	Bal-A	104	196	38	61	8	0	4	27	32	29	.311	.408	.413	127	8	9	36	7	3	0	.992	-11	O/D	-0.4
1981	Bal-A	83	189	19	47	7	0	6	20	22	32	.249	.330	.381	105	1	1	22	7	6	-2	.990	-12	O/D	-1.5
1982	Bal-A	122	322	69	103	15	2	24	66	54	59	.320	.419	.602	177	35	35	81	7	6	-2	**1.000**	-7	*O	2.4
1983	*Bal-A	122	310	52	87	13	2	15	60	49	55	.281	.381	.481	138	16	17	61	2	1	0	.982	-11	*O/2D	0.3
1984	Bal-A	105	270	34	64	13	0	8	28	33	54	.237	.322	.374	94	-3	-2	34	1	0	0	.971	-8	OD/1	-1.1
1985	Bal-A	12	26	0	2	0	0	0	2	2	3	.077	.143	.077	-39	-5	-5	0	0	0	0	1.000	-0	/OD	-0.5
Total	16	1368	3476	510	881	137	18	116	441	446	596	.253	.340	.403	108	41	43	496	128	78	-8	.984	-96	OD/321S	-8.7

■ PEANUTS LOWREY Lowrey, Harry Lee b: 8/27/18, Culver City, Cal. d: 7/2/86, Inglewood, Cal. BR/TR, 5'8.5", 170 lbs. Deb: 4/14/42 C

YEAR	TM/L	G	AB	R	H	2B	3B	HR	RBI	BB	SO	AVG	OBP	SLG	PRO+	BR	/A	RC	SB	CS	SBR	FA	FR	POS	TPR
1942	Chi-N	27	58	4	11	0	0	1	4	4	4	.190	.242	.241	43	-4	-4	4	0			.978	-1	O	-0.6
1943	Chi-N	130	480	59	140	25	12	1	63	35	24	.292	.340	.400	115	7	8	64	13			.982	14	*OS/2	1.7
1945	*Chi-N	143	523	72	148	22	7	7	89	48	27	.283	.343	.392	106	2	4	73	11			.987	4	*O/S	0.0
1946	Chi-N★	144	540	75	139	24	5	4	54	56	22	.257	.328	.343	92	-7	-5	63	10			.979	8	*O3	-0.3
1947	Chi-N	115	448	56	126	17	5	5	37	38	26	.281	.339	.375	93	-7	-5	58	2			.945	9	3O/2	0.4
1948	Chi-N	129	435	47	128	12	3	2	54	34	31	.294	.347	.349	93	-6	-4	52	2			.983	-1	*O/32S	-1.1
1949	Chi-N	38	111	18	30	5	0	2	10	9	8	.270	.325	.369	88	-2	-2	13	3			.966	-4	O/3	-0.8
	Cin-N	89	309	48	85	16	2	2	25	37	11	.275	.354	.359	91	-3	-3	39	1			.995	8	O	0.1
	Yr	127	420	66	115	21	2	4	35	46	19	.274	.347	.362	90	-5	-5	52	4			.989	4	*O/3	-0.7
1950	Cin-N	91	264	34	60	14	0	1	11	36	7	.227	.320	.292	62	-14	-14	25	0			.987	1	O/2	-1.6
	StL-N	17	56	10	15	0	0	1	4	6	1	.268	.349	.321	74	-2	-2	7	0			1.000	1	/23O	-0.1
	Yr	108	320	44	75	14	0	2	15	42	8	.234	.325	.297	64	-15	-16	31	0			.982	2	O/23	-1.7
1951	StL-N	114	370	52	112	19	5	5	40	35	12	.303	.366	.422	111	6	6	57	0	1	-1	.983	-1	O3/2	0.1
1952	StL-N	132	374	48	107	18	2	1	48	34	13	.286	.352	.353	96	-1	-1	48	3	2	-0	.978	-9	*O/3	-1.5
1953	StL-N	104	182	26	49	9	2	5	27	15	21	.269	.325	.423	93	-2	-2	24	1	0	0	1.000	-10	O2/3	-1.2
1954	StL-N	74	61	6	7	1	2	0	5	9	9	.115	.229	.197	12	-8	-8	3	0	0	0	1.000	-5	O	-1.3
1955	Phi-N	54	106	9	20	4	0	0	8	7	10	.189	.239	.226	25	-11	-11	5	2	0	1	.973	-6	O/21	-1.7
Total	13	1401	4317	564	1177	186	45	37	479	403	226	.273	.336	.362	92	-52	-44	533	48	3		.983	9	O3/2S1	-7.9

■ DWIGHT LOWRY Lowry, Dwight (b: Dwight Lowery) b: 10/23/57, Lumberton, N.C. BL/TR, 6'3", 210 lbs. Deb: 4/03/84

YEAR	TM/L	G	AB	R	H	2B	3B	HR	RBI	BB	SO	AVG	OBP	SLG	PRO+	BR	/A	RC	SB	CS	SBR	FA	FR	POS	TPR
1984	Det-A	32	45	8	11	2	0	2	7	3	11	.244	.292	.422	95	-0	-0	5	0	0	0	1.000	5	C	0.5
1986	Det-A	56	150	21	46	4	0	3	18	17	19	.307	.392	.393	115	4	4	24	0	0	0	.992	-1	C/1O	0.6
1987	Det-A	13	25	0	5	2	0	0	1	0	6	.200	.200	.280	27	-3	-3	1	0	0	0	1.000	1	C/1	-0.2
1988	Min-A	7	7	0	0	0	0	0	0	0	2	.000	.000	.000	-97	-2	-2	0	0	0	0	1.000	2	/CD	0.0
Total	4	108	227	29	62	8	0	5	26	20	38	.273	.343	.374	96	-1	-1	30	0	0	0	.995	7	C/D1O	0.9

■ JOHN LOWRY Lowry, John D. b: Baltimore, Md. Deb: 6/12/1875

YEAR	TM/L	G	AB	R	H	2B	3B	HR	RBI	BB	SO	AVG	OBP	SLG	PRO+	BR	/A	RC	SB	CS	SBR	FA	FR	POS	TPR
1875	Was-n	6	21	2	3	0	0	0		1		.143	.182	.143	14	-2	-2	1						/O	-0.1

■ WILLIE LOZADO Lozado, William b: 5/12/59, New York, N.Y. BR/TR, 6', 166 lbs. Deb: 7/16/84

YEAR	TM/L	G	AB	R	H	2B	3B	HR	RBI	BB	SO	AVG	OBP	SLG	PRO+	BR	/A	RC	SB	CS	SBR	FA	FR	POS	TPR
1984	Mil-A	43	107	15	29	8	2	1	20	12	23	.271	.345	.411	113	1	2	15	0	3	-2	.925	-1	3/S2D	-0.1

■ STEVE LUBRATICH Lubratich, Steven George b: 5/1/55, Oakland, Cal. BR/TR, 6', 170 lbs. Deb: 9/27/81

YEAR	TM/L	G	AB	R	H	2B	3B	HR	RBI	BB	SO	AVG	OBP	SLG	PRO+	BR	/A	RC	SB	CS	SBR	FA	FR	POS	TPR
1981	Cal-A	7	21	2	3	1	0	0	1	0	2	.143	.143	.190	-5	-3	-3	0	1	0	0	1.000	2	/3	-0.1

YEAR	TM/L	G	AB	R	H	2B	3B	HR	RBI	BB	SO	AVG	OBP	SLG	PRO+	BR	/A	RC	SB	CS	SBR	FA	FR	POS	TPR
1983	Cal-A	57	156	12	34	9	0	0	7	4	17	.218	.237	.276	41	-13	-12	10	0	1	-1	.949	16	S32	0.5
Total	2	64	177	14	37	10	0	0	8	4	19	.209	.227	.266	36	-15	-15	10	1	1	-0	.988	18	/3S2	0.4

■ HAL LUBY

Luby, Hugh Max b: 6/13/13, Blackfoot, Idaho d: 5/4/86, Eugene, Oregon BR/TR, 5′10″, 185 lbs. Deb: 9/10/36

YEAR	TM/L	G	AB	R	H	2B	3B	HR	RBI	BB	SO	AVG	OBP	SLG	PRO+	BR	/A	RC	SB	CS	SBR	FA	FR	POS	TPR
1936	Phi-A	9	38	3	7	1	0	0	3	0	7	.184	.205	.211	3	-6	-6	2	2	0	1	.880	-4	/2	-0.8
1944	NY-N	111	323	30	82	10	2	2	35	52	15	.254	.364	.316	93	-1	-1	40	2			.943	16	32/1	1.9
Total	2	120	361	33	89	11	2	2	38	52	22	.247	.349	.305	83	-7	-6	42	4	0		.954	12	/321	1.1

■ JOHNNY LUCADELLO

Lucadello, John b: 2/22/19, Thurber, Tex. BB/TR, 5′11″, 160 lbs. Deb: 9/24/38

YEAR	TM/L	G	AB	R	H	2B	3B	HR	RBI	BB	SO	AVG	OBP	SLG	PRO+	BR	/A	RC	SB	CS	SBR	FA	FR	POS	TPR
1938	StL-A	7	20	1	3	1	0	0	0	0	0	.150	.150	.200	-13	-4	-4	1	0	0	0	.909	-1	/3	-0.5
1939	StL-A	9	30	0	7	2	0	0	4	2	4	.233	.281	.300	48	-2	-2	3	0	0	0	.912	-4	/2	-0.6
1940	StL-A	17	63	15	20	4	2	2	10	6	4	.317	.394	.540	137	4	3	15	1	0	0	.968	0	2	0.5
1941	StL-A	107	351	58	98	22	4	2	31	48	23	.279	.366	.382	95	-0	-2	54	5	2	0	.962	-16	2S/3O	-1.1
1946	StL-A	87	210	21	52	7	1	1	15	36	20	.248	.358	.305	82	-2	-4	26	0	1	-1	.942	-7	32	-1.0
1947	NY-A	12	12	0	1	0	0	0	0	1	5	.083	.154	.083	-33	-2	-2	0	0	0	0	1.000	-2	/2	-0.4
Total	6	239	686	95	181	36	7	5	60	93	56	.264	.353	.359	88	-7	-10	98	6	3	0	.965	-29	2/3SO	-3.1

■ RED LUCAS

Lucas, Charles Frederick "The Nashville Narcissus" b: 4/28/02, Columbia, Tenn. d: 7/9/86, Nashville, Tenn. BL/TR, 5′9.5″, 170 lbs. Deb: 4/19/23

YEAR	TM/L	G	AB	R	H	2B	3B	HR	RBI	BB	SO	AVG	OBP	SLG	PRO+	BR	/A	RC	SB	CS	SBR	FA	FR	POS	TPR
1923	NY-N	3	2	0	0	0	0	0	0	0	1	.000	.000	.000	-99	-1	-1	0	0	0	0	1.000	1	/P	0.0
1924	Bos-N	33	33	5	11	1	0	0	5	1	4	.333	.353	.364	96	-0	-0	4	0	0	0	1.000	1	P/3	0.0
1925	Bos-N	6	20	1	3	0	0	0	2	2	4	.150	.227	.150	-2	-3	-3	1	0	0	0	.968	0	/2	-0.2
1926	Cin-N	66	76	15	23	4	4	0	14	10	13	.303	.384	.461	130	3	3	13	0			1.000	-1	P/2	0.0
1927	Cin-N	80	150	14	47	5	2	0	28	12	10	.313	.368	.373	102	0	1	21	0			.983	-6	P/2SO	-0.4
1928	Cin-N	39	73	8	23	2	1	0	7	4	6	.315	.351	.370	90	-1	-1	9	0			1.000	-0	P	0.0
1929	Cin-N	76	140	15	41	6	0	0	13	13	15	.293	.353	.336	75	-6	-5	17	1			.949	0	P	0.0
1930	Cin-N	80	113	18	38	4	1	2	19	17	4	.336	.423	.442	115	3	4	22	0			1.000	-3	P	0.0
1931	Cin-N	97	153	15	43	4	0	0	17	12	9	.281	.333	.307	78	-5	-4	17	0			.984	1	P	0.0
1932	Cin-N	76	150	13	43	11	2	0	19	10	9	.287	.335	.387	97	-1	-1	20	0			.973	-0	P	0.0
1933	Cin-N	75	122	14	35	6	1	1	15	12	6	.287	.356	.377	111	2	2	17	0			1.000	0	P	0.0
1934	Pit-N	68	105	11	23	5	1	0	8	6	16	.219	.261	.286	45	-8	-8	8	1			.939	-3	P	0.0
1935	Pit-N	47	66	6	21	6	0	0	10	7	11	.318	.392	.409	112	2	1	11	0			.968	-1	P	0.0
1936	Pit-N	69	108	11	26	4	1	0	14	8	17	.241	.293	.296	58	-6	-6	9	0			.976	-1	P	0.0
1937	Pit-N	59	82	8	22	3	0	0	17	7	6	.268	.326	.305	72	-3	-3	8	0			1.000	-2	P	0.0
1938	Pit-N	33	46	1	5	0	0	0	2	3	2	.109	.163	.109	-24	-8	-8	1	0			1.000	-1	P	0.0
Total	16	907	1439	155	404	61	13	3	190	124	133	.281	.340	.347	84	-33	-29	177	2	0		.981	-14	P/2S3O	-0.6

■ FRED LUCAS

Lucas, Frederick Warrington "Fritz" b: 1/19/03, Vineland, N.J. d: 3/11/87, Cambridge, Md. BR/TR, 5′10″, 165 lbs. Deb: 7/15/35

YEAR	TM/L	G	AB	R	H	2B	3B	HR	RBI	BB	SO	AVG	OBP	SLG	PRO+	BR	/A	RC	SB	CS	SBR	FA	FR	POS	TPR
1935	Phi-N	20	34	1	9	0	0	0	2	3	6	.265	.324	.265	55	-2	-2	3	0			.944	-2	O	-0.4

■ JOHNNY LUCAS

Lucas, John Charles "Buster" b: 2/10/03, Glen Carbon, Ill. d: 10/31/70, Maryville, Ill. BR/TL, 5′10″, 186 lbs. Deb: 4/15/31

YEAR	TM/L	G	AB	R	H	2B	3B	HR	RBI	BB	SO	AVG	OBP	SLG	PRO+	BR	/A	RC	SB	CS	SBR	FA	FR	POS	TPR
1931	Bos-A	3	2	0	0	0	0	0	0	0	1	.000	.000	.000	-99	-1	-1	0	0	0	0	.000	-1	/O	-0.2
1932	Bos-A	1	1	0	0	0	0	0	0	0	0	.000	.000	.000	-99	-0	-0	0	0	0	0	.000	0	H	0.0
Total	2	4	3	0	0	0	0	0	0	0	1	.000	.000	.000	-99	-1	-1	0	0	0	0	.979	-1	/O	-0.2

■ FRANK LUCE

Luce, Frank Edward b: 12/6/1896, Spencer, Ohio d: 2/3/42, Milwaukee, Wis. BL/TR, 5′11″, 180 lbs. Deb: 9/17/23

YEAR	TM/L	G	AB	R	H	2B	3B	HR	RBI	BB	SO	AVG	OBP	SLG	PRO+	BR	/A	RC	SB	CS	SBR	FA	FR	POS	TPR
1923	Pit-N	9	12	2	6	0	0	0	3	2	2	.500	.571	.500	181	2	2	4	2	1	0	1.000	-2	/O	0.0

■ JOE LUCEY

Lucey, Joseph Earl "Scootch" b: 3/27/1897, Holyoke, Mass. d: 7/30/80, Holyoke, Mass. BR/TR, 6′, 168 lbs. Deb: 7/06/20

YEAR	TM/L	G	AB	R	H	2B	3B	HR	RBI	BB	SO	AVG	OBP	SLG	PRO+	BR	/A	RC	SB	CS	SBR	FA	FR	POS	TPR
1920	NY-A	3	3	0	0	0	0	0	0	0	0	.000	.000	.000	-97	-1	-1	0	0	0	0	1.000	0	/2S	0.0
1925	Bos-A	10	15	0	2	0	0	0	0	0	4	.133	.133	.133	-32	-3	-3	0	0	0	0	.889	-1	/PS	-0.3
Total	2	13	18	0	2	0	0	0	0	0	4	.111	.111	.111	-43	-4	-4	0	0	0	0	.778	-0	/PS2	-0.3

■ FRED LUDERUS

Luderus, Frederick William b: 9/12/1885, Milwaukee, Wis. d: 1/4/61, Milwaukee, Wis. BL/TR, 5′11.5″, 185 lbs. Deb: 9/23/09

YEAR	TM/L	G	AB	R	H	2B	3B	HR	RBI	BB	SO	AVG	OBP	SLG	PRO+	BR	/A	RC	SB	CS	SBR	FA	FR	POS	TPR
1909	Chi-N	11	37	8	11	1	1	1	9	3		.297	.366	.459	152	2	2	6	0			.950	-2	1	0.1
1910	Chi-N	24	54	5	11	1	1	0	3	4	3	.204	.259	.259	52	-3	-3	4	0			.975	-0	1	-0.4
	Phi-N	21	68	10	20	5	2	0	14	9	5	.294	.385	.426	132	3	3	12	2			.985	1	1	0.4
	Yr	45	122	15	31	6	3	0	17	13	8	.254	.331	.352	98	-0	-0	15	2			.981	0	1	0.0
1911	Phi-N	146	551	69	166	24	11	16	99	40	76	.301	.353	.472	128	19	18	93	6			.985	-2	*1	1.6
1912	Phi-N	148	572	77	147	31	5	10	69	44	65	.257	.318	.381	85	-9	-14	70	8			.990	10	*1	-0.6
1913	Phi-N	155	588	67	154	32	7	18	86	34	51	.262	.304	.432	105	3	1	75	5			.984	1	*1	0.0
1914	Phi-N	121	443	55	110	16	5	12	55	33	31	.248	.308	.388	100	2	-1	51	2			.975	1	*1	-0.3
1915	*Phi-N	141	499	55	157	36	7	7	62	42	36	.315	.376	.457	150	30	30	87	9	7	-2	.993	10	*1	3.8
1916	Phi-N	146	508	52	143	26	3	5	53	41	32	.281	.341	.374	115	12	10	69	8			.982	-2	*1	0.3
1917	Phi-N	154	522	57	136	24	4	5	72	65	35	.261	.349	.351	110	11	9	64	5			.991	5	*1	0.9
1918	Phi-N	125	468	54	135	23	2	5	67	42	33	.288	.351	.378	115	13	9	61	4			.988	7	*1	1.2
1919	Phi-N	138	509	60	149	30	6	5	49	54	48	.293	.365	.405	123	20	16	75	6			.985	10	*1	2.3
1920	Phi-N	16	32	1	5	2	0	0	4	3	6	.156	.229	.219	28	-3	-3	2	0	1	-1	.983	0	/1	-0.4
Total	12	1346	4851	570	1344	251	54	84	642	414	421	.277	.340	.403	113	101	75	669	55	8		.986	39	*1	8.9

■ BILL LUDWIG

Ludwig, William Lawrence b: 5/27/1882, Louisville, Ky. d: 9/5/47, Louisville, Ky. BR/TR, Deb: 4/16/08

YEAR	TM/L	G	AB	R	H	2B	3B	HR	RBI	BB	SO	AVG	OBP	SLG	PRO+	BR	/A	RC	SB	CS	SBR	FA	FR	POS	TPR
1908	StL-N	66	187	15	34	2	2	0	8	16		.182	.246	.214	50	-11	-10	11	3			.952	-3	C	-0.9

■ ROY LUEBBE

Luebbe, Roy John b: 9/17/1900, Parkersburg, Iowa d: 8/21/85, Papillion, Neb. BB/TR, 6′, 175 lbs. Deb: 8/22/25

YEAR	TM/L	G	AB	R	H	2B	3B	HR	RBI	BB	SO	AVG	OBP	SLG	PRO+	BR	/A	RC	SB	CS	SBR	FA	FR	POS	TPR
1925	NY-A	8	15	1	0	0	0	0	3	2	6	.000	.118	.000	-69	-4	-4	0	0	0	0	1.000	1	/C	-0.2

■ HENRY LUFF

Luff, Henry T. b: 9/14/1856, Philadelphia, Pa. d: 10/11/16, Philadelphia, Pa. 5′11″, 175 lbs. Deb: 4/21/1875

YEAR	TM/L	G	AB	R	H	2B	3B	HR	RBI	BB	SO	AVG	OBP	SLG	PRO+	BR	/A	RC	SB	CS	SBR	FA	FR	POS	TPR
1875	NH-n	38	165	15	46	11	3	2		0		.279	.279	.418	158	6	9	20						3/PO	0.7
1882	Det-N	3	11	1	3	2	0	0	1	0	0	.273	.273	.455	129	0	0	1				.667	-1	/2O	-0.1
	Cin-a	28	120	16	28	2	2	0		2		.233	.246	.283	74	-3	-4	9				.922	-2	1/O	-0.8
1883	Lou-a	6	23	1	4	0	0	0		0		.174	.174	.174	13	-2	-2	1				.868	-1	/1O	-0.3
1884	Phi-U	26	111	9	30	4	2	0		4		.270	.296	.342	124	2	3	12				.733	-3	O/132	-0.1
	KC-U	5	19	0	1	0	0	0		1		.053	.100	.053	-54	-3	-2	0				.444	-4	/3O	-0.6
	Yr	31	130	9	31	4	2	0		5		.238	.267	.300	100	-1	1	11				.706	-7	O/312	-0.7
Total	3	68	284	27	66	8	4	0	1	7	0	.232	.251	.289	82	-6	-5	22				.911	-12	/1O32	-1.9

■ EDDIE LUKON

Lukon, Edward Paul "Mongoose" b: 8/5/20, Burgettstown, Pa. BL/TL, 5′10″, 168 lbs. Deb: 8/06/41

YEAR	TM/L	G	AB	R	H	2B	3B	HR	RBI	BB	SO	AVG	OBP	SLG	PRO+	BR	/A	RC	SB	CS	SBR	FA	FR	POS	TPR
1941	Cin-N	23	86	6	23	3	0	0	3	6	6	.267	.315	.302	74	-3	-3	8	1			.980	2	O	-0.2
1945	Cin-N	2	8	1	1	0	0	0	0	0	1	.125	.125	.125	-31	-1	-1	0	0			1.000	0	/O	-0.2
1946	Cin-N	102	312	31	78	8	8	12	34	26	29	.250	.310	.442	116	3	4	43	3			.985	2	O	0.3
1947	Cin-N	86	200	26	41	6	1	11	33	28	36	.205	.306	.410	89	-4	-4	26	0			1.000	-2	O	-0.8
Total	4	213	606	64	143	17	9	23	70	60	72	.236	.307	.408	99	-5	-4	77	4			.989	3	O	-0.9

■ MIKE LUM

Lum, Michael Ken-Wai b: 10/27/45, Honolulu, Hawaii BL/TL, 6′, 180 lbs. Deb: 9/12/67 C

YEAR	TM/L	G	AB	R	H	2B	3B	HR	RBI	BB	SO	AVG	OBP	SLG	PRO+	BR	/A	RC	SB	CS	SBR	FA	FR	POS	TPR
1967	Atl-N	9	26	1	6	0	0	0	1	1	4	.231	.259	.231	42	-2	-2	1	0	1	-1	.944	1	/O	-0.2
1968	Atl-N	122	232	22	52	7	3	3	21	14	35	.224	.280	.319	79	-6	-6	19	3	5	-2	.976	-11	O	-2.6
1969	*Atl-N	121	168	20	45	8	0	1	22	16	18	.268	.332	.333	86	-3	-3	18	0	0	0	.992	10	O	0.5

YEAR	TM/L	G	AB	R	H	2B	3B	HR	RBI	BB	SO	AVG	OBP	SLG	PRO+	BR	/A	RC	SB	CS	SBR	FA	FR	POS	TPR
1970	Atl-N	123	291	25	74	17	2	7	28	17	43	.254	.307	.399	83	-6	-8	36	3	2	-0	.988	6	O	-0.6
1971	Atl-N	145	454	56	122	14	1	13	55	47	43	.269	.344	.390	101	5	2	61	0	3	-2	.990	10	*O/1	0.4
1972	Atl-N	123	369	40	84	14	2	9	38	50	52	.228	.325	.350	84	-3	-7	43	1	4	-2	.976	5	*O/1	-1.0
1973	Atl-N	138	513	74	151	26	6	16	82	41	89	.294	.354	.462	116	16	11	84	2	5	-2	.991	-3	1O	-0.3
1974	Atl-N	106	361	50	84	11	2	11	50	45	49	.233	.321	.366	88	-4	-6	42	0	2	-1	.994	-6	1O	-2.0
1975	Atl-N	124	364	32	83	8	2	8	36	39	38	.228	.303	.327	72	-13	-14	34	2	4	-2	.992	-1	1O	-2.3
1976	*Cin-N	84	136	15	31	5	1	3	20	22	24	.228	.340	.346	93	-0	-1	17	0	1	-1	1.000	-4	O	-0.7
1977	Cin-N	81	125	14	20	1	0	5	16	9	33	.160	.222	.288	35	-12	-12	8	2	0	1	1.000	-1	O/1	-1.4
1978	Cin-N	86	146	15	39	7	1	6	23	22	18	.267	.363	.452	126	5	5	24	0	0	0	.987	5	O/1	0.9
1979	Atl-N	111	217	27	54	6	0	6	27	18	34	.249	.306	.359	75	-6	-8	22	0	2	-1	.998	2	1/O	-1.0
1980	Atl-N	93	83	7	17	3	0	0	5	18	19	.205	.347	.241	65	-3	-3	8	0	0	0	1.000	1	O1	-0.2
1981	Atl-N	10	11	1	1	0	0	0	0	2	2	.091	.231	.091	-6	-1	-2	0	0	0	0	1.000	0	/O	-0.2
	Chi-N	41	58	5	14	1	0	2	7	5	5	.241	.313	.362	87	-1	-1	7	0	0	0	.923	-2	O/1	-0.4
	Yr	51	69	6	15	1	0	2	7	7	7	.217	.299	.319	72	-2	-3	7	0	0	0	.938	-2	O/1	-0.6
Total	15	1517	3554	404	877	128	20	90	431	366	506	.247	.322	.370	89	-34	-55	426	13	29	-14	.986	12	O1	-11.1

■ HARRY LUMLEY
Lumley, Harry G "Judge" b: 9/29/1880, Forest City, Pa. d: 5/22/38, Binghamton, N.Y. BL/TL, 5'10", 183 lbs. Deb: 4/14/04 M

YEAR	TM/L	G	AB	R	H	2B	3B	HR	RBI	BB	SO	AVG	OBP	SLG	PRO+	BR	/A	RC	SB	CS	SBR	FA	FR	POS	TPR
1904	Bro-N	150	577	79	161	23	**18**	**9**	78	41		.279	.328	.428	137	20	22	94	30			.955	4	*O	1.7
1905	Bro-N	130	505	50	148	19	10	7	47	36		.293	.340	.412	134	13	18	82	22			.912	-1	*O	1.1
1906	Bro-N	133	484	72	157	23	12	9	61	48		.324	.386	**.477**	**184**	38	**42**	107	35			.949	1	*O	4.0
1907	Bro-N	127	454	47	121	23	11	9	66	31		.267	.316	.425	144	14	18	70	18			.959	-4	*O	1.1
1908	Bro-N	127	440	36	95	13	12	4	39	29		.216	.264	.327	92	-7	-5	39	4			.955	-5	*O	-1.8
1909	Bro-N	55	172	13	43	8	3	0	14	16		.250	.314	.331	104	-0	1	19	1			.948	2	OM	0.1
1910	Bro-N	8	21	3	3	0	0	0	0	3	6	.143	.280	.143	25	-2	-2	1	0			.833	-1	/O	-0.3
Total	7	730	2653	300	728	109	66	38	305	204	<u>6</u>	.274	.327	.408	135	76	93	412	110			.946	-5	O	5.9

■ JERRY LUMPE
Lumpe, Jerry Dean b: 6/2/33, Lincoln, Mo. BL/TR, 6'2", 185 lbs. Deb: 4/17/56 C

YEAR	TM/L	G	AB	R	H	2B	3B	HR	RBI	BB	SO	AVG	OBP	SLG	PRO+	BR	/A	RC	SB	CS	SBR	FA	FR	POS	TPR
1956	NY-A	20	62	12	16	3	0	0	4	5	11	.258	.313	.306	66	-3	-3	6	1	1	-0	.916	3	S/3	0.1
1957	*NY-A	40	103	15	35	6	2	0	11	9	13	.340	.393	.437	128	4	4	18	2	2	-1	.956	-2	3/S	0.2
1958	*NY-A	81	232	34	59	8	4	3	32	23	21	.254	.324	.362	92	-3	-2	26	1	2	-1	.943	4	3/S	0.1
1959	NY-A	18	45	2	10	0	0	0	2	6	7	.222	.314	.222	52	-3	-3	3	0	0	0	1.000	2	3/S2	0.0
	KC-A	108	403	47	98	11	5	3	28	41	32	.243	.313	.318	72	-14	-15	41	2	1	0	.986	-10	2S/3	-1.6
	Yr	126	448	49	108	11	5	3	30	47	39	.241	.313	.308	70	-17	-18	44	2	1	0	.987	-8	2S3	-1.6
1960	KC-A	146	574	69	156	19	3	8	53	48	49	.272	.328	.357	85	-12	-12	67	1	1	-0	.982	-7	*2S	-0.6
1961	KC-A	148	569	81	167	29	9	3	54	48	39	.293	.351	.392	98	-1	-1	79	1	0	0	.979	16	*2	3.0
1962	KC-A	156	641	89	193	34	10	10	83	44	38	.301	.346	.432	105	6	4	94	0	2	-1	.986	-4	*2/S	1.5
1963	KC-A	157	595	75	161	26	7	5	59	58	44	.271	.335	.363	92	-3	-5	74	3	2	-0	.988	2	*2	1.2
1964	Det-A☆	158	624	75	160	21	6	6	46	50	61	.256	.314	.338	80	-15	-16	67	2	1	0	.983	-21	*2	-2.6
1965	Det-A	145	502	72	129	15	3	4	39	56	34	.257	.335	.323	87	-7	-7	58	7	0	2	.985	-18	*2	-1.2
1966	Det-A	113	385	30	89	14	3	1	26	24	44	.231	.276	.291	62	-18	-19	31	0	3	-2	.991	-6	2	-2.2
1967	Det-A	81	177	19	41	4	0	4	17	16	18	.232	.295	.322	80	-4	-4	17	0	0	0	.963	-3	2/3	-0.5
Total	12	1371	4912	620	1314	190	52	47	454	428	411	.268	.327	.356	87	-73	-81	581	20	15	-3	.984	-44	*23S	-2.6

■ DON LUND
Lund, Donald Andrew b: 5/18/23, Detroit, Mich. BR/TR, 6', 200 lbs. Deb: 7/03/45 C

YEAR	TM/L	G	AB	R	H	2B	3B	HR	RBI	BB	SO	AVG	OBP	SLG	PRO+	BR	/A	RC	SB	CS	SBR	FA	FR	POS	TPR
1945	Bro-N	4	3	0	0	0	0	0	0	1	1	.000	.250	.000	-27	-0	-0	0	0			.000	0	H	0.0
1947	Bro-N	11	20	5	6	2	0	2	5	3	7	.300	.391	.700	178	2	2	6	0			1.000	-0	/O	0.2
1948	Bro-N	27	69	9	13	4	0	1	5	5	16	.188	.243	.290	42	-6	-6	5	1			.977	-2	O	-0.9
	StL-A	63	161	21	40	7	4	3	25	10	17	.248	.305	.398	84	-4	-5	21	0	0	0	1.000	-4	O	-1.1
1949	Det-A	2	2	0	0	0	0	0	0	0	1	.000	.000	.000	-99	-1	-1	0	0	0	0	.000	0	H	-0.1
1952	Det-A	8	23	1	7	0	0	0	1	3	3	.304	.385	.304	93	-0	-0	3	0	1	-1	1.000	0	/O	-0.1
1953	Det-A	131	421	51	108	21	4	9	47	39	65	.257	.323	.390	93	-6	-5	53	3	3	-1	.980	1	*O	-0.9
1954	Det-A	35	54	4	7	2	0	0	3	4	3	.130	.190	.167	-2	-8	-8	2	1	0	0	.971	-8	O	-1.6
Total	7	281	753	91	181	36	8	15	86	65	113	.240	.305	.369	81	-22	-22	89	5	<u>4</u>		.983	-12	O	-4.5

■ GORDY LUND
Lund, Gordon Thomas b: 2/23/41, Iron Mountain, Mich BR/TR, 5'11", 170 lbs. Deb: 8/01/67

YEAR	TM/L	G	AB	R	H	2B	3B	HR	RBI	BB	SO	AVG	OBP	SLG	PRO+	BR	/A	RC	SB	CS	SBR	FA	FR	POS	TPR
1967	Cle-A	3	8	1	2	1	0	0	0	0	2	.250	.250	.375	82	-0	-0	1	0	0	0	.667	-2	/S	-0.2
1969	Sea-A	20	38	4	10	0	0	0	1	5	7	.263	.349	.263	75	-1	-1	4	1	1	-0	.927	-1	S/23	-0.1
Total	2	23	46	5	12	1	0	0	1	5	9	.261	.333	.283	76	-1	-1	5	1	1	-0	.902	-2	/S32	-0.3

■ TOM LUNDSTEDT
Lundstedt, Thomas Robert b: 4/10/49, Davenport, Iowa BB/TR, 6'4", 195 lbs. Deb: 8/31/73

YEAR	TM/L	G	AB	R	H	2B	3B	HR	RBI	BB	SO	AVG	OBP	SLG	PRO+	BR	/A	RC	SB	CS	SBR	FA	FR	POS	TPR
1973	Chi-N	4	5	0	0	0	0	0	0	0	1	.000	.000	.000	-93	-1	-1	0	0	0	0	1.000	1	/C	-0.1
1974	Chi-N	22	32	1	3	0	0	0	0	5	7	.094	.216	.094	-11	-5	-5	1	0	0	0	.987	2	C	-0.3
1975	Min-A	18	28	2	3	0	0	0	1	4	5	.107	.219	.107	-5	-4	-4	1	0	0	0	1.000	1	C/D	-0.2
Total	3	44	65	3	6	0	0	0	1	9	13	.092	.203	.092	-14	-10	-10	2	0	0	0	.993	4	/CD	-0.6

■ HARRY LUNTE
Lunte, Harry August b: 9/15/1892, St.Louis, Mo. d: 7/27/65, St.Louis, Mo. BR/TR, 5'11.5", 165 lbs. Deb: 5/19/19

YEAR	TM/L	G	AB	R	H	2B	3B	HR	RBI	BB	SO	AVG	OBP	SLG	PRO+	BR	/A	RC	SB	CS	SBR	FA	FR	POS	TPR
1919	Cle-A	26	77	2	15	2	0	0	2	1	7	.195	.215	.221	21	-8	-9	4	0			.935	-2	S	-1.0
1920	*Cle-A	23	71	6	14	0	0	0	7	5	6	.197	.250	.197	19	-8	-8	3	0	1	-1	.979	3	S/2	-0.4
Total	2	49	148	8	29	2	0	0	9	6	13	.196	.232	.209	20	-16	-17	7	0	<u>1</u>		.955	1	/S2	-1.4

■ TONY LUPIEN
Lupien, Ulysses John b: 4/23/17, Chelmsford, Mass. BL/TL, 5'10.5", 185 lbs. Deb: 9/12/40

YEAR	TM/L	G	AB	R	H	2B	3B	HR	RBI	BB	SO	AVG	OBP	SLG	PRO+	BR	/A	RC	SB	CS	SBR	FA	FR	POS	TPR
1940	Bos-A	10	19	5	9	3	2	0	4	1	1	.474	.500	.842	232	4	4	8	0	0	0	1.000	-0	/1	0.3
1942	Bos-A	128	463	63	130	25	7	3	70	50	20	.281	.351	.384	103	4	2	65	10	12	-4	.992	-7	*1	-1.7
1943	Bos-A	154	608	65	155	21	9	4	47	54	23	.255	.317	.339	90	-7	-8	70	16	9	-1	.993	4	*1	-1.5
1944	Phi-N	153	597	82	169	23	9	5	52	56	29	.283	.347	.377	107	3	6	82	18			.992	1	*1	-0.1
1945	Phi-N	15	54	1	17	1	0	0	3	6	0	.315	.383	.333	103	0	1	8	2			1.000	3	1	0.2
1948	Chi-A	154	617	69	152	19	3	6	54	74	38	.246	.327	.316	74	-25	-22	71	11	7	-1	.993	-4	*1	-2.8
Total	6	614	2358	285	632	92	30	18	230	241	111	.268	.337	.355	94	-20	-18	304	57	<u>28</u>		.993	-4	1	-5.6

■ AL LUPLOW
Luplow, Alvin David b: 3/13/39, Saginaw, Mich. BL/TR, 5'11", 180 lbs. Deb: 9/16/61

YEAR	TM/L	G	AB	R	H	2B	3B	HR	RBI	BB	SO	AVG	OBP	SLG	PRO+	BR	/A	RC	SB	CS	SBR	FA	FR	POS	TPR
1961	Cle-A	5	18	0	1	0	0	0	0	2	6	.056	.150	.056	-44	-4	-4	0	0	0	0	1.000	2	/O	-0.2
1962	Cle-A	97	318	54	88	15	3	14	45	36	44	.277	.361	.475	127	10	12	57	1	0	0	.960	-3	O	0.4
1963	Cle-A	100	295	34	69	6	2	7	27	33	62	.234	.317	.339	85	-6	-5	32	4	4	-1	.994	3	O	-0.8
1964	Cle-A	19	18	1	2	0	0	0	1	1	8	.111	.158	.111	-24	-3	-3	0	0	0	0	1.000	-1	/O	-0.4
1965	Cle-A	53	45	3	6	2	0	1	4	3	14	.133	.188	.244	22	-5	-5	2	0	1	-1	1.000	-2	/O	-0.7
1966	NY-N	111	334	31	84	9	1	7	31	38	46	.251	.332	.347	91	-4	-3	37	2	6	-3	.987	-7	*O	-1.9
1967	NY-N	41	112	11	23	1	0	3	9	8	19	.205	.264	.295	61	-6	-6	9	0	0	0	.966	-1	O	-0.8
	Pit-N	55	103	13	19	1	0	1	8	6	14	.184	.236	.223	32	-9	-9	6	1	0	0	.961	3	O	-0.7
	Yr	96	215	24	42	2	0	4	17	14	33	.195	.251	.260	47	-15	-15	14	1	0	0	.963	3	O	-1.5
Total	7	481	1243	147	292	34	6	33	125	127	213	.235	.312	.352	85	-26	-23	142	8	11	-4	.977	-5	O	-5.1

■ SCOTT LUSADER
Lusader, Scott Edward b: 9/30/64, Chicago, Ill. BL/TL, 5'10", 165 lbs. Deb: 9/01/87

YEAR	TM/L	G	AB	R	H	2B	3B	HR	RBI	BB	SO	AVG	OBP	SLG	PRO+	BR	/A	RC	SB	CS	SBR	FA	FR	POS	TPR
1987	Det-A	23	47	8	15	3	1	1	8	5	7	.319	.385	.489	135	2	2	9	1	0	0	.967	-5	O/D	-0.2
1988	Det-A	16	16	3	1	0	0	1	3	1	4	.063	.118	.250	-0	-2	-2	0	0	0	0	1.000	-1	/O	-0.4
1989	Det-A	40	103	15	26	4	0	1	8	9	21	.252	.313	.320	81	-3	-3	11	3	0	1	.933	-6	O/D	-0.8

YEAR	TM/L	G	AB	R	H	2B	3B	HR	RBI	BB	SO	AVG	OBP	SLG	PRO+	BR	/A	RC	SB	CS	SBR	FA	FR	POS	TPR
1990	Det-A	45	87	13	21	2	0	2	16	12	8	.241	.333	.333	86	-1	-1	10	0	0	0	.982	-7	O/D	-0.9
1991	NY-A	11	7	2	1	0	0	0	1	1	3	.143	.250	.143	12	-1	-1	0	0	1	-1	1.000	-1	/OD	-0.3
Total	5	135	260	41	64	9	1	5	36	28	43	.246	.319	.346	86	-5	-4	31	4	1	1	.961	-20	O/D	-2.6

■ ERNIE LUSH Lush, Ernest Benjamin b: 10/31/1884, Bridgeport, Conn. d: 2/26/37, Detroit, Mich. BR/TL, Deb: 4/20/10 F

YEAR	TM/L	G	AB	R	H	2B	3B	HR	RBI	BB	SO	AVG	OBP	SLG	PRO+	BR	/A	RC	SB	CS	SBR	FA	FR	POS	TPR
1910	StL-N	1	4	0	0	0	0	0	0	1	1	.000	.200	.000	-42	-1	-1	0	0			1.000	-0	/O	-0.1

■ JOHNNY LUSH Lush, John Charles b: 10/8/1885, Williamsport, Pa. d: 11/18/46, Beverly Hills, Cal BL/TL, 5'9.5", 165 lbs. Deb: 4/22/04

YEAR	TM/L	G	AB	R	H	2B	3B	HR	RBI	BB	SO	AVG	OBP	SLG	PRO+	BR	/A	RC	SB	CS	SBR	FA	FR	POS	TPR
1904	Phi-N	106	369	39	102	22	3	2	42	27		.276	.334	.369	122	7	9	51	12			.950	-10	1O/P	-0.6
1905	Phi-N	6	16	3	5	0	0	0	1	1		.313	.389	.313	114	0	0	2	0			.667	-1	/OP	-0.1
1906	Phi-N	76	212	28	56	7	1	0	15	14		.264	.310	.307	92	-2	-2	23	6			.907	5	PO/1	0.0
1907	Phi-N	17	40	5	8	1	1	0	5	1		.200	.220	.275	56	-2	-2	3	1			1.000	0	/PO	-0.2
	StL-N	27	82	6	23	2	3	0	5	5		.280	.322	.378	124	1	2	12	4			.917	-3	P/O	-0.3
	Yr	44	122	11	31	3	4	0	10	6		.254	.289	.344	101	-1	-0	14	5			.941	-3	PO	-0.5
1908	StL-N	45	89	7	15	2	0	0	2	7		.169	.229	.191	36	-6	-6	4	1			.926	0	P	0.0
1909	StL-N	45	92	11	22	5	0	0	14	6		.239	.293	.293	87	-2	-1	8	2			.945	-1	P/O	-0.1
1910	StL-N	47	93	8	21	1	3	0	10	8	11	.226	.287	.301	74	-4	-3	8	2			.928	-2	P	0.0
Total	7	369	993	107	252	40	11	2	94	69	11	.254	.307	.322	98	-7	-4	111	28			.926	-12	P/O1	-1.3

■ BILLY LUSH Lush, William Lucas b: 11/10/1873, Bridgeport, Conn. d: 8/28/51, Hawthorne, N.Y. BB/TR, 5'8", 165 lbs. Deb: 9/03/1895 F

YEAR	TM/L	G	AB	R	H	2B	3B	HR	RBI	BB	SO	AVG	OBP	SLG	PRO+	BR	/A	RC	SB	CS	SBR	FA	FR	POS	TPR
1895	Was-N	5	18	2	6	0	0	0	2	2	1	.333	.400	.333	94	-0	-0	2	0			.692	-1	/O	-0.1
1896	Was-N	97	352	74	87	9	11	4	45	66	49	.247	.369	.369	97	0	1	60	28			.885	-2	*O/2	-0.7
1897	Was-N	3	12	1	0	0	0	0	0	2		.000	.143	.000	-61	-3	-3	0	0			1.000	1	/O	-0.2
1901	Bos-N	7	27	2	5	1	1	0	3	3		.185	.267	.296	58	-1	-2	2	0			.960	3	/O	0.0
1902	Bos-N	120	413	68	92	8	1	2	19	76		.223	.346	.262	87	-2	-2	51	30			.952	11	*O/3	0.1
1903	Det-A	119	423	71	116	18	14	1	33	70		.274	.379	.390	135	19	21	76	14			.968	11	*O3/2S	2.6
1904	Cle-A	138	477	76	123	13	8	1	50	72		.258	.359	.325	118	13	13	65	12			.959	3	*O	0.9
Total	7	489	1722	294	429	49	35	8	152	291	50	.249	.360	.332	107	27	28	257	84			.943	24	O/32S	2.6

■ CHARLIE LUSKEY Luskey, Charles Melton b: 4/6/1876, Washington, D.C. d: 12/20/62, Bethesda, Md. BR/TR, 5'7", 165 lbs. Deb: 9/12/01

YEAR	TM/L	G	AB	R	H	2B	3B	HR	RBI	BB	SO	AVG	OBP	SLG	PRO+	BR	/A	RC	SB	CS	SBR	FA	FR	POS	TPR
1901	Was-A	11	41	8	8	3	1	0	3	2		.195	.233	.317	52	-3	-3	3	0			.818	-1	/OC	-0.4

■ LUKE LUTENBERG Lutenberg, Charles William b: 10/4/1864, Quincy, Ill. d: 12/24/38, Quincy, Ill. BR/TR, 6'2", 225 lbs. Deb: 7/07/1894

YEAR	TM/L	G	AB	R	H	2B	3B	HR	RBI	BB	SO	AVG	OBP	SLG	PRO+	BR	/A	RC	SB	CS	SBR	FA	FR	POS	TPR
1894	Lou-N	69	250	42	48	10	4	0	23	23	21	.192	.284	.264	36	-27	-24	21	4			.977	1	1/2	-1.7

■ LYLE LUTTRELL Luttrell, Lyle Kenneth b: 2/22/30, Bloomington, Ill. d: 7/11/84, Chattanooga, Tenn BR/TR, 6', 180 lbs. Deb: 5/15/56

YEAR	TM/L	G	AB	R	H	2B	3B	HR	RBI	BB	SO	AVG	OBP	SLG	PRO+	BR	/A	RC	SB	CS	SBR	FA	FR	POS	TPR
1956	Was-A	38	122	17	23	5	3	2	9	8	19	.189	.256	.328	53	-9	-9	9	5	1	1	.939	-7	S	-1.1
1957	Was-A	19	45	4	9	4	0	0	5	3	8	.200	.250	.289	47	-3	-3	3	0	0	0	.927	-5	S	-0.8
Total	2	57	167	21	32	9	3	2	14	11	27	.192	.254	.317	52	-12	-12	12	5	1	1	.936	-12	/S	-1.9

■ RED LUTZ Lutz, Louis William b: 12/17/1898, Cincinnati, Ohio d: 2/22/84, Cincinnati, Ohio BR/TR, 5'10", 170 lbs. Deb: 5/31/22

YEAR	TM/L	G	AB	R	H	2B	3B	HR	RBI	BB	SO	AVG	OBP	SLG	PRO+	BR	/A	RC	SB	CS	SBR	FA	FR	POS	TPR
1922	Cin-N	1	1	0	1	1	0	0	0	0	0	1.000	1.000	2.000	669	1	1	2	0	0	0	.000	0	/C	0.1

■ JOE LUTZ Lutz, Rollin Joseph b: 2/18/25, Keokuk, Iowa BL/TL, 6', 195 lbs. Deb: 4/17/51 C

YEAR	TM/L	G	AB	R	H	2B	3B	HR	RBI	BB	SO	AVG	OBP	SLG	PRO+	BR	/A	RC	SB	CS	SBR	FA	FR	POS	TPR
1951	StL-A	14	36	7	6	0	1	0	2	6	9	.167	.286	.222	38	-3	-3	3	0	0	0	1.000	-1	1	-0.5

■ RUBE LUTZKE Lutzke, Walter John b: 11/17/1897, Milwaukee, Wis. d: 3/6/38, Granville, Wis. BR/TR, 5'11", 175 lbs. Deb: 4/18/23

YEAR	TM/L	G	AB	R	H	2B	3B	HR	RBI	BB	SO	AVG	OBP	SLG	PRO+	BR	/A	RC	SB	CS	SBR	FA	FR	POS	TPR
1923	Cle-A	143	511	71	131	20	6	3	65	59	57	.256	.338	.337	78	-16	-16	62	10	6	-1	.940	20	*3	1.6
1924	Cle-A	106	341	37	83	18	3	0	42	38	46	.243	.328	.314	65	-17	-17	39	4	0	1	.947	19	*3/2	1.0
1925	Cle-A	81	238	31	52	9	0	1	16	26	29	.218	.295	.269	44	-20	-21	20	2	4	-2	.936	-0	32	-1.7
1926	Cle-A	142	475	42	124	28	6	0	59	34	35	.261	.313	.345	71	-21	-21	53	6	3	0	.960	-1	*3	-1.3
1927	Cle-A	100	311	35	78	12	3	0	41	22	29	.251	.307	.309	60	-18	-19	30	2	1	0	.938	6	3	-0.8
Total	5	572	1876	216	468	87	18	4	223	179	196	.249	.319	.321	66	-92	-93	204	24	14	-1	.945	45	3/2	-1.2

■ GREG LUZINSKI Luzinski, Gregory Michael b: 11/22/50, Chicago, Ill. BR/TR, 6'1", 225 lbs. Deb: 9/09/70

YEAR	TM/L	G	AB	R	H	2B	3B	HR	RBI	BB	SO	AVG	OBP	SLG	PRO+	BR	/A	RC	SB	CS	SBR	FA	FR	POS	TPR
1970	Phi-N	8	12	0	2	0	0	0	0	3	5	.167	.333	.167	39	-1	-1	1	0	1	-1	1.000	1	/1	-0.1
1971	Phi-N	28	100	13	30	8	0	3	15	12	32	.300	.386	.470	141	6	6	19	2	0	1	.996	6	1	1.1
1972	Phi-N	150	563	66	158	33	5	18	68	42	114	.281	.334	.453	119	14	13	81	0	4	-2	.960	-2	*O/1	0.1
1973	Phi-N	161	610	76	174	26	4	29	97	51	135	.285	.347	.484	125	21	19	101	3	3	-1	**.993**	-9	*O	0.2
1974	Phi-N	85	302	29	82	14	1	7	48	29	76	.272	.335	.394	99	1	-0	40	3	0	1	.981	-2	O	-0.5
1975	Phi-N★	161	596	85	179	35	3	34	**120**	89	151	.300	.398	.540	152	47	44	128	3	6	-3	.966	-10	*O	2.6
1976	*Phi-N★	149	533	74	162	28	1	21	95	50	107	.304	.375	.478	137	28	26	96	1	2	-1	.964	-16	*O	0.4
1977	*Phi-N★	149	554	99	171	35	3	39	130	80	140	.309	.399	.594	155	49	45	132	3	2	-0	.964	-15	*O	2.4
1978	*Phi-N★	155	540	85	143	32	2	35	101	100	135	.265	.390	.526	152	41	40	114	8	7	-2	.984	-15	*O	1.8
1979	Phi-N	137	452	47	114	23	1	18	81	56	103	.252	.347	.427	107	7	5	68	3	3	-1	.946	-21	*O	-2.3
1980	*Phi-N	106	368	44	84	19	1	19	56	60	100	.228	.346	.440	112	9	7	60	3	0	1	.993	-18	*O	-1.5
1981	Chi-A	104	378	55	100	15	1	21	62	58	80	.265	.367	.476	144	21	22	67	0	0	0	.000	0	*D	2.3
1982	Chi-A	159	583	87	170	37	1	18	102	89	120	.292	.391	.451	130	27	27	103	1	1	-0	.000	0	*D	2.7
1983	*Chi-A	144	502	73	128	26	1	32	95	70	117	.255	.358	.502	129	24	21	93	2	1	0	1.000	0	*D/1	2.1
1984	Chi-A	125	412	47	98	13	0	13	58	56	80	.238	.333	.364	89	-3	-5	52	5	1	1	.000	0	*D	-0.5
Total	15	1821	6505	880	1795	344	24	307	1128	845	1495	.276	.366	.478	129	291	269	1154	37	31	-8	.972	-101	*OD/1	10.8

■ JERRY LYNCH Lynch, Gerald Thomas b: 7/17/30, Bay City, Mich. BL/TR, 6'1", 189 lbs. Deb: 4/15/54

YEAR	TM/L	G	AB	R	H	2B	3B	HR	RBI	BB	SO	AVG	OBP	SLG	PRO+	BR	/A	RC	SB	CS	SBR	FA	FR	POS	TPR
1954	Pit-N	98	284	27	68	4	5	8	36	20	43	.239	.292	.373	73	-12	-12	29	2	2	-1	.965	-4	O	-2.0
1955	Pit-N	88	282	43	80	18	6	5	28	22	33	.284	.336	.443	106	1	2	40	2	2	-1	.950	-2	O/C	-0.4
1956	Pit-N	19	19	1	3	0	1	0	0	1	4	.158	.200	.263	24	-2	-2	1	0	0	0	1.000	0	/O	-0.2
1957	Cin-N	67	124	11	32	4	1	4	13	6	18	.258	.292	.403	79	-3	-4	15	0	0	0	1.000	-2	O/C	-0.7
1958	Cin-N	122	420	58	131	20	5	16	68	18	54	.312	.340	.498	112	10	7	67	1	4	-2	.970	-7	*O	-0.8
1959	Cin-N	117	379	49	102	16	3	17	58	29	50	.269	.323	.462	103	2	1	56	2	0	1	.979	2	O	-0.2
1960	Cin-N	102	159	23	46	8	2	6	27	16	25	.289	.358	.478	124	6	5	28	0	0	0	.913	-4	O	0.0
1961	*Cin-N	96	181	33	57	13	2	13	50	27	25	.315	.407	.624	166	18	18	46	2	2	-1	.948	-6	O	0.9
1962	Cin-N	114	288	41	81	15	4	12	57	24	38	.281	.339	.486	115	7	5	46	3	3	-1	.970	-5	O	-0.4
1963	Cin-N	22	32	5	8	3	0	2	9	1	5	.250	.294	.531	129	1	1	5	0	0	0	1.000	-1	/O	0.0
	Pit-N	88	237	26	63	6	3	10	36	22	28	.266	.331	.443	120	6	6	34	0	1	-1	.960	-9	O	-0.8
	Yr	110	269	31	71	9	3	12	45	23	33	.264	.327	.454	121	7	7	39	0	1	-1	.962	-10	O	-0.8
1964	Pit-N	114	297	35	81	14	2	16	66	26	57	.273	.333	.495	130	11	11	48	0	1	-1	.983	-17	O	-1.1
1965	Pit-N	73	121	7	34	1	0	5	16	8	26	.281	.331	.413	108	1	1	14	0	2	-1	.903	-3	O	-0.4
1966	Pit-N	64	56	5	12	1	0	1	6	4	10	.214	.267	.286	54	-3	-3	4	0	0	0	1.000	1	/O	-0.3
Total	13	1184	2879	364	798	123	34	115	470	224	416	.277	.331	.463	110	42	35	434	12	17	-7	.964	-58	O/C	-6.4

■ HENRY LYNCH Lynch, Henry W. b: 4/8/1866, Worcester, Mass. d: 11/23/25, Worcester, Mass. 5'7", 143 lbs. Deb: 9/21/1893

YEAR	TM/L	G	AB	R	H	2B	3B	HR	RBI	BB	SO	AVG	OBP	SLG	PRO+	BR	/A	RC	SB	CS	SBR	FA	FR	POS	TPR
1893	Chi-N	4	14	0	3	2	0	0	2	1	1	.214	.267	.357	68	-1	-1	1	0			.833	-1	/O	-0.1

■ DANNY LYNCH Lynch, Matt Dan "Dummy" b: 2/7/26, Dallas, Tex. d: 6/30/78, Plano, Tex. BR/TR, 5'11", 174 lbs. Deb: 9/14/48

YEAR	TM/L	G	AB	R	H	2B	3B	HR	RBI	BB	SO	AVG	OBP	SLG	PRO+	BR	/A	RC	SB	CS	SBR	FA	FR	POS	TPR
1948	Chi-N	7	7	3	2	0	0	1	1	1	1	.286	.375	.714	197	1	1	2	0			1.000	0	/2	0.1

YEAR	TM/L	G	AB	R	H	2B	3B	HR	RBI	BB	SO	AVG	OBP	SLG	PRO+	BR	/A	RC	SB	CS	SBR	FA	FR	POS	TPR
■ **MIKE LYNCH**	Lynch, Michael Joseph b: 9/10/1875, St.Paul, Minn. d: 4/1/47, Jennings Lodge, Ore TR , 6'2", 170 lbs. Deb: 4/24/02																								
1902	Chi-N	7	28	4	4	0	0	0	0	2		.143	.200	.143	6	-3	-3	1	0			.929	-1	/O	-0.4
■ **TOM LYNCH**	Lynch, Thomas James b: 4/3/1860, Bennington, Vt. d: 3/28/55, Cohoes, N.Y. BL/TR, 5'10.5", 170 lbs. Deb: 8/18/1884 U																								
1884	Wil-U	16	58	6	16	3	1	0		5		.276	.333	.362	131	2	2	7				.846	-3	/CO1	-0.1
	Phi-N	13	48	7	15	4	2	0	3	4	5	.313	.365	.479	171	3	4	9				.860	-2	/CO	0.2
1885	Phi-N	13	53	7	10	3	0	0	1	10	3	.189	.317	.245	86	-0	-0	4				.838	3	O	0.2
Total	2	42	159	20	41	10	3	0	4	19	8	.258	.337	.358	128	5	6	20				.887	-2	/OC1	0.3
■ **WALT LYNCH**	Lynch, Walter Edward "Jabber" b: 4/15/1897, Buffalo, N.Y. d: 12/21/76, Daytona Beach, Fla TR , 6', 176 lbs. Deb: 7/08/22																								
1922	Bos-A	3	2	1	1	0	0	0	0	0	0	.500	.500	.500	163	0	0	0	0	0	0	1.000	0	/C	0.0
■ **BYRD LYNN**	Lynn, Byrd "Birdie" b: 3/13/1889, Unionville, Ill. d: 2/5/40, Napa, Cal. BR/TR, 5'11", 165 lbs. Deb: 4/16/16																								
1916	Chi-A	31	40	4	9	1	0	0	3	4	7	.225	.311	.250	68	-1	-1	4	2			.952	8	C	0.8
1917	*Chi-A	35	72	7	16	2	0	0	5	7	11	.222	.300	.250	67	-3	-3	6	1			.959	-2	C	-0.3
1918	Chi-A	5	8	0	2	0	0	0	0	2	1	.250	.400	.250	95	0	0	1	0			1.000	-1	/C	-0.1
1919	*Chi-A	29	66	4	15	4	0	0	4	4	9	.227	.271	.288	57	-4	-4	5	0			.982	1	C	-0.2
1920	Chi-A	16	25	0	8	2	1	0	3	1	3	.320	.346	.480	117	0	0	4	0	0	0	1.000	-1	C	0.0
Total	5	116	211	15	50	9	1	0	15	18	31	.237	.303	.289	72	-7	-8	20	3	0		.969	5	/C	0.2
■ **FRED LYNN**	Lynn, Fredric Michael b: 2/3/52, Chicago, Ill. BL/TL, 6'1", 190 lbs. Deb: 9/05/74																								
1974	Bos-A	15	43	5	18	2	2	2	10	6	6	.419	.500	.698	226	8	8	16	0	0	0	1.000	-0	O/D	0.7
1975	*Bos-A★	145	528	**103**	175	**47**	7	21	105	62	90	.331	.405	**.566**	158	49	44	120	10	5	0	.983	13	*O	5.1
1976	Bos-A★	132	507	76	159	32	8	10	65	48	67	.314	.374	.467	130	28	21	88	14	9	-1	.984	14	*O/D	2.9
1977	Bos-A★	129	497	81	129	29	5	18	76	51	63	.260	.332	.447	98	6	-2	72	2	3	-1	.994	8	*O/D	0.0
1978	Bos-A★	150	541	75	161	33	3	22	82	75	50	.298	.384	.492	131	33	25	103	3	6	-3	.984	8	*O	2.5
1979	Bos-A★	147	531	116	177	42	1	39	122	82	79	**.333**	.426	**.637**	**173**	**62**	**58**	**147**	2	2	-1	.987	7	*O	5.5
1980	Bos-A★	110	415	67	125	32	3	12	61	58	39	.301	.387	.480	129	21	19	80	12	0	4	.994	9	*O	2.6
1981	Cal-A★	76	256	28	56	8	1	5	31	38	42	.219	.327	.316	86	-4	-4	27	1	2	-1	.978	1	O	-0.6
1982	*Cal-A★	138	472	89	141	38	1	21	86	58	72	.299	.379	.517	143	28	28	91	7	8	-3	.991	-3	*O	1.9
1983	Cal-A★	117	437	56	119	20	3	22	74	55	83	.272	.356	.483	130	17	18	76	2	2	-1	.993	-2	*O/D	1.2
1984	Cal-A	142	517	84	140	28	4	23	79	77	97	.271	.367	.474	132	23	23	90	2	2	-1	.982	-10	*O	0.8
1985	Bal-A	124	448	59	118	12	1	23	68	53	100	.263	.343	.449	118	9	11	70	7	3	0	.994	2	*O	0.8
1986	Bal-A	112	397	67	114	13	1	23	67	53	59	.287	.374	.499	137	20	20	69	2	2	-1	.984	-4	*O/D	1.2
1987	Bal-A	111	396	49	100	24	0	23	60	39	72	.253	.321	.487	113	5	6	58	3	7	-3	.991	-3	*O/D	-0.3
1988	Bal-A	87	301	37	76	13	1	18	37	28	66	.252	.316	.482	123	7	8	44	2	2	-1	.991	0	O/D	0.5
	Det-A	27	90	9	20	1	0	7	19	5	16	.222	.271	.467	106	-0	0	11	0	0	0	1.000	0	O/D	0.0
	Yr	114	391	46	96	14	1	25	56	33	82	.246	.306	.478	120	7	8	55	2	2	-1	.992	1	*O/D	0.5
1989	Det-A	117	353	44	85	11	1	11	46	47	71	.241	.332	.371	100	-0	1	46	1	1	-0	.992	-1	OD	-0.2
1990	SD-N	90	196	18	47	3	1	6	23	22	44	.240	.320	.357	85	-4	-4	24	2	0	1	1.000	-4	O	-0.9
Total	17	1969	6925	1063	1960	388	43	306	1111	857	1116	.283	.364	.484	129	309	280	1233	72	54	-11	.988	35	*O/D	23.7
■ **JERRY LYNN**	Lynn, Jerome Edward b: 4/14/16, Scranton, Pa. d: 9/25/72, Scranton, Pa. BR/TR, 5'10", 164 lbs. Deb: 9/19/37																								
1937	Was-A	1	3	0	2	1	0	0	0	0	0	.667	.667	1.000	329	1	1	2	0	0	0	1.000	1	/2	0.2
■ **RUSS LYON**	Lyon, Russell Mayo b: 6/26/13, Ball Ground, Ga. d: 12/24/75, Charleston, S.C. BR/TR, 6'1", 230 lbs. Deb: 4/21/44																								
1944	Cle-A	7	11	1	2	0	0	0	0	1	1	.182	.250	.182	25	-1	-1	0	0	0	0	.909	0	/C	-0.1
■ **BARRY LYONS**	Lyons, Barry Stephen b: 6/3/60, Biloxi, Miss. BR/TR, 6'1", 205 lbs. Deb: 4/19/86																								
1986	NY-N	6	9	1	0	0	0	0	2	1	2	.000	.100	.000	-72	-2	-2	0	0	0	0	.941	0	/C	-0.2
1987	NY-N	53	130	15	33	4	1	4	24	8	24	.254	.307	.392	88	-3	-2	16	0	0	0	.984	0	C	0.0
1988	NY-N	50	91	5	21	7	1	0	11	3	12	.231	.255	.330	70	-4	-4	7	0	0	0	.979	-2	C/1	-0.5
1989	NY-N	79	235	15	58	13	0	3	27	11	28	.247	.286	.340	82	-7	-6	21	0	1	-1	.980	1	C	-0.2
1990	NY-N	24	80	8	19	0	0	2	7	2	9	.237	.265	.313	58	-5	-5	6	0	0	0	.980	3	C	0.0
	LA-N	3	5	1	1	0	0	1	2	0	1	.200	.200	.800	166	0	0	1	0	0	0	1.000	-1	/C	0.0
	Yr	27	85	9	20	0	0	3	9	2	10	.235	.261	.341	65	-4	-4	7	0	0	0	.980	3	C	0.0
1991	LA-N	9	9	0	0	0	0	0	0	0	2	.000	.000	.000	-99	-2	-2	0	0	0	0	1.000	1	/C	-0.1
	Cal-A	2	5	0	1	0	0	0	0	0	0	.200	.200	.200	11	-1	-1	0	0	0	0	1.000	0	/1	-0.1
Total	6	226	564	45	133	24	2	10	73	25	78	.236	.274	.339	73	-24	-21	52	0	1	-1	.980	3	C/1	-1.1
■ **DENNY LYONS**	Lyons, Dennis Patrick Aloysius b: 3/12/1866, Cincinnati, Ohio d: 1/2/29, W.Covington, Ky. BR/TR, 5'10", 185 lbs. Deb: 9/18/1885																								
1885	Pro-N	4	16	3	2	1	0	0	1	0	3	.125	.125	.188	-0	-2	-2	0				.824	-0	/3	-0.2
1886	Phi-a	32	123	22	26	3	1	0		8		.211	.281	.252	69	-4	-4	11	7			.807	-7	3	-0.9
1887	Phi-a	137	570	128	209	43	14	6		47		.367	.421	.523	165	48	48	160	73			.866	-6	*3	3.6
1888	Phi-a	111	456	93	135	22	5	6	83	41		.296	.363	.406	151	26	26	83	39			.878	-13	*3	1.4
1889	Phi-a	131	510	135	168	36	4	9	82	79	44	.329	.426	.469	159	41	42	109	10			.860	9	*3/1	4.6
1890	Phi-a	88	339	79	120	29	5	7		57		.354	**.461**	**.531**	**200**	43	44	95	21			.909	9	3	4.9
1891	StL-a	120	451	124	142	24	3	11	84	88	58	.315	.445	.455	140	41	29	98	9			.871	-6	*3	2.4
1892	NY-N	108	389	71	100	16	7	8	51	59	36	.257	.359	.396	132	15	16	61	11			.871	-6	*3	1.3
1893	Pit-N	131	490	103	150	19	16	3	105	97	29	.306	.430	.429	133	26	28	101	19			.918	5	*3	2.9
1894	Pit-N	71	254	51	82	14	4	4	50	42	12	.323	.427	.457	116	8	8	58	14			.898	7	3	1.2
1895	StL-N	33	129	24	38	6	0	2	25	14	5	.295	.377	.388	101	0	1	21	3			.894	-4	3	-0.3
1896	Pit-N	118	436	77	134	25	6	4	71	67	25	.307	.406	.420	125	15	18	83	13			.893	-15	*3	0.5
1897	Pit-N	37	131	22	27	6	4	2	17	22		.206	.346	.359	89	-2	-1	19	5			.989	-0	1/3	-0.1
Total	13	1121	4294	932	1333	244	69	62	569	621	212	.310	.407	.443	141	256	254	898	224			.882	-26	*3/1	21.3
■ **ED LYONS**	Lyons, Edward Hoyte "Mouse" b: 5/12/23, Winston-Salem, N.C BR/TR, 5'9", 165 lbs. Deb: 9/15/47 C																								
1947	Was-A	7	26	2	4	0	0	0	0	2	2	.154	.214	.154	3	-3	-3	1	0	0	0	1.000	4	/2	0.1
■ **HARRY LYONS**	Lyons, Harry P. b: 3/25/1866, Chester, Pa. d: 6/30/12, Mauricetown, N.J. BR/TR, 5'10.5", 157 lbs. Deb: 8/29/1887																								
1887	Phi-N	1	4	0	0	0	0	0	0	1	0	.000	.200	.000	-37	-1	-1	0	0			.500	-0	/O	-0.1
	*StL-a	2	8	2	1	0	0	0		0		.125	.125	.125	-27	-1	-1	0	2			1.000	1	/2O	-0.1
1888	*StL-a	123	499	66	97	10	5	4	63	20		.194	.230	.259	53	-23	-31	39	36			.891	6	*O/3S2	-2.6
1889	NY-N	5	20	1	2	0	1	0	2	2	0	.100	.182	.200	7	-3	-3	1	0			1.000	-1	/O	-0.3
1890	Roc-a	133	584	83	152	11	11	3		27		.260	.294	.332	94	-12	-5	73	47			.920	11	*O/3CP	0.1
1892	NY-N	96	411	67	98	5	2	0	53	33	29	.238	.297	.260	72	-14	-13	40	25			.910	3	O	-1.4
1893	NY-N	47	187	27	51	5	2	0	21	14	6	.273	.323	.321	73	-7	-7	23	10			.917	2	O	-0.6
Total	6	407	1713	246	401	31	21	7	139	97	35	.234	.277	.289	71	-60	-60	176	120			.908	21	O/32PCS	-5.0
■ **PAT LYONS**	Lyons, Patrick Jerry b: 1860, Canada d: 1/20/14, Springfield, Ohio TR , Deb: 7/21/1890																								
1890	Cle-N	11	38	2	2	1	0	0	1	4	4	.053	.143	.079	-35	-6	-6	0	0			.839	-5	2	-1.0
■ **STEVE LYONS**	Lyons, Stephen John b: 6/3/60, Tacoma, Wash. BL/TR, 6'3", 192 lbs. Deb: 4/15/85																								
1985	Bos-A	133	371	52	98	14	3	5	30	32	64	.264	.324	.358	83	-6	-8	44	12	9	-2	.973	-8	*O/3SD	-2.1
1986	Bos-A	59	124	20	31	7	2	1	14	12	23	.250	.316	.363	84	-3	-3	13	2	3	-1	.972	-5	O	-1.0

YEAR	TM/L	G	AB	R	H	2B	3B	HR	RBI	BB	SO	AVG	OBP	SLG	PRO+	BR	/A	RC	SB	CS	SBR	FA	FR	POS	TPR
	Chi-A	42	123	10	25	2	1	0	6	7	24	.203	.252	.236	33	-11	-12	7	2	3	-1	.987	1	O/31D	-1.3
	Yr	101	247	30	56	9	3	1	20	19	47	.227	.285	.300	58	-14	-14	21	4	6	-2	.978	-4	O/31D	-2.3
1987	Chi-A	76	193	26	54	11	1	1	19	12	37	.280	.322	.363	79	-5	-6	22	3	1	0	.971	11	3O/2D	0.4
1988	Chi-A	146	472	59	127	28	3	5	45	32	59	.269	.317	.373	93	-5	-5	57	1	2	-1	.927	10	*3O/2C1	0.3
1989	Chi-A	140	443	51	117	21	3	2	50	35	68	.264	.319	.339	88	-8	-7	50	9	6	-1	.982	-9	213O/SCD	-1.7
1990	Chi-A	94	146	22	28	6	1	1	11	10	41	.192	.248	.267	45	-11	-11	11	1	0	0	.991	-1	12/O3SDP	-1.3
1991	Bos-A	87	212	15	51	10	1	4	17	11	35	.241	.278	.354	70	-8	-9	22	10	3	1	1.000	1	O23/1SDP	-0.8
1992	Atl-N	11	14	0	1	0	1	0	1	0	4	.071	.071	.214	-20	-2	-2	0	0	0	0	1.000	-2	/O2	-0.4
	Mon-N	16	13	2	3	0	0	0	1	1	3	.231	.286	.231	48	-1	-1	0	1	2	-1	1.000	-2	/O1	-0.4
	Yr	27	27	2	4	0	1	0	2	1	7	.148	.179	.222	12	-3	-3	0	1	2	-1	1.000	-3	O/21	-0.8
	Bos-A	21	28	3	7	0	1	0	2	2	1	.250	.300	.321	71	-1	-1	3	0	1	-1	1.000	-0	/1O2	-0.2
Total	8	825	2139	260	542	99	17	19	196	154	359	.253	.305	.342	78	-62	-65	229	41	30	-6	.979	-3	O312/DSC	-8.5

■ TERRY LYONS

Lyons, Terence Hilbert b: 12/14/08, New Holland, Ohio d: 9/9/59, Dayton, Ohio BR/TR, 6'0.5", 165 lbs. Deb: 4/19/29

YEAR	TM/L	G	AB	R	H	2B	3B	HR	RBI	BB	SO	AVG	OBP	SLG	PRO+	BR	/A	RC	SB	CS	SBR	FA	FR	POS	TPR
1929	Phi-N	1	0	0	0	0	0	0	0	0	0	—	—	—	—	0	0	0	0			.000	0	/1	0.0

■ TED LYONS

Lyons, Theodore Amar b: 12/28/1900, Lake Charles, La. d: 7/25/86, Sulphur, La. BB/TR, 5'11", 200 lbs. Deb: 7/02/23 MCH

YEAR	TM/L	G	AB	R	H	2B	3B	HR	RBI	BB	SO	AVG	OBP	SLG	PRO+	BR	/A	RC	SB	CS	SBR	FA	FR	POS	TPR
1923	Chi-A	9	5	0	1	0	0	0	1	1	3	.200	.333	.200	43	-0	-0	0	0	0	0	1.000	1	/P	0.0
1924	Chi-A	41	77	10	17	0	1	0	6	5	13	.221	.277	.247	37	-7	-7	6	0	0	0	.902	-3	P	0.0
1925	Chi-A	43	97	6	18	3	0	0	7	3	13	.186	.218	.216	11	-13	-13	5	0	0	0	.957	2	P	0.0
1926	Chi-A	41	104	7	22	1	1	0	3	1	10	.212	.219	.240	20	-12	-12	6	0	0	0	.955	4	P	0.0
1927	Chi-A	41	110	16	28	6	2	1	9	6	17	.255	.293	.373	74	-5	-5	12	0	0	0	.979	0	P	0.0
1928	Chi-A	49	91	10	23	2	0	0	8	1	9	.253	.261	.275	41	-8	-8	7	0	0	0	.920	2	P	0.0
1929	Chi-A	40	91	7	20	4	0	0	11	9	13	.220	.290	.264	44	-8	-7	8	0	0	0	.946	2	P/O	0.0
1930	Chi-A	57	122	20	38	6	3	1	15	2	18	.311	.323	.434	93	-2	-2	17	0	0	0	.938	3	P	0.0
1931	Chi-A	42	33	6	5	0	0	0	3	2	1	.152	.200	.152	-7	-5	-5	1	0	0	0	.957	-1	P	0.0
1932	Chi-A	49	73	11	19	2	1	1	10	4	10	.260	.308	.356	76	-3	-2	8	0	0	0	.964	-1	P	0.0
1933	Chi-A	51	91	11	26	2	1	1	11	4	6	.286	.316	.363	83	-3	-2	10	0	1	-1	.983	0	P	0.0
1934	Chi-A	50	97	9	20	4	0	1	16	3	19	.206	.245	.278	34	-10	-10	7	0	0	0	.939	2	P	0.0
1935	Chi-A	29	82	5	18	4	0	0	6	3	4	.220	.256	.268	35	-8	-8	6	0	0	0	1.000	-1	P	0.0
1936	Chi-A	26	70	2	11	0	0	0	5	5	12	.157	.213	.157	-7	-12	-12	3	0	0	0	1.000	1	P	0.0
1937	Chi-A	23	57	6	12	0	0	0	3	9	14	.211	.318	.211	36	-5	-5	5	0	0	0	1.000	0	P	0.0
1938	Chi-A	24	72	9	14	2	0	0	4	2	9	.194	.216	.222	10	-10	-10	4	0	0	0	.982	2	P	0.0
1939	Chi-A☆	21	61	5	18	3	0	0	8	5	7	.295	.348	.344	76	-2	-2	8	0	0	0	.912	-1	P	0.0
1940	Chi-A	22	75	4	18	4	0	0	7	2	7	.240	.260	.293	43	-6	-6	5	0	0	0	.923	-2	P	0.0
1941	Chi-A	22	74	8	20	2	0	0	6	2	6	.270	.289	.297	56	-5	-5	6	0	0	0	.981	1	P	0.0
1942	Chi-A	20	67	10	16	4	0	0	10	3	7	.239	.282	.299	65	-3	-3	6	0	0	0	.980	1	P	0.0
1946	Chi-A	5	14	0	0	0	0	0	0	1	3	.000	.067	.000	-83	-3	-3	0	0	0	0	1.000	0	/PM	0.0
Total	21	705	1563	162	364	49	9	5	149	73	201	.233	.270	.285	44	-132	-129	128	0	1	-1	.958	11	P/O	0.0

■ BILL LYONS

Lyons, William Allen b: 4/26/58, Alton, Ill. BR/TR, 6'1", 175 lbs. Deb: 7/20/83

YEAR	TM/L	G	AB	R	H	2B	3B	HR	RBI	BB	SO	AVG	OBP	SLG	PRO+	BR	/A	RC	SB	CS	SBR	FA	FR	POS	TPR
1983	StL-N	42	60	3	10	1	1	0	3	1	11	.167	.180	.217	10	-7	-7	2	3	2	-0	.985	2	2/3S	-0.5
1984	StL-N	46	73	13	16	3	0	0	3	9	13	.219	.305	.260	62	-4	-3	7	3	1	0	.991	14	2S/3	1.2
Total	2	88	133	16	26	4	1	0	6	10	24	.195	.252	.241	39	-11	-11	9	6	3	0	.989	16	/2S3	0.7

■ DAD LYTLE

Lytle, Edward Benson "Pop" b: 3/10/1862, Racine, Wis. d: 12/21/50, Long Beach, Cal. BR/TR, 5'11", 160 lbs. Deb: 8/11/1890

YEAR	TM/L	G	AB	R	H	2B	3B	HR	RBI	BB	SO	AVG	OBP	SLG	PRO+	BR	/A	RC	SB	CS	SBR	FA	FR	POS	TPR
1890	Chi-N	1	4	1	0	0	0	0	0	0	1	.000	.000	.000	-96	-1	-1	0	0			1.000	1	/O	0.0
	Pit-N	15	55	2	8	1	0	0	0	8	9	.145	.254	.164	27	-5	-4	2	0			.837	-6	/2O	-0.9
	Yr	16	59	3	8	1	0	0	0	8	10	.136	.239	.153	18	-6	-5	2	0			.824	-5	/O2	-0.9

■ JIM LYTTLE

Lyttle, James Lawrence b: 5/20/46, Hamilton, Ohio BL/TR, 6', 186 lbs. Deb: 5/17/69

YEAR	TM/L	G	AB	R	H	2B	3B	HR	RBI	BB	SO	AVG	OBP	SLG	PRO+	BR	/A	RC	SB	CS	SBR	FA	FR	POS	TPR
1969	NY-A	28	83	7	15	4	0	0	4	4	19	.181	.218	.229	26	-8	-8	4	1	2	-1	.983	1	O	-1.0
1970	NY-A	87	126	20	39	7	1	3	14	10	26	.310	.360	.452	129	4	4	18	3	6	-3	.989	-9	O	-1.0
1971	NY-A	49	86	7	17	5	0	1	7	8	18	.198	.274	.291	64	-5	-4	6	0	2	-1	1.000	-3	O	-0.9
1972	Chi-A	44	82	8	19	5	2	0	5	1	28	.232	.241	.341	70	-3	-3	7	0	1	-1	1.000	-2	O	-0.7
1973	Mon-N	49	116	12	30	5	1	4	19	9	14	.259	.312	.422	98	-0	-1	14	0	2	-1	.974	4	O	0.1
1974	Mon-N	25	9	1	3	0	0	0	2	1	3	.333	.400	.333	101	0	0	1	0	0	0	1.000	2	O	0.2
1975	Mon-N	44	55	7	15	4	0	0	6	13	6	.273	.412	.345	107	2	1	9	0	1	-1	1.000	-1	O	0.0
1976	Mon-N	42	85	6	23	4	1	1	8	7	13	.271	.326	.376	95	-0	-1	10	0	0	0	.977	1	O	-0.1
	LA-N	23	68	3	15	3	0	0	5	8	12	.221	.303	.265	63	-3	-3	6	0	1	-1	1.000	5	O	0.1
	Yr	65	153	9	38	7	1	1	13	15	25	.248	.315	.327	81	-3	-4	16	0	1	-1	.990	6	O	0.0
Total	8	391	710	71	176	37	5	9	70	61	139	.248	.308	.352	86	-14	-14	75	4	15	-8	.988	-2	O	-3.3

■ KEVIN MAAS

Maas, Kevin Christian b: 1/20/65, Castro Valley, Cal. BL/TL, 6'3", 195 lbs. Deb: 6/29/90

YEAR	TM/L	G	AB	R	H	2B	3B	HR	RBI	BB	SO	AVG	OBP	SLG	PRO+	BR	/A	RC	SB	CS	SBR	FA	FR	POS	TPR
1990	NY-A	79	254	42	64	9	0	21	41	43	76	.252	.367	.535	149	17	17	52	1	2	-1	.983	-3	1D	0.9
1991	NY-A	148	500	69	110	14	1	23	63	83	128	.220	.336	.390	100	1	1	72	5	1	1	.983	-1	*D1	-0.2
1992	NY-A	98	286	35	71	12	0	11	35	25	63	.248	.309	.406	97	-1	-2	37	3	1	0	.986	-3	D1	-0.6
Total	3	325	1040	146	245	35	1	55	139	151	267	.236	.336	.430	111	17	16	161	9	4	0	.983	-7	D1	0.1

■ HARVEY MacDONALD

MacDonald, Harvey Forsyth b: 5/18/1898, New York, N.Y. d: 10/4/65, Manoa, Pa. BL/TL, 5'11", 170 lbs. Deb: 6/12/28

YEAR	TM/L	G	AB	R	H	2B	3B	HR	RBI	BB	SO	AVG	OBP	SLG	PRO+	BR	/A	RC	SB	CS	SBR	FA	FR	POS	TPR
1928	Phi-N	13	16	0	4	0	0	0	2	2	3	.250	.333	.250	53	-1	-1	1	0			1.000	-0	/O	-0.1

■ MACEY

Macey b: Columbus, Ohio Deb: 10/02/1890

YEAR	TM/L	G	AB	R	H	2B	3B	HR	RBI	BB	SO	AVG	OBP	SLG	PRO+	BR	/A	RC	SB	CS	SBR	FA	FR	POS	TPR
1890	Phi-a	1	1	0	0	0	0	0		0		.000	.000	.000	-99	-0	-0	0	0			1.000	-1	/C	-0.1

■ MIKE MACFARLANE

Macfarlane, Michael Andrew b: 4/12/64, Stockton, Cal. BR/TR, 6'1", 200 lbs. Deb: 7/23/87

YEAR	TM/L	G	AB	R	H	2B	3B	HR	RBI	BB	SO	AVG	OBP	SLG	PRO+	BR	/A	RC	SB	CS	SBR	FA	FR	POS	TPR
1987	KC-A	8	19	0	4	1	0	0	3	2	2	.211	.286	.263	46	-1	-1	1	0	0	0	1.000	-1	/C	-0.2
1988	KC-A	70	211	25	56	15	0	4	26	21	37	.265	.335	.393	102	1	1	28	0	0	0	.994	-15	C	-0.9
1989	KC-A	69	157	13	35	6	0	2	19	7	27	.223	.265	.299	59	-9	-9	11	0	0	0	.996	3	C/D	-0.4
1990	KC-A	124	400	37	102	24	4	6	58	25	69	.255	.310	.380	94	-5	-4	47	1	0	0	.991	-19	*C/D	-1.6
1991	KC-A	84	267	34	74	18	2	13	41	17	52	.277	.334	.506	128	9	9	45	1	0	0	.993	-12	C/D	0.1
1992	KC-A	129	402	51	94	28	3	17	48	30	89	.234	.311	.445	109	4	3	54	1	5	-3	.993	-2	*CD	0.5
Total	6	484	1456	160	365	92	9	42	195	102	276	.251	.313	.413	101	-1	-1	186	3	5	-2	.993	-47	C/D	-2.5

■ ED MacGAMWELL

MacGamwell, Edward M. b: 1/10/1879, Buffalo, N.Y. d: 5/26/24, Albany, N.Y. BL/TL, Deb: 4/14/05

YEAR	TM/L	G	AB	R	H	2B	3B	HR	RBI	BB	SO	AVG	OBP	SLG	PRO+	BR	/A	RC	SB	CS	SBR	FA	FR	POS	TPR
1905	Bro-N	4	16	0	4	0	0	0	0	1		.250	.294	.250	68	-1	-1	1	0			.951	-1	/1	-0.1

■ KEN MACHA

Macha, Kenneth Edward b: 9/29/50, Monroeville, Pa. BR/TR, 6'2", 217 lbs. Deb: 9/14/74 FC

YEAR	TM/L	G	AB	R	H	2B	3B	HR	RBI	BB	SO	AVG	OBP	SLG	PRO+	BR	/A	RC	SB	CS	SBR	FA	FR	POS	TPR
1974	Pit-N	5	5	1	3	1	0	0	1	0	0	.600	.600	.800	300	1	1	2	0	0	0	1.000	-0	/C	0.1
1977	Pit-N	35	95	2	26	4	0	0	11	6	17	.274	.317	.316	68	-4	-4	8	1	1	-0	.964	-4	31/O	-0.9
1978	Pit-N	29	52	5	11	1	1	0	5	12	10	.212	.359	.269	75	-1	-1	6	2	0	1	.970	-3	3	-0.5
1979	Mon-N	25	36	8	10	3	1	0	4	2	9	.278	.333	.417	104	0	0	4	0	0	0	1.000	2	3/1OC	0.2
1980	Mon-N	49	107	10	31	5	1	1	8	11	17	.290	.361	.383	108	1	1	13	0	2	-1	.910	-5	3/1CO	-0.6
1981	Tor-A	37	85	4	17	2	0	0	6	8	15	.200	.269	.224	41	-6	-7	5	1	1	-0	.892	-1	31/CD	-0.9
Total	6	180	380	30	98	16	3	1	35	39	68	.258	.330	.324	80	-8	-9	39	4	4	-1	.938	-11	3/1OCD	-2.6

YEAR	TM/L	G	AB	R	H	2B	3B	HR	RBI	BB	SO	AVG	OBP	SLG	PRO+	BR	/A	RC	SB	CS	SBR	FA	FR	POS	TPR

■ MIKE MACHA   Macha, Michael William   b: 2/17/54, Victoria, Tex.   BR/TR, 5'11", 180 lbs.   Deb: 4/20/79   F

1979	Atl-N	6	13	2	2	0	0	0	1	1	5	.154	.214	.154	2	-2	-2	0	0	0	0	.769	0	/3	-0.2
1980	Tor-A	5	8	0	0	0	0	0	0	0	1	.000	.000	.000	-96	-2	-2	0	0	0	0	.778	1	/3C	-0.2
Total	2	11	21	2	2	0	0	0	1	1	6	.095	.136	.095	-33	-4	-4	0	0	0	0	.773	1	/3C	-0.4

■ DAVE MACHEMER   Machemer, David Ritchie   b: 5/24/51, St.Joseph, Mo.   BR/TR, 5'11.5", 180 lbs.   Deb: 6/21/78

1978	Cal-A	10	22	6	6	1	0	1	2	2	1	.273	.333	.455	124	1	1	3	0	1	-1	1.000	-2	/23S	-0.2
1979	Det-A	19	26	8	5	1	0	0	2	3	2	.192	.276	.231	37	-2	-2	1	0	3	-2	.972	4	2/O	0.0
Total	2	29	48	14	11	2	0	1	4	5	3	.229	.302	.333	74	-2	-2	4	0	4	-2	.978	2	/23OS	-0.2

■ CONNIE MACK   Mack, Cornelius Alexander "The Tall Tactician" (b: Cornelius Alexander McGillicuddy)   b: 12/22/1862, E.Brookfield, Mass.   d: 2/8/56, Philadelphia, Pa.   BR/TR, 6'1", 150 lbs.   Deb: 9/11/1886   FMH

1886	Was-N	10	36	4	13	2	1	0	5	0	2	.361	.361	.472	161	2	2	6				.957	9	C	1.1
1887	Was-N	82	314	35	63	6	1	0	20	8	17	.201	.228	.226	29	-30	-27	23		26		.906	3	C/O2	-1.5
1888	Was-N	85	300	49	56	5	6	3	29	17	18	.187	.249	.273	72	-10	-8	29		31		.916	5	CO1	0.5
1889	Was-N	98	386	51	113	16	1	0	42	15	12	.293	.333	.330	95	-5	-2	54		26		.891	5	CO1	0.4
1890	Buf-P	123	503	95	134	15	12	0	53	47	13	.266	.353	.344	96	-7	1	68		16		.925	-11	*C/O1	0.0
1891	Pit-N	75	280	43	60	10	0	0	29	19	11	.214	.286	.250	60	-14	-13	22		4		.926	9	C/1	0.2
1892	Pit-N	97	346	39	84	9	4	1	31	21	22	.243	.298	.301	82	-7	-7	35		11		**.951**	24	C/O1	2.1
1893	Pit-N	37	133	22	38	3	1	0	15	10	9	.286	.358	.323	85	-3	-2	17		4		.941	6	C	-0.5
1894	Pit-N	69	228	32	57	7	1	1	21	20	14	.250	.321	.303	53	-17	-17	27		8		.947	6	CM	-0.4
1895	Pit-N	14	49	12	15	2	0	0	4	7	1	.306	.404	.347	102	0	1	8		1		.962	-2	C/1M	0.0
1896	Pit-N	33	120	9	26	4	1	0	16	5	8	.217	.248	.267	39	-11	-10	8		0		.974	1	/CM	-0.7
Total	11	723	2695	391	659	79	28	5	265	169	127	.245	.305	.300	74	-102	-82	297		127		.927	54	C/102S	2.2

■ DENNY MACK   Mack, Dennis Joseph (b: Dennis Joseph McGee)   b: 1851, Easton, Pa.   d: 4/10/1888, Wilkes-Barre, Pa.   BR/TR, 5'7", 164 lbs.   Deb: 5/06/1871   MU

1871	Rok-n	25	122	34	30	7	1	0	17	8	7	.246	.292	.320	79	-4	-2	15	12					*1/PS	0.0
1872	Ath-n	47	205	68	59	9	1	0	34	**23**	9	.288	.360	.341	116	5	5	27						1S	0.4
1873	Phi-n	48	205	55	60	5	0	0	19	15	9	.293	.341	.317	92	-0	-2	24						*1/OS2	0.0
1874	Phi-n	56	248	48	51	7	4	0			1	.206	.209	.266	48	-13	-15	14						*1	-1.2
1876	StL-N	48	180	32	39	5	0	0	7	11	5	.217	.262	.261	79	-4	-3	13				.886	-8	S/2O	-1.0
1880	Buf-N	17	59	5	12	0	0	0	3	5	7	.203	.266	.203	60	-2	-2	3				.940	-2	S/2	-0.3
1882	Lou-a	72	264	41	48	3	1	0		16		.182	.229	.201	49	-14	-12	12				.898	-3	S/2/OM	-1.1
1883	Pit-a	60	224	26	44	5	3	0		13		.196	.241	.246	60	-10	-9	14		4		.844	4	S1/2	-0.5
Total	4 n	176	780	205	200	28	6	0	70	47	25	.256	.299	.308	83	-12	-14	81						1/SOP2	-0.8
Total	4	197	727	104	143	13	4	1	10	45	12	.197	.244	.230	60	-31	-26	42				.886	-8	S/21O	-2.9

■ EARLE MACK   Mack, Earle Thaddeus (b: Earle Thaddeus McGillicuddy)   b: 2/1/1890, Spencer, Mass.   d: 2/4/67, Upper Darby Township, Pa.   BL/TR, 5'8", 140 lbs.   Deb: 10/05/10   FMC

1910	Phi-A	1	4	0	2	0	1	0	0	0		.500	.500	1.000	372	1	1	2	0			1.000	-1	/C	0.1
1911	Phi-A	2	4	0	0	0	0	0	0	0		.000	.000	.000	-99	-1	-1	0	0			.000	0	/3	-0.1
1914	Phi-A	2	8	0	0	0	0	0	1	0	0	.000	.000	.000	-99	-2	-2	0	1			1.000	0	/1	-0.2
Total	3	5	16	0	2	0	1	0	1	0	0	.125	.125	.250	11	-2	-2	2	1			.974	-1	/13C	-0.2

■ REDDY MACK   Mack, Joseph (b: Joseph McNamara)   b: 5/2/1866, Ireland   d: 12/30/16, Newport, Ky.   Deb: 9/16/1885

1885	Lou-a	11	41	7	10	1	0	0		2		.244	.295	.268	82	-1	-1	3				.885	0	2	0.0
1886	Lou-a	137	483	82	118	23	11	1		68		.244	.342	.344	111	12	7	63	13			.900	6	*2	1.6
1887	Lou-a	128	478	117	147	23	8	1		83		.308	.415	.395	127	23	22	90	22			.912	5	*2	2.4
1888	Lou-a	112	446	77	97	13	5	3	34	52		.217	.320	.289	101	2	4	48	18			.907	4	*2	1.5
1889	Bal-a	136	519	84	125	24	7	1	87	60	69	.241	.329	.320	86	-7	-9	64	23			.897	-11	*2/O	-1.1
1890	Bal-a	26	95	14	27	3	5	0		10		.284	.370	.421	130	4	4	18	7			.932	1	2	0.5
Total	6	550	2062	381	524	87	36	6	121	275	69	.254	.352	.340	107	34	26	286	83			.905	5	2/O	4.5

■ JOE MACK   Mack, Joe John (b: Joseph John Maciarz)   b: 1/4/12, Chicago, Ill.   BB/TL, 5'11.5", 185 lbs.   Deb: 4/17/45

| 1945 | Bos-N | 66 | 260 | 30 | 60 | 13 | 1 | 3 | 44 | 34 | 39 | .231 | .320 | .323 | 79 | -7 | -7 | 29 | 1 | | | .991 | 0 | 1 | -1.1 |

■ RAY MACK   Mack, Raymond James (b: Raymond James Mickovsky)   b: 8/31/16, Cleveland, Ohio   d: 5/7/69, Bucyrus, Ohio   BR/TR, 6', 200 lbs.   Deb: 9/09/38

1938	Cle-A	2	6	2	2	0	1	0	2	0	1	.333	.333	.667	147	0	0	1	0	0	0	1.000	2	/2	0.2
1939	Cle-A	36	112	12	17	4	1	1	6	12	19	.152	.240	.232	22	-14	-13	9	0	2	-1	.976	2	2/3	-1.0
1940	Cle-A★	146	530	60	150	21	5	12	69	51	77	.283	.346	.409	98	-4	-2	76	4	2	0	.965	-9	*2	-0.1
1941	Cle-A	145	500	54	114	22	4	4	44	54	69	.228	.303	.342	74	-22	-19	55	4	3	0	.970	-5	*2	-1.3
1942	Cle-A	143	481	43	108	14	6	2	45	41	51	.225	.288	.291	67	-24	-20	42	9	3	1	.969	-4	*2	-1.5
1943	Cle-A	153	545	56	120	25	2	7	62	44	61	.220	.285	.312	79	-19	-15	49	8	3	1	.967	-2	*2	-0.8
1944	Cle-A	83	284	24	66	15	3	0	29	28	45	.232	.301	.306	77	-10	-8	28	4	1	1	.951	10	2	0.7
1946	Cle-A	61	171	13	35	6	2	1	9	23	27	.205	.299	.281	67	-8	-7	16	2	2	-1	.970	1	2	-0.3
1947	NY-A	1	0	0	0	0	0	0	0	0	0	—	—	—		0	0	0	0	0	0	.000	0	R	0.0
	Chi-N	21	78	9	17	6	0	2	12	5	15	.218	.274	.372	73	-4	-3	7	0			.965	7	2	0.5
Total	9	791	2707	273	629	113	24	34	278	261	365	.232	.301	.330	76	-103	-87	281	35	17		.966	3	2/3	-3.6

■ SHANE MACK   Mack, Shane Lee   b: 12/7/63, Los Angeles, Cal.   BR/TR, 6', 185 lbs.   Deb: 5/25/87

1987	SD-N	105	238	28	57	11	3	4	25	18	47	.239	.301	.361	77	-9	-8	22	4	6	-2	.982	-8	O	-2.0
1988	SD-N	56	119	13	29	3	0	0	12	14	21	.244	.338	.269	78	-3	-3	13	5	1	1	.983	-3	O	-0.6
1990	Min-A	125	313	50	102	10	4	8	44	29	69	.326	.392	.460	129	16	14	58	13	4	2	.988	1	*O/D	1.4
1991	*Min-A	143	442	79	137	27	8	18	74	34	79	.310	.367	.529	139	26	23	82	13	9	-2	.977	-9	*O/D	1.0
1992	Min-A	156	600	101	189	31	6	16	75	64	106	.315	.395	.467	136	34	31	114	26	14	-1	.988	1	*O	2.8
Total	5	585	1712	271	514	82	21	46	230	159	322	.300	.370	.453	124	64	57	288	61	34	-2	.984	-18	O/D	2.6

■ PETE MACKANIN   Mackanin, Peter   b: 8/1/51, Chicago, Ill.   BR/TR, 6'2", 190 lbs.   Deb: 7/03/73

1973	Tex-A	44	90	3	9	2	0	0	2	4	26	.100	.147	.122	-24	-15	-14	2	0	0	0	.947	2	S3	-1.0
1974	Tex-A	2	6	0	1	0	1	0	0	0	2	.167	.167	.500	88	-0	-0	1	0	0	0	1.000	2	/S	0.2
1975	Mon-N	130	448	59	101	19	6	12	44	31	99	.225	.279	.375	77	-14	-16	46	11	5	0	.966	18	*2/S3	0.9
1976	Mon-N	114	380	36	85	15	2	8	33	15	66	.224	.257	.337	65	-17	-19	31	6	2	1	.965	-2	*2/3SO	-1.6
1977	Mon-N	55	85	9	19	2	2	1	6	4	17	.224	.258	.329	58	-5	-5	7	3	1	0	1.000	4	/2S3O	0.1
1978	Phi-N	5	8	0	2	0	0	0	1	0	4	.250	.250	.250	40	-1	-1	1	0	0	0	1.000	0	/13	-0.1
1979	Phi-N	13	9	2	1	0	0	1	2	1	2	.111	.200	.444	69	-0	-0	1	0	0	0	1.000	3	/2S3	0.0
1980	Min-A	108	319	31	85	18	0	4	35	14	34	.266	.297	.361	74	-10	-12	33	6	2	1	.968	16	2S/13D	1.0
1981	Min-A	77	225	21	52	7	1	4	18	7	40	.231	.258	.324	63	-10	-12	18	1	2	-1	.980	-5	2S1/3D	-1.5
Total	9	548	1570	161	355	63	12	30	141	76	290	.226	.265	.339	65	-72	-80	138	27	12		.968	38	2S/31DO	-1.8

■ ERIC MacKENZIE   MacKenzie, Eric Hugh   b: 8/29/32, Glendon, Alt., Can.   BL/TR, 6', 185 lbs.   Deb: 4/23/55

| 1955 | KC-A | 1 | 1 | 0 | 0 | 0 | 0 | 0 | 0 | 0 | 0 | .000 | .000 | .000 | -99 | -0 | -0 | 0 | | 0 | | .000 | 0 | /C | 0.0 |

■ GORDON MacKENZIE   MacKenzie, Henry Gordon   b: 7/9/37, St.Petersburg, Fla   BR/TR, 5'11", 175 lbs.   Deb: 8/13/61   C

| 1961 | KC-A | 11 | 24 | 1 | 3 | 0 | 0 | 0 | 1 | 1 | 6 | .125 | .160 | .125 | -23 | -4 | -4 | 0 | 0 | | | 1.000 | -1 | /C | -0.4 |

YEAR	TM/L	G	AB	R	H	2B	3B	HR	RBI	BB	SO	AVG	OBP	SLG	PRO+	BR	/A	RC	SB	CS	SBR	FA	FR	POS	TPR

■ FELIX MACKIEWICZ   Mackiewicz, Felix Thaddeus b: 11/20/17, Chicago, Ill.   BR/TR, 6'2", 195 lbs.   Deb: 9/07/41

1941	Phi-A	5	14	3	4	0	1	0	0	1	0	.286	.333	.429	103	-0	-0	2	0	0	0	1.000	-1	/O	-0.1
1942	Phi-A	6	14	3	3	2	0	0	2	0	4	.214	.214	.357	59	-1	-1	1	0	0	0	1.000	0	/O	-0.1
1943	Phi-A	9	16	1	1	0	0	0	0	2	8	.063	.167	.063	-32	-3	-3	0	0	0	0	1.000	0	/O	-0.3
1945	Cle-A	120	359	42	98	14	7	2	37	44	41	.273	.356	.368	115	5	7	47	5	5	-2	.987	5	*O	0.6
1946	Cle-A	78	258	35	67	15	4	0	16	16	32	.260	.305	.349	88	-7	-5	28	5	1	1	.983	-2	O	-0.9
1947	Cle-A	2	5	0	0	0	0	0	0	0	2	.000	.000	.000	-99	-1	-1	-0	0	0	0	1.000	-0	/O	-0.2
	Was-A	3	6	1	1	1	0	0	0	0	1	.167	.167	.333	38	-1	-1	0	0	0	0	1.000	-1	/O	-0.2
	Yr	5	11	1	1	1	0	0	0	0	3	.091	.091	.182	-26	-2	-2	-0	0	0	0	1.000	-1	/O	-0.4
Total	6	223	672	85	174	32	12	2	55	63	88	.259	.325	.351	97	-7	-3	79	10	6	-1	.986	2	O	-1.2

■ STEVE MACKO   Macko, Steven Joseph b: 9/6/54, Burlington, Iowa d: 11/15/81, Arlington, Tex.   BL/TR, 5'10", 160 lbs.   Deb: 8/18/79

1979	Chi-N	19	40	2	9	1	0	0	3	4	8	.225	.295	.250	46	-3	-3	3	0	0	0	1.000	4	2/3	0.2
1980	Chi-N	6	20	2	6	2	0	0	2	0	3	.300	.300	.400	87	-0	-0	2	0	0	0	1.000	1	/S32	0.1
Total	2	25	60	4	15	3	0	0	5	4	11	.250	.297	.350	59	-3	-4	6	0	0	0	1.000	6	/23S	0.3

■ MAX MACON   Macon, Max Cullen b: 10/14/15, Pensacola, Fla. d: 8/5/89, Jupiter, Fla.   BL/TL, 6'3", 175 lbs.   Deb: 4/21/38

1938	StL-N	46	36	5	11	0	0	0	3	2	4	.306	.342	.306	75	-1	-1	4	0			.946	0	P/O	0.0
1940	Bro-N	2	1	0	1	0	0	0	0	0	0	1.000	1.000	1.000	427	0	0	1	0			.000	-0	/P	0.0
1942	Bro-N	26	43	4	12	2	1	0	1	2	4	.279	.311	.372	98	-0	-0	5	1			.960	-0	P	0.5
1943	Bro-N	45	55	7	9	0	0	0	6	0	1	.164	.164	.164	-5	-7	-7	1	1			1.000	0	P/1	-0.8
1944	Bos-N	106	366	38	100	15	3	3	36	12	23	.273	.296	.355	79	-9	-11	38	7			.977	-2	1O/P	-1.8
1947	Bos-N	1	1	0	0	0	0	0	0	0	0	.000	.000	.000	-99	-0	-0	0	0			1.000	0	/P	0.0
Total	6	226	502	54	133	17	4	3	46	16	32	.265	.288	.333	72	-18	-20	49	9			.965	-2	/P1O	-2.0

■ WADDY MacPHEE   MacPhee, Walter Scott b: 12/23/1899, Brooklyn, N.Y. d: 1/20/80, Charlotte, N.C.   BR/TR, 5'8", 140 lbs.   Deb: 9/27/22

| 1922 | NY-N | 2 | 7 | 2 | 2 | 0 | 1 | 0 | 1 | 0 | 1 | .286 | .375 | .571 | 140 | 0 | 0 | 2 | 0 | 0 | 0 | .889 | 1 | /3 | 0.1 |

■ JIMMY MACULLAR   Macullar, James F. "Little Mac" b: 1/16/1855, Boston, Mass. d: 4/8/24, Baltimore, Md.   BR/TL, 5'6", 155 lbs.   Deb: 5/05/1879   MU

1879	Syr-N	64	246	24	52	9	0	0	13	3	27	.211	.221	.248	61	-12	-8	14				.864	1	SO/23M	-0.5
1882	Cin-a	79	299	44	70	6	6	0		14		.234	.268	.294	85	-3	-5	24				.922	-0	*O	-0.5
1883	Cin-a	14	48	4	8	2	0	0		4		.167	.231	.208	40	-3	-3	2				.900	-4	O/S	-0.6
1884	Bal-a	107	360	73	73	16	6	4		36		.203	.290	.314	96	1	-1	34				.866	1	*S	0.1
1885	Bal-a	100	320	52	61	7	6	3		49		.191	.306	.278	89	-2	-1	28				.877	1	*S/OP	0.1
1886	Bal-a	85	268	49	55	7	1	0		49		.205	.332	.239	84	-3	-2	30	23			.852	-10	S/O2P	-0.9
Total	6	449	1541	246	319	47	19	7	13	155	27	.207	.285	.276	84	-21	-20	131	23			.865	-11	SO/2P3	-2.3

■ GENE MADDEN   Madden, Eugene b: 6/5/1890, Elm Grove, W.Va. d: 4/6/49, Utica, N.Y.   BL/TR, 5'10", 155 lbs.   Deb: 4/20/16

| 1916 | Pit-N | 1 | 1 | 0 | 0 | 0 | 0 | 0 | 0 | 0 | 0 | .000 | .000 | .000 | -99 | -0 | -0 | 0 | 0 | | | .000 | 0 | H | 0.0 |

■ FRANK MADDEN   Madden, Francis A. "Red" b: 10/17/1892, Pittsburgh, Pa. d: 4/30/52, Pittsburgh, Pa.   Deb: 7/04/14

| 1914 | Pit-F | 2 | 2 | 0 | 1 | 0 | 0 | 0 | 1 | 0 | 0 | .500 | .500 | .500 | 186 | 0 | 0 | 1 | 0 | | | .000 | 0 | /C | 0.0 |

■ BUNNY MADDEN   Madden, Thomas Francis b: 9/14/1882, Boston, Mass. d: 1/20/54, Cambridge, Mass.   BR/TR, 5'10", 190 lbs.   Deb: 6/03/09

1909	Bos-A	10	17	0	4	0	0	0	1	0		.235	.235	.235	48	-1	-1	1	0			.941	0	/C	0.1
1910	Bos-A	14	35	4	13	3	0	0	4	3		.371	.436	.457	175	3	3	7	0			.938	-3	C	0.1
1911	Bos-A	4	15	2	3	0	0	0	2	2		.200	.294	.200	39	-1	-1	1	0			1.000	-2	C	-0.3
	Phi-N	28	76	4	21	1	1	0		0	13	.276	.276	.316	65	-4	-4	6	0			.924	3	C	0.1
Total	3	56	143	10	41	4	1	0	11	5	13	.287	.315	.329	87	-3	-3	15	0			.935	-1	/C	-0.0

■ TOMMY MADDEN   Madden, Thomas Joseph b: 7/31/1883, Philadelphia, Pa. d: 7/26/30, Philadelphia, Pa.   BL/TL, 5'11", 160 lbs.   Deb: 9/10/06

1906	Bos-N	4	15	1	4	0	0	0	0	1		.267	.313	.267	83	-0	-0	1	0			1.000	-0	/O	-0.1
1910	NY-A	1	1	0	0	0	0	0	0	0		.000	.000	.000	-95	-0	-0	0	0			.000	-0	H	-0.1
Total	2	5	16	1	4	0	0	0	0	1		.250	.294	.250	72	-1	-1	1	0			.907	-1	/O	-0.2

■ CLARENCE MADDERN   Maddern, Clarence James b: 9/26/21, Bisbee, Ariz. d: 8/9/86, Tucson, Ariz.   BR/TR, 6'1", 185 lbs.   Deb: 9/19/46

1946	Chi-N	3	3	0	0	0	0	0	0	0	0	.000	.250	.000	-27	-0	-0	0	0			1.000	-0	/O	-0.1
1948	Chi-N	80	214	16	54	12	1	4	27	10	25	.252	.301	.374	85	-6	-5	25	0			.981	-2	O	-1.0
1949	Chi-N	10	9	1	3	0	0	1	2	2	0	.333	.455	.667	202	1	1	3	0			1.000	-0	/1	0.2
1951	Cle-A	11	12	0	2	0	0	0	0	0	1	.167	.167	.167	-10	-2	-2	0	0	0	0	.667	-0	/O	-0.2
Total	4	104	238	17	59	12	1	5	29	12	26	.248	.301	.370	84	-7	-6	28	0	0	0	.973	-2	/O1	-1.1

■ ELLIOTT MADDOX   Maddox, Elliott b: 12/21/47, East Orange, N.J.   BR/TR, 5'11", 181 lbs.   Deb: 4/07/70

1970	Det-A	109	258	30	64	13	4	3	24	30	42	.248	.333	.364	92	-2	-3	31	2	5	-1	.919	0	3OS/2	-0.5
1971	Was-A	128	258	38	56	8	2	1	18	51	42	.217	.346	.275	83	-5	-4	28	10	4	1	.990	-3	*O3	-1.0
1972	Tex-A	98	294	40	74	7	2	0	10	49	53	.252	.362	.289	100	1	2	34	20	10	0	.990	4	O	0.2
1973	Tex-A	100	172	24	41	1	0	1	17	29	28	.238	.358	.262	80	-4	-3	18	5	4	-1	.981	-7	O/3D	-1.4
1974	NY-A	137	466	75	141	26	2	3	45	69	48	.303	.397	.386	130	19	21	74	6	5	-1	.986	9	*O/23	2.3
1975	NY-A	55	218	36	67	10	3	1	23	21	24	.307	.386	.394	124	7	8	33	9	3	1	1.000	8	O/2	1.4
1976	*NY-A	18	46	4	10	2	0	0	3	4	3	.217	.280	.261	60	-2	-2	3	0	1	-1	1.000	-1	O/D	-0.4
1977	Bal-A	49	107	14	28	7	0	2	9	13	9	.262	.363	.383	110	1	2	14	2	1	-1	.990	-4	O/3	-0.4
1978	NY-N	119	389	43	100	18	2	2	39	71	38	.257	.374	.329	102	2	4	50	2	11	-6	.988	-2	O3/1	-0.7
1979	NY-N	86	224	21	60	13	0	1	12	20	27	.268	.336	.339	88	-4	-3	26	3	2	-0	.985	5	O3	0.0
1980	NY-N	41	154	35	101	16	1	4	34	52	44	.246	.339	.319	87	-7	-5	44	1	9	-5	.956	-1	*3/O1	-1.5
Total	11	1029	2843	360	742	121	16	18	234	409	358	.261	.361	.334	100	5	17	357	60	54	-14	.989	8	O3/S21D	-2.0

■ GARRY MADDOX   Maddox, Garry Lee b: 9/1/49, Cincinnati, Ohio   BR/TR, 6'3", 184 lbs.   Deb: 4/25/72

1972	SF-N	125	458	62	122	26	7	12	58	14	97	.266	.294	.432	103	0	-1	57	13	6	0	.979	-4	*O	-1.0
1973	SF-N	144	587	81	187	30	10	11	76	24	73	.319	.352	.460	118	16	14	94	24	10	1	.969	3	*O	1.1
1974	SF-N	135	538	74	153	31	3	8	50	29	64	.284	.325	.398	97	-1	-4	68	21	9	1	.986	-2	*O	-1.0
1975	SF-N	17	52	4	7	1	0	1	4	6	3	.135	.237	.212	24	-5	-6	3	1	1	-0	1.000	4	O	-0.3
	Phi-N	99	374	50	109	25	8	4	46	36	54	.291	.361	.433	115	10	8	64	24	3	5	.983	14	O	2.4
	Yr	116	426	54	116	26	8	5	50	42	57	.272	.346	.406	104	4	2	65	25	4	5	.985	18	*O	2.1
1976	*Phi-N	146	531	75	175	37	6	6	68	42	59	.330	.383	.456	133	26	24	92	29	12	6	.989	18	*O	3.9
1977	*Phi-N	139	571	85	167	27	10	14	74	24	58	.292	.326	.448	101	2	-1	84	22	6	3	.977	7	O	0.4
1978	*Phi-N	155	598	62	172	34	3	11	68	39	89	.288	.333	.410	106	4	3	83	33	7	6	.983	14	O	1.7
1979	Phi-N	148	548	70	154	28	6	13	61	17	71	.281	.308	.425	95	-4	-6	68	26	13	0	.996	20	*O	0.9
1980	*Phi-N	143	549	59	142	31	3	11	73	18	52	.259	.282	.386	80	-13	-16	58	25	5	5	.976	5	*O	-1.3
1981	*Phi-N	94	323	37	85	7	1	5	40	17	42	.263	.302	.337	78	-8	-10	33	9	4	0	.977	4	O	-0.9
1982	Phi-N	119	412	39	117	27	2	8	61	12	32	.284	.304	.417	98	-2	-3	47	7	5	-1	**.992**	2	O	-0.5
1983	*Phi-N	97	324	27	89	14	2	4	32	17	31	.275	.313	.367	89	-6	-5	34	7	6	-2	.977	-5	O	-1.5
1984	Phi-N	77	241	29	68	11	0	5	19	13	29	.282	.319	.390	97	-1	-2	30	3	2	1	1.000	0	O	-0.4
1985	Phi-N	105	218	22	52	8	1	4	23	13	26	.239	.284	.339	72	-8	-9	21	2	4	0	.980	-12	O	-2.4
1986	Phi-N	6	7	1	3	0	0	1	2	1		.429	.556	.429	169	1	1	2	0	1	-1	1.000	-1	/O	-0.1
Total	15	1749	6331	777	1802	337	62	117	754	323	781	.285	.323	.413	100	12	-11	838	248	92	19	.983	67	*O	1.0

YEAR	TM/L	G	AB	R	H	2B	3B	HR	RBI	BB	SO	AVG	OBP	SLG	PRO+	BR	/A	RC	SB	CS	SBR	FA	FR	POS	TPR
■ **JERRY MADDOX**	Maddox, Jerry Glenn b: 7/28/53, Whittier, Cal. BR/TR, 6'2", 200 lbs. Deb: 6/03/78																								
1978	Atl-N	7	14	1	3	0	0	0	1	1	2	.214	.267	.214	32	-1	-1	1	0	0	0	.909	-0	/3	-0.2
■ **ART MADISON**	Madison, Arthur b: 1/14/1872, Clarksburg, Mass. d: 1/27/33, N.Adams, Mass. BR/TR, 5'9", 165 lbs. Deb: 9/09/1895																								
1895	Phi-N	11	34	6	12	3	0	0	8	1	1	.353	.371	.441	111	0	0	7	4			.955	-1	/S23	0.0
1899	Pit-N	42	118	20	32	2	4	0	19	11		.271	.338	.356	91	-2	-1	15	1			.953	-6	2S/3	-0.5
Total	2	53	152	26	44	5	4	0	27	12	1	.289	.345	.375	95	-1	-1	22	5			.926	-7	/2S3	-0.5
■ **SCOTTI MADISON**	Madison, Charles Scott b: 9/12/59, Pensacola, Fla. BB/TR, 5'11", 195 lbs. Deb: 7/06/85																								
1985	Det-A	6	11	0	0	0	0	0	1	2	0	.000	.154	.000	-54	-2	-2	0	0	0	0	1.000	-0	/CD	-0.2
1986	Det-A	2	7	0	0	0	0	0	1	0	3	.000	.000	.000	-99	-2	-2	0	0	0	0	.667	-1	/3D	-0.3
1987	KC-A	7	15	4	4	3	0	0	0	1	5	.267	.313	.467	100	0	-0	2	0	0	0	1.000	-1	/1C	-0.1
1988	KC-A	16	35	4	6	2	0	0	2	4	5	.171	.256	.229	37	-3	-3	2	1	0	0	1.000	-2	/CO1D	-0.4
1989	Cin-N	40	98	13	17	7	0	1	7	8	9	.173	.243	.276	46	-7	-7	6	0	1	-1	1.000	2	3	-0.6
Total	5	71	166	21	27	12	0	1	11	15	22	.163	.236	.253	37	-14	-14	11	1	1	-0	.985	-1	/3DC1O	-1.6
■ **ED MADJESKI**	Madjeski, Edward William (b: Edward William Majewski) b: 7/24/09, Far Rockaway, N.Y BR/TR, 5'11", 178 lbs. Deb: 5/02/32																								
1932	Phi-A	17	35	4	8	0	0	0	3	3	6	.229	.289	.229	35	-3	-3	2	0	0	0	1.000	2	/C	-0.1
1933	Phi-A	51	142	17	40	4	0	0	17	4	21	.282	.301	.310	62	-8	-8	13	0	0	0	.958	-4	C	-0.9
1934	Phi-A	8	8	1	3	1	0	0	2	0	1	.375	.375	.500	129	0	0	1	0	0	0	.000	-1	/C	0.0
	Chi-A	85	281	36	62	14	2	5	32	14	31	.221	.260	.338	52	-21	-22	25	2	0	1	.973	2	C	-1.4
	Yr	93	289	37	65	15	2	5	34	14	32	.225	.263	.343	54	-21	-22	26	2	0	1	.971	2	C	-1.4
1937	NY-N	5	15	0	3	0	0	0	2	0	2	.200	.200	.200	9	-2	-2	1	0			1.000	-2	/C	-0.4
Total	4	166	481	58	116	19	2	5	56	21	61	.241	.274	.320	53	-33	-35	43	2	0		.970	-2	C	-2.8
■ **BILL MADLOCK**	Madlock, Bill b: 1/2/51, Memphis, Tenn. BR/TR, 5'11", 185 lbs. Deb: 9/07/73																								
1973	Tex-A	21	77	16	27	5	3	1	5	7	9	.351	.412	.532	171	7	7	17	3	2	-0	.918	-6	3	0.1
1974	Chi-N	128	453	65	142	21	5	9	54	42	39	.313	.378	.442	124	17	15	72	11	7	-1	.946	-12	*3	0.2
1975	Chi-N★	130	514	77	182	29	7	7	64	42	34	**.354**	.406	.479	139	31	28	98	9	7	-2	.943	-11	*3	1.6
1976	Chi-N	142	514	68	174	36	1	15	84	56	27	**.339**	.415	.500	146	41	35	100	15	11	-2	.961	-20	*3	1.3
1977	SF-N	140	533	70	161	28	1	12	46	43	33	.302	.361	.426	111	8	8	73	13	10	-2	.949	-17	*3/2	-1.2
1978	SF-N	122	447	76	138	26	3	15	44	48	39	.309	.380	.481	145	23	25	84	16	5	2	.974	-24	*2/1	1.2
1979	SF-N	69	249	37	65	9	2	7	41	18	19	.261	.311	.398	99	-3	-1	31	11	3	2	.976	-14	2/1	-1.0
	*Pit-N	85	311	48	102	17	3	7	44	34	22	.328	.396	.469	129	16	14	55	21	8	2	.969	-6	3	0.8
	Yr	154	560	85	167	26	5	14	85	52	41	.298	.359	.438	117	12	13	86	32	11	3	.969	-20	32/1	-0.2
1980	Pit-N	137	494	62	137	22	4	10	53	45	33	.277	.343	.399	105	4	3	64	16	10	-1	.955	-17	*31	-1.8
1981	Pit-N★	82	279	35	95	23	1	6	45	34	17	**.341**	.418	.495	153	22	21	59	18	6	2	.956	-4	3	1.9
1982	Pit-N	154	568	92	181	33	3	19	95	48	39	.319	.376	.488	136	29	27	103	18	6	2	.952	-6	*3/1	2.0
1983	Pit-N★	130	473	68	153	21	0	12	68	49	24	**.323**	.389	.444	127	20	19	78	3	4	-2	.958	-14	*3	0.2
1984	Pit-N	103	403	38	102	16	0	4	44	26	29	.253	.300	.323	75	-14	-14	38	3	1	0	.942	-8	3/1	-2.4
1985	Pit-N	110	399	49	100	23	1	10	41	39	42	.251	.325	.388	100	-1	-0	49	3	3	-1	.940	-16	31	-2.0
	*LA-N	34	114	20	41	4	0	2	15	10	11	.360	.425	.447	149	7	8	23	7	1	2	.948	3	3	1.2
	Yr	144	513	69	141	27	1	12	56	49	53	.275	.347	.402	110	6	7	71	10	4	1	.943	-13	*31	-0.8
1986	LA-N	111	379	38	106	17	0	10	60	30	43	.280	.341	.404	112	2	5	52	3	3	-1	.910	-8	*3/1	-0.6
1987	LA-N	21	61	5	11	1	0	3	7	6	5	.180	.265	.344	61	-4	-3	5	0	0	0	.912	-4	3/1	-0.8
	*Det-A	87	326	56	91	17	0	14	50	28	45	.279	.354	.460	119	7	9	52	4	3	-1	.989	-2	D1/3	0.4
Total	15	1806	6594	920	2008	348	34	163	860	605	510	.305	.369	.442	123	213	206	1053	174	90	-2	.948	-185	*32/D1	1.1
■ **SAL MADRID**	Madrid, Salvador b: 6/9/20, ElPaso, Tex. d: 2/24/77, Ft.Wayne, Ind. BR/TR, 5'9", 165 lbs. Deb: 9/17/47																								
1947	Chi-N	8	24	0	3	1	0	0	1	1	6	.125	.160	.167	-14	-4	-4	1	0			.956	4	/S	0.0
■ **DAVE MAGADAN**	Magadan, David Joseph b: 9/30/62, Tampa, Fla. BL/TR, 6'3", 190 lbs. Deb: 9/07/86																								
1986	NY-N	10	18	3	8	0	0	0	3	3	1	.444	.524	.444	175	2	2	4	0	0	0	1.000	1	/1	0.3
1987	NY-N	85	192	21	61	13	1	3	24	22	22	.318	.388	.443	126	6	7	33	0	0	0	.981	3	31	0.9
1988	*NY-N	112	314	39	87	15	0	1	35	60	39	.277	.396	.334	117	8	10	45	0	1	-1	.988	-1	13	0.4
1989	NY-N	127	374	47	107	22	3	4	41	49	37	.286	.370	.393	124	10	12	58	1	0	0	.991	3	13	1.0
1990	NY-N	144	451	74	148	28	6	6	72	74	55	.328	**.425**	.457	143	30	30	91	2	1	0	**.998**	3	*13	2.5
1991	NY-N	124	418	58	108	23	0	4	51	83	50	.258	.384	.342	106	7	8	62	1	1	-0	.996	2	*1	0.1
1992	NY-N	99	321	33	91	9	1	3	28	56	44	.283	.390	.346	111	7	7	47	1	0	0	.941	-13	3/1	-0.5
Total	7	701	2088	275	610	110	11	21	254	347	248	.292	.395	.386	122	70	77	341	5	3	-0	.994	-3	13	4.7
■ **EVER MAGALLANES**	Magallanes, Everado (Espinoza) b: 11/6/65, Chihuahua, Mexico BL/TR, 5'10", 165 lbs. Deb: 5/17/91																								
1991	Cle-A	3	2	0	0	0	0	0	0	1	1	.000	.333	.000	1	-0	-0	0	0	0	0	1.000	-1	/S	-0.1
■ **LEE MAGEE**	Magee, Leo Christopher (b: Leopold Christopher Hoernschemeyer) b: 6/4/1889, Cincinnati, Ohio d: 3/14/66, Columbus, Ohio BB/TR, 5'11", 165 lbs. Deb: 7/04/11 M																								
1911	StL-N	26	69	9	18	1	1	0	8	8	8	.261	.338	.304	82	-2	-1	8	4			.975	-2	2/S	-0.4
1912	StL-N	128	458	60	133	13	8	0	40	39	29	.290	.347	.354	94	-5	-3	63	16			.956	7	O2/1S	-0.1
1913	StL-N	137	531	54	142	13	7	2	31	34	30	.267	.314	.330	85	-11	-11	61	23			.982	13	*O2/1S	-0.2
1914	StL-N	142	529	59	150	23	4	2	40	42	24	.284	.337	.353	107	3	4	74	36			.970	5	*O1/2	0.4
1915	Bro-F	121	452	87	146	19	10	4	49	22	19	.323	.356	.436	133	16	17	86	34			.937	-1	*2/1M	1.8
1916	NY-A	131	510	57	131	18	4	3	45	50	31	.257	.324	.325	93	-3	-4	56	29	25	-6	.975	5	*O/2	-1.4
1917	NY-A	51	173	17	38	4	1	0	8	13	18	.220	.278	.254	62	-8	-8	14	3			.938	-8	O	-2.1
	StL-A	36	112	11	19	1	0	0	4	6	6	.170	.212	.179	20	-11	-10	5	3			.971	6	3/21O	-0.5
	Yr	87	285	28	57	5	1	0	12	19	24	.200	.252	.225	46	-19	-18	19	6			.938	-2	O3/21	-2.6
1918	Cin-N	119	459	61	133	22	13	0	28	28	19	.290	.331	.394	123	10	11	65	19			.956	9	*2/3	3.0
1919	Bro-N	45	181	16	43	7	2	0	7	5	8	.238	.262	.298	67	-7	-8	16	5			.938	-1	2/3	-0.7
	Chi-N	79	267	36	78	12	4	1	17	18	16	.292	.339	.378	115	5	5	38	14			.978	-6	OS3/2	-0.4
	Yr	124	448	52	121	19	6	1	24	23	24	.270	.309	.346	96	-2	-3	53	19			.978	-7	O23S	-1.1
Total	9	1015	3741	467	1031	133	54	12	277	265	208	.276	.325	.350	99	-13	-9	486	186	25		.969	27	O2/13S	-0.6
■ **SHERRY MAGEE**	Magee, Sherwood Robert b: 8/6/1884, Clarendon, Pa. d: 3/13/29, Philadelphia, Pa. BR/TR, 5'11", 179 lbs. Deb: 6/29/04 U																								
1904	Phi-N	95	364	51	101	15	12	3	57	14		.277	.306	.409	125	7	8	51	11			.921	5	O/1	0.8
1905	Phi-N	155	603	100	180	24	17	5	98	44		.299	.353	.420	135	21	24	110	48			.963	10	*O	2.7
1906	Phi-N	154	563	77	159	36	8	6	67	52		.282	.346	.407	135	22	22	102	55			.982	11	*O	2.8
1907	Phi-N	140	503	75	165	28	12	4	**85**	53		.328	.396	.455	170	39	39	113	46			.978	7	*O	4.6
1908	Phi-N	143	508	79	144	30	16	2	57	49		.283	.359	.417	143	27	26	90	40			.970	2	*O	2.5
1909	Phi-N	143	522	60	141	33	14	2	66	43		.270	.339	.398	128	16	16	83	38			.970	-6	*O	0.4
1910	Phi-N	154	519	**110**	172	39	17	6	**123**	94	36	**.331**	**.445**	**.507**	**172**	**55**	**53**	**139**	49			.974	-13	*O	3.3
1911	Phi-N	121	445	79	128	32	5	15	94	49	33	.288	.366	.483	135	20	19	86	22			**.981**	3	*O	1.6
1912	Phi-N	132	464	79	142	25	9	6	66	55	54	.306	.388	.438	118	17	13	91	30			.963	-11	*O/1	-0.5
1913	Phi-N	138	470	92	144	36	6	11	70	38	36	.306	.369	.479	136	24	21	89	23			.968	-10	*O/1	0.7
1914	Phi-N	146	544	96	**171**	**39**	11	15	**103**	55	42	.314	.380	**.509**	154	41	37	110	25			.940	9	OS1/2	4.8
1915	Bos-N	156	571	72	160	34	12	2	87	54	39	.280	.350	.392	130	17	20	82	15	12	-3	.981	15	*O1	2.8
1916	Bos-N	122	419	44	101	17	5	3	54	44	52	.241	.322	.327	104	1	3	50	10			.978	-5	*O/1S	-1.0

YEAR	TM/L	G	AB	R	H	2B	3B	HR	RBI	BB	SO	AVG	OBP	SLG	PRO+	BR	/A	RC	SB	CS	SBR	FA	FR	POS	TPR
1917	Bos-N	72	246	24	63	8	4	1	29	13	23	.256	.302	.333	100	-2	-0	27	7			.954	2	O/1	-0.2
	Cin-N	45	137	17	44	8	4	0	23	16	7	.321	.400	.438	164	10	10	25	4			.989	4	O/1	1.4
	Yr	117	383	41	107	16	8	1	52	29	30	.279	.338	.371	124	8	10	51	11			.967	6	*O/1	1.2
1918	Cin-N	115	400	46	119	15	13	2	**76**	37	18	.298	.370	.415	142	19	20	64	14			.981	-2	1O/2	1.4
1919	*Cin-N	56	163	11	35	6	1	0	21	26	19	.215	.337	.264	84	-2	-2	16	4			.990	-3	O/23	-0.9
Total	16	2087	7441	1112	2169	425	166	83	1176	736	359	.291	.363	.427	137	331	328	1327	441	12		.970	16	*O1/S23	27.2
■ HARL MAGGERT	Maggert, Harl Vestin b: 2/13/1883, Cromwell, Ind. d: 1/7/63, Fresno, Cal. BL/TR, 5'8", 155 lbs. Deb: 9/04/07 F																								
1907	Pit-N	3	6	1	0	0	0	0	0	2		.000	.250	.000	-21	-1	-1	0	1			1.000	0	/O	-0.1
1912	Phi-A	74	242	39	62	8	6	1	13	36		.256	.357	.351	107	2	3	34	10			.939	-6	O	-0.6
Total	2	77	248	40	62	8	6	1	13	38		.250	.354	.343	104	1	2	34	11			.942	-6	/O	-0.7
■ HARL MAGGERT	Maggert, Harl Warren b: 5/4/14, Los Angeles, Cal. d: 7/10/86, Citrus Heights, Cal. BR/TR, 6', 190 lbs. Deb: 4/19/38 F																								
1938	Bos-N	66	89	12	25	3	0	3	19	10	20	.281	.354	.416	123	1	2	13	0			.944	-0	O/3	0.2
■ STUBBY MAGNER	Magner, Edmund Burke b: 2/20/1888, Kalamazoo, Mich. d: 9/6/56, Chillicother, Ohio BR/TR, 5'3", 135 lbs. Deb: 7/12/11																								
1911	NY-A	13	33	3	7	0	0	0	4	4		.212	.297	.212	40	-2	-3	3	1			.970	-0	/S2	-0.3
■ JOHN MAGNER	Magner, John T. b: 1855, St.Louis, Mo. Deb: 7/14/1879 U																								
1879	Cin-N	1	4	0	0	0	0	0	1	0	1	.000	.000	.000	-99	-1	-1	0				.500	-0	/O	-0.1
■ GEORGE MAGOON	Magoon, George Henry "Maggie" or "Topsy" b: 3/27/1875, St.Albans, Maine d: 12/6/43, Rochester, N.H. BR/TR, 5'10", 160 lbs. Deb: 6/29/1898																								
1898	Bro-N	93	343	35	77	7	0	1	39	30		.224	.293	.254	57	-19	-18	28	7			.925	13	S	-0.1
1899	Bal-N	62	207	26	53	8	3	0	31	26		.256	.353	.324	82	-3	-5	28	7			.923	6	S	0.5
	Chi-N	59	189	24	43	5	1	0	21	24		.228	.333	.265	67	-8	-7	21	5			.896	7	S	0.4
	Yr	121	396	50	96	13	4	0	52	50		.242	.344	.295	75	-11	-12	48	12			.909	13	*S	0.9
1901	Cin-N	127	460	47	116	16	7	1	53	52		.252	.331	.324	97	-4	-0	57	15			.919	-20	*S2	-1.0
1902	Cin-N	45	162	29	44	9	2	0	23	13		.272	.344	.352	105	3	1	24	7			.930	4	2/S	0.7
1903	Cin-N	42	139	6	30	6	0	0	9	19		.216	.314	.259	58	-6	-8	13	2			.971	5	2/3	-0.2
	Chi-A	94	334	32	76	11	3	0	25	30		.228	.303	.278	79	-9	-7	31	4			.936	-21	2	-2.6
Total	5	522	1834	199	439	62	16	2	201	194		.239	.321	.294	79	-46	-45	201	47			.916	-7	S2/3	-2.3
■ TOM MAGRANN	Magrann, Thomas Joseph b: 12/9/63, Hollywood, Fla. BR/TR, 6'3", 177 lbs. Deb: 9/07/89																								
1989	Cle-A	9	10	0	0	0	0	0	0	0	4	.000	.000	.000	-98	-3	-3	0	0	0	0	1.000	3	/C	0.1
■ FREDDIE MAGUIRE	Maguire, Frederick Edward b: 5/10/1899, Roxbury, Mass. d: 11/3/61, Boston, Mass. BR/TR, 5'11", 155 lbs. Deb: 9/22/22																								
1922	NY-N	5	12	4	4	0	0	0	1	0	1	.333	.333	.333	72	-0	-0	1	1	0	0	.944	2	/2	0.1
1923	*NY-N	41	30	11	6	1	0	0	2	2	4	.200	.250	.233	29	-3	-3	2	1	0	0	.881	12	2/3	0.9
1928	Chi-N	140	574	67	160	24	7	1	41	25	38	.279	.312	.350	74	-23	-22	62	6			.976	**51**	*2	3.1
1929	Bos-N	138	496	54	125	26	8	0	41	19	40	.252	.284	.337	55	-37	-34	46	8			.971	8	*2/S	-1.9
1930	Bos-N	146	516	54	138	21	5	0	52	20	22	.267	.297	.328	53	-41	-38	49	4			.969	-4	*2	-3.0
1931	Bos-N	148	492	36	112	18	2	0	26	16	26	.228	.259	.272	45	-39	-37	37	3			**.976**	9	*2	-1.9
Total	6	618	2120	226	545	90	22	1	163	82	131	.257	.289	.322	57	-144	-135	197	23	0		.971	77	2/S3	-2.7
■ JACK MAGUIRE	Maguire, Jack b: 2/5/25, St.Louis, Mo. BR/TR, 5'11", 165 lbs. Deb: 4/18/50																								
1950	NY-N	29	40	3	7	2	0	0	3	3	13	.175	.233	.225	21	-5	-5	2	0			1.000	1	/O1	-0.3
1951	NY-N	16	20	6	8	1	1	1	4	2	2	.400	.455	.700	204	3	3	7	0	0	0	1.000	-0	/O	0.2
	Pit-N	8	5	1	0	0	0	0	0	1	0	.000	.167	.000	-50	-1	-1	0	0	0	0	1.000	1	/23	0.0
	Yr	24	25	7	8	1	1	1	4	3	2	.320	.393	.560	151	2	2	6	0	0	0	1.000	0	/O23	0.2
	StL-A	41	127	15	31	2	1	1	14	12	21	.244	.309	.299	63	-6	-7	12	1	0	0	.969	-0	O/32	-0.7
Total	2	94	192	25	46	5	2	2	21	18	36	.240	.305	.318	66	-9	-9	20	1	0		.979	2	/O321	-0.8
■ JIM MAHADY	Mahady, James Bernard b: 4/22/01, Cortland, N.Y. d: 8/9/36, Cortland, N.Y. BR/TR, 5'11", 170 lbs. Deb: 10/02/21																								
1921	NY-N	1	0	0	0	0	0	0	0	0	0	—	—	—	—	0	0	0	0	0	0	1.000	0	/2	0.0
■ ART MAHAN	Mahan, Arthur Leo b: 6/8/13, Somerville, Mass. BL/TL, 5'11", 178 lbs. Deb: 4/30/40																								
1940	Phi-N	146	544	55	133	24	5	2	39	40	37	.244	.297	.318	73	-22	-20	52	4			.992	4	*1/P	-3.0
■ FRANK MAHAR	Mahar, Frank Edward b: 12/4/1878, Natick, Mass. d: 12/5/61, Somerville, Mass. TR, 5'10.5", Deb: 8/29/02																								
1902	Phi-N	1	1	0	0	0	0	0	0	0		.000	.000	.000	-99	-0	-0	0	0			.000	0	H	0.0
■ BILLY MAHARG	Maharg, William Joseph b: 3/19/1881, Philadelphia, Pa. d: 11/20/53, Philadelphia, Pa. BR/TR, 5'4.5", Deb: 5/18/12																								
1912	Det-A	1	1	0	0	0	0	0	0	0		.000	.000	.000	-99	-0	-0	0	0			1.000	1	/3	0.0
1916	Phi-N	1	1	0	0	0	0	0	0	0	0	.000	.000	.000	-97	-0	-0	0	0			.000	-0	/O	-0.1
Total	2	2	2	0	0	0	0	0	0	0	0	.000	.000	.000	-99	-0	-0	0	0			.935	0	/O3	-0.1
■ TOM MAHER	Maher, Thomas Francis b: 7/6/1870, Philadelphia, Pa. d: 8/25/29, Philadelphia, Pa. Deb: 4/24/02																								
1902	Phi-N	1	0	0	0	0	0	0	0	0		—	—	—	—	0	0	0	0			.000	0	R	0.0
■ GREG MAHLBERG	Mahlberg, Gregory John b: 8/8/52, Milwaukee, Wis. BR/TR, 5'10", 180 lbs. Deb: 9/24/78																								
1978	Tex-A	1	1	0	0	0	0	0	0	0	0	.000	.000	.000	-99	-0	-0	0	0	0	0	1.000	0	/C	0.0
1979	Tex-A	7	17	2	2	0	0	1	1	2	4	.118	.211	.294	35	-2	-2	1	0	0	0	1.000	-2	/C	-0.3
Total	2	8	18	2	2	0	0	1	1	2	4	.111	.200	.278	28	-2	-2	1	0	0	0	1.000	-2	/C	-0.3
■ DAN MAHONEY	Mahoney, Daniel J. b: 3/20/1864, Springfield, Mass. d: 2/1/04, Springfield, Mass. BR/TR, 5'9.5", 165 lbs. Deb: 8/20/1892																								
1892	Cin-N	5	21	1	4	0	1	0	1	1	4	.190	.227	.286	57	-1	-1	1	0			.943	2	/C	0.1
1895	Was-N	6	12	2	2	0	0	0	1	0	0	.167	.167	.167	-13	-2	-2	0	0			1.000	-1	/C1	-0.2
Total	2	11	33	3	6	0	1	0	2	1	4	.182	.206	.242	29	-3	-3	2	0			.949	1	/C1	-0.1
■ DANNY MAHONEY	Mahoney, Daniel Joseph b: 9/6/1888, Haverhill, Mass. d: 9/28/60, Utica, N.Y. BR/TR, 5'6.5", 145 lbs. Deb: 5/15/11																								
1911	Cin-N	1	0	0	0	0	0	0	0	0	0	—	—	—	—	0	0	0	0			.000	0	R	0.0
■ MIKE MAHONEY	Mahoney, George W. "Big Mike" b: 12/5/1873, Boston, Mass. d: 1/3/40, Boston, Mass. BR, 6'4", 220 lbs. Deb: 5/18/1897																								
1897	Bos-N	2	2	1	1	0	0	0	1	0		.500	.500	.500	155	0	0	1	0			1.000	0	/CP	0.0
1898	StL-N	2	7	0	0	0	0	0	1	0		.000	.000	.000	-98	-2	-2	0	0			.920	-0	/1	-0.2
Total	2	4	9	1	1	0	0	0	1	0		.111	.111	.111	-36	-2	-2	1	0			.980	-0	/1PC	-0.2
■ JIM MAHONEY	Mahoney, James Thomas "Moe" b: 5/26/34, Englewood, N.J. BR/TR, 6', 175 lbs. Deb: 7/28/59 C																								
1959	Bos-A	31	23	10	3	0	0	1	4	3	7	.130	.231	.261	33	-2	-2	2	0	0	0	.940	10	S	0.9
1961	Was-A	43	108	10	26	0	1	0	6	5	23	.241	.274	.259	44	-9	-8	7	1	2	-1	.968	12	S/2	0.5
1962	Cle-A	41	74	12	18	4	0	3	5	3	14	.243	.273	.419	86	-2	-2	8	0	0	0	.964	8	S/23	0.8
1965	Hou-N	5	5	0	1	0	0	0	0	0	3	.200	.200	.200	14	-1	-1	0	0	0	0	1.000	0	/S	0.0
Total	4	120	210	32	48	4	1	4	15	11	47	.229	.267	.314	57	-13	-13	17	1	2	-1	.962	31	/S23	2.2
■ BOB MAIER	Maier, Robert Phillip b: 9/5/15, Dunellen, N.J. BR/TR, 5'8", 180 lbs. Deb: 4/17/45																								
1945	*Det-A	132	486	58	128	25	7	1	34	38	32	.263	.317	.350	88	-5	-8	52	7	11	-5	.936	-13	*3/O	-2.4

YEAR	TM/L	G	AB	R	H	2B	3B	HR	RBI	BB	SO	AVG	OBP	SLG	PRO+	BR	/A	RC	SB	CS	SBR	FA	FR	POS	TPR

■ EMIL MAILHO Mailho, Emil Pierre "Lefty" b: 12/16/09, Berkeley, Cal. BL/TL, 5'10", 165 lbs. Deb: 4/14/36

| 1936 | Phi-A | 21 | 18 | 5 | 1 | 0 | 0 | 0 | 0 | 5 | 3 | .056 | .261 | .056 | -18 | -3 | -3 | 1 | 0 | 0 | 0 | 1.000 | -0 | /O | -0.3 |

■ CHARLIE MAISEL Maisel, Charles Louis b: 4/21/1894, Catonsville, Md. d: 8/25/53, Baltimore, Md. BR/TR, 6', Deb: 10/02/15 F

| 1915 | Bal-F | 1 | 4 | 0 | 0 | 0 | 0 | 0 | 0 | 0 | 0 | .000 | .000 | .000 | -97 | -1 | -1 | 0 | 0 | | | 1.000 | 0 | /C | -0.1 |

■ FRITZ MAISEL Maisel, Frederick Charles "Flash" b: 12/23/1889, Catonsville, Md. d: 4/22/67, Baltimore, Md. BR/TR, 5'7.5", 170 lbs. Deb: 8/11/13 F

1913	NY-A	51	187	33	48	4	3	0	12	34	20	.257	.371	.310	99	2	1	29	25			.950	-5	3	-0.3
1914	NY-A	150	548	78	131	23	9	2	47	76	69	.239	.334	.325	98	-0	-0	74	**74**	17	**12**	.928	-18	*3	-0.1
1915	NY-A	135	530	77	149	16	6	4	46	48	35	.281	.342	.357	109	5	5	76	51	12	**8**	.940	-9	*3	1.0
1916	NY-A	53	158	18	36	5	0	0	7	20	18	.228	.318	.259	72	-4	-5	15	4			.980	-5	O3/2	-1.2
1917	NY-A	113	404	46	80	4	4	0	20	36	18	.198	.267	.228	51	-23	-24	32	29			.967	-1	*2/3	-2.2
1918	StL-A	90	284	43	66	4	2	0	16	46	17	.232	.341	.261	84	-4	-3	31	11			.949	-4	3/O	-0.6
Total	6	592	2111	295	510	56	24	6	148	260	177	.242	.327	.299	88	-25	-25	258	194	29		.938	-43	32/O	-3.4

■ GEORGE MAISEL Maisel, George John b: 3/12/1892, Catonsville, Md. d: 11/20/68, Baltimore, Md. BR/TR, 5'10.5", 180 lbs. Deb: 5/01/13

1913	StL-A	11	18	2	3	2	0	0	1	1	7	.167	.211	.278	44	-1	-1	1	0			.833	-2	/O	-0.4
1916	Det-A	8	5	2	0	0	0	0	0	0	2	.000	.000	.000	-97	-1	-1	0	0			.857	2	/3	0.1
1921	Chi-N	111	393	54	122	7	2	0	43	11	13	.310	.334	.338	78	-12	-12	45	17	7	1	.978	0	*O	-1.8
1922	Chi-N	38	84	9	16	1	1	0	6	8	2	.190	.261	.226	26	-9	-9	5	1	3	-2	1.000	-2	O	-1.4
Total	4	168	500	67	141	10	3	0	50	20	24	.282	.314	.314	66	-23	-24	51	18	10		.979	-2	O/3	-3.5

■ HANK MAJESKI Majeski, Henry "Heeney" b: 12/13/16, Staten Island, N.Y. d: 8/9/91, Staten Island, N.Y. BR/TR, 5'9", 180 lbs. Deb: 5/17/39

1939	Bos-N	106	367	35	100	16	1	7	54	18	30	.272	.310	.379	91	-9	-6	41	2			.945	12	3	0.7
1940	Bos-N	3	3	0	0	0	0	0	0	0	0	.000	.000	.000	-99	-1	-1	0	0			.000	0	H	-0.1
1941	Bos-N	19	55	5	8	5	0	0	3	1	13	.145	.161	.236	11	-7	-6	2	0			.911	1	3	-0.6
1946	NY-A	8	12	1	1	0	1	0	0	0	3	.083	.083	.250	-9	-2	-2	0	0	0	0	.750	-1	/3	-0.3
	Phi-A	78	264	25	66	14	3	1	25	26	13	.250	.320	.337	84	-6	-6	29	3	2	-0	.967	8	3	0.3
	Yr	86	276	26	67	14	4	1	25	26	16	.243	.310	.333	80	-8	-7	29	3	2	-0	.964	7	3	0.0
1947	Phi-A	141	479	54	134	26	5	8	72	53	31	.280	.358	.405	110	8	6	70	1	0	0	**.988**	7	*3/S2	1.5
1948	Phi-A	148	590	88	183	41	4	12	120	48	43	.310	.368	.454	118	13	13	98	2	1	0	**.975**	1	*3/S	1.3
1949	Phi-A	114	448	62	124	26	5	9	67	29	23	.277	.326	.417	99	-5	-3	58	0	1	-1	.957	-4	*3	-1.0
1950	Chi-A	122	414	47	128	18	2	6	46	42	34	.309	.377	.406	103	1	2	62	1	4	-2	.970	10	*3	0.8
1951	Chi-A	12	35	4	9	4	0	0	6	1	0	.257	.278	.371	76	-1	-1	3	0	1		.950	-0	/3	-0.2
	Phi-A	89	323	41	92	19	4	5	42	35	24	.285	.358	.415	106	4	3	48	1	2	-1	.974	14	3	1.4
	Yr	101	358	45	101	23	4	5	48	36	24	.282	.351	.411	104	2	2	52	1	3	-1	.972	14	3	1.2
1952	Phi-A	34	117	14	30	2	2	2	20	19	10	.256	.365	.359	96	1	-0	15	0	1	-1	.976	4	3	0.3
	Cle-A	36	54	7	16	2	0	0	9	7	7	.296	.377	.333	106	0	1	6	0	0	0	.913	-0	3/2	0.0
	Yr	70	171	21	46	4	2	2	29	26	17	.269	.369	.351	101	1	1	21	0	1	-1	.966	4	3/2	0.3
1953	Cle-A	50	50	6	15	1	0	2	12	3	8	.300	.352	.440	116	1	1	8	0	0	0	1.000	-2	2/3O	-0.1
1954	*Cle-A	57	121	10	34	4	0	3	17	7	14	.281	.320	.388	92	-1	-2	14	0	0	0	.990	4	23	0.4
1955	Cle-A	36	48	3	9	2	0	2	6	8	3	.188	.328	.354	80	-1	-1	6	0	0	0	1.000	-2	/32	-0.3
	Bal-A	16	41	2	7	1	0	0	2	2	4	.171	.209	.195	10	-5	-5	2	0	0	0	1.000	-2	/32	-0.8
	Yr	52	89	5	16	3	0	2	8	10	7	.180	.277	.281	50	-6	-6	7	0	0	0	1.000	-5	3/2	-1.1
Total	13	1069	3421	404	956	181	27	57	501	299	260	.279	.342	.398	100	-11	-7	462	10	11		.968	49	3/2SO	3.3

■ MIKE MAKSUDIAN Maksudian, Michael Bryant b: 5/28/66, Belleville, Ill. BL/TR, 5'11", 220 lbs. Deb: 9/02/92

| 1992 | Tor-A | 3 | 3 | 0 | 0 | 0 | 0 | 0 | 0 | 0 | 0 | .000 | .000 | .000 | -96 | -1 | -1 | 0 | 0 | 0 | 0 | .000 | 0 | /1 | -0.1 |

■ CHARLIE MALAY Malay, Charles Francis b: 6/13/1879, Brooklyn, N.Y. d: 9/18/49, Brooklyn, N.Y. BB/TR, 5'11.5", 175 lbs. Deb: 4/24/05 F

| 1905 | Bro-N | 102 | 349 | 33 | 88 | 7 | 2 | 1 | 31 | 22 | | .252 | .300 | .292 | 83 | -10 | -6 | 37 | 13 | | | .932 | -9 | 2O/S | -1.7 |

■ JOE MALAY Malay, Joseph Charles b: 10/25/05, Brooklyn, N.Y. d: 3/19/89, Bridgeport, Conn. BL/TL, 6', 175 lbs. Deb: 9/07/33 F

1933	NY-N	8	24	0	3	0	0	0	2	0	0	.125	.125	.125	-29	-4	-4	0	0			1.000	2	/1	-0.3
1935	NY-N	1	1	0	1	0	0	0	0	0	0	1.000	1.000	1.000	447	0	0	1	0			.000	0	H	0.0
Total	2	9	25	0	4	0	0	0	2	0	0	.160	.160	.160	-9	-3	-3	1	0			.932	2	/1	-0.3

■ CANDY MALDONADO Maldonado, Candido (Guadarrama) b: 9/5/60, Humacao, P.R. BR/TR, 6', 190 lbs. Deb: 9/07/81

1981	LA-N	11	12	0	1	0	0	0	0	0	5	.083	.083	.083	-55	-2	-2	0	0	0	0	1.000	0	/O	-0.2
1982	LA-N	6	4	0	0	0	0	0	0	0	2	.000	.200	.000	-41	-1	-1	0	0	0	0	1.000	1	/O	0.0
1983	*LA-N	42	62	5	12	1	1	1	6	5	14	.194	.254	.290	51	-4	-4	5	0	0	0	1.000	-1	O	-0.6
1984	LA-N	116	254	25	68	14	0	5	28	19	29	.268	.321	.382	98	-1	-1	30	0	3	-2	.955	-16	*O/3	-2.2
1985	*LA-N	121	213	20	48	7	1	5	19	19	40	.225	.289	.338	77	-7	-7	21	1	1	-0	.984	-22	*O	-3.3
1986	SF-N	133	405	49	102	31	3	18	85	20	77	.252	.292	.477	114	2	4	51	4	4	-1	.983	-4	*O/3	-0.4
1987	*SF-N	118	442	69	129	28	4	20	85	34	78	.292	.351	.509	131	14	17	75	8	8	-2	.973	-6	*O	0.5
1988	SF-N	142	499	53	127	23	1	12	68	37	89	.255	.315	.377	102	-2	1	57	6	5	-1	.962	-3	*O	-0.8
1989	*SF-N	129	345	39	75	23	0	9	41	37	69	.217	.299	.362	91	-6	-4	38	4	1	1	.974	-6	*O	-1.3
1990	Cle-A	155	590	76	161	32	2	22	95	49	134	.273	.334	.446	117	11	12	86	3	5	-2	.993	7	*OD	1.3
1991	Mil-N	34	111	11	23	6	0	5	20	13	23	.207	.290	.396	90	-2	-2	12	1	0	0	.976	-2	O	-0.4
	*Tor-A	52	177	26	49	9	4	7	28	23	53	.277	.379	.446	123	7	6	31	3	0	1	.990	0	O/D	0.7
	Yr	86	288	37	72	15	4	12	48	36	76	.250	.345	.427	111	5	5	43	4	0	1	.986	-2	*O/D	0.3
1992	*Tor-A	137	489	64	133	25	4	20	66	59	112	.272	.359	.462	123	18	16	81	2	2	-1	.978	5	*O/D	1.7
Total	12	1196	3603	437	928	199	16	124	541	316	725	.258	.324	.425	109	28	35	486	32	29	-8	.978	-46	*O/D3	-5.0

■ JIM MALER Maler, James Michael b: 8/16/58, New York, N.Y. BR/TR, 6'4", 230 lbs. Deb: 9/03/81

1981	Sea-A	12	23	1	8	1	0	0	2	1	1	.348	.423	.391	131	1	1	4	1	0	0	1.000	-0	/1D	0.1
1982	Sea-A	64	221	18	50	8	3	4	26	12	35	.226	.275	.344	67	-10	-11	21	0	0	0	.991	3	1/D	-1.0
1983	Sea-A	26	66	5	12	1	0	1	3	5	11	.182	.260	.242	38	-5	-6	3	0	3	-2	1.000	0	1/D	-0.8
Total	3	102	310	24	70	10	3	5	31	19	47	.226	.284	.326	65	-14	-15	28	1	3	-2	.994	3	/1D	-1.7

■ TONY MALINOSKY Malinosky, Anthony Francis b: 10/5/09, Collinsville, Ill. BR/TR, 5'10.5", 165 lbs. Deb: 4/26/37

| 1937 | Bro-N | 35 | 79 | 7 | 18 | 2 | 0 | 0 | 3 | 9 | 11 | .228 | .307 | .253 | 53 | -5 | -5 | 7 | 0 | | | .833 | -9 | 3S | -1.4 |

■ BOBBY MALKMUS Malkmus, Robert Edward b: 7/4/31, Newark, N.J. BR/TR, 5'9", 180 lbs. Deb: 6/01/57

1957	Mil-N	13	22	6	2	1	0	0	0	3	3	.091	.200	.182	4	-3	-3	1	0	0	0	.972	4	/2	0.1
1958	Was-A	41	70	5	13	2	1	0	3	4	15	.186	.230	.243	31	-7	-7	3	0	0	0	.964	8	2/3S	0.2
1959	Was-A	6	0	0	0	0	0	0	0	0	0	—	—	—	—	0	0	0	0	0	0	.000	0	R	—
1960	Phi-N	79	133	16	28	4	1	1	12	11	28	.211	.271	.278	51	-9	-9	10	2	2	-1	1.000	7	S23	-0.1
1961	Phi-N	121	342	39	79	8	2	7	31	20	43	.231	.277	.327	61	-20	-19	30	1	3	-2	.988	16	2S3	0.4
1962	Phi-N	5	5	3	1	0	1	0	0	0	1	.200	.200	.400	58	-0	0	0	0	0	0	1.000	3	/S	0.3
Total	6	268	572	69	123	15	5	8	46	38	90	.215	.266	.301	53	-39	-38	45	3	5	-2	.982	37	2/S3	0.9

■ JERRY MALLETT Mallett, Gerald Gordon b: 9/18/35, Bonne Terre, Mo. BR/TR, 6'5", 208 lbs. Deb: 9/19/59

| 1959 | Bos-A | 4 | 15 | 1 | 4 | 0 | 0 | 0 | 1 | 1 | 3 | .267 | .313 | .267 | 58 | -1 | -1 | 1 | 0 | 0 | 0 | 1.000 | 3 | /O | 0.2 |

YEAR	TM/L	G	AB	R	H	2B	3B	HR	RBI	BB	SO	AVG	OBP	SLG	PRO+	BR	/A	RC	SB	CS	SBR	FA	FR	POS	TPR

■ LES MALLON Mallon, Leslie Clyde b: 11/21/05, Sweetwater, Tex. d: 4/17/91, Granbury, Tex. BR/TR, 5'8", 160 lbs. Deb: 4/14/31

1931	Phi-N	122	375	41	116	19	2	1	45	29	40	.309	.359	.379	91	-0	-4	53	0			.956	6	2/1S3	0.8
1932	Phi-N	103	347	44	90	16	0	5	31	28	28	.259	.318	.349	71	-10	-15	40	1			.955	-31	2/3	-4.2
1934	Bos-N	42	166	23	49	6	1	0	18	15	12	.295	.354	.343	95	-4	2	20	0			.967	-4	2	-0.3
1935	Bos-N	116	412	48	113	24	2	2	25	28	37	.274	.322	.357	89	-10	-6	47	3			.975	-14	23/O	-1.2
Total	4	383	1300	156	368	65	5	8	119	100	117	.283	.336	.359	85	-23	-26	161	4			.962	-43	2/31SO	-4.8

■ BEN MALLONEE Mallonee, Howard Bennett "Lefty" b: 3/31/1894, Baltimore, Md. d: 2/19/78, Baltimore, Md. BL/TL, 5'6", 150 lbs. Deb: 9/14/21

| 1921 | Phi-A | 7 | 25 | 2 | 6 | 1 | 0 | 0 | 4 | 1 | 2 | .240 | .269 | .280 | 40 | -2 | -2 | 2 | 1 | 0 | 0 | 1.000 | 0 | /O | -0.2 |

■ JULE MALLONEE Mallonee, Julius Norris b: 4/4/1900, Charlotte, N.C. d: 12/26/34, Charlotte, N.C. BL/TR, 6'2", 180 lbs. Deb: 8/04/25

| 1925 | Chi-A | 2 | 3 | 1 | 0 | 0 | 0 | 0 | 0 | 1 | 0 | .000 | .250 | .000 | -34 | -1 | -1 | 0 | 0 | 0 | 0 | 1.000 | -0 | /O | -0.1 |

■ JIM MALLORY Mallory, James Baugh "Sunny Jim" b: 9/1/18, Lawrenceville, Va. BR/TR, 6'1", 170 lbs. Deb: 9/08/40

1940	Was-A	4	12	2	2	0	0	0	0	1	1	.167	.231	.167	5	-2	-2	1	0	0		1.000	1	/O	-0.1
1945	StL-N	13	43	3	10	2	0	0	5	0	2	.233	.233	.279	41	-3	-4	3	0			.923	-2	O	-0.6
	NY-N	37	94	10	28	1	0	0	9	6	7	.298	.340	.309	80	-2	-2	10	1			.979	-0	O	-0.4
	Yr	50	137	13	38	3	0	0	14	6	9	.277	.308	.299	68	-6	-6	13	1			.959	-2	O	-1.0
Total	2	54	149	15	40	3	0	0	14	7	10	.268	.301	.289	63	-7	-8	14	1	0		.964	-1	/O	-1.1

■ SHELDON MALLORY Mallory, Sheldon b: 7/16/53, Argo, Ill. BL/TL, 6'2", 175 lbs. Deb: 4/10/77

| 1977 | Oak-A | 64 | 126 | 19 | 27 | 4 | 1 | 0 | 5 | 11 | 18 | .214 | .293 | .262 | 53 | -8 | -8 | 11 | 12 | 5 | 1 | .977 | -3 | O/1D | -1.1 |

■ HARRY MALMBERG Malmberg, Harry William "Swede" b: 7/31/26, Fairfield, Ala. d: 10/29/76, San Francisco, Cal. BR/TR, 6'1", 170 lbs. Deb: 4/12/55 C

| 1955 | Det-A | 67 | 208 | 25 | 45 | 5 | 2 | 0 | 19 | 29 | 19 | .216 | .312 | .260 | 56 | -13 | -12 | 17 | 0 | 1 | -1 | .985 | 6 | 2 | -0.2 |

■ EDDIE MALONE Malone, Edward Russell b: 6/16/20, Chicago, Ill. BR/TR, 5'10", 175 lbs. Deb: 7/17/49

1949	Chi-A	55	170	17	46	7	2	1	16	29	19	.271	.377	.353	97	-1	-0	25	2	1		.990	-3	C	0.0
1950	Chi-A	31	71	2	16	2	0	0	10	10	8	.225	.321	.254	50	-5	-5	5	0	0	0	1.000	2	C	-0.2
Total	2	86	241	19	62	9	2	1	26	39	27	.257	.361	.324	83	-6	-5	30	2	1	0	.993	-2	/C	-0.2

■ FERGY MALONE Malone, Ferguson G. b: 1842, Ireland d: 1/1/05, Seattle, Wash. BR/TL, 5'8", 156 lbs. Deb: 6/03/1871 MU

1871	Ath-n	27	134	33	46	7	1	1	33	9	4	.343	.385	.433	136	6	7	26	9					*C	0.4
1872	Ath-n	41	213	46	61	6	2	0	39	4	5	.286	.300	.333	94	-1	-1	23						C1	0.0
1873	Phi-n	53	259	59	75	11	2	0	42	14	7	.290	.326	.347	95	-0	-2	30						*C/SM	-0.1
1874	Chi-n	47	222	32	55	5	0	0		5		.248	.264	.270	70	-7	-7	16						*CM	-0.5
1875	Phi-n	29	122	15	28	2	1	0		1		.230	.236	.262	69	-3	-4	8						1/CO	-0.3
1876	Phi-N	22	96	14	22	0	0	0	6	0	1	.229	.229	.250	60	-4	-4	6				.777	-2	C/OS	-0.5
1884	Phi-U	1	4	0	1	0	0	0		0		.250	.250	.250	75	-0	-0	0				.818	-1	/CM	-0.1
Total	5 n	197	950	185	265	31	6	1	114	33	16	.279	.303	.327	92	-5	-8	104						C/1OS	-0.5
Total	2	23	100	14	23	2	0	0		6	0	.230	.230	.250	61	-4	-4	6				.780	-3	/COS	-0.6

■ LEW MALONE Malone, Lewis Aloysius b: 3/13/1897, Baltimore, Md. d: 2/17/72, Brooklyn, N.Y. BR/TR, 5'11", 175 lbs. Deb: 5/31/15

1915	Phi-A	76	201	17	41	4	4	1	17	21	40	.204	.283	.279	70	-8	-7	18	7	1	2	.919	-4	23/OS	-1.0
1916	Phi-A	5	4	1	0	0	0	0	0	1	2	.000	.200	.000	-42	-1	-1	0	0			1.000	-0	/S	-0.1
1917	Bro-N	1	0	1	0	0	0	0	0	0	0	—	—	—		0	0	0	0			.000	0	R	0.0
1919	Bro-N	51	162	9	33	7	3	0	11	6	18	.204	.232	.284	54	-9	-10	11	1			.934	-6	3/2S	-1.6
Total	4	133	367	28	74	11	7	1	28	28	60	.202	.260	.278	62	-18	-17	29	8	1		.910	-11	/32SO	-2.7

■ JOHN MALONEY Maloney, John d: 7/21/1890, Deb: 9/15/1876

1876	NY-N	2	7	1	2	0	1	0	2	0	1	.286	.286	.571	206	1	1	1				.800	-0	/O	0.0
1877	Har-N	1	4	0	1	0	0	0	0	0	0	.250	.250	.250	65	-0	-0	0				.250	-1	/O	-0.1
Total	2	3	11	1	3	0	1	0	2	0	1	.273	.273	.455	152	0	1	1				.556	-1	/O	-0.1

■ PAT MALONEY Maloney, Patrick William b: 1/19/1888, Grosvenordale, Conn. d: 6/27/74, Pawtucket, R.I. BR/TR, 6', 150 lbs. Deb: 6/19/12

| 1912 | NY-A | 25 | 79 | 9 | 17 | 1 | 0 | 0 | 4 | 6 | | .215 | .279 | .228 | 43 | -5 | -6 | 6 | 3 | | | .926 | 2 | O | -0.5 |

■ BILLY MALONEY Maloney, William Alphonse b: 6/5/1878, Lewiston, Me. d: 9/2/60, Breckenridge, Tex. BL/TR, 5'10", 177 lbs. Deb: 5/02/01

1901	Mil-A	86	290	42	85	3	4	0	22	7		.293	.323	.393	86	-7	-5	37	11			.952	8	C/O	0.9
1902	StL-A	30	112	8	23	3	0	0	11	6		.205	.258	.232	37	-9	-9	7	0			.906	-4	O/C	-1.3
	Cin-N	27	89	13	22	4	0	1	7	2		.247	.272	.326	77	-2	-3	11	8			.848	-3	O/C	-0.6
1905	Chi-N	145	558	78	145	17	14	2	56	43		.260	.325	.351	98	1	-2	87	59			.954	3	*O	-0.6
1906	Bro-N	151	566	71	125	15	7	0	32	49		.221	.286	.272	81	-16	-12	58	38			.966	11	*O	-0.9
1907	Bro-N	144	502	51	115	7	10	0	32	31		.229	.279	.283	83	-14	-10	51	25			.967	5	*O	-1.2
1908	Bro-N	113	359	31	70	5	3	0	17	24		.195	.257	.273	72	-13	-11	29	14			.947	4	*O/C	-1.2
Total	6	696	2476	294	585	54	42	6	177	162		.236	.292	.299	83	-61	-51	279	155			.954	25	O/C	-4.9

■ FRANK MALZONE Malzone, Frank James b: 2/28/30, Bronx, N.Y. BR/TR, 5'10", 180 lbs. Deb: 9/17/55

1955	Bos-A	6	20	2	7	1	0	1		3		.350	.381	.400	101	0	0	3	0	0	0	1.000	2	/3	0.2
1956	Bos-A	27	103	15	17	3	1	2	11	9	8	.165	.232	.272	29	-10	-12	6	1	0	0	.931	1	3	-1.0
1957	Bos-A★	153	634	82	185	31	5	15	103	31	41	.292	.326	.427	98	2	-3	85	2	1	0	.954	14	*3	1.5
1958	Bos-A★	155	627	76	185	30	2	15	87	33	53	.295	.334	.421	94	-1	-4	82	1	3	-2	.950	17	*3	1.6
1959	Bos-A★	154	604	90	169	34	2	19	92	42	58	.280	.328	.437	103	5	2	85	6	0	2	.953	8	*3	1.2
1960	Bos-A★	152	595	60	161	30	2	14	79	36	42	.271	.317	.398	89	-8	-10	70	2	3	-1	.948	8	*3	-0.5
1961	Bos-A	151	590	74	157	21	4	14	87	44	49	.266	.318	.386	85	-11	-13	68	1	3	-2	.950	-5	*3	-1.9
1962	Bos-A	156	619	74	175	20	3	21	95	35	43	.283	.321	.426	96	-2	-8	80	0	1	-1	.967	5	*3	0.1
1963	Bos-A★	151	580	66	169	25	2	15	71	31	45	.291	.331	.419	105	3	5	73	0	2	-1	.964	7	*3	0.6
1964	Bos-A☆	148	537	62	142	19	0	13	56	37	43	.264	.314	.372	86	-7	-10	64	0	0	0	.959	-0	*3	-1.3
1965	Bos-A	106	364	40	87	20	0	3	34	28	38	.239	.295	.319	70	-12	-15	31	1	1	-0	.969	-3	3	-2.2
1966	Cal-A	82	155	6	32	5	0	2	12	10	11	.206	.255	.277	54	-9	-9	10	0	0	0	.925	-1	3	-1.2
Total	12	1441	5428	647	1486	239	21	133	728	337	434	.274	.318	.399	91	-44	-73	656	14	14	-4	.955	47	*3	-2.9

■ GUS MANCUSO Mancuso, August Rodney "Blackie" b: 12/5/05, Galveston, Tex. d: 10/26/84, Houston, Tex. BR/TR, 5'10", 185 lbs. Deb: 4/30/28 FC

1928	StL-N	11	38	2	7	1	0	0	3	0	5	.184	.184	.237	9	-5	-5	2	0			.984	4	C	0.0
1930	*StL-N	76	227	39	83	17	2	6	59	18	16	.366	.415	.551	127	11	10	50	1			.969	1	C	1.4
1931	*StL-N	67	187	13	49	16	1	1	23	18	13	.262	.327	.374	85	-3	-4	24	2			.972	6	C	0.6
1932	*StL-N	103	310	25	88	23	1	5	43	30	15	.284	.347	.413	100	2	1	46	0			.977	8	C	1.3
1933	*NY-N	144	481	39	127	17	2	6	56	48	21	.264	.331	.345	95	-3	-2	56	0			.972	2	*C	0.8
1934	NY-N	122	383	32	94	17	0	7	46	27	19	.245	.295	.337	70	-17	-16	39	0			.977	6	C	-0.4
1935	NY-N★	128	447	33	133	18	2	5	56	30	16	.298	.342	.380	95	-4	-3	57	1			.972	-5	*C	-0.1
1936	*NY-N	139	519	55	156	21	3	9	63	39	28	.301	.351	.405	104	2	3	73	0			.977	5	*C	1.4
1937	*NY-N★	86	287	30	80	17	1	4	39	17	20	.279	.319	.387	90	-4	-5	36	1			.982	16	C	1.5
1938	NY-N	52	158	19	55	8	2	0	13	18	16	.348	.411	.437	132	8	8	29	0			.977	4	C	1.5
1939	Chi-N	80	251	17	58	10	0	2	17	24	19	.231	.298	.295	59	-14	-15	23	0			.981	5	C	-0.6
1940	Bro-N	60	144	16	33	6	0	0	16	13	7	.229	.293	.285	56	-8	-9	12	0			.982	7	C	0.1

YEAR	TM/L	G	AB	R	H	2B	3B	HR	RBI	BB	SO	AVG	OBP	SLG	PRO+	BR	/A	RC	SB	CS	SBR	FA	FR	POS	TPR
1941	StL-N	106	328	25	75	13	1	2	37	37	19	.229	.309	.293	66	-12	-15	31	0			.989	11	*C	0.3
1942	StL-N	5	13	0	1	0	0	0	1	0	0	.077	.077	.077	-51	-3	-3	0	0			.917	-1	/C	-0.4
	NY-N	39	109	4	21	1	1	0	8	14	7	.193	.285	.220	48	-7	-7	7	1			.982	3	C	-0.2
	Yr	44	122	4	22	1	1	0	9	14	7	.180	.265	.205	38	-9	-9	7	1			.977	1	C	-0.6
1943	NY-N	94	252	11	50	5	0	2	20	28	16	.198	.284	.242	52	-15	-15	17	0			.974	-0	C	-1.1
1944	NY-N	78	195	15	49	4	1	1	25	30	20	.251	.351	.297	84	-3	-3	22	0			.976	5	C	0.5
1945	Phi-N	70	176	11	35	5	0	0	16	28	10	.199	.309	.227	52	-11	-10	13	2			.988	1	C	-0.6
Total	17	1460	4505	386	1194	197	16	53	543	418	264	.265	.328	.351	85	-85	-90	536	8			.977	75	*C	5.9
■ FRANK MANCUSO Mancuso, Frank Octavius b: 5/23/18, Houston, Tex. BR/TR, 6', 195 lbs. Deb: 4/18/44 F																									
1944	*StL-A	88	244	19	50	11	0	1	24	20	32	.205	.271	.262	50	-15	-17	17	1	0	0	.953	-6	C	-1.9
1945	StL-A	119	365	39	98	13	3	1	38	46	44	.268	.354	.329	94	1	-1	43	0	2	-1	.989	-6	*C	-0.2
1946	StL-A	87	262	22	63	8	3	3	23	30	31	.240	.323	.328	78	-6	-7	29	1	0	0	.973	-18	C	-2.1
1947	Was-A	43	131	5	30	5	1	0	13	5	11	.229	.257	.282	51	-9	-9	8	0	0	0	.958	-4	C	-1.1
Total	4	337	1002	85	241	37	7	5	98	101	118	.241	.314	.306	74	-29	-34	96	2	2	-1	.972	-34	C	-5.3
■ CARL MANDA Manda, Carl Alan b: 11/16/1888, Little River, Kan. d: 3/9/83, Artesia, N.Mex. BR/TR, 5'10", 170 lbs. Deb: 9/11/14																									
1914	Chi-A	9	15	2	4	0	0	0	1	3	3	.267	.389	.267	99	0	0	2	1			.971	4	/2	0.5
■ JIM MANGAN Mangan, James Daniel b: 9/24/29, San Francisco, Cal. BR/TR, 5'10", 190 lbs. Deb: 4/16/52																									
1952	Pit-N	11	13	1	2	0	0	0	2	1	3	.154	.214	.154	4	-2	-2	0	0	0	0	.833	-1	/C	-0.2
1954	Pit-N	14	26	2	5	0	0	0	2	4	9	.192	.300	.192	32	-3	-2	2	0	0	0	1.000	0	/C	-0.2
1956	NY-N	20	20	2	2	0	0	0	1	4	6	.100	.250	.100	-1	-3	-3	1	0	0	0	1.000	0	C	-0.2
Total	3	45	59	5	9	0	0	0	5	9	18	.153	.265	.153	15	-7	-7	3	0	0	0	.985	-0	/C	-0.6
■ ANGEL MANGUAL Mangual, Angel Luis (Guilbe) b: 3/19/47, Juana Diaz, P.R. BR/TR, 5'10", 180 lbs. Deb: 9/15/69 F																									
1969	Pit-N	6	4	1	1	1	0	0	0	0	0	.250	.250	.500	108	-0	0	1	0	0	0	.000	-0	/O	0.0
1971	*Oak-A	94	287	32	82	8	1	4	30	17	27	.286	.326	.362	97	-2	-2	31	1	4	-2	.988	-2	O	-1.0
1972	*Oak-A	91	272	19	67	13	2	5	32	14	48	.246	.286	.364	97	-3	-2	26	0	1	-1	.971	3	O	-0.3
1973	*Oak-A	74	192	20	43	4	1	3	13	8	34	.224	.259	.302	61	-11	-10	15	1	1	-0	.947	-5	OD/12	-1.8
1974	*Oak-A	115	365	37	85	14	4	9	43	17	59	.233	.267	.367	87	-10	-8	36	3	0	1	.961	-7	OD/3	-1.7
1975	Oak-A	62	109	13	24	3	0	1	6	3	18	.220	.241	.275	47	-8	-8	7	0	1	-1	.978	-9	OD	-1.8
1976	Oak-A	8	12	0	2	1	0	0	1	0	1	.167	.167	.250	22	-1	-1	0	0	1	-1	1.000	-2	/O	-0.4
Total	7	450	1241	122	304	44	8	22	125	59	187	.245	.280	.346	83	-36	-30	116	5	8	-3	.969	-22	O/D132	-7.0
■ PEPE MANGUAL Mangual, Jose Manuel (Guilbe) b: 5/23/52, Ponce, P.R. BR/TR, 5'10", 165 lbs. Deb: 9/06/72 F																									
1972	Mon-N	8	11	2	3	0	0	0	0	1	5	.273	.333	.273	73	-0	-0	1	0	1	-1	1.000	-0	/O	-0.2
1973	Mon-N	33	62	9	11	2	1	3	7	6	18	.177	.250	.387	71	-3	-3	5	2	4	-2	.966	-1	O	-0.7
1974	Mon-N	23	61	10	19	3	0	0	4	5	15	.311	.364	.361	98	0	-0	10	5	0	2	1.000	-3	O	-0.3
1975	Mon-N	140	514	84	126	16	2	9	45	74	115	.245	.345	.337	86	-5	-8	65	33	11	3	.972	-9	*O	-2.0
1976	Mon-N	66	215	34	56	9	1	3	16	50	49	.260	.404	.353	112	8	6	37	17	7	1	.968	-3	O	0.2
	NY-N	41	102	15	19	5	2	1	9	10	32	.186	.259	.304	63	-6	-5	9	7	3	0	.985	2	O	-0.4
	Yr	107	317	49	75	14	3	4	25	60	81	.237	.361	.338	99	2	2	46	24	10	1	.973	-1	*O	-0.2
1977	NY-N	8	7	1	1	0	0	0	2	1	4	.143	.250	.143	9	-1	-1	0	0	0	0	.833	0	/O	-0.1
Total	6	319	972	155	235	35	6	16	83	147	238	.242	.345	.340	89	-7	-11	127	64	26	4	.972	-15	O	-3.5
■ GEORGE MANGUS Mangus, George Graham b: 5/22/1890, Red Creek, N.Y. d: 8/10/33, Rutland, Mass. BL/TR, 5'11.5", 165 lbs. Deb: 8/20/12																									
1912	Phi-N	10	25	2	5	3	0	0	3	1	6	.200	.231	.320	47	-2	-2	2	0			.750	-1	/O	-0.4
■ CLYDE MANION Manion, Clyde Jennings "Pete" b: 10/30/1896, Jefferson City, Mo d: 9/4/67, Detroit, Mich. BR/TR, 5'11", 175 lbs. Deb: 5/05/20																									
1920	Det-A	32	80	4	22	4	1	0	8	4	7	.275	.318	.350	79	-3	-2	9	0	0	0	.940	-2	C	-0.2
1921	Det-A	12	10	0	2	0	0	0	2	2	2	.200	.385	.200	53	-1	-1	1	0	0	0	1.000	1	/C	0.0
1922	Det-A	42	69	9	19	4	1	0	12	4	6	.275	.315	.362	79	-3	-2	8	0	1	-1	.932	-2	C/1	-0.4
1923	Det-A	23	22	0	3	0	0	0	2	2	2	.136	.208	.136	-8	-3	-3	1	0	0	0	.857	-0	/C1	-0.4
1924	Det-A	14	13	1	3	0	0	0	2	1	1	.231	.286	.231	35	-1	-1	1	0	0	0	.750	-1	/C1	-0.2
1926	Det-A	75	176	15	35	4	0	0	14	24	16	.199	.295	.222	36	-16	-16	13	1	1	-0	.972	-0	C	-1.3
1927	Det-A	1	0	0	0	0	0	0	0	1	0	—	1.000	—	174	0	0	0	0	0	0	.000	0	H	0.0
1928	StL-A	76	243	25	55	5	1	2	31	15	18	.226	.274	.280	44	-19	-20	20	3	0	1	.980	12	C	-0.2
1929	StL-A	35	111	16	27	2	0	0	11	15	3	.243	.333	.261	53	-7	-8	11	1	0	0	.976	5	C	0.0
1930	StL-A	57	148	12	32	1	0	1	11	24	17	.216	.326	.243	45	-11	-12	13	0	1	-1	.985	11	C	0.3
1932	Cin-N	49	135	7	28	4	0	0	12	14	16	.207	.282	.237	43	-11	-10	10	0			.970	4	C	-0.4
1933	Cin-N	36	84	3	14	1	0	0	3	8	7	.167	.239	.179	21	-8	-8	4	0			.981	4	C	-0.3
1934	Cin-N	25	54	4	10	0	0	0	4	4	7	.185	.241	.185	16	-6	-6	3	0			1.000	3	C	-0.3
Total	13	477	1145	96	250	25	3	3	112	118	102	.218	.293	.253	45	-89	-90	94	5	3		.973	33	C/1	-3.4
■ PHIL MANKOWSKI Mankowski, Philip Anthony b: 1/9/53, Buffalo, N.Y. BL/TR, 6', 180 lbs. Deb: 8/30/76																									
1976	Det-A	24	85	9	23	2	1	1	4	4	8	.271	.303	.353	88	-1	-1	8	0	0	0	.971	2	3	0.1
1977	Det-A	94	286	21	79	7	3	3	27	16	41	.276	.319	.353	79	-7	-9	32	1	2	-1	.964	13	3/2	0.2
1978	Det-A	88	222	28	61	8	0	4	20	22	28	.275	.346	.365	97	0	-0	26	2	3	-1	.972	-1	3/D	-0.3
1979	Det-A	42	99	11	22	4	0	0	8	10	16	.222	.294	.263	50	-7	-7	8	0	0	0	.963	-1	3	-0.8
1980	NY-N	8	12	1	2	1	0	0	1	2	4	.167	.286	.250	52	-1	-1	1	0	0	0	.571	-1	/3	-0.2
1982	NY-N	13	35	2	8	1	0	0	4	1	6	.229	.250	.257	42	-3	-3	2	0	1	-1	.957	-1	3	-0.4
Total	6	269	739	72	195	23	4	8	64	55	103	.264	.318	.338	79	-17	-21	76	3	6	-3	.962	12	3/D2	-1.4
■ CHARLIE MANLOVE Manlove, Charles Henry "Chick" b: 10/8/1862, Philadelphia, Pa. d: 2/12/52, Altoona, Pa. BR/TR, 5'9", 165 lbs. Deb: 5/31/1884																									
1884	Alt-U	2	7	1	3	0	0	0		0		.429	.429	.429	188	1	1	1				1.000	-1	/CO	0.0
	NY-N	3	10	0	0	0	0	0	0	0	4	.000	.000	.000	-98	-2	-2	0				.833	-1	/CO	-0.3
Total	1	5	17	1	3	0	0	0	0	0	4	.176	.176	.176	14	-2	-2	1				.880	-2	/CO	-0.3
■ GARTH MANN Mann, Ben Garth "Red" b: 11/16/15, Brandon, Tex. d: 9/11/80, Italy, Tex. BR/TR, 6', 155 lbs. Deb: 5/14/44																									
1944	Chi-N	1	0	1	0	0	0	0	0	0	0	—	—	—	—	0	0	0	0			.000	0	R	0.0
■ FRED MANN Mann, Fred J. b: 4/1/1858, Sutton, Vt. d: 4/6/16, Springfield, Mass. BL, 5'10.5", 178 lbs. Deb: 5/01/1882																									
1882	Wor-N	19	77	12	18	5	0	0	7	2	15	.234	.253	.299	74	-2	-2	6				.703	-6	3/1	-0.8
	Phi-a	29	121	13	28	7	4	0		4		.231	.256	.355	93	0	-2	11				.798	-10	3	-1.1
1883	Col-a	96	394	61	98	18	13	1		18		.249	.282	.368	117	3	8	42				.854	-3	*O/13S	0.4
1884	Col-a	99	366	70	101	12	18	7		25		.276	.341	.464	178	25	30	59				.857	-6	*O/2	2.0
1885	Pit-a	99	391	60	99	17	6	0		31		.253	.318	.327	108	4	5	42				.908	-8	*O/3	-0.5
1886	Pit-a	116	440	85	110	16	14	2		45		.250	.335	.364	121	11	12	64	26			.878	-3	*O	0.5
1887	Cle-a	64	259	45	80	15	7	2		23		.309	.385	.444	137	12	13	55	25			.879	1	O	1.1
	Phi-a	55	229	42	63	14	6	0		15		.275	.336	.389	104	1	1	36	16			.916	-4	O	-0.3
	Yr	119	488	87	143	29	13	2		38		.293	.362	.418	121	13	14	91	41			.896	-3	*O	0.8
Total	6	577	2277	388	597	104	68	12	7	163	15	.262	.323	.383	124	55	65	315	67			.881	-39	O/312S	1.3
■ JOHNNY MANN Mann, John Leo b: 2/4/1898, Fontanet, Ind. d: 3/31/77, Terre Haute, Ind. BR/TR, 5'11", 160 lbs. Deb: 4/18/28																									
1928	Chi-A	6	6	0	2	0	0	0	1	1	0	.333	.429	.333	104	0	0	1	0	0	0	1.000	0	/3	0.0

■ KELLY MANN Mann, Kelly John b: 8/17/67, Santa Monica, Cal. BR/TR, 6'3", 215 lbs. Deb: 9/04/89

YEAR	TM/L	G	AB	R	H	2B	3B	HR	RBI	BB	SO	AVG	OBP	SLG	PRO+	BR	/A	RC	SB	CS	SBR	FA	FR	POS	TPR
1989	Atl-N	7	24	1	5	2	0	0	1	0	6	.208	.240	.292	50	-2	-2	1	0	0	0	1.000	2	/C	0.1
1990	Atl-N	11	28	2	4	1	0	1	2	0	6	.143	.143	.286	14	-3	-4	1	0	0	0	1.000	-1	C	-0.4
Total	2	18	52	3	9	3	0	1	3	0	12	.173	.189	.288	30	-5	-5	2	0	0	0	1.000	1	/C	-0.3

■ LES MANN Mann, Leslie "Major" b: 11/18/1893, Lincoln, Neb. d: 1/14/62, Pasadena, Cal. BR/TR, 5'9", 172 lbs. Deb: 4/30/13

YEAR	TM/L	G	AB	R	H	2B	3B	HR	RBI	BB	SO	AVG	OBP	SLG	PRO+	BR	/A	RC	SB	CS	SBR	FA	FR	POS	TPR
1913	Bos-N	120	407	54	103	24	7	3	51	18	73	.253	.291	.369	86	-8	-9	43	7			.960	-2	*O	-1.7
1914	*Bos-N	126	389	44	96	16	11	4	40	24	50	.247	.292	.375	99	-3	-2	43	9			.952	13	*O	0.7
1915	Chi-F	135	470	74	144	12	**19**	4	58	36	40	.306	.357	.438	142	18	21	83	18			.969	5	*O/S	2.2
1916	Chi-N	127	415	46	113	13	9	2	29	19	31	.272	.307	.361	95	1	-3	48	11	7	-1	.972	-8	*O	-1.9
1917	Chi-N	117	444	63	121	19	10	1	44	27	46	.273	.316	.367	101	4	0	54	14			.953	0	*O	-0.7
1918	*Chi-N	129	489	69	141	27	7	2	55	38	45	.288	.342	.384	119	12	11	70	21			.961	-3	*O	0.1
1919	Chi-N	80	299	31	68	8	8	1	22	11	29	.227	.257	.318	72	-11	-11	26	12			.982	2	O	-1.7
	Bos-N	40	145	15	41	6	4	3	20	9	14	.283	.329	.441	136	5	5	22	7			.929	3	O	0.6
	Yr	120	444	46	109	14	12	4	42	20	43	.245	.281	.358	92	-6	-5	48	19			.962	4	*O	-1.1
1920	Bos-N	115	424	48	117	7	8	3	32	38	42	.276	.341	.351	104	0	2	52	7	7	-2	.980	3	*O	-0.5
1921	StL-N	97	256	57	84	12	7	7	30	23	28	.328	.390	.512	140	13	14	50	5	5	-2	.969	0	O	0.8
1922	StL-N	84	147	42	51	14	1	2	20	16	12	.347	.415	.497	141	8	9	30	0	1	-1	.978	-11	O	-0.5
1923	StL-N	38	89	20	33	5	2	5	11	9	5	.371	.434	.640	184	10	10	25	0	0	0	.979	-3	O	0.6
	Cin-N	8	1	1	0	0	0	0	0	0	0	.000	.000	.000	-99	-0	-0	0	0	0	0	.000	0	H	0.0
	Yr	46	90	21	33	5	2	5	11	9	5	.367	.430	.633	181	10	10	25	0	0	0	.979	-3	O	0.6
1924	Bos-N	32	102	13	28	7	4	0	10	8	10	.275	.333	.422	105	-0	1	15	1	0	0	1.000	2	O	0.1
1925	Bos-N	60	184	27	63	11	4	2	20	5	11	.342	.373	.478	127	4	6	33	6	1	1	.992	-2	O	0.3
1926	Bos-N	50	129	23	39	8	2	1	20	9	9	.302	.348	.419	116	1	2	18	5			.966	-6	O	-0.6
1927	Bos-N	29	66	8	17	3	1	0	6	8	3	.258	.338	.333	87	-2	-1	8	2			.955	-2	O	-0.4
	NY-N	29	67	13	22	4	1	2	10	8	7	.328	.400	.507	142	4	4	13	2			1.000	-4	O	-0.1
	Yr	58	133	21	39	7	2	2	16	16	10	.293	.369	.421	116	2	3	21	4			.973	-6	O	-0.5
1928	NY-N	82	193	29	51	7	1	2	25	18	9	.264	.330	.342	76	-7	-7	22	2			.952	-19	O	-2.8
Total	16	1498	4716	677	1332	203	106	44	503	324	464	.282	.332	.398	110	51	53	656	129	21		.966	-32	*O/S	-5.5

■ JIM MANNING Manning, James H. b: 1/31/1862, Fall River, Mass. d: 10/22/29, Edinburg, Tex. TR , 157 lbs. Deb: 5/16/1884 M

YEAR	TM/L	G	AB	R	H	2B	3B	HR	RBI	BB	SO	AVG	OBP	SLG	PRO+	BR	/A	RC	SB	CS	SBR	FA	FR	POS	TPR
1884	Bos-N	89	345	52	83	8	6	2	35	19	47	.241	.280	.316	88	-5	-5	31				.878	1	O/S23	-0.4
1885	Bos-N	84	306	34	63	8	9	2	27	19	36	.206	.252	.310	84	-6	-5	25				.898	9	*O/S	0.2
	Det-N	20	78	15	21	4	0	1	9	4	10	.269	.305	.359	114	1	1	9				.802	-7	S	-0.5
	Yr	104	384	49	84	12	9	3	36	23	46	.219	.263	.320	90	-5	-4	33				.898	3	OS	-0.3
1886	Det-N	26	97	14	18	2	3	0	7	6	10	.186	.233	.268	51	-6	-6	8	7			.947	-1	O/S	-0.7
1887	Det-N	13	52	5	10	1	0	0	3	5	4	.192	.276	.212	37	-4	-4	4	3			.867	-4	O/S	-0.8
1889	KC-a	132	506	68	103	16	7	3	68	54	61	.204	.297	.281	63	-21	-26	61	58			.927	-10	O2/S3	-2.9
Total	5	364	1384	188	298	39	25	8	149	107	168	.215	.278	.297	74	-41	-45	137	68			.979	-11	O/2S3	-5.1

■ JACK MANNING Manning, John E. b: 12/20/1853, Braintree, Mass. d: 8/15/29, Boston, Mass. BR/TR, 5'8.5", 158 lbs. Deb: 4/23/1873 M

YEAR	TM/L	G	AB	R	H	2B	3B	HR	RBI	BB	SO	AVG	OBP	SLG	PRO+	BR	/A	RC	SB	CS	SBR	FA	FR	POS	TPR
1873	Bos-n	32	159	29	43	5	2	0	22	1	11	.270	.275	.327	71	-5	-7	15						1/O	-0.4
1874	Bal-n	42	168	33	59	10	1	0		3		.351	.363	.423	150	9	9	26						P2/S	0.6
	Har-n	1	5	1	1	0	0	0		0		.200	.200	.200	26	-0	-0	0						/3	0.0
	Yr	43	173	34	60	10	1	0		3		.347	.358	.416	146	9	9	26						P2/S3	0.6
1875	Bos-n	77	343	71	94	8	2	1		2		.274	.278	.318	102	2	-0	31						*OP13	0.3
1876	Bos-N	70	288	52	76	13	0	2	25	7	5	.264	.281	.330	101	1	0	27				.777	-5	*OP/S2	-0.5
1877	Cin-N	57	252	47	80	16	7	0	36	5	6	.317	.331	.437	157	11	15	37				.742	-13	S1OP/2M	0.1
1878	Bos-N	60	248	41	63	10	1	0	23	10	16	.254	.283	.302	86	-2	-4	22				.753	-13	*O/P	-2.0
1880	Cin-N	48	190	20	41	6	3	2	17	7	15	.216	.244	.311	87	-3	-2	15				.798	-3	O/1	-0.6
1881	Buf-N	1	1	0	0	0	0	0	0	0	0	.000	.000	.000	-99	-0	-0	0				1.000	0	/O	0.0
1883	Phi-N	98	420	60	112	31	5	0	37	20	37	.267	.300	.364	110	0	6	47				.853	10	*O	1.3
1884	Phi-N	104	424	71	115	29	4	5	52	40	67	.271	.334	.394	134	14	17	57				.847	-1	*O	1.3
1885	Phi-N	107	445	61	114	24	4	3	40	37	27	.256	.313	.348	116	7	9	50				.896	-6	*O	0.0
1886	Bal-a	137	556	78	124	18	7	1		50		.223	.291	.286	85	-10	-8	55	24			.887	-10	*O	-1.8
Total	3 n	152	675	134	197	23	5	1	22	6	11	.292	.298	.345	105	6	1	73	1					/OP12S3	0.5
Total	9	682	2824	430	725	147	31	13	230	176	173	.257	.301	.345	109	19	33	310	24			.844	-40	O/PS12	-2.2

■ RICK MANNING Manning, Richard Eugene b: 9/2/54, Niagara Falls, N.Y. BL/TR, 6'1", 180 lbs. Deb: 5/23/75

YEAR	TM/L	G	AB	R	H	2B	3B	HR	RBI	BB	SO	AVG	OBP	SLG	PRO+	BR	/A	RC	SB	CS	SBR	FA	FR	POS	TPR
1975	Cle-A	120	480	69	137	16	5	3	35	44	62	.285	.348	.358	100	1	1	60	19	11	-1	.974	13	*O/D	0.8
1976	Cle-A	138	552	73	161	24	7	6	43	41	75	.292	.341	.393	116	9	10	72	16	10	-1	.987	8	*O	1.2
1977	Cle-A	68	252	33	57	7	3	5	18	21	35	.226	.286	.337	71	-11	-10	24	9	5	-0	.990	5	O	-0.8
1978	Cle-A	148	566	65	149	27	3	3	50	38	62	.263	.311	.337	83	-13	-13	57	12	12	-4	.995	5	*O	-1.8
1979	Cle-A	144	560	67	145	12	2	3	51	55	48	.259	.326	.304	71	-21	-22	59	30	8	4	.986	15	*O	-0.8
1980	Cle-A	140	471	55	110	17	4	3	52	63	66	.234	.326	.306	74	-15	-15	49	12	6	0	.990	8	*O	-1.3
1981	Cle-A	103	360	47	88	15	3	4	33	40	57	.244	.320	.336	90	-4	-4	44	25	3	6	.987	13	*O	1.2
1982	Cle-A	152	562	71	152	18	2	8	44	54	60	.270	.334	.352	89	-8	-7	66	12	8	-1	.978	6	*O	-0.7
1983	Cle-A	50	194	20	54	6	0	1	10	12	22	.278	.320	.325	75	-6	-7	20	7	3	0	.987	3	O	-0.5
	Mil-A	108	375	40	86	14	4	3	33	26	40	.229	.281	.312	68	-19	-15	33	11	2	2	.991	6	*O	-1.0
	Yr	158	569	60	140	20	4	4	43	38	62	.246	.294	.316	71	-25	-22	53	18	5	2	.990	9	*O	-1.5
1984	Mil-A	119	341	53	85	10	5	7	31	34	32	.249	.319	.370	94	-5	-3	39	5	7	-3	.987	-14	*O/D	-2.2
1985	Mil-A	79	216	19	47	9	1	2	18	14	19	.218	.265	.296	54	-14	-14	18	1	0	0	.976	-6	O/D	-2.1
1986	Mil-A	89	205	31	52	7	3	8	27	17	20	.254	.314	.434	98	-0	-1	27	5	3	-0	.988	-5	O/D	-0.8
1987	Mil-A	97	114	21	26	7	1	0	13	12	18	.228	.302	.307	60	-6	-7	11	4	0	1	.958	-19	O/D	-2.4
Total	13	1555	5248	664	1349	189	43	56	458	471	616	.257	.319	.341	84	-112	-106	580	168	78	4	.985	40	*O/D	-11.2

■ TIM MANNING Manning, Timothy Edward b: 12/3/1853, Henley-On-The- Thames, England d: 6/11/34, Oak Park, Ill. BR/TR, 5'10", 170 lbs. Deb: 5/01/1882

YEAR	TM/L	G	AB	R	H	2B	3B	HR	RBI	BB	SO	AVG	OBP	SLG	PRO+	BR	/A	RC	SB	CS	SBR	FA	FR	POS	TPR
1882	Pro-N	21	76	7	8	0	0	0	8	5	13	.105	.160	.105	-13	-9	-9	1				.787	-10	S/C	-1.7
1883	Bal-a	35	121	23	26	5	0	0		14		.215	.296	.256	77	-2	-3	9				.913	3	2	0.1
1884	Bal-a	91	341	49	70	14	5	2		26		.205	.275	.293	85	-3	-5	28				.907	-2	*2	-0.5
1885	Bal-a	43	157	17	32	8	1	0		10		.204	.265	.268	72	-5	-4	11				.919	3	2/3	0.0
	Pro-N	10	35	3	2	1	0	0	0	1	11	.057	.083	.086	-47	-5	-5	0				.854	-3	S	-0.8
Total	4	200	730	99	138	28	6	2	8	56	24	.189	.256	.252	65	-25	-27	51				.911	-9	2/SC3	-2.9

■ DON MANNO Manno, Donald D. b: 5/15/15, Williamsport, Pa. BR/TR, 6'1", 190 lbs. Deb: 9/22/40

YEAR	TM/L	G	AB	R	H	2B	3B	HR	RBI	BB	SO	AVG	OBP	SLG	PRO+	BR	/A	RC	SB	CS	SBR	FA	FR	POS	TPR
1940	Bos-N	3	7	1	2	0	0	1	4	0	2	.286	.286	.714	177	1	1	1	0			1.000	0	/O	0.1
1941	Bos-N	22	30	2	5	1	0	0	4	3	7	.167	.242	.200	27	-3	-3	1	0			1.000	-1	/O31	-0.5
Total	2	25	37	3	7	1	0	1	8	3	9	.189	.250	.297	56	-2	-2	3	0			1.000	-1	/O31	-0.4

■ FRED MANRIQUE Manrique, Fred Eloy (Reyes) b: 5/11/61, Edo Bolivar, Venez. BR/TR, 6'1", 175 lbs. Deb: 8/23/81

YEAR	TM/L	G	AB	R	H	2B	3B	HR	RBI	BB	SO	AVG	OBP	SLG	PRO+	BR	/A	RC	SB	CS	SBR	FA	FR	POS	TPR
1981	Tor-A	14	28	1	4	0	0	0	1	0	12	.143	.172	.143	-8	-4	-4	1	0	1	-1	.949	3	S/3D	-0.1
1984	Tor-A	10	9	0	3	0	0	0	1	0	1	.333	.333	.333	82	-0	-0	1	0	0	0	.938	3	/2D	0.2
1985	Mon-N	9	13	5	4	1	1	1	1	1	3	.308	.357	.769	219	2	2	4	0	0	0	1.000	2	/2S3	0.4
1986	StL-N	13	17	2	3	0	0	1	1	1	1	.176	.222	.353	57	-1	-1	1	1	0	0	1.000	-2	/32	-0.2

YEAR	TM/L	G	AB	R	H	2B	3B	HR	RBI	BB	SO	AVG	OBP	SLG	PRO+	BR	/A	RC	SB	CS	SBR	FA	FR	POS	TPR
1987	Chi-A	115	298	30	77	13	3	4	29	19	69	.258	.305	.362	74	-10	-11	33	5	3	-0	.984	19	2S/D	1.1
1988	Chi-A	140	345	43	81	10	6	5	37	21	54	.235	.285	.342	75	-12	-12	33	6	5	-1	.985	12	*2S/D	0.4
1989	Chi-A	65	187	23	56	13	1	2	30	8	30	.299	.335	.412	112	2	2	23	0	4	-2	.961	-5	2/S3	-0.4
	Tex-A	54	191	23	55	12	0	2	22	9	33	.288	.320	.382	96	-1	-1	24	4	1	1	.963	-11	S2/3D	-0.9
	Yr	119	378	46	111	25	1	4	52	17	63	.294	.327	.397	104	1	1	46	4	5	-2	.952	-17	2S/3D	-1.3
1990	Min-A	69	228	22	54	10	0	5	29	4	35	.237	.256	.346	63	-11	-12	18	2	0	1	.974	-10	2/D	-2.1
1991	Oak-A	9	21	2	3	0	0	0	0	2	1	.143	.217	.143	2	-3	-3	1	0	0	0	.955	-0	/S2	-0.3
Total	9	498	1337	151	340	59	11	20	151	65	239	.254	.293	.360	79	-39	-41	137	18	14	-3	.976	10	2/S3D	-1.9

■ JOHN MANSELL Mansell, John b: 1861, Auburn, N.Y. d: 2/20/25, Romulus, N.Y. BL , Deb: 5/09/1882 F

YEAR	TM/L	G	AB	R	H	2B	3B	HR	RBI	BB	SO	AVG	OBP	SLG	PRO+	BR	/A	RC	SB	CS	SBR	FA	FR	POS	TPR
1882	Phi-a	31	126	17	30	3	1	0		4		.238	.262	.278	73	-2	-4	9				.791	-4	O	-0.8

■ MIKE MANSELL Mansell, Michael R. b: 1/15/1858, Auburn, N.Y. d: 12/4/02, Auburn, N.Y. BL , Deb: 5/01/1879 F

YEAR	TM/L	G	AB	R	H	2B	3B	HR	RBI	BB	SO	AVG	OBP	SLG	PRO+	BR	/A	RC	SB	CS	SBR	FA	FR	POS	TPR
1879	Syr-N	67	242	24	52	4	2	1	13	5	45	.215	.231	.260	69	-10	-6	15				.881	15	*O	0.6
1880	Cin-N	53	187	22	36	6	2	2	12	4	37	.193	.209	.278	64	-7	-7	11				.865	12	O	0.4
1882	Pit-a	79	347	59	96	**18**	**16**	2		7		.277	.291	.438	150	14	17	45				.829	3	*O	1.7
1883	Pit-a	96	412	90	106	12	13	3		25		.257	.300	.371	120	7	10	47				.883	4	*O	1.1
1884	Pit-a	27	100	15	14	0	3	1		7		.140	.204	.230	42	-6	-6	5				.796	-1	O	-0.7
	Phi-a	20	70	6	14	1	1	0		5		.200	.253	.243	61	-2	-3	4				.762	-1	O	-0.4
	Ric-a	29	113	21	34	2	5	0		8		.301	.363	.407	156	7	7	17				.763	-5	O	0.1
	Yr	76	283	42	62	3	9	1		20		.219	.280	.304	91	-1	-2	25				.775	-7	O	-1.0
Total	5	371	1471	237	352	43	42	9	25	61	82	.239	.271	.344	106	3	12	145				.854	26	O	2.8

■ TOM MANSELL Mansell, Thomas E. "Brick" b: 1/1/1855, Auburn, N.Y. d: 10/6/34, Auburn, N.Y. BL/TL, 5'8", 160 lbs. Deb: 5/01/1879 F

YEAR	TM/L	G	AB	R	H	2B	3B	HR	RBI	BB	SO	AVG	OBP	SLG	PRO+	BR	/A	RC	SB	CS	SBR	FA	FR	POS	TPR
1879	Tro-N	40	177	29	43	6	0	0	11	3	9	.243	.256	.277	81	-5	-3	13				.742	-6	O	-1.0
	Syr-N	1	4	0	1	0	0	0	0	0	0	.250	.250	.250	74	-0	-0	0				1.000	-0	/O	0.0
	Yr	41	181	29	44	6	0	0	11	3	9	.243	.255	.276	81	-5	-3	13				.747	-6	O	-1.0
1883	Det-N	34	131	22	29	4	1	0	10	8	13	.221	.266	.267	66	-6	-5	10				.758	-2	O/P	-0.6
	StL-a	28	112	23	45	8	1	0		7		.402	.437	.491	188	12	11	25				.786	-6	O	0.5
1884	Cin-a	65	266	49	66	4	6	0		15		.248	.301	.308	97	1	-1	25				.752	-11	O	-1.2
	Col-a	23	77	9	15	1	3	0		6		.195	.262	.286	88	-1	-0	6				.667	-4	O	-0.4
	Yr	88	343	58	81	5	9	0		21		.236	.292	.303	96	-0	-1	31				.739	-15	O	-1.6
Total	3	191	767	132	199	23	11	0	21	39	22	.259	.300	.318	101	2	2	78				.751	-28	O/P	-2.7

■ FELIX MANTILLA Mantilla, Felix (Lamela) b: 7/29/34, Isabela, P.R. BR/TR, 6', 160 lbs. Deb: 6/21/56

YEAR	TM/L	G	AB	R	H	2B	3B	HR	RBI	BB	SO	AVG	OBP	SLG	PRO+	BR	/A	RC	SB	CS	SBR	FA	FR	POS	TPR
1956	Mil-N	35	53	9	15	1	1	0	3	1	8	.283	.309	.340	79	-2	-2	5	0	1	-1	1.000	9	S/3	0.8
1957	*Mil-N	71	182	28	43	9	1	4	21	14	34	.236	.298	.363	82	-6	-5	20	2	0	1	.931	6	S2/3O	0.6
1958	*Mil-N	85	226	37	50	5	1	7	19	20	20	.221	.285	.345	72	-11	-9	22	2	0	1	.987	-6	O2/S3	-1.5
1959	Mil-N	103	251	26	54	5	0	3	19	16	31	.215	.268	.271	48	-20	-17	18	6	1	1	.970	4	2S/3O	-0.8
1960	Mil-N	63	148	21	38	7	0	3	11	7	16	.257	.295	.365	86	-4	-3	16	3	1	0	.956	-12	2S/O	-1.2
1961	Mil-N	45	93	13	20	3	0	1	5	10	16	.215	.298	.280	58	-6	-5	8	1	1	-0	.933	-3	S2O/3	-0.7
1962	NY-N	141	466	54	128	17	4	11	59	37	51	.275	.335	.399	94	-3	-4	62	3	1	0	.948	-7	3S2	-0.7
1963	Bos-A	66	178	27	56	8	0	6	15	20	14	.315	.384	.461	131	9	8	31	2	1	0	.965	-5	SO/2	0.5
1964	Bos-A	133	425	69	123	20	1	30	64	41	46	.289	.357	.553	142	27	24	81	0	1	-1	.984	-6	O2/3S	2.1
1965	Bos-A★	150	534	60	147	17	2	18	92	79	84	.275	.377	.416	118	20	16	83	7	3	0	.976	-22	*2O/1	0.4
1966	Hou-N	77	151	16	33	5	0	6	22	11	32	.219	.280	.371	85	-4	-3	15	1	0	0	.990	-2	13/2O	-0.6
Total	11	969	2707	360	707	97	10	89	330	256	352	.261	.331	.403	100	-1	1	361	27	10	2	.977	-43	2SO3/1	-1.1

■ MICKEY MANTLE Mantle, Mickey Charles "The Commerce Comet" b: 10/20/31, Spavinaw, Okla. BB/TR, 5'11", 198 lbs. Deb: 4/17/51 CH

YEAR	TM/L	G	AB	R	H	2B	3B	HR	RBI	BB	SO	AVG	OBP	SLG	PRO+	BR	/A	RC	SB	CS	SBR	FA	FR	POS	TPR
1951	*NY-A	96	341	61	91	11	5	13	65	43	74	.267	.349	.443	117	5	7	55	8	7	-2	.959	-6	O	-0.3
1952	*NY-A☆	142	549	94	171	37	7	23	87	75	111	.311	.394	.530	166	**40**	**44**	**123**	4	1	1	.968	3	*O/3	4.3
1953	*NY-A★	127	461	105	136	24	3	21	92	79	90	.295	.398	.497	145	27	29	100	8	4	0	.982	1	*O/S	2.6
1954	NY-A★	146	543	**129**	163	17	12	27	102	102	107	.300	.411	.525	160	43	45	127	5	2	0	.975	-1	*O/S2	3.9
1955	*NY-A★	147	517	121	158	25	**11**	**37**	99	**113**	97	.306	**.433**	**.611**	**181**	59	**60**	**148**	8	1	2	.995	8	*O/S	**6.2**
1956	*NY-A★	150	533	**132**	188	22	5	**52**	**130**	112	99	**.353**	.467	**.705**	**213**	**83**	**86**	**188**	10	1	2	.990	8	*O	**8.4**
1957	*NY-A★	144	474	**121**	173	28	6	34	94	**146**	75	.365	.515	.665	223	89	**90**	**178**	16	3	3	.979	0	*O	**8.5**
1958	*NY-A★	150	519	**127**	158	21	1	**42**	97	**129**	120	.304	.445	.592	**189**	**64**	**67**	**147**	18	3	4	.977	-0	*O	**6.3**
1959	NY-A★	144	541	104	154	23	4	31	75	93	126	.285	.392	.514	**152**	36	38	**117**	21	3	5	**.995**	8	*O	**4.4**
1960	*NY-A★	153	527	**119**	145	17	6	**40**	94	111	125	.275	.402	.558	**166**	**44**	**48**	**125**	14	3	2	.991	-1	*O	**4.2**
1961	*NY-A★	153	514	**132**	163	16	6	54	128	**126**	112	.317	.452	**.687**	**210**	76	80	174	12	1	3	.983	4	*O	**7.6**
1962	*NY-A★	123	377	96	121	15	1	30	89	**122**	78	.321	**.488**	**.605**	**198**	**57**	**59**	126	9	0	3	.978	-6	*O	**4.8**
1963	*NY-A	65	172	40	54	8	0	15	35	40	32	.314	.443	.622	197	23	24	49	2	1	0	.990	-2	O	2.0
1964	*NY-A★	143	465	92	141	25	2	35	111	99	102	.303	**.426**	.591	**177**	**53**	**52**	121	6	3	0	.978	-13	*O	3.4
1965	NY-A	122	361	44	92	12	1	19	46	73	76	.255	.380	.452	136	19	19	64	4	1	1	.966	-4	*O	1.2
1966	NY-A	108	333	40	96	12	1	23	56	57	76	.288	.392	.538	171	29	30	71	1	1	-0	1.000	-7	O	2.0
1967	NY-A★	144	440	63	108	17	0	22	55	107	113	.245	.394	.434	150	29	31	82	1	1	-0	.993	0	*1	2.5
1968	NY-A★	144	435	57	103	14	1	18	54	106	97	.237	.387	.398	143	25	27	74	6	2	1	.988	-3	*1	1.6
Total	18	2401	8102	1677	2415	344	72	536	1509	1733	1710	.298	.423	.557	173	803	838	2069	153	38	23	.982	-9	*O1/S23	73.6

■ JEFF MANTO Manto, Jeffrey Paul b: 8/23/64, Bristol, Pa. BR/TR, 6'3", 210 lbs. Deb: 6/07/90

YEAR	TM/L	G	AB	R	H	2B	3B	HR	RBI	BB	SO	AVG	OBP	SLG	PRO+	BR	/A	RC	SB	CS	SBR	FA	FR	POS	TPR
1990	Cle-A	30	76	12	17	5	1	2	14	21	18	.224	.392	.395	121	3	3	13	0	1	-1	.990	1	1/3	0.2
1991	Cle-A	47	128	15	27	7	0	2	13	14	22	.211	.308	.313	72	-5	-5	13	2	0	1	.929	1	31/CO	-0.3
Total	2	77	204	27	44	12	1	4	27	35	40	.216	.342	.343	91	-2	-2	27	2	1	0	.986	3	/13CO	-0.1

■ CHUCK MANUEL Manuel, Charles Fuqua b: 1/4/44, North Fork, W.Va. BL/TR, 6'4", 200 lbs. Deb: 4/08/69 C

YEAR	TM/L	G	AB	R	H	2B	3B	HR	RBI	BB	SO	AVG	OBP	SLG	PRO+	BR	/A	RC	SB	CS	SBR	FA	FR	POS	TPR
1969	*Min-A	83	164	14	34	6	0	2	24	28	33	.207	.323	.280	69	-6	-6	16	1	0	0	.967	-6	O	-1.4
1970	*Min-A	59	64	4	12	0	0	1	7	6	17	.188	.268	.234	39	-5	-5	4	0	0	0	1.000	-3	O	-0.8
1971	Min-A	18	16	1	2	1	0	0	1	1	8	.125	.176	.188	3	-2	-2	1	0	0	0	.000	-0	/O	-0.3
1972	Min-A	63	122	6	25	5	0	1	8	4	16	.205	.236	.270	48	-8	-8	8	0	0	0	.977	-1	O	-1.1
1974	LA-N	4	3	0	1	0	0	0	1	1	0	.333	.500	.333	142	0	0	1	0	0	0	.000	0	H	0.0
1975	LA-N	15	15	0	2	0	0	0	2	0	3	.133	.133	.133	-27	-3	-2	0	0	0	0	.000	0	H	-0.3
Total	6	242	384	25	76	12	0	4	43	40	77	.198	.277	.260	52	-23	-24	30	1	0	0	.973	-9	/O	-3.9

■ JERRY MANUEL Manuel, Jerry b: 12/23/53, Hahira, Ga. BB/TR, 6', 165 lbs. Deb: 9/18/75 C

YEAR	TM/L	G	AB	R	H	2B	3B	HR	RBI	BB	SO	AVG	OBP	SLG	PRO+	BR	/A	RC	SB	CS	SBR	FA	FR	POS	TPR
1975	Det-A	6	18	0	1	0	0	0	0	0	4	.056	.056	.056	-66	-4	-4	0	0	0	0	.944	3	/2	-0.1
1976	Det-A	54	43	4	6	1	0	0	2	3	9	.140	.213	.163	11	-5	-5	2	1	0	0	.921	10	2/SD	0.7
1980	Mon-N	7	6	0	0	0	0	0	0	0	2	.000	.000	.000	-99	-2	-2	0	0	0	0	.941	3	/S	0.1
1981	*Mon-N	27	55	10	11	5	0	3	10	6	11	.200	.279	.455	104	0	-0	7	0	0	0	.987	-0	2/S	0.0
1982	SD-N	2	5	0	1	0	1	0	1	1	0	.200	.333	.600	165	0	0	1	0	0	0	1.000	-1	/2S3	-0.1
Total	5	96	127	14	19	6	1	3	13	10	26	.150	.217	.283	42	-10	-10	10	1	0	0	.949	14	/2S3D	0.6

■ FRANK MANUSH Manush, Frank Benjamin b: 9/18/1883, Tuscumbia, Ala. d: 1/5/65, Laguna Beach, Cal. BR/TR, 5'10.5", 175 lbs. Deb: 8/31/08 F

YEAR	TM/L	G	AB	R	H	2B	3B	HR	RBI	BB	SO	AVG	OBP	SLG	PRO+	BR	/A	RC	SB	CS	SBR	FA	FR	POS	TPR
1908	Phi-A	23	77	6	12	2	1	0	0	2		.156	.188	.208	27	-6	-7	3	2			.933	-5	3/2	-1.3

YEAR	TM/L	G	AB	R	H	2B	3B	HR	RBI	BB	SO	AVG	OBP	SLG	PRO+	BR	/A	RC	SB	CS	SBR	FA	FR	POS	TPR
■ HEINIE MANUSH	Manush, Henry Emmett b: 7/20/01, Tuscumbia, Ala. d: 5/12/71, Sarasota, Fla. BL/TL, 6'1", 200 lbs. Deb: 4/20/23 FCH																								
1923	Det-A	109	308	59	103	20	5	4	54	20	21	.334	.406	.471	133	14	15	59	3	5	-2	.953	-4	O	0.3
1924	Det-A	120	422	83	122	24	8	9	68	27	30	.289	.355	.448	108	2	3	69	14	5	1	.979	-6	*O/1	-0.8
1925	Det-A	99	278	46	84	14	3	5	47	24	21	.302	.362	.428	101	-1	0	44	8	3	1	.982	-5	O	-0.8
1926	Det-A	136	498	95	188	35	8	14	86	31	28	**.378**	.421	.564	153	38	37	116	11	5	0	.967	-4	*O	2.5
1927	Det-A	151	593	102	177	31	18	6	90	47	29	.298	.354	.442	104	3	2	88	12	8	-1	.971	-3	*O	-1.1
1928	StL-A	154	638	104	**241**	**47**	20	13	108	39	14	.378	.414	.575	153	50	48	150	17	5	2	.992	2	*O	3.9
1929	StL-A	142	574	85	204	**45**	10	6	81	43	24	.355	.401	.500	126	26	23	113	9	8	-2	.987	-2	*O	0.8
1930	StL-A	49	198	26	65	16	4	2	29	5	7	.328	.345	.480	103	1	0	32	3	1	0	.990	2	O	-0.1
	Was-A	88	356	74	129	33	8	7	65	26	17	.362	.406	.559	141	22	22	79	4	3	-1	.988	-2	O	1.2
	Yr	137	554	100	194	49	12	9	94	31	24	.350	.385	.531	128	23	22	111	7	4	-0	.989	0	*O	1.1
1931	Was-A	146	616	110	189	41	11	6	70	36	27	.307	.351	.438	106	4	4	94	3	3	-1	.977	-11	*O	-1.6
1932	Was-A	149	625	121	214	41	14	14	116	36	29	.342	.383	.520	133	27	28	124	7	2	1	.988	-0	*O	1.8
1933	*Was-A	153	658	115	**221**	32	**17**	5	95	36	18	.336	.372	.459	120	17	18	111	6	4	-1	.982	-2	*O	0.7
1934	Was-A★	137	556	88	194	42	11	11	89	36	23	.349	.392	.523	140	26	29	113	7	3	0	.980	-0	*O	2.2
1935	Was-A	119	479	68	131	26	9	4	56	35	17	.273	.328	.390	88	-12	-9	62	2	0	1	.985	3	*O	-0.9
1936	Bos-A	82	313	43	91	15	5	0	45	17	11	.291	.329	.371	69	-14	-17	37	1	3	-2	.966	-8	O	-2.6
1937	Bro-N	132	466	57	155	25	7	4	73	40	24	.333	.389	.442	123	17	16	84	6			.970	-12	*O	0.0
1938	Bro-N	17	51	9	12	3	1	0	6	5	4	.235	.304	.333	73	-2	-2	5	1			1.000	1	O	-0.1
	Pit-N	15	13	2	4	1	1	0	4	2	0	.308	.400	.538	155	1	1	3	0			.000	0	H	0.1
	Yr	32	64	11	16	4	2	0	10	7	4	.250	.324	.375	90	-1	-1	7	1			1.000	1	O	0.0
1939	Pit-N	10	12	0	0	0	0	0	1	1	1	.000	.077	.000	-79	-3	-3	0	0			1.000	-0	/O	-0.3
Total	17	2008	7654	1287	2524	491	160	110	1183	506	345	.330	.377	.479	121	218	215	1383	114	58		.979	-50	*O/1	5.2
■ KIRT MANWARING	Manwaring, Kirt Dean b: 7/15/65, Elmira, N.Y. BR/TR, 5'11", 185 lbs. Deb: 9/15/87																								
1987	SF-N	6	7	0	1	0	0	0	0	0	1	.143	.250	.143	8	-1	-1	0	0	0	0	.909	-1	/C	-0.2
1988	SF-N	40	116	12	29	7	0	1	15	2	21	.250	.281	.336	80	-4	-3	11	0	1	-1	.979	-2	C	-0.3
1989	*SF-N	85	200	14	42	4	2	0	18	11	28	.210	.265	.250	49	-13	-13	13	2	1	0	.982	-0	C	-1.0
1990	SF-N	8	13	0	2	0	1	0	1	0	3	.154	.154	.308	25	-1	-1	1	0	0	0	1.000	2	/C	0.1
1991	SF-N	67	178	16	40	9	0	0	19	9	22	.225	.274	.275	57	-11	-10	14	1	1	-0	.988	1	C	-0.6
1992	SF-N	109	349	24	85	10	5	4	26	29	42	.244	.311	.335	87	-8	-6	35	2	1	0	.994	1	*C	0.1
Total	6	315	863	66	199	30	8	5	79	51	117	.231	.286	.301	70	-38	-34	75	5	4	-1	.988	1	C	-1.9
■ CLIFF MAPES	Mapes, Clifford Franklin b: 3/13/22, Sutherland, Neb. BL/TR, 6'3", 205 lbs. Deb: 4/20/48																								
1948	NY-A	53	88	19	22	11	1	1	12	6	13	.250	.298	.432	94	-2	-2	11	1	1	-0	.958	1	O	-0.1
1949	*NY-A	111	304	56	75	13	3	7	38	58	50	.247	.369	.378	98	0	0	49	6	0	**2**	.976	3	*O	0.0
1950	*NY-A	108	356	60	88	14	6	12	61	47	61	.247	.338	.421	96	-5	-3	49	1	6	-3	.950	-7	*O	-1.7
1951	NY-A	45	51	6	11	3	1	2	8	4	14	.216	.273	.431	92	-1	-1	6	0	0	0	1.000	-9	O	-1.0
	StL-A	56	201	32	55	7	2	7	30	26	33	.274	.360	.433	110	4	3	32	0	1	-1	.983	-1	O	-0.1
	Yr	101	252	38	66	10	3	9	38	30	47	.262	.343	.433	109	2	2	38	0	1	-1	.986	-10	O	-1.1
1952	Det-A	86	193	26	38	7	0	9	23	27	42	.197	.295	.373	84	-4	-5	23	0	1	-1	.967	-10	O	-1.8
Total	5	459	1193	199	289	55	13	38	172	168	213	.242	.338	.406	97	-8	-7	169	8	9	-3	.969	-23	O	-4.7
■ HOWARD MAPLE	Maple, Howard Albert "Mape" b: 7/20/03, Adrian, Mo. d: 11/9/70, Portland, Ore. BL/TR, 5'7", 175 lbs. Deb: 5/19/32																								
1932	Was-A	44	41	6	10	0	1	0	7	7	7	.244	.367	.293	74	-1	-1	5	0	0	0	1.000	-3	C	-0.3
■ GEORGE MAPPES	Mappes, George Richard "Dick" b: 12/25/1865, St.Louis, Mo. d: 2/20/34, St.Louis, Mo. Deb: 9/23/1885																								
1885	Bal-a	6	19	2	4	0	1	0		1		.211	.250	.316	81	-0	-0	2				.875	-2	/2	-0.2
1886	StL-N	6	14	1	2	0	0	0	0	1	5	.143	.200	.143	6	-2	-1	0	0			1.000	-1	/C32	-0.2
Total	2	12	33	3	6	0	1	0	0	2	5	.182	.229	.242	49	-2	-2	2	0			.848	-3	/2C3	-0.4
■ RABBIT MARANVILLE	Maranville, Walter James Vincent b: 11/11/1891, Springfield, Mass. d: 1/5/54, New York, N.Y. BR/TR, 5'5", 155 lbs. Deb: 9/10/12 MH																								
1912	Bos-N	26	86	8	18	2	0	0	8	9	14	.209	.292	.233	44	-6	-7	7	1			.929	5	S	0.1
1913	Bos-N	143	571	68	141	13	8	2	48	68	62	.247	.330	.308	81	-11	-12	64	25			.949	15	*S	1.7
1914	*Bos-N	156	586	74	144	23	6	4	78	45	56	.246	.306	.326	88	-9	-9	66	28			.938	**52**	*S	**5.9**
1915	Bos-N	149	509	51	124	23	6	2	43	45	65	.244	.308	.324	96	-5	-3	55	18	12	-2	.941	21	*S	3.1
1916	Bos-N	155	604	79	142	16	13	4	38	50	69	.235	.296	.325	94	-7	-4	64	32	15	1	**.947**	22	*S	3.0
1917	Bos-N	142	561	69	146	19	13	3	43	40	47	.260	.312	.357	111	2	6	67	27			.947	14	*S	3.0
1918	Bos-N	11	38	3	12	0	1	0	3	4	0	.316	.381	.368	134	1	2	5	0			.932	2	S	0.4
1919	Bos-N	131	480	44	128	18	10	5	43	36	23	.267	.319	.377	113	5	7	59	12			.941	**29**	*S	**4.7**
1920	Bos-N	134	493	48	131	19	15	1	43	28	24	.266	.305	.371	98	-5	-3	54	14	11	-2	.948	14	*S	2.1
1921	Pit-N	153	612	90	180	25	12	1	70	47	38	.294	.347	.379	90	-6	-8	82	25	12	0	.962	-11	*S	-0.4
1922	Pit-N	155	672	115	198	26	15	0	63	61	43	.295	.355	.378	88	-10	-11	92	24	13	-1	.961	11	*S2	1.4
1923	Pit-N	141	581	78	161	19	9	1	41	42	34	.277	.327	.346	76	-18	-20	66	14	11	-2	**.965**	12	*S	0.3
1924	Pit-N	152	594	62	158	33	20	2	71	35	53	.266	.307	.399	86	-12	-13	70	18	14	-3	**.973**	4	*2	-1.0
1925	Chi-N	75	266	37	62	10	3	0	23	29	20	.233	.308	.293	54	-18	-18	25	6	5	-1	.955	4	SM	-0.7
1926	Bro-N	78	234	32	55	8	5	0	24	26	24	.235	.312	.312	69	-10	-10	23	7			.948	10	S2	0.6
1927	StL-N	9	29	0	7	1	0	0	0	2	2	.241	.290	.276	51	-2	-2	2	0			.962	3	/S	0.2
1928	*StL-N	112	366	40	88	14	10	1	34	36	27	.240	.310	.342	69	-16	-17	39	3			.969	-5	*S/2	-1.0
1929	Bos-N	146	560	87	159	26	10	0	55	47	33	.284	.344	.366	79	-21	-17	70	13			.961	20	*S/2	1.8
1930	Bos-N	142	558	85	157	26	8	2	43	48	23	.281	.344	.367	75	-25	-21	70	9			**.965**	-13	*S/3	-1.6
1931	Bos-N	145	562	69	146	22	5	0	33	56	34	.260	.329	.317	77	-19	-16	63	9			.949	-24	*S2	-2.6
1932	Bos-N	149	571	67	134	20	4	0	37	46	28	.235	.295	.284	59	-34	-31	51	4			**.975**	6	*2	-1.8
1933	Bos-N	143	478	46	104	15	4	0	38	36	34	.218	.274	.266	59	-28	-23	35	2			.971	-27	*2	-4.5
1935	Bos-N	23	67	3	10	2	0	0	5	3	3	.149	.186	.179	-2	-10	-9	2	0			.963	-5	2	-1.2
Total	23	2670	10078	1255	2605	380	177	28	884	839	756	.258	.318	.340	82	-263	-240	1132	291	93		.952	158	*S2/3	13.5
■ JOHNNY MARCUM	Marcum, John Alfred "Footsie" b: 9/9/09, Campbellsburg, Ky. d: 9/10/84, Louisville, Ky. BL/TR, 5'11", 197 lbs. Deb: 9/07/33																								
1933	Phi-A	5	12	2	2	0	0	0	0	2	1	.167	.286	.167	22	-1	-1	1	0	0	0	1.000	0	/P	0.0
1934	Phi-A	58	112	10	30	4	0	1	13	3	5	.268	.287	.330	61	-7	-7	10	0	1	-1	.949	-0	P	0.0
1935	Phi-A	64	119	13	37	2	1	2	17	9	5	.311	.359	.395	96	-1	-1	17	0	0	0	.896	-3	P	0.0
1936	Bos-A	48	88	6	18	3	0	2	7	3	5	.205	.231	.307	30	-10	-11	6	0	0	0	.950	0	P	0.0
1937	Bos-A	51	86	12	23	8	0	0	13	7	4	.267	.323	.360	69	-4	-4	10	0	0	0	.981	1	P	0.0
1938	Bos-A	19	37	3	5	0	0	0	3	6	9	.135	.256	.135	1	-6	-6	2	0	0	0	1.000	-1	P	0.0
1939	StL-A	16	22	3	10	1	0	0	5	1	2	.455	.478	.500	147	2	2	5	0	0	0	1.000	-0	P	0.0
	Chi-A	38	57	7	16	0	0	0	12	5	1	.281	.339	.281	58	-3	-3	6	0	0	0	.941	-1	P	0.0
	Yr	54	79	10	26	1	0	0	17	6	3	.329	.376	.342	83	-1	-2	10	0	0	0	.962	-1	P	0.0
Total	7	299	533	56	141	18	1	5	70	36	32	.265	.311	.330	62	-30	-31	57	0	1	-1	.953	-4	P	0.0
■ RED MARION	Marion, John Wyeth b: 3/14/14, Richburg, S.C. d: 3/13/75, San Jose, Cal. BR/TR, 6'2", 175 lbs. Deb: 9/16/35 F																								
1935	Was-A	4	11	1	2	1	0	1	1	0	2	.182	.182	.545	85	-0	-0	1	0	0	0	.833	-0	/O	-0.1
1943	Was-A	14	17	2	3	0	0	0	1	3	1	.176	.300	.176	42	-1	-1	1	0	0	0	1.000	-1	/O	-0.2
Total	2	18	28	3	5	1	0	1	2	3	3	.179	.258	.321	63	-2	-1	2	0	0	0	.923	-1	/O	-0.3

■ **MARTY MARION** Marion, Martin Whitford "Slats" or "The Octopus" b: 12/1/17, Richburg, S.C. BR/TR, 6'2", 170 lbs. Deb: 4/16/40 FMC

YEAR	TM/L	G	AB	R	H	2B	3B	HR	RBI	BB	SO	AVG	OBP	SLG	PRO+	BR	/A	RC	SB	CS	SBR	FA	FR	POS	TPR
1940	StL-N	125	435	44	121	18	1	3	46	21	34	.278	.311	.345	76	-12	-15	45	9			.949	-6	*S	-1.1
1941	StL-N	155	547	50	138	22	3	3	58	42	48	.252	.308	.320	72	-17	-21	56	8			.954	7	*S	-0.3
1942	*StL-N	147	485	66	134	**38**	5	0	54	48	50	.276	.343	.375	102	6	2	64	8			.960	7	*S	1.9
1943	*StL-N★	129	418	38	117	15	3	1	52	32	37	.280	.334	.337	90	-3	-5	49	1			.970	25	*S	3.1
1944	*StL-N★	144	506	50	135	26	2	6	63	43	50	.267	.324	.362	91	-5	-6	61	1			**.972**	5	*S	1.0
1945	StL-N	123	430	63	119	27	5	1	59	39	39	.277	.340	.370	95	-2	-3	56	2			.967	-2	*S	0.5
1946	*StL-N★	146	498	51	116	29	4	3	46	59	53	.233	.318	.325	79	-11	-14	55	1			.973	**19**	*S	1.4
1947	StL-N★	149	540	57	147	19	6	4	74	49	58	.272	.334	.352	79	-13	-17	63	3			**.981**	**20**	*S	1.1
1948	StL-N	144	567	70	143	26	4	4	43	37	54	.252	.298	.333	67	-24	-28	55	1			**.974**	9	*S	-1.0
1949	StL-N☆	134	515	61	140	31	2	5	70	37	42	.272	.323	.369	81	-11	-14	59	0			.976	17	*S	1.1
1950	StL-N★	106	372	36	92	10	2	4	40	44	55	.247	.327	.317	67	-15	-18	39	1			.978	-1	*S	-1.1
1952	StL-A	67	186	16	46	11	0	2	19	19	17	.247	.320	.339	81	-4	-5	20	0	2	-1	.980	-7	SM	-0.9
1953	StL-A	3	7	0	0	0	0	0	0	0	0	.000	.000	.000	-98	-2	-2	0	0	0	0	1.000	-1	/3M	-0.4
Total	13	1572	5506	602	1448	272	37	36	624	470	537	.263	.323	.345	81	-113	-145	623	35	2		.969	92	*S/3	5.3

■ **ROGER MARIS** Maris, Roger Eugene (b: Roger Eugene Maras) b: 9/10/34, Hibbing, Minn. d: 12/14/85, Houston, Tex. BL/TR, 6', 204 lbs. Deb: 4/16/57

YEAR	TM/L	G	AB	R	H	2B	3B	HR	RBI	BB	SO	AVG	OBP	SLG	PRO+	BR	/A	RC	SB	CS	SBR	FA	FR	POS	TPR
1957	Cle-A	116	358	61	84	9	5	14	51	60	79	.235	.346	.405	106	3	3	53	8	4	0	.975	5	*O	0.3
1958	Cle-A	51	182	26	41	5	1	9	27	17	33	.225	.291	.412	94	-3	-2	23	4	2	0	.967	5	O	0.0
	KC-A	99	401	61	99	14	3	19	53	28	52	.247	.299	.439	99	-1	-2	54	0	0	0	.975	-4	O	-1.2
	Yr	150	583	87	140	19	4	28	80	45	85	.240	.297	.431	97	-4	-4	77	4	2	0	.972	1	*O	-1.2
1959	KC-A★	122	433	69	118	21	7	16	72	58	53	.273	.362	.464	123	15	14	76	2	1	0	.975	6	*O	1.5
1960	*NY-A★	136	499	98	141	18	7	39	**112**	70	65	.283	.374	**.581**	164	36	40	111	2	2	-1	.985	3	*O	3.6
1961	*NY-A★	161	590	**132**	159	16	4	**61**	**142**	94	67	.269	.376	.620	170	50	54	138	0	0	0	.968	-11	*O	3.3
1962	*NY-A★	157	590	92	151	34	1	33	100	87	78	.256	.357	.485	128	20	23	107	1	0	0	.991	-4	*O	0.9
1963	*NY-A	90	312	53	84	14	1	23	53	35	40	.269	.347	.542	146	18	18	61	1	0	0	.988	2	O	1.7
1964	*NY-A	141	513	86	144	12	2	26	71	62	78	.281	.365	.464	127	21	20	91	3	0	1	.996	-0	*O	1.4
1965	NY-A	46	155	22	37	7	0	8	27	29	29	.239	.359	.439	126	6	6	25	0	0	0	.971	-2	O	0.2
1966	NY-A	119	348	37	81	9	2	13	43	36	60	.233	.310	.382	101	-1	0	41	0	0	0	.993	-7	O	-1.1
1967	*StL-N	125	410	64	107	18	7	9	55	52	61	.261	.350	.405	117	9	10	59	0	0	0	.991	2	*O	0.7
1968	*StL-N	100	310	25	79	18	2	5	45	24	38	.255	.310	.374	106	1	2	37	0	0	0	.983	2	O	0.0
Total	12	1463	5101	826	1325	195	42	275	851	652	733	.260	.348	.476	128	174	185	878	21	9	1	.982	-2	*O	11.3

■ **GENE MARKLAND** Markland, Cleneth Eugene "Mousey" b: 12/26/19, Detroit, Mich. BR/TR, 5'10", 160 lbs. Deb: 4/25/50

YEAR	TM/L	G	AB	R	H	2B	3B	HR	RBI	BB	SO	AVG	OBP	SLG	PRO+	BR	/A	RC	SB	CS	SBR	FA	FR	POS	TPR
1950	Phi-A	5	8	2	1	0	0	0	0	3	0	.125	.364	.125	30	-1	-1	1	0	0	0	1.000	0	/2	0.0

■ **HAL MARNIE** Marnie, Harry Sylvester b: 7/6/18, Philadelphia, Pa. BR/TR, 6'1", 178 lbs. Deb: 9/15/40

YEAR	TM/L	G	AB	R	H	2B	3B	HR	RBI	BB	SO	AVG	OBP	SLG	PRO+	BR	/A	RC	SB	CS	SBR	FA	FR	POS	TPR
1940	Phi-N	11	34	4	6	0	0	0	4	4	2	.176	.263	.176	24	-3	-3	2	0			.984	6	2	0.3
1941	Phi-N	61	158	12	38	3	3	0	11	13	25	.241	.298	.297	71	-7	-6	13	0			.990	5	2S/3	0.2
1942	Phi-N	24	30	3	5	0	0	0	0	1	2	.167	.194	.167	6	-4	-3	1	1			.971	8	2/S3	0.6
Total	3	96	222	19	49	3	3	0	15	18	29	.221	.279	.261	55	-14	-13	16	1			.987	19	/2S3	1.1

■ **FRED MAROLEWSKI** Marolewski, Fred Daniel "Fritz" b: 10/6/28, Chicago, Ill. BR/TR, 6'2.5", 205 lbs. Deb: 9/19/53

YEAR	TM/L	G	AB	R	H	2B	3B	HR	RBI	BB	SO	AVG	OBP	SLG	PRO+	BR	/A	RC	SB	CS	SBR	FA	FR	POS	TPR
1953	StL-N	1	0	0	0	0	0	0	0	0	0	—	—	—	—	0	0	0	0	0	0	.000	0	/1	0.0

■ **OLLIE MARQUARDT** Marquardt, Albert Ludwig b: 9/22/02, Toledo, Ohio d: 2/7/68, Fort Clinton, Ohio BR/TR, 5'9", 156 lbs. Deb: 4/14/31

YEAR	TM/L	G	AB	R	H	2B	3B	HR	RBI	BB	SO	AVG	OBP	SLG	PRO+	BR	/A	RC	SB	CS	SBR	FA	FR	POS	TPR
1931	Bos-A	17	39	4	7	1	0	0	2	3	4	.179	.238	.205	18	-5	-4	2	0	1	-1	.946	-3	2/S3	-0.7

■ **GONZALO MARQUEZ** Marquez, Gonzalo Enrique (Moya) b: 3/31/46, Carupano, Venez. d: 12/20/84, Valencia, Venez. BL/TL, 5'11", 180 lbs. Deb: 8/11/72

YEAR	TM/L	G	AB	R	H	2B	3B	HR	RBI	BB	SO	AVG	OBP	SLG	PRO+	BR	/A	RC	SB	CS	SBR	FA	FR	POS	TPR
1972	*Oak-A	23	21	2	8	0	0	0	4	3	4	.381	.480	.381	167	2	2	4	1	1	-0	.929	-0	/1	0.2
1973	Oak-A	23	25	1	6	1	0	0	2	0	4	.240	.240	.280	49	-2	-2	1	0	0	0	.000	-1	/21OD	-0.3
	Chi-N	19	58	5	13	2	0	1	4	3	4	.224	.274	.310	57	-3	-4	5	0	0	0	.994	2	1	-0.3
1974	Chi-N	11	11	1	0	0	0	0	0	1	2	.000	.083	.000	-72	-3	-3	0	0	0	0	1.000	-0	/1	-0.3
Total	3	76	115	9	27	3	0	1	10	7	14	.235	.290	.287	62	-6	-6	11	1	1	-0	.989	1	/12DO	-0.7

■ **LUIS MARQUEZ** Marquez, Luis Angel (Sanchez) "Canena" b: 10/28/25, Aguadilla, P.R. d: 3/1/88, Aguadilla, P.R. BR/TR, 5'10.5", 174 lbs. Deb: 4/18/51

YEAR	TM/L	G	AB	R	H	2B	3B	HR	RBI	BB	SO	AVG	OBP	SLG	PRO+	BR	/A	RC	SB	CS	SBR	FA	FR	POS	TPR
1951	Bos-N	68	122	19	24	5	1	0	11	10	20	.197	.274	.254	46	-10	-9	9	4	4	-1	1.000	-2	O	-1.3
1954	Chi-N	17	12	2	1	0	0	0	0	2	4	.083	.214	.083	-19	-2	-2	1	3	0	1	1.000	-4	O	-0.6
	Pit-N	14	9	3	1	0	0	0	0	4	0	.111	.385	.111	37	-1	-1	1	0	0	0	1.000	-1	/O	-0.2
	Yr	31	21	5	2	0	0	0	0	6	4	.095	.296	.095	7	-3	-3	2	3	0	1	1.000	-5	O	-0.8
Total	2	99	143	24	26	5	1	0	11	16	24	.182	.278	.231	40	-12	-11	10	7	4	-0	1.000	-7	/O	-2.1

■ **BOB MARQUIS** Marquis, Robert Rudolph b: 12/23/24, Oklahoma City, Okla. BL/TL, 6'1", 170 lbs. Deb: 4/17/53

YEAR	TM/L	G	AB	R	H	2B	3B	HR	RBI	BB	SO	AVG	OBP	SLG	PRO+	BR	/A	RC	SB	CS	SBR	FA	FR	POS	TPR
1953	Cin-N	40	44	9	12	1	1	2	3	4	11	.273	.333	.477	107	0	0	8	0	0	0	.905	-2	O	-0.2

■ **ROGER MARQUIS** Marquis, Roger Julian "Noonie" b: 4/5/37, Holyoke, Mass. BL/TL, 6', 190 lbs. Deb: 9/25/55

YEAR	TM/L	G	AB	R	H	2B	3B	HR	RBI	BB	SO	AVG	OBP	SLG	PRO+	BR	/A	RC	SB	CS	SBR	FA	FR	POS	TPR
1955	Bal-A	1	1	0	0	0	0	0	0	0	0	.000	.000	.000	-99	-0	-0	0	0	0	0	.000	-0	/O	-0.1

■ **LEFTY MARR** Marr, Charles W. b: 9/19/1862, Cincinnati, Ohio d: 1/11/12, New Britain, Conn. BL/TL, Deb: 10/03/1886

YEAR	TM/L	G	AB	R	H	2B	3B	HR	RBI	BB	SO	AVG	OBP	SLG	PRO+	BR	/A	RC	SB	CS	SBR	FA	FR	POS	TPR
1886	Cin-a	8	29	2	8	1	1	0		1		.276	.323	.379	118	1	1	4	1			.696	-1	/O	-0.1
1889	Col-a	139	546	110	167	26	**15**	1	75	87	32	.306	.407	.414	144	30	35	106	29			.856	12	3OS/1C	4.1
1890	Cin-N	130	527	91	158	17	12	1	73	46	29	.300	.363	.383	120	13	14	91	44			.930	-11	O3/S	0.2
1891	Cin-N	72	286	32	74	9	7	0	32	25	15	.259	.323	.339	94	-2	-2	37	16			.835	-10	O	-1.3
	Cin-a	14	57	9	11	1	0	0	4	7	4	.193	.281	.211	40	-4	-5	4	2			.923	-1	O	-0.5
Total	4	363	1445	244	418	54	35	2	184	166	80	.289	.368	.379	120	38	42	243	92			.853	-10	O3/S1C	2.4

■ **WILLIAM MARRIOTT** Marriott, William Earl b: 4/18/1893, Pratt, Kan. d: 8/11/69, Berkeley, Cal. BL/TR, 6', 170 lbs. Deb: 9/06/17

YEAR	TM/L	G	AB	R	H	2B	3B	HR	RBI	BB	SO	AVG	OBP	SLG	PRO+	BR	/A	RC	SB	CS	SBR	FA	FR	POS	TPR
1917	Chi-N	3	6	0	0	0	0	0	0	0	1	.000	.000	.000	-93	-1	-1	0	0			.667	-0	/O	-0.2
1920	Chi-N	14	43	7	12	4	2	0	5	6	5	.279	.367	.465	135	2	2	7	1	1	-0	.892	-4	2	-0.2
1921	Chi-N	30	38	3	12	1	1	0	7	4	1	.316	.381	.395	105	0	0	6	0	1	-1	.826	-1	/2S3O	-0.1
1925	Bos-N	103	370	37	99	9	1	1	40	28	26	.268	.322	.305	67	-21	-16	36	3	8	-4	.928	3	3/O	-1.0
1926	Bro-N	109	360	39	96	13	9	3	42	17	20	.267	.303	.378	84	-10	-9	40	12			.927	-8	*3	-1.0
1927	Bro-N	6	9	0	1	0	1	0	1	2	2	.111	.273	.333	61	-1	-1	1	0			.889	1	/3	0.0
Total	6	265	826	86	220	27	14	4	95	57	55	.266	.317	.347	78	-30	-25	90	16	10		.925	-9	3/2OS	-2.5

■ **ARMANDO MARSANS** Marsans, Armando b: 10/3/1887, Matanzas, Cuba d: 9/3/60, Havana, Cuba BR/TR, 5'10", 157 lbs. Deb: 7/04/11

YEAR	TM/L	G	AB	R	H	2B	3B	HR	RBI	BB	SO	AVG	OBP	SLG	PRO+	BR	/A	RC	SB	CS	SBR	FA	FR	POS	TPR
1911	Cin-N	58	138	17	36	2	2	0	11	15	11	.261	.346	.304	86	-3	-2	18	11			.968	-5	O/13	-0.9
1912	Cin-N	110	416	59	132	19	7	1	38	20	17	.317	.353	.404	110	3	4	70	35			.975	-3	O/1	-0.3
1913	Cin-N	118	435	49	129	7	6	0	38	17	25	.297	.327	.340	91	-6	-5	57	37			.963	-5	O1/3S	-1.5
1914	Cin-N	36	124	16	37	3	0	0	22	14	6	.298	.374	.323	105	2	1	19	13			.916	1	O	0.1
	StL-F	9	40	5	14	0	2	0	2	3	0	.350	.395	.450	133	2	2	9	4			.927	0	/2S	0.2
1915	StL-F	36	124	16	22	3	0	0	6	14	5	.177	.261	.202	35	-10	-10	9	5			.975	3	O	-1.0
1916	StL-A	151	528	51	134	12	1	1	60	57	41	.254	.333	.286	91	-7	-4	58	46	26	-2	.977	5	*O	-0.9
1917	StL-A	75	257	31	59	12	0	0	20	20	6	.230	.285	.276	74	-9	-8	23	11			.963	-4	O/32	-1.7
	NY-A	25	88	10	20	4	0	0	15	8	3	.227	.292	.273	72	-3	-3	9	6			.974	3	O	-0.1

YEAR	TM/L	G	AB	R	H	2B	3B	HR	RBI	BB	SO	AVG	OBP	SLG	PRO+	BR	/A	RC	SB	CS	SBR	FA	FR	POS	TPR
	Yr	100	345	41	79	16	0	0	35	28	9	.229	.287	.275	73	-12	-11	31	17			.967	-1	O/32	-1.8
1918	NY-A	37	123	13	29	5	1	0	9	5	3	.236	.266	.293	67	-5	-5	10	3			.943	-6	O	-1.5
Total	8	655	2273	267	612	67	19	2	221	173	117	.269	.325	.318	89	-35	-31	283	171	26		.967	-11	O/123S	-7.6

■ **FRED MARSH** Marsh, Fred Francis b: 1/5/24, Valley Falls, Kan. BR/TR, 5'10", 180 lbs. Deb: 4/19/49

YEAR	TM/L	G	AB	R	H	2B	3B	HR	RBI	BB	SO	AVG	OBP	SLG	PRO+	BR	/A	RC	SB	CS	SBR	FA	FR	POS	TPR
1949	Cle-A	1	0	0	0	0	0	0	0	0	0	—	—	—	—	0	0	0	0	0	0	.000	0	R	0.0
1951	StL-A	130	445	44	108	21	4	4	43	36	56	.243	.299	.335	69	-19	-20	45	4	4	-1	.928	3	*3/S2	-2.0
1952	StL-A	11	24	3	5	1	0	0	1	5	4	.208	.345	.250	65	-1	-1	2	0	1	-1	.963	2	/2S	0.1
	Was-A	9	24	1	1	0	0	0	1	1	4	.042	.080	.042	-68	-5	-5	0	0	0	0	1.000	-2	/2O	-0.8
	StL-A	76	223	25	64	8	1	2	26	22	29	.287	.351	.359	95	-0	-1	29	3	2	-0	.945	-15	S3	-1.4
	Yr	96	271	29	70	9	1	2	28	28	37	.258	.328	.321	79	-7	-7	29	3	3	-1	.945	-15	S32/O	-2.1
1953	Chi-A	67	95	22	19	1	0	2	2	13	26	.200	.303	.274	55	-6	-6	8	0	3	-2	.940	7	3S/12	-0.1
1954	Chi-A	62	98	21	30	5	2	0	4	9	16	.306	.364	.398	105	1	1	14	4	2	0	.975	18	3/S1O	1.9
1955	Bal-A	89	303	30	66	7	1	2	19	35	33	.218	.301	.267	58	-19	-17	25	1	2	-1	.983	-15	23S	-2.7
1956	Bal-A	20	24	2	3	0	0	0	0	4	3	.125	.250	.125	2	-3	-3	1	1	0	0	.929	0	/S32	-0.2
Total	7	465	1236	148	296	43	8	10	96	125	171	.239	.310	.311	69	-52	-53	125	13	14	-5	.928	-2	3S/210	-5.2

■ **TOM MARSH** Marsh, Thomas Owen b: 12/27/65, Toledo, Ohio BR/TR, 6'2", 180 lbs. Deb: 6/05/92

YEAR	TM/L	G	AB	R	H	2B	3B	HR	RBI	BB	SO	AVG	OBP	SLG	PRO+	BR	/A	RC	SB	CS	SBR	FA	FR	POS	TPR
1992	Phi-N	42	125	7	25	3	2	2	16	2	23	.200	.219	.304	47	-9	-9	8	0	1	-1	.971	-1	O	-1.2

■ **CHARLIE MARSHALL** Marshall, Charles Anthony (b: Charles Anthony Marczlewicz) b: 8/28/19, Wilmington, Del. BR/TR, 5'10.5", 178 lbs. Deb: 6/14/41

YEAR	TM/L	G	AB	R	H	2B	3B	HR	RBI	BB	SO	AVG	OBP	SLG	PRO+	BR	/A	RC	SB	CS	SBR	FA	FR	POS	TPR
1941	StL-N	1	0	0	0	0	0	0	0	0	0	—	—	—	—	0	0	0	0			1.000	-0	/C	0.0

■ **DAVE MARSHALL** Marshall, David Lewis b: 1/14/43, Artesia, Cal. BL/TR, 6'1", 190 lbs. Deb: 9/07/67

YEAR	TM/L	G	AB	R	H	2B	3B	HR	RBI	BB	SO	AVG	OBP	SLG	PRO+	BR	/A	RC	SB	CS	SBR	FA	FR	POS	TPR
1967	SF-N	1	0	0	0	0	0	0	0	0	0	—	—	—	—	0	0	0	0	0	0	.000	0	R	0.0
1968	SF-N	76	174	17	46	5	1	1	16	20	37	.264	.344	.322	101	1	1	21	2	1	0	.924	-4	O	-0.7
1969	SF-N	110	267	32	62	7	1	2	33	40	68	.232	.343	.288	80	-6	-5	28	1	8	-5	.956	-7	O	-2.2
1970	NY-N	92	189	21	46	10	1	6	29	17	43	.243	.306	.402	88	-4	-4	23	4	1	1	.973	0	O	-0.5
1971	NY-N	100	214	28	51	9	1	3	21	26	54	.238	.326	.332	88	-3	-3	24	3	1	0	.989	-2	O	-0.8
1972	NY-N	72	156	21	39	5	0	4	11	22	28	.250	.346	.359	103	1	1	19	3	3	-1	.972	-2	O	-0.4
1973	SD-N	39	49	4	14	5	0	0	4	8	9	.286	.397	.388	128	2	2	7	0	1	-1	1.000	-0	/O	0.1
Total	7	490	1049	123	258	41	4	16	114	133	239	.246	.336	.338	92	-10	-8	123	13	15	-5	.966	-16	O	-4.5

■ **ED MARSHALL** Marshall, Edward Herbert b: 6/4/06, New Albany, Miss. BR/TR, 5'11", 150 lbs. Deb: 9/28/29

YEAR	TM/L	G	AB	R	H	2B	3B	HR	RBI	BB	SO	AVG	OBP	SLG	PRO+	BR	/A	RC	SB	CS	SBR	FA	FR	POS	TPR
1929	NY-N	5	15	6	6	2	0	0	2	1	0	.400	.438	.533	140	1	1	3	0			1.000	-2	/2	-0.1
1930	NY-N	78	223	33	69	5	3	0	21	13	9	.309	.350	.359	73	-10	-9	27	0			.947	-3	S2/3	-0.6
1931	NY-N	68	194	15	39	6	2	0	10	8	8	.201	.233	.253	31	-19	-18	12	1			.956	4	2S/3	-1.1
1932	NY-N	68	226	18	56	8	1	0	28	6	11	.248	.270	.292	52	-15	-15	18	1			.922	-3	S	-1.2
Total	4	219	658	72	170	21	6	0	61	28	28	.258	.291	.309	56	-43	-41	61	2			.931	-4	S/23	-3.0

■ **JOE MARSHALL** Marshall, Joseph Hanley "Home Run Joe" b: 2/19/1876, Audubon, Minn. d: 9/11/31, Santa Monica, Cal BR/TR, Deb: 9/07/03

YEAR	TM/L	G	AB	R	H	2B	3B	HR	RBI	BB	SO	AVG	OBP	SLG	PRO+	BR	/A	RC	SB	CS	SBR	FA	FR	POS	TPR
1903	Pit-N	10	23	2	6	1	2	0	2	0		.261	.261	.478	106	0	-0	3	0			1.000	-4	/SO2	-0.4
1906	StL-N	33	95	2	15	1	2	0	7	6		.158	.216	.211	35	-7	-7	4	0			.903	-1	O/1	-1.0
Total	2	43	118	4	21	2	4	0	9	6		.178	.224	.263	51	-7	-7	7	0			.903	-5	/O1S2	-1.4

■ **KEITH MARSHALL** Marshall, Keith Alan b: 7/2/51, San Francisco, Cal. BR/TR, 6'2", 175 lbs. Deb: 4/07/73

YEAR	TM/L	G	AB	R	H	2B	3B	HR	RBI	BB	SO	AVG	OBP	SLG	PRO+	BR	/A	RC	SB	CS	SBR	FA	FR	POS	TPR
1973	KC-A	8	9	0	2	1	0	0	3	1	4	.222	.300	.333	73	-0	-0	1	0	0	0	1.000	-3	/O	-0.3

■ **MIKE MARSHALL** Marshall, Michael Allen b: 1/12/60, Libertyville, Ill. BR/TR, 6'5", 220 lbs. Deb: 9/07/81

YEAR	TM/L	G	AB	R	H	2B	3B	HR	RBI	BB	SO	AVG	OBP	SLG	PRO+	BR	/A	RC	SB	CS	SBR	FA	FR	POS	TPR
1981	*LA-N	14	25	2	5	3	0	0	1	1	4	.200	.259	.320	66	-1	-1	2	0	0	0	1.000	-1	/13O	-0.3
1982	LA-N	49	95	10	23	3	0	5	9	13	23	.242	.339	.432	117	2	2	15	2	0	1	1.000	-2	O1	0.0
1983	*LA-N	140	465	47	132	17	1	17	65	43	127	.284	.351	.434	117	10	10	72	7	3	0	.976	-12	*O1	-0.7
1984	LA-N☆	134	495	68	127	27	0	21	65	40	93	.257	.316	.438	111	5	6	66	4	3	-1	.981	4	*O1	0.5
1985	*LA-N	135	518	72	152	27	2	28	95	37	137	.293	.344	.515	141	23	25	87	3	10	-5	.991	-0	*O/1	1.6
1986	LA-N	103	330	47	77	11	0	19	53	27	90	.233	.299	.439	109	-1	2	42	4	4	-1	.963	-2	O	-0.4
1987	LA-N	104	402	45	118	19	0	16	72	18	79	.294	.330	.460	109	3	4	55	0	5	-3	.987	-6	*O	-0.8
1988	*LA-N	144	542	63	150	27	2	20	82	24	93	.277	.316	.445	120	9	11	71	4	1	1	.966	-1	O1	0.4
1989	LA-N	105	377	41	98	21	1	11	42	33	78	.260	.328	.408	111	4	5	49	2	5	-2	.978	-2	*O	-0.2
1990	NY-N	53	163	24	39	8	1	6	27	7	40	.239	.283	.411	89	-3	-3	18	0	2	-1	.993	-1	1/O	-0.8
	*Bos-A	30	112	10	32	6	1	4	12	4	26	.286	.316	.464	111	2	1	16	0	0	0	1.000	1	D/1O	0.1
1991	Bos-A	22	62	4	18	4	0	1	7	0	19	.290	.290	.403	86	-1	-1	6	0	0	0	.979	-3	/1OD	-0.4
	Cal-A	2	7	0	0	0	0	0	0	0	1	.000	.000	.000	-99	-2	-2	0	0	0	0	1.000	0	/1D	-0.2
	Yr	24	69	4	18	4	0	1	7	0	20	.261	.261	.362	67	-3	-3	6	0	0	0	.984	-2	/D1O	-0.6
Total	11	1035	3593	433	971	173	8	148	530	247	810	.270	.324	.446	115	50	59	499	26	33	-12	.978	-24	O1/D3	-1.2

■ **MAX MARSHALL** Marshall, Milo Max b: 9/18/13, Shenandoah, Iowa BL/TR, 6'1", 180 lbs. Deb: 5/10/42

YEAR	TM/L	G	AB	R	H	2B	3B	HR	RBI	BB	SO	AVG	OBP	SLG	PRO+	BR	/A	RC	SB	CS	SBR	FA	FR	POS	TPR
1942	Cin-N	131	530	49	135	17	6	7	43	34	38	.255	.301	.349	90	-8	-8	56	4			.976	-10	*O	-2.7
1943	Cin-N	132	508	55	120	11	8	4	39	34	52	.236	.287	.313	74	-18	-17	47	8			.981	-5	*O	-3.2
1944	Cin-N	66	229	36	56	13	2	4	23	21	10	.245	.308	.371	94	-3	-2	27	3			.965	2	O	-0.4
Total	3	329	1267	140	311	41	16	15	105	89	100	.245	.297	.339	84	-30	-28	131	15			.975	-14	O	-6.3

■ **JIM MARSHALL** Marshall, Rufus James b: 5/25/31, Danville, Ill. BL/TL, 6'1", 190 lbs. Deb: 4/15/58 MC

YEAR	TM/L	G	AB	R	H	2B	3B	HR	RBI	BB	SO	AVG	OBP	SLG	PRO+	BR	/A	RC	SB	CS	SBR	FA	FR	POS	TPR
1958	Bal-A	85	191	17	41	4	3	5	19	18	30	.215	.282	.346	76	-8	-6	18	3	2	-0	1.000	-5	1/O	-1.5
	Chi-N	26	81	12	22	2	0	5	11	12	13	.272	.372	.481	126	3	3	16	1	0	0	.992	-4	1O	-0.1
1959	Chi-N	108	294	39	74	10	1	11	40	33	39	.252	.327	.405	95	-3	-2	39	0	1	-1	.997	1	1/O	-0.7
1960	SF-N	75	118	19	28	2	2	2	13	17	24	.237	.333	.339	90	-2	-1	13	0	1	-1	.968	-3	1/O	-0.7
1961	SF-N	44	36	5	8	0	0	1	7	3	8	.222	.282	.306	58	-2	-2	3	0	0	0	1.000	0	/1O	-0.2
1962	NY-N	17	32	6	11	1	0	3	4	3	6	.344	.400	.656	175	3	3	9	0	0	0	1.000	0	/1O	0.3
	Pit-N	55	100	13	22	5	1	2	12	15	19	.220	.322	.350	80	-3	-3	12	1	0	0	1.000	1	1	-0.3
	Yr	72	132	19	33	6	1	5	16	18	25	.250	.340	.424	103	1	1	20	1	0	0	1.000	1	1/O	0.0
Total	5	410	852	111	206	24	7	29	106	101	139	.242	.323	.388	93	-11	-8	111	5	4	-1	.994	-10	1/O	-3.2

■ **WILLARD MARSHALL** Marshall, Willard Warren b: 2/8/21, Richmond, Va. BL/TR, 6'1", 205 lbs. Deb: 4/14/42

YEAR	TM/L	G	AB	R	H	2B	3B	HR	RBI	BB	SO	AVG	OBP	SLG	PRO+	BR	/A	RC	SB	CS	SBR	FA	FR	POS	TPR
1942	NY-N★	116	401	41	103	9	2	11	59	26	20	.257	.307	.372	98	-2	-2	46	1			.975	-0	*O	-0.9
1946	NY-N	131	510	63	144	18	3	13	48	33	29	.282	.327	.406	107	3	3	65	3			.978	2	*O	-0.2
1947	NY-N★	155	587	102	171	19	6	36	107	67	30	.291	.366	.528	134	27	27	113	3			.972	12	*O	3.0
1948	NY-N	143	537	72	146	21	8	14	86	64	34	.272	.350	.419	107	6	5	80	2			.983	4	*O	0.1
1949	NY-N★	141	499	81	153	19	3	12	70	78	20	.307	.401	.429	123	19	19	90	4			.974	6	*O	1.8
1950	Bos-N	105	298	38	70	10	2	5	40	36	5	.235	.319	.332	77	-12	-9	32	1			.958	1	O	-1.1
1951	Bos-N	136	469	65	132	24	7	11	62	48	18	.281	.351	.433	118	6	10	69	0	3	-2	**1.000**	-8	*O	-0.4
1952	Bos-N	21	66	5	15	4	1	2	11	4	4	.227	.271	.409	89	-2	-1	7	0	0	0	.938	1	O	-0.1
	Cin-N	107	397	52	106	23	1	8	46	37	21	.267	.333	.390	100	-0	-0	53	0	1	-1	.985	2	*O	-0.3
	Yr	128	463	57	121	27	2	10	57	41	25	.261	.324	.393	99	-2	-1	59	0	1	-1	.979	3	*O	-0.4
1953	Cin-N	122	357	51	95	14	6	17	62	41	28	.266	.342	.482	111	5	5	59	0	0	0	.995	6	O	0.8
1954	Chi-A	47	71	7	18	2	0	1	7	11	9	.254	.354	.324	84	-1	-1	9	0	0	0	.960	-7	O	-0.9

YEAR	TM/L	G	AB	R	H	2B	3B	HR	RBI	BB	SO	AVG	OBP	SLG	PRO+	BR	/A	RC	SB	CS	SBR	FA	FR	POS	TPR
1955	Chi-A	22	41	6	7	0	0	0	6	13	1	.171	.370	.171	48	-2	-2	4	0	0	0	.957	-1	O	-0.4
Total	11	1246	4233	583	1160	163	39	130	604	458	219	.274	.347	.423	109	47	52	625	14	4		.979	20	*O	1.4
■ BILL MARSHALL	Marshall, William Henry b: 2/14/11, Dorchester, Mass. d: 5/5/77, Sacramento, Cal. BR/TR, 5'8.5", 156 lbs. Deb: 6/20/31																								
1931	Bos-A	1	0	1	0	0	0	0	0	0	0	—	—	—	—	0	0	0	0	0	0	.000	0	R	0.0
1934	Cin-N	6	8	0	1	0	0	0	0	0	2	.125	.125	.125	-34	-1	-1	0	0			.875	1	/2	-0.1
Total	2	7	8	1	1	0	0	0	0	0	2	.125	.125	.125	-34	-1	-1	0	0	0		.889	1	/2	-0.1
■ DOC MARSHALL	Marshall, William Riddle b: 9/22/1875, Butler, Pa. d: 12/11/59, Clinton, Ill. BR/TR, 6', 185 lbs. Deb: 4/15/04																								
1904	Phi-N	8	20	1	2	0	0	0	1	0		.100	.100	.100	-39	-3	-3	0	0			.944	2	/C	-0.1
	NY-N	1	0	0	0	0	0	0	0	0		—	—	—	—	0	0	0	0			.000	0	/C	0.0
	Bos-N	13	43	3	9	0	1	0	2	2		.209	.244	.256	57	-2	-2	3	2			.955	1	C/O	0.0
	NY-N	10	17	3	6	1	0	0	2	1		.353	.389	.412	142	1	1	3	0			.917	2	/CO2	0.3
	Yr	32	80	7	17	1	1	0	5	3		.213	.241	.250	52	-5	-4	5	2			.945	5	C/O2	0.2
1906	NY-N	38	102	8	17	3	2	0	7	7		.167	.234	.235	46	-6	-7	8	7			1.000	-2	OC/1	-0.9
	StL-N	39	123	6	34	4	1	0	10	6		.276	.315	.325	104	-0	0	13	1			.961	9	C	1.4
	Yr	77	225	14	51	7	3	0	17	13		.227	.278	.284	76	-7	-6	21	8			.969	7	CO/1	0.5
1907	StL-N	84	268	19	54	8	2	2	18	12		.201	.244	.269	63	-13	-12	19	2			.952	6	C	0.2
1908	StL-N	6	14	0	1	0	0	0	1	0		.071	.071	.071	-57	-2	-2	0	0			1.000	2	/C	0.0
	Chi-N	12	20	4	6	0	1	0	3	0		.300	.300	.400	118	0	0	2	0			1.000	5	/CO	0.6
	Yr	18	34	4	7	0	1	0	4	0		.206	.206	.265	50	-2	-2	2	0			1.000	7	C/O	0.6
1909	Bro-N	50	149	7	30	7	1	0	10	6		.201	.232	.262	55	-9	-8	9	3			.968	-5	C/O	-1.0
Total	5	261	756	51	159	23	8	2	54	34		.210	.250	.270	64	-35	-33	58	15			.960	20	C/O12	0.5
■ DOC MARTEL	Martel, Leon Alphonse "Marty" b: 1/29/1883, Weymouth, Mass. d: 10/11/47, Washington, D.C. BR/TR, 6', 185 lbs. Deb: 7/06/09																								
1909	Phi-N	24	41	1	11	3	1	0	7	4		.268	.333	.390	123	1	1	5	0			.974	4	C	0.7
1910	Bos-N	10	31	0	4	0	0	0	1	2	3	.129	.182	.129	-9	-4	-4	1	0			.980	-0	1	-0.5
Total	2	34	72	1	15	3	1	0	8	6	3	.208	.269	.278	64	-3	-3	6	0			.927	4	/C1	0.2
■ AL MARTIN	Martin, Albert (a.k.a. Albert May In 1872) Deb: 5/07/1872																								
1872	Eck-n	4	18	2	5	0	0	0	2	0	0	.278	.278	.278	84	-1	-0	1						/2	0.0
1874	Atl-n	7	30	1	4	0	0	0		0		.133	.133	.133	-17	-4	-3	1						/2O	-0.3
1875	Atl-n	6	26	1	3	0	0	0		0		.115	.115	.115	-23	-3	-2	0						/O	-0.2
Total	3 n	17	74	4	12	0	0	0		0		.162	.162	.162	6	-7	-6	2						/2O	-0.5
■ ALBERT MARTIN	Martin, Albert Lee b: 11/24/67, West Covina, Cal. BL/TL, 6'2", 220 lbs. Deb: 7/28/92																								
1992	Pit-N	12	12	1	2	0	1	0	2	0	5	.167	.167	.333	39	-1	-1	1	0	0	0	1.000	-2	/O	-0.3
■ BILLY MARTIN	Martin, Alfred Manuel b: 5/16/28, Berkeley, Cal. d: 12/25/89, Johnson City, N.Y. BR/TR, 5'11.5", 165 lbs. Deb: 4/18/50 MC																								
1950	NY-A	34	36	10	9	1	0	1	8	3	3	.250	.308	.361	73	-2	-2	4	0	0	0	.976	-1	2/3	-0.2
1951	*NY-A	51	58	10	15	1	2	0	2	4	9	.259	.328	.345	85	-1	-1	5	0	1	-1	.988	16	2/S3O	1.4
1952	*NY-A	109	363	32	97	13	3	3	33	22	31	.267	.323	.344	91	-7	-5	40	3	6	-3	.984	18	*2	1.7
1953	*NY-A	149	587	72	151	24	6	15	75	43	56	.257	.314	.395	94	-9	-7	70	6	7	-2	.985	-1	*2S	-0.2
1955	*NY-A	20	70	8	21	2	0	1	9	7	9	.300	.364	.371	100	-0	0	9	1	2	-1	.977	1	2/S	0.2
1956	*NY-A★	121	458	76	121	24	5	9	49	30	56	.264	.314	.397	90	-10	-8	57	7	3	0	.980	-14	*23	-1.3
1957	NY-A	43	145	12	35	5	2	1	12	3	14	.241	.262	.324	60	-8	-8	11	2	1	0	.947	-3	23	-0.9
	KC-A	73	265	33	68	9	3	9	27	12	20	.257	.296	.415	91	-4	-4	32	7	1	2	.987	-20	23/S	-1.9
	Yr	116	410	45	103	14	5	10	39	15	34	.251	.284	.383	80	-12	-13	42	9	2	2	.973	-23	23/S	-2.8
1958	Det-A	131	498	56	127	19	1	7	42	16	62	.255	.282	.339	65	-21	-25	44	5	3	-0	.958	-18	S3	-3.7
1959	Cle-A	73	242	37	63	7	0	9	24	8	18	.260	.292	.401	92	-5	-4	27	0	2	-1	.997	-11	2/3	-1.1
1960	Cin-N	103	317	34	78	17	1	3	16	27	34	.246	.305	.334	74	-11	-11	30	0	1	-1	.975	-13	2	-1.8
1961	Mil-N	6	6	1	0	0	0	0	0	0	1	.000	.000	.000	-99	-2	-2	0	0	0	0	.000	0	H	-0.2
	Min-A	108	374	44	92	15	5	6	36	13	42	.246	.277	.361	65	-17	-20	35	3	2	-0	.963	-15	*2/S	-2.5
Total	11	1021	3419	425	877	137	28	64	333	188	355	.257	.301	.369	81	-98	-97	364	34	29	-7	.980	-61	2S/3O	-10.5
■ PHONNEY MARTIN	Martin, Alphonse Case b: 8/4/1845, New York, N.Y. d: 5/24/33, Hollis, N.Y. 5'7", 148 lbs. Deb: 4/26/1872																								
1872	Tro-n	25	120	27	34	3	1	0	14	0	1	.283	.283	.325	86	-2	-2	11						O/P	0.0
	Eck-n	18	79	12	14	0	0	0	9	1	2	.177	.188	.177	15	-8	-5	3						P/O	0.0
	Yr	43	199	39	48	3	1	0	23	1	3	.241	.245	.266	61	-10	-7	14						OP	0.0
1873	Mut-n	31	139	12	30	2	0	0	14	0	4	.216	.216	.230	32	-11	-11	7						O/P	-0.6
Total	2 n	74	338	51	78	5	1	0	37	1	7	.231	.233	.251	48	-21	-19	21						/OP	-0.6
■ BABE MARTIN	Martin, Boris Michael (b: Boris Michael Martinovich) b: 3/28/20, Seattle, Wash. BR/TR, 5'11.5", 194 lbs. Deb: 9/25/44																								
1944	StL-A	2	4	0	3	1	0	0	1	0	0	.750	.750	1.000	376	1	1	3	0	0	0	1.000	-0	/O	0.1
1945	StL-A	54	185	13	37	5	2	2	16	11	24	.200	.245	.281	50	-12	-13	12	0	1	-1	.992	6	O/1	-1.1
1946	StL-A	3	9	0	2	0	0	0	1	1	2	.222	.300	.222	45	-1	-1	1	0	0	0	1.000	1	/C	0.0
1948	Bos-A	4	4	0	2	0	0	0	0	0	1	.500	.500	.500	158	0	0	1	0	0	0	.000	0	/C	0.0
1949	Bos-A	2	2	0	0	0	0	0	0	0	0	.000	.000	.000	-93	-1	-1	0	0	0	0	.000	0	/C	-0.1
1953	StL-A	4	2	0	0	0	0	0	0	1	0	.000	.333	.000	-4	-0	-0	0	0	0	0	.000	0	/C	0.0
Total	6	69	206	13	44	6	2	2	18	13	27	.214	.260	.291	56	-11	-13	17	0	1	-1	.992	6	/O1C	-1.1
■ FRANK MARTIN	Martin, Frank b: 1877, Chicago, Ill. Deb: 6/30/1897																								
1897	Lou-N	2	8	1	2	0	0	0	0	0		.250	.250	.250	33	-1	-1	1	0			.813	0	/2	0.0
1898	Chi-N	1	4	0	0	0	0	0	0	0		.000	.000	.000	-99	-1	-1	0	0			1.000	0	/2	-0.1
1899	NY-N	17	54	5	14	2	0	0	1	2		.259	.298	.296	66	-3	-2	5	0			.824	2	3	0.0
Total	3	20	66	6	16	2	0	0	1	2		.242	.275	.273	52	-5	-4	5	0			.870	3	/32	-0.1
■ HERSH MARTIN	Martin, Hershel Ray b: 9/19/09, Birmingham, Ala. d: 11/17/80, Cuba, Mo. BB/TR, 6'2", 190 lbs. Deb: 4/23/37																								
1937	Phi-N	141	579	102	164	35	7	8	49	69	66	.283	.362	.409	101	8	2	92	11			.978	5	*O	0.2
1938	Phi-N☆	120	466	58	139	36	6	3	39	34	48	.298	.347	.421	113	6	8	67	8			.965	1	*O	0.5
1939	Phi-N	111	393	59	111	28	5	1	22	42	27	.282	.355	.387	102	0	2	56	4			.976	11	O	0.9
1940	Phi-N	33	83	10	21	6	1	0	5	9	9	.253	.326	.349	90	-1	-1	10	1			.979	-0	O	-0.2
1944	NY-A	85	328	49	99	12	4	9	47	34	26	.302	.371	.445	128	14	12	57	5	2	0	.964	3	O	1.2
1945	NY-A	117	408	53	109	18	6	7	53	65	31	.267	.368	.392	115	12	10	66	4	1	1	.984	3	*O	0.8
Total	6	607	2257	331	643	135	29	28	215	253	207	.285	.359	.408	109	38	32	350	33	3		.974	23	O	3.4
■ JERRY MARTIN	Martin, Jerry Lindsey b: 5/11/49, Columbia, S.C. BR/TR, 6'1", 195 lbs. Deb: 9/07/74 F																								
1974	Phi-N	13	14	2	3	1	0	0	1	1	5	.214	.267	.286	52	-1	-1	1	0	0	0	1.000	-1	O	-0.2
1975	Phi-N	57	113	15	24	7	1	2	11	11	16	.212	.288	.345	72	-4	-5	11	2	2	-1	.979	7	O	0.0
1976	*Phi-N	130	121	30	30	7	0	2	15	7	28	.248	.289	.355	80	-3	-4	11	3	2	-0	.975	3	*O/1	-0.2
1977	*Phi-N	116	215	34	56	16	3	6	28	18	42	.260	.329	.447	101	1	0	31	6	4	-1	.984	1	*O/1	-0.1
1978	*Phi-N	128	266	40	72	13	4	9	36	28	65	.271	.342	.451	119	7	6	42	9	5	-0	.987	4	*O	0.8
1979	Chi-N	150	534	74	145	34	3	19	73	38	85	.272	.323	.453	100	5	-1	74	2	4	-2	.981	-9	*O	-1.8
1980	Chi-N	141	494	57	112	22	2	23	73	38	107	.227	.285	.419	88	-6	-10	57	8	3	1	.978	-13	*O	-3.0
1981	SF-N	72	241	23	58	5	3	4	25	21	52	.241	.309	.336	85	-5	-5	24	6	2	1	.993	-6	O	-1.3

YEAR	TM/L	G	AB	R	H	2B	3B	HR	RBI	BB	SO	AVG	OBP	SLG	PRO+	BR	/A	RC	SB	CS	SBR	FA	FR	POS	TPR
1982	KC-A	147	519	52	138	22	1	15	65	38	138	.266	.318	.399	95	-4	-4	66	1	1	-0	.980	4	*O/D	-0.4
1983	KC-A	13	44	4	14	2	0	2	13	1	7	.318	.333	.500	125	1	1	8	1	0	0	.957	-2	O	0.0
1984	NY-N	51	91	6	14	1	0	3	5	6	29	.154	.206	.264	32	-9	-8	4	0	0	0	1.000	-1	O/1	-1.1
Total	11	1018	2652	337	666	130	17	85	345	207	574	.251	.309	.409	93	-17	-29	329	38	23	-2	.982	-12	O/1D	-7.3

■ JACK MARTIN

Martin, John Christopher b: 4/19/1887, Plainfield, N.J. d: 7/4/80, Plainfield, N.J. BR/TR, 5'9", 159 lbs. Deb: 4/25/12

1912	NY-A	71	231	30	52	6	1	0	17	37		.225	.347	.260	70	-6	-8	26	14			.898	-4	S/32	-0.5
1914	Bos-N	33	85	10	18	2	0	0	5	6	7	.212	.264	.235	49	-5	-5	5	0			.949	0	3/12	-0.5
	Phi-N	83	292	26	74	5	3	0	21	27	29	.253	.319	.291	77	-6	-8	29	6			.930	-3	S	-0.4
	Yr	116	377	36	92	7	3	0	26	33	36	.244	.307	.279	71	-11	-13	34	6			.930	-3	S3/12	-0.9
Total	2	187	608	66	144	13	4	0	43	70	36	.237	.323	.271	71	-17	-21	61	20			.915	-6	S/321	-1.4

■ PEPPER MARTIN

Martin, John Leonard Roosevelt "The Wild Horse Of The Osage"
b: 2/29/04, Temple, Okla. d: 3/5/65, McAlester, Okla. BR/TR, 5'8", 170 lbs. Deb: 4/16/28 C

1928	*StL-N	39	13	11	4	0	0	0	0	1	2	.308	.400	.308	86	-0	-0	2	2			1.000	-2	/O	-0.1
1930	StL-N	6	1	5	0	0	0	0	0	0	0	.000	.000	.000	-97	-0	-0	0	0			.000	0	H	0.0
1931	*StL-N	123	413	68	124	32	8	7	75	30	40	.300	.351	.467	114	9	7	69	16			.967	0	*O	0.1
1932	StL-N	85	323	47	77	19	6	4	34	30	31	.238	.305	.372	79	-9	-10	38	9			.976	-1	O3	-1.4
1933	StL-N★	145	599	**122**	189	36	12	8	57	67	46	.316	.387	.456	133	32	29	111	**26**			.943	-3	*3	3.7
1934	*StL-N★	110	454	74	131	25	11	5	49	32	41	.289	.337	.425	96	1	-3	69	**23**			.936	-5	*3/P	-0.3
1935	StL-N★	135	539	121	161	41	6	9	54	33	58	.299	.341	.447	106	7	4	84	20			.904	-14	*3O	-0.7
1936	StL-N	143	572	121	177	36	11	11	76	58	66	.309	.373	.469	126	20	20	103	**23**			.976	-10	*O3/P	0.5
1937	StL-N☆	98	339	60	103	27	8	5	38	33	50	.304	.366	.475	124	12	11	62	9			.973	11	O/3	1.9
1938	StL-N	91	269	34	79	18	2	2	38	18	34	.294	.340	.398	97	1	-1	38	4			.986	-3	O/3	-0.6
1939	StL-N	88	281	48	86	17	7	3	37	30	35	.306	.375	.448	113	8	6	47	6			.975	-4	O3	0.0
1940	StL-N	86	228	28	72	15	4	3	39	22	24	.316	.378	.456	122	9	8	41	6			.974	-3	O/3	0.2
1944	StL-N	40	86	15	24	4	0	2	4	15	11	.279	.386	.395	118	3	3	14	2			.980	-4	O	-0.2
Total	13	1189	4117	754	1227	270	75	59	501	369	438	.298	.358	.443	112	93	73	679	146			.973	-36	O3/P	3.1

■ J. C. MARTIN

Martin, Joseph Clifton b: 12/13/36, Axton, Va. BL/TR, 6'2", 200 lbs. Deb: 9/10/59 C

1959	Chi-A	3	4	0	1	0	0	0	1	0	1	.250	.250	.250	38	-0	-0	0	0	0	0	.667	-0	/3	0.0
1960	Chi-A	7	20	0	2	1	0	0	2	0	6	.100	.100	.150	-34	-4	-4	0	0	0	0	1.000	-0	/31	-0.4
1961	Chi-A	110	274	26	63	8	3	5	32	21	31	.230	.290	.336	68	-13	-13	27	1	2	-1	.988	9	13	-0.7
1962	Chi-A	18	26	0	2	0	0	0	2	0	3	.077	.077	.077	-59	-6	-6	0	0	0	0	1.000	-1	/C13	-0.6
1963	Chi-A	105	259	25	53	11	1	5	28	26	35	.205	.280	.313	67	-12	-11	24	0	0	0	.983	14	C/13	0.6
1964	Chi-A	122	294	23	58	10	1	4	22	16	30	.197	.244	.279	46	-22	-21	20	0	0	0	.986	8	*C	-0.9
1965	Chi-A	119	230	21	60	12	0	2	21	24	29	.261	.336	.339	98	-2	-0	28	2	1	0	.982	1	*C/13	0.4
1966	Chi-A	67	157	13	40	5	3	2	20	14	24	.255	.320	.363	103	-1	0	18	0	0	0	.982	-1	C	0.3
1967	Chi-A	101	252	22	59	12	1	4	22	30	41	.234	.318	.337	97	-2	-0	27	4	4	-1	.987	3	C/1	0.6
1968	NY-N	78	244	20	55	9	2	3	31	21	31	.225	.300	.316	84	-4	-4	24	0	0	0	.994	-3	C1	-0.5
1969	*NY-N	66	177	12	37	5	1	4	21	12	32	.209	.259	.316	59	-10	-10	14	0	0	0	.996	-6	C/1	-1.5
1970	Chi-N	40	77	11	12	1	0	1	4	20	11	.156	.337	.208	44	-5	-6	6	0	0	0	.983	2	C/1	-0.3
1971	Chi-N	47	125	13	33	5	0	2	17	12	16	.264	.338	.352	84	-0	-3	15	1	1	-0	.996	2	C/O	0.1
1972	Chi-N	25	50	3	12	3	0	0	7	5	9	.240	.309	.300	67	-2	-2	4	1	0	0	.970	-3	C	-0.5
Total	14	908	2189	189	487	82	12	32	230	201	299	.222	.293	.315	72	-82	-80	207	9	8	-2	.987	26	C/13O	-3.4

■ MIKE MARTIN

Martin, Joseph Michael b: 12/3/58, Portland, Ore. BL/TR, 6'2", 193 lbs. Deb: 8/15/86

1986	Chi-N	8	13	1	1	1	0	0	0	2	4	.077	.200	.154	-1	-2	-2	0	0	0	0	1.000	0	/C	-0.2

■ JOE MARTIN

Martin, Joseph Samuel "Silent Joe" b: 1/1/1876, Hollidaysburg, Pa. d: 5/25/64, Altoona, Pa. BL/TR, 5'9.5", 155 lbs. Deb: 4/28/03

1903	Was-A	35	119	11	27	4	5	0	7	5		.227	.258	.345	78	-3	-3	12	2			.892	-4	23/O	-0.8
	StL-A	44	173	18	37	6	4	0	7	6		.214	.249	.295	64	-8	-7	14	0			.983	-3	O/23	-1.3
	Yr	79	292	29	64	10	9	0	14	11		.219	.252	.315	70	-11	-11	26	2			.959	-7	O23	-2.1

■ STU MARTIN

Martin, Stuart McGuire b: 11/17/13, Rich Square, N.C. BL/TR, 6', 155 lbs. Deb: 4/14/36

1936	StL-N☆	92	332	63	99	21	4	6	41	29	27	.298	.356	.440	114	6	6	53	17			.949	-13	2/S	-0.1
1937	StL-N	90	223	34	58	6	1	1	17	32	18	.260	.353	.309	80	-5	-5	26	3			.946	-6	2/1S	-0.9
1938	StL-N	114	417	54	116	26	2	1	27	30	28	.278	.328	.357	84	-7	-10	52	4			.967	-10	2	-1.3
1939	StL-N	120	425	60	114	26	7	3	30	33	40	.268	.325	.384	85	-7	-10	54	4			**.977**	-3	*2/1	-0.7
1940	StL-N	112	369	45	88	12	6	4	32	33	35	.238	.301	.336	71	-12	-15	39	4			.972	-25	32	-3.9
1941	Pit-N	88	233	37	71	13	2	0	19	10	17	.305	.341	.378	103	0	1	29	2			.972	-4	2/31	0.0
1942	Pit-N	42	120	16	27	4	2	1	12	8	10	.225	.273	.317	71	-4	-5	11	1			.979	-11	2/1S	-1.5
1943	Chi-N	64	118	13	26	4	0	0	5	15	10	.220	.308	.254	64	-5	-5	10	1			.980	2	2/31	-0.2
Total	8	722	2237	322	599	112	24	16	183	190	185	.268	.327	.361	86	-33	-43	273	36			.966	-70	2/31S	-8.6

■ GENE MARTIN

Martin, Thomas Eugene b: 1/12/47, Americus, Ga. BL/TR, 6'0.5", 190 lbs. Deb: 7/28/68

1968	Was-A	9	11	1	4	1	0	1	1	0	1	.364	.364	.727	232	1	2	2	0	0	0	.000	-1	/O	0.1

■ BILLY MARTIN

Martin, William Lloyd b: 2/13/1894, Washington, D.C. d: 9/14/49, Arlington, Va. BR/TR, 5'8.5", 170 lbs. Deb: 10/06/14

1914	Bos-N	1	3	0	0	0	0	0	0	0	0	.000	.000	.000	-99	-1	-1	0	0			.500	-1	/S	-0.2

■ JOE MARTIN

Martin, William Joseph "Smokey Joe" b: 8/28/11, Seymour, Mo. d: 9/28/60, Buffalo, N.Y. BR/TR, 5'11.5", 181 lbs. Deb: 5/05/36

1936	NY-N	7	15	0	4	1	0	0	2	0	4	.267	.313	.333	75	-1	-1	1	0			1.000	1	/3	0.0
1938	Chi-A	1	0	0	0	0	0	0	0	0	0	—	—	—	—	0	0	0	0	0	0	.000	0	R	0.0
Total	2	8	15	0	4	1	0	0	2	0	4	.267	.313	.333	75	-1	-1	1	0	0		.895	1	/3	0.0

■ CARLOS MARTINEZ

Martinez, Carlos Alberto Escobar (b: Carlos Alberto Escobar (Martinez))
b: 8/11/64, LaGuaira, Venez. BR/TR, 6'5", 175 lbs. Deb: 9/02/88

1988	Chi-A	17	55	5	9	1	0	0	0	0	12	.164	.164	.182	-3	-7	-7	2	1	0	0	.909	3	3/D	-0.5
1989	Chi-A	109	350	44	105	22	0	5	32	21	57	.300	.341	.406	112	4	5	45	4	1	1	.912	-6	31O/D	-0.2
1990	Chi-A	92	272	18	61	6	5	4	24	10	40	.224	.252	.327	62	-15	-14	19	0	4	-2	.988	-5	1/OD	-2.8
1991	Cle-A	72	257	22	73	14	0	5	30	10	43	.284	.316	.397	95	-2	-2	29	3	2	-0	.968	-4	D1	-0.9
1992	Cle-A	69	228	23	60	9	1	5	35	7	21	.263	.288	.377	84	-5	-6	23	1	2	-1	.996	-5	13/D	-1.4
Total	5	359	1162	112	308	52	6	19	121	48	173	.265	.297	.369	86	-26	-24	118	9	9	-3	.987	-18	13/DO	-5.8

■ CARMELO MARTINEZ

Martinez, Carmelo (Salgado) b: 7/28/60, Dorado, P.R. BR/TR, 6'2", 220 lbs. Deb: 8/22/83

1983	Chi-N	29	89	8	23	3	0	6	16	4	19	.258	.290	.494	108	1	1	12	0	0	0	.992	-0	1/3O	-0.1
1984	*SD-N	149	488	64	122	28	2	13	66	68	82	.250	.346	.395	108	6	6	70	1	3	-2	.976	21	*O/1	2.2
1985	SD-N	150	514	64	130	28	1	21	72	87	82	.253	.364	.434	124	17	18	84	0	4	-2	.978	13	*O/1	2.5
1986	SD-N	113	244	28	58	10	0	9	25	35	46	.238	.336	.389	101	0	1	31	1	1	-0	.978	-0	O1/3	-0.2
1987	SD-N	139	447	59	122	21	2	15	70	70	82	.273	.375	.430	117	10	12	73	5	5	-2	.968	-3	O1	0.1
1988	SD-N	121	365	48	86	12	0	18	65	35	57	.236	.303	.416	106	1	2	44	1	1	-0	.993	10	O1	0.7
1989	SD-N	111	267	23	59	12	2	6	39	32	54	.221	.304	.348	86	-5	-5	27	0	0	0	.982	1	O1	-0.7
1990	Phi-N	71	198	23	48	8	0	8	31	29	37	.242	.339	.404	104	1	1	28	2	1	0	.994	-2	1O	-0.4
	*Pit-N	12	19	3	4	1	0	2	4	1	5	.211	.250	.579	126	0	0	3	0	0	0	1.000	0	/1O	0.1
	Yr	83	217	26	52	9	0	10	35	30	42	.240	.332	.419	106	2	2	32	2	1	0	.995	-2	1O	-0.3

YEAR	TM/L	G	AB	R	H	2B	3B	HR	RBI	BB	SO	AVG	OBP	SLG	PRO+	BR	/A	RC	SB	CS	SBR	FA	FR	POS	TPR
1991	Pit-N	11	16	1	4	0	0	0	0	1	2	.250	.294	.250	55	-1	-1	1	0	0	0	.945	-1	/1	-0.2
	KC-A	44	121	17	25	6	0	4	17	27	25	.207	.351	.355	96	0	0	16	0	1	-1	.991	4	1/D	0.1
	Cin-N	53	138	12	32	5	0	6	19	15	37	.232	.307	.399	93	-1	-1	18	0	0	0	.985	0	1O	-0.3
Total	9	1003	2906	350	713	134	7	108	424	404	528	.245	.340	.408	108	30	34	407	10	16	-7	.980	42	O1/3D	3.8

■ TINO MARTINEZ

Martinez, Constantino b: 12/7/67, Tampa, Fla. BL/TR, 6'2", 205 lbs. Deb: 8/20/90

YEAR	TM/L	G	AB	R	H	2B	3B	HR	RBI	BB	SO	AVG	OBP	SLG	PRO+	BR	/A	RC	SB	CS	SBR	FA	FR	POS	TPR
1990	Sea-A	24	68	4	15	4	0	0	5	9	9	.221	.312	.279	66	-3	-3	7	0	0	0	1.000	0	1	-0.4
1991	Sea-A	36	112	11	23	2	0	4	9	11	24	.205	.276	.330	67	-5	-5	10	0	0	0	.993	2	1/D	-0.5
1992	Sea-A	136	460	53	118	19	2	16	66	42	77	.257	.321	.411	103	1	1	54	2	1	0	.995	1	1D	-0.3
Total	3	196	640	68	156	25	2	20	80	62	110	.244	.313	.383	93	-7	-7	72	2	1	0	.995	3	1/D	-1.2

■ DAVE MARTINEZ

Martinez, David b: 9/26/64, New York, N.Y. BL/TL, 5'10", 150 lbs. Deb: 6/15/86

YEAR	TM/L	G	AB	R	H	2B	3B	HR	RBI	BB	SO	AVG	OBP	SLG	PRO+	BR	/A	RC	SB	CS	SBR	FA	FR	POS	TPR
1986	Chi-N	53	108	13	15	1	1	1	7	6	22	.139	.191	.194	6	-14	-15	4	4	2	0	.988	-4	O	-2.0
1987	Chi-N	142	459	70	134	18	8	8	36	57	96	.292	.373	.418	105	7	5	75	16	8	0	.980	1	*O	0.2
1988	Chi-N	75	256	27	65	10	1	4	34	21	46	.254	.315	.348	86	-3	-4	29	7	3	0	.970	-1	O	-0.8
	Mon-N	63	191	24	49	3	5	2	12	17	48	.257	.317	.356	89	-2	-3	23	16	6	1	.992	-5	O	-0.8
	Yr	138	447	51	114	13	6	6	46	38	94	.255	.316	.351	87	-5	-7	52	23	9	2	.979	-5	*O	-1.6
1989	Mon-N	126	361	41	99	16	7	3	27	27	57	.274	.325	.382	100	0	-0	49	23	4	5	.967	-18	*O	-1.8
1990	Mon-N	118	391	60	109	13	5	11	39	24	48	.279	.322	.422	107	1	2	49	13	11	-3	.989	-3	*O/P	-0.5
1991	Mon-N	124	396	47	117	18	5	7	42	20	54	.295	.334	.419	112	5	5	56	16	7	1	.982	-1	*O	0.4
1992	Cin-N	135	393	47	100	20	5	3	31	42	54	.254	.326	.354	88	-3	-6	46	12	8	-1	.991	-4	*O1	-1.5
Total	7	836	2555	329	688	99	37	39	228	214	425	.269	.328	.383	96	-9	-15	332	107	49	3	.982	-33	O/1P	-6.8

■ DOMINGO MARTINEZ

Martinez, Domingo Emelio b: 8/4/67, Santo Domingo, D.R. BR/TR, 6'2", 215 lbs. Deb: 9/11/92

YEAR	TM/L	G	AB	R	H	2B	3B	HR	RBI	BB	SO	AVG	OBP	SLG	PRO+	BR	/A	RC	SB	CS	SBR	FA	FR	POS	TPR
1992	Tor-A	7	8	2	5	0	0	1	3	0	1	.625	.625	1.000	333	2	2	5	0	0	0	1.000	-1	/1	0.2

■ EDGAR MARTINEZ

Martinez, Edgar b: 1/2/63, New York, N.Y. BR/TR, 6' ", 175 lbs. Deb: 9/12/87

YEAR	TM/L	G	AB	R	H	2B	3B	HR	RBI	BB	SO	AVG	OBP	SLG	PRO+	BR	/A	RC	SB	CS	SBR	FA	FR	POS	TPR
1987	Sea-A	13	43	6	16	5	2	0	5	2	5	.372	.413	.581	152	4	3	11	0	0	0	1.000	1	3/D	0.4
1988	Sea-A	14	32	0	9	4	0	0	5	4	7	.281	.361	.406	110	1	1	5	0	0	0	.929	-4	3	-0.4
1989	Sea-A	65	171	20	41	5	0	2	20	17	26	.240	.319	.304	74	-5	-6	18	2	1	0	.949	-6	3	-1.2
1990	Sea-A	144	487	71	147	27	2	11	49	74	62	.302	.399	.433	131	24	23	86	1	4	-2	.928	-1	*3/D	2.1
1991	Sea-A	150	544	98	167	35	1	14	52	84	72	.307	.407	.452	137	31	31	100	0	3	-2	.962	3	*3/D	3.2
1992	Sea-A★	135	528	100	181	**46**	3	18	73	54	61	**.343**	.408	.544	163	45	44	116	14	4	2	.943	1	*3D/1	**4.8**
Total	6	521	1805	295	561	122	8	45	204	235	233	.311	.396	.462	137	100	97	335	17	12	-2	.947	-7	3/D1	8.9

■ TONY MARTINEZ

Martinez, Gabriel Antonio (Diaz) b: 3/18/40, Perico, Cuba d: 8/24/91, Miami, Fla. BR/TR, 5'10", 165 lbs. Deb: 4/09/63

YEAR	TM/L	G	AB	R	H	2B	3B	HR	RBI	BB	SO	AVG	OBP	SLG	PRO+	BR	/A	RC	SB	CS	SBR	FA	FR	POS	TPR
1963	Cle-A	43	141	10	22	4	0	0	8	5	18	.156	.185	.184	4	-18	-18	4	1	1	-0	.961	-6	S	-2.4
1964	Cle-A	9	14	1	3	1	0	0	2	0	2	.214	.214	.286	38	-1	-1	0	0	1	-1	1.000	4	/2S	0.2
1965	Cle-A	4	3	0	0	0	0	0	0	0	0	.000	.000	.000	-99	-1	-1	0	0	0	0	.000	0	H	-0.1
1966	Cle-A	17	17	2	5	0	0	0	0	1	6	.294	.333	.294	82	-0	-0	2	1	1	-0	.833	1	/S2	0.1
Total	4	73	175	13	30	5	0	0	10	6	26	.171	.199	.200	13	-20	-20	6	2	3	-1	.958	-1	/S2	-2.2

■ BUCK MARTINEZ

Martinez, John Albert b: 11/7/48, Redding, Cal. BR/TR, 5'10", 190 lbs. Deb: 6/18/69

YEAR	TM/L	G	AB	R	H	2B	3B	HR	RBI	BB	SO	AVG	OBP	SLG	PRO+	BR	/A	RC	SB	CS	SBR	FA	FR	POS	TPR
1969	KC-A	72	205	14	47	6	1	4	23	8	25	.229	.258	.327	62	-11	-11	16	0	0	0	.972	-1	C/O	-1.0
1970	KC-A	6	9	1	1	0	0	0	0	2	1	.111	.273	.111	10	-1	-1	0	0	0	0	.958	2	/C	0.1
1971	KC-A	22	46	3	7	2	0	0	1	5	9	.152	.235	.196	23	-5	-5	2	0	1	-1	.968	2	C	-0.3
1973	KC-A	14	32	2	8	1	0	1	6	4	5	.250	.333	.375	92	-0	-0	4	0	0	0	.966	-1	C	-0.1
1974	KC-A	43	107	10	23	3	1	1	8	14	19	.215	.317	.290	71	-3	-4	11	0	1	-1	.977	1	C	-0.2
1975	KC-A	80	226	15	51	9	2	3	23	21	28	.226	.294	.323	72	-8	-8	22	1	0	0	.980	-0	C	-0.6
1976	*KC-A	95	267	24	61	13	3	5	34	16	45	.228	.272	.356	82	-7	-7	27	0	0	0	.991	5	C	0.1
1977	KC-A	29	80	3	18	4	0	1	9	3	12	.225	.253	.313	53	-5	-5	6	0	1	-1	.993	3	C	-0.3
1978	Mil-A	89	256	26	56	10	1	1	20	14	42	.219	.259	.277	51	-17	-17	19	1	1	-0	.978	-3	C	-1.9
1979	Mil-A	69	196	17	53	8	0	4	26	8	25	.270	.299	.372	80	-6	-6	21	0	1	-1	.967	-2	C/P	-0.6
1980	Mil-A	76	219	16	49	9	0	3	17	12	33	.224	.267	.306	58	-13	-12	18	1	0	0	.985	11	C	0.1
1981	Tor-A	45	128	13	29	8	1	4	21	11	16	.227	.293	.398	92	-1	-2	14	1	0	0	.991	2	C	0.2
1982	Tor-A	96	260	26	63	17	0	10	37	24	34	.242	.306	.423	90	-1	-4	31	1	1	-0	.988	6	C	0.4
1983	Tor-A	88	221	27	56	14	0	10	33	29	39	.253	.340	.452	109	5	3	33	0	1	-1	.989	-3	C	0.3
1984	Tor-A	102	232	24	51	13	1	5	37	29	49	.220	.312	.349	80	-5	-6	27	0	3	-2	.995	-4	C/D	-0.9
1985	Tor-A	42	99	11	16	3	0	4	14	10	12	.162	.245	.313	50	-7	-7	8	0	0	0	.988	4	C	-0.2
1986	Tor-A	81	160	13	29	8	0	2	12	20	25	.181	.272	.269	47	-11	-12	12	0	0	0	.994	-1	C/D	-1.0
Total	17	1049	2743	245	618	128	10	58	321	230	419	.225	.287	.343	73	-96	-105	272	5	10	-5	.984	19	*C/DPO	-5.9

■ JOSE MARTINEZ

Martinez, Jose (Azcuiz) b: 7/26/41, Cardenas, Cuba BR/TR, 5'10", 190 lbs. Deb: 6/18/69 C

YEAR	TM/L	G	AB	R	H	2B	3B	HR	RBI	BB	SO	AVG	OBP	SLG	PRO+	BR	/A	RC	SB	CS	SBR	FA	FR	POS	TPR
1969	Pit-N	77	168	20	45	6	0	1	16	9	32	.268	.309	.321	78	-5	-5	15	1	3	-2	.975	10	2S/3O	0.7
1970	Pit-N	19	20	1	1	0	0	0	0	1	5	.050	.095	.050	-61	-5	-4	0	0	0	0	1.000	3	/32S	-0.1
Total	2	96	188	21	46	6	0	1	16	10	37	.245	.286	.293	63	-10	-9	16	1	3	-2	.966	13	/2S3O	0.6

■ MARTY MARTINEZ

Martinez, Orlando (Oliva) b: 8/23/41, Havana, Cuba BB/TR, 6'1", 175 lbs. Deb: 5/02/62 MC

YEAR	TM/L	G	AB	R	H	2B	3B	HR	RBI	BB	SO	AVG	OBP	SLG	PRO+	BR	/A	RC	SB	CS	SBR	FA	FR	POS	TPR
1962	Min-A	37	18	13	3	0	1	0	3	3	4	.167	.286	.278	51	-1	-1	2	0	0	0	.920	13	S/3	1.1
1967	Atl-N	44	73	14	21	2	1	0	5	11	11	.288	.388	.342	112	2	2	10	0	1	-1	.920	4	S/2C31	0.8
1968	Atl-N	113	356	34	82	5	3	0	12	29	28	.230	.292	.261	67	-14	-14	27	6	6	-2	.955	-5	S32C	-1.6
1969	Hou-N	78	198	14	61	5	4	0	15	10	21	.308	.341	.374	102	-0	0	24	0	0	0	1.000	-8	OS3/CP2	-0.7
1970	Hou-N	75	150	12	33	3	0	0	12	9	22	.220	.264	.240	38	-13	-13	9	0	0	0	.990	-6	S3/C2	-1.5
1971	Hou-N	32	62	4	16	3	1	0	4	3	6	.258	.292	.339	80	-2	-2	5	1	0	0	.968	1	/2S13	0.0
1972	StL-N	9	7	0	3	0	0	0	2	0	1	.429	.429	.429	146	0	0	1	0	0	0	1.000	0	/S23	0.1
	Oak-A	22	40	3	5	0	0	0	1	3	6	.125	.186	.125	-7	-5	-5	1	0	0	0	.944	3	2/S3	-0.1
	Tex-A	26	41	3	6	1	1	0	3	2	8	.146	.186	.220	21	-4	-4	1	0	1	-1	.944	-2	/S32	-0.6
	Yr	48	81	6	11	1	1	0	4	5	14	.136	.186	.173	8	-9	-9	2	0	1	-1	.946	2	2S/3	-0.7
Total	7	436	945	97	230	19	11	0	57	70	107	.243	.298	.287	70	-37	-36	82	7	8	-3	.950	1	S/32CO1P	-2.5

■ CHITO MARTINEZ

Martinez, Reyenaldo Ignacio b: 12/19/65, Belize City, British Honduras (Now Belize) BL/TL, 5'10", 180 lbs. Deb: 7/05/91

YEAR	TM/L	G	AB	R	H	2B	3B	HR	RBI	BB	SO	AVG	OBP	SLG	PRO+	BR	/A	RC	SB	CS	SBR	FA	FR	POS	TPR
1991	Bal-A	67	216	32	58	12	1	13	33	11	51	.269	.304	.514	127	5	6	33	1	1	-0	.982	2	O/1D	0.7
1992	Bal-A	83	198	26	53	10	1	5	25	31	47	.268	.372	.404	118	6	6	29	0	1	-1	.973	1	O/D	0.5
Total	2	150	414	58	111	22	2	18	58	42	98	.268	.338	.461	123	11	12	62	1	2	-1	.978	4	O/D1	1.2

■ HECTOR MARTINEZ

Martinez, Rodolfo Hector (Santos) b: 5/11/39, Las Villas, Cuba BR/TR, 5'10", 160 lbs. Deb: 9/30/62

YEAR	TM/L	G	AB	R	H	2B	3B	HR	RBI	BB	SO	AVG	OBP	SLG	PRO+	BR	/A	RC	SB	CS	SBR	FA	FR	POS	TPR
1962	KC-A	1	1	0	0	0	0	0	0	0	1	.000	.000	.000	-97	-0	-0	0	0	0	0	.000	0	H	0.0
1963	KC-A	6	14	2	4	0	0	1	3	1	3	.286	.375	.500	137	1	1	2	0	1	-1	1.000	0	/O	0.0
Total	2	7	15	2	4	0	0	1	3	1	4	.267	.353	.467	122	1	0	2	0	1	-1	.931	0	/O	0.0

■ TED MARTINEZ

Martinez, Teodoro Noel (Encarnacion) b: 12/10/47, Central Barahona, D.R. BR/TR, 6', 165 lbs. Deb: 7/18/70

YEAR	TM/L	G	AB	R	H	2B	3B	HR	RBI	BB	SO	AVG	OBP	SLG	PRO+	BR	/A	RC	SB	CS	SBR	FA	FR	POS	TPR
1970	NY-N	4	16	0	1	0	0	0	0	0	3	.063	.063	.063	-66	-4	-4	0	0	0	0	1.000	1	/2S	-0.3
1971	NY-N	38	125	16	36	5	2	1	10	4	22	.288	.326	.384	102	-0	0	17	6	0	2	.976	-7	S2/3O	-0.2
1972	NY-N	103	330	22	74	5	5	1	19	12	49	.224	.254	.279	52	-21	-20	21	7	4	-0	.994	1	2SO/3	-1.5
1973	*NY-N	92	263	34	67	11	0	1	14	13	38	.255	.295	.308	68	-12	-11	22	3	5	-2	.941	-2	SO3/2	-1.2

YEAR	TM/L	G	AB	R	H	2B	3B	HR	RBI	BB	SO	AVG	OBP	SLG	PRO+	BR	/A	RC	SB	CS	SBR	FA	FR	POS	TPR
1974	NY-N	116	334	32	73	15	7	2	43	14	40	.219	.250	.323	61	-19	-19	23	3	2	-0	.952	15	S32O	0.4
1975	StL-N	16	21	1	4	2	0	0	2	0	2	.190	.190	.286	30	-2	-2	1	0	0	0	1.000	0	/O2S3	-0.2
	*Oak-A	86	87	7	15	0	0	0	3	2	9	.172	.200	.172	6	-11	-10	3	1	1	-0	.955	4	S23	-0.5
1977	LA-N	67	137	21	41	6	1	1	10	2	20	.299	.309	.380	84	-3	-3	15	3	4	-2	.992	14	2S3	1.1
1978	LA-N	54	55	13	14	1	0	1	5	4	14	.255	.317	.327	80	-1	-1	6	3	2	-0	.912	10	S32	1.0
1979	LA-N	81	112	19	30	5	1	0	2	4	16	.268	.293	.330	71	-5	-5	10	3	2	-0	.769	-1	3S2	-0.4
Total	9	657	1480	165	355	50	16	7	108	55	213	.240	.271	.309	62	-78	-76	118	29	20	-3	.956	35	S2/3O	-1.8

■ JOE MARTY Marty, Joseph Anton b: 9/1/13, Sacramento, Cal. d: 10/4/84, Sacramento, Cal. BR/TR, 6', 182 lbs. Deb: 4/22/37

YEAR	TM/L	G	AB	R	H	2B	3B	HR	RBI	BB	SO	AVG	OBP	SLG	PRO+	BR	/A	RC	SB	CS	SBR	FA	FR	POS	TPR
1937	Chi-N	88	290	41	84	17	2	5	44	28	30	.290	.356	.414	104	4	2	41	3			.976	-2	O	-0.2
1938	*Chi-N	76	235	32	57	8	3	7	35	18	26	.243	.305	.391	88	-4	-5	27	0			.987	-4	O	-1.0
1939	Chi-N	23	76	6	10	1	0	2	10	4	13	.132	.175	.224	6	-10	-10	2	2			.933	-2	O	-1.3
	Phi-N	91	299	32	76	12	6	9	44	24	27	.254	.310	.425	98	-3	-2	38	1			.974	3	O/P	-0.2
	Yr	114	375	38	86	13	6	11	54	28	40	.229	.283	.384	79	-13	-12	38	3			.968	1	*O/P	-1.5
1940	Phi-N	123	455	52	123	21	8	13	50	17	50	.270	.298	.437	105	-2	0	54	2			.974	2	*O	-0.3
1941	Phi-N	137	477	60	128	19	3	8	39	51	41	.268	.344	.371	105	1	4	63	6			.964	-6	*O	-1.1
Total	5	538	1832	223	478	78	22	44	222	142	187	.261	.318	.400	97	-14	-11	225	14			.972	-9	O/P	-4.1

■ BOB MARTYN Martyn, Robert Gordon b: 8/15/30, Weiser, Idaho BL/TR, 6', 176 lbs. Deb: 6/18/57

YEAR	TM/L	G	AB	R	H	2B	3B	HR	RBI	BB	SO	AVG	OBP	SLG	PRO+	BR	/A	RC	SB	CS	SBR	FA	FR	POS	TPR
1957	KC-A	58	131	10	35	2	4	1	12	11	20	.267	.324	.366	87	-2	-2	15	1	3	-2	.976	-3	O	-1.0
1958	KC-A	95	226	25	59	10	7	2	23	26	36	.261	.337	.394	99	0	-0	30	1	4	-2	.967	-5	O	-1.0
1959	KC-A	1	1	0	0	0	0	0	0	0	0	.000	.000	.000	-98	-0	-0	0	0	0	0	.000	0	R	0.0
Total	3	154	358	35	94	12	11	3	35	37	56	.263	.332	.383	94	-2	-3	45	2	7	-4	.970	-8	O	-2.0

■ GARY MARTZ Martz, Gary Arthur b: 1/10/51, Spokane, Wash. BR/TR, 6'4", 210 lbs. Deb: 7/08/75

YEAR	TM/L	G	AB	R	H	2B	3B	HR	RBI	BB	SO	AVG	OBP	SLG	PRO+	BR	/A	RC	SB	CS	SBR	FA	FR	POS	TPR
1975	KC-A	1	1	0	0	0	0	0	0	0	0	.000	.000	.000	-97	-0	-0	0	0	0	0	1.000	-0	/O	-0.1

■ JOHN MARZANO Marzano, John Robert b: 2/14/63, Philadelphia, Pa. BR/TR, 5'11", 197 lbs. Deb: 7/31/87

YEAR	TM/L	G	AB	R	H	2B	3B	HR	RBI	BB	SO	AVG	OBP	SLG	PRO+	BR	/A	RC	SB	CS	SBR	FA	FR	POS	TPR
1987	Bos-A	52	168	20	41	11	0	5	24	7	41	.244	.287	.399	77	-5	-6	19	0	1	-1	.986	1	C	-0.2
1988	Bos-A	10	29	3	4	1	0	0	1	1	3	.138	.167	.172	-5	-4	-4	1	0	0	0	1.000	5	C	0.2
1989	Bos-A	7	18	5	8	3	0	1	3	0	2	.444	.444	.778	224	3	3	5	0	0	0	1.000	-0	/C	0.3
1990	Bos-A	32	83	8	20	4	0	0	6	5	10	.241	.284	.289	58	-4	-5	7	0	1	-1	1.000	4	C	0.0
1991	Bos-A	49	114	10	30	8	0	0	9	1	16	.263	.276	.333	64	-5	-6	9	0	0	0	.985	-3	C	-0.7
1992	Bos-A	19	50	4	4	2	1	0	1	2	12	.080	.132	.160	-18	-8	-8	1	0	0	0	.968	0	C/D	-0.8
Total	6	169	462	50	107	29	1	6	44	16	84	.232	.265	.338	61	-24	-26	42	0	2	-1	.988	8	C/D	-1.2

■ CLYDE MASHORE Mashore, Clyde Wayne b: 5/29/45, Concord, Cal. BR/TR, 5'11", 184 lbs. Deb: 7/11/69

YEAR	TM/L	G	AB	R	H	2B	3B	HR	RBI	BB	SO	AVG	OBP	SLG	PRO+	BR	/A	RC	SB	CS	SBR	FA	FR	POS	TPR
1969	Cin-N	2	1	1	0	0	0	0	0	0	0	.000	.000	.000	-95	-0	-0	0	0	0	0	.000	0	H	0.0
1970	Mon-N	13	25	2	4	0	0	1	3	4	11	.160	.276	.280	49	-2	-2	2	0	0	0	1.000	-0	O	-0.2
1971	Mon-N	66	114	20	22	5	0	1	7	10	22	.193	.258	.263	48	-8	-8	8	1	0	0	.967	-1	O/3	-1.0
1972	Mon-N	93	176	23	40	7	1	3	23	14	41	.227	.284	.330	73	-6	-7	18	6	1	1	.988	-2	O	-1.1
1973	Mon-N	67	103	12	21	3	0	3	14	15	28	.204	.305	.320	71	-4	-4	11	4	3	-1	.958	4	O/2	-0.2
Total	5	241	419	58	87	15	1	8	47	43	102	.208	.281	.305	64	-20	-21	38	11	4	1	.974	1	O/23	-2.5

■ PHIL MASI Masi, Philip Samuel b: 1/6/17, Chicago, Ill. d: 3/29/90, Mt.Prospect, Ill. BR/TR, 5'10", 180 lbs. Deb: 4/23/39

YEAR	TM/L	G	AB	R	H	2B	3B	HR	RBI	BB	SO	AVG	OBP	SLG	PRO+	BR	/A	RC	SB	CS	SBR	FA	FR	POS	TPR
1939	Bos-N	46	114	14	29	7	2	1	14	9	15	.254	.315	.377	92	-3	-2	13	0			.960	-3	C	-0.2
1940	Bos-N	63	138	11	27	4	1	1	14	14	14	.196	.270	.261	50	-10	-9	9	0			.966	-1	C	-0.7
1941	Bos-N	87	180	17	40	8	2	3	18	16	13	.222	.286	.339	79	-6	-5	18	4			.978	-7	C	-0.7
1942	Bos-N	57	87	14	19	3	1	0	9	12	4	.218	.313	.276	74	-3	-2	8	2			.961	2	C/O	0.1
1943	Bos-N	80	238	27	65	9	1	2	28	27	20	.273	.347	.345	102	1	1	28	7			.991	-6	C	0.0
1944	Bos-N	89	251	33	69	13	5	3	23	31	20	.275	.355	.402	108	4	3	37	4			.977	-0	C1/3	0.6
1945	Bos-N†	114	371	55	101	25	4	7	46	42	32	.272	.348	.418	112	6	5	54	9			.980	1	C/1	1.1
1946	Bos-N★	133	397	52	106	17	5	3	62	55	41	.267	.358	.358	102	3	2	53	5			.981	-5	*C	0.4
1947	Bos-N★	126	411	54	125	22	4	9	50	47	27	.304	.377	.443	120	10	12	69	7			**.989**	-6	*C	1.3
1948	*Bos-N★	113	376	43	95	19	0	5	44	35	26	.253	.318	.343	80	-11	-10	40	2			.988	1	*C	-0.2
1949	Bos-N	37	105	13	22	2	0	0	6	14	10	.210	.303	.229	47	-8	-7	7	1			.993	-2	C	-0.7
	Pit-N	48	135	16	37	6	1	2	13	17	16	.274	.355	.378	94	-0	-1	18	1			.994	-2	C/1	0.0
	Yr	85	240	29	59	8	1	2	19	31	26	.246	.332	.313	74	-8	-8	25	2			**.994**	-3	C/1	-0.7
1950	Chi-A	122	377	38	105	17	2	7	55	49	36	.279	.366	.390	96	-3	-2	54	2	1	0	**.996**	-1	*C	0.2
1951	Chi-A	84	225	24	61	11	2	4	28	32	27	.271	.367	.391	107	2	3	34	1	0	0	.979	-0	C	0.6
1952	Chi-A	30	63	9	16	1	1	0	7	10	10	.254	.356	.302	84	-1	-1	8	0	0	0	.956	0	C	0.0
Total	14	1229	3468	420	917	164	31	47	417	410	311	.264	.344	.370	97	-19	-13	450	45	1		.983	-27	*C/1O3	1.8

■ HARRY MASKREY Maskrey, Harry H. b: 12/21/1861, Mercer, Pa. d: 8/17/30, Mercer, Pa. Deb: 9/21/1882 F

YEAR	TM/L	G	AB	R	H	2B	3B	HR	RBI	BB	SO	AVG	OBP	SLG	PRO+	BR	/A	RC	SB	CS	SBR	FA	FR	POS	TPR
1882	Lou-a	1	4	0	0	0	0	0		0		.000	.000	.000	-99	-1	-1	0				.000	-1	/O	-0.1

■ LEECH MASKREY Maskrey, Samuel Leech b: 2/11/1854, Mercer, Pa. d: 4/1/22, Mercer, Pa. BR/TR, 5'8", 150 lbs. Deb: 5/02/1882 F

YEAR	TM/L	G	AB	R	H	2B	3B	HR	RBI	BB	SO	AVG	OBP	SLG	PRO+	BR	/A	RC	SB	CS	SBR	FA	FR	POS	TPR
1882	Lou-a	76	288	30	65	14	2	0		9		.226	.249	.288	85	-6	-3	21				.902	-1	*O/2	-0.4
1883	Lou-a	96	361	50	73	13	8	1		10		.202	.224	.291	70	-14	-10	24				.914	9	*O/S	-0.1
1884	Lou-a	105	412	48	103	13	4	0		17		.250	.281	.301	97	-3	-0	36				.896	2	*O/3S	0.0
1885	Lou-a	109	423	54	97	8	11	1		19		.229	.269	.307	84	-7	-7	36				.899	-3	*O/3	-1.2
1886	Lou-a	5	19	1	3	1	0	0		1		.158	.200	.211	28	-2	-2	1	0			.800	-1	/O	-0.3
	Cin-a	27	98	7	19	3	1	0		5		.194	.240	.245	52	-5	-6	7	4			.926	1	O/3	-0.5
	Yr	32	117	8	22	4	1	0		6		.188	.234	.239	48	-7	-7	8	4			.915	-0	O/3	-0.8
Total	5	418	1601	190	360	52	26	2		61		.225	.256	.294	82	-37	-28	125	4			.904	7	O/3S2	-2.5

■ CHARLIE MASON Mason, Charles E. b: 6/25/1853, New Orleans, La. d: 10/21/36, Philadelphia, Pa. TR, 175 lbs. Deb: 4/26/1875 M

YEAR	TM/L	G	AB	R	H	2B	3B	HR	RBI	BB	SO	AVG	OBP	SLG	PRO+	BR	/A	RC	SB	CS	SBR	FA	FR	POS	TPR
1875	Cen-n	12	47	5	11	1	0	0		0		.234	.234	.255	75	-1	-1	3						/O1	-0.1
	Was-n	8	34	2	3	0	0	0		0		.088	.088	.088	-40	-5	-4	0						/OP	-0.4
	Yr	20	81	7	14	1	0	0		0		.173	.173	.185	25	-6	-5	3						O/1P	-0.5
1883	Phi-a	1	2	0	1	0	0	0		0		.500	.500	.500	206	0	0	1				.000	-0	/O	0.0

■ DON MASON Mason, Donald Stetson b: 12/20/44, Boston, Mass. BL/TR, 5'11", 160 lbs. Deb: 4/14/66

YEAR	TM/L	G	AB	R	H	2B	3B	HR	RBI	BB	SO	AVG	OBP	SLG	PRO+	BR	/A	RC	SB	CS	SBR	FA	FR	POS	TPR
1966	SF-N	42	25	8	3	0	0	1	1	0	2	.120	.120	.240	-3	-3	-4	1	0	1	-1	.905	9	/2	0.4
1967	SF-N	4	3	0	0	0	0	0	0	0	0	.000	.000	.000	-99	-1	-1	0	0	0	0	1.000	1	/2	0.0
1968	SF-N	10	19	3	3	0	0	0	1	1	4	.158	.200	.158	9	-2	-2	1	1	1	-0	1.000	-1	/2S3	-0.4
1969	SF-N	104	250	43	57	4	2	0	13	36	29	.228	.325	.260	67	-10	-10	24	1	5	-3	.956	10	23/S	0.1
1970	SF-N	46	36	4	5	0	0	0	1	5	7	.139	.244	.139	5	-5	-5	1	0	0	0	.950	2	2	-0.3
1971	SD-N	113	344	43	73	12	1	2	11	27	35	.212	.270	.270	57	-21	-18	24	6	4	-1	.965	-12	2/3	-2.6
1972	SD-N	9	11	1	2	0	0	0	0	1	1	.182	.250	.182	26	-1	-1	1	0	0	0	.692	-0	/2	-0.1
1973	SD-N	8	8	0	0	0	0	0	0	0	2	.000	.000	.000	-99	-2	-2	0	0	0	0	.750	1	/2	-0.2
Total	8	336	696	102	143	16	3	3	27	70	80	.205	.278	.250	52	-45	-42	50	8	11	-4	.955	8	2/3S	-3.1

■ JIM MASON Mason, James Percy b: 8/14/50, Mobile, Ala. BL/TR, 6'2", 190 lbs. Deb: 9/26/71

YEAR	TM/L	G	AB	R	H	2B	3B	HR	RBI	BB	SO	AVG	OBP	SLG	PRO+	BR	/A	RC	SB	CS	SBR	FA	FR	POS	TPR
1971	Was-A	3	9	0	3	0	0	0	0	1	3	.333	.400	.333	116	0	0	1	0	0	0	.955	2	/S	0.3

YEAR	TM/L	G	AB	R	H	2B	3B	HR	RBI	BB	SO	AVG	OBP	SLG	PRO+	BR	/A	RC	SB	CS	SBR	FA	FR	POS	TPR
1972	Tex-A	46	147	10	29	3	0	0	10	9	39	.197	.248	.218	41	-11	-10	8	0	0	0	.948	-6	S3	-1.3
1973	Tex-A	92	238	23	49	7	2	3	19	23	48	.206	.276	.290	62	-13	-12	20	0	1	-1	.947	9	S2/3	0.5
1974	NY-A	152	440	41	110	18	6	5	37	35	87	.250	.305	.352	91	-7	-5	48	1	2	-1	.964	-4	*S	0.8
1975	NY-A	94	223	17	34	3	2	2	16	22	49	.152	.229	.211	26	-22	-21	10	0	2	-1	.955	-10	S/2	-2.5
1976	*NY-A	93	217	17	39	7	1	1	14	9	37	.180	.212	.235	31	-19	-19	11	0	0	0	.966	7	S	-0.3
1977	Tor-A	22	79	10	13	3	0	0	2	7	10	.165	.233	.203	20	-9	-9	4	1	1	-0	.971	-5	S	-1.2
	Tex-A	36	55	9	12	3	0	1	7	6	10	.218	.295	.327	69	-2	-2	6	0	0	0	.976	7	S/3D	0.6
	Yr	58	134	19	25	6	0	1	9	13	20	.187	.259	.254	40	-11	-11	9	1	1	-0	.973	3	S/3D	-0.6
1978	Tex-A	55	105	10	20	4	0	0	3	5	17	.190	.227	.229	28	-10	-10	6	0	0	0	.938	1	S3/2D	-0.7
1979	Mon-N	40	71	3	13	5	1	0	6	7	16	.183	.256	.282	47	-5	-5	4	0	2	-1	.966	0	S/3	-0.4
Total	9	633	1584	140	322	53	12	12	114	124	316	.203	.262	.275	54	-98	-93	117	2	8	-4	.959	2	S/32D	-4.2
■ GORDON MASSA	Massa, Gordon Richard "Moose" or "Duke" b: 9/2/35, Cincinnati, Ohio BL/TR, 6'3", 210 lbs. Deb: 9/24/57																								
1957	Chi-N	6	15	2	7	1	0	0	3	4	3	.467	.579	.533	205	3	3	5	0	0	0	1.000	-3	/C	0.0
1958	Chi-N	2	2	0	0	0	0	0	0	0	2	.000	.000	.000	-99	-1	-1	0	0	0	0	.000	0	H	-0.1
Total	2	8	17	2	7	1	0	0	3	4	5	.412	.524	.471	172	2	2	5	0	0	0	.952	-3	/C	-0.1
■ RED MASSEY	Massey, Roy Hardee "Roy" or "Red" b: 10/9/1890, Sevierville, Tenn. d: 6/23/54, Atlanta, Ga. BL/TR, 5'11", 170 lbs. Deb: 4/16/18																								
1918	Bos-N	66	203	20	59	6	2	0	18	23	20	.291	.363	.340	120	4	5	25	1			.954	-3	O/31S	-0.1
■ BILL MASSEY	Massey, William Harry "Big Bill" b: 1/1871, Philadelphia, Pa. d: 10/9/40, Manila, Philippines BR , 5'11", 168 lbs. Deb: 9/18/1894																								
1894	Cin-N	13	53	7	15	3	0	0	5	3	2	.283	.321	.340	59	-3	-4	6	0			.991	-1	1/23	-0.4
■ MIKE MASSEY	Massey, William Herbert b: 9/28/1893, Galveston, Tex. d: 10/17/71, Shreveport, La. BB/TR, 6', 195 lbs. Deb: 4/12/17																								
1917	Bos-N	31	91	12	18	0	0	0	2	15	15	.198	.318	.198	63	-3	-3	7	2			.900	-8	2	-1.1
■ VICTOR MATA	Mata, Victor Jose (Abreu) b: 6/17/61, Santiago, D.R. BR/TR, 6'1", 165 lbs. Deb: 7/22/84																								
1984	NY-A	30	70	8	23	5	0	1	6	0	12	.329	.338	.443	119	1	1	10	1	1	-0	.942	-6	O	-0.5
1985	NY-A	6	7	1	1	0	0	0	0	0	0	.143	.143	.143	-22	-1	-1	0	0	0	0	1.000	-2	/O	-0.3
Total	2	36	77	9	24	5	0	1	6	0	12	.312	.321	.416	106	-0	0	10	1	1	-0	.943	-7	/O	-0.8
■ TOM MATCHICK	Matchick, John Thomas b: 9/7/43, Hazleton, Pa. BL/TR, 6', 175 lbs. Deb: 9/02/67																								
1967	Det-A	8	6	1	1	0	0	0	0	0	2	.167	.167	.167	-1	-1	-1	0	0	0	0	1.000	1	/S	0.0
1968	*Det-A	80	227	18	46	6	2	3	14	10	46	.203	.249	.286	60	-11	-11	16	0	2	-1	.950	-14	S2/1	-2.4
1969	Det-A	94	298	25	72	11	2	0	32	15	51	.242	.278	.292	57	-16	-18	23	3	0	1	.972	-7	23/S1	-2.1
1970	Bos-A	10	14	2	1	0	0	0	0	2	2	.071	.188	.071	-24	-2	-3	0	0	1	-1	1.000	-1	/32S	-0.4
	KC-A	55	158	11	31	3	2	0	11	5	23	.196	.226	.241	29	-15	-15	7	0	0	0	.985	13	S2/3	0.2
	Yr	65	172	13	32	3	2	0	11	7	25	.186	.222	.227	24	-18	-18	7	0	1	-1	.985	12	S2/3	-0.2
1971	Mil-A	42	114	6	25	1	0	1	7	7	23	.219	.264	.254	48	-8	-8	8	3	2	-0	.979	1	3/2	-0.8
1972	Bal-A	3	9	0	2	0	0	0	0	0	1	.222	.222	.222	32	-1	-1	0	0	1	-1	.857	-1	/3	-0.2
Total	6	292	826	63	178	21	6	4	64	39	148	.215	.255	.270	49	-54	-56	54	6	6	-2	.967	-7	S/321	-5.7
■ JOE MATHES	Mathes, Joseph John b: 7/28/1891, Milwaukee, Wis. d: 12/21/78, St.Louis, Mo. BB/TR, 6'0.5", 180 lbs. Deb: 9/19/12																								
1912	Phi-A	4	14	0	2	0	0	0	0	0		.143	.200	.143	-2	-2	-2	0	0			.889	-1	/3	-0.3
1914	StL-F	26	85	10	25	3	0	0	6	9	11	.294	.362	.329	92	0	-1	11	1			.938	-4	2	-0.5
1916	Bos-N	2	0	0	0	0	0	0	0	0	0	—	—	—	—	0	0	0	0			.000	-1	/2	-0.1
Total	3	32	99	10	27	3	0	0	6	9	11	.273	.339	.303	80	-2	-2	11	1			.921	-6	/23	-0.9
■ EDDIE MATHEWS	Mathews, Edwin Lee b: 10/13/31, Texarkana, Tex. BL/TR, 6'1", 200 lbs. Deb: 4/15/52 MCH																								
1952	Bos-N	145	528	80	128	23	5	25	58	59	115	.242	.320	.447	114	6	8	78	6	4	-1	.957	-10	*3	-0.5
1953	Mil-N★	157	579	110	175	31	8	**47**	135	99	83	.302	.406	.627	**175**	55	60	157	1	3	-2	.939	3	*3	5.5
1954	Mil-N	138	476	96	138	21	4	40	103	113	61	.290	.428	.603	**177**	49	53	131	10	3	1	.966	-2	*3O	4.8
1955	Mil-N★	141	499	108	144	23	5	41	101	**109**	98	.289	.417	.601	175	50	54	131	3	4	-2	.952	-4	*3	4.7
1956	Mil-N☆	151	552	103	150	21	2	37	95	91	86	.272	.376	.518	146	30	34	114	6	0	2	.944	-12	*3	2.6
1957	*Mil-N★	148	572	109	167	28	9	32	94	90	79	.292	.388	.540	157	38	44	126	3	1	0	.964	-2	*3	4.5
1958	*Mil-N☆	149	546	97	137	18	1	31	77	85	85	.251	.354	.458	123	11	17	94	5	0	2	.955	5	*3	2.5
1959	Mil-N★	148	594	118	182	16	8	**46**	114	80	71	.306	.391	.593	172	48	55	143	2	1	0	.961	3	*3	5.7
1960	Mil-N★	153	548	108	152	19	7	39	124	111	113	.277	.401	.551	**170**	46	**52**	**128**	7	3	0	.950	-13	*3	3.9
1961	Mil-N★	152	572	103	175	23	6	32	91	**93**	95	.306	.405	.535	156	40	45	128	12	7	-1	.961	-6	*3	3.9
1962	Mil-N★	152	536	106	142	25	6	29	90	**101**	90	.265	.383	.496	138	28	30	106	4	2	0	.964	2	*3/1	3.2
1963	Mil-N	158	547	82	144	27	4	23	84	**124**	119	.263	**.400**	.453	147	37	38	106	3	4	-2	**.968**	12	*3O	5.0
1964	Mil-N	141	502	83	117	19	1	23	74	85	100	.233	.345	.412	112	10	9	75	2	2	-1	.962	2	*3/1	0.9
1965	Mil-N	156	546	77	137	23	0	32	95	73	110	.251	.342	.469	125	19	18	89	1	0	0	.956	9	*3	2.6
1966	Atl-N	134	452	72	113	21	4	16	53	63	82	.250	.342	.420	109	7	6	67	1	1	-0	.946	-2	*3	0.1
1967	Hou-N	101	328	39	78	13	2	10	38	48	65	.238	.337	.381	109	3	4	43	2	4	-2	.987	-4	13	-0.7
	Det-A	36	108	14	25	3	0	6	19	15	23	.231	.336	.426	121	3	3	17	0	0	0	.933	-2	31	0.0
1968	*Det-A	31	52	4	11	0	0	3	8	5	12	.212	.281	.385	97	-0	-0	6	0	0	0	.974	-1	/13	-0.1
Total	17	2391	8537	1509	2315	354	72	512	1453	1444	1487	.271	.378	.509	145	480	531	1738	68	39	-3	.956	-22	*31/O	48.6
■ NELSON MATHEWS	Mathews, Nelson Elmer b: 7/21/41, Columbia, Ill. BR/TR, 6'4", 195 lbs. Deb: 9/09/60																								
1960	Chi-N	3	8	1	2	0	0	0	0	0	2	.250	.250	.250	38	-1	-1	1	0	0	0	1.000	0	/O	-0.1
1961	Chi-N	3	9	0	1	0	0	0	0	0	2	.111	.111	.111	-40	-2	-2	0	0	0	0	1.000	0	/O	-0.2
1962	Chi-N	15	49	5	15	2	0	2	13	5	4	.306	.393	.469	126	2	2	8	3	3	-1	.962	-1	O	-0.1
1963	Chi-N	61	155	12	24	3	2	4	10	16	48	.155	.234	.277	44	-11	-12	9	3	4	-2	.979	2	O	-1.4
1964	KC-A	157	573	58	137	27	5	14	60	43	143	.239	.293	.377	82	-13	-15	59	2	3	-1	.968	9	*O	-1.5
1965	KC-A	67	184	17	39	7	7	2	15	24	49	.212	.303	.359	89	-3	-3	20	0	2	-1	.981	-2	O	-0.8
Total	6	306	978	93	218	39	14	22	98	88	248	.223	.289	.359	78	-27	-29	96	8	12	-5	.972	9	O	-4.1
■ BOBBY MATHEWS	Mathews, Robert T. b: 11/21/1851, Baltimore, Md. d: 4/17/1898, Baltimore, Md. BR/TR, 5'5.5", 140 lbs. Deb: 5/04/1871 U																								
1871	Kek-n	19	89	15	24	3	1	0	10	2	0	.270	.286	.326	74	-3	-3	9	2					P	0.0
1872	Bal-n	50	221	35	50	2	1	0	21	3	2	.226	.237	.244	46	-13	-15	13						*P/O3	0.4
1873	Mut-n	52	223	40	43	4	3	0	13	10	3	.193	.227	.238	37	-17	-17	12						*P/O	0.6
1874	Mut-n	65	297	47	70	8	1	0		4		.236	.246	.269	62	-12	-13	20						*P	0.0
1875	Mut-n	70	268	23	47	5	2	0		0		.175	.175	.209	31	-17	-20	10						*P	0.0
1876	NY-N	56	218	19	40	4	1	0	9	3	2	.183	.195	.211	40	-14	-10	9				.810	-3	*P/O	0.0
1877	Cin-N	15	59	5	10	0	0	0	0	1	2	.169	.183	.169	13	-6	-5	2				.862	-3	P/OS	-0.2
1879	Pro-N	43	173	25	35	2	0	1	10	7	12	.202	.233	.231	55	-8	-8	10				.956	-5	PO/3	-0.9
1881	Pro-N	16	57	6	11	1	0	0	4	5	6	.193	.258	.211	50	-3	-3	3				.810	-3	P/O	-0.2
	Bos-N	19	71	2	12	2	0	0	4	0	5	.169	.169	.197	15	-7	-6	2				.818	-4	O/P	-0.9
	Yr	35	128	8	23	3	0	0	8	5	11	.180	.211	.203	32	-10	-9	6				.811	-7	OP	-1.1
1882	Bos-N	45	169	17	38	6	0	0	13	8	18	.225	.260	.260	67	-6	-6	12				.867	-10	PO/S	-0.6
1883	Phi-a	45	167	15	31	2	0	0		4		.186	.205	.198	28	-13	-15	7				.874	-2	P/O	-0.1
1884	Phi-a	49	184	26	34	5	1	0		7		.185	.215	.223	42	-11	-12	9				.775	-1	P/O	0.1
1885	Phi-a	48	179	22	30	3	0	0		10		.168	.212	.184	26	-14	-16	7				.881	-0	P/O	0.0
1886	Phi-a	24	88	16	21	3	0	0		3		.239	.264	.273	69	-3	-3	7	1			.843	-0	P/O	-0.1

YEAR	TM/L	G	AB	R	H	2B	3B	HR	RBI	BB	SO	AVG	OBP	SLG	PRO+	BR	/A	RC	SB	CS	SBR	FA	FR	POS	TPR
1887	Phi-a	7	25	5	5	0	0	0		4		.200	.310	.200	46	-2	-2	2	0			.889	0	/P	0.0
Total	5 n	256	1098	160	234	22	8	0	44	19	5	.213	.226	.248	47	-62	-68	65	4					P/O3	1.0
Total	10	367	1390	158	267	28	2	1	40	52	45	.192	.221	.217	42	-86	-85	69	1			.845	-30	P/O3S	-2.9

■ **JIMMY MATHISON** Mathison, James I. b: 11/1878, Baltimore, Md. d: 7/4/11, Baltimore, Md. TR , Deb: 8/29/02

YEAR	TM/L	G	AB	R	H	2B	3B	HR	RBI	BB	SO	AVG	OBP	SLG	PRO+	BR	/A	RC	SB	CS	SBR	FA	FR	POS	TPR
1902	Bal-A	29	91	12	24	2	1	0	7	9		.264	.374	.308	86	-0	-1	12	2			.889	-1	3/S	-0.2

■ **JOHN MATIAS** Matias, John Roy b: 8/15/44, Honolulu, Hawaii BL/TL, 5'11", 170 lbs. Deb: 4/07/70

YEAR	TM/L	G	AB	R	H	2B	3B	HR	RBI	BB	SO	AVG	OBP	SLG	PRO+	BR	/A	RC	SB	CS	SBR	FA	FR	POS	TPR
1970	Chi-A	58	117	7	22	2	0	2	6	3	22	.188	.215	.256	28	-11	-12	6	1	0	0	.941	-4	O1	-1.8

■ **C. V. MATTERSON** Matterson, C. V. b: Ohio Deb: 6/13/1884

YEAR	TM/L	G	AB	R	H	2B	3B	HR	RBI	BB	SO	AVG	OBP	SLG	PRO+	BR	/A	RC	SB	CS	SBR	FA	FR	POS	TPR
1884	StL-U	1	4	0	0	0	0	0		0		.000	.000	.000	-97	-1	-1	0				.000	-1	/OP	-0.1

■ **GARY MATTHEWS** Matthews, Gary Nathaniel b: 7/5/50, San Fernando, Cal. BR/TR, 6'3", 190 lbs. Deb: 9/06/72

YEAR	TM/L	G	AB	R	H	2B	3B	HR	RBI	BB	SO	AVG	OBP	SLG	PRO+	BR	/A	RC	SB	CS	SBR	FA	FR	POS	TPR
1972	SF-N	20	62	11	18	1	1	4	14	7	13	.290	.362	.532	149	4	4	11	0	1	-1	.971	-2	O	0.1
1973	SF-N	148	540	74	162	22	10	12	58	58	83	.300	.369	.444	119	18	15	90	17	5	2	.983	-0	*O	1.1
1974	SF-N	154	561	87	161	27	6	16	82	70	69	.287	.369	.442	120	20	17	90	11	9	-2	.970	-1	*O	0.8
1975	SF-N	116	425	67	119	22	3	12	58	65	53	.280	.378	.431	119	15	13	71	13	4	2	.967	6	*O	1.6
1976	SF-N	156	587	79	164	28	4	20	84	75	94	.279	.362	.443	124	21	19	98	12	5	1	.975	-12	*O	0.2
1977	Atl-N	148	555	89	157	25	5	17	64	67	90	.283	.362	.438	101	11	3	89	22	8	2	.965	-2	*O	-0.3
1978	Atl-N	129	474	75	135	20	5	18	62	61	92	.285	.369	.462	118	20	13	78	8	7	-2	.969	-1	*O	0.6
1979	Atl-N★	156	631	97	192	34	5	27	90	60	75	.304	.365	.502	125	28	23	118	18	6	2	.974	1	*O	1.9
1980	Atl-N	155	571	79	159	17	3	19	75	42	93	.278	.328	.419	104	4	2	76	11	3	2	.960	-9	*O	-1.2
1981	•Phi-N	101	359	62	108	21	3	9	67	59	42	.301	.404	.451	136	22	20	71	15	2	3	.963	-2	*O	1.9
1982	Phi-N	162	616	89	173	31	1	19	83	66	87	.281	.352	.427	114	14	12	91	21	4	4	.966	-2	*O	1.0
1983	•Phi-N	132	446	66	115	18	2	10	50	69	81	.258	.357	.374	104	3	4	62	13	9	-2	.974	-5	*O	-0.7
1984	•Chi-N	147	491	101	143	21	2	14	82	**103**	97	.291	**.417**	.428	126	30	24	96	17	8	0	.955	-4	*O	1.7
1985	Chi-N	97	298	45	70	12	0	13	40	59	64	.235	.365	.406	104	8	4	47	2	0	1	.977	-2	O	0.0
1986	Chi-N	123	370	49	96	16	1	21	46	60	59	.259	.363	.478	121	15	12	63	3	2	-0	.940	-8	*O	0.1
1987	Chi-N	44	42	3	11	3	0	0	8	4	11	.262	.326	.333	72	-1	-2	4	0	0	0	1.000	-0	/O	-0.2
	Sea-A	45	119	10	28	1	0	3	15	15	22	.235	.321	.319	67	-5	-6	11	0	1	-1	.000	0	D	-0.6
Total	16	2033	7147	1083	2011	319	51	234	978	940	1125	.281	.367	.439	116	229	178	1167	183	74	11	.968	-42	*O/D	8.0

■ **BOB MATTHEWS** Matthews, Robert b: Camden, N.J. Deb: 9/25/1891

YEAR	TM/L	G	AB	R	H	2B	3B	HR	RBI	BB	SO	AVG	OBP	SLG	PRO+	BR	/A	RC	SB	CS	SBR	FA	FR	POS	TPR
1891	Phi-a	1	3	1	1	0	0	0	0	0	1	.333	.600	.333	168	1	1	1	0			.000	-0	/O	0.0

■ **WID MATTHEWS** Matthews, Wid Curry "Matty" b: 10/20/1896, Raleigh, Ill d: 10/5/65, Hollywood, Cal. BL/TL, 5'8.5", 155 lbs. Deb: 4/18/23

YEAR	TM/L	G	AB	R	H	2B	3B	HR	RBI	BB	SO	AVG	OBP	SLG	PRO+	BR	/A	RC	SB	CS	SBR	FA	FR	POS	TPR
1923	Phi-A	129	485	52	133	11	6	1	25	50	27	.274	.343	.328	76	-15	-16	54	16	17	-5	.947	-8	*O	-3.7
1924	Was-A	53	169	25	51	10	4	0	13	11	4	.302	.355	.408	100	-1	-0	23	3	8	-4	.985	5	O	-0.2
1925	Was-A	10	9	2	4	0	0	0	1	0	1	.444	.444	.444	129	0	0	2	0	0	0	1.000	-0	/O	0.0
Total	3	192	663	79	188	21	10	1	39	61	32	.284	.348	.350	83	-16	-16	79	19	25	-9	.957	-4	O	-3.9

■ **STEVE MATTHIAS** Matthias, Stephen J. b: 1860, Mitchellville, Md. BR/TR, 5'8", 160 lbs. Deb: 4/20/1884

YEAR	TM/L	G	AB	R	H	2B	3B	HR	RBI	BB	SO	AVG	OBP	SLG	PRO+	BR	/A	RC	SB	CS	SBR	FA	FR	POS	TPR
1884	CP-U	37	142	24	39	7	1	0		5		.275	.299	.338	116	2	2	15				.840	2	S/O	0.4

■ **BOBBY MATTICK** Mattick, Robert James b: 12/5/15, Sioux City, Iowa BR/TR, 5'11", 178 lbs. Deb: 5/05/38 FM

YEAR	TM/L	G	AB	R	H	2B	3B	HR	RBI	BB	SO	AVG	OBP	SLG	PRO+	BR	/A	RC	SB	CS	SBR	FA	FR	POS	TPR
1938	Chi-N	1	1	0	1	0	0	0	1	0	0	1.000	1.000	1.000	439	0	0	1	0			.000	0	/S	0.0
1939	Chi-N	51	178	16	51	12	1	0	23	6	19	.287	.314	.365	80	-5	-5	20	1			.927	7	S	0.6
1940	Chi-N	128	441	30	96	15	0	0	33	19	33	.218	.250	.252	39	-37	-36	27	5			.946	10	*S/3	-1.6
1941	Cin-N	20	60	8	11	3	0	0	7	8	7	.183	.279	.233	45	-4	-4	4	1			.982	-2	S/32	-0.5
1942	Cin-N	6	10	0	2	1	0	0	0	0	1	.200	.200	.300	45	-1	-1	1	0			1.000	1	/S	0.1
Total	5	206	690	54	161	31	1	0	64	33	60	.233	.269	.281	52	-46	-45	53	7			.943	17	S/32	-1.4

■ **WALLY MATTICK** Mattick, Walter Joseph "Chink" b: 3/12/1887, St.Louis, Mo. d: 11/5/68, Los Altos, Cal. BR/TR, 5'10", 180 lbs. Deb: 4/11/12 F

YEAR	TM/L	G	AB	R	H	2B	3B	HR	RBI	BB	SO	AVG	OBP	SLG	PRO+	BR	/A	RC	SB	CS	SBR	FA	FR	POS	TPR
1912	Chi-A	90	285	45	74	7	9	1	35	27		.260	.334	.358	101	-1	0	40	15			.982	-3	O	-0.6
1913	Chi-A	71	207	15	39	8	1	0	11	18	16	.188	.253	.237	44	-15	-15	14	3			.977	2	O	-1.7
1918	StL-N	8	14	0	2	0	0	0	1	2	3	.143	.333	.143	49	-1	-1	1	0			1.000	0	/O	0.0
Total	3	169	506	60	115	15	10	1	47	47	19	.227	.302	.302	77	-16	-15	54	18			.980	-1	O	-2.3

■ **MIKE MATTIMORE** Mattimore, Michael Joseph b: 1859, Renovo, Pa. d: 4/28/31, Butte, Mont. BL/TL, 5'8.5", 160 lbs. Deb: 5/03/1887

YEAR	TM/L	G	AB	R	H	2B	3B	HR	RBI	BB	SO	AVG	OBP	SLG	PRO+	BR	/A	RC	SB	CS	SBR	FA	FR	POS	TPR
1887	NY-N	8	32	5	8	1	0	0	4	0	6	.250	.250	.281	51	-2	-2	3	1			.889	-1	/PO	0.0
1888	Phi-a	41	142	22	38	6	5	0	12	12		.268	.333	.380	133	5	5	24	16			.915	5	PO	0.3
1889	Phi-a	23	73	10	17	1	2	1	8	9	7	.233	.333	.342	96	-0	-0	11	6			.944	-3	O/1P	-0.3
	KC-a	19	75	6	12	1	1	0	5	3	16	.160	.192	.200	12	-8	-9	3	0			.844	-2	O/P	-0.9
	Yr	42	148	16	29	2	3	1	13	12	23	.196	.265	.270	53	-9	-9	13	6			.873	-5	O/1P	-1.2
1890	Bro-a	33	129	14	17	1	1	0		16		.132	.238	.155	18	-13	-12	8	11			.887	-6	PO	-0.9
Total	4	124	451	57	92	10	9	1	29	40	29	.204	.278	.273	67	-19	-18	48	34			.853	-7	/OP1	-1.8

■ **DON MATTINGLY** Mattingly, Donald Arthur b: 4/20/61, Evansville, Ind. BL/TL, 6', 175 lbs. Deb: 9/08/82

YEAR	TM/L	G	AB	R	H	2B	3B	HR	RBI	BB	SO	AVG	OBP	SLG	PRO+	BR	/A	RC	SB	CS	SBR	FA	FR	POS	TPR
1982	NY-A	7	12	0	2	0	0	0	1	0	1	.167	.167	.167	-8	-2	-2	0	0	0	0	1.000	1	/O1	-0.1
1983	NY-A	91	279	34	79	15	4	4	32	21	31	.283	.336	.409	108	1	3	37	0	0	0	.974	-10	O1/2	-1.1
1984	NY-A★	153	603	91	**207**	**44**	2	23	110	41	33	**.343**	.386	.537	**159**	41	44	120	1	1	-0	**.996**	13	*1O	4.7
1985	NY-A★	159	652	107	211	**48**	3	35	**145**	56	41	.324	.379	.567	159	48	50	136	2	2	-1	**.995**	-11	*1	2.7
1986	NY-A★	162	677	117	**238**	**53**	2	31	113	53	35	.352	.399	**.573**	**163**	**56**	**57**	**150**	0	0	0	**.996**	-7	*1/3D	3.6
1987	NY-A★	141	569	93	186	38	2	30	115	51	38	.327	.383	.559	147	36	37	115	1	4	-2	**.996**	-4	*1/D	2.0
1988	NY-A★	144	599	94	186	37	0	18	88	41	29	.311	.358	.462	129	21	22	96	1	0	0	.993	-4	*1/OD	0.6
1989	NY-A★	158	631	79	191	37	2	23	113	51	30	.303	.356	.477	134	26	27	104	3	0	1	.995	-5	*1D/O	1.1
1990	NY-A	102	394	40	101	16	0	5	42	28	20	.256	.311	.335	80	-10	-10	39	1	0	0	.997	6	1D/O	-1.1
1991	NY-A	152	587	64	169	35	0	9	68	46	42	.288	.344	.394	103	3	3	76	2	0	1	.996	-4	*1D	-0.9
1992	NY-A	157	640	89	184	40	0	14	86	39	43	.287	.329	.416	105	5	3	87	3	0	1	**.997**	7	*1D	0.1
Total	11	1426	5643	808	1754	363	15	192	913	427	343	.311	.361	.483	132	225	233	960	14	7	0	.996	-19	*1/OD32	11.6

■ **RALPH MATTIS** Mattis, Ralph "Matty" b: 8/24/1890, Roxborough, Pa. d: 9/13/60, Williamsport, Pa. BR/TR, 5'11", 172 lbs. Deb: 4/22/14

YEAR	TM/L	G	AB	R	H	2B	3B	HR	RBI	BB	SO	AVG	OBP	SLG	PRO+	BR	/A	RC	SB	CS	SBR	FA	FR	POS	TPR
1914	Pit-F	36	85	14	21	4	1	0	8	9	11	.247	.326	.318	84	-2	-2	10	2			.938	2	O	-0.1

■ **CLOY MATTOX** Mattox, Cloy Mitchell "Monk" b: 11/24/02, Leesville, Va. d: 8/3/85, Danville, Va. BL/TR, 5'8", 168 lbs. Deb: 9/01/29 F

YEAR	TM/L	G	AB	R	H	2B	3B	HR	RBI	BB	SO	AVG	OBP	SLG	PRO+	BR	/A	RC	SB	CS	SBR	FA	FR	POS	TPR
1929	Phi-A	3	6	0	1	0	0	0	0	1	1	.167	.286	.167	19	-1	-1	0	0	0	0	.875	-0	/C	-0.1

■ **JIM MATTOX** Mattox, James Powell b: 12/17/1896, Leesville, Va. d: 10/12/73, Myrtle Beach, S.C. BL/TR, 5'9.5", 168 lbs. Deb: 4/30/22 F

YEAR	TM/L	G	AB	R	H	2B	3B	HR	RBI	BB	SO	AVG	OBP	SLG	PRO+	BR	/A	RC	SB	CS	SBR	FA	FR	POS	TPR
1922	Pit-N	29	51	11	15	1	1	0	3	1	3	.294	.308	.353	69	-2	-2	5	0	0	0	.984	1	C	0.0
1923	Pit-N	22	32	4	6	1	1	0	1	0	5	.188	.235	.281	35	-3	-3	2	0	0	0	.960	1	/C	-0.2
Total	2	51	83	15	21	2	2	0	4	1	8	.253	.279	.325	56	-5	-6	8	0	0	0	.978	2	/C	-0.2

■ **LEN MATUSZEK** Matuszek, Leonard James b: 9/27/54, Toledo, Ohio BL/TR, 6'2", 195 lbs. Deb: 9/03/81

YEAR	TM/L	G	AB	R	H	2B	3B	HR	RBI	BB	SO	AVG	OBP	SLG	PRO+	BR	/A	RC	SB	CS	SBR	FA	FR	POS	TPR
1981	Phi-N	13	11	1	3	1	0	0	1	3	1	.273	.429	.364	121	1	1	2	0	1	-1	1.000	2	/13	0.1
1982	Phi-N	25	39	1	3	1	0	0	3	1	10	.077	.122	.103	-36	-7	-7	0	0	1	-1	.750	-2	/31	-1.1

YEAR	TM/L	G	AB	R	H	2B	3B	HR	RBI	BB	SO	AVG	OBP	SLG	PRO+	BR	/A	RC	SB	CS	SBR	FA	FR	POS	TPR
1983	Phi-N	28	80	12	22	6	1	4	16	4	14	.275	.310	.525	129	2	2	12	0	1	-1	1.000	-1	1	0.0
1984	Phi-N	101	262	40	65	17	1	12	43	39	54	.248	.354	.458	125	10	9	43	4	3	-1	.990	4	1/O	0.9
1985	Tor-A	62	151	23	32	6	2	2	15	11	24	.212	.265	.318	57	-9	-9	12	2	1	0	1.000	0	D/1	-0.9
	*LA-N	43	63	10	14	2	1	3	13	8	14	.222	.319	.429	111	1	1	9	0	1	-1	1.000	-1	O1/3	-0.2
1986	LA-N	91	199	26	52	7	0	9	28	21	47	.261	.335	.432	118	2	4	29	2	2	-1	1.000	-4	O1	-0.3
1987	LA-N	16	15	0	1	0	0	0	0	1	4	.067	.125	.067	-49	-3	-3	0	0	0	0	1.000	0	/1	-0.3
Total	7	379	820	113	192	40	5	30	119	88	168	.234	.314	.405	99	-3	-3	107	8	10	-4	.990	-2	1/OD3	-1.8

■ GENE MAUCH
Mauch, Gene William "Skip" b: 11/18/25, Salina, Kan. BR/TR, 5'10", 165 lbs. Deb: 4/18/44 M

YEAR	TM/L	G	AB	R	H	2B	3B	HR	RBI	BB	SO	AVG	OBP	SLG	PRO+	BR	/A	RC	SB	CS	SBR	FA	FR	POS	TPR
1944	Bro-N	5	15	2	2	1	0	0	2	2	3	.133	.235	.200	24	-2	-1	1	0			1.000	-2	/S	-0.3
1947	Pit-N	16	30	8	9	0	0	0	1	7	6	.300	.432	.300	95	0	0	5	0			.963	-2	/2S	-0.1
1948	Bro-N	12	13	1	2	0	0	0	0	1	4	.154	.214	.154	1	-2	-2	1	0			.950	1	/2S	0.0
	Chi-N	53	138	18	28	3	2	1	7	26	10	.203	.329	.275	68	-6	-5	15	1			.925	-6	2S	-0.9
	Yr	65	151	19	30	3	2	1	7	27	14	.199	.320	.265	62	-8	-7	15	1			.929	-5	2S	-0.9
1949	Chi-N	72	150	15	37	6	2	1	7	21	15	.247	.339	.333	83	-4	-3	17	3			.971	12	2S/3	1.0
1950	Bos-N	48	121	17	28	5	0	1	15	14	9	.231	.316	.298	67	-6	-5	11	1			.968	-1	2/3S	-0.5
1951	Bos-N	19	20	5	2	0	0	0	1	7	4	.100	.333	.100	24	-2	-2	1	0	0	0	1.000	-0	S/32	-0.1
1952	StL-N	7	3	0	0	0	0	0	0	1	2	.000	.250	.000	-25	-0	-0	0	0	0	0	.500	0	/S	0.0
1956	Bos-A	7	25	4	8	0	0	0	1	3	3	.320	.393	.320	80	-0	-1	3	0	0	0	.935	-2	/2	-0.2
1957	Bos-A	65	222	23	60	10	3	2	28	22	26	.270	.339	.369	88	-2	-3	27	1	0	0	.962	-10	2	-0.9
Total	9	304	737	93	176	25	7	5	62	104	82	.239	.335	.312	75	-23	-23	80	6	0		.958	-10	2/S3	-2.0

■ AL MAUL
Maul, Albert Joseph "Smiling Al" b: 10/9/1865, Philadelphia, Pa. d: 5/3/58, Philadelphia, Pa. BR/TR, 6', 175 lbs. Deb: 6/20/1884

YEAR	TM/L	G	AB	R	H	2B	3B	HR	RBI	BB	SO	AVG	OBP	SLG	PRO+	BR	/A	RC	SB	CS	SBR	FA	FR	POS	TPR
1884	Phi-U	1	4	0	0	0	0	0		0		.000	.000	.000	-99	-1	-1	0				1.000	-0	/P	0.0
1887	Phi-N	16	56	15	17	2	2	1	4	15	10	.304	.451	.464	148	5	5	14	5			.897	2	/OP1	0.4
1888	Pit-N	74	259	21	54	9	4	0	31	21	45	.208	.276	.274	84	-6	-3	23	9			.975	-1	1O/P	-0.8
1889	Pit-N	68	257	37	71	6	6	4	44	29	41	.276	.356	.393	123	4	8	43	18			.946	11	O/P	1.3
1890	Pit-P	45	162	31	42	6	2	0	21	22	12	.259	.348	.321	88	-4	-1	20	5			.904	4	PO/S	-0.1
1891	Pit-N	47	149	15	28	2	4	0	14	20	28	.188	.284	.255	61	-7	-7	12	4			.877	-2	O/P	-0.8
1893	Was-N	44	134	10	34	8	4	0	12	33	14	.254	.405	.373	112	3	4	21	1			.889	1	P/O	0.1
1894	Was-N	42	125	23	30	3	3	2	20	14	11	.240	.349	.360	75	-5	-5	17	1			.877	2	PO	-0.1
1895	Was-N	22	72	9	18	5	2	0	16	6	7	.250	.308	.375	78	-3	-2	9	0			.933	1	P/O	-0.1
1896	Was-N	8	28	6	8	1	1	0	5	3	2	.286	.355	.393	99	-0	-0	4	0			.923	-1	/P	0.0
1897	Was-N	1	1	0	0	0	0	0	0	0		.000	.000	.000	-99	-0	-0	0	0			1.000	0	/P	0.0
	Bal-N	2	3	0	1	0	0	0	0	0		.333	.333	.333	76	-0	-0	0	0			1.000	-0	/P	0.0
	Yr	3	4	0	1	0	0	0	0	0		.250	.250	.250	32	-0	-0	0	0			1.000	-0	/P	0.0
1898	Bal-N	29	93	21	19	3	2	0	10	16		.204	.333	.280	75	-2	-3	9	1			.978	-5	P/O	0.0
1899	Bro-N	4	11	2	3	0	0	0	0	1		.273	.333	.273	66	-0	-0	1	0			.900	0	/P	0.0
1900	Phi-N	5	15	2	3	0	0	0	1	2		.200	.294	.200	38	-1	-1	1	0			.917	0	/P	0.0
1901	NY-N	3	8	1	3	0	0	0	1	0		.375	.375	.375	123	0	0	1	0			1.000	0	/P	0.0
Total	15	411	1377	193	331	45	30	7	179	182	170	.240	.336	.332	92	-17	-6	176	44			.910	13	PO/1S	-0.1

■ MARK MAULDIN
Mauldin, Marshall Reese b: 11/5/14, Atlanta, Ga. d: 9/2/90, Union City, Ga. BR/TR, 5'11", 170 lbs. Deb: 9/10/34

YEAR	TM/L	G	AB	R	H	2B	3B	HR	RBI	BB	SO	AVG	OBP	SLG	PRO+	BR	/A	RC	SB	CS	SBR	FA	FR	POS	TPR
1934	Chi-A	10	38	3	10	2	0	1	3	0	3	.263	.263	.395	66	-2	-2	4	0	0	0	.906	-0	3	-0.2

■ ROB MAURER
Maurer, Robert John b: 1/7/67, Evansville, Ind. BL/TL, 6'3", 210 lbs. Deb: 9/08/91

YEAR	TM/L	G	AB	R	H	2B	3B	HR	RBI	BB	SO	AVG	OBP	SLG	PRO+	BR	/A	RC	SB	CS	SBR	FA	FR	POS	TPR
1991	Tex-A	13	16	0	1	1	0	0	2	2	6	.063	.211	.125	-5	-2	-2	1	0	0	0	1.000	1	/1D	-0.1
1992	Tex-A	8	9	1	2	0	0	0	1	1	2	.222	.300	.222	50	-1	-1	1	0	0	0	1.000	0	/1D	0.0
Total	2	21	25	1	3	1	0	0	3	3	8	.120	.241	.160	14	-3	-3	1	0	0	0	1.000	1	/1D	-0.1

■ CARMEN MAURO
Mauro, Carmen Louis b: 11/10/26, St.Paul, Minn. BL/TR, 6', 167 lbs. Deb: 10/01/48

YEAR	TM/L	G	AB	R	H	2B	3B	HR	RBI	BB	SO	AVG	OBP	SLG	PRO+	BR	/A	RC	SB	CS	SBR	FA	FR	POS	TPR
1948	Chi-N	3	5	2	1	0	0	1	1	2	0	.200	.429	.800	235	1	1	2	0			1.000	1	/O	0.1
1950	Chi-N	62	185	19	42	4	3	1	10	13	31	.227	.285	.297	54	-13	-12	16	3			.946	-3	O	-1.7
1951	Chi-N	13	29	3	5	1	0	0	3	2	6	.172	.250	.207	24	-3	-3	2	0	0	0	.900	1	/O	-0.3
1953	Bro-N	8	9	1	0	0	0	0	0	0	4	.000	.000	.000	-98	-3	-3	0	0	0	0	1.000	-0	/O	-0.3
	Was-A	17	23	1	4	0	1	0	2	1	3	.174	.208	.261	27	-2	-2	1	0	0	0	1.000	-0	/O	-0.3
	Phi-A	64	165	14	44	4	4	0	17	19	21	.267	.342	.339	81	-3	-4	18	3	4	-2	.969	-1	O/3	-0.8
	Yr	81	188	15	48	4	5	0	19	20	24	.255	.327	.330	76	-6	-6	20	3	4	-2	.971	-1	O/3	-1.1
Total	4	167	416	40	96	9	8	2	33	37	65	.231	.298	.305	61	-23	-23	39	6	4		.958	-4	O/3	-3.3

■ BOB MAVIS
Mavis, Robert Henry b: 4/8/18, Milwaukee, Wis. BL/TR, 5'7", 160 lbs. Deb: 9/17/49

YEAR	TM/L	G	AB	R	H	2B	3B	HR	RBI	BB	SO	AVG	OBP	SLG	PRO+	BR	/A	RC	SB	CS	SBR	FA	FR	POS	TPR
1949	Det-A	1	0	0	0	0	0	0	0	0	0	—	—	—	—	0	0	0	0	0	0	.000	0	R	0.0

■ DAL MAXVILL
Maxvill, Charles Dallan b: 2/18/39, Granite City, Ill. BR/TR, 5'11", 160 lbs. Deb: 6/10/62 C

YEAR	TM/L	G	AB	R	H	2B	3B	HR	RBI	BB	SO	AVG	OBP	SLG	PRO+	BR	/A	RC	SB	CS	SBR	FA	FR	POS	TPR
1962	StL-N	79	189	20	42	3	1	1	18	17	39	.222	.290	.265	46	-13	-15	15	1	2	-1	.962	-2	S/3	-1.3
1963	StL-N	53	51	12	12	2	0	0	3	6	11	.235	.316	.275	66	-2	-2	5	0	0	0	.974	7	S/23	0.6
1964	*StL-N	37	26	4	6	0	0	0	4	0	7	.231	.231	.231	28	-2	-3	2	1	0	0	.972	6	2S/3O	0.4
1965	StL-N	68	89	10	12	2	2	0	10	7	15	.135	.206	.202	14	-10	-11	4	0	0	0	.993	13	2S	0.4
1966	StL-N	134	394	25	96	14	3	0	24	37	61	.244	.312	.294	69	-15	-15	36	3	0	1	.967	24	*S/2O	2.1
1967	*StL-N	152	476	37	108	14	4	1	41	48	66	.227	.299	.279	67	-20	-19	39	0	2	-1	.974	3	*S/2	-0.3
1968	*StL-N	151	459	51	116	8	5	1	24	52	71	.253	.330	.298	91	-4	-3	46	0	2	-1	.969	-9	*S	0.2
1969	StL-N	132	372	27	65	10	2	2	32	44	52	.175	.264	.228	39	-30	-30	23	1	1	-0	.969	21	*S	0.4
1970	StL-N	152	399	35	80	5	2	0	28	51	56	.201	.291	.223	39	-33	-34	29	0	0	0	**.982**	**38**	*S2	1.8
1971	StL-N	142	356	31	80	10	1	0	24	43	45	.225	.310	.258	60	-16	-18	28	1	2	-1	.979	**29**	*S	2.6
1972	StL-N	105	276	22	61	6	1	1	23	31	47	.221	.300	.261	61	-14	-13	21	0	1	-1	.980	9	S2	0.7
	*Oak-A	27	36	2	9	1	0	0	1	1	11	.250	.270	.278	67	-2	-1	3	0	1	-1	.983	4	2/S	0.3
1973	Oak-A	29	19	0	4	0	0	0	1	1	3	.211	.250	.211	33	-2	-2	1	0	0	0	.966	4	S2/3	0.3
	Pit-N	74	217	19	41	4	3	0	17	22	40	.189	.264	.235	40	-18	-17	14	0	0	0	.971	4	S	-0.4
1974	Pit-N	8	22	3	4	0	0	0	0	2	4	.182	.250	.182	23	-2	-2	1	0	0	0	.946	1	/S	-0.1
	*Oak-A	60	52	3	10	0	0	0	2	8	10	.192	.300	.192	47	-3	-3	4	0	0	0	1.000	9	2S/3	0.8
1975	Oak-A	20	10	1	2	0	0	0	0	0	0	.200	.200	.200	14	-1	-1	0	0	0	0	.955	2	S/2	0.2
Total	14	1423	3443	302	748	79	24	6	252	370	538	.217	.295	.259	57	-186	-190	270	7	11	-5	.973	161	*S2/3O	8.7

■ CHARLIE MAXWELL
Maxwell, Charles Richard "Smokey" b: 4/8/27, Lawton, Mich. BL/TL, 5'11", 185 lbs. Deb: 9/20/50

YEAR	TM/L	G	AB	R	H	2B	3B	HR	RBI	BB	SO	AVG	OBP	SLG	PRO+	BR	/A	RC	SB	CS	SBR	FA	FR	POS	TPR
1950	Bos-A	3	8	1	0	0	0	0	0	1	3	.000	.111	.000	-63	-2	-2	0	0	0	0	1.000	1	/O	-0.1
1951	Bos-A	49	80	8	15	1	0	3	12	9	18	.188	.270	.313	52	-5	-6	7	0	1	-1	.926	-1	O	-0.8
1952	Bos-A	8	15	0	1	1	0	0	0	3	11	.067	.222	.133	0	-2	-2	1	0	0	0	.966	2	/1O	-0.1
1954	Bos-A	74	104	9	26	4	1	0	5	12	21	.250	.328	.308	67	-3	-5	11	3	0	1	1.000	-7	O	-1.2
1955	Bal-A	4	4	0	0	0	0	0	0	0	1	.000	.000	.000	-99	-1	-1	0	0	0	0	.000	0	H	-0.1
	Det-A	55	109	19	29	7	1	7	18	8	20	.266	.328	.541	134	4	4	19	0	0	0	.967	2	O/1	0.5
	Yr	59	113	19	29	7	1	7	18	8	21	.257	.317	.522	126	3	3	19	0	0	0	.967	2	O/1	0.4
1956	Det-A☆	141	500	96	163	14	3	28	87	79	74	.326	.420	.534	150	38	37	118	1	1	-0	.987	13	*O	4.2
1957	Det-A★	138	492	75	136	23	3	24	82	76	84	.276	.379	.482	130	24	22	94	3	2	-0	**.997**	14	*O	2.8
1958	Det-A	131	397	56	108	14	4	13	65	64	54	.272	.373	.426	111	12	8	68	6	1	1	.986	-1	*O1	0.2
1959	Det-A	145	518	81	130	12	2	31	95	81	91	.251	.359	.461	117	17	14	89	0	2	-1	.986	10	*O	1.6

YEAR	TM/L	G	AB	R	H	2B	3B	HR	RBI	BB	SO	AVG	OBP	SLG	PRO+	BR	/A	RC	SB	CS	SBR	FA	FR	POS	TPR
1960	Det-A	134	482	70	114	16	5	24	81	58	75	.237	.326	.440	102	2	1	73	5	0	2	**.996**	8	*O	0.4
1961	Det-A	79	131	11	30	4	2	5	18	20	24	.229	.336	.405	94	-1	-1	19	0	0	0	.965	2	O	-0.1
1962	Det-A	30	67	5	13	2	0	1	9	8	10	.194	.280	.269	47	-5	-5	5	0	0	0	.966	-1	O/1	-0.7
	Chi-A	69	206	30	61	8	3	9	43	34	32	.296	.396	.495	139	12	12	42	0	0	0	.990	-1	O/1	0.8
	Yr	99	273	35	74	10	3	10	52	42	42	.271	.368	.440	115	7	7	46	0	0	0	.985	-1	O/1	0.1
1963	Chi-A	71	130	17	30	4	2	3	17	31	27	.231	.379	.362	111	3	3	20	0	0	0	1.000	-4	O1	-0.2
1964	Chi-A	2	2	0	0	0	0	0	0	0	0	.000	.000	.000	-99	-1	-1	0	0	0	0	.000	0	H	-0.1
Total	14	1133	3245	478	856	110	26	148	532	484	545	.264	.363	.451	116	92	78	566	18	7	1	.988	37	O/1	7.1

■ CARLOS MAY
May, Carlos b: 5/17/48, Birmingham, Ala. BL/TR, 6', 215 lbs. Deb: 9/06/68 F

YEAR	TM/L	G	AB	R	H	2B	3B	HR	RBI	BB	SO	AVG	OBP	SLG	PRO+	BR	/A	RC	SB	CS	SBR	FA	FR	POS	TPR
1968	Chi-A	17	67	4	12	1	0	0	1	3	15	.179	.214	.194	24	-6	-6	3	0	0	0	.960	-2	O	-1.0
1969	Chi-A★	100	367	62	103	18	2	18	62	58	66	.281	.387	.488	137	22	20	69	1	4	-2	.982	-1	*O	1.2
1970	Chi-A	150	555	83	158	28	4	12	68	79	96	.285	.377	.414	114	16	13	84	12	5	1	.991	1	*O/1	0.7
1971	Chi-A	141	500	64	147	21	7	7	70	62	61	.294	.379	.406	119	16	14	77	16	7	1	.986	-5	*1/O	-0.2
1972	Chi-A☆	148	523	83	161	26	3	12	68	79	70	.308	.408	.438	149	37	36	96	23	14	-2	.983	-1	*O/1	3.0
1973	Chi-A	149	553	62	148	20	0	20	96	53	73	.268	.337	.412	106	7	5	75	8	6	-1	.992	1	DO/1	0.2
1974	Chi-A	149	551	66	137	19	2	8	58	46	76	.249	.308	.334	82	-11	-13	56	8	9	-3	.988	6	*OD	-1.6
1975	Chi-A	128	454	55	123	19	2	8	53	67	46	.271	.375	.374	111	10	9	66	12	7	-1	.989	1	1OD	0.3
1976	Chi-A	20	63	7	11	2	0	0	3	9	5	.175	.278	.206	43	-4	-4	5	4	0	1	1.000	-1	D/O	-0.5
	*NY-A	87	288	38	80	11	2	3	40	34	32	.278	.364	.361	114	6	6	39	1	1	-0	.950	0	D/O1	0.6
	Yr	107	351	45	91	13	2	3	43	43	37	.259	.348	.333	101	2	2	44	5	1	1	.970	-1	DO/1	0.1
1977	NY-A	65	181	21	41	7	1	2	16	17	24	.227	.296	.309	66	-9	-8	16	0	0	0	1.000	-1	D/O	-0.9
	Cal-A	11	18	0	6	0	0	0	1	5	1	.333	.478	.333	131	1	1	3	0	0	0	1.000	0	/1D	0.1
	Yr	76	199	21	47	7	1	2	17	22	25	.236	.315	.312	73	-7	-7	19	0	0	0	1.000	-1	D/O1	-0.8
Total	10	1165	4120	545	1127	172	23	90	536	512	565	.274	.360	.392	111	85	73	589	85	53	-6	.984	-1	OD1	1.9

■ DAVE MAY
May, David La France b: 12/23/43, New Castle, Del. BL/TR, 5'10.5", 186 lbs. Deb: 7/28/67 F

YEAR	TM/L	G	AB	R	H	2B	3B	HR	RBI	BB	SO	AVG	OBP	SLG	PRO+	BR	/A	RC	SB	CS	SBR	FA	FR	POS	TPR
1967	Bal-A	36	85	12	20	1	1	1	7	6	13	.235	.286	.306	75	-3	-3	8	0	0	0	.969	-0	O	-0.4
1968	Bal-A	84	152	15	29	6	3	0	7	19	27	.191	.285	.270	69	-5	-5	11	3	3	-1	.984	-11	O	-2.2
1969	*Bal-A	78	120	8	29	6	0	3	10	9	23	.242	.305	.367	86	-2	-2	12	2	1	0	.940	-4	O	-0.8
1970	Bal-A	25	31	6	6	0	1	1	6	4	4	.194	.286	.355	75	-1	-1	2	0	0	0	1.000	-2	/O	-0.4
	Mil-A	100	342	36	82	8	1	7	31	44	56	.240	.330	.330	82	-7	-8	37	8	6	-1	.989	8	O	-0.6
	Yr	125	373	42	88	8	2	8	37	48	60	.236	.326	.332	81	-8	-9	40	8	6	-1	.989	6	*O	-1.0
1971	Mil-A	144	501	74	139	20	3	16	65	50	59	.277	.347	.425	119	11	12	70	15	9	-1	.975	10	*O	1.5
1972	Mil-A	143	500	49	119	20	2	9	45	47	56	.238	.307	.340	94	-5	-4	49	11	13	-5	.985	15	*O	0.0
1973	Mil-A★	156	624	96	189	23	4	25	93	44	78	.303	.354	.473	134	24	25	100	6	7	-2	.979	3	*O/D	2.0
1974	Mil-A	135	477	56	108	15	1	10	42	28	73	.226	.274	.325	72	-18	-18	41	4	3	-1	.989	-3	*O/D	-2.8
1975	Atl-N	82	203	28	56	8	0	12	40	25	27	.276	.361	.493	130	9	8	36	1	1	-0	.964	-1	O	0.5
1976	Atl-N	105	214	27	46	5	3	3	23	26	31	.215	.303	.308	69	-7	-9	21	5	1	1	.972	0	O	-1.0
1977	Tex-A	120	340	46	82	14	1	7	42	32	43	.241	.314	.350	80	-9	-9	38	4	3	-1	.969	-4	*O/D	-1.8
1978	Mil-A	39	77	9	15	4	0	2	11	9	10	.195	.295	.325	74	-3	-3	7	0	0	0	.944	0	O/D	-0.3
	Pit-N	5	4	0	0	0	0	0	0	1	1	.000	.200	.000	-38	-1	-1	0	1	0	0	.000	0	H	0.0
Total	12	1252	3670	462	920	130	20	96	422	344	501	.251	.320	.375	97	-17	-17	435	60	47	-10	.978	11	*O/D	-6.3

■ DERRICK MAY
May, Derrick Brant b: 7/14/68, Rochester, N.Y. BL/TR, 6'4", 210 lbs. Deb: 9/06/90 F

YEAR	TM/L	G	AB	R	H	2B	3B	HR	RBI	BB	SO	AVG	OBP	SLG	PRO+	BR	/A	RC	SB	CS	SBR	FA	FR	POS	TPR
1990	Chi-N	17	61	8	15	3	0	1	11	2	7	.246	.270	.344	63	-3	-3	6	1	0	0	.972	0	O	-0.3
1991	Chi-N	15	22	4	5	2	0	1	3	2	1	.227	.292	.455	102	0	-0	3	0	0	0	1.000	0	/O	0.0
1992	Chi-N	124	351	33	96	11	0	8	45	14	40	.274	.307	.373	90	-4	-5	37	5	3	-0	.969	-11	*O	-2.0
Total	3	156	434	45	116	16	0	10	59	18	48	.267	.301	.373	86	-7	-9	46	6	3	0	.971	-10	O	-2.3

■ JERRY MAY
May, Jerry Lee b: 12/14/43, Staunton, Va. BR/TR, 6'2.5", 195 lbs. Deb: 9/19/64

YEAR	TM/L	G	AB	R	H	2B	3B	HR	RBI	BB	SO	AVG	OBP	SLG	PRO+	BR	/A	RC	SB	CS	SBR	FA	FR	POS	TPR
1964	Pit-N	11	31	1	8	0	0	0	3	3	9	.258	.324	.258	66	-1	-1	3	0	0	0	.988	4	C	0.3
1965	Pit-N	4	2	0	1	0	0	0	1	0	0	.500	.500	.500	182	0	0	1	0	0	0	1.000	-0	/C	0.0
1966	Pit-N	42	52	6	13	4	0	1	2	2	15	.250	.291	.385	86	-1	-1	6	0	1	-1	.984	8	C	0.7
1967	Pit-N	110	325	23	88	13	2	3	22	36	55	.271	.349	.351	100	1	1	37	0	0	0	.993	-0	*C	0.7
1968	Pit-N	137	416	26	91	15	2	1	33	41	80	.219	.293	.272	72	-14	-13	33	0	0	0	.988	4	*C	-0.1
1969	Pit-N	62	190	21	44	8	0	7	23	9	53	.232	.274	.384	84	-5	-5	20	1	1	-0	.994	-5	C	-0.8
1970	Pit-N	51	139	13	29	4	2	1	16	21	25	.209	.317	.288	65	-7	-6	13	0	0	0	.994	13	C	0.8
1971	KC-A	71	218	16	55	13	2	1	24	27	37	.252	.335	.344	93	-2	-1	25	0	0	0	.997	0	C	0.1
1972	KC-A	53	116	10	22	5	1	1	4	14	13	.190	.277	.276	65	-5	-5	9	0	0	0	.979	-1	C	-0.5
1973	KC-A	11	30	4	4	1	1	0	2	3	5	.133	.235	.233	30	-3	-3	2	0	0	0	.940	-2	C	-0.4
	NY-N	4	8	0	2	0	0	0	0	1	1	.250	.333	.250	65	-0	-0	1	0	0	0	1.000	-1	/C	-0.1
Total	10	556	1527	120	357	63	10	15	130	157	293	.234	.310	.318	81	-36	-35	148	1	2	-1	.990	20	C	0.7

■ LEE MAY
May, Lee Andrew b: 3/23/43, Birmingham, Ala. BR/TR, 6'3", 205 lbs. Deb: 9/01/65 FC

YEAR	TM/L	G	AB	R	H	2B	3B	HR	RBI	BB	SO	AVG	OBP	SLG	PRO+	BR	/A	RC	SB	CS	SBR	FA	FR	POS	TPR
1965	Cin-N	5	4	1	0	0	0	0	0	0	1	.000	.000	.000	-94	-1	-1	0	0	0	0	.000	0	H	-0.1
1966	Cin-N	25	75	14	25	5	1	2	10	0	14	.333	.333	.507	119	3	2	12	0	1	-1	.972	-1	1	0.0
1967	Cin-N	127	438	54	116	29	2	12	57	19	80	.265	.310	.422	97	3	-2	53	4	8	-4	.994	2	1O	-1.2
1968	Cin-N	146	559	78	162	32	1	22	80	34	100	.290	.337	.469	132	25	22	79	4	7	-3	.996	1	*1O	1.1
1969	Cin-N★	158	607	85	169	32	3	38	110	45	142	.278	.334	.529	132	28	24	104	5	4	-1	.993	1	*1/O	1.1
1970	*Cin-N	153	605	78	153	34	2	34	94	38	125	.253	.299	.484	106	2	1	81	1	1	-0	.993	0	*1	-1.2
1971	Cin-N★	147	553	85	154	17	3	39	98	42	135	.278	.334	.532	145	27	28	96	3	0	1	.994	-7	*1	1.0
1972	Hou-N★	148	592	87	168	31	2	29	98	52	145	.284	.344	.490	137	25	26	97	3	1	0	.996	-3	*1	1.2
1973	Hou-N	148	545	65	147	24	3	28	105	34	122	.270	.315	.479	117	10	10	78	1	1	-0	.993	-3	*1	-0.5
1974	Hou-N	152	556	59	149	26	0	24	85	17	97	.268	.298	.444	110	1	3	71	1	0	0	.994	1	*1	-0.5
1975	Bal-A	146	580	67	152	28	3	20	99	36	91	.262	.311	.424	113	2	7	68	1	2	-1	.993	3	*1/D	-0.1
1976	Bal-A	148	530	61	137	17	4	25	**109**	41	104	.258	.315	.447	130	12	16	73	4	1	1	.996	0	1D	1.1
1977	Bal-A	150	585	75	148	16	2	27	99	38	119	.253	.299	.426	101	-6	-1	68	2	2	-1	.995	-7	*1D	-1.5
1978	Bal-A	148	556	56	137	16	1	25	80	31	110	.246	.287	.414	101	-6	-2	61	5	2	0	.973	-0	*D/1	-0.2
1979	*Bal-A	124	456	59	116	15	0	19	69	28	100	.254	.299	.412	93	-8	-6	50	3	4	-2	.913	-1	*D/1	-0.8
1980	Bal-A	78	222	20	54	10	2	7	31	15	53	.243	.291	.401	88	-4	-4	23	2	0	1	1.000	-0	D/1	-0.4
1981	*KC-A	26	55	3	16	3	0	0	8	3	14	.291	.328	.345	95	-0	-0	5	0	1	-1	1.000	-1	/1D	-0.2
1982	KC-A	42	91	12	28	5	2	3	12	14	18	.308	.400	.505	147	6	6	20	0	0	0	.989	-2	1/D	0.3
Total	18	2071	7609	959	2031	340	31	354	1244	487	1570	.267	.315	.459	116	117	129	1039	39	35	-9	.994	-18	*1D/O	-0.9

■ PINKY MAY
May, Merrill Glend b: 1/18/11, Laconia, Ind. BR/TR, 5'11.5", 165 lbs. Deb: 4/21/39 F

YEAR	TM/L	G	AB	R	H	2B	3B	HR	RBI	BB	SO	AVG	OBP	SLG	PRO+	BR	/A	RC	SB	CS	SBR	FA	FR	POS	TPR
1939	Phi-N	135	464	49	133	27	3	2	62	41	20	.287	.346	.371	95	-4	-3	59	4			**.956**	8	*3	0.7
1940	Phi-N★	136	501	59	147	24	2	1	48	58	33	.293	.371	.355	105	3	6	69	2			.954	13	*3/S	2.1
1941	Phi-N	142	490	46	131	17	4	0	39	55	30	.267	.344	.318	91	-7	-4	54	2			**.972**	**25**	*3	2.4
1942	Phi-N	115	345	25	82	15	0	0	18	51	17	.238	.338	.281	86	-6	-4	36	3			.963	17	*3	1.6
1943	Phi-N	137	415	31	117	19	2	1	48	56	21	.282	.369	.345	111	6	7	53	2			**.963**	11	*3	2.1
Total	5	665	2215	210	610	102	11	4	215	261	121	.275	.354	.337	98	-8	2	270	13			.962	74	3/S	8.9

■ MILT MAY May, Milton Scott b: 8/1/50, Gary, Ind. BL/TR, 6', 190 lbs. Deb: 9/08/70 FC

YEAR	TM/L	G	AB	R	H	2B	3B	HR	RBI	BB	SO	AVG	OBP	SLG	PRO+	BR	/A	RC	SB	CS	SBR	FA	FR	POS	TPR
1970	Pit-N	5	4	1	2	1	0	0	2	0	0	.500	.600	.750	265	1	1	2	0	0	0	.000	0	H	0.1
1971	*Pit-N	49	126	15	35	1	0	6	25	9	16	.278	.326	.429	113	2	2	16	0	0	0	1.000	3	C	0.6
1972	*Pit-N	57	139	12	39	10	0	0	14	10	13	.281	.329	.353	96	-1	-1	16	0	0	0	.985	5	C	0.5
1973	Pit-N	101	283	29	76	8	1	7	31	34	26	.269	.351	.378	105	1	2	36	0	1	-1	.973	-6	C	-0.1
1974	Hou-N	127	405	47	117	17	4	7	54	39	33	.289	.353	.402	116	6	8	57	0	1	-1	**.993**	2	*C	1.4
1975	Hou-N	111	386	29	93	15	1	4	52	26	41	.241	.289	.316	73	-17	-14	35	1	2	-1	.986	1	*C	-1.0
1976	Det-A	6	25	2	7	1	0	0	1	0	1	.280	.280	.320	73	-1	-1	2	0	0	0	1.000	1	/C	0.0
1977	Det-A	115	397	32	99	9	3	12	46	26	31	.249	.296	.378	78	-11	-13	42	0	0	0	.986	7	*C	-0.3
1978	Det-A	105	352	24	88	9	0	10	37	27	26	.250	.307	.361	85	-6	-8	37	0	0	0	.979	1	C	-0.4
1979	Det-A	6	11	1	3	2	0	0	3	1	1	.273	.333	.455	107	0	0	1	0	0	0	1.000	1	/C	0.1
	Chi-A	65	202	23	51	13	0	7	28	14	27	.252	.307	.421	94	-2	-2	26	0	0	0	.981	1	C	0.1
	Yr	71	213	24	54	15	0	7	31	15	28	.254	.309	.423	95	-2	-2	28	0	0	0	.982	2	C	0.2
1980	SF-N	111	358	27	93	16	2	6	50	25	40	.260	.310	.366	90	-6	-5	38	0	1	-1	.986	-4	*C	-0.7
1981	SF-N	97	316	20	98	17	0	2	33	34	29	.310	.377	.383	118	8	8	44	1	4	-2	.989	-1	C	0.9
1982	SF-N	114	395	29	104	19	0	9	39	28	38	.263	.312	.380	93	-5	-4	47	0	1	-1	.987	-1	*C	-0.2
1983	SF-N	66	186	18	46	6	0	6	20	21	23	.247	.324	.376	96	-2	-1	21	2	2	-1	.981	-2	C	-0.1
	Pit-N	7	12	0	3	0	0	0	0	1	1	.250	.308	.250	55	-1	-1	1	0	0	0	1.000	2	/C	0.1
	Yr	73	198	18	49	6	0	6	20	22	24	.247	.323	.369	94	-2	-2	23	2	2	-1	.983	0	C	0.0
1984	Pit-N	50	96	4	17	3	0	1	8	10	15	.177	.255	.240	40	-8	-8	6	0	1	-1	.993	5	C	-0.3
Total	15	1192	3693	313	971	147	11	77	443	305	361	.263	.321	.371	93	-41	-37	426	4	13	-7	.986	14	*C	0.7

■ JOHN MAYBERRY Mayberry, John Claiborn b: 2/18/49, Detroit, Mich. BL/TL, 6'3", 220 lbs. Deb: 9/10/68 C

YEAR	TM/L	G	AB	R	H	2B	3B	HR	RBI	BB	SO	AVG	OBP	SLG	PRO+	BR	/A	RC	SB	CS	SBR	FA	FR	POS	TPR
1968	Hou-N	4	9	0	0	0	0	0	0	0	2	.000	.100	.000	-69	-2	-2	0	0	0	0	1.000	-0	/1	-0.3
1969	Hou-N	5	4	0	0	0	0	0	0	1	1	.000	.200	.000	-41	-1	-1	0	0	0	0	.000	0	H	-0.1
1970	Hou-N	50	148	23	32	3	2	5	14	21	33	.216	.322	.365	87	-3	-3	17	1	1	-0	.995	3	1	-0.3
1971	Hou-N	46	137	16	25	0	1	7	14	13	32	.182	.263	.350	74	-5	-5	13	0	0	0	.997	-3	1	-1.2
1972	KC-A	149	503	65	150	24	3	25	100	78	74	.298	.396	.507	168	43	43	101	0	2	-1	**.995**	-0	*1	3.3
1973	KC-A★	152	510	87	142	20	2	26	100	**122**	79	.278	**.420**	.478	141	**41**	36	113	3	0	1	.994	-5	*1/D	2.0
1974	KC-A★	126	427	63	100	13	1	22	69	77	72	.234	.359	.424	118	15	12	70	4	2	0	.990	-2	*1D	0.3
1975	KC-A	156	554	95	161	38	1	34	106	**119**	73	.291	.419	.547	**167**	**56**	**54**	**135**	5	3	-0	.988	3	*1D	4.8
1976	*KC-A	161	594	76	138	22	2	13	95	82	73	.232	.327	.342	95	-1	-2	70	3	2	-0	.996	-3	*1/D	-1.7
1977	*KC-A	153	543	73	125	22	1	23	82	83	86	.230	.340	.401	100	2	1	76	1	3	-2	**.995**	-6	*1/D	-1.5
1978	Tor-A	152	515	51	129	15	2	22	70	60	57	.250	.333	.416	107	6	5	71	1	2	-1	.993	-14	*1/D	-1.9
1979	Tor-A	137	464	61	127	22	1	21	74	69	60	.274	.374	.461	122	17	16	82	1	1	-0	.995	-8	*1	0.0
1980	Tor-A	149	501	62	124	19	2	30	82	77	80	.248	.351	.473	118	16	13	86	0	0	0	.994	-4	*1/D	0.1
1981	Tor-A	94	290	34	72	6	1	17	43	44	45	.248	.363	.452	125	13	11	49	1	1	-0	.993	-6	1D	0.0
1982	Tor-A	17	33	7	9	0	0	2	3	7	5	.273	.415	.455	127	2	2	7	0	0	0	1.000	-1	D/1	0.1
	NY-A	69	215	20	45	7	0	8	27	28	38	.209	.315	.353	84	-5	-4	24	0	0	0	.996	-4	1/D	-1.1
	Yr	86	248	27	54	7	0	10	30	35	43	.218	.329	.367	90	-3	-3	31	0	0	0	.996	-4	1D	-1.0
Total	15	1620	5447	733	1379	211	19	255	879	881	810	.253	.363	.439	122	195	177	913	20	17	-4	.994	-49	*1/D	2.5

■ LEE MAYE Maye, Arthur Lee b: 12/11/34, Tuscaloosa, Ala. BL/TR, 6'2", 190 lbs. Deb: 7/17/59

YEAR	TM/L	G	AB	R	H	2B	3B	HR	RBI	BB	SO	AVG	OBP	SLG	PRO+	BR	/A	RC	SB	CS	SBR	FA	FR	POS	TPR
1959	Mil-N	51	140	17	42	5	1	4	16	7	26	.300	.338	.436	114	1	2	20	2	2	-1	.976	1	O	0.0
1960	Mil-N	41	83	14	25	6	0	0	2	7	21	.301	.363	.373	110	0	1	12	5	0	2	.968	-1	O	0.1
1961	Mil-N	110	373	68	101	11	5	14	41	36	50	.271	.340	.440	112	2	5	60	10	1	2	.972	-4	O	-0.1
1962	Mil-N	99	349	40	85	10	0	10	41	25	58	.244	.296	.358	77	-13	-12	39	9	3	1	.977	5	O	-1.1
1963	Mil-N	124	442	67	120	22	7	11	34	36	52	.271	.331	.428	118	9	10	65	14	2	3	.983	5	*O	1.2
1964	Mil-N	153	588	96	179	**44**	5	10	74	34	54	.304	.347	.447	121	16	16	86	5	10	-5	.961	5	*O/3	1.0
1965	Mil-N	15	53	8	16	2	0	2	7	2	6	.302	.339	.453	120	1	1	8	0	0	0	.962	1	O	0.2
	Hou-N	108	415	38	104	17	7	3	36	20	37	.251	.287	.347	83	-13	-10	40	1	5	-3	.953	-2	*O	-2.0
	Yr	123	468	46	120	19	7	5	43	22	43	.256	.293	.359	88	-11	-8	48	1	5	-3	.954	-1	*O	-1.8
1966	Hou-N	115	358	38	103	12	4	9	36	20	26	.288	.325	.419	113	2	5	47	4	3	-1	.949	-6	O	-0.6
1967	Cle-A	115	297	43	77	20	4	9	27	26	47	.259	.321	.444	123	8	8	43	3	3	-1	.981	-10	O/2	-0.7
1968	Cle-A	109	299	20	84	13	2	4	26	15	24	.281	.317	.378	112	3	3	36	0	0	0	.984	1	O/1	0.0
1969	Cle-A	43	108	9	27	5	0	1	15	8	15	.250	.308	.324	74	-3	-4	11	1	0	0	.982	1	O	-0.5
	Was-A	71	238	41	69	9	3	9	26	20	25	.290	.345	.466	132	7	9	35	1	3	-2	.944	-6	O	-0.2
	Yr	114	346	50	96	14	3	10	41	28	40	.277	.333	.422	112	4	5	46	2	3	-1	.957	-5	O	-0.7
1970	Was-A	96	255	28	67	12	1	7	30	21	32	.263	.321	.400	103	-1	0	33	4	2	0	1.000	-8	O/3	-1.1
	Chi-A	6	6	0	1	0	0	0	1	0	1	.167	.167	.167	-8	-1	-1	0	0	0	0	.000	0	H	-0.1
	Yr	102	261	28	68	12	1	7	31	21	33	.261	.318	.395	100	-2	-1	33	4	2	0	1.000	-8	O/3	-1.2
1971	Chi-A	32	44	6	9	2	0	1	7	5	7	.205	.286	.318	69	-2	-2	4	0	0	0	1.000	-1	O	-0.3
Total	13	1288	4048	533	1109	190	39	94	419	282	481	.274	.324	.410	108	17	32	539	59	34	-3	.970	-19	*O/312	-4.2

■ ED MAYER Mayer, Edward H. b: 8/16/1866, Marshall, Ill. d: 5/18/13, Chicago, Ill. 5'8.5", 155 lbs. Deb: 4/19/1890

YEAR	TM/L	G	AB	R	H	2B	3B	HR	RBI	BB	SO	AVG	OBP	SLG	PRO+	BR	/A	RC	SB	CS	SBR	FA	FR	POS	TPR
1890	Phi-N	117	484	49	117	25	5	1	70	22	36	.242	.286	.320	77	-14	-16	51	20			.878	-6	*3/O	-1.6
1891	Phi-N	68	268	24	50	2	4	0	31	14	29	.187	.238	.224	35	-21	-22	16	7			.895	-6	3O/S2	-2.5
Total	2	185	752	73	167	27	9	1	101	36	65	.222	.269	.286	62	-36	-38	68	27			.882	-12	3/OS2	-4.1

■ SAM MAYER Mayer, Samuel Frankel (b: Samuel Frankel Erskine) b: 2/28/1893, Atlanta, Ga. d: 7/1/62, Atlanta, Ga. BR/TL, 5'10", 164 lbs. Deb: 9/14/15 F

YEAR	TM/L	G	AB	R	H	2B	3B	HR	RBI	BB	SO	AVG	OBP	SLG	PRO+	BR	/A	RC	SB	CS	SBR	FA	FR	POS	TPR
1915	Was-A	11	29	5	7	0	0	1	4	4	2	.241	.333	.345	101	0	0	3	1	2	-1	1.000	0	/OP1	-0.1

■ WALLY MAYER Mayer, Walter A. b: 7/8/1890, Cincinnati, Ohio d: 11/18/51, Minneapolis, Minn. BR/TR, 5'11", 168 lbs. Deb: 9/28/11

YEAR	TM/L	G	AB	R	H	2B	3B	HR	RBI	BB	SO	AVG	OBP	SLG	PRO+	BR	/A	RC	SB	CS	SBR	FA	FR	POS	TPR
1911	Chi-A	1	3	0	0	0	0	0	0	2		.000	.400	.000	16	-0	-0	0	0			.900	-1	/C	-0.1
1912	Chi-A	9	9	1	0	0	0	0	0	1		.000	.100	.000	-73	-2	-2	0	0			1.000	-0	/C	-0.2
1914	Chi-A	40	85	7	14	3	1	0	5	14	23	.165	.290	.224	55	-4	-4	6	1	1	-0	.968	5	C/3	0.3
1915	Chi-A	22	54	3	12	3	1	0	5	5	8	.222	.288	.315	78	-1	-2	5	0	2	-1	.990	-1	C	-0.3
1917	Bos-A	4	12	2	2	0	0	0	0	5	2	.167	.412	.167	78	0	0	1	0			.964	2	/C	0.2
1918	Bos-A	26	49	7	11	4	0	0	5	7	7	.224	.321	.306	91	-1	-0	5	0			.964	-1	C	0.0
1919	StL-A	30	62	2	14	4	1	0	5	8	11	.226	.314	.323	77	-2	-2	7	0			.959	6	C	0.5
Total	7	132	274	22	53	14	3	0	20	42	51	.193	.303	.266	68	-10	-10	23	1	3		.969	10	C/3	0.4

■ PADDY MAYES Mayes, Adair Bushyhead b: 3/17/1885, Locust Grove, Okla. d: 5/28/62, Fayetteville, Ark. BL/TR, 5'11", 160 lbs. Deb: 6/11/11

YEAR	TM/L	G	AB	R	H	2B	3B	HR	RBI	BB	SO	AVG	OBP	SLG	PRO+	BR	/A	RC	SB	CS	SBR	FA	FR	POS	TPR
1911	Phi-N	5	5	1	0	0	0	0	0	1	2	.000	.286	.000	-17	-1	-1	0	0			1.000	-0	/O	-0.1

■ BUSTER MAYNARD Maynard, James Walter b: 3/25/13, Henderson, S.C. d: 9/7/77, Durham, N.C. BR/TR, 5'11", 170 lbs. Deb: 9/17/40

YEAR	TM/L	G	AB	R	H	2B	3B	HR	RBI	BB	SO	AVG	OBP	SLG	PRO+	BR	/A	RC	SB	CS	SBR	FA	FR	POS	TPR
1940	NY-N	7	29	6	8	2	2	1	2	2	6	.276	.323	.586	145	2	2	6	0			.929	-1	/O	0.0
1942	NY-N	89	190	17	47	4	1	4	32	19	19	.247	.319	.342	93	-2	-2	20	3			.982	-0	O3/2	-0.4
1943	NY-N	121	393	43	81	8	2	9	32	24	27	.206	.252	.305	60	-21	-21	30	3			.965	-6	O3	-3.4
1946	NY-N	7	4	2	0	0	0	0	0	1	1	.000	.200	.000	-41	-1	-1	0	0			.750	-1	/O	-0.2
Total	4	224	616	68	136	14	5	14	66	46	53	.221	.276	.328	74	-22	-22	56	6			.967	-8	O/32	-4.0

■ CHICK MAYNARD Maynard, Le Roy Evans b: 11/2/1896, Turners Falls, Mass. d: 1/31/57, Bangor, Maine BL/TR, 5'9", 150 lbs. Deb: 6/27/22

YEAR	TM/L	G	AB	R	H	2B	3B	HR	RBI	BB	SO	AVG	OBP	SLG	PRO+	BR	/A	RC	SB	CS	SBR	FA	FR	POS	TPR
1922	Bos-A	12	24	1	3	0	0	0	0	3	2	.125	.222	.125	-8	-4	-4	1	0	1	-1	.872	-2	S	-0.6

■ BRENT MAYNE Mayne, Brent Danem b: 4/19/68, Loma Linda, Cal. BL/TR, 6'1", 195 lbs. Deb: 9/18/90

YEAR	TM/L	G	AB	R	H	2B	3B	HR	RBI	BB	SO	AVG	OBP	SLG	PRO+	BR	/A	RC	SB	CS	SBR	FA	FR	POS	TPR
1990	KC-A	5	13	2	3	0	0	0	1	3	3	.231	.375	.231	74	-0	-0	1	0	1	-1	.970	1	/C	0.0
1991	KC-A	85	231	22	58	8	0	3	31	23	42	.251	.319	.325	78	-6	-7	23	2	4	-2	.987	4	C/D	0.0
1992	KC-A	82	213	16	48	10	0	0	18	11	26	.225	.263	.272	50	-14	-14	14	0	4	-2	.990	2	C/3	-1.2
Total	3	172	457	40	109	18	0	3	50	37	71	.239	.296	.298	65	-21	-21	38	2	9	-5	.988	6	C/3D	-1.2

■ EDDIE MAYO Mayo, Edward Joseph "Hotshot" (b: Edward Joseph Mayoski) b: 4/15/10, Holyoke, Mass. BL/TR, 5'11", 178 lbs. Deb: 5/29/36 C

YEAR	TM/L	G	AB	R	H	2B	3B	HR	RBI	BB	SO	AVG	OBP	SLG	PRO+	BR	/A	RC	SB	CS	SBR	FA	FR	POS	TPR
1936	*NY-N	46	141	11	28	4	1	1	8	11	12	.199	.257	.262	40	-12	-12	10	0			.981	5	3	-0.6
1937	Bos-N	65	172	19	39	6	1	1	18	15	20	.227	.293	.291	65	-10	-8	15	1			.956	-4	3	-1.0
1938	Bos-N	8	14	2	3	0	0	1	4	1	0	.214	.267	.429	98	-0	-0	1	0			.923	2	/3S	0.2
1943	Phi-A	128	471	49	103	10	1	0	28	34	32	.219	.278	.244	54	-27	-27	36	2	0	1	**.976**	-3	*3	-3.0
1944	Det-A	154	607	76	151	18	3	5	63	57	23	.249	.317	.313	76	-15	-19	62	9	13	-5	.978	**29**	*2S	1.5
1945	*Det-A†	134	501	71	143	24	3	10	54	47	29	.285	.347	.405	111	10	7	72	7	7	-2	**.980**	18	*2	3.2
1946	Det-A	51	202	21	51	9	2	0	22	14	12	.252	.301	.317	68	-8	-9	19	6	2	1	.965	-11	2	-1.7
1947	Det-A	142	535	66	149	28	4	6	48	48	28	.279	.338	.379	96	-1	-3	67	3	7	-3	.983	-23	*2	-2.1
1948	Det-A	106	370	35	92	20	1	2	42	30	19	.249	.310	.324	67	-17	-18	35	1	9	-5	.975	-10	23	-2.8
Total	9	834	3013	350	759	119	16	26	287	257	175	.252	.313	.328	78	-79	-89	316	29	<u>38</u>		.978	3	23/S	-6.3

■ JACKIE MAYO Mayo, John Lewis b: 7/26/25, Litchfield, Ill. BL/TR, 6'1", 190 lbs. Deb: 9/19/48

YEAR	TM/L	G	AB	R	H	2B	3B	HR	RBI	BB	SO	AVG	OBP	SLG	PRO+	BR	/A	RC	SB	CS	SBR	FA	FR	POS	TPR
1948	Phi-N	12	35	7	8	2	1	0	3	7	7	.229	.386	.343	101	0	0	6	1			1.000	1	O	0.1
1949	Phi-N	45	39	3	5	0	0	0	2	4	5	.128	.209	.128	-8	-6	-6	1	0			.889	-7	O	-1.3
1950	*Phi-N	18	36	1	8	3	0	0	3	2	5	.222	.263	.306	50	-3	-3	3	0			.958	-3	O	-0.5
1951	Phi-N	9	7	1	1	0	0	0	0	0	0	.143	.143	.143	-23	-1	-1	0	0	0	0	1.000	-2	/O	-0.3
1952	Phi-N	50	119	13	29	5	0	1	4	12	17	.244	.313	.311	74	-4	-4	11	1	3	-2	1.000	4	O/1	-0.3
1953	Phi-N	5	4	0	0	0	0	0	0	0	1	.000	.000	.000	-99	-1	-1	0	0	0	0	.000	-0	/O	-0.2
Total	6	139	240	25	51	10	1	1	12	25	35	.213	.292	.275	56	-15	-14	21	2	<u>3</u>		.972	-7	/O1	-2.5

■ WILLIE MAYS Mays, Willie Howard "Say Hey" b: 5/6/31, Westfield, Ala. BR/TR, 5'11", 180 lbs. Deb: 5/25/51 CH

YEAR	TM/L	G	AB	R	H	2B	3B	HR	RBI	BB	SO	AVG	OBP	SLG	PRO+	BR	/A	RC	SB	CS	SBR	FA	FR	POS	TPR
1951	*NY-N	121	464	59	127	22	5	20	68	57	60	.274	.356	.472	120	13	13	80	7	4	-0	.976	11	*O	1.9
1952	NY-N	34	127	17	30	2	4	4	23	16	17	.236	.326	.409	102	0	0	18	4	1	1	.991	8	O	0.7
1954	*NY-N★	151	565	119	195	33	**13**	41	110	66	57	**.345**	.415	**.667**	176	62	61	155	8	5	-1	.985	16	*O	**6.8**
1955	NY-N★	152	580	123	185	18	**13**	**51**	127	79	60	.319	.404	**.659**	**176**	**62**	**62**	**157**	24	4	**5**	.982	**20**	*O	**7.7**
1956	NY-N★	152	578	101	171	27	8	36	84	68	65	.296	.371	.557	146	36	36	118	**40**	10	**6**	.979	12	*O	**4.7**
1957	NY-N★	152	585	112	195	26	**20**	35	97	76	62	.333	.411	**.626**	**174**	**61**	**61**	**145**	**38**	19	0	.980	11	*O	**6.3**
1958	SF-N★	152	600	**121**	208	33	11	29	96	78	56	.347	.423	.583	**167**	**55**	**57**	**152**	**31**	6	**6**	.980	17	*O	**7.0**
1959	SF-N★	151	575	125	180	43	5	34	104	65	58	.313	.385	.583	157	43	44	131	**27**	4	**6**	.984	7	*O	4.9
1960	SF-N★	153	595	107	**190**	29	12	29	103	61	70	.319	.386	.555	164	44	48	124	25	10	2	.981	14	*O	5.6
1961	SF-N★	154	572	**129**	176	32	3	40	123	81	77	.308	.395	.584	162	46	49	130	18	9	0	.980	4	*O	4.2
1962	*SF-N★	162	621	130	189	36	5	**49**	141	78	85	.304	.385	.615	167	54	55	146	18	2	4	.991	7	*O	5.5
1963	SF-N★	157	596	115	187	32	7	38	103	66	83	.314	.384	.582	176	56	57	131	8	3	1	.981	8	*O/S	6.0
1964	SF-N★	157	578	121	171	21	9	**47**	111	82	72	.296	.384	**.607**	**171**	**57**	**55**	**136**	19	5	3	.984	8	*O/1S3	6.0
1965	SF-N★	157	558	118	177	21	3	**52**	112	76	71	.317	**.399**	**.645**	**184**	**65**	**63**	**143**	9	4	0	.983	10	*O	**6.9**
1966	SF-N★	152	552	99	159	29	4	37	103	70	81	.288	.370	.556	149	39	37	113	5	1	1	.982	5	*O	3.7
1967	SF-N★	141	486	83	128	22	2	22	70	51	92	.263	.336	.453	125	14	15	74	6	0	2	.976	-5	*O	0.6
1968	SF-N★	148	498	84	144	20	5	23	79	67	81	.289	.376	.488	158	36	36	91	12	6	0	.978	-3	*O/1	2.9
1969	SF-N★	117	403	64	114	17	3	13	58	49	71	.283	.365	.437	126	13	14	66	6	2	1	.976	-12	*O/1	-0.4
1970	SF-N★	139	478	94	139	15	2	28	83	79	90	.291	.395	.506	141	28	29	101	5	0	2	.975	-2	*O/1	2.1
1971	*SF-N★	136	417	82	113	24	5	18	61	**112**	123	.271	**.429**	.482	160	38	38	98	23	3	5	.970	-6	O1	3.2
1972	SF-N	19	49	8	9	2	0	0	3	17	5	.184	.394	.224	79	-0	-0	6	3	0	1	1.000	-1	O	-0.1
	NY-N★	69	195	27	52	9	1	8	19	43	43	.267	.402	.446	144	12	13	35	1	5	-3	.974	2	O1	1.0
	Yr	88	244	35	61	11	1	8	22	60	48	.250	.400	.402	131	12	13	41	4	5	-2	.979	1	O1	0.9
1973	*NY-N★	66	209	24	44	10	0	6	25	27	47	.211	.304	.344	81	-6	-5	22	1	0	0	.991	0	O1	-0.8
Total	22	2992	10881	2062	3283	523	140	660	1903	1464	1526	.302	.387	.557	157	827	838	2372	338	103	40	.981	131	*O/1S3	86.4

■ BILL MAZEROSKI Mazeroski, William Stanley "Maz" b: 9/5/36, Wheeling, W.Va. BR/TR, 5'11.5", 183 lbs. Deb: 7/07/56 C

YEAR	TM/L	G	AB	R	H	2B	3B	HR	RBI	BB	SO	AVG	OBP	SLG	PRO+	BR	/A	RC	SB	CS	SBR	FA	FR	POS	TPR
1956	Pit-N	81	255	30	62	8	1	3	14	18	24	.243	.293	.318	66	-13	-12	24	0	0	0	.981	11	2	0.6
1957	Pit-N	148	526	59	149	27	7	8	54	27	49	.283	.319	.407	96	-6	-4	68	3	3	-1	.978	4	*2	1.1
1958	Pit-N★	152	567	69	156	24	6	19	68	25	71	.275	.309	.439	98	-6	-4	73	1	1	-0	.980	19	*2	2.6
1959	Pit-N★	135	493	50	119	15	6	7	59	29	54	.241	.285	.339	66	-25	-24	44	1	3	-2	.981	-9	*2	-2.5
1960	*Pit-N★	151	538	58	147	21	5	11	64	40	50	.273	.325	.392	95	-4	-4	68	4	0	1	**.989**	**25**	*2	3.8
1961	Pit-N	152	558	71	148	21	2	13	59	26	55	.265	.302	.380	79	-17	-17	62	2	1	0	.975	**31**	*2	2.9
1962	Pit-N★	159	572	55	155	24	9	14	81	37	47	.271	.318	.418	95	-5	-5	71	0	3	-2	.985	**41**	*2	5.0
1963	Pit-N†	142	534	43	131	22	3	8	52	32	46	.245	.288	.343	80	-14	-14	50	2	0	1	.984	**57**	*2	6.0
1964	Pit-N☆	162	601	66	161	22	8	10	64	29	52	.268	.302	.381	91	-8	-8	63	1	1	-0	.975	**34**	*2	4.1
1965	Pit-N	130	494	52	134	17	1	6	54	18	34	.271	.300	.346	81	-13	-13	47	2	1	0	**.988**	26	*2	2.5
1966	Pit-N	162	621	56	163	22	7	16	82	31	62	.262	.299	.398	91	-8	-8	69	4	3	-1	**.992**	**41**	*2	4.5
1967	Pit-N★	163	639	62	167	25	3	9	77	30	55	.261	.294	.352	84	-14	-14	62	1	2	-1	.981	17	*2	1.4
1968	Pit-N	143	506	36	127	18	2	3	42	38	38	.251	.306	.312	87	-8	-8	45	3	4	-2	.981	**26**	*2	2.8
1969	Pit-N	67	227	13	52	7	1	3	25	22	16	.229	.303	.308	73	-8	-8	21	1	1	-0	.988	14	2	1.1
1970	*Pit-N	112	367	29	84	14	0	7	39	27	40	.229	.285	.324	64	-20	-19	34	2	0	1	.987	24	*2	1.4
1971	*Pit-N	70	193	17	49	3	1	1	16	15	8	.254	.308	.295	72	-7	-7	18	0	0	0	.986	-1	2/3	-0.5
1972	*Pit-N	34	64	3	12	4	0	0	3	3	5	.188	.224	.250	35	-6	-5	3	0	0	0	.986	3	2/3	-0.2
Total	17	2163	7755	769	2016	294	62	138	853	447	706	.260	.302	.367	84	-180	-174	824	27	23	-6	.983	362	*2/3	36.6

■ MEL MAZZERA Mazzera, Melvin Leonard "Mike" b: 1/31/14, Stockton, Cal. BL/TL, 5'11", 180 lbs. Deb: 9/09/35

YEAR	TM/L	G	AB	R	H	2B	3B	HR	RBI	BB	SO	AVG	OBP	SLG	PRO+	BR	/A	RC	SB	CS	SBR	FA	FR	POS	TPR
1935	StL-A	12	30	4	7	2	0	1	2	4	9	.233	.324	.400	82	-1	-1	4	0	0	0	.950	-1	O	-0.2
1937	StL-A	7	7	1	2	2	0	0	0	0	2	.286	.286	.571	110	0	0	1	0	0	0	.000	0	H	0.0
1938	StL-A	86	204	33	57	8	2	6	29	12	25	.279	.329	.426	88	-5	-5	29	1	1	-0	.976	-1	O	-0.7
1939	StL-A	33	110	21	33	5	2	3	22	10	20	.300	.364	.464	108	1	1	19	0	0	0	.983	0	O	0.0
1940	Phi-N	69	156	16	37	5	4	0	13	19	15	.237	.320	.321	80	-5	-4	16	1			.985	-4	O1	-1.0
Total	5	207	507	75	136	22	8	10	66	45	71	.268	.333	.402	90	-8	-8	69	2	<u>1</u>		.978	-6	O/1	-1.9

■ LEE MAZZILLI Mazzilli, Lee Louis b: 3/25/55, New York, N.Y. BB/TR, 6'1", 185 lbs. Deb: 9/07/76

YEAR	TM/L	G	AB	R	H	2B	3B	HR	RBI	BB	SO	AVG	OBP	SLG	PRO+	BR	/A	RC	SB	CS	SBR	FA	FR	POS	TPR
1976	NY-N	24	77	9	15	2	0	2	7	14	10	.195	.326	.299	83	-2	-1	8	5	4	-1	.983	3	O	0.0
1977	NY-N	159	537	66	134	24	3	6	46	72	72	.250	.342	.339	87	-11	-8	66	22	15	-2	.992	3	*O	-1.3
1978	NY-N	148	542	78	148	28	5	16	61	69	82	.273	.356	.432	124	14	17	85	20	13	-2	.987	7	*O	1.6
1979	NY-N★	158	597	78	181	34	4	15	79	93	74	.303	.397	.449	135	28	31	115	34	12	3	.989	1	*O1	2.8
1980	NY-N	152	578	82	162	31	4	16	76	82	92	.280	.373	.431	127	20	22	98	41	15	3	.983	-3	1O	1.5
1981	NY-N	95	324	36	74	14	5	6	34	46	53	.228	.328	.358	96	-2	-1	41	17	7	1	.970	2	O	-0.2
1982	Tex-A	58	195	23	47	8	0	4	17	28	26	.241	.339	.344	93	-2	-1	24	11	6	-0	.945	-3	OD	-0.5
	NY-A	37	128	20	34	2	0	6	17	15	15	.266	.347	.422	112	2	2	19	2	3	-1	.995	-3	1/OD	-0.3
	Yr	95	323	43	81	10	0	10	34	43	41	.251	.342	.375	100	-1	1	42	13	9	-2	.949	-6	DO1	-0.8
1983	Pit-N	109	246	37	59	9	0	5	24	49	43	.240	.370	.337	95	1	0	34	15	5	2	.985	1	O/1	0.1
1984	Pit-N	111	266	37	63	11	1	4	21	40	42	.237	.339	.331	89	-3	-3	33	8	1	2	.989	-7	O/1	-1.1

YEAR	TM/L	G	AB	R	H	2B	3B	HR	RBI	BB	SO	AVG	OBP	SLG	PRO+	BR	/A	RC	SB	CS	SBR	FA	FR	POS	TPR
1985	Pit-N	92	117	20	33	8	0	1	9	29	17	.282	.425	.376	127	6	6	21	4	1	1	.986	-1	1/O	0.4
1986	Pit-N	61	93	18	21	2	1	1	8	26	25	.226	.395	.301	93	1	1	13	3	3	-1	1.000	-3	O/1	-0.4
	*NY-N	39	58	10	16	3	0	2	7	12	11	.276	.417	.431	138	3	4	11	1	1	-0	1.000	-1	O/1	0.1
	Yr	100	151	28	37	5	1	3	15	38	36	.245	.403	.351	109	4	4	24	4	4	-1	1.000	-4	O1	-0.3
1987	NY-N	88	124	26	38	8	1	3	24	21	14	.306	.407	.460	136	6	7	24	5	3	-0	1.000	-6	O1	0.0
1988	*NY-N	68	116	9	17	2	0	0	12	12	16	.147	.233	.164	16	-12	-12	5	4	1	1	1.000	-4	O1	-1.8
1989	NY-N	48	60	10	11	2	0	2	7	17	19	.183	.364	.317	101	0	1	9	3	0	1	.889	-4	O/1	-0.3
	*Tor-A	28	66	12	15	3	0	4	11	17	16	.227	.400	.455	143	4	5	14	2	0	1	.944	-1	D/1O	0.4
Total	14	1475	4124	571	1068	191	24	93	460	642	627	.259	.361	.385	109	54	69	618	197	90	5	.986	-18	O1/D	1.0
■ **JIMMY McALEER** McAleer, James Robert "Loafer" b: 7/10/1864, Youngstown, Ohio d: 4/29/31, Youngstown, Ohio BR/TR, 6', 175 lbs. Deb: 4/24/1889 M																									
1889	Cle-N	110	447	66	105	6	6	1	35	30	49	.235	.289	.282	62	-23	-21	48	37			.955	9	*O	-1.3
1890	Cle-P	86	341	58	91	8	7	1	42	37	33	.267	.340	.340	91	-7	-2	48	21			.940	11	O	0.5
1891	Cle-N	136	565	97	134	16	11	1	61	49	47	.237	.304	.310	77	-14	-17	70	51			.924	5	*O	-1.5
1892	*Cle-N	149	571	92	136	26	7	4	70	63	54	.238	.318	.329	94	-1	-4	74	40			.948	12	*O	0.1
1893	Cle-N	91	350	63	83	5	1	2	41	35	21	.237	.314	.274	55	-20	-24	41	32			.928	4	*O	-2.0
1894	Cle-N	64	253	36	73	15	1	2	40	13	17	.289	.331	.379	70	-12	-14	38	14			.953	3	O	-1.1
1895	*Cle-N	131	528	84	143	17	2	0	68	38	37	.271	.327	.311	63	-25	-30	67	32			.934	3	*O	-3.1
1896	*Cle-N	116	455	70	131	16	4	1	54	47	32	.288	.361	.347	84	-5	-10	70	24			.958	7	*O	-1.1
1897	Cle-N	24	91	6	20	2	0	0	10	7		.220	.283	.242	37	-8	-9	8	4			.947	-1	O	-1.0
1898	Cle-N	106	366	47	87	3	0	0	48	46		.238	.331	.246	67	-14	-13	34	7			.965	3	*O/2	-1.6
1901	Cle-A	3	7	0	1	0	0	0	0	0		.143	.143	.143	-22	-1	-1	0	0			1.000	-1	/OP3M	-0.2
1902	StL-A	2	3	0	2	0	0	0	0	0		.667	.667	.667	274	1	1	1	0			.000	-1	/OM	0.0
1907	StL-A	2	0	0	0	0	0	0	0	0		—	—	—	—	0	0	0	0			.000	0	RM	0.0
Total	13	1020	3977	619	1006	114	39	12	469	365	290	.253	.322	.310	73	-129	-145	499	262			.944	54	*O/23P	-12.3
■ **JACK McALEESE** McAleese, John James b: 1877, Sharon, Pa. d: 11/15/50, New York, N.Y. BR/TR, 5'8", Deb: 8/10/01																									
1901	Chi-A	1	1	0	0	0	0	0	0	0		.000	.000	.000	-99	-0	-0	0	0			1.000	0	/P	0.0
1909	StL-A	85	267	33	57	7	0	0	12	32		.213	.318	.240	82	-5	-3	26	18			.910	-3	O/3	-1.0
Total	2	86	268	33	57	7	0	0	12	32		.213	.317	.239	82	-6	-3	26	18			.983	-3	/O3P	-1.0
■ **BILL McALLESTER** McAllester, William Lusk b: 12/29/1888, Chattanooga, Tenn. d: 3/3/70, Chattanooga, Tenn. BR/TR, 5'11.5", 170 lbs. Deb: 5/02/13																									
1913	StL-A	49	85	3	13	4	0	0	6	11	12	.153	.250	.200	33	-7	-7	5	2			.908	-4	C	-0.9
■ **SPORT McALLISTER** McAllister, Lewis William b: 7/23/1874, Austin, Miss. d: 7/17/62, Wyandotte, Mich. BB/TR, 5'11", 180 lbs. Deb: 8/07/1896																									
1896	Cle-N	8	27	2	6	2	0	0	1	0	2	.222	.250	.296	43	-2	-2	2	1			.500	-6	/OCP	-0.8
1897	Cle-N	43	137	23	30	5	1	0	11	12		.219	.287	.270	45	-10	-12	12	3			.894	-6	O/SP1C2	-1.6
1898	Cle-N	17	57	8	13	3	1	0	9	5		.228	.290	.316	75	-2	-2	5	0			.941	1	/PO	0.0
1899	Cle-N	113	418	29	99	6	8	1	31	19		.237	.273	.297	61	-26	-21	38	5			.943	-16	OC/31SP2	-3.7
1901	Det-A	90	306	45	92	9	4	3	57	15		.301	.344	.386	98	1	-2	49	17			.898	-20	C1O3/S	-1.7
1902	Det-A	21	67	8	14	1	0	1	8	2		.209	.243	.269	41	-5	-6	5	0			1.000	1	/1S2C3O	-0.4
	Bal-A	3	11	0	1	0	0	0	1	1		.091	.167	.091	-26	-2	-2	0	0			.923	-0	/21	-0.2
	Det-A	45	162	11	34	4	2	0	24	3		.210	.229	.259	34	-14	-15	10	1			.991	-1	1O/C3S	-1.5
	Yr	69	240	19	49	5	2	1	33	6		.204	.230	.254	33	-22	-22	15	1			.992	-1	1O/CS32D	-2.1
1903	Det-A	78	265	31	69	8	2	0	22	10		.260	.295	.306	83	-6	-5	27	5			.888	-8	SC/O31	-1.0
Total	7	418	1450	157	358	38	18	5	164	67	2	.247	.287	.308	66	-68	-67	148	32			.914	-56	O/C1S3P2	-10.9
■ **JIM McANANY** McAnany, James b: 9/4/36, Los Angeles, Cal. BR/TR, 5'10", 196 lbs. Deb: 9/19/58																									
1958	Chi-A	5	13	0	0	0	0	0	0	0	5	.000	.000	.000	-99	-3	-3	0	0	0	0	1.000	1	/O	-0.3
1959	*Chi-A	67	210	22	58	9	3	0	27	19	26	.276	.339	.348	90	-3	-2	26	2	1	0	.966	-1	O	-0.6
1960	Chi-A	3	2	0	0	0	0	0	0	0	2	.000	.000	.000	-99	-1	-1	0	0	0	0	.000	0	H	-0.1
1961	Chi-N	11	10	1	3	1	0	0	0	1	3	.300	.364	.400	101	0	0	2	0	0	0	.000	0	/O	0.0
1962	Chi-N	7	6	0	0	0	0	0	0	1	2	.000	.143	.000	-56	-1	-1	0	0	0	0	.000	0	H	-0.1
Total	5	93	241	23	61	10	3	0	27	21	38	.253	.316	.320	75	-8	-8	27	2	1	0	.968	-0	/O	-1.1
■ **BUB McATEE** McAtee, Michael James "Butch" b: 3/1845, Troy, N.Y. d: 10/18/1876, Troy, N.Y. TR, 5'9", 160 lbs. Deb: 5/08/1871																									
1871	Chi-n	26	135	34	37	8	2	0	10	5	2	.274	.300	.363	81	-2	-5	17	5					*1	-0.3
1872	Tro-n	25	130	30	29	4	1	0	15	1	2	.223	.229	.269	52	-7	-7	8						1	-0.5
Total	2 n	51	265	64	66	12	3	0	25	6	4	.249	.266	.317	68	-9	-13	24						/1	-0.8
■ **IKE McAULEY** McAuley, James Earl b: 8/19/1891, Wichita, Kan. d: 4/6/28, Des Moines, Iowa BR/TR, 5'9.5", 150 lbs. Deb: 9/10/14																									
1914	Pit-N	15	24	3	3	0	0	0	0	0	8	.125	.125	.125	-27	-4	-4	0	0			.900	1	/S32	-0.3
1915	Pit-N	5	15	0	2	1	0	0	0	0	6	.133	.133	.200	0	-2	-2	0	0			.917	-3	/S	-0.5
1916	Pit-N	4	8	1	2	0	0	0	1	0	1	.250	.250	.250	53	-0	-0	1	0			.938	1	/S	0.0
1917	StL-N	3	7	0	2	0	0	0	1	0	1	.286	.286	.286	78	-0	-0	1	0			.833	-2	/S	-0.3
1925	Chi-N	37	125	10	35	7	2	0	11	11	12	.280	.343	.368	80	-3	-4	17	1	0	0	.949	-8	S	-0.7
Total	5	64	179	14	44	8	2	0	13	11	28	.246	.293	.313	62	-9	-10	19	1	0		.940	-12	/S32	-1.8
■ **GENE McAULIFFE** McAuliffe, Eugene Leo b: 2/28/1872, Randolph, Mass. d: 4/29/53, Randolph, Mass. BR/TR, 6'1", 180 lbs. Deb: 8/17/04																									
1904	Bos-N	1	2	0	1	0	0	0	0	0		.500	.500	.500	218	0	0	1	0			.667	-0	/C	0.0
■ **DICK McAULIFFE** McAuliffe, Richard John b: 11/29/39, Hartford, Conn. BL/TR, 5'11", 176 lbs. Deb: 9/17/60																									
1960	Det-A	8	27	2	7	0	1	0	1	2	6	.259	.310	.333	72	-1	-1	3	0	0	0	.884	1	/S	0.1
1961	Det-A	80	285	36	73	12	4	6	33	24	39	.256	.323	.389	87	-5	-6	36	2	3	-1	.933	-29	S3	-3.1
1962	Det-A	139	471	50	124	20	5	12	63	64	76	.263	.351	.403	99	2	0	68	4	2	0	.965	-21	23S	-1.2
1963	Det-A	150	568	77	149	18	6	13	61	64	75	.262	.337	.384	98	2	-0	75	11	5	0	.963	-24	*S2	-1.4
1964	Det-A	162	557	85	134	18	7	24	66	77	96	.241	.336	.427	109	8	7	81	8	5	-1	.958	-8	*S	1.1
1965	Det-A★	113	404	61	105	13	6	15	54	49	62	.260	.343	.433	118	10	10	60	6	9	-4	.956	-15	*S	-0.1
1966	Det-A★	124	430	83	118	16	8	23	56	66	80	.274	.375	.509	148	29	28	83	5	7	-3	.964	-11	*S3	2.6
1967	Det-A★	153	557	92	133	16	7	22	65	105	118	.239	.366	.411	126	24	22	93	6	5	-1	.965	-14	*2S	2.0
1968	*Det-A	151	570	**95**	142	24	10	16	56	82	99	.249	.346	.411	125	21	19	87	8	7	-2	.986	-20	*2/S	0.7
1969	Det-A	74	271	49	71	10	5	11	33	47	41	.262	.371	.458	125	12	10	48	2	5	-2	.976	-0	2	1.4
1970	Det-A	146	530	73	124	21	1	12	50	101	62	.234	.360	.345	95	0	-1	74	5	6	-2	.975	-6	*2S3	0.4
1971	Det-A	128	477	67	99	16	6	18	57	53	67	.208	.293	.379	86	-8	-10	55	4	1	1	.987	7	*2/S	0.9
1972	*Det-A	122	408	47	98	16	3	8	30	59	59	.240	.339	.353	103	4	3	53	0	0	0	.975	-7	*2/S3	0.2
1973	Det-A	106	343	39	94	18	1	12	47	49	52	.274	.366	.437	118	12	9	57	0	4	-2	.986	-5	*2/SD	1.8
1974	Bos-A	100	272	32	57	13	1	5	24	39	40	.210	.311	.320	76	-6	-8	28	2	0	1	.971	-8	23/SD	-1.4
1975	Bos-A	7	15	0	2	0	0	0	1	1	2	.133	.188	.133	-7	-2	-2	0	0	0	0	.769	-2	/3	-0.4
Total	16	1763	6185	888	1530	231	71	197	697	882	974	.247	.344	.403	108	104	81	899	63	59	-17	.977	-150	2S3/D	3.6
■ **GEORGE McAVOY** McAvoy, George H. Deb: 7/17/14																									
1914	Phi-N	1	1	0	0	0	0	0	0	0	0	.000	.000	.000	-94	-0	-0	0	0			.000	0	H	0.0
■ **WICKEY McAVOY** McAvoy, James Eugene b: 10/22/1894, Rochester, N.Y. d: 7/6/73, Rochester, N.Y. BR/TR, 5'11", 172 lbs. Deb: 9/29/13																									
1913	Phi-A	4	9	0	1	0	0	0	0	0	4	.111	.200	.111	-9	-1	-1	0	0			1.000	1	/C	0.0

YEAR	TM/L	G	AB	R	H	2B	3B	HR	RBI	BB	SO	AVG	OBP	SLG	PRO+	BR	/A	RC	SB	CS	SBR	FA	FR	POS	TPR
1914	Phi-A	8	16	1	2	0	1	0	0	0	4	.125	.125	.250	13	-2	-2	1	0			.971	1	/C	-0.1
1915	Phi-A	68	184	12	35	7	2	0	6	11	32	.190	.236	.250	47	-13	-12	11	0	2	-1	.931	5	C	-0.5
1917	Phi-A	10	24	1	6	1	0	1	4	0	3	.250	.250	.417	105	-0	-0	2	0			.955	3	/C	0.4
1918	Phi-A	83	271	14	66	5	3	0	32	13	23	.244	.283	.284	70	-10	-10	23	5			.960	5	C/P1O	0.1
1919	Phi-A	62	170	10	24	5	2	0	11	14	21	.141	.207	.194	13	-20	-20	7	1			.973	-3	C	-1.9
Total	6	235	674	38	134	18	8	1	53	38	87	.199	.245	.254	47	-46	-46	43	6	2		.954	13	C/O1P	-2.0

■ ALGIE McBRIDE McBride, Algernon Griggs b: 5/23/1869, Washington, D.C. d: 1/10/56, Georgetown, Ohio BL/TL, 5'9", 152 lbs. Deb: 5/12/1896

YEAR	TM/L	G	AB	R	H	2B	3B	HR	RBI	BB	SO	AVG	OBP	SLG	PRO+	BR	/A	RC	SB	CS	SBR	FA	FR	POS	TPR
1896	Chi-N	9	29	2	7	1	1	1	7	7	3	.241	.389	.448	118	1	1	5	0			.917	0	/O	0.0
1898	Cin-N	120	486	94	147	14	12	2	43	51		.302	.380	.393	114	15	10	82	16			.959	7	*O	0.8
1899	Cin-N	64	251	57	87	12	5	1	23	30		.347	.431	.446	138	16	15	52	5			.950	-2	O	0.7
1900	Cin-N	112	436	59	120	15	8	4	59	25		.275	.320	.374	94	-6	-5	58	12			.915	-9	*O	-2.0
1901	Cin-N	30	123	19	29	7	0	2	18	7		.236	.282	.341	86	-3	-2	12	0			.968	-2	O	-0.7
	NY-N	68	264	27	74	11	0	2	29	12		.280	.312	.345	94	-4	-2	31	3			.948	-4	O	-1.1
	Yr	98	387	46	103	18	0	4	47	19		.266	.302	.344	91	-7	-5	43	3			.956	-6	O	-1.8
Total	5	403	1589	258	464	60	26	12	179	132	3	.292	.355	.385	108	18	16	240	36			.946	-10	O	-2.3

■ BAKE McBRIDE McBride, Arnold Ray b: 2/3/49, Fulton, Mo. BL/TR, 6'2", 190 lbs. Deb: 7/26/73

YEAR	TM/L	G	AB	R	H	2B	3B	HR	RBI	BB	SO	AVG	OBP	SLG	PRO+	BR	/A	RC	SB	CS	SBR	FA	FR	POS	TPR
1973	StL-N	40	63	8	19	3	0	0	5	4	10	.302	.362	.349	98	0	0	8	0	1	-1	.976	3	O	0.2
1974	StL-N	150	559	81	173	19	5	6	56	43	57	.309	.372	.394	115	12	12	85	30	11	2	.990	5	*O	1.3
1975	StL-N	116	413	70	124	10	9	5	36	34	52	.300	.355	.404	107	5	4	62	26	8	3	.990	4	*O	0.6
1976	StL-N☆	72	272	40	91	13	4	3	24	18	28	.335	.389	.445	135	13	13	48	10	5	0	.981	9	O	2.0
1977	StL-N	43	122	21	32	5	1	4	20	7	19	.262	.302	.418	93	-2	-2	16	9	3	1	1.000	-3	O	-0.5
	*Phi-N	85	280	55	95	20	5	11	41	25	25	.339	.399	.564	149	21	20	67	27	4	6	.986	-0	O	2.2
	Yr	128	402	76	127	25	6	15	61	32	44	.316	.371	.520	133	20	18	81	36	7	7	.990	-3	*O	1.7
1978	*Phi-N	122	472	68	127	20	4	10	49	28	68	.269	.317	.392	96	-3	-3	63	28	3	7	**.996**	2	*O	0.0
1979	Phi-N	151	582	82	163	16	12	12	60	41	77	.280	.332	.411	98	0	-2	79	25	14	-1	.989	15	*O	0.6
1980	*Phi-N	137	554	68	171	33	10	9	87	26	58	.309	.345	.453	115	14	11	79	13	10	-2	.990	2	*O	0.5
1981	*Phi-N	58	221	26	60	17	1	2	21	11	25	.271	.306	.385	91	-2	-3	25	5	0	2	.987	-9	O	-1.4
1982	Cle-A	27	85	8	31	3	3	0	13	2	12	.365	.379	.471	132	3	4	14	2	2	-1	1.000	-2	O	0.0
1983	Cle-A	70	230	21	67	8	1	1	18	9	26	.291	.321	.348	81	-5	-6	24	8	2	1	.977	0	OD	-0.6
Total	11	1071	3853	548	1153	167	55	63	430	248	457	.299	.348	.420	109	57	46	570	183	63	17	.989	25	O/D	4.9

■ GEORGE McBRIDE McBride, George Florian b: 11/20/1880, Milwaukee, Wis. d: 7/2/73, Milwaukee, Wis. BR/TR, 5'11", 170 lbs. Deb: 9/12/01 MC

YEAR	TM/L	G	AB	R	H	2B	3B	HR	RBI	BB	SO	AVG	OBP	SLG	PRO+	BR	/A	RC	SB	CS	SBR	FA	FR	POS	TPR
1901	Mil-A	3	12	0	2	0	0	0	0	1		.167	.231	.167	12	-1	-1	0	0			1.000	-1	/S	-0.2
1905	Pit-N	27	87	9	19	4	0	0	7	6		.218	.277	.264	60	-4	-4	8	2			.902	-4	3/S	-0.8
	StL-N	81	281	22	61	1	2	2	34	14		.217	.264	.256	57	-15	-14	23	10			.938	-2	S/1	-1.5
	Yr	108	368	31	80	5	2	2	41	20		.217	.267	.258	58	-19	-19	31	12			.935	-6	S3/1	-2.3
1906	StL-N	90	313	24	53	8	2	0	13	17		.169	.215	.208	33	-25	-24	16	5			.944	9	S	-1.3
1908	Was-A	155	518	47	120	10	6	0	34	41		.232	.292	.274	92	-8	-4	45	12			.948	33	*S	3.6
1909	Was-A	156	504	38	118	16	0	0	34	36		.234	.294	.266	81	-12	-10	46	17			**.935**	11	*S	0.4
1910	Was-A	154	514	54	118	19	4	1	55	61		.230	.321	.288	95	-4	-1	53	11			.939	27	*S	3.5
1911	Was-A	154	557	58	131	11	4	0	59	52		.235	.312	.269	64	-27	-25	52	15			.941	24	*S	0.9
1912	Was-A	152	521	56	118	13	7	1	52	38		.226	.288	.284	63	-25	-25	48	17			**.941**	**31**	*S	1.9
1913	Was-A	150	499	52	107	18	7	1	52	43	46	.214	.286	.285	66	-21	-22	43	12			**.960**	11	*S	0.3
1914	Was-A	156	503	49	102	12	4	0	24	43	70	.203	.274	.243	53	-27	-29	36	12	14	-5	**.958**	12	*S	-1.0
1915	Was-A	146	476	54	97	8	6	1	30	29	60	.204	.251	.252	50	-30	-31	34	10	5	0	**.968**	9	*S	-1.1
1916	Was-A	139	466	36	106	15	4	1	36	23	58	.227	.271	.283	67	-20	-20	41	8			.957	13	*S	0.1
1917	Was-A	50	141	6	27	3	0	0	9	10	17	.191	.265	.213	46	-9	-9	9	1			.943	-1	S/32	-0.9
1918	Was-A	18	53	2	7	0	0	0	1	0	11	.132	.132	.132	-21	-8	-8	1	1			.986	2	S/2	-0.6
1919	Was-A	15	40	3	8	1	1	0	4	3	6	.200	.256	.275	49	-3	-3	3	0			.932	1	S	-0.1
1920	Was-A	13	41	6	9	1	0	0	3	2	3	.220	.256	.244	34	-4	-4	3	0	0	0	.966	-3	S	-0.6
Total	16	1659	5526	516	1203	140	47	7	447	419	271	.218	.281	.264	65	-244	-234	461	133	19		.948	170	*S/321	2.6

■ JOHN McBRIDE McBride, John F. Deb: 10/12/1890

YEAR	TM/L	G	AB	R	H	2B	3B	HR	RBI	BB	SO	AVG	OBP	SLG	PRO+	BR	/A	RC	SB	CS	SBR	FA	FR	POS	TPR
1890	Phi-a	1	2	0	0	0	0	0		0		.000	.000	.000	-99	-0	-0	0	0			1.000	1	/O	0.0

■ TOM McBRIDE McBride, Thomas Raymond b: 11/2/14, Bonham, Tex. BR/TR, 6', 190 lbs. Deb: 4/23/43

YEAR	TM/L	G	AB	R	H	2B	3B	HR	RBI	BB	SO	AVG	OBP	SLG	PRO+	BR	/A	RC	SB	CS	SBR	FA	FR	POS	TPR
1943	Bos-A	26	96	11	23	3	1	0	7	7	3	.240	.291	.292	70	-4	-4	7	2	0	1	.984	0	O	-0.5
1944	Bos-A	71	216	29	53	7	3	0	24	8	13	.245	.276	.306	67	-10	-10	18	4	0	1	.992	-1	O/1	-1.2
1945	Bos-A	100	344	38	105	11	7	1	47	26	17	.305	.354	.387	112	6	5	47	2	2	-1	.984	-0	O1	-0.1
1946	*Bos-A	61	153	21	46	5	2	0	19	9	6	.301	.340	.359	90	-1	-2	18	0	1	-1	1.000	-7	O	-1.2
1947	Bos-A	2	5	0	1	0	0	0	0	0	0	.200	.200	.200	11	-1	-1	0	0	0	0	1.000	1	/O	0.0
	Was-A	56	166	19	45	4	2	0	15	15	9	.271	.331	.319	84	-4	-3	17	3	1	0	.972	-4	O/3	-1.0
	Yr	58	171	19	46	4	2	0	15	15	9	.269	.328	.316	81	-5	-4	17	3	1	0	.973	-3	O/3	-1.0
1948	Was-A	92	206	22	53	9	1	1	29	28	15	.257	.346	.325	81	-6	-5	23	2	2	-1	.983	2	O	-0.6
Total	6	408	1186	140	326	39	16	2	141	93	63	.275	.328	.340	88	-19	-19	130	13	6	0	.985	-9	O/13	-4.6

■ SWAT McCABE McCabe, James Arthur b: 11/20/1881, Towanda, Pa. d: 12/9/44, Bristol, Conn. BL/TR, 5'10", Deb: 9/23/09

YEAR	TM/L	G	AB	R	H	2B	3B	HR	RBI	BB	SO	AVG	OBP	SLG	PRO+	BR	/A	RC	SB	CS	SBR	FA	FR	POS	TPR
1909	Cin-N	3	11	2	6	1	0	0	0	0		.545	.545	.636	269	2	2	4	1			.625	-1	/O	0.1
1910	Cin-N	13	35	3	9	1	0	0	5	1	2	.257	.297	.286	73	-1	-1	3	0			1.000	1	/O	-0.1
Total	2	16	46	5	15	2	0	0	5	1	2	.326	.354	.370	118	1	1	7	1			.875	-1	/O	0.0

■ JOE McCABE McCabe, Joseph Robert b: 8/27/38, Indianapolis, Ind. BR/TR, 6', 190 lbs. Deb: 4/18/64

YEAR	TM/L	G	AB	R	H	2B	3B	HR	RBI	BB	SO	AVG	OBP	SLG	PRO+	BR	/A	RC	SB	CS	SBR	FA	FR	POS	TPR
1964	Min-A	14	19	1	3	0	0	0	2	0	8	.158	.158	.158	-12	-3	-3	1	0	0	0	1.000	0	C	-0.2
1965	Was-A	14	27	1	5	0	0	1	5	4	13	.185	.290	.296	68	-1	-1	3	1	0	0	.972	-3	C	-0.3
Total	2	28	46	2	8	0	0	1	7	4	21	.174	.240	.239	36	-4	-4	3	1	0	0	.986	-2	/C	-0.5

■ BILL McCABE McCabe, William Francis b: 10/28/1892, Chicago, Ill. d: 9/2/66, Chicago, Ill. BB/TR, 5'9.5", 180 lbs. Deb: 4/16/18

YEAR	TM/L	G	AB	R	H	2B	3B	HR	RBI	BB	SO	AVG	OBP	SLG	PRO+	BR	/A	RC	SB	CS	SBR	FA	FR	POS	TPR
1918	*Chi-N	29	45	9	8	0	1	0	5	4	7	.178	.245	.222	42	-3	-3	3	2			.939	5	2/O	0.3
1919	Chi-N	33	84	8	13	3	1	0	5	9	15	.155	.253	.214	41	-6	-6	5	3			.950	-1	O/S3	-0.9
1920	Chi-N	3	2	1	1	0	0	0	0	0	0	.500	.500	.500	184	0	0	0	0	0	0	.000	0	H	0.0
	*Bro-N	41	68	10	10	0	0	0	3	2	6	.147	.171	.147	-8	-9	-10	2	1	2	-1	.882	4	S/O23	-0.7
	Yr	44	70	11	11	0	0	0	3	2	6	.157	.181	.157	-2	-9	-9	2	1	2	-1	.882	4	S/O23	-0.7
Total	3	106	199	28	32	3	2	0	13	15	28	.161	.227	.196	26	-18	-18	10	6	2		.943	8	/OS23	-1.3

■ HARRY McCAFFERY McCaffery, Harry Charles b: 11/25/1858, St.Louis, Mo. d: 4/19/28, St.Louis, Mo. BR/TR, 5'10.5", 185 lbs. Deb: 6/15/1882 U

YEAR	TM/L	G	AB	R	H	2B	3B	HR	RBI	BB	SO	AVG	OBP	SLG	PRO+	BR	/A	RC	SB	CS	SBR	FA	FR	POS	TPR
1882	Lou-a	1	4	1	1	0	0	0		0		.250	.250	.250	73	-0	-0	0				1.000	-1	/2	-0.1
	StL-a	38	153	23	42	8	6	0		3		.275	.288	.405	127	5	4	18				.891	4	O/231	0.7
	Yr	39	157	24	43	8	6	0		3		.274	.287	.401	125	5	4	19				.891	3	O/231	0.6
1883	StL-a	5	18	0	1	0	0	0		1		.056	.105	.056	-44	-3	-3	0				.889	1	/O	-0.2
1885	Cin-a	1	5	0	0	0	0	0		0		.000	.000	.000	-98	-1	-1	0				.000	-0	/P	0.0
Total	3	45	180	24	44	8	6	0		4		.244	.261	.356	101	1	-0	19				.891	4	/O23P1	0.4

YEAR	TM/L	G	AB	R	H	2B	3B	HR	RBI	BB	SO	AVG	OBP	SLG	PRO+	BR	/A	RC	SB	CS	SBR	FA	FR	POS	TPR

■ SPARROW McCAFFREY McCaffrey, Charles P. b: 1868, Philadelphia, Pa. d: 4/29/1894, Philadelphia, Pa. 120 lbs. Deb: 8/13/1889

| 1889 | Col-a | 2 | 1 | 1 | 1 | 0 | 0 | 0 | 0 | 1 | 0 | 1.000 | 1.000 | 1.000 | 501 | 1 | 1 | 1 | 0 | | | .000 | 0 | /C | 0.1 |

■ BRIAN McCALL McCall, Brian Allen "Bam" b: 1/25/43, Kentfield, Cal. BL/TL, 5'10", 170 lbs. Deb: 9/18/62

1962	Chi-A	4	8	2	3	0	0	2	3	0	2	.375	.375	1.125	287	2	2	3	0	0	0	1.000	0	/O	0.2
1963	Chi-A	3	7	1	0	0	0	0	0	1	2	.000	.125	.000	-62	-2	-2	0	0	0	0	1.000	-0	/O	-0.2
Total	2	7	15	3	3	0	0	2	3	1	4	.200	.250	.600	126	0	0	3	0	0	0	1.000	0	/O	0.0

■ JACK McCANDLESS McCandless, Scott Cook b: 5/5/1891, Pittsburgh, Pa. d: 8/17/61, Pittsburgh, Pa. BL/TR, 6', 170 lbs. Deb: 9/10/14

1914	Bal-F	11	31	5	8	0	1	0	1	3	0	.258	.343	.323	87	-0	-0	4	0			1.000	-0	/O	-0.1
1915	Bal-F	117	406	47	87	6	7	5	34	41	99	.214	.296	.300	73	-12	-14	41	9			.945	3	*O	-1.7
Total	2	128	437	52	95	6	8	5	35	44	99	.217	.299	.302	74	-13	-14	44	9			.948	3	O	-1.8

■ EMMETT McCANN McCann, Robert Emmett b: 3/4/02, Philadelphia, Pa. d: 4/15/37, Philadelphia, Pa. BR/TR, 5'11", 150 lbs. Deb: 4/19/20

1920	Phi-A	13	34	4	9	1	1	0	3	3	1	.265	.342	.353	84	-1	-1	4	0	1	-1	.907	-0	S	-0.1
1921	Phi-A	52	157	15	35	5	0	0	15	4	6	.223	.242	.255	27	-17	-18	10	2	1	0	.949	-0	S/321	-1.4
1926	Bos-A	6	3	0	0	0	0	0	0	1	1	.000	.250	.000	-32	-1	-1	0	0	0	0	1.000	-0	S3	-0.1
Total	3	71	194	19	44	6	1	0	18	8	8	.227	.261	.268	36	-19	-19	14	2	2	-1	.939	-1	/S321	-1.6

■ ROGER McCARDELL McCardell, Roger Morton b: 8/29/32, Gorsuch Mills, Md. BR/TR, 6', 200 lbs. Deb: 5/08/59

| 1959 | SF-N | 4 | 4 | 0 | 0 | 0 | 0 | 0 | 0 | 0 | 0 | .000 | .000 | .000 | -99 | -1 | -1 | 0 | 0 | 0 | 0 | 1.000 | 0 | /C | -0.1 |

■ BILL McCARREN McCarren, William Joseph b: 11/4/1895, Fortenia, Pa. d: 9/11/83, Denver, Colo. BR/TR, 5'11.5", 170 lbs. Deb: 5/04/23

| 1923 | Bro-N | 69 | 216 | 28 | 53 | 10 | 1 | 3 | 27 | 22 | 39 | .245 | .326 | .343 | 79 | -7 | -6 | 25 | 0 | 1 | -1 | .927 | -2 | 3/O | -0.3 |

■ ALEX McCARTHY McCarthy, Alexander George b: 5/12/1888, Chicago, Ill. d: 3/12/78, Salisbury, Md. BR/TR, 5'9", 150 lbs. Deb: 10/07/10

1910	Pit-N	3	12	1	1	0	1	0	0	0	2	.083	.083	.250	-3	-2	-2	0	0			.875	0	/S	-0.2
1911	Pit-N	50	150	18	36	5	1	2	31	14	24	.240	.305	.327	74	-5	-6	16	4			.981	-1	S2/3O	-0.4
1912	Pit-N	111	401	53	111	12	4	1	41	30	26	.277	.332	.334	84	-10	-9	48	8			.962	3	*2/3	-0.8
1913	Pit-N	31	74	7	15	5	0	0	10	7	7	.203	.298	.270	66	-3	-3	7	1			.902	-2	S3/2	-0.5
1914	Pit-N	57	173	14	26	0	1	1	14	6	17	.150	.192	.179	11	-19	-18	6	2			.975	11	32/S	-0.7
1915	Pit-N	21	49	3	10	0	1	0	3	5	10	.204	.291	.245	64	-2	-2	4	1	2	-1	.950	1	/2S31	-0.2
	Chi-N	23	72	4	19	3	0	1	6	5	7	.264	.329	.347	105	-0	0	8	2	3	-1	.972	11	23/S	1.2
	Yr	44	121	7	29	3	1	1	9	10	17	.240	.313	.306	88	-2	-1	12	3	5	-2	.964	12	23/S1	1.0
1916	Chi-N	37	107	10	26	2	3	0	6	11	7	.243	.341	.318	93	1	-0	12	1			.931	-2	2/S	-0.2
	Pit-N	50	146	11	29	3	0	0	3	15	10	.199	.282	.219	54	-7	-7	11	3			.955	-5	S/23	-1.2
	Yr	87	253	21	55	5	3	0	9	26	17	.217	.308	.261	72	-6	-8	24	4			.951	-7	S2/3	-1.4
1917	Pit-N	49	151	15	33	4	0	0	8	11	13	.219	.276	.245	58	-7	-7	11	1			.964	7	32/S	0.1
Total	8	432	1335	136	306	34	11	5	122	104	123	.229	.295	.282	67	-53	-54	124	23	5		.957	23	2S3/10	-2.9

■ JERRY McCARTHY McCarthy, Jerome Francis b: 5/23/23, Brooklyn, N.Y. d: 10/3/65, Oceanside, N.Y. BL/TL, 6'1", 205 lbs. Deb: 6/19/48

| 1948 | StL-A | 2 | 3 | 0 | 1 | 0 | 0 | 0 | 0 | 0 | 0 | .333 | .333 | .333 | 76 | -0 | -0 | 0 | 0 | 0 | 0 | .600 | -1 | /1 | -0.1 |

■ JACK McCARTHY McCarthy, John Arthur b: 3/26/1869, Gilbertville, Mass d: 9/11/31, Chicago, Ill. BL/TL, 5'9", 155 lbs. Deb: 8/03/1893

1893	Cin-N	49	195	28	55	8	3	0	22	22	7	.282	.355	.354	88	-2	-3	27	6			.887	-1	O/1	-0.5
1894	Cin-N	40	167	29	45	9	1	0	21	17	6	.269	.348	.335	64	-9	-10	22	3			.895	2	O1	-0.7
1898	Pit-N	137	537	75	155	13	12	4	78	34		.289	.336	.380	107	2	4	75	7			.935	4	*O	-0.3
1899	Pit-N	138	560	108	171	22	17	3	67	39		.305	.355	.421	113	8	8	99	28			.961	-5	*O	-0.7
1900	Chi-N	124	503	68	148	16	7	0	48	24		.294	.329	.354	92	-9	-6	69	22			.944	-1	O	-1.4
1901	Cle-A	86	343	60	110	14	7	0	32	30		.321	.382	.402	123	9	11	60	9			.949	-1	O	0.4
1902	Cle-A	95	359	45	102	31	5	0	41	24		.284	.328	.398	105	-0	2	54	12			.944	-5	O	-0.9
1903	Cle-A	108	415	47	110	20	8	0	43	19		.265	.299	.352	96	-3	-2	52	15			.964	-3	*O	-1.3
	Chi-N	24	101	11	28	5	0	0	14	4		.277	.305	.327	83	-3	-2	13	8			.947	-3	O	-0.7
1904	Chi-N	115	432	36	114	14	2	0	51	23		.264	.307	.306	90	-5	-5	48	14			.961	-5	*O	-1.8
1905	Chi-N	59	170	16	47	4	3	0	14	10		.276	.320	.335	92	-1	-2	22	8			.986	2	O/1	-0.2
1906	Bro-N	91	322	23	98	13	1	0	35	20		.304	.347	.351	128	6	9	45	9			.924	2	O	0.7
1907	Bro-N	25	91	4	20	2	0	0	8	2		.220	.237	.242	54	-5	-5	7	4			1.000	-4	O	-1.1
Total	12	1091	4195	550	1203	171	66	7	474	268	13	.287	.333	.364	101	-12	-1	591	145			.946	-17	*O/1	-8.5

■ JOHNNY McCARTHY McCarthy, John Joseph b: 1/7/10, Chicago, Ill. d: 9/13/73, Mundelein, Ill. BL/TL, 6'1.5", 185 lbs. Deb: 9/02/34

1934	Bro-N	17	39	7	7	2	0	1	5	2	2	.179	.220	.308	42	-3	-3	3	0			.961	1	1	-0.3
1935	Bro-N	22	48	9	12	1	1	0	4	2	9	.250	.280	.313	60	-3	-3	4	1			.982	-3	1	-0.7
1936	NY-N	4	16	1	7	0	0	1	2	0	1	.438	.438	.625	185	2	2	4	1			.981	1	/1	0.3
1937	*NY-N	114	420	53	117	19	3	10	65	24	37	.279	.322	.410	96	-2	-3	56	2			.987	-2	*1	-1.3
1938	NY-N	134	470	55	128	13	4	8	59	39	28	.272	.329	.368	91	-5	-6	60	3			.993	-3	*1	-2.4
1939	NY-N	50	80	12	21	6	1	1	11	3	8	.262	.298	.400	85	-2	-2	9	0			1.000	-4	1/OP	-0.7
1940	NY-N	51	67	6	16	4	0	0	5	2	8	.239	.261	.299	53	-4	-4	4	0			1.000	1	/1	-0.4
1941	NY-N	14	40	1	13	3	0	0	12	3	0	.325	.372	.400	115	1	1	6	0			.987	-0	/1O	0.1
1943	Bos-N	78	313	32	95	24	6	2	33	10	19	.304	.327	.438	122	6	7	41	1			.996	1	1	0.3
1946	Bos-N	2	7	0	1	0	0	0	1	2	0	.143	.333	.143	37	-0	-0	1	0			1.000	-1	/1	-0.1
1948	Bos-N	56	57	6	15	0	1	2	12	3	2	.263	.300	.404	88	-1	-1	7	0			.966	-0	1	-0.2
Total	11	542	1557	182	432	72	16	25	209	90	114	.277	.319	.392	95	-13	-14	194	8			.990	-5	1/OP	-5.4

■ JOE McCARTHY McCarthy, Joseph N. b: 12/25/1881, Syracuse, N.Y. d: 1/12/37, Syracuse, N.Y. BR/TR, Deb: 9/27/05

1905	NY-A	1	2	0	0	0	0	0	0	0	0	.000	.000	.000	-90	-0	-0	0	0			1.000	0	/C	0.0
1906	StL-N	15	37	3	9	2	0	0	2	2		.243	.282	.297	84	-1	-1	3	0			.984	-0	C	0.0
Total	2	16	39	3	9	2	0	0	2	2		.231	.268	.282	75	-1	-1	3	0			.985	-0	/C	0.0

■ TOMMY McCARTHY McCarthy, Thomas Francis Michael b: 7/24/1863, Boston, Mass. d: 8/5/22, Boston, Mass. BR/TR, 5'7", 170 lbs. Deb: 7/10/1884 MH

1884	Bos-U	53	209	37	45	2	2	0		6		.215	.234	.244	64	-8	-7	12				.794	-2	O/P	-0.9
1885	Bos-N	40	148	16	27	2	0	0	11	5	25	.182	.209	.196	33	-11	-10	6				.865	3	O	-0.8
1886	Phi-N	8	27	6	5	2	1	0	3	2	3	.185	.241	.333	73	-1	-1	2	1			.818	-1	/OP	-0.2
1887	Phi-N	18	70	7	13	4	0	0	6	2	5	.186	.219	.243	28	-7	-7	7	15			.818	-9	/O2S3	-1.4
1888	*StL-a	131	511	107	140	20	3	1	68	38		.274	.328	.331	103	9	8	88	93			.932	30	*O/P	2.5
1889	StL-a	140	604	136	176	24	7	2	63	46	26	.291	.348	.364	93	4	-9	99	57			.893	14	*O/2P	0.1
1890	StL-a	133	548	137	192	28	9	6		66		.350	.430	.467	147	**48**	35	**150**	**83**			.893	7	*O3/2M	3.5
1891	StL-a	136	578	127	179	21	6	8	95	50	19	.310	.375	.408	110	20	5	105	37			.895	-1	*O2S/3P	-0.8
1892	*Bos-N	152	603	119	146	19	5	4	63	93	29	.242	.347	.310	93	4	-5	85	53			.883	2	*O	-0.8
1893	Bos-N	116	462	107	160	28	6	5	111	64	10	.346	.429	.465	130	28	21	115	46			.902	3	*O/2S	1.6
1894	Bos-N	127	539	118	188	21	8	13	126	59	17	.349	.419	.490	111	19	10	133	43			.904	11	*O/S2P	0.9
1895	Bos-N	117	452	90	131	13	2	2	73	72	12	.290	.391	.341	85	-2	-9	71	18			.885	-10	*O/2	-2.2
1896	Bro-N	104	377	62	94	8	4	3	47	34	17	.249	.316	.316	73	-17	-13	47	22			.920	-2	*O	-2.0
Total	13	1275	5128	1069	1496	192	53	44	666	537	163	.292	.364	.376	102	87	12	920	468			.897	45	*O/23SP	0.5

■ **BILL McCARTHY** McCarthy, William John b: Boston, Mass. d: 2/4/28, Washington, D.C. TR , Deb: 6/05/05

YEAR	TM/L	G	AB	R	H	2B	3B	HR	RBI	BB	SO	AVG	OBP	SLG	PRO+	BR	/A	RC	SB	CS	SBR	FA	FR	POS	TPR
1905	Bos-N	1	3	0	0	0	0	0	0	0		.000	.000	.000	-99	-1	-1	0	0			.667	-0	/C	-0.1
1907	Cin-N	3	8	1	1	0	0	0	0	0		.125	.125	.125	-21	-1	-1	0	0			1.000	-1	/C	-0.2
Total	2	4	11	1	1	0	0	0	0	0		.091	.091	.091	-43	-2	-2	0	0			.842	-1	/C	-0.3

■ **FRANK McCARTON** McCarton, Francis b: 10/6/1854, Middleton, Conn. d: 6/17/07, New York, N.Y. Deb: 4/26/1872

YEAR	TM/L	G	AB	R	H	2B	3B	HR	RBI	BB	SO	AVG	OBP	SLG	PRO+	BR	/A	RC	SB	CS	SBR	FA	FR	POS	TPR
1872	Man-n	19	83	19	31	5	0	0	9	1	3	.373	.381	.434	159	5	6	14						O	0.4

■ **LEW McCARTY** McCarty, George Lewis b: 11/17/1888, Milton, Pa. d: 6/9/30, Reading, Pa. BR/TR, 5'11.5", 192 lbs. Deb: 8/30/13

YEAR	TM/L	G	AB	R	H	2B	3B	HR	RBI	BB	SO	AVG	OBP	SLG	PRO+	BR	/A	RC	SB	CS	SBR	FA	FR	POS	TPR
1913	Bro-N	9	26	1	6	0	0	0	2	2	2	.231	.286	.231	47	-2	-2	2	0			1.000	1	/C	0.0
1914	Bro-N	90	284	20	72	14	2	1	30	14	22	.254	.293	.327	83	-6	-7	27	1			.970	1	C	0.1
1915	Bro-N	84	276	19	66	9	4	0	19	7	23	.239	.261	.301	68	-11	-11	23	7	4	-0	.969	-8	C	-1.5
1916	Bro-N	55	150	17	47	6	1	0	13	14	16	.313	.383	.367	127	6	6	24	4			.985	-4	C1	0.4
	NY-N	25	68	6	27	3	4	0	9	7	9	.397	.453	.559	222	9	9	18	0			.993	0	C	1.2
	Yr	80	218	23	74	9	5	0	22	21	25	.339	.405	.427	155	15	15	41	4			.989	-3	C1	1.6
1917	*NY-N	56	162	15	40	3	2	2	19	14	6	.247	.311	.327	99	-1	-0	16	1			.979	-3	C	0.1
1918	NY-N	86	257	16	69	7	3	0	24	17	13	.268	.321	.319	97	-1	-1	27	3			.975	-7	C	-0.2
1919	NY-N	85	210	17	59	5	4	2	21	18	15	.281	.341	.371	115	4	4	27	2			.970	-8	C	0.1
1920	NY-N	36	38	2	5	0	0	0	0	4	2	.132	.214	.132	1	-5	-5	1	2	0	1	1.000	2	/C	-0.2
	StL-N	5	7	0	2	0	0	0	0	5	0	.286	.583	.286	160	1	1	2	0	0	0	1.000	-1	/C	0.1
	Yr	41	45	2	7	0	0	0	0	9	2	.156	.296	.156	33	-4	-3	3	2	0	1	1.000	1	/C	-0.1
1921	StL-N	1	1	0	0	0	0	0	0	0	1	.000	.000	.000	-99	-0	-0	0	0	0	0	.000	0	H	0.0
Total	9	532	1479	113	393	47	20	5	137	102	109	.266	.318	.335	97	-6	-6	167	20	4		.975	-27	C/1	0.1

■ **TIM McCARVER** McCarver, James Timothy b: 10/16/41, Memphis, Tenn. BL/TR, 6'1", 195 lbs. Deb: 9/10/59

YEAR	TM/L	G	AB	R	H	2B	3B	HR	RBI	BB	SO	AVG	OBP	SLG	PRO+	BR	/A	RC	SB	CS	SBR	FA	FR	POS	TPR
1959	StL-N	8	24	3	4	1	0	0	0	2	1	.167	.231	.208	17	-3	-3	1	0	0	0	.971	-2	/C	-0.5
1960	StL-N	10	10	3	2	0	0	0	0	0	2	.200	.200	.200	9	-1	-1	0	0	0	0	1.000	-0	/C	-0.1
1961	StL-N	22	67	5	16	2	1	1	6	0	5	.239	.239	.343	47	-5	-5	5	0	0	0	.969	-2	C	-0.6
1963	StL-N	127	405	39	117	12	7	4	51	27	43	.289	.336	.383	97	3	-1	53	5	2	0	.994	-0	*C	0.4
1964	*StL-N	143	465	53	134	19	3	9	52	40	44	.288	.346	.400	101	6	1	64	2	0	1	.987	-9	*C	-0.1
1965	StL-N	113	409	48	113	17	2	11	48	31	26	.276	.329	.408	97	3	-1	55	5	1	1	**.995**	-4	*C	0.1
1966	StL-N★	150	543	50	149	19	**13**	12	68	36	38	.274	.322	.424	105	3	3	71	9	6	-1	.992	-4	*C	0.8
1967	*StL-N★	138	471	68	139	26	3	14	69	54	32	.295	.374	.452	137	22	23	78	8	8	-2	**.997**	4	*C	3.4
1968	*StL-N	128	434	35	110	15	6	5	48	26	31	.253	.297	.350	95	-4	-3	44	4	3	-1	.986	3	*C	0.8
1969	StL-N	138	515	46	134	27	3	7	51	49	26	.260	.327	.365	93	-4	-5	60	4	9	-4	.986	9	*C	0.8
1970	Phi-N	44	164	16	47	11	1	4	14	14	10	.287	.346	.439	112	2	2	24	2	2	-1	.991	0	C	0.4
1971	Phi-N	134	474	51	132	20	5	8	46	43	26	.278	.340	.392	107	4	4	62	5	3	-0	.985	-8	*C	0.1
1972	Phi-N	45	152	14	36	8	0	2	14	17	15	.237	.322	.329	83	-3	-3	17	1	2	-1	.989	-3	C	-0.6
	Mon-N	77	239	19	60	5	1	5	20	19	14	.251	.309	.343	84	-5	-5	24	4	4	-1	.990	0	CO/3	-0.5
	Yr	122	391	33	96	13	1	7	34	36	29	.246	.314	.338	83	-7	-8	40	5	6	-2	.990	-3	CO/3	-1.1
1973	StL-N	130	331	30	88	16	4	3	49	38	31	.266	.345	.366	97	-1	-1	44	2	0	1	.986	-6	1C	-1.2
1974	StL-N	74	106	13	23	0	1	0	11	22	6	.217	.366	.236	72	-3	-3	11	0	1	-1	.969	-1	C/1	-0.4
	Bos-A	11	28	3	7	1	0	0	1	4	1	.250	.344	.286	77	-0	-1	3	1	0	0	1.000	1	/CD	0.1
1975	Bos-A	12	21	1	8	2	1	0	3	1	3	.381	.409	.571	161	2	2	5	0	0	0	.957	-0	/C1	0.2
	Phi-N	47	59	6	15	2	0	1	7	14	7	.254	.397	.339	102	1	1	9	0	0	0	.984	1	C/1	0.3
1976	*Phi-N	90	155	26	43	11	2	3	29	35	14	.277	.414	.432	136	10	9	31	2	1	0	1.000	5	C/1	1.7
1977	*Phi-N	93	169	28	54	13	2	6	30	28	11	.320	.422	.527	146	14	13	37	3	5	-2	.988	2	C/1	1.3
1978	*Phi-N	90	146	18	36	9	1	1	14	28	24	.247	.375	.342	101	2	1	20	2	2	-1	.995	2	C1	0.3
1979	Phi-N	79	137	13	33	5	1	1	12	19	12	.241	.338	.314	76	-3	-4	14	2	0	1	.989	3	C/O	0.1
1980	Phi-N	6	5	2	1	1	0	0	2	1	0	.200	.333	.400	98	0	-0	0	0	0	0	1.000	-0	/1	0.0
Total	21	1909	5529	590	1501	242	57	97	645	548	422	.271	.340	.388	102	41	24	735	61	49	-11	.990	-10	*C1/O3D	6.8

■ **AL McCAULEY** McCauley, Allen A. b: 3/4/1863, Indianapolis, Ind. d: 8/24/17, Wayne Twnshp., Ind BL/TL, 6', 180 lbs. Deb: 6/21/1884

YEAR	TM/L	G	AB	R	H	2B	3B	HR	RBI	BB	SO	AVG	OBP	SLG	PRO+	BR	/A	RC	SB	CS	SBR	FA	FR	POS	TPR
1884	Ind-a	17	53	7	10	0	1	0		12		.189	.358	.226	101	1	1	4				1.000	0	P/1O	-0.2
1890	Phi-N	112	418	63	102	25	7	1	42	57	38	.244	.346	.344	101	3	2	54	8			.973	-6	*1	-0.9
1891	Was-a	59	206	36	58	5	8	1	31	30	13	.282	.378	.398	131	7	9	35	9			.969	-2	1	0.4
Total	3	188	677	106	170	30	16	2	73	99	51	.251	.357	.352	110	12	12	94	17			.971	-7	1/PO	-0.7

■ **JIM McCAULEY** McCauley, James A. b: 3/24/1863, Stanley, N.Y. d: 9/14/30, Canandaigua , N.Y. BL/TR, 6', 180 lbs. Deb: 9/17/1884

YEAR	TM/L	G	AB	R	H	2B	3B	HR	RBI	BB	SO	AVG	OBP	SLG	PRO+	BR	/A	RC	SB	CS	SBR	FA	FR	POS	TPR
1884	StL-a	1	2	0	0	0	0	0		0		.000	.000	.000	-97	-0	-0	0				.818	1	/C	0.0
1885	Buf-N	24	84	4	15	2	1	0	7	11	12	.179	.274	.226	61	-3	-3	5				.936	-1	C/O	-0.2
	Chi-N	3	6	1	1	0	0	0	0	2	3	.167	.375	.167	70	0	-0	0				.800	-3	/CO	-0.3
	Yr	27	90	5	16	2	1	0	7	13	15	.178	.282	.222	62	-3	-4	6				.927	-3	C/O	-0.5
1886	Bro-a	11	30	5	7	1	0	0		11		.233	.439	.267	124	2	2	5	2			.846	-1	C	0.2
Total	3	39	122	10	23	3	1	0	7	24	15	.189	.322	.230	77	-1	-2	10	2			.893	-3	/CO	-0.3

■ **PAT McCAULEY** McCauley, Patrick M. b: 6/10/1870, Ware, Mass. d: 1/23/17, Newark, N.J. TR , Deb: 9/05/1893

YEAR	TM/L	G	AB	R	H	2B	3B	HR	RBI	BB	SO	AVG	OBP	SLG	PRO+	BR	/A	RC	SB	CS	SBR	FA	FR	POS	TPR
1893	StL-N	5	16	0	1	0	0	0	0	0	1	.063	.063	.063	-66	-4	-4	0	0			.808	1	/C	-0.2
1896	Was-N	26	84	14	21	3	0	3	11	7	8	.250	.315	.393	88	-2	-2	12	3			.917	0	C/O	0.1
1903	NY-A	6	19	0	1	0	0	0	1	0		.053	.053	.053	-64	-4	-4	0	0			.920	-2	/C	-0.6
Total	3	37	119	14	23	3	0	3	12	7	9	.193	.244	.294	45	-9	-9	12	3			.900	-1	/CO	-0.7

■ **BILL McCAULEY** McCauley, William H. b: 12/20/1869, Washington, D.C. d: 1/27/26, Washington, D.C. Deb: 8/31/1895

YEAR	TM/L	G	AB	R	H	2B	3B	HR	RBI	BB	SO	AVG	OBP	SLG	PRO+	BR	/A	RC	SB	CS	SBR	FA	FR	POS	TPR
1895	Was-N	1	2	0	0	0	0	0	0	0	0	.000	.000	.000	-99	-1	-1	0	0			.714	0	/S	0.0

■ **HARRY McCHESNEY** McChesney, Harry Vincent "Pud" b: 6/1/1880, Pittsburgh, Pa. d: 8/11/60, Pittsburgh, Pa. BR/TR, 5'9", 165 lbs. Deb: 9/17/04

YEAR	TM/L	G	AB	R	H	2B	3B	HR	RBI	BB	SO	AVG	OBP	SLG	PRO+	BR	/A	RC	SB	CS	SBR	FA	FR	POS	TPR
1904	Chi-N	22	88	9	23	6	2	0	11	4		.261	.293	.375	106	0	0	11	2			.967	-2	O	-0.3

■ **PETE McCLANAHAN** McClanahan, Robert Hugh b: 10/24/06, Coldspring, Tex. d: 10/28/87, Mont Belvieu, Tex. BR/TR, 5'9", 170 lbs. Deb: 4/24/31

YEAR	TM/L	G	AB	R	H	2B	3B	HR	RBI	BB	SO	AVG	OBP	SLG	PRO+	BR	/A	RC	SB	CS	SBR	FA	FR	POS	TPR
1931	Pit-N	7	4	2	2	0	0	0	0	2	0	.500	.667	.500	220	1	1	2	0			.000	0	H	0.1

■ **HARVEY McCLELLAN** McClellan, Harvey McDowell "Little Mac" b: 12/22/1894, Cynthiana, Ky. d: 11/6/25, Cynthiana, Ky. BR/TR, 5'9.5", 143 lbs. Deb: 5/31/19

YEAR	TM/L	G	AB	R	H	2B	3B	HR	RBI	BB	SO	AVG	OBP	SLG	PRO+	BR	/A	RC	SB	CS	SBR	FA	FR	POS	TPR
1919	Chi-A	7	12	2	4	0	0	0	1	1	1	.333	.385	.333	102	0	0	1	0			1.000	1	/3S	0.1
1920	Chi-A	10	18	4	6	1	1	0	5	4	1	.333	.455	.500	153	2	2	5	2	0	1	.917	-3	/S3	-0.1
1921	Chi-A	63	196	20	35	4	1	1	14	14	18	.179	.237	.224	18	-24	-24	11	2	3	-1	.968	18	2SO/3	-0.6
1922	Chi-A	91	301	28	68	17	3	2	28	16	32	.226	.272	.322	55	-21	-21	27	3	2	-0	.971	-4	3/S2O	-1.9
1923	Chi-A	141	550	67	129	29	3	1	41	27	44	.235	.270	.304	52	-41	-40	45	14	11	-2	.958	-18	*S/2	-4.6
1924	Chi-A	32	85	9	15	3	0	0	9	6	7	.176	.239	.212	17	-11	-10	5	2	0	1	.938	3	S/23O	-0.4
Total	6	344	1162	130	257	54	8	4	98	68	103	.221	.267	.292	46	-95	-93	95	23	16		.952	-4	S/32O	-7.5

■ **BILL McCLELLAN** McClellan, William Henry b: 3/22/1856, Chicago, Ill. d: 7/3/29, Chicago, Ill. BL/TL, 156 lbs. Deb: 5/20/1878

YEAR	TM/L	G	AB	R	H	2B	3B	HR	RBI	BB	SO	AVG	OBP	SLG	PRO+	BR	/A	RC	SB	CS	SBR	FA	FR	POS	TPR
1878	Chi-N	48	205	26	46	6	1	0	29	2	13	.224	.232	.263	59	-8	-10	13				.866	-9	*2/SO	-1.5
1881	Pro-N	68	259	30	43	3	1	0	16	15	21	.166	.212	.185	26	-21	-21	10				.855	-8	SO/2	-2.4
1883	Phi-N	80	326	42	75	21	4	1	33	19	18	.230	.272	.328	89	-7	-2	30				.849	5	*S/O3	0.4
1884	Phi-N	111	450	71	116	13	2	3	33	28	43	.258	.301	.316	99	-3	1	44				.852	-12	*S/O	-0.9

YEAR	TM/L	G	AB	R	H	2B	3B	HR	RBI	BB	SO	AVG	OBP	SLG	PRO+	BR	/A	RC	SB	CS	SBR	FA	FR	POS	TPR
1885	Bro-a	112	464	85	124	22	7	0		28		.267	.317	.345	111	7	6	52				.837	-5	32	0.4
1886	Bro-a	141	595	131	152	33	9	1		56		.255	.322	.346	110	8	7	82	43			.907	-7	*2	0.5
1887	Bro-a	136	548	109	144	24	6	1		80		.263	.363	.334	96	2	0	94	70			.879	-23	*2	-1.5
1888	Bro-a	74	278	33	57	7	3	0	21	40		.205	.307	.252	83	-3	-3	26	13			.905	-7	2O	-0.8
	Cle-a	22	72	6	16	0	0	0	5	6		.222	.282	.222	67	-3	-2	6	6			.875	-4	O/2S	-0.5
	Yr	96	350	39	73	7	3	0	26	46		.209	.302	.246	80	-6	-5	33	19			.897	-11	2O/S	-1.3
Total	8	792	3197	533	773	129	33	6	137	274	95	.242	.305	.308	91	-28	-24	358	132			.893	-68	2S/3O	-6.3

■ LLOYD McCLENDON McClendon, Lloyd Glenn b: 1/11/59, Gary, Ind. BR/TR, 5'11", 195 lbs. Deb: 4/06/87

YEAR	TM/L	G	AB	R	H	2B	3B	HR	RBI	BB	SO	AVG	OBP	SLG	PRO+	BR	/A	RC	SB	CS	SBR	FA	FR	POS	TPR
1987	Cin-N	45	72	8	15	5	0	2	13	4	15	.208	.250	.361	57	-4	-5	7	1	0	0	.981	-2	C/13O	-0.6
1988	Cin-N	72	137	9	30	4	0	3	14	15	22	.219	.305	.314	75	-4	-4	13	4	0	1	1.000	-3	CO1/3	-0.7
1989	*Chi-N	92	259	47	74	12	1	12	40	37	31	.286	.377	.479	133	15	13	48	6	4	-1	.962	-7	O1/3C	0.2
1990	Chi-N	49	107	5	17	3	0	1	10	14	21	.159	.256	.215	29	-10	-11	6	1	0	0	.980	1	O/C1	-1.0
	Pit-N	4	3	1	1	0	0	1	2	0	1	.333	.333	1.333	349	1	1	1	0	0	0	.000	-0	/O	0.0
	Yr	53	110	6	18	3	0	2	12	14	22	.164	.258	.245	37	-9	-10	8	1	0	0	.980	1	O/C1	-1.0
1991	*Pit-N	85	163	24	47	7	0	7	24	18	23	.288	.366	.460	133	7	7	28	2	1	0	.966	-7	O1/C	-0.2
1992	*Pit-N	84	190	26	48	8	1	3	20	28	24	.253	.355	.353	102	1	1	24	1	3	-2	.964	-7	O1	-1.0
Total	6	431	931	120	232	39	2	29	123	116	137	.249	.337	.389	101	6	2	129	15	8	-0	.966	-25	O/1C3	-3.3

■ JEFF McCLESKEY McCleskey, Jefferson Lamar b: 11/6/1891, Americus, Ga. d: 5/11/71, Americus, Ga. BL/TR, 5'11", 160 lbs. Deb: 9/08/13

YEAR	TM/L	G	AB	R	H	2B	3B	HR	RBI	BB	SO	AVG	OBP	SLG	PRO+	BR	/A	RC	SB	CS	SBR	FA	FR	POS	TPR
1913	Bos-N	2	3	0	0	0	0	0	0	1	0	.000	.250	.000	-25	-0	-0	0	0			.750	-0	/3	-0.1

■ MC CLOSKEY McCloskey b: Brooklyn, N.Y. Deb: 5/25/1875

YEAR	TM/L	G	AB	R	H	2B	3B	HR	RBI	BB	SO	AVG	OBP	SLG	PRO+	BR	/A	RC	SB	CS	SBR	FA	FR	POS	TPR
1875	Was-n	11	40	1	7	0	0	0		1		.175	.195	.175	30	-3	-2	1						C	-0.2

■ BILL McCLOSKEY McCloskey, William George b: 5/1854, Pennsylvania 5'8", 155 lbs. Deb: 8/18/1884

YEAR	TM/L	G	AB	R	H	2B	3B	HR	RBI	BB	SO	AVG	OBP	SLG	PRO+	BR	/A	RC	SB	CS	SBR	FA	FR	POS	TPR
1884	Wil-U	9	30	0	3	0	0	0		0		.100	.100	.100	-31	-4	-4	0				.588	1	/OC	-0.2

■ HALL McCLURE McClure, Harold Murray "Mac" b: 8/8/1859, Lewisburg, Pa. d: 3/1/19, Lewisburg, Pa. BR/TR, 6', 165 lbs. Deb: 5/10/1882

YEAR	TM/L	G	AB	R	H	2B	3B	HR	RBI	BB	SO	AVG	OBP	SLG	PRO+	BR	/A	RC	SB	CS	SBR	FA	FR	POS	TPR
1882	Bos-N	2	6	1	2	0	0	0	0	0	1	.333	.333	.333	115	0	0	1				.750	-0	/O	0.0

■ LARRY McCLURE McClure, Lawrence Ledwith b: 10/3/1885, Wayne, W.Va. d: 8/31/49, Huntington, W.Va. BR/TR, 5'6.5", 130 lbs. Deb: 7/26/10

YEAR	TM/L	G	AB	R	H	2B	3B	HR	RBI	BB	SO	AVG	OBP	SLG	PRO+	BR	/A	RC	SB	CS	SBR	FA	FR	POS	TPR
1910	NY-A	1	1	0	0	0	0	0	0	0		.000	.000	.000	-95	-0	-0	0	0			.000	0	/O	0.0

■ AMBY McCONNELL McConnell, Ambrose Moses b: 4/29/1883, N.Pownal, Vt. d: 5/20/42, Utica, N.Y. BL/TR, 5'7", 150 lbs. Deb: 4/17/08

YEAR	TM/L	G	AB	R	H	2B	3B	HR	RBI	BB	SO	AVG	OBP	SLG	PRO+	BR	/A	RC	SB	CS	SBR	FA	FR	POS	TPR
1908	Bos-A	140	502	77	140	10	6	2	43	38		.279	.342	.335	117	12	10	67	31			.939	-20	*2/S	-1.2
1909	Bos-A	121	453	61	108	7	8	0	36	34		.238	.300	.289	84	-7	-8	47	26			.954	14	*2	0.5
1910	Bos-A	11	35	6	6	0	0	0	1	5		.171	.310	.171	50	-2	-2	3	4			.959	-1	2	-0.3
	Chi-A	33	120	13	33	2	3	0	5	7		.275	.320	.342	112	1	1	14	4			.952	-1	2	0.0
	Yr	44	155	19	39	2	3	0	6	12		.252	.318	.303	97	-1	-0	17	8			.954	-2	2	-0.3
1911	Chi-A	104	396	45	111	11	5	1	34	23		.280	.331	.341	90	-7	-5	47	7			**.973**	-7	*2	-1.4
Total	4	409	1506	202	398	30	22	3	119	107		.264	.324	.319	98	-3	-3	179	72			.954	-13	2/S	-2.4

■ GEORGE McCONNELL McConnell, George Neely "Slats" b: 9/16/1877, Shelbyville, Tenn d: 5/10/64, Chattanooga, Tenn. BR/TR, 6'3", 190 lbs. Deb: 4/13/09

YEAR	TM/L	G	AB	R	H	2B	3B	HR	RBI	BB	SO	AVG	OBP	SLG	PRO+	BR	/A	RC	SB	CS	SBR	FA	FR	POS	TPR
1909	NY-A	13	43	4	9	0	1	0	5	1		.209	.227	.256	52	-2	-2	3	1			.964	2	1/P	-0.2
1912	NY-A	42	91	11	27	4	2	0	8	4		.297	.333	.385	99	0	-0	11	0			.913	5	P/1	0.0
1913	NY-A	39	67	4	12	2	0	0	2	0	11	.179	.179	.209	13	-7	-7	3	0			.965	5	P/1	0.0
1914	Chi-N	1	2	0	0	0	0	0	0	0	1	.000	.000	.000	-99	-0	-0	0	0			1.000	0	/P	0.0
1915	Chi-F	53	125	14	31	6	2	1	18	0	16	.248	.254	.352	82	-4	-3	12	2			.974	3	P	0.0
1916	Chi-N	28	57	2	9	0	0	0	0	2	4	.158	.200	.158	10	-6	-7	2	0			.952	2	P	0.0
Total	6	176	385	35	88	12	5	1	33	7	32	.229	.248	.294	59	-20	-21	31	3			.953	15	P/1	-0.2

■ SAM McCONNELL McConnell, Samuel Faulkner b: 6/8/1895, Philadelphia, Pa. d: 6/27/81, Phoenixville, Pa. BL/TR, 5'6.5", 150 lbs. Deb: 4/19/15

YEAR	TM/L	G	AB	R	H	2B	3B	HR	RBI	BB	SO	AVG	OBP	SLG	PRO+	BR	/A	RC	SB	CS	SBR	FA	FR	POS	TPR
1915	Phi-A	6	11	1	2	1	0	0	0	1	3	.182	.250	.273	58	-1	-1	1	0			.842	2	/3	0.1

■ DON McCORMACK McCormack, Donald Ross b: 9/18/55, Omak, Wash. BR/TR, 6'3", 205 lbs. Deb: 9/30/80

YEAR	TM/L	G	AB	R	H	2B	3B	HR	RBI	BB	SO	AVG	OBP	SLG	PRO+	BR	/A	RC	SB	CS	SBR	FA	FR	POS	TPR
1980	Phi-N	2	1	0	1	0	0	0	0	0	0	1.000	1.000	1.000	436	0	0	1	0	0	0	1.000	1	/C	0.1
1981	Phi-N	3	4	0	1	0	0	0	0	0	1	.250	.250	.250	40	-0	-0	0	0	0	0	1.000	0	/C	0.0
Total	2	5	5	0	2	0	0	0	0	0	1	.400	.400	.400	121	0	0	1	0	0	0	1.000	1	/C	0.1

■ FRANK McCORMICK McCormick, Frank Andrew "Buck" b: 6/9/11, New York, N.Y. d: 11/21/82, Manhassett, N.Y. BR/TR, 6'4", 205 lbs. Deb: 9/11/34 C

YEAR	TM/L	G	AB	R	H	2B	3B	HR	RBI	BB	SO	AVG	OBP	SLG	PRO+	BR	/A	RC	SB	CS	SBR	FA	FR	POS	TPR
1934	Cin-N	12	16	1	5	2	1	0	5	0	1	.313	.313	.563	132	1	1	2	0			.941	-1	/1	0.0
1937	Cin-N	24	83	5	27	5	0	0	9	2	4	.325	.341	.386	102	-0	0	9	1			1.000	1	1/2O	-0.2
1938	Cin-N★	151	640	89	**209**	40	4	5	106	18	17	.327	.348	.425	115	8	10	93	1			.995	-3	*1	-1.0
1939	*Cin-N★	156	630	99	**209**	41	4	18	**128**	40	16	.332	.374	.495	131	26	26	110	1			**.996**	2	*1	1.1
1940	*Cin-N★	155	618	93	**191**	**44**	3	19	127	52	26	.309	.367	.482	131	26	26	104	2			**.995**	1	*1	1.1
1941	Cin-N★	154	603	77	162	31	5	17	97	40	13	.269	.318	.421	107	3	3	76	2			**.995**	1	*1	-0.8
1942	Cin-N★	145	564	58	156	24	0	13	89	45	18	.277	.332	.388	111	6	6	72	1			.993	6	*1	0.3
1943	Cin-N†	126	472	56	143	28	0	8	56	29	15	.303	.345	.413	120	10	10	67	2			.995	4	*1	0.8
1944	Cin-N☆	153	581	85	177	37	3	20	102	57	17	.305	.371	.482	144	29	31	101	7			.992	12	*1	3.6
1945	Cin-N†	152	580	68	160	33	0	10	81	56	22	.276	.345	.384	105	2	3	75	6			.994	5	*1	-0.1
1946	Phi-N★	135	504	46	143	20	2	11	66	36	21	.284	.333	.397	110	3	4	66	2			**.999**	4	*1	0.1
1947	Phi-N	15	40	7	9	2	0	1	8	3	2	.225	.279	.350	69	-2	-2	3	0			.989	-1	1	-0.3
	Bos-N	81	212	24	75	18	2	2	43	11	8	.354	.386	.486	133	9	9	37	2			.996	-1	1	0.6
	Yr	96	252	31	84	20	2	3	51	14	10	.333	.368	.464	123	6	7	40	2			.995	-2	1	0.3
1948	*Bos-N	75	180	14	45	9	2	4	34	10	9	.250	.289	.389	84	-5	-5	19	0			.987	3	1	-0.2
Total	13	1534	5723	722	1711	334	26	128	951	399	189	.299	.348	.434	118	115	124	834	27			.995	31	*1/2O	5.0

■ MOOSE McCORMICK McCormick, Harry Elwood b: 2/28/1881, Philadelphia, Pa. d: 7/9/62, Lewisburg, Pa. BL/TL, 5'11", 180 lbs. Deb: 4/14/04

YEAR	TM/L	G	AB	R	H	2B	3B	HR	RBI	BB	SO	AVG	OBP	SLG	PRO+	BR	/A	RC	SB	CS	SBR	FA	FR	POS	TPR
1904	NY-N	59	203	28	54	9	5	1	26	13		.266	.320	.374	110	3	2	29	13			.916	-5	O	-0.6
	Pit-N	66	238	25	69	10	6	2	23	13		.290	.332	.408	125	7	6	36	6			.940	-6	O	-0.3
	Yr	125	441	53	123	19	11	3	49	26		.279	.326	.392	118	10	8	65	19			.928	-11	*O	-0.9
1908	Phi-N	11	22	0	2	0	0	0	2	2		.091	.167	.091	-17	-3	-3	0	0			1.000	-0	/O	-0.4
	NY-N	73	252	31	76	16	3	0	32	4		.302	.315	.389	119	5	4	32	6			.901	-11	O	-1.1
	Yr	84	274	31	78	16	3	0	34	6		.285	.302	.365	108	3	1	31	6			.910	-11	O	-1.5
1909	NY-N	110	413	68	120	21	8	3	27	49		.291	.373	.402	138	20	19	63	4			.924	-14	*O	0.1
1912	*NY-N	42	39	4	13	4	1	0	8	6	9	.333	.422	.487	144	3	3	8	1			.667	-3	/O1	0.0
1913	*NY-N	57	80	9	22	2	3	0	15	5	13	.275	.318	.375	97	-0	-1	9	0			.909	-2	O	-0.3
Total	5	418	1247	165	356	62	26	6	133	92	22	.285	.340	.391	122	35	31	178	30			.920	-40	O/1	-2.6

■ JIM McCORMICK McCormick, James Ambrose b: 11/2/1868, Spencer, Mass. d: 2/1/48, Saco, Maine BR/TR, 6'1", 160 lbs. Deb: 9/10/1892

YEAR	TM/L	G	AB	R	H	2B	3B	HR	RBI	BB	SO	AVG	OBP	SLG	PRO+	BR	/A	RC	SB	CS	SBR	FA	FR	POS	TPR
1892	StL-N	3	11	0	0	0	0	0	0	1	5	.000	.083	.000	-78	-2	-2	0	0			1.000	-0	/23	-0.2

■ JERRY McCORMICK McCormick, John b: Philadelphia, Pa. d: 9/19/05, Philadelphia, Pa. Deb: 5/01/1883

YEAR	TM/L	G	AB	R	H	2B	3B	HR	RBI	BB	SO	AVG	OBP	SLG	PRO+	BR	/A	RC	SB	CS	SBR	FA	FR	POS	TPR
1883	Bal-a	93	389	40	102	16	6	0		2		.262	.266	.334	89	-4	-6	35				.799	1	*3	-0.5
1884	Phi-U	67	295	41	84	12	2	0		4		.285	.294	.339	123	4	7	30				.811	14	3/2OSP	1.8

YEAR	TM/L	G	AB	R	H	2B	3B	HR	RBI	BB	SO	AVG	OBP	SLG	PRO+	BR	/A	RC	SB	CS	SBR	FA	FR	POS	TPR
	Was-U	42	157	23	34	8	2	0		1		.217	.222	.293	75	-5	-4	10				.792	-6	3/S	-0.8
	Yr	109	452	64	118	20	4	0		5		.261	.269	.323	106	-1	3	40				**.806**	8	3/S2OP	1.0
Total	2	202	841	104	220	36	10	0		7		.262	.268	.328	98	-5	-2	76				.802	9	3/SO2P	0.5

■ MIKE McCORMICK McCormick, Michael J. "Kid" or "Dude" b: 5/1883, Scotland d: 11/18/53, Jersey City, N.J. BR/TR, 5'9", Deb: 4/14/04

YEAR	TM/L	G	AB	R	H	2B	3B	HR	RBI	BB	SO	AVG	OBP	SLG	PRO+	BR	/A	RC	SB	CS	SBR	FA	FR	POS	TPR
1904	Bro-N	105	347	28	64	5	4	0	27	43		.184	.276	.222	56	-17	-16	29	22			**.914**	-3	*3/2	-1.7

■ MIKE McCORMICK McCormick, Myron Winthrop b: 5/6/17, Angels Camp, Cal. d: 4/14/76, Ventura, Cal. BR/TR, 6', 200 lbs. Deb: 4/16/40

YEAR	TM/L	G	AB	R	H	2B	3B	HR	RBI	BB	SO	AVG	OBP	SLG	PRO+	BR	/A	RC	SB	CS	SBR	FA	FR	POS	TPR
1940	*Cin-N	110	417	48	125	20	0	1	30	13	36	.300	.326	.355	87	-7	-8	48	8			.986	8	*O	-0.6
1941	Cin-N	110	369	52	106	17	3	4	31	30	24	.287	.341	.382	103	1	1	48	4			.976	7	*O	0.3
1942	Cin-N	40	135	18	32	2	3	1	11	13	7	.237	.304	.319	82	-3	-3	13	0			.990	1	O	-0.4
1943	Cin-N	4	15	0	2	0	0	0	0	2	0	.133	.235	.133	8	-2	-2	1	0			.909	-0	/O	-0.3
1946	Cin-N	23	74	10	16	2	0	0	5	8	4	.216	.293	.243	55	-4	-4	6	0			1.000	1	O	-0.5
	Bos-N	59	164	23	43	6	2	1	16	11	7	.262	.309	.341	83	-4	-4	18	0			.973	-2	O	-0.8
	Yr	82	238	33	59	8	2	1	21	19	11	.248	.304	.311	75	-8	-8	23	0			.982	-1	O	-1.3
1947	Bos-N	92	284	42	81	13	7	3	36	20	21	.285	.332	.412	99	-2	-1	37	1			.981	-12	O	-1.6
1948	*Bos-N	115	343	45	104	22	7	1	39	32	34	.303	.363	.417	112	5	6	52	1			.975	-11	*O	-1.0
1949	*Bro-N	55	139	17	29	5	1	2	14	14	12	.209	.281	.302	54	-9	-9	12	1			1.000	-6	O	-1.7
1950	NY-N	4	4	0	0	0	0	0	0	0	2	.000	.000	.000	-99	-1	-1	0	0			.000	0	H	-0.1
	Chi-A	55	138	16	32	4	3	0	10	16	6	.232	.312	.304	60	-9	-8	12	0	1	-1	.982	-1	O	-1.1
1951	Was-A	81	243	31	70	9	3	1	23	29	20	.288	.364	.362	98	-0	0	30	1	2	-1	.966	1	O	-0.2
Total	10	748	2325	302	640	100	29	14	215	188	173	.275	.330	.361	90	-35	-33	277	16	3		.976	-14	O	-8.0

■ BARRY McCORMICK McCormick, William J. b: 12/25/1874, Maysville, Ky. d: 1/28/56, Cincinnati, Ohio TR, 5'9", Deb: 9/25/1895 U

YEAR	TM/L	G	AB	R	H	2B	3B	HR	RBI	BB	SO	AVG	OBP	SLG	PRO+	BR	/A	RC	SB	CS	SBR	FA	FR	POS	TPR
1895	Lou-N	3	12	2	3	0	1	0	0	0	0	.250	.250	.417	76	-1	-0	2	1			1.000	-1	/S2	-0.1
1896	Chi-N	45	168	22	37	3	1	1	23	14	30	.220	.280	.268	45	-13	-14	16	9			.835	-6	3/S2O	-1.6
1897	Chi-N	101	419	87	112	8	10	2	55	33		.267	.324	.348	75	-14	-17	63	44			.851	-3	3S/2	-1.5
1898	Chi-N	137	530	76	131	15	9	2	78	47		.247	.314	.321	82	-12	-12	61	15			.888	4	*3/S2	-0.7
1899	Chi-N	102	376	48	97	15	2	2	52	25		.258	.311	.324	76	-14	-12	45	14			.941	4	2/S	-0.2
1900	Chi-N	110	379	35	83	13	5	3	48	38		.219	.292	.303	67	-19	-16	39	8			.907	-8	S3/2	-1.6
1901	Chi-N	115	427	45	100	15	6	1	32	31		.234	.288	.304	75	-15	-13	42	12			.911	0	*S/3	-0.4
1902	StL-A	139	504	55	124	14	4	3	51	37		.246	.304	.308	71	-20	-19	53	10			.905	-12	*3/SO	-2.8
1903	StL-A	61	207	13	45	6	1	1	16	18		.217	.283	.271	69	-8	-7	18	5			.969	-4	23/S	-1.0
	Was-A	63	219	14	47	10	2	0	23	10		.215	.255	.279	59	-11	-11	17	3			.960	8	2	-0.1
	Yr	124	426	27	92	16	3	1	39	28		.216	.269	.275	64	-18	-18	35	8			.962	5	23/S	-1.1
1904	Was-A	113	404	36	88	11	1	0	39	27		.218	.274	.250	67	-15	-14	32	9			.938	-1	*2	-1.3
Total	10	989	3645	433	867	110	42	15	417	280	30	.238	.297	.303	71	-141	-137	388	130			.885	-18	32S/O	-11.3

■ BARNEY McCOSKY McCosky, William Barney b: 4/11/17, Coal Run, Pa. BL/TR, 6'1", 184 lbs. Deb: 4/18/39

YEAR	TM/L	G	AB	R	H	2B	3B	HR	RBI	BB	SO	AVG	OBP	SLG	PRO+	BR	/A	RC	SB	CS	SBR	FA	FR	POS	TPR
1939	Det-A	147	611	120	190	33	14	4	58	70	45	.311	.384	.430	100	8	1	108	20	4	4	.986	9	*O	0.8
1940	*Det-A	143	589	123	**200**	39	**19**	4	57	67	41	.340	.408	.491	120	29	21	123	13	9	-2	.983	-1	*O	1.0
1941	Det-A	127	494	80	160	25	8	3	55	61	33	.324	.401	.425	108	15	8	92	8	3	1	.985	5	*O	0.6
1942	Det-A	154	600	75	176	28	11	7	50	68	37	.293	.365	.412	109	15	9	94	11	5	0	.981	3	*O	0.4
1946	Det-A	25	91	11	18	5	0	1	11	17	9	.198	.324	.286	67	-3	-4	10	0	0	0	.966	-1	O	-0.6
	Phi-A	92	308	33	109	17	4	1	34	43	13	.354	.433	.445	146	21	21	63	2	2	-1	.981	-4	O	1.3
	Yr	117	399	44	127	22	4	2	45	60	22	.318	.407	.409	127	18	17	72	2	2	-1	.978	-4	*O	0.7
1947	Phi-A	137	546	77	179	22	7	1	52	57	29	.328	.395	.399	119	17	16	92	1	4	-2	.983	4	*O	1.1
1948	Phi-A	135	515	95	168	21	5	0	46	68	22	.326	.405	.386	111	11	11	86	1	3	-2	.990	-3	*O	-0.1
1950	Phi-A	66	179	19	43	10	1	0	11	22	12	.240	.323	.307	63	-10	-10	19	0	0	0	.987	-5	O	-1.6
1951	Phi-A	12	27	4	8	2	0	1	1	3	4	.296	.367	.481	125	1	1	5	0	0	0	1.000	-1	/O	0.0
	Cin-N	25	50	2	16	2	1	1	11	4	2	.320	.370	.460	120	1	1	9	0	0	0	1.000	-3	O	-0.2
	Cle-A	31	61	8	13	3	0	0	2	8	5	.213	.304	.262	57	-4	-3	5	1	0	0	1.000	-1	O	-0.5
1952	Cle-A	54	80	14	17	4	1	1	6	8	5	.213	.284	.325	74	-3	-3	7	1	1	-0	.944	-5	O	-0.9
1953	Cle-A	22	21	3	4	3	0	0	3	1	4	.190	.227	.333	51	-2	-2	2	0	0	0	.000	0	H	-0.2
Total	11	1170	4172	664	1301	214	71	24	397	497	261	.312	.386	.414	109	96	68	715	58	31	-1	.984	-1	*O	1.1

■ WILLIE McCOVEY McCovey, Willie Lee "Stretch" b: 1/10/38, Mobile, Ala. BL/TL, 6'4", 210 lbs. Deb: 7/30/59 H

YEAR	TM/L	G	AB	R	H	2B	3B	HR	RBI	BB	SO	AVG	OBP	SLG	PRO+	BR	/A	RC	SB	CS	SBR	FA	FR	POS	TPR
1959	SF-N	52	192	32	68	9	5	13	38	22	35	.354	.431	.656	189	23	24	53	2	0	1	.989	-2	1	1.9
1960	SF-N	101	260	37	62	15	3	13	51	45	53	.238	.351	.469	130	8	10	45	1	1	-0	.985	-3	1	0.2
1961	SF-N	106	328	59	89	12	3	18	50	37	60	.271	.354	.491	126	10	11	56	1	2	-1	.985	-2	1	0.2
1962	*SF-N	91	229	41	67	6	1	20	54	29	35	.293	.372	.590	156	17	17	48	3	3	-1	.976	-2	O1	1.0
1963	SF-N★	152	564	103	158	19	5	**44**	102	50	119	.280	.350	.566	161	41	42	111	1	1	-0	.942	-6	*O1	3.0
1964	SF-N	130	364	55	80	14	1	18	54	61	73	.220	.340	.412	108	6	5	53	2	1	0	.935	-9	O1	-0.9
1965	SF-N	160	540	93	149	17	4	39	92	88	118	.276	.383	.539	152	42	40	115	0	4	-2	.991	-3	*1	2.8
1966	SF-N★	150	502	85	148	26	6	36	96	76	100	.295	.394	.586	163	47	45	119	2	1	0	.984	-3	*1	3.4
1967	SF-N	135	456	73	126	17	4	31	91	71	110	.276	.381	.535	162	36	37	94	3	3	-1	.989	1	*1	3.1
1968	SF-N★	148	523	81	153	16	4	**36**	**105**	72	71	.293	.383	**.545**	**176**	**49**	**49**	110	4	2	0	.985	3	*1	4.6
1969	SF-N★	149	491	101	157	26	2	**45**	**126**	121	66	.320	**.458**	**.656**	**212**	**76**	**77**	**151**	0	0	0	.992	-6	*1	**6.2**
1970	SF-N★	152	495	98	143	39	2	39	126	**137**	75	.289	.446	**.612**	**183**	**62**	**63**	140	0	0	0	.989	13	*1	**6.1**
1971	*SF-N★	105	329	45	91	13	0	18	70	64	57	.277	.401	.480	151	23	24	65	0	2	-1	.983	-2	1	1.3
1972	SF-N	81	263	30	56	8	0	14	35	38	45	.213	.317	.403	102	1	1	35	0	0	0	.986	-5	1	-1.2
1973	SF-N	130	383	52	102	14	3	29	75	105	78	.266	.425	.546	161	39	37	95	1	0	0	.988	1	*1	3.0
1974	SD-N	128	344	53	87	19	1	22	63	96	76	.253	.417	.506	164	30	32	79	1	0	0	.987	-6	*1	2.1
1975	SD-N	122	413	43	104	17	0	23	68	57	80	.252	.347	.460	130	12	15	66	1	0	0	.986	-1	*1	0.8
1976	SD-N	71	202	20	41	9	0	7	36	21	39	.203	.281	.351	86	-6	-4	20	0	0	0	.991	5	1	-0.3
	Oak-A	11	24	0	5	0	0	0	0	3	4	.208	.296	.208	52	-1	-1	2	0	0	0	.000	0	/D	-0.1
1977	SF-N	141	478	54	134	21	0	28	86	67	106	.280	.369	.500	131	21	21	86	3	0	1	.989	-7	*1	0.7
1978	SF-N	108	351	32	80	19	2	12	64	36	57	.228	.300	.396	97	-4	-3	40	1	0	0	.987	-4	1	-1.2
1979	SF-N	117	353	34	88	9	0	15	57	36	70	.249	.321	.402	103	-2	1	45	0	2	-1	.987	-1	1	-0.7
1980	SF-N	48	113	8	23	8	0	1	16	13	23	.204	.291	.301	67	-5	-5	10	0	0	0	.992	-2	1	-0.9
Total	22	2588	8197	1229	2211	353	46	521	1555	1345	1550	.270	.377	.515	148	524	538	1638	26	22	-5	.987	-41	*1O/D	35.1

■ ART McCOY McCoy, Arthur Gray b: 7/1864, Danville, Pa. d: 3/22/04, Danville, Pa. 168 lbs. Deb: 7/08/1889

YEAR	TM/L	G	AB	R	H	2B	3B	HR	RBI	BB	SO	AVG	OBP	SLG	PRO+	BR	/A	RC	SB	CS	SBR	FA	FR	POS	TPR
1889	Was-N	2	6	0	0	0	0	0	0	2	1	.000	.250	.000	-28	-1	-1	0	0			.889	-2	/2	-0.2

■ BENNY McCOY McCoy, Benjamin Jenison b: 11/9/15, Jenison, Mich. BL/TR, 5'9", 170 lbs. Deb: 9/14/38

YEAR	TM/L	G	AB	R	H	2B	3B	HR	RBI	BB	SO	AVG	OBP	SLG	PRO+	BR	/A	RC	SB	CS	SBR	FA	FR	POS	TPR
1938	Det-A	7	15	2	3	1	0	0	0	1	2	.200	.250	.267	28	-2	-2	1	0	0	0	.963	2	/23	0.1
1939	Det-A	55	192	38	58	13	6	1	33	29	26	.302	.394	.448	107	5	3	35	3	1	0	.958	-2	2S	0.4
1940	Phi-A	134	490	56	126	26	5	7	62	65	44	.257	.345	.373	88	-9	-8	65	2	2	-1	.951	-16	*2/3	-1.5
1941	Phi-A	141	517	86	140	12	7	8	61	95	50	.271	.384	.368	102	3	5	80	3	3	-1	.963	-13	*2	0.1
Total	4	337	1214	182	327	52	18	16	156	190	122	.269	.369	.381	97	-3	-2	182	8	6	-1	.957	-28	2/S3	-0.9

■ TOMMY McCRAW McCraw, Tommy Lee b: 11/21/40, Malvern, Ark. BL/TL, 6', 183 lbs. Deb: 6/04/63 C

YEAR	TM/L	G	AB	R	H	2B	3B	HR	RBI	BB	SO	AVG	OBP	SLG	PRO+	BR	/A	RC	SB	CS	SBR	FA	FR	POS	TPR
1963	Chi-A	102	280	38	71	11	3	6	33	21	46	.254	.313	.379	94	-3	-2	34	15	4	2	.993	-1	1	-0.5
1964	Chi-A	125	368	47	96	11	5	6	36	32	65	.261	.327	.367	95	-3	-2	46	15	7	0	.992	-7	1O	-1.4

YEAR	TM/L	G	AB	R	H	2B	3B	HR	RBI	BB	SO	AVG	OBP	SLG	PRO+	BR	/A	RC	SB	CS	SBR	FA	FR	POS	TPR
1965	Chi-A	133	273	38	65	12	1	5	21	25	48	.238	.309	.344	91	-5	-3	28	12	7	-1	.993	-8	1O	-1.6
1966	Chi-A	151	389	49	89	16	4	5	48	29	40	.229	.291	.329	83	-11	-8	37	20	11	-1	.990	-2	*1O	-1.8
1967	Chi-A	125	453	55	107	18	3	11	45	33	55	.236	.290	.362	95	-6	-4	46	24	10	1	.991	11	*1/O	0.2
1968	Chi-A	136	477	51	112	16	12	9	44	36	58	.235	.295	.375	101	0	-0	53	20	5	3	.986	2	*1	-0.5
1969	Chi-A	93	240	21	62	12	2	2	25	21	24	.258	.326	.350	85	-3	-5	26	1	3	-2	.989	-10	1O	-2.2
1970	Chi-A	129	332	39	73	11	2	6	31	21	50	.220	.275	.319	61	-17	-19	31	12	3	2	.987	-3	1O	-2.6
1971	Was-A	122	207	33	44	6	4	7	25	19	38	.213	.294	.382	96	-3	-2	23	3	3	-1	.958	-9	O1	-1.5
1972	Cle-A	129	391	43	101	13	5	7	33	41	47	.258	.335	.371	106	5	4	47	12	10	-2	1.000	-1	O1	-0.7
1973	Cal-A	99	264	25	70	7	0	3	24	30	42	.265	.345	.326	97	-3	-0	32	3	2	-0	1.000	2	O1/D	-0.2
1974	Cal-A	56	119	21	34	8	0	3	17	12	13	.286	.351	.429	131	4	4	18	2	1	0	1.000	2	1O/D	0.4
	Cle-A	45	112	17	34	8	0	3	17	5	11	.304	.339	.455	128	3	4	16	0	1	-1	.990	2	1/O	0.3
	Yr	101	231	38	68	16	0	6	34	17	24	.294	.345	.442	130	7	8	33	2	2	-1	.994	4	1O/D	0.7
1975	Cle-A	23	51	7	14	1	1	2	5	7	7	.275	.362	.451	129	2	2	9	4	1	1	1.000	-2	1/O	0.0
Total	13	1468	3956	484	972	150	42	75	404	332	544	.246	.311	.362	94	-40	-32	446	143	68	2	.991	-22	1O/D	-12.1

■ **RODNEY McCRAY** McCray, Rodney Duncan b: 9/13/63, Detroit, Mich. BR/TR, 5′10″, 175 lbs. Deb: 4/30/90

YEAR	TM/L	G	AB	R	H	2B	3B	HR	RBI	BB	SO	AVG	OBP	SLG	PRO+	BR	/A	RC	SB	CS	SBR	FA	FR	POS	TPR
1990	Chi-A	32	6	8	0	0	0	0	0	1	4	.000	.143	.000	-58	-1	-1	0	6	0	2	1.000	-5	O/D	-0.4
1991	Chi-A	17	7	2	2	0	0	0	0	0	2	.286	.286	.286	60	-0	-0	0	1	1	-0	1.000	-2	/OD	-0.2
1992	NY-N	18	1	3	1	0	0	0	1	0	0	1.000	1.000	1.000	471	0	0	2	2	0	1	1.000	-4	O	-0.3
Total	3	67	14	13	3	0	0	0	1	1	6	.214	.267	.214	36	-1	-1	3	9	1	2	1.000	-10	/OD	-0.9

■ **FRANK McCREA** McCrea, Francis William b: 9/6/1896, Jersey City, N.J. d: 2/25/81, Dover, N.J. BR/TR, 5′9″, 155 lbs. Deb: 9/26/25

YEAR	TM/L	G	AB	R	H	2B	3B	HR	RBI	BB	SO	AVG	OBP	SLG	PRO+	BR	/A	RC	SB	CS	SBR	FA	FR	POS	TPR
1925	Cle-A	1	5	1	1	0	0	0	0	0	0	.200	.200	.200	2	-1	-1	0	0	0	0	1.000	-1	/C	-0.1

■ **JUDGE McCREDIE** McCredie, Walter Henry b: 11/29/1876, Manchester, Iowa d: 7/29/34, Portland, Ore. BL/TR, 6′2″, 195 lbs. Deb: 4/20/03

YEAR	TM/L	G	AB	R	H	2B	3B	HR	RBI	BB	SO	AVG	OBP	SLG	PRO+	BR	/A	RC	SB	CS	SBR	FA	FR	POS	TPR
1903	Bro-N	56	213	40	69	5	0	0	20	24		.324	.395	.347	116	5	6	34	10			.925	-4	O	-0.2

■ **TOM McCREERY** McCreery, Thomas Livingston b: 10/19/1874, Beaver, Pa. d: 7/3/41, Beaver, Pa. BB/TR, 5′11″, 180 lbs. Deb: 6/08/1895

YEAR	TM/L	G	AB	R	H	2B	3B	HR	RBI	BB	SO	AVG	OBP	SLG	PRO+	BR	/A	RC	SB	CS	SBR	FA	FR	POS	TPR
1895	Lou-N	31	108	18	35	3	1	0	10	8	15	.324	.376	.370	101	-0	1	17	3			.875	-6	O/PS31	-0.6
1896	Lou-N	115	441	87	155	23	**21**	7	65	42	58	.351	.409	.546	159	32	35	113	26			.916	1	*O/2P	2.2
1897	Lou-N	89	338	55	96	5	6	4	40	38		.284	.356	.370	95	-4	-2	53	13			.856	-5	*O	-1.2
	NY-N	49	177	36	53	8	5	1	27	22		.299	.380	.418	114	3	4	35	15			.900	-1	O/2	-0.1
	Yr	138	515	91	149	13	11	5	67	60		.289	.365	.386	101	-1	2	88	28			.869	-7	*O/2	-1.3
1898	NY-N	35	121	15	24	4	3	1	17	19		.198	.307	.306	78	-4	-3	13	3			.820	-5	O	-1.0
	Pit-N	53	190	33	59	5	7	2	20	26		.311	.394	.442	142	10	11	36	3			.934	-1	O	0.6
	Yr	88	311	48	83	9	10	3	37	45		.267	.360	.389	117	6	8	48	6			.901	-6	O	-0.4
1899	Pit-N	118	455	76	147	21	9	2	64	47		.323	.390	.422	123	15	15	82	11			.911	-8	O/S2	0.1
1900	Pit-N	43	132	20	29	4	3	1	13	16		.220	.304	.318	71	-5	-5	14	2			.887	2	O/P	-0.5
1901	Bro-N	91	335	47	97	11	14	3	53	32		.290	.353	.433	124	11	10	57	13			.947	4	O/1S	0.8
1902	Bro-N	112	430	49	105	8	4	4	57	29		.244	.295	.309	86	-7	-8	46	16			.979	-1	*1/O	-1.1
1903	Bro-N	40	141	13	37	5	2	0	10	20		.262	.354	.326	97	-0	0	19	5			.892	-2	O	-0.4
	Bos-N	23	83	15	18	2	1	1	10	9		.217	.293	.301	73	-3	-3	9	6			.900	0	O	-0.4
	Yr	63	224	28	55	7	3	1	20	29		.246	.332	.317	88	-4	-2	28	11			.896	-2	O	-0.8
Total	9	799	2951	464	855	99	76	26	386	308	73	.290	.359	.401	113	47	55	495	116			.905	-22	O1/S2P3	-1.6

■ **FRANK McCUE** McCue, Frank Aloysius b: 10/4/1898, Chicago, Ill. d: 7/5/53, Chicago, Ill. BB/TR, 5′9″, 150 lbs. Deb: 9/15/22

YEAR	TM/L	G	AB	R	H	2B	3B	HR	RBI	BB	SO	AVG	OBP	SLG	PRO+	BR	/A	RC	SB	CS	SBR	FA	FR	POS	TPR
1922	Phi-A	2	5	0	0	0	0	0	0	0	0	.000	.000	.000	-97	-1	-1	0	0	0	0	.000	0	/3	-0.1

■ **CLYDE McCULLOUGH** McCullough, Clyde Edward b: 3/4/17, Nashville, Tenn. d: 9/18/82, San Francisco, Cal. BR/TR, 5′11.5″, 180 lbs. Deb: 4/28/40 C

YEAR	TM/L	G	AB	R	H	2B	3B	HR	RBI	BB	SO	AVG	OBP	SLG	PRO+	BR	/A	RC	SB	CS	SBR	FA	FR	POS	TPR
1940	Chi-N	9	26	4	4	1	0	0	1	5	5	.154	.290	.192	36	-2	-2	2	0			1.000	3	/C	0.1
1941	Chi-N	125	418	41	95	9	2	9	53	34	67	.227	.289	.323	75	-16	-14	39	5			.982	-8	*C	-1.3
1942	Chi-N	109	337	39	95	22	1	5	31	25	47	.282	.331	.398	117	4	6	43	7			.980	-1	C	1.3
1943	Chi-N	87	266	20	63	5	2	2	23	24	33	.237	.302	.293	73	-9	-9	24	6			.977	-14	C	-1.9
1946	Chi-N	95	307	38	88	18	5	4	34	22	39	.287	.338	.417	116	4	5	42	2			.991	-2	C	0.8
1947	Chi-N	86	234	25	59	12	4	3	30	20	20	.252	.314	.376	86	-6	-5	27	1			.984	7	C	0.6
1948	Chi-N☆	69	172	10	36	4	2	1	7	15	25	.209	.273	.273	50	-12	-12	12	0			.973	5	C	-0.4
1949	Pit-N	91	241	30	57	9	3	4	21	24	30	.237	.316	.349	76	-7	-8	28	1			.985	8	C	0.4
1950	Pit-N	103	279	28	71	16	4	6	34	31	35	.254	.340	.405	92	-2	-3	40	3			.985	-8	*C	-0.7
1951	Pit-N	92	259	26	77	9	2	8	39	27	31	.297	.366	.440	113	6	5	40	2	0	1	.988	10	C	1.8
1952	Pit-N	66	172	10	40	5	1	1	15	10	18	.233	.283	.291	58	-9	-10	14	0	1	-1	.981	7	C/1	-0.2
1953	Chi-N☆	77	229	21	59	3	2	6	23	15	23	.258	.303	.367	72	-9	-10	24	0	0	0	.987	-3	C	-1.0
1954	Chi-N	31	81	9	21	7	0	3	17	5	5	.259	.310	.457	96	-1	-1	12	0	0	0	.981	-2	C/3	-0.1
1955	Chi-N	44	81	7	16	0	0	0	10	8	15	.198	.278	.198	29	-8	-8	5	0	0	0	.989	7	C	0.0
1956	Chi-N	14	19	0	4	1	0	0	1	0	5	.211	.211	.263	27	-2	-2	1	0	0	0	1.000	1	/C	-0.1
Total	15	1098	3121	308	785	121	28	52	339	265	398	.252	.314	.358	85	-70	-68	352	27	1		.984	8	C/31	-0.7

■ **HARRY McCURDY** McCurdy, Harry Henry "Hank" b: 9/15/1899, Stevens Point, Wis. d: 7/21/72, Houston, Tex. BL/TR, 5′11″, 187 lbs. Deb: 7/04/22

YEAR	TM/L	G	AB	R	H	2B	3B	HR	RBI	BB	SO	AVG	OBP	SLG	PRO+	BR	/A	RC	SB	CS	SBR	FA	FR	POS	TPR
1922	StL-N	13	27	3	8	2	2	0	5	1	1	.296	.321	.519	119	0	0	4	0	0	0	.967	-1	/C1	0.0
1923	StL-N	67	185	17	49	11	2	0	15	11	11	.265	.306	.346	73	-8	-7	20	3	1	0	.969	-7	C	-1.1
1926	Chi-A	44	86	16	28	7	2	1	11	6	10	.326	.370	.488	127	2	3	15	0	1	-1	.974	-4	C/1	0.0
1927	Chi-A	86	262	34	75	19	3	1	27	32	24	.286	.366	.393	99	-1	0	37	6	4	-1	.972	-3	C	0.2
1928	Chi-A	49	103	12	27	10	0	2	13	8	15	.262	.315	.417	92	-2	-2	13	1	3	-2	.964	-4	C	-0.4
1930	Phi-N	80	148	23	49	6	2	1	25	15	12	.331	.393	.419	90	-0	-2	24	0			.966	-5	C	-0.4
1931	Phi-N	66	150	21	43	9	0	1	25	23	16	.287	.382	.367	95	1	-0	23	2			.968	-1	C	0.2
1932	Phi-N	62	136	13	32	6	1	1	14	17	13	.235	.325	.316	65	-5	-7	15	0			.974	-1	C	-0.5
1933	Phi-N	73	54	9	15	1	0	2	12	16	6	.278	.451	.407	130	5	4	12	0			.000	0	/C	0.4
1934	Cin-N	3	6	0	0	0	0	0	1	0	0	.000	.000	.000	-99	-2	-2	0	0			1.000	1	/1	-0.1
Total	10	543	1157	148	326	71	12	9	148	129	108	.282	.355	.387	92	-8	-12	163	12	9		.970	-24	C/1	-1.7

■ **TERRY McDANIEL** McDaniel, Terrence Keith b: 12/6/66, Kansas City, Mo. BR/TR, 5′9″, 205 lbs. Deb: 8/31/91

YEAR	TM/L	G	AB	R	H	2B	3B	HR	RBI	BB	SO	AVG	OBP	SLG	PRO+	BR	/A	RC	SB	CS	SBR	FA	FR	POS	TPR
1991	NY-N	23	29	3	6	1	0	0	2	1	11	.207	.233	.241	34	-3	-3	2	2	0	1	1.000	-3	O	-0.5

■ **RED McDERMOTT** McDermott, Frank A. b: 11/12/1889, Philadelphia, Pa. d: 9/11/64, Philadelphia, Pa. BR/TR, 5′6″, 150 lbs. Deb: 8/06/12

YEAR	TM/L	G	AB	R	H	2B	3B	HR	RBI	BB	SO	AVG	OBP	SLG	PRO+	BR	/A	RC	SB	CS	SBR	FA	FR	POS	TPR
1912	Det-A	5	15	2	4	1	0	0	0	0		.267	.313	.333	87	-0	-0	2	1			1.000	-0	/O	-0.1

■ **JOE McDERMOTT** McDermott, Joseph Deb: 5/04/1871

YEAR	TM/L	G	AB	R	H	2B	3B	HR	RBI	BB	SO	AVG	OBP	SLG	PRO+	BR	/A	RC	SB	CS	SBR	FA	FR	POS	TPR
1871	Kek-n	2	8	3	2	0	0	0	1	1	1	.250	.333	.250	69	-0	-0	1	1					/O	0.0
1872	Eck-n	7	33	3	9	3	0	0	3	1	2	.273	.294	.364	119	0	1	4						/P	0.0
Total	2 n	9	41	6	11	3	0	0	4	2	3	.268	.302	.341	107	-0	1	5						/PO	0.0

■ **MICKEY McDERMOTT** McDermott, Maurice Joseph "Maury" b: 8/29/28, Poughkeepsie, N.Y. BL/TL, 6′2″, 170 lbs. Deb: 4/24/48 C

YEAR	TM/L	G	AB	R	H	2B	3B	HR	RBI	BB	SO	AVG	OBP	SLG	PRO+	BR	/A	RC	SB	CS	SBR	FA	FR	POS	TPR
1948	Bos-A	7	8	2	3	1	0	0	0	0	0	.375	.375	.500	125	0	0	2	0	0	0	1.000	1	/P	0.0
1949	Bos-A	12	33	3	7	3	0	0	6	3	6	.212	.278	.303	50	-2	-3	3	0	0	0	.941	-0	P	0.0
1950	Bos-A	39	44	11	16	5	0	0	12	9	3	.364	.472	.477	131	3	3	11	0	0	0	.938	1	P	0.0
1951	Bos-A	43	66	8	18	1	1	1	6	3	14	.273	.314	.364	76	-2	-3	7	0	1	-1	.950	1	P	0.0

YEAR	TM/L	G	AB	R	H	2B	3B	HR	RBI	BB	SO	AVG	OBP	SLG	PRO+	BR	/A	RC	SB	CS	SBR	FA	FR	POS	TPR
1952	Bos-A	36	62	10	14	1	1	1	7	4	11	.226	.273	.323	60	-3	-4	6	0	0	0	.944	-0	P	0.0
1953	Bos-A	45	93	9	28	8	0	1	13	2	13	.301	.316	.419	92	-1	-1	12	0	1	-1	.957	1	P	0.0
1954	Was-A	54	95	7	19	3	0	0	4	7	12	.200	.255	.232	36	-9	-8	5	0	0	0	.955	1	P	0.0
1955	Was-A	70	95	10	25	4	0	1	10	6	16	.263	.314	.337	79	-3	-3	11	1	0	0	.943	0	P	0.0
1956	*NY-A	46	52	4	11	0	0	1	4	8	13	.212	.317	.269	58	-3	-3	4	0	0	0	1.000	-0	P	0.0
1957	KC-A	58	49	6	12	1	0	4	7	9	16	.245	.362	.510	133	2	2	9	0	0	0	.960	1	P/1	0.0
1958	Det-A	4	3	0	1	0	0	0	1	0	2	.333	.333	.333	78	-0	-0	0	0	0	0	.000	-0	/P	0.0
1961	StL-N	22	14	1	1	1	0	0	3	0	4	.071	.071	.143	-41	-3	-3	0	0	0	0	1.000	-0	P	0.0
	KC-A	7	5	0	1	1	0	0	1	1	2	.200	.333	.400	95	-0	-0	1	0	0	0	.500	-0	/P	0.0
Total	12	443	619	71	156	29	2	9	74	52	112	.252	.312	.349	76	-20	-22	69	1	2	-1	.951	4	P/1	0.0

■ TERRY McDERMOTT McDermott, Terrence Michael b: 3/20/51, Rockville Cen., N.Y BR/TR, 6'3", 205 lbs. Deb: 9/12/72

YEAR	TM/L	G	AB	R	H	2B	3B	HR	RBI	BB	SO	AVG	OBP	SLG	PRO+	BR	/A	RC	SB	CS	SBR	FA	FR	POS	TPR
1972	LA-N	9	23	2	3	0	0	0	0	2	8	.130	.200	.130	-5	-3	-3	1	0	0	0	1.000	-1	/1	-0.4

■ SANDY McDERMOTT McDermott, Thomas Nathaniel b: 3/15/1856, Zanesville, Ohio d: 11/23/22, Mansfield, Ohio Deb: 6/18/1885

YEAR	TM/L	G	AB	R	H	2B	3B	HR	RBI	BB	SO	AVG	OBP	SLG	PRO+	BR	/A	RC	SB	CS	SBR	FA	FR	POS	TPR
1885	Bal-a	1	0	0	0	0	0	0		0		—	—	—	—	0	0	0				.000	0	/2	0.0

■ MC DONALD McDonald Deb: 5/18/1872

YEAR	TM/L	G	AB	R	H	2B	3B	HR	RBI	BB	SO	AVG	OBP	SLG	PRO+	BR	/A	RC	SB	CS	SBR	FA	FR	POS	TPR
1872	Eck-n	1	4	0	0	0	0	0	0	0	0	.000	.000	.000	-99	-1	-1	0						/S	-0.1

■ TEX McDONALD McDonald, Charles E. (b: Charles C. Crabtree) b: 1/31/1891, Farmersville, Tex. d: 3/31/43, Houston, Tex. BL/TR, 5'10", 160 lbs. Deb: 4/11/12

YEAR	TM/L	G	AB	R	H	2B	3B	HR	RBI	BB	SO	AVG	OBP	SLG	PRO+	BR	/A	RC	SB	CS	SBR	FA	FR	POS	TPR
1912	Cin-N	61	140	16	36	3	4	1	15	13	24	.257	.329	.357	90	-2	-2	18	5			.915	-9	S	-0.7
1913	Cin-N	11	10	1	3	0	0	0	2	0	1	.300	.300	.300	72	-0	-0	1	0			.000	0	/S	0.0
	Bos-N	62	145	24	52	4	4	0	18	15	17	.359	.422	.441	144	9	9	28	4			.869	-2	3/2O	0.8
	Yr	73	155	25	55	4	4	0	20	15	18	.355	.415	.432	140	9	9	29	4			.869	-2	3/2SO	0.8
1914	Pit-F	67	223	27	71	16	7	3	29	13	23	.318	.361	.493	143	11	11	44	9			.925	-3	O2/S	0.7
	Buf-F	69	250	32	74	13	6	3	32	20	26	.296	.353	.432	120	7	6	44	11			.953	-3	O2	0.1
	Yr	136	473	59	145	29	13	6	61	33	49	.307	.357	.461	131	18	17	88	20			.943	-6	O2/S	0.8
1915	Buf-F	87	251	31	68	9	6	6	39	27	34	.271	.346	.426	124	8	7	40	5			.924	-7	O	-0.2
Total	4	357	1019	131	304	45	27	13	135	88	125	.298	.359	.434	125	32	31	175	34			.936	-23	O/S23	0.7

■ JACK McDONALD McDonald, Daniel b: 1847, Brooklyn, N.Y. d: 11/23/1880, Brooklyn, N.Y. Deb: 5/02/1872

YEAR	TM/L	G	AB	R	H	2B	3B	HR	RBI	BB	SO	AVG	OBP	SLG	PRO+	BR	/A	RC	SB	CS	SBR	FA	FR	POS	TPR
1872	Atl-n	15	61	9	15	4	1	0	5	0	1	.246	.246	.344	68	-1	-4	5						O	-0.2

■ DAVE McDONALD McDonald, David Bruce b: 5/20/43, New Albany, Ind. BL/TR, 6'3", 215 lbs. Deb: 9/15/69

YEAR	TM/L	G	AB	R	H	2B	3B	HR	RBI	BB	SO	AVG	OBP	SLG	PRO+	BR	/A	RC	SB	CS	SBR	FA	FR	POS	TPR
1969	NY-A	9	23	0	5	1	0	0	2	2	5	.217	.280	.261	54	-1	-1	2	0	1	-1	.960	-1	/1	-0.3
1971	Mon-N	24	39	3	4	2	0	1	4	4	14	.103	.186	.231	17	-4	-4	1	0	0	0	.983	-1	/1O	-0.6
Total	2	33	62	3	9	3	0	1	6	6	19	.145	.221	.242	31	-6	-6	3	0	1	-1	.972	-1	/1O	-0.9

■ ED McDONALD McDonald, Edward C. b: 10/28/1886, Albany, N.Y. d: 3/11/46, Albany, N.Y. BR/TR, 6', 180 lbs. Deb: 8/05/11

YEAR	TM/L	G	AB	R	H	2B	3B	HR	RBI	BB	SO	AVG	OBP	SLG	PRO+	BR	/A	RC	SB	CS	SBR	FA	FR	POS	TPR
1911	Bos-N	54	175	28	36	7	3	1	21	40	39	.206	.359	.297	78	-2	-4	23	11			.955	-6	3/S	-0.9
1912	Bos-N	121	459	70	119	23	6	2	34	70	91	.259	.363	.349	94	-1	-2	65	22			.940	-2	*3	-0.3
1913	Chi-N	1	0	0	0	0	0	0	0	0	0	—	—	—	—	0	0	0	0			.000	0	R	0.0
Total	3	176	634	98	155	30	9	3	55	110	130	.244	.362	.334	89	-3	-6	88	33			.945	-7	3/S	-1.2

■ JIM McDONALD McDonald, James b: Philadelphia, Pa. BR/TR, 6', 180 lbs. Deb: 6/02/02

YEAR	TM/L	G	AB	R	H	2B	3B	HR	RBI	BB	SO	AVG	OBP	SLG	PRO+	BR	/A	RC	SB	CS	SBR	FA	FR	POS	TPR
1902	NY-N	2	9	0	3	0	0	0	1	0		.333	.333	.333	107	0	0	1	0			1.000	-0	/O	-0.1

■ JIM McDONALD McDonald, James A. b: 8/6/1860, San Francisco, Cal. d: 9/14/14, San Francisco, Cal. Deb: 10/02/1884

YEAR	TM/L	G	AB	R	H	2B	3B	HR	RBI	BB	SO	AVG	OBP	SLG	PRO+	BR	/A	RC	SB	CS	SBR	FA	FR	POS	TPR
1884	Was-U	2	6	0	1	0	0	0		0		.167	.167	.167	13	-1	-0	0				.700	-1	/CO	-0.1
	Pit-a	38	145	11	23	3	0	0		2		.159	.170	.179	15	-13	-13	5				.795	-6	3O/2	-1.8
1885	Buf-N	5	14	0	0	0	0	0	0	0	4	.000	.000	.000	-97	-3	-3	0				.875	2	/SO	-0.1
Total	2	45	165	11	24	3	0	0	0	2	4	.145	.156	.164	6	-16	-17	5				.976	-6	/3OS2C	-2.0

■ JOE McDONALD McDonald, Malcolm Joseph b: 4/9/1888, Texas d: 5/30/63, Baytown, Tex. BR/TR, 5'11", 175 lbs. Deb: 9/06/10

YEAR	TM/L	G	AB	R	H	2B	3B	HR	RBI	BB	SO	AVG	OBP	SLG	PRO+	BR	/A	RC	SB	CS	SBR	FA	FR	POS	TPR
1910	StL-A	10	32	4	5	0	0	0	1	1		.156	.182	.156	6	-3	-3	1	0			.821	-3	3	-0.7

■ JIM McDONNELL McDonnell, James William "Mack" b: 8/15/22, Gagetown, Mich. BL/TR, 5'11", 165 lbs. Deb: 9/23/43

YEAR	TM/L	G	AB	R	H	2B	3B	HR	RBI	BB	SO	AVG	OBP	SLG	PRO+	BR	/A	RC	SB	CS	SBR	FA	FR	POS	TPR
1943	Cle-A	2	1	1	0	0	0	0	0	2	1	.000	.667	.000	108	0	0	0	0	0	0	1.000	-0	/C	0.0
1944	Cle-A	20	43	5	10	0	0	0	4	4	3	.233	.298	.233	55	-3	-2	3	0	0	0	.900	-2	C	-0.4
1945	Cle-A	28	51	3	10	2	0	0	8	2	4	.196	.226	.235	36	-4	-4	3	0	0	0	.980	8	C	0.5
Total	3	50	95	9	20	2	0	0	12	8	8	.211	.272	.232	48	-7	-6	6	0	0	0	.953	6	/C	0.1

■ ED McDONOUGH McDonough, Edward Sebastian b: 9/11/1886, Elgin, Ill. d: 9/2/26, Elgin, Ill. BR/TR, 6', 160 lbs. Deb: 8/03/09

YEAR	TM/L	G	AB	R	H	2B	3B	HR	RBI	BB	SO	AVG	OBP	SLG	PRO+	BR	/A	RC	SB	CS	SBR	FA	FR	POS	TPR
1909	Phi-N	1	1	0	0	0	0	0	0	0		.000	.000	.000	-99	-0	-0	0	0			1.000	0	/C	0.0
1910	Phi-N	5	9	1	1	0	0	0	0	0	1	.111	.111	.111	-34	-2	-2	0	0			1.000	-1	/C	-0.2
Total	2	6	10	1	1	0	0	0	0	0	1	.100	.100	.100	-40	-2	-2	0	0			1.000	-1	/C	-0.2

■ GIL McDOUGALD McDougald, Gilbert James b: 5/19/28, San Francisco, Cal BR/TR, 6'1", 180 lbs. Deb: 4/20/51

YEAR	TM/L	G	AB	R	H	2B	3B	HR	RBI	BB	SO	AVG	OBP	SLG	PRO+	BR	/A	RC	SB	CS	SBR	FA	FR	POS	TPR
1951	*NY-A	131	402	72	123	23	4	14	63	56	54	.306	.396	.488	143	22	24	81	14	5	1	.949	-16	32	1.1
1952	*NY-A★	152	555	65	146	16	5	11	78	57	73	.263	.336	.369	102	-3	1	71	6	5	-1	.968	12	*32	1.2
1953	*NY-A	141	541	82	154	27	7	10	83	60	65	.285	.361	.416	113	7	10	85	3	4	-2	.953	6	*32	1.2
1954	NY-A	126	394	66	102	22	2	12	48	62	64	.259	.367	.416	118	9	10	64	3	4	-2	.989	1	23	1.6
1955	*NY-A	141	533	79	152	10	8	13	53	65	77	.285	.365	.407	109	6	7	83	6	4	-1	**.985**	19	*23	3.5
1956	*NY-A☆	120	438	79	136	13	3	13	56	68	59	.311	.407	.443	128	18	20	82	3	8	-4	.970	3	S2/3	2.8
1957	*NY-A★	141	539	87	156	25	**9**	13	62	59	71	.289	.364	.442	121	14	15	86	2	5	-2	.976	15	*S2/3	4.2
1958	*NY-A★	138	503	69	126	19	1	14	65	59	75	.250	.333	.376	98	-3	-1	64	6	2	1	.977	-3	*2S	0.6
1959	NY-A★	127	434	44	109	16	8	4	34	35	40	.251	.311	.353	85	-11	-9	46	0	3	-2	.989	8	2S3	0.5
1960	*NY-A	119	337	54	87	16	4	8	34	38	45	.258	.339	.401	105	-0	2	47	2	4	-2	.945	-3	32	0.0
Total	10	1336	4676	697	1291	187	51	112	576	559	623	.276	.358	.410	112	58	79	708	45	44	-13	.984	42	23S	16.7

■ ODDIBE McDOWELL McDowell, Oddibe b: 8/25/62, Hollywood, Fla. BL/TL, 5'9", 165 lbs. Deb: 5/19/85

YEAR	TM/L	G	AB	R	H	2B	3B	HR	RBI	BB	SO	AVG	OBP	SLG	PRO+	BR	/A	RC	SB	CS	SBR	FA	FR	POS	TPR
1985	Tex-A	111	406	63	97	14	5	18	42	36	85	.239	.306	.431	98	-1	-2	55	25	7	3	.993	10	*O/D	0.8
1986	Tex-A	154	572	105	152	24	7	18	49	65	112	.266	.342	.427	105	6	4	83	33	15	1	.991	3	*O/D	0.3
1987	Tex-A	128	407	65	98	26	4	14	52	51	99	.241	.325	.428	97	-2	-2	61	24	2	6	.989	-2	*O	-0.1
1988	Tex-A	120	437	55	108	19	5	6	37	41	89	.247	.315	.355	85	-7	-9	53	33	10	4	.989	-3	*O/D	-1.2
1989	Cle-A	69	239	33	53	5	2	3	22	25	36	.222	.298	.297	67	-10	-10	23	12	5	1	.992	2	O/D	-1.0
	Atl-N	76	280	56	85	18	4	7	24	27	37	.304	.365	.471	134	13	12	49	15	10	-2	.978	5	O	1.4
1990	Atl-N	113	305	47	74	14	0	7	25	21	53	.243	.296	.357	74	-9	-11	34	13	2	3	.971	-6	O	-1.7
Total	6	771	2646	424	667	120	27	73	251	266	511	.252	.322	.401	95	-10	-18	357	155	51	16	.988	9	O/D	-1.5

■ PRYOR McELVEEN McElveen, Pryor Mynatt "Humpty" b: 11/5/1883, Atlanta, Ga. d: 10/27/51, Pleasant Hill, Tenn. BR/TR, 5'10", 168 lbs. Deb: 4/26/09

YEAR	TM/L	G	AB	R	H	2B	3B	HR	RBI	BB	SO	AVG	OBP	SLG	PRO+	BR	/A	RC	SB	CS	SBR	FA	FR	POS	TPR
1909	Bro-N	81	258	22	51	8	1	3	25	14		.198	.242	.271	61	-13	-12	18	6			.938	-5	3OS/12	-1.8
1910	Bro-N	74	213	19	48	8	3	1	26	22	47	.225	.307	.305	81	-6	-5	22	6			.943	-5	3/S2C	-0.9
1911	Bro-N	16	31	1	6	0	0	0	5	0	3	.194	.194	.194	9	-4	-4	1	0			.929	-1	/2S	-0.5
Total	3	171	502	42	105	16	4	4	56	36	50	.209	.268	.281	67	-23	-21	41	12			.941	-11	/3S2O1C	-3.2

YEAR	TM/L	G	AB	R	H	2B	3B	HR	RBI	BB	SO	AVG	OBP	SLG	PRO+	BR	/A	RC	SB	CS	SBR	FA	FR	POS	TPR

■ LEE McELWEE
McElwee, Leland Stanford b: 5/23/1894, LaMesa, Cal. d: 2/8/57, Union, Maine BR/TR, 5'10.5", 160 lbs. Deb: 7/03/16

| 1916 | Phi-A | 54 | 155 | 9 | 41 | 3 | 0 | 0 | 10 | 8 | 17 | .265 | .301 | .284 | 79 | -5 | -4 | 14 | 0 | | | .883 | -2 | 3/021S | -0.6 |

■ FRANK McELYEA
McElyea, Frank b: 8/4/18, Hawthorne Twsp., Ill. d: 4/19/87, Evansville, Ill. BR/TR, 6'6", 221 lbs. Deb: 9/10/42

| 1942 | Bos-N | 7 | 4 | 2 | 0 | 0 | 0 | 0 | 0 | 0 | 0 | .000 | .000 | .000 | -99 | -1 | -1 | 0 | 0 | | | 1.000 | -0 | /O | -0.1 |

■ GUY McFADDEN
McFadden, Guy G. b: 9/3/1872, Topeka, Kan. d: 3/10/11, Topeka, Kan. Deb: 8/24/1895

| 1895 | StL-N | 4 | 14 | 1 | 3 | 0 | 0 | 0 | 2 | 0 | 2 | .214 | .214 | .214 | 12 | -2 | -2 | 1 | 0 | | | .968 | -1 | /1 | -0.2 |

■ LEON McFADDEN
McFadden, Leon b: 4/26/44, Little Rock, Ark. BR/TR, 6'2", 195 lbs. Deb: 9/06/68

1968	Hou-N	16	47	2	13	1	0	0	1	6	10	.277	.358	.298	101	0	0	6	1	0	0	.968	-1	S	0.2
1969	Hou-N	44	74	3	13	2	0	0	3	4	9	.176	.218	.203	19	-8	-8	3	1	2	-1	.944	-1	O/S	-1.0
1970	Hou-N	2	0	0	0	0	0	0	0	0	0	—	—	—	—	0	0	0	0	0	0	.000	0	R	0.0
Total	3	62	121	5	26	3	0	0	4	10	19	.215	.275	.240	50	-8	-8	9	2	2	-1	.966	-1	/SO	-0.8

■ ALEX McFARLAN
McFarlan, Alexander Shepherd b: 11/11/1866, Kentucky d: 3/2/39, Peewee Valley, Ky. Deb: 6/19/1892 F

| 1892 | Lou-N | 14 | 42 | 2 | 7 | 0 | 0 | 0 | 1 | 8 | 11 | .167 | .300 | .167 | 47 | -2 | -2 | 2 | 1 | | | .773 | -3 | O/2 | -0.5 |

■ CHRIS McFARLAND
McFarland, Christopher b: 8/17/1861, Fall River, Mass. d: 5/24/18, New Bedford, Mass. 5'9", 170 lbs. Deb: 4/19/1884

| 1884 | Bal-U | 3 | 14 | 2 | 3 | 1 | 0 | 0 | | 0 | | .214 | .214 | .286 | 61 | -0 | -1 | 1 | | | | .571 | -1 | /OP | -0.2 |

■ ED McFARLAND
McFarland, Edward William b: 8/3/1874, Cleveland, Ohio d: 11/28/59, Cleveland, Ohio BR/TR, 5'10", 180 lbs. Deb: 7/07/1893

1893	Cle-N	8	22	5	9	2	1	0	6	1	2	.409	.458	.591	170	2	2	6	0			1.000	-4	/O3C	-0.1
1896	StL-N	83	290	48	70	13	4	3	36	15	17	.241	.281	.345	69	-15	-13	32	7			.961	8	C/O	0.3
1897	StL-N	31	107	14	35	5	2	1	17	8		.327	.374	.439	116	2	2	19	2			.965	2	C/1O2	0.6
	Phi-N	38	130	18	29	3	5	1	16	14		.223	.308	.346	74	-5	-5	16	2			.951	-1	C	-0.1
	Yr	69	237	32	64	8	7	2	33	22		.270	.337	.388	93	-3	-3	35	4			.957	2	C/1O2	0.5
1898	Phi-N	121	429	65	121	21	5	3	71	44		.282	.352	.375	113	5	7	61	4			.960	-2	*C	1.7
1899	Phi-N	96	324	59	108	22	9	2	57	36		.333	.403	.475	146	18	20	68	9			.968	14	C	3.6
1900	Phi-N	94	344	50	105	14	8	0	38	29		.305	.364	.392	110	4	5	55	9			.963	-2	C/3	1.0
1901	Phi-N	74	295	33	84	14	2	1	32	18		.285	.326	.356	96	-1	-2	39	11			.970	2	C	0.7
1902	Chi-A	75	246	29	56	9	2	1	25	19		.228	.291	.293	65	-12	-11	25	8			.967	1	C/O1	-0.2
1903	Chi-A	61	201	15	42	7	2	1	19	14		.209	.264	.279	66	-9	-8	17	3			.968	0	C/1	-0.2
1904	Chi-A	50	160	22	44	11	3	0	20	17		.275	.348	.381	136	6	7	23	2			.975	-11	C	0.1
1905	Chi-A	80	250	24	70	13	4	0	31	23		.280	.345	.364	131	7	9	35	5			.973	6	C	2.4
1906	*Chi-A	12	23	0	4	1	0	0	3	3		.174	.269	.217	55	-1	-1	2	0			.973	-1	/C	-0.1
1907	Chi-A	52	138	11	39	9	1	0	8	12		.283	.340	.362	129	4	4	19	3			.972	-1	C	0.7
1908	Bos-A	19	48	5	10	2	1	0	4	1		.208	.224	.292	66	-2	-2	3	0			.978	4	C	0.3
Total	14	894	3007	398	826	146	49	13	383	254	19	.275	.335	.369	104	3	14	419	65			.967	16	C/O132	10.7

■ HERM McFARLAND
McFarland, Hermas Walter b: 3/11/1870, Des Moines, Iowa d: 9/21/35, Richmond, Va. BL/TR, 5'6", 150 lbs. Deb: 4/21/1896

1896	Lou-N	30	110	11	21	4	1	1	12	9	14	.191	.252	.273	41	-10	-9	9	4			.833	-3	O/C	-1.2
1898	Cin-N	19	64	10	18	1	3	0	11	7		.281	.361	.391	108	1	1	10	3			.968	-2	O	-0.2
1901	Chi-A	132	473	83	130	21	9	4	59	75		.275	.384	.383	116	12	14	86	33			.946	5	*O	0.8
1902	Chi-A	7	27	5	5	0	0	0	4	2		.185	.241	.185	20	-3	-3	2	1			1.000	-0	/O	-0.3
	Bal-A	61	242	54	78	19	6	3	36	36		.322	.420	.488	145	18	16	55	10			.965	6	O	1.7
	Yr	68	269	59	83	19	6	3	40	38		.309	.404	.457	133	15	14	56	11			.967	6	O	1.4
1903	NY-A	103	362	41	88	16	9	5	45	46		.243	.332	.378	106	7	4	52	13			.939	-3	*O	-0.6
Total	5	352	1278	204	340	61	28	13	167	175	14	.266	.362	.388	110	25	23	214	64			.941	2	O/C	0.2

■ HOWIE McFARLAND
McFarland, Howard Alexander b: 3/7/11, ElReno, Okla. BR/TR, 6', 175 lbs. Deb: 7/16/45

| 1945 | Was-A | 6 | 11 | 0 | 1 | 0 | 0 | 0 | 0 | 0 | 3 | .091 | .091 | .091 | -52 | -2 | -2 | 0 | 0 | 0 | 0 | 1.000 | -0 | /O | -0.3 |

■ ORLANDO McFARLANE
McFarlane, Orlando Dejesus (Quesada) b: 6/28/38, Oriente, Cuba BR/TR, 6', 180 lbs. Deb: 4/23/62

1962	Pit-N	8	23	0	2	0	0	0	1	1	4	.087	.125	.087	-42	-5	-5	0	0	0	0	1.000	2	/C	-0.2
1964	Pit-N	37	78	5	19	5	0	0	1	4	27	.244	.280	.308	66	-4	-4	7	0	0	0	.983	-6	C/O	-0.9
1966	Det-A	49	138	16	35	7	0	5	13	9	46	.254	.304	.413	102	0	0	17	0	0	0	.991	2	C	0.0
1967	Cal-A	12	22	0	5	0	0	0	3	1	7	.227	.261	.227	47	-1	-1	1	0	0	0	.935	-1	/C	-0.2
1968	Cal-A	18	31	1	9	0	0	0	2	5	9	.290	.389	.290	112	1	1	4	0	0	0	.977	-0	/C	0.1
Total	5	124	292	22	70	12	0	5	20	20	93	.240	.291	.332	78	-9	-9	29	0	0	0	.985	-7	/CO	-1.2

■ PATSY McGAFFIGAN
McGaffigan, Mark Andrew b: 9/12/1888, Carlyle, Ill. d: 12/22/40, Carlyle, Ill. BR/TR, 5'8", 140 lbs. Deb: 4/16/17

1917	Phi-N	19	60	5	10	1	0	0	6	0	7	.167	.167	.183	7	-7	-7	2	1			.920	-1	S/O	-0.8
1918	Phi-N	54	192	17	39	3	2	1	8	16	23	.203	.268	.255	56	-9	-10	14	3			.948	-12	2/S	-2.2
Total	2	73	252	22	49	4	2	1	14	16	30	.194	.245	.238	45	-16	-17	17	4			.923	-12	/2SO	-3.0

■ EDDIE McGAH
McGah, Edward Joseph b: 9/30/21, Oakland, Cal. BR/TR, 6', 183 lbs. Deb: 4/26/46

1946	Bos-A	15	37	2	8	1	1	0	1	7	7	.216	.341	.297	75	-1	-1	5	0	0	0	.981	-2	C	-0.3
1947	Bos-A	9	14	1	0	0	0	0	2	3	0	.000	.176	.000	-45	-3	-3	0	0	0	0	.964	2	/C	-0.1
Total	2	24	51	3	8	1	1	0	3	10	7	.157	.295	.216	41	-4	-4	5	0	0	0	.975	-0	/C	-0.4

■ AMBROSE McGANN
McGann, Ambrose b: Baltimore, Md. Deb: 5/02/1895

| 1895 | Lou-N | 20 | 73 | 9 | 21 | 5 | 2 | 0 | 9 | 8 | 6 | .288 | .358 | .411 | 107 | -0 | 1 | 13 | 6 | | | .852 | -3 | /S3O | -0.1 |

■ DAN McGANN
McGann, Dennis Lawrence "Cap" b: 7/15/1871, Shelbyville, Ky. d: 12/13/10, Louisville, Ky. BB/TR, 6', 190 lbs. Deb: 8/08/1896

1896	Bos-N	43	171	25	55	6	7	2	30	12	10	.322	.383	.474	120	6	5	33	2			.905	-17	2	-0.8
1898	Bal-N	145	535	99	161	18	8	5	106	53		.301	.404	.393	126	24	22	102	33			.983	2	*1	2.2
1899	Bro-N	63	214	49	52	11	4	2	32	21		.243	.362	.360	96	1	-0	35	16			.985	2	1	0.1
	Was-N	76	280	65	96	9	8	5	58	14		.343	.410	.486	147	17	18	62	11			.990	2	1	1.8
	Yr	139	494	114	148	20	12	7	90	35		.300	.389	.431	124	18	18	97	27			.988	4	*1	1.9
1900	StL-N	121	444	79	132	10	9	4	58	32		.297	.373	.387	111	7	8	77	26			.990	-1	*1/2	0.6
1901	StL-N	103	423	73	115	15	9	6	56	16		.272	.332	.392	116	5	8	63	17			.984	-3	*1	0.3
1902	Bal-A	68	250	40	79	10	8	0	42	19		.316	.380	.442	116	8	6	49	17			.987	3	1	0.7
	NY-N	61	227	25	68	5	7	0	21	12		.300	.351	.383	128	7	7	36	12			.981	2	1	0.8
1903	NY-N	129	482	75	130	21	6	3	50	32		.270	.328	.357	92	-3	-6	73	36			.988	-0	*1	-0.8
1904	NY-N	141	517	81	148	22	6	6	71	36		.286	.348	.387	122	17	14	89	42			.991	3	*1	1.4
1905	*NY-N	136	491	88	147	23	14	5	75	55		.299	.391	.434	143	30	28	97	22			.991	3	*1	3.0
1906	NY-N	134	451	62	107	14	8	0	37	60		.237	.341	.304	99	3	2	61	30			.995	3	*1	0.1
1907	NY-N	81	262	29	78	9	1	2	36	29		.298	.380	.363	129	11	10	42	9			.994	5	1	1.5
1908	Bos-N	135	475	52	114	18	5	5	55	38		.240	.319	.291	96	-1	-0	48	9			.988	5	*1/2	0.2
Total	12	1436	5222	842	1482	181	100	42	727	429	10	.284	.362	.381	117	131	121	866	282			.989	10	*1/2	11.1

■ CHIPPY McGARR
McGarr, James B. b: 5/10/1863, Worcester, Mass. d: 6/6/04, Worcester, Mass. BR/TR, 5'7", 168 lbs. Deb: 7/11/1884 U

1884	CP-U	19	70	10	11	2	0	0		0		.157	.157	.186	16	-6	-6	2				.905	-6	2/O	-1.0
1886	Phi-a	71	267	41	71	9	3	2		9		.266	.295	.345	101	-0	-1	33	17			.850	1	S	0.0
1887	Phi-a	137	536	93	158	23	6	1		23		.295	.326	.366	95	-4	-4	94	84			.875	-1	*S	-0.3

YEAR	TM/L	G	AB	R	H	2B	3B	HR	RBI	BB	SO	AVG	OBP	SLG	PRO+	BR	/A	RC	SB	CS	SBR	FA	FR	POS	TPR
1888	StL-a	34	132	17	31	1	0	0	13	6		.235	.268	.242	60	-5	-7	16	25			.895	-3	2/S	-0.7
1889	KC-a	25	108	22	31	3	0	0	16	6	11	.287	.330	.315	81	-2	-3	16	12			.857	-2	3/O2S	-0.3
	Bal-a	3	7	1	1	0	0	0	0	1	1	.143	.250	.143	14	-1	-1	0	0			.583	-2	/S	-0.2
	Yr	28	115	23	32	3	0	0	16	7	12	.278	.325	.304	77	-3	-4	16	12			.857	-4	3/OS2	-0.5
1890	Bos-N	121	487	68	115	12	7	1	51	34	38	.236	.291	.296	68	-17	-23	55	39			**.933**	-2	*3/SO	-1.8
1893	Cle-N	63	249	38	77	12	0	0	28	20	15	.309	.363	.357	88	-2	-5	42	24			.886	0	3	-0.3
1894	Cle-N	128	523	94	144	24	6	2	74	28	29	.275	.316	.356	61	-32	-36	71	31			.902	-7	*3	-3.3
1895	*Cle-N	112	419	85	111	14	2	2	59	34	33	.265	.322	.322	64	-19	-24	53	19			.870	-5	*3/2	-2.2
1896	*Cle-N	113	455	68	122	16	4	1	53	22	30	.268	.302	.327	64	-22	-26	52	16			.924	-7	*3/C	-2.6
Total	10	826	3253	537	872	116	28	9	294	183	157	.268	.310	.329	73	-109	-134	432	267			.903	-32	3S/2OC	-12.7

■ JIM McGARR

McGarr, James Vincent "Reds" b: 11/9/1888, Philadelphia, Pa. d: 7/21/81, Miami, Fla. BR/TR, 5'9.5", 170 lbs. Deb: 5/18/12

YEAR	TM/L	G	AB	R	H	2B	3B	HR	RBI	BB	SO	AVG	OBP	SLG	PRO+	BR	/A	RC	SB	CS	SBR	FA	FR	POS	TPR
1912	Det-A	1	4	0	0	0	0	0	0	0		.000	.000	.000	-99	-1	-1	0	0			.800	-0	/2	-0.2

■ DAN McGARVEY

McGarvey, Daniel Francis b: 12/2/1887, Philadelphia, Pa. d: 3/7/47, Philadelphia, Pa. Deb: 5/18/12

YEAR	TM/L	G	AB	R	H	2B	3B	HR	RBI	BB	SO	AVG	OBP	SLG	PRO+	BR	/A	RC	SB	CS	SBR	FA	FR	POS	TPR
1912	Det-A	1	3	0	0	0	0	0	0	1		.000	.400	.000	18	-0	-0	0	0			.667	0	/O	0.0

■ JACK McGEACHEY

McGeachey, John Charles b: 5/23/1864, Clinton, Mass. d: 4/5/30, Cambridge, Mass. BR/TR, 5'8", 165 lbs. Deb: 6/17/1886

YEAR	TM/L	G	AB	R	H	2B	3B	HR	RBI	BB	SO	AVG	OBP	SLG	PRO+	BR	/A	RC	SB	CS	SBR	FA	FR	POS	TPR
1886	Det-N	6	27	3	9	0	1	0	4	0	3	.333	.333	.407	121	1	1	4	2			.875	-1	/O	0.0
	StL-N	59	226	31	46	12	3	2	24	1	37	.204	.207	.310	59	-12	-10	17	8			.880	2	O/23	-0.9
	Yr	65	253	34	55	12	4	2	28	1	40	.217	.220	.320	66	-12	-10	21	10			.880	1	O/23	-0.9
1887	Ind-N	99	405	49	109	17	3	1	56	5	16	.269	.280	.333	74	-16	-14	46	27			.894	7	*O/3P	-0.7
1888	Ind-N	118	452	45	99	15	2	0	30	5	21	.219	.231	.261	57	-21	-22	40	49			.932	5	*O/SP	-2.0
1889	Ind-N	131	532	83	142	32	1	2	63	9	39	.267	.282	.342	74	-19	-21	63	37			.918	9	*O/P	-1.3
1890	Bro-P	104	443	84	108	24	4	1	65	19	12	.244	.278	.323	58	-25	-30	47	21			.906	-1	*O	-2.8
1891	Phi-a	50	201	24	46	4	3	2	13	6	12	.229	.255	.308	61	-10	-11	19	9			.920	2	O	-0.9
	Bos-a	41	178	26	45	2	1	1	21	12	8	.253	.304	.292	74	-6	-6	20	11			.910	-4	O	-1.0
	Yr	91	379	50	91	6	4	3	34	18	20	.240	.278	.301	67	-17	-17	38	20			.916	-2	O	-1.9
Total	6	608	2464	345	604	106	18	9	276	57	148	.245	.265	.314	66	-110	-113	255	164			.909	18	O/P32S	-9.6

■ MIKE McGEARY

McGeary, Michael Henry b: 1851, Philadelphia, Pa. BR/TR, 5'7", 138 lbs. Deb: 5/09/1871 M

YEAR	TM/L	G	AB	R	H	2B	3B	HR	RBI	BB	SO	AVG	OBP	SLG	PRO+	BR	/A	RC	SB	CS	SBR	FA	FR	POS	TPR
1871	Tro-n	29	148	42	39	4	0	0	12	6	0	.264	.292	.291	67	-6	-6	19	**20**					*C/S	-0.5
1872	Ath-n	47	226	68	81	9	2	0	35	2	1	.358	.364	.416	139	10	10	36						CS/O	0.6
1873	Ath-n	52	275	63	83	9	1	0	30	1	1	.302	.304	.342	84	-3	-8	28						*SC/3	-0.8
1874	Ath-n	54	270	61	87	11	2	0		2		.322	.327	.378	114	7	3	34						SC/O	0.2
1875	Phi-n	68	309	71	89	6	2	0		1		.288	.290	.320	107	3	1	29						32S/OCM	0.0
1876	StL-N	61	276	48	72	3	0	0	30	2	1	.261	.266	.272	84	-6	-4	20				.889	5	*2/CO3	0.1
1877	StL-N	57	258	35	65	3	2	0	20	2	6	.252	.258	.279	73	-9	-7	19				.883	7	23	0.2
1879	Pro-N	85	374	62	103	7	2	0	35	5	13	.275	.285	.305	96	-2	-1	33				.884	1	*23	0.5
1880	Pro-N	18	59	5	8	0	0	0	1	0	6	.136	.136	.136	-8	-6	-6	1				.887	3	3/2SM	-0.2
	Cle-N	31	111	14	28	2	1	0	6	4	3	.252	.278	.288	94	-1	-1	9				.887	-4	3/O	-0.4
	Yr	49	170	19	36	2	1	0	7	4	9	.212	.230	.235	60	-7	-7	9				.887	-1	3/2OS	-0.6
1881	Cle-N	11	41	1	9	0	0	0	5	0	6	.220	.220	.220	41	-3	-3	2				.724	-7	3M	-0.9
1882	Det-N	34	133	14	19	4	1	0	2	2	20	.143	.156	.188	10	-13	-13	4				.928	8	S/2	-0.3
Total	5 n	250	1228	305	379	39	7	0	77	12	2	.309	.315	.352	103	11	-0	147						S/C32O	-0.5
Total	6	297	1252	179	304	19	6	0	99	15	55	.243	.252	.268	72	-40	-34	89				.885	14	2/3SCO	-1.0

■ DAN McGEE

McGee, Daniel Aloysius b: 9/29/13, New York, N.Y. BR/TR, 5'8.5", 152 lbs. Deb: 7/14/34

YEAR	TM/L	G	AB	R	H	2B	3B	HR	RBI	BB	SO	AVG	OBP	SLG	PRO+	BR	/A	RC	SB	CS	SBR	FA	FR	POS	TPR
1934	Bos-N	7	22	2	3	0	0	0	1	3	6	.136	.240	.136	4	-3	-3	1	0			.951	3	/S	0.1

■ FRANK McGEE

McGee, Francis De Sales b: 4/28/1899, Columbus, Ohio d: 1/30/34, Columbus, Ohio BR/TR, 5'11.5", 175 lbs. Deb: 9/19/25

YEAR	TM/L	G	AB	R	H	2B	3B	HR	RBI	BB	SO	AVG	OBP	SLG	PRO+	BR	/A	RC	SB	CS	SBR	FA	FR	POS	TPR
1925	Was-A	2	3	0	0	0	0	0	0	0	1	.000	.000	.000	-99	-1	-1	0	0	0	0	1.000	0	/1	-0.1

■ PAT McGEE

McGee, Patrick b: Philadelphia, Pa. d: 6/21/1889, New York, N.Y. Deb: 9/24/1874

YEAR	TM/L	G	AB	R	H	2B	3B	HR	RBI	BB	SO	AVG	OBP	SLG	PRO+	BR	/A	RC	SB	CS	SBR	FA	FR	POS	TPR
1874	Atl-n	16	65	4	11	2	0	0		0		.169	.169	.200	19	-6	-4	2						O/S2	-0.3
1875	Mut-n	25	94	4	16	3	0	0		0		.170	.170	.202	27	-6	-7	3						O	-0.6
	Atl-n	18	63	3	9	4	1	0		1		.143	.156	.238	39	-4	-3	2						O/2	-0.2
	Yr	43	157	7	25	7	1	0		1		.159	.165	.217	31	-10	-10	6						O/2	-0.8
Total	2 n	59	222	11	36	9	1	0		1		.162	.166	.212	28	-16	-14	8						/O2S	-1.1

■ WILLIE McGEE

McGee, Willie Dean b: 11/2/58, San Francisco, Cal. BB/TR, 6'1", 175 lbs. Deb: 5/10/82

YEAR	TM/L	G	AB	R	H	2B	3B	HR	RBI	BB	SO	AVG	OBP	SLG	PRO+	BR	/A	RC	SB	CS	SBR	FA	FR	POS	TPR
1982	*StL-N	123	422	43	125	12	8	4	56	12	58	.296	.319	.391	97	-2	-3	49	24	12	0	.958	-15	*O	-2.2
1983	StL-N★	147	601	75	172	22	8	5	75	26	98	.286	.316	.374	90	-9	-9	73	39	8	7	.987	0	*O	-0.7
1984	StL-N	145	571	82	166	19	11	6	50	29	80	.291	.326	.394	104	-0	2	74	43	10	7	.985	11	*O	1.6
1985	*StL-N★	152	612	114	**216**	26	**18**	10	82	34	86	**.353**	.387	.503	148	37	37	123	56	16	7	.978	13	*O	5.4
1986	StL-N	124	497	65	127	22	7	7	48	37	82	.256	.308	.370	87	-10	-9	53	19	16	-4	**.991**	15	*O	-0.2
1987	*StL-N★	153	620	76	177	37	11	11	105	24	90	.285	.314	.434	94	-6	-7	77	16	4	2	.981	8	*O/S	-0.2
1988	StL-N★	137	562	73	164	24	6	3	50	32	84	.292	.331	.372	100	1	0	72	41	6	9	.975	10	*O	1.6
1989	StL-N	58	199	23	47	10	2	3	17	10	34	.236	.276	.352	76	-6	-7	18	8	6	-1	.976	2	O	-0.8
1990	StL-N	125	501	76	168	32	5	3	62	38	86	**.335**	.383	.437	125	17	17	85	28	9	3	.957	16	*O	3.4
	*Oak-A	29	113	23	31	3	2	0	15	10	18	.274	.333	.336	91	-2	-1	13	3	0	1	.986	1	O/D	0.0
1991	SF-N	131	497	67	155	30	3	4	43	34	74	.312	.358	.408	119	10	12	71	17	9	-0	.978	-2	*O	0.7
1992	SF-N	138	474	56	141	20	2	1	36	29	88	.297	.339	.354	102	-2	1	58	13	4	2	.976	3	*O	0.3
Total	11	1462	5669	773	1689	257	83	57	639	315	878	.298	.336	.403	106	28	33	767	307	100	32	.977	62	*O/DS	8.9

■ DAN McGEEHAN

McGeehan, Daniel De Sales b: 6/7/1885, Jeddo, Pa. d: 7/12/55, Hazleton, Pa. BR/TR, 5'6", 135 lbs. Deb: 4/22/11 F

YEAR	TM/L	G	AB	R	H	2B	3B	HR	RBI	BB	SO	AVG	OBP	SLG	PRO+	BR	/A	RC	SB	CS	SBR	FA	FR	POS	TPR
1911	StL-N	3	9	0	2	0	0	0	1	0	1	.222	.222	.222	25	-1	-1	0	0			.818	-1	/2	-0.2

■ ED McGHEE

McGhee, Warren Edward b: 9/29/24, Perry, Ark. d: 2/13/86, Memphis, Tenn. BR/TR, 5'11", 170 lbs. Deb: 9/20/50

YEAR	TM/L	G	AB	R	H	2B	3B	HR	RBI	BB	SO	AVG	OBP	SLG	PRO+	BR	/A	RC	SB	CS	SBR	FA	FR	POS	TPR
1950	Chi-A	3	6	0	1	0	1	0	0	0	1	.167	.167	.500	67	-0	-0	1	0	0	0	1.000	-0	/O	-0.1
1953	Phi-A	104	358	36	94	11	4	1	29	32	43	.263	.328	.324	74	-11	-13	38	4	3	-1	.982	7	O	-1.0
1954	Phi-A	21	53	5	11	2	0	2	9	4	8	.208	.263	.358	69	-3	-3	5	0	1	-1	.933	1	O	-0.3
	Chi-A	42	75	12	17	1	0	0	5	12	8	.227	.333	.240	57	-4	-4	7	5	0	2	.982	-3	O	-0.7
	Yr	63	128	17	28	3	0	2	14	16	16	.219	.306	.289	62	-6	-7	12	5	1	1	.960	-3	O	-1.0
1955	Chi-A	26	13	6	1	0	0	0	0	6	1	.077	.368	.077	24	-1	-1	1	2	1	0	.923	-6	O	-0.7
Total	4	196	505	59	124	14	5	3	43	54	61	.246	.322	.311	70	-19	-21	51	11	5	0	.975	-2	O	-2.8

■ BILL McGHEE

McGhee, William Mac "Fibber" b: 9/5/08, Shawmut, Ala. BL/TL, 5'10.5", 185 lbs. Deb: 7/05/44

YEAR	TM/L	G	AB	R	H	2B	3B	HR	RBI	BB	SO	AVG	OBP	SLG	PRO+	BR	/A	RC	SB	CS	SBR	FA	FR	POS	TPR
1944	Phi-A	77	287	27	83	12	0	1	19	21	20	.289	.338	.341	96	-2	-2	32	2	1	0	.989	-0	1	-0.6
1945	Phi-A	93	250	24	63	6	1	0	19	24	16	.252	.320	.284	76	-7	-7	24	3	2	-0	.989	-5	O/1	-1.6
Total	2	170	537	51	146	18	1	1	38	45	36	.272	.329	.315	87	-9	-9	57	5	3	-0	.990	-5	/1O	-2.2

■ BILL McGILVRAY

McGilvray, William Alexander "Big Bill" b: 4/29/1883, Portland, Ore. d: 5/23/52, Denver, Colo. BL/TL, 6', 160 lbs. Deb: 4/17/08

YEAR	TM/L	G	AB	R	H	2B	3B	HR	RBI	BB	SO	AVG	OBP	SLG	PRO+	BR	/A	RC	SB	CS	SBR	FA	FR	POS	TPR
1908	Cin-N	2	2	0	0	0	0	0	0	0		.000	.000	.000	-99	-0	-0	0	0			.000	0	H	-0.1

YEAR	TM/L	G	AB	R	H	2B	3B	HR	RBI	BB	SO	AVG	OBP	SLG	PRO+	BR	/A	RC	SB	CS	SBR	FA	FR	POS	TPR

■ TIM McGINLEY
McGinley, Timothy S. b: Philadelphia, Pa. d: 11/2/1899, Oakland, Cal. 5'9.5", 155 lbs. Deb: 4/30/1875

1875	Cen-n	13	51	5	13	1	1	0		1		.255	.269	.314	110	0		4						C/O	0.1
	NH-n	32	130	13	36	3	1	0		1		.277	.282	.315	122	1	3	12						C	0.4
	Yr	45	181	18	49	4	2	0		2		.271	.279	.315	118	1	4	16						C/O	0.5
1876	Bos-N	9	40	5	6	0	0	0	2	0	1	.150	.150	.150	0	-4	-4	1				.600	-3	/OC	-0.7

■ FRANK McGINN
McGinn, Frank J. b: 1869, Cincinnati, Ohio d: 11/19/1897, Cincinnati, Ohio Deb: 6/09/1890

| 1890 | Pit-N | 1 | 4 | 0 | 0 | 0 | 0 | 0 | 0 | 0 | 2 | .000 | .000 | .000 | -99 | -1 | -1 | 0 | 0 | | | 1.000 | -0 | /O | -0.1 |

■ RUSS McGINNIS
McGinnis, Russell Brent b: 6/18/63, Coffeyville, Kan. BR/TR, 6'3", 225 lbs. Deb: 6/03/92

| 1992 | Tex-A | 14 | 33 | 2 | 8 | 4 | 0 | 0 | 4 | 3 | 7 | .242 | .306 | .364 | 90 | -1 | -0 | 4 | 0 | 0 | 0 | 1.000 | -3 | C/13 | -0.4 |

■ JOHN McGLONE
McGlone, John T. b: 1864, Brooklyn, N.Y. d: 11/24/27, Brooklyn, N.Y. Deb: 10/07/1886

1886	Was-N	4	15	2	1	0	0	0	1	0	3	.067	.067	.067	-63	-3	-3	0	0			.846	-1	/3	-0.4
1887	Cle-a	21	79	14	20	2	1	0		7		.253	.337	.304	84	-2	-1	13	15			.854	1	3	0.0
1888	Cle-a	55	203	22	37	1	3	1	22	16		.182	.249	.242	58	-9	-8	19	26			.787	-6	3/O	-1.3
Total	3	80	297	38	58	3	4	1	23	23	3	.195	.265	.242	60	-14	-12	32	41			.810	-7	/3O	-1.7

■ ART McGOVERN
McGovern, Arthur John b: 2/27/1882, St.John, N.B., Can. d: 11/14/15, Thornton, R.I. BR/TR, 5'10", 160 lbs. Deb: 4/21/05

| 1905 | Bos-A | 15 | 44 | 1 | 5 | 1 | 0 | 0 | 1 | 4 | | .114 | .204 | .136 | 9 | -4 | -4 | 1 | 0 | | | .951 | -4 | C | -0.8 |

■ BEAUTY McGOWAN
McGowan, Frank Bernard b: 11/8/01, Branford, Conn. d: 5/6/82, Hamden, Conn. BL/TR, 5'11", 190 lbs. Deb: 4/12/22

1922	Phi-A	99	300	36	69	10	5	1	20	40	46	.230	.323	.307	63	-15	-16	32	6	5	-1	.965	9	O	-1.4
1923	Phi-A	95	287	41	73	9	1	1	19	36	25	.254	.340	.303	69	-12	-12	32	4	3	-1	.971	-0	O	-1.7
1928	StL-A	47	168	35	61	13	4	2	18	16	15	.363	.425	.524	143	12	11	38	2	1	0	.962	-1	O	0.7
1929	StL-A	125	441	62	112	26	6	2	51	61	34	.254	.346	.354	78	-12	-14	58	5	2	0	.975	7	*O	-1.4
1937	Bos-N	9	12	0	1	0	0	0	0	1	2	.083	.154	.083	-37	-2	-2	0	0			1.000	-1	/O	-0.3
Total	5	375	1208	174	316	58	16	6	108	154	122	.262	.347	.351	80	-29	-34	160	17	11		.970	14	O	-4.1

■ JOHN McGRAW
McGraw, John Joseph "Mugsy" or "Little Napoleon"
b: 4/7/1873, Truxton, N.Y. d: 2/25/34, New Rochelle, N.Y. BL/TR, 5'7", 155 lbs. Deb: 8/26/1891 MH

1891	Bal-a	33	115	17	31	3	5	0	14	12	17	.270	.359	.383	114	2		18	4			.811	-15	S/O2	-1.0
1892	Bal-N	79	286	41	77	13	2	1	26	32	21	.269	.355	.339	109	5	4	41	15			.897	1	O2/S3	0.4
1893	Bal-N	127	480	123	154	9	10	5	64	101	11	.321	.454	.452	131	31	29	110	38			.894	-23	*SO	0.9
1894	*Bal-N	124	512	156	174	18	14	1	92	91	12	.340	.451	.436	112	20	15	141	78			.892	-3	*3/2	1.1
1895	*Bal-N	96	388	110	143	13	6	2	48	60	9	.369	.459	.448	133	26	23	111	61			.878	9	*3/2	2.7
1896	*Bal-N	23	77	20	25	2	2	0	14	11	4	.325	.422	.403	119	3	3	19	13			.833	-2	3/1	0.1
1897	*Bal-N	106	391	90	127	15	3	0	48	99		.325	.471		126	24	24	94	44			.886	-13	*3	1.2
1898	Bal-N	143	515	143	176	8	10	0	53	112		.342	.475	.396	148	45	44	121	43			.900	-12	*3/O	3.0
1899	Bal-N	117	399	140	156	13	3	1	33	124		.391	.547	.446	165	57	53	141	73			.945	2	*3M	5.0
1900	StL-N	99	334	84	115	10	4	2	33	85		.344	.503	.407	156	36	36	88	29			.909	-8	*3	2.6
1901	Bal-A	73	232	71	81	14	9	0	28	61		.349	.508	.487	169	31	29	72	24			.890	-18	3M	1.0
1902	Bal-A	20	63	14	18	3	2	1	3	17		.286	.458	.444	144	6	5	16	5			.864	-8	3M	-0.2
	NY-N	35	107	13	25	0	0	0	5	26		.234	.397	.234	96	2	2	13	7			.926	-2	SM	0.2
1903	NY-N	12	11	2	3	0	0	0	1	1		.273	.429	.273	98	0	0	2	1			.000	-2	/20S3M	-0.2
1904	NY-N	5	12	0	4	0	0	0	0	3		.333	.467	.333	143	1	1	0	0			.947	3	/2SM	0.4
1905	NY-N	3	0	0	0	0	0	0	0	0		—	—	—	—	0	0	0	1			.000	-0	/OM	0.0
1906	NY-N.	4	2	0	0	0	0	0	0	1		.000	.333	.000	5	-0	-0	0	0			.000	0	/3M	0.0
Total	16	1099	3924	1024	1309	121	70	13	462	836	74	.334	.465	.410	136	289	271	988	436			.900	-88	3S/O21	17.2

■ FRED McGRIFF
McGriff, Frederick Stanley b: 10/31/63, Tampa, Fla. BL/TL, 6'3", 215 lbs. Deb: 5/17/86

1986	Tor-A	3	5	1	1	0	0	0	0	0	0	.200	.200	.200	9	-1	-1	0	0	0	0	1.000	-0	/1D	-0.1
1987	Tor-A	107	295	58	73	16	0	20	43	60	104	.247	.376	.505	128	14	13	60	3	2	-0	.983	-1	D1	1.0
1988	Tor-A	154	536	100	151	35	4	34	82	79	149	.282	.378	.552	156	41	41	113	6	1	1	.997	-5	*1	2.4
1989	*Tor-A	161	551	98	148	27	3	36	92	119	132	.269	.402	.525	162	47	48	121	7	4	-0	.989	-1	*1/D	3.4
1990	Tor-A	153	557	91	167	21	1	35	88	94	108	.300	.403	.530	156	46	44	124	5	3	-0	.996	9	*1/D	4.2
1991	SD-N	153	528	84	147	19	1	31	106	105	135	.278	.400	.494	146	38	36	107	4	1	1	.990	-11	*1	1.7
1992	SD-N★	152	531	79	152	30	4	35	104	96	108	.286	.396	.556	161	48	46	116	8	6	-1	.991	-1	*1	3.5
Total	7	883	3003	511	839	148	13	191	515	553	738	.279	.394	.528	153	233	228	641	33	17	-0	.992	-11	1D	16.1

■ TERRY McGRIFF
McGriff, Terence Roy b: 9/23/63, Fort Pierce, Fla. BR/TR, 6'2", 190 lbs. Deb: 7/11/87

1987	Cin-N	34	89	6	20	3	0	2	11	8	17	.225	.289	.326	60	-5	-5	8	0	0	0	.983	4	C	0.0
1988	Cin-N	35	96	9	19	3	0	1	4	12	31	.198	.287	.260	56	-5	-5	7	1	0	0	.990	3	C	0.0
1989	Cin-N	6	11	1	3	0	0	0	2	2	3	.273	.385	.273	88	-0	-0	1	0	0	0	.929	1	/C	0.1
1990	Cin-N	2	4	0	0	0	0	0	0	0	1	.000	.000	.000	-96	-1	-1	0	0	0	0	1.000	0	/C	0.0
	Hou-N	4	5	0	0	0	0	0	0	0	0	.000	.000	.000	-99	-1	-1	0	0	0	0	.900	0	/C	-0.1
	Yr	6	9	0	0	0	0	0	0	0	1	.000	.000	.000	-99	-2	-2	0	0	0	0	.938	1	/C	-0.1
Total	4	81	205	16	42	6	0	3	17	22	52	.205	.282	.278	53	-12	-13	17	1	0	0	.981	8	/C	0.0

■ MARK McGRILLIS
McGrillis, Mark A. b: 10/22/1872, Philadelphia, Pa. d: 5/16/35, Philadelphia, Pa. Deb: 9/17/1892

| 1892 | StL-N | 1 | 3 | 0 | 0 | 0 | 0 | 0 | 0 | 0 | 1 | .000 | .000 | .000 | -99 | -1 | -1 | 0 | 0 | | | 1.000 | -0 | /3 | -0.1 |

■ JOE McGUCKIN
McGuckin, Joseph W. b: 3/13/1862, Paterson, N.J. d: 12/31/03, Yonkers, N.Y. Deb: 8/27/1890

| 1890 | Bal-a | 11 | 37 | 2 | 4 | 0 | 0 | 0 | | 6 | | .108 | .250 | .108 | 7 | -4 | -4 | 2 | 3 | | | .962 | 3 | O | -0.1 |

■ JOHN McGUINNESS
McGuinness, John James b: 1857, Ireland d: 12/19/16, Binghamton, N.Y. Deb: 5/06/1876

1876	NY-N	1	4	0	0	0	0	0	0	0		.000	.000	.000	-99	-1	-1	0				.500	-2	/2C	-0.2
1879	Syr-N	12	51	7	15	1	1	0	4	0	6	.294	.294	.353	126	1	1	5				.928	-1	1	0.0
1884	Phi-U	53	220	25	52	8	1	0		5		.236	.253	.282	87	-4	-2	16				.959	-0	1/2S	-0.7
Total	3	66	275	32	67	9	2	0	4	5	6	.244	.257	.291	91	-5	-1	22				.954	-2	/12SC	-0.9

■ JIM McGUIRE
McGuire, James A. b: 2/4/1875, Dunkirk, N.Y. d: 1/26/17, Buffalo, N.Y. TR, Deb: 9/10/01

| 1901 | Cle-A | 18 | 69 | 4 | 16 | 2 | 0 | 0 | 3 | 0 | | .232 | .232 | .261 | 38 | -6 | -6 | 4 | 0 | | | .913 | 1 | S | -0.3 |

■ DEACON McGUIRE
McGuire, James Thomas b: 11/18/1863, Youngstown, Ohio d: 10/31/36, Albion, Mich. BR/TR, 6'1", 185 lbs. Deb: 6/21/1884 MC

1884	Tol-a	45	151	12	28	7	0	1		5		.185	.217	.252	52	-7	-8	8				.906	-8	C/OS	-1.2
1885	Det-N	34	121	11	23	4	2	0	9	5	23	.190	.222	.256	54	-6	-6	7				.920	14	C/O	1.0
1886	Phi-N	50	167	25	33	7	1	2	18	19	25	.198	.280	.287	72	-5	-5	14	2			.899	-6	C/O	-0.5
1887	Phi-N	41	150	22	46	6	6	2	23	11	8	.307	.362	.467	123	6	5	27	3			.884	-1	C	0.6
1888	Phi-N	12	51	7	17	4	0	2	11	4	9	.333	.382	.490	170	4	4	10	0			.800	-5	C/3	-0.3
	Det-N	3	13	0	0	0	0	0	0	0	4	.000	.000	.000	-99	-3	-3	0	0			.810	-2	/C	-0.5
	Yr	15	64	7	17	4	0	2	11	4	13	.266	.309	.391	119	2	1	8	0			.802	-7	C/3	-0.5
	Cle-a	26	94	15	24	1	3	1	13	7		.255	.333	.362	130	3	3	12	2			.891	-1	C/1O	0.7
1890	Roc-a	87	331	46	99	16	4	4		21		.299	.356	.408	138	10	14	52	8			.938	8	C1/OP	2.4
1891	Was-a	114	413	55	125	22	10	3	66	43	34	.303	.382	.426	141	18	22	73	10			.911	-12	*CO/31	1.6
1892	Was-N	97	315	46	73	14	4	4	43	61	48	.232	.360	.340	117	8	9	42	7			.936	-1	C/1O	1.3

YEAR	TM/L	G	AB	R	H	2B	3B	HR	RBI	BB	SO	AVG	OBP	SLG	PRO+	BR	/A	RC	SB	CS	SBR	FA	FR	POS	TPR
1893	Was-N	63	237	29	62	14	3	1	26	26	12	.262	.342	.359	90	-4	-3	31	3			.889	-5	C1	-0.4
1894	Was-N	104	425	67	130	18	6	6	78	33	19	.306	.366	.419	93	-7	-4	71	11			.918	-1	*C	0.4
1895	Was-N	132	533	89	179	30	8	10	97	40	18	.336	.388	.478	126	18	20	108	16			.936	11	*C/S	3.5
1896	Was-N	108	389	60	125	25	3	2	70	30	14	.321	.379	.416	112	7	7	68	12			.936	-1	*C/1	1.4
1897	Was-N	93	327	51	112	17	7	4	53	21		.343	.386	.474	127	11	12	65	9			.947	7	C/1	2.3
1898	Was-N	131	489	59	131	18	3	1	57	24		.268	.310	.323	82	-12	-12	55	10			.967	4	C1M	0.1
1899	Was-N	59	199	25	54	3	1	1	12	16		.271	.335	.312	79	-6	-5	22	3			.973	-5	C/1	-0.5
	Bro-N	46	157	22	50	12	4	0	23	12		.318	.385	.446	125	6	5	29	4			.971	2	C	1.0
	Yr	105	356	47	104	15	5	1	35	28		.292	.357	.371	99	0	0	51	7			.972	-3	*C/1	0.5
1900	*Bro-N	71	241	20	69	15	2	0	34	19		.286	.348	.365	92	-1	-3	32	2			.952	-7	C	-0.3
1901	Bro-N	85	301	28	89	16	4	0	40	18		.296	.340	.375	105	3	2	41	4			.960	-5	C/1	0.5
1902	Det-A	73	229	27	52	14	1	2	23	24		.227	.300	.323	71	-8	-9	23	0			.952	-5	C	-0.6
1903	Det-A	72	248	15	62	12	1	0	21	19		.250	.306	.306	87	-4	-3	25	3			.960	-6	C/1	-0.2
1904	NY-A	101	322	17	67	12	2	0	20	27		.208	.276	.258	66	-11	-12	25	2			.970	13	C/1	1.3
1905	NY-A	72	228	9	50	7	2	0	33	18		.219	.288	.268	69	-6	-9	19	3			.975	-6	C	-0.8
1906	NY-A	51	144	11	43	5	0	0	14	12		.299	.361	.333	107	3	2	19	3			.962	-1	C/1	0.5
1907	NY-A	1	1	0	0	0	0	0	0	0		.000	.000	.000	-93	-0	-0	0	0			1.000	1	/C	0.0
	Bos-A	6	4	1	3	0	0	1	1	0		.750	.750	1.500	621	2	2	5	0			.000	0	HM	0.2
	Yr	7	5	1	3	0	0	1	1	0		.600	.600	1.200	470	2	2	4	0			1.000	1	/C	0.2
1908	Bos-A	1	1	0	0	0	0	0	0	0		.000	.000	.000	-97	-0	-0	0	0			.000	0	HM	0.0
	Cle-A	1	4	0	1	1	0	0	2	0		.250	.250	.500	142	0	0	0	0			1.000	-0	/1	0.0
	Yr	2	5	0	1	1	0	0	2	0		.200	.200	.400	93	-0	-0	0	0			1.000	-0	/1	0.0
1910	Cle-A	1	3	0	1	0	0	0	0	0		.333	.500	.333	159	0	0	0	0			1.000	-1	/CM	-0.1
1912	Det-A	1	2	1	1	0	0	0	0	0		.500	.500	.500	192	0	0	0	0			.714	0	/C	0.1
Total	26	1781	6290	770	1749	300	79	45	787	515	214	.278	.341	.372	102	21	24	887	117			.938	-19	*C/1O3SP	13.4

■ MICKEY McGUIRE McGuire, M C Adolphus b: 1/18/41, Dayton, Ohio BR/TR, 5'10", 170 lbs. Deb: 9/07/62

YEAR	TM/L	G	AB	R	H	2B	3B	HR	RBI	BB	SO	AVG	OBP	SLG	PRO+	BR	/A	RC	SB	CS	SBR	FA	FR	POS	TPR
1962	Bal-A	6	4	0	0	0	0	0	0	0	0	.000	.000	.000	-99	-1	-1	0	0	0	0	1.000	-0	/S	-0.1
1967	Bal-A	10	17	2	4	0	0	0	2	0	2	.235	.235	.235	40	-1	-1	1	0	0	0	1.000	-2	/2	-0.4
Total	2	16	21	2	4	0	0	0	2	0	2	.190	.190	.190	11	-2	-2	1	0	0	0	.956	-3	/S2	-0.5

■ BILL McGUIRE McGuire, William Patrick b: 2/14/64, Omaha, Neb. BR/TR, 6'3", 205 lbs. Deb: 8/02/88

YEAR	TM/L	G	AB	R	H	2B	3B	HR	RBI	BB	SO	AVG	OBP	SLG	PRO+	BR	/A	RC	SB	CS	SBR	FA	FR	POS	TPR
1988	Sea-A	9	16	1	3	0	0	0	2	3	2	.188	.316	.188	43	-1	-1	1	0	0	0	1.000	-0	/C	-0.1
1989	Sea-A	14	28	2	5	0	0	1	4	2	6	.179	.233	.286	44	-2	-2	1	0	0	0	1.000	4	C	0.3
Total	2	23	44	3	8	0	0	1	6	5	8	.182	.265	.250	44	-3	-3	3	0	0	0	1.000	4	/C	0.2

■ BILL McGUNNIGLE McGunnigle, William Henry "Gunner" b: 1/1/1855, Boston, Mass. d: 3/9/1899, Brockton, Mass. BR/TR, 5'9", 155 lbs. Deb: 5/02/1879 M

YEAR	TM/L	G	AB	R	H	2B	3B	HR	RBI	BB	SO	AVG	OBP	SLG	PRO+	BR	/A	RC	SB	CS	SBR	FA	FR	POS	TPR
1879	Buf-N	47	171	22	30	0	1	0	5	5	24	.175	.199	.187	27	-13	-13	7				.918	1	OP	-1.0
1880	Buf-N	7	22	0	4	0	0	0	1	0	4	.182	.182	.182	23	-2	-2	1				1.000	-2	/PO	-0.2
	Wor-N	1	4	0	0	0	0	0	0	0	2	.000	.000	.000	-92	-1	-1	0				1.000	-1	/O	-0.2
	Yr	8	26	0	4	0	0	0	1	0	6	.154	.154	.154	5	-2	-3	1				1.000	-2	/PO	-0.4
1882	Cle-N	1	5	2	1	0	0	0	0	0	1	.200	.200	.200	30	-0	-0	0				.000	-1	/O	-0.1
Total	3	56	202	24	35	0	1	0	6	5	31	.173	.193	.183	25	-16	-16	7				.900	-1	/OP	-1.5

■ MARK McGWIRE McGwire, Mark David b: 10/1/63, Pomona, Cal. BR/TR, 6'5", 225 lbs. Deb: 8/22/86

YEAR	TM/L	G	AB	R	H	2B	3B	HR	RBI	BB	SO	AVG	OBP	SLG	PRO+	BR	/A	RC	SB	CS	SBR	FA	FR	POS	TPR
1986	Oak-A	18	53	10	10	1	0	3	9	4	18	.189	.259	.377	76	-2	-2	5	0	1	-1	.833	-3	3	-0.5
1987	Oak-A★	151	557	97	161	28	4	**49**	118	71	131	.289	.374	**.618**	168	44	50	131	1	1	-0	.992	-7	*1/3O	3.0
1988	*Oak-A★	155	550	87	143	22	1	32	99	76	117	.260	.354	.478	135	23	25	93	0	0	0	.993	-8	*1/O	0.5
1989	*Oak-A★	143	490	74	113	17	0	33	95	83	94	.231	.345	.467	132	18	20	76	1	1	-0	.995	7	*1/D	1.6
1990	*Oak-A★	156	523	87	123	16	0	39	108	**110**	116	.235	.375	.489	146	30	33	101	2	1	0	.997	-5	*1/D	1.7
1991	Oak-A†	154	483	62	97	22	0	22	75	93	116	.201	.333	.383	103	-0	4	65	2	1	0	.997	2	*1	-0.4
1992	*Oak-A★	139	467	87	125	22	0	42	104	90	105	.268	.391	**.585**	177	44	47	110	0	1	-1	.995	-10	*1	2.8
Total	7	916	3123	504	772	128	5	220	608	527	697	.247	.361	.503	143	157	177	582	6	6	-2	.995	-23	1/3DO	8.7

■ JIM McHALE McHale, James Bernard "J.B." b: 12/17/1875, Miners Mills, Pa. d: 6/17/59, Los Angeles, Cal. BR/TR, 5'11", 165 lbs. Deb: 4/14/08

YEAR	TM/L	G	AB	R	H	2B	3B	HR	RBI	BB	SO	AVG	OBP	SLG	PRO+	BR	/A	RC	SB	CS	SBR	FA	FR	POS	TPR
1908	Bos-A	21	67	9	15	2	2	0	7	4		.224	.278	.313	90	-1	-1	7	4			.970	-2	O	-0.4

■ JOHN McHALE McHale, John Joseph b: 9/21/21, Detroit, Mich. BL/TR, 6', 200 lbs. Deb: 5/28/43

YEAR	TM/L	G	AB	R	H	2B	3B	HR	RBI	BB	SO	AVG	OBP	SLG	PRO+	BR	/A	RC	SB	CS	SBR	FA	FR	POS	TPR
1943	Det-A	4	3	0	0	0	0	0	0	1	1	.000	.250	.000	-23	-0	-0	0	0	0	0	.000	0	H	-0.1
1944	Det-A	1	1	0	0	0	0	0	0	0	0	.000	.000	.000	-95	-0	-0	0	0	0	0	.000	0	H	0.0
1945	*Det-A	19	14	0	2	0	0	0	1	1	4	.143	.250	.143	14	-1	-2	1	0	0	0	1.000	0	/1	-0.1
1947	Det-A	39	95	10	20	1	0	3	11	7	24	.211	.265	.316	59	-5	-6	8	1	1	-0	.995	-1	1	-0.8
1948	Det-A	1	1	0	0	0	0	0	0	0	0	.000	.000	.000	-97	-0	-0	0	0	0	0	.000	0	H	0.0
Total	5	64	114	10	22	1	0	3	12	9	29	.193	.258	.281	49	-8	-8	9	1	1	-0	.995	-1	/1	-1.0

■ BOB McHALE McHale, Robert Emmet "Rabbit" b: 2/25/1872, Michigan Bluff, Cal. d: 6/9/52, Sacramento, Cal. Deb: 5/09/1898

YEAR	TM/L	G	AB	R	H	2B	3B	HR	RBI	BB	SO	AVG	OBP	SLG	PRO+	BR	/A	RC	SB	CS	SBR	FA	FR	POS	TPR
1898	Was-N	11	33	5	6	2	0	0	7	1		.182	.270	.242	47	-2	-2	3	1			.900	-1	/OS1	-0.4

■ AUSTIN McHENRY McHenry, Austin Bush "Mac" b: 9/22/1895, Wrightsville, O. d: 11/27/22, Jefferson, Ohio BR/TR, 5'11", 152 lbs. Deb: 6/22/18

YEAR	TM/L	G	AB	R	H	2B	3B	HR	RBI	BB	SO	AVG	OBP	SLG	PRO+	BR	/A	RC	SB	CS	SBR	FA	FR	POS	TPR
1918	StL-N	80	272	32	71	12	6	1	29	21	24	.261	.319	.360	111	2	3	33	8			.952	2	O	0.0
1919	StL-N	110	371	41	106	19	11	1	47	19	57	.286	.322	.404	125	7	9	49	7			.985	1	*O	0.4
1920	StL-N	137	504	66	142	19	11	10	65	25	73	.282	.316	.423	115	5	7	64	8	11	-4	.952	2	*O	-0.4
1921	StL-N	152	574	92	201	37	8	17	102	38	48	.350	.393	.531	145	33	35	111	10	20	-9	.965	7	*O	2.2
1922	StL-N	64	238	31	72	18	3	5	43	14	27	.303	.344	.466	112	2	3	37	2	2	-1	.935	7	O	0.5
Total	5	543	1959	262	592	105	39	34	286	117	229	.302	.343	.448	126	49	58	294	35	33		.960	18	O	2.7

■ VANCE McHENRY McHenry, Vance Loren b: 7/10/56, Chico, Cal. BR/TR, 5'9", 165 lbs. Deb: 8/13/81

YEAR	TM/L	G	AB	R	H	2B	3B	HR	RBI	BB	SO	AVG	OBP	SLG	PRO+	BR	/A	RC	SB	CS	SBR	FA	FR	POS	TPR
1981	Sea-A	15	18	3	4	0	0	0	2	1	1	.222	.263	.222	39	-1	-1	1	0	0	0	.893	0	S/D	-0.1
1982	Sea-A	3	1	0	0	0	0	0	0	0	0	.000	.000	.000	-97	-0	-0	0	0	0	0	.500	-0	/SD	-0.1
Total	2	18	19	3	4	0	0	0	2	1	1	.211	.250	.211	32	-2	-2	1	0	0	0	.867	-0	/SD	-0.2

■ IRISH McILVEEN McIlveen, Henry Cooke b: 7/27/1880, Belfast, Ireland d: 10/18/60, Lorain, Ohio BL/TL, 5'11.5", 180 lbs. Deb: 7/10/06

YEAR	TM/L	G	AB	R	H	2B	3B	HR	RBI	BB	SO	AVG	OBP	SLG	PRO+	BR	/A	RC	SB	CS	SBR	FA	FR	POS	TPR
1906	Pit-N	5	5	1	2	0	0	0	0	0		.400	.400	.400	144	0	0	1	0			1.000	0	/P	0.0
1908	NY-A	44	169	17	36	3	3	0	8	14		.213	.277	.266	76	-4	-4	14	6			.949	0	O	-0.7
1909	NY-A	4	3	0	0	0	0	0	0	1		.000	.250	.000	-20	-0	-0	0	0			.000	0	H	0.0
Total	3	53	177	18	38	3	3	0	8	15		.215	.280	.266	76	-4	-4	15	6				0	/OP	-0.7

■ STUFFY McINNIS McInnis, John Phalen "Jack" b: 9/19/1890, Gloucester, Mass. d: 2/16/60, Ipswich, Mass. BR/TR, 5'9.5", 162 lbs. Deb: 4/12/09 M

YEAR	TM/L	G	AB	R	H	2B	3B	HR	RBI	BB	SO	AVG	OBP	SLG	PRO+	BR	/A	RC	SB	CS	SBR	FA	FR	POS	TPR
1909	Phi-A	19	46	4	11	0	0	1	4	2		.239	.286	.304	85	-1	-1	4	0			.886	4	S	0.4
1910	Phi-A	38	73	10	22	2	4	0	12	7		.301	.363	.438	152	4	4	12	3			.927	-5	S/23O	0.0
1911	*Phi-A	126	468	76	150	20	10	3	77	25		.321	.361	.425	121	10	12	80	23			.982	-15	1S	-0.1
1912	Phi-A	153	568	83	186	25	13	3	101	49		.327	.384	.433	139	24	27	105	27			.984	3	*1	2.7
1913	*Phi-A	148	543	79	176	30	4	4	90	45	31	.324	.382	.416	137	23	24	91	16			**.992**	-2	*1	2.2
1914	*Phi-A	149	576	74	181	12	8	1	95	19	27	.314	.341	.368	118	7	9	76	25	19	-4	**.995**	0	*1	0.2
1915	Phi-A	119	456	44	143	14	4	0	49	14	17	.314	.337	.362	113	3	5	57	8	8	-2	.989	5	*1	0.5

YEAR	TM/L	G	AB	R	H	2B	3B	HR	RBI	BB	SO	AVG	OBP	SLG	PRO+	BR	/A	RC	SB	CS	SBR	FA	FR	POS	TPR
1916	Phi-A	140	512	42	151	25	3	1	60	25	19	.295	.331	.361	114	3	6	67	7			.992	7	*1	0.8
1917	Phi-A	150	567	50	172	19	4	0	44	33	19	.303	.342	.351	113	6	7	72	18			.993	2	*1	0.3
1918	*Bos-A	117	423	40	115	11	5	0	56	19	10	.272	.306	.322	91	-7	-6	46	10			**.992**	4	13	-0.6
1919	Bos-A	120	440	32	134	12	5	1	58	23	11	.305	.341	.361	103	-2	1	57	8			.995	3	*1	-0.1
1920	Bos-A	148	559	50	166	21	3	2	71	18	19	.297	.321	.356	83	-17	-14	62	6	11	-5	**.996**	-1	*1	-2.3
1921	Bos-A	152	584	72	179	31	10	0	76	21	9	.307	.335	.394	88	-14	-12	76	2	4	-2	**.999**	4	*1	-1.2
1922	Cle-A	142	537	58	164	28	7	1	78	15	5	.305	.325	.389	85	-13	-13	66	1	5	-3	**.997**	-5	*1	-2.6
1923	Bos-N	154	607	70	191	23	9	2	95	26	12	.315	.343	.392	97	-6	-3	80	7	8	-3	.991	4	*1	-1.0
1924	Bos-N	146	581	57	169	23	7	1	59	15	6	.291	.311	.360	83	-18	-15	65	9	3	1	.994	7	*1	-1.6
1925	*Pit-N	59	155	19	57	10	4	0	24	17	1	.368	.437	.484	126	9	7	33	1	1	-0	.993	1	1	0.6
1926	Pit-N	47	127	12	38	6	1	0	13	7	3	.299	.336	.362	83	-2	-3	15	1			.988	-1	1	-0.6
1927	Phi-N	1	0	0	0	0	0	0	0	0	0	—	—	—	—	0	0	0	0			1.000	-0	/1M	0.0
Total	19	2128	7822	872	2405	312	101	20	1062	380	189	.307	.343	.381	106	9	36	1065	172	59		.993	17	*1/S320	-2.4

■ TIM McINTOSH McIntosh, Timothy Allen b: 3/21/65, Minneapolis, Minn. BR/TR, 5'11", 195 lbs. Deb: 9/03/90

YEAR	TM/L	G	AB	R	H	2B	3B	HR	RBI	BB	SO	AVG	OBP	SLG	PRO+	BR	/A	RC	SB	CS	SBR	FA	FR	POS	TPR
1990	Mil-A	5	5	1	1	0	0	1	1	0	2	.200	.200	.800	168	0	0	1	0	0	0	.875	-0	/C	0.0
1991	Mil-A	7	11	2	4	1	0	1	1	0	4	.364	.364	.727	199	1	1	3	0	0	0	.000	-2	/O1D	0.0
1992	Mil-A	35	77	7	14	3	0	0	6	3	9	.182	.232	.221	28	-7	-7	4	1	3	-2	.983	1	CO/1D	-0.8
Total	3	47	93	10	19	4	0	2	8	3	15	.204	.245	.312	56	-6	-6	7	1	3	-2	.970	-1	/CO1D	-0.8

■ MATTY McINTYRE McIntyre, Matthew W. b: 6/12/1880, Stonington, Conn. d: 4/2/20, Detroit, Mich. BL/TL, 5'11", 175 lbs. Deb: 7/03/01

YEAR	TM/L	G	AB	R	H	2B	3B	HR	RBI	BB	SO	AVG	OBP	SLG	PRO+	BR	/A	RC	SB	CS	SBR	FA	FR	POS	TPR
1901	Phi-A	82	308	38	85	12	4	0	46	30		.276	.344	.341	87	-3	-5	42	11			.921	-3	O	-1.3
1904	Det-A	152	578	74	146	11	10	2	46	44		.253	.310	.317	102	-0	2	65	11			.959	12	*O	0.5
1905	Det-A	131	495	59	130	21	5	0	30	48		.263	.330	.325	108	6	5	58	9			.968	16	*O	1.7
1906	Det-A	133	493	63	128	19	11	0	39	56		.260	.336	.343	110	9	7	69	29			.982	12	*O	1.4
1907	Det-A	20	81	6	23	1	1	0	9	7		.284	.341	.321	108	1	1	10	3			1.000	3	O	0.3
1908	*Det-A	151	569	**105**	168	24	13	0	28	83		.295	.392	.383	146	37	34	93	20			**.977**	15	*O	4.8
1909	*Det-A	125	476	65	116	18	9	1	34	54		.244	.325	.326	101	4	2	54	13			.975	-0	*O	-0.4
1910	Det-A	83	305	40	72	15	5	0	25	39		.236	.323	.318	94	1	-1	32	4			.946	4	O	-0.2
1911	Chi-A	146	569	102	184	19	11	1	52	64		.323	.397	.401	127	19	22	96	17			.948	-2	*O	1.2
1912	Chi-A	49	84	10	14	0	0	0	10	14		.167	.300	.167	36	-6	-6	5	3			1.000	-1	O	-0.8
Total	10	1072	3958	562	1066	140	69	4	319	439		.269	.346	.343	110	66	59	526	120			.964	56	*O	7.2

■ OTTO McIVOR McIvor, Edward Otto b: 7/26/1884, Greenville, Tex. d: 5/4/54, Dallas, Tex. BB/TL, 5'11.5", 175 lbs. Deb: 4/18/11

YEAR	TM/L	G	AB	R	H	2B	3B	HR	RBI	BB	SO	AVG	OBP	SLG	PRO+	BR	/A	RC	SB	CS	SBR	FA	FR	POS	TPR
1911	StL-N	30	62	11	14	2	1	1	9	9	14	.226	.333	.339	91	-1	-1	7	0			.926	-3	O	-0.4

■ DAVE McKAY McKay, David Lawrence b: 3/14/50, Vancouver, B.C., Can BB/TR, 6'1", 195 lbs. Deb: 8/22/75 C

YEAR	TM/L	G	AB	R	H	2B	3B	HR	RBI	BB	SO	AVG	OBP	SLG	PRO+	BR	/A	RC	SB	CS	SBR	FA	FR	POS	TPR
1975	Min-A	33	125	8	32	4	1	2	16	6	14	.256	.295	.352	81	-3	-3	12	1	1	-0	.923	2	3	-0.2
1976	Min-A	45	138	8	28	2	0	0	8	9	27	.203	.272	.217	43	-9	-10	8	1	2	-1	.911	-1	3/SD	-1.3
1977	Tor-A	95	274	18	54	4	3	3	22	7	51	.197	.223	.266	32	-26	-26	15	2	1	0	.968	7	23S/D	-1.6
1978	Tor-A	145	504	59	120	20	8	7	45	20	91	.238	.269	.351	71	-19	-21	43	4	4	-1	.984	-7	*2/S3D	-1.9
1979	Tor-A	47	156	19	34	9	0	0	12	7	19	.218	.256	.276	43	-12	-13	10	1	1	-0	.974	6	2/3	-0.4
1980	Oak-A	123	295	29	72	16	1	1	29	10	57	.244	.283	.315	68	-15	-12	27	1	1	-0	.977	-6	23S	-1.5
1981	*Oak-A	79	224	25	59	11	1	4	21	16	43	.263	.318	.375	104	-0	1	27	4	1	1	.926	-4	32/S	-0.1
1982	Oak-A	78	212	25	42	4	1	4	17	11	35	.198	.238	.283	44	-17	-16	16	6	1	1	.968	-3	23/S	-1.6
Total	8	645	1928	191	441	70	15	21	170	86	337	.229	.268	.313	62	-102	-100	157	20	12	-1	.976	-6	23/SD	-8.6

■ ED McKEAN McKean, Edwin John "Mack" b: 6/6/1864, Grafton, Ohio d: 8/16/19, Cleveland, Ohio BR/TR, 5'9", 160 lbs. Deb: 4/16/1887

YEAR	TM/L	G	AB	R	H	2B	3B	HR	RBI	BB	SO	AVG	OBP	SLG	PRO+	BR	/A	RC	SB	CS	SBR	FA	FR	POS	TPR
1887	Cle-a	132	539	97	154	16	13	2		60		.286	.358	.375	110	6	9	102	76			.847	-8	*S/2O	0.2
1888	Cle-a	131	548	94	164	21	15	6	68	28		.299	.340	.425	152	28	30	99	52			.909	3	SO/23	3.1
1889	Cle-N	123	500	88	159	22	8	4	75	42	25	.318	.375	.418	126	15	17	94	35			.907	6	*S/2	2.6
1890	Cle-N	136	530	95	157	15	14	7	61	87	25	.296	.401	.417	144	31	32	100	23			.903	-18	*S/2	2.0
1891	Cle-N	141	603	115	170	13	12	6	69	64	19	.282	.352	.373	109	11	7	86	14			.887	-12	*S	0.2
1892	*Cle-N	129	531	76	139	14	10	0	93	49	28	.262	.325	.326	95	-0	-3	64	19			.862	-45	*S	-4.0
1893	Cle-N	125	545	103	169	29	24	4	133	50	14	.310	.372	.473	119	18	12	105	16			.902	-4	*S	1.2
1894	Cle-N	130	554	116	198	30	15	8	128	49	12	.357	.412	.509	118	20	16	134	33			.905	-21	*S	0.2
1895	*Cle-N	131	565	131	193	32	17	8	119	45	25	.342	.397	.501	125	26	20	121	12			.909	-19	*S	0.6
1896	*Cle-N	133	571	100	193	29	12	7	112	45	9	.338	.388	.468	120	21	16	113	13			.915	-33	*S	-1.1
1897	Cle-N	125	523	83	143	21	14	2	78	40		.273	.330	.379	82	-11	-16	73	15			.920	-30	*S	-3.7
1898	Cle-N	151	604	89	172	23	1	9	94	56		.285	.346	.371	107	4	5	85	11			.932	-36	*S	-2.2
1899	StL-N	67	277	40	72	7	3	3	40	20		.260	.310	.339	76	-9	-10	32	4			.886	-17	S12	-2.1
Total	13	1654	6890	1227	2083	272	158	66	1070	635	157	.302	.364	.416	115	160	135	1208	323			.900	-232	*S/O213	-3.0

■ BILL McKECHNIE McKechnie, William Boyd "Deacon" b: 8/7/1886, Wilkinsburg, Pa. d: 10/29/65, Bradenton, Fla. BB/TR, 5'10", 160 lbs. Deb: 9/08/07 MCH

YEAR	TM/L	G	AB	R	H	2B	3B	HR	RBI	BB	SO	AVG	OBP	SLG	PRO+	BR	/A	RC	SB	CS	SBR	FA	FR	POS	TPR
1907	Pit-N	3	8	0	1	0	0	0	0	0		.125	.125	.125	-21	-1	-1	0	0			1.000	-1	/32	-0.2
1910	Pit-N	71	212	23	46	1	2	0	12	11	23	.217	.256	.241	42	-15	-17	14	4			.971	8	2S/31	-0.9
1911	Pit-N	104	321	40	73	8	7	2	37	28	18	.227	.293	.315	68	-13	-15	34	9			.975	-0	12S/3	-1.5
1912	Pit-N	24	73	8	18	0	1	0	4	4	5	.247	.286	.274	54	-5	-5	6	2			.978	2	3/S21	-0.3
1913	Bos-N	1	4	1	0	0	0	0	0	0	1	.000	.200	.000	-39	-1	-1	0	0			1.000	0	/O	-0.1
	NY-A	45	112	7	15	0	0	0	8	8	17	.134	.198	.134	-2	-14	-14	3	2			.950	5	2/S3	-1.0
1914	Ind-F	149	570	107	173	24	6	2	38	53	36	.304	.368	.377	101	10	2	103	47			.939	23	*3	3.1
1915	New-F	127	451	49	113	22	5	1	43	41	31	.251	.316	.328	95	-6	-3	59	28			.956	2	*3/OM	0.4
1916	NY-N	71	260	22	64	9	1	0	17	7	20	.246	.269	.288	75	-9	-8	22	7			.940	-3	3	-1.0
	Cin-N	37	130	4	36	3	0	0	10	3	12	.277	.293	.300	84	-3	-3	13	4			.960	-4	3	-0.6
	Yr	108	390	26	100	12	1	0	27	10	32	.256	.277	.292	78	-12	-11	36	11			.947	-8	*3	-1.6
1917	Cin-N	48	134	11	34	3	1	0	15	7	7	.254	.296	.291	84	-3	-3	12	5			.943	-7	2S/3	-0.9
1918	Pit-N	126	435	34	111	13	9	2	43	24	22	.255	.297	.340	91	-4	-6	47	12			.966	-1	*3	-0.4
1920	Pit-N	40	133	13	29	3	1	1	13	4	7	.218	.241	.278	47	-9	-9	9	7	4	-0	.943	-1	3S/21	-1.0
Total	11	846	2843	319	713	86	33	8	240	190	199	.251	.301	.313	78	-73	-81	324	127	4		.952	22	32/1SO	-4.4

■ FRANK McKEE McKee, Frank b: Philadelphia, Pa. Deb: 6/11/1884

YEAR	TM/L	G	AB	R	H	2B	3B	HR	RBI	BB	SO	AVG	OBP	SLG	PRO+	BR	/A	RC	SB	CS	SBR	FA	FR	POS	TPR
1884	Was-U	4	17	2	3	0	0	0		1		.176	.222	.176	38	-1	-1	1				.200	-2	/O3C	-0.2

■ RED McKEE McKee, Raymond Ellis b: 7/20/1890, Shawnee, Ohio d: 8/5/72, Saginaw, Mich. BL/TR, 5'11", 180 lbs. Deb: 4/19/13

YEAR	TM/L	G	AB	R	H	2B	3B	HR	RBI	BB	SO	AVG	OBP	SLG	PRO+	BR	/A	RC	SB	CS	SBR	FA	FR	POS	TPR
1913	Det-A	68	187	18	53	3	4	1	20	21	21	.283	.359	.358	112	3	3	27	7			.950	-5	C	0.4
1914	Det-A	34	64	7	12	1	1	0	8	14	16	.188	.342	.234	71	-1	-2	5	1	2	-1	.964	-6	C	-0.7
1915	Det-A	55	106	10	29	5	0	1	17	13	16	.274	.353	.349	105	1	1	14	1			.954	-6	C	-0.3
1916	Det-A	32	76	3	16	1	2	0	4	6	11	.211	.268	.276	61	-4	-4	6	0			.955	-5	C	-0.8
Total	4	189	433	38	110	10	7	2	49	54	64	.254	.339	.323	95	-1	-2	52	9	2		.954	-22	C	-1.4

■ JIM McKEEVER McKeever, James b: 4/19/1861, St.John's, Newfoundland, Can. d: 8/19/1897, Boston, Mass. Deb: 4/17/1884

YEAR	TM/L	G	AB	R	H	2B	3B	HR	RBI	BB	SO	AVG	OBP	SLG	PRO+	BR	/A	RC	SB	CS	SBR	FA	FR	POS	TPR
1884	Bos-U	16	66	13	9	0	0	0		0		.136	.136	.136	-8	-7	-7	1				.869	-6	C/O	-1.0

■ JOHN McKELVEY McKelvey, John Wellington b: 8/27/1847, Rochester, N.Y. d: 5/31/44, Rochester, N.Y. BR/TR, 5'7.5", 175 lbs. Deb: 4/21/1875

YEAR	TM/L	G	AB	R	H	2B	3B	HR	RBI	BB	SO	AVG	OBP	SLG	PRO+	BR	/A	RC	SB	CS	SBR	FA	FR	POS	TPR
1875	NH-n	43	187	26	43	4	1	0		4		.230	.246	.262	87	-4	-0	12						O/3	0.0

YEAR	TM/L	G	AB	R	H	2B	3B	HR	RBI	BB	SO	AVG	OBP	SLG	PRO+	BR	/A	RC	SB	CS	SBR	FA	FR	POS	TPR

■ RUSS McKELVY   McKelvy, Russell Errett   b: 9/8/1856, Meadville, Pa.   d: 10/19/15, Omaha, Neb.   BR/TR,   Deb: 5/01/1878

1878	Ind-N	63	253	33	57	4	3	2	36	5	38	.225	.240	.289	84	-7	-2	18				.846	6	*O/P	0.0
1882	Pit-a	1	4	0	0	0	0	0		0		.000	.000	.000	-99	-1	-1	0				.000	-0	/O	-0.1
Total	2	64	257	33	57	4	3	2	36	5	38	.222	.237	.284	81	-8	-3	18				.846	5	/OP	-0.1

■ ED McKENNA   McKenna, Edward J.   b: St.Louis, Mo.   Deb: 7/29/1874

1874	Phi-n	1	4	0	0	0	0	0			0	.000	.000	.000	-97	-1	-1	0						/1	-0.1
1877	StL-N	1	5	0	1	0	0	0	0	0	1	.200	.200	.200	28	-0	-0	0				1.000	-0	/O	-0.1
1884	Was-U	32	117	19	22	1	0	0			4	.188	.215	.197	41	-7	-6	5				.876	-14	CO/3	-1.7
Total	2	33	122	19	23	1	0	0	0	4	1	.189	.214	.197	41	-7	-7	5				.556	-14	/CO3	-1.8

■ DAVE McKEOUGH   McKeough, David J.   b: 12/1/1863, Utica, N.Y.   d: 7/11/01, Utica, N.Y.   5'7", 158 lbs.   Deb: 4/22/1890

1890	Roc-a	62	218	38	49	5	0	0			29	.225	.316	.248	74	-7	-5	22	14			.929	-4	CS/23	-0.4
1891	Phi-a	15	54	4	14	1	1	0	3	8	6	.259	.355	.315	92	-0	-0	6	0			.854	-4	C/S	-0.3
Total	2	77	272	42	63	6	1	0	3	37	6	.232	.324	.261	78	-8	-5	28	14			.912	-9	/CS23	-0.7

■ RICH McKINNEY   McKinney, Charles Richard   b: 11/22/46, Piqua, Ohio   BR/TR, 5'11", 185 lbs.   Deb: 6/26/70

1970	Chi-A	43	119	12	20	5	0	4	17	11	25	.168	.244	.311	50	-8	-9	8	3	2	-0	.931	2	3S	-0.6
1971	Chi-A	114	369	35	100	11	2	8	46	35	37	.271	.337	.377	99	1	-0	46	0	0	0	.968	-9	2O/3	-0.6
1972	NY-A	37	121	10	26	2	0	1	7	7	13	.215	.258	.256	55	-7	-7	7	1	0	0	.917	-3	3	-1.0
1973	Oak-A	48	65	9	16	3	0	1	7	7	4	.246	.319	.338	90	-1	-1	6	0	0	0	.900	-1	3/2OD	-0.1
1974	Oak-A	5	7	0	1	0	0	0	0	0	0	.143	.143	.143	-19	-1	-1	0	0	0	0	1.000	-2	/2	-0.4
1975	Oak-A	8	7	0	1	0	0	0	2	1	2	.143	.250	.143	14	-1	-1	0	0	0	0	1.000	-0	/1D	-0.1
1977	Oak-A	86	198	13	35	7	0	6	21	16	43	.177	.238	.303	47	-15	-15	12	0	1	-1	.978	-4	1D/3O2	-2.1
Total	7	341	886	79	199	28	2	20	100	77	124	.225	.289	.328	73	-32	-33	80	4	3	-1	.911	-17	/3210DS	-4.9

■ BOB McKINNEY   McKinney, Robert Francis   b: 10/4/1875, McSherrystown, Pa.   d: 8/19/46, Hanover, Pa.   BR/TR, 5'7", 165 lbs.   Deb: 7/23/01

| 1901 | Phi-A | 2 | 2 | 0 | 0 | 0 | 0 | 0 | | | 0 | .000 | .000 | .000 | -96 | -1 | -1 | 0 | 0 | | | .000 | -1 | /23 | -0.2 |

■ ALEX McKINNON   McKinnon, Alexander J.   b: 8/14/1856, Boston, Mass.   d: 7/24/1887, Charlestown, Mass   BR , 5'11.5",   Deb: 5/01/1884   M

1884	NY-N	116	470	66	128	21	12	4	73	8	62	.272	.285	.394	108	5	3	54				.955	-2	*1	-1.1
1885	StL-N	100	411	42	121	21	6	1	44	8	31	.294	.308	.382	130	9	12	50				.978	-2	*1M	-0.1
1886	StL-N	122	491	75	148	24	7	8	72	21	23	.301	.330	.428	138	16	20	74	10			.963	-6	*1/O	0.1
1887	Pit-N	48	200	26	68	16	4	1	30	8	9	.340	.365	.475	142	8	10	38	6			.977	3	1	0.7
Total	4	386	1572	209	465	82	29	14	219	45	125	.296	.315	.412	127	37	46	216	16			.967	-7	1/O	-0.4

■ JIM McKNIGHT   McKnight, James Arthur   b: 6/1/36, Bee Branch, Ark.   BR/TR, 6'1", 185 lbs.   Deb: 9/22/60   F

1960	Chi-N	3	6	0	2	0	0	0	1	0	1	.333	.333	.333	84	-0	-0	1	0	0	0	.667	-2	/2O	-0.2
1962	Chi-N	60	85	6	19	0	1	0	5	2	13	.224	.241	.247	30	-8	-9	4	0	0	0	.955	3	/3O2	-0.5
Total	2	63	91	6	21	0	1	0	6	2	14	.231	.247	.253	34	-8	-9	5	0	0	0	.875	1	/3O2	-0.7

■ JEFF McKNIGHT   McKnight, Jefferson Alan   b: 2/18/63, Conway, Ark.   BB/TR, 6', 170 lbs.   Deb: 6/06/89   F

1989	NY-N	6	12	2	3	0	0	0	2	1	2	.250	.357	.250	80	-0	-0	1	0	0	0	1.000	-3	/213S	-0.3
1990	Bal-A	29	75	11	15	2	0	1	4	5	17	.200	.259	.267	49	-5	-5	6	0	0	0	1.000	-3	1/O2SD	-0.9
1991	Bal-A	16	41	2	7	1	0	0	2	2	7	.171	.209	.195	13	-5	-5	1	1	0	0	1.000	-0	/O1D	-0.5
1992	NY-N	31	85	10	23	3	1	2	13	2	8	.271	.287	.400	93	-1	-1	9	0	1	-1	.980	-5	2/13SO	-0.5
Total	4	82	213	25	48	6	1	3	19	11	33	.225	.267	.305	62	-12	-11	17	1	1	-0	.995	-8	/120DS3	-2.2

■ ED McLANE   McLane, Edward Cameron   b: 8/20/1881, Weston, Mass.   d: 8/21/21, Baltimore, Md.   5'10", 179 lbs.   Deb: 10/06/07

| 1907 | Bro-N | 1 | 2 | 0 | 0 | 0 | 0 | 0 | 0 | | 0 | .000 | .333 | .000 | 6 | -0 | -0 | 0 | | | | .333 | -1 | /O | -0.1 |

■ ART McLARNEY   McLarney, Arthur James   b: 12/20/08, Ft.Worden, Wash.   d: 12/20/84, Seattle, Wash.   BB/TR, 6', 168 lbs.   Deb: 8/23/32

| 1932 | NY-N | 9 | 23 | 2 | 3 | 1 | 0 | 0 | 3 | 1 | 3 | .130 | .167 | .174 | -8 | -3 | -3 | 1 | 0 | | | 1.000 | -1 | /S | -0.4 |

■ POLLY McLARRY   McLarry, Howard Zell   b: 3/25/1891, Leonard, Tex.   d: 11/4/71, Bonham, Tex.   BL/TR, 6', 185 lbs.   Deb: 9/02/12

1912	Chi-A	2	2	0	0	0	0	0	0	0		.000	.000	.000	-99	-1	-1	0	0			.000	0	H	-0.1
1915	Chi-N	68	127	16	25	3	0	1	12	14	20	.197	.277	.244	58	-6	-6	9	2	2	-1	.957	3	21	-0.4
Total	2	70	129	16	25	3	0	1	12	14	20	.194	.273	.240	56	-7	-7	9	2	2		.971	3	/21	-0.5

■ BARNEY McLAUGHLIN   McLaughlin, Bernard   b: 1857, Ireland   d: 2/13/21, Lowell, Mass.   BR/TR,   Deb: 8/02/1884   F

1884	KC-U	42	162	15	37	7	3	0			9	.228	.269	.309	109	-1	3	14				.762	-4	O2/PS	-0.1
1887	Phi-N	50	205	26	45	8	3	1	26	11	27	.220	.263	.302	55	-12	-14	17	2			.879	-11	2	-2.0
1890	Syr-a	86	329	43	87	8	1	2			47	.264	.360	.313	113	2	8	43	13			.902	-12	S	0.1
Total	3	178	696	84	169	23	7	3	26	67	27	.243	.312	.309	93	-10	-3	74	15			.900	-27	/S2OP	-2.0

■ FRANK McLAUGHLIN   McLaughlin, Francis Edward   b: 6/19/1856, Lowell, Mass.   d: 4/5/17, Lowell, Mass.   BR/TR, 5'9", 160 lbs.   Deb: 8/09/1882   F

1882	Wor-N	15	55	7	12	0	2	1	4	0	11	.218	.218	.345	76	-1	-2	4				.760	-3	S/O	-0.4
1883	Pit-a	29	114	15	25	2	0	1		6		.219	.258	.263	72	-4	-3	8				.802	-1	S/O2P	-0.3
1884	Cin-U	16	67	10	16	4	1	2			2	.239	.261	.418	117	2	1	7				.740	-7	S	-0.5
	CP-U	15	67	11	16	4	1	0			1	.239	.250	.358	95	-0	-0	6				.888	6	2/SO	-0.5
	KC-U	32	123	17	28	11	0	1			9	.228	.280	.341	126	1	4	12				.847	-9	2O/3SP	-0.4
	Yr	63	257	38	60	19	2	3			12	.233	.268	.358	115	3	5	25				.873	-10	2SO/3P	-0.4
Total	3	107	426	60	97	21	4	5	4	18	11	.228	.259	.331	98	-3	-0	37				.769	-15	/S2O3P	-1.1

■ JAMES McLAUGHLIN   McLaughlin, James   b: San Francisco, Cal.   Deb: 5/03/1884

| 1884 | Was-U | 10 | 37 | 3 | 7 | 3 | 0 | 0 | | | 0 | .189 | .189 | .270 | 56 | -2 | -2 | 2 | | | | .696 | -3 | /S3 | -0.4 |

■ KID McLAUGHLIN   McLaughlin, James Anson "Sunshine"   b: 4/12/1888, Randolph, N.Y.   d: 11/13/34, Allegheny, N.Y.   BL/TR, 5'8.5", 158 lbs.   Deb: 6/30/14

| 1914 | Cin-N | 3 | 2 | 1 | 0 | 0 | 0 | 0 | 0 | 0 | 4 | .000 | .000 | .000 | -97 | -0 | -0 | 0 | 0 | | | 1.000 | -1 | /O | -0.1 |

■ JIM McLAUGHLIN   McLaughlin, James Robert   b: 1/3/02, St.Louis, Mo.   d: 12/18/68, Mount Vernon, Ill.   BR/TR, 5'8.5", 168 lbs.   Deb: 4/18/32

| 1932 | StL-A | 1 | 1 | 0 | 0 | 0 | 0 | 0 | 1 | 0 | 0 | .000 | .000 | .000 | -95 | -0 | -0 | 0 | 0 | 0 | 0 | .000 | 0 | /3 | 0.0 |

■ TOM McLAUGHLIN   McLaughlin, Thomas   b: 3/28/1860, Louisville, Ky.   d: 7/21/21, Louisville, Ky.   TR ,   Deb: 7/17/1883

1883	Lou-a	42	146	16	28	1	2	0			5	.192	.219	.226	47	-9	-7	7				.844	4	SO/132	-0.3
1884	Lou-a	98	335	41	67	11	6	0			22	.200	.262	.269	79	-8	-6	24				.892	19	*S/32	1.3
1885	Lou-a	112	411	49	87	13	9	0			15	.212	.245	.302	74	-12	-12	31				.883	1	*2S	-0.6
1886	NY-a	74	250	27	34	3	1	0			26	.136	.220	.156	21	-22	-20	12	13			.886	7	S2/O	-1.1
1891	Was-a	14	41	9	11	0	1	0	3	7	6	.268	.400	.317	114	1	1	7	3			.871	-0	S	0.2
Total	5	340	1183	142	227	28	19	0	3	75	6	.192	.247	.253	63	-50	-43	81	16			.886	30	S2/O31	-0.5

■ RALPH McLAURIN   McLaurin, Ralph Edgar   b: 5/23/1885, Kissimmee, Fla.   d: 2/11/43, McColl, S.C.   Deb: 9/05/08

| 1908 | StL-N | 8 | 22 | 2 | 5 | 0 | 0 | 0 | 0 | 0 | | .227 | .227 | .227 | 48 | -1 | -1 | 1 | 0 | | | .875 | -0 | /O | -0.2 |

■ LARRY McLEAN   McLean, John Bannerman   b: 7/18/1881, Cambridge, Mass.   d: 3/24/21, Boston, Mass.   BR/TR, 6'5", 228 lbs.   Deb: 4/26/01

| 1901 | Bos-A | 9 | 19 | 4 | 4 | 1 | 0 | 0 | 2 | 0 | | .211 | .211 | .263 | 31 | -2 | -2 | 1 | | 1 | | 1.000 | 0 | /1 | -0.1 |
| 1903 | Chi-N | 1 | 4 | 0 | 0 | 0 | 0 | 0 | 0 | 0 | | .000 | .200 | .000 | -42 | -1 | -1 | 0 | | 0 | | .889 | -0 | /C | -0.1 |

YEAR	TM/L	G	AB	R	H	2B	3B	HR	RBI	BB	SO	AVG	OBP	SLG	PRO+	BR	/A	RC	SB	CS	SBR	FA	FR	POS	TPR
1904	StL-N	27	84	5	14	2	1	0	4	4		.167	.205	.214	31	-7	-7	4	1			.954	-2	C	-0.6
1906	Cin-N	12	35	3	7	2	0	0	2	4		.200	.282	.257	66	-1	-1	3	0			.954	-2	C	-0.2
1907	Cin-N	113	374	35	108	9	9	0	54	13		.289	.313	.361	107	3	1	45	4			.975	-3	C1	0.7
1908	Cin-N	99	309	24	67	9	4	1	28	15		.217	.255	.282	74	-10	-10	22	2			.963	-6	C1	-1.1
1909	Cin-N	95	324	26	83	12	2	2	36	21		.256	.307	.324	97	-2	-2	33	1			.978	-6	C	0.1
1910	Cin-N	127	423	27	126	14	7	2	71	26	23	.298	.340	.378	114	4	6	55	4			.983	-4	*C	1.4
1911	Cin-N	107	328	24	94	7	2	0	34	20	18	.287	.330	.320	85	-8	-6	34	1			.968	8	C	1.0
1912	Cin-N	102	333	17	81	15	1	1	27	18	15	.243	.284	.303	63	-19	-17	28	1			.973	-2	C	-1.0
1913	StL-N	48	152	7	41	9	0	0	12	6	9	.270	.297	.329	80	-4	-4	14	0			.981	-6	C	-0.7
	*NY-N	30	75	3	24	4	0	0	9	4	4	.320	.354	.373	107	1	1	10	1			.953	-2	C	0.0
	Yr	78	227	10	65	13	0	0	21	10	13	.286	.316	.344	89	-4	-4	23	1			.970	-9	C	-0.7
1914	NY-N	79	154	8	40	6	0	0	14	4	9	.260	.283	.299	76	-5	-5	13	4			.973	-4	C	-0.5
1915	NY-N	13	33	0	5	0	0	0	4	0	1	.152	.152	.152	-9	-4	-4	1	0			.985	2	C	-0.1
Total	13	862	2647	183	694	90	26	6	298	136	79	.262	.300	.323	86	-57	-51	263	20			.973	-26	C/1	-1.2

■ MARK McLEMORE

McLemore, Mark Tremell b: 10/4/64, San Diego, Cal. BB/TR, 5'11", 195 lbs. Deb: 9/13/86

YEAR	TM/L	G	AB	R	H	2B	3B	HR	RBI	BB	SO	AVG	OBP	SLG	PRO+	BR	/A	RC	SB	CS	SBR	FA	FR	POS	TPR
1986	Cal-A	5	4	0	0	0	0	0	0	1	2	.000	.200	.000	-40	-1	-1	0	0	1	-1	1.000	4	/2	0.2
1987	Cal-A	138	433	61	102	13	3	3	41	48	72	.236	.312	.300	66	-22	-20	45	25	8	3	.974	-5	*2/SD	-1.5
1988	Cal-A	77	233	38	56	11	2	2	16	25	28	.240	.314	.330	83	-6	-5	24	13	7	-0	.979	7	2/3D	0.4
1989	Cal-A	32	103	12	25	3	1	0	14	7	19	.243	.297	.291	68	-4	-4	10	6	1	1	.966	3	2/D	0.0
1990	Cal-A	20	48	4	7	2	0	0	2	4	9	.146	.212	.188	13	-6	-5	2	1	0	0	1.000	-2	/2SD	-0.7
	Cle-A	8	12	2	2	0	0	0	0	0	6	.167	.167	.167	-7	-2	-2	0	0	0	0	1.000	2	/32D	0.0
	Yr	28	60	6	9	2	0	0	2	4	15	.150	.203	.183	9	-7	-7	2	1	0	0	1.000	0	2/S3D	-0.7
1991	Hou-N	21	61	6	9	1	0	0	2	6	13	.148	.224	.164	11	-7	-7	2	0	1	-1	.975	1	2	-0.6
1992	Bal-A	101	228	40	56	7	2	0	27	21	26	.246	.309	.294	70	-9	-9	21	11	5	0	.978	9	2D	0.2
Total	7	402	1122	163	257	37	8	5	102	112	175	.229	.300	.290	64	-56	-52	104	56	23	3	.976	18	2/DS3	-2.0

■ RALPH McLEOD

McLeod, Ralph Alton b: 10/19/16, N.Quincy, Mass. BL/TL, 6', 170 lbs. Deb: 9/14/38

YEAR	TM/L	G	AB	R	H	2B	3B	HR	RBI	BB	SO	AVG	OBP	SLG	PRO+	BR	/A	RC	SB	CS	SBR	FA	FR	POS	TPR
1938	Bos-N	6	7	1	2	1	0	0	0	0	2	.286	.286	.429	105	-0	-0	0	0			1.000	-0	/O	0.0

■ JIM McLEOD

McLeod, Soule James b: 9/12/08, Jones, La. d: 8/3/81, Little Rock, Ark. BR/TR, 6', 187 lbs. Deb: 5/22/30

YEAR	TM/L	G	AB	R	H	2B	3B	HR	RBI	BB	SO	AVG	OBP	SLG	PRO+	BR	/A	RC	SB	CS	SBR	FA	FR	POS	TPR
1930	Was-A	18	34	3	9	1	0	0	1	1	5	.265	.306	.294	53	-2	-2	3	1	1	-0	1.000	-1	3/S	-0.2
1932	Was-A	7	0	1	0	0	0	0	0	1	0	—	1.000	—	183	0	0	0	0	0	0	1.000	3	/S	0.2
1933	Phi-N	67	232	20	45	6	1	0	15	12	25	.194	.237	.228	30	-20	-23	13	1			.914	-6	3/S	-2.7
Total	3	92	266	24	54	7	1	0	16	14	30	.203	.248	.237	33	-22	-25	16	2	1		.922	-4	/3S	-2.7

■ JACK McMAHON

McMahon, John Henry b: 10/15/1869, Waterbury, Conn. d: 12/30/1894, Bridgeport, Conn. BR/TL, 5'10", 165 lbs. Deb: 8/08/1892

YEAR	TM/L	G	AB	R	H	2B	3B	HR	RBI	BB	SO	AVG	OBP	SLG	PRO+	BR	/A	RC	SB	CS	SBR	FA	FR	POS	TPR
1892	NY-N	40	147	21	33	5	7	1	24	10	9	.224	.278	.374	100	-1	-1	17	3			.973	-2	1/C	-0.4
1893	NY-N	11	30	5	10	2	1	0	4	2	0	.333	.375	.467	125	1	1	5	0			.891	-1	C	0.1
Total	2	51	177	26	43	7	8	1	28	12	9	.243	.295	.390	105	-0	0	22	3			.900	-3	/1C	-0.3

■ FRANK McMANUS

McManus, Francis E. b: 9/21/1875, Lawrence, Mass. d: 9/1/23, Syracuse, N.Y. TR , 5'10", Deb: 9/14/1899

YEAR	TM/L	G	AB	R	H	2B	3B	HR	RBI	BB	SO	AVG	OBP	SLG	PRO+	BR	/A	RC	SB	CS	SBR	FA	FR	POS	TPR
1899	Was-N	7	21	3	8	1	0	0	2	2		.381	.435	.429	139	1	1	5	3			.931	0	/C	0.2
1903	Bro-N	2	7	0	0	0	0	0	0	0		.000	.000	.000	-99	-2	-2	0	0			.929	1	/C	-0.1
1904	Det-A	1	0	0	0	0	0	0	0	0		—	—	—	—	0	0	0	0			.000	0	/C	0.0
	NY-A	4	7	0	0	0	0	0	0	0		.000	.000	.000	-96	-2	-2	0	0			.900	-1	/C	-0.3
	Yr	5	7	0	0	0	0	0	0	0		.000	.000	.000	-97	-2	-2	0	0			.900	-1	/C	-0.3
Total	3	14	35	3	8	1	0	0	2	2		.229	.270	.257	50	-2	-2	5	3			.925	-0	/C	-0.2

■ JIM McMANUS

McManus, James Michael b: 7/20/36, Brookline, Mass. BL/TL, 6'4", 215 lbs. Deb: 9/21/60

YEAR	TM/L	G	AB	R	H	2B	3B	HR	RBI	BB	SO	AVG	OBP	SLG	PRO+	BR	/A	RC	SB	CS	SBR	FA	FR	POS	TPR
1960	KC-A	5	13	3	4	0	0	1	2	1	2	.308	.357	.538	138	1	1	2	0	0	0	1.000	-0	/1	0.0

■ MARTY McMANUS

McManus, Martin Joseph b: 3/14/1900, Chicago, Ill. d: 2/18/66, St.Louis, Mo. BR/TR, 5'10.5", 160 lbs. Deb: 9/26/20 M

YEAR	TM/L	G	AB	R	H	2B	3B	HR	RBI	BB	SO	AVG	OBP	SLG	PRO+	BR	/A	RC	SB	CS	SBR	FA	FR	POS	TPR
1920	StL-A	1	3	0	1	0	1	0	1	0	0	.333	.333	1.000	237	1	1	1	0	0	0	.667	-0	/3	0.0
1921	StL-A	121	412	49	107	19	8	3	64	27	30	.260	.308	.367	68	-19	-22	48	5	3	-0	.952	-11	23/1S	-2.8
1922	StL-A	154	606	88	189	34	11	11	109	38	41	.312	.358	.459	108	9	6	99	9	6	-1	.964	3	*2/1	1.1
1923	StL-A	154	582	86	180	35	10	15	94	49	50	.309	.367	.481	116	16	12	102	14	10	-2	.960	-1	*21	0.9
1924	StL-A	123	442	71	147	23	5	5	80	55	40	.333	.409	.441	112	14	10	82	13	9	-2	.972	7	*2	1.5
1925	StL-A	154	587	108	169	**44**	8	13	90	73	69	.288	.371	.457	104	7	3	99	5	11	-5	.967	4	*2/O	0.4
1926	StL-A	149	549	102	156	30	10	9	68	55	62	.284	.350	.424	97	-0	-4	82	5	7	-3	.958	15	32/1	1.5
1927	Det-A	108	369	60	99	19	7	9	69	34	38	.268	.332	.431	95	-3	-4	49	8	7	-2	.960	-2	S23/1	-0.1
1928	Det-A	139	500	78	144	37	5	8	73	51	32	.288	.355	.430	104	3	2	75	11	13	-5	.955	0	31/S	0.0
1929	Det-A	154	599	99	168	32	8	18	90	60	52	.280	.347	.451	103	2	2	93	16	11	-2	.972	8	*3/S	1.4
1930	Det-A	132	484	74	155	40	4	9	89	59	28	.320	.396	.475	118	16	14	95	**23**	8	2	**.966**	6	*3/S1	2.7
1931	Det-A	107	362	39	98	17	3	3	53	49	22	.271	.361	.359	87	-4	-6	50	7	3	0	.950	13	32/1	1.2
	Bos-A	17	62	8	18	4	0	1	9	8	1	.290	.371	.403	110	0	1	9	1	1	-0	1.000	8	3/2	0.9
	Yr	124	424	47	116	21	3	4	62	57	23	.274	.362	.366	90	-4	-5	59	8	4	0	.956	21	32/1	2.1
1932	Bos-A	93	302	39	71	19	4	5	24	36	30	.235	.317	.374	80	-10	-9	37	1	2	-1	.969	6	23/S1M	0.0
1933	Bos-A	106	366	51	104	30	4	3	36	49	21	.284	.369	.413	108	4	5	59	3	0	1	.957	-5	32/1M	0.6
1934	Bos-N	119	435	56	120	18	0	8	47	32	42	.276	.330	.372	95	-7	-3	53	5			.964	-5	23	-0.2
Total	15	1831	6660	1008	1926	401	88	120	996	675	558	.289	.357	.430	101	29	7	1033	126	91		.965	44	23/1SO	9.1

■ JIMMY McMATH

McMath, Jimmy Lee b: 8/10/49, Tuscaloosa, Ala. BL/TL, 6'1.5", 195 lbs. Deb: 9/07/68

YEAR	TM/L	G	AB	R	H	2B	3B	HR	RBI	BB	SO	AVG	OBP	SLG	PRO+	BR	/A	RC	SB	CS	SBR	FA	FR	POS	TPR
1968	Chi-N	6	14	0	2	0	0	0	2	0	6	.143	.143	.143	-13	-2	-2	0	0	0	0	1.000	-0	/O	-0.3

■ GEORGE McMILLAN

McMillan, George A. "Reddy" b: Evansville, Ind. 5'8", 175 lbs. Deb: 8/11/1890

YEAR	TM/L	G	AB	R	H	2B	3B	HR	RBI	BB	SO	AVG	OBP	SLG	PRO+	BR	/A	RC	SB	CS	SBR	FA	FR	POS	TPR
1890	NY-N	10	35	4	5	0	0	0	1	7	4	.143	.286	.143	28	-3	-3	2	1			.800	-1	O	-0.4

■ NORM McMILLAN

McMillan, Norman Alexis "Bub" b: 10/5/1895, Latta, S.C. d: 9/28/69, Marion, S.C. BR/TR, 6', 175 lbs. Deb: 4/12/22

YEAR	TM/L	G	AB	R	H	2B	3B	HR	RBI	BB	SO	AVG	OBP	SLG	PRO+	BR	/A	RC	SB	CS	SBR	FA	FR	POS	TPR
1922	*NY-A	33	78	7	20	1	2	0	11	6	10	.256	.310	.321	63	-4	-4	8	4	1	1	.921	-8	O/3	-1.3
1923	Bos-A	131	459	37	116	24	5	0	42	28	44	.253	.299	.327	64	-24	-25	46	13	5	1	.942	12	32S	-0.2
1924	StL-A	76	201	25	56	12	2	0	27	12	17	.279	.332	.358	73	-7	-9	24	6	4	-1	.966	-3	23/S1	-1.0
1928	Chi-N	49	123	11	27	2	2	1	12	13	19	.220	.299	.293	56	-8	-8	11	0			.977	-1	23	-0.7
1929	*Chi-N	124	495	77	134	35	5	5	55	36	43	.271	.324	.392	76	-19	-19	62	13			.944	6	*3	-0.8
Total	5	413	1356	157	353	74	16	6	147	95	133	.260	.313	.352	69	-62	-65	152	36	10		.944	7	3/2SO1	-4.0

■ ROY McMILLAN

McMillan, Roy David b: 7/17/30, Bonham, Tex. BR/TR, 5'11", 170 lbs. Deb: 4/17/51 MC

YEAR	TM/L	G	AB	R	H	2B	3B	HR	RBI	BB	SO	AVG	OBP	SLG	PRO+	BR	/A	RC	SB	CS	SBR	FA	FR	POS	TPR
1951	Cin-N	85	199	21	42	4	0	1	8	17	26	.211	.273	.246	40	-16	-17	15	0	0	0	.963	5	S3/2	-0.9
1952	Cin-N	154	540	60	132	32	2	7	57	45	81	.244	.306	.350	82	-14	-14	57	4	5	-2	.971	11	*S	0.7
1953	Cin-N	155	557	51	130	15	4	5	43	43	52	.233	.290	.302	54	-37	-38	49	2	4	-2	.972	14	*S	-1.4
1954	Cin-N	154	588	86	147	21	2	4	42	47	54	.250	.311	.313	61	-31	-34	61	4	2	0	.959	6	*S	-1.5
1955	Cin-N	151	470	50	126	21	2	1	37	66	33	.268	.366	.328	81	-7	-10	60	4	4	-1	.969	17	*S	1.8
1956	Cin-N★	150	479	51	126	16	7	3	62	76	54	.263	.370	.344	88	-1	-5	64	4	3	-1	**.975**	**30**	*S	3.7
1957	Cin-N★	151	448	50	122	25	5	1	55	66	44	.272	.373	.357	91	1	-3	64	5	1	1	**.977**	-8	*S	0.4
1958	Cin-N	145	393	48	90	18	3	1	25	47	33	.229	.313	.298	60	-20	-23	38	5	2	0	**.980**	4	*S	-0.7

YEAR	TM/L	G	AB	R	H	2B	3B	HR	RBI	BB	SO	AVG	OBP	SLG	PRO+	BR	/A	RC	SB	CS	SBR	FA	FR	POS	TPR
1959	Cin-N	79	246	38	65	14	2	9	24	27	27	.264	.347	.447	106	3	2	35	0	2	-1	.974	-7	S	0.0
1960	Cin-N	124	399	42	94	12	2	10	42	35	40	.236	.304	.351	77	-12	-13	43	2	0	1	.964	-13	*S2	-1.7
1961	Mil-N	154	505	42	111	16	0	7	48	61	86	.220	.309	.293	65	-27	-23	46	2	4	-2	**.975**	-0	*S	-1.2
1962	Mil-N	137	468	66	115	13	0	12	41	60	53	.246	.338	.350	87	-9	-7	57	2	2	-1	.972	1	*S	0.6
1963	Mil-N	100	320	35	80	10	1	4	29	17	25	.250	.292	.325	78	-9	-9	29	1	5	-3	.979	7	S	0.2
1964	Mil-N	8	13	1	4	0	0	0	2	0	2	.308	.308	.308	73	-0	-0	1	1	0	0	.933	-1	/S	-0.1
	NY-N	113	379	30	80	8	2	1	25	14	16	.211	.247	.251	42	-30	-29	20	3	1	0	.976	1	*S	-2.1
	Yr	121	392	31	84	8	2	1	27	14	18	.214	.249	.253	43	-30	-29	22	4	1	1	.975	-0	*S	-2.2
1965	NY-N	157	528	44	128	19	2	1	42	24	60	.242	.281	.292	64	-27	-25	44	1	0	0	.964	-4	*S	-1.9
1966	NY-N	76	220	24	47	9	1	1	12	20	25	.214	.285	.277	59	-12	-12	18	1	1	-0	.975	6	S	-0.1
Total	16	2093	6752	739	1639	253	35	68	594	665	711	.243	.316	.321	72	-249	-258	702	41	36	-9	.972	67	*S/32	-4.2
■ **TOM McMILLAN** McMillan, Thomas Erwin b: 9/13/51, Richmond, Va. BR/TR, 5'9", 165 lbs. Deb: 9/17/77																									
1977	Sea-A	2	5	0	0	0	0	0	0	0	0	.000	.000	.000	-99	-1	-1	0	0	0	0	1.000	-0	/S	-0.2
■ **TOMMY McMILLAN** McMillan, Thomas Law "Rebel" b: 4/18/1888, Pittston, Pa. d: 7/15/66, Orlando, Fla. BR/TR, 5'5", 130 lbs. Deb: 8/19/08																									
1908	Bro-N	43	147	9	35	3	0	0	3	9		.238	.291	.259	79	-4	-3	13	5			.873	-5	SO	-1.0
1909	Bro-N	108	373	18	79	15	1	0	24	20		.212	.254	.257	61	-19	-17	26	11			.914	-10	*S/23	-2.9
1910	Bro-N	23	74	2	13	1	0	0	2	6	10	.176	.237	.189	26	-7	-7	4	4			.898	-1	S	-0.8
	Cin-N	82	248	20	46	0	3	0	13	31	23	.185	.281	.210	46	-17	-15	18	7			.927	10	S	-0.3
	Yr	105	322	22	59	1	3	0	15	37	33	.183	.271	.205	41	-24	-22	22	11			.921	8	*S	-1.1
1912	NY-A	41	149	24	34	2	0	0	12	15		.228	.303	.242	53	-8	-9	17	18			.948	-8	S	-1.4
Total	4	297	991	73	207	21	4	0	54	81	33	.209	.273	.238	55	-54	-52	78	45			.917	-14	S/O23	-6.4
■ **HUGH McMULLEN** McMullen, Hugh Raphael b: 12/16/01, LaCygne, Kan. d: 5/23/86, Whittier, Cal. BB/TR, 6'1", 180 lbs. Deb: 9/19/25																									
1925	NY-N	5	15	1	2	1	0	0	0	0	3	.133	.133	.200	-17	-3	-3	0	0	0	0	1.000	-2	/C	-0.4
1926	NY-N	57	91	5	17	2	0	0	6	2	18	.187	.204	.209	11	-11	-11	4	1			.942	-0	C	-0.9
1928	Was-A	1	1	0	0	0	0	0	0	0	1	.000	.000	.000	-99	-0	-0	0	0	0	0	.000	0	H	0.0
1929	Cin-N	1	1	0	0	0	0	0	0	0	0	.000	.000	.000	-99	-0	-0	0	0			1.000	0	/C	0.0
Total	4	64	108	6	19	3	0	0	6	2	22	.176	.191	.204	5	-15	-14	4	1	0		.947	-2	/C	-1.3
■ **KEN McMULLEN** McMullen, Kenneth Lee b: 6/1/42, Oxnard, Cal. BR/TR, 6'3", 195 lbs. Deb: 9/17/62																									
1962	LA-N	6	11	0	3	0	0	0	0	0	3	.273	.273	.273	50	-1	-1	1	0	0	0	1.000	-1	/O	-0.1
1963	LA-N	79	233	16	55	9	0	5	28	20	46	.236	.299	.339	89	-5	-3	22	1	2	-1	.933	7	3/2O	0.3
1964	LA-N	24	67	3	14	0	0	1	2	3	7	.209	.243	.254	43	-5	-5	3	0	1	-1	.991	-2	1/3O	-0.9
1965	Was-A	150	555	75	146	18	6	18	54	47	90	.263	.325	.414	110	6	7	74	2	0	1	.954	6	*3/O1	1.0
1966	Was-A	147	524	48	122	19	4	13	54	44	89	.233	.292	.359	87	-10	-9	53	3	1	0	.951	-1	*3/1O	-1.4
1967	Was-A	146	563	73	138	22	2	16	67	46	84	.245	.303	.377	104	-1	1	62	5	3	-0	.965	12	*3	1.3
1968	Was-A	151	557	66	138	11	2	20	62	63	66	.248	.327	.382	118	10	12	70	1	3	-2	.962	5	*3S	1.8
1969	Was-A	158	562	83	153	25	2	19	87	70	103	.272	.354	.425	123	13	16	86	4	5	-2	.976	13	*3	3.0
1970	Was-A	15	59	5	12	2	0	0	3	5	10	.203	.266	.237	42	-5	-4	4	0	0	0	.971	6	3	0.1
	Cal-A	124	422	50	98	9	3	14	61	59	81	.232	.331	.367	96	-4	-2	52	1	0	0	.959	9	*3	0.6
	Yr	139	481	55	110	11	3	14	64	64	91	.229	.323	.351	89	-9	-6	55	1	0	0	.960	15	*3	0.7
1971	Cal-A	160	593	63	148	19	2	21	68	53	74	.250	.314	.395	107	-1	3	71	1	1	-0	.966	-1	*3	0.1
1972	Cal-A	137	472	36	127	18	1	9	34	48	59	.269	.337	.369	116	6	9	58	1	2	-1	.970	2	*3	1.0
1973	LA-N	42	85	6	21	5	0	5	18	6	13	.247	.297	.482	118	1	1	12	0	0	0	.922	5	3	0.6
1974	*LA-N	44	60	5	15	1	0	3	12	2	12	.250	.274	.417	95	-1	-1	7	0	0	0	1.000	-1	/32	-0.1
1975	LA-N	39	46	4	11	1	1	2	14	7	12	.239	.340	.435	119	1	1	7	0	0	0	1.000	1	3/1	0.2
1976	Oak-A	98	186	20	41	6	2	5	23	22	33	.220	.306	.355	97	-2	-1	20	1	1	-0	.952	-1	31D/O2	-0.4
1977	Mil-A	63	136	15	31	7	1	5	19	15	33	.228	.305	.404	91	-2	-2	16	0	0	0	.978	2	D1/3	-0.1
Total	16	1583	5131	568	1273	172	26	156	606	510	815	.248	.318	.383	105	-1	23	617	20	19	-5	.961	61	*3/1DOS2	7.0
■ **FRED McMULLIN** McMullin, Frederick William b: 10/13/1891, Scammon, Kan. d: 11/21/52, Los Angeles, Cal. BR/TR, 5'11", 170 lbs. Deb: 8/27/14																									
1914	Det-A	1	1	0	0	0	0	0	0	0	1	.000	.000	.000	-97	-0	-0	0	0			.667	0	/S	0.0
1916	Chi-A	68	187	8	48	3	0	0	10	19	30	.257	.332	.273	81	-4	-4	22	9			.950	-4	3/S2	-0.6
1917	*Chi-A	59	194	35	46	2	1	0	12	27	17	.237	.339	.258	81	-3	-3	22	9			.932	-13	3/S	-1.7
1918	Chi-A	70	235	32	65	7	0	1	16	25	26	.277	.356	.319	103	2	2	30	7			.941	-2	3/2	0.2
1919	*Chi-A	60	170	31	50	8	4	0	19	11	18	.294	.355	.388	108	2	2	25	4			.931	-0	3/2	0.3
1920	Chi-A	46	127	14	25	1	4	0	13	9	13	.197	.255	.268	39	-11	-11	9	1	1	-0	.962	-5	3/2S	-1.5
Total	6	304	914	120	234	21	9	1	70	91	105	.256	.333	.302	85	-14	-15	108	30	1		.942	-24	3/2S	-3.3
■ **JOHN McMULLIN** McMullin, John F. "Lefty" b: 1848, Philadelphia, Pa. d: 4/11/1881, Philadelphia, Pa. BR/TL, 5'9", 160 lbs. Deb: 5/09/1871																									
1871	Tro-n	29	136	38	38	0	5	0	32	8	6	.279	.319	.353	92	-1	-1	19	11					*P	0.0
1872	Mut-n	54	237	48	60	7	1	0	24	11	6	.253	.286	.291	83	-6	-2	22						*O/P	0.1
1873	Ath-n	52	227	54	62	8	1	0	29	8	4	.273	.298	.317	76	-5	-9	24						*O/P	-0.3
1874	Ath-n	55	262	61	89	10	2	2		7		.340	.357	.416	134	13	9	40						*O/C	0.8
1875	Phi-n	54	223	34	56	9	4	2		5		.251	.268	.354	109	3	2	22						*O/P	0.2
Total	5 n	244	1085	235	305	34	13	4		39		.281	.306	.347	100	5	-2	127						O/PC	0.8
■ **CARL McNABB** McNabb, Carl Mac "Skinny" b: 1/25/17, Stevenson, Ala. BR/TR, 5'9", 155 lbs. Deb: 4/20/45																									
1945	Det-A	1	1	0	0	0	0	0	0	0	1	.000	.000	.000	-94	-0	-0	0	0	0	0	.000	0	H	0.0
■ **ERIC McNAIR** McNair, Donald Eric "Boob" b: 4/12/09, Meridian, Miss. d: 3/11/49, Meridian, Miss. BR/TR, 5'8", 160 lbs. Deb: 9/20/29																									
1929	Phi-A	4	8	2	4	1	0	0	3	0	0	.500	.500	.625	181	1	1	3	1	0	0	1.000	-0	/S	0.1
1930	*Phi-A	78	237	27	63	12	2	0	34	9	19	.266	.296	.333	57	-15	-16	23	5	2	0	.915	-7	S3/2O	-1.7
1931	*Phi-A	79	280	41	76	10	1	5	33	11	19	.271	.306	.368	72	-10	-13	30	1	4	-2	.915	-6	32S	-1.5
1932	Phi-A	135	554	87	158	**47**	3	18	95	28	29	.285	.323	.478	101	1	-2	84	8	4	0	.953	-7	*S	0.3
1933	Phi-A	89	310	57	81	15	4	7	48	15	32	.261	.302	.403	85	-8	-8	38	2	1	0	.966	-2	S2	-0.5
1934	Phi-A	151	599	80	168	20	4	17	82	35	42	.280	.321	.412	91	-13	-10	77	7	8	-3	.951	4	*S	0.0
1935	Phi-A	137	526	55	142	22	2	4	57	35	33	.270	.319	.342	72	-23	-22	57	3	7	-3	.955	-21	*S3/1	-3.8
1936	Bos-A	128	494	68	141	36	2	4	74	27	34	.285	.329	.391	73	-19	-23	63	2	3	-1	.966	-12	S23	-2.5
1937	Bos-A	126	455	60	133	29	4	12	76	30	33	.292	.340	.453	94	-3	-6	69	10	7	-1	.969	-6	*2/S31	-0.4
1938	Bos-A	46	96	9	15	1	1	0	7	3	6	.156	.182	.188	-7	-16	-17	3	0	1	-1	.870	3	S2/3	-1.2
1939	Chi-A	129	479	62	155	18	5	7	82	38	41	.324	.375	.426	102	3	1	74	17	9	-0	.937	4	*32/S	0.7
1940	Chi-A	66	251	26	57	13	1	7	31	12	26	.227	.265	.371	62	-15	-15	21	1	7	-4	.958	-17	2/3	-3.1
1941	Det-A	23	59	5	11	1	0	0	3	4	4	.186	.250	.203	19	-7	-7	2	0	0	0	.970	-2	3/S	-0.9
1942	Det-A	26	68	5	11	2	0	1	4	3	5	.162	.197	.235	20	-7	-8	2	0	1	-1	.881	-8	S	-1.6
	Phi-A	34	103	8	25	2	0	0	4	11	5	.243	.316	.262	64	-5	-5	9	1	0	0	.952	-6	S/2	-0.9
	Yr	60	171	13	36	4	0	1	8	14	10	.211	.270	.251	46	-12	-13	11	1	1	-0	.927	-13	S/2	-2.5
Total	14	1251	4519	592	1240	229	29	82	633	261	328	.274	.318	.392	80	-135	-150	556	58	54	-15	.949	-83	S23/10	-17.0
■ **MIKE McNALLY** McNally, Michael Joseph "Minooka Mike" b: 9/9/1892, Minooka, Pa. d: 5/29/65, Bethlehem, Pa. BR/TR, 5'11", 150 lbs. Deb: 4/21/15																									
1915	Bos-A	23	53	7	8	0	1	0	0	3	7	.151	.196	.189	16	-6	-5	2	0	2	-1	.891	1	3/2	-0.6
1916	*Bos-A	87	135	28	23	0	0	0	9	10	19	.170	.228	.170	20	-13	-13	8	9			.964	7	23/SO	-0.6
1917	Bos-A	42	50	9	15	1	0	0	2	6	3	.300	.375	.320	113	1	1	8	3			.935	6	3/S2	0.8

YEAR	TM/L	G	AB	R	H	2B	3B	HR	RBI	BB	SO	AVG	OBP	SLG	PRO+	BR	/A	RC	SB	CS	SBR	FA	FR	POS	TPR
1919	Bos-A	33	42	10	11	4	0	0	6	1	2	.262	.279	.357	83	-1	-1	5	4			.950	9	S3/2	0.9
1920	Bos-A	93	312	42	80	5	1	0	23	31	24	.256	.326	.279	64	-16	-14	30	13	10	-2	.930	-9	2/S1	-2.3
1921	*NY-A	71	215	36	56	4	2	1	24	14	15	.260	.306	.312	57	-14	-14	20	5	6	-2	.974	18	32	0.4
1922	*NY-A	52	143	20	36	2	2	0	18	16	14	.252	.331	.294	63	-7	-8	16	2	0	1	.983	-0	3/2S1	-0.4
1923	NY-A	30	38	5	8	0	0	0	1	3	4	.211	.268	.211	27	-4	-4	3	2	0	1	1.000	0	S/32	-0.3
1924	NY-A	49	69	11	17	0	0	0	2	7	5	.246	.316	.246	46	-5	-5	6	1	1	-0	.985	10	23/S	0.4
1925	Was-A	12	21	1	3	0	0	0	0	1	4	.143	.182	.143	-17	-4	-4	1	0	0	0	1.000	1	/3S2	-0.3
Total	10	492	1078	169	257	16	6	1	85	92	97	.238	.299	.267	54	-69	-68	98	39	19		.946	41	23/S10	-2.0

■ JIM McNAMARA McNamara, James Patrick b: 6/10/65, Nashua, N.H. BL/TR, 6'4", 210 lbs. Deb: 4/09/92

YEAR	TM/L	G	AB	R	H	2B	3B	HR	RBI	BB	SO	AVG	OBP	SLG	PRO+	BR	/A	RC	SB	CS	SBR	FA	FR	POS	TPR
1992	SF-N	30	74	6	16	1	0	1	9	6	25	.216	.275	.270	58	-4	-4	6	0	0	0	.993	-0	C	-0.3

■ GEORGE McNAMARA McNamara, George Francis b: 1/11/01, Chicago, Ill. d: 6/12/90, Hinsdale, Ill. BL/TR, 6', 175 lbs. Deb: 9/28/22

YEAR	TM/L	G	AB	R	H	2B	3B	HR	RBI	BB	SO	AVG	OBP	SLG	PRO+	BR	/A	RC	SB	CS	SBR	FA	FR	POS	TPR
1922	Was-A	3	11	3	3	0	0	0	1	1	2	.273	.333	.273	63	-1	-1	1	0	0	0	1.000	-1	/O	-0.1

■ DINNY McNAMARA McNamara, John Raymond b: 9/16/05, Lexington, Mass. d: 12/20/63, Arlington, Mass. BL/TR, 5'9", 165 lbs. Deb: 7/02/27

YEAR	TM/L	G	AB	R	H	2B	3B	HR	RBI	BB	SO	AVG	OBP	SLG	PRO+	BR	/A	RC	SB	CS	SBR	FA	FR	POS	TPR
1927	Bos-N	11	9	3	0	0	0	0	0	0	3	.000	.000	.000	-99	-3	-2	0	0			1.000	0	/O	-0.2
1928	Bos-N	9	4	2	1	0	0	0	0	0	1	.250	.250	.250	33	-0	-0	0	0			1.000	-0	/O	0.0
Total	2	20	13	5	1	0	0	0	0	0	4	.077	.077	.077	-63	-3	-3	0	0			1.000	0	/O	-0.2

■ BOB McNAMARA McNamara, Robert Maxey b: 9/19/16, Denver, Colo. BR/TR, 5'10", 170 lbs. Deb: 5/27/39

YEAR	TM/L	G	AB	R	H	2B	3B	HR	RBI	BB	SO	AVG	OBP	SLG	PRO+	BR	/A	RC	SB	CS	SBR	FA	FR	POS	TPR
1939	Phi-A	9	9	0	2	1	0	0	3	1	1	.222	.300	.333	63	-1	-1	1	0	0	0	1.000	0	/3S12	0.0

■ TOM McNAMARA McNamara, Thomas Henry b: 11/5/1895, Roxbury, Mass. d: 5/5/74, Danvers, Mass. BR/TR, 6'2", 200 lbs. Deb: 6/25/22

YEAR	TM/L	G	AB	R	H	2B	3B	HR	RBI	BB	SO	AVG	OBP	SLG	PRO+	BR	/A	RC	SB	CS	SBR	FA	FR	POS	TPR
1922	Pit-N	1	1	0	0	0	0	0	0	0	0	.000	.000	.000	-99	-0	-0	0	0	0	0	.000	0	H	0.0

■ RUSTY McNEALY McNealy, Robert Lee b: 8/12/58, Sacramento, Cal. BL/TL, 5'8", 160 lbs. Deb: 9/04/83

YEAR	TM/L	G	AB	R	H	2B	3B	HR	RBI	BB	SO	AVG	OBP	SLG	PRO+	BR	/A	RC	SB	CS	SBR	FA	FR	POS	TPR
1983	Oak-A	15	4	5	0	0	0	0	0	0	0	.000	.000	.000	-99	-1	-1	0	0	1	-1	1.000	-2	/OD	-0.4

■ EARL McNEELY McNeely, George Earl b: 5/12/1898, Sacramento, Cal. d: 7/16/71, Sacramento, Cal. BR/TR, 5'9", 155 lbs. Deb: 8/09/24 C

YEAR	TM/L	G	AB	R	H	2B	3B	HR	RBI	BB	SO	AVG	OBP	SLG	PRO+	BR	/A	RC	SB	CS	SBR	FA	FR	POS	TPR
1924	*Was-A	43	179	31	59	5	6	0	15	5	21	.330	.355	.425	104	-0	0	27	3	1	0	.973	-2	O	-0.4
1925	*Was-A	122	385	76	110	14	2	3	37	48	54	.286	.378	.356	89	-6	-5	53	14	16	-5	.975	-2	*O/1	-1.7
1926	Was-A	124	442	84	134	20	12	0	48	44	28	.303	.373	.403	105	2	3	70	18	6	2	.969	0	*O	-0.2
1927	Was-A	73	185	40	51	10	4	0	16	11	13	.276	.320	.373	80	-6	-6	20	11	4	1	.977	-7	O/1	-1.4
1928	StL-A	127	496	66	117	27	7	0	44	37	39	.236	.299	.319	61	-27	-29	49	8	6	-1	.984	7	*O	-3.1
1929	StL-A	69	230	27	56	8	1	1	18	7	13	.243	.272	.300	45	-18	-20	19	2	1	0	.980	-7	O	-2.9
1930	StL-A	76	235	33	64	19	1	0	20	22	14	.272	.340	.362	75	-8	-9	30	8	3	1	.939	-7	O1	-1.8
1931	StL-A	49	102	12	23	4	0	0	15	9	5	.225	.288	.265	45	-8	-8	8	4	4	-1	.969	-5	O/1	-1.6
Total	8	683	2254	369	614	107	33	4	213	183	187	.272	.335	.354	78	-71	-73	275	68	41	-4	.974	-21	O/1	-13.1

■ NORM McNEIL McNeil, Norman Francis b: 10/22/1892, Chicago, Ill. d: 4/11/42, Buffalo, N.Y. BR/TR, 5'11", 180 lbs. Deb: 6/21/19

YEAR	TM/L	G	AB	R	H	2B	3B	HR	RBI	BB	SO	AVG	OBP	SLG	PRO+	BR	/A	RC	SB	CS	SBR	FA	FR	POS	TPR
1919	Bos-A	5	9	0	3	0	0	0	1	1	0	.333	.400	.333	113	0	0	1	0			.818	-2	/C	-0.1

■ JERRY McNERTNEY McNertney, Gerald Edward b: 8/7/36, Boone, Iowa BR/TR, 6'1", 195 lbs. Deb: 4/16/64 C

YEAR	TM/L	G	AB	R	H	2B	3B	HR	RBI	BB	SO	AVG	OBP	SLG	PRO+	BR	/A	RC	SB	CS	SBR	FA	FR	POS	TPR
1964	Chi-A	73	186	16	40	5	0	3	23	19	24	.215	.298	.290	66	-9	-8	16	0	0	0	.987	8	C	0.2
1966	Chi-A	44	59	3	13	0	0	0	1	7	6	.220	.303	.220	57	-3	-3	4	1	1	-0	.969	5	C	0.4
1967	Chi-A	56	123	8	28	6	0	3	13	6	14	.228	.275	.350	87	-3	-2	11	0	0	0	.996	13	C	1.4
1968	Chi-A	74	169	18	37	4	1	3	18	18	29	.219	.302	.308	84	-3	-3	17	0	0	0	.985	14	C/1	1.6
1969	Sea-A	128	410	39	99	18	1	8	55	29	63	.241	.292	.349	80	-13	-12	40	1	0	0	.988	2	*C	-0.4
1970	Mil-A	111	296	27	72	11	1	6	22	22	33	.243	.304	.348	79	-9	-9	27	1	4	-2	.984	-9	C1	-1.7
1971	StL-N	56	128	15	37	4	2	4	22	12	14	.289	.350	.445	119	4	3	19	0	0	0	.985	-3	C	0.2
1972	StL-N	39	48	3	10	3	1	0	9	6	16	.208	.296	.313	74	-2	-2	5	0	0	0	.982	2	C	0.0
1973	Pit-N	9	4	0	1	0	0	0	0	0	0	.250	.250	.250	40	-0	-0	0	0	0	0	1.000	1	/C	0.1
Total	9	590	1423	129	337	51	6	27	163	119	199	.237	.301	.338	81	-37	-35	140	3	5	-2	.987	33	C/1	1.8

■ PAT McNULTY McNulty, Patrick Howard b: 2/27/1899, Cleveland, Ohio d: 5/4/63, Hollywood, Cal. BL/TR, 5'11", 160 lbs. Deb: 9/05/22

YEAR	TM/L	G	AB	R	H	2B	3B	HR	RBI	BB	SO	AVG	OBP	SLG	PRO+	BR	/A	RC	SB	CS	SBR	FA	FR	POS	TPR
1922	Cle-A	22	59	10	16	2	1	0	5	9	5	.271	.368	.339	85	-1	-1	8	4	1	1	.956	-3	O	-0.5
1924	Cle-A	101	291	46	78	13	5	0	26	33	22	.268	.347	.347	78	-9	-9	36	10	8	-2	.961	-4	O	-1.9
1925	Cle-A	118	373	70	117	18	2	6	43	47	23	.314	.392	.421	105	5	4	63	7	7	-2	.965	-2	*O	-0.5
1926	Cle-A	48	56	3	14	2	1	0	6	5	9	.250	.311	.321	65	-3	-3	6	0	1	-1	.909	-2	/O	-0.6
1927	Cle-A	19	41	3	13	1	0	0	4	4	3	.317	.378	.341	87	-1	-1	5	1	2	-1	.906	-1	O	-0.2
Total	5	308	820	132	238	36	9	6	84	98	62	.290	.368	.378	91	-9	-10	118	22	19	-5	.957	-11	O	-3.7

■ BILL McNULTY McNulty, William Francis b: 8/29/46, Sacramento, Cal. BR/TR, 6'4", 205 lbs. Deb: 7/09/69

YEAR	TM/L	G	AB	R	H	2B	3B	HR	RBI	BB	SO	AVG	OBP	SLG	PRO+	BR	/A	RC	SB	CS	SBR	FA	FR	POS	TPR
1969	Oak-A	5	17	0	0	0	0	0	0	0	10	.000	.000	.000	-99	-4	-4	0	0	0	0	1.000	1	/O	-0.3
1972	Oak-A	4	10	0	1	0	0	0	0	2	1	.100	.250	.100	7	-1	-1	0	0	0	0	.800	-2	/3	-0.3
Total	2	9	27	0	1	0	0	0	0	2	11	.037	.103	.037	-61	-6	-5	0	0	0	0	.000	-0	/O3	-0.6

■ BID McPHEE McPhee, John Alexander b: 11/1/1859, Massena, N.Y. d: 1/3/43, San Diego, Cal. BR/TR, 5'8", 152 lbs. Deb: 5/02/1882 M

YEAR	TM/L	G	AB	R	H	2B	3B	HR	RBI	BB	SO	AVG	OBP	SLG	PRO+	BR	/A	RC	SB	CS	SBR	FA	FR	POS	TPR
1882	Cin-a	78	311	43	71	8	7	1		11		.228	.255	.309	84	-3	-6	25				**.920**	-1	*2	-0.5
1883	Cin-a	96	367	61	90	10	10	2		18		.245	.281	.343	95	0	-3	36				**.928**	3	*2	0.1
1884	Cin-a	112	450	107	125	8	7	5		27		.278	.327	.360	121	14	10	54				.924	16	*2	2.6
1885	Cin-a	110	431	78	114	12	4	0		19		.265	.306	.311	96	-1	-2	42				**.936**	6	*2	0.7
1886	Cin-a	140	560	139	150	23	12	**8**		59		.268	.343	.395	129	21	18	92	40			**.939**	31	*2	4.7
1887	Cin-a	129	540	137	156	20	**19**	2		55		.289	.360	.407	113	12	10	116	95			.924	26	*2	3.2
1888	Cin-a	111	458	88	110	12	10	4	51	43		.240	.312	.336	105	6	3	67	54			**.940**	31	*2	3.5
1889	Cin-a	135	540	109	145	25	7	5	57	60	29	.269	.346	.369	103	5	2	93	63			**.946**	**41**	*2/3	4.2
1890	Cin-N	132	528	125	135	16	22	3	39	82	26	.256	.362	.386	121	15	16	96	55			.942	30	*2	4.7
1891	Cin-N	138	562	107	144	14	16	6	38	74	35	.256	.345	.370	109	8	8	85	33			**.954**	23	*2	3.3
1892	Cin-N	144	573	111	157	19	12	4	60	84	48	.274	.373	.370	129	22	23	98	44			.948	25	*2	4.6
1893	Cin-N	127	491	101	138	17	11	3	68	94	20	.281	.401	.379	107	11	9	87	25			.954	**34**	*2	3.7
1894	Cin-N	126	474	107	144	21	9	5	88	90	23	.304	.420	.418	101	7	3	100	33			.945	31	*2	3.0
1895	Cin-N	115	432	107	129	24	12	1	75	73	30	.299	.409	.417	111	13	10	89	30			.955	15	*2	2.4
1896	Cin-N	117	433	81	132	18	7	1	87	51	18	.305	.391	.386	101	7	2	87	48			**.978**	6	*2	1.2
1897	Cin-N	81	282	45	85	13	7	1	39	35		.301	.386	.408	103	5	1	51	9			.966	13	2	1.6
1898	Cin-N	133	486	72	121	26	9	1	60	66		.249	.341	.346	91	-1	-6	68	21			.956	-12	*2/O	-0.9
1899	Cin-N	111	373	60	104	17	7	1	65	40		.279	.360	.370	98	1	-0	59	18			.955	-4	*2/O	0.2
Total	18	2135	8291	1678	2250	303	188	53	727	981	229	.271	.355	.372	108	143	97	1345	568			.944	315	*2/O3	42.3

■ MART McQUAID McQuaid, Mortimer Martin b: 6/28/1861, Chicago, Ill. d: 3/5/28, Chicago, Ill. Deb: 8/15/1891

YEAR	TM/L	G	AB	R	H	2B	3B	HR	RBI	BB	SO	AVG	OBP	SLG	PRO+	BR	/A	RC	SB	CS	SBR	FA	FR	POS	TPR
1891	StL-a	4	11	1	4	2	0	0	1	0	1	.364	.364	.545	141	1	0	3	1			1.000	-1	/2O	0.0
1898	Was-N	1	4	0	0	0	0	0	0	0		.000	.000	.000	-99	-1	-1	0	0			.333	-1	/O	-0.2
Total	2	5	15	1	4	2	0	0	1	0	1	.267	.267	.400	83	-0	-1	3	1			.333	-1	/2O	-0.2

■ JERRY McQUAIG McQuaig, Gerald Joseph b: 1/31/12, Douglas, Ga. BR/TR, 5'11", 183 lbs. Deb: 8/25/34

YEAR	TM/L	G	AB	R	H	2B	3B	HR	RBI	BB	SO	AVG	OBP	SLG	PRO+	BR	/A	RC	SB	CS	SBR	FA	FR	POS	TPR
1934	Phi-A	7	16	2	1	0	0	0	1	2	4	.063	.167	.063	-40	-3	-3	0	0	0	0	.889	-1	/O	-0.5

YEAR	TM/L	G	AB	R	H	2B	3B	HR	RBI	BB	SO	AVG	OBP	SLG	PRO+	BR	/A	RC	SB	CS	SBR	FA	FR	POS	TPR
■ MOX McQUERY		McQuery, William Thomas b: 6/28/1861, Garrard Co., Ky. d: 6/12/1900, Covington, Ky. 6'4", Deb: 8/20/1884																							
1884	Cin-U	35	132	31	37	5	0	2		8		.280	.321	.364	122	4	3	16				.978	1	1	0.0
1885	Det-N	70	278	34	76	15	4	3	30	8	29	.273	.294	.388	119	5	5	33				.976	5	1/O	0.2
1886	KC-N	122	449	62	111	27	4	4	38	36	44	.247	.303	.352	93	-1	-5	50	4			.969	1	*1	-1.7
1890	Syr-a	122	461	64	142	17	6	2		53		.308	.383	.384	144	18	25	80	26			.972	-1	*1	1.6
1891	Was-a	68	261	40	63	9	4	2	37	18	19	.241	.305	.330	88	-6	-4	28	3			.977	1	1	-0.5
Total	5	417	1581	231	429	73	18	13	105	123	92	.271	.327	.365	113	21	24	206	33			.973	7	1/O	-0.4
■ GLENN McQUILLEN		McQuillen, Glenn Richard "Red" b: 4/19/15, Strasburg, Va. d: 6/8/89, Gardenville, Md. BR/TR, 6', 198 lbs. Deb: 6/16/38																							
1938	StL-A	43	116	14	33	4	0	0	13	4	12	.284	.308	.319	57	-8	-8	11	0	1	-1	.971	-0	O	-0.8
1941	StL-A	7	21	4	7	2	1	0	3	1	2	.333	.364	.524	128	1	1	3	0	1	-1	.933	-0	/O	0.0
1942	StL-A	100	339	40	96	15	12	3	47	10	17	.283	.306	.425	103	-0	-1	37	1	1	-0	.969	-5	O	-1.1
1946	StL-A	59	166	24	40	3	3	1	12	19	18	.241	.319	.313	73	-5	-6	16	0	2	-1	.977	-2	O	-1.1
1947	StL-A	1	1	0	0	0	0	0	0	0	0	.000	.000	.000	-98	-0	-0	0	0	0	0	.000	0	H	0.0
Total	5	210	643	82	176	24	16	4	75	34	49	.274	.311	.379	87	-12	-14	67	1	5	-3	.970	-7	O	-3.0
■ GEORGE McQUINN		McQuinn, George Hartley b: 5/29/10, Arlington, Va. d: 12/24/78, Alexandria, Va. BL/TL, 5'11", 165 lbs. Deb: 4/14/36																							
1936	Cin-N	38	134	5	27	3	4	0	13	10	22	.201	.262	.284	50	-10	-9	11	0			.992	1	1	-1.2
1938	StL-A	148	602	100	195	42	7	12	82	58	49	.324	.384	.477	115	13	13	110	4	5	-2	.992	-0	*1	-0.6
1939	StL-A☆	154	617	101	195	37	13	20	94	65	42	.316	.383	.515	125	24	22	122	6	5	-1	.993	10	*1	1.3
1940	StL-A☆	151	594	78	166	39	10	16	84	57	58	.279	.343	.460	104	4	2	95	3	3	-1	**.992**	10	*1	-0.3
1941	StL-A	130	495	93	147	28	4	18	80	74	30	.297	.388	.479	124	21	18	96	5	4	-1	**.995**	8	*1	1.6
1942	StL-A☆	145	554	86	145	32	5	12	78	60	77	.262	.335	.403	105	4	3	78	1	1	-0	.991	1	*1	-0.5
1943	StL-A	125	449	53	109	19	2	12	74	56	65	.243	.327	.374	103	2	1	58	4	3	-1	.992	2	*1	-0.4
1944	*StL-A★	146	516	83	129	26	3	11	72	85	74	.250	.357	.376	103	8	4	79	4	3	-1	**.994**	-5	*1	-0.9
1945	StL-A	139	483	69	134	31	3	7	61	65	51	.277	.364	.398	115	14	11	75	1	1	-0	.991	4	*1	0.6
1946	Phi-A	136	484	47	109	23	6	3	35	64	62	.225	.317	.316	78	-14	-14	54	4	2	0	.988	3	*1	-1.9
1947	*NY-A★	144	517	84	157	24	3	13	80	78	66	.304	.395	.437	132	23	24	97	0	2	-1	.994	-2	*1	1.7
1948	NY-A★	94	302	33	75	11	4	11	41	40	38	.248	.336	.421	102	-1	-0	45	0	2	-1	.993	-1	1	-0.3
Total	12	1550	5747	832	1588	315	64	135	794	712	634	.276	.357	.424	109	88	76	920	32	31		.992	31	*1	-0.9
■ BRIAN McRAE		McRae, Brian Wesley b: 8/27/67, Bradenton, Fla. BB/TR, 6', 175 lbs. Deb: 8/07/90 F																							
1990	KC-A	46	168	21	48	8	3	2	23	9	29	.286	.322	.405	104	0	0	20	4	3	-1	1.000	4	O	0.2
1991	KC-A	152	629	86	164	28	9	8	64	24	99	.261	.290	.372	81	-17	-17	64	20	11	-1	.993	8	*O	-1.4
1992	KC-A	149	533	63	119	23	5	4	52	42	88	.223	.287	.308	66	-24	-24	49	18	5	2	.993	10	*O	-1.6
Total	3	347	1330	170	331	59	17	14	139	75	216	.249	.293	.350	78	-41	-41	134	42	19	1	.994	22	O	-2.8
■ HAL McRAE		McRae, Harold Abraham b: 7/10/45, Avon Park, Fla. BR/TR, 5'11", 180 lbs. Deb: 7/11/68 FCM																							
1968	Cin-N	17	51	1	10	1	0	0	2	4	14	.196	.255	.216	40	-3	-4	2	1	1	-0	.926	-4	2	-0.8
1970	*Cin-N	70	165	18	41	6	1	8	23	15	23	.248	.315	.442	100	-0	-1	21	0	2	-1	.981	-5	O/32	-0.8
1971	Cin-N	99	337	39	89	24	2	9	34	11	35	.264	.291	.427	103	-1	-0	39	3	2	-0	.966	-3	O	-0.8
1972	*Cin-N	61	97	9	27	4	0	5	26	2	10	.278	.307	.474	126	2	2	12	0	0	0	.867	-4	O3	-0.3
1973	KC-A	106	338	36	79	18	3	9	50	34	38	.234	.315	.385	89	-2	-5	41	2	2	-1	.963	-4	OD/3	-1.3
1974	KC-A	148	539	71	167	36	4	15	88	54	68	.310	.378	.475	136	30	27	95	11	8	-2	.950	2	DO/3	2.6
1975	KC-A★	126	480	58	147	38	6	5	71	47	47	.306	.373	.442	126	19	17	75	11	8	-2	.986	-1	*OD/3	1.0
1976	*KC-A★	149	527	75	175	34	5	8	73	64	43	.332	**.412**	.461	154	39	**38**	101	22	12	-1	.970	-0	*DO	3.8
1977	*KC-A	162	641	104	191	**54**	11	21	92	59	43	.298	.369	.515	137	33	32	119	18	14	-3	.958	4	*DO	3.1
1978	*KC-A	156	623	90	170	39	5	16	72	51	62	.273	.334	.429	110	10	8	87	17	8	0	1.000	0	*D/O	0.8
1979	KC-A	101	393	55	113	32	4	10	74	38	46	.288	.356	.466	117	11	10	66	5	4	-1	.000	0	*D	0.8
1980	*KC-A	124	489	73	145	39	5	14	83	29	56	.297	.346	.483	123	15	15	79	10	2	2	1.000	-1	*D/O	1.5
1981	*KC-A	101	389	38	106	23	2	7	36	34	33	.272	.334	.396	111	5	5	49	3	4	-2	.909	0	D/O	0.4
1982	KC-A★	159	613	91	189	**46**	8	27	**133**	55	61	.308	.370	.542	146	38	38	123	4	4	-1	.500	-0	*D/O	3.6
1983	KC-A	157	589	84	183	41	6	12	82	50	68	.311	.374	.462	128	24	23	98	2	3	-1	.000	0	*D	2.2
1984	*KC-A	106	317	30	96	13	4	3	42	34	47	.303	.372	.397	112	7	6	45	0	3	-2	.000	0	D	0.4
1985	*KC-A	112	320	41	83	19	0	14	70	44	45	.259	.351	.450	117	8	8	49	0	1	-1	.000	0	*D	0.7
1986	KC-A	112	278	22	70	14	0	7	37	18	39	.252	.300	.378	81	-7	-8	29	0	0	0	.000	0	D	-0.8
1987	KC-A	18	32	5	10	3	0	1	9	5	1	.313	.405	.500	135	2	2	6	0	0	0	.000	0	/D	0.2
Total	19	2084	7218	940	2091	484	66	191	1097	648	779	.290	.355	.454	122	227	213	1138	109	78	-14	.966	-16	*DO/32	16.3
■ MC REMER		McRemer Deb: 6/20/1884																							
1884	Was-U	1	3	0	0	0	0	0		0		.000	.000	.000	-99	-1	-1	0				1.000	0	/O	0.0
■ KEVIN McREYNOLDS		McReynolds, Walter Kevin b: 10/16/59, Little Rock, Ark. BR/TR, 6'1", 210 lbs. Deb: 6/02/83																							
1983	SD-N	39	140	15	31	3	1	4	14	12	29	.221	.283	.343	75	-5	-5	14	2	1	0	.989	3	O	-0.3
1984	*SD-N	147	525	68	146	26	6	20	75	34	69	.278	.322	.465	119	11	11	72	3	6	-3	.991	18	*O	2.3
1985	SD-N	152	564	61	132	24	4	15	75	43	81	.234	.292	.371	85	-13	-12	59	4	0	1	.993	23	*O	0.7
1986	SD-N	158	560	89	161	31	6	26	96	66	83	.287	.364	.504	140	27	29	103	8	6	-1	.977	-14	*O	0.9
1987	NY-N	151	590	86	163	32	5	29	95	39	70	.276	.322	.495	119	8	12	93	14	1	4	.987	9	*O	1.9
1988	*NY-N	147	552	82	159	30	2	27	99	38	56	.288	.338	.496	144	24	27	97	21	0	6	.985	10	*O	4.1
1989	NY-N	148	545	74	148	25	3	22	85	46	74	.272	.329	.450	127	13	16	80	15	7	0	.969	15	*O	2.9
1990	NY-N	147	521	75	140	23	1	24	82	71	61	.269	.358	.455	122	16	16	88	9	2	2	.988	5	*O	2.0
1991	NY-N	143	522	65	135	32	1	16	74	49	46	.259	.325	.416	108	4	4	70	6	6	-2	.993	2	*O	0.1
1992	KC-A	109	373	45	92	25	0	13	49	67	48	.247	.361	.418	117	10	10	61	7	1	2	.986	-3	*O/D	0.6
Total	10	1341	4892	660	1307	251	29	196	744	465	617	.267	.332	.451	119	95	108	736	89	30	9	.986	69	*O/D	15.2
■ PETE McSHANNIC		McShannic, Peter Robert b: 3/20/1864, Pittsburgh, Pa. d: 11/30/46, Toledo, Ohio BB/TR, 5'7", 190 lbs. Deb: 9/15/1888																							
1888	Pit-N	26	98	5	19	1	0	0	5	1	9	.194	.218	.204	40	-7	-6	5	3			.907	-0	3	-0.5
■ TRICK McSORLEY		McSorley, John Bernard b: 12/6/1858, St.Louis, Mo. d: 2/9/36, St.Louis, Mo. TR , 5'4", 142 lbs. Deb: 5/06/1875																							
1875	RS-n	15	52	4	11	0	0	0		0		.212	.212	.212	52	-3	-2	2						/3O	-0.2
1884	Tol-a	21	68	12	17	1	0	0		3		.250	.282	.265	79	-1	-2	5				.974	1	1/O3P	-0.2
1885	StL-N	2	6	2	3	1	0	0	1	2	1	.500	.625	.667	340	2	2	3				.400	-2	/3	0.0
1886	StL-a	5	20	1	3	3	0	0		0		.150	.150	.300	39	-1	-2	1	0			.765	-3	/S	-0.4
Total	3	28	94	15	23	5	0	0	1	5	1	.245	.283	.298	87	-1	-1	9	0			.400	-4	/1SO3P	-0.6
■ PAUL McSWEENEY		McSweeney, Paul A. b: 4/3/1867, St.Louis, Mo. d: 8/12/51, St.Louis, Mo. Deb: 9/20/1891																							
1891	StL-a	3	12	2	3	1	0	0	2	0	0	.250	.308	.333	75	-0	-1	2	1			.643	-2	/23	-0.2
■ JIM McTAMANY		McTamany, James Edward b: 7/1/1863, Philadelphia, Pa. d: 4/16/16, Lenni, Pa. BR/TR, 5'8", 190 lbs. Deb: 8/15/1885																							
1885	Bro-a	35	131	21	36	7	2	1		9		.275	.321	.382	123	4	3	16				.896	-5	O	-0.3
1886	Bro-a	111	418	86	106	23	10	2		54		.254	.353	.371	128	16	15	63	18			.893	14	*O	2.3
1887	Bro-a	134	520	123	134	22	10	1		76		.258	.365	.344	99	4	3	92	66			.918	8	*O	0.6
1888	KC-a	130	516	94	127	12	10	4	41	67		.246	.345	.331	113	15	10	80	55			.913	6	*O	1.1
1889	Col-a	139	529	113	146	21	7	4	52	116	66	.276	.407	.365	129	22	28	97	40			.902	-5	*O	1.6
1890	Col-a	125	466	**140**	120	27	7	1		**112**		.258	.405	.352	136	22	28	86	43			.940	2	*O	2.3

YEAR	TM/L	G	AB	R	H	2B	3B	HR	RBI	BB	SO	AVG	OBP	SLG	PRO+	BR	/A	RC	SB	CS	SBR	FA	FR	POS	TPR
1891	Col-a	81	304	59	76	17	9	3	35	58	48	.250	.374	.395	130	10	14	54	20			.929	-3	O	0.7
	Phi-a	58	218	57	49	6	3	3	21	43	44	.225	.365	.321	96	2	1	31	13			.901	0	O	-0.1
	Yr	139	522	116	125	23	12	6	56	101	92	.239	.370	.364	115	12	14	85	33			.917	-2	*O	0.6
Total	7	813	3102	693	794	135	58	19	149	535	158	.256	.373	.355	119	95	101	519	255			.913	16	O	8.2
■ **BILL McTIGUE**	McTigue, William Patrick "Rebel" b: 1/3/1891, Nashville, Tenn. d: 5/8/20, Nashville, Tenn. BL/TL, 6'1.5", 175 lbs. Deb: 5/02/11																								
1911	Bos-N	14	12	1	1	1	0	0	0	0	5	.083	.083	.167	-28	-2	-2	0	0			.875	-1	P	0.0
1912	Bos-N	10	13	2	1	0	0	0	1	1	5	.077	.143	.077	-38	-2	-3	0	0			1.000	1	P	0.0
1913	Bos-N	1	0	0	0	0	0	0	0	0	0	—	—	—	—	0	0	0	0			.000	0	R	0.0
1916	Det-A	3	1	0	0	0	0	0	0	0	0	.000	.000	.000	-97	-0	-0	0	0			1.000	0	/P	0.0
Total	4	28	26	3	2	1	0	0	1	1	10	.077	.111	.115	-36	-5	-5	0	0			.957	0	/P	0.0
■ **CAL McVEY**	McVey, Calvin Alexander b: 8/30/1850, Montrose, Iowa d: 8/20/26, San Francisco, Cal BR/TR, 5'9", 170 lbs. Deb: 5/05/1871 M																								
1871	Bos-n	29	153	43	**66**	9	5	0	43	1	2	.431	.435	.556	177	16	14	41	6					*C/O	0.9
1872	Bos-n	46	237	56	73	11	3	0	41	0	1	.308	.308	.380	105	3	-0	30						*C/O	0.0
1873	Bal-n	38	192	49	73	8	5	3	33	3	2	.380	.390	.521	166	15	15	40						C/OS213M	1.1
1874	Bos-n	70	341	**91**	**124**	22	4	4		0		.364	.364	.487	159	**25**	21	**62**						*OC	**1.7**
1875	Bos-n	82	389	88	137	**33**	9	3		1		.352	.354	**.506**	187	**35**	**33**	**71**						*1OC/P	**2.8**
1876	Chi-N	63	308	62	107	15	0	1	53	2	4	.347	.352	.406	136	16	10	45				.959	4	*1P/CO3	1.0
1877	Chi-N	60	266	58	98	9	7	0	36	8	11	.368	.387	.455	147	19	14	48				.859	-13	*C3P/21	0.1
1878	Cin-N	61	271	43	83	10	4	2	28	5	10	.306	.319	.395	147	9	13	35				.814	-10	*3/CM	0.5
1879	Cin-N	81	354	64	105	18	6	0	55	8	13	.297	.312	.381	134	10	12	43				.946	-7	*1/OP3CM	0.2
Total	5 n	265	1312	327	473	83	26	10	117	5	5	.361	.363	.486	160	93	84	244						C/O1S2P3	6.5
Total	4	265	1199	227	393	52	17	3	172	23	38	.328	.340	.407	140	54	50	171				.951	-26	1/3CPO2	1.8
■ **GEORGE McVEY**	McVey, George W. b: 1864, Port Jervis, N.Y. d: 5/3/1896, Quincy, Ill. BR/TR, 6'1", 185 lbs. Deb: 9/19/1885																								
1885	Bro-a	6	21	2	3	0	0	0		2		.143	.217	.143	17	-2	-2	1				.967	-0	/1C	-0.2
■ **BILL McWILLIAMS**	McWilliams, William Henry b: 11/28/10, Dubuque, Iowa BR/TR, 6', 185 lbs. Deb: 7/08/31																								
1931	Bos-A	2	2	0	0	0	0	0	0	0	1	.000	.000	.000	-99	-1	-1	0	0	0	0	.000	0	H	-0.1
■ **BOB MEACHAM**	Meacham, Robert Andrew b: 8/25/60, Los Angeles, Cal. BB/TR, 6'1", 180 lbs. Deb: 6/30/83																								
1983	NY-A	22	51	5	12	2	0	0	4	4	10	.235	.304	.275	63	-3	-2	6	8	0	2	.929	9	S/3	1.0
1984	NY-A	99	360	62	91	13	4	2	25	32	70	.253	.319	.328	83	-10	-8	41	9	5	-0	.955	-12	S/2	-1.1
1985	NY-A	156	481	70	105	16	2	1	47	54	102	.218	.304	.266	59	-27	-25	45	25	7	3	.963	-17	*S	-2.3
1986	NY-A	56	161	19	36	7	1	0	10	17	39	.224	.309	.280	62	-8	-8	13	3	6	-3	.948	-5	S	-1.0
1987	NY-A	77	203	28	55	11	1	5	21	19	33	.271	.351	.409	102	1	1	30	6	5	-1	.961	-1	S2/D	0.3
1988	NY-A	47	115	18	25	9	0	0	7	14	22	.217	.313	.296	72	-4	-4	13	7	1	2	.959	-7	S2/3	-0.8
Total	6	457	1371	202	324	58	8	8	114	140	276	.236	.316	.308	73	-50	-46	147	58	24	3	.957	-32	S/23D	-3.9
■ **CHARLIE MEAD**	Mead, Charles Richard b: 4/9/21, Vermilion, Alt., Canada BL/TR, 6'1.5", 185 lbs. Deb: 8/28/43																								
1943	NY-N	37	146	9	40	6	1	1	13	10	15	.274	.321	.349	93	-1	-2	16	3			.976	1	O	-0.3
1944	NY-N	39	78	5	14	1	0	1	8	5	7	.179	.229	.231	30	-7	-7	4	0			.981	2	O	-0.7
1945	NY-N	11	37	4	10	1	0	1	6	5	2	.270	.357	.378	103	0	0	5	0			.962	1	O	0.1
Total	3	87	261	18	64	8	1	3	27	20	24	.245	.299	.318	75	-8	-9	26	3			.975	3	/O	-0.9
■ **LOUIE MEADOWS**	Meadows, Michael Ray b: 4/29/61, Maysville, N.C. BL/TL, 5'11", 190 lbs. Deb: 7/03/86																								
1986	Hou-N	6	6	1	2	0	0	0	0	0	0	.333	.333	.333	87	-0	-0	1	1	0	0	.000	-0	/O	0.0
1988	Hou-N	35	42	5	8	0	1	2	3	6	8	.190	.292	.381	95	-0	-0	5	4	2	0	1.000	0	O	0.0
1989	Hou-N	31	51	5	9	0	0	3	10	1	14	.176	.192	.353	55	-3	-3	3	1	2	-1	1.000	-4	O/1	-0.9
1990	Hou-N	15	14	3	2	0	0	0	0	2	4	.143	.250	.143	11	-2	-2	1	0	0	0	1.000	-2	/O	-0.4
	Phi-N	15	14	1	1	0	0	0	0	1	2	.071	.133	.071	-42	-3	-3	0	0	0	0	1.000	-2	/O	-0.5
	Yr	30	28	4	3	0	0	0	0	3	6	.107	.194	.107	-15	-4	-4	1	0	0	0	1.000	-4	O	-0.9
Total	4	102	127	15	22	0	1	5	13	10	28	.173	.234	.307	54	-8	-8	9	6	4	-1	1.000	-9	/O1	-1.8
■ **PAT MEANEY**	Meaney, Patrick J. b: 1870, Philadelphia, Pa. d: 10/20/22, Philadelphia, Pa. TL , Deb: 5/18/12																								
1912	Det-A	1	2	0	0	0	0	0	0	1		.000	.500	.000	48	0	0	0	0			.833	-0	/S	0.0
■ **CHARLIE MEARA**	Meara, Charles Edward "Goggy" b: 4/13/1891, New York, N.Y. d: 2/8/62, Bronx, N.Y. BL/TR, 5'10", 160 lbs. Deb: 6/01/14																								
1914	NY-A	4	7	2	2	0	0	0	1	2	2	.286	.444	.286	120	0	0	1	0	1	-1	1.000	-1	/O	-0.1
■ **RAY MEDEIROS**	Medeiros, Ray Antone "Pep" b: 5/9/26, Oakland, Cal. BR/TR, 5'10", 163 lbs. Deb: 4/25/45																								
1945	Cin-N	1	0	0	0	0	0	0	0	0	0	—	—	—	—	0	0	0	0			.000	0	R	0.0
■ **LUIS MEDINA**	Medina, Luis Main b: 3/26/63, Santa Monica, Cal. BR/TL, 6'4", 200 lbs. Deb: 9/02/88																								
1988	Cle-A	16	51	10	13	0	0	6	8	2	18	.255	.309	.608	146	3	3	10	0	0	0	1.000	-0	1	0.2
1989	Cle-A	30	83	8	17	1	0	4	8	6	35	.205	.258	.361	72	-3	-3	7	0	1	-1	.500	-1	D/O1	-0.6
1991	Cle-A	5	16	0	1	0	0	0	0	1	7	.063	.118	.063	-48	-3	-3	0	0	0	0	.000	0	/D	-0.3
Total	3	51	150	18	31	1	0	10	16	9	60	.207	.261	.413	85	-3	-4	17	0	1	-1	1.000	-2	/D1O	-0.7
■ **JOE MEDWICK**	Medwick, Joseph Michael "Ducky" or "Muscles" b: 11/24/11, Carteret, N.J. d: 3/21/75, St.Petersburg, Fla BR/TR, 5'10", 187 lbs. Deb: 9/02/32 H																								
1932	StL-N	26	106	13	37	12	1	2	12	2	10	.349	.367	.538	136	5	5	21	3			.970	0	O	0.4
1933	StL-N	148	595	92	182	40	10	18	98	26	56	.306	.337	.497	129	25	21	97	5			.980	8	*O	2.2
1934	*StL-N★	149	620	110	198	40	**18**	18	106	21	83	.319	.343	.529	122	23	18	109	3			.960	4	*O	1.5
1935	StL-N★	154	634	132	224	46	13	23	126	30	59	.353	.386	.576	149	46	43	139	4			.965	3	*O	3.8
1936	StL-N★	155	636	115	**223**	**64**	13	18	**138**	34	33	.351	.387	.577	157	47	47	141	3			.985	14	*O	5.3
1937	StL-N★	156	633	**111**	**237**	**56**	10	**31**	**154**	41	50	**.374**	.414	**.641**	**179**	**69**	**67**	**170**	4			**.988**	4	*O	**6.3**
1938	StL-N★	146	590	100	190	**47**	8	21	**122**	42	41	.322	.369	.536	138	34	30	113	0			.974	8	*O	3.4
1939	StL-N★	150	606	98	201	48	8	14	117	45	44	.332	.380	.507	128	29	25	114	6			.976	5	*O	2.4
1940	StL-N	37	158	21	48	12	0	3	20	6	8	.304	.329	.437	104	1	0	20	0			.988	-0	O	-0.2
	Bro-N	106	423	62	127	18	12	14	66	26	28	.300	.345	.499	123	16	12	70	2			.980	5	*O	1.2
	Yr	143	581	83	175	30	12	17	86	32	36	.301	.341	.482	118	17	13	90	2			.982	5	*O	1.0
1941	*Bro-N★	133	538	100	171	33	10	18	88	38	35	.318	.364	.517	140	30	27	95	2			.983	1	*O	2.1
1942	Bro-N★	142	553	69	166	37	4	4	96	32	25	.300	.338	.403	115	10	9	72	2			.990	-3	*O	-0.1
1943	Bro-N	48	173	13	47	10	0	0	25	10	8	.272	.315	.329	86	-3	-3	18	1			.971	-5	O	-1.1
	NY-N	78	324	41	91	20	3	5	45	9	14	.281	.300	.407	103	-1	-1	35	0			.988	5	O/1	0.0
	Yr	126	497	54	138	30	3	5	70	19	22	.278	.306	.380	97	-4	-4	53	1			.983	-0	*O/1	-1.1
1944	NY-N★	128	490	64	165	24	3	7	85	38	24	.337	.386	.441	133	21	21	82	2			.993	8	*O	2.3
1945	NY-N	26	92	14	28	4	0	3	11	2	2	.304	.319	.446	110	1	1	12	2			.979	-1	O	-0.1
	Bos-N	66	218	17	62	13	0	0	26	12	12	.284	.325	.344	85	-4	-4	23	3			1.000	1	O1	-0.7
	Yr	92	310	31	90	17	0	3	37	14	14	.290	.323	.374	93	-4	-4	36	5			.992	-0	O1	-0.8
1946	Bro-N	41	77	7	24	4	0	2	18	6	5	.312	.369	.442	128	3	3	13	0			1.000	-3	O/1	-0.1
1947	StL-N	75	150	19	46	12	0	4	28	16	12	.307	.373	.467	117	5	4	26	0			1.000	-5	O	-0.3
1948	StL-N	20	19	0	4	0	0	0	2	1	2	.211	.250	.211	24	-2	-2	1	0			.000	-0	/O	-0.3
Total	17	1984	7635	1198	2471	540	113	205	1383	437	551	.324	.362	.505	133	354	322	1372	42			.980	49	*O/1	28.0

YEAR	TM/L	G	AB	R	H	2B	3B	HR	RBI	BB	SO	AVG	OBP	SLG	PRO+	BR	/A	RC	SB	CS	SBR	FA	FR	POS	TPR

■ TOMMY MEE   Mee, Thomas William "Judge"   b: 3/18/1890, Chicago, Ill.   d: 5/16/81, Chicago, Ill.   BR/TR, 5'8", 165 lbs.   Deb: 6/14/10

| 1910 | StL-A | 8 | 19 | 1 | 3 | 2 | 0 | 0 | 1 | 0 | | .158 | .158 | .263 | 34 | -2 | -1 | 1 | 0 | | | .828 | -1 | /S23 | -0.3 |

■ DAD MEEK   Meek, Frank J.   b: St.Louis, Mo.   d: 12/26/22, St.Louis, Mo.   Deb: 5/10/1889

1889	StL-a	2	2	2	1	0	0	0	1	0	0	.500	.500	.500	166	0	0	1	1			.667	0	/C	0.0
1890	StL-a	4	16	3	5	0	0	0		0		.313	.313	.313	76	-0	-1	2	1			.913	3	/C	0.2
Total	2	6	18	5	6	0	0	0	1	0	0	.333	.333	.333	86	-0	-0	3	2			.898	3	/C	0.2

■ SAMMY MEEKS   Meeks, Samuel Mack   b: 4/23/23, Anderson, S.C.   BR/TR, 5'9", 160 lbs.   Deb: 4/29/48

1948	Was-A	24	33	4	4	1	0	0	2	1	12	.121	.147	.152	-21	-6	-6	1	0	0	0	.939	-0	S/2	-0.6
1949	Cin-N	16	36	10	11	2	0	2	6	2	6	.306	.342	.528	128	1	1	6	1			1.000	6	/2S	0.7
1950	Cin-N	39	95	7	27	5	0	1	8	6	14	.284	.327	.368	82	-2	-2	11	1			.951	-4	S/3	-0.5
1951	Cin-N	23	35	4	8	0	0	0	2	0	4	.229	.229	.229	23	-4	-4	1	1	0	0	.929	-1	/3S	-0.5
Total	4	102	199	25	50	8	0	3	18	9	36	.251	.284	.337	64	-11	-11	20	3	0		.953	0	/S23	-0.9

■ DUTCH MEIER   Meier, Arthur Ernst   b: 3/30/1879, St.Louis, Mo.   d: 3/23/48, Chicago, Ill.   BR/TR, 5'10", 175 lbs.   Deb: 5/12/06

| 1906 | Pit-N | 82 | 273 | 32 | 70 | 11 | 4 | 0 | 16 | 13 | | .256 | .298 | .326 | 91 | -2 | -4 | 29 | 4 | | | .975 | -12 | OS | -1.9 |

■ DAVE MEIER   Meier, David Keith   b: 8/8/59, Helena, Mont.   BR/TR, 6', 185 lbs.   Deb: 4/03/84

1984	Min-A	59	147	18	35	8	1	0	13	6	9	.238	.273	.306	57	-8	-9	11	0	1	-1	.978	-4	O/3D	-1.5
1985	Min-A	71	104	15	27	6	0	1	8	18	12	.260	.374	.346	93	1	-0	13	0	6	-4	.987	-9	O/D	-1.4
1987	Tex-A	13	21	4	6	1	0	0	0	0	5	.286	.286	.333	63	-1	-1	1	0	0	0	.917	-1	/O	-0.2
1988	Chi-N	2	5	0	2	0	0	0	1	0	1	.400	.400	.400	125	0	0	1	0	0	0	1.000	-1	/3	-0.1
Total	4	145	277	37	70	15	1	1	22	24	26	.253	.317	.325	73	-8	-10	27	0	7	-4	.978	-15	O/D3	-3.2

■ WALT MEINERT   Meinert, Walter Henry   b: 12/11/1890, New York, N.Y.   d: 11/9/58, Decatur, Ill.   BL/TL, 5'7.5", 150 lbs.   Deb: 9/06/13

| 1913 | StL-A | 4 | 8 | 1 | 3 | 0 | 0 | 0 | 0 | 1 | 3 | .375 | .444 | .375 | 144 | 0 | 0 | 2 | 1 | | | 1.000 | -0 | /O | 0.0 |

■ FRANK MEINKE   Meinke, Frank Louis   b: 10/18/1863, Chicago, Ill.   d: 11/8/31, Chicago, Ill.   5'10.5", 172 lbs.   Deb: 5/01/1884   F

1884	Det-N	92	341	28	56	5	7	6	24	6	89	.164	.179	.273	42	-23	-20	17				.839	-3	SP/O32	-1.2
1885	Det-N	1	3	0	0	0	0	0	0	0	1	.000	.000	.000	-99	-1	-1	0				1.000	-0	/OP	0.0
Total	2	93	344	28	56	5	7	6	24	6	90	.163	.177	.270	41	-24	-21	17				1.000	-3	/SPO23	-1.2

■ BOB MEINKE   Meinke, Robert Bernard   b: 6/25/1887, Chicago, Ill.   d: 12/29/52, Chicago, Ill.   BR/TR, 5'10", 135 lbs.   Deb: 8/22/10   F

| 1910 | Cin-N | 2 | 1 | 0 | 0 | 0 | 0 | 0 | 0 | 1 | 0 | .000 | .500 | .000 | 51 | 0 | 0 | 0 | 0 | | | 1.000 | 1 | /S | 0.1 |

■ GEORGE MEISTER   Meister, George B.   b: 6/5/1864, Dorzbach, Germany   d: 8/24/08, Pittsburgh, Pa.   Deb: 8/15/1884

| 1884 | Tol-a | 34 | 119 | 9 | 23 | 6 | 0 | 0 | | 3 | | .193 | .244 | .244 | 60 | -5 | -5 | 7 | | | | .817 | -9 | 3 | -1.3 |

■ JOHN MEISTER   Meister, John F.   b: 5/10/1863, Allentown, Pa.   d: 1/17/23, Philadelphia, Pa.   Deb: 8/24/1886

1886	NY-a	45	186	35	44	7	3	2		4		.237	.253	.339	90	-4	-2	17	1			.906	-8	2	-0.8
1887	NY-a	39	157	24	35	6	2	1		16		.223	.303	.306	75	-6	-4	18	9			.930	-9	O2/3S	-1.1
Total	2	84	343	59	79	13	5	3		20		.230	.277	.324	83	-9	-7	34	10			.905	-17	/2O3S	-1.9

■ KARL MEISTER   Meister, Karl Daniel "Dutch"   b: 5/15/1891, Marietta, Ohio   d: 8/15/67, Marietta, Ohio   BR/TR, 6', 178 lbs.   Deb: 8/10/13

| 1913 | Cin-N | 4 | 7 | 1 | 2 | 1 | 0 | 0 | | 0 | 4 | .286 | .286 | .429 | 103 | -0 | -0 | 1 | 0 | | | .667 | -2 | /O | -0.2 |

■ MOXIE MEIXELL   Meixell, Merton Merrill   b: 10/18/1887, Lake Crystal, Minn   d: 8/17/82, Los Angeles, Cal.   BL/TR, 5'10", 168 lbs.   Deb: 7/07/12

| 1912 | Cle-A | 3 | 2 | 0 | 1 | 0 | 0 | 0 | 0 | 0 | | .500 | .500 | .500 | 180 | 0 | 0 | 0 | 0 | | | .000 | 0 | /O | 0.0 |

■ ROMAN MEJIAS   Mejias, Roman (Gomez)   b: 8/9/30, Abreus, Las Villas, Cuba   BR/TR, 6', 175 lbs.   Deb: 4/13/55

1955	Pit-N	71	167	14	36	8	1	3	21	9	13	.216	.256	.329	55	-11	-11	13	1	3	-2	.926	-0	O	-1.4
1957	Pit-N	58	142	12	39	7	4	2	15	6	13	.275	.309	.423	97	-2	-1	17	2	2	-1	1.000	-2	O	-0.5
1958	Pit-N	76	157	17	42	3	2	5	19	2	27	.268	.281	.408	82	-5	-5	17	2	0	1	.973	-1	O	-0.7
1959	Pit-N	96	276	28	65	6	1	7	28	21	48	.236	.301	.341	71	-12	-11	28	2	1	-1	.970	-0	O	-1.6
1960	Pit-N	3	1	1	0	0	0	0	0	0	1	.000	.000	.000	-99	-0	-0	0	0	0	0	.000	0	H	0.0
1961	Pit-N	4	1	1	0	0	0	0	0	0	0	.000	.000	.000	-99	-0	-0	0	0	0	0	1.000	0	/O	0.0
1962	Hou-N	146	566	82	162	12	3	24	76	30	83	.286	.329	.445	114	3	8	81	12	4	1	.946	-4	*O	-0.3
1963	Bos-A	111	357	43	81	18	0	11	39	14	36	.227	.262	.370	72	-13	-14	32	4	1	1	.973	2	O	-1.7
1964	Bos-A	62	101	14	24	3	1	2	4	7	16	.238	.294	.347	74	-3	-4	9	0	0	0	.962	-3	O	-0.8
Total	9	627	1768	212	449	57	12	54	202	89	238	.254	.296	.391	86	-43	-38	197	22	12	-1	.963	-8	O	-7.0

■ SAM MEJIAS   Mejias, Samuel Elias   b: 5/9/52, Santiago, D.R.   BR/TR, 6', 170 lbs.   Deb: 9/06/76

1976	StL-N	18	21	1	3	1	0	0	0	2	2	.143	.217	.190	16	-2	-2	1	2	0	1	1.000	2	O	0.0
1977	Mon-N	74	101	14	23	4	1	3	8	2	17	.228	.243	.376	65	-5	-5	9	1	0	0	.966	3	O	-0.3
1978	Mon-N	67	56	9	13	1	0	0	6	2	5	.232	.259	.250	43	-4	-4	3	0	0	0	.949	3	O/P	-0.2
1979	Chi-N	31	11	4	2	0	0	0	0	2	5	.182	.308	.182	34	-1	-1	1	0	0	0	.875	1	O	-0.1
	Cin-N	7	2	1	1	0	0	0	0	0	0	.500	.500	.500	173	0	0	1	0	0	0	1.000	0	/O	0.0
	Yr	38	13	5	3	0	0	0	0	2	5	.231	.333	.231	53	-1	-1	1	0	0	0	.889	1	O	-0.1
1980	Cin-N	71	108	16	30	5	1	1	10	6	13	.278	.322	.370	93	-1	-1	13	4	2	0	.989	8	O	0.6
1981	Cin-N	66	49	6	14	2	0	0	7	2	9	.286	.314	.327	80	-1	-1	5	1	0	0	.972	2	O	0.1
Total	6	334	348	51	86	13	2	4	31	16	51	.247	.282	.330	69	-15	-15	32	8	2	1	.973	18	O/P	0.1

■ DUTCH MELE   Mele, Albert Ernest   b: 1/11/15, New York, N.Y.   d: 2/12/75, Hollywood, Fla.   BL/TL, 6'0.5", 195 lbs.   Deb: 9/14/37

| 1937 | Cin-N | 6 | 14 | 1 | 2 | 1 | 0 | 0 | 1 | 1 | 1 | .143 | .200 | .214 | 13 | -2 | -2 | 1 | 0 | | | 1.000 | -2 | /O | -0.4 |

■ SAM MELE   Mele, Sabath Anthony   b: 1/21/23, Astoria, N.Y.   BR/TR, 6'1", 187 lbs.   Deb: 4/15/47   MC

1947	Bos-A	123	453	71	137	14	8	12	73	37	35	.302	.356	.448	114	12	8	72	0	3	-2	.992	-3	*O/1	-0.2
1948	Bos-A	66	180	25	42	12	1	2	25	13	21	.233	.292	.344	66	-9	-10	18	1	1	-0	.971	-4	O	-1.6
1949	Bos-A	18	46	1	9	1	1	0	7	7	14	.196	.302	.261	46	-3	-4	4	2	0	1	.955	-0	O	-0.4
	Was-A	78	264	21	64	12	2	3	25	17	34	.242	.288	.337	67	-14	-14	24	2	1	0	.966	-8	O1	-2.5
	Yr	96	310	22	73	13	3	3	32	24	48	.235	.290	.326	63	-18	-18	28	4	1	1	.964	-9	O1	-2.9
1950	Was-A	126	435	57	119	21	6	12	86	51	40	.274	.351	.432	105	-1	2	64	2	0	1	.990	-5	O1	-0.7
1951	Was-A	143	558	58	153	36	7	5	94	32	31	.274	.315	.391	92	-10	-9	64	2	3	-1	.993	3	*O1	-1.2
1952	Was-A	9	28	2	12	3	0	2	10	1	2	.429	.448	.750	237	4	5	10	0	0	0	.917	-1	/O	0.3
	Chi-A	123	423	46	105	18	2	14	59	48	40	.248	.328	.400	101	0	-0	53	1	2	-1	1.000	-6	*O/1	-1.2
	Yr	132	451	48	117	21	2	16	69	49	42	.259	.335	.421	109	5	4	62	1	2	-1	.994	-7	*O/1	-0.9
1953	Chi-A	140	481	64	132	26	8	12	82	58	47	.274	.353	.437	109	8	6	75	3	1	0	.996	-8	*O/1	-0.7
1954	Bal-A	72	230	17	55	9	4	5	32	18	26	.239	.294	.378	90	-6	-4	23	1	0	0	.962	-4	O1	-1.1
	Bos-A	42	132	22	42	6	0	7	23	12	12	.318	.384	.523	132	8	6	25	0	1	-1	.994	-4	1O	0.0
	Yr	114	362	39	97	15	4	12	55	30	38	.268	.327	.431	107	2	2	47	1	1	-0	.961	-4	O1	-1.1
1955	Bos-A	14	31	1	4	2	0	1	1	0	7	.129	.129	.194	-13	-5	-5	1	0	1	0	1.000	2	O	-0.3
	Cin-N	35	62	4	13	1	0	2	7	5	13	.210	.279	.323	56	-4	-4	4	0	1	-1	.960	-1	O/1	-0.6
1956	Cle-A	57	114	17	29	7	0	4	20	12	20	.254	.325	.421	94	-1	-1	15	0	1	-1	.969	-0	O/1	-0.3
Total	10	1046	3437	406	916	168	39	80	544	311	342	.267	.329	.408	97	-21	-25	451	15	14	-4	.985	-39	O/1	-10.5

■ FRANCISCO MELENDEZ
Melendez, Francisco Javier (Villegas) b: 1/25/64, Rio Piedras, P.R. BL/TL, 6', 190 lbs. Deb: 8/26/84

YEAR	TM/L	G	AB	R	H	2B	3B	HR	RBI	BB	SO	AVG	OBP	SLG	PRO+	BR	/A	RC	SB	CS	SBR	FA	FR	POS	TPR
1984	Phi-N	21	23	0	3	0	0	0	2	1	5	.130	.167	.130	-15	-3	-4	0	0	0	0	1.000	1	1	-0.3
1986	Phi-N	9	8	0	2	0	0	0	0	0	2	.250	.250	.250	37	-1	-1	1	0	0	0	1.000	-0	/1	-0.1
1987	SF-N	12	16	2	5	0	0	1	1	0	3	.313	.313	.500	117	0	0	3	0	0	0	1.000	-1	/1	0.0
1988	SF-N	23	26	1	5	0	0	0	3	3	2	.192	.276	.192	38	-2	-2	1	0	0	0	1.000	-1	/1O	-0.4
1989	Bal-A	9	11	1	3	0	0	0	3	1	2	.273	.333	.273	75	-0	-0	1	0	0	0	1.000	0	/1	0.0
Total	5	74	84	4	18	0	0	1	9	5	14	.214	.258	.250	43	-6	-6	6	0	0	0	1.000	-1	/1O	-0.8

■ LUIS MELENDEZ
Melendez, Luis Antonio (Santana) b: 8/11/49, Aibonito, P.R. BR/TR, 6', 165 lbs. Deb: 9/07/70

YEAR	TM/L	G	AB	R	H	2B	3B	HR	RBI	BB	SO	AVG	OBP	SLG	PRO+	BR	/A	RC	SB	CS	SBR	FA	FR	POS	TPR
1970	StL-N	21	70	11	21	1	0	0	8	2	12	.300	.319	.314	69	-3	-3	7	3	0	1	1.000	1	O	-0.2
1971	StL-N	88	173	25	39	3	1	0	11	24	29	.225	.320	.254	62	-7	-8	15	2	0	1	.959	1	O	-0.9
1972	StL-N	118	332	32	79	11	3	5	28	25	34	.238	.293	.334	79	-10	-9	31	5	4	-1	.959	1	*O	-1.5
1973	StL-N	121	341	35	91	18	1	2	35	27	50	.267	.321	.343	84	-7	-7	34	2	7	-4	.990	5	O	-1.0
1974	StL-N	83	124	15	27	4	3	0	8	11	9	.218	.287	.298	64	-6	-6	11	2	2	-1	.977	5	O/S	-0.3
1975	StL-N	110	291	33	77	8	5	2	27	16	25	.265	.303	.347	77	-8	-10	28	3	2	-0	.983	3	O	-1.0
1976	StL-N	20	24	0	3	0	0	0	0	0	3	.125	.125	.125	-29	-4	-4	0	0	0	0	1.000	1	/O	-0.3
	SD-N	72	119	15	29	5	0	0	5	3	12	.244	.262	.286	60	-7	-6	8	1	1	-0	.988	4	O	-0.4
	Yr	92	143	15	32	5	0	0	5	3	15	.224	.240	.259	44	-11	-10	7	1	1	-0	.990	5	O	-0.7
1977	SD-N	8	3	1	0	0	0	0	0	1	1	.000	.250	.000	-29	-1	-0	0	0	0	0	1.000	0	/O	0.0
Total	8	641	1477	167	366	50	13	9	122	109	175	.248	.300	.318	73	-53	-54	135	18	16	-4	.977	20	O/S	-5.6

■ SKI MELILLO
Melillo, Oscar Donald "Spinach" b: 8/4/1899, Chicago, Ill. d: 11/14/63, Chicago, Ill. BR/TR, 5'8", 150 lbs. Deb: 4/18/26 C

YEAR	TM/L	G	AB	R	H	2B	3B	HR	RBI	BB	SO	AVG	OBP	SLG	PRO+	BR	/A	RC	SB	CS	SBR	FA	FR	POS	TPR
1926	StL-A	99	385	54	98	18	5	1	30	32	31	.255	.315	.335	66	-18	-20	41	6	7	-2	.965	8	23	-1.1
1927	StL-A	107	356	45	80	18	2	0	26	25	28	.225	.276	.287	45	-29	-30	27	3	6	-3	.935	-2	*2	-3.1
1928	StL-A	51	132	9	25	2	0	0	9	9	11	.189	.241	.205	18	-16	-16	7	2	1	0	.961	4	23	-1.1
1929	StL-A	141	494	57	146	17	10	5	67	29	30	.296	.337	.401	86	-9	-11	67	11	6	-0	.973	23	*2	1.6
1930	StL-A	149	574	62	147	30	10	5	59	23	44	.256	.287	.369	63	-32	-35	60	15	9	-1	.979	**27**	*2	-0.1
1931	StL-A	151	617	88	189	34	11	2	75	37	29	.306	.346	.407	94	-3	-6	84	7	11	-5	.968	**33**	*2	2.9
1932	StL-A	154	612	71	148	19	11	3	66	36	42	.242	.286	.324	54	-39	-44	57	6	6	-2	.981	11	*2	-2.6
1933	StL-A	132	496	50	145	23	6	3	79	29	18	.292	.333	.381	83	-9	-13	61	12	10	-2	**.991**	**23**	*2	1.5
1934	StL-A	144	552	54	133	19	3	2	55	28	27	.241	.279	.297	45	-43	-49	45	4	6	-2	**.981**	18	*2	-2.3
1935	StL-A	19	62	8	13	3	0	0	5	8	4	.210	.300	.258	43	-5	-5	5	0	0	0	.970	0	2	-0.4
	Bos-A	106	400	45	104	13	2	1	39	38	22	.260	.327	.310	61	-20	-24	42	3	2	-0	.973	18	*2	0.2
	Yr	125	462	53	117	16	2	1	44	46	26	.253	.324	.303	59	-25	-29	48	3	2	-0	.973	19	*2	-0.2
1936	Bos-A	98	327	39	74	12	4	0	32	28	16	.226	.287	.287	40	-30	-33	29	0	0	0	.980	-8	2	-3.1
1937	Bos-A	26	56	8	14	2	0	0	6	5	4	.250	.311	.286	50	-4	-4	5	0	1	-1	.939	-3	2/S3	-0.7
Total	12	1377	5063	590	1316	210	64	22	548	327	306	.260	.306	.340	64	-256	-292	530	69	65	-18	.973	151	*2/3S	-8.3

■ JOE MELLANA
Mellana, Joseph Peter b: 3/11/05, Oakland, Cal. d: 11/1/69, Larkspur, Cal. BR/TR, 5'10", 180 lbs. Deb: 9/21/27

YEAR	TM/L	G	AB	R	H	2B	3B	HR	RBI	BB	SO	AVG	OBP	SLG	PRO+	BR	/A	RC	SB	CS	SBR	FA	FR	POS	TPR
1927	Phi-A	4	7	1	2	0	0	0	2	0	1	.286	.286	.286	46	-1	-1	1	0	0	0	.889	2	/3	0.1

■ BILL MELLOR
Mellor, William Harpin b: 6/6/1874, Camden, N.J. d: 11/5/40, Bridgeton, R.I. BR/TR, 6', 190 lbs. Deb: 7/28/02

YEAR	TM/L	G	AB	R	H	2B	3B	HR	RBI	BB	SO	AVG	OBP	SLG	PRO+	BR	/A	RC	SB	CS	SBR	FA	FR	POS	TPR
1902	Bal-A	10	36	4	13	3	0	0	5	3		.361	.410	.444	131	2	2	7	1			.978	-1	1	0.0

■ PAUL MELOAN
Meloan, Paul B. "Molly" b: 8/23/1888, Paynesville, Mo. d: 2/11/50, Taft, Cal. BR/TL, 5'10.5", 175 lbs. Deb: 8/02/10

YEAR	TM/L	G	AB	R	H	2B	3B	HR	RBI	BB	SO	AVG	OBP	SLG	PRO+	BR	/A	RC	SB	CS	SBR	FA	FR	POS	TPR
1910	Chi-A	65	222	23	54	6	6	0	23	17		.243	.314	.324	104	0	1	24	4			.948	3	O	0.2
1911	Chi-A	1	3	0	1	0	0	0	1	0		.333	.333	.333	89	-0	-0	0	0			.000	-1	/O	-0.1
	StL-A	64	206	30	54	11	2	3	14	15		.262	.318	.379	98	-2	-1	27	7			.904	-6	O	-1.0
	Yr	65	209	30	55	11	2	3	15	15		.263	.319	.378	98	-2	-1	27	7			.893	-6	O	-1.1
Total	2	130	431	53	109	17	8	3	38	32		.253	.316	.350	101	-2	-0	51	11			.923	-3	O	-0.9

■ DAVE MELTON
Melton, David Olin b: 10/3/28, Pampa, Tex. BR/TR, 6', 185 lbs. Deb: 4/17/56

YEAR	TM/L	G	AB	R	H	2B	3B	HR	RBI	BB	SO	AVG	OBP	SLG	PRO+	BR	/A	RC	SB	CS	SBR	FA	FR	POS	TPR
1956	KC-A	3	3	0	1	0	0	0	0	0	0	.333	.333	.333	76	-0	-0	0	0	0	0	1.000	-1	/O	-0.1
1958	KC-A	9	6	0	0	0	0	0	0	0	5	.000	.000	.000	-98	-2	-2	0	0	0	0	1.000	-0	/O	-0.2
Total	2	12	9	0	1	0	0	0	0	0	5	.111	.111	.111	-39	-2	-2	0	0	0	0	1.000	-1	/O	-0.3

■ BILL MELTON
Melton, William Edwin b: 7/7/45, Gulfport, Miss. BR/TR, 6'2", 200 lbs. Deb: 5/04/68

YEAR	TM/L	G	AB	R	H	2B	3B	HR	RBI	BB	SO	AVG	OBP	SLG	PRO+	BR	/A	RC	SB	CS	SBR	FA	FR	POS	TPR
1968	Chi-A	34	109	5	29	8	0	2	16	10	32	.266	.328	.394	117	2	2	14	1	1	-0	.968	3	3	0.6
1969	Chi-A	157	556	67	142	26	2	23	87	56	106	.255	.329	.433	106	7	4	79	1	2	-1	.952	7	*3O	1.1
1970	Chi-A	141	514	74	135	15	1	33	96	56	107	.263	.345	.488	123	18	16	88	2	4	-2	1.000	8	O3	1.9
1971	Chi-A☆	150	543	72	146	18	2	**33**	86	61	87	.269	.354	.492	133	26	24	96	3	3	-1	.968	27	*3	5.1
1972	Chi-A	57	208	22	51	5	0	7	30	23	31	.245	.320	.370	103	1	1	26	1	1	-0	.935	3	3	0.3
1973	Chi-A	152	560	83	155	29	1	20	87	75	66	.277	.364	.439	121	20	17	87	4	4	-1	.953	14	*3/D	3.0
1974	Chi-A	136	495	63	120	17	0	21	63	59	60	.242	.329	.404	107	6	5	65	3	2	-0	.939	-3	*3D	0.0
1975	Chi-A	149	512	62	123	16	0	15	70	78	106	.240	.349	.359	99	3	2	67	5	4	-1	.945	1	*3D	0.1
1976	Cal-A	118	341	31	71	17	3	6	42	44	53	.208	.302	.328	90	-6	-4	36	2	0	1	.992	-3	D13	-0.9
1977	Cle-A	50	133	17	32	11	0	0	14	17	21	.241	.336	.323	83	-3	-2	13	1	3	-2	1.000	1	1D3	-0.4
Total	10	1144	3971	496	1004	162	9	160	591	479	669	.253	.340	.419	112	74	64	571	23	24	-8	.949	57	3/DO1	10.8

■ BOB MELVIN
Melvin, Robert Paul b: 10/28/61, Palo Alto, Cal. BR/TR, 6'4", 205 lbs. Deb: 5/25/85

YEAR	TM/L	G	AB	R	H	2B	3B	HR	RBI	BB	SO	AVG	OBP	SLG	PRO+	BR	/A	RC	SB	CS	SBR	FA	FR	POS	TPR
1985	Det-A	41	82	10	18	4	1	0	4	3	21	.220	.247	.293	47	-6	-6	6	0	0	0	.989	8	C	0.3
1986	SF-N	89	268	24	60	14	2	5	25	15	69	.224	.265	.347	71	-13	-11	23	3	2	-0	.988	7	C/3	0.1
1987	*SF-N	84	246	31	49	8	0	11	31	17	44	.199	.251	.366	64	-15	-13	20	0	4	-2	.998	4	C/1	-0.7
1988	SF-N	92	273	23	64	13	1	8	27	13	46	.234	.269	.377	87	-7	-5	26	0	2	-1	.984	-8	C/1	-0.9
1989	Bal-A	85	278	22	67	10	1	1	32	15	53	.241	.280	.295	64	-14	-13	20	1	4	-2	.991	-9	C/D	-2.1
1990	Bal-A	93	301	30	73	14	1	5	37	11	53	.243	.269	.346	73	-13	-11	26	0	1	-1	.997	1	CD/1	-0.7
1991	Bal-A	79	228	11	57	10	0	1	23	11	46	.250	.285	.307	66	-11	-10	19	0	0	0	.998	6	C/D	-0.1
1992	KC-A	32	70	5	22	5	0	0	6	5	13	.314	.360	.386	108	1	1	9	0	0	0	1.000	-0	C/1	0.1
Total	8	595	1746	156	410	78	6	31	185	90	345	.235	.272	.340	71	-77	-69	150	4	13	-7	.993	9	C/D13	-4.0

■ MINNIE MENDOZA
Mendoza, Cristobal Rigoberto (Carreras) b: 11/16/33, Ceiba Del Agua, Cuba BR/TR, 6', 180 lbs. Deb: 4/09/70

YEAR	TM/L	G	AB	R	H	2B	3B	HR	RBI	BB	SO	AVG	OBP	SLG	PRO+	BR	/A	RC	SB	CS	SBR	FA	FR	POS	TPR
1970	Min-A	16	16	2	3	0	0	0	2	0	1	.188	.188	.188	4	-2	-2	1	0	0	0	1.000	0	/32	-0.2

■ MARIO MENDOZA
Mendoza, Mario (Aizpuru) b: 12/26/50, Chihuahua, Mex. BR/TR, 5'11", 187 lbs. Deb: 4/26/74 C

YEAR	TM/L	G	AB	R	H	2B	3B	HR	RBI	BB	SO	AVG	OBP	SLG	PRO+	BR	/A	RC	SB	CS	SBR	FA	FR	POS	TPR
1974	*Pit-N	91	163	10	36	1	2	0	15	8	35	.221	.262	.252	46	-12	-11	10	1	1	-0	.964	5	S	-0.1
1975	Pit-N	56	50	8	9	1	0	0	2	3	17	.180	.226	.200	19	-5	-5	2	0	0	0	.952	8	S/3	0.4
1976	Pit-N	50	92	6	17	5	0	0	12	4	15	.185	.219	.239	30	-9	-9	4	0	1	-1	.967	12	S/32	0.6
1977	Pit-N	70	81	5	16	3	0	0	4	3	10	.198	.226	.235	23	-9	-9	4	0	0	0	.928	12	S3/P	0.5
1978	Pit-N	57	55	5	12	1	0	1	3	2	9	.218	.283	.291	58	-3	-3	5	3	1	0	.980	9	23S	0.8
1979	Sea-A	148	373	26	74	10	3	1	29	9	62	.198	.219	.249	26	-39	-40	19	3	0	1	.968	28	*S	0.2
1980	Sea-A	114	277	27	68	6	3	2	14	16	42	.245	.287	.310	63	-14	-14	24	3	4	-2	.959	12	*S	0.6
1981	Tex-A	88	229	18	53	6	1	0	22	7	25	.231	.257	.266	54	-14	-13	15	2	1	0	.970	3	S	-0.2
1982	Tex-A	12	17	1	2	0	0	0	0	0	4	.118	.118	.118	-37	-3	-3	0	0	0	0	.882	2	S/D	-0.1
Total	9	686	1337	106	287	33	9	4	101	52	219	.215	.247	.262	41	-108	-107	84	12	8	-1	.961	91	S/32DP	2.7

YEAR	TM/L	G	AB	R	H	2B	3B	HR	RBI	BB	SO	AVG	OBP	SLG	PRO+	BR	/A	RC	SB	CS	SBR	FA	FR	POS	TPR

■ MIKE MENDOZA
Mendoza, Michael Joseph b: 11/26/55, Inglewood, Cal. BR/TR, 6'5", 215 lbs. Deb: 9/07/79

| 1979 | Hou-N | 2 | 0 | 0 | 0 | 0 | 0 | 0 | 0 | 0 | 0 | — | — | — | — | 0 | 0 | 0 | 0 | 0 | 0 | .000 | 0 | /P | 0.0 |

■ JOCK MENEFEE
Menefee, John b: 1/15/1868, West Virginia d: 3/11/53, Belle Vernon, Pa. BR/TR, 6', 165 lbs. Deb: 8/17/1892

1892	Pit-N	2	3	0	0	0	0	0	0	0	0	.000	.000	.000	-99	-1	-1	0	0			1.000	0	/OP	-0.1
1893	Lou-N	22	73	10	20	2	1	0	12	13	5	.274	.391	.329	102	0	1	10	2			.913	3	P/O	0.1
1894	Lou-N	29	79	7	13	1	0	0	4	8	7	.165	.250	.177	6	-12	-11	5	2			.940	3	P/2	0.0
	Pit-N	13	47	6	12	1	2	0	7	3	3	.255	.300	.362	61	-3	-3	6	2			.909	2	P	0.0
	Yr	42	126	13	25	2	2	0	11	11	10	.198	.268	.246	27	-15	-14	11	4			.928	5	P/2	0.0
1895	Pit-N	0	0	0	0	0	0	0	0	0	0	—	—	—	—	0	0	0	0			.667	0	/P	0.0
1898	NY-N	1	5	0	0	0	0	0	0	0	0	.000	.000	.000	-99	-1	-1	0	0			.750	0	/P	0.0
1900	Chi-N	17	46	5	5	0	0	0	4	2		.109	.180	.109	-20	-7	-7	1	0			.889	-2	P	0.0
1901	Chi-N	48	152	19	39	5	3	0	13	8		.257	.327	.329	94	-1	-1	19	4			.913	-2	OP/12	-0.3
1902	Chi-N	65	216	24	50	4	1	0	15	15		.231	.303	.259	76	-6	-5	21	4			.952	-4	OP1/32	-0.1
1903	Chi-N	22	64	3	13	3	0	0	2	3		.203	.239	.250	41	-5	-5	4	0			.896	3	P/1	-0.1
Total	9	221	685	74	152	16	7	0	57	52	15	.222	.295	.266	61	-37	-33	67	14			.918	3	P/O123	-1.2

■ DENIS MENKE
Menke, Denis John b: 7/21/40, Algona, Iowa BR/TR, 6', 190 lbs. Deb: 4/14/62 C

1962	Mil-N	50	146	12	28	3	1	2	16	16	38	.192	.280	.267	49	-11	-10	11	0	1	-1	.980	5	23/S10	-0.3
1963	Mil-N	146	518	58	121	16	4	11	50	37	106	.234	.292	.344	83	-12	-11	51	6	7	-2	.976	12	S32/10	0.6
1964	Mil-N	151	505	79	143	29	5	20	65	68	77	.283	.373	.479	137	26	26	91	4	2	0	.964	2	*S2/3	4.0
1965	Mil-N	71	181	16	44	13	1	4	18	18	28	.243	.315	.392	97	-1	-1	22	1	3	-2	.967	-7	S/13	-0.7
1966	Atl-N	138	454	55	114	20	4	15	60	71	87	.251	.360	.412	112	10	10	68	0	7	-4	.955	-22	*S3/1	-0.9
1967	Atl-N	129	418	37	95	14	3	7	39	65	62	.227	.335	.325	91	-3	-3	48	5	7	-3	.965	-23	*S/3	-1.8
1968	Hou-N	150	542	56	135	23	6	6	56	64	81	.249	.335	.347	107	5	6	65	5	8	-3	.982	-17	*2S/13	-0.5
1969	Hou-N★	154	553	72	149	25	5	10	90	87	87	.269	.373	.387	115	12	14	81	2	7	-4	.956	-9	*S2/13	1.7
1970	Hou-N★	154	562	82	171	26	6	13	92	82	80	.304	.384	.441	130	22	25	103	6	5	-1	.954	-15	*S2/130	2.5
1971	Hou-N	146	475	57	117	26	3	1	43	59	68	.246	.332	.320	88	-8	-6	51	4	5	-2	.997	-3	*13S/2	-1.9
1972	*Cin-N	140	447	41	104	19	2	9	50	58	76	.233	.327	.345	97	-4	-1	53	0	1	-1	.955	0	*31	-0.3
1973	*Cin-N	139	241	38	46	10	0	3	26	69	53	.191	.375	.270	86	-2	-1	29	1	1	-0	.966	16	*3/S21	1.6
1974	Hou-N	30	29	2	3	1	0	0	1	4	10	.103	.212	.138	-1	-4	-4	1	0	0	0	1.000	3	1/32S	0.1
Total	13	1598	5071	605	1270	225	40	101	606	698	853	.250	.346	.370	104	32	45	675	34	54	-22	.961	-57	S321/O	3.9

■ MIKE MENOSKY
Menosky, Michael William "Leaping Mike" b: 10/16/1894, Glen Campbell, Pa. d: 4/11/83, Detroit, Mich. BL/TR, 5'10", 163 lbs. Deb: 4/18/14

1914	Pit-F	68	140	26	37	4	1	2	9	16	30	.264	.352	.350	101	0	1	20	5			.942	-3	O	-0.4
1915	Pit-F	17	21	3	2	0	0	0	1	2	0	.095	.208	.095	-10	-3	-3	1	2			.917	-2	/O	-0.6
1916	Was-A	11	37	5	6	1	1	0	3	1	10	.162	.184	.243	29	-3	-3	2	1			.952	1	/O	-0.3
1917	Was-A	114	322	46	83	12	10	1	34	45	55	.258	.359	.366	123	9	10	48	22			.982	7	O	1.4
1919	Was-A	116	342	62	98	15	3	6	39	44	46	.287	.379	.401	120	10	10	54	13			.979	0	*O	0.4
1920	Bos-A	141	532	80	158	24	9	3	64	65	52	.297	.383	.393	111	7	10	82	23	19	-5	.961	-3	*O	-0.8
1921	Bos-A	133	477	77	143	18	5	3	45	60	45	.300	.388	.377	99	0	2	75	12	6	-0	.970	-4	*O	-1.1
1922	Bos-A	126	406	61	115	16	5	3	32	40	33	.283	.355	.369	90	-6	-5	55	9	5	-0	.977	6	*O	-0.7
1923	Bos-A	84	188	22	43	8	4	0	25	22	19	.229	.310	.314	64	-10	-10	18	3	6	-3	.920	3	O	-1.2
Total	9	810	2465	382	685	98	38	18	252	295	290	.278	.364	.370	100	4	11	356	90	36		.967	7	O	-3.3

■ ED MENSOR
Mensor, Edward "The Midget" b: 11/7/1886, Woodville, Ore. d: 4/20/70, Salem, Ore. BB/TR, 5'6", 145 lbs. Deb: 7/15/12

1912	Pit-N	39	99	19	26	3	2	0	1	23	12	.263	.402	.333	104	2	2	17	10			.955	-2	O	-0.2
1913	Pit-N	44	56	9	10	1	0	0	1	8	13	.179	.292	.196	43	-4	-4	4	2			.971	-1	O/2S	-0.5
1914	Pit-N	44	89	15	18	2	1	1	6	22	13	.202	.372	.281	99	1	1	11	2			.969	2	O	0.2
Total	3	127	244	43	54	6	3	1	8	53	38	.221	.367	.283	89	-2	-0	31	14			.964	-1	/OS2	-0.5

■ TED MENZE
Menze, Theodore Charles b: 11/4/1897, St.Louis, Mo. d: 12/23/69, St.Louis, Mo. BR/TR, 5'9", 172 lbs. Deb: 4/23/18

| 1918 | StL-N | 1 | 3 | 0 | 0 | 0 | 0 | 0 | 0 | 0 | 2 | .000 | .000 | .000 | -99 | -1 | -1 | 0 | 0 | | | 1.000 | -0 | /O | -0.1 |

■ RUDY MEOLI
Meoli, Rudolph Bartholomew b: 5/1/51, Troy, N.Y. BL/TR, 5'9", 165 lbs. Deb: 9/09/71

1971	Cal-A	7	3	0	0	0	0	0	0	0	0	.000	.000	.000	-99	-1	-1	0	0	0	0	.000	0	H	-0.1
1973	Cal-A	120	305	36	68	12	1	2	23	31	38	.223	.295	.289	70	-14	-11	26	2	4	-2	.933	-2	S3/2	-0.4
1974	Cal-A	36	90	9	22	2	0	0	3	8	10	.244	.306	.267	70	-4	-3	6	2	4	-2	.946	2	3/S12	-0.2
1975	Cal-A	70	126	12	27	2	1	0	6	15	20	.214	.298	.246	59	-7	-6	10	3	0	1	.976	0	S32/D	-0.2
1978	Chi-N	47	29	10	3	0	1	0	2	6	4	.103	.257	.172	20	-3	-3	2	1	0	0	.900	3	/23	0.4
1979	Phi-N	30	73	2	13	4	1	0	6	9	15	.178	.268	.260	43	-6	-6	7	2	0	1	.984	3	S2/3	0.0
Total	6	310	626	69	133	20	4	2	40	69	88	.212	.291	.267	61	-34	-30	51	10	8	-2	.944	11	S/32D1	-0.5

■ ORLANDO MERCADO
Mercado, Orlando (Rodriguez) b: 11/7/61, Arecibo, P.R. BR/TR, 6', 195 lbs. Deb: 9/13/82

1982	Sea-A	9	17	1	2	0	0	1	6	0	5	.118	.118	.294	8	-2	-2	1	0	0	0	1.000	1	/C	-0.1
1983	Sea-A	66	178	10	35	11	2	1	16	14	27	.197	.259	.298	51	-12	-12	14	2	2	-1	.995	4	C	-0.6
1984	Sea-A	30	78	5	17	3	1	0	5	4	12	.218	.265	.282	52	-5	-5	6	1	0	0	.992	-6	C	-1.0
1986	Tex-A	46	102	7	24	1	1	1	7	6	13	.235	.284	.294	56	-6	-6	7	0	1	-1	.996	16	C	1.0
1987	Det-A	10	22	2	3	0	0	0	2	0	1	.136	.208	.136	-6	-3	-3	1	0	0	0	.980	3	C	0.1
	LA-N	7	5	1	3	1	0	0	1	1	1	.600	.667	.800	294	1	1	3	0	0	0	1.000	0	/C	0.2
1988	Oak-A	16	24	3	3	0	0	0	1	3	8	.125	.222	.250	33	-2	-2	2	0	0	0	.959	1	C	-0.1
1989	Min-A	19	38	1	4	0	0	0	1	4	4	.105	.190	.105	-14	-6	-6	1	1	0	0	1.000	4	C	-0.1
1990	NY-N	42	90	10	19	1	0	3	7	8	11	.211	.290	.322	68	-4	-4	8	0	0	0	.991	2	C	-0.1
	Mon-N	8	8	0	2	0	0	0	0	1	1	.250	.250	.250	39	-1	-1	0	0	0	0	1.000	3	/C	0.2
	Yr	50	98	10	21	1	0	3	7	8	12	.214	.287	.316	66	-5	-4	8	0	0	0	.992	4	C	0.1
Total	8	253	562	40	112	17	4	7	45	42	82	.199	.261	.281	48	-39	-40	42	4	3	-1	.993	27	C	-0.5

■ ORLANDO MERCED
Merced, Orlando Luis (Villanueva) b: 11/2/66, Hato Rey, P.R. BB/TR, 6', 180 lbs. Deb: 6/27/90

1990	Pit-N	25	24	3	5	0	0	0	1	0	9	.208	.240	.250	36	-2	-2	1	0	0	0	.000	-0	/CO	-0.3
1991	*Pit-N	120	411	83	113	17	2	10	50	64	81	.275	.374	.399	119	11	12	65	8	4	0	.988	-8	*1/O	-0.2
1992	*Pit-N	134	405	50	100	28	5	6	60	52	63	.247	.336	.385	105	2	3	54	5	4	-1	.995	1	*1O	-0.4
Total	3	279	840	136	218	46	7	16	110	117	153	.260	.352	.388	110	12	13	120	13	8	-1	.991	-7	1/OC	-0.9

■ HENRY MERCEDES
Mercedes, Henry Felipe (Perez) b: 7/23/69, Santo Domingo, D.R. BR/TR, 5'11", 185 lbs. Deb: 4/22/92

| 1992 | Oak-A | 9 | 5 | 1 | 4 | 0 | 0 | 1 | 0 | 1 | 1 | .800 | .800 | 1.200 | 472 | 2 | 2 | 5 | 0 | 0 | 0 | .875 | -0 | /C | 0.2 |

■ LUIS MERCEDES
Mercedes, Luis Roberto (Santana) b: 2/15/68, San Pedro De Macoris, D.R. BR/TR, 6', 180 lbs. Deb: 9/08/91

1991	Bal-A	19	54	10	11	2	0	0	2	4	9	.204	.259	.241	41	-4	-4	3	0	0	0	1.000	-2	O/D	-0.7
1992	Bal-A	23	50	7	7	2	0	0	4	8	9	.140	.271	.180	29	-5	-5	3	0	1	-1	.956	2	O/D	-0.3
Total	2	42	104	17	18	4	0	0	6	12	18	.173	.265	.212	35	-9	-9	6	0	1	-1	.969	-0	OD	-1.0

■ WIN MERCER
Mercer, George Barclay b: 6/20/1874, Chester, W.Va. d: 1/12/03, San Francisco, Cal BR/TR, 5'7", 140 lbs. Deb: 4/21/1894

1894	Was-N	53	164	29	48	5	2	1	29	9	20	.293	.329	.384	75	-7	-6	24	9			.944	2	P/O	-0.1
1895	Was-N	63	196	26	50	9	1	1	26	12	32	.255	.308	.327	66	-10	-10	23	7			.874	-8	P/SO32	-0.8
1896	Was-N	49	156	23	38	1	1	1	14	9	18	.244	.302	.282	56	-10	-10	17	9			.856	1	P/O	0.0

YEAR	TM/L	G	AB	R	H	2B	3B	HR	RBI	BB	SO	AVG	OBP	SLG	PRO+	BR	/A	RC	SB	CS	SBR	FA	FR	POS	TPR
1897	Was-N	49	135	22	43	2	5	0	19	6		.319	.357	.407	102	-0	0	23	7			.865	-1	P	0.0
1898	Was-N	80	249	38	80	3	5	2	25	18		.321	.369	.398	120	6	6	44	14			.863	-9	PSO/32	-0.4
1899	Was-N	108	375	73	112	6	7	1	35	32		.299	.360	.360	99	-1	0	57	16			.846	-14	3PO/S1	-1.6
1900	NY-N	76	248	32	73	4	0	0	27	26		.294	.366	.310	92	-3	-1	35	15			.931	-1	P3O/S2	-0.3
1901	Was-A	51	140	26	42	7	2	0	16	23		.300	.399	.379	118	4	5	26	10			.944	-2	PO/1S3	-0.1
1902	Det-A	35	100	8	18	2	0	0	6	6		.180	.226	.200	18	-11	-11	5	1			.935	4	P	0.0
Total	9	564	1763	277	504	39	23	7	197	141	70	.286	.344	.346	88	-31	-27	254	88			.903	-29	P/3OS12	-3.3

■ JOHN MERCER
Mercer, John Locke b: 6/22/1892, Taylortown, La. d: 12/22/82, Shreveport, La. BL/TL, 5'10.5", 155 lbs. Deb: 6/25/12

YEAR	TM/L	G	AB	R	H	2B	3B	HR	RBI	BB	SO	AVG	OBP	SLG	PRO+	BR	/A	RC	SB	CS	SBR	FA	FR	POS	TPR
1912	StL-N	1	1	0	0	0	0	0	0	0	0	.000	.000	.000	-99	-0	-0	0	0			.500	-0	/1	-0.1

■ ANDY MERCHANT
Merchant, James Anderson b: 8/30/50, Mobile, Ala. BL/TR, 5'11", 185 lbs. Deb: 9/28/75

YEAR	TM/L	G	AB	R	H	2B	3B	HR	RBI	BB	SO	AVG	OBP	SLG	PRO+	BR	/A	RC	SB	CS	SBR	FA	FR	POS	TPR
1975	Bos-A	1	4	1	2	0	0	0	0	1	0	.500	.600	.500	197	1	1	1	0	0	0	1.000	-1	/C	0.0
1976	Bos-A	2	2	0	0	0	0	0	0	0	2	.000	.000	.000	-89	-0	-1	0	0	0	0	1.000	-0	/C	-0.1
Total	2	3	6	1	2	0	0	0	0	1	2	.333	.429	.333	109	0	0	1	0	0	0	1.000	-1	/C	-0.1

■ ART MEREWETHER
Merewether, Arthur Francis "Merry" b: 7/1/02, E.Providence, R.I. BR/TR, 5'9.5", 155 lbs. Deb: 7/10/22

YEAR	TM/L	G	AB	R	H	2B	3B	HR	RBI	BB	SO	AVG	OBP	SLG	PRO+	BR	/A	RC	SB	CS	SBR	FA	FR	POS	TPR
1922	Pit-N	1	1	0	0	0	0	0	0	0	0	.000	.000	.000	-99	-0	-0	0	0	0	0	.000	0	H	0.0

■ FRED MERKLE
Merkle, Frederick Charles b: 12/20/1888, Watertown, Wis. d: 3/2/56, Daytona Beach, Fla. BR/TR, 6'1", 190 lbs. Deb: 9/21/07 C

YEAR	TM/L	G	AB	R	H	2B	3B	HR	RBI	BB	SO	AVG	OBP	SLG	PRO+	BR	/A	RC	SB	CS	SBR	FA	FR	POS	TPR
1907	NY-N	15	47	0	12	1	0	0	5	1		.255	.271	.277	70	-2	-2	4	0			.949	-1	1	-0.4
1908	NY-N	38	41	6	11	2	1	1	7	4		.268	.333	.439	140	2	2	6	0			1.000	-2	1/O23	0.0
1909	NY-N	79	236	15	45	9	1	0	20	16		.191	.245	.237	49	-14	-14	15	8			.976	-3	1/2	-2.0
1910	NY-N	144	506	75	148	35	14	4	70	44	59	.292	.353	.441	131	18	18	86	23			.981	1	*1	1.9
1911	*NY-N	149	541	80	153	24	10	12	84	43	60	.283	.342	.431	112	9	7	95	49			.985	15	*1	2.2
1912	*NY-N	129	479	82	148	22	6	11	84	42	70	.309	.374	.449	121	16	14	93	37			.980	-1	*1	1.0
1913	*NY-N	153	563	78	147	30	13	2	69	41	60	.261	.315	.371	95	-5	-5	72	35			.986	-3	*1	-1.0
1914	NY-N	146	512	71	132	25	7	7	63	52	80	.258	.327	.375	112	5	7	66	23			.990	3	*1	0.8
1915	NY-N	140	505	52	151	25	3	4	62	36	39	.299	.348	.384	129	13	16	70	20	15	-3	.989	-1	*1O	0.9
1916	NY-N	112	401	45	95	19	3	7	44	33	46	.237	.308	.352	108	1	3	49	17			.984	0	*1	-0.1
	*Bro-N	23	69	6	16	1	0	0	2	7	4	.232	.312	.246	70	-2	-2	6	2			.992	-1	1/O	-0.4
	Yr	135	470	51	111	20	3	7	46	40	50	.236	.308	.336	102	-1	1	55	19			.985	-1	*1/O	-0.5
1917	Bro-N	2	8	1	1	1	0	0	0	0	1	.125	.125	.250	13	-1	-1	0	0			1.000	0	/1	-0.1
	Chi-N	146	549	65	146	30	9	3	57	42	60	.266	.323	.370	104	7	3	67	13			.983	-3	*1/O	-0.7
	Yr	148	557	66	147	31	9	3	57	42	61	.264	.320	.368	103	7	2	67	13			.983	-3	*1/O	-0.8
1918	*Chi-N	129	482	55	143	25	5	3	65	35	36	.297	.349	.388	122	14	13	71	21			.990	1	*1	0.9
1919	Chi-N	133	498	52	133	20	6	3	62	33	35	.267	.315	.349	99	-1	-1	58	20			.985	-10	*1/2	-1.7
1920	Chi-N	92	330	33	94	20	4	3	38	24	32	.285	.335	.397	108	4	3	43	3	5	-2	.985	-0	1/O	-0.1
1925	NY-A	7	13	4	5	1	0	0	1	1	1	.385	.429	.462	128	1	1	3	1	0	0	1.000	-0	/1	0.0
1926	NY-A	1	2	0	0	0	0	0	0	0	0	.000	.000	.000	-99	-1	-1	0	0	0	0	1.000	-0	/1	-0.1
Total	16	1638	5782	720	1580	290	82	60	733	454	583	.273	.331	.383	109	64	59	804	272	20		.985	-5	*1/O23	1.1

■ ED MERRILL
Merrill, Edward Mason b: 5/1860, Kentucky d: 8/18/24, Chicago, Ill. 5'11", 176 lbs. Deb: 6/20/1882

YEAR	TM/L	G	AB	R	H	2B	3B	HR	RBI	BB	SO	AVG	OBP	SLG	PRO+	BR	/A	RC	SB	CS	SBR	FA	FR	POS	TPR
1882	Wor-N	2	8	0	1	0	0	0	4	0	1	.125	.125	.125	-19	-1	-1	0				.714	-1	/3	-0.1
1884	Ind-a	55	196	14	35	3	1	0		6		.179	.207	.204	37	-13	-12	8				.900	-4	2	-1.4
Total	2	57	204	14	36	3	1	0	4	6	1	.176	.204	.201	35	-14	-13	9				.984	-5	/23	-1.5

■ LLOYD MERRIMAN
Merriman, Lloyd Archer "Citation" b: 8/2/24, Clovis, Cal. BL/TL, 6', 195 lbs. Deb: 4/24/49

YEAR	TM/L	G	AB	R	H	2B	3B	HR	RBI	BB	SO	AVG	OBP	SLG	PRO+	BR	/A	RC	SB	CS	SBR	FA	FR	POS	TPR
1949	Cin-N	103	287	35	66	12	5	4	26	21	36	.230	.285	.348	68	-13	-14	28	2			.969	-1	O	-1.8
1950	Cin-N	92	298	44	77	15	3	2	31	30	23	.258	.330	.349	79	-9	-9	36	6			.989	-4	O	-1.6
1951	Cin-N	114	359	34	87	23	2	5	36	31	34	.242	.303	.359	76	-12	-13	41	8	4	0	.997	9	*O	-0.7
1954	Cin-N	73	112	12	30	8	1	0	16	23	10	.268	.406	.357	98	1	1	19	3	0	1	.981	-1	O	0.0
1955	Chi-A	1	1	0	0	0	0	0	0	0	0	.000	.000	.000	-97	-0	-0	0	0	0	0	.000	0	H	0.0
	Chi-N	72	145	15	31	6	1	1	8	21	21	.214	.313	.290	62	-8	-8	15	1	0	0	.977	-6	O	-1.5
Total	5	455	1202	140	291	64	12	12	117	126	124	.242	.317	.345	75	-40	-42	140	20	4		.985	-2	O	-5.6

■ GEORGE MERRITT
Merritt, George Washington b: 4/14/1880, Paterson, N.J. d: 2/21/38, Memphis, Tenn. TR , 6', 160 lbs. Deb: 9/06/01

YEAR	TM/L	G	AB	R	H	2B	3B	HR	RBI	BB	SO	AVG	OBP	SLG	PRO+	BR	/A	RC	SB	CS	SBR	FA	FR	POS	TPR
1901	Pit-N	4	11	2	3	0	1	0	0	0		.273	.385	.455	139	1	1	2	0			1.000	-0	/P	0.0
1902	Pit-N	2	9	2	3	1	0	0	2	0		.333	.333	.444	135	0	0	1	0			1.000	1	/O	0.1
1903	Pit-N	9	27	4	4	0	1	0	3	2		.148	.233	.222	29	-2	-3	2	1			.889	-2	/OP	-0.4
Total	3	15	47	8	10	1	2	0	5	2		.213	.288	.319	74	-1	-2	5	1			.929	-1	/OP	-0.3

■ HERM MERRITT
Merritt, Herman G. b: 11/12/1900, Independence, Kan. d: 5/26/27, Kansas City, Mo. BR/TR, Deb: 8/25/21

YEAR	TM/L	G	AB	R	H	2B	3B	HR	RBI	BB	SO	AVG	OBP	SLG	PRO+	BR	/A	RC	SB	CS	SBR	FA	FR	POS	TPR
1921	Det-A	20	46	3	17	1	2	0	6	1	5	.370	.396	.478	123	1	2	9	1	0	0	.882	-6	S	-0.3

■ JOHN MERRITT
Merritt, John Howard b: 10/12/1894, Tupelo, Miss. d: 11/3/55, Tupelo, Miss. BR/TL, 5'11", 170 lbs. Deb: 9/27/13

YEAR	TM/L	G	AB	R	H	2B	3B	HR	RBI	BB	SO	AVG	OBP	SLG	PRO+	BR	/A	RC	SB	CS	SBR	FA	FR	POS	TPR
1913	NY-N	1	0	0	0	0	0	0	0	0	0	—	—	—	—	0	0	0	0			.000	-0	/O	0.0

■ BILL MERRITT
Merritt, William Henry b: 7/30/1870, Lowell, Mass. d: 11/17/37, Lowell, Mass. BR/TR, 5'7", 160 lbs. Deb: 8/08/1891

YEAR	TM/L	G	AB	R	H	2B	3B	HR	RBI	BB	SO	AVG	OBP	SLG	PRO+	BR	/A	RC	SB	CS	SBR	FA	FR	POS	TPR
1891	Chi-N	11	42	4	9	1	0	0	4	2	2	.214	.250	.238	44	-3	-3	3	0			.955	-3	C/1	-0.5
1892	Lou-N	46	168	22	33	4	2	1	13	11	15	.196	.246	.262	60	-9	-7	12	3			.940	-3	C	-0.7
1893	Bos-N	39	141	30	49	6	3	3	26	13	13	.348	.403	.496	130	8	6	30	3			.945	-4	C/O	0.4
1894	Bos-N	10	26	3	6	1	0	0	6	8	0	.231	.412	.269	64	-1	-1	3	0			.881	1	/CO	0.0
	Pit-N	36	109	18	30	1	2	1	18	15	7	.275	.363	.349	75	-4	-4	15	2			.952	-2	C/1O	-0.3
	Cin-N	29	113	17	37	6	1	1	21	9	3	.327	.387	.425	94	-0	-1	21	4			.953	-3	C/31O	-0.2
	Yr	75	248	38	73	8	3	2	45	32	10	.294	.379	.375	82	-5	-6	39	6			.941	-4	C/1O3	-0.5
1895	Cin-N	22	79	9	14	2	0	0	12	6	5	.177	.235	.203	14	-10	-10	5	2			.955	-1	C/2	-0.8
	Pit-N	67	239	32	68	5	1	0	27	18	16	.285	.340	.314	75	-10	-7	27	2			.935	-3	C/1	-0.3
	Yr	89	318	41	82	7	1	0	39	24	21	.258	.314	.286	59	-19	-18	32	4			.939	-4	C/12	-1.1
1896	Pit-N	77	282	26	82	8	2	1	42	18	10	.291	.336	.344	84	-7	-6	36	3			.941	1	C/321S	0.3
1897	Pit-N	62	209	21	55	6	1	1	26	9		.263	.297	.316	64	-12	-11	21	2			.946	-4	C/1	-0.8
1899	Bos-N	1	2	0	0	0	0	0	0	0		.000	.333	.000	-5	-0	-0	0	0			1.000	0	/C	0.0
Total	8	400	1410	182	383	40	12	8	195	109	71	.272	.327	.334	77	-49	-45	173	21			.942	-21	C/13O2S	-2.9

■ JACK MERSON
Merson, John Warren b: 1/17/22, Elk Ridge, Md. BR/TR, 5'11", 175 lbs. Deb: 9/14/51

YEAR	TM/L	G	AB	R	H	2B	3B	HR	RBI	BB	SO	AVG	OBP	SLG	PRO+	BR	/A	RC	SB	CS	SBR	FA	FR	POS	TPR
1951	Pit-N	13	50	6	18	2	2	1	14	1	7	.360	.373	.540	138	3	3	10	0	0	0	.987	2	2	0.5
1952	Pit-N	111	398	41	98	20	2	5	38	22	38	.246	.287	.344	72	-15	-16	38	1	1	-0	.978	-6	23	-1.9
1953	Bos-A	1	4	0	0	0	0	0	0	0	0	.000	.000	.000	-95	-1	-1	0	0	0	0	.875	0	/2	-0.1
Total	3	125	452	47	116	22	4	6	52	23	45	.257	.294	.363	78	-13	-14	49	1	1	-0	.978	-3	/23	-1.5

■ SAM MERTES
Mertes, Samuel Blair "Sandow" b: 8/6/1872, San Francisco, Cal. d: 3/11/45, San Francisco, Cal BR/TR, 5'10", 185 lbs. Deb: 6/30/1896

YEAR	TM/L	G	AB	R	H	2B	3B	HR	RBI	BB	SO	AVG	OBP	SLG	PRO+	BR	/A	RC	SB	CS	SBR	FA	FR	POS	TPR
1896	Phi-N	37	143	20	34	4	4	0	14	8	10	.238	.288	.322	63	-8	-8	20	19			.907	-1	O/S2	-0.9
1898	Chi-N	83	269	45	80	4	8	1	47	34		.297	.388	.383	121	9	9	53	27			.880	2	OS/21	0.7
1899	Chi-N	117	426	83	127	13	16	9	81	33		.298	.349	.467	126	11	13	88	45			.923	-1	*O/1S	0.4
1900	Chi-N	127	481	72	142	25	4	7	60	42		.295	.356	.407	114	6	9	87	38			.923	-5	O1/S	-0.2
1901	Chi-A	137	545	94	151	16	17	5	98	52		.277	.347	.396	109	4	7	95	46			.940	-6	*2/O	0.5

YEAR	TM/L	G	AB	R	H	2B	3B	HR	RBI	BB	SO	AVG	OBP	SLG	PRO+	BR	/A	RC	SB	CS	SBR	FA	FR	POS	TPR
1902	Chi-A	129	497	60	140	23	7	1	79	37		.282	.334	.362	97	-5	-2	78	46			.922	6	*O/SCP123	-0.3
1903	NY-N	138	517	100	145	**32**	14	7	**104**	61		.280	.360	.437	122	18	15	101	45			**.973**	8	*O/C1	1.4
1904	NY-N	148	532	83	147	28	11	4	78	54		.276	.345	.393	123	18	15	93	47			.956	-1	*O/S	0.6
1905	*NY-N	150	551	81	154	27	17	5	108	56		.279	.350	.417	126	19	17	103	52			.960	-11	*O	-0.1
1906	NY-N	71	253	37	60	9	6	1	33	29		.237	.323	.332	102	2	1	35	21			.970	1	O	-0.1
	StL-N	53	191	20	47	7	4	0	19	16		.246	.304	.325	101	-1	-0	23	10			.890	-6	O	-1.0
	Yr	124	444	57	107	16	10	1	52	45		.241	.315	.329	102	1	1	59	31			.938	-5	*O	-1.1
Total	10	1190	4405	695	1227	188	108	40	721	422	10	.279	.346	.398	114	72	76	777	396			.938	-14	O2/1SC3P	1.0

■ LENNIE MERULLO Merullo, Leonard Richard b: 5/5/17, Boston, Mass. BR/TR, 5'11", 168 lbs. Deb: 9/12/41 F

YEAR	TM/L	G	AB	R	H	2B	3B	HR	RBI	BB	SO	AVG	OBP	SLG	PRO+	BR	/A	RC	SB	CS	SBR	FA	FR	POS	TPR
1941	Chi-N	7	17	3	6	1	0	0	1	2	0	.353	.421	.412	140	1	1	3	1			.968	2	/S	0.3
1942	Chi-N	143	515	53	132	23	3	2	37	35	45	.256	.310	.324	89	-10	-7	52	14			.946	-1	*S	0.0
1943	Chi-N	129	453	37	115	18	3	1	25	26	42	.254	.297	.313	78	-14	-13	42	7			.940	-12	*S	-1.8
1944	Chi-N	66	193	20	41	8	1	1	16	16	18	.212	.276	.280	57	-11	-11	16	3			.937	2	S/1	-0.5
1945	*Chi-N	121	394	40	94	18	0	2	37	31	30	.239	.297	.299	68	-18	-17	34	7			.948	-4	*S	-1.3
1946	Chi-N	65	126	14	19	8	0	0	7	11	13	.151	.219	.214	24	-13	-13	6	2			.946	18	S	0.7
1947	Chi-N	108	373	24	90	16	1	0	29	15	26	.241	.274	.290	52	-27	-25	28	4			.949	7	*S	-1.3
Total	7	639	2071	191	497	92	8	6	152	136	174	.240	.291	.301	69	-92	-86	180	38			.945	11	S/1	-3.9

■ MATT MERULLO Merullo, Matthew Bates b: 8/4/65, Winchester, Mass. BL/TR, 6'2", 200 lbs. Deb: 4/12/89 F

YEAR	TM/L	G	AB	R	H	2B	3B	HR	RBI	BB	SO	AVG	OBP	SLG	PRO+	BR	/A	RC	SB	CS	SBR	FA	FR	POS	TPR
1989	Chi-A	31	81	5	18	1	0	1	8	6	14	.222	.276	.272	56	-5	-5	6	0	1	-1	.973	-4	C/D	-0.8
1991	Chi-A	80	140	8	32	1	0	5	21	9	18	.229	.275	.343	72	-6	-6	14	0	0	0	.989	-1	C1/D	-0.6
1992	Chi-A	24	50	3	9	1	1	0	3	1	8	.180	.212	.240	27	-5	-5	3	0	0	0	.971	-1	C/D	-0.5
Total	3	135	271	16	59	3	1	6	32	16	40	.218	.264	.303	59	-16	-15	22	0	1	-1	.978	-5	/C1D	-1.9

■ STEVE MESNER Mesner, Stephan Mathias b: 1/13/18, Los Angeles, Cal. d: 4/6/81, San Diego, Cal. BR/TR, 5'9", 178 lbs. Deb: 9/23/38

YEAR	TM/L	G	AB	R	H	2B	3B	HR	RBI	BB	SO	AVG	OBP	SLG	PRO+	BR	/A	RC	SB	CS	SBR	FA	FR	POS	TPR
1938	Chi-N	2	4	2	1	0	0	0	0	1	1	.250	.400	.250	80	-0	-0	1	0			.667	-1	/S	-0.1
1939	Chi-N	17	43	7	12	4	0	0	6	3	4	.279	.340	.372	90	-0	-1	5	0			.927	1	S/23	0.2
1941	StL-N	24	69	8	10	1	0	0	10	5	6	.145	.203	.159	3	-9	-9	2	0			.958	5	3	-0.4
1943	Cin-N	137	504	53	137	26	1	0	52	26	20	.272	.309	.327	85	-11	-10	50	6			.944	1	*3	-0.8
1944	Cin-N	121	414	31	100	17	4	1	47	34	20	.242	.301	.309	75	-15	-14	38	1			.951	-7	*3	-2.0
1945	Cin-N	150	540	52	137	19	1	1	52	52	18	.254	.322	.298	74	-19	-17	52	4			.971	12	*3/2	-0.2
Total	6	451	1574	153	397	67	6	2	167	121	69	.252	.308	.306	75	-55	-51	149	11			.956	10	3/S2	-3.3

■ BOBBY MESSENGER Messenger, Charles Walter b: 3/19/1884, Bangor, Me. d: 7/10/51, Bath, Maine BB/TR, 5'10.5", 165 lbs. Deb: 8/30/09

YEAR	TM/L	G	AB	R	H	2B	3B	HR	RBI	BB	SO	AVG	OBP	SLG	PRO+	BR	/A	RC	SB	CS	SBR	FA	FR	POS	TPR
1909	Chi-A	31	112	18	19	1	1	0	0	13		.170	.268	.196	49	-6	-6	8	7			.950	-2	O	-1.0
1910	Chi-A	9	26	7	6	0	1	0	4	4		.231	.375	.308	119	1	1	4	3			.846	-0	/O	0.0
1911	Chi-A	13	17	4	2	0	1	0	0	3		.118	.250	.235	37	-1	-1	1	0			.875	-1	/O	-0.2
1914	StL-A	1	2	0	0	0	0	0	0	0	0	.000	.000	.000	-99	-0	-0	0	0			.000	-0	/O	-0.1
Total	4	54	157	29	27	1	3	0	4	20	0	.172	.282	.217	57	-7	-7	13	10			.918	-3	/O	-1.3

■ TOM MESSITT Messitt, Thomas John b: 7/27/1874, Frankfort, Pa. d: 9/22/34, Chicago, Ill. 5'9", 177 lbs. Deb: 9/14/1899

YEAR	TM/L	G	AB	R	H	2B	3B	HR	RBI	BB	SO	AVG	OBP	SLG	PRO+	BR	/A	RC	SB	CS	SBR	FA	FR	POS	TPR
1899	Lou-N	3	11	0	1	0	0	0	0	0		.091	.091	.091	-50	-2	-2	0	0			1.000	1	/C	-0.1

■ AL METCALF Metcalf, Al b: Brooklyn, N.Y. Deb: 5/27/1875

YEAR	TM/L	G	AB	R	H	2B	3B	HR	RBI	BB	SO	AVG	OBP	SLG	PRO+	BR	/A	RC	SB	CS	SBR	FA	FR	POS	TPR
1875	Mut-n	8	31	2	7	0	0	0		1		.226	.250	.226	62	-1	-1	2						/3OS	-0.1

■ SCAT METHA Metha, Frank Joseph b: 12/13/13, Los Angeles, Cal. d: 3/2/75, Fountain Valley, Cal. BR/TR, 5'11", 165 lbs. Deb: 4/22/40

YEAR	TM/L	G	AB	R	H	2B	3B	HR	RBI	BB	SO	AVG	OBP	SLG	PRO+	BR	/A	RC	SB	CS	SBR	FA	FR	POS	TPR
1940	Det-A	26	37	6	9	0	1	0	3	2	8	.243	.282	.297	46	-3	-3	3	0	1	-1	.960	4	2/3	0.0

■ BUD METHENY Metheny, Arthur Beauregard b: 6/1/15, St.Louis, Mo. BL/TL, 5'11", 190 lbs. Deb: 4/27/43

YEAR	TM/L	G	AB	R	H	2B	3B	HR	RBI	BB	SO	AVG	OBP	SLG	PRO+	BR	/A	RC	SB	CS	SBR	FA	FR	POS	TPR
1943	*NY-A	103	360	51	94	18	2	9	36	39	34	.261	.333	.397	113	5	5	49	2	3	-1	.963	-12	O	-1.4
1944	NY-A	137	518	72	124	16	1	14	67	56	57	.239	.316	.355	89	-6	-8	59	5	5	-2	.956	-8	*O	-2.6
1945	NY-A	133	509	64	126	18	2	8	53	54	31	.248	.325	.338	88	-5	-8	60	5	2	0	.984	-6	*O	-2.2
1946	NY-A	3	3	0	0	0	0	0	0	0	0	.000	.000	.000	-99	-1	-1	0	0	0	0	.000	0	H	-0.1
Total	4	376	1390	187	344	52	5	31	156	149	122	.247	.323	.359	94	-6	-11	169	12	10	-2	.968	-26	O	-6.3

■ CATFISH METKOVICH Metkovich, George Michael b: 10/8/21, Angel's Camp, Cal. BL/TL, 6'1", 185 lbs. Deb: 7/16/43

YEAR	TM/L	G	AB	R	H	2B	3B	HR	RBI	BB	SO	AVG	OBP	SLG	PRO+	BR	/A	RC	SB	CS	SBR	FA	FR	POS	TPR
1943	Bos-A	78	321	34	79	14	4	5	27	19	38	.246	.294	.361	90	-5	-5	34	1	3	-2	.955	-3	O/1	-1.5
1944	Bos-A	134	549	94	152	28	8	9	59	31	57	.277	.319	.406	108	2	3	73	13	4	2	.962	5	O1	0.3
1945	Bos-A	138	539	65	140	26	3	5	62	51	70	.260	.331	.347	94	-2	-4	67	19	6	2	.985	-4	1O	-1.6
1946	*Bos-A	86	281	42	69	15	2	4	25	36	39	.246	.333	.356	88	-2	-4	37	8	3	1	.948	-11	O	-1.9
1947	Cle-A	126	473	68	120	22	7	5	40	32	51	.254	.302	.362	86	-12	-10	52	5	3	-0	.989	1	*O/1	-1.6
1949	Chi-A	93	338	50	80	9	4	5	45	41	24	.237	.321	.331	75	-14	-12	34	5	4	-1	.968	-7	O	-2.4
1951	Pit-N	120	423	51	124	21	3	3	40	28	23	.293	.338	.378	90	-5	-6	54	3	2	-0	.994	1	O1	-0.9
1952	Pit-N	125	373	41	101	18	3	7	41	32	29	.271	.335	.391	98	0	-1	50	5	2	0	.988	-7	1O	-1.1
1953	Pit-N	26	41	5	6	0	1	1	7	6	3	.146	.255	.268	37	-4	-4	3	0	0	0	1.000	-1	/1O	-0.5
	Chi-N	61	124	19	29	9	0	2	12	16	10	.234	.326	.355	76	-4	-4	14	2	1	0	1.000	-5	O/1	-1.0
	Yr	87	165	24	35	9	1	3	19	22	13	.212	.309	.333	66	-8	-8	17	2	1	0	1.000	-6	O1	-1.5
1954	Mil-N	68	123	7	34	5	1	1	15	15	15	.276	.360	.358	94	-2	-1	15	0	0	0	1.000	1	1O	-0.1
Total	10	1055	3585	476	934	167	36	47	373	307	359	.261	.323	.367	91	-47	-49	434	61	28	2	.976	-28	O1	-12.3

■ CHARLIE METRO Metro, Charles (b: Charles Moreskonich) b: 4/28/19, Nanty-Glo, Pa. BR/TR, 5'11.5", 178 lbs. Deb: 5/04/43 MC

YEAR	TM/L	G	AB	R	H	2B	3B	HR	RBI	BB	SO	AVG	OBP	SLG	PRO+	BR	/A	RC	SB	CS	SBR	FA	FR	POS	TPR
1943	Det-A	44	40	12	8	0	0	0	2	3	6	.200	.256	.200	32	-3	-4	2	1	1	-0	.966	-2	O	-0.7
1944	Det-A	38	78	8	15	0	1	0	5	3	10	.192	.222	.218	25	-8	-8	4	1	0	0	1.000	-2	O	-1.1
	Phi-A	24	40	4	4	0	0	0	1	7	6	.100	.234	.100	-3	-5	-5	1	0	0	0	1.000	-1	O/32	-0.6
	Yr	62	118	12	19	0	1	0	6	10	16	.161	.227	.178	16	-13	-13	5	1	0	0	1.000	-2	O/32	-1.7
1945	Phi-A	65	200	18	42	10	1	3	15	23	33	.210	.291	.315	76	-6	-6	20	1	1	-0	.972	-5	O	-1.5
Total	3	171	358	42	69	10	2	3	23	36	55	.193	.266	.257	51	-22	-23	27	3	2	-0	.980	-9	O/32	-3.9

■ LENNY METZ Metz, Leonard Raymond b: 7/6/1899, Louisville, Colo. d: 2/24/53, Denver, Colo. BR/TR, 5'10.5", 170 lbs. Deb: 9/11/23

YEAR	TM/L	G	AB	R	H	2B	3B	HR	RBI	BB	SO	AVG	OBP	SLG	PRO+	BR	/A	RC	SB	CS	SBR	FA	FR	POS	TPR
1923	Phi-N	12	37	4	8	0	0	0	3	4	3	.216	.310	.216	37	-3	-4	3	0	0	0	.969	1	/2S	-0.2
1924	Phi-N	7	7	1	2	0	0	0	1	1	0	.286	.375	.286	71	-0	-0	1	0	0	0	.846	0	/S	0.0
1925	Phi-N	11	14	1	0	0	0	0	0	0	2	.000	.000	.000	-92	-4	-4	0	0	0	0	1.000	2	/S2	-0.2
Total	3	30	58	6	10	0	0	0	4	5	5	.172	.250	.172	11	-7	-8	4	0	0	0	.951	3	/S2	-0.4

■ ROGER METZGER Metzger, Roger Henry b: 10/10/47, Fredericksburg, Tex BB/TR, 6', 165 lbs. Deb: 6/16/70

YEAR	TM/L	G	AB	R	H	2B	3B	HR	RBI	BB	SO	AVG	OBP	SLG	PRO+	BR	/A	RC	SB	CS	SBR	FA	FR	POS	TPR
1970	Chi-N	1	2	0	0	0	0	0	0	0	0	.000	.000	.000	-89	-1	-1	0	0	0	0	.833	1	/S	0.1
1971	Hou-N	150	562	64	132	14	**11**	0	26	44	50	.235	.295	.299	70	-23	-21	52	15	6	1	.977	-5	*S	-0.6
1972	Hou-N	153	641	84	142	12	3	2	38	60	71	.222	.289	.259	58	-35	-34	52	23	9	2	.971	5	*S	-0.6
1973	Hou-N	154	580	67	145	11	**14**	1	35	39	70	.250	.301	.322	73	-22	-21	57	10	4	1	**.982**	-19	*S	-2.1
1974	Hou-N	143	572	66	145	18	10	0	30	37	73	.253	.299	.320	76	-21	-18	54	9	7	-2	.976	-11	*S	-1.2
1975	Hou-N	127	450	54	102	7	9	2	26	41	39	.227	.291	.296	68	-22	-19	40	4	5	-2	.977	11	*S	0.4
1976	Hou-N	152	481	37	101	13	8	0	29	52	63	.210	.287	.270	65	-25	-20	38	1	1	-0	**.986**	-3	*S/2	-0.6
1977	Hou-N	97	269	24	50	9	6	0	16	32	24	.186	.272	.264	49	-21	-18	20	2	0	1	.973	-4	S/2	-1.2
1978	Hou-N	45	123	11	27	4	1	0	6	12	9	.220	.289	.268	61	-7	-6	8	0	0	0	.964	-4	S/2	-0.6

YEAR	TM/L	G	AB	R	H	2B	3B	HR	RBI	BB	SO	AVG	OBP	SLG	PRO+	BR	/A	RC	SB	CS	SBR	FA	FR	POS	TPR
	SF-N	75	235	17	61	6	1	0	17	12	17	.260	.296	.294	68	-11	-10	21	8	1	2	.974	-12	S	-1.2
	Yr	120	358	28	88	10	2	0	23	24	26	.246	.293	.285	66	-18	-16	30	8	1	2	.970	-16	*S/2	-1.8
1979	SF-N	94	259	24	65	7	8	0	31	23	31	.251	.312	.340	83	-8	-6	28	11	3	2	.956	2	S2/3	0.6
1980	SF-N	28	27	5	2	0	0	0	0	3	2	.074	.167	.074	-31	-5	-5	0	0	0	0	.971	3	S/2	-0.2
Total	11	1219	4201	453	972	101	71	5	254	355	449	.231	.293	.293	67	-200	-178	372	83	36	3	.976	-36	*S/23	-7.2

■ WILLIAM METZIG Metzig, William Andrew b: 12/4/18, Ft.Dodge, Iowa BR/TR, 6'1", 180 lbs. Deb: 9/19/44

YEAR	TM/L	G	AB	R	H	2B	3B	HR	RBI	BB	SO	AVG	OBP	SLG	PRO+	BR	/A	RC	SB	CS	SBR	FA	FR	POS	TPR
1944	Chi-A	5	16	1	2	0	0	0	1	1	4	.125	.176	.125	-13	-2	-2	0	0	0	0	1.000	2	/2	0.0

■ ALEX METZLER Metzler, Alexander b: 1/4/03, Fresno, Cal. d: 11/30/73, Fresno, Cal. BL/TR, 5'9", 167 lbs. Deb: 9/16/25

YEAR	TM/L	G	AB	R	H	2B	3B	HR	RBI	BB	SO	AVG	OBP	SLG	PRO+	BR	/A	RC	SB	CS	SBR	FA	FR	POS	TPR
1925	Chi-N	9	38	2	7	2	0	0	2	3	7	.184	.244	.237	23	-4	-4	2	0	0	0	1.000	2	/O	-0.3
1926	Phi-A	20	67	8	16	3	0	0	12	7	5	.239	.311	.284	53	-4	-5	6	1	0	0	1.000	2	O	-0.4
1927	Chi-A	134	543	87	173	29	11	3	61	61	39	.319	.396	.429	117	13	15	89	15	11	-2	.965	16	*O	1.9
1928	Chi-A	139	464	71	141	18	14	3	55	77	30	.304	.410	.422	121	16	17	86	16	8	0	.968	-4	*O	0.4
1929	Chi-A	146	568	80	156	23	13	2	49	80	45	.275	.367	.371	92	-6	-5	82	9	5	-0	.960	1	*O	-1.3
1930	Chi-A	56	79	12	14	4	0	0	5	11	6	.177	.278	.228	31	-8	-8	5	0	2	-1	.969	-5	O	-1.4
	StL-A	56	209	30	54	6	3	1	23	21	12	.258	.326	.330	65	-10	-11	24	5	1	1	.951	-5	O	-1.8
	Yr	112	288	42	68	10	3	1	28	32	18	.236	.313	.302	57	-19	-19	29	5	3	-0	.955	-10	O	-3.2
Total	6	560	1968	290	561	85	41	9	207	260	144	.285	.374	.384	97	-4	-1	295	46	27	-2	.965	6	O	-2.9

■ HENSLEY MEULENS Meulens, Hensley Filemon Acasio "Bam-Bam" b: 6/23/67, Curaco, Neth.Antilles BR/TR, 6'4", 200 lbs. Deb: 8/23/89

YEAR	TM/L	G	AB	R	H	2B	3B	HR	RBI	BB	SO	AVG	OBP	SLG	PRO+	BR	/A	RC	SB	CS	SBR	FA	FR	POS	TPR
1989	NY-A	8	28	2	5	0	0	0	1	2	8	.179	.233	.179	18	-3	-3	1	0	1	-1	.875	2	/3	-0.1
1990	NY-A	23	83	12	20	7	0	3	10	9	25	.241	.337	.434	113	2	1	12	1	0	0	.963	3	O	0.4
1991	NY-A	96	288	37	64	8	1	6	29	18	97	.222	.277	.319	64	-14	-14	25	3	0	1	.967	2	OD/1	-1.3
1992	NY-A	2	5	1	3	0	0	1	1	1	0	.600	.667	1.200	404	2	2	3	0	0	0	1.000	0	/3	0.2
Total	4	129	404	52	92	15	1	10	41	30	130	.228	.293	.344	76	-13	-14	41	4	1	1	.966	7	/OD31	-0.8

■ IRISH MEUSEL Meusel, Emil Frederick b: 6/9/1893, Oakland, Cal. d: 3/1/63, Long Beach, Cal. BR/TR, 5'11.5", 178 lbs. Deb: 10/01/14 FC

YEAR	TM/L	G	AB	R	H	2B	3B	HR	RBI	BB	SO	AVG	OBP	SLG	PRO+	BR	/A	RC	SB	CS	SBR	FA	FR	POS	TPR
1914	Was-A	1	2	0	0	0	0	0	0	0	0	.000	.000	.000	-96	-0	-0	0	0			1.000	-0	/O	-0.1
1918	Phi-N	124	473	48	132	25	6	4	62	30	21	.279	.323	.383	108	7	4	61	18			.972	8	*O/2	0.6
1919	Phi-N	135	521	65	159	26	7	5	59	15	13	.305	.327	.411	113	11	7	74	24			.968	-2	*O	-0.3
1920	Phi-N	138	518	75	160	27	8	14	69	32	27	.309	.349	.473	129	21	18	83	17	11	-2	.929	-5	*O/1	0.3
1921	Phi-N	84	343	59	121	21	7	12	51	18	17	.353	.385	.560	136	22	18	72	8	4	0	.929	2	O	1.3
	*NY-N	62	243	37	80	12	6	2	36	15	12	.329	.373	.453	117	6	6	38	5	9	-4	.971	-1	O	-0.3
	Yr	146	586	96	201	33	13	14	87	33	29	.343	.380	.515	129	28	24	110	13	13	-4	.947	1	*O	1.0
1922	*NY-N	154	617	100	204	28	17	16	132	35	33	.331	.369	.509	123	20	19	112	12	10	-2	.980	-9	*O	-0.3
1923	*NY-N	146	595	102	177	22	14	19	**125**	38	16	.297	.341	.477	115	9	10	94	8	8	-2	.949	-8	*O	-0.9
1924	*NY-N	139	549	75	170	26	9	6	102	33	18	.310	.351	.423	109	4	6	81	11	7	-1	.967	-7	*O	-1.1
1925	NY-N	135	516	82	169	35	8	21	111	26	19	.328	.363	.548	135	20	23	100	5	4	-1	.959	1	*O	1.4
1926	NY-N	129	449	51	131	25	10	6	65	16	18	.292	.322	.432	103	-1	-0	60	5			.958	-5	*O	-1.3
1927	Bro-N	42	74	7	18	3	1	1	7	11	5	.243	.341	.351	85	-1	-1	9	0			1.000	-0	O	-0.3
Total	11	1289	4900	701	1521	250	93	106	819	269	199	.310	.348	.464	118	118	110	783	113	53		.959	-25	*O/21	-1.0

■ BOB MEUSEL Meusel, Robert William "Long Bob" b: 7/19/1896, San Jose, Cal. d: 11/28/77, Downey, Cal. BR/TR, 6'3", 190 lbs. Deb: 4/14/20 F

YEAR	TM/L	G	AB	R	H	2B	3B	HR	RBI	BB	SO	AVG	OBP	SLG	PRO+	BR	/A	RC	SB	CS	SBR	FA	FR	POS	TPR
1920	NY-A	119	460	75	151	40	7	11	83	20	72	.328	.359	.517	126	17	15	83	4	4	-1	.947	-10	O3/1	0.0
1921	*NY-A	149	598	104	190	40	16	24	135	34	88	.318	.356	.559	128	22	21	117	17	6	2	.934	5	*O	1.5
1922	*NY-A	121	473	61	151	26	11	16	84	40	58	.319	.376	.522	129	20	19	91	13	9	-2	.950	0	*O	0.9
1923	*NY-A	132	460	59	144	29	10	9	91	31	52	.313	.359	.478	117	10	9	74	13	15	-5	.953	-7	*O	-0.9
1924	NY-A	143	579	93	188	40	11	12	120	32	43	.325	.365	.494	120	14	14	102	26	14	-1	.951	-7	*O/3	-0.3
1925	NY-A	156	624	101	181	34	12	**33**	**138**	54	55	.290	.348	.542	125	16	18	112	10	14	-5	.985	-9	*O3	-0.3
1926	*NY-A	108	413	73	130	22	3	12	81	37	32	.315	.373	.470	120	10	11	68	16	17	-5	.960	-6	*O	-0.7
1927	*NY-A	135	516	75	174	47	9	8	103	45	58	.337	.393	.510	137	24	26	96	24	10	1	.950	-4	*O	1.4
1928	*NY-A	131	518	77	154	45	5	11	113	39	56	.297	.349	.467	116	8	10	82	6	9	-4	.975	4	*O	0.2
1929	NY-A	100	391	46	102	15	3	10	57	17	42	.261	.292	.391	79	-16	-13	43	1	5	-3	.968	3	O	-1.8
1930	Cin-N	113	443	62	128	30	8	10	62	26	63	.289	.330	.460	93	-10	-6	65	9			.962	-4	*O	-1.6
Total	11	1407	5475	826	1693	368	95	156	1067	375	619	.309	.356	.497	119	116	123	932	139	103		.958	-34	*O/31	-1.6

■ BENNY MEYER Meyer, Bernhard "Earache" b: 1/1/1888, Hematite, Mo. d: 2/6/74, Festus, Mo. BR/TR, 5'9", 170 lbs. Deb: 4/09/13 C

YEAR	TM/L	G	AB	R	H	2B	3B	HR	RBI	BB	SO	AVG	OBP	SLG	PRO+	BR	/A	RC	SB	CS	SBR	FA	FR	POS	TPR
1913	Bro-N	38	87	12	17	0	1	1	10	10	14	.195	.278	.253	51	-5	-6	8	8			.943	-2	O/C	-0.9
1914	Bal-F	143	500	76	152	18	10	5	40	71	53	.304	.395	.410	125	21	19	95	23			.916	-11	*O/S	0.4
1915	Bal-F	35	120	20	29	2	0	0	5	37	13	.242	.424	.258	99	4	3	17	6			.931	-3	O	-0.2
	Buf-F	93	333	37	77	8	6	1	29	40	37	.231	.316	.300	80	-7	-8	36	9			.947	-6	O	-2.0
	Yr	128	453	57	106	10	6	1	34	77	50	.234	.348	.289	86	-3	-5	53	15			.943	-10	*O	-2.2
1925	Phi-N	1	1	1	1	1	0	0	0	0	0	1.000	1.000	2.000	594	1	1	2	0	0	0	.000	0	/2	0.1
Total	4	310	1041	146	276	29	17	7	84	158	117	.265	.365	.346	103	14	10	157	46	0		.931	-22	O/S2C	-2.6

■ DAN MEYER Meyer, Daniel Thomas b: 8/3/52, Hamilton, Ohio BL/TR, 5'11", 180 lbs. Deb: 9/14/74

YEAR	TM/L	G	AB	R	H	2B	3B	HR	RBI	BB	SO	AVG	OBP	SLG	PRO+	BR	/A	RC	SB	CS	SBR	FA	FR	POS	TPR
1974	Det-A	13	50	5	10	1	1	3	7	1	1	.200	.231	.440	86	-1	-1	4	1	0	0	.967	1	O	-0.1
1975	Det-A	122	470	56	111	17	3	8	47	26	25	.236	.279	.336	70	-18	-20	41	8	3	1	.950	-0	O1	-2.7
1976	Det-A	105	294	37	74	8	4	2	16	17	22	.252	.293	.327	78	-7	-9	28	10	0	3	.988	-4	O1/D	-1.3
1977	Sea-A	159	582	75	159	24	4	22	90	43	51	.273	.324	.442	107	4	5	77	11	8	-2	.992	1	*1	-0.6
1978	Sea-A	123	444	38	101	18	1	8	56	24	39	.227	.267	.327	66	-21	-20	38	7	3	0	.989	-2	*1/OD	-3.0
1979	Sea-A	144	525	72	146	21	7	20	74	29	35	.278	.321	.459	106	4	3	72	11	7	-1	.936	-14	*3O1	-1.4
1980	Sea-A	146	531	56	146	25	6	11	71	31	42	.275	.316	.407	96	-4	-4	66	8	4	0	.961	-10	*O/31D	-1.9
1981	Sea-A	83	252	26	66	10	1	3	22	10	16	.262	.293	.345	80	-6	-7	24	4	3	-1	.961	-2	3O/1D	-1.1
1982	Oak-A	120	383	28	92	17	3	8	59	18	33	.240	.274	.363	77	-15	-13	37	1	1	-0	.990	-3	1DO	-2.0
1983	Oak-A	69	169	15	32	9	0	1	13	19	11	.189	.271	.260	50	-12	-11	11	0	0	0	.987	-6	1DO/3	-1.9
1984	Oak-A	20	22	1	7	3	1	0	4	0	2	.318	.318	.545	143	1	1	3	0	0	0	.944	0	/1D	0.1
1985	Oak-A	14	12	2	0	0	0	0	0	1	0	.000	.077	.000	-83	-3	-3	0	0	0	0	.000	-0	/3OD	-0.3
Total	12	1118	3734	411	944	153	31	86	459	219	277	.253	.296	.379	86	-77	-80	402	61	29	1	.991	-38	1O3/D	-16.2

■ GEORGE MEYER Meyer, George Francis b: 8/3/09, Chicago, Ill. d: 1/3/92, Hoffman Estates, Ill. BR/TR, 5'9", 160 lbs. Deb: 9/03/38

YEAR	TM/L	G	AB	R	H	2B	3B	HR	RBI	BB	SO	AVG	OBP	SLG	PRO+	BR	/A	RC	SB	CS	SBR	FA	FR	POS	TPR
1938	Chi-A	24	81	10	24	2	2	0	9	11	17	.296	.387	.370	89	-1	-1	13	3	1	0	.967	6	2	0.6

■ DUTCH MEYER Meyer, Lambert Dalton b: 10/6/15, Waco, Tex. BR/TR, 5'10.5", 181 lbs. Deb: 6/23/37

YEAR	TM/L	G	AB	R	H	2B	3B	HR	RBI	BB	SO	AVG	OBP	SLG	PRO+	BR	/A	RC	SB	CS	SBR	FA	FR	POS	TPR
1937	Chi-N	1	0	0	0	0	0	0	0	0	0	—	—	—	—	0	0	0	0			.000	0	R	0.0
1940	Det-A	23	58	12	15	3	0	0	6	4	10	.259	.317	.310	58	-3	-4	7	2	0	1	.960	0	2	-0.2
1941	Det-A	46	153	12	29	9	1	1	14	8	13	.190	.230	.281	31	-15	-17	10	1	1	-0	.972	6	2	-0.8
1942	Det-A	14	52	5	17	3	0	2	9	4	4	.327	.386	.500	137	3	3	9	0	1	-1	.989	6	2	0.9
1945	Cle-A	130	524	71	153	29	8	7	48	40	32	.292	.342	.418	125	12	14	74	2	4	-2	.978	-32	*2	-1.2
1946	Cle-A	72	207	13	48	5	3	0	16	26	16	.232	.321	.285	75	-8	-6	20	0	1	-1	.977	-13	2	-1.7
Total	6	286	994	113	262	49	12	10	93	82	75	.264	.322	.367	94	-11	-10	119	5	7		.977	-32	2	-3.0

■ LEE MEYER Meyer, Lee TR, Deb: 9/27/09

YEAR	TM/L	G	AB	R	H	2B	3B	HR	RBI	BB	SO	AVG	OBP	SLG	PRO+	BR	/A	RC	SB	CS	SBR	FA	FR	POS	TPR
1909	Bro-N	7	23	1	3	0	0	0	0	2		.130	.200	.130	3	-3	-2	1	0			.882	2	/S	-0.1

YEAR	TM/L	G	AB	R	H	2B	3B	HR	RBI	BB	SO	AVG	OBP	SLG	PRO+	BR	/A	RC	SB	CS	SBR	FA	FR	POS	TPR

■ SCOTT MEYER Meyer, Scott William b: 8/19/57, Evergreen Park, Ill BR/TR, 6'1", 195 lbs. Deb: 9/10/78

| 1978 | Oak-A | 8 | 9 | 1 | 1 | 1 | 0 | 0 | 0 | 0 | 4 | .111 | .111 | .222 | -9 | -1 | -1 | 0 | 0 | 0 | 0 | 1.000 | -1 | /C | -0.2 |

■ JOEY MEYER Meyer, Tanner Joe b: 5/10/62, Honolulu, Hawaii BR/TR, 6'3", 260 lbs. Deb: 4/04/88

1988	Mil-A	103	327	22	86	18	0	11	45	23	88	.263	.313	.419	102	1	0	41	0	1	-1	.986	-0	D1	-0.3
1989	Mil-A	53	147	13	33	6	0	7	29	12	36	.224	.283	.408	93	-2	-2	17	1	0	0	.982	-1	D1	-0.3
Total	2	156	474	35	119	24	0	18	74	35	124	.251	.304	.416	100	-1	-2	58	1	1	-0	.984	-1	/D1	-0.6

■ BILLY MEYER Meyer, William Adam b: 1/14/1892, Knoxville, Tenn. d: 3/31/57, Knoxville, Tenn. BR/TR, 5'9.5", 170 lbs. Deb: 9/06/13 M

1913	Chi-A	1	1	0	1	0	0	0	0	0	0	1.000	1.000	1.000	490	0	0	1	0			.857	1	/C	0.1
1916	Phi-A	50	138	6	32	2	2	1	12	8	11	.232	.274	.297	75	-5	-5	13	3			.961	7	C	0.7
1917	Phi-A	62	162	9	38	5	1	0	9	7	14	.235	.271	.278	68	-7	-6	12	0			.962	9	C	0.7
Total	3	113	301	15	71	7	3	1	21	15	25	.236	.274	.289	73	-11	-11	25	3			.960	18	C	1.5

■ LEVI MEYERLE Meyerle, Levi Samuel "Long Levi" b: 7/1845, Philadelphia, Pa. d: 11/4/21, Philadelphia, Pa. BR/TR, 6'1", 177 lbs. Deb: 5/20/1871

1871	Ath-n	26	130	45	64	9	3	**4**	40	2	1	**.492**	**.500**	**.700**	**243**	**23**	**23**	49	4					*3/P	**1.3**
1872	Ath-n	27	146	31	48	7	6	1	31	0	1	.329	.329	.479	145	7	7	24						O/S3	0.6
1873	Phi-n	48	238	53	83	14	4	3	56	2	0	.349	.354	.479	138	12	10	43						*3/S	0.7
1874	Chi-n	53	253	66	102	20	0	1			3	.403	.410	.494	185	24	23	53						23/OS	1.7
1875	Phi-n	68	300	55	96	13	9	1			0	.320	.320	.433	152	17	15	43						231	1.2
1876	Phi-N	55	256	46	87	12	8	0	34	3	2	.340	.347	.449	165	16	17	41				.791	-3	*3/O2P	1.2
1877	Cin-N	27	107	11	35	7	2	0	15	0	4	.327	.327	.430	154	4	6	15				.822	1	S2/O	0.6
1884	Phi-U	3	11	0	1	1	0	0			0	.091	.091	.182	-1	-1	-1	0				.789	-1	/1O	-0.2
Total	5 n	222	1067	250	393	63	22	10	127	7	2	.368	.372	.497	167	82	78	211						3/2O1SP	5.5
Total	3	85	374	57	123	20	10	0	49	3	6	.329	.334	.436	157	19	21	57				.891	-4	/3S2O1P	1.6

■ HENRY MEYERS Meyers, Henry L. b: 1860, Philadelphia, Pa. d: 6/28/1898, Harrisburg, Pa. Deb: 8/30/1890

| 1890 | Phi-a | 5 | 19 | 2 | 3 | 0 | 0 | 0 | | | 1 | .158 | .238 | .158 | 19 | -2 | -2 | 1 | 2 | | | .684 | -3 | /3 | -0.4 |

■ CHIEF MEYERS Meyers, John Tortes b: 7/29/1880, Riverside, Cal. d: 7/25/71, San Bernardino, Cal. BR/TR, 5'11", 194 lbs. Deb: 4/16/09

1909	NY-N	90	220	15	61	10	5	1	30	22		.277	.359	.382	128	8	8	31	3			.963	2	C	1.6
1910	NY-N	127	365	25	104	18	0	1	62	40	18	.285	.362	.342	106	4	4	48	5			.969	5	*C	2.0
1911	*NY-N	133	391	48	130	18	9	1	61	25	33	.332	.392	.432	126	16	14	69	7			.979	-3	*C	2.3
1912	*NY-N	126	371	60	133	16	5	6	54	47	20	.358	.441	.477	147	28	27	82	8			.973	-10	*C	2.7
1913	*NY-N	120	378	37	118	18	5	3	47	37	22	.312	.387	.410	127	15	14	60	7			.967	9	*C	3.4
1914	NY-N	134	381	33	109	13	5	1	55	34	25	.286	.357	.354	116	6	8	48	4			.970	-12	*C	0.6
1915	NY-N	110	289	24	67	10	5	1	26	26	18	.232	.311	.311	94	-4	-2	28	4	4	-1	.986	-4	*C	0.0
1916	*Bro-N	80	239	21	59	10	3	0	21	26	15	.247	.336	.314	97	1	0	26	2			.984	7	C	1.5
1917	Bro-N	47	132	8	28	3	0	0	3	13	7	.212	.283	.235	58	-6	-6	10	4			.974	-6	C	-1.0
	Bos-N	25	68	5	17	4	0	0	4	4	4	.250	.311	.426	133	2	2	9	0			1.000	7	C	1.2
	Yr	72	200	13	45	7	0	0	7	17	11	.225	.292	.300	82	-4	-4	18	4			.984	1	C	0.2
Total	9	992	2834	276	826	120	41	14	363	274	162	.291	.367	.378	117	70	69	409	44	4		.974	-6	C	14.3

■ LOU MEYERS Meyers, Lewis Henry "Crazy Horse" b: 12/9/1859, Cincinnati, Ohio d: 11/30/20, Cincinnati, Ohio BR/TR, 5'11", 165 lbs. Deb: 5/10/1884

| 1884 | Cin-U | 2 | 3 | 1 | 0 | 0 | 0 | 0 | | | 1 | .000 | .250 | .000 | -8 | -0 | -0 | 0 | | | | .667 | -2 | /CO | -0.2 |

■ MICKEY MICELOTTA Micelotta, Robert Peter b: 10/20/28, Corona, N.Y. BR/TR, 5'11", 185 lbs. Deb: 4/20/54

1954	Phi-N	13	3	2	0	0	0	0	0	1	1	.000	.250	.000	-28	-1	-1	0	0	0	0	1.000	4	/S	0.3
1955	Phi-N	4	4	0	0	0	0	0	0	0	0	.000	.000	.000	-99	-1	-1	0	0	0	0	1.000	0	/S	-0.1
Total	2	17	7	2	0	0	0	0	0	1	1	.000	.125	.000	-64	-2	-2	0	0	0	0	1.000	4	/S	0.2

■ GENE MICHAEL Michael, Eugene Richard "Stick" b: 6/2/38, Kent, Ohio BB/TR, 6'2", 183 lbs. Deb: 7/15/66 MC

1966	Pit-N	30	33	9	5	2	1	0	2	0	7	.152	.152	.273	15	-4	-4	1	0	0	0	.903	5	/S23	0.2
1967	LA-N	98	223	20	45	3	1	0	7	11	30	.202	.246	.224	39	-18	-16	12	1	3	-2	.950	5	S	-0.8
1968	NY-A	61	116	8	23	3	0	1	8	2	23	.198	.218	.250	43	-8	-8	6	3	2	-0	.939	-1	S/P	-0.7
1969	NY-A	119	412	41	112	24	4	2	31	43	56	.272	.342	.364	101	-1	1	52	7	4	-0	.968	-1	*S	1.3
1970	NY-A	134	435	42	93	10	1	2	38	50	93	.214	.295	.255	56	-27	-24	35	3	1	0	.957	2	*S/32	-0.8
1971	NY-A	139	456	36	102	15	0	3	35	48	64	.224	.302	.276	69	-20	-17	37	3	3	-1	.973	17	*S	1.7
1972	NY-A	126	391	29	91	7	4	1	32	32	45	.233	.292	.279	73	-14	-12	31	4	2	0	.969	24	*S	3.1
1973	NY-A	129	418	30	94	11	1	3	47	26	51	.225	.270	.278	56	-25	-24	29	1	3	-2	.965	5	*S	-0.4
1974	NY-A	81	177	19	46	9	0	0	13	14	24	.260	.314	.311	83	-4	-4	17	0	0	0	.970	5	2S/3	0.5
1975	Det-A	56	145	15	31	2	0	3	13	8	28	.214	.255	.290	51	-9	-10	11	0	0	0	.938	-4	S/23	-1.0
Total	10	973	2806	249	642	86	12	15	226	234	421	.229	.290	.284	66	-131	-118	231	22	18	-4	.962	55	S/23P	3.1

■ CASS MICHAELS Michaels, Casimir Eugene (Played In 1943 Under Real Name Of Casimir Eugene Kwietniewski) b: 3/4/26, Detroit, Mich. d: 11/12/82, Grosse Pointe, Mich. BR/TR, 5'11", 175 lbs. Deb: 8/19/43

1943	Chi-A	2	7	0	0	0	0	0	0	0	0	.000	.000	.000	-99	-2	-2	0	0	0	0	1.000	-1	/3	-0.4
1944	Chi-A	27	68	4	12	4	1	0	5	2	5	.176	.200	.265	33	-6	-6	4	0	0	0	.930	6	S/3	0.1
1945	Chi-A	129	445	47	109	8	5	2	54	37	28	.245	.307	.299	78	-13	-12	41	8	7	-2	.936	10	*S/2	0.6
1946	Chi-A	91	291	37	75	8	0	1	22	29	36	.258	.333	.296	80	-8	-7	32	9	3	1	.957	3	23/S	0.2
1947	Chi-A	110	355	31	97	15	4	3	34	39	28	.273	.350	.363	102	-0	1	45	10	5	1	.982	11	23/S	1.7
1948	Chi-A	145	484	47	120	12	6	5	56	69	42	.248	.344	.329	82	-13	-11	60	8	2	1	.957	13	S2/O	1.1
1949	Chi-A★	154	561	73	173	27	9	6	83	101	50	.308	.417	.421	126	21	24	102	5	7	-3	.976	12	*2	3.9
1950	Chi-A	36	138	21	43	6	3	4	19	13	8	.312	.375	.486	122	3	4	25	0	0	0	.964	-6	2	-0.1
	Was-A	106	388	48	97	8	4	4	47	55	39	.250	.345	.322	75	-16	-13	45	2	3	-1	.975	8	*2	-0.2
	Yr	142	526	69	140	14	7	8	66	68	47	.266	.352	.365	88	-12	-9	70	2	3	-1	.972	2	*2	-0.3
1951	Was-A	138	485	59	125	20	4	4	45	61	41	.258	.342	.340	86	-9	-8	58	1	1	-0	.964	-23	*2	-2.5
1952	Was-A	22	86	10	20	4	1	1	7	7	15	.233	.290	.337	77	-3	-3	7	0	0	0	.977	1	2	-0.1
	StL-A	55	166	21	44	8	2	3	25	23	16	.265	.354	.392	104	2	1	25	1	0	0	.916	-0	3/2	0.1
	Phi-A	55	200	22	50	4	2	1	18	23	11	.250	.330	.335	80	-4	-5	24	3	0	1	.993	-13	2	-1.6
	Yr	132	452	53	114	16	5	5	50	53	42	.252	.332	.356	89	-5	-7	56	4	0	1	.989	-13	23	-1.6
1953	Phi-A	117	411	53	103	10	6	12	42	51	56	.251	.335	.363	85	-6	-9	55	7	0	2	.970	-11	*2	-1.1
1954	Chi-A	101	282	35	74	13	2	7	44	56	31	.262	.392	.397	113	9	7	50	10	4	1	.958	-4	3/2	0.3
Total	12	1288	4367	508	1142	147	46	53	501	566	406	.262	.349	.353	92	-46	-37	572	64	32	0	.973	3	2S3/O	2.0

■ RALPH MICHAELS Michaels, Ralph Joseph b: 5/3/02, Etna, Pa. d: 8/5/88, Monroeville, Pa. BR/TR, 5'10.5", 178 lbs. Deb: 4/16/24

1924	Chi-N	8	11	0	4	0	0	0	2	0	1	.364	.364	.364	95	-0	-0	1	0	0	0	.929	1	/S	0.1
1925	Chi-N	22	50	10	14	1	0	0	6	6	9	.280	.357	.300	69	-2	-2	6	1	0	0	.975	3	3/12S	0.2
1926	Chi-N	2	0	1	0	0	0	0	0	0	0	—	—	—	—	0	0	0	0			.000	0	/H	0.0
Total	3	32	61	11	18	1	0	0	8	6	10	.295	.358	.311	73	-2	-2	7	1	0	0	.933	3	/3S21	0.3

■ ED MICKELSON Mickelson, Edward Allen b: 9/9/26, Ottawa, Ill. BR/TR, 6'3", 205 lbs. Deb: 9/18/50

1950	StL-N	5	10	1	1	0	0	0	1	1	3	.100	.250	.100	-4	-1	-2	0	0	0	0	1.000	1	/1	-0.1
1953	StL-A	7	15	0	2	0	0	0	1	0	4	.133	.235	.200	18	-2	-2	1	0	0	0	1.000	0	/1	-0.2
1957	Chi-N	6	12	0	0	0	0	0	0	2	6	.000	.000	.000	-99	-3	-3	0	0	0	0	1.000	1	/1	-0.3

YEAR	TM/L	G	AB	R	H	2B	3B	HR	RBI	BB	SO	AVG	OBP	SLG	PRO+	BR	/A	RC	SB	CS	SBR	FA	FR	POS	TPR
Total	3	18	37	2	3	1	0	0	3	4	13	.081	.171	.108	-23	-7	-7	1	0	0		1.000	2	/1	-0.6

■ EZRA MIDKIFF Midkiff, Ezra Millington "Salt Rock" b: 11/13/1882, Salt Rock, W.Va. d: 3/20/57, Huntington, W.Va. BL/TR, 5'10", 180 lbs. Deb: 10/05/09

YEAR	TM/L	G	AB	R	H	2B	3B	HR	RBI	BB	SO	AVG	OBP	SLG	PRO+	BR	/A	RC	SB	CS	SBR	FA	FR	POS	TPR
1909	Cin-N	1	2	0	0	0	0	0	0	0		.000	.000	.000	-99	-0	-0	0	0			.000	-1	/3	-0.1
1912	NY-A	21	86	9	21	1	0	0	9	7		.244	.301	.256	56	-4	-5	8	4			.901	2	3	-0.3
1913	NY-A	83	284	22	56	9	1	0	14	12	33	.197	.232	.236	37	-23	-23	17	9			.957	18	3/S2	-0.5
Total	3	105	372	31	77	10	1	0	23	19	33	.207	.247	.239	41	-28	-29	25	13			.942	19	/3S2	-0.9

■ ED MIERKOWICZ Mierkowicz, Edward Frank "Butch" or "Mouse" b: 3/6/24, Wyandotte, Mich. BR/TR, 6'4", 205 lbs. Deb: 8/31/45

YEAR	TM/L	G	AB	R	H	2B	3B	HR	RBI	BB	SO	AVG	OBP	SLG	PRO+	BR	/A	RC	SB	CS	SBR	FA	FR	POS	TPR
1945	*Det-A	10	15	0	2	2	0	0	2	1	3	.133	.188	.267	29	-1	-2	1	0	0	0	1.000	-1	/O	-0.3
1947	Det-A	21	42	6	8	1	0	1	1	1	12	.190	.209	.286	36	-4	-4	2	1	0	0	.947	-1	O	-0.6
1948	Det-A	3	5	0	1	0	0	0	1	2	2	.200	.429	.200	69	-0	-0	0	0	0	0	1.000	0	/O	0.0
1950	StL-N	1	1	0	0	0	0	0	0	0	1	.000	.000	.000	-95	-0	-0	0	0			.000	0	H	0.0
Total	4	35	63	6	11	3	0	1	4	4	18	.175	.224	.270	36	-5	-6	3	1	0		.968	-2	/O	-0.9

■ LARRY MIGGINS Miggins, Lawrence Edward "Irish" b: 8/20/25, Bronx, N.Y. BR/TR, 6'4", 198 lbs. Deb: 10/03/48

YEAR	TM/L	G	AB	R	H	2B	3B	HR	RBI	BB	SO	AVG	OBP	SLG	PRO+	BR	/A	RC	SB	CS	SBR	FA	FR	POS	TPR
1948	StL-N	1	1	1	0	0	0	0	0	0	0	.000	.000	.000	-95	-0	-0	0	0			.000	0	H	0.0
1952	StL-N	42	96	7	22	5	1	2	10	3	19	.229	.253	.365	69	-4	-4	9	0	1	-1	.967	-4	O/1	-1.1
Total	2	43	97	8	22	5	1	2	10	3	19	.227	.250	.361	67	-5	-5	9	0	1		.983	-4	/O1	-1.1

■ JOHN MIHALIC Mihalic, John Michael b: 11/13/11, Cleveland, Ohio d: 4/24/87, Ft.Oglethorpe, Ga. BR/TR, 5'11", 172 lbs. Deb: 9/18/35

YEAR	TM/L	G	AB	R	H	2B	3B	HR	RBI	BB	SO	AVG	OBP	SLG	PRO+	BR	/A	RC	SB	CS	SBR	FA	FR	POS	TPR
1935	Was-A	6	22	4	5	3	0	0	6	2	3	.227	.292	.364	71	-1	-1	3	1	0	0	.966	-1	/S	-0.1
1936	Was-A	25	88	15	21	2	1	0	8	14	14	.239	.343	.284	60	-6	-5	10	2	1	0	.972	1	2	-0.2
1937	Was-A	38	107	13	27	5	2	0	8	17	9	.252	.355	.336	79	-4	-3	14	2	1	0	.981	4	2/S	0.3
Total	3	69	217	32	53	10	3	0	22	33	26	.244	.344	.318	70	-10	-9	26	5	2	0	.977	4	/2S	0.0

■ EDDIE MIKSIS Miksis, Edward Thomas b: 9/11/26, Burlington, N.J. BR/TR, 6'0.5", 185 lbs. Deb: 6/17/44

YEAR	TM/L	G	AB	R	H	2B	3B	HR	RBI	BB	SO	AVG	OBP	SLG	PRO+	BR	/A	RC	SB	CS	SBR	FA	FR	POS	TPR
1944	Bro-N	26	91	12	20	2	0	0	11	6	11	.220	.268	.242	45	-7	-6	6	4			.896	-4	3S	-1.0
1946	Bro-N	23	48	3	7	0	0	0	5	3	3	.146	.212	.146	2	-6	-6	1	0			.970	0	3/2	-0.6
1947	*Bro-N	45	86	18	23	1	0	4	10	9	8	.267	.337	.419	96	-0	-1	12	0			1.000	3	2O/3S	0.3
1948	Bro-N	86	221	28	47	7	1	2	16	19	27	.213	.278	.281	50	-15	-16	19	5			.967	4	23/S	-1.0
1949	*Bro-N	50	113	17	25	5	0	1	6	7	8	.221	.267	.292	48	-8	-9	8	3			.978	6	3/S21	-0.3
1950	Bro-N	51	76	13	19	2	1	2	10	5	10	.250	.296	.382	75	-3	-3	8	3			.964	5	2S/3	0.3
1951	Bro-N	19	10	6	2	1	0	0	0	1	2	.200	.333	.300	70	-0	-0	1	0	0	0	1.000	2	/32	0.2
	Chi-N	102	421	48	112	13	3	4	35	33	36	.266	.319	.340	76	-13	-14	46	11	5	0	.969	3	*2	-0.6
	Yr	121	431	54	114	14	3	4	35	34	38	.265	.320	.339	76	-14	-15	48	11	5	0	.969	5	*2/3	-0.4
1952	Chi-N	93	383	44	89	20	1	2	19	20	32	.232	.272	.305	59	-21	-22	31	4	4	-1	.950	-13	2S	-3.2
1953	Chi-N	142	577	61	145	17	6	8	39	33	59	.251	.293	.343	64	-30	-32	57	13	4	2	.954	-13	2S	-3.3
1954	Chi-N	38	99	9	20	3	0	2	3	3	9	.202	.225	.293	33	-10	-10	6	1	0	0	.961	4	2/3O	-0.4
1955	Chi-N	131	481	52	113	14	2	9	41	32	55	.235	.283	.328	62	-27	-27	42	3	6	-3	**.989**	5	*O3	-3.0
1956	Chi-N	114	356	54	85	10	3	9	27	32	40	.239	.303	.360	79	-11	-11	38	4	2	0	.975	-3	3O2/S	-1.3
1957	StL-N	49	38	3	8	0	0	1	2	7	7	.211	.333	.289	68	-1	-2	4	0	0	0	1.000	-11	O	-1.3
	Bal-A	1	1	0	0	0	0	0	0	0	0	.000	.000	.000	-99	-0	-0	0	0	0	0	.000	0	H	0.0
1958	Bal-A	3	2	0	0	0	0	0	0	0	1	.000	.000	.000	-99	-1	-1	0	0	0	0	.000	0	/S	-0.1
	Cin-N	69	50	15	7	0	0	0	4	5	5	.140	.218	.140	-2	-7	-8	2	1	1	-0	1.000	-4	O3/2S1	-1.2
Total	14	1042	3053	383	722	95	17	44	228	215	313	.236	.288	.322	62	-161	-166	283	52	22		.962	-17	2O3S/1	-16.5

■ HORACE MILAN Milan, Horace Robert b: 4/7/1894, Linden, Tenn. d: 6/29/55, Texarkana, Ark. BR/TR, 5'9", 175 lbs. Deb: 8/29/15 F

YEAR	TM/L	G	AB	R	H	2B	3B	HR	RBI	BB	SO	AVG	OBP	SLG	PRO+	BR	/A	RC	SB	CS	SBR	FA	FR	POS	TPR
1915	Was-A	11	27	6	11	1	1	0	7	8	7	.407	.543	.519	214	5	5	9	2			1.000	-3	O	0.2
1917	Was-A	31	73	8	21	3	1	0	9	4	9	.288	.342	.356	114	1	1	10	4			.932	-4	O	-0.4
Total	2	42	100	14	32	4	2	0	16	12	16	.320	.404	.400	144	6	6	18	6			.944	-6	/O	-0.2

■ CLYDE MILAN Milan, Jesse Clyde "Deerfoot" b: 3/25/1887, Linden, Tenn. d: 3/3/53, Orlando, Fla. BL/TR, 5'9", 168 lbs. Deb: 8/19/07 FMC

YEAR	TM/L	G	AB	R	H	2B	3B	HR	RBI	BB	SO	AVG	OBP	SLG	PRO+	BR	/A	RC	SB	CS	SBR	FA	FR	POS	TPR
1907	Was-A	48	183	22	51	3	3	0	9	8		.279	.320	.328	116	1	3	23	8			.929	4	O	0.5
1908	Was-A	130	485	55	116	10	12	1	32	38		.239	.304	.315	111	1	5	54	29			.959	9	*O	1.1
1909	Was-A	130	400	36	80	12	4	1	15	31		.200	.268	.257	69	-15	-13	32	10			.972	5	*O	-1.5
1910	Was-A	142	531	89	148	17	6	0	16	71		.279	.379	.333	129	18	21	83	44			.946	11	*O	2.8
1911	Was-A	154	616	109	194	24	8	3	35	74		.315	.395	.394	123	19	21	117	58			.957	11	*O	2.3
1912	Was-A	154	601	105	184	19	11	1	79	63		.306	.377	.379	116	14	13	117	**88**			.935	8	*O	1.4
1913	Was-A	154	579	92	174	18	9	3	54	58	25	.301	.367	.378	116	14	12	102	**75**			.932	-7	*O	-0.2
1914	Was-A	115	437	63	129	19	11	1	39	32	26	.295	.346	.396	118	11	9	63	38	21	-1	.949	-4	*O	-0.1
1915	Was-A	153	573	83	165	13	7	2	66	53	32	.288	.353	.346	107	7	5	77	40	19	1	.946	-0	*O	-0.2
1916	Was-A	150	565	58	154	14	3	1	45	56	31	.273	.343	.313	98	-1	-0	66	34	21	-2	.961	17	*O	0.7
1917	Was-A	155	579	60	170	15	4	0	48	58	26	.294	.364	.333	114	10	11	76	20			.962	-5	*O	-0.2
1918	Was-A	128	503	56	146	18	5	0	56	36	14	.290	.344	.346	110	4	5	65	26			.972	2	*O	0.1
1919	Was-A	88	321	43	92	12	6	0	37	40	16	.287	.371	.361	107	4	4	46	11			.953	-3	O	-0.5
1920	Was-A	126	506	70	163	22	5	3	41	28	12	.322	.364	.403	106	2	4	72	10	12	-4	.971	8	*O	-0.2
1921	Was-A	113	406	55	117	19	11	1	40	37	13	.288	.351	.397	95	-6	-3	57	4	5	-2	.931	2	O	-1.0
1922	Was-A	42	74	8	17	5	0	0	5	2	2	.230	.250	.297	44	-6	-6	5	0	0	0	1.000	1	OM	-0.6
Total	16	1982	7359	1004	2100	240	105	17	617	685	197	.285	.353	.353	109	77	92	1055	495	78		.953	58	*O	4.4

■ LARRY MILBOURNE Milbourne, Lawrence William b: 2/14/51, Port Norris, N.J. BB/TR, 6', 165 lbs. Deb: 4/06/74

YEAR	TM/L	G	AB	R	H	2B	3B	HR	RBI	BB	SO	AVG	OBP	SLG	PRO+	BR	/A	RC	SB	CS	SBR	FA	FR	POS	TPR
1974	Hou-N	112	136	31	38	2	1	0	9	10	14	.279	.329	.309	83	-4	-3	15	6	2	1	.974	18	2/SO	1.8
1975	Hou-N	73	151	17	32	1	2	1	9	6	14	.212	.247	.265	45	-12	-11	9	1	2	-1	.968	10	2S	0.1
1976	Hou-N	59	145	22	36	4	0	0	7	14	10	.248	.319	.276	77	-5	-4	14	6	1	1	.965	-1	2	-0.1
1977	Sea-A	86	242	24	53	10	0	2	21	6	20	.219	.244	.285	44	-19	-19	17	3	1	0	.982	4	2S/3D	-0.9
1978	Sea-A	93	234	31	53	6	2	2	20	9	6	.226	.255	.295	55	-14	-14	15	5	7	-3	.989	16	3S2D	0.1
1979	Sea-A	123	356	40	99	13	4	2	26	19	20	.278	.315	.354	79	-10	-11	38	5	3	-0	.981	-17	S23	-2.0
1980	Sea-A	106	258	31	68	6	6	0	26	19	13	.264	.317	.333	78	-8	-8	26	7	6	-2	.976	0	2S/3D	-0.4
1981	*NY-A	61	163	24	51	7	2	1	12	9	14	.313	.353	.399	118	3	3	23	2	0	1	.955	-7	S2/3D	0.2
1982	NY-A	14	27	2	4	1	0	0	0	1	4	.148	.179	.185	0	-4	-4	1	0	1	-1	.917	1	/S23	-0.3
	Min-A	29	98	9	23	1	1	0	1	7	8	.235	.286	.265	51	-6	-7	7	1	1	-0	.981	-10	2	-1.6
	Cle-A	82	291	29	80	11	4	2	25	12	20	.275	.308	.361	83	-7	-7	29	2	5	-2	.981	-6	2S/3D	-1.1
	Yr	125	416	40	107	13	5	2	26	20	32	.257	.295	.327	70	-17	-17	36	3	7	-3	.979	-15	2S3/D	-3.0
1983	Phi-N	41	66	3	16	0	1	0	4	4	7	.242	.286	.273	56	-4	-4	5	2	1	0	.963	1	2/S3	-0.3
	NY-A	31	70	5	14	4	0	0	2	5	10	.200	.263	.257	46	-5	-5	5	1	1	-0	1.000	3	2/S3	-0.1
1984	Sea-A	79	211	22	56	5	1	1	22	12	16	.265	.305	.313	72	-8	-8	19	0	2	-1	.900	-9	32/SD	-1.8
Total	11	989	2448	290	623	71	24	11	184	133	176	.254	.295	.317	70	-103	-99	222	41	33	-8	.974	3	2S3/DO	-6.4

■ DON MILES Miles, Donald Ray b: 3/13/36, Indianapolis, Ind. BL/TR, 6'1", 210 lbs. Deb: 9/09/58

YEAR	TM/L	G	AB	R	H	2B	3B	HR	RBI	BB	SO	AVG	OBP	SLG	PRO+	BR	/A	RC	SB	CS	SBR	FA	FR	POS	TPR
1958	LA-N	8	22	2	4	0	0	0	0	0	6	.182	.217	.182	7	-3	-3	1	0	0	0	1.000	2	/O	-0.2

■ DEE MILES Miles, Wilson Daniel b: 2/15/09, Kellerman, Ala. d: 11/2/76, Birmingham, Ala. BL/TR, 6', 175 lbs. Deb: 7/07/35

YEAR	TM/L	G	AB	R	H	2B	3B	HR	RBI	BB	SO	AVG	OBP	SLG	PRO+	BR	/A	RC	SB	CS	SBR	FA	FR	POS	TPR
1935	Was-A	60	215	28	57	5	2	0	29	7	13	.265	.291	.307	57	-14	-14	19	6	4	-1	.970	2	O	-1.3
1936	Was-A	25	59	8	14	1	2	0	7	1	5	.237	.250	.322	43	-6	-5	4	0	1	-1	.958	0	O	-0.5

YEAR	TM/L	G	AB	R	H	2B	3B	HR	RBI	BB	SO	AVG	OBP	SLG	PRO+	BR	/A	RC	SB	CS	SBR	FA	FR	POS	TPR
1939	Phi-A	106	320	49	96	17	6	1	37	15	17	.300	.331	.400	88	-7	-6	42	3	4	-2	.968	-7	O	-1.6
1940	Phi-A	88	236	26	71	9	6	1	23	8	18	.301	.327	.403	90	-5	-4	32	1	1	-0	.945	-1	O	-0.8
1941	Phi-A	80	170	14	53	7	1	0	15	4	8	.312	.331	.365	86	-4	-4	20	0	1	-1	1.000	0	O	-0.6
1942	Phi-A	99	346	41	94	12	5	0	22	12	10	.272	.300	.335	79	-11	-11	36	5	3	-0	.984	-3	O	-1.9
1943	Bos-A	45	121	9	26	2	2	0	10	3	3	.215	.234	.264	45	-9	-9	7	0	2	-1	.968	-1	O	-1.3
Total	7	503	1467	175	411	53	24	2	143	50	74	.280	.306	.353	76	-56	-52	159	15	16	-5	.971	-10	O	-8.0

■ **MIKE MILEY** Miley, Michael Wilfred b: 3/30/53, Yazoo City, Miss. d: 1/6/77, Baton Rouge, La. BB/TR, 6'1", 185 lbs. Deb: 7/06/75

YEAR	TM/L	G	AB	R	H	2B	3B	HR	RBI	BB	SO	AVG	OBP	SLG	PRO+	BR	/A	RC	SB	CS	SBR	FA	FR	POS	TPR
1975	Cal-A	70	224	17	39	3	2	4	26	16	54	.174	.232	.259	42	-18	-16	13	0	1	-1	.939	-9	S	-1.9
1976	Cal-A	14	38	4	7	2	0	0	4	4	8	.184	.262	.237	50	-2	-2	3	1	0	0	.981	-2	S	-0.2
Total	2	84	262	21	46	5	2	4	30	20	62	.176	.237	.256	43	-21	-19	16	1	1	-0	.945	-11	/S	-2.1

■ **FELIX MILLAN** Millan, Felix Bernardo (Martinez) b: 8/21/43, Yabucoa, P.R. BR/TR, 5'11", 172 lbs. Deb: 6/02/66

YEAR	TM/L	G	AB	R	H	2B	3B	HR	RBI	BB	SO	AVG	OBP	SLG	PRO+	BR	/A	RC	SB	CS	SBR	FA	FR	POS	TPR
1966	Atl-N	37	91	20	25	6	0	0	5	2	6	.275	.290	.341	74	-3	-3	8	3	1	0	.973	-2	2/S3	-0.4
1967	Atl-N	41	136	13	32	3	3	2	6	4	10	.235	.268	.346	75	-5	-5	11	0	3	-2	.972	3	2	-0.1
1968	Atl-N	149	570	49	165	22	2	1	33	22	26	.289	.323	.340	99	-1	-1	58	6	6	-2	.980	3	*2	1.0
1969	*Atl-N★	162	652	98	174	23	5	6	57	34	35	.267	.311	.345	83	-15	-15	69	14	3	2	**.980**	-16	*2	-1.6
1970	Atl-N†	142	590	100	183	25	5	2	37	35	23	.310	.354	.380	91	-2	-7	79	16	5	2	.979	-19	*2	-1.2
1971	Atl-N★	143	577	65	167	20	8	2	45	37	22	.289	.335	.362	92	-2	-6	69	11	7	-1	.982	6	*2	1.2
1972	Atl-N	125	498	46	128	19	3	1	38	23	28	.257	.294	.313	66	-18	-23	46	6	4	-1	.987	-16	*2	-3.6
1973	*NY-N	153	638	82	185	23	4	3	37	35	22	.290	.333	.353	91	-8	-7	72	2	2	-1	.989	-4	*2	-0.3
1974	NY-N	136	518	50	139	15	2	1	33	31	14	.268	.320	.311	78	-16	-15	53	5	1	1	.979	-20	*2	-2.8
1975	NY-N	162	676	81	191	37	2	1	56	36	28	.283	.330	.348	92	-11	-7	75	1	6	-3	.972	-25	*2	-2.8
1976	NY-N	139	531	55	150	25	2	1	35	41	19	.282	.342	.343	101	-3	1	60	2	4	-2	.977	-24	*2	-1.8
1977	NY-N	91	314	40	78	11	2	2	21	18	9	.248	.296	.315	67	-16	-14	28	1	1	-0	.977	-16	2	-2.5
Total	12	1480	5791	699	1617	229	38	22	403	318	242	.279	.324	.343	87	-100	-103	628	67	43	-6	.980	-129	*2/3S	-14.9

■ **FRANK MILLARD** Millard, Frank E. b: 7/4/1865, E.St.Louis, Ill. d: 7/4/1892, Galveston, Tex. Deb: 5/04/1890

YEAR	TM/L	G	AB	R	H	2B	3B	HR	RBI	BB	SO	AVG	OBP	SLG	PRO+	BR	/A	RC	SB	CS	SBR	FA	FR	POS	TPR
1890	StL-a	1	1	0	0	0	0	0		1		.000	.500	.000	45	0	0	0	0			.625	1	/2	0.0

■ **DUSTY MILLER** Miller, Charles Bradley b: 9/10/1868, Oil City, Pa. d: 9/3/45, Memphis, Tenn. BL/TR, 5'11.5", 170 lbs. Deb: 9/23/1889

YEAR	TM/L	G	AB	R	H	2B	3B	HR	RBI	BB	SO	AVG	OBP	SLG	PRO+	BR	/A	RC	SB	CS	SBR	FA	FR	POS	TPR
1889	Bal-a	11	40	4	6	1	1	0	6	2	11	.150	.209	.225	25	-4	-4	3	3			.636	-7	/SO	-1.0
1890	StL-a	26	96	17	21	5	3	1		8		.219	.279	.365	80	-1	-4	11	4			.872	3	O/S	-0.2
1895	Cin-N	132	529	103	177	31	16	10	112	33	34	.335	.378	.510	125	21	17	122	43			.937	11	*O	1.4
1896	Cin-N	125	504	91	162	38	12	4	93	33	30	.321	.368	.468	114	14	8	119	76			.902	-2	*O	-0.3
1897	Cin-N	119	440	83	139	27	1	4	70	48		.316	.392	.409	105	9	4	86	29			.929	2	*O	-0.3
1898	Cin-N	152	586	99	175	24	12	3	90	38		.299	.350	.396	106	9	3	97	32			.929	8	*O	0.1
1899	Cin-N	80	323	44	81	12	5	0	37	9		.251	.275	.319	62	-17	-18	35	18			.927	7	O	-1.6
	StL-N	10	39	3	8	1	0	0	3	3		.205	.279	.231	40	-3	-3	3	1			.875	-1	O	-0.5
	Yr	90	362	47	89	13	5	0	40	12		.246	.276	.309	59	-21	-22	38	19			.921	6	O	-2.1
Total	7	655	2557	444	769	139	50	22	411	174	75	.301	.352	.420	103	26	3	475	206			.923	21	O/S	-2.4

■ **BRUCE MILLER** Miller, Charles Bruce b: 3/4/47, Fort Wayne, Ind. BR/TR, 6'1", 185 lbs. Deb: 8/04/73

YEAR	TM/L	G	AB	R	H	2B	3B	HR	RBI	BB	SO	AVG	OBP	SLG	PRO+	BR	/A	RC	SB	CS	SBR	FA	FR	POS	TPR
1973	SF-N	12	21	1	3	0	0	0	2	2	3	.143	.217	.143	2	-3	-3	1	0	0	0	.900	1	/32S	-0.2
1974	SF-N	73	198	19	55	7	1	0	16	11	15	.278	.319	.323	76	-5	-6	19	1	1	-0	.938	13	3S/2	0.8
1975	SF-N	99	309	22	74	6	3	1	31	15	26	.239	.277	.288	55	-18	-20	21	0	1	-1	.949	10	32/S	-1.0
1976	SF-N	12	25	1	4	1	0	0	2	2	5	.160	.222	.200	20	-3	-3	1	0	0	0	.920	-1	/23	-0.4
Total	4	196	553	43	136	14	4	1	51	30	49	.246	.287	.291	59	-29	-32	42	1	2	-1	.944	22	3/2S	-0.8

■ **CHARLIE MILLER** Miller, Charles Elmer b: 1/4/1892, Warrensburg, Mo. d: 4/23/72, Warrensburg, Mo. TR , Deb: 9/18/12

YEAR	TM/L	G	AB	R	H	2B	3B	HR	RBI	BB	SO	AVG	OBP	SLG	PRO+	BR	/A	RC	SB	CS	SBR	FA	FR	POS	TPR
1912	StL-A	1	2	0	0	0	0	0	0	0		.000	.000	.000	-99	-1	-1	0	0			1.000	-0	/S	-0.1

■ **CHARLIE MILLER** Miller, Charles Hess b: 12/30/1877, Contestoga Center, Pa. d: 1/13/51, Millersville, Pa. BR/TR, 6', 190 lbs. Deb: 10/02/15

YEAR	TM/L	G	AB	R	H	2B	3B	HR	RBI	BB	SO	AVG	OBP	SLG	PRO+	BR	/A	RC	SB	CS	SBR	FA	FR	POS	TPR
1915	Bal-F	1	1	0	0	0	0	0	0	0	0	.000	.000	.000	-97	-0	-0	0	0			.000	0	H	0.0

■ **CHUCK MILLER** Miller, Charles Marion b: 9/18/1889, Woodville, Ohio d: 6/16/61, Houston, Tex. BL/TL, 5'8.5", 155 lbs. Deb: 9/19/13

YEAR	TM/L	G	AB	R	H	2B	3B	HR	RBI	BB	SO	AVG	OBP	SLG	PRO+	BR	/A	RC	SB	CS	SBR	FA	FR	POS	TPR
1913	StL-N	4	12	0	2	0	0	0	1	0	2	.167	.167	.167	-5	-2	-2	0	0			1.000	-1	/O	-0.3
1914	StL-N	36	36	4	7	1	0	0	2	3	9	.194	.256	.222	43	-3	-2	2	2			1.000	-3	O	-0.6
Total	2	40	48	4	9	1	0	0	3	3	11	.188	.235	.208	31	-4	-4	3	2			1.000	-4	/O	-0.9

■ **DUSTY MILLER** Miller, Dakin Evans b: 9/2/1877, Malvern, Iowa d: 4/20/50, Stockton, Cal. BL/TR, 5'10", 175 lbs. Deb: 4/17/02

YEAR	TM/L	G	AB	R	H	2B	3B	HR	RBI	BB	SO	AVG	OBP	SLG	PRO+	BR	/A	RC	SB	CS	SBR	FA	FR	POS	TPR
1902	Chi-N	51	187	17	46	4	1	0	13	7		.246	.299	.278	80	-5	-4	20	10			.955	1	O	-0.7

■ **DARRELL MILLER** Miller, Darrell Keith b: 2/26/58, Washington, D.C. BR/TR, 6'2", 200 lbs. Deb: 8/14/84

YEAR	TM/L	G	AB	R	H	2B	3B	HR	RBI	BB	SO	AVG	OBP	SLG	PRO+	BR	/A	RC	SB	CS	SBR	FA	FR	POS	TPR
1984	Cal-A	17	41	5	7	0	0	0	1	4	9	.171	.244	.171	17	-5	-4	2	0	0	0	.990	-1	1/O	-0.6
1985	Cal-A	51	48	8	18	2	1	2	7	1	10	.375	.400	.583	166	4	4	11	0	1	-1	.952	-11	O/C3D	-0.7
1986	Cal-A	33	57	6	13	2	1	0	4	4	8	.228	.279	.298	58	-3	-3	4	0	0	0	1.000	-10	OC/D	-1.3
1987	Cal-A	53	108	14	26	5	0	4	16	9	13	.241	.311	.398	89	-2	-2	13	1	0	0	.984	-6	CO/3D	-0.6
1988	Cal-A	70	140	21	31	4	1	2	7	9	29	.221	.292	.307	70	-6	-5	13	2	1	0	.987	3	C/OD	0.0
Total	5	224	394	54	95	13	3	8	35	27	69	.241	.303	.350	80	-12	-11	43	3	2	-0	.987	-25	/CO1D3	-3.2

■ **BING MILLER** Miller, Edmund John b: 8/30/1894, Vinton, Iowa d: 5/7/66, Philadelphia, Pa. BR/TR, 6', 185 lbs. Deb: 4/16/21 FC

YEAR	TM/L	G	AB	R	H	2B	3B	HR	RBI	BB	SO	AVG	OBP	SLG	PRO+	BR	/A	RC	SB	CS	SBR	FA	FR	POS	TPR
1921	Was-A	114	420	57	121	28	8	9	71	25	50	.288	.334	.457	105	-2	1	63	3	4	-2	.945	2	*O	-0.6
1922	Phi-A	143	535	90	179	29	12	21	90	24	42	.335	.371	.551	134	26	24	104	10	10	-3	.977	5	*O	1.5
1923	Phi-A	123	458	68	137	25	4	12	64	27	34	.299	.344	.450	106	3	2	71	9	3	1	.978	-1	*O	-0.5
1924	Phi-A	113	398	62	136	22	4	6	62	12	24	.342	.376	.462	114	8	7	69	11	5	0	.973	-2	O/1	-0.1
1925	Phi-A	124	474	78	151	29	10	10	81	19	14	.319	.355	.485	105	6	1	80	11	6	-0	.975	-10	*O1	-1.6
1926	Phi-A	38	110	13	32	6	2	2	13	11	6	.291	.355	.436	100	1	-0	18	4	1	1	1.000	-5	O/1	-0.6
	StL-A	94	353	60	117	27	5	4	50	22	12	.331	.382	.470	116	10	8	60	7	11	-5	.939	4	O	0.1
	Yr	132	463	73	149	33	7	6	63	33	18	.322	.376	.462	112	11	8	78	11	12	-4	.950	-1	*O/1	-0.5
1927	StL-A	143	492	83	160	32	7	5	75	30	26	.325	.375	.449	109	9	6	78	9	7	-2	.970	4	*O	0.1
1928	Phi-A	139	510	76	168	34	7	8	85	27	24	.329	.372	.471	117	14	12	88	10	6	-1	.968	0	*O	0.3
1929	*Phi-A	147	556	84	186	32	16	8	93	40	25	.335	.383	.493	120	19	16	105	24	9	2	.970	6	*O	1.3
1930	*Phi-A	154	585	89	177	38	7	9	100	47	22	.303	.357	.438	96	0	-4	90	13	13	-4	.976	5	*O	-1.2
1931	*Phi-A	137	534	75	150	43	5	8	77	36	16	.281	.338	.425	94	-2	-6	77	5	3	-0	.987	6	*O	-0.9
1932	Phi-A	95	305	40	90	17	4	7	58	20	11	.295	.343	.446	99	0	-1	47	7	3	0	.979	1	O	-0.4
1933	Phi-A	67	120	22	33	7	1	2	17	12	7	.275	.346	.400	96	-1	-1	17	4	2	0	1.000	-6	O/1	-0.8
1934	Phi-A	81	177	22	43	10	2	1	22	16	14	.243	.309	.339	70	-9	-8	19	1	0	0	1.000	-3	O	-1.2
1935	Bos-A	78	138	18	42	8	1	3	26	10	8	.304	.356	.442	99	1	-1	22	0	1	-1	.962	-2	O	-0.4
1936	Bos-A	30	47	9	14	2	1	1	6	5	5	.298	.377	.447	97	0	-0	8	0	0	0	1.000	-3	O	-0.3
Total	16	1820	6212	946	1936	389	96	116	990	383	340	.312	.359	.461	108	83	57	1017	128	84	-12	.971	2	*O/1	-5.3

■ **EDDIE MILLER** Miller, Edward Lee b: 6/29/57, San Pablo, Cal. BB/TR, 5'9", 175 lbs. Deb: 9/05/77

YEAR	TM/L	G	AB	R	H	2B	3B	HR	RBI	BB	SO	AVG	OBP	SLG	PRO+	BR	/A	RC	SB	CS	SBR	FA	FR	POS	TPR
1977	Tex-A	17	6	7	2	0	0	0	1	1	1	.333	.429	.333	110	0	0	1	3	1	0	1.000	-0	/OD	0.0
1978	Atl-N	6	21	5	3	1	0	0	2	2	4	.143	.250	.190	22	-2	-2	2	3	0	1	1.000	-1	/O	-0.3
1979	Atl-N	27	113	12	35	1	0	0	5	5	24	.310	.350	.319	78	-2	-3	15	15	2	3	.988	3	O	0.2

YEAR	TM/L	G	AB	R	H	2B	3B	HR	RBI	BB	SO	AVG	OBP	SLG	PRO+	BR	/A	RC	SB	CS	SBR	FA	FR	POS	TPR
1980	Atl-N	11	19	3	3	0	0	0	0	0	5	.158	.158	.158	-11	-3	-3	0	1	2	-1	1.000	-1	/O	-0.5
1981	Atl-N	50	134	29	31	3	1	0	7	7	29	.231	.285	.269	56	-7	-8	12	23	5	4	.985	-1	O	-0.7
1982	Det-A	14	25	3	1	0	0	0	0	4	4	.040	.250	.040	-14	-4	-4	1	0	3	-2	1.000	-0	/OD	-0.6
1984	SD-N	13	14	4	4	0	1	1	2	0	4	.286	.286	.643	155	1	1	3	4	0	1	1.000	-1	/O	0.1
Total	7	138	332	63	79	5	2	1	17	19	71	.238	.297	.274	57	-17	-19	34	49	13	7	.989	-2	/OD	-1.8

■ EDDIE MILLER
Miller, Edward Robert "Eppie" b: 11/26/16, Pittsburgh, Pa. BR/TR, 5'9", 180 lbs. Deb: 9/09/36

YEAR	TM/L	G	AB	R	H	2B	3B	HR	RBI	BB	SO	AVG	OBP	SLG	PRO+	BR	/A	RC	SB	CS	SBR	FA	FR	POS	TPR
1936	Cin-N	5	10	0	1	0	0	0	0	1	1	.100	.182	.100	-24	-2	-2	0	0			.938	-0	/S2	-0.2
1937	Cin-N	36	60	3	9	3	1	0	5	3	8	.150	.190	.233	15	-7	-7	2	0			.926	7	S/3	0.2
1939	Bos-N	77	296	32	79	12	2	4	31	16	21	.267	.315	.361	88	-8	-5	33	4			.970	12	S	1.4
1940	Bos-N★	151	569	78	157	33	3	14	79	41	43	.276	.330	.418	111	3	7	76	8			**.970**	15	*S	3.4
1941	Bos-N★	154	585	54	140	27	3	6	68	35	72	.239	.288	.326	76	-22	-19	54	8			**.966**	12	*S	0.5
1942	Bos-N★	142	534	47	130	28	2	6	47	22	42	.243	.279	.337	81	-15	-14	47	11			**.983**	4	*S	-0.2
1943	Cin-N★	154	576	49	129	26	4	2	71	33	43	.224	.271	.293	64	-28	-27	47	8			**.979**	**27**	*S	1.1
1944	Cin-N†	155	536	48	112	21	5	4	55	41	41	.209	.269	.289	59	-31	-29	43	9			.971	12	*S	-0.4
1945	Cin-N	115	421	46	100	27	2	13	49	18	38	.238	.275	.404	89	-10	-9	44	4			**.975**	5	*S	0.5
1946	Cin-N†	91	299	30	58	10	0	6	36	25	34	.194	.258	.288	57	-18	-17	22	5			.970	24	S	1.2
1947	Cin-N†	151	545	69	146	**38**	4	19	87	49	40	.268	.333	.457	109	4	4	81	5			.972	-5	*S	0.7
1948	Phi-N	130	468	45	115	20	1	14	61	19	40	.246	.281	.382	79	-16	-15	47	1			.966	-14	*S	-2.2
1949	Phi-N	85	266	21	55	10	1	6	29	29	21	.207	.294	.320	66	-13	-13	26	1			.986	-10	2/S	-1.9
1950	StL-N	64	172	17	39	8	0	3	22	19	21	.227	.307	.326	64	-8	-9	18	0			.980	14	S/2	0.7
Total	14	1510	5337	539	1270	263	28	97	640	351	465	.238	.290	.352	80	-173	-155	540	64			.972	102	*S/23	4.8

■ ED MILLER
Miller, Edwin J. "Big Ed" b: 11/24/1888, Annville, Pa. d: 4/17/80, S.Lebanon Twsp, Pa BR/TR, 6', 180 lbs. Deb: 6/29/12

YEAR	TM/L	G	AB	R	H	2B	3B	HR	RBI	BB	SO	AVG	OBP	SLG	PRO+	BR	/A	RC	SB	CS	SBR	FA	FR	POS	TPR
1912	StL-A	13	46	4	9	1	0	0	5	2		.196	.245	.217	34	-4	-4	3	1			.951	-4	/1S	-0.8
1914	StL-A	41	58	8	8	0	1	0	4	4	13	.138	.219	.172	18	-6	-6	2	1	3	-2	.981	-1	/12O3	-1.0
1918	Cle-A	32	96	9	22	4	3	0	3	12	10	.229	.321	.333	89	-0	-1	11	2			.977	1	1/O	-0.2
Total	3	86	200	21	39	5	4	0	12	18	23	.195	.275	.260	58	-10	-11	16	4	3		.972	-5	/1O2S3	-2.0

■ ELMER MILLER
Miller, Elmer b: 7/28/1890, Sandusky, Ohio d: 11/28/44, Beloit, Wis. BR/TR, 6', 175 lbs. Deb: 4/27/12

YEAR	TM/L	G	AB	R	H	2B	3B	HR	RBI	BB	SO	AVG	OBP	SLG	PRO+	BR	/A	RC	SB	CS	SBR	FA	FR	POS	TPR
1912	StL-N	12	37	5	7	1	0	0	3	4	9	.189	.268	.216	34	-3	-3	2	1			1.000	0	O	-0.4
1915	NY-A	26	83	4	12	1	0	0	3	4	14	.145	.193	.157	5	-10	-10	3	0			.955	-4	O	-1.7
1916	NY-A	43	152	12	34	3	2	1	18	11	18	.224	.280	.289	70	-6	-6	15	8			.969	5	O	-0.4
1917	NY-A	114	379	43	95	11	3	3	35	40	44	.251	.336	.319	99	1	1	45	11			.961	-6	*O	-1.2
1918	NY-A	67	202	18	49	9	2	1	22	19	17	.243	.317	.322	91	-2	-2	22	2			.947	4	O	-0.2
1921	*NY-A	56	242	41	72	9	8	4	36	19	16	.298	.356	.450	102	1	0	39	2	2	-1	.947	3	O	-0.1
1922	NY-A	51	172	31	46	7	2	3	18	11	12	.267	.311	.384	79	-5	-6	20	2	3	-1	.982	-2	O	-1.2
	Bos-A	44	147	16	28	2	3	4	16	5	10	.190	.222	.327	42	-13	-13	11	3	1	0	.957	-0	O	-1.6
	Yr	95	319	47	74	9	5	7	34	16	22	.232	.271	.357	62	-19	-19	30	5	4	-1	.970	-2	O	-2.8
Total	7	413	1414	170	343	43	20	16	151	113	140	.243	.307	.335	80	-37	-40	157	29	6		.960	-0	O	-6.8

■ ELMER MILLER
Miller, Elmer Joseph "Lefty" b: 4/17/03, Detroit, Mich. d: 1/8/87, Corona, Cal. BL/TL, 5'11", 189 lbs. Deb: 6/21/29

YEAR	TM/L	G	AB	R	H	2B	3B	HR	RBI	BB	SO	AVG	OBP	SLG	PRO+	BR	/A	RC	SB	CS	SBR	FA	FR	POS	TPR
1929	Phi-N	31	38	3	9	1	0	1	4	1	5	.237	.256	.342	44	-3	-4	3	0			.750	2	/PO	-0.1

■ KOHLY MILLER
Miller, Frank A. b: Philadelphia, Pa. Deb: 10/03/1892

YEAR	TM/L	G	AB	R	H	2B	3B	HR	RBI	BB	SO	AVG	OBP	SLG	PRO+	BR	/A	RC	SB	CS	SBR	FA	FR	POS	TPR
1892	Was-N	1	3	0	0	0	0	0	0	0	1	.000	.000	.000	-99	-1	-1	0	0			.400	-1	/S	-0.2
	StL-N	1	4	0	0	0	0	0	0	0	0	.000	.000	.000	-99	-1	-1	0	0			.500	-1	/3	-0.2
	Yr	2	7	0	0	0	0	0	0	0	1	.000	.000	.000	-99	-2	-2	0	0			.400	-2	/S3	-0.4
1897	Phi-N	3	11	2	2	0	0	0	1	2		.182	.308	.182	32	-1	-1	1	0			.857	-2	/2	-0.3
Total	2	5	18	2	2	0	0	0	1	2	1	.111	.200	.111	-13	-3	-3	1	0			.953	-5	/23S	-0.7

■ GEORGE MILLER
Miller, George C. b: 2/19/1853, Newport, Ky. d: 7/24/29, Norwood, Ohio BR/TR, 5'5", 160 lbs. Deb: 9/06/1877

YEAR	TM/L	G	AB	R	H	2B	3B	HR	RBI	BB	SO	AVG	OBP	SLG	PRO+	BR	/A	RC	SB	CS	SBR	FA	FR	POS	TPR
1877	Cin-N	11	37	4	6	1	0	0	3	5	2	.162	.262	.189	50	-2	-1	2				.918	0	C	-0.1
1884	Cin-a	6	20	6	5	1	1	0		1		.250	.318	.400	130	1	1	3				.975	2	/C	0.3
Total	2	17	57	10	11	2	1	0	3	6	2	.193	.281	.263	80	-1	-1	4				.938	2	/C	0.2

■ DOGGIE MILLER
Miller, George Frederick "Foghorn" or "Calliope" b: 8/15/1864, Brooklyn, N.Y. d: 4/6/09, Brooklyn, N.Y. BR/TR, 5'6", Deb: 5/01/1884 M

YEAR	TM/L	G	AB	R	H	2B	3B	HR	RBI	BB	SO	AVG	OBP	SLG	PRO+	BR	/A	RC	SB	CS	SBR	FA	FR	POS	TPR
1884	Pit-a	89	347	46	78	10	2	0		13		.225	.257	.265	72	-10	-11	24				.798	-5	OC/32	-1.2
1885	Pit-a	42	166	19	27	3	1	0		4		.163	.182	.193	20	-14	-14	6				.893	-5	C/OS3	-1.5
1886	Pit-a	83	317	70	80	15	1	2		43		.252	.343	.325	112	6	6	49	35			.918	-22	CO/2	-0.8
1887	Pit-N	87	342	58	83	17	4	1	34	35	13	.243	.317	.325	85	-8	-5	47	33			.928	-22	CO/3	-1.7
1888	Pit-N	103	404	50	112	17	5	0	36	18	16	.277	.319	.344	123	6	10	54	27			.908	-15	CO/3	0.1
1889	Pit-N	104	422	77	113	25	3	6	56	31	11	.268	.321	.384	108	-2	4	59	16			.889	-5	CO/3	0.5
1890	Pit-N	138	549	85	150	24	3	4	66	68	11	.273	.357	.350	123	8	18	82	32			.850	1	3OSC/2	2.1
1891	Pit-N	135	548	80	156	19	6	4	57	59	26	.285	.357	.363	115	9	12	86	35			.938	-16	CS3O/1	0.2
1892	Pit-N	149	623	103	158	15	12	2	59	69	14	.254	.335	.326	101	3	3	79	28			.906	-11	OCS/3	-0.6
1893	Pit-N	41	154	23	28	6	1	0	17	17	8	.182	.284	.234	40	-13	-12	11	3			.916	-0	C	-0.8
1894	StL-N	127	481	93	163	9	11	8	86	58	9	.339	.414	.453	111	10	10	101	17			.832	-14	3C21/OSM	0.0
1895	StL-N	121	490	81	143	15	4	5	74	25	12	.292	.334	.369	84	-13	-11	68	18			.829	-24	3CO/S1	-2.6
1896	Lou-N	98	324	54	89	17	4	1	33	27	9	.275	.334	.361	89	-7	-5	46	16			.922	-16	C2/O31S	-1.2
Total	13	1317	5167	839	1380	192	57	33	518	467	129	.267	.333	.345	99	-25	5	712	260			.918	-155	CO3/S21	-7.5

■ HUGHIE MILLER
Miller, Hugh Stanley "Cotton" b: 12/28/1887, St.Louis, Mo. d: 12/24/45, Jefferson Barracks, Mo. BR/TR, 6'1.5", 175 lbs. Deb: 6/18/11

YEAR	TM/L	G	AB	R	H	2B	3B	HR	RBI	BB	SO	AVG	OBP	SLG	PRO+	BR	/A	RC	SB	CS	SBR	FA	FR	POS	TPR
1911	Phi-N	1	0	0	0	0	0	0	0	0	0	—	—	—	—	0	0	0	0			.000	0	R	0.0
1914	StL-F	132	490	51	109	20	5	0	46	27	57	.222	.264	.284	53	-29	-32	41	4			.990	0	*1	-3.7
1915	StL-F	7	6	0	3	1	0	0	3	0	0	.500	.500	.667	230	1	1	2	0			1.000	-0	/1	0.1
Total	3	140	496	51	112	21	5	0	49	27	57	.226	.267	.288	55	-28	-31	43	4			.990	0	1	-3.6

■ JAKE MILLER
Miller, Jacob George (b: Jacob George Munzing) b: 12/1/1895, Baltimore, Md. d: 8/24/74, Towson, Md. BR/TR, 5'10", 170 lbs. Deb: 7/16/22

YEAR	TM/L	G	AB	R	H	2B	3B	HR	RBI	BB	SO	AVG	OBP	SLG	PRO+	BR	/A	RC	SB	CS	SBR	FA	FR	POS	TPR
1922	Pit-N	3	11	0	1	0	0	0	0	2	0	.091	.231	.091	-14	-2	-2	0	1	0	0	.889	0	/O	-0.2

■ HACK MILLER
Miller, James Eldridge b: 2/13/13, Celeste, Tex. d: 11/21/66, Dallas, Tex. BR/TR, 5'11.5", 215 lbs. Deb: 4/18/44

YEAR	TM/L	G	AB	R	H	2B	3B	HR	RBI	BB	SO	AVG	OBP	SLG	PRO+	BR	/A	RC	SB	CS	SBR	FA	FR	POS	TPR
1944	Det-A	5	5	1	1	0	0	1	3	1	1	.200	.333	.800	207	1	1	1	0	0	0	1.000	0	/C	0.1
1945	Det-A	2	4	0	3	0	0	0	1	0	0	.750	.750	.750	315	1	1	1	0	0	0	1.000	-0	/C	0.1
Total	2	7	9	1	4	0	0	1	4	1	1	.444	.500	.778	250	2	2	3	0	0	0	1.000	-0	/C	0.2

■ JIM MILLER
Miller, James McCurdy "Rabbit" b: 10/2/1880, Pittsburgh, Pa. d: 2/7/37, Pittsburgh, Pa. BR/TR, 5'8", 165 lbs. Deb: 9/09/01

YEAR	TM/L	G	AB	R	H	2B	3B	HR	RBI	BB	SO	AVG	OBP	SLG	PRO+	BR	/A	RC	SB	CS	SBR	FA	FR	POS	TPR
1901	NY-N	18	58	3	8	0	0	0	3	6		.138	.219	.138	5	-7	-7	2	1			.936	-3	2	-0.8

■ JOHN MILLER
Miller, John Allen b: 3/14/44, Alhambra, Cal. BR/TR, 5'11", 195 lbs. Deb: 9/11/66

YEAR	TM/L	G	AB	R	H	2B	3B	HR	RBI	BB	SO	AVG	OBP	SLG	PRO+	BR	/A	RC	SB	CS	SBR	FA	FR	POS	TPR
1966	NY-A	6	23	1	2	0	0	1	2	0	9	.087	.087	.217	-16	-3	-3	0	0	0	0	1.000	-1	/1O	-0.5
1969	LA-N	26	38	3	8	1	0	1	1	2	9	.211	.250	.316	62	-2	-2	3	0	0	0	1.000	-0	/O132	-0.3
Total	2	32	61	4	10	1	0	2	3	2	18	.164	.190	.279	33	-6	-5	4	0	0	0	1.000	-1	/O132	-0.8

■ DOTS MILLER
Miller, John Barney b: 9/9/1886, Kearny, N.J. d: 9/5/23, Saranac Lake, N.Y. BR/TR, 5'11.5", 170 lbs. Deb: 4/16/09

YEAR	TM/L	G	AB	R	H	2B	3B	HR	RBI	BB	SO	AVG	OBP	SLG	PRO+	BR	/A	RC	SB	CS	SBR	FA	FR	POS	TPR
1909	*Pit-N	151	560	71	156	31	13	3	87	39		.279	.329	.396	115	14	9	78	14			**.953**	-11	*2	-0.6

YEAR	TM/L	G	AB	R	H	2B	3B	HR	RBI	BB	SO	AVG	OBP	SLG	PRO+	BR	/A	RC	SB	CS	SBR	FA	FR	POS	TPR
1910	Pit-N	120	444	45	101	13	10	1	48	33	41	.227	.284	.309	69	-17	-20	43	11			.946	-19	*2/1S	-4.3
1911	Pit-N	137	470	82	126	17	8	6	78	51	48	.268	.348	.377	99	2	-1	69	17			.943	-6	*2	-1.0
1912	Pit-N	148	567	74	156	33	12	4	87	37	45	.275	.324	.397	98	-5	-4	78	18			.985	1	*1	-0.5
1913	Pit-N	154	580	75	158	24	20	7	90	37	52	.272	.317	.419	114	4	8	81	20			.985	-4	*1/S	0.2
1914	StL-N	155	573	67	166	27	10	4	88	34	52	.290	.339	.393	119	11	12	79	16			.993	0	1S/2	1.6
1915	StL-N	150	553	73	146	17	10	2	72	43	48	.264	.324	.342	101	1	1	65	27	19	-3	.991	4	12/3S	0.1
1916	StL-N	143	505	47	120	22	7	1	46	40	49	.238	.300	.315	89	-6	-6	54	18			.993	2	12S/3	-0.6
1917	StL-N	148	544	61	135	15	9	2	45	33	52	.248	.295	.320	91	-8	-6	54	14			.960	19	21S	1.8
1919	StL-N	101	346	38	80	10	4	1	24	13	23	.231	.265	.292	72	-14	-12	28	6			.981	2	12	-1.3
1920	Phi-N	98	343	41	87	12	2	1	27	16	17	.254	.289	.309	68	-13	-14	31	13	6	0	.948	-9	23S/10	-2.2
1921	Phi-N	84	320	37	95	11	3	0	23	15	27	.297	.330	.350	74	-9	-12	36	3	5	-2	.940	1	31/2	-1.1
Total	12	1589	5805	711	1526	232	108	32	715	391	454	.263	.314	.357	95	-39	-46	696	177	30		.988	-21	12S/30	-7.9

■ JOE MILLER Miller, Joseph A. b: 2/17/1861, Baltimore, Md. d: 4/23/28, Wheeling, W.V.A 5'9.5", 165 lbs. Deb: 5/01/1884

YEAR	TM/L	G	AB	R	H	2B	3B	HR	RBI	BB	SO	AVG	OBP	SLG	PRO+	BR	/A	RC	SB	CS	SBR	FA	FR	POS	TPR
1884	Tol-a	105	423	46	101	12	8	1		26		.239	.284	.312	94	-1	-3	38				.864	1	*S	-0.1
1885	Lou-a	98	339	44	62	9	5	0		28		.183	.249	.239	57	-15	-15	21				.891	3	*S3/2	-0.9
Total	2	203	762	90	163	21	13	1		54		.214	.269	.280	77	-16	-18	59				.876	4	S/32	-1.0

■ JOE MILLER Miller, Joseph Wick b: 7/24/1850, Germany d: 8/30/1891, White Bear Lake, Minn. 5'10.5", 169 lbs. Deb: 6/26/1872 M

YEAR	TM/L	G	AB	R	H	2B	3B	HR	RBI	BB	SO	AVG	OBP	SLG	PRO+	BR	/A	RC	SB	CS	SBR	FA	FR	POS	TPR
1872	Nat-n	1	4	0	1	0	0	0	0	0	0	.250	.250	.250	47	-0	-0	0						/1M	0.0
1875	Wes-n	13	50	4	6	1	0	0		0		.120	.120	.140	-10	-5	-6	1						2	-0.5
	Chi-n	15	53	1	8	0	0	0		0		.151	.151	.151	5	-5	-5	1						2/O	-0.4
	Yr	28	103	5	14	1	0	0		0		.136	.136	.146	-3	-10	-11	2						2/O	-0.9
Total	2 n	29	107	5	15	1	0	0		0		.140	.140	.150	-0	-10	-11	2						/2O1	-0.9

■ KEITH MILLER Miller, Keith Alan b: 6/12/63, Midland, Mich. BR/TR, 5'11", 180 lbs. Deb: 6/16/87

YEAR	TM/L	G	AB	R	H	2B	3B	HR	RBI	BB	SO	AVG	OBP	SLG	PRO+	BR	/A	RC	SB	CS	SBR	FA	FR	POS	TPR
1987	NY-N	25	51	14	19	2	2	0	1	2	6	.373	.407	.490	144	3	3	11	8	1	2	.967	2	2	0.7
1988	NY-N	40	70	9	15	1	1	1	5	6	10	.214	.276	.300	69	-3	-3	5	0	5	-3	.946	-7	2/S3O	-1.4
1989	NY-N	57	143	15	33	7	0	1	7	5	27	.231	.262	.301	63	-8	-7	12	6	0	2	.967	-4	2O/S3	-0.9
1990	NY-N	88	233	42	60	8	0	1	12	23	46	.258	.329	.305	76	-7	-7	27	16	3	3	.980	5	O2/S	0.0
1991	NY-N	98	275	41	77	22	1	4	23	23	44	.280	.347	.411	113	4	5	42	14	4	2	.972	0	2O/3S	0.8
1992	KC-A	106	416	57	118	24	4	4	38	31	46	.284	.354	.389	107	5	4	62	16	6	1	.971	-20	2O/D	-1.3
Total	6	414	1188	178	322	64	8	11	86	90	179	.271	.334	.366	97	-6	-4	157	60	19	7	.970	-23	2O/S3D	-2.1

■ ED MILLER Miller, L. Edward b: Tecumseh, Mich. Deb: 7/18/1884

YEAR	TM/L	G	AB	R	H	2B	3B	HR	RBI	BB	SO	AVG	OBP	SLG	PRO+	BR	/A	RC	SB	CS	SBR	FA	FR	POS	TPR
1884	Tol-a	8	24	2	6	0	0	0		1		.250	.280	.250	74	-1	-1	2				.615	-1	/O	-0.1

■ HACK MILLER Miller, Lawrence H. b: 1/1/1894, New York, N.Y. d: 9/17/71, Oakland, Cal. BR/TR, 5'9", 195 lbs. Deb: 9/22/16

YEAR	TM/L	G	AB	R	H	2B	3B	HR	RBI	BB	SO	AVG	OBP	SLG	PRO+	BR	/A	RC	SB	CS	SBR	FA	FR	POS	TPR
1916	Bro-N	3	3	0	1	0	1	0	1	1	1	.333	.500	1.000	345	1	1	2	0			1.000	-1	/O	0.0
1918	*Bos-A	12	29	2	8	2	0	0	4	0	4	.276	.276	.345	89	-1	-1	3	0			1.000	-3	O	-0.4
1922	Chi-N	122	466	61	164	28	5	12	78	26	39	.352	.389	.511	128	20	18	91	3	3	-1	.959	-3	*O	0.6
1923	Chi-N	135	485	74	146	24	2	20	88	27	39	.301	.343	.482	116	9	9	79	6	5	-1	.978	6	*O	0.4
1924	Chi-N	53	131	17	44	8	1	4	25	8	11	.336	.379	.504	133	6	6	25	1	0	0	.948	-4	O	0.0
1925	Chi-N	24	86	10	24	3	2	2	9	2	9	.279	.303	.430	84	-2	-2	11	0	1	-1	.878	-3	O	-0.7
Total	6	349	1200	164	387	65	11	38	205	64	103	.322	.361	.490	120	33	31	209	10	9		.962	-8	O	-0.1

■ LEMMIE MILLER Miller, Lemmie Earl b: 6/2/60, Dallas, Tex. BR/TR, 6'1", 190 lbs. Deb: 5/22/84

YEAR	TM/L	G	AB	R	H	2B	3B	HR	RBI	BB	SO	AVG	OBP	SLG	PRO+	BR	/A	RC	SB	CS	SBR	FA	FR	POS	TPR
1984	LA-N	8	12	1	2	0	0	0	0	1	2	.167	.231	.167	13	-1	-1	1	0	0	0	1.000	-1	/O	-0.3

■ OTTO MILLER Miller, Lowell Otto "Moonie" b: 6/1/1889, Minden, Neb. d: 3/29/62, Brooklyn, N.Y. BR/TR, 6', 196 lbs. Deb: 7/16/10 C

YEAR	TM/L	G	AB	R	H	2B	3B	HR	RBI	BB	SO	AVG	OBP	SLG	PRO+	BR	/A	RC	SB	CS	SBR	FA	FR	POS	TPR
1910	Bro-N	31	66	5	11	3	0	0	2	2	19	.167	.203	.212	22	-7	-7	3	1			.987	9	C	0.4
1911	Bro-N	25	62	7	13	2	2	0	8	0	4	.210	.210	.306	46	-5	-5	4	2			.927	-3	C	-0.6
1912	Bro-N	98	316	35	88	18	1	1	31	18	50	.278	.325	.351	88	-7	-5	39	11			.975	13	C	1.7
1913	Bro-N	104	320	26	87	11	7	0	26	10	31	.272	.294	.350	81	-8	-9	34	7			.962	-37	*C/1	-4.0
1914	Bro-N	54	169	17	39	6	1	0	9	7	20	.231	.261	.278	59	-9	-9	12	0			.964	0	C/1	-0.5
1915	Bro-N	84	254	20	57	4	6	0	25	6	28	.224	.245	.287	60	-13	-13	20	3			.981	8	C	0.2
1916	*Bro-N	73	216	16	55	9	2	1	17	7	29	.255	.281	.329	85	-4	-4	22	6			.968	4	C	0.5
1917	Bro-N	92	274	19	63	5	4	1	17	14	29	.230	.272	.288	70	-9	-10	23	5			.979	1	C	-0.2
1918	Bro-N	75	228	8	44	6	1	0	8	9	20	.193	.230	.228	40	-16	-16	11	1			.972	4	C/1	-0.8
1919	Bro-N	51	164	18	37	5	0	0	5	7	14	.226	.257	.256	53	-9	-9	11	2			.966	2	C	-0.3
1920	*Bro-N	90	301	16	87	9	2	0	33	9	18	.289	.312	.332	82	-6	-7	30	0	5	-3	**.986**	-2	C	-0.7
1921	Bro-N	91	286	22	67	8	6	1	27	9	26	.234	.260	.315	50	-20	-22	24	2	1	0	.972	9	C	-0.8
1922	Bro-N	59	180	20	47	11	1	1	23	6	13	.261	.285	.350	63	-10	-10	18	0	0	0	.968	3	C	-0.4
Total	13	927	2836	229	695	97	33	5	231	104	301	.245	.275	.308	67	-123	-126	250	40	6		.973	11	C/1	-5.5

■ KEITH MILLER Miller, Neal Keith b: 3/7/63, Dallas, Tex. BB/TR, 5'11", 175 lbs. Deb: 4/23/88

YEAR	TM/L	G	AB	R	H	2B	3B	HR	RBI	BB	SO	AVG	OBP	SLG	PRO+	BR	/A	RC	SB	CS	SBR	FA	FR	POS	TPR
1988	Phi-N	47	48	4	8	3	0	0	6	5	13	.167	.245	.229	36	-4	-4	3	0	0	0	1.000	-3	/O3S	-0.8
1989	Phi-N	8	10	0	3	1	0	0	0	0	3	.300	.300	.400	98	-0	-0	1	0	0	0	1.000	-1	/O	-0.1
Total	2	55	58	4	11	4	0	0	6	5	16	.190	.254	.259	47	-4	-4	4	0	0	0	1.000	-4	/O3S	-0.9

■ NORM MILLER Miller, Norman Calvin b: 2/5/46, Los Angeles, Cal. BL/TR, 5'11", 195 lbs. Deb: 9/11/65

YEAR	TM/L	G	AB	R	H	2B	3B	HR	RBI	BB	SO	AVG	OBP	SLG	PRO+	BR	/A	RC	SB	CS	SBR	FA	FR	POS	TPR
1965	Hou-N	11	15	2	3	0	1	0	1	1	7	.200	.250	.333	67	-1	-1	1	0	0	0	1.000	-0	/O	-0.1
1966	Hou-N	11	34	1	5	0	0	1	3	2	8	.147	.194	.235	20	-4	-3	2	0	0	0	1.000	0	/O3	-0.4
1967	Hou-N	64	190	15	39	9	3	1	14	19	42	.205	.278	.300	68	-8	-8	14	2	0	1	.967	-1	O	-1.1
1968	Hou-N	79	257	35	61	18	2	6	28	22	48	.237	.310	.393	112	3	3	31	6	5	-1	.971	-3	O	-0.5
1969	Hou-N	119	409	58	108	21	4	4	50	47	77	.264	.350	.364	102	1	2	54	4	4	-1	.984	-0	*O	-0.6
1970	Hou-N	90	226	29	54	9	0	4	29	41	33	.239	.358	.332	90	-3	-2	29	3	1	0	.947	-1	O/C	-0.5
1971	Hou-N	45	74	5	19	5	0	2	10	5	13	.257	.313	.405	105	0	0	9	0	0	0	1.000	-2	O/C	-0.3
1972	Hou-N	67	107	18	26	4	0	4	13	13	23	.243	.331	.393	107	1	1	14	1	0	0	1.000	-1	O	-0.1
1973	Hou-N	3	3	0	0	0	0	0	0	0	2	.000	.000	.000	-99	-1	-1	0	0	0	0	.000	0	/O	-0.1
	Atl-N	9	8	2	3	1	0	1	6	3	3	.375	.545	.875	267	2	2	4	0	0	0	.667	-0	/O	0.2
	Yr	12	11	2	3	1	0	1	6	3	5	.273	.429	.636	181	1	1	3	0	0	0	.667	-0	/O	0.1
1974	Atl-N	42	41	1	7	1	0	1	5	7	9	.171	.292	.268	55	-2	-2	4	0	0	0	1.000	0	/O	-0.2
Total	10	540	1364	166	325	68	10	24	159	160	265	.238	.325	.356	95	-12	-8	162	16	10	-1	.972	-7	O/C3	-3.7

■ OTTO MILLER Miller, Otis Louis b: 2/2/01, Belleville, Ill. d: 7/26/59, Belleville, Ill. BR/TR, 5'10.5", 168 lbs. Deb: 4/17/27

YEAR	TM/L	G	AB	R	H	2B	3B	HR	RBI	BB	SO	AVG	OBP	SLG	PRO+	BR	/A	RC	SB	CS	SBR	FA	FR	POS	TPR
1927	StL-A	51	76	8	17	5	0	0	8	8	5	.224	.306	.289	53	-5	-5	7	0	1	-1	.938	-4	S3	-0.8
1930	Bos-A	112	370	49	106	22	5	0	40	26	21	.286	.333	.373	82	-12	-10	46	2	4	-2	.948	-6	32	-1.1
1931	Bos-A	107	389	38	106	12	1	0	43	15	20	.272	.301	.308	64	-22	-19	36	1	1	-0	.953	-1	32	-1.3
1932	Bos-A	2	2	0	0	0	0	0	0	0	0	.000	.000	.000	-99	-1	-1	0	0	0	0	.000	0	H	-0.1
Total	4	272	837	95	229	39	6	0	91	49	46	.274	.315	.335	71	-40	-35	89	3	6	-3	.949	-11	3/2S	-3.3

■ RALPH MILLER Miller, Ralph Joseph b: 2/29/1896, Ft.Wayne, Ind. d: 3/18/39, Ft.Wayne, Ind. BR/TR, 6', 190 lbs. Deb: 4/14/20

YEAR	TM/L	G	AB	R	H	2B	3B	HR	RBI	BB	SO	AVG	OBP	SLG	PRO+	BR	/A	RC	SB	CS	SBR	FA	FR	POS	TPR
1920	Phi-N	97	338	28	74	14	1	0	28	11	32	.219	.246	.266	45	-23	-25	22	3	4	-2	.940	0	3/1SO	-2.4
1921	Phi-N	57	204	19	62	10	0	3	26	6	10	.304	.327	.397	84	-3	-5	25	3	5	-2	.910	0	S3	-0.2

YEAR	TM/L	G	AB	R	H	2B	3B	HR	RBI	BB	SO	AVG	OBP	SLG	PRO+	BR	/A	RC	SB	CS	SBR	FA	FR	POS	TPR
1924	*Was-A	9	15	1	2	0	0	0	0	1	1	.133	.188	.133	-17	-3	-3	0	0	0	0	.941	0	/2	-0.2
Total	3	163	557	48	138	24	1	3	54	18	43	.248	.274	.311	59	-29	-33	47	6	9	-4	.904	1	3/S21O	-2.8

■ RAY MILLER Miller, Raymond Peter b: 2/12/1888, Pittsburgh, Pa. d: 4/7/27, Pittsburgh, Pa. BL/TL, 5'10", 168 lbs. Deb: 4/14/17

YEAR	TM/L	G	AB	R	H	2B	3B	HR	RBI	BB	SO	AVG	OBP	SLG	PRO+	BR	/A	RC	SB	CS	SBR	FA	FR	POS	TPR
1917	Cle-A	19	21	1	4	1	0	0	2	8	3	.190	.414	.238	92	1	0	2	0			1.000	1	/1	0.2
	Pit-N	6	27	1	4	1	0	0	0	2	3	.148	.207	.185	20	-3	-3	1	0			1.000	0	/1	-0.3
Total	1	25	48	2	8	2	0	0	2	10	6	.167	.310	.208	56	-2	-2	3	0			1.000	2	/1	-0.1

■ RICK MILLER Miller, Richard Alan b: 4/19/48, Grand Rapids, Mich. BL/TL, 6', 185 lbs. Deb: 9/04/71

YEAR	TM/L	G	AB	R	H	2B	3B	HR	RBI	BB	SO	AVG	OBP	SLG	PRO+	BR	/A	RC	SB	CS	SBR	FA	FR	POS	TPR
1971	Bos-A	15	33	9	11	5	0	1	7	8	8	.333	.463	.576	180	4	4	9	0	2	-1	.969	1	O	0.3
1972	Bos-A	89	98	13	21	4	1	3	15	11	27	.214	.294	.367	91	-1	-1	10	0	2	-1	.967	-11	O	-1.7
1973	Bos-A	143	441	65	115	17	7	6	43	51	59	.261	.341	.372	95	1	-2	58	12	7	-1	.978	-4	*O	-1.3
1974	Bos-A	114	280	41	73	8	1	5	22	37	47	.261	.347	.350	94	1	-1	38	13	2	3	.989	2	*O	0.0
1975	*Bos-A	77	108	21	21	2	1	0	15	21	20	.194	.326	.231	55	-5	-6	9	3	2	-0	.981	-8	O	-1.7
1976	Bos-A	105	269	40	76	15	3	0	27	34	47	.283	.363	.361	100	5	1	36	11	10	-3	.991	5	O/D	0.0
1977	Bos-A	86	189	34	48	9	3	0	24	22	30	.254	.341	.333	76	-3	-6	23	11	5	0	.992	-7	O/D	-1.5
1978	Cal-A	132	475	66	125	25	4	1	37	54	70	.263	.343	.339	96	-3	-1	53	3	13	-7	.989	15	*O	0.2
1979	*Cal-A	120	427	60	125	15	5	2	28	50	69	.293	.368	.365	102	1	3	60	5	4	-1	.989	10	*O	0.7
1980	Cal-A	129	412	52	113	14	3	2	38	48	71	.274	.351	.337	92	-4	-3	53	7	3	0	.984	5	*O	-0.2
1981	Bos-A	97	316	38	92	17	2	2	33	28	36	.291	.351	.377	103	4	2	41	3	5	-2	.987	-3	O	-0.7
1982	Bos-A	135	409	50	104	13	2	4	38	40	41	.254	.324	.325	75	-11	-14	43	5	6	-2	.983	-6	*O	-2.6
1983	Bos-A	104	262	41	75	10	2	2	21	28	30	.286	.357	.363	92	0	-2	34	3	3	-1	.993	0	O/1D	-0.5
1984	Bos-A	95	123	17	32	5	1	0	12	17	22	.260	.350	.317	82	-2	-2	14	1	1	-0	.974	-7	O/1	-1.1
1985	Bos-A	41	45	5	15	2	0	0	9	5	6	.333	.400	.378	110	1	1	7	1	0	0	1.000	-2	/OD	0.0
Total	15	1482	3887	552	1046	161	35	28	369	454	583	.269	.348	.350	92	-11	-29	488	78	65	-16	.986	-10	*O/D1	-10.1

■ ROD MILLER Miller, Rodney Carter b: 1/16/40, Portland, Ore. BL/TR, 5'10", 160 lbs. Deb: 9/28/57

YEAR	TM/L	G	AB	R	H	2B	3B	HR	RBI	BB	SO	AVG	OBP	SLG	PRO+	BR	/A	RC	SB	CS	SBR	FA	FR	POS	TPR
1957	Bro-N	1	1	0	0	0	0	0	0	0	1	.000	.000	.000	-91	-0	-0	0	0	0	0	.000	0	H	0.0

■ DOC MILLER Miller, Roy Oscar b: 1883, Chatham, Ont., Canada d: 7/31/38, Jersey City, N.J. BL/TL, 5'10.5", 170 lbs. Deb: 5/04/10

YEAR	TM/L	G	AB	R	H	2B	3B	HR	RBI	BB	SO	AVG	OBP	SLG	PRO+	BR	/A	RC	SB	CS	SBR	FA	FR	POS	TPR
1910	Chi-N	1	1	0	0	0	0	0	0	0	0	.000	.000	.000	-99	-0	-0	0	0			.000	0	H	0.0
	Bos-N	130	482	48	138	27	4	3	55	33	52	.286	.333	.378	103	3	0	66	17			.951	-12	*O	-1.9
	Yr	131	483	48	138	27	4	3	55	33	52	.286	.333	.377	102	3	-0	66	17			.951	-12	*O	-1.9
1911	Bos-N	146	577	69	**192**	36	3	7	91	43	43	.333	.379	.442	120	21	15	107	32			.961	2	*O	0.9
1912	Bos-N	51	201	26	47	8	1	2	24	14	17	.234	.287	.313	63	-10	-11	20	6			.948	3	O	-1.1
	Phi-N	67	177	24	51	12	5	0	21	9	13	.288	.323	.412	94	-1	-2	24	3			.986	2	O	-0.2
	Yr	118	378	50	98	20	6	2	45	23	30	.259	.303	.360	78	-11	-13	44	9			.964	5	O	-1.3
1913	Phi-N	69	87	9	30	6	0	0	11	6	6	.345	.400	.414	127	4	3	14	2			.800	-4	O	-0.1
1914	Cin-N	93	192	8	49	7	2	0	33	16	18	.255	.313	.313	83	-3	-4	19	4			.976	-4	O	-1.1
Total	5	557	1717	184	507	96	15	12	235	121	149	.295	.343	.390	102	13	1	251	64			.958	-13	O	-3.5

■ RUDY MILLER Miller, Rudel Charles b: 7/12/1900, Kalamazoo, Mich. BR/TR, 6'1", 180 lbs. Deb: 9/19/29

YEAR	TM/L	G	AB	R	H	2B	3B	HR	RBI	BB	SO	AVG	OBP	SLG	PRO+	BR	/A	RC	SB	CS	SBR	FA	FR	POS	TPR
1929	Phi-A	2	4	1	1	0	0	0	1	3	0	.250	.571	.250	115	1	0	1	0	0	0	.750	-0	/3	0.0

■ TOM MILLER Miller, Thomas P. "Reddy" b: Philadelphia, Pa. d: 5/29/1876, Philadelphia, Pa. Deb: 10/24/1874

YEAR	TM/L	G	AB	R	H	2B	3B	HR	RBI	BB	SO	AVG	OBP	SLG	PRO+	BR	/A	RC	SB	CS	SBR	FA	FR	POS	TPR
1874	Ath-n	4	16	1	8	0	0	0		0		.500	.500	.500	202	2	2	4						C	0.1
1875	StL-n	55	212	17	34	2	0	0		2		.160	.168	.170	19	-17	-14	6						*C/3	-1.0
Total	2 n	59	228	18	42	2	0	0		2		.184	.191	.193	35	-15	-12	10						/C3	-0.9

■ TOM MILLER Miller, Thomas Royall b: 7/5/1897, Powhatan Court House, Va. d: 8/13/80, Richmond, Va. BL/TR, 5'11", 180 lbs. Deb: 7/29/18

YEAR	TM/L	G	AB	R	H	2B	3B	HR	RBI	BB	SO	AVG	OBP	SLG	PRO+	BR	/A	RC	SB	CS	SBR	FA	FR	POS	TPR
1918	Bos-N	2	2	0	0	0	0	0	0	0	0	.000	.000	.000	-99	-0	-0	-0	1			.000	0	H	-0.1
1919	Bos-N	7	6	2	2	0	0	0	0	0	1	.333	.333	.333	105	-0	0	1	0			.000	0	H	0.0
Total	2	9	8	2	2	0	0	0	0	0	1	.250	.250	.250	53	-0	-0	1	1				0		-0.1

■ WARD MILLER Miller, Ward Taylor "Windy" or "Grump" b: 7/5/1884, Mt.Carroll, Ill. d: 9/4/58, Dixon, Ill. BL/TR, 5'11", 177 lbs. Deb: 4/14/09

YEAR	TM/L	G	AB	R	H	2B	3B	HR	RBI	BB	SO	AVG	OBP	SLG	PRO+	BR	/A	RC	SB	CS	SBR	FA	FR	POS	TPR
1909	Pit-N	15	56	2	8	0	1	0	4	4		.143	.213	.179	20	-5	-6	3	2			.967	-1	O	-0.8
	Cin-N	43	113	17	35	3	1	0	4	6		.310	.345	.354	118	2	2	17	9			.981	-7	O	-0.6
	Yr	58	169	19	43	3	2	0	8	10		.254	.300	.296	84	-3	-3	18	11			.976	-8	O	-1.4
1910	Cin-N	81	126	21	30	6	0	0	10	22	13	.238	.356	.286	92	-1	-0	17	10			.944	2	O	0.0
1912	Chi-N	86	241	45	74	11	4	0	22	26	18	.307	.377	.386	109	3	4	39	11			.943	-8	O	-0.8
1913	Chi-N	80	203	23	48	5	7	1	16	34	33	.236	.349	.345	98	1	1	27	13			.980	3	O	0.2
1914	StL-F	121	402	49	118	17	7	4	50	59	36	.294	.397	.400	121	17	14	74	18			.953	10	*O	2.0
1915	StL-F	154	536	80	164	19	9	1	63	79	39	.306	.400	.381	123	24	20	101	33			.963	3	*O	1.7
1916	StL-A	146	485	72	129	17	5	1	50	72	76	.266	.371	.328	116	9	12	65	25	21	-5	.943	-5	*O	-0.6
1917	StL-A	43	82	13	17	1	1	1	2	16	15	.207	.350	.280	96	0	0	10	7			.966	-4	O	-0.6
Total	8	769	2244	322	623	79	35	8	221	318	230	.278	.375	.355	112	50	47	353	128	21		.957	-8	O	0.5

■ WARREN MILLER Miller, Warren Lemuel "Gitz" b: 7/14/1885, Philadelphia, Pa. d: 8/12/56, Philadelphia, Pa. BL/TL, 5'10", 160 lbs. Deb: 7/29/09

YEAR	TM/L	G	AB	R	H	2B	3B	HR	RBI	BB	SO	AVG	OBP	SLG	PRO+	BR	/A	RC	SB	CS	SBR	FA	FR	POS	TPR
1909	Was-A	26	51	5	11	0	0	0	1	4		.216	.273	.216	57	-3	-2	3	0			1.000	-1	O	-0.5
1911	Was-A	21	34	3	5	0	0	0	0	0		.147	.147	.147	-18	-5	-5	1	0			.778	-2	/O	-0.7
Total	2	47	85	8	16	0	0	0	1	4		.188	.225	.188	25	-8	-8	4	0			.931	-3	/O	-1.2

■ BILL MILLER Miller, William Alexander b: 5/23/1879, Germany d: 9/8/57, Ashtabula, Ohio BL/TL, 6'2", 170 lbs. Deb: 8/23/02

YEAR	TM/L	G	AB	R	H	2B	3B	HR	RBI	BB	SO	AVG	OBP	SLG	PRO+	BR	/A	RC	SB	CS	SBR	FA	FR	POS	TPR
1902	Pit-N	1	5	0	1	0	0	0	2	0		.200	.200	.200	23	-0	-0	0				.000	-0	/O	-0.1

■ JOE MILLETTE Millette, Joseph Anthony b: 8/12/66, Walnut Creek, Cal. BR/TR, 6'1", 180 lbs. Deb: 7/16/92

YEAR	TM/L	G	AB	R	H	2B	3B	HR	RBI	BB	SO	AVG	OBP	SLG	PRO+	BR	/A	RC	SB	CS	SBR	FA	FR	POS	TPR
1992	Phi-N	33	78	5	16	0	0	0	2	5	10	.205	.271	.205	37	-6	-6	3	1	0	0	.974	10	S/32	0.6

■ WALLY MILLIES Millies, Walter Louis b: 10/18/06, Chicago, Ill. BR/TR, 5'10.5", 170 lbs. Deb: 9/23/34

YEAR	TM/L	G	AB	R	H	2B	3B	HR	RBI	BB	SO	AVG	OBP	SLG	PRO+	BR	/A	RC	SB	CS	SBR	FA	FR	POS	TPR
1934	Bro-N	2	7	0	0	0	0	0	0	0	0	.000	.000	.000	-99	-2	-2	0	0			1.000	1	/C	-0.1
1936	Was-A	74	215	26	67	10	2	0	25	11	8	.312	.345	.377	83	-7	-6	28	1	0	0	.968	1	C	-0.2
1937	Was-A	59	179	21	40	7	1	0	28	9	15	.223	.261	.274	36	-18	-17	13	1	0	0	.971	2	C	-1.2
1939	Phi-N	84	205	12	48	3	0	0	12	9	5	.234	.270	.249	41	-17	-16	13	0			.964	-7	C	-2.0
1940	Phi-N	26	43	1	3	0	0	0	0	4	4	.070	.149	.070	-39	-8	-8	0	0			.958	2	C	-0.5
1941	Phi-N	1	2	0	0	0	0	0	0	0	0	.000	.000	.000	-99	-1	-1	0	0			.800	0	/C	0.0
Total	6	246	651	60	158	20	3	0	65	33	32	.243	.280	.283	47	-53	-49	55	2	0		.966	-2	C	-4.0

■ JOCKO MILLIGAN Milligan, John b: 8/8/1861, Philadelphia, Pa. d: 8/29/23, Philadelphia, Pa. BR/TR, 6', 192 lbs. Deb: 5/01/1884

YEAR	TM/L	G	AB	R	H	2B	3B	HR	RBI	BB	SO	AVG	OBP	SLG	PRO+	BR	/A	RC	SB	CS	SBR	FA	FR	POS	TPR
1884	Phi-a	66	268	39	77	20	3	3		8		.287	.308	.418	129	10	8	35				**.939**	13	C/O	2.4
1885	Phi-a	67	265	35	71	15	4	2		7		.268	.289	.377	106	3	1	30				.935	11	C/1O	1.5
1886	Phi-a	75	301	52	76	17	3	5		21		.252	.301	.379	113	4	4	41	18			.919	5	C1/O3	0.8
1887	Phi-a	95	377	54	114	27	4	2		21		.302	.344	.411	112	5	5	57	8			.966	3	1C/O	0.7
1888	*StL-a	63	219	19	55	6	2	5	37	17		.251	.311	.365	108	5	1	26	3			.941	8	C/1	1.2
1889	StL-a	72	273	53	100	30	2	12	76	16	19	.366	.408	.623	172	31	25	72	2			.933	14	C/1	3.7
1890	Phi-P	62	234	38	69	9	3	3	57	19	19	.295	.363	.397	103	2	1	35	2			.893	4	C/1	0.8
1891	Phi-a	118	455	75	138	**35**	12	11	106	56	51	.303	.397	.505	157	35	33	94	2			.939	0	C1	3.4

YEAR	TM/L	G	AB	R	H	2B	3B	HR	RBI	BB	SO	AVG	OBP	SLG	PRO+	BR	/A	RC	SB	CS	SBR	FA	FR	POS	TPR
1892	Was-N	88	323	40	89	20	9	4	43	26	24	.276	.335	.430	137	12	13	48	2			.947	5	C1	1.9
1893	Bal-N	24	102	19	25	5	2	1	19	5	7	.245	.294	.363	74	-4	-4	12	2			.981	1	1/C	-0.3
	NY-N	42	147	16	34	5	6	1	25	14	13	.231	.302	.367	79	-5	-5	17	2			.934	14	C	1.0
	Yr	66	249	35	59	10	8	2	44	19	20	.237	.299	.365	77	-9	-9	29	4			.932	15	C1	0.7
Total	10	772	2964	440	848	189	50	49	363	210	133	.286	.341	.433	124	98	81	469	41			.930	78	C1/O3	17.1

■ RANDY MILLIGAN

Milligan, Randy Andre b: 11/27/61, San Diego, Cal. BR/TR, 6'2", 230 lbs. Deb: 9/12/87

YEAR	TM/L	G	AB	R	H	2B	3B	HR	RBI	BB	SO	AVG	OBP	SLG	PRO+	BR	/A	RC	SB	CS	SBR	FA	FR	POS	TPR
1987	NY-N	3	1	0	0	0	0	0	0	1	1	.000	.500	.000	49	0	0	0	0	0	0	.000	0	/H	0.0
1988	Pit-N	40	82	10	18	5	0	3	8	20	24	.220	.379	.390	123	3	3	13	1	2	-1	.987	-1	1/O	0.0
1989	Bal-A	124	365	56	98	23	5	12	45	74	75	.268	.396	.458	144	22	24	68	9	5	-0	.995	2	*1/D	1.7
1990	Bal-A	109	362	64	96	20	1	20	60	88	68	.265	.412	.492	157	29	30	78	6	3	0	.990	5	1/D	2.8
1991	Bal-A	141	483	57	127	17	2	16	70	84	108	.263	.374	.406	121	13	16	71	0	5	-3	.990	3	*1D/O	0.8
1992	Bal-A	137	462	71	111	21	1	11	53	106	81	.240	.386	.361	111	12	12	70	0	1	-1	.994	-6	*1/D	-0.3
Total	6	554	1755	258	450	86	9	62	236	373	357	.256	.390	.422	130	78	85	300	16	16	-5	.992	3	1/DO	5.0

■ JACK MILLS

Mills, Abbott Paige b: 10/23/1889, S.Williamstown, Mass. d: 6/3/73, Washington, D.C. BL/TR, 6', 165 lbs. Deb: 7/01/11

YEAR	TM/L	G	AB	R	H	2B	3B	HR	RBI	BB	SO	AVG	OBP	SLG	PRO+	BR	/A	RC	SB	CS	SBR	FA	FR	POS	TPR
1911	Cle-A	13	17	5	5	0	0	0	1	1		.294	.368	.294	85	-0	-0	2	1			1.000	2	/3	0.1

■ CHARLIE MILLS

Mills, Charles b: Brooklyn, N.Y. d: 4/10/1874, Brooklyn, N.Y. 6', Deb: 5/18/1871 U

YEAR	TM/L	G	AB	R	H	2B	3B	HR	RBI	BB	SO	AVG	OBP	SLG	PRO+	BR	/A	RC	SB	CS	SBR	FA	FR	POS	TPR
1871	Mut-n	32	146	27	36	4	3	0	22	1	0	.247	.252	.315	68	-7	-4	12	2					*C/O2	-0.3
1872	Mut-n	6	31	6	4	0	0	0	2	0	0	.129	.129	.129	-22	-4	-4	1						/OC	-0.3
Total	2 n	38	177	33	40	4	3	0	24	1		.226	.230	.282	53	-11	-8	13						/CO2	-0.6

■ BUSTER MILLS

Mills, Colonel Buster "Bus" b: 9/16/08, Ranger, Tex. d: 12/1/91, Arlington, Tex. BR/TR, 5'11.5", 195 lbs. Deb: 4/18/34 MC

YEAR	TM/L	G	AB	R	H	2B	3B	HR	RBI	BB	SO	AVG	OBP	SLG	PRO+	BR	/A	RC	SB	CS	SBR	FA	FR	POS	TPR
1934	StL-N	29	72	7	17	4	1	1	8	4	11	.236	.295	.361	70	-3	-3	8	0			1.000	-0	O	-0.4
1935	Bro-N	17	56	12	12	2	1	1	7	5	11	.214	.323	.339	80	-2	-1	6	0			.971	-2	O	-0.4
1937	Bos-A	123	505	85	149	25	8	7	58	46	41	.295	.361	.418	92	-3	-6	77	11	8	-2	.946	-5	*O	-1.5
1938	StL-A	123	466	66	133	24	4	3	46	43	46	.285	.350	.373	81	-13	-13	61	7	8	-3	.964	3	*O	-1.5
1940	NY-A	34	63	10	25	3	3	1	15	7	5	.397	.457	.587	176	7	7	15	0	0	0	1.000	-2	O	0.4
1942	Cle-A	80	195	19	54	4	2	1	26	23	18	.277	.353	.333	99	-1	0	23	5	4	-1	.973	2	O	-0.1
1946	Cle-A	9	22	1	6	0	0	0	3	3	5	.273	.360	.273	84	-0	-0	2	0	1	-1	1.000	-0	/O	-0.2
Total	7	415	1379	200	396	62	19	14	163	131	137	.287	.355	.390	91	-16	-17	191	23	21		.964	-5	O	-3.7

■ EVERETT MILLS

Mills, Everett b: 1/1846, Newark, N.J. d: 6/22/08, Newark, N.J. 6'1", 174 lbs. Deb: 5/05/1871 M

YEAR	TM/L	G	AB	R	H	2B	3B	HR	RBI	BB	SO	AVG	OBP	SLG	PRO+	BR	/A	RC	SB	CS	SBR	FA	FR	POS	TPR
1871	Oly-n	32	157	38	43	6	4	1	24	3	1	.274	.287	.382	95	-2	-0	18	2					*1	0.1
1872	Bal-n	55	267	55	76	13	3	0	35	3	2	.285	.293	.356	94	-1	-3	28						*1M	-0.1
1873	Bal-n	54	263	64	87	16	6	0	57	2	1	.331	.336	.437	126	8	8	40						*1/O	0.8
1874	Har-n	53	241	40	70	6	2	0		6		.290	.308	.332	99	1	-1	25						*1	-0.1
1875	Har-n	80	341	59	91	10	4	1		0		.267	.267	.328	100	1	-1	31						*1	-0.2
1876	Har-N	63	254	28	66	8	1	0	23	1	3	.260	.263	.299	80	-4	-7	20				.939	-2	*1	-0.9
Total	5 n	274	1269	256	367	51	19	2	116	14	4	.289	.297	.364	103	8	3	142						1/O	0.5

■ FRANK MILLS

Mills, Frank Le Moyne b: 5/13/1895, Knoxville, Ohio d: 8/31/83, Youngstown, Ohio BL/TR, 6', 180 lbs. Deb: 9/22/14

YEAR	TM/L	G	AB	R	H	2B	3B	HR	RBI	BB	SO	AVG	OBP	SLG	PRO+	BR	/A	RC	SB	CS	SBR	FA	FR	POS	TPR
1914	Cle-A	4	8	0	1	0	0	0	0	1	2	.125	.222	.125	4	-1	-1	0	0			.900	-1	/C	-0.2

■ BRAD MILLS

Mills, James Bradley b: 1/19/57, Exeter, Cal. BL/TR, 6', 195 lbs. Deb: 6/08/80

YEAR	TM/L	G	AB	R	H	2B	3B	HR	RBI	BB	SO	AVG	OBP	SLG	PRO+	BR	/A	RC	SB	CS	SBR	FA	FR	POS	TPR
1980	Mon-N	21	60	1	18	1	0	0	8	5	6	.300	.354	.317	88	-1	-1	7	0	1	-1	.977	-1	3	-0.3
1981	*Mon-N	17	21	3	5	1	0	0	1	2	1	.238	.304	.286	67	-1	-1	2	0	0	0	1.000	0	/32	-0.1
1982	Mon-N	54	67	6	15	3	0	1	2	5	11	.224	.278	.313	64	-3	-3	5	0	0	0	.867	-3	3	-0.7
1983	Mon-N	14	20	1	5	0	0	0	1	2	3	.250	.318	.250	60	-1	-1	2	0	0	0	1.000	-1	/31	-0.2
Total	4	106	168	11	43	5	0	1	12	14	21	.256	.313	.304	73	-6	-6	16	0	1	-1	.959	-5	/321	-1.3

■ RUPERT MILLS

Mills, Rupert Frank b: 10/12/1892, Newark, N.J. d: 7/20/29, Lake Hopatcong, N.J. BR/TR, 6'2", 185 lbs. Deb: 6/23/15

YEAR	TM/L	G	AB	R	H	2B	3B	HR	RBI	BB	SO	AVG	OBP	SLG	PRO+	BR	/A	RC	SB	CS	SBR	FA	FR	POS	TPR
1915	New-F	41	134	12	27	5	1	0	16	6	21	.201	.241	.254	48	-9	-8	10	6			.976	0	1	-1.0

■ BILL MILLS

Mills, William Henry b: 11/2/20, Boston, Mass. BR/TR, 5'10", 175 lbs. Deb: 5/19/44

YEAR	TM/L	G	AB	R	H	2B	3B	HR	RBI	BB	SO	AVG	OBP	SLG	PRO+	BR	/A	RC	SB	CS	SBR	FA	FR	POS	TPR
1944	Phi-A	5	4	0	1	0	0	0	0	1	1	.250	.400	.250	89	0	0	0	0	0	0	.000	0	/C	0.0

■ PETE MILNE

Milne, William James b: 4/10/25, Mobile, Ala. BL/TR, 6'1", 180 lbs. Deb: 9/15/48

YEAR	TM/L	G	AB	R	H	2B	3B	HR	RBI	BB	SO	AVG	OBP	SLG	PRO+	BR	/A	RC	SB	CS	SBR	FA	FR	POS	TPR
1948	NY-N	12	27	0	6	0	1	0	2	1	6	.222	.250	.296	47	-2	-2	2	0			.867	-2	/O	-0.5
1949	NY-N	31	29	5	7	1	0	1	6	3	6	.241	.313	.379	85	-1	-1	3	0			1.000	-0	/O	-0.1
1950	NY-N	4	4	1	1	0	1	0	1	0	1	.250	.250	.750	151	0	0	1	0			.000	0	H	0.0
Total	3	47	60	6	14	1	2	1	9	4	13	.233	.281	.367	73	-2	-2	6	0			.882	-2	/O	-0.6

■ BRIAN MILNER

Milner, Brian Tate b: 11/17/59, Fort Worth, Tex. BR/TR, 6'2", 200 lbs. Deb: 6/23/78

YEAR	TM/L	G	AB	R	H	2B	3B	HR	RBI	BB	SO	AVG	OBP	SLG	PRO+	BR	/A	RC	SB	CS	SBR	FA	FR	POS	TPR
1978	Tor-A	2	9	3	4	0	1	0	2	0	1	.444	.444	.667	204	1	1	3	0	0	0	.800	-3	/C	-0.1

■ EDDIE MILNER

Milner, Eddie James b: 5/21/55, Columbus, Ohio BL/TL, 5'11", 173 lbs. Deb: 9/02/80

YEAR	TM/L	G	AB	R	H	2B	3B	HR	RBI	BB	SO	AVG	OBP	SLG	PRO+	BR	/A	RC	SB	CS	SBR	FA	FR	POS	TPR
1980	Cin-N	6	3	1	0	0	0	0	0	0	0	.000	.000	.000	-99	-1	-1	0	0	0	0	.000	0	/H	-0.1
1981	Cin-N	8	5	0	1	1	0	0	1	1	1	.200	.333	.400	106	0	0	1	0	0	0	1.000	0	/O	0.0
1982	Cin-N	113	407	61	109	23	5	4	31	41	40	.268	.338	.378	98	0	-1	52	18	12	-2	.987	6	*O	0.0
1983	Cin-N	146	502	77	131	23	6	9	33	68	60	.261	.350	.384	100	3	1	72	41	12	5	.990	13	*O	1.5
1984	Cin-N	117	336	44	78	8	4	7	29	51	50	.232	.337	.342	87	-3	-5	42	21	13	-2	.983	10	*O	0.1
1985	Cin-N	145	453	82	115	19	7	3	33	61	31	.254	.344	.347	89	-2	-5	60	35	13	3	.983	15	*O	0.9
1986	Cin-N	145	424	70	110	22	6	15	47	36	56	.259	.317	.446	104	3	1	59	18	11	-1	.990	7	*O	0.3
1987	*SF-N	101	214	38	54	14	0	4	19	24	33	.252	.328	.374	90	-4	-3	26	10	9	-2	.993	-9	O	-1.7
1988	Cin-N	23	51	3	9	1	0	0	2	4	9	.176	.236	.196	24	-5	-5	2	2	2	-1	.968	-0	O	-0.7
Total	9	804	2395	376	607	111	28	42	195	286	280	.253	.335	.376	94	-8	-17	314	145	72	0	.987	40	O	0.3

■ JOHN MILNER

Milner, John David "The Hammer" b: 12/28/49, Atlanta, Ga. BL/TL, 6', 185 lbs. Deb: 9/15/71

YEAR	TM/L	G	AB	R	H	2B	3B	HR	RBI	BB	SO	AVG	OBP	SLG	PRO+	BR	/A	RC	SB	CS	SBR	FA	FR	POS	TPR
1971	NY-N	9	18	1	3	1	0	0	1	0	3	.167	.167	.222	9	-2	-2	1	0	0	0	1.000	1	/O	-0.1
1972	NY-N	117	362	52	86	12	2	17	38	51	74	.238	.340	.423	118	8	9	54	2	1	0	.965	1	O1	0.5
1973	*NY-N	129	451	69	108	12	3	23	72	62	84	.239	.333	.432	112	6	7	64	1	1	-0	.989	-5	1O	-0.8
1974	NY-N	137	507	70	128	19	0	20	63	66	77	.252	.339	.408	110	5	6	69	10	2	2	.994	-1	*1	-0.2
1975	NY-N	91	220	24	42	11	0	7	29	33	22	.191	.302	.336	81	-7	-6	23	1	1	-0	.985	5	O1	-0.4
1976	NY-N	127	443	56	120	25	4	15	78	65	53	.271	.364	.447	137	17	21	70	0	7	-4	.985	-2	*O1	1.0
1977	NY-N	131	388	43	99	20	3	12	57	61	55	.255	.356	.415	111	4	7	59	6	2	1	.994	1	1O	0.2
1978	Pit-N	108	295	39	80	17	0	6	38	34	25	.271	.347	.390	101	2	1	41	5	0	2	1.000	-2	O1	-0.4
1979	*Pit-N	128	326	52	90	9	4	16	60	53	37	.276	.379	.475	126	15	13	60	3	5	-2	.958	-5	O1	0.1
1980	Pit-N	114	238	31	58	6	0	8	34	52	29	.244	.379	.370	108	5	5	36	2	2	-1	.991	-3	1O	-0.2
1981	Pit-N	34	59	6	14	1	0	2	9	5	3	.237	.297	.356	82	-1	-2	6	0	0	0	.980	-2	/1O	-0.4
	*Mon-N	31	76	6	18	5	0	3	9	12	6	.237	.341	.421	114	2	1	11	0	1	-1	.978	1	1	0.1
	Yr	65	135	12	32	6	0	5	18	17	9	.237	.322	.393	100	0	-0	17	0	1	-1	.979	-1	1/O	-0.3
1982	Mon-N	26	28	1	3	0	0	0	2	4	2	.107	.219	.107	-6	-4	-4	1	1	0	0	1.000	0	/1	-0.4
	Pit-N	33	25	5	6	2	0	2	8	6	3	.240	.406	.560	163	2	2	7	1	0	0	1.000	-0	/1	0.3
	Yr	59	53	6	9	2	0	2	10	10	5	.170	.313	.321	76	-1	-2	6	1	0	0	1.000	0	/1	-0.1

YEAR	TM/L	G	AB	R	H	2B	3B	HR	RBI	BB	SO	AVG	OBP	SLG	PRO+	BR	/A	RC	SB	CS	SBR	FA	FR	POS	TPR
Total	12	1215	3436	455	855	140	16	131	498	504	473	.249	.347	.413	112	53	59	501	31	22	-4	.991	-12	1O	-0.7

■ MIKE MILOSEVICH Milosevich, Michael "Mollie" b: 1/13/15, Zeigler, Ill. d: 2/3/66, E.Chicago, Ind. BR/TR, 5'10.5", 172 lbs. Deb: 4/30/44

YEAR	TM/L	G	AB	R	H	2B	3B	HR	RBI	BB	SO	AVG	OBP	SLG	PRO+	BR	/A	RC	SB	CS	SBR	FA	FR	POS	TPR
1944	NY-A	94	312	27	77	11	4	0	32	30	37	.247	.313	.308	75	-9	-10	29	1	2	-1	.954	7	S	0.3
1945	NY-A	30	69	5	15	2	0	0	7	6	6	.217	.289	.246	54	-4	-4	5	0	0	0	.957	1	S/2	-0.2
Total	2	124	381	32	92	13	4	0	39	36	43	.241	.309	.297	71	-13	-14	34	1	2	-1	.954	8	S/2	0.1

■ DON MINCHER Mincher, Donald Ray b: 6/24/38, Huntsville, Ala. BL/TR, 6'3", 213 lbs. Deb: 4/18/60

YEAR	TM/L	G	AB	R	H	2B	3B	HR	RBI	BB	SO	AVG	OBP	SLG	PRO+	BR	/A	RC	SB	CS	SBR	FA	FR	POS	TPR
1960	Was-A	27	79	10	19	4	1	2	5	11	11	.241	.333	.392	96	-0	-0	9	0	1	-1	.977	-4	1	-0.7
1961	Min-A	35	101	18	19	5	1	5	11	22	11	.188	.333	.406	91	-0	-1	13	0	1	-1	.969	-2	1	-0.6
1962	Min-A	86	121	20	29	1	1	9	29	34	24	.240	.406	.488	134	8	7	26	0	0	0	.978	-1	1	0.5
1963	Min-A	82	225	41	58	8	0	17	42	30	51	.258	.353	.520	138	12	12	44	0	0	0	.983	-5	1	0.5
1964	Min-A	120	287	45	68	12	4	23	56	27	51	.237	.303	.547	130	10	10	45	0	0	0	.992	-0	1	0.7
1965	*Min-A	128	346	43	87	17	3	22	65	49	73	.251	.348	.509	134	18	16	62	1	3	-2	.992	-5	1/O	0.5
1966	Min-A	139	431	53	108	30	0	14	62	58	68	.251	.342	.418	110	10	7	61	3	2	-0	.992	3	*1	0.2
1967	Cal-A★	147	487	81	133	23	3	25	76	69	69	.273	.368	.487	157	31	33	87	0	3	-2	.994	-2	*1/O	2.3
1968	Cal-A	120	399	35	94	12	1	13	48	43	65	.236	.316	.368	111	3	5	47	0	2	-1	.991	-3	*1	-0.9
1969	Sea-A★	140	427	53	105	14	0	25	78	78	69	.246	.369	.454	131	18	19	72	10	11	-4	.995	8	*1	1.4
1970	Oak-A	140	463	62	114	18	0	27	74	56	71	.246	.331	.460	120	9	11	70	5	4	-1	.990	2	*1	0.1
1971	Oak-A	28	92	9	22	6	1	2	8	20	14	.239	.375	.391	120	3	3	14	1	1	-0	.996	3	1	0.3
	Was-A	100	323	35	94	15	1	10	45	53	52	.291	.394	.437	143	17	19	58	2	1	0	.990	3	1	1.5
	Yr	128	415	44	116	21	2	12	53	73	66	.280	.390	.427	138	19	22	73	3	2	-0	.991	6	*1	1.8
1972	Tex-A	61	191	23	45	10	0	6	39	46	23	.236	.389	.382	136	9	10	33	2	1	0	.994	6	1	1.3
	*Oak-A	47	54	2	8	1	0	0	5	10	16	.148	.281	.167	37	-4	-4	2	0	2	-1	.988	-1	1	-0.7
	Yr	108	245	25	53	11	0	6	44	56	39	.216	.366	.335	115	6	7	33	2	3	-1	.993	5	1	0.6
Total	13	1400	4026	530	1003	176	16	200	643	606	668	.249	.351	.450	127	144	147	644	24	32	-12	.990	2	*1/O	6.4

■ ED MINCHER Mincher, Edward John b: Baltimore, Md. Deb: 5/04/1871

YEAR	TM/L	G	AB	R	H	2B	3B	HR	RBI	BB	SO	AVG	OBP	SLG	PRO+	BR	/A	RC	SB	CS	SBR	FA	FR	POS	TPR
1871	Kek-n	9	36	4	8	0	0	0	5	0	0	.222	.222	.222	28	-3	-3	2	1					/O	-0.2
1872	Nat-n	11	54	4	5	0	0	0	3	0	1	.093	.093	.093	-37	-9	-11	0						O	-0.7
Total	2 n	20	90	8	13	0	0	0	8	0	1	.144	.144	.144	-12	-12	-14	3						/O	-0.9

■ DAN MINNEHAN Minnehan, Daniel Joseph b: 11/28/1865, Troy, N.Y. d: 8/8/29, Troy, N.Y. BR/TR, 5'10", 145 lbs. Deb: 9/20/1895

YEAR	TM/L	G	AB	R	H	2B	3B	HR	RBI	BB	SO	AVG	OBP	SLG	PRO+	BR	/A	RC	SB	CS	SBR	FA	FR	POS	TPR
1895	Lou-N	8	34	6	13	0	0	0	6	1	1	.382	.400	.382	112	0	1	5	0			.920	-0	/3O	0.0

■ MINNIE MINOSO Minoso, Saturnino Orestes Armas (Arrieta) b: 11/29/22, Havana, Cuba BR/TR, 5'10", 175 lbs. Deb: 4/19/49 C

YEAR	TM/L	G	AB	R	H	2B	3B	HR	RBI	BB	SO	AVG	OBP	SLG	PRO+	BR	/A	RC	SB	CS	SBR	FA	FR	POS	TPR
1949	Cle-A	9	16	2	3	0	0	1	1	2	2	.188	.350	.375	94	-0	-0	1	0	1	-1	1.000	-1	/O	-0.2
1951	Cle-A	8	14	3	6	2	0	0	2	1	1	.429	.529	.571	209	2	2	5	0	0	0	.952	-0	/1	0.2
	Chi-A	138	516	109	167	32	14	10	74	71	41	.324	.419	.498	150	36	38	115	31	10	3	.961	-12	O3/S	2.5
	Yr	146	530	112	173	34	**14**	10	76	72	42	.326	.422	.500	152	38	40	120	**31**	10	3	.961	-12	O3/1S	2.7
1952	Chi-A★	147	569	96	160	24	9	13	61	71	46	.281	.375	.424	121	18	17	92	**22**	16	-3	.979	4	*O/3S	1.2
1953	Chi-A★	151	556	104	174	24	8	15	104	74	43	.313	.410	.466	132	31	28	106	**25**	16	-2	.967	6	*O3	2.6
1954	Chi-A★	153	568	119	182	29	**18**	19	116	77	46	.320	.416	.535	154	47	45	125	18	11	-1	.978	13	*O/3	5.1
1955	Chi-A	139	517	79	149	26	7	10	70	76	43	.288	.390	.424	115	16	14	87	19	8	1	.971	12	*O/3	2.0
1956	Chi-A	151	545	106	172	29	**11**	21	88	86	40	.316	.430	.525	149	43	42	130	12	6	0	.974	3	*O/31	3.7
1957	Chi-A★	153	568	96	176	**36**	5	12	103	79	54	.310	.413	.454	136	33	32	106	18	15	-4	.984	6	*O/3	2.6
1958	Cle-A	149	556	94	168	25	2	24	80	59	53	.302	.384	.484	141	29	31	101	14	14	-4	.975	13	*O/3	3.3
1959	Cle-A★	148	570	92	172	32	0	21	92	54	46	.302	.379	.468	136	25	28	100	8	10	-4	.985	16	*O	3.3
1960	Chi-A★	154	591	89	**184**	32	4	20	105	52	63	.311	.380	.481	132	26	26	104	17	13	-3	.980	5	*O	2.0
1961	Chi-A	152	540	91	151	28	3	14	82	67	46	.280	.376	.420	114	11	13	89	9	4	0	.956	3	*O	0.7
1962	StL-N	39	97	14	19	5	0	1	10	7	17	.196	.271	.278	44	-7	-8	8	4	0	1	.972	-2	O	-1.1
1963	Was-A	109	315	38	72	12	2	4	30	33	38	.229	.317	.317	79	-8	-8	30	8	6	-1	.955	-5	O/3	-1.9
1964	Chi-A	30	31	4	7	0	0	1	5	5	3	.226	.351	.323	91	-0	-0	4	0	0	0	1.000	0	/O	0.0
1976	Chi-A	3	8	0	1	0	0	0	0	0	2	.125	.125	.125	-27	-1	-1	0	0	0	0	.000	0	/D	-0.1
1980	Chi-A	2	2	0	0	0	0	0	0	0	0	.000	.000	.000	-99	-1	-1	0	0	0	0	.000	0	/H	-0.1
Total	17	1835	6579	1136	1963	336	83	186	1023	814	584	.298	.391	.459	130	299	298	1204	205	130	-16	.974	60	*O3/1DS	25.8

■ WILLIE MIRANDA Miranda, Guillermo (Perez) b: 5/24/26, Velasco, Cuba BB/TR, 5'9.5", 150 lbs. Deb: 5/06/51

YEAR	TM/L	G	AB	R	H	2B	3B	HR	RBI	BB	SO	AVG	OBP	SLG	PRO+	BR	/A	RC	SB	CS	SBR	FA	FR	POS	TPR
1951	Was-A	7	9	2	4	0	0	0	0	0	0	.444	.444	.444	143	0	1	2	0	0	0	.818	-0	/S1	0.0
1952	Chi-A	12	8	1	2	1	0	0	0	3	0	.250	.455	.375	131	1	1	2	0	0	0	1.000	4	/S32	0.5
	StL-A	7	11	2	1	0	1	0	1	3	1	.091	.286	.273	54	-1	-1	1	0	0	0	.900	-1	/S	-0.1
	Chi-A	58	142	13	31	3	1	0	7	10	14	.218	.275	.254	47	-10	-10	11	1	0	0	.975	10	S/23	0.3
	Yr	77	161	16	34	4	2	0	8	16	15	.211	.287	.261	52	-10	-10	14	1	0	0	.970	14	S/32	0.7
1953	StL-A	17	6	2	1	0	0	0	0	1	1	.167	.286	.167	24	-1	-1	0	1	1	-0	.933	3	/S3	0.3
	NY-A	48	58	12	13	0	0	1	5	5	10	.224	.286	.276	54	-4	-4	4	1	1	-0	.984	17	S	1.4
	Yr	65	64	14	14	0	0	1	5	6	11	.219	.286	.266	51	-4	-4	4	2	2	-1	.979	20	S/3	1.7
1954	NY-A	92	116	12	29	4	2	1	12	10	10	.250	.310	.345	82	-4	-3	12	0	3	-2	.948	16	S/23	1.5
1955	Bal-A	153	487	42	124	12	6	1	38	42	58	.255	.315	.310	74	-21	-17	48	4	3	-1	.958	19	*S/2	1.4
1956	Bal-A	148	461	38	100	16	4	2	34	46	73	.217	.288	.282	55	-33	-28	38	3	6	-3	.962	2	*S	-1.8
1957	Bal-A	115	314	29	61	3	0	0	20	24	42	.194	.251	.204	28	-32	-29	17	2	1	0	.966	-3	*S	-2.4
1958	Bal-A	102	214	15	43	6	0	1	8	14	25	.201	.250	.243	38	-19	-17	13	1	1	-0	.962	-2	*S	-1.3
1959	Bal-A	65	88	8	14	5	0	0	7	7	16	.159	.221	.216	21	-10	-9	4	0	0	0	.974	22	S3/2	1.4
Total	9	824	1914	176	423	50	14	6	132	165	250	.221	.284	.271	54	-131	-118	152	13	16	-6	.962	88	S/321	1.2

■ JOHN MISSE Misse, John Beverly b: 5/30/1885, Highland, Kan. d: 3/18/70, St.Joseph, Mo. BR/TR, 5'8", 150 lbs. Deb: 5/26/14

YEAR	TM/L	G	AB	R	H	2B	3B	HR	RBI	BB	SO	AVG	OBP	SLG	PRO+	BR	/A	RC	SB	CS	SBR	FA	FR	POS	TPR
1914	StL-F	99	306	28	60	8	1	0	22	36	52	.196	.281	.229	43	-21	-23	24	3			.948	14	2S/3	-0.6

■ CLARENCE MITCHELL Mitchell, Clarence Elmer b: 2/22/1891, Franklin, Neb. d: 11/6/63, Grand Island, Neb. BL/TL, 5'11.5", 190 lbs. Deb: 6/02/11 C

YEAR	TM/L	G	AB	R	H	2B	3B	HR	RBI	BB	SO	AVG	OBP	SLG	PRO+	BR	/A	RC	SB	CS	SBR	FA	FR	POS	TPR
1911	Det-A	5	4	2	2	0	0	0	0	1		.500	.600	.500	198	1	1	1	0			1.000	-1	/P	0.0
1916	Cin-N	56	117	11	28	2	1	0	11	4	6	.239	.264	.274	67	-5	-5	9	1			.985	-2	P/1O	-0.5
1917	Cin-N	47	90	13	25	3	0	0	5	5	5	.278	.316	.311	97	-1	-0	9	0			.982	-0	P/1O	-0.1
1918	Bro-N	10	24	2	6	1	1	0	2	0	3	.250	.250	.375	90	-0	-0	2	0			.750	-2	/O1P	-0.4
1919	Bro-N	34	49	7	18	1	0	1	2	4	4	.367	.415	.449	156	4	3	9	0			.976	1	P	0.0
1920	*Bro-N	55	107	9	25	2	2	0	11	8	9	.234	.287	.290	64	-5	-5	9	1	0	0	1.000	1	P1/O	-0.4
1921	Bro-N	46	91	11	24	5	0	0	12	5	7	.264	.316	.319	66	-4	-4	10	3	1	0	.945	3	P/1	0.0
1922	Bro-N	56	155	21	45	6	3	3	28	19	6	.290	.371	.426	106	1	2	25	0	0	0	.992	3	1/P	0.2
1923	Phi-N	53	78	10	21	3	2	1	9	4	11	.269	.305	.397	75	-2	-3	9	0	0	0	.880	-3	P	0.0
1924	Phi-N	69	102	7	26	3	0	0	13	2	7	.255	.276	.284	45	-7	-9	8	1	0	0	1.000	3	P	0.0
1925	Phi-N	52	92	7	18	2	0	0	13	5	9	.196	.237	.217	16	-11	-13	5	2	0	1	1.000	4	P/1	0.0
1926	Phi-N	39	78	8	19	4	0	0	6	5	5	.244	.289	.295	55	-5	-5	7	0			.986	4	P/1	0.0
1927	Phi-N	18	42	5	10	2	0	1	6	2	1	.238	.273	.357	67	-2	-2	4	0			.963	1	P	0.0
1928	Phi-N	5	4	0	1	0	0	0	0	0	0	.250	.250	.250	30	-0	-0	0	0			1.000	0	/P	0.0
	*StL-N	19	56	0	7	1	0	0	1	0	3	.125	.125	.143	-30	-11	-11	1	0			.982	2	P	0.0
	Yr	24	60	0	8	1	0	0	1	0	3	.133	.133	.150	-26	-11	-11	1	0			.983	3	P	0.0
1929	StL-N	26	66	9	18	3	1	0	9	4	6	.273	.314	.348	63	-4	-4	7	1			.974	-1	P	0.0

YEAR	TM/L	G	AB	R	H	2B	3B	HR	RBI	BB	SO	AVG	OBP	SLG	PRO+	BR	/A	RC	SB	CS	SBR	FA	FR	POS	TPR
1930	StL-N	1	2	0	1	0	0	0	0	0	0	.500	.500	.500	138	0	0	0	0			.000	-0	/P	0.0
	NY-N	24	47	9	12	1	0	0	1	1	5	.255	.271	.277	33	-5	-5	3	0			1.000	2	P	0.0
	Yr	25	49	9	13	1	0	0	1	1	5	.265	.280	.286	38	-5	-5	4	0			1.000	2	P	0.0
1931	NY-N	27	73	5	16	2	0	1	4	2	4	.219	.240	.288	42	-6	-6	5	0			.885	-2	P	0.0
1932	NY-N	8	10	2	2	0	0	0	0	1	1	.200	.273	.200	30	-1	-1	1	0			.833	-1	/P	0.0
Total	18	650	1287	138	324	41	10	7	133	72	92	.252	.293	.315	64	-63	-67	125	9	1		.972	14	P/1O	-1.2

■ FRED MITCHELL Mitchell, Frederick Francis (b: Frederick Francis Yapp)
b: 6/5/1878, Cambridge, Mass. d: 10/13/70, Newton, Mass. BR/TR, 5'9.5", 185 lbs. Deb: 4/27/01 M

YEAR	TM/L	G	AB	R	H	2B	3B	HR	RBI	BB	SO	AVG	OBP	SLG	PRO+	BR	/A	RC	SB	CS	SBR	FA	FR	POS	TPR
1901	Bos-A	20	44	5	7	0	2	0	4	2		.159	.196	.250	23	-5	-5	2	0			.875	-0	P/2S	-0.1
1902	Bos-A	1	1	0	0	0	0	0	0	0		.000	.000	.000	-97	-0	-0	0	0			.667	0	/P	0.0
	Phi-A	19	48	7	9	1	1	0	3	1		.188	.204	.250	24	-5	-5	3	1			.942	2	P/O	-0.1
	Yr	20	49	7	9	1	1	0	3	1		.184	.200	.245	22	-5	-5	3	1			.927	2	P/O	-0.1
1903	Phi-N	29	95	11	19	4	0	0	10	0		.200	.200	.242	27	-9	-9	5	0			.857	-3	P	0.0
1904	Phi-N	25	82	9	17	3	1	0	3	5		.207	.253	.268	64	-4	-3	6	1			.981	3	P/13O	-0.2
	Bro-N	8	24	3	7	1	1	0	6	1		.292	.346	.417	139	1	1	4	0			.906	1	/P	0.0
	Yr	33	106	12	24	4	2	0	9	6		.226	.274	.302	81	-3	-2	10	1			.952	4	P/13O	-0.2
1905	Bro-N	27	79	4	15	0	0	0	8	4		.190	.238	.190	30	-7	-6	4	0			.881	-2	P/13SO	-0.6
1910	NY-A	68	196	16	45	7	2	0	18	9		.230	.274	.286	71	-6	-7	16	6			.968	-14	C	-1.8
1913	Bos-N	4	3	0	1	0	0	0	0	0	2	.333	.333	.333	89	-0	-0	0	0			.000	0	H	0.0
Total	7	201	572	55	120	16	7	0	52	22	2	.210	.245	.262	52	-35	-35	41	8			.904	-13	/PC13OS2	-2.8

■ JOHNNY MITCHELL Mitchell, John Franklin b: 8/9/1894, Detroit, Mich. d: 11/4/65, Birmingham, Mich. BB/TR, 5'8", 155 lbs. Deb: 5/21/21

YEAR	TM/L	G	AB	R	H	2B	3B	HR	RBI	BB	SO	AVG	OBP	SLG	PRO+	BR	/A	RC	SB	CS	SBR	FA	FR	POS	TPR
1921	NY-A	13	42	4	11	1	0	0	2	4	4	.262	.326	.286	56	-3	-3	4	1	0	0	.958	-6	/S2	-0.8
1922	NY-A	4	4	1	0	0	0	0	0	0	1	.000	.000	.000	-98	-1	-1	0	0	0	0	1.000	-1	/S	-0.2
	Bos-A	59	203	20	51	4	1	1	8	16	17	.251	.318	.296	61	-11	-11	20	1	2	-1	.962	-4	S	-1.0
	Yr	63	207	21	51	4	1	1	8	16	18	.246	.313	.290	58	-12	-12	20	1	2	-1	.963	-5	S	-1.2
1923	Bos-A	92	347	40	78	15	4	0	19	34	18	.225	.296	.291	55	-23	-23	29	7	11	-5	.961	-0	S/2	-1.9
1924	Bro-N	64	243	42	64	10	0	1	16	37	22	.263	.361	.317	86	-4	-3	31	3	1	0	.951	-1	S	0.4
1925	Bro-N	97	336	45	84	8	3	0	18	28	19	.250	.308	.292	55	-23	-21	32	2	0	1	.947	-4	S	-1.5
Total	5	329	1175	152	288	38	8	2	63	119	81	.245	.317	.296	62	-65	-63	117	14	14	-4	.955	-16	S/2	-5.0

■ KEITH MITCHELL Mitchell, Keith Alexander b: 8/6/69, San Diego, Cal. BR/TR, 5'10", 180 lbs. Deb: 7/23/91

YEAR	TM/L	G	AB	R	H	2B	3B	HR	RBI	BB	SO	AVG	OBP	SLG	PRO+	BR	/A	RC	SB	CS	SBR	FA	FR	POS	TPR
1991	*Atl-N	48	66	11	21	0	0	2	5	8	12	.318	.392	.409	118	2	2	11	3	1	0	.970	-7	O	-0.5

■ KEVIN MITCHELL Mitchell, Kevin Darnell b: 1/13/62, San Diego, Cal. BR/TR, 5'11", 210 lbs. Deb: 9/04/84

YEAR	TM/L	G	AB	R	H	2B	3B	HR	RBI	BB	SO	AVG	OBP	SLG	PRO+	BR	/A	RC	SB	CS	SBR	FA	FR	POS	TPR
1984	NY-N	7	14	0	3	0	0	0	1	0	3	.214	.214	.214	21	-1	-1	0	0	1	-1	.833	-1	/3	-0.3
1986	*NY-N	108	328	51	91	22	2	12	43	33	61	.277	.345	.466	125	9	10	52	3	3	-1	.983	-11	OS/31	-0.1
1987	SD-N	62	196	19	48	7	1	7	26	20	38	.245	.315	.398	91	-4	-3	24	0	0	0	.945	4	3/O	0.0
	*SF-N	69	268	49	82	13	1	15	44	28	50	.306	.376	.530	144	14	16	52	9	6	-1	.962	-5	3/OS	0.8
	Yr	131	464	68	130	20	2	22	70	48	88	.280	.350	.474	121	10	13	76	9	6	-1	.954	-2	*3/OS	0.8
1988	SF-N	148	505	60	127	25	7	19	80	48	85	.251	.323	.442	123	10	13	71	5	5	-2	.943	-5	*3O	0.5
1989	*SF-N★	154	543	100	158	34	6	**47**	**125**	87	115	.291	.392	**.635**	**194**	**62**	**64**	136	3	4	-2	.978	7	*O/3	**6.8**
1990	SF-N★	140	524	90	152	24	2	35	93	58	87	.290	.363	.544	151	31	34	101	4	7	-3	.971	7	*O	3.5
1991	SF-N	113	371	52	95	13	1	27	69	43	57	.256	.341	.515	142	17	19	65	2	3	-1	.970	3	*O/1	1.9
1992	Sea-A	99	360	48	103	24	0	9	67	35	46	.286	.354	.428	117	9	8	55	0	2	-1	1.000	-0	OD	0.5
Total	8	900	3109	469	859	162	20	171	548	352	542	.276	.354	.506	141	148	159	557	26	31	-11	.974	-2	O3/DS1	13.6

■ DALE MITCHELL Mitchell, Loren Dale b: 8/23/21, Colony, Okla. d: 1/5/87, Tulsa, Okla. BL/TL, 6'1", 195 lbs. Deb: 9/15/46

YEAR	TM/L	G	AB	R	H	2B	3B	HR	RBI	BB	SO	AVG	OBP	SLG	PRO+	BR	/A	RC	SB	CS	SBR	FA	FR	POS	TPR
1946	Cle-A	11	44	7	19	3	0	0	5	1	2	.432	.444	.500	175	4	4	10	1	0	0	1.000	-0	O	0.4
1947	Cle-A	123	493	69	156	16	10	1	34	23	14	.316	.347	.396	109	3	4	69	2	5	-2	.977	-9	*O	-1.4
1948	*Cle-A	141	608	82	204	30	8	4	56	45	17	.336	.383	.431	119	13	15	98	13	18	-7	**.991**	4	*O	0.4
1949	Cle-A★	149	640	81	**203**	16	**23**	3	56	43	11	.317	.360	.428	110	5	7	102	10	3	1	**.994**	3	*O	0.3
1950	Cle-A	130	506	81	156	27	5	3	49	67	21	.308	.390	.399	106	4	6	83	3	7	-3	.972	-11	*O	-1.3
1951	Cle-A	134	510	83	148	21	7	11	62	53	16	.290	.358	.424	117	7	11	79	7	7	-2	.992	-6	*O	-0.1
1952	Cle-A★	134	511	61	165	26	3	5	58	52	9	.323	.387	.415	132	17	21	82	6	6	-2	.992	-5	*O	0.9
1953	Cle-A	134	500	76	150	26	4	13	60	42	20	.300	.354	.446	118	9	11	80	3	1	0	.970	-6	*O	0.1
1954	*Cle-A	53	60	6	17	1	0	1	6	9	1	.283	.377	.350	98	0	0	8	0	0	0	.889	-1	/O1	-0.1
1955	Cle-A	61	58	4	15	2	1	0	10	4	3	.259	.306	.328	68	-2	-3	5	0	0	0	1.000	-1	/1O	-0.4
1956	Cle-A	38	30	2	4	0	0	0	6	7	2	.133	.297	.133	17	-3	-3	2	0	0	0	.000	-0	/O	-0.4
	*Bro-N	19	24	3	7	1	0	0	1	0	3	.292	.292	.333	63	-1	-1	2	0	0	0	1.000	-0	/O	-0.2
Total	11	1127	3984	555	1244	169	61	41	403	346	119	.312	.368	.416	114	54	71	622	45	47	-15	.985	-32	O/1	-1.8

■ MIKE MITCHELL Mitchell, Michael Francis b: 12/12/1879, Springfield, Ohio d: 7/16/61, Phoenix, Ariz. BR/TR, 6'1", 185 lbs. Deb: 4/11/07

YEAR	TM/L	G	AB	R	H	2B	3B	HR	RBI	BB	SO	AVG	OBP	SLG	PRO+	BR	/A	RC	SB	CS	SBR	FA	FR	POS	TPR
1907	Cin-N	148	558	64	163	17	12	3	47	37		.292	.338	.382	121	15	12	82	17			.962	22	*O/1	3.2
1908	Cin-N	119	406	41	90	9	6	1	37	46		.222	.304	.281	90	-5	-4	40	18			.959	1	*O/1	-0.9
1909	Cin-N	145	523	83	162	17	**17**	4	86	57		.310	.378	.430	152	30	31	98	37			.962	6	*O/1	3.4
1910	Cin-N	156	583	79	167	16	**18**	5	88	59	56	.286	.356	.401	126	14	18	96	35			.958	-3	*O/1	0.8
1911	Cin-N	142	529	74	154	22	22	2	84	44	34	.291	.348	.427	121	10	12	90	35			.971	11	*O	1.6
1912	Cin-N	147	552	60	156	14	13	4	78	41	43	.283	.333	.377	97	-6	-3	76	23			.947	-0	*O	-1.1
1913	Chi-N	82	279	37	73	11	6	4	35	32	33	.262	.340	.387	107	3	3	41	15			.941	4	O	0.3
	Pit-N	54	199	25	54	8	2	1	16	14	15	.271	.319	.347	94	-3	-2	23	8			.946	7	O	0.3
	Yr	136	478	62	127	19	8	5	51	46	48	.266	.331	.370	102	-0	1	63	23			.943	11	*O	0.6
1914	Pit-N	76	273	31	64	11	5	2	23	16	16	.234	.279	.333	86	-7	-6	26	5			.984	9	O	0.0
	Was-A	55	193	20	55	5	3	1	20	22	19	.285	.361	.358	112	4	3	27	9	7	-2	.957	4	O	0.4
Total	8	1124	4095	514	1138	130	104	27	514	368	216	.278	.340	.380	114	56	65	598	202	7		.959	61	*O/1	8.0

■ BOBBY MITCHELL Mitchell, Robert McKasha b: 2/6/1856, Cincinnati, Ohio d: 5/1/33, Springfield, Ohio BL/TL, 5'5", 135 lbs. Deb: 9/06/1877

YEAR	TM/L	G	AB	R	H	2B	3B	HR	RBI	BB	SO	AVG	OBP	SLG	PRO+	BR	/A	RC	SB	CS	SBR	FA	FR	POS	TPR
1877	Cin-N	13	49	5	10	3	0	0	5	1	2	.204	.220	.265	59	-3	-2	3				.920	-1	P/O	-0.1
1878	Cin-N	13	49	4	12	0	0	0	8	1	4	.245	.260	.245	74	-2	-1	3				.944	0	/PSO	0.0
1879	Cle-N	30	109	11	16	2	2	0	6	0	14	.147	.147	.202	14	-10	-10	3				.714	-6	P/O	-0.5
1882	StL-a	1	4	0	0	0	0	0		0		.000	.000	.000	-96	-1	-1	0				.000	-1	/OP	-0.1
Total	4	57	211	20	38	5	2	0	19	2	20	.180	.188	.223	35	-15	-13	9				.811	-7	/POS	-0.7

■ BOBBY MITCHELL Mitchell, Robert Van b: 4/7/55, Salt Lake City, Utah BL/TL, 5'10", 170 lbs. Deb: 9/01/80

YEAR	TM/L	G	AB	R	H	2B	3B	HR	RBI	BB	SO	AVG	OBP	SLG	PRO+	BR	/A	RC	SB	CS	SBR	FA	FR	POS	TPR
1980	LA-N	9	3	1	1	0	0	0	0	1	0	.333	.500	.333	139	0	0	1	0	0	0	1.000	1	/O	0.1
1981	LA-N	10	8	0	1	0	0	0	0	1	4	.125	.222	.125	1	-1	-1	0	0	0	0	1.000	1	/O	-0.1
1982	Min-A	124	454	48	113	11	6	2	28	54	53	.249	.331	.313	76	-12	-14	48	8	9	-3	.997	14	*O	-0.7
1983	Min-A	59	152	26	35	4	2	1	15	28	21	.230	.354	.303	80	-2	-3	18	1	1	-0	.990	-3	O	-0.8
Total	4	202	617	75	150	15	8	3	43	84	78	.243	.337	.308	76	-15	-18	67	9	10	-3	.996	12	O	-1.5

■ BOBBY MITCHELL Mitchell, Robert Vance b: 10/22/43, Norristown, Pa. BR/TR, 6'4", 190 lbs. Deb: 7/05/70

YEAR	TM/L	G	AB	R	H	2B	3B	HR	RBI	BB	SO	AVG	OBP	SLG	PRO+	BR	/A	RC	SB	CS	SBR	FA	FR	POS	TPR
1970	NY-A	10	22	1	5	2	0	0	4	2	3	.227	.320	.318	81	-1	-1	2	0	2	-1	1.000	1	/O	-0.1
1971	Mil-A	35	55	7	10	1	1	2	6	6	18	.182	.262	.345	72	-2	-2	5	0	2	-1	.974	1	O	-0.4
1973	Mil-A	47	130	12	29	6	0	5	20	5	32	.223	.252	.385	79	-5	-4	13	4	1	1	.960	-4	OD	-0.8

YEAR	TM/L	G	AB	R	H	2B	3B	HR	RBI	BB	SO	AVG	OBP	SLG	PRO+	BR	/A	RC	SB	CS	SBR	FA	FR	POS	TPR
1974	Mil-A	88	173	27	42	6	2	5	20	18	46	.243	.318	.387	103	0	0	20	7	6	-2	.969	-5	DO	-0.7
1975	Mil-A	93	229	39	57	14	3	9	41	25	69	.249	.323	.454	117	5	4	32	3	4	-2	.992	-4	OD	-0.3
Total	5	273	609	86	143	29	6	21	91	56	168	.235	.301	.406	100	-3	-2	72	14	15	-5	.984	-11	O/D	-2.3

■ **RALPH MITTERLING** Mitterling, Ralph "Sarge" b: 4/19/1890, Freeburg, Pa. d: 1/22/56, Pittsburgh, Pa. BR/TR, 5'10", 165 lbs. Deb: 7/07/16

YEAR	TM/L	G	AB	R	H	2B	3B	HR	RBI	BB	SO	AVG	OBP	SLG	PRO+	BR	/A	RC	SB	CS	SBR	FA	FR	POS	TPR
1916	Phi-A	13	39	1	6	0	0	0	2	3	6	.154	.214	.154	11	-4	-4	1	0			.944	-2	O	-0.8

■ **GEORGE MITTERWALD** Mitterwald, George Eugene b: 6/7/45, Berkeley, Cal. BR/TR, 6'2", 206 lbs. Deb: 9/15/66 C

YEAR	TM/L	G	AB	R	H	2B	3B	HR	RBI	BB	SO	AVG	OBP	SLG	PRO+	BR	/A	RC	SB	CS	SBR	FA	FR	POS	TPR
1966	Min-A	3	5	1	1	0	0	0	0	0	0	.200	.200	.200	14	-1	-1	0	0	0	0	1.000	1	/C	0.0
1968	Min-A	11	34	1	7	1	0	0	1	3	8	.206	.270	.235	52	-2	-2	2	0	0	0	.961	0	C	-0.1
1969	*Min-A	69	187	18	48	8	0	5	13	17	47	.257	.329	.380	96	-1	-1	23	0	1	-1	.987	11	C/O	1.2
1970	*Min-A	117	369	36	82	12	2	15	46	34	84	.222	.291	.388	84	-8	-9	39	3	5	-2	.996	24	*C	1.9
1971	Min-A	125	388	38	97	13	1	13	44	39	104	.250	.319	.389	97	-1	-2	47	3	3	-1	.986	-10	*C	-0.9
1972	Min-A	64	163	12	30	4	1	1	8	9	37	.184	.227	.239	37	-12	-13	8	0	1	-1	.984	6	C	-0.6
1973	Min-A	125	432	50	112	15	0	16	64	39	111	.259	.328	.405	101	3	0	57	3	1	0	.992	-1	*C/D	0.5
1974	Chi-N	78	215	17	54	7	0	7	28	18	42	.251	.315	.381	90	-2	-3	25	1	3	-2	.974	-4	C	-0.6
1975	Chi-N	84	200	19	44	4	3	5	26	19	42	.220	.288	.345	72	-7	-8	20	0	0	0	.976	-1	C1	-0.8
1976	Chi-N	101	303	19	65	7	0	5	28	16	63	.215	.254	.287	49	-19	-22	20	1	2	-1	.981	0	C1	-2.4
1977	Chi-N	110	349	40	83	22	0	9	43	28	69	.238	.296	.378	72	-11	-16	34	3	1	0	.989	12	*C/1	0.0
Total	11	887	2645	251	623	93	7	76	301	222	607	.236	.298	.362	80	-61	-77	275	14	17	-6	.987	40	C/1DO	-1.8

■ **JOHNNY MIZE** Mize, John Robert "The Big Cat" b: 1/7/13, Demorest, Ga. BL/TR, 6'2", 215 lbs. Deb: 4/16/36 CH

YEAR	TM/L	G	AB	R	H	2B	3B	HR	RBI	BB	SO	AVG	OBP	SLG	PRO+	BR	/A	RC	SB	CS	SBR	FA	FR	POS	TPR
1936	StL-N	126	414	76	136	30	8	19	93	50	32	.329	.402	.577	162	35	35	102	1			.994	1	1/O	2.5
1937	StL-N★	145	560	103	204	40	7	25	113	56	57	.364	.427	.595	171	57	56	150	2			.988	-13	*1	2.6
1938	StL-N	149	531	85	179	34	**16**	27	102	74	47	.337	.422	**.614**	172	59	55	141	0			.989	-2	*1	3.7
1939	StL-N★	153	564	104	197	44	14	**28**	108	92	49	**.349**	.444	**.626**	**174**	**69**	**64**	**162**	0			.987	-4	*1	**4.3**
1940	StL-N★	155	579	111	182	31	13	**43**	**137**	82	49	.314	.404	**.636**	**173**	**64**	**60**	**152**	7			.990	-7	*1	3.8
1941	StL-N★	126	473	67	150	**39**	8	16	100	70	45	.317	.406	.535	153	40	36	106	4			.994	3	*1	3.0
1942	NY-N★	142	541	97	165	25	7	26	**110**	60	39	.305	.380	**.521**	161	41	40	110	3			**.995**	-3	*1	3.1
1946	NY-N★	101	377	70	127	18	3	22	70	62	26	.337	.437	.576	185	44	43	100	3			.989	5	*1	4.4
1947	NY-N★	154	586	**137**	177	26	2	**51**	**138**	74	42	.302	.384	.614	160	48	48	143	2			**.996**	9	*1	4.9
1948	NY-N★	152	560	110	162	26	4	**40**	125	94	37	.289	.395	.564	156	45	44	131	4			.991	4	*1	4.6
1949	NY-N★	106	388	59	102	15	0	18	62	50	19	.263	.351	.441	111	6	6	63	1			.994	2	*1	0.7
	*NY-A	13	23	4	6	1	0	1	2	4	2	.261	.393	.435	119	1	1	5	0	0	0	.980	-0	/1	0.0
1950	*NY-A	90	274	43	76	12	0	25	72	29	24	.277	.351	.595	143	13	14	59	0	1	-1	.996	-3	1	0.8
1951	*NY-A	113	332	37	86	14	1	10	49	36	24	.259	.339	.398	102	-1	1	47	1	0	0	.994	-4	1	-0.7
1952	*NY-A	78	137	9	36	9	0	4	29	11	15	.263	.327	.416	112	1	2	18	0	0	0	.987	1	1	0.1
1953	*NY-A★	81	104	6	26	3	0	4	27	12	17	.250	.339	.394	101	-0	0	15	0	0	0	1.000	-0	1	-0.1
Total	15	1884	6443	1118	2011	367	83	359	1337	856	524	.312	.397	.562	157	520	505	1502	28	1		.992	-14	*1/O	37.7

■ **JOHN MIZEROCK** Mizerock, John Joseph b: 12/8/60, Punxsutawney, Pa. BL/TR, 5'11", 190 lbs. Deb: 4/12/83

YEAR	TM/L	G	AB	R	H	2B	3B	HR	RBI	BB	SO	AVG	OBP	SLG	PRO+	BR	/A	RC	SB	CS	SBR	FA	FR	POS	TPR
1983	Hou-N	33	85	8	13	4	1	1	10	12	15	.153	.265	.259	49	-6	-6	6	0	0	0	.967	1	C	-0.4
1985	Hou-N	15	38	6	9	4	0	0	6	2	8	.237	.293	.342	79	-1	-1	3	0	0	0	.966	3	C	0.3
1986	Hou-N	44	81	9	15	1	1	1	6	24	16	.185	.377	.259	81	-1	-1	9	0	0	0	.987	4	C	0.5
1989	Atl-N	11	27	1	6	0	0	0	2	0	3	.222	.222	.222	27	-3	-3	1	0	0	0	1.000	1	C	-0.2
Total	4	103	231	24	43	9	2	2	24	38	42	.186	.309	.268	64	-11	-10	19	0	0	0	.979	8	C	0.2

■ **BILL MIZEUR** Mizeur, William Francis "Bad Bill" b: 6/22/1897, Nokomis, Ill. d: 8/27/76, Decatur, Ill. BL/TR, 6', 180 lbs. Deb: 9/30/23

YEAR	TM/L	G	AB	R	H	2B	3B	HR	RBI	BB	SO	AVG	OBP	SLG	PRO+	BR	/A	RC	SB	CS	SBR	FA	FR	POS	TPR
1923	StL-A	1	1	0	0	0	0	0	0	0	0	.000	.000	.000	-95	-0	-0	0	0	0	0	.000	0	H	0.0
1924	StL-A	1	1	0	0	0	0	0	0	0	0	.000	.000	.000	-94	-0	-0	0	0	0	0	.000	0	H	0.0
Total	2	2	2	0	0	0	0	0	0	0	0	.000	.000	.000	-94	-1	-1	0	0	0	0		0		0.0

■ **DAVE MOATES** Moates, David Allan b: 1/30/48, Great Lakes, Ill. BL/TL, 5'9", 163 lbs. Deb: 9/21/74

YEAR	TM/L	G	AB	R	H	2B	3B	HR	RBI	BB	SO	AVG	OBP	SLG	PRO+	BR	/A	RC	SB	CS	SBR	FA	FR	POS	TPR
1974	Tex-A	1	0	0	0	0	0	0	0	0	0	—	—	—	—	0	0	0	0	0	0	.000	0	R	0.0
1975	Tex-A	54	175	21	48	9	0	3	14	13	15	.274	.324	.377	99	-1	-1	20	9	2	2	.984	1	O/D	0.0
1976	Tex-A	85	137	21	33	7	1	0	13	11	18	.241	.297	.307	75	-4	-4	13	6	3	0	.991	-10	O/D	-1.7
Total	3	140	312	42	81	16	1	3	27	24	33	.260	.313	.346	88	-5	-5	33	15	5	2	.987	-9	O/D	-1.7

■ **DANNY MOELLER** Moeller, Daniel Edward b: 3/23/1885, DeWitt, Iowa d: 4/14/51, Florence, Ala. BB/TR, 5'11", 165 lbs. Deb: 9/24/07

YEAR	TM/L	G	AB	R	H	2B	3B	HR	RBI	BB	SO	AVG	OBP	SLG	PRO+	BR	/A	RC	SB	CS	SBR	FA	FR	POS	TPR
1907	Pit-N	11	42	4	12	1	1	0	3	4		.286	.348	.357	119	1	1	6	2			.800	-2	O	-0.2
1908	Pit-N	36	109	14	21	3	1	0	9	9		.193	.254	.239	58	-5	-5	7	4			.950	-5	O	-1.3
1912	Was-A	132	519	90	143	26	10	6	46	52		.276	.346	.399	112	8	7	81	30			.944	11	*O	1.1
1913	Was-A	153	589	88	139	15	10	5	42	72	103	.236	.322	.321	86	-8	-10	75	62			.926	6	*O	-1.1
1914	Was-A	151	571	83	143	19	10	1	45	71	89	.250	.341	.324	96	1	-1	65	26	25	-7	.930	-1	*O	-1.8
1915	Was-A	118	438	65	99	11	10	2	23	59	63	.226	.319	.311	87	-6	-7	51	32	10	4	.952	-3	*O	-1.2
1916	Was-A	78	240	30	59	8	1	1	23	30	35	.246	.335	.300	92	-2	-2	29	13			.963	2	O	-0.4
	Cle-A	25	30	5	2	0	0	0	1	5	6	.067	.200	.067	-19	-4	-4	1	2			1.000	-2	/O2	-0.8
	Yr	103	270	35	61	8	1	1	24	35	41	.226	.319	.274	78	-6	-6	29	15			.966	-1	O/2	-1.2
Total	7	704	2538	379	618	83	43	15	192	302	296	.243	.328	.328	93	-15	-21	314	171	35		.938	6	O/2	-5.7

■ **JOE MOFFETT** Moffett, Joseph W. b: 6/1859, Wheeling, W.Va. 6', Deb: 5/06/1884 F

YEAR	TM/L	G	AB	R	H	2B	3B	HR	RBI	BB	SO	AVG	OBP	SLG	PRO+	BR	/A	RC	SB	CS	SBR	FA	FR	POS	TPR
1884	Tol-a	56	204	17	41	5	3	0		2		.201	.209	.255	51	-10	-11	11				.957	-5	13/2O	-1.9

■ **SAM MOFFETT** Moffett, Samuel R. b: 3/14/1857, Wheeling, W.Va. d: 5/5/07, Butte, Mont. TR , 6', 175 lbs. Deb: 5/15/1884 F

YEAR	TM/L	G	AB	R	H	2B	3B	HR	RBI	BB	SO	AVG	OBP	SLG	PRO+	BR	/A	RC	SB	CS	SBR	FA	FR	POS	TPR
1884	Cle-N	67	256	26	47	12	2	0	15	8	56	.184	.208	.246	41	-17	-18	13				.827	6	OP/132	-0.8
1887	Ind-N	11	41	6	5	1	0	0	1	1	6	.122	.143	.146	-19	-6	-6	1	2			.857	-3	/PO	-0.4
1888	Ind-N	10	35	6	4	0	0	0	0	5	4	.114	.225	.114	12	-3	-3	1	0			.750	-3	/PO	-0.2
Total	3	88	332	38	56	13	2	0	16	14	66	.169	.202	.220	30	-26	-27	16	2			.821	1	/OP123	-1.4

■ **JOHN MOHARDT** Mohardt, John Henry b: 1/21/1898, Pittsburgh, Pa. d: 11/24/61, LaJolla, Cal. BR/TR, 5'10", 165 lbs. Deb: 4/15/22

YEAR	TM/L	G	AB	R	H	2B	3B	HR	RBI	BB	SO	AVG	OBP	SLG	PRO+	BR	/A	RC	SB	CS	SBR	FA	FR	POS	TPR
1922	Det-A	5	1	2	1	0	0	0	0	1	0	1.000	1.000	1.000	436	1	1	1	0	1	-1	1.000	-1	/O	-0.1

■ **KID MOHLER** Mohler, Ernest Follette b: 12/13/1874, Oneida, Ill. d: 11/4/61, San Francisco, Cal. BL/TL, 5'4.5", 145 lbs. Deb: 9/29/1894

YEAR	TM/L	G	AB	R	H	2B	3B	HR	RBI	BB	SO	AVG	OBP	SLG	PRO+	BR	/A	RC	SB	CS	SBR	FA	FR	POS	TPR
1894	Was-N	3	9	0	1	0	0	0	0	2	4	.111	.273	.111	-3	-1	-1	0	0			.952	2	/2	0.0

■ **JOHNNY MOKAN** Mokan, John Leo b: 9/23/1895, Buffalo, N.Y. d: 2/10/85, Buffalo, N.Y. BR/TR, 5'7", 165 lbs. Deb: 4/15/21

YEAR	TM/L	G	AB	R	H	2B	3B	HR	RBI	BB	SO	AVG	OBP	SLG	PRO+	BR	/A	RC	SB	CS	SBR	FA	FR	POS	TPR
1921	Pit-N	19	52	7	14	3	2	0	9	5	3	.269	.333	.404	92	-0	-1	7	0	0	0	.946	0	O	-0.1
1922	Pit-N	31	89	9	23	3	1	0	8	9	3	.258	.327	.315	65	-4	-4	9	0	1	-1	.903	-4	O	-1.0
	Phi-N	47	151	20	38	7	1	3	27	16	25	.252	.327	.371	73	-5	-7	19	1	0	0	.905	-6	O/3	-1.4
	Yr	78	240	29	61	10	2	3	35	25	28	.254	.327	.350	70	-9	-11	29	1	1	-0	.905	-10	O/3	-2.4
1923	Phi-N	113	400	76	125	23	3	10	48	53	31	.313	.401	.460	113	17	10	73	6	11	-5	.969	7	*O/3	0.6
1924	Phi-N	96	366	50	95	15	1	7	44	30	27	.260	.321	.363	74	-9	-15	43	7	5	-1	.986	-0	O	-2.2
1925	Phi-N	75	209	30	69	11	2	6	42	27	9	.330	.417	.488	120	10	8	43	3	5	-2	.984	-12	O	-1.0
1926	Phi-N	127	456	68	138	23	5	6	62	41	31	.303	.365	.414	104	6	3	69	4			.967	-8	*O	-1.3
1927	Phi-N	74	213	22	61	13	2	0	33	25	21	.286	.361	.366	94	-1	-1	29	5			.962	-9	O	-1.4
Total	7	582	1936	282	563	98	17	32	273	206	150	.291	.364	.409	97	15	-7	292	26	22		.966	-32	O/3	-7.8

YEAR	TM/L	G	AB	R	H	2B	3B	HR	RBI	BB	SO	AVG	OBP	SLG	PRO+	BR	/A	RC	SB	CS	SBR	FA	FR	POS	TPR
■ **FENTON MOLE** Mole, Fenton Le Roy "Muscles" b: 6/14/25, San Leandro, Cal. BL/TL, 6'1.5", 200 lbs. Deb: 9/01/49																									
1949	NY-A	10	27	2	5	2	1	0	2	3	5	.185	.267	.333	58	-2	-2	2	0	0	0	1.000	1	/1	-0.1
■ **BOB MOLINARO** Molinaro, Robert Joseph b: 5/21/50, Newark, N.J. BL/TR, 6', 190 lbs. Deb: 9/18/75																									
1975	Det-A	6	19	2	5	0	1	0	1	1	0	.263	.300	.368	84	-0	-0	2	0	0	0	1.000	-0	/O	-0.1
1977	Det-A	4	4	0	1	1	0	0	0	0	2	.250	.250	.500	94	-0	-0	1	0	0	0	.000	0	H	0.0
	Chi-A	1	2	0	1	0	0	0	0	0	1	.500	.500	.500	174	0	0	1	1	0	0	1.000	-0	/O	0.0
	Yr	5	6	0	2	1	0	0	0	0	3	.333	.333	.500	119	0	0	1	1	0	0	1.000	-0	/O	0.0
1978	Chi-A	105	286	39	75	5	5	6	27	19	12	.262	.315	.378	93	-3	-3	35	22	6	3	1.000	-7	OD	-0.9
1979	Bal-A	8	6	0	0	0	0	0	0	1	3	.000	.143	.000	-60	-1	-1	0	1	0	0	1.000	-1	/O	-0.2
1980	Chi-A	119	344	48	100	16	4	5	36	26	29	.291	.353	.404	107	4	4	50	18	7	1	.957	-2	OD	0.1
1981	Chi-A	47	42	7	11	1	1	1	9	8	1	.262	.392	.405	133	2	2	7	1	0	0	1.000	-0	/OD	0.2
1982	Chi-N	65	66	6	13	1	0	1	12	6	5	.197	.264	.258	45	-5	-5	5	1	1	-0	1.000	-1	/O	-0.7
	Phi-N	19	14	0	4	0	0	0	2	3	1	.286	.412	.286	96	0	0	2	1	0	0	.000	0	H	0.0
	Yr	84	80	6	17	1	0	1	14	9	6	.213	.292	.262	55	-5	-5	7	2	1	0	1.000	-1	/O	-0.7
1983	Phi-N	19	18	1	2	1	0	1	3	0	2	.111	.111	.333	19	-2	-2	1	0	0	0	.000	0	H	-0.2
	Det-A	8	2	3	0	0	0	0	0	1	1	.000	.333	.000	1	-0	-0	0	1	1	-0	.000	0	/D	-0.1
Total	8	401	803	106	212	25	11	14	90	65	57	.264	.328	.375	95	-5	-6	104	46	15	5	.980	-12	O/D	-1.9
■ **PAUL MOLITOR** Molitor, Paul Leo b: 8/22/56, St.Paul, Minn. BR/TR, 6', 185 lbs. Deb: 4/07/78																									
1978	Mil-A	125	521	73	142	26	4	6	45	19	54	.273	.303	.372	89	-9	-9	59	30	12	2	.976	-5	2S/3D	-0.1
1979	Mil-A	140	584	88	188	27	16	9	62	48	48	.322	.375	.469	126	21	21	103	33	13	2	.979	1	*2S/D	3.3
1980	Mil-A†	111	450	81	137	29	2	9	37	48	48	.304	.375	.438	126	14	16	78	34	7	6	.971	-2	2S/3D	2.8
1981	*Mil-A	64	251	45	67	11	0	2	19	25	29	.267	.341	.335	100	-1	1	30	10	6	-1	.976	2	OD	0.0
1982	*Mil-A	160	666	**136**	201	26	8	19	71	69	93	.302	.368	.450	132	22	27	117	41	9	7	.942	-1	*3/SD	3.0
1983	Mil-A	152	608	95	164	28	6	15	47	59	74	.270	.336	.410	113	3	10	88	41	8	8	.966	2	*3/D	1.7
1984	Mil-A	13	46	3	10	1	0	0	6	2	8	.217	.250	.239	38	-4	-4	3	1	0	0	.933	4	/3D	0.0
1985	Mil-A★	140	576	93	171	28	3	10	48	54	80	.297	.358	.408	110	8	8	85	21	7	2	.953	-2	*3/D	0.6
1986	Mil-A	105	437	62	123	24	6	9	55	40	81	.281	.342	.426	104	4	2	65	20	5	3	.944	2	3D/O	0.6
1987	Mil-A	118	465	**114**	164	**41**	5	16	75	69	67	.353	.438	.566	159	45	43	125	45	10	8	.947	-10	D32	3.8
1988	Mil-A★	154	609	115	190	34	6	13	60	71	54	.312	.386	.452	132	29	28	112	41	10	6	.941	-8	*3D/2	2.5
1989	Mil-A	155	615	84	194	35	4	11	56	64	67	.315	.384	.439	133	27	27	106	27	11	2	.950	4	*3D2	3.4
1990	Mil-A	103	418	64	119	27	6	12	45	37	51	.285	.344	.464	125	12	13	68	18	3	4	.988	-1	21/3D	1.4
1991	Mil-A★	158	665	**133**	**216**	32	**13**	17	75	77	62	.325	.400	.489	148	41	44	132	19	8	1	.986	-1	*D1	4.0
1992	Mil-A★	158	609	89	195	36	7	12	89	73	66	.320	.396	.461	142	33	35	116	31	6	6	.996	-4	*D1	3.4
Total	15	1856	7520	1275	2281	405	86	160	790	755	882	.303	.369	.444	126	247	264	1287	412	115	55	.950	-20	3D21/SO	30.4
■ **FRED MOLLENKAMP** Mollenkamp, Frederick Henry b: 3/15/1890, Cincinnati, Ohio d: 11/1/48, Cincinnati, Ohio Deb: 8/29/14																									
1914	Phi-N	3	8	0	1	0	0	0	0	2	0	.125	.300	.125	26	-1	-1	0	0			1.000	2	/1	0.1
■ **FRITZ MOLLWITZ** Mollwitz, Frederick August b: 6/16/1890, Coburg, Germany d: 10/3/67, Bradenton, Fla. BR/TR, 6'2", 170 lbs. Deb: 9/26/13																									
1913	Chi-N	2	7	1	3	0	0	0	0	0	0	.429	.429	.429	145	0	0	1	0			1.000	-0	/1	0.0
1914	Chi-N	13	20	0	3	0	0	0	1	0	3	.150	.150	.150	-11	-3	-3	1	1			.962	-1	/1O	-0.4
	Cin-N	32	111	12	18	2	0	0	5	3	9	.162	.198	.180	12	-12	-12	4	2			.991	1	1	-1.3
	Yr	45	131	12	21	2	0	0	6	3	12	.160	.191	.176	9	-15	-15	5	3			.989	0	1/O	-1.7
1915	Cin-N	153	525	36	136	21	3	1	51	15	49	.259	.281	.316	79	-14	-15	50	19	11	-1	**.996**	0	*1	-2.2
1916	Cin-N	65	183	12	41	4	4	0	16	5	12	.224	.245	.290	65	-8	-8	15	6			.981	-1	1	-1.1
	Chi-N	33	71	1	19	2	0	0	11	7	6	.268	.333	.296	85	-0	-1	8	4			.976	-1	1/O	-0.3
	Yr	98	254	13	60	6	4	0	27	12	18	.236	.271	.291	71	-9	-9	24	10			.980	-2	1/O	-1.4
1917	Pit-N	36	140	15	36	4	1	0	12	8	8	.257	.297	.300	81	-3	-3	14	4			.994	-1	1/2	-0.7
1918	Pit-N	119	432	43	116	12	7	0	45	23	24	.269	.305	.329	90	-4	-6	50	23			.990	-0	*1	-1.2
1919	Pit-N	56	168	11	29	2	4	0	12	15	18	.173	.249	.232	43	-11	-12	11	9			.994	-3	1/O	-1.9
	StL-N	25	83	7	19	3	0	0	5	7	3	.229	.289	.265	71	-3	-3	7	2			.994	1	1	-0.3
	Yr	81	251	18	48	5	4	0	17	22	21	.191	.262	.243	52	-14	-14	18	11			.994	-3	1/O	-2.2
Total	7	534	1740	138	420	50	19	1	158	83	132	.241	.278	.294	72	-57	-61	162	70	11		.991	-6	1/O2	-9.4
■ **BLAS MONACO** Monaco, Blas b: 11/16/15, San Antonio, Tex. BB/TR, 5'11", 170 lbs. Deb: 8/18/37																									
1937	Cle-A	5	7	0	2	0	1	0	2	0	2	.286	.375	.571	134	0	0	2	0	0	0	1.000	0	/2	0.1
1946	Cle-A	12	6	2	0	0	0	0	0	1	1	.000	.143	.000	-62	-1	-1	0	0	0	0	.000	0	H	-0.1
Total	2	17	13	2	2	0	1	0	2	1	3	.154	.267	.308	53	-1	-1	2	0	0	0	1.000	0	/2	0.0
■ **FREDDIE MONCEWICZ** Moncewicz, Frederick Alfred b: 9/1/03, Brockton, Mass. d: 4/23/69, Brockton, Mass. BR/TR, 5'8.5", 175 lbs. Deb: 6/19/28																									
1928	Bos-A	3	1	0	0	0	0	0	0	0	1	.000	.000	.000	-99	-0	-0	0	0	0	0	1.000	0	/S	0.0
■ **ALEX MONCHAK** Monchak, Alex b: 12/22/19, Bayonne, N.J. BR/TR, 6', 180 lbs. Deb: 6/22/40 C																									
1940	Phi-N	19	14	1	2	0	0	0	0	0	6	.143	.143	.143	-22	-2	-2	0	1			.833	0	/S2	-0.2
■ **RICK MONDAY** Monday, Robert James b: 11/20/45, Batesville, Ark. BL/TL, 6'3", 200 lbs. Deb: 9/03/66																									
1966	KC-A	17	41	4	4	1	1	0	2	6	16	.098	.213	.171	12	-5	-5	2	1	1	-0	.964	-1	O	-0.7
1967	KC-A	124	406	52	102	14	6	14	58	42	107	.251	.324	.419	122	9	10	55	3	6	-3	.972	15	*O	1.9
1968	Oak-A★	148	482	56	132	24	7	8	49	72	143	.274	.373	.402	142	22	25	78	14	6	1	.978	-0	*O	2.0
1969	Oak-A	122	399	57	108	17	4	12	54	72	100	.271	.389	.424	133	17	19	71	12	3	2	.964	-2	*O	1.4
1970	Oak-A	112	376	63	109	19	7	10	37	58	99	.290	.388	.457	137	18	20	68	17	11	-2	.981	1	*O	1.4
1971	*Oak-A	116	355	53	87	9	3	18	56	49	93	.245	.337	.439	121	8	9	52	6	9	-4	.984	-0	*O	0.1
1972	Chi-N	138	434	68	108	22	5	11	42	78	102	.249	.365	.399	105	12	6	67	12	9	-2	**.996**	-12	*O	-1.5
1973	Chi-N	149	554	93	148	24	5	26	56	92	124	.267	.372	.469	123	25	20	100	5	12	-6	.973	-4	*O	0.3
1974	Chi-N	142	538	84	158	19	7	20	58	70	94	.294	.377	.467	130	25	23	97	7	9	-3	.984	-7	*O	0.7
1975	Chi-N	136	491	89	131	29	4	17	60	83	95	.267	.374	.446	121	19	16	86	8	3	1	.973	-3	*O	0.9
1976	Chi-N	137	534	107	145	20	5	32	77	60	125	.272	.347	.507	129	26	21	92	5	9	-4	.993	2	*O1	1.3
1977	*LA-N	118	392	47	90	13	1	15	48	60	109	.230	.332	.383	91	-4	-4	52	1	4	-2	.991	-17	*O/1	-2.9
1978	*LA-N★	119	342	54	87	14	1	19	57	49	100	.254	.349	.468	127	12	12	56	2	4	-2	.995	-1	*O/1	0.6
1979	LA-N	12	33	2	10	0	0	0	2	5	6	.303	.395	.303	94	0	0	4	0	0	0	.964	1	O	0.1
1980	LA-N	96	194	35	52	7	1	10	25	28	49	.268	.363	.469	133	8	9	35	2	2	-1	.969	-2	O	0.5
1981	*LA-N	66	130	24	41	1	2	11	25	24	42	.315	.426	.608	198	16	16	35	1	2	-1	.962	-5	O	1.0
1982	LA-N	104	210	37	54	6	4	11	42	39	51	.257	.376	.481	142	11	12	40	2	1	0	.943	-6	O/1	0.5
1983	*LA-N	99	178	21	44	7	1	6	20	29	42	.247	.353	.399	108	2	3	26	0	0	0	.969	0	O/1	-0.3
1984	LA-N	31	47	4	9	2	0	1	7	8	16	.191	.309	.298	72	-2	-2	5	0	0	0	.987	-1	1/O	-0.4
Total	19	1986	6136	950	1619	248	64	241	775	924	1513	.264	.362	.443	124	220	210	1020	98	91	-25	.979	-46	*O/1	6.9
■ **DON MONEY** Money, Donald Wayne "Brooks" b: 6/7/47, Washington, D.C. BR/TR, 6'1", 190 lbs. Deb: 4/10/68																									
1968	Phi-N	4	13	1	3	2	0	0	2	2	4	.231	.333	.385	115	0	0	1	0	1	-1	1.000	-1	/S	-0.1
1969	Phi-N	127	450	41	103	22	2	6	42	43	83	.229	.298	.327	77	-15	-14	41	1	3	-2	.969	17	*S	1.7
1970	Phi-N	120	447	66	132	25	4	14	66	43	68	.295	.366	.463	124	13	15	75	4	7	-3	.961	11	*3/S	2.1
1971	Phi-N	121	439	40	98	22	8	7	38	31	80	.223	.279	.358	79	-13	-13	44	4	1	1	.953	3	3O2	-1.1
1972	Phi-N	152	536	54	119	16	2	15	52	41	92	.222	.280	.343	74	-18	-19	50	5	7	-3	**.978**	20	*3/S	-0.3

YEAR	TM/L	G	AB	R	H	2B	3B	HR	RBI	BB	SO	AVG	OBP	SLG	PRO+	BR	/A	RC	SB	CS	SBR	FA	FR	POS	TPR
1973	Mil-A	145	556	75	158	28	2	11	61	53	53	.284	.350	.401	113	8	10	80	22	5	4	**.971**	-23	*3S	-0.8
1974	Mil-A☆	159	629	85	178	32	3	15	65	62	80	.283	.349	.415	120	15	16	93	19	6	2	**.989**	-10	*3/2D	0.8
1975	Mil-A	109	405	58	112	16	1	15	43	31	51	.277	.333	.432	114	7	7	58	7	9	-3	.951	-21	3/S	-1.8
1976	Mil-A★	117	439	51	117	18	4	12	62	47	50	.267	.337	.408	120	9	10	59	6	5	-1	.958	-4	*3D/S	0.5
1977	Mil-A†	152	570	86	159	28	3	25	83	57	70	.279	.352	.470	122	17	17	92	8	5	-1	.981	-3	*2O3/D	2.0
1978	Mil-A★	137	518	88	152	30	2	14	54	48	70	.293	.361	.440	124	17	17	84	3	0	1	.994	-2	123D/S	1.5
1979	Mil-A	92	350	52	83	20	1	6	38	40	47	.237	.319	.351	81	-9	-9	40	1	0	0	1.000	-2	D312	-1.1
1980	Mil-A	86	289	39	74	17	1	17	46	40	36	.256	.348	.498	133	11	12	52	0	0	0	.940	0	31D/2	1.1
1981	*Mil-A	60	185	17	40	7	0	2	14	19	27	.216	.293	.286	71	-7	-6	17	0	0	0	.977	-5	3/1D	-1.2
1982	*Mil-A	96	275	40	78	14	3	16	55	32	38	.284	.360	.531	150	15	17	53	0	2	-1	.923	5	D31/2	2.0
1983	Mil-A	43	114	5	17	5	0	1	8	11	17	.149	.224	.219	24	-12	-11	6	0	0	0	.980	4	D3/1	-0.7
Total	16	1720	6215	798	1623	302	36	176	729	600	866	.261	.330	.406	106	38	48	847	80	51	-7	.968	-9	*32DS1/O	4.6
■ **FRANK MONROE**	Monroe, Frank W. b: Hamilton, Ohio Deb: 7/18/1884																								
1884	Ind-a	2	8	1	0	0	0	0		0		.000	.000	.000	-99	-2	-2	0				1.000	-1	/OC	-0.3
■ **JOHN MONROE**	Monroe, John Allen b: 8/24/1898, Farmersville, Tex. d: 6/19/56, Conroe, Tex. BL/TR, 5'10", 160 lbs. Deb: 4/16/21																								
1921	NY-N	19	21	4	3	0	0	1	3	3	6	.143	.280	.286	50	-2	-2	2	0	0	0	.846	2	/2S	0.0
	Phi-N	41	133	13	38	4	2	1	8	11	9	.286	.345	.368	82	-2	-3	17	2	2	-1	.938	5	2/3	0.3
	Yr	60	154	17	41	4	2	2	11	14	15	.266	.335	.357	79	-3	-5	19	2	2	-1	.920	7	2/3S	0.3
■ **ED MONTAGUE**	Montague, Edward Francis b: 7/24/05, San Francisco, Cal. d: 6/17/88, Daly City, Cal. BR/TR, 5'10", 165 lbs. Deb: 5/14/28																								
1928	Cle-A	32	51	12	12	0	1	0	3	6	7	.235	.339	.275	62	-2	-3	5	0	0	0	.914	5	S/3	0.4
1930	Cle-A	58	179	37	47	5	2	1	16	37	38	.263	.392	.330	82	-2	-3	25	1	5	-3	.917	-15	S3	-1.4
1931	Cle-A	64	193	27	55	8	3	1	26	21	22	.285	.358	.373	87	-2	-3	26	3	4	-2	.924	16	S	1.5
1932	Cle-A	66	192	29	47	5	1	0	24	21	24	.245	.326	.281	55	-11	-13	19	3	3	-1	.891	-13	S3	-2.1
Total	4	220	615	105	161	18	7	2	69	85	91	.262	.357	.324	74	-18	-22	76	7	12	-5	.912	-7	S/3	-1.6
■ **WILLIE MONTANEZ**	Montanez, Guillermo (Naranjo) b: 4/1/48, Catano, P.R. BL/TL, 6'1", 193 lbs. Deb: 4/12/66																								
1966	Cal-A	8	2	2	0	0	0	0	0	0	2	.000	.000	.000	-99	-1	-0	0	1	0	0	1.000	0	/1	0.0
1970	Phi-N	18	25	3	6	0	0	0	3	1	4	.240	.269	.240	39	-2	-2	2	0	0	0	1.000	1	O/1	-0.1
1971	Phi-N	158	599	78	153	27	6	30	99	67	105	.255	.333	.471	126	19	19	89	4	7	-3	.972	-2	*O/1	0.6
1972	Phi-N	147	531	60	131	**39**	3	13	64	58	108	.247	.322	.405	103	3	2	70	1	3	-2	.985	8	*O1	0.2
1973	Phi-N	146	552	69	145	16	5	11	65	46	80	.263	.326	.370	90	-6	-7	65	2	6	-3	.994	-2	1O	-2.4
1974	Phi-N	143	527	55	160	33	1	7	79	32	57	.304	.347	.410	107	7	4	72	3	6	-3	.992	-1	*1/O	-0.9
1975	Phi-N	21	84	9	24	8	0	2	16	4	12	.286	.318	.452	108	1	0	11	1	0	0	.990	2	1	0.1
	SF-N	135	518	52	158	26	2	8	85	45	50	.305	.365	.409	110	10	8	72	5	3	-0	.994	-1	*1	-0.3
	Yr	156	602	61	182	34	2	10	101	49	62	.302	.359	.415	110	11	8	84	6	3	0	.993	0	*1	-0.2
1976	SF-N	60	230	22	71	15	2	2	20	15	15	.309	.354	.417	115	5	4	31	2	1	0	.989	4	1	0.5
	Atl-N	103	420	52	135	14	0	9	64	21	32	.321	.354	.419	112	9	6	56	0	4	-2	.986	-6	*1	-0.9
	Yr	163	650	74	206	29	2	11	84	36	47	.317	.354	.418	113	14	11	87	2	5	-2	.987	-1	*1	-0.4
1977	Atl-N★	136	544	70	156	31	1	20	68	35	60	.287	.330	.458	97	5	-3	77	1	1	-0	.992	-4	*1	-1.6
1978	NY-N	159	609	66	156	32	0	17	96	60	92	.256	.324	.392	103	-1	1	76	9	4	0	.995	3	*1	-0.6
1979	NY-N	109	410	36	96	19	0	5	47	25	48	.234	.280	.317	65	-22	-20	33	0	1	-1	.989	3	*1	-2.5
	Tex-A	38	144	19	46	6	0	8	24	8	14	.319	.359	.528	137	7	7	26	0	1	-1	.995	1	1D	0.6
1980	SD-N	128	481	39	132	12	4	6	63	36	52	.274	.329	.353	96	-6	-3	55	3	4	-2	.994	1	*1	-1.1
	Mon-N	14	19	1	4	0	0	0	1	3	3	.211	.318	.211	50	-1	-1	1	0	1	-1	1.000	0	/1	-0.2
	Yr	142	500	40	136	12	4	6	64	39	55	.272	.328	.348	94	-7	-4	57	3	5	-2	.994	1	*1	-1.3
1981	Mon-N	26	62	6	11	0	1	0	5	4	9	.177	.227	.210	24	-6	-6	2	0	0	0	.992	1	1	-0.6
	Pit-N	29	38	2	10	0	0	1	1	1	2	.263	.282	.342	74	-1	-1	3	0	0	0	1.000	-1	1	-0.3
	Yr	55	100	8	21	0	1	1	6	5	11	.210	.248	.260	43	-7	-8	5	0	0	0	.995	0	1	-0.9
1982	Pit-N	36	32	4	9	1	0	0	1	3	3	.281	.343	.313	82	-1	-1	3	0	0	0	1.000	0	/1O	-0.1
	Phi-N	18	16	0	1	0	0	0	1	1	3	.063	.118	.063	-47	-3	-3	0	0	0	0	1.000	1	/1	-0.3
	Yr	54	48	4	10	1	0	0	2	4	6	.208	.269	.229	40	-4	-4	3	0	0	0	1.000	1	/1O	-0.4
Total	14	1632	5843	645	1604	279	25	139	802	465	751	.275	.331	.402	101	16	4	744	32	42	-16	.992	8	*1O/D	-9.9
■ **RENE MONTEAGUDO**	Monteagudo, Rene (Miranda) b: 3/12/16, Havana, Cuba d: 9/14/73, Hialeah, Fla. BL/TL, 5'7", 165 lbs. Deb: 9/06/38 F																								
1938	Was-A	5	6	0	3	0	0	0	1	0	0	.500	.500	.500	162	0	1	1	0	0	0	1.000	-1	/P	0.0
1940	Was-A	27	33	4	6	1	1	0	1	1	4	.182	.206	.273	24	-4	-4	2	0	0	0	.941	-1	P	0.0
1944	Was-A	10	38	2	11	2	0	0	4	0	1	.289	.289	.342	84	-1	-1	4	0	0	0	.929	-1	/O	-0.3
1945	Phi-N	114	193	26	58	6	0	0	15	28	7	.301	.389	.332	104	2	3	26	2			.918	-1	OP	0.0
Total	4	156	270	32	78	9	1	0	21	29	12	.289	.358	.330	94	-3	-1	33	2	0		.889	-4	/PO	-0.3
■ **FELIPE MONTEMAYOR**	Montemayor, Felipe Angel "Monty" b: 2/7/30, Monterrey, Mexico BL/TL, 6'2", 185 lbs. Deb: 4/14/53																								
1953	Pit-N	28	55	5	6	4	0	0	2	4	13	.109	.210	.182	3	-8	-8	2	0	0	0	1.000	1	O	-0.7
1955	Pit-N	36	95	10	20	1	3	2	8	18	24	.211	.342	.347	85	-2	-2	12	1	0	0	.957	-5	O	-0.8
Total	2	64	150	15	26	5	3	2	10	22	37	.173	.295	.287	55	-10	-10	15	1	0	0	.974	-5	/O	-1.5
■ **AL MONTGOMERY**	Montgomery, Alvin Atlas b: 7/3/20, Loving, N.Mex. d: 4/26/42, Waverly, Va. BR/TR, 5'10.5", 185 lbs. Deb: 6/20/41																								
1941	Bos-N	42	52	4	10	1	0	0	4	9	8	.192	.323	.212	55	-3	-3	4	0			.976	-6	C	-0.8
■ **BOB MONTGOMERY**	Montgomery, Robert Edward b: 4/16/44, Nashville, Tenn. BR/TR, 6'1", 203 lbs. Deb: 9/06/70																								
1970	Bos-A	22	78	8	14	2	0	1	4	6	20	.179	.247	.244	33	-7	-8	4	0	0	0	.981	0	C	-0.6
1971	Bos-A	67	205	19	49	11	2	2	24	16	43	.239	.304	.341	77	-5	-7	21	1	0	0	.989	-3	C	-0.7
1972	Bos-A	24	77	7	22	1	0	2	7	3	17	.286	.313	.377	99	0	-0	9	0	0	0	.985	-2	C	-0.2
1973	Bos-A	34	128	18	41	6	2	7	25	7	36	.320	.356	.563	146	8	8	23	0	0	0	.974	1	C	0.9
1974	Bos-A	88	254	26	64	10	0	4	38	13	50	.252	.291	.339	75	-7	-9	24	3	0	1	.977	-6	C/D	-1.2
1975	*Bos-A	62	195	16	44	10	1	2	26	4	37	.226	.245	.318	53	-11	-13	15	1	1	-0	.987	-5	C/1D	-1.7
1976	Bos-A	31	93	10	23	3	1	3	13	5	20	.247	.286	.398	88	-1	-2	10	0	1	-1	.983	-1	C/D	-0.2
1977	Bos-A	17	40	6	12	2	0	2	7	4	9	.300	.378	.500	123	2	1	8	0	0	0	.982	-0	C	0.1
1978	Bos-A	10	29	2	7	1	1	0	5	2	12	.241	.290	.345	70	-1	-1	3	0	0	0	.976	0	C	-0.1
1979	Bos-A	32	86	13	30	4	1	0	7	4	24	.349	.378	.419	109	2	1	13	1	0	0	.984	-4	C	-0.2
Total	10	387	1185	125	306	50	8	23	156	64	268	.258	.300	.372	83	-19	-29	129	6	2	1	.983	-19	C/D1	-3.9
■ **AL MONTREUIL**	Montreuil, Allan Arthur b: 8/23/43, New Orleans, La. BR/TR, 5'5", 158 lbs. Deb: 9/01/72																								
1972	Chi-N	5	11	0	1	0	0	0	0	1	4	.091	.167	.091	-23	-2	-2	0	0	0	0	1.000	0	/2	-0.2
■ **DAN MONZON**	Monzon, Daniel Francisco b: 5/17/46, Bronx, N.Y. BR/TR, 5'10", 182 lbs. Deb: 4/25/72																								
1972	Min-A	55	55	13	15	1	0	0	5	8	12	.273	.365	.291	92	0	-0	7	1	0	0	.977	9	2/3SO	1.1
1973	Min-A	39	76	10	17	1	1	0	4	11	9	.224	.330	.263	66	-3	-3	8	1	0	0	.968	9	23/O	0.7
Total	2	94	131	23	32	2	1	0	9	19	21	.244	.344	.275	77	-3	-3	15	2	0	1	.971	18	/23SO	1.8
■ **JOE MOOCK**	Moock, Joseph Geoffrey b: 3/12/44, Plaquemine, La. BL/TR, 6'1", 180 lbs. Deb: 9/01/67																								
1967	NY-N	13	40	2	9	2	0	0	5	0	7	.225	.225	.275	43	-3	-3	2	0	0	0	.917	2	3	-0.2

■ GEORGE MOOLIC

Moolic, George Henry "Prunes" b: 3/12/1865, Lawrence, Mass. d: 2/19/15, Metheun, Mass. BR/TR, 5'7", 145 lbs. Deb: 5/01/1886

YEAR	TM/L	G	AB	R	H	2B	3B	HR	RBI	BB	SO	AVG	OBP	SLG	PRO+	BR	/A	RC	SB	CS	SBR	FA	FR	POS	TPR
1886	Chi-N	16	56	9	8	3	0	0	2	2	17	.143	.172	.196	10	-6	-7	2	0			.945	3	C/O	-0.2

■ WALLY MOON

Moon, Wallace Wade b: 4/3/30, Bay, Ark. BL/TR, 6', 175 lbs. Deb: 4/13/54 C

YEAR	TM/L	G	AB	R	H	2B	3B	HR	RBI	BB	SO	AVG	OBP	SLG	PRO+	BR	/A	RC	SB	CS	SBR	FA	FR	POS	TPR
1954	StL-N	151	635	106	193	29	9	12	76	71	73	.304	.375	.435	109	10	10	106	18	10	-1	.978	2	*O	0.4
1955	StL-N	152	593	86	175	24	8	19	76	47	65	.295	.350	.459	113	10	10	91	11	11	-3	.975	-9	*O1	-1.0
1956	StL-N	149	540	86	161	22	11	16	68	80	50	.298	.390	.469	129	24	24	99	12	9	-2	.988	0	O1	1.5
1957	StL-N★	142	516	86	152	28	5	24	73	62	57	.295	.371	.508	131	24	23	94	5	6	-2	.966	-9	*O	0.4
1958	StL-N	108	290	36	69	10	3	7	38	47	30	.238	.344	.366	85	-4	-6	37	2	3	-1	.984	-8	O	-2.0
1959	*LA-N★	145	543	93	164	26	**11**	19	74	81	64	.302	.396	.495	126	29	24	111	15	6	1	.983	-4	*O/1	1.4
1960	LA-N	138	469	74	140	21	6	13	69	67	53	.299	.387	.452	121	20	16	77	6	10	-4	.986	4	*O	1.1
1961	LA-N	134	463	79	152	25	3	17	88	89	79	.328	**.438**	.505	137	37	31	107	7	5	-1	.970	-9	*O	1.3
1962	LA-N	95	244	36	59	9	1	4	31	30	33	.242	.327	.336	84	-7	-5	28	5	2	0	.981	-2	O1	-1.0
1963	LA-N	122	343	41	90	13	2	8	48	45	43	.262	.350	.382	119	6	8	45	5	5	-2	.962	-12	O	-1.1
1964	LA-N	68	118	8	26	2	1	2	9	12	22	.220	.292	.305	74	-5	-4	10	1	1	-0	1.000	-2	O	-0.8
1965	*LA-N	53	89	6	18	3	0	1	11	13	22	.202	.304	.270	67	-4	-3	8	2	0	1	1.000	-2	O	-0.6
Total	12	1457	4843	737	1399	212	60	142	661	644	591	.289	.374	.445	117	142	130	810	89	68	-14	.978	-50	*O1	-0.4

■ AL MOORE

Moore, Albert James b: 8/4/02, Brooklyn, N.Y. d: 11/29/74, AtSea N.Y.To P.R BR/TR, 5'10", 174 lbs. Deb: 9/27/25

YEAR	TM/L	G	AB	R	H	2B	3B	HR	RBI	BB	SO	AVG	OBP	SLG	PRO+	BR	/A	RC	SB	CS	SBR	FA	FR	POS	TPR
1925	NY-N	2	8	0	1	0	0	0	0	1	2	.125	.222	.125	-9	-1	-1	0	0	1	-1	1.000	-0	/O	-0.2
1926	NY-N	28	81	12	18	4	0	0	10	5	7	.222	.267	.272	46	-6	-6	6	2			.966	3	O	-0.5
Total	2	30	89	12	19	4	0	0	10	6	9	.213	.263	.258	41	-8	-7	6	2	1		.968	3	/O	-0.7

■ JUNIOR MOORE

Moore, Alvin Earl b: 1/25/53, Waskom, Tex. BR/TR, 5'11", 185 lbs. Deb: 8/02/76

YEAR	TM/L	G	AB	R	H	2B	3B	HR	RBI	BB	SO	AVG	OBP	SLG	PRO+	BR	/A	RC	SB	CS	SBR	FA	FR	POS	TPR
1976	Atl-N	20	26	1	7	1	0	0	2	4	4	.269	.387	.308	93	0	0	4	0	0	0	.929	1	/32O	0.1
1977	Atl-N	112	361	41	94	9	3	5	34	33	29	.260	.324	.343	71	-10	-16	38	4	5	-2	.942	-4	*3/2	-2.3
1978	Chi-A	24	65	8	19	0	1	0	4	6	7	.292	.352	.323	90	-1	-1	7	1	1	-0	.857	-0	D/3O	-0.1
1979	Chi-A	88	201	24	53	6	2	1	23	12	20	.264	.305	.328	71	-8	-8	18	0	2	-1	.966	-9	OD/2	-1.9
1980	Chi-A	45	121	9	31	4	1	1	10	7	11	.256	.297	.331	72	-5	-5	10	0	2	-1	.929	-2	3/O1D	-0.9
Total	5	289	774	83	204	20	7	7	73	62	71	.264	.320	.335	73	-23	-29	77	5	10	-5	.936	-14	3/OD21	-5.1

■ ANSE MOORE

Moore, Anselm Winn b: 9/22/17, Delhi, La. BL/TR, 6'1", 190 lbs. Deb: 4/17/46

YEAR	TM/L	G	AB	R	H	2B	3B	HR	RBI	BB	SO	AVG	OBP	SLG	PRO+	BR	/A	RC	SB	CS	SBR	FA	FR	POS	TPR
1946	Det-A	51	134	16	28	4	0	1	8	12	9	.209	.279	.261	48	-9	-10	11	1	1	-0	.971	1	O	-1.1

■ ARCHIE MOORE

Moore, Archie Francis b: 8/30/41, Upper Darby, Pa. BL/TL, 6'2", 190 lbs. Deb: 4/20/64

YEAR	TM/L	G	AB	R	H	2B	3B	HR	RBI	BB	SO	AVG	OBP	SLG	PRO+	BR	/A	RC	SB	CS	SBR	FA	FR	POS	TPR
1964	NY-A	31	23	4	4	2	0	0	1	2	9	.174	.240	.261	39	-2	-2	2	0	0	0	1.000	-2	/O1	-0.4
1965	NY-A	9	17	1	7	2	0	1	4	4	4	.412	.524	.706	248	4	4	6	0	0	0	.889	-0	/O	0.3
Total	2	40	40	5	11	4	0	1	5	6	13	.275	.370	.450	128	2	2	8	0	0	0	.929	-2	/O1	-0.1

■ CHARLEY MOORE

Moore, Charles Wesley b: 12/1/1884, Jackson Co., Ind. d: 7/29/70, Portland, Ore. BR/TR, 5'10", 160 lbs. Deb: 4/16/12

YEAR	TM/L	G	AB	R	H	2B	3B	HR	RBI	BB	SO	AVG	OBP	SLG	PRO+	BR	/A	RC	SB	CS	SBR	FA	FR	POS	TPR
1912	Chi-N	5	9	2	2	0	1	0	2	0	1	.222	.222	.444	80	-0	-0	1	0			.800	1	/S23	0.0

■ CHARLIE MOORE

Moore, Charles William b: 6/21/53, Birmingham, Ala. BR/TR, 5'11", 180 lbs. Deb: 9/08/73

YEAR	TM/L	G	AB	R	H	2B	3B	HR	RBI	BB	SO	AVG	OBP	SLG	PRO+	BR	/A	RC	SB	CS	SBR	FA	FR	POS	TPR
1973	Mil-A	8	27	0	5	0	1	0	3	2	4	.185	.241	.259	42	-2	-2	2	0	0	0	.981	3	/C	0.1
1974	Mil-A	72	204	17	50	10	4	0	19	21	34	.245	.316	.333	87	-3	-3	21	3	4	-2	.985	3	C/D	0.0
1975	Mil-A	73	241	26	70	20	1	1	29	17	31	.290	.337	.394	106	2	1	30	1	5	-3	.960	-6	CO/D	-0.6
1976	Mil-A	87	241	33	46	7	4	3	16	43	45	.191	.316	.290	80	-5	-5	24	1	2	-1	.969	-3	CO/3D	-0.9
1977	Mil-A	138	375	42	93	15	6	5	45	31	39	.248	.307	.360	81	-10	-10	38	1	7	-4	.980	-7	*C	-1.7
1978	Mil-A	96	268	30	72	7	1	5	31	12	24	.269	.300	.358	84	-6	-6	28	4	2	0	.983	-2	C	-0.6
1979	Mil-A	111	337	45	101	16	2	5	38	29	32	.300	.357	.404	105	3	3	46	8	5	-1	.979	9	*C	1.4
1980	Mil-A	111	320	42	93	13	2	2	30	24	28	.291	.340	.363	96	-3	-2	39	10	5	0	.989	-15	*C	-1.3
1981	*Mil-A	48	156	16	47	8	3	1	9	12	13	.301	.351	.410	125	4	5	21	1	4	-2	.970	-0	C/OD	0.3
1982	*Mil-A	133	456	53	116	22	4	6	45	29	49	.254	.300	.360	86	-13	-9	45	2	10	-5	.988	5	*OC/2	-1.1
1983	Mil-A	151	529	65	150	27	6	2	49	55	42	.284	.355	.369	108	1	7	71	11	4	1	.978	0	*O/CD	0.3
1984	Mil-A	70	188	13	44	7	1	2	17	10	26	.234	.276	.314	66	-10	-9	14	0	4	-2	.984	-3	O/C	-1.5
1985	Mil-A	105	349	35	81	13	4	0	31	27	53	.232	.289	.292	60	-19	-19	29	4	0	1	.977	5	*C/O	-0.8
1986	Mil-A	80	235	24	61	12	3	3	39	21	38	.260	.320	.374	86	-4	-5	27	5	5	-2	.992	13	C/O2D	1.0
1987	Tor-A	51	107	15	23	10	1	1	7	13	12	.215	.306	.355	73	-4	-4	12	0	0	0	.984	6	C/O	0.4
Total	15	1334	4033	456	1052	187	43	36	408	346	470	.261	.321	.355	89	-70	-58	447	51	57	-19	.980	9	CO/D23	-5.0

■ DEE MOORE

Moore, D C b: 4/6/14, Hedley, Tex. BR/TR, 5'11", 190 lbs. Deb: 9/12/36

YEAR	TM/L	G	AB	R	H	2B	3B	HR	RBI	BB	SO	AVG	OBP	SLG	PRO+	BR	/A	RC	SB	CS	SBR	FA	FR	POS	TPR
1936	Cin-N	6	10	4	4	2	1	0	1	0	3	.400	.400	.800	230	1	2	3	0			1.000	-0	/PC	0.0
1937	Cin-N	7	13	2	1	0	0	0	0	1	2	.077	.200	.077	-23	-2	-2	0	0			.931	2	/C	0.0
1943	Bro-N	37	79	8	20	3	0	0	12	11	8	.253	.344	.291	84	-1	-1	9	1			.982	-6	C/3	-0.7
	Phi-N	37	113	13	27	4	1	1	8	15	8	.239	.328	.319	91	-2	-1	12	0			.960	-0	C/O31	0.0
	Yr	74	192	21	47	7	1	1	20	26	16	.245	.335	.307	88	-3	-2	21	1			.968	-7	C3/O1	-0.7
1946	Phi-N	11	13	2	1	0	0	0	1	7	3	.077	.400	.077	41	-0	-0	1	0			1.000	0	/C1	0.0
Total	4	98	228	29	53	9	2	1	22	34	24	.232	.335	.303	85	-4	-3	25	1			.962	-5	/C3O1P	-0.7

■ GENE MOORE

Moore, Eugene Jr. "Rowdy" b: 8/26/09, Lancaster, Tex. d: 3/12/78, Jackson, Miss. BL/TL, 5'11", 175 lbs. Deb: 9/20/31 F

YEAR	TM/L	G	AB	R	H	2B	3B	HR	RBI	BB	SO	AVG	OBP	SLG	PRO+	BR	/A	RC	SB	CS	SBR	FA	FR	POS	TPR
1931	Cin-N	4	14	2	2	1	0	0	1	0	0	.143	.143	.214	-6	-2	-2	0	0			1.000	0	/O	-0.2
1933	StL-N	11	38	6	15	3	2	0	8	4	10	.395	.452	.579	183	5	4	10	1			.967	0	O	0.4
1934	StL-N	9	18	2	5	1	0	0	1	2	2	.278	.350	.333	79	-0	-0	2	0			.923	1	/O	0.0
1935	StL-N	3	3	0	0	0	0	0	0	0	1	.000	.000	.000	-96	-1	-1	0	0			.000	0	H	-0.1
1936	Bos-N	151	637	91	185	38	12	13	67	40	80	.290	.335	.449	117	6	12	100	6			.977	15	*O	2.0
1937	Bos-N☆	148	561	88	159	29	10	16	70	61	73	.283	.358	.456	132	15	22	96	11			.978	14	*O	3.0
1938	Bos-N	54	180	27	49	8	3	3	19	16	20	.272	.338	.400	114	1	3	25	1			.981	1	O	0.2
1939	Bro-N	107	306	45	69	13	6	3	39	40	50	.225	.315	.337	73	-11	-12	35	4			.961	-6	O/1	-2.1
1940	Bro-N	10	26	3	7	2	0	0	2	1	3	.269	.296	.346	72	-1	-1	3	0			1.000	-1	/O	-0.2
	Bos-N	103	363	46	106	24	1	5	39	25	32	.292	.338	.405	110	2	4	48	2			.986	6	O	0.6
	Yr	113	389	49	113	26	1	5	41	26	35	.290	.335	.401	107	1	3	51	2			.986	5	*O	0.4
1941	Bos-N	129	397	42	108	17	8	5	43	45	37	.272	.349	.393	114	5	7	57	5			.968	4	*O	0.5
1942	Was-A	1	2	0	0	0	0	0	0	0	1	.000	.000	.000	-99	-1	-1	0	0	0	0	.000	-1	/O	-0.1
1943	Was-A	92	254	41	68	14	3	2	39	19	29	.268	.321	.370	106	-0	1	29	0	2	-1	.985	0	O/1	-0.3
1944	*StL-A	110	390	56	93	13	6	6	58	24	37	.238	.284	.349	76	-11	-14	37	0	5	-3	.968	2	O/1	-2.2
1945	StL-A	110	354	48	92	16	2	5	50	40	26	.260	.337	.359	97	1	-1	46	1	3	-2	.970	-3	*O	-1.2
Total	14	1042	3543	497	958	179	53	58	436	317	401	.270	.333	.400	105	7	21	489	31	10		.975	32	O/1	0.3

■ FERDIE MOORE

Moore, Ferdinand Depage b: 2/21/1896, Camden, N.J. d: 5/6/47, Atlantic City, N.J. Deb: 10/02/14

YEAR	TM/L	G	AB	R	H	2B	3B	HR	RBI	BB	SO	AVG	OBP	SLG	PRO+	BR	/A	RC	SB	CS	SBR	FA	FR	POS	TPR
1914	Phi-A	2	4	1	2	0	0	0	1	0	2	.500	.500	.500	209	0	0	1	0			.895	-1	/1	0.0

■ GARY MOORE

Moore, Gary Douglas b: 2/24/45, Tulsa, Okla. BR/TL, 5'10", 175 lbs. Deb: 5/03/70

YEAR	TM/L	G	AB	R	H	2B	3B	HR	RBI	BB	SO	AVG	OBP	SLG	PRO+	BR	/A	RC	SB	CS	SBR	FA	FR	POS	TPR
1970	LA-N	7	16	2	3	0	2	0	0	0	1	.188	.188	.438	65	-1	-1	0	1	0	0	1.000	-1	/O1	-0.1

YEAR	TM/L	G	AB	R	H	2B	3B	HR	RBI	BB	SO	AVG	OBP	SLG	PRO+	BR	/A	RC	SB	CS	SBR	FA	FR	POS	TPR

■ EDDIE MOORE   Moore, Graham Edward   b: 1/18/1899, Barlow, Ky.   d: 2/10/76, Ft.Myers, Fla.   BR/TR, 5'7", 165 lbs.   Deb: 9/25/23

1923	Pit-N	6	26	6	7	1	0	0	1	2	3	.269	.321	.308	65	-1	-1	3	1	0	0	.923	-5	/S	-0.6
1924	Pit-N	72	209	47	75	8	4	2	13	27	12	.359	.437	.464	139	14	13	42	6	7	-2	.988	4	O3/2	1.3
1925	*Pit-N	142	547	106	163	29	8	6	77	73	26	.298	.383	.413	97	-5	-1	92	19	7	2	.952	-6	*2O/3	-0.4
1926	Pit-N	43	132	19	30	8	1	0	19	12	6	.227	.292	.303	57	-7	-8	12	3			.911	-11	2/3S	-1.8
	Bos-N	54	184	17	49	3	2	0	15	16	12	.266	.325	.304	77	-7	-5	19	6			.973	-3	2S/3	-0.6
	Yr	97	316	36	79	11	3	0	34	28	18	.250	.311	.304	68	-15	-14	31	9			.950	-14	2S3	-2.4
1927	Bos-N	112	411	53	124	14	4	1	32	39	17	.302	.364	.363	103	-2	3	54	5			.947	-2	32O/S	0.3
1928	Bos-N	68	215	27	51	9	0	2	18	19	12	.237	.299	.307	62	-13	-11	20	7			.958	6	O/2	-0.9
1929	Bro-N	111	402	48	119	18	6	0	48	44	16	.296	.370	.371	86	-9	-7	56	5			.955	-18	2S/O3	-1.6
1930	Bro-N	76	196	24	55	13	1	1	20	21	7	.281	.356	.372	77	-7	-7	26	1			.991	3	2OS/3	-0.2
1932	NY-N	37	87	9	23	3	0	1	6	9	6	.264	.340	.333	84	-2	-2	10	1			.930	3	S/32	0.3
1934	Cle-A	27	65	4	10	2	0	0	8	10	4	.154	.267	.185	18	-8	-8	4	0	0	0	.932	1	2/3S	-0.6
Total	10	748	2474	360	706	108	26	13	257	272	121	.285	.359	.366	89	-37	-35	338	52	14		.956	-29	2O/OS3	-4.8

■ HARRY MOORE   Moore, Henry S.   Deb: 4/17/1884

| 1884 | Was-U | 111 | 461 | 77 | 155 | 23 | 5 | 1 | | | 19 | .336 | .363 | .414 | 168 | 29 | 31 | 71 | | | | .820 | -9 | *O/S | 1.8 |

■ JACKIE MOORE   Moore, Jackie Spencer   b: 2/19/39, Jay, Fla.   BR/TR, 6', 180 lbs.   Deb: 4/18/65   MC

| 1965 | Det-A | 21 | 53 | 2 | 5 | 0 | 0 | 0 | 2 | 6 | 12 | .094 | .186 | .094 | -17 | -8 | -8 | 1 | 0 | 0 | 0 | .985 | 4 | C | -0.4 |

■ JIMMY MOORE   Moore, James William   b: 4/24/03, Paris, Tenn.   d: 3/7/86, Memphis, Tenn.   BR/TR, 6'0.5", 187 lbs.   Deb: 8/31/30

1930	Chi-A	16	39	4	8	2	0	0	2	6	3	.205	.326	.256	52	-3	-3	4	0	0	0	.900	0	O	-0.3
	*Phi-A	15	50	10	19	3	0	2	12	2	4	.380	.404	.560	136	3	3	11	1	1	-0	.958	-0	O	0.1
	Yr	31	89	14	27	5	0	2	14	8	7	.303	.367	.427	100	0	0	14	1	1	-0	.932	-0	O	-0.2
1931	*Phi-A	49	143	18	32	5	1	2	21	11	13	.224	.284	.315	54	-9	-10	13	0	1	-1	.973	0	O	-1.2
Total	2	80	232	32	59	10	1	4	35	19	20	.254	.316	.358	71	-9	-10	27	1	2	-1	.958	0	/O	-1.4

■ JERRIE MOORE   Moore, Jeremiah S.   b: Detroit, Mich.   d: 9/26/1890, Wayne, Mich.   BL,   Deb: 4/17/1884

1884	Alt-U	20	80	10	25	3	1	1		0		.313	.313	.412	141	3	3	11				.800	-8	C/O	-0.4
	Cle-N	9	30	1	6	0	0	0	10	0	5	.200	.200	.200	25	-2	-3	1				.887	-1	/C	-0.3
1885	Det-N	6	23	2	4	1	0	0	.0	1	3	.174	.208	.217	38	-2	-2	1				.800	-3	/C	-0.4
Total	2	35	133	13	35	4	1	1	10	1	8	.263	.269	.331	95	-1	-1	13				.830	-13	/CO	-1.1

■ JOHNNY MOORE   Moore, John Francis   b: 3/23/02, Waterville, Conn.   d: 4/4/91, Bradenton, Fla.   BL/TR, 5'10.5", 175 lbs.   Deb: 9/15/28

1928	Chi-N	4	4	0	0	0	0	0	0	0	0	.000	.000	.000	-99	-1	-1	0	0			.000	0	H	-0.1
1929	Chi-N	37	63	13	18	1	0	2	8	4	6	.286	.338	.397	81	-2	-2	8	0			.971	-0	O	-0.3
1931	Chi-N	39	104	19	25	3	1	2	16	7	5	.240	.288	.346	69	-5	-5	11	1			.964	1	O	-0.5
1932	*Chi-N	119	443	59	135	24	5	13	64	22	38	.305	.342	.470	117	9	9	71	4			.983	1	*O	0.3
1933	Cin-N	135	514	60	135	19	5	1	44	29	16	.263	.306	.325	81	-13	-12	52	4			.974	5	*O	-1.5
1934	Cin-N	16	42	5	8	1	1	0	5	3	2	.190	.244	.262	36	-4	-4	3	0			1.000	-0	O	-0.4
	Phi-N	116	458	68	157	'34	6	11	93	40	18	.343	.397	.515	125	27	19	97	7			.981	7	*O	2.0
	Yr	132	500	73	165	35	7	11	98	43	20	.330	.384	.494	120	23	16	98	7			.983	6	*O	1.6
1935	Phi-N	153	600	84	194	33	3	19	93	45	50	.323	.375	.483	117	24	16	114	4			.973	-10	*O	0.1
1936	Phi-N	124	472	85	155	24	3	16	68	26	22	.328	.365	.494	117	18	12	83	1			.948	-8	*O	-0.1
1937	Phi-N	96	307	46	98	16	2	9	59	18	18	.319	.357	.472	114	9	6	52	2			.943	-2	O	0.1
1945	Chi-N	7	6	0	1	0	0	0	2	1	1	.167	.286	.167	28	-1	-1	0	0			.000	0	H	-0.1
Total	10	846	3013	439	926	155	26	73	452	195	176	.307	.352	.449	109	62	38	492	23			.970	-7	O	-0.5

■ JO-JO MOORE   Moore, Joseph Gregg "The Gause Ghost"   b: 12/25/08, Gause, Tex.   BL/TR, 5'11", 155 lbs.   Deb: 9/17/30

1930	NY-N	3	5	1	1	0	0	0	0	0	1	.200	.200	.200	-3	-1	-1	0	0			1.000	-0	/O	-0.1
1931	NY-N	4	8	0	2	1	0	0	3	0	1	.250	.250	.375	68	-0	-0	1	1			1.000	-0	/O	-0.1
1932	NY-N	86	361	53	110	15	2	2	27	20	18	.305	.341	.374	94	-4	-3	47	4			.982	-4	O	-1.2
1933	*NY-N	132	524	56	153	16	5	0	42	21	27	.292	.323	.342	91	-7	-6	59	4			.966	3	*O	-1.0
1934	NY-N†	139	580	106	192	37	4	15	61	31	23	.331	.370	.486	130	21	23	109	5			.954	-10	O	0.8
1935	NY-N★	155	681	108	201	28	9	5	71	53	24	.295	.353	.429	111	9	10	110	5			.972	2	*O	0.6
1936	*NY-N★	152	649	110	205	29	9	7	63	37	27	.316	.358	.421	110	8	9	103	2			.981	8	*O	1.0
1937	*NY-N★	142	580	89	180	37	10	6	57	46	37	.310	.364	.440	116	14	13	96	7			.975	-7	*O	0.1
1938	NY-N★	125	506	76	153	23	6	11	56	22	27	.302	.335	.437	110	6	5	77	2			.978	-5	O	-0.3
1939	NY-N	138	562	80	151	23	2	10	47	45	17	.269	.324	.370	85	-11	-12	69	5			.986	3	*O	-1.4
1940	NY-N★	138	543	83	150	33	4	6	46	43	30	.276	.337	.385	98	-1	-1	72	7			.982	-1	*O	-1.0
1941	NY-N	121	428	57	117	16	2	7	40	30	15	.273	.322	.369	93	-4	-5	52	4			.972	-4	*O	-1.6
Total	12	1335	5427	809	1615	258	53	79	513	348	247	.298	.344	.408	105	29	32	795	46			.975	-14	*O	-4.2

■ KELVIN MOORE   Moore, Kelvin Orlando   b: 9/26/57, LeRoy, Ala.   BR/TL, 6'1", 195 lbs.   Deb: 8/28/81

1981	*Oak-A	14	47	5	12	0	1	3	5	15	.255	.327	.362	103	-0	0	6	1	0	0	1.000	-1	1	-0.1
1982	Oak-A	21	67	6	15	1	1	2	6	3	23	.224	.257	.358	70	-3	-3	5	0	1	-1	.971	-2	1	-0.6
1983	Oak-A	41	124	12	26	4	0	5	16	10	39	.210	.274	.363	78	-5	-4	11	2	4	-2	.994	-3	1	-1.0
Total	3	76	238	23	53	5	2	8	25	18	77	.223	.280	.361	81	-8	-6	22	3	5	-2	.989	-5	/1	-1.7

■ MOLLY MOORE   Moore, Maurice   b: 2/24/1881, New York, N.Y.   Deb: 6/30/1875

| 1875 | Atl-n | 22 | 88 | 5 | 20 | 5 | 0 | 0 | | 0 | | .227 | .227 | .284 | 87 | -2 | -0 | 6 | | | | | | S/13 | -0.1 |

■ RANDY MOORE   Moore, Randolph Edward   b: 6/21/06, Naples, Tex.   d: 6/12/92, Mt.Pleasant, Tex.   BL/TR, 6', 185 lbs.   Deb: 4/12/27

1927	Chi-A	6	15	0	0	0	0	0	0	0	2	.000	.000	.000	-99	-4	-4	0	0	0	0	1.000	1	/O	-0.4
1928	Chi-A	24	61	6	13	4	1	0	5	3	5	.213	.250	.311	47	-5	-5	5	0	1	-1	.946	0	O	-0.6
1930	Bos-N	83	191	24	55	9	0	2	34	10	13	.288	.323	.366	69	-10	-9	22	3			.986	-2	O3	-1.1
1931	Bos-N	83	192	19	50	8	1	3	34	13	3	.260	.311	.359	83	-6	-5	22	1			.952	0	O3/2	-0.7
1932	Bos-N	107	351	41	103	21	2	3	43	15	11	.293	.322	.390	94	-5	-3	44	1			.987	-7	O31/C	-1.3
1933	Bos-N	135	497	64	150	23	7	8	70	40	16	.302	.356	.425	133	14	19	74	3			.979	-0	*O1	1.2
1934	Bos-N	123	422	55	120	21	2	7	64	40	16	.284	.346	.393	105	-1	3	59	2			.965	-2	O1	-0.4
1935	Bos-N	125	407	42	112	20	4	4	42	26	16	.275	.319	.373	93	-9	-4	48	1			.950	0	O1	-0.9
1936	Bro-N	42	88	4	21	3	0	0	14	6	1	.239	.302	.273	55	-5	-5	7	0			.964	-4	O	-1.0
1937	Bro-N	13	22	3	3	1	0	0	2	4	2	.136	.240	.182	16	-3	-3	1	0			.889	0	C	-0.2
	StL-N	8	7	0	0	0	0	0	0	0	0	.000	.000	.000	-98	-2	-2	0	0			.000	-0	/O	-0.2
	Yr	21	29	3	3	1	0	0	2	5	2	.103	.188	.138	-10	-4	-5	1	0			.889	-0	C/O	-0.4
Total	10	749	2253	258	627	110	17	27	308	158	85	.278	.326	.378	95	-35	-19	283	11	1		.969	-15	O/13C2	-5.4

■ BOBBY MOORE   Moore, Robert Vincent   b: 10/27/65, Cincinnati, Ohio   BR/TR, 5'9", 165 lbs.   Deb: 9/05/91

| 1991 | KC-A | 18 | 14 | 3 | 5 | 1 | 0 | 0 | 0 | 1 | 2 | .357 | .400 | .429 | 129 | 1 | 1 | 2 | 3 | 2 | -0 | 1.000 | -4 | O | -0.4 |

■ TERRY MOORE   Moore, Terry Bluford   b: 5/27/12, Vernon, Ala.   BR/TR, 5'11", 195 lbs.   Deb: 4/16/35   MC

1935	StL-N	119	456	63	131	34	3	6	53	15	40	.287	.314	.414	90	-5	-7	60	13			.984	14	*O	0.2
1936	StL-N	143	590	85	156	39	4	5	47	37	52	.264	.309	.369	82	-16	-16	70	9			.977	22	*O	0.1
1937	StL-N	115	461	76	123	17	3	5	43	32	41	.267	.317	.349	79	-12	-13	53	13			.988	14	*O	-0.4

YEAR	TM/L	G	AB	R	H	2B	3B	HR	RBI	BB	SO	AVG	OBP	SLG	PRO+	BR	/A	RC	SB	CS	SBR	FA	FR	POS	TPR
1938	StL-N	94	312	49	85	21	3	4	21	46	19	.272	.366	.397	104	5	3	49	9			.987	9	O/3	1.0
1939	StL-N★	130	417	65	123	25	2	17	77	43	38	.295	.362	.487	119	15	11	73	6			**.994**	11	*O/P	1.8
1940	StL-N★	136	537	92	163	33	4	17	64	42	44	.304	.356	.475	121	19	15	92	18			.987	17	*O	2.5
1941	StL-N★	122	493	86	145	26	4	6	68	52	31	.294	.364	.400	108	10	6	74	3			.984	7	*O	0.6
1942	*StL-N★	130	489	80	141	26	3	6	49	56	26	.288	.364	.391	112	13	9	72	10			.986	-3	*O/3	0.0
1946	*StL-N	91	278	32	73	14	1	3	28	18	26	.263	.312	.353	85	-5	-6	32	0			.982	1	O	-0.8
1947	StL-N	127	460	61	130	17	1	7	45	38	39	.283	.339	.370	84	-8	-11	58	1			.983	1	*O	-1.5
1948	StL-N	91	207	30	48	11	0	4	18	27	12	.232	.321	.343	75	-6	-7	24	0			.993	-10	O	-2.0
Total	11	1298	4700	719	1318	263	28	80	513	406	368	.280	.340	.399	98	11	-16	656	82			.985	83	*O/3P	1.5

■ SCRAPPY MOORE
Moore, William Allen b: 12/16/1892, St.Louis, Mo. d: 10/13/64, Little Rock, Ark. BR/TR, 5'8", 153 lbs. Deb: 6/21/17

YEAR	TM/L	G	AB	R	H	2B	3B	HR	RBI	BB	SO	AVG	OBP	SLG	PRO+	BR	/A	RC	SB	CS	SBR	FA	FR	POS	TPR
1917	StL-A	4	8	1	1	0	0	0	0	1	0	.125	.222	.125	6	-1	-1	0	0			.750	0	/3	-0.1

■ BILL MOORE
Moore, William Henry "Willie" b: 12/12/01, Kansas City, Mo. d: 5/24/72, Kansas City, Mo. BL/TR, 5'11", 170 lbs. Deb: 9/07/26

YEAR	TM/L	G	AB	R	H	2B	3B	HR	RBI	BB	SO	AVG	OBP	SLG	PRO+	BR	/A	RC	SB	CS	SBR	FA	FR	POS	TPR
1926	Bos-A	5	18	2	3	0	0	0	0	0	2	.167	.167	.167	-13	-3	-3	0	0	0	0	1.000	0	/C	-0.2
1927	Bos-A	44	69	7	15	2	0	0	4	13	8	.217	.341	.246	56	-4	-4	7	0	0	0	.938	2	C	0.0
Total	2	49	87	9	18	2	0	0	4	13	10	.207	.310	.230	43	-7	-7	7	0	0	0	.939	2	/C	-0.2

■ BILL MOORE
Moore, William Ross b: 10/10/60, Los Angeles, Cal. BR/TL, 6'1", 185 lbs. Deb: 7/19/86

YEAR	TM/L	G	AB	R	H	2B	3B	HR	RBI	BB	SO	AVG	OBP	SLG	PRO+	BR	/A	RC	SB	CS	SBR	FA	FR	POS	TPR
1986	Mon-N	6	12	0	2	0	0	0	0	0	4	.167	.167	.167	-8	-2	-2	0	0	0	0	1.000	-1	/1O	-0.3

■ ANDRES MORA
Mora, Andres (Ibarra) b: 5/25/55, Rio Bravo, Mex. BR/TR, 6', 180 lbs. Deb: 4/13/76

YEAR	TM/L	G	AB	R	H	2B	3B	HR	RBI	BB	SO	AVG	OBP	SLG	PRO+	BR	/A	RC	SB	CS	SBR	FA	FR	POS	TPR
1976	Bal-A	73	220	18	48	11	0	6	25	13	49	.218	.262	.350	83	-7	-5	20	1	0	0	.951	-2	DO	-0.8
1977	Bal-A	77	233	32	57	8	2	13	44	5	53	.245	.264	.464	100	-3	-2	27	0	0	0	1.000	-9	O/3D	-1.3
1978	Bal-A	76	229	21	49	8	0	8	14	13	47	.214	.259	.354	75	-10	-8	20	0	1	-1	.978	1	O/D	-1.0
1980	Cle-A	9	18	0	2	0	0	0	0	0	0	.111	.111	.111	-39	-3	-3	0	0	0	0	1.000	0	/O	-0.4
Total	4	235	700	71	156	27	2	27	83	31	149	.223	.258	.383	83	-23	-18	67	1	1	-0	.978	-10	O/D3	-3.5

■ JOSE MORALES
Morales, Jose Manuel (Hernandez) b: 12/30/44, Frederiksted, V.I. BR/TR, 6', 195 lbs. Deb: 8/13/73 C

YEAR	TM/L	G	AB	R	H	2B	3B	HR	RBI	BB	SO	AVG	OBP	SLG	PRO+	BR	/A	RC	SB	CS	SBR	FA	FR	POS	TPR
1973	Oak-A	6	14	0	4	1	0	0	1	1	5	.286	.333	.357	100	-0	-0	1	0	1	-1	.000	0	/D	-0.1
	Mon-N	5	5	0	2	0	0	0	0	0	0	.400	.400	.400	118	0	0	1	0	0	0	.000	0	H	0.0
1974	Mon-N	25	26	3	7	4	0	1	5	1	7	.269	.296	.538	123	1	1	3	0	0	0	.800	-1	/C	0.0
1975	Mon-N	93	163	18	49	6	1	2	24	14	21	.301	.356	.387	102	1	1	20	0	2	-1	.983	4	1/OC	0.2
1976	Mon-N	104	158	12	50	11	0	4	37	3	20	.316	.337	.462	120	4	4	23	0	0	0	.977	1	1C	0.4
1977	Mon-N	65	74	3	15	4	1	1	9	5	12	.203	.253	.324	55	-5	-5	5	0	0	0	1.000	-2	/C1	-0.6
1978	Min-A	101	242	22	76	13	1	2	38	20	35	.314	.369	.401	114	6	5	34	0	1	-1	.000	0	D/C1O	0.4
1979	Min-A	92	191	21	51	5	1	2	27	14	27	.267	.324	.335	75	-6	-7	19	0	0	0	1.000	-0	D/1	-0.7
1980	Min-A	97	241	36	73	17	2	8	36	22	19	.303	.364	.490	123	10	8	40	0	0	0	1.000	-1	D/C1	0.7
1981	Bal-A	38	86	6	21	3	0	2	14	3	13	.244	.270	.349	77	-3	-3	6	0	0	0	1.000	-0	D/1	-0.3
1982	Bal-A	3	3	0	0	0	0	0	0	0	2	.000	.000	.000	-99	-1	-1	0	0	0	0	.000	0	/H	-0.1
	LA-N	35	30	1	9	1	0	1	8	4	8	.300	.382	.433	131	1	1	5	0	0	0	.000	0	H	0.1
1983	*LA-N	47	53	4	15	3	0	3	8	1	11	.283	.296	.509	120	1	1	7	0	0	0	.951	-0	/1	0.1
1984	LA-N	22	19	0	3	0	0	0	0	1	2	.158	.200	.158	2	-2	-2	1	0	0	0	.000	0	H	-0.3
Total	12	733	1305	126	375	68	6	26	207	89	182	.287	.336	.408	102	8	3	164	0	4	-2	.981	2	D/1CO	-0.2

■ JERRY MORALES
Morales, Julio Ruben (Torres) b: 2/18/49, Yabucao, P.R. BR/TR, 5'10", 175 lbs. Deb: 9/05/69

YEAR	TM/L	G	AB	R	H	2B	3B	HR	RBI	BB	SO	AVG	OBP	SLG	PRO+	BR	/A	RC	SB	CS	SBR	FA	FR	POS	TPR
1969	SD-N	19	41	5	8	2	0	1	6	5	7	.195	.283	.317	71	-2	-2	3	0	2	-1	1.000	2	O	-0.1
1970	SD-N	28	58	6	9	0	1	1	4	3	11	.155	.197	.241	17	-7	-7	2	0	0	0	.926	-2	O	-0.9
1971	SD-N	12	17	1	2	0	0	0	1	2	2	.118	.211	.118	-5	-2	-2	0	1	0	0	1.000	0	/O	-0.2
1972	SD-N	115	347	38	83	15	7	4	18	35	54	.239	.309	.357	96	-5	-2	38	4	6	-2	.987	9	O/3	0.0
1973	SD-N	122	388	47	109	23	2	9	34	27	55	.281	.328	.420	115	2	6	49	6	5	-1	.991	4	*O	0.5
1974	Chi-N	151	534	70	146	21	7	15	82	46	63	.273	.333	.423	106	6	3	69	2	12	-7	.975	-2	*O	-1.2
1975	Chi-N	153	578	62	156	21	0	12	91	50	65	.270	.333	.369	91	-4	-7	69	3	7	-3	.979	-0	*O	-1.8
1976	Chi-N	140	537	66	147	17	0	16	67	41	49	.274	.325	.395	95	1	-4	62	3	8	-4	.983	5	*O	-0.9
1977	Chi-N★	136	490	56	142	34	5	11	69	43	75	.290	.350	.447	101	8	1	75	0	3	-2	.985	-12	*O	-1.8
1978	StL-N	130	457	44	109	19	8	4	46	33	44	.239	.291	.341	77	-15	-14	43	4	4	-1	.977	-0	*O	-2.3
1979	Det-A	129	440	50	93	23	1	14	56	30	56	.211	.265	.364	65	-21	-23	39	10	4	1	.986	-9	*O/D	-3.6
1980	NY-N	94	193	19	49	7	1	3	30	13	31	.254	.304	.347	84	-5	-4	20	2	3	-1	.973	3	O	-0.5
1981	Chi-N	84	245	27	70	6	2	1	25	22	29	.286	.347	.339	91	-1	-2	29	1	1	-0	.986	-3	O	-0.8
1982	Chi-N	65	116	14	33	2	2	4	30	9	7	.284	.336	.440	112	2	2	15	1	2	-1	1.000	7	O	0.7
1983	Chi-N	63	87	11	17	9	0	0	11	7	19	.195	.255	.299	51	-6	-6	7	0	0	0	1.000	-0	O	-0.7
Total	15	1441	4528	516	1173	199	36	95	570	366	567	.259	.316	.382	91	-49	-63	520	37	57	-23	.983	2	*O/D3	-13.6

■ RICH MORALES
Morales, Richard Angelo b: 9/20/43, San Francisco, Cal. BR/TR, 5'11", 170 lbs. Deb: 8/08/67 C

YEAR	TM/L	G	AB	R	H	2B	3B	HR	RBI	BB	SO	AVG	OBP	SLG	PRO+	BR	/A	RC	SB	CS	SBR	FA	FR	POS	TPR
1967	Chi-A	8	10	0	0	0	0	0	0	0	2	.000	.000	.000	-99	-2	-2	0	0	0	0	.944	2	/S	-0.1
1968	Chi-A	10	29	2	5	0	0	0	0	2	5	.172	.226	.172	22	-3	-3	1	0	0	0	.966	2	/S2	0.0
1969	Chi-A	55	121	12	26	0	1	0	6	7	18	.215	.269	.231	39	-9	-10	8	1	0	0	.976	10	2S/3	0.3
1970	Chi-A	62	112	6	18	2	0	1	2	9	16	.161	.230	.205	20	-12	-13	6	1	0	0	.967	6	S32	-0.5
1971	Chi-A	84	185	19	45	8	0	2	14	22	26	.243	.336	.319	84	-3	-3	20	2	3	-1	.976	-1	S3/2O	0.0
1972	Chi-A	110	287	24	59	7	1	2	20	19	49	.206	.262	.258	54	-16	-16	17	2	3	-1	.968	-1	S23	-0.9
1973	Chi-A	7	4	1	0	0	0	0	1	1	1	.000	.200	.000	-38	-1	-1	0	0	0	0	1.000	1	/32	0.0
	SD-N	90	244	9	40	6	1	0	16	27	36	.164	.247	.197	27	-25	-22	13	0	1	-1	.988	22	2S	0.4
1974	SD-N	54	61	8	12	3	0	1	5	8	6	.197	.290	.295	67	-3	-3	6	1	0	0	.933	7	S2/31	0.6
Total	8	480	1053	81	205	26	3	6	64	95	159	.195	.268	.242	46	-73	-73	70	7	7	-2	.970	47	S2/310	-0.2

■ CHARLIE MORAN
Moran, Charles Barthell "Uncle Charlie" b: 2/22/1878, Nashville, Tenn. d: 6/14/49, Horse Cave, Ky. BR/TR, 5'8", 180 lbs. Deb: 9/09/03 U

YEAR	TM/L	G	AB	R	H	2B	3B	HR	RBI	BB	SO	AVG	OBP	SLG	PRO+	BR	/A	RC	SB	CS	SBR	FA	FR	POS	TPR
1903	StL-N	4	14	2	6	0	0	0	1	0		.429	.429	.429	150	1	1	3	1			1.000	-1	/PS	0.0
1908	StL-N	21	63	2	11	1	2	0	2	0		.175	.175	.254	38	-5	-4	3	0			.903	-3	C	-0.7
Total	2	25	77	4	17	1	2	0	3	0		.221	.221	.286	61	-4	-4	6	1			.974	-4	/CPS	-0.7

■ CHARLES MORAN
Moran, Charles Vincent b: 3/26/1879, Washington, D.C. d: 4/11/34, Washington, D.C. TR , Deb: 4/29/03

YEAR	TM/L	G	AB	R	H	2B	3B	HR	RBI	BB	SO	AVG	OBP	SLG	PRO+	BR	/A	RC	SB	CS	SBR	FA	FR	POS	TPR
1903	Was-A	98	373	41	84	14	5	1	24	33		.225	.297	.298	77	-9	-10	37	8			**.943**	5	S/2	0.0
1904	Was-A	62	243	27	54	10	0	0	7	23		.222	.289	.263	77	-6	-6	22	7			.919	-13	S/3	-2.0
	StL-A	82	272	15	47	3	1	0	14	25		.173	.242	.191	41	-18	-16	15	2			.937	-3	3/O	-2.0
	Yr	144	515	42	101	13	1	0	21	48		.196	.265	.225	58	-24	-22	36	9			.938	-17	3S/O	-4.0
1905	StL-A	27	82	6	16	1	0	0	5	10		.195	.290	.207	62	-3	-3	7	3			.954	-4	2/3	-0.7
Total	3	269	970	89	201	28	6	1	50	91		.207	.279	.252	66	-36	-35	81	20			.935	-16	S/32O	-4.7

■ HERBIE MORAN
Moran, John Herbert b: 2/16/1884, Costello, Pa. d: 9/21/54, Clarkson, N.Y. BL/TR, 5'5", 150 lbs. Deb: 4/16/08

YEAR	TM/L	G	AB	R	H	2B	3B	HR	RBI	BB	SO	AVG	OBP	SLG	PRO+	BR	/A	RC	SB	CS	SBR	FA	FR	POS	TPR
1908	Phi-A	19	59	4	9	0	0	0	4	6		.153	.242	.153	27	-4	-5	3	1			.952	1	O	-0.6
	Bos-N	8	29	3	8	0	0	0	2	2		.276	.364	.276	107	0	0	3	1			1.000	2	/O	0.3
1909	Bos-N	8	31	8	7	1	0	0	0	5		.226	.333	.258	80	-0	-1	3	0			1.000	-1	/O	-0.1
1910	Bos-N	20	67	11	8	0	0	0	3	13	14	.119	.280	.119	17	-6	-7	4	6			.958	4	O	-0.4
1912	Bro-N	130	508	77	140	18	10	1	40	69	38	.276	.368	.356	102	1	4	76	28			.961	8	*O	0.5
1913	Bro-N	132	515	71	137	15	5	0	26	45	29	.266	.333	.315	83	-8	-10	58	21			.950	2	*O	-1.4

YEAR	TM/L	G	AB	R	H	2B	3B	HR	RBI	BB	SO	AVG	OBP	SLG	PRO+	BR	/A	RC	SB	CS	SBR	FA	FR	POS	TPR
1914	Cin-N	107	395	43	93	10	5	1	35	41	29	.235	.312	.294	78	-9	-10	42	26			.954	-5	*O	-2.2
	*Bos-N	41	154	24	41	3	1	0	4	17	11	.266	.347	.299	93	-1	-1	17	4			.940	-8	O	-1.1
	Yr	148	549	67	134	13	6	1	39	58	40	.244	.322	.295	82	-10	-11	59	30			.950	-13	*O	-3.3
1915	Bos-N	130	419	59	84	13	5	0	21	66	41	.200	.320	.255	79	-10	-7	38	16	10	-1	.964	-6	*O	-2.2
Total	7	595	2177	300	527	60	26	2	135	264	162	.242	.332	.296	83	-37	-36	244	103	10		.957	-2	O	-7.2

■ PAT MORAN Moran, Patrick Joseph b: 2/7/1876, Fitchburg, Mass. d: 3/7/24, Orlando, Fla. BR/TR, 5'10", 180 lbs. Deb: 5/15/01 M

YEAR	TM/L	G	AB	R	H	2B	3B	HR	RBI	BB	SO	AVG	OBP	SLG	PRO+	BR	/A	RC	SB	CS	SBR	FA	FR	POS	TPR
1901	Bos-N	52	180	12	38	5	1	2	18	3		.211	.228	.283	44	-12	-14	13	3			.973	-5	C1/3SO2	-1.7
1902	Bos-N	80	251	22	60	5	5	1	24	17		.239	.305	.311	89	-3	-3	27	6			**.982**	2	C/1O	0.7
1903	Bos-N	109	389	40	102	25	5	7	54	29		.262	.329	.406	114	4	6	57	8			.967	19	*C/1	3.5
1904	Bos-N	113	398	26	90	11	3	4	34	18		.226	.263	.299	77	-13	-11	35	10			.957	4	C3/1	0.2
1905	Bos-N	85	267	22	64	11	5	2	22	8		.240	.267	.341	83	-7	-7	26	3			**.986**	13	C	1.4
1906	*Chi-N	70	226	22	57	13	1	0	35	7		.252	.281	.319	82	-4	-6	23	6			.979	3	C	0.4
1907	*Chi-N	65	198	8	45	5	1	1	19	10		.227	.271	.278	68	-7	-8	17	5			.973	1	C	-0.2
1908	Chi-N	50	150	12	39	5	1	0	12	13		.260	.323	.307	97	0	-0	17	6			.968	1	C	0.6
1909	Chi-N	77	246	18	54	11	1	1	23	16		.220	.278	.285	73	-8	-8	20	2			.984	1	C	0.0
1910	Phi-N	68	199	13	47	7	1	0	11	17	16	.236	.306	.281	69	-7	-8	19	6			.989	0	C	-0.2
1911	Phi-N	34	103	2	19	3	0	0	8	3	13	.184	.208	.214	18	-11	-12	5	0			.984	-1	C	-1.0
1912	Phi-N	13	26	1	3	1	0	0	1	1	7	.115	.148	.154	-16	-4	-4	1	0			.955	-2	C	-0.5
1913	Phi-N	1	1	0	0	0	0	0	0	0	0	.000	.000	.000	-96	-0	-0	0	0			.000	0	H	0.0
1914	Phi-N	1	0	0	0	0	0	0	1	0	0	—	—	—	—	0	0	0	0			.000	0	/C	0.0
Total	14	818	2634	198	618	102	24	18	262	142	36	.235	.283	.312	78	-73	-76	259	55			.976	35	C/31OS2	3.2

■ AL MORAN Moran, Richard Alan b: 12/5/38, Detroit, Mich. BR/TR, 6'1.5", 190 lbs. Deb: 4/09/63

YEAR	TM/L	G	AB	R	H	2B	3B	HR	RBI	BB	SO	AVG	OBP	SLG	PRO+	BR	/A	RC	SB	CS	SBR	FA	FR	POS	TPR
1963	NY-N	119	331	26	64	5	2	1	23	36	60	.193	.274	.230	46	-22	-22	21	3	7	-3	.951	6	*S/3	-1.3
1964	NY-N	16	22	2	5	0	0	0	4	2	2	.227	.292	.227	50	-1	-1	1	0	0	0	.957	4	S/3	0.4
Total	2	135	353	28	69	5	2	1	27	38	62	.195	.276	.229	46	-23	-24	22	3	7	-3	.951	11	S/3	-0.9

■ ROY MORAN Moran, Roy Ellis "Deedle" b: 9/17/1884, Vincennes, Ind. d: 7/18/66, Atlanta, Ga. BR/TR, 5'8", 155 lbs. Deb: 9/03/12

YEAR	TM/L	G	AB	R	H	2B	3B	HR	RBI	BB	SO	AVG	OBP	SLG	PRO+	BR	/A	RC	SB	CS	SBR	FA	FR	POS	TPR
1912	Was-A	7	13	1	2	0	0	0	0	8		.154	.476	.154	82	1	1	3	3			.889	-0	/O	0.0

■ BILL MORAN Moran, William L. b: 10/10/1869, Joliet, Ill. d: 4/8/16, Joliet, Ill. 175 lbs. Deb: 5/07/1892

YEAR	TM/L	G	AB	R	H	2B	3B	HR	RBI	BB	SO	AVG	OBP	SLG	PRO+	BR	/A	RC	SB	CS	SBR	FA	FR	POS	TPR
1892	StL-N	24	81	2	11	1	0	0	5	2	12	.136	.157	.148	-7	-10	-10	2	0			.891	-5	C/O	-1.2
1895	Chi-N	15	55	8	9	2	1	1	9	3	2	.164	.220	.291	30	-6	-6	4	2			.827	-2	C	-0.6
Total	2	39	136	10	20	3	1	1	14	5	14	.147	.183	.206	11	-16	-16	6	2			.866	-6	/CO	-1.8

■ BILLY MORAN Moran, William Nelson b: 11/27/33, Montgomery, Ala. BR/TR, 5'11", 185 lbs. Deb: 4/15/58

YEAR	TM/L	G	AB	R	H	2B	3B	HR	RBI	BB	SO	AVG	OBP	SLG	PRO+	BR	/A	RC	SB	CS	SBR	FA	FR	POS	TPR
1958	Cle-A	115	257	26	58	11	0	1	18	13	23	.226	.263	.280	51	-18	-17	18	3	2	-0	.960	13	2S	0.1
1959	Cle-A	11	17	1	5	0	0	0	2	0	1	.294	.294	.294	64	-1	-1	1	0	0	0	1.000	-1	/2S	-0.1
1961	LA-A	54	173	17	45	7	1	2	22	17	16	.260	.330	.347	73	-4	-7	20	0	0	0	.966	-5	2/S	-0.6
1962	LA-A★	160	659	90	186	25	3	17	74	39	80	.282	.326	.407	99	-5	-2	89	5	1	1	.986	19	*2	3.4
1963	LA-A	153	597	67	164	29	5	7	65	31	57	.275	.314	.375	98	-7	-3	68	1	1	-0	.973	15	*2	2.8
1964	LA-A	50	198	26	53	10	1	0	11	13	20	.268	.316	.328	88	-5	-3	18	1	3	-2	.929	-7	3/2S	-1.2
	Cle-A	69	151	14	31	6	0	1	10	18	16	.205	.294	.265	57	-8	-8	12	0	1	-1	.972	3	32/1	-0.6
	Yr	119	349	40	84	16	1	1	21	31	36	.241	.306	.301	73	-14	-12	30	1	4	-2	.947	-4	32/1S	-1.8
1965	Cle-A	22	24	1	3	0	0	0	0	2	5	.125	.222	.125	1	-3	-3	1	0	0	0	1.000	1	/2S	-0.2
Total	7	634	2076	242	545	88	10	28	202	133	218	.263	.310	.355	85	-51	-44	227	10	8	-2	.976	39	2/3S1	3.6

■ MICKEY MORANDINI Morandini, Michael Robert b: 4/22/66, Kittanning, Pa. BL/TR, 5'11", 170 lbs. Deb: 9/01/90

YEAR	TM/L	G	AB	R	H	2B	3B	HR	RBI	BB	SO	AVG	OBP	SLG	PRO+	BR	/A	RC	SB	CS	SBR	FA	FR	POS	TPR
1990	Phi-N	25	79	9	19	4	0	1	3	6	19	.241	.294	.329	71	-3	-3	8	3	0	1	.990	1	2	-0.1
1991	Phi-N	98	325	38	81	11	4	1	20	29	45	.249	.315	.317	79	-9	-9	35	13	2	3	.986	8	2	0.4
1992	Phi-N	127	422	47	112	8	8	3	30	25	64	.265	.306	.344	84	-9	-9	46	8	3	1	.991	11	*2/S	0.6
Total	3	250	826	94	212	23	12	5	53	60	128	.257	.309	.332	81	-21	-21	88	24	5	4	.989	21	2/S	0.9

■ RAY MOREHART Morehart, Raymond Anderson b: 12/2/1899, Near Abner, Tex. d: 1/13/89, Dallas, Tex. BL/TR, 5'9", 157 lbs. Deb: 8/09/24

YEAR	TM/L	G	AB	R	H	2B	3B	HR	RBI	BB	SO	AVG	OBP	SLG	PRO+	BR	/A	RC	SB	CS	SBR	FA	FR	POS	TPR
1924	Chi-A	31	100	10	20	4	2	0	8	17	7	.200	.316	.280	56	-7	-6	10	3	1	0	.873	-12	S/2	-1.4
1926	Chi-A	73	192	27	61	10	3	0	21	11	15	.318	.358	.401	101	-1	0	24	3	11	-6	.950	-5	2	-0.9
1927	NY-A	73	195	45	50	7	2	1	20	29	18	.256	.353	.328	80	-6	-5	23	4	4	-1	.945	4	2	-0.1
Total	3	177	487	82	131	21	7	1	49	57	40	.269	.347	.347	83	-13	-11	57	10	16	-7	.946	-13	2/S	-2.4

■ DANNY MOREJON Morejon, Daniel (Torres) b: 7/21/30, Havana, Cuba BR/TR, 6'1", 175 lbs. Deb: 7/11/58

YEAR	TM/L	G	AB	R	H	2B	3B	HR	RBI	BB	SO	AVG	OBP	SLG	PRO+	BR	/A	RC	SB	CS	SBR	FA	FR	POS	TPR
1958	Cin-N	12	26	4	5	0	0	0	1	9	2	.192	.400	.192	60	-1	-1	3	1	0	0	1.000	-2	O	-0.4

■ KEITH MORELAND Moreland, Bobby Keith b: 5/2/54, Dallas, Tex. BR/TR, 6', 200 lbs. Deb: 10/01/78

YEAR	TM/L	G	AB	R	H	2B	3B	HR	RBI	BB	SO	AVG	OBP	SLG	PRO+	BR	/A	RC	SB	CS	SBR	FA	FR	POS	TPR
1978	Phi-N	1	2	0	0	0	0	0	0	0	0	.000	.000	.000	-99	-1	-1	0	0	0	0	1.000	0	/C	0.0
1979	Phi-N	14	48	3	18	3	2	0	8	3	5	.375	.412	.521	148	3	3	10	0	0	0	1.000	-0	C	0.3
1980	*Phi-N	62	159	13	50	8	0	4	29	8	14	.314	.347	.440	112	4	3	22	3	1	0	.967	-1	C/3O	0.3
1981	*Phi-N	61	196	16	50	7	0	6	37	15	13	.255	.311	.383	92	-1	-2	20	1	2	-1	.982	-7	C/31O	-0.9
1982	Chi-N	138	476	50	124	17	2	15	68	46	71	.261	.330	.399	100	2	0	61	0	6	-4	.989	-2	OC/3	-0.6
1983	Chi-N	154	533	76	161	30	3	16	70	68	73	.302	.384	.460	127	25	22	93	0	3	-2	.976	-13	*O/C	0.3
1984	*Chi-N	140	495	59	138	17	3	16	80	34	71	.279	.329	.422	101	5	0	64	1	4	-2	.976	-7	*O1/3C	-1.5
1985	Chi-N	161	587	74	180	30	3	14	106	68	58	.307	.380	.440	116	23	16	100	12	3	2	.976	-9	*O13/C	0.3
1986	Chi-N	156	586	72	159	30	0	12	79	53	48	.271	.332	.384	90	-3	-8	72	3	6	-3	.980	-9	*O3C1	-2.5
1987	Chi-N	153	563	63	150	29	1	27	88	39	66	.266	.314	.465	99	0	-2	78	3	3	-1	.934	4	*3/1	-0.1
1988	SD-N	143	511	40	131	23	0	5	64	40	51	.256	.310	.331	86	-10	-9	50	2	3	-1	.994	-3	1O/3	-2.3
1989	Det-A	90	318	34	95	16	0	5	35	27	33	.299	.357	.396	115	5	6	42	3	2	-0	1.000	-6	D13/C	-0.3
	Bal-A	33	107	11	23	4	0	1	10	4	12	.215	.243	.280	49	-8	-7	6	0	0	0	.000	0	D	-0.7
	Yr	123	425	45	118	20	0	6	45	31	45	.278	.330	.367	99	-2	-1	46	3	2	-0	1.000	-6	D13/C	-1.0
Total	12	1306	4581	511	1279	214	14	121	674	405	515	.279	.339	.411	103	45	19	616	28	33	-11	.979	-52	O3C1/D	-7.7

■ HARRY MORELOCK Morelock, A. Harry b: Philadelphia, Pa. Deb: 8/21/1891

YEAR	TM/L	G	AB	R	H	2B	3B	HR	RBI	BB	SO	AVG	OBP	SLG	PRO+	BR	/A	RC	SB	CS	SBR	FA	FR	POS	TPR
1891	Phi-N	4	14	1	1	0	0	0	0	3	3	.071	.235	.071	-8	-2	-2	0	0			.824	-4	/S	-0.5
1892	Phi-N	1	3	0	0	0	0	0	0	1	0	.000	.250	.000	-22	-0	-0	0	0			.600	-1	/3	-0.1
Total	2	5	17	1	1	0	0	0	0	4	3	.059	.238	.059	-10	-2	-2	0	0			1.000	-4	/S3	-0.6

■ JOSE MORENO Moreno, Jose De Los Santos (b: Jose De Los Santos Mauricio (Moreno)) b: 11/1/57, Santo Domingo, D.R. BB/TR, 6', 175 lbs. Deb: 5/24/80

YEAR	TM/L	G	AB	R	H	2B	3B	HR	RBI	BB	SO	AVG	OBP	SLG	PRO+	BR	/A	RC	SB	CS	SBR	FA	FR	POS	TPR
1980	NY-N	37	46	6	9	2	1	2	9	3	12	.196	.245	.413	83	-1	-1	4	1	0	0	.917	0	/23	-0.1
1981	SD-N	34	48	5	11	2	0	0	6	1	8	.229	.245	.271	50	-3	-3	3	4	1	1	1.000	1	/O2	-0.2
1982	Cal-A	11	3	3	0	0	0	0	0	2	0	.000	.400	.000	21	-0	-0	0	0	2	-1	1.000	2	/2D	0.0
Total	3	82	97	14	20	4	1	2	15	6	20	.206	.252	.330	66	-5	-5	7	5	3	-0	.947	2	/O23D	-0.3

■ OMAR MORENO Moreno, Omar Renan (Quintero) b: 10/24/52, Puerto Armuelles, Panama BL/TL, 6'2", 180 lbs. Deb: 9/06/75

YEAR	TM/L	G	AB	R	H	2B	3B	HR	RBI	BB	SO	AVG	OBP	SLG	PRO+	BR	/A	RC	SB	CS	SBR	FA	FR	POS	TPR
1975	Pit-N	6	6	1	1	0	0	0	0	1	1	.167	.286	.167	28	-1	-1	1	1	0	0	.000	-0	/O	-0.1
1976	Pit-N	48	122	24	33	4	1	2	12	16	24	.270	.360	.369	106	2	1	19	15	5	2	.960	4	O	0.6
1977	Pit-N	150	492	69	118	19	9	7	34	38	102	.240	.296	.358	72	-18	-20	55	53	16	6	.977	1	*O	-1.9
1978	Pit-N	155	515	95	121	15	7	2	33	81	104	.235	.342	.303	78	-10	-13	65	**71**	22	8	.984	10	*O	-0.1

YEAR	TM/L	G	AB	R	H	2B	3B	HR	RBI	BB	SO	AVG	OBP	SLG	PRO+	BR	/A	RC	SB	CS	SBR	FA	FR	POS	TPR
1979	*Pit-N	162	695	110	196	21	12	8	69	51	104	.282	.334	.381	90	-5	-9	94	**77**	21	11	.975	15	*O	0.9
1980	Pit-N	162	676	87	168	20	**13**	2	36	57	101	.249	.309	.325	76	-20	-21	71	96	33	9	.990	18	*O	-0.1
1981	Pit-N	103	434	62	120	18	8	1	35	26	76	.276	.322	.362	91	-4	-6	53	39	14	3	.997	5	*O	-0.1
1982	Pit-N	158	645	82	158	18	9	3	44	44	121	.245	.294	.315	68	-26	-28	61	60	26	2	.983	5	*O	-2.6
1983	Hou-N	97	405	48	98	12	11	0	25	22	72	.242	.283	.326	73	-18	-15	38	30	13	1	.977	4	O	-1.4
	NY-A	48	152	17	38	9	1	1	17	8	31	.250	.287	.342	75	-6	-5	14	7	3	0	.992	-0	O	-0.6
1984	NY-A	117	355	37	92	12	6	4	38	18	48	.259	.297	.361	84	-10	-8	37	20	11	-1	.985	3	*O/D	-0.8
1985	NY-A	34	66	12	13	4	1	1	4	1	16	.197	.209	.333	47	-5	-5	4	1	1	-0	1.000	0	O/D	-0.6
	KC-A	24	70	9	17	1	3	2	12	3	8	.243	.284	.429	91	-1	-1	8	0	1	-1	1.000	-3	O	-0.6
	Yr	58	136	21	30	5	4	3	16	4	24	.221	.248	.382	70	-6	-6	12	1	2	-1	1.000	-3	O/D	-1.2
1986	Atl-N	118	359	46	84	18	6	4	27	21	77	.234	.276	.351	68	-15	-17	32	17	16	-5	.970	-3	O	-2.8
Total	12	1382	4992	699	1257	171	87	37	386	387	885	.252	.308	.343	79	-137	-147	553	487	182	37	.982	59	*O/D	-10.2

■ CHET MORGAN Morgan, Chester Collins "Chick" b: 6/6/10, Cleveland, Miss. d: 9/20/91, Pasadena, Tex. BL/TR, 5'9", 160 lbs. Deb: 4/19/35

YEAR	TM/L	G	AB	R	H	2B	3B	HR	RBI	BB	SO	AVG	OBP	SLG	PRO+	BR	/A	RC	SB	CS	SBR	FA	FR	POS	TPR
1935	Det-A	14	23	2	4	1	0	0	1	5	0	.174	.321	.217	43	-2	-2	2	0	0	0	.909	-0	/O	-0.2
1938	Det-A	74	306	50	87	6	1	0	27	20	12	.284	.330	.310	58	-18	-20	31	5	6	-2	.980	0	O	-2.3
Total	2	88	329	52	91	7	1	0	28	25	12	.277	.330	.304	57	-20	-22	33	5	6	-2	.977	0	/O	-2.5

■ ED MORGAN Morgan, Edward Carre b: 5/22/04, Cairo, Ill. d: 4/9/80, New Orleans, La. BR/TR, 6'0.5", 180 lbs. Deb: 4/11/28

YEAR	TM/L	G	AB	R	H	2B	3B	HR	RBI	BB	SO	AVG	OBP	SLG	PRO+	BR	/A	RC	SB	CS	SBR	FA	FR	POS	TPR
1928	Cle-A	76	265	42	83	24	6	4	54	21	17	.313	.366	.494	123	8	8	47	5	5	-2	.968	1	1O3	0.4
1929	Cle-A	93	318	60	101	19	10	3	37	37	24	.318	.392	.469	116	10	9	59	4	3	-1	.908	-11	O	-0.8
1930	Cle-A	150	584	122	204	47	11	26	136	62	66	.349	.413	.601	148	46	43	144	8	4	0	.987	-3	*1O	2.4
1931	Cle-A	131	462	87	162	33	4	11	86	83	46	.351	.451	.511	144	39	35	110	4	5	-2	.984	2	*1/3	2.3
1932	Cle-A	144	532	96	156	32	7	4	68	94	44	.293	.402	.402	102	11	6	92	7	6	-2	.985	-8	*1/3	-1.4
1933	Cle-A	39	121	10	32	3	3	1	13	7	9	.264	.305	.364	73	-4	-5	13	1	1	-0	.997	2	1/O	-0.6
1934	Bos-A	138	528	95	141	28	4	3	79	81	46	.267	.367	.352	80	-9	-14	74	7	1	2	.988	-7	*1	-3.0
Total	7	771	2810	512	879	186	45	52	473	385	252	.313	.398	.467	117	102	81	540	36	25	-4	.986	-23	1O/3	-0.7

■ EDDIE MORGAN Morgan, Edwin Willis "Pepper" b: 11/19/14, Brady Lake, Ohio d: 6/27/82, Lakewood, Ohio BL/TL, 5'10", 160 lbs. Deb: 4/14/36

YEAR	TM/L	G	AB	R	H	2B	3B	HR	RBI	BB	SO	AVG	OBP	SLG	PRO+	BR	/A	RC	SB	CS	SBR	FA	FR	POS	TPR
1936	StL-N	8	18	4	5	0	0	1	3	2	4	.278	.350	.444	113	0	0	3	0			.889	-0	/O	0.0
1937	Bro-N	31	48	4	9	3	0	0	5	9	7	.188	.316	.250	55	-3	-3	5	0			.984	-3	/1O	-0.6
Total	2	39	66	8	14	3	0	1	8	11	11	.212	.325	.303	70	-2	-3	8	0			.842	-3	/O1	-0.6

■ BILL MORGAN Morgan, Henry William b: 10/1857, Washington, D.C. Deb: 5/04/1875

YEAR	TM/L	G	AB	R	H	2B	3B	HR	RBI	BB	SO	AVG	OBP	SLG	PRO+	BR	/A	RC	SB	CS	SBR	FA	FR	POS	TPR
1875	RS-n	19	69	11	18	4	0	0		5		.261	.311	.319	131	1	3	7						/OP3	0.2
1878	Mil-N	14	56	2	11	0	0	0	5	3	9	.196	.237	.196	41	-3	-4	3				.769	-6	O/32	-1.0
1882	Pit-a	17	66	10	17	2	1	0		4		.258	.300	.318	114	1	1	6				.688	-8	O/C	-0.6
1884	Ric-a	6	20	0	2	0	0	0		1		.100	.143	.100	-18	-2	-2	0				.850	-2	/CO2	-0.4
	Bal-U	2	9	1	2	0	0	0		1		.222	.300	.222	72	-0	-0	1				.909	0	/C2O	0.0
Total	3	39	151	13	32	2	1	0	5	9	9	.212	.256	.238	65	-5	-5	10				.743	-16	/OC23	-2.0

■ RED MORGAN Morgan, James Edward b: 10/6/1883, Neola, Iowa d: 3/25/81, New York, N.Y. TR , Deb: 6/20/06

YEAR	TM/L	G	AB	R	H	2B	3B	HR	RBI	BB	SO	AVG	OBP	SLG	PRO+	BR	/A	RC	SB	CS	SBR	FA	FR	POS	TPR
1906	Bos-A	88	307	20	66	6	3	1	21	16		.215	.270	.264	68	-11	-11	26	7			.866	-13	3	-2.4

■ JOE MORGAN Morgan, Joe Leonard b: 9/19/43, Bonham, Tex. BL/TR, 5'7", 160 lbs. Deb: 9/21/63 H

YEAR	TM/L	G	AB	R	H	2B	3B	HR	RBI	BB	SO	AVG	OBP	SLG	PRO+	BR	/A	RC	SB	CS	SBR	FA	FR	POS	TPR
1963	Hou-N	8	25	5	6	0	1	0	3	5	5	.240	.367	.320	106	0	0	4	1	0	0	.909	-3	/2	-0.2
1964	Hou-N	10	37	4	7	0	0	0	0	6	7	.189	.302	.189	44	-3	-2	2	0	1	-1	.949	-0	2	-0.2
1965	Hou-N	157	601	100	163	22	12	14	40	**97**	77	.271	.375	.418	132	21	27	103	20	9	1	.969	-2	*2	4.1
1966	Hou-N†	122	425	60	121	14	8	5	42	89	43	.285	.412	.391	134	19	23	77	11	8	-2	.965	-16	*2	1.4
1967	Hou-N	133	494	73	136	27	11	6	42	81	51	.275	.380	.411	131	20	22	88	29	5	**6**	.979	-5	*2/O	3.4
1968	Hou-N	10	20	6	5	0	1	0	0	7	4	.250	.444	.350	144	2	2	5	3	0	1	.882	-4	/2O	-0.1
1969	Hou-N	147	535	94	126	18	5	15	43	110	74	.236	.367	.372	110	9	10	86	49	14	6	.972	-2	*2O	2.6
1970	Hou-N★	144	548	102	147	28	9	8	52	102	55	.268	.384	.396	114	11	14	92	42	13	5	.979	11	*2	4.1
1971	Hou-N	160	583	87	149	27	**11**	13	56	88	52	.256	.354	.407	118	13	15	95	40	8	7	.986	-3	*2	3.4
1972	*Cin-N★	149	552	**122**	161	23	4	16	73	**115**	44	.292	**.419**	.435	152	37	41	117	58	17	7	**.990**	-7	*2	**5.3**
1973	*Cin-N★	157	576	116	167	35	2	26	82	111	61	.290	.408	.493	157	42	46	128	67	15	**11**	.990	-8	*2	**5.9**
1974	Cin-N★	149	512	107	150	31	3	22	67	120	69	.293	**.430**	.494	160	45	46	125	58	12	10	.982	-13	*2	5.1
1975	*Cin-N★	146	498	107	163	27	6	17	94	**132**	52	.327	**.471**	.508	**169**	**57**	**56**	**145**	67	10	14	**.986**	-7	*2	**7.2**
1976	*Cin-N★	141	472	113	151	30	5	27	111	114	41	.320	**.453**	**.576**	**186**	**61**	**60**	**144**	60	9	13	.981	-23	*2	6.0
1977	Cin-N★	153	521	113	150	21	6	22	78	117	58	.288	.420	.478	138	35	34	121	49	10	9	**.993**	-18	*2	3.5
1978	Cin-N★	132	441	68	104	27	0	13	75	79	40	.236	.354	.385	107	6	6	67	19	5	3	.980	-31	*2	-1.4
1979	*Cin-N★	127	436	70	109	26	1	9	32	93	45	.250	.383	.376	107	9	8	72	28	6	5	.980	-13	*2	0.9
1980	*Hou-N	141	461	66	112	17	5	11	49	**93**	47	.243	.370	.373	117	8	13	73	24	6	4	.988	-12	*2	1.3
1981	SF-N	90	308	47	74	16	1	8	31	66	37	.240	.374	.377	116	8	9	49	14	5	1	.991	-11	2	0.5
1982	SF-N	134	463	68	134	19	4	14	61	85	60	.289	.402	.438	135	25	25	92	24	4	5	.989	-6	*2/3	3.1
1983	*Phi-N	123	404	72	93	20	1	16	59	89	54	.230	.374	.403	117	11	12	68	18	2	4	.971	-2	*2	2.1
1984	Oak-A	116	365	50	89	21	0	6	43	66	39	.244	.361	.351	105	1	5	51	8	3	1	.977	-31	*2/D	-2.3
Total	22	2649	9277	1650	2517	449	96	268	1133	1865	1015	.271	.395	.427	133	438	470	1804	689	162	110	.981	-205	*2/OD3	55.7

■ JOE MORGAN Morgan, Joseph Michael b: 11/19/30, Walpole, Mass. BL/TR, 5'10", 170 lbs. Deb: 4/14/59 MC

YEAR	TM/L	G	AB	R	H	2B	3B	HR	RBI	BB	SO	AVG	OBP	SLG	PRO+	BR	/A	RC	SB	CS	SBR	FA	FR	POS	TPR
1959	Mil-N	13	23	2	5	1	0	0	1	2	4	.217	.280	.261	49	-2	-2	2	0	0	0	.913	-2	/2	-0.3
	KC-A	20	21	2	4	0	1	0	3	3	7	.190	.292	.286	58	-1	-1	2	0	0	0	1.000	-1	/3	-0.2
1960	Phi-N	26	83	5	11	2	2	0	2	6	11	.133	.191	.205	8	-11	-11	3	0	0	0	.971	1	3	-1.0
	Cle-A	22	47	6	14	2	0	2	4	6	4	.298	.377	.468	131	2	2	8	0	0	0	.889	-2	3/O	0.0
1961	Cle-A	4	10	0	2	0	0	0	0	1	3	.200	.273	.200	29	-1	-1	1	0	0	0	1.000	0	/O	-0.1
1964	StL-N	3	3	0	0	0	0	0	0	0	2	.000	.000	.000	-92	-1	-1	0	0	0	0	.000	0	H	-0.1
Total	4	88	187	15	36	5	3	2	10	18	31	.193	.263	.283	49	-13	-13	15	0	0	0	.944	-3	/32O	-1.7

■ RAY MORGAN Morgan, Raymond Caryll b: 6/14/1889, Baltimore, Md. d: 2/15/40, Baltimore, Md. BR/TR, 5'8.5", 155 lbs. Deb: 8/07/11

YEAR	TM/L	G	AB	R	H	2B	3B	HR	RBI	BB	SO	AVG	OBP	SLG	PRO+	BR	/A	RC	SB	CS	SBR	FA	FR	POS	TPR
1911	Was-A	25	89	11	19	2	0	0	5	4		.213	.247	.236	36	-8	-8	6	2			.900	-3	3	-1.1
1912	Was-A	81	273	40	65	10	7	1	30	29		.238	.318	.337	87	-5	-5	33	11			.939	-7	2/S3	-1.3
1913	Was-A	138	481	58	131	19	8	0	57	68	63	.272	.369	.345	107	8	7	66	19			.950	-6	*2/S	0.0
1914	Was-A	147	491	50	126	22	8	1	49	62	34	.257	.352	.340	104	6	4	63	24	17	-3	.948	-9	*2	-1.0
1915	Was-A	62	193	21	45	5	4	0	21	30	15	.233	.342	.301	91	-1	-1	22	6	5	-1	.965	-4	2/S3	-0.6
1916	Was-A	99	315	41	84	12	4	1	29	59	29	.267	.398	.340	123	12	13	50	14			.957	-17	2/S13	-0.1
1917	Was-A	101	338	32	90	9	1	1	33	40	29	.266	.346	.308	101	1	1	38	7			.961	-8	2/3	-0.2
1918	Was-A	88	300	25	70	11	1	0	30	28	14	.233	.311	.277	79	-8	-7	27	4			.959	-5	2/O	-0.8
Total	8	741	2480	278	630	90	33	4	254	320	184	.254	.348	.322	98	7	4	304	87	22		.953	-58	2/3S10	-5.1

■ BOBBY MORGAN Morgan, Robert Morris b: 6/29/26, Oklahoma City, Okla. BR/TR, 5'9", 175 lbs. Deb: 4/18/50

YEAR	TM/L	G	AB	R	H	2B	3B	HR	RBI	BB	SO	AVG	OBP	SLG	PRO+	BR	/A	RC	SB	CS	SBR	FA	FR	POS	TPR
1950	Bro-N	67	199	38	45	10	3	7	21	32	43	.226	.342	.412	95	-1	-1	29	0			.969	6	3S	0.5
1952	*Bro-N	67	191	36	45	8	0	7	16	46	35	.236	.392	.387	115	6	6	33	2	2	-1	.968	3	3/2S	0.8
1953	*Bro-N	69	196	35	51	6	2	7	33	33	47	.260	.370	.418	103	2	2	31	2	2	-1	.920	-2	3S	0.0
1954	Phi-N	135	455	58	119	25	2	14	50	70	68	.262	.360	.418	102	2	2	70	3	1	0	.954	-22	*S/32	-0.9
1955	Phi-N	136	483	61	112	20	2	10	49	73	72	.232	.333	.344	81	-13	-11	57	6	4	-1	.980	-13	2S/31	-1.5

YEAR	TM/L	G	AB	R	H	2B	3B	HR	RBI	BB	SO	AVG	OBP	SLG	PRO+	BR	/A	RC	SB	CS	SBR	FA	FR	POS	TPR
1956	Phi-N	8	25	1	5	0	0	0	1	6	4	.200	.355	.200	56	-1	-1	2	0	0	0	.857	1	/32	0.0
	StL-N	61	113	14	22	7	0	3	20	15	24	.195	.289	.336	67	-5	-5	10	0	2	-1	.980	1	23/S	-0.5
	Yr	69	138	15	27	7	0	3	21	21	28	.196	.302	.312	65	-7	-7	13	0	2	-1	.877	1	32/S	-0.5
1957	Phi-N	2	0	0	0	0	0	0	0	0	0	—	—	—	—	0	0	0	0	0	0	1.000	1	/2	0.1
	Chi-N	125	425	43	88	20	2	5	27	52	87	.207	.295	.299	61	-23	-23	41	5	0	2	.976	8	*23	-0.4
	Yr	127	425	43	88	20	2	5	27	52	87	.207	.295	.299	61	-23	-23	41	5	0	2	.976	9	*23	-0.3
1958	Chi-N	1	1	0	0	0	0	0	0	0	1	.000	.000	.000	-99	-0	-0	0	0	0	0	.000	0	H	0.0
Total	8	671	2088	286	487	96	11	53	217	327	381	.233	.339	.366	88	-33	-32	272	18	11		.978	-17	2S3/1	-1.9

■ VERN MORGAN Morgan, Vernon Thomas b: 8/8/28, Emporia, Va. d: 11/8/75, Minneapolis, Minn. BL/TR, 6'1", 190 lbs. Deb: 8/10/54 C

YEAR	TM/L	G	AB	R	H	2B	3B	HR	RBI	BB	SO	AVG	OBP	SLG	PRO+	BR	/A	RC	SB	CS	SBR	FA	FR	POS	TPR
1954	Chi-N	24	64	3	15	2	0	0	2	1	10	.234	.246	.266	33	-6	-6	4	0	0	0	.895	-4	3	-1.1
1955	Chi-N	7	7	1	1	0	0	0	1	3	4	.143	.400	.143	52	-0	-0	1	0	0	0	.667	-1	/3	-0.1
Total	2	31	71	4	16	2	0	0	3	4	14	.225	.267	.254	36	-7	-7	5	0	0	0	.864	-5	/3	-1.2

■ BILL MORGAN Morgan, William Deb: 8/06/1883

YEAR	TM/L	G	AB	R	H	2B	3B	HR	RBI	BB	SO	AVG	OBP	SLG	PRO+	BR	/A	RC	SB	CS	SBR	FA	FR	POS	TPR
1883	Pit-a	32	114	12	18	2	1	0		7		.158	.207	.193	31	-9	-8	5				.825	-2	S/OC2	-0.8
1884	Was-a	45	162	8	28	1	1	0		8		.173	.216	.191	41	-11	-8	7				.781	-5	OC/2S	-1.1
Total	2	77	276	20	46	3	2	0		15		.167	.212	.192	36	-19	-16	12				.771	-6	/OSC2	-1.9

■ MOE MORHARDT Morhardt, Meredith Goodwin b: 1/16/37, Manchester, Conn. BL/TL, 6'1", 185 lbs. Deb: 9/07/61

YEAR	TM/L	G	AB	R	H	2B	3B	HR	RBI	BB	SO	AVG	OBP	SLG	PRO+	BR	/A	RC	SB	CS	SBR	FA	FR	POS	TPR
1961	Chi-N	7	18	3	5	0	0	0	1	3	5	.278	.381	.278	78	-0	-0	2	0	0	0	.962	-1	/1	-0.2
1962	Chi-N	18	16	1	2	0	0	0	2	2	8	.125	.222	.125	-4	-2	-2	1	0	0	0	.000	0	H	-0.2
Total	2	25	34	4	7	0	0	0	3	5	13	.206	.308	.206	39	-3	-3	3	0	0	0	.939	-1	/1	-0.4

■ ED MORIARTY Moriarty, Edward Jerome b: 10/12/12, Holyoke, Mass. d: 9/29/91, Holyoke, Mass. BR/TR, 5'10.5", 180 lbs. Deb: 6/21/35

YEAR	TM/L	G	AB	R	H	2B	3B	HR	RBI	BB	SO	AVG	OBP	SLG	PRO+	BR	/A	RC	SB	CS	SBR	FA	FR	POS	TPR
1935	Bos-N	8	34	4	11	2	1	1	1	0	6	.324	.324	.529	136	1	1	6	0			.923	-4	/2	-0.2
1936	Bos-N	6	6	1	1	0	0	0	0	0	1	.167	.167	.167	-11	-1	-1	0	0			.000	0	H	-0.1
Total	2	14	40	5	12	2	1	1	1	0	7	.300	.300	.475	114	0	0	6	0			.953	-4	/2	-0.3

■ GENE MORIARITY Moriarity, Eugene John b: Holyoke, Mass. BL/TL, 5'8", 130 lbs. Deb: 6/18/1884

YEAR	TM/L	G	AB	R	H	2B	3B	HR	RBI	BB	SO	AVG	OBP	SLG	PRO+	BR	/A	RC	SB	CS	SBR	FA	FR	POS	TPR
1884	Bos-N	4	16	1	1	0	0	0	0	0	8	.063	.063	.063	-61	-3	-3	0				.714	-1	/O	-0.3
	Ind-a	10	37	4	8	0	2	0		0		.216	.216	.324	78	-1	-1	3				.769	-1	/OP3	-0.2
1885	Det-N	11	39	1	1	1	0	0	0	0	10	.026	.026	.051	-75	-7	-7	0				.905	2	/O3SP	-0.5
1892	StL-N	47	177	20	31	4	1	3	19	4	37	.175	.207	.260	44	-13	-12	11	7			.820	2	O	-1.1
Total	3	72	269	26	41	5	3	3	19	4	55	.152	.174	.227	25	-24	-23	14	7			.822	2	/O3PS	-2.1

■ GEORGE MORIARTY Moriarty, George Joseph b: 6/7/1884, Chicago, Ill. d: 4/8/64, Miami, Fla. BR/TR, 6', 185 lbs. Deb: 9/27/03 FMU

YEAR	TM/L	G	AB	R	H	2B	3B	HR	RBI	BB	SO	AVG	OBP	SLG	PRO+	BR	/A	RC	SB	CS	SBR	FA	FR	POS	TPR
1903	Chi-N	1	5	1	0	0	0	0	0	0		.000	.000	.000	-99	-1	-1	0	0			1.000	-0	/3	-0.2
1904	Chi-N	4	13	0	0	0	0	0	0	1		.000	.071	.000	-77	-3	-3	0	0			.778	-0	/3O	-0.3
1906	NY-A	65	197	22	46	7	7	0	23	17		.234	.294	.340	90	-0	-3	24	8			.912	2	3O/12	-0.1
1907	NY-A	126	437	51	121	16	5	0	43	25		.277	.319	.336	101	4	0	58	28			.899	-9	31/O2S	-0.8
1908	NY-A	101	348	25	82	12	1	0	27	11		.236	.269	.276	76	-9	-10	31	22			.976	8	13O/2	-0.2
1909	*Det-A	133	473	43	129	20	4	1	39	24		.273	.309	.338	100	1	-1	59	34			**.939**	2	*31	0.5
1910	Det-A	136	490	53	123	24	3	2	60	33		.251	.308	.324	92	-2	-6	58	33			.927	-1	*3	-0.3
1911	Det-A	130	478	51	116	20	4	1	60	27		.243	.287	.308	63	-23	-26	51	28			.929	-4	*3/1	-2.8
1912	Det-A	105	375	38	93	23	1	0	54	26		.248	.316	.315	83	-10	-8	46	27			.987	-8	13	-1.6
1913	Det-A	105	347	29	83	5	2	0	30	24	25	.239	.302	.265	67	-14	-14	36	33			.938	-3	3/O	-1.7
1914	Det-A	132	465	56	118	19	5	1	40	39	27	.254	.318	.323	90	-4	-6	55	34	15	1	.956	17	*3/1	1.8
1915	Det-A	31	38	2	8	1	0	0	0	5	7	.211	.318	.237	63	-1	-2	3	1	1	-0	.875	-0	3/12O	-0.2
1916	Chi-A	7	5	1	1	0	0	0	0	2	0	.200	.429	.200	88	0	0	0	0			1.000	1	/13	0.1
Total	13	1076	3671	372	920	147	32	5	376	234	59	.251	.303	.312	84	-63	-78	424	248	16		.931	5	31/O2S	-5.8

■ BILL MORIARTY Moriarty, William Joseph b: 1883, Chicago, Ill. d: 12/25/16, Elgin, Ill. BR/TR, 6'2", 180 lbs. Deb: 4/29/09 F

YEAR	TM/L	G	AB	R	H	2B	3B	HR	RBI	BB	SO	AVG	OBP	SLG	PRO+	BR	/A	RC	SB	CS	SBR	FA	FR	POS	TPR
1909	Cin-N	6	20	1	4	1	0	0	1	0		.200	.200	.250	40	-1	-1	1	2			.944	0	/S	-0.1

■ BILL MORLEY Morley, William M. (b: William Morley Jennings) b: 1/23/1890, Holland, Mich. d: 5/14/85, Lubbock, Tex. BR/TR, 5'11", 170 lbs. Deb: 9/08/13

YEAR	TM/L	G	AB	R	H	2B	3B	HR	RBI	BB	SO	AVG	OBP	SLG	PRO+	BR	/A	RC	SB	CS	SBR	FA	FR	POS	TPR
1913	Was-A	2	3	0	0	0	0	0	0	0	0	.000	.000	.000	-98	-1	-1	0	0			.000	0	/2	-0.1

■ RUSS MORMAN Morman, Russell Lee b: 4/28/62, Independence, Mo. BR/TR, 6'4", 215 lbs. Deb: 8/03/86

YEAR	TM/L	G	AB	R	H	2B	3B	HR	RBI	BB	SO	AVG	OBP	SLG	PRO+	BR	/A	RC	SB	CS	SBR	FA	FR	POS	TPR
1986	Chi-A	49	159	18	40	5	0	4	17	16	36	.252	.328	.358	84	-3	-3	19	1	0	0	.989	-3	1	-0.9
1988	Chi-A	40	75	8	18	2	0	0	3	3	17	.240	.269	.267	51	-5	-5	4	0	0	0	.981	-3	1O/D	-0.9
1989	Chi-A	37	58	5	13	2	0	0	8	6	16	.224	.297	.259	59	-3	-3	5	1	0	0	.988	1	1/D	-0.3
1990	KC-A	12	37	5	10	4	2	1	3	3	3	.270	.325	.568	147	2	2	7	0	0	0	1.000	-0	/O1D	0.1
1991	KC-A	12	23	1	6	0	0	0	1	1	5	.261	.292	.261	54	-1	-1	2	0	0	0	1.000	0	/1OD	-0.2
Total	5	150	352	37	87	13	2	5	32	29	77	.247	.308	.338	78	-10	-11	37	2	0	1	.989	-6	1/OD	-2.2

■ JEFF MORONKO Moronko, Jeffrey Robert b: 8/17/59, Houston, Tex. BR/TR, 6'2", 190 lbs. Deb: 9/01/84

YEAR	TM/L	G	AB	R	H	2B	3B	HR	RBI	BB	SO	AVG	OBP	SLG	PRO+	BR	/A	RC	SB	CS	SBR	FA	FR	POS	TPR
1984	Cle-A	7	19	1	3	1	0	0	3	3	5	.158	.273	.211	35	-2	-2	1	0	0	0	.895	-0	/3D	-0.2
1987	NY-A	7	11	0	1	0	0	0	0	0	2	.091	.167	.091	-29	-2	-2	0	0	0	0	1.000	-0	/3SO	-0.2
Total	2	14	30	1	4	1	0	0	3	3	7	.133	.235	.167	12	-4	-4	2	0	0	0	.926	-0	/3OSD	-0.4

■ JOHN MORRILL Morrill, John Francis "Honest John" b: 2/19/1855, Boston, Mass. d: 4/2/32, Boston, Mass. BR/TR, 5'10.5", 155 lbs. Deb: 4/24/1876 M

YEAR	TM/L	G	AB	R	H	2B	3B	HR	RBI	BB	SO	AVG	OBP	SLG	PRO+	BR	/A	RC	SB	CS	SBR	FA	FR	POS	TPR
1876	Bos-N	66	278	38	73	5	2	0	26	3	5	.263	.270	.295	87	-3	-4	23				.857	7	2C/O1	0.3
1877	Bos-N	61	242	47	73	5	1	0	28	6	15	.302	.319	.331	101	1	0	26				.864	-9	31O/2	-0.8
1878	Bos-N	60	233	26	56	5	1	0	23	5	16	.240	.256	.270	68	-7	-9	17				.957	2	*1/O3	-0.8
1879	Bos-N	84	348	56	98	18	5	0	49	14	32	.282	.309	.362	118	8	7	40				.878	3	31	0.8
1880	Bos-N	86	342	51	81	16	8	2	44	11	37	.237	.261	.348	108	1	3	32				.966	0	13/P	0.0
1881	Bos-N	81	311	47	90	19	3	1	39	12	30	.289	.316	.379	123	6	8	38				.969	9	*1/2P3	1.0
1882	Bos-N	83	349	73	101	19	11	2	54	18	29	.289	.324	.424	137	14	14	49				.964	-3	*1/S2O3PM	0.3
1883	Bos-N	97	404	83	129	33	16	6	68	15	68	.319	.344	.525	155	28	26	75				**.974**	-1	*1/O3S2PM	1.5
1884	Bos-N	111	438	80	114	19	7	3	61	30	87	.260	.308	.356	109	4	5	49				.971	3	*12/P3OM	-0.2
1885	Bos-N	111	394	74	89	20	7	4	44	64	78	.226	.334	.343	124	11	13	46				.969	2	*12/3M	0.5
1886	Bos-N	117	430	86	106	25	6	7	69	56	81	.247	.333	.381	121	10	12	59	9			.895	-3	S12/PM	0.5
1887	Bos-N	127	504	79	141	32	6	12	81	37	86	.280	.330	.438	113	8	8	81	19			.984	4	*1M	0.0
1888	Bos-N	135	486	60	96	18	7	4	39	55	68	.198	.282	.288	83	-7	-8	46	21			.979	9	*1/2M	-1.1
1889	Was-N	44	146	20	27	5	0	2	16	30	23	.185	.328	.260	71	-5	-4	17	12			.980	-1	1/32PM	-0.6
1890	Bos-P	2	7	1	1	0	0	0	2	2	1	.143	.333	.143	29	-1	-1	0	0			.750	-1	/S1	-0.1
Total	15	1265	4912	821	1275	239	80	43	643	358	656	.260	.310	.367	112	69	71	599	61			.971	22	132/SOCP	1.3

■ DOYT MORRIS Morris, Doyt Theodore b: 7/15/16, Stanley, N.C. d: 7/4/84, Gastonia, N.C. BR/TR, 6'4", 195 lbs. Deb: 6/06/37

YEAR	TM/L	G	AB	R	H	2B	3B	HR	RBI	BB	SO	AVG	OBP	SLG	PRO+	BR	/A	RC	SB	CS	SBR	FA	FR	POS	TPR
1937	Phi-A	6	13	0	2	0	0	0	0	0	3	.154	.154	.154	-23	-2	-2	0	0	0	0	1.000	-0	/O	-0.2

■ E. MORRIS Morris, E. b: Trenton, N.J. Deb: 9/11/1884

YEAR	TM/L	G	AB	R	H	2B	3B	HR	RBI	BB	SO	AVG	OBP	SLG	PRO+	BR	/A	RC	SB	CS	SBR	FA	FR	POS	TPR
1884	Bal-U	1	3	0	0	0	0	0		0		.000	.000	.000	-91	-1	-1	0				.500	-1	/OP	-0.1

■ JOHN MORRIS Morris, John Daniel b: 2/23/61, N.Bellmore, N.Y. BL/TL, 6'1", 185 lbs. Deb: 8/05/86

YEAR	TM/L	G	AB	R	H	2B	3B	HR	RBI	BB	SO	AVG	OBP	SLG	PRO+	BR	/A	RC	SB	CS	SBR	FA	FR	POS	TPR
1986	StL-N	39	100	8	24	0	1	1	14	7	15	.240	.290	.290	61	-5	-5	8	6	2	1	.986	-1	O	-0.7
1987	*StL-N	101	157	22	41	6	4	3	23	11	22	.261	.314	.408	88	-3	-3	20	5	2	0	.989	-15	O	-1.9
1988	StL-N	20	38	3	11	2	1	0	3	1	7	.289	.308	.395	99	-0	-0	5	0	0	0	.857	-5	O	-0.6
1989	StL-N	96	117	8	28	4	1	2	14	4	22	.239	.264	.342	70	-5	-5	10	1	0	0	1.000	-13	O	-1.9
1990	StL-N	18	18	0	2	0	0	0	0	3	6	.111	.238	.111	-1	-2	-2	1	0	0	0	1.000	-2	/O	-0.4
1991	Phi-N	85	127	15	28	2	1	1	6	12	25	.220	.293	.276	61	-6	-6	11	2	0	1	.974	-10	O	-1.8
1992	Cal-A	43	57	4	11	1	0	1	3	4	11	.193	.258	.263	47	-4	-4	4	1	0	0	1.000	-3	O/D	-0.7
Total	7	402	614	60	145	15	8	8	63	42	108	.236	.288	.326	69	-26	-26	59	15	4	2	.981	-49	O/D	-8.0

■ WALTER MORRIS Morris, John Walter b: 1/31/1880, Rockwall, Tex. d: 8/2/61, Dallas, Tex. BR/TR, 5'11", Deb: 8/31/08

YEAR	TM/L	G	AB	R	H	2B	3B	HR	RBI	BB	SO	AVG	OBP	SLG	PRO+	BR	/A	RC	SB	CS	SBR	FA	FR	POS	TPR
1908	StL-N	23	73	1	13	1	1	0	2	0		.178	.178	.219	28	-6	-6	3	1			.938	4	S	-0.2

■ P. MORRIS Morris, P. b: Rockford, Ill. Deb: 5/14/1884

YEAR	TM/L	G	AB	R	H	2B	3B	HR	RBI	BB	SO	AVG	OBP	SLG	PRO+	BR	/A	RC	SB	CS	SBR	FA	FR	POS	TPR
1884	Was-U	1	3	0	0	0	0	0		0		.000	.000	.000	-99	-1	-1	0				.750	0	/S	0.0

■ HAL MORRIS Morris, William Harold b: 4/9/65, Fort Rucker, Ala. BL/TL, 6'3", 200 lbs. Deb: 7/29/88

YEAR	TM/L	G	AB	R	H	2B	3B	HR	RBI	BB	SO	AVG	OBP	SLG	PRO+	BR	/A	RC	SB	CS	SBR	FA	FR	POS	TPR
1988	NY-A	15	20	1	2	0	0	0	0	0	9	.100	.100	.100	-44	-4	-4	0	0	0	0	1.000	-1	/OD	-0.5
1989	NY-A	15	18	2	5	0	0	0	4	1	4	.278	.316	.278	69	-1	-1	1	0	0	0	1.000	-2	/O1D	-0.2
1990	*Cin-N	107	309	50	105	22	3	7	36	21	32	.340	.384	.498	135	17	15	55	9	3	1	.995	-0	1/O	1.0
1991	Cin-N	136	478	72	152	33	1	14	59	46	61	.318	.379	.479	135	25	23	89	10	4	1	.992	4	*1/O	2.0
1992	Cin-N	115	395	41	107	21	3	6	53	45	53	.271	.348	.385	102	5	2	51	6	6	-2	**.999**	5	*1	-0.1
Total	5	388	1220	166	371	76	7	27	152	113	159	.304	.365	.444	121	42	36	197	25	13	-0	.995	7	1/OD	2.2

■ JIM MORRISON Morrison, James Forrest b: 9/23/52, Pensacola, Fla. BR/TR, 5'11", 182 lbs. Deb: 9/18/77

YEAR	TM/L	G	AB	R	H	2B	3B	HR	RBI	BB	SO	AVG	OBP	SLG	PRO+	BR	/A	RC	SB	CS	SBR	FA	FR	POS	TPR
1977	Phi-N	5	7	3	3	0	0	0	1	1	1	.429	.500	.429	145	1	1	2	0	0	0	.875	1	/3	0.1
1978	*Phi-N	53	108	12	17	1	1	3	10	10	21	.157	.235	.269	40	-9	-9	7	1	1	-0	.968	13	2/3O	0.6
1979	Chi-A	67	240	38	66	14	0	14	35	15	48	.275	.328	.508	122	6	6	41	11	3	2	.982	0	23	1.0
1980	Chi-A	162	604	66	171	40	0	15	57	36	74	.283	.332	.424	106	4	4	80	9	6	-1	.969	-3	*2/SD	1.1
1981	Chi-A	90	290	27	68	8	1	10	34	10	29	.234	.265	.372	84	-8	-7	26	3	2	-0	.956	8	3/2D	-0.1
1982	Chi-A	51	166	17	37	7	3	7	19	13	15	.223	.279	.428	91	-3	-3	18	0	1	-1	.914	-14	3/D	-1.9
	Pit-N	44	86	10	24	4	1	4	15	5	14	.279	.319	.488	119	2	2	12	2	0	1	.964	2	3/O2S	0.4
1983	Pit-N	66	158	16	48	7	2	6	25	9	25	.304	.349	.487	126	6	5	24	2	6	-3	.973	3	23/S	0.6
1984	Pit-N	100	304	38	87	14	2	11	45	20	52	.286	.332	.454	119	7	7	43	0	1	-1	.938	0	32/S1	0.7
1985	Pit-N	92	244	17	62	10	0	4	22	8	44	.254	.281	.344	75	-9	-9	23	3	0	1	.961	1	32/O	-0.8
1986	Pit-N	154	537	58	147	35	4	23	88	47	88	.274	.337	.482	120	15	14	86	9	8	-2	.946	-13	*3/2S	-0.5
1987	Pit-N	96	348	41	92	22	1	9	46	27	57	.264	.319	.411	91	-5	-5	44	8	5	-1	.975	1	3S/2	-0.5
	*Det-A	34	117	15	24	1	1	4	19	2	26	.205	.225	.333	47	-9	-9	9	2	1	0	.962	3	3/2SO1D	-0.6
1988	Det-A	24	74	7	16	5	0	0	6	0	14	.216	.216	.284	40	-6	-6	3	0	2	-1	1.000	-0	D/13OS	-0.8
	Atl-N	51	92	6	14	2	0	2	13	10	13	.152	.235	.239	35	-8	-8	5	0	1	-1	.933	0	3/OP	-0.9
Total	12	1089	3375	371	876	170	16	112	435	213	521	.260	.308	.419	98	-16	-17	424	50	37	-7	.949	1	32/SDO1P	-1.6

■ JON MORRISON Morrison, Jonathan W. b: 1859, Port Huron, Mich. Deb: 8/01/1884

YEAR	TM/L	G	AB	R	H	2B	3B	HR	RBI	BB	SO	AVG	OBP	SLG	PRO+	BR	/A	RC	SB	CS	SBR	FA	FR	POS	TPR
1884	Ind-a	44	182	26	48	6	8	1		7		.264	.306	.401	135	6	7	23				.784	3	O	0.8
1887	NY-a	9	34	7	4	0	0	0		6		.118	.268	.118	12	-4	-3	1	0			.600	-4	/O	-0.6
Total	2	53	216	33	52	6	8	1		13		.241	.299	.356	113	2	3	24	0			.756	-1	/O	0.2

■ TOM MORRISON Morrison, Thomas J. b: 1875, St.Louis, Mo. 5'3", 145 lbs. Deb: 9/18/1895

YEAR	TM/L	G	AB	R	H	2B	3B	HR	RBI	BB	SO	AVG	OBP	SLG	PRO+	BR	/A	RC	SB	CS	SBR	FA	FR	POS	TPR
1895	Lou-N	6	22	3	6	0	2	0	4	1	1	.273	.304	.455	102	-0	-0	3	0			1.000	-2	/S3	-0.2
1896	Lou-N	8	27	3	4	1	0	0	0	4	4	.148	.258	.185	20	-3	-3	1	0			.864	-1	/3OS	-0.3
Total	2	14	49	6	10	1	2	0	4	5	5	.204	.278	.306	57	-3	-3	5	0			.839	-3	/3SO	-0.5

■ JACK MORRISSEY Morrissey, John Albert "King" b: 5/2/1876, Lansing, Mich. d: 10/30/36, Lansing, Mich. BB/TR, 5'10", 160 lbs. Deb: 9/18/02

YEAR	TM/L	G	AB	R	H	2B	3B	HR	RBI	BB	SO	AVG	OBP	SLG	PRO+	BR	/A	RC	SB	CS	SBR	FA	FR	POS	TPR
1902	Cin-N	12	39	5	11	1	1	0	3	4		.282	.349	.359	108	1	0	5	0			.941	-2	2/O	-0.1
1903	Cin-N	29	89	14	22	1	0	0	9	14		.247	.350	.258	67	-2	-4	10	3			.922	-10	2/OS	-1.4
Total	2	41	128	19	33	2	1	0	12	18		.258	.349	.289	79	-1	-3	15	3			.930	-12	/2OS	-1.5

■ JOHN MORRISSEY Morrissey, John J. b: 1856, Janesville, Wis. d: 4/29/1884, Janesville, Wis. Deb: 5/02/1881 F

YEAR	TM/L	G	AB	R	H	2B	3B	HR	RBI	BB	SO	AVG	OBP	SLG	PRO+	BR	/A	RC	SB	CS	SBR	FA	FR	POS	TPR
1881	Buf-N	12	47	3	10	2	0	0	3	0	3	.213	.213	.255	47	-3	-3	3				.865	-2	3	-0.4
1882	Det-N	2	7	1	2	0	0	0	0	0	2	.286	.286	.286	84	-0	-0	1				.714	-1	/3	-0.1
Total	2	14	54	4	12	2	0	0	3	0	5	.222	.222	.259	52	-3	-3	3				.841	-3	/3	-0.5

■ JO-JO MORRISSEY Morrissey, Joseph Anselm b: 1/16/04, Warren, R.I. d: 5/2/50, Worcester, Mass. BR/TR, 6'1.5", 178 lbs. Deb: 4/12/32

YEAR	TM/L	G	AB	R	H	2B	3B	HR	RBI	BB	SO	AVG	OBP	SLG	PRO+	BR	/A	RC	SB	CS	SBR	FA	FR	POS	TPR
1932	Cin-N	89	269	15	65	10	1	0	13	14	15	.242	.282	.286	55	-17	-16	22	2			.967	8	S23/O	-0.3
1933	Cin-N	148	534	43	123	20	0	0	26	20	22	.230	.261	.268	52	-34	-33	35	5			.964	-9	2S3	-3.5
1936	Chi-A	17	38	3	7	1	0	0	6	2	3	.184	.225	.211	8	-6	-6	2	0	0	0	.895	0	/3S2	-0.5
Total	3	254	841	61	195	31	1	0	45	36	40	.232	.266	.271	51	-57	-55	59	7	0		.971	-0	2S/3O	-4.3

■ TOM MORRISSEY Morrissey, Thomas J. b: 1861, Janesville, Wis. d: 9/23/41, Janesville, Wis. Deb: 9/27/1884 F

YEAR	TM/L	G	AB	R	H	2B	3B	HR	RBI	BB	SO	AVG	OBP	SLG	PRO+	BR	/A	RC	SB	CS	SBR	FA	FR	POS	TPR
1884	Mil-U	12	47	3	8	2	0	0		0		.170	.170	.213	53	-3	-0	2				.710	-1	3	-0.1

■ BUD MORSE Morse, Newell Obediah b: 9/4/04, Berkeley, Cal. d: 4/6/87, Sparks, Nev. BL/TR, 5'9", 150 lbs. Deb: 9/14/29

YEAR	TM/L	G	AB	R	H	2B	3B	HR	RBI	BB	SO	AVG	OBP	SLG	PRO+	BR	/A	RC	SB	CS	SBR	FA	FR	POS	TPR
1929	Phi-A	8	27	1	2	0	0	0	0	0	2	.074	.074	.074	-60	-6	-7	0	0	0	0	.975	2	/2	-0.4

■ HAP MORSE Morse, Peter Raymond "Pete" b: 12/6/1886, St.Paul, Minn. d: 6/19/74, St.Paul, Minn. BR/TR, 5'8", 160 lbs. Deb: 4/18/11

YEAR	TM/L	G	AB	R	H	2B	3B	HR	RBI	BB	SO	AVG	OBP	SLG	PRO+	BR	/A	RC	SB	CS	SBR	FA	FR	POS	TPR
1911	StL-N	4	8	0	0	0	0	0	0	1	2	.000	.111	.000	-70	-2	-2	0	0			.750	-0	/SO	-0.2

■ CHARLIE MORTON Morton, Charles Hazen b: 10/12/1854, Kingsville, Ohio d: 12/9/21, Massillon, Ohio TR , Deb: 5/02/1882 MU

YEAR	TM/L	G	AB	R	H	2B	3B	HR	RBI	BB	SO	AVG	OBP	SLG	PRO+	BR	/A	RC	SB	CS	SBR	FA	FR	POS	TPR
1882	Pit-a	25	103	12	29	0	3	0		5		.282	.315	.340	127	2	3	11				.816	1	O/3S	0.4
	StL-a	9	32	2	2	0	1	0		2		.063	.118	.125	-17	-4	-4	0				.708	-4	/2O	-0.8
	Yr	34	135	14	31	0	4	0		7		.230	.268	.289	90	-2	-1	11				.821	-3	O/23S	-0.4
1884	Tol-a	32	111	11	18	6	2	0		7		.162	.212	.252	51	-5	-6	6				.861	-1	3O/P2M	-0.5
1885	Det-N	22	79	9	14	1	2	0	3	5	10	.177	.226	.241	51	-4	-4	4				.750	2	3/SM	-0.2
Total	3	88	325	34	63	7	8	0	3	19	10	.194	.238	.265	66	-11	-11	22				.841	-3	/O32SP	-1.1

■ GUY MORTON Morton, Guy Jr. "Moose" b: 11/4/30, Tuscaloosa, Ala. BR/TR, 6'2", 200 lbs. Deb: 9/17/54 F

YEAR	TM/L	G	AB	R	H	2B	3B	HR	RBI	BB	SO	AVG	OBP	SLG	PRO+	BR	/A	RC	SB	CS	SBR	FA	FR	POS	TPR
1954	Bos-A	1	1	0	0	0	0	0	0	0	1	.000	.000	.000	-90	-0	-0	0	0	0	0	.000	0	H	0.0

■ BUBBA MORTON Morton, Wycliffe Nathaniel b: 12/13/31, Washington, D.C. BR/TR, 5'10.5", 180 lbs. Deb: 4/19/61

YEAR	TM/L	G	AB	R	H	2B	3B	HR	RBI	BB	SO	AVG	OBP	SLG	PRO+	BR	/A	RC	SB	CS	SBR	FA	FR	POS	TPR
1961	Det-A	77	108	26	31	5	1	2	19	9	25	.287	.347	.407	98	0	-0	16	3	1	0	.952	-4	O	-0.5
1962	Det-A	90	195	30	51	6	3	4	17	32	32	.262	.366	.385	99	1	1	28	1	1	-0	.991	-2	O/1	-0.4
1963	Det-A	6	11	2	1	0	0	0	2	2	1	.091	.231	.091	-5	-2	-2	0	0	0	0	.875	-0	/O	-0.2
	Mil-N	15	28	1	5	0	0	0	4	2	3	.179	.258	.179	28	-2	-2	1	0	0	0	1.000	0	/O	-0.3
1966	Cal-A	15	50	4	11	1	0	0	4	2	6	.220	.250	.240	43	-4	-4	3	1	1	-0	1.000	0	O	-0.4
1967	Cal-A	80	201	23	63	9	3	0	32	22	29	.313	.387	.388	135	8	9	29	0	3	-2	1.000	-6	O	-0.2
1968	Cal-A	81	163	13	44	6	0	1	18	14	18	.270	.343	.325	107	1	2	18	2	1	0	.985	-4	O/3	-0.5

YEAR	TM/L	G	AB	R	H	2B	3B	HR	RBI	BB	SO	AVG	OBP	SLG	PRO+	BR	/A	RC	SB	CS	SBR	FA	FR	POS	TPR
1969	Cal-A	87	172	18	42	10	1	7	32	28	29	.244	.360	.436	128	5	6	28	0	0	0	1.000	-0	O/1	0.4
Total	7	451	928	117	248	37	8	14	128	111	143	.267	.352	.370	106	8	10	124	7	7	-2	.988	-16	O/13	-2.1

■ WALT MORYN Moryn, Walter Joseph "Moose" b: 4/12/26, St.Paul, Minn. BL/TR, 6'2", 205 lbs. Deb: 6/29/54

YEAR	TM/L	G	AB	R	H	2B	3B	HR	RBI	BB	SO	AVG	OBP	SLG	PRO+	BR	/A	RC	SB	CS	SBR	FA	FR	POS	TPR
1954	Bro-N	48	91	16	25	4	2	2	14	7	11	.275	.333	.429	94	-1	-1	13	0	0	0	.881	-0	O	-0.2
1955	Bro-N	11	19	3	5	1	0	1	3	5	4	.263	.417	.474	132	1	1	4	0	0	0	.833	-2	/O	-0.1
1956	Chi-N	147	529	69	151	27	3	23	67	50	67	.285	.351	.478	122	14	16	89	4	2	0	.983	10	*O	1.8
1957	Chi-N	149	568	76	164	33	0	19	88	50	90	.289	.349	.447	114	10	11	88	0	2	-1	.960	7	*O	0.8
1958	Chi-N☆	143	512	77	135	26	7	26	77	62	83	.264	.352	.494	123	15	16	91	1	2	-1	.978	5	*O	1.3
1959	Chi-N	117	381	41	89	14	1	14	48	44	66	.234	.318	.386	87	-8	-7	46	0	0	0	.989	0	*O	-1.2
1960	Chi-N	38	109	12	32	4	0	2	11	13	19	.294	.369	.385	108	1	2	16	2	1	0	.964	0	O	0.1
	StL-N	75	200	24	49	4	3	11	35	17	38	.245	.304	.460	97	1	-1	26	0	0	0	.990	-3	O	-0.7
	Yr	113	309	36	81	8	3	13	46	30	57	.262	.327	.434	101	2	0	43	2	1	0	.981	-3	O	-0.6
1961	StL-N	17	32	0	4	2	0	0	2	1	5	.125	.152	.188	-10	-5	-5	1	0	0	0	.889	-1	/O	-0.7
	Pit-N	40	65	6	13	1	0	3	9	2	10	.200	.235	.354	53	-5	-5	4	0	0	0	.950	1	O	-0.4
	Yr	57	97	6	17	3	0	3	11	3	15	.175	.208	.299	31	-10	-10	4	0	0	0	.931	-0	O	-1.1
Total	8	785	2506	324	667	116	16	101	354	251	393	.266	.338	.446	108	25	26	377	7	7	-2	.972	18	O	0.7

■ ROSS MOSCHITTO Moschitto, Rosaire Allen b: 2/15/45, Fresno, Cal. BR/TR, 6'2", 175 lbs. Deb: 4/15/65

YEAR	TM/L	G	AB	R	H	2B	3B	HR	RBI	BB	SO	AVG	OBP	SLG	PRO+	BR	/A	RC	SB	CS	SBR	FA	FR	POS	TPR
1965	NY-A	96	27	12	5	0	0	1	3	0	12	.185	.185	.296	35	-2	-2	2	0	0	0	.941	-26	O	-3.1
1967	NY-A	14	9	1	1	0	0	0	0	1	2	.111	.200	.111	-6	-1	-1	0	0	0	0	1.000	-2	/O	-0.4
Total	2	110	36	13	6	0	0	1	3	1	14	.167	.189	.250	25	-4	-3	2	0	0	0	.944	-28	/O	-3.5

■ LLOYD MOSEBY Moseby, Lloyd Anthony b: 11/5/59, Portland, Ark. BL/TR, 6'3", 200 lbs. Deb: 5/24/80

YEAR	TM/L	G	AB	R	H	2B	3B	HR	RBI	BB	SO	AVG	OBP	SLG	PRO+	BR	/A	RC	SB	CS	SBR	FA	FR	POS	TPR
1980	Tor-A	114	389	44	89	24	1	9	46	25	85	.229	.282	.365	73	-14	-16	37	4	6	-2	.982	6	*O/D	-1.7
1981	Tor-A	100	378	36	88	16	2	9	43	24	86	.233	.280	.357	78	-9	-12	37	11	8	-2	.989	3	*O	-1.5
1982	Tor-A	147	487	51	115	20	9	9	52	33	106	.236	.295	.370	74	-13	-19	52	11	7	-1	.992	-1	*O	-2.4
1983	Tor-A	151	539	104	170	31	7	18	81	51	85	.315	.380	.499	132	29	25	104	27	8	3	.983	10	*O	3.3
1984	Tor-A	158	592	97	166	28	**15**	18	92	78	122	.280	.372	.470	126	26	23	110	39	9	6	.990	17	*O	4.1
1985	*Tor-A	152	584	92	151	30	7	18	70	76	91	.259	.348	.426	108	9	7	89	37	15	2	.980	1	*O	0.5
1986	Tor-A★	152	589	89	149	24	5	21	86	64	122	.253	.332	.418	100	2	0	86	32	11	3	.984	3	*O/D	0.1
1987	Tor-A	155	592	106	167	27	4	26	96	70	124	.282	.360	.473	116	16	14	106	39	7	8	.980	-8	*O/D	0.8
1988	Tor-A	128	472	77	113	17	7	10	42	70	93	.239	.345	.369	99	2	1	66	31	8	5	.984	-6	*O/D	-0.4
1989	*Tor-A	135	502	72	111	25	3	11	43	56	101	.221	.307	.349	86	-10	-9	58	24	7	3	.986	-3	*OD	-1.3
1990	Det-A	122	431	64	107	16	5	14	51	48	77	.248	.331	.406	104	3	2	57	17	5	2	.983	8	*O/D	1.0
1991	Det-A	74	260	37	68	15	1	6	35	21	43	.262	.324	.396	97	-1	-1	35	8	1	2	.955	-1	O/D	-0.2
Total	12	1588	5815	869	1494	273	66	169	737	616	1135	.257	.334	.414	102	40	16	836	280	92	29	.984	28	*O/D	2.3

■ ARNIE MOSER Moser, Arnold Robert b: 8/9/15, Houston, Tex. BR/TR, 5'11", 165 lbs. Deb: 6/20/37

YEAR	TM/L	G	AB	R	H	2B	3B	HR	RBI	BB	SO	AVG	OBP	SLG	PRO+	BR	/A	RC	SB	CS	SBR	FA	FR	POS	TPR
1937	Cin-N	5	5	0	0	0	0	0	0	0	2	.000	.000	.000	-99	-1	-1	0	0			.000	0	H	-0.1

■ JERRY MOSES Moses, Gerald Braheen b: 8/9/46, Yazoo City, Miss. BR/TR, 6'3", 210 lbs. Deb: 5/09/65

YEAR	TM/L	G	AB	R	H	2B	3B	HR	RBI	BB	SO	AVG	OBP	SLG	PRO+	BR	/A	RC	SB	CS	SBR	FA	FR	POS	TPR
1965	Bos-A	4	4	1	1	0	0	1	1	0	2	.250	.250	1.000	224	1	1	1	0	0	0	.000	0	H	0.1
1968	Bos-A	6	18	2	6	0	0	2	4	1	4	.333	.368	.667	196	2	2	3	0	1	-1	.963	-3	/C	-0.1
1969	Bos-A	53	135	13	41	9	1	4	17	5	23	.304	.333	.474	117	4	3	21	0	1	-1	.981	-5	C	-0.2
1970	Bos-A☆	92	315	26	83	18	1	6	35	21	45	.263	.314	.384	85	-4	-7	37	1	1	-0	.990	2	C/O	-0.1
1971	Cal-A	69	181	12	41	8	2	4	15	10	34	.227	.267	.359	82	-6	-5	15	0	0	0	.977	5	C/O	0.2
1972	Cle-A	52	141	9	31	3	0	4	14	11	29	.220	.290	.326	81	-3	-3	14	0	0	0	.982	1	C/1	-0.2
1973	NY-A	21	59	5	15	2	0	0	3	2	6	.254	.279	.288	62	-3	-3	4	0	0	0	1.000	5	C/D	0.3
1974	Det-A	74	198	19	47	6	3	4	19	11	38	.237	.284	.359	81	-5	-5	19	0	1	-1	.985	0	C	-0.3
1975	SD-N	13	19	1	3	2	0	0	1	2	3	.158	.238	.263	42	-2	-1	1	0	0	0	.900	-1	/C	-0.2
	Chi-A	2	2	1	1	0	1	0	0	0	0	.500	.500	1.500	441	1	1	2	0	0	0	1.000	-0	/1D	0.1
Total	9	386	1072	89	269	48	8	25	109	63	184	.251	.297	.381	89	-16	-19	116	1	4	-2	.984	3	C/1DO	-0.4

■ JOHN MOSES Moses, John William b: 8/9/57, Los Angeles, Cal. BB/TL, 5'10", 170 lbs. Deb: 8/23/82

YEAR	TM/L	G	AB	R	H	2B	3B	HR	RBI	BB	SO	AVG	OBP	SLG	PRO+	BR	/A	RC	SB	CS	SBR	FA	FR	POS	TPR
1982	Sea-A	22	44	7	14	5	1	1	3	4	5	.318	.375	.545	145	3	3	10	5	1	1	.947	-4	O	-0.1
1983	Sea-A	93	130	19	27	4	1	0	6	12	20	.208	.280	.254	46	-9	-10	9	11	5	0	.979	-9	OD	-1.9
1984	Sea-A	19	35	3	12	1	1	0	2	2	5	.343	.395	.429	129	1	1	6	1	0	0	1.000	-4	O/D	-0.3
1985	Sea-A	33	62	4	12	0	0	0	3	2	8	.194	.219	.194	14	-7	-7	2	5	2	0	1.000	-7	O	-1.5
1986	Sea-A	103	399	56	102	16	3	3	34	34	65	.256	.314	.333	76	-13	-13	40	25	18	-3	.987	2	O/1D	-1.8
1987	Sea-A	116	390	58	96	16	4	3	38	29	49	.246	.303	.331	65	-18	-21	38	23	15	-2	.987	-2	*O/1D	-2.7
1988	Min-A	105	206	33	65	10	3	2	12	15	21	.316	.368	.422	117	6	5	31	11	6	-0	1.000	-14	O/D	-1.1
1989	Min-A	129	242	33	68	12	3	1	31	19	23	.281	.336	.368	92	-1	-3	30	14	7	0	.988	-24	*O/1PD	-2.9
1990	Min-A	115	172	26	38	3	1	1	14	19	19	.221	.306	.267	58	-8	-10	14	2	3	-1	1.000	-17	OD/1P	-3.0
1991	Det-A	13	21	5	1	1	0	0	1	2	7	.048	.130	.095	-36	-4	-4	1	4	0	1	1.000	-2	O	-0.5
1992	Sea-A	21	22	3	3	1	0	0	1	5	4	.136	.296	.182	36	-2	-2	2	0	0	0	1.000	-4	O	-0.7
Total	11	769	1723	247	438	69	17	11	145	143	226	.254	.315	.333	75	-51	-59	183	101	57	-4	.990	-86	O/D1P	-16.5

■ WALLY MOSES Moses, Wallace b: 10/8/10, Uvalda, Ga. d: 10/10/90, Vidalia, Ga. BL/TL, 5'10", 160 lbs. Deb: 4/17/35 C

YEAR	TM/L	G	AB	R	H	2B	3B	HR	RBI	BB	SO	AVG	OBP	SLG	PRO+	BR	/A	RC	SB	CS	SBR	FA	FR	POS	TPR
1935	Phi-A	85	345	60	112	21	3	5	35	25	18	.325	.375	.446	113	6	6	57	3	4	-2	.943	0	O	0.2
1936	Phi-A	146	585	98	202	35	11	7	66	62	32	.345	.410	.479	121	18	20	117	12	6	0	.974	3	*O	1.5
1937	Phi-A☆	154	649	113	208	48	13	25	86	54	38	.320	.374	.550	132	27	28	132	9	7	-2	.958	6	*O	2.5
1938	Phi-A	142	589	86	181	29	8	8	49	58	31	.307	.369	.424	101	-2	1	95	15	5	2	.966	5	*O	0.2
1939	Phi-A	115	437	68	134	28	7	3	33	44	23	.307	.370	.423	105	2	3	71	7	4	-0	.965	-1	*O	-0.1
1940	Phi-A	142	537	91	166	41	9	9	50	75	44	.309	.396	.469	126	20	22	108	6	4	-1	.974	4	*O	1.7
1941	Phi-A	116	438	78	132	31	4	4	35	62	27	.301	.388	.418	116	10	11	76	3	3	-1	.975	9	*O	1.2
1942	Chi-A	146	577	73	156	28	4	7	49	74	27	.270	.353	.369	106	4	5	81	16	10	-1	.980	7	*O	0.3
1943	Chi-A	150	599	82	147	22	**12**	3	48	55	47	.245	.310	.337	89	-9	-9	69	56	14	8	.979	9	*O	0.1
1944	Chi-A	136	535	82	150	26	9	3	34	52	22	.280	.345	.379	108	5	6	77	21	7	2	.975	-2	*O	-0.2
1945	Chi-A	140	569	79	168	**35**	15	2	50	69	33	.295	.373	.420	134	22	24	97	11	5	0	.977	9	*O	2.7
1946	Chi-A	56	168	20	46	9	1	4	16	17	20	.274	.344	.411	115	2	3	24	2	2	-1	1.000	-1	O	0.0
	*Bos-A	48	175	23	36	11	3	2	17	14	15	.206	.268	.337	65	-8	-9	16	2	4	-2	.979	0	O	-1.4
	Yr	104	343	43	82	20	4	6	33	31	35	.239	.306	.373	88	-6	-6	40	4	6	-2	.989	-0	O	-1.4
1947	Bos-A	90	255	32	70	18	2	2	27	27	16	.275	.344	.384	95	1	-2	35	3	0	1	.974	-3	O	-0.7
1948	Bos-A	78	189	26	49	12	1	2	29	21	19	.259	.340	.365	83	-4	-5	27	5	0	2	.981	1	O	-0.4
1949	Phi-A	110	308	49	85	19	3	1	25	51	19	.276	.381	.367	102	1	2	48	1	3	-2	.983	-3	O	-0.6
1950	Phi-A	88	265	47	70	16	5	2	21	40	17	.264	.365	.385	94	-3	-2	40	0	1	-1	.987	5	O	0.0
1951	Phi-A	70	136	17	26	6	0	0	9	21	9	.191	.304	.235	46	-10	-10	10	2	2	-1	.984	2	O	-0.9
Total	17	2012	7356	1124	2138	435	110	89	679	821	457	.291	.364	.416	109	81	94	1179	174	81	4	.973	51	*O	6.1

■ DOC MOSKIMAN Moskiman, William Bankhead b: 12/20/1879, Oakland, Cal. d: 1/11/53, San Leandro, Cal. BR/TR, 6', 170 lbs. Deb: 8/23/10

YEAR	TM/L	G	AB	R	H	2B	3B	HR	RBI	BB	SO	AVG	OBP	SLG	PRO+	BR	/A	RC	SB	CS	SBR	FA	FR	POS	TPR
1910	Bos-A	5	9	1	1	0	0	0	1	2		.111	.273	.111	20	-1	-1	0	0			1.000	0	/1O	0.0

■ JIM MOSOLF Mosolf, James Frederick b: 8/21/05, Puyallup, Wash. d: 12/28/79, Dallasyore. BL/TR, 5'10", 186 lbs. Deb: 9/09/29

YEAR	TM/L	G	AB	R	H	2B	3B	HR	RBI	BB	SO	AVG	OBP	SLG	PRO+	BR	/A	RC	SB	CS	SBR	FA	FR	POS	TPR
1929	Pit-N	8	13	3	6	1	1	0	2	1	1	.462	.500	.692	188	2	2	4	0			1.000	0	/O	0.2

YEAR	TM/L	G	AB	R	H	2B	3B	HR	RBI	BB	SO	AVG	OBP	SLG	PRO+	BR	/A	RC	SB	CS	SBR	FA	FR	POS	TPR
1930	Pit-N	40	51	16	17	2	1	0	9	8	7	.333	.424	.412	103	1	1	9	0			.765	-3	O/P	-0.3
1931	Pit-N	39	44	7	11	1	0	1	8	8	5	.250	.365	.341	92	-0	-0	6	0			1.000	-1	/O	-0.1
1933	Chi-N	31	82	13	22	5	1	1	9	5	8	.268	.326	.390	104	0	0	11	0			.964	1	O	0.0
Total	4	118	190	39	56	9	3	2	28	22	21	.295	.374	.405	107	3	3	31	0			.929	-4	/OP	-0.2
■ CHARLIE MOSS	Moss, Charles Crosby b: 3/20/11, Meridian, Miss. BR/TR, 5'10", 160 lbs. Deb: 5/19/34																								
1934	Phi-A	10	10	3	2	0	0	0	1	0	0	.200	.200	.200	4	-1	-1	0	0	0	0	1.000	-1	/C	-0.2
1935	Phi-A	4	3	1	1	0	0	0	1	1	0	.333	.500	.333	120	0	0	1	0	0	0	.000	0	/C	0.0
1936	Phi-A	33	44	2	11	1	1	0	10	6	5	.250	.340	.318	65	-2	-2	5	1	0	0	.929	-2	C	-0.3
Total	3	47	57	6	14	1	1	0	12	7	5	.246	.328	.298	58	-4	-3	6	1	0	0	.935	-2	/C	-0.5
■ HOWIE MOSS	Moss, Howard Glenn b: 10/17/19, Gastonia, N.C. d: 5/7/89, Baltimore, Md. BR/TR, 5'11.5", 185 lbs. Deb: 4/14/42																								
1942	NY-N	7	14	0	0	0	0	0	0	0	4	.000	.000	.000	-99	-3	-3	0	0			1.000	0	/O	-0.4
1946	Cin-N	7	26	1	5	0	0	0	1	0	4	.192	.222	.192	19	-3	-3	1	0			1.000	0	/O	-0.3
	Cle-A	8	32	2	2	0	0	0	0	3	9	.063	.143	.063	-44	-6	-6	0	0	1	-1	.857	0	/3	-0.7
Total	2	22	72	3	7	0	0	0	1	3	17	.097	.145	.097	-32	-12	-12	1	0	1		1.000	0	/O3	-1.4
■ LES MOSS	Moss, John Lester b: 5/14/25, Tulsa, Okla. BR/TR, 5'11", 205 lbs. Deb: 9/10/46 MC																								
1946	StL-A	12	35	4	13	3	0	0	5	3	5	.371	.436	.457	142	2	2	8	1	0	0	.968	1	C	0.4
1947	StL-A	96	274	17	43	5	2	6	27	35	48	.157	.255	.255	41	-22	-23	20	0	0	0	.983	-5	C	-2.3
1948	StL-A	107	335	35	86	12	1	14	46	39	50	.257	.334	.424	98	-1	-2	46	0	0	0	.988	-9	*C	-0.4
1949	StL-A	97	278	28	81	11	0	10	39	49	32	.291	.399	.439	117	10	8	51	0	1	-1	.970	-5	C	0.7
1950	StL-A	84	222	24	59	6	0	8	34	26	32	.266	.343	.401	87	-4	-5	30	0	1	-1	.957	-1	C	-0.4
1951	StL-A	16	47	5	8	2	0	1	7	6	8	.170	.264	.277	45	-4	-4	3	0	0	0	.967	-0	C	-0.4
	Bos-A	71	202	18	40	6	0	3	26	25	34	.198	.289	.272	48	-13	-16	16	0	0	0	.984	-1	C	-1.4
	Yr	87	249	23	48	8	0	4	33	31	42	.193	.285	.273	47	-17	-20	19	0	0	0	.981	-1	C	-1.8
1952	StL-A	52	118	11	29	3	0	3	12	15	13	.246	.331	.347	86	-2	-2	13	0	1	-1	.957	-3	C	-0.5
1953	StL-A	78	239	21	66	14	1	2	28	18	31	.276	.329	.368	86	-4	-5	27	0	1	-1	.978	-6	C	-0.8
1954	Bal-A	50	126	7	31	3	0	0	5	14	16	.246	.321	.270	68	-6	-5	11	0	0	0	.972	-2	C	-0.5
1955	Bal-A	29	56	5	19	1	0	2	6	7	4	.339	.413	.464	146	3	3	10	0	1	-1	1.000	2	C	0.5
	Chi-A	32	59	5	15	2	0	2	7	6	10	.254	.333	.390	91	-1	-1	8	0	0	0	.990	-0	C	0.0
	Yr	61	115	10	34	3	0	4	13	13	14	.296	.372	.426	116	2	3	19	0	1	-1	.994	2	C	0.5
1956	Chi-A	56	127	20	31	4	0	10	22	18	15	.244	.338	.512	120	3	3	20	0	0	0	.994	-6	C	-0.2
1957	Chi-A	42	115	10	31	3	0	2	12	20	18	.270	.378	.348	99	1	1	16	0	0	0	.980	-7	C	-0.5
1958	Chi-A	2	1	0	0	0	0	0	0	1	0	.000	.500	.000	51	0	0	0	0	0	0	.000	0	H	0.0
Total	13	824	2234	210	552	75	4	63	276	282	316	.247	.333	.369	86	-37	-45	280	1	5	-3	.978	-42	C	-5.8
■ JOHNNY MOSTIL	Mostil, John Anthony "Bananas" b: 6/1/1896, Chicago, Ill. d: 12/10/70, Midlothian, Ill. BR/TR, 5'8.5", 168 lbs. Deb: 6/20/18																								
1918	Chi-A	10	33	4	9	2	2	0	4	1	6	.273	.294	.455	125	1	1	4	1			.923	-2	/2	-0.1
1921	Chi-A	100	326	43	98	21	7	3	42	28	35	.301	.379	.436	109	4	5	53	10	12	-4	.946	0	O/2	-0.5
1922	Chi-A	132	458	74	139	28	14	7	70	38	39	.303	.375	.472	120	12	13	81	14	10	-2	.966	5	*O	0.7
1923	Chi-A	153	546	91	159	37	15	3	64	62	51	.291	.376	.430	113	10	11	92	41	17	**2**	.974	22	*O/3S	2.5
1924	Chi-A	118	385	75	125	22	5	4	49	45	41	.325	.401	.439	120	10	12	67	7	11	-5	.974	7	*O	0.8
1925	Chi-A	153	605	**135**	181	36	16	2	50	**90**	52	.299	.400	.421	115	11	16	108	**43**	21	0	**.985**	7	*O	1.2
1926	Chi-A	148	600	120	197	41	15	4	42	79	55	.328	.415	.467	134	28	31	122	**35**	14	**2**	.968	17	*O	3.9
1927	Chi-A	13	16	3	2	0	0	0	1	0	1	.125	.176	.125	-21	-3	-3	0	1	0	0	.857	-2	/O	-0.4
1928	Chi-A	133	503	69	136	19	8	0	51	66	54	.270	.360	.340	86	-9	-8	63	23	21	-6	.976	18	*O	-0.5
1929	Chi-A	12	35	4	8	3	0	0	3	6	2	.229	.341	.314	71	-1	-1	4	1	1	-0	.963	-1	O	-0.3
Total	10	972	3507	618	1054	209	82	23	376	415	336	.301	.386	.427	113	63	76	595	176	107		.971	72	O/23S	7.3
■ ANDY MOTA	Mota, Andres Alberto (Matos) b: 3/4/66, Santo Domingo, D.R. BR/TR, 5'10", 180 lbs. Deb: 8/31/91 F																								
1991	Hou-N	27	90	4	17	2	0	1	6	1	17	.189	.198	.244	25	-9	-9	5	2	0	1	.970	-3	2	-1.1
■ JOSE MOTA	Mota, Jose Manuel (Matos) b: 3/16/65, Santo Domingo, D.R. BB/TR, 5'9", 155 lbs. Deb: 5/25/91 F																								
1991	SD-N	17	36	4	8	0	0	0	2	2	7	.222	.282	.222	42	-3	-3	3	0	0	0	.962	0	2/S	-0.2
■ MANNY MOTA	Mota, Manuel Rafael (Geronimo) b: 2/18/38, Santo Domingo, D.R. BR/TR, 5'11", 168 lbs. Deb: 4/16/62 FC																								
1962	SF-N	47	74	9	13	1	0	0	9	7	8	.176	.256	.189	22	-8	-8	4	3	2	-0	1.000	4	O/32	-0.5
1963	Pit-N	59	126	20	34	2	3	0	7	7	18	.270	.313	.333	86	-2	-2	12	0	2	-1	.953	-4	O/2	-0.9
1964	Pit-N	115	271	43	75	8	3	5	32	10	31	.277	.310	.384	94	-2	-2	32	4	1	1	.961	-9	O/C2	-1.5
1965	Pit-N	121	294	47	82	7	6	4	29	22	32	.279	.333	.384	101	1	0	37	2	2	-1	.985	-1	O	-0.4
1966	Pit-N	116	322	54	107	16	7	5	46	25	28	.332	.387	.472	137	17	17	57	7	7	-2	.994	-2	O/3	0.9
1967	Pit-N	120	349	53	112	14	8	4	56	14	46	.321	.351	.441	125	11	10	52	3	2	-0	.988	-2	O/3	0.4
1968	Pit-N	111	331	35	93	10	2	1	33	20	19	.281	.324	.332	99	-1	-1	36	4	2	0	.981	-5	O/23	-1.1
1969	Mon-N	31	89	6	28	1	1	0	0	6	11	.315	.358	.348	98	-0	-0	10	1	3	-2	.907	-2	O	-0.5
	LA-N	85	294	35	95	6	4	3	30	26	25	.323	.380	.401	128	8	11	45	5	4	-1	.969	-3	O	0.2
	Yr	116	383	41	123	7	5	3	30	32	36	.321	.375	.389	120	8	10	55	6	7	-2	.954	-5	*O	-0.3
1970	LA-N	124	417	63	127	12	6	3	37	47	37	.305	.379	.384	110	4	7	61	11	6	-0	.973	-6	*O/3	-0.5
1971	LA-N	91	269	24	84	13	5	0	34	20	20	.312	.362	.398	122	5	7	37	4	3	-1	.965	-9	O	-0.6
1972	LA-N	118	371	57	120	16	5	5	48	27	15	.323	.377	.434	133	15	16	58	4	4	-1	.993	-11	O	0.0
1973	LA-N★	89	293	33	92	11	2	0	23	25	12	.314	.370	.365	109	2	4	37	1	3	-2	1.000	-10	O	-1.1
1974	*LA-N	66	57	5	16	2	0	0	16	5	4	.281	.349	.316	91	-1	-0	7	0	0	0	1.000	-1	/O	-0.1
1975	LA-N	52	49	3	13	1	0	0	10	5	1	.265	.357	.286	84	-1	-1	5	0	0	0	1.000	1	/O	0.0
1976	LA-N	50	52	1	15	3	0	0	13	7	5	.288	.373	.346	107	1	1	7	0	0	0	1.000	1	/O	0.2
1977	*LA-N	49	38	5	15	1	0	1	4	10	0	.395	.521	.500	176	5	5	10	1	1	-0	1.000	0	/O	0.5
1978	*LA-N	37	33	2	10	1	0	0	6	3	4	.303	.361	.333	95	-0	-0	4	0	0	0	.000	0	H	0.0
1979	LA-N	47	42	1	15	0	0	0	3	3	4	.357	.400	.357	110	1	1	6	0	0	0	.000	0	/O	0.1
1980	LA-N	7	7	0	3	0	0	0	2	0	0	.429	.429	.429	143	0	0	1	0	0	0	.000	0	/H	0.0
1982	LA-N	1	1	0	0	0	0	0	0	0	0	.000	.000	.000	-99	-0	-0	0	0	0	0	.000	0	/H	0.0
Total	20	1536	3779	496	1149	125	52	31	438	289	320	.304	.358	.389	112	53	64	517	50	42	-10	.979	-57	*O/32C	-4.9
■ DARRYL MOTLEY	Motley, Darryl De Wayne b: 1/21/60, Muskogee, Okla. BR/TR, 5'9", 196 lbs. Deb: 8/10/81																								
1981	KC-A	42	125	15	29	4	0	2	8	7	15	.232	.278	.312	70	-5	-5	10	1	3	-2	.968	3	O	-0.5
1983	KC-A	19	68	9	16	1	2	3	11	2	8	.235	.268	.441	91	-1	-1	7	2	1	0	.978	1	O/D	-0.1
1984	*KC-A	146	522	64	148	25	6	15	70	28	73	.284	.321	.441	108	5	4	63	10	12	-4	.984	-2	*O	-0.6
1985	*KC-A	123	383	45	85	20	1	17	49	18	57	.222	.261	.413	81	-12	-12	35	6	4	-1	.967	-8	*O/D	-2.4
1986	KC-A	72	217	22	44	9	1	7	20	11	31	.203	.241	.350	57	-13	-14	16	0	2	-1	.979	-8	O/D	-2.4
	Atl-N	5	10	1	2	1	0	0	0	1	1	.200	.273	.300	55	-1	-1	1	0	0	0	1.000	-0	/O	-0.1
1987	Atl-N	6	8	0	0	0	0	0	1	0	1	.000	.000	.000	-95	-2	-2	0	0	0	0	1.000	-0	/O	-0.3
Total	6	413	1333	156	324	60	10	44	159	67	186	.243	.282	.402	86	-29	-30	130	19	22	-8	.976	-15	O/D	-6.4
■ BITSY MOTT	Mott, Elisha Matthew b: 6/12/18, Arcadia, Fla. BR/TR, 5'8", 155 lbs. Deb: 4/17/45																								
1945	Phi-N	90	289	21	64	8	0	0	22	27	25	.221	.290	.249	52	-19	-18	22	2			.944	13	S2/3	0.1

YEAR	TM/L	G	AB	R	H	2B	3B	HR	RBI	BB	SO	AVG	OBP	SLG	PRO+	BR	/A	RC	SB	CS	SBR	FA	FR	POS	TPR

■ CURT MOTTON   Motton, Curtell Howard   b: 9/24/40, Darnell, La.   BR/TR, 5'7.5", 175 lbs.   Deb: 7/05/67   C

1967	Bal-A	27	65	5	13	2	0	2	9	5	14	.200	.278	.323	78	-2	-2	6	0	1	-1	.973	1	O	-0.3
1968	Bal-A	83	217	27	43	7	0	8	25	31	43	.198	.301	.341	94	-1	-1	22	1	3	-2	.989	2	O	-0.4
1969	*Bal-A	56	89	15	27	6	0	6	21	13	10	.303	.398	.573	167	8	8	22	3	1	0	1.000	-3	O	0.5
1970	Bal-A	52	84	16	19	3	1	3	19	18	20	.226	.369	.393	109	2	2	14	1	2	-1	1.000	-1	O	-0.1
1971	*Bal-A	38	53	13	10	1	0	4	8	10	12	.189	.317	.434	112	1	1	8	0	0	0	1.000	-2	O	-0.2
1972	Mil-A	6	6	1	1	0	0	1	2	1	2	.167	.286	.667	181	1	1	1	0	0	0	.000	-1	/O	-0.1
	Cal-A	42	39	6	6	1	0	0	1	5	12	.154	.250	.179	31	-3	-3	2	0	0	0	1.000	-0	/O	-0.4
	Yr	48	45	7	7	1	0	1	3	6	14	.156	.255	.244	52	-3	-3	3	0	0	0	1.000	-1	O	-0.5
1973	Bal-A	5	6	2	2	0	0	1	4	1	1	.333	.429	.833	250	1	1	2	0	0	0	.000	-0	/OD	0.1
1974	*Bal-A	7	8	0	0	0	0	0	0	2	2	.000	.200	.000	-40	-1	-1	0	0	0	0	1.000	-0	/OD	-0.2
Total	8	316	567	85	121	20	1	25	89	86	116	.213	.322	.384	105	4	5	76	5	7	-3	.991	-5	O/D	-1.1

■ FRANK MOTZ   Motz, Frank H.   b: 10/1/1868, Freeburg, Pa.   d: 3/18/44, Akron, Ohio   6', 160 lbs.   Deb: 8/27/1890

1890	Phi-N	1	2	1	0	0	0	0	3	1		.000	.333	.000	1	-0	-0	0	1			1.000	0	/1	0.0
1893	Cin-N	43	156	16	40	7	1	2	25	19	10	.256	.352	.353	87	-2	-3	21	3			.981	6	1	0.2
1894	Cin-N	18	69	8	14	4	0	0	12	9	1	.203	.304	.261	37	-7	-7	6	2			.995	4	1	-0.3
Total	3	62	227	25	54	11	1	2	40	29	12	.238	.337	.322	70	-9	-10	27	6			.985	10	/1	-0.1

■ ALLIE MOULTON   Moulton, Albert Theodore   b: 1/16/1886, Medway, Mass.   d: 7/10/68, Peabody, Mass.   BR/TR, 5'6", 155 lbs.   Deb: 9/25/11

| 1911 | StL-A | 4 | 15 | 4 | 1 | 0 | 0 | 0 | 1 | 4 | | .067 | .263 | .067 | -6 | -2 | -2 | 0 | 0 | | | .938 | -1 | /2 | -0.3 |

■ FRANK MOUNTAIN   Mountain, Frank Henry   b: 5/17/1860, Ft.Edward, N.Y.   d: 11/19/39, Schenectady, N.Y.   BR/TR, 5'11", 185 lbs.   Deb: 7/19/1880

1880	Tro-N	2	9	1	2	0	0	0	0	0	4	.222	.222	.222	49	-0	-1	0				1.000	0	/P	0.0
1881	Det-N	7	25	0	4	1	1	0	4	2	8	.160	.222	.280	55	-1	-1	2				.923	-1	/P	0.0
1882	Wor-N	5	16	1	1	0	0	0	1	0	5	.063	.063	.063	-58	-3	-3	0				.889	-1	/P	0.0
	Phi-N	9	36	5	12	3	0	0		2		.333	.368	.417	147	2	2	6				.917	1	/PO	0.0
	Wor-N	20	70	8	19	2	2	2	5	3	18	.271	.301	.443	132	3	2	10				.870	-3	P/O1S	-0.1
1883	Col-a	70	276	36	60	14	5	3		9		.217	.242	.337	92	-5	-1	23				.848	2	PO	0.0
1884	Col-a	58	210	26	50	7	3	4		9		.238	.283	.357	120	2	5	22				.919	2	PO	0.0
1885	Pit-a	5	20	1	2	0	1	0		1		.100	.143	.200	9	-2	-2	1				.846	0	/P	0.0
1886	Pit-a	18	55	6	8	1	1	0		13		.145	.319	.200	66	-1	-1	5	3			.959	-0	1/P	-0.3
Total	7	194	717	84	158	28	13	9	10	39	35	.220	.265	.333	97	-5	-0	67	3			.880	0	P/O1S	-0.4

■ RAY MOWE   Mowe, Raymond Benjamin   b: 7/12/1889, Rochester, Ind.   d: 8/14/68, Sarasota, Fla.   BL/TR, 5'7.5", 160 lbs.   Deb: 9/25/13

| 1913 | Bro-N | 5 | 9 | 0 | 1 | 0 | 0 | 0 | 0 | 0 | 1 | .111 | .200 | .111 | -10 | -1 | -1 | 0 | 0 | | | .941 | 1 | /S | 0.0 |

■ MIKE MOWREY   Mowrey, Harry Harlan   b: 4/20/1884, Browns Mill, Pa.   d: 3/20/47, Chambersburg, Pa.   BR/TR, 5'10", 180 lbs.   Deb: 9/24/05

1905	Cin-N	7	30	4	8	1	0	0	6	1		.267	.290	.300	69	-1	-1	3	0			.759	-0	/3	-0.2
1906	Cin-N	21	53	3	17	3	0	0	6	5		.321	.379	.377	131	2	2	9	2			.930	4	3/2S	0.7
1907	Cin-N	138	448	43	113	16	6	1	44	35		.252	.308	.321	93	-2	-4	51	10			.929	-19	*3S	-2.1
1908	Cin-N	77	227	17	50	9	1	0	23	12		.220	.266	.269	73	-8	-7	18	5			.936	-7	3/SO2	-1.4
1909	Cin-N	38	115	10	22	5	0	0	5	20		.191	.311	.235	70	-3	-3	9	2			.947	0	3S	-0.2
	StL-N	12	29	3	7	1	0	0	4	4		.241	.333	.276	95	-0	0	3	1			.921	-1	/23	-0.1
	Yr	50	144	13	29	6	0	0	9	24		.201	.315	.243	75	-4	-3	13	3			.948	-1	3S/2	-0.3
1910	StL-N	143	489	69	138	24	6	2	70	67	38	.282	.375	.368	121	13	16	76	21			.927	12	*3	3.1
1911	StL-N	137	471	59	126	29	7	0	61	59	46	.268	.355	.359	103	1	3	66	15			.944	7	*3/S	1.1
1912	StL-N	114	408	59	104	13	8	2	50	46	29	.255	.335	.341	87	-8	-7	54	19			.931	3	*3	-0.3
1913	StL-N	132	450	61	117	18	4	0	33	53	40	.260	.342	.318	90	-5	-4	55	21			.953	14	*3	1.2
1914	Pit-N	79	284	24	72	7	5	1	25	22	20	.254	.316	.324	94	-3	-2	31	8			.960	-2	3	-0.2
1915	Pit-F	151	521	56	146	26	6	1	49	66	39	.280	.367	.359	115	11	11	88	40			**.959**	-19	*3	-0.1
1916	*Bro-N	144	495	57	121	22	6	0	60	50	60	.244	.320	.313	92	-2	-3	59	16			**.965**	0	*3	0.2
1917	Bro-N	83	271	20	58	9	5	0	25	29	25	.214	.292	.284	75	-7	-8	24	7			.952	-3	3/2	-1.0
Total	13	1276	4291	485	1099	183	54	7	461	469	297	.256	.334	.329	97	-12	-8	546	167			.944	-12	*3/S2O	0.7

■ JOE MOWRY   Mowry, Joseph Aloysius   b: 4/6/08, St.Louis, Mo.   BB/TR, 6', 198 lbs.   Deb: 5/13/33

1933	Bos-N	86	249	25	55	8	5	0	20	15	22	.221	.273	.293	67	-12	-10	21	1			.994	1	O	-1.4
1934	Bos-N	25	79	9	17	3	0	1	4	3	13	.215	.244	.291	46	-6	-6	6	0			.976	0	O/2	-0.6
1935	Bos-N	81	136	17	36	8	1	1	13	11	13	.265	.324	.360	91	-3	-2	17	0			.970	-7	O	-1.0
Total	3	192	464	51	108	19	6	2	37	29	48	.233	.284	.313	71	-22	-17	44	1			.985	-7	O/2	-3.0

■ MIKE MOYNAHAN   Moynahan, Michael   b: 1856, Chicago, Ill.   d: 4/9/1899, Chicago, Ill.   BL/TR,   Deb: 8/20/1880

1880	Buf-N	27	100	12	33	5	1	0	14	6	9	.330	.368	.400	157	6	6	15				.862	-6	S	0.1
1881	Cle-N	33	135	12	31	5	1	0	8	3	14	.230	.246	.281	69	-5	-4	10				.883	-2	O/3	-0.7
	Det-N	1	4	1	1	0	0	0	0	0	1	.250	.250	.250	55	-0	-0	0				.857	1	/3	0.0
	Yr	34	139	13	32	5	1	0	8	3	15	.230	.246	.281	69	-5	-4	10				.883	-2	O/3	-0.7
1883	Phi-a	95	400	90	123	18	10	1		30		.308	.356	.410	135	21	15	60				.833	0	*S	1.5
1884	Phi-a	1	4	0	0	0	0	0		0		.000	.000	.000	-94	-1	-1	0				.000	-0	/O	-0.1
	Cle-N	12	45	9	13	2	1	0	6	7	11	.289	.337	.378	136	2	2	7				.852	-0	/2SO	0.2
Total	4	169	688	124	201	30	13	1	28	46	35	.292	.337	.378	124	23	18	91				.837	-9	S/O23	1.0

■ HEINIE MUELLER   Mueller, Clarence Francis   b: 9/16/1899, Creve Coeur, Mo.   d: 1/23/75, DeSoto, Mo.   BL/TL, 5'8", 158 lbs.   Deb: 9/25/20

1920	StL-N	4	22	0	7	1	0	0	1	2	4	.318	.375	.364	117	0	1	3	1	0	0	1.000	0	/O	0.1
1921	StL-N	55	176	25	62	10	6	1	34	11	22	.352	.397	.494	137	9	9	33	2	4	-2	.976	-3	O	0.1
1922	StL-N	61	159	20	43	7	2	3	26	14	18	.270	.329	.396	91	-3	-2	21	2	1	0	.947	-3	O	-0.8
1923	StL-N	78	265	39	91	16	9	5	41	18	16	.343	.392	.528	144	15	16	54	4	3	-1	.963	2	O	1.2
1924	StL-N	92	296	39	78	12	6	2	37	19	16	.264	.312	.365	82	-8	-8	33	8	7	-2	.962	-2	O1	-1.6
1925	StL-N	78	243	33	76	16	4	1	26	17	11	.313	.365	.424	99	-0	-0	37	0	3	-2	.955	-3	O	-0.9
1926	StL-N	52	191	36	51	7	5	3	28	11	6	.267	.330	.403	93	-1	-2	25	8			.950	-1	O	-0.6
	NY-N	85	305	36	76	6	2	4	29	21	17	.249	.300	.321	68	-14	-14	29	7			.950	5	O	-1.5
	Yr	137	496	72	127	13	7	7	57	32	23	.256	.312	.353	78	-15	-16	54	15			.950	4	*O	-2.1
1927	NY-N	84	190	33	55	6	1	3	19	25	12	.289	.384	.379	105	2	2	29	2			.944	-7	O/1	-0.7
1928	Bos-N	42	151	25	34	3	1	0	19	17	9	.225	.316	.258	54	-10	-9	14	1			.985	-0	O	-0.5
1929	Bos-N	46	93	10	19	2	1	0	11	12	12	.204	.302	.247	39	-9	-8	8	0			1.000	-4	O	-1.2
1935	StL-A	16	27	0	5	1	0	0	1	1	4	.185	.214	.222	12	-4	-4	1	0	0	0	.955	-1	/1O	-0.4
Total	11	693	2118	296	597	87	37	22	272	168	147	.282	.342	.389	94	-23	-20	287	37	18		.960	-11	O/1	-6.8

■ DON MUELLER   Mueller, Donald Frederick "Mandrake The Magician"   b: 4/14/27, St.Louis, Mo.   BL/TR, 6', 185 lbs.   Deb: 8/02/48   F

1948	NY-N	36	81	12	29	4	1	0	9	0	3	.358	.358	.469	121	2	2	12	0			.973	-1	O	0.0
1949	NY-N	51	56	5	13	4	0	1	1	5	6	.232	.295	.304	61	-3	-3	3	0			1.000	-1	/O	-0.4
1950	NY-N	132	525	60	153	15	6	7	84	10	26	.291	.309	.383	80	-16	-16	60	1			.986	-5	*O	-2.5
1951	NY-N	122	469	58	130	10	7	16	69	19	13	.277	.307	.431	95	-4	-5	63	1	1	-0	.983	-2	*O	-1.1
1952	NY-N	126	456	61	128	14	7	12	49	34	24	.281	.333	.421	107	4	4	65	2	1	0	.987	-1	*O	-0.2
1953	NY-N	131	480	56	160	12	2	6	60	19	13	.333	.360	.404	97	-1	-2	71	2	0	1	.972	-4	*O	-1.0
1954	*NY-N★	153	619	90	**212**	35	8	4	71	22	17	.342	.367	.444	110	8	8	94	2	3	-1	.979	-0	*O	0.0

YEAR	TM/L	G	AB	R	H	2B	3B	HR	RBI	BB	SO	AVG	OBP	SLG	PRO+	BR	/A	RC	SB	CS	SBR	FA	FR	POS	TPR
1955	NY-N★	147	605	67	185	21	4	8	83	19	12	.306	.330	.393	91	-8	-8	75	1	2	-1	.976	-11	*O	-2.7
1956	NY-N	138	453	38	122	12	1	5	41	15	7	.269	.293	.333	68	-21	-20	39	0	1	-1	.989	-9	*O	-3.6
1957	NY-N	135	450	45	116	7	1	6	37	13	16	.258	.280	.318	60	-25	-25	39	2	0	1	.989	-1	*O	-3.2
1958	Chi-A	70	166	7	42	5	0	0	16	11	9	.253	.299	.283	62	-9	-8	14	0	0	0	.968	-5	O	-1.5
1959	Chi-A	4	4	0	2	0	0	0	0	0	0	.500	.500	.500	178	0	0	1	0	0	0	.000	0	H	0.0
Total	12	1245	4364	499	1292	139	37	65	520	167	146	.296	.324	.390	89	-72	-74	538	11	8		.982	-38	*O	-16.2

■ HEINIE MUELLER

Mueller, Emmett Jerome b: 7/20/12, St.Louis, Mo. d: 10/3/86, Orlando, Fla. BB/TR, 5'6", 167 lbs. Deb: 4/19/38

YEAR	TM/L	G	AB	R	H	2B	3B	HR	RBI	BB	SO	AVG	OBP	SLG	PRO+	BR	/A	RC	SB	CS	SBR	FA	FR	POS	TPR
1938	Phi-N	136	444	53	111	12	4	4	34	64	43	.250	.346	.322	87	-7	-6	55	2			.967	-27	*23	-2.7
1939	Phi-N	115	341	46	95	19	4	9	43	33	34	.279	.342	.437	111	3	5	49	4			.964	-14	23O/S	-0.7
1940	Phi-N	97	263	24	65	13	2	3	28	37	23	.247	.344	.346	95	-2	-1	33	2			.966	-9	2O3/1	-0.9
1941	Phi-N	93	233	21	53	11	1	1	22	22	24	.227	.302	.296	72	-9	-8	21	2			.980	-4	2O3	-1.2
Total	4	441	1281	144	324	55	11	17	127	156	124	.253	.337	.353	93	-16	-10	159	10			.968	-54	2/3O1S	-5.5

■ RAY MUELLER

Mueller, Ray Coleman "Iron Man" b: 3/8/12, Pittsburg, Kan. BR/TR, 5'9", 175 lbs. Deb: 5/11/35 C

YEAR	TM/L	G	AB	R	H	2B	3B	HR	RBI	BB	SO	AVG	OBP	SLG	PRO+	BR	/A	RC	SB	CS	SBR	FA	FR	POS	TPR
1935	Bos-N	42	97	10	22	5	0	3	11	3	11	.227	.250	.371	70	-5	-4	9	0			.978	-2	C	-0.5
1936	Bos-N	24	71	5	14	4	0	0	5	5	17	.197	.250	.254	38	-6	-6	5	0			.986	-4	C	-0.8
1937	Bos-N	64	187	21	47	9	2	2	26	18	36	.251	.317	.353	90	-5	-2	21	1			.995	2	C	0.3
1938	Bos-N	83	274	23	65	8	6	4	35	16	28	.237	.282	.354	82	-10	-7	27	3			.993	-2	C	-0.6
1939	Pit-N	86	180	14	42	8	1	2	18	14	22	.233	.289	.322	65	-9	-9	18	0			.971	-3	C	-0.9
1940	Pit-N	4	3	1	1	0	0	0	1	2	0	.333	.600	.333	165	1	1	1	0			1.000	1	/C	0.1
1943	Cin-N	141	427	50	111	19	4	8	52	56	42	.260	.347	.379	111	6	7	59	1			.988	20	*C	3.8
1944	Cin-N★	155	555	54	159	24	4	10	73	53	47	.286	.353	.398	115	8	11	79	4			.983	-5	*C	1.6
1946	Cin-N	114	378	35	96	18	4	8	48	27	37	.254	.309	.386	100	-3	-2	45	0			**.994**	10	*C	1.5
1947	Cin-N	71	192	17	48	11	0	6	33	16	25	.250	.311	.401	88	-4	-4	22	1			.984	-1	C	-0.2
1948	Cin-N	14	34	2	7	1	0	0	2	4	3	.206	.289	.235	45	-3	-2	2	0			.982	1	C	0.0
1949	Cin-N	32	106	7	29	4	0	1	13	5	13	.274	.319	.340	76	-4	-4	12	1			1.000	-3	C	-0.4
	NY-N	56	170	17	38	2	2	5	23	13	14	.224	.279	.347	67	-8	-8	15	1			.982	1	C	-0.5
	Yr	88	276	24	67	6	2	6	36	18	27	.243	.294	.344	70	-12	-12	27	2			.988	-2	C	-0.9
1950	NY-N	4	11	0	1	1	0	0	0	0	2	.091	.091	.182	-30	-2	-2	0	0			1.000	2	/C	0.0
	Pit-N	67	156	17	42	7	0	6	24	11	14	.269	.321	.429	92	-1	-2	19	2			.996	2	C	0.2
	Yr	71	167	17	43	8	0	6	24	11	16	.257	.307	.413	85	-4	-4	18	2			.996	4	C	0.2
1951	Bos-N	28	70	8	11	2	0	1	9	7	11	.157	.234	.229	27	-7	-7	4	0	0	0	1.000	3	C	-0.3
Total	14	985	2911	281	733	123	23	56	373	250	322	.252	.314	.368	91	-54	-41	337	14	0		.988	21	C	3.3

■ WALTER MUELLER

Mueller, Walter John b: 12/6/1894, Central, Mo. d: 8/16/71, St.Louis, Mo. BR/TR, 5'8", 160 lbs. Deb: 5/07/22 F

YEAR	TM/L	G	AB	R	H	2B	3B	HR	RBI	BB	SO	AVG	OBP	SLG	PRO+	BR	/A	RC	SB	CS	SBR	FA	FR	POS	TPR
1922	Pit-N	32	122	21	33	5	1	2	18	5	7	.270	.305	.377	74	-5	-5	14	1	0	0	.976	7	O	0.0
1923	Pit-N	40	111	11	34	4	4	0	20	4	6	.306	.336	.414	95	-1	-1	15	2	2	-1	.941	1	O	-0.2
1924	Pit-N	30	50	6	13	1	1	0	8	4	4	.260	.327	.320	73	-2	-2	6	1	0	0	1.000	-1	O	-0.3
1926	Pit-N	19	62	8	15	0	1	0	3	0	2	.242	.242	.274	37	-5	-6	4	0			.969	0	O	-0.6
Total	4	121	345	46	95	10	7	2	49	13	19	.275	.307	.362	74	-13	-14	39	4	2		.966	8	/O	-1.1

■ BILL MUELLER

Mueller, William Lawrence "Hawk" b: 11/9/20, Bay City, Mich. BR/TR, 6'1.5", 180 lbs. Deb: 8/29/42

YEAR	TM/L	G	AB	R	H	2B	3B	HR	RBI	BB	SO	AVG	OBP	SLG	PRO+	BR	/A	RC	SB	CS	SBR	FA	FR	POS	TPR
1942	Chi-A	26	85	5	14	1	0	0	5	12	9	.165	.276	.176	29	-8	-7	4	2	1	0	.978	7	O	-0.2
1945	Chi-A	13	9	3	0	0	0	0	0	2	1	.000	.182	.000	-47	-2	-2	0	1	0	0	.778	-3	/O	-0.4
Total	2	39	94	8	14	1	0	0	5	14	10	.149	.266	.160	22	-9	-9	4	3	1	0	.960	4	/O	-0.6

■ MIKE MULDOON

Muldoon, Michael D. b: 1858, Ireland 5'8", 165 lbs. Deb: 5/01/1882

YEAR	TM/L	G	AB	R	H	2B	3B	HR	RBI	BB	SO	AVG	OBP	SLG	PRO+	BR	/A	RC	SB	CS	SBR	FA	FR	POS	TPR
1882	Cle-N	84	341	50	84	17	5	6	45	10	28	.246	.268	.378	108	1	3	35				.880	3	*3O	0.7
1883	Cle-N	98	378	54	86	22	3	0	29	10	39	.228	.247	.302	67	-15	-14	29				.825	-9	*3/O	-2.1
1884	Cle-N	110	422	46	101	16	6	2	38	18	67	.239	.270	.320	82	-7	-10	37				.833	-7	*3/O2	-1.4
1885	Bal-a	102	410	47	103	20	6	2		20		.251	.293	.344	105	1	2	42				.870	-3	*3/2	0.1
1886	Bal-a	101	381	57	76	13	8	0		34		.199	.269	.276	74	-12	-10	32	12			.912	2	23	-0.4
Total	5	495	1932	254	450	88	28	10	112	92	134	.233	.270	.323	87	-31	-29	176	12			.846	-14	3/2O	-3.1

■ TONY MULLANE

Mullane, Anthony John "Count" or "The Apollo Of The Box"
b: 1/20/1859, Cork, Ireland d: 4/25/44, Chicago, Ill. BB/TB, 5'10.5", 165 lbs. Deb: 8/27/1881

YEAR	TM/L	G	AB	R	H	2B	3B	HR	RBI	BB	SO	AVG	OBP	SLG	PRO+	BR	/A	RC	SB	CS	SBR	FA	FR	POS	TPR
1881	Det-N	5	19	0	5	0	0	0	1	0	0	.263	.263	.263	63	-1	-1	1				.882	0	/P	0.0
1882	Lou-a	77	303	46	78	13	1	0		13		.257	.288	.307	107	0	3	27				.959	10	*P1O/2	-0.1
1883	StL-a	83	307	38	69	11	6	0		13		.225	.256	.300	74	-7	-10	24				.851	2	PO/21	-0.3
1884	Tol-a	95	352	49	97	19	3	3		33		.276	.339	.372	131	14	12	46				.885	7	PO/13S2	0.1
1886	Cin-a	91	324	59	73	12	5	0		25		.225	.283	.293	80	-6	-8	33	20			.899	-0	PO/13S2	-0.5
1887	Cin-a	56	199	35	44	6	3	3		16		.221	.292	.327	73	-7	-8	25	20			.944	-2	P/O	-0.2
1888	Cin-a	51	175	27	44	4	4	1	16	8		.251	.296	.337	100	1	-0	22	12			.888	-2	P/1O2	-0.2
1889	Cin-a	63	196	53	58	16	4	0	29	27	21	.296	.387	.418	128	9	8	42	24			.920	-1	P3O/1	0.4
1890	Cin-N	81	286	41	79	9	8	0	34	39	30	.276	.375	.364	118	8	8	47	19			.941	-2	OP3S/1	0.3
1891	Cin-N	64	209	16	31	1	2	0	10	18	33	.148	.229	.172	19	-21	-21	9	4			.958	-3	PO/3	-0.6
1892	Cin-N	39	118	14	20	3	1	0	9	9	8	.169	.246	.212	41	-8	-8	7	4			.926	5	P/1	0.0
1893	Cin-N	16	52	11	15	0	0	1	6	5	3	.288	.383	.346	94	0	-0	7	1			.939	0	P/3	0.0
	Bal-N	38	114	15	26	2	1	0	14	5	14	.228	.261	.263	40	-10	-10	9	5			.943	2	P/O1	-0.1
	Yr	54	166	26	41	2	1	1	20	10	17	.247	.302	.289	58	-10	-10	17	6			.942	2	P/O31	-0.1
1894	Bal-N	21	53	3	21	3	0	0	9	6	3	.396	.475	.453	121	3	2	13	2			.889	-1	P	0.0
	Cle-N	4	13	0	1	0	0	0	0	4	2	.077	.294	.077	-5	-2	-2	1	1			.944	2	/P	0.0
	Yr	25	66	3	22	3	0	0	9	10	5	.333	.436	.379	96	1	0	13	3			.911	1	P	0.0
Total	13	784	2720	407	661	99	38	8	128	221	114	.243	.307	.316	89	-27	-35	315	112			.918	18	PO/31S2	-1.2

■ GREG MULLEAVY

Mulleavy, Gregory Thomas "Moe" b: 9/25/05, Detroit, Mich. d: 2/1/80, Arcadia, Cal. BR/TR, 5'9", 167 lbs. Deb: 7/04/30 C

YEAR	TM/L	G	AB	R	H	2B	3B	HR	RBI	BB	SO	AVG	OBP	SLG	PRO+	BR	/A	RC	SB	CS	SBR	FA	FR	POS	TPR
1930	Chi-A	77	289	27	76	14	5	0	28	20	23	.263	.311	.346	69	-15	-13	32	5	2	0	.918	-5	S	-0.9
1932	Chi-A	1	3	0	0	0	0	0	0	0	0	.000	.000	.000	-99	-1	-1	0	0	0	0	1.000	0	/2	-0.1
1933	Bos-A	1	0	1	0	0	0	0	0	0	0	—	—	—	—	0	0	0	0	0	0	.000	0	R	0.0
Total	3	79	292	28	76	14	5	0	28	20	23	.260	.308	.342	67	-16	-14	32	5	2	0	.956	-5	/S2	-1.0

■ MULLEN

Mullen Deb: 8/17/1872

YEAR	TM/L	G	AB	R	H	2B	3B	HR	RBI	BB	SO	AVG	OBP	SLG	PRO+	BR	/A	RC	SB	CS	SBR	FA	FR	POS	TPR
1872	Cle-n	1	4	1	0	0	0	0	0	0	0	.000	.000	.000	-99	-1	-1	0						/O	-0.1

■ CHARLIE MULLEN

Mullen, Charles George b: 3/15/1889, Seattle, Wash. d: 6/6/63, Seattle, Wash. BR/TR, 5'10.5", 155 lbs. Deb: 5/18/10

YEAR	TM/L	G	AB	R	H	2B	3B	HR	RBI	BB	SO	AVG	OBP	SLG	PRO+	BR	/A	RC	SB	CS	SBR	FA	FR	POS	TPR
1910	Chi-A	41	123	15	24	2	1	0	13	4		.195	.220	.228	42	-9	-8	8	4			.982	1	1/O	-0.8
1911	Chi-A	20	59	7	12	2	1	0	5	5		.203	.266	.271	51	-4	-4	5	1			.969	0	1	-0.4
1914	NY-A	93	323	33	84	8	0	0	44	33	55	.260	.332	.285	86	-5	-5	32	11	17	-7	.994	3	1	-1.2
1915	NY-A	40	90	11	24	1	0	0	7	10	12	.267	.340	.278	85	-1	-1	10	5	2	0	.982	1	1	-0.1
1916	NY-A	59	146	11	39	9	1	0	18	9	13	.267	.310	.342	94	-1	-2	18	7			.943	-4	21/O	-0.7
Total	5	253	741	77	183	22	3	0	87	61	80	.247	.306	.285	78	-20	-19	72	28	19		.988	0	1/2O	-3.2

■ MOON MULLEN

Mullen, Ford Parker b: 2/9/17, Olympia, Wash. BL/TR, 5'9", 165 lbs. Deb: 4/18/44

YEAR	TM/L	G	AB	R	H	2B	3B	HR	RBI	BB	SO	AVG	OBP	SLG	PRO+	BR	/A	RC	SB	CS	SBR	FA	FR	POS	TPR
1944	Phi-N	118	464	51	124	9	4	0	31	28	32	.267	.315	.304	77	-15	-13	46	4			.963	-7	*2/3	-1.4

YEAR	TM/L	G	AB	R	H	2B	3B	HR	RBI	BB	SO	AVG	OBP	SLG	PRO+	BR	/A	RC	SB	CS	SBR	FA	FR	POS	TPR
■ JOHN MULLEN Mullen, John b: Philadelphia, Pa. BL/TL, Deb: 9/09/1876																									
1876	Phi-N	1	3	0	0	0	0	0	0	0	0	.000	.000	.000	-99	-1	-1	0				.714	0	/C	0.0
■ BILLY MULLEN Mullen, William John b: 1/23/1896, St.Louis, Mo. d: 5/4/71, St.Louis, Mo. BR/TR, 5'8", 160 lbs. Deb: 10/02/20																									
1920	StL-A	2	4	0	0	0	0	0	0	0	0	.000	.000	.000	-97	-1	-1	0	0	0	0	1.000	-1	/2	-0.2
1921	StL-A	4	4	0	0	0	0	0	0	2	1	.000	.333	.000	-8	-1	-1	0	0	0	0	1.000	0	/3	0.0
1923	Bro-N	4	11	1	3	0	0	0	0	0	0	.273	.273	.273	46	-1	-1	1	0	0	0	.875	-0	/3	-0.1
1926	Det-A	11	13	2	1	0	0	0	0	5	1	.077	.333	.077	11	-1	-2	1	1	0	0	.875	-0	/3	-0.1
1928	StL-A	15	18	2	7	1	0	0	2	3	4	.389	.476	.444	139	1	1	4	0	0	0	.867	1	/3	0.2
Total	5	36	50	5	11	1	0	0	2	10	6	.220	.350	.240	56	-3	-3	6	1	0	0	.884	-1	/32	-0.2
■ FREDDIE MULLER Muller, Frederick William b: 12/21/07, Newark, Cal. d: 10/20/76, Davis, Cal. BR/TR, 5'10", 170 lbs. Deb: 7/08/33																									
1933	Bos-A	15	48	6	9	1	1	0	3	5	5	.188	.264	.250	37	-4	-4	4	1	0	0	.923	-4	2	-0.7
1934	Bos-A	2	1	1	0	0	0	0	0	1	0	.000	.500	.000	36	0	-0	0	0	0	0	.800	-0	/23	0.0
Total	2	17	49	7	9	1	1	0	3	6	5	.184	.273	.245	38	-4	-4	4	1	0	0	.914	-5	/23	-0.7
■ MULLIGAN Mulligan Deb: 6/14/1884																									
1884	Was-U	1	4	2	1	0	0	0		0		.250	.250	.250	72	-0	-0	0				1.000	1	/3	0.1
■ EDDIE MULLIGAN Mulligan, Edward Joseph b: 8/27/1894, St.Louis, Mo. d: 3/15/82, San Rafael, Cal. BR/TR, 5'9", 152 lbs. Deb: 9/23/15																									
1915	Chi-N	11	22	5	8	1	0	0	2	5	1	.364	.481	.409	170	2	2	5	2	2	-1	.907	3	S/3	0.5
1916	Chi-N	58	189	13	29	3	4	0	9	8	30	.153	.200	.212	24	-16	-19	9	1			.888	3	S	-1.4
1921	Chi-A	151	609	82	153	21	12	1	45	32	53	.251	.293	.330	59	-39	-38	57	13	18	-7	.955	-13	*3/S	-4.5
1922	Chi-A	103	372	39	87	14	8	0	31	22	32	.234	.278	.315	55	-26	-25	33	7	7	-2	.971	4	3/S	-1.6
1928	Pit-N	27	43	4	10	2	0	0	1	3	4	.233	.283	.279	45	-3	-4	4	0			.929	0	/32	-0.3
Total	5	350	1235	143	287	41	24	1	88	70	120	.232	.278	.307	54	-82	-83	107	23	27		.961	-3	3/S2	-7.3
■ GEORGE MULLIN Mullin, George Joseph "Wabash George" b: 7/4/1880, Toledo, Ohio d: 1/7/44, Wabash, Ind. BR/TR, 5'11", 188 lbs. Deb: 5/04/02																									
1902	Det-A	40	120	20	39	4	3	0	11	8		.325	.367	.408	112	2	2	19	1			.921	1	P/O	-0.1
1903	Det-A	46	126	11	35	9	1	1	12	2		.278	.295	.389	107	0	1	16	1			.936	5	P/O	0.0
1904	Det-A	53	155	14	45	10	2	0	8	10		.290	.337	.381	131	5	5	21	1			.936	7	P/O	-0.1
1905	Det-A	47	135	15	35	4	0	0	12	12		.259	.320	.289	93	-1	-1	15	4			.962	7	P/O	0.0
1906	Det-A	50	142	13	32	6	4	0	6	4		.225	.247	.324	76	-4	-4	12	2			.957	2	P/2O	-0.1
1907	*Det-A	70	157	16	34	5	3	0	13	12		.217	.276	.287	77	-4	-4	13	2			.961	4	P/1	0.0
1908	*Det-A	55	125	13	32	2	2	1	8	7		.256	.306	.328	102	1	0	13	2			.961	3	P	0.0
1909	*Det-A	53	126	13	27	7	0	0	17	13		.214	.288	.270	73	-3	-4	10	2			.973	0	P/O	-0.1
1910	Det-A	50	129	15	33	6	2	1	11	8		.256	.299	.357	99	0	-1	14	1			.944	-0	P/O	-0.1
1911	Det-A	40	98	4	28	7	2	0	5	10		.286	.352	.398	104	1	0	14	1			.941	-2	P	0.0
1912	Det-A	38	90	13	25	5	1	0	12	17		.278	.393	.356	118	2	3	13	0			.929	0	P	0.0
1913	Det-A	12	20	1	7	0	0	0	1	4	1	.350	.458	.350	139	1	1	3	0			.952	1	/P	0.0
	Was-A	11	21	4	4	0	0	0	0	2	5	.190	.292	.190	41	-1	-1	1	1			.958	1	P	0.0
	Yr	23	41	5	11	0	0	0	1	6	6	.268	.375	.268	89	-0	-0	4	1			.956	1	P	0.0
1914	Ind-F	43	77	11	24	5	3	0	21	11	15	.312	.404	.455	130	5	4	15	0			.915	-4	P	0.0
1915	New-F	6	10	0	1	0	0	0	0	2	0	.100	.250	.100	5	-1	-1	0	0			1.000	-1	/P	0.0
Total	14	614	1531	163	401	70	23	3	137	122	21	.262	.319	.344	100	4	-0	179	18			.947	24	P/O12	-0.5
■ HENRY MULLIN Mullin, Henry J. b: 4/1862, St.John, N.B., Canada d: 11/8/27, Beverly, Mass. BR , Deb: 6/04/1884																									
1884	Was-a	34	120	13	17	3	1	0		8		.142	.195	.183	29	-9	-7	4				.869	-1	O/3	-0.8
	Bos-U	2	8	1	0	0	0	0		0		.000	.000	.000	-99	-2	-2	0				1.000	3	/O	0.1
Total	1	36	128	14	17	3	1	0		8		.133	.184	.172	21	-11	-9	4				.882	2	/O3	-0.7
■ JIM MULLIN Mullin, James Henry b: 10/16/1883, New York, N.Y. d: 1/24/25, Philadelphia, Pa. BR/TR, 5'10", 173 lbs. Deb: 6/01/04																									
1904	Phi-A	22	52	5	14	1	0	1	5	3		.269	.321	.346	106	1	0	7	2			.985	-5	/12SO	-0.6
	Was-A	27	102	10	19	2	2	0	4	4		.186	.224	.245	49	-6	-6	7	3			.981	5	2	0.0
	Phi-A	19	58	4	10	0	0	0	4	2		.172	.238	.172	30	-4	-5	3	2			.984	-1	1	-0.6
	Yr	68	212	19	43	3	2	1	13	9		.203	.252	.250	58	-10	-10	16	7			.965	-1	21/SO	-1.2
1905	Was-A	50	163	18	31	7	6	0	13	5		.190	.214	.307	67	-7	-6	13	5			.928	-4	2/1	-1.1
Total	2	118	375	37	74	10	8	1	26	14		.197	.236	.275	62	-17	-17	29	12			.946	-4	/21SO	-2.3
■ PAT MULLIN Mullin, Patrick Joseph b: 11/1/17, Trotter, Pa. BL/TR, 6'2", 190 lbs. Deb: 9/18/40 C																									
1940	Det-A	4	4	0	0	0	0	0	0	0	0	.000	.000	.000	-91	-1	-1	0	0	0	0	.000	-1	/O	-0.2
1941	Det-A	54	220	42	76	11	5	5	23	18	18	.345	.400	.509	126	12	9	48	5	1	1	.944	-4	O	0.2
1946	Det-A	93	276	34	68	13	4	3	35	25	36	.246	.311	.355	81	-6	-8	31	3	5	-2	.949	-3	O	-1.7
1947	Det-A☆	116	398	62	102	28	6	15	62	63	66	.256	.359	.470	126	15	14	69	3	8	-4	.988	8	*O	1.2
1948	Det-A★	138	496	91	143	16	11	23	80	77	57	.288	.385	.504	132	24	22	103	1	2	-1	.972	0	*O	1.3
1949	Det-A	104	310	55	83	8	6	12	59	42	29	.268	.357	.448	112	4	4	52	1	2	-1	.989	-4	O	-0.4
1950	Det-A	69	142	16	31	5	0	6	23	20	23	.218	.315	.380	75	-5	-6	18	1	4	-2	1.000	-1	O	-0.9
1951	Det-A	110	295	41	83	11	6	12	51	40	38	.281	.367	.481	128	11	11	55	2	2	-1	.939	-9	O	-0.2
1952	Det-A	97	255	29	64	13	5	7	35	31	30	.251	.332	.424	108	3	2	36	4	2	0	.979	2	O	0.2
1953	Det-A	79	97	11	26	1	0	4	17	14	15	.268	.360	.402	107	1	1	14	0	1	-1	.944	-2	O	-0.2
Total	10	864	2493	381	676	106	43	87	385	330	312	.271	.358	.453	115	58	48	426	20	27	-10	.970	-14	O	-0.7
■ RANCE MULLINIKS Mulliniks, Steven Rance b: 1/15/56, Tulare, Cal. BL/TR, 6', 170 lbs. Deb: 6/18/77																									
1977	Cal-A	78	271	36	73	13	2	3	21	23	36	.269	.329	.365	93	-4	-3	34	1	1	-0	.963	2	S	0.8
1978	Cal-A	50	119	6	22	3	1	1	6	8	23	.185	.242	.252	41	-10	-9	7	2	0	1	.953	2	S/D	-0.3
1979	Cal-A	22	68	7	10	0	0	1	8	4	14	.147	.205	.191	8	-9	-8	3	0	0	0	.957	-7	S	-1.3
1980	KC-A	36	54	8	14	3	0	0	6	7	10	.259	.344	.315	81	-1	-1	6	0	0	0	.981	2	S2	0.3
1981	KC-A	24	44	6	10	3	0	0	5	2	7	.227	.261	.295	61	-2	-2	3	0	1	-1	.900	3	2/S3	0.1
1982	Tor-A	112	311	32	76	25	0	4	35	37	49	.244	.327	.363	82	-4	-8	36	3	2	-0	.938	-16	*3S	-2.6
1983	Tor-A	129	364	54	100	34	3	10	49	57	43	.275	.374	.467	122	16	13	62	0	2	-1	.971	-18	*3S/2	-0.7
1984	Tor-A	125	343	41	111	21	5	3	42	33	44	.324	.385	.440	123	13	12	58	2	3	-1	**.968**	-13	*3/S2	-0.4
1985	*Tor-A	129	366	55	108	26	1	10	57	55	54	.295	.387	.454	126	16	15	66	2	0	1	**.971**	-16	*3	-0.2
1986	Tor-A	117	348	50	90	22	0	11	45	43	60	.259	.342	.417	103	3	2	48	1	1	-0	**.975**	-1	*3/2D	-0.2
1987	Tor-A	124	332	37	103	28	1	11	44	34	55	.310	.374	.500	127	14	13	60	1	1	-0	.927	-6	3D/S	0.5
1988	Tor-A	119	337	49	101	21	1	12	48	56	57	.300	.399	.475	143	21	21	65	1	0	0	1.000	-0	*D/3	2.1
1989	*Tor-A	103	273	25	65	11	2	3	29	34	40	.238	.322	.326	85	-5	-5	27	0	0	0	.985	1	D3	-0.3
1990	Tor-A	57	97	11	28	4	0	2	16	22	19	.289	.420	.392	126	5	5	18	2	1	0	.949	-0	3D/1	0.5
1991	*Tor-A	97	240	27	60	12	1	2	24	44	44	.250	.366	.333	92	0	-1	31	0	0	0	1.000	0	D/3	-0.1
1992	Tor-A	3	2	1	1	0	0	0	0	1	0	.500	.667	.500	221	1	1	1	0	0	0	.000	0	/D	0.1
Total	16	1325	3569	445	972	226	17	73	435	460	555	.272	.357	.407	107	54	43	526	15	12	-3	.961	-67	3DS/21	-1.7
■ FRAN MULLINS Mullins, Francis Joseph b: 5/14/57, Oakland, Cal. BR/TR, 6', 180 lbs. Deb: 9/01/80																									
1980	Chi-A	21	62	9	12	4	0	0	3	9	8	.194	.296	.258	53	-4	-4	4	0	1	-1	.981	-2	3	-0.7
1984	SF-N	57	110	8	24	8	0	2	10	9	29	.218	.277	.345	77	-4	-4	10	3	1	0	.969	9	S3/2	0.8
1986	Cle-A	28	40	3	7	4	0	0	5	2	11	.175	.214	.275	33	-4	-4	3	0	0	0	.953	8	2S/1D	0.5

YEAR	TM/L	G	AB	R	H	2B	3B	HR	RBI	BB	SO	AVG	OBP	SLG	PRO+	BR	/A	RC	SB	CS	SBR	FA	FR	POS	TPR
Total	3	106	212	20	43	16	0	2	18	20	48	.203	.272	.307	61	-12	-11	17	3	2	-0	.968	15	/3S2D1	0.6

■ JOE MULVEY
Mulvey, Joseph H. b: 10/27/1858, Providence, R.I. d: 8/21/28, Philadelphia, Pa. BR/TR, 5'11.5", 178 lbs. Deb: 5/31/1883

YEAR	TM/L	G	AB	R	H	2B	3B	HR	RBI	BB	SO	AVG	OBP	SLG	PRO+	BR	/A	RC	SB	CS	SBR	FA	FR	POS	TPR
1883	Pro-N	4	16	1	2	1	0	0	2	0	1	.125	.125	.188	-6	-2	-2	0				.692	-3	/S	-0.4
	Phi-N	3	12	2	6	1	0	0	3	0	1	.500	.500	.583	250	2	2	4				.750	-1	/3	0.1
	Yr	7	28	3	8	2	0	0	5	0	2	.286	.286	.357	96	-0	-0	3				.692	-3	/S3	-0.3
1884	Phi-N	100	401	47	92	11	2	2	32	4	49	.229	.237	.282	66	-17	-15	27				.834	11	*3	-0.2
1885	Phi-N	107	443	74	119	25	6	6	64	3	18	.269	.274	.393	116	5	6	49				.848	-7	*3	0.1
1886	Phi-N	107	430	71	115	16	10	2	53	15	31	.267	.292	.365	98	-1	-2	55	27			.879	-19	*3/O	-1.7
1887	Phi-N	111	474	93	136	21	6	2	78	21	14	.287	.321	.369	88	-5	-9	72	43			.865	-15	*3	-1.9
1888	Phi-N	100	398	37	86	12	3	0	39	9	33	.216	.235	.261	57	-18	-20	29	18			.891	-13	*3	-3.2
1889	Phi-N	129	544	77	157	21	9	6	77	23	25	.289	.319	.393	92	-2	-9	77	23			.893	1	*3	-0.4
1890	Phi-P	120	519	96	149	26	15	6	87	27	36	.287	.326	.430	100	-1	-3	81	20			.857	-16	*3	-1.2
1891	Phi-a	113	453	62	115	9	13	5	66	17	32	.254	.287	.364	86	-9	-11	52	11			.894	2	*3	-0.3
1892	Phi-N	25	98	9	14	1	1	0	4	6	9	.143	.200	.173	14	-10	-10	4	2			.883	3	3	-0.6
1893	Was-N	55	226	21	53	9	4	0	19	7	8	.235	.264	.310	55	-16	-15	19	2			.874	5	3	-0.7
1895	Bro-N	13	49	8	15	4	1	0	8	2	0	.306	.333	.429	106	-0	0	8	1			.917	2	3	0.2
Total	12	987	4063	598	1059	157	70	29	532	134	257	.261	.287	.355	86	-74	-88	478	147			.871	-48	3/SO	-10.2

■ JERRY MUMPHREY
Mumphrey, Jerry Wayne b: 9/9/52, Tyler, Tex. BB/TR, 6'2", 185 lbs. Deb: 9/10/74

YEAR	TM/L	G	AB	R	H	2B	3B	HR	RBI	BB	SO	AVG	OBP	SLG	PRO+	BR	/A	RC	SB	CS	SBR	FA	FR	POS	TPR
1974	StL-N	5	2	2	0	0	0	0	0	0	0	.000	.000	.000	-99	-1	-1	0	0	0	0	.000	0	/O	-0.1
1975	StL-N	11	16	2	6	2	0	0	1	4	3	.375	.500	.500	172	2	2	5	0	0	0	1.000	0	/O	0.2
1976	StL-N	112	384	51	99	15	5	1	26	37	53	.258	.325	.331	86	-6	-7	46	22	6	3	.993	4	O	-0.4
1977	StL-N	145	463	73	133	20	10	2	38	47	70	.287	.354	.387	100	-0	1	64	22	15	-2	.971	-9	*O	-1.6
1978	StL-N	125	367	41	96	13	4	2	37	30	40	.262	.319	.335	84	-8	-8	37	14	10	-2	.995	-6	*O	-2.1
1979	StL-N	124	339	53	100	10	3	3	32	26	39	.295	.345	.369	94	-2	-2	41	8	11	-4	.984	-13	*O	-2.4
1980	SD-N	160	564	61	168	24	3	4	59	49	90	.298	.354	.372	109	3	7	79	52	5	13	.974	-2	*O	1.3
1981	*NY-A	80	319	44	98	11	5	6	32	24	27	.307	.356	.429	127	10	10	47	14	9	-1	.966	7	O	1.4
1982	NY-A	123	477	76	143	24	10	9	68	50	66	.300	.366	.449	124	15	16	76	11	3	2	.986	9	*O	2.3
1983	NY-A	83	267	41	70	11	4	7	36	28	33	.262	.332	.412	107	1	3	34	2	3	-1	.983	7	O	0.6
	Hou-N	44	143	17	48	10	2	1	17	22	23	.336	.428	.455	154	10	11	31	5	0	2	.990	3	O	1.4
1984	Hou-N★	151	524	66	152	20	3	9	83	56	79	.290	.359	.391	119	8	13	74	15	7	0	.988	0	*O	0.9
1985	Hou-N	130	444	52	123	25	2	8	61	37	57	.277	.333	.396	106	1	3	56	6	7	-2	.969	-0	*O	-0.3
1986	Chi-N	111	309	37	94	11	2	5	32	26	45	.304	.358	.401	101	4	1	45	2	3	-1	.982	-16	O	-1.9
1987	Chi-N	118	309	41	103	19	2	13	44	35	47	.333	.401	.534	140	20	19	66	1	1	-0	.992	-2	O	1.4
1988	Chi-N	63	66	3	9	2	0	0	9	7	16	.136	.219	.167	12	-7	-8	2	0	0	0	1.000	-1	/O	-0.9
Total	15	1585	4993	660	1442	217	55	70	575	478	688	.289	.351	.396	109	50	60	702	174	80	4	.981	-18	*O	-0.2

■ JOHN MUNCE
Munce, John Lewis "Big John" b: 11/18/1857, Philadelphia, Pa. d: 3/15/17, Philadelphia, Pa. 6', Deb: 8/19/1884

YEAR	TM/L	G	AB	R	H	2B	3B	HR	RBI	BB	SO	AVG	OBP	SLG	PRO+	BR	/A	RC	SB	CS	SBR	FA	FR	POS	TPR
1884	Wil-U	7	21	1	4	0	0	0		1		.190	.227	.190	41	-1	-1	1				.667	-1	/O	-0.2

■ JAKE MUNCH
Munch, Jacob Ferdinand b: 11/16/1890, Morton, Pa. d: 6/8/66, Lansdowne, Pa. BL/TL, 6'2.5", 170 lbs. Deb: 5/27/18

YEAR	TM/L	G	AB	R	H	2B	3B	HR	RBI	BB	SO	AVG	OBP	SLG	PRO+	BR	/A	RC	SB	CS	SBR	FA	FR	POS	TPR
1918	Phi-A	22	30	3	8	0	1	0	0	0	5	.267	.267	.333	80	-1	-1	2	0			.667	-2	/O1	-0.3

■ GEORGE MUNDINGER
Mundinger, George b: 11/20/1854, New Orleans, La. d: 10/12/10, Covington, La. BR/TR, 6'2", 200 lbs. Deb: 5/09/1884

YEAR	TM/L	G	AB	R	H	2B	3B	HR	RBI	BB	SO	AVG	OBP	SLG	PRO+	BR	/A	RC	SB	CS	SBR	FA	FR	POS	TPR
1884	Ind-a	3	8	1	2	0	0	0		0		.250	.250	.250	68	-0	-0	1				.750	-3	/C	-0.3

■ BILL MUNDY
Mundy, William Edward b: 6/28/1889, Salineville, Ohio d: 9/23/58, Kalamazoo, Mich. BL/TL, 5'10", 154 lbs. Deb: 8/17/13

YEAR	TM/L	G	AB	R	H	2B	3B	HR	RBI	BB	SO	AVG	OBP	SLG	PRO+	BR	/A	RC	SB	CS	SBR	FA	FR	POS	TPR
1913	Bos-A	16	47	4	12	0	0	0	4	4	12	.255	.314	.255	65	-2	-2	4	0			.952	-2	1	-0.5

■ HORATIO MUNN
Munn, Horatio Deb: 9/06/1875

YEAR	TM/L	G	AB	R	H	2B	3B	HR	RBI	BB	SO	AVG	OBP	SLG	PRO+	BR	/A	RC	SB	CS	SBR	FA	FR	POS	TPR
1875	Atl-n	1	4	0	0	0	0	0		0		.000	.000	.000	-99	-1	-1	0						/2	-0.1

■ PEDRO MUNOZ
Munoz, Pedro Javier (Gonzalez) b: 9/19/68, Ponce, P.R. BR/TR, 5'11", 170 lbs. Deb: 9/01/90

YEAR	TM/L	G	AB	R	H	2B	3B	HR	RBI	BB	SO	AVG	OBP	SLG	PRO+	BR	/A	RC	SB	CS	SBR	FA	FR	POS	TPR
1990	Min-A	22	85	13	23	4	1	0	5	2	16	.271	.287	.341	70	-3	-4	8	3	0	1	.972	-1	O/D	-0.5
1991	Min-A	51	138	15	39	7	1	7	26	9	31	.283	.331	.500	121	4	4	23	3	0	1	.989	0	O/D	0.4
1992	Min-A	127	418	44	113	16	3	12	71	17	90	.270	.300	.409	94	-3	-5	44	4	5	-2	.987	-1	*O/D	-1.0
Total	3	200	641	72	175	27	5	19	102	28	137	.273	.306	.420	97	-2	-5	75	10	5	0	.986	-2	O/D	-1.1

■ RED MUNSON
Munson, Clarence Hanford b: 7/31/1883, Cincinnati, Ohio d: 2/19/57, Mishawaka, Ind. TR, Deb: 8/28/05

YEAR	TM/L	G	AB	R	H	2B	3B	HR	RBI	BB	SO	AVG	OBP	SLG	PRO+	BR	/A	RC	SB	CS	SBR	FA	FR	POS	TPR
1905	Phi-N	9	26	1	3	1	0	0	2	0		.115	.115	.154	-21	-4	-4	1	0			.857	-1	/C	-0.4

■ JOE MUNSON
Munson, Joseph Martin Napoleon (b: Joseph Martin Napoleon Carlson)
b: 11/6/1899, Renovo, Pa. d: 2/24/91, Drexel Hill, Pa. BL/TR, 5'9", 184 lbs. Deb: 9/18/25

YEAR	TM/L	G	AB	R	H	2B	3B	HR	RBI	BB	SO	AVG	OBP	SLG	PRO+	BR	/A	RC	SB	CS	SBR	FA	FR	POS	TPR
1925	Chi-N	9	35	5	13	3	1	0	3	3	1	.371	.436	.514	140	2	2	8	1	1	-0	1.000	-0	/O	0.1
1926	Chi-N	33	101	17	26	2	2	3	15	8	4	.257	.318	.406	93	-1	-1	13	0			.898	-2	O	-0.5
Total	2	42	136	22	39	5	3	3	18	11	5	.287	.349	.434	105	1	1	21	1	1		.922	-2	/O	-0.4

■ THURMAN MUNSON
Munson, Thurman Lee b: 6/7/47, Akron, Ohio d: 8/2/79, Canton, Ohio BR/TR, 5'11", 191 lbs. Deb: 8/08/69

YEAR	TM/L	G	AB	R	H	2B	3B	HR	RBI	BB	SO	AVG	OBP	SLG	PRO+	BR	/A	RC	SB	CS	SBR	FA	FR	POS	TPR
1969	NY-A	26	86	6	22	1	2	1	9	10	10	.256	.333	.349	94	-1	-1	9	0	1	-1	.986	-1	C	0.0
1970	NY-A	132	453	59	137	25	4	6	53	57	56	.302	.389	.415	128	15	18	72	5	7	-3	.989	6	*C	2.9
1971	NY-A★	125	451	71	113	15	4	10	42	52	65	.251	.337	.368	106	0	4	57	6	5	-1	**.998**	-1	*C/O	0.6
1972	NY-A	140	511	54	143	16	3	7	46	47	58	.280	.344	.364	115	7	9	62	6	7	-2	.977	-5	*C	0.8
1973	NY-A★	147	519	80	156	29	4	20	74	48	64	.301	.364	.487	143	25	27	89	4	6	-2	.984	6	*C/D	3.7
1974	NY-A★	144	517	64	135	19	2	13	60	44	66	.261	.320	.381	104	0	2	61	2	0	1	.974	2	*C/D	1.1
1975	NY-A★	157	597	83	190	24	3	12	102	45	52	.318	.372	.429	129	20	22	90	3	2	-0	.972	9	*CD/103	3.6
1976	*NY-A★	152	616	79	186	27	1	17	105	29	38	.302	.343	.432	127	18	19	85	14	11	-2	.981	-6	*CDO	1.4
1977	*NY-A★	149	595	85	183	28	5	18	100	39	55	.308	.352	.462	121	15	16	90	5	6	-2	.984	-5	*CD	1.3
1978	*NY-A†	154	617	73	183	27	1	6	71	35	70	.297	.337	.373	102	-1	1	73	2	3	-1	.986	-0	*CDO	0.2
1979	NY-A	97	382	42	110	18	3	3	39	32	37	.288	.343	.374	95	-3	-2	46	1	2	-1	.978	-6	C/1D	-0.5
Total	11	1423	5344	696	1558	229	32	113	701	438	571	.292	.350	.410	117	97	116	735	48	50	-16	.982	-2	*C/DO13	15.1

■ JOHN MUNYAN
Munyan, John B. b: 11/14/1860, Chester, Pa. d: 2/18/45, Endicott, N.Y. Deb: 7/12/1887

YEAR	TM/L	G	AB	R	H	2B	3B	HR	RBI	BB	SO	AVG	OBP	SLG	PRO+	BR	/A	RC	SB	CS	SBR	FA	FR	POS	TPR
1887	Cle-a	16	58	9	14	1	1	0		3		.241	.279	.293	63	-3	-3	6	4			.762	-2	O/C3	-0.3
1890	Col-a	2	7	1	1	0	0	0		0		.143	.250	.143	19	-1	-1	0	0			.667	0	/O	0.0
	StL-a	96	342	61	91	15	7	4		32		.266	.341	.386	102	7	-1	50	11			.939	-3	C/O23S	0.3
	Yr	98	349	62	92	15	7	4		32		.264	.339	.381	101	6	-2	50	11			.939	-3	C/O23S	0.3
1891	StL-a	62	182	44	42	4	3	0	20	43	39	.231	.389	.286	84	2	-3	26	13			.943	-6	CO/S3	-0.5
Total	3	176	589	115	148	20	11	4	20	78	39	.251	.351	.343	92	5	-7	82	28			.937	-10	C/O3S2	-0.5

■ BOBBY MURCER
Murcer, Bobby Ray b: 5/20/46, Oklahoma City, Okla BL/TR, 5'11", 180 lbs. Deb: 9/08/65

YEAR	TM/L	G	AB	R	H	2B	3B	HR	RBI	BB	SO	AVG	OBP	SLG	PRO+	BR	/A	RC	SB	CS	SBR	FA	FR	POS	TPR
1965	NY-A	11	37	2	9	0	1	1	4	5	12	.243	.333	.378	102	0	0	5	0	0	0	.932	7	S	0.8
1966	NY-A	21	69	3	12	1	1	0	5	4	5	.174	.219	.217	27	-7	-6	3	2	2	-1	.931	-4	S	-1.0
1969	NY-A	152	564	82	146	24	4	26	82	50	103	.259	.323	.454	120	9	12	82	7	5	-1	.964	-5	*O3	-0.2
1970	NY-A	159	581	95	146	23	3	23	78	87	100	.251	.351	.420	118	10	14	89	15	10	-2	.992	10	*O	1.4
1971	NY-A★	146	529	94	175	25	6	25	94	91	60	.331	**.429**	.543	**185**	**54**	**58**	**126**	14	8	-1	.985	-1	*O	5.2

YEAR	TM/L	G	AB	R	H	2B	3B	HR	RBI	BB	SO	AVG	OBP	SLG	PRO+	BR	/A	RC	SB	CS	SBR	FA	FR	POS	TPR
1972	NY-A★	153	585	**102**	171	30	7	33	96	63	67	.292	.363	.537	171	45	47	114	11	9	-2	.992	10	*O	5.3
1973	NY-A★	160	616	83	187	29	2	22	95	50	67	.304	.359	.464	135	23	26	100	6	7	-2	.985	2	*O	1.8
1974	NY-A★	156	606	69	166	25	4	10	88	57	59	.274	.338	.378	109	5	7	79	14	5	1	.978	0	*O	0.2
1975	SF-N★	147	526	80	157	29	4	11	91	91	45	.298	.404	.432	127	26	23	97	9	5	-0	.981	-11	*O	0.6
1976	SF-N	147	533	73	138	20	2	23	90	84	78	.259	.364	.433	122	19	17	86	12	7	-1	.961	-2	*O	0.9
1977	Chi-N	154	554	90	147	18	3	27	89	80	77	.265	.361	.455	106	14	6	95	16	7	1	.980	-8	*O/2S	-0.8
1978	Chi-N	146	499	66	140	22	6	9	64	80	57	.281	.380	.403	106	15	8	79	14	5	1	.979	-11	*O	-0.9
1979	Chi-N	58	190	22	49	4	1	7	22	36	20	.258	.379	.400	103	5	2	31	2	3	-1	1.000	-1	O	-0.2
	NY-A	74	264	42	72	12	0	8	33	25	32	.273	.340	.409	103	0	1	35	1	1	-0	.983	-4	O	-0.6
1980	*NY-A	100	297	41	80	9	1	13	57	34	28	.269	.348	.438	116	6	6	45	2	0	1	.955	-9	OD	-0.4
1981	*NY-A	50	117	14	31	6	0	6	24	12	15	.265	.333	.470	131	4	4	18	0	0	0	.000	0	D	0.4
1982	NY-A	65	141	12	32	6	0	7	30	12	15	.227	.292	.418	94	-2	-2	16	2	1	0	.000	0	D	-0.2
1983	NY-A	9	22	2	4	2	0	1	1	1	1	.182	.217	.409	71	-1	-1	1	0	0	0	.000	0	/D	-0.1
Total	17	1908	6730	972	1862	285	45	252	1043	862	841	.277	.361	.445	124	226	222	1103	127	75	-7	.981	-26	*OD/3S2	12.2

■ SIMMY MURCH Murch, Simeon Augustus b: 11/21/1880, Castine, Me. d: 6/6/39, Exeter, N.H. BR/TR, 6'4", 220 lbs. Deb: 9/20/04

YEAR	TM/L	G	AB	R	H	2B	3B	HR	RBI	BB	SO	AVG	OBP	SLG	PRO+	BR	/A	RC	SB	CS	SBR	FA	FR	POS	TPR
1904	StL-N	13	51	3	7	1	0	0	1	1		.137	.154	.157	-4	-6	-6	1	0			.905	-3	/23S	-0.9
1905	StL-N	4	9	0	1	0	0	0	0	0		.111	.111	.111	-35	-1	-1	0	0			.750	-3	/2S	-0.5
1908	Bro-N	6	11	1	2	1	0	0	0	1		.182	.250	.273	70	-0	-0	1	0			.964	-1	/1	-0.1
Total	3	23	71	4	10	2	0	0	1	2		.141	.164	.169	3	-8	-8	2	0			.880	-6	/231S	-1.5

■ WILBUR MURDOCH Murdoch, Wilbur Edwin b: 3/14/1875, Avon, N.Y. d: 10/29/41, Los Angeles, Cal. Deb: 8/29/08

YEAR	TM/L	G	AB	R	H	2B	3B	HR	RBI	BB	SO	AVG	OBP	SLG	PRO+	BR	/A	RC	SB	CS	SBR	FA	FR	POS	TPR
1908	StL-N	27	62	5	16	3	0	0	5	3		.258	.292	.306	96	-1	-0	7	4			.913	-5	O	-0.6

■ TIM MURNANE Murnane, Timothy Hayes b: 6/4/1852, Naugatuck, Conn. d: 2/7/17, Boston, Mass. BL/TR, 5'9.5", 172 lbs. Deb: 4/26/1872 M

YEAR	TM/L	G	AB	R	H	2B	3B	HR	RBI	BB	SO	AVG	OBP	SLG	PRO+	BR	/A	RC	SB	CS	SBR	FA	FR	POS	TPR
1872	Man-n	24	115	29	39	3	0	0	13	0	1	.339	.339	.365	124	2	4	15						1	0.3
1873	Ath-n	41	176	53	39	3	1	1	10	8	13	.222	.255	.267	50	-10	-12	14						O/12	-0.8
1874	Ath-n	21	81	11	18	2	0	0		2		.222	.241	.247	51	-4	-5	5						O/21	-0.4
1875	Phi-n	69	311	70	85	4	0	1		8		.273	.292	.296	100	1	-1	27						1O2	-0.1
1876	Bos-N	69	308	60	87	4	3	2	34	8	12	.282	.301	.334	109	4	3	32				.927	-4	*1/O2	-0.2
1877	Bos-N	35	140	23	39	7	1	1	15	6	7	.279	.308	.364	107	2	1	16				.815	-1	O/1	-0.1
1878	Pro-N	49	188	35	45	6	1	0	14	8	12	.239	.270	.282	82	-3	-3	15				.940	1	*1/O	-0.4
1884	Bos-U	76	311	55	73	5	2	0		22		.235	.285	.264	88	-4	-3	24				.950	-5	1OM	-1.3
Total	4 n	155	683	163	181	12	1	2	23	18	14	.265	.284	.294	83	-10	-15	61						/O12	-1.0
Total	4	229	947	173	244	22	7	3	63	44	31	.258	.291	.305	97	-1	-2	87				.938	-8	1/O2	-2.0

■ MURPHY Murphy Deb: 8/16/1884

YEAR	TM/L	G	AB	R	H	2B	3B	HR	RBI	BB	SO	AVG	OBP	SLG	PRO+	BR	/A	RC	SB	CS	SBR	FA	FR	POS	TPR
1884	Bos-U	1	3	0	0	0	0	0		1		.000	.250	.000	-9	-0	-0	0				.333	-3	/CO	-0.3

■ CLARENCE MURPHY Murphy, Clarence Deb: 6/17/1886

YEAR	TM/L	G	AB	R	H	2B	3B	HR	RBI	BB	SO	AVG	OBP	SLG	PRO+	BR	/A	RC	SB	CS	SBR	FA	FR	POS	TPR
1886	Lou-a	1	3	0	0	0	0	0		0		.000	.000	.000	-95	-1	-1	0	0			1.000	0	/O	-0.1

■ CONNIE MURPHY Murphy, Cornelius David "Stone Face" b: 11/1/1870, Northfield, Mass. d: 12/14/45, New Bedford, Mass. BL/TR, 5'8", 155 lbs. Deb: 9/17/1893

YEAR	TM/L	G	AB	R	H	2B	3B	HR	RBI	BB	SO	AVG	OBP	SLG	PRO+	BR	/A	RC	SB	CS	SBR	FA	FR	POS	TPR
1893	Cin-N	6	17	3	3	1	0	0	2	1	2	.176	.222	.235	22	-2	-2	1	0			.917	-2	/C	-0.3
1894	Cin-N	1	4	0	0	0	0	0	0	1	1	.000	.200	.000	-46	-1	-1	0	0			.500	-1	/C	-0.2
Total	2	7	21	3	3	1	0	0	2	2	3	.143	.217	.190	7	-3	-3	1	0			.857	-3	/C	-0.5

■ DALE MURPHY Murphy, Dale Bryan b: 3/12/56, Portland, Ore. BR/TR, 6'5", 215 lbs. Deb: 9/13/76

YEAR	TM/L	G	AB	R	H	2B	3B	HR	RBI	BB	SO	AVG	OBP	SLG	PRO+	BR	/A	RC	SB	CS	SBR	FA	FR	POS	TPR
1976	Atl-N	19	65	3	17	6	0	0	9	7	9	.262	.333	.354	89	-0	-1	8	0	0	0	.974	-0	C	0.0
1977	Atl-N	18	76	5	24	8	1	2	14	0	8	.316	.316	.526	108	2	1	11	0	1	-1	.954	-2	C	-0.1
1978	Atl-N	151	530	66	120	14	3	23	79	42	145	.226	.287	.394	80	-10	-17	56	11	7	-1	.984	4	*1C	-2.3
1979	Atl-N	104	384	53	106	7	2	21	57	38	67	.276	.344	.469	111	10	6	60	6	1	1	.980	-9	1C	-0.5
1980	Atl-N★	156	569	98	160	27	2	33	89	59	133	.281	.350	.510	133	26	24	101	9	6	-1	.985	-1	*O/1	1.7
1981	Atl-N	104	369	43	91	12	1	13	50	44	72	.247	.327	.390	100	1	0	47	14	5	1	.981	-1	*O/1	-0.3
1982	*Atl-N★	162	598	113	168	23	2	36	**109**	93	134	.281	.380	.507	140	38	35	118	23	11	0	.979	-2	*O	3.0
1983	Atl-N★	162	589	131	178	24	4	36	**121**	90	110	.302	.396	**.540**	146	**46**	41	**131**	30	4	7	.985	-3	*O	4.1
1984	Atl-N★	162	607	94	176	32	8	**36**	100	79	134	.290	.374	**.547**	145	**44**	38	123	19	7	2	.987	1	*O	3.7
1985	Atl-N★	162	616	**118**	185	32	2	**37**	111	**90**	141	.300	.390	.539	148	48	43	**131**	10	3	1	.980	-5	*O	3.6
1986	Atl-N★	160	614	89	163	29	7	29	83	75	141	.265	.347	.477	118	20	16	102	7	7	-2	.981	-4	*O	0.5
1987	Atl-N★	159	566	115	167	27	1	44	105	115	136	.295	.420	.580	154	53	49	**143**	16	6	1	.977	12	*O	5.6
1988	Atl-N	156	592	77	134	35	4	24	77	74	125	.226	.314	.421	104	6	3	72	3	5	-2	.992	18	*O	1.4
1989	Atl-N	154	574	60	131	16	0	20	84	65	142	.228	.309	.361	88	-7	-9	64	3	2	-0	.985	4	*O	-0.9
1990	Atl-N	97	349	38	81	14	0	17	55	41	84	.232	.315	.418	94	-1	-3	45	9	2	2	.981	4	O	0.0
	Phi-N	57	214	22	57	9	1	7	28	20	46	.266	.329	.416	104	1	1	26	0	1	-1	.992	3	O	0.2
	Yr	154	563	60	138	23	1	24	83	61	130	.245	.320	.417	98	0	-2	72	9	3	1	.985	7	*O	0.2
1991	Phi-N	153	544	66	137	33	1	18	81	48	93	.252	.313	.415	104	1	2	67	1	0	0	.983	4	*O	0.2
1992	Phi-N	18	62	5	10	1	0	2	7	1	13	.161	.175	.274	25	-6	-6	2	0	0	0	.950	-3	O	-1.1
Total	17	2154	7918	1196	2105	349	39	398	1259	981	1733	.266	.349	.471	120	272	223	1306	161	68	8	.983	21	*O1/C	18.8

■ DANNY MURPHY Murphy, Daniel Francis b: 8/11/1876, Philadelphia, Pa. d: 11/22/55, Jersey City, N.J. BR/TR, 5'9", 175 lbs. Deb: 9/17/00 C

YEAR	TM/L	G	AB	R	H	2B	3B	HR	RBI	BB	SO	AVG	OBP	SLG	PRO+	BR	/A	RC	SB	CS	SBR	FA	FR	POS	TPR
1900	NY-N	22	74	11	20	1	0	0	6	8		.270	.341	.284	77	-2	-2	9	4			.888	-6	2	-0.6
1901	NY-N	5	20	0	4	0	0	0	0	1		.200	.238	.200	29	-2	-2	1	0			.895	-3	/2	-0.5
1902	Phi-A	76	291	48	91	11	8	1	48	13		.313	.351	.416	107	4	2	48	12			.963	-12	2	-0.6
1903	Phi-A	133	513	66	140	31	11	1	60	13		.273	.295	.382	97	-0	-3	66	17			.949	-13	*2	-1.1
1904	Phi-A	150	557	78	160	30	17	7	77	22		.287	.320	.440	133	22	19	89	22			.941	13	*2	4.0
1905	*Phi-A	151	537	71	149	34	4	6	71	42		.277	.338	.389	128	18	17	83	23			.955	-9	*2	1.0
1906	Phi-A	119	448	48	135	28	6	2	60	21		.301	.335	.404	128	15	13	69	17			.955	-11	*2	0.4
1907	Phi-A	124	469	51	127	23	3	2	57	30		.271	.316	.345	108	5	4	58	11			.965	13	*2	1.7
1908	Phi-A	142	525	51	139	28	7	4	66	32		.265	.309	.368	112	10	6	65	16			.963	10	O2/1	1.4
1909	Phi-A	149	541	61	152	28	14	5	69	35		.281	.332	.412	132	19	18	81	19			**.977**	-2	*O	1.2
1910	*Phi-A	151	560	70	168	28	18	4	64	31		.300	.338	.436	143	24	24	88	18			.974	-2	*O	1.7
1911	*Phi-A	141	508	104	167	27	11	6	66	50		.329	.398	.461	142	27	28	102	22			.961	6	*O/2	2.6
1912	Phi-A	36	130	27	42	6	2	2	20	16		.323	.401	.446	148	7	8	26	8			.891	-6	O	0.0
1913	Phi-A	40	59	3	19	5	1	0	6	4	8	.322	.365	.441	139	2	3	9	0			1.000	-2	/O	0.0
1914	Bro-F	52	161	16	49	9	0	4	32	17	16	.304	.374	.435	131	6	6	30	4			.986	1	O	0.5
1915	Bro-F	5	6	0	1	0	0	0	0	0	0	.167	.167	.167	-2	-1	-1	0	0			1.000	-1	/2O	-0.2
Total	16	1496	5399	705	1563	289	102	44	702	335	24	.289	.336	.405	124	155	142	823	193			.953	-24	2O/1	11.5

■ DANNY MURPHY Murphy, Daniel Francis b: 8/23/42, Beverly, Mass. BL/TR, 5'11", 185 lbs. Deb: 6/18/60

YEAR	TM/L	G	AB	R	H	2B	3B	HR	RBI	BB	SO	AVG	OBP	SLG	PRO+	BR	/A	RC	SB	CS	SBR	FA	FR	POS	TPR
1960	Chi-N	31	75	7	9	2	0	1	6	4	13	.120	.175	.187	-1	-10	-10	2	0	0	0	.976	-1	O	-1.3
1961	Chi-N	4	13	3	5	0	0	2	3	1	5	.385	.429	.846	225	2	2	5	0	0	0	1.000	0	/O	0.2
1962	Chi-N	14	35	5	7	3	1	0	3	2	9	.200	.243	.343	53	-2	-2	3	0	0	0	1.000	-1	/O	-0.4
1969	Chi-A	17	1	0	0	0	0	0	0	2	0	.000	.667	.000	95	0	0	0	0	0	0	1.000	-0	P	0.0
1970	Chi-A	51	6	3	2	0	0	1	1	2	2	.333	.500	.833	252	1	1	2	0	0	0	.933	-1	P	0.0
Total	5	117	130	18	23	5	1	4	13	11	29	.177	.246	.323	53	-9	-9	13	0	0	0	.947	-3	/PO	-1.5

YEAR	TM/L	G	AB	R	H	2B	3B	HR	RBI	BB	SO	AVG	OBP	SLG	PRO+	BR	/A	RC	SB	CS	SBR	FA	FR	POS	TPR

■ DANNY MURPHY   Murphy, Daniel Joseph "Handsome Dan"   b: 9/10/1864, Brooklyn, N.Y.   d: 12/14/15, Brooklyn, N.Y.   156 lbs.   Deb: 4/26/1892

| 1892 | NY-N | 8 | 26 | 2 | 3 | 0 | 0 | 0 | 0 | 5 | 4 | .115 | .258 | .115 | 15 | -2 | -2 | 1 | 0 | | | .900 | -2 | /C | -0.4 |

■ DAVE MURPHY   Murphy, David Francis "Dirty Dave"   b: 5/4/1876, Adams, Mass.   d: 4/8/40, Adams, Mass.   TR ,   Deb: 8/28/05

| 1905 | Bos-N | 3 | 11 | 0 | 2 | 0 | 0 | 0 | 1 | 0 | | .182 | .182 | .182 | 9 | -1 | -1 | 0 | 0 | | | 1.000 | -2 | /S3 | -0.4 |

■ DWAYNE MURPHY   Murphy, Dwayne Keith   b: 3/18/55, Merced, Cal.   BL/TR, 6'1", 185 lbs.   Deb: 4/08/78

1978	Oak-A	60	52	15	10	2	0	0	5	7	14	.192	.288	.231	50	-3	-3	4	0	1	-1	1.000	-10	O/D	-1.5
1979	Oak-A	121	388	57	99	10	4	11	40	84	80	.255	.389	.387	116	9	12	62	15	11	-2	.988	8	*O	1.3
1980	Oak-A	159	573	86	157	18	2	13	68	102	96	.274	.386	.380	119	13	18	90	26	15	-1	.990	24	*O	3.4
1981	*Oak-A	107	390	58	98	10	3	15	60	73	91	.251	.372	.408	131	15	17	64	10	4	1	.985	12	*O/D	2.7
1982	Oak-A	151	543	84	129	15	1	27	94	94	122	.238	.353	.418	116	10	13	88	26	8	3	.983	22	*O/SD	3.4
1983	Oak-A	130	471	55	107	17	2	17	75	62	105	.227	.317	.380	97	-6	-2	55	7	5	-1	.979	10	*O/D	0.3
1984	Oak-A	153	559	93	143	18	2	33	88	74	111	.256	.346	.472	133	18	23	90	4	5	-2	.988	21	*O	3.7
1985	Oak-A	152	523	77	122	21	3	20	59	84	123	.233	.343	.400	111	3	9	73	4	5	-2	.989	9	*O	1.0
1986	Oak-A	98	329	50	83	11	3	9	39	56	80	.252	.368	.386	114	4	8	51	3	1	0	.993	11	O/D	1.6
1987	Oak-A	82	219	39	51	7	0	8	35	58	61	.233	.394	.374	113	4	7	36	4	4	-1	.984	0	O/12	0.3
1988	Det-A	49	144	14	36	5	0	4	19	24	26	.250	.361	.368	109	2	2	21	1	1	-0	1.000	1	O/D	0.2
1989	Phi-N	98	156	20	34	5	0	9	27	29	44	.218	.341	.423	117	4	4	24	0	1	-1	.986	-6	O	-0.4
Total	12	1360	4347	648	1069	139	20	166	609	747	953	.246	.359	.402	116	72	109	659	100	61	-7	.987	102	*O/D21S	16.0

■ ED MURPHY   Murphy, Edward Joseph   b: 8/23/18, Joliet, Ill.   d: 12/10/91, Joliet, Ill.   BR/TR, 5'11", 190 lbs.   Deb: 9/10/42

| 1942 | Phi-N | 13 | 28 | 2 | 7 | 2 | 0 | 0 | 4 | 2 | 4 | .250 | .300 | .321 | 86 | -1 | -1 | 3 | 0 | | | 1.000 | -0 | /1 | -0.1 |

■ TONY MURPHY   Murphy, Frank J.   b: Brooklyn, N.Y.   Deb: 10/15/1884

| 1884 | NY-a | 1 | 3 | 1 | 1 | 0 | 0 | 0 | | 0 | | .333 | .333 | .333 | 125 | 0 | 0 | 0 | | | | 1.000 | -1 | /C | -0.1 |

■ FRANK MURPHY   Murphy, Frank Morton   b: 1880, Hackensack, N.J.   d: 11/2/12, New York, N.Y.   Deb: 7/02/01

1901	Bos-N	45	176	13	46	5	3	1	18	4		.261	.282	.341	74	-5	-7	19	6			.939	4	O	-0.6
	NY-N	35	130	10	21	3	0	0	8	6		.162	.199	.185	12	-15	-14	5	2			.847	-10	2O	-2.4
	Yr	80	306	23	67	8	3	1	26	10		.219	.246	.275	49	-19	-21	24	8			.940	-5	O2	-3.0

■ DUMMY MURPHY   Murphy, Herbert Courtland   b: 12/18/1886, Olney, Ill.   d: 8/10/62, Tallahassee, Fla.   BR/TR, 5'10", 165 lbs.   Deb: 4/14/14

| 1914 | Phi-N | 9 | 26 | 1 | 4 | 1 | 0 | 0 | 3 | 0 | 4 | .154 | .185 | .192 | 12 | -3 | -3 | 1 | 0 | | | .864 | 3 | /S | 0.1 |

■ HOWARD MURPHY   Murphy, Howard   b: 1/1/1882, Birmingham, Ala.   d: 10/5/26, Fort Worth, Tex.   BL/TR, 5'8.5", 150 lbs.   Deb: 8/04/09

| 1909 | StL-N | 25 | 60 | 3 | 12 | 0 | 0 | 0 | 3 | 4 | | .200 | .250 | .200 | 42 | -4 | -4 | 3 | 1 | | | .925 | -2 | O | -0.7 |

■ EDDIE MURPHY   Murphy, John Edward   b: 10/2/1891, Hancock, N.Y.   d: 2/21/69, Dunmore, Pa.   BL/TR, 5'9", 155 lbs.   Deb: 8/26/12

1912	Phi-A	33	142	24	45	4	1	0	6	11		.317	.370	.359	113	2	3	21	7			.947	0	O	0.1
1913	*Phi-A	137	508	105	150	14	7	1	30	70	44	.295	.391	.356	122	16	17	76	21			.942	-12	*O	-0.1
1914	*Phi-A	148	573	101	156	12	9	3	43	87	46	.272	.379	.340	121	16	19	77	36	32	-8	.941	-5	*O	-0.2
1915	Phi-A	68	260	37	60	3	4	0	17	29	15	.231	.315	.273	79	-7	-6	25	13	3	2	.899	-5	O/3	-1.2
	Chi-A	70	273	51	86	11	5	0	26	39	12	.315	.410	.392	136	15	14	47	20	12	-1	.952	-1	O	0.9
	Yr	138	533	88	146	14	9	0	43	68	27	.274	.365	.334	109	8	8	71	33	15	1	.933	-6	*O/3	-0.3
1916	Chi-A	51	105	14	22	5	1	0	4	9	5	.210	.284	.276	68	-4	-4	9	3			1.000	-3	O/3	-0.9
1917	Chi-A	53	51	9	16	2	1	0	16	5	1	.314	.386	.392	135	2	2	9	4			1.000	-4	/O	-0.2
1918	Chi-A	91	286	36	85	9	3	0	23	22	18	.297	.350	.350	110	4	3	37	6			.958	-10	O/2	-1.1
1919	*Chi-A	30	35	8	17	4	0	0	5	7	0	.486	.571	.600	228	7	7	12	0			.917	-0	/O	0.6
1920	Chi-A	58	118	22	40	2	1	0	19	12	4	.339	.405	.373	107	2	2	18	1	3	-2	.886	1	O/3	0.0
1921	Chi-A	6	5	1	1	0	0	0	0	0	0	.200	.200	.200	2	-1	-1	0	0	0	0	.000	0	H	-0.1
1926	Pit-N	16	17	3	2	0	0	0	6	3	0	.118	.250	.118	2	-2	-2	1	0			1.000	-0	/O	-0.3
Total	11	761	2373	411	680	66	32	4	195	294	145	.287	.374	.346	114	49	53	331	111	50		.942	-39	O/32	-2.5

■ JOHN MURPHY   Murphy, John Patrick   b: 1879, New Haven, Conn.   d: 4/20/49, Andover, Mass.   5'7.5", 160 lbs.   Deb: 9/10/02

1902	StL-N	1	3	1	2	1	0	0	1	1		.667	.750	1.000	458	1	1	2	0			1.000	-1	/3	0.1
1903	Det-A	5	22	1	4	1	0	0	1	0		.182	.182	.227	23	-2	-2	1	0			.852	-1	/S	-0.3
Total	2	6	25	2	6	2	0	0	2	1		.240	.269	.320	79	-2	-1	3	0			.926	-2	/S3	-0.2

■ LARRY MURPHY   Murphy, Lawrence Patrick   BL ,   Deb: 5/30/1891

| 1891 | Was-a | 101 | 400 | 73 | 106 | 15 | 3 | 1 | 35 | 63 | 27 | .265 | .372 | .325 | 107 | 4 | 7 | 61 | 29 | | | .874 | -5 | *O | -0.1 |

■ LEO MURPHY   Murphy, Leo Joseph "Red"   b: 1/7/1889, Terre Haute, Ind.   d: 8/12/60, Racine, Wis.   BR/TR, 6'1", 179 lbs.   Deb: 5/02/15

| 1915 | Pit-N | 31 | 41 | 4 | 4 | 0 | 0 | 0 | 4 | 4 | 12 | .098 | .178 | .098 | -16 | -6 | -6 | 1 | 0 | | | .932 | -3 | C | -0.9 |

■ MIKE MURPHY   Murphy, Michael Jerome   b: 8/19/1888, Forestville, Pa.   d: 10/26/52, Johnson City, N.Y.   BR/TR, 5'9", 170 lbs.   Deb: 5/17/12

1912	StL-N	1	1	0	0	0	0	0	1	0	0	.000	.000	.000	-99	-0	-0	0	0			.000	0	/C	0.0
1916	Phi-A	14	27	0	3	0	0	0	1	1	3	.111	.143	.111	-25	-4	-4	1	0			.973	-3	C	-0.8
Total	2	15	28	0	3	0	0	0	2	1	3	.107	.138	.107	-28	-4	-4	1	0			.973	-3	/C	-0.8

■ MORGAN MURPHY   Murphy, Morgan Edward   b: 2/14/1867, E.Providence, R.I.   d: 10/3/38, Providence, R.I.   BR/TR, 5'8", 160 lbs.   Deb: 4/22/1890

1890	Bos-P	68	246	38	56	10	2	2	32	24	31	.228	.301	.309	61	-12	-15	28	16			.903	4	C/SO3	-0.5
1891	Bos-a	106	402	60	87	11	4	4	54	36	58	.216	.289	.294	70	-16	-15	40	17			.954	11	*C/O	0.4
1892	Cin-N	74	234	29	46	8	2	2	24	25	57	.197	.277	.274	69	-9	-8	19	4			.955	0	C	-0.3
1893	Cin-N	57	200	25	47	5	1	1	19	14	35	.235	.295	.285	55	-13	-13	18	1			.932	-5	C/1	-1.2
1894	Cin-N	75	255	42	70	9	0	1	37	26	34	.275	.344	.322	60	-15	-17	32	6			.901	-4	C/S3	-1.1
1895	Cin-N	25	82	15	22	2	0	0	16	11	8	.268	.355	.293	67	-3	-4	11	6			.907	-2	C	-0.4
1896	StL-N	49	175	12	45	5	2	0	11	8	14	.257	.290	.309	62	-10	-9	17	1			.926	-2	C	-0.5
1897	StL-N	62	207	13	35	2	0	0	12	6		.169	.196	.179	-1	-30	-30	8	1			.950	-3	C/1	-2.3
1898	Pit-N	5	16	0	2	0	0	0	2	1		.125	.176	.125	-14	-2	-2	0	1			.957	1	/C	-0.1
	Phi-N	25	86	6	17	3	0	0	11	6		.198	.258	.233	43	-7	-6	6	0			.964	1	C	-0.3
	Yr	30	102	6	19	3	0	0	13	7		.186	.245	.216	34	-9	-8	6	1			.963	2	C	-0.4
1900	Phi-N	11	36	2	10	0	1	0	3	0		.278	.278	.333	69	-2	-2	4	0			.980	2	C	0.1
1901	Phi-A	9	28	5	6	1	0	0	6	0		.214	.214	.250	27	-3	-3	2	1			.929	0	/C1	-0.2
Total	11	566	1967	247	443	56	12	10	227	157	237	.225	.287	.281	55	-121	-124	185	53			.936	2	C/1OS3	-6.4

■ PAT MURPHY   Murphy, Patrick J.   b: 1/2/1857, Auburn, Mass.   d: 5/16/27, Worcester, Mass.   TR , 5'10", 160 lbs.   Deb: 9/02/1887

1887	NY-N	17	56	4	12	2	0	0	4	2	4	.214	.241	.250	40	-5	-4	4	1			.847	2	C	-0.1
1888	*NY-N	28	106	11	18	1	0	0	4	6	11	.170	.214	.179	28	-8	-8	5	3			.913	3	C	-0.2
1889	NY-N	9	28	5	10	1	1	1	4	2	0	.357	.400	.571	171	2	2	7	0			.872	-2	/C	0.1
1890	NY-N	32	119	14	28	5	1	0	9	14	13	.235	.321	.294	81	-2	-2	12	3			.905	-5	C/OS	-0.5
Total	4	86	309	34	68	9	2	1	21	24	28	.220	.278	.272	66	-13	-12	28	7			.895	-3	/COS	-0.7

■ DICK MURPHY   Murphy, Richard Lee   b: 10/25/31, Cincinnati, Ohio   BL/TL, 5'11", 170 lbs.   Deb: 6/13/54

| 1954 | Cin-N | 6 | 1 | 1 | 0 | 0 | 0 | 0 | 1 | 1 | | .000 | .000 | .000 | -97 | -0 | 0 | 0 | 0 | 0 | 0 | .000 | 0 | H | 0.0 |

YEAR	TM/L	G	AB	R	H	2B	3B	HR	RBI	BB	SO	AVG	OBP	SLG	PRO+	BR	/A	RC	SB	CS	SBR	FA	FR	POS	TPR

■ BUZZ MURPHY
Murphy, Robert R. b: 4/26/1895, Denver, Colo. d: 5/11/38, Denver, Colo.   BL/TL, 5'8.5", 155 lbs. Deb: 7/14/18

1918	Bos-N	9	32	6	12	2	3	1	9	3	5	.375	.429	.719	259	5	5	10				1.000	-2	/O	0.4
1919	Was-A	79	252	19	66	7	4	0	28	19	32	.262	.326	.321	83	-6	-5	28	5			.959	2	O	-0.9
Total	2	88	284	25	78	9	7	1	37	22	37	.275	.338	.366	101	-0	0	38	5			.961	0	/O	-0.5

■ BILLY MURPHY
Murphy, William Eugene b: 5/7/44, Pineville, La.   BR/TR, 6'1", 190 lbs. Deb: 4/15/66

| 1966 | NY-N | 84 | 135 | 15 | 31 | 4 | 1 | 3 | 17 | 34 | | .230 | .273 | .341 | 71 | -6 | -5 | 12 | 1 | 2 | -1 | .955 | 3 | O | -0.5 |

■ YALE MURPHY
Murphy, William Henry "Tot" or "Midget" b: 11/11/1869, Southville, Mass. d: 2/14/06, Southville, Mass.   BL/TR, 5'3", 125 lbs. Deb: 4/19/1894

1894	*NY-N	74	280	64	76	6	2	0	28	51	23	.271	.384	.307	70	-11	-11	45	28			.898	-11	SO/321	-1.5
1895	NY-N	51	184	35	37	6	2	0	16	27	13	.201	.303	.255	48	-14	-13	17	7			.944	-4	O/S32	-1.6
1897	NY-N	5	8	1	0	0	0	0	1	2		.000	.200	.000	-46	-2	-2	0	0			.800	-2	/S2	-0.3
Total	3	130	472	100	113	12	4	0	45	80	36	.239	.350	.282	60	-27	-25	62	35			.890	-17	/SO321	-3.4

■ WILLIE MURPHY
Murphy, William N. "Gentle Willie" b: 1865, Boston, Mass.   BL, 5'11", 198 lbs. Deb: 5/01/1884

1884	Cle-N	42	168	18	38	3	3	1	9	1	23	.226	.231	.298	63	-7	-8	12				.720	-5	O	-1.2
	Was-a	5	21	3	10	0	0	0		1		.476	.542	.476	271	3	4	6				.700	-0	/O2	0.3
Total	1	47	189	21	48	3	3	1	9	2	23	.254	.269	.317	84	-3	-4	17				.718	-5	/O2	-0.9

■ TONY MURRAY
Murray, Anthony Joseph b: 4/30/04, Chicago, Ill. d: 3/19/74, Chicago, Ill.   BR/TR, 5'10.5", 154 lbs. Deb: 10/06/23

| 1923 | Chi-N | 2 | 4 | 0 | 1 | 0 | 0 | 0 | 0 | 0 | 0 | .250 | .400 | .250 | 75 | -0 | -0 | 0 | 0 | 0 | 0 | 1.000 | -2 | /O | -0.2 |

■ EDDIE MURRAY
Murray, Eddie Clarence b: 2/24/56, Los Angeles, Cal.   BB/TR, 6'2", 200 lbs. Deb: 4/07/77 F

1977	Bal-A	160	611	81	173	29	2	27	88	48	104	.283	.336	.470	125	13	18	90	0	1	-1	.992	-4	*D1/O	1.0
1978	Bal-A☆	161	610	85	174	32	3	27	95	70	97	.285	.360	.480	143	27	32	104	6	5	-1	.997	1	*1/3D	2.2
1979	*Bal-A	159	606	90	179	30	2	25	99	72	78	.295	.372	.475	132	23	26	107	10	2	2	.994	-1	*1	1.6
1980	Bal-A	158	621	100	186	36	2	32	116	54	71	.300	.357	.519	138	30	30	111	7	2	1	.994	-9	*1/D	1.3
1981	Bal-A★	99	378	57	111	21	2	22	78	40	43	.294	.363	.534	156	26	26	70	2	3	-1	.999	10	1	3.0
1982	Bal-A★	151	550	87	174	30	1	32	110	70	82	.316	.395	.549	157	42	43	116	7	2	1	.997	1	*1/D	3.6
1983	*Bal-A★	156	582	115	178	30	3	33	111	86	90	.306	.398	.538	**158**	45	**46**	**133**	5	1	1	.993	4	*1/D	4.1
1984	Bal-A★	162	588	97	180	26	3	29	110	**107**	87	.306	**.415**	.509	157	**47**	**49**	130	10	2	2	.992	8	*1/D	4.8
1985	Bal-A★	156	583	111	173	37	1	31	124	84	68	.297	.387	.523	151	38	41	122	5	2	0	.987	13	*1/D	4.3
1986	Bal-A☆	137	495	61	151	25	1	17	84	78	49	.305	.400	.463	136	26	27	92	3	0	1	.989	-3	*1D	1.6
1987	Bal-A	160	618	89	171	28	3	30	91	73	80	.277	.353	.477	121	15	18	103	1	2	-1	.993	12	*1/D	1.6
1988	Bal-A	161	603	75	171	27	2	28	84	75	78	.284	.361	.474	136	26	28	101	5	2	0	.989	10	*1D	3.0
1989	LA-N	160	594	66	147	29	1	20	88	87	85	.247	.346	.401	115	11	12	85	7	2	1	**.996**	13	*1/3	1.4
1990	LA-N	155	558	96	184	22	3	26	95	82	64	.330	.417	.520	160	45	47	118	8	5	-1	.992	4	*1	3.9
1991	LA-N★	153	576	69	150	23	1	19	96	55	74	.260	.325	.403	106	2	4	73	10	3	1	.995	9	*1/D	-0.3
1992	NY-N	156	551	64	144	37	2	16	93	66	74	.261	.340	.423	116	11	11	79	4	2	0	.991	-4	*1	0.8
Total	16	2444	9124	1343	2646	462	32	414	1562	1147	1224	.290	.370	.484	137	427	457	1632	90	36	5	.993	62	*1D/3O	37.5

■ ED MURRAY
Murray, Edward Francis b: 5/8/1895, Mystic, Conn. d: 11/8/70, Cheyenne, Wyoming   BR/TR, 5'6", 145 lbs. Deb: 6/24/17

| 1917 | StL-A | 1 | 1 | 0 | 0 | 0 | 0 | 0 | 0 | 0 | 1 | .000 | .000 | .000 | -99 | -0 | -0 | 0 | 0 | | | .000 | 0 | /S | 0.0 |

■ JIM MURRAY
Murray, James Oscar b: 1/16/1878, Galveston, Tex. d: 4/25/45, Galveston, Tex.   BR/TL, 5'10", 180 lbs. Deb: 9/02/02

1902	Chi-N	12	47	3	8	0	0	0		1	2	.170	.204	.170	16	-5	-4	2	0			1.000	-1	O	-0.6
1911	StL-A	31	102	8	19	5	0	3	11	5		.186	.224	.324	54	-7	-7	7	0			.935	-0	O	-0.8
1914	Bos-N	39	112	10	26	4	2	0	12	6	24	.232	.277	.304	73	-4	-4	10	2			.941	-8	O	-1.4
Total	3	82	261	21	53	9	2	3	24	13	24	.203	.244	.287	56	-16	-15	18	2			.600	-9	/O	-2.8

■ MIAH MURRAY
Murray, Jeremiah J. b: 1/1/1865, Boston, Mass. d: 1/11/22, Boston, Mass.   BR/TR, 5'11.5", 170 lbs. Deb: 5/17/1884 U

1884	Pro-N	8	27	1	5	0	0	0		1	8	.185	.214	.185	28	-5	-2	1				.836	-4	/CO1	-0.6
1885	Lou-a	12	43	4	8	0	0	0		2		.186	.239	.186	38	-3	-3	2		0		.863	1	C/1	-0.1
1888	Was-N	12	42	1	4	1	0	0	3	1	7	.095	.116	.119	-25	-6	-5	1	0			.912	0	C/1	-0.5
1891	Was-a	2	8	0	0	0	0	0	1	0	1	.000	.000	.000	-99	-2	-2	0	0			1.000	3	/C	0.1
Total	4	34	120	6	17	1	0	0	4	4	16	.142	.176	.150	4	-13	-12	4	0			.884	-1	/C1O	-1.1

■ RED MURRAY
Murray, John Joseph b: 3/4/1884, Arnot, Pa. d: 12/4/58, Sayre, Pa.   BR/TR, 5'10.5", 190 lbs. Deb: 6/16/06

1906	StL-N	46	144	18	37	9	7	1	16	9		.257	.301	.438	136	4	5	21	5			.962	-3	O/C	0.1
1907	StL-N	132	485	46	127	10	10	7	46	24		.262	.299	.367	113	3	4	63	23			.935	5	*O	0.5
1908	StL-N	154	593	64	167	19	15	7	62	37		.282	.332	.400	140	21	23	92	48			.914	-4	*O	1.5
1909	NY-N	149	570	74	150	15	12	**7**	91	45		.263	.319	.368	112	7	6	81	48			.947	3	*O	0.4
1910	NY-N	149	553	78	153	27	8	4	87	52	51	.277	.345	.376	110	7	7	91	57			.948	4	*O	0.4
1911	*NY-N	140	488	70	142	27	15	3	78	43	37	.291	.354	.426	114	10	8	89	48			.954	-11	*O	-0.9
1912	*NY-N	143	549	83	152	26	20	3	92	27	45	.277	.320	.413	97	-3	-5	83	38			**.968**	2	*O	-1.0
1913	*NY-N	147	520	70	139	21	3	2	59	34	28	.267	.320	.331	85	-10	-10	63	35			.965	10	*O	-0.7
1914	NY-N	86	139	19	31	5	3	0	23	9	7	.223	.270	.309	75	-5	-5	14	11			1.000	-10	O	-1.7
1915	NY-N	45	127	12	28	1	2	3	11	7	15	.220	.261	.331	83	-4	-3	10	2	3	-1	.959	-1	O	-0.7
	Chi-N	51	144	20	43	6	1	0	11	8	8	.299	.340	.354	110	2	2	18	6	5	-1	.966	1	O/2	0.0
	Yr	96	271	32	71	7	3	3	22	15	23	.262	.303	.343	98	-2	-1	28	8	8	-2	.963	1	O/C	-0.7
1917	NY-N	22	22	1	1	0	0	0	3	4	3	.045	.192	.091	-12	-3	-3	0				1.000	-3	O/C	-0.7
Total	11	1264	4334	555	1170	168	96	37	579	299	194	.270	.323	.379	108	29	30	627	321	8		.950	-6	*O/C2	-2.8

■ LARRY MURRAY
Murray, Larry b: 4/1/53, Chicago, Ill.   BB/TR, 5'11", 179 lbs. Deb: 9/07/74

1974	NY-A	6	1	1	0	0	0	0	0	0	0	.000	.000	.000	-99	-0	-0	0	0	1	-1	.000	-2	/O	-0.3
1975	NY-A	6	1	1	0	0	0	0	0	0	0	.000	.000	.000	-99	-0	-0	0	0	0	0	1.000	-2	/O	-0.2
1976	NY-A	8	10	2	1	0	0	0	2	1	2	.100	.182	.100	-16	-1	-1	0	2	0	0	1.000	-1	/O	-0.2
1977	Oak-A	90	162	19	29	5	2	1	9	17	36	.179	.257	.253	40	-13	-13	12	12	3	2	.992	-13	O/SD	-2.6
1978	Oak-A	11	12	1	1	0	0	0	0	3	2	.083	.267	.083	3	-1	-1	0	2	0	0	1.000	-1	/O	-0.3
1979	Oak-A	105	226	25	42	11	2	2	20	28	34	.186	.276	.279	53	-16	-14	18	6	6	-2	.963	-1	O/2	-1.9
Total	6	226	412	49	73	16	4	3	31	49	74	.177	.265	.257	44	-33	-31	31	20	10	0	.975	-20	O/2DS	-5.5

■ RAY MURRAY
Murray, Raymond Lee "Deacon" b: 10/12/17, Spring Hope, N.C.   BR/TR, 6'3", 204 lbs. Deb: 4/25/48

1948	Cle-A	4	4	0	0	0	0	0	0	0	0	.000	.000	.000	-99	-1	-1	0	0			.000	0	H	-0.1
1950	Cle-A	55	139	16	38	8	2	1	13	12	13	.273	.331	.381	85	-4	-3	16	1	0		.972	-5	C	-0.6
1951	Cle-A	1	1	0	1	0	0	0	1	0		1.000	1.000	1.000	468	1	1	1	0	0		1.000	1	/C	0.1
	Phi-A	40	122	10	26	6	0	0	13	14	9	.213	.294	.262	50	-8	-9	10	0	0		.985	-3	C	-0.9
	Yr	41	123	10	27	6	0	0	14	14	9	.220	.299	.268	53	-8	-8	10	0	0		.986	-2	C	-0.8
1952	Phi-A	44	136	14	28	5	1	0	10	9	13	.206	.255	.265	42	-10	-11	9	0	0		.995	7	C	-0.2
1953	Phi-A	84	268	25	76	14	3	6	41	18	25	.284	.331	.425	99	-0	-1	38	0	0		.989	4	C	0.6
1954	Phi-A	22	61	4	15	4	0	0	2	2	7	.246	.270	.344	73	-3	-2	6	0	0		.989	1	C	-0.1
Total	6	250	731	69	184	37	6	8	80	55	67	.252	.305	.352	75	-26	-27	79	1	0		.987	6	C	-1.2

■ RICH MURRAY
Murray, Richard Dale b: 7/6/57, Los Angeles, Cal.   BR/TR, 6'4", 195 lbs. Deb: 6/07/80 F

| 1980 | SF-N | 53 | 194 | 19 | 42 | 8 | 2 | 4 | 24 | 11 | 48 | .216 | .259 | .340 | 67 | -9 | -9 | 15 | 2 | 1 | 0 | .987 | 0 | 1 | -1.3 |

YEAR	TM/L	G	AB	R	H	2B	3B	HR	RBI	BB	SO	AVG	OBP	SLG	PRO+	BR	/A	RC	SB	CS	SBR	FA	FR	POS	TPR
1983	SF-N	4	10	0	2	0	0	0	1	0	3	.200	.200	.200	11	-1	-1	0	0	0	0	1.000	-0	/1	-0.2
Total	2	57	204	19	44	8	2	4	25	11	51	.216	.256	.333	65	-11	-10	15	2	1	0	.988	0	/1	-1.5

■ BOBBY MURRAY Murray, Robert Hayes b: 7/4/1894, St.Albans, Vt. d: 1/4/79, Nashua, N.H. BL/TR, 5'7", 155 lbs. Deb: 9/24/23

YEAR	TM/L	G	AB	R	H	2B	3B	HR	RBI	BB	SO	AVG	OBP	SLG	PRO+	BR	/A	RC	SB	CS	SBR	FA	FR	POS	TPR
1923	Was-A	10	37	2	7	1	0	0	2	1	4	.189	.211	.216	13	-5	-4	2	1	0	0	1.000	2	3	-0.1

■ TOM MURRAY Murray, Thomas W. b: 1866, Savannah, Ga. Deb: 6/20/1894

YEAR	TM/L	G	AB	R	H	2B	3B	HR	RBI	BB	SO	AVG	OBP	SLG	PRO+	BR	/A	RC	SB	CS	SBR	FA	FR	POS	TPR
1894	Phi-N	1	2	0	0	0	0	0	0	0	2	.000	.000	.000	-99	-1	-1	0	0			.833	0	/S	0.0

■ BILL MURRAY Murray, William Allenwood "Dasher" b: 9/6/1893, Vinalhaven, Me. d: 9/14/43, Boston, Mass. BB/TR, 5'11", 165 lbs. Deb: 6/27/17

YEAR	TM/L	G	AB	R	H	2B	3B	HR	RBI	BB	SO	AVG	OBP	SLG	PRO+	BR	/A	RC	SB	CS	SBR	FA	FR	POS	TPR
1917	Was-A	8	21	2	3	0	1	0	4	2	2	.143	.217	.238	39	-2	-2	1	1			.889	-2	/2S	-0.3

■ IVAN MURRELL Murrell, Ivan Augustus (Peters) b: 4/24/45, Almirante, Panama BR/TR, 6'2", 196 lbs. Deb: 9/28/63

YEAR	TM/L	G	AB	R	H	2B	3B	HR	RBI	BB	SO	AVG	OBP	SLG	PRO+	BR	/A	RC	SB	CS	SBR	FA	FR	POS	TPR
1963	Hou-N	2	5	1	1	0	0	0	0	0	2	.200	.200	.200	17	-1	-1	0	0	0	0	1.000	0	/O	-0.1
1964	Hou-N	10	14	1	2	1	0	0	1	0	6	.143	.143	.214	-1	-2	-2	0	0	0	0	1.000	-1	/O	-0.3
1967	Hou-N	10	29	2	9	0	0	0	1	1	9	.310	.333	.310	88	-1	-0	3	1	0	0	.846	-1	/O	-0.1
1968	Hou-N	32	59	3	6	1	1	0	3	1	17	.102	.117	.153	-20	-9	-8	1	0	0	0	.931	3	O	-0.7
1969	SD-N	111	247	19	63	10	6	3	25	11	65	.255	.292	.381	91	-5	-4	26	3	4	-2	.959	-0	O/1	-0.9
1970	SD-N	125	347	43	85	9	3	12	35	17	93	.245	.288	.392	84	-11	-9	36	9	7	-2	.970	1	*O/1	-1.4
1971	SD-N	103	255	23	60	6	3	7	24	7	60	.235	.264	.365	82	-9	-7	22	5	2	0	.978	1	O	-0.9
1972	SD-N	5	7	0	1	0	0	0	1	0	3	.143	.143	.143	-20	-1	-1	0	0	0	0	1.000	0	/O	-0.1
1973	SD-N	93	210	23	48	13	1	9	21	2	52	.229	.236	.429	87	-7	-5	20	2	0	1	.959	3	O1	-0.4
1974	Atl-N	73	133	11	33	1	1	2	12	5	35	.248	.275	.316	62	-7	-7	11	0	0	0	.983	5	O1	-0.4
Total	10	564	1306	126	308	41	15	33	123	44	342	.236	.266	.366	77	-51	-44	120	20	13	-2	.965	11	O/1	-5.3

■ DANNY MURTAUGH Murtaugh, Daniel Edward b: 10/8/17, Chester, Pa. d: 12/2/76, Chester, Pa. BR/TR, 5'9", 165 lbs. Deb: 7/06/41 MC

YEAR	TM/L	G	AB	R	H	2B	3B	HR	RBI	BB	SO	AVG	OBP	SLG	PRO+	BR	/A	RC	SB	CS	SBR	FA	FR	POS	TPR
1941	Phi-N	85	347	34	76	8	1	0	11	26	31	.219	.275	.248	50	-24	-22	25	**18**			.978	2	2/S	-1.4
1942	Phi-N	144	506	48	122	16	4	0	27	49	39	.241	.311	.289	80	-15	-12	47	13			.939	6	S32	0.1
1943	Phi-N	113	451	65	123	17	4	1	35	57	23	.273	.357	.335	104	2	4	57	4			.974	0	*2	1.2
1946	Phi-N	6	19	1	4	1	0	1	3	2	2	.211	.286	.421	102	-0	-0	2	0			.958	-4	/2	-0.4
1947	Bos-N	3	8	0	1	0	0	0	0	1	2	.125	.222	.125	-6	-1	-1	0	0			1.000	-0	/23	-0.1
1948	Pit-N	146	514	56	149	21	5	1	71	60	40	.290	.365	.356	94	-1	-2	70	10			.979	1	*2	0.7
1949	Pit-N	75	236	16	48	7	2	2	24	29	17	.203	.291	.275	51	-16	-16	21	2			.975	3	2	-1.0
1950	Pit-N	118	367	34	108	20	5	2	37	47	42	.294	.376	.392	99	3	1	56	2			.976	3	*2	0.8
1951	Pit-N	77	151	9	30	7	0	1	11	16	19	.199	.284	.265	47	-11	-11	11	0	0	0	.970	-2	2/3	-1.2
Total	9	767	2599	263	661	97	21	8	219	287	215	.254	.331	.317	81	-62	-60	290	49	0		.975	10	2/S3	-1.3

■ TONY MUSER Muser, Anthony Joseph b: 8/1/47, Van Nuys, Cal. BL/TL, 6'2", 190 lbs. Deb: 9/14/69 C

YEAR	TM/L	G	AB	R	H	2B	3B	HR	RBI	BB	SO	AVG	OBP	SLG	PRO+	BR	/A	RC	SB	CS	SBR	FA	FR	POS	TPR
1969	Bos-A	2	9	0	1	0	0	0	1	1	1	.111	.200	.111	-10	-1	-1	0	0	0	0	1.000	1	/1	-0.1
1971	Chi-A	11	16	2	5	0	1	0	0	1	1	.313	.353	.438	119	0	0	2	0	0	0	.963	0	/1	0.1
1972	Chi-A	44	61	6	17	2	2	1	9	2	6	.279	.302	.426	113	1	1	7	1	1	-0	.986	-0	1/O	-0.1
1973	Chi-A	109	309	38	88	14	3	4	30	33	36	.285	.354	.388	105	4	3	43	8	4	0	.992	-3	1D/O	-0.6
1974	Chi-A	103	206	16	60	5	1	1	18	6	22	.291	.315	.340	86	-3	-4	20	1	4	-2	.998	-4	1D	-1.3
1975	Chi-A	43	111	11	27	3	0	0	6	7	8	.243	.288	.270	58	-6	-6	8	2	1	0	.993	2	1	-0.6
	Bal-A	80	82	11	26	3	0	0	11	8	9	.317	.378	.354	115	1	2	11	0	0	0	.996	1	1	0.2
	Yr	123	193	22	53	6	0	0	17	15	17	.275	.327	.306	83	-5	-4	18	2	1	0	.994	3	*1	-0.4
1976	Bal-A	136	326	25	74	7	1	1	30	21	34	.227	.274	.264	62	-17	-15	23	1	1	-0	.991	1	*1OD	-2.1
1977	Bal-A	120	118	14	27	6	0	0	7	13	16	.229	.305	.280	65	-6	-5	9	1	2	-1	.992	1	1O/D	-0.6
1978	Mil-A	15	30	0	4	1	1	0	5	3	5	.133	.212	.233	25	-3	-3	1	0	0	0	.988	-0	1	-0.4
Total	9	663	1268	123	329	41	9	7	117	95	138	.259	.312	.323	82	-31	-29	124	14	13	-4	.992	-1	1/DO	-5.5

■ STAN MUSIAL Musial, Stanley Frank "Stan The Man" b: 11/21/20, Donora, Pa. BL/TL, 6', 175 lbs. Deb: 9/17/41 H

YEAR	TM/L	G	AB	R	H	2B	3B	HR	RBI	BB	SO	AVG	OBP	SLG	PRO+	BR	/A	RC	SB	CS	SBR	FA	FR	POS	TPR
1941	StL-N	12	47	8	20	4	0	1	7	2	1	.426	.449	.574	175	5	5	12	1			1.000	0	O	0.4
1942	*StL-N	140	467	87	147	32	10	10	72	62	25	.315	.397	.490	148	35	31	96	6			.984	1	*O	2.7
1943	*StL-N★	157	617	108	**220**	**48**	**20**	13	81	72	18	**.357**	**.425**	**.562**	**176**	**66**	**62**	**147**	9			.982	11	*O	**6.7**
1944	*StL-N★	146	568	112	**197**	**51**	14	12	94	90	28	.347	**.440**	**.549**	**174**	**61**	**60**	**145**	7			.987	3	*O	**5.5**
1946	*StL-N★	156	624	**124**	**228**	**50**	**20**	16	103	73	31	**.365**	.434	**.587**	**180**	**71**	**68**	**164**	7			.989	-1	*1O	**6.0**
1947	StL-N★	149	587	113	183	30	13	19	95	80	24	.312	.398	.504	132	33	29	118	4			.994	-7	*1	1.6
1948	StL-N★	155	611	**135**	**230**	**46**	**18**	39	**131**	79	34	**.376**	**.450**	**.702**	**196**	**90**	**86**	**191**	7			.981	-8	*O/1	**6.8**
1949	StL-N★	157	612	128	**207**	**41**	**13**	36	123	107	38	.338	**.438**	.624	174	**72**	**68**	**173**	3			**.991**	-19	*O/1	4.1
1950	StL-N★	146	555	105	192	41	7	28	109	87	36	**.346**	.437	**.596**	**161**	**57**	**54**	**149**	5			.964	-13	O1	3.4
1951	StL-N★	152	578	**124**	205	30	**12**	32	108	98	40	**.355**	.449	.614	**182**	70	**70**	**169**	4	5	-2	.974	4	O1	6.4
1952	StL-N★	154	578	**105**	**194**	**42**	6	21	91	96	29	**.336**	.432	**.538**	**167**	**56**	**56**	**141**	7	7	-2	.987	-7	*O1/P	4.2
1953	StL-N★	157	593	127	200	**53**	9	30	113	**105**	32	.337	**.437**	.609	169	**63**	**63**	**166**	3	4	-2	.984	-9	*O	4.4
1954	StL-N★	153	591	**120**	195	**41**	9	35	126	103	39	.330	.433	.607	166	61	60	153	1	7	-4	**.990**	-2	*O1	4.7
1955	StL-N★	154	562	97	179	30	5	33	108	80	39	.319	.411	.566	156	46	47	131	5	4	-1	.992	1	*1O	3.8
1956	StL-N★	156	594	87	184	33	6	27	**109**	75	39	.310	.390	.522	142	36	36	119	2	0	1	.993	6	*1O	3.3
1957	StL-N★	134	502	82	176	38	3	29	102	66	34	**.351**	**.428**	.612	172	54	53	129	1	1	-0	.992	2	*1	4.6
1958	StL-N★	135	472	64	159	35	2	17	62	72	26	.337	.426	.528	145	37	34	102	0	0	0	.989	8	*1	3.5
1959	StL-N★	115	341	37	87	13	2	14	44	60	25	.255	.367	.428	104	7	4	53	0	2	-1	.990	2	1/O	-0.1
1960	StL-N★	116	331	49	91	17	1	17	63	41	34	.275	.358	.486	118	13	9	59	1	1	-0	.990	-1	O1	0.3
1961	StL-N★	123	372	46	107	22	4	15	70	52	35	.288	.376	.489	116	15	10	69	0	0	0	**.994**	-5	*O	0.0
1962	StL-N★	135	433	57	143	18	1	19	82	64	46	.330	.420	.508	135	31	26	94	3	0	1	.977	-10	*O	1.0
1963	StL-N★	124	337	34	86	10	2	12	58	35	43	.255	.329	.404	100	4	1	47	2	0	1	.968	-12	O	-1.6
Total	22	3026	10972	1949	3630	725	177	475	1951	1599	696	.331	.418	.559	157	983	930	2625	78	31		.984	-53	*O1/P	71.7

■ DANNY MUSSER Musser, William Daniel b: 9/5/05, Zion, Pa. BL/TR, 5'9.5", 160 lbs. Deb: 9/18/32

YEAR	TM/L	G	AB	R	H	2B	3B	HR	RBI	BB	SO	AVG	OBP	SLG	PRO+	BR	/A	RC	SB	CS	SBR	FA	FR	POS	TPR
1932	Was-A	1	2	0	1	0	0	0	0	0	0	.500	.500	.500	162	0	0	0	0	0	0	.000	0	/3	0.0

■ GEORGE MYATT Myatt, George Edward "Mercury', "Stud" or "Foghorn" b: 6/14/14, Denver, Colo. BL/TR, 5'11", 167 lbs. Deb: 8/16/38 MC

YEAR	TM/L	G	AB	R	H	2B	3B	HR	RBI	BB	SO	AVG	OBP	SLG	PRO+	BR	/A	RC	SB	CS	SBR	FA	FR	POS	TPR
1938	NY-N	43	170	27	52	2	1	3	10	14	13	.306	.362	.382	104	1	1	24	10			.919	7	S3	1.1
1939	NY-N	22	53	7	10	2	0	0	3	6	6	.189	.271	.226	35	-5	-5	4	2			.907	1	3	-0.4
1943	Was-A	42	53	11	13	3	0	0	3	13	7	.245	.394	.302	109	1	1	9	3	0	1	.930	-1	2/S3	0.2
1944	Was-A	140	538	86	153	19	6	0	40	54	44	.284	.357	.342	105	2	5	72	26	10	2	.957	-22	*2S/O	-0.8
1945	Was-A	133	490	81	145	17	7	1	39	63	43	.296	.378	.365	127	12	17	77	30	11	2	.972	-19	2O/3S	0.5
1946	Was-A	15	34	7	8	1	0	0	4	2	3	.235	.297	.265	61	-2	-2	3	1	1	-0	.900	-2	/32	-0.4
1947	Was-A	12	7	1	0	0	0	0	0	4	4	.000	.364	.000	6	-1	-1	0	0	0	0	1.000	0	/2	-0.1
Total	7	407	1345	220	381	44	14	4	99	156	120	.283	.362	.346	108	9	17	188	72	22		.962	-35	2/3SO	0.1

■ GLENN MYATT Myatt, Glenn Calvin b: 7/9/1897, Argenta, Ark. d: 8/9/69, Houston, Tex. BL/TR, 5'11", 165 lbs. Deb: 4/15/20

YEAR	TM/L	G	AB	R	H	2B	3B	HR	RBI	BB	SO	AVG	OBP	SLG	PRO+	BR	/A	RC	SB	CS	SBR	FA	FR	POS	TPR
1920	Phi-A	70	196	14	49	8	3	0	18	12	22	.250	.293	.321	62	-11	-11	18	1	3	-2	.900	-5	OC	-1.9
1921	Phi-A	44	69	6	14	2	0	0	5	6	7	.203	.267	.232	28	-7	-8	5	0	0	0	.939	2	C	-0.5
1923	Cle-A	92	220	36	63	7	6	3	40	16	18	.286	.338	.414	97	-2	-2	30	0	2	-1	.934	-8	C	-0.8
1924	Cle-A	105	342	55	117	22	7	8	73	33	12	.342	.402	.518	134	17	17	72	6	1	1	.978	-15	C	0.8
1925	Cle-A	106	358	51	97	15	9	11	54	29	24	.271	.329	.455	97	-4	-4	54	2	1	0	.973	-18	C/O	-1.6

YEAR	TM/L	G	AB	R	H	2B	3B	HR	RBI	BB	SO	AVG	OBP	SLG	PRO+	BR	/A	RC	SB	CS	SBR	FA	FR	POS	TPR
1926	Cle-A	56	117	14	29	5	2	0	13	13	13	.248	.323	.325	69	-5	-5	13	1	0	0	1.000	-1	C	-0.4
1927	Cle-A	55	94	15	23	6	0	2	8	12	7	.245	.336	.372	83	-2	-2	12	1	1	-0	.978	2	C	0.0
1928	Cle-A	58	125	9	36	7	2	1	15	13	13	.288	.355	.400	97	-0	-0	17	0	2	-1	.967	-9	C	-0.8
1929	Cle-A	59	129	14	30	4	1	1	17	7	5	.233	.277	.302	47	-10	-11	11	0	1	-1	.976	-1	C	-0.9
1930	Cle-A	86	265	30	78	23	2	2	37	18	17	.294	.342	.419	88	-4	-5	37	2	3	-1	.977	-7	C	-0.6
1931	Cle-A	65	195	21	48	14	2	1	29	21	13	.246	.319	.354	73	-7	-8	23	2	1	0	.991	-4	C	-0.8
1932	Cle-A	82	252	45	62	12	1	8	46	27	21	.246	.326	.397	81	-5	-8	34	2	2	-1	.988	-8	C	-1.2
1933	Cle-A	40	77	10	18	4	0	0	7	15	8	.234	.372	.286	73	-2	-2	9	0	1	-1	.965	-1	C	-0.2
1934	Cle-A	36	107	18	34	6	1	0	12	13	5	.318	.392	.393	101	1	1	17	1	0	0	.980	-1	C	0.2
1935	Cle-A	10	36	1	3	1	0	0	2	4	3	.083	.175	.111	-24	-7	-7	1	0	0	0	1.000	-1	C	-0.7
	NY-N	13	18	2	4	0	1	1	6	0	3	.222	.222	.500	90	-0	-0	2	0			1.000	-1	/C	-0.1
1936	Det-A	27	78	5	17	1	0	0	5	9	4	.218	.299	.231	32	-8	-8	6	0	0	0	1.000	-2	C	-0.8
Total	16	1004	2678	346	722	137	37	38	387	248	195	.270	.334	.391	85	-56	-65	362	18	18		.974	-78	C/O	-10.3

■ BUDDY MYER Myer, Charles Solomon b: 3/16/04, Ellisville, Miss. d: 10/31/74, Baton Rouge, La. BL/TR, 5'10.5", 163 lbs. Deb: 9/26/25

YEAR	TM/L	G	AB	R	H	2B	3B	HR	RBI	BB	SO	AVG	OBP	SLG	PRO+	BR	/A	RC	SB	CS	SBR	FA	FR	POS	TPR
1925	*Was-A	4	8	1	2	0	0	0	0	0	1	.250	.250	.250	28	-1	-1	0	0	0	0	1.000	-2	/S	-0.3
1926	Was-A	132	434	66	132	18	6	1	62	45	19	.304	.370	.380	98	-2	-0	61	10	11	-4	.928	-18	*S/3	-1.0
1927	Was-A	15	51	7	11	1	0	0	7	8	3	.216	.322	.235	47	-4	-4	4	3	1	0	.933	-3	S	-0.4
	Bos-A	133	469	59	135	22	11	2	47	48	15	.288	.359	.394	97	-3	-1	65	9	5	-0	.940	7	*S3O/2	1.4
	Yr	148	520	66	146	23	11	2	54	56	18	.281	.355	.379	92	-7	-5	69	12	6	0	.939	4	*S3O/2	1.0
1928	Bos-A	147	536	78	168	26	6	1	44	53	28	.313	.379	.390	104	4	5	82	**30**	16	-1	.967	4	*3	1.5
1929	Was-A	141	563	80	169	29	10	3	82	63	33	.300	.373	.403	99	1	0	88	18	7	1	.958	-15	23	-0.7
1930	Was-A	138	541	97	164	18	8	2	61	58	31	.303	.373	.377	90	-6	-6	78	14	11	-2	.965	-19	*2/O	-1.8
1931	Was-A	139	591	114	173	33	11	4	56	58	42	.293	.360	.406	100	1	1	85	11	14	-5	**.984**	-17	*2	-1.1
1932	Was-A	143	577	120	161	38	16	5	52	69	33	.279	.360	.426	104	3	4	91	12	7	-1	.975	-18	*2	-0.7
1933	*Was-A	131	530	95	160	29	15	4	61	60	29	.302	.374	.436	115	11	12	87	6	8	-3	.978	-1	*2	1.4
1934	Was-A	139	524	103	160	33	8	3	57	102	32	.305	.419	.416	121	17	21	98	6	6	-2	.975	-13	*2	1.3
1935	Was-A☆	151	616	115	215	36	11	5	100	96	40	**.349**	.440	.468	139	37	40	132	7	6	-2	.979	8	*2	5.3
1936	Was-A	51	156	31	42	5	2	0	15	42	11	.269	.427	.327	94	-0	1	27	7	2	1	.985	3	2	0.8
1937	Was-A☆	125	430	54	126	16	10	1	65	78	41	.293	.407	.384	105	4	7	72	2	6	-3	.966	-17	*2/O	-0.4
1938	Was-A	127	437	79	147	22	8	6	71	93	32	.336	.454	.465	140	26	31	99	9	5	-0	**.982**	2	*2	3.5
1939	Was-A	83	258	33	78	10	3	1	32	40	18	.302	.396	.376	106	1	4	42	4	1	1	.968	-1	2	0.7
1940	Was-A	71	210	28	61	14	4	0	29	34	10	.290	.389	.395	111	2	4	34	6	3	0	.967	4	2	1.1
1941	Was-A	53	107	14	27	3	1	0	9	18	10	.252	.360	.299	80	-3	-2	13	2	0	1	.982	-8	2	-0.8
Total	17	1923	7038	1174	2131	353	130	38	850	965	428	.303	.389	.406	108	89	115	1158	156	109	-19	.974	-103	*2S3/O	9.8

■ GEORGE MYERS Myers, George D. b: 11/13/1860, Buffalo, N.Y. d: 12/14/26, Buffalo, N.Y. BR/TR, Deb: 5/02/1884

YEAR	TM/L	G	AB	R	H	2B	3B	HR	RBI	BB	SO	AVG	OBP	SLG	PRO+	BR	/A	RC	SB	CS	SBR	FA	FR	POS	TPR
1884	Buf-N	78	325	34	59	9	2	2	32	13	33	.182	.213	.240	41	-21	-23	17				.837	-10	CO	-2.7
1885	Buf-N	89	326	40	67	7	2	0	19	23	40	.206	.258	.239	60	-13	-15	21				.899	-6	CO	-1.5
1886	StL-N	79	295	26	56	7	3	0	27	18	42	.190	.236	.234	46	-20	-17	18	6			.928	-13	C/O3	-2.0
1887	Ind-N	69	235	25	51	8	1	1	20	22	7	.217	.298	.272	63	-12	-10	27	26			.929	-13	CO/13	-1.7
1888	Ind-N	66	248	36	59	9	0	2	16	16	14	.238	.292	.298	89	-2	-3	31	28			.929	-8	C3O/1	-0.6
1889	Ind-N	43	149	22	29	3	0	0	12	17	13	.195	.294	.215	44	-10	-11	13	12			.909	4	OC/1	-0.5
Total	6	424	1578	183	321	43	8	5	126	109	149	.203	.260	.250	57	-78	-78	127	72			.901	-46	CO/31	-9.0

■ GREG MYERS Myers, Gregory Richard b: 4/14/66, Riverside, Cal. BL/TR, 6'1", 200 lbs. Deb: 9/12/87

YEAR	TM/L	G	AB	R	H	2B	3B	HR	RBI	BB	SO	AVG	OBP	SLG	PRO+	BR	/A	RC	SB	CS	SBR	FA	FR	POS	TPR
1987	Tor-A	7	9	1	1	0	0	0	0	0	3	.111	.111	.111	-40	-2	-2	-0	0	0	0	1.000	2	/C	0.0
1989	Tor-A	17	44	0	5	2	0	0	1	2	9	.114	.152	.159	-12	-7	-6	1	0	1	-1	1.000	2	C/D	-0.5
1990	Tor-A	87	250	33	59	7	1	5	22	22	33	.236	.298	.332	75	-8	-9	22	0	1	-1	.993	-0	C	-0.5
1991	Tor-A	107	309	25	81	22	0	8	36	21	45	.262	.309	.411	94	-2	-3	36	0	0	0	.979	-4	*C	-0.2
1992	Tor-A	22	61	4	14	6	0	1	13	5	5	.230	.288	.377	81	-1	-2	6	0	0	0	.991	0	C	0.0
	Cal-A	8	17	0	4	1	0	0	0	0	6	.235	.235	.294	48	-1	-1	1	0	0	0	1.000	2	/CD	0.1
	Yr	30	78	4	18	7	0	1	13	5	11	.231	.277	.359	75	-3	-3	8	0	0	0	.993	2	C/D	0.1
Total	5	248	690	63	164	38	1	14	72	50	101	.238	.289	.357	77	-21	-23	66	0	2	-1	.987	2	C/D	-1.1

■ HENRY MYERS Myers, Henry C. b: 5/1858, Philadelphia, Pa. d: 4/18/1895, Philadelphia, Pa. BR/TR, 5'9", 159 lbs. Deb: 8/20/1881 M

YEAR	TM/L	G	AB	R	H	2B	3B	HR	RBI	BB	SO	AVG	OBP	SLG	PRO+	BR	/A	RC	SB	CS	SBR	FA	FR	POS	TPR
1881	Pro-N	1	4	0	0	0	0	0	0	0	2	.000	.000	.000	-99	-1	-1	0				1.000	-0	/S	-0.1
1882	Bal-a	69	294	43	53	3	0	0		12		.180	.212	.190	40	-19	-15	12				.822	-7	*S/PM	-1.7
1884	Wil-U	6	24	3	3	0	0	0		0		.125	.125	.125	-15	-3	-3	0				.875	4	/S2	0.1
Total	3	76	322	46	56	3	0	0	0	12	2	.174	.204	.183	34	-22	-19	13				.826	-3	/SP2	-1.7

■ HY MYERS Myers, Henry Harrison b: 4/27/1889, E.Liverpool, Ohio d: 5/1/65, Minerva, Ohio BR/TR, 5'9.5", 175 lbs. Deb: 8/30/09

YEAR	TM/L	G	AB	R	H	2B	3B	HR	RBI	BB	SO	AVG	OBP	SLG	PRO+	BR	/A	RC	SB	CS	SBR	FA	FR	POS	TPR
1909	Bro-N	6	22	1	5	1	0	0	6	2		.227	.292	.273	78	-1	-1	2	1			1.000	-1	/O	-0.2
1911	Bro-N	13	43	2	7	1	0	0	0	2	3	.163	.200	.186	9	-5	-5	2	1			.889	-2	O	-0.8
1914	Bro-N	70	227	35	65	3	9	0	17	7	24	.286	.316	.379	104	1	0	27	2			.964	-6	O	-0.9
1915	Bro-N	153	605	69	150	21	7	2	46	17	51	.248	.275	.316	77	-17	-18	52	19	22	-8	.964	7	*O	-3.0
1916	*Bro-N	113	412	54	108	12	14	3	36	21	35	.262	.308	.381	108	4	3	55	17			.969	1	*O	-0.1
1917	Bro-N	120	471	37	126	15	10	1	41	18	25	.268	.294	.348	94	-3	-4	49	5			.982	-3	O123	-1.2
1918	Bro-N	107	407	36	104	9	8	4	40	20	26	.256	.292	.346	95	-4	-4	44	17			.975	13	*O	0.3
1919	Bro-N	133	512	62	157	23	**14**	5	**73**	23	34	.307	.339	**.436**	129	18	17	78	13			.979	9	*O	1.9
1920	*Bro-N	154	582	83	177	36	**22**	4	80	35	54	.304	.345	.462	126	21	18	88	9	13	-5	.978	4	*O/3	0.7
1921	Bro-N	144	549	51	158	14	4	4	68	22	51	.288	.318	.350	74	-18	-21	61	8	6	-1	.968	7	*O2/3	-2.4
1922	Bro-N	153	618	82	196	20	9	6	89	13	26	.317	.331	.408	90	-11	-10	79	9	10	-3	.974	6	*O/2	-1.8
1923	StL-N	96	330	29	99	18	2	2	48	12	19	.300	.330	.385	90	-6	-5	42	5	3	-0	.977	6	O	-0.4
1924	StL-N	43	124	12	26	5	1	1	15	3	10	.210	.228	.290	39	-11	-11	8	1	2	-1	.945	-3	O3/2	-1.5
1925	StL-N	1	1	0	0	0	0	0	0	0	0	.000	.000	.000	-98	-0	-0	0	0	0	0	.000	0	H	0.0
	Cin-N	3	6	1	1	1	0	0	0	0	0	.167	.167	.333	25	-1	-1	0	0	0	0	1.000	-1	/O	-0.1
	StL-N	1	1	1	1	0	0	0	0	0	0	1.000	1.000	1.000	403	0	0	1	0	0	0	.000	0	H	0.0
	Yr	5	8	2	2	1	0	0	0	0	0	.250	.250	.375	58	-1	-1	1	0	0	0	1.000	-1	/O	-0.1
Total	14	1310	4910	555	1380	179	100	32	559	195	358	.281	.312	.378	95	-34	-41	587	107	56		.972	39	*O/231	-9.5

■ BERT MYERS Myers, James Albert b: 4/8/1874, Frederick, Md. d: 10/12/15, Washington, D.C. BR/TR, 5'10", Deb: 4/25/1896

YEAR	TM/L	G	AB	R	H	2B	3B	HR	RBI	BB	SO	AVG	OBP	SLG	PRO+	BR	/A	RC	SB	CS	SBR	FA	FR	POS	TPR
1896	StL-N	122	454	47	116	12	8	0	37	40	32	.256	.320	.317	73	-19	-16	51	8			.867	-9	*3/S	-1.9
1898	Was-N	31	110	14	29	1	4	0	13	13		.264	.341	.345	97	-0	-0	14	2			.835	-3	3	-0.3
1900	Phi-N	7	28	5	5	1	0	0	2	3		.179	.258	.214	31	-3	-3	2	1			.909	2	/3	-0.1
Total	3	160	592	66	150	14	12	0	52	56	32	.253	.321	.318	75	-22	-19	67	11			.863	-10	3/S	-2.3

■ AL MYERS Myers, James Albert "Cod" b: 10/22/1863, Danville, Ill. d: 12/24/27, Marshall, Ill. BR/TR, 5'8.5", 165 lbs. Deb: 9/27/1884

YEAR	TM/L	G	AB	R	H	2B	3B	HR	RBI	BB	SO	AVG	OBP	SLG	PRO+	BR	/A	RC	SB	CS	SBR	FA	FR	POS	TPR
1884	Mil-U	12	46	6	15	6	0	0		0		.326	.326	.457	299	3	6	7				.848	2	2	0.7
1885	Phi-N	93	357	25	73	13	2	1	28	11	41	.204	.228	.261	59	-17	-16	22				.884	-17	*2	-2.8
1886	KC-N	118	473	69	131	22	9	4	51	22	42	.277	.309	.387	104	5	1	59	3			.913	2	*2	0.7
1887	Was-N	105	362	45	84	9	5	2	36	40	26	.232	.312	.301	77	-12	-9	41	18			.909	-5	2S	-0.9
1888	Was-N	132	502	46	104	12	7	2	46	37	46	.207	.270	.271	79	-13	-9	43	20			.918	-25	*2	-2.9
1889	Was-N	46	176	24	46	3	0	0	20	22	7	.261	.347	.278	82	-4	-2	21	10			.942	3	2	0.3

YEAR	TM/L	G	AB	R	H	2B	3B	HR	RBI	BB	SO	AVG	OBP	SLG	PRO+	BR	/A	RC	SB	CS	SBR	FA	FR	POS	TPR
	Phi-N	75	305	52	82	14	2	0	28	36	9	.269	.354	.328	85	-2	-6	39	8			.853	-8	2	-0.8
	Yr	121	481	76	128	17	2	0	48	58	16	.266	.351	.310	84	-6	-8	60	18			.886	-4	*2	-0.5
1890	Phi-N	117	487	95	135	29	7	2	81	57	46	.277	.365	.378	116	13	11	85	44			.948	14	*2	2.8
1891	Phi-N	135	514	67	118	27	2	2	69	69	46	.230	.331	.302	84	-6	-8	55	8			.937	-10	*2	-1.1
Total	8	833	3222	429	788	135	34	13	359	294	263	.245	.314	.320	90	-33	-33	372	111			.914	-42	2/S	-4.0

■ LYNN MYERS Myers, Lynnwood Lincoln b: 2/23/14, Enola, Pa. BR/TR, 5'6.5", 145 lbs. Deb: 7/13/38 F

YEAR	TM/L	G	AB	R	H	2B	3B	HR	RBI	BB	SO	AVG	OBP	SLG	PRO+	BR	/A	RC	SB	CS	SBR	FA	FR	POS	TPR
1938	StL-N	70	227	18	55	10	2	1	19	9	25	.242	.271	.317	58	-12	-14	20	9			.944	-1	S	-1.0
1939	StL-N	74	117	24	28	6	1	0	10	12	23	.239	.310	.308	63	-5	-6	12	1			.897	5	S3/2	0.1
Total	2	144	344	42	83	16	3	1	29	21	48	.241	.285	.314	60	-18	-20	32	10			.930	4	S/32	-0.9

■ HAP MYERS Myers, Ralph Edward b: 4/8/1888, San Francisco, Cal. d: 6/30/67, San Francisco, Cal. BR/TR, 6'3", 175 lbs. Deb: 4/16/10

YEAR	TM/L	G	AB	R	H	2B	3B	HR	RBI	BB	SO	AVG	OBP	SLG	PRO+	BR	/A	RC	SB	CS	SBR	FA	FR	POS	TPR
1910	Bos-A	3	6	0	2	0	0	0	0	0		.333	.333	.333	106	0	0	1	0			1.000	0	/O	0.0
1911	StL-A	11	37	4	11	1	0	0	1	1		.297	.316	.324	82	-1	-1	4	0			.976	-2	1	-0.3
	Bos-A	13	38	3	14	2	0	0	0	4		.368	.429	.421	139	2	2	8	4			.947	-1	1	0.1
	Yr	24	75	7	25	3	0	0	1	5		.333	.375	.373	111	1	1	12	4			.963	-3	1	-0.2
1913	Bos-N	140	524	74	143	20	1	2	50	38	48	.273	.333	.326	87	-7	-8	73	57			.987	5	*1	-0.5
1914	Bro-F	92	305	61	67	10	5	1	29	44	43	.220	.322	.295	77	-8	-8	45	43			.989	1	1	-1.0
1915	Bro-F	118	341	61	98	9	1	1	36	32	39	.287	.352	.328	101	1	1	54	28			.990	1	*1	0.0
Total	5	377	1251	203	335	42	7	4	116	119	130	.268	.338	.322	90	-13	-14	184	132			.987	4	1/O	-1.7

■ RICHIE MYERS Myers, Richard b: 4/7/30, Sacramento, Cal. BR/TR, 5'6", 150 lbs. Deb: 4/21/56

YEAR	TM/L	G	AB	R	H	2B	3B	HR	RBI	BB	SO	AVG	OBP	SLG	PRO+	BR	/A	RC	SB	CS	SBR	FA	FR	POS	TPR
1956	Chi-N	4	1	1	0	0	0	0	0	0	0	.000	.000	.000	-99	-0	-0	0	0	0	0	.000	0	H	0.0

■ BILLY MYERS Myers, William Harrison b: 8/14/10, Enola, Pa. BR/TR, 5'8", 168 lbs. Deb: 4/16/35 F

YEAR	TM/L	G	AB	R	H	2B	3B	HR	RBI	BB	SO	AVG	OBP	SLG	PRO+	BR	/A	RC	SB	CS	SBR	FA	FR	POS	TPR
1935	Cin-N	117	445	60	119	15	10	5	36	29	81	.267	.315	.380	89	-9	-7	55	10			.939	3	*S	0.2
1936	Cin-N	98	323	45	87	9	6	6	27	28	56	.269	.328	.390	99	-4	-1	43	6			.938	8	S	1.3
1937	Cin-N	124	335	35	84	13	3	7	43	44	57	.251	.339	.370	97	-3	-1	46	0			.948	4	*S/2	1.1
1938	Cin-N	134	442	57	112	18	6	12	47	41	80	.253	.317	.403	99	-3	-1	58	2			.939	2	*S2	1.1
1939	*Cin-N	151	509	79	143	18	6	9	56	71	90	.281	.369	.393	104	5	5	81	4			.951	6	*S	2.4
1940	*Cin-N	90	282	33	57	14	2	5	30	30	56	.202	.283	.319	65	-13	-14	27	0			.961	-5	S	-1.1
1941	Chi-N	24	63	10	14	1	0	1	4	7	25	.222	.310	.286	71	-2	-2	6	1			.939	4	S/2	0.3
Total	7	738	2399	319	616	88	33	45	243	250	445	.257	.328	.377	93	-29	-21	316	23			.946	23	S/2	5.3

■ TIM NAEHRING Naehring, Timothy James b: 2/1/67, Cincinnati, Ohio BR/TR, 6'2", 190 lbs. Deb: 7/15/90

YEAR	TM/L	G	AB	R	H	2B	3B	HR	RBI	BB	SO	AVG	OBP	SLG	PRO+	BR	/A	RC	SB	CS	SBR	FA	FR	POS	TPR
1990	Bos-A	24	85	10	23	6	0	2	12	8	15	.271	.333	.412	102	1	0	11	0	0	0	.918	-1	S/32	0.1
1991	Bos-A	20	55	1	6	1	0	0	3	6	15	.109	.197	.127	-8	-8	-8	2	0	0	0	.956	-1	S/32	-0.9
1992	Bos-A	72	186	12	43	8	0	3	14	18	31	.231	.309	.323	73	-5	-7	20	0	0	0	.992	16	S23/OD	1.1
Total	3	116	326	23	72	15	0	5	29	32	61	.221	.296	.313	67	-13	-15	34	0	0	0	.958	13	/S23DO	0.3

■ BILL NAGEL Nagel, William Taylor b: 8/19/15, Memphis, Tenn. d: 10/8/81, Freehold, N.J. BR/TR, 6'1", 190 lbs. Deb: 4/20/39

YEAR	TM/L	G	AB	R	H	2B	3B	HR	RBI	BB	SO	AVG	OBP	SLG	PRO+	BR	/A	RC	SB	CS	SBR	FA	FR	POS	TPR
1939	Phi-A	105	341	39	86	19	4	12	39	25	86	.252	.307	.437	90	-8	-7	42	2	1	0	.944	-15	23/P	-1.7
1941	Phi-N	17	56	2	8	1	1	0	6	3	14	.143	.186	.196	8	-7	-7	2	0			.935	3	2/O3	-0.3
1945	Chi-A	67	220	21	46	10	3	3	27	15	41	.209	.263	.323	71	-9	-9	18	3	1	0	.984	-3	1/3	-1.7
Total	3	189	617	62	140	30	8	15	72	43	141	.227	.281	.374	77	-24	-22	61	5	2		.942	-15	/213OP	-3.7

■ LOU NAGELSEN Nagelsen, Louis Marcellus (b: Louis Marcellus Nageleisen)
b: 6/29/1887, Piqua, Ohio d: 10/22/65, Fort Wayne, Ind. BR/TR, 6'2", 180 lbs. Deb: 9/10/12

YEAR	TM/L	G	AB	R	H	2B	3B	HR	RBI	BB	SO	AVG	OBP	SLG	PRO+	BR	/A	RC	SB	CS	SBR	FA	FR	POS	TPR
1912	Cle-A	2	3	0	0	0	0	0	0	0		.000	.000	.000	-97	-1	-1	0	0			1.000	-1	/C	-0.2

■ RUSS NAGELSON Nagelson, Russell Charles b: 9/19/44, Cincinnati, Ohio BL/TR, 6', 205 lbs. Deb: 9/11/68

YEAR	TM/L	G	AB	R	H	2B	3B	HR	RBI	BB	SO	AVG	OBP	SLG	PRO+	BR	/A	RC	SB	CS	SBR	FA	FR	POS	TPR
1968	Cle-A	5	3	0	1	0	0	0	0	2	2	.333	.600	.333	192	1	1	1	0	0	0	.000	0	H	0.1
1969	Cle-A	12	17	1	6	0	0	0	0	3	3	.353	.450	.353	123	1	1	3	0	0	0	1.000	-1	/O1	0.0
1970	Cle-A	17	24	3	3	1	0	1	2	3	9	.125	.222	.292	39	-2	-2	2	0	0	0	1.000	-0	/O	-0.3
	Det-A	28	32	5	6	0	0	0	2	5	6	.188	.297	.188	36	-3	-3	2	0	0	0	1.000	-1	/O1	-0.4
	Yr	45	56	8	9	1	0	1	4	8	15	.161	.266	.232	38	-5	-5	4	0	0	0	1.000	-2	/O1	-0.7
Total	3	62	76	9	16	1	0	1	4	13	20	.211	.326	.263	64	-3	-3	8	0	0	0	1.000	-2	/O1	-0.6

■ TOM NAGLE Nagle, Thomas Edward b: 10/30/1865, Milwaukee, Wis. d: 3/9/46, Milwaukee, Wis. BR/TR, 5'10", 150 lbs. Deb: 4/22/1890

YEAR	TM/L	G	AB	R	H	2B	3B	HR	RBI	BB	SO	AVG	OBP	SLG	PRO+	BR	/A	RC	SB	CS	SBR	FA	FR	POS	TPR
1890	Chi-N	38	144	21	39	5	1	1	11	7	24	.271	.318	.340	90	-1	-2	17	4			.939	-7	C/O	-0.6
1891	Chi-N	8	25	3	3	0	0	0	1	1	3	.120	.154	.120	-19	-4	-4	0	0			.906	-3	/CO	-0.6
Total	2	46	169	24	42	5	1	1	12	8	27	.249	.294	.308	75	-5	-6	18	4			.935	-11	/CO	-1.2

■ BILL NAHORODNY Nahorodny, William Gerard b: 8/31/53, Hamtramck, Mich. BR/TR, 6'2", 200 lbs. Deb: 9/27/76

YEAR	TM/L	G	AB	R	H	2B	3B	HR	RBI	BB	SO	AVG	OBP	SLG	PRO+	BR	/A	RC	SB	CS	SBR	FA	FR	POS	TPR
1976	Phi-N	3	5	0	1	1	0	0	0	0	0	.200	.200	.400	65	-0	-0	0	0	0	0	1.000	0	/C	0.0
1977	Chi-A	7	23	3	6	1	0	1	4	2	3	.261	.320	.435	104	0	0	3	0	0	0	1.000	-1	/C	-0.1
1978	Chi-A	107	347	29	82	11	2	8	35	23	52	.236	.288	.349	77	-11	-11	35	1	0	0	.980	-3	*C/1D	-1.2
1979	Chi-A	65	179	20	46	10	0	6	29	18	23	.257	.325	.413	98	-1	-1	23	0	1	-1	.973	-0	C/D	0.0
1980	Atl-N	59	157	14	38	12	0	5	18	8	21	.242	.287	.414	91	-2	-3	17	0	2	-1	.990	-7	C/1	-1.0
1981	Atl-N	14	13	0	3	1	0	0	2	1	3	.231	.286	.308	67	-1	-1	1	0	0	0	1.000	0	/C1	-0.1
1982	Cle-A	39	94	6	21	5	1	4	18	2	9	.223	.240	.426	79	-3	-3	8	0	0	0	1.000	-3	C	-0.6
1983	Det-A	2	1	0	0	0	0	0	0	1	0	.000	.500	.000	53	0	0	0	0	0	0	.000	0	/H	0.0
1984	Sea-A	12	25	2	6	0	0	1	3	1	7	.240	.321	.360	89	-0	-0	3	0	1	-1	.976	-3	C/1	-0.3
Total	9	308	844	74	203	41	3	25	109	56	118	.241	.292	.385	85	-18	-19	91	1	4	-2	.983	-17	C/1D	-3.3

■ FRANK NALEWAY Naleway, Frank "Chick" b: 7/5/02, Chicago, Ill. d: 1/28/49, Chicago, Ill. BR/TR, 5'9.5", 165 lbs. Deb: 9/16/24

YEAR	TM/L	G	AB	R	H	2B	3B	HR	RBI	BB	SO	AVG	OBP	SLG	PRO+	BR	/A	RC	SB	CS	SBR	FA	FR	POS	TPR
1924	Chi-A	1	2	0	0	0	0	0	0	1	0	.000	.333	.000	-10	-0	-0	0	0	0	0	.750	-1	/S	-0.1

■ DOC NANCE Nance, William G. "Kid" (b: Willie G. Cooper) b: 8/2/1876, Ft.Worth, Tex. d: 5/28/58, Fort Worth, Tex. BR/TR, Deb: 8/19/1897

YEAR	TM/L	G	AB	R	H	2B	3B	HR	RBI	BB	SO	AVG	OBP	SLG	PRO+	BR	/A	RC	SB	CS	SBR	FA	FR	POS	TPR
1897	Lou-N	35	120	25	29	5	3	3	17	20		.242	.355	.408	105	0	1	19	3			.986	4	O	0.2
1898	Lou-N	22	76	13	24	5	0	1	16	12		.316	.416	.421	142	4	5	15	2			.946	2	O	0.5
1901	Det-A	132	461	72	129	24	5	3	66	51		.280	.355	.373	98	2	-1	69	9			.932	1	*O	-0.9
Total	3	189	657	110	182	34	8	7	99	83		.277	.362	.385	104	7	5	103	14			.943	6	O	-0.2

■ AL NAPLES Naples, Aloysius Francis b: 8/29/27, St.George, S.I., N.Y. BR/TR, 5'9", 168 lbs. Deb: 6/25/49

YEAR	TM/L	G	AB	R	H	2B	3B	HR	RBI	BB	SO	AVG	OBP	SLG	PRO+	BR	/A	RC	SB	CS	SBR	FA	FR	POS	TPR
1949	StL-A	2	7	0	1	1	0	0	0	0	1	.143	.143	.286	12	-1	-1	0	0	0	0	.875	-1	/S	-0.2

■ DANNY NAPOLEON Napoleon, Daniel b: 1/11/42, Claysburg, Pa. BR/TR, 5'11", 190 lbs. Deb: 4/14/65

YEAR	TM/L	G	AB	R	H	2B	3B	HR	RBI	BB	SO	AVG	OBP	SLG	PRO+	BR	/A	RC	SB	CS	SBR	FA	FR	POS	TPR
1965	NY-N	68	97	5	14	1	1	0	7	8	23	.144	.224	.175	15	-11	-10	4	0	0	0	.941	-0	O/3	-1.2
1966	NY-N	12	33	2	7	2	0	0	0	1	10	.212	.235	.273	42	-3	-3	2	0	1	-1	.929	-1	O	-0.4
Total	2	80	130	7	21	3	1	0	7	9	33	.162	.227	.200	22	-14	-13	5	0	1	-1	.938	-1	/O3	-1.6

■ HAL NARAGON Naragon, Harold Richard b: 10/1/28, Zanesville, Ohio BL/TR, 6', 175 lbs. Deb: 9/23/51 C

YEAR	TM/L	G	AB	R	H	2B	3B	HR	RBI	BB	SO	AVG	OBP	SLG	PRO+	BR	/A	RC	SB	CS	SBR	FA	FR	POS	TPR
1951	Cle-A	3	8	0	2	0	0	0	0	1	0	.250	.400	.250	83	-0	-0	1	0	0	0	.929	0	/C	0.0
1954	*Cle-A	46	101	10	24	2	2	0	12	9	12	.238	.300	.297	63	-5	-5	10	0	0	0	1.000	-2	C	-0.5
1955	Cle-A	57	127	12	41	9	2	1	14	15	8	.323	.394	.449	122	5	4	23	1	0	0	.991	-4	C	0.2

YEAR	TM/L	G	AB	R	H	2B	3B	HR	RBI	BB	SO	AVG	OBP	SLG	PRO+	BR	/A	RC	SB	CS	SBR	FA	FR	POS	TPR
1956	Cle-A	53	122	11	35	3	1	3	18	13	9	.287	.360	.402	99	0	-0	18	0	0	0	.988	-12	C	-1.0
1957	Cle-A	57	121	12	31	1	1	0	8	12	9	.256	.328	.281	69	-5	-5	11	0	0	0	.990	-2	C	-0.6
1958	Cle-A	9	9	2	3	0	1	0	0	0	0	.333	.333	.556	144	0	0	2	0	0	0	.000	0	H	0.0
1959	Cle-A	14	36	6	10	4	1	0	5	3	2	.278	.350	.444	121	1	1	6	0	0	0	1.000	-1	C	0.0
	Was-A	71	195	12	47	3	2	0	11	8	9	.241	.275	.277	52	-13	-13	14	0	1	-1	.993	-2	C	-1.2
	Yr	85	231	18	57	7	3	0	16	11	11	.247	.287	.303	63	-12	-12	20	0	1	-1	.994	-3	C	-1.2
1960	Was-A	33	92	7	19	2	0	0	5	8	4	.207	.277	.228	39	-8	-8	6	0	0	0	.978	-2	C	-0.9
1961	Min-A	57	139	10	42	2	1	2	11	4	8	.302	.326	.374	82	-3	-4	16	0	0	0	.994	-5	C	-0.7
1962	Min-A	24	35	1	8	1	0	0	3	3	1	.229	.289	.257	47	-2	-3	3	0	0	0	1.000	0	/C	-0.2
Total	10	424	985	83	262	27	11	6	87	76	62	.266	.323	.334	77	-29	-31	109	1	1	-0	.991	-29	C	-4.9

■ BILL NARLESKI Narleski, William Edward "Cap" b: 6/9/1899, Perth Amboy, N.J. d: 7/22/64, Laurel Springs, N.J. BR/TR, 5'9", 160 lbs. Deb: 4/18/29 F

YEAR	TM/L	G	AB	R	H	2B	3B	HR	RBI	BB	SO	AVG	OBP	SLG	PRO+	BR	/A	RC	SB	CS	SBR	FA	FR	POS	TPR
1929	Bos-A	96	260	30	72	16	1	0	25	21	22	.277	.333	.346	77	-9	-8	30	4	4	-1	.957	-17	S2/3	-1.9
1930	Bos-A	39	98	11	23	9	0	0	7	7	5	.235	.306	.327	63	-6	-5	10	0	0	0	.915	-8	S3/2	-1.1
Total	2	135	358	41	95	25	1	0	32	28	27	.265	.326	.341	73	-15	-14	41	4	4	-1	.949	-25	/S23	-3.0

■ JERRY NARRON Narron, Jerry Austin b: 1/15/56, Goldsboro, N.C. BL/TR, 6'3", 205 lbs. Deb: 4/13/79

YEAR	TM/L	G	AB	R	H	2B	3B	HR	RBI	BB	SO	AVG	OBP	SLG	PRO+	BR	/A	RC	SB	CS	SBR	FA	FR	POS	TPR
1979	NY-A	61	123	17	21	3	1	4	18	9	26	.171	.227	.309	44	-10	-10	9	0	0	0	.973	-5	C	-1.3
1980	Sea-A	48	107	7	21	3	0	4	18	13	18	.196	.283	.336	68	-5	-5	11	0	0	0	.992	-10	C/D	-1.3
1981	Sea-A	76	203	13	45	5	0	3	17	16	35	.222	.285	.291	64	-9	-10	17	0	0	0	.996	-14	C	-2.3
1983	Cal-A	10	22	1	3	0	0	1	4	1	3	.136	.174	.273	21	-2	-2	1	0	0	0	.895	-1	/CD	-0.3
1984	Cal-A	69	150	9	37	5	0	3	17	8	12	.247	.289	.340	74	-6	-5	13	0	0	0	.994	-8	C/1	-1.2
1985	Cal-A	67	132	12	29	4	0	5	14	11	17	.220	.280	.364	75	-5	-5	13	0	0	0	1.000	2	C/1D	-0.1
1986	*Cal-A	57	95	5	21	3	1	1	8	9	14	.221	.295	.305	65	-5	-5	8	0	0	0	.988	1	C/D	-0.1
1987	Sea-A	4	8	0	0	0	0	0	0	0	2	.000	.000	.000	-95	-2	-2	0	0	0	0	1.000	-0	/C	-0.2
Total	8	392	840	64	177	23	2	21	96	67	127	.211	.272	.318	62	-43	-44	72	0	0	0	.989	-34	C/D1	-6.8

■ SAM NARRON Narron, Samuel b: 8/25/13, Middlesex, N.C. BR/TR, 5'10", 180 lbs. Deb: 9/15/35 C

YEAR	TM/L	G	AB	R	H	2B	3B	HR	RBI	BB	SO	AVG	OBP	SLG	PRO+	BR	/A	RC	SB	CS	SBR	FA	FR	POS	TPR
1935	StL-N	4	7	0	3	0	0	0	0	0	0	.429	.429	.429	126	0	0	1	0			1.000	-0	/C	0.0
1942	StL-N	10	10	0	4	0	0	0	1	0	0	.400	.400	.400	125	0	0	2	0			1.000	-0	/C	0.0
1943	*StL-N	10	11	0	1	0	0	0	0	1	2	.091	.167	.091	-24	-2	-2	0	0			1.000	1	/C	-0.1
Total	3	24	28	0	8	0	0	0	1	1	2	.286	.310	.286	67	-1	-1	3	0			1.000	1	/C	-0.1

■ COTTON NASH Nash, Charles Francis b: 7/24/42, Jersey City, N.J. BR/TR, 6'6", 220 lbs. Deb: 9/01/67

YEAR	TM/L	G	AB	R	H	2B	3B	HR	RBI	BB	SO	AVG	OBP	SLG	PRO+	BR	/A	RC	SB	CS	SBR	FA	FR	POS	TPR
1967	Chi-A	3	3	1	0	0	0	0	0	1	0	.000	.250	.000	-21	-0	-0	0	0	0	0	.833	-1	/1	-0.1
1969	Min-A	6	9	0	2	0	0	0	0	1	2	.222	.300	.222	47	-1	-1	1	0	0	0	1.000	1	/1O	0.0
1970	Min-A	4	4	1	1	0	0	0	2	1	1	.250	.400	.250	82	-0	-0	0	0	1	-1	1.000	-0	/1	-0.1
Total	3	13	16	2	3	0	0	0	2	3	3	.188	.316	.188	45	-1	-1	1	0	1	-1	.965	0	/1O	-0.2

■ KEN NASH Nash, Kenneth Leland (Played One Game In 1912 Under Name Of Costello)
b: 7/14/1888, Weymouth, Mass. d: 2/16/77, Epsom, N.H. BB/TR, 5'8", 140 lbs. Deb: 7/04/12

YEAR	TM/L	G	AB	R	H	2B	3B	HR	RBI	BB	SO	AVG	OBP	SLG	PRO+	BR	/A	RC	SB	CS	SBR	FA	FR	POS	TPR
1912	Cle-A	11	23	2	4	0	0	0	0	3		.174	.269	.174	27	-2	-2	1	0			.826	-3	/S	-0.5
1914	StL-N	24	51	4	14	3	1	0	6	6	10	.275	.351	.373	116	1	1	6	0			.875	-6	3/2S	-0.6
Total	2	35	74	6	18	3	1	0	6	9	10	.243	.325	.311	87	-1	-1	8	0			.760	-10	/S32	-1.1

■ BILLY NASH Nash, William Mitchell b: 6/24/1865, Richmond, Va. d: 11/15/29, E.Orange, N.J. BR/TR, 5'8.5", 167 lbs. Deb: 8/05/1884 MU

YEAR	TM/L	G	AB	R	H	2B	3B	HR	RBI	BB	SO	AVG	OBP	SLG	PRO+	BR	/A	RC	SB	CS	SBR	FA	FR	POS	TPR
1884	Ric-a	45	166	31	33	8	8	1		12		.199	.281	.361	112	2	3	17				.828	8	3	1.0
1885	Bos-N	26	94	9	24	4	0	0	11	2	9	.255	.271	.298	87	-2	-1	8				.864	-4	3/2	-0.4
1886	Bos-N	109	417	61	117	11	8	1	45	24	28	.281	.320	.353	108	2	4	53	16			.863	-5	*3S/O	0.2
1887	Bos-N	121	475	100	140	24	12	6	94	60	30	.295	.376	.434	126	18	18	96	43			.884	9	*3/O	2.4
1888	Bos-N	135	526	71	149	18	15	4	75	50	46	.283	.350	.397	138	25	23	82	20			**.913**	26	*32	**5.0**
1889	Bos-N	128	481	84	132	20	2	3	76	79	44	.274	.379	.343	98	6	1	74	26			.905	12	*3/P	1.5
1890	Bos-P	129	488	103	130	28	6	5	90	88	43	.266	.383	.379	99	7	0	83	26			.866	18	*3/P	1.9
1891	Bos-N	140	537	92	148	24	9	5	95	74	50	.276	.369	.382	108	16	6	88	28			.900	-12	*3	0.0
1892	*Bos-N	135	526	94	137	25	5	4	95	59	41	.260	.338	.350	101	7	0	75	31			**.898**	24	*3/O	2.7
1893	Bos-N	128	485	115	141	27	6	10	123	85	29	.291	.399	.433	114	18	11	98	30			**.923**	3	*3	1.3
1894	Bos-N	132	512	132	148	23	6	8	87	91	23	.289	.399	.404	89	-0	-9	93	20			**.933**	6	*3	-0.2
1895	Bos-N	132	508	97	147	23	6	10	108	74	19	.289	.383	.417	100	8	0	92	18			.882	-8	*3	-0.5
1896	Phi-N	65	227	29	56	9	1	3	30	34	21	.247	.355	.335	85	-4	-4	29	3			.911	7	3M	0.4
1897	Phi-N	104	337	45	87	20	2	0	39	60		.258	.373	.329	89	-4	-3	46	4			.919	-7	3S/2	-0.6
1898	Phi-N	20	70	9	17	2	1	0	9	11		.243	.346	.300	89	-1	-0	7	0			.958	-1	3	-0.1
Total	15	1549	5849	1072	1606	266	87	60	977	803	383	.275	.366	.381	105	98	50	942	265			.897	75	*3/2SOP	14.6

■ ROB NATAL Natal, Robert Marcilino b: 11/13/65, Long Beach, Cal. BR/TR, 5'11", 190 lbs. Deb: 7/18/92

YEAR	TM/L	G	AB	R	H	2B	3B	HR	RBI	BB	SO	AVG	OBP	SLG	PRO+	BR	/A	RC	SB	CS	SBR	FA	FR	POS	TPR
1992	Mon-N	5	6	0	0	0	0	0	0	1	1	.000	.143	.000	-57	-1	-1	0	0	0	0	.909	-0	/C	-0.2

■ PETE NATON Naton, Peter Alphonsus b: 9/9/31, Flushing, N.Y. BR/TR, 6'1", 200 lbs. Deb: 6/16/53

YEAR	TM/L	G	AB	R	H	2B	3B	HR	RBI	BB	SO	AVG	OBP	SLG	PRO+	BR	/A	RC	SB	CS	SBR	FA	FR	POS	TPR
1953	Pit-N	6	12	2	2	0	0	0	1	2	1	.167	.286	.167	22	-1	-1	1	0	0	0	1.000	-1	/C	-0.2

■ SANDY NAVA Nava, Vincent P. (b: Irwin Sandy) b: 4/12/1850, San Francisco, Cal d: 6/15/06, Baltimore, Md. 5'6", 155 lbs. Deb: 5/05/1882

YEAR	TM/L	G	AB	R	H	2B	3B	HR	RBI	BB	SO	AVG	OBP	SLG	PRO+	BR	/A	RC	SB	CS	SBR	FA	FR	POS	TPR
1882	Pro-N	28	97	15	20	2	0	0	7	1	13	.206	.214	.227	42	-6	-6	5				.867	-7	C/O	-1.1
1883	Pro-N	29	100	18	24	4	2	0	16	3	17	.240	.262	.320	74	-3	-3	9				.813	-4	C/O	-0.5
1884	Pro-N	34	116	10	11	0	0	0	6	11	35	.095	.173	.095	-14	-15	-14	2				.887	1	C/S2	-0.9
1885	Bal-a	8	27	2	5	1	0	0		1		.185	.214	.222	41	-2	-2	1				.825	-5	/C	-0.6
1886	Bal-a	2	5	0	1	0	0	0		0		.200	.200	.200	27	-0	-0	0	1			.500	-1	/SC	-0.1
Total	5	101	345	45	61	7	2	0	29	16	65	.177	.213	.209	33	-26	-26	17	1			.857	-16	/CSO2	-3.2

■ EARL NAYLOR Naylor, Earl Eugene b: 5/19/19, Kansas City, Mo. d: 1/16/90, Winter Haven, Fla. BR/TR, 6', 190 lbs. Deb: 4/15/42

YEAR	TM/L	G	AB	R	H	2B	3B	HR	RBI	BB	SO	AVG	OBP	SLG	PRO+	BR	/A	RC	SB	CS	SBR	FA	FR	POS	TPR
1942	Phi-N	76	168	9	33	4	1	0	14	11	18	.196	.246	.232	42	-13	-12	9	1			.984	-5	OP	-1.8
1943	Phi-N	33	120	12	21	2	0	3	14	12	16	.175	.256	.267	53	-8	-7	7	1			.964	6	O	-0.3
1946	Bro-N	3	2	1	0	0	0	0	0	0	1	.000	.000	.000	-99	-1	-1	0	0			.000	0	H	-0.1
Total	3	112	290	22	54	6	1	3	28	23	35	.186	.248	.245	46	-21	-19	16	2			.971	1	/OP	-2.2

■ JACK NEAGLE Neagle, John Henry b: 1/2/1858, Syracuse, N.Y. d: 9/20/04, Syracuse, N.Y. BR/TR, 5'6", 155 lbs. Deb: 7/08/1879

YEAR	TM/L	G	AB	R	H	2B	3B	HR	RBI	BB	SO	AVG	OBP	SLG	PRO+	BR	/A	RC	SB	CS	SBR	FA	FR	POS	TPR
1879	Cin-N	3	12	1	2	0	0	0	2	0	0	.167	.167	.167	11	-1	-1	0				.000	-1	/OP	-0.1
1883	Phi-N	18	73	6	12	1	0	0	4	1	9	.164	.176	.178	9	-8	-7	2				.840	-2	O/P	-0.5
	Bal-a	9	35	3	10	4	0	0		2		.286	.324	.400	128	1	1	5				.769	-3	/PO	-0.2
	Pit-a	27	101	14	19	0	1	0		5		.188	.226	.208	43	-6	-6	5				.839	-3	PO	-0.4
	Yr	36	136	17	29	4	1	0		7		.213	.252	.257	66	-5	-5	9				.818	-6	PO	-0.6
1884	Pit-a	43	148	13	22	6	0	0		6		.149	.187	.189	24	-12	-12	5				.760	-5	P/O	-0.3
Total	3	100	369	37	65	11	1	0	6	14	9	.176	.208	.211	36	-26	-24	18				.785	-14	/PO	-1.5

■ CHARLIE NEAL Neal, Charles Lenard b: 1/30/31, Longview, Tex. BR/TR, 5'10", 165 lbs. Deb: 4/17/56

YEAR	TM/L	G	AB	R	H	2B	3B	HR	RBI	BB	SO	AVG	OBP	SLG	PRO+	BR	/A	RC	SB	CS	SBR	FA	FR	POS	TPR
1956	*Bro-N	62	136	22	39	5	1	2	14	14	19	.287	.353	.382	91	-0	-1	18	2	2	-1	.972	2	2/S	0.2
1957	Bro-N	128	448	62	121	13	7	12	62	53	83	.270	.358	.411	96	5	-1	69	11	4	1	.949	-3	*S3/2	0.8
1958	LA-N	140	473	87	120	9	6	22	65	61	91	.254	.345	.438	102	4	2	71	7	6	-2	.976	12	*2/S	2.2

YEAR	TM/L	G	AB	R	H	2B	3B	HR	RBI	BB	SO	AVG	OBP	SLG	PRO+	BR	/A	RC	SB	CS	SBR	FA	FR	POS	TPR
1959	*LA-N★	151	616	103	177	30	**11**	19	83	43	86	.287	.338	.464	103	8	3	91	17	6	2	**.989**	20	*2/S	3.5
1960	LA-N★	139	477	60	122	23	2	8	40	48	75	.256	.325	.363	83	-8	-11	54	5	5	-2	.977	-16	*2/S	-1.7
1961	LA-N	108	341	40	80	6	1	10	48	30	49	.235	.298	.346	65	-15	-18	35	3	2	-0	.976	2	*2	-0.7
1962	NY-N	136	508	59	132	14	9	11	58	56	90	.260	.333	.388	91	-5	-6	62	2	8	-4	.970	-8	2S3	-0.6
1963	NY-N	72	253	26	57	12	1	3	18	27	49	.225	.302	.316	77	-7	-7	25	1	2	-1	.961	0	3/S	-0.8
	Cin-N	34	64	2	10	1	0	0	3	5	15	.156	.217	.172	13	-7	-7	3	0	1	-1	.927	-2	3/2S	-1.1
	Yr	106	317	28	67	13	1	3	21	32	64	.211	.286	.287	64	-14	-14	28	1	3	-2	.955	-2	3/S2	-1.9
Total	8	970	3316	461	858	113	38	87	391	337	557	.259	.331	.394	90	-24	-48	429	48	36	-7	.978	7	2S3	1.8
■ **OFFA NEAL**	Neal, Theophilus Fountain b: 6/5/1876, Logan, Ill. d: 4/12/50, Mt.Vernon, Ill. BL/TR, 6', 185 lbs. Deb: 9/30/05																								
1905	NY-N	4	13	0	0	0	0	0	0	0		.000	.000	.000	-98	-3	-3	0	0			1.000	-1	/32	-0.4
■ **GREASY NEALE**	Neale, Alfred Earle b: 11/5/1891, Parkersburg, W.Va. d: 11/2/73, Lake Worth, Fla. BL/TR, 6', 170 lbs. Deb: 4/12/16 C																								
1916	Cin-N	138	530	53	139	13	5	0	20	19	79	.262	.295	.306	87	-10	-9	54	17			.973	11	*O	-0.5
1917	Cin-N	121	385	40	113	14	9	3	33	24	36	.294	.343	.400	133	12	14	58	25			.979	-5	*O	0.3
1918	Cin-N	107	371	57	100	11	11	1	32	24	38	.270	.324	.367	112	4	5	50	23			**.981**	10	*O	1.0
1919	*Cin-N	139	500	57	121	10	12	1	54	47	51	.242	.316	.316	93	-5	-3	59	28			.959	2	*O	-1.2
1920	Cin-N	150	530	55	135	10	7	3	46	45	48	.255	.322	.317	85	-10	-9	58	29	12	2	.987	14	*O	-0.4
1921	Phi-N	22	57	7	12	1	0	0	1	14	9	.211	.366	.228	56	-2	-3	5	3	4	-2	.842	-5	O	-1.1
	Cin-N	63	241	39	58	10	5	0	12	22	16	.241	.307	.324	70	-11	-10	24	9	6	-1	.964	1	O	-1.4
	Yr	85	298	46	70	11	5	0	13	36	25	.235	.319	.305	67	-14	-13	30	12	10	-2	.950	-4	O	-2.5
1922	Cin-N	25	43	11	10	2	1	0	2	6	3	.233	.353	.326	77	-1	-1	6	5	2	0	.864	-4	O	-0.5
1924	Cin-N	3	4	0	0	0	0	0	0	0	1	.000	.000	.000	-99	-1	-1	0	0	0	0	1.000	-0	/O	-0.2
Total	8	768	2661	319	688	71	50	8	200	201	281	.259	.319	.332	94	-25	-18	314	139	24		.972	24	O	-4.0
■ **JOE NEALE**	Neale, Joseph Hunt b: 5/7/1866, Wadsworth, Ohio d: 12/30/13, Akron, Ohio BR/TR, 5'8", 153 lbs. Deb: 6/21/1886																								
1886	Lou-a	2	5	0	0	0	0	0		0		.000	.000	.000	-95	-1	-1	0	0			1.000	0	/OP	-0.1
1887	Lou-a	5	19	3	1	0	0	0		3		.053	.182	.053	-31	-3	-3	0	1			.833	0	/P	0.0
1890	StL-a	11	30	4	2	0	0	0		3		.067	.152	.067	-30	-5	-6	0	0			1.000	-2	P/O	0.0
1891	StL-a	15	51	6	6	0	1	1	8	3	11	.118	.167	.216	9	-6	-7	2	1			.933	2	P	0.0
Total	4	33	105	13	9	0	1	1	8	9	11	.086	.158	.133	-13	-15	-17	3	2			.930	0	/PO	-0.1
■ **JIM NEALON**	Nealon, James Joseph b: 12/15/1884, Sacramento, Cal. d: 4/2/10, San Francisco, Cal. BR/TR, 6'1.5", Deb: 4/12/06																								
1906	Pit-N	154	556	82	142	21	12	3	**83**	53		.255	.325	.353	107	7	4	73	15			.987	1	*1	0.1
1907	Pit-N	105	381	29	98	10	8	0	47	23		.257	.301	.325	95	-2	-3	43	11			.978	0	*1	-0.7
Total	2	259	937	111	240	31	20	3	130	76		.256	.315	.342	102	5	1	116	26			.983	1	1	-0.6
■ **TOM NEEDHAM**	Needham, Thomas J. "Deerfoot" b: 4/7/1879, Ireland d: 12/13/26, Steubenville, Ohio BR/TR, 5'10", 180 lbs. Deb: 5/12/04																								
1904	Bos-N	84	269	18	70	12	3	4	19	11		.260	.292	.372	109	0	2	31	3			.945	4	C/O	1.4
1905	Bos-N	83	271	21	59	6	1	2	17	24		.218	.293	.269	70	-10	-9	23	3			.949	-8	C/O1	-1.0
1906	Bos-N	83	285	11	54	8	2	1	12	13		.189	.230	.242	49	-18	-17	17	3			.959	-2	C/2130	-1.3
1907	Bos-N	86	260	19	51	6	2	1	19	18		.196	.264	.246	60	-12	-12	19	4			.967	-11	C/1	-1.8
1908	NY-N	54	91	8	19	3	0	0	11	12		.209	.339	.242	82	-0	-1	8	0			.975	7	C	1.0
1909	Chi-N	13	28	3	4	0	0	0	0	0		.143	.143	.143	-11	-4	-4	1	0			.980	1	/C	-0.2
1910	*Chi-N	31	76	9	14	3	1	0	10	10	10	.184	.287	.250	57	-4	-4	6	1			.982	3	C/1	0.2
1911	Chi-N	27	62	4	12	2	0	0	5	9	14	.194	.315	.226	52	-4	-4	5	2			.984	6	C	0.4
1912	Chi-N	33	90	12	16	5	0	0	10	7	13	.178	.260	.233	36	-8	-8	6	3			.994	-1	C	-0.6
1913	Chi-N	20	42	5	10	4	1	0	11	4	8	.238	.304	.381	95	-0	-0	5	0			.962	5	C/1	0.5
1914	Chi-N	9	17	3	2	1	0	0	3	1	4	.118	.167	.176	2	-2	-2	1	1			.943	1	/C	0.0
Total	11	523	1491	113	311	50	10	8	117	109	49	.209	.274	.272	67	-61	-59	122	20			.962	6	C/1203	-1.4
■ **TROY NEEL**	Neel, Troy Lee b: 9/14/65, Freeport, Tex. BL/TR, 6'4", 210 lbs. Deb: 5/30/92																								
1992	Oak-A	24	53	8	14	3	0	3	9	5	15	.264	.339	.491	135	2	2	8	0	1	-1	.846	-2	/O1D	0.0
■ **CAL NEEMAN**	Neeman, Calvin Amandus b: 2/18/29, Valmeyer, Ill. BR/TR, 6'1", 192 lbs. Deb: 4/16/57																								
1957	Chi-N	122	415	37	107	17	1	10	39	22	87	.258	.300	.376	81	-12	-11	46	0	0	0	.990	1	*C	-0.6
1958	Chi-N	76	201	30	52	7	0	12	29	21	41	.259	.338	.473	113	3	3	32	0	0	0	.992	1	C	0.8
1959	Chi-N	44	105	7	17	2	0	3	9	11	23	.162	.241	.267	36	-10	-10	7	0	0	0	.994	-1	C	-1.0
1960	Chi-N	9	13	0	2	1	0	0	0	0	5	.154	.154	.231	4	-2	-2	0	0	0	0	1.000	4	/C	0.2
	Phi-N	59	160	13	29	6	2	4	13	16	42	.181	.264	.319	59	-9	-9	13	0	0	0	.979	5	C	-0.2
	Yr	68	173	13	31	7	2	4	13	16	47	.179	.257	.312	55	-11	-11	13	0	0	0	.982	8	C	0.0
1961	Phi-N	19	31	0	7	1	0	0	2	4	8	.226	.314	.258	55	-2	-2	2	1	0	0	.986	2	C	0.1
1962	Pit-N	24	50	5	9	1	1	1	5	3	10	.180	.226	.300	40	-4	-4	3	0	0	0	.983	8	C	0.4
1963	Cle-A	9	9	0	0	0	0	0	0	1	5	.000	.100	.000	-70	-2	-2	0	0	0	0	1.000	3	/C	0.1
	Was-A	14	18	1	1	0	0	0	0	1	0	.056	.105	.056	-54	-4	-4	0	0	0	0	.970	2	C	-0.2
	Yr	23	27	1	1	0	0	0	0	2	5	.037	.103	.037	-59	-6	-6	0	0	0	0	.985	5	C	-0.1
Total	7	376	1002	93	224	35	4	30	97	79	221	.224	.286	.356	72	-42	-41	104	1	0	0	.988	24	C	-0.4
■ **DOUG NEFF**	Neff, Douglas Williams b: 10/8/1891, Harrisonburg, Va. d: 5/23/32, Cape Charles, Va. BR/TR, 5'9", 141 lbs. Deb: 6/26/14																								
1914	Was-A	3	2	0	0	0	0	0	0	0	0	.000	.000	.000	-96	-0	-0	0	0			.889	2	/S	0.1
1915	Was-A	30	60	1	10	1	0	0	4	4	6	.167	.219	.183	20	-6	-6	3	1	2	-1	.867	-4	32/S	-1.1
Total	2	33	62	1	10	1	0	0	4	4	6	.161	.212	.177	16	-6	-7	3	1	2		.900	-2	/32S	-1.0
■ **CY NEIGHBORS**	Neighbors, Flemon Cecil b: 9/23/1880, Fayetteville, Mo. d: 5/20/64, Tacoma, Wash. BR , Deb: 4/29/08																								
1908	Pit-N	1	0	0	0	0	0	0	0	0		—	—	—	—	0	0	0	0			.000	-1	/O	-0.1
■ **BOB NEIGHBORS**	Neighbors, Robert Otis b: 11/9/17, Talahina, Okla. d: 8/8/52, North Korea (Mia) BR/TR, 5'11", 165 lbs. Deb: 9/16/39																								
1939	StL-A	7	11	3	2	0	0	1	1	0	1	.182	.182	.455	56	-1	-1	1	0	0	0	.917	-0	/S	-0.1
■ **TOMMY NEILL**	Neill, Thomas White b: 11/7/19, Hartselle, Ala. d: 9/22/80, Houston, Tex. BL/TR, 6'2", 200 lbs. Deb: 9/10/46																								
1946	Bos-N	13	45	8	12	2	0	0	7	2	1	.267	.298	.311	72	-2	-2	4	0			1.000	-1	O	-0.4
1947	Bos-N	7	10	1	2	0	1	0	0	1	2	.200	.333	.400	96	-0	-0	1	0			1.000	-1	/O	-0.1
Total	2	20	55	9	14	2	1	0	7	3	3	.255	.305	.327	77	-2	-2	5	0			1.000	-2	/O	-0.5
■ **BERNIE NEIS**	Neis, Bernard Edmund b: 9/26/1895, Bloomington, Ill. d: 11/29/72, Inverness, Fla. BB/TR, 5'7", 160 lbs. Deb: 4/14/20																								
1920	*Bro-N	95	249	38	63	11	2	2	22	26	35	.253	.329	.337	89	-2	-3	28	9	9	-3	.957	-2	O	-1.3
1921	Bro-N	102	230	34	59	5	4	4	34	25	41	.257	.332	.365	81	-5	-6	28	9	7	-2	.946	-6	O/2	-1.7
1922	Bro-N	61	70	15	16	4	1	1	9	13	8	.229	.349	.357	83	-2	-1	9	3	2	-0	.897	-5	O	-0.7
1923	Bro-N	126	445	78	122	17	4	5	37	36	38	.274	.330	.364	85	-11	-9	53	8	8	-2	.941	6	*O	-1.2
1924	Bro-N	80	211	43	64	8	3	4	26	27	17	.303	.385	.427	121	6	7	36	4	2	0	.937	-4	O	-0.1
1925	Bos-N	106	355	47	101	20	2	5	45	38	19	.285	.354	.394	100	-4	0	49	8	10	-4	.970	11	O	0.1
1926	Bos-N	30	93	16	20	5	2	0	8	8	10	.215	.277	.312	64	-6	-4	8	4			.925	2	O	-0.4
1927	Cle-A	32	96	17	29	9	0	4	18	18	9	.302	.412	.521	140	6	6	20	0	1	-1	.978	5	O	0.8
	Chi-A	45	76	9	22	5	0	0	11	10	9	.289	.372	.355	92	-1	-1	10	1	0	0	.927	-3	O	-0.4
	Yr	77	172	26	51	14	0	4	29	28	18	.297	.395	.448	120	5	6	31	1	1	-0	.962	2	O	0.4
Total	8	677	1825	297	496	84	18	25	210	201	186	.272	.346	.379	94	-19	-12	242	46	39		.950	3	O/2	-4.9

YEAR	TM/L	G	AB	R	H	2B	3B	HR	RBI	BB	SO	AVG	OBP	SLG	PRO+	BR	/A	RC	SB	CS	SBR	FA	FR	POS	TPR

■ ERNIE NEITZKE Neitzke, Ernest Fredrich b: 11/13/1894, Toledo, Ohio d: 4/27/77, Sylvania, Ohio BR/TR, 5'10", 180 lbs. Deb: 6/02/21

| 1921 | Bos-A | 11 | 25 | 3 | 6 | 0 | 0 | 0 | 2 | 4 | 4 | .240 | .345 | .240 | 53 | -2 | -2 | 2 | 0 | 0 | 0 | .875 | -1 | /OP | -0.3 |

■ DAVE NELSON Nelson, David Earl b: 6/20/44, Fort Sill, Okla. BR/TR, 5'10", 160 lbs. Deb: 4/11/68 C

1968	Cle-A	88	189	26	44	4	5	0	19	17	35	.233	.300	.307	85	-4	-3	20	23	7	3	.987	-2	2S	0.2
1969	Cle-A	52	123	11	25	0	0	0	6	9	26	.203	.263	.203	31	-11	-11	7	4	3	-1	.966	4	2/O	-0.5
1970	Was-A	47	107	5	17	1	0	0	4	7	24	.159	.211	.168	6	-14	-13	4	2	1	0	.986	1	2	-1.0
1971	Was-A	85	329	47	92	11	3	5	33	23	29	.280	.329	.377	105	-1	1	39	17	8	0	.938	-13	3/2	-1.3
1972	Tex-A	145	499	68	113	16	3	2	28	67	81	.226	.324	.283	85	-9	-7	54	51	17	5	.945	-12	*3O	-1.7
1973	Tex-A★	142	576	71	165	24	4	7	48	34	78	.286	.326	.378	102	-2	1	70	43	16	3	.984	-12	*2	0.0
1974	Tex-A	121	474	71	112	13	1	3	42	34	72	.236	.293	.287	69	-20	-18	38	25	13	-0	.969	1	*2/D	-1.2
1975	Tex-A	28	80	9	17	1	0	2	10	8	10	.213	.292	.300	68	-3	-3	8	6	0	2	.959	1	2/D	0.1
1976	*KC-A	78	153	24	36	4	2	1	17	14	26	.235	.299	.307	77	-4	-4	16	15	5	2	.975	2	2D/1	0.1
1977	KC-A	27	48	8	9	3	1	0	4	7	11	.188	.291	.292	59	-3	-3	4	1	3	-2	.926	-2	2/D	-0.6
Total	10	813	2578	340	630	77	19	20	211	220	392	.244	.307	.312	81	-70	-61	259	187	73	12	.976	-31	23/DOS1	-5.9

■ ROCKY NELSON Nelson, Glenn Richard b: 11/18/24, Portsmouth, Ohio BL/TL, 5'11", 178 lbs. Deb: 4/27/49

1949	StL-N	82	244	28	54	8	4	3	32	11	12	.221	.258	.336	55	-15	-17	20	1			1.000	-4	1	-2.1
1950	StL-N	76	235	27	58	10	4	1	20	26	9	.247	.324	.336	71	-9	-10	27	4			.992	3	1	-0.8
1951	StL-N	9	18	3	4	1	0	0	1	1	0	.222	.263	.278	45	-1	-1	1	0	0	0	1.000	-0	/1O	-0.3
	Pit-N	71	195	29	52	7	4	1	14	10	7	.267	.302	.359	75	-7	-7	21	1	1	-0	.990	1	1O	-0.9
	Yr	80	213	32	56	8	4	1	15	11	7	.263	.299	.352	73	-8	-9	22	1	1	-0	.991	-0	1O	-1.2
	Chi-A	6	5	0	0	0	0	0	0	1	0	.000	.167	.000	-53	-1	-1	0	0	0	0	.000	0	H	-0.1
1952	*Bro-N	37	39	6	10	0	0	0	3	7	4	.256	.370	.282	82	-1	-1	5	0	0	0	1.000	-1	/1	-0.2
1954	Cle-A	4	4	0	0	0	0	0	0	0	1	.000	.000	.000	-98	-1	-1	0	0	0	0	1.000	-0	/1	-0.1
1956	Bro-N	31	96	7	20	2	0	4	15	14	10	.208	.240	.354	53	-6	-7	8	0	0	0	.991	2	1	-0.7
	StL-N	38	56	6	13	5	0	3	8	6	6	.232	.306	.482	108	0	0	8	0	0	0	1.000	1	1/O	0.0
	Yr	69	152	13	33	7	0	7	23	20	16	.217	.265	.401	73	-6	-6	15	0	0	0	.993	2	1/O	-0.7
1959	Pit-N	98	175	31	51	11	0	6	32	23	19	.291	.383	.457	124	6	6	32	0	0	0	.994	-4	1/O	0.0
1960	*Pit-N	93	200	34	60	11	1	7	35	24	15	.300	.389	.470	133	10	10	38	1	2	-1	.996	1	1	0.6
1961	Pit-N	75	127	15	25	5	1	5	13	17	11	.197	.301	.370	77	-4	-4	14	0	0	0	.996	-1	1/O	-0.7
Total	9	620	1394	186	347	61	14	31	173	130	94	.249	.318	.379	84	-28	-33	174	7	3		.995	-3	1/O	-5.3

■ JAMIE NELSON Nelson, James Victor b: 9/5/59, Clinton Okla. BR/TR, 5'11", 180 lbs. Deb: 7/21/83

| 1983 | Sea-A | 40 | 96 | 9 | 21 | 3 | 0 | 1 | 5 | 13 | 12 | .219 | .312 | .281 | 62 | -4 | -5 | 9 | 4 | 2 | 0 | .978 | 3 | C | 0.0 |

■ CANDY NELSON Nelson, John W b: 3/12/1854, Portland, Maine d: 9/4/10, Brooklyn, N.Y. BL/TR, 5'6", 145 lbs. Deb: 6/11/1872

1872	Tro-n	4	17	1	6	0	0	0	4	0	2	.353	.353	.353	116	0	0	2						/OS	0.0
	Eck-n	18	76	12	19	2	0	0	7	2	2	.250	.269	.276	80	-3	-0	6						/2O3	0.0
	Yr	22	93	13	25	2	0	0	11	2	4	.269	.284	.290	88	-2	0	8						O/23S	0.0
1873	Mut-n	36	168	28	55	6	1	0	22	1	2	.327	.331	.375	108	1	2	22						2/03C1	0.0
1874	Mut-n	65	295	55	71	8	5	0		9		.241	.263	.302	77	-6	-8	24						*2S	-0.9
1875	Mut-n	70	276	29	56	8	0	0		10		.203	.231	.232	57	-10	-13	15						23/O	0.0
1878	Ind-N	19	84	12	11	1	0	0	5	5	11	.131	.180	.143	8	-8	-6	2				.841	-6	S	-1.1
1879	Tro-N	28	106	17	28	7	1	0	10	8	4	.264	.316	.349	127	2	3	12				.834	4	S/O	0.8
1881	Wor-N	24	103	13	29	1	0	1	15	5	6	.282	.315	.320	95	0	-1	11				.898	2	S	0.3
1883	NY-a	97	417	75	127	19	6	0		31		.305	.353	.379	131	17	14	57				.875	0	*S	1.0
1884	*NY-a	111	432	114	110	15	3	1		74		.255	.375	.310	133	19	21	51				.879	-17	*S/2	0.5
1885	NY-a	107	420	98	107	12	4	1		61		.255	.353	.310	124	10	15	47				.892	13	*S/3	2.7
1886	NY-a	109	413	89	93	7	2	0		64		.225	.332	.252	90	-3	-0	40	14			.855	-8	SO	-0.8
1887	NY-a	68	257	61	63	5	1	0		48		.245	.380	.272	90	-1	1	39	29			.895	10	OS/2	0.9
	NY-N	1	2	0	0	0	0	0	0	0	1	.000	.000	.000	-99	-1	-1	0	0			.000	-0	/3	0.0
1890	Bro-a	60	223	44	56	3	2	0		35		.251	.365	.283	97	0	2	28	12			.866	-8	S/O	-0.3
Total	4 n	193	832	125	207	24	6	0	33	22	6	.249	.268	.292	78	-18	-19	69	3					2/3OS1C	-2.1
Total	9	624	2457	523	624	70	19	3	30	331	22	.254	.349	.302	110	35	49	287	55			.875	-16	S/O32	4.0

■ LYNN NELSON Nelson, Lynn Bernard "Line Drive" b: 2/24/05, Sheldon, N.Dak. d: 2/15/55, Kansas City, Mo. BL/TR, 5'10.5", 170 lbs. Deb: 4/18/30

1930	Chi-N	37	18	0	4	1	1	0	2	0	1	.222	.222	.389	44	-2	-2	1	0			.966	1	P	0.0
1933	Chi-N	29	21	5	5	1	1	0	1	1	3	.238	.273	.381	85	-0	-0	2	0			1.000	1	P	0.0
1934	Chi-N	2	0	0	0	0	0	0	0	0	0	—	—	—		0	0	0	0			.000	-0	/P	0.0
1937	Phi-A	74	113	18	40	6	2	4	29	6	13	.354	.387	.549	135	5	5	24	1	0	0	1.000	-0	P/O	0.3
1938	Phi-A	67	112	12	31	0	0	0	15	7	12	.277	.319	.277	52	-8	-8	10	0	0	0	.952	-0	P	0.0
1939	Phi-A	40	80	3	15	2	0	0	5	2	13	.188	.217	.213	10	-11	-11	3	0	1	-1	.950	-1	P	0.0
1940	Det-A	19	23	4	8	0	0	1	3	0	6	.348	.348	.478	102	0	0	5	0	0	0	1.000	0	/P	0.0
Total	7	268	367	42	103	10	4	5	55	16	48	.281	.313	.371	74	-16	-15	45	1	1		.967	1	P/O	0.3

■ RAY NELSON Nelson, Raymond "Kell" (b: Raymond Nelson Kellogg) b: 8/4/1875, Holyoke, Mass. d: 1/8/61, Mt.Vernon, N.Y. BR/TR, 5'9", 150 lbs. Deb: 5/06/01

| 1901 | NY-N | 39 | 130 | 12 | 26 | 2 | 0 | 0 | 7 | 10 | | .200 | .262 | .215 | 41 | -10 | -9 | 9 | 3 | | | .885 | -3 | 2 | -1.0 |

■ RICKY NELSON Nelson, Ricky Lee b: 5/8/59, Eloy, Ariz. BL/TR, 6', 200 lbs. Deb: 5/17/83

1983	Sea-A	98	291	32	74	13	5	6	36	17	50	.254	.295	.371	79	-8	-9	31	7	4	-0	.971	-8	O/D	-1.9
1984	Sea-A	9	15	2	3	0	0	1	2	2	4	.200	.294	.400	91	-0	-0	2	0	0	0	1.000	-0	OD	-0.1
1985	Sea-A	6	2	2	0	0	0	0	0	0	1	.000	.000	.000	-99	-1	-1	0	0	0	0	1.000	-1	O/	-0.2
1986	Sea-A	10	12	2	2	0	0	0	1	0	4	.167	.167	.167	-9	-2	-2	0	1	0	0	.667	-0	/OD	-0.2
Total	4	123	320	38	79	13	6	6	39	19	59	.247	.289	.363	75	-10	-11	34	8	4	0	.965	-9	/OD	-2.4

■ ROB NELSON Nelson, Robert Augustus b: 5/17/64, Pasadena, Cal. BL/TL, 6'4", 215 lbs. Deb: 9/09/86

1986	Oak-A	5	9	1	2	1	0	0	0	1	4	.222	.300	.333	78	-0	-0	1	0	0	0	.800	0	/1D	0.0
1987	Oak-A	7	24	1	4	0	0	0	0	0	12	.167	.167	.208	-2	-3	-3	0	0	0	0	.968	3	/1	-0.1
	SD-N	10	11	0	1	0	0	0	1	1	8	.091	.167	.091	-31	-2	-2	0	0	0	0	1.000	-0	/1	-0.2
1988	SD-N	7	21	4	4	0	0	1	3	2	9	.190	.261	.333	71	-1	-1	2	0	0	0	.981	1	/1	-0.1
1989	SD-N	42	82	6	16	0	1	3	7	20	29	.195	.353	.329	96	0	0	10	1	3	-2	.991	3	1	0.1
1990	SD-N	5	5	0	0	0	0	0	0	0	4	.000	.000	.000	-99	-1	-1	0	0	0	0	.000	0	/H	-0.1
Total	5	76	152	12	27	2	1	4	11	24	66	.178	.290	.283	62	-8	-7	14	2	3	-2	.983	6	/1D	-0.4

■ TEX NELSON Nelson, Robert Sidney "Babe" b: 8/7/36, Dallas, Tex. BL/TR, 6'3", 205 lbs. Deb: 6/22/55

1955	Bal-A	25	31	4	6	0	0	0	1	7	13	.194	.342	.194	50	-2	-2	3	0	0	0	.889	0	/O1	-0.2
1956	Bal-A	39	68	5	14	2	0	0	5	7	22	.206	.280	.235	40	-6	-5	5	0	0	0	.939	-3	O	-0.9
1957	Bal-A	15	23	2	5	0	0	0	5	1	5	.217	.280	.391	87	-1	-1	3	0	0	0	1.000	-1	/O1	-0.3
Total	3	79	122	11	25	2	0	0	11	15	40	.205	.297	.254	52	-9	-8	10	0	0	0	.938	-5	/O1	-1.4

■ TOMMY NELSON Nelson, Tom Cousineau b: 5/1/17, Chicago, Ill. d: 9/24/73, San Diego, Cal. BR/TR, 5'11.5", 180 lbs. Deb: 4/17/45

| 1945 | Bos-N | 40 | 121 | 6 | 20 | 2 | 0 | 0 | 6 | 4 | 13 | .165 | .192 | .182 | 4 | -16 | -16 | 3 | 1 | | | .910 | -3 | 32 | -1.8 |

YEAR	TM/L	G	AB	R	H	2B	3B	HR	RBI	BB	SO	AVG	OBP	SLG	PRO+	BR	/A	RC	SB	CS	SBR	FA	FR	POS	TPR

■ DICK NEN Nen, Richard Le Roy b: 9/24/39, South Gate, Cal. BL/TL, 6'2", 205 lbs. Deb: 9/18/63

1963	LA-N	7	8	2	1	0	0	1	3	3	3	.125	.364	.500	157	1	1	1	0	0	0	1.000	-1	/1	0.0
1965	Was-A	69	246	18	64	7	1	6	31	19	47	.260	.316	.370	96	-2	-2	29	1	2	-1	.993	8	1	0.2
1966	Was-A	94	235	20	50	8	0	6	30	28	46	.213	.297	.323	79	-6	-6	21	0	2	-1	.990	-2	1	-1.5
1967	Was-A	110	238	21	52	7	1	6	29	21	39	.218	.282	.332	84	-6	-5	21	0	1	-1	.995	1	1/O	-0.9
1968	Chi-N	81	94	8	17	1	1	2	16	6	17	.181	.230	.277	48	-6	-6	6	0	0	0	.987	-1	1	-1.0
1970	Was-A	6	5	1	1	0	0	0	0	0	0	.200	.200	.200	11	-1	-1	0	0	0	0	1.000	0	/1	0.0
Total	6	367	826	70	185	23	3	21	107	77	152	.224	.291	.335	82	-20	-19	79	1	5	-3	.992	7	1/O	-3.2

■ JACK NESS Ness, John Charles b: 11/11/1885, Chicago, Ill. d: 12/3/57, DeLand, Fla. BR/TR, 6'2", 165 lbs. Deb: 5/09/11

1911	Det-A	12	39	6	6	0	0	0	2	2		.154	.195	.154	-2	-5	-6	-1	0			.977	1	1	-0.5
1916	Chi-A	75	258	32	69	7	5	1	34	9	32	.267	.310	.345	96	-2	-2	30	4			.979	-5	1	-1.1
Total	2	87	297	38	75	7	5	1	36	11	32	.253	.295	.320	82	-7	-8	31	4			.978	-4	/1	-1.6

■ GRAIG NETTLES Nettles, Graig b: 8/20/44, San Diego, Cal. BL/TR, 6', 186 lbs. Deb: 9/06/67 FC

1967	Min-A	3	3	0	1	1	0	0	0	0	0	.333	.333	.667	175	0	0	1	0	0	0	.000	0	H	0.0
1968	Min-A	22	76	13	17	2	1	5	8	7	20	.224	.298	.474	125	2	2	10	0	0	0	.968	1	O/31	0.3
1969	*Min-A	96	225	27	50	9	2	7	26	32	47	.222	.322	.373	92	-2	-2	27	1	2	-1	.987	-5	O3	-1.1
1970	Cle-A	157	549	81	129	13	1	26	62	81	77	.235	.336	.404	99	3	-0	77	3	1	0	**.967**	28	*3/O	2.7
1971	Cle-A	158	598	78	156	18	1	28	86	82	56	.261	.353	.435	112	18	11	93	7	4	-0	.973	42	*3	**5.5**
1972	Cle-A	150	557	65	141	28	0	17	70	57	50	.253	.327	.395	110	9	7	73	2	3	-1	.956	5	*3	1.1
1973	NY-A	160	552	65	129	18	1	22	81	78	76	.234	.336	.386	107	3	5	73	1	0	0	.953	26	*3/D	3.1
1974	NY-A	155	566	74	139	21	1	22	75	59	75	.246	.320	.403	110	4	6	75	1	0	0	.961	16	*3/S	2.2
1975	NY-A★	157	581	71	155	24	4	21	91	51	88	.267	.328	.430	116	8	10	82	1	3	-2	.964	1	*3	2.0
1976	*NY-A★	158	583	88	148	29	2	**32**	93	62	94	.254	.330	.475	135	23	23	92	11	6	-0	.965	17	*3/S	**4.1**
1977	*NY-A★	158	589	99	150	23	4	37	107	68	79	.255	.335	.496	124	17	18	98	2	5	-2	.974	-3	*3/D	1.1
1978	*NY-A★	159	587	81	162	23	2	27	93	59	69	.276	.348	.460	128	19	21	91	1	1	-0	.975	-3	*3/S	1.3
1979	NY-A★	145	521	71	132	15	1	20	73	59	53	.253	.329	.401	98	-3	-2	68	1	2	-1	.966	9	*3	0.5
1980	*NY-A★	89	324	52	79	14	0	16	45	42	42	.244	.332	.435	110	4	4	47	0	0	0	.960	-3	*3/S	1.1
1981	*NY-A	103	349	46	85	7	1	15	46	47	49	.244	.335	.398	112	5	6	48	0	2	-1	.972	8	3/D	1.1
1982	NY-A	122	405	47	94	11	2	18	55	51	49	.232	.319	.402	98	-2	-1	50	1	5	-3	.934	3	3/D	0.1
1983	NY-A	129	462	56	123	17	3	20	75	51	49	.266	.343	.446	120	10	12	71	0	1	-1	.956	1	*3/D	1.0
1984	*SD-N	124	395	56	90	11	1	20	65	58	55	.228	.334	.413	109	5	5	55	0	0	0	.936	-10	*3	-0.7
1985	SD-N★	137	440	66	115	23	1	15	61	72	59	.261	.365	.420	121	13	14	70	0	0	0	.959	-9	*3	0.3
1986	SD-N	126	354	36	77	9	0	16	55	41	66	.218	.302	.379	88	-7	-6	41	0	1	-1	.941	-2	*3	-1.1
1987	Atl-N	112	177	16	37	8	1	5	33	22	25	.209	.296	.350	67	-8	-9	18	1	0	0	.951	-0	3/1	-1.0
1988	Mon-N	80	93	5	16	4	0	1	14	9	19	.172	.245	.247	40	-7	-7	5	0	0	0	.818	-2	3/1	-1.0
Total	22	2700	8986	1193	2225	328	28	390	1314	1088	1209	.248	.332	.421	110	115	118	1264	32	36	-12	.961	132	*3/O1DS	21.5

■ JIM NETTLES Nettles, James William b: 3/2/47, San Diego, Cal. BL/TL, 6', 186 lbs. Deb: 9/07/70 F

1970	Min-A	13	20	3	5	0	0	0	1	5		.250	.286	.250	48	-1	-1	1	0	1	-1	1.000	-2	O	-0.5
1971	Min-A	70	168	17	42	5	1	6	24	19	24	.250	.326	.399	101	1	0	22	3	2	-0	.986	2	O	-0.1
1972	Min-A	102	235	28	48	5	2	4	15	32	52	.204	.302	.294	74	-6	-7	21	4	3	-1	.982	-1	O/1	-1.3
1974	Det-A	43	141	20	32	5	1	6	17	15	26	.227	.306	.404	99	-0	-0	17	3	4	-2	1.000	-1	O	-0.5
1979	KC-A	11	23	0	2	0	0	0	1	3	2	.087	.192	.087	-21	-4	-4	1	0	0	0	1.000	-0	/O1	-0.4
1981	Oak-A	1	0	0	0	0	0	0	0	0	0	—	—	—		0	0	0	0	0	0	.000	-0	/O	0.0
Total	6	240	587	68	129	15	4	16	57	70	109	.220	.305	.341	83	-10	-13	63	10	10	-3	.988	-3	O/1	-2.8

■ MORRIS NETTLES Nettles, Morris b: 1/26/52, Los Angeles, Cal. BL/TL, 6'1", 170 lbs. Deb: 4/26/74

1974	Cal-A	56	175	27	48	4	0	0	8	16	38	.274	.335	.297	88	-3	-2	18	20	11	-1	.990	-6	O	-1.1
1975	Cal-A	112	294	50	68	11	0	0	23	26	57	.231	.296	.269	65	-15	-12	24	22	15	-2	.974	-2	O/D	-2.0
Total	2	168	469	77	116	15	0	0	31	42	95	.247	.311	.279	74	-18	-14	41	42	26	-3	.980	-8	O/D	-3.1

■ MILO NETZEL Netzel, Miles A. b: 5/12/1886, Eldred, Pa. d: 3/18/38, Oxnard, Cal. TL, Deb: 9/16/09

| 1909 | Cle-A | 10 | 37 | 2 | 7 | 1 | 0 | 0 | 3 | 3 | | .189 | .250 | .216 | 46 | -2 | -2 | 2 | 1 | | | .800 | -3 | /3O | -0.6 |

■ OTTO NEU Neu, Otto Adam b: 9/24/1894, Springfield, Ohio d: 9/19/32, Kenton, Ohio BR/TR, 5'11", 170 lbs. Deb: 7/10/17

| 1917 | StL-A | 1 | 0 | 0 | 0 | 0 | 0 | 0 | 0 | 0 | 0 | — | — | — | | 0 | 0 | 0 | 0 | 0 | 0 | .000 | 0 | /S | 0.0 |

■ JOHNNY NEUN Neun, John Henry b: 10/28/1900, Baltimore, Md. d: 3/28/90, Baltimore, Md. BB/TL, 5'10.5", 175 lbs. Deb: 4/14/25 MC

1925	Det-A	60	75	15	20	3	3	0	4	9	12	.267	.345	.387	87	-2	-2	10	2	3	-1	.990	-1	1	-0.4
1926	Det-A	97	242	47	72	14	4	0	15	27	26	.298	.370	.388	97	-0	-1	34	4	7	-3	.993	-3	1	-0.9
1927	Det-A	79	204	38	66	9	4	0	27	35	13	.324	.427	.407	116	7	7	35	22	7	2	.980	-3	1	0.3
1928	Det-A	36	108	15	23	3	1	0	5	7	10	.213	.261	.259	36	-10	-10	7	2	2	-1	.975	-1	1	-1.3
1930	Bos-N	81	212	39	69	12	2	0	23	21	18	.325	.389	.429	101	-0	1	35	9			.991	0	1	-0.4
1931	Bos-N	79	104	17	23	1	3	0	11	11	14	.221	.302	.288	62	-6	-5	10	2			.994	-1	1	-0.7
Total	6	432	945	171	273	42	17	2	85	110	93	.289	.366	.376	91	-11	-10	131	41	19		.987	-7	1	-3.4

■ ALEXANDER NEVIN Nevin, Alexander Brown b: 10/3/1850, Alegheny City, Pa. d: 10/10/21, Pensacola, Fla. Deb: 6/17/1873

| 1873 | Res-n | 13 | 54 | 7 | 11 | 0 | 2 | 0 | 2 | 0 | 3 | .204 | .204 | .278 | 44 | -4 | -3 | 3 | | | | | | 3/O | -0.3 |

■ DON NEWCOMBE Newcombe, Donald "Newk" b: 6/14/26, Madison, N.J. BL/TR, 6'4", 225 lbs. Deb: 5/20/49

1949	*Bro-N★	39	96	8	22	4	0	0	10	5	16	.229	.267	.271	43	-8	-8	6	0			1.000	1	P	0.0
1950	Bro-N★	40	97	8	24	3	1	1	8	10	19	.247	.318	.330	69	-4	-4	10	0			.969	-0	P	0.0
1951	Bro-N★	40	103	11	23	3	1	0	8	8	9	.223	.286	.272	50	-7	-7	9	0	0	0	.958	1	P	0.0
1954	Bro-N	31	47	6	15	1	0	0	4	4	6	.319	.373	.340	85	-1	-1	7	0	0	0	.931	-1	P	0.0
1955	*Bro-N★	57	117	18	42	9	1	7	23	6	18	.359	.395	.632	163	11	10	30	1	0	0	.907	-2	P	0.0
1956	*Bro-N	52	111	13	26	6	0	2	16	12	18	.234	.315	.342	71	-4	-5	12	1	0	0	.985	0	P	0.0
1957	Bro-N	34	74	8	17	2	0	1	7	11	11	.230	.329	.297	64	-3	-4	7	0	1	-1	.964	1	P	0.0
1958	LA-N	11	12	2	5	0	0	0	2	0	2	.417	.500	.417	141	1	1	3	0	0	0	1.000	0	P	0.0
	Cin-N	39	60	9	21	1	0	1	9	9	8	.350	.426	.417	118	3	3	12	0	0	0	1.000	-2	P	0.0
	Yr	50	72	11	26	1	0	1	9	10	12	.361	.439	.417	122	4	3	14	0	0	0	1.000	-2	P	0.0
1959	Cin-N	61	105	10	32	2	0	3	21	17	23	.305	.402	.410	113	3	3	19	0	0	0	.978	-1	P	0.0
1960	Cin-N	24	36	0	5	1	0	0	1	3	8	.139	.205	.167	3	-5	-5	2	0	0	0	.895	-1	P	0.0
	Cle-A	24	20	1	6	1	0	1	1	7	.300	.333	.350	88	-0	-0	2	0	0	0	.889	-1	P	0.0
Total	10	452	878	94	238	33	3	15	108	87	147	.271	.339	.367	85	-13	-18	117	2	1		.963	-6	P	0.0

■ JOHN NEWELL Newell, John A. b: 1/14/1868, Wilmington, Del. d: 1/28/19, Wilmington, Del. BR/TL, Deb: 7/22/1891

| 1891 | Pit-N | 5 | 18 | 1 | 2 | 0 | 0 | 0 | 2 | 0 | | .111 | .158 | .111 | -21 | -3 | -3 | 0 | 0 | | | .846 | -2 | /3 | -0.4 |

■ T. E. NEWELL Newell, T. E. b: St.Louis, Mo. Deb: 8/08/1877

| 1877 | StL-N | 1 | 3 | 0 | 0 | 0 | 0 | 0 | 0 | 0 | 0 | .000 | .000 | .000 | -99 | -1 | -1 | 0 | | | | .833 | 0 | /S | 0.0 |

■ AL NEWMAN Newman, Albert Dwayne b: 6/30/60, Kansas City, Mo. BB/TR, 5'9", 183 lbs. Deb: 6/14/85

| 1985 | Mon-N | 25 | 29 | 7 | 5 | 1 | 0 | 0 | 1 | 3 | 4 | .172 | .250 | .207 | 31 | -3 | -3 | 2 | 2 | 1 | 0 | 1.000 | 10 | 2/S | 0.8 |

YEAR	TM/L	G	AB	R	H	2B	3B	HR	RBI	BB	SO	AVG	OBP	SLG	PRO+	BR	/A	RC	SB	CS	SBR	FA	FR	POS	TPR
1986	Mon-N	95	185	23	37	3	0	1	8	21	20	.200	.282	.232	44	-14	-14	12	11	11	-3	.967	9	2S	-0.6
1987	*Min-A	110	307	44	68	15	5	0	29	34	27	.221	.299	.303	58	-17	-19	28	15	11	-2	.982	-11	S23/OD	-2.6
1988	Min-A	105	260	35	58	7	0	0	19	29	34	.223	.301	.250	54	-14	-15	22	12	3	2	.966	-4	3S2/D	-1.6
1989	Min-A	141	446	62	113	18	2	0	38	59	46	.253	.343	.303	78	-8	-12	52	25	12	0	.980	-21	23S/OD	-2.9
1990	Min-A	144	388	43	94	14	0	0	30	33	34	.242	.305	.278	60	-18	-21	35	13	6	0	.993	-2	2S3/O	-1.9
1991	*Min-A	118	246	25	47	5	0	0	19	23	21	.191	.263	.211	31	-22	-23	14	4	5	-2	.987	-1	S23/1OD	-2.3
1992	Tex-A	116	246	25	54	5	0	0	12	34	26	.220	.317	.240	60	-13	-11	21	9	6	-1	.983	12	23S/O	0.1
Total	8	854	2107	264	476	68	7	1	156	236	212	.226	.306	.266	58	-108	-118	185	91	55	-6	.984	-9	2S3/DO1	-11.0

■ CHARLIE NEWMAN

Newman, Charles "Decker" b: 11/5/1868, Juda, Wis. d: 11/23/47, San Diego, Cal. BR/TR, Deb: 9/11/1892

YEAR	TM/L	G	AB	R	H	2B	3B	HR	RBI	BB	SO	AVG	OBP	SLG	PRO+	BR	/A	RC	SB	CS	SBR	FA	FR	POS	TPR
1892	NY-N	3	12	1	4	0	0	0	1	2	0	.333	.429	.333	136	1	1	3	3			.750	-0	/O	0.0
	Chi-N	16	61	4	10	0	0	0	2	1	6	.164	.177	.164	4	-7	-7	2	2			.950	-3	O	-1.0
	Yr	19	73	5	14	0	0	0	3	3	6	.192	.224	.192	27	-6	-6	4	5			.917	-3	O	-1.0

■ JEFF NEWMAN

Newman, Jeffrey Lynn b: 9/11/48, Fort Worth, Tex. BR/TR, 6'2", 218 lbs. Deb: 6/30/76 MC

YEAR	TM/L	G	AB	R	H	2B	3B	HR	RBI	BB	SO	AVG	OBP	SLG	PRO+	BR	/A	RC	SB	CS	SBR	FA	FR	POS	TPR
1976	Oak-A	43	77	5	15	4	0	0	4	4	12	.195	.235	.247	43	-6	-5	5	0	0	0	.981	6	C	0.2
1977	Oak-A	94	162	17	36	9	0	4	15	4	24	.222	.246	.352	61	-9	-9	14	2	0	1	.970	10	C/P	0.3
1978	Oak-A	105	268	25	64	7	1	9	32	18	40	.239	.289	.373	90	-6	-4	28	0	3	-2	.969	-5	C1/D	-1.2
1979	Oak-A☆	143	516	53	119	17	2	22	71	27	88	.231	.270	.399	82	-18	-14	51	2	1	0	.977	-1	C1/3D	-1.5
1980	Oak-A	127	438	37	102	19	1	15	56	25	81	.233	.276	.384	85	-14	-10	43	3	4	-2	.982	-9	1C/32D	-2.2
1981	*Oak-A	68	216	17	50	12	0	3	15	9	28	.231	.262	.329	73	-9	-8	16	0	2	-1	.995	2	C1	-0.7
1982	Oak-A	72	251	19	50	11	0	6	30	14	49	.199	.242	.315	54	-17	-16	18	0	1	-1	.989	-1	C/13D	-1.5
1983	Bos-A	59	132	11	25	4	0	3	7	10	31	.189	.257	.288	46	-9	-10	9	0	1	-1	.990	2	C/D	-0.8
1984	Bos-A	24	63	5	14	2	0	1	3	5	16	.222	.279	.302	58	-3	-4	6	0	0	0	.992	2	C	-0.1
Total	9	735	2123	189	475	85	4	63	233	116	369	.224	.266	.357	73	-92	-81	190	7	12	-5	.981	7	C1/D32P	-7.5

■ PATRICK NEWNAM

Newnam, Patrick Henry b: 12/10/1880, Hempstead, Tex. d: 6/20/38, San Antonio, Tex. BL/TR, 6', 180 lbs. Deb: 5/29/10

YEAR	TM/L	G	AB	R	H	2B	3B	HR	RBI	BB	SO	AVG	OBP	SLG	PRO+	BR	/A	RC	SB	CS	SBR	FA	FR	POS	TPR
1910	StL-A	103	384	45	83	3	8	2	26	29		.216	.275	.281	79	-12	-9	33	16			.972	-4	*1	-1.5
1911	StL-A	20	62	11	12	4	0	0	5	12		.194	.351	.258	74	-2	-1	7	4			.986	1	1	-0.1
Total	2	123	446	56	95	7	8	2	31	41		.213	.287	.278	78	-14	-11	40	20			.974	-3	1	-1.6

■ SKEETER NEWSOME

Newsome, Lamar Ashby b: 10/18/10, Phenix City, Ala. d: 8/31/89, Columbus, Ga. BR/TR, 5'9", 155 lbs. Deb: 4/19/35

YEAR	TM/L	G	AB	R	H	2B	3B	HR	RBI	BB	SO	AVG	OBP	SLG	PRO+	BR	/A	RC	SB	CS	SBR	FA	FR	POS	TPR
1935	Phi-A	59	145	18	30	7	1	1	10	5	9	.207	.233	.290	35	-15	-14	10	2	1	0	.956	8	S2/3O	-0.5
1936	Phi-A	127	471	41	106	15	2	0	46	25	27	.225	.266	.265	32	-51	-50	35	13	4	2	.957	7	*S/23O	-3.0
1937	Phi-A	122	438	53	111	22	1	1	30	37	22	.253	.312	.315	59	-28	-27	45	11	5	0	.954	7	*S	-1.0
1938	Phi-A	17	48	7	13	4	0	0	7	1	4	.271	.286	.354	61	-3	-3	5	1	1	-0	.971	1	S	-0.1
1939	Phi-A	99	248	22	55	9	1	0	17	19	12	.222	.277	.266	40	-23	-22	17	5	7	-3	.950	1	S/2	-1.6
1941	Bos-A	93	227	28	51	6	0	2	17	22	11	.225	.296	.278	51	-15	-16	20	10	4	1	.958	15	S2	0.4
1942	Bos-A	29	95	7	26	6	0	0	9	9	5	.274	.337	.337	87	-1	-2	11	2	1	0	.925	3	32/S	0.2
1943	Bos-A	114	449	48	119	21	2	1	22	21	21	.265	.301	.327	82	-10	-11	43	5	6	-2	.962	14	S3	0.9
1944	Bos-A	136	472	41	114	26	3	0	41	33	21	.242	.291	.309	72	-18	-17	43	4	3	-1	.963	11	*S/23	0.4
1945	Bos-A	125	438	45	127	30	1	1	48	20	15	.290	.322	.370	98	-1	-2	51	6	3	0	.963	22	2S3	2.9
1946	Phi-N	112	375	35	87	10	2	1	23	30	23	.232	.289	.277	63	-19	-18	33	4			.955	-12	*S/23	-2.5
1947	Phi-N	95	310	36	71	8	2	2	22	24	24	.229	.284	.287	54	-21	-20	26	4			.969	2	S/23	-1.4
Total	12	1128	3716	381	910	164	15	9	292	246	194	.245	.293	.304	62	-206	-202	338	67	35		.959	78	S2/3O	-5.3

■ WARREN NEWSON

Newson, Warren Dale b: 7/3/64, Newnan, Ga. BL/TL, 5'7", 190 lbs. Deb: 5/29/91

YEAR	TM/L	G	AB	R	H	2B	3B	HR	RBI	BB	SO	AVG	OBP	SLG	PRO+	BR	/A	RC	SB	CS	SBR	FA	FR	POS	TPR
1991	Chi-A	71	132	20	39	5	0	4	25	28	34	.295	.419	.424	137	8	8	24	2	2	-1	.962	-10	O/D	-0.3
1992	Chi-A	63	136	19	30	3	0	1	11	37	38	.221	.387	.265	88	-0	0	17	3	0	1	1.000	-4	O/D	-0.4
Total	2	134	268	39	69	8	0	5	36	65	72	.257	.402	.343	112	7	8	41	5	2	0	.984	-13	O/D	-0.7

■ GUS NIARHOS

Niarhos, Constantine Gregory b: 12/6/20, Birmingham, Ala. BR/TR, 6', 165 lbs. Deb: 6/09/46 C

YEAR	TM/L	G	AB	R	H	2B	3B	HR	RBI	BB	SO	AVG	OBP	SLG	PRO+	BR	/A	RC	SB	CS	SBR	FA	FR	POS	TPR
1946	NY-A	37	40	11	9	1	1	0	2	11	2	.225	.392	.300	94	0	0	6	1	0	0	.989	6	C	0.8
1948	NY-A	83	228	41	61	12	2	0	19	52	15	.268	.404	.338	99	2	3	36	1	3	-2	.990	11	C	1.6
1949	*NY-A	32	43	7	12	2	1	0	6	13	8	.279	.456	.372	120	2	2	9	0	0	0	1.000	4	C	0.7
1950	NY-A	1	0	0	0	0	0	0	0	0	0	—	—	—	—	0	0	0	0	0	0	.000	0	R	0.0
	Chi-A	41	105	17	34	4	0	0	16	14	6	.324	.408	.362	101	1	1	16	0	0	0	.978	8	C	1.0
	Yr	42	105	17	34	4	0	0	16	14	6	.324	.408	.362	101	1	1	16	0	0	0	.978	8	C	1.0
1951	Chi-A	66	168	27	43	6	0	1	10	47	9	.256	.419	.310	101	3	3	26	4	3	-1	.985	4	C	0.9
1952	Bos-A	29	58	4	6	0	0	0	4	12	9	.103	.268	.103	6	-7	-8	3	0	0	0	.992	6	C	-0.1
1953	Bos-A	16	35	6	7	1	1	0	2	4	4	.200	.300	.286	56	-2	-2	3	0	1	-1	.985	4	C	0.1
1954	Phi-N	3	5	0	1	0	0	0	0	0	1	.200	.200	.200	5	-1	-1	0	0	0	0	1.000	1	/C	0.0
1955	Phi-N	7	9	1	1	0	0	0	0	0	2	.111	.111	.111	-42	-2	-2	0	0	0	0	1.000	1	/C	-0.1
Total	9	315	691	114	174	26	5	1	59	153	56	.252	.390	.308	89	-3	-3	99	6	7	-2	.988	45	C	4.9

■ SAM NICHOL

Nichol, Samuel Anderson b: 4/20/1869, Ireland d: 4/19/37, Steubenville, Ohio BR/TR, 5'10", 178 lbs. Deb: 10/05/1888

YEAR	TM/L	G	AB	R	H	2B	3B	HR	RBI	BB	SO	AVG	OBP	SLG	PRO+	BR	/A	RC	SB	CS	SBR	FA	FR	POS	TPR
1888	Pit-N	8	22	3	1	0	0	0	0	2	2	.045	.125	.045	-47	-3	-3	0	0			.952	0	/O	-0.3
1890	Col-a	14	56	7	9	0	0	0		2		.161	.190	.161	5	-7	-6	2	3			.903	3	O	-0.3
Total	2	22	78	10	10	0	0	0	0	4	2	.128	.171	.128	-9	-10	-9	2	3			.923	3	/O	-0.6

■ DON NICHOLAS

Nicholas, Donald Leigh b: 10/30/30, Phoenix, Ariz. BL/TR, 5'7", 150 lbs. Deb: 4/16/52

YEAR	TM/L	G	AB	R	H	2B	3B	HR	RBI	BB	SO	AVG	OBP	SLG	PRO+	BR	/A	RC	SB	CS	SBR	FA	FR	POS	TPR
1952	Chi-A	3	2	0	0	0	0	0	0	0	0	.000	.000	.000	-99	-1	-1	0	0	0	0	.000	0	H	-0.1
1954	Chi-A	7	0	3	0	0	0	0	0	1	0	—	1.000	—	185	0	0	0	0	1	-1	.000	0	H	0.0
Total	2	10	2	3	0	0	0	0	0	1	0	.000	.333	.000	-2	-0	-0	0	0	1	-1		0		-0.1

■ SIMON NICHOLLS

Nicholls, Simon Burdette b: 7/18/1882, Germantown, Md. d: 3/12/11, Baltimore, Md. BL/TR, Deb: 9/18/03

YEAR	TM/L	G	AB	R	H	2B	3B	HR	RBI	BB	SO	AVG	OBP	SLG	PRO+	BR	/A	RC	SB	CS	SBR	FA	FR	POS	TPR
1903	Det-A	2	8	0	3	0	0	0	0	0		.375	.375	.375	129	0	0	1	0			.600	-2	/S	-0.2
1906	Phi-A	12	44	1	8	1	0	0	1	3		.182	.234	.205	37	-3	-3	2	0			.965	-2	S	-0.6
1907	Phi-A	124	460	75	139	12	2	0	23	24		.302	.338	.337	113	8	6	62	13			.930	-20	S23	-1.2
1908	Phi-A	150	550	58	119	17	3	4	31	35		.216	.263	.280	72	-15	-19	45	14			.913	-21	*S2/3	-4.2
1909	Phi-A	21	71	10	15	2	1	0	3	3		.211	.243	.268	60	-3	-3	5	0			.889	0	S/31	-0.3
1910	Cle-A	3	0	0	0	0	0	0	0	0		—	—	—	—	0	0	0	0			.000	-1	/S	-0.1
Total	6	312	1133	144	284	32	6	4	58	65		.251	.292	.300	86	-13	-19	116	27			.917	-45	S/231	-6.6

■ AL NICHOLS

Nichols, Albert H. b: Brooklyn, N.Y. 5'11", 180 lbs. Deb: 4/24/1875

YEAR	TM/L	G	AB	R	H	2B	3B	HR	RBI	BB	SO	AVG	OBP	SLG	PRO+	BR	/A	RC	SB	CS	SBR	FA	FR	POS	TPR
1875	Atl-n	32	129	4	20	3	0	0		0		.155	.155	.178	17	-11	-8	4						3	-0.7
1876	NY-N	57	212	20	38	4	0	0	9	2	3	.179	.187	.198	33	-15	-11	8				.779	5	*3	-0.4
1877	Lou-N	6	19	1	4	0	1	0	0	0	2	.211	.211	.316	54	-1	-1	1				.706	4	/2S31	0.2
Total	2	63	231	21	42	4	1	0	9	2	5	.182	.189	.208	35	-16	-13	9				.785	9	/321S	-0.2

■ ART NICHOLS

Nichols, Arthur Francis (b: Arthur Francis Meikle)
b: 7/14/1871, Manchester, N.H. d: 8/9/45, Willimantic, Conn. BR/TR, 5'10", 175 lbs. Deb: 9/16/1898

YEAR	TM/L	G	AB	R	H	2B	3B	HR	RBI	BB	SO	AVG	OBP	SLG	PRO+	BR	/A	RC	SB	CS	SBR	FA	FR	POS	TPR
1898	Chi-N	14	42	7	12	1	0	0	6	4		.286	.388	.310	101	0	0	8	6			.968	1	C	0.2
1899	Chi-N	17	47	5	12	2	0	1	11	0		.255	.286	.362	79	-2	-2	6	3			.931	-1	C	-0.2
1900	Chi-N	8	25	1	5	0	0	0	0	3		.200	.286	.200	37	-2	-2	2	1			.938	-2	/C	-0.3

YEAR	TM/L	G	AB	R	H	2B	3B	HR	RBI	BB	SO	AVG	OBP	SLG	PRO+	BR	/A	RC	SB	CS	SBR	FA	FR	POS	TPR
1901	StL-N	93	308	50	75	11	3	1	33	10		.244	.285	.308	76	-11	-9	33	14			.960	-3	CO	-1.0
1902	StL-N	73	251	36	67	12	0	1	31	21		.267	.331	.327	107	1	2	35	18			.984	-7	1C/O	-0.5
1903	StL-N	36	120	13	23	2	0	0	9	12		.192	.271	.208	39	-9	-9	10	9			.972	-5	1/OC	-1.4
Total	6	241	793	112	194	28	3	3	90	50		.245	.303	.299	80	-23	-19	93	51			.952	-17	/C1O	-3.2

■ CARL NICHOLS

Nichols, Carl Edward b: 10/14/62, Los Angeles, Cal. BR/TR, 6', 208 lbs. Deb: 9/14/86

YEAR	TM/L	G	AB	R	H	2B	3B	HR	RBI	BB	SO	AVG	OBP	SLG	PRO+	BR	/A	RC	SB	CS	SBR	FA	FR	POS	TPR
1986	Bal-A	5	5	0	0	0	0	0	0	1	4	.000	.167	.000	-51	-1	-1	0	0	0	0	1.000	-0	/C	-0.1
1987	Bal-A	13	21	4	8	1	0	0	3	1	4	.381	.409	.429	126	1	1	4	0	0	0	1.000	1	C	0.2
1988	Bal-A	18	47	2	9	1	0	0	1	3	10	.191	.240	.213	29	-4	-4	2	0	0	0	.987	6	C/O	0.2
1989	Hou-N	8	13	0	1	0	0	0	2	0	3	.077	.077	.077	-58	-3	-3	0	0	0	0	1.000	-0	/C	-0.3
1990	Hou-N	32	49	7	10	3	0	0	11	8	11	.204	.328	.265	67	-2	-2	5	0	0	0	.986	3	C/1O	0.1
1991	Hou-N	20	51	3	10	3	0	0	1	5	17	.196	.268	.255	51	-3	-3	4	0	0	0	.971	3	C	0.1
Total	6	96	186	16	38	8	0	0	18	18	49	.204	.278	.247	49	-13	-12	15	0	0	0	.985	12	/CO1	0.2

■ ROY NICHOLS

Nichols, Roy b: 3/3/21, Little Rock, Ark. BR/TR, 5'11", 155 lbs. Deb: 5/06/44

YEAR	TM/L	G	AB	R	H	2B	3B	HR	RBI	BB	SO	AVG	OBP	SLG	PRO+	BR	/A	RC	SB	CS	SBR	FA	FR	POS	TPR
1944	NY-N	11	9	3	2	1	0	0	0	2	2	.222	.364	.333	97	0	0	1	0			1.000	2	/23	0.2

■ REID NICHOLS

Nichols, Thomas Reid b: 8/5/58, Ocala, Fla. BR/TR, 5'11", 165 lbs. Deb: 9/16/80

YEAR	TM/L	G	AB	R	H	2B	3B	HR	RBI	BB	SO	AVG	OBP	SLG	PRO+	BR	/A	RC	SB	CS	SBR	FA	FR	POS	TPR
1980	Bos-A	12	36	5	8	0	1	0	3	3	8	.222	.282	.278	51	-2	-2	3	0	1	-1	.962	0	/OD	-0.3
1981	Bos-A	39	48	13	9	0	1	0	3	2	6	.188	.220	.229	28	-4	-5	3	0	1	-1	1.000	-4	O/3D	-1.1
1982	Bos-A	92	245	35	74	16	1	7	33	14	28	.302	.342	.461	112	6	4	38	5	3	-0	.989	-2	O/D	0.0
1983	Bos-A	100	274	35	78	22	1	6	22	26	36	.285	.353	.438	108	6	4	42	7	5	-1	.994	2	OD/S	0.3
1984	Bos-A	74	124	14	28	5	1	1	14	12	18	.226	.309	.306	68	-5	-5	13	2	1	0	.988	-4	O/D	-1.0
1985	Bos-A	21	32	3	6	1	0	1	3	2	4	.188	.257	.313	53	-2	-2	3	1	0	0	.933	-2	O/2D	-0.4
	Chi-A	51	118	20	35	7	1	1	15	15	13	.297	.376	.398	108	2	2	18	5	5	-2	1.000	-12	O/D	-1.2
	Yr	72	150	23	41	8	1	2	18	17	17	.273	.351	.380	96	0	-0	20	6	5	-1	.988	-14	O/D2	-1.6
1986	Chi-A	74	136	9	31	4	0	2	18	11	23	.228	.286	.301	58	-8	-8	12	5	4	-1	.989	-4	O/2D	-1.4
1987	Mon-N	77	147	22	39	8	2	4	20	14	13	.265	.333	.429	97	-0	-1	21	2	1	0	.990	-4	O/3	-0.5
Total	8	540	1160	156	308	63	8	22	131	99	149	.266	.328	.391	91	-7	-14	151	27	21	-5	.990	-29	O/D23S	-5.6

■ DAVE NICHOLSON

Nicholson, David Lawrence b: 8/29/39, St.Louis, Mo. BR/TR, 6'2", 215 lbs. Deb: 5/24/60

YEAR	TM/L	G	AB	R	H	2B	3B	HR	RBI	BB	SO	AVG	OBP	SLG	PRO+	BR	/A	RC	SB	CS	SBR	FA	FR	POS	TPR
1960	Bal-A	54	113	17	21	1	1	5	11	20	55	.186	.308	.345	77	-4	-3	12	0	2	-1	.982	-5	O	-1.1
1962	Bal-A	97	173	25	30	4	1	9	15	27	76	.173	.289	.364	78	-7	-5	19	3	4	-2	.983	-7	O	-1.7
1963	Chi-A	126	449	53	103	11	4	22	70	63	175	.229	.324	.419	108	4	5	65	2	1	0	.970	2	*O	0.0
1964	Chi-A	97	294	40	60	6	1	13	39	52	126	.204	.330	.364	95	-2	-1	38	0	2	-1	.972	-2	O	-0.9
1965	Chi-A	54	85	11	13	2	1	2	12	9	40	.153	.234	.271	46	-6	-6	6	0	0	0	1.000	-9	O	-1.7
1966	Hou-N	100	280	36	69	8	4	10	31	46	92	.246	.359	.411	122	6	9	45	1	1	-0	.968	3	O	0.8
1967	Atl-N	10	25	2	5	0	0	0	1	2	9	.200	.259	.200	34	-2	-2	2	0	0	0	1.000	0	/O	-0.3
Total	7	538	1419	184	301	32	12	61	179	219	573	.212	.320	.381	97	-11	-4	186	6	10	-4	.974	-19	O	-4.9

■ FRED NICHOLSON

Nicholson, Fred "Shoemaker" b: 9/1/1894, Honey Grove, Tex. d: 1/23/72, Kilgore, Tex. BR/TR, 5'10.5", 173 lbs. Deb: 4/11/17

YEAR	TM/L	G	AB	R	H	2B	3B	HR	RBI	BB	SO	AVG	OBP	SLG	PRO+	BR	/A	RC	SB	CS	SBR	FA	FR	POS	TPR
1917	Det-A	13	14	4	4	1	0	0	1	1	2	.286	.333	.357	111	0	0	2	0			1.000	-1	/O	-0.1
1919	Pit-N	30	66	8	18	2	2	1	6	6	11	.273	.333	.409	118	2	1	9	2			.939	-1	O/1	-0.1
1920	Pit-N	99	247	33	89	16	7	4	30	18	31	.360	.404	.530	162	21	20	51	9	6	-1	.957	2	O	1.8
1921	Bos-N	83	245	36	80	11	7	5	41	17	29	.327	.370	.490	133	9	10	43	5	4	-1	.983	-7	O/12	-0.1
1922	Bos-N	78	222	31	56	4	5	2	29	23	24	.252	.336	.342	79	-8	-6	26	5	7	-3	.915	-4	O	-1.6
Total	5	303	794	112	247	34	21	12	107	65	97	.311	.367	.452	124	23	25	131	21	17		.950	-11	O/12	-0.1

■ OVID NICHOLSON

Nicholson, Ovid Edward b: 12/30/1888, Salem, Ind. d: 3/24/68, Salem, Ind. BL/TR, 5'9.5", 155 lbs. Deb: 9/17/12

YEAR	TM/L	G	AB	R	H	2B	3B	HR	RBI	BB	SO	AVG	OBP	SLG	PRO+	BR	/A	RC	SB	CS	SBR	FA	FR	POS	TPR
1912	Pit-N	6	11	2	5	0	0	0	3	1	2	.455	.500	.455	165	1	1	3	0			1.000	-1	/O	0.0

■ PARSON NICHOLSON

Nicholson, Thomas C. "Deacon" b: 4/14/1863, Blaine, Ohio d: 2/28/17, Bellaire, Ohio 6'6", 190 lbs. Deb: 9/14/1888

YEAR	TM/L	G	AB	R	H	2B	3B	HR	RBI	BB	SO	AVG	OBP	SLG	PRO+	BR	/A	RC	SB	CS	SBR	FA	FR	POS	TPR
1888	Det-N	24	85	11	22	2	3	1	9	2	7	.259	.284	.388	115	1	1	11	6			.935	-2	2	0.0
1890	Tol-a	134	523	78	140	16	11	4		42		.268	.333	.363	105	4	2	80	46			.929	-8	*2/C	0.2
1895	Was-N	10	38	7	7	2	1	0	5	7	4	.184	.311	.289	58	-2	-2	5	6			.797	-2	S	-0.3
Total	3	168	646	96	169	20	15	5	14	51	11	.262	.325	.362	103	3	1	97	58			.930	-11	2/SC	-0.1

■ BILL NICHOLSON

Nicholson, William Beck "Swish" b: 12/11/14, Chestertown, Md. BL/TR, 6', 205 lbs. Deb: 6/13/36

YEAR	TM/L	G	AB	R	H	2B	3B	HR	RBI	BB	SO	AVG	OBP	SLG	PRO+	BR	/A	RC	SB	CS	SBR	FA	FR	POS	TPR
1936	Phi-A	11	12	2	0	0	0	0	0	0	5	.000	.000	.000	-99	-4	-4	0	0	0	0	1.000	-0	/O	-0.4
1939	Chi-N	58	220	37	65	12	5	5	38	20	29	.295	.354	.464	116	5	5	38	0			.955	1	O	0.4
1940	Chi-N★	135	491	78	146	27	7	25	98	50	67	.297	.366	.534	148	29	30	97	2			.950	-2	*O	2.2
1941	Chi-N★	147	532	74	135	26	1	26	98	82	91	.254	.357	.453	132	19	22	90	1			.971	6	*O	1.9
1942	Chi-N	152	588	83	173	22	11	21	78	76	80	.294	.382	.476	156	38	40	112	8			.986	11	*O	**4.6**
1943	Chi-N★	154	608	95	188	30	9	**29**	**128**	71	86	.309	.386	.531	166	48	49	129	4			.978	6	*O	4.9
1944	Chi-N★	156	582	**116**	167	35	8	**33**	**122**	93	71	.287	.391	.545	162	47	48	132	3			.979	2	*O	4.2
1945	*Chi-N†	151	559	82	136	28	4	13	88	92	73	.243	.356	.377	106	5	7	81	4			.990	1	*O	-0.1
1946	Chi-N	105	296	36	65	13	2	8	41	44	44	.220	.325	.358	95	-2	-2	37	1			.973	2	O	-0.3
1947	Chi-N	148	487	69	119	28	1	26	75	87	83	.244	.364	.466	124	14	16	90	1			**.990**	-1	*O	0.8
1948	Chi-N	143	494	68	129	24	5	19	67	81	60	.261	.371	.445	125	15	18	88	2			.980	-3	*O	0.7
1949	Phi-N	98	299	42	70	8	3	11	40	45	53	.234	.344	.391	99	-1	0	44	1			.995	3	O	-0.1
1950	Phi-N	41	58	3	13	2	1	3	10	8	16	.224	.318	.448	101	-0	-0	8	0			.952	-2	O	-0.3
1951	Phi-N	85	170	23	41	9	2	8	30	25	24	.241	.342	.459	115	3	3	29	0	1	-1	.987	-3	O	-0.2
1952	Phi-N	55	88	17	24	3	0	6	19	14	26	.273	.390	.511	150	6	6	20	0	0	0	1.000	-2	O	0.4
1953	Phi-N	38	62	12	13	5	1	2	16	12	20	.210	.338	.419	97	-0	-0	9	0	0	0	1.000	-2	O	-0.3
Total	16	1677	5546	837	1484	272	60	235	948	800	828	.268	.365	.465	133	221	238	1005	27	1		.979	17	*O	18.4

■ GEORGE NICOL

Nicol, George Edward b: 10/17/1870, Barry, Ill. d: 8/10/24, Milwaukee, Wis. TL, 5'7", 155 lbs. Deb: 9/23/1890

YEAR	TM/L	G	AB	R	H	2B	3B	HR	RBI	BB	SO	AVG	OBP	SLG	PRO+	BR	/A	RC	SB	CS	SBR	FA	FR	POS	TPR
1890	StL-a	3	7	4	2	1	0	0		4		.286	.545	.429	168	1	1	2	0			1.000	-0	/P	0.0
1891	Chi-N	3	6	0	2	0	1	0	3	0	1	.333	.333	.667	191	1	1	1	0			.000	-1	/P	0.0
1894	Pit-N	8	20	8	9	1	0	0	3	0	1	.450	.450	.500	132	1	1	5	0			.800	-1	/P	0.0
	Lou-N	27	108	12	38	6	4	0	19	2	3	.352	.375	.481	115	1	2	22	4			.791	-5	O/P	-0.4
	Yr	35	128	20	47	7	4	0	22	2	4	.367	.386	.484	117	2	3	26	4			.791	-6	O/P	-0.4
Total	3	41	141	24	51	8	5	0	25	6	5	.362	.396	.489	123	4	5	29	4			.692	-7	/OP	-0.4

■ HUGH NICOL

Nicol, Hugh b: 1/1/1858, Campsie, Scotland d: 6/27/21, Lafayette, Ind. BR/TR, 5'4", 145 lbs. Deb: 5/03/1881 M

YEAR	TM/L	G	AB	R	H	2B	3B	HR	RBI	BB	SO	AVG	OBP	SLG	PRO+	BR	/A	RC	SB	CS	SBR	FA	FR	POS	TPR
1881	Chi-N	26	108	13	22	2	0	0	7	4	12	.204	.232	.222	42	-7	-7	6				.932	3	O/S	-0.4
1882	Chi-N	47	186	19	37	9	1	1	16	7	29	.199	.228	.274	58	-8	-9	12				.887	10	O/S	0.0
1883	StL-a	94	368	73	106	13	3	0		18		.288	.321	.340	107	5	2	41				.916	12	*O2	1.2
1884	StL-a	110	442	79	115	14	5	0		22		.260	.300	.314	100	2	-0	43				.873	23	*O2/S3	2.0
1885	*StL-a	112	425	59	88	11	1	0		34		.207	.271	.238	61	-16	-19	28				.888	13	*O/3	-0.7
1886	StL-a	67	253	44	52	6	3	0		26		.206	.280	.253	66	-8	-10	29	38			.942	-4	O/S2	-1.3
1887	Cin-a	125	475	122	102	18	2	1		86		.215	.341	.267	71	-13	-15	93	**138**			.918	-3	*O	-1.6
1888	Cin-a	135	548	112	131	10	2	1	35	67		.239	.330	.270	91	1	-3	85	103			.957	-3	*O2/S	-0.9
1889	Cin-a	122	474	82	121	7	8	2	58	54	35	.255	.338	.316	86	-5	-8	80	80			.918	1	*O/23	-0.8
1890	Cin-N	50	186	28	39	1	4	0	19	19	12	.210	.283	.258	60	-9	-9	21	24			.921	-6	O/S2	-1.4

YEAR	TM/L	G	AB	R	H	2B	3B	HR	RBI	BB	SO	AVG	OBP	SLG	PRO+	BR	/A	RC	SB	CS	SBR	FA	FR	POS	TPR
Total	10	888	3465	631	813	91	29	5	135	337	88	.235	.307	.282	80	-58	-79	437	383			.912	49	O/2S3	-3.9

■ STEVE NICOSIA

Nicosia, Steven Richard b: 8/6/55, Paterson, N.J. BR/TR, 5'10", 185 lbs. Deb: 7/08/78

YEAR	TM/L	G	AB	R	H	2B	3B	HR	RBI	BB	SO	AVG	OBP	SLG	PRO+	BR	/A	RC	SB	CS	SBR	FA	FR	POS	TPR
1978	Pit-N	3	5	0	0	0	0	0	0	1	0	.000	.167	.000	-48	-1	-1	0	0	0	0	1.000	1	/C	0.0
1979	*Pit-N	70	191	22	55	16	0	4	13	23	17	.288	.364	.435	112	5	4	29	0	2	-1	.991	4	C	0.9
1980	Pit-N	60	176	16	38	8	0	1	22	19	16	.216	.296	.278	60	-9	-9	14	0	1	-1	.984	-1	C	-0.9
1981	Pit-N	54	169	21	39	10	1	2	18	13	10	.231	.286	.337	74	-6	-6	15	3	1	0	.982	1	C	-0.4
1982	Pit-N	39	100	6	28	3	0	1	7	11	13	.280	.351	.340	91	-0	-1	12	0	1	-1	.990	4	C/O	0.4
1983	Pit-N	21	46	4	6	2	0	1	1	1	7	.130	.149	.239	6	-6	-6	1	0	0	0	.988	-1	C	-0.7
	SF-N	15	33	4	11	0	0	0	6	3	2	.333	.389	.333	105	0	0	4	0	0	0	.984	2	/C	0.3
	Yr	36	79	8	17	2	0	1	7	4	9	.215	.253	.278	47	-6	-6	4	0	0	0	.986	1	C	-0.4
1984	SF-N	48	132	9	40	11	2	2	19	8	14	.303	.343	.462	129	4	4	20	1	1	-0	.985	-5	C	0.0
1985	Mon-N	42	71	4	12	2	0	0	1	7	11	.169	.244	.197	26	-7	-7	4	1	0	0	.988	-5	C/1	-1.1
	Tor-A	6	15	0	4	0	0	0	1	0	0	.267	.267	.267	46	-1	-1	1	0	0	0	1.000	1	/C	0.0
Total	8	358	938	86	233	52	3	11	88	86	90	.248	.312	.345	82	-21	-23	99	5	6	-2	.987	0	C/O1	-1.5

■ CHARLIE NIEBERGALL

Niebergall, Charles Arthur "Nig" b: 5/23/1899, New York, N.Y. d: 8/29/82, Holiday, Fla. BR/TR, 5'10", 160 lbs. Deb: 6/17/21

YEAR	TM/L	G	AB	R	H	2B	3B	HR	RBI	BB	SO	AVG	OBP	SLG	PRO+	BR	/A	RC	SB	CS	SBR	FA	FR	POS	TPR
1921	StL-N	5	6	1	1	0	0	0	0	0	0	.167	.167	.167	-12	-1	-1	0	0	0	0	1.000	-1	/C	-0.1
1923	StL-N	9	28	2	3	1	0	0	1	2	2	.107	.167	.143	-18	-5	-5	1	0	0	0	1.000	-0	/C	-0.4
1924	StL-N	40	58	6	17	6	0	0	7	3	9	.293	.339	.397	98	-0	-0	8	0	0	0	.951	1	C	0.2
Total	3	54	92	9	21	7	0	0	8	5	11	.228	.276	.304	55	-6	-6	9	0	0	0	.966	1	/C	-0.3

■ AL NIEHAUS

Niehaus, Albert Bernard b: 6/1/1899, Cincinnati, Ohio d: 10/14/31, Cincinnati, Ohio BR/TR, 5'11", 175 lbs. Deb: 4/22/25

YEAR	TM/L	G	AB	R	H	2B	3B	HR	RBI	BB	SO	AVG	OBP	SLG	PRO+	BR	/A	RC	SB	CS	SBR	FA	FR	POS	TPR
1925	Pit-N	17	64	7	14	8	0	0	7	1	5	.219	.242	.344	45	-5	-6	5	0	0	0	.962	-1	1	-0.8
	Cin-N	51	147	16	44	10	2	0	14	13	10	.299	.360	.395	95	-1	-1	20	1	4	-2	.988	2	1	-0.3
	Yr	68	211	23	58	18	2	0	21	14	15	.275	.326	.379	80	-7	-7	25	1	4	-2	.981	1	1	-1.1

■ BERT NIEHOFF

Niehoff, John Albert b: 5/13/1884, Louisville, Colo. d: 12/8/74, Inglewood, Cal. BR/TR, 5'10.5", 170 lbs. Deb: 10/04/13 C

YEAR	TM/L	G	AB	R	H	2B	3B	HR	RBI	BB	SO	AVG	OBP	SLG	PRO+	BR	/A	RC	SB	CS	SBR	FA	FR	POS	TPR
1913	Cin-N	2	8	0	0	0	0	0	0	0	2	.000	.000	.000	-99	-2	-2	0	0			.917	2	/3	0.0
1914	Cin-N	142	484	46	117	16	9	4	49	38	77	.242	.298	.337	86	-8	-9	52	20			.924	7	*3/2	0.2
1915	*Phi-N	148	529	61	126	27	2	2	49	30	63	.238	.280	.308	77	-15	-15	50	21	11	-0	.946	-7	*2	-2.3
1916	Phi-N	146	548	65	133	**42**	4	4	61	37	57	.243	.292	.356	95	-2	-4	60	20	14	-2	.936	-2	*2/3	-0.4
1917	Phi-N	114	361	30	92	17	4	2	42	23	29	.255	.303	.341	93	-2	-3	39	8			.945	18	2/13	2.2
1918	StL-N	22	84	5	15	2	0	0	5	3	10	.179	.207	.202	26	-8	-7	4	2			.975	2	2	-0.5
	NY-N	7	23	3	6	0	0	0	1	0	4	.261	.261	.261	60	-1	-1	1	0			.871	-2	/2	-0.4
	Yr	29	107	8	21	2	0	0	6	3	14	.196	.218	.215	33	-9	-8	5	2			.954	-1	2	-0.9
Total	6	581	2037	210	489	104	19	12	207	131	242	.240	.288	.327	84	-37	-43	206	71	25		.943	18	23/1	-1.2

■ MILT NIELSEN

Nielsen, Milton Robert b: 2/8/25, Tyler, Minn. BL/TL, 5'11", 190 lbs. Deb: 9/27/49

YEAR	TM/L	G	AB	R	H	2B	3B	HR	RBI	BB	SO	AVG	OBP	SLG	PRO+	BR	/A	RC	SB	CS	SBR	FA	FR	POS	TPR
1949	Cle-A	3	9	1	1	0	0	0	0	2	4	.111	.273	.111	4	-1	-1	0	0	0	0	1.000	-0	/O	-0.2
1951	Cle-A	16	6	1	0	0	0	0	0	1	1	.000	.143	.000	-63	-1	-1	0	0	0	0	.000	0	H	-0.1
Total	2	19	15	2	1	0	0	0	0	3	5	.067	.222	.067	-22	-3	-2	0	0	0	0		-0	/O	-0.3

■ BUTCH NIEMAN

Nieman, Elmer Le Roy b: 2/8/18, Herkimer, Kan. BL/TL, 6'2", 195 lbs. Deb: 5/02/43

YEAR	TM/L	G	AB	R	H	2B	3B	HR	RBI	BB	SO	AVG	OBP	SLG	PRO+	BR	/A	RC	SB	CS	SBR	FA	FR	POS	TPR
1943	Bos-N	101	335	39	84	15	8	7	46	39	39	.251	.331	.406	114	5	5	47	4			.963	1	O	0.2
1944	Bos-N	134	468	65	124	16	6	16	65	47	47	.265	.332	.427	108	7	4	69	5			.975	-2	*O	-0.4
1945	Bos-N	97	247	43	61	15	0	14	56	43	33	.247	.361	.478	131	10	10	44	11			.932	0	O	0.7
Total	3	332	1050	147	269	46	14	37	167	129	119	.256	.339	.432	116	22	20	161	20			.961	-0	O	0.5

■ BOB NIEMAN

Nieman, Robert Charles b: 1/26/27, Cincinnati, Ohio d: 3/10/85, Corona, Cal. BR/TR, 5'11", 195 lbs. Deb: 9/14/51

YEAR	TM/L	G	AB	R	H	2B	3B	HR	RBI	BB	SO	AVG	OBP	SLG	PRO+	BR	/A	RC	SB	CS	SBR	FA	FR	POS	TPR
1951	StL-A	12	43	6	16	3	1	2	8	3	5	.372	.413	.628	174	4	4	11	0	0	0	.962	0	O	0.4
1952	StL-A	131	478	66	138	22	2	18	74	46	73	.289	.352	.456	120	14	12	75	0	4	-2	.976	1	*O	0.6
1953	Det-A	142	508	72	143	32	5	15	69	57	57	.281	.354	.453	118	11	12	82	0	3	-2	.979	3	*O	0.8
1954	Det-A	91	251	24	66	14	1	8	35	22	32	.263	.322	.422	105	-0	1	31	0	2	-1	.984	-2	O	-0.5
1955	Chi-A	99	272	36	77	11	2	11	53	36	37	.283	.371	.460	119	8	7	46	1	0	0	.976	-7	O	-0.2
1956	Chi-A	14	40	3	12	1	0	2	4	4	4	.300	.364	.475	118	1	1	5	0	1	-1	1.000	1	O	0.0
	Bal-A	114	388	60	125	20	6	12	64	86	59	.322	.445	.497	161	31	36	89	1	5	-3	.980	7	*O	3.3
	Yr	128	428	63	137	21	6	14	68	90	63	.320	.438	.495	156	32	36	94	1	6	-3	.982	7	*O	3.3
1957	Bal-A	129	445	61	123	17	6	13	70	63	86	.276	.369	.429	125	12	15	70	4	4	-1	.980	5	*O	1.2
1958	Bal-A	105	366	56	119	20	2	16	60	44	57	.325	.398	.522	159	26	28	71	2	8	-4	.961	-7	*O	1.2
1959	Bal-A	118	360	49	105	18	2	21	60	42	55	.292	.369	.528	146	21	22	67	1	2	-1	.973	-0	O	1.6
1960	StL-N	81	188	19	54	13	5	4	31	24	31	.287	.374	.473	120	8	6	33	0	1	-1	.940	-8	O	-0.5
1961	StL-N	6	17	0	8	1	0	0	2	0	2	.471	.471	.529	150	2	1	4	0	0	0	1.000	-1	/O	0.0
	Cle-A	39	65	2	23	6	0	2	10	7	4	.354	.417	.538	157	5	5	16	1	0	0	.960	0	O	0.5
1962	Cle-A	2	1	0	0	0	0	0	1	0	1	.000	.000	.000	-99	-0	-0	0	0	0	0	.000	0	H	0.0
	*SF-N	30	30	1	9	2	0	1	3	1	9	.300	.323	.467	111	0	0	5	0	0	0	1.000	0	/O	0.0
Total	12	1113	3452	455	1018	180	32	125	544	435	512	.295	.375	.474	132	142	150	605	10	30	-15	.975	-8	O	8.4

■ AL NIEMIEC

Niemiec, Alfred Joseph b: 5/18/11, Meriden, Conn. BR/TR, 5'11", 158 lbs. Deb: 9/19/34

YEAR	TM/L	G	AB	R	H	2B	3B	HR	RBI	BB	SO	AVG	OBP	SLG	PRO+	BR	/A	RC	SB	CS	SBR	FA	FR	POS	TPR
1934	Bos-A	9	32	2	7	0	0	0	3	3	4	.219	.286	.219	30	-3	-4	2	0	0	0	1.000	4	/2	0.1
1936	Phi-A	69	203	22	40	3	2	1	20	26	16	.197	.291	.246	35	-21	-20	16	2	2	-1	.972	10	2/S	-0.6
Total	2	78	235	24	47	3	2	1	23	29	20	.200	.291	.243	34	-24	-24	18	2	2	-1	.976	15	/2S	-0.5

■ TOM NIETO

Nieto, Thomas Andrew b: 10/27/60, Downey, Cal. BR/TR, 6'1", 205 lbs. Deb: 5/10/84

YEAR	TM/L	G	AB	R	H	2B	3B	HR	RBI	BB	SO	AVG	OBP	SLG	PRO+	BR	/A	RC	SB	CS	SBR	FA	FR	POS	TPR
1984	StL-N	33	86	7	24	4	0	3	12	5	18	.279	.319	.430	112	1	1	11	0	0	0	.994	4	C	0.6
1985	*StL-N	95	253	15	57	10	2	0	34	26	37	.225	.305	.281	65	-11	-11	21	0	2	-1	.990	-4	C	-1.3
1986	Mon-N	30	65	5	13	3	1	1	7	6	21	.200	.278	.323	66	-3	-3	5	0	1	-1	.978	-3	C	-0.5
1987	Min-A	41	105	7	21	7	1	1	12	8	24	.200	.276	.314	54	-7	-7	10	0	0	0	.996	2	C/D	-0.3
1988	Min-A	24	60	1	4	0	0	0	0	1	17	.067	.097	.067	-52	-12	-12	0	0	0	0	.991	3	C	-0.9
1989	Phi-N	11	20	1	3	0	0	0	0	6	7	.150	.370	.150	54	-1	-1	2	0	0	0	1.000	3	C	0.3
1990	Phi-N	17	30	1	5	0	0	0	4	3	11	.167	.265	.167	21	-3	-3	1	0	0	0	.984	2	C	0.0
Total	7	251	619	37	127	24	4	5	69	55	135	.205	.281	.281	56	-37	-37	50	0	3	-2	.991	7	C/D	-2.1

■ MELVIN NIEVES

Nieves, Melvin Ramos b: 12/28/71, San Juan, P.R. BB/TR, 6'2", 186 lbs. Deb: 9/01/92

YEAR	TM/L	G	AB	R	H	2B	3B	HR	RBI	BB	SO	AVG	OBP	SLG	PRO+	BR	/A	RC	SB	CS	SBR	FA	FR	POS	TPR
1992	Atl-N	12	19	0	4	1	0	0	1	2	7	.211	.286	.263	52	-1	-1	2	0	0	0	.727	-1	/O	-0.3

■ TOM NILAND

Niland, Thomas James "Honest Tom" b: 4/14/1870, Brookfield, Mass. d: 4/30/50, Lynn, Mass. BR/TR, 5'11", 160 lbs. Deb: 4/19/1896

YEAR	TM/L	G	AB	R	H	2B	3B	HR	RBI	BB	SO	AVG	OBP	SLG	PRO+	BR	/A	RC	SB	CS	SBR	FA	FR	POS	TPR
1896	StL-N	18	68	3	12	0	1	0	3	5	4	.176	.243	.206	21	-8	-7	4	0			.913	-4	O/S	-1.1

■ HARRY NILES

Niles, Herbert Clyde b: 9/10/1880, Buchanan, Mich. d: 4/18/53, Sturgis, Mich. BR/TR, 5'8", 175 lbs. Deb: 4/24/06

YEAR	TM/L	G	AB	R	H	2B	3B	HR	RBI	BB	SO	AVG	OBP	SLG	PRO+	BR	/A	RC	SB	CS	SBR	FA	FR	POS	TPR
1906	StL-A	142	541	71	124	14	4	2	31	46		.229	.297	.281	85	-10	-8	57	30			.967	6	*O3	-0.7
1907	StL-A	120	492	65	142	9	5	2	35	28		.289	.331	.339	114	7	7	64	19			.949	-6	*2/O	0.1
1908	NY-A	96	362	43	90	14	6	4	24	25		.249	.303	.354	112	5	4	44	18			.928	-24	2/O	-2.4
	Bos-A	17	32	4	8	0	0	1	3	6		.250	.385	.344	133	2	2	6	3			1.000	-1	/2S	0.1
	Yr	113	394	47	98	14	6	5	27	31		.249	.310	.353	114	6	6	49	21			.934	-24	2/OS	-2.3
1909	Bos-A	145	546	64	134	12	5	1	38	39		.245	.311	.291	88	-5	-7	58	27			.952	-0	*O3/S2	-1.2

YEAR	TM/L	G	AB	R	H	2B	3B	HR	RBI	BB	SO	AVG	OBP	SLG	PRO+	BR	/A	RC	SB	CS	SBR	FA	FR	POS	TPR
1910	Bos-A	18	57	6	12	3	0	1	3	4		.211	.262	.316	79	-1	-2	5	1			.920	-0	O	-0.3
	Cle-A	70	240	25	51	6	4	1	18	15		.213	.267	.283	72	-8	-8	20	9			.975	-4	O/S3	-1.6
	Yr	88	297	31	63	9	4	2	21	19		.212	.266	.290	73	-9	-10	25	10			.962	-4	O/S3	-1.9
Total	5	608	2270	278	561	58	24	12	152	163		.247	.306	.310	95	-12	-11	254	107			.960	-29	O2/3S	-6.0

■ **BILL NILES** Niles, William A. b: 1/1874, Vermont d: 7/3/36, Springfield, Ohio 160 lbs. Deb: 5/13/1895

YEAR	TM/L	G	AB	R	H	2B	3B	HR	RBI	BB	SO	AVG	OBP	SLG	PRO+	BR	/A	RC	SB	CS	SBR	FA	FR	POS	TPR
1895	Pit-N	11	37	2	8	0	0	0	0	5	2	.216	.310	.216	41	-3	-3	3	2			.930	1	3/2	-0.2

■ **RABBIT NILL** Nill, George Charles b: 7/14/1881, Ft.Wayne, Ind. d: 5/24/62, Fort Wayne, Ind. BR/TR, 5'7", 160 lbs. Deb: 9/27/04

YEAR	TM/L	G	AB	R	H	2B	3B	HR	RBI	BB	SO	AVG	OBP	SLG	PRO+	BR	/A	RC	SB	CS	SBR	FA	FR	POS	TPR
1904	Was-A	15	48	4	8	0	1	0	3	5		.167	.259	.208	50	-3	-3	3	0			.878	-4	2	-0.7
1905	Was-A	103	319	46	58	7	3	3	31	33		.182	.269	.251	68	-12	-10	27	12			.897	-3	32/S	-1.2
1906	Was-A	89	315	37	74	8	2	0	15	47		.235	.338	.273	97	-0	1	37	16			.882	4	S23O	0.7
1907	Was-A	66	215	21	47	7	3	0	25	15		.219	.282	.279	86	-5	-3	20	6			.962	-2	2O/3	-0.6
	Cle-A	12	43	5	12	1	0	0	2	3		.279	.326	.302	100	0	0	5	2			.815	-4	/3S	-0.4
	Yr	78	258	26	59	8	3	0	27	18		.229	.289	.283	89	-5	-3	25	8			.962	-5	2O/3S	-1.0
1908	Cle-A	11	23	3	5	0	0	0	1	0		.217	.217	.217	41	-2	-2	1	0			.833	0	/SO2	-0.1
Total	5	296	963	116	204	23	9	3	77	103		.212	.296	.264	81	-21	-16	93	36			.943	-7	2/3SO	-2.3

■ **DAVE NILSSON** Nilsson, David Wayne b: 12/14/69, Brisbane, Queensland, Australia BL/TR, 6'3", 185 lbs. Deb: 5/18/92

YEAR	TM/L	G	AB	R	H	2B	3B	HR	RBI	BB	SO	AVG	OBP	SLG	PRO+	BR	/A	RC	SB	CS	SBR	FA	FR	POS	TPR
1992	Mil-A	51	164	15	38	8	0	4	25	17	18	.232	.304	.354	85	-4	-3	18	2	2	-1	.992	0	C/1D	-0.1

■ **AL NIXON** Nixon, Albert Richard "Humpty Dumpty" b: 4/11/1886, Atlantic City, N.J d: 11/9/60, Opelousas, La. BR/TL, 5'7.5", 164 lbs. Deb: 9/04/15

YEAR	TM/L	G	AB	R	H	2B	3B	HR	RBI	BB	SO	AVG	OBP	SLG	PRO+	BR	/A	RC	SB	CS	SBR	FA	FR	POS	TPR
1915	Bro-N	14	26	3	6	1	0	0	2	2	4	.231	.286	.269	67	-1	-1	2	1	1	-0	1.000	-2	O	-0.4
1916	Bro-N	1	2	0	2	0	0	0	0	0	0	1.000	1.000	1.000	501	1	1	2	0			.000	-0	/O	0.1
1918	Bro-N	6	11	1	5	0	0	0	0	0	0	.455	.455	.455	178	1	1	2	0			1.000	-0	/O	0.1
1921	Bos-N	55	138	25	33	6	3	1	9	7	11	.239	.281	.348	69	-7	-6	13	3	2	-0	.980	-2	O	-1.1
1922	Bos-N	86	318	35	84	14	4	2	22	9	19	.264	.284	.352	66	-18	-16	30	6	6	-2	.975	1	O	-2.2
1923	Bos-N	88	321	53	88	12	4	0	19	24	14	.274	.334	.336	81	-10	-8	37	2	3	-1	.987	9	O	-0.5
1926	Phi-N	93	311	38	91	18	2	4	41	13	20	.293	.323	.402	90	-3	-5	39	5			.977	-2	O	-1.3
1927	Phi-N	54	154	18	48	7	0	0	18	5	5	.312	.333	.357	84	-3	-4	18	1			.969	-1	O	-0.6
1928	Phi-N	25	64	7	15	2	0	0	7	6	4	.234	.300	.266	47	-5	-5	5	1			1.000	-0	O	-0.6
Total	9	422	1345	180	372	60	13	7	118	66	77	.277	.314	.356	78	-46	-43	148	19	12		.980	2	O	-6.5

■ **OTIS NIXON** Nixon, Otis Junior b: 1/9/59, Columbus Co., N.C. BB/TR, 6'2", 180 lbs. Deb: 9/09/83 F

YEAR	TM/L	G	AB	R	H	2B	3B	HR	RBI	BB	SO	AVG	OBP	SLG	PRO+	BR	/A	RC	SB	CS	SBR	FA	FR	POS	TPR
1983	NY-A	13	14	2	2	0	0	0	0	1	5	.143	.200	.143	-4	-2	-2	1	2	0	1	.938	-1	/O	-0.2
1984	Cle-A	49	91	16	14	0	0	0	1	8	11	.154	.222	.154	6	-11	-12	3	12	6	0	1.000	-2	O	-1.5
1985	Cle-A	104	162	34	38	4	0	3	9	8	27	.235	.271	.315	60	-9	-9	12	20	11	-1	.971	-7	OD	-1.7
1986	Cle-A	105	95	33	25	4	1	0	8	13	12	.263	.352	.326	88	-1	-1	13	23	6	3	.969	-23	O/D	-2.2
1987	Cle-A	19	17	2	1	0	0	0	1	3	4	.059	.200	.059	-26	-3	-3	0	2	3	-1	1.000	-4	O/D	-0.8
1988	Mon-N	90	271	47	66	8	2	0	15	28	42	.244	.314	.288	71	-8	-10	30	46	13	6	.994	-2	O	-0.9
1989	Mon-N	126	258	41	56	7	2	0	21	33	36	.217	.306	.260	62	-11	-12	24	37	12	4	.988	-15	O	-2.6
1990	Mon-N	119	231	46	58	6	2	1	20	28	33	.251	.332	.307	80	-6	-5	29	50	13	7	.994	-9	O/S	-0.8
1991	Atl-N	124	401	81	119	10	1	0	26	47	40	.297	.373	.327	93	1	-2	57	72	21	9	.987	1	*O	0.6
1992	*Atl-N	120	456	79	134	14	2	2	22	39	54	.294	.349	.346	90	-1	-5	58	41	18	2	.991	13	*O	0.7
Total	10	869	1996	381	513	53	10	6	123	208	264	.257	.328	.303	76	-52	-60	228	305	103	30	.987	-49	O/DS	-9.4

■ **DONELL NIXON** Nixon, Robert Donell b: 12/31/61, Evergreen, N.C. BR/TR, 6'1", 185 lbs. Deb: 4/07/87 F

YEAR	TM/L	G	AB	R	H	2B	3B	HR	RBI	BB	SO	AVG	OBP	SLG	PRO+	BR	/A	RC	SB	CS	SBR	FA	FR	POS	TPR
1987	Sea-A	46	132	17	33	4	0	3	12	13	28	.250	.327	.348	75	-4	-5	16	21	7	2	1.000	0	O/D	-0.3
1988	SF-N	59	78	15	27	3	0	0	6	10	12	.346	.420	.385	138	4	4	12	11	8	-2	.983	-8	O	-0.7
1989	*SF-N	95	166	23	44	2	0	1	15	11	30	.265	.311	.295	76	-5	-5	15	10	3	1	.967	-14	O	-2.0
1990	Bal-A	8	20	1	5	2	0	0	2	1	7	.250	.286	.350	79	-1	-1	3	5	0	2	1.000	-1	/OD	0.0
Total	4	208	396	56	109	11	0	4	35	35	77	.275	.337	.333	88	-6	-6	46	47	18	3	.983	-23	O/D	-3.0

■ **RUSS NIXON** Nixon, Russell Eugene b: 2/19/35, Cleves, Ohio BL/TR, 6'1", 200 lbs. Deb: 4/20/57 MC

YEAR	TM/L	G	AB	R	H	2B	3B	HR	RBI	BB	SO	AVG	OBP	SLG	PRO+	BR	/A	RC	SB	CS	SBR	FA	FR	POS	TPR
1957	Cle-A	62	185	15	52	7	1	2	18	12	12	.281	.325	.362	88	-3	-3	20	0	1	-1	.984	-6	C	-0.8
1958	Cle-A	113	376	42	113	17	4	9	46	13	38	.301	.324	.439	111	3	4	47	0	3	-2	.991	-10	*C	-0.3
1959	Cle-A	82	258	23	62	10	3	1	29	15	28	.240	.282	.314	66	-13	-12	21	0	0	0	.985	-7	C	-1.5
1960	Cle-A	25	82	6	20	5	0	1	6	6	6	.244	.311	.341	79	-3	-2	8	0	1	-1	.993	-0	C	-0.2
	Bos-A	80	272	24	81	17	3	5	33	13	23	.298	.330	.438	102	1	0	36	0	1	-1	.987	-17	C	-1.3
	Yr	105	354	30	101	22	3	6	39	19	29	.285	.325	.415	97	-1	-2	44	0	2	-1	.989	-17	C	-1.5
1961	Bos-A	87	242	24	70	12	2	1	19	13	19	.289	.331	.368	84	-5	-5	29	0	1	-1	.975	-3	C	-0.6
1962	Bos-A	65	151	11	42	7	2	1	19	8	14	.278	.314	.371	81	-4	-4	17	0	0	0	1.000	-2	C	-0.5
1963	Bos-A	98	287	27	77	18	1	5	30	22	32	.268	.329	.390	98	0	-1	36	0	0	0	.992	-10	C	-0.8
1964	Bos-A	81	163	10	38	7	0	1	20	14	29	.233	.302	.294	64	-7	-8	14	0	0	0	.990	-4	C	-1.1
1965	Bos-A	59	137	11	37	5	1	0	11	6	23	.270	.301	.321	72	-4	-5	11	0	0	0	.981	-6	C	-1.0
1966	Min-A	51	96	5	25	2	1	0	7	7	13	.260	.317	.302	74	-2	-3	9	0	0	0	.986	-4	C	-0.6
1967	Min-A	74	170	16	40	6	1	1	22	18	29	.235	.309	.300	74	-4	-5	16	0	0	0	.994	-12	C	-1.6
1968	Bos-A	29	85	1	13	2	0	0	6	7	13	.153	.217	.176	19	-8	-9	3	0	0	0	.994	-5	C	-1.4
Total	12	906	2504	215	670	115	19	27	266	154	279	.268	.313	.361	84	-49	-54	266	0	7	-4	.988	-85	C	-11.7

■ **RAY NOBLE** Noble, Rafael Miguel (Magee) b: 3/15/19, Central Hatillo, Cuba BR/TR, 5'11", 210 lbs. Deb: 4/18/51

YEAR	TM/L	G	AB	R	H	2B	3B	HR	RBI	BB	SO	AVG	OBP	SLG	PRO+	BR	/A	RC	SB	CS	SBR	FA	FR	POS	TPR
1951	*NY-N	55	141	16	33	6	0	5	26	6	26	.234	.265	.383	72	-6	-6	13	0	0	0	.974	-5	C	-0.9
1952	NY-N	6	5	0	0	0	0	0	0	0	1	.000	.000	.000	-99	-1	-1	0	0	0	0	1.000	0	/C	-0.1
1953	NY-N	46	97	15	20	0	1	4	14	19	14	.206	.353	.351	83	-2	-2	14	1	0	0	.982	-1	C	-0.1
Total	3	107	243	31	53	6	1	9	40	25	41	.218	.299	.362	74	-9	-10	27	1	0	0	.979	-5	/C	-1.1

■ **JUNIOR NOBOA** Noboa, Miliciades Arturo (Diaz) b: 11/10/64, Azua, D.R. BR/TR, 5'10", 160 lbs. Deb: 8/22/84

YEAR	TM/L	G	AB	R	H	2B	3B	HR	RBI	BB	SO	AVG	OBP	SLG	PRO+	BR	/A	RC	SB	CS	SBR	FA	FR	POS	TPR
1984	Cle-A	23	11	3	4	0	0	0	0	0	2	.364	.364	.364	100	0	-0	1	1	0	0	1.000	4	2/D	0.4
1987	Cle-A	39	80	7	18	2	1	0	7	3	6	.225	.253	.275	40	-7	-7	6	1	0	0	.983	4	2/S3D	-0.2
1988	Cal-A	21	16	4	1	0	0	0	0	0	1	.063	.063	.063	-67	-3	-3	-0	0	0	0	.967	9	/2S3	0.5
1989	Mon-N	21	44	3	10	0	0	0	1	1	3	.227	.244	.227	35	-4	-4	3	0	0	0	1.000	7	2/S3	0.4
1990	Mon-N	81	158	15	42	7	2	0	14	7	14	.266	.301	.335	78	-6	-5	16	4	1	1	1.000	-17	2/O3SP	-2.2
1991	Mon-N	67	95	5	23	3	0	1	2	1	8	.242	.250	.305	56	-6	-6	6	2	3	-1	1.000	-3	/O23S1	-1.0
1992	NY-N	46	47	7	7	0	0	0	3	3	8	.149	.216	.149	5	-6	-6	1	0	0	0	.977	6	2/3S	0.0
Total	7	298	451	44	105	12	3	1	27	15	42	.233	.261	.279	50	-31	-30	34	8	4	0	.987	9	2/S3OD1P	-2.1

■ **PAUL NOCE** Noce, Paul David b: 12/16/59, San Francisco, Cal. BR/TR, 5'10", 175 lbs. Deb: 6/01/87

YEAR	TM/L	G	AB	R	H	2B	3B	HR	RBI	BB	SO	AVG	OBP	SLG	PRO+	BR	/A	RC	SB	CS	SBR	FA	FR	POS	TPR
1987	Chi-N	70	180	17	41	9	2	3	14	6	49	.228	.261	.350	58	-11	-12	16	5	3	-0	.983	19	2S/3	1.0
1990	Cin-N	1	1	0	1	0	0	0	0	0	0	1.000	1.000	1.000	434	0	0	1	0	0	0	.000	0	/H	0.0
Total	2	71	181	17	42	9	2	3	14	6	49	.232	.265	.354	60	-10	-11	17	5	3	-0		19	/2S3	1.0

■ **GEORGE NOFTSKER** Noftsker, George Washington b: 8/24/1859, Shippensburg, Pa. d: 5/8/31, Shippensburg, Pa. BR/TR, 5'8", 135 lbs. Deb: 4/17/1884

YEAR	TM/L	G	AB	R	H	2B	3B	HR	RBI	BB	SO	AVG	OBP	SLG	PRO+	BR	/A	RC	SB	CS	SBR	FA	FR	POS	TPR
1884	Alt-U	7	25	0	1	0	0	0		0		.040	.040	.040	-72	-4	-4	0				.818	1	/OC	-0.3

■ **MATT NOKES** Nokes, Matthew Dodge b: 10/31/63, San Diego, Cal. BL/TR, 6'1", 185 lbs. Deb: 9/03/85

YEAR	TM/L	G	AB	R	H	2B	3B	HR	RBI	BB	SO	AVG	OBP	SLG	PRO+	BR	/A	RC	SB	CS	SBR	FA	FR	POS	TPR
1985	SF-N	19	53	3	11	2	0	2	5	1	9	.208	.236	.358	67	-3	-2	4	0	0	0	.977	-1	C	-0.3

YEAR	TM/L	G	AB	R	H	2B	3B	HR	RBI	BB	SO	AVG	OBP	SLG	PRO+	BR	/A	RC	SB	CS	SBR	FA	FR	POS	TPR
1986	Det-A	7	24	2	8	1	0	1	2	1	1	.333	.360	.500	132	1	1	4	0	0	0	1.000	2	/C	0.3
1987	*Det-A★	135	461	69	133	14	2	32	87	35	70	.289	.347	.536	135	18	21	82	2	1	0	.992	-9	*CD/O3	1.8
1988	Det-A	122	382	53	96	18	0	16	53	34	58	.251	.314	.424	109	2	3	49	0	1	-1	.989	-3	*C/D	0.8
1989	Det-A	87	268	15	67	10	0	9	39	17	37	.250	.300	.388	95	-3	-3	30	1	0	0	.978	-6	CD	-0.6
1990	Det-A	44	111	12	30	5	1	3	8	4	14	.270	.308	.414	99	-0	-0	12	0	0	0	.984	-3	DC	-0.2
	NY-A	92	240	21	57	4	0	8	32	20	33	.237	.307	.354	84	-5	-5	25	2	2	-1	.995	-7	CD/O	-1.0
	Yr	136	351	33	87	9	1	11	40	24	47	.248	.307	.373	89	-5	-6	38	2	2	-1	.993	-9	CD/O	-1.2
1991	NY-A	135	456	52	122	20	0	24	77	25	49	.268	.313	.469	113	6	6	66	3	2	-0	.992	-15	*C/D	-0.2
1992	NY-A	121	384	42	86	9	1	22	59	37	62	.224	.297	.424	98	-1	-2	45	0	1	-1	.993	-9	*C	-0.6
Total	8	762	2379	269	610	83	4	117	362	174	333	.256	.314	.442	108	14	18	318	8	7	-2	.990	-50	CD/O3	-0.0

■ JOE NOLAN
Nolan, Joseph William b: 5/12/51, St.Louis, Mo. BL/TR, 6', 190 lbs. Deb: 9/21/72

YEAR	TM/L	G	AB	R	H	2B	3B	HR	RBI	BB	SO	AVG	OBP	SLG	PRO+	BR	/A	RC	SB	CS	SBR	FA	FR	POS	TPR
1972	NY-N	4	10	0	0	0	0	0	0	1	3	.000	.091	.000	-74	-2	-2	0	0	0	0	.938	-1	/C	-0.3
1975	Atl-N	4	4	0	1	0	0	0	0	1	0	.250	.400	.250	80	-0	-0	1	0	0	0	1.000	-0	/C	0.0
1977	Atl-N	62	82	13	23	3	0	3	9	13	12	.280	.379	.427	103	2	1	14	1	0	0	1.000	-1	C	0.1
1978	Atl-N	95	213	22	49	7	3	4	22	34	28	.230	.339	.347	83	-2	-4	27	3	2	-0	.979	-6	C	-1.0
1979	Atl-N	89	230	28	57	9	3	4	21	27	28	.248	.335	.365	85	-3	-5	28	1	3	-2	.983	-7	C	-1.2
1980	Atl-N	17	22	2	6	1	0	0	2	2	4	.273	.333	.318	80	-0	-1	2	0	0	0	1.000	1	/C	0.1
	Cin-N	53	154	14	48	7	0	3	24	13	8	.312	.365	.416	117	4	4	24	0	0	0	.982	1	C	0.7
	Yr	70	176	16	54	8	0	3	26	15	12	.307	.361	.403	112	3	3	26	0	0	0	.983	2	C	0.8
1981	Cin-N	81	236	25	73	18	1	1	26	24	19	.309	.375	.407	120	7	7	35	1	2	-1	**.995**	-11	C	-0.3
1982	Bal-A	77	219	24	51	7	1	6	35	16	35	.233	.285	.356	75	-8	-8	22	1	1	-0	.978	-3	C	-0.9
1983	*Bal-A	73	184	25	51	11	1	5	24	16	31	.277	.342	.429	113	3	3	26	0	0	0	.980	-10	C	-0.5
1984	Bal-A	35	62	2	18	1	1	1	9	12	10	.290	.405	.387	123	2	3	11	0	0	0	.962	-1	D/C	0.2
1985	Bal-A	31	38	1	5	2	0	0	6	5	5	.132	.233	.184	16	-4	-4	2	0	0	0	1.000	1	/CD	-0.3
Total	11	621	1454	156	382	66	10	27	178	164	183	.263	.340	.378	95	-1	-7	190	7	8	-3	.984	-37	C/D	-3.4

■ RED NONNENKAMP
Nonnenkamp, Leo William b: 7/7/11, St.Louis, Mo. BL/TL, 5'11", 165 lbs. Deb: 9/06/33

YEAR	TM/L	G	AB	R	H	2B	3B	HR	RBI	BB	SO	AVG	OBP	SLG	PRO+	BR	/A	RC	SB	CS	SBR	FA	FR	POS	TPR
1933	Pit-N	1	1	0	0	0	0	0	0	0	1	.000	.000	.000	-99	-0	-0	0	0			.000	0	H	0.0
1938	Bos-A	87	180	37	51	4	1	0	18	21	13	.283	.358	.317	67	-7	-9	22	6	1	1	.968	2	O/1	-0.7
1939	Bos-A	58	75	12	18	2	1	0	5	12	6	.240	.345	.293	62	-4	-4	8	0	1	-1	.962	-3	O	-0.7
1940	Bos-A	9	7	0	0	0	0	0	1	0	4	.000	.125	.000	-62	-2	-2	0	0	0	0	.000	0	H	-0.2
Total	4	155	263	49	69	6	2	0	24	33	24	.262	.347	.300	62	-13	-15	30	6	2		.966	-1	/O1	-1.6

■ PETE NOONAN
Noonan, Peter John b: 11/24/1881, W.Stockbridge, Mass. d: 2/11/65, Great Barrington, Mass. BR/TR, 6', 180 lbs. Deb: 6/20/04

YEAR	TM/L	G	AB	R	H	2B	3B	HR	RBI	BB	SO	AVG	OBP	SLG	PRO+	BR	/A	RC	SB	CS	SBR	FA	FR	POS	TPR
1904	Phi-A	39	114	13	23	3	1	2	13	1		.202	.209	.298	57	-6	-6	8	1			.969	-4	C1	-0.9
1906	Chi-N	5	3	0	1	0	0	0	0	0		.333	.333	.333	102	0	-0	0	0			1.000	0	/1	0.0
	StL-N	44	125	8	21	1	3	1	9	11		.168	.235	.248	53	-7	-7	8	1			.957	3	C1	-0.2
	Yr	49	128	8	22	1	3	1	9	11		.172	.237	.250	54	-7	-7	9	1			.957	3	C1	-0.2
1907	StL-N	74	237	19	53	7	3	1	16	9		.224	.252	.291	73	-9	-8	19	3			.951	4	C	0.2
Total	3	162	479	40	98	11	7	4	38	21		.205	.238	.282	64	-22	-21	36	5			.955	3	C/1	-0.9

■ TIM NORDBROOK
Nordbrook, Timothy Charles b: 7/7/49, Baltimore, Md. BR/TR, 6'1", 180 lbs. Deb: 9/13/74

YEAR	TM/L	G	AB	R	H	2B	3B	HR	RBI	BB	SO	AVG	OBP	SLG	PRO+	BR	/A	RC	SB	CS	SBR	FA	FR	POS	TPR
1974	Bal-A	6	15	4	4	0	0	0	1	2	2	.267	.353	.267	83	-0	-0	2	1	0	0	1.000	1	/S2	0.2
1975	Bal-A	40	34	6	4	1	0	0	0	7	7	.118	.268	.147	21	-3	-3	2	0	0	0	.970	5	S/2	0.4
1976	Bal-A	27	22	4	5	0	0	0	0	3	5	.227	.320	.227	66	-1	-1	2	0	0	0	1.000	3	2S	0.3
	Cal-A	5	8	1	0	0	0	0	0	1	3	.000	.111	.000	-70	-2	-2	0	1	0	0	.941	2	/S2D	0.1
	Yr	32	30	5	5	0	0	0	0	4	8	.167	.265	.167	30	-3	-2	2	1	0	0	.978	5	S2/D	0.4
1977	Chi-A	15	20	2	5	0	0	0	1	7	4	.250	.444	.250	95	0	0	3	1	0	0	.850	-2	S/3D	0.0
	Tor-A	24	63	9	11	0	1	0	1	4	11	.175	.224	.206	18	-7	-7	3	1	0	0	.989	1	S	-0.4
	Yr	39	83	11	16	0	1	0	2	11	15	.193	.287	.217	39	-7	-7	6	2	0	1	.947	-1	S/D3	-0.4
1978	Tor-A	7	0	1	0	0	0	0	0	0	0	—	1.000	—	200	0	0	0	0	0	0	1.000	2	/S	0.2
	Mil-A	2	5	0	0	0	0	0	0	1	1	.000	.167	.000	-49	-1	-1	0	0	0	0	.909	0	/S	0.0
	Yr	9	5	1	0	0	0	0	0	1	1	.000	.286	.000	-13	-1	-1	0	0	0	0	.941	2	/S	0.2
1979	Mil-A	2	2	0	1	0	0	0	0	0	0	.500	.500	.500	171	0	0	1	0	0	0	1.000	-1	/S	0.0
Total	6	128	169	27	30	1	1	0	3	25	33	.178	.287	.195	38	-13	-13	12	4	0	1	.961	12	S/2D3	0.8

■ WAYNE NORDHAGEN
Nordhagen, Wayne Oren b: 7/4/48, Thief River Falls, Minn. BR/TR, 6'2", 205 lbs. Deb: 7/16/76

YEAR	TM/L	G	AB	R	H	2B	3B	HR	RBI	BB	SO	AVG	OBP	SLG	PRO+	BR	/A	RC	SB	CS	SBR	FA	FR	POS	TPR
1976	Chi-A	22	53	6	10	2	0	0	5	4	12	.189	.246	.226	39	-4	-4	3	0	0	0	1.000	0	O/CD	-0.4
1977	Chi-A	52	124	16	39	7	3	4	22	2	12	.315	.325	.516	125	4	4	20	1	0	0	.944	-10	O/CD	-0.7
1978	Chi-A	68	206	28	62	16	0	5	35	5	18	.301	.318	.451	113	3	3	27	0	1	-1	.941	-8	ODC	-0.7
1979	Chi-A	78	193	20	54	15	0	7	25	13	22	.280	.325	.466	111	2	2	26	0	0	0	1.000	0	DO/CP	0.2
1980	Chi-A	123	415	45	115	22	4	15	59	10	45	.277	.296	.458	104	-0	0	51	0	1	-1	.969	-5	OD	-0.8
1981	Chi-A	65	208	19	64	8	1	6	33	10	25	.308	.342	.442	127	6	6	29	0	1	-1	.947	-7	O	-0.3
1982	Tor-A	44	115	8	32	3	0	1	14	9	13	.278	.331	.330	75	-3	-4	11	0	2	-1	1.000	-1	DO	-0.6
	Pit-N	1	4	0	2	0	0	0	2	0	1	.500	.500	.500	175	0	0	1	0	0	0	1.000	0	/O	0.0
	Tor-A	28	70	4	18	3	0	0	6	1	9	.257	.268	.300	51	-4	-5	5	0	0	0	.000	0	D	-0.5
1983	Chi-N	21	35	1	5	1	0	1	4	0	5	.143	.167	.257	15	-4	-4	1	0	0	0	1.000	-1	/O	-0.6
Total	8	502	1423	147	401	77	8	39	205	54	162	.282	.309	.429	101	-0	-2	174	1	5	-3	.962	-30	OD/CP	-4.4

■ LOU NORDYKE
Nordyke, Louis Ellis b: 8/7/1876, Brighton, Iowa d: 9/27/45, Los Angeles, Cal. BR/TR, 6', 185 lbs. Deb: 4/18/06

YEAR	TM/L	G	AB	R	H	2B	3B	HR	RBI	BB	SO	AVG	OBP	SLG	PRO+	BR	/A	RC	SB	CS	SBR	FA	FR	POS	TPR
1906	StL-A	25	53	4	13	1	0	0	7	10		.245	.365	.264	103	1	1	7	3			.942	-3	1	-0.2

■ IRV NOREN
Noren, Irving Arnold b: 11/29/24, Jamestown, N.Y. BL/TL, 6', 190 lbs. Deb: 4/18/50 C

YEAR	TM/L	G	AB	R	H	2B	3B	HR	RBI	BB	SO	AVG	OBP	SLG	PRO+	BR	/A	RC	SB	CS	SBR	FA	FR	POS	TPR
1950	Was-A	138	542	80	160	27	10	14	98	67	77	.295	.375	.459	118	10	13	98	5	2	0	.984	16	*O1	2.2
1951	Was-A	129	509	82	142	33	5	8	86	51	35	.279	.345	.411	105	2	3	72	10	7	-1	.978	21	*O	1.8
1952	Was-A	12	49	4	12	3	1	0	2	6	3	.245	.327	.347	91	-1	-1	6	1	0	0	1.000	3	O	0.2
	*NY-A	93	272	36	64	13	2	5	21	26	34	.235	.316	.353	91	-5	-3	33	4	2	0	1.000	-7	O1	-1.4
	Yr	105	321	40	76	16	3	5	23	32	37	.237	.318	.352	91	-6	-4	39	5	2	0	1.000	-4	O1	-1.2
1953	*NY-A	109	345	55	92	12	6	6	46	42	39	.267	.350	.388	103	-0	1	50	3	3	-1	.991	-1	O	-0.4
1954	NY-A★	125	426	70	136	21	6	12	66	43	38	.319	.383	.481	140	20	22	79	4	6	-2	.980	-1	*O/1	1.4
1955	*NY-A	132	371	49	94	19	1	8	59	43	33	.253	.336	.375	92	-5	-4	48	5	2	0	.980	-0	*O	-0.9
1956	NY-A	29	37	4	8	1	0	0	6	12	7	.216	.408	.243	78	-1	-0	4	0	0	0	.875	-2	O/1	-0.3
1957	KC-A	81	160	8	34	8	0	2	16	11	19	.213	.267	.300	54	-10	-10	12	0	0	0	.990	-2	1/O	-1.4
	StL-N	17	30	3	11	4	1	1	10	4	6	.367	.441	.667	189	4	4	8	0	1	-1	1.000	-2	/O	0.1
1958	StL-N	117	178	24	47	9	1	4	22	13	21	.264	.328	.393	87	-3	-3	23	0	1	-1	.974	-17	O	-2.4
1959	StL-N	8	8	0	1	1	0	0	0	0	2	.125	.125	.250	-3	-1	-1	0	0	0	0	.000	-1	/O1	-0.2
	Chi-N	65	156	27	50	6	2	4	19	13	24	.321	.384	.462	125	6	6	29	2	0	1	1.000	3	O/1	0.8
	Yr	73	164	27	51	7	2	4	19	13	26	.311	.372	.451	118	4	4	29	2	0	1	1.000	2	O/1	0.6
1960	Chi-N	12	11	0	1	0	0	0	1	3	4	.091	.286	.091	9	-1	-1	0	0	0	0	.833	-1	/1O	-0.2
	LA-N	26	25	1	5	0	0	1	1	1	8	.200	.231	.320	46	-2	-2	2	0	0	0	.000	0	H	-0.2
	Yr	38	36	1	6	0	0	1	2	4	12	.167	.250	.250	36	-3	-3	2	0	0	0	1.000	-1	/1O	-0.4
Total	11	1093	3119	443	857	157	35	65	453	335	350	.275	.349	.410	106	12	22	464	34	24	-4	.984	10	O/1	-0.9

YEAR	TM/L	G	AB	R	H	2B	3B	HR	RBI	BB	SO	AVG	OBP	SLG	PRO+	BR	/A	RC	SB	CS	SBR	FA	FR	POS	TPR
■ **DAN NORMAN** Norman, Daniel Edmund b: 1/11/55, Los Angeles, Cal. BR/TR, 6'2", 195 lbs. Deb: 9/27/77																									
1977	NY-N	7	16	2	4	1	0	0	0	4	2	.250	.400	.313	99	0	0	2	0	0	0	1.000	-1	/O	-0.1
1978	NY-N	19	64	7	17	0	1	4	10	2	14	.266	.288	.484	116	1	1	9	1	0	0	1.000	-0	O	0.0
1979	NY-N	44	110	9	27	3	1	3	11	10	26	.245	.314	.373	90	-2	-2	14	2	0	1	.967	1	O	-0.2
1980	NY-N	69	92	5	17	1	1	2	9	6	14	.185	.235	.283	45	-7	-7	7	5	0	2	1.000	-1	O	-0.7
1982	Mon-N	53	66	6	14	3	0	2	7	7	20	.212	.288	.348	76	-2	-2	7	0	1	-1	.969	1	O	-0.2
Total	5	192	348	29	79	8	3	11	37	29	76	.227	.288	.362	81	-11	-10	39	8	1	2	.981	-0	O	-1.2
■ **BILL NORMAN** Norman, Henry Willis Patrick b: 7/16/10, St.Louis, Mo. d: 4/21/62, Milwaukee, Wis. BR/TR, 6'2", 190 lbs. Deb: 8/08/31 MC																									
1931	Chi-A	24	55	7	10	2	0	0	6	4	10	.182	.237	.218	22	-6	-6	3	0	1	-1	.933	-1	O	-0.8
1932	Chi-A	13	48	6	11	3	1	0	2	2	3	.229	.260	.333	56	-4	-3	4	0	0	0	.917	-2	O	-0.6
Total	2	37	103	13	21	5	1	0	8	6	13	.204	.248	.272	38	-10	-9	7	0	1	-1	.928	-3	/O	-1.4
■ **NELSON NORMAN** Norman, Nelson Augusto b: 5/23/58, San Pedro De Macoris, D.R. BB/TR, 6'2", 160 lbs. Deb: 5/20/78																									
1978	Tex-A	23	34	1	9	2	0	0	1	0	5	.265	.265	.324	64	-2	-2	3	0	0	0	.984	10	S/3	0.9
1979	Tex-A	147	343	36	76	9	3	0	21	19	41	.222	.262	.265	43	-27	-27	25	4	1	1	.952	-15	*S/2	-2.9
1980	Tex-A	17	32	4	7	0	0	0	1	1	1	.219	.242	.219	28	-3	-3	1	0	1	-1	.943	7	S	0.4
1981	Tex-A	7	13	1	3	1	0	0	2	1	2	.231	.286	.308	75	-0	-0	1	0	0	0	.963	3	/S	0.3
1982	Pit-N	3	3	0	0	0	0	0	0	0	0	.000	.000	.000	-97	-1	-1	0	0	0	0	.000	-1	/2S	-0.2
1987	Mon-N	1	4	0	0	0	0	0	0	0	1	.000	.000	.000	-97	-1	-1	0	0	0	0	.667	-1	/S	-0.2
Total	6	198	429	42	95	12	3	0	25	21	50	.221	.258	.263	42	-35	-34	30	4	2	0	.954	3	S/32	-1.7
■ **JIM NORRIS** Norris, James Francis b: 12/20/48, Brooklyn, N.Y. BL/TL, 5'10", 175 lbs. Deb: 4/07/77																									
1977	Cle-A	133	440	59	119	23	6	2	37	64	57	.270	.363	.364	102	1	3	59	26	17	-2	.982	12	*O/1	0.8
1978	Cle-A	113	315	41	89	14	5	2	27	42	20	.283	.367	.378	111	5	6	45	12	7	-1	.988	0	OD/1	0.2
1979	Cle-A	124	353	50	87	15	6	3	30	44	35	.246	.330	.348	83	-8	-8	39	15	10	-2	.982	0	OD	-1.2
1980	Tex-A	119	174	23	43	5	0	0	16	23	16	.247	.335	.276	72	-6	-6	15	6	3	0	1.000	-18	O1/D	-2.6
Total	4	489	1282	173	338	57	17	7	110	173	128	.264	.351	.351	95	-7	-5	159	59	37	-5	.985	-5	O/D1	-2.8
■ **LEO NORRIS** Norris, Leo John b: 5/17/08, Bay St.Louis, Miss d: 2/13/87, Zachary, La. BR/TR, 5'11", 165 lbs. Deb: 4/14/36																									
1936	Phi-N	154	581	64	154	27	4	11	76	39	79	.265	.315	.382	79	-12	-19	69	4			.936	-8	*S2	-1.7
1937	Phi-N	116	381	45	98	24	3	9	36	21	53	.257	.296	.407	82	-7	-11	48	3			.949	-11	23S	-1.6
Total	2	270	962	109	252	51	7	20	112	60	132	.262	.307	.392	80	-19	-31	117	7			.940	-20	S2/3	-3.3
■ **BILLY NORTH** North, William Alex b: 5/15/48, Seattle, Wash. BB/TR, 5'11", 185 lbs. Deb: 9/03/71																									
1971	Chi-N	8	16	3	6	0	0	0	0	4	6	.375	.524	.375	138	2	1	4	1	1	-0	1.000	-1	/O	-0.1
1972	Chi-N	66	127	22	23	2	3	0	4	13	33	.181	.262	.244	40	-9	-11	9	6	0	2	.955	0	O	-1.1
1973	Oak-A	146	554	98	158	10	5	5	34	78	89	.285	.376	.348	111	7	11	81	53	20	4	.980	24	*O/D	3.2
1974	*Oak-A	149	543	79	141	20	5	4	33	69	86	.260	.348	.337	105	1	5	68	**54**	26	1	.991	18	*O/D	1.9
1975	*Oak-A	140	524	74	143	17	5	1	43	81	80	.273	.374	.330	103	4	6	73	30	12	2	.975	20	*O/D	2.2
1976	Oak-A	154	590	91	163	20	5	2	31	73	95	.276	.358	.337	109	6	9	78	**75**	29	5	.978	6	*O/D	1.5
1977	Oak-A	56	184	32	48	3	3	1	9	32	25	.261	.376	.326	95	-0	0	24	17	13	-3	.983	-4	O/D	-0.8
1978	Oak-A	24	52	5	11	4	0	0	5	9	13	.212	.349	.288	86	-1	-0	6	3	2	-0	1.000	-2	O	-0.3
	*LA-N	110	304	54	71	10	0	0	10	65	48	.234	.372	.266	81	-4	-4	38	27	8	3	.975	-7	*O	-1.2
1979	SF-N	142	460	87	119	15	4	5	30	96	84	.259	.388	.341	108	5	9	71	58	24	3	.987	-4	*O	0.4
1980	SF-N	128	415	73	104	12	1	1	19	81	78	.251	.374	.292	90	-2	-1	54	45	19	2	.982	3	*O	-0.1
1981	SF-N	46	131	22	29	7	0	1	12	26	28	.221	.354	.298	88	-1	-1	18	26	8	3	.966	-1	O	0.0
Total	11	1169	3900	640	1016	120	31	20	230	627	665	.261	.366	.323	99	7	25	524	395	162	21	.981	53	*O/D	5.6
■ **HUB NORTHEN** Northen, Hubbard Elwin b: 8/16/1885, Atlanta, Tex. d: 10/1/47, Shreveport, La. BL/TL, 5'8", 175 lbs. Deb: 9/10/10																									
1910	StL-A	26	96	6	19	1	0	0	16	5		.198	.238	.208	42	-7	-6	5	2			.926	-2	O	-1.1
1911	Cin-N	1	0	0	0	0	0	0	0	0	0	—	—	—	—	0	0	0	0			.000	0	H	0.0
	Bro-N	19	76	16	24	2	2	0	1	14	9	.316	.429	.395	137	4	4	14	4			.911	2	O	0.5
	Yr	20	76	16	24	2	2	0	1	14	9	.316	.429	.395	137	4	4	14	4			.911	2	O	0.5
1912	Bro-N	118	412	54	116	26	6	3	46	41	46	.282	.352	.396	109	2	4	60	8			.950	-7	*O	-0.8
Total	3	164	584	76	159	29	8	3	63	60	55	.272	.345	.365	103	-0	3	79	14			.939	-7	O	-1.4
■ **RON NORTHEY** Northey, Ronald James b: 4/26/20, Mahanoy City, Pa. d: 4/16/71, Pittsburgh, Pa. BL/TR, 5'10", 195 lbs. Deb: 4/14/42 FC																									
1942	Phi-N	127	402	31	101	13	2	5	31	28	33	.251	.300	.331	89	-9	-6	41	2			.952	1	*O	-1.2
1943	Phi-N	147	586	72	163	31	5	16	68	51	52	.278	.339	.430	127	14	17	88	2			.978	3	*O	1.3
1944	Phi-N	152	570	72	164	35	9	22	104	67	51	.288	.367	.496	146	30	32	107	1			.981	4	*O	2.9
1946	Phi-N	128	438	55	109	24	6	16	62	39	59	.249	.313	.441	116	5	6	61	1			.971	-6	*O	-0.6
1947	Phi-N	13	47	7	12	3	0	0	3	6	3	.255	.340	.319	79	-1	-1	6	1			1.000	-1	O	-0.3
	StL-N	110	311	52	91	19	3	15	63	48	29	.293	.391	.518	133	18	16	65	0			.949	-12	O/3	0.0
	Yr	123	358	59	103	22	3	15	66	54	32	.288	.384	.492	127	16	14	70	1			.955	-13	*O/3	-0.3
1948	StL-N	96	246	40	79	10	1	13	64	38	25	.321	.420	.528	147	20	18	55	0			.989	-10	O	0.5
1949	StL-N	90	265	28	69	18	2	7	50	31	15	.260	.338	.423	98	1	-1	37	0			.980	-11	O	-1.5
1950	Cin-N	27	77	11	20	5	0	5	9	15	6	.260	.380	.519	134	4	4	16	0			.955	-5	O	-0.2
	Chi-N	53	114	11	32	9	0	4	20	10	9	.281	.339	.465	110	1	1	18	0			.976	-1	O	-0.1
	Yr	80	191	22	52	14	0	9	29	25	15	.272	.356	.487	120	5	5	33	0			.969	-6	O	-0.3
1952	Chi-N	1	1	0	0	0	0	0	0	0	0	.000	.000	.000	-99	-0	-0	0	0	0	0	.000	0	H	0.0
1955	Chi-A	14	14	1	5	2	0	1	4	3	3	.357	.471	.714	209	2	2	4	0	0	0	1.000	-1	/O	0.2
1956	Chi-A	53	48	4	17	2	0	3	23	8	1	.354	.446	.583	168	5	5	12	0	0	0	1.000	-1	/O	0.4
1957	Chi-A	40	27	0	5	1	0	0	7	11	5	.185	.421	.222	80	0	0	4	0	0	0	.000	0	H	0.0
	Phi-N	33	26	1	7	0	0	1	5	6	6	.269	.406	.385	118	1	1	5	0	0	0	.000	0	H	0.1
Total	12	1084	3172	385	874	172	28	108	513	361	297	.276	.352	.450	124	90	94	517	7	0		.972	-38	O/3	1.5
■ **SCOTT NORTHEY** Northey, Scott Richard b: 10/15/46, Philadelphia, Pa. BR/TR, 6', 175 lbs. Deb: 9/02/69 F																									
1969	KC-A	20	61	11	16	2	2	1	7	7	19	.262	.338	.410	108	1	1	9	6	3	0	.973	-0	O	-0.1
■ **JIM NORTHRUP** Northrup, James Thomas b: 11/24/39, Breckenridge, Mich. BL/TR, 6'3", 190 lbs. Deb: 9/30/64																									
1964	Det-A	5	12	1	1	1	0	0	0	0	3	.083	.083	.167	-32	-2	-2	0	1	0	0	1.000	-1	/O	-0.3
1965	Det-A	80	219	20	45	12	3	2	16	12	50	.205	.253	.315	60	-12	-12	16	1	1	-0	.976	-4	O	-1.9
1966	Det-A	123	419	53	111	24	6	16	58	33	52	.265	.325	.465	121	12	11	56	4	7	-3	.980	10	*O	1.3
1967	Det-A	144	495	63	134	18	6	10	61	43	83	.271	.333	.392	110	8	7	63	7	1	2	.972	-20	*O	-2.0
1968	*Det-A	154	580	76	153	29	7	21	90	50	87	.264	.326	.447	129	21	19	82	4	5	-2	.979	8	*O	2.0
1969	Det-A	148	543	79	160	31	5	25	66	52	83	.295	.360	.508	135	27	25	100	4	2	0	.985	4	*O	2.1
1970	Det-A	139	504	71	132	21	3	24	80	58	68	.262	.346	.458	119	13	13	78	3	6	-3	.993	3	*O	0.6
1971	Det-A	136	459	72	124	27	2	16	71	60	43	.270	.357	.442	121	15	13	71	7	4	-0	.981	-20	*O1	-1.6
1972	*Det-A	134	426	40	111	15	2	8	42	38	47	.261	.324	.362	101	2	0	45	4	7	-3	.978	-16	*O/1	-2.7
1973	Det-A	119	404	55	124	14	7	12	44	38	41	.307	.368	.465	125	17	14	68	4	4	-1	.982	-9	*O	-0.1
1974	Det-A	97	376	41	89	12	1	11	42	36	46	.237	.303	.362	88	-5	-6	42	0	0	0	.973	3	O	-0.8
	Mon-N	21	54	3	13	1	0	2	8	5	9	.241	.305	.370	84	-1	-1	5	0	0	0	1.000	-3	O	-0.5
	Bal-A	8	7	2	4	0	0	1	3	2	1	.571	.667	1.000	386	3	3	5	0	0	0	1.000	-1	/OD	0.2
1975	Bal-A	84	194	27	53	13	0	5	29	22	22	.273	.353	.418	125	4	6	27	0	1	-1	.979	-12	O/D	-0.8

YEAR	TM/L	G	AB	R	H	2B	3B	HR	RBI	BB	SO	AVG	OBP	SLG	PRO+	BR	/A	RC	SB	CS	SBR	FA	FR	POS	TPR
Total	12	1392	4692	603	1254	218	42	153	610	449	635	.267	.335	.429	115	104	89	659	39	38	-11	.981	-58	*O/1D	-4.5

■ FRANK NORTON
Norton, Frank Prescott   Deb: 5/05/1871

| 1871 | Oly-n | 1 | 1 | 0 | 0 | 0 | 0 | 0 | 0 | 0 | 1 | .000 | .000 | .000 | -99 | -0 | -0 | 0 | 0 | | | | | /O | 0.0 |

■ WILLIE NORWOOD
Norwood, Willie b: 11/7/50, Green County, Ala.   BR/TR, 6', 185 lbs.   Deb: 4/21/77

1977	Min-A	39	83	15	19	3	0	3	9	6	17	.229	.281	.373	78	-3	-3	9	6	1	1	.952	-4	O/D	-0.6
1978	Min-A	125	428	56	109	22	3	8	46	28	64	.255	.305	.376	89	-6	-7	46	25	10	2	.944	-2	*O/D	-1.3
1979	Min-A	96	270	32	67	13	3	6	30	20	51	.248	.300	.385	80	-7	-8	29	9	5	-0	.974	-4	OD	-1.5
1980	Min-A	34	73	6	12	2	0	1	8	3	13	.164	.197	.233	16	-8	-9	3	1	1	-0	1.000	-1	O/D	-1.1
Total	4	294	854	109	207	40	6	18	93	57	145	.242	.292	.367	79	-24	-27	87	41	17	2	.959	-12	O/D	-4.5

■ JOE NOSSEK
Nossek, Joseph Rudolph b: 11/8/40, Cleveland, Ohio   BR/TR, 6', 178 lbs.   Deb: 4/18/64   C

1964	Min-A	7	1	1	0	0	0	0	0	0	0	.000	.000	.000	-99	-0	-0	0	0	0	0	.000	-1	/O	-0.1
1965	*Min-A	87	170	19	37	9	0	2	16	7	22	.218	.253	.306	55	-10	-10	13	2	0	1	.970	-6	O/3	-1.8
1966	Min-A	4	0	0	0	0	0	0	0	0	0	—	—	—	—	-0	-0	0	0	0	0	.000	-0	/O	-0.1
	KC-A	87	230	13	60	10	3	1	27	8	21	.261	.286	.343	83	-6	-6	21	4	2	0	.983	3	O/3	-0.5
	Yr	91	230	13	60	10	3	1	27	8	21	.261	.286	.343	82	-6	-6	21	4	2	0	.983	2	O/3	-0.6
1967	KC-A	87	166	12	34	6	1	0	10	4	26	.205	.224	.253	42	-12	-12	9	4	2	0	.982	-3	O	-1.8
1969	Oak-A	13	6	0	0	0	0	0	0	0	0	.000	.000	.000	-99	-2	-2	0	0	0	0	1.000	-4	O	-0.5
	StL-N	9	5	2	1	0	0	0	0	0	3	.200	.200	.200	12	-1	-1	0	0	0	0	1.000	1	/O	0.0
1970	StL-N	1	1	0	0	0	0	0	0	0	0	.000	.000	.000	-98	-0	-0	0	0	0	0	.000	-0	H	0.0
Total	6	295	579	47	132	25	4	3	53	19	72	.228	.254	.301	60	-31	-30	43	8	2	1	.980	-10	O/3	-4.8

■ LOU NOVIKOFF
Novikoff, Louis Alexander "The Mad Russian" b: 10/12/15, Glendale, Ariz.   d: 9/30/70, South Gate, Cal.   BR/TR, 5'10", 185 lbs.   Deb: 4/15/41

1941	Chi-N	62	203	22	49	8	0	5	24	11	15	.241	.284	.355	82	-6	-5	19	0			1.000	-4	O	-1.3
1942	Chi-N	128	483	48	145	25	5	7	64	24	28	.300	.337	.416	125	10	12	64	3			.964	-2	*O	0.4
1943	Chi-N	78	233	22	65	7	3	0	28	18	15	.279	.333	.335	95	-2	-2	24	0			.980	-8	O	-1.4
1944	Chi-N	71	139	15	39	4	2	3	19	10	11	.281	.329	.403	106	1	1	19	1			.976	-5	O	-0.6
1946	Phi-N	17	23	0	7	1	0	0	3	1	2	.304	.333	.348	96	-0	-0	2	0			1.000	0	/O	0.0
Total	5	356	1081	107	305	45	10	15	138	64	71	.282	.325	.384	107	2	6	129	4			.976	-19	O	-2.9

■ RUBE NOVOTNEY
Novotney, Ralph Joseph b: 8/5/24, Streator, Ill.   d: 7/16/87, Redondo Beach, Cal.   BR/TR, 6', 187 lbs.   Deb: 4/29/49

| 1949 | Chi-N | 22 | 67 | 4 | 18 | 2 | 1 | 0 | 6 | 3 | 11 | .269 | .300 | .328 | 70 | -3 | -3 | 6 | 0 | | | .958 | 0 | C | -0.1 |

■ LES NUNAMAKER
Nunamaker, Leslie Grant b: 1/25/1889, Malcolm, Neb.   d: 11/14/38, Hastings, Neb.   BR/TR, 6'2", 190 lbs.   Deb: 4/28/11

1911	Bos-A	62	183	18	47	4	3	0	19	12		.257	.303	.311	72	-7	-7	18	1			.972	6	C	0.4
1912	Bos-A	35	103	15	26	5	2	0	6	6		.252	.313	.340	82	-2	-3	12	2			.971	-3	C	-0.3
1913	Bos-A	29	65	9	14	5	2	0	9	8	8	.215	.311	.354	92	-1	-1	8	2			.977	3	C	0.5
1914	Bos-A	5	5	0	1	0	0	0	0	1	0	.200	.333	.200	61	-0	-0	0	0			1.000	0	/C1	0.0
	NY-A	87	257	19	68	10	3	2	29	22	34	.265	.327	.350	104	1	1	30	11	9	-2	.971	4	C/1	1.0
	Yr	92	262	19	69	10	3	2	29	23	34	.263	.328	.347	103	1	1	30	11	9	-2	.971	4	C/1	1.0
1915	NY-A	87	249	24	56	6	3	0	17	23	24	.225	.293	.273	70	-9	-9	21	3	2	-0	.964	-4	C/1	-0.8
1916	NY-A	91	260	25	77	14	7	0	28	34	21	.296	.380	.404	133	12	11	41	4			.983	-6	C	1.2
1917	NY-A	104	310	22	81	9	2	0	33	21	25	.261	.311	.303	86	-5	-5	30	5			.976	-4	C	-0.3
1918	StL-N	85	274	22	71	9	2	0	22	28	16	.259	.339	.307	98	-1	-0	30	6			.979	0	C/1O	0.1
1919	Cle-A	26	56	6	14	1	1	0	7	2	6	.250	.276	.304	59	-3	-3	5	0			.927	-3	C	-0.7
1920	*Cle-A	34	54	10	18	3	3	0	14	4	5	.333	.379	.500	128	2	2	10	1	0	0	.963	1	C/1	0.4
1921	Cle-A	46	131	16	47	7	2	0	25	11	8	.359	.408	.443	115	4	3	24	1	1	-0	.970	4	C	0.8
1922	Cle-A	25	43	8	13	2	0	0	7	4	3	.302	.362	.349	85	-1	-1	6	0	0	0	.936	-2	C	-0.3
Total	12	716	1990	194	533	75	30	2	216	176	150	.268	.332	.339	95	-11	-12	234	36	12		.972	-6	C/1O	2.7

■ EMORY NUSZ
Nusz, Emory Moberly b: 4/2/1866, Frederick, Md.   d: 8/3/1893, Point Of Rocks, Md.   Deb: 4/26/1884

| 1884 | Was-U | 1 | 4 | 1 | 0 | 0 | 0 | 0 | 0 | | | .000 | .000 | .000 | -99 | -1 | -1 | 0 | | | | .500 | -0 | /O | -0.1 |

■ DIZZY NUTTER
Nutter, Everett Clarence b: 8/27/1893, Roseville, Ohio   d: 7/25/58, Battle Creek, Mich.   BL/TR, 5'9", 160 lbs.   Deb: 9/07/19

| 1919 | Bos-N | 18 | 52 | 4 | 11 | 0 | 0 | 0 | 3 | 4 | 5 | .212 | .268 | .212 | 47 | -3 | -3 | 3 | 1 | | | 1.000 | 2 | O | -0.3 |

■ CHARLIE NYCE
Nyce, Charles Reiff (b: Charles Reiff Nice) b: 7/1/1870, Philadelphia, Pa.   d: 5/9/08, Philadelphia, Pa.   5'8", 160 lbs.   Deb: 5/28/1895

| 1895 | Bos-N | 9 | 35 | 7 | 8 | 5 | 0 | 2 | 9 | 4 | 2 | .229 | .325 | .543 | 114 | 1 | 0 | 6 | 0 | | | .889 | -1 | /S | 0.0 |

■ CHRIS NYMAN
Nyman, Christopher Curtis b: 6/6/55, Pomona, Cal.   BR/TR, 6'4", 200 lbs.   Deb: 7/28/82   F

1982	Chi-A	28	65	6	16	1	0	0	2	3	9	.246	.279	.262	50	-4	-4	4	3	2	-0	.994	0	1/O	-0.6
1983	Chi-A	21	28	12	8	0	0	2	4	4	7	.286	.394	.500	139	2	2	5	2	2	-1	1.000	1	1D	0.2
Total	2	49	93	18	24	1	0	2	6	7	16	.258	.317	.333	78	-3	-3	10	5	4	-1	.996	1	/1DO	-0.4

■ NYLS NYMAN
Nyman, Nyls Wallace Rex b: 3/7/54, Detroit, Mich.   BL/TR, 6', 170 lbs.   Deb: 9/06/74   F

1974	Chi-A	5	14	5	9	2	1	0	4	0	1	.643	.667	.929	347	5	4	8	1	0	0	1.000	1	/O	0.6
1975	Chi-A	106	327	36	74	6	3	2	28	11	34	.226	.256	.281	51	-21	-22	23	10	4	1	.958	-4	O/D	-3.0
1976	Chi-A	8	15	2	2	1	0	0	1	0	3	.133	.133	.200	-3	-2	-2	0	1	0	0	1.000	-1	/O	-0.3
1977	Chi-a	1	1	0	0	0	0	0	0	0	0	.000	.000	.000	-99	-0	-0	0	0	0	0	.000	0	H	0.0
Total	4	120	357	43	85	9	4	2	33	11	38	.238	.267	.303	60	-19	-19	32	12	4	1	.962	-4	O/D	-2.7

■ REBEL OAKES
Oakes, Ennis Telfair b: 12/17/1886, Homer, La.   d: 2/29/48, Rocky Springs, Lisbon, La.   BL/TR, 5'8", 170 lbs.   Deb: 4/14/09   M

1909	Cin-N	120	415	55	112	10	5	3	31	40		.270	.341	.340	112	6	6	56	23			.979	-2	*O	0.0
1910	StL-N	131	468	50	118	14	6	0	43	38	38	.252	.315	.308	85	-11	-9	51	18			.939	-7	*O	-2.3
1911	StL-N	154	551	69	145	13	6	2	59	41	35	.263	.320	.319	81	-16	-14	64	25			.961	11	*O	-1.1
1912	StL-N	136	495	57	139	19	5	0	58	31	24	.281	.328	.358	90	-9	-8	66	26			.947	-2	*O	-1.6
1913	StL-N	147	539	60	158	14	5	0	49	43	32	.293	.350	.358	98	-1	-0	71	22			.968	-2	*O	-1.0
1914	Pit-F	145	571	80	178	18	10	7	75	35	22	.312	.359	.415	121	14	14	100	28			.960	6	*OM	1.5
1915	Pit-F	153	580	55	161	24	5	0	82	37	19	.278	.323	.336	95	-5	-4	75	21			.973	-3	*OM	-1.6
Total	7	986	3619	428	1011	112	42	15	397	265	170	.279	.334	.346	97	-22	-14	483	163			.961	1	O	-6.1

■ PRINCE OANA
Oana, Henry Kauhane b: 1/22/08, Waipahu, Hawaii   d: 6/19/76, Austin, Tex.   BR/TR, 6'2", 193 lbs.   Deb: 4/22/34

1934	Phi-N	6	21	3	5	1	0	0	3	0	1	.238	.238	.286	35	-2	-2	1	0			1.000	1	/O	-0.1
1943	Det-A	20	26	5	10	2	1	1	7	1	2	.385	.407	.654	193	3	3	6	0	0	0	.750	-0	P	0.0
1945	Det-A	4	5	0	1	0	0	0	0	0	0	.200	.200	.200	15	-1	-1	0	0	0	0	1.000	-0	/P	0.0
Total	3	30	52	8	16	3	1	1	10	1	3	.308	.321	.462	108	1	0	7	0	0	0	.778	0	/PO	-0.1

■ JOHNNY OATES
Oates, Johnny Lane b: 1/21/46, Sylva, N.C.   BL/TR, 5'11", 188 lbs.   Deb: 9/17/70   MC

1970	Bal-A	5	18	2	5	0	1	0	2	2	0	.278	.350	.389	102	0	0	3	0	0		.939	1	/C	0.1
1972	Bal-A	85	253	20	66	12	1	4	21	28	31	.261	.335	.360	105	3	2	29	5	7	-3	**.995**	-3	C	0.0
1973	Atl-N	93	322	27	80	6	0	4	27	22	31	.248	.299	.304	63	-14	-17	28	1	4	-2	.981	-6	C	-2.2
1974	Atl-N	100	291	22	65	10	0	1	21	20	24	.223	.280	.268	52	-18	-19	22	2	4	-1	.992	12	C	-0.6
1975	Atl-N	8	18	0	4	1	0	0	0	1	4	.222	.263	.278	48	-1	-1	1	0	0	0	1.000	-0	/C	-0.2
	Phi-N	90	269	28	77	14	0	1	25	33	29	.286	.364	.349	95	1	-1	35	0	2	C	.990	2	C	0.5

YEAR	TM/L	G	AB	R	H	2B	3B	HR	RBI	BB	SO	AVG	OBP	SLG	PRO+	BR	/A	RC	SB	CS	SBR	FA	FR	POS	TPR
	Yr	98	287	28	81	15	0	1	25	34	33	.282	.358	.345	92	-1	-2	36	1	0	0	.990	1	C	0.3
1976	*Phi-N	37	99	10	25	2	0	0	8	8	12	.253	.308	.273	64	-4	-5	7	0	1	-1	.994	2	C	-0.3
1977	*LA-N	60	156	18	42	4	0	3	11	11	11	.269	.317	.353	80	-5	-4	17	1	0	0	.987	5	C	0.2
1978	*LA-N	40	75	5	23	1	0	0	6	5	3	.307	.350	.320	89	-1	-1	8	0	1	-1	.956	-2	C	-0.3
1979	LA-N	26	46	4	6	2	0	0	2	4	1	.130	.200	.174	3	-6	-6	2	0	1	-1	.975	3	C	-0.4
1980	NY-A	39	64	6	12	3	0	1	3	2	3	.188	.224	.281	38	-6	-5	3	1	2	-1	.991	3	C	-0.3
1981	NY-A	10	26	4	5	1	0	0	0	2	0	.192	.250	.231	40	-2	-2	2	0	0	0	.963	1	C	-0.1
Total	11	593	1637	146	410	56	2	14	126	141	149	.250	.311	.313	73	-53	-60	158	11	19	-8	.987	16	C	-3.6

■ HENRY OBERBECK Oberbeck, Henry A. b: 5/17/1858, Missouri d: 8/26/21, St.Louis, Mo. Deb: 5/07/1883

YEAR	TM/L	G	AB	R	H	2B	3B	HR	RBI	BB	SO	AVG	OBP	SLG	PRO+	BR	/A	RC	SB	CS	SBR	FA	FR	POS	TPR
1883	Pit-a	2	9	1	2	1	0	0		0		.222	.222	.333	80	-0	-0	1				1.000	0	/1	0.0
	StL-a	4	14	0	0	0	0	0		0		.000	.000	.000	-95	-3	-3	0				.833	1	/O	-0.2
	Yr	6	23	1	2	1	0	0		0		.087	.087	.130	-30	-3	-3	0				.833	1	/O1	-0.2
1884	Bal-U	33	125	19	23	4	0	0		3		.184	.203	.216	38	-7	-9	6				.878	2	O/3P	-0.7
	KC-U	27	90	7	17	3	0	0		7		.189	.247	.222	69	-3	-2	5				.823	7	3/OP1	0.5
	Yr	60	215	26	40	7	0	0		10		.186	.222	.219	50	-11	-11	11				.908	9	O3/P1	-0.2
Total	2	66	238	27	42	8	0	0		10		.176	.210	.210	41	-14	-14	11				.901	9	/O3P1	-0.4

■ KEN OBERKFELL Oberkfell, Kenneth Ray b: 5/4/56, Highland, Ill. BL/TR, 6', 210 lbs. Deb: 8/22/77

YEAR	TM/L	G	AB	R	H	2B	3B	HR	RBI	BB	SO	AVG	OBP	SLG	PRO+	BR	/A	RC	SB	CS	SBR	FA	FR	POS	TPR
1977	StL-N	9	9	0	1	0	0	0	1	0	3	.111	.111	.111	-41	-2	-2	0	0	0	0	1.000	-1	/2	-0.2
1978	StL-N	24	50	7	6	1	0	0	0	3	1	.120	.170	.140	-13	-8	-7	1	0	0	0	.987	3	2/3	-0.3
1979	StL-N	135	369	53	111	19	5	1	35	57	35	.301	.400	.388	115	11	11	60	4	1	1	**.985**	-4	*23/S	1.4
1980	StL-N	116	422	58	128	27	6	3	46	51	23	.303	.380	.417	118	14	12	66	4	4	-1	.989	-8	*23	1.0
1981	StL-N	102	376	43	110	12	6	2	45	37	28	.293	.356	.372	104	4	3	49	13	5	1	.956	11	*3/S	1.3
1982	*StL-N	137	470	55	136	22	5	2	34	40	31	.289	.346	.370	99	1	0	58	11	9	-2	**.972**	11	*3/2	0.7
1983	StL-N	151	488	62	143	26	5	3	38	61	27	.293	.373	.385	110	9	9	71	12	6	0	**.960**	3	*32/S	1.2
1984	StL-N	50	152	17	47	11	1	0	11	16	10	.309	.379	.395	121	4	4	22	1	2	-1	.967	4	3/2S	0.7
	Atl-N	50	172	21	40	8	1	1	10	15	17	.233	.294	.308	65	-7	-8	15	1	3	-2	.964	-5	3/2	-1.7
	Yr	100	324	38	87	19	2	1	21	31	27	.269	.334	.349	90	-3	-4	37	2	5	-2	.966	-1	3/2S	-1.0
1985	Atl-N	134	412	30	112	19	4	3	35	51	38	.272	.360	.359	96	3	-0	54	1	2	-1	.963	-1	*32	-0.4
1986	Atl-N	151	503	62	136	24	3	5	48	83	40	.270	.376	.360	98	6	2	72	7	4	-0	.976	9	*32	1.0
1987	Atl-N	135	508	59	142	29	2	3	48	48	29	.280	.344	.362	83	-8	-12	63	3	3	-1	.979	-4	*32	-1.8
1988	Atl-N	120	422	42	117	20	4	3	40	32	28	.277	.331	.365	95	-0	-3	51	4	5	-2	.951	-7	*3/2	-1.3
	Pit-N	20	54	7	12	2	0	0	2	5	6	.222	.288	.259	59	-3	-3	4	0	0	0	1.000	-4	2/S31	-0.6
	Yr	140	476	49	129	22	4	3	42	37	34	.271	.326	.353	91	-3	-5	55	4	5	-2	.952	-10	*32/S1	-1.9
1989	Pit-N	14	40	2	5	1	0	0	2	2	2	.125	.167	.150	-9	-6	-5	1	0	0	0	.988	-1	/12	-0.7
	SF-N	83	116	17	37	5	1	2	15	8	8	.319	.373	.431	133	4	5	18	0	1	-1	.971	-4	3/12	0.0
	Yr	97	156	19	42	6	1	2	17	10	10	.269	.321	.359	97	-1	-1	17	0	1	-1	.971	-5	312	-0.7
1990	Hou-N	77	150	10	31	6	1	1	12	15	17	.207	.283	.280	57	-9	-8	12	1	1	-0	.935	-2	312	-1.2
1991	Hou-N	53	70	7	16	4	0	0	14	14	8	.229	.357	.286	88	-1	-0	8	0	0	0	1.000	0	1/3	-0.1
1992	Cal-A	41	91	6	24	1	0	0	10	8	5	.264	.323	.275	70	-3	-3	8	0	1	-1	.986	-7	2/1D	-1.1
Total	16	1602	4874	558	1354	237	44	29	446	546	356	.278	.353	.362	97	9	-6	636	62	47	-10	.965	-5	*32/1SD	-2.1

■ MIKE O'BERRY O'Berry, Preston Michael b: 4/20/54, Birmingham, Ala. BR/TR, 6'2", 195 lbs. Deb: 4/08/79

YEAR	TM/L	G	AB	R	H	2B	3B	HR	RBI	BB	SO	AVG	OBP	SLG	PRO+	BR	/A	RC	SB	CS	SBR	FA	FR	POS	TPR
1979	Bos-A	43	59	8	10	1	0	1	4	5	16	.169	.246	.237	29	-6	-6	3	0	0	0	.957	0	C	-0.5
1980	Chi-N	19	48	7	10	1	0	0	5	5	13	.208	.283	.229	41	-3	-4	4	0	0	0	.982	4	C	0.1
1981	Cin-N	55	111	6	20	3	1	1	5	14	19	.180	.272	.252	49	-7	-7	8	0	0	0	.983	3	C	-0.3
1982	Cin-N	21	45	5	10	2	0	0	3	10	13	.222	.364	.267	77	-1	-1	5	0	0	0	.990	-1	C	-0.1
1983	Cal-A	26	60	7	10	1	0	1	5	3	11	.167	.206	.233	21	-7	-6	3	0	0	0	1.000	-1	C	-0.6
1984	NY-A	13	32	3	8	2	0	0	5	2	2	.250	.294	.313	71	-1	-1	3	0	0	0	1.000	1	C/3	0.0
1985	Mon-N	20	21	2	4	0	0	0	0	4	3	.190	.320	.190	49	-1	-1	2	1	0	0	1.000	3	C	0.3
Total	7	197	376	38	72	10	1	3	27	43	77	.191	.276	.247	46	-26	-27	28	1	0	0	.984	10	C/3	-1.1

■ JIM OBRADOVICH Obradovich, James Thomas b: 9/13/49, Fort Campbell, Ky. BL/TL, 6'2", 200 lbs. Deb: 9/12/78

YEAR	TM/L	G	AB	R	H	2B	3B	HR	RBI	BB	SO	AVG	OBP	SLG	PRO+	BR	/A	RC	SB	CS	SBR	FA	FR	POS	TPR
1978	Hou-N	10	17	3	3	0	1	0	2	1	3	.176	.222	.294	47	-1	-1	1	0	0	0	1.000	-0	/1	-0.2

■ CHARLIE O'BRIEN O'Brien, Charles Hugh b: 5/1/60, Tulsa, Okla. BR/TR, 6'2", 195 lbs. Deb: 6/02/85

YEAR	TM/L	G	AB	R	H	2B	3B	HR	RBI	BB	SO	AVG	OBP	SLG	PRO+	BR	/A	RC	SB	CS	SBR	FA	FR	POS	TPR
1985	Oak-A	16	11	3	3	1	0	0	1	3	3	.273	.429	.364	129	0	1	2	0	0	0	.958	-0	C	0.1
1987	Mil-A	10	35	2	7	3	1	0	0	4	4	.200	.282	.343	63	-2	-2	3	0	1	-1	1.000	6	C	0.4
1988	Mil-A	40	118	12	26	6	0	2	9	5	16	.220	.252	.322	59	-7	-7	9	0	1	-1	.991	12	C	0.7
1989	Mil-A	62	188	22	44	10	0	6	35	21	11	.234	.339	.383	104	1	2	23	0	0	0	.986	7	C	1.1
1990	Mil-A	46	145	11	27	7	2	0	11	11	26	.186	.253	.262	45	-11	-11	10	0	0	0	.992	5	C	-0.3
	NY-N	28	68	6	11	3	0	0	9	10	8	.162	.278	.206	36	-6	-6	5	0	0	0	.986	9	C	0.5
1991	NY-N	69	168	16	31	6	0	2	14	17	25	.185	.275	.256	51	-11	-11	12	0	2	-1	.991	19	C	1.0
1992	NY-N	68	156	15	33	12	0	2	13	16	18	.212	.289	.327	75	-5	-5	15	0	1	-1	.979	5	C	0.2
Total	7	339	889	87	182	48	3	12	92	87	111	.205	.288	.306	67	-39	-39	78	0	5	-3	.988	62	C	3.7

■ EDDIE O'BRIEN O'Brien, Edward Joseph b: 12/11/30, S.Amboy, N.J. BR/TR, 5'9", 165 lbs. Deb: 4/25/53 FC

YEAR	TM/L	G	AB	R	H	2B	3B	HR	RBI	BB	SO	AVG	OBP	SLG	PRO+	BR	/A	RC	SB	CS	SBR	FA	FR	POS	TPR
1953	Pit-N	89	261	21	62	5	3	0	14	17	30	.238	.289	.280	50	-19	-19	23	6	1	1	.935	-14	S	-2.6
1955	Pit-N	75	236	26	55	3	1	0	8	18	13	.233	.290	.254	47	-18	-17	18	4	5	-2	.993	1	O/3S	-2.1
1956	Pit-N	63	53	17	14	2	0	0	3	2	2	.264	.291	.302	61	-3	-3	5	1	1	-0	.978	9	S/O32P	0.7
1957	Pit-N	3	4	0	0	0	0	0	0	0	0	.000	.000	.000	-99	-1	-1	0	0	0	0	1.000	0	/P	0.0
1958	Pit-N	1	0	0	0	0	0	0	0	0	0	—	—	—	—	0	0	0	0	0	0	.000	-0	/P	0.0
Total	5	231	554	64	131	10	4	0	25	37	45	.236	.288	.269	48	-41	-40	45	11	7	-1	.942	-4	S/O3P2	-4.0

■ MICKEY O'BRIEN O'Brien, Frank Aloysius b: 9/13/1894, San Francisco, Cal. d: 11/4/71, Monterey Park, Cal. BR/TR, 5'8", 160 lbs. Deb: 4/26/23

YEAR	TM/L	G	AB	R	H	2B	3B	HR	RBI	BB	SO	AVG	OBP	SLG	PRO+	BR	/A	RC	SB	CS	SBR	FA	FR	POS	TPR
1923	Phi-N	15	21	3	7	2	0	0	0	2	1	.333	.391	.429	104	1	0	4	0	0	0	.909	0	/C	0.1

■ GEORGE O'BRIEN O'Brien, George Joseph b: 11/4/1889, Cleveland, Ohio d: 3/24/66, Columbus, Ohio BR/TR, 6', 185 lbs. Deb: 8/16/15

YEAR	TM/L	G	AB	R	H	2B	3B	HR	RBI	BB	SO	AVG	OBP	SLG	PRO+	BR	/A	RC	SB	CS	SBR	FA	FR	POS	TPR
1915	StL-A	3	9	1	2	0	0	0	0	1	2	.222	.300	.222	59	-0	-0	1	0			.933	-1	/C	-0.1

■ JERRY O'BRIEN O'Brien, Jeremiah b: 2/2/1864, New York d: 7/4/11, Binghamton, N.Y. Deb: 7/30/1887

YEAR	TM/L	G	AB	R	H	2B	3B	HR	RBI	BB	SO	AVG	OBP	SLG	PRO+	BR	/A	RC	SB	CS	SBR	FA	FR	POS	TPR
1887	Was-N	1	4	0	0	0	0	0	0	0	2	.000	.000	.000	-99	-1	-1	0	0			.714	-0	/2	-0.1

■ JOHN O'BRIEN O'Brien, John E. b: 10/22/1851, Columbus, Ohio d: 12/31/14, Fall River, Mass. TR, 5'11.5", 187 lbs. Deb: 4/19/1884

YEAR	TM/L	G	AB	R	H	2B	3B	HR	RBI	BB	SO	AVG	OBP	SLG	PRO+	BR	/A	RC	SB	CS	SBR	FA	FR	POS	TPR
1884	Bal-U	18	77	7	19	1	1	0		2		.247	.266	.286	78	-1	-2	6				.865	0	O	-0.2

■ JOHN O'BRIEN O'Brien, John J. "Chewing Gum" b: 7/14/1870, St.John, N.B., Can d: 5/13/13, Lewiston, Maine BL/TR, 175 lbs. Deb: 4/22/1891

YEAR	TM/L	G	AB	R	H	2B	3B	HR	RBI	BB	SO	AVG	OBP	SLG	PRO+	BR	/A	RC	SB	CS	SBR	FA	FR	POS	TPR
1891	Bro-N	43	167	22	41	4	2	0	26	12	17	.246	.308	.293	78	-5	-4	17	4			.854	-22	2	-2.2
1893	Chi-N	4	14	3	5	0	1	0	1	2	2	.357	.471	.500	163	1	1	3	0			.900	-2	/2	0.0
1895	Lou-N	128	539	82	138	10	4	1	50	45	20	.256	.325	.295	66	-28	-22	61	15			.938	3	*2/1	-1.0
1896	Lou-N	49	186	24	63	9	1	2	24	13	7	.339	.385	.430	121	4	6	33	4			.919	-1	2	0.6
	Was-N	73	270	38	72	6	3	4	33	27	12	.267	.344	.356	87	-5	-5	36	4			.952	2	2	0.2
	Yr	122	456	62	135	15	4	6	57	40	19	.296	.361	.386	100	-0	1	69	8			.938	1	*2	0.8
1897	Was-N	86	320	37	78	12	2	3	45	19		.244	.309	.322	67	-16	-16	35	6			.942	3	2	-0.7

YEAR	TM/L	G	AB	R	H	2B	3B	HR	RBI	BB	SO	AVG	OBP	SLG	PRO+	BR	/A	RC	SB	CS	SBR	FA	FR	POS	TPR
1899	Bal-N	39	135	14	26	4	0	1	17	15		.193	.283	.244	43	-10	-11	11	4			.966	7	2	-0.2
	Pit-N	79	279	26	63	2	4	1	33	21		.226	.285	.272	53	-18	-18	26	8			.946	3	2	-0.9
	Yr	118	414	40	89	6	4	2	50	36		.215	.284	.263	50	-28	-29	37	12			.953	10	*2	-1.1
Total	6	501	1910	246	486	47	17	12	229	154	58	.254	.322	.316	73	-76	-68	222	45			.978	-7	2/1	-4.2
■ JACK O'BRIEN	O'Brien, John Joseph b: 2/5/1873, Watervliet, N.Y. d: 6/10/33, Watervliet, N.Y. BL/TR, 6'1", 165 lbs. Deb: 4/14/1899																								
1899	Was-N	127	468	68	132	11	5	6	51	31		.282	.329	.365	91	-7	-6	65	17			.926	4	*O/3	-1.0
1901	Was-A	11	45	5	8	0	0	0	5	3		.178	.245	.178	19	-5	-5	3	2			.929	-0	O	-0.5
	Cle-A	92	375	54	106	14	5	0	39	22		.283	.329	.347	91	-6	-4	49	13			.941	-3	O/3	-1.2
	Yr	103	420	59	114	14	5	0	44	25		.271	.320	.329	83	-11	-9	51	15			.939	-3	*O/3	-1.7
1903	*Bos-A	96	338	44	71	14	4	3	38	21		.210	.262	.302	65	-13	-15	32	10			.958	-6	O3/2S	-2.7
Total	3	326	1226	171	317	39	14	9	133	77		.259	.308	.335	81	-31	-30	148	42			.937	-5	O/32S	-5.4
■ JACK O'BRIEN	O'Brien, John K. (b: John K. Bryne) b: 6/12/1860, Philadelphia, Pa. d: 11/20/10, Philadelphia, Pa. BR/TR, 5'10", 184 lbs. Deb: 5/02/1882																								
1882	Phi-a	62	241	44	73	13	3	3		13		.303	.339	.419	138	13	9	35				**.925**	11	CO/31	2.0
1883	Phi-a	94	390	74	113	14	10	0		25		.290	.333	.377	118	12	7	50				.876	-1	CO3/S	0.8
1884	Phi-a	36	138	25	39	6	1	1		9		.283	.340	.362	124	5	4	17				.930	-0	C/O1	0.5
1885	Phi-a	62	225	35	60	9	1	2		20		.267	.340	.342	112	6	3	27				.903	-8	C/S1O3	-0.2
1886	Phi-a	105	423	65	107	25	7	0		38		.253	.325	.345	111	6	6	56	23			.918	-15	C31S/2O	-0.6
1887	Bro-a	30	123	18	28	4	1	1		6		.228	.264	.301	58	-7	-7	12	8			.839	-8	C/O2	-1.0
1888	Bal-a	57	196	25	44	11	5	0	18	17		.224	.300	.332	108	1	2	24	14			.925	-15	CO/1	-0.9
1890	Phi-a	109	433	80	113	24	14	4		52		.261	.356	.409	131	15	17	76	31			.976	4	*1/OC	1.4
Total	8	555	2169	366	577	106	42	11	18	180		.266	.331	.369	116	53	41	298	76			.903	-31	C1/O3S2	2.0
■ JOHNNY O'BRIEN	O'Brien, John Thomas b: 12/11/30, S.Amboy, N.J. BR/TR, 5'9", 170 lbs. Deb: 4/19/53 F																								
1953	Pit-N	89	279	28	69	13	2	2	22	21	36	.247	.309	.330	67	-13	-13	28	1	1	-0	.982	-5	2/S	-1.4
1955	Pit-N	84	278	22	83	15	2	1	25	20	19	.299	.348	.378	94	-3	-2	36	1	1	-0	.969	5	2	0.8
1956	Pit-N	73	104	13	18	1	0	0	3	5	7	.173	.211	.183	7	-13	-13	4	0	0	0	.959	5	2/PS	-0.4
1957	Pit-N	34	35	7	11	2	1	0	1	1	4	.314	.368	.429	117	1	1	5	0	0	0	.857	-2	P/S2	-0.1
1958	Pit-N	3	1	1	0	0	0	0	0	0	1	.000	.000	.000	-99	-0	-0	0	0	0	0	.000	0	H	0.0
	StL-N	12	2	3	0	0	0	0	0	1	0	.000	.333	.000	-2	-0	-0	0	0	0	0	1.000	0	/SP2	0.0
	Yr	15	3	4	0	0	0	0	0	1	1	.000	.250	.000	-26	-1	-1	0	0	0	0	1.000	0	/SP2	0.0
1959	Mil-N	44	116	16	23	4	0	1	8	11	15	.198	.273	.259	47	-9	-8	9	0	0	0	.987	-3	2	-0.8
Total	6	339	815	90	204	35	5	4	59	59	82	.250	.307	.320	68	-39	-36	82	2	2	-1	.974	0	2/PS	-1.9
■ PETE O'BRIEN	O'Brien, Peter J. b: 6/17/1877, Binghamton, N.Y. d: 1/31/17, Jersey City, N.J. BL/TR, 5'7", 170 lbs. Deb: 9/21/01																								
1901	Cin-N	16	54	1	11	1	0	1	3	2		.204	.232	.278	51	-4	-3	4	0			.889	-2	2	-0.5
1906	StL-A	151	524	44	122	9	4	2	57	42		.233	.293	.277	83	-12	-9	53	25			.933	-41	*23S	-5.4
1907	Cle-A	43	145	9	33	5	2	0	6	7		.228	.263	.290	76	-4	-4	12	1			.943	-11	23S	-1.7
	Was-A	39	134	6	25	3	1	0	12	12		.187	.259	.224	59	-7	-5	9	4			.912	4	3S/2	0.0
	Yr	82	279	15	58	8	3	0	18	19		.208	.261	.258	68	-11	-10	22	5			.905	-7	3S2	-1.7
Total	3	249	857	60	191	18	7	3	78	63		.223	.279	.271	76	-26	-22	79	30			.929	-50	2/3S	-7.6
■ PETE O'BRIEN	O'Brien, Peter James b: 6/16/1867, Chicago, Ill. d: 6/30/37, York Township, Du Page County, Ill. BR/TR, 5'9.5", 165 lbs. Deb: 4/29/1890																								
1890	Chi-N	27	106	15	30	7	0	3	16	5	10	.283	.315	.434	115	2	1	16	4			.929	-2	2	0.1
■ PETE O'BRIEN	O'Brien, Peter Michael b: 2/9/58, Santa Monica, Cal. BL/TL, 6'1", 198 lbs. Deb: 9/03/82																								
1982	Tex-A	20	67	13	16	4	1	4	13	6	8	.239	.301	.507	124	1	2	11	1	0	0	1.000	-0	O/1D	0.1
1983	Tex-A	154	524	53	124	24	5	8	53	58	62	.237	.314	.347	83	-13	-11	57	5	4	-1	.993	13	*1O/D	-0.7
1984	Tex-A	142	520	57	149	26	2	18	80	53	50	.287	.353	.448	116	14	12	80	3	5	-2	.992	1	*1/O	0.1
1985	Tex-A	159	573	69	153	34	3	22	92	69	53	.267	.347	.452	115	13	12	85	5	10	-5	.995	-6	*1	-0.7
1986	Tex-A	156	551	86	160	23	3	23	90	87	66	.290	.387	.468	128	26	24	98	4	4	-1	.992	2	*1	1.4
1987	Tex-A	159	569	84	163	26	1	23	88	59	61	.286	.354	.457	113	10	10	91	0	4	-2	.992	16	*1/OD	1.2
1988	Tex-A	156	547	57	149	24	1	16	71	72	73	.272	.357	.408	111	11	9	80	1	4	-2	.995	13	*1/D	0.8
1989	Cle-A	155	554	75	144	24	1	12	55	83	48	.260	.358	.372	104	7	6	77	3	1	0	.994	3	*1/D	-0.4
1990	Sea-A	108	366	32	82	18	0	5	27	44	33	.224	.311	.314	74	-12	-12	36	0	0	0	.995	4	1/OD	-1.6
1991	Sea-A	152	560	58	139	29	3	17	88	44	61	.248	.304	.402	93	-6	-6	66	0	1	-1	**.997**	2	*1DO	-1.4
1992	Sea-A	134	396	40	88	15	1	14	52	40	27	.222	.294	.371	84	-9	-9	43	2	1	0	.996	2	1D	-1.2
Total	11	1495	5227	624	1367	247	21	162	709	615	542	.262	.340	.410	105	44	37	725	24	34	-13		48	*1/DO	-2.4
■ RAY O'BRIEN	O'Brien, Raymond Joseph b: 10/31/1892, St.Louis, Mo. d: 3/31/42, St.Louis, Mo. BL/TL, 5'9", 175 lbs. Deb: 6/27/16																								
1916	Pit-N	16	57	5	12	3	2	0	3	1	14	.211	.224	.333	69	-2	-2	5	0			.864	-1	O	-0.4
■ SYD O'BRIEN	O'Brien, Sydney Lloyd b: 12/18/44, Compton, Cal. BR/TR, 6'1", 185 lbs. Deb: 4/15/69																								
1969	Bos-A	100	263	47	64	10	5	9	29	15	37	.243	.287	.422	91	-3	-4	31	2	3	-1	.939	-1	3S2	-0.5
1970	Chi-A	121	441	48	109	13	2	8	44	22	62	.247	.286	.340	69	-18	-20	41	3	3	-1	.938	-6	32/S	-2.4
1971	Cal-A	90	251	25	50	8	1	5	21	15	33	.199	.247	.299	58	-16	-14	16	0	2	-1	.961	-1	S/231O	-1.1
1972	Cal-A	36	39	10	7	2	0	1	1	6	10	.179	.289	.308	82	-1	-1	4	0	0	0	.889	1	/3S21	0.0
	Mil-A	31	58	5	12	2	0	1	5	2	13	.207	.233	.293	57	-3	-3	3	0	1	-1	.852	-1	/32	-0.5
	Yr	67	97	15	19	4	0	2	6	8	23	.196	.257	.299	68	-4	-4	7	0	1	-1	.861	0	32/S1	-0.5
Total	4	378	1052	135	242	35	8	24	100	60	155	.230	.274	.347	72	-40	-42	95	5	9	-4	.934	-8	3/S21O	-4.5
■ TOMMY O'BRIEN	O'Brien, Thomas Edward "Obie" b: 12/19/18, Anniston, Ala. d: 11/5/78, Anniston, Ala. BR/TR, 5'11", 195 lbs. Deb: 4/24/43																								
1943	Pit-N	89	232	35	72	12	7	2	26	15	24	.310	.352	.448	126	8	7	35	0			.964	-6	O/3	-0.1
1944	Pit-N	85	156	27	39	6	2	3	20	21	12	.250	.343	.372	97	1	-0	19	1			.965	-9	O/3	-1.2
1945	Pit-N	58	161	23	54	6	5	0	18	9	13	.335	.374	.435	120	5	4	27	0			.961	-6	O	-0.3
1949	Bos-A	49	125	24	28	5	0	3	10	21	12	.224	.336	.336	73	-4	-5	15	1	0	0	.984	-2	O	-0.9
1950	Bos-A	9	31	0	4	1	0	0	3	3	5	.129	.206	.161	-5	-5	-5	1	0	0	0	1.000	-1	/O	-0.7
	Was-A	3	9	1	1	0	0	0	1	1	0	.111	.200	.111	-20	-2	-2	0	0	0	0	1.000	1	/O	-0.1
	Yr	12	40	1	5	1	0	0	4	4	5	.125	.205	.150	-8	-7	-7	1	0	0	0	1.000	-0	O	-0.8
Total	5	293	714	110	198	30	14	8	78	70	66	.277	.344	.392	100	3	-1	97	2	0		.970	-23	O/3	-3.3
■ TOM O'BRIEN	O'Brien, Thomas H. b: 6/22/1860, Salem, Mass. d: 4/21/21, Worcester, Mass. BR/TR, Deb: 6/14/1882																								
1882	Wor-N	22	89	9	18	1	1	0	7	1	10	.202	.211	.236	42	-6	-6	5				.789	-2	O/23	-0.8
1883	Bal-a	33	138	16	37	6	4	0		5		.268	.294	.370	109	2	1	15				.825	-4	2/O	-0.2
1884	Bos-U	103	449	80	118	31	8	4		12		.263	.282	.394	128	12	13	51				.853	1	*2/O1C	1.4
1885	Bal-a	8	33	4	7	3	0	0		2		.212	.257	.303	80	-1	-1	3				.932	1	/12	0.0
1887	NY-a	31	129	13	25	3	2	0		2		.194	.212	.248	31	-12	-11	9	10			.963	-2	1/O32P	-1.2
1890	Roc-a	73	273	36	52	6	5	0		30		.190	.273	.249	60	-15	-11	21	6			.971	-4	1/2	-1.6
Total	6	270	1111	158	257	50	20	4	7	52	10	.231	.267	.323	88	-20	-15	104	16			.846	-10	2/1O3PC	-2.4
■ TOM O'BRIEN	O'Brien, Thomas J. b: 2/20/1873, Verona, Pa. d: 2/4/01, Phoenix, Arizona Deb: 5/10/1897																								
1897	Bal-N	50	147	25	37	6	0	0	32	20		.252	.349	.293	70	-6	-6	18	7			.968	0	1O	-0.6
1898	Bal-N	18	60	9	13	0	0	0	14	10		.217	.338	.217	59	-3	-3	5	0			.833	0	O	-0.3
	Pit-N	107	413	53	107	10	8	1	45	25		.259	.318	.329	87	-8	-7	51	13			.924	-3	O1/32S	-1.3

YEAR	TM/L	G	AB	R	H	2B	3B	HR	RBI	BB	SO	AVG	OBP	SLG	PRO+	BR	/A	RC	SB	CS	SBR	FA	FR	POS	TPR
	Yr	125	473	62	120	10	8	1	59	35		.254	.321	.315	84	-10	-9	57	13			.911	-3	O1/32S	-1.6
1899	NY-N	150	573	100	170	21	10	6	77	44		.297	.351	.400	110	4	7	91	23			.933	-1	*O3/S21	-0.4
1900	Pit-N	102	376	61	109	22	6	3	61	21		.290	.349	.404	107	3	3	59	12			.961	-11	1O/2S	-0.9
Total	4	427	1569	248	436	59	24	10	229	120		.278	.341	.365	97	-9	-5	225	55			.928	-15	O1/32S	-3.5

■ DARBY O'BRIEN

O'Brien, William D. b: 9/1/1863, Peoria, Ill. d: 6/15/1893, Peoria, Ill. BR/TR, 6'1", 186 lbs. Deb: 4/16/1887

YEAR	TM/L	G	AB	R	H	2B	3B	HR	RBI	BB	SO	AVG	OBP	SLG	PRO+	BR	/A	RC	SB	CS	SBR	FA	FR	POS	TPR
1887	NY-a	127	522	97	157	30	13	5		40		.301	.355	.437	128	15	19	101	49			.913	6	*O1/S3P	1.8
1888	Bro-a	136	532	105	149	27	6	2	65	30		.280	.327	.365	125	14	14	83	55			.932	2	*O	1.1
1889	*Bro-a	136	567	146	170	30	11	5	80	61	76	.300	.384	.418	130	24	24	129	91			.906	-7	*O	1.2
1890	*Bro-N	85	350	78	110	28	6	2	63	32	43	.314	.378	.446	142	18	18	75	38			.960	4	O	1.6
1891	Bro-N	103	395	79	100	18	6	5	57	39	53	.253	.331	.367	106	3	3	60	31			.951	2	*O	0.2
1892	Bro-N	122	490	72	119	14	5	1	56	29	52	.243	.289	.298	82	-13	-10	60	57			.956	4	*O	-1.1
Total	6	709	2856	577	805	147	47	20	321	231	224	.282	.344	.387	119	61	68	508	321			.934	11	O/1SP3	4.8

■ BILLY O'BRIEN

O'Brien, William Smith b: 3/14/1860, Albany, N.Y. d: 5/26/11, Kansas City, Mo. BR , 6', 185 lbs. Deb: 9/27/1884

YEAR	TM/L	G	AB	R	H	2B	3B	HR	RBI	BB	SO	AVG	OBP	SLG	PRO+	BR	/A	RC	SB	CS	SBR	FA	FR	POS	TPR
1884	StP-U	8	30	1	7	3	0	0		0		.233	.233	.333	165	-0	2	2				.840	1	/3P	0.2
	KC-U	4	17	2	4	0	0	0		0		.235	.235	.235	68	-1	-0	1				.714	1	/31	0.0
	Yr	12	47	3	11	3	0	0		0		.234	.234	.298	121	-1	1	3				.795	2	3/P1	0.2
1887	Was-N	113	453	71	126	16	12	**19**	73	21	17	.278	.317	.492	130	12	16	76	11			.974	-3	*1/O32	0.2
1888	Was-N	133	528	42	119	15	2	9	66	9	70	.225	.238	.313	81	-15	-11	43	10			.975	-4	*1/3	-2.6
1889	Was-N	2	8	1	0	0	0	0	0	1	1	.000	.111	.000	-72	-2	-2	0	0			1.000	-0	/1	-0.2
1890	Bro-a	96	388	47	108	25	8	4		28		.278	.332	.415	127	9	11	56	5			.973	-2	*1	0.3
Total	5	356	1424	164	364	59	22	32	139	59	88	.256	.289	.395	111	4	16	179	26			.974	-8	1/3O2P	-2.1

■ WHITEY OCK

Ock, Harold David b: 3/17/12, Brooklyn, N.Y. d: 3/18/75, Mt.Kisco, N.Y. BR/TR, 5'11", 180 lbs. Deb: 9/29/35

YEAR	TM/L	G	AB	R	H	2B	3B	HR	RBI	BB	SO	AVG	OBP	SLG	PRO+	BR	/A	RC	SB	CS	SBR	FA	FR	POS	TPR
1935	Bro-N	1	3	0	0	0	0	0	0	1	2	.000	.250	.000	-27	-1	-1	0	0			1.000	-0	/C	-0.1

■ DANNY O'CONNELL

O'Connell, Daniel Francis b: 1/21/27, Paterson, N.J. d: 10/2/69, Clifton, N.J. BR/TR, 6', 180 lbs. Deb: 7/14/50 C

YEAR	TM/L	G	AB	R	H	2B	3B	HR	RBI	BB	SO	AVG	OBP	SLG	PRO+	BR	/A	RC	SB	CS	SBR	FA	FR	POS	TPR
1950	Pit-N	79	315	39	92	16	1	8	32	24	33	.292	.342	.425	97	-0	-2	45	7			.977	17	S3	2.0
1953	Pit-N	149	588	88	173	26	8	7	55	57	42	.294	.361	.401	99	-0	0	87	3	4	-2	.958	8	*32	0.7
1954	Mil-N	146	541	61	151	28	4	2	37	38	46	.279	.329	.357	84	-17	-12	64	2	2	-1	.979	9	*23/1S	0.2
1955	Mil-N	124	453	47	102	15	4	6	40	28	43	.225	.278	.316	60	-28	-25	40	2	2	-1	.981	16	*2/3S	-0.1
1956	Mil-N	139	498	71	119	17	9	2	42	76	42	.239	.344	.321	86	-11	-7	61	3	3	-1	.985	-6	*2/3S	-0.3
1957	Mil-N	48	183	29	43	9	1	1	8	19	20	.235	.314	.311	74	-8	-6	20	1	0	0	.982	7	2	0.5
	NY-N	95	364	57	97	18	3	7	28	33	30	.266	.331	.390	93	-4	-3	47	8	3	1	.980	6	23	0.9
	Yr	143	547	86	140	27	4	8	36	52	50	.256	.325	.364	87	-11	-9	66	9	3	1	.981	12	*23	1.4
1958	SF-N	107	306	44	71	12	2	3	23	51	35	.232	.342	.314	77	-10	-9	36	2	1	0	.986	3	*2/3	0.1
1959	SF-N	34	58	6	11	3	0	0	0	5	15	.190	.254	.241	34	-6	-5	4	0	1	-1	.927	7	3/2	0.1
1961	Was-A	138	493	61	128	30	1	1	37	77	62	.260	.363	.331	88	-6	-5	67	15	5	2	.939	1	32	0.5
1962	Was-A	84	236	24	62	7	2	2	18	23	28	.263	.328	.335	80	-7	-6	27	5	1	1	.961	-1	32	-0.4
Total	10	1143	4035	527	1049	181	35	39	320	431	396	.260	.335	.351	84	-96	-81	496	48	22		.980	67	23/S1	4.2

■ JIMMY O'CONNELL

O'Connell, James Joseph b: 2/11/01, Sacramento, Cal. d: 11/11/76, Bakersfield, Cal. BL/TR, 5'10.5", 175 lbs. Deb: 4/17/23

YEAR	TM/L	G	AB	R	H	2B	3B	HR	RBI	BB	SO	AVG	OBP	SLG	PRO+	BR	/A	RC	SB	CS	SBR	FA	FR	POS	TPR
1923	*NY-N	87	252	42	63	9	2	6	39	34	32	.250	.351	.373	92	-3	-2	35	7	3	0	.980	-8	O/1	-1.4
1924	NY-N	52	104	24	33	4	2	2	18	11	16	.317	.388	.452	128	4	4	19	2	1	0	.952	-7	O/2	-0.4
Total	2	139	356	66	96	13	4	8	57	45	48	.270	.361	.396	102	1	2	54	9	4	0	.974	-15	/O12	-1.8

■ JOHN O'CONNELL

O'Connell, John Charles b: 6/13/04, Berona, Pa. d: 10/17/92 Canton, Ohio BR/TR, 6', 170 lbs. Deb: 8/16/28

YEAR	TM/L	G	AB	R	H	2B	3B	HR	RBI	BB	SO	AVG	OBP	SLG	PRO+	BR	/A	RC	SB	CS	SBR	FA	FR	POS	TPR
1928	Pit-N	1	1	0	0	0	0	0	0	0	0	.000	.000	.000	-96	-0	-0	0	0			1.000	1	/C	0.0
1929	Pit-N	2	7	1	1	1	0	0	0	1	1	.143	.250	.286	32	-1	-1	1	0			1.000	-0	/C	-0.1
Total	2	3	8	1	1	1	0	0	0	1	1	.125	.222	.250	17	-1	-1	1	0			1.000	0	/C	-0.1

■ JOHN O'CONNELL

O'Connell, John Joseph b: 5/16/1872, Lawrence, Mass. d: 5/14/08, Derry, N.H. Deb: 8/22/1891

YEAR	TM/L	G	AB	R	H	2B	3B	HR	RBI	BB	SO	AVG	OBP	SLG	PRO+	BR	/A	RC	SB	CS	SBR	FA	FR	POS	TPR
1891	Bal-a	8	29	2	5	1	0	0	7	3	6	.172	.250	.207	33	-2	-3	2	2			.938	-3	/S2O	-0.5
1902	Det-A	8	22	1	4	0	0	0	0	3		.182	.280	.182	29	-2	-2	1	0			.919	1	/21	-0.1
Total	2	16	51	3	9	1	0	0	7	6	6	.176	.263	.196	31	-4	-5	3	2			.885	-2	/2S1O	-0.6

■ PAT O'CONNELL

O'Connell, Patrick H. b: 6/10/1861, Bangor, Me. d: 1/24/43, Lewiston, Maine BR/TR, 5'10", 175 lbs. Deb: 7/22/1886

YEAR	TM/L	G	AB	R	H	2B	3B	HR	RBI	BB	SO	AVG	OBP	SLG	PRO+	BR	/A	RC	SB	CS	SBR	FA	FR	POS	TPR
1886	Bal-a	42	166	20	30	3	2	0		11		.181	.236	.223	47	-10	-9	11	10			.782	-4	O/1P	-1.3
1890	Bro-a	11	40	7	9	2	1	0		7		.225	.340	.325	102	0	0	6	3			.830	-1	3/1	0.0
Total	2	53	206	27	39	5	3	0		18		.189	.258	.243	58	-10	-9	17	13			1.000	-5	/O31P	-1.3

■ DAN O'CONNOR

O'Connor, Daniel Cornelius b: 8/1868, Guelph, Ont., Canada d: 3/3/42, Guelph, Ont., Canada BL/TR, 6'2", 185 lbs. Deb: 6/03/1890

YEAR	TM/L	G	AB	R	H	2B	3B	HR	RBI	BB	SO	AVG	OBP	SLG	PRO+	BR	/A	RC	SB	CS	SBR	FA	FR	POS	TPR
1890	Lou-a	6	26	3	12	1	1	0		1		.462	.481	.577	220	3	4	10	5			1.000	-1	/1	0.2

■ JOHNNY O'CONNOR

O'Connor, John Charles "Bucky" b: 12/1/1891, Cahersiveen, Ire. d: 5/30/82, Bonner Springs, Kan. BR/TR, 5'9", Deb: 9/16/16

YEAR	TM/L	G	AB	R	H	2B	3B	HR	RBI	BB	SO	AVG	OBP	SLG	PRO+	BR	/A	RC	SB	CS	SBR	FA	FR	POS	TPR
1916	Chi-N	1	0	0	0	0	0	0	0	0	0	—	—	—	—	0	0	0	0			.000	0	/C	0.0

■ JACK O'CONNOR

O'Connor, John Joseph "Rowdy Jack" or "Peach Pie"
b: 6/2/1869, St.Louis, Mo. d: 11/14/37, St.Louis, Mo. BR/TR, 5'10", 170 lbs. Deb: 4/20/1887 M

YEAR	TM/L	G	AB	R	H	2B	3B	HR	RBI	BB	SO	AVG	OBP	SLG	PRO+	BR	/A	RC	SB	CS	SBR	FA	FR	POS	TPR
1887	Cin-a	12	40	4	4	0	0	0		2		.100	.143	.100	-30	-7	-7	1	3			.947	3	/OC	-0.3
1888	Cin-a	36	137	14	28	3	1	1	17	6		.204	.243	.263	61	-5	-6	12	12			.795	-0	O/C	-0.7
1889	Col-a	107	398	69	107	17	7	4	60	33	37	.269	.331	.377	109	1	5	60	26			**.955**	-1	CO/21	0.9
1890	Col-a	121	457	89	148	14	10	2		38		.324	.377	.411	145	19	24	84	29			**.962**	10	*C/OS23	3.7
1891	Col-a	56	229	28	61	12	3	0	37	11	14	.266	.300	.345	92	-5	-3	27	10			.878	3	OC	0.0
1892	*Cle-N	140	572	71	142	22	5	1	58	25	48	.248	.282	.309	77	-15	-18	56	17			.935	9	*OC	-1.1
1893	Cle-N	96	384	72	110	23	1	4	75	29	12	.286	.341	.383	89	-4	-8	62	29			.949	-2	CO	-0.6
1894	Cle-N	86	330	67	104	23	7	2	51	15	7	.315	.345	.445	88	-6	-8	58	15			.942	7	CO/1	0.0
1895	Cle-N	89	340	51	99	14	10	0	58	30	22	.291	.354	.391	89	-3	-7	54	11			.923	-5	C1/3	-0.5
1896	*Cle-N	68	256	41	76	11	1	1	43	15	12	.297	.343	.359	82	-5	-7	38	15			.966	-7	C1O	-0.8
1897	Cle-N	103	397	49	115	21	4	2	69	26		.290	.338	.378	84	-7	-11	60	20			.941	-12	O1C	-2.2
1898	Cle-N	131	478	50	119	17	4	1	56	26		.249	.292	.308	73	-18	-17	48	8			.983	2	1CO	-1.1
1899	StL-N	84	289	33	73	5	6	0	43	15		.253	.299	.311	66	-13	-14	30	7			.943	2	C1	-0.7
1900	StL-N	10	32	4	7	0	0	0	6	2		.219	.306	.219	46	-2	-2	2	0			.957	-0	C	-0.1
	*Pit-N	43	147	15	35	4	1	0	19	3		.238	.263	.279	49	-10	-10	13	5			.944	-11	C/1	-1.6
	Yr	53	179	19	42	4	1	0	25	5		.235	.271	.268	49	-12	-13	15	5			.947	-11	C/1	-1.7
1901	Pit-N	61	202	16	39	7	3	0	22	10		.193	.238	.257	43	-15	-15	14	2			.978	-1	C	-1.0
1902	Pit-N	49	170	13	50	1	2	1	28	3		.294	.306	.341	96	-1	-1	19	2			.979	-4	C/1O	-0.1
1903	NY-A	64	212	13	43	4	1	0	12	8		.203	.232	.231	37	-15	-17	13	4			.988	1	C/1	-1.0
1904	StL-A	14	47	4	10	1	0	0	2	2		.213	.245	.234	55	-3	-2	3	0			.943	-4	C	-0.6
1906	StL-A	55	174	8	33	0	0	0	11	2		.190	.199	.190	23	-16	-15	8	4			.990	10	C	0.0
1907	StL-A	25	89	2	14	2	0	0	4	0		.157	.176	.180	14	-9	-9	3	0			.991	-2	C	-1.0
1910	StL-A	1	0	0	0	0	0	0	0	0		—	—	—	—	0	0	0	0			1.000	-0	/CM	0.0
Total	21	1451	5380	713	1417	201	66	19	671	301	152	.263	.307	.336	81	-137	-149	664	219			.917	-3	CO1/S23	-8.8

YEAR	TM/L	G	AB	R	H	2B	3B	HR	RBI	BB	SO	AVG	OBP	SLG	PRO+	BR	/A	RC	SB	CS	SBR	FA	FR	POS	TPR
■ PADDY O'CONNOR		O'Connor, Patrick Francis b: 8/4/1879, County Kerry, Ireland d: 8/17/50, Springfield, Mass. BR/TR, 5'8", 168 lbs. Deb: 4/17/08																							
1908	Pit-N	12	16	1	3	0	0	0	2	0		.188	.188	.188	20	-1	-1	1	0			.889	-2	/C	-0.3
1909	★Pit-N	9	16	1	5	1	0	0	3	0		.313	.313	.375	104	0	-0	2	0			.700	-2	/C3	-0.2
1910	Pit-N	6	4	0	1	0	0	0	0	1	1	.250	.400	.250	85	0	-0	0	0			1.000	-0	/C	0.0
1914	StL-N	10	9	0	0	0	0	0	0	2	2	.000	.250	.000	-24	-1	-1	0	0			1.000	-0	/C	-0.2
1915	Pit-F	70	219	15	50	10	1	0	16	14	30	.228	.278	.283	66	-10	-10	20	4			.987	4	C	0.0
1918	NY-A	1	3	0	1	0	0	0	0	0	1	.333	.333	.333	99	-0	-0	0	0			1.000	-0	/C	0.0
Total	6	108	267	17	60	11	1	0	21	17	34	.225	.276	.273	63	-12	-12	23	4			.979	-0	/C3	-0.7
■ KEN O'DEA		O'Dea, James Kenneth b: 3/16/13, Lima, N.Y. d: 12/17/85, Lima, N.Y. BL/TR, 6', 180 lbs. Deb: 4/21/35																							
1935	★Chi-N	76	202	30	52	13	2	6	38	26	18	.257	.345	.431	106	2	2	31	0			.964	-2	C	0.3
1936	Chi-N	80	189	36	58	10	3	2	38	38	18	.307	.423	.423	126	10	9	37	0			.979	-3	C	0.8
1937	Chi-N	83	219	31	66	7	5	4	32	24	26	.301	.370	.434	113	6	4	38	1			.985	-6	C	0.1
1938	★Chi-N	86	247	22	65	12	1	3	33	12	18	.263	.297	.356	77	-8	-8	25	1			.970	4	C	-0.1
1939	NY-N	52	97	7	17	1	0	3	11	10	16	.175	.252	.278	42	-8	-8	7	0			.947	-2	C	-0.9
1940	NY-N	48	96	9	23	4	1	0	12	16	15	.240	.348	.302	80	-2	-2	11	0			.992	2	C	0.2
1941	NY-N	59	89	13	19	5	1	3	17	8	20	.213	.278	.393	86	-2	-2	10	0			1.000	1	C	0.0
1942	★StL-N	58	192	22	45	7	1	5	32	17	23	.234	.297	.359	85	-3	-4	20	0			.979	10	C	1.1
1943	★StL-N	71	203	15	57	11	2	3	25	19	25	.281	.345	.399	110	4	3	29	0			.989	6	C	1.2
1944	★StL-N	85	265	35	66	11	2	6	37	37	29	.249	.343	.374	100	1	1	37	1			.994	7	C	1.2
1945	StL-N†	100	307	36	78	18	2	4	43	50	31	.254	.359	.365	99	2	1	43	0			**.995**	3	C	0.9
1946	StL-N	22	57	2	7	2	0	1	3	8	8	.123	.231	.211	25	-6	-6	3	0			.991	5	C	0.0
	Bos-N	12	32	4	7	0	0	0	2	8	4	.219	.375	.219	70	-1	-1	3	0			1.000	-1	C	-0.1
	Yr	34	89	6	14	2	0	1	5	16	12	.157	.286	.213	41	-6	-7	6	0			.994	4	C	-0.1
Total	12	832	2195	262	560	101	20	40	323	273	251	.255	.338	.374	95	-5	-12	292	3			.983	26	C	4.7
■ PAUL O'DEA		O'Dea, Paul "Lefty" b: 7/3/20, Cleveland, Ohio d: 12/11/78, Cleveland, Ohio BL/TL, 6', 200 lbs. Deb: 4/19/44																							
1944	Cle-A	76	173	25	55	9	0	0	13	23	21	.318	.401	.370	126	6	7	24	2	2	-1	.949	-5	O/P1	0.0
1945	Cle-A	87	221	21	52	2	2	1	21	20	26	.235	.299	.276	70	-9	-8	18	3	0	1	.992	2	O/P	-0.8
Total	2	163	394	46	107	11	2	1	34	43	47	.272	.345	.317	95	-3	-1	43	5	2	0	.975	-2	/OP1	-0.8
■ HEINIE ODOM		Odom, Herman Boyd b: 10/13/1900, Rusk, Tex. d: 8/31/70, Rusk, Tex. BB/TR, 6', 170 lbs. Deb: 4/22/25																							
1925	NY-A	1	1	0	1	0	0	0	0	0	0	1.000	1.000	1.000	416	0	0	1	0	0	0	1.000	0	/3	0.1
■ BLUE MOON ODOM		Odom, Johnny Lee b: 5/29/45, Macon, Ga. BR/TR, 6', 185 lbs. Deb: 9/05/64																							
1964	KC-A	5	5	1	0	0	0	0	0	1	4	.000	.167	.000	-47	-1	-1	0	0	0	0	.800	0	/P	0.0
1965	KC-A	1	0	0	0	0	0	0	0	0	0	—	—	—	—	0	0	0	0	0	0	1.000	0	/P	0.0
1966	KC-A	17	31	1	3	0	0	0	2	3	16	.097	.176	.097	-20	-5	-5	1	0	0	0	.970	2	P	0.0
1967	KC-A	33	28	4	8	1	0	0	0	1	14	.286	.310	.321	90	-0	-0	3	0	1	-1	.897	0	P	0.0
1968	Oak-A★	42	78	14	17	2	0	1	2	6	29	.218	.282	.282	75	-3	-2	7	0	0	0	.964	1	P	0.0
1969	Oak-A★	43	79	15	21	2	1	5	16	2	24	.266	.293	.506	125	1	2	12	0	0	0	.937	1	P	0.0
1970	Oak-A	37	54	8	13	2	0	3	7	3	18	.241	.281	.444	100	-1	-0	7	1	0	0	.929	2	P	0.0
1971	Oak-A	37	50	8	8	0	1	1	1	2	24	.160	.192	.260	28	-5	-5	2	0	0	0	.850	-1	P	0.0
1972	★Oak-A	59	66	16	8	1	0	2	2	1	29	.121	.134	.227	7	-8	-7	2	4	2	0	.873	0	P	0.0
1973	★Oak-A	51	1	5	0	0	0	0	0	0	0	.000	.000	.000	-99	-0	-0	-1	1	2	-1	.875	-1	P	0.0
1974	★Oak-A	43	0	3	0	0	0	0	0	0	0	—	—	—	—	0	0	0	0	0	0	.821	1	P	0.0
1975	Oak-A	8	0	1	0	0	0	0	0	0	0	—	—	—	—	0	0	0	0	0	0	.750	0	/P	0.0
	Cle-A	3	0	0	0	0	0	0	0	0	0	—	—	—	—	0	0	0	0	0	0	1.000	-0	/P	0.0
	Yr	11	0	1	0	0	0	0	0	0	0	—	—	—	—	0	0	0	0	0	0	.800	-0	P	0.0
	Atl-N	15	13	0	1	1	0	0	1	0	5	.077	.077	.154	-36	-2	-2	0	0	0	0	.944	0	P	0.0
1976	Chi-A	8	0	0	0	0	0	0	0	0	0	—	—	—	—	0	0	0	0	0	0	.600	-1	/P	0.0
Total	13	402	405	76	79	9	2	12	31	19	163	.195	.235	.316	60	-23	-22	32	6	5	-1	.904	5	P	0.0
■ O'DONNELL		O'Donnell b: Littlestown, Pa. Deb: 7/16/1884																							
1884	Phi-U	1	4	0	1	0	0	0		0		.250	.250	.250	75	-0	-0	0				.545	-2	/C	-0.1
■ HARRY O'DONNELL		O'Donnell, Harry Herman "Butch" b: 4/2/1894, Philadelphia, Pa. d: 1/31/58, Philadelphia, Pa. BR/TR, 5'8", 175 lbs. Deb: 4/30/27																							
1927	Phi-N	16	16	1	1	0	0	0	2	2	2	.063	.167	.063	-36	-3	-3	0	0			1.000	1	C	-0.2
■ LEFTY O'DOUL		O'Doul, Francis Joseph b: 3/4/1897, San Francisco, Cal. d: 12/7/69, San Francisco, Cal. BL/TL, 6', 180 lbs. Deb: 4/29/19																							
1919	NY-A	19	16	2	4	0	0	0	1	1	2	.250	.294	.250	53	-1	-1	1	1			.500	-1	/PO	-0.1
1920	NY-A	13	12	2	2	1	0	0	1	1	1	.167	.231	.250	26	-1	-1	1	0	0	0	.000	-1	/PO	-0.1
1922	NY-A	8	9	0	3	1	0	0	4	0	2	.333	.333	.444	99	-0	-0	1	0	0	0	1.000	0	/P	0.0
1923	Bos-A	36	35	2	5	0	0	0	4	2	3	.143	.189	.143	-12	-6	-6	1	0	0	0	.958	1	P/O	-0.1
1928	NY-N	114	354	67	113	19	4	8	46	30	8	.319	.372	.463	117	8	8	60	9			.962	-12	O	-0.9
1929	Phi-N	154	638	152	**254**	35	6	32	122	76	19	**.398**	**.465**	.622	157	69	62	180	2			.971	5	*O	5.0
1930	Phi-N	140	528	122	202	37	7	22	97	63	21	.383	.453	.604	142	47	41	141	3			.953	-5	*O	2.3
1931	Bro-N	134	512	85	172	32	11	7	75	48	16	.336	.396	.482	136	26	26	100	5			.954	-1	*O	1.6
1932	Bro-N	148	595	120	219	32	8	21	90	50	20	**.368**	.423	.555	164	51	53	142	11			.979	-5	*O	3.8
1933	Bro-N	43	159	14	40	5	1	5	21	15	6	.252	.320	.390	106	0	1	21	2			.947	-3	O	-0.4
	★NY-N★	78	229	31	70	9	1	9	35	29	17	.306	.388	.472	147	14	14	43	1			.974	-6	O	0.6
	Yr	121	388	45	110	14	2	14	56	44	23	.284	.361	.438	130	14	15	63	3			.962	-8	*O	0.2
1934	NY-N	83	177	27	56	4	3	9	46	18	7	.316	.383	.525	144	10	11	38	2			.968	-5	O	0.4
Total	11	970	3264	624	1140	175	41	113	542	333	122	.349	.413	.532	142	217	208	730	36	0		.964	-33	O/P	12.1
■ FRED ODWELL		Odwell, Frederick William "Fritz" b: 9/25/1872, Downsville, N.Y. d: 8/19/48, Downsville, N.Y. BL/TR, 5'9.5", 160 lbs. Deb: 4/16/04																							
1904	Cin-N	129	468	75	133	22	10	1	58	26		.284	.329	.380	109	9	5	71	30			.956	14	*O/2	1.2
1905	Cin-N	130	468	79	113	10	9	**9**	65	26		.241	.291	.359	84	-5	-12	58	21			.967	4	*O	-1.4
1906	Cin-N	58	202	20	45	5	4	0	21	15		.223	.286	.287	76	-5	-6	21	11			.963	3	O	-0.6
1907	Cin-N	94	274	24	74	5	7	0	24	22		.270	.336	.339	107	4	3	37	10			.975	5	O/2	0.5
Total	4	411	1412	198	365	42	30	10	168	89		.258	.312	.352	96	3	-10	188	72			.964	26	O/2	-0.3
■ CHUCK OERTEL		Oertel, Charles Frank "Ducky" or "Snuffy" b: 3/12/31, Coffeyville, Kan. BL/TR, 5'8", 165 lbs. Deb: 9/01/58																							
1958	Bal-A	14	12	4	2	0	0	1	1	1	1	.167	.231	.417	78	-1	-0	1	0	0	0	1.000	-1	/O	-0.1
■ RON OESTER		Oester, Ronald John b: 5/5/56, Cincinnati, Ohio BB/TR, 6'2", 190 lbs. Deb: 9/10/78																							
1978	Cin-N	6	8	1	3	0	0	0	1	0	2	.375	.375	.375	110	0	0	1	0	0	0	1.000	1	/S	0.1
1979	Cin-N	6	3	0	0	0	0	0	0	0	1	.000	.000	.000	-99	-1	-1	0	0	0	0	1.000	1	/S	0.1
1980	Cin-N	100	303	40	84	16	2	2	20	26	44	.277	.336	.363	95	-2	-2	37	6	2	1	.980	-14	2S/3	-1.0
1981	Cin-N	105	354	45	96	16	7	5	42	42	49	.271	.348	.398	110	6	5	48	2	5	-2	.980	5	*2/S	1.5
1982	Cin-N	151	549	63	143	19	4	9	47	35	82	.260	.305	.359	83	-12	-13	56	5	6	-2	.972	4	*2S3	-0.4
1983	Cin-N	157	549	63	145	23	5	11	58	49	106	.264	.326	.384	93	-3	-6	66	2	2	-1	.977	-25	*2	-2.5
1984	Cin-N	150	553	54	134	26	3	3	38	41	97	.242	.296	.316	69	-21	-23	50	7	2	1	.980	-16	*2/S	-3.5
1985	Cin-N	152	526	59	155	26	3	1	34	51	65	.295	.357	.361	97	2	-1	68	5	0	2	.989	5	*2	1.1
1986	Cin-N	153	523	52	135	23	2	8	44	52	84	.258	.326	.356	84	-8	-11	59	9	2	2	.978	18	*2	1.5

YEAR	TM/L	G	AB	R	H	2B	3B	HR	RBI	BB	SO	AVG	OBP	SLG	PRO+	BR	/A	RC	SB	CS	SBR	FA	FR	POS	TPR
1987	Cin-N	69	237	28	60	9	6	2	23	22	51	.253	.317	.367	77	-7	-8	26	2	3	-1	.974	6	2	0.0
1988	Cin-N	54	150	20	42	7	0	0	10	9	24	.280	.321	.327	83	-3	-3	15	0	2	-1	.995	2	2/S	0.0
1989	Cin-N	109	305	23	75	15	0	1	14	32	47	.246	.318	.305	76	-8	-9	29	1	0	0	.985	8	*2/S	0.2
1990	*Cin-N	64	154	10	46	10	1	0	13	10	29	.299	.341	.377	93	-1	-1	20	1	2	-1	.982	-8	2/3	-1.0
Total	13	1276	4214	458	1118	190	33	42	344	369	681	.265	.325	.356	87	-56	-73	474	40	26	-4	.980	-14	*2/S3	-3.9

■ BOB O'FARRELL O'Farrell, Robert Arthur b: 10/19/1896, Waukegan, Ill. d: 2/20/88, Waukegan, Ill. BR/TR, 5'9.5", 180 lbs. Deb: 9/05/15 M

1915	Chi-N	2	3	0	1	0	0	0	0	0	0	.333	.333	.333	102	-0	-0	0	0			.667	-1	/C	-0.1
1916	Chi-N	1	0	0	0	0	0	0	0	0	0	—	—	—	—	0	0	0	0			.000	0	/C	0.0
1917	Chi-N	3	8	1	3	2	0	0	1	1	0	.375	.444	.625	210	1	1	2	1			1.000	-1	/C	0.0
1918	*Chi-N	52	113	9	32	7	3	1	14	10	15	.283	.347	.425	132	5	4	16	0			.974	-6	C	0.1
1919	Chi-N	49	125	11	27	4	2	0	9	7	10	.216	.258	.280	61	-6	-6	9	2			.965	-4	C	-0.7
1920	Chi-N	94	270	29	67	11	4	3	19	34	23	.248	.332	.352	95	-1	-1	34	1	0	0	.956	-6	C	-0.1
1921	Chi-N	96	260	32	65	12	7	4	32	18	14	.250	.299	.396	82	-7	-7	31	2	0	1	.967	-5	C	-0.7
1922	Chi-N	128	392	68	127	18	8	4	60	79	34	.324	.439	.441	125	21	19	82	5	3	-0	.977	16	*C	3.8
1923	Chi-N	131	452	73	144	25	4	12	84	67	38	.319	.408	.471	131	22	22	91	10	3	1	.976	1	*C	2.9
1924	Chi-N	71	183	25	44	6	2	3	28	30	13	.240	.347	.344	85	-3	-3	24	2	0	1	.984	-2	C	-0.1
1925	Chi-N	17	22	2	4	0	1	0	3	2	5	.182	.250	.273	33	-2	-2	2	0	0	0	1.000	-1	/C	-0.3
	StL-N	94	317	37	88	13	2	3	32	46	26	.278	.373	.360	86	-4	-5	45	0	1	-1	.975	-5	C	-0.5
	Yr	111	339	39	92	13	3	3	35	48	31	.271	.365	.354	83	-6	-7	46	0	1	-1	.975	-6	C	-0.8
1926	*StL-N	147	492	63	144	30	9	7	68	61	44	.293	.371	.433	111	11	9	79	1			.983	10	*C	2.7
1927	StL-N	61	178	19	47	10	1	0	18	23	22	.264	.348	.331	80	-4	-4	21	3			.979	-0	CM	-0.1
1928	StL-N	16	52	6	11	1	0	0	4	13	9	.212	.369	.231	59	-2	-2	5	2			.985	0	C	-0.1
	NY-N	75	133	23	26	6	0	2	20	34	16	.195	.359	.286	70	-4	-5	16	2			.988	-1	C	-0.2
	Yr	91	185	29	37	7	0	2	24	47	25	.200	.362	.270	67	-7	-7	21	4			.987	-1	C	-0.3
1929	NY-N	91	248	35	76	14	3	4	42	28	30	.306	.384	.435	103	2	2	41	3			.979	-5	C	0.3
1930	NY-N	94	249	37	75	16	4	4	54	31	21	.301	.381	.446	101	0	1	42	1			.973	0	C	0.6
1931	NY-N	85	174	11	39	8	3	1	19	21	23	.224	.311	.322	72	-7	-6	19	0			.980	1	C	-0.2
1932	NY-N	50	67	7	16	3	0	0	8	11	10	.239	.354	.284	76	-2	-2	8	0			.969	2	C	0.1
1933	StL-N	55	163	16	39	4	2	2	20	15	25	.239	.303	.325	76	-4	-5	16	0			.970	-5	C	-0.8
1934	Cin-N	44	123	10	30	8	3	1	9	11	19	.244	.306	.382	85	-3	-3	14	0			.993	1	CM	0.0
	Chi-N	22	67	3	15	3	0	0	5	3	11	.224	.257	.269	42	-6	-5	5	0			1.000	2	C	-0.3
	Yr	66	190	13	45	11	3	1	14	14	30	.237	.289	.342	70	-9	-8	19	0			.996	2	C	-0.3
1935	StL-N	14	10	0	0	0	0	0	0	2	0	.000	.167	.000	-49	-2	-2	0	0			1.000	1	/C	-0.1
Total	21	1492	4101	517	1120	201	58	51	549	547	408	.273	.360	.388	97	4	-2	604	35	7		.976	-10	*C	6.2

■ JOSE OFFERMAN Offerman, Jose Antonio (Dono) b: 11/8/68, San Pedro De Macoris, D.R. BB/TR, 6', 150 lbs. Deb: 8/19/90

1990	LA-N	29	58	7	9	0	0	1	7	4	14	.155	.210	.207	15	-7	-7	3	1	0	0	.946	-2	S	-0.7
1991	LA-N	52	113	10	22	2	0	0	3	25	32	.195	.345	.212	62	-5	-4	9	3	2	-0	.945	2	S	0.0
1992	LA-N	149	534	67	139	20	8	1	30	57	98	.260	.332	.333	90	-7	-6	61	23	16	-3	.935	-18	*S	-1.6
Total	3	230	705	84	170	22	8	2	40	86	144	.241	.324	.304	80	-18	-17	73	27	18	-3	.938	-18	S	-2.3

■ ROWLAND OFFICE Office, Rowland Johnie b: 10/25/52, Sacramento, Cal. BL/TL, 6', 170 lbs. Deb: 8/05/72

1972	Atl-N	2	5	1	2	0	0	0	0	1	2	.400	.500	.400	145	0	0	1	0	0	0	1.000	0	/O	0.0
1974	Atl-N	131	248	20	61	16	1	3	31	16	30	.246	.292	.355	77	-7	-9	23	5	3	-0	.994	-16	*O	-2.9
1975	Atl-N	126	355	30	103	14	1	3	30	23	41	.290	.339	.361	91	-3	-4	42	2	2	-1	.967	3	*O	-0.6
1976	Atl-N	99	359	51	101	17	1	4	34	37	49	.281	.352	.368	98	3	-0	46	2	8	-4	.986	-7	O	-1.6
1977	Atl-N	124	428	42	103	13	1	5	39	23	58	.241	.284	.311	53	-25	-31	36	2	4	-2	.988	2	*O/1	-3.6
1978	Atl-N	146	404	40	101	13	1	9	40	22	52	.250	.299	.354	73	-11	-16	41	8	6	-1	.990	-9	*O	-3.2
1979	Atl-N	124	277	35	69	14	2	2	37	27	33	.249	.320	.336	74	-8	-10	30	5	4	-1	.988	3	O	-1.2
1980	Mon-N	116	292	36	78	13	4	6	30	36	39	.267	.348	.401	108	4	4	42	3	3	-1	.987	-5	O	-0.5
1981	Mon-N	26	40	4	7	0	0	0	0	4	6	.175	.250	.175	22	-4	-4	2	0	0	0	.938	-1	O	-0.6
1982	Mon-N	3	3	0	1	1	0	0	0	0	1	.333	.333	.667	170	0	0	1	0	0	0	1.000	0	/O	0.1
1983	NY-A	2	2	0	0	0	0	0	1	0	0	.000	.000	.000	-99	-1	-1	0	0	0	0	1.000	-1	/O	-0.1
Total	11	899	2413	259	626	101	11	32	242	189	311	.259	.317	.350	79	-50	-70	264	27	30	-10	.985	-31	O/1	-14.2

■ JIM OGLESBY Oglesby, James Dorn b: 8/10/05, Schofield, Mo. d: 9/1/55, Tulsa, Okla. BL/TL, 6', 190 lbs. Deb: 4/14/36

1936	Phi-A	3	11	0	2	0	0	0	2	2	0	.182	.308	.182	24	-1	-1	1	0	0	0	1.000	0	/1	-0.1

■ BEN OGLIVIE Oglivie, Benjamin Ambrosio (Palmer) b: 2/11/49, Colon, Panama BL/TL, 6'2", 170 lbs. Deb: 9/04/71

1971	Bos-A	14	38	2	10	3	0	0	4	0	5	.263	.263	.342	66	-2	-2	3	0	0	0	.958	1	O	-0.1
1972	Bos-A	94	253	27	61	10	2	8	30	18	61	.241	.294	.391	97	0	-1	29	1	1	-0	.981	-1	O	-0.6
1973	Bos-A	58	147	16	32	9	1	2	9	9	32	.218	.272	.333	66	-6	-7	13	1	1	-0	.983	0	OD	-0.9
1974	Det-A	92	252	28	68	11	3	4	29	34	38	.270	.357	.385	109	5	4	36	12	3	2	.947	-5	O1/D	-0.2
1975	Det-A	100	332	45	95	14	1	9	36	16	62	.286	.323	.416	103	2	0	40	11	8	-2	.975	6	O/1D	0.1
1976	Det-A	115	305	36	87	12	3	15	47	11	44	.285	.317	.492	129	11	10	43	9	4	0	.986	1	O/1D	0.8
1977	Det-A	132	450	63	118	24	2	21	61	40	80	.262	.327	.464	107	7	4	64	9	9	-3	.976	7	*O/D	0.4
1978	Mil-A	128	469	71	142	29	4	18	72	52	69	.303	.372	.497	142	26	26	85	11	7	-1	.980	1	OD1	2.2
1979	Mil-A	139	514	88	145	30	4	29	81	48	56	.282	.346	.525	131	21	21	91	12	5	1	.985	-0	*OD/1	1.5
1980	Mil-A★	156	592	94	180	26	2	**41**	118	54	71	.304	.367	.563	156	39	42	121	11	9	-2	.978	21	*O/D	5.3
1981	*Mil-A	107	400	53	97	15	2	14	72	37	49	.243	.316	.395	109	2	4	49	2	2	-1	.982	-3	*O/D	-0.3
1982	*Mil-A★	159	602	92	147	22	1	34	102	70	81	.244	.327	.453	119	9	14	90	3	5	-2	.982	13	*O	2.0
1983	Mil-A★	125	411	49	115	19	3	13	66	60	64	.280	.377	.436	133	14	19	67	4	6	-2	.985	6	*O/D	1.9
1984	Mil-A	131	461	49	121	16	2	12	60	44	56	.262	.328	.384	100	-2	0	55	0	6	-4	.970	-4	*O/D	-1.1
1985	Mil-A	101	341	40	99	17	2	10	61	37	51	.290	.363	.440	119	9	9	54	0	2	-1	.965	-3	O/D	0.2
1986	Mil-A	103	346	31	98	20	1	5	53	30	33	.283	.340	.390	95	-1	-2	45	1	2	-1	.991	4	OD	-0.1
Total	16	1754	5913	784	1615	277	33	235	901	560	852	.273	.340	.450	119	134	139	886	87	70	-16	.978	44	*OD/1	11.1

■ BRUCE OGRODOWSKI Ogrodowski, Ambrose Francis "Brusie" b: 2/17/12, Hoytville, Pa. d: 3/5/56, San Francisco, Cal. BR/TR, 5'11", 175 lbs. Deb: 4/14/36

1936	StL-N	94	237	28	54	15	1	1	20	10	20	.228	.259	.312	53	-16	-16	18	0			.989	4	C	-0.8
1937	StL-N	90	279	37	65	10	3	3	31	11	17	.233	.267	.323	58	-16	-17	22	2			.984	2	C	-1.0
Total	2	184	516	65	119	25	4	4	51	21	37	.231	.263	.318	56	-32	-33	39	2			.986	6	C	-1.8

■ HAL O'HAGEN O'Hagen, Harry P. b: 9/30/1873, Washington, D.C. d: 1/14/13, Newark, N.J. 6', 173 lbs. Deb: 9/24/1892

1892	Was-N	1	4	1	1	0	0	0	0	0	2	.250	.250	.250	54	-0	-0	0	0			1.000	1	/C	0.0
1902	Chi-N	31	108	10	21	1	3	0	10	11		.194	.269	.259	65	-5	-4	10	8			.982	3	1	-0.2
	NY-N	4	11	0	1	0	0	0	0	0		.091	.091	.091	-44	-2	-2	0	0			1.000	-1	/O	-0.3
	Cle-A	3	13	2	5	2	0	0	1	0		.385	.385	.538	160	1	1	4	2			1.000	1	/1	0.1
	NY-N	22	73	5	11	2	1	0	8	2		.151	.195	.205	24	-7	-7	4	3			.973	-0	1/O	-0.8
	Yr	57	192	15	33	2	4	0	18	13		.172	.232	.224	45	-14	-13	14	11			.979	2	1/O	-1.3
Total	2	61	209	18	39	5	4	0	19	13	2	.187	.241	.249	51	-12	-12	18	13			.981	3	/1OC	-1.2

■ KID O'HARA O'Hara, James Francis b: 12/19/1875, Wilkes-Barre, Pa. d: 12/1/54, Canton, Ohio BB/TR, 5'7.5", 152 lbs. Deb: 9/15/04

1904	Bos-N	8	29	3	6	0	0	0	0	4		.207	.303	.207	61	-1	-1	2	1			.923	0	/O	-0.1

YEAR	TM/L	G	AB	R	H	2B	3B	HR	RBI	BB	SO	AVG	OBP	SLG	PRO+	BR	/A	RC	SB	CS	SBR	FA	FR	POS	TPR

■ TOM O'HARA
O'Hara, Thomas F. b: 7/13/1885, Waverly, N.Y. d: 6/8/54, Denver, Colo. Deb: 9/19/06

1906	StL-N	14	53	8	16	1	0	0	0	3		.302	.339	.321	111	0	1	7	3			.889	-2	O	-0.2
1907	StL-N	48	173	11	41	2	1	0	5	12		.237	.286	.260	74	-6	-5	14	1			.943	-1	O	-0.9
Total	2	62	226	19	57	3	1	0	5	15		.252	.299	.274	83	-5	-4	21	4			.930	-3	/O	-1.1

■ BILL O'HARA
O'Hara, William Alexander b: 8/14/1883, Toronto, Ont., Can. d: 6/15/31, Jersey City, N.J. BL/TR, 5'10", Deb: 4/15/09

1909	NY-N	115	360	48	85	9	3	1	30	41		.236	.318	.286	86	-4	-5	42	31			.978	2	*O	-0.8
1910	StL-N	9	20	1	3	0	0	0	2	1	3	.150	.190	.150	-0	-3	-2	1	0			1.000	-0	/OP1	-0.3
Total	2	124	380	49	88	9	3	1	32	42	3	.232	.311	.279	82	-7	-7	43	31			.979	2	O/1P	-1.1

■ LEN OKRIE
Okrie, Leonard Joseph b: 7/16/23, Detroit, Mich. BR/TR, 6', 185 lbs. Deb: 6/16/48 FC

1948	Was-A	19	42	1	10	0	0	0	1	1	7	.238	.256	.286	45	-3	-3	2	0	0	0	.981	1	C	0.0
1950	Was-A	17	27	1	6	0	0	0	2	6	7	.222	.382	.222	61	-1	-1	3	0	0	0	1.000	1	C	0.0
1951	Was-A	5	8	1	1	1	0	0	0	2	1	.125	.300	.250	51	-1	-1	1	0	0	0	.850	1	/C	0.0
1952	Bos-A	1	1	0	0	0	0	0	0	0	1	.000	.000	.000	-93	-0	-0	0	0	0	0	1.000	-0	/C	0.0
Total	4	42	78	3	17	1	1	0	3	9	16	.218	.307	.256	51	-6	-5	6	0	0	0	.965	4	/C	0.0

■ JIM OLANDER
Olander, James Bentley b: 2/21/63, Tucson, Ariz. BR/TR, 6'1", 185 lbs. Deb: 9/20/91

| 1991 | Mil-A | 12 | 9 | 2 | 0 | 0 | 0 | 0 | 0 | 2 | 5 | .000 | .182 | .000 | -46 | -2 | -2 | 0 | 0 | 0 | 0 | 1.000 | -2 | /OD | -0.4 |

■ DAVE OLDFIELD
Oldfield, David b: 12/18/1864, Philadelphia, Pa. d: 8/28/39, Philadelphia, Pa. BB/TL, 5'7", 175 lbs. Deb: 6/28/1883

1883	Bal-a	1	4	0	0	0	0	0		0		.000	.000	.000	-97	-1	-1	0				.667	-1	/C	-0.2
1885	Bro-a	10	25	2	8	1	0	0		3		.320	.414	.360	149	2	2	4				.873	1	/CO	0.3
1886	Bro-a	14	55	7	13	1	0	0		2		.236	.263	.255	63	-2	-2	4	1			.833	-3	C/SO	-0.3
	Was-N	21	71	2	10	2	0	0	2	5	15	.141	.197	.169	13	-7	-7	2	0			.899	-4	C/O	-0.8
Total	3	46	155	11	31	4	0	0	2	10	15	.200	.253	.226	51	-9	-8	10	1			.857	-7	/COS	-1.0

■ JOHN OLDHAM
Oldham, John Hardin b: 11/6/32, Salinas, Cal. BR/TL, 6'3", 198 lbs. Deb: 9/02/56

| 1956 | Cin-N | 1 | 0 | 0 | 0 | 0 | 0 | 0 | 0 | 0 | 0 | — | — | — | | 0 | 0 | 0 | 0 | 0 | 0 | .000 | 0 | R | 0.0 |

■ BOB OLDIS
Oldis, Robert Carl b: 1/5/28, Preston, Iowa BR/TR, 6'1", 185 lbs. Deb: 4/28/53 C

1953	Was-A	7	16	0	4	0	0	0	3	1	2	.250	.294	.250	49	-1	-1	1	0	0	0	1.000	2	/C	0.1
1954	Was-A	11	24	1	8	1	0	0	0	1	3	.333	.360	.375	107	0	0	3	0	0	0	.941	-1	/C3	0.0
1955	Was-A	6	6	1	0	0	0	0	0	1	1	.000	.143	.000	-62	-1	-1	0	0	0	0	1.000	0	/C	-0.1
1960	*Pit-N	22	20	1	4	1	0	0	1	1	2	.200	.238	.250	34	-2	-2	1	0	0	0	1.000	3	C	0.1
1961	Pit-N	4	5	0	0	0	0	0	0	0	0	.000	.000	.000	-99	-1	-1	0	0	0	0	1.000	1	/C	0.1
1962	Phi-N	38	80	9	21	1	0	1	10	13	10	.262	.366	.313	87	-1	-1	10	0	1	-1	.987	1	C	0.0
1963	Phi-N	47	85	8	19	3	0	0	8	3	5	.224	.250	.259	47	-6	-6	5	0	0	0	.979	5	C	0.2
Total	7	135	236	20	56	6	0	1	22	20	22	.237	.297	.275	60	-13	-12	21	0	1	-1	.983	12	C/3	0.2

■ RUBE OLDRING
Oldring, Reuben Henry b: 5/30/1884, New York, N.Y. d: 9/9/61, Bridgeton, N.J. BR/TR, 5'10", 186 lbs. Deb: 10/02/05

1905	NY-A	8	30	2	9	0	1	1	6	2		.300	.344	.467	140	2	1	6	4			.967	5	/S	0.7
1906	Phi-A	59	174	15	42	10	1	0	19	2		.241	.263	.310	77	-5	-5	17	7			.897	2	3/S21	-0.2
1907	Phi-A	117	441	48	126	27	8	1	40	7		.286	.302	.390	118	7	6	63	29			.974	-10	*O	-0.9
1908	Phi-A	116	434	38	96	14	2	1	39	18		.221	.265	.270	69	-13	-16	35	13			.941	3	*O	-2.1
1909	Phi-A	90	326	39	75	13	8	1	28	20		.230	.287	.328	92	-3	-4	36	17			.963	-1	O/1	-0.9
1910	Phi-A	134	546	79	168	27	14	4	57	23		.308	.340	.430	143	22	23	85	17			**.978**	-1	*O	1.7
1911	*Phi-A	121	495	84	147	11	14	3	59	21		.297	.332	.394	104	-0	1	72	21			**.979**	-9	*O	-1.4
1912	Phi-A	99	395	61	119	14	5	1	24	10		.301	.324	.370	102	-3	-1	53	17			.974	-3	O	-0.9
1913	*Phi-A	137	538	101	152	27	9	5	71	34	37	.283	.328	.394	114	5	6	78	40			.968	-7	*O/S	-0.6
1914	*Phi-A	119	466	68	129	21	7	4	49	18	35	.277	.308	.371	108	-0	2	53	14	16	-5	.965	-6	*O	-1.6
1915	Phi-A	107	408	49	101	23	3	6	42	22	21	.248	.293	.363	100	-5	-3	45	11	6	-0	.982	5	O/3	-0.2
1916	Phi-A	40	146	10	36	8	3	0	14	9	9	.247	.290	.342	95	-2	-2	15	1			.897	-2	O	-0.7
	NY-A	43	158	17	37	8	0	1	12	12	13	.234	.288	.304	76	-5	-5	16	6			.957	-3	O	-1.2
	Yr	83	304	27	73	16	3	1	26	21	22	.240	.289	.322	85	-7	-7	31	7			.926	-5	O	-1.9
1918	Phi-A	49	133	5	31	2	1	0	11	8	10	.233	.282	.263	64	-6	-6	10	0			.949	-8	O/23	-1.8
Total	13	1239	4690	616	1268	205	76	27	471	206	125	.270	.307	.364	103	-4	-1	582	197	22		.966	-35	*O/3S21	-10.1

■ CHARLEY O'LEARY
O'Leary, Charles Timothy b: 10/15/1882, Chicago, Ill. d: 1/6/41, Chicago, Ill. BR/TR, 5'7", 165 lbs. Deb: 4/14/04 C

1904	Det-A	135	456	39	97	10	3	1	16	21		.213	.252	.254	62	-20	-19	34	9			.933	6	*S	-1.1
1905	Det-A	148	512	47	109	13	1	0	33	29		.213	.259	.242	59	-23	-24	40	13			.933	-8	*S	-3.2
1906	Det-A	128	443	34	97	13	2	2	34	17		.219	.253	.271	62	-19	-20	36	8			.926	-8	*S	-2.6
1907	*Det-A	139	465	61	112	19	1	0	34	32		.241	.297	.286	83	-7	-9	46	11			.943	-4	*S	-1.0
1908	*Det-A	65	211	21	53	9	3	0	17	9		.251	.295	.322	96	-0	-1	21	4			.920	-12	S/2	-1.4
1909	*Det-A	76	261	29	53	10	0	0	13	6		.203	.224	.241	45	-16	-17	16	9			.922	-4	32/SO	-2.2
1910	Det-A	65	211	23	51	7	1	0	9	9		.242	.276	.284	71	-6	-8	19	7			.935	1	2S/3	-0.7
1911	Det-A	74	256	29	68	8	2	0	25	21		.266	.336	.313	77	-6	-6	32	10			.966	4	2/3	-0.5
1912	Det-A	3	10	1	2	0	0	0	1	0		.200	.200	.200	15	-1	-1	0	0			1.000	2	/2	0.1
1913	StL-N	121	406	32	88	15	5	0	31	20	34	.217	.260	.278	55	-25	-24	30	3			.951	-8	*S2	-2.5
1934	StL-A	1	1	1	1	0	0	0	0	0	0	1.000	1.000	1.000	385	0	0	1	0	0	0	.000	0	H	0.0
Total	11	955	3232	317	731	104	18	3	213	164	34	.226	.270	.272	67	-123	-130	275	74	0		.935	-31	S2/3O	-15.1

■ DAN O'LEARY
O'Leary, Daniel "Hustling Dan" b: 10/22/1856, Detroit, Mich. d: 6/24/22, Chicago, Ill. BL, 5'10", 165 lbs. Deb: 9/03/1879 M

1879	Pro-N	2	7	1	3	0	0	0	2	0	0	.429	.429	.429	187	1	1	1				.000	-1	/O	0.0
1880	Bos-N	3	12	1	3	2	0	0	1	0	3	.250	.250	.417	126	0	0	1				1.000	-1	/O	-0.1
1881	Det-N	2	8	0	0	0	0	0	0	0	2	.000	.000	.000	-96	-2	-2	0				.714	-1	/O	-0.2
1882	Wor-N	6	22	2	4	1	0	0	2	5	5	.182	.333	.227	82	-0	-0	2				.800	-2	/O	-0.2
1884	Cin-U	32	132	14	34	0	2	1		5		.258	.285	.311	94	0	-1	12				.862	2	OM	0.0
Total	5	45	181	18	44	3	2	1	5	10	10	.243	.283	.298	89	-1	-3	16				.843	-2	/O	-0.5

■ JOHN OLERUD
Olerud, John Garrett b: 8/5/68, Seattle, Wash. BL/TL, 6'5", 205 lbs. Deb: 9/03/89

1989	Tor-A	6	8	2	3	0	0	0	0	0	1	.375	.375	.375	114	0	0	1	0	0	0	1.000	0	/1D	0.0
1990	Tor-A	111	358	43	95	15	1	14	48	57	75	.265	.368	.430	120	12	11	59	0	2	-1	.986	-1	D1	0.8
1991	*Tor-A	139	454	64	116	30	1	17	68	68	84	.256	.360	.438	115	13	11	72	0	2	-1	.996	-4	*1/D	-0.3
1992	*Tor-A	138	458	68	130	28	0	16	66	70	61	.284	.380	.450	126	21	18	78	1	0	0	.994	-2	*1/D	0.8
Total	4	394	1278	177	344	73	2	47	182	195	221	.269	.369	.440	120	46	40	211	1	4	-2	.994	-7	1/D	1.3

■ FRANK OLIN
Olin, Franklin Walter b: 1/9/1860, Woodford, Vt. d: 5/21/51, St.Louis, Mo. BL, Deb: 7/04/1884

1884	Was-a	21	83	12	32	4	4	0		8		.386	.440	.458	223	9	10	17				.775	-7	2O	0.3
	Was-U	1	4	0	0	0	0	0		0		.000	.000	.000	-99	-1	-1	0				.000	-0	/O	-0.1
	Tol-a	26	86	16	22	0	1	1		5		.256	.304	.314	101	1	0	8				.875	0	O	0.0
1885	Det-N	1	4	1	2	0	0	0	0	0	0	.500	.500	.500	224	1	1	1				.667	-0	/3	0.0
Total	2	49	177	29	56	4	2	1	0	13	0	.316	.366	.379	153	9	10	27				.849	-7	/O23	0.2

YEAR	TM/L	G	AB	R	H	2B	3B	HR	RBI	BB	SO	AVG	OBP	SLG	PRO+	BR	/A	RC	SB	CS	SBR	FA	FR	POS	TPR
■ TONY OLIVA Oliva, Pedro (Lopez) b: 7/20/40, Pinar Del Rio, Cuba BL/TR, 6'2", 190 lbs. Deb: 9/09/62 C																									
1962	Min-A	9	9	3	4	1	0	0	3	3	2	.444	.583	.556	201	2	2	3	0	0	0	1.000	-0	/O	0.1
1963	Min-A	7	7	0	3	0	0	0	1	0	2	.429	.429	.429	138	0	0	1	0	0	0	.000	0	H	0.0
1964	Min-A★	161	672	**109**	**217**	**43**	9	32	94	34	68	**.323**	.361	.557	150	43	42	**132**	12	6	0	.981	5	*O	4.1
1965	*Min-A★	149	576	107	**185**	40	5	16	98	55	64	**.321**	.384	.491	141	35	32	109	19	9	0	.964	7	*O	3.4
1966	Min-A★	159	622	99	**191**	32	7	25	87	42	72	.307	.356	.502	135	33	29	106	13	7	-0	.972	14	*O	3.7
1967	Min-A★	146	557	76	161	**34**	6	17	83	44	61	.289	.350	.463	128	26	21	91	11	3	2	.987	12	*O	2.9
1968	Min-A★	128	470	54	136	24	5	18	68	45	61	.289	.360	.477	145	29	26	77	10	9	-2	.983	8	*O	2.8
1969	*Min-A†	153	637	97	**197**	**39**	4	24	101	45	66	.309	.358	.496	134	29	27	107	10	13	-5	.982	13	*O	2.8
1970	*Min-A★	157	628	96	**204**	**36**	7	23	107	38	67	.325	.366	.514	138	32	31	112	5	4	-1	.968	21	*O	4.3
1971	Min-A†	126	487	73	164	30	3	22	81	25	44	**.337**	.372	**.546**	152	34	32	90	4	1	1	.969	-1	*O	2.7
1972	Min-A	10	28	1	9	1	0	0	1	2	5	.321	.367	.357	111	1	0	4	0	0	0	.857	-3	/O	-0.3
1973	Min-A	146	571	63	166	20	0	16	92	45	44	.291	.347	.410	108	9	6	79	2	1	0	.000	0	*D	0.6
1974	Min-A	127	459	43	131	16	2	13	57	27	31	.285	.328	.414	108	6	4	58	0	1	-1	.000	0	*D	0.4
1975	Min-A	131	455	46	123	10	0	13	58	41	45	.270	.348	.378	103	4	3	60	0	1	-1	.000	0	*D	0.2
1976	Min-A	67	123	3	26	3	0	1	16	2	13	.211	.236	.260	44	-9	-9	7	0	0	0	.000	0	D	-1.0
Total	15	1676	6301	870	1917	329	48	220	947	448	645	.304	.356	.476	130	272	246	1036	86	55	-7	.975	76	*OD	26.7
■ ED OLIVARES Olivares, Edward (Balzac) b: 11/5/38, Mayaguez, P.R. BR/TR, 5'11", 180 lbs. Deb: 9/16/60 F																									
1960	StL-N	3	5	0	0	0	0	0	0	0	3	.000	.000	.000	-92	-1	-1	0	0	0	0	.500	-0	/3	-0.2
1961	StL-N	21	30	2	5	0	0	0	1	0	4	.167	.167	.167	-10	-5	-5	1	1	0	0	1.000	-1	O	-0.6
Total	2	24	35	2	5	0	0	0	1	0	7	.143	.143	.143	-21	-6	-6	1	1	0	0	.981	-1	/O3	-0.8
■ AL OLIVER Oliver, Albert b: 10/14/46, Portsmouth, Ohio BL/TL, 6', 195 lbs. Deb: 9/23/68																									
1968	Pit-N	4	8	1	1	0	0	0	0	0	4	.125	.125	.125	-25	-1	-1	0	0	0	0	1.000	0	/O	-0.1
1969	Pit-N	129	463	55	132	19	2	17	70	21	38	.285	.334	.445	119	9	10	62	8	5	-1	.991	-3	*1O	-0.3
1970	*Pit-N	151	551	63	149	33	5	12	83	35	35	.270	.330	.414	100	-2	-1	75	1	1	-0	.986	-3	O1	-1.4
1971	*Pit-N	143	529	69	149	31	7	14	64	27	72	.282	.323	.446	116	9	9	72	4	3	-1	.981	3	*O1	0.5
1972	*Pit-N★	140	565	88	176	27	4	12	89	34	44	.312	.356	.437	127	17	18	85	2	4	-2	.985	-6	*O/1	0.4
1973	Pit-N	158	654	90	191	38	7	20	99	22	52	.292	.320	.463	118	10	12	92	6	0	2	.964	-6	*O1	-0.2
1974	*Pit-N	147	617	96	198	38	12	11	85	33	58	.321	.360	.475	137	24	27	101	10	1	2	.986	1	O1	2.3
1975	*Pit-N★	155	628	90	176	39	8	18	84	25	73	.280	.313	.454	112	5	6	83	4	2	0	.987	-3	*O/1	-0.4
1976	Pit-N★	121	443	62	143	22	5	12	61	26	29	.323	.367	.476	137	21	20	74	6	2	1	.984	2	*O/1	1.9
1977	Pit-N	154	568	75	175	29	6	19	82	40	38	.308	.358	.481	119	17	15	91	13	16	-6	.981	0	*O	0.4
1978	Tex-A	133	525	65	170	35	5	14	89	31	41	.324	.364	.490	138	25	25	90	8	9	-3	.987	6	*OD	2.3
1979	Tex-A	136	492	69	159	28	4	12	76	34	34	.323	.372	.470	127	17	18	81	4	5	-2	.975	0	*OD	1.1
1980	Tex-A★	163	656	96	209	43	3	19	117	39	47	.319	.361	.480	132	24	27	108	5	7	-3	.973	4	*O/1D	2.2
1981	Tex-A★	102	421	53	130	29	1	4	55	24	28	.309	.349	.411	125	9	12	56	3	0	1	1.000	-0	*D/1	1.3
1982	Mon-N★	160	617	90	**204**	**43**	2	22	**109**	61	59	**.331**	.394	.514	149	43	41	**125**	5	2	0	.986	-9	*1	2.6
1983	Mon-N★	157	614	70	184	**38**	3	8	84	44	44	.300	.348	.410	110	7	8	81	1	3	-2	.990	3	*1/O	0.0
1984	SF-N	91	339	27	101	19	2	0	34	20	27	.298	.339	.366	101	-1	0	36	2	2	-1	.985	-1	1	-0.7
	Phi-N	28	93	9	29	7	0	0	14	7	9	.312	.360	.387	108	1	1	11	1	2	-1	.987	-3	1/O	-0.5
	Yr	119	432	36	130	26	2	0	48	27	36	.301	.343	.370	103	0	1	48	3	4	-2	.985	-4	*1/O	-1.2
1985	LA-N	35	79	1	20	5	0	0	8	5	11	.253	.298	.316	74	-3	-3	7	1	0	0	.882	-2	O	-0.6
	*Tor-A	61	187	20	47	6	1	5	23	7	13	.251	.282	.374	76	-6	-7	17	0	0	0	1.000	-0	D/1	-0.7
Total	18	2368	9049	1189	2743	529	77	219	1326	535	756	.303	.348	.451	122	224	237	1348	84	64	-13	.980	-18	*O1D	10.1
■ DAVE OLIVER Oliver, David Jacob b: 4/7/51, Stockton, Cal. BL/TR, 5'11", 175 lbs. Deb: 9/25/77 C																									
1977	Cle-A	7	22	2	7	0	1	0	3	4	0	.318	.444	.409	139	1	1	5	0	0	0	.949	1	/2	0.2
■ GENE OLIVER Oliver, Eugene George b: 3/22/35, Moline, Ill. BR/TR, 6'2", 225 lbs. Deb: 6/06/59																									
1959	StL-N	68	172	14	42	9	0	6	28	7	41	.244	.274	.401	72	-6	-8	17	3	2	-0	.955	-5	O/C1	-1.5
1961	StL-N	22	52	8	14	2	0	4	9	6	10	.269	.367	.538	124	3	2	10	0	0	0	1.000	1	C/O	0.4
1962	StL-N	122	345	42	89	19	1	14	45	50	59	.258	.354	.441	102	6	2	54	5	2	0	.991	-3	C/O1	0.2
1963	StL-N	39	102	10	23	4	0	6	18	13	19	.225	.313	.441	105	2	1	13	0	0	0	.981	1	C	0.3
	Mil-N	95	296	34	74	12	2	11	47	27	59	.250	.323	.416	112	4	4	38	4	4	-1	.985	-11	1O/C	-1.2
	Yr	134	398	44	97	16	2	17	65	40	78	.244	.321	.422	110	6	5	52	4	4	-1	.985	-9	1CO	-0.9
1964	Mil-N	93	279	45	77	15	1	13	49	17	41	.276	.320	.477	120	7	7	37	3	7	-3	.982	-6	1/C	-0.6
1965	Mil-N	122	392	56	106	20	0	21	58	36	61	.270	.336	.482	127	14	13	60	5	4	-1	.976	1	C1/O	1.5
1966	Atl-N	76	191	19	37	9	1	8	24	16	43	.194	.256	.377	72	-7	-8	19	2	0	1	.990	11	C/1O	0.7
1967	Atl-N	17	51	8	10	2	0	3	6	6	8	.196	.281	.412	97	-0	-0	5	0	0	0	.968	2	C	0.3
	Phi-N	85	263	29	59	16	0	7	34	29	56	.224	.304	.365	90	-3	-4	29	2	2	-1	.987	-12	C/1	-1.3
	Yr	102	314	37	69	18	0	10	40	35	64	.220	.300	.373	91	-4	-4	35	2	2	-1	.984	-10	C/1	-1.0
1968	Bos-A	16	35	2	5	0	0	0	1	4	12	.143	.250	.143	20	-3	-3	2	0	0	0	.984	-2	C/O	-0.5
	Chi-N	8	11	1	4	0	0	0	1	3	2	.364	.500	.364	152	1	1	2	0	0	0	1.000	0	/1CO	0.2
1969	Chi-N	23	27	0	6	3	0	0	0	1	9	.222	.276	.333	62	-1	-2	2	0	0	0	1.000	2	/C	0.1
Total	10	786	2216	268	546	111	5	93	320	215	420	.246	.317	.427	103	15	6	289	24	21	-5	.985	-19	C1/O	-1.4
■ JOE OLIVER Oliver, Joseph Melton b: 7/24/65, Memphis, Tenn. BR/TR, 6'3", 215 lbs. Deb: 7/15/89																									
1989	Cin-N	49	151	13	41	8	0	3	23	6	28	.272	.304	.384	92	-1	-2	17	0	0	0	.986	-1	C	0.0
1990	*Cin-N	121	364	34	84	23	0	8	52	37	75	.231	.305	.360	79	-9	-11	40	1	1	-0	**.992**	2	*C	-0.3
1991	Cin-N	94	269	21	58	11	0	11	41	18	53	.216	.265	.379	76	-8	-10	23	0	0	0	.980	-1	C	-0.6
1992	Cin-N	143	485	42	131	25	1	10	57	35	75	.270	.321	.388	95	-1	-4	57	2	3	-1	.992	-0	*C/1	0.3
Total	4	407	1269	110	314	67	1	32	173	96	231	.247	.302	.377	86	-20	-26	137	3	4	-2	.989	-0	C/1	-0.6
■ NATE OLIVER Oliver, Nathaniel "Peewee" b: 12/13/40, St.Petersburg, Fla. BR/TR, 5'10", 160 lbs. Deb: 4/09/63																									
1963	LA-N	65	163	23	39	2	3	1	9	13	25	.239	.299	.307	80	-5	-4	14	3	4	-2	.961	5	2/S	0.4
1964	LA-N	99	321	28	78	9	0	0	21	31	57	.243	.310	.271	70	-14	-11	26	7	4	-0	.967	-10	2/S	-1.5
1965	LA-N	8	1	3	1	0	0	0	0	0	0	1.000	1.000	1.000	498	0	0	1	1	0	0	1.000	3	/2	0.3
1966	*LA-N	80	119	17	23	2	0	0	3	13	17	.193	.278	.210	41	-10	-8	7	3	3	-1	.977	11	2/S3	0.5
1967	LA-N	77	232	18	55	6	2	0	7	13	50	.237	.283	.280	67	-11	-9	18	3	2	-0	.973	-8	2S/O	-1.4
1968	SF-N	36	73	3	13	2	0	0	1	1	13	.178	.189	.205	18	-7	-7	3	0	1	-1	.950	1	2S/3	-0.7
1969	NY-A	1	1	0	0	0	0	0	0	0	0	.000	.000	.000	-99	-0	-0	0	0	0	0	.000	0	H	0.0
	Chi-N	44	44	15	7	3	0	1	4	1	10	.159	.196	.295	32	-4	-5	2	0	1	-1	1.000	11	2	0.6
Total	7	410	954	107	216	24	5	2	45	72	172	.226	.284	.268	62	-51	-44	71	17	15	-4	.969	12	2/S3O	-1.8
■ BOB OLIVER Oliver, Robert Lee b: 2/8/43, Shreveport, La. BR/TR, 6'2", 215 lbs. Deb: 9/10/65																									
1965	Pit-N	3	2	1	0	0	0	0	0	0	0	.000	.000	.000	-99	-1	-1	0	0	0	0	1.000	0	/O	0.0
1969	KC-A	118	394	43	100	8	4	13	43	21	74	.254	.295	.393	91	-6	-7	39	5	5	-2	.977	5	O1/3	-0.9
1970	KC-A	160	612	83	159	24	6	27	99	42	126	.260	.311	.451	108	4	4	82	3	3	-1	.993	-8	*13	-1.6
1971	KC-A	128	373	35	91	12	2	8	52	14	88	.244	.281	.351	79	-12	-11	34	0	0	0	.988	-0	1O/3	-2.0
1972	KC-A	16	63	7	17	2	1	1	6	2	12	.270	.292	.381	100	-0	-0	7	1	0	0	.979	3	O	0.3
	Cal-A	134	509	47	137	20	4	19	70	27	97	.269	.310	.436	127	10	13	64	4	3	-1	.994	-6	*1/O	-0.5
	Yr	150	572	54	154	22	5	20	76	29	109	.269	.308	.430	124	10	13	70	5	3	-0	.994	-3	*1O	-0.2

YEAR	TM/L	G	AB	R	H	2B	3B	HR	RBI	BB	SO	AVG	OBP	SLG	PRO+	BR	/A	RC	SB	CS	SBR	FA	FR	POS	TPR
1973	Cal-A	151	544	51	144	24	1	18	89	33	100	.265	.313	.412	111	0	5	66	1	1	-0	.952	-1	3O1D	-0.1
1974	Cal-A	110	359	22	89	9	1	8	55	16	51	.248	.282	.345	84	-10	-8	29	2	1	0	.985	-12	13/OD	-2.5
	Bal-A	9	20	1	3	2	0	0	4	0	5	.150	.150	.250	14	-2	-2	1	1	1	-0	.974	1	/1D	-0.2
	Yr	119	379	23	92	11	1	8	59	16	56	.243	.275	.340	81	-12	-10	30	3	2	-0	.984	-11	13/OD	-2.7
1975	NY-A	18	38	3	5	1	0	0	1	1	9	.132	.154	.158	-12	-6	-5	1	0	0	0	1.000	-0	/13D	-0.6
Total	8	847	2914	293	745	102	19	94	419	156	562	.256	.298	.400	100	-23	-12	322	17	14	-3	.991	-18	1O3/D	-8.1
■ **TOM OLIVER**	Oliver, Thomas Noble "Rebel" b: 1/15/03, Montgomery, Ala. d: 2/26/88, Montgomery, Ala. BR/TR, 6', 168 lbs. Deb: 4/14/30 C																								
1930	Bos-A	154	646	86	189	34	2	0	46	42	25	.293	.339	.351	78	-23	-20	77	6	6	-2	.982	15	*O	-1.6
1931	Bos-A	148	586	52	162	35	5	0	70	25	17	.276	.307	.353	77	-24	-19	62	4	6	-2	**.993**	13	*O	-1.7
1932	Bos-A	122	455	39	120	23	3	0	37	25	12	.264	.305	.327	66	-24	-23	45	1	6	-3	.983	8	*O	-2.3
1933	Bos-A	90	244	25	63	9	1	0	23	13	7	.258	.296	.303	60	-14	-14	22	1	1	-0	.985	-1	O	-1.8
Total	4	514	1931	202	534	101	11	0	176	105	61	.277	.316	.340	73	-86	-76	206	12	19	-8	.986	35	O	-7.4
■ **LUIS OLMO**	Olmo, Luis Francisco (Rodriguez) (b: Luis Francisco Rodriquez (Olmo)) b: 8/11/19, Arecibo, P.R. BR/TR, 5'11.5", 190 lbs. Deb: 7/23/43																								
1943	Bro-N	57	238	39	72	6	4	4	37	8	20	.303	.325	.412	112	2	2	29	3			.957	-2	O	-0.2
1944	Bro-N	136	520	65	134	20	5	9	85	17	37	.258	.284	.367	84	-14	-13	53	10			.971	-8	O23	-2.3
1945	Bro-N	141	556	62	174	27	**13**	10	110	36	33	.313	.356	.462	127	17	18	90	15			.971	-9	*O3/2	0.4
1949	*Bro-N	38	105	15	32	4	1	1	14	5	11	.305	.336	.390	91	-1	-2	12	2			.950	-4	O	-0.7
1950	Bos-N	69	154	23	35	7	1	5	22	18	23	.227	.308	.383	86	-5	-3	17	3			.974	-9	O/3	-1.3
1951	Bos-N	21	56	4	11	1	1	0	4	4	4	.196	.250	.250	38	-5	-5	4	0	1	-1	1.000	-3	O	-0.9
Total	6	462	1629	208	458	65	25	29	272	88	128	.281	.319	.405	102	-5	-2	204	33	1		.968	-34	O/32	-5.0
■ **BARNEY OLSEN**	Olsen, Bernard Charles b: 9/11/19, Everett, Mass. d: 3/30/77, Everett, Mass. BR/TR, 5'11", 179 lbs. Deb: 4/17/41																								
1941	Chi-N	24	73	13	21	6	1	1	4	4	11	.288	.325	.438	118	1	1	10	0			.947	1	O	0.1
■ **GREG OLSON**	Olson, Gregory William b: 9/6/60, Marshall, Minn. BR/TR, 6', 200 lbs. Deb: 6/27/89																								
1989	Min-A	3	2	0	1	0	0	0	0	0	0	.500	.500	.500	171	0	0	1	0	0	0	1.000	0	/C	0.0
1990	Atl-N★	100	298	36	78	12	1	7	36	30	51	.262	.333	.379	90	-2	-4	37	1	1	-0	.987	-7	C/3	-0.5
1991	*Atl-N	133	411	46	99	25	0	6	44	44	48	.241	.319	.345	82	-7	-10	45	1	1	-0	.995	2	*C	-0.1
1992	Atl-N	95	302	27	72	14	2	3	27	34	31	.238	.318	.328	77	-6	-9	32	2	1	0	.998	8	C	0.4
Total	4	331	1013	109	250	51	3	16	107	108	130	.247	.323	.350	83	-14	-22	114	4	3	-1	.994	4	C/3	-0.2
■ **IVY OLSON**	Olson, Ivan Massie b: 10/14/1885, Kansas City, Mo. d: 9/1/65, Inglewood, Cal. BR/TR, 5'10.5", 175 lbs. Deb: 4/12/11 C																								
1911	Cle-A	140	545	89	142	20	8	1	50	34		.261	.311	.332	78	-16	-17	63	20			.909	-16	*S/3	-2.4
1912	Cle-A	125	467	68	118	13	1	0	33	21		.253	.291	.285	63	-22	-24	45	16			.917	6	S32/O	-1.3
1913	Cle-A	104	370	47	92	13	3	0	32	22	28	.249	.296	.300	72	-12	-14	35	7			.953	4	31/2	-1.0
1914	Cle-A	89	310	22	75	6	2	1	20	13	24	.242	.275	.284	65	-13	-14	26	15	9	-1	.942	12	S23/O1	-0.1
1915	Cin-N	63	207	18	48	5	4	0	14	12	13	.232	.274	.295	71	-7	-8	18	10	6	-1	.938	13	23/1	0.6
	Bro-N	18	26	2	2	0	1	0	3	1	0	.077	.111	.154	-20	-4	-4	1	0			.909	-1	/S23O	-0.5
	Yr	81	233	20	50	5	5	0	17	13	13	.215	.256	.279	61	-11	-11	18	10	6	-1	.938	12	23/1SO	0.1
1916	*Bro-N	108	351	29	89	13	4	1	38	21	27	.254	.298	.322	88	-4	-5	40	14			.920	-12	*S/21	-1.4
1917	Bro-N	139	580	64	156	18	5	2	38	14	34	.269	.291	.328	87	-9	-10	55	6			.941	-6	*S/3	-1.1
1918	Bro-N	126	506	63	121	16	4	1	17	27	18	.239	.286	.292	77	-14	-14	46	21			.918	-25	*S	-3.8
1919	Bro-N	140	590	73	**164**	14	9	1	38	30	12	.278	.316	.337	94	-3	-4	67	26			.947	-2	*S	0.3
1920	*Bro-N	143	637	71	162	13	11	1	46	20	19	.254	.278	.314	68	-26	-28	54	4	7	-3	.935	-7	*S2	-2.9
1921	Bro-N	151	652	88	174	22	10	3	35	28	26	.267	.301	.345	68	-28	-31	66	4	9	-4	.943	5	*S2	-1.7
1922	Bro-N	136	551	63	150	26	6	1	47	25	10	.272	.306	.347	69	-27	-26	58	8	5	-1	.960	-6	2S	-2.3
1923	Bro-N	82	292	33	76	11	1	1	35	14	10	.260	.296	.315	63	-16	-15	29	5	0	2	.974	5	2/31S	-0.7
1924	Bro-N	10	27	0	6	1	0	0	0	3	1	.222	.300	.259	53	-2	-2	2	0	0	0	.941	-2	/S2	-0.3
Total	14	1574	6111	730	1575	191	69	13	446	285	222	.258	.295	.318	74	-203	-216	605	156	36		.932	-34	*S23/1O	-18.6
■ **KARL OLSON**	Olson, Karl Arthur "Ole" b: 7/6/30, Kentfield, Cal. BR/TR, 6'3", 205 lbs. Deb: 6/30/51																								
1951	Bos-A	5	10	0	1	0	0	0	0	0	3	.100	.100	.100	-42	-2	-2	0	0	0	0	1.000	-1	/O	-0.3
1953	Bos-A	25	57	5	7	2	0	1	6	1	9	.123	.138	.211	-7	-9	-9	1	0	0	0	.970	-4	O	-1.4
1954	Bos-A	101	227	25	59	12	2	1	20	12	23	.260	.297	.344	68	-8	-11	21	2	1	0	.957	-8	O	-2.2
1955	Bos-A	26	48	7	12	1	2	0	1	1	10	.250	.265	.354	60	-3	-3	4	0	0	0	1.000	-5	O	-0.8
1956	Was-A	106	313	34	77	10	2	4	22	28	41	.246	.310	.329	69	-14	-14	30	1	1	-0	.990	-10	*O	-2.8
1957	Was-A	8	12	2	2	0	0	0	0	1	2	.167	.231	.167	10	-1	-1	1	0	0	0	1.000	-1	/O	-0.2
	Det-A	8	14	1	2	0	0	0	1	0	6	.143	.143	.143	-21	-2	-2	0	0	0	0	1.000	-1	/O	-0.4
	Yr	16	26	3	4	0	0	0	1	1	8	.154	.185	.154	-6	-4	-4	1	0	0	0	1.000	-2	O	-0.6
Total	6	279	681	74	160	25	6	6	50	43	94	.235	.281	.316	57	-40	-44	56	3	2	-0	.979	-28	O	-8.1
■ **MARV OLSON**	Olson, Marvin Clement "Sparky" b: 5/28/07, Gayville, S.Dak. BR/TR, 5'7", 160 lbs. Deb: 9/13/31																								
1931	Bos-A	15	53	8	10	1	0	0	5	9	3	.189	.306	.208	40	-5	-4	4	0	0	0	.963	3	2	0.0
1932	Bos-A	115	403	58	100	14	6	0	25	61	26	.248	.347	.313	74	-15	-13	47	1	5	-3	.955	-15	*2/3	-2.4
1933	Bos-A	3	1	1	0	0	0	0	0	0	1	.000	.000	.000	-99	-0	-0	0	0	0	0	.000	0	/2	0.0
Total	3	133	457	67	110	15	6	0	30	70	30	.241	.342	.300	70	-20	-17	51	1	5	-3	.956	-12	2/3	-2.4
■ **TOM O'MALLEY**	O'Malley, Thomas Patrick b: 12/25/60, Orange, N.J. BL/TR, 6', 190 lbs. Deb: 5/08/82																								
1982	SF-N	92	291	26	80	12	4	2	27	33	39	.275	.351	.364	100	1	1	35	0	3	-2	.965	0	3/2S	-0.3
1983	SF-N	135	410	40	106	16	1	5	45	52	47	.259	.348	.339	94	-3	-2	49	2	4	-2	.940	1	*3	-0.5
1984	SF-N	13	25	2	3	0	0	0	0	2	2	.120	.185	.120	-13	-4	-4	1	0	0	0	1.000	-0	/3	-0.4
	Chi-A	12	16	0	2	0	0	0	3	0	5	.125	.125	.125	-29	-3	-3	0	0	0	0	1.000	-2	/3	-0.5
1985	Bal-A	8	14	1	1	0	0	1	2	0	2	.071	.071	.286	-8	-2	-2	0	0	0	0	.833	-1	/3	-0.3
1986	Bal-A	56	181	19	46	9	0	1	18	17	21	.254	.318	.320	76	-6	-6	18	0	1	-1	.938	-1	3	-0.9
1987	Tex-A	45	117	10	32	8	0	1	12	15	9	.274	.356	.368	92	-1	-1	14	0	0	0	.962	-4	3/2	-0.6
1988	Mon-N	14	27	3	7	0	0	0	2	3	4	.259	.333	.259	69	-1	-1	3	0	0	0	.905	1	/3	0.0
1989	NY-N	9	11	2	6	2	0	0	8	0	2	.545	.545	.727	274	2	2	4	0	0	0	1.000	-0	/3	0.2
1990	NY-N	82	121	14	27	7	0	3	14	11	20	.223	.288	.355	76	-4	-4	13	0	0	0	.983	2	3/1	-0.2
Total	9	466	1213	117	310	54	5	13	131	133	151	.256	.332	.340	87	-21	-19	136	2	8	-4	.951	-5	3/12S	-3.5
■ **OLLIE O'MARA**	O'Mara, Oliver Edward b: 3/8/1891, St.Louis, Mo. d: 10/24/89, Reno, Nev. BR/TR, 5'9", 155 lbs. Deb: 9/08/12																								
1912	Det-A	1	4	0	0	0	0	0	0	0		.000	.000	.000	-99	-1	-1	0	0			.857	0	/S	-0.1
1914	Bro-N	67	247	41	65	10	2	1	7	16	26	.263	.316	.332	91	-2	-3	29	14			.918	-12	S	-1.1
1915	Bro-N	149	577	77	141	26	3	0	31	51	40	.244	.308	.300	83	-10	-11	56	11	12	-4	.906	-34	*S	-4.2
1916	*Bro-N	72	193	18	39	5	2	0	15	12	20	.202	.249	.249	52	-11	-11	15	10			.898	-5	S	-1.6
1918	Bro-N	121	450	29	96	8	1	1	24	7	18	.213	.242	.242	48	-28	-28	29	11			.951	-2	*3	-3.1
1919	Bro-N	2	7	1	0	0	0	0	0	0	0	.000	.000	.000	-98	-2	-2	-0	0			.875	-0	/3	-0.2
Total	6	412	1478	166	341	49	8	2	77	86	104	.231	.280	.279	69	-54	-56	129	46	12		.907	-53	S3	-10.3
■ **TOM O'MEARA**	O'Meara, Thomas Edward b: 12/12/1872, Chicago, Ill. d: 2/16/02, Fort Wayne, Ind. Deb: 9/29/1895																								
1895	Cle-N	1	1	1	0	0	0	0	0	1	0	.000	.500	.000	36	0	-0	0	0			.500	-0	/C	0.0
1896	Cle-N	12	33	5	5	0	0	0	0	5	7	.152	.263	.152	12	-4	-4	1	0			.914	-1	/C1	-0.4
Total	2	13	34	6	5	0	0	0	0	6	7	.147	.275	.147	14	-4	-4	1	0			.892	-1	/C1	-0.4

YEAR	TM/L	G	AB	R	H	2B	3B	HR	RBI	BB	SO	AVG	OBP	SLG	PRO+	BR	/A	RC	SB	CS	SBR	FA	FR	POS	TPR

■ O'NEAL   O'Neal   Deb: 10/23/1874

| 1874 | Har-n | 1 | 3 | 0 | 0 | 0 | 0 | 0 | | 0 | | .000 | .000 | .000 | -95 | -1 | -1 | 0 | | | | | | /O | -0.1 |

■ DENNY O'NEIL   O'Neil, Dennis   b: 11/22/1866, Holyoke, Mass.   d: 11/15/22, Rushville, Ind.   BL/TL, 6'2.5", 200 lbs.   Deb: 6/18/1893

| 1893 | StL-N | 7 | 25 | 3 | 3 | 0 | 0 | 0 | 2 | 4 | 0 | .120 | .241 | .120 | -2 | -4 | -4 | 1 | 3 | | | .986 | -1 | /1 | -0.4 |

■ MICKEY O'NEIL   O'Neil, George Michael   b: 4/12/1900, St.Louis, Mo.   d: 4/8/64, St.Louis, Mo.   BR/TR, 5'10", 185 lbs.   Deb: 9/12/19   C

1919	Bos-N	11	28	3	6	0	0	0	1	1	7	.214	.241	.214	39	-2	-2	2	0			.981	3	C	0.2
1920	Bos-N	112	304	19	86	5	4	0	28	20	21	.283	.339	.326	96	-3	-1	35	4	4	-1	.962	8	*C/2	1.3
1921	Bos-N	98	277	26	69	9	4	2	29	23	21	.249	.307	.332	73	-12	-10	29	2	2	-1	.968	8	C	0.1
1922	Bos-N	83	251	18	56	5	2	0	26	14	11	.223	.267	.259	38	-24	-22	18	1	0	0	.978	8	C	-1.7
1923	Bos-N	96	306	29	65	7	4	0	20	17	14	.212	.258	.261	39	-28	-26	21	3	2	-0	.973	14	C	-0.8
1924	Bos-N	106	362	32	89	4	1	0	22	14	27	.246	.276	.262	47	-28	-26	26	4	3	-1	.985	1	*C	-1.9
1925	Bos-N	70	222	29	57	6	5	2	30	21	16	.257	.327	.356	81	-8	-6	26	1	2	-1	.972	-8	C	-1.1
1926	Bro-N	75	201	19	42	5	3	0	20	23	8	.209	.293	.264	52	-14	-13	17	3			.965	-3	C	-1.2
1927	Was-A	5	6	0	0	0	0	0	0	0	1	.000	.000	.000	-99	-2	-2	0	0	0	0	1.000	-0	/C	-0.2
	NY-N	16	38	2	5	0	0	0	3	5	2	.132	.233	.132	-0	-5	-5	1	0			.969	3	C	-0.1
Total	9	672	1995	177	475	41	23	4	179	139	127	.238	.292	.288	58	-125	-113	175	18	13		.972	26	C/2	-5.4

■ JOHN O'NEIL   O'Neil, John Francis   b: 4/19/20, Shelbiana, Ky.   BR/TR, 5'9", 155 lbs.   Deb: 4/16/46

| 1946 | Phi-N | 46 | 94 | 12 | 25 | 3 | 0 | 0 | 9 | 5 | 12 | .266 | .303 | .298 | 73 | -4 | -3 | 9 | 0 | | | .940 | 4 | S | 0.2 |

■ FRED O'NEILL   O'Neill, Frederick James "Tip"   b: 1865, London, Ontario, Canada   d: 3/7/1892, London, Ont., Can.   5'7", 142 lbs.   Deb: 5/03/1887

| 1887 | NY-a | 6 | 26 | 4 | 8 | 1 | 1 | 0 | | 1 | | .308 | .357 | .423 | 125 | 1 | 1 | 5 | 3 | | | .800 | -1 | /O | -0.1 |

■ HARRY O'NEILL   O'Neill, Harry Mink   b: 5/8/17, Philadelphia, Pa.   d: 3/6/45, Iwo Jima, Marianas Islands   BR/TR, 6'3", 205 lbs.   Deb: 7/23/39

| 1939 | Phi-A | 1 | 0 | 0 | 0 | 0 | 0 | 0 | 0 | 0 | 0 | — | — | — | — | 0 | 0 | 0 | 0 | 0 | 0 | .000 | 0 | /C | 0.0 |

■ TIP O'NEILL   O'Neill, James Edward   b: 5/25/1858, Woodstock, Ont., Canada   d: 12/31/15, Montreal, Que., Can   BR/TR, 6'1.5", 167 lbs.   Deb: 5/05/1883

1883	NY-N	23	76	8	15	3	0	0	5	3	15	.197	.228	.237	42	-5	-5	4				.917	-2	P/O	-0.2
1884	StL-a	78	297	49	82	13	11	3		12		.276	.324	.424	135	12	11	40				.811	-6	OP/1	0.1
1885	*StL-a	52	206	44	72	7	4	3		13		.350	.399	.466	168	18	16	39				.881	-1	O	1.2
1886	*StL-a	138	579	106	190	28	14	3		47		.328	.385	.440	153	40	36	104	9			.927	8	*O	3.5
1887	*StL-a	124	517	167	225	52	19	14		50		.435	.490	.691	208	88	78	194	30			.895	-6	*O	5.5
1888	*StL-a	130	529	96	177	24	10	5	98	44		.335	.390	.446	155	42	33	105	26			.937	-1	O	2.6
1889	StL-a	134	534	123	179	33	8	9	110	72	37	.335	.419	.478	139	42	29	122	28			.936	-2	*O	2.0
1890	Chi-P	137	577	112	174	20	16	3	75	65	36	.302	.377	.407	107	10	6	102	29			.926	-12	*O	-0.9
1891	StL-a	129	521	112	167	28	4	10	95	62	33	.321	.402	.447	127	32	18	106	25			.935	-13	*O	0.1
1892	Cin-N	109	419	63	105	14	6	2	52	53	25	.251	.339	.327	105	3	4	52	14			.922	-3	*O	-0.4
Total	10	1054	4255	880	1386	222	92	52	435	421	146	.326	.392	.458	142	281	225	869	161			.917	-38	*O/P1	13.5

■ JIM O'NEILL   O'Neill, James Leo   b: 2/23/1893, Minooka, Pa.   d: 9/5/76, Chambersburg, Pa.   BR/TR, 5'10.5", 165 lbs.   Deb: 4/15/20   F

1920	Was-A	86	294	27	85	17	7	1	40	13	30	.289	.324	.405	95	-4	-3	38	7	3	0	.943	-5	S/2	-0.1
1923	Was-A	23	33	6	9	1	0	0	3	1	3	.273	.294	.303	60	-2	-2	3	0	0	0	.946	3	/23SO	0.1
Total	2	109	327	33	94	18	7	1	43	14	33	.287	.321	.394	91	-6	-5	41	7	3	0	.943	-3	/S23O	0.0

■ JOHN O'NEILL   O'Neill, John J.   b: New York, N.Y.   TR ,   Deb: 9/06/1899

1899	NY-N	2	7	0	0	0	0	0	0	0	0	.000	.000	.000	-99	-2	-2	0	0			.929	1	/C	-0.1
1902	NY-N	2	8	0	0	0	0	0	0	0	0	.000	.000	.000	-99	-2	-2	0	0			.933	1	/C	-0.1
Total	2	4	15	0	0	0	0	0	0	0	0	.000	.000	.000	-99	-4	-4	0	0			.931	2	/C	-0.2

■ JACK O'NEILL   O'Neill, John Joseph   b: 1/10/1873, Galway, Ireland   d: 6/29/35, Scranton, Pa.   BR/TR, 5'10", 165 lbs.   Deb: 4/21/02   F

1902	StL-N	63	192	13	27	1	1	0	12	13		.141	.211	.156	14	-19	-18	7	2			.973	1	C	-1.2
1903	StL-N	75	246	23	58	9	1	0	27	13		.236	.285	.280	64	-12	-11	24	11			.972	16	C	1.2
1904	Chi-N	51	168	8	36	5	0	1	19	6		.214	.258	.262	61	-8	-8	12	1			.981	5	C	0.3
1905	Chi-N	53	172	16	34	4	2	0	12	8		.198	.277	.244	54	-9	-10	14	6			.974	7	C	0.2
1906	Bos-N	61	167	14	30	5	1	0	4	12		.180	.243	.222	46	-11	-10	10	0			.971	12	C/1O	0.7
Total	5	303	945	74	185	24	5	1	74	52		.196	.256	.235	49	-59	-57	68	20			.974	40	C/1O	1.2

■ MIKE O'NEILL   O'Neill, Michael Joyce (a.k.a. Michael Joyce In 1901)   b: 9/7/1877, Galway, Ireland   d: 8/12/59, Scranton, Pa.   BR/TR, 5'11", 185 lbs.   Deb: 9/20/01   F

1901	StL-N	6	15	3	6	0	0	0	2	3		.400	.526	.400	180	2	2	3	0			.875	-1	/P	0.0
1902	StL-N	51	135	21	43	5	3	2	15	2		.319	.333	.444	145	5	6	21	0			.920	-0	P/O	0.0
1903	StL-N	41	110	12	25	2	2	0	6	8		.227	.303	.282	70	-5	-4	11	3			.882	4	PO	-0.3
1904	StL-N	30	91	9	21	7	2	0	16	5		.231	.286	.352	101	-1	-0	10	0			.910	1	P/O	0.0
1907	Cin-N	9	29	5	2	0	0	0	2	2		.069	.129	.207	5	-3	-3	1	1			.864	-0	/O	-0.5
Total	5	137	380	50	97	14	9	2	41	20		.255	.306	.355	102	-1	0	45	4			.907	-1	/PO	-0.8

■ PAUL O'NEILL   O'Neill, Paul Andrew   b: 2/25/63, Columbus, Ohio   BL/TL, 6'4", 205 lbs.   Deb: 9/03/85

1985	Cin-N	5	12	1	4	1	0	0	1	0	0	.333	.333	.417	103	0	0	2	0	0	0	1.000	1	/O	0.1
1986	Cin-N	3	2	0	0	0	0	0	0	0	1	.000	.333	.000	-0	-0	-0	0	0	0	0	.000	0	/H	0.0
1987	Cin-N	84	160	24	41	14	1	7	28	18	29	.256	.331	.488	109	3	2	26	2	1	0	.949	-3	O/1P	-0.3
1988	Cin-N	145	485	58	122	25	3	16	73	38	65	.252	.309	.414	102	2	0	61	8	6	-1	.984	1	*O1	-0.6
1989	Cin-N	117	428	49	118	24	2	15	74	46	64	.276	.349	.446	122	14	12	69	20	5	3	.983	4	*O	1.8
1990	*Cin-N	145	503	59	136	28	0	16	78	53	103	.270	.342	.421	104	6	3	69	13	11	-3	.993	6	*O	0.4
1991	Cin-N★	152	532	71	136	36	0	28	91	73	107	.256	.347	.481	126	21	18	89	12	7	-1	.994	13	*O	2.9
1992	Cin-N	148	496	59	122	19	1	14	66	77	85	.246	.350	.373	100	5	2	67	6	3	0	.997	15	*O	1.5
Total	8	799	2618	321	679	147	7	96	411	306	456	.259	.339	.431	110	51	38	383	61	33	-2	.988	37	O/1P	5.8

■ PEACHES O'NEILL   O'Neill, Philip Bernard   b: 8/30/1879, Anderson, Ind.   d: 8/2/55, Anderson, Ind.   BR/TR, 5'11", 165 lbs.   Deb: 4/16/04

| 1904 | Cin-N | 8 | 15 | 0 | 4 | 0 | 0 | 0 | 1 | 1 | | .267 | .313 | .267 | 73 | -0 | -0 | 1 | 0 | | | .900 | -3 | /C1 | -0.4 |

■ STEVE O'NEILL   O'Neill, Stephen Francis   b: 7/6/1891, Minooka, Pa.   d: 1/26/62, Cleveland, Ohio   BR/TR, 5'10", 165 lbs.   Deb: 9/18/11   FMC

1911	Cle-A	9	27	1	4	1	0	0	1	4		.148	.281	.185	31	-2	-2	2	2			.986	4	/C	0.2
1912	Cle-A	69	215	17	49	4	0	0	14	12		.228	.272	.247	47	-14	-15	15	2			.961	9	C	0.0
1913	Cle-A	80	234	19	69	13	3	0	29	10	24	.295	.329	.376	103	1	0	30	5			.973	3	C	1.1
1914	Cle-A	87	269	28	68	12	0	0	20	15	35	.253	.292	.312	79	-7	-8	24	1	3	-2	.956	5	C/1	-0.2
1915	Cle-A	121	386	32	91	14	2	1	34	26	41	.236	.293	.298	75	-12	-13	35	2	3	-1	.968	5	*C	0.1
1916	Cle-A	130	378	30	89	23	0	0	29	24	33	.235	.288	.296	71	-12	-15	35	2			.971	5	*C	-0.1
1917	Cle-A	129	370	21	68	10	2	0	29	41	55	.184	.272	.222	47	-21	-24	24	2			.980	1	*C	-1.4
1918	Cle-A	114	359	34	87	8	7	1	35	48	22	.242	.343	.312	89	0	-3	39	5			.983	1	*C	0.8
1919	Cle-A	125	398	46	115	35	7	2	47	48	21	.289	.373	.427	117	13	10	63	4			.977	-7	*C	1.4
1920	*Cle-A	149	489	63	157	39	5	3	55	69	39	.321	.408	.440	121	20	17	91	3	5	-0	.976	-8	*C	1.8
1921	Cle-A	106	335	39	108	22	1	1	50	57	22	.322	.424	.403	110	9	8	61	0	1	-1	.982	3	*C	1.6
1922	Cle-A	133	392	33	122	27	4	0	65	73	25	.311	.423	.416	118	15	14	74	2	2	-1	.974	-14	*C	0.6
1923	Cle-A	113	330	31	82	12	0	0	50	64	34	.248	.374	.285	75	-9	-9	39	0	4	-2	.968	-12	*C	-1.7

YEAR	TM/L	G	AB	R	H	2B	3B	HR	RBI	BB	SO	AVG	OBP	SLG	PRO+	BR	/A	RC	SB	CS	SBR	FA	FR	POS	TPR
1924	Bos-A	106	307	29	73	15	1	0	38	63	23	.238	.371	.293	73	-10	-10	38	0	2	-1	.970	0	C	-0.5
1925	NY-A	35	91	7	26	5	0	1	13	10	3	.286	.363	.374	89	-2	-1	13	0	0	0	.946	3	C	0.3
1927	StL-A	74	191	14	44	7	0	1	22	20	6	.230	.303	.283	51	-13	-14	17	0	3	-2	.983	1	C	-1.1
1928	StL-A	10	24	4	7	1	0	0	6	8	0	.292	.485	.333	115	2	1	5	0	0	0	.958	-4	C	-0.2
Total	17	1590	4795	448	1259	248	34	13	537	592	383	.263	.349	.337	88	-42	-63	604	30	23		.972	-9	*C/1	2.7

■ BILL O'NEILL O'Neill, William John b: 1/22/1880, St.John, N.B., Can. d: 7/27/20, St.John, N.B., Can BB/TR, 5'11", 175 lbs. Deb: 5/07/04

YEAR	TM/L	G	AB	R	H	2B	3B	HR	RBI	BB	SO	AVG	OBP	SLG	PRO+	BR	/A	RC	SB	CS	SBR	FA	FR	POS	TPR
1904	Bos-A	17	51	7	10	1	0	0	5	2		.196	.226	.216	38	-3	-4	3	0			.933	-2	/OS	-0.8
	Was-A	95	365	33	89	10	1	1	16	22		.244	.294	.285	85	-6	-6	39	22			.899	-10	O/2	-2.4
	Yr	112	416	40	99	11	1	1	21	24		.238	.286	.276	79	-10	-10	41	22			.902	-12	*O/2S	-3.2
1906	*Chi-A	94	330	37	82	4	1	1	21	22		.248	.301	.276	83	-7	-6	35	19			.949	-6	O	-1.8
Total	2	206	746	77	181	15	2	2	42	46		.243	.293	.276	81	-16	-15	77	41			.921	-18	O/2S	-5.0

■ RALPH ONIS Onis, Manuel Dominguez "Curly" b: 10/24/08, Tampa, Fla. BR/TR, 5'9", 180 lbs. Deb: 4/27/35

YEAR	TM/L	G	AB	R	H	2B	3B	HR	RBI	BB	SO	AVG	OBP	SLG	PRO+	BR	/A	RC	SB	CS	SBR	FA	FR	POS	TPR
1935	Bro-N	1	1	0	1	0	0	0	0	0	0	1.000	1.000	1.000	449	0	0	1	0			.500	-0	/C	0.0

■ EDDIE ONSLOW Onslow, Edward Joseph b: 2/17/1893, Meadville, Pa. d: 5/8/81, Dennison, Ohio BL/TL, 6', 170 lbs. Deb: 8/07/12 F

YEAR	TM/L	G	AB	R	H	2B	3B	HR	RBI	BB	SO	AVG	OBP	SLG	PRO+	BR	/A	RC	SB	CS	SBR	FA	FR	POS	TPR
1912	Det-A	36	128	11	29	1	2	1	13	3		.227	.250	.289	56	-8	-8	10	3			.972	-3	1	-1.1
1913	Det-A	17	55	7	14	1	0	0	8	5	9	.255	.328	.273	77	-1	-1	5	1			.990	-1	1	-0.3
1918	Cle-A	2	6	0	1	0	0	0	0	0	1	.167	.167	.167	1	-1	-1	0	0			.000	-1	/O	-0.2
1927	Was-A	9	18	1	4	1	0	0	1	1	0	.222	.263	.278	41	-2	-2	1	0	0	0	1.000	0	/1	-0.2
Total	4	64	207	19	48	3	2	1	22	9	10	.232	.271	.280	59	-12	-11	16	4	0		.979	-5	/1O	-1.8

■ JACK ONSLOW Onslow, John James b: 10/13/1888, Scottdale, Pa. d: 12/22/60, Concord, Mass. BR/TR, 5'11", 180 lbs. Deb: 5/02/12 FMC

YEAR	TM/L	G	AB	R	H	2B	3B	HR	RBI	BB	SO	AVG	OBP	SLG	PRO+	BR	/A	RC	SB	CS	SBR	FA	FR	POS	TPR
1912	Det-A	36	69	7	11	1	0	0	4	10		.159	.284	.174	33	-6	-5	4	1			.948	1	C/O	-0.2
1917	NY-N	9	8	1	2	1	0	0	0	0	1	.250	.333	.375	121	0	0	1	0			.929	-0	/C	0.0
Total	2	45	77	8	13	2	0	0	4	10	1	.169	.289	.195	41	-6	-5	5	1			.947	0	/CO	-0.2

■ STEVE ONTIVEROS Ontiveros, Steven Robert b: 10/26/51, Bakersfield, Cal. BB/TR, 6', 185 lbs. Deb: 8/05/73

YEAR	TM/L	G	AB	R	H	2B	3B	HR	RBI	BB	SO	AVG	OBP	SLG	PRO+	BR	/A	RC	SB	CS	SBR	FA	FR	POS	TPR
1973	SF-N	24	33	3	8	0	0	1	5	4	7	.242	.324	.333	79	-1	-1	4	0	0	0	1.000	1	/1O	0.0
1974	SF-N	120	343	45	91	15	1	4	33	57	41	.265	.375	.350	99	4	2	46	0	0	0	.929	-5	31/O	-0.5
1975	SF-N	108	325	21	94	16	0	3	31	55	44	.289	.395	.366	108	8	6	50	2	0	1	.923	0	3/O1	0.7
1976	SF-N	59	74	8	13	3	0	0	5	6	11	.176	.247	.216	31	-7	-7	4	0	0	0	1.000	-2	/3O1	-1.0
1977	Chi-N	156	546	54	163	32	3	10	68	81	69	.299	.392	.423	107	17	9	92	3	3	-1	.955	-2	*3	0.5
1978	Chi-N	82	276	34	67	14	4	1	22	34	33	.243	.326	.333	75	-5	-9	31	0	2	-1	.965	10	3/1	-0.2
1979	Chi-N	152	519	58	148	28	2	4	57	58	68	.285	.365	.370	92	3	-4	69	0	1	-1	.941	-4	*3/1	-1.0
1980	Chi-N	31	77	7	16	3	0	1	3	14	17	.208	.330	.286	68	-2	-3	8	0	0	0	.929	-1	3	-0.4
Total	8	732	2193	230	600	111	10	24	224	309	290	.274	.367	.366	94	17	-6	305	5	6	-2	.982	-3	3/1O	-1.9

■ JOSE OQUENDO Oquendo, Jose Manuel (Contreras) b: 7/4/63, Rio Piedras, P.R. BB/TR, 5'10", 160 lbs. Deb: 5/02/83

YEAR	TM/L	G	AB	R	H	2B	3B	HR	RBI	BB	SO	AVG	OBP	SLG	PRO+	BR	/A	RC	SB	CS	SBR	FA	FR	POS	TPR
1983	NY-N	120	328	29	70	7	0	1	17	19	60	.213	.261	.244	41	-26	-26	19	8	9	-3	.960	6	*S	-1.4
1984	NY-N	81	189	23	42	5	0	0	10	15	26	.222	.286	.249	52	-12	-11	16	10	1	2	.972	2	S	-0.3
1986	StL-N	76	138	20	41	4	1	0	13	15	20	.297	.366	.341	97	-0	-0	17	2	3	-1	.956	-6	S2/3O	-0.5
1987	*StL-N	116	248	43	71	9	0	1	24	54	29	.286	.414	.335	99	4	3	38	4	4	-1	1.000	3	O2S/31P	0.5
1988	StL-N	148	451	36	125	10	1	7	46	52	40	.277	.352	.350	101	3	2	57	4	6	-2	.997	8	23S1O/PC	1.2
1989	StL-N	163	556	59	162	28	7	1	48	79	59	.291	.380	.372	112	14	12	81	3	5	-2	**.994**	20	*2/S1	3.8
1990	StL-N	156	469	38	118	17	5	1	37	74	46	.252	.354	.316	85	-7	-7	57	1	1	-0	**.996**	-1	*2/S	-0.5
1991	StL-N	127	366	37	88	11	4	1	26	67	48	.240	.359	.301	87	-3	-3	43	1	2	-1	.988	15	*2S/1P	1.5
1992	StL-N	14	35	3	9	3	1	0	3	5	3	.257	.350	.400	114	1	1	5	0	0	0	1.000	0	/2S	0.1
Total	9	1001	2780	288	726	94	19	12	224	380	331	.261	.351	.322	89	-26	-29	332	33	31	-9	.993	48	2S/O31PC	4.4

■ TOM ORAN Oran, Thomas b: 1845, d: 9/22/1886, St.Louis, Mo. Deb: 5/04/1875

YEAR	TM/L	G	AB	R	H	2B	3B	HR	RBI	BB	SO	AVG	OBP	SLG	PRO+	BR	/A	RC	SB	CS	SBR	FA	FR	POS	TPR
1875	RS-n	19	81	7	16	5	1	0		1		.198	.207	.284	75	-2	-1	5						O	-0.1

■ ERNIE ORAVETZ Oravetz, Ernest Eugene b: 1/24/32, Johnstown, Pa. BB/TL, 5'4", 145 lbs. Deb: 4/11/55

YEAR	TM/L	G	AB	R	H	2B	3B	HR	RBI	BB	SO	AVG	OBP	SLG	PRO+	BR	/A	RC	SB	CS	SBR	FA	FR	POS	TPR
1955	Was-A	100	263	24	71	5	1	0	25	26	19	.270	.338	.297	76	-10	-8	27	1	2	-1	.967	-3	O	-1.5
1956	Was-A	88	137	20	34	3	2	0	11	27	20	.248	.372	.299	79	-3	-3	18	1	0	0	.946	-2	O	-0.6
Total	2	188	400	44	105	8	3	0	36	53	39	.262	.350	.298	77	-13	-11	45	2	2	-1	.961	-5	/O	-2.1

■ TONY ORDENANA Ordenana, Antonio (Rodriguez) "Mosquito" b: 10/30/18, Guanabacoa, Havana, Cuba d: 9/29/88, Miami, Fla. BR/TR, 5'9", 158 lbs. Deb: 10/03/43

YEAR	TM/L	G	AB	R	H	2B	3B	HR	RBI	BB	SO	AVG	OBP	SLG	PRO+	BR	/A	RC	SB	CS	SBR	FA	FR	POS	TPR
1943	Pit-N	1	4	0	2	0	0	0	3	0	0	.500	.500	.500	183	0	0	1	0			1.000	1	/S	0.1

■ JOE ORENGO Orengo, Joseph Charles b: 11/29/14, San Francisco, Cal d: 7/24/88, San Francisco, Cal. BR/TR, 6', 185 lbs. Deb: 4/18/39

YEAR	TM/L	G	AB	R	H	2B	3B	HR	RBI	BB	SO	AVG	OBP	SLG	PRO+	BR	/A	RC	SB	CS	SBR	FA	FR	POS	TPR
1939	StL-N	7	3	0	0	0	0	0	0	0	1	.000	.000	.000	-94	-1	-1	0	0			.667	-0	/S	-0.1
1940	StL-N	129	415	58	119	23	4	7	56	65	90	.287	.383	.412	113	13	10	72	9			.952	5	23S	2.2
1941	NY-N	77	252	23	54	11	2	4	25	28	49	.214	.298	.321	73	-9	-9	24	1			.958	18	3/S2	1.1
1943	NY-N	83	266	28	58	8	2	6	29	36	46	.218	.311	.331	85	-5	-5	28	1			.992	4	1	-0.5
	Bro-N	7	15	1	3	2	0	0	1	4	2	.200	.368	.333	103	0	0	2	0			1.000	-0	/3	0.0
	Yr	90	281	29	61	10	2	6	30	40	48	.217	.315	.331	86	-5	-5	30	1			.992	4	1/3	-0.5
1944	Det-A	46	154	14	31	10	0	0	10	20	29	.201	.297	.266	58	-7	-8	13	1	1	-0	.903	6	S3/12	-0.1
1945	Chi-A	17	15	5	1	0	0	0	1	3	2	.067	.222	.067	-15	-2	-2	0	0	0	0	.923	1	/32	-0.1
Total	6	366	1120	129	266	54	8	17	122	156	219	.237	.332	.346	88	-10	-16	139	12	1		.957	35	3/12S	2.5

■ GEORGE ORME Orme, George William b: 9/16/1891, Lebanon, Ind. d: 3/16/62, Indianapolis, Ind. BR/TR, 5'10", 160 lbs. Deb: 9/14/20

YEAR	TM/L	G	AB	R	H	2B	3B	HR	RBI	BB	SO	AVG	OBP	SLG	PRO+	BR	/A	RC	SB	CS	SBR	FA	FR	POS	TPR
1920	Bos-A	4	6	4	2	0	0	0	1	3	0	.333	.556	.333	146	1	1	1	0	0	0	1.000	0	/O	0.1

■ JESS ORNDORFF Orndorff, Jesse Walworth Thayer b: 1/15/1881, Chicago, Ill. d: 9/28/60, Cardiff-By-The- Sea, Cal. BB/TR, 6', 168 lbs. Deb: 4/18/07

YEAR	TM/L	G	AB	R	H	2B	3B	HR	RBI	BB	SO	AVG	OBP	SLG	PRO+	BR	/A	RC	SB	CS	SBR	FA	FR	POS	TPR
1907	Bos-N	5	17	0	2	0	0	0	0	0		.118	.118	.118	-26	-2	-2	0	0			.900	-2	/C	-0.5

■ FRANK O'ROURKE O'Rourke, James Francis "Blackie" b: 11/28/1894, Hamilton, Ont., Can d: 5/14/86, Chatham, N.J. BR/TR, 5'10.5", 165 lbs. Deb: 6/12/12

YEAR	TM/L	G	AB	R	H	2B	3B	HR	RBI	BB	SO	AVG	OBP	SLG	PRO+	BR	/A	RC	SB	CS	SBR	FA	FR	POS	TPR
1912	Bos-N	61	196	11	24	3	1	0	16	11	50	.122	.177	.148	-10	-30	-31	6	1			.915	-7	S/3	-3.3
1917	Bro-N	64	198	18	47	7	1	0	15	14	25	.237	.294	.283	75	-5	-6	19	11			.954	7	3	0.3
1918	Bro-N	4	12	0	2	0	0	0	2	1	3	.167	.231	.167	22	-1	-1	0	0			.857	1	/2O	0.0
1920	Was-A	14	54	8	16	1	0	0	5	2	5	.296	.321	.315	71	-2	-2	6	2	1	0	.952	4	S/3	0.3
1921	Was-A	123	444	51	104	17	8	3	54	26	56	.234	.287	.329	60	-30	-27	42	6	7	-2	.922	-7	*S	-2.4
1922	Bos-A	67	216	28	57	14	3	1	17	20	28	.264	.335	.370	84	-5	-5	27	6	6	-2	.909	-11	S3	-1.2
1924	Det-A	47	181	28	50	11	2	0	19	12	19	.276	.332	.359	79	-6	-6	22	7	4	-0	.970	11	2/S	0.6
1925	Det-A	124	482	88	141	40	7	5	57	32	37	.293	.350	.436	100	-3	-1	73	5	8	-3	**.971**	15	*2/3	1.1
1926	Det-A	111	363	43	88	16	1	1	41	35	33	.242	.321	.300	62	-19	-20	37	8	6	-1	.936	10	32S	-0.6
1927	StL-A	140	538	85	144	25	3	1	39	64	43	.268	.358	.331	77	-14	-16	64	19	8	1	.955	11	*32/1	0.2
1928	StL-A	99	391	54	103	24	3	1	62	21	19	.263	.303	.348	68	-17	-19	43	10	2	2	.954	-9	3/S	-2.1
1929	StL-A	154	585	81	147	23	9	2	62	41	28	.251	.306	.332	62	-32	-35	62	14	7	0	.943	-18	*3/2S	-4.4
1930	StL-A	115	400	52	107	15	4	1	41	35	30	.268	.326	.333	65	-19	-21	44	11	9	-2	.950	10	3S/1	-0.6
1931	StL-A	8	9	0	2	0	0	0	0	0	1	.222	.222	.222	17	-1	-1	0	1	1	-0	1.000	1	/S1	-0.1
Total	14	1131	4069	547	1032	196	42	15	430	314	377	.254	.315	.333	68	-185	-191	444	101	59		.949	17	3S2/1O	-12.2

■ **JIM O'ROURKE** O'Rourke, James Henry "Orator Jim" b: 9/1/1850, Bridgeport, Conn. d: 1/8/19, Bridgeport, Conn. BR/TR, 5'8", 185 lbs. Deb: 4/26/1872 FMUH

YEAR	TM/L	G	AB	R	H	2B	3B	HR	RBI	BB	SO	AVG	OBP	SLG	PRO+	BR	/A	RC	SB	CS	SBR	FA	FR	POS	TPR
1872	Man-n	23	100	27	33	3	0	0	15	2	0	.330	.343	.360	124	2	3	13						S/C3	0.2
1873	Bos-n	57	280	79	98	22	3	1	46	14	1	.350	.381	.461	135	16	11	51						1O/C	0.9
1874	Bos-n	70	332	82	105	12	6	**5**		2		.316	.320	.434	130	13	10	47						*1	0.7
1875	Bos-n	75	364	98	106	16	8	**6**		10		.291	.310	.429	147	19	17	50						O3/1	1.5
1876	Bos-N	70	312	61	102	17	3	2	43	15	17	.327	.358	.420	156	19	18	48				.856	-3	*O/1C	1.3
1877	Bos-N	61	265	**68**	96	14	4	0	23	**20**	9	.362	**.407**	.445	162	21	20	49				.846	-0	*O/1	1.5
1878	Bos-N	60	255	44	71	17	7	1	29	5	21	.278	.292	.412	120	7	5	31				.860	4	*O/1C	0.5
1879	Pro-N	81	362	69	126	19	9	1	46	13	10	.348	**.371**	.459	174	27	28	63				.785	-9	*O1/C3	1.4
1880	Bos-N	86	363	71	100	20	11	**6**	45	21	8	.275	.315	.441	158	20	21	52				.907	-3	O1S3/C	1.7
1881	Buf-N	83	348	71	105	21	7	0	30	27	18	.302	.352	.402	139	15	16	51				.821	-20	*3O/CS1M	-0.2
1882	Buf-N	84	370	62	104	15	6	2	37	13	13	.281	.305	.370	114	6	5	43				.866	-0	*O/SC3M	0.4
1883	Buf-N	94	436	102	143	29	8	1	38	15	13	.328	.350	.438	135	19	18	69				.866	-12	OC/3SPM	0.6
1884	Buf-N	108	467	119	**162**	33	7	5	63	35	17	.347	.392	.480	167	39	36	90				.894	-9	*O1C/P3M	2.1
1885	NY-N	112	477	119	143	21	**16**	5	42	40	21	.300	.354	.442	158	30	30	77				.940	-16	*O/C	1.2
1886	NY-N	105	440	106	136	26	6	1	34	39	21	.309	.365	.402	132	18	17	72	14			.926	8	OC/1	2.6
1887	NY-N	103	397	73	113	15	13	3	88	36	11	.285	.352	.411	118	7	11	75	46			.890	-8	C3O/2	0.5
1888	*NY-N	107	409	50	112	16	6	4	50	24	30	.274	.319	.372	123	10	10	58	25			.960	-1	OC/13	0.8
1889	*NY-N	128	502	89	161	36	7	3	81	40	34	.321	.372	.438	127	18	18	96	33			.893	-9	*O/C	0.5
1890	NY-P	111	478	112	172	37	5	9	115	33	20	.360	.410	.515	136	31	24	113	23			.930	5	*O	1.9
1891	NY-N	136	555	92	164	28	7	5	95	26	29	.295	.334	.398	120	8	12	82	19			.906	-1	*OC	0.7
1892	NY-N	115	448	62	136	28	5	0	56	30	30	.304	.354	.388	128	14	15	69	16			.913	-10	*O/C1	0.0
1893	Was-N	129	547	75	157	22	5	2	95	49	26	.287	.354	.356	93	-6	-4	76	15			.927	5	O1/CM	-0.2
1904	NY-N	1	4	1	1	0	0	0	0	0		.250	.250	.250	53	-0	-0	0	0			.800	-1	/C	-0.1
Total	4 n	225	1076	286	342	53	17	12	61	28	1	.318	.335	.432	137	50	41	161	5					1/O3SC	3.3
Total	19	1774	7435	1446	2304	414	132	50	1010	481	348	.310	.355	.421	134	303	300	1214	191			.898	-80	*OC31/SP2	17.2

■ **CHARLIE O'ROURKE** O'Rourke, James Patrick b: 6/22/37, Walla Walla, Wash BR/TR, 6'2", 195 lbs. Deb: 6/16/59

YEAR	TM/L	G	AB	R	H	2B	3B	HR	RBI	BB	SO	AVG	OBP	SLG	PRO+	BR	/A	RC	SB	CS	SBR	FA	FR	POS	TPR
1959	StL-N	2	2	0	0	0	0	0	0	0	0	.000	.000	.000	-94	-1	-1	0	0	0	0	.000	0	H	-0.1

■ **QUEENIE O'ROURKE** O'Rourke, James Stephen b: 12/26/1883, Bridgeport, Conn. d: 12/22/55, Sparrows Point, Md BR/TR, 5'7", 150 lbs. Deb: 8/15/08 F

YEAR	TM/L	G	AB	R	H	2B	3B	HR	RBI	BB	SO	AVG	OBP	SLG	PRO+	BR	/A	RC	SB	CS	SBR	FA	FR	POS	TPR
1908	NY-A	34	108	5	25	1	0	0	3	4		.231	.259	.241	62	-4	-5	8	4			1.000	-6	OS/23	-1.3

■ **JOHN O'ROURKE** O'Rourke, John b: 8/23/1849, Bridgeport, Conn. d: 6/23/11, Boston, Mass. BL/TL, 6', 190 lbs. Deb: 5/01/1879 F

YEAR	TM/L	G	AB	R	H	2B	3B	HR	RBI	BB	SO	AVG	OBP	SLG	PRO+	BR	/A	RC	SB	CS	SBR	FA	FR	POS	TPR
1879	Bos-N	72	317	69	108	17	11	6	**62**	8	32	.341	.357	**.521**	181	28	27	60				.882	2	*O	2.3
1880	Bos-N	81	313	30	86	22	8	3	36	18	32	.275	.314	.425	153	16	17	43				.871	5	*O	1.9
1883	NY-a	77	315	49	85	19	5	2		21		.270	.315	.381	119	8	6	39				.856	-3	*O/1	0.2
Total	3	230	945	148	279	58	24	11	98	47	64	.295	.329	.442	150	52	50	142				.871	4	O/1	4.4

■ **JOE O'ROURKE** O'Rourke, Joseph Leo Jr. b: 10/28/04, Philadelphia, Pa. d: 6/27/90, Philadelphia, Pa. BL/TR, 5'7", 145 lbs. Deb: 4/19/29 F

YEAR	TM/L	G	AB	R	H	2B	3B	HR	RBI	BB	SO	AVG	OBP	SLG	PRO+	BR	/A	RC	SB	CS	SBR	FA	FR	POS	TPR
1929	Phi-N	3	3	0	0	0	0	0	0	0	1	.000	.000	.000	-94	-1	-1	0	0			.000	0	H	-0.1

■ **PATSY O'ROURKE** O'Rourke, Joseph Leo Sr. b: 4/13/1881, Philadelphia, Pa. d: 4/18/56, Philadelphia, Pa. BR/TR, 5'7", 160 lbs. Deb: 4/16/08 F

YEAR	TM/L	G	AB	R	H	2B	3B	HR	RBI	BB	SO	AVG	OBP	SLG	PRO+	BR	/A	RC	SB	CS	SBR	FA	FR	POS	TPR
1908	StL-N	53	164	8	32	4	2	0	16	14		.195	.263	.244	65	-7	-6	11	2			.860	-7	S	-1.4

■ **TOM O'ROURKE** O'Rourke, Thomas Joseph b: 10/1865, New York, N.Y. d: 7/19/29, New York, N.Y. TR, 5'9", 158 lbs. Deb: 5/11/1887

YEAR	TM/L	G	AB	R	H	2B	3B	HR	RBI	BB	SO	AVG	OBP	SLG	PRO+	BR	/A	RC	SB	CS	SBR	FA	FR	POS	TPR
1887	Bos-N	22	78	12	12	3	0	0	10	7	6	.154	.233	.192	20	-8	-8	5	4			.777	-5	C/O3	-1.0
1888	Bos-N	20	74	3	13	0	0	0	4	1	9	.176	.187	.176	17	-7	-7	3	2			.881	1	C/O	-0.4
1890	NY-N	2	7	1	0	0	0	0	0	1	0	.000	.125	.000	-62	-1	-1	0	0			.864	1	/C	0.0
	Syr-a	41	153	16	33	8	0	0		12		.216	.277	.268	70	-7	-5	12	2			.907	-12	C/1	-1.1
Total	3	85	312	32	58	11	0	0	14	21	15	.186	.242	.221	40	-23	-21	20	8			.867	-15	/CO13	-2.5

■ **TIM O'ROURKE** O'Rourke, Timothy Patrick "Voiceless Tim" b: 5/18/1864, Chicago, Ill. d: 4/20/38, Seattle, Wash. BL/TR, 5'10", 170 lbs. Deb: 5/27/1890

YEAR	TM/L	G	AB	R	H	2B	3B	HR	RBI	BB	SO	AVG	OBP	SLG	PRO+	BR	/A	RC	SB	CS	SBR	FA	FR	POS	TPR
1890	Syr-a	87	332	48	94	13	6	1		36		.283	.360	.367	131	8	13	53	22			.866	-11	3	0.5
1891	Col-a	34	136	22	38	1	3	0	12	15	7	.279	.359	.331	107	1	2	20	9			.879	0	3	0.3
1892	Bal-N	63	239	40	74	8	4	0	35	24	19	.310	.373	.377	125	9	8	39	12			.869	-14	S/O3	-0.3
1893	Bal-N	31	135	22	49	4	1	0	19	12	4	.363	.423	.407	121	5	5	26	5			.980	-4	O/3S	-0.1
	Lou-N	92	352	80	99	8	4	0	53	77	15	.281	.421	.327	111	7	12	59	22			.865	-21	SO/3	-0.5
	Yr	123	487	102	148	12	5	0	72	89	19	.304	.422	.349	114	12	17	85	27			.861	-25	SO3	-0.6
1894	Lou-N	55	220	46	61	3	3	0	27	23	9	.277	.351	.318	68	-12	-9	29	9			.977	-1	1O/S32	-0.8
	StL-N	18	71	10	20	4	1	0	10	8	3	.282	.354	.366	76	-3	-3	10	2			.861	-2	3	-0.4
	Was-N	7	25	4	5	2	1	0	2	2	1	.200	.259	.360	51	-2	-2	2	0			.909	1	/2S	0.0
	Yr	80	316	60	86	9	5	0	39	33	13	.272	.345	.332	69	-17	-14	42	11			.977	-2	13O/S2	-1.2
Total	5	387	1510	272	440	43	23	1	158	197	58	.291	.380	.352	108	11	26	239	81			.861	-51	3S/O12	-1.3

■ **DAVE ORR** Orr, David L. b: 9/29/1859, New York, N.Y. d: 6/3/15, Brooklyn, N.Y. BR/TR, 5'11", 250 lbs. Deb: 5/17/1883 M

YEAR	TM/L	G	AB	R	H	2B	3B	HR	RBI	BB	SO	AVG	OBP	SLG	PRO+	BR	/A	RC	SB	CS	SBR	FA	FR	POS	TPR
1883	NY-a	1	4	1	1	1	0	0		0		.250	.250	.500	131	0	0	1				1.000	0	/1	0.0
	NY-N	1	3	0	0	0	0	0	0	0	1	.000	.000	.000	-99	-1	-1	0				1.000	0	/O	-0.1
	NY-a	12	46	5	15	3	3	2		0		.326	.326	.652	200	5	5	10				.938	-2	1	0.2
1884	*NY-a	110	458	82	**162**	32	13	9		5		**.354**	.362	.539	**199**	43	**45**	92				.960	-5	*1/O	2.5
1885	NY-a	107	444	76	152	29	**21**	6		8		.342	.358	**.543**	**201**	39	45	88				.966	-3	*1/P	2.6
1886	NY-a	136	571	93	**193**	25	**31**	7		17		.338	.363	**.527**	**188**	**47**	**51**	**118**	16			**.981**	-0	*1	3.0
1887	NY-a	84	345	63	127	25	10	2		22		.368	.408	.516	166	26	29	81	17			.969	-1	1/OM	1.6
1888	Bro-a	99	394	57	120	20	5	1	59	7		.305	.330	.388	134	13	13	55	11			.979	4	*1	0.8
1889	Col-a	134	560	70	183	31	12	4	87	9	38	.327	.340	.446	132	15	19	91	12			.983	9	*1	1.7
1890	Bro-P	107	464	89	173	32	13	6	124	30	11	.373	.416	.537	147	34	29	110	10			.972	-5	*1	1.6
Total	8	791	3289	536	1126	198	108	37	270	98	50	.342	.366	.502	165	223	236	647	66			.973	-3	1/OP	13.9

■ **BILLY ORR** Orr, William John b: 4/22/1891, San Francisco, Cal d: 3/10/67, Santarium, Cal. BR/TR, 5'11", 168 lbs. Deb: 5/03/13

YEAR	TM/L	G	AB	R	H	2B	3B	HR	RBI	BB	SO	AVG	OBP	SLG	PRO+	BR	/A	RC	SB	CS	SBR	FA	FR	POS	TPR
1913	Phi-A	30	67	6	13	1	1	0	7	4	10	.194	.239	.239	41	-5	-5	4	1			.967	-2	S/132	-0.6
1914	Phi-A	10	24	3	4	1	1	0	1	2	5	.167	.231	.292	59	-1	-1	2	1	1	-0	.810	-4	/S3	-0.6
Total	2	40	91	9	17	2	2	0	8	6	15	.187	.237	.253	46	-7	-6	5	2	1		.927	-6	/S312	-1.2

■ **ERNIE ORSATTI** Orsatti, Ernest Ralph b: 9/8/02, Los Angeles, Cal. d: 9/4/68, Canoga Park, Cal. BL/TL, 5'7.5", 154 lbs. Deb: 9/04/27

YEAR	TM/L	G	AB	R	H	2B	3B	HR	RBI	BB	SO	AVG	OBP	SLG	PRO+	BR	/A	RC	SB	CS	SBR	FA	FR	POS	TPR
1927	StL-N	27	92	15	29	7	3	0	12	11	12	.315	.388	.457	122	3	3	16	2			.922	-1	O	0.1
1928	*StL-N	27	69	10	21	6	0	3	15	10	11	.304	.400	.522	137	4	4	14	0			1.000	-2	O/1	0.1
1929	StL-N	113	346	64	115	21	7	3	39	33	43	.332	.394	.460	110	6	6	62	7			.974	4	O1	0.4
1930	*StL-N	48	131	24	42	8	4	1	15	12	18	.321	.382	.466	100	1	0	23	1			.985	4	1O	0.1
1931	*StL-N	70	158	27	46	16	6	0	19	14	16	.291	.349	.468	113	4	3	26	1			.988	-5	O/1	-0.4
1932	StL-N	101	375	44	126	27	6	2	44	18	29	.336	.368	.456	117	10	9	63	5			.976	-9	O/1	-0.6
1933	StL-N	120	436	55	130	21	6	0	38	33	33	.298	.348	.374	101	4	1	58	14			.986	2	*O/1	-0.3
1934	*StL-N	105	337	39	101	14	4	0	31	27	31	.300	.353	.365	87	-3	-6	45	6			.986	-2	O	-1.1
1935	StL-N	90	221	28	53	9	3	1	24	18	25	.240	.297	.321	64	-10	-12	21	10			.975	-5	O	-1.8
Total	9	701	2165	306	663	129	39	10	237	176	218	.306	.360	.416	102	19	9	328	46			.979	-14	O/1	-3.5

■ JOHN ORSINO Orsino, John Joseph "Horse" b: 4/22/38, Teaneck, N.J. BR/TR, 6'3", 215 lbs. Deb: 7/14/61

YEAR	TM/L	G	AB	R	H	2B	3B	HR	RBI	BB	SO	AVG	OBP	SLG	PRO+	BR	/A	RC	SB	CS	SBR	FA	FR	POS	TPR
1961	SF-N	25	83	5	23	3	2	4	12	3	13	.277	.310	.506	116	1	1	13	0	0	0	.959	-3	C	0.0
1962	*SF-N	18	48	4	13	2	0	0	4	5	11	.271	.340	.313	78	-1	-1	5	0	0	0	.963	-2	C	-0.2
1963	Bal-A	116	379	53	103	18	1	19	56	38	53	.272	.352	.475	132	15	16	63	2	3	-1	.990	-6	*C/1	1.3
1964	Bal-A	81	248	21	55	10	0	8	23	23	55	.222	.293	.359	81	-7	-7	26	0	0	0	.976	1	C/1	-0.4
1965	Bal-A	77	232	30	54	10	2	9	28	23	51	.233	.315	.409	102	1	1	26	1	0	0	.987	-8	C/1	-0.4
1966	Was-A	14	23	1	4	1	0	0	0	0	7	.174	.174	.217	12	-3	-3	1	0	0	0	1.000	-0	/1C	-0.3
1967	Was-A	1	1	0	0	0	0	0	0	0	1	.000	.000	.000	-99	-0	-0	0	0	0	0	.000	0	H	0.0
Total	7	332	1014	114	252	44	5	40	123	92	191	.249	.321	.420	106	6	7	135	3	3	-1	.982	-18	C/1	-0.0

■ JOE ORSULAK Orsulak, Joseph Michael b: 5/31/62, Glen Ridge, N, J. BL/TL, 6'1", 186 lbs. Deb: 9/01/83

YEAR	TM/L	G	AB	R	H	2B	3B	HR	RBI	BB	SO	AVG	OBP	SLG	PRO+	BR	/A	RC	SB	CS	SBR	FA	FR	POS	TPR
1983	Pit-N	7	11	0	2	0	0	0	1	0	2	.182	.182	.182	1	-1	-1	0	0	1	-1	1.000	1	/O	-0.1
1984	Pit-N	32	67	12	17	1	2	0	3	1	7	.254	.275	.328	69	-3	-3	6	3	1	0	1.000	-1	O	-0.5
1985	Pit-N	121	397	54	119	14	6	0	21	26	27	.300	.344	.365	100	-1	-0	51	24	11	1	.976	-0	*O	-0.3
1986	Pit-N	138	401	60	100	19	6	2	19	28	38	.249	.300	.342	75	-13	-14	42	24	11	1	.981	-5	*O	-2.3
1988	Bal-A	125	379	48	109	21	3	8	27	23	30	.288	.333	.422	113	4	6	51	9	8	-2	.979	-6	*O	-0.5
1989	Bal-A	123	390	59	111	22	5	7	55	41	35	.285	.356	.421	122	10	11	59	5	3	-0	.985	7	*O/D	1.5
1990	Bal-A	124	413	49	111	14	3	11	57	46	48	.269	.343	.397	110	4	6	55	6	8	-3	.989	11	*O/D	1.1
1991	Bal-A	143	486	57	135	22	1	5	43	28	45	.278	.322	.358	92	-8	-6	56	6	2	1	.997	10	*O/D	0.2
1992	Bal-A	117	391	45	113	18	3	4	39	28	34	.289	.343	.381	103	1	2	52	5	4	-1	.983	4	*O/D	0.2
Total	9	930	2935	384	817	131	29	37	265	221	266	.278	.332	.381	100	-7	-0	372	82	49	-5	.985	21	O/D	-0.7

■ JORGE ORTA Orta, Jorge (Nunez) b: 11/26/50, Mazatlan, Mexico BL/TR, 5'10", 175 lbs. Deb: 4/15/72

YEAR	TM/L	G	AB	R	H	2B	3B	HR	RBI	BB	SO	AVG	OBP	SLG	PRO+	BR	/A	RC	SB	CS	SBR	FA	FR	POS	TPR
1972	Chi-A	51	124	20	25	3	1	3	11	6	37	.202	.244	.315	64	-6	-6	9	3	3	-1	.958	-0	S2/3	-0.5
1973	Chi-A	128	425	46	113	9	10	6	40	37	87	.266	.326	.376	94	-2	-4	51	8	8	-2	.969	-27	*2/S	-2.6
1974	Chi-A	139	525	73	166	31	2	10	67	40	88	.316	.368	.440	128	21	19	85	9	5	-0	.971	-13	*2D/S	1.3
1975	Chi-A†	140	542	64	165	26	10	11	83	48	67	.304	.365	.450	128	20	20	85	16	9	-1	.978	-12	*2/D	1.5
1976	Chi-A	158	636	74	174	29	8	14	72	38	77	.274	.320	.410	112	8	8	81	24	8	2	.971	2	O3D	0.8
1977	Chi-A	144	564	71	159	27	8	11	84	46	49	.282	.338	.417	105	3	3	78	4	4	-1	.970	-47	*2	-3.5
1978	Chi-A	117	420	45	115	19	2	13	53	42	39	.274	.345	.421	114	8	8	61	1	2	-1	.984	-22	*2/D	-0.7
1979	Chi-A	113	325	49	85	18	3	11	46	44	33	.262	.351	.437	111	5	5	50	1	5	-3	.978	-10	D2	-0.5
1980	Cle-A☆	129	481	78	140	18	3	10	64	71	44	.291	.384	.403	116	13	13	78	6	5	-1	.982	13	*O/D	2.0
1981	Cle-A	88	338	50	92	14	3	5	34	21	43	.272	.317	.376	100	-1	-0	38	4	3	-1	.994	4	O	0.0
1982	LA-N	86	115	13	25	5	0	2	8	12	13	.217	.297	.313	73	-4	-4	11	0	1	-1	.947	1	O	-0.4
1983	Tor-A	103	245	30	58	6	3	10	38	19	29	.237	.292	.408	85	-4	-6	28	1	2	-1	1.000	-3	DO	-1.0
1984	*KC-A	122	403	50	120	23	7	9	50	28	39	.298	.346	.457	119	10	10	63	0	1	-1	.980	-3	DO/2	0.6
1985	*KC-A	110	300	32	80	21	1	4	45	22	28	.267	.321	.383	92	-3	-4	36	2	1	0	.000	0	D	-0.4
1986	KC-A	106	336	35	93	14	2	9	46	23	34	.277	.323	.411	96	-1	-2	42	0	3	-2	.000	0	D	-0.4
1987	KC-A	21	50	3	9	4	0	2	4	3	8	.180	.226	.380	55	-3	-3	4	0	0	0	.000	0	D	-0.3
Total	16	1755	5829	733	1619	267	63	130	745	500	715	.278	.338	.412	108	65	57	800	79	60	-12	.974	-117	2DO/3S	-4.1

■ FRANK ORTENZIO Ortenzio, Frank Joseph b: 2/24/51, Fresno, Cal. BR/TR, 6'2", 215 lbs. Deb: 9/09/73

YEAR	TM/L	G	AB	R	H	2B	3B	HR	RBI	BB	SO	AVG	OBP	SLG	PRO+	BR	/A	RC	SB	CS	SBR	FA	FR	POS	TPR
1973	KC-A	9	25	1	7	2	0	1	6	2	6	.280	.333	.480	118	1	1	4	0	0	0	.983	1	/1D	0.1

■ AL ORTH Orth, Albert Lewis "Smiling Al" or "The Curveless Wonder" b: 9/5/1872, Tipton, Ind. d: 10/8/48, Lynchburg, Va. BL/TR, 6', 200 lbs. Deb: 8/15/1895 U

YEAR	TM/L	G	AB	R	H	2B	3B	HR	RBI	BB	SO	AVG	OBP	SLG	PRO+	BR	/A	RC	SB	CS	SBR	FA	FR	POS	TPR
1895	Phi-N	11	45	8	16	4	0	1	13	1	6	.356	.370	.511	127	2	2	9	0			.842	-2	P	0.0
1896	Phi-N	25	82	12	21	3	3	1	13	3	11	.256	.282	.402	82	-3	-3	10	2			.901	1	P	0.0
1897	Phi-N	53	152	26	50	7	4	1	17	3		.329	.342	.447	110	1	1	26	5			.929	0	P/O	0.0
1898	Phi-N	39	123	17	36	6	4	1	14	3		.293	.310	.431	117	1	2	18	1			.959	1	P/O	0.1
1899	Phi-N	22	62	5	13	3	1	1	5	1		.210	.222	.339	55	-4	-4	5	2			.793	-4	P/O	0.0
1900	Phi-N	39	129	6	40	4	1	1	21	2		.310	.326	.380	95	-1	-1	17	2			.943	1	P/O	0.0
1901	Phi-N	41	128	14	36	6	0	1	15	3		.281	.303	.352	88	-2	-2	15	3			.945	1	P/O	-0.1
1902	Was-A	56	175	20	38	3	2	2	10	9		.217	.259	.291	52	-11	-12	14	2			.923	-0	PO/1S	-0.4
1903	Was-A	55	162	19	49	9	7	0	11	4		.302	.323	.444	126	5	5	25	3			.920	-2	P/SO1	-0.1
1904	Was-A	31	102	7	22	3	1	0	11	1		.216	.238	.265	60	-5	-5	7	2			.816	-2	OP	-0.8
	NY-A	24	64	6	19	1	1	0	7	0		.297	.308	.344	101	0	-0	8	2			.968	1	P/O	0.0
	Yr	55	166	13	41	4	2	0	18	1		.247	.265	.295	76	-5	-5	14	4			.969	-2	PO	-0.8
1905	NY-A	55	131	13	24	3	1	1	8	4		.183	.213	.244	40	-8	-10	8	2			.940	-0	P/1O	-0.1
1906	NY-A	47	135	12	37	2	2	1	17	6		.274	.305	.341	93	0	-1	15	2			.934	0	P/O	0.1
1907	NY-A	44	105	11	34	6	0	1	13	4		.324	.355	.410	133	5	4	16	1			.920	2	P/O	0.0
1908	NY-A	38	69	4	20	1	2	0	4	2		.290	.310	.362	117	1	1	8	0			.980	-1	P	0.0
1909	NY-A	22	34	3	9	0	1	0	5	5		.265	.359	.324	115	1	1	4	1			1.000	-2	/2P	-0.1
Total	15	602	1698	183	464	61	30	12	184	51	17	.273	.298	.366	92	-20	-23	205	30			.932	-5	P/OS21	-1.4

■ JUNIOR ORTIZ Ortiz, Adalberto Colon b: 10/24/59, Humacao, P.R. BR/TR, 5'11", 176 lbs. Deb: 9/20/82

YEAR	TM/L	G	AB	R	H	2B	3B	HR	RBI	BB	SO	AVG	OBP	SLG	PRO+	BR	/A	RC	SB	CS	SBR	FA	FR	POS	TPR
1982	Pit-N	7	15	1	3	1	0	0	0	1	3	.200	.250	.267	43	-1	-1	1	0	0	0	1.000	1	/C	0.0
1983	Pit-N	5	8	1	1	0	0	0	0	1	0	.125	.222	.125	-1	-1	-1	0	0	0	0	1.000	0	/C	-0.1
	NY-N	68	185	10	47	5	0	0	12	3	34	.254	.270	.281	53	-12	-12	14	1	0	0	.965	1	C	-0.8
	Yr	73	193	11	48	5	0	0	12	4	34	.249	.268	.275	51	-13	-13	15	1	0	0	.967	1	C	-0.9
1984	NY-N	40	91	6	18	3	0	0	11	5	15	.198	.240	.231	33	-8	-8	5	1	0	0	.980	-4	C	-1.1
1985	Pit-N	23	72	4	21	2	0	1	5	3	17	.292	.320	.361	91	-1	-1	8	1	0	0	.985	1	C	0.1
1986	Pit-N	49	110	11	37	6	0	0	14	9	13	.336	.387	.391	112	2	2	16	0	1	-1	.983	-1	C	0.3
1987	Pit-N	75	192	16	52	8	1	1	22	15	23	.271	.324	.339	75	-6	-7	20	0	2	-1	.975	-0	C	-0.4
1988	Pit-N	49	118	8	33	6	0	2	18	9	9	.280	.341	.381	109	1	1	13	1	4	-2	.983	-2	C	0.0
1989	Pit-N	91	230	16	50	6	1	1	22	20	20	.217	.286	.265	61	-12	-11	17	2	2	-1	.995	-10	C	-1.9
1990	Min-A	71	170	18	57	7	1	0	18	12	16	.335	.386	.388	110	4	3	24	0	4	-2	1.000	2	C/D	0.5
1991	*Min-A	61	134	9	28	5	1	0	11	15	12	.209	.293	.261	52	-8	-9	10	0	1	-1	.995	0	C	-0.7
1992	Cle-A	86	244	20	61	7	0	0	24	12	23	.250	.296	.279	61	-12	-12	19	1	3	-2	.989	-0	C	-1.0
Total	11	625	1569	120	408	56	4	5	157	105	185	.260	.311	.310	73	-54	-55	146	7	17	-8	.985	-12	C/D	-5.1

■ JAVIER ORTIZ Ortiz, Javier Victor b: 1/22/63, Boston, Mass. BR/TR, 6'4", 220 lbs. Deb: 6/15/90

YEAR	TM/L	G	AB	R	H	2B	3B	HR	RBI	BB	SO	AVG	OBP	SLG	PRO+	BR	/A	RC	SB	CS	SBR	FA	FR	POS	TPR
1990	Hou-N	30	77	7	21	5	1	1	10	12	11	.273	.371	.403	116	2	2	12	1	1	-0	.978	-3	O	-0.2
1991	Hou-N	47	83	7	23	4	1	1	5	14	14	.277	.381	.386	123	2	3	12	0	0	0	1.000	-3	O	0.0
Total	2	77	160	14	44	9	2	2	15	26	25	.275	.376	.394	120	4	5	25	1	1	-0	.987	-6	/O	-0.2

■ JOSE ORTIZ Ortiz, Jose Luis (Irizarry) b: 6/25/47, Ponce, P.R. BR/TR, 5'9.5", 155 lbs. Deb: 9/04/69

YEAR	TM/L	G	AB	R	H	2B	3B	HR	RBI	BB	SO	AVG	OBP	SLG	PRO+	BR	/A	RC	SB	CS	SBR	FA	FR	POS	TPR
1969	Chi-A	16	11	0	3	1	0	0	2	1	0	.273	.333	.364	90	-0	-0	1	0	0	0	1.000	-2	/O	-0.3
1970	Chi-A	15	24	4	8	1	0	0	1	2	2	.333	.407	.375	113	1	1	4	1	0	0	1.000	1	/O	0.2
1971	Chi-N	36	88	10	26	7	1	0	3	4	10	.295	.347	.398	96	1	-0	12	2	2	-1	1.000	1	O	-0.1
Total	3	67	123	14	37	9	1	0	6	7	12	.301	.358	.390	99	2	0	18	3	2	-0	1.000	-0	/O	-0.2

■ ROBERTO ORTIZ Ortiz, Roberto Gonzalo (Nunez) b: 6/30/15, Camaguey, Cuba d: 9/15/71, Miami, Fla. BR/TR, 6'4", 200 lbs. Deb: 9/06/41 F

YEAR	TM/L	G	AB	R	H	2B	3B	HR	RBI	BB	SO	AVG	OBP	SLG	PRO+	BR	/A	RC	SB	CS	SBR	FA	FR	POS	TPR
1941	Was-A	22	79	10	26	1	2	1	17	3	10	.329	.354	.430	112	1	1	11	0	1	-1	.860	-2	O	-0.2
1942	Was-A	20	42	4	7	1	3	1	4	5	11	.167	.271	.405	89	-1	-1	5	0	0	0	.941	-1	/O	-0.2

YEAR	TM/L	G	AB	R	H	2B	3B	HR	RBI	BB	SO	AVG	OBP	SLG	PRO+	BR	/A	RC	SB	CS	SBR	FA	FR	POS	TPR
1943	Was-A	1	4	0	1	0	0	0	0	0	0	.250	.250	.250	48	-0	-0	0	0	1	-1	1.000	0	/O	-0.1
1944	Was-A	85	316	36	80	11	4	5	35	19	47	.253	.312	.361	96	-4	-2	38	4	1	1	.949	-3	O	-0.9
1949	Was-A	40	129	12	36	3	0	1	11	9	12	.279	.326	.326	74	-5	-5	13	0	0	0	.946	-1	O	-0.8
1950	Was-A	39	75	4	17	2	1	0	8	7	12	.227	.301	.280	52	-6	-5	7	0	0	0	1.000	-3	O	-0.8
	Phi-A	6	14	1	1	0	0	0	3	0	3	.071	.071	.071	-65	-3	-3	0	0	0	0	1.000	-1	/O	-0.4
	Yr	45	89	5	18	2	1	0	11	7	15	.202	.268	.247	34	-9	-9	6	0	0	0	1.000	-3	O	-1.2
Total	6	213	659	67	168	18	10	8	78	43	95	.255	.310	.349	84	-19	-16	75	4	3	-1	.942	-10	O	-3.4

■ JOHN ORTON Orton, John Andrew b: 12/8/65, Santa Cruz, Cal. BR/TR, 6'1", 195 lbs. Deb: 8/20/89

YEAR	TM/L	G	AB	R	H	2B	3B	HR	RBI	BB	SO	AVG	OBP	SLG	PRO+	BR	/A	RC	SB	CS	SBR	FA	FR	POS	TPR
1989	Cal-A	16	39	4	7	1	0	0	4	2	17	.179	.220	.205	21	-4	-4	2	0	0	0	.988	5	C	0.1
1990	Cal-A	31	84	8	16	5	0	1	6	5	31	.190	.244	.286	49	-6	-6	5	0	1	-1	.987	1	C	-0.4
1991	Cal-A	29	69	7	14	4	0	0	3	10	17	.203	.313	.261	60	-3	-3	6	0	1	-1	.994	8	C/D	0.5
1992	Cal-A	43	114	11	25	3	0	2	12	7	32	.219	.276	.298	62	-6	-6	10	1	1	-0	.981	7	C	0.4
Total	4	119	306	30	62	13	0	3	25	24	97	.203	.269	.275	53	-19	-19	23	1	3	-2	.987	22	C/D	0.6

■ OSSIE ORWOLL Orwoll, Oswald Christian b: 11/17/1900, Portland, Ore. d: 5/8/67, Decorah, Iowa BL/TL, 6', 174 lbs. Deb: 4/13/28

YEAR	TM/L	G	AB	R	H	2B	3B	HR	RBI	BB	SO	AVG	OBP	SLG	PRO+	BR	/A	RC	SB	CS	SBR	FA	FR	POS	TPR
1928	Phi-A	64	170	28	52	13	2	0	22	16	24	.306	.366	.406	100	1	0	26	3	1	0	.983	-1	1P	-0.3
1929	Phi-A	30	51	6	13	2	1	0	6	2	11	.255	.283	.333	56	-3	-4	5	0	0	0	1.000	-2	P/O	-0.4
Total	2	94	221	34	65	15	3	0	28	18	35	.294	.347	.389	90	-3	-3	31	3	1	0	.970	-3	/P1O	-0.7

■ FRED OSBORN Osborn, Wilfred Pearl "Ossie" b: 11/28/1883, Nevada, Ohio d: 9/2/54, Upper Sandusky, O. BL/TR, 5'9", 178 lbs. Deb: 6/08/07

YEAR	TM/L	G	AB	R	H	2B	3B	HR	RBI	BB	SO	AVG	OBP	SLG	PRO+	BR	/A	RC	SB	CS	SBR	FA	FR	POS	TPR
1907	Phi-N	56	163	22	45	2	3	0	9	3		.276	.298	.325	97	-2	-1	17	4			1.000	-4	O/1	-0.7
1908	Phi-N	152	555	62	148	19	12	2	44	30		.267	.305	.355	107	5	3	64	16			.969	2	*O	-0.1
1909	Phi-N	58	189	14	35	4	1	0	19	12		.185	.238	.217	41	-13	-13	12	6			.979	10	O	-0.6
Total	3	266	907	98	228	25	16	2	72	45		.251	.290	.321	91	-10	-11	94	26			.975	8	O/1	-1.4

■ FRED OSBORNE Osborne, Frederick W. b: Hampton, Iowa TL, Deb: 7/14/1890

YEAR	TM/L	G	AB	R	H	2B	3B	HR	RBI	BB	SO	AVG	OBP	SLG	PRO+	BR	/A	RC	SB	CS	SBR	FA	FR	POS	TPR
1890	Pit-N	41	168	24	40	8	3	1	14	6	18	.238	.269	.339	89	-5	-2	16	0			.828	1	O/P	-0.2

■ BOBO OSBORNE Osborne, Lawrence Sidney b: 10/12/35, Chattahoochee, Ga. BL/TR, 6'1", 205 lbs. Deb: 6/27/57 F

YEAR	TM/L	G	AB	R	H	2B	3B	HR	RBI	BB	SO	AVG	OBP	SLG	PRO+	BR	/A	RC	SB	CS	SBR	FA	FR	POS	TPR
1957	Det-A	11	27	4	4	1	0	0	1	3	7	.148	.233	.185	15	-3	-3	1	0	0	0	1.000	-1	/O1	-0.4
1958	Det-A	2	2	0	0	0	0	0	0	0	0	.000	.000	.000	-93	-1	-1	0	0	0	0	.000	0	H	-0.1
1959	Det-A	86	209	27	40	7	1	3	21	16	41	.191	.256	.278	44	-16	-17	15	1	0	0	.983	-1	1/O	-2.2
1961	Det-A	71	93	8	20	7	0	2	13	20	15	.215	.354	.355	88	-1	-1	13	1	0	0	.957	-2	/31	-0.4
1962	Det-A	64	74	12	17	1	0	0	7	16	25	.230	.374	.243	68	-2	-3	8	0	0	0	.857	-2	3/1C	-0.4
1963	Was-A	125	358	42	76	14	1	12	44	49	83	.212	.312	.358	87	-6	-6	42	0	0	0	.988	-3	13	-1.3
Total	6	359	763	93	157	30	2	17	86	104	171	.206	.306	.317	71	-28	-30	81	2	0	1	.987	-9	1/3OC	-4.8

■ HARRY OSTDIEK Ostdiek, Henry Girard b: 4/12/1881, Ottumwa, Iowa d: 5/6/56, Minneapolis, Minn. BR/TR, 5'11", 185 lbs. Deb: 9/10/04

YEAR	TM/L	G	AB	R	H	2B	3B	HR	RBI	BB	SO	AVG	OBP	SLG	PRO+	BR	/A	RC	SB	CS	SBR	FA	FR	POS	TPR
1904	Cle-A	7	18	1	3	0	1	0	3	3		.167	.318	.278	90	-0	-0	2	1			.946	-0	/C	0.0
1908	Bos-A	1	3	0	0	0	0	0	0	0		.000	.000	.000	-97	-1	-1	0	0			.889	0	/C	0.0
Total	2	8	21	1	3	0	1	0	3	3		.143	.280	.238	66	-1	-1	2	1			.935	-0	/C	0.0

■ CHAMP OSTEEN Osteen, James Champlin b: 2/24/1877, Hendersonville, N.C. d: 12/14/62, Greenville, S.C. BL/TR, 5'8", 150 lbs. Deb: 9/18/03

YEAR	TM/L	G	AB	R	H	2B	3B	HR	RBI	BB	SO	AVG	OBP	SLG	PRO+	BR	/A	RC	SB	CS	SBR	FA	FR	POS	TPR
1903	Was-A	10	40	4	8	0	2	0	4	2		.200	.256	.300	65	-2	-2	3	0			.938	1	S	0.0
1904	NY-A	28	107	15	21	1	4	2	9	1		.196	.218	.336	71	-4	-4	8	0			.930	-2	3/S1	-0.6
1908	StL-N	29	112	2	22	4	0	0	11	0		.196	.204	.232	41	-8	-7	5	0			.847	-6	S3	-1.6
1909	StL-N	16	45	6	9	1	0	0	7	7		.200	.308	.222	69	-2	-1	4	1			.879	-6	S	-0.8
Total	4	83	304	27	60	6	6	2	31	10		.197	.233	.276	60	-15	-14	20	1			.890	-13	/S31	-3.0

■ RED OSTERGARD Ostergard, Roy Lund b: 5/16/1896, Denmark, Wis. d: 1/13/77, Hemet, Cal. BR/TR, 5'10.5", 175 lbs. Deb: 6/14/21

YEAR	TM/L	G	AB	R	H	2B	3B	HR	RBI	BB	SO	AVG	OBP	SLG	PRO+	BR	/A	RC	SB	CS	SBR	FA	FR	POS	TPR
1921	Chi-A	12	11	2	4	0	0	0	0	0	2	.364	.364	.364	87	-0	-0	1	0	0	0	.000	0	H	0.0

■ CHARLIE OSTERHOUT Osterhout, Charles H. b: 1856, Syracuse, N.Y. d: 5/21/33, Syracuse, N.Y. TR, Deb: 6/23/1879

YEAR	TM/L	G	AB	R	H	2B	3B	HR	RBI	BB	SO	AVG	OBP	SLG	PRO+	BR	/A	RC	SB	CS	SBR	FA	FR	POS	TPR
1879	Syr-N	2	8	0	0	0	0	0	0	0	0	.000	.000	.000	-99	-2	-2	0				1.000	-0	/OC	-0.2

■ BRIAN OSTROSSER Ostrosser, Brian Leonard b: 6/17/49, Hamilton, Ont., Can BL/TR, 6', 175 lbs. Deb: 8/05/73

YEAR	TM/L	G	AB	R	H	2B	3B	HR	RBI	BB	SO	AVG	OBP	SLG	PRO+	BR	/A	RC	SB	CS	SBR	FA	FR	POS	TPR
1973	NY-N	4	5	0	0	0	0	0	0	0	2	.000	.000	.000	-99	-1	-1	0	0	0	0	1.000	-0	/S	-0.1

■ JOHNNY OSTROWSKI Ostrowski, John Thaddeus b: 10/17/17, Chicago, Ill. BR/TR, 5'10.5", 170 lbs. Deb: 9/24/43

YEAR	TM/L	G	AB	R	H	2B	3B	HR	RBI	BB	SO	AVG	OBP	SLG	PRO+	BR	/A	RC	SB	CS	SBR	FA	FR	POS	TPR
1943	Chi-N	10	29	2	6	0	1	0	3	3	8	.207	.303	.276	69	-1	-1	2	0			1.000	-2	/O3	-0.4
1944	Chi-N	8	13	2	2	1	0	0	2	1	4	.154	.214	.231	25	-1	-1	1	0			.500	-1	/O	-0.2
1945	Chi-N	7	10	4	3	2	0	0	1	0	0	.300	.300	.500	123	0	0	2	0			.750	-1	/3	-0.1
1946	Chi-N	64	160	20	34	4	2	3	12	20	31	.213	.300	.319	77	-5	-5	16	1			.934	1	3/2	-0.3
1948	Bos-A	1	1	0	0	0	0	0	0	0	1	.000	.000	.000	-95	-0	-0	0	0	0	0	.000	0	H	0.0
1949	Chi-A	49	158	19	42	9	4	5	31	15	41	.266	.333	.468	115	1	2	24	4	3	-1	.944	-4	O/3	-0.4
1950	Chi-A	21	45	9	10	1	1	2	2	9	8	.222	.364	.422	104	0	0	8	0	0	0	1.000	-1	O	-0.1
	Was-A	55	141	16	32	2	1	4	23	20	31	.227	.327	.340	75	-6	-5	17	2	0	1	.947	-0	O	-0.6
	Chi-A	1	4	1	2	1	0	0	0	0	1	.500	.500	.750	223	1	1	2	0	0	0	1.000	-0	/O	0.0
	Yr	77	190	26	44	4	2	6	25	29	40	.232	.339	.368	85	-5	-4	26	2	0	1	.958	-2	O	-0.7
Total	7	216	561	73	131	20	9	14	74	68	125	.234	.321	.376	89	-12	-10	71	7	3		.950	-9	O/32	-2.1

■ REGGIE OTERO Otero, Regino Jose (Gomez) b: 9/7/15, Havana, Cuba d: 10/21/88, Hialeah, Fla. BL/TR, 6', 165 lbs. Deb: 9/02/45 C

YEAR	TM/L	G	AB	R	H	2B	3B	HR	RBI	BB	SO	AVG	OBP	SLG	PRO+	BR	/A	RC	SB	CS	SBR	FA	FR	POS	TPR
1945	Chi-N	14	23	1	9	0	0	0	5	2	2	.391	.440	.391	135	1	1	4	0			.967	0	/1	0.1

■ AMOS OTIS Otis, Amos Joseph b: 4/26/47, Mobile, Ala. BR/TR, 5'11", 166 lbs. Deb: 9/06/67 C

YEAR	TM/L	G	AB	R	H	2B	3B	HR	RBI	BB	SO	AVG	OBP	SLG	PRO+	BR	/A	RC	SB	CS	SBR	FA	FR	POS	TPR
1967	NY-N	19	59	6	13	2	0	0	1	5	13	.220	.292	.254	59	-3	-3	4	0	4	-2	1.000	-1	O/3	-0.7
1969	NY-N	48	93	6	14	3	1	0	4	6	27	.151	.202	.204	14	-11	-11	4	1	0	0	1.000	3	O/3	-0.9
1970	KC-A★	159	620	91	176	**36**	9	11	58	68	67	.284	.356	.424	114	12	12	102	33	2	**9**	.990	14	*O	2.7
1971	KC-A★	147	555	80	167	26	4	15	79	40	74	.301	.350	.443	125	16	16	87	**52**	8	**11**	.990	20	*O	4.2
1972	KC-A†	143	540	75	158	28	2	11	54	50	59	.293	.356	.413	129	19	19	82	28	12	1	.992	10	*O	2.6
1973	KC-A★	148	583	89	175	21	4	26	93	63	47	.300	.369	.484	129	29	23	103	13	9	-2	.986	3	*OD	1.9
1974	KC-A	146	552	87	157	31	9	12	73	58	67	.284	.355	.438	120	19	15	86	18	5	2	.986	10	*O/D	2.2
1975	KC-A	132	470	87	116	26	6	9	46	66	48	.247	.344	.385	103	5	3	68	39	11	5	.988	3	*O	0.6
1976	*KC-A★	153	592	93	165	**40**	2	18	86	55	100	.279	.345	.444	129	21	21	92	26	7	4	.992	-5	*O	1.4
1977	*KC-A	142	478	85	120	20	8	17	78	71	88	.251	.348	.433	110	8	8	74	23	7	3	.991	1	*O	0.6
1978	*KC-A	141	486	74	145	30	7	22	96	66	54	.298	.387	.525	150	35	34	102	32	8	5	**.995**	10	*O/D	4.3
1979	KC-A	151	577	100	170	28	2	18	90	68	92	.295	.372	.444	117	16	15	100	30	5	6	**.992**	5	*O/D	1.9
1980	*KC-A	107	394	56	99	16	3	10	53	39	70	.251	.323	.383	92	-4	-4	52	16	1	4	.988	7	*O	0.2
1981	*KC-A	99	372	49	100	22	3	9	57	31	59	.269	.328	.417	114	6	6	51	16	7	1	.993	11	O/D	1.4
1982	KC-A	125	475	73	136	25	3	11	88	37	65	.286	.340	.421	108	5	5	64	9	5	-0	.997	-1	*O	0.0
1983	KC-A	98	356	35	93	16	3	4	41	27	63	.261	.313	.357	84	-8	-8	39	5	2	0	.996	3	O/D	-0.7
1984	Pit-N	40	97	6	16	4	0	0	10	7	15	.165	.221	.206	21	-10	-10	4	0	0	0	.964	2	O	-1.0
Total	17	1998	7299	1092	2020	374	66	193	1007	757	1008	.277	.347	.425	114	155	140	1114	341	93	47	.991	94	*O/D3	20.7

YEAR	TM/L	G	AB	R	H	2B	3B	HR	RBI	BB	SO	AVG	OBP	SLG	PRO+	BR	/A	RC	SB	CS	SBR	FA	FR	POS	TPR

■ BILL OTIS
Otis, Paul Franklin b: 12/24/1889, Scituate, Mass. d: 12/15/90, Duluth, Minn. BL/TR, 5'10.5", 150 lbs. Deb: 7/04/12

| 1912 | NY-A | 4 | 17 | 1 | 1 | 0 | 0 | 0 | 2 | 3 | | .059 | .200 | .059 | -24 | -3 | -3 | 0 | 0 | | | .917 | 1 | /O | -0.3 |

■ MEL OTT
Ott, Melvin Thomas "Master Melvin" b: 3/2/09, Gretna, La. d: 11/21/58, New Orleans, La. BL/TR, 5'9", 170 lbs. Deb: 4/27/26 MH

1926	NY-N	35	60	7	23	2	0	0	4	1	9	.383	.393	.417	120	1	1	9	1			.913	1	O	0.2
1927	NY-N	82	163	23	46	7	3	1	19	13	9	.282	.335	.380	91	-2	-2	20	2			.982	-7	O	-1.1
1928	NY-N	124	435	69	140	26	4	18	77	52	36	.322	.397	.524	138	24	24	89	3			.970	-3	*O/23	1.4
1929	NY-N	150	545	138	179	37	2	42	151	113	38	.328	.449	.635	166	58	59	157	6			.973	9	*O/2	5.2
1930	NY-N	148	521	122	182	34	5	25	119	103	35	.349	.458	.578	152	45	47	139	9			.969	6	*O	3.7
1931	NY-N	138	497	104	145	23	8	29	115	80	44	.292	.392	.545	153	35	37	111	10			.981	8	*O	3.5
1932	NY-N	154	566	119	180	30	8	38	123	100	39	.318	.424	.601	175	60	62	151	6			.984	2	*O	5.2
1933	*NY-N	152	580	98	164	36	1	23	103	75	48	.283	.367	.467	139	28	29	105	1			.983	-14	*O	0.8
1934	NY-N★	153	582	119	190	29	10	35	135	85	43	.326	.415	.591	170	55	57	150	0			.974	-9	*O	4.0
1935	NY-N★	152	593	113	191	33	6	31	114	82	58	.322	.407	.555	159	48	49	144	7			.990	6	*O3	4.8
1936	*NY-N★	150	534	120	175	28	6	33	135	111	41	.328	.448	.588	179	62	63	153	6			.985	-3	*O	5.1
1937	*NY-N★	151	545	99	160	28	2	31	95	102	69	.294	.408	.523	149	41	40	128	7			.939	-0	3O	3.8
1938	NY-N★	150	527	116	164	23	6	36	116	118	47	.311	.442	.583	178	62	61	149	2			.957	1	*3O	6.2
1939	NY-N	125	396	85	122	23	2	27	80	100	50	.308	.449	.581	173	46	45	112	2			.973	5	O3	3.6
1940	NY-N	151	536	89	155	27	3	19	79	100	50	.289	.407	.457	137	32	31	107	6			.982	2	*O3	2.8
1941	NY-N★	148	525	89	150	29	0	27	90	100	68	.286	.403	.495	149	39	37	115	5			.968	5	O	3.4
1942	NY-N★	152	549	118	162	21	0	30	93	109	61	.295	.415	.497	165	49	49	122	6			.990	-1	*OM	4.2
1943	NY-N★	125	380	65	89	12	2	18	47	95	48	.234	.391	.418	133	20	20	71	7			.975	1	*O/3M	1.5
1944	NY-N★	120	399	91	115	16	4	26	82	90	47	.288	.423	.544	171	40	41	101	2			.986	-4	*O/3M	3.2
1945	NY-N†	135	451	73	139	23	0	21	79	71	41	.308	.411	.499	150	33	33	98	1			.983	-4	*OM	2.3
1946	NY-N	31	68	2	5	1	0	1	4	8	15	.074	.171	.132	-13	-10	-10	2	0			1.000	0	OM	-1.3
1947	NY-N	4	4	0	0	0	0	0	0	0	0	.000	.000	.000	-99	-1	-1	0	0			.000	0	HM	-0.1
Total	22	2730	9456	1859	2876	488	72	511	1860	1708	896	.304	.414	.533	155	767	773	2235	89			.980	-10	*O3/2	62.4

■ ED OTT
Ott, Nathan Edward b: 7/11/51, Muncy, Pa. BL/TR, 5'10", 198 lbs. Deb: 6/10/74 C

1974	Pit-N	7	5	1	0	0	0	0	0	0	1	.000	.000	.000	-99	-1	-1	0	0	0	0	1.000	0	/O	-0.1
1975	Pit-N	5	5	0	1	0	0	0	0	0	0	.200	.200	.200	11	-1	-1	0	0	0	0	1.000	-0	/C	-0.1
1976	Pit-N	27	39	2	12	2	0	0	5	3	5	.308	.357	.359	103	0	0	5	0	0	0	1.000	-1	/C	0.0
1977	Pit-N	104	311	40	82	14	3	7	38	32	41	.264	.336	.395	93	-2	-3	41	7	7	-2	.982	-5	C	-0.8
1978	Pit-N	112	379	49	102	18	4	9	38	27	56	.269	.318	.409	97	-0	-2	49	4	1	1	.975	-9	C/O	-0.9
1979	*Pit-N	117	403	49	110	20	2	7	51	26	62	.273	.317	.385	86	-6	-8	48	0	1	-1	.994	-3	*C	-0.8
1980	Pit-N	120	392	35	102	14	0	8	41	33	47	.260	.318	.357	87	-6	-7	42	1	6	-3	.983	-3	*C/O	-1.0
1981	Cal-A	75	258	20	56	8	1	2	22	17	42	.217	.268	.279	58	-14	-14	19	2	1	0	.979	1	C	-1.1
Total	8	567	1792	196	465	76	10	33	195	138	254	.259	.314	.368	86	-30	-36	203	14	16	-5	.983	-20	C/O	-4.8

■ BILLY OTT
Ott, William Joseph b: 11/23/40, New York, N.Y. BB/TR, 6'1", 180 lbs. Deb: 9/04/62

1962	Chi-N	12	28	3	4	0	0	1	2	2	10	.143	.200	.250	19	-3	-3	1	0	0	0	1.000	0	/O	-0.4
1964	Chi-N	20	39	4	7	3	0	0	1	3	10	.179	.238	.256	38	-3	-3	2	0	1	-1	1.000	-1	O	-0.6
Total	2	32	67	7	11	3	0	1	3	5	20	.164	.222	.254	30	-6	-7	4	0	1	-1	1.000	-1	/O	-1.0

■ JOE OTTEN
Otten, Joseph G. b: Murphysboro, Ill. TR, Deb: 7/05/1895

| 1895 | StL-N | 26 | 87 | 8 | 21 | 0 | 0 | 0 | 8 | 5 | 8 | .241 | .283 | .241 | 38 | -8 | -8 | 7 | 2 | | | .947 | -4 | C/O | -0.8 |

■ BILLY OTTERSON
Otterson, William John b: 5/4/1862, Pittsburgh, Pa. d: 9/21/40, Pittsburgh, Pa. BR/TR, 5'7", 124 lbs. Deb: 9/04/1887

| 1887 | Bro-a | 30 | 100 | 16 | 20 | 4 | 1 | 2 | | 8 | | .200 | .259 | .320 | 62 | -5 | -5 | 11 | 8 | | | .859 | 1 | S | -0.4 |

■ PHIL OUELLETTE
Ouellette, Philip Roland b: 11/10/61, Salem, Ore. BB/TR, 6', 190 lbs. Deb: 9/10/86

| 1986 | SF-N | 10 | 23 | 1 | 4 | 0 | 0 | 0 | 0 | 3 | 3 | .174 | .269 | .174 | 26 | -2 | -2 | 1 | 0 | 0 | 0 | 1.000 | 0 | /C | -0.2 |

■ JOHNNY OULLIBER
Oulliber, John Andrew b: 2/24/11, New Orleans, La. d: 12/26/80, New Orleans, La. BR/TR, 5'11", 165 lbs. Deb: 7/25/33

| 1933 | Cle-A | 22 | 75 | 9 | 20 | 1 | 0 | 0 | 3 | 4 | 5 | .267 | .313 | .280 | 55 | -4 | -5 | 7 | 0 | 0 | 0 | 1.000 | -3 | O | -0.9 |

■ CHINK OUTEN
Outen, William Austin b: 6/17/05, Mt.Holly, N.C. d: 9/11/61, Durham, N.C. BL/TR, 6', 200 lbs. Deb: 4/16/33

| 1933 | Bro-N | 93 | 153 | 20 | 38 | 10 | 0 | 4 | 17 | 20 | 15 | .248 | .335 | .392 | 112 | 2 | 2 | 22 | 1 | | | .982 | -13 | C | -0.9 |

■ JIMMY OUTLAW
Outlaw, James Paulus b: 1/20/13, Orme, Tenn. BR/TR, 5'8", 168 lbs. Deb: 4/20/37

1937	Cin-N	49	165	18	45	7	3	0	11	3	31	.273	.290	.352	77	-6	-5	17	2			.914	4	3	0.0
1938	Cin-N	4	0	1	0	0	0	0	0	0	0	—	—	—	—	0	0	0	0			.000	0	R	0.0
1939	Bos-N	65	133	15	35	2	0	0	5	10	14	.263	.315	.278	65	-7	-6	13	1			.964	-3	O/3	-1.0
1943	Det-A	20	67	8	18	1	0	1	6	8	4	.269	.347	.328	91	-0	-1	8	0	0	0	1.000	0	O	-0.1
1944	Det-A	139	535	69	146	20	6	3	57	41	40	.273	.327	.350	88	-5	-8	60	7	8	-3	.964	-3	*O	-2.2
1945	*Det-A	132	446	56	121	16	5	0	34	45	33	.271	.338	.330	88	-3	-6	52	6	7	-2	.967	-4	*O3	-1.8
1946	Det-A	92	299	36	78	14	2	2	31	29	24	.261	.328	.341	82	-5	-7	33	5	4	-1	1.000	-8	O3	-1.8
1947	Det-A	70	127	20	29	7	1	0	15	21	14	.228	.338	.299	76	-3	-4	15	3	1	0	.983	-7	O/3	-1.2
1948	Det-A	74	198	33	56	12	0	0	25	31	15	.283	.383	.343	91	-0	-1	27	0	1	-1	.920	1	3O	-0.2
1949	Det-A	5	4	1	1	0	0	0	0	0	1	.250	.250	.250	32	-0	-0	0	0	0	0	.000	0	H	0.0
Total	10	650	1974	257	529	79	17	6	184	188	176	.268	.333	.334	85	-30	-39	225	24	21		.972	-19	O3	-8.3

■ MICKEY OWEN
Owen, Arnold Malcolm b: 4/4/16, Nixa, Mo. BR/TR, 5'10", 190 lbs. Deb: 5/02/37 C

1937	StL-N	80	234	17	54	4	2	0	20	15	13	.231	.277	.265	47	-17	-17	17	1			.974	-3	C	-1.7
1938	StL-N	122	397	45	106	25	2	4	36	32	14	.267	.325	.370	86	-5	-8	46	2			.980	1	*C	-0.1
1939	StL-N	131	344	32	89	18	2	3	35	43	28	.259	.344	.349	82	-6	-8	42	6			.982	4	*C	0.2
1940	StL-N	117	307	27	81	16	2	0	27	34	13	.264	.341	.329	81	-5	-7	35	4			.980	3	*C	0.2
1941	*Bro-N★	128	386	32	89	15	2	1	44	34	14	.231	.296	.288	62	-18	-20	33	1			.995	6	*C	-0.4
1942	Bro-N★	133	421	53	109	16	3	0	44	44	17	.259	.330	.311	87	-5	-6	43	10			.987	5	*C	0.9
1943	Bro-N☆	106	365	31	95	11	2	0	54	25	15	.260	.309	.301	77	-11	-11	34	4			.987	-6	*C/3S	-1.0
1944	Bro-N☆	130	461	43	126	20	3	1	42	36	17	.273	.326	.336	88	-8	-7	48	4			.979	-11	*C/2	-1.1
1945	Bro-N	24	84	5	24	9	0	0	11	10	2	.286	.368	.393	113	2	2	11	0			.963	-3	C	0.0
1949	Chi-N	62	198	15	54	9	3	2	18	12	13	.273	.318	.379	88	-4	-4	24	1			.969	-1	C	-0.1
1950	Chi-N	86	259	22	63	11	0	2	21	13	16	.243	.282	.309	56	-17	-17	21	2			.978	3	C	-1.0
1951	Chi-N	58	125	10	23	6	0	1	15	19	13	.184	.292	.232	42	-10	-10	9	1	0	0	.969	8	C	0.0
1954	Bos-A	32	68	6	16	3	0	1	9	9	6	.235	.325	.324	70	-2	-3	7	0	1	-1	.989	-2	C	-0.5
Total	13	1209	3649	338	929	163	21	14	378	326	181	.255	.318	.322	76	-106	-116	371	36	1		.982	3	*C/32S	-4.6

■ DAVE OWEN
Owen, Dave b: 4/25/58, Cleburne, Tex. BB/TR, 6'2", 170 lbs. Deb: 9/06/83 F

1983	Chi-N	16	22	1	2	0	1	0	2	2	7	.091	.167	.182	-3	-3	-3	1	1	0	0	1.000	4	S/3	0.1
1984	Chi-N	47	93	8	18	2	2	1	10	8	15	.194	.272	.290	53	-5	-6	8	1	2	-1	.969	1	S/32	-0.4
1985	Chi-N	22	19	6	7	0	0	0	4	1	5	.368	.400	.368	105	0	0	3	1	1	-0	.917	2	/S32	0.2
1988	KC-A	7	5	0	0	0	0	0	0	0	3	.000	.000	.000	-99	-1	-1	0	0	0	0	.941	4	/S	0.3
Total	4	92	139	15	27	2	3	1	16	11	30	.194	.263	.273	47	-9	-11	12	3	3	-1	.969	10	/S32	0.2

YEAR	TM/L	G	AB	R	H	2B	3B	HR	RBI	BB	SO	AVG	OBP	SLG	PRO+	BR	/A	RC	SB	CS	SBR	FA	FR	POS	TPR

■ LARRY OWEN Owen, Lawrence Thomas b: 5/31/55, Cleveland, Ohio BR/TR, 5'11", 185 lbs. Deb: 8/14/81

1981	Atl-N	13	16	0	0	0	0	0	0	1	4	.000	.059	.000	-80	-4	-4	0	0	0	0	.964	2	C	-0.2
1982	Atl-N	2	3	1	1	1	0	0	0	0	1	.333	.333	.667	167	0	0	1	0	0	0	1.000	-0	/C	0.0
1983	Atl-N	17	17	0	2	0	0	0	1	0	2	.118	.118	.118	-32	-3	-3	0	0	1	-1	.970	1	C	-0.3
1985	Atl-N	26	71	7	17	3	0	2	12	8	17	.239	.316	.366	85	-1	-1	8	0	0	0	.966	3	C	0.2
1987	KC-A	76	164	17	31	6	0	5	14	16	51	.189	.261	.317	51	-11	-12	13	0	0	0	.983	19	C	1.0
1988	KC-A	37	81	5	17	1	0	1	3	9	23	.210	.304	.259	59	-4	-4	7	0	0	0	.989	5	C	0.3
Total	6	171	352	30	68	11	0	8	30	34	98	.193	.268	.293	51	-23	-25	30	0	1	-1	.980	29	C	1.0

■ MARV OWEN Owen, Marvin James "Freck" b: 3/22/06, Agnew, Cal. d: 6/22/91, Mountain View, Cal. BR/TR, 6'1", 175 lbs. Deb: 4/16/31

1931	Det-A	105	377	35	84	11	6	3	39	29	38	.223	.282	.308	53	-25	-27	34	2	2	-1	.937	1	S31/2	-2.1
1933	Det-A	138	550	77	144	24	9	2	65	44	56	.262	.321	.349	76	-18	-19	63	2	2	-1	.944	-11	*3	-2.1
1934	*Det-A	154	565	79	179	34	9	8	96	59	37	.317	.385	.451	115	13	13	100	3	3	-1	.956	-7	*3	1.0
1935	*Det-A	134	483	52	127	24	5	2	71	43	37	.263	.326	.346	76	-19	-16	56	1	4	-2	.958	-10	*3	-2.2
1936	Det-A	154	583	72	172	20	4	9	105	53	41	.295	.361	.389	85	-13	-13	84	9	6	-1	.952	-4	*3/1	-1.1
1937	Det-A	107	396	48	114	22	5	1	45	41	24	.288	.358	.376	83	-8	-10	54	3	4	-2	.970	0	*3	-0.8
1938	Chi-A	141	577	84	162	23	6	6	55	45	31	.281	.337	.373	76	-20	-22	74	6	4	-1	.948	0	*3	-1.9
1939	Chi-A	58	194	22	46	9	0	0	15	16	15	.237	.302	.284	49	-14	-15	17	4	5	-2	.953	-2	3	-1.7
1940	Bos-A	20	57	4	12	0	0	0	6	8	4	.211	.308	.211	36	-5	-5	4	0	0	0	.962	2	/31	-0.4
Total	9	1011	3782	473	1040	167	44	31	497	338	283	.275	.339	.367	80	-110	-116	485	30	30	-9	.953	-30	3/1S2	-11.3

■ SPIKE OWEN Owen, Spike Dee b: 4/19/61, Cleburne, Tex. BB/TR, 5'10", 170 lbs. Deb: 6/25/83 F

1983	Sea-A	80	306	36	60	11	3	2	21	24	44	.196	.259	.271	44	-22	-24	23	10	6	-1	.970	-0	S	-1.7
1984	Sea-A	152	530	67	130	18	8	3	43	46	63	.245	.309	.326	77	-17	-16	56	16	8	0	.977	16	*S	1.5
1985	Sea-A	118	352	41	91	10	6	6	37	34	27	.259	.324	.372	89	-5	-5	44	11	5	0	.975	30	*S	3.5
1986	Sea-A	112	402	46	99	22	6	0	35	34	42	.246	.307	.331	73	-15	-15	40	1	3	-2	.972	34	*S	2.7
	*Bos-A	42	126	21	23	2	1	1	10	17	9	.183	.285	.238	44	-9	-10	10	3	1	0	.976	-2	S	-0.7
	Yr	154	528	67	122	24	7	1	45	51	51	.231	.301	.309	66	-24	-24	49	4	4	-1	.973	32	*S	2.0
1987	Bos-A	132	437	50	113	17	7	2	48	53	43	.259	.340	.343	80	-10	-12	52	11	8	-2	.975	-14	*S	-1.6
1988	*Bos-A	89	257	40	64	14	1	5	18	27	27	.249	.325	.370	90	-2	-3	31	0	1	-1	.967	-1	S/D	0.1
1989	Mon-N	142	437	52	102	17	4	6	41	76	44	.233	.351	.332	95	1	-0	53	3	2	-0	.979	11	*S	2.2
1990	Mon-N	149	453	55	106	24	5	5	35	70	60	.234	.337	.342	91	-6	-4	55	8	6	-1	.989	-13	*S	-0.8
1991	Mon-N	139	424	39	108	22	8	3	26	42	61	.255	.323	.366	95	-4	-3	48	2	6	-3	.986	8	*S	1.1
1992	Mon-N	122	386	52	104	16	3	7	40	50	30	.269	.353	.381	108	5	5	53	9	4	0	.982	-11	*S	0.4
Total	10	1277	4110	499	1000	173	52	40	354	473	450	.243	.323	.340	83	-84	-86	464	74	50	-8	.978	59	*S/D	6.7

■ FRANK OWENS Owens, Frank Walter "Yip" b: 1/26/1886, Toronto, Ont., Can. d: 7/2/58, Minneapolis, Minn. BR/TR, 6', 170 lbs. Deb: 9/11/05

1905	Bos-A	1	2	0	0	0	0	0	0	0	0	.000	.000	.000	-99	-0	-0	0	0			1.000	-0	/C	-0.1
1909	Chi-A	64	174	12	35	4	1	0	17	8		.201	.245	.236	54	-10	-9	11	3			.959	-6	C	-1.2
1914	Bro-F	58	184	15	51	7	3	2	20	9	16	.277	.314	.380	98	-1	-1	23	2			.967	-14	C	-1.1
1915	Bal-F	99	334	32	84	14	7	3	28	17	34	.251	.290	.362	88	-5	-6	38	4			.976	2	C	0.4
Total	4	222	694	59	170	25	11	5	65	34	50	.245	.284	.334	83	-16	-17	73	9			.969	-19	C	-2.0

■ JACK OWENS Owens, Furman Lee b: 5/6/08, Converse, S.C. d: 11/14/58, Greenville, S.C. BR/TR, 6'1", 186 lbs. Deb: 9/21/35

| 1935 | Phi-A | 2 | 8 | 0 | 2 | 0 | 0 | 0 | 1 | 0 | 1 | .250 | .250 | .250 | 30 | -1 | -1 | 0 | 0 | 0 | 0 | .900 | -0 | /C | -0.1 |

■ RED OWENS Owens, Thomas Llewellyn b: 11/1/1874, Pottsville, Pa. d: 8/20/52, Harrisburg, Pa. BR/TR, Deb: 7/28/1899

1899	Phi-N	8	21	0	1	0	0	0	1	2		.048	.130	.048	-52	-4	-4	0	0			.914	-0	/2	-0.4
1905	Bro-N	43	168	14	36	6	2	1	20	6		.214	.241	.292	63	-9	-7	13	1			.929	4	2	-0.3
Total	2	51	189	14	37	6	2	1	21	8		.196	.228	.265	49	-13	-12	13	1			.927	3	/2	-0.7

■ HENRY OXLEY Oxley, Henry Havelock b: 1/4/1858, Covehead, P.E.I., Canada. d: 10/12/45, Somerville, Mass. Deb: 7/30/1884

1884	NY-N	3	4	0	0	0	0	0	0	1	2	.000	.200	.000	-31	-1	-1	0				.900	1	/C	0.0
	NY-a	1	3	0	0	0	0	0	0	0		.000	.000	.000	-99	-1	-1	0				.889	0	/C	0.0
Total	1	4	7	0	0	0	0	0	0	1	2	.000	.125	.000	-56	-1	-1	0				.895	1	/C	0.0

■ ANDY OYLER Oyler, Andrew Paul "Pepper" b: 5/5/1880, Newville, Pa. d: 10/24/70, E.Pennsboro Twp., Cumberland County, Pa. BR/TR, 5'6.5", 138 lbs. Deb: 5/08/02

| 1902 | Bal-A | 27 | 77 | 9 | 17 | 1 | 0 | 1 | 6 | 8 | | .221 | .310 | .273 | 60 | -4 | -4 | 8 | 3 | | | .947 | -8 | 3/OS2 | -1.1 |

■ RAY OYLER Oyler, Raymond Francis b: 8/4/38, Indianapolis, Ind. d: 1/26/81, Seattle, Wash. BR/TR, 5'11", 165 lbs. Deb: 4/18/65

1965	Det-A	82	194	22	36	6	0	5	13	21	61	.186	.265	.294	58	-11	-11	14	1	0	0	.955	6	S2/13	-0.1
1966	Det-A	71	210	16	36	8	3	1	9	23	62	.171	.263	.252	48	-14	-14	14	0	0	0	.965	15	S	0.6
1967	Det-A	148	367	33	76	14	2	1	29	37	91	.207	.283	.264	61	-16	-18	28	0	2	-1	.964	15	*S	0.8
1968	*Det-A	111	215	13	29	6	1	1	12	20	59	.135	.215	.186	22	-20	-21	8	0	2	-1	.977	9	*S	-0.6
1969	Sea-A	106	255	24	42	5	0	7	22	31	80	.165	.260	.267	48	-18	-18	17	1	2	-1	.965	9	*S	-0.1
1970	Cal-A	24	24	2	2	0	0	0	1	3	6	.083	.185	.083	-24	-4	-4	1	0	0	0	1.000	-1	S/3	-0.5
Total	6	542	1265	110	221	39	6	15	86	135	359	.175	.259	.251	48	-83	-85	83	2	6	-3	.966	52	S/231	0.1

■ CHARLIE PABOR Pabor, Charles Henry b: 9/24/1846, New York, N.Y. d: 4/22/13, New Haven, Conn. BL/TL, 5'8", 155 lbs. Deb: 5/04/1871 M

1871	Cle-n	29	142	24	42	2	4	0	18	1	3	.296	.301	.366	96	-2	0	16	1					*O/PM	0.2
1872	Cle-n	21	90	12	19	0	0	0	7	0	0	.211	.211	.211	32	-7	-6	4						O/P	-0.3
1873	Atl-n	55	228	36	82	7	4	0	41	6	3	.360	.376	.425	151	10	15	38						*O	1.2
1874	Phi-n	17	77	11	18	0	0	1	0			.234	.234	.273	59	-3	-4	5						/O	-0.3
1875	Atl-n	42	153	15	36	1	3	0	1			.235	.240	.281	91	-3	0	11						O/PM	0.0
	NH-n	6	23	4	8	0	2	0	0			.348	.348	.522	225	2	3	4						OM	0.2
	Yr	48	176	19	44	1	5	0	1			.250	.254	.313	109	-1	3	14						O/P	0.2
Total	5 n	170	713	102	205	10	13	1		8		.288	.295	.342	104	-3	8	79						O/P	1.0

■ ED PABST Pabst, Edward D. A. b: 1868, St.Louis, Mo. d: 6/19/40, St.Louis, Mo. 5'11", 170 lbs. Deb: 9/26/1890

1890	Phi-a	8	25	7	10	2	0	0	5			.400	.500	.480	197	3	3	8	3			.963	4	/O	0.6
	StL-a	4	14	1	2	0	1	0	0			.143	.143	.286	24	-1	-2	1	0			1.000	1	/O	0.0
	Yr	12	39	8	12	2	1	0	5			.308	.386	.410	133	2	2	8	3			.972	5	O	0.6

■ JIM PACIOREK Paciorek, James Joseph b: 6/7/60, Detroit, Mich. BR/TR, 6'3", 203 lbs. Deb: 4/09/87 F

| 1987 | Mil-A | 48 | 101 | 16 | 23 | 5 | 0 | 2 | 10 | 12 | 20 | .228 | .310 | .337 | 69 | -4 | -4 | 11 | 1 | 0 | 0 | .980 | -4 | 13/OD | -0.9 |

■ JOHN PACIOREK Paciorek, John Francis b: 2/11/45, Detroit, Mich. BR/TR, 6'2", 200 lbs. Deb: 9/29/63 F

| 1963 | Hou-N | 1 | 3 | 4 | 3 | 0 | 0 | 0 | 3 | 2 | 0 | 1.000 | 1.000 | 1.000 | 509 | 2 | 2 | 4 | 0 | 0 | 0 | 1.000 | -0 | /O | 0.2 |

■ TOM PACIOREK Paciorek, Thomas Marian b: 11/2/46, Detroit, Mich. BR/TR, 6'4", 215 lbs. Deb: 9/12/70 F

1970	LA-N	8	9	2	2	1	0	0	0	0	3	.222	.300	.333	73	-0	-0	1	0	0	0	1.000	-0	/O	-0.1
1971	LA-N	2	2	0	1	0	0	0	1	0	0	.500	.500	.500	196	0	0	1	0	0	0	1.000	0	/O	0.0
1972	LA-N	11	47	4	12	4	0	1	6	1	9	.255	.271	.404	92	-1	-1	5	1	0	0	.979	1	/1O	-0.1
1973	LA-N	96	195	26	51	8	0	5	18	11	35	.262	.304	.379	92	-3	-2	20	3	3	-1	.979	-1	O/1	-0.7
1974	*LA-N	85	175	23	42	8	6	1	24	10	32	.240	.285	.371	86	-5	-4	17	3	5	-2	.944	-3	O/1	-1.1

YEAR	TM/L	G	AB	R	H	2B	3B	HR	RBI	BB	SO	AVG	OBP	SLG	PRO+	BR	/A	RC	SB	CS	SBR	FA	FR	POS	TPR
1975	LA-N	62	145	14	28	8	0	1	5	11	29	.193	.250	.269	46	-11	-10	9	4	3	-1	.972	-3	O	-1.6
1976	Atl-N	111	324	39	94	10	4	4	36	19	57	.290	.335	.383	97	1	-1	40	2	3	-1	.983	-8	O1/3	-1.5
1977	Atl-N	72	155	20	37	8	0	3	15	6	46	.239	.267	.348	57	-8	-11	15	1	0	0	.984	-1	1/O3	-1.3
1978	Atl-N	5	9	2	3	0	0	0	0	0	1	.333	.333	.333	78	-0	-0	1	0	0	0	1.000	-0	/1	-0.1
	Sea-A	70	251	32	75	20	3	4	30	15	39	.299	.338	.450	121	6	6	36	2	2	-1	.980	-3	OD/1	0.0
1979	Sea-A	103	310	38	89	23	4	6	42	28	62	.287	.356	.445	113	6	6	49	6	4	-1	1.000	-2	O1	-0.1
1980	Sea-A	126	418	44	114	19	1	15	59	17	67	.273	.303	.431	98	-2	-3	50	3	2	-0	1.000	-3	O1D	-0.9
1981	Sea-A★	104	405	50	132	28	2	14	66	35	50	.326	.385	.509	150	28	26	76	13	10	-2	.974	6	*O	2.8
1982	Chi-A	104	382	49	119	27	4	11	55	24	53	.312	.366	.490	133	17	17	68	3	3	-1	.993	-1	*1/O	0.9
1983	*Chi-A	115	420	65	129	32	3	9	63	25	58	.307	.350	.462	117	12	10	67	6	1	1	1.000	-10	1O/D	-0.5
1984	Chi-A	111	363	35	93	21	2	4	29	25	69	.256	.311	.358	81	-8	-10	42	6	0	2	.993	-13	1O	-2.6
1985	Chi-A	46	122	14	30	2	0	0	9	8	22	.246	.298	.262	53	-7	-8	10	2	0	1	.970	-2	OD/1	-1.0
	NY-N	46	116	14	33	3	1	1	11	6	14	.284	.325	.353	92	-2	-1	13	1	0	0	1.000	-5	O/1	-0.7
1986	Tex-A	88	213	17	61	7	0	4	22	3	41	.286	.306	.376	82	-5	-6	22	1	3	-2	.967	-1	O13/SD	-1.0
1987	Tex-A	27	60	6	17	3	0	3	12	1	19	.283	.306	.483	105	0	0	7	0	1	-1	1.000	-0	1O/D	-0.1
Total	18	1392	4121	494	1162	232	30	86	503	245	704	.282	.328	.415	102	17	7	548	55	38	-6	.979	-49	O1/D3S	-9.7

■ **FRANKIE PACK** Pack, Frank b: 4/10/28, Morristown, Tenn. BL/TR, 6′, 190 lbs. Deb: 6/05/49

YEAR	TM/L	G	AB	R	H	2B	3B	HR	RBI	BB	SO	AVG	OBP	SLG	PRO+	BR	/A	RC	SB	CS	SBR	FA	FR	POS	TPR
1949	StL-A	1	1	0	0	0	0	0	0	0	1	.000	.000	.000	-96	-0	-0	0	0	0	0	.000	0	H	0.0

■ **DICK PADDEN** Padden, Richard Joseph "Brains" b: 9/17/1870, Martins Ferry, O. d: 10/31/22, Martins Ferry, O. BR/TR, 5′10″, 165 lbs. Deb: 7/15/1896

YEAR	TM/L	G	AB	R	H	2B	3B	HR	RBI	BB	SO	AVG	OBP	SLG	PRO+	BR	/A	RC	SB	CS	SBR	FA	FR	POS	TPR
1896	Pit-N	61	219	33	53	4	8	2	24	14	9	.242	.294	.361	77	-9	-7	27	8			.931	-12	2	-1.4
1897	Pit-N	134	517	84	146	16	10	2	58	38		.282	.350	.364	92	-8	-5	77	18			.941	2	*2	0.3
1898	Pit-N	128	463	61	119	7	6	2	43	35		.257	.335	.311	87	-8	-6	54	11			.947	-3	*2	-0.1
1899	Was-N	134	451	66	125	20	7	2	61	24		.277	.337	.366	94	-5	-4	67	27			.913	9	S2	1.2
1901	StL-N	123	489	71	125	17	7	2	62	31		.256	.313	.331	92	-8	-5	62	26			.950	-0	*2/S	0.1
1902	StL-A	117	413	54	109	26	3	1	40	30		.264	.333	.349	90	-6	-5	54	11			**.967**	18	*2	1.6
1903	StL-A	29	94	7	19	3	0	0	6	9		.202	.306	.234	66	-4	-3	9	5			.955	6	2	0.4
1904	StL-A	132	453	42	108	19	4	0	36	40		.238	.322	.298	103	0	3	53	23			.959	-9	*2	-0.2
1905	StL-A	16	58	5	10	1	1	0	4	3		.172	.213	.224	41	-4	-4	4	3			.950	-0	2	-0.4
Total	9	874	3157	423	814	113	46	11	334	224	9	.258	.327	.333	90	-50	-35	406	132			.950	10	2/S	1.5

■ **TOM PADDEN** Padden, Thomas Francis b: 10/6/08, Manchester, N.H. d: 6/10/73, Manchester, N.H. BR/TR, 5′11.5″, 170 lbs. Deb: 5/29/32

YEAR	TM/L	G	AB	R	H	2B	3B	HR	RBI	BB	SO	AVG	OBP	SLG	PRO+	BR	/A	RC	SB	CS	SBR	FA	FR	POS	TPR
1932	Pit-N	47	118	13	31	6	1	0	10	9	7	.263	.315	.331	75	-4	-4	13	0			.985	-1	C	-0.3
1933	Pit-N	30	90	5	19	2	0	0	8	2	6	.211	.237	.233	35	-8	-8	5	0			.984	6	C	0.0
1934	Pit-N	82	237	27	76	12	2	0	22	30	23	.321	.399	.388	109	5	5	37	3			.978	-5	C	0.3
1935	Pit-N	97	302	35	82	9	1	1	30	48	26	.272	.371	.318	84	-3	-5	39	1			.966	14	C	1.3
1936	Pit-N	88	281	22	70	9	2	1	31	22	41	.249	.304	.306	63	-14	-15	27	0			.976	2	C	-0.8
1937	Pit-N	35	98	14	28	2	0	0	8	13	11	.286	.369	.306	85	-1	-1	12	1			.983	6	C	0.6
1943	Phi-N	17	41	5	12	0	0	0	1	2	6	.293	.341	.293	87	-1	-1	4	0			1.000	4	C	0.4
	Was-A	3	3	1	0	0	0	0	0	1	1	.000	.250	.000	-25	-0	-0	0	0	0	0	1.000	0	/C	0.0
Total	7	399	1170	122	318	40	6	2	110	127	121	.272	.345	.321	80	-26	-28	136	5	0		.977	27	C	1.5

■ **DEL PADDOCK** Paddock, Delmar Harold b: 6/8/1887, Volga, S.Dak. d: 2/6/52, Remer, Minn BL/TR, 5′9″, 165 lbs. Deb: 4/14/12

YEAR	TM/L	G	AB	R	H	2B	3B	HR	RBI	BB	SO	AVG	OBP	SLG	PRO+	BR	/A	RC	SB	CS	SBR	FA	FR	POS	TPR
1912	Chi-A	1	1	0	0	0	0	0	0	0		.000	.000	.000	-99	-0	-0	0	0			.000	0	H	0.0
	NY-A	46	156	26	45	5	3	1	14	23		.288	.393	.378	114	5	4	27	9			.894	-10	3/2O	-0.6
	Yr	47	157	26	45	5	3	1	14	23		.287	.391	.376	113	5	4	26	9			.894	-10	3/2O	-0.6

■ **DON PADGETT** Padgett, Don Wilson b: 12/5/11, Caroleen, N.C. d: 12/9/80, High Point, N.C. BL/TR, 6′, 190 lbs. Deb: 4/23/37

YEAR	TM/L	G	AB	R	H	2B	3B	HR	RBI	BB	SO	AVG	OBP	SLG	PRO+	BR	/A	RC	SB	CS	SBR	FA	FR	POS	TPR
1937	StL-N	123	446	62	140	22	6	10	74	30	43	.314	.357	.457	117	11	10	75	4			.955	3	*O	0.9
1938	StL-N	110	388	59	105	26	5	8	65	18	28	.271	.303	.425	93	-3	-5	48	0			.962	5	O1/C	-0.4
1939	StL-N	92	233	38	93	15	3	5	53	18	11	.399	.444	.554	157	22	20	54	1			.978	-3	C/1	1.9
1940	StL-N	93	240	24	58	15	1	6	41	26	14	.242	.321	.387	89	-2	-4	30	1			.962	-8	C/1	-0.7
1941	StL-N	107	324	39	80	18	0	5	44	21	16	.247	.293	.349	75	-9	-12	32	0			.959	-9	OC/1	-2.4
1946	Bro-N	19	30	2	5	1	0	1	9	4	4	.167	.265	.300	59	-2	-2	2	0			1.000	-1	C	-0.3
	Bos-N	44	98	6	25	3	0	2	21	5	7	.255	.291	.347	80	-3	-3	10	0			.939	-6	C	-0.8
	Yr	63	128	8	30	4	0	3	30	9	11	.234	.285	.336	75	-4	-5	13	0			.954	-7	C	-1.1
1947	Phi-N	75	158	14	50	8	1	0	24	16	5	.316	.383	.380	107	1	2	22	0			.962	-7	C	-0.3
1948	Phi-N	36	74	3	17	3	0	0	7	3	2	.230	.260	.270	44	-6	-6	5	0			.957	-4	C	-0.9
Total	8	699	1991	247	573	111	16	37	338	141	130	.288	.336	.415	101	10	1	279	6			.962	-32	CO/1	-3.0

■ **ERNIE PADGETT** Padgett, Ernest Kitchen "Red" b: 3/1/1899, Philadelphia, Pa. d: 4/15/57, E.Orange, N.J. BR/TR, 5′8″, 155 lbs. Deb: 10/03/23

YEAR	TM/L	G	AB	R	H	2B	3B	HR	RBI	BB	SO	AVG	OBP	SLG	PRO+	BR	/A	RC	SB	CS	SBR	FA	FR	POS	TPR
1923	Bos-N	4	11	3	2	0	0	0	0	2	0	.182	.308	.182	33	-1	-1	1	0	0	0	.947	2	/S2	0.1
1924	Bos-N	138	502	42	128	25	9	1	46	37	56	.255	.310	.347	79	-17	-15	53	4	9	-4	.967	-10	*32	-2.0
1925	Bos-N	86	256	31	78	9	7	0	29	14	14	.305	.341	.395	96	-5	-2	33	3	5	-2	.964	-20	2S/3	-2.0
1926	Cle-A	36	62	7	13	0	1	0	6	8	3	.210	.300	.242	42	-5	-5	5	1	0	0	.930	2	3/S	-0.2
1927	Cle-A	7	7	1	2	0	0	0	0	0	2	.286	.286	.286	48	-1	-1	1	0	0	0	1.000	-0	/2	-0.1
Total	5	271	838	84	223	34	17	1	81	61	75	.266	.318	.351	80	-29	-23	92	8	14	-6	.957	-26	3/2S	-4.2

■ **DENNIS PAEPKE** Paepke, Dennis Ray b: 4/17/45, Long Beach, Cal. BR/TR, 6′, 202 lbs. Deb: 6/02/69

YEAR	TM/L	G	AB	R	H	2B	3B	HR	RBI	BB	SO	AVG	OBP	SLG	PRO+	BR	/A	RC	SB	CS	SBR	FA	FR	POS	TPR
1969	KC-A	12	27	2	3	1	0	0	0	2	3	.111	.172	.148	-10	-4	-4	1	0	0	0	1.000	3	/C	-0.1
1971	KC-A	60	152	11	31	6	0	2	14	8	29	.204	.244	.283	49	-10	-10	9	0	0	0	.994	-3	CO	-1.4
1972	KC-A	2	6	0	0	0	0	0	0	1	2	.000	.143	.000	-55	-1	-1	0	0	0	0	.842	1	/C	0.0
1974	KC-A	6	12	0	2	0	0	0	0	1	2	.167	.231	.167	15	-1	-1	0	0	1	-1	1.000	-1	/CO	-0.3
Total	4	80	197	13	36	7	0	2	14	12	36	.183	.230	.249	36	-17	-17	10	0	1	-1	.984	-1	/CO	-1.8

■ **ANDY PAFKO** Pafko, Andrew "Handy Andy" or "Pruschka" b: 2/25/21, Boyceville, Wis. BR/TR, 6′, 190 lbs. Deb: 9/24/43 C

YEAR	TM/L	G	AB	R	H	2B	3B	HR	RBI	BB	SO	AVG	OBP	SLG	PRO+	BR	/A	RC	SB	CS	SBR	FA	FR	POS	TPR
1943	Chi-N	13	58	7	22	3	0	0	10	2	5	.379	.400	.431	142	3	3	9	1			1.000	-2	O	0.0
1944	Chi-N	128	469	47	126	16	2	6	62	28	23	.269	.315	.350	87	-9	-8	50	2			.983	15	*O	0.0
1945	*Chi-N	144	534	64	159	24	12	12	110	45	36	.298	.361	.455	129	17	19	92	5			**.995**	3	*O	1.4
1946	Chi-N	65	234	18	66	6	4	3	39	27	15	.282	.366	.380	114	4	5	33	4			.978	11	O	1.3
1947	Chi-N★	129	513	68	155	25	7	13	66	31	39	.302	.346	.454	115	6	9	75	4			.985	7	*O	0.9
1948	Chi-N★	142	548	82	171	30	2	26	101	50	50	.312	.375	.516	145	28	31	105	3			.938	13	*3	4.2
1949	Chi-N★	144	519	79	146	29	2	18	69	63	33	.281	.369	.449	121	14	16	86	4			.987	-7	O3	0.3
1950	Chi-N★	146	514	95	156	24	8	36	92	69	32	.304	.397	.591	158	41	42	124	4			.978	-1	*O	3.4
1951	Chi-N	49	178	26	47	5	3	12	35	17	10	.264	.342	.528	128	7	6	31	1	1	-0	.992	2	O	0.6
	Bro-N	84	277	42	69	11	0	18	58	35	27	.249	.350	.484	120	8	7	47	1	4	-2	.993	-2	O	0.1
	Yr	133	455	68	116	16	3	30	93	52	37	.255	.347	.501	123	15	14	78	2	5	-2	.993	0	*O	0.7
1952	*Bro-N	150	551	76	158	17	5	19	85	64	48	.287	.366	.439	121	17	16	91	4	3	-1	.988	-7	*O3	0.3
1953	Mil-N	140	516	70	153	23	4	17	72	37	33	.297	.347	.455	114	5	9	81	2	1	0	.976	-4	*O	0.0
1954	Mil-N	138	510	61	146	22	4	14	69	37	36	.286	.339	.427	105	-2	2	72	1	2	-1	.969	-4	*O	-0.8
1955	Mil-N	86	252	29	67	3	5	5	34	7	23	.266	.297	.377	81	-9	-7	26	1	2	-1	.980	-8	O3	-1.8
1956	Mil-N	45	93	15	24	5	0	2	9	10	13	.258	.330	.376	95	-1	-1	12	0	0	0	.978	-5	O	-0.7
1957	*Mil-N	83	220	31	61	6	1	8	27	10	22	.277	.312	.423	102	-2	-0	28	1	0	0	.982	-6	O	-0.9
1958	*Mil-N	95	164	17	39	7	1	3	23	15	17	.238	.309	.348	80	-6	-4	18	0	0	0	1.000	-14	O	-2.1

YEAR	TM/L	G	AB	R	H	2B	3B	HR	RBI	BB	SO	AVG	OBP	SLG	PRO+	BR	/A	RC	SB	CS	SBR	FA	FR	POS	TPR
1959	Mil-N	71	142	17	31	8	2	1	15	14	15	.218	.293	.324	70	-7	-6	13	0	0	0	.978	-12	O	-2.0
Total	17	1852	6292	844	1796	264	62	213	976	561	477	.285	.351	.449	118	115	140	992	38	13		.984	-21	*O3	4.2

■ JOSE PAGAN

Pagan, Jose Antonio (Rodriguez) b: 5/5/35, Barceloneta, P.R. BR/TR, 5'9", 165 lbs. Deb: 8/04/59 C

YEAR	TM/L	G	AB	R	H	2B	3B	HR	RBI	BB	SO	AVG	OBP	SLG	PRO+	BR	/A	RC	SB	CS	SBR	FA	FR	POS	TPR
1959	SF-N	31	46	7	8	1	0	0	1	2	8	.174	.208	.196	9	-6	-6	2	1	0	0	.900	3	3/S2	-0.2
1960	SF-N	18	49	8	14	2	2	0	2	1	6	.286	.300	.408	97	-1	-0	5	2	2	-1	.917	-8	S/3	-0.9
1961	SF-N	134	434	38	110	15	2	5	46	31	45	.253	.306	.332	72	-19	-17	42	8	5	-1	.964	-17	*S/O	-2.4
1962	*SF-N	164	580	73	150	25	6	7	57	47	77	.259	.315	.359	82	-16	-15	63	13	9	-2	**.973**	-25	*S	-2.6
1963	SF-N	148	483	46	113	12	1	6	39	26	67	.234	.279	.300	67	-21	-20	40	10	7	-1	.970	-18	*S/2O	-3.2
1964	SF-N	134	367	33	82	10	1	1	28	35	66	.223	.293	.264	57	-19	-20	29	5	4	-1	.958	-17	*S/O	-3.2
1965	SF-N	26	83	10	17	4	0	0	5	8	9	.205	.275	.253	48	-5	-6	6	1	0	0	.941	-5	S	-1.0
	Pit-N	42	38	6	9	1	0	0	1	1	7	.237	.275	.263	52	-2	-2	3	1	0	0	.923	8	3/S	0.6
	Yr	68	121	16	26	5	0	0	6	9	16	.215	.275	.256	50	-8	-8	8	2	0	1	.923	3	S3	-0.4
1966	Pit-N	109	368	44	97	15	6	4	54	13	38	.264	.296	.370	84	-8	-9	38	0	2	-1	.949	3	3S/2O	-0.8
1967	Pit-N	81	211	17	61	6	2	1	19	10	28	.289	.330	.351	95	-1	-1	24	1	1	-0	.938	10	3OS/2C	0.9
1968	Pit-N	80	163	24	36	7	1	4	21	11	32	.221	.282	.350	90	-2	-2	15	2	3	-1	.924	-2	3O/S21	-0.6
1969	Pit-N	108	274	29	78	11	4	9	42	17	46	.285	.329	.453	119	5	6	41	1	0	0	.954	-3	3O/2	0.2
1970	*Pit-N	95	230	21	61	14	1	7	29	20	24	.265	.324	.426	101	-1	-0	31	1	1	-0	.957	-2	3/O12	-0.2
1971	*Pit-N	57	158	16	38	1	0	5	15	16	25	.241	.314	.342	86	-3	-3	17	0	0	0	.980	-2	3/O1	-0.5
1972	Pit-N	53	127	11	32	9	0	3	8	5	17	.252	.286	.394	93	-2	-2	14	0	0	0	.899	-8	3/O	-1.1
1973	Phi-N	46	78	4	16	5	0	0	5	1	15	.205	.215	.269	33	-7	-7	3	0	1	-1	.958	-1	3/1O2	-1.0
Total	15	1326	3689	387	922	138	26	52	372	244	510	.250	.300	.344	79	-109	-105	373	46	35	-7	.963	-84	S3/O21C	-16.0

■ MIKE PAGE

Page, Michael Randy b: 7/12/40, Woodruff, S.C. BL/TR, 6'2.5", 210 lbs. Deb: 6/30/68

YEAR	TM/L	G	AB	R	H	2B	3B	HR	RBI	BB	SO	AVG	OBP	SLG	PRO+	BR	/A	RC	SB	CS	SBR	FA	FR	POS	TPR
1968	Atl-N	20	28	1	5	0	0	0	1	1	9	.179	.207	.179	16	-3	-3	1	0	0	0	1.000	-1	/O	-0.4

■ MITCHELL PAGE

Page, Mitchell Otis b: 10/15/51, Los Angeles, Cal. BL/TR, 6'2", 205 lbs. Deb: 4/09/77

YEAR	TM/L	G	AB	R	H	2B	3B	HR	RBI	BB	SO	AVG	OBP	SLG	PRO+	BR	/A	RC	SB	CS	SBR	FA	FR	POS	TPR
1977	Oak-A	145	501	85	154	28	8	21	75	78	95	.307	.407	.521	153	37	38	117	42	5	**10**	.954	7	*O/D	4.8
1978	Oak-A	147	516	62	147	25	7	17	70	53	95	.285	.356	.459	135	19	22	82	23	19	-5	.973	-1	*OD	1.2
1979	Oak-A	133	478	51	118	11	2	9	42	52	93	.247	.325	.335	83	-14	-10	51	17	16	-5	1.000	-0	*D/O	-1.5
1980	Oak-A	110	348	58	85	10	4	17	51	35	87	.244	.315	.443	113	2	5	47	14	7	0	.000	0	*D	0.5
1981	Oak-A	34	92	9	13	1	0	4	13	7	29	.141	.202	.283	40	-8	-7	5	2	1	0	.000	0	D	-0.7
1982	Oak-A	31	78	14	20	5	0	4	7	7	24	.256	.333	.474	124	2	2	10	3	4	-2	.000	0	D	0.1
1983	Oak-A	57	79	16	19	3	0	0	1	10	22	.241	.341	.278	77	-2	-2	8	3	3	-1	1.000	-2	DO	-0.5
1984	Pit-N	16	12	2	4	1	0	0	0	3	4	.333	.467	.417	150	1	1	3	0	0	0	.000	0	H	0.1
Total	8	673	2104	297	560	84	21	72	259	245	449	.266	.348	.429	118	37	49	322	104	55	-2	.963	3	DO	4.0

■ KARL PAGEL

Pagel, Karl Douglas b: 3/29/55, Madison, Wis. BL/TL, 6'2", 190 lbs. Deb: 9/21/78

YEAR	TM/L	G	AB	R	H	2B	3B	HR	RBI	BB	SO	AVG	OBP	SLG	PRO+	BR	/A	RC	SB	CS	SBR	FA	FR	POS	TPR
1978	Chi-N	2	2	0	0	0	0	0	0	0	2	.000	.000	.000	-89	-1	-1	0	0	0	0	.000	0	H	-0.1
1979	Chi-N	1	1	0	0	0	0	0	0	0	1	.000	.000	.000	-91	-0	-0	0	0	0	0	.000	0	/H	0.0
1981	Cle-A	14	15	3	4	0	2	1	4	4	1	.267	.421	.733	230	3	3	5	0	0	0	1.000	2	/1D	0.4
1982	Cle-A	23	18	3	3	0	0	0	2	7	11	.167	.400	.167	63	-0	-0	2	0	0	0	.970	0	1/D	-0.1
1983	Cle-A	8	20	1	6	0	0	0	1	0	5	.300	.300	.300	63	-1	-1	2	0	0	0	.000	-1	/OD	-0.2
Total	5	48	56	7	13	0	2	1	7	11	20	.232	.358	.357	99	0	0	9	0	0	0	.985	1	/1DO	0.0

■ JIM PAGLIARONI

Pagliaroni, James Vincent "Pag" b: 12/8/37, Dearborn, Mich. BR/TR, 6'4", 210 lbs. Deb: 8/13/55

YEAR	TM/L	G	AB	R	H	2B	3B	HR	RBI	BB	SO	AVG	OBP	SLG	PRO+	BR	/A	RC	SB	CS	SBR	FA	FR	POS	TPR
1955	Bos-A	1	0	0	0	0	0	0	1	0	0	—	—	—	—	0	-0	0	0	0	0	.000	0	/C	0.0
1960	Bos-A	28	62	7	19	5	2	2	9	13	11	.306	.434	.548	158	6	6	16	0	0	0	.990	-3	C	0.4
1961	Bos-A	120	376	50	91	17	0	16	58	55	74	.242	.345	.415	100	1	0	56	1	1	-0	.984	-4	*C	0.2
1962	Bos-A	90	260	39	67	14	0	11	37	36	55	.258	.359	.438	110	5	4	43	2	1	0	.987	-3	C	0.4
1963	Pit-N	92	252	27	58	5	0	11	26	36	57	.230	.331	.381	104	2	2	31	0	0	0	.988	4	C	1.0
1964	Pit-N	97	302	33	89	12	3	10	36	41	56	.295	.383	.454	135	15	15	52	1	0	0	.992	1	C	2.1
1965	Pit-N	134	403	42	108	15	0	17	65	41	84	.268	.340	.432	115	8	8	57	0	0	0	.994	-4	*C	1.1
1966	Pit-N	123	374	37	88	20	0	11	49	50	71	.235	.332	.377	96	-1	-1	47	0	5	-3	**.997**	-14	*C	-1.1
1967	Pit-N	44	100	4	20	1	1	0	9	16	26	.200	.316	.230	59	-5	-5	7	0	0	0	.984	-0	C	-0.3
1968	Oak-A	66	199	19	49	4	0	6	20	24	42	.246	.333	.357	115	3	4	25	0	0	0	.997	-9	C	-0.1
1969	Oak-A	14	27	1	4	1	0	1	2	5	2	.148	.303	.296	71	-1	-1	3	0	0	0	.981	2	/C	0.1
	Sea-A	40	110	10	29	4	1	5	14	13	16	.264	.341	.455	123	3	3	18	0	0	0	.988	-6	C/1O	-0.2
	Yr	54	137	11	33	5	1	6	16	18	18	.241	.333	.423	113	2	2	21	0	0	0	.987	-4	C/1O	-0.1
Total	11	849	2465	269	622	98	7	90	326	330	494	.252	.346	.407	109	37	35	355	4	7	-3	.991	-36	C/1O	3.6

■ MIKE PAGLIARULO

Pagliarulo, Michael Timothy b: 3/15/60, Medford, Mass. BL/TR, 6'1", 205 lbs. Deb: 7/07/84

YEAR	TM/L	G	AB	R	H	2B	3B	HR	RBI	BB	SO	AVG	OBP	SLG	PRO+	BR	/A	RC	SB	CS	SBR	FA	FR	POS	TPR
1984	NY-A	67	201	24	48	15	3	7	34	15	46	.239	.292	.448	105	-0	1	25	0	0	0	.955	6	3	0.6
1985	NY-A	138	380	55	91	16	2	19	62	45	86	.239	.326	.442	111	4	5	56	0	0	0	.951	-17	*3	-1.3
1986	NY-A	149	504	71	120	24	3	28	71	54	120	.238	.317	.464	111	5	6	74	4	1	1	.953	6	*3/S	1.0
1987	NY-A	150	522	76	122	26	3	32	87	53	111	.234	.307	.479	105	1	2	75	1	3	-2	.959	4	*3/1	0.3
1988	NY-A	125	444	46	96	20	1	15	67	37	104	.216	.280	.367	80	-13	-13	46	1	0	0	.943	-0	*3	-1.4
1989	NY-A	74	223	19	44	10	0	4	16	19	43	.197	.266	.296	59	-12	-12	18	1	1	-0	.936	-4	3/D	-1.7
	SD-N	50	148	12	29	7	0	3	14	18	39	.196	.287	.304	69	-6	-6	14	2	0	1	.936	0	3	-0.5
1990	SD-N	128	398	29	101	23	2	7	38	39	66	.254	.325	.374	91	-4	-5	47	1	3	-2	.955	1	*3	-0.4
1991	*Min-A	121	365	38	102	20	0	6	36	21	55	.279	.324	.384	91	-3	-5	43	1	2	-1	.965	13	*3/2	0.7
1992	Min-A	42	105	10	21	4	0	0	9	1	17	.200	.215	.238	26	-10	-11	5	1	0	0	.962	3	3/D	-0.8
Total	9	1044	3290	380	774	165	14	121	434	302	687	.235	.304	.404	93	-39	-37	404	12	10	-2	.953	11	*3/DS21	-3.5

■ TOM PAGNOZZI

Pagnozzi, Thomas Alan b: 7/30/62, Tucson, Ariz. BR/TR, 6', 190 lbs. Deb: 4/12/87

YEAR	TM/L	G	AB	R	H	2B	3B	HR	RBI	BB	SO	AVG	OBP	SLG	PRO+	BR	/A	RC	SB	CS	SBR	FA	FR	POS	TPR
1987	*StL-N	27	48	8	9	1	0	2	9	4	13	.188	.250	.333	52	-3	-4	4	1	0	0	1.000	-4	C/1	-0.6
1988	StL-N	81	195	17	55	9	0	0	15	11	32	.282	.320	.328	86	-3	-4	20	0	0	0	.971	-2	C1/3	-0.6
1989	StL-N	52	80	3	12	2	0	0	3	6	19	.150	.218	.175	13	-9	-9	2	0	0	0	.982	-3	C/13	-1.2
1990	StL-N	69	220	20	61	15	0	2	23	14	37	.277	.323	.373	91	-3	-3	28	1	1	-0	.989	10	C/1	1.0
1991	StL-N	140	459	38	121	24	5	2	57	36	63	.264	.323	.351	89	-6	-7	49	9	13	-5	.991	-7	*C/1	-1.1
1992	StL-N★	139	485	33	121	26	3	7	44	28	64	.249	.292	.359	85	-12	-11	46	2	5	-2	**.999**	-16	*C	-2.2
Total	6	508	1487	119	379	77	8	13	151	99	228	.255	.304	.344	82	-36	-37	149	13	19	-8	.992	-22	C/13	-4.7

■ REY PALACIOS

Palacios, Robert Rey b: 11/8/62, Brooklyn, N.Y. BR/TR, 5'10", 190 lbs. Deb: 9/08/88

YEAR	TM/L	G	AB	R	H	2B	3B	HR	RBI	BB	SO	AVG	OBP	SLG	PRO+	BR	/A	RC	SB	CS	SBR	FA	FR	POS	TPR
1988	KC-A	5	11	2	1	0	0	0	0	0	4	.091	.091	.091	-48	-2	-2	0	0	0	0	1.000	1	/C3D	-0.1
1989	KC-A	55	47	12	8	2	0	1	8	2	14	.170	.220	.277	39	-4	-4	3	0	1	-1	.958	3	31C/OD	-0.1
1990	KC-A	41	56	8	13	3	0	2	9	5	24	.232	.295	.393	92	-1	-1	6	2	2	-1	.992	4	C/13O	0.4
Total	3	101	114	22	22	5	0	3	17	7	42	.193	.246	.316	57	-7	-7	9	2	3	-1	.994	8	/C13DO	0.2

■ ERV PALICA

Palica, Ervin Martin (b: Ervin Martin Pavliecivich)
b: 2/9/28, Lomita, Cal. d: 5/29/82, Huntington Beach, Cal. BR/TR, 6'1.5", 180 lbs. Deb: 4/21/45

YEAR	TM/L	G	AB	R	H	2B	3B	HR	RBI	BB	SO	AVG	OBP	SLG	PRO+	BR	/A	RC	SB	CS	SBR	FA	FR	POS	TPR
1945	Bro-N	2	0	0	0	0	0	0	0	0	0	—	—	—	—	0	0	0	0			.000	0	R	0.0
1947	Bro-N	3	0	0	0	0	0	0	0	0	0	—	—	—	—	0	0	0	0			.000	-0	/P	0.0
1948	Bro-N	45	39	6	5	1	1	0	3	4	12	.128	.209	.205	12	-5	-5	2	0			1.000	-1	P	0.0
1949	*Bro-N	49	19	2	3	1	0	0	2	2	6	.158	.238	.211	20	-2	-2	1	0			.875	-0	P	0.0

YEAR	TM/L	G	AB	R	H	2B	3B	HR	RBI	BB	SO	AVG	OBP	SLG	PRO+	BR	/A	RC	SB	CS	SBR	FA	FR	POS	TPR
1950	Bro-N	48	68	4	15	4	0	1	8	0	8	.221	.221	.324	40	-6	-6	5	2			.889	-4	P	0.0
1951	Bro-N	20	13	1	2	0	0	0	0	2	5	.154	.267	.154	16	-1	-2	1	0	0	0	1.000	1	P	0.0
1953	Bro-N	4	1	0	1	0	0	0	0	0	0	1.000	1.000	1.000	414	0	0	1	0	0	0	1.000	0	/P	0.0
1954	Bro-N	28	16	2	4	1	0	0	1	1	4	.250	.294	.313	56	-1	-1	2	0	0	0	.875	-2	P	0.0
1955	Bal-A	33	55	3	13	1	0	0	3	4	18	.236	.288	.255	50	-4	-4	4	0	0	0	.905	-1	P	0.0
1956	Bal-A	30	32	4	5	0	0	0	0	0	10	.156	.156	.156	-19	-5	-5	1	0	0	0	.917	-0	P	0.0
Total	10	262	243	22	48	8	1	1	17	13	63	.198	.238	.251	31	-24	-24	16	2	0		.921	-7	P	0.0

■ RAFAEL PALMEIRO Palmeiro, Rafael (Corrales) b: 9/24/64, Havana, Cuba BL/TL, 6', 180 lbs. Deb: 9/08/86

YEAR	TM/L	G	AB	R	H	2B	3B	HR	RBI	BB	SO	AVG	OBP	SLG	PRO+	BR	/A	RC	SB	CS	SBR	FA	FR	POS	TPR
1986	Chi-N	22	73	9	18	4	0	3	12	4	6	.247	.295	.425	89	-1	-1	8	1	1	-0	.900	-0	O	-0.3
1987	Chi-N	84	221	32	61	15	1	14	30	20	26	.276	.339	.543	124	8	7	40	2	2	-1	1.000	-4	O1	0.1
1988	Chi-N★	152	580	75	178	41	5	8	53	38	34	.307	.353	.436	120	18	15	89	12	2	2	.983	4	*O/1	1.8
1989	Tex-A	156	559	76	154	23	4	8	64	63	48	.275	.355	.374	104	6	5	74	4	3	-1	.991	10	*1/D	0.2
1990	Tex-A	154	598	72	**191**	35	6	14	89	40	59	.319	.365	.468	131	24	24	94	3	3	-1	.995	-2	*1/D	1.1
1991	Tex-A★	159	631	115	203	**49**	3	26	88	68	72	.322	.393	.532	156	46	47	129	4	3	-1	.992	-4	*1/D	3.2
1992	Tex-A	159	608	84	163	27	4	22	85	72	83	.268	.355	.434	124	17	19	96	2	3	-1	.995	15	*1/D	2.2
Total	7	886	3270	463	968	194	23	95	421	305	328	.296	.361	.457	127	117	115	530	28	17	-2	.993	19	1O/D	8.3

■ DEAN PALMER Palmer, Dean William b: 12/27/68, Tallahassee, Fla. BR/TR, 6'1", 175 lbs. Deb: 9/01/89

YEAR	TM/L	G	AB	R	H	2B	3B	HR	RBI	BB	SO	AVG	OBP	SLG	PRO+	BR	/A	RC	SB	CS	SBR	FA	FR	POS	TPR
1989	Tex-A	16	19	0	2	2	0	0	1	0	12	.105	.105	.211	-13	-3	-3	0	0	0	0	.667	-0	/3SOD	-0.3
1991	Tex-A	81	268	38	50	9	2	15	37	32	98	.187	.281	.403	88	-6	-5	31	0	2	-1	.944	-10	3O/D	-1.7
1992	Tex-A	152	541	74	124	25	0	26	72	62	154	.229	.313	.420	107	1	4	73	10	4	1	.945	-10	*3	-0.6
Total	3	249	828	112	176	36	2	41	110	94	264	.213	.298	.409	98	-7	-4	104	10	6	-1	.942	-20	3/ODS	-2.6

■ EDDIE PALMER Palmer, Edwin Henry "Baldy" b: 6/1/1893, Petty, Tex. d: 1/9/83, Marlow, Okla. BR/TR, 5'9.5", 175 lbs. Deb: 9/06/17

YEAR	TM/L	G	AB	R	H	2B	3B	HR	RBI	BB	SO	AVG	OBP	SLG	PRO+	BR	/A	RC	SB	CS	SBR	FA	FR	POS	TPR
1917	Phi-A	16	52	7	11	1	0	0	5	7	7	.212	.305	.231	65	-2	-2	4	1			.898	0	3/S	-0.2

■ JOE PALMISANO Palmisano, Joseph b: 11/19/02, West Point, Ga. d: 11/5/71, Albuquerque, N.Mex. BR/TR, 5'8", 160 lbs. Deb: 5/31/31

YEAR	TM/L	G	AB	R	H	2B	3B	HR	RBI	BB	SO	AVG	OBP	SLG	PRO+	BR	/A	RC	SB	CS	SBR	FA	FR	POS	TPR
1931	Phi-A	19	44	5	10	2	0	0	4	6	3	.227	.320	.273	54	-3	-3	4	0	0	0	.960	-2	C/2	-0.4

■ STAN PALYS Palys, Stanley Francis b: 5/1/30, Blakely, Pa. BR/TR, 6'2", 190 lbs. Deb: 9/20/53

YEAR	TM/L	G	AB	R	H	2B	3B	HR	RBI	BB	SO	AVG	OBP	SLG	PRO+	BR	/A	RC	SB	CS	SBR	FA	FR	POS	TPR
1953	Phi-N	2	2	0	0	0	0	0	0	1	0	.000	.333	.000	-4	-0	-0	0	0	0	0	.000	-0	/O	-0.1
1954	Phi-N	2	4	0	1	0	0	0	0	1	1	.250	.400	.250	74	-0	-0	1	0	0	0	1.000	0	/O	0.0
1955	Phi-N	15	52	8	15	3	0	1	8	6	5	.288	.362	.404	105	0	0	8	1	0	0	1.000	-0	O	0.0
	Cin-N	79	222	29	51	14	0	7	30	12	35	.230	.272	.387	69	-9	-11	23	1	1	-0	.992	2	O/1	-1.2
	Yr	94	274	37	66	17	0	8	38	18	40	.241	.290	.391	75	-9	-11	31	2	1	0	.993	2	O/1	-1.2
1956	Cin-N	40	53	5	12	0	0	2	5	6	13	.226	.305	.340	69	-2	-2	6	0	0	0	.929	-2	O	-0.5
Total	4	138	333	42	79	17	0	10	43	26	54	.237	.294	.378	74	-11	-13	37	2	1	0	.988	-1	/O1	-1.8

■ JIM PANKOVITS Pankovits, James Franklin b: 8/6/55, Pennington Gap, Va. BR/TR, 5'10", 195 lbs. Deb: 5/27/84

YEAR	TM/L	G	AB	R	H	2B	3B	HR	RBI	BB	SO	AVG	OBP	SLG	PRO+	BR	/A	RC	SB	CS	SBR	FA	FR	POS	TPR
1984	Hou-N	53	81	6	23	7	0	1	14	2	20	.284	.301	.407	105	-1	0	10	2	1	0	.925	-5	2/S/O	-0.5
1985	Hou-N	75	172	24	42	3	0	4	14	17	29	.244	.316	.331	84	-4	-4	19	1	0	0	.983	0	O2/S3	-0.4
1986	*Hou-N	70	113	12	32	6	1	1	7	11	25	.283	.347	.381	103	0	1	14	1	1	-0	.969	3	2/OC	0.4
1987	Hou-N	50	61	7	14	2	0	1	8	6	13	.230	.299	.311	64	-3	-3	6	2	0	1	1.000	5	/2O3	0.2
1988	Hou-N	68	140	13	31	7	1	2	12	8	28	.221	.273	.329	75	-5	-5	13	2	1	0	.939	-2	23/1	-0.7
1990	Bos-A	2	0	0	0	0	0	0	0	0	0	—	—	—	—	0	0	0	0	0	0	.000	0	/2	0.0
Total	6	318	567	62	142	25	2	9	55	44	115	.250	.308	.349	86	-13	-11	61	8	3	1	.961	1	2/O3S1C	-1.0

■ KEN PAPE Pape, Kenneth Wayne b: 10/1/51, San Antonio, Tex. BR/TR, 5'11", 195 lbs. Deb: 5/17/76

YEAR	TM/L	G	AB	R	H	2B	3B	HR	RBI	BB	SO	AVG	OBP	SLG	PRO+	BR	/A	RC	SB	CS	SBR	FA	FR	POS	TPR
1976	Tex-A	21	23	7	5	1	0	1	4	3	2	.217	.357	.391	117	1	1	3	0	1	-1	.968	4	/S32D	0.5

■ STAN PAPI Papi, Stanley Gerard b: 2/4/51, Fresno, Cal. BR/TR, 6', 178 lbs. Deb: 4/11/74

YEAR	TM/L	G	AB	R	H	2B	3B	HR	RBI	BB	SO	AVG	OBP	SLG	PRO+	BR	/A	RC	SB	CS	SBR	FA	FR	POS	TPR
1974	StL-N	8	4	0	1	0	0	0	1	0	0	.250	.250	.250	40	-0	-0	0	0	0	0	1.000	1	/S2	0.0
1977	Mon-N	13	43	5	10	2	1	0	4	1	9	.233	.250	.326	55	-3	-3	3	1	0	0	.952	-5	3/S2	-0.7
1978	Mon-N	67	152	15	35	11	0	0	11	10	28	.230	.287	.303	65	-7	-7	12	0	0	0	.976	-3	S3/2	-0.8
1979	Bos-A	50	117	9	22	8	0	1	6	5	20	.188	.221	.282	33	-11	-12	8	0	0	0	.982	12	2S	0.3
1980	Bos-A	1	0	0	0	0	0	0	0	0	0	—	—	—	—	0	0	0	0	0	0	.000	0	/3	0.0
	Det-A	46	114	12	27	3	4	3	17	5	24	.237	.269	.412	82	-3	-3	12	0	0	0	.973	-2	23/S/1	-0.4
	Yr	47	114	12	27	3	4	3	17	5	24	.237	.269	.412	82	-3	-3	12	0	0	0	.973	-2	23/S1	-0.4
1981	Det-A	40	93	8	19	2	1	3	12	3	18	.204	.229	.344	61	-5	-5	7	1	0	0	.941	-1	3/12OD	-0.7
Total	6	225	523	49	114	26	6	7	51	24	99	.218	.255	.331	60	-29	-30	42	2	0	1	.931	2	/32SD1O	-2.3

■ ERIK PAPPAS Pappas, Erik Daniel b: 4/25/66, Chicago, Ill. BR/TR, 6', 190 lbs. Deb: 4/19/91

YEAR	TM/L	G	AB	R	H	2B	3B	HR	RBI	BB	SO	AVG	OBP	SLG	PRO+	BR	/A	RC	SB	CS	SBR	FA	FR	POS	TPR
1991	Chi-N	7	17	1	3	0	0	0	2	1	5	.176	.222	.176	13	-2	-2	1	0	0	0	1.000	1	/C	0.0

■ AL PARDO Pardo, Alberto Judas b: 9/8/62, Oviedo, Spain BB/TR, 6'2", 187 lbs. Deb: 7/03/85

YEAR	TM/L	G	AB	R	H	2B	3B	HR	RBI	BB	SO	AVG	OBP	SLG	PRO+	BR	/A	RC	SB	CS	SBR	FA	FR	POS	TPR
1985	Bal-A	34	75	3	10	1	0	0	1	3	15	.133	.167	.147	-14	-12	-11	2	0	0	0	.979	3	C	-0.7
1986	Bal-A	16	51	3	7	1	0	1	3	0	14	.137	.137	.216	-6	-7	-7	1	0	0	0	.987	-2	C/D	-0.9
1988	Phi-N	2	2	0	0	0	0	0	0	0	2	.000	.000	.000	-98	-1	-1	0	0	0	0	1.000	-0	/C	-0.1
1989	Phi-N	1	1	0	0	0	0	0	0	0	0	.000	.000	.000	-99	-0	-0	0	0	0	0	1.000	0	/C	0.0
Total	4	53	129	6	17	2	0	1	4	3	31	.132	.152	.171	-12	-20	-19	3	0	0	0	.982	1	/CD	-1.7

■ JOHNNY PAREDES Paredes, Johnny Alfonso (Isambert) b: 9/2/62, Maracaibo, Venez. BR/TR, 5'11", 165 lbs. Deb: 4/29/88

YEAR	TM/L	G	AB	R	H	2B	3B	HR	RBI	BB	SO	AVG	OBP	SLG	PRO+	BR	/A	RC	SB	CS	SBR	FA	FR	POS	TPR
1988	Mon-N	35	91	6	17	2	0	1	10	9	17	.187	.282	.242	49	-5	-6	7	5	2	0	.976	0	2/O	-0.5
1990	Det-A	6	8	2	1	0	0	0	0	1	0	.125	.222	.125	-0	-1	-1	0	0	0	0	.917	1	/2	0.0
	Mon-N	3	6	0	2	1	0	0	1	1	0	.333	.429	.500	161	0	1	1	0	0	0	.889	1	/2	0.1
1991	Det-A	16	18	4	6	0	0	0	0	0	1	.333	.333	.333	84	-0	-0	2	1	1	-0	.958	4	/23SD	0.3
Total	3	60	123	12	26	3	0	1	11	11	18	.211	.292	.260	56	-6	-7	10	6	3	0	.965	6	/2DS3O	-0.1

■ FREDDY PARENT Parent, Frederick Alfred b: 11/25/1875, Biddeford, Me. d: 11/2/72, Sanford, Maine BR/TR, 5'7", 154 lbs. Deb: 7/14/1899

YEAR	TM/L	G	AB	R	H	2B	3B	HR	RBI	BB	SO	AVG	OBP	SLG	PRO+	BR	/A	RC	SB	CS	SBR	FA	FR	POS	TPR
1899	StL-N	2	8	0	1	0	0	0	1	0		.125	.125	.125	-31	-1	-1	0	0			.889	-1	/2	-0.2
1901	Bos-A	138	517	87	158	23	9	4	59	41		.306	.367	.408	117	11	12	88	16			.918	-0	*S	2.1
1902	Bos-A	138	567	91	156	31	8	3	62	24		.275	.310	.374	87	-10	-12	74	16			.932	4	*S	0.0
1903	*Bos-A	139	560	83	170	31	17	4	80	13		.304	.326	.441	122	17	14	92	24			.930	9	*S	3.0
1904	Bos-A	155	591	85	172	22	9	6	77	28		.291	.330	.389	120	17	13	87	20			.929	-8	*S	1.1
1905	Bos-A	153	602	55	141	16	5	0	33	47		.234	.296	.277	81	-11	-12	63	25			.920	-7	*S	-1.8
1906	Bos-A	149	600	67	141	14	10	1	49	31		.235	.276	.297	80	-15	-15	57	16			.933	-7	*S/2	-1.8
1907	Bos-A	114	409	51	113	19	5	1	26	22		.276	.321	.355	117	6	7	54	12			.978	-0	OS/32	0.7
1908	Chi-A	119	391	28	81	7	5	0	35	50		.207	.300	.251	81	-7	-6	33	9			.930	5	*S	0.2
1909	Chi-A	136	472	61	123	10	5	0	30	46		.261	.335	.303	106	2	5	60	32			.929	17	SO/2	2.4
1910	Chi-A	81	258	23	46	6	1	1	16	29		.178	.266	.221	55	-13	-12	19	14			.970	-2	O2/S3	-2.0
1911	Chi-A	3	9	2	4	1	0	0	3	2		.444	.545	.556	214	1	2	3	0			1.000	1	/2	0.2
Total	12	1327	4984	633	1306	180	74	20	471	333		.262	.315	.340	99	-2	-6	631	184			.927	9	*SO/23	3.9

■ MARK PARENT Parent, Mark Allen b: 9/16/61, Ashland, Ore. BR/TR, 6'5", 224 lbs. Deb: 9/20/86

YEAR	TM/L	G	AB	R	H	2B	3B	HR	RBI	BB	SO	AVG	OBP	SLG	PRO+	BR	/A	RC	SB	CS	SBR	FA	FR	POS	TPR
1986	SD-N	8	14	1	2	0	0	0	0	1	3	.143	.200	.143	-4	-2	-2	0	0	0	0	.889	-1	/C	-0.3

YEAR	TM/L	G	AB	R	H	2B	3B	HR	RBI	BB	SO	AVG	OBP	SLG	PRO+	BR	/A	RC	SB	CS	SBR	FA	FR	POS	TPR
1987	SD-N	12	25	0	2	0	0	0	2	0	9	.080	.080	.080	-60	-6	-5	0	0	0	0	1.000	0	C	-0.5
1988	SD-N	41	118	9	23	3	0	6	15	6	23	.195	.234	.373	73	-5	-5	10	0	0	0	.986	5	C	0.3
1989	SD-N	52	141	12	27	4	0	7	21	8	34	.191	.235	.369	70	-6	-6	11	1	0	0	1.000	6	C/1	0.2
1990	SD-N	65	189	13	42	11	0	3	16	16	29	.222	.283	.328	67	-9	-9	18	1	0	0	.992	8	C	0.3
1991	Tex-A	3	1	0	0	0	0	0	0	0	1	.000	.000	.000	-99	-0	-0	0	0	0	0	1.000	1	/C	0.0
1992	Bal-A	17	34	4	8	1	0	2	4	3	7	.235	.316	.441	110	0	0	5	0	0	0	.988	4	C	0.5
Total	7	198	522	39	104	19	0	18	58	34	106	.199	.250	.339	64	-27	-27	45	2	0	1	.991	24	C/1	0.5

■ KELLY PARIS Paris, Kelly Jay b: 10/17/57, Encino, Cal. BR/TR, 6′, 180 lbs. Deb: 9/01/82

YEAR	TM/L	G	AB	R	H	2B	3B	HR	RBI	BB	SO	AVG	OBP	SLG	PRO+	BR	/A	RC	SB	CS	SBR	FA	FR	POS	TPR
1982	StL-N	12	29	1	3	0	0	0	1	0	7	.103	.103	.103	-42	-5	-5	0	0	0	0	.867	2	/3S	-0.3
1983	Cin-N	56	120	13	30	6	0	0	7	15	22	.250	.338	.300	75	-3	-4	13	8	2	1	1.000	-2	32/S1	-0.4
1985	Bal-A	5	9	0	0	0	0	0	0	0	1	.000	.000	.000	-99	-2	-2	0	0	0	0	.857	-0	/2D	-0.3
1986	Bal-A	5	10	0	2	0	0	0	0	0	3	.200	.200	.200	9	-1	-1	0	0	1	-1	.857	1	/3D	-0.1
1988	Chi-A	14	44	6	11	0	0	3	6	0	6	.250	.250	.455	93	-1	-1	5	0	0	0	1.000	-0	/13D	-0.1
Total	5	92	212	20	46	6	0	3	14	15	39	.217	.272	.288	54	-13	-13	18	8	3	1	.944	1	/312SD	-1.2

■ TONY PARISSE Parisse, Louis Peter b: 6/25/11, Philadelphia, Pa. d: 6/2/56, Philadelphia, Pa. BR/TR, 5′10″, 165 lbs. Deb: 9/22/43

YEAR	TM/L	G	AB	R	H	2B	3B	HR	RBI	BB	SO	AVG	OBP	SLG	PRO+	BR	/A	RC	SB	CS	SBR	FA	FR	POS	TPR
1943	Phi-A	6	17	0	3	0	0	0	1	2	2	.176	.263	.176	30	-1	-1	1	0	0	0	1.000	0	/C	-0.1
1944	Phi-A	4	4	0	0	0	0	0	0	0	1	.000	.000	.000	-99	-1	-1	0	0	0	0	.500	-1	/C	-0.2
Total	2	10	21	0	3	0	0	0	1	2	3	.143	.217	.143	6	-2	-2	1	0	0	0	.960	-0	/C	-0.3

■ ACE PARKER Parker, Clarence McKay b: 5/17/12, Portsmouth, Va. BR/TR, 6′, 180 lbs. Deb: 4/24/37

YEAR	TM/L	G	AB	R	H	2B	3B	HR	RBI	BB	SO	AVG	OBP	SLG	PRO+	BR	/A	RC	SB	CS	SBR	FA	FR	POS	TPR
1937	Phi-A	38	94	8	11	0	1	2	13	4	17	.117	.153	.202	-11	-16	-16	3	0	0	0	.905	-5	S/2O	-1.9
1938	Phi-A	56	113	12	26	5	0	0	12	10	16	.230	.293	.274	44	-10	-10	9	1	2	-1	.972	-5	S/23	-1.3
Total	2	94	207	20	37	5	1	2	25	14	33	.179	.231	.242	19	-26	-26	12	1	2	-1	.934	-10	/S23O	-3.2

■ PAT PARKER Parker, Clarence Perkins b: 5/22/1893, Somerville, Mass. d: 3/21/67, Claremont, N.H. BR/TR, 5′7″, 160 lbs. Deb: 8/10/15

YEAR	TM/L	G	AB	R	H	2B	3B	HR	RBI	BB	SO	AVG	OBP	SLG	PRO+	BR	/A	RC	SB	CS	SBR	FA	FR	POS	TPR
1915	StL-A	3	6	0	1	0	0	0	1	0	3	.167	.167	.167	-0	-1	-1	0	0	1	-1	1.000	-0	/O	-0.2

■ DAVE PARKER Parker, David Gene b: 6/9/51, Calhoun, Miss. BL/TR, 6′5″, 230 lbs. Deb: 7/12/73

YEAR	TM/L	G	AB	R	H	2B	3B	HR	RBI	BB	SO	AVG	OBP	SLG	PRO+	BR	/A	RC	SB	CS	SBR	FA	FR	POS	TPR
1973	Pit-N	54	139	17	40	9	1	4	14	2	27	.288	.308	.453	111	1	1	18	1	1	-0	.964	3	O	0.3
1974	*Pit-N	73	220	27	62	10	3	4	29	10	53	.282	.322	.409	107	0	1	28	3	3	-1	.964	2	O/1	0.0
1975	*Pit-N	148	558	75	172	35	10	25	101	38	89	.308	.358	**.541**	148	32	32	101	8	6	-1	.972	7	*O	3.3
1976	Pit-N	138	537	82	168	28	10	13	90	30	80	.313	.351	.475	132	21	20	85	19	7	2	.956	6	*O	2.3
1977	Pit-N★	159	637	107	**215**	**44**	8	21	88	58	107	**.338**	.399	.531	143	42	40	130	17	19	-6	.965	28	*O/2	5.5
1978	Pit-N	148	581	102	194	32	12	30	117	57	92	**.334**	.395	**.585**	163	**53**	**50**	**134**	20	7	2	.960	5	*O	**5.2**
1979	*Pit-N★	158	622	109	193	45	7	25	94	67	101	.310	.385	.526	140	39	36	131	20	4	4	.960	9	*O	4.2
1980	Pit-N★	139	518	71	153	31	1	17	79	25	69	.295	.330	.458	116	10	9	75	10	7	-1	.965	-1	*O	0.2
1981	Pit-N★	67	240	29	62	14	3	9	48	9	25	.258	.291	.454	106	1	0	30	6	2	1	.941	-8	O	-1.0
1982	Pit-N	73	244	41	66	19	3	6	29	22	45	.270	.333	.447	113	5	4	34	7	5	-1	.957	-6	O	-0.5
1983	Pit-N	144	552	68	154	29	4	12	69	28	89	.279	.314	.411	97	-2	-4	67	12	9	-2	.973	1	*O	-1.0
1984	Cin-N	156	607	73	173	28	0	16	94	41	89	.285	.331	.410	103	5	2	80	11	10	-3	.974	5	*O	-0.1
1985	Cin-N★	160	635	88	198	**42**	4	34	**125**	52	80	.312	.367	.551	146	43	39	112	5	13	-6	.972	13	*O	4.1
1986	Cin-N★	162	637	89	174	31	3	31	116	56	126	.273	.333	.477	116	16	12	94	1	6	-3	.970	-2	*O	0.2
1987	Cin-N	153	589	77	149	28	0	26	97	44	104	.253	.314	.433	91	-5	-9	77	7	3	0	.967	8	*O/1	-0.6
1988	*Oak-A	101	377	43	97	18	1	12	55	32	70	.257	.315	.406	104	-0	1	49	0	1	-1	.953	-0	DO/1	-0.1
1989	*Oak-A	144	553	56	146	27	0	22	97	38	91	.264	.313	.432	112	4	6	68	0	0	0	1.000	0	*D/O	0.6
1990	Mil-A☆	157	610	71	176	30	3	21	92	41	102	.289	.337	.451	119	13	14	86	4	7	-3	.960	-1	*D/1	1.0
1991	Cal-A	119	466	45	108	22	2	11	56	29	91	.232	.281	.358	76	-16	-16	46	3	2	-0	.000	0	*D	-1.7
	Tor-A	13	36	2	12	4	0	0	3	4	7	.333	.400	.444	128	2	2	6	0	1	-1	.000	0	D	0.1
	Yr	132	502	47	120	26	2	11	59	33	98	.239	.290	.365	80	-15	-15	52	3	3	-1	.000	0	*D	-1.6
Total	19	2466	9358	1272	2712	526	75	339	1493	683	1537	.290	.342	.471	121	262	241	1452	154	113	-22	.965	66	*OD/12	22.0

■ DIXIE PARKER Parker, Douglas Woolley b: 4/24/1895, Forest Home, Ala. d: 5/15/72, Tuscaloosa, Ala. BL/TR, 5′11″, 160 lbs. Deb: 7/28/23

YEAR	TM/L	G	AB	R	H	2B	3B	HR	RBI	BB	SO	AVG	OBP	SLG	PRO+	BR	/A	RC	SB	CS	SBR	FA	FR	POS	TPR
1923	Phi-N	4	5	0	1	0	0	0	1	0	1	.200	.200	.200	5	-1	-1	0	0	0	0	.500	-1	/C	-0.2

■ SALTY PARKER Parker, Francis James b: 7/8/13, E.St.Louis, Ill. d: 7/27/92, Houston, Tex. BR/TR, 6′, 173 lbs. Deb: 8/13/36 MC

YEAR	TM/L	G	AB	R	H	2B	3B	HR	RBI	BB	SO	AVG	OBP	SLG	PRO+	BR	/A	RC	SB	CS	SBR	FA	FR	POS	TPR
1936	Det-A	11	25	6	7	2	0	0	4	2	3	.280	.333	.360	71	-1	-1	2	0	2	-1	.906	3	/S1	0.1

■ WES PARKER Parker, Maurice Wesley b: 11/13/39, Evanston, Ill. BB/TL, 6′1″, 180 lbs. Deb: 4/19/64

YEAR	TM/L	G	AB	R	H	2B	3B	HR	RBI	BB	SO	AVG	OBP	SLG	PRO+	BR	/A	RC	SB	CS	SBR	FA	FR	POS	TPR
1964	LA-N	124	214	29	55	7	1	3	10	14	45	.257	.306	.341	88	-5	-3	23	5	4	-1	.971	6	O1	-0.1
1965	*LA-N	154	542	80	129	24	7	8	51	75	95	.238	.336	.352	101	-2	2	70	13	7	-0	**.997**	-0	*1/O	-0.7
1966	*LA-N	156	475	67	120	17	5	12	51	69	83	.253	.353	.385	114	5	10	67	7	3	0	.992	0	*1O	0.2
1967	LA-N	139	413	56	102	16	5	5	31	65	83	.247	.359	.346	112	4	8	55	10	5	0	**.996**	5	*1O	0.7
1968	LA-N	135	468	42	112	22	2	3	27	49	87	.239	.314	.314	96	-5	-2	49	4	6	-2	**.999**	2	*1O	-1.3
1969	LA-N	132	471	76	131	23	4	13	68	56	46	.278	.357	.427	128	12	16	73	4	1	1	.995	1	*1/O	0.8
1970	LA-N	161	614	84	196	**47**	4	10	111	79	70	.319	.397	.458	134	26	30	113	8	2	1	**.996**	4	*1	2.0
1971	LA-N	157	533	69	146	24	1	6	62	63	63	.274	.352	.356	107	2	6	69	6	1	1	.996	5	*1O	-0.1
1972	LA-N	130	427	45	119	14	3	4	59	62	43	.279	.371	.354	110	6	7	57	3	5	-2	**.997**	1	*1/O	-0.4
Total	9	1288	4157	548	1110	194	32	64	470	532	615	.267	.353	.375	112	44	75	575	60	34	-2	.996	23	*1O	1.1

■ RICK PARKER Parker, Richard Allen b: 3/20/63, Kansas City, Mo. BR/TR, 6′, 185 lbs. Deb: 5/04/90

YEAR	TM/L	G	AB	R	H	2B	3B	HR	RBI	BB	SO	AVG	OBP	SLG	PRO+	BR	/A	RC	SB	CS	SBR	FA	FR	POS	TPR
1990	SF-N	54	107	19	26	5	0	2	14	10	15	.243	.314	.346	84	-3	-2	13	6	1	1	.978	-10	O/23S	-1.2
1991	SF-N	13	14	0	1	0	0	0	1	1	5	.071	.133	.071	-42	-3	-3	0	0	0	0	1.000	-1	/O	-0.4
Total	2	67	121	19	27	5	0	2	15	11	20	.223	.293	.314	70	-5	-5	13	6	1	1	.980	-11	/O2S3	-1.6

■ BILLY PARKER Parker, William David b: 1/14/47, Hayneville, Ala. BR/TR, 5′8″, 168 lbs. Deb: 9/09/71

YEAR	TM/L	G	AB	R	H	2B	3B	HR	RBI	BB	SO	AVG	OBP	SLG	PRO+	BR	/A	RC	SB	CS	SBR	FA	FR	POS	TPR
1971	Cal-A	20	70	4	16	0	1	1	6	2	20	.229	.250	.300	59	-4	-4	5	1	1	-0	.958	-1	2	-0.4
1972	Cal-A	36	80	11	17	2	0	2	8	9	17	.213	.292	.313	85	-2	-1	7	0	2	-1	.951	-0	3/2OS	-0.3
1973	Cal-A	38	102	14	23	2	1	0	7	8	23	.225	.288	.265	61	-6	-5	8	0	1	-1	.959	-3	2/SD	-0.7
Total	3	94	252	29	56	4	2	3	21	19	60	.222	.279	.290	68	-12	-10	19	1	4	-2	.963	-5	/23OSD	-1.4

■ FRANK PARKINSON Parkinson, Frank Joseph "Parky" b: 3/23/1895, Dickson City, Pa. d: 7/4/60, Trenton, N.J. BR/TR, 5′11″, 175 lbs. Deb: 4/13/21

YEAR	TM/L	G	AB	R	H	2B	3B	HR	RBI	BB	SO	AVG	OBP	SLG	PRO+	BR	/A	RC	SB	CS	SBR	FA	FR	POS	TPR
1921	Phi-N	108	391	36	99	20	2	5	32	13	81	.253	.277	.353	61	-20	-24	37	3	4	-2	.931	9	*S/3	-0.6
1922	Phi-N	141	545	86	150	18	6	15	70	55	93	.275	.344	.413	86	-5	-13	79	3	4	-2	.963	**31**	*2	1.9
1923	Phi-N	67	219	21	53	12	0	3	28	13	31	.242	.288	.338	58	-12	-15	20	0	4	-2	.950	3	2S3	-1.2
1924	Phi-N	62	156	14	33	7	0	1	19	14	28	.212	.281	.276	44	-11	-14	13	3	1	0	.952	7	3S2	-0.3
Total	4	378	1311	157	335	57	8	24	149	95	233	.256	.308	.366	69	-48	-65	149	9	13	-5	.962	50	2S/3	-0.2

■ ART PARKS Parks, Artie William b: 11/1/11, Paris, Ark. d: 12/6/89, Little Rock, Ark. BL/TR, 5′9″, 170 lbs. Deb: 9/25/37

YEAR	TM/L	G	AB	R	H	2B	3B	HR	RBI	BB	SO	AVG	OBP	SLG	PRO+	BR	/A	RC	SB	CS	SBR	FA	FR	POS	TPR
1937	Bro-N	7	16	2	5	2	0	0	0	2	2	.313	.389	.438	122	1	1	3	0			1.000	0	/O	0.0
1939	Bro-N	71	239	27	65	13	2	1	19	28	14	.272	.348	.356	86	-3	-4	30	2			.977	-4	O	-1.0
Total	2	78	255	29	70	15	2	1	19	30	16	.275	.351	.361	89	-2	-4	33	2			.978	-4	/O	-1.0

■ DEREK PARKS Parks, Derek Gavin b: 9/29/68, Covina, Cal. BR/TR, 6′, 205 lbs. Deb: 9/11/92

YEAR	TM/L	G	AB	R	H	2B	3B	HR	RBI	BB	SO	AVG	OBP	SLG	PRO+	BR	/A	RC	SB	CS	SBR	FA	FR	POS	TPR
1992	Min-A	7	6	1	2	0	0	0	0	1	1	.333	.500	.333	133	1	0	1	0	0	0	1.000	1	/C	0.2

YEAR	TM/L	G	AB	R	H	2B	3B	HR	RBI	BB	SO	AVG	OBP	SLG	PRO+	BR	/A	RC	SB	CS	SBR	FA	FR	POS	TPR

■ BILL PARKS Parks, William Robert b: 6/4/1849, Easton, Pa. d: 10/10/11, Easton, Pa. BR/TR, 5'8", 150 lbs. Deb: 4/26/1875 M

1875	Was-n	26	112	13	20	1	0	0		0		.179	.179	.188	28	-8	-7	4						OPM	-0.2
	Phi-n	2	6	0	1	0	0	0		0		.167	.167	.167	15	-0	-1	0						/PO	0.0
	Yr	28	118	13	21	1	0	0		0		.178	.178	.186	27	-8	-8	4						OP	-0.2
1876	Bos-N	1	4	0	0	0	0	0	0	0	0	.000	.000	.000	-98	-1	-1	0				.750	-0	/O	-0.1

■ SAM PARRILLA Parrilla, Samuel b: 6/12/43, Santurce, P.R. BR/TR, 5'11", 185 lbs. Deb: 4/11/70

| 1970 | Phi-N | 11 | 16 | 0 | 2 | 1 | 0 | 0 | 1 | 0 | 4 | .125 | .176 | .188 | -3 | -2 | -2 | 1 | 0 | 0 | 0 | 1.000 | 0 | /O | -0.2 |

■ LANCE PARRISH Parrish, Lance Michael b: 6/15/56, Clairton, Pa. BR/TR, 6'3", 220 lbs. Deb: 9/05/77

1977	Det-A	12	46	10	9	2	0	3	7	5	12	.196	.275	.435	85	-1	-1	5	0	0	0	1.000	2	C	0.1
1978	Det-A	85	288	37	63	11	3	14	41	11	71	.219	.255	.424	85	-6	-7	29	0	0	0	.987	5	C	-0.1
1979	Det-A	143	493	65	136	26	3	19	65	49	105	.276	.344	.456	110	9	7	73	6	7	-2	.989	4	*C	1.3
1980	Det-A★	144	553	79	158	34	6	24	82	31	109	.286	.327	.499	120	15	13	80	6	4	-1	.990	-5	*CD/1O	1.2
1981	Det-A	96	348	39	85	18	2	10	46	34	52	.244	.312	.394	98	0	-1	38	2	3	-1	.993	-2	C/D	-0.1
1982	Det-A★	133	486	75	138	19	2	32	87	40	99	.284	.340	.529	134	21	21	86	3	4	-2	.989	9	*C/O	3.3
1983	Det-A★	155	605	80	163	42	3	27	114	44	106	.269	.320	.483	120	12	14	86	1	3	-2	.995	0	*CD	1.9
1984	*Det-A★	147	578	75	137	16	2	33	98	41	120	.237	.290	.443	100	-3	-2	71	2	3	-1	.991	1	*CD	0.4
1985	Det-A†	140	549	64	150	27	1	28	98	41	90	.273	.326	.479	118	11	12	82	2	6	-3	.993	-6	*CD	0.9
1986	Det-A	91	327	53	84	6	1	22	62	38	83	.257	.343	.483	122	10	10	57	0	0	0	.989	2	C/D	1.7
1987	Phi-N	130	466	42	114	21	0	17	67	47	104	.245	.315	.399	85	-9	-11	53	0	1	-1	.989	-3	*C	-0.6
1988	Phi-N★	123	424	44	91	17	2	15	60	47	93	.215	.296	.370	88	-6	-7	46	0	0	0	.988	-4	*C/1	-0.2
1989	Cal-A	124	433	48	103	12	1	17	50	42	104	.238	.308	.388	97	-3	-2	51	1	1	-0	.993	-2	*C/D	0.2
1990	Cal-A★	133	470	54	126	14	0	24	70	46	107	.268	.340	.451	122	11	13	71	2	2	-1	.993	10	*C/1D	3.0
1991	Cal-A	119	402	38	87	12	1	19	51	35	117	.216	.287	.388	85	-9	-9	45	0	1	-1	.997	-5	*C/1D	-0.4
1992	Cal-A	24	83	7	19	2	0	4	11	5	22	.229	.273	.398	87	-2	-2	9	0	0	0	.975	-5	C/D	-0.6
	Sea-A	69	192	19	45	11	1	8	21	19	48	.234	.307	.427	103	0	0	24	1	1	-0	.995	-4	C1D	-0.3
	Yr	93	275	26	64	13	1	12	32	24	70	.233	.297	.418	98	-2	-2	33	1	1	-0	.987	-10	CD1	-0.9
Total	16	1868	6743	829	1708	290	27	316	1030	575	1442	.253	.315	.445	107	51	47	906	26	36	-14	.991	3	*CD/1O	11.7

■ LARRY PARRISH Parrish, Larry Alton b: 11/10/53, Winter Haven, Fla. BR/TR, 6'3", 215 lbs. Deb: 9/06/74

1974	Mon-N	25	69	9	14	5	0	4	4	6	19	.203	.286	.275	54	-4	-4	6	0	0	0	.986	8	3	0.3
1975	Mon-N	145	532	50	146	32	5	10	65	28	74	.274	.316	.410	96	-2	-5	64	4	5	-2	.919	-3	*3/2S	-1.0
1976	Mon-N	154	543	65	126	28	5	11	61	41	91	.232	.288	.363	81	-13	-16	54	2	6	-3	.945	5	*3	-1.6
1977	Mon-N	123	402	50	99	19	2	11	46	37	71	.246	.316	.386	90	-8	-6	47	2	4	-2	.936	-9	*3	-1.9
1978	Mon-N	144	520	68	144	39	4	15	70	32	103	.277	.321	.454	116	8	9	69	2	3	-1	.947	-5	*3	0.0
1979	Mon-N★	153	544	83	167	39	2	30	82	41	101	.307	.358	.551	146	31	31	106	5	1	1	.947	-9	3	2.2
1980	Mon-N	126	452	55	115	27	3	15	72	36	80	.254	.315	.427	105	2	2	57	2	6	-3	.949	-8	*3	-1.1
1981	*Mon-N	97	349	41	85	19	3	8	44	28	73	.244	.300	.384	92	-4	-5	39	0	0	0	.935	-17	3	-2.6
1982	Tex-A	128	440	59	116	15	0	17	62	30	84	.264	.316	.414	104	-2	1	56	5	2	0	.962	-7	*O/3D	-0.9
1983	Tex-A	145	555	76	151	26	4	26	88	46	91	.272	.331	.474	121	13	14	82	0	0	0	.962	-5	*OD	0.5
1984	Tex-A	156	613	72	175	42	1	22	101	42	116	.285	.337	.465	116	15	12	89	2	4	-2	.982	4	OD3	1.2
1985	Tex-A	94	346	44	86	11	1	17	51	33	77	.249	.316	.434	101	1	1	44	0	2	-1	.991	-3	OD/3	-0.6
1986	Tex-A	129	464	67	128	22	1	28	94	52	114	.276	.351	.509	127	19	17	80	3	1	0	.935	-5	D3	1.2
1987	Tex-A★	152	557	79	149	22	1	32	100	49	154	.268	.330	.483	112	8	8	88	3	1	0	.918	-9	*D3/O	-0.1
1988	Tex-A	68	248	22	47	9	1	7	26	20	79	.190	.256	.319	58	-14	-15	20	0	0	0	.000	0	D	-1.5
	*Bos-A	52	158	10	41	5	0	7	26	8	32	.259	.299	.424	96	-0	-1	19	0	1	-1	.988	3	1D	-0.2
	Yr	120	406	32	88	14	1	14	52	28	111	.217	.272	.360	73	-14	-16	39	0	1	-1	.988	3	D1	-1.7
Total	15	1891	6792	850	1789	360	33	256	992	529	1359	.263	.321	.439	106	49	44	919	30	36	-13	.941	-62	*3OD/1S2	-6.1

■ TOM PARROTT Parrott, Thomas William "Tacky Tom" b: 4/10/1868, Portland, Ore. d: 1/1/32, Dundee, Ore. BR/TR, 5'10.5", 170 lbs. Deb: 6/18/1893 F

1893	Chi-N	7	27	4	7	1	0	0	3	1	2	.259	.286	.296	57	-2	-2	2	0			.800	-1	/P32	-0.1
	Cin-N	24	68	5	13	1	1	1	9	1	9	.191	.203	.279	28	-7	-7	4	0			.915	1	P/O	-0.1
	Yr	31	95	9	20	2	1	1	12	2	11	.211	.227	.284	36	-9	-9	6	0			.906	-0	P/32O	-0.2
1894	Cin-N	68	229	51	74	12	6	4	40	17	10	.323	.372	.480	102	2	-0	44	4			.929	5	PO1/S32	0.1
1895	Cin-N	64	201	35	69	13	7	3	41	11	8	.343	.377	.522	127	9	7	45	0			.922	1	P1/O	0.1
1896	StL-N	118	474	62	138	13	12	7	70	11	24	.291	.307	.414	94	-9	-6	67	12			.951	13	*O/P1	-0.1
Total	4	281	999	157	301	40	26	15	163	41	53	.301	.329	.438	98	-8	-8	162	26			.940	19	OP/132S	-0.1

■ JIGGS PARROTT Parrott, Walter Edward b: 7/14/1871, Portland, Ore. d: 4/16/1898, Phoenix, Ariz. 5'11", 160 lbs. Deb: 7/11/1892 F

1892	Chi-N	78	333	38	67	8	5	2	22	8	30	.201	.222	.273	50	-21	-21	22	7			.891	-2	3	-1.9
1893	Chi-N	110	455	54	111	10	9	1	65	13	25	.244	.267	.312	56	-31	-29	46	25			.904	9	*3/2O	-1.5
1894	Chi-N	124	517	82	128	17	9	3	64	16	35	.248	.274	.333	45	-46	-51	58	30			.931	-6	*2/3	-4.1
1895	Chi-N	3	4	0	1	0	0	0	0	0	0	.250	.250	.250	29	-0	-0	0	0			.000	-1	/OS1	-0.1
Total	4	315	1309	174	307	35	23	6	151	37	90	.235	.258	.310	49	-97	-102	126	62			.899	-0	32/O1S	-7.6

■ CASEY PARSONS Parsons, Casey Robert b: 4/14/54, Wenatchee, Wash. BL/TR, 6'1", 180 lbs. Deb: 5/31/81

1981	Sea-A	36	22	6	5	1	0	1	5	1	4	.227	.320	.409	105	0	0	3	0	0	0	1.000	-5	O/1	-0.5
1983	Chi-A	8	5	1	1	0	0	0	0	2	1	.200	.429	.200	77	0	-0	1	0	0	0	1.000	-1	/OD	-0.1
1984	Chi-A	1	1	0	0	0	0	0	0	0	1	.000	.000	.000	-96	-0	-0	0	0	0	0	.000	0	/H	-0.1
1987	Cle-A	18	25	2	4	0	0	1	5	0	5	.160	.160	.280	13	-3	-3	1	0	0	0	1.000	-1	/O1D	-0.4
Total	4	63	53	9	10	1	0	2	10	3	11	.189	.259	.321	57	-3	-3	4	0	0	0	1.000	-6	/OD1	-1.0

■ DIXIE PARSONS Parsons, Edward Dixon b: 5/12/16, Talladega, Ala. d: 10/31/91, Longview, Tex. BR/TR, 6'2", 180 lbs. Deb: 8/16/39

1939	Det-A	5	1	0	0	0	0	0	0	1	1	.000	.500	.000	36	0	-0	0	0	0	0	1.000	0	/C	0.0
1942	Det-A	63	188	8	37	4	0	2	11	13	22	.197	.249	.250	37	-15	-17	12	1	0	0	.981	10	C	-0.3
1943	Det-A	40	106	2	15	3	0	0	4	6	16	.142	.188	.170	4	-13	-14	3	0	0	0	.975	5	C	-0.7
Total	3	108	295	10	52	7	0	2	15	20	39	.176	.229	.220	26	-28	-31	15	1	0	0	.979	15	C	-1.0

■ JOHN PARSONS Parsons, John S. b: Napoleon, Ohio Deb: 10/15/1884

| 1884 | Cin-a | 1 | 3 | 0 | 0 | 0 | 0 | 0 | | 0 | | .000 | .000 | .000 | -95 | -1 | -1 | 0 | | | | 1.000 | -1 | /O | -0.1 |

■ ROY PARTEE Partee, Roy Robert b: 9/7/17, Los Angeles, Cal. BR/TR, 5'10", 180 lbs. Deb: 4/23/43

1943	Bos-A	96	299	30	84	14	2	0	31	39	33	.281	.368	.341	106	4	4	40	0	0	0	.983	-6	C	0.4
1944	Bos-A	89	280	18	68	12	0	2	41	37	29	.243	.333	.307	85	-5	-5	30	0	1	-1	.989	-6	C	-0.7
1946	*Bos-A	40	111	13	35	5	2	0	9	13	14	.315	.387	.396	113	3	2	17	0	0	0	.974	-6	C	-0.2
1947	Bos-A	60	169	14	39	2	0	0	16	18	23	.231	.305	.243	50	-10	-12	14	0	0	0	.975	-1	C	-0.9
1948	StL-A	82	231	14	47	8	1	0	17	25	21	.203	.284	.247	41	-19	-20	16	2	2	-1	.982	1	C	-1.5
Total	5	367	1090	89	273	41	5	2	114	132	120	.250	.334	.303	78	-27	-30	116	2	3	-1	.982	-18	C	-2.9

■ STEVE PARTENHEIMER Partenheimer, Harold Philip b: 8/30/1891, Greenfield, Mass. d: 6/16/71, Mansfield, Ohio BR/TR, 5'8.5", 145 lbs. Deb: 6/18/13 F

| 1913 | Det-A | 1 | 2 | 0 | 0 | 0 | 0 | 0 | 0 | 0 | 0 | .000 | .333 | .000 | -1 | -0 | -0 | 0 | | | | .750 | 0 | /3 | 0.0 |

■ JAY PARTRIDGE Partridge, James Bugg b: 11/15/02, Mountville, Ga. d: 1/14/74, Nashville, Tenn. BL/TR, 5'11", 160 lbs. Deb: 4/12/27

| 1927 | Bro-N | 146 | 572 | 72 | 149 | 17 | 6 | 7 | 40 | 20 | 36 | .260 | .289 | .348 | 70 | -25 | -26 | 56 | 9 | | | .938 | -16 | *2 | -3.6 |

YEAR	TM/L	G	AB	R	H	2B	3B	HR	RBI	BB	SO	AVG	OBP	SLG	PRO+	BR	/A	RC	SB	CS	SBR	FA	FR	POS	TPR
1928	Bro-N	37	73	18	18	0	1	0	12	13	6	.247	.368	.274	71	-2	-2	8	2			.908	-5	2/3	-0.7
Total	2	183	645	90	167	17	7	7	52	33	42	.259	.299	.340	70	-28	-28	64	11			.935	-20	2/3	-4.3
■ BEN PASCHAL	Paschal, Benjamin Edwin b: 10/13/1895, Enterprise, Ala. d: 11/10/74, Charlotte, N.C. BR/TR, 5'11", 185 lbs. Deb: 8/16/15																								
1915	Cle-A	9	9	0	1	0	0	0	0	0	3	.111	.111	.111	-33	-1	-1	0	0			.000	0	H	-0.2
1920	Bos-A	9	28	5	10	0	0	0	5	5	2	.357	.455	.357	122	1	1	5	1	0	0	1.000	-0	/O	0.1
1924	NY-A	4	12	2	3	1	0	0	3	1	0	.250	.308	.333	65	-1	-1	1	0	0	0	1.000	-0	/O	-0.1
1925	NY-A	89	247	49	89	16	5	12	56	22	29	.360	.417	.611	161	21	21	60	14	9	-1	.953	-4	O	1.1
1926	*NY-A	96	258	46	74	12	3	7	32	26	35	.287	.354	.438	107	2	2	40	7	6	-2	.935	-3	O	-0.7
1927	NY-A	50	82	16	26	9	2	2	16	4	10	.317	.349	.549	134	3	3	14	0	2	-1	.976	-5	O	-0.3
1928	*NY-A	65	79	12	25	6	1	1	15	8	11	.316	.379	.456	122	2	2	14	1	0	0	1.000	-6	O	-0.4
1929	NY-A	42	72	13	15	3	0	2	11	6	3	.208	.269	.333	58	-5	-4	7	1	1	-0	.951	-1	O	-0.7
Total	8	364	787	143	243	47	11	24	138	72	93	.309	.369	.488	123	21	24	141	24	18		.953	-19	O	-1.2
■ JOHNNY PASEK	Pasek, John Paul b: 6/25/05, Niagara Falls, N.Y. d: 3/13/76, Niagara Falls, N.Y BR/TR, 5'10", 175 lbs. Deb: 7/28/33																								
1933	Det-A	28	61	6	15	4	0	0	4	7	7	.246	.324	.311	68	-3	-3	7	2	0	1	.989	-1	C	-0.1
1934	Chi-A	4	9	1	3	0	0	0	0	1	1	.333	.400	.333	88	-0	-0	1	0	0	0	1.000	0	/C	0.0
Total	2	32	70	7	18	4	0	0	4	8	8	.257	.333	.314	70	-3	-3	8	2	0	1	.990	-1	/C	-0.1
■ DODE PASKERT	Paskert, George Henry b: 8/28/1881, Cleveland, Ohio d: 2/12/59, Cleveland, Ohio BR/TR, 5'11", 165 lbs. Deb: 9/21/07																								
1907	Cin-N	16	50	10	14	4	0	1	8	2		.280	.321	.420	127	2	1	8	2			.973	1	O	0.2
1908	Cin-N	118	395	40	96	14	4	1	36	27		.243	.298	.306	96	-3	-2	44	25			.953	5	*O	-0.2
1909	Cin-N	104	322	49	81	7	4	0	33	34		.252	.327	.298	95	-2	-1	39	23			.968	0	O/1	-0.5
1910	Cin-N	144	506	63	152	21	5	2	46	70	60	.300	.389	.374	128	17	20	93	51			.957	14	*O/1	2.8
1911	Phi-N	153	560	96	153	18	5	4	47	70	70	.273	.358	.345	96	-1	-2	81	28			.979	8	*O	-0.2
1912	Phi-N	145	540	102	170	37	5	2	43	91	67	.315	.420	.413	120	26	21	108	36			.967	5	*O/23	1.8
1913	Phi-N	124	454	83	119	21	9	4	29	65	69	.262	.358	.374	105	7	5	65	12			.972	18	*O	1.7
1914	Phi-N	132	451	59	119	25	6	3	44	56	68	.264	.349	.366	106	8	4	64	23			.958	12	*O/S	1.2
1915	*Phi-N	109	328	51	80	17	4	3	39	35	38	.244	.319	.348	100	1	0	41	9	6	-1	.970	-2	O/1	-0.8
1916	Phi-N	149	555	82	155	30	7	8	46	54	76	.279	.346	.402	125	19	17	77	22	21	-6	.983	1	*O/S	0.6
1917	Phi-N	141	546	78	137	27	11	4	43	62	63	.251	.331	.363	108	9	6	68	19			**.984**	-2	*O	-0.4
1918	*Chi-N	127	461	69	132	24	3	3	59	53	49	.286	.362	.371	121	14	13	68	20			.980	-3	*O/3	0.4
1919	Chi-N	88	270	21	53	11	3	2	29	28	33	.196	.274	.281	67	-10	-11	22	7			.969	-6	O	-2.5
1920	Chi-N	139	487	57	136	22	10	5	71	64	58	.279	.366	.396	117	14	12	72	16	14	-4	.956	1	*O	0.0
1921	Cin-N	27	92	8	16	1	1	0	4	4	8	.174	.208	.207	11	-12	-11	4	0	2	-1	.984	1	O	-1.3
Total	15	1716	6017	868	1613	279	77	42	577	715	659	.268	.350	.361	108	88	73	855	293	43		.969	52	*O/13S2	2.8
■ KEVIN PASLEY	Pasley, Kevin Patrick b: 7/22/53, Bronx, N.Y. BR/TR, 6', 185 lbs. Deb: 10/02/74																								
1974	LA-N	1	0	0	0	0	0	0	0	0	0	—	—	—	—	0	0	0	0	0	0	1.000	-0	/C	0.0
1976	LA-N	23	52	4	12	2	0	0	2	3	7	.231	.273	.269	55	-3	-3	4	0	0	0	.971	5	C	0.2
1977	LA-N	2	3	0	1	0	0	0	0	0	0	.333	.333	.333	80	-0	-0	0	0	0	0	1.000	1	/C	0.0
	Sea-A	4	13	1	5	0	0	0	2	1	2	.385	.429	.385	125	0	1	2	0	0	0	1.000	-2	/C	-0.1
1978	Sea-A	25	54	3	13	5	0	1	5	2	4	.241	.268	.389	83	-1	-1	5	0	0	0	1.000	-0	C	-0.1
Total	4	55	122	8	31	7	0	1	9	6	13	.254	.289	.336	76	-4	-4	12	0	0	0	.986	3	/C	0.0
■ DAN PASQUA	Pasqua, Daniel Anthony b: 10/17/61, Yonkers, N.Y. BL/TL, 6', 203 lbs. Deb: 5/30/85																								
1985	NY-A	60	148	17	31	3	1	9	25	16	38	.209	.291	.426	96	-2	-1	19	0	0	0	1.000	1	OD	-0.1
1986	NY-A	102	280	44	82	17	0	16	45	47	78	.293	.400	.525	151	20	21	62	2	0	1	.987	-2	O/1D	1.6
1987	NY-A	113	318	42	74	7	1	17	42	40	99	.233	.320	.421	96	-3	-2	43	0	2	-1	.985	-2	OD1	-0.8
1988	Chi-A	129	422	48	96	16	2	20	50	46	100	.227	.308	.417	101	-0	0	54	1	0	0	**.996**	7	*O/1D	0.4
1989	Chi-A	73	246	26	61	9	1	11	47	25	58	.248	.320	.427	111	2	3	35	1	2	-1	.993	2	O/D	0.2
1990	Chi-A	112	325	43	89	27	3	13	58	37	66	.274	.352	.495	137	14	15	57	1	1	-0	.962	0	DO	1.4
1991	Chi-A	134	417	71	108	22	5	18	66	62	86	.259	.359	.465	129	15	17	71	0	2	-1	.991	-8	1O/D	0.2
1992	Chi-A	93	265	26	56	16	1	6	33	36	57	.211	.308	.347	85	-6	-5	30	0	1	-1	.963	-2	O/1D	-1.0
Total	8	816	2421	317	597	117	14	110	366	309	582	.247	.336	.443	115	42	47	371	5	8	-3	.986	-4	O1D	1.9
■ MIKE PASQUELLA	Pasquella, Michael John "Toney" (b: Michael John Pasquariello) b: 11/7/1898, Philadelphia, Pa. d: 4/5/65, Bridgeport, Conn. BR/TR, 5'11", 167 lbs. Deb: 7/09/19																								
1919	Phi-N	1	1	1	1	0	0	0	0	0	0	1.000	1.000	1.000	469	0	0	1	0			.000	0	/1	0.0
	StL-N	1	1	0	0	0	0	0	0	0	1	.000	.000	.000	-99	-0	-0	0	0			.000	0	H	0.0
	Yr	2	2	1	1	0	0	0	0	0	1	.500	.500	.500	200	0	0	0	0			.000	0	/1	0.0
■ CLIFF PASTORNICKY	Pastornicky, Clifford Scott b: 11/18/58, Seattle, Was. BR/TR, 5'10", 170 lbs. Deb: 6/14/83																								
1983	KC-A	10	32	4	4	0	0	2	5	0	3	.125	.125	.313	16	-4	-4	0	0	0	0	.929	-0	3	-0.4
■ BOB PATE	Pate, Robert Wayne b: 12/3/53, Los Angeles, Cal. BR/TR, 6'3.5", 200 lbs. Deb: 6/02/80																								
1980	Mon-N	23	39	3	10	2	0	0	5	3	6	.256	.310	.308	73	-1	-1	4	0	1	-1	1.000	-1	O	-0.4
1981	Mon-N	8	6	0	2	0	0	0	0	1	0	.333	.429	.333	117	0	0	1	0	0	0	1.000	0	/O	0.0
Total	2	31	45	3	12	2	0	0	5	4	6	.267	.327	.311	79	-1	-1	5	0	1	-1	1.000	-1	/O	-0.4
■ FREDDIE PATEK	Patek, Frederick Joseph "The Flea" b: 10/9/44, Seguin, Tex. BR/TR, 5'5", 148 lbs. Deb: 6/03/68																								
1968	Pit-N	61	208	31	53	4	2	2	18	12	37	.255	.302	.322	89	-3	-3	22	18	7	1	.976	-2	S/O3	0.2
1969	Pit-N	147	460	48	110	9	1	5	32	53	86	.239	.319	.296	75	-15	-14	43	15	8	-0	.954	-2	*S	-0.1
1970	*Pit-N	84	237	42	58	10	5	1	19	29	46	.245	.327	.342	81	-7	-6	29	8	2	1	.971	11	S	1.3
1971	KC-A	147	591	86	158	21	**11**	6	36	44	80	.267	.323	.371	97	-4	-3	75	49	14	6	.968	10	*S	3.4
1972	KC-A†	136	518	59	110	25	4	0	32	47	64	.212	.282	.276	67	-21	-21	44	33	7	6	.971	**30**	*S	3.8
1973	KC-A	135	501	82	117	19	5	5	45	54	63	.234	.312	.321	73	-14	-19	53	36	14	2	.966	**35**	*S	3.7
1974	KC-A	149	537	72	121	18	6	3	38	77	69	.225	.326	.298	76	-11	-15	58	33	15	1	.967	4	*S	0.9
1975	KC-A	136	483	58	110	14	5	5	45	42	65	.228	.292	.308	68	-19	-21	47	32	7	5	.959	-7	*S/D	-0.7
1976	*KC-A★	144	432	58	104	19	3	1	43	50	63	.241	.322	.306	84	-7	-8	48	51	15	6	.962	-6	*S/D	1.0
1977	*KC-A	154	497	72	130	26	6	5	60	41	84	.262	.324	.368	88	-8	-8	65	**53**	13	8	.958	-19	*S	-0.2
1978	*KC-A★	138	440	54	109	23	1	2	46	42	56	.248	.315	.318	76	-12	-13	48	38	11	5	.949	-25	*S	-1.7
1979	KC-A	106	306	30	77	17	0	1	37	16	42	.252	.295	.317	64	-15	-16	26	11	12	-4	.955	-28	*S	-3.7
1980	Cal-A	86	273	41	72	10	5	5	34	15	26	.264	.304	.392	92	-5	-4	28	7	6	-2	.953	-18	S	-1.5
1981	Cal-A	27	47	3	11	1	1	0	5	1	6	.234	.250	.298	57	-3	-3	3	1	0	0	.983	2	2/3S	0.0
Total	14	1650	5530	736	1340	216	55	41	490	523	787	.242	.311	.324	79	-143	-152	592	385	131	37	.962	-15	*S/23OD	6.4
■ BOB PATRICK	Patrick, Robert Lee b: 10/27/17, Ft.Smith, Ark. BR/TR, 6'2", 190 lbs. Deb: 9/20/41																								
1941	Det-A	5	7	2	2	0	0	0	0	0	1	.286	.286	.286	47	-0	-1	1	0	0	0	.750	-1	/O	-0.2
1942	Det-A	4	8	1	2	1	0	1	3	1	0	.250	.333	.750	185	1	1	2	0	0	0	1.000	-0	/O	0.0
Total	2	9	15	3	4	1	0	1	3	1	1	.267	.313	.533	118	0	0	3	0	0	0	.889	-1	/O	-0.2
■ HARRY PATTEE	Pattee, Harry Ernest b: 1/17/1882, Charlestown, Mass. d: 7/17/71, Lynchburg, Va. BL/TR, 5'8", 149 lbs. Deb: 4/14/08																								
1908	Bro-N	80	264	19	57	5	2	0	9	25		.216	.284	.250	74	-8	-7	26	24			.964	12	2	0.5

YEAR	TM/L	G	AB	R	H	2B	3B	HR	RBI	BB	SO	AVG	OBP	SLG	PRO+	BR	/A	RC	SB	CS	SBR	FA	FR	POS	TPR

■ DAN PATTERSON Patterson, Daniel Thomas b: 1846, New York, N.Y. TL , 5'9", 143 lbs. Deb: 5/18/1871

1871	Mut-n	32	151	31	31	2	0	0	13	1	0	.205	.211	.219	26	-14	-11	8	2					*O/2	-0.7
1872	Eck-n	12	47	6	8	1	0	0	3	0	1	.170	.170	.191	13	-5	-3	2						O/1	-0.2
1874	Mut-n	1	5	1	2	0	0	0		0	0	.400	.400	.400	151	0	0	1						/1O	0.0
1875	Atl-n	11	41	3	8	0	0	0		0	0	.195	.195	.195	41	-3	-2	2						/2O	-0.2
Total	4 n	56	244	41	49	3	0	0			1	.201	.204	.213	28	-21	-16	12						/O21	-1.1

■ HAM PATTERSON Patterson, Hamilton b: 10/13/1877, Belleville, Ill. d: 11/25/45, E.St.Louis, Ill. BR/TR, 6'2", 185 lbs. Deb: 5/18/09 F

1909	StL-A	17	49	2	10	1	0	0	5	0		.204	.204	.224	38	-4	-3	2	1			1.000	-1	/1O	-0.5
	Chi-A	1	3	2	0	0	0	0	0	1		.000	.250	.000	-21	-0	-0	0	0			1.000	1	/1	0.0
	Yr	18	52	4	10	1	0	0	5	1		.192	.208	.212	35	-4	-4	2	1			1.000	0	/1O	-0.5

■ HANK PATTERSON Patterson, Henry Joseph Colquit b: 7/17/07, San Francisco, Cal. d: 9/30/70, Panorama City, Cal. BR/TR, 5'11.5", 170 lbs. Deb: 9/05/32

| 1932 | Bos-A | 1 | 1 | 0 | 0 | 0 | 0 | 0 | 0 | 0 | 0 | .000 | .000 | .000 | -99 | -0 | -0 | 0 | 0 | 0 | 0 | .000 | 0 | /C | 0.0 |

■ JOHN PATTERSON Patterson, John Allen b: 2/11/67, Key West, Fla. BB/TR, 5'9", 160 lbs. Deb: 4/06/92

| 1992 | SF-N | 32 | 103 | 10 | 19 | 1 | 1 | 0 | 4 | 5 | 24 | .184 | .229 | .214 | 28 | -10 | -9 | 5 | 5 | 1 | 1 | .960 | 6 | 2/O | -0.2 |

■ CLAIRE PATTERSON Patterson, Lorenzo Claire b: 10/5/1887, Arkansas City, Kan. d: 3/28/13, Mojave, Cal. BL/TR, 6' ", 180 lbs. Deb: 9/05/09

| 1909 | Cin-N | 4 | 8 | 0 | 1 | 0 | 0 | 0 | 1 | 0 | | .125 | .125 | .125 | -23 | -1 | -1 | 0 | 0 | | | 1.000 | -0 | /O | -0.2 |

■ MIKE PATTERSON Patterson, Michael Lee b: 1/26/58, Santa Monica, Cal. BL/TR, 5'10", 170 lbs. Deb: 4/15/81

1981	Oak-A	12	23	4	8	1	1	0	1	2	5	.348	.400	.478	160	2	2	4	0	1	-1	1.000	-1	/OD	0.0
	NY-A	4	9	2	2	0	2	0	0	0	0	.222	.222	.667	150	0	0	1	0	0	0	1.000	-1	/O	0.0
	Yr	16	32	6	10	1	3	0	1	2	5	.313	.353	.531	158	2	2	6	0	1	-1	1.000	-1	/OD	0.0
1982	NY-A	11	16	3	3	1	0	1	1	2	6	.188	.278	.438	94	-0	-0	2	1	0	0	1.000	-3	/OD	-0.3
Total	2	27	48	9	13	2	3	1	2	4	11	.271	.327	.500	135	2	2	8	1	1	-0	1.000	-5	/OD	-0.3

■ PAT PATTERSON Patterson, William Jennings Bryan b: 1/29/01, Belleville, Ill. d: 10/1/77, St.Louis, Mo. BR/TR, 6', 175 lbs. Deb: 4/14/21 F

| 1921 | NY-N | 23 | 35 | 5 | 14 | 0 | 0 | 1 | 5 | 2 | 5 | .400 | .432 | .486 | 142 | 2 | 2 | 7 | 0 | 1 | -1 | .970 | 4 | 3/S | 0.6 |

■ GEORGE PATTISON Pattison, George Deb: 4/24/1884

| 1884 | Phi-U | 2 | 7 | 0 | 1 | 0 | 0 | 0 | | 0 | | .143 | .143 | .143 | -3 | -1 | -1 | 0 | | | | .500 | -0 | /O | -0.1 |

■ GENE PATTON Patton, Gene Tunney b: 7/8/26, Coatesville, Pa. BL/TR, 5'10", 165 lbs. Deb: 6/17/44

| 1944 | Bos-N | 1 | 0 | 0 | 0 | 0 | 0 | 0 | 0 | 0 | 0 | — | — | — | — | 0 | 0 | 0 | 0 | | | .000 | 0 | R | 0.0 |

■ BILL PATTON Patton, George William b: 10/7/12, Cornwall, Pa. d: 3/15/86, Philadelphia, Pa. BR/TR, 6'2", 180 lbs. Deb: 6/29/35

| 1935 | Phi-A | 9 | 10 | 1 | 3 | 1 | 0 | 0 | 2 | 2 | 3 | .300 | .417 | .400 | 113 | 0 | 0 | 2 | 0 | 0 | 0 | 1.000 | 0 | /C | 0.1 |

■ TOM PATTON Patton, Thomas Allen b: 9/5/35, Honey Brook, Pa. BR/TR, 5'9.5", 185 lbs. Deb: 4/30/57

| 1957 | Bal-A | 1 | 2 | 0 | 0 | 0 | 0 | 0 | 0 | 0 | 2 | .000 | .000 | .000 | -99 | -1 | -1 | 0 | 0 | 0 | 0 | 1.000 | 1 | /C | 0.1 |

■ LOU PAUL Paul, Louis BR/TR, Deb: 9/05/1876

| 1876 | Phi-N | 3 | 12 | 2 | 2 | 0 | 0 | 0 | 0 | 0 | 0 | .167 | .167 | .250 | 37 | -1 | -1 | 1 | | | | .643 | -2 | /C | -0.3 |

■ CARLOS PAULA Paula, Carlos (Conill) b: 11/28/27, Havana, Cuba d: 4/25/83, Miami, Fla. BR/TR, 6'3", 195 lbs. Deb: 9/06/54

1954	Was-A	9	24	2	4	1	0	0	2	2	4	.167	.231	.208	22	-3	-2	1	0	0	0	1.000	1	/O	-0.2
1955	Was-A	115	351	34	105	20	7	6	45	17	43	.299	.335	.447	115	3	5	49	2	3	-1	.941	-2	O	-0.2
1956	Was-A	33	82	8	15	2	1	3	13	8	15	.183	.256	.341	56	-6	-6	6	0	2	-1	.974	-1	O	-0.9
Total	3	157	457	44	124	23	8	9	60	27	62	.271	.315	.416	99	-6	-3	56	2	5	-2	.950	-2	O	-1.3

■ GENE PAULETTE Paulette, Eugene Edward b: 5/26/1891, Centralia, Ill. d: 2/8/66, Little Rock, Ark. BR/TR, 6', 150 lbs. Deb: 6/16/11

1911	NY-N	10	12	1	2	0	0	0	1	0	1	.167	.167	.167	-6	-2	-2	0	0			.938	-1	/1S3	-0.3
1916	StL-A	5	4	1	2	0	0	0	1	1	1	.500	.600	.500	242	1	1	1	0			.000	0	H	0.1
1917	StL-A	12	22	3	4	0	0	0	0	3	3	.182	.280	.182	43	-1	-1	1	0			.982	0	/123	-0.1
	StL-N	95	332	32	88	21	7	0	34	16	16	.265	.303	.370	109	1	2	38	9			.993	-1	1	-0.3
1918	StL-N	125	461	33	126	15	3	0	52	27	16	.273	.316	.319	97	-3	-2	49	11			.983	5	1S/203P	-0.3
1919	StL-N	43	144	11	31	6	0	0	11	9	6	.215	.261	.257	60	-8	-7	10	4			.990	2	1/S	-0.7
	Phi-N	67	243	20	63	8	3	1	31	19	10	.259	.316	.329	88	-2	-3	27	10			.957	0	2O/1	-0.1
	Yr	110	387	31	94	14	3	1	42	28	16	.243	.296	.302	78	-9	-10	36	14			.957	2	21O/S	-0.8
1920	Phi-N	143	562	59	162	16	6	1	36	33	16	.288	.332	.343	90	-4	-7	64	9	8	-2	.988	6	*1/S	-0.7
Total	6	500	1780	160	478	66	19	2	165	108	69	.269	.314	.330	92	-18	-19	191	43	8		.988	11	1/2SO3P	-2.1

■ SI PAUXTIS Pauxtis, Simon Francis b: 7/20/1885, Pittston, Pa. d: 3/13/61, Philadelphia, Pa. BR/TR, 6' ", 175 lbs. Deb: 9/18/09

| 1909 | Cin-N | 4 | 8 | 2 | 1 | 0 | 0 | 0 | 0 | 0 | | .125 | .222 | .125 | 8 | -1 | -1 | 0 | 0 | | | 1.000 | -1 | /C | -0.2 |

■ DON PAVLETICH Pavletich, Donald Stephen b: 7/13/38, Milwaukee, Wis. BR/TR, 5'11", 209 lbs. Deb: 4/20/57

1957	Cin-N	1	1	0	0	0	0	0	0	0	0	.000	.000	.000	-93	-0	-0	0	0	0	0	.000	0	H	0.0
1959	Cin-N	1	0	1	0	0	0	0	0	0	0	—	—	—	—	0	0	0	0	0	0	.000	0	R	0.0
1962	Cin-N	34	63	7	14	3	0	1	7	8	18	.222	.310	.317	67	-3	-3	7	0	0	0	1.000	1	1/C	-0.3
1963	Cin-N	71	183	18	38	11	0	5	18	17	12	.208	.275	.350	76	-5	-6	18	0	0	0	.991	-3	1C	-1.1
1964	Cin-N	34	91	12	22	4	0	5	11	10	17	.242	.317	.451	109	1	1	13	0	0	0	.983	-3	C/1	-0.1
1965	Cin-N	68	191	25	61	11	1	8	32	23	27	.319	.395	.513	144	14	12	38	1	1	-0	.986	-2	C/1	1.2
1966	Cin-N	83	235	29	69	13	2	12	38	18	37	.294	.346	.519	126	11	9	41	0	1	0	.975	-10	C1	-0.4
1967	Cin-N	74	231	25	55	14	3	6	34	21	38	.238	.313	.403	93	1	-2	26	2	1	0	.986	-5	C/13	-0.4
1968	Cin-N	46	98	11	28	3	1	2	11	8	23	.286	.352	.398	117	3	2	12	0	0	0	1.000	-0	1/C	0.1
1969	Chi-A	78	188	26	46	12	0	6	33	28	45	.245	.343	.404	103	2	1	28	0	0	0	.974	-6	C1	-0.4
1970	Bos-A	32	65	4	9	1	1	0	6	10	15	.138	.253	.185	21	-7	-7	3	1	0	0	1.000	1	1C	-0.7
1971	Bos-A	14	27	5	7	1	0	1	3	5	5	.259	.375	.407	113	1	1	5	0	0	0	.973	-2	/C	-0.1
Total	12	536	1373	163	349	73	8	46	193	148	237	.254	.330	.420	103	18	7	190	5	2	0	.983	-31	C1/3	-1.7

■ TED PAWELEK Pawelek, Theodore John "Porky" b: 8/15/19, Chicago Heights, Ill. d: 2/12/64, Chicago Heights, Ill. BL/TR, 5'10.5", 202 lbs. Deb: 9/13/46

| 1946 | Chi-N | 4 | 4 | 0 | 1 | 1 | 0 | 0 | 0 | 0 | 0 | .250 | .250 | .500 | 112 | 0 | 0 | 1 | 0 | | | .000 | -0 | /C | 0.0 |

■ STAN PAWLOSKI Pawloski, Stanley Walter b: 9/6/31, Wanamie, Pa. BR/TR, 6'1", 175 lbs. Deb: 9/24/55

| 1955 | Cle-A | 2 | 8 | 0 | 1 | 0 | 0 | 0 | 0 | 0 | 2 | .125 | .125 | .125 | -31 | -1 | -2 | 0 | 0 | 0 | 0 | 1.000 | 1 | /2 | 0.0 |

■ FRED PAYNE Payne, Frederick Thomas b: 9/2/1880, Camden, N.Y. d: 1/16/54, Camden, N.Y. BR/TR, 5'10", 162 lbs. Deb: 4/21/06

1906	Det-A	72	222	23	60	5	5	0	20	13		.270	.316	.338	102	1	0	27	4			.966	-1	CO	0.4
1907	*Det-A	53	169	17	28	2	2	0	14	7		.166	.221	.201	34	-12	-13	9	4			.981	3	C/O	-0.7
1908	Det-A	20	45	3	3	0	0	0	2	3		.067	.176	.067	-20	-6	-6	1	1			.954	-3	C/O	-1.0
1909	Chi-A	32	82	8	20	2	0	0	12	5		.244	.295	.268	82	-2	-5	7	0			.987	-3	C/O	-0.1
1910	Chi-A	91	252	17	56	5	4	0	19	11		.222	.260	.274	70	-10	-9	20	6			.974	-3	C/O	-0.6
1911	Chi-A	66	133	14	27	2	1	1	19	8		.203	.259	.256	45	-10	-10	10	6			.963	-4	C	-0.9
Total	6	334	903	82	194	16	12	1	86	47		.215	.265	.262	64	-39	-38	74	21			.972	-10	C/O	-2.9

YEAR	TM/L	G	AB	R	H	2B	3B	HR	RBI	BB	SO	AVG	OBP	SLG	PRO+	BR	/A	RC	SB	CS	SBR	FA	FR	POS	TPR

■ GEORGE PAYNTER Paynter, George Washington (b: George Washington Paner)
b: 7/6/1871, Cincinnati, Ohio d: 10/1/50, Cincinnati, Ohio BR/TR, 5'9", 125 lbs. Deb: 8/12/1894

| 1894 | StL-N | 1 | 4 | 0 | 0 | 0 | 0 | 0 | 0 | 1 | 0 | .000 | .200 | .000 | -47 | -1 | -1 | 0 | 1 | | | 1.000 | 1 | /O | 0.0 |

■ JOHNNY PEACOCK Peacock, John Gaston b: 1/10/10, Fremont, N.C. d: 10/17/81, Wilson, N.C. BL/TR, 5'11", 165 lbs. Deb: 9/23/37

1937	Bos-A	9	32	3	10	2	1	0	6	1	0	.313	.333	.438	89	-0	-1	5	0	0	0	.980	1	/C	0.1
1938	Bos-A	72	195	29	59	7	1	1	39	17	4	.303	.358	.364	78	-5	-7	26	4	1	1	.984	-9	C/1O	-1.1
1939	Bos-A	92	274	33	76	11	4	0	36	29	11	.277	.347	.347	75	-9	-10	35	1	1	-0	.972	-8	C	-1.3
1940	Bos-A	63	131	20	37	4	1	0	13	23	10	.282	.390	.328	85	-1	-2	17	1	1	-0	.994	-6	C	-0.6
1941	Bos-A	79	261	28	74	20	1	0	27	21	3	.284	.339	.368	85	-5	-6	34	2	1	0	.988	-4	C	-0.4
1942	Bos-A	88	286	17	76	7	3	0	25	21	11	.266	.316	.311	74	-9	-10	29	1	1	-0	.988	-6	C	-1.1
1943	Bos-A	48	114	7	23	3	1	0	7	10	9	.202	.266	.246	49	-7	-7	8	1	1	-0	.972	-1	C	-0.7
1944	Bos-A	4	4	0	0	0	0	0	0	0	0	.000	.000	.000	-99	-1	-1	0	0	0	0	1.000	0	/C	-0.1
	Phi-N	83	253	21	57	9	3	0	21	31	15	.225	.310	.285	70	-10	-9	23	1			.990	1	C/2	-0.4
1945	Phi-N	33	74	6	15	6	0	0	6	6	0	.203	.262	.284	53	-5	-5	5	1			.969	-5	C	-0.9
	Bro-N	48	110	11	28	5	1	0	14	24	10	.255	.388	.318	98	1	1	16	2			.975	1	C	0.3
	Yr	81	184	17	43	11	1	0	20	30	10	.234	.341	.304	82	-4	-4	21	3			.973	-5	C	-0.6
Total	9	619	1734	175	455	74	16	1	194	183	73	.262	.333	.325	76	-51	-56	197	14	6		.983	-37	C/2O1	-6.2

■ ELIAS PEAK Peak, Elias b: 5/23/1859, Philadelphia, Pa. d: 12/17/16, Philadelphia, Pa. Deb: 4/19/1884

1884	Bos-U	1	3	2	2	0	0	0			1	.667	.750	.667	389	1	1	2				1.000	-0	/O	0.1
	Phi-U	54	215	35	42	6	4	0			7	.195	.221	.260	67	-8	-6	13				.825	-6	2/OS	-1.0
	Yr	55	218	37	44	6	4	0			8	.202	.230	.266	73	-7	-5	14				.825	-6	2/OS	-0.9

■ HARRY PEARCE Pearce, Harry James b: 7/12/1889, Philadelphia, Pa. d: 1/8/42, Philadelphia, Pa. BR/TR, 5'9", 158 lbs. Deb: 10/02/17

1917	Phi-N	7	16	2	4	3	0	0	2	0		.250	.294	.438	118	0	0	2	0			.967	5	/S	0.5
1918	Phi-N	60	164	16	40	3	2	0	18	9	31	.244	.295	.287	73	-4	-5	15	5			.944	5	2/S13	0.3
1919	Phi-N	68	244	24	44	3	3	0	9	8	27	.180	.209	.217	26	-21	-23	12	6			.948	-1	2S/3	-2.4
Total	3	135	424	42	88	9	5	0	29	17	62	.208	.247	.252	48	-25	-28	29	11			.946	9	/2S31	-1.6

■ DICKEY PEARCE Pearce, Richard J. b: 2/29/1836, Brooklyn, N.Y. d: 10/12/08, Wareham, Mass. BR/TR, 5'3.5", 161 lbs. Deb: 5/18/1871 MU

1871	Mut-n	33	163	31	44	5	0	0	20	4	1	.270	.287	.301	76	-6	-3	14	0					*S	-0.2
1872	Mut-n	44	206	32	40	1	1	0	24	4	1	.194	.210	.223	36	-16	-13	10						*S/OM	-0.9
1873	Atl-n	55	262	42	72	6	0	1	25	8	2	.275	.296	.309	88	-7	-1	25						*S/12	-0.1
1874	Atl-n	56	254	48	75	4	0	0			7	.295	.314	.311	113	0	6	25						*S/3	0.3
1875	StL-n	70	312	51	77	5	3	0			7	.247	.263	.282	98	-3	1	24						*S/PM	-0.1
1876	StL-N	25	102	12	21	1	0	0	10	3	5	.206	.229	.216	51	-5	-4	5				.902	5	S/O2	0.0
1877	StL-N	8	29	1	5	0	0	0	4	1	4	.172	.200	.172	19	-3	-2	1				.950	3	/S	0.0
Total	5 n	258	1197	204	308	21	4	2	69	30	4	.257	.275	.287	84	-31	-9	99						S/P3210	-1.0
Total	2	33	131	13	26	1	0	0	14	4	9	.198	.222	.206	44	-8	-7	6				.914	8	/S2O	0.0

■ DUCKY PEARCE Pearce, William C. b: 3/17/1885, Corning, Ohio d: 5/22/33, Brownstown, Ind. BR/TR, 6'1", 185 lbs. Deb: 7/01/08

1908	Cin-N	2	2	0	0	0	0	0	0	0		.000	.000	.000	-99	-0	-0	-0	0			1.000	1	/C	0.1
1909	Cin-N	2	2	0	0	0	0	0	0	0		.000	.000	.000	-99	-0	-0	0	0			1.000	-0	/C	-0.1
Total	2	4	4	0	0	0	0	0	0	0		.000	.000	.000	-99	-1	-1	-0	0			1.000	1	/C	0.0

■ ALBIE PEARSON Pearson, Albert Gregory b: 9/12/34, Alhambra, Cal. BL/TL, 5'5", 141 lbs. Deb: 4/14/58

1958	Was-A	146	530	63	146	25	5	3	33	64	31	.275	.356	.358	99	-0	1	69	7	8	-3	.980	6	*O	-0.4
1959	Was-A	25	80	9	15	1	0	0	2	14	3	.188	.309	.200	43	-6	-6	6	1	1	-0	.974	-2	O	-1.0
	Bal-A	80	138	22	32	4	2	0	6	13	5	.232	.298	.290	64	-7	-7	12	4	0	1	.987	-7	O	-1.4
	Yr	105	218	31	47	5	2	0	8	27	8	.216	.302	.257	56	-13	-12	19	5	1	1	.983	-9	O	-2.4
1960	Bal-A	48	82	17	20	2	0	1	6	17	3	.244	.374	.305	87	-1	-1	11	4	0	1	.975	-5	O	-0.6
1961	LA-A	144	427	92	123	21	3	7	41	96	40	.288	.422	.400	109	18	11	84	11	3	2	.956	-1	*O	0.5
1962	LA-A	160	614	**115**	160	29	6	5	42	95	36	.261	.361	.352	96	-3	-1	85	15	6	1	.989	9	*O	-0.1
1963	LA-A★	154	578	92	176	26	5	6	47	92	37	.304	.403	.398	133	24	28	100	17	10	-1	.983	7	*O	2.7
1964	LA-A	107	265	34	59	5	1	2	16	35	22	.223	.316	.272	72	-11	-8	25	6	4	-1	.978	-3	O	-1.5
1965	Cal-A	122	360	41	100	17	2	4	21	51	17	.278	.370	.369	114	7	8	55	12	1	3	.988	-4	*O	0.3
1966	Cal-A	2	3	0	0	0	0	0	0	0	1	.000	.000	.000	-99	-1	-1	0	0	0	0	.000	-0	/O	-0.1
Total	9	988	3077	485	831	130	24	28	214	477	195	.270	.370	.355	102	20	26	447	77	33	3	.980	1	O	-1.6

■ CHARLIE PECHOUS Pechous, Charles Edward b: 10/5/1896, Chicago, Ill. d: 9/13/80, Kenosha, Wis. BR/TR, 6', 170 lbs. Deb: 9/14/15

1915	Chi-F	18	51	4	9	3	0	0	4	4	15	.176	.236	.235	41	-4	-4	4	1			.938	-1	3	-0.4
1916	Chi-N	22	69	5	10	1	1	0	4	3	21	.145	.181	.188	12	-7	-8	3	1			.940	8	3	0.1
1917	Chi-N	13	41	2	10	0	0	0	1	2	9	.244	.295	.244	61	-2	-2	3	1			1.000	-2	/3S	-0.4
Total	3	53	161	11	29	4	1	0	9	9	45	.180	.228	.217	34	-13	-13	9	3			.947	6	/3S	-0.7

■ HAL PECK Peck, Harold Arthur b: 4/20/17, Big Bend, Wis. BL/TL, 5'11", 175 lbs. Deb: 5/13/43

1943	Bro-N	1	1	0	0	0	0	0	0	0	0	.000	.000	.000	-99	-0	-0	0	0			.000	0	H	0.0
1944	Phi-A	2	8	0	2	0	0	0	1	0	2	.250	.250	.250	44	-1	-1	0	0	2	-1	1.000	-0	/O	-0.2
1945	Phi-A	112	449	51	124	22	9	5	39	37	28	.276	.331	.399	112	5	5	61	5	3	-0	.943	-9	*O	-1.1
1946	Phi-A	48	150	14	37	8	2	2	11	16	14	.247	.319	.367	92	-2	-2	18	1	2	-1	.981	-3	O	-0.8
1947	Cle-A	114	392	58	115	18	2	8	44	27	31	.293	.342	.411	112	3	5	56	3	3	-1	.983	-7	O	-0.8
1948	*Cle-A	45	63	12	18	3	0	0	8	4	8	.286	.328	.333	78	-2	-2	8	1	0		1.000	-2	/O	-0.4
1949	Cle-A	33	29	1	9	1	0	0	9	3	3	.310	.375	.345	93	-0	-0	4	0	0	0	1.000	-1	/O	-0.1
Total	7	355	1092	136	305	52	13	15	112	87	86	.279	.334	.392	106	3	5	147	10	10		.965	-21	O	-3.4

■ ROGER PECKINPAUGH Peckinpaugh, Roger Thorpe b: 2/5/1891, Wooster, Ohio d: 11/17/77, Cleveland, Ohio BR/TR, 5'10.5", 165 lbs. Deb: 9/15/10 M

1910	Cle-A	15	45	1	9	0	0	0	6	1		.200	.234	.200	36	-3	-3	3	3			.906	-6	S	-1.0
1912	Cle-A	70	236	18	50	4	1	1	22	16		.212	.262	.250	45	-17	-18	18	11			.924	-2	S	-1.4
1913	Cle-A	1	0	1	0	0	0	0	0	0	0	—	—	—	—	0	0	0	0			.000	0	H	0.0
	NY-A	95	340	35	91	10	7	1	32	24	47	.268	.316	.347	94	-4	-4	41	19			.931	-6	S	-0.1
	Yr	96	340	36	91	10	7	1	32	24	47	.268	.316	.347	94	-4	-4	41	19			.931	-6	S	-0.1
1914	NY-A	157	570	55	127	14	6	3	51	51	73	.223	.288	.284	72	-20	-20	52	38	17	1	.956	4	*SM	-0.2
1915	NY-A	142	540	67	119	18	7	5	44	49	72	.220	.289	.307	79	-16	-16	53	19	12	-2	.942	11	*S	0.5
1916	NY-A	145	552	65	141	22	8	4	58	62	50	.255	.332	.346	101	2	1	72	18			.946	1	*S	1.1
1917	NY-A	148	543	63	141	24	7	0	41	64	46	.260	.340	.330	103	4	3	66	17			.934	10	*S	2.2
1918	NY-A	122	446	59	103	15	3	0	43	43	41	.231	.303	.278	74	-13	-14	42	12			.961	**25**	*S	1.8
1919	NY-A	122	453	89	138	20	2	7	33	59	37	.305	.390	.404	122	16	15	75	10			.943	28	*S	5.1
1920	NY-A	139	534	109	144	26	6	8	54	72	47	.270	.356	.386	93	-2	-5	75	8	12	-5	.962	3	*S	0.6
1921	*NY-A	149	577	128	166	25	7	8	71	84	44	.288	.380	.397	96	1	-1	93	2	2	-1	.948	-5	*S	0.7
1922	Was-A	147	520	62	132	14	4	2	48	55	36	.254	.329	.308	70	-24	-21	57	11	6	-0	.951	22	*S	1.6
1923	Was-A	154	568	73	150	18	4	2	62	64	30	.264	.340	.320	78	-20	-16	66	10	8	-2	.948	**23**	*S	2.0
1924	*Was-A	155	523	72	142	20	6	2	73	72	45	.272	.363	.340	84	-13	-11	69	11	7	-1	.963	9	*S	1.4
1925	*Was-A	126	422	67	124	16	6	4	64	49	23	.294	.367	.379	91	-6	-5	63	13	4	2	.952	-16	*S/1	-0.5
1926	Was-A	57	147	19	35	4	1	1	14	28	12	.238	.360	.299	75	-5	-4	18	3	0	1	.960	-1	S/1	0.0

YEAR	TM/L	G	AB	R	H	2B	3B	HR	RBI	BB	SO	AVG	OBP	SLG	PRO+	BR	/A	RC	SB	CS	SBR	FA	FR	POS	TPR
1927	Chi-A	68	217	23	64	6	3	0	23	21	6	.295	.360	.350	87	-4	-3	27	2	3	-1	.964	-1	S	0.0
Total	17	2012	7233	1006	1876	256	75	48	739	814	609	.259	.336	.335	87	-124	-120	889	207	71		.949	99	*S/1	13.8
■ BILL PECOTA Pecota, William Joseph b: 2/16/60, Redwood City, Cal. BR/TR, 6'2", 195 lbs. Deb: 9/19/86																									
1986	KC-A	12	29	3	6	2	0	0	2	3	3	.207	.303	.276	58	-2	-2	2	0	2	-1	.974	6	3/SD	0.3
1987	KC-A	66	156	22	43	5	1	3	14	15	25	.276	.343	.378	89	-2	-2	21	5	0	2	.977	7	S32/D	0.9
1988	KC-A	90	178	25	37	3	3	1	15	18	34	.208	.288	.275	58	-10	-10	16	7	2	1	.976	11	S31/OD2C	0.4
1989	KC-A	65	83	21	17	4	2	3	5	7	9	.205	.275	.410	91	-1	-1	9	5	0	2	.988	3	SO2/31D	0.4
1990	KC-A	87	240	43	58	15	2	5	20	33	39	.242	.336	.383	102	1	1	32	8	5	-1	.986	7	2S3/O1D	1.0
1991	KC-A	125	398	53	114	23	2	6	45	41	45	.286	.356	.399	108	5	5	56	16	7	1	.983	-13	*32/S1DOP	-0.6
1992	NY-N	117	269	28	61	13	0	2	26	25	40	.227	.295	.297	69	-11	-11	24	9	3	1	.926	10	3S2/P1	0.2
Total	7	562	1353	195	336	65	10	20	127	142	195	.248	.324	.356	88	-20	-20	160	50	19	4	.966	30	3S2/O1DP	2.6
■ LES PEDEN Peden, Leslie Earl "Gooch" b: 9/17/23, Azle, Tex. BR/TR, 6'1.5", 212 lbs. Deb: 4/17/53																									
1953	Was-A	9	28	4	7	1	0	1	1	4	3	.250	.344	.393	101	-0	0	4	0	0	0	1.000	-1	/C	0.0
■ STU PEDERSON Pederson, Stuart Russell b: 1/28/60, Palo Alto, Cal. BL/TL, 6', 185 lbs. Deb: 9/08/85																									
1985	LA-N	8	4	1	0	0	0	0	1	0	2	.000	.000	.000	-99	-1	-1	0	0	0	0	1.000	-1	/O	-0.3
■ JORGE PEDRE Pedre, Jorge Enrique b: 10/12/66, Culver City, Cal. BR/TR, 5'11", 210 lbs. Deb: 9/07/91																									
1991	KC-A	10	19	2	5	1	1	0	3	3	5	.263	.364	.421	116	0	0	3	0	0	0	.971	-0	/C1	0.1
1992	Chi-N	4	4	0	0	0	0	0	0	0	1	.000	.000	.000	-98	-1	-1	0	0	0	0	1.000	-1	/C	-0.2
Total	2	14	23	2	5	1	1	0	3	3	6	.217	.308	.348	81	-1	-1	3	0	0	0	.973	-1	/C1	-0.1
■ AL PEDRIQUE Pedrique, Alfredo Jose (Garcia) b: 8/11/60, Aragua, Venez. BR/TR, 6' ", 155 lbs. Deb: 4/14/87																									
1987	NY-N	5	6	1	0	0	0	0	0	1	2	.000	.143	.000	-61	-1	-1	0	0	0	0	1.000	1	/S2	0.0
	Pit-N	88	246	23	74	10	1	1	27	18	27	.301	.356	.362	90	-3	-3	31	5	4	-1	.968	-12	S/32	-0.9
	Yr	93	252	24	74	10	1	1	27	19	29	.294	.350	.353	87	-4	-4	30	5	4	-1	.969	-10	S/23	-0.9
1988	Pit-N	50	128	7	23	5	0	0	4	8	17	.180	.234	.219	31	-11	-11	6	0	0	0	.974	2	S/3	-0.6
1989	Det-A	31	69	1	14	3	0	0	5	2	15	.203	.225	.246	34	-6	-6	3	0	0	0	.960	8	3S/2	0.2
Total	3	174	449	32	111	18	1	1	36	29	61	.247	.299	.298	64	-22	-21	39	5	4	-1	.971	-1	S/32	-1.3
■ CHICK PEDROES Pedroes, Charles P. b: 10/27/1869, Chicago, Ill. d: 8/6/27, Chicago, Ill. Deb: 8/21/02																									
1902	Chi-N	2	6	0	0	0	0	0	0	0		.000	.000	.000	-99	-1	-1	0	0			1.000	-0	/O	-0.2
■ HOMER PEEL Peel, Homer Hefner b: 10/10/02, Port Sullivan, Tex BR/TR, 5'9.5", 170 lbs. Deb: 9/13/27																									
1927	StL-N	2	2	0	0	0	0	0	0	0	1	.000	.000	.000	-97	-1	-1	0	0			.000	-1	/O	-0.1
1929	Phi-N	53	156	16	42	12	1	0	19	12	7	.269	.329	.359	66	-7	-9	18	1			.990	-2	O/1	-1.2
1930	StL-N	26	73	9	12	2	0	0	10	3	4	.164	.197	.192	-5	-13	-13	3	0			.968	-4	O	-1.7
1933	*NY-N	84	148	16	38	1	1	1	12	14	10	.257	.325	.297	80	-4	-3	15	0			.962	-12	O	-1.8
1934	NY-N	21	41	7	8	0	0	1	3	1	2	.195	.214	.268	29	-4	-4	2	0			.929	-3	O	-0.7
Total	5	186	420	48	100	15	2	2	44	30	24	.238	.294	.298	53	-28	-30	38	1			.974	-22	O/1	-5.5
■ JACK PEERSON Peerson, Jack Chiles b: 8/28/10, Brunswick, Ga. d: 10/23/66, Ft.Walton Beach, Fla. BR/TR, 5'11", 175 lbs. Deb: 9/07/35																									
1935	Phi-A	10	19	3	6	1	0	0	1	1	1	.316	.350	.368	87	-0	-0	2	0	0	0	.952	0	/S	0.0
1936	Phi-A	8	34	7	11	1	1	0	5	0	3	.324	.324	.412	82	-1	-1	4	0	1	-1	.942	4	/S2	0.2
Total	2	18	53	10	17	2	1	0	6	1	4	.321	.333	.396	84	-2	-1	6	0	1	-1	.945	4	/S2	0.2
■ CHARLIE PEETE Peete, Charles "Mule" b: 2/22/29, Franklin, Va. d: 11/27/56, Caracas, Venez. BL/TR, 5'9.5", 190 lbs. Deb: 7/17/56																									
1956	StL-N	23	52	3	10	2	2	0	6	6	10	.192	.288	.308	60	-3	-3	3	0	2	-1	1.000	-1	O	-0.7
■ MONTE PEFFER Peffer, Monte (b: Montague Pfeiffer) b: 10/8/1891, New York, N.Y. d: 9/27/41, New York, N.Y. BR/TR, 5'4.5", 147 lbs. Deb: 9/29/13																									
1913	Phi-A	1	3	0	0	0	0	0	0	0	1	.000	.250	.000	-26	-0	-0	0	0			.800	-0	/S	-0.1
■ JULIO PEGUERO Peguero, Julio Cesar b: 9/7/68, San Isidro, D.R. BB/TR, 6', 160 lbs. Deb: 4/08/92																									
1992	Phi-N	14	9	3	2	0	0	0	0	3	3	.222	.417	.222	86	0	0	1	0	0	0	1.000	-5	O	-0.5
■ HEINIE PEITZ Peitz, Henry Clement b: 11/28/1870, St.Louis, Mo. d: 10/23/43, Cincinnati, Ohio BR/TR, 5'11", 165 lbs. Deb: 10/15/1892 FC																									
1892	StL-N	1	3	0	0	0	0	0	0	0	0	.000	.000	.000	-99	-1	-1	0	0			1.000	-0	/C	-0.1
1893	StL-N	96	362	53	92	12	9	1	45	54	20	.254	.353	.345	87	-5	-5	50	12			.948	9	CSO/1	0.8
1894	StL-N	99	338	52	89	19	9	3	49	43	21	.263	.348	.399	81	-11	-11	54	14			.897	4	3C1/P	-0.2
1895	StL-N	90	334	44	95	14	12	2	65	29	20	.284	.345	.416	99	-2	-1	53	9			.937	1	C13	0.6
1896	Cin-N	68	211	33	63	12	5	2	34	30	15	.299	.386	.431	110	6	3	40	7			.968	1	C	0.9
1897	Cin-N	77	266	35	78	11	7	1	44	18		.293	.340	.398	89	-3	-6	39	3			**.979**	7	C/P	0.8
1898	Cin-N	105	330	49	90	15	5	1	43	35		.273	.344	.358	95	1	-3	46	9			.945	-3	*C	0.4
1899	Cin-N	93	290	45	79	13	2	1	43	45		.272	.374	.341	95	1	-0	44	11			.977	-1	C/P	0.5
1900	Cin-N	91	294	34	75	14	1	2	34	20		.255	.313	.330	80	-9	-8	33	5			.958	5	C/1	0.4
1901	Cin-N	82	269	24	82	13	5	1	24	23		.305	.362	.401	130	7	10	41	3			.982	2	C2/31	1.7
1902	Cin-N	112	387	54	122	22	5	1	60	24		.315	.371	.406	127	18	13	63	7			.919	-0	2C/13	2.1
1903	Cin-N	105	358	45	93	15	3	0	42	37		.260	.331	.318	77	-6	-12	42	7			.970	-2	C1/32	-0.5
1904	Cin-N	84	272	32	66	13	2	1	30	14		.243	.282	.316	78	-5	-8	26	1			.975	4	C1/3	0.3
1905	Pit-N	88	278	18	62	10	0	0	27	24		.223	.287	.259	62	-12	-13	24	2			.965	-11	C/2	-1.6
1906	Pit-N	40	125	13	30	8	0	0	20	13		.240	.317	.304	90	-1	-1	13	1			.979	-0	C	0.3
1913	StL-N	3	4	1	1	0	1	0	0	0	0	.250	.250	.750	182	0	0	1	0			.625	-2	/CO	-0.1
Total	16	1234	4121	532	1117	191	66	16	560	409	76	.271	.341	.361	93	-22	-42	567	91			.963	15	C/312OSP	6.3
■ JOE PEITZ Peitz, Joseph b: 11/8/1869, St.Louis, Mo. d: 12/4/19, St.Louis, Mo. Deb: 7/05/1894 F																									
1894	StL-N	7	26	10	11	2	3	0	3	6	1	.423	.531	.731	204	5	5	11	2			.818	1	/O	0.3
■ EDDIE PELLAGRINI Pellagrini, Edward Charles b: 3/13/18, Boston, Mass. BR/TR, 5'9", 165 lbs. Deb: 4/22/46																									
1946	Bos-A	22	71	7	15	3	1	2	4	3	18	.211	.253	.366	68	-3	-4	6	1	0	0	.891	-0	3/S	-0.3
1947	Bos-A	74	231	29	47	8	1	4	19	23	35	.203	.281	.299	57	-12	-15	21	2	2	-1	.926	-6	3S	-2.1
1948	StL-A	105	290	31	69	8	3	2	27	34	40	.238	.320	.307	65	-13	-14	30	1	2	-1	.964	**24**	S	1.3
1949	StL-A	79	235	26	56	8	1	2	15	14	24	.238	.284	.306	54	-16	-17	21	2	1	0	.961	7	S	-0.5
1951	Phi-N	86	197	31	46	4	5	5	30	23	25	.234	.326	.381	91	-3	-3	26	5	1	1	.990	-17	2/S3	-1.6
1952	Cin-N	46	100	15	17	2	0	1	3	8	18	.170	.231	.220	26	-10	-10	5	1	0	0	.983	10	2/1S3	0.1
1953	Pit-N	78	174	16	44	3	2	4	19	14	20	.253	.309	.362	75	-7	-7	21	1	1	-0	.972	-4	23/S	-0.9
1954	Pit-N	73	125	12	27	6	0	0	16	9	21	.216	.290	.264	46	-10	-10	11	0	0	0	.968	2	3/2S	-0.8
Total	8	563	1423	167	321	42	13	20	133	128	201	.226	.295	.316	62	-74	-78	140	13	7	-0	.956	15	S23/1	-4.8
■ BILL PELOUZE Pelouze, William Nelson b: 9/12/1865, Washington, D.C. d: 6/20/43, Lake Geneva, Wis. BR/TR, 5'8", 170 lbs. Deb: 7/22/1886																									
1886	StL-N	1	3	0	0	0	0	0	0	0	2	.000	.000	.000	-99	-1	-1	0	0			1.000	0	/O	0.0
■ DAN PELTIER Peltier, Daniel Edward b: 6/30/68, Clifton Park, N.Y. BL/TL, 6'1", 200 lbs. Deb: 6/26/92																									
1992	Tex-A	12	24	1	4	0	0	0	2	0	3	.167	.167	.167	-7	-3	-3	1	0	0	0	.857	-3	O	-0.7

YEAR	TM/L	G	AB	R	H	2B	3B	HR	RBI	BB	SO	AVG	OBP	SLG	PRO+	BR	/A	RC	SB	CS	SBR	FA	FR	POS	TPR

■ JOHN PELTZ   Peltz, John   b: 4/23/1861, New Orleans, La.   d: 2/27/06, New Orleans, La.   BR/TR,   Deb: 5/01/1884

1884	Ind-a	106	393	40	86	13	17	3			7	.219	.236	.361	97	-3	-1	34				.818	4	*O	0.1
1888	Bal-a	1	4	1	1	0	0	0	0	0		.250	.250	.250	65	-0	-0	1	1			.500	-0	/O	-0.1
1890	Bro-a	98	384	55	87	9	6	1			32	.227	.289	.289	75	-13	-11	36	10			.904	3	*O	-1.0
	Syr-a	5	17	2	3	1	1	0			3	.176	.300	.353	106	-0	-0	2	0			.857	0	O	0.0
	Tol-a	20	73	8	18	2	2	0			3	.247	.286	.329	81	-2	-2	9	7			.886	-2	O	-0.4
	Yr	123	474	65	108	12	9	1			38	.228	.289	.297	77	-15	-13	47	17			.900	1	*O	-1.4
Total	3	230	871	106	195	25	26	4	0		45	.224	.266	.326	86	-18	-14	82	18			.865	5	O	-1.4

■ BROCK PEMBERTON   Pemberton, Brock   b: 11/5/53, Tulsa, Okla.   BB/TL, 6'3", 190 lbs.   Deb: 9/10/74

1974	NY-N	11	22	0	4	0	0	0	1	0	3	.182	.182	.182	2	-3	-3	1	0	1	-1	1.000	1	/1	-0.3
1975	NY-N	2	2	0	0	0	0	0	0	0	1	.000	.000	.000	-99	-1	-1	0	0	0	0	.000	0	H	-0.1
Total	2	13	24	0	4	0	0	0	1	0	4	.167	.167	.167	-7	-3	-3	1	0	1	-1	.902	1	/1	-0.4

■ BERT PENA   Pena, Adalberto (Rivera)   b: 7/11/59, Santurce, P.R.   BR/TR, 5'11", 165 lbs.   Deb: 9/14/81

1981	Hou-N	4	2	0	1	0	0	0	0	0	0	.500	.500	.500	194	0	0	1	0	0	0	1.000	0	/S	0.0
1983	Hou-N	4	8	0	1	0	0	0	0	2	2	.125	.300	.125	23	-1	-1	0	0	0	0	1.000	-1	/S	-0.2
1984	Hou-N	24	39	3	8	1	0	1	4	3	8	.205	.262	.308	64	-2	-2	2	0	0	0	.956	6	S	0.5
1985	Hou-N	20	29	7	8	2	0	0	4	1	6	.276	.300	.345	82	-1	-1	3	0	0	0	1.000	1	/3S2	-0.1
1986	Hou-N	15	29	3	6	1	0	0	2	5	9	.207	.324	.241	60	-1	-1	2	1	0	0	.907	1	S/32	0.1
1987	Hou-N	21	46	5	7	0	0	0	2	2	7	.152	.204	.152	-4	-7	-7	1	0	0	0	.982	-1	S/3	-0.7
Total	6	88	153	18	31	4	0	1	10	13	28	.203	.269	.248	45	-12	-11	9	1	0	0	.953	3	/S32	-0.4

■ TONY PENA   Pena, Antonio Francisco (Padilla)   b: 6/4/57, Monte Cristi, D.R.   BR/TR, 6', 181 lbs.   Deb: 9/01/80   F

1980	Pit-N	8	21	1	9	1	1	0	1	0	4	.429	.429	.571	174	2	2	4	0	1	-1	.952	2	/C	0.3
1981	Pit-N	66	210	16	63	9	1	2	17	8	23	.300	.329	.381	98	-0	-1	25	1	2	-1	.985	2	C	0.2
1982	Pit-N★	138	497	53	147	28	4	11	63	17	57	.296	.324	.435	107	5	4	63	2	5	-2	.982	-7	*C	0.0
1983	Pit-N	151	542	51	163	22	3	15	70	31	73	.301	.339	.435	110	8	6	75	6	7	-2	.992	-0	*C	1.1
1984	Pit-N★	147	546	77	156	27	2	15	78	36	79	.286	.334	.425	112	8	8	74	12	8	-1	.991	13	*C	2.8
1985	Pit-N★	147	546	53	136	27	2	10	59	29	67	.249	.287	.361	81	-16	-15	51	12	8	-1	.988	9	*C/1	0.0
1986	Pit-N★	144	510	56	147	26	2	10	52	53	69	.288	.356	.406	107	7	6	68	9	10	-3	.981	5	*C/1	1.7
1987	*StL-N	116	384	40	82	13	4	5	44	36	54	.214	.283	.307	55	-24	-25	30	6	1	1	.988	-1	*C/1O	-1.7
1988	StL-N	149	505	55	133	23	1	10	51	33	60	.263	.310	.372	94	-4	-5	56	6	2	1	.994	6	*C/1	1.3
1989	StL-N★	141	424	36	110	17	2	4	37	35	33	.259	.319	.337	85	-7	-8	41	5	3	-0	.997	11	*C/O	1.0
1990	*Bos-A	143	491	62	129	19	1	7	56	43	71	.263	.323	.348	84	-8	-11	50	8	6	-1	.995	11	*C/1	0.8
1991	Bos-A	141	464	45	107	23	2	5	48	37	53	.231	.293	.321	66	-19	-22	40	8	3	1	.995	8	*C	-0.5
1992	Bos-A	133	410	39	99	21	1	1	38	24	61	.241	.285	.305	62	-19	-22	35	3	2	-0	.993	11	*C	-0.4
Total	13	1624	5550	584	1481	256	26	95	614	382	704	.267	.316	.374	90	-67	-83	611	78	58	-11	.990	70	*C/1O	6.6

■ GERONIMO PENA   Pena, Geronimo (Martinez)   b: 3/29/67, Distrito Nacional, D.R.   BB/TR, 6'1", 170 lbs.   Deb: 9/05/90

1990	StL-N	18	45	5	11	2	0	0	2	4	14	.244	.320	.289	69	-2	-2	5	1	1	-0	.982	-1	2	-0.3
1991	StL-N	104	185	38	45	8	3	5	17	18	45	.243	.327	.400	103	1	1	27	15	5	2	.976	-3	2/O	0.0
1992	StL-N	62	203	31	62	12	1	7	31	24	37	.305	.392	.478	147	13	13	39	13	8	-1	.984	8	2	2.2
Total	3	184	433	74	118	22	4	12	50	46	96	.273	.357	.425	120	12	12	71	29	14	0	.981	4	2/O	1.9

■ ROBERTO PENA   Pena, Roberto Cesar "Baby" (b: Roberto Cesar Zapata (Pena))   b: 4/17/37, Santo Domingo, D.R.   d: 7/23/82, Santiago, D.R.   BR/TR, 5'8", 175 lbs.   Deb: 4/12/65

1965	Chi-N	51	170	17	37	5	1	2	12	16	19	.218	.293	.294	64	-7	-8	14	1	2	-1	.930	-10	S	-1.6
1966	Chi-N	6	17	0	3	2	0	0	1	0	4	.176	.176	.294	28	-2	-2	1	0	0	0	.957	0	/S	-0.1
1968	Phi-N	138	500	56	130	13	2	1	38	34	63	.260	.310	.300	84	-9	-9	45	3	5	-2	.954	6	*S	1.0
1969	SD-N	139	472	44	118	16	3	4	30	21	63	.250	.286	.322	73	-19	-17	40	0	3	-2	.977	-23	S231	-3.6
1970	Oak-A	19	58	4	15	1	0	0	3	3	4	.259	.295	.276	61	-3	-3	4	1	1	-0	.961	-1	S/3	-0.3
	Mil-A	121	416	36	99	19	1	3	42	25	45	.238	.284	.310	63	-21	-21	34	3	5	-2	.981	-16	S2/1	-2.8
	Yr	140	474	40	114	20	1	3	45	28	49	.241	.286	.306	63	-24	-24	38	4	6	-2	.979	-17	*S2/13	-3.1
1971	Mil-A	113	274	17	65	9	3	3	28	15	37	.237	.279	.325	71	-11	-11	24	2	1	0	.996	-5	13S/2	-1.8
Total	6	587	1907	174	467	65	10	13	154	114	235	.245	.291	.310	72	-73	-71	164	10	17	-7	.962	-49	S/132	-9.2

■ ELMER PENCE   Pence, Elmer Clair   b: 8/17/1900, Valley Springs, Cal.   d: 9/17/68, San Francisco, Cal.   BR/TR, 6', 185 lbs.   Deb: 8/23/22

| 1922 | Chi-A | 1 | 0 | 0 | 0 | 0 | 0 | 0 | 0 | 0 | 0 | — | — | — | 0 | 0 | 0 | 0 | 0 | 0 | 0 | 1.000 | -0 | /O | 0.0 |

■ JIM PENDLETON   Pendleton, James Edward   b: 1/7/24, St.Charles, Mo.   BR/TR, 6', 185 lbs.   Deb: 4/17/53

1953	Mil-N	120	251	48	75	12	4	7	27	7	36	.299	.323	.462	108	-0	2	35	6	5	-1	.961	-13	*O/S	-1.4
1954	Mil-N	71	173	20	38	3	1	1	16	4	21	.220	.237	.266	33	-18	-16	11	2	1	0	.950	-4	O	-2.1
1955	Mil-N	8	10	0	0	0	0	0	0	0	2	.000	.000	.000	-99	-3	-3	0	0	0	0	1.000	-0	/S3O	-0.3
1956	Mil-N	14	11	0	0	0	0	0	0	1	3	.000	.083	.000	-80	-3	-3	0	0	0	0	1.000	-0	/S312	-0.3
1957	Pit-N	46	59	9	18	1	1	0	9	9	14	.305	.406	.356	110	1	1	9	0	0	0	.917	-3	/O3S	-0.2
1958	Pit-N	3	3	0	1	0	0	0	0	0	0	.333	.333	.333	79	-0	-0	0	0	0	0	.000	0	H	0.0
1959	Cin-N	65	113	13	29	2	0	3	9	9	18	.257	.311	.354	75	-4	-4	12	3	0	1	.971	0	O3/S	-0.4
1962	Hou-N	117	321	30	79	12	2	8	36	14	57	.246	.282	.371	79	-13	-10	33	0	0	0	.963	-4	O/13S	-1.9
Total	8	444	941	120	240	30	8	19	97	43	151	.255	.292	.365	76	-39	-32	100	11	6	0	.959	-25	O/3S12	-6.6

■ TERRY PENDLETON   Pendleton, Terry Lee   b: 7/16/60, Los Angeles, Cal.   BB/TR, 5'9", 180 lbs.   Deb: 7/18/84

1984	StL-N	67	262	37	85	16	3	1	33	16	32	.324	.363	.420	123	6	7	40	20	5	3	.943	9	3	1.9
1985	*StL-N	149	559	56	134	16	3	5	69	37	75	.240	.287	.306	66	-26	-25	45	17	12	-2	.965	23	*3	-0.7
1986	StL-N	159	578	56	138	26	5	1	59	34	59	.239	.282	.306	63	-30	-29	50	24	6	4	.962	24	*3/O	-0.5
1987	*StL-N	159	583	82	167	29	4	12	96	70	74	.286	.365	.412	103	6	4	86	19	12	-2	.949	16	*3	1.6
1988	StL-N	110	391	44	99	20	2	6	53	21	51	.253	.295	.361	86	-7	-8	39	3	3	-1	.963	11	*3	0.2
1989	StL-N	162	613	83	162	28	5	13	74	44	81	.264	.314	.390	97	-1	-3	72	9	5	-0	.971	30	*3	2.9
1990	StL-N	121	447	46	103	20	2	6	58	30	58	.230	.280	.324	66	-21	-22	38	7	5	-1	.947	7	*3	-1.5
1991	*Atl-N	153	586	94	187	34	8	22	86	43	70	.319	.367	.517	138	34	29	107	10	2	2	.950	28	*3	6.1
1992	*Atl-N★	160	640	98	199	39	1	21	105	37	67	.311	.349	.473	121	24	18	101	5	2	0	.960	13	*3	3.4
Total	9	1240	4659	596	1274	228	33	87	633	332	567	.273	.323	.393	96	-16	-28	578	114	52	3	.958	161	*3/O	13.4

■ WILL PENNYFEATHER   Pennyfeather, William Nathaniel   b: 5/25/68, Perth Amboy, N.J.   BR/TR, 6'2", 195 lbs.   Deb: 6/27/92

| 1992 | Pit-N | 15 | 9 | 2 | 2 | 0 | 0 | 0 | 0 | 0 | 0 | .222 | .222 | .222 | 27 | -1 | -1 | 0 | 0 | 0 | 0 | 1.000 | -4 | O | -0.5 |

■ JIMMY PEOPLES   Peoples, James Elsworth   b: 10/8/1863, Big Beaver, Mich.   d: 8/29/20, Detroit, Mich.   TR, 5'8", 200 lbs.   Deb: 5/29/1884   U

1884	Cin-a	69	267	28	45	2	2	1			6	.169	.187	.202	27	-20	-22	10				.829	0	SCO/31	-1.9
1885	Cin-a	7	22	1	4	0	0	0			1	.182	.182	.182	28	-2	-2	1				.826	-1	/CPO	-0.2
	Bro-a	41	151	21	30	4	1	1			5	.199	.229	.258	55	-7	-7	9				.895	-2	C/S130	-0.6
	Yr	48	173	22	34	4	1	1			6	.197	.228	.249	52	-9	-9	10				.889	-4	C/POS13	-0.8
1886	Bro-a	93	340	45	74	7	3	3			20	.218	.261	.282	71	-11	-12	30	20			.879	19	C/S03	1.3
1887	Bro-a	73	268	36	68	14	2	1			16	.254	.306	.332	79	-7	-8	35	22			.853	-6	C/OS12	-0.7
1888	Bro-a	32	103	15	20	5	3	0	17	8		.194	.259	.301	82	-2	-2	11	10			.904	10	C/SO	0.9
1889	Col-a	29	100	13	23	6	2	1	16	6	8	.230	.274	.360	86	-3	-2	11	3			.922	-4	C/O2S	-0.3

YEAR	TM/L	G	AB	R	H	2B	3B	HR	RBI	BB	SO	AVG	OBP	SLG	PRO+	BR	/A	RC	SB	CS	SBR	FA	FR	POS	TPR
Total	6	344	1251	157	264	38	13	7	33	62	8	.211	.252	.279	63	-52	-54	108	55			.886	15	C/SO123P	-1.5
■ **JOE PEPITONE** Pepitone, Joseph Anthony "Pepi" b: 10/9/40, Brooklyn, N.Y. BL/TL, 6'2", 200 lbs. Deb: 4/10/62 C																									
1962	NY-A	63	138	14	33	3	2	7	17	3	21	.239	.255	.442	86	-4	-3	13	1	1	-0	1.000	-9	O1	-1.5
1963	*NY-A★	157	580	79	157	16	3	27	89	23	63	.271	.307	.448	109	5	5	76	3	5	-2	.995	4	*1O	0.0
1964	*NY-A★	160	613	71	154	12	3	28	100	24	63	.251	.283	.418	90	-9	-10	67	2	1	0	.988	-6	*1O	-2.4
1965	NY-A★	143	531	51	131	18	3	18	62	43	59	.247	.306	.394	98	-3	-2	62	4	2	0	**.997**	-3	*1O	-1.4
1966	NY-A	152	585	85	149	21	4	31	83	29	58	.255	.292	.463	118	8	10	74	4	3	-1	**.995**	1	*1O	0.1
1967	NY-A	133	501	45	126	18	3	13	64	34	62	.251	.303	.377	104	-1	1	53	1	3	-2	.976	6	*O/1	-0.2
1968	NY-A	108	380	41	93	9	3	15	56	37	45	.245	.313	.403	119	7	8	48	8	2	1	.980	-6	O1	-0.3
1969	NY-A	135	513	49	124	16	3	27	70	30	42	.242	.285	.442	105	-3	-0	59	8	6	-1	**.995**	-6	*1	-1.9
1970	Hou-N	75	279	44	70	9	5	14	35	18	28	.251	.299	.470	107	-1	1	37	5	2	0	.995	-1	1O	-0.5
	Chi-N	56	213	38	57	9	2	12	44	15	15	.268	.316	.498	102	3	-0	33	0	2	-1	.992	2	O1	-0.3
	Yr	131	492	82	127	18	7	26	79	33	43	.258	.306	.482	105	2	1	70	5	4	-1	.989	1	O1	-0.8
1971	Chi-N	115	427	50	131	19	4	16	61	24	41	.307	.349	.482	117	17	10	67	1	2	-1	.990	-1	1O	-0.1
1972	Chi-N	66	214	23	56	5	0	8	21	13	22	.262	.313	.397	91	-0	-3	26	1	2	-1	.997	-0	1	-0.9
1973	Chi-N	31	112	16	30	3	0	3	18	8	6	.268	.322	.375	86	-1	-2	14	3	1	0	.985	0	1	-0.4
	Atl-N	3	11	0	4	0	0	0	1	1	1	.364	.417	.364	110	0	0	1	0	0	0	.963	-1	/1	-0.1
	Yr	34	123	16	34	3	0	3	19	9	7	.276	.331	.374	88	-1	-2	15	3	1	0	.983	-1	1	-0.5
Total	12	1397	5097	606	1315	158	35	219	721	302	526	.258	.303	.432	105	18	14	629	41	32	-7	.993	-18	1O	-9.9
■ **HENRY PEPLOSKI** Peploski, Henry Stephen "Pep" b: 9/15/05, Garlin, Poland d: 1/28/82, Dover, N.J. BL/TR, 5'9", 155 lbs. Deb: 9/19/29 F																									
1929	Bos-N	6	10	1	2	0	0	0	1	1	3	.200	.273	.200	20	-1	-1	1	0			1.000	-0	/3	-0.1
■ **PEPPER PEPLOSKI** Peploski, Joseph Aloysius b: 9/12/1891, Brooklyn, N.Y. d: 7/13/72, New York, N.Y. BR/TR, 5'8", 155 lbs. Deb: 6/24/13 F																									
1913	Det-A	2	4	1	2	0	0	0	0	0	0	.500	.500	.500	196	0	0	1	0			1.000	-1	/3	0.0
■ **DON PEPPER** Pepper, Donald Hoyte b: 10/8/43, Saratoga Sprgs., N.Y BL/TR, 6'4.5", 215 lbs. Deb: 9/10/66																									
1966	Det-A	4	3	0	0	0	0	0	0	0	1	.000	.000	.000	-98	-1	-1	0	0	0	0	1.000	-0	/1	-0.1
■ **ROY PEPPER** Pepper, Raymond Watson b: 8/5/05, Decatur, Ala. BR/TR, 6'2", 195 lbs. Deb: 4/15/32																									
1932	StL-N	21	57	3	14	2	1	0	7	5	13	.246	.306	.316	66	-3	-3	6	1			.971	-0	O	-0.4
1933	StL-N	3	9	2	2	0	0	1	2	0	1	.222	.222	.556	110	0	0	1	0			1.000	-0	/O	0.0
1934	StL-A	148	564	71	168	24	6	7	101	29	67	.298	.333	.399	81	-11	-18	73	1	4	-2	.963	5	*O	-2.0
1935	StL-A	92	261	20	66	15	3	4	37	20	32	.253	.306	.379	73	-10	-12	30	0	2	-1	.982	-3	O	-1.7
1936	StL-A	75	124	13	35	5	0	2	23	5	23	.282	.310	.371	66	-7	-7	13	0	2	-1	.941	-2	O	-1.0
Total	5	339	1015	109	285	46	10	14	170	59	136	.281	.321	.387	77	-30	-39	123	2	8		.967	-1	O	-5.1
■ **JACK PERCONTE** Perconte, John Patrick b: 8/31/54, Joliet, Ill. BL/TR, 5'10", 160 lbs. Deb: 9/13/80																									
1980	LA-N	14	17	2	4	0	0	0	2	2	1	.235	.316	.235	57	-1	-1	2	3	0	1	1.000	3	/2	0.4
1981	LA-N	8	9	2	2	0	1	0	1	2	2	.222	.364	.444	133	0	0	1	1	1	-0	1.000	5	/2	0.5
1982	Cle-A	93	219	27	52	4	4	0	15	22	25	.237	.307	.292	66	-10	-10	22	9	3	1	.976	8	2/D	0.2
1983	Cle-A	14	26	1	7	1	0	0	0	5	2	.269	.387	.308	91	0	-0	4	3	1	0	.950	8	2	0.8
1984	Sea-A	155	612	93	180	24	4	0	31	57	47	.294	.359	.346	97	-1	-0	84	29	6	5	.981	0	*2	1.1
1985	Sea-A	125	485	60	128	17	7	2	23	50	36	.264	.336	.340	85	-8	-9	62	31	2	8	.986	0	*2	0.4
1986	Chi-A	24	73	6	16	1	0	0	4	11	10	.219	.321	.233	52	-4	-5	6	2	0	1	.990	-7	2	-1.0
Total	7	433	1441	191	389	47	16	2	76	149	123	.270	.342	.329	86	-24	-23	181	78	13	16	.982	18	2/D	2.4
■ **TONY PEREZ** Perez, Atanacio (Rigal) b: 5/14/42, Camaguey, Cuba BR/TR, 6'2", 205 lbs. Deb: 7/26/64 C																									
1964	Cin-N	12	25	1	2	1	0	0	1	3	9	.080	.179	.120	-14	-4	-4	1	0	0	0	.981	-1	/1	-0.6
1965	Cin-N	104	281	40	73	14	4	12	47	21	67	.260	.316	.466	110	6	3	38	0	2	-1	.989	-2	1	-0.4
1966	Cin-N	99	257	25	68	10	4	4	39	14	44	.265	.308	.381	83	-4	-6	27	1	0	0	.989	-5	1	-1.6
1967	Cin-N★	156	600	78	174	28	7	26	102	33	102	.290	.331	.490	119	22	15	91	0	3	-2	.963	-22	*31/2	-1.2
1968	Cin-N★	160	625	93	176	25	7	18	92	51	92	.282	.342	.430	123	23	19	88	3	2	-0	.952	5	*3	2.7
1969	Cin-N★	160	629	103	185	31	2	37	122	63	131	.294	.360	.526	138	36	32	114	4	2	0	.937	1	*3	3.4
1970	*Cin-N★	158	587	107	186	28	6	40	129	83	134	.317	.405	.589	162	52	52	140	8	3	1	.923	-7	*3/1	4.3
1971	Cin-N	158	609	72	164	22	3	25	91	51	120	.269	.327	.438	117	10	12	86	4	1	1	.959	7	*31	1.7
1972	*Cin-N	136	515	64	146	33	7	21	90	55	121	.283	.353	.497	148	25	28	90	4	2	0	.993	-6	*1	1.2
1973	*Cin-N	151	564	73	177	33	3	27	101	74	117	.314	.396	.527	162	41	45	118	3	1	0	.991	-4	*1	3.0
1974	Cin-N★	158	596	81	158	28	2	28	101	61	112	.265	.335	.460	123	14	15	88	1	3	-2	**.996**	-6	*1	-0.2
1975	*Cin-N★	137	511	74	144	28	3	20	109	54	101	.282	.354	.466	124	17	16	83	1	2	-1	.993	-5	*1	0.1
1976	*Cin-N★	139	527	77	137	32	6	19	91	50	88	.260	.330	.452	117	12	11	78	10	5	0	.996	-4	*1	-0.2
1977	Mon-N	154	559	71	158	32	6	19	91	63	111	.283	.357	.463	122	14	16	91	4	3	-1	.992	9	*1	1.6
1978	Mon-N	148	544	63	158	38	3	14	78	38	104	.290	.339	.449	120	12	13	82	2	0	1	.991	-1	*1	0.4
1979	Mon-N	132	489	58	132	29	4	13	73	38	82	.270	.326	.425	104	1	2	65	2	1	0	.991	-6	*1	-1.3
1980	Bos-A	151	585	73	161	31	3	25	105	41	93	.275	.324	.467	108	9	5	80	1	0	0	.993	-1	*1D	-0.4
1981	Bos-A	84	306	35	77	11	3	9	39	27	66	.252	.312	.395	97	1	-2	37	0	0	0	.993	0	1D	-0.5
1982	Bos-A	69	196	18	51	14	2	6	31	19	48	.260	.326	.444	103	2	1	27	0	1	-1	.857	0	D/1	0.0
1983	*Phi-N	91	253	18	61	11	2	6	43	28	57	.241	.319	.372	92	-3	-3	29	1	0	0	.998	1	1	-0.5
1984	Cin-N	71	137	9	33	6	1	2	15	11	21	.241	.297	.343	76	-4	-5	12	0	0	0	.990	-2	1	-0.8
1985	Cin-N	72	183	25	60	8	0	6	33	22	22	.328	.400	.470	136	11	10	35	0	2	-1	.995	-2	1	0.4
1986	Cin-N	77	200	14	51	12	1	2	29	25	25	.255	.338	.355	87	-2	-3	24	0	0	0	.984	-3	1	-1.0
Total	23	2777	9778	1272	2732	505	79	379	1652	925	1867	.279	.344	.463	122	292	272	1523	49	33	-5	.992	-54	*13/D2	10.1
■ **MARTY PEREZ** Perez, Martin Roman b: 2/28/47, Visalia, Cal. BR/TR, 5'11", 160 lbs. Deb: 9/09/69																									
1969	Cal-A	13	13	3	3	0	0	0	0	2	1	.231	.333	.231	63	-1	-1	1	0	0	0	1.000	6	/S23	0.6
1970	Cal-A	3	3	0	0	0	0	0	1	0	0	.000	.000	.000	-99	-1	-1	0	0	0	0	.833	1	/S	0.0
1971	Atl-N	130	410	28	93	15	3	4	32	25	44	.227	.273	.307	60	-20	-23	32	1	2	-1	.955	-14	*S/2	-2.4
1972	Atl-N	141	479	33	109	13	1	1	28	30	55	.228	.277	.265	50	-28	-33	32	0	3	-2	.957	-34	*S	-5.4
1973	Atl-N	141	501	66	125	15	5	8	57	49	66	.250	.319	.347	79	-10	-15	54	2	3	-1	.962	-9	*S	-0.8
1974	Atl-N	127	447	51	116	20	5	2	34	35	51	.260	.315	.340	80	-10	-13	47	2	0	1	.985	-9	*2S/3	-1.6
1975	Atl-N	120	461	50	127	14	2	2	34	37	44	.275	.329	.328	80	-10	-12	48	2	2	-1	.985	-8	*2/S	-1.5
1976	Atl-N	31	96	12	24	4	0	1	6	8	9	.250	.308	.323	74	-3	-3	9	0	0	0	.976	-2	2S/3	-0.3
	SF-N	93	332	37	86	13	1	2	26	30	28	.259	.320	.322	80	-7	-8	36	3	4	-2	.979	7	2/S	0.3
	Yr	124	428	49	110	17	1	3	32	38	37	.257	.318	.322	79	-10	-12	45	3	4	-2	.978	5	*2S/3	0.0
1977	NY-A	1	4	0	2	0	0	0	0	0	1	.500	.500	.500	175	0	0	1	0	0	0	1.000	1	/3	0.1
	Oak-A	115	373	32	86	14	5	2	23	29	65	.231	.291	.311	65	-18	-18	33	1	3	-2	.974	0	*23/S	-1.2
	Yr	116	377	32	88	14	5	2	23	29	66	.233	.293	.313	66	-18	-17	34	1	3	-2	.974	1	*23/S	-1.1
1978	Oak-A	16	12	1	0	0	0	0	0	0	5	.000	.000	.000	-99	-3	-3	0	0	0	0	1.000	2	3/S2	-0.1
Total	10	931	3131	313	771	108	22	22	241	245	369	.246	.303	.316	70	-111	-129	291	11	17	-7	.958	-59	S2/3	-12.3
■ **TONY PEREZCHICA** Perezchica, Antonio Llamas (Gonzales) b: 4/20/66, Mexicali, Mex. BR/TR, 5'11", 165 lbs. Deb: 9/07/88																									
1988	SF-N	7	8	1	1	0	0	0	1	2	1	.125	.300	.125	27	-1	-1	1	0	0	0	1.000	-1	/2	-0.2
1990	SF-N	4	3	1	1	0	0	0	0	1	2	.333	.500	.333	139	0	0	1	0	0	0	1.000	-2	/2S	-0.1
1991	SF-N	23	48	2	11	4	1	0	3	2	12	.229	.260	.354	73	-2	-2	4	0	1	-1	.947	-3	S/2	-0.5

YEAR	TM/L	G	AB	R	H	2B	3B	HR	RBI	BB	SO	AVG	OBP	SLG	PRO+	BR	/A	RC	SB	CS	SBR	FA	FR	POS	TPR
	Cle-A	17	22	4	8	2	0	0	0	3	5	.364	.440	.455	147	2	2	5	0	0	0	1.000	-2	/S32D	0.0
1992	Cle-A	18	20	2	2	1	0	0	1	2	6	.100	.182	.150	-6	-3	-3	1	0	0	0	.875	-1	/32SD	-0.4
Total	4	69	101	10	23	7	1	0	5	10	26	.228	.297	.317	73	-4	-3	11	0	1	-1	.944	-9	/S23D	-1.2

■ BRODERICK PERKINS Perkins, Broderick Phillip b: 11/23/54, Pittsburg, Cal. BL/TL, 5'10", 180 lbs. Deb: 7/07/78

YEAR	TM/L	G	AB	R	H	2B	3B	HR	RBI	BB	SO	AVG	OBP	SLG	PRO+	BR	/A	RC	SB	CS	SBR	FA	FR	POS	TPR
1978	SD-N	62	217	14	52	14	1	2	33	5	29	.240	.257	.341	71	-11	-9	18	4	0	1	.993	3	1	-0.8
1979	SD-N	57	87	8	23	0	0	0	8	8	12	.264	.326	.264	67	-4	-3	7	0	0	0	.982	-1	1	-0.5
1980	SD-N	43	100	18	37	9	0	2	14	11	10	.370	.432	.520	175	9	10	24	2	1	0	.988	-2	1O	0.6
1981	SD-N	92	254	27	71	18	3	2	40	14	16	.280	.317	.398	110	-0	2	29	0	4	-2	.997	-2	1/O	-0.7
1982	SD-N	125	347	32	94	10	4	2	34	26	20	.271	.327	.340	92	-6	-4	39	2	1	0	.994	1	1O	-0.8
1983	Cle-A	79	184	23	50	10	0	0	24	9	19	.272	.306	.326	71	-6	-7	17	1	5	-3	.991	0	1OD	-1.1
1984	Cle-A	58	66	5	13	1	0	0	4	7	10	.197	.284	.212	39	-5	-5	4	0	0	0	1.000	-0	D/1	-0.6
Total	7	516	1255	127	340	62	8	8	157	80	116	.271	.317	.352	90	-23	-17	138	9	11	-4	.993	-1	1/OD	-3.9

■ CY PERKINS Perkins, Ralph Foster b: 2/27/1896, Gloucester, Mass. d: 10/2/63, Philadelphia, Pa. BR/TR, 5'10.5", 158 lbs. Deb: 9/25/15 MC

YEAR	TM/L	G	AB	R	H	2B	3B	HR	RBI	BB	SO	AVG	OBP	SLG	PRO+	BR	/A	RC	SB	CS	SBR	FA	FR	POS	TPR
1915	Phi-A	7	20	2	4	1	0	0	0	3	3	.200	.304	.250	68	-1	-1	2	0			.920	1	/C	0.0
1917	Phi-A	6	18	1	3	0	0	0	2	2	1	.167	.250	.167	28	-2	-1	1	0			.978	4	/C	0.3
1918	Phi-A	68	218	9	41	4	1	1	14	8	15	.188	.217	.229	34	-18	-18	11	1			.990	12	C	-0.1
1919	Phi-A	101	305	22	77	12	7	2	29	27	22	.252	.313	.357	87	-5	-6	33	2			.971	7	C/S	1.0
1920	Phi-A	148	492	40	128	24	6	5	52	28	35	.260	.303	.364	75	-18	-19	53	5	6	-2	.979	**23**	*C/2	1.2
1921	Phi-A	141	538	58	155	31	4	12	73	32	32	.288	.329	.428	91	-9	-9	73	5	9	-4	.971	5	*C	0.0
1922	Phi-A	148	505	58	135	20	6	6	69	40	30	.267	.322	.366	77	-16	-18	59	1	7	-4	.984	-4	*C	-1.7
1923	Phi-A	143	500	53	135	34	5	2	65	65	30	.270	.356	.370	90	-5	-6	69	1	3	-2	.971	-7	*C	-0.8
1924	Phi-A	128	392	31	95	19	4	0	32	31	20	.242	.304	.311	58	-24	-25	38	3	4	-2	.983	-0	*C	-1.8
1925	Phi-A	65	140	21	43	10	0	1	18	26	6	.307	.426	.400	104	4	2	26	0	0	0	.980	11	C/3	1.5
1926	Phi-A	63	148	14	43	6	0	0	19	18	7	.291	.371	.331	80	-3	-4	19	0	2	-1	.984	9	C	0.6
1927	Phi-A	59	137	11	35	7	2	1	15	12	8	.255	.315	.358	70	-5	-7	15	0	2	-1	.979	1	C/1	-0.4
1928	Phi-A	19	29	1	5	0	0	0	1	1	1	.172	.200	.172	-1	-4	-4	1	0	1	-1	.982	4	C	-0.1
1929	Phi-A	38	76	4	16	4	0	0	9	5	4	.211	.259	.263	34	-7	-8	5	0	0	0	.990	2	C	-0.4
1930	Phi-A	20	38	1	6	2	0	0	4	2	3	.158	.200	.211	4	-6	-6	2	0	0	0	.964	0	C/1	-0.4
1931	NY-A	16	47	3	12	1	0	0	7	1	4	.255	.286	.277	51	-3	-3	4	0	0	0	1.000	-5	C	-0.7
1934	Det-A	1	1	0	0	0	0	0	0	0	0	.000	.000	.000	-99	-0	-0	0	0	0	0	.000	0	H	0.0
Total	17	1171	3604	329	933	175	35	30	409	301	221	.259	.319	.352	75	-124	-133	411	18	34		.978	63	*C/S132	-1.8

■ SAM PERLOZZO Perlozzo, Samuel Benedict b: 3/4/51, Cumberland, Md. BR/TR, 5'9", 170 lbs. Deb: 9/13/77 C

YEAR	TM/L	G	AB	R	H	2B	3B	HR	RBI	BB	SO	AVG	OBP	SLG	PRO+	BR	/A	RC	SB	CS	SBR	FA	FR	POS	TPR
1977	Min-A	10	24	6	7	0	2	0	0	2	3	.292	.346	.458	119	1	1	4	0	0	0	1.000	-3	2/3	-0.2
1979	SD-N	2	2	0	0	0	0	0	0	1	0	.000	.333	.000	-1	-0	-0	0	0	0	0	.500	-1	/2	-0.2
Total	2	12	26	6	7	0	2	0	0	3	3	.269	.345	.423	110	0	0	4	0	0	0	.967	-5	/23	-0.4

■ JOHN PERRIN Perrin, John Stephenson b: 2/4/1898, Escanaba, Mich. d: 6/24/69, Detroit, Mich. BL/TR, 5'9", 160 lbs. Deb: 7/11/21

YEAR	TM/L	G	AB	R	H	2B	3B	HR	RBI	BB	SO	AVG	OBP	SLG	PRO+	BR	/A	RC	SB	CS	SBR	FA	FR	POS	TPR
1921	Bos-A	4	13	3	3	0	0	0	1	0	3	.231	.231	.231	19	-2	-2	1	0	0	0	1.000	-2	/O	-0.3

■ NIG PERRINE Perrine, John Grover b: 1/14/1885, Clinton, Wis. d: 8/13/48, Kansas City, Mo. BR/TR, 5'9", 160 lbs. Deb: 4/11/07

YEAR	TM/L	G	AB	R	H	2B	3B	HR	RBI	BB	SO	AVG	OBP	SLG	PRO+	BR	/A	RC	SB	CS	SBR	FA	FR	POS	TPR
1907	Was-A	44	146	13	25	4	1	0	15	13		.171	.248	.212	51	-8	-7	11	10			.946	-3	2S/3	-1.1

■ GEORGE PERRING Perring, George Wilson b: 8/13/1884, Sharon, Wis. d: 8/20/60, Beloit, Wis. BR/TR, 6', 190 lbs. Deb: 4/25/08

YEAR	TM/L	G	AB	R	H	2B	3B	HR	RBI	BB	SO	AVG	OBP	SLG	PRO+	BR	/A	RC	SB	CS	SBR	FA	FR	POS	TPR
1908	Cle-A	89	310	23	67	8	5	0	19	16		.216	.255	.274	72	-10	-10	23	8			.928	-6	S3	-1.6
1909	Cle-A	88	283	26	63	10	9	0	20	19		.223	.283	.322	87	-3	-5	27	6			.932	6	3S/2	0.5
1910	Cle-A	39	122	14	27	6	3	0	8	3		.221	.240	.320	74	-4	-4	10	3			.931	2	3/1	-0.2
1914	KC-F	144	496	68	138	28	10	2	69	59	39	.278	.355	.387	116	8	10	74	7			.934	9	*31/PS	2.3
1915	KC-F	153	553	67	143	23	7	7	67	57	30	.259	.329	.363	108	2	5	74	10			.958	15	*312/S	2.5
Total	5	513	1764	198	438	75	34	9	183	154	69	.248	.311	.345	99	-8	-4	208	34			.939	26	3/1S2P	3.5

■ BOYD PERRY Perry, Boyd Glenn b: 3/21/14, Snow Camp, N.C. d: 6/29/90, Burlington, N.C. BR/TR, 5'10", 158 lbs. Deb: 5/23/41

YEAR	TM/L	G	AB	R	H	2B	3B	HR	RBI	BB	SO	AVG	OBP	SLG	PRO+	BR	/A	RC	SB	CS	SBR	FA	FR	POS	TPR
1941	Det-A	36	83	9	15	5	0	0	11	10	9	.181	.269	.241	32	-8	-9	6	1	0	0	.974	-0	S2	-0.7

■ CLAY PERRY Perry, Clayton Shields b: 12/18/1881, Rice Lake, Wis. d: 1/16/54, Rice Lake, Wis. BR/TR, 5'10.5", 175 lbs. Deb: 9/02/08

YEAR	TM/L	G	AB	R	H	2B	3B	HR	RBI	BB	SO	AVG	OBP	SLG	PRO+	BR	/A	RC	SB	CS	SBR	FA	FR	POS	TPR
1908	Det-A	7	17	0	2	0	0	0	0	0		.118	.167	.118	-7	-2	-2	0	0			.917	-1	/3	-0.4

■ GERALD PERRY Perry, Gerald June b: 10/30/60, Savannah, Ga. BL/TR, 6', 190 lbs. Deb: 8/11/83

YEAR	TM/L	G	AB	R	H	2B	3B	HR	RBI	BB	SO	AVG	OBP	SLG	PRO+	BR	/A	RC	SB	CS	SBR	FA	FR	POS	TPR
1983	Atl-N	27	39	5	14	2	0	1	6	5	4	.359	.432	.487	144	3	3	8	0	1	-1	.982	-2	/1O	0.0
1984	Atl-N	122	347	52	92	12	2	7	47	61	38	.265	.378	.372	104	8	5	50	15	12	-3	.988	-8	1O	-1.1
1985	Atl-N	110	238	22	51	5	0	3	13	23	28	.214	.284	.273	53	-14	-15	18	9	5	-0	.985	-0	1/O	-2.0
1986	Atl-N	29	70	6	19	2	0	2	11	8	4	.271	.346	.386	96	0	-0	8	0	1	-1	.889	-5	O/1	-0.7
1987	Atl-N	142	533	77	144	35	2	12	74	48	63	.270	.332	.411	91	-4	-7	69	42	16	3	.990	-10	*1/O	-2.4
1988	Atl-N★	141	547	61	164	29	1	8	74	36	49	.300	.344	.400	108	9	6	70	29	14	0	.988	1	*1	-0.6
1989	Atl-N	72	266	24	67	11	0	4	21	32	28	.252	.339	.338	92	-1	-2	31	10	6	-1	.987	1	1	-0.7
1990	KC-A	133	465	57	118	22	2	8	57	39	56	.254	.316	.361	90	-7	-6	53	17	4	3	.986	2	D1	-0.5
1991	StL-N	109	242	29	58	8	4	6	36	22	34	.240	.303	.380	90	-3	-3	28	15	8	-0	.989	-4	1/O	-1.1
1992	StL-N	87	143	13	34	8	0	1	18	15	23	.238	.314	.315	80	-4	-4	13	3	6	-3	.987	-4	1	-1.2
Total	10	972	2890	346	761	134	11	52	357	289	327	.263	.333	.371	93	-13	-25	348	140	73	-2	.988	-28	1/OD	-10.3

■ BOB PERRY Perry, Melvin Gray b: 9/14/34, New Bern, N.C. BR/TR, 6'2", 180 lbs. Deb: 5/17/63

YEAR	TM/L	G	AB	R	H	2B	3B	HR	RBI	BB	SO	AVG	OBP	SLG	PRO+	BR	/A	RC	SB	CS	SBR	FA	FR	POS	TPR
1963	LA-A	61	166	16	42	9	0	3	14	9	31	.253	.303	.361	91	-3	-2	18	1	1	-0	.946	-7	O	-1.2
1964	LA-A	70	221	19	61	8	1	3	16	14	52	.276	.319	.362	99	-3	-1	25	1	1	-0	.975	-4	O	-0.9
Total	2	131	387	35	103	17	1	6	30	23	83	.266	.312	.362	95	-7	-3	43	2	2	-1	.962	-11	O	-2.1

■ HANK PERRY Perry, William Henry "Socks" b: 7/28/1886, Howell, Mich. d: 7/18/56, Pontiac, Mich. BL/TR, 5'11", 190 lbs. Deb: 4/12/12

YEAR	TM/L	G	AB	R	H	2B	3B	HR	RBI	BB	SO	AVG	OBP	SLG	PRO+	BR	/A	RC	SB	CS	SBR	FA	FR	POS	TPR
1912	Det-A	13	36	3	6	1	0	0	0	3		.167	.231	.194	23	-4	-3	2	0			1.000	2	/O	-0.2

■ JOHNNY PESKY Pesky, John Michael (b: John Michael Paveskovich) b: 9/27/19, Portland, Ore. BL/TR, 5'9", 168 lbs. Deb: 4/14/42 MC

YEAR	TM/L	G	AB	R	H	2B	3B	HR	RBI	BB	SO	AVG	OBP	SLG	PRO+	BR	/A	RC	SB	CS	SBR	FA	FR	POS	TPR
1942	Bos-A	147	620	105	**205**	29	9	2	51	42	36	.331	.375	.416	118	18	15	100	12	7	-1	.955	18	*S	4.1
1946	•Bos-A★	153	621	115	**208**	43	4	2	55	65	29	.335	.401	.427	124	27	23	111	9	8	-2	.969	12	*S	4.3
1947	Bos-A	155	638	106	**207**	27	8	0	39	72	22	.324	.393	.392	110	18	12	103	12	9	-2	.976	-11	*S3	0.7
1948	Bos-A	143	565	124	159	26	6	3	55	99	32	.281	.394	.365	98	6	2	90	3	5	-2	.951	6	*3	0.4
1949	Bos-A	148	604	111	185	27	7	2	69	100	19	.306	.408	.384	103	13	7	104	8	4	0	.970	21	*3	2.5
1950	Bos-A	127	490	112	153	22	6	1	49	104	31	.312	.437	.388	103	16	9	93	2	1	0	.974	22	*3/S	2.7
1951	Bos-A	131	480	93	150	20	6	3	41	84	15	.313	.417	.398	110	18	12	87	2	2	-1	.961	9	*S3/2	2.7
1952	Bos-A	25	67	10	10	2	0	0	2	15	5	.149	.313	.179	36	-5	-6	4	0	3	-2	.917	-6	3/S	-1.4
	Det-A	69	177	26	45	4	0	1	9	41	11	.254	.394	.294	93	1	1	25	1	2	-1	.952	-6	S2/3	-0.2
	Yr	94	244	36	55	6	0	1	11	56	16	.225	.372	.262	77	-4	-5	28	1	5	-3	.953	-11	S32	-1.6
1953	Det-A	103	308	43	90	22	1	2	24	27	10	.292	.353	.390	102	0	1	43	3	7	-3	.991	-14	2	-1.2
1954	Det-A	20	17	5	3	0	0	1	1	3	1	.176	.300	.353	80	-1	-0	1	0	0	0	.000	0	H	-0.1
	Was-A	49	158	17	40	4	3	0	9	10	7	.253	.298	.316	72	-7	-6	15	1	1	-0	.979	-8	2/S	-1.3
	Yr	69	175	22	43	4	3	1	10	13	8	.246	.298	.320	72	-8	-7	16	1	1	-0	.979	-8	2/S	-1.4
Total	10	1270	4745	867	1455	226	50	17	404	662	218	.307	.394	.386	106	105	69	777	53	49	-14	.964	43	S32	13.2

YEAR	TM/L	G	AB	R	H	2B	3B	HR	RBI	BB	SO	AVG	OBP	SLG	PRO+	BR	/A	RC	SB	CS	SBR	FA	FR	POS	TPR

■ BILL PETERMAN   Peterman, William David   b: 3/20/21, Philadelphia, Pa.   BR/TR, 6'2", 185 lbs.   Deb: 4/26/42

| 1942 | Phi-N | 1 | 1 | 0 | 1 | 0 | 0 | 0 | 0 | 0 | 0 | 1.000 | 1.000 | 1.000 | 512 | 0 | 0 | 1 | 0 | | | .000 | 0 | /C | 0.0 |

■ JOHN PETERS   Peters, John Paul   b: 4/8/1850, Louisiana, Mo.   d: 1/4/24, St.Louis, Mo.   BR/TR, 5'7", 180 lbs.   Deb: 5/23/1874

1874	Chi-n	55	240	39	69	10	0	1		0	2	.287	.293	.342	101	0	-0	25						S2/3	-0.2
1875	Chi-n	69	298	40	86	18	0	0		0		.289	.289	.349	118	5	5	31						*S/2	0.2
1876	Chi-N	66	316	70	111	14	2	1	47	3	2	.351	.357	.418	141	18	13	48				.932	-1	*S/P	1.0
1877	Chi-N	60	265	45	84	10	3	0	41	1	7	.317	.320	.377	106	5	1	33				.883	19	*S	1.8
1878	Mil-N	55	246	33	76	6	1	0	22	5	8	.309	.323	.341	111	5	2	28				.853	5	2S	0.9
1879	Chi-N	83	379	45	93	13	2	1	31	1	19	.245	.247	.298	74	-9	-12	29				.837	-8	*S	-1.4
1880	Pro-N	86	359	30	82	5	0	0	24	5	15	.228	.239	.242	66	-13	-12	21				.900	-1	*S	-0.7
1881	Buf-N	54	229	21	49	8	1	0	25	3	12	.214	.224	.258	52	-13	-12	14				.869	7	S/O	-0.2
1882	Pit-a	78	333	46	96	10	1	0		4		.288	.297	.324	115	3	5	33				.883	6	*S/2	1.3
1883	Pit-a	8	28	3	3	0	0	0		0		.107	.107	.107	-32	-4	-4	0				.818	3	/S	0.0
1884	Pit-a	1	4	0	0	0	0	0		0		.000	.000	.000	-98	-1	-1	0				.667	-2	/S	-0.2
Total	2 n	124	538	79	155	28	0	1		2		.288	.291	.346	110	6	5	55						/S23	0.0
Total	9	491	2159	293	594	66	10	2	190	22	63	.275	.282	.318	94	-8	-20	206				.881	27	S/2OP	2.5

■ JOHN PETERS   Peters, John William "Big Pete" or "Shotgun"   b: 7/14/1893, Kansas City, Kan.   d: 2/21/32, Kansas City, Mo.   BR/TR, 6', 192 lbs.   Deb: 5/01/15

1915	Det-A	1	3	0	0	0	0	0	0	0	1	.000	.000	.000	-95	-1	-1	0	0			1.000	1	/C	0.1
1918	Cle-A	1	1	0	0	0	0	0	0	0	1	.000	.500	.000	46	0	0	0	0			.500	1	/C	-0.1
1921	Phi-N	55	155	7	45	4	0	3	23	6	13	.290	.329	.374	79	-3	-5	19	1	0	0	.933	-13	C	-1.5
1922	Phi-N	55	143	15	35	9	1	4	24	9	18	.245	.308	.406	75	-4	-6	18	0	1	-1	.953	-5	C	-0.9
Total	4	112	302	22	80	13	1	7	47	16	33	.265	.317	.384	76	-8	-12	37	1	1		.934	-18	/C	-2.4

■ RICK PETERS   Peters, Richard Devin   b: 11/21/55, Lynwood, Cal.   BB/TR, 5'9", 170 lbs.   Deb: 9/08/79

1979	Det-A	12	19	3	5	0	0	0	2	5	3	.263	.417	.263	85	0	-0	3	0	0	0	.000	-1	/32OD	-0.1
1980	Det-A	133	477	79	139	19	7	2	42	54	48	.291	.371	.373	102	5	3	66	13	7	-0	.977	0	*OD	-0.1
1981	Det-A	63	207	26	53	7	3	0	15	29	28	.256	.353	.319	91	-0	-1	22	1	6	-3	.991	3	OD	-0.2
1983	Oak-A	55	178	20	51	7	0	0	20	12	21	.287	.335	.326	88	-4	-2	18	4	9	-4	.986	5	O/D	-0.3
1986	Oak-A	44	38	7	7	1	0	0	1	7	7	.184	.311	.211	49	-3	-2	2	2	2	-1	1.000	-5	O/2	-0.8
Total	5	307	919	135	255	34	10	2	80	107	107	.277	.358	.343	95	-2	-3	111	20	24	-8	.983	1	O/D23	-1.5

■ RUSTY PETERS   Peters, Russell Dixon   b: 12/14/14, Roanoke, Va.   BR/TR, 5'11", 170 lbs.   Deb: 4/14/36

1936	Phi-A	45	119	12	26	3	2	3	16	4	28	.218	.244	.353	47	-11	-11	10	1	1	-0	.898	1	S3/O2	-0.8
1937	Phi-A	116	339	39	88	17	6	3	43	41	59	.260	.339	.372	80	-11	-10	44	4	4	-1	.966	-13	23S	-1.8
1938	Phi-A	2	7	0	0	0	0	0	0	0	1	.000	.000	.000	-99	-2	-2	0	0	0	0	.714	-2	/S	-0.4
1940	Cle-A	30	71	5	17	3	2	0	7	4	14	.239	.280	.338	61	-4	-4	7	1	0	0	.922	0	/2S31	-0.3
1941	Cle-A	29	63	6	13	2	0	0	2	7	10	.206	.286	.238	42	-5	-5	4	0	1	-1	.891	2	S/32	-0.3
1942	Cle-A	34	58	6	13	5	1	0	2	2	14	.224	.250	.345	70	-3	-3	4	0	0	0	.944	2	S/23	0.0
1943	Cle-A	79	215	22	47	6	2	1	19	18	29	.219	.282	.279	69	-10	-8	18	1	1	-0	.913	-6	3S/2O	-1.5
1944	Cle-A	88	282	23	63	13	3	1	24	15	35	.223	.268	.301	65	-14	-13	23	2	1	0	.976	-3	2S/3	-1.3
1946	Cle-A	9	21	0	6	0	0	0	2	1	1	.286	.318	.286	74	-1	-1	2	0	1	-1	1.000	1	/S	-0.1
1947	StL-A	39	47	10	16	4	0	0	2	6	8	.340	.415	.426	131	2	2	9	0	0	0	.955	7	2/S	0.2
Total	10	471	1222	123	289	53	16	8	117	98	199	.236	.295	.326	69	-59	-54	120	9	9	-3	.966	-13	2S3/01	-5.5

■ BUDDY PETERSON   Peterson, Carl Francis   b: 4/23/25, Portland, Ore.   BR/TR, 5'9.5", 170 lbs.   Deb: 9/14/55

1955	Chi-A	6	21	7	6	1	0	0	2	3	1	.286	.400	.333	96	0	0	3	0	0	0	.962	-1	/S	0.0
1957	Bal-A	7	17	1	3	2	0	0	0	2	2	.176	.263	.294	55	-1	-1	1	0	0	0	.963	-1	/S	-0.2
Total	2	13	38	8	9	3	0	0	2	5	3	.237	.341	.316	80	-1	-1	4	0	0	0	.962	-2	/S	-0.2

■ CAP PETERSON   Peterson, Charles Andrew   b: 8/15/42, Tacoma, Wash.   d: 5/16/80, Tacoma, Wash.   BR/TR, 6'2", 195 lbs.   Deb: 9/12/62

1962	SF-N	4	6	1	1	0	0	0	0	1	4	.167	.286	.167	25	-1	-1	0	0	0	0	1.000	-1	/S	-0.1
1963	SF-N	22	54	7	14	2	0	1	2	2	13	.259	.286	.352	83	-1	-1	6	0	0	0	.917	-6	/23OS	-0.7
1964	SF-N	66	74	8	15	1	1	1	8	3	20	.203	.234	.284	44	-5	-6	5	0	0	0	1.000	-1	O/123	-0.7
1965	SF-N	63	105	14	26	7	0	3	15	10	16	.248	.313	.400	97	-0	-1	12	0	0	0	1.000	-3	O	-0.4
1966	SF-N	89	190	13	45	6	1	2	19	11	32	.237	.282	.311	63	-9	-10	15	2	0	1	1.000	0	O/1	-1.4
1967	Was-A	122	405	35	97	17	2	8	46	32	61	.240	.300	.351	95	-5	-3	41	0	3	-2	.970	0	*O	-1.0
1968	Was-A	94	226	20	46	8	1	3	18	18	31	.204	.265	.288	70	-9	-8	18	2	1	0	1.000	-1	O	-1.4
1969	Cle-A	76	110	8	25	3	0	1	14	24	18	.227	.370	.282	82	-1	-2	12	0	0	0	.977	2	O/3	-0.5
Total	8	536	1170	106	269	44	5	19	122	101	195	.230	.294	.325	80	-31	-30	109	4	4	-1	.983	-15	O/321S	-6.2

■ HARDY PETERSON   Peterson, Harding William   b: 10/17/29, Perth Amboy, N.J.   BR/TR, 6', 205 lbs.   Deb: 5/05/55

1955	Pit-N	32	81	7	20	6	0	1	10	7	7	.247	.315	.358	79	-3	-2	9	0	0	0	.965	6	C	0.4
1957	Pit-N	30	73	10	22	2	1	2	11	9	10	.301	.378	.438	122	2	2	10	0	1	-1	.985	2	C	0.4
1958	Pit-N	2	6	0	2	0	0	0	0	1	0	.333	.429	.333	108	0	0	1	0	0	0	1.000	-0	/C	0.0
1959	Pit-N	2	1	0	0	0	0	0	0	0	0	.000	.000	.000	-99	-0	-0	0	0	0	0	1.000	1	/C	0.0
Total	4	66	161	17	44	8	1	3	21	17	17	.273	.346	.391	99	-1	-0	20	0	1	-1	.976	7	/C	0.8

■ BOB PETERSON   Peterson, Robert A.   b: 7/16/1884, Philadelphia, Pa.   d: 11/27/62, Eveshan Township, N.J.   BR/TR, 6'1", 160 lbs.   Deb: 4/18/06

1906	Bos-A	39	118	10	24	1	1	1	9	11		.203	.277	.254	67	-4	-4	9	1			.899	-7	C/21O	-0.9
1907	Bos-A	4	13	1	1	0	0	0	0	0		.077	.077	.077	-51	-2	-2	0	0			1.000	0	/C	-0.2
Total	2	43	131	11	25	1	1	1	9	11		.191	.259	.237	56	-6	-6	9	1			.910	-7	/C21O	-1.1

■ TED PETOSKEY   Petoskey, Frederick Lee   b: 1/5/11, St.Charles, Mich.   BR/TR, 5'11.5", 183 lbs.   Deb: 9/09/34

1934	Cin-N	6	7	0	0	0	0	0	0	0	5	.000	.000	.000	-99	-2	-2	0	0			1.000	1	/O	-0.1
1935	Cin-N	4	5	0	2	0	0	0	0	0	1	.400	.400	.400	119	0	0	1	1			1.000	-1	/O	-0.1
Total	2	10	12	0	2	0	0	0	1	0	6	.167	.167	.167	-11	-2	-2	1	1			1.000	0	/O	-0.2

■ GENO PETRALLI   Petralli, Eugene James   b: 9/25/59, Sacramento, Cal.   BL/TR, 6'2", 185 lbs.   Deb: 9/04/82

1982	Tor-A	16	44	3	16	2	0	0	1	4	6	.364	.417	.409	117	2	1	8	0	0	0	.981	-2	C/3	0.0
1983	Tor-A	6	4	0	0	0	0	0	0	1	1	.000	.000	.000	-37	-1	-1	0	0	0	0	1.000	0	/CD	0.0
1984	Tor-A	3	3	0	0	0	0	0	0	0	0	.000	.000	.000	-97	-1	-1	0	0	0	0	1.000	0	/CD	0.0
1985	Tex-A	42	100	7	27	2	0	0	11	8	12	.270	.330	.290	71	-4	-4	10	1	0	0	.990	2	C	0.0
1986	Tex-A	69	137	17	35	9	3	2	18	5	14	.255	.282	.409	83	-3	-4	14	3	0	1	.988	-1	C3/2D	-0.9
1987	Tex-A	101	202	28	61	11	2	7	31	27	29	.302	.390	.480	129	9	9	38	0	2	-1	.995	-0	C3/120D	1.0
1988	Tex-A	129	351	35	99	14	2	7	36	41	52	.282	.360	.393	108	6	5	49	0	1	-1	.981	-1	CD/312	0.9
1989	Tex-A	70	184	18	56	7	0	4	23	17	24	.304	.369	.408	117	5	5	28	0	0	0	.989	-12	CD	-0.5
1990	Tex-A	133	325	28	83	13	1	0	21	50	49	.255	.360	.302	87	-3	-4	36	0	2	-1	.991	-4	*C/32	-0.7
1991	Tex-A	87	199	21	54	8	1	2	20	21	25	.271	.341	.352	94	-2	-1	25	2	1	0	.972	-10	C/3D	-0.8
1992	Tex-A	94	192	11	38	12	0	1	18	20	34	.198	.274	.276	56	-12	-11	14	0	1	-1	.990	4	CD/32	-0.5
Total	11	750	1741	168	469	78	9	23	179	194	246	.269	.346	.364	96	-3	-5	220	6	8	-5	.987	-30	C/D3210	-1.0

■ RICO PETROCELLI   Petrocelli, Americo Peter   b: 6/27/43, Brooklyn, N.Y.   BR/TR, 6', 185 lbs.   Deb: 9/21/63

| 1963 | Bos-A | 1 | 4 | 0 | 1 | 1 | 0 | 0 | 1 | 0 | 1 | .250 | .250 | .500 | 101 | -0 | -0 | 1 | 0 | 0 | 0 | .833 | -0 | /S | 0.0 |

YEAR	TM/L	G	AB	R	H	2B	3B	HR	RBI	BB	SO	AVG	OBP	SLG	PRO+	BR	/A	RC	SB	CS	SBR	FA	FR	POS	TPR
1965	Bos-A	103	323	38	75	15	2	13	33	36	71	.232	.311	.412	98	1	-1	41	0	2	-1	.958	10	S	1.5
1966	Bos-A	139	522	58	124	20	1	18	59	41	99	.238	.297	.383	85	-5	-11	60	1	1	-0	.954	1	*S/3	0.1
1967	*Bos-A★	142	491	53	127	24	2	17	66	49	93	.259	.332	.420	112	12	8	70	2	4	-2	.970	3	*S	2.4
1968	Bos-A	123	406	41	95	17	2	12	46	31	73	.234	.295	.374	95	0	-3	45	0	1	-1	**.978**	11	*S/1	2.2
1969	Bos-A★	154	535	92	159	32	2	40	97	98	68	.297	.407	.589	167	55	51	129	3	5	-2	**.981**	5	*S/3	**7.2**
1970	Bos-A	157	583	82	152	31	3	29	103	67	82	.261	.339	.473	114	16	11	92	1	1	-0	.970	-10	*S3	1.8
1971	Bos-A	158	553	82	139	24	4	28	89	91	108	.251	.359	.461	122	23	18	92	2	0	1	**.976**	-1	*3	1.8
1972	Bos-A	147	521	62	125	15	2	15	75	78	91	.240	.341	.363	104	8	5	68	0	1	-1	.970	-1	*3	0.2
1973	Bos-A	100	356	44	87	13	1	13	45	47	64	.244	.334	.396	99	3	-0	47	0	0	0	.980	5	3	0.4
1974	Bos-A	129	454	53	121	23	1	15	76	48	74	.267	.339	.421	110	10	6	65	1	0	0	.962	-19	*3/D	-1.4
1975	*Bos-A	115	402	31	96	15	1	7	59	41	66	.239	.314	.333	76	-9	-13	40	0	2	-1	.960	-18	*3/D	-3.4
1976	Bos-A	85	240	17	51	7	1	3	24	34	36	.213	.310	.287	67	-7	-10	20	0	5	-3	.967	-4	3/21SD	-1.9
Total	13	1553	5390	653	1352	237	22	210	773	661	926	.251	.336	.420	108	107	61	769	10	22	-10	.969	-18	S3/D21	10.9

■ PAT PETTEE
Pettee, Patrick E. b: 1/10/1863, Natick, Mass. d: 10/9/34, Natick, Mass. BR/TR, 5'10", 170 lbs. Deb: 4/08/1891

YEAR	TM/L	G	AB	R	H	2B	3B	HR	RBI	BB	SO	AVG	OBP	SLG	PRO+	BR	/A	RC	SB	CS	SBR	FA	FR	POS	TPR
1891	Lou-a	2	5	1	0	0	0	0	0	3	1	.000	.375	.000	12	-0	-0	0	1			.818	-1	/2	-0.1

■ NED PETTIGREW
Pettigrew, Jim Ned b: 8/25/1881, Honey Grove, Tex. d: 8/20/52, Duncan, Okla. BR/TR, 5'11", 175 lbs. Deb: 4/23/14

YEAR	TM/L	G	AB	R	H	2B	3B	HR	RBI	BB	SO	AVG	OBP	SLG	PRO+	BR	/A	RC	SB	CS	SBR	FA	FR	POS	TPR
1914	Buf-F	2	2	0	0	0	0	0	0	0	0	.000	.000	.000	-98	-1	-1	0	0			.000	0	H	-0.1

■ JOE PETTINI
Pettini, Joseph Paul b: 1/26/55, Wheeling, W.Va. BR/TR, 5'9", 165 lbs. Deb: 7/10/80

YEAR	TM/L	G	AB	R	H	2B	3B	HR	RBI	BB	SO	AVG	OBP	SLG	PRO+	BR	/A	RC	SB	CS	SBR	FA	FR	POS	TPR
1980	SF-N	63	190	19	44	3	1	1	9	17	33	.232	.295	.274	61	-10	-9	17	5	2	0	.955	-13	S3/2	-1.9
1981	SF-N	35	29	3	2	1	0	0	2	4	5	.069	.182	.103	-18	-4	-4	1	1	0	0	.920	4	2S/3	0.0
1982	SF-N	29	39	5	8	1	0	0	2	3	4	.205	.262	.231	39	-3	-3	2	0	1	-1	.934	-1	S/3	-0.3
1983	SF-N	61	86	11	16	0	1	0	7	9	11	.186	.263	.209	33	-8	-7	5	4	1	1	.949	11	S23	0.6
Total	4	188	344	38	70	5	2	1	20	33	53	.203	.273	.238	45	-25	-24	25	10	4	1	.943	2	S/32	-1.6

■ GARY PETTIS
Pettis, Gary George b: 4/3/58, Oakland, Cal. BB/TR, 6'1", 165 lbs. Deb: 9/13/82

YEAR	TM/L	G	AB	R	H	2B	3B	HR	RBI	BB	SO	AVG	OBP	SLG	PRO+	BR	/A	RC	SB	CS	SBR	FA	FR	POS	TPR
1982	Cal-A	10	5	5	1	0	0	1	1	0	2	.200	.200	.800	159	0	0	1	0	0	0	1.000	-2	/O	-0.2
1983	Cal-A	22	85	19	25	2	3	3	6	7	15	.294	.348	.494	130	3	3	15	8	3	1	.982	2	O	0.5
1984	Cal-A	140	397	63	90	11	6	2	29	60	115	.227	.333	.300	77	-11	-10	46	48	17	4	.983	1	*O	-0.9
1985	Cal-A	125	443	67	114	10	8	1	32	62	125	.257	.349	.323	86	-7	-7	61	56	9	11	.990	17	*O	1.7
1986	*Cal-A	154	539	93	139	23	4	5	58	69	132	.258	.342	.343	88	-8	-7	71	50	13	7	.985	21	*O/D	1.6
1987	Cal-A	133	394	49	82	13	2	1	17	52	124	.208	.302	.259	53	-27	-25	35	24	5	4	.980	6	*O	-1.8
1988	Det-A	129	458	65	96	14	4	3	36	47	85	.210	.285	.277	60	-25	-23	42	44	10	7	.987	10	*O/D	-0.9
1989	Det-A	119	444	77	114	8	6	1	18	84	106	.257	.375	.309	97	1	2	58	43	15	4	.988	5	*O	0.8
1990	Tex-A	136	423	66	101	16	8	3	31	57	118	.239	.335	.336	88	-5	-6	52	38	15	2	.993	4	*O/D	-0.2
1991	Tex-A	137	282	37	61	7	5	0	19	54	91	.216	.342	.277	75	-8	-7	32	29	13	1	.977	-11	*O/D	-1.9
1992	SD-N	30	30	0	6	1	0	0	0	2	11	.200	.250	.233	36	-2	-3	2	1	0	0	.952	-3	O	-0.6
	Det-A	48	129	27	26	4	3	1	12	27	34	.202	.340	.302	80	-2	-3	16	13	4	2	.993	5	O	0.3
Total	11	1183	3629	568	855	109	49	21	259	521	958	.236	.333	.310	80	-91	-84	432	354	104	44	.986	54	*O/D	-1.6

■ BOB PETTIT
Pettit, Robert Henry b: 7/19/1861, Williamstown, Mass. d: 11/1/10, Derby, Conn. BL/TR, 5'9", 160 lbs. Deb: 9/03/1887

YEAR	TM/L	G	AB	R	H	2B	3B	HR	RBI	BB	SO	AVG	OBP	SLG	PRO+	BR	/A	RC	SB	CS	SBR	FA	FR	POS	TPR
1887	Chi-N	32	138	29	36	3	3	2	12	8	15	.261	.301	.370	77	-3	-6	21	16			.894	-1	O/CP	-0.6
1888	Chi-N	43	169	23	43	1	4	4	23	7	9	.254	.288	.379	106	2	1	21	7			.931	-4	O	-0.4
1891	Mil-a	21	80	10	14	4	0	1	5	7	7	.175	.267	.262	45	-5	-8	6	2			.932	-7	/2O3	-1.2
Total	3	96	387	62	93	8	7	7	40	22	31	.240	.288	.351	81	-5	-12	48	25			.919	-11	/O23PC	-2.2

■ MARTY PEVEY
Pevey, Marty Ashley b: 12/25/62, Savannah, Ga. BL/TR, 6'1", 185 lbs. Deb: 5/16/89

YEAR	TM/L	G	AB	R	H	2B	3B	HR	RBI	BB	SO	AVG	OBP	SLG	PRO+	BR	/A	RC	SB	CS	SBR	FA	FR	POS	TPR
1989	Mon-N	13	41	2	9	1	1	0	3	0	8	.220	.220	.293	45	-3	-3	2	0	0	0	.985	-2	C/O	-0.5

■ LARRY PEZOLD
Pezold, Lorenz Johannes b: 6/22/1893, New Orleans, La. d: 10/22/57, Baton Rouge, La. BR/TR, 5'9.5", 175 lbs. Deb: 7/27/14

YEAR	TM/L	G	AB	R	H	2B	3B	HR	RBI	BB	SO	AVG	OBP	SLG	PRO+	BR	/A	RC	SB	CS	SBR	FA	FR	POS	TPR
1914	Cle-A	23	71	4	16	0	1	0	5	9	6	.225	.313	.254	68	-2	-3	6	2	3	-1	.827	-1	3/O	-0.5

■ FRED PFEFFER
Pfeffer, Nathaniel Frederick "Fritz" or "Dandelion"
b: 3/17/1860, Louisville, Ky. d: 4/10/32, Chicago, Ill. BR/TR, 5'10.5", 184 lbs. Deb: 5/01/1882 M

YEAR	TM/L	G	AB	R	H	2B	3B	HR	RBI	BB	SO	AVG	OBP	SLG	PRO+	BR	/A	RC	SB	CS	SBR	FA	FR	POS	TPR
1882	Tro-N	85	330	26	72	7	4	1	43	1	24	.218	.221	.273	60	-16	-13	20				.857	11	*S/2	0.1
1883	Chi-N	96	371	41	87	22	7	1	45	8	50	.235	.251	.340	73	-10	-13	32				.887	17	*2S/31	0.5
1884	Chi-N	112	467	105	135	10	10	25	101	25	47	.289	.325	.514	147	30	25	80				.903	**46**	*2/P	**6.3**
1885	*Chi-N	112	469	90	113	12	7	5	73	26	47	.241	.281	.328	84	-2	-12	44				.893	25	*2/PO	1.7
1886	*Chi-N	118	474	88	125	17	8	7	95	36	46	.264	.316	.378	96	6	-5	68	30			.903	7	*2/1	0.6
1887	Chi-N	123	479	95	133	21	6	16	89	34	20	.278	.327	.447	101	8	-2	91	57			.917	25	*2/O	2.2
1888	Chi-N	135	517	90	129	22	10	8	57	32	38	.250	.297	.377	108	9	4	79	64			.931	**38**	*2	4.6
1889	Chi-N	134	531	85	121	15	7	7	77	53	51	.228	.302	.322	72	-17	-22	67	45			.943	20	*2	0.4
1890	Chi-P	124	499	86	128	21	8	5	80	44	23	.257	.319	.361	80	-13	-17	68	27			.916	24	*2	1.2
1891	Chi-N	137	498	93	123	12	9	7	77	79	60	.247	.353	.349	107	7	7	78	40			.921	25	*2	3.3
1892	Lou-N	124	470	78	121	14	9	2	76	67	36	.257	.353	.338	121	8	14	67	27			.933	12	*21/PM	2.5
1893	Lou-N	125	508	85	129	29	12	3	75	51	18	.254	.322	.376	94	-11	-4	74	32			.939	6	*2	0.4
1894	Lou-N	104	409	68	126	12	14	5	59	30	14	.308	.357	.443	100	-5	0	79	31			.937	12	*2S/P	1.3
1895	Lou-N	11	45	8	13	1	0	0	5	5	3	.289	.360	.311	81	-1	-1	6	2			.742	-3	/S21	-0.3
1896	NY-N	4	14	1	2	0	0	0	4	1	1	.143	.250	.143	7	-2	-2	1	0			.760	-2	/2	-0.3
	Chi-N	94	360	45	88	16	7	2	52	23	20	.244	.294	.344	67	-17	-19	44	22			.947	10	*2	-0.3
	Yr	98	374	46	90	16	7	2	56	24	21	.241	.292	.337	65	-18	-21	45	22			.939	8	2	-0.6
1897	Chi-N	32	114	10	26	0	1	0	11	12		.228	.318	.246	48	-8	-9	11	5			.883	-6	2	-1.2
Total	16	1670	6555	1094	1671	231	119	94	1019	527	498	.255	.312	.369	93	-33	-69	908	382			.920	266	*2S/1PO3	23.0

■ BOBBY PFEIL
Pfeil, Robert Raymond b: 11/13/43, Passaic, N.J. BR/TR, 6'1", 180 lbs. Deb: 6/26/69

YEAR	TM/L	G	AB	R	H	2B	3B	HR	RBI	BB	SO	AVG	OBP	SLG	PRO+	BR	/A	RC	SB	CS	SBR	FA	FR	POS	TPR
1969	NY-N	62	211	20	49	9	0	0	10	7	27	.232	.260	.275	49	-14	-15	14	0	1	-1	.976	-3	32/O	-1.9
1971	Phi-N	44	70	5	19	3	0	2	9	6	9	.271	.329	.400	106	0	0	8	1	1	-0	1.000	-1	3/CO12S	-0.1
Total	2	106	281	25	68	12	0	2	19	13	36	.242	.278	.306	63	-14	-14	22	1	2	-1	.980	-4	/32OCS1	-2.0

■ GEORGE PFISTER
Pfister, George Edward b: 9/4/18, Bound Brook, N.J. BR/TR, 6', 200 lbs. Deb: 9/27/41

YEAR	TM/L	G	AB	R	H	2B	3B	HR	RBI	BB	SO	AVG	OBP	SLG	PRO+	BR	/A	RC	SB	CS	SBR	FA	FR	POS	TPR
1941	Bro-N	1	2	0	0	0	0	0	0	0	0	.000	.000	.000	-96	-1	-1	0	0			.000	0	/C	-0.1

■ MONTE PFYL
Pfyl, Meinhard Charles b: 5/11/1884, St.Louis, Mo. d: 10/18/45, San Francisco, Cal BL/TL, 6'3", 190 lbs. Deb: 7/30/07

YEAR	TM/L	G	AB	R	H	2B	3B	HR	RBI	BB	SO	AVG	OBP	SLG	PRO+	BR	/A	RC	SB	CS	SBR	FA	FR	POS	TPR
1907	NY-N	1	0	0	0	0	0	0	0	0		—	—	—	—	0	-0	0	0			.000	0	/1	0.0

■ ART PHELAN
Phelan, Arthur Thomas "Dugan" b: 8/14/1887, Niantic, Ill. d: 12/27/64, Ft.Worth, Tex. BR/TR, 5'8", 160 lbs. Deb: 6/25/10

YEAR	TM/L	G	AB	R	H	2B	3B	HR	RBI	BB	SO	AVG	OBP	SLG	PRO+	BR	/A	RC	SB	CS	SBR	FA	FR	POS	TPR
1910	Cin-N	23	42	7	9	0	0	0	4	7	6	.214	.327	.214	61	-2	-2	5	5			1.000	-2	/32OS	-0.4
1912	Cin-N	130	461	56	112	9	11	3	54	46	37	.243	.314	.330	79	-15	-13	56	25			.924	-2	*3/2	-1.4
1913	Chi-N	91	261	41	65	11	6	2	35	29	26	.249	.331	.360	97	-1	-1	33	8			.931	-9	23/S	-1.0
1914	Chi-N	25	46	5	13	2	1	0	3	4	3	.283	.340	.370	111	1	1	6	0			.905	-0	/32S	0.1
1915	Chi-N	133	448	41	98	16	7	3	35	55	42	.219	.307	.306	86	-7	-7	45	12	9	-2	.939	-2	*32	-0.6
Total	5	402	1258	150	297	38	25	8	131	141	114	.236	.317	.325	85	-24	-22	144	50	9		.931	-14	3/2SO	-3.3

YEAR	TM/L	G	AB	R	H	2B	3B	HR	RBI	BB	SO	AVG	OBP	SLG	PRO+	BR	/A	RC	SB	CS	SBR	FA	FR	POS	TPR
■ DAN PHELAN Phelan, Daniel T. b: 7/1865, Thomaston, Conn. d: 12/7/45, West Haven, Conn. Deb: 4/18/1890																									
1890	Lou-a	8	32	4	8	1	1	0		0		.250	.250	.344	79	-1	-1	3	1			.975	0	/1	-0.1
■ DICK PHELAN Phelan, James Dickson b: 12/10/1854, Towanda, Pa. d: 2/13/31, San Antonio, Tex. Deb: 4/17/1884																									
1884	Bal-U	101	402	63	99	13	3	3		12		.246	.268	.316	88	-1	-8	35				.872	-9	*2/3O	-1.3
1885	Buf-N	4	16	2	2	0	0	1	3	0	3	.125	.125	.313	37	-1	-1	1				.808	-1	/2	-0.2
	StL-N	2	4	1	1	1	0	0	1	0	2	.250	.250	.500	147	0	0	1				1.000	-1	/3	0.0
	Yr	6	20	3	3	1	0	1	4	0	5	.150	.150	.350	58	-1	-1	1				.808	-2	/23	-0.2
Total	2	107	422	66	102	14	3	4	4	12	5	.242	.263	.318	86	-2	-9	36				.869	-10	2/3O	-1.5
■ NEALY PHELPS Phelps, Cornelius Carman b: 11/19/1840, New York, N.Y. d: 2/12/1885, New York, N.Y. Deb: 7/01/1871																									
1871	Kek-n	1	3	0	0	0	0	0	0	1	0	.000	.250	.000	-20	-0	-0	0	0					/1	0.0
1873	Mut-n	1	6	0	0	0	0	0	0	0	0	.000	.000	.000	-99	-1	-1	0						/O	-0.1
1874	Mut-n	6	24	5	3	0	0	0		0		.125	.125	.125	-20	-3	-3	0						/O	-0.2
1875	Mut-n	2	6	1	2	0	0	0		0		.333	.333	.333	125	0	0	1						/O	0.0
1876	NY-N	1	3	0	0	0	0	0	0	0	1	.000	.000	.000	-99	-1	-1	0				.667	-0	/O	-0.1
	Phi-N	1	4	0	0	0	0	0	0	0	0	.000	.000	.000	-99	-1	-1	0				.571	-1	/C	-0.2
	Yr	2	7	0	0	0	0	0	0	0	1	.000	.000	.000	-99	-1	-1	0				.667	-2	/OC	-0.3
Total	4 n	10	39	6	5	0	0	0		1		.128	.150	.128	-11	-5	-5	1						/O1	-0.3
■ ED PHELPS Phelps, Edward Jaykill "Yaller" b: 3/3/1879, Albany, N.Y. d: 1/31/42, E.Greenbush, N.Y. BR/TR, 5'11", 185 lbs. Deb: 9/03/02																									
1902	Pit-N	18	61	5	13	1	0	0	6	4		.213	.284	.230	57	-3	-3	5	2			.968	-6	C/1	-0.8
1903	*Pit-N	81	273	32	77	7	3	2	31	17		.282	.333	.352	93	-2	-3	35	2			.980	-8	C/1	-0.3
1904	Pit-N	94	302	29	73	5	3	0	28	15		.242	.289	.278	74	-8	-9	27	2			.964	-10	C/1	-1.1
1905	Cin-N	44	156	18	36	5	3	0	18	12		.231	.298	.301	71	-4	-6	16	4			.949	-6	C	-0.8
1906	Cin-N	12	40	3	11	0	2	1	5	3		.275	.326	.450	136	2	1	7	2			.987	-1	C	0.2
	Pit-N	43	118	9	28	3	1	0	12	9		.237	.302	.280	78	-2	-3	11	1			.971	-4	C	-0.3
	Yr	55	158	12	39	3	3	1	17	12		.247	.308	.323	93	-1	-1	18	3			.975	-4	C	-0.1
1907	Pit-N	43	113	11	24	1	0	0	12	9		.212	.282	.221	57	-5	-5	8	1			.979	-3	C/1	-0.6
1908	Pit-N	34	64	3	15	2	2	0	11	2		.234	.269	.328	90	-1	-1	5	0			.977	-0	C	0.0
1909	StL-N	104	306	43	76	13	1	0	22	39		.248	.350	.297	108	2	5	35	7			.954	-9	C	0.2
1910	StL-N	93	270	25	71	4	2	0	37	36	29	.263	.356	.293	93	-2	-1	32	9			.976	-15	C	-0.9
1912	Bro-N	52	111	8	32	4	3	0	23	16	15	.288	.388	.378	114	2	3	17	1			.976	-4	C	0.1
1913	Bro-N	15	18	0	4	0	0	0	0	1	2	.222	.263	.222	38	-1	-1	1	0			.875	-2	/C	-0.3
Total	11	633	1832	186	460	45	20	3	205	163	46	.251	.323	.302	88	-22	-24	199	31			.968	-68	C/1	-4.6
■ BABE PHELPS Phelps, Ernest Gordon "Blimp" b: 4/19/08, Odenton, Md. BL/TR, 6'2", 225 lbs. Deb: 9/17/31																									
1931	Was-A	3	3	0	1	0	0	0	0	0	0	.333	.333	.333	75	-0	-0	0	0	0	0	.000	0	H	0.0
1933	Chi-N	3	7	0	2	0	0	0	2	0	1	.286	.286	.286	64	-0	-0	1	0			1.000	1	/C	0.0
1934	Chi-N	44	70	7	20	5	2	2	12	1	8	.286	.296	.500	111	0	1	10	0			.981	-2	C	-0.1
1935	Bro-N	47	121	17	44	7	2	5	22	9	10	.364	.408	.579	165	10	11	28	0			.957	-2	C	1.0
1936	Bro-N	115	319	36	117	23	2	5	57	27	18	.367	.421	.498	145	21	21	69	1			.977	-16	C/O	0.9
1937	Bro-N	121	409	42	128	37	3	7	58	25	28	.313	.357	.469	121	12	11	67	2			.971	-7	*C	1.0
1938	Bro-N†	66	208	33	64	12	2	5	46	23	15	.308	.379	.457	126	8	8	35	2			.980	-4	C	0.7
1939	Bro-N★	98	323	33	92	21	2	6	42	24	24	.285	.336	.418	98	0	-1	43	0			.980	2	C	0.5
1940	Bro-N★	118	370	47	109	24	5	13	61	30	27	.295	.349	.492	122	14	11	59	2			.977	-9	C/1	0.9
1941	Bro-N	16	30	3	7	3	0	2	4	1	2	.233	.258	.533	114	0	0	4	0			.971	-1	C	0.0
1942	Pit-N	95	257	21	73	11	1	9	41	20	24	.284	.345	.440	126	9	8	39	2			.959	-3	C	1.1
Total	11	726	2117	239	657	143	19	54	345	160	157	.310	.362	.472	124	75	68	356	9	0		.974	-41	C/1O	6.0
■ KEN PHELPS Phelps, Kenneth Allen b: 8/6/54, Seattle, Wash. BL/TL, 6'1", 209 lbs. Deb: 9/20/80																									
1980	KC-A	3	4	0	0	0	0	0	0	0	2	.000	.000	.000	-99	-1	-1	0	0	0	0	1.000	-0	/1	-0.1
1981	KC-A	21	22	1	3	0	1	0	1	1	13	.136	.174	.227	15	-2	-2	1	0	0	0	1.000	0	/1D	-0.2
1982	Mon-N	10	8	0	2	0	0	0	0	0	3	.250	.333	.250	64	-0	-0	1	0	0	0	.000	0	H	0.0
1983	Sea-A	50	127	10	30	4	1	7	16	13	25	.236	.307	.449	101	1	-0	19	0	0	0	1.000	2	1D	0.1
1984	Sea-A	101	290	52	70	9	0	24	51	61	73	.241	.382	.521	149	20	21	63	3	3	-1	.987	-1	D/1	1.8
1985	Sea-A	61	116	18	24	3	0	9	24	24	33	.207	.343	.466	118	3	3	20	2	0	1	1.000	-0	D/1	0.3
1986	Sea-A	125	344	69	85	16	4	24	64	88	96	.247	.409	.526	151	28	28	81	2	3	-1	.983	-4	1D	1.9
1987	Sea-A	120	332	68	86	13	1	27	68	80	75	.259	.414	.548	145	28	25	81	1	1	-0	1.000	-0	*D/1	2.3
1988	Sea-A	72	190	37	54	8	0	14	32	51	35	.284	.438	.547	167	21	20	50	1	0	0	.952	0	D/1	2.0
	NY-A	45	107	17	24	5	0	10	22	19	26	.224	.341	.551	147	6	6	20	0	0	0	.000	-0	D/1	0.6
	Yr	117	297	54	78	13	0	24	54	70	61	.263	.405	.549	160	28	27	70	1	0	0	.952	-0	D/1	2.6
1989	NY-A	86	185	26	46	3	0	7	29	27	47	.249	.344	.378	105	1	2	26	0	0	0	.980	-1	D/1	0.0
	*Oak-A	11	9	0	1	1	0	0	0	4	0	.111	.385	.222	78	-0	-0	1	0	0	0	.000	-0	/1D	0.0
	Yr	97	194	26	47	4	0	7	29	31	47	.242	.347	.371	104	1	2	27	0	0	0	.980	-1	D/1	0.0
1990	Oak-A	32	59	6	11	2	0	1	6	12	10	.186	.324	.271	71	-2	-2	6	0	0	0	.964	0	D/1	-0.2
	Cle-A	24	61	4	7	0	0	0	0	10	11	.115	.239	.115	2	-8	-8	2	1	0	0	1.000	0	1/D	-0.9
	Yr	56	120	10	18	2	0	1	6	22	21	.150	.282	.192	36	-10	-10	7	1	0	0	.992	0	D1	-1.1
Total	11	761	1854	308	443	64	7	123	313	390	449	.239	.377	.480	132	95	92	369	10	7	-1	.987	-4	D1	7.6
■ DAVE PHILLEY Philley, David Earl b: 5/16/20, Paris, Tex. BB/TR, 6', 188 lbs. Deb: 9/06/41																									
1941	Chi-A	7	9	4	2	1	0	0	0	3	3	.222	.417	.333	102	0	0	2	0	0	0	.000	-1	/O	-0.1
1946	Chi-A	17	68	10	24	2	3	0	17	4	4	.353	.389	.471	145	3	4	14	5	0	2	.983	5	O	0.9
1947	Chi-A	143	551	55	142	25	11	2	45	35	39	.258	.303	.354	85	-15	-12	56	21	16	-3	.986	2	*O/3	-2.2
1948	Chi-A	137	488	51	140	28	3	5	42	50	33	.287	.353	.387	100	-3	-0	67	8	10	-4	.978	15	*O	0.4
1949	Chi-A	146	598	84	171	20	8	0	44	54	51	.286	.347	.346	86	-14	-12	76	13	4	2	.977	2	*O	-1.5
1950	Chi-A	156	619	69	150	21	5	14	80	52	57	.242	.302	.360	71	-31	-29	67	6	3	0	.980	1	*O	-3.3
1951	Chi-A	7	25	0	6	2	0	0	2	2	3	.240	.296	.320	68	-1	-1	2	0	0	0	.938	-0	/O	-0.1
	Phi-A	125	468	71	123	18	7	7	59	63	38	.263	.354	.376	95	-1	-2	68	9	6	-1	.978	2	*O/3	-0.6
	Yr	132	493	71	129	20	7	7	61	65	41	.262	.351	.373	94	-2	-3	70	9	6	-1	.976	2	*O/3	-0.7
1952	Phi-A	151	586	80	154	25	4	7	71	59	35	.263	.334	.355	86	-6	-11	67	11	4	1	.991	13	*O/3	-0.3
1953	Phi-A	157	620	80	188	30	9	9	59	51	35	.303	.358	.424	106	8	5	92	13	5	1	.981	-4	*O/3	-0.4
1954	*Cle-A	133	452	48	102	13	3	12	60	57	48	.226	.312	.347	79	-12	-13	48	2	4	-2	.984	-4	*O	-2.5
1955	Cle-A	43	104	15	31	4	2	2	9	12	10	.298	.371	.433	111	2	2	15	0	2	-1	1.000	-3	O	-0.3
	Bal-A	83	311	50	93	13	3	6	41	34	38	.299	.368	.418	119	5	8	47	1	2	-1	.970	-7	O/3	-0.3
	Yr	126	415	65	124	17	5	8	50	46	48	.299	.369	.422	116	7	9	62	1	4	-2	.976	-9	*O/3	-0.6
1956	Bal-A	32	117	13	24	4	2	1	17	18	13	.205	.311	.299	67	-6	-5	10	3	1	0	.935	-4	O/3	-1.0
	Chi-A	86	279	44	74	14	2	4	47	28	27	.265	.334	.373	85	-6	-6	33	1	3	-2	.978	-9	1O	-2.0
	Yr	118	396	57	98	18	4	5	64	46	40	.247	.327	.351	80	-12	-11	44	4	4	-1	.965	-13	O1/3	-3.0
1957	Chi-A	22	71	9	23	4	0	0	9	4	10	.324	.360	.380	102	0	0	10	1	1	-0	.975	1	O/1	-0.1
	Det-A	65	173	15	49	8	1	2	16	7	16	.283	.311	.376	85	-4	-4	19	3	1	0	.996	1	1O/3	-0.5
	Yr	87	244	24	72	12	1	2	25	11	26	.295	.325	.377	90	-3	-4	29	4	2	0	.965	2	O1/3	-0.6
1958	Phi-N	91	207	30	64	11	4	3	31	15	20	.309	.359	.444	113	3	4	31	1	1	-0	1.000	-4	O1	-0.2
1959	Phi-N	99	254	32	74	18	2	7	37	18	27	.291	.341	.461	109	3	3	40	0	0	0	1.000	1	O1	0.1

YEAR	TM/L	G	AB	R	H	2B	3B	HR	RBI	BB	SO	AVG	OBP	SLG	PRO+	BR	/A	RC	SB	CS	SBR	FA	FR	POS	TPR
1960	Phi-N	14	15	2	5	2	0	0	4	3	2	.333	.444	.467	149	1	1	3	0	0	0	.000	-2	/O1	-0.1
	SF-N	39	61	5	10	0	0	1	7	6	14	.164	.239	.213	26	-6	-6	3	0	0	0	.941	-1	O/3	-0.7
	Yr	53	76	7	15	2	0	1	11	9	16	.197	.282	.263	53	-5	-5	6	0	0	0	.941	-3	O/31	-0.8
	Bal-A	14	34	6	9	2	1	1	5	4	5	.265	.342	.471	119	1	1	6	1	0	0	1.000	-0	/O3	0.0
1961	Bal-A	99	144	13	36	9	2	1	23	10	20	.250	.299	.361	77	-5	-5	13	2	0	1	1.000	-6	O/1	-1.1
1962	Bos-A	38	42	3	6	2	0	0	4	5	3	.143	.250	.190	20	-5	-5	1	0	0	0	1.000	-0	/O	-0.5
Total	18	1904	6296	789	1700	276	72	84	729	594	551	.270	.335	.377	91	-87	-84	790	101	63	-8	.981	-0	*O1/3	-16.4

■ ADOLFO PHILLIPS Phillips, Adolfo Emilio (Lopez) b: 12/16/41, Bethania, Panama BR/TR, 6', 177 lbs. Deb: 9/02/64

YEAR	TM/L	G	AB	R	H	2B	3B	HR	RBI	BB	SO	AVG	OBP	SLG	PRO+	BR	/A	RC	SB	CS	SBR	FA	FR	POS	TPR
1964	Phi-N	13	13	4	3	0	0	0	0	3	3	.231	.375	.231	76	-0	-0	2	0	0	0	1.000	1	/O	0.1
1965	Phi-N	41	87	14	20	4	0	3	5	5	34	.230	.272	.379	83	-2	-2	9	3	3	-1	1.000	1	O	-0.3
1966	Phi-N	2	3	1	0	0	0	0	0	0	0	.000	.000	.000	-99	-1	-1	0	0	0	0	1.000	0	/O	-0.1
	Chi-N	116	416	68	109	29	1	16	36	43	135	.262	.348	.452	119	12	11	66	32	15	1	.978	7	*O	1.4
	Yr	118	419	69	109	29	1	16	36	43	135	.260	.346	.449	118	11	10	66	32	15	1	.979	7	*O	1.3
1967	Chi-N	144	448	66	120	20	7	17	70	80	93	.268	.386	.458	134	26	24	82	24	10	1	.981	12	*O	3.2
1968	Chi-N	143	439	49	106	20	5	13	33	47	90	.241	.322	.399	108	8	5	55	9	7	-2	.979	3	*O	0.0
1969	Chi-N	28	49	5	11	3	1	0	1	16	15	.224	.424	.327	100	2	1	7	1	3	-2	.956	1	O	0.0
	Mon-N	58	199	25	43	4	4	4	7	19	62	.216	.288	.337	74	-7	-7	19	6	5	-1	.981	-3	O	-1.5
	Yr	86	248	30	54	7	5	4	8	35	77	.218	.319	.335	80	-5	-6	27	7	8	-3	.973	-2	O	-1.5
1970	Mon-N	92	214	36	51	6	3	6	21	36	51	.238	.353	.379	96	-0	-0	31	7	1	2	.985	-8	O	-1.0
1972	Cle-A	12	7	2	0	0	0	0	0	2	2	.000	.222	.000	-29	-1	-1	0	0	0	0	1.000	-3	O	-0.4
Total	8	649	1875	270	463	86	21	59	173	251	485	.247	.344	.410	110	36	29	270	82	44	-2	.980	12	O	1.4

■ DAMON PHILLIPS Phillips, Damon Roswell "Dee" b: 6/8/19, Corsicana, Tex. BR/TR, 6', 176 lbs. Deb: 7/19/42

YEAR	TM/L	G	AB	R	H	2B	3B	HR	RBI	BB	SO	AVG	OBP	SLG	PRO+	BR	/A	RC	SB	CS	SBR	FA	FR	POS	TPR
1942	Cin-N	28	84	4	17	2	0	0	6	7	5	.202	.264	.226	44	-6	-6	5	0			.964	7	S	0.3
1944	Bos-N	140	489	35	126	30	1	1	53	28	34	.258	.301	.329	74	-15	-18	49	1			.932	-4	3S	-1.7
1946	Bos-N	2	2	0	1	0	0	0	0	0	0	.500	.500	.500	182	0	0	1	0			.000	0	H	0.0
Total	3	170	575	39	144	32	1	1	59	35	39	.250	.296	.315	70	-21	-23	55	1			.956	3	/3S	-1.4

■ EDDIE PHILLIPS Phillips, Edward David b: 2/17/01, Worcester, Mass. d: 1/26/68, Buffalo, N.Y. BR/TR, 6', 178 lbs. Deb: 5/04/24

YEAR	TM/L	G	AB	R	H	2B	3B	HR	RBI	BB	SO	AVG	OBP	SLG	PRO+	BR	/A	RC	SB	CS	SBR	FA	FR	POS	TPR
1924	Bos-N	3	3	0	0	0	0	0	0	0	2	.000	.000	.000	-99	-1	-1	0	0	0	0	1.000	0	/C	-0.1
1929	Det-A	68	221	24	52	13	1	2	21	20	16	.235	.302	.330	62	-13	-13	23	0	1	-1	.967	-5	C	-1.2
1931	Pit-N	106	353	30	82	18	3	7	44	41	49	.232	.317	.360	82	-9	-9	43	1			.986	-7	*C	-0.8
1932	NY-A	9	31	4	9	1	0	2	4	2	3	.290	.333	.516	123	1	1	5	1	0	0	1.000	1	/C	0.2
1934	Was-A	56	169	6	33	6	1	2	16	26	24	.195	.306	.278	54	-12	-11	16	1	0	0	.984	-7	C	-1.4
1935	Cle-A	70	220	18	60	16	1	1	41	15	21	.273	.319	.368	76	-8	-8	26	0	0	0	.980	-8	C	-1.3
Total	6	312	997	82	236	54	6	14	126	104	115	.237	.312	.345	72	-42	-41	113	3	1		.980	-27	C	-4.6

■ EDDIE PHILLIPS Phillips, Howard Edward b: 7/8/31, St.Louis, Mo. BB/TR, 6'1", 180 lbs. Deb: 9/10/53

YEAR	TM/L	G	AB	R	H	2B	3B	HR	RBI	BB	SO	AVG	OBP	SLG	PRO+	BR	/A	RC	SB	CS	SBR	FA	FR	POS	TPR
1953	StL-N	9	0	4	0	0	0	0	0	0	0	—	—	—	—	0	0	0	0	0	0	.000	0	R	0.0

■ JACK PHILLIPS Phillips, Jack Dorn "Stretch" b: 9/6/21, Clarence, N.Y. BR/TR, 6'4", 193 lbs. Deb: 8/22/47

YEAR	TM/L	G	AB	R	H	2B	3B	HR	RBI	BB	SO	AVG	OBP	SLG	PRO+	BR	/A	RC	SB	CS	SBR	FA	FR	POS	TPR
1947	*NY-A	16	36	5	10	0	1	1	2	3	5	.278	.333	.417	109	0	0	5	0	0	0	.986	-2	1	-0.2
1948	NY-A	1	2	0	0	0	0	0	0	0	1	.000	.000	.000	-99	-1	-1	0	0	0	0	.889	-0	/1	-0.1
1949	NY-A	45	91	16	28	4	1	1	10	12	9	.308	.388	.407	110	2	2	15	1	0	0	.977	-2	1	0.0
	Pit-N	18	56	6	13	3	1	0	3	4	6	.232	.283	.321	60	-3	-3	5	1			1.000	-0	1/3	-0.4
1950	Pit-N	69	208	25	61	7	6	5	34	20	17	.293	.355	.457	108	3	2	35	1			.986	2	1/3P	0.3
1951	Pit-N	70	156	12	37	7	3	0	12	15	17	.237	.304	.321	66	-7	-8	15	1	2	-1	.991	-1	1/3	-1.1
1952	Pit-N	1	1	0	0	0	0	0	0	0	0	.000	.000	.000	-97	-0	-0	0	0	0	0	1.000	-0	/1	0.0
1955	Det-A	55	117	15	37	8	2	1	20	10	12	.316	.370	.444	121	3	3	19	0	0	0	.992	-1	1/3	0.0
1956	Det-A	67	224	31	66	13	2	1	20	21	19	.295	.355	.384	95	-1	-2	28	1	1	-0	.981	-1	1/2O	-0.7
1957	Det-A	1	1	1	0	0	0	0	0	0	0	.000	.000	.000	-97	-0	-0	0	0	0	0	.000	0	H	0.0
Total	9	343	892	111	252	42	16	9	101	85	86	.283	.345	.396	95	-5	-6	122	5	3		.986	-6	1/3O2P	-2.2

■ BUBBA PHILLIPS Phillips, John Melvin b: 2/24/30, West Point, Miss. BR/TR, 5'9", 180 lbs. Deb: 4/30/55

YEAR	TM/L	G	AB	R	H	2B	3B	HR	RBI	BB	SO	AVG	OBP	SLG	PRO+	BR	/A	RC	SB	CS	SBR	FA	FR	POS	TPR
1955	Det-A	95	184	18	43	4	0	3	23	14	20	.234	.295	.304	63	-10	-10	17	2	1	0	.992	-1	O/3	-1.2
1956	Chi-A	67	99	16	27	6	0	2	11	6	12	.273	.321	.394	87	-2	-2	13	1	2	-1	1.000	-1	O/3	-0.5
1957	Chi-A	121	393	38	106	13	3	7	42	28	32	.270	.323	.372	89	-6	-6	48	5	3	-0	.958	16	3O	1.0
1958	Chi-A	84	260	26	71	10	0	5	30	15	14	.273	.315	.369	89	-5	-4	29	3	0	1	.954	7	3O	0.3
1959	*Chi-A	117	379	43	100	27	1	5	40	27	28	.264	.320	.380	92	-5	-4	45	1	1	-0	.951	3	*3O	-0.3
1960	Cle-A	113	304	34	63	14	1	4	33	14	37	.207	.252	.299	50	-23	-21	23	1	0	0	.953	-8	3O/S	-3.1
1961	Cle-A	143	546	64	144	23	1	18	72	29	61	.264	.307	.408	92	-10	-8	66	1	0	0	.958	-18	*3	-2.5
1962	Cle-A	148	562	53	145	26	0	10	54	20	55	.258	.292	.358	76	-22	-19	56	4	0	1	.977	-15	*3/O2	-3.2
1963	Det-A	128	464	42	114	11	2	5	45	19	42	.246	.281	.310	63	-21	-23	38	6	2	1	.961	1	*3/O	-2.3
1964	Det-A	46	87	14	22	1	0	3	6	10	13	.253	.330	.368	92	-1	-1	10	1	2	-1	.983	2	3/O	0.0
Total	10	1062	3278	348	835	135	8	62	356	182	314	.255	.300	.358	79	-104	-99	343	25	11	1	.960	-16	3O/2S	-11.8

■ JACK PHILLIPS Phillips, John Stephen b: 5/24/19, St.Louis, Mo. d: 6/16/58, St.Louis, Mo. BR/TR, 6'1", 185 lbs. Deb: 7/13/45

YEAR	TM/L	G	AB	R	H	2B	3B	HR	RBI	BB	SO	AVG	OBP	SLG	PRO+	BR	/A	RC	SB	CS	SBR	FA	FR	POS	TPR
1945	NY-N	2	2	1	1	0	0	0	0	0	0	.500	.500	.500	176	0	0	1	0			1.000	-0	/P	0.0

■ TONY PHILLIPS Phillips, Keith Anthony b: 4/25/59, Atlanta, Ga. BB/TR, 5'10", 160 lbs. Deb: 5/10/82

YEAR	TM/L	G	AB	R	H	2B	3B	HR	RBI	BB	SO	AVG	OBP	SLG	PRO+	BR	/A	RC	SB	CS	SBR	FA	FR	POS	TPR
1982	Oak-A	40	81	11	17	2	2	0	8	12	26	.210	.326	.284	73	-3	-2	8	2	3	-1	.953	-5	S	-0.5
1983	Oak-A	148	412	54	102	12	3	4	35	48	70	.248	.329	.320	85	-10	-7	48	16	5	2	.941	1	*S2/3D	0.6
1984	Oak-A	154	451	62	120	24	3	4	37	42	86	.266	.329	.359	97	-6	-2	55	10	6	-1	.941	-11	S2/O	-0.4
1985	Oak-A	42	161	23	45	12	2	4	17	13	34	.280	.333	.453	122	3	4	25	3	2	-0	.980	-0	32	0.4
1986	Oak-A	118	441	76	113	14	5	5	52	76	82	.256	.369	.345	103	0	5	63	15	10	-2	.976	1	23/OSD	0.7
1987	Oak-A	111	379	48	91	20	0	10	46	57	76	.240	.339	.372	95	-5	-2	49	7	6	-2	.974	-3	23/SOD	-0.1
1988	*Oak-A	79	212	32	43	8	4	2	17	36	50	.203	.321	.307	80	-6	-5	22	0	2	-1	.913	-20	3O2S/1D	-2.6
1989	*Oak-A	143	451	48	118	15	6	4	47	58	66	.262	.350	.348	101	0	2	53	3	8	-4	.985	-24	23SO/1	-2.3
1990	Det-A	152	573	97	144	23	5	8	55	99	85	.251	.365	.351	100	5	4	81	19	9	0	.931	6	*32S/OD	1.3
1991	Det-A	146	564	87	160	28	4	17	72	79	95	.284	.375	.438	122	20	19	97	10	5	0	.992	6	O32DS	2.5
1992	Det-A	159	606	**114**	167	32	3	10	64	114	93	.276	.391	.388	117	20	19	98	12	10	-2	.968	4	O2D3/S	2.0
Total	11	1292	4331	652	1120	190	37	68	450	634	763	.259	.356	.367	103	18	36	598	97	66	-11	.982	-45	23SO/D1	1.6

■ MARR PHILLIPS Phillips, Marr B. b: 6/16/1857, Pittsburgh, Pa. d: 4/1/28, Pittsburgh, Pa. 5'6.5", 164 lbs. Deb: 5/01/1884

YEAR	TM/L	G	AB	R	H	2B	3B	HR	RBI	BB	SO	AVG	OBP	SLG	PRO+	BR	/A	RC	SB	CS	SBR	FA	FR	POS	TPR
1884	Ind-a	97	413	41	111	18	8	0		5		.269	.279	.351	110	2	4	42				.862	14	*S	1.7
1885	Det-N	33	139	13	29	5	0	0	17	0	13	.209	.209	.245	46	-8	-8	7				.881	2	S	-0.5
	Pit-a	4	15	1	4	0	0	0		2		.267	.353	.267	102	0	0	1				.875	-1	/S	-0.1
1890	Roc-a	64	257	18	53	8	0	0		16		.206	.261	.237	53	-16	-13	19	10			.918	6	S	-0.3
Total	3	198	824	73	197	31	8	0	17	23	13	.239	.263	.296	80	-22	-17	69	10			.884	21	S	0.8

■ MIKE PHILLIPS Phillips, Michael Dwaine b: 8/19/50, Beaumont, Tex. BL/TR, 6'1", 185 lbs. Deb: 4/15/73

YEAR	TM/L	G	AB	R	H	2B	3B	HR	RBI	BB	SO	AVG	OBP	SLG	PRO+	BR	/A	RC	SB	CS	SBR	FA	FR	POS	TPR
1973	SF-N	63	104	18	25	3	4	1	9	6	17	.240	.288	.375	79	-3	-3	10	0	3	-2	.931	-0	3S/2	-0.4
1974	SF-N	100	283	19	62	6	1	2	20	14	37	.219	.258	.269	45	-20	-22	19	4	5	-2	.909	4	32S	-1.7
1975	SF-N	10	31	3	6	0	0	0	1	6	4	.194	.324	.194	44	-2	-2	2	1	0	0	.969	4	/23	0.2

YEAR	TM/L	G	AB	R	H	2B	3B	HR	RBI	BB	SO	AVG	OBP	SLG	PRO+	BR	/A	RC	SB	CS	SBR	FA	FR	POS	TPR
	NY-N	116	383	31	98	10	7	1	28	25	47	.256	.303	.326	78	-13	-11	38	3	0	1	.944	1	*S/2	0.2
	Yr	126	414	34	104	10	7	1	29	31	51	.251	.305	.316	76	-15	-14	40	4	0	1	.944	4	*S/23	0.4
1976	NY-N	87	262	30	67	4	6	4	29	25	29	.256	.321	.363	99	-2	-1	31	2	2	-1	.955	-9	S23	-0.4
1977	NY-N	38	86	5	18	2	1	1	3	2	15	.209	.244	.291	45	-7	-7	6	0	1	-1	1.000	-5	S/32	-1.0
	StL-N	48	87	17	21	3	2	0	9	9	13	.241	.320	.322	74	-3	-3	10	1	0	0	.971	5	2/S3	0.4
	Yr	86	173	22	39	5	3	1	12	11	28	.225	.283	.306	60	-10	-10	15	1	1	-0	.973	1	2S3	-0.6
1978	StL-N	76	164	14	44	8	1	1	28	13	25	.268	.330	.348	91	-2	-2	19	0	0	0	.971	-1	2S/3	0.1
1979	StL-N	44	97	10	22	3	1	1	6	10	9	.227	.306	.309	68	-4	-4	9	0	0	0	.973	13	S2/3	1.1
1980	StL-N	63	128	13	30	5	0	0	7	9	17	.234	.285	.273	55	-7	-8	9	0	0	0	.971	13	S/23	0.8
1981	SD-N	14	29	1	6	0	1	0	0	0	3	.207	.207	.276	39	-2	-2	1	1	0	0	.979	4	/2S	0.2
	*Mon-N	34	55	5	12	2	0	0	4	5	15	.218	.283	.255	53	-3	-3	4	0	1	-1	.974	0	S/2	-0.2
	Yr	48	84	6	18	2	1	0	4	5	18	.214	.258	.262	49	-6	-6	5	1	1	-0	.974	4	S2	0.0
1982	Mon-N	14	8	0	1	0	0	0	1	0	3	.125	.125	.125	-29	-1	-1	0	0	0	0	1.000	3	2/S	0.1
1983	Mon-N	5	2	0	0	0	0	0	0	0	0	.000	.000	.000	-99	-1	-1	0	0	0	0	.000	-1	/S3	-0.2
Total	11	712	1719	166	412	46	24	11	145	124	234	.240	.294	.314	70	-72	-70	156	12	12	-4	.956	29	S23	-0.8

■ DICK PHILLIPS Phillips, Richard Eugene b: 11/24/31, Racine, Wis. BL/TR, 6', 180 lbs. Deb: 4/15/62 C

YEAR	TM/L	G	AB	R	H	2B	3B	HR	RBI	BB	SO	AVG	OBP	SLG	PRO+	BR	/A	RC	SB	CS	SBR	FA	FR	POS	TPR
1962	SF-N	5	3	1	0	0	0	0	1	1	1	.000	.250	.000	-27	-1	-1	0	0	0	0	1.000	-0	/1	-0.1
1963	Was-A	124	321	33	76	8	0	10	32	29	35	.237	.304	.355	84	-7	-7	36	1	0	0	.994	4	1/23	-0.6
1964	Was-A	109	234	17	54	6	1	2	23	27	22	.231	.313	.291	70	-9	-9	23	1	2	-1	.994	2	1/3	-1.1
1966	Was-A	25	37	3	6	0	0	0	4	2	5	.162	.225	.162	13	-4	-4	1	0	0	0	1.000	-1	/1	-0.5
Total	4	263	595	54	136	14	1	12	60	59	63	.229	.302	.316	74	-21	-20	60	2	2	-1	.995	5	1/32	-2.3

■ BILL PHILLIPS Phillips, William B. b: 1857, St.John, N.B., Canada d: 10/7/1900, Chicago, Ill. BR/TR, 202 lbs. Deb: 5/01/1879

YEAR	TM/L	G	AB	R	H	2B	3B	HR	RBI	BB	SO	AVG	OBP	SLG	PRO+	BR	/A	RC	SB	CS	SBR	FA	FR	POS	TPR
1879	Cle-N	81	365	58	99	15	4	0	29	2	20	.271	.275	.334	101	-0	0	34				.954	-5	*1C/O	-0.6
1880	Cle-N	85	334	41	85	14	10	1	36	6	29	.254	.268	.365	115	4	5	33				.963	2	*1	-0.1
1881	Cle-N	85	357	51	97	18	10	1	44	5	19	.272	.282	.387	114	3	5	40				.966	-1	*1	-0.3
1882	Cle-N	78	335	40	87	17	7	4	47	7	18	.260	.275	.388	114	3	5	37				.971	3	*1/C	-0.1
1883	Cle-N	97	382	42	94	29	8	2	40	8	49	.246	.262	.380	93	-4	-3	39				.967	-2	*1	-1.3
1884	Cle-N	111	464	58	128	25	12	3	46	18	80	.276	.303	.401	115	9	7	58				.959	-2	*1	-0.6
1885	Bro-a	99	391	65	118	16	11	3		27		.302	.364	.422	150	23	23	62				**.973**	0	*1	1.0
1886	Bro-a	141	585	68	160	26	15	0		33		.274	.313	.369	114	9	8	74	13			.978	-2	*1	-0.9
1887	Bro-a	132	533	82	142	34	11	2		45		.266	.330	.383	99	0	-1	75	16			**.982**	4	*1	-0.8
1888	KC-a	129	509	57	120	20	10	1	56	27		.236	.284	.320	90	-2	-7	50	10			.980	3	*1	-1.4
Total	10	1038	4255	562	1130	214	98	17	298	178	215	.266	.299	.374	110	45	41	501	39			.971	1	*1/CO	-5.1

■ BILL PHYLE Phyle, William Joseph b: 6/25/1875, Duluth, Minn. d: 8/6/53, Los Angeles, Cal. TR , Deb: 9/17/1898

YEAR	TM/L	G	AB	R	H	2B	3B	HR	RBI	BB	SO	AVG	OBP	SLG	PRO+	BR	/A	RC	SB	CS	SBR	FA	FR	POS	TPR
1898	Chi-N	4	9	1	1	0	0	0	0	2		.111	.273	.111	11	-1	-1	0	0			.800	-1	/P	0.0
1899	Chi-N	10	34	2	6	0	0	0	1	0		.176	.176	.176	-3	-5	-5	1	0			.935	1	P	0.0
1901	NY-N	25	66	8	12	2	0	0	3	2		.182	.206	.212	22	-7	-6	3	0			.903	1	P/S	0.0
1906	StL-N	22	73	6	13	3	1	0	4	5		.178	.231	.247	51	-4	-4	5	2			.935	2	3	-0.2
Total	4	61	182	17	32	5	1	0	8	9		.176	.215	.214	28	-17	-16	9	2			.907	3	/P3S	-0.2

■ MIKE PIAZZA Piazza, Michael Joseph b: 9/4/68, Norristown, Pa. BR/TR, 6'3", 200 lbs. Deb: 9/01/92

YEAR	TM/L	G	AB	R	H	2B	3B	HR	RBI	BB	SO	AVG	OBP	SLG	PRO+	BR	/A	RC	SB	CS	SBR	FA	FR	POS	TPR
1992	LA-N	21	69	5	16	3	0	1	7	4	12	.232	.284	.319	71	-3	-3	6	0	0	0	.990	-2	C	-0.4

■ ROB PICCIOLO Picciolo, Robert Michael b: 2/4/53, Santa Monica, Cal. BR/TR, 6'2", 185 lbs. Deb: 4/09/77 C

YEAR	TM/L	G	AB	R	H	2B	3B	HR	RBI	BB	SO	AVG	OBP	SLG	PRO+	BR	/A	RC	SB	CS	SBR	FA	FR	POS	TPR
1977	Oak-A	148	419	35	84	12	3	2	22	9	55	.200	.219	.258	30	-41	-40	22	1	4	-2	.966	7	*S	-2.2
1978	Oak-A	78	93	16	21	1	0	2	7	2	13	.226	.242	.301	55	-6	-6	6	1	1	-0	.958	12	S23	0.9
1979	Oak-A	115	348	37	88	16	2	2	27	3	45	.253	.261	.328	61	-21	-19	27	2	1	0	.964	-3	*S/23O	-1.0
1980	Oak-A	95	271	32	65	9	2	5	18	2	63	.240	.245	.343	64	-16	-13	21	1	1	-0	.977	-23	S2/O	-3.0
1981	*Oak-A	82	179	23	48	5	3	4	13	5	22	.268	.292	.397	102	-1	-0	19	0	1	-1	.981	-15	S	-1.0
1982	Oak-A	18	49	3	11	1	0	0	3	1	10	.224	.240	.245	35	-4	-4	3	1	0	0	.979	3	S	0.1
	Mil-A	22	21	7	6	1	0	0	1	1	4	.286	.318	.333	84	-1	-0	2	0	0	0	1.000	2	2/SD	0.1
	Yr	40	70	10	17	2	0	0	4	2	14	.243	.264	.271	50	-5	-5	6	1	0	0	.973	5	S2/D	0.2
1983	Mil-A	14	27	2	6	3	0	0	1	0	4	.222	.222	.333	55	-2	-2	2	0	0	0	1.000	2	/S231D	0.1
1984	Cal-A	87	119	18	24	6	0	1	9	0	21	.202	.202	.277	31	-11	-11	6	0	1	-1	.974	13	S3/2O	0.4
1985	Oak-A	71	102	19	28	2	0	1	8	2	17	.275	.288	.324	73	-5	-4	9	3	2	-0	.889	6	321D/S	0.3
Total	9	730	1628	192	381	56	10	17	109	25	254	.234	.247	.312	55	-108	-99	118	9	11	-4	.970	6	S2/31DO	-5.3

■ NICK PICCIUTO Picciuto, Nicholas Thomas b: 8/27/21, Newark, N.J. BR/TR, 5'8.5", 165 lbs. Deb: 5/11/45

YEAR	TM/L	G	AB	R	H	2B	3B	HR	RBI	BB	SO	AVG	OBP	SLG	PRO+	BR	/A	RC	SB	CS	SBR	FA	FR	POS	TPR
1945	Phi-N	36	89	7	12	6	0	0	6	6	17	.135	.189	.202	9	-11	-11	4	0			.839	-6	3/2	-1.6

■ VAL PICINICH Picinich, Valentine John b: 9/8/1896, New York, N.Y. d: 12/5/42, Nobleboro, Maine BR/TR, 5'9", 165 lbs. Deb: 7/25/16 C

YEAR	TM/L	G	AB	R	H	2B	3B	HR	RBI	BB	SO	AVG	OBP	SLG	PRO+	BR	/A	RC	SB	CS	SBR	FA	FR	POS	TPR
1916	Phi-A	40	118	8	23	3	1	0	5	6	33	.195	.234	.237	44	-9	-8	7	1			.967	-0	C	-0.6
1917	Phi-A	2	6	0	2	0	0	0	0	1	2	.333	.429	.333	135	0	0	1	0			.786	-1	/C	-0.1
1918	Was-A	47	148	13	34	3	3	0	12	9	25	.230	.274	.291	72	-6	-5	12	0			.960	-2	C	-0.4
1919	Was-A	80	212	18	58	12	3	3	22	17	43	.274	.330	.401	106	1	1	30	6			.978	15	C	2.1
1920	Was-A	48	133	14	27	6	2	3	14	9	33	.203	.259	.346	61	-8	-8	12	0	0	0	.978	9	C	0.4
1921	Was-A	45	141	10	39	9	0	0	12	16	21	.277	.354	.340	82	-4	-3	17	0	3	-2	.966	3	C	0.1
1922	Was-A	76	210	16	48	12	2	0	19	23	33	.229	.311	.305	64	-12	-10	22	1	0	0	.976	7	C	0.0
1923	Bos-A	87	268	33	74	21	1	2	31	46	32	.276	.386	.384	103	3	3	42	3	5	-2	.957	-2	C	0.3
1924	Bos-A	69	161	25	44	6	3	1	24	29	19	.273	.394	.366	97	1	0	26	5	1	1	.951	-4	C	0.0
1925	Bos-A	90	251	31	64	21	0	1	25	33	21	.255	.344	.351	77	-9	-9	33	2	0	1	.968	-8	C/1	-1.1
1926	Cin-N	89	240	33	63	16	1	2	31	29	22	.262	.342	.363	92	-3	-2	30	4			.967	-0	C	0.2
1927	Cin-N	65	173	16	44	8	3	0	12	24	15	.254	.345	.335	85	-4	-3	21	3			.980	5	C	0.6
1928	Cin-N	96	324	29	98	15	1	7	35	20	25	.302	.343	.420	100	-1	-1	45	1			.983	-3	C	0.4
1929	Bro-N	93	273	28	71	16	6	4	31	34	24	.260	.342	.407	86	-7	-6	38	3			.979	-4	C	-0.2
1930	Bro-N	23	46	4	10	3	0	0	3	5	6	.217	.294	.283	41	-4	-4	4	1			.944	-2	C	-0.4
1931	Bro-N	24	45	5	12	4	0	1	4	4	9	.267	.327	.422	100	-0	-0	6	1			.967	1	C	0.1
1932	Bro-N	41	70	8	18	6	0	1	11	4	8	.257	.297	.386	84	-2	-2	8	0			.985	-2	C	-0.3
1933	Bro-N	6	6	1	1	1	0	0	0	0	1	.167	.167	.333	42	-0	-0	0	0			.889	0	/C	0.0
	Pit-N	16	52	6	13	4	0	1	7	5	10	.250	.316	.385	99	-0	-0	7	0			.982	-3	C	-0.2
	Yr	22	58	7	14	5	0	1	7	5	11	.241	.302	.379	95	-1	-0	7	0			.969	-3	C	-0.2
Total	18	1037	2877	298	743	166	26	26	298	314	382	.258	.334	.361	86	-65	-58	362	31	9		.970	11	C/1	0.9

■ CHARLIE PICK Pick, Charles Thomas b: 4/10/1888, Brookneal, Va. d: 6/26/54, Lynchburg, Va. BL/TR, 5'10", 160 lbs. Deb: 9/20/14

YEAR	TM/L	G	AB	R	H	2B	3B	HR	RBI	BB	SO	AVG	OBP	SLG	PRO+	BR	/A	RC	SB	CS	SBR	FA	FR	POS	TPR
1914	Was-A	10	23	0	9	0	0	0	1	4	4	.391	.481	.391	157	2	2	4	1	2	-1	.833	-0	/O	0.1
1915	Was-A	3	2	0	0	0	0	0	0	0	0	.000	.000	.000	-98	-0	-0	0	0			.000	0	H	-0.1
1916	Phi-A	121	398	29	96	10	3	0	20	40	24	.241	.315	.281	83	-9	-7	39	25	16	-2	.899	4	*3/O	-0.2
1918	*Chi-N	29	89	13	29	4	1	0	12	14	4	.326	.417	.393	144	6	6	17	7			.964	-0	2/3	0.8
1919	Chi-N	75	269	27	65	8	6	0	18	14	12	.242	.292	.316	82	-6	-6	29	17			.946	12	2/3	1.0
	Bos-N	34	114	12	29	1	1	1	7	7	5	.254	.325	.307	94	-1	-0	12	4			.924	-2	2/3O1	-0.2
	Yr	109	383	39	94	9	7	1	25	21	17	.245	.302	.313	86	-7	-6	41	21			.942	10	2/3O1	0.8
1920	Bos-N	95	383	34	105	16	6	2	28	23	11	.274	.320	.363	100	-2	-0	41	10	16	-7	.952	0	2	-0.4

YEAR	TM/L	G	AB	R	H	2B	3B	HR	RBI	BB	SO	AVG	OBP	SLG	PRO+	BR	/A	RC	SB	CS	SBR	FA	FR	POS	TPR
Total	6	367	1278	115	333	39	17	3	86	102	60	.261	.323	.325	95	-11	-7	143	64	34		.949	14	23/O1	1.0

■ **EDDIE PICK** Pick, Edgar Everett b: 5/7/1899, Attleboro, Mass. d: 5/13/67, Santa Monica, Cal. BB/TR, 6', 185 lbs. Deb: 9/13/23

YEAR	TM/L	G	AB	R	H	2B	3B	HR	RBI	BB	SO	AVG	OBP	SLG	PRO+	BR	/A	RC	SB	CS	SBR	FA	FR	POS	TPR
1923	Cin-N	9	8	2	3	0	0	0	2	3	3	.375	.545	.375	150	1	1	2	0	0	0	1.000	-1	/O	-0.1
1924	Cin-N	3	2	0	0	0	0	0	0	0	1	.000	.000	.000	-99	-1	-1	0	0	0	0	1.000	-0	/O	-0.1
1927	Chi-N	54	181	23	31	5	2	2	15	20	26	.171	.254	.254	36	-16	-17	12	0			.910	-6	3/2O	-2.0
Total	3	66	191	25	34	5	2	2	17	23	30	.178	.266	.257	40	-16	-16	15	0	0		1.000	-8	/3O2	-2.2

■ **OLLIE PICKERING** Pickering, Oliver Daniel b: 4/9/1870, Olney, Ill. d: 1/20/52, Vincennes, Ind. BL/TR, 5'11", 170 lbs. Deb: 8/09/1896

YEAR	TM/L	G	AB	R	H	2B	3B	HR	RBI	BB	SO	AVG	OBP	SLG	PRO+	BR	/A	RC	SB	CS	SBR	FA	FR	POS	TPR
1896	Lou-N	45	165	28	50	6	4	1	22	12	11	.303	.350	.406	105	0	1	29	13			.901	3	O	0.1
1897	Lou-N	63	246	34	62	5	2	1	20	25		.252	.326	.301	68	-12	-10	32	20			.937	5	O	-0.9
	Cle-N	46	182	33	64	5	2	1	22	11		.352	.392	.418	108	4	2	38	18			.950	-0	O/2	-0.1
	Yr	109	428	67	126	10	4	2	42	36		.294	.353	.350	86	-8	-8	69	38			.943	4	*O/2	-1.0
1901	Cle-A	137	547	102	169	25	6	0	40	58		.309	.383	.377	116	11	14	96	36			.949	15	*O	1.7
1902	Cle-A	69	293	46	75	5	2	3	26	19		.256	.306	.317	76	-11	-9	36	22			.979	-2	O/1	-1.5
1903	Phi-A	137	512	93	144	18	6	1	36	53		.281	.353	.346	106	8	5	82	40			.970	4	*O	0.1
1904	Phi-A	124	455	56	103	10	3	0	30	45		.226	.299	.262	74	-10	-12	44	17			.939	-1	*O	-2.2
1907	StL-A	151	576	63	159	15	10	0	60	35		.276	.321	.337	110	6	6	71	15			.949	-11	*O	-1.2
1908	Was-A	113	373	45	84	7	4	2	30	28		.225	.285	.282	92	-6	-3	33	13			.940	-7	O	-1.6
Total	8	885	3349	500	910	96	39	9	286	286	11	.272	.334	.332	97	-10	-6	460	194			.949	5	O/12	-5.6

■ **URBANE PICKERING** Pickering, Urbane Henry "Pick" b: 6/3/1899, Hoxie, Kan. d: 5/13/70, Modesto, Cal. BR/TR, 5'10", 180 lbs. Deb: 4/18/31

YEAR	TM/L	G	AB	R	H	2B	3B	HR	RBI	BB	SO	AVG	OBP	SLG	PRO+	BR	/A	RC	SB	CS	SBR	FA	FR	POS	TPR
1931	Bos-A	103	341	48	86	13	4	9	52	33	53	.252	.318	.393	91	-8	-5	43	3	4	-2	.967	-2	32	-0.3
1932	Bos-A	132	457	47	119	28	5	2	40	39	71	.260	.320	.357	77	-17	-15	53	3	4	-2	.941	-7	*3/C	-1.4
Total	2	235	798	95	205	41	9	11	92	72	124	.257	.319	.372	83	-25	-20	95	6	8	-3	.951	-9	3/2C	-1.7

■ **DAVE PICKETT** Pickett, David T. b: 5/26/1874, Brookline, Mass. d: 4/22/50, Easton, Mass. 5'7.5", 170 lbs. Deb: 6/21/1898

YEAR	TM/L	G	AB	R	H	2B	3B	HR	RBI	BB	SO	AVG	OBP	SLG	PRO+	BR	/A	RC	SB	CS	SBR	FA	FR	POS	TPR
1898	Bos-N	14	43	3	12	1	0	0	3	6		.279	.380	.302	91	0	-0	6	2			.955	-2	O	-0.3

■ **JOHN PICKETT** Pickett, John Thomas b: 2/20/1866, Chicago, Ill. d: 7/4/22, Chicago, Ill. BR/TR, Deb: 6/06/1889

YEAR	TM/L	G	AB	R	H	2B	3B	HR	RBI	BB	SO	AVG	OBP	SLG	PRO+	BR	/A	RC	SB	CS	SBR	FA	FR	POS	TPR
1889	KC-a	53	201	20	45	7	0	0	12	11	21	.224	.271	.259	50	-12	-14	16	7			.900	-16	O32	-2.6
1890	Phi-P	100	407	82	114	7	9	4	64	40	17	.280	.347	.371	92	-4	-5	58	12			.893	-22	*2	-1.7
1892	Bal-N	36	141	13	30	2	3	1	12	7	10	.213	.260	.291	66	-6	-6	11	2			.915	-5	2	-1.0
Total	3	189	749	115	189	16	12	5	88	58	48	.252	.311	.326	76	-21	-26	86	21			.900	-42	2/O3	-5.3

■ **TY PICKUP** Pickup, Clarence William b: 10/29/1897, Philadelphia, Pa. d: 8/2/74, Philadelphia, Pa. BR/TR, 6', 180 lbs. Deb: 4/30/18

YEAR	TM/L	G	AB	R	H	2B	3B	HR	RBI	BB	SO	AVG	OBP	SLG	PRO+	BR	/A	RC	SB	CS	SBR	FA	FR	POS	TPR
1918	Phi-N	1	1	0	1	0	0	0	0	0	0	1.000	1.000	1.000	478	0	0	1	0			1.000	-0	/O	0.0

■ **GRACIE PIERCE** Pierce, Grayson S. b: New York, N.Y. d: 8/28/1894, New York, N.Y. BR/TR, Deb: 5/02/1882 U

YEAR	TM/L	G	AB	R	H	2B	3B	HR	RBI	BB	SO	AVG	OBP	SLG	PRO+	BR	/A	RC	SB	CS	SBR	FA	FR	POS	TPR
1882	Lou-a	9	33	3	10	1	0	0		1		.303	.324	.333	129	1	1	4				.864	1	/2	0.2
	Bal-a	41	151	8	30	2	1	0		3		.199	.214	.225	52	-8	-6	7				.796	-10	2/OS	-1.4
	Yr	50	184	11	40	3	1	0		4		.217	.234	.245	66	-7	-5	11				.808	-9	2/OS	-1.2
1883	Col-a	11	41	5	7	0	0	0		0		.171	.171	.171	11	-4	-3	1				.744	-1	/2O	-0.4
	NY-N	18	62	3	5	0	1	0	2	1	9	.081	.095	.113	-37	-10	-10	1				.850	-2	O/2	-1.1
1884	NY-a	5	20	2	5	1	0	0		0		.250	.250	.300	83	-0	-0	2				1.000	-5	/O2	-0.5
Total	3	84	307	21	57	4	2	0	2	5	9	.186	.199	.212	37	-21	-19	15				.795	-17	/2OS	-3.2

■ **JACK PIERCE** Pierce, Lavern Jack b: 6/2/48, Laurel, Miss. BL/TR, 6', 210 lbs. Deb: 4/27/73

YEAR	TM/L	G	AB	R	H	2B	3B	HR	RBI	BB	SO	AVG	OBP	SLG	PRO+	BR	/A	RC	SB	CS	SBR	FA	FR	POS	TPR
1973	Atl-N	11	20	0	1	0	0	0	0	1	8	.050	.095	.050	-55	-4	-4	0	0	0	0	1.000	1	/1	-0.4
1974	Atl-N	6	9	1	1	0	0	0	0	1	0	.111	.200	.111	-11	-1	-1	0	0	0	0	.958	0	/1	-0.1
1975	Det-A	53	170	19	40	6	1	8	22	20	40	.235	.323	.424	105	2	1	24	0	0	0	.971	-4	1	-0.7
Total	3	70	199	20	42	6	1	8	22	22	48	.211	.296	.372	83	-4	-5	25	0	0	0	.973	-3	/1	-1.2

■ **MAURY PIERCE** Pierce, Maurice b: Baltimore, Md. Deb: 4/23/1884

YEAR	TM/L	G	AB	R	H	2B	3B	HR	RBI	BB	SO	AVG	OBP	SLG	PRO+	BR	/A	RC	SB	CS	SBR	FA	FR	POS	TPR
1884	Was-U	2	7	0	1	0	0	0		0		.143	.143	.143	-3	-1	-1	0				.778	0	/3	-0.1

■ **ANDY PIERCY** Piercy, Andrew J. b: 8/1856, San Jose, Cal. d: 12/27/32, San Jose, Cal. TR , Deb: 5/12/1881

YEAR	TM/L	G	AB	R	H	2B	3B	HR	RBI	BB	SO	AVG	OBP	SLG	PRO+	BR	/A	RC	SB	CS	SBR	FA	FR	POS	TPR
1881	Chi-N	2	8	1	2	0	0	0	0	0	1	.250	.250	.250	55	-0	-0	1				.750	-1	/32	-0.2

■ **DICK PIERRE** Pierre, Richard J. b: Grand Haven, Mich. Deb: 9/25/1883

YEAR	TM/L	G	AB	R	H	2B	3B	HR	RBI	BB	SO	AVG	OBP	SLG	PRO+	BR	/A	RC	SB	CS	SBR	FA	FR	POS	TPR
1883	Phi-N	5	19	1	3	0	0	0	0	0	2	.158	.158	.158	-4	-2	-2	0				.577	-4	/S	-0.5

■ **JIM PIERSALL** Piersall, James Anthony b: 11/14/29, Waterbury, Conn. BR/TR, 6', 175 lbs. Deb: 9/07/50 C

YEAR	TM/L	G	AB	R	H	2B	3B	HR	RBI	BB	SO	AVG	OBP	SLG	PRO+	BR	/A	RC	SB	CS	SBR	FA	FR	POS	TPR
1950	Bos-A	6	7	4	2	0	0	0	0	4	0	.286	.545	.286	107	1	1	2	0	0	0	1.000	1	/O	0.1
1952	Bos-A	56	161	28	43	8	0	1	16	28	26	.267	.379	.335	93	1	-0	23	3	3	-1	.928	-6	SO/3	-0.6
1953	Bos-A	151	585	76	159	21	9	3	52	41	52	.272	.329	.354	80	-13	-17	69	11	10	-3	.987	16	*O	-0.9
1954	Bos-A★	133	474	77	135	24	2	8	38	36	42	.285	.339	.395	90	-0	-7	63	5	1	1	.985	0	*O	-1.1
1955	Bos-A	149	515	68	146	25	5	13	62	67	52	.283	.368	.427	104	10	4	82	6	1	1	.993	13	*O	1.1
1956	Bos-A★	155	601	91	176	**40**	6	14	87	58	48	.293	.356	.449	99	9	-1	92	7	7	-2	**.991**	**18**	*O	0.6
1957	Bos-A	151	609	103	159	27	5	19	63	62	54	.261	.333	.415	98	2	-2	83	14	6	1	.990	13	*O	0.2
1958	Bos-A	130	417	55	99	13	5	8	48	42	43	.237	.307	.350	75	-11	-15	46	12	2	2	.985	9	*O	-0.9
1959	Cle-A	100	317	42	78	13	2	4	30	25	31	.246	.305	.338	79	-10	-9	34	6	3	0	.982	0	O/3	-1.3
1960	Cle-A	138	486	70	137	12	4	18	66	24	38	.282	.316	.434	104	-1	0	62	18	5	2	.992	10	*O	0.7
1961	Cle-A	121	484	81	156	26	7	6	40	43	46	.322	.380	.442	122	13	15	79	8	2	1	**.991**	16	*O	2.5
1962	Was-A	135	471	38	115	20	4	4	31	39	53	.244	.302	.329	70	-20	-20	45	12	7	-1	**.997**	7	*O	-2.1
1963	Was-A	29	94	9	23	1	0	1	5	6	11	.245	.290	.287	63	-5	-5	8	4	0	1	1.000	1	O	-0.4
	NY-N	40	124	13	24	4	1	1	10	10	14	.194	.254	.266	49	-8	-8	8	1	2	-1	1.000	1	O	-1.1
	LA-A	20	52	4	16	1	0	0	4	5	5	.308	.368	.327	103	-0	0	6	0	1	-1	1.000	-2	O	-0.4
1964	LA-A	87	255	28	80	11	0	2	13	16	32	.314	.354	.380	116	2	5	34	5	3	-0	1.000	-6	O	-0.5
1965	Cal-A	53	112	10	30	5	2	2	12	5	15	.268	.305	.402	101	-0	-0	13	2	2	-1	.984	-4	O	-0.6
1966	Cal-A	75	123	14	26	5	0	0	14	13	19	.211	.287	.252	58	-7	-6	8	1	2	-1	.973	-10	O	-2.1
1967	Cal-A	5	3	0	0	0	0	0	0	0	2	.000	.000	.000	-99	-1	-1	0	0	0	0	1.000	-0	/O	-0.1
Total	17	1734	5890	811	1604	256	52	104	591	524	583	.272	.334	.386	92	-39	-66	756	115	57	0	.990	76	*O/S3	-6.9

■ **DAVE PIERSON** Pierson, David P. b: 8/20/1855, Wilkes-Barre, Pa. d: 11/11/22, Trenton, N.J. BR/TR, 5'7", 142 lbs. Deb: 4/25/1876 F

YEAR	TM/L	G	AB	R	H	2B	3B	HR	RBI	BB	SO	AVG	OBP	SLG	PRO+	BR	/A	RC	SB	CS	SBR	FA	FR	POS	TPR
1876	Cin-N	57	233	33	55	4	1	0	13	1	9	.236	.239	.262	78	-8	-3	15				.760	-2	CO/S32P	-0.4

■ **DICK PIERSON** Pierson, Edmund Dana b: 10/24/1857, Wilkes-Barre, Pa. d: 7/20/22, Newark, N.J. TR , Deb: 6/23/1885 F

YEAR	TM/L	G	AB	R	H	2B	3B	HR	RBI	BB	SO	AVG	OBP	SLG	PRO+	BR	/A	RC	SB	CS	SBR	FA	FR	POS	TPR
1885	NY-a	3	9	1	1	0	0	0		2		.111	.273	.111	29	-1	-1	0				.682	-2	/2	-0.2

■ **TONY PIET** Piet, Anthony Francis (b: Anthony Francis Pietruszka) b: 12/7/06, Berwick, Pa. d: 12/1/81, Hinsdale, Ill. BR/TR, 6', 175 lbs. Deb: 8/15/31

YEAR	TM/L	G	AB	R	H	2B	3B	HR	RBI	BB	SO	AVG	OBP	SLG	PRO+	BR	/A	RC	SB	CS	SBR	FA	FR	POS	TPR
1931	Pit-N	44	167	22	50	12	4	0	24	13	24	.299	.354	.419	108	2	2	25	10			.987	-4	2/S	0.0
1932	Pit-N	154	574	66	162	25	8	7	85	46	56	.282	.343	.390	98	-2	-1	80	19			.970	-28	*2	-2.0
1933	Pit-N	107	362	45	117	21	5	1	42	19	28	.323	.367	.417	124	11	11	57	12			.955	-5	2	1.2
1934	Cin-N	106	421	58	109	20	5	1	38	23	44	.259	.307	.337	74	-16	-15	43	6			.934	-10	32	-2.0
1935	Cin-N	6	5	2	1	1	0	0	2	0	0	.200	.200	.400	59	-0	-0	0	0			1.000	-0	/O	-0.1

YEAR	TM/L	G	AB	R	H	2B	3B	HR	RBI	BB	SO	AVG	OBP	SLG	PRO+	BR	/A	RC	SB	CS	SBR	FA	FR	POS	TPR
	Chi-A	77	292	47	87	17	5	3	27	33	27	.298	.375	.421	103	3	2	48	2	1	0	.975	4	23	1.0
1936	Chi-A	109	352	69	96	15	2	7	42	66	48	.273	.400	.386	92	0	-2	61	15	5	2	.966	6	23	0.9
1937	Chi-A	100	332	34	78	15	1	4	38	32	36	.235	.314	.322	61	-20	-20	36	14	6	1	.939	2	32	-1.4
1938	Det-A	41	80	9	17	6	0	0	14	15	11	.213	.351	.287	58	-4	-5	8	2	4	-2	.919	0	3/2	-0.6
Total	8	744	2585	352	717	132	30	23	312	247	274	.277	.350	.378	91	-28	-29	359	80	16		.967	-37	23/OS	-3.0

■ SANDY PIEZ Piez, Charles William b: 10/13/1892, New York, N.Y. d: 12/29/30, Atlantic City, N.J BR/TR, 5'10", 170 lbs. Deb: 4/17/14

YEAR	TM/L	G	AB	R	H	2B	3B	HR	RBI	BB	SO	AVG	OBP	SLG	PRO+	BR	/A	RC	SB	CS	SBR	FA	FR	POS	TPR
1914	NY-N	37	8	9	3	0	1	0	3	0	1	.375	.375	.625	202	1	1	3	4			1.000	-1	/O	0.1

■ JOE PIGNATANO Pignatano, Joseph Benjamin b: 8/4/29, Brooklyn, N.Y. BR/TR, 5'10", 180 lbs. Deb: 4/28/57 C

YEAR	TM/L	G	AB	R	H	2B	3B	HR	RBI	BB	SO	AVG	OBP	SLG	PRO+	BR	/A	RC	SB	CS	SBR	FA	FR	POS	TPR
1957	Bro-N	8	14	0	3	1	0	0	1	0	5	.214	.214	.286	30	-1	-1	1	0	0	0	1.000	3	/C	0.2
1958	LA-N	63	142	18	31	4	0	9	17	16	26	.218	.306	.437	91	-2	-2	19	4	1	1	1.000	10	C	1.0
1959	*LA-N	52	139	17	33	4	1	1	11	21	15	.237	.346	.302	69	-4	-6	16	1	0	0	.997	7	C	0.4
1960	LA-N	58	90	11	21	4	0	2	9	15	17	.233	.343	.344	83	-1	-2	12	1	1	-0	.984	15	C	1.5
1961	KC-A	92	243	31	59	10	3	4	22	36	42	.243	.350	.358	89	-3	-3	34	2	2	-1	.979	1	C/3	0.1
1962	SF-N	7	5	2	1	0	0	0	0	4	0	.200	.556	.200	114	1	1	1	0	0	0	1.000	-1	/C	0.0
	NY-N	27	56	2	13	2	0	0	2	2	11	.232	.259	.268	41	-5	-5	3	0	0	0	.991	4	C	0.0
	Yr	34	61	4	14	2	0	0	2	6	11	.230	.299	.262	51	-4	-4	4	0	0	0	.992	4	C	0.0
Total	6	307	689	81	161	25	4	16	62	94	116	.234	.332	.351	80	-15	-18	86	8	4	0	.990	39	C/3	3.2

■ JAY PIKE Pike, Jacob Emanuel b: Brooklyn, N.Y. BL/TL, Deb: 8/27/1877 F

YEAR	TM/L	G	AB	R	H	2B	3B	HR	RBI	BB	SO	AVG	OBP	SLG	PRO+	BR	/A	RC	SB	CS	SBR	FA	FR	POS	TPR
1877	Har-N	1	4	0	1	0	0	0	0	0	0	.250	.250	.250	65	-0	-0	0				.000	-1	/O	-0.1

■ JESS PIKE Pike, Jess Willard b: 7/31/15, Dustin, Okla. d: 3/28/84, San Diego, Cal. BL/TR, 6'3", 175 lbs. Deb: 4/18/46

YEAR	TM/L	G	AB	R	H	2B	3B	HR	RBI	BB	SO	AVG	OBP	SLG	PRO+	BR	/A	RC	SB	CS	SBR	FA	FR	POS	TPR
1946	NY-N	16	41	4	7	1	1	1	6	6	9	.171	.277	.317	68	-2	-2	4	0			.929	-2	O	-0.5

■ LIP PIKE Pike, Lipman Emanuel b: 5/25/1845, New York, N.Y. d: 10/10/1893, Brooklyn, N.Y. BL/TL, 5'8", 158 lbs. Deb: 5/09/1871 FM

YEAR	TM/L	G	AB	R	H	2B	3B	HR	RBI	BB	SO	AVG	OBP	SLG	PRO+	BR	/A	RC	SB	CS	SBR	FA	FR	POS	TPR
1871	Tro-n	28	130	43	49	10	7	**4**	39	5	7	.377	.400	.654	194	16	15	36	3					O/21M	1.0
1872	Bal-n	56	285	68	84	10	4	**6**	**62**	3	5	.295	.302	.421	115	6	3	39						O2/3	0.3
1873	Bal-n	56	287	71	90	18	8	**4**	48	6	4	.314	.328	.474	133	11	11	48						*O/2	1.0
1874	Har-n	52	238	58	81	**24**	5	1		0		.340	.340	**.496**	155	16	14	41						OS/2M	1.0
1875	StL-n	70	312	61	107	21	10	0		3		.343	.349	.474	**200**	25	29	53						*O/2	2.5
1876	StL-N	63	282	55	91	19	10	1	50	8	9	.323	.341	.472	178	20	22	47				.896	-4	*O/2	1.5
1877	Cin-N	58	262	45	78	12	4	**4**	23	9	7	.298	.321	.420	148	9	14	36				.802	-3	O2/SM	0.9
1878	Cin-N	31	145	28	47	5	1	0	11	4	9	.324	.342	.372	149	5	7	19				.824	-4	O	0.1
	Pro-N	5	22	4	5	0	1	0	4	1	1	.227	.261	.318	90	-0	-0	2				.788	-3	/2	-0.3
	Yr	36	167	32	52	5	2	0	15	5	10	.311	.331	.365	140	5	7	21				.824	-7	O/2	-0.2
1881	Wor-N	5	18	1	2	0	0	0	0	4	3	.111	.273	.111	24	-1	-2	1				.647	-1	/O	-0.3
1887	NY-a	1	4	0	0	0	0	0		0		.000	.000	.000	-99	-1	-1	0	0			1.000	-0	/O	-0.1
Total	5 n	262	1252	301	411	83	34	15	149	17	16	.328	.337	.485	154	73	73	217	18					O/2S31	5.8
Total	5	163	733	133	223	36	16	5	88	26	29	.304	.328	.417	152	31	40	104	0			.833	-15	O/2S	1.8

■ AL PILARCIK Pilarcik, Alfred James b: 7/3/30, Whiting, Ind. BL/TL, 5'10", 180 lbs. Deb: 7/13/56

YEAR	TM/L	G	AB	R	H	2B	3B	HR	RBI	BB	SO	AVG	OBP	SLG	PRO+	BR	/A	RC	SB	CS	SBR	FA	FR	POS	TPR
1956	KC-A	69	239	28	60	10	1	4	22	30	32	.251	.335	.351	81	-6	-6	31	9	2	2	.976	3	O	-0.6
1957	Bal-A	142	407	52	113	16	3	9	49	53	28	.278	.366	.398	116	6	9	62	14	7	0	.996	0	*O	0.3
1958	Bal-A	141	379	40	92	21	0	1	24	42	37	.243	.322	.306	78	-13	-10	39	7	3	0	.986	-14	*O	-3.0
1959	Bal-A	130	273	37	77	12	1	3	16	30	25	.282	.355	.366	101	0	1	37	9	3	1	.978	-16	*O	-1.7
1960	Bal-A	104	194	30	48	5	1	4	17	15	16	.247	.315	.345	79	-6	-6	21	0	2	-1	1.000	-11	O	-2.0
1961	KC-A	35	60	9	12	1	1	0	9	6	7	.200	.273	.250	41	-5	-5	4	1	0	0	1.000	-1	O	-0.7
	Chi-A	47	62	9	11	1	0	1	6	9	5	.177	.282	.242	42	-5	-5	4	1	1	-0	.944	-0	O	-0.6
	Yr	82	122	18	23	2	1	1	15	15	12	.189	.277	.246	41	-10	-10	8	2	1	0	.971	-1	O	-1.3
Total	6	668	1614	205	413	66	7	22	143	185	150	.256	.336	.346	89	-29	-22	198	41	18	2	.986	-39	O	-8.3

■ ANDY PILNEY Pilney, Antone James b: 1/19/13, Frontenac, Kan. BR/TR, 5'11", 174 lbs. Deb: 6/12/36

YEAR	TM/L	G	AB	R	H	2B	3B	HR	RBI	BB	SO	AVG	OBP	SLG	PRO+	BR	/A	RC	SB	CS	SBR	FA	FR	POS	TPR
1936	Bos-N	3	2	0	0	0	0	0	0	0	1	.000	.000	.000	-99	-1	-1	0	0			.000	0	H	-0.1

■ BABE PINELLI Pinelli, Ralph Arthur (b: Rinaldo Angelo Paolinelli)
b: 10/18/1895, San Francisco, Cal d: 10/22/84, Daly City, Cal. BR/TR, 5'9", 165 lbs. Deb: 8/03/18 U

YEAR	TM/L	G	AB	R	H	2B	3B	HR	RBI	BB	SO	AVG	OBP	SLG	PRO+	BR	/A	RC	SB	CS	SBR	FA	FR	POS	TPR
1918	Chi-A	24	78	7	18	1	1	1	7	7	8	.231	.302	.308	83	-2	-2	8	3			.847	-7	3	-0.9
1920	Det-A	102	284	33	65	9	3	0	21	25	16	.229	.296	.282	55	-19	-18	24	6	8	-3	.954	20	3S/2	0.3
1922	Cin-N	156	547	77	167	19	7	1	72	48	37	.305	.368	.371	93	-6	-4	73	17	22	-8	.945	21	*3	1.9
1923	Cin-N	117	423	44	117	14	5	0	51	27	29	.277	.320	.333	74	-17	-15	43	10	14	-5	.938	9	*3	-0.2
1924	Cin-N	144	510	61	156	16	7	0	70	32	32	.306	.353	.365	94	-4	-3	65	23	17	-3	.956	**27**	*3	3.1
1925	Cin-N	130	492	68	139	33	6	2	49	22	28	.283	.316	.386	80	-17	-15	55	8	19	-9	.945	21	*3S	0.6
1926	Cin-N	71	207	26	46	7	4	0	24	15	5	.222	.284	.295	58	-13	-12	18	2			.978	1	3S/2	-0.7
1927	Cin-N	30	76	11	15	2	0	1	4	6	7	.197	.265	.263	43	-6	-6	5	2			.968	-1	3/S2	-0.6
Total	8	774	2617	327	723	101	33	5	298	182	162	.276	.328	.346	79	-83	-75	292	71	80		.947	91	3/S2	3.5

■ LOU PINIELLA Piniella, Louis Victor b: 8/28/43, Tampa, Fla. BR/TR, 6'2", 198 lbs. Deb: 9/04/64 MC

YEAR	TM/L	G	AB	R	H	2B	3B	HR	RBI	BB	SO	AVG	OBP	SLG	PRO+	BR	/A	RC	SB	CS	SBR	FA	FR	POS	TPR
1964	Bal-A	4	1	0	0	0	0	0	0	0	0	.000	.000	.000	-99	-0	-0	0	0	0	0	.000	0	H	0.0
1968	Cle-A	6	5	1	0	0	0	0	1	0	0	.000	.000	.000	-99	-1	-1	0	0	0	0	1.000	-0	/O	-0.2
1969	KC-A	135	493	43	139	21	6	11	68	33	56	.282	.331	.416	107	4	3	65	2	4	-2	.977	15	*O	1.0
1970	KC-A	144	542	54	163	24	5	11	88	35	42	.301	.345	.424	111	7	7	74	3	6	-3	.984	4	*O/1	0.2
1971	KC-A	126	448	43	125	21	5	3	51	21	43	.279	.314	.368	94	-5	-5	49	5	3	-0	.986	1	*O	-1.1
1972	KC-A★	151	574	65	179	**33**	4	11	72	34	59	.312	.359	.441	138	25	25	84	7	2	1	.976	3	*O	2.5
1973	KC-A	144	513	53	128	28	1	9	69	30	65	.250	.294	.361	77	-12	-17	47	5	7	-3	.986	-5	*O/D	-3.2
1974	NY-A	140	518	71	158	26	0	9	70	32	58	.305	.348	.407	120	10	12	66	1	8	-5	.989	11	*O/1D	1.4
1975	NY-A	74	199	7	39	4	1	0	22	16	22	.196	.266	.226	41	-15	-15	10	0	0	0	.986	-3	OD	-1.9
1976	*NY-A	100	327	36	92	16	6	3	38	18	34	.281	.323	.394	110	3	3	41	0	1	-1	.982	2	OD	0.2
1977	*NY-A	103	339	47	112	19	3	12	45	20	31	.330	.369	.510	138	16	17	59	2	2	-1	.975	-4	OD/1	1.1
1978	*NY-A	130	472	67	148	34	5	6	69	34	36	.314	.362	.445	129	16	17	74	3	1	0	.969	2	*OD	1.5
1979	NY-A	130	461	49	137	22	2	11	69	17	31	.297	.325	.425	103	-1	1	58	3	2	-0	.982	3	*OD	-0.1
1980	*NY-A	116	321	39	92	18	0	2	27	29	20	.287	.346	.361	96	-2	-1	36	0	2	-1	.971	-7	*O/D	-1.3
1981	*NY-A	60	159	16	44	9	0	5	18	13	9	.277	.331	.428	119	3	3	20	0	1	-1	.986	1	OD	0.3
1982	NY-A	102	261	33	80	17	1	6	37	18	18	.307	.354	.448	120	6	7	37	0	1	-1	1.000	-1	DO	0.4
1983	NY-A	53	148	19	43	9	1	2	16	11	12	.291	.344	.405	109	1	2	20	1	1	-0	.959	-2	O/D	-0.1
1984	NY-A	29	86	8	26	4	1	1	6	7	5	.302	.355	.407	115	1	2	10	0	0	0	1.000	1	O/D	0.2
Total	18	1747	5867	651	1705	305	41	102	766	368	541	.291	.336	.409	109	56	60	750	32	41	-15	.981	21	*OD/1	0.9

■ ED PINKHAM Pinkham, Edward b: 1849, Brooklyn, N.Y. TL, 5'7", 142 lbs. Deb: 5/08/1871

YEAR	TM/L	G	AB	R	H	2B	3B	HR	RBI	BB	SO	AVG	OBP	SLG	PRO+	BR	/A	RC	SB	CS	SBR	FA	FR	POS	TPR
1871	Chi-n	24	95	27	25	5	5	1	17	**18**	3	.263	.381	.453	125	5	3	19	5					3/OP	0.1

■ GEORGE PINKNEY Pinkney, George Burton b: 1/11/1862, Orange Prairie, Ill. d: 11/10/26, Peoria, Ill. BR/TR, 5'7", 160 lbs. Deb: 8/16/1884

YEAR	TM/L	G	AB	R	H	2B	3B	HR	RBI	BB	SO	AVG	OBP	SLG	PRO+	BR	/A	RC	SB	CS	SBR	FA	FR	POS	TPR
1884	Cle-N	36	144	18	45	9	0	0	16	10	7	.313	.357	.375	126	5	4	20				.848	-8	2S	-0.3
1885	Bro-a	110	447	77	124	16	5	0		27		.277	.328	.336	112	7	7	51				.904	-11	23/S	-0.1

YEAR	TM/L	G	AB	R	H	2B	3B	HR	RBI	BB	SO	AVG	OBP	SLG	PRO+	BR	/A	RC	SB	CS	SBR	FA	FR	POS	TPR
1886	Bro-a	141	597	119	156	22	7	0		**70**		.261	.339	.322	108	8	8	78	32			.858	-16	*3/P	-0.4
1887	Bro-a	138	580	133	155	26	6	3		61		.267	.343	.348	94	-2	-4	92	59			**.890**	13	*3/S	1.0
1888	Bro-a	143	575	**134**	156	18	8	4	52	66		.271	.358	.351	132	23	23	93	51			.898	-26	*3	0.0
1889	*Bro-a	138	545	103	134	25	7	4	82	59	43	.246	.327	.339	92	-5	-5	78	47			**.897**	-8	*3	-0.7
1890	*Bro-N	126	485	115	150	20	9	7	83	80	19	.309	.411	.431	148	32	32	108	47			.933	-15	*3	2.0
1891	Bro-N	135	501	80	137	19	6	2	71	66	32	.273	.366	.347	111	9	10	82	44			.904	-20	*3/S	-0.4
1892	StL-N	78	290	31	50	3	2	0	25	36	26	.172	.268	.197	45	-19	-17	17	4			.888	-8	3	-2.1
1893	Lou-N	118	446	64	105	12	6	1	62	50	8	.235	.323	.296	72	-20	-14	48	12			.923	-2	*3	-1.1
Total	10	1163	4610	874	1212	170	56	21	391	525	135	.263	.345	.338	105	39	45	665	296			.897	-99	*3/2SP	-2.1

■ VADA PINSON Pinson, Vada Edward b: 8/11/36, Memphis, Tenn. BL/TL, 5'11", 181 lbs. Deb: 4/15/58 C

YEAR	TM/L	G	AB	R	H	2B	3B	HR	RBI	BB	SO	AVG	OBP	SLG	PRO+	BR	/A	RC	SB	CS	SBR	FA	FR	POS	TPR
1958	Cin-N	27	96	20	26	7	0	1	8	11	18	.271	.352	.375	88	-1	-1	13	2	1	0	1.000	2	O	-0.1
1959	Cin-N★	154	648	**131**	205	**47**	9	20	84	55	98	.316	.371	.509	128	28	26	124	21	6	3	.984	20	*O	4.0
1960	Cin-N★	154	652	107	187	**37**	12	20	61	47	96	.287	.339	.472	117	16	15	104	32	12	2	.981	9	*O	1.9
1961	*Cin-N	154	607	101	**208**	34	8	16	87	39	63	.343	.383	.504	131	28	27	116	23	10	1	.976	13	*O	3.1
1962	Cin-N	155	619	107	181	31	7	23	100	45	68	.292	.344	.477	114	14	11	101	26	8	3	.989	0	*O	0.6
1963	Cin-N	162	652	96	**204**	37	**14**	22	106	36	80	.313	.350	.514	141	35	33	113	27	8	3	.979	3	*O	3.3
1964	Cin-N	156	625	99	166	23	11	23	84	42	99	.266	.317	.448	109	9	7	89	8	2	1	.972	-2	*O	-0.2
1965	Cin-N	159	669	97	204	34	10	22	94	43	81	.305	.353	.484	125	28	23	112	21	8	2	**.992**	8	*O	2.6
1966	Cin-N	156	618	70	178	35	6	16	76	33	83	.288	.329	.442	103	9	3	87	18	10	-1	.964	1	*O	-0.5
1967	Cin-N	158	650	90	187	28	**13**	18	66	26	86	.288	.318	.454	106	13	5	94	26	8	3	.986	1	*O	0.1
1968	Cin-N	130	499	60	135	29	6	5	48	32	59	.271	.315	.383	102	4	1	59	17	11	-2	.978	-3	*O	-1.1
1969	StL-N	132	495	58	126	22	6	10	70	35	63	.255	.308	.384	92	-6	-6	56	4	4	-1	**.996**	1	*O	-1.4
1970	Cle-A	148	574	74	164	28	6	24	82	28	69	.286	.322	.481	113	12	8	84	7	6	-2	.982	5	*O/1	0.5
1971	Cle-A	146	566	60	149	23	4	11	35	21	58	.263	.297	.376	82	-10	-15	63	25	6	4	.978	4	*O/1	-1.6
1972	Cal-A	136	484	56	133	24	2	7	49	30	54	.275	.324	.376	114	4	7	59	17	6	2	.991	-5	*O/1	-0.3
1973	Cal-A	124	466	56	121	14	6	8	57	20	55	.260	.290	.367	91	-11	-7	46	5	5	-2	.965	-4	*O	-1.9
1974	KC-A	115	406	46	112	18	2	6	41	21	45	.276	.315	.374	92	-2	-5	49	21	5	3	.980	-5	*O/1D	-1.2
1975	KC-A	103	319	38	71	14	5	4	22	10	21	.223	.251	.335	63	-16	-17	24	5	6	-2	.993	-3	O/1D	-2.6
Total	18	2469	9645	1366	2757	485	127	256	1170	574	1196	.286	.330	.442	110	155	114	1394	305	122	18	.981	45	*O/1D	5.2

■ WALLY PIPP Pipp, Walter Clement b: 2/17/1893, Chicago, Ill. d: 1/11/65, Grand Rapids, Mich BL/TL, 6'1", 180 lbs. Deb: 6/29/13

YEAR	TM/L	G	AB	R	H	2B	3B	HR	RBI	BB	SO	AVG	OBP	SLG	PRO+	BR	/A	RC	SB	CS	SBR	FA	FR	POS	TPR
1913	Det-A	12	31	3	5	0	3	0	5	2	6	.161	.235	.355	73	-1	-1	2	0			.977	-1	1	-0.2
1915	NY-A	136	479	59	118	20	13	4	60	66	81	.246	.339	.367	112	6	7	65	18	7	1	**.992**	3	*1	0.8
1916	NY-A	151	545	70	143	20	14	**12**	93	54	82	.262	.331	.417	122	14	12	82	16			.992	6	*1	1.4
1917	NY-A	155	587	82	143	29	12	**9**	70	60	66	.244	.320	.380	112	8	7	72	11			.990	4	*1	0.7
1918	NY-A	91	349	48	106	15	9	2	44	22	34	.304	.345	.415	127	10	10	52	11			.988	0	1	0.7
1919	NY-A	138	523	74	144	23	10	7	50	39	42	.275	.330	.398	103	1	1	71	9			.991	1	*1	-0.3
1920	NY-A	153	610	109	171	30	14	11	76	48	54	.280	.339	.430	99	0	-3	87	4	10	-5	.991	0	*1	-1.1
1921	*NY-A	153	588	96	174	35	9	8	97	45	28	.296	.347	.427	94	-4	-6	87	17	10	-1	.991	-4	*1	-1.4
1922	*NY-A	152	577	96	190	32	10	9	90	56	32	.329	.392	.466	120	20	18	104	7	12	-5	.993	-5	*1	0.1
1923	*NY-A	144	569	79	173	19	8	6	108	36	28	.304	.352	.397	95	-3	-5	77	6	13	-6	.992	-4	*1	-2.1
1924	NY-A	153	589	88	174	30	**19**	9	113	51	36	.295	.352	.457	108	4	4	95	12	6	0	**.994**	2	*1	-0.4
1925	NY-A	62	178	19	41	6	3	3	24	13	12	.230	.286	.348	61	-11	-11	18	3	3	-1	.991	4	1	-1.0
1926	Cin-N	155	574	72	167	22	15	6	99	49	26	.291	.352	.413	108	4	6	83	8			.992	2	*1	-0.2
1927	Cin-N	122	443	49	115	19	6	2	41	32	11	.260	.309	.343	77	-16	-14	47	2			**.996**	0	*1	-2.2
1928	Cin-N	95	272	30	77	11	3	2	26	23	13	.283	.341	.368	87	-6	-5	34	1			.989	1	1	-1.0
Total	15	1872	6914	974	1941	311	148	90	996	596	551	.281	.341	.408	104	25	19	976	125	61		.992	9	*1	-6.2

■ JIM PISONI Pisoni, James Pete b: 8/14/29, St.Louis, Mo. BR/TR, 5'10", 169 lbs. Deb: 9/25/53

YEAR	TM/L	G	AB	R	H	2B	3B	HR	RBI	BB	SO	AVG	OBP	SLG	PRO+	BR	/A	RC	SB	CS	SBR	FA	FR	POS	TPR
1953	StL-A	3	12	1	1	0	0	1	1	0	5	.083	.083	.333	8	-2	-2	0	0	0	0	1.000	-0	/O	-0.2
1956	KC-A	10	30	4	8	0	0	2	5	2	8	.267	.313	.467	103	-0	-0	4	0	0	0	.966	4	/O	0.4
1957	KC-A	44	97	14	23	2	2	3	12	10	17	.237	.321	.392	92	-1	-1	13	0	0	0	.989	-3	O	-0.6
1959	Mil-N	9	24	4	4	1	0	0	0	2	6	.167	.231	.208	20	-3	-3	1	0	0	0	.941	-1	/O	-0.4
	NY-A	17	17	2	3	0	1	0	1	1	9	.176	.222	.294	42	-1	-1	1	0	0	0	1.000	-3	O	-0.4
1960	NY-A	20	9	1	1	0	0	0	1	1	2	.111	.200	.111	-14	-1	-1	0	0	0	0	.938	-5	O	-0.7
Total	5	103	189	26	40	3	3	6	20	16	47	.212	.280	.354	71	-8	-8	20	0	0	0	.978	-7	/O	-1.9

■ ALEX PITKO Pitko, Alexander "Spunk" b: 11/22/14, Burlington, N.J. BR/TR, 5'10", 180 lbs. Deb: 9/11/38

YEAR	TM/L	G	AB	R	H	2B	3B	HR	RBI	BB	SO	AVG	OBP	SLG	PRO+	BR	/A	RC	SB	CS	SBR	FA	FR	POS	TPR
1938	Phi-N	7	19	2	6	1	0	0	2	3	3	.316	.409	.368	118	1	1	3	1			.889	-2	/O	-0.1
1939	Was-A	4	8	0	1	0	0	0	1	1	3	.125	.222	.125	-10	-1	-1	0	0	0	0	1.000	-1	/O	-0.2
Total	2	11	27	2	7	1	0	0	3	4	6	.259	.355	.296	80	-1	-1	3	1	0		.917	-3	/O	-0.3

■ JAKE PITLER Pitler, Jacob Albert b: 4/22/1894, New York, N.Y. d: 2/3/68, Binghamton, N.Y. BR/TR, 5'8", 150 lbs. Deb: 5/30/17 C

YEAR	TM/L	G	AB	R	H	2B	3B	HR	RBI	BB	SO	AVG	OBP	SLG	PRO+	BR	/A	RC	SB	CS	SBR	FA	FR	POS	TPR
1917	Pit-N	109	382	39	89	8	5	0	23	30	24	.233	.297	.280	75	-9	-11	34	6			**.966**	-12	*2/O	-2.0
1918	Pit-N	2	1	1	0	0	0	0	0	1	0	.000	.500	.000	55	0	0	1	2			.667	0	/2	0.1
Total	2	111	383	40	89	8	5	0	23	31	24	.232	.298	.279	75	-9	-11	35	8			.962	-11	2/O	-1.9

■ CHRIS PITTARO Pittaro, Christopher Francis b: 9/16/61, Trenton, N.J. BB/TR, 5'11", 170 lbs. Deb: 4/08/85

YEAR	TM/L	G	AB	R	H	2B	3B	HR	RBI	BB	SO	AVG	OBP	SLG	PRO+	BR	/A	RC	SB	CS	SBR	FA	FR	POS	TPR
1985	Det-A	28	62	10	15	3	1	0	7	5	13	.242	.299	.323	71	-3	-2	6	1	1	-0	.881	-1	3/2D	-0.3
1986	Min-A	11	21	0	2	0	0	0	0	0	8	.095	.095	.095	-47	-4	-4	0	0	0	0	.969	2	/2S	-0.2
1987	Min-A	14	12	6	4	0	0	0	0	1	0	.333	.385	.333	90	-0	-0	2	1	0	0	1.000	2	/2D	0.2
Total	3	53	95	16	21	3	1	0	7	6	21	.221	.267	.274	48	-7	-7	8	2	1	0	.968	4	/32SD	-0.3

■ PINKY PITTINGER Pittinger, Clarke Alonzo b: 2/24/1899, Hudson, Mich. d: 11/4/77, Ft.Lauderdale, Fla. BR/TR, 5'10", 160 lbs. Deb: 4/15/21

YEAR	TM/L	G	AB	R	H	2B	3B	HR	RBI	BB	SO	AVG	OBP	SLG	PRO+	BR	/A	RC	SB	CS	SBR	FA	FR	POS	TPR
1921	Bos-A	40	91	6	18	1	0	0	5	4	13	.198	.232	.209	13	-12	-12	5	3	2	-0	.985	3	O/3S2	-1.0
1922	Bos-A	66	186	16	48	3	0	0	7	9	10	.258	.299	.274	51	-13	-13	15	2	5	-2	.920	5	3S	-0.6
1923	Bos-A	60	177	15	38	5	0	0	15	5	10	.215	.236	.243	26	-19	-19	10	3	1	0	.959	-11	2S/3	-2.8
1925	Chi-N	59	173	21	54	7	2	0	15	12	7	.312	.364	.376	88	-2	-3	24	5	4	-1	.940	4	S3	0.4
1927	Cin-N	31	84	17	23	5	0	1	10	2	5	.274	.291	.369	78	-3	-3	9	4			.963	3	2/S3	0.1
1928	Cin-N	40	38	12	9	0	1	0	4	0	1	.237	.237	.289	37	-4	-3	2	2			.892	8	S/23	0.5
1929	Cin-N	77	210	31	62	11	0	0	27	5	4	.295	.318	.348	68	-12	-10	22	8			.956	2	S/32	-0.2
Total	7	373	959	118	252	32	3	1	83	37	50	.263	.294	.306	55	-65	-63	87	27	12		.938	14	S/32O	-3.6

■ JOE PITTMAN Pittman, Joseph Wayne b: 1/1/54, Houston, Tex. BR/TR, 6'1", 180 lbs. Deb: 4/25/81

YEAR	TM/L	G	AB	R	H	2B	3B	HR	RBI	BB	SO	AVG	OBP	SLG	PRO+	BR	/A	RC	SB	CS	SBR	FA	FR	POS	TPR
1981	*Hou-N	52	135	11	38	4	2	0	7	11	16	.281	.336	.341	97	-1	-0	15	4	4	-1	.980	-9	2/3	-1.0
1982	Hou-N	15	10	0	2	1	0	0	0	0	2	.200	.200	.300	41	-1	-1	1	0	0	0	1.000	1	/3O	0.0
	SD-N	55	118	16	30	2	0	0	7	9	13	.254	.307	.271	66	-6	-5	10	8	3	1	.964	-3	2S	-0.5
	Yr	70	128	16	32	3	0	0	7	9	15	.250	.299	.273	65	-6	-6	11	8	3	1	.964	-2	2S/3O	-0.5
1984	SF-N	17	22	2	5	0	0	0	2	0	6	.227	.227	.227	29	-2	-2	1	1	1	-0	.900	-2	/S23	-0.4
Total	3	139	285	29	75	7	2	0	16	20	37	.263	.311	.302	77	-10	-8	26	13	8	-1	.974	-14	/2S3O	-1.9

■ GAYLEN PITTS Pitts, Gaylen Richard b: 6/6/46, Wichita, Kan. BR/TR, 6'1", 175 lbs. Deb: 5/12/74 C

YEAR	TM/L	G	AB	R	H	2B	3B	HR	RBI	BB	SO	AVG	OBP	SLG	PRO+	BR	/A	RC	SB	CS	SBR	FA	FR	POS	TPR
1974	Oak-A	18	41	4	10	3	0	0	3	5	4	.244	.326	.317	92	-1	-0	4	0	0	0	.909	0	3/21	0.0
1975	Oak-A	10	3	1	1	1	0	0	1	0	0	.333	.333	.667	181	0	0	0	0	0	0	.800	2	/3S2	0.2

YEAR	TM/L	G	AB	R	H	2B	3B	HR	RBI	BB	SO	AVG	OBP	SLG	PRO+	BR	/A	RC	SB	CS	SBR	FA	FR	POS	TPR
Total	2	28	44	5	11	4	0	0	4	5	4	.250	.327	.341	98	-0	-0	4	0	0	0	.895	2	/32S1	0.2
■ **HERMAN PITZ**	Pitz, Herman b: 7/18/1865, Brooklyn, N.Y. d: 9/3/24, Far Rockaway, N.Y. 5'6", 140 lbs. Deb: 4/18/1890																								
1890	Bro-a	61	189	26	26	0	0	0		45		.138	.312	.138	36	-12	-11	16	25			.885	-7	C3/OS2	-1.3
	Syr-a	29	95	17	21	0	0	0		13		.221	.321	.221	70	-4	-2	12	14			.929	-5	C/SO	-0.4
	Yr	90	284	43	47	0	0	0		58		.165	.315	.165	47	-16	-13	28	39			.906	-11	C3O/S2	-1.7
■ **PHIL PLANTIER**	Plantier, Phillip Alan b: 1/27/69, Manchester, N.H. BL/TR, 6', 175 lbs. Deb: 8/21/90																								
1990	Bos-A	14	15	1	2	1	0	0	3	4	6	.133	.350	.200	55	-1	-1	1	0	0	0	.000	-0	/OD	-0.1
1991	Bos-A	53	148	27	49	7	1	11	35	23	38	.331	.424	.615	175	17	16	40	1	0	0	.976	-0	O/D	1.5
1992	Bos-A	108	349	46	86	19	0	7	30	44	83	.246	.334	.361	90	-2	-4	42	2	3	-1	.975	2	OD	-0.5
Total	3	175	512	74	137	27	1	18	68	71	127	.268	.361	.430	114	15	11	83	3	3	-1	.975	2	O/D	0.9
■ **DON PLARSKI**	Plarski, Donald Joseph b: 11/9/29, Chicago, Ill. d: 12/29/81, St.Louis, Mo. BR/TR, 5'6", 160 lbs. Deb: 7/20/55																								
1955	KC-A	8	11	0	1	0	0	0	0	0	2	.091	.091	.091	-50	-2	-2	0	1	0	0	1.000	-2	/O	-0.4
■ **ELMO PLASKETT**	Plaskett, Elmo Alexander b: 6/27/38, Frederiksted, V.I. BR/TR, 5'10", 195 lbs. Deb: 9/08/62																								
1962	Pit-N	7	14	2	4	0	0	1	3	1	3	.286	.333	.500	120	0	0	2	0	0	0	1.000	-1	/C	-0.1
1963	Pit-N	10	21	1	3	0	0	0	2	0	5	.143	.143	.143	-17	-3	-3	0	0	0	0	1.000	-2	/C3	-0.5
Total	2	17	35	3	7	0	0	1	5	1	8	.200	.222	.286	41	-3	-3	3	0	0	0	1.000	-3	/C3	-0.6
■ **WHITEY PLATT**	Platt, Mizell George b: 8/21/20, W.Palm Beach, Fla. d: 7/27/70, W.Palm Beach, Fla BR/TR, 6'2", 195 lbs. Deb: 9/16/42																								
1942	Chi-N	4	16	1	1	0	0	0	2	0	3	.063	.063	.063	-66	-3	-3	-0	0			1.000	0	/O	-0.4
1943	Chi-N	20	41	2	7	3	0	0	2	1	7	.171	.190	.244	25	-4	-4	2	0			.952	-3	O	-0.9
1946	Chi-A	84	247	28	62	8	5	3	32	17	34	.251	.307	.360	89	-5	-4	24	1	7	-4	.971	-3	O	-1.4
1948	StL-A	123	454	57	123	22	10	7	82	39	51	.271	.331	.410	94	-4	-6	60	1	4	-2	.948	-6	*O	-2.0
1949	StL-A	102	244	29	63	8	2	3	29	24	27	.258	.325	.344	74	-9	-10	27	0	1	-1	.986	0	O/1	-1.3
Total	5	333	1002	117	256	41	17	13	147	81	122	.255	.314	.369	83	-25	-27	112	2	12		.964	-12	O/1	-6.0
■ **AL PLATTE**	Platte, Alfred Frederick Joseph b: 4/13/1890, Grand Rapids, Mich d: 8/29/76, Grand Rapids, Mich BL/TL, 5'7", 160 lbs. Deb: 9/01/13																								
1913	Det-A	9	18	1	2	1	0	0	0	1	1	.111	.158	.167	-5	-2	-2	1	0			.800	-1	/O	-0.4
■ **RANCE PLESS**	Pless, Rance b: 12/6/25, Greeneville, Tenn. BR/TR, 6', 145 lbs. Deb: 4/21/56																								
1956	KC-A	48	85	4	23	3	1	0	9	10	13	.271	.354	.329	81	-2	-2	9	0	1	-1	1.000	2	1/3	-0.1
■ **HERB PLEWS**	Plews, Herbert Eugene b: 6/14/28, Helena, Mont. BL/TR, 5'11", 160 lbs. Deb: 4/18/56																								
1956	Was-A	91	256	24	69	10	7	1	25	26	40	.270	.339	.375	88	-4	-4	32	1	2	-1	.947	-3	2/S3	-0.4
1957	Was-A	104	329	51	89	19	4	1	26	28	39	.271	.331	.362	90	-5	-4	38	0	3	-2	.979	-15	23/S	-1.5
1958	Was-A	111	380	46	98	12	6	2	29	17	45	.258	.291	.337	74	-15	-14	36	2	3	-1	.976	-21	23	-3.2
1959	Was-A	27	40	4	9	0	0	0	2	3	5	.225	.279	.225	40	-3	-3	2	0	1	-1	.971	1	/2	-0.2
	Bos-A	13	12	0	1	1	0	0	0	0	4	.083	.083	.167	-32	-2	-2	0	0	0	0	.833	1	/2	-0.1
	Yr	40	52	4	10	1	0	0	2	3	9	.192	.236	.212	24	-5	-5	2	0	1	-1	.951	2	/2	-0.3
Total	4	346	1017	125	266	42	17	4	82	74	133	.262	.314	.348	80	-29	-28	107	3	9	-5	.967	-36	2/3S	-5.4
■ **WALTER PLOCK**	Plock, Walter S. b: 7/2/1869, Philadelphia, Pa. d: 4/28/1900, Richmond, Va. 6'3", Deb: 8/21/1891																								
1891	Phi-N	2	5	2	2	0	0	0	0	0	1	.400	.500	.400	162	1	0	1	0			.000	-1	/O	-0.1
■ **BILL PLUMMER**	Plummer, William Francis b: 3/21/47, Oakland, Cal. BR/TR, 6'1", 200 lbs. Deb: 4/19/68 MC																								
1968	Chi-N	2	2	0	0	0	0	0	0	0	1	.000	.000	.000	-94	-0	-0	0	0	0	0	1.000	0	/C	0.0
1970	Cin-N	4	8	0	1	0	0	0	0	0	2	.125	.222	.125	-4	-1	-1	0	0	0	0	.857	-2	/C	-0.3
1971	Cin-N	10	19	0	0	0	0	0	0	0	4	.000	.000	.000	-99	-5	-5	0	0	0	0	1.000	0	/C3	-0.5
1972	Cin-N	38	102	8	19	4	0	2	9	4	20	.186	.217	.284	44	-8	-7	6	0	0	0	.994	0	C/13	-0.7
1973	Cin-N	50	119	8	18	3	0	2	11	18	26	.151	.268	.227	41	-10	-9	8	1	0	0	.994	-1	C/3	-0.8
1974	Cin-N	50	120	7	27	7	0	2	10	6	21	.225	.262	.333	67	-6	-6	10	1	0	0	.974	5	C/3	0.1
1975	Cin-N	65	159	17	29	7	0	1	19	24	28	.182	.297	.245	51	-10	-10	14	1	0	0	.990	-3	C	-1.1
1976	Cin-N	56	153	16	38	6	1	4	19	14	36	.248	.311	.379	93	-1	-2	16	0	2	-1	.977	6	C	0.5
1977	Cin-N	51	117	10	16	5	0	1	7	17	34	.137	.246	.205	22	-13	-13	7	1	1	-0	.986	-1	C	-1.4
1978	Sea-A	41	93	6	20	5	0	2	7	12	19	.215	.305	.333	80	-2	-2	9	0	0	0	.978	-5	C	-0.7
Total	10	367	892	72	168	37	1	14	82	95	191	.188	.269	.279	53	-57	-56	70	4	3	-1	.984	1	C/31	-4.9
■ **BIFF POCOROBA**	Pocoroba, Biff b: 7/25/53, Burbank, Cal. BB/TR, 5'10", 180 lbs. Deb: 4/25/75																								
1975	Atl-N	67	188	15	48	7	1	1	22	20	11	.255	.327	.319	77	-5	-6	20	0	0	0	.970	-4	C	-0.8
1976	Atl-N	54	174	16	42	7	0	0	14	19	12	.241	.316	.282	66	-6	-8	15	1	0	0	.978	4	C	-0.2
1977	Atl-N	113	321	46	93	24	1	8	44	57	27	.290	.398	.445	113	14	9	57	3	4	-2	.989	2	*C	1.2
1978	Atl-N★	92	289	21	70	8	0	6	34	29	14	.242	.316	.332	73	-7	-11	27	0	3	-2	.990	1	C	-1.0
1979	Atl-N	28	38	6	12	4	0	0	4	7	0	.316	.422	.421	122	2	2	6	1	1	-0	.933	0	/C	0.2
1980	Atl-N	70	83	7	22	4	0	2	8	11	11	.265	.351	.386	102	1	0	12	1	0	0	.934	-1	C	0.1
1981	Atl-N	57	122	4	22	4	0	0	8	12	15	.180	.265	.213	36	-10	-10	7	0	0	0	.938	-5	3/C	-1.7
1982	*Atl-N	56	120	5	33	7	0	2	22	13	12	.275	.351	.383	101	1	0	16	0	0	0	.988	-4	C/3	-0.3
1983	Atl-N	55	120	11	32	6	0	2	16	12	7	.267	.333	.367	87	-1	-2	14	0	0	0	.983	-3	C	-0.3
1984	Atl-N	4	2	1	0	0	0	0	0	2	0	.000	.500	.000	48	0	0	0	0	0	0	.000	0	/H	0.0
Total	10	596	1457	132	374	71	2	21	172	182	109	.257	.342	.351	86	-11	-25	175	6	8	-3	.982	-9	C/3	-2.8
■ **MIKE POEPPING**	Poepping, Michael Harold b: 8/7/50, Little Falls, Minn. BR/TR, 6'6", 230 lbs. Deb: 9/06/75																								
1975	Min-A	14	37	0	5	1	0	0	1	5	7	.135	.238	.162	15	-4	-4	1	0	0	0	.950	-2	O	-0.7
■ **JIMMY POFAHL**	Pofahl, James Willard b: 6/18/17, Faribault, Minn. d: 9/14/84, Owatonna, Minn. BR/TR, 5'11", 185 lbs. Deb: 4/16/40																								
1940	Was-A	119	406	34	95	23	5	2	36	37	55	.234	.298	.330	67	-23	-19	41	2	0	1	.952	-5	*S/2	-1.3
1941	Was-A	22	75	9	14	3	2	0	6	10	11	.187	.282	.280	52	-6	-5	7	1	0	0	.934	-4	S	-0.7
1942	Was-A	84	283	22	59	7	2	0	28	29	30	.208	.282	.247	50	-19	-18	20	4	3	-1	.956	1	S23	-1.5
Total	3	225	764	65	168	33	9	2	70	76	96	.220	.290	.295	59	-47	-42	67	7	3	0	.951	-8	S/23	-3.5
■ **JOHN POFF**	Poff, John William b: 10/23/52, Chillicothe, Ohio BL/TL, 6'2", 190 lbs. Deb: 9/08/79																								
1979	Phi-N	12	19	2	2	1	0	0	1	1	4	.105	.150	.158	-15	-3	-3	0	0	0	0	.875	-0	/O1	-0.4
1980	Mil-A	19	68	7	17	1	2	1	7	3	7	.250	.282	.368	79	-2	-2	7	0	0	0	1.000	-1	/O1D	-0.3
Total	2	31	87	9	19	2	2	1	8	4	11	.218	.253	.322	57	-5	-5	7	0	0	0	.957	-1	/OD1	-0.7
■ **AARON POINTER**	Pointer, Aaron Elton "Hawk" b: 4/19/42, Little Rock, Ark. BR/TR, 6'2", 185 lbs. Deb: 9/22/63																								
1963	Hou-N	2	5	0	1	0	0	0	0	0	1	.200	.200	.200	17	-1	-1	0	0	0	0	1.000	-0	/O	-0.1
1966	Hou-N	11	26	5	9	1	0	1	5	5	6	.346	.469	.500	182	3	3	7	1	1	-0	1.000	2	O	0.4
1967	Hou-N	27	70	6	11	4	0	1	10	13	26	.157	.298	.257	62	-3	-3	6	1	0	0	.951	1	O	-0.3
Total	3	40	101	11	21	5	0	2	15	18	33	.208	.339	.317	91	-1	-0	13	2	1	0	.966	2	/O	0.0
■ **HUGH POLAND**	Poland, Hugh Reid b: 1/19/13, Tompkinsville, Ky. d: 3/30/84, Guthrie, Ky. BL/TR, 5'11.5", 185 lbs. Deb: 4/22/43																								
1943	NY-N	4	12	1	1	0	1	0	2	1	0	.083	.154	.250	16	-1	-1	1	0			.889	-2	/C	-0.3
	Bos-N	44	141	5	27	7	0	0	13	4	11	.191	.214	.241	32	-13	-12	7	0			.973	-2	C	-1.3

YEAR	TM/L	G	AB	R	H	2B	3B	HR	RBI	BB	SO	AVG	OBP	SLG	PRO+	BR	/A	RC	SB	CS	SBR	FA	FR	POS	TPR
	Yr	48	153	6	28	7	1	0	15	5	11	.183	.209	.242	30	-14	-14	7	0			.969	-4	C	-1.6
1944	Bos-N	8	23	1	3	1	0	0	2	0	1	.130	.130	.174	-14	-3	-4	0	0			.939	1	/C	-0.2
1946	Bos-N	4	6	0	1	1	0	0	0	0	0	.167	.167	.333	40	-1	-1	0	0			1.000	0	/C	0.0
1947	Phi-N	4	8	0	0	0	0	0	0	0	0	.000	.000	.000	-99	-2	-2	0	0			1.000	1	/C	-0.2
	Cin-N	16	18	1	6	1	0	0	2	1	4	.333	.368	.389	102	0	0	3	0			.667	-1	/C	-0.1
	Yr	20	26	1	6	1	0	0	2	1	4	.231	.259	.269	41	-2	-2	2	0			.867	-1	/C	-0.3
1948	Cin-N	3	3	0	1	0	0	0	0	0	0	.333	.333	.333	84	-0	-0	0	0			.000	0	H	0.0
Total	5	83	211	8	39	10	1	0	19	6	16	.185	.207	.242	28	-20	-20	11	0			.958	-4	/C	-2.1
■ MARK POLHEMUS	Polhemus, Mark S. "Humpty Dumpty" b: 10/4/1862, Brooklyn, N.Y. d: 11/12/23, Lynn, Mass. 5'6.5", 185 lbs. Deb: 7/13/1887																								
1887	Ind-N	20	75	6	18	1	0	0	8	2	9	.240	.260	.253	46	-5	-5	6	4			.744	0	O	-0.4
■ GUS POLIDOR	Polidor, Gustavo Adolfo (Gonzalez) b: 10/26/61, Caracas, Venezuela BR/TR, 6', 170 lbs. Deb: 9/07/85																								
1985	Cal-A	2	1	1	1	0	0	0	0	0	0	1.000	1.000	1.000	452	0	0	1	0	0	0	1.000	0	/SO	0.0
1986	Cal-A	6	19	1	5	1	0	0	1	1	0	.263	.300	.316	69	-1	-1	1	0	0	0	1.000	0	/2S3	-0.1
1987	Cal-A	63	137	12	36	3	0	2	15	2	15	.263	.279	.328	62	-8	-7	12	0	0	0	.983	-6	S3/2	-1.0
1988	Cal-A	54	81	4	12	3	0	0	4	3	11	.148	.179	.185	2	-11	-10	3	0	0	0	.984	0	S3/2D	-0.9
1989	Mil-A	79	175	15	34	7	0	0	14	6	18	.194	.230	.234	31	-16	-16	9	3	0	1	.923	3	32S/D	-1.1
1990	Mil-A	18	15	0	1	0	0	0	1	0	1	.067	.067	.067	-63	-3	-3	0	0	0	0	1.000	2	3/2S	-0.2
Total	6	222	428	33	89	14	0	2	35	12	45	.208	.235	.255	35	-38	-37	26	3	0	1	.970	-1	/S32DO	-3.3
■ NICK POLLY	Polly, Nicholas (b: Nicholas Joseph Polachanin) b: 4/18/17, Chicago, Ill. BR/TR, 5'11", 190 lbs. Deb: 9/11/37																								
1937	Bro-N	10	18	2	4	0	0	0	2	0	1	.222	.222	.222	21	-2	-2	1	0			.850	2	/3	0.0
1945	Bos-A	4	7	0	1	0	0	0	1	0	0	.143	.143	.143	-17	-1	-1	0	0	0	0	1.000	-0	/3	-0.1
Total	2	14	25	2	5	0	0	0	3	0	1	.200	.200	.200	11	-3	-3	1	0	0		.870	2	/3	-0.1
■ LUIS POLONIA	Polonia, Luis Andrew (Almonte) b: 12/10/64, Santiago, D.R. BL/TL, 5'8", 155 lbs. Deb: 4/24/87																								
1987	Oak-A	125	435	78	125	16	10	4	49	32	64	.287	.336	.398	100	-4	0	61	29	7	5	.979	-1	*OD	0.0
1988	*Oak-A	84	288	51	84	11	4	2	27	21	40	.292	.340	.378	104	0	2	38	24	9	2	.988	1	O/D	0.2
1989	Oak-A	59	206	31	59	6	4	1	17	9	15	.286	.316	.369	96	-2	-1	23	13	4	2	.985	5	O	0.4
	NY-A	66	227	39	71	11	2	2	29	16	29	.313	.363	.405	118	5	5	32	9	4	0	.982	4	O/D	0.8
	Yr	125	433	70	130	17	6	3	46	25	44	.300	.341	.388	108	3	4	55	22	8	2	.984	8	*O/D	1.2
1990	NY-A	11	22	2	7	0	0	0	3	0	1	.318	.318	.318	78	-1	-1	2	1	0	0	.000	0	/D	0.0
	Cal-A	109	381	50	128	7	9	2	32	25	42	.336	.378	.417	125	11	12	57	20	14	-2	.980	-5	OD	0.3
	Yr	120	403	52	135	7	9	2	35	25	43	.335	.375	.412	122	11	12	59	21	14	-2	.980	-5	OD/H	0.3
1991	Cal-A	150	604	92	179	28	8	2	50	52	74	.296	.353	.379	103	3	3	81	48	23	1	.981	1	*O/D	0.1
1992	Cal-A	149	577	83	165	17	4	0	35	45	64	.286	.339	.329	89	-8	-7	63	51	21	3	.980	2	OD	-0.5
Total	6	753	2740	426	818	96	41	13	242	200	329	.299	.347	.378	103	4	13	358	195	82	9	.982	6	O/D	1.3
■ CARLOS PONCE	Ponce, Carlos Antonio (Diaz) b: 2/7/59, Rio Piedras, P.R. BR/TR, 5'10", 170 lbs. Deb: 8/14/85																								
1985	Mil-A	21	62	4	10	2	0	1	5	1	9	.161	.175	.242	13	-7	-7	2	0	0	0	1.000	-0	1/OD	-0.9
■ RALPH POND	Pond, Ralph Benjamin b: 5/4/1888, Eau Claire, Wis. d: 9/8/47, Cleveland, Ohio Deb: 6/08/10																								
1910	Bos-A	1	4	0	1	0	0	0	0	0		.250	.250	.250	55	-0	-0	0	1			.000	-1	/O	-0.1
■ HARLIN POOL	Pool, Harold G "Samson" b: 3/12/08, Lakeport, Cal. d: 2/15/63, Rodeo, Cal. BL/TR, 5'10", 195 lbs. Deb: 5/30/34																								
1934	Cin-N	99	358	38	117	22	5	2	50	17	18	.327	.369	.433	117	7	8	58	3			.953	0	O	0.4
1935	Cin-N	28	68	8	12	6	2	0	11	2	2	.176	.200	.324	39	-6	-6	4	0			.962	-3	O	-0.9
Total	2	127	426	46	129	28	7	2	61	19	20	.303	.343	.415	105	1	2	62	3			.954	-3	O	-0.5
■ ED POOLE	Poole, Edward I. b: 9/7/1874, Canton, Ohio d: 3/11/19, Malvern, Ohio BR/TR, 5'10", 175 lbs. Deb: 10/06/00																								
1900	Pit-N	2	4	1	2	0	1	1	3	0		.500	.500	1.750	504	2	2	4	0			.500	-0	/OP	0.0
1901	Pit-N	26	78	6	16	4	0	1	4	4		.205	.244	.295	54	-5	-5	6	1			.933	-2	PO/23	-0.5
1902	Pit-N	1	4	0	1	0	0	0	0	0		.250	.250	.250	52	-0	-0	0	0			.667	-0	/P	0.0
	Cin-N	17	61	7	7	2	0	0	1	0		.115	.115	.148	-17	-9	-9	1	0			1.000	-1	P/O	-0.1
	Yr	18	65	7	8	2	0	0	1	0		.123	.123	.154	-13	-9	-9	1	0			.976	-1	P/O	-0.1
1903	Cin-N	25	70	7	17	1	0	0	7	2		.243	.264	.257	44	-5	-6	5	0			.929	2	P	0.0
1904	Bro-N	25	62	3	8	1	0	0	0	0		.129	.129	.145	-16	-8	-8	1	0			.973	3	P	0.0
Total	5	96	279	24	51	8	1	2	15	6		.183	.200	.240	29	-24	-26	18	1			.954	3	/PO32	-0.6
■ JIM POOLE	Poole, James Robert "Easy" b: 5/12/1895, Taylorsville, N.C. d: 1/2/75, Hickory, N.C. BL/TR, 6', 175 lbs. Deb: 4/14/25																								
1925	Phi-A	133	480	65	143	29	8	5	67	27	37	.298	.338	.423	86	-8	-12	68	5	4	-1	.982	-7	*1	-2.6
1926	Phi-A	112	361	49	106	23	5	8	63	23	25	.294	.339	.452	99	1	-2	55	4	3	-1	.992	0	*1/O	-0.8
1927	Phi-A	38	99	4	22	2	0	0	10	9	6	.222	.287	.242	36	-9	-10	7	0	0	0	.993	0	1	-1.1
Total	3	283	940	118	271	54	13	13	140	59	68	.288	.333	.415	86	-16	-24	130	9	7	-2	.917	-7	1/O	-4.5
■ RAY POOLE	Poole, Raymond Herman b: 1/16/20, Salisbury, N.C. BL/TR, 6', 180 lbs. Deb: 9/09/41																								
1941	Phi-A	2	2	0	0	0	0	0	0	0	1	.000	.000	.000	-99	-1	-1	0	0	0	0	.000	0	H	-0.1
1947	Phi-A	13	13	1	3	0	0	0	1	1	4	.231	.286	.231	44	-1	-1	1	0	0	0	.000	0	H	-0.1
Total	2	15	15	1	3	0	0	0	1	1	5	.200	.250	.200	25	-2	-2	1	0	0	0		0		-0.2
■ TOM POORMAN	Poorman, Thomas Iverson b: 10/14/1857, Lock Haven, Pa. d: 2/18/05, Lock Haven, Pa. BL/TR, 5'7", 135 lbs. Deb: 5/05/1880																								
1880	Buf-N	19	70	5	11	1	0	0	1	0	13	.157	.157	.171	11	-6	-6	2				.879	-2	PO	-0.6
	Chi-N	7	25	3	5	1	2	0	0	0	2	.200	.200	.400	92	-0	-0	2				.778	-2	/OP	-0.1
	Yr	26	95	8	16	2	2	0	1	0	15	.168	.168	.232	33	-6	-7	4				.750	-4	OP	-0.7
1884	Tol-a	94	382	56	89	8	7	0		10		.233	.254	.291	77	-8	-10	29				.845	4	*O/P	-0.7
1885	Bos-N	56	227	44	54	5	3	3	25	7	32	.238	.261	.326	92	-3	-2	20				.867	-2	O	-0.5
1886	Bos-N	88	371	72	97	16	6	3	41	19	52	.261	.297	.361	103	-1	1	50	31			.902	6	*O	0.4
1887	Phi-a	135	585	140	155	18	**19**	4		35		.265	.317	.381	96	-4	-4	101	88			.911	3	*O/2P	-0.3
1888	Phi-a	97	383	76	87	16	6	2	44	31		.227	.294	.316	99	-0	0	50	46			.898	-10	*O	-1.2
Total	6	496	2043	396	498	65	43	12	111	102	99	.244	.285	.335	91	-22	-21	254	165			.885	-4	O/P2	-3.0
■ DAVE POPE	Pope, David b: 6/17/25, Talladega, Ala. BL/TR, 5'10.5", 170 lbs. Deb: 7/01/52																								
1952	Cle-A	12	34	9	10	1	1	1	4	1	7	.294	.314	.471	124	0	1	5	0	0	0	1.000	-1	O	-0.1
1954	*Cle-A	60	102	21	30	2	1	4	13	10	22	.294	.357	.451	118	3	2	16	2	1	0	1.000	-4	O	-0.2
1955	Cle-A	35	104	17	31	5	0	6	22	12	31	.298	.376	.519	134	5	5	21	0	0	0	.954	-3	O	0.1
	Bal-A	86	222	21	55	8	4	1	30	16	34	.248	.304	.333	77	-9	-7	22	5	2	0	1.000	-8	O	-1.8
	Yr	121	326	38	86	13	4	7	52	28	65	.264	.328	.393	97	-4	-2	42	5	2	0	.986	-11	*O	-1.7
1956	Bal-A	12	19	1	3	0	0	0	1	0	7	.158	.200	.158	-5	-3	-3	1	0	0	0	1.000	-1	/O	-0.4
	Cle-A	25	70	6	17	3	1	0	3	1	12	.243	.254	.314	48	-5	-6	6	0	0	0	1.000	-1	O	-0.7
	Yr	37	89	7	20	3	1	0	4	1	19	.225	.242	.281	38	-8	-8	6	0	0	0	1.000	-2	O	-1.1
Total	4	230	551	75	146	19	7	12	73	40	113	.265	.319	.390	92	-9	-7	71	7	3	0	.990	-18	O	-3.1
■ PAUL POPOVICH	Popovich, Paul Edward b: 8/18/40, Flemington, W.Va. BB/TR, 6', 175 lbs. Deb: 4/19/64																								
1964	Chi-N	1	1	0	1	0	0	0	0	0	0	1.000	1.000	1.000	447	0	0	1	0	0	0	.000	0	H	0.0
1966	Chi-N	2	6	0	0	0	0	0	0	0	2	.000	.000	.000	-99	-2	-2	0	0	0	0	.889	-1	/2	-0.3

YEAR	TM/L	G	AB	R	H	2B	3B	HR	RBI	BB	SO	AVG	OBP	SLG	PRO+	BR	/A	RC	SB	CS	SBR	FA	FR	POS	TPR
1967	Chi-N	49	159	18	34	4	0	0	2	9	12	.214	.265	.239	43	-11	-12	9	0	1	-1	.967	-4	S2/3	-1.4
1968	LA-N	134	418	35	97	8	1	2	25	29	37	.232	.283	.270	72	-16	-13	32	1	3	-2	.983	3	2S/3	-0.3
1969	LA-N	28	50	5	10	0	0	0	4	1	4	.200	.216	.200	18	-5	-5	2	0	0	0	.985	0	2/S	-0.4
	Chi-N	60	154	26	48	6	0	1	14	18	14	.312	.387	.370	100	3	1	24	0	1	-1	.974	-6	2/S3O	-0.3
	Yr	88	204	31	58	6	0	1	18	19	18	.284	.348	.328	85	-2	-4	25	0	1	-1	.978	-6	2S/3O	-0.7
1970	Chi-N	78	186	22	47	5	1	4	20	18	18	.253	.325	.355	73	-5	-8	22	0	1	-1	.990	-6	2S3	-1.1
1971	Chi-N	89	226	24	49	7	1	4	28	14	17	.217	.262	.310	54	-12	-15	17	0	1	-1	.985	4	23/S	-1.0
1972	Chi-N	58	129	8	25	3	2	1	11	12	8	.194	.262	.271	47	-8	-10	9	0	1	-1	.981	19	2/S3	1.1
1973	Chi-N	99	280	24	66	6	3	2	24	18	27	.236	.284	.300	58	-14	-17	23	3	2	-0	.981	26	2/S3	1.4
1974	*Pit-N	59	83	9	18	2	1	0	5	5	10	.217	.261	.265	49	-6	-6	6	0	0	0	.962	-1	2S	-0.6
1975	Pit-N	25	40	5	8	1	0	0	1	3	2	.200	.273	.225	40	-3	-3	3	0	0	0	1.000	-3	/2S	-0.6
Total	11	682	1732	176	403	42	9	14	134	127	151	.233	.288	.292	62	-79	-89	147	4	10	-5	.982	31	2S/3O	-3.5

■ GEORGE POPPLEIN
Popplein, George J. b: Baltimore, Md. Deb: 7/11/1873

YEAR	TM/L	G	AB	R	H	2B	3B	HR	RBI	BB	SO	AVG	OBP	SLG	PRO+	BR	/A	RC	SB	CS	SBR	FA	FR	POS	TPR
1873	Mar-n	1	4	0	0	0	0	0	0	0	0	.000	.000	.000	-99	-1	-1	0						/3O	-0.1

■ TOM POQUETTE
Poquette, Thomas Arthur b: 10/30/51, Eau Claire, Wis. BL/TR, 5'10", 175 lbs. Deb: 9/01/73

YEAR	TM/L	G	AB	R	H	2B	3B	HR	RBI	BB	SO	AVG	OBP	SLG	PRO+	BR	/A	RC	SB	CS	SBR	FA	FR	POS	TPR
1973	KC-A	21	28	4	6	1	0	0	3	1	4	.214	.267	.250	43	-2	-2	2	1	1	-0	.870	-4	O	-0.7
1976	*KC-A	104	344	43	104	18	10	2	34	29	31	.302	.363	.430	131	14	13	52	6	5	-1	.979	-8	O/D	0.1
1977	*KC-A	106	342	43	100	23	6	2	33	19	21	.292	.339	.412	103	1	1	47	1	4	-2	1.000	-2	O	-0.6
1978	*KC-A	80	204	16	44	9	2	4	30	14	9	.216	.266	.338	67	-9	-10	18	2	0	1	.955	4	O/D	-0.8
1979	KC-A	21	26	1	5	0	0	0	3	1	4	.192	.222	.192	13	-3	-3	1	0	0	0	1.000	-2	O	-0.5
	Bos-A	63	154	14	51	9	0	2	23	8	7	.331	.376	.429	110	4	2	25	2	2	-1	.949	-7	O/D	-0.6
	Yr	84	180	15	56	9	0	2	26	9	11	.311	.354	.394	97	0	-1	25	2	2	-1	.954	-9	O/D	-1.1
1981	Bos-A	3	2	0	0	0	0	0	0	0	0	.000	.000	.000	-94	-1	-1	0	0	0	0	.000	-1	/O	-0.2
	Tex-A	30	64	2	10	1	0	0	7	5	1	.156	.229	.172	18	-7	-6	2	0	1	-1	.963	-3	O	-1.2
	Yr	33	66	2	10	1	0	0	7	5	1	.152	.222	.167	14	-7	-7	2	0	1	-1	.963	-4	O	-1.4
1982	KC-A	24	62	4	9	1	0	0	3	4	5	.145	.209	.161	3	-8	-8	3	1	0	0	.957	-1	O	-0.9
Total	7	452	1226	127	329	62	18	10	136	81	82	.268	.321	.373	92	-11	-13	149	13	13	-4	.971	-24	O/D	-5.4

■ DAN PORTER
Porter, Daniel Edward b: 10/17/31, Decatur, Ill. BL/TL, 6', 164 lbs. Deb: 8/16/51

YEAR	TM/L	G	AB	R	H	2B	3B	HR	RBI	BB	SO	AVG	OBP	SLG	PRO+	BR	/A	RC	SB	CS	SBR	FA	FR	POS	TPR
1951	Was-A	13	19	2	4	0	0	0	0	2	4	.211	.286	.211	36	-2	-2	1	0	0	0	1.000	-0	/O	-0.2

■ DARRELL PORTER
Porter, Darrell Ray b: 1/17/52, Joplin, Mo. BL/TR, 6', 193 lbs. Deb: 9/02/71

YEAR	TM/L	G	AB	R	H	2B	3B	HR	RBI	BB	SO	AVG	OBP	SLG	PRO+	BR	/A	RC	SB	CS	SBR	FA	FR	POS	TPR
1971	Mil-A	22	70	4	15	2	0	2	9	9	20	.214	.304	.329	80	-2	-2	7	2	2	-1	.977	2	C	0.1
1972	Mil-A	18	56	2	7	1	0	1	2	5	21	.125	.210	.196	22	-5	-5	2	0	0	0	.976	5	C	0.0
1973	Mil-A	117	350	50	89	19	2	16	67	57	85	.254	.365	.457	133	15	16	61	5	2	0	.977	-4	CD	1.7
1974	Mil-A☆	131	432	59	104	15	4	12	56	50	88	.241	.326	.377	103	1	2	54	8	7	-2	.978	-3	*C/D	0.2
1975	Mil-A	130	409	66	95	12	5	18	60	89	77	.232	.376	.418	123	16	16	68	2	5	-2	.979	-2	*C/D	1.7
1976	Mil-A	119	389	43	81	14	1	5	32	51	61	.208	.302	.288	75	-12	-11	37	2	0	1	.975	-5	*C/D	-1.4
1977	*KC-A	130	425	61	117	21	3	16	60	53	70	.275	.357	.452	118	11	11	71	1	0	0	.982	1	*C/D	1.5
1978	*KC-A★	150	520	77	138	27	6	18	78	75	75	.265	.360	.444	122	18	16	82	0	5	-3	.988	-6	*C/D	1.2
1979	KC-A★	157	533	101	155	23	10	20	112	**121**	65	.291	**.429**	.484	143	41	39	119	3	4	-2	.982	-2	*CD	4.0
1980	*KC-A★	118	418	51	104	14	2	7	51	69	50	.249	.358	.342	92	-2	-2	54	1	1	-0	.978	2	CD	0.2
1981	StL-N	61	174	22	39	10	2	6	31	39	32	.224	.369	.408	117	6	5	28	1	2	-1	.979	-3	C	0.4
1982	*StL-N	120	373	46	86	18	5	12	48	66	66	.231	.349	.402	109	6	6	55	1	1	-0	.983	-5	*C	0.4
1983	StL-N	145	443	57	116	24	3	15	66	68	94	.262	.365	.431	120	13	13	71	1	3	-2	.989	-7	*C	1.0
1984	StL-N	127	422	56	98	16	3	11	68	60	79	.232	.335	.363	98	-1	0	52	5	3	-0	.984	-12	*C	-0.6
1985	*StL-N	84	240	30	53	12	2	10	36	41	48	.221	.337	.412	109	3	3	36	6	1	1	.990	-2	C	0.7
1986	Tex-A	68	155	21	41	6	0	12	29	22	51	.265	.360	.535	136	8	8	30	1	1	-0	.994	2	CD	1.1
1987	Tex-A	85	130	19	31	3	0	7	21	30	43	.238	.389	.423	115	4	4	24	0	0	0	1.000	-0	D/C1	0.4
Total	17	1782	5539	765	1369	237	48	188	826	905	1025	.247	.357	.409	113	120	118	853	39	37	-11	.982	-38	*CD/1	12.6

■ IRV PORTER
Porter, Irving Marble b: 5/17/1888, Lynn, Mass. d: 2/20/71, Lynn, Mass. BB/TR, 5'9", 155 lbs. Deb: 8/20/14

YEAR	TM/L	G	AB	R	H	2B	3B	HR	RBI	BB	SO	AVG	OBP	SLG	PRO+	BR	/A	RC	SB	CS	SBR	FA	FR	POS	TPR
1914	Chi-A	1	4	1	1	0	0	0	0	0	1	.250	.250	.250	51	-0	-0	0	0			1.000	-0	/O	-0.1

■ JAY PORTER
Porter, J W "J W" b: 1/17/33, Shawnee, Okla. BR/TR, 6'2", 180 lbs. Deb: 7/30/52

YEAR	TM/L	G	AB	R	H	2B	3B	HR	RBI	BB	SO	AVG	OBP	SLG	PRO+	BR	/A	RC	SB	CS	SBR	FA	FR	POS	TPR
1952	StL-A	33	104	12	26	4	1	0	7	10	10	.250	.316	.308	72	-4	-4	11	4	0	1	.973	-1	O/3	-0.5
1955	Det-A	24	55	6	13	2	0	0	3	8	15	.236	.333	.273	66	-3	-2	5	0	0	0	1.000	-3	/1CO	-0.6
1956	Det-A	14	21	0	2	0	0	0	3	0	8	.095	.095	.095	-49	-4	-5	0	0	0	0	1.000	-1	/CO	-0.5
1957	Det-A	58	140	14	35	8	0	2	18	14	20	.250	.323	.350	82	-3	-4	17	0	0	0	.953	-3	OC/1	-0.8
1958	Cle-A	40	85	13	17	1	0	4	19	9	23	.200	.284	.353	76	-3	-3	8	0	0	0	1.000	-3	C/13	-0.5
1959	Was-A	37	106	8	24	4	0	1	10	11	16	.226	.305	.292	65	-5	-5	10	0	0	0	.993	-1	C/1	-0.5
	StL-N	23	33	5	7	3	0	1	2	1	4	.212	.257	.394	66	-2	-2	3	0	0	0	1.000	0	C/1	-0.1
Total	6	229	544	58	124	22	1	8	62	53	96	.228	.301	.316	68	-23	-24	54	4	0	1	.990	-12	/CO13	-3.5

■ MATTHEW PORTER
Porter, Matthew Sheldon b: Kansas City, Mo. Deb: 6/27/1884 M

YEAR	TM/L	G	AB	R	H	2B	3B	HR	RBI	BB	SO	AVG	OBP	SLG	PRO+	BR	/A	RC	SB	CS	SBR	FA	FR	POS	TPR
1884	KC-U	3	12	1	1	1	0	0		0		.083	.083	.167	-20	-1	-1	0				.750	1	/OM	0.0

■ DICK PORTER
Porter, Richard Twilley "Wiggles" or "Twitches"
b: 12/30/01, Princess Anne, Md. d: 9/24/74, Philadelphia, Pa. BL/TR, 5'10", 170 lbs. Deb: 4/16/29

YEAR	TM/L	G	AB	R	H	2B	3B	HR	RBI	BB	SO	AVG	OBP	SLG	PRO+	BR	/A	RC	SB	CS	SBR	FA	FR	POS	TPR
1929	Cle-A	71	192	26	63	16	5	1	24	17	14	.328	.386	.479	117	6	5	34	3	5	-2	.941	-5	O2	-0.3
1930	Cle-A	119	480	100	168	43	8	4	57	55	31	.350	.420	.498	127	25	22	102	3	3	-1	.962	-4	*O	0.8
1931	Cle-A	114	414	82	129	24	3	1	38	56	36	.312	.395	.391	102	7	3	65	6	9	-4	.970	-6	*O/2	-1.3
1932	Cle-A	146	621	106	191	42	8	4	60	64	43	.308	.373	.420	99	6	-0	99	2	4	-2	.982	-11	*O	-2.1
1933	Cle-A	132	499	73	133	19	6	0	41	51	42	.267	.335	.329	73	-16	-19	57	4	4	-1	**.996**	-1	*O	-2.7
1934	Cle-A	13	44	9	10	2	1	1	6	4	5	.227	.292	.386	73	-2	-2	5	0	0	0	1.000	-1	O	-0.4
	Bos-A	80	265	30	80	13	6	0	56	21	15	.302	.355	.396	87	-3	-5	38	5	2	0	.940	-6	O	-1.3
	Yr	93	309	39	90	15	7	1	62	25	20	.291	.346	.395	85	-5	-7	43	5	2	0	.947	-7	O	-1.7
Total	6	675	2515	426	774	159	37	11	282	268	186	.308	.376	.414	99	22	3	400	23	27	-9	.973	-35	O/2	-7.3

■ BOB PORTER
Porter, Robert Lee b: 7/22/59, Yuma, Ariz. BL/TL, 5'10", 180 lbs. Deb: 5/13/81

YEAR	TM/L	G	AB	R	H	2B	3B	HR	RBI	BB	SO	AVG	OBP	SLG	PRO+	BR	/A	RC	SB	CS	SBR	FA	FR	POS	TPR
1981	Atl-N	17	14	2	4	1	0	0	4	2	1	.286	.375	.357	106	0	0	2	0	0	0	.000	0	/H	0.0
1982	Atl-N	24	27	1	3	0	0	0	0	1	9	.111	.143	.111	-27	-5	-5	1	0	0	0	1.000	-0	/O1	-0.5
Total	2	41	41	3	7	1	0	0	4	3	10	.171	.227	.195	19	-4	-5	3	0	0	0	.986	-0	/O1	-0.5

■ LEO POSADA
Posada, Leopoldo Jesus (Hernandez) b: 4/15/36, Havana, Cuba BR/TR, 5'11", 175 lbs. Deb: 9/21/60

YEAR	TM/L	G	AB	R	H	2B	3B	HR	RBI	BB	SO	AVG	OBP	SLG	PRO+	BR	/A	RC	SB	CS	SBR	FA	FR	POS	TPR
1960	KC-A	10	36	8	13	0	2	1	2	3	7	.361	.410	.556	158	3	3	8	1	0	0	1.000	-2	/O	0.1
1961	KC-A	116	344	37	87	10	4	7	53	36	84	.253	.331	.366	86	-7	-7	43	0	0	0	.973	-3	*O	-1.5
1962	KC-A	29	46	6	9	1	1	0	3	7	14	.196	.302	.261	51	-3	-3	4	0	0	0	1.000	-0	O	-0.4
Total	3	155	426	51	109	11	7	8	58	46	105	.256	.334	.371	88	-7	-7	55	1	0	0	.976	-5	O	-1.8

■ LEW POST
Post, Lewis G. b: 4/12/1875, Hastings, Mich. d: 8/21/44, Chicago, Ill. Deb: 9/21/02

YEAR	TM/L	G	AB	R	H	2B	3B	HR	RBI	BB	SO	AVG	OBP	SLG	PRO+	BR	/A	RC	SB	CS	SBR	FA	FR	POS	TPR
1902	Det-A	3	12	2	1	0	0	0	2	0		.083	.083	.083	-53	-2	-2	0	0			.800	-1	/O	-0.3

YEAR	TM/L	G	AB	R	H	2B	3B	HR	RBI	BB	SO	AVG	OBP	SLG	PRO+	BR	/A	RC	SB	CS	SBR	FA	FR	POS	TPR

■ SAM POST Post, Samuel Gilbert b: 11/17/1896, Richmond, Va. d: 3/31/71, Portsmouth, Va. BL/TL, 6'1.5", 170 lbs. Deb: 4/22/22

| 1922 | Bro-N | 9 | 25 | 3 | 7 | 0 | 0 | 0 | 4 | 1 | 4 | .280 | .308 | .280 | 53 | -2 | -2 | 2 | 1 | 0 | 0 | .982 | -1 | /1 | -0.3 |

■ WALLY POST Post, Walter Charles b: 7/9/29, St.Wendelin, Ohio d: 1/6/82, St.Henry, Ohio BR/TR, 6'1", 203 lbs. Deb: 9/18/49

1949	Cin-N	6	8	1	2	0	0	0	1	0	3	.250	.250	.250	34	-1	-1	0	0			.750	-1	/O	-0.2
1951	Cin-N	15	41	6	9	3	0	1	7	3	4	.220	.273	.366	69	-2	-2	4	0	0	0	.963	1	O	-0.2
1952	Cin-N	19	58	5	9	1	0	2	7	4	20	.155	.222	.276	37	-5	-5	4	0	0	0	1.000	2	O	-0.4
1953	Cin-N	11	33	3	8	1	0	1	4	4	6	.242	.324	.364	78	-1	-1	4	1	0	0	.960	1	O	-0.1
1954	Cin-N	130	451	46	115	21	3	18	83	26	70	.255	.300	.435	86	-9	-11	56	2	2	-1	.957	5	*O	-1.1
1955	Cin-N	154	601	116	186	33	3	40	109	60	102	.309	.374	.574	139	39	34	125	7	4	-0	.978	2	*O	2.8
1956	Cin-N	143	539	94	134	25	3	36	83	37	124	.249	.302	.506	105	7	3	81	6	0	2	.969	12	*O	0.9
1957	Cin-N	134	467	68	114	26	2	20	74	33	84	.244	.294	.437	87	-6	-10	57	2	2	-1	.985	10	*O	-0.7
1958	Phi-N	110	379	51	107	21	3	12	62	32	74	.282	.343	.449	100	4	4	59	0	2	-1	.952	8	O	0.6
1959	Phi-N	132	468	62	119	17	6	22	94	36	101	.254	.312	.457	100	-0	-1	67	0	0	0	.992	9	O	0.1
1960	Phi-N	34	84	11	24	6	1	2	12	9	24	.286	.355	.452	119	2	2	14	0	0	0	1.000	1	O	0.2
	Cin-N	77	249	36	70	14	0	17	38	28	51	.281	.354	.542	139	13	13	43	0	2	-1	.985	4	O	1.3
	Yr	111	333	47	94	20	1	19	50	37	75	.282	.354	.520	134	16	15	58	0	2	-1	.989	5	O	1.5
1961	*Cin-N	99	282	44	83	16	3	20	57	22	61	.294	.348	.585	140	15	15	55	0	1	-1	.959	-1	O	0.9
1962	Cin-N	109	285	43	75	10	3	17	62	32	67	.263	.342	.498	118	8	7	48	0	0	0	.935	-11	O	-0.7
1963	Cin-N	5	7	1	0	0	0	0	0	1	0	.000	.125	.000	-59	-1	-1	-0	0	0	0	1.000	0	O	-0.1
	Min-A	21	47	6	9	0	1	2	6	2	17	.191	.224	.362	60	-3	-3	4	0	0	0	1.000	-2	O	-0.5
1964	Cle-A	5	8	1	0	0	0	0	0	3	4	.000	.273	.000	-16	-1	-1	0	0	0	0	.667	-1	/O	-0.2
Total	15	1204	4007	594	1064	194	28	210	699	331	813	.266	.325	.485	109	59	42	620	19	13		.970	38	*O	2.6

■ MIKE POTTER Potter, Michael Gary b: 5/16/51, Montebello, Cal. BR/TR, 6'1", 195 lbs. Deb: 9/06/76

1976	StL-N	9	16	0	0	0	0	0	0	1	6	.000	.059	.000	-82	-4	-4	0	0	0	0	1.000	0	/O	-0.4
1977	StL-N	5	7	0	0	0	0	0	0	0	2	.000	.000	.000	-99	-2	-2	0	0	0	0	1.000	0	/O	-0.2
Total	2	14	23	0	0	0	0	0	0	1	8	.000	.042	.000	-87	-6	-6	0	0	0	0	1.000	0	/O	-0.6

■ DAN POTTS Potts, Daniel b: Kent, Ohio Deb: 10/03/1892

| 1892 | Was-N | 1 | 4 | 0 | 1 | 0 | 0 | 0 | | 0 | 1 | .250 | .250 | .250 | 54 | -0 | -0 | 0 | 0 | | | 1.000 | 1 | /C | 0.0 |

■ JOHN POTTS Potts, John Frederick "Fred" b: 2/6/1887, Tipp City, Ohio d: 9/5/62, Cleveland, Ohio BL/TR, 5'7", 165 lbs. Deb: 4/18/14

| 1914 | KC-F | 41 | 102 | 14 | 27 | 4 | 0 | 1 | 9 | 25 | 13 | .265 | .414 | .333 | 119 | 4 | 4 | 18 | 7 | | | .933 | -4 | O | -0.1 |

■ KEN POULSEN Poulsen, Ken Sterling b: 8/4/47, Van Nuys, Cal. BL/TR, 6'1", 190 lbs. Deb: 7/03/67

| 1967 | Bos-A | 5 | 5 | 0 | 1 | 1 | 0 | 0 | 0 | 0 | 2 | .200 | .200 | .400 | 68 | -0 | -0 | 0 | 0 | 0 | 0 | .667 | -1 | /3S | -0.1 |

■ ALONZO POWELL Powell, Alonzo Sidney b: 12/12/64, San Francisco, Cal. BR/TR, 6'2", 190 lbs. Deb: 4/06/87

1987	Mon-N	14	41	3	8	3	0	0	4	5	17	.195	.283	.268	46	-3	-3	3	0	0	0	1.000	-1	O	-0.5
1991	Sea-A	57	111	16	24	6	1	3	12	11	24	.216	.293	.369	82	-3	-3	12	0	2	-1	.960	-9	O/1D	-1.4
Total	2	71	152	19	32	9	1	3	16	16	41	.211	.290	.342	71	-6	-6	15	0	2	-1	.968	-10	/OD1	-1.9

■ JAKE POWELL Powell, Alvin Jacob b: 7/15/08, Silver Spring, Md d: 11/4/48, Washington, D.C. BR/TR, 5'11.5", 180 lbs. Deb: 8/03/30

1930	Was-A	3	4	1	0	0	0	0	0	0	1	.000	.000	.000	-99	-1	-1	0	0	0	0	1.000	-0	/O	-0.1
1934	Was-A	9	35	6	10	2	0	0	1	4	2	.286	.359	.343	85	-1	-1	4	1	1	-0	.955	1	/O	0.0
1935	Was-A	139	551	88	172	26	10	6	98	37	37	.312	.360	.428	107	2	4	85	15	7	0	.976	0	*O/2	0.0
1936	Was-A	53	210	40	62	11	5	1	30	18	21	.295	.357	.410	94	-4	-2	31	10	4	1	.951	-7	O	-1.0
	*NY-A	87	328	62	99	13	3	7	48	33	30	.302	.366	.424	98	-3	-1	52	16	7	1	.976	0	O	-0.3
	Yr	140	538	102	161	24	8	8	78	51	51	.299	.362	.418	96	-7	-3	83	26	11	1	.967	-7	*O	-1.3
1937	*NY-A	97	365	54	96	22	3	3	45	25	36	.263	.314	.364	70	-17	-18	42	7	5	-1	.981	1	O	-1.9
1938	*NY-A	45	164	27	42	12	1	2	20	15	20	.256	.326	.378	76	-6	-6	21	3	1	0	.978	-3	O	-0.9
1939	NY-A	31	86	12	21	4	1	1	9	3	8	.244	.270	.349	58	-6	-6	7	1	2	-1	.983	0	O	-0.6
1940	NY-A	12	27	3	5	0	0	0	2	1	4	.185	.214	.185	5	-4	-4	1	0	0	0	1.000	0	/O	-0.3
1943	Was-A	37	132	14	35	10	2	0	20	5	13	.265	.297	.371	99	-1	-1	13	3	5	-2	.978	2	O	-0.3
1944	Was-A	96	367	29	88	9	1	1	37	16	26	.240	.272	.278	60	-21	-19	29	7	2	1	.980	-4	O/3	-2.4
1945	Was-A	31	98	4	19	2	0	0	3	8	8	.194	.255	.214	40	-8	-7	6	1	1	-0	.950	-1	O	-1.1
	Phi-N	48	173	13	40	5	0	1	14	8	13	.231	.265	.277	52	-12	-11	11	1			.986	-4	O	-1.7
Total	11	688	2540	353	689	116	26	22	327	173	219	.271	.320	.363	81	-82	-72	303	65	35		.975	-9	O/23	-10.6

■ ABNER POWELL Powell, Charles Abner "Ab" b: 12/15/1860, Shenandoah, Pa. d: 8/7/53, New Orleans, La. BR/TR, 5'7", 160 lbs. Deb: 8/04/1884

1884	Was-U	48	191	36	54	10	5	0			3	.283	.294	.387	133	5	6	22				.875	-2	OP/3S2	0.0
1886	Bal-a	11	39	4	7	2	1	0			1	.179	.200	.282	53	-2	-2	3	4			.917	1	/PO	-0.2
	Cin-a	19	74	13	17	1	1	0			4	.230	.269	.270	69	-2	-3	6	0			.760	0	O/SP	-0.2
	Yr	30	113	17	24	3	2	0			5	.212	.246	.274	64	-5	-5	9	4			.735	1	OP/S	-0.4
Total	2	78	304	53	78	13	7	0			8	.257	.276	.345	105	0	1	31	4			.817	-1	/OPS32	-0.4

■ HOSKEN POWELL Powell, Hosken b: 5/14/55, Selma, Ala. BL/TL, 6'1", 185 lbs. Deb: 4/05/78

1978	Min-A	121	381	55	94	20	2	3	31	45	31	.247	.326	.333	84	-6	-7	44	11	5	0	.983	-1	*O	-1.3
1979	Min-A	104	338	49	99	17	3	2	36	33	25	.293	.361	.379	96	1	-1	47	5	1	1	.977	-2	O/D	-0.6
1980	Min-A	137	485	58	127	17	5	6	35	32	46	.262	.312	.355	76	-12	-17	53	14	3	2	.968	7	*O	-1.2
1981	Min-A	80	264	30	63	11	3	2	25	17	31	.239	.287	.326	71	-8	-10	24	7	4	-0	.970	2	O/D	-1.2
1982	Tor-A	112	265	43	73	13	4	3	26	12	23	.275	.307	.389	82	-4	-7	30	4	4	-1	.974	-9	OD	-1.9
1983	Tor-A	40	83	6	14	0	0	1	7	5	8	.169	.216	.205	16	-9	-10	4	2	0	1	.981	-4	O/1D	-1.4
Total	6	594	1816	241	470	78	17	17	160	144	164	.259	.316	.349	79	-40	-52	202	43	17	3	.975	-8	O/D1	-7.6

■ JIM POWELL Powell, James Edwin b: 8/30/1859, Richmond, Va. d: 11/20/29, Butte, Mon. 5'10", 170 lbs. Deb: 8/05/1884

| 1884 | Ric-a | 41 | 151 | 23 | 37 | 8 | 4 | 0 | | | 7 | .245 | .296 | .351 | 115 | 2 | 3 | 16 | | | | .943 | 1 | 1 | -0.1 |

■ BOOG POWELL Powell, John Wesley b: 8/17/41, Lakeland, Fla. BL/TR, 6'4", 240 lbs. Deb: 9/26/61

1961	Bal-A	4	13	0	1	0	0	0	1	0	2	.077	.077	.077	-60	-3	-3	0	0	0	0	1.000	-1	/O	-0.4
1962	Bal-A	124	400	44	97	13	2	15	53	38	79	.243	.311	.398	94	-7	-4	47	1	1	-0	.969	-7	*O/1	-1.8
1963	Bal-A	140	491	67	130	22	2	25	82	49	70	.265	.331	.470	124	13	15	74	1	2	-1	.969	-8	*O1	-0.1
1964	Bal-A	134	424	74	123	17	0	39	99	76	91	.290	.400	.606	176	44	44	105	0	0	0	.974	4	*O/1	4.4
1965	Bal-A	144	472	54	117	20	2	17	72	71	93	.248	.351	.407	112	10	9	71	1	1	-0	.992	3	1O	0.6
1966	*Bal-A	140	491	78	141	18	0	34	109	67	125	.287	.374	.532	159	36	37	97	0	4	-2	.989	-7	*1	2.0
1967	Bal-A	125	415	53	97	14	1	13	55	55	94	.234	.326	.366	105	3	3	51	1	3	-2	.986	-4	*1	-1.0
1968	Bal-A★	154	550	60	137	21	0	22	85	73	97	.249	.340	.411	127	18	18	79	7	1	2	.990	-5	*1	0.4
1969	*Bal-A★	152	533	83	162	25	0	37	121	72	76	.304	.388	.559	161	43	43	112	1	1	-0	.995	-2	*1	3.0
1970	*Bal-A★	154	526	82	156	28	0	35	114	104	80	.297	.417	.549	163	49	48	123	1	1	0	.992	-2	*1	3.4
1971	*Bal-A†	128	418	59	107	19	0	22	92	82	64	.256	.383	.459	139	23	23	77	1	0	1	.995	-3	*1	1.0
1972	*Bal-A	140	465	53	117	20	1	21	81	65	92	.252	.348	.434	129	19	17	71	4	0	1	.988	-3	*1	0.6
1973	*Bal-A	114	370	50	98	13	1	11	54	85	64	.265	.402	.395	126	17	17	62	0	2	-1	.989	2	*1	0.9
1974	*Bal-A	110	344	37	91	13	0	12	45	52	58	.265	.361	.413	126	11	10	49	0	3	-1	.996	1	*1/D	0.7
1975	Cle-A	134	435	64	129	18	0	27	86	59	72	.297	.382	.524	154	31	31	89	1	3	-2	.997	-2	*1/D	2.0

YEAR	TM/L	G	AB	R	H	2B	3B	HR	RBI	BB	SO	AVG	OBP	SLG	PRO+	BR	/A	RC	SB	CS	SBR	FA	FR	POS	TPR
1976	Cle-A	95	293	29	63	9	0	9	33	41	43	.215	.311	.338	91	-3	-3	31	1	1	-0	.987	1	1	-0.9
1977	LA-N	50	41	0	10	0	0	0	5	12	9	.244	.415	.244	82	-0	-0	5	0	0	0	.938	-1	/1	-0.1
Total	17	2042	6681	889	1776	270	11	339	1187	1001	1226	.266	.364	.462	134	305	309	1145	20	21	-7	.991	-33	*1O/D	14.7

■ MARTIN POWELL
Powell, Martin J. b: 3/25/1856, Fitchburg, Mass. d: 2/5/1888, Fitchburg, Mass. BL/TL, 6', 170 lbs. Deb: 6/18/1881

YEAR	TM/L	G	AB	R	H	2B	3B	HR	RBI	BB	SO	AVG	OBP	SLG	PRO+	BR	/A	RC	SB	CS	SBR	FA	FR	POS	TPR
1881	Det-N	55	219	47	74	9	4	1	38	15	9	.338	.380	.429	148	14	12	37				.947	-3	1/C	0.4
1882	Det-N	80	338	44	81	13	0	0	29	19	27	.240	.280	.278	80	-7	-7	27				.940	-5	*1	-1.9
1883	Det-N	101	421	76	115	17	5	1	48	28	23	.273	.318	.344	106	1	5	47				.950	-3	*1	-0.7
1884	Cin-U	43	185	46	59	4	2	1		13		.319	.364	.378	140	10	8	26				.940	-2	1	0.1
1885	Phi-a	19	75	5	12	0	3	0		1		.160	.192	.240	35	-5	-6	4				.973	-0	1	-0.8
Total	5	298	1238	218	341	43	14	3	115	76	59	.275	.318	.340	108	13	12	141				.947	-13	1/C	-2.9

■ PAUL POWELL
Powell, Paul Ray b: 3/19/48, San Angelo, Tex. BR/TR, 5'11", 185 lbs. Deb: 4/07/71

YEAR	TM/L	G	AB	R	H	2B	3B	HR	RBI	BB	SO	AVG	OBP	SLG	PRO+	BR	/A	RC	SB	CS	SBR	FA	FR	POS	TPR
1971	Min-A	20	31	7	5	0	0	1	2	3	12	.161	.235	.258	38	-3	-3	2	0	0	0	1.000	-2	O	-0.6
1973	LA-N	2	1	0	0	0	0	0	0	0	1	.000	.000	.000	-99	-0	-0	0	0	0	0	.000	0	/O	0.0
1975	LA-N	8	10	2	2	1	0	0	0	1	2	.200	.273	.300	61	-1	-1	1	0	0	0	.955	1	/CO	0.1
Total	3	30	42	9	7	1	0	1	2	4	15	.167	.239	.262	41	-3	-3	2	0	0	0	1.000	-1	/OC	-0.5

■ RAY POWELL
Powell, Raymond Reath "Rabbit" b: 11/20/1888, Siloam Springs, Ark. d: 10/16/62, Chillicothe, Mo. BL/TR, 5'9", 160 lbs. Deb: 4/16/13

YEAR	TM/L	G	AB	R	H	2B	3B	HR	RBI	BB	SO	AVG	OBP	SLG	PRO+	BR	/A	RC	SB	CS	SBR	FA	FR	POS	TPR
1913	Det-A	2	0	0	0	0	0	0	0	0	0	—	—	—	—	0	0	0	0			.000	0	/O	0.0
1917	Bos-N	88	357	42	97	10	4	4	30	24	54	.272	.318	.356	113	2	4	42	12			.976	9	O	0.9
1918	Bos-N	53	188	31	40	7	5	0	20	29	30	.213	.321	.303	95	-1	-0	19	2			.949	-0	O	-0.4
1919	Bos-N	123	470	51	111	12	12	2	33	41	79	.236	.303	.326	93	-6	-4	49	16			.951	1	*O	-1.3
1920	Bos-N	147	609	69	137	12	12	6	29	44	83	.225	.282	.314	74	-23	-20	51	10	18	-8	.956	5	*O	-3.7
1921	Bos-N	149	624	114	191	25	**18**	12	74	58	85	.306	.369	.462	125	16	21	102	6	17	-8	.954	3	*O	0.4
1922	Bos-N	142	550	82	163	22	11	6	37	59	66	.296	.369	.409	105	1	5	82	3	12	-6	.980	12	*O	0.0
1923	Bos-N	97	338	57	102	20	4	4	38	45	36	.302	.385	.420	117	7	9	55	1	6	-3	.941	-4	O	-0.3
1924	Bos-N	74	188	21	49	9	1	1	15	21	28	.261	.338	.335	85	-5	-3	22	1	3	-2	.947	4	O	-0.3
Total	9	875	3324	467	890	117	67	35	276	321	461	.268	.336	.375	102	-8	12	421	51	56		.959	29	O	-4.7

■ LEROY POWELL
Powell, Robert Leroy b: 10/17/33, Flint, Mich. BR/TR, 6'1", 190 lbs. Deb: 9/16/55

YEAR	TM/L	G	AB	R	H	2B	3B	HR	RBI	BB	SO	AVG	OBP	SLG	PRO+	BR	/A	RC	SB	CS	SBR	FA	FR	POS	TPR
1955	Chi-A	1	0	0	0	0	0	0	0	0	0	—	—	—	—	0	0	0	0	0	0	.000	0	R	0.0
1957	Chi-A	1	0	1	0	0	0	0	0	0	0	—	—	—	—	0	0	0	0	0	0	.000	0	R	0.0
Total	2	2	0	1	0	0	0	0	0	0	0	—	—	—	—	0	0	0	0	0	0		0		0.0

■ TOM POWER
Power, Thomas E. b: San Francisco, Cal. d: 2/25/1898, San Francisco, Cal 5'11", 164 lbs. Deb: 8/27/1890

YEAR	TM/L	G	AB	R	H	2B	3B	HR	RBI	BB	SO	AVG	OBP	SLG	PRO+	BR	/A	RC	SB	CS	SBR	FA	FR	POS	TPR
1890	Bal-a	38	125	11	26	3	1	0		13		.208	.293	.248	59	-6	-7	11	6			.960	-4	12	-0.9

■ VIC POWER
Power, Victor Pellot (b: Victor Pellot (Power)) b: 11/1/31, Arecibo, P.R. BR/TR, 5'11", 195 lbs. Deb: 4/13/54

YEAR	TM/L	G	AB	R	H	2B	3B	HR	RBI	BB	SO	AVG	OBP	SLG	PRO+	BR	/A	RC	SB	CS	SBR	FA	FR	POS	TPR
1954	Phi-A	127	462	36	118	17	5	8	38	19	19	.255	.288	.366	78	-16	-16	44	2	1	0	.985	10	*O1/S3	-1.1
1955	KC-A★	147	596	91	190	34	10	19	76	35	27	.319	.357	.505	128	21	20	103	0	2	-1	.993	14	*1	2.4
1956	KC-A★	127	530	77	164	21	5	14	63	24	16	.309	.341	.447	106	3	3	80	2	2	-1	.993	8	12/O	0.8
1957	KC-A	129	467	48	121	15	1	14	42	19	21	.259	.292	.385	82	-12	-13	50	3	2	-0	**.998**	12	*1/O2	-0.8
1958	KC-A	52	205	35	62	13	4	4	27	7	3	.302	.325	.463	112	3	3	28	1	1	-0	.992	6	1/2	0.5
	Cle-A	93	385	63	122	24	6	12	53	13	11	.317	.341	.504	133	13	15	65	2	1	0	.977	6	312/SO	2.0
	Yr	145	590	98	184	37	**10**	16	80	20	14	.312	.336	.490	125	17	17	92	3	2	-0	.992	11	132/SO	2.5
1959	Cle-A★	147	595	102	172	31	6	10	60	40	22	.289	.336	.412	108	3	5	75	9	13	-5	**.995**	10	*12/3	0.4
1960	Cle-A★	147	580	69	167	26	3	10	84	24	20	.288	.316	.395	94	-9	-6	69	9	5	-0	**.996**	21	*1/S3	0.3
1961	Cle-A	147	563	64	151	34	4	5	63	38	16	.268	.316	.369	85	-15	-13	62	4	3	-1	.994	18	*1/2	-0.6
1962	Min-A	144	611	80	177	28	2	16	63	22	35	.290	.318	.421	93	-4	-7	79	7	1	2	.993	9	*1/2	-0.6
1963	Min-A	138	541	65	146	28	2	10	52	22	24	.270	.298	.384	88	-8	-10	59	3	1	0	.992	-1	*12/3	-1.4
1964	Min-A	19	45	6	10	2	0	0	1	1	3	.222	.239	.267	40	-4	-4	3	0	0	0	.990	1	1/2	-0.3
	LA-A	68	221	17	55	6	0	3	13	8	14	.249	.278	.317	72	-11	-8	18	1	1	-0	1.000	2	13/2	-0.8
	Yr	87	266	23	65	8	0	3	14	9	17	.244	.272	.308	66	-14	-12	21	1	1	-0	.998	4	13/2	-1.1
	Phi-N	18	48	1	10	4	0	0	3	2	3	.208	.240	.292	50	-3	-3	3	0	0	0	.993	1	1	-0.2
1965	Cal-A	124	197	11	51	7	1	1	20	5	13	.259	.281	.320	72	-8	-7	17	2	2	-1	.996	6	*1/23	-0.5
Total	12	1627	6046	765	1716	290	49	126	658	279	247	.284	.317	.411	97	-46	-41	755	45	35	-7	.994	123	*120/3S	0.1

■ MIKE POWERS
Powers, Ellis Foree b: 3/2/06, Crestwood, Ky. d: 12/2/83, Louisville, Ky. BL/TL, 6'1", 185 lbs. Deb: 8/19/32

YEAR	TM/L	G	AB	R	H	2B	3B	HR	RBI	BB	SO	AVG	OBP	SLG	PRO+	BR	/A	RC	SB	CS	SBR	FA	FR	POS	TPR
1932	Cle-A	14	33	4	6	4	0	0	5	2	2	.182	.229	.303	34	-3	-4	2	0	0	0	.917	-2	/O	-0.5
1933	Cle-A	24	47	6	13	2	1	0	2	6	6	.277	.358	.362	87	-0	-1	6	2	1	0	.952	-2	O	-0.3
Total	2	38	80	10	19	6	1	0	7	8	8	.237	.307	.338	65	-4	-4	9	2	1	0	.939	-3	/O	-0.8

■ JOHN POWERS
Powers, John Calvin b: 7/8/29, Birmingham, Ala. BL/TR, 6', 190 lbs. Deb: 9/24/55

YEAR	TM/L	G	AB	R	H	2B	3B	HR	RBI	BB	SO	AVG	OBP	SLG	PRO+	BR	/A	RC	SB	CS	SBR	FA	FR	POS	TPR
1955	Pit-N	2	4	0	1	0	0	0	0	0	0	.250	.250	.250	34	-0	-0	0	0	0	0	1.000	-0	/O	0.0
1956	Pit-N	11	21	0	1	0	0	0	0	1	4	.048	.091	.048	-63	-5	-5	0	0	0	0	1.000	-0	/O	-0.5
1957	Pit-N	20	35	7	10	3	0	2	8	5	9	.286	.419	.543	161	3	3	9	0	0	0	1.000	0	/O	0.3
1958	Pit-N	57	82	6	15	1	0	2	2	8	19	.183	.256	.268	40	-7	-7	5	0	0	0	1.000	0	O	-0.7
1959	Cin-N	43	43	8	11	2	1	2	4	3	13	.256	.319	.488	108	1	0	7	0	0	0	1.000	-1	/O	-0.1
1960	Bal-A	10	18	3	2	0	0	0	0	3	1	.111	.238	.111	-2	-3	-3	1	0	0	0	.833	-1	/O	-0.4
	Cle-A	8	12	2	2	1	1	0	0	2	2	.167	.286	.417	90	-0	-0	1	0	0	0	1.000	-1	/O	-0.1
	Yr	18	30	5	4	1	1	0	0	5	3	.133	.257	.233	34	-3	-3	2	0	0	0	.929	-1	/O	-0.5
Total	6	151	215	26	42	7	2	6	14	22	48	.195	.282	.330	64	-12	-11	23	0	0	0	.986	-2	/O	-1.5

■ LES POWERS
Powers, Leslie Edwin b: 11/5/09, Ballard, Wash. d: 11/13/78, Santa Monica, Cal. BL/TL, 6', 175 lbs. Deb: 9/17/38

YEAR	TM/L	G	AB	R	H	2B	3B	HR	RBI	BB	SO	AVG	OBP	SLG	PRO+	BR	/A	RC	SB	CS	SBR	FA	FR	POS	TPR
1938	NY-N	2	3	0	0	0	0	0	0	0	1	.000	.000	.000	-99	-1	-1	0	0			.000	0	H	-0.1
1939	Phi-N	19	52	7	18	1	1	0	2	4	6	.346	.393	.404	118	1	1	9	0			.983	-2	1	-0.2
Total	2	21	55	7	18	1	1	0	2	4	7	.327	.373	.382	106	0	1	9	0			.988	-2	/1	-0.3

■ MIKE POWERS
Powers, Michael Riley "Doc" b: 9/22/1870, Pittsfield, Mass. d: 4/26/09, Philadelphia, Pa. BR/TR, Deb: 6/12/1898

YEAR	TM/L	G	AB	R	H	2B	3B	HR	RBI	BB	SO	AVG	OBP	SLG	PRO+	BR	/A	RC	SB	CS	SBR	FA	FR	POS	TPR
1898	Lou-N	34	99	13	27	4	3	1	19	5		.273	.308	.404	105	-0	0	13	1			.962	-3	C/1O	-0.1
1899	Lou-N	49	169	15	35	8	2	0	22	6		.207	.239	.278	42	-14	-14	12	1			.942	-7	C/1	-1.7
	Was-N	14	38	3	10	2	0	0	3	1		.263	.282	.316	65	-2	-2	4	0			.942	-0	C/1	-0.1
	Yr	63	207	18	45	10	2	0	25	7		.217	.247	.285	46	-16	-16	16	1			.942	-8	C/1	-1.8
1901	Phi-A	116	431	53	108	26	5	1	47	18		.251	.292	.341	72	-15	-18	47	10			.952	-5	*C/1	-1.1
1902	Phi-A	71	246	35	65	7	1	2	39	14		.264	.312	.325	74	-8	-9	27	3			.950	4	C/1	0.2
1903	Phi-A	75	247	19	56	11	1	0	23	5		.227	.242	.279	54	-13	-15	18	1			.982	-2	C/1	-1.0
1904	Phi-A	57	184	11	35	3	0	0	11	6		.190	.220	.207	34	-13	-14	10	3			.965	-5	C/O	-1.4
1905	*Phi-A	21	60	6	10	0	0	0	5	0		.167	.180	.167	10	-6	-6	2	2			.928	3	C	-0.1
	NY-A	11	33	3	6	1	0	0	2	1		.182	.206	.212	29	-3	-3	1	0			.975	-0	/1C	-0.3
	*Phi-A	19	61	2	8	0	0	0	5	3		.131	.172	.131	-3	-7	-7	2	2			.991	-5	C	-1.2
	Yr	51	154	11	24	1	0	0	12	4		.156	.182	.162	9	-16	-16	6	4			.957	-2	C/1	-1.6
1906	Phi-A	58	185	5	29	1	0	0	7	1		.157	.170	.162	4	-20	-21	6	2			.974	9	C/1	-0.7
1907	Phi-A	59	159	9	29	3	0	0	9	7		.182	.217	.201	33	-12	-12	9	1			.983	14	C	0.7
1908	Phi-A	62	172	8	31	6	1	0	7	5		.180	.217	.227	41	-11	-12	9	1			.967	7	C/1	0.0

YEAR	TM/L	G	AB	R	H	2B	3B	HR	RBI	BB	SO	AVG	OBP	SLG	PRO+	BR	/A	RC	SB	CS	SBR	FA	FR	POS	TPR
1909	Phi-A	1	4	1	1	0	0	0	0	0		.250	.250	.250	57	-0	-0	0	0			1.000	0	/C	0.0
Total	11	647	2088	183	450	72	13	4	199	72		.216	.248	.268	51	-124	-133	161	27			.965	12	C/1O	-6.8
■ PHIL POWERS Powers, Phillip B. "Grandmother" b: 7/26/1854, New York, N.Y. d: 12/22/14, New York, N.Y. BR/TR, 5'7", 166 lbs. Deb: 8/31/1878 U																									
1878	Chi-N	8	31	2	5	1	1	0	2	1	5	.161	.188	.258	42	-2	-2	2				.930	5	/C	0.3
1880	Bos-N	37	126	11	18	5	0	0	10	5	15	.143	.176	.183	22	-10	-9	4				.851	-5	C/O	-1.3
1881	Cle-N	5	15	1	1	0	0	0	0	1	2	.067	.125	.067	-40	-2	-2	0				.955	-1	/C3	-0.2
1882	Cin-a	16	60	4	13	1	1	0		3		.217	.254	.267	72	-1	-2	4				.921	3	C/1O	0.0
1883	Cin-a	30	114	16	28	1	4	0		3		.246	.265	.325	84	-1	-2	10				.893	-2	CO	-0.3
1884	Cin-a	34	130	10	18	1	0	0		5		.138	.170	.146	6	-13	-14	3				.891	5	C/O1	-0.6
1885	Cin-a	15	60	6	16	2	0	0		0		.267	.267	.300	80	-1	-2	5				.833	-3	C	-0.3
	Bal-a	9	34	6	4	1	0	0		1		.118	.143	.147	-7	-4	-4	1				.844	-4	/CO	-0.7
	Yr	24	94	12	20	3	0	0		1		.213	.221	.245	49	-5	-5	5				.837	-7	C/O	-1.0
Total	7	154	570	56	103	12	6	0	12	19	22	.181	.207	.223	41	-35	-37	29				.877	-2	C/O13	-3.1
■ CARL POWIS Powis, Carl Edgar "Jug" b: 1/11/28, Philadelphia, Pa. BR/TR, 6', 185 lbs. Deb: 4/15/57																									
1957	Bal-A	15	41	4	8	3	1	0	2	7	9	.195	.327	.317	82	-1	-1	5	2	0	1	.909	-1	O	-0.2
■ JOHNNY PRAMESA Pramesa, John Steven b: 8/28/25, Barton, Ohio BR/TR, 6'2", 210 lbs. Deb: 4/24/49																									
1949	Cin-N	17	25	2	6	1	0	1	2	3	5	.240	.321	.400	91	-0	-0	3	0			.966	-1	C	-0.1
1950	Cin-N	74	228	14	70	10	1	5	30	19	15	.307	.363	.425	106	2	2	34	0			.981	0	C	0.5
1951	Cin-N	72	227	12	52	5	2	6	22	5	17	.229	.246	.348	57	-14	-15	18	0	0	0	.968	-7	C	-1.9
1952	Chi-N	22	46	1	13	1	0	1	5	4	4	.283	.340	.370	96	-0	-0	6	0	0	0	.958	2	C	0.2
Total	4	185	526	29	141	17	3	13	59	31	41	.268	.310	.386	84	-12	-13	61	0	0		.973	-6	C	-1.3
■ DEL PRATT Pratt, Derrill Burnham b: 1/10/1888, Walhalla, S.C. d: 9/30/77, Texas City, Tex. BR/TR, 5'11", 175 lbs. Deb: 4/11/12																									
1912	StL-A	152	570	76	172	26	15	5	69	36		.302	.348	.426	125	13	16	91	24			.943	14	*2S/O3	2.8
1913	StL-A	155	592	60	175	31	13	2	87	40	57	.296	.341	.402	121	10	12	89	37			.951	5	*2/1	1.6
1914	StL-A	158	584	85	165	34	13	5	65	50	45	.283	.341	.411	131	16	19	83	37	28	-6	.944	-2	*2	1.1
1915	StL-A	159	602	61	175	31	11	3	78	26	43	.291	.323	.394	119	7	9	80	32	23	-4	.965	12	*2	2.0
1916	StL-A	158	596	64	159	35	12	5	**103**	54	56	.267	.331	.391	123	10	13	80	26	17	-2	.966	22	*2	4.2
1917	StL-A	123	450	40	111	22	8	1	53	33	36	.247	.301	.338	98	-4	-2	49	18			.959	15	*2/1	2.0
1918	NY-A	126	477	65	131	19	7	2	55	35	26	.275	.327	.356	104	2	1	59	12			.969	12	*2	2.3
1919	NY-A	140	527	69	154	27	7	4	56	36	24	.292	.342	.393	105	3	3	75	22			.969	**28**	*2	3.8
1920	NY-A	154	574	84	180	37	8	4	97	50	24	.314	.372	.427	107	9	6	91	12	10	-2	.971	12	*2	2.0
1921	Bos-A	135	521	80	169	36	10	5	102	44	10	.324	.378	.461	116	10	12	89	8	10	-4	.961	-1	*2	0.9
1922	Bos-A	154	607	73	183	44	7	6	86	53	20	.301	.361	.427	106	4	4	93	7	10	-4	.966	-13	*2	-0.8
1923	Det-A	101	297	43	92	18	3	0	40	25	9	.310	.375	.391	104	1	2	46	5	1	1	.947	-10	213	-0.6
1924	Det-A	121	429	56	130	32	3	1	77	31	10	.303	.353	.399	95	-5	-4	59	6	9	-4	.948	-2	21/3O	-1.1
Total	13	1836	6826	856	1996	392	117	43	968	513	360	.292	.345	.403	112	76	91	984	246	108		.960	91	*2/1S3O	20.2
■ FRANK PRATT Pratt, Francis Bruce "Truckhorse" b: 8/24/1897, Blocton, Ala. d: 3/8/74, Centreville, Ala. BL/TR, 5'9.5", 155 lbs. Deb: 5/13/21																									
1921	Chi-A	1	1	0	0	0	0	0	0	0	0	.000	.000	.000	-99	-0	-0	0	0	0	0	.000	0	H	0.0
■ LARRY PRATT Pratt, Lester John b: 10/8/1886, Gibson City, Ill. d: 1/8/69, Peoria, Ill. BR/TR, 6' ", 183 lbs. Deb: 9/19/14																									
1914	Bos-A	5	4	0	0	0	0	0	0	0	4	.000	.000	.000	-99	-1	-1	0	0			.923	2	/C	0.1
1915	Bro-F	20	49	5	9	1	0	1	2	2	18	.184	.216	.265	41	-4	-4	3	2			.949	-1	C	-0.3
	New-F	5	4	2	2	2	0	0	0	3	1	.500	.714	1.000	426	2	2	4	2			1.000	-1	/C	0.2
	Yr	25	53	7	11	3	0	1	2	5	19	.208	.276	.321	76	-2	-2	6	4			.953	-1	C	-0.1
Total	2	30	57	7	11	3	0	1	2	5	23	.193	.258	.298	64	-3	-3	8	4			.949	0	/C	-0.0
■ TOM PRATT Pratt, Thomas J. b: 1844, Chelsea, Mass. d: 9/28/08, Philadelphia, Pa. TL , 5'7.5", 150 lbs. Deb: 10/18/1871 U																									
1871	Ath-n	1	6	2	2	0	0	0	1	0	0	.333	.333	.333	93	-0	-0	1	0					/1	0.0
■ TODD PRATT Pratt, Todd Alan b: 2/9/67, Bellevue, Neb. BR/TR, 6'3", 195 lbs. Deb: 7/29/92																									
1992	Phi-N	16	46	6	13	1	0	2	10	4	12	.283	.340	.435	119	1	1	6	0	0	0	.972	-1	C	0.1
■ MEL PREIBISCH Preibisch, Melvin Adolphus "Primo" b: 11/23/14, Sealy, Tex. d: 4/12/80, Sealy, Tex. BR/TR, 5'11", 185 lbs. Deb: 9/17/40																									
1940	Bos-N	11	40	3	9	2	0	0	5	2	4	.225	.262	.275	51	-3	-3	3	0			1.000	1	O	-0.2
1941	Bos-N	5	4	0	0	0	0	0	0	1	2	.000	.200	.000	-42	-1	-1	0	0			1.000	-1	/O	-0.2
Total	2	16	44	3	9	2	0	0	5	3	6	.205	.255	.250	42	-4	-3	3	0			1.000	-0	/O	-0.4
■ BOBBY PRESCOTT Prescott, George Bertrand b: 3/27/31, Colon, Panama BR/TR, 5'11", 180 lbs. Deb: 6/17/61																									
1961	KC-A	10	12	0	1	0	0	0	0	2	5	.083	.214	.083	-17	-2	-2	0	0	0	0	.000	-1	/O	-0.3
■ JIM PRESLEY Presley, James Arthur b: 10/23/61, Pensacola, Fla. BR/TR, 6'1", 200 lbs. Deb: 6/24/84																									
1984	Sea-A	70	251	27	57	12	1	10	36	6	63	.227	.248	.402	78	-9	-9	24	1	1	-0	.958	-3	3/D	-1.3
1985	Sea-A	155	570	71	157	33	1	28	84	44	100	.275	.328	.484	118	13	13	80	2	2	-1	.961	7	*3	1.7
1986	Sea-A☆	155	616	83	163	33	4	27	107	32	172	.265	.305	.463	105	2	2	80	0	4	-2	.965	6	*3	0.2
1987	Sea-A	152	575	78	142	23	6	24	88	38	157	.247	.298	.433	86	-9	-13	72	2	0	1	.953	11	*3/SD	-0.4
1988	Sea-A	150	544	50	125	26	0	14	62	36	114	.230	.283	.355	74	-17	-20	52	3	5	-2	.940	-13	*3/D	-3.7
1989	Sea-A	117	390	42	92	20	1	12	41	21	107	.236	.277	.385	82	-9	-11	39	0	0	0	.924	-4	31/D	-1.6
1990	Atl-N	140	541	59	131	34	1	19	72	29	130	.242	.284	.414	85	-10	-13	62	1	1	-0	.930	-2	*31	-1.7
1991	SD-N	20	59	3	8	0	0	1	5	4	16	.136	.203	.186	10	-7	-7	2	0	1	-1	.923	-3	3	-1.2
Total	8	959	3546	413	875	181	14	135	495	210	859	.247	.292	.420	90	-46	-59	409	9	14	-6	.949	-1	3/1DS	-8.0
■ WALT PRESTON Preston, Walter B. b: 1870, Richmond, Va. BL/TR, 6', 175 lbs. Deb: 4/18/1895																									
1895	Lou-N	50	197	42	55	6	4	1	24	17	17	.279	.366	.365	97	-2	0	31	11			.893	-7	O3	-0.6
■ JIM PRICE Price, Jimmie William b: 10/13/41, Harrisburg, Pa. BR/TR, 6', 195 lbs. Deb: 4/11/67																									
1967	Det-A	44	92	9	24	4	0	0	8	4	10	.261	.292	.304	74	-3	-3	7	0	0	0	.974	0	C	-0.2
1968	*Det-A	64	132	12	23	4	0	3	13	13	14	.174	.253	.273	58	-6	-7	8	0	0	0	.996	2	C	-0.4
1969	Det-A	72	192	21	45	8	0	9	28	18	20	.234	.300	.417	95	-1	-2	24	0	0	0	.989	4	C	0.4
1970	Det-A	52	132	12	24	4	0	5	15	21	23	.182	.294	.326	70	-5	-5	13	0	0	0	.979	-1	C	-0.5
1971	Det-A	29	54	4	13	2	0	1	7	6	3	.241	.328	.333	84	-1	-1	6	0	0	0	.981	1	C	0.1
Total	5	261	602	58	129	22	0	18	71	62	70	.214	.290	.341	78	-16	-18	58	0	0	0	.985	5	C	-0.6
■ JACKIE PRICE Price, John Thomas Reid "Johnny" b: 11/13/12, Windborn, Miss. d: 10/2/67, San Francisco, Cal. BL/TR, 5'10.5", 150 lbs. Deb: 8/18/46																									
1946	Cle-A	7	13	1	3	0	0	0	0	0	0	.231	.231	.231	31	-1	-1	1	0	0	0	.947	2	/S	0.1
■ JOE PRICE Price, Joseph Preston "Lumber" b: 4/10/1897, Milligan College, Tenn. d: 1/15/61, Washington, D.C. BR/TR, 6'1.5", 187 lbs. Deb: 9/05/28																									
1928	NY-N	1	1	0	0	0	0	0	0	0	1	.000	.000	.000	-99	-0	-0	0	0			.000	-1	/O	-0.1
■ BOB PRICHARD Prichard, Robert Alexander b: 10/21/17, Paris, Tex. BL/TL, 6'1", 195 lbs. Deb: 6/14/39																									
1939	Was-A	26	85	8	20	5	0	0	8	19	16	.235	.375	.294	79	-3	-2	11	0	2	-1	.992	-1	1	-0.6

■ JERRY PRIDDY Priddy, Gerald Edward b: 11/9/19, Los Angeles, Cal. d: 3/3/80, N.Hollywood, Cal. BR/TR, 5'11.5", 180 lbs. Deb: 4/17/41

YEAR	TM/L	G	AB	R	H	2B	3B	HR	RBI	BB	SO	AVG	OBP	SLG	PRO+	BR	/A	RC	SB	CS	SBR	FA	FR	POS	TPR
1941	NY-A	56	174	18	37	7	0	1	26	18	16	.213	.290	.270	50	-13	-12	14	4	2	0	.968	9	231	-0.1
1942	*NY-A	59	189	23	53	9	2	2	28	31	27	.280	.385	.381	118	5	6	31	0	1	-1	.944	5	31/2S	1.1
1943	Was-A	149	560	68	152	31	3	4	62	67	76	.271	.350	.359	112	6	9	72	5	5	-2	.971	4	*2S/3	2.1
1946	Was-A	138	511	54	130	22	8	6	58	57	73	.254	.332	.364	100	-4	-0	64	9	3	1	.962	2	*2	1.2
1947	Was-A	147	505	42	108	20	3	3	49	62	79	.214	.301	.283	65	-25	-23	44	7	6	-2	.980	-2	*2	-1.7
1948	StL-A	151	560	96	166	40	9	8	79	86	71	.296	.391	.443	118	18	16	101	6	5	-1	.968	24	*2	4.5
1949	StL-A	145	544	83	158	26	4	11	63	80	81	.290	.382	.414	106	9	6	89	5	3	-0	.968	-3	*2	0.9
1950	Det-A	157	618	104	171	26	6	13	75	95	95	.277	.376	.401	96	0	-3	95	2	7	-4	.981	**31**	*2	3.0
1951	Det-A	154	584	73	152	22	6	8	57	69	73	.260	.338	.360	88	-9	-9	73	4	3	-1	.980	10	*2/S	0.7
1952	Det-A	75	279	37	79	23	3	4	20	42	29	.283	.379	.430	124	10	10	46	1	8	-5	.968	-1	2	0.8
1953	Det-A	65	196	14	46	6	2	1	24	17	19	.235	.299	.301	63	-10	-10	18	1	1	-0	.977	4	21/3	-0.5
Total	11	1296	4720	612	1252	232	46	61	541	624	639	.265	.353	.373	97	-12	-11	646	44	44	-13	.973	82	*2/31S	12.0

■ JOHNNY PRIEST Priest, John Gooding b: 6/23/1886, St.Joseph, Mo. d: 11/4/79, Washington, D.C. BR/TR, 5'11", 170 lbs. Deb: 5/30/11

YEAR	TM/L	G	AB	R	H	2B	3B	HR	RBI	BB	SO	AVG	OBP	SLG	PRO+	BR	/A	RC	SB	CS	SBR	FA	FR	POS	TPR
1911	NY-A	8	21	2	3	0	0	0	2	2		.143	.250	.143	10	-2	-3	1	3			.824	-3	/23	-0.6
1912	NY-A	2	2	1	1	0	0	0	1	0		.500	.500	.500	176	0	0	0	0			.000	0	H	0.0
Total	2	10	23	3	4	0	0	0	3	2		.174	.269	.174	23	-2	-2	2	3			.962	-3	/23	-0.6

■ TOM PRINCE Prince, Thomas Albert b: 8/13/64, Kankakee, Ill. BR/TR, 5'11", 185 lbs. Deb: 9/22/87

YEAR	TM/L	G	AB	R	H	2B	3B	HR	RBI	BB	SO	AVG	OBP	SLG	PRO+	BR	/A	RC	SB	CS	SBR	FA	FR	POS	TPR
1987	Pit-N	4	9	1	2	1	0	1	2	0	2	.222	.222	.667	123	0	0	1	0	0	0	1.000	1	/C	0.1
1988	Pit-N	29	74	3	13	2	0	0	6	4	15	.176	.218	.203	22	-7	-7	3	0	0	0	.983	-2	C	-0.9
1989	Pit-N	21	52	1	7	4	0	0	5	6	12	.135	.224	.212	26	-5	-5	2	1	1	-0	.960	-0	C	-0.5
1990	Pit-N	4	10	1	1	0	0	0	0	1	2	.100	.182	.100	-21	-2	-2	0	0	1	-1	1.000	0	/C	-0.2
1991	Pit-N	26	34	4	9	3	0	1	2	7	3	.265	.405	.441	140	2	2	6	0	0	0	.984	1	C/1	0.4
1992	Pit-N	27	44	1	4	2	0	0	5	6	9	.091	.200	.136	-3	-6	-6	1	1	1	-0	.977	3	C/3	-0.3
Total	6	111	223	11	36	12	0	2	20	24	43	.161	.246	.242	40	-18	-17	13	2	3	-1	.978	3	/C31	-1.4

■ WALTER PRINCE Prince, Walter Farr b: 5/9/1861, Amherst, N.H. d: 3/2/38, Bristol, N.H. BL/TR, 5'9", 150 lbs. Deb: 8/07/1883

YEAR	TM/L	G	AB	R	H	2B	3B	HR	RBI	BB	SO	AVG	OBP	SLG	PRO+	BR	/A	RC	SB	CS	SBR	FA	FR	POS	TPR
1883	Lou-a	4	11	1	2	0	0	0		0		.182	.182	.182	19	-1	-1	0				.500	-2	/O1S	-0.3
1884	Det-N	7	21	0	3	0	0	0	1	3	4	.143	.250	.143	29	-2	-1	1				.375	-3	/O	-0.5
	Was-a	43	166	22	36	3	2	1		13		.217	.286	.277	98	-2	1	13				.940	-6	1	-0.8
	Was-U	1	4	0	1	0	0	0		0		.250	.250	.250	72	-0	-0	0				.818	-0	/1	-0.1
Total	2	55	202	23	42	3	2	1	1	16	4	.208	.276	.257	86	-5	-1	15				.935	-11	/1OS	-1.7

■ BUDDY PRITCHARD Pritchard, Harold William b: 1/25/36, South Gate, Cal. BR/TR, 6'1", 195 lbs. Deb: 4/21/57

YEAR	TM/L	G	AB	R	H	2B	3B	HR	RBI	BB	SO	AVG	OBP	SLG	PRO+	BR	/A	RC	SB	CS	SBR	FA	FR	POS	TPR
1957	Pit-N	23	11	1	1	0	0	0	0	0	4	.091	.091	.091	-53	-2	-2	0	0	0	0	.947	5	S/2	0.2

■ GEORGE PROESER Proeser, George "Yatz" b: 5/30/1864, Cincinnati, Ohio d: 10/13/41, New Burlington, O. BL/TL, 5'10", 190 lbs. Deb: 9/15/1888

YEAR	TM/L	G	AB	R	H	2B	3B	HR	RBI	BB	SO	AVG	OBP	SLG	PRO+	BR	/A	RC	SB	CS	SBR	FA	FR	POS	TPR
1888	Cle-a	7	23	5	7	2	0	0	1	1		.304	.333	.391	139	1	1	3	0			.846	-1	/P	0.0
1890	Syr-a	13	53	11	13	1	1	1		10		.245	.365	.358	129	1	2	7	1			.895	-2	O	0.0
Total	2	20	76	16	20	3	1	1	1	11		.263	.356	.368	132	2	3	11	1			.931	-3	/OP	0.0

■ JAKE PROPST Propst, William Jacob b: 3/10/1895, Kennedy, Ala. d: 2/24/67, Columbus, Miss. BL/TR, 5'10", 165 lbs. Deb: 8/07/23

YEAR	TM/L	G	AB	R	H	2B	3B	HR	RBI	BB	SO	AVG	OBP	SLG	PRO+	BR	/A	RC	SB	CS	SBR	FA	FR	POS	TPR
1923	Was-A	1	1	0	0	0	0	0	0	0	0	.000	.000	.000	-99	-0	-0	0	0	0	0	.000	0	H	0.0

■ DOC PROTHRO Prothro, James Thompson b: 7/16/1893, Memphis, Tenn. d: 10/14/71, Memphis, Tenn. BR/TR, 5'10.5", 170 lbs. Deb: 9/26/20 M

YEAR	TM/L	G	AB	R	H	2B	3B	HR	RBI	BB	SO	AVG	OBP	SLG	PRO+	BR	/A	RC	SB	CS	SBR	FA	FR	POS	TPR
1920	Was-A	6	13	2	5	0	0	0	2	0	4	.385	.385	.385	107	0	0	2	0	0	0	1.000	-1	/S3	0.0
1923	Was-A	6	8	2	2	0	1	0	3	1	3	.250	.333	.500	124	0	0	1	0	0	0	1.000	3	/3	0.3
1924	Was-A	46	159	17	53	11	5	0	24	15	11	.333	.394	.465	125	5	6	29	4	4	-1	.915	-11	3	-0.3
1925	Bos-A	119	415	44	130	23	3	0	51	52	21	.313	.390	.383	97	-0	-0	62	9	11	-4	.945	-6	*3/S	-0.2
1926	Cin-N	3	5	1	1	0	1	0	1	1	1	.200	.333	.600	151	0	0	1	0			1.000	-0	/3	0.0
Total	5	180	600	66	191	34	10	0	81	69	40	.318	.390	.408	105	5	6	95	13	15		.940	-14	3/S	-0.2

■ EARL PRUESS Pruess, Earl Henry "Gibby" b: 4/2/1895, Chicago, Ill. d: 8/28/79, Branson, Mo. BR/TR, 5'10.5", 170 lbs. Deb: 9/15/20

YEAR	TM/L	G	AB	R	H	2B	3B	HR	RBI	BB	SO	AVG	OBP	SLG	PRO+	BR	/A	RC	SB	CS	SBR	FA	FR	POS	TPR
1920	StL-A	1	0	1	0	0	0	0	0	1	0	—	1.000	—	176	0	0	1	1	0	0	1.000	0	/O	0.1

■ JIM PRUETT Pruett, James Calvin b: 12/16/17, Nashville, Tenn. BR/TR, 5'10", 178 lbs. Deb: 9/26/44

YEAR	TM/L	G	AB	R	H	2B	3B	HR	RBI	BB	SO	AVG	OBP	SLG	PRO+	BR	/A	RC	SB	CS	SBR	FA	FR	POS	TPR
1944	Phi-A	3	4	1	1	0	0	0	0	1	0	.250	.500	.250	119	0	0	1	0	0	0	1.000	1	/C	0.1
1945	Phi-A	6	9	1	2	0	0	0	0	1	2	.222	.300	.222	53	-1	-1	0	0	1	-1	1.000	1	/C	-0.1
Total	2	9	13	2	3	0	0	0	0	2	2	.231	.375	.231	77	-0	-0	1	0	1	-1	1.000	1	/C	0.0

■ RON PRUITT Pruitt, Ronald Ralph b: 10/21/51, Flint, Mich. BR/TR, 6', 185 lbs. Deb: 6/25/75

YEAR	TM/L	G	AB	R	H	2B	3B	HR	RBI	BB	SO	AVG	OBP	SLG	PRO+	BR	/A	RC	SB	CS	SBR	FA	FR	POS	TPR
1975	Tex-A	14	17	2	3	0	0	0	0	1	3	.176	.222	.176	14	-2	-2	1	0	0	0	1.000	-1	C/O	-0.3
1976	Cle-A	47	86	7	23	1	1	0	5	16	8	.267	.382	.302	103	1	1	11	2	3	-1	1.000	2	O/C31D	0.2
1977	Cle-A	78	219	29	63	10	2	2	32	28	22	.288	.373	.379	109	3	4	30	2	3	-1	.972	-8	O/C3D	-0.7
1978	Cle-A	71	187	17	44	6	1	6	17	16	20	.235	.296	.374	88	-4	-3	21	2	1	0	.984	-6	CO/3D	-1.0
1979	Cle-A	64	166	23	47	7	0	2	21	19	21	.283	.357	.361	94	-1	-1	22	2	0	1	.957	-5	ODC/3	-0.6
1980	Cle-A	23	36	1	11	1	0	0	4	4	6	.306	.375	.333	95	-0	-0	5	0	0	0	1.000	0	/O3D	0.0
	Chi-A	33	70	8	21	2	0	2	11	8	7	.300	.372	.414	116	2	2	10	0	0	0	1.000	-1	O/C31D	0.0
	Yr	56	106	9	32	3	0	2	15	12	13	.302	.373	.387	109	2	2	15	0	0	0	1.000	-1	O/D3C1	0.0
1981	Cle-A	5	9	0	0	0	0	0	0	1	2	.000	.100	.000	-70	-2	-2	0	0	0	0	1.000	-1	/OCD	-0.3
1982	SF-N	5	4	1	2	1	0	0	2	1	1	.500	.600	.750	276	1	1	2	0	0	0	1.000	0	/CO	0.1
1983	SF-N	1	1	0	0	0	0	0	0	0	0	.000	.000	.000	-99	-0	-0	0	0	0	0	.000	0	/H	0.0
Total	9	341	795	88	214	28	4	12	92	94	90	.269	.348	.360	97	-2	-1	100	8	7	-2	.977	-19	O/CD31	-2.6

■ GREG PRYOR Pryor, Gregory Russell b: 10/2/49, Marietta, Ohio BR/TR, 6', 186 lbs. Deb: 6/04/76

YEAR	TM/L	G	AB	R	H	2B	3B	HR	RBI	BB	SO	AVG	OBP	SLG	PRO+	BR	/A	RC	SB	CS	SBR	FA	FR	POS	TPR
1976	Tex-A	5	8	2	3	0	0	0	1	0	1	.375	.375	.375	118	0	0	1	0	0	0	1.000	0	/2S3	0.1
1978	Chi-A	82	222	27	58	11	0	2	15	11	18	.261	.299	.338	78	-6	-7	22	3	1	0	.966	6	2S3	0.4
1979	Chi-A	143	476	60	131	23	3	3	34	35	41	.275	.327	.355	84	-10	-10	52	3	4	-2	.961	-5	*S23	-0.4
1980	Chi-A	122	338	32	81	18	4	1	29	12	35	.240	.270	.325	63	-18	-18	28	2	2	-1	.975	22	S3/2D	1.1
1981	Chi-A	47	76	4	17	1	0	0	6	6	8	.224	.298	.237	57	-4	-4	6	0	0	0	.931	4	3S/2	0.0
1982	KC-A	73	152	23	41	10	1	2	12	10	20	.270	.315	.388	92	-2	-2	18	2	0	1	.951	8	321/S	0.6
1983	KC-A	68	115	9	25	4	0	1	14	7	8	.217	.262	.278	49	-8	-8	8	0	0	0	.958	11	3/12	0.2
1984	*KC-A	123	270	32	71	11	1	4	25	12	28	.263	.302	.356	80	-7	-7	26	0	3	-2	.970	17	*32/S1D	0.8
1985	*KC-A	63	114	8	25	3	0	1	3	8	12	.219	.270	.272	49	-8	-8	7	0	1	-1	.946	2	32S/1D	-0.5
1986	KC-A	63	112	7	19	4	0	0	7	3	14	.170	.191	.205	8	-14	-14	3	1	1	-0	.935	6	3S2/1	-0.9
Total	10	789	1883	204	471	85	9	14	146	104	185	.250	.293	.327	70	-78	-78	172	11	12	-4	.952	70	3S2/1D	1.4

■ GEORGE PUCCINELLI Puccinelli, George Lawrence "Pooch" or "Count"
b: 6/22/07, San Francisco, Cal. d: 4/16/56, San Francisco, Cal BR/TR, 6'0.5", 190 lbs. Deb: 7/17/30

YEAR	TM/L	G	AB	R	H	2B	3B	HR	RBI	BB	SO	AVG	OBP	SLG	PRO+	BR	/A	RC	SB	CS	SBR	FA	FR	POS	TPR
1930	*StL-N	11	16	5	9	1	0	3	8	0	1	.563	.563	1.188	298	5	5	10	0			1.000	-1	/O	0.3
1932	StL-N	31	108	17	30	8	0	3	11	12	13	.278	.350	.435	107	2	1	17	1			.942	2	O	0.2
1934	StL-A	10	26	4	6	1	0	2	5	1	8	.231	.286	.500	92	-0	-1	4	0	0	0	.941	1	/O	0.0
1936	Phi-A	135	457	83	127	30	3	11	78	65	70	.278	.369	.429	98	-3	-1	75	2	3	-1	.948	0	*O	-0.6

YEAR	TM/L	G	AB	R	H	2B	3B	HR	RBI	BB	SO	AVG	OBP	SLG	PRO+	BR	/A	RC	SB	CS	SBR	FA	FR	POS	TPR
Total	4	187	607	109	172	40	3	19	102	78	92	.283	.367	.453	105	4	4	105	3	3		.947	2	O	-0.1
■ KIRBY PUCKETT	Puckett, Kirby b: 3/14/61, Chicago, Ill. BR/TR, 5'8", 210 lbs. Deb: 5/08/84																								
1984	Min-A	128	557	63	165	12	5	0	31	16	69	.296	.321	.336	78	-14	-17	58	14	7	0	.993	30	*O	0.9
1985	Min-A	161	691	80	199	29	13	4	74	41	87	.288	.332	.385	90	-4	-9	88	21	12	-1	.984	21	*O	0.5
1986	Min-A★	161	680	119	223	37	6	31	96	34	99	.328	.366	.537	138	37	35	127	20	12	-1	.986	11	*O	3.8
1987	*Min-A★	157	624	96	**207**	32	5	28	99	32	91	.332	.370	.534	131	30	27	116	12	7	-1	.986	5	*O/D	2.6
1988	Min-A★	158	657	109	**234**	42	5	24	121	23	83	.356	.380	.545	151	46	43	126	6	7	-2	.994	20	*O	5.5
1989	Min-A★	159	635	75	**215**	45	4	9	85	41	59	**.339**	.381	.465	129	30	25	107	11	4	1	.991	18	*O/D	4.0
1990	Min-A★	146	551	82	164	40	3	12	80	57	73	.298	.367	.446	119	20	15	88	5	4	-1	.989	8	*O/23SD	1.9
1991	*Min-A★	152	611	92	195	29	6	15	89	31	78	.319	.356	.460	118	18	15	91	11	5	0	.985	4	*O	1.6
1992	Min-A★	160	639	104	**210**	38	4	19	110	44	97	.329	.377	.490	137	34	31	114	17	7	1	.993	6	*O/23SD	3.5
Total	9	1382	5645	820	1812	304	51	142	785	319	736	.321	.361	.468	122	197	166	914	117	65	-4	.989	124	*O/D32S	24.3
■ JOHN PUHL	Puhl, John G. b: 1875, New York, N.Y. d: 8/24/1900, Bayonne, N.J. Deb: 10/13/1898																								
1898	NY-N	2	9	1	2	0	0	0	1	0		.222	.222	.222	28	-1	-1	0	0			.667	-1	/3	-0.1
1899	NY-N	1	2	0	0	0	0	0	0	0		.000	.333	.000	-5	-0	-0	0	0			.667	-0	/3	0.0
Total	2	3	11	1	2	0	0	0	1	0		.182	.250	.182	24	-1	-1	0	0			.667	-1	/3	-0.1
■ TERRY PUHL	Puhl, Terry Stephen b: 7/8/56, Melville, Sask., Can BL/TR, 6'2", 200 lbs. Deb: 7/12/77																								
1977	Hou-N	60	229	40	69	13	5	0	10	30	31	.301	.385	.402	122	5	7	39	10	1	2	.992	1	O	0.8
1978	Hou-N☆	149	585	87	169	25	6	3	35	48	46	.289	.347	.368	108	0	5	75	32	14	1	.992	20	*O	2.1
1979	Hou-N	157	600	87	172	22	4	8	49	58	46	.287	.353	.377	105	1	5	80	30	22	-4	**1.000**	-6	*O	-1.3
1980	*Hou-N	141	535	75	151	24	5	13	55	60	52	.282	.359	.419	126	12	18	85	27	11	2	.991	14	*O	2.9
1981	*Hou-N	96	350	43	88	19	4	3	28	31	49	.251	.319	.354	96	-4	-2	44	22	4	4	**1.000**	3	O	0.2
1982	Hou-N	145	507	64	133	17	9	8	50	51	49	.262	.332	.379	106	-1	4	66	17	9	-0	.989	-2	*O	-0.3
1983	Hou-N	137	465	66	136	25	7	8	44	36	48	.292	.346	.428	121	8	11	70	24	11	1	.991	-5	*O	0.3
1984	Hou-N	132	449	66	135	19	7	9	55	59	45	.301	.383	.434	139	19	23	77	13	8	-1	.986	-2	*O	1.7
1985	Hou-N	57	194	34	55	14	3	2	23	18	23	.284	.347	.418	116	3	4	30	6	2	1	1.000	0	O	0.3
1986	*Hou-N	81	172	17	42	10	0	3	14	15	24	.244	.305	.355	84	-5	-4	18	3	2	-0	1.000	-4	O	-1.0
1987	Hou-N	90	122	9	28	5	0	2	15	11	16	.230	.293	.320	65	-7	-6	11	1	1	-0	.980	-6	O	-1.3
1988	Hou-N	113	234	42	71	7	2	3	19	35	30	.303	.396	.389	131	10	11	42	22	4	4	.983	-7	O	0.6
1989	Hou-N	121	354	41	96	25	4	0	27	45	39	.271	.355	.364	110	4	5	46	9	8	-2	1.000	-2	*O/1	-0.1
1990	Hou-N	37	41	5	12	1	0	0	8	5	7	.293	.383	.317	98	0	0	5	1	2	-1	1.000	-2	/O1	-0.3
1991	KC-A	15	18	0	4	0	0	0	3	3	2	.222	.333	.222	57	-1	-1	1	0	0	0	.000	-0	/OD	-0.1
Total	15	1531	4855	676	1361	226	56	62	435	505	507	.280	.351	.388	113	44	80	690	217	99	6	.993	1	*O/1D	4.5
■ RICH PUIG	Puig, Richard Gerald b: 3/16/53, Tampa, Fla. BL/TR, 5'10", 165 lbs. Deb: 9/13/74																								
1974	NY-N	4	10	0	0	0	0	0	0	1	2	.000	.091	.000	-74	-2	-2	0	0	0	0	.923	-0	/23	-0.3
■ LUIS PUJOLS	Pujols, Luis Bienvenido (Toribio) b: 11/18/55, Santiago, D.R. BR/TR, 6'1", 195 lbs. Deb: 9/22/77																								
1977	Hou-N	6	15	0	1	0	0	0	0	0	5	.067	.067	.067	-70	-3	-3	0	0	0	0	1.000	0	/C	-0.3
1978	Hou-N	56	153	11	20	8	1	1	11	12	45	.131	.199	.216	17	-18	-16	6	0	0	0	.981	0	C/1	-1.6
1979	Hou-N	26	75	7	17	2	1	0	8	2	14	.227	.247	.280	46	-6	-5	5	0	0	0	.993	1	C	-0.4
1980	*Hou-N	78	221	15	44	6	1	0	20	13	29	.199	.247	.235	38	-19	-17	13	0	0	0	.990	-3	C/3	-1.9
1981	*Hou-N	40	117	5	28	3	1	1	14	10	17	.239	.299	.308	76	-4	-4	10	1	0	0	.995	-1	C	-0.3
1982	Hou-N	65	176	8	35	6	2	4	15	10	40	.199	.242	.324	62	-11	-9	12	0	3	-2	.991	5	C	-0.4
1983	Hou-N	40	87	4	17	2	0	0	12	5	14	.195	.239	.218	29	-8	-8	4	0	0	0	.971	5	C	-0.2
1984	KC-A	4	5	0	1	0	0	0	1	0	0	.200	.200	.200	11	-1	-1	0	0	0	0	1.000	0	/C	0.0
1985	Tex-A	1	1	0	1	0	0	0	0	0	0	1.000	1.000	1.000	444	0	0	1	0	0	0	1.000	-0	/C	0.0
Total	9	316	850	50	164	27	6	6	81	52	164	.193	.241	.260	43	-69	-62	51	1	3	-2	.987	7	C/31	-5.1
■ HARVEY PULLIAM	Pulliam, Harvey Jerome b: 10/20/67, San Francisco, Cal. BR/TR, 6', 210 lbs. Deb: 8/10/91																								
1991	KC-A	18	33	4	9	1	0	3	4	3	9	.273	.333	.576	146	2	2	6	0	0	0	.917	-2	O	0.0
1992	KC-A	4	5	2	1	1	0	0	0	1	3	.200	.333	.400	104	0	0	1	0	0	0	1.000	0	/OD	0.0
Total	2	22	38	6	10	2	0	3	4	4	12	.263	.333	.553	140	2	2	7	0	0	0	.926	-1	/OD	0.0
■ BLONDIE PURCELL	Purcell, William Aloysius b: Paterson, N.J. BR/TR, 5'9.5", 159 lbs. Deb: 5/01/1879 M																								
1879	Syr-N	63	277	32	72	6	3	0	25	3	13	.260	.268	.303	99	-4	1	23				.773	-13	OP/C	-1.2
	Cin-N	12	50	10	11	0	0	0	4	0	3	.220	.220	.220	48	-3	-2	2				.750	1	O/P	-0.2
	Yr	75	327	42	83	6	3	0	29	3	16	.254	.261	.291	91	-6	-2	25				.767	-13	OP/C	-1.4
1880	Cin-N	77	325	48	95	13	6	1	24	5	13	.292	.303	.378	131	9	10	38				.814	-2	OP/S	0.4
1881	Cle-N	20	80	3	14	2	1	0	4	5	8	.175	.224	.225	44	-5	-5	4				.786	-2	O	-0.7
	Buf-N	30	113	15	33	7	2	0	17	8	8	.292	.339	.389	130	4	4	15				.706	-6	O/P	-0.3
	Yr	50	193	18	47	9	3	0	21	13	16	.244	.291	.321	95	-1	-1	19				.748	-8	O/P	-1.0
1882	Buf-N	84	380	79	105	18	6	2	40	14	27	.276	.302	.371	113	6	5	44				.820	-5	*O/P	-0.1
1883	Phi-N	97	425	70	114	20	5	1	32	13	26	.268	.290	.346	101	-4	2	44				.777	5	3OPM	0.5
1884	Phi-N	103	428	67	108	11	7	1	31	29	30	.252	.300	.318	99	-2	1	42				.874	-0	*O/P	-0.1
1885	Phi-a	66	304	71	90	15	5	0		16		.296	.337	.378	121	10	7	40				.858	-1	O/P	0.4
	Bos-N	21	87	9	19	1	1	0	3	3	15	.218	.244	.253	63	-4	-3	6				.840	-3	O	-0.7
1886	Bal-a	26	85	17	19	0	1	0		17		.224	.365	.247	98	1	1	13	13			.867	-1	O/SP	0.0
1887	Bal-a	140	567	101	142	25	8	4		46		.250	.318	.344	92	-10	-4	92	88			.925	-4	*O/P	-0.8
1888	Bal-a	101	406	53	96	9	4	2	39	27		.236	.289	.293	92	-4	-3	40	16			.906	-6	*O/S1	-1.1
	Phi-a	18	66	10	11	3	1	0	6	5		.167	.236	.242	56	-3	-3	6	10			.903	0	O/3	-0.3
	Yr	119	472	63	107	12	5	2	45	32		.227	.281	.286	87	-7	-6	46	26			.905	-6	*O/S13	-1.4
1889	Phi-a	129	507	72	160	19	7	0	85	50	27	.316	.383	.381	122	15	16	84	22			.903	-10	*O	0.2
1890	Phi-a	110	463	110	128	28	3	2		43		.276	.343	.363	113	6	8	76	48			.949	-1	*O	0.2
Total	12	1097	4563	767	1217	177	60	13	310	284	170	.267	.314	.340	105	11	34	569	197			.869	-49	O/P3S1C	-3.8
■ PID PURDY	Purdy, Everett Virgil b: 6/15/04, Beatrice, Neb. d: 1/16/51, Beatrice, Neb. BL/TR, 5'6", 150 lbs. Deb: 9/07/26																								
1926	Chi-A	11	33	5	6	2	1	0	6	2	1	.182	.229	.303	39	-3	-3	2	0	1	-1	1.000	0	/O	-0.4
1927	Cin-N	18	62	15	22	2	4	1	12	4	3	.355	.412	.565	164	5	5	14	0			.946	-3	O	0.1
1928	Cin-N	70	223	32	69	11	1	0	25	23	13	.309	.377	.368	97	-1	-0	31	1			.966	0	O	-0.4
1929	Cin-N	82	181	22	49	7	5	1	16	19	8	.271	.350	.381	85	-5	-4	24	2			.978	-1	O	-0.7
Total	4	181	499	74	146	22	11	2	59	48	25	.293	.362	.393	97	-4	-2	72	3	1		.969	-4	O	-1.4
■ JESSE PURNELL	Purnell, Jesse Rhoades b: 5/11/1881, Glenside, Pa. d: 7/4/66, Philadelphia, Pa. BL/TR, 5'5.5", 140 lbs. Deb: 10/01/04																								
1904	Phi-N	7	19	2	2	0	0	0	1	4		.105	.292	.105	26	-1	-1	1	1			.864	-1	/3	-0.2
■ BILLY PURTELL	Purtell, William Patrick b: 1/6/1886, Columbus, Ohio d: 3/17/62, Bradenton, Fla. BR/TR, 5'9", 170 lbs. Deb: 4/16/08																								
1908	Chi-A	26	69	3	9	2	0	0	3	2		.130	.155	.159	2	-7	-7	2	2			.940	6	3	0.0
1909	Chi-A	103	361	34	93	9	3	0	40	19		.258	.302	.299	94	-4	-3	39	14			.929	5	32	0.4
1910	Chi-A	102	368	21	82	5	3	1	36	21		.223	.272	.261	70	-14	-12	28	5			.907	4	*3	-0.6
	Bos-A	49	168	15	35	1	2	1	15	18		.208	.289	.256	69	-5	-6	14	2			.908	-5	3/S	-1.1
	Yr	151	536	36	117	6	5	2	51	39		.218	.278	.259	70	-19	-18	43	7			.907	-1	*3/S	-1.7

YEAR	TM/L	G	AB	R	H	2B	3B	HR	RBI	BB	SO	AVG	OBP	SLG	PRO+	BR	/A	RC	SB	CS	SBR	FA	FR	POS	TPR
1911	Bos-A	27	82	5	23	5	3	0	7	1		.280	.298	.415	99	-1	-1	10	1			.867	-1	3/2SO	-0.1
1914	Det-A	28	76	4	13	4	0	0	3	2	7	.171	.203	.224	27	-7	-7	3	0	2	-1	.946	-1	3/S2	-0.9
Total	5	335	1124	82	255	26	11	2	104	63	7	.227	.275	.275	73	-39	-36	97	24	2		.915	9	3/2SO	-2.3

■ ED PUTMAN Putman, Eddy William b: 9/25/53, Los Angeles, Cal. BR/TR, 6'1", 190 lbs. Deb: 9/07/76

1976	Chi-N	5	7	0	3	0	0	0	0	0	0	.429	.429	.429	132	0	0	0	0	0	0	1.000	0	/C1	0.0
1978	Chi-N	17	25	2	5	0	0	0	3	4	6	.200	.310	.200	40	-2	-2	2	0	0	0	.950	-0	/31C	-0.2
1979	Det-A	21	39	4	9	3	0	2	4	4	12	.231	.302	.462	99	-0	-0	5	0	1	-1	1.000	1	C/1	0.0
Total	3	43	71	6	17	3	0	2	7	8	18	.239	.316	.366	81	-1	-2	7	0	1	-1	1.000	1	/C13	-0.2

■ PAT PUTNAM Putnam, Patrick Edward b: 12/3/53, Bethel, Vt. BL/TR, 6'1", 214 lbs. Deb: 9/02/77

1977	Tex-A	11	26	3	8	4	0	0	3	1	4	.308	.333	.462	113	0	0	3	0	1	-1	1.000	-1	/1D	-0.1
1978	Tex-A	20	46	4	7	1	0	1	2	2	5	.152	.188	.239	19	-5	-5	2	0	0	0	1.000	0	D/1	-0.5
1979	Tex-A	139	426	57	118	19	2	18	64	23	50	.277	.323	.458	109	3	4	57	1	6	-3	.994	0	1D	-0.4
1980	Tex-A	147	410	42	108	16	2	13	55	36	49	.263	.323	.407	102	-1	0	51	0	2	-1	.992	5	*1/3D	-0.3
1981	Tex-A	95	297	33	79	17	2	8	35	17	38	.266	.306	.418	113	1	3	37	4	2	0	.993	3	1/O	0.2
1982	Tex-A	43	122	14	28	8	0	2	9	10	18	.230	.293	.344	78	-4	-4	11	0	2	-1	.990	1	1/3O	-0.6
1983	Sea-A	144	469	58	126	23	2	19	67	39	57	.269	.329	.448	107	6	4	67	2	1	0	.994	4	*1D	0.1
1984	Sea-A	64	155	11	31	6	0	2	16	12	27	.200	.257	.277	49	-11	-11	11	3	0	1	1.000	-1	DO/1	-1.2
	Min-A	14	38	1	3	1	0	0	4	4	12	.079	.167	.105	-22	-6	-7	1	0	0	0	.000	0	D	-0.7
	Yr	78	193	12	34	7	0	2	20	16	39	.176	.239	.244	34	-17	-17	12	3	0	1	1.000	-1	DO/1	-1.9
Total	8	677	1989	223	508	95	8	63	255	144	260	.255	.309	.406	96	-16	-14	241	10	14	-5	.993	10	1D/O3	-3.5

■ JIM PYBURN Pyburn, James Edward b: 11/1/32, Fairfield, Ala. BR/TR, 6', 190 lbs. Deb: 4/17/55

1955	Bal-A	39	98	5	20	2	2	0	7	8	24	.204	.271	.265	48	-8	-7	7	1	1	-0	1.000	-5	3/O	-1.2
1956	Bal-A	84	156	23	27	3	3	2	11	17	26	.173	.254	.269	41	-14	-13	11	4	1	1	.975	-11	O	-2.5
1957	Bal-A	35	40	8	9	0	0	1	2	9	6	.225	.367	.300	90	-0	-0	5	1	0	0	1.000	-2	O/C	-0.3
Total	3	158	294	36	56	5	5	3	20	34	56	.190	.277	.272	51	-22	-20	23	6	2	1	.982	-18	O/3C	-4.0

■ FRANKIE PYTLAK Pytlak, Frank Anthony b: 7/30/08, Buffalo, N.Y. d: 5/8/77, Buffalo, N.Y. BR/TR, 5'7.5", 160 lbs. Deb: 4/22/32

1932	Cle-A	12	29	5	7	1	1	0	4	3	2	.241	.333	.345	71	-1	-1	4	0	0	0	1.000	3	C	0.2
1933	Cle-A	80	248	36	77	10	6	2	33	17	10	.310	.355	.423	101	2	0	36	3	4	-2	1.000	11	C	1.2
1934	Cle-A	91	289	46	75	12	4	0	35	36	11	.260	.352	.329	75	-9	-10	37	11	2	2	.989	-10	C	-1.3
1935	Cle-A	55	149	14	44	6	1	1	12	11	4	.295	.348	.369	84	-3	-4	19	3	2	-0	.984	-1	C	-0.2
1936	Cle-A	75	224	35	72	15	4	0	31	24	11	.321	.394	.424	101	1	1	39	5	2	0	.996	-6	C	-0.1
1937	Cle-A	125	397	60	125	15	6	1	44	52	15	.315	.404	.390	100	3	3	68	16	5	2	.986	10	*C	1.9
1938	Cle-A	113	364	46	112	14	7	1	43	36	15	.308	.376	.393	95	-3	-2	55	9	5	-0	.987	-8	C	-0.4
1939	Cle-A	63	183	20	49	2	5	0	14	20	5	.268	.343	.333	76	-7	-6	22	4	1	1	1.000	3	C	0.0
1940	Cle-A	62	149	16	21	2	1	0	16	17	5	.141	.234	.168	6	-21	-20	7	0	1	-1	.996	7	C/O	-1.0
1941	Bos-A	106	336	36	91	23	1	2	39	28	19	.271	.329	.363	81	-9	-10	40	5	7	-3	.991	1	C	-0.4
1945	Bos-A	9	17	1	2	0	0	0	0	3	0	.118	.250	.118	8	-2	-2	1	0	0	0	1.000	1	/C	-0.1
1946	Bos-A	4	14	1	2	0	0	0	1	0	0	.143	.143	.143	-19	-2	-2	0	0	0	0	1.000	2	/C	0.0
Total	12	795	2399	316	677	100	36	7	272	247	97	.282	.355	.363	84	-51	-53	328	56	29	-1	.991	12	C/O	-0.2

■ TIM PYZNARSKI Pyznarski, Timothy Matthew b: 2/4/60, Chicago, Ill. BR/TR, 6'2", 195 lbs. Deb: 9/14/86

1986	SD-N	15	42	3	10	1	0	0	0	4	11	.238	.319	.262	63	-2	-2	4	2	0	1	.977	-0	1	-0.2

■ JIM QUALLS Qualls, James Robert b: 10/9/46, Exeter, Cal. BB/TR, 5'10", 158 lbs. Deb: 4/10/69

1969	Chi-N	43	120	12	30	5	3	0	9	2	14	.250	.268	.342	62	-5	-7	11	2	1	0	1.000	-1	O/2	-0.9
1970	Mon-N	9	9	1	1	0	0	0	1	0	0	.111	.111	.111	-40	-2	-2	0	0	0	0	1.000	-0	/2O	-0.2
1972	Chi-A	11	10	0	0	0	0	0	0	0	2	.000	.000	.000	-98	-2	-2	0	0	0	0	1.000	0	/O	-0.3
Total	3	63	139	13	31	5	3	0	10	2	16	.223	.239	.302	46	-9	-11	11	2	1	0	1.000	-1	/O2	-1.4

■ MEL QUEEN Queen, Melvin Douglas b: 3/26/42, Johnson City, N.Y. BL/TR, 6'1", 197 lbs. Deb: 4/13/64 FC

1964	Cin-N	48	95	7	19	2	0	2	12	4	19	.200	.232	.284	43	-7	-7	5	0	1	-1	.977	2	O	-0.8
1965	Cin-N	5	3	0	0	0	0	0	0	0	1	.000	.000	.000	-94	-1	-1	0	0	0	0	1.000	0	/O	-0.1
1966	Cin-N	56	55	4	7	1	0	0	5	10	12	.127	.262	.145	16	-6	-7	3	0	0	0	1.000	3	O/P	-0.4
1967	Cin-N	49	81	6	17	4	0	0	5	4	10	.210	.247	.259	40	-6	-7	5	2	0	1	.941	-2	P	0.0
1968	Cin-N	10	8	2	1	0	0	0	0	1	3	.125	.222	.125	6	-1	-1	0	0	0	0	1.000	0	/P	0.0
1969	Cin-N	2	6	0	1	0	0	0	1	0	2	.167	.167	.167	-6	-1	-1	0	0	0	0	1.000	-0	/P	0.0
1970	Cal-A	37	16	1	4	0	0	0	1	0	2	.250	.250	.250	40	-1	-1	1	0	0	0	1.000	-1	P	0.0
1971	Cal-A	45	8	0	0	0	0	0	1	1	0	.000	.111	.000	-71	-2	-2	0	0	0	0	.900	-1	P	0.0
1972	Cal-A	17	2	0	0	0	0	0	0	1	1	.000	.333	.000	5	-0	-0	0	0	0	0	1.000	-0	P	0.0
Total	9	269	274	20	49	7	0	2	25	21	50	.179	.237	.226	30	-25	-27	15	2	1	0	.951	0	P/O	-1.3

■ BILLY QUEEN Queen, William Eddleman "Doc" b: 11/28/28, Gastonia, N.C. BR/TR, 6'1", 185 lbs. Deb: 4/13/54

1954	Mil-N	3	2	0	0	0	0	0	0	0	2	.000	.000	.000	-99	-1	-1	0	0	0	0	1.000	-0	/O	-0.1

■ GEORGE QUELLICH Quellich, George William b: 2/10/06, Johnsville, Cal. d: 8/31/58, Johnsville, Cal. BR/TR, 6'1", 180 lbs. Deb: 8/01/31

1931	Det-A	13	54	6	12	5	0	1	11	3	4	.222	.263	.370	63	-3	-3	5	1	0	0	1.000	1	O	-0.3

■ JOE QUEST Quest, Joseph S. b: 11/3/1851, New Castle, Pa. d: 4/7/23, Cleveland, Ohio BR/TR, 5'6", 150 lbs. Deb: 8/30/1871 U

1871	Cle-n	3	13	1	3	1	0	0	2	1	0	.231	.286	.308	75	-0	-0	1	0					/2S	0.0
1878	Ind-N	62	278	45	57	3	2	0	13	12	24	.205	.238	.230	63	-13	-8	16				.876	2	*2	-0.2
1879	Chi-N	83	334	38	69	16	1	0	22	9	33	.207	.227	.260	57	-14	-17	20				**.925**	14	*2	0.3
1880	Chi-N	82	300	37	71	12	1	0	27	8	16	.237	.256	.283	78	-5	-8	22				.895	4	*2/S3	0.1
1881	Chi-N	78	293	35	72	6	0	1	26	2	29	.246	.251	.276	63	-11	-13	21				**.929**	6	*2/S	-0.5
1882	Chi-N	42	159	24	32	5	2	0	15	8	16	.201	.240	.258	57	-7	-8	10				.879	-5	2/S	-1.1
1883	Det-N	37	137	22	32	8	2	0	25	10	18	.234	.286	.321	88	-2	-1	13				.897	0	2	0.0
	StL-a	19	78	12	20	3	1	0		1		.256	.266	.321	83	-1	-2	7				.890	-6	2	-0.7
1884	StL-a	81	310	46	64	9	5	0		19		.206	.257	.268	71	-8	-10	22				.894	-9	*2	-1.6
	Pit-a	12	43	2	9	3	0	0		0		.209	.227	.279	65	-2	-2	3				.938	0	/2S	-0.1
	Yr	93	353	48	73	12	5	0		19		.207	.253	.269	71	-10	-11	25				.898	-9	2/S	-1.7
1885	Det-N	55	200	24	39	8	2	0	21	14	25	.195	.248	.255	63	-8	-8	13				.898	-2	2S/O	-0.8
1886	Phi-a	42	150	14	31	4	1	0		20		.207	.300	.247	73	-4	-4	13	5			.847	2	S/2	-0.2
Total	9	593	2282	299	496	77	17	1	149	103	161	.217	.252	.267	68	-75	-80	159	5			.902	5	2/SO3	-4.8

■ HAL QUICK Quick, James Harold "Blondie" b: 10/4/17, Rome, Ga. d: 3/9/74, Swansea, Ill. BR/TR, 5'10.5", 163 lbs. Deb: 9/07/39

1939	Was-A	12	41	3	10	1	0	0	2	1	1	.244	.279	.268	44	-4	-3	3	1	0	0	.927	1	S	-0.1

■ FRANK QUILICI Quilici, Francis Ralph "Guido" b: 5/11/39, Chicago, Ill. BR/TR, 6', 175 lbs. Deb: 7/18/65 MC

1965	*Min-A	56	149	16	31	5	1	0	7	15	33	.208	.280	.255	51	-9	-10	11	1	1	-0	.990	3	2/S	-0.3
1967	Min-A	23	19	2	2	1	0	0	0	3	4	.105	.227	.158	14	-2	-2	1	0	0	0	1.000	1	2/3S	-0.1
1968	Min-A	97	229	22	56	11	4	1	22	21	45	.245	.311	.341	93	-1	-2	25	0	0	0	1.000	17	23/S1	2.0
1969	Min-A	118	144	19	25	3	1	2	12	12	22	.174	.237	.250	36	-12	-13	9	2	0	1	.935	24	32/S	1.4
1970	*Min-A	111	141	19	32	3	0	2	12	15	16	.227	.301	.291	63	-7	-7	11	0	2	-1	.987	15	23/S	1.0

YEAR	TM/L	G	AB	R	H	2B	3B	HR	RBI	BB	SO	AVG	OBP	SLG	PRO+	BR	/A	RC	SB	CS	SBR	FA	FR	POS	TPR
Total	5	405	682	78	146	23	6	5	53	66	120	.214	.284	.287	63	-31	-33	57	3	3	-1	.993	60	23/S1	4.0
■ LEE QUILLEN	Quillen, Leon Abner b: 5/5/1882, North Branch, Minn. d: 5/14/65, St.Paul, Minn. BR/TR, 5'10", 165 lbs. Deb: 9/30/06																								
1906	Chi-A	4	9	1	3	0	0	0	0	0		.333	.333	.333	112	0	0	1	1			.600	-2	/S	-0.2
1907	Chi-A	49	151	17	29	5	0	0	14	10		.192	.256	.225	56	-8	-7	12	8			.871	-0	3	-0.6
Total	2	53	160	18	32	5	0	0	14	10		.200	.260	.231	59	-7	-7	13	9			.965	-2	/3S	-0.8
■ QUINLAN	Quinlan Deb: 9/07/1874																								
1874	Phi-n	1	4	0	1	0	0	0		0		.250	.250	.250	58	-0	-0	0						S	0.0
■ FRANK QUINLAN	Quinlan, Francis Patrick b: 3/9/1869, Marlboro, Mass. d: 5/4/04, Brockton, Mass. Deb: 10/05/1891																								
1891	Bos-a	2	5	0	0	0	0	0	0	0	2	.000	.000	.000	-99	-1	-1	0	0			1.000	-1	/CO	-0.2
■ FINNERS QUINLAN	Quinlan, Thomas Finners b: 10/21/1887, Scranton, Pa. d: 2/17/66, Scranton, Pa. BL/TL, 5'8", 154 lbs. Deb: 9/06/13																								
1913	StL-N	13	50	1	8	0	0	0	1	1	9	.160	.176	.160	-4	-7	-7	1	0			.897	2	O	-0.6
1915	Chi-A	42	114	11	22	3	0	0	7	4	11	.193	.270	.219	45	-7	-8	7	3	4	-2	1.000	-2	O	-1.3
Total	2	55	164	12	30	3	0	0	8	5	20	.183	.243	.201	31	-14	-14	9	3	4		.961	0	/O	-1.9
■ TOM QUINLAN	Quinlan, Thomas Raymond b: 3/27/68, St.Paul, Minn. BR/TR, 6'3", 200 lbs. Deb: 9/04/90																								
1990	Tor-A	1	2	0	1	0	0	0	0	0	1	.500	.667	.500	227	1	1	1	0	0	0	1.000	-0	/3	0.0
1992	Tor-A	13	15	2	1	1	0	0	2	2	9	.067	.176	.133	-12	-2	-2	0	0	0	0	.909	-1	3	-0.3
Total	2	14	17	2	2	1	0	0	2	2	10	.118	.250	.176	20	-2	-2	1	0	0	0	.917	-1	/3	-0.3
■ QUINN	Quinn Deb: 6/21/1877																								
1877	Chi-N	4	14	1	1	0	0	0	0	1	0	.071	.133	.071	-30	-2	-2	0				.667	0	/O	-0.2
■ QUINN	Quinn Deb: 9/07/1881																								
1881	Bos-N	1	4	0	0	0	0	0	0	0	0	.000	.000	.000	-99	-1	-1	0				1.000	-0	/1	-0.1
	Wor-N	2	7	0	1	0	0	0	1	1	2	.143	.250	.143	25	-1	-1	0				.714	-3	/C	-0.3
	Yr	3	11	0	1	0	0	0	1	1	2	.091	.167	.091	-16	-1	-1	0				.714	-3	/C1	-0.4
■ FRANK QUINN	Quinn, Frank J. b: 1876, Grand Rapids, Mich. d: 2/17/20, Camden, Ind. 5'8", Deb: 8/09/1899																								
1899	Chi-N	12	34	6	6	0	1	0	1	6		.176	.300	.235	49	-2	-2	3	1			.909	-4	O/2	-0.6
■ JOHN QUINN	Quinn, John Edward "Pick" b: 9/12/1885, Framingham, Mass. d: 4/9/56, Marlboro, Mass. BR/TR, 5'11", 150 lbs. Deb: 10/09/11																								
1911	Phi-N	1	2	0	0	0	0	0	0	0	0	.000	.000	.000	-99	-1	-1	0	0			1.000	-0	/C	-0.1
■ JOE QUINN	Quinn, Joseph C. b: 8/1849, Chicago, Ill. d: 1/2/09, Chicago, Ill. 5'8.5", 148 lbs. Deb: 7/26/1871																								
1871	Kek-n	5	17	8	4	0	0	0	2	4	0	.235	.381	.235	81	-0	-0	3	3					/C	0.0
1875	Wes-n	11	43	4	14	2	0	0		0		.326	.326	.372	133	2	1	5						/CO	0.1
	Har-n	5	13	1	3	0	0	0		1		.231	.286	.231	77	-0	-0	1						/CO	0.0
	Chi-n	17	59	12	14	0	0	0		0		.237	.237	.237	64	-2	-2	3						C/O	-0.1
	Yr	33	115	17	31	2	0	0		1		.270	.276	.287	92	-1	-1	9						CO	0.0
Total	2 n	38	132	25	35	2	0	0		5		.265	.292	.280	91	-1	-1	12						/CO	0.0
■ JOE QUINN	Quinn, Joseph J. b: 12/25/1864, Sydney, Australia d: 11/12/40, St.Louis, Mo. BR/TR, 5'7", 158 lbs. Deb: 4/26/1884 M																								
1884	StL-U	103	429	74	116	21	1	0		9		.270	.285	.324	102	2	-0	41				.945	-1	*1/OS	-1.1
1885	StL-N	97	343	27	73	8	2	0	15	9	38	.213	.233	.248	59	-17	-14	20				.875	-6	O31	-2.1
1886	StL-N	75	271	33	63	11	3	1	21	8	31	.232	.254	.306	75	-10	-7	25	12			.895	-1	O2/13S	-0.9
1888	Bos-N	38	156	19	47	8	3	4	29	2	5	.301	.310	.468	145	7	7	27	12			.914	-7	2	0.2
1889	Bos-N	112	444	57	116	13	5	2	69	25	21	.261	.308	.327	74	-13	-17	53	24			.860	-29	S2/3	-3.5
1890	Bos-P	130	509	87	153	19	8	7	82	44	24	.301	.359	.411	100	4	-2	87	29			**.942**	15	*2	1.6
1891	Bos-N	124	508	70	122	8	10	3	63	28	28	.240	.288	.313	69	-16	-25	54	24			.938	-23	*2	-3.9
1892	*Bos-N	143	532	63	116	14	1	1	59	35	40	.218	.275	.254	57	-24	-31	43	17			**.951**	2	*2	-2.5
1893	StL-N	135	547	68	126	18	6	0	71	33	7	.230	.279	.285	51	-38	-39	51	24			.942	-30	*2	-5.5
1894	StL-N	106	405	59	116	18	1	4	61	24	8	.286	.328	.365	68	-21	-21	60	25			.952	22	*2	0.4
1895	StL-N	134	543	84	169	19	9	2	74	36	6	.311	.356	.390	96	-4	-3	87	22			.946	-2	*2M	0.1
1896	StL-N	48	191	19	40	6	1	1	17	9	5	.209	.252	.267	40	-17	-16	16	8			.956	3	2	-0.9
	*Bal-N	24	82	22	27	1	1	0	5	6	1	.329	.375	.366	96	-0	-0	14	6			.951	-3	/2O3S	-0.3
	Yr	72	273	41	67	7	2	1	22	15	6	.245	.290	.297	58	-17	-16	29	14			.955	-1	2/O3S	-1.2
1897	Bal-N	75	285	33	74	11	4	1	45	13		.260	.299	.337	68	-14	-14	33	12			.946	9	3S2/O1	-0.3
1898	Bal-N	12	32	5	8	1	0	0	5	1		.250	.273	.281	58	-2	-2	3	0			.893	1	/32O	-0.1
	StL-N	103	375	35	94	10	5	0	36	24		.251	.301	.304	72	-13	-14	40	13			.962	-2	2S/O	-1.0
	Yr	115	407	40	102	11	5	0	41	25		.251	.299	.302	71	-15	-16	43	13			.960	-1	2S/3O	-1.1
1899	Cle-N	147	615	73	176	24	6	0	72	21		.286	.312	.345	86	-18	-12	75	22			**.962**	3	*2M	-0.1
1900	StL-N	22	80	12	21	2	0	1	11	10		.262	.344	.325	86	-1	-1	11	4			.933	-9	2/S3	-0.8
	Cin-N	74	266	18	73	5	2	0	25	16		.274	.316	.308	74	-10	-9	30	7			.950	-18	2	-2.2
	Yr	96	346	30	94	7	2	1	36	26		.272	.323	.312	77	-11	-10	40	11			.947	-27	2/S3	-3.0
1901	Was-A	66	266	33	67	11	2	2	34	11		.252	.287	.331	72	-11	-10	28	7			.954	-14	2	-2.0
Total	17	1768	6879	891	1797	228	70	29	794	364	214	.261	.302	.327	76	-216	-230	799	268			.946	-91	*2SO1/3	-24.9
■ PATRICK QUINN	Quinn, Patrick 5'8", 162 lbs. Deb: 9/09/1875																								
1875	Atl-n	2	7	2	1	0	0	0		0		.143	.143	.143	-1	-1	-1	0						/O	0.0
■ TOM QUINN	Quinn, Thomas Oscar b: 4/25/1864, Annapolis, Md. d: 7/24/32, Pittsburgh, Pa. BR/TR, 5'8", 180 lbs. Deb: 9/02/1886																								
1886	Pit-a	3	11	1	0	0	0	0		0		.000	.000	.000	-99	-2	-2	0	1			.929	-2	/C	-0.3
1889	Bal-a	55	194	18	34	2	1	1	15	19	22	.175	.252	.211	34	-16	-17	12	6			.925	8	C	-0.3
1890	Pit-P	55	207	23	44	4	3	1	15	17	8	.213	.282	.275	55	-14	-11	17	1			.888	-4	C	-0.9
Total	3	113	412	42	78	6	4	2	30	36	30	.189	.261	.238	41	-33	-30	29	8			.910	2	C	-1.5
■ LUIS QUINONES	Quinones, Luis Raul b: 4/28/62, Ponce, P.R. BB/TR, 5'11", 175 lbs. Deb: 5/27/83																								
1983	Oak-A	19	42	5	8	2	1	0	4	1	4	.190	.209	.286	37	-4	-3	2	1	1	-0	1.000	1	/23OSD	-0.2
1986	SF-N	71	106	13	19	1	3	0	11	3	17	.179	.209	.245	26	-11	-10	6	3	1	0	.922	-7	S3/2	-1.7
1987	Chi-N	49	101	12	22	6	0	0	8	10	16	.218	.288	.277	49	-7	-8	9	0	0	0	.965	-7	S/23	-1.2
1988	Cin-N	23	52	4	12	3	0	1	11	2	11	.231	.259	.346	70	-2	-2	5	1	1	-0	.974	1	S/23	-0.1
1989	Cin-N	97	340	43	83	13	4	12	34	25	46	.244	.302	.412	99	-0	-1	42	2	4	-2	.979	-5	23/S	-0.7
1990	*Cin-N	83	145	10	35	7	0	2	17	13	29	.241	.308	.331	73	-5	-5	15	1	0	0	.981	9	32/S1	0.5
1991	Cin-N	97	212	15	47	4	3	4	20	21	31	.222	.298	.325	72	-7	-8	21	1	2	-1	.975	-4	23/S	-1.2
1992	Min-A	3	5	0	1	0	0	0	1	0	0	.200	.200	.200	12	-1	-1	0	0	0	0	.714	-0	/3SD	-0.1
Total	8	442	1003	102	227	36	11	19	106	75	154	.226	.285	.341	72	-36	-39	100	9	9	-3	.937	-11	32/SDO1	-4.7
■ REY QUINONES	Quinones, Rey Francisco (Santiago) b: 11/11/63, Rio Pedras, P.R. BR/TR, 5'11", 160 lbs. Deb: 5/17/86																								
1986	Bos-A	62	190	26	45	12	1	2	15	19	26	.237	.316	.342	79	-5	-5	20	3	2	-0	.940	-8	S	-0.8
	Sea-A	36	122	6	23	4	0	0	7	5	31	.189	.220	.221	21	-13	-13	6	1	1	-0	.945	1	S	-1.0
	Yr	98	312	32	68	16	1	2	22	24	57	.218	.280	.295	56	-19	-19	26	4	3	-1	.942	-7	S	-1.8
1987	Sea-A	135	478	55	132	18	2	12	56	26	71	.276	.319	.397	84	-8	-12	57	1	3	-2	.959	-10	*S	-1.1

YEAR	TM/L	G	AB	R	H	2B	3B	HR	RBI	BB	SO	AVG	OBP	SLG	PRO+	BR	/A	RC	SB	CS	SBR	FA	FR	POS	TPR
1988	Sea-A	140	499	63	124	30	3	12	52	23	71	.248	.286	.393	84	-9	-12	52	0	3	-2	.963	3	*S/D	0.0
1989	Sea-A	7	19	2	2	0	0	0	0	1	1	.105	.150	.105	-26	-3	-3	0	0	0	0	.889	-2	/S	-0.5
	Pit-N	71	225	21	47	11	0	3	29	15	40	.209	.261	.298	62	-12	-11	17	0	2	-1	.934	-11	S	-2.0
Total	4	451	1533	173	373	75	6	29	159	89	240	.243	.290	.357	74	-52	-57	153	5	11	-5	.952	-27	S/D	-5.4

■ CARLOS QUINTANA Quintana, Carlos Narcis (Hernandez) b: 8/26/65, Estado Miranda, Ven. BR/TR, 6', 175 lbs. Deb: 9/16/88

YEAR	TM/L	G	AB	R	H	2B	3B	HR	RBI	BB	SO	AVG	OBP	SLG	PRO+	BR	/A	RC	SB	CS	SBR	FA	FR	POS	TPR
1988	Bos-A	5	6	1	2	0	0	0	2	2	3	.333	.500	.333	133	1	0	1	0	0	0	1.000	-0	/OD	0.0
1989	Bos-A	34	77	6	16	5	0	0	6	7	12	.208	.274	.273	51	-5	-5	5	0	0	0	.926	-5	O/1D	-1.1
1990	*Bos-A	149	512	56	147	28	0	7	67	52	74	.287	.355	.383	102	5	2	67	1	2	-1	.987	15	*1/O	0.5
1991	Bos-A	149	478	69	141	21	1	11	71	61	66	.295	.377	.412	113	13	10	74	1	0	0	.993	7	*1O/D	0.9
Total	4	337	1073	132	306	54	1	18	146	122	155	.285	.360	.388	103	15	8	148	2	2	-1	.990	16	1/OD	0.3

■ MARSHALL QUINTON Quinton, Marshall J. b: Philadelphia, Pa. 5'11", 190 lbs. Deb: 8/07/1884

YEAR	TM/L	G	AB	R	H	2B	3B	HR	RBI	BB	SO	AVG	OBP	SLG	PRO+	BR	/A	RC	SB	CS	SBR	FA	FR	POS	TPR
1884	Ric-a	26	94	12	22	5	0	0		0		.234	.242	.287	75	-3	-2	7				.878	-9	CO/S	-0.9
1885	Phi-a	7	29	6	6	1	0	0		1		.207	.258	.241	57	-1	-1	2				.869	-2	/C	-0.3
Total	2	33	123	18	28	6	0	0		1		.228	.246	.276	71	-4	-4	9				.874	-11	/COS	-1.2

■ JAMIE QUIRK Quirk, James Patrick b: 10/22/54, Whittier, Cal. BL/TR, 6'4", 200 lbs. Deb: 9/04/75 C

YEAR	TM/L	G	AB	R	H	2B	3B	HR	RBI	BB	SO	AVG	OBP	SLG	PRO+	BR	/A	RC	SB	CS	SBR	FA	FR	POS	TPR
1975	KC-A	14	39	2	10	0	0	1	5	2	7	.256	.293	.333	75	-1	-1	4	0	0	0	.909	0	O/3D	-0.1
1976	*KC-A	64	114	11	28	6	0	1	15	2	22	.246	.259	.325	70	-5	-5	8	0	0	0	1.000	-1	DS3/1	-0.6
1977	Mil-A	93	221	16	48	14	1	3	13	8	47	.217	.251	.330	57	-14	-14	17	0	1	-1	.950	0	DO/3	-1.4
1978	KC-A	17	29	3	6	2	0	0	2	5	4	.207	.324	.276	68	-1	-1	3	0	0	0	.926	2	3/SD	0.1
1979	KC-A	51	79	8	24	6	1	1	11	5	13	.304	.353	.443	111	1	1	13	0	0	0	.944	-1	/CS3D	0.1
1980	KC-A	62	163	13	45	5	0	5	21	7	24	.276	.310	.399	92	-2	-2	18	3	2	-0	.929	-1	3C/O1D	-0.3
1981	KC-A	46	100	8	25	7	0	0	10	6	17	.250	.299	.320	79	-3	-3	8	0	2	-1	.985	-3	C/32O	-0.7
1982	KC-A	36	78	8	18	3	0	1	5	3	15	.231	.259	.308	55	-5	-5	6	0	0	0	1.000	2	C/13O	-0.3
1983	StL-N	48	86	3	18	2	1	2	11	6	27	.209	.269	.326	64	-4	-4	7	0	0	0	.929	-5	C/3S	-0.9
1984	Chi-A	3	2	0	0	0	0	0	1	0	2	.000	.000	.000	-96	-1	-1	0	0	0	0	1.000	0	/3	-0.1
	Cle-A	1	1	1	1	0	0	1	1	0	0	1.000	1.000	4.000	1189	1	1	4	0	0	0	.000	0	/C	0.1
	Yr	4	3	1	1	0	0	1	2	0	2	.333	.333	1.333	324	1	1	1	0	0	0	1.000	0	/3C	0.0
1985	*KC-A	19	57	3	16	3	1	0	4	2	9	.281	.305	.368	83	-1	-1	6	0	0	0	.986	-3	C/1	-0.3
1986	KC-A	80	219	24	47	10	0	8	26	17	41	.215	.274	.370	72	-9	-9	22	0	1	-1	.989	11	C3/1O	0.3
1987	KC-A	109	296	24	70	17	0	5	33	28	56	.236	.311	.345	72	-11	-12	32	1	0	0	.986	-4	*C/S	-0.9
1988	KC-A	84	196	22	47	7	1	8	25	28	41	.240	.338	.408	107	2	2	27	1	5	-3	.982	14	C/13	1.8
1989	NY-A	13	24	0	2	0	0	0	0	3	5	.083	.185	.083	-22	-4	-4	0	0	1	-1	1.000	1	/CSD	-0.3
	Oak-A	9	10	1	2	0	0	1	1	0	4	.200	.200	.500	95	-0	-0	1	0	0	0	.500	-0	/3C1O	-0.1
	Bal-A	25	51	5	11	2	0	0	9	9	11	.216	.333	.255	70	-2	-2	4	0	1	-1	1.000	5	C	0.4
	Yr	47	85	6	15	2	0	1	10	12	20	.176	.278	.235	47	-6	-6	5	0	2	-1	1.000	6	C/3SD1O	0.0
1990	*Oak-A	56	121	12	34	5	1	3	26	14	34	.281	.360	.413	121	3	3	19	0	0	0	.977	-2	C/13OD	0.4
1991	Oak-A	76	203	16	53	4	0	1	17	16	28	.261	.321	.296	76	-7	-6	18	0	3	-2	.982	5	C/13D	0.0
1992	*Oak-A	78	177	13	39	7	1	2	11	16	28	.220	.296	.305	71	-7	-6	16	0	0	0	.973	5	C/13D	0.1
Total	18	984	2266	193	544	100	7	43	247	177	435	.240	.300	.347	78	-69	-68	234	5	16	-8	.982	27	C3/D1OS2	-2.7

■ JOHN RABB Rabb, John Andrew b: 6/23/60, Los Angeles, Cal. BR/TR, 6'1", 180 lbs. Deb: 9/04/82

YEAR	TM/L	G	AB	R	H	2B	3B	HR	RBI	BB	SO	AVG	OBP	SLG	PRO+	BR	/A	RC	SB	CS	SBR	FA	FR	POS	TPR
1982	SF-N	2	2	0	1	0	1	0	0	0	1	.500	.500	1.500	441	1	1	2	0	0	0	1.000	0	/O	0.1
1983	SF-N	40	104	10	24	9	0	1	14	9	17	.231	.292	.346	79	-3	-3	10	1	0	0	.973	4	C/O	0.2
1984	SF-N	54	82	10	16	1	0	3	9	10	33	.195	.283	.317	71	-3	-3	8	1	1	-0	.988	-2	1/OC	-0.6
1985	Atl-N	3	2	0	0	0	0	0	0	0	1	.000	.000	.000	-94	-1	-1	0	0	0	0	.000	-0	/O	-0.1
1988	Sea-A	9	14	2	5	2	0	0	4	0	1	.357	.357	.500	131	1	1	3	0	0	0	1.000	0	/O1D	0.1
Total	5	108	204	22	46	12	1	4	27	19	53	.225	.291	.353	81	-6	-5	22	2	1	0	.966	2	/C1OD	-0.3

■ JOE RABBITT Rabbitt, Joseph Patrick b: 1/16/1900, Frontenac, Kan. d: 12/5/69, Norwalk, Conn. BL/TR, 5'10", 165 lbs. Deb: 9/15/22

YEAR	TM/L	G	AB	R	H	2B	3B	HR	RBI	BB	SO	AVG	OBP	SLG	PRO+	BR	/A	RC	SB	CS	SBR	FA	FR	POS	TPR
1922	Cle-A	2	3	1	1	0	0	0	0	0	0	.333	.333	.333	74	-0	-0	0	0	0	0	.000	-1	/O	-0.1

■ MARV RACKLEY Rackley, Marvin Eugene b: 7/25/21, Seneca, S.C. BL/TL, 5'10", 170 lbs. Deb: 4/15/47

YEAR	TM/L	G	AB	R	H	2B	3B	HR	RBI	BB	SO	AVG	OBP	SLG	PRO+	BR	/A	RC	SB	CS	SBR	FA	FR	POS	TPR
1947	Bro-N	18	9	2	2	0	0	0	2	1	0	.222	.300	.222	39	-1	-1	1	0			1.000	0	/O	0.0
1948	Bro-N	88	281	55	92	13	5	0	15	19	25	.327	.370	.409	107	4	3	44	8			.949	-5	O	-0.6
1949	*Bro-N	9	9	2	4	1	0	0	1	1	0	.444	.500	.556	175	1	1	3	0			1.000	-0	/O	0.1
	Pit-N	11	35	5	11	2	0	0	2	2	3	.314	.351	.371	92	-0	-0	5	1			1.000	0	/O	-0.1
	*Bro-N	54	141	23	41	4	1	1	14	13	8	.291	.351	.355	86	-2	-3	18	1			.986	-8	O	-1.2
	Yr	74	185	30	56	7	1	1	17	16	11	.303	.358	.368	91	-1	-2	25	2			.990	-8	O	-1.2
1950	Cin-N	5	2	0	1	0	0	0	1	0	0	.500	.500	.500	163	0	0	1	0			.000	0	H	0.0
Total	4	185	477	87	151	20	6	1	35	36	36	.317	.365	.390	100	3	1	71	10			.966	-13	O	-1.8

■ CHARLEY RADBOURN Radbourn, Charles Gardner "Old Hoss"
b: 12/11/1854, Rochester, N.Y. d: 2/5/1897, Bloomington, Ill. BR/TR, 5'9", 168 lbs. Deb: 5/05/1880 H

YEAR	TM/L	G	AB	R	H	2B	3B	HR	RBI	BB	SO	AVG	OBP	SLG	PRO+	BR	/A	RC	SB	CS	SBR	FA	FR	POS	TPR
1880	Buf-N	6	21	1	3	0	0	0	1	0	1	.143	.143	.143	-3	-2	-2	0				.900	4	/O2	0.2
1881	Pro-N	72	270	27	59	9	0	0	28	10	15	.219	.246	.252	58	-13	-12	17				.906	-2	POS	-0.9
1882	Pro-N	83	326	30	78	11	0	1	32	12	22	.239	.266	.282	76	-8	-8	25				.912	1	PO/S	-0.2
1883	Pro-N	89	381	59	108	11	3	3	48	14	16	.283	.309	.352	98	0	-1	42				.920	2	*PO/1	-0.3
1884	*Pro-N	87	361	48	83	7	1	1	37	26	42	.230	.282	.263	74	-11	-9	27				.892	-6	*P/O1S2	-0.3
1885	Pro-N	66	249	34	58	9	2	0	22	36	27	.233	.330	.285	104	2	3	24				.937	0	PO/2	-0.2
1886	Bos-N	66	253	30	60	5	1	2	22	17	36	.237	.285	.289	78	-7	-6	23	5			.924	1	P/O	-0.2
1887	Bos-N	51	175	25	40	2	2	1	24	18	21	.229	.308	.280	66	-7	-7	17	6			.848	-4	P/O	-0.1
1888	Bos-N	24	79	6	17	1	0	0	6	3	14	.215	.262	.228	58	-3	-4	6	4			.895	-1	P	0.0
1889	Bos-N	35	122	17	23	1	0	1	13	9	19	.189	.256	.221	33	-10	-12	8	3			.975	1	P/O3	-0.1
1890	Bos-P	45	154	20	39	6	0	0	16	9	20	.253	.299	.292	56	-9	-11	16	7			.935	0	P/O1	-0.2
1891	Cin-N	29	96	11	17	2	2	0	10	4	11	.177	.225	.240	37	-8	-8	6	1			.880	-3	P/O3	-0.1
Total	12	653	2487	308	585	64	11	9	259	158	244	.235	.283	.281	73	-77	-77	212	26			.913	-6	PO/S123	-2.4

■ JOHN RADCLIFF Radcliff, John Y. b: 6/1848, Pennsylvania d: 7/26/11, Ocean City, N.J. 5'6", 140 lbs. Deb: 5/20/1871

YEAR	TM/L	G	AB	R	H	2B	3B	HR	RBI	BB	SO	AVG	OBP	SLG	PRO+	BR	/A	RC	SB	CS	SBR	FA	FR	POS	TPR
1871	Ath-n	28	145	47	44	7	5	0	22	6	1	.303	.331	.421	115	3	3	22	5					*S	0.2
1872	Bal-n	56	298	70	87	10	4	1	46	0	2	.292	.292	.362	96	-0	-3	32						*S/32	-0.3
1873	Bal-n	45	245	59	70	10	1	0	33	3	2	.286	.294	.335	85	-5	-4	25						3S/2	-0.4
1874	Phi-n	23	102	20	26	6	0	1		2		.255	.269	.343	90	-1	-1	10						O/2S13	-0.1
1875	Cen-n	5	24	2	4	0	0	0		0		.167	.167	.167	17	-2	-2	1						/S	-0.2
Total	5 n	157	814	198	231	33	10	2		11		.284	.293	.356	94	-5	-7	90						S/3O21	-0.8

■ RIP RADCLIFF Radcliff, Raymond Allen b: 1/19/06, Kiowa, Okla. d: 5/23/62, Enid, Okla. BL/TL, 5'10", 170 lbs. Deb: 9/17/34

YEAR	TM/L	G	AB	R	H	2B	3B	HR	RBI	BB	SO	AVG	OBP	SLG	PRO+	BR	/A	RC	SB	CS	SBR	FA	FR	POS	TPR
1934	Chi-A	14	56	7	15	2	1	0	5	0	2	.268	.268	.339	54	-4	-4	5	1	0	0	.946	1	O	-0.3
1935	Chi-A	146	623	95	178	28	8	10	68	53	21	.286	.346	.404	91	-7	-9	88	4	4	-1	.968	-18	*O	-3.1
1936	Chi-A★	138	618	120	207	31	7	8	82	44	12	.335	.381	.447	100	3	-0	105	6	3	0	.936	-17	*O	-2.0
1937	Chi-A	144	584	105	190	38	10	4	79	53	25	.325	.383	.445	108	8	8	102	6	1	1	.966	-4	*O	0.0
1938	Chi-A	129	503	64	166	23	6	5	81	36	17	.330	.376	.429	99	1	-1	80	5	7	-3	.979	-1	O1	-0.9
1939	Chi-A	113	397	49	105	25	2	2	53	26	21	.264	.313	.353	68	-18	-20	44	6	4	-1	.970	-10	O1	-3.3

YEAR	TM/L	G	AB	R	H	2B	3B	HR	RBI	BB	SO	AVG	OBP	SLG	PRO+	BR	/A	RC	SB	CS	SBR	FA	FR	POS	TPR
1940	StL-A	150	584	83	**200**	33	9	7	81	47	20	.342	.392	.466	119	19	17	109	6	4	-1	.973	-6	*O/1	0.3
1941	StL-A	19	71	12	20	2	2	2	14	10	1	.282	.370	.451	112	2	1	12	1	1	-0	1.000	-2	O/1	-0.2
	Det-A	96	379	47	120	14	5	3	40	19	13	.317	.351	.404	90	-1	-6	53	4	4	-1	.970	-5	O	-1.8
	Yr	115	450	59	140	16	7	5	54	29	14	.311	.354	.411	94	1	-5	66	5	5	-2	.974	-8	*O/1	-2.0
1942	Det-A	62	144	13	36	5	0	1	20	9	6	.250	.294	.306	64	-6	-8	13	0	1	-1	.978	-0	O/1	-1.0
1943	Det-A	70	115	3	30	4	0	0	10	13	3	.261	.341	.296	81	-1	-2	12	1	1	-0	1.000	0	O/1	-0.4
Total	10	1081	4074	598	1267	205	50	42	533	310	141	.311	.362	.417	96	-5	-24	623	40	30	-6	.967	-62	O/1	-12.7
■ DAVE RADER	Rader, David Martin b: 12/26/48, Claremore, Okla. BL/TR, 5'11", 165 lbs. Deb: 9/05/71																								
1971	SF-N	3	4	0	0	0	0	0	0	0	0	.000	.000	.000	-99	-1	-1	0	0	0	0	1.000	-0	/C	-0.1
1972	SF-N	133	459	44	119	14	1	6	41	29	31	.259	.308	.333	81	-11	-12	45	1	2	-1	.985	-13	*C	-2.2
1973	SF-N	148	462	59	106	15	4	9	41	63	22	.229	.330	.338	82	-8	-10	51	0	0	0	.991	-12	*C	-1.7
1974	SF-N	113	323	26	94	16	2	1	26	31	21	.291	.353	.362	96	1	-1	41	1	0	0	.984	-9	*C	-0.6
1975	SF-N	98	292	39	85	15	0	5	31	32	30	.291	.363	.394	106	4	3	41	1	0	0	.984	-3	C	0.4
1976	SF-N	88	255	25	67	15	0	1	22	27	21	.263	.333	.333	87	-3	-4	27	2	0	1	.984	-9	C	-1.0
1977	StL-N	66	114	15	30	7	1	1	16	9	10	.263	.317	.368	85	-3	-2	15	1	0	0	.976	4	C	0.2
1978	Chi-N	116	305	29	62	13	3	3	36	34	26	.203	.285	.295	56	-15	-20	24	1	1	-0	.977	-13	*C	-3.2
1979	Phi-N	31	54	3	11	1	1	1	5	6	7	.204	.283	.315	61	-3	-3	4	0	0	0	.932	-4	C	-0.6
1980	Bos-A	50	137	14	45	11	0	3	17	14	12	.328	.391	.474	129	7	6	25	1	1	-0	.981	3	C/D	0.9
Total	10	846	2405	254	619	107	12	30	235	245	180	.257	.329	.349	86	-32	-45	272	8	4	0	.983	-56	C/D	-7.9
■ DON RADER	Rader, Donald Russell b: 9/5/1893, Wolcott, Ind. d: 6/26/83, Walla Walla, Wash BL/TR, 5'10", 164 lbs. Deb: 7/25/13																								
1913	Chi-A	4	3	1	1	1	0	0	0	0	0	.333	.333	.667	193	0	0	1	0			.000	-1	/3O	0.0
1921	Phi-N	9	32	4	9	2	0	0	3	3	5	.281	.343	.344	76	-1	-1	4	0	0	0	1.000	-6	/S	-0.6
Total	2	13	35	5	10	3	0	0	3	3	5	.286	.342	.371	84	-0	-1	5	0	0			-6	/SO3	-0.6
■ DOUG RADER	Rader, Douglas Lee "Rojo" or "The Red Rooster" b: 7/30/44, Chicago, Ill. BR/TR, 6'3", 215 lbs. Deb: 7/31/67 MC																								
1967	Hou-N	47	162	24	54	10	4	2	26	7	31	.333	.368	.481	146	8	9	27	0	3	-2	.972	-1	1/3	0.4
1968	Hou-N	98	333	42	89	16	4	6	43	31	51	.267	.332	.393	119	7	8	43	2	2	-1	.930	1	3/1	0.9
1969	Hou-N	155	569	62	140	25	3	11	83	62	103	.246	.327	.359	94	-6	-4	65	1	5	-3	.945	14	*3/1	0.8
1970	Hou-N	156	576	90	145	25	3	25	87	57	102	.252	.323	.436	106	-0	3	76	3	2	-0	**.966**	24	*3/1	2.5
1971	Hou-N	135	484	51	118	21	4	12	56	40	112	.244	.306	.378	95	-5	-4	56	5	1	1	.946	2	*3	-0.3
1972	Hou-N	152	553	70	131	24	7	22	90	57	120	.237	.314	.425	110	5	6	70	5	5	-2	.958	18	*3	2.2
1973	Hou-N	154	574	79	146	26	0	21	89	46	97	.254	.313	.409	99	-2	-2	73	4	3	-1	.945	-5	*3	-0.9
1974	Hou-N	152	533	61	137	27	3	17	78	60	131	.257	.337	.415	114	6	9	74	7	2	1	.965	5	*3	1.4
1975	Hou-N	129	448	41	100	23	2	12	48	42	101	.223	.297	.364	89	-12	-8	47	5	4	-1	**.971**	8	*3/S	-0.1
1976	SD-N	139	471	45	121	22	4	9	55	55	102	.257	.338	.378	112	2	7	60	3	4	-2	.955	14	*3	1.9
1977	SD-N	52	170	19	46	8	3	5	27	33	40	.271	.392	.441	137	7	9	30	0	1	-1	.961	1	3	0.9
	Tor-A	96	313	47	75	18	2	13	40	38	65	.240	.328	.435	104	2	2	44	2	1	0	.966	1	3D/1O	0.1
Total	11	1465	5186	631	1302	245	39	155	722	528	1055	.251	.325	.403	106	11	33	665	37	33	-9	.956	82	*3/1DSO	9.8
■ PAUL RADFORD	Radford, Paul Revere "Shorty" b: 10/14/1861, Roxbury, Mass. d: 2/21/45, Boston, Mass. BR/TR, 5'6", 148 lbs. Deb: 5/01/1883																								
1883	Bos-N	72	258	46	53	6	3	0	14	9	26	.205	.232	.252	46	-16	-17	15				.836	-5	*O	-1.9
1884	*Pro-N	97	355	56	70	11	2	1	29	25	43	.197	.250	.248	59	-17	-15	23				.882	5	*O/P	-1.1
1885	Pro-N	105	371	55	90	12	5	0	32	33	43	.243	.304	.302	101	-1	2	35				.852	1	*OS/P2	0.0
1886	KC-N	122	493	78	113	17	5	0	20	58	48	.229	.310	.284	77	-9	-14	57	39			.890	10	*OS/2	-0.5
1887	NY-a	128	486	127	129	15	5	4		**106**		.265	.403	.342	116	14	19	99	73			.833	-2	SO2/P	1.4
1888	Bro-a	90	308	48	67	9	3	2	29	35		.218	.305	.286	93	-1	-1	38	33			.944	9	O/2	0.5
1889	Cle-N	136	487	94	116	21	5	1	46	91	37	.238	.365	.308	92	-2	-0	67	30			.942	-0	*O/3	-0.3
1890	Cle-P	122	466	98	136	24	12	2	62	82	28	.292	.406	.408	131	17	24	90	25			.895	8	OS/32P	2.5
1891	Bos-a	133	456	102	118	11	5	0	65	96	36	.259	.393	.305	105	8	9	78	55			.906	20	*S/OP	3.1
1892	Was-N	137	510	93	130	19	4	1	37	86	47	.255	.366	.314	111	9	11	73	35			.933	-7	O3S/2	0.4
1893	Was-N	124	464	87	106	18	3	2	34	105	42	.228	.380	.293	84	-6	-4	65	32			.901	7	*O/2P	-0.2
1894	Was-N	95	325	61	78	13	5	0	49	65	23	.240	.378	.311	71	-14	-11	49	24			.852	-1	S2O	-0.8
Total	12	1361	4979	945	1206	176	57	13	417	791	373	.242	.351	.308	94	-17	3	689	346			.901	46	OS/32P	3.1
■ JACK RADTKE	Radtke, Jack William b: 4/14/13, Denver, Colo. BB/TR, 5'7", 160 lbs. Deb: 8/01/36																								
1936	Bro-N	33	31	8	3	0	0	0	2	4	9	.097	.200	.097	-18	-5	-5	1	3			1.000	5	2/3S	0.0
■ JACK RAFTER	Rafter, John Cornelius b: 2/20/1875, Troy, N.Y. d: 1/5/43, Troy, N.Y. BR/TR, 5'8", 165 lbs. Deb: 9/24/04																								
1904	Pit-N	1	3	0	0	0	0	0	0	0		.000	.000	.000	-97	-1	-1	0	0			1.000	0	/C	-0.1
■ TOM RAFTERY	Raftery, Thomas Francis b: 10/5/1881, Boston, Mass. d: 12/31/54, Boston, Mass. BR/TR, 5'10.5", 175 lbs. Deb: 4/18/09																								
1909	Cle-A	8	32	6	7	2	1	0	0	4		.219	.306	.344	101	0	0	4	1			1.000	-1	/O	-0.1
■ TOM RAGLAND	Ragland, Thomas b: 6/16/46, Talladega, Ala. BR/TR, 5'10", 155 lbs. Deb: 4/05/71																								
1971	Was-A	10	23	1	4	0	0	0	0	0	5	.174	.208	.174	10	-3	-3	0	0	0	0	1.000	-1	2	-0.3
1972	Tex-A	25	58	3	10	2	0	0	2	5	11	.172	.238	.207	35	-5	-4	3	0	1	-1	.982	-3	2/3S	-0.8
1973	Cle-A	67	183	16	47	7	1	0	12	8	31	.257	.292	.306	67	-8	-8	16	2	3	-1	.984	13	2/S	0.7
Total	3	102	264	20	61	9	1	0	14	13	47	.231	.272	.273	56	-15	-15	19	2	4	-2	.985	10	/2S3	-0.4
■ LARRY RAINES	Raines, Lawrence Glenn Hope b: 3/9/30, St.Albans, W.Va. d: 1/28/78, Lansing, Mich. BR/TR, 5'10", 165 lbs. Deb: 4/16/57																								
1957	Cle-A	96	244	39	64	14	0	2	16	19	40	.262	.318	.344	82	-6	-6	27	5	2	0	.922	-5	3S2/O	-0.9
1958	Cle-A	7	9	1	0	0	0	0	0	0	5	.000	.000	.000	-99	-2	-2	0	0	1	-1	.933	4	/2	0.1
Total	2	103	253	40	64	14	0	2	16	19	45	.253	.308	.332	76	-9	-8	27	5	3	-0	.963	-2	/3S2O	-0.8
■ TIM RAINES	Raines, Timothy "Rock" b: 9/16/59, Sanford, Fla. BB/TR, 5'8", 178 lbs. Deb: 9/11/79																								
1979	Mon-N	6	0	3	0	0	0	0	0	0	0	—	—	—	—	0	0	0	2	0	1	.000	0	/R	0.1
1980	Mon-N	15	20	5	1	0	0	0	0	6	3	.050	.269	.050	-6	-3	-3	1	5	0	2	1.000	2	/2O	0.2
1981	*Mon-N★	88	313	61	95	13	7	5	37	45	31	.304	.394	.438	134	16	16	64	**71**	11	**15**	.976	-1	O/2	2.8
1982	Mon-N★	156	647	90	179	32	8	4	43	75	83	.277	.354	.369	101	4	2	96	**78**	16	**14**	.992	-1	*O2	1.4
1983	Mon-N★	156	615	**133**	183	32	8	11	71	97	70	.298	.395	.429	129	27	27	120	**90**	14	**19**	.988	11	*O/2	5.4
1984	Mon-N★	160	622	106	192	**38**	9	8	60	87	69	.309	.395	.437	140	30	34	124	**75**	10	**17**	.988	10	*O/2	5.7
1985	Mon-N★	150	575	115	184	30	13	11	41	81	60	.320	.407	.475	155	38	42	124	70	9	16	.993	10	*O	**6.4**
1986	Mon-N★	151	580	91	194	35	10	9	62	78	60	**.334**	**.415**	.476	146	38	39	**130**	70	9	16	.979	11	*O	**6.2**
1987	Mon-N★	139	530	**123**	175	34	8	18	68	90	52	.330	.431	.526	148	43	41	132	50	5	12	.987	16	*O	6.2
1988	Mon-N	109	429	66	116	19	7	12	48	53	44	.270	.353	.431	119	14	12	69	33	7	6	.988	7	*O	2.3
1989	Mon-N	145	517	76	148	29	6	9	60	93	48	.286	.398	.418	132	26	26	96	41	9	7	.996	3	*O	3.3
1990	Mon-N	130	457	65	131	11	5	9	62	70	43	.287	.385	.392	119	12	14	75	49	16	5	.976	-1	*O	1.5
1991	Chi-A	155	609	102	163	20	6	5	50	83	68	.268	.360	.345	98	-0	2	85	51	15	6	.990	10	*OD	1.5
1992	Chi-A	144	551	102	162	22	9	7	54	81	48	.294	.384	.405	124	18	20	98	45	6	10	.994	14	*OD	4.1
Total	14	1704	6465	1138	1923	315	96	108	656	939	679	.297	.389	.426	128	263	270	1214	730	127	143	.988	92	*O/2D	47.1
■ JOHN RAINEY	Rainey, John Paul b: 7/26/1864, Birmingham, Mich. d: 11/11/12, Detroit, Mich. BL/TR, 6'1.5", 164 lbs. Deb: 8/25/1887																								
1887	NY-N	17	58	6	17	3	0	0	12	5	6	.293	.349	.345	100	-0	0	7	0			.818	-3	3	-0.2

YEAR	TM/L	G	AB	R	H	2B	3B	HR	RBI	BB	SO	AVG	OBP	SLG	PRO+	BR	/A	RC	SB	CS	SBR	FA	FR	POS	TPR
1890	Buf-P	42	166	29	39	5	1	1	20	24	15	.235	.349	.295	81	-5	-2	22	12			.870	0	O/S32	-0.2
Total	2	59	224	35	56	8	1	1	32	29	21	.250	.349	.308	86	-5	-2	29	12			.827	-3	/O3S2	-0.4

■ GARY RAJSICH Rajsich, Gary Louis b: 10/28/54, Youngstown, Ohio BL/TL, 6'2", 210 lbs. Deb: 4/09/82 F

YEAR	TM/L	G	AB	R	H	2B	3B	HR	RBI	BB	SO	AVG	OBP	SLG	PRO+	BR	/A	RC	SB	CS	SBR	FA	FR	POS	TPR
1982	NY-N	80	162	17	42	8	3	2	12	17	40	.259	.333	.383	100	0	0	20	1	3	-2	1.000	-3	O/1	-0.6
1983	NY-N	11	36	5	12	3	0	1	3	3	1	.333	.400	.500	149	2	2	7	0	0	0	1.000	-0	1	0.2
1984	StL-N	7	7	1	1	0	0	0	2	2	1	.143	.333	.143	39	-0	-0	1	0	0	0	1.000	-0	/1	-0.1
1985	SF-N	51	91	5	15	6	0	0	10	17	22	.165	.296	.231	52	-6	-5	7	0	1	-1	.990	-1	1	-0.9
Total	4	149	296	28	70	17	3	3	27	39	64	.236	.329	.345	90	-4	-3	35	1	4	-2	.994	-5	/1O	-1.4

■ DOC RALSTON Ralston, Samuel Beryl b: 8/3/1885, Pierpont, Ohio d: 8/29/50, Lancaster, Pa. BR/TR, 6', 185 lbs. Deb: 9/08/10

YEAR	TM/L	G	AB	R	H	2B	3B	HR	RBI	BB	SO	AVG	OBP	SLG	PRO+	BR	/A	RC	SB	CS	SBR	FA	FR	POS	TPR
1910	Was-A	21	73	4	15	1	0	0	3	3		.205	.256	.219	52	-4	-4	5	2			.976	2	O	-0.4

■ BOB RAMAZZOTTI Ramazzotti, Robert Louis b: 1/16/17, Elanora, Pa. BR/TR, 5'8.5", 175 lbs. Deb: 4/20/46

YEAR	TM/L	G	AB	R	H	2B	3B	HR	RBI	BB	SO	AVG	OBP	SLG	PRO+	BR	/A	RC	SB	CS	SBR	FA	FR	POS	TPR
1946	Bro-N	62	120	10	25	4	0	0	7	9	13	.208	.264	.242	43	-9	-9	8	0			.939	5	32	-0.4
1948	Bro-N	4	3	0	0	0	0	0	0	0	1	.000	.000	.000	-97	-1	-1	0	0			1.000	0	/32	-0.1
1949	Bro-N	5	13	1	2	0	0	1	3	0	3	.154	.154	.385	38	-1	-1	1	0			.833	-1	/3	-0.3
	Chi-N	65	190	14	34	3	1	0	6	5	33	.179	.200	.205	9	-24	-24	6	9			.972	6	3S/2	-1.7
	Yr	70	203	15	36	3	1	1	9	5	36	.177	.197	.217	11	-26	-25	7	9			.965	5	3S/2	-2.0
1950	Chi-N	61	145	19	38	3	3	1	6	4	16	.262	.287	.345	66	-8	-7	14	3			.961	-2	23/S	-0.8
1951	Chi-N	73	158	13	39	5	2	1	15	10	23	.247	.292	.323	64	-8	-8	15	0	0	0	.950	13	S/23	0.7
1952	Chi-N	50	183	26	52	5	3	1	12	14	14	.284	.338	.361	93	-1	-2	22	3	1	0	.979	-2	2	-0.1
1953	Chi-N	26	39	3	6	2	0	0	4	3	4	.154	.214	.205	10	-5	-5	2	0	0	0	.911	-0	2	-0.5
Total	7	346	851	86	196	22	9	4	53	45	107	.230	.271	.291	52	-57	-57	68	15	1		.966	18	2/3S	-3.2

■ MARIO RAMIREZ Ramirez, Mario (Torres) b: 9/12/57, Yauco, P.R. BR/TR, 5'9", 159 lbs. Deb: 4/25/80

YEAR	TM/L	G	AB	R	H	2B	3B	HR	RBI	BB	SO	AVG	OBP	SLG	PRO+	BR	/A	RC	SB	CS	SBR	FA	FR	POS	TPR
1980	NY-N	18	24	2	5	0	0	0	0	1	7	.208	.240	.208	27	-2	-2	1	0	0	0	1.000	3	/S/23	0.1
1981	SD-N	13	13	1	1	0	0	0	1	2	5	.077	.200	.077	-21	-2	-2	0	0	0	0	1.000	4	/S3	0.2
1982	SD-N	13	23	1	4	1	0	0	1	2	4	.174	.240	.217	30	-2	-2	1	0	0	0	.963	2	/S23	0.0
1983	SD-N	55	107	11	21	6	3	0	12	20	23	.196	.328	.308	80	-3	-2	12	0	0	0	.985	-2	S/3	-0.2
1984	*SD-N	48	59	12	7	1	0	2	9	13	14	.119	.278	.237	46	-4	-4	4	0	0	0	.971	-1	S/32	-0.3
1985	SD-N	37	60	6	17	0	0	2	5	3	11	.283	.317	.383	97	-1	-0	8	0	0	0	.918	-5	S/2	-0.4
Total	6	184	286	33	55	8	3	4	28	41	64	.192	.296	.283	64	-14	-13	27	0	0	0	.970	1	S/23	-0.6

■ MILT RAMIREZ Ramirez, Milton (Barboza) b: 4/2/50, Mayaguez, P.R. BR/TR, 5'9", 150 lbs. Deb: 4/11/70

YEAR	TM/L	G	AB	R	H	2B	3B	HR	RBI	BB	SO	AVG	OBP	SLG	PRO+	BR	/A	RC	SB	CS	SBR	FA	FR	POS	TPR
1970	StL-N	62	79	8	15	2	1	0	3	8	9	.190	.264	.241	36	-7	-7	4	0	1	-1	.923	10	S/3	0.5
1971	StL-N	4	11	2	3	0	0	0	0	2	1	.273	.385	.273	86	-0	-0	1	0	0	0	.947	-1	/S	-0.1
1979	Oak-A	28	62	4	10	1	1	0	3	3	8	.161	.200	.210	11	-8	-7	3	0	0	0	.923	-5	32/S	-1.1
Total	3	94	152	14	28	3	2	0	6	13	18	.184	.248	.230	30	-15	-15	8	0	1	-1	.920	4	/S32	-0.7

■ ORLANDO RAMIREZ Ramirez, Orlando (Leal) b: 12/18/51, Cartagena, Colombia BR/TR, 5'10", 175 lbs. Deb: 7/06/74

YEAR	TM/L	G	AB	R	H	2B	3B	HR	RBI	BB	SO	AVG	OBP	SLG	PRO+	BR	/A	RC	SB	CS	SBR	FA	FR	POS	TPR
1974	Cal-A	31	86	4	14	0	0	0	7	6	23	.163	.217	.163	11	-10	-9	4	2	1	0	.956	5	S	0.0
1975	Cal-A	44	100	10	24	4	1	0	4	11	22	.240	.315	.300	80	-3	-2	9	9	6	-1	.905	0	S	0.1
1976	Cal-A	30	70	3	14	1	0	0	5	6	11	.200	.263	.214	44	-5	-5	4	3	2	-0	.966	4	S	0.2
1977	Cal-A	25	13	6	1	0	0	0	0	0	3	.077	.077	.077	-60	-3	-3	0	1	0	0	1.000	9	/2SD	0.6
1979	Cal-A	13	12	1	0	0	0	0	0	1	6	.000	.143	.000	-60	-3	-3	0	1	0	0	.844	4	S	0.2
Total	5	143	281	24	53	5	1	0	16	24	65	.189	.255	.214	37	-23	-21	17	16	9	-1	.931	22	S/2D	1.1

■ RAFAEL RAMIREZ Ramirez, Rafael Emilio (Peguero) b: 2/18/58, San Pedro De Macoris, D.R. BR/TR, 6', 185 lbs. Deb: 8/04/80

YEAR	TM/L	G	AB	R	H	2B	3B	HR	RBI	BB	SO	AVG	OBP	SLG	PRO+	BR	/A	RC	SB	CS	SBR	FA	FR	POS	TPR
1980	Atl-N	50	165	17	44	6	1	2	11	2	33	.267	.292	.352	76	-5	-6	17	2	1	0	.949	-10	S	-1.1
1981	Atl-N	95	307	30	67	16	2	2	20	24	47	.218	.277	.303	63	-15	-15	27	7	3	0	.942	-2	S	-0.8
1982	*Atl-N	157	609	74	169	24	4	10	52	36	49	.278	.321	.379	91	-5	-8	73	27	14	-0	.956	17	*S	2.4
1983	Atl-N	152	622	82	185	13	5	7	58	36	48	.297	.338	.368	89	-4	-9	76	16	12	-2	.949	8	*S	1.2
1984	Atl-N☆	145	591	51	157	22	4	2	48	26	70	.266	.298	.327	70	-20	-25	53	14	17	-6	.959	-3	*S	-2.1
1985	Atl-N	138	568	54	141	25	4	5	58	20	63	.248	.274	.333	65	-25	-29	45	2	6	-3	.954	9	*S	-1.1
1986	Atl-N	134	496	57	119	21	1	8	33	21	60	.240	.275	.335	64	-23	-26	42	19	8	1	.952	13	S3/O	-0.6
1987	Atl-N	56	179	22	47	12	0	1	21	8	16	.263	.302	.346	68	-8	-9	18	6	3	0	.946	-6	S3	-1.2
1988	Hou-N	155	566	51	156	30	5	6	59	18	61	.276	.302	.378	98	-6	-3	60	3	2	-0	.965	-10	*S	-0.1
1989	Hou-N	151	537	46	132	20	2	6	54	29	64	.246	.284	.324	76	-19	-17	49	3	1	0	.945	-41	*S	-5.0
1990	Hou-N	132	445	44	116	19	3	2	37	24	46	.261	.300	.330	75	-16	-15	43	10	5	0	.953	-18	*S	-2.4
1991	Hou-N	101	233	17	55	10	0	1	20	13	40	.236	.276	.292	64	-12	-11	18	3	3	-1	.953	-14	S2/3	-2.4
1992	Hou-N	73	176	17	44	6	0	1	13	7	24	.250	.283	.301	69	-8	-7	14	0	0	0	.961	-6	S/3	-1.0
Total	13	1539	5494	562	1432	224	31	53	484	264	621	.261	.297	.342	77	-165	-179	536	112	75	-11	.953	-64	*S/32O	-14.2

■ DOMINGO RAMOS Ramos, Domingo Antonio (De Ramos) b: 3/29/58, Santiago, D.R. BR/TR, 5'10", 155 lbs. Deb: 9/08/78

YEAR	TM/L	G	AB	R	H	2B	3B	HR	RBI	BB	SO	AVG	OBP	SLG	PRO+	BR	/A	RC	SB	CS	SBR	FA	FR	POS	TPR
1978	NY-A	1	0	0	0	0	0	0	0	0	0	—	—	—	—	0	0	0	0	0	0	.000	0	/S	0.0
1980	Tor-A	5	16	0	2	0	0	0	0	2	5	.125	.222	.125	-2	-2	-2	1	0	0	0	1.000	-0	/2SD	-0.2
1982	Sea-A	8	26	3	4	2	0	0	1	3	2	.154	.241	.231	30	-2	-3	2	0	0	0	.920	-5	/S	-0.8
1983	Sea-A	53	127	14	36	4	0	2	10	7	12	.283	.326	.362	86	-2	-2	14	3	1	0	.948	8	S/23D	0.8
1984	Sea-A	59	81	6	15	2	0	0	2	5	12	.185	.233	.210	24	-8	-8	3	2	2	-1	.911	4	3S/12	-0.4
1985	Sea-A	75	168	19	33	6	0	1	15	17	23	.196	.270	.250	43	-13	-13	12	0	1	-1	.951	-8	S21/3	-1.8
1986	Sea-A	49	99	8	18	2	0	0	5	8	13	.182	.250	.202	25	-10	-10	4	0	1	-1	.966	13	S2/3D	0.3
1987	Sea-A	42	103	9	32	6	0	2	11	3	12	.311	.336	.427	96	-0	-1	14	0	1	-1	.953	7	S/32D	0.7
1988	Cle-A	22	46	7	12	1	0	0	5	3	7	.261	.320	.283	68	-2	-2	5	0	0	0	1.000	2	2/1S3	0.0
	Cal-A	10	15	3	2	0	0	0	0	0	0	.133	.133	.133	-26	-2	-2	0	0	0	0	1.000	-0	/3O	-0.3
	Yr	32	61	10	14	1	0	0	5	3	7	.230	.277	.246	47	-4	-4	4	0	0	0	1.000	2	23/1SO	-0.3
1989	*Chi-N	85	179	18	47	6	2	1	19	17	23	.263	.333	.335	85	-2	-3	18	1	1	-0	.959	3	S3	0.2
1990	Chi-N	98	226	22	60	5	0	2	17	27	29	.265	.346	.314	77	-4	-6	25	0	2	-1	.932	-15	3S/2	-2.1
Total	11	507	1086	109	261	34	2	8	85	92	138	.240	.304	.297	64	-48	-53	97	6	9	-4	.955	7	S3/21DO	-3.6

■ CHUCHO RAMOS Ramos, Jesus Manuel (Garcia) b: 4/12/18, Maturin, Venez. d: 9/2/77, Caracas, Venez. BR/TL, 5'10.5", 167 lbs. Deb: 5/07/44

YEAR	TM/L	G	AB	R	H	2B	3B	HR	RBI	BB	SO	AVG	OBP	SLG	PRO+	BR	/A	RC	SB	CS	SBR	FA	FR	POS	TPR
1944	Cin-N	4	10	1	5	1	0	0	0	0	0	.500	.500	.600	217	1	1	3	0			1.000	-1	/O	0.0

■ JOHN RAMOS Ramos, John Joseph b: 8/6/65, Tampa, Fla. BR/TR, 6', 190 lbs. Deb: 9/18/91

YEAR	TM/L	G	AB	R	H	2B	3B	HR	RBI	BB	SO	AVG	OBP	SLG	PRO+	BR	/A	RC	SB	CS	SBR	FA	FR	POS	TPR
1991	NY-A	10	26	4	8	1	0	0	3	1	3	.308	.333	.346	88	-0	-0	3	0	0	0	1.000	-0	/CD	0.0

■ PEDRO RAMOS Ramos, Pedro (Guerra) "Pete" b: 4/28/35, Pinar Del Rio, Cuba BB/TR, 6', 185 lbs. Deb: 4/11/55

YEAR	TM/L	G	AB	R	H	2B	3B	HR	RBI	BB	SO	AVG	OBP	SLG	PRO+	BR	/A	RC	SB	CS	SBR	FA	FR	POS	TPR
1955	Was-A	59	38	6	3	0	0	0	0	2	18	.079	.125	.079	-47	-8	-7	0	0	1	-1	.964	-1	P	0.0
1956	Was-A	56	44	9	9	0	2	0	2	2	16	.205	.239	.295	40	-4	-4	3	0	1	-1	1.000	-0	P	0.0
1957	Was-A	56	76	6	13	0	0	1	10	2	27	.171	.192	.211	10	-9	-9	3	0	0	0	1.000	-0	P	0.0
1958	Was-A	53	88	9	21	1	0	0	10	0	33	.239	.239	.250	35	-8	-8	6	0	0	0	.982	-1	P	0.0
1959	Was-A☆	45	75	7	11	1	1	1	2	4	38	.147	.190	.227	14	-9	-9	4	1	0	0	1.000	-1	P	0.0
1960	Was-A	53	86	6	10	3	0	2	4	1	36	.116	.126	.221	-8	-13	-13	3	0	0	0	1.000	0	P	0.0
1961	Min-A	53	93	8	16	1	0	3	11	3	42	.172	.206	.280	27	-10	-10	5	0	0	0	.955	-3	P	0.0
1962	Cle-A	39	68	6	10	3	0	3	8	1	29	.147	.171	.324	31	-7	-7	3	0	0	0	.962	0	P	0.0

YEAR	TM/L	G	AB	R	H	2B	3B	HR	RBI	BB	SO	AVG	OBP	SLG	PRO+	BR	/A	RC	SB	CS	SBR	FA	FR	POS	TPR
1963	Cle-A	54	55	13	6	0	0	3	7	3	32	.109	.155	.273	17	-6	-6	3	0	0	0	.963	-2	P	0.0
1964	Cle-A	44	39	6	7	0	0	2	2	2	22	.179	.220	.333	52	-3	-3	3	0	0	0	.960	-1	P	0.0
	NY-A	13	5	0	0	0	0	0	0	0	2	.000	.000	.000	-98	-1	-1	0	0	0	0	.000	-1	P	0.0
	Yr	57	44	6	7	0	0	2	2	2	24	.159	.196	.295	34	-4	-4	3	0	0	0	.960	-2	P	0.0
1965	NY-A	65	12	0	1	0	0	0	0	0	8	.083	.083	.083	-53	-2	-2	0	1	0	0	.895	-1	P	0.0
1966	NY-A	52	13	0	2	0	0	0	0	0	8	.154	.154	.154	-12	-2	-2	0	0	0	0	.952	-0	P	0.0
1967	Phi-N	6	1	0	0	0	0	0	0	0	0	.000	.000	.000	-99	-0	-0	0	0	0	0	1.000	1	/P	0.0
1969	Pit-N	5	1	0	0	0	0	0	0	0	1	.000	.000	.000	-99	-0	-0	0	0	0	0	1.000	0	/P	0.0
	Cin-N	38	8	0	0	0	0	0	0	1	4	.000	.111	.000	-63	-2	-2	0	0	0	0	1.000	-0	P	0.0
	Yr	43	9	0	0	0	0	0	0	1	5	.000	.100	.000	-67	-2	-2	0	0	0	0	1.000	-0	P	0.0
1970	Was-A	5	1	0	0	0	0	0	0	1	0	.000	.500	.000	52	0	0	0	0	0	0	1.000	0	/P	0.0
Total	15	696	703	76	109	9	3	15	56	22	316	.155	.183	.240	14	-84	-84	34	2	2	-1	.977	-9	P	0.0

■ **BOBBY RAMOS** Ramos, Roberto b: 11/5/55, Havana, Cuba BR/TR, 5'11", 208 lbs. Deb: 9/26/78

YEAR	TM/L	G	AB	R	H	2B	3B	HR	RBI	BB	SO	AVG	OBP	SLG	PRO+	BR	/A	RC	SB	CS	SBR	FA	FR	POS	TPR
1978	Mon-N	2	4	0	0	0	0	0	0	0	1	.000	.000	.000	-99	-1	-1	0	0	0	0	1.000	0	/C	-0.1
1980	Mon-N	13	32	5	5	2	0	0	2	5	5	.156	.270	.219	38	-3	-3	2	0	0	0	.964	0	C	-0.2
1981	Mon-N	26	41	4	8	1	0	1	3	3	5	.195	.250	.293	53	-3	-3	3	0	0	0	.974	4	C	0.1
1982	NY-A	4	11	1	1	0	0	1	2	0	3	.091	.091	.364	18	-1	-1	0	0	0	0	1.000	1	/C	0.0
1983	Mon-N	27	61	2	14	3	1	0	5	8	11	.230	.329	.311	79	-2	-2	7	0	0	0	.984	4	C	0.4
1984	Mon-N	31	83	8	16	1	0	2	5	6	13	.193	.247	.277	49	-6	-5	5	0	0	0	.982	7	C	0.2
Total	6	103	232	20	44	7	1	4	17	22	38	.190	.263	.280	53	-15	-15	17	0	0	0	.980	15	/C	0.4

■ **FERNANDO RAMSEY** Ramsey, Fernando David b: 12/20/65, Rainbow, Panama BR/TR, 6'1", 175 lbs. Deb: 9/07/92

YEAR	TM/L	G	AB	R	H	2B	3B	HR	RBI	BB	SO	AVG	OBP	SLG	PRO+	BR	/A	RC	SB	CS	SBR	FA	FR	POS	TPR
1992	Chi-N	18	25	0	3	0	0	0	2	0	6	.120	.120	.120	-31	-4	-4	0	0	0	0	1.000	-5	O	-1.0

■ **MIKE RAMSEY** Ramsey, Michael James b: 7/8/60, Thomson, Ga. BB/TL, 6', 170 lbs. Deb: 4/06/87

YEAR	TM/L	G	AB	R	H	2B	3B	HR	RBI	BB	SO	AVG	OBP	SLG	PRO+	BR	/A	RC	SB	CS	SBR	FA	FR	POS	TPR
1987	LA-N	48	125	18	29	4	2	0	12	10	32	.232	.289	.296	57	-8	-8	10	2	4	-2	.973	-3	O	-1.4

■ **MIKE RAMSEY** Ramsey, Michael Jeffrey b: 3/29/54, Roanoke, Va. BB/TR, 6'1", 170 lbs. Deb: 9/04/78

YEAR	TM/L	G	AB	R	H	2B	3B	HR	RBI	BB	SO	AVG	OBP	SLG	PRO+	BR	/A	RC	SB	CS	SBR	FA	FR	POS	TPR
1978	StL-N	12	5	4	1	0	0	0	0	0	1	.200	.200	.200	12	-1	-1	0	0	0	0	.909	5	/S	0.5
1980	StL-N	59	126	11	33	8	1	0	8	3	17	.262	.279	.341	70	-5	-5	11	0	0	0	.960	0	2S/3	-0.3
1981	StL-N	47	124	19	32	3	0	0	9	8	16	.258	.303	.282	65	-5	-6	10	4	0	1	.966	13	S/32O	1.2
1982	*StL-N	112	256	18	59	8	2	1	21	22	34	.230	.294	.289	63	-12	-12	21	6	5	-1	.963	9	23S/O	-0.1
1983	StL-N	97	175	25	46	4	3	1	16	12	23	.263	.314	.337	80	-5	-5	18	4	2	0	.968	3	2S/3O	0.0
1984	StL-N	21	15	1	1	1	0	0	0	1	3	.067	.125	.133	-28	-3	-3	0	0	0	0	1.000	4	/2S3	0.2
	Mon-N	37	70	2	15	1	0	0	3	0	13	.214	.214	.229	26	-7	-7	3	0	0	0	.975	1	S2	-0.4
	Yr	58	85	3	16	2	0	0	3	1	16	.188	.198	.212	16	-10	-9	3	0	0	0	.978	5	S2/3	-0.2
1985	LA-N	9	15	1	2	1	0	0	0	2	4	.133	.235	.200	24	-2	-1	1	0	0	0	.923	-0	/S2	-0.1
Total	7	394	786	81	189	26	6	2	57	48	111	.240	.286	.296	63	-39	-39	65	14	7	0	.973	36	2S/3O	1.0

■ **BILL RAMSEY** Ramsey, William Thrace "Square Jaw" b: 2/20/21, Osceola, Ark. BR/TR, 6'1", 190 lbs. Deb: 4/19/45

YEAR	TM/L	G	AB	R	H	2B	3B	HR	RBI	BB	SO	AVG	OBP	SLG	PRO+	BR	/A	RC	SB	CS	SBR	FA	FR	POS	TPR
1945	Bos-N	78	137	16	40	8	0	1	12	4	22	.292	.326	.372	93	-1	-2	16	1			.963	-7	O	-1.0

■ **DICK RAND** Rand, Richard Hilton b: 3/7/31, South Gate, Cal. BR/TR, 6'2", 185 lbs. Deb: 9/16/53

YEAR	TM/L	G	AB	R	H	2B	3B	HR	RBI	BB	SO	AVG	OBP	SLG	PRO+	BR	/A	RC	SB	CS	SBR	FA	FR	POS	TPR
1953	StL-N	9	31	3	9	1	0	0	1	2	6	.290	.333	.323	72	-1	-1	4	0	0	0	.984	3	/C	0.2
1955	StL-N	3	10	1	3	0	0	1	3	1	1	.300	.364	.600	150	1	1	2	0	1	-1	1.000	-2	/C	-0.1
1957	Pit-N	60	105	7	23	2	1	1	9	11	24	.219	.293	.286	58	-6	-6	10	0	0	0	.973	0	C	-0.4
Total	3	72	146	11	35	3	1	2	13	14	31	.240	.306	.315	68	-7	-6	15	0	1	-1	.977	2	/C	-0.3

■ **SAP RANDALL** Randall, James Odell b: 8/19/60, Mobile, Ala. BB/TR, 5'11", 195 lbs. Deb: 8/02/88

YEAR	TM/L	G	AB	R	H	2B	3B	HR	RBI	BB	SO	AVG	OBP	SLG	PRO+	BR	/A	RC	SB	CS	SBR	FA	FR	POS	TPR
1988	Chi-A	4	12	1	0	0	0	0	1	2	3	.000	.143	.000	-57	-3	-3	0	0	0	0	1.000	0	/1OD	-0.3

■ **NEWT RANDALL** Randall, Newton J. b: 2/3/1880, New Lowell, Ont., Canada d: 5/3/55, Duluth, Minn. BR/TR, 5'10", Deb: 4/18/07

YEAR	TM/L	G	AB	R	H	2B	3B	HR	RBI	BB	SO	AVG	OBP	SLG	PRO+	BR	/A	RC	SB	CS	SBR	FA	FR	POS	TPR
1907	Chi-N	22	78	6	16	4	2	0	4	8		.205	.279	.308	79	-2	-2	8	2			.904	1	O	-0.2
	Bos-N	75	258	16	55	6	3	0	15	19		.213	.285	.260	71	-8	-8	21	4			.920	-8	O	-2.1
	Yr	97	336	22	71	10	5	0	19	27		.211	.284	.271	73	-10	-10	28	6			.915	-7	O	-2.3

■ **BOB RANDALL** Randall, Robert Lee b: 6/10/48, Norton, Kan. BR/TR, 6'3", 180 lbs. Deb: 4/13/76 C

YEAR	TM/L	G	AB	R	H	2B	3B	HR	RBI	BB	SO	AVG	OBP	SLG	PRO+	BR	/A	RC	SB	CS	SBR	FA	FR	POS	TPR
1976	Min-A	153	475	55	127	18	4	1	34	28	38	.267	.319	.328	87	-6	-8	51	3	5	-2	.969	-4	*2	-0.5
1977	Min-A	103	306	36	73	13	2	0	22	15	25	.239	.290	.294	60	-17	-16	27	1	4	-2	.985	10	*2/13D	-0.2
1978	Min-A	119	330	36	89	11	3	0	21	24	22	.270	.331	.321	82	-6	-7	36	5	3	-0	.983	10	*2/3D	1.0
1979	Min-A	80	199	25	49	7	0	0	14	15	17	.246	.299	.281	55	-12	-13	18	2	2	-1	.983	7	2/3SO	-0.3
1980	Min-A	5	15	2	3	1	0	0	0	1	0	.200	.250	.267	39	-1	-1	1	0	0	0	.909	0	/32	-0.1
Total	5	460	1325	154	341	50	9	1	91	83	102	.257	.311	.311	74	-42	-45	132	11	14	-5	.979	22	2/3DOS1	-0.1

■ **LEN RANDLE** Randle, Leonard Shenoff b: 2/12/49, Long Beach, Cal. BB/TR, 5'10", 169 lbs. Deb: 6/16/71

YEAR	TM/L	G	AB	R	H	2B	3B	HR	RBI	BB	SO	AVG	OBP	SLG	PRO+	BR	/A	RC	SB	CS	SBR	FA	FR	POS	TPR
1971	Was-A	75	215	27	47	11	0	2	13	24	56	.219	.300	.298	74	-8	-7	21	1	1	-0	.967	5	2	0.4
1972	Tex-A	74	249	23	48	13	0	2	21	13	51	.193	.236	.269	52	-16	-15	14	4	5	-2	.952	1	2/SO	-1.4
1973	Tex-A	10	29	3	6	1	1	1	1	0	2	.207	.207	.414	74	-1	-1	2	0	2	-1	.964	-2	/2O	-0.5
1974	Tex-A	151	520	65	157	17	4	1	49	29	43	.302	.341	.356	103	0	2	61	26	17	-2	.935	1	32O/SD	0.1
1975	Tex-A	156	601	85	166	24	7	4	57	57	80	.276	.343	.359	99	-0	0	73	16	19	-7	.973	15	2O3/CSD	1.0
1976	Tex-A	142	539	53	121	11	6	1	51	46	63	.224	.288	.273	63	-23	-25	45	30	15	0	.971	-4	*2O/3D	-2.4
1977	NY-N	136	513	78	156	22	7	5	27	65	70	.304	.384	.404	117	11	14	78	33	21	-3	.961	-6	*32/OS	0.5
1978	NY-N	132	437	53	102	16	8	2	35	64	57	.233	.333	.320	86	-8	-6	49	14	11	-2	.967	-7	*3/2	-1.8
1979	NY-A	20	39	2	7	0	0	0	3	3	2	.179	.238	.179	15	-5	-4	2	0	0	0	1.000	-0	O	-0.5
1980	Chi-N	130	489	67	135	19	6	5	39	50	55	.276	.344	.370	93	0	-4	61	19	13	-2	.929	-5	*32/O	-1.2
1981	Sea-A	82	273	22	63	9	1	4	25	17	22	.231	.278	.315	68	-11	-12	24	11	6	-0	.986	7	32/OS	-0.5
1982	Sea-A	30	46	10	8	2	0	0	1	4	4	.174	.240	.217	26	-5	-5	2	2	2	-1	.964	6	D/32	0.0
Total	12	1138	3950	488	1016	145	40	27	322	372	505	.257	.323	.335	87	-65	-63	430	156	112	-20	.953	11	32O/DSC	-6.3

■ **WILLIE RANDOLPH** Randolph, Willie Larry b: 7/6/54, Holly Hill, S.C. BR/TR, 5'11", 166 lbs. Deb: 7/29/75

YEAR	TM/L	G	AB	R	H	2B	3B	HR	RBI	BB	SO	AVG	OBP	SLG	PRO+	BR	/A	RC	SB	CS	SBR	FA	FR	POS	TPR
1975	*Pit-N	30	61	9	10	1	0	0	3	7	6	.164	.250	.180	21	-6	-6	3	1	0	0	.962	4	2/3	-0.2
1976	*NY-A†	125	430	59	115	15	4	1	40	58	39	.267	.358	.328	103	3	4	55	37	12	4	.974	15	*2	3.2
1977	*NY-A★	147	551	91	151	28	11	4	40	64	53	.274	.351	.387	102	2	3	77	13	6	0	.980	6	*2	1.9
1978	NY-A	134	499	87	139	18	6	3	42	82	51	.279	.385	.357	112	10	12	78	36	7	7	.978	-8	*2	2.1
1979	NY-A	153	574	98	155	15	13	5	61	95	39	.270	.376	.368	104	5	7	82	33	12	3	.985	9	*2	2.8
1980	*NY-A★	138	513	99	151	23	7	7	46	**119**	45	.294	.429	.407	133	29	30	105	30	5	6	.976	-7	*2	3.8
1981	*NY-A★	93	357	59	83	14	3	2	24	57	24	.232	.338	.305	88	-4	-4	40	14	5	1	.977	-2	2	0.2
1982	NY-A	144	553	85	155	21	4	3	36	75	35	.280	.369	.349	100	2	3	75	16	9	-1	.981	-3	*2/D	0.7
1983	NY-A	104	420	73	117	21	1	2	38	53	32	.279	.361	.348	100	-0	2	55	12	4	1	.979	3	*2	1.1
1984	NY-A	142	564	86	162	24	2	2	31	86	42	.287	.382	.348	108	6	9	79	10	6	-1	.983	11	*2	2.5
1985	NY-A	143	497	75	137	21	2	5	40	85	39	.276	.386	.356	107	7	9	69	16	9	-1	.985	-3	*2	1.1
1986	NY-A	141	492	76	136	15	2	5	50	94	49	.276	.396	.346	105	8	8	77	15	2	3	.972	-12	*2/D	0.5
1987	NY-A★	120	449	96	137	24	2	7	67	82	25	.305	.415	.414	122	18	18	82	11	1	3	.981	-2	*2/D	2.4
1988	NY-A	110	404	43	93	20	1	2	34	55	39	.230	.325	.300	77	-11	-11	42	8	4	0	.988	8	*2	0.1

YEAR	TM/L	G	AB	R	H	2B	3B	HR	RBI	BB	SO	AVG	OBP	SLG	PRO+	BR	/A	RC	SB	CS	SBR	FA	FR	POS	TPR
1989	LA-N★	145	549	62	155	18	0	2	36	71	51	.282	.369	.326	102	3	4	69	7	6	-2	.987	-1	*2	0.7
1990	LA-N	26	96	15	26	4	0	1	9	13	9	.271	.364	.344	98	-0	0	13	1	0	0	.969	-2	2	-0.1
	*Oak-A	93	292	37	75	9	3	1	21	32	25	.257	.332	.318	86	-6	-4	31	6	1	1	.982	-12	2/D	-1.4
1991	Mil-A	124	431	60	141	14	3	0	54	75	38	.327	.427	.374	127	18	20	72	4	2	0	.969	10	*2/D	3.2
1992	NY-N	90	286	29	72	11	1	2	15	40	34	.252	.352	.318	92	-2	-2	34	1	3	-2	.977	-14	2	-1.6
Total	18	2202	8018	1239	2210	316	65	54	687	1243	675	.276	.375	.351	105	82	103	1138	271	94	25	.980	0	*2/D3	23.0
■ MERRITT RANEW	Ranew, Merritt Thomas b: 5/10/38, Albany, Ga. BL/TR, 5'10", 180 lbs. Deb: 4/13/62																								
1962	Hou-N	71	218	26	51	6	8	4	24	14	43	.234	.289	.390	87	-7	-5	24	2	2	-1	.980	-6	C	-0.9
1963	Chi-N	78	154	18	52	8	1	3	15	9	32	.338	.382	.461	134	8	7	27	1	0	0	.980	-5	C/1	0.4
1964	Chi-N	16	33	0	3	0	0	0	1	2	6	.091	.167	.091	-24	-5	-6	1	0	0	0	1.000	2	/C	-0.3
	Mil-N	9	17	1	2	0	0	0	0	0	3	.118	.118	.118	-33	-3	-3	0	0	1	-1	1.000	-1	/C	-0.5
	Yr	25	50	1	5	0	0	0	1	2	9	.100	.151	.100	-27	-8	-9	1	0	1	-1	1.000	1	C	-0.8
1965	Cal-A	41	91	12	19	4	0	1	10	7	22	.209	.265	.286	58	-5	-5	7	0	0	0	.988	-10	C	-1.5
1969	Sea-A	54	81	11	20	2	0	0	4	10	14	.247	.330	.272	71	-3	-3	7	0	0	0	.969	-6	C/O3	-0.8
Total	5	269	594	68	147	20	9	8	54	42	120	.247	.304	.352	83	-15	-14	66	3	3	-1	.982	-25	C/1O3	-3.6
■ JEFF RANSOM	Ransom, Jeffrey Dean b: 11/11/60, Fresno, Cal. BR/TR, 5'11", 185 lbs. Deb: 9/05/81																								
1981	SF-N	5	15	2	4	1	0	0	0	1	1	.267	.313	.333	85	-0	-0	1	0	0	0	1.000	2	/C	0.2
1982	SF-N	15	44	5	7	0	0	0	3	6	7	.159	.260	.159	20	-5	-5	2	0	0	0	.988	2	C	-0.3
1983	SF-N	6	20	3	4	0	0	1	3	4	7	.200	.333	.350	92	-0	-0	2	0	0	0	.946	-2	/C	-0.1
Total	3	26	79	10	15	1	0	1	6	11	15	.190	.289	.241	50	-5	-5	5	0	0	0	.980	2	/C	-0.2
■ EARL RAPP	Rapp, Earl Wellington b: 5/20/21, Corunna, Mich. d: 2/13/92, Swedesboro, N.J. BL/TR, 6'2", 185 lbs. Deb: 4/28/49																								
1949	Det-A	1	0	0	0	0	0	0	0	1	0	—	1.000	—	175	0	0	0	0	0	0	.000	0	H	0.0
	Chi-A	19	54	3	14	1	1	0	11	5	6	.259	.322	.315	71	-2	-2	6	1	1	-0	.974	2	O	-0.1
	Yr	20	54	3	14	1	1	0	11	6	6	.259	.333	.315	74	-2	-2	6	1	1	-0	.974	2	O	-0.1
1951	NY-N	13	11	0	1	0	0	0	1	2	3	.091	.231	.091	-10	-2	-2	0	0	0	0	.000	0	H	-0.2
	StL-A	26	98	14	32	5	3	2	14	11	11	.327	.394	.500	137	5	5	21	1	0	0	.979	0	O	0.5
1952	StL-A	30	49	3	7	4	0	0	4	0	8	.143	.143	.224	1	-7	-7	1	0	0	0	1.000	-1	/O	-0.8
	Was-A	46	67	7	19	6	0	0	9	6	13	.284	.351	.373	105	0	0	10	0	0	0	.917	-2	O	-0.2
	Yr	76	116	10	26	10	0	0	13	6	21	.224	.268	.310	61	-6	-6	10	0	0	0	.958	-3	O	-1.0
Total	3	135	279	27	73	16	4	2	39	25	41	.262	.325	.369	89	-5	-5	38	2	1	0	.973	-0	/O	-0.8
■ GOLDIE RAPP	Rapp, Joseph Aloysius b: 2/6/1892, Cincinnati, Ohio d: 7/1/66, LaMesa, Cal. BB/TR, 5'10", 165 lbs. Deb: 4/13/21																								
1921	NY-N	58	181	21	39	9	1	0	15	15	13	.215	.276	.276	46	-14	-14	12	3	11	-6	.941	13	3	-0.3
	Phi-N	52	202	28	56	7	1	1	10	14	8	.277	.324	.337	70	-7	-9	21	6	7	-2	.950	-2	3/2	-1.0
	Yr	110	383	49	95	16	2	1	25	29	21	.248	.301	.308	59	-21	-23	33	9	18	-8	.945	10	*3/2	-1.3
1922	Phi-N	119	502	58	127	26	3	0	38	32	29	.253	.299	.317	54	-31	-37	46	6	12	-5	.948	5	*3/S	-2.8
1923	Phi-N	47	179	27	47	5	0	1	10	14	14	.263	.320	.307	59	-8	-11	18	1	1	-0	.947	-1	3	-0.8
Total	3	276	1064	134	269	47	5	2	73	75	64	.253	.303	.312	57	-60	-72	97	16	31	-14	.947	14	3/S2	-4.9
■ BILL RARIDEN	Rariden, William Angel "Bedford Bill" b: 2/4/1888, Bedford, Ind. d: 8/28/42, Bedford, Ind. BR/TR, 5'10", 168 lbs. Deb: 8/12/09																								
1909	Bos-N	13	42	1	6	1	0	0	1	4		.143	.217	.167	18	-4	-4	2	1			.912	-3	C	-0.7
1910	Bos-N	49	137	15	31	5	1	1	14	12	22	.226	.293	.299	70	-5	-6	13	1			.962	3	C	0.1
1911	Bos-N	70	246	22	56	9	0	0	21	21	18	.228	.288	.264	51	-15	-17	19	3			.952	1	C/32	-0.9
1912	Bos-N	79	247	27	55	3	1	1	14	18	35	.223	.281	.255	46	-18	-18	19	3			.964	-5	C	-1.6
1913	Bos-N	95	246	31	58	9	2	3	30	30	21	.236	.324	.325	84	-4	-5	27	5			.976	3	C	0.6
1914	Ind-F	131	396	44	93	15	5	0	47	61	43	.235	.337	.298	73	-8	-13	47	12			.981	20	*C	1.9
1915	New-F	142	444	49	120	30	7	0	40	60	29	.270	.361	.369	122	10	13	65	8			.978	23	*C	5.0
1916	NY-N	120	351	23	78	9	3	1	29	55	32	.222	.333	.274	92	-3	-1	34	4			.972	-9	*C	0.0
1917	*NY-N	101	266	20	72	10	1	0	25	42	17	.271	.372	.316	116	6	7	32	3			.971	-17	*C	-0.3
1918	NY-N	69	183	15	41	5	1	0	17	15	15	.224	.283	.262	68	-7	-7	14	1			**.984**	-9	C	-1.3
1919	*Cin-N	74	218	16	47	6	3	1	24	17	19	.216	.275	.284	70	-8	-8	18	4			.983	3	C	0.1
1920	Cin-N	39	101	9	25	3	0	0	10	5	0	.248	.283	.277	62	-5	-5	8	2	0	1	.972	-0	C	-0.3
Total	12	982	2877	272	682	105	24	7	272	340	251	.237	.320	.298	81	-61	-64	297	47	0		.973	11	C/32	2.6
■ MORRIE RATH	Rath, Morris Charles b: 12/25/1886, Mobeetie, Tex. d: 11/18/45, Upper Darby, Pa. BL/TR, 5'8.5", 160 lbs. Deb: 9/28/09																								
1909	Phi-A	7	26	4	7	1	0	0	3	2		.269	.387	.308	117	1	1	3	1			.846	2	/S3	0.3
1910	Phi-A	18	26	3	4	0	0	0	1	5		.154	.290	.154	40	-2	-2	2	0			.950	-2	3/2	-0.4
	Cle-A	24	67	5	13	3	0	0	0	10		.194	.299	.239	68	-2	-2	5	2			.950	2	3/S	0.1
	Yr	42	93	8	17	3	0	0	1	15		.183	.296	.215	60	-4	-4	7	2			.950	0	3/2S	-0.3
1912	Chi-A	157	591	104	161	10	2	1	19	95		.272	.380	.301	98	2	5	80	30			**.963**	18	*2	1.9
1913	Chi-A	92	295	37	59	2	0	0	12	46	22	.200	.310	.207	52	-16	-16	26	22			.962	-2	2	-2.0
1919	*Cin-N	138	537	77	142	13	1	1	29	64	24	.264	.343	.298	96	-2	0	61	17			.974	13	*2	2.2
1920	Cin-N	129	506	61	135	7	4	2	28	36	24	.267	.319	.308	82	-12	-11	51	10	11	-4	**.977**	-7	*2/3O	-1.8
Total	6	565	2048	291	521	36	7	4	92	258	70	.254	.342	.285	86	-30	-24	227	82	11		.970	25	2/3SO	0.3
■ GENE RATLIFF	Ratliff, Kelly Eugene b: 9/28/45, Macon, Ga. BR/TR, 6'5", 185 lbs. Deb: 5/15/65																								
1965	Hou-N	4	4	0	0	0	0	0	0	0	4	.000	.000	.000	-99	-1	-1	0	0	0	0	.000	0	H	-0.1
■ PAUL RATLIFF	Ratliff, Paul Hawthorne b: 1/23/44, San Diego, Cal. BL/TR, 6'2", 190 lbs. Deb: 4/14/63																								
1963	Min-A	10	21	2	4	1	0	1	3	2	7	.190	.292	.381	85	-0	-0	3	0	0	0	.976	2	/C	0.2
1970	*Min-A	69	149	19	40	7	2	5	22	15	51	.268	.363	.443	119	4	4	25	0	0	0	.980	-15	C	-1.0
1971	Min-A	21	44	3	7	1	0	2	6	4	17	.159	.229	.318	52	-3	-3	3	0	0	0	1.000	1	C	-0.2
	Mil-A	23	41	3	7	1	0	3	7	5	21	.171	.277	.415	95	-1	-0	5	0	0	0	.966	-1	C	-0.1
	Yr	44	85	6	14	2	0	5	13	9	38	.165	.253	.365	72	-3	-3	8	0	0	0	.985	0	C	-0.3
1972	Mil-A	22	42	1	3	0	0	1	4	2	23	.071	.114	.143	-25	-6	-6	1	0	0	0	1.000	-2	C	-1.0
Total	4	145	297	28	61	10	2	12	42	28	119	.205	.293	.374	86	-6	-6	37	0	0	0	.983	-16	C	-2.1
■ TOMMY RAUB	Raub, Thomas Jefferson b: 12/1/1870, Raubsville, Pa. d: 2/16/49, Phillipsburg, N.J. BR/TR, 5'10", 155 lbs. Deb: 5/03/03																								
1903	Chi-N	36	84	6	19	3	2	0	7	5		.226	.278	.310	69	-4	-3	8	3			.900	-4	C/1O3	-0.7
1906	StL-N	24	78	9	22	2	4	0	2	4		.282	.325	.410	135	2	3	11	2			.957	-4	C	0.1
Total	2	60	162	15	41	5	6	0	9	9		.253	.301	.358	99	-1	-1	20	5			.940	-8	/C1O3	-0.6
■ BOB RAUDMAN	Raudman, Robert Joyce "Shorty" b: 3/14/42, Erie, Pa. BL/TL, 5'9.5", 185 lbs. Deb: 9/13/66																								
1966	Chi-N	8	29	1	7	2	0	0	2	1	4	.241	.267	.310	59	-2	-2	2	0	0	0	.909	-0	/O	-0.2
1967	Chi-N	8	26	0	4	0	0	0	1	1	4	.154	.185	.154	-2	-3	-4	0	0	0	0	.875	0	/O	-0.4
Total	2	16	55	1	11	2	0	0	3	2	8	.200	.228	.236	30	-5	-5	3	0	0	0	.889	0	/O	-0.6
■ JOHNNY RAWLINGS	Rawlings, John William "Red" b: 8/17/1892, Bloomfield, Iowa d: 10/16/72, Inglewood, Cal. BR/TR, 5'8", 158 lbs. Deb: 4/14/14																								
1914	Cin-N	33	60	9	13	1	0	0	8	6	8	.217	.288	.233	54	-3	-3	5	1			.885	0	3/2S	-0.3
	KC-F	61	193	19	41	3	0	0	15	22	25	.212	.296	.228	52	-12	-11	16	6			.937	17	S	1.1
1915	KC-F	120	399	40	86	9	2	2	24	27	40	.216	.269	.263	59	-22	-20	37	17			.926	-4	*S	-1.6
1917	Bos-N	122	371	37	95	9	4	2	31	38	32	.256	.337	.318	107	2	4	43	12			.977	11	2S/3O	2.3

YEAR	TM/L	G	AB	R	H	2B	3B	HR	RBI	BB	SO	AVG	OBP	SLG	PRO+	BR	/A	RC	SB	CS	SBR	FA	FR	POS	TPR
1918	Bos-N	111	410	32	85	7	3	0	21	30	31	.207	.265	.239	56	-22	-20	29	10			.956	2	S2O	-1.7
1919	Bos-N	77	275	30	70	8	2	1	16	16	20	.255	.298	.309	86	-6	-5	28	10			.961	-12	2O/S	-1.6
1920	Bos-N	5	3	0	0	0	0	0	2	0	1	.000	.000	.000	-99	-1	-1	0	0	0	0	1.000	-1	/2	-0.1
	Phi-N	98	384	39	90	19	2	3	30	22	25	.234	.278	.318	67	-15	-17	34	9	6	-1	.970	-2	2	-1.8
	Yr	103	387	39	90	19	2	3	32	22	26	.233	.276	.315	67	-16	-18	34	9	6	-1	.970	-2	2	-1.9
1921	Phi-N	60	254	20	74	14	2	1	16	8	12	.291	.318	.374	76	-7	-9	29	4	5	-2	.954	5	2	-0.5
	*NY-N	86	307	40	82	8	1	1	30	18	19	.267	.316	.309	66	-14	-14	31	4	4	-1	.970	-1	2/S	-1.5
	Yr	146	561	60	156	22	3	2	46	26	31	.278	.317	.339	71	-21	-23	60	8	9	-3	.963	3	*2/S	-2.0
1922	NY-N	88	308	46	87	13	8	1	30	23	15	.282	.342	.386	87	-6	-6	41	7	6	-2	.984	-4	2/3	-0.9
1923	Pit-N	119	461	53	131	18	4	1	45	25	29	.284	.322	.347	75	-16	-17	54	9	0	3	.958	-8	*2	-2.0
1924	Pit-N	3	3	0	1	0	0	0	2	0	0	.333	.333	.333	78	-0	-0	0	0	0	0	.000	0	H	0.0
1925	Pit-N	36	110	17	31	7	0	2	13	8	8	.282	.336	.400	82	-2	-3	15	0	1	-1	.981	3	2	0.0
1926	Pit-N	61	181	27	42	6	0	0	20	14	10	.232	.287	.265	47	-13	-14	15	3			.970	-3	2	-1.5
Total	12	1080	3719	409	928	122	28	14	303	257	275	.250	.303	.309	72	-135	-136	375	92	22		.968	3	2S/O3	-10.1

■ IRV RAY

Ray, Irving Burton "Stubby" b: 1/22/1864, Harrington, Me. d: 2/21/48, Harrington, Me. BL/TR, 5'6", 165 lbs. Deb: 7/07/1888

YEAR	TM/L	G	AB	R	H	2B	3B	HR	RBI	BB	SO	AVG	OBP	SLG	PRO+	BR	/A	RC	SB	CS	SBR	FA	FR	POS	TPR
1888	Bos-N	50	206	26	51	2	3	2	26	6	11	.248	.272	.316	87	-3	-3	20	7			.879	-11	S/2	-1.3
1889	Bos-N	9	33	8	10	1	0	0	2	4	0	.303	.378	.333	96	0	-0	5	1			.875	-4	/S3	-0.3
	Bal-a	26	106	20	36	4	1	0	17	7	6	.340	.397	.396	126	4	4	22	12			.784	-7	S/O	-0.2
1890	Bal-a	38	139	28	50	6	2	1		15		.360	.433	.453	157	12	10	33	11			.894	-10	S	0.2
1891	Bal-a	103	418	72	116	17	5	0	58	54	18	.278	.366	.342	104	5	4	64	28			.885	-14	OS	-0.8
Total	4	226	902	154	263	30	11	3	103	86	35	.292	.360	.359	112	18	15	144	59			.863	-46	S/O32	-2.4

■ JOHNNY RAY

Ray, John Cornelius b: 3/1/57, Chouteau, Okla. BB/TR, 5'11", 185 lbs. Deb: 9/02/81

YEAR	TM/L	G	AB	R	H	2B	3B	HR	RBI	BB	SO	AVG	OBP	SLG	PRO+	BR	/A	RC	SB	CS	SBR	FA	FR	POS	TPR
1981	Pit-N	31	102	10	25	11	0	0	6	6	9	.245	.287	.353	78	-3	-3	10	0	0	0	.987	2	2	0.0
1982	Pit-N	162	647	79	182	30	7	7	63	36	34	.281	.320	.382	93	-5	-7	80	16	7	1	.977	8	*2	1.0
1983	Pit-N	151	576	68	163	**38**	7	5	53	35	26	.283	.324	.399	97	-2	-3	73	18	9	0	.983	17	*2	2.2
1984	Pit-N	155	555	75	173	**38**	6	6	67	37	31	.312	.358	.434	122	15	15	83	11	6	-0	.984	-9	*2	1.1
1985	Pit-N	154	594	67	163	33	3	7	70	46	24	.274	.328	.375	97	-3	-3	71	13	9	-2	.976	-15	*2	-1.4
1986	Pit-N	155	579	67	174	33	0	7	78	58	47	.301	.367	.394	107	9	7	79	6	9	-4	.993	5	*2	1.5
1987	Pit-N	123	472	48	129	19	3	5	54	41	36	.273	.331	.358	82	-11	-12	53	4	2	0	.981	4	*2	-0.2
	Cal-A	30	127	16	44	11	0	0	15	3	10	.346	.362	.433	113	2	2	19	0	0	0	.986	-1	2/D	0.3
1988	Cal-A★	153	602	75	184	42	7	6	83	36	38	.306	.349	.429	120	12	15	90	4	1	1	.972	-7	*2O/D	1.1
1989	Cal-A	134	530	52	153	16	3	5	62	36	30	.289	.334	.358	97	-3	-2	62	6	3	0	.984	4	*2	0.6
1990	Cal-A	105	404	47	112	23	0	5	43	19	44	.277	.310	.371	91	-6	-5	44	2	3	-1	.987	12	*2/D	0.8
Total	10	1353	5188	604	1502	294	36	53	594	353	329	.290	.336	.391	101	5	4	662	80	49	-5	.982	20	*2/OD	7.0

■ LARRY RAY

Ray, Larry Dale b: 3/11/58, Madison, Ind. BL/TR, 6'1", 195 lbs. Deb: 9/10/82

YEAR	TM/L	G	AB	R	H	2B	3B	HR	RBI	BB	SO	AVG	OBP	SLG	PRO+	BR	/A	RC	SB	CS	SBR	FA	FR	POS	TPR
1982	Hou-N	5	6	0	1	0	0	0	1	0	4	.167	.167	.167	-7	-1	-1	0	0	0	0	1.000	-0	/O	-0.1

■ FLOYD RAYFORD

Rayford, Floyd Kinnard b: 7/27/57, Memphis, Tenn. BR/TR, 5'10", 195 lbs. Deb: 4/17/80

YEAR	TM/L	G	AB	R	H	2B	3B	HR	RBI	BB	SO	AVG	OBP	SLG	PRO+	BR	/A	RC	SB	CS	SBR	FA	FR	POS	TPR
1980	Bal-A	8	18	1	4	0	0	0	1	0	5	.222	.222	.222	22	-2	-2	1	0	0	0	.900	0	/32D	-0.2
1982	Bal-A	34	53	7	7	0	0	3	5	6	14	.132	.220	.302	42	-4	-4	4	0	1	-1	.898	5	3/CD	-0.1
1983	StL-N	56	104	5	22	4	0	3	14	10	27	.212	.281	.337	70	-4	-4	10	1	0	0	.883	-4	3	-0.9
1984	Bal-A	86	250	24	64	14	0	4	27	12	51	.256	.298	.360	83	-7	-6	25	0	3	-2	.991	11	C3/1	0.6
1985	Bal-A	105	359	55	110	21	1	18	48	10	69	.306	.325	.521	131	12	13	56	3	1	0	.972	-2	3C/D	1.1
1986	Bal-A	81	210	15	37	4	0	8	19	15	50	.176	.231	.310	46	-16	-16	14	0	0	0	.912	4	3C/D	-1.2
1987	Bal-A	20	50	5	11	0	0	2	3	2	9	.220	.250	.340	56	-3	-3	4	0	0	0	.980	6	C/3D	0.4
Total	7	390	1044	112	255	43	1	38	117	55	225	.244	.284	.397	86	-25	-23	113	4	5	-2	.931	21	3C/D12	-0.3

■ FRED RAYMER

Raymer, Frederick Charles b: 11/12/1875, Leavenworth, Kan. d: 6/11/57, Los Angeles, Cal. BR/TR, 5'11", 185 lbs. Deb: 4/24/01

YEAR	TM/L	G	AB	R	H	2B	3B	HR	RBI	BB	SO	AVG	OBP	SLG	PRO+	BR	/A	RC	SB	CS	SBR	FA	FR	POS	TPR
1901	Chi-N	120	463	41	108	14	2	0	43	11		.233	.256	.272	55	-28	-26	39	18			.881	-18	3S/12	-4.0
1904	Bos-N	114	419	28	88	12	3	1	27	13		.210	.236	.260	55	-23	-22	32	17			**.958**	7	*2	-1.2
1905	Bos-N	137	498	26	105	14	2	0	31	8		.211	.231	.247	44	-36	-34	34	15			.949	-18	*2/1O	-5.4
Total	3	371	1380	95	301	40	7	1	101	32		.218	.241	.259	51	-87	-82	105	50			.954	-29	2/3S1O	-10.6

■ HARRY RAYMOND

Raymond, Harry H. "Jack" b: 2/20/1862, Utica, N.Y. d: 3/21/25, San Diego, Cal. 5'9", 179 lbs. Deb: 9/09/1888

YEAR	TM/L	G	AB	R	H	2B	3B	HR	RBI	BB	SO	AVG	OBP	SLG	PRO+	BR	/A	RC	SB	CS	SBR	FA	FR	POS	TPR
1888	Lou-a	32	123	8	26	2	0	0	13	1		.211	.218	.228	46	-7	-7	8	7			.884	-1	3/O	-0.7
1889	Lou-a	130	515	58	123	12	9	0	47	19	45	.239	.270	.297	64	-25	-24	48	19			.886	-1	*3/OP	-1.7
1890	*Lou-a	123	521	91	135	7	4	2		22		.259	.293	.299	79	-16	-14	52	18			.874	-2	*3/S	-1.0
1891	Lou-a	14	59	4	12	2	0	0	2	5	6	.203	.288	.237	54	-3	-3	5	3			.898	5	S	0.2
1892	Pit-N	12	49	4	4	0	1	0	2	4	8	.082	.151	.122	-16	-7	-7	1	1			.867	-2	3	-0.8
	Was-N	4	15	2	1	0	0	0	0	3	2	.067	.222	.067	-11	-2	-2	0	1			.783	1	/3	-0.1
	Yr	16	64	6	5	0	1	0	2	7	10	.078	.169	.109	-15	-9	-9	2	2			.838	-1	3	-0.9
Total	5	315	1282	167	301	23	14	2	64	54	61	.235	.270	.279	64	-61	-57	114	49			.878	1	3/SOP	-4.1

■ LOU RAYMOND

Raymond, Louis Anthony (b: Louis Anthony Raymondjack)
b: 12/11/1894, Buffalo, N.Y. d: 5/2/79, Rochester, N.Y. BR/TR, 5'10.5", 187 lbs. Deb: 5/02/19

YEAR	TM/L	G	AB	R	H	2B	3B	HR	RBI	BB	SO	AVG	OBP	SLG	PRO+	BR	/A	RC	SB	CS	SBR	FA	FR	POS	TPR
1919	Phi-N	1	2	0	1	0	0	0	0	0	0	.500	.500	.500	188	0	0	0	0			.000	0	/2	0.0

■ AL REACH

Reach, Alfred James b: 5/25/1840, London, England d: 1/14/28, Atlantic City, N.J BL/TL, 5'6", 155 lbs. Deb: 5/20/1871 FM

YEAR	TM/L	G	AB	R	H	2B	3B	HR	RBI	BB	SO	AVG	OBP	SLG	PRO+	BR	/A	RC	SB	CS	SBR	FA	FR	POS	TPR
1871	Ath-n	26	133	43	47	7	6	0	34	5	6	.353	.377	.496	150	8	8	26	2					*2	0.4
1872	Ath-n	24	118	21	23	0	0	0	11	4	0	.195	.221	.195	29	-9	-9	5						O/1	-0.6
1873	Ath-n	13	73	13	16	5	1	0	9	0	0	.219	.219	.315	51	-4	-5	6						/O2	-0.3
1874	Ath-n	14	55	8	7	2	0	0		0		.127	.127	.164	-7	-6	-7	1						O	-0.5
1875	Ath-n	3	14	4	4	1	0	0		0		.286	.286	.357	109	0	0	1						/O2	0.0
Total	5 n	80	393	89	97	15	7	0		9		.247	.264	.321	73	-11	-13	40						/O21	-1.0

■ BOB REACH

Reach, Robert b: 8/28/1843, Williamsburg, N.Y. d: 5/19/22, Springfield, Mass. 5'5", 155 lbs. Deb: 4/23/1872 F

YEAR	TM/L	G	AB	R	H	2B	3B	HR	RBI	BB	SO	AVG	OBP	SLG	PRO+	BR	/A	RC	SB	CS	SBR	FA	FR	POS	TPR
1872	Oly-n	2	8	1	2	0	0	0	0	0	0	.250	.250	.250	57	-0	-0	1						/S	0.0
1873	Was-n	1	5	1	1	0	0	0	0	0	0	.200	.200	.200	19	-0	-0	0						/S	0.0
Total	2 n	3	13	2	3	0	0	0		0		.231	.231	.231	42	-1	-1	1						/S	0.0

■ RANDY READY

Ready, Randy Max b: 1/8/60, Fremont, Cal. BR/TR, 5'11", 180 lbs. Deb: 9/04/83

YEAR	TM/L	G	AB	R	H	2B	3B	HR	RBI	BB	SO	AVG	OBP	SLG	PRO+	BR	/A	RC	SB	CS	SBR	FA	FR	POS	TPR
1983	Mil-A	12	37	8	15	3	2	1	6	6	3	.405	.488	.676	234	6	7	12	0	1	-1	1.000	0	/3D	0.6
1984	Mil-A	37	123	13	23	6	1	3	13	14	18	.187	.270	.325	66	-6	-6	11	0	0	0	.946	3	3	-0.3
1985	Mil-A	48	181	29	48	9	5	1	21	14	23	.265	.321	.387	93	-2	-2	22	0	0	0	.989	4	O/32D	0.1
1986	Mil-A	23	79	8	15	4	0	1	4	9	9	.190	.273	.278	49	-5	-6	6	2	0	1	.950	-4	O/23D	-0.9
	SD-N	1	3	0	0	0	0	0	0	0	1	.000	.000	.000	-99	-1	-1	0	0	0	0	.667	-0	/3	-0.1
1987	SD-N	124	350	69	108	26	6	12	54	67	44	.309	.424	.520	154	27	29	81	7	3	0	.912	2	32O	3.1
1988	SD-N	114	331	43	88	16	2	7	39	39	38	.266	.349	.390	114	6	6	48	6	2	1	.952	-10	32O	-0.3
1989	SD-N	28	67	4	17	2	1	0	5	11	6	.254	.359	.313	94	-0	-0	8	0	0	0	.963	1	3/2O	0.2
	Phi-N	72	187	33	50	11	1	8	21	31	31	.267	.377	.465	140	10	10	35	4	3	-1	.962	-6	O3/2	0.4
	Yr	100	254	37	67	13	2	8	26	42	37	.264	.372	.425	127	10	10	43	4	3	-1	.962	-4	O3/2	0.6
1990	Phi-N	101	217	26	53	9	1	1	26	29	35	.244	.336	.309	79	-5	-5	25	3	2	-0	1.000	-6	O2	-1.2

YEAR	TM/L	G	AB	R	H	2B	3B	HR	RBI	BB	SO	AVG	OBP	SLG	PRO+	BR	/A	RC	SB	CS	SBR	FA	FR	POS	TPR
1991	Phi-N	76	205	32	51	10	1	1	20	47	25	.249	.391	.322	104	3	4	29	2	1	0	.989	-7	2	-0.2
1992	*Oak-A	61	125	17	25	2	0	3	17	25	23	.200	.333	.288	79	-3	-3	14	1	0	0	1.000	-3	OD/312	-0.6
Total	10	697	1905	282	493	98	20	38	226	292	256	.259	.361	.391	110	29	34	292	25	12	0	.940	-26	320/D1	0.8

■ LEROY REAMS Reams, Leroy b: 8/11/43, Pine Bluff, Ark. BL/TR, 6'2", 175 lbs. Deb: 5/07/69

YEAR	TM/L	G	AB	R	H	2B	3B	HR	RBI	BB	SO	AVG	OBP	SLG	PRO+	BR	/A	RC	SB	CS	SBR	FA	FR	POS	TPR
1969	Phi-N	1	1	0	0	0	0	0	0	0	1	.000	.000	.000	-99	-0	-0	0	0	0	0	.000	0	H	0.0

■ PHIL REARDON Reardon, Philip Michael b: 10/3/1883, Brooklyn, N.Y. d: 9/28/20, Brooklyn, N.Y. BR/TR, Deb: 9/19/06

YEAR	TM/L	G	AB	R	H	2B	3B	HR	RBI	BB	SO	AVG	OBP	SLG	PRO+	BR	/A	RC	SB	CS	SBR	FA	FR	POS	TPR
1906	Bro-N	5	14	0	1	0	0	0	0	0		.071	.133	.071	-39	-2	-2	0	0			.917	1	/O	-0.1

■ ART REBEL Rebel, Arthur Anthony b: 3/4/15, Cincinnati, Ohio BL/TL, 5'8", 180 lbs. Deb: 4/19/38

YEAR	TM/L	G	AB	R	H	2B	3B	HR	RBI	BB	SO	AVG	OBP	SLG	PRO+	BR	/A	RC	SB	CS	SBR	FA	FR	POS	TPR
1938	Phi-N	7	9	2	2	0	0	0	1	1	1	.222	.300	.222	47	-1	-1	0	0			1.000	-1	/O	-0.1
1945	StL-N	26	72	12	25	4	0	0	5	6	4	.347	.397	.403	120	2	2	11	1			.976	2	O	0.3
Total	2	33	81	14	27	4	0	0	6	7	5	.333	.386	.383	112	2	2	11	1			.978	1	/O	0.2

■ JEFF REBOULET Reboulet, Jeffrey Allen b: 4/30/64, Dayton, Ohio BR/TR, 6', 167 lbs. Deb: 5/12/92

YEAR	TM/L	G	AB	R	H	2B	3B	HR	RBI	BB	SO	AVG	OBP	SLG	PRO+	BR	/A	RC	SB	CS	SBR	FA	FR	POS	TPR
1992	Min-A	73	137	15	26	7	1	1	16	23	26	.190	.311	.277	64	-6	-6	14	3	2	-0	.971	20	S32/OD	1.5

■ JOHN RECCIUS Reccius, John b: 6/7/1862, Louisville, Ky. d: 9/1/30, Louisville, Ky. 5'6.5", Deb: 5/02/1882 F

YEAR	TM/L	G	AB	R	H	2B	3B	HR	RBI	BB	SO	AVG	OBP	SLG	PRO+	BR	/A	RC	SB	CS	SBR	FA	FR	POS	TPR
1882	Lou-a	74	266	46	63	12	3	1		23		.237	.298	.316	113	3	5	26				.857	-3	*OP	0.2
1883	Lou-a	18	63	10	9	2	0	0		7		.143	.229	.175	34	-4	-4	3				.833	-1	O/P	-0.5
Total	2	92	329	56	72	14	3	1		30		.219	.284	.289	98	-2	1	28				.851	-4	/OP	-0.3

■ PHIL RECCIUS Reccius, Phillip b: 6/7/1862, Louisville, Ky. d: 2/15/03, Louisville, Ky. 5'9", 163 lbs. Deb: 9/25/1882 F

YEAR	TM/L	G	AB	R	H	2B	3B	HR	RBI	BB	SO	AVG	OBP	SLG	PRO+	BR	/A	RC	SB	CS	SBR	FA	FR	POS	TPR
1882	Lou-a	4	15	0	2	0	0	0		0		.133	.133	.133	-10	-2	-2	0				.778	-0	/O	-0.2
1883	Lou-a	1	3	1	1	1	0	0		0		.333	.333	.667	231	0	0	1				1.000	-0	/O	0.0
1884	Lou-a	73	263	23	63	9	2	3		5		.240	.267	.323	99	-2	0	23				.845	-2	3PS	-0.1
1885	Lou-a	102	402	57	97	8	10	1		13		.241	.267	.318	87	-6	-6	35				.829	-2	*3/P	-0.6
1886	Lou-a	5	13	4	4	1	1	0		3		.308	.471	.538	207	2	2	3	0			.889	1	/OP	0.2
1887	Lou-a	11	37	9	9	2	0	0		8		.243	.391	.297	94	0	0	6	3			.926	2	O/S	0.1
	Cle-a	62	229	23	47	6	3	0		24		.205	.295	.258	58	-12	-11	21	9			.877	8	3/P	-0.2
	Yr	73	266	32	56	8	3	0		32		.211	.309	.263	64	-12	-11	26	12			.877	10	3O/SP	-0.1
1888	Lou-a	2	9	0	2	1	0	0	4	1		.222	.300	.333	108	0	0	1	0			.750	-2	/3	-0.1
1890	Roc-a	1	4	0	0	0	0	0		0		.000	.000	.000	-99	-1	-1	0	0			.000	-0	/O	-0.1
Total	8	261	975	117	225	28	16	4	4	54		.231	.280	.305	83	-20	-17	90	12			.848	5	3/POS	-1.0

■ JOHNNY REDER Reder, John Anthony b: 9/24/09, Lublin, Poland BR/TR, 6', 184 lbs. Deb: 4/16/32

YEAR	TM/L	G	AB	R	H	2B	3B	HR	RBI	BB	SO	AVG	OBP	SLG	PRO+	BR	/A	RC	SB	CS	SBR	FA	FR	POS	TPR
1932	Bos-A	17	37	4	5	1	0	0	3	6	6	.135	.256	.162	11	-5	-5	2	0	0	0	.990	0	1/3	-0.5

■ BUCK REDFERN Redfern, George Howard b: 4/7/02, Asheville, N.C. d: 9/8/64, Asheville, N.C. BR/TR, 5'11", 165 lbs. Deb: 4/11/28

YEAR	TM/L	G	AB	R	H	2B	3B	HR	RBI	BB	SO	AVG	OBP	SLG	PRO+	BR	/A	RC	SB	CS	SBR	FA	FR	POS	TPR
1928	Chi-A	86	261	22	61	6	3	0	35	12	19	.234	.267	.280	44	-21	-21	21	8	2	1	.953	6	2S/3	-0.9
1929	Chi-A	21	46	0	6	0	0	0	3	3	3	.130	.184	.130	-18	-8	-8	1	1	1	-0	.967	-5	2/3S	-1.2
Total	2	107	307	22	67	6	3	0	38	15	22	.218	.255	.257	35	-29	-29	22	9	3	1	.955	1	/2S3	-2.1

■ JOE REDFIELD Redfield, Joseph Randall b: 1/14/61, Doylestown, Pa. BR/TR, 6'2", 190 lbs. Deb: 6/04/88

YEAR	TM/L	G	AB	R	H	2B	3B	HR	RBI	BB	SO	AVG	OBP	SLG	PRO+	BR	/A	RC	SB	CS	SBR	FA	FR	POS	TPR
1988	Cal-A	1	2	0	0	0	0	0	0	0	0	.000	.000	.000	-99	-1	-1	0	0	0	0	1.000	0	/3	0.0
1991	Pit-N	11	18	1	2	0	0	0	0	4	1	.111	.273	.111	12	-2	-2	1	0	1	-1	.917	-1	/3	-0.3
Total	2	12	20	1	2	0	0	0	0	4	1	.100	.250	.100	2	-3	-2	1	0	1	-1	.923	-0	/3	-0.3

■ GLENN REDMON Redmon, Glenn Vincent b: 1/11/48, Detroit, Mich. BR/TR, 5'11", 180 lbs. Deb: 9/08/74

YEAR	TM/L	G	AB	R	H	2B	3B	HR	RBI	BB	SO	AVG	OBP	SLG	PRO+	BR	/A	RC	SB	CS	SBR	FA	FR	POS	TPR
1974	SF-N	7	17	0	4	3	0	0	4	1	3	.235	.278	.412	87	-0	-0	2	0	0	0	.955	-1	/2	-0.1

■ HARRY REDMOND Redmond, Harry John b: 9/13/1887, Cleveland, Ohio d: 7/10/60, Cleveland, Ohio TR, Deb: 9/07/09

YEAR	TM/L	G	AB	R	H	2B	3B	HR	RBI	BB	SO	AVG	OBP	SLG	PRO+	BR	/A	RC	SB	CS	SBR	FA	FR	POS	TPR
1909	Bro-N	6	19	3	0	0	0	0	1	0		.000	.000	.000	-99	-4	-4	-0	0			.892	4	/2	-0.1

■ WAYNE REDMOND Redmond, Howard Wayne b: 11/25/45, Athens, Ala. BR/TR, 5'10", 165 lbs. Deb: 9/07/65

YEAR	TM/L	G	AB	R	H	2B	3B	HR	RBI	BB	SO	AVG	OBP	SLG	PRO+	BR	/A	RC	SB	CS	SBR	FA	FR	POS	TPR
1965	Det-A	4	4	1	0	0	0	0	0	1	1	.000	.200	.000	-38	-1	-1	0	0	0	0	1.000	-0	/O	-0.1
1969	Det-A	5	3	0	0	0	0	0	0	0	2	.000	.000	.000	-96	-1	-1	0	0	0	0	.000	0	H	-0.1
Total	2	9	7	1	0	0	0	0	0	1	3	.000	.125	.000	-60	-2	-2	0	0	0	0	.932	-0	/O	-0.2

■ JACK REDMOND Redmond, John McKittrick "Red" b: 9/3/10, Florence, Ariz. d: 7/27/68, Garland, Tex. BL/TR, 5'11", 185 lbs. Deb: 4/22/35

YEAR	TM/L	G	AB	R	H	2B	3B	HR	RBI	BB	SO	AVG	OBP	SLG	PRO+	BR	/A	RC	SB	CS	SBR	FA	FR	POS	TPR
1935	Was-A	22	34	8	6	1	0	1	7	3	1	.176	.243	.294	40	-3	-3	3	0	0	0	.978	2	C	-0.1

■ BILLY REDMON Redmon, William T. b: Brooklyn, N.Y. BL/TL, Deb: 5/04/1875

YEAR	TM/L	G	AB	R	H	2B	3B	HR	RBI	BB	SO	AVG	OBP	SLG	PRO+	BR	/A	RC	SB	CS	SBR	FA	FR	POS	TPR
1875	RS-n	19	82	12	16	2	0	0		2		.195	.214	.220	56	-4	-3	4						S/3	-0.3
1877	Cin-N	3	12	1	3	1	0	0	3	1	1	.250	.308	.333	115	0	0	1				.833	2	/S	0.2
1878	Mil-N	48	187	16	43	8	0	0	21	8	13	.230	.262	.273	71	-5	-6	14				.785	-17	S/O3C	-2.1
Total	2	51	199	17	46	9	0	0	24	9	14	.231	.264	.276	73	-5	-6	15				.791	-16	/SO3C	-1.9

■ GARY REDUS Redus, Gary Eugene b: 11/1/56, Athens, Ala. BR/TR, 6'1", 185 lbs. Deb: 9/07/82

YEAR	TM/L	G	AB	R	H	2B	3B	HR	RBI	BB	SO	AVG	OBP	SLG	PRO+	BR	/A	RC	SB	CS	SBR	FA	FR	POS	TPR
1982	Cin-N	20	83	12	18	3	2	1	7	5	21	.217	.261	.337	65	-4	-4	8	11	2	2	.970	-1	O	-0.4
1983	Cin-N	125	453	90	112	20	9	17	51	71	111	.247	.353	.444	115	12	10	76	39	14	3	.972	5	*O	1.6
1984	Cin-N	123	394	69	100	21	3	7	22	52	71	.254	.342	.376	97	2	-1	58	48	11	8	.967	-2	*O	0.3
1985	Cin-N	101	246	51	62	14	4	6	28	44	52	.252	.368	.415	113	7	6	45	48	12	7	.986	-10	O	0.1
1986	Phi-N	90	340	62	84	22	4	11	33	47	78	.247	.344	.432	109	6	4	55	25	7	3	.980	10	O	1.6
1987	Chi-A	130	475	78	112	26	6	12	48	69	90	.236	.333	.392	89	-5	-7	69	52	11	9	.979	4	*O/D	0.1
1988	Chi-A	77	262	42	69	10	4	6	34	33	52	.263	.350	.401	110	4	4	42	26	2	7	.987	1	O/D	0.9
	Pit-N	30	71	12	14	2	0	2	4	15	19	.197	.345	.310	90	-0	-0	9	5	2	0	.957	2	O	0.1
1989	Pit-N	98	279	42	79	18	7	6	33	40	51	.283	.375	.462	143	14	16	52	25	6	4	.987	0	1O	1.5
1990	*Pit-N	96	227	32	56	15	3	6	23	33	38	.247	.347	.419	114	3	4	36	11	5	0	.988	-2	1/O	-0.2
1991	*Pit-N	98	252	45	62	12	2	7	24	28	39	.246	.329	.393	104	1	1	37	17	3	3	.990	-11	1O	-1.1
1992	*Pit-N	76	176	26	45	7	3	3	12	17	25	.256	.321	.381	99	-1	-0	23	11	4	1	1.000	-4	1O	-0.6
Total	11	1064	3258	561	813	170	47	84	319	454	647	.250	.344	.408	106	39	34	509	318	79	48	.974	-8	O1/D	3.9

■ BOB REECE Reece, Robert Scott b: 1/5/51, Sacramento, Cal. BR/TR, 6'1", 190 lbs. Deb: 4/22/78

YEAR	TM/L	G	AB	R	H	2B	3B	HR	RBI	BB	SO	AVG	OBP	SLG	PRO+	BR	/A	RC	SB	CS	SBR	FA	FR	POS	TPR
1978	Mon-N	9	11	2	2	1	0	0	3	0	4	.182	.182	.273	26	-1	-1	1	0	0	0	.947	1	/C	0.0

■ DARREN REED Reed, Darren A. Douglass b: 10/16/65, Ojai, Cal. BR/TR, 6'1", 190 lbs. Deb: 5/01/90

YEAR	TM/L	G	AB	R	H	2B	3B	HR	RBI	BB	SO	AVG	OBP	SLG	PRO+	BR	/A	RC	SB	CS	SBR	FA	FR	POS	TPR
1990	NY-N	26	39	5	8	4	1	1	2	3	11	.205	.262	.436	89	-1	-1	5	1	0	0	.955	-1	O	-0.2
1992	Mon-N	42	81	10	14	2	0	5	10	6	23	.173	.239	.383	74	-3	-3	7	0	0	0	1.000	-3	O	-0.7
	Min-A	14	33	2	6	2	0	0	4	2	11	.182	.229	.242	31	-3	-3	2	0	0	0	1.000	-2	O/D	-0.6
Total	2	82	153	17	28	8	1	6	16	11	45	.183	.242	.366	68	-7	-7	13	1	0	0	.987	-6	/OD	-1.5

■ HUGH REED Reed, Hugh b: 1837, Chicago, Ill. d: 11/3/1883, Chicago, Ill. Deb: 8/26/1874

YEAR	TM/L	G	AB	R	H	2B	3B	HR	RBI	BB	SO	AVG	OBP	SLG	PRO+	BR	/A	RC	SB	CS	SBR	FA	FR	POS	TPR
1874	Bal-n	1	4	0	0	0	0	0		0		.000	.000	.000	-99	-1	-1	0						/O	-0.1

YEAR	TM/L	G	AB	R	H	2B	3B	HR	RBI	BB	SO	AVG	OBP	SLG	PRO+	BR	/A	RC	SB	CS	SBR	FA	FR	POS	TPR

■ JEFF REED Reed, Jeffrey Scott b: 11/12/62, Joliet, Ill. BL/TR, 6'2", 190 lbs. Deb: 4/05/84

1984	Min-A	18	21	3	3	3	0	0	1	2	6	.143	.217	.286	36	-2	-2	1	0	0	0	.977	2	C	0.1
1985	Min-A	7	10	2	2	0	0	0	0	0	3	.200	.200	.200	9	-1	-1	0	0	0	0	1.000	-0	/C	-0.1
1986	Min-A	68	165	13	39	6	1	2	9	16	19	.236	.308	.321	70	-6	-7	17	1	0	0	.994	8	C	0.4
1987	Mon-N	75	207	15	44	11	0	1	21	12	20	.213	.259	.280	42	-17	-18	14	0	1	-1	.970	-4	C	-1.8
1988	Mon-N	43	123	10	27	3	2	0	9	13	22	.220	.294	.276	62	-5	-6	10	1	0	0	.995	2	C	-0.1
	Cin-N	49	142	10	33	6	0	1	7	15	19	.232	.306	.296	71	-5	-5	13	0	0	0	.993	5	C	0.3
	Yr	92	265	20	60	9	2	1	16	28	41	.226	.300	.287	66	-10	-11	24	1	0	0	.994	8	C	0.2
1989	Cin-N	102	287	16	64	11	0	3	23	34	46	.223	.310	.293	71	-9	-10	27	0	0	0	.988	-5	C	-1.1
1990	*Cin-N	72	175	12	44	8	1	3	16	24	26	.251	.342	.360	89	-1	-2	22	0	0	0	.987	2	C	0.3
1991	Cin-N	91	270	20	72	15	2	3	31	23	38	.267	.327	.370	92	-2	-3	32	0	1	-1	.991	-2	C	0.0
1992	Cin-N	15	25	2	4	0	0	0	2	1	4	.160	.192	.160	1	-3	-3	-1	0	0	0	1.000	-0	/C	-0.3
Total	9	540	1425	103	332	63	6	13	119	140	203	.233	.304	.313	70	-52	-58	139	2	2	-1	.988	2	C	-2.3

■ JODY REED Reed, Jody Eric b: 7/26/62, Tampa, Fla. BR/TR, 5'9", 170 lbs. Deb: 9/12/87

1987	Bos-A	9	30	4	9	1	0	0	8	4	0	.300	.382	.400	105	0	0	5	1	1	-0	1.000	5	/S23	0.5
1988	*Bos-A	109	338	60	99	23	1	1	28	45	21	.293	.382	.376	109	8	6	51	1	3	-2	.971	3	S2/3D	1.5
1989	Bos-A	146	524	76	151	42	2	3	40	73	44	.288	.379	.393	111	15	11	81	4	5	-2	.967	1	S2/30D	1.8
1990	*Bos-A	155	598	70	173	**45**	0	5	51	75	65	.289	.372	.390	108	13	9	87	4	4	-1	.990	-6	*2S/D	0.9
1991	Bos-A	153	618	87	175	42	2	5	60	60	53	.283	.350	.382	98	3	-1	83	6	5	-1	.982	2	*2/S	0.3
1992	Bos-A	143	550	64	136	27	1	3	40	62	44	.247	.324	.316	76	-14	-17	55	7	8	-3	.982	**24**	*2/D	0.7
Total	6	715	2658	361	743	180	7	17	227	319	227	.280	.360	.372	100	26	8	362	23	26	-9	.984	29	2S/3DO	5.7

■ JACK REED Reed, John Burwell b: 2/2/33, Silver City, Miss. BR/TR, 6', 185 lbs. Deb: 4/23/61

1961	*NY-A	28	13	4	2	0	0	1	1	1	1	.154	.214	.154	0	-2	-2	0	0	0	0	.933	-9	O	-1.1
1962	NY-A	88	43	17	13	2	1	1	4	4	7	.302	.362	.465	125	1	1	7	2	1	0	.941	-23	O	-2.2
1963	NY-A	106	73	18	15	3	1	0	1	9	14	.205	.293	.274	60	-4	-4	7	5	1	1	1.000	-21	O	-2.6
Total	3	222	129	39	30	5	2	1	6	14	22	.233	.308	.326	76	-4	-4	14	7	2	1	.972	-53	O	-5.9

■ MILT REED Reed, Milton D. b: 7/4/1890, Atlanta, Ga. d: 7/27/38, Atlanta, Ga. BL/TR, 5'9.5", 150 lbs. Deb: 9/09/11

1911	StL-N	1	1	0	0	0	0	0	0	0	0	.000	.000	.000	-99	-0	-0	0	0			.000	0	H	0.0
1913	Phi-N	13	24	4	6	1	0	0	0	1	5	.250	.280	.292	61	-1	-1	2	1			.900	-4	/S2	-0.5
1914	Phi-N	44	107	10	22	2	1	0	2	10	13	.206	.280	.243	52	-6	-6	8	4			.887	-17	S2/3	-2.5
1915	Bro-F	10	31	2	9	1	1	0	8	2	0	.290	.353	.387	88	1	1	5	2			.864	-4	S	-0.3
Total	4	68	163	16	37	4	2	0	10	13	18	.227	.292	.276	65	-6	-7	16	7			.880	-25	/S23	-3.3

■ TED REED Reed, Ralph Edwin b: 10/18/1890, Beaver, Pa. d: 2/16/59, Beaver, Pa. BR/TR, 5'11", 190 lbs. Deb: 9/10/15

| 1915 | New-F | 20 | 77 | 5 | 20 | 1 | 2 | 0 | 4 | 2 | 7 | .260 | .287 | .325 | 85 | -2 | -2 | 9 | 1 | | | .863 | -3 | 3 | -0.4 |

■ BILLY REED Reed, William Joseph b: 11/12/22, Shawano, Wis. BL/TR, 5'10.5", 175 lbs. Deb: 4/15/52

| 1952 | Bos-N | 15 | 52 | 4 | 13 | 0 | 0 | 0 | 0 | 0 | 5 | .250 | .264 | .250 | 45 | -4 | -4 | 3 | 0 | 0 | 0 | .931 | -7 | 2 | -1.0 |

■ ICICLE REEDER Reeder, James Edward b: 1865, Cincinnati, Ohio BR , Deb: 6/24/1884

1884	Cin-a	3	14	0	2	0	0	0				.143	.143	.143	-5	-2	-2	0				1.000	-0	/O	-0.2
	Was-U	3	12	0	2	0	0	0				.167	.167	.167	13	-1	-1	0				.500	-1	/O	-0.2
Total	1	6	26	0	4	0	0	0				.154	.154	.154	3	-3	-3	1				.714	-1	/O	-0.4

■ NICK REEDER Reeder, Nicholas (b: Nicholas Herchenroeder) b: 3/22/1867, Louisville, Ky. d: 9/26/1894, Louisville, Ky. BR/TR, 5'9", 189 lbs. Deb: 4/11/1891

| 1891 | Lou-a | 2 | 2 | 0 | 0 | 0 | 0 | 0 | | | 1 | .000 | .000 | .000 | -99 | -1 | -1 | 0 | 0 | | | 1.000 | -0 | /3 | -0.1 |

■ RANDY REESE Reese, Andrew Jackson b: 2/7/04, Tupelo, Miss. d: 1/10/66, Tupelo, Miss. BR/TR, 5'11", 180 lbs. Deb: 4/15/27

1927	NY-N	97	355	43	94	14	2	4	21	13	52	.265	.298	.349	73	-14	-14	36	5			.912	-1	3O/1	-1.3
1928	NY-N	109	406	61	125	18	4	6	44	13	24	.308	.331	.416	94	-5	-5	53	7			.941	-10	O2/1S3	-1.7
1929	NY-N	58	209	36	55	11	3	0	21	15	19	.263	.316	.344	64	-12	-12	23	8			.960	1	2/O3	-0.9
1930	NY-N	67	172	26	47	4	2	4	25	10	12	.273	.313	.390	70	-9	-8	20	1			.957	-3	O3/1	-1.2
Total	4	331	1142	166	321	47	11	14	111	51	107	.281	.315	.378	78	-40	-39	132	21			.954	-14	O/321S	-5.1

■ PEE WEE REESE Reese, Harold Henry b: 7/23/18, Ekron, Ky. BR/TR, 5'9", 175 lbs. Deb: 4/23/40 CH

1940	Bro-N	84	312	58	85	8	4	5	28	45	42	.272	.366	.372	98	3	1	47	15			.960	-14	S	-0.7
1941	*Bro-N	152	595	76	136	23	5	2	46	68	56	.229	.311	.294	68	-22	-25	59	10			.946	8	*S	-0.6
1942	Bro-N★	151	564	87	144	24	5	3	53	82	55	.255	.350	.332	98	2	1	71	15			.959	17	*S	2.9
1946	Bro-N†	152	542	79	154	16	10	5	60	87	71	.284	.384	.378	116	15	14	85	10			.966	-4	*S	2.1
1947	*Bro-N★	142	476	81	135	24	4	12	73	**104**	67	.284	.414	.426	119	21	18	93	7			.966	-2	*S	2.3
1948	Bro-N★	151	566	96	155	31	4	9	75	79	63	.274	.363	.390	100	5	2	82	25			.962	10	*S	2.1
1949	*Bro-N★	155	617	**132**	172	27	3	16	73	116	58	.279	.396	.410	112	19	15	111	26			**.977**	2	*S	2.8
1950	Bro-N★	141	531	97	138	21	5	11	52	91	62	.260	.369	.380	96	1	-1	81	17			.963	2	*S/3	1.1
1951	Bro-N★	154	616	94	176	20	8	10	84	81	57	.286	.371	.393	103	7	5	91	20	14	-2	.953	-8	*S	0.6
1952	Bro-N★	149	559	94	152	18	8	6	58	86	59	.272	.369	.365	103	6	5	84	**30**	5	6	.969	-11	*S	1.1
1953	*Bro-N★	140	524	108	142	25	7	13	61	82	61	.271	.374	.420	104	7	5	88	22	6	3	.966	-1	*S	1.7
1954	Bro-N☆	141	554	98	171	35	8	10	69	90	62	.309	.408	.455	121	23	21	104	8	5	-1	.965	-4	*S	2.8
1955	*Bro-N	145	553	99	156	29	4	10	61	78	60	.282	.374	.403	103	7	5	82	8	7	-2	.965	-13	*S	0.2
1956	*Bro-N	147	572	85	147	19	2	9	46	56	69	.257	.324	.344	74	-15	-15	66	13	4	2	.965	-9	*S3	-0.3
1957	Bro-N	103	330	33	74	3	1	1	29	39	32	.224	.308	.248	47	-21	-25	27	5	2	0	.943	10	3S	-1.1
1958	LA-N	59	147	21	33	7	2	4	17	26	15	.224	.341	.381	88	-2	-2	20	1	2	-1	.929	-8	S3	-0.9
Total	16	2166	8058	1338	2170	330	80	126	885	1210	890	.269	.366	.377	98	56	19	1191	232	45		.962	-25	*S3	14.6

■ JIMMIE REESE Reese, James Herman (b: James Herman Soloman) b: 10/1/01, New York, N.Y. BL/TR, 5'11.5", 165 lbs. Deb: 4/19/30 C

1930	NY-A	77	188	44	65	14	2	3	18	11	9	.346	.382	.489	125	5	6	35	1	1	-0	.974	-9	2/3	-0.1
1931	NY-A	65	245	41	59	10	2	3	26	17	10	.241	.293	.335	68	-13	-11	24	2	3	-1	.972	5	2	-0.4
1932	StL-N	90	309	38	82	15	0	2	26	20	19	.265	.314	.333	72	-11	-12	33	4			.979	9	2	0.0
Total	3	232	742	123	206	39	4	8	70	48	37	.278	.324	.373	84	-19	-17	92	7	4		.975	4	2/3	-0.5

■ RICH REESE Reese, Richard Benjamin b: 9/29/41, Leipsic, Ohio BL/TL, 6'3", 200 lbs. Deb: 9/04/64

1964	Min-A	10	7	0	0	0	0	0	0	0	1	.000	.000	.000	-99	-2	-2	0	0	0	0	1.000	0	/1	-0.2
1965	Min-A	14	7	0	2	1	0	0	0	2	2	.286	.444	.429	143	1	1	1	0	0	0	1.000	-0	/1O	0.0
1966	Min-A	3	2	0	0	0	0	0	0	0	2	.000	.333	.000	5	-0	-0	0	0	0	0	.000	0	H	0.0
1967	Min-A	95	101	13	25	5	0	4	20	9	17	.248	.303	.416	102	1	0	13	0	0	0	.990	-1	1O	-0.2
1968	Min-A	126	332	40	86	15	2	4	28	18	36	.259	.303	.352	93	-1	-3	35	3	1	0	.991	-2	1O	-1.2
1969	*Min-A	132	419	52	135	24	4	16	69	23	57	.322	.365	.513	140	22	21	76	1	5	-3	.993	-4	*1/O	0.7
1970	*Min-A	153	501	63	131	15	5	10	56	48	70	.261	.335	.371	93	-3	-4	64	5	4	-1	.992	-2	*1	-2.0
1971	Min-A	120	329	40	72	8	3	10	39	20	35	.219	.274	.353	74	-11	-12	30	7	4	-0	.994	-3	1/O	-2.5
1972	Min-A	132	197	23	43	3	2	5	26	25	27	.218	.306	.330	85	-2	-2	20	0	1	-1	.992	-3	1/O	-0.5
1973	Det-A	59	102	10	14	1	0	2	4	7	17	.137	.193	.206	11	-12	-13	2	0	0	0	1.000	-3	1O	-1.8
	Min-A	22	23	7	4	1	1	3	6	6	.174	.345	.435	114	1	1	4	0	0	0	1.000	1	1	0.1
	Yr	81	125	17	18	2	1	3	7	13	23	.144	.225	.248	31	-11	-12	7	0	0	0	1.000	-2	1O	-1.7

YEAR	TM/L	G	AB	R	H	2B	3B	HR	RBI	BB	SO	AVG	OBP	SLG	PRO+	BR	/A	RC	SB	CS	SBR	FA	FR	POS	TPR
Total	10	866	2020	248	512	73	17	52	245	158	270	.253	.314	.384	95	-8	-16	247	16	15	-4	.992	-10	1/O	-7.6

■ BOBBY REEVES Reeves, Robert Edwin "Gunner" b: 6/24/04, Hill City, Tenn. BR/TR, 5'11", 170 lbs. Deb: 6/09/26

YEAR	TM/L	G	AB	R	H	2B	3B	HR	RBI	BB	SO	AVG	OBP	SLG	PRO+	BR	/A	RC	SB	CS	SBR	FA	FR	POS	TPR
1926	Was-A	20	49	4	11	0	1	0	7	6	9	.224	.321	.265	56	-3	-3	4	1	1	-0	.940	1	3/2S	-0.1
1927	Was-A	112	380	37	97	11	5	1	39	21	53	.255	.296	.318	60	-23	-23	35	3	1	0	.923	-7	S3/2	-1.8
1928	Was-A	102	353	44	107	16	8	3	42	24	47	.303	.351	.419	102	0	1	50	4	8	-4	.908	-4	S2/3O	0.2
1929	Bos-A	140	460	66	114	19	2	2	28	60	57	.248	.343	.311	71	-19	-17	52	7	8	-3	.912	1	*3/2S1	-1.4
1930	Bos-A	92	272	41	59	7	4	2	18	50	36	.217	.345	.294	66	-14	-12	32	6	2	1	.895	5	3S2	-0.1
1931	Bos-A	36	84	11	14	2	2	0	1	14	16	.167	.293	.238	43	-7	-6	7	0	1	-1	.912	-8	2/P	-1.2
Total	6	502	1598	203	402	55	22	8	135	175	218	.252	.331	.329	73	-66	-60	180	21	21	-6	.906	-11	3S/2P1O	-4.4

■ RUDY REGALADO Regalado, Rudolph Valentino b: 5/21/30, Los Angeles, Cal. BR/TR, 6'1", 185 lbs. Deb: 4/13/54

YEAR	TM/L	G	AB	R	H	2B	3B	HR	RBI	BB	SO	AVG	OBP	SLG	PRO+	BR	/A	RC	SB	CS	SBR	FA	FR	POS	TPR
1954	*Cle-A	65	180	21	45	5	0	2	24	19	16	.250	.335	.311	76	-5	-5	19	0	2	-1	.967	-5	3/2	-1.3
1955	Cle-A	10	26	2	7	2	0	0	5	2	4	.269	.321	.346	77	-1	-1	3	0	0	0	.955	2	/32	0.1
1956	Cle-A	16	47	4	11	1	0	0	2	4	1	.234	.308	.255	49	-3	-3	4	0	0	0	.783	-7	3/1	-1.0
Total	3	91	253	27	63	8	0	2	31	25	21	.249	.329	.304	71	-9	-10	26	0	2	-1	.944	-10	/321	-2.2

■ JOE REGAN Regan, Joseph Charles b: 7/12/1872, Seymour, Conn. d: 11/18/48, Hartford, Conn. BR/TR, 6'1", Deb: 9/21/1898

YEAR	TM/L	G	AB	R	H	2B	3B	HR	RBI	BB	SO	AVG	OBP	SLG	PRO+	BR	/A	RC	SB	CS	SBR	FA	FR	POS	TPR
1898	NY-N	2	5	1	1	0	0	0	2	0		.200	.200	.200	15	-1	-1	0	0			1.000	-1	/O	-0.1

■ BILL REGAN Regan, William Wright b: 1/23/1899, Pittsburgh, Pa. d: 6/11/68, Pittsburgh, Pa. BR/TR, 5'10", 155 lbs. Deb: 6/02/26

YEAR	TM/L	G	AB	R	H	2B	3B	HR	RBI	BB	SO	AVG	OBP	SLG	PRO+	BR	/A	RC	SB	CS	SBR	FA	FR	POS	TPR
1926	Bos-A	108	403	40	106	21	3	4	34	23	37	.263	.309	.360	76	-16	-15	45	6	3	0	.965	17	*2	0.6
1927	Bos-A	129	468	43	128	37	10	2	66	26	51	.274	.315	.408	88	-11	-10	55	10	10	-3	.960	3	*2	-0.6
1928	Bos-A	138	511	53	135	30	6	7	75	21	40	.264	.296	.387	80	-18	-17	58	9	6	-1	.963	15	*2/O	0.0
1929	Bos-A	104	371	38	107	27	7	1	54	22	38	.288	.328	.407	90	-7	-6	49	7	5	-1	.962	-16	23/1	-1.8
1930	Bos-A	134	507	54	135	35	10	3	53	25	60	.266	.303	.393	78	-21	-18	60	4	2	0	.963	-10	*2/3	-1.9
1931	Pit-N	28	104	8	21	8	0	1	10	5	19	.202	.239	.308	46	-8	-8	8	2			.944	-0	2	-0.7
Total	6	641	2364	236	632	158	36	18	292	122	245	.267	.306	.387	81	-82	-73	275	38	26		.962	8	2/31O	-4.4

■ TONY REGO Rego, Antone (b: Antone Do Rego) b: 10/31/1897, Wailuku, Hawaii d: 1/6/78, Tulsa, Okla. BR/TR, 5'4", 165 lbs. Deb: 6/21/24

YEAR	TM/L	G	AB	R	H	2B	3B	HR	RBI	BB	SO	AVG	OBP	SLG	PRO+	BR	/A	RC	SB	CS	SBR	FA	FR	POS	TPR
1924	StL-A	24	59	5	13	1	0	0	5	1	3	.220	.233	.237	20	-7	-7	3	0	0	0	.972	0	C	-0.6
1925	StL-A	20	32	5	13	2	1	0	3	3	2	.406	.472	.531	147	3	3	8	0	0	0	.979	2	C	0.5
Total	2	44	91	10	26	3	1	0	8	4	5	.286	.323	.341	66	-4	-5	11	0	0	0	.975	2	/C	-0.1

■ WALLY REHG Rehg, Walter Phillip b: 8/31/1888, Summerfield, Ill. d: 4/5/46, Burbank, Cal. BR/TR, 5'8", 160 lbs. Deb: 4/14/12

YEAR	TM/L	G	AB	R	H	2B	3B	HR	RBI	BB	SO	AVG	OBP	SLG	PRO+	BR	/A	RC	SB	CS	SBR	FA	FR	POS	TPR
1912	Pit-N	8	9	1	0	0	0	0	0	0	1	.000	.000	.000	-99	-2	-2	0	0			1.000	-1	/O	-0.3
1913	Bos-A	30	101	13	28	3	2	0	9	2	7	.277	.291	.347	84	-2	-3	11	4			.943	-3	O	-0.7
1914	Bos-A	88	151	14	33	4	2	0	11	18	11	.219	.306	.272	74	-5	-5	12	5	8	-3	.980	-5	O	-1.6
1915	Bos-A	5	5	2	1	0	0	0	0	0	1	.200	.200	.200	20	-1	-0	0	1			1.000	-0	/O	0.0
1917	Bos-N	87	341	48	92	12	6	1	31	24	32	.270	.320	.349	111	2	4	41	13			.956	-5	O	-0.6
1918	Bos-N	40	133	6	32	5	1	1	12	5	14	.241	.268	.316	81	-4	-3	11	3			.988	2	O	-0.3
1919	Cin-N	5	12	1	2	0	0	0	3	1	0	.167	.231	.167	21	-1	-1	1	0			.875	0	/O	-0.1
Total	7	263	752	85	188	24	11	2	66	50	66	.250	.299	.319	90	-13	-10	76	26	8		.965	-11	O	-3.6

■ FRANK REIBER Reiber, Frank Bernard "Tubby" b: 9/19/09, Huntington, W.Va. BR/TR, 5'8.5", 169 lbs. Deb: 4/13/33

YEAR	TM/L	G	AB	R	H	2B	3B	HR	RBI	BB	SO	AVG	OBP	SLG	PRO+	BR	/A	RC	SB	CS	SBR	FA	FR	POS	TPR
1933	Det-A	13	18	3	5	0	1	1	3	2	3	.278	.350	.556	134	1	1	4	0	0	0	.929	-2	/C	-0.1
1934	Det-A	3	1	0	0	0	0	0	0	2	0	.000	.667	.000	84	0	0	0	0	0	0	.000	0	H	0.0
1935	Det-A	8	11	3	3	0	0	0	1	3	3	.273	.429	.273	88	-0	0	2	0	0	0	1.000	-1	/C	0.0
1936	Det-A	20	55	7	15	2	0	1	5	5	7	.273	.333	.364	72	-2	-2	7	0	1	-1	.982	-4	C/O	-0.5
Total	4	44	85	13	23	2	1	2	9	12	13	.271	.361	.388	89	-1	-1	12	0	1	-1	.975	-6	/CO	-0.6

■ HERMAN REICH Reich, Herman Charles b: 11/23/17, Bell, Cal. BR/TL, 6'2", 200 lbs. Deb: 5/03/49

YEAR	TM/L	G	AB	R	H	2B	3B	HR	RBI	BB	SO	AVG	OBP	SLG	PRO+	BR	/A	RC	SB	CS	SBR	FA	FR	POS	TPR
1949	Was-A	2	2	0	0	0	0	0	0	0	1	.000	.000	.000	-99	-1	-1	0	0	0	0	.000	0	H	-0.1
	Cle-A	1	2	0	1	0	0	0	0	1	0	.500	.667	.500	215	0	0	1	0	0	0	.000	-0	/O	0.0
	Yr	3	4	0	1	0	0	0	0	1	1	.250	.400	.250	75	-0	-0	1	0	0	0	.000	-0	/O	-0.1
	Chi-N	108	386	43	108	18	2	3	34	13	32	.280	.305	.360	80	-13	-12	41	4			.989	14	1O	0.1
Total	1	111	390	43	109	18	2	3	34	14	33	.279	.306	.359	80	-13	-12	41	4	0		.969	14	/1O	0.0

■ RICK REICHARDT Reichardt, Frederic Carl b: 3/16/43, Madison, Wis. BR/TR, 6'3", 215 lbs. Deb: 9/01/64

YEAR	TM/L	G	AB	R	H	2B	3B	HR	RBI	BB	SO	AVG	OBP	SLG	PRO+	BR	/A	RC	SB	CS	SBR	FA	FR	POS	TPR
1964	LA-A	11	37	0	6	0	0	0	0	1	12	.162	.184	.162	-3	-5	-5	1	1	0	0	1.000	0	O	-0.5
1965	Cal-A	20	75	8	20	4	0	1	6	5	12	.267	.321	.360	95	-1	-0	9	4	1	1	.975	1	O	0.0
1966	Cal-A	89	319	48	92	5	4	16	44	27	61	.288	.368	.480	145	17	18	57	8	4	0	.976	-1	O	1.4
1967	Cal-A	146	498	56	132	14	2	17	69	35	90	.265	.322	.404	118	7	9	61	5	3	-0	.974	10	*O	1.4
1968	Cal-A	151	534	62	136	20	3	21	73	42	118	.255	.330	.421	131	17	19	72	8	7	-2	.989	9	*O	2.1
1969	Cal-A	137	493	60	125	11	4	13	68	43	100	.254	.324	.371	99	-4	-1	56	3	6	-3	.981	8	*O/1	-0.4
1970	Cal-A	9	6	1	1	0	0	0	1	3	0	.167	.444	.167	78	0	0	1	0	0	0	1.000	-0	/O	0.0
	Was-A	107	277	42	70	14	2	15	46	23	69	.253	.330	.480	127	7	9	39	2	4	-2	.985	-8	O/3	-0.5
	Yr	116	283	43	71	14	2	15	47	26	69	.251	.333	.473	126	7	9	40	2	4	-2	.985	-8	O/3	-0.5
1971	Chi-A	138	496	53	138	14	2	19	62	37	90	.278	.336	.429	112	9	7	68	5	10	-5	.981	-7	*O/1	-1.2
1972	Chi-A	101	291	31	73	14	4	8	43	28	63	.251	.323	.409	114	6	5	39	2	2	-1	.981	-10	O	-1.1
1973	Chi-A	46	153	15	42	8	1	3	16	8	29	.275	.315	.399	96	-0	-1	18	2	3	-1	1.000	-2	O/D	-0.6
	KC-A	41	127	15	28	5	2	3	17	11	28	.220	.283	.362	75	-4	-5	12	0	1	-1	1.000	-1	D/O	-0.6
	Yr	87	280	30	70	13	3	6	33	19	57	.250	.300	.382	86	-4	-6	30	2	4	-2	1.000	-3	OD	-1.2
1974	KC-A	1	1	0	1	0	0	0	0	0	0	1.000	1.000	1.000	451	0	0	1	0	0	0	.000	0	H	0.0
Total	11	997	3307	391	864	109	24	116	445	263	672	.261	.328	.414	115	49	55	434	40	41	-13	.982	-2	O/D13	-0.0

■ DICK REICHLE Reichle, Richard Wendell b: 11/23/1896, Lincoln, Ill. d: 6/13/67, St.Louis, Mo. BL/TR, 6', 185 lbs. Deb: 9/19/22

YEAR	TM/L	G	AB	R	H	2B	3B	HR	RBI	BB	SO	AVG	OBP	SLG	PRO+	BR	/A	RC	SB	CS	SBR	FA	FR	POS	TPR
1922	Bos-A	6	24	3	6	1	0	0	0	0	2	.250	.280	.292	50	-2	-2	2	0	0	0	1.000	-0	/O	-0.3
1923	Bos-A	122	361	40	93	17	3	1	39	22	34	.258	.315	.330	69	-16	-16	37	3	6	-3	.976	-7	O/1	-3.1
Total	2	128	385	43	99	18	3	1	39	22	36	.257	.313	.327	68	-18	-18	39	3	6	-3	.977	-7	/O1	-3.4

■ JESSIE REID Reid, Jessie Thomas b: 6/1/62, Honolulu, Hawaii BL/TL, 6'1", 200 lbs. Deb: 9/09/87

YEAR	TM/L	G	AB	R	H	2B	3B	HR	RBI	BB	SO	AVG	OBP	SLG	PRO+	BR	/A	RC	SB	CS	SBR	FA	FR	POS	TPR
1987	SF-N	6	8	1	1	0	0	1	1	1	5	.125	.222	.500	89	-0	-0	1	0	0	0	1.000	-1	/O	-0.1
1988	SF-N	2	2	0	0	0	0	0	0	0	1	.000	.000	.000	-99	-1	-0	0	0	0	0	.000	0	H	-0.1
Total	2	8	10	1	1	0	0	1	1	1	6	.100	.182	.400	54	-1	-1	1	0	0	0	1.000	-1	/O	-0.2

■ SCOTT REID Reid, Scott Donald b: 1/7/47, Chicago, Ill. BL/TR, 6'1", 195 lbs. Deb: 9/10/69

YEAR	TM/L	G	AB	R	H	2B	3B	HR	RBI	BB	SO	AVG	OBP	SLG	PRO+	BR	/A	RC	SB	CS	SBR	FA	FR	POS	TPR
1969	Phi-N	13	19	5	4	0	0	0	0	7	5	.211	.423	.211	85	0	0	2	0	1	-1	1.000	-1	/O	-0.1
1970	Phi-N	25	49	5	6	1	0	0	1	11	22	.122	.283	.143	18	-5	-5	3	0	0	0	1.000	5	O	-0.1
Total	2	38	68	10	10	1	0	0	1	18	27	.147	.326	.162	37	-5	-5	5	0	1	-1	1.000	5	/O	-0.2

■ BILLY REID Reid, William Alexander b: 5/17/1857, London, Ont., Can. d: 6/26/40, London, Ont., Can. BR/TR, 6', 170 lbs. Deb: 5/01/1883

YEAR	TM/L	G	AB	R	H	2B	3B	HR	RBI	BB	SO	AVG	OBP	SLG	PRO+	BR	/A	RC	SB	CS	SBR	FA	FR	POS	TPR
1883	Bal-a	24	97	14	27	3	0	0		4		.278	.307	.309	96	-0	-1	9				.842	-8	2/S	-0.7
1884	Pit-a	19	70	11	17	2	0	0		4		.243	.293	.271	87	-1	-1	6				.724	-4	O/32	-0.5
Total	2	43	167	25	44	5	0	0		8		.263	.301	.293	92	-1	-1	15				.839	-12	/2O3S	-1.2

YEAR	TM/L	G	AB	R	H	2B	3B	HR	RBI	BB	SO	AVG	OBP	SLG	PRO+	BR	/A	RC	SB	CS	SBR	FA	FR	POS	TPR

■ **DUKE REILLEY** Reilley, Alexander Aloysius "Midget" b: 8/25/1884, Chicago, Ill. d: 3/4/68, Indianapolis, Ind. BB/TR, 5'4.5", 148 lbs. Deb: 8/28/09

| 1909 | Cle-A | 20 | 62 | 10 | 13 | 0 | 0 | 0 | 4 | | | .210 | .258 | .210 | 46 | -4 | -4 | 5 | 5 | | | .979 | 3 | O | -0.2 |

■ **CHARLIE REILLEY** Reilley, Charles E. b: 1856, Hartford, Conn. d: 1888. BR/TR, 5'10", 165 lbs. Deb: 5/01/1879

1879	Tro-N	62	236	17	54	5	1	0	19	1	20	.229	.232	.258	66	-10	-7	15				.867	-16	C1/O	-2.1
1880	Cin-N	30	103	8	21	1	0	0	9	0	5	.204	.204	.214	42	-6	-6	5				.759	-5	OC/3	-1.1
1881	Det-N	19	70	8	12	2	0	0	3	0	10	.171	.171	.200	16	-7	-7	2				.889	-4	C/OS31	-1.0
	Wor-N	2	8	2	3	0	0	0	1	0	1	.375	.375	.375	129	0	0	1				1.000	-2	/C	-0.2
	Yr	21	78	10	15	2	0	0	4	0	11	.192	.192	.218	28	-6	-7	3				.897	-6	C/OS31	-1.2
1882	Pro-N	3	11	0	2	0	0	0	2	1	2	.182	.250	.182	41	-1	-1	1				.714	-2	/C	-0.3
Total	4	116	428	35	92	8	1	0	34	2	38	.215	.219	.238	52	-23	-21	23				.867	-29	/CO13S	-4.7

■ **ARCH REILLY** Reilly, Archer Edwin b: 8/17/1891, Alton, Ill. d: 11/29/63, Columbus, Ohio BR/TR, 5'10", 163 lbs. Deb: 6/01/17

| 1917 | Pit-N | 1 | 0 | 0 | 0 | 0 | 0 | 0 | 0 | 0 | 0 | — | — | — | — | 0 | 0 | 0 | 0 | | | 1.000 | 0 | /3 | 0.0 |

■ **BARNEY REILLY** Reilly, Bernard Eugene b: 2/7/1885, Brockton, Mass. d: 11/15/34, St.Joseph, Mo. BR/TR, 6' , 175 lbs. Deb: 7/02/09

| 1909 | Chi-A | 12 | 25 | 3 | 5 | 0 | 0 | 0 | 3 | 3 | | .200 | .286 | .200 | 56 | -1 | -1 | 2 | 2 | | | .962 | 4 | 2/O | 0.2 |

■ **JOSH REILLY** Reilly, Charles b: 1868, San Francisco, Cal. d: 6/13/38, San Francisco, Cal. Deb: 5/02/1896

| 1896 | Chi-N | 9 | 42 | 6 | 9 | 1 | 0 | 0 | 1 | 1 | | .214 | .233 | .238 | 24 | -4 | -5 | 3 | 2 | | | .857 | -1 | /2S | -0.4 |

■ **CHARLIE REILLY** Reilly, Charles Thomas "Princeton Charlie" (b: Charles Thomas O'Reilly)
b: 2/15/1867, Princeton, N.J. d: 12/16/37, Los Angeles, Cal. BB/TR, 5'11", 190 lbs. Deb: 10/09/1889

1889	Col-a	6	23	5	11	1	0	3	6	2	2	.478	.538	.913	330	6	6	17	9			.923	2	/3	0.7
1890	Col-a	137	530	75	141	23	3	4		35		.266	.319	.343	105	-3	3	74	43			**.893**	28	*3	3.2
1891	Pit-N	114	415	43	91	8	5	3	44	29	58	.219	.277	.284	67	-18	-17	39	20			.857	2	*3S/O	-0.9
1892	Phi-N	91	331	42	65	7	3	1	24	18	43	.196	.242	.245	49	-21	-20	23	13			.905	10	3O/2	-0.8
1893	Phi-N	104	416	64	102	16	7	4	56	33	36	.245	.314	.346	77	-14	-14	51	13			.895	-1	*3	-1.0
1894	Phi-N	39	135	21	40	1	2	0	19	16	10	.296	.364	.333	78	-4	-4	21	9			.874	2	3/O2S1	-0.1
1895	Phi-N	49	179	28	48	6	1	0	25	13	12	.268	.335	.313	69	-8	-8	23	7			.900	-1	S3/2O	-0.6
1897	Was-N	101	351	64	97	18	3	2	60	34		.276	.359	.362	91	-4	-4	54	18			.905	18	*3	1.4
Total	8	641	2380	342	595	80	24	17	234	180	161	.250	.314	.325	81	-66	-57	302	132			.890	60	3/SO21	1.9

■ **HAL REILLY** Reilly, Harold J. Deb: 6/19/19

| 1919 | Chi-N | 1 | 3 | 0 | 0 | 0 | 0 | 0 | 0 | 0 | 1 | .000 | .000 | .000 | -99 | -1 | -1 | 0 | 0 | | | .000 | -1 | /O | -0.1 |

■ **JOHN REILLY** Reilly, John Good "Long Jong" b: 10/5/1858, Cincinnati, Ohio d: 5/31/37, Cincinnati, Ohio BR/TR, 6'3", 178 lbs. Deb: 5/18/1880

1880	Cin-N	73	272	21	56	8	4	0	16	3	36	.206	.215	.265	62	-11	-10	16				.947	-4	*1/O	-2.0
1883	Cin-a	98	437	103	136	21	14	9			9	.311	.325	.485	149	26	22	71				.961	-1	*1/O	1.0
1884	Cin-a	105	448	114	152	24	19	**11**			5	.339	.366	**.551**	190	46	43	**93**				.971	-2	*1/OS	2.6
1885	Cin-a	111	482	92	143	18	11	5			11	.297	.322	.411	131	17	15	65				.963	-5	*1/O	-0.2
1886	Cin-a	115	441	92	117	12	11	6			31	.265	.321	.383	118	10	8	62	19			.967	-1	*1/O	-0.5
1887	Cin-a	134	551	106	170	35	14	10			22	.309	.352	.477	129	21	19	113	50			.980	-0	*1/O	0.5
1888	Cin-a	127	527	112	169	28	14	**13**	103	17		.321	.363	**.501**	170	44	40	**129**	82			.977	-0	*1O	2.6
1889	Cin-a	111	427	84	111	24	13	5	66	34	37	.260	.340	.412	113	8	6	76	43			**.984**	-2	*1/O	-0.2
1890	Cin-N	133	553	114	166	25	**26**	6	86	16	41	.300	.328	.472	135	19	20	98	29			.977	-3	*1/O	0.9
1891	Cin-N	135	546	60	132	20	13	4	64	9	42	.242	.267	.348	80	-16	-16	58	22			.982	-7	*1O	-2.6
Total	10	1142	4684	898	1352	215	139	69	335	157	156	.289	.325	.438	130	165	147	780	245			.972	-25	*1/OS	2.1

■ **JOE REILLY** Reilly, Joseph J. b: 1861, New York, N.Y. 5'10", 140 lbs. Deb: 4/21/1884

1884	Bos-U	3	11	1	0	0	0	0			1	.000	.083	.000	-71	-2	-2	0				1.000	-1	/O3	-0.3
1885	NY-a	10	40	6	7	3	0	0			2	.175	.214	.250	52	-2	-2	2				.848	1	/23	0.0
Total	2	13	51	7	7	3	0	0			3	.137	.185	.196	25	-4	-4	2				.778	0	/23O	-0.3

■ **TOM REILLY** Reilly, Thomas Henry b: 8/3/1884, St.Louis, Mo. d: 10/18/18, New Orleans, La. BR/TR, 5'10", Deb: 7/27/08

1908	StL-N	29	81	5	14	1	0	1	3	2		.173	.193	.222	34	-6	-6	4	4			.866	-6	S	-1.3
1909	StL-N	5	7	0	2	0	1	0	2	0		.286	.286	.571	176	0	0	1	0			1.000	0	/S	0.1
1914	Cle-A	1	1	0	0	0	0	0	0	0	0	.000	.000	.000	-96	-0	-0	0	0			.000	0	H	0.0
Total	3	35	89	5	16	1	1	1	5	2	0	.180	.198	.247	44	-6	-6	5	4			.875	-6	/S	-1.2

■ **KEVIN REIMER** Reimer, Kevin Michael b: 6/28/64, Macon, Ga. BL/TR, 6'2", 215 lbs. Deb: 9/13/88

1988	Tex-A	12	25	2	3	0	0	0	0	2	6	.120	.120	.240	-2	-3	-3	1	0	0	0	.000	-0	/OD	-0.4
1989	Tex-A	3	5	0	0	0	0	0	0	0	1	.000	.000	.000	-98	-1	-1	0	0	0	0	.000	0	/D	-0.1
1990	Tex-A	64	100	5	26	9	1	2	15	10	22	.260	.333	.430	112	1	1	14	0	1	-1	.857	-2	D/O	-0.1
1991	Tex-A	136	394	46	106	22	6	20	69	33	93	.269	.336	.477	125	11	12	60	0	3	-2	.948	-5	OD	0.4
1992	Tex-A	148	494	56	132	32	2	16	58	42	103	.267	.337	.437	119	9	11	71	2	4	-2	.949	-3	*OD	0.5
Total	5	363	1018	109	267	63	3	39	144	85	225	.262	.330	.445	117	17	20	146	2	8	-4	.945	-10	OD	0.3

■ **MIKE REINBACH** Reinbach, Michael Wayne b: 8/6/49, San Diego, Cal. BL/TR, 6'2", 195 lbs. Deb: 4/07/74

| 1974 | Bal-A | 12 | 20 | 2 | 5 | 1 | 0 | 0 | 2 | 2 | 5 | .250 | .318 | .300 | 81 | -1 | -0 | 2 | 0 | 0 | 0 | 1.000 | -1 | /OD | -0.1 |

■ **ART REINHOLZ** Reinholz, Arthur August b: 1/27/03, Detroit, Mich. d: 12/29/80, Newport Richey, Fla. BR/TR, 5'10.5", 175 lbs. Deb: 9/27/28

| 1928 | Cle-A | 2 | 3 | 0 | 1 | 0 | 0 | 0 | 0 | 1 | 0 | .333 | .500 | .333 | 122 | 0 | 0 | 1 | 0 | 0 | 0 | .833 | 1 | /3 | 0.1 |

■ **WALLY REINECKER** Reinecker, Walter (b: Walter Joseph Smith) b: 4/21/1890, Pittsburgh, Pa. d: 4/18/57, Pittsburgh, Pa. BR/TR, 5'6", 150 lbs. Deb: 9/17/15

| 1915 | Bal-F | 3 | 8 | 0 | 1 | 0 | 0 | 0 | 0 | 0 | 0 | .125 | .222 | .125 | 3 | -1 | -1 | 0 | 0 | | | .571 | -2 | /3 | -0.3 |

■ **CHARLIE REIPSCHLAGER** Reipschlager, Charles W. BR/TR, 5'6.5", 160 lbs. Deb: 5/02/1883

1883	NY-a	37	145	8	27	4	2	0			4	.186	.208	.241	43	-9	-10	7				.936	5	C/O	-0.3
1884	*NY-a	59	233	21	56	13	2	0			1	.240	.250	.313	87	-4	-3	19				.925	19	C/O	1.8
1885	NY-a	72	268	29	65	11	1	0			9	.243	.270	.291	86	-6	-3	22				.879	-8	C/O3S2	-0.5
1886	NY-a	65	232	21	49	4	6	0			9	.211	.244	.280	68	-9	-8	17	2			.880	-6	C/O	-0.7
1887	Cle-a	63	231	20	49	8	3	0			11	.212	.251	.273	49	-16	-15	18	7			.888	3	C1	-0.7
Total	5	296	1109	99	246	40	14	0			34	.222	.248	.283	68	-44	-38	82	9			.900	12	C/O132S	-0.4

■ **BOBBY REIS** Reis, Robert Joseph Thomas b: 1/2/09, Woodside, N.Y. d: 5/1/73, St.Paul, Minn. BR/TR, 6'1", 175 lbs. Deb: 9/19/31

1931	Bro-N	6	17	3	5	0	0	0	0	2		.294	.368	.294	81	-0	-0	2	0			.933	-1	/3	-0.1
1932	Bro-N	1	4	0	1	0	0	0	0	0	1	.250	.250	.250	36	-0	-0	0	0			.500	-1	/3	-0.1
1935	Bro-N	52	85	10	21	3	2	0	4	6	13	.247	.297	.329	70	-4	-4	8	2			.950	2	OP/213	-0.2
1936	Bos-N	37	60	3	13	2	0	0	5	3	6	.217	.254	.250	39	-5	-5	4	0			1.000	3	P/O	-0.1
1937	Bos-N	45	86	10	21	5	0	0	6	13	12	.244	.343	.302	84	-2	-1	10	2			1.000	-4	O/P1	-0.6
1938	Bos-N	34	49	6	9	0	0	0	4	1	3	.184	.200	.184	7	-6	-6	2	1			1.000	-3	PO/SC2	-0.6
Total	6	175	301	32	70	10	2	0	21	25	35	.233	.291	.279	59	-18	-16	26	5			1.000	-2	/PO312SC	-1.7

■ **PETE REISER** Reiser, Harold Patrick b: 3/17/19, St.Louis, Mo. d: 10/25/81, Palm Springs, Cal. BL/TR, 5'11", 185 lbs. Deb: 7/23/40 C

| 1940 | Bro-N | 58 | 225 | 34 | 66 | 11 | 4 | 3 | 20 | 15 | 33 | .293 | .338 | .418 | 101 | 2 | 0 | 31 | 2 | | | .960 | -4 | 3O/S | -0.3 |

YEAR	TM/L	G	AB	R	H	2B	3B	HR	RBI	BB	SO	AVG	OBP	SLG	PRO+	BR	/A	RC	SB	CS	SBR	FA	FR	POS	TPR
1941	*Bro-N★	137	536	**117**	184	**39**	**17**	14	76	46	71	**.343**	.406	**.558**	**163**	48	45	124	4			.981	12	*O	**4.9**
1942	Bro-N★	125	480	89	149	33	5	10	64	48	45	.310	.375	.463	142	26	25	88	**20**			.969	-2	*O	1.8
1946	Bro-N☆	122	423	75	117	21	5	11	73	55	58	.277	.361	.428	122	13	12	70	**34**			.978	7	O3	1.6
1947	*Bro-N	110	388	68	120	23	2	5	46	68	41	.309	.415	.418	117	15	13	74	14			.988	-5	*O	0.2
1948	Bro-N	64	127	17	30	8	2	1	19	29	21	.236	.382	.354	97	1	1	20	4			.981	-5	O/3	-0.6
1949	Bos-N	84	221	32	60	8	3	8	40	33	42	.271	.369	.443	123	6	7	38	3			.980	-1	O/3	0.4
1950	Bos-N	53	78	12	16	2	0	1	10	18	22	.205	.367	.269	75	-2	-2	9	1			.979	-2	O/3	-0.4
1951	Pit-N	74	140	22	38	9	3	2	13	27	20	.271	.389	.421	115	4	4	25	4	2	0	.982	-2	O/3	0.1
1952	Cle-A	34	44	7	6	1	0	3	7	4	16	.136	.208	.364	61	-3	-3	3	1	1	-0	1.000	-1	O	-0.5
Total	10	861	2662	473	786	155	41	58	368	343	369	.295	.380	.450	127	110	103	483	87	3		.979	-1	O/3S	7.2
■ CHARLIE REISING Reising, Charles "Pop" b: 8/28/1861, Indiana d: 7/26/15, Louisville, Ky. Deb: 7/19/1884																									
1884	Ind-a	2	8	0	0	0	0	0		1		.000	.111	.000	-61	-1	-1	0				.400	-1	/O	-0.3
■ AL REISS Reiss, Albert Allen b: 1/8/09, Elizabeth, N.J. d: 5/13/89, Red Bank, N.J. BB/TR, 5'10.5", 165 lbs. Deb: 6/22/32																									
1932	Phi-A	9	5	0	1	0	0	0	1	1	1	.200	.333	.200	40	-0	-0	0	0	0	0	1.000	0	/S	0.0
■ HEINIE REITZ Reitz, Henry P. b: 6/29/1867, Chicago, Ill. d: 11/10/14, Sacramento, Cal BL/TR, 5'7", 158 lbs. Deb: 4/27/1893																									
1893	Bal-N	130	490	90	140	17	13	1	76	65	32	.286	.377	.380	102	4	3	81	24			.939	-1	*2	0.4
1894	*Bal-N	108	446	86	135	22	**31**	2	105	42	24	.303	.372	.504	106	6	2	93	18			**.968**	26	*23	2.5
1895	Bal-N	71	245	45	72	15	5	0	29	18	11	.294	.350	.396	91	-2	-4	41	15			.938	-3	23/S	-0.4
1896	*Bal-N	120	464	76	133	15	6	4	106	49	32	.287	.357	.371	93	-3	-4	75	28			.952	-17	*2/S	-1.2
1897	*Bal-N	128	477	76	138	15	6	2	84	50		.289	.370	.358	93	-3	-3	74	23			**.962**	21	*2	2.1
1898	Was-N	132	489	62	148	20	2	2	47	32		.303	.357	.364	107	4	4	71	11			**.959**	6	*2	1.8
1899	Pit-N	34	130	11	34	4	2	0	15	10		.262	.314	.323	75	-5	-4	15	3			.975	1	2	-0.1
Total	7	723	2741	446	800	108	65	11	462	266	99	.292	.363	.391	98	1	-6	451	122			.955	34	2/3S	5.1
■ KEN REITZ Reitz, Kenneth John b: 6/24/51, San Francisco, Cal BR/TR, 6', 185 lbs. Deb: 9/05/72																									
1972	StL-N	21	78	5	28	4	0	0	10	2	4	.359	.375	.410	125	2	2	10	0	1	-1	.956	-4	3	-0.2
1973	StL-N	147	426	40	100	20	2	6	42	9	25	.235	.257	.333	63	-23	-23	31	0	1	-1	**.974**	-6	*3/S	-3.1
1974	StL-N	154	579	48	157	28	2	7	54	23	63	.271	.301	.363	86	-13	-13	56	0	0	0	**.974**	-17	*3/S2	-3.3
1975	StL-N	161	592	43	159	25	1	5	63	22	54	.269	.300	.340	75	-19	-22	56	1	1	-0	.946	-21	*3	-4.6
1976	SF-N	155	577	40	154	21	1	5	66	24	48	.267	.297	.333	76	-17	-19	51	5	4	-1	.959	2	*3/S	-2.1
1977	StL-N	157	587	58	153	36	1	17	79	19	74	.261	.292	.412	88	-13	-12	64	2	6	-3	**.980**	-2	*3	-1.9
1978	StL-N	150	540	41	133	26	2	10	75	23	61	.246	.283	.357	79	-17	-16	52	1	0	0	**.973**	1	*3	-1.8
1979	StL-N	159	605	42	162	41	2	8	73	25	85	.268	.301	.382	84	-14	-14	67	1	0	0	.972	-13	*3	-2.9
1980	StL-N★	151	523	39	141	33	0	8	58	22	44	.270	.303	.379	86	-9	-11	56	0	1	-1	**.979**	-4	*3	-1.9
1981	Chi-N	82	260	10	56	9	1	2	28	15	56	.215	.266	.281	53	-15	-17	18	0	0	0	**.977**	5	3	-1.4
1982	Pit-N	7	10	0	0	0	0	0	0	0	4	.000	.091	.000	-70	-2	-2	0	0	0	0	1.000	1	/3	-0.2
Total	11	1344	4777	366	1243	243	12	68	548	184	518	.260	.293	.359	79	-141	-146	461	10	14	-5	.970	-58	*3/S2	-23.4
■ BUTCH REMENTER Rementer, Willis J. H. b: 3/14/1878, Philadelphia, Pa. d: 9/23/22, Philadelphia, Pa. TR , Deb: 10/08/04																									
1904	Phi-N	1	2	0	0	0	0	0	0	0		.000	.000	.000	-99	-0	-0	0	0			1.000	-0	/C	-0.1
■ JACK REMSEN Remsen, John J. b: 4/1850, Brooklyn, N.Y. BR/TR, 5'11", 189 lbs. Deb: 5/02/1872																									
1872	Atl-n	37	164	26	40	6	5	0	13	2	5	.244	.253	.341	69	-4	-10	14						*O	-0.6
1873	Atl-n	50	207	29	61	7	6	1	29	2	2	.295	.301	.401	117	1	6	25						*O	0.4
1874	Mut-n	64	285	52	65	11	4	2		0		.228	.228	.316	69	-9	-11	21						*O/1	-0.7
1875	Har-n	86	354	69	96	10	4	0		5		.271	.281	.322	103	3	0	33						*O	0.1
1876	Har-N	69	324	62	89	12	5	1	30	1	15	.275	.277	.352	100	2	-2	32				.887	8	*O	0.5
1877	StL-N	33	123	14	32	3	4	0	13	4	3	.260	.283	.350	104	-0	1	12				.906	2	O	0.1
1878	Chi-N	56	224	32	52	11	1	1	19	**17**	33	.232	.286	.304	88	-1	-3	20				**.944**	6	*O	0.0
1879	Chi-N	42	152	14	33	4	2	0	8	2	23	.217	.227	.270	60	-6	-7	10				.862	-2	O1	-1.0
1881	Cle-N	48	172	14	30	4	3	0	13	9	31	.174	.215	.233	43	-11	-10	9				.873	-1	O	-1.2
1884	Phi-N	12	43	9	9	2	0	0	3	6	9	.209	.306	.256	83	-1	-0	3				.952	0	O	-0.1
	Bro-a	81	301	45	67	6	6	3		23		.223	.278	.312	94	-1	-1	27				.914	4	*O	0.1
Total	4 n	237	1010	176	262	34	19	3	42	9	7	.259	.266	.340	90	-9	-15	93						O/1	-0.8
Total	6	341	1339	190	312	42	21	5	86	62	114	.233	.267	.307	85	-18	-23	113				.900	17	O/1	-1.6
■ JERRY REMY Remy, Gerald Peter b: 11/8/52, Fall River, Mass. BL/TR, 5'9", 165 lbs. Deb: 4/07/75																									
1975	Cal-A	147	569	82	147	17	5	1	46	45	55	.258	.313	.311	82	-17	-12	53	34	21	-2	.982	10	*2	0.3
1976	Cal-A	143	502	64	132	14	3	0	28	38	43	.263	.315	.303	87	-11	-8	50	35	16	1	.977	15	*2/D	1.8
1977	Cal-A	154	575	74	145	19	10	4	44	59	59	.252	.324	.341	85	-14	-11	67	41	17	2	.975	-12	*2/3	-1.0
1978	Bos-A☆	148	583	87	162	24	6	2	44	40	55	.278	.324	.350	81	-8	-16	66	30	13	1	.983	2	*2/SD	-0.2
1979	Bos-A	80	306	49	91	11	2	0	29	26	25	.297	.352	.346	85	-4	-6	39	14	9	-1	.970	-21	2	-2.3
1980	Bos-A	63	230	24	72	7	2	0	9	10	14	.313	.342	.361	88	-2	-4	27	14	6	1	.977	-3	2/O	-0.3
1981	Bos-A	88	358	55	110	9	1	0	31	36	30	.307	.371	.338	99	4	1	48	9	2	2	.984	-7	2	0.1
1982	Bos-A	155	636	89	178	22	3	0	47	55	77	.280	.339	.324	79	-13	-18	71	16	9	-1	.982	-16	*2	-2.7
1983	Bos-A	146	592	73	163	16	5	0	43	40	35	.275	.321	.319	72	-18	-23	62	11	3	2	.990	-31	*2	-4.6
1984	Bos-A	30	104	8	26	1	1	0	8	7	11	.250	.297	.279	58	-5	-6	9	4	3	-1	.973	-3	2	-0.9
Total	10	1154	4455	605	1226	140	38	7	329	356	404	.275	.329	.328	82	-89	-102	492	208	99	3	.981	-67	*2/DOS3	-9.8
■ RICK RENICK Renick, Warren Richard b: 3/16/44, London, Ohio BR/TR, 6', 190 lbs. Deb: 7/11/68 C																									
1968	Min-A	42	97	16	21	5	2	3	13	9	42	.216	.283	.402	101	0	-0	11	0	0	0	.946	-0	S	0.3
1969	*Min-A	71	139	21	34	3	0	5	17	12	32	.245	.309	.374	88	-2	-2	15	0	1	-1	.913	-8	3O/S	-1.1
1970	*Min-A	81	179	20	41	8	0	7	25	22	29	.229	.317	.391	93	-2	-2	21	0	2	-1	.987	-3	3O/S	-0.8
1971	Min-A	27	45	4	10	2	0	1	8	5	14	.222	.314	.333	81	-1	-1	5	0	0	0	.846	-3	/3O	-0.5
1972	Min-A	55	93	10	16	2	0	4	8	15	25	.172	.287	.323	77	-2	-3	8	0	1	-1	1.000	-4	O/13S	-0.9
Total	5	276	553	71	122	20	2	20	71	63	142	.221	.304	.373	89	-6	-8	60	0	4	-2	.940	-18	/3OS1	-3.0
■ BILL RENNA Renna, William Beneditto "Big Bill" b: 10/14/24, Hanford, Cal. BR/TR, 6'3", 218 lbs. Deb: 4/14/53																									
1953	NY-A	61	121	19	38	6	3	2	13	13	31	.314	.385	.463	133	5	5	22	0	1	-1	.983	-6	O	-0.3
1954	Phi-A	123	422	52	98	15	4	13	53	41	60	.232	.305	.379	86	-9	-9	49	1	3	-2	.972	6	*O	-1.0
1955	KC-A	100	249	33	53	7	3	7	28	31	42	.213	.305	.349	75	-9	-9	27	0	3	-2	.992	-6	O	-2.1
1956	KC-A	33	48	12	13	3	0	2	5	3	10	.271	.314	.458	101	-0	-0	7	1	0	0	.950	-6	O	-0.6
1958	Bos-A	39	56	5	15	5	0	4	18	6	14	.268	.339	.571	136	3	3	11	0	0	0	1.000	-1	O	0.2
1959	Bos-A	14	22	2	2	0	0	0	2	5	9	.091	.259	.091	0	-3	-3	1	0	0	0	1.000	-2	/O	-0.5
Total	6	370	918	123	219	36	10	28	119	99	166	.239	.317	.391	91	-13	-14	117	2	7	-4	.979	-15	O	-4.3
■ TONY RENSA Rensa, George Anthony "Pug" b: 9/29/01, Parsons, Pa. d: 1/4/87, Wilkes-Barre, Pa. BR/TR, 5'10", 180 lbs. Deb: 5/05/30																									
1930	Det-A	20	37	6	10	2	1	1	3	6	7	.270	.386	.459	111	1	1	7	1	0	0	.964	-1	C	0.1
	Phi-N	54	172	31	49	11	2	3	31	10	18	.285	.328	.424	75	-6	-8	23	0			.932	-11	C	-1.3
1931	Phi-N	19	29	2	3	1	0	0	2	6	2	.103	.257	.138	8	-4	-4	1	0			.958	2	C	-0.1
1933	NY-A	8	29	4	9	2	1	0	3	1	3	.310	.333	.448	112	0	0	4	0	1	-1	.977	-1	/C	-0.1
1937	Chi-A	26	57	10	17	5	1	0	5	8	6	.298	.385	.421	103	0	0	10	3	0	1	.975	1	C	0.3

YEAR	TM/L	G	AB	R	H	2B	3B	HR	RBI	BB	SO	AVG	OBP	SLG	PRO+	BR	/A	RC	SB	CS	SBR	FA	FR	POS	TPR
1938	Chi-A	59	165	15	41	5	0	3	19	25	16	.248	.351	.333	71	-7	-7	21	1	1	-0	.982	6	C	0.1
1939	Chi-A	14	25	3	5	0	0	0	2	1	2	.200	.231	.200	11	-3	-3	1	0	0	0	.972	1	C	-0.2
Total	6	200	514	71	134	26	5	7	65	57	54	.261	.338	.372	74	-18	-21	67	5	2		.965	-4	C	-1.2

■ RICH RENTERIA   Renteria, Richard Avina b: 12/25/61, Harbor City, Cal. BR/TR, 5'9", 172 lbs. Deb: 9/14/86

1986	Pit-N	10	12	2	3	1	0	0	1	0	4	.250	.250	.333	58	-1	-1	1	0	0	0	.600	0	/3	-0.1
1987	Sea-A	12	10	2	1	1	0	0	0	1	2	.100	.182	.200	1	-1	-2	0	1	0	0	.833	1	/2SD	-0.2
1988	Sea-A	31	88	6	18	9	0	0	6	2	8	.205	.222	.307	45	-6	-7	4	1	3	-2	.958	4	DS/32	-0.3
Total	3	53	110	10	22	11	0	0	7	3	14	.200	.221	.300	42	-9	-9	6	2	3	-1	.960	5	/DS23	-0.4

■ BOB REPASS   Repass, Robert Willis b: 11/6/17, W.Pittston, Pa. BR/TR, 6'1", 185 lbs. Deb: 9/18/39

1939	StL-N	3	6	0	2	1	0	1	0	2	.333	.333	.500	114	0	0	1	0			1.000	0	/2	0.1
1942	Was-A	81	259	30	62	11	1	2	23	33	30	.239	.328	.313	81	-6	-6	29	6	1	1	.973	-3	23S	-0.4
Total	2	84	265	30	64	12	1	2	24	33	32	.242	.328	.317	82	-6	-6	29	6	1		.973	-2	/23S	-0.3

■ ROGER REPOZ   Repoz, Roger Allen b: 8/3/40, Bellingham, Wash. BL/TL, 6'3", 195 lbs. Deb: 9/11/64

1964	NY-A	11	1	1	0	0	0	0	0	1	1	.000	.500	.000	52	0	0	0	0	0	0	1.000	-3	/O	-0.3
1965	NY-A	79	218	34	48	7	4	12	28	25	57	.220	.300	.454	112	3	3	30	1	1	-0	.993	-2	O	-0.3
1966	NY-A	37	43	4	15	4	1	0	9	4	8	.349	.404	.488	161	3	3	9	0	0	0	1.000	-10	O	-0.8
	KC-A	101	319	40	69	10	3	11	34	44	80	.216	.315	.370	99	-1	0	38	3	3	-1	.991	-3	O1	-1.0
	Yr	138	362	44	84	14	4	11	43	48	88	.232	.325	.384	106	2	3	47	3	3	-1	.992	-13	O1	-1.8
1967	KC-A	40	87	9	21	1	2	8	12	10	21	.241	.340	.402	122	2	3	12	4	2	0	1.000	1	O	0.3
	Cal-A	74	176	25	44	9	1	5	20	19	37	.250	.323	.398	116	3	3	24	2	2	-1	.959	-3	O	-0.3
	Yr	114	263	34	65	15	2	7	28	31	57	.247	.329	.399	118	5	6	36	6	4	-1	.972	-1	O	0.0
1968	Cal-A	133	375	30	90	8	1	13	54	38	83	.240	.315	.371	111	3	5	46	8	7	-2	.987	-5	*O	-0.8
1969	Cal-A	103	219	25	36	1	1	8	19	32	52	.164	.271	.288	59	-13	-12	19	1	3	-2	.985	-5	O1	-2.4
1970	Cal-A	137	407	50	97	17	6	18	47	45	90	.238	.319	.442	112	3	5	60	4	2	0	.995	-4	*O1	-0.6
1971	Cal-A	113	297	39	59	11	1	13	41	60	69	.199	.335	.374	108	1	4	40	3	5	-2	1.000	-4	O1	-0.8
1972	Cal-A	3	3	0	1	0	0	0	0	0	2	.333	.333	.333	105	-0	0	0	0	0	0	.000	0	H	0.0
Total	9	831	2145	257	480	73	19	82	260	280	499	.224	.325	.390	106	4	14	279	26	25	-7	.989	-39	O1	-7.0

■ RIP REPULSKI   Repulski, Eldon John b: 10/4/27, Sauk Rapids, Minn. BR/TR, 6', 195 lbs. Deb: 4/14/53

1953	StL-N	153	567	75	156	25	4	15	66	33	71	.275	.325	.413	91	-8	-8	74	3	6	-3	.987	-7	*O	-2.3
1954	StL-N	152	619	99	175	39	5	19	79	43	75	.283	.333	.454	102	1	0	88	8	10	-4	.975	-5	*O	-1.5
1955	StL-N	147	512	64	138	28	2	23	73	49	66	.270	.338	.467	111	7	7	75	5	7	-3	.974	-5	*O	-0.7
1956	StL-N★	112	376	44	104	18	3	11	55	24	46	.277	.332	.428	102	1	1	50	2	2	-1	.974	-0	*O	-0.5
1957	Phi-N	134	516	65	134	23	4	20	68	19	74	.260	.293	.436	95	-7	-5	64	7	1	2	.968	3	*O	-0.8
1958	Phi-N	85	238	33	58	9	4	13	40	15	47	.244	.300	.479	103	-0	-0	31	0	1	0	.949	-2	O	-0.5
1959	*LA-N	53	94	11	24	4	0	2	14	13	23	.255	.346	.362	83	-1	-2	11	0	1	-1	1.000	-5	O	-0.9
1960	LA-N	4	5	0	1	0	0	0	0	0	1	.200	.200	.200	9	-1	-1	0	0	0	0	1.000	-1	/O	-0.1
	Bos-A	73	136	14	33	6	1	3	20	10	25	.243	.295	.368	75	-4	-5	13	0	0	0	1.000	-2	O	-0.8
1961	Bos-A	15	25	2	7	1	0	1	1	1	5	.280	.308	.320	66	-1	-1	2	0	2	-1	1.000	-1	/O	-0.3
Total	9	928	3088	407	830	153	23	106	416	207	433	.269	.322	.436	98	-15	-14	409	25	29	-10	.976	-24	O	-8.4

■ LARRY RESSLER   Ressler, Lawrence P. b: 8/10/1848, France d: 6/12/18, Reading, Pa. Deb: 4/26/1875

| 1875 | Was-n | 27 | 106 | 17 | 21 | 1 | 0 | 0 | | 1 | | .198 | .206 | .208 | 45 | -6 | -5 | 5 | | | | | | O/2 | -0.4 |

■ DINO RESTELLI   Restelli, Dino Paul "Dingo" b: 9/23/24, St.Louis, Mo. BR/TR, 6'1.5", 191 lbs. Deb: 6/14/49

1949	Pit-N	72	232	41	58	11	0	12	40	35	26	.250	.358	.453	113	5	5	38	3			.961	5	O/1	0.6
1951	Pit-N	21	38	1	7	1	0	1	3	2	4	.184	.225	.289	36	-3	-4	3	0	0	0	.920	-1	O	-0.5
Total	2	93	270	42	65	12	0	13	43	37	30	.241	.341	.430	103	2	1	41	3	0		.956	4	/O1	0.1

■ MERV RETTENMUND   Rettenmund, Mervin Weldon b: 6/6/43, Flint, Mich. BR/TR, 5'10", 195 lbs. Deb: 4/14/68 C

1968	Bal-A	31	64	10	19	5	0	2	7	18	20	.297	.458	.469	181	8	8	16	1	1	-0	1.000	-5	O	0.1
1969	*Bal-A	95	190	27	47	10	3	4	25	28	28	.247	.344	.395	105	2	2	27	6	1	1	.991	-10	O	-1.0
1970	*Bal-A	106	338	60	109	17	2	18	58	38	59	.322	.396	.544	155	26	25	72	13	7	-0	.976	-1	O	2.0
1971	*Bal-A	141	491	81	156	23	4	11	75	87	60	.318	.424	.448	149	35	35	99	15	6	1	.977	-3	*O	2.8
1972	Bal-A	102	301	40	70	10	2	6	21	41	37	.233	.325	.339	95	-0	-1	33	6	4	-1	.989	-6	O	-1.3
1973	*Bal-A	95	321	59	84	17	2	9	44	57	38	.262	.380	.411	124	12	12	56	11	2	2	.985	3	O	1.4
1974	Cin-N	80	208	30	45	6	0	6	28	37	39	.216	.340	.303	90	-2	-2	25	5	1	1	1.000	-4	O	-0.8
1975	*Cin-N	93	188	24	45	6	1	2	19	35	22	.239	.359	.314	86	-2	-2	23	5	0	2	1.000	-3	O/3	-0.5
1976	SD-N	86	140	16	32	7	0	2	11	29	23	.229	.361	.321	103	0	2	19	4	1	1	.977	5	O	0.6
1977	SD-N	107	126	23	36	6	1	4	17	33	28	.286	.438	.444	153	9	11	27	1	2	-1	1.000	-4	O/3	0.5
1978	Cal-A	50	108	16	29	5	1	1	14	30	13	.269	.436	.361	131	6	7	19	0	3	-2	.968	-3	OD	0.1
1979	*Cal-A	35	76	7	20	2	0	1	10	11	14	.263	.364	.329	91	-1	-0	9	1	0	0	1.000	-3	D/O	-0.3
1980	Cal-A	2	4	0	1	0	0	0	1	0	1	.250	.400	.250	84	-0	-0	1	0	0	0	.000	0	H	0.0
Total	13	1023	2555	393	693	114	16	66	329	445	382	.271	.383	.406	124	92	95	425	68	28	4	.985	-34	O/D3	3.6

■ KEN RETZER   Retzer, Kenneth Leo b: 4/30/34, Wood River, Ill. BL/TR, 6', 185 lbs. Deb: 9/09/61

1961	Was-A	16	53	7	18	4	1	0	3	4	5	.340	.386	.472	130	2	2	10	1	0	0	.988	1	C	0.4
1962	Was-A	109	340	36	97	11	2	8	37	26	21	.285	.336	.400	98	-2	-1	45	2	0	1	.985	0	C	0.3
1963	Was-A	95	265	21	64	10	0	5	31	17	20	.242	.292	.336	76	-9	-9	26	2	0	1	.981	-11	C	-1.7
1964	Was-A	17	32	1	3	0	0	1	1	5	4	.094	.237	.094	3	-4	-4	1	0	0	0	.971	4	C	-0.2
Total	4	237	690	65	182	25	2	14	72	52	50	.264	.318	.367	87	-13	-12	82	5	0	2	.983	-6	C	-1.0

■ DAVE REVERING   Revering, David Alvin b: 2/12/53, Roseville, Cal. BL/TR, 6'4", 210 lbs. Deb: 4/08/78

1978	Oak-A	152	521	49	141	21	3	16	46	26	55	.271	.305	.415	106	-1	2	63	0	1	-1	.989	9	*1/D	0.3
1979	Oak-A	125	472	63	136	25	5	19	77	34	65	.288	.337	.483	125	11	14	75	1	4	-2	.986	2	*1D	0.7
1980	Oak-A	106	376	48	109	21	5	15	62	32	37	.290	.346	.492	136	13	16	64	1	0	0	.989	3	1/D	1.4
1981	Oak-A	31	87	12	20	1	1	2	10	11	12	.230	.323	.333	94	-1	-0	9	0	1	-1	.995	-1	1/D	-0.4
	*NY-A	45	119	8	28	4	1	2	7	11	20	.235	.300	.336	84	-3	-2	12	0	1	-1	.994	3	1	-0.2
	Yr	76	206	20	48	5	2	4	17	22	32	.233	.310	.335	88	-4	-3	21	0	2	-1	.994	2	1/D	-0.6
1982	NY-A	14	40	2	6	2	0	0	2	3	4	.150	.209	.200	13	-5	-5	1	0	0	0	1.000	-2	1/D	-0.7
	Tor-A	55	135	15	29	6	0	5	18	22	30	.215	.325	.370	83	-2	-3	16	0	3	-1	1.000	-0	D/1	-0.6
	Sea-A	29	82	8	17	3	1	3	12	9	17	.207	.286	.378	74	-2	-3	8	0	0	0	.986	-1	1	-0.5
	Yr	98	257	25	52	11	1	8	32	34	51	.202	.296	.346	71	-9	-11	25	0	3	-1	.992	-3	D1	-1.8
Total	5	557	1832	205	486	83	16	62	234	148	240	.265	.321	.430	110	10	18	248	2	10	-5	.989	13	1/D	-0.0

■ HENRY REVILLE   Reville, Henry b: Baltimore, Md. Deb: 10/14/1874

| 1874 | Bal-n | 1 | 4 | 0 | 0 | 0 | 0 | 0 | | 0 | 0 | .000 | .000 | .000 | -99 | -1 | -1 | 0 | | | | | | /O | -0.1 |

■ WILLIAM REXTER   Rexter, William H. b: Brooklyn, N.Y. Deb: 9/25/1875

| 1875 | Atl-n | 1 | 4 | 0 | 0 | 0 | 0 | 0 | | 0 | 0 | .000 | .000 | .000 | -99 | -1 | -1 | 0 | | | | | | /O | -0.1 |

■ GILBERTO REYES   Reyes, Gilberto R. (Polanco) b: 12/10/63, Santo Domingo, D.R. BR/TR, 6'2", 203 lbs. Deb: 6/11/83

| 1983 | LA-N | 19 | 31 | 1 | 5 | 2 | 0 | 0 | 0 | 0 | 5 | .161 | .188 | .226 | 14 | -4 | -4 | 1 | 0 | 0 | 0 | .944 | 2 | C | -0.1 |

YEAR	TM/L	G	AB	R	H	2B	3B	HR	RBI	BB	SO	AVG	OBP	SLG	PRO+	BR	/A	RC	SB	CS	SBR	FA	FR	POS	TPR
1984	LA-N	4	5	0	0	0	0	0	0	0	3	.000	.000	.000	-99	-1	-1	0	0	0	0	1.000	-0	/C	-0.2
1985	LA-N	6	1	0	0	0	0	0	0	1	1	.000	.667	.000	105	0	0	0	0	0	0	1.000	2	/C	0.2
1987	LA-N	1	0	0	0	0	0	0	0	0	0	—	—	—	—	0	0	0	0	0	0	.000	-0	/C	0.0
1988	LA-N	5	9	1	1	0	0	0	0	0	3	.111	.111	.111	-37	-2	-2	0	0	0	0	1.000	0	/C	-0.1
1989	Mon-N	4	5	0	1	0	0	0	1	0	1	.200	.200	.200	14	-1	-1	0	0	0	0	1.000	1	/C	0.0
1991	Mon-N	83	207	11	45	9	0	0	13	19	51	.217	.286	.261	56	-12	-12	15	2	4	-2	.975	14	C	0.4
Total	7	122	258	13	52	11	0	0	14	20	64	.202	.267	.244	45	-19	-18	17	2	4	-2	.973	17	C	0.2

■ NAP REYES

Reyes, Napoleon Aguilera b: 11/24/19, Santiago De Cuba, Cuba BR/TR, 6′1″, 205 lbs. Deb: 5/19/43

YEAR	TM/L	G	AB	R	H	2B	3B	HR	RBI	BB	SO	AVG	OBP	SLG	PRO+	BR	/A	RC	SB	CS	SBR	FA	FR	POS	TPR
1943	NY-N	40	125	13	32	4	2	0	13	4	12	.256	.290	.320	76	-4	-4	12	2			.994	-5	1/3	-1.2
1944	NY-N	116	374	38	108	16	5	8	53	15	24	.289	.325	.422	109	3	3	49	2			.990	2	13/O	0.3
1945	NY-N	122	431	39	124	15	4	5	44	25	26	.288	.338	.376	97	-1	-2	53	1			.961	-4	*3/1	-0.3
1950	NY-N	1	1	0	0	0	0	0	0	0	0	.000	.000	.000	-99	-0	-0	0	0			.667	-0	/1	-0.1
Total	4	279	931	90	264	35	11	13	110	44	62	.284	.326	.387	99	-3	-4	113	5			.960	-7	31/O	-1.3

■ CARL REYNOLDS

Reynolds, Carl Nettles b: 2/1/03, LaRue, Tex. d: 5/29/78, Houston, Tex. BR/TR, 6′, 194 lbs. Deb: 9/01/27

YEAR	TM/L	G	AB	R	H	2B	3B	HR	RBI	BB	SO	AVG	OBP	SLG	PRO+	BR	/A	RC	SB	CS	SBR	FA	FR	POS	TPR
1927	Chi-A	14	42	5	9	3	0	1	7	5	7	.214	.313	.357	75	-2	-2	4	1	2	-1	1.000	2	O	-0.1
1928	Chi-A	84	291	51	94	21	11	2	36	17	13	.323	.371	.491	126	10	10	54	15	3	3	.979	-2	O	0.6
1929	Chi-A	131	517	81	164	24	12	11	67	20	37	.317	.348	.474	111	5	6	83	19	9	0	.949	-2	*O	-0.4
1930	Chi-A	138	563	103	202	25	18	22	104	20	39	.359	.388	.584	148	34	37	126	16	4	2	.975	10	*O	3.5
1931	Chi-A	118	462	71	134	24	14	6	77	24	26	.290	.333	.442	108	-0	4	68	17	6	2	.949	-4	*O	-0.6
1932	Was-A	102	406	53	124	28	7	9	63	13	19	.305	.332	.475	108	2	3	62	8	4	0	.983	5	O	0.1
1933	StL-A	135	475	81	136	26	14	8	71	49	25	.286	.357	.451	106	8	4	77	5	4	-1	.965	-2	*O	-0.5
1934	Bos-A	113	413	61	125	26	9	4	86	27	28	.303	.350	.438	95	0	-4	63	5	3	-0	.977	3	*O	-0.5
1935	Bos-A	78	244	33	66	13	4	6	35	24	20	.270	.336	.430	91	-2	-4	36	4	1	1	.975	6	O	0.0
1936	Was-A	89	293	41	81	18	2	4	41	21	22	.276	.329	.392	82	-11	-9	38	8	4	0	.968	-0	O	-1.1
1937	Chi-N	7	11	0	3	1	0	0	1	2	2	.273	.385	.364	100	0	0	1	0			.800	-0	/O	0.0
1938	*Chi-N	125	497	59	150	28	10	3	67	22	32	.302	.335	.416	103	3	1	69	9			.983	-3	*O	-0.5
1939	Chi-N	88	281	33	69	10	6	4	44	16	38	.246	.298	.367	76	-9	-10	30	5			.972	2	O	-1.1
Total	13	1222	4495	672	1357	247	107	80	699	260	308	.302	.346	.458	107	37	35	713	112	40		.970	15	*O	-0.6

■ CHARLIE REYNOLDS

Reynolds, Charles Lawrence b: 5/1/1865, Williamsburg, Ind. d: 7/3/44, Denver, Colo. 5′9″, 175 lbs. Deb: 5/08/1889

YEAR	TM/L	G	AB	R	H	2B	3B	HR	RBI	BB	SO	AVG	OBP	SLG	PRO+	BR	/A	RC	SB	CS	SBR	FA	FR	POS	TPR
1889	KC-a	1	4	1	1	0	0	0	1	0	1	.250	.250	.250	42	-0	-0	0	0			1.000	-1	/C	-0.1
	Bro-a	12	42	5	9	1	1	0	3	1	6	.214	.233	.286	49	-3	-3	3	2			.892	1	C	-0.1
	Yr	13	46	6	10	1	1	0	4	1	7	.217	.234	.283	48	-3	-3	4	2			.893	-1	C	-0.2

■ DANNY REYNOLDS

Reynolds, Daniel Vance "Squirrel" b: 11/27/19, Stony Point, N.C. BR/TR, 5′11″, 158 lbs. Deb: 5/26/45

YEAR	TM/L	G	AB	R	H	2B	3B	HR	RBI	BB	SO	AVG	OBP	SLG	PRO+	BR	/A	RC	SB	CS	SBR	FA	FR	POS	TPR
1945	Chi-A	29	72	6	12	2	1	0	4	3	8	.167	.200	.222	23	-7	-7	2	1	2	-1	.947	2	S2	-0.5

■ DON REYNOLDS

Reynolds, Donald Edward b: 4/16/53, Arkadelphia, Ark. BR/TR, 5′8″, 178 lbs. Deb: 4/07/78 F

YEAR	TM/L	G	AB	R	H	2B	3B	HR	RBI	BB	SO	AVG	OBP	SLG	PRO+	BR	/A	RC	SB	CS	SBR	FA	FR	POS	TPR
1978	SD-N	57	87	8	22	2	0	0	10	15	14	.253	.363	.276	87	-1	-1	10	1	0	0	.923	-2	O	-0.4
1979	SD-N	30	45	6	10	1	2	0	6	7	6	.222	.327	.333	86	-1	-1	4	0	1	-1	.950	1	O	-0.1
Total	2	87	132	14	32	3	2	0	16	22	20	.242	.351	.295	87	-3	-1	14	1	1	-0	.935	-2	/O	-0.5

■ CRAIG REYNOLDS

Reynolds, Gordon Craig b: 12/27/52, Houston, Tex. BL/TR, 6′1″, 175 lbs. Deb: 8/01/75

YEAR	TM/L	G	AB	R	H	2B	3B	HR	RBI	BB	SO	AVG	OBP	SLG	PRO+	BR	/A	RC	SB	CS	SBR	FA	FR	POS	TPR
1975	*Pit-N	31	76	8	17	3	0	0	4	3	5	.224	.253	.263	44	-6	-6	5	0	1	-1	.969	4	S	0.0
1976	Pit-N	7	4	1	1	0	0	1	1	0	0	.250	.250	1.000	241	1	1	1	0	0	0	.889	2	/S2	0.2
1977	Sea-A	135	420	41	104	12	3	4	28	15	23	.248	.279	.319	63	-22	-21	36	6	6	-2	.955	8	*S	-0.1
1978	Sea-A☆	148	548	57	160	16	7	5	44	36	41	.292	.339	.374	101	0	1	71	9	6	-1	.960	4	*S	2.2
1979	Hou-N★	146	555	63	147	20	9	0	39	21	49	.265	.294	.333	75	-23	-19	57	12	6	0	.965	-16	*S	-2.0
1980	*Hou-N	137	381	34	86	9	6	3	28	20	39	.226	.264	.304	63	-22	-18	32	2	1	0	.969	12	*S	0.6
1981	*Hou-N	87	323	43	84	10	**12**	4	31	12	31	.260	.287	.402	99	-4	-2	35	3	3	-1	.973	-5	S	0.1
1982	Hou-N	54	118	16	30	2	3	1	7	11	9	.254	.323	.347	95	-2	-1	14	3	1	0	.958	2	S/3	0.5
1983	Hou-N	65	98	10	21	3	0	1	6	6	10	.214	.260	.276	52	-7	-6	7	0	1	-1	.956	-4	23/SO	-1.0
1984	Hou-N	146	527	61	137	15	11	6	60	22	53	.260	.290	.364	89	-13	-9	57	7	1	2	.965	18	*S/3	2.4
1985	Hou-N	107	379	43	103	18	8	4	32	12	30	.272	.294	.393	93	-6	-5	42	4	4	-1	.977	10	*S/2	1.4
1986	*Hou-N	114	313	32	78	7	3	6	41	12	31	.249	.277	.348	73	-13	-12	28	3	1	0	.978	-12	S/13OP	-1.7
1987	Hou-N	135	374	35	95	17	3	4	28	30	44	.254	.309	.348	77	-14	-12	42	5	1	1	.970	-12	*S/3	-1.4
1988	Hou-N	78	161	20	41	7	0	1	14	8	23	.255	.290	.317	77	-5	-5	15	3	0	1	.970	-5	S321	-0.8
1989	Hou-N	101	189	16	38	4	0	2	14	19	18	.201	.274	.254	54	-12	-11	14	1	0	0	.979	8	2S3/1PO	0.0
Total	15	1491	4466	480	1142	143	65	42	377	227	406	.256	.293	.345	80	-148	-126	457	58	32	-2	.966	16	*S/231OP	0.4

■ HAROLD REYNOLDS

Reynolds, Harold Craig b: 11/26/60, Eugene, Ore. BB/TR, 5′11″, 165 lbs. Deb: 9/02/83 F

YEAR	TM/L	G	AB	R	H	2B	3B	HR	RBI	BB	SO	AVG	OBP	SLG	PRO+	BR	/A	RC	SB	CS	SBR	FA	FR	POS	TPR
1983	Sea-A	20	59	8	12	4	1	0	1	2	9	.203	.230	.305	44	-4	-5	3	0	2	-1	.975	-1	2	-0.6
1984	Sea-A	10	10	3	3	0	0	0	0	0	1	.300	.364	.300	87	-0	-0	1	1	1	-0	1.000	4	/2	0.4
1985	Sea-A	67	104	15	15	3	1	0	6	17	14	.144	.264	.192	27	-10	-10	7	3	2	-0	.960	19	2	1.0
1986	Sea-A	126	445	46	99	19	4	1	24	29	42	.222	.275	.290	53	-28	-29	37	30	12	2	.977	29	*2	0.7
1987	Sea-A★	160	530	73	146	31	8	1	35	39	34	.275	.327	.370	80	-12	-15	67	**60**	20	6	.977	19	*2	1.7
1988	Sea-A★	158	598	61	169	26	**11**	4	41	51	51	.283	.341	.383	98	2	-1	74	35	29	-7	.977	6	*2	0.5
1989	Sea-A	153	613	87	184	24	9	0	43	55	45	.300	.361	.369	103	6	4	83	25	18	-3	.980	**27**	*2/D	3.2
1990	Sea-A	160	642	100	162	36	5	5	55	81	52	.252	.339	.347	91	-5	-6	80	31	16	-0	.978	16	*2	1.3
1991	Sea-A	161	631	95	160	34	6	3	57	72	63	.254	.335	.341	87	-9	-9	78	28	8	4	.978	5	*2/D	0.3
1992	Sea-A	140	458	55	113	23	3	3	33	45	41	.247	.318	.330	81	-11	-11	47	15	12	-3	.982	2	*2/OD	-0.9
Total	10	1155	4090	543	1063	200	48	17	295	391	352	.260	.328	.345	84	-71	-83	477	228	120	-4	.978	126	*2/DO	7.6

■ R. J. REYNOLDS

Reynolds, Robert James b: 4/19/59, Sacramento, Cal. BB/TR, 6′, 190 lbs. Deb: 9/01/83

YEAR	TM/L	G	AB	R	H	2B	3B	HR	RBI	BB	SO	AVG	OBP	SLG	PRO+	BR	/A	RC	SB	CS	SBR	FA	FR	POS	TPR
1983	LA-N	24	55	5	13	0	0	2	11	3	11	.236	.276	.345	72	-2	-2	6	5	0	2	.931	0	O	-0.1
1984	LA-N	73	240	24	62	12	2	2	24	14	38	.258	.302	.350	84	-6	-6	24	7	5	-1	.973	-7	O	-1.6
1985	LA-N	73	207	22	55	10	4	0	25	13	31	.266	.312	.353	88	-4	-3	23	6	3	0	.970	-2	O	-0.7
	Pit-N	31	130	22	40	5	3	3	17	9	18	.308	.357	.462	129	4	5	22	12	2	2	.958	1	O	0.7
	Yr	104	337	44	95	15	7	3	42	22	49	.282	.330	.395	104	0	1	45	18	5	2	.965	-1	O	0.0
1986	Pit-N	118	402	63	108	30	2	9	48	40	78	.269	.336	.420	105	4	3	55	16	9	-1	.955	-15	*O	-1.7
1987	Pit-N	117	335	47	87	24	1	7	51	34	80	.260	.328	.400	91	-4	-4	46	14	1	4	.993	-6	O	-1.0
1988	Pit-N	130	323	35	80	14	2	6	51	20	62	.248	.292	.359	87	-6	-6	35	15	2	3	.974	-6	O	-1.2
1989	Pit-N	125	363	45	98	16	2	6	48	34	66	.270	.334	.375	106	1	3	45	22	5	4	.990	-1	O	0.4
1990	*Pit-N	95	215	25	62	10	1	0	19	23	35	.288	.357	.344	98	-1	-0	26	12	2	2	.972	-6	O	-0.5
Total	8	786	2270	288	605	121	17	35	294	190	419	.267	.325	.381	97	-15	-12	282	109	29	15	.973	-41	O	-5.7

■ RONN REYNOLDS

Reynolds, Ronn Dwayne b: 8/28/58, Wichita, Kan. BR/TR, 6′, 200 lbs. Deb: 9/29/82

YEAR	TM/L	G	AB	R	H	2B	3B	HR	RBI	BB	SO	AVG	OBP	SLG	PRO+	BR	/A	RC	SB	CS	SBR	FA	FR	POS	TPR
1982	NY-N	2	4	0	0	0	0	0	0	1	1	.000	.200	.000	-40	-1	-1	0	0	0	0	1.000	-1	/C	-0.2
1983	NY-N	24	66	4	13	1	0	0	2	8	12	.197	.284	.212	40	-5	-5	4	0	0	0	.942	-1	C	-0.5
1985	NY-N	28	43	4	9	2	0	0	1	0	18	.209	.227	.256	36	-4	-4	2	0	0	0	.990	6	C	0.3
1986	Phi-N	43	126	8	27	4	0	3	10	5	30	.214	.244	.317	52	-8	-9	9	0	0	0	.991	1	C	-0.6
1987	Hou-N	38	102	5	17	4	0	1	7	3	29	.167	.190	.235	12	-13	-12	4	0	1	-1	.975	4	C	-0.7
1990	SD-N	8	15	1	1	1	0	0	1	1	6	.067	.125	.133	-29	-3	-3	0	0	0	0	1.000	1	/C	-0.2

YEAR	TM/L	G	AB	R	H	2B	3B	HR	RBI	BB	SO	AVG	OBP	SLG	PRO+	BR	/A	RC	SB	CS	SBR	FA	FR	POS	TPR
Total	6	143	356	22	67	12	0	4	21	18	96	.188	.229	.256	32	-34	-33	20	0	1	-1	.977	10	C	-1.9
■ TOMMIE REYNOLDS	Reynolds, Tommie D b: 8/15/41, Arizona, La. BR/TR, 6'2", 190 lbs. Deb: 9/05/63 C																								
1963	KC-A	8	19	1	1	1	0	0	0	1	7	.053	.143	.105	-28	-3	-3	0	0	0	0	.800	-1	/O	-0.5
1964	KC-A	31	94	11	19	1	0	2	9	10	22	.202	.292	.277	58	-5	-5	7	0	0	0	.976	-0	O/3	-0.7
1965	KC-A	90	270	34	64	11	3	1	22	36	41	.237	.327	.311	83	-5	-5	28	9	2	2	.982	7	O/3	0.0
1967	NY-N	101	136	16	28	1	0	2	9	11	26	.206	.280	.257	56	-8	-7	10	1	1	-0	.971	2	O/3C	-0.8
1969	Oak-A	107	315	51	81	10	0	2	20	34	29	.257	.345	.308	87	-6	-4	34	1	3	-2	.979	6	O	-0.5
1970	Cal-A	59	120	11	30	3	1	1	6	6	10	.250	.291	.317	70	-5	-5	10	1	1	-0	.969	0	O/3	-0.6
1971	Cal-A	45	86	4	16	3	0	2	8	9	6	.186	.286	.291	68	-4	-3	6	0	1	-1	.978	-2	O/3	-0.7
1972	Mil-A	72	130	13	26	5	1	2	13	10	25	.200	.262	.300	68	-5	-5	10	0	0	0	.961	-1	O/13	-0.9
Total	8	513	1170	141	265	35	5	12	87	117	166	.226	.307	.296	73	-42	-38	106	12	8	-1	.973	11	O/31C	-4.7
■ BILL REYNOLDS	Reynolds, William Dee b: 8/14/1884, Eastland, Tex. d: 6/5/24, Carnegie, Okla. BR/TR, 6', 185 lbs. Deb: 9/15/13																								
1913	NY-A	5	5	0	0	0	0	0	0	0	1	.000	.000	.000	-99	-1	-1	0	0			.917	0	/C	-0.1
1914	NY-A	4	5	0	2	0	0	0	0	0	3	.400	.400	.400	141	0	0	1	0			1.000	0	/C	0.1
Total	2	9	10	0	2	0	0	0	0	0	4	.200	.200	.200	19	-1	-1	1	0			.941	0	/C	0.0
■ ROCKY RHAWN	Rhawn, Robert John b: 2/13/19, Catawissa, Pa. d: 6/9/84, Danville, Pa. BR/TR, 5'8", 180 lbs. Deb: 9/17/47																								
1947	NY-N	13	45	7	14	3	0	1	3	8	1	.311	.415	.444	128	2	2	9	0			.913	0	/23	0.3
1948	NY-N	36	44	11	12	2	1	1	8	8	6	.273	.385	.432	120	1	1	7	3			.872	1	S/3	0.2
1949	NY-N	14	29	8	5	0	0	0	2	7	2	.172	.333	.172	40	-2	-2	2	1			.959	4	/2	0.2
	Pit-N	3	7	0	1	0	0	0	0	0	0	.143	.143	.143	-23	-1	-1	0	0			.889	1	/3	-0.1
	Yr	17	36	8	6	0	0	0	2	7	2	.167	.302	.167	29	-3	-3	2	1			.959	4	/23	0.1
	Chi-A	24	73	12	15	4	1	0	5	12	8	.205	.318	.288	63	-4	-4	7	0	1	-1	.959	3	3/S	-0.2
Total	3	90	198	38	47	9	2	2	18	35	17	.237	.352	.333	84	-4	-4	26	4	1		.963	8	/3S2	0.4
■ CY RHEAM	Rheam, Kenneth Johnston b: 9/28/1893, Pittsburgh, Pa. d: 10/23/47, Pittsburgh, Pa. BR/TR, 6' ", 175 lbs. Deb: 5/20/14																								
1914	Pit-F	73	214	15	45	5	3	0	20	9	33	.210	.242	.262	44	-16	-16	16	6			.976	-4	132/O	-2.2
1915	Pit-F	34	69	10	12	0	0	1	5	1	7	.174	.186	.217	18	-7	-7	4	4			.959	0	O/1	-0.9
Total	2	107	283	25	57	5	3	1	25	10	40	.201	.229	.251	38	-23	-23	20	10			.976	-4	/1O32	-3.1
■ BILLY RHIEL	Rhiel, William Joseph b: 8/16/1900, Youngstown, Ohio d: 8/16/46, Youngstown, Ohio BR/TR, 5'11", 175 lbs. Deb: 4/20/29																								
1929	Bro-N	76	205	27	57	9	4	4	25	19	25	.278	.339	.420	89	-5	-4	29	0			.979	1	2/3S	-0.1
1930	Bos-N	20	47	3	8	4	0	0	4	2	5	.170	.204	.255	11	-7	-7	2	0			.947	-4	3/2	-0.9
1932	Det-A	85	250	30	70	13	3	3	38	17	23	.280	.328	.392	82	-6	-7	33	2	0	1	.956	-5	31/O2	-1.0
1933	Det-A	19	17	1	3	0	1	0	1	5	4	.176	.364	.294	75	-0	-0	2	0	0	0	1.000	0	/O	0.0
Total	4	200	519	61	138	26	8	7	68	43	57	.266	.323	.387	78	-18	-18	66	2	0		.949	-8	/321OS	-2.0
■ DUSTY RHODES	Rhodes, James Lamar b: 5/13/27, Mathews, Ala. BL/TR, 6', 180 lbs. Deb: 7/15/52																								
1952	NY-N	67	176	34	44	8	1	10	36	23	33	.250	.340	.477	123	5	5	29	1	0	0	.917	-4	O	0.0
1953	NY-N	76	163	18	38	7	0	11	30	10	28	.233	.277	.479	91	-3	-3	21	0	1	-1	.965	1	O	-0.4
1954	*NY-N	82	164	31	56	7	3	15	50	18	25	.341	.410	.695	181	19	19	47	1	0	0	.984	-3	O	1.5
1955	NY-N	94	187	22	57	5	2	6	32	27	26	.305	.393	.449	122	7	7	35	1	1	-0	.986	-4	O	0.1
1956	NY-N	111	244	20	53	10	3	8	33	30	41	.217	.303	.381	83	-6	-6	27	0	0	0	.958	-5	O	-1.4
1957	NY-N	92	190	20	39	5	1	4	19	18	34	.205	.278	.305	57	-12	-12	15	0	0	0	1.000	-6	O	-2.0
1959	SF-N	54	48	1	9	2	0	0	7	5	9	.188	.264	.229	34	-5	-4	3	0	0	0	.000	0	H	-0.4
Total	7	576	1172	146	296	44	10	54	207	131	196	.253	.329	.445	104	6	6	178	3	2	-0	.963	-20	O	-2.6
■ KARL RHODES	Rhodes, Karl Derrick b: 8/21/68, Cincinnati, Ohio BL/TL, 6', 175 lbs. Deb: 8/07/90																								
1990	Hou-N	38	86	12	21	6	1	1	3	13	12	.244	.343	.372	100	-0	0	12	4	1	1	.955	-1	O	-0.1
1991	Hou-N	44	136	7	29	3	1	1	12	14	26	.213	.291	.272	63	-7	-6	11	2	2	-1	.958	3	O	-0.5
1992	Hou-N	5	4	0	0	0	0	0	0	0	2	.000	.000	.000	-99	-1	-1	0	0	0	0	.000	-1	/O	-0.2
Total	3	87	226	19	50	9	2	2	15	27	40	.221	.307	.305	75	-8	-7	23	6	3	0	.957	1	/O	-0.8
■ KEVIN RHOMBERG	Rhomberg, Kevin Jay b: 11/22/55, Dubuque, Iowa BR/TR, 6', 175 lbs. Deb: 9/01/82																								
1982	Cle-A	16	18	3	6	0	0	1	1	2	4	.333	.400	.500	146	1	1	3	0	2	-1	.900	-0	/O3D	0.0
1983	Cle-A	12	21	2	10	0	0	0	2	2	4	.476	.522	.476	170	2	2	5	1	1	-0	1.000	-2	/OD	0.0
1984	Cle-A	13	8	0	2	0	0	0	0	0	3	.250	.250	.250	38	-1	-1	1	0	0	0	1.000	-2	/O12D	-0.2
Total	3	41	47	5	18	0	0	1	3	4	11	.383	.431	.447	140	3	3	9	1	3	-2	.963	-4	/OD213	-0.2
■ HAL RHYNE	Rhyne, Harold J. b: 3/30/1899, Paso Robles, Cal. d: 1/7/71, Orangeville, Cal. BR/TR, 5'8.5", 163 lbs. Deb: 4/18/26																								
1926	Pit-N	109	366	46	92	14	3	2	39	35	21	.251	.327	.322	71	-12	-15	40	1			.967	8	2S/3	-0.1
1927	*Pit-N	62	168	21	46	5	0	0	17	14	9	.274	.330	.304	66	-7	-8	17	0			.963	-7	23/S	-1.3
1929	Bos-A	120	346	41	87	24	5	0	38	25	14	.251	.309	.350	71	-16	-15	39	4	1	1	.935	-3	*S/3O	-0.5
1930	Bos-A	107	296	34	60	8	5	0	23	25	19	.203	.269	.264	37	-29	-27	22	1	4	-2	.944	4	*S	-1.4
1931	Bos-A	147	565	75	154	34	3	0	51	57	41	.273	.341	.343	85	-15	-11	68	3	3	-1	**.963**	17	*S	1.8
1932	Bos-A	71	207	26	47	12	5	0	14	23	14	.227	.310	.333	69	-10	-9	22	3	2	-0	.966	-2	S/32	-0.6
1933	Chi-A	39	83	9	22	1	1	0	10	5	9	.265	.315	.301	67	-4	-4	8	1	1	-0	.955	5	23/S	0.2
Total	7	655	2031	252	508	98	22	2	192	184	127	.250	.318	.323	69	-93	-89	217	13	11		.950	23	S2/3O	-1.9
■ DEL RICE	Rice, Delbert b: 10/27/22, Portsmouth, Ohio d: 1/26/83, Buena Park, Cal. BR/TR, 6'2", 190 lbs. Deb: 5/02/45 MC																								
1945	StL-N	83	253	27	66	17	3	1	28	16	33	.261	.313	.364	86	-5	-6	28	0			.994	9	C	0.7
1946	*StL-N	55	139	10	38	8	1	1	12	8	16	.273	.313	.367	89	-2	-2	15	0			.977	-0	C	0.0
1947	StL-N	97	261	28	57	7	3	12	44	36	40	.218	.315	.406	87	-4	-6	35	1			.981	4	C	0.3
1948	StL-N	100	290	24	57	10	1	4	34	37	46	.197	.298	.279	54	-17	-19	26	1			**.996**	8	C	-0.5
1949	StL-N	92	284	25	67	16	1	4	29	30	40	.236	.320	.342	74	-9	-11	32	0			.992	-3	C	-0.8
1950	StL-N	130	414	39	101	20	3	9	54	43	65	.244	.323	.372	78	-11	-14	50	0			.984	6	*C	-0.2
1951	StL-N	122	374	34	94	13	1	9	47	34	26	.251	.319	.364	83	-9	-9	44	0	0	0	.985	2	*C	-0.2
1952	StL-N	147	495	43	128	27	2	11	65	33	38	.259	.313	.388	93	-6	-6	60	0	1	-1	.992	-4	*C	-0.4
1953	StL-N†	135	419	32	99	22	1	6	37	48	49	.236	.323	.337	72	-16	-16	47	0	0	0	.988	-5	*C	-1.5
1954	StL-N	56	147	13	37	10	1	2	16	16	21	.252	.325	.374	81	-4	-4	18	0	1	-1	.985	6	C	0.3
1955	StL-N	20	59	6	12	3	0	1	7	7	6	.203	.288	.305	58	-4	-4	5	0	0	0	.964	-5	C	-0.8
	Mil-N	27	71	5	14	0	1	2	7	6	12	.197	.260	.310	53	-5	-5	6	0	0	0	.981	1	C	-0.4
	Yr	47	130	11	26	3	1	3	14	13	18	.200	.273	.308	55	-9	-8	11	0	0	0	.973	-5	C	-1.2
1956	Mil-N	71	188	15	40	9	1	3	17	18	34	.213	.282	.319	65	-10	-9	16	0	0	0	.983	2	C	-0.5
1957	*Mil-N	54	144	15	33	1	1	9	20	17	37	.229	.311	.438	106	-1	1	18	0	0	0	.992	6	C	0.9
1958	Mil-N	43	121	10	27	7	0	1	8	8	30	.223	.271	.306	57	-8	-7	10	0	0	0	.995	-0	C	-0.6
1959	Mil-N	13	29	3	6	0	0	0	1	2	3	.207	.258	.207	28	-3	-3	1	0	0	0	.956	-0	/C	-0.3
1960	Chi-N	18	52	2	12	3	0	0	4	2	7	.231	.259	.288	50	-4	-4	3	0	0	0	.968	-2	C	-0.5
	StL-N	1	2	0	0	0	0	0	0	1	0	.000	.333	.000	1	-0	-0	0	0	0	0	1.000	-0	/C	-0.1
	Yr	19	54	2	12	3	0	0	4	3	7	.222	.263	.278	49	-4	-4	3	0	0	0	.970	-2	C	-0.6
	Bal-A	1	1	0	0	0	0	0	0	0	0	.000	.000	.000	-99	-0	-0	0	0	0	0	1.000	-0	/C	0.0
1961	LA-A	44	83	11	20	4	0	4	11	20	19	.241	.388	.434	107	3	1	15	0	1	-1	.994	2	C	0.4
Total	17	1309	3826	342	908	177	20	79	441	382	522	.237	.312	.356	78	-115	-122	430	2	3		.987	25	*C	-4.2

■ **SAM RICE** Rice, Edgar Charles b: 2/20/1890, Morocco, Ind. d: 10/13/74, Rossmor, Md. BL/TR, 5'9", 150 lbs. Deb: 8/07/15 H

YEAR	TM/L	G	AB	R	H	2B	3B	HR	RBI	BB	SO	AVG	OBP	SLG	PRO+	BR	/A	RC	SB	CS	SBR	FA	FR	POS	TPR
1915	Was-A	4	8	0	3	0	0	0	0	0	1	.375	.375	.375	122	0	0	1	0			.889	0	/P	0.0
1916	Was-A	58	197	26	59	8	3	1	17	15	13	.299	.352	.386	123	5	5	28	4			.957	2	O/P	0.5
1917	Was-A	155	586	77	177	25	7	0	69	50	41	.302	.360	.369	124	15	16	86	35			.960	8	*O	1.8
1918	Was-A	7	23	3	8	1	0	0	3	2	0	.348	.400	.391	141	1	1	4	1			1.000	3	/O	0.4
1919	Was-A	141	557	80	179	23	9	3	71	42	26	.321	.376	.411	122	16	16	91	26			.962	8	*O	1.5
1920	Was-A	153	624	83	211	29	9	3	80	39	23	.338	.381	.428	117	12	15	100	**63**	30	1	.960	21	*O	2.4
1921	Was-A	143	561	83	185	39	13	4	79	38	10	.330	.382	.467	121	12	16	100	25	12	0	.964	11	*O	1.5
1922	Was-A	154	633	91	187	37	13	6	69	48	13	.295	.347	.423	105	-1	3	93	20	9	1	.951	9	*O	0.1
1923	Was-A	148	595	117	188	35	**18**	3	75	57	12	.316	.381	.450	125	15	20	105	20	8	1	.970	8	*O	1.8
1924	*Was-A	154	646	106	**216**	39	14	1	76	46	24	.334	.382	.443	116	11	14	109	24	13	-1	.967	4	*O	0.6
1925	*Was-A	152	649	111	227	31	13	1	87	37	10	.350	.388	.442	113	10	12	112	26	11	1	.968	9	*O	1.1
1926	Was-A	152	641	98	**216**	32	14	3	76	42	20	.337	.380	.445	117	13	15	103	25	23	-6	.961	7	*O	0.5
1927	Was-A	142	603	98	179	33	14	2	65	36	11	.297	.336	.408	93	-8	-7	78	19	6	2	.975	-0	*O	-1.4
1928	Was-A	148	616	95	202	32	15	2	55	49	15	.328	.379	.438	115	13	13	105	16	3	**3**	.973	-8	*O	-0.2
1929	Was-A	150	616	119	199	39	10	1	62	55	9	.323	.382	.424	106	8	7	102	16	8	0	.970	7	*O	0.3
1930	Was-A	147	593	121	207	35	13	1	73	55	14	.349	.407	.457	118	19	18	111	13	8	-1	.963	4	*O	1.0
1931	Was-A	120	413	81	128	21	8	0	42	35	11	.310	.365	.400	100	1	1	61	6	5	-1	.970	1	*O	-0.6
1932	Was-A	106	288	58	93	16	7	1	34	32	6	.323	.391	.438	116	7	7	50	7	4	-0	.972	-3	O	0.0
1933	*Was-A	73	85	19	25	4	3	1	12	2	7	.294	.326	.447	104	-0	0	11	0	2	-1	1.000	-8	O	-0.9
1934	Cle-A	97	335	48	98	19	1	1	33	28	9	.293	.351	.364	83	-7	-8	44	5	1	1	.963	-7	O	-1.6
Total	20	2404	9269	1514	2987	498	184	34	1078	708	275	.322	.374	.427	113	140	163	1495	351	143		.965	76	*O/P	8.8

■ **HAL RICE** Rice, Harold Housten "Hoot" b: 2/11/24, Morganette, W.Va. BL/TR, 6'1", 195 lbs. Deb: 4/29/48

YEAR	TM/L	G	AB	R	H	2B	3B	HR	RBI	BB	SO	AVG	OBP	SLG	PRO+	BR	/A	RC	SB	CS	SBR	FA	FR	POS	TPR
1948	StL-N	8	31	3	10	1	2	0	3	2	4	.323	.364	.484	121	1	1	6	0			1.000	-1	/O	0.0
1949	StL-N	40	46	3	9	2	1	1	9	3	7	.196	.245	.348	55	-3	-3	4	0			1.000	-2	O	-0.6
1950	StL-N	44	128	12	27	3	1	2	11	10	10	.211	.268	.297	46	-10	-11	11	0			.972	-1	O	-1.3
1951	StL-N	69	236	20	60	12	1	4	38	24	22	.254	.323	.364	84	-5	-5	27	0	1	-1	.953	-3	O	-1.1
1952	StL-N	98	295	37	85	14	5	7	45	16	26	.288	.325	.441	110	3	3	39	1	3	-2	.972	-5	O	-0.7
1953	StL-N	8	8	0	2	0	0	0	0	0	3	.250	.250	.250	31	-1	-1	1	0	0	0	.000	0	H	-0.1
	Pit-N	78	286	39	89	16	1	4	42	17	22	.311	.350	.416	99	-1	-0	42	0	1	-1	.973	14	O	1.0
	Yr	86	294	39	91	16	1	4	42	17	25	.310	.347	.412	97	-1	-1	42	0	1	-1	.973	14	O	0.9
1954	Pit-N	28	81	10	14	4	1	1	9	14	24	.173	.295	.284	52	-6	-6	7	0	2	-1	1.000	3	O	-0.5
	Chi-N	51	72	5	11	0	0	0	5	8	15	.153	.237	.153	4	-10	-10	3	0	0	0	.897	-4	O	-1.5
	Yr	79	153	15	25	4	1	1	14	22	39	.163	.269	.222	29	-16	-16	10	0	2	-1	.966	-2	O	-2.0
Total	7	424	1183	129	307	52	12	19	162	94	133	.260	.314	.372	82	-31	-32	139	1	7		.969	0	O	-4.8

■ **HARRY RICE** Rice, Harry Francis b: 11/22/01, Ware Station, Ill. d: 1/1/71, Portland, Ore. BL/TR, 5'9", 185 lbs. Deb: 4/18/23

YEAR	TM/L	G	AB	R	H	2B	3B	HR	RBI	BB	SO	AVG	OBP	SLG	PRO+	BR	/A	RC	SB	CS	SBR	FA	FR	POS	TPR
1923	StL-A	4	3	0	0	0	0	0	0	0	0	.000	.000	.000	-95	-1	-1	0	0	0	0	.000	0	H	-0.1
1924	StL-A	54	93	19	26	7	0	0	15	7	5	.280	.350	.355	77	-2	-3	11	1	3	-2	.917	-0	3/21SO	-0.4
1925	StL-A	103	354	87	127	25	8	11	47	54	15	.359	.450	.568	149	32	29	92	8	7	-2	.984	6	O/1C23	2.5
1926	StL-A	148	578	86	181	27	10	9	59	63	40	.313	.384	.441	110	13	9	98	10	11	-4	.970	7	*O/32S	0.4
1927	StL-A	137	520	90	149	26	9	7	68	50	21	.287	.351	.412	94	-3	-5	73	6	4	-1	.938	12	*O/3	-0.2
1928	Det-A	131	510	87	154	21	12	6	81	44	27	.302	.360	.425	104	4	3	78	20	13	-2	.962	1	*O/3	-0.7
1929	Det-A	130	536	97	163	33	7	6	69	61	23	.304	.379	.425	106	7	6	87	6	10	-4	.960	6	*O/3	-0.1
1930	Det-A	37	128	16	39	6	0	2	24	19	8	.305	.403	.398	102	2	1	21	0	3	-2	.944	-0	O	-0.3
	NY-A	100	346	62	103	17	5	7	74	31	21	.298	.361	.436	106	0	3	55	3	3	-1	.969	8	O/13	0.4
	Yr	137	474	78	142	23	5	9	98	50	29	.300	.372	.426	105	2	4	76	3	6	-3	.964	7	*O/13	0.1
1931	Was-A	47	162	32	43	5	6	0	15	12	10	.265	.320	.370	81	-5	-5	20	2	1	0	.968	-1	O	-0.8
1933	Cin-N	143	510	44	133	19	6	0	54	35	24	.261	.316	.322	84	-11	-10	53	4			**.991**	3	*O/3	-1.6
Total	10	1034	3740	620	1118	186	63	48	506	376	194	.299	.368	.421	104	36	28	587	60	55		.966	39	O/312SC	-0.9

■ **JIM RICE** Rice, James Edward b: 3/8/53, Anderson, S.C. BR/TR, 6'2", 205 lbs. Deb: 8/19/74

YEAR	TM/L	G	AB	R	H	2B	3B	HR	RBI	BB	SO	AVG	OBP	SLG	PRO+	BR	/A	RC	SB	CS	SBR	FA	FR	POS	TPR
1974	Bos-A	24	67	6	18	2	1	1	13	4	12	.269	.319	.373	92	-0	-1	8	0	0	0	.800	-1	D/O	-0.2
1975	Bos-A	144	564	92	174	29	4	22	102	36	122	.309	.354	.491	126	25	19	92	10	5	0	1.000	-1	OD	1.5
1976	Bos-A	153	581	75	164	25	8	25	85	28	123	.282	.320	.482	118	20	12	83	8	5	-1	.967	0	OD	0.8
1977	Bos-A★	160	644	104	206	29	15	**39**	114	53	120	.320	.379	**.593**	143	51	42	136	5	4	-1	.956	1	*DO	3.9
1978	Bos-A★	163	677	121	**213**	25	**15**	**46**	**139**	58	126	.315	.373	**.600**	153	**59**	**50**	**147**	7	5	-1	.989	10	*OD	**5.5**
1979	Bos-A★	158	619	117	201	39	6	39	130	57	97	.325	.385	.596	152	50	46	138	9	4	0	.984	2	*OD	4.1
1980	Bos-A†	124	504	81	148	22	6	24	86	30	87	.294	.338	.504	121	17	14	81	8	3	1	.988	7	*OD	1.6
1981	Bos-A	108	451	51	128	18	1	17	62	34	76	.284	.338	.441	116	12	9	64	2	2	-1	.988	5	*O	1.0
1982	Bos-A	145	573	86	177	24	5	24	97	55	98	.309	.376	.494	129	29	25	98	0	1	-1	.969	-1	*O	1.9
1983	Bos-A★	155	626	90	191	34	1	**39**	**126**	52	102	.305	.364	.550	137	39	33	113	0	2	-1	.984	17	*O/D	4.3
1984	Bos-A★	159	657	98	184	25	7	28	122	44	102	.280	.326	.467	111	13	9	88	4	0	1	.989	12	*O/D	1.8
1985	Bos-A★	140	546	85	159	20	3	27	103	51	75	.291	.354	.487	122	20	17	83	2	0	1	.964	0	*O/D	1.3
1986	*Bos-A★	157	618	98	200	39	2	20	110	62	78	.324	.389	.490	137	33	32	115	0	1	-1	.977	17	*O/D	4.2
1987	Bos-A	108	404	66	112	14	0	13	62	45	77	.277	.360	.408	100	3	1	55	1	1	-0	.977	4	OD	0.2
1988	*Bos-A	135	485	57	128	18	3	15	72	48	89	.264	.334	.406	102	4	1	63	1	1	-0	.968	-2	*DO	-0.1
1989	Bos-A	56	209	22	49	10	2	3	28	13	39	.234	.283	.344	71	-7	-9	20	1	0	0	.000	0	D	-0.9
Total	16	2089	8225	1249	2452	373	79	382	1451	670	1423	.298	.356	.502	127	367	300	1382	58	34	-3	.980	71	*OD	30.9

■ **LEN RICE** Rice, Leonard Oliver b: 9/2/18, Lead, S.Dak. d: 6/13/92, Sonora, Cal. BR/TR, 6', 175 lbs. Deb: 4/26/44

YEAR	TM/L	G	AB	R	H	2B	3B	HR	RBI	BB	SO	AVG	OBP	SLG	PRO+	BR	/A	RC	SB	CS	SBR	FA	FR	POS	TPR
1944	Cin-N	10	4	1	0	0	0	0	0	0	0	.000	.000	.000	-99	-1	-1	0	0			1.000	1	/C	0.0
1945	Chi-N	32	99	10	23	3	0	0	7	5	8	.232	.269	.263	49	-7	-7	6	2			.976	-1	C	-0.6
Total	2	42	103	11	23	3	0	0	7	5	8	.223	.259	.252	44	-8	-8	6	2			.977	1	/C	-0.6

■ **BOB RICE** Rice, Robert Turnbull b: 5/28/1899, Philadelphia, Pa. d: 2/20/86, Elizabethtown, Pa BR/TR, 5'10", 170 lbs. Deb: 9/01/26

YEAR	TM/L	G	AB	R	H	2B	3B	HR	RBI	BB	SO	AVG	OBP	SLG	PRO+	BR	/A	RC	SB	CS	SBR	FA	FR	POS	TPR
1926	Phi-N	19	54	3	8	0	1	0	10	3	4	.148	.193	.185	2	-7	-8	2	0			.864	1	3/2S	-0.6

■ **LEE RICHARD** Richard, Lee Edward "Bee Bee" b: 9/18/48, Lafayette, La. BR/TR, 5'11", 165 lbs. Deb: 4/07/71

YEAR	TM/L	G	AB	R	H	2B	3B	HR	RBI	BB	SO	AVG	OBP	SLG	PRO+	BR	/A	RC	SB	CS	SBR	FA	FR	POS	TPR
1971	Chi-A	87	260	38	60	7	3	2	17	20	46	.231	.288	.304	66	-11	-12	21	8	9	-3	.920	-0	SO	-0.8
1972	Chi-A	11	29	5	7	0	0	0	1	0	7	.241	.241	.241	43	-2	-2	2	1	0	0	1.000	-0	/OS	-0.2
1974	Chi-A	32	67	5	11	1	0	0	1	5	8	.164	.222	.179	16	-7	-7	3	0	0	0	.821	3	3/S2OD	-0.4
1975	Chi-A	43	45	11	9	0	1	0	5	4	7	.200	.265	.244	44	-3	-3	3	2	3	-1	1.000	6	3/S2D	0.2
1976	StL-N	66	91	12	16	4	2	0	5	4	9	.176	.211	.264	34	-8	-8	4	1	0	0	.975	12	2S/3	0.5
Total	5	239	492	71	103	12	6	2	29	33	77	.209	.260	.270	50	-32	-33	33	12	12	-4	.923	20	/S23OD	-0.7

■ **GENE RICHARDS** Richards, Eugene b: 9/29/53, Monticello, S.C. BL/TL, 6', 175 lbs. Deb: 4/06/77

YEAR	TM/L	G	AB	R	H	2B	3B	HR	RBI	BB	SO	AVG	OBP	SLG	PRO+	BR	/A	RC	SB	CS	SBR	FA	FR	POS	TPR
1977	SD-N	146	525	79	152	16	11	5	32	60	80	.290	.365	.390	114	3	10	81	56	12	10	.963	1	*O1	1.5
1978	SD-N	154	555	90	171	26	12	4	45	64	80	.308	.384	.420	135	20	25	92	37	17	1	.965	-11	*O1	0.9
1979	SD-N	150	545	77	152	17	9	4	41	47	62	.279	.345	.365	100	-4	0	72	24	8	2	.973	-6	*O	-0.9
1980	SD-N	158	642	91	193	26	8	4	41	61	73	.301	.363	.385	116	9	13	96	61	16	9	.979	6	*O	2.3
1981	SD-N	104	393	47	113	14	**12**	3	42	53	44	.288	.374	.407	131	12	16	63	20	8	1	.975	-2	*O	1.2
1982	SD-N	132	521	63	149	13	8	3	28	36	52	.286	.335	.359	99	-4	-1	62	30	20	-3	.977	-3	*O/1	-1.2

YEAR	TM/L	G	AB	R	H	2B	3B	HR	RBI	BB	SO	AVG	OBP	SLG	PRO+	BR	/A	RC	SB	CS	SBR	FA	FR	POS	TPR
1983	SD-N	95	233	37	64	11	3	3	22	17	17	.275	.327	.386	100	-1	-0	28	14	5	1	.980	-4	O	-0.4
1984	SF-N	87	135	18	34	4	0	0	4	18	28	.252	.340	.281	79	-4	-3	13	5	3	-0	.940	-1	O	-0.5
Total	8	1026	3549	502	1028	127	63	26	255	356	436	.290	.358	.383	113	32	60	508	247	89	21	.972	-20	O/1	2.9

■ FRED RICHARDS Richards, Fred Charles "Fuzzy" b: 11/3/27, Warren, Ohio BL/TL, 6'1.5", 185 lbs. Deb: 9/15/51

YEAR	TM/L	G	AB	R	H	2B	3B	HR	RBI	BB	SO	AVG	OBP	SLG	PRO+	BR	/A	RC	SB	CS	SBR	FA	FR	POS	TPR
1951	Chi-N	10	27	1	8	2	0	0	4	2	3	.296	.345	.370	91	-0	-0	4	0	0	0	1.000	1	/1	0.1

■ PAUL RICHARDS Richards, Paul Rapier b: 11/21/08, Waxahachie, Tex. d: 5/4/86, Waxahachie, Tex. BR/TR, 6'1.5", 180 lbs. Deb: 4/17/32 M

YEAR	TM/L	G	AB	R	H	2B	3B	HR	RBI	BB	SO	AVG	OBP	SLG	PRO+	BR	/A	RC	SB	CS	SBR	FA	FR	POS	TPR
1932	Bro-N	3	8	0	0	0	0	0	0	0	2	.000	.000	.000	-99	-2	-2	0	0			1.000	4	/C	0.1
1933	NY-N	51	87	4	17	3	0	0	10	3	12	.195	.222	.230	30	-8	-8	4	0			.989	1	C	-0.6
1934	NY-N	42	75	10	12	1	0	0	3	13	8	.160	.284	.173	26	-8	-7	4	0			1.000	2	C	-0.4
1935	NY-N	7	4	0	1	0	0	0	0	2	1	.250	.500	.250	110	0	0	1	0			1.000	1	/C	0.2
	Phi-A	85	257	31	63	10	1	4	29	24	12	.245	.310	.339	68	-13	-12	28	0	0	0	.977	-3	C	-1.1
1943	Det-A	100	313	32	69	7	1	5	33	38	35	.220	.307	.297	71	-9	-11	31	1	0	0	**.986**	21	*C	1.8
1944	Det-A	95	300	24	71	13	0	3	37	35	30	.237	.318	.310	76	-7	-9	30	8	3	1	.979	16	C	1.3
1945	*Det-A	83	234	26	60	12	1	3	32	19	31	.256	.315	.355	88	-2	-4	29	4	0	1	**.995**	12	C	1.4
1946	Det-A	57	139	13	28	5	2	0	11	23	18	.201	.315	.266	60	-6	-7	13	2	0	1	.997	15	C	1.1
Total	8	523	1417	140	321	51	5	15	155	157	149	.227	.305	.301	68	-55	-61	139	15	3		.987	69	C	3.8

■ HARDY RICHARDSON Richardson, Abram Harding "Old True Blue"
b: 4/21/1855, Clarksboro, N.J. d: 1/14/31, Utica, N.Y. BR/TR, 5'9.5", 170 lbs. Deb: 5/01/1879

YEAR	TM/L	G	AB	R	H	2B	3B	HR	RBI	BB	SO	AVG	OBP	SLG	PRO+	BR	/A	RC	SB	CS	SBR	FA	FR	POS	TPR
1879	Buf-N	79	336	54	95	18	10	0	37	16	30	.283	.315	.396	130	12	11	43				.843	-6	*3/C	0.6
1880	Buf-N	83	343	48	89	18	8	0	17	14	37	.259	.289	.359	116	6	5	36				.848	-7	*3/C	0.1
1881	Buf-N	83	344	62	100	18	9	2	53	12	27	.291	.315	.413	129	10	11	46				.914	25	*O/2S3	3.1
1882	Buf-N	83	354	61	96	20	8	2	57	11	33	.271	.293	.390	115	6	5	41				.898	16	*2	2.1
1883	Buf-N	92	399	73	124	34	7	1	56	22	20	.311	.347	.439	134	17	16	62				.903	19	*2	3.1
1884	Buf-N	102	439	85	132	27	9	6	60	22	41	.301	.334	.444	138	21	18	67				.897	8	2O/31	2.4
1885	Buf-N	96	426	90	136	19	11	6	44	20	22	.319	.350	.458	154	27	25	70				.905	13	2O/SP	3.5
1886	Det-N	125	538	125	**189**	27	11	**11**	61	46	27	.351	.402	.504	169	47	45	129	42			.899	11	O2/PS3	4.9
1887	*Det-N	120	543	131	178	25	18	8	94	31	40	.328	.366	.484	132	25	22	110	29			.941	17	2O	3.3
1888	Det-N	58	266	60	77	18	2	6	32	17	23	.289	.335	.440	148	14	14	45	13			.925	4	2	1.9
1889	Bos-N	132	536	122	163	33	10	6	79	48	44	.304	.367	.437	119	18	12	106	47			.924	13	2O	2.5
1890	Bos-P	130	555	126	181	26	14	13	**146**	52	46	.326	.384	.494	127	26	19	124	42			.950	2	*O/S1	1.4
1891	Bos-a	74	278	45	71	9	4	7	52	40	26	.255	.351	.392	117	6	6	45	16			.955	-0	O/3S1	0.4
1892	Was-N	10	37	2	4	0	0	0	0	5	3	.108	.214	.108	-1	-4	-4	1	2			.941	-0	/O32	-0.4
	NY-N	64	248	36	53	11	5	2	34	21	26	.214	.278	.323	84	-6	-5	27	14			.931	-1	2O/1S	-0.5
	Yr	74	285	38	57	11	5	2	34	26	29	.200	.269	.295	73	-10	-9	28	16			.933	-1	2O/1S3	-0.9
Total	14	1331	5642	1120	1688	303	126	70	822	377	445	.299	.344	.435	131	225	201	952	205			.915	113	2O3/S1CP	28.4

■ ART RICHARDSON Richardson, Arthur L. b: 1862, Hamilton, Ont., Can. d: 25, Deb: 7/10/1884

YEAR	TM/L	G	AB	R	H	2B	3B	HR	RBI	BB	SO	AVG	OBP	SLG	PRO+	BR	/A	RC	SB	CS	SBR	FA	FR	POS	TPR
1884	CP-U	1	4	0	0	0	0	0		0		.000	.000	.000	-99	-1	-1	0				.667	-1	/2	-0.2

■ NOLEN RICHARDSON Richardson, Clifford Nolen b: 1/18/03, Chattanooga, Tenn. d: 9/25/51, Athens, Ga. BR/TR, 6'1.5", 170 lbs. Deb: 4/16/29

YEAR	TM/L	G	AB	R	H	2B	3B	HR	RBI	BB	SO	AVG	OBP	SLG	PRO+	BR	/A	RC	SB	CS	SBR	FA	FR	POS	TPR
1929	Det-A	13	21	2	4	0	0	0	2	2	1	.190	.261	.190	18	-3	-3	1	1	1	-0	.839	-4	S	-0.6
1931	Det-A	38	148	13	40	9	2	0	16	6	3	.270	.299	.358	70	-6	-7	16	2	1	0	.946	-2	3	-0.6
1932	Det-A	69	155	13	34	5	2	0	12	9	13	.219	.262	.277	38	-14	-15	12	5	2	0	.986	11	3/S	-0.1
1935	NY-A	12	46	3	10	1	1	0	5	3	1	.217	.265	.283	44	-4	-4	4	0	0	0	.922	-6	S	-0.9
1938	Cin-N	35	100	8	29	4	0	0	10	3	4	.290	.311	.330	78	-3	-3	10	0			.966	-1	S	-0.2
1939	Cin-N	1	3	0	0	0	0	0	0	0	0	.000	.000	.000	-99	-1	-1	0	0			1.000	1	/S	0.0
Total	6	168	473	39	117	19	5	0	45	23	22	.247	.282	.309	55	-31	-32	42	8	4		.969	-2	3/S	-2.4

■ DANNY RICHARDSON Richardson, Daniel b: 1/25/1863, Elmira, N.Y. d: 9/12/26, New York, N.Y. BR/TR, 5'8", 165 lbs. Deb: 5/22/1884 M

YEAR	TM/L	G	AB	R	H	2B	3B	HR	RBI	BB	SO	AVG	OBP	SLG	PRO+	BR	/A	RC	SB	CS	SBR	FA	FR	POS	TPR
1884	NY-N	74	277	36	70	8	1	1	27	16	17	.253	.294	.300	85	-4	-5	25				.907	2	OS	-0.3
1885	NY-N	49	198	26	52	9	3	0	25	10	14	.263	.298	.338	107	1	1	20				.950	-1	O3/P	0.1
1886	NY-N	68	237	43	55	9	1	1	27	17	21	.232	.283	.291	74	-7	-7	24	12			.953	-0	O/PS32	-0.9
1887	NY-N	122	450	79	125	19	10	3	62	36	25	.278	.337	.384	107	1	5	74	41			.928	14	*23/P	1.9
1888	*NY-N	135	561	82	127	16	7	8	61	15	35	.226	.248	.323	83	-11	-11	55	35			**.942**	9	*2	0.4
1889	*NY-N	125	497	88	139	22	8	7	100	46	37	.280	.342	.398	108	5	5	81	32			.934	12	*2	2.0
1890	NY-P	123	528	102	135	12	9	4	80	37	19	.256	.307	.335	67	-21	-29	67	37			.900	25	S2	0.2
1891	NY-N	123	516	85	139	18	5	4	51	33	27	.269	.313	.347	98	-5	-2	66	28			.952	**49**	*2/S	**4.6**
1892	Was-N	142	551	48	132	13	4	3	58	25	45	.240	.274	.294	75	-19	-16	52	25			.931	**58**	S2/3M	4.2
1893	Bro-N	54	206	36	46	6	2	0	27	13	18	.223	.279	.272	50	-15	-14	18	7			.949	-17	2/3S	-2.4
1894	Lou-N	116	430	51	109	17	2	1	40	35	31	.253	.317	.309	57	-32	-27	46	8			.916	2	*S2	-1.4
Total	11	1131	4451	676	1129	149	52	32	558	283	289	.254	.301	.332	83	-107	-99	529	225			.940	153	2SO/3P	8.4

■ JEFF RICHARDSON Richardson, Jeffrey Scott b: 8/26/65, Grand Island, Neb. BR/TR, 6'2", 175 lbs. Deb: 7/14/89

YEAR	TM/L	G	AB	R	H	2B	3B	HR	RBI	BB	SO	AVG	OBP	SLG	PRO+	BR	/A	RC	SB	CS	SBR	FA	FR	POS	TPR
1989	Cin-N	53	125	10	21	4	0	2	11	10	23	.168	.235	.248	37	-10	-11	8	1	0	0	.969	-2	S/3	-1.0
1991	Pit-N	6	4	0	1	0	0	0	0	0	3	.250	.250	.250	42	-0	-0	0	0	0	0	.000	-1	/3S	-0.1
Total	2	59	129	10	22	4	0	2	11	10	26	.171	.236	.248	37	-10	-11	8	1	0	0	.969	-3	/S3	-1.1

■ KEN RICHARDSON Richardson, Kenneth Franklin b: 5/2/15, Orleans, Ind. d: 12/7/87, Woodland Hills, Cal BR/TR, 5'10.5", 187 lbs. Deb: 4/14/42

YEAR	TM/L	G	AB	R	H	2B	3B	HR	RBI	BB	SO	AVG	OBP	SLG	PRO+	BR	/A	RC	SB	CS	SBR	FA	FR	POS	TPR
1942	Phi-A	6	15	1	1	0	0	0	0	2	0	.067	.176	.067	-30	-3	-3	0	0	0	0	1.000	0	/O13	-0.3
1946	Phi-N	6	20	1	3	1	0	0	2	0	2	.150	.150	.200	-1	-3	-3	0	0			.939	-0	/2	-0.3
Total	2	12	35	2	4	1	0	0	2	2	2	.114	.162	.143	-14	-5	-5	1	0	0		.929	-0	/2O31	-0.6

■ BOBBY RICHARDSON Richardson, Robert Clinton b: 8/19/35, Sumter, S.C. BR/TR, 5'9", 170 lbs. Deb: 8/05/55

YEAR	TM/L	G	AB	R	H	2B	3B	HR	RBI	BB	SO	AVG	OBP	SLG	PRO+	BR	/A	RC	SB	CS	SBR	FA	FR	POS	TPR
1955	NY-A	11	26	2	4	0	0	0	3	2	0	.154	.214	.154	0	-4	-4	1	1	1	-0	.864	-5	/2S	-0.9
1956	NY-A	5	7	1	1	0	0	0	0	0	1	.143	.143	.143	-25	-1	-1	0	0	0	0	1.000	2	/2	0.1
1957	*NY-A☆	97	305	36	78	11	1	0	19	9	26	.256	.277	.298	58	-18	-18	23	1	3	-2	.979	5	2	-0.8
1958	*NY-A	73	182	18	45	6	2	0	14	8	5	.247	.279	.302	62	-10	-9	15	1	3	-2	.973	8	23/S	0.0
1959	NY-A☆	134	469	53	141	18	6	2	33	26	20	.301	.337	.377	99	-3	-1	60	5	5	-2	.970	2	*2S3	0.9
1960	*NY-A	150	460	45	116	12	3	1	26	35	19	.252	.305	.298	68	-23	-20	42	6	6	-2	.973	-4	*23	-1.4
1961	*NY-A	162	662	80	173	17	5	3	49	30	23	.261	.295	.316	67	-35	-30	59	9	7	-2	.978	-9	*2	-2.4
1962	*NY-A★	161	692	99	**209**	38	5	8	59	37	24	.302	.338	.406	103	-1	1	92	11	9	-2	.982	-3	*2	1.3
1963	*NY-A★	151	630	72	167	20	6	3	48	25	22	.265	.295	.330	76	-21	-21	63	15	1	4	.984	7	*2	0.5
1964	*NY-A★	159	679	90	181	25	4	4	50	28	36	.267	.296	.333	73	-24	-25	66	11	2	2	.982	-14	*2/S	-2.4
1965	NY-A★	160	664	76	164	28	2	6	47	37	39	.247	.288	.322	74	-24	-23	61	7	5	-1	.981	-3	*2	-1.4
1966	NY-A★	149	610	71	153	21	3	7	42	25	28	.251	.281	.330	78	-20	-18	52	6	6	-2	.980	3	*2/3	-0.7
Total	12	1412	5386	643	1432	196	37	34	390	262	243	.266	.301	.335	77	-184	-168	534	73	48	-7	.979	-11	*2/3S	-7.2

■ TOM RICHARDSON Richardson, Thomas Mitchell b: 8/7/1883, Louisville, Ill. d: 11/15/39, Onawa, Iowa BR/TR, 6', 190 lbs. Deb: 8/02/17

YEAR	TM/L	G	AB	R	H	2B	3B	HR	RBI	BB	SO	AVG	OBP	SLG	PRO+	BR	/A	RC	SB	CS	SBR	FA	FR	POS	TPR
1917	StL-A	1	1	0	0	0	0	0	0	0	0	.000	.000	.000	-99	-0	-0	0	0			.000	0	H	0.0

■ BILL RICHARDSON Richardson, William Henry b: 9/24/1878, Salem, Ind. d: 11/6/49, Sullivan, Ind. BR/TR, 5'11", 200 lbs. Deb: 9/20/01

YEAR	TM/L	G	AB	R	H	2B	3B	HR	RBI	BB	SO	AVG	OBP	SLG	PRO+	BR	/A	RC	SB	CS	SBR	FA	FR	POS	TPR
1901	StL-N	15	52	7	11	2	0	2	7	6		.212	.293	.365	95	-1	-0	6	1			.981	-1	1	-0.2

YEAR	TM/L	G	AB	R	H	2B	3B	HR	RBI	BB	SO	AVG	OBP	SLG	PRO+	BR	/A	RC	SB	CS	SBR	FA	FR	POS	TPR

■ MIKE RICHARDT Richardt, Michael Anthony b: 5/24/58, Los Angeles, Cal. BR/TR, 6', 170 lbs. Deb: 8/30/80

1980	Tex-A	22	71	2	16	2	0	0	8	1	7	.225	.236	.254	35	-6	-6	4	0	0	0	.978	-1	2/D	-0.6
1982	Tex-A	119	402	34	97	10	0	3	43	23	42	.241	.284	.289	61	-23	-20	32	9	1	2	.988	4	2D/O	-0.9
1983	Tex-A	22	83	9	13	2	1	1	7	2	11	.157	.176	.241	14	-10	-10	3	2	1	0	.992	2	2	-0.7
1984	Tex-A	6	9	0	1	0	0	0	0	1	1	.111	.200	.111	-11	-1	-1	0	0	1	-1	1.000	1	/2	-0.1
	Hou-N	16	15	1	4	1	0	0	2	0	1	.267	.267	.333	73	-1	-1	1	0	0	0	.000	0	H	-0.1
Total	4	185	580	46	131	15	1	4	60	27	62	.226	.262	.276	50	-41	-38	41	11	3	2	.988	6	2/DO	-2.4

■ LANCE RICHBOURG Richbourg, Lance Clayton b: 12/18/1897, DeFuniak Springs Fla. d: 9/10/75, Crestview, Fla. BL/TR, 5'10.5", 160 lbs. Deb: 7/04/21

1921	Phi-N	10	5	2	1	1	0	0	0	0	3	.200	.200	.400	51	-0	-0	0	1	1	-0	1.000	3	/2	0.2
1924	Was-A	15	32	3	9	2	1	0	1	2	0	.281	.324	.406	90	-1	-1	4	0	0	0	1.000	1	/O	0.0
1927	Bos-N	115	450	57	139	12	9	2	34	22	30	.309	.342	.389	104	-3	1	58	24			.953	-4	*O	-0.9
1928	Bos-N	148	612	105	206	26	12	2	52	62	39	.337	.399	.428	123	17	21	104	11			.972	7	*O	1.7
1929	Bos-N	139	557	76	170	24	13	3	56	42	26	.305	.355	.411	93	-9	-6	80	7			.971	5	*O	-1.0
1930	Bos-N	130	529	81	161	23	8	3	54	19	31	.304	.331	.395	77	-22	-19	66	13			.971	-3	*O	-2.8
1931	Bos-N	97	286	32	82	11	6	2	29	19	14	.287	.331	.388	96	-3	-2	38	9			.981	-3	O	-1.0
1932	Chi-N	44	148	22	38	2	2	1	21	8	4	.257	.295	.318	65	-7	-7	14	0			.986	-1	O	-1.0
Total	8	698	2619	378	806	101	51	13	247	174	147	.308	.352	.400	97	-30	-13	364	65	1		.970	4	O/2	-4.8

■ ROB RICHIE Richie, Robert Eugene b: 9/5/65, Reno, Nev. BL/TR, 6'2", 190 lbs. Deb: 8/19/89

| 1989 | Det-A | 19 | 49 | 6 | 13 | 4 | 1 | 1 | 10 | 5 | 10 | .265 | .333 | .490 | 132 | 2 | 2 | 7 | 0 | 1 | -1 | .917 | -1 | O/D | 0.0 |

■ DON RICHMOND Richmond, Donald Lester b: 10/27/19, Gillett, Pa. d: 5/24/81, Elmira, N.Y. BL/TR, 6'1", 175 lbs. Deb: 9/16/41

1941	Phi-A	9	35	3	7	1	1	0	5	0	1	.200	.200	.286	28	-4	-4	1	0	2	-1	.957	-2	/3	-0.7
1946	Phi-A	16	62	3	18	3	0	1	9	0	10	.290	.290	.387	89	-1	-1	7	1	0	0	.940	-3	3	-0.4
1947	Phi-A	19	21	2	4	1	1	0	4	3	3	.190	.292	.333	72	-1	-1	2	0	0	0	.500	-3	/32	-0.4
1951	StL-N	12	34	3	3	1	0	1	4	3	3	.088	.162	.206	-2	-5	-5	1	0	1	-1	1.000	5	3	-0.1
Total	4	56	152	11	32	6	2	2	22	6	17	.211	.241	.316	51	-11	-11	11	1	3	-2	.957	-4	/32	-1.6

■ JOHN RICHMOND Richmond, John H. b: 1854, Pennsylvania TR, Deb: 4/22/1875

1875	Ath-n	29	126	29	25	1	0				0	.198	.198	.206	36	-7	-9	5						2O/C	-0.8
1879	Syr-N	62	254	31	54	8	4	1	23	4	24	.213	.225	.287	76	-9	-5	17				.874	-7	OS/C	-1.1
1880	Bos-N	32	129	12	32	3	1	0	9	2	18	.248	.260	.287	88	-2	-2	10				.844	-12	S/O	-1.1
1881	Bos-N	27	98	13	27	2	2	1	12	6	7	.276	.317	.367	120	2	2	12				.969	2	O/S	0.2
1882	Cle-N	41	140	12	24	6	2	0	11	11	27	.171	.232	.243	54	-7	-6	8				.917	3	O	-0.4
	Phi-n	18	65	8	12	2	2	0		11		.185	.303	.277	87	-0	-1	6				.892	0	O	-0.1
1883	Col-a	92	385	63	109	7	8	0		25		.283	.327	.343	126	7	12	44				.877	26	*S/O	3.4
1884	Col-a	105	398	57	100	13	7	3		35		.251	.317	.342	128	9	14	44				.866	-9	*S	0.5
1885	Pit-a	34	131	14	27	2	2	0		8		.206	.262	.252	66	-5	-4	9				.849	-10	SO	-1.3
Total	7	411	1600	210	385	43	28	5	55	102	76	.241	.288	.312	102	-5	10	149				.866	-10	SO/C	0.1

■ LEE RICHMOND Richmond, J. Lee b: 5/5/1857, Sheffield, Ohio d: 10/1/29, Toledo, Ohio TL, 5'10", 142 lbs. Deb: 9/27/1879

1879	Bos-N	1	6	0	2	0	0	0	1	0	1	.333	.333	.333	118	-0	1	1				1.000	0	/P	0.0
1880	Wor-N	77	309	44	70	8	4	0	34	9	32	.227	.248	.278	72	-7	-10	22				.827	-13	*PO	-0.7
1881	Wor-N	61	252	31	63	5	1	0	28	10	10	.250	.279	.278	71	-7	-9	20				.937	-1	PO	-0.4
1882	Wor-N	55	228	50	64	8	9	2	28	9	11	.281	.308	.421	128	8	7	30				.889	2	PO	0.0
1883	Pro-N	49	194	41	55	8	6	1	19	15	19	.284	.335	.402	120	6	5	27				.714	-10	OP	-0.5
1886	Cin-a	8	29	3	8	0	0	0		3		.276	.344	.276	94	0	-0	3	0			.400	-4	/OP	-0.3
Total	6	251	1018	169	262	29	20	3	110	46	73	.257	.289	.334	95	-0	-7	102	0			.886	-26	P/O	-1.9

■ AL RICHTER Richter, Allen Gordon b: 2/7/27, Norfolk, Va. BR/TR, 5'11", 165 lbs. Deb: 9/23/51

1951	Bos-A	5	11	1	1	0	0	0	0	3	0	.091	.286	.091	5	-1	-2	0	0	0	0	1.000	2	/S	0.1
1953	Bos-A	1	0	0	0	0	0	0	0	0	0	—	—	—	—	0	0	0	0	0	0	1.000	0	/S	0.0
Total	2	6	11	1	1	0	0	0	0	3	0	.091	.286	.091	5	-1	-2	0	0	0	0	1.000	3	/S	0.1

■ JOHN RICHTER Richter, John M. b: 2/8/1873, Louisville, Ky. d: 10/4/27, Louisville, Ky. Deb: 10/06/1898

| 1898 | Lou-N | 3 | 13 | 1 | 2 | 0 | 0 | 0 | 0 | 0 | 0 | .154 | .154 | .154 | -12 | -2 | -2 | 0 | 0 | | | .929 | 1 | /3 | -0.1 |

■ JOE RICKERT Rickert, Joseph Francis "Diamond Joe" b: 12/12/1876, London, Ohio d: 10/15/43, Springfield, Ohio BR/TR, 5'10.5", 165 lbs. Deb: 10/12/1898

1898	Pit-N	2	6	0	1	0	0	0	0	0	0	.167	.167	.167	-5	-1	-1	0	0			1.000	1	O	0.0
1901	Bos-N	13	60	6	10	1	2	0	1	3		.167	.206	.250	29	-5	-6	3	1			.974	2	O	-0.5
Total	2	15	66	6	11	1	2	0	1	3		.167	.203	.242	27	-6	-7	4	1			.979	3	/O	-0.5

■ MARV RICKERT Rickert, Marvin August "Twitch" b: 1/8/21, Long Branch, Wash. d: 6/3/78, Oakville, Wash. BL/TR, 6'2", 195 lbs. Deb: 9/10/42

1942	Chi-N	8	26	5	7	0	0	0	1	1	5	.269	.296	.269	69	-1	-1	2	0			1.000	1	/O	0.0
1946	Chi-N	111	392	44	103	18	3	7	47	28	54	.263	.314	.378	98	-4	-3	46	3			.972	-6	*O	-1.4
1947	Chi-N	71	137	7	20	0	0	2	15	15	17	.146	.230	.190	13	-17	-16	6	0			.982	-1	O/1	-1.9
1948	Cin-N	8	6	0	1	0	0	0	0	0	0	.167	.167	.167	-10	-1	-1	0	0			.000	0	H	-0.1
	*Bos-N	3	13	1	3	0	1	0	2	0	1	.231	.286	.385	81	-0	-0	2	0			1.000	1	/O	0.1
	Yr	11	19	1	4	0	1	0	2	0	1	.211	.250	.316	54	-1	-1	2	0			1.000	1	/O	0.0
1949	Bos-N	100	277	44	81	18	3	6	49	23	38	.292	.347	.444	117	4	5	42	1			.981	-0	O1	0.2
1950	Pit-N	17	20	0	3	0	0	0	4	0	4	.150	.150	.150	-20	-3	-4	0	0			.000	0	/O	-0.5
	Chi-A	84	278	38	66	9	2	4	27	21	42	.237	.291	.327	60	-18	-17	25	0	1	-1	.968	-6	O/1	-2.5
Total	6	402	1149	139	284	45	9	19	145	88	161	.247	.302	.352	79	-41	-37	122	4	1		.976	-12	O/1	-6.1

■ DAVE RICKETTS Ricketts, David William b: 7/12/35, Pottstown, Pa. BB/TR, 6'2", 195 lbs. Deb: 9/25/63 FC

1963	StL-N	3	8	0	2	0	0	0	0	0	2	.250	.250	.250	41	-1	-1	1	0	0	0	1.000	-0	/C	-0.1
1965	StL-N	11	29	1	7	0	0	0	0	1	3	.241	.267	.241	40	-2	-2	2	0	0	0	.977	-2	C	-0.5
1967	*StL-N	52	99	11	27	8	0	1	14	4	7	.273	.301	.384	96	-1	-1	11	0	0	0	1.000	-0	/C	-0.3
1968	*StL-N	20	22	1	3	0	0	0	1	0	3	.136	.136	.136	-18	-3	-3	0	0	0	0	1.000	-0	/C	-0.4
1969	StL-N	30	44	2	12	1	0	0	5	4	5	.273	.333	.295	77	-1	-1	5	0	0	0	.983	1	/C	0.0
1970	Pit-N	14	11	0	2	0	0	0	0	1	3	.182	.250	.182	18	-1	-1	0	0	0	0	.909	0	/C	-0.1
Total	6	130	213	15	53	9	0	1	20	10	23	.249	.283	.305	67	-9	-9	19	0	0	0	.988	-1	/C	-1.1

■ BRANCH RICKEY Rickey, Wesley Branch "The Mahatma" b: 12/20/1881, Lucasville, Ohio d: 12/9/65, Columbia, Mo. BL/TR, 5'9", 175 lbs. Deb: 6/16/05 MH

1905	StL-A	1	3	0	0	0	0	0	0	0	0	.000	.000	.000	-99	-1	-1	0	0			1.000	0	/C	-0.1
1906	StL-A	65	201	22	57	7	3	3	24	16		.284	.345	.393	137	7	8	30	4			.954	-8	C/O	0.6
1907	NY-A	52	137	16	25	1	3	0	15	11		.182	.253	.234	51	-7	-8	10	4			.846	-5	OC/1	-1.4
1914	StL-A	2	2	0	0	0	0	0	0	0	1	.000	.000	.000	-99	-0	-0	0	0			.000	0	HM	-0.1
Total	4	120	343	38	82	8	6	3	39	27	1	.239	.304	.324	97	-1	-1	39	8			.940	-13	/CO1	-1.0

■ CHRIS RICKLEY Rickley, Christian b: 10/7/1859, Philadelphia, Pa. d: 10/25/11, Philadelphia, Pa. 5'8", 160 lbs. Deb: 6/09/1884

| 1884 | Phi-U | 6 | 25 | 5 | 5 | 2 | 0 | 0 | | 2 | | .200 | .259 | .280 | 89 | -0 | -0 | 2 | | | | .757 | 0 | /S | 0.0 |

YEAR	TM/L	G	AB	R	H	2B	3B	HR	RBI	BB	SO	AVG	OBP	SLG	PRO+	BR	/A	RC	SB	CS	SBR	FA	FR	POS	TPR
■ JOHN RICKS Ricks, John Deb: 9/21/1891																									
1891	StL-a	5	18	3	3	0	0	0	0	0	2	.167	.167	.167	-3	-2	-3	1	0			.810	-1	/3	-0.3
1894	StL-N	1	1	0	0	0	0	0	0	0	0	.000	.000	.000	-99	-0	-0	0	0			.250	-1	/3	-0.1
Total	2	6	19	3	3	0	0	0	0	0	2	.158	.158	.158	-8	-3	-3	1	0			.720	-2	/3	-0.4
■ FRED RICO Rico, Alfredo (Cruz) b: 7/4/44, Jerome, Ariz. BR/TR, 5'10", 180 lbs. Deb: 9/01/69																									
1969	KC-A	12	26	2	6	2	0	0	2	9	10	.231	.429	.308	108	1	1	4	0	1	-1	1.000	4	/O3	0.4
■ ART RICO Rico, Arthur Raymond b: 7/23/1896, Roxbury, Mass. d: 1/3/19, Boston, Mass. BR/TR, 5'9.5", 185 lbs. Deb: 7/31/16																									
1916	Bos-N	4	4	0	0	0	0	0	0	0	0	.000	.000	.000	-99	-1	-1	0	0			1.000	-0	/C	-0.1
1917	Bos-N	13	14	1	4	1	0	0	2	0	2	.286	.286	.357	102	-0	-0	1	0			.950	-2	C/O	-0.1
Total	2	17	18	1	4	1	0	0	2	0	2	.222	.222	.278	56	-1	-1	1	0			.962	-2	/CO	-0.2
■ HARRY RICONDA Riconda, Henry Paul b: 3/17/1897, New York, N.Y. d: 11/15/58, Mahopac, N.Y. BR/TR, 5'10", 175 lbs. Deb: 4/19/23																									
1923	Phi-A	55	175	23	46	11	4	0	12	12	18	.263	.317	.371	80	-5	-6	21	4	2	0	.911	4	3/S	0.2
1924	Phi-A	83	281	34	71	16	3	1	21	27	43	.253	.323	.342	71	-12	-13	32	3	4	-2	.927	1	3/S	-0.7
1926	Bos-N	4	12	1	2	0	0	0	0	2	2	.167	.286	.167	27	-1	-1	1	0			.818	-1	/3	-0.2
1928	Bro-N	92	281	22	63	15	4	3	35	20	28	.224	.285	.338	63	-16	-16	27	6			.957	3	23S	-0.9
1929	Pit-N	8	15	3	7	2	0	0	2	0	0	.467	.467	.600	158	1	1	4	0			.840	-0	/S	0.1
1930	Cin-N	1	1	0	0	0	0	0	0	0	0	.000	.000	.000	-99	-0	-0	0	0			.000	0	H	0.0
Total	6	243	765	83	189	44	11	4	70	61	91	.247	.309	.349	71	-34	-34	84	13	6		.922	6	3/2S	-1.5
■ JOHN RIDDLE Riddle, John H. b: 2/1864, Pennsylvania BR/TR, Deb: 9/18/1889																									
1889	Was-N	11	37	3	8	3	0	0	3	2	8	.216	.256	.297	59	-2	-2	3	0			.841	1	/CO	-0.1
1890	Phi-a	27	85	7	7	0	1	0		17		.082	.243	.106	5	-9	-9	3	4			.914	-2	CO/23	-0.9
Total	2	38	122	10	15	3	1	0	3	19	8	.123	.246	.164	22	-12	-11	6	4			.880	-2	/CO23	-1.0
■ JOHNNY RIDDLE Riddle, John Ludy "Mutt" b: 10/3/05, Clinton, S.C. BR/TR, 5'11", 190 lbs. Deb: 4/17/30 FC																									
1930	Chi-A	25	58	7	14	3	1	0	4	3	6	.241	.290	.328	58	-4	-4	6	0	0	0	1.000	-3	C	-0.4
1937	Was-A	8	26	2	7	0	0	0	3	0	2	.269	.296	.269	46	-2	-2	2	0	0	0	.971	0	/C	-0.1
	Bos-N	2	3	0	0	0	0	0	0	1	0	.000	.250	.000	-29	-1	-0	0	0			1.000	1	/C	0.0
1938	Bos-N	19	57	6	16	1	0	0	2	4	2	.281	.328	.298	81	-2	-1	6	0			.951	4	C	0.4
1941	Cin-N	10	10	2	3	0	0	0	0	0	1	.300	.300	.300	69	-0	-0	1	0			1.000	1	C	0.1
1944	Cin-N	1	0	0	0	0	0	0	0	0	0	—	—	—	—	0	0	0	0			.000	0	/C	0.0
1945	Cin-N	23	45	0	8	0	0	0	2	4	6	.178	.245	.178	19	-5	-5	2	0			1.000	4	C	0.0
1948	Pit-N	10	15	1	3	0	0	0	0	1	2	.200	.250	.200	23	-2	-2	1	0			1.000	0	C	-0.1
Total	7	98	214	18	51	4	1	0	11	13	19	.238	.288	.266	51	-15	-14	18	0	0		.983	7	/C	-0.1
■ HANK RIEBE Riebe, Harvey Donald b: 10/10/21, Cleveland, Ohio BR/TR, 5'9.5", 175 lbs. Deb: 8/26/42																									
1942	Det-A	11	35	1	11	2	0	0	2	0	6	.314	.314	.371	85	-1	-1	4	0	0	0	1.000	-1	C	-0.1
1947	Det-A	8	7	0	0	0	0	0	2	0	2	.000	.000	.000	-97	-2	-2	0	0	0	0	1.000	-0	/C	-0.2
1948	Det-A	25	62	0	12	0	0	0	5	3	5	.194	.231	.194	13	-8	-8	2	0	1	-1	1.000	1	C	-0.7
1949	Det-A	17	33	1	6	2	0	0	2	0	5	.182	.182	.242	12	-4	-4	1	1	0	0	.960	-2	C	-0.5
Total	4	61	137	2	29	4	0	0	11	3	18	.212	.229	.241	26	-14	-15	7	1	1	-0	.994	-3	/C	-1.5
■ NIKCO RIESGO Riesgo, Damon Nikco b: 1/11/67, Long Beach, Cal. BR/TR, 6'2", 185 lbs. Deb: 4/20/91																									
1991	Mon-N	4	7	1	1	0	0	0	0	3	1	.143	.400	.143	60	-0	-0	1	0	0	0	.500	-0	/O	0.0
■ JOE RIGGERT Riggert, Joseph Aloysius b: 12/11/1886, Janesville, Wis. d: 12/10/73, Kansas City, Mo. BR/TR, 5'9.5", 170 lbs. Deb: 5/12/11																									
1911	Bos-A	50	146	19	31	4	4	2	13	12		.212	.290	.336	75	-5	-5	16	5			.929	-4	O	-1.1
1914	Bro-N	27	83	6	16	1	3	2	6	4	20	.193	.230	.349	70	-3	-4	7	2			.972	-1	O	-0.6
	StL-N	34	89	9	19	5	2	0	8	5	14	.213	.255	.315	70	-4	-4	8	4			.961	-3	O	-0.9
	Yr	61	172	15	35	6	5	2	14	9	34	.203	.243	.331	70	-7	-7	15	6			.966	-4	O	-1.5
1919	Bos-N	63	240	34	68	8	5	4	17	25	30	.283	.356	.408	135	9	10	36	9			.950	2	O	0.8
Total	3	174	558	68	134	18	14	8	44	46	64	.240	.305	.366	98	-4	-3	66	20			.950	-6	O	-1.8
■ LEW RIGGS Riggs, Lewis Sidney b: 4/22/10, Mebane, N.C. d: 8/12/75, Durham, N.C. BL/TR, 6', 175 lbs. Deb: 4/28/34																									
1934	StL-N	2	1	0	0	0	0	0	0	0	1	.000	.000	.000	-94	-0	-0	0	0			.000	0	H	0.0
1935	Cin-N	142	532	73	148	26	8	5	46	43	32	.278	.334	.385	96	-5	-3	72	8			.928	8	*3	1.0
1936	Cin-N★	141	538	69	138	20	12	6	57	38	33	.257	.314	.372	90	-13	-8	63	5			.968	12	*3	0.9
1937	Cin-N	122	384	43	93	17	5	6	45	24	17	.242	.289	.359	79	-14	-12	40	4			.941	20	*3/2S	1.0
1938	Cin-N	142	531	53	134	21	13	2	55	40	28	.252	.311	.352	84	-13	-12	60	3			.947	-1	*3	-1.1
1939	Cin-N	22	38	5	6	1	0	0	1	5	4	.158	.256	.184	20	-4	-4	2	1			.957	-1	3	-0.5
1940	*Cin-N	41	72	8	21	7	1	1	9	2	4	.292	.311	.458	109	1	0	10	0			.943	2	3	0.2
1941	*Bro-N	77	197	27	60	13	4	5	36	16	12	.305	.357	.487	131	9	8	35	1			.932	-7	3/12	0.1
1942	Bro-N	70	180	20	50	5	0	3	22	13	9	.278	.333	.356	100	0	-0	22	0			.944	-6	3/1	-0.6
1946	Bro-N	1	4	0	0	0	0	0	0	0	0	.000	.000	.000	-99	-1	-1	0	0			1.000	0	/3	-0.1
Total	10	760	2477	298	650	110	43	28	271	181	140	.262	.317	.375	91	-42	-32	304	22			.945	27	3/21S	0.9
■ TOPPER RIGNEY Rigney, Emory Elmo b: 1/7/1897, Groveton, Tex. d: 6/6/72, San Antonio, Tex. BR/TR, 5'9", 150 lbs. Deb: 4/12/22																									
1922	Det-A	155	536	68	161	17	7	2	63	68	44	.300	.380	.369	99	-1	2	81	17	8	0	.938	-11	*S	0.7
1923	Det-A	129	470	63	148	24	11	1	74	55	35	.315	.389	.419	115	10	11	80	7	5	-1	.944	-16	*S	0.6
1924	Det-A	147	499	81	144	29	9	4	94	102	39	.289	.410	.407	113	12	14	90	11	11	-3	**.967**	10	*S	3.4
1925	Det-A	62	146	21	36	5	2	2	18	21	15	.247	.341	.349	77	-5	-5	18	2	2	-1	.934	-14	S/3	-1.5
1926	Bos-A	148	525	71	142	32	6	4	53	108	31	.270	.395	.377	105	6	8	85	6	8	-3	**.969**	20	*S	3.9
1927	Bos-A	8	18	0	2	1	0	0	0	1	2	.111	.158	.167	-16	-3	-3	1	0	0	0	1.000	-1	/3S	-0.4
	Was-A	45	132	20	36	5	4	0	13	22	10	.273	.381	.371	97	-0	0	19	1	2	-1	.929	-3	S/3	0.0
	Yr	53	150	20	38	6	4	0	13	23	12	.253	.356	.347	84	-3	-3	19	1	2	-1	.932	-4	S3	-0.4
Total	6	694	2326	324	669	113	39	13	315	377	176	.288	.388	.387	104	19	27	374	44	36	-8	.953	-16	S/3	6.7
■ BILL RIGNEY Rigney, William Joseph "Specs" or "The Cricket" b: 1/29/18, Alameda, Cal. BR/TR, 6'1", 178 lbs. Deb: 4/16/46 MC																									
1946	NY-N	110	360	38	85	9	1	3	31	36	29	.236	.307	.292	70	-14	-14	34	9			.965	3	3S	-0.9
1947	NY-N	130	531	84	142	24	3	17	59	51	54	.267	.337	.420	99	-1	-1	76	7			.974	1	23S	0.5
1948	NY-N★	113	424	72	112	17	3	10	43	47	54	.264	.342	.389	97	-1	-2	58	4			.967	-11	*2/S	-0.7
1949	NY-N	122	389	53	108	19	6	6	47	47	38	.278	.356	.404	103	2	2	56	3			.928	-17	S23	-0.8
1950	NY-N	56	83	8	15	2	0	0	8	8	13	.181	.253	.205	22	-9	-9	4	0			.966	6	23	-0.3
1951	*NY-N	44	69	9	16	2	0	4	9	8	7	.232	.321	.435	100	-0	-0	10	0	1	-1	.953	5	3/2	0.5
1952	NY-N	60	90	15	27	5	1	1	14	11	6	.300	.388	.411	121	3	3	14	2	3	-1	.889	-1	3/2S1	0.1
1953	NY-N	19	20	2	5	0	0	0	1	0	5	.250	.250	.250	30	-2	-2	1	0	0	0	1.000	0	/32	-0.2
Total	8	654	1966	281	510	78	14	41	212	208	206	.259	.334	.376	91	-22	-23	254	25	4		.971	-13	23S/1	-1.8
■ CULLEY RIKARD Rikard, Culley b: 5/9/14, Oxford, Miss. BL/TR, 5'11", 183 lbs. Deb: 9/20/41																									
1941	Pit-N	6	20	1	4	1	0	0	0	1	1	.200	.238	.250	38	-2	-2	1	0			1.000	1	/O	-0.1
1942	Pit-N	38	52	6	10	2	1	0	5	7	8	.192	.288	.269	62	-2	-2	4	0			.958	-4	O	-0.7
1947	Pit-N	109	324	57	93	16	4	4	32	50	39	.287	.384	.398	105	5	4	51	1			.978	-1	O	-0.1

YEAR	TM/L	G	AB	R	H	2B	3B	HR	RBI	BB	SO	AVG	OBP	SLG	PRO+	BR	/A	RC	SB	CS	SBR	FA	FR	POS	TPR
Total	3	153	396	64	107	19	5	4	37	58	48	.270	.365	.374	97	1	-0	57	1			.978	-4	O	-0.9
■ **ERNIE RILES** Riles, Ernest b: 10/2/60, Cairo, Ga. BL/TR, 6'1", 180 lbs. Deb: 5/14/85																									
1985	Mil-A	116	448	54	128	12	7	5	45	36	54	.286	.342	.377	97	-2	-1	55	2	2	-1	.957	-19	*S/D	-0.9
1986	Mil-A	145	524	69	132	24	2	9	47	54	80	.252	.323	.357	82	-11	-13	59	7	7	-2	.964	-30	*S	-3.2
1987	Mil-A	83	276	38	72	11	1	4	38	30	47	.261	.336	.351	80	-6	-7	33	3	4	-2	.935	-6	3S	-1.3
1988	Mil-A	41	127	7	32	6	1	1	9	7	26	.252	.291	.339	75	-4	-4	12	2	2	-1	.958	1	3/SD	-0.3
	SF-N	79	187	26	55	7	2	3	28	10	33	.294	.330	.401	114	2	3	23	1	2	-1	.975	8	32S	1.2
1989	*SF-N	122	302	43	84	13	2	7	40	28	50	.278	.343	.404	116	5	6	39	0	6	-4	.962	-10	32/SO	-0.7
1990	SF-N	92	155	22	31	2	1	8	21	26	26	.200	.315	.381	94	-2	-1	20	0	0	0	.986	-4	S23	-0.4
1991	Oak-A	108	281	30	60	8	4	5	32	31	42	.214	.294	.324	75	-11	-9	27	3	2	-0	.939	-10	3S/21	-1.9
1992	Hou-N	39	61	5	16	1	0	1	4	2	11	.262	.286	.328	78	-2	-2	6	1	0	0	1.000	-2	/S312	-0.4
Total	8	825	2361	294	610	84	20	43	264	224	369	.258	.324	.366	91	-31	-29	274	19	25	-9	.964	-71	S3/21DO	-7.9
■ **JIM RILEY** Riley, James Joseph b: 11/10/1886, Buffalo, N.Y. d: 3/25/49, Buffalo, N.Y. BR/TR, 6', 165 lbs. Deb: 8/02/10																									
1910	Bos-N	1	1	0	0	0	0	0	0	1	1	.000	.500	.000	46	0	0	0	0			.600	-0	/O	0.0
■ **JIM RILEY** Riley, James Norman b: 5/25/1895, Bayfield, N.B., Can d: 5/25/69, Seguin, Tex. BL/TR, 5'10.5", 185 lbs. Deb: 7/03/21																									
1921	StL-A	4	11	0	0	0	0	0	0	1	3	.000	.083	.000	-73	-3	-3	0	0	0	0	.818	-3	/2	-0.6
1923	Was-A	2	3	1	0	0	0	0	0	2	0	.000	.400	.000	12	-0	-0	0	0	0	0	.882	-1	/1	-0.1
Total	2	6	14	1	0	0	0	0	0	3	3	.000	.176	.000	-50	-3	-3	0	0	0	0	.929	-4	/21	-0.7
■ **LEE RILEY** Riley, Leon Francis b: 8/20/06, Princeton, Neb. d: 9/13/70, Schenectady, N.Y. BL/TR, 6'1", 185 lbs. Deb: 4/19/44																									
1944	Phi-N	4	12	1	1	1	0	0	1	0	0	.083	.083	.167	-32	-2	-2	0	0			1.000	-1	/O	-0.3
■ **BILLY RILEY** Riley, William James "Pigtail Billy" b: 1855, Cincinnati, Ohio d: 11/9/1887, Cincinnati, Ohio BR/TR, 5'10", 160 lbs. Deb: 5/05/1875																									
1875	Wes-n	8	33	4	5	1	0	0		1		.152	.176	.182	23	-2	-3	1						/O	-0.2
1879	Cle-N	44	165	14	24	2	0	0	9	2	26	.145	.156	.158	4	-16	-16	4				.850	4	O/1C	-1.3
■ **FRANK RINGO** Ringo, Frank C. b: 10/12/1860, Parkville, Mo. d: 4/12/1889, Kansas City, Mo. 5'11", 175 lbs. Deb: 5/01/1883																									
1883	Phi-N	60	221	24	42	10	1	0	12	6	34	.190	.211	.244	42	-16	-13	12				.847	-9	CO/S32	-1.7
1884	Phi-N	26	91	4	12	2	0	0	6	3	19	.132	.160	.154	-1	-10	-10	2				.783	-16	C	-2.2
	Phi-a	2	6	0	0	0	0	0		0		.000	.000	.000	-94	-1	-1	0				.762	1	/C	0.0
1885	Det-N	17	65	12	16	3	0	0	2	0	7	.246	.246	.292	73	-2	-2	5				.852	2	/C3O	0.1
	Pit-a	3	11	0	2	0	0	0		0		.182	.182	.182	17	-1	-1	0				.941	3	/C	0.2
1886	Pit-a	15	56	3	12	2	2	0		1		.214	.228	.321	73	-2	-2	4	0			.934	-0	/1C	-0.2
	KC-N	16	56	6	13	7	0	0	7	5	10	.232	.295	.357	92	-0	-1	6	0			.904	-6	C/O3	-0.5
Total	4	139	506	49	97	24	3	0	27	15	70	.192	.215	.251	46	-33	-29	29	0			.844	-24	/C3O1S2	-4.3
■ **BOB RINKER** Rinker, Robert John b: 4/21/21, Audenried, Pa. BR/TR, 6', 190 lbs. Deb: 9/06/50																									
1950	Phi-A	3	3	0	1	0	0	0	0	0	0	.333	.333	.333	72	-0	-0	0	0	0	0	.000	0	/C	0.0
■ **JUAN RIOS** Rios, Juan Onofre Velez (b: Juan Onofre Velez (Rios)) b: 6/14/42, Mayaguez, P.R. BR/TR, 6'3", 185 lbs. Deb: 4/09/69																									
1969	KC-A	87	196	20	44	5	1	1	5	7	19	.224	.262	.276	50	-13	-13	12	1	3	-2	.967	-16	2S/3	-2.8
■ **CAL RIPKEN** Ripken, Calvin Edwin Jr. b: 8/24/60, Havre De Grace, Md. BR/TR, 6'4", 215 lbs. Deb: 8/10/81 F																									
1981	Bal-A	23	39	1	5	0	0	0	0	1	8	.128	.150	.128	-19	-6	-6	0	0	0	0	.946	0	S/3	-0.6
1982	Bal-A	160	598	90	158	32	5	28	93	46	95	.264	.320	.475	115	10	11	87	3	3	-1	.972	-7	S3	1.0
1983	*Bal-A★	162	663	**121**	**211**	**47**	2	27	102	58	97	.318	.373	.517	145	37	39	120	0	4	-2	.970	16	*S	**6.6**
1984	Bal-A★	162	641	103	195	37	7	27	86	71	89	.304	.375	.510	146	37	38	122	2	1	0	.971	**39**	*S	**9.1**
1985	Bal-A★	161	642	116	181	32	5	26	110	67	68	.282	.351	.469	125	19	21	96	2	3	-1	.967	7	*S	4.2
1986	Bal-A★	162	627	98	177	35	1	25	81	70	60	.282	.358	.461	123	18	20	102	4	2	0	.982	10	*S	4.3
1987	Bal-A★	162	624	97	157	28	3	27	98	81	77	.252	.339	.436	106	3	6	90	3	5	-2	.973	-4	*S	1.3
1988	Bal-A★	161	575	87	152	25	1	23	81	102	69	.264	.377	.431	129	23	25	99	2	2	-1	.973	-2	*S	3.6
1989	Bal-A★	162	646	80	166	30	0	21	93	57	72	.257	.320	.401	105	1	3	79	3	2	-0	.990	4	*S	2.0
1990	Bal-A★	161	600	78	150	28	4	21	84	82	66	.250	.345	.415	115	10	13	88	3	1	0	**.996**	-30	*S	-0.5
1991	Bal-A★	162	650	99	210	46	5	34	114	53	46	.323	.379	.566	164	48	52	134	6	1	1	**.986**	18	*S	**8.1**
1992	Bal-A★	162	637	73	160	29	1	14	72	64	50	.251	.326	.366	94	-5	-5	76	4	3	-1	.984	-12	*S	-0.5
Total	12	1800	6942	1043	1922	369	34	273	1014	752	797	.277	.350	.458	124	196	216	1093	32	27	-7	.978	37	*S/3	38.6
■ **BILLY RIPKEN** Ripken, William Oliver b: 12/16/64, Havre De Grace, Md. BR/TR, 6'1", 183 lbs. Deb: 7/11/87 F																									
1987	Bal-A	58	234	27	72	9	0	2	20	21	23	.308	.365	.372	99	-1	0	33	4	1	1	.990	-3	2	0.0
1988	Bal-A	150	512	52	106	18	1	2	34	33	63	.207	.262	.258	47	-37	-35	35	8	2	1	.984	2	*2/3D	-2.6
1989	Bal-A	115	318	31	76	11	2	2	26	22	53	.239	.288	.305	69	-14	-12	27	1	2	-1	.985	12	*2/D	0.2
1990	Bal-A	129	406	48	118	28	1	3	38	28	43	.291	.342	.387	107	2	4	55	5	2	0	.987	-9	*2	-0.2
1991	Bal-A	104	287	24	62	11	1	0	14	15	31	.216	.255	.261	45	-22	-21	17	0	1	-1	.986	4	*2	-1.6
1992	Bal-A	111	330	35	76	15	0	4	36	18	26	.230	.276	.312	65	-16	-16	27	2	3	-1	**.993**	-0	*2	-1.5
Total	6	667	2087	217	510	92	5	13	168	137	239	.244	.295	.312	71	-87	-80	193	20	11	-1	.987	6	2/D3	-5.7
■ **JIMMY RIPPLE** Ripple, James Albert b: 10/14/09, Export, Pa. d: 7/16/59, Greensburg, Pa. BL/TR, 5'10", 170 lbs. Deb: 4/20/36																									
1936	*NY-N	96	311	42	95	17	2	7	47	28	15	.305	.365	.441	117	7	7	51	1			.980	-0	O	0.4
1937	*NY-N	121	426	70	135	23	3	5	66	29	20	.317	.362	.420	110	7	6	65	3			.980	-9	*O	-0.7
1938	NY-N	134	501	68	131	21	3	10	60	49	21	.261	.333	.375	94	-4	-4	62	2			.976	-3	*O	-1.1
1939	NY-N	66	123	10	28	4	0	1	12	8	7	.228	.286	.285	53	-8	-8	10	0			1.000	-2	O	-1.1
	Bro-N	28	106	18	35	8	4	0	22	11	8	.330	.398	.481	131	5	5	19	0			1.000	-2	O	0.2
	Yr	94	229	28	63	12	4	1	34	19	15	.275	.339	.376	90	-3	-3	28	0			1.000	-3	O	-0.9
1940	Bro-N	7	13	0	3	0	0	0	0	2	2	.231	.333	.231	55	-1	-1	1	0			1.000	1	/O	0.0
	*Cin-N	32	101	15	31	10	0	4	20	13	5	.307	.397	.525	151	7	7	22	1			1.000	-5	O	0.1
	Yr	39	114	15	34	10	0	4	20	15	7	.298	.389	.491	139	7	6	23	1			1.000	-4	O	0.1
1941	Cin-N	38	102	10	22	6	1	1	9	9	4	.216	.279	.324	69	-4	-4	10	0			1.000	-2	O	-0.9
1943	Phi-A	32	126	8	30	3	1	0	15	7	7	.238	.284	.278	65	-6	-6	11	0	0	0	1.000	-4	O	-1.3
Total	7	554	1809	241	510	92	14	28	251	156	89	.282	.343	.395	101	4	3	252	7	0		.984	-27	O	-4.4
■ **SWEDE RISBERG** Risberg, Charles August b: 10/13/1894, San Francisco, Cal d: 10/13/75, Red Bluff, Cal. BR/TR, 6', 175 lbs. Deb: 4/11/17																									
1917	*Chi-A	149	474	59	96	20	8	1	45	59	65	.203	.297	.285	76	-12	-13	45	16			.913	-39	*S	-5.2
1918	Chi-A	82	273	36	70	12	3	1	27	23	32	.256	.321	.333	97	-1	-2	30	5			.944	-8	S32/1O	-0.8
1919	*Chi-A	119	414	48	106	19	6	2	38	35	38	.256	.317	.345	86	-8	-8	49	19			.934	-13	S1	-1.7
1920	Chi-A	126	458	53	122	21	10	2	65	31	45	.266	.316	.369	81	-14	-14	53	12	10	-2	.934	-4	*S	-0.9
Total	4	476	1619	196	394	72	27	6	175	148	180	.243	.311	.332	83	-35	-37	177	52	10		.928	-64	S/132O	-8.6
■ **POP RISING** Rising, Percival Sumner b: 1/2/1872, Industry, Pa. d: 1/28/38, Rochester, Pa. Deb: 8/10/05																									
1905	Bos-A	11	29	2	3	1	1	0	2	2		.103	.161	.207	16	-3	-3	1	0			1.000	0	/O3	-0.3
■ **CLAUDE RITCHEY** Ritchey, Claude Cassius "Little All Right" b: 10/5/1873, Emlenton, Pa. d: 11/8/51, Emlenton, Pa. BB/TR, 5'6.5", 167 lbs. Deb: 4/22/1897																									
1897	Cin-N	101	337	58	95	12	4	0	41	42		.282	.368	.341	82	-4	-8	49	11			.897	-16	SO/2	-2.0
1898	Lou-N	151	551	65	140	10	4	5	51	46		.254	.322	.314	84	-12	-11	67	19			.919	-16	S2	-1.7

YEAR	TM/L	G	AB	R	H	2B	3B	HR	RBI	BB	SO	AVG	OBP	SLG	PRO+	BR	/A	RC	SB	CS	SBR	FA	FR	POS	TPR
1899	Lou-N	147	536	65	161	15	7	4	71	49		.300	.370	.377	105	5	5	87	21			.938	-6	*2S	0.6
1900	*Pit-N	123	476	62	139	17	8	1	67	29		.292	.339	.368	94	-4	-4	69	18			.952	7	*2	0.8
1901	Pit-N	140	540	66	160	20	4	1	74	47		.296	.357	.354	103	6	4	78	15			.941	3	*2/S	1.2
1902	Pit-N	115	405	54	112	13	1	2	55	53		.277	.370	.328	112	10	8	57	10			**.966**	6	*2/O	1.9
1903	*Pit-N	138	506	66	145	28	10	0	59	55		.287	.360	.381	108	8	6	78	15			**.961**	19	*2	2.8
1904	Pit-N	156	544	79	143	22	12	0	51	59		.263	.338	.347	109	9	7	72	12			.958	-2	*2/S	1.0
1905	Pit-N	153	533	54	136	29	6	0	52	51		.255	.324	.332	93	-2	-4	64	12			**.961**	-5	*2/S	-0.7
1906	Pit-N	152	484	46	130	21	5	1	62	68		.269	.369	.339	116	15	12	68	6			**.966**	1	*2	1.6
1907	Bos-N	144	499	45	127	17	4	2	51	50		.255	.329	.317	103	2	2	58	8			**.971**	14	*2	1.7
1908	Bos-N	121	421	44	115	10	3	2	36	50		.273	.361	.325	122	12	12	54	7			.967	16	*2	3.1
1909	Bos-N	30	87	4	15	1	0	0	3	8		.172	.242	.184	31	-7	-7	4	1			.959	0	2	-0.9
Total	13	1671	5919	708	1618	215	68	18	673	607		.273	.348	.342	101	38	23	807	155			.957	21	*2S/O	9.4

■ **CHARLIE RITTER** Ritter, Charles J. Deb: 9/21/1885

YEAR	TM/L	G	AB	R	H	2B	3B	HR	RBI	BB	SO	AVG	OBP	SLG	PRO+	BR	/A	RC	SB	CS	SBR	FA	FR	POS	TPR
1885	Buf-N	2	6	0	1	0	0	0	0	0	2	.167	.167	.167	8	-1	-1	0				.813	0	/2	0.0

■ **FLOYD RITTER** Ritter, Floyd Alexander b: 6/1/1870, Dorset, Ohio d: 2/7/43, Stevenson, Wash. BR/TR, 5'8", 155 lbs. Deb: 6/04/1890

YEAR	TM/L	G	AB	R	H	2B	3B	HR	RBI	BB	SO	AVG	OBP	SLG	PRO+	BR	/A	RC	SB	CS	SBR	FA	FR	POS	TPR
1890	Tol-a	1	3	0	0	0	0	0		0		.000	.000	.000	-97	-1	-1	0	0			.778	0	/C	-0.1

■ **LEW RITTER** Ritter, Lewis Elmer "Old Dog" b: 9/7/1875, Liverpool, Pa. d: 5/27/52, Harrisburg, Pa. BR/TR, 5'9", 150 lbs. Deb: 9/10/02

YEAR	TM/L	G	AB	R	H	2B	3B	HR	RBI	BB	SO	AVG	OBP	SLG	PRO+	BR	/A	RC	SB	CS	SBR	FA	FR	POS	TPR
1902	Bro-N	16	57	5	12	1	0	0	2	1		.211	.224	.228	39	-4	-4	4	2			.973	3	C	0.0
1903	Bro-N	78	259	26	61	9	6	0	37	19		.236	.290	.317	75	-9	-8	28	9			.940	-17	C/O	-1.7
1904	Bro-N	72	214	23	53	4	1	0	19	20		.248	.315	.276	85	-4	-3	25	17			.966	6	C/23	1.0
1905	Bro-N	92	311	32	68	10	5	1	28	15		.219	.255	.293	68	-15	-12	29	16			.951	-14	C/O3	-1.8
1906	Bro-N	73	226	22	47	1	3	0	15	16		.208	.260	.239	61	-12	-10	17	6			.978	-8	C/O13	-1.5
1907	Bro-N	93	271	15	55	6	1	0	17	18		.203	.253	.232	57	-15	-13	19	5			.969	-1	C	-0.6
1908	Bro-N	38	99	6	19	2	1	0	2	7		.192	.245	.232	55	-5	-5	6	0			.961	-3	C	-0.6
Total	7	462	1437	129	315	33	17	1	120	96		.219	.269	.268	67	-64	-54	127	55			.960	-36	C/O321	-5.2

■ **WHITEY RITTERSON** Ritterson, Edward West b: 4/26/1855, Philadelphia, Pa. d: 7/28/17, Sellersville, Pa. BR/TR, 5'8", Deb: 5/03/1876

YEAR	TM/L	G	AB	R	H	2B	3B	HR	RBI	BB	SO	AVG	OBP	SLG	PRO+	BR	/A	RC	SB	CS	SBR	FA	FR	POS	TPR
1876	Phi-N	16	52	8	13	3	0	0	4	0	2	.250	.250	.308	86	-1	-1	4				.671	-8	C/O3	-0.7

■ **JIM RITZ** Ritz, James L. b: 1874, Pittsburgh, Pa. d: 11/10/1896, Pittsburgh, Pa. Deb: 7/20/1894

YEAR	TM/L	G	AB	R	H	2B	3B	HR	RBI	BB	SO	AVG	OBP	SLG	PRO+	BR	/A	RC	SB	CS	SBR	FA	FR	POS	TPR
1894	Pit-N	1	4	1	0	0	0	0	0	0	0	.000	.200	.000	-48	-1	-1	0	1			.750	-0	/3	-0.1

■ **GERMAN RIVERA** Rivera, German (Diaz) b: 7/6/60, Santurce, P.R. BR/TR, 6'2", 195 lbs. Deb: 9/02/83

YEAR	TM/L	G	AB	R	H	2B	3B	HR	RBI	BB	SO	AVG	OBP	SLG	PRO+	BR	/A	RC	SB	CS	SBR	FA	FR	POS	TPR
1983	LA-N	13	17	1	6	1	0	0	0	2	2	.353	.421	.412	132	1	1	3	0	1	-1	.929	2	/3	0.2
1984	LA-N	94	227	20	59	12	2	2	17	21	30	.260	.325	.357	92	-2	-2	23	1	0	0	.937	16	3	1.4
1985	Hou-N	13	36	3	7	2	1	0	2	4	8	.194	.275	.306	64	-2	-2	3	0	0	0	.941	3	3	0.1
Total	3	120	280	24	72	15	3	2	19	27	40	.257	.325	.354	91	-3	-3	28	1	1	-0	.937	20	3	1.7

■ **BOMBO RIVERA** Rivera, Jesus Manuel (Torres) b: 8/2/52, Ponce, Pr. BR/TR, 5'10", 187 lbs. Deb: 4/17/75

YEAR	TM/L	G	AB	R	H	2B	3B	HR	RBI	BB	SO	AVG	OBP	SLG	PRO+	BR	/A	RC	SB	CS	SBR	FA	FR	POS	TPR
1975	Mon-N	5	9	1	1	0	0	0	0	2	3	.111	.273	.111	9	-1	-1	0	0	0	0	.889	0	/O	-0.1
1976	Mon-N	68	185	22	51	11	4	2	19	13	32	.276	.323	.411	103	1	0	24	1	0	0	.950	0	O	-0.1
1978	Min-A	101	251	35	68	8	2	3	23	35	47	.271	.365	.355	101	2	2	35	5	3	-0	.982	-9	O/D	-1.1
1979	Min-A	112	263	37	74	13	5	2	31	17	40	.281	.325	.392	89	-3	-4	32	5	5	-2	.989	-4	*O	-1.3
1980	Min-A	44	113	13	25	7	0	3	10	4	20	.221	.248	.363	61	-6	-7	9	0	0	0	.922	-4	O/D	-1.2
1982	KC-A	5	10	1	1	0	0	0	0	0	2	.100	.100	.100	-45	-2	-2	0	0	0	0	1.000	-1	/O	-0.3
Total	6	335	831	109	220	39	11	10	83	71	144	.265	.324	.374	90	-8	-12	100	11	8	-2	.970	-18	O/D	-4.1

■ **LUIS RIVERA** Rivera, Luis Antonio (Pedraza) b: 1/3/64, Cidra, P.R. BR/TR, 5'9", 170 lbs. Deb: 8/03/86

YEAR	TM/L	G	AB	R	H	2B	3B	HR	RBI	BB	SO	AVG	OBP	SLG	PRO+	BR	/A	RC	SB	CS	SBR	FA	FR	POS	TPR
1986	Mon-N	55	166	20	34	11	1	0	13	17	33	.205	.286	.283	58	-9	-9	15	1	1	-0	.953	-9	S	-1.5
1987	Mon-N	18	32	0	5	2	0	0	1	1	8	.156	.182	.219	5	-4	-4	1	0	0	0	.923	2	S	-0.2
1988	Mon-N	123	371	35	83	17	3	4	30	24	69	.224	.273	.318	66	-15	-17	30	3	4	-2	.962	-6	*S	-1.7
1989	Bos-A	93	323	35	83	17	1	5	29	20	60	.257	.302	.362	81	-6	-9	34	2	3	-1	.958	-3	S/2D	-0.7
1990	*Bos-A	118	346	38	78	20	0	7	45	25	58	.225	.280	.344	70	-13	-15	32	4	3	-1	.965	11	*S/23	0.3
1991	Bos-A	129	414	64	107	22	3	8	40	35	86	.258	.321	.384	90	-4	-6	50	4	4	-1	.959	4	*S	0.6
1992	Bos-A	102	288	17	62	11	1	0	29	26	56	.215	.287	.260	52	-17	-19	22	4	3	-1	.966	14	S/23OD	0.1
Total	7	638	1940	209	452	100	9	24	187	148	370	.233	.291	.331	71	-69	-80	185	18	18	-5	.961	12	S/2D3O	-3.1

■ **JIM RIVERA** Rivera, Manuel Joseph "Jungle Jim" b: 7/22/22, New York, N.Y. BL/TL, 6', 196 lbs. Deb: 4/15/52

YEAR	TM/L	G	AB	R	H	2B	3B	HR	RBI	BB	SO	AVG	OBP	SLG	PRO+	BR	/A	RC	SB	CS	SBR	FA	FR	POS	TPR
1952	StL-A	97	336	45	86	13	6	4	30	29	59	.256	.319	.366	88	-5	-6	40	8	7	-2	.976	9	O	-0.3
	Chi-A	53	201	27	50	7	3	3	18	21	27	.249	.320	.358	88	-3	-4	26	13	2	3	.988	4	O	0.1
	Yr	150	537	72	136	20	9	7	48	50	86	.253	.319	.363	88	-8	-10	67	21	9	1	.980	12	*O	-0.2
1953	Chi-A	156	567	79	147	26	**16**	11	78	53	70	.259	.329	.420	98	-1	-3	76	22	15	-2	.976	-1	*O	-1.2
1954	Chi-A	145	490	62	140	16	8	13	61	49	68	.286	.358	.431	111	10	8	77	18	10	-1	.959	-17	*O	-1.6
1955	Chi-A	147	454	71	120	24	4	10	52	62	59	.264	.354	.401	100	2	0	66	**25**	16	-2	.981	2	*O	-0.6
1956	Chi-A	139	491	76	125	23	5	12	66	49	75	.255	.326	.395	88	-8	-9	66	20	9	1	.976	1	*O	-1.4
1957	Chi-A	125	402	51	103	21	6	14	52	40	80	.256	.328	.443	108	4	4	59	18	2	**4**	.974	-7	O1	-0.6
1958	Chi-A	116	276	37	62	8	4	9	35	24	49	.225	.289	.380	84	-7	-7	31	21	3	5	.994	-3	O	-1.0
1959	*Chi-A	80	177	18	39	9	4	4	19	11	19	.220	.270	.384	78	-6	-6	18	5	3	-0	.976	-8	O	-1.6
1960	Chi-A	48	17	17	5	0	0	1	1	3	3	.294	.400	.471	136	1	1	4	4	0	1	1.000	-6	O	-0.4
1961	Chi-A	1	0	0	0	0	0	0	0	0	0	—	—	—	—	0	0	0	0	1	-1	.000	0	H	-0.1
	KC-A	64	141	20	34	8	0	2	10	24	14	.241	.352	.340	86	-2	-2	18	6	2	1	.981	-9	O	-1.2
	Yr	65	141	20	34	8	0	2	10	24	14	.241	.352	.340	86	-2	-2	18	6	3	0	.981	-9	O	-1.3
Total	10	1171	3552	503	911	155	56	83	422	365	523	.256	.330	.402	96	-17	-24	484	160	70	6	.977	-36	*O/1	-9.9

■ **MICKEY RIVERS** Rivers, John Milton b: 10/31/48, Miami, Fla. BL/TL, 5'10", 165 lbs. Deb: 8/04/70

YEAR	TM/L	G	AB	R	H	2B	3B	HR	RBI	BB	SO	AVG	OBP	SLG	PRO+	BR	/A	RC	SB	CS	SBR	FA	FR	POS	TPR
1970	Cal-A	17	25	6	8	2	0	0	3	3	5	.320	.414	.400	130	1	1	5	1	0	0	1.000	0	/O	0.1
1971	Cal-A	79	268	31	71	12	2	1	12	19	38	.265	.316	.336	91	-5	-3	32	13	1	3	.976	-3	O	-0.7
1972	Cal-A	58	159	18	34	6	2	0	7	8	26	.214	.256	.277	62	-8	-7	11	4	3	-1	.981	-1	O	-1.3
1973	Cal-A	30	129	26	45	6	4	0	16	8	11	.349	.391	.457	150	6	8	24	8	3	1	.909	-4	O	0.3
1974	Cal-A	118	466	69	133	19	**11**	3	31	39	47	.285	.342	.393	118	6	10	64	30	13	1	.994	10	*O	1.6
1975	Cal-A	155	616	70	175	17	**13**	1	53	43	42	.284	.333	.359	103	-4	1	81	**70**	14	**13**	.977	11	*O/D	1.9
1976	*NY-A★	137	590	95	184	31	8	8	67	13	51	.312	.330	.432	123	13	14	88	43	7	9	.986	9	*O	2.8
1977	*NY-A	138	565	79	184	18	5	12	69	18	45	.326	.351	.439	115	10	10	86	22	14	-2	.982	13	*O/D	1.6
1978	*NY-A	141	559	78	148	25	8	11	48	29	51	.265	.305	.397	98	-5	-3	69	25	5	5	.980	10	*O	0.5
1979	NY-A	74	286	37	82	18	5	3	25	13	21	.287	.320	.416	99	-2	-1	36	3	7	-3	.974	-6	O	-1.3
	Tex-A	58	247	35	74	9	3	6	25	9	18	.300	.327	.433	104	0	1	35	7	2	1	.981	3	O	0.2
	Yr	132	533	72	156	27	8	9	50	22	39	.293	.323	.424	101	-2	-0	71	10	9	-2	.978	-3	*O	-1.1
1980	Tex-A	147	630	96	210	32	6	7	60	20	34	.333	.355	.437	119	12	14	98	18	7	1	.978	10	*O/D	1.9
1981	Tex-A	99	399	62	114	21	2	3	26	24	31	.286	.328	.371	107	0	3	49	9	5	-0	.996	4	O	0.3
1982	Tex-A	19	68	6	16	1	1	1	4	0	7	.235	.235	.324	54	-5	-4	5	0	0	0	.000	0	D	-0.4
1983	Tex-A	96	309	37	88	17	0	1	20	11	21	.285	.312	.350	83	-8	-7	35	9	4	0	.980	0	DO	-0.7
1984	Tex-A	102	313	40	94	13	1	4	33	9	23	.300	.320	.387	91	-3	-4	38	5	5	-2	1.000	-0	DO	-0.7

YEAR	TM/L	G	AB	R	H	2B	3B	HR	RBI	BB	SO	AVG	OBP	SLG	PRO+	BR	/A	RC	SB	CS	SBR	FA	FR	POS	TPR
Total	15	1468	5629	785	1660	247	71	61	499	266	471	.295	.329	.397	106	10	32	756	267	90	26	.982	57	*OD	6.1

■ JOHNNY RIZZO Rizzo, John Costa b: 7/30/12, Houston, Tex. d: 12/4/77, Houston, Tex. BR/TR, 6', 190 lbs. Deb: 4/19/38

YEAR	TM/L	G	AB	R	H	2B	3B	HR	RBI	BB	SO	AVG	OBP	SLG	PRO+	BR	/A	RC	SB	CS	SBR	FA	FR	POS	TPR
1938	Pit-N	143	555	97	167	31	9	23	111	54	61	.301	.368	.514	139	29	29	105	1			.951	-8	*O	1.6
1939	Pit-N	94	330	49	86	23	3	6	55	42	27	.261	.349	.403	103	1	2	46	0			.974	-0	O	-0.2
1940	Pit-N	9	28	1	5	1	0	0	2	5	5	.179	.324	.214	51	-2	-2	2	0			.818	-2	/O	-0.4
	Cin-N	31	110	17	31	6	0	4	17	14	14	.282	.363	.445	121	3	3	19	1			.974	5	O	0.6
	Phi-N	103	367	53	107	12	2	20	53	37	31	.292	.358	.499	139	16	18	67	2			.968	6	O/3	2.0
	Yr	143	505	71	143	19	2	24	72	56	50	.283	.357	.471	130	18	19	88	3			.964	9	*O/3	2.2
1941	Phi-N	99	235	20	51	9	2	4	24	24	34	.217	.295	.323	77	-8	-7	22	1			.968	0	O/3	-1.0
1942	Bro-N	78	217	31	50	8	0	4	27	24	25	.230	.307	.323	83	-4	-5	21	2			.977	-2	O	-1.0
Total	5	557	1842	268	497	90	16	61	289	200	197	.270	.345	.435	116	35	38	282	7			.964	-1	O/3	1.6

■ PHIL RIZZUTO Rizzuto, Philip Francis "Scooter" b: 9/25/17, Brooklyn, N.Y. BR/TR, 5'6", 160 lbs. Deb: 4/15/41

YEAR	TM/L	G	AB	R	H	2B	3B	HR	RBI	BB	SO	AVG	OBP	SLG	PRO+	BR	/A	RC	SB	CS	SBR	FA	FR	POS	TPR
1941	*NY-A	133	515	65	158	20	9	3	46	27	36	.307	.343	.398	97	-4	-3	70	14	5	1	.957	16	*S	2.2
1942	*NY-A☆	144	553	79	157	24	7	4	68	44	40	.284	.343	.374	104	1	2	74	22	6	3	.962	**25**	*S	4.0
1946	NY-A	126	471	53	121	17	1	2	38	34	39	.257	.315	.310	74	-15	-16	48	14	7	0	.961	13	*S	0.5
1947	*NY-A	153	549	78	150	26	9	2	60	57	31	.273	.350	.364	100	-0	0	76	11	6	-0	.969	16	*S	2.5
1948	NY-A	128	464	65	117	13	2	6	50	60	24	.252	.340	.328	79	-14	-13	57	6	5	-1	.973	-11	*S	-1.8
1949	*NY-A	153	614	110	169	22	7	5	65	72	34	.275	.352	.358	88	-10	-10	82	18	6	**2**	**.971**	3	*S	0.5
1950	*NY-A★	155	617	125	200	36	7	7	66	92	39	.324	.418	.439	123	22	24	124	12	8	-1	**.982**	9	*S	**4.1**
1951	*NY-A★	144	540	87	148	21	6	2	43	58	27	.274	.350	.346	92	-7	-5	73	18	3	**4**	.968	6	*S	1.5
1952	*NY-A★	152	578	89	147	24	10	2	43	67	42	.254	.337	.341	95	-8	-3	73	17	6	2	.976	19	*S	2.9
1953	*NY-A★	134	413	54	112	21	3	2	54	71	39	.271	.383	.351	103	3	5	63	4	3	-1	.963	-3	*S	1.0
1954	NY-A	127	307	47	60	11	0	2	15	41	23	.195	.292	.251	51	-21	-19	25	3	2	-0	.968	-1	*S/2	-1.2
1955	*NY-A	81	143	19	37	4	1	1	9	22	18	.259	.369	.322	88	-2	-1	20	7	1	2	.957	-9	S/2	-0.5
1956	NY-A	31	52	6	12	0	0	0	6	6	6	.231	.310	.231	46	-4	-4	5	3	0	1	.934	3	S	0.2
Total	13	1661	5816	877	1588	239	62	38	563	651	398	.273	.351	.355	93	-60	-43	789	149	58	10	.968	86	*S/2	15.9

■ MIKE ROACH Roach, James Michael b: 1876, New York, N.Y. d: 11/12/16, Binghamton, N.Y. Deb: 8/10/1899

YEAR	TM/L	G	AB	R	H	2B	3B	HR	RBI	BB	SO	AVG	OBP	SLG	PRO+	BR	/A	RC	SB	CS	SBR	FA	FR	POS	TPR
1899	Was-N	24	78	7	17	1	0	0	7	3		.218	.265	.231	37	-7	-7	6	3			.964	-5	C/1	-0.9

■ MEL ROACH Roach, Melvin Earl b: 1/25/33, Richmond, Va. BR/TR, 6'1", 190 lbs. Deb: 7/31/53

YEAR	TM/L	G	AB	R	H	2B	3B	HR	RBI	BB	SO	AVG	OBP	SLG	PRO+	BR	/A	RC	SB	CS	SBR	FA	FR	POS	TPR
1953	Mil-N	5	2	1	0	0	0	0	0	0	1	.000	.000	.000	-99	-1	-1	0	0	0	0	.000	0	/2	-0.1
1954	Mil-N	3	4	0	0	0	0	0	0	0	1	.000	.000	.000	-99	-1	-1	0	0	0	0	1.000	-0	/1	-0.1
1957	Mil-N	7	6	1	1	0	0	0	0	0	3	.167	.167	.167	-11	-1	-1	0	0	0	0	1.000	0	/2	-0.1
1958	Mil-N	44	136	14	42	7	0	3	10	6	15	.309	.338	.426	110	-0	1	20	0	0	0	.993	-2	2/O1	0.2
1959	Mil-N	19	31	1	3	0	0	0	0	2	4	.097	.152	.097	-35	-6	-6	1	0	0	0	.880	1	/2O3	-0.5
1960	Mil-N	48	140	12	42	12	0	3	18	6	19	.300	.333	.450	121	2	3	17	0	0	0	.975	-8	O2/13	-0.4
1961	Mil-N	13	36	3	6	0	0	1	6	2	4	.167	.250	.250	35	-3	-3	3	0	0	0	1.000	-2	/O1	-0.6
	Chi-N	23	39	1	5	2	0	0	1	3	9	.128	.190	.179	-1	-6	-6	1	1	0	0	.981	-1	/12	-0.7
	Yr	36	75	4	11	2	0	1	7	5	13	.147	.220	.213	16	-9	-9	3	1	0	0	1.000	-3	/O12	-1.3
1962	Phi-N	65	105	9	20	4	0	0	8	5	19	.190	.227	.229	23	-11	-11	5	0	0	0	.951	-1	3/21O	-1.2
Total	8	227	499	42	119	25	0	7	43	24	75	.238	.278	.331	66	-27	-23	47	1	0	0	.969	-12	/2O31	-3.5

■ ROXEY ROACH Roach, Wilbur Charles b: 11/28/1882, Anita, Pa. d: 12/26/47, Bay City, Mich. BR/TR, 5'11", 160 lbs. Deb: 5/02/10

YEAR	TM/L	G	AB	R	H	2B	3B	HR	RBI	BB	SO	AVG	OBP	SLG	PRO+	BR	/A	RC	SB	CS	SBR	FA	FR	POS	TPR
1910	NY-A	70	220	27	47	9	2	0	20	29		.214	.313	.273	79	-3	-5	24	15			.913	-7	S/O	-1.1
1911	NY-A	13	40	4	10	2	1	0	2	6		.250	.348	.350	89	-0	-1	5	0			.891	-1	/S2	-0.1
1912	Was-A	2	2	1	1	0	0	1	1	0		.500	.500	2.000	600	1	1	2	0			.500	-1	/S	0.1
1915	Buf-F	92	346	35	93	20	3	2	31	17	34	.269	.303	.361	93	-3	-4	43	11			.959	16	S	2.0
Total	4	177	608	67	151	31	6	3	54	52	34	.248	.311	.334	90	-6	-8	74	26			.938	8	S/O2	0.9

■ MIKE ROARKE Roarke, Michael Thomas b: 11/8/30, West Warwick, R.I. BR/TR, 6'2", 195 lbs. Deb: 4/19/61 C

YEAR	TM/L	G	AB	R	H	2B	3B	HR	RBI	BB	SO	AVG	OBP	SLG	PRO+	BR	/A	RC	SB	CS	SBR	FA	FR	POS	TPR
1961	Det-A	86	229	21	51	6	1	2	22	20	31	.223	.285	.284	51	-15	-16	18	0	0	0	.988	4	C	-0.9
1962	Det-A	56	136	11	29	4	1	4	14	13	17	.213	.287	.346	67	-6	-7	13	0	0	0	.982	6	C	0.1
1963	Det-A	23	44	5	14	0	0	0	1	2	3	.318	.362	.318	89	-0	-0	5	0	0	0	.986	1	C	0.1
1964	Det-A	29	82	4	19	1	0	0	7	10	10	.232	.315	.244	57	-4	-4	7	0	0	0	.994	3	C	0.0
Total	4	194	491	41	113	11	2	6	44	45	61	.230	.297	.297	60	-26	-28	43	0	0	0	.987	14	C	-0.7

■ FRED ROAT Roat, Frederick R. b: 11/10/1867, Oregon, Ill. d: 9/24/13, Oregon, Ill. TR , Deb: 5/10/1890

YEAR	TM/L	G	AB	R	H	2B	3B	HR	RBI	BB	SO	AVG	OBP	SLG	PRO+	BR	/A	RC	SB	CS	SBR	FA	FR	POS	TPR
1890	Pit-N	57	215	18	48	2	0	2	17	16	22	.223	.286	.260	70	-10	-6	18	7			.847	2	3/1O	-0.3
1892	Chi-N	8	31	4	6	0	1	0	2	2	3	.194	.242	.258	52	-2	-2	2	2			.897	-3	/2	-0.5
Total	2	65	246	22	54	2	1	2	19	18	25	.220	.281	.260	67	-12	-8	21	9			.944	-1	/312O	-0.8

■ TOMMY ROBELLO Robello, Thomas Vardasco "Tony" b: 2/9/13, San Leandro, Cal. BR/TR, 5'10.5", 175 lbs. Deb: 8/13/33

YEAR	TM/L	G	AB	R	H	2B	3B	HR	RBI	BB	SO	AVG	OBP	SLG	PRO+	BR	/A	RC	SB	CS	SBR	FA	FR	POS	TPR
1933	Cin-N	14	30	1	7	3	0	0	3	1	5	.233	.258	.333	69	-1	-1	3	0			1.000	2	2/3	0.1
1934	Cin-N	2	2	0	0	0	0	0	0	0	1	.000	.000	.000	-99	-1	-1	0	0			.000	0	H	-0.1
Total	2	16	32	1	7	3	0	0	3	1	6	.219	.242	.313	58	-2	-2	3	0			.852	2	/23	0.0

■ SKIPPY ROBERGE Roberge, Joseph Albert Armand b: 5/19/17, Lowell, Mass. BR/TR, 5'11", 185 lbs. Deb: 7/18/41

YEAR	TM/L	G	AB	R	H	2B	3B	HR	RBI	BB	SO	AVG	OBP	SLG	PRO+	BR	/A	RC	SB	CS	SBR	FA	FR	POS	TPR
1941	Bos-N	55	167	12	36	6	0	0	15	9	18	.216	.256	.251	45	-13	-12	12	0			.978	5	2/3S	-0.4
1942	Bos-N	74	172	10	37	7	0	1	12	9	19	.215	.258	.273	57	-10	-9	13	1			.977	8	23/S	0.0
1946	Bos-N	48	169	13	39	6	2	2	20	7	12	.231	.270	.325	68	-8	-8	15	1			.973	2	3	-0.5
Total	3	177	508	35	112	19	2	3	47	25	49	.220	.261	.283	57	-30	-29	39	2			.967	15	/32S	-0.9

■ RED ROBERTS Roberts, Charles Emory b: 8/8/18, Carrollton, Ga. BR/TR, 6', 170 lbs. Deb: 9/03/43

YEAR	TM/L	G	AB	R	H	2B	3B	HR	RBI	BB	SO	AVG	OBP	SLG	PRO+	BR	/A	RC	SB	CS	SBR	FA	FR	POS	TPR
1943	Was-A	9	23	1	6	1	0	1	3	4	2	.261	.370	.435	140	1	1	4	0	0	0	.778	-5	/S3	-0.3

■ SKIPPER ROBERTS Roberts, Clarence Ashley b: 1/11/1888, Wardner, Idaho d: 12/24/63, Long Beach, Cal. BL/TR, 5'10.5", 175 lbs. Deb: 6/12/13

YEAR	TM/L	G	AB	R	H	2B	3B	HR	RBI	BB	SO	AVG	OBP	SLG	PRO+	BR	/A	RC	SB	CS	SBR	FA	FR	POS	TPR
1913	StL-N	26	41	4	6	2	0	0	3	3	13	.146	.205	.195	15	-5	-5	2	1			.859	-2	C	-0.6
1914	Pit-F	33	55	7	12	2	1	0	4	1	11	.218	.246	.291	53	-4	-4	5	2			.941	-1	C	-0.4
	Chi-F	4	3	0	1	0	0	0	1	1	1	.333	.500	.333	148	0	0	1	0			.000	0	H	0.0
	Pit-F	19	39	5	10	2	1	1	4	1	8	.256	.293	.436	107	0	0	5	1			.923	-4	/CO	-0.3
	Yr	56	97	12	23	4	2	1	9	3	20	.237	.275	.351	78	-3	-3	11	3			.935	-5	C/O	-0.7
Total	2	82	138	16	29	6	2	1	12	6	33	.210	.253	.304	59	-8	-8	12	4			.906	-7	/CO	-1.3

■ CURT ROBERTS Roberts, Curtis Benjamin b: 8/16/29, Pineland, Tex. d: 11/14/69, Oakland, Cal. BR/TR, 5'8", 165 lbs. Deb: 4/13/54

YEAR	TM/L	G	AB	R	H	2B	3B	HR	RBI	BB	SO	AVG	OBP	SLG	PRO+	BR	/A	RC	SB	CS	SBR	FA	FR	POS	TPR
1954	Pit-N	134	496	47	115	18	7	1	36	55	49	.232	.311	.302	62	-28	-27	50	6	3	0	.969	2	*2	-1.6
1955	Pit-N	6	17	1	2	1	0	0	0	2	1	.118	.211	.176	4	-2	-2	1	0	0	0	.913	-1	/2	-0.3
1956	Pit-N	31	62	6	11	5	2	0	4	5	12	.177	.239	.323	50	-5	-4	5	1	0	0	.988	-2	2	-0.4
Total	3	171	575	54	128	24	9	1	40	62	62	.223	.300	.301	59	-35	-34	56	7	3	0	.969	0	2	-2.3

■ DAVE ROBERTS Roberts, David Leonard b: 6/30/33, Panama City, Pan. BL/TL, 6', 172 lbs. Deb: 9/05/62

YEAR	TM/L	G	AB	R	H	2B	3B	HR	RBI	BB	SO	AVG	OBP	SLG	PRO+	BR	/A	RC	SB	CS	SBR	FA	FR	POS	TPR
1962	Hou-N	16	53	3	13	3	0	1	10	8	8	.245	.355	.358	99	-0	0	8	0	0	0	1.000	-2	O/1	-0.2
1964	Hou-N	61	125	9	23	4	1	1	7	14	28	.184	.271	.256	52	-8	-7	9	0	1	-1	.983	4	1/O	-0.6
1966	Pit-N	14	16	3	2	1	0	0	0	0	7	.125	.125	.188	-15	-2	-2	0	0	0	0	.950	0	/1	-0.2

YEAR	TM/L	G	AB	R	H	2B	3B	HR	RBI	BB	SO	AVG	OBP	SLG	PRO+	BR	/A	RC	SB	CS	SBR	FA	FR	POS	TPR
Total	3	91	194	15	38	8	1	2	17	22	43	.196	.284	.278	60	-11	-10	17	0	1	-1	.967	2	/1O	-1.0

■ DAVE ROBERTS Roberts, David Wayne b: 2/17/51, Lebanon, Ore. BR/TR, 6'3", 215 lbs. Deb: 6/07/72 C

YEAR	TM/L	G	AB	R	H	2B	3B	HR	RBI	BB	SO	AVG	OBP	SLG	PRO+	BR	/A	RC	SB	CS	SBR	FA	FR	POS	TPR
1972	SD-N	100	418	38	102	17	0	5	33	18	64	.244	.275	.321	74	-18	-15	37	7	2	1	.931	-6	32/SC	-2.1
1973	SD-N	127	479	56	137	20	3	21	64	17	83	.286	.312	.472	124	7	11	70	11	2	2	.942	3	*32	1.7
1974	SD-N	113	318	26	53	10	1	5	18	32	69	.167	.247	.252	41	-26	-24	20	2	0	1	.955	-4	*3/SO	-3.0
1975	SD-N	33	113	7	32	2	0	2	12	13	19	.283	.367	.354	107	1	1	16	3	1	0	.925	-4	3/2	-0.2
1977	SD-N	82	186	15	41	14	1	1	23	11	32	.220	.268	.323	64	-11	-9	16	2	1	0	.982	-4	C/23S	-1.2
1978	SD-N	54	97	7	21	4	1	1	7	12	25	.216	.309	.309	79	-3	-2	9	0	0	0	.980	-1	C/1O	-0.3
1979	Tex-A	44	84	12	22	2	1	3	14	7	17	.262	.319	.417	98	-1	-0	11	1	0	0	.980	1	CO/213	0.1
1980	Tex-A	101	235	27	56	4	0	10	30	13	38	.238	.281	.383	83	-7	-6	24	0	1	-1	.930	-21	3SC/O12	-2.6
1981	*Hou-N	27	54	4	13	3	0	1	5	3	6	.241	.281	.352	83	-2	-1	5	1	0	0	.958	0	1/32C	-0.2
1982	Phi-N	28	33	2	6	1	0	0	2	2	8	.182	.229	.212	23	-3	-3	2	0	1	-1	.818	1	3C/2	-0.3
Total	10	709	2017	194	483	77	7	49	208	128	361	.239	.288	.357	83	-64	-49	210	27	8	3	.983	-35	3C/2S1O	-8.1

■ BIP ROBERTS Roberts, Leon Joseph b: 10/27/63, Berkeley, Cal. BB/TR, 5'7", 160 lbs. Deb: 4/07/86

YEAR	TM/L	G	AB	R	H	2B	3B	HR	RBI	BB	SO	AVG	OBP	SLG	PRO+	BR	/A	RC	SB	CS	SBR	FA	FR	POS	TPR
1986	SD-N	101	241	34	61	5	2	1	12	14	29	.253	.294	.303	66	-11	-11	20	14	12	-3	.971	4	2	-0.8
1988	SD-N	5	9	1	3	0	0	0	0	1	2	.333	.400	.333	115	0	0	1	0	2	-1	.500	-1	/32	-0.2
1989	SD-N	117	329	81	99	15	8	3	25	49	45	.301	.393	.422	133	16	16	58	21	11	-0	.976	-8	O3S/2	0.8
1990	SD-N	149	556	104	172	36	3	9	44	55	65	.309	.378	.433	122	18	18	97	46	12	7	.982	-0	O3S/2	2.4
1991	SD-N	117	424	66	119	13	3	3	32	37	71	.281	.344	.347	92	-2	-4	53	26	11	1	.978	-7	2O	-0.9
1992	Cin-N★	147	532	92	172	34	6	4	45	62	54	.323	.396	.432	128	26	23	96	44	16	4	.993	-14	O23	1.3
Total	6	636	2091	378	626	103	22	20	158	218	266	.299	.369	.398	113	46	42	325	151	64	7	.982	-26	O23/S	2.6

■ LEON ROBERTS Roberts, Leon Kauffman b: 1/22/51, Vicksburg, Mich. BR/TR, 6'3", 200 lbs. Deb: 9/03/74

YEAR	TM/L	G	AB	R	H	2B	3B	HR	RBI	BB	SO	AVG	OBP	SLG	PRO+	BR	/A	RC	SB	CS	SBR	FA	FR	POS	TPR
1974	Det-A	17	63	5	17	3	2	0	7	3	10	.270	.303	.381	92	-1	-1	6	0	2	-1	.926	-3	O	-0.6
1975	Det-A	129	447	51	115	17	5	10	38	36	94	.257	.318	.385	94	-2	-4	53	3	7	-3	.982	8	*O/D	-0.5
1976	Hou-N	87	235	31	68	11	2	7	33	19	43	.289	.350	.443	136	7	9	38	1	0	0	.980	-7	O	0.1
1977	Hou-N	19	27	1	2	0	0	0	2	1	8	.074	.107	.074	-55	-6	-5	0	0	0	0	1.000	0	/O	-0.6
1978	Sea-A	134	472	78	142	21	7	22	92	41	52	.301	.367	.515	146	27	28	90	6	3	0	.975	10	*O/D	3.2
1979	Sea-A	140	450	61	122	24	6	15	54	56	64	.271	.354	.451	114	10	9	73	3	3	-1	.983	4	*O	0.7
1980	Sea-A	119	374	48	94	18	3	10	33	43	59	.251	.330	.396	97	-1	-1	48	8	4	0	.984	3	*O/D	-0.2
1981	Tex-A	72	233	26	65	17	2	4	31	25	38	.279	.351	.421	128	7	8	33	3	4	-2	.992	-4	O	0.0
1982	Tex-A	31	73	7	17	3	0	1	6	4	14	.233	.282	.315	67	-4	-3	6	0	0	0	1.000	-5	O/D	-0.9
	Tor-A	40	105	6	24	4	0	1	5	7	16	.229	.277	.295	52	-6	-7	8	1	1	-0	1.000	-2	DO	-1.0
	Yr	71	178	13	41	7	0	2	11	11	30	.230	.279	.303	58	-10	-10	14	1	1	-0	1.000	-7	OD	-1.9
1983	KC-A	84	213	24	55	7	0	8	24	17	27	.258	.316	.404	96	-1	-1	26	1	1	-0	.979	-6	O/D	-1.0
1984	KC-A	29	45	4	10	1	1	0	3	4	3	.222	.300	.289	63	-2	-2	4	0	0	0	1.000	-3	O/PD	-0.5
Total	11	901	2737	342	731	126	28	78	328	256	428	.267	.335	.419	108	28	28	383	26	25	-7	.982	-5	O/DP	-1.3

■ JIM ROBERTSON Robertson, Alfred James b: 1/29/28, Chicago, Ill. BR/TR, 5'9", 183 lbs. Deb: 4/15/54

YEAR	TM/L	G	AB	R	H	2B	3B	HR	RBI	BB	SO	AVG	OBP	SLG	PRO+	BR	/A	RC	SB	CS	SBR	FA	FR	POS	TPR
1954	Phi-A	63	147	9	27	8	0	0	8	23	25	.184	.298	.238	48	-10	-10	12	0	0	0	.974	-2	C	-1.0
1955	KC-A	6	8	1	2	0	0	0	0	1	2	.250	.333	.250	58	-0	-0	1	0	0	0	1.000	0	/C	0.0
Total	2	69	155	10	29	8	0	0	8	24	27	.187	.300	.239	49	-10	-10	13	0	0	0	.975	-2	/C	-1.0

■ ANDRE ROBERTSON Robertson, Andre Levett b: 10/2/57, Orange, Tex. BR/TR, 5'10", 160 lbs. Deb: 9/03/81

YEAR	TM/L	G	AB	R	H	2B	3B	HR	RBI	BB	SO	AVG	OBP	SLG	PRO+	BR	/A	RC	SB	CS	SBR	FA	FR	POS	TPR
1981	*NY-A	10	19	1	5	1	0	0	0	0	3	.263	.263	.316	67	-1	-1	1	1	1	-0	1.000	4	/S2	0.3
1982	NY-A	44	118	16	26	5	0	2	9	8	19	.220	.270	.314	61	-7	-6	9	0	0	0	.966	8	S2/3	0.4
1983	NY-A	98	322	37	80	16	3	1	22	8	54	.248	.273	.326	67	-16	-15	28	2	4	-2	.960	22	S2	1.2
1984	NY-A	52	140	10	30	5	1	0	6	4	20	.214	.236	.264	40	-12	-11	6	0	1	-1	.930	11	S/2	0.3
1985	NY-A	50	125	16	41	5	0	2	17	6	24	.328	.364	.416	116	2	3	18	1	2	-1	.867	-6	3S/2	-0.4
Total	5	254	724	80	182	32	4	5	54	26	120	.251	.281	.327	69	-33	-30	62	4	8	-4	.953	38	S/23	1.8

■ DARYL ROBERTSON Robertson, Daryl Berdene b: 1/5/36, Cripple Creek, Colo BR/TR, 6', 184 lbs. Deb: 5/04/62

YEAR	TM/L	G	AB	R	H	2B	3B	HR	RBI	BB	SO	AVG	OBP	SLG	PRO+	BR	/A	RC	SB	CS	SBR	FA	FR	POS	TPR
1962	Chi-N	9	19	0	2	0	0	0	2	2	10	.105	.190	.105	-18	-3	-3	1	0	0	0	1.000	-1	/S3	-0.4

■ DAVE ROBERTSON Robertson, Davis Aydelotte b: 9/25/1889, Portsmouth, Va. d: 11/5/70, Virginia Beach, Va. BL/TL, 6', 186 lbs. Deb: 6/05/12

YEAR	TM/L	G	AB	R	H	2B	3B	HR	RBI	BB	SO	AVG	OBP	SLG	PRO+	BR	/A	RC	SB	CS	SBR	FA	FR	POS	TPR
1912	NY-N	3	2	0	1	0	0	0	1	0	1	.500	.500	.500	169	0	0	1	1			1.000	-1	/1O	0.0
1914	NY-N	82	256	25	68	12	3	2	32	10	26	.266	.299	.359	99	-3	-2	29	9			.950	-2	O	-0.7
1915	NY-N	141	544	72	160	17	10	3	58	22	52	.294	.326	.379	120	7	10	71	22	10	1	.956	-1	*O	0.4
1916	NY-N	150	587	88	180	18	8	**12**	69	14	56	.307	.326	.426	137	18	21	82	21	17	-4	.960	5	*O	1.6
1917	*NY-N	142	532	64	138	16	9	**12**	54	10	47	.259	.276	.391	107	-1	1	59	17			.942	1	*O	-0.7
1919	NY-N	1	0	0	0	0	0	0	0	0	0	—	—	—	—	0	0	0	0			.000	0	R	0.0
	Chi-N	27	96	8	20	2	0	1	10	1	10	.208	.224	.260	45	-6	-7	6	3			.932	-2	O	-1.2
	Yr	28	96	8	20	2	0	1	10	1	10	.208	.224	.260	45	-6	-6	6	3			.932	-2	O	-1.2
1920	Chi-N	134	500	68	150	29	11	10	75	40	44	.300	.353	.462	130	20	19	75	17	23	-9	.968	-9	*O	-0.9
1921	Chi-N	22	36	7	8	3	0	0	14	1	3	.222	.243	.306	44	-3	-3	2	0	2	-1	1.000	-2	/O	-0.7
	Pit-N	60	230	29	74	18	3	6	48	12	16	.322	.361	.504	123	8	7	40	4	5	-2	.960	-4	O	-0.2
	Yr	82	266	36	82	21	3	6	62	13	19	.308	.345	.477	113	5	4	41	4	7	-3	.962	-6	O	-0.9
1922	NY-N	42	47	5	13	2	0	1	3	3	7	.277	.320	.383	80	-1	-1	6	0	0	0	.909	-2	/O	-0.3
Total	9	804	2830	366	812	117	44	47	364	113	262	.287	.318	.409	117	38	45	370	94	57		.955	-16	O/1	-2.7

■ DON ROBERTSON Robertson, Donald Alexander b: 10/15/30, Harvey, Ill. BL/TL, 5'10", 180 lbs. Deb: 4/13/54

YEAR	TM/L	G	AB	R	H	2B	3B	HR	RBI	BB	SO	AVG	OBP	SLG	PRO+	BR	/A	RC	SB	CS	SBR	FA	FR	POS	TPR
1954	Chi-N	14	6	2	0	0	0	0	0	0	2	.000	.000	.000	-99	-2	-2	0	0	0	0	1.000	-2	/O	-0.4

■ GENE ROBERTSON Robertson, Eugene Edward b: 12/25/1898, St.Louis, Mo. d: 10/21/81, Fallon, Nev. BL/TR, 5'7", 152 lbs. Deb: 7/04/19

YEAR	TM/L	G	AB	R	H	2B	3B	HR	RBI	BB	SO	AVG	OBP	SLG	PRO+	BR	/A	RC	SB	CS	SBR	FA	FR	POS	TPR
1919	StL-A	5	7	1	1	0	0	0	0	1	2	.143	.250	.143	11	-1	-1	0	0			.750	-2	/S	-0.2
1922	StL-A	18	27	2	8	2	1	0	1	1	1	.296	.321	.444	95	-0	-0	4	1	0	0	.875	1	/3S2	0.1
1923	StL-A	78	251	36	62	10	1	0	17	21	7	.247	.310	.295	57	-14	-16	25	4	2	0	.935	-15	3/2	-2.4
1924	StL-A	121	439	70	140	25	4	4	52	36	14	.319	.373	.421	99	3	-1	69	3	5	-2	.958	-11	*3/2	-0.5
1925	StL-A	154	582	97	158	26	5	14	76	81	30	.271	.364	.405	90	-4	-9	90	10	7	-1	.939	-2	*3/S	-0.1
1926	StL-A	78	247	23	62	12	6	1	19	17	10	.251	.302	.360	69	-11	-12	28	5	1	1	.924	-5	3S/2	-1.2
1928	*NY-A	83	251	29	73	9	0	1	36	14	6	.291	.328	.339	78	-9	-8	28	2	4	-2	.926	-8	3/2	-1.3
1929	NY-A	90	309	45	92	15	6	0	35	28	6	.298	.358	.385	98	-4	-1	43	3	3	-1	.966	-11	3	-0.9
	Bos-N	8	28	1	8	0	0	0	6	1	0	.286	.310	.286	51	-2	-2	2	1			.875	-2	/3S	-0.3
1930	Bos-N	21	59	7	11	1	0	0	7	5	3	.186	.250	.203	12	-8	-8	3	0			.949	-2	3	-0.8
Total	9	656	2200	311	615	100	23	20	249	205	79	.280	.344	.373	83	-51	-58	292	29	22		.941	-56	3/S2	-7.6

■ BOB ROBERTSON Robertson, Robert Eugene b: 10/2/46, Frostburg, Md. BR/TR, 6'1", 210 lbs. Deb: 9/18/67

YEAR	TM/L	G	AB	R	H	2B	3B	HR	RBI	BB	SO	AVG	OBP	SLG	PRO+	BR	/A	RC	SB	CS	SBR	FA	FR	POS	TPR
1967	Pit-N	9	35	4	6	0	0	2	4	3	12	.171	.237	.343	64	-2	-2	3	0	0	0	.990	-0	/1	-0.3
1969	Pit-N	32	96	7	20	4	1	1	9	8	30	.208	.269	.302	61	-5	-5	7	1	0	0	.996	1	1	-0.6
1970	*Pit-N	117	390	69	112	19	4	27	82	51	98	.287	.372	.564	150	25	26	83	4	1	1	.995	3	1/3O	2.1
1971	*Pit-N	131	469	65	127	18	2	26	72	60	101	.271	.358	.484	137	22	23	83	1	2	-1	.993	15	*1	2.6
1972	*Pit-N	115	306	25	59	11	0	12	41	41	84	.193	.294	.346	83	-8	-7	33	1	1	-0	.993	10	1O3	-0.2
1973	Pit-N	119	397	43	95	16	0	14	40	55	77	.239	.333	.385	101	-0	1	50	0	4	-2	.995	5	*1	-0.5

YEAR	TM/L	G	AB	R	H	2B	3B	HR	RBI	BB	SO	AVG	OBP	SLG	PRO+	BR	/A	RC	SB	CS	SBR	FA	FR	POS	TPR
1974	*Pit-N	91	236	25	54	11	0	16	48	33	48	.229	.323	.479	127	6	7	36	0	0	0	.991	-1	1	0.2
1975	*Pit-N	75	124	17	34	4	0	6	18	23	25	.274	.396	.452	136	7	7	25	0	0	0	.996	1	1	0.6
1976	Pit-N	61	129	10	28	5	1	2	25	16	23	.217	.303	.318	76	-4	-4	13	0	1	-1	.996	-0	1	-0.7
1978	Sea-A	64	174	17	40	5	2	8	28	24	39	.230	.327	.420	109	2	2	24	0	0	0	1.000	-1	D1	0.0
1979	Tor-A	15	29	1	3	0	0	1	1	3	9	.103	.188	.207	6	-4	-4	1	0	0	0	1.000	1	/1	-0.3
Total	11	829	2385	283	578	93	10	115	368	317	546	.242	.334	.434	115	39	44	357	7	9	-3	.994	35	1/DO3	2.9
■ **SHERRY ROBERTSON**	Robertson, Sherrard Alexander b: 1/1/19, Montreal, Que., Can. d: 10/23/70, Houghton, S.Dak. BL/TR, 6', 180 lbs. Deb: 9/08/40 C																								
1940	Was-A	10	33	4	7	0	1	0	0	5	6	.212	.316	.273	58	-2	-2	3	0	0	0	.940	1	S	0.0
1941	Was-A	1	3	0	0	0	0	0	0	0	3	.000	.000	.000	-99	-1	-1	0	0	0	0	.750	0	/3	-0.1
1943	Was-A	59	120	22	26	4	1	3	14	17	19	.217	.319	.342	97	-1	-0	14	0	2	-1	.897	-4	3/S	-0.6
1946	Was-A	74	230	30	46	6	3	6	19	30	42	.200	.292	.330	78	-8	-7	25	6	2	1	.902	-6	32S/O	-1.1
1947	Was-A	95	266	25	62	9	3	1	23	32	52	.233	.318	.301	74	-9	-9	27	4	5	-2	.949	0	O3/2	-1.4
1948	Was-A	71	187	19	46	11	3	2	22	24	26	.246	.335	.369	90	-4	-3	27	8	0	**2**	.939	-1	O	-0.4
1949	Was-A	110	374	59	94	17	3	11	42	42	35	.251	.329	.401	95	-6	-5	52	10	3	1	.947	-8	23O	-0.9
1950	Was-A	71	123	19	32	3	3	2	16	22	18	.260	.372	.382	98	-1	0	19	1	1	-0	.952	-9	O2/3	-0.8
1951	Was-A	62	111	14	21	2	1	1	10	9	22	.189	.256	.252	38	-10	-10	8	2	1	0	.949	3	O	-0.7
1952	Was-A	1	0	0	0	0	0	0	0	0	0	—	—	—	—	0	0	0	0	0	0	.000	0	R	0.0
	Phi-A	43	60	8	12	3	0	0	5	21	15	.200	.407	.250	81	0	-0	8	1	2	-1	.958	-3	/2O3	-0.5
	Yr	44	60	8	12	3	0	0	5	21	15	.200	.407	.250	81	0	-0	8	1	2	-1	.958	-3	/2O3	-0.5
Total	10	597	1507	200	346	55	18	26	151	202	238	.230	.323	.342	83	-41	-36	184	32	16	0	.946	-27	O2/3S	-6.5
■ **BILLY JO ROBIDOUX**	Robidoux, William Joseph b: 1/13/64, Ware, Mass. BL/TR, 6'1", 200 lbs. Deb: 9/11/85																								
1985	Mil-A	18	51	5	9	2	0	3	8	12	16	.176	.333	.392	98	0	0	7	0	0	0	1.000	-1	O/1D	-0.1
1986	Mil-A	56	181	15	41	8	0	1	21	33	36	.227	.346	.287	72	-5	-6	19	0	0	0	.986	-2	1D	-1.1
1987	Mil-A	23	62	9	12	0	0	0	4	8	17	.194	.286	.194	30	-6	-6	4	0	1	-1	.983	-0	1D	-0.7
1988	Mil-A	33	91	9	23	5	0	0	5	8	14	.253	.313	.308	74	-3	-3	8	1	1	-0	.983	2	1/D	-0.3
1989	Chi-A	16	39	2	5	2	0	0	1	4	9	.128	.209	.179	11	-5	-4	2	0	0	0	.990	-1	1/O	-0.6
1990	Bos-A	27	44	3	8	4	0	1	4	6	14	.182	.294	.341	74	-1	-2	4	0	0	0	.981	-0	1/D	-0.2
Total	6	173	468	43	98	21	0	5	43	71	106	.209	.315	.286	65	-20	-21	44	1	2	-1	.986	-1	1/DO	-3.0
■ **AARON ROBINSON**	Robinson, Aaron Andrew b: 6/23/15, Lancaster, S.C. d: 3/9/66, Lancaster, S.C. BL/TR, 6'2", 205 lbs. Deb: 5/06/43																								
1943	NY-A	1	1	0	0	0	0	0	0	0	1	.000	.000	.000	-99	-0	-0	0	0	0	0	.000	0	H	0.0
1945	NY-A	50	160	19	45	6	1	8	24	21	23	.281	.368	.481	139	9	8	30	0	0	0	1.000	-3	C	0.8
1946	NY-A	100	330	32	98	17	2	16	64	48	39	.297	.388	.506	146	21	21	69	0	1	-1	.983	-11	C	1.5
1947	*NY-A☆	82	252	23	68	11	5	5	36	40	26	.270	.370	.413	119	6	7	41	0	1	-1	.997	-0	C	1.1
1948	Chi-A	98	326	47	82	14	2	8	39	46	30	.252	.344	.380	96	-4	-2	45	0	1	-1	.989	-5	C	-0.1
1949	Det-A	110	331	38	89	12	0	13	56	73	21	.269	.402	.423	118	11	11	60	0	2	-1	.986	-1	*C	1.4
1950	Det-A	107	283	37	64	7	0	9	37	75	35	.226	.388	.346	86	-2	-3	45	0	1	-1	.993	-3	*C	-0.2
1951	Det-A	36	82	3	17	6	0	0	9	17	9	.207	.343	.280	70	-3	-3	8	0	0	0	1.000	-2	C	-0.4
	Bos-A	26	74	9	15	1	1	2	7	17	10	.203	.352	.324	76	-1	-2	10	0	0	0	.983	-1	C	-0.2
	Yr	62	156	12	32	7	1	2	16	34	19	.205	.347	.301	73	-4	-5	18	0	0	0	.991	-3	C	-0.6
Total	8	610	1839	208	478	74	11	61	272	337	194	.260	.375	.412	112	38	36	307	0	6	-4	.990	-26	C	3.9
■ **VAL ROBINSON**	Robinson, Alfred Valentine Deb: 5/01/1872																								
1872	Oly-n	7	32	6	6	0	0	0	4	1	1	.188	.212	.188	25	-3	-2	1						/O	-0.1
■ **BROOKS ROBINSON**	Robinson, Brooks Calbert b: 5/18/37, Little Rock, Ark. BR/TR, 6'1", 190 lbs. Deb: 9/17/55 CH																								
1955	Bal-A	6	22	0	2	0	0	0	1	0	10	.091	.091	.091	-55	-5	-4	0	0	0	0	.833	-2	/3	-0.7
1956	Bal-A	15	44	5	10	4	0	1	1	1	5	.227	.244	.386	70	-3	-2	4	0	0	0	.944	0	3/2	-0.2
1957	Bal-A	50	117	13	28	6	1	2	14	7	10	.239	.288	.359	81	-4	-3	11	1	0	0	.971	4	3	0.1
1958	Bal-A	145	463	31	110	16	3	3	32	31	51	.238	.293	.305	68	-22	-19	38	1	2	-1	.953	10	*32	-0.9
1959	Bal-A	88	313	29	89	15	2	4	24	17	37	.284	.325	.383	96	-3	-2	38	2	2	-1	.955	7	3/2	0.5
1960	Bal-A★	152	595	74	175	27	9	14	88	35	49	.294	.333	.440	109	4	5	78	2	2	-1	**.977**	12	*3/2	1.6
1961	Bal-A★	163	668	89	192	38	7	7	61	47	57	.287	.338	.397	98	-5	-3	85	1	3	-2	**.972**	-6	*3/2S	-0.8
1962	Bal-A★	162	634	77	192	29	9	23	86	42	70	.303	.347	.486	127	17	21	102	3	1	0	**.979**	7	*3/S2	3.0
1963	Bal-A★	161	589	67	148	26	4	11	67	46	84	.251	.307	.365	89	-10	-9	66	2	3	-1	**.976**	9	*3/S	-0.1
1964	Bal-A★	163	612	82	194	35	3	28	**118**	51	64	.317	.373	.521	146	37	37	115	1	0	0	**.972**	-2	*3	3.5
1965	Bal-A★	144	559	81	166	25	2	18	80	47	47	.297	.354	.445	123	18	17	86	3	0	1	.967	-6	*3	0.9
1966	*Bal-A★	157	620	91	167	35	2	23	100	56	36	.269	.335	.444	123	17	18	88	2	3	-1	**.976**	4	*3	1.8
1967	Bal-A★	158	610	88	164	25	5	22	77	54	54	.269	.332	.434	126	18	18	83	1	3	-2	**.980**	**31**	*3	5.0
1968	Bal-A★	162	608	65	154	36	6	17	75	44	55	.253	.308	.416	118	11	11	76	1	1	-0	**.970**	17	*3	3.2
1969	*Bal-A★	156	598	73	140	21	3	23	84	56	55	.234	.303	.395	93	-7	-7	69	2	1	0	**.976**	19	*3	1.3
1970	*Bal-A★	158	608	84	168	31	4	18	94	53	53	.276	.338	.429	109	8	7	85	1	1	-0	.966	-1	*3	0.5
1971	*Bal-A★	156	589	67	160	21	1	20	92	63	50	.272	.345	.413	115	11	11	83	0	0	0	.968	7	*3	1.8
1972	Bal-A★	153	556	48	139	23	2	8	64	43	45	.250	.306	.342	90	-6	-7	58	1	0	0	**.977**	6	*3	-0.3
1973	*Bal-A★	155	549	53	141	17	2	9	72	55	50	.257	.328	.344	90	-7	-6	61	2	0	1	.970	9	*3	0.2
1974	*Bal-A★	153	553	46	159	27	0	7	59	56	47	.288	.356	.374	114	8	10	74	2	0	1	.967	21	*3	3.1
1975	Bal-A	144	482	50	97	15	1	6	53	44	33	.201	.269	.274	57	-29	-25	37	0	0	0	**.979**	4	*3	-2.3
1976	Bal-A	71	218	16	46	8	2	3	11	8	24	.211	.242	.307	64	-12	-10	16	0	0	0	.969	0	3	-1.1
1977	Bal-A	24	47	3	7	2	0	1	4	4	4	.149	.216	.255	30	-5	-4	2	0	0	0	1.000	2	3	-0.3
Total	23	2896	10654	1232	2848	482	68	268	1357	860	990	.267	.325	.401	105	32	52	1358	28	22	-5	.971	151	*3/2S	19.8
■ **BRUCE ROBINSON**	Robinson, Bruce Philip b: 4/16/54, LaJolla, Cal. BL/TR, 6'1", 185 lbs. Deb: 8/19/78 F																								
1978	Oak-A	28	84	5	21	3	1	0	8	3	8	.250	.276	.310	68	-4	-4	7	0	0	0	.965	7	C	0.5
1979	NY-A	6	12	0	2	0	0	0	2	1	0	.167	.231	.167	9	-2	-1	1	0	0	0	.943	2	/C	0.1
1980	NY-A	4	5	0	0	0	0	0	0	0	4	.000	.000	.000	-99	-1	-1	0	0	0	0	1.000	-0	/C	-0.2
Total	3	38	101	5	23	3	1	0	10	4	12	.228	.257	.277	52	-7	-6	7	0	0	0	.962	9	/C	0.4
■ **CHARLIE ROBINSON**	Robinson, Charles Henry b: 7/27/1856, Westerly, R.I. d: 5/18/13, BL/TR, Deb: 8/02/1884																								
1884	Ind-a	20	80	11	23	2	0	0		3		.287	.313	.313	111	1	1	8				.967	-1	C/SO	0.1
1885	Bro-a	11	40	5	6	2	1	0		3		.150	.209	.250	46	-2	-2	2				.840	-4	C	-0.5
Total	2	31	120	16	29	4	1	0		6		.242	.278	.292	88	-2	-1	10				.919	-5	/CSO	-0.4
■ **RABBIT ROBINSON**	Robinson, Clyde b: 3/5/1882, Wellsburg, W.Va. d: 4/9/15, Waterbury, Conn. BR/TR, 5'6", 148 lbs. Deb: 4/22/03																								
1903	Was-A	103	373	41	79	10	8	1	20	33		.212	.279	.290	70	-13	-14	36	16			.917	2	2OS/3	-1.1
1904	Det-A	101	320	30	77	13	6	0	37	29		.241	.314	.319	103	1	2	39	14			.925	1	S3O2	0.5
1910	Cin-N	2	7	0	0	0	0	0	1	1	0	.000	.125	.000	-66	-1	-1	0	0			1.000	-1	/3	-0.3
Total	3	206	700	71	156	23	14	1	58	63	0	.223	.294	.300	83	-13	-13	75	30			.940	3	/2SO3	-0.9
■ **CRAIG ROBINSON**	Robinson, Craig George b: 8/21/48, Abington, Pa. BR/TR, 5'10", 165 lbs. Deb: 9/09/72																								
1972	Phi-N	5	15	0	3	1	0	0	0	1	2	.200	.250	.267	46	-1	-1	1	0	0	0	1.000	2	/S	0.2
1973	Phi-N	46	146	11	33	7	0	0	7	0	25	.226	.226	.274	37	-12	-13	8	1	1	-0	.945	1	S/2	-0.8
1974	Atl-N	145	452	52	104	4	6	0	29	30	57	.230	.282	.265	52	-28	-30	34	11	2	2	.956	-17	*S	-2.9
1975	Atl-N	10	17	1	1	0	0	0	0	0	5	.059	.059	.059	-65	-4	-4	0	0	0	0	1.000	1	/S	-0.2

YEAR	TM/L	G	AB	R	H	2B	3B	HR	RBI	BB	SO	AVG	OBP	SLG	PRO+	BR	/A	RC	SB	CS	SBR	FA	FR	POS	TPR
	SF-N	29	29	4	2	1	0	0	0	2	6	.069	.129	.103	-34	-5	-5	0	0	0	0	.941	5	S/2	0.0
	Yr	39	46	5	3	1	0	0	0	2	11	.065	.104	.087	-45	-9	-9	0	0	0	0	.967	6	S/2	-0.2
1976	SF-N	15	13	4	4	1	0	0	2	3	4	.308	.438	.385	131	1	1	2	0	1	-1	.952	4	/23S	0.4
	Atl-N	15	17	4	4	0	0	0	3	5	2	.235	.409	.235	81	0	-0	2	0	0	0	.952	2	/2S3	0.2
	Yr	30	30	8	8	1	0	0	5	8	6	.267	.421	.300	102	1	1	5	0	1	-1	.952	6	2/3S	0.6
1977	Atl-N	27	29	4	6	1	0	0	1	1	6	.207	.233	.241	25	-3	-3	2	0	0	0	1.000	6	S	0.3
Total	6	292	718	80	157	15	6	0	42	42	107	.219	.265	.256	44	-52	-56	50	12	4	1	.956	3	S/23	-2.8

■ DAVE ROBINSON

Robinson, David Tanner b: 5/22/46, Minneapolis, Minn. BB/TL, 6'1", 186 lbs. Deb: 9/10/70 F

YEAR	TM/L	G	AB	R	H	2B	3B	HR	RBI	BB	SO	AVG	OBP	SLG	PRO+	BR	/A	RC	SB	CS	SBR	FA	FR	POS	TPR
1970	SD-N	15	38	5	12	2	0	2	6	5	4	.316	.395	.526	151	2	3	8	2	0	1	1.000	1	O	0.4
1971	SD-N	7	6	0	0	0	0	0	0	1	3	.000	.143	.000	-61	-1	-1	0	0	0	0	.000	0	H	-0.1
Total	2	22	44	5	12	2	0	2	6	6	7	.273	.360	.455	124	1	1	8	2	0	1	.907	1	/O	0.3

■ EARL ROBINSON

Robinson, Earl John b: 11/3/36, New Orleans, La. BR/TR, 6'1", 190 lbs. Deb: 9/10/58

YEAR	TM/L	G	AB	R	H	2B	3B	HR	RBI	BB	SO	AVG	OBP	SLG	PRO+	BR	/A	RC	SB	CS	SBR	FA	FR	POS	TPR
1958	LA-N	8	15	3	3	0	0	0	0	1	4	.200	.250	.200	20	-2	-2	0	0	0	0	1.000	1	/3	0.0
1961	Bal-A	96	222	37	59	12	3	8	30	31	54	.266	.356	.455	117	5	5	36	4	3	-1	.973	-3	O	-0.2
1962	Bal-A	29	63	12	18	3	1	1	4	8	10	.286	.366	.413	115	1	1	10	2	0	1	1.000	0	O	0.1
1964	Bal-A	37	121	11	33	5	1	3	10	7	24	.273	.313	.405	98	-1	-1	15	1	2	-1	.986	1	O	-0.2
Total	4	170	421	63	113	20	5	12	44	47	92	.268	.342	.425	108	3	4	61	7	5	-1	.980	-1	O/3	-0.3

■ FLOYD ROBINSON

Robinson, Floyd Andrew b: 5/9/36, Prescott, Ark. BL/TR, 5'9", 175 lbs. Deb: 8/10/60

YEAR	TM/L	G	AB	R	H	2B	3B	HR	RBI	BB	SO	AVG	OBP	SLG	PRO+	BR	/A	RC	SB	CS	SBR	FA	FR	POS	TPR
1960	Chi-A	22	46	7	13	0	0	0	1	11	8	.283	.431	.283	98	1	1	7	2	3	-1	.960	-2	O	-0.4
1961	Chi-A	132	432	69	134	20	7	11	59	52	32	.310	.389	.465	129	18	19	82	7	4	-0	.991	4	*O	1.6
1962	Chi-A	156	600	89	187	**45**	10	11	109	72	47	.312	.387	.475	131	27	27	113	4	2	0	.973	-9	*O	0.8
1963	Chi-A	146	527	71	149	21	6	13	71	62	43	.283	.363	.419	120	14	15	81	4	3	-1	.984	-7	*O	0.1
1964	Chi-A	141	525	83	158	17	3	11	59	70	41	.301	.388	.408	125	18	20	87	9	5	-0	.987	-12	*O	0.0
1965	Chi-A	156	577	70	153	15	6	14	66	76	51	.265	.356	.385	117	10	14	83	4	1	1	.985	-4	*O	0.4
1966	Chi-A	127	342	44	81	11	2	5	35	44	32	.237	.332	.325	96	-3	-1	41	8	2	1	.962	-14	*O	-1.9
1967	Cin-N	55	130	19	31	6	2	1	10	14	14	.238	.313	.338	77	-2	-4	14	3	1	0	.981	-3	O	-0.8
1968	Oak-A	53	81	5	20	5	0	1	14	4	10	.247	.282	.346	94	-1	-1	8	0	0	0	1.000	-1	O	-0.3
	Bos-A	23	24	1	3	0	0	0	2	3	4	.125	.250	.125	15	-2	-2	1	1	0	0	.833	-3	O	-0.6
	Yr	76	105	6	23	5	0	1	16	7	14	.219	.274	.295	74	-4	-3	9	1	0	0	.963	-4	O	-0.9
Total	9	1011	3284	458	929	140	36	67	426	408	282	.283	.367	.409	118	78	88	517	42	21	0	.981	-51	O	-1.1

■ FRANK ROBINSON

Robinson, Frank b: 8/31/35, Beaumont, Tex. BR/TR, 6'1", 195 lbs. Deb: 4/17/56 MCH

YEAR	TM/L	G	AB	R	H	2B	3B	HR	RBI	BB	SO	AVG	OBP	SLG	PRO+	BR	/A	RC	SB	CS	SBR	FA	FR	POS	TPR
1956	Cin-N★	152	572	**122**	166	27	6	38	83	64	95	.290	.381	.558	139	39	34	121	8	4	0	.976	6	*O	3.2
1957	Cin-N★	150	611	97	197	29	5	29	75	44	92	.322	.379	.529	131	34	29	122	10	2	2	.989	19	*O1	4.1
1958	Cin-N	148	554	90	149	25	6	31	83	62	80	.269	.350	.504	116	17	13	99	10	1	2	.991	9	*O3	1.8
1959	Cin-N★	146	540	106	168	31	4	36	125	69	93	.311	.397	.583	152	44	42	122	18	8	1	.984	-9	*1O	2.4
1960	Cin-N	139	464	86	138	33	6	31	83	82	67	.297	.413	**.595**	169	**48**	47	113	13	6	0	.993	7	1O/3	4.6
1961	*Cin-N★	153	545	117	176	32	7	37	124	71	64	.323	.411	**.611**	164	**52**	**51**	**137**	22	3	**5**	.990	8	*O/3	**5.4**
1962	Cin-N★	162	609	**134**	208	**51**	2	39	136	76	62	.342	**.424**	**.624**	**172**	**67**	**64**	**160**	18	9	0	.994	9	*O	**6.2**
1963	Cin-N	140	482	79	125	19	3	21	91	81	69	.259	.381	.442	132	26	24	87	26	10	2	.984	5	*O/1	2.5
1964	Cin-N	156	568	103	174	38	6	29	96	79	67	.306	.399	.548	158	50	47	127	23	5	4	.986	4	*O	4.9
1965	Cin-N★	156	582	109	172	33	5	33	113	70	100	.296	.388	.540	148	46	41	120	13	9	-2	.990	3	*O	3.7
1966	*Bal-A★	155	576	**122**	182	34	2	**49**	**122**	87	90	**.316**	**.415**	**.637**	**200**	**74**	**75**	**146**	8	5	-1	.985	-4	*O/1	**6.6**
1967	Bal-A†	129	479	83	149	23	7	30	94	71	84	.311	.408	.576	189	53	54	113	2	3	-1	.990	-2	*O/1	4.8
1968	Bal-A	130	421	69	113	27	1	15	52	73	84	.268	.391	.444	153	30	30	77	11	2	2	.962	-8	*O/1	2.0
1969	*Bal-A★	148	539	111	166	19	5	32	100	88	62	.308	.417	.540	164	50	49	126	9	3	1	.987	-1	*O1	4.2
1970	*Bal-A★	132	471	88	144	24	1	25	78	69	70	.306	.402	.520	151	35	34	99	2	1	0	.987	6	*O/1	3.4
1971	*Bal-A★	133	455	82	128	16	2	28	99	72	62	.281	.390	.510	154	33	34	88	3	0	1	.973	-4	O1	2.4
1972	LA-N	103	342	41	86	6	1	19	59	55	76	.251	.358	.442	129	12	13	55	2	3	-1	.967	-2	O	0.7
1973	Cal-A	147	534	85	142	29	0	30	97	82	93	.266	.374	.489	153	30	36	99	1	1	-0	.976	4	*DO	3.8
1974	Cal-A★	129	427	75	107	26	2	20	63	75	85	.251	.375	.461	148	24	27	77	5	1	1	.000	-0	*D/O	2.8
	Cle-A	15	50	6	10	1	1	2	5	10	10	.200	.333	.380	106	0	1	7	0	1	-1	.958	-1	D/1	-0.1
	Yr	144	477	81	117	27	3	22	68	85	95	.245	.371	.453	143	24	27	85	5	2	0	.958	-1	*D/1O	2.7
1975	Cle-A	49	118	19	28	5	0	9	24	29	15	.237	.388	.508	152	9	9	25	0	0	0	.000	0	DM	0.9
1976	Cle-A	36	67	5	15	0	0	3	10	11	12	.224	.333	.358	104	0	1	8	0	0	0	1.000	-1	D/1OM	0.0
Total	21	2808	10006	1829	2943	528	72	586	1812	1420	1532	.294	.392	.537	154	773	754	2126	204	77	15	.984	47	*OD1/3	70.3

■ FRED ROBINSON

Robinson, Frederic Henry b: 7/6/1856, South Acton, Mass. d: 12/18/33, Hudson, Mass. BR/TR, Deb: 4/17/1884 F

YEAR	TM/L	G	AB	R	H	2B	3B	HR	RBI	BB	SO	AVG	OBP	SLG	PRO+	BR	/A	RC	SB	CS	SBR	FA	FR	POS	TPR
1884	Cin-U	3	13	1	3	0	0	0		0		.231	.231	.231	52	-1	-1	1				.727	-3	/2	-0.3

■ JACKIE ROBINSON

Robinson, Jack Roosevelt b: 1/31/19, Cairo, Ga. d: 10/24/72, Stamford, Conn. BR/TR, 5'11", 204 lbs. Deb: 4/15/47 H

YEAR	TM/L	G	AB	R	H	2B	3B	HR	RBI	BB	SO	AVG	OBP	SLG	PRO+	BR	/A	RC	SB	CS	SBR	FA	FR	POS	TPR
1947	*Bro-N	151	590	125	175	31	5	12	48	74	36	.297	.383	.427	111	14	11	104	**29**			.989	-3	*1	0.3
1948	Bro-N	147	574	108	170	38	8	12	85	57	37	.296	.367	.453	117	16	14	99	22			**.980**	1	*21/3	2.1
1949	*Bro-N★	156	593	122	203	38	12	16	124	86	27	**.342**	.432	.528	150	50	46	135	**37**			.981	-1	*2	5.1
1950	Bro-N★	144	518	99	170	39	4	14	81	80	24	.328	.423	.500	139	34	33	114	12			**.986**	11	*2	**4.7**
1951	Bro-N★	153	548	106	185	33	7	19	88	79	27	.338	.429	.527	153	46	44	133	25	8	3	**.992**	17	*2	**6.9**
1952	*Bro-N★	149	510	104	157	17	3	19	75	106	40	.308	**.440**	.465	149	42	41	116	24	7	3	.974	4	*2	**5.6**
1953	*Bro-N★	136	484	109	159	34	7	12	95	74	30	.329	.425	.502	137	32	30	111	17	4	3	.981	8	O3/21S	3.6
1954	Bro-N★	124	386	62	120	22	4	15	59	63	20	.311	.417	.505	135	24	22	83	7	3	0	1.000	-9	O3/2	1.1
1955	*Bro-N	105	317	51	81	6	2	8	36	61	18	.256	.381	.363	96	2	1	49	12	3	2	.966	7	3O/12	0.9
1956	*Bro-N	117	357	61	98	15	2	10	43	60	32	.275	.383	.412	106	9	5	60	12	5	1	.967	15	32/1O	2.3
Total	10	1382	4877	947	1518	273	54	137	734	740	291	.311	.410	.474	131	269	248	1002	197	30		.983	49	231O/S	32.6

■ JACK ROBINSON

Robinson, John W. "Bridgeport" b: 7/15/1880, Portland, Maine d: 7/22/21, Macon, Ga. TR , Deb: 9/06/02

YEAR	TM/L	G	AB	R	H	2B	3B	HR	RBI	BB	SO	AVG	OBP	SLG	PRO+	BR	/A	RC	SB	CS	SBR	FA	FR	POS	TPR
1902	NY-N	4	9	0	0	0	0	0	0	0		.000	.000	.000	-99	-2	-2	0	0			1.000	1	/C	-0.1

■ WILBERT ROBINSON

Robinson, Wilbert "Uncle Robby" b: 6/29/1863, Bolton, Mass. d: 8/8/34, Atlanta, Ga. BR/TR, 5'8.5", 215 lbs. Deb: 4/19/1886 FMCH

YEAR	TM/L	G	AB	R	H	2B	3B	HR	RBI	BB	SO	AVG	OBP	SLG	PRO+	BR	/A	RC	SB	CS	SBR	FA	FR	POS	TPR
1886	Phi-a	87	342	57	69	11	3	1		21		.202	.254	.260	62	-14	-15	32	33			.893	-10	C1/O	-1.8
1887	Phi-a	68	264	28	60	6	2	1		14		.227	.269	.277	54	-16	-16	24	15			.901	1	C/1O	-0.7
1888	Phi-a	66	254	32	62	7	2	1	31	9		.244	.270	.299	86	-4	-4	24	11			.938	25	C/1	2.5
1889	Phi-a	69	264	31	61	13	2	0	28	6	34	.231	.251	.295	58	-15	-15	22	9			.943	4	C	-0.4
1890	Phi-a	82	329	32	78	13	4	4		16		.237	.279	.337	86	-8	-7	37	20			.930	-9	C	-0.8
	Bal-a	14	48	7	13	1	0	0		3		.271	.314	.292	77	-1	-1	5	1			.989	6	C/1	0.5
	Yr	96	377	39	91	14	4	4		19		.241	.283	.332	84	-9	-8	42	21			.938	-3	C/1	-0.3
1891	Bal-a	93	334	25	72	8	5	2	46	16	37	.216	.251	.287	56	-20	-20	29	18			.954	3	C/O	-0.8
1892	Bal-N	90	330	36	88	14	4	2	57	15	35	.267	.303	.352	97	-1	-3	38	5			.921	-18	C/1O	-1.4
1893	Bal-N	95	359	49	120	21	3	3	57	26	22	.334	.382	.435	117	9	8	68	17			.942	-8	*C/1	0.7
1894	*Bal-N	109	414	69	146	21	4	1	98	46	18	.353	.421	.430	103	7	4	84	12			.944	-5	*C	0.7
1895	*Bal-N	77	282	38	74	19	1	0	48	12	19	.262	.295	.337	62	-15	-17	33	11			**.979**	14	C	0.4
1896	*Bal-N	67	245	43	85	9	6	2	38	14	13	.347	.385	.457	122	8	7	48	9			.948	2	C	1.4
1897	Bal-N	48	181	25	57	9	0	0	23	8		.315	.347	.365	88	-3	-3	24	0			.965	-2	C	0.0
1898	Bal-N	79	289	29	80	12	2	0	38	16		.277	.317	.332	85	-6	-6	33	3			.965	-5	C	-0.3

YEAR	TM/L	G	AB	R	H	2B	3B	HR	RBI	BB	SO	AVG	OBP	SLG	PRO+	BR	/A	RC	SB	CS	SBR	FA	FR	POS	TPR
1899	Bal-N	108	356	40	101	15	2	0	47	31		.284	.344	.337	83	-6	-9	45	5			.949	-18	*C	-1.7
1900	StL-N	60	210	26	52	5	1	0	28	11		.248	.291	.281	59	-12	-12	20	7			.974	-1	C	-0.7
1901	Bal-A	68	239	32	72	12	3	0	26	10		.301	.335	.377	93	-1	-3	34	9			.949	-1	C	0.2
1902	Bal-A	91	335	38	98	16	7	1	57	12		.293	.323	.391	93	-2	-4	47	11			.949	-15	CM	-0.9
Total	17	1371	5075	637	1388	212	51	18	622	286	178	.273	.316	.346	84	-102	-116	647	196			.941	-35	*C/1O	-3.1

■ EDDIE ROBINSON

Robinson, William Edward b: 12/15/20, Paris, Tex. BL/TR, 6'2.5", 210 lbs. Deb: 9/09/42 C

YEAR	TM/L	G	AB	R	H	2B	3B	HR	RBI	BB	SO	AVG	OBP	SLG	PRO+	BR	/A	RC	SB	CS	SBR	FA	FR	POS	TPR
1942	Cle-A	8	8	1	1	0	0	0	2	1	0	.125	.222	.125	-1	-1	-1	0	0	0	0	1.000	-0	/1	-0.1
1946	Cle-A	8	30	6	12	1	0	3	4	2	4	.400	.438	.733	238	5	5	10	0	0	0	.988	-2	/1	0.3
1947	Cle-A	95	318	52	78	10	1	14	52	30	18	.245	.314	.415	105	-1	0	41	1	0	0	.994	-2	1	-0.4
1948	*Cle-A	134	493	53	125	18	5	16	83	36	42	.254	.307	.408	91	-11	-9	61	1	0	0	**.995**	-1	*1	-1.0
1949	Was-A★	143	527	66	155	27	3	18	78	67	30	.294	.381	.459	125	16	17	93	3	4	-2	.987	-2	*1	1.2
1950	Was-A	36	129	21	30	4	2	1	13	25	4	.233	.365	.318	80	-4	-3	17	0	0	0	1.000	0	1	-0.4
	Chi-A	119	424	62	133	11	2	20	73	60	28	.314	.405	.491	132	19	20	90	0	0	0	.987	-7	*1	1.0
	Yr	155	553	83	163	15	4	21	86	85	32	.295	.395	.450	120	15	17	106	0	0	0	.990	-7	*1	0.6
1951	Chi-A★	151	564	85	159	23	5	29	117	77	54	.282	.371	.495	135	25	26	107	2	5	-2	.988	-6	*1	1.1
1952	Chi-A★	155	594	79	176	33	1	22	104	70	49	.296	.382	.466	134	28	28	113	2	0	1	.990	-8	*1	1.5
1953	Phi-A★	156	615	64	152	28	4	22	102	63	56	.247	.322	.413	94	-4	-7	84	1	2	-1	.988	-14	*1	-2.9
1954	NY-A	85	142	11	37	9	0	3	27	19	21	.261	.348	.387	105	0	1	21	0	0	0	.980	1	1	0.0
1955	*NY-A	88	173	25	36	1	0	16	42	36	26	.208	.360	.491	129	7	7	31	0	0	0	.995	-2	1	0.3
1956	NY-A	26	54	7	12	1	0	5	11	5	3	.222	.323	.519	123	1	1	9	0	1	-1	1.000	-0	1	0.0
	KC-A	75	172	13	34	5	1	2	12	26	20	.198	.310	.273	55	-11	-11	15	0	0	0	.977	-4	1	-1.7
	Yr	101	226	20	46	6	1	7	23	31	23	.204	.313	.332	71	-10	-10	24	0	1	-1	.983	-4	1	-1.7
1957	Det-A	13	9	0	0	0	0	0	0	3	0	.000	.308	.000	-9	-1	-1	0	0	0	0	1.000	0	/1	-0.1
	Cle-A	19	27	1	6	1	0	1	3	0	3	.222	.250	.370	68	-1	-1	2	0	0	0	1.000	0	/1	-0.1
	Bal-A	4	3	0	0	0	0	0	0	1	1	.000	.250	.000	-28	-1	-0	0	0	0	0	.000	0	H	0.0
	Yr	36	39	1	6	1	0	1	3	4	4	.154	.267	.256	44	-3	-3	2	0	0	0	1.000	1	/1	-0.2
Total	13	1315	4282	546	1146	172	24	172	723	521	359	.268	.354	.440	113	65	72	694	10	12	-4	.990	-45	*1	-1.3

■ YANK ROBINSON

Robinson, William H. b: 9/19/1859, Philadelphia, Pa. d: 8/25/1894, St.Louis, Mo. BR/TR, 5'6.5", 170 lbs. Deb: 8/24/1882

YEAR	TM/L	G	AB	R	H	2B	3B	HR	RBI	BB	SO	AVG	OBP	SLG	PRO+	BR	/A	RC	SB	CS	SBR	FA	FR	POS	TPR
1882	Det-N	11	39	1	7	1	0	0	2	1	13	.179	.200	.205	30	-3	-3	2				.800	-4	S/OP	-0.6
1884	Bal-U	102	415	101	111	24	4	2		**37**		.267	.327	.359	120	15	8	50				.831	16	3SCP/2	2.4
1885	*StL-a	78	287	63	75	8	8	0		29		.261	.344	.345	116	8	6	35				.862	-6	O2/C31	0.0
1886	*StL-a	133	481	89	132	26	9	3		64		.274	.377	.385	135	26	22	91	51			.888	-4	*2/3OSP	2.0
1887	*StL-a	125	430	102	131	32	4	1		92		.305	.445	.405	127	31	21	114	75			.899	-13	*2/3OSCP	0.9
1888	*StL-a	134	455	111	105	17	6	3	53	**116**		.231	**.400**	.314	121	27	18	82	56			.895	-44	*2S	-2.0
1889	StL-a	132	452	97	94	17	3	5	70	**118**	55	.208	.378	.292	83	4	-8	66	39			.887	-35	*2	-3.1
1890	Pit-P	98	306	59	70	10	3	0	38	101	33	.229	.434	.281	104	7	12	46	17			.887	-19	*2	-0.1
1891	Cin-a	97	342	48	61	9	4	1	37	68	51	.178	.328	.237	59	-12	-18	35	23			.867	-11	*2	-2.2
	StL-a	1	3	0	0	0	0	0	0	0	0	.000	.000	.000	-87	-1	-1	0	0			.750	-1	/2	-0.1
	Yr	98	345	48	61	9	4	1	37	68	51	.177	.325	.235	58	-13	-19	35	23			.866	-12	2	-2.3
1892	Was-N	67	218	26	39	4	3	0	19	38	28	.179	.301	.225	63	-9	-8	18	11			.852	-4	3/S2	-0.9
Total	10	978	3428	697	825	148	44	15	219	664	180	.241	.375	.323	105	92	49	538	272			.887	-125	23/SOCP1	-3.7

■ BILL ROBINSON

Robinson, William Henry b: 6/26/43, McKeesport, Pa. BR/TR, 6'3", 205 lbs. Deb: 9/20/66 C

YEAR	TM/L	G	AB	R	H	2B	3B	HR	RBI	BB	SO	AVG	OBP	SLG	PRO+	BR	/A	RC	SB	CS	SBR	FA	FR	POS	TPR
1966	Atl-N	6	11	1	3	0	1	0	3	0	1	.273	.273	.455	96	-0	-0	1	0	0	0	.800	-0	/O	-0.1
1967	NY-A	116	342	31	67	6	1	7	29	28	56	.196	.261	.281	62	-17	-16	24	2	2	-1	.968	-2	*O	-2.5
1968	NY-A	107	342	34	82	16	7	6	40	26	54	.240	.297	.380	107	1	2	36	7	6	-2	.985	-3	O	-0.8
1969	NY-A	87	222	23	38	11	2	3	21	16	39	.171	.227	.279	42	-18	-17	13	3	1	0	.963	-3	O/1	-2.5
1972	Phi-N	82	188	19	45	9	1	8	21	5	30	.239	.259	.426	89	-3	-4	16	2	3	-1	.982	-6	O	-1.4
1973	Phi-N	124	452	62	130	32	1	25	65	27	91	.288	.329	.529	131	18	17	74	5	4	-1	.979	2	*O3	1.3
1974	Phi-N	100	280	32	66	14	1	5	29	17	61	.236	.282	.346	72	-10	-12	24	5	3	-0	.971	3	O	-1.3
1975	*Pit-N	92	200	26	56	12	2	6	33	11	36	.280	.318	.450	112	2	2	27	3	1	0	.991	2	O	0.3
1976	Pit-N	122	393	55	119	22	3	21	64	16	73	.303	.332	.534	142	19	18	62	2	4	-2	.993	-8	O3/1	0.6
1977	Pit-N	137	507	74	154	32	1	26	104	25	92	.304	.340	.525	125	18	16	88	12	6	0	.992	-11	1O3	-0.2
1978	Pit-N	136	499	70	123	36	2	14	80	35	105	.246	.302	.411	93	-3	-6	60	14	11	-2	.988	-4	*O3/1	-1.9
1979	*Pit-N	148	421	59	111	17	6	24	75	24	81	.264	.305	.504	111	7	5	60	13	2	3	.982	-19	*O1/3	-1.8
1980	Pit-N	100	272	28	78	10	1	12	36	15	45	.287	.324	.463	116	5	5	36	1	4	-2	.985	-5	1O	-0.6
1981	Pit-N	39	88	8	19	3	0	2	8	5	18	.216	.258	.318	61	-5	-5	7	1	0	0	1.000	-1	1/O3	-0.7
1982	Pit-N	31	71	8	17	3	0	4	12	5	19	.239	.289	.451	101	0	-0	8	0	1	-1	1.000	0	O	-0.1
	Phi-N	35	69	6	18	6	0	3	19	7	15	.261	.329	.478	121	2	2	10	1	1	-0	.960	-0	O/1	0.1
	Yr	66	140	14	35	9	0	7	31	12	34	.250	.309	.464	111	2	2	18	1	2	-1	.984	0	O/1	0.0
1983	Phi-N	10	7	0	1	0	0	0	2	1	4	.143	.250	.143	12	-1	-1	0	0	0	0	1.000	-1	/13O	-0.2
Total	16	1472	4364	536	1127	229	29	166	641	263	820	.258	.303	.438	104	14	6	545	71	49	-8	.979	-55	*O13	-11.8

■ RAFAEL ROBLES

Robles, Rafael Orlando (Natera) b: 10/20/47, San Pedro De Macoris, D.R. BR/TR, 6', 170 lbs. Deb: 4/08/69

YEAR	TM/L	G	AB	R	H	2B	3B	HR	RBI	BB	SO	AVG	OBP	SLG	PRO+	BR	/A	RC	SB	CS	SBR	FA	FR	POS	TPR
1969	SD-N	6	20	1	2	0	0	0	0	1	3	.100	.143	.100	-32	-3	-3	0	1	1	-0	.895	-4	/S	-0.8
1970	SD-N	23	89	5	19	1	0	0	3	5	11	.213	.263	.225	33	-8	-8	6	3	0	1	.968	2	S	-0.3
1972	SD-N	18	24	1	4	0	0	0	0	0	3	.167	.167	.167	-5	-3	-3	1	0	0	0	.952	-2	S/3	-0.5
Total	3	47	133	7	25	1	0	0	3	6	17	.188	.229	.195	17	-15	-14	7	4	1	1	.958	-4	/S3	-1.6

■ SERGIO ROBLES

Robles, Sergio (Valenzuela) b: 4/16/46, Magdalena, Mexico BR/TR, 6'2", 190 lbs. Deb: 8/27/72

YEAR	TM/L	G	AB	R	H	2B	3B	HR	RBI	BB	SO	AVG	OBP	SLG	PRO+	BR	/A	RC	SB	CS	SBR	FA	FR	POS	TPR
1972	Bal-A	2	5	0	1	0	0	0	0	0	0	.200	.200	.200	19	-0	-1	0	0	0	0	1.000	-1	/C	-0.2
1973	Bal-A	8	13	0	1	0	0	0	0	3	1	.077	.250	.077	-4	-2	-2	0	0	0	0	1.000	3	/C	0.1
1976	LA-N	6	3	0	0	0	0	0	0	0	2	.000	.000	.000	-99	-1	-1	0	0	0	0	1.000	1	/C	0.0
Total	3	16	21	0	2	0	0	0	0	3	3	.095	.208	.095	-11	-3	-3	1	0	0	0	1.000	2	/C	-0.1

■ TOM ROBSON

Robson, Thomas James b: 1/15/46, Rochester, N.Y. BR/TR, 6'3", 215 lbs. Deb: 9/14/74 C

YEAR	TM/L	G	AB	R	H	2B	3B	HR	RBI	BB	SO	AVG	OBP	SLG	PRO+	BR	/A	RC	SB	CS	SBR	FA	FR	POS	TPR
1974	Tex-A	6	13	2	3	1	0	0	2	4	3	.231	.412	.308	112	0	0	2	0	0	0	1.000	-0	/1D	0.0
1975	Tex-A	17	35	3	7	0	0	0	2	1	3	.200	.222	.200	20	-4	-4	1	0	0	0	1.000	-0	/1D	-0.4
Total	2	23	48	5	10	1	0	0	4	5	6	.208	.283	.229	48	-3	-3	3	0	0	0	1.000	-0	/D1	-0.4

■ ADAM ROCAP

Rocap, Adam b: 1854, Philadelphia, Pa. d: 3/29/1892, Philadelphia, Pa. 5'9", 170 lbs. Deb: 5/05/1875

YEAR	TM/L	G	AB	R	H	2B	3B	HR	RBI	BB	SO	AVG	OBP	SLG	PRO+	BR	/A	RC	SB	CS	SBR	FA	FR	POS	TPR
1875	Ath-n	16	70	13	12	0	0	0		0		.171	.171	.171	17	-5	-7	2						O/2	-0.6

■ MIKE ROCCO

Rocco, Michael Dominick b: 3/2/16, St.Paul, Minn. BL/TL, 5'11", 188 lbs. Deb: 6/05/43

YEAR	TM/L	G	AB	R	H	2B	3B	HR	RBI	BB	SO	AVG	OBP	SLG	PRO+	BR	/A	RC	SB	CS	SBR	FA	FR	POS	TPR
1943	Cle-A	108	405	43	97	14	4	5	46	51	40	.240	.328	.331	99	-3	-0	47	1	2	-1	**.995**	-5	*1	-1.4
1944	Cle-A	155	653	87	174	29	7	13	70	56	51	.266	.325	.392	108	2	5	84	4	8	-4	.993	17	*1	1.1
1945	Cle-A	143	565	81	149	28	6	10	56	52	40	.264	.326	.388	111	3	6	72	0	4	-2	**.992**	4	*1	-0.2
1946	Cle-A	34	98	8	24	2	0	2	14	15	15	.245	.345	.327	94	-1	-0	12	1	1	-0	.996	5	1	0.3
Total	4	440	1721	219	444	73	17	30	186	174	146	.258	.327	.372	106	1	11	215	6	15	-7	.994	21	1	-0.2

■ JACK ROCHE

Roche, John Joseph "Red" b: 11/22/1890, Los Angeles, Cal. d: 3/30/83, Peoria, Ariz. BR/TR, 6'1", 178 lbs. Deb: 5/24/14

YEAR	TM/L	G	AB	R	H	2B	3B	HR	RBI	BB	SO	AVG	OBP	SLG	PRO+	BR	/A	RC	SB	CS	SBR	FA	FR	POS	TPR
1914	StL-N	12	9	1	6	2	1	0	3	0	1	.667	.700	1.111	441	4	4	7	1			.667	-2	/C	0.2
1915	StL-N	46	39	2	8	0	1	0	6	4	8	.205	.295	.256	68	-1	-1	3	1			1.000	0	/C	-0.1

YEAR	TM/L	G	AB	R	H	2B	3B	HR	RBI	BB	SO	AVG	OBP	SLG	PRO+	BR	/A	RC	SB	CS	SBR	FA	FR	POS	TPR
1917	StL-N	1	1	0	0	0	0	0	0	0	0	.000	.000	.000	-99	-0	-0	0	0			.000	-1	/C	-0.1
Total	3	59	49	3	14	2	2	0	9	4	9	.286	.364	.408	133	2	2	11	2			.750	-2	/C	0.0

■ BEN ROCHEFORT Rochefort, Bennett Harold (b: Bennett Harold Rochefort Gilbert) b: 8/15/1896, Camden, N.J. d: 4/2/81, Red Bank, N.J. BL/TR, 6'2", 185 lbs. Deb: 10/03/14

YEAR	TM/L	G	AB	R	H	2B	3B	HR	RBI	BB	SO	AVG	OBP	SLG	PRO+	BR	/A	RC	SB	CS	SBR	FA	FR	POS	TPR
1914	Phi-A	1	2	0	1	0	0	0	0	0	1	.500	.500	.500	209	0	0	1	0			1.000	0	/1	0.1

■ LOU ROCHELLI Rochelli, Louis Joseph b: 1/11/19, Williamson, Ill. BR/TR, 6'1", 175 lbs. Deb: 8/25/44

YEAR	TM/L	G	AB	R	H	2B	3B	HR	RBI	BB	SO	AVG	OBP	SLG	PRO+	BR	/A	RC	SB	CS	SBR	FA	FR	POS	TPR
1944	Bro-N	5	17	0	3	0	1	0	2	2	6	.176	.263	.294	58	-1	-1	1	0			.964	-0	/2	-0.1

■ LES ROCK Rock, Lester Henry (b: Lester Henry Schwarzrock) b: 8/19/12, Springfield, Minn. d: 9/9/91, Davis, Cal. BL/TR, 6'2", 184 lbs. Deb: 9/11/36

YEAR	TM/L	G	AB	R	H	2B	3B	HR	RBI	BB	SO	AVG	OBP	SLG	PRO+	BR	/A	RC	SB	CS	SBR	FA	FR	POS	TPR
1936	Chi-A	2	1	0	0	0	0	0	1	0	0	.000	.000	.000	-97	-0	-0	0	0	0	0	.000	0	/1	0.0

■ IKE ROCKENFIELD Rockenfield, Isaac Broc b: 11/3/1876, Omaha, Neb. d: 2/21/27, San Diego, Cal. BR/TR, 5'7", 150 lbs. Deb: 5/05/05

YEAR	TM/L	G	AB	R	H	2B	3B	HR	RBI	BB	SO	AVG	OBP	SLG	PRO+	BR	/A	RC	SB	CS	SBR	FA	FR	POS	TPR
1905	StL-A	95	322	40	70	12	0	0	16	46		.217	.339	.255	94	-1	1	36	11			.926	-9	2	-0.7
1906	StL-A	27	89	3	21	4	0	0	8	1		.236	.277	.281	78	-3	-2	8	0			.956	-5	2	-0.8
Total	2	122	411	43	91	16	0	0	24	47		.221	.326	.260	91	-3	-1	44	11			.933	-14	2	-1.5

■ PAT ROCKETT Rockett, Patrick Edward b: 1/9/55, San Antonio, Tex. BR/TR, 5'11", 170 lbs. Deb: 9/17/76

YEAR	TM/L	G	AB	R	H	2B	3B	HR	RBI	BB	SO	AVG	OBP	SLG	PRO+	BR	/A	RC	SB	CS	SBR	FA	FR	POS	TPR
1976	Atl-N	4	5	0	1	0	0	0	0	0	1	.200	.200	.200	13	-1	-1	0	0	0	0	1.000	-1	/S	-0.2
1977	Atl-N	93	264	27	67	10	0	1	24	27	32	.254	.330	.303	64	-10	-14	26	1	2	-1	.940	-11	S	-1.7
1978	Atl-N	55	142	6	20	2	0	0	4	13	12	.141	.213	.155	4	-18	-20	4	1	2	-1	.970	-10	S	-2.8
Total	3	152	411	33	88	12	0	1	28	40	45	.214	.289	.251	43	-29	-34	31	2	4	-2	.949	-21	S	-4.7

■ ANDRE RODGERS Rodgers, Kenneth Andre Ian "Andy" b: 12/2/34, Nassau, Bahamas BR/TR, 6'3", 200 lbs. Deb: 4/16/57

YEAR	TM/L	G	AB	R	H	2B	3B	HR	RBI	BB	SO	AVG	OBP	SLG	PRO+	BR	/A	RC	SB	CS	SBR	FA	FR	POS	TPR
1957	NY-N	32	86	8	21	2	1	3	9	9	21	.244	.323	.395	92	-1	-1	12	0	0	0	.950	5	S/3	0.6
1958	SF-N	22	63	7	13	3	1	2	11	4	14	.206	.254	.381	67	-3	-3	6	0	0	0	.972	-3	S	-0.5
1959	SF-N	71	228	32	57	12	1	6	24	32	50	.250	.345	.390	98	-1	-0	32	2	1	0	.933	-9	S	-0.4
1960	SF-N	81	217	22	53	8	5	2	22	24	44	.244	.328	.355	92	-4	-2	25	1	1	-0	.953	-4	S3/1O	-0.4
1961	Chi-N	73	214	27	57	17	0	6	23	25	54	.266	.346	.430	103	1	1	31	1	1	-0	.983	1	1S/O2	0.0
1962	Chi-N	138	461	40	128	20	8	5	44	44	93	.278	.344	.388	93	-2	-4	60	5	6	-2	.960	7	*S/1	1.3
1963	Chi-N	150	516	51	118	17	4	5	33	65	90	.229	.325	.306	79	-9	-13	52	5	7	-3	.954	-3	*S	-0.8
1964	Chi-N	129	448	50	107	17	3	12	46	53	88	.239	.319	.371	90	-3	-5	55	5	1	1	.965	19	*S	2.4
1965	Pit-N	75	178	17	51	12	0	2	25	18	28	.287	.352	.388	108	2	2	24	2	1	0	.950	-6	S3/12	-0.2
1966	Pit-N	36	49	6	9	1	0	0	4	8	7	.184	.298	.204	43	-4	-4	3	0	1	-1	.913	-1	/S3O1	-0.5
1967	Pit-N	47	61	8	14	3	0	2	4	8	18	.230	.319	.377	98	-0	-0	7	1	1	-0	1.000	2	/13S2	0.2
Total	11	854	2521	268	628	112	23	45	245	290	507	.249	.331	.365	90	-23	-29	305	22	20	-5	.956	9	S/13O2	1.7

■ BOB RODGERS Rodgers, Robert Leroy b: 8/16/38, Delaware, Ohio BB/TR, 6'2", 195 lbs. Deb: 9/08/61 MC

YEAR	TM/L	G	AB	R	H	2B	3B	HR	RBI	BB	SO	AVG	OBP	SLG	PRO+	BR	/A	RC	SB	CS	SBR	FA	FR	POS	TPR
1961	LA-A	16	56	8	18	2	0	2	13	1	6	.321	.333	.464	99	1	-0	7	0	0	0	.965	-1	C	0.0
1962	LA-A	155	565	65	146	34	6	6	61	45	68	.258	.313	.372	86	-14	-11	61	1	8	-5	.989	1	*C	-0.9
1963	LA-A	100	300	24	70	6	0	4	23	29	35	.233	.305	.293	73	-12	-10	28	2	2	-1	.979	-14	C	-2.3
1964	LA-A	148	514	38	125	18	3	4	54	40	71	.243	.303	.313	80	-19	-13	47	4	3	-1	.987	14	*C	0.7
1965	Cal-A	132	411	33	86	14	3	1	32	35	61	.209	.276	.265	56	-24	-23	28	4	5	-2	.991	6	*C	-1.4
1966	Cal-A	133	454	45	107	20	3	7	48	29	57	.236	.285	.339	81	-13	-12	41	3	4	-2	.992	-4	*C	-1.0
1967	Cal-A	139	429	29	94	13	3	6	41	34	55	.219	.280	.305	76	-15	-13	35	1	4	-2	.991	2	*C/O	-0.6
1968	Cal-A	91	258	13	49	6	0	1	14	16	48	.190	.245	.225	45	-17	-16	15	2	1	0	.985	0	C	-1.3
1969	Cal-A	18	46	4	9	1	0	0	2	5	8	.196	.288	.217	46	-3	-3	3	0	0	0	1.000	-0	C	-0.3
Total	9	932	3033	259	704	114	18	31	288	234	409	.232	.291	.312	74	-117	-101	265	17	27	-11	.988	3	C/O	-7.1

■ BILL RODGERS Rodgers, Wilbur Kincaid "Rawmeat Bill" b: 4/18/1887, Pleasant Ridge, O. d: 12/24/78, Goliad, Tex. BL/TR, 5'9.5", 170 lbs. Deb: 4/15/15

YEAR	TM/L	G	AB	R	H	2B	3B	HR	RBI	BB	SO	AVG	OBP	SLG	PRO+	BR	/A	RC	SB	CS	SBR	FA	FR	POS	TPR
1915	Cle-A	16	45	8	14	2	0	0	7	8	7	.311	.415	.356	128	2	2	7	3	3	-1	.945	-4	2	-0.3
	Bos-A	11	6	2	0	0	0	0	0	3	2	.000	.333	.000	-0	-1	-0	0	0			.900	1	/2	0.1
	Yr	27	51	10	14	2	0	0	7	11	9	.275	.403	.314	115	2	2	7	3	3	-1	.938	-3	2	-0.2
	Cin-N	72	213	20	51	13	4	0	12	11	29	.239	.299	.338	91	-2	-3	22	8	5	-1	.947	5	2/S3O	0.3
1916	Cin-N	3	4	0	0	0	0	0	0	0	2	.000	.000	.000	-99	-1	-1	0	0			1.000	-0	/S	-0.2
Total	2	102	268	30	65	15	4	0	19	22	40	.243	.316	.328	93	-1	-2	29	11	8		.945	2	/2SO3	-0.1

■ BILL RODGERS Rodgers, William Sherman b: 12/5/22, Harrisburg, Pa. BL/TL, 6', 162 lbs. Deb: 9/27/44

YEAR	TM/L	G	AB	R	H	2B	3B	HR	RBI	BB	SO	AVG	OBP	SLG	PRO+	BR	/A	RC	SB	CS	SBR	FA	FR	POS	TPR
1944	Pit-N	2	4	1	1	0	0	0	0	0	1	.250	.250	.250	39	-0	-0	0	0			.000	-1	/O	-0.1
1945	Pit-N	1	1	0	1	0	0	0	0	0	0	1.000	1.000	1.000	440	0	0	1	0			.000	0	H	0.0
Total	2	3	5	1	2	0	0	0	0	0	1	.400	.400	.400	120	0	0	1	0			.963	-1	/O	-0.1

■ ERIC RODIN Rodin, Eric Chapman b: 2/5/30, Orange, N.J. d: 1/4/91, Somerville, N.J. BR/TR, 6'2", 215 lbs. Deb: 9/07/54

YEAR	TM/L	G	AB	R	H	2B	3B	HR	RBI	BB	SO	AVG	OBP	SLG	PRO+	BR	/A	RC	SB	CS	SBR	FA	FR	POS	TPR
1954	NY-N	5	6	0	0	0	0	0	0	0	2	.000	.000	.000	-99	-2	-2	0	0	0	0	1.000	-1	/O	-0.3

■ AURELIO RODRIGUEZ Rodriguez, Aurelio (Ituarte) b: 12/28/47, Cananea, Sonora, Mex BR/TR, 5'10", 180 lbs. Deb: 9/01/67

YEAR	TM/L	G	AB	R	H	2B	3B	HR	RBI	BB	SO	AVG	OBP	SLG	PRO+	BR	/A	RC	SB	CS	SBR	FA	FR	POS	TPR
1967	Cal-A	29	130	14	31	3	1	1	8	2	21	.238	.250	.300	64	-6	-6	10	1	0	0	.989	5	3	-0.2
1968	Cal-A	76	223	14	54	10	1	1	16	17	36	.242	.299	.309	88	-4	-3	19	0	2	-1	.921	-7	3/2	-1.2
1969	Cal-A	159	561	47	130	17	2	7	49	32	88	.232	.276	.307	66	-29	-26	45	5	3	-0	.954	8	*3	-1.8
1970	Cal-A	17	63	6	17	2	2	0	7	3	6	.270	.313	.365	90	-1	-1	6	0	1	-1	1.000	4	3	0.2
	Was-A	142	547	64	135	31	5	19	76	37	81	.247	.303	.426	104	-3	0	67	15	5	2	.961	13	*3/S	1.5
	Yr	159	610	70	152	33	7	19	83	40	87	.249	.304	.420	102	-4	-1	73	15	6	1	.965	17	*3/S	1.7
1971	Det-A	154	604	68	153	30	7	15	39	27	93	.253	.289	.401	90	-8	-10	65	4	6	-2	.953	15	*3/S	0.1
1972	*Det-A	153	601	65	142	23	5	13	56	28	104	.236	.273	.356	83	-12	-14	55	2	3	-1	.969	24	*3/S	0.8
1973	Det-A	160	555	46	123	27	3	9	58	31	85	.222	.267	.330	63	-25	-30	48	3	1	0	.971	10	*3/S	-2.1
1974	Det-A	159	571	54	127	23	5	5	49	26	70	.222	.258	.306	60	-29	-31	43	2	0	1	.961	22	*3	-1.1
1975	Det-A	151	507	47	124	20	6	13	60	30	63	.245	.287	.385	85	-10	-12	55	1	1	-0	.953	21	*3	0.8
1976	Det-A	128	480	40	115	13	2	8	50	19	61	.240	.270	.325	71	-17	-19	37	0	4	-2	**.978**	13	*3	-1.0
1977	Det-A	96	306	30	67	14	1	10	32	16	36	.219	.258	.369	65	-14	-16	27	1	1	-0	.972	16	3/S	-0.1
1978	Det-A	134	385	40	102	25	2	7	43	19	37	.265	.305	.395	93	-3	-5	44	0	1	-1	**.987**	2	*3	-0.5
1979	Det-A	106	343	27	87	18	0	5	36	11	40	.254	.279	.350	66	-16	-17	31	0	2	-1	.956	6	*3/1	-1.3
1980	SD-N	89	175	7	35	7	2	2	13	6	26	.200	.227	.297	48	-13	-12	11	1	1	-0	.965	10	3/S	-0.3
	*NY-A	52	164	14	36	6	1	3	14	7	35	.220	.251	.323	57	-10	-10	12	0	0	0	.954	-5	3/2	-1.5
1981	*NY-A	27	52	4	18	2	0	2	8	2	10	.346	.370	.500	151	3	3	9	0	0	0	.951	4	3/21D	0.7
1982	Chi-A	118	257	24	62	15	1	3	31	11	35	.241	.275	.342	68	-11	-11	23	0	0	0	.969	19	*3/2S	0.6
1983	Bal-A	45	67	0	8	0	0	0	2	0	13	.119	.132	.119	-31	-12	-12	1	0	0	0	.969	2	3	-1.0
	*Chi-A	22	20	1	4	1	0	1	1	0	3	.200	.200	.400	58	-1	-1	1	0	0	0	1.000	4	3	0.3
	Yr	67	87	1	12	1	0	1	3	0	16	.138	.148	.184	-9	-13	-13	2	0	0	0	.978	6	3	-0.7
Total	17	2017	6611	612	1570	287	46	124	648	324	943	.237	.276	.351	75	-223	-234	610	35	31	-8	.964	184	*3/S2D1	-7.1

■ CARLOS RODRIGUEZ Rodriguez, Carlos (Marquez) b: 11/1/67, Mexico City, Mexico BB/TR, 5'9", 160 lbs. Deb: 6/16/91

YEAR	TM/L	G	AB	R	H	2B	3B	HR	RBI	BB	SO	AVG	OBP	SLG	PRO+	BR	/A	RC	SB	CS	SBR	FA	FR	POS	TPR
1991	NY-A	15	37	1	7	0	0	0	2	1	2	.189	.211	.189	11	-4	-4	1	0	0	0	.957	1	S/2	-0.3

■ EDWIN RODRIGUEZ Rodriguez, Edwin (Morales) b: 8/14/60, Ponce, P.R. BR/TR, 5'11", 175 lbs. Deb: 9/28/82

YEAR	TM/L	G	AB	R	H	2B	3B	HR	RBI	BB	SO	AVG	OBP	SLG	PRO+	BR	/A	RC	SB	CS	SBR	FA	FR	POS	TPR
1982	NY-A	3	9	2	3	0	0	0	1	1	1	.333	.400	.333	106	0	0	1	0	0	0	.875	1	/2	0.1

YEAR	TM/L	G	AB	R	H	2B	3B	HR	RBI	BB	SO	AVG	OBP	SLG	PRO+	BR	/A	RC	SB	CS	SBR	FA	FR	POS	TPR
1983	SD-N	7	12	1	2	1	0	0	0	1	3	.167	.231	.250	34	-1	-1	1	0	0	0	1.000	-1	/2S3	-0.2
1985	SD-N	1	1	0	0	0	0	0	0	0	0	.000	.000	.000	-99	-0	-0	0	0	0	0	.000	0	/H	0.0
Total	3	11	22	3	5	1	0	0	1	2	4	.227	.292	.273	58	-1	-1	2	0	0	0	.935	0	/2S3	-0.1
■ ELLIE RODRIGUEZ	Rodriguez, Eliseo (Delgado) b: 5/24/46, Fajardo, P.R. BR/TR, 5'11", 185 lbs. Deb: 5/26/68																								
1968	NY-A	9	24	1	5	0	0	0	1	3	3	.208	.296	.208	57	-1	-1	2	0	0	0	1.000	0	/C	0.0
1969	KC-A☆	95	267	27	63	10	0	2	20	31	26	.236	.333	.296	77	-7	-7	27	3	2	-0	.990	-8	C	-1.2
1970	KC-A	80	231	25	52	8	2	1	15	27	35	.225	.317	.290	68	-9	-9	21	2	1	0	.988	12	C	0.6
1971	Mil-A	115	319	28	67	10	1	1	30	41	51	.210	.315	.257	64	-14	-13	27	1	1	-0	.992	6	*C	-0.4
1972	Mil-A☆	116	355	31	101	14	2	2	35	52	43	.285	.386	.352	123	12	13	51	1	4	-2	.983	-11	*C	0.5
1973	Mil-A	94	290	30	78	8	1	0	30	41	28	.269	.378	.303	96	0	1	36	4	3	-1	.986	4	CD	0.8
1974	Cal-A	140	395	48	100	20	0	7	36	69	56	.253	.376	.357	119	9	12	56	4	5	-2	.992	-10	*C/D	0.7
1975	Cal-A	90	226	20	53	6	0	3	27	49	37	.235	.384	.301	103	2	4	30	2	2	-1	.991	-7	C	0.0
1976	LA-N	36	66	10	14	0	0	0	9	19	12	.212	.409	.212	82	-0	0	8	0	0	0	.986	4	C	0.6
Total	9	775	2173	220	533	76	6	16	203	332	291	.245	.359	.308	94	-8	-0	258	17	18	-6	.989	-10	C/D	1.6
■ HECTOR RODRIGUEZ	Rodriguez, Hector Antonio (Ordenana) b: 6/13/20, Alquizar, Cuba BR/TR, 5'8", 165 lbs. Deb: 4/15/52																								
1952	Chi-A	124	407	55	108	14	0	1	40	47	22	.265	.346	.307	82	-8	-8	45	7	6	-2	.959	3	*3	-1.0
■ HENRY RODRIGUEZ	Rodriguez, Henry Anderson (Lorenzo) b: 11/8/67, Santo Domingo, D.R. BL/TL, 6'1", 180 lbs. Deb: 7/05/92																								
1992	LA-N	53	146	11	32	7	0	3	14	8	30	.219	.260	.329	67	-7	-7	12	0	0	0	.960	1	O/1	-0.7
■ IVAN RODRIGUEZ	Rodriguez, Ivan (Torres) b: 11/27/71, Manati, P.R. BR/TR, 5'9", 165 lbs. Deb: 6/20/91																								
1991	Tex-A	88	280	24	74	16	0	3	27	5	42	.264	.277	.354	75	-11	-10	24	0	1	-1	.983	14	C	0.8
1992	Tex-A★	123	420	39	109	16	1	8	37	24	73	.260	.301	.360	87	-10	-8	42	0	0	0	.983	8	*C/D	0.7
Total	2	211	700	63	183	32	1	11	64	29	115	.261	.292	.357	82	-20	-18	66	0	1	-1	.983	22	C/D	1.5
■ JOSE RODRIGUEZ	Rodriguez, Jose "El Hombre Goma" b: 2/23/1894, Havana, Cuba d: 1/21/53, Havana, Cuba BR/TR, 5'8", 150 lbs. Deb: 10/05/16																								
1916	NY-N	1	0	0	0	0	0	0	0	0	0	—	—	—	—	0	0	0	0			.000	0	R	0.0
1917	NY-N	7	20	2	4	0	1	0	2	2	1	.200	.273	.300	78	-1	-1	2	2			1.000	-1	/1	-0.2
1918	NY-N	50	125	15	20	0	2	0	15	12	3	.160	.239	.192	33	-10	-10	7	6			.978	4	2/13	-0.4
Total	3	58	145	17	24	0	3	0	17	14	4	.166	.244	.207	39	-10	-10	9	8			.989	3	/213	-0.6
■ RUBEN RODRIGUEZ	Rodriguez, Ruben Dario (Martinez) b: 8/4/64, Cabrera, D.R. BR/TR, 6'3", 190 lbs. Deb: 9/17/86																								
1986	Pit-N	2	3	0	0	0	0	0	0	0	1	.000	.000	.000	-98	-1	-1	0	0	0	0	1.000	1	/C	0.0
1988	Pit-N	2	5	1	1	0	1	0	1	0	2	.200	.200	.600	123	0	0	1	0	0	0	1.000	0	/C	0.0
Total	2	4	8	1	1	0	1	0	1	0	3	.125	.125	.375	36	-1	-1	1	0	0	0	1.000	1	/C	0.0
■ VIC RODRIGUEZ	Rodriguez, Victor Manuel (Rivera) b: 7/14/61, New York, N.Y. BR/TR, 5'11", 173 lbs. Deb: 9/05/84																								
1984	Bal-A	11	17	4	7	3	0	0	2	0	2	.412	.412	.588	177	2	2	4	0	0	0	.958	2	/2D	0.3
1989	Min-A	6	11	2	5	2	0	0	0	0	1	.455	.455	.636	191	1	1	3	0	0	0	.900	1	/3D	0.2
Total	2	17	28	6	12	5	0	0	2	0	3	.429	.429	.607	183	3	3	7	0	0	0	.916	3	/23D	0.5
■ GARY ROENICKE	Roenicke, Gary Steven b: 12/5/54, Covina, Cal. BR/TR, 6'3", 205 lbs. Deb: 6/08/76 F																								
1976	Mon-N	29	90	9	20	3	1	2	5	4	18	.222	.263	.344	69	-4	-4	8	0	0	0	.955	-1	O	-0.7
1978	Bal-A	27	58	5	15	3	0	3	15	8	3	.259	.358	.466	138	2	3	9	0	1	-1	1.000	-3	O	-0.1
1979	*Bal-A	133	376	60	98	16	1	25	64	61	74	.261	.381	.508	143	21	23	73	1	3	-2	.981	-8	*O	0.9
1980	Bal-A	118	297	40	71	13	0	10	28	41	49	.239	.343	.384	100	0	1	40	2	0	1	**1.000**	-13	*O	-1.5
1981	Bal-A	85	219	31	59	16	0	3	20	23	29	.269	.344	.384	110	3	3	26	1	2	-1	.983	-13	O	-1.4
1982	Bal-A	137	393	58	106	25	1	21	74	70	73	.270	.392	.499	143	25	25	79	6	7	-2	.990	-9	*O1	1.1
1983	*Bal-A	115	323	45	84	13	0	19	64	30	35	.260	.331	.477	121	8	9	49	2	2	-1	.982	-14	*O/13D	-0.9
1984	Bal-A	121	326	36	73	19	1	10	44	58	43	.224	.348	.380	104	2	3	45	1	2	-1	.995	-10	*O	-1.1
1985	Bal-A	114	225	36	49	9	0	15	43	44	36	.218	.346	.458	121	6	7	37	2	2	-1	.993	-8	OD	-0.3
1986	NY-A	69	136	11	36	5	0	3	18	27	30	.265	.390	.368	109	3	3	22	1	1	-0	1.000	-6	OD/31	-0.4
1987	Atl-N	67	151	25	33	8	0	9	28	32	23	.219	.359	.450	107	3	2	26	0	0	0	.968	-4	O/1	-0.3
1988	Atl-N	49	114	11	26	5	0	1	7	8	15	.228	.279	.298	63	-5	-6	9	0	0	0	1.000	-4	O/1	-1.2
Total	12	1064	2708	367	670	135	4	121	410	406	428	.247	.354	.434	117	65	69	424	16	20	-7	.988	-93	O/D13	-5.9
■ RON ROENICKE	Roenicke, Ronald Jon b: 8/19/56, Covina, Cal. BB/TL, 6', 180 lbs. Deb: 9/02/81 F																								
1981	LA-N	22	47	6	11	0	0	0	0	6	8	.234	.321	.234	62	-2	-2	4	1	1	-0	1.000	3	O	0.0
1982	LA-N	109	143	18	37	8	0	1	12	21	32	.259	.361	.336	99	0	1	20	5	0	2	.984	-2	O	-0.1
1983	LA-N	81	145	12	32	4	0	2	12	14	26	.221	.289	.290	61	-8	-7	12	3	2	-0	.987	-0	O	-1.0
	Sea-A	59	198	23	50	12	0	4	23	33	22	.253	.365	.374	100	2	1	30	6	2	1	.993	7	O/1D	0.7
1984	*SD-N	12	20	4	6	1	0	1	2	2	5	.300	.364	.500	141	1	1	4	0	0	0	1.000	-2	O	-0.2
1985	SF-N	65	133	23	34	9	1	3	13	35	27	.256	.411	.406	136	7	8	26	6	2	1	.984	-1	O	0.7
1986	Phi-N	102	275	42	68	13	1	5	42	61	52	.247	.384	.356	102	5	3	42	2	2	-1	.989	-2	O	-0.1
1987	Phi-N	63	78	9	13	3	1	1	4	14	15	.167	.293	.269	49	-5	-6	7	1	0	0	.964	-6	O	-1.2
1988	Cin-N	14	37	4	5	1	0	0	5	4	8	.135	.238	.162	16	-4	-4	2	0	0	0	1.000	-2	O	-0.7
Total	8	527	1076	141	256	51	3	17	113	190	195	.238	.355	.338	92	-4	-5	146	24	9	2	.989	-6	O/1D	-1.9
■ OSCAR ROETTGER	Roettger, Oscar Frederick Louis "Okkie" b: 2/19/1900, St.Louis, Mo. d: 7/4/86, St.Louis, Mo. BR/TR, 6', 170 lbs. Deb: 7/07/23 F																								
1923	NY-A	5	2	0	0	0	0	0	0	0	0	.000	.000	.000	-98	-1	-1	0	0	0	0	1.000	0	/P	0.0
1924	NY-A	1	0	0	0	0	0	0	0	0	0	—	—	—	—	0	0	0	0	0	0	.000	0	/P	0.0
1927	Bro-N	5	4	0	0	0	0	0	0	1	1	.000	.333	.000	-4	-0	-0	0	0			.000	-1	/O	-0.1
1932	Phi-A	26	60	7	14	1	0	0	6	5	4	.233	.292	.250	40	-5	-5	5	0	0	0	.978	-2	1	-0.7
Total	4	37	66	7	14	1	0	0	6	6	5	.212	.288	.227	34	-6	-6	5	0	0		1.000	-2	/1PO	-0.8
■ WALLY ROETTGER	Roettger, Walter Henry b: 8/28/02, St.Louis, Mo. d: 9/14/51, Champaign, Ill. BR/TR, 6'1.5", 190 lbs. Deb: 5/01/27 F																								
1927	StL-N	5	1	0	0	0	0	0	0	1	0	.000	.500	.000	42	0	0	0	0			.500	-1	/O	-0.1
1928	StL-N	68	261	27	89	17	4	6	44	10	22	.341	.372	.506	125	9	9	47	2			.981	-1	O	0.4
1929	StL-N	79	269	27	68	11	3	3	42	13	27	.253	.287	.349	56	-19	-19	26	0			.993	-4	O	-2.6
1930	NY-N	121	420	51	119	15	5	5	51	25	29	.283	.330	.379	72	-20	-19	51	1			**.992**	-6	*O	-2.8
1931	Cin-N	44	185	25	65	11	4	1	20	7	9	.351	.378	.470	135	7	8	33	1			.990	-1	O	0.4
	*StL-N	45	151	16	43	12	2	0	17	9	14	.285	.337	.391	92	-1	-2	21	0			.974	-6	O	-1.1
	Yr	89	336	41	108	23	6	1	37	16	23	.321	.360	.435	114	6	6	53	1			.983	-7	O	-0.7
1932	Cin-N	106	347	26	96	18	3	3	43	23	24	.277	.323	.372	89	-7	-5	43	0			.991	-1	O	-1.2
1933	Cin-N	84	209	13	50	7	1	1	17	8	10	.239	.267	.297	62	-11	-10	15	0			.977	0	O	-1.4
1934	Pit-N	47	106	7	26	5	1	0	11	3	8	.245	.266	.311	53	-7	-7	8	0			1.000	1	O	-0.7
Total	8	599	1949	192	556	96	23	19	245	99	143	.285	.324	.387	85	-48	-45	244	4			.986	-19	O	-9.1
■ ED ROETZ	Roetz, Edward Bernard b: 8/6/05, Philadelphia, Pa. d: 3/16/65, Philadelphia, Pa. BR/TR, 5'10", 160 lbs. Deb: 5/26/29																								
1929	StL-A	16	45	7	11	4	1	0	5	4	6	.244	.306	.378	72	-2	-2	5	0	0	0	.909	-1	/S123	-0.2
■ BILLY ROGELL	Rogell, William George b: 11/24/04, Springfield, Ill. BB/TR, 5'10.5", 163 lbs. Deb: 4/14/25																								
1925	Bos-A	58	169	12	33	5	1	0	17	11	17	.195	.244	.237	22	-20	-20	10	0	3	-2	.935	6	2/S	-1.4
1927	Bos-A	82	207	35	55	14	6	2	28	24	28	.266	.342	.420	99	-1	-1	29	3	1	0	.966	6	3/2O	0.7

YEAR	TM/L	G	AB	R	H	2B	3B	HR	RBI	BB	SO	AVG	OBP	SLG	PRO+	BR	/A	RC	SB	CS	SBR	FA	FR	POS	TPR
1928	Bos-A	102	296	33	69	10	4	0	29	22	47	.233	.295	.294	56	-19	-18	26	2	6	-3	.935	-13	S2/O3	-2.7
1930	Det-A	54	144	20	24	4	2	0	9	15	23	.167	.250	.222	20	-17	-18	9	1	2	-1	.938	4	S3/O	-1.0
1931	Det-A	48	185	21	56	12	3	2	24	24	17	.303	.383	.432	110	4	3	30	8	8	-2	.958	11	S	1.5
1932	Det-A	144	554	88	150	29	6	9	61	50	38	.271	.332	.394	84	-11	-14	74	14	6	1	.944	8	*S/3	0.6
1933	Det-A	155	587	67	173	42	11	0	57	79	33	.295	.381	.404	106	9	7	93	6	9	-4	.944	20	*S	3.2
1934	*Det-A	154	592	114	175	32	8	3	100	74	36	.296	.374	.392	97	-1	-1	92	13	3	2	.962	9	*S	1.8
1935	*Det-A	150	560	88	154	23	11	6	71	80	29	.275	.367	.387	99	-3	0	83	3	6	-3	**.971**	12	*S	1.7
1936	Det-A	146	585	85	160	27	5	6	68	73	41	.274	.357	.368	79	-18	-19	80	14	10	-2	**.965**	-1	*S/3	-1.1
1937	Det-A	146	536	85	148	30	7	8	64	83	48	.276	.376	.403	94	-1	-3	86	5	5	-2	**.967**	2	*S	0.7
1938	Det-A	136	501	76	130	22	8	3	55	86	37	.259	.373	.353	78	-11	-15	73	9	2	2	.959	8	*S	0.4
1939	Det-A	74	174	24	40	6	3	2	23	26	14	.230	.330	.333	65	-8	-10	21	3	1	0	.931	2	S3/2	-0.4
1940	Chi-N	33	59	7	8	0	0	1	3	2	8	.136	.164	.186	-4	-8	-8	2	1			.900	-5	S/32	-1.3
Total	14	1482	5149	755	1375	256	75	42	609	649	416	.267	.351	.370	84	-106	-116	707	82	62		.956	68	*S3/2O	2.7

■ **EMMETT ROGERS** Rogers, Emmett b: 1865, Rome, N.Y. BB, 5'10", 165 lbs. Deb: 4/19/1890

YEAR	TM/L	G	AB	R	H	2B	3B	HR	RBI	BB	SO	AVG	OBP	SLG	PRO+	BR	/A	RC	SB	CS	SBR	FA	FR	POS	TPR
1890	Tol-a	35	110	18	19	3	3	0		14		.173	.266	.255	54	-6	-7	8	2			.924	5	C/O	0.1

■ **FRALEY ROGERS** Rogers, Fraley W. b: 1850, Brooklyn, N.Y. d: 5/10/1881, New York, N.Y. 5'8", 184 lbs. Deb: 4/30/1872

YEAR	TM/L	G	AB	R	H	2B	3B	HR	RBI	BB	SO	AVG	OBP	SLG	PRO+	BR	/A	RC	SB	CS	SBR	FA	FR	POS	TPR
1872	Bos-n	45	204	39	58	10	1	1	28	1	4	.284	.288	.358	93	-1	-3	22						O/1	0.0
1873	Bos-n	1	6	1	2	2	0	0	2	0	1	.333	.333	.667	172	1	0	1						/1	0.0
Total	2 n	46	210	40	60	12	1	1	30	1	5	.286	.289	.367	95	-0	-3	23						/O1	0.0

■ **JIM ROGERS** Rogers, James F. b: 4/9/1872, Hartford, Conn. 5'7.5", 180 lbs. Deb: 4/17/1896 M

YEAR	TM/L	G	AB	R	H	2B	3B	HR	RBI	BB	SO	AVG	OBP	SLG	PRO+	BR	/A	RC	SB	CS	SBR	FA	FR	POS	TPR
1896	Was-N	38	154	21	43	6	4	1	30	10	9	.279	.323	.390	89	-3	-3	21	3			.882	-6	3/2O	-0.7
	Lou-N	72	290	39	75	8	6	0	38	15	14	.259	.297	.328	69	-14	-12	33	13			.971	-2	1S	-1.2
	Yr	110	444	60	118	14	10	1	68	25	23	.266	.306	.349	76	-17	-15	54	16			.971	-8	13S/2O	-1.9
1897	Lou-N	41	150	22	22	3	2	2	22	22		.147	.260	.233	32	-15	-14	11	4			.933	-5	2/1M	-1.5
Total	2	151	594	82	140	17	12	3	90	47	23	.236	.294	.320	65	-32	-30	66	20			.970	-14	/123SO	-3.4

■ **JAY ROGERS** Rogers, Jay Lewis b: 8/3/1888, Sandusky, N.Y. d: 7/1/64, Carlisle, N.Y. BR/TR, 5'11.5", 178 lbs. Deb: 5/22/14

YEAR	TM/L	G	AB	R	H	2B	3B	HR	RBI	BB	SO	AVG	OBP	SLG	PRO+	BR	/A	RC	SB	CS	SBR	FA	FR	POS	TPR
1914	NY-A	5	8	0	0	0	0	0	0	0	4	.000	.000	.000	-99	-2	-2	0	0			.923	-0	/C	-0.2

■ **PACKY ROGERS** Rogers, Stanley Frank (b: Stanley Frank Hazinski) b: 4/26/13, Swoyersville, Pa. BR/TR, 5'8", 175 lbs. Deb: 7/12/38

YEAR	TM/L	G	AB	R	H	2B	3B	HR	RBI	BB	SO	AVG	OBP	SLG	PRO+	BR	/A	RC	SB	CS	SBR	FA	FR	POS	TPR
1938	Bro-N	23	37	3	7	1	1	0	5	6	6	.189	.302	.270	57	-2	-2	3	0			1.000	-1	/S32O	-0.2

■ **MIKE ROGODZINSKI** Rogodzinski, Michael George b: 2/22/48, Evanston, Ill. BL/TR, 6', 185 lbs. Deb: 5/04/73

YEAR	TM/L	G	AB	R	H	2B	3B	HR	RBI	BB	SO	AVG	OBP	SLG	PRO+	BR	/A	RC	SB	CS	SBR	FA	FR	POS	TPR
1973	Phi-N	66	80	13	19	3	0	2	7	12	19	.237	.337	.350	88	-1	-1	10	0	0	0	.947	-0	O	-0.2
1974	Phi-N	17	15	1	1	0	0	0	1	2	3	.067	.176	.067	-29	-3	-3	0	0	0	0	.000	0	/O	-0.3
1975	Phi-N	16	19	3	5	1	0	0	4	3	2	.263	.364	.316	86	-0	-0	2	0	1	-1	.667	-1	/O	-0.2
Total	3	99	114	17	25	4	0	2	12	17	24	.219	.321	.307	73	-4	-4	12	0	1	-1	.909	-1	/O	-0.7

■ **DAVE ROHDE** Rohde, David Grant b: 5/8/64, Los Altos, Cal. BB/TR, 6'2", 180 lbs. Deb: 4/09/90

YEAR	TM/L	G	AB	R	H	2B	3B	HR	RBI	BB	SO	AVG	OBP	SLG	PRO+	BR	/A	RC	SB	CS	SBR	FA	FR	POS	TPR
1990	Hou-N	59	98	8	18	4	0	0	5	9	20	.184	.286	.224	44	-7	-7	7	0	0	0	1.000	-1	2/3S	-0.7
1991	Hou-N	29	41	3	5	0	0	0	0	5	8	.122	.217	.122	-2	-5	-5	1	0	0	0	1.000	1	/23S1	-0.4
1992	Cle-A	5	7	0	0	0	0	0	0	2	3	.000	.222	.000	-33	-1	-1	0	0	0	0	.900	1	/3	-0.1
Total	3	93	146	11	23	4	0	0	5	16	31	.158	.263	.185	27	-14	-13	8	0	0	0	1.000	1	/23S1	-1.2

■ **GEORGE ROHE** Rohe, George Anthony "Whitey" b: 9/15/1875, Cincinnati, Ohio d: 6/10/57, Cincinnati, Ohio BR/TR, 5'9", 165 lbs. Deb: 5/07/01

YEAR	TM/L	G	AB	R	H	2B	3B	HR	RBI	BB	SO	AVG	OBP	SLG	PRO+	BR	/A	RC	SB	CS	SBR	FA	FR	POS	TPR
1901	Bal-A	14	36	7	10	2	0	0	4	5		.278	.381	.333	95	0	0	5	1			.912	-3	/13	-0.2
1905	Chi-A	34	113	14	24	1	0	1	12	12		.212	.310	.248	81	-2	-2	10	2			.934	-4	23	-0.5
1906	*Chi-A	77	225	14	58	5	1	0	25	16		.258	.316	.289	92	-2	-1	25	8			.926	2	3/2O	0.3
1907	Chi-A	144	494	46	105	11	2	2	51	39		.213	.274	.255	72	-16	-15	42	16			.898	-5	32S	-1.9
Total	4	269	868	81	197	19	3	3	92	72		.227	.294	.266	79	-21	-18	82	27			.917	-10	3/2S1O	-2.3

■ **DAN ROHN** Rohn, Daniel Jay b: 1/10/56, Alpena, Mich. BL/TR, 5'7", 165 lbs. Deb: 9/02/83

YEAR	TM/L	G	AB	R	H	2B	3B	HR	RBI	BB	SO	AVG	OBP	SLG	PRO+	BR	/A	RC	SB	CS	SBR	FA	FR	POS	TPR
1983	Chi-N	23	31	3	12	3	2	0	6	2	2	.387	.424	.613	176	3	3	8	1	0	0	.923	-0	/2S	0.3
1984	Chi-N	25	31	1	4	0	0	1	3	1	6	.129	.156	.226	6	-4	-4	1	0	0	0	1.000	0	/32S	-0.4
1986	Cle-A	6	10	1	2	0	0	0	2	1	1	.200	.273	.200	32	-1	-1	1	0	0	0	.900	1	/23S	0.0
Total	3	54	72	5	18	3	2	1	11	4	9	.250	.289	.389	82	-1	-2	10	1	0	0	.930	1	/23S	-0.1

■ **RAY ROHWER** Rohwer, Ray b: 6/5/1895, Dixon, Cal. d: 1/24/88, Davis, Cal. BL/TL, 5'10", 155 lbs. Deb: 4/13/21

YEAR	TM/L	G	AB	R	H	2B	3B	HR	RBI	BB	SO	AVG	OBP	SLG	PRO+	BR	/A	RC	SB	CS	SBR	FA	FR	POS	TPR
1921	Pit-N	30	40	6	10	3	2	0	6	4	8	.250	.318	.425	93	-0	-1	5	0	1	-1	.842	-1	O	-0.3
1922	Pit-N	53	129	19	38	6	3	3	22	10	17	.295	.350	.457	105	1	1	21	1	0	0	.938	0	O	-0.1
Total	2	83	169	25	48	9	5	3	28	14	25	.284	.342	.450	102	1	0	26	1	1	-0	.917	-1	/O	-0.4

■ **TONY ROIG** Roig, Anton Ambrose b: 12/23/27, New Orleans, La. BR/TR, 6'1", 180 lbs. Deb: 9/13/53

YEAR	TM/L	G	AB	R	H	2B	3B	HR	RBI	BB	SO	AVG	OBP	SLG	PRO+	BR	/A	RC	SB	CS	SBR	FA	FR	POS	TPR
1953	Was-A	3	8	0	1	1	0	0	0	0	1	.125	.125	.250	-1	-1	-1	0	0	0	0	1.000	2	/2	0.0
1955	Was-A	29	57	3	13	1	1	0	4	2	15	.228	.254	.281	46	-5	-4	4	0	0	0	.932	1	S/32	-0.3
1956	Was-A	44	119	11	25	5	2	0	7	20	29	.210	.324	.286	62	-6	-6	11	2	0	1	.973	7	2S	0.4
Total	3	76	184	14	39	7	3	0	11	22	45	.212	.296	.283	55	-12	-12	15	2	0	1	.927	9	/S23	0.1

■ **COOKIE ROJAS** Rojas, Octavio Victor (Rivas) b: 3/6/39, Havana, Cuba BR/TR, 5'10", 170 lbs. Deb: 4/10/62 MC

YEAR	TM/L	G	AB	R	H	2B	3B	HR	RBI	BB	SO	AVG	OBP	SLG	PRO+	BR	/A	RC	SB	CS	SBR	FA	FR	POS	TPR
1962	Cin-N	39	86	9	19	2	0	0	6	9	4	.221	.302	.244	47	-6	-6	6	1	1	-0	.949	-2	2/3	-0.6
1963	Phi-N	64	77	18	17	0	1	1	2	3	8	.221	.259	.286	57	-4	-4	5	4	1	1	.991	17	2/O	1.5
1964	Phi-N	109	340	58	99	19	5	2	31	22	17	.291	.338	.394	107	2	3	42	1	3	-2	.967	-7	O2S/C3	-0.6
1965	Phi-N★	142	521	78	158	25	3	3	42	42	33	.303	.359	.380	110	7	8	71	5	5	-2	.986	1	2OS/C1	1.4
1966	Phi-N	156	626	77	168	18	1	6	55	35	46	.268	.311	.329	78	-18	-18	63	4	6	-2	.983	-9	*2O/S	-2.6
1967	Phi-N	147	528	60	137	21	2	4	45	30	58	.259	.299	.330	79	-14	-15	50	8	4	0	.977	-3	*2/OCSP3	-1.0
1968	Phi-N	152	621	53	144	19	0	9	48	16	55	.232	.251	.306	67	-26	-26	43	4	8	-4	**.987**	11	*2/C	-1.2
1969	Phi-N	110	391	35	89	11	1	4	30	23	28	.228	.272	.292	60	-22	-21	28	1	6	-3	.980	-3	2/O	-2.1
1970	StL-N	23	47	2	5	0	0	0	2	3	4	.106	.176	.106	-22	-8	-8	1	0	0	0	1.000	1	2/OS	-0.6
	KC-A	98	384	36	100	13	3	2	28	20	29	.260	.297	.326	72	-15	-15	34	3	7	-3	.982	-1	2	-1.1
1971	KC-A★	115	414	56	124	22	2	6	59	39	35	.300	.363	.406	118	10	10	60	8	3	1	**.991**	-12	*2/SO	0.9
1972	KC-A★	137	487	49	127	25	0	3	53	41	35	.261	.319	.331	94	-4	-3	47	2	8	-4	.986	-2	*2/3S	-0.2
1973	KC-A★	139	551	78	152	29	3	6	69	37	38	.276	.323	.372	88	-4	-9	65	18	4	3	.982	9	*2	1.1
1974	KC-A☆	144	542	52	147	17	1	6	60	30	43	.271	.313	.339	83	-9	-13	52	8	4	0	**.987**	-24	*2	-3.2
1975	KC-A	120	406	34	103	18	2	2	37	30	24	.254	.305	.323	75	-12	-13	37	4	5	-2	.980	-15	*2/D	-2.5
1976	*KC-A	63	132	11	32	6	0	0	16	8	15	.242	.286	.288	68	-5	-5	11	2	0	1	1.000	-13	2/31D	-1.7
1977	*KC-A	64	156	8	39	9	1	0	10	8	17	.250	.287	.321	65	-8	-8	12	1	3	-2	.944	3	32/D	-0.5
Total	16	1822	6309	714	1660	254	25	54	593	396	489	.263	.309	.337	83	-137	-145	630	74	68	-19	.984	-48	*2O/3SDC1	-13.0

■ **STAN ROJEK** Rojek, Stanley Andrew b: 4/21/19, N.Tonawanda, N.Y. BR/TR, 5'10", 170 lbs. Deb: 9/22/42

YEAR	TM/L	G	AB	R	H	2B	3B	HR	RBI	BB	SO	AVG	OBP	SLG	PRO+	BR	/A	RC	SB	CS	SBR	FA	FR	POS	TPR
1942	Bro-N	1	0	1	0	0	0	0	0	0	0	—	—	—	—	0	0	0	0			.000	0	R	0.0
1946	Bro-N	45	47	11	13	2	1	0	2	4	1	.277	.333	.362	96	-0	-0	5	1			.974	5	S/23	0.6
1947	Bro-N	32	80	7	21	0	1	0	7	7	3	.262	.322	.287	61	-4	-4	7	1			.971	8	S/32	0.4
1948	Pit-N	156	641	85	186	27	5	4	51	61	41	.290	.355	.367	94	-3	-5	87	24			.962	-9	*S	-0.4

YEAR	TM/L	G	AB	R	H	2B	3B	HR	RBI	BB	SO	AVG	OBP	SLG	PRO+	BR	/A	RC	SB	CS	SBR	FA	FR	POS	TPR
1949	Pit-N	144	557	72	136	19	2	0	31	50	31	.244	.309	.285	59	-30	-32	52	4			.966	1	*S	-2.1
1950	Pit-N	76	230	28	59	12	1	0	17	18	13	.257	.313	.317	64	-11	-12	23	2			.967	-15	S/2	-2.2
1951	Pit-N	8	16	0	3	0	0	0	0	0	1	.188	.188	.188	1	-2	-2	1	0	0	0	.900	-1	/S	-0.3
	StL-N	51	186	21	51	7	3	0	14	10	10	.274	.318	.344	78	-6	-6	19	0	3	-2	.974	1	S	-0.4
	Yr	59	202	21	54	7	3	0	14	10	11	.267	.308	.332	72	-8	-8	19	0	3	-2	.968	-1	S	-0.7
1952	StL-A	9	7	0	1	0	0	0	0	2	0	.143	.333	.143	35	-1	-1	0	0	0	0	1.000	2	/S2	0.1
Total	8	522	1764	225	470	67	13	4	122	152	100	.266	.327	.326	74	-57	-62	193	32	3		.965	-9	S/23	-4.3
■ **RED ROLFE**	Rolfe, Robert Abial b: 10/17/08, Penacook, N.H. d: 7/8/69, Guilford, N.H. BL/TR, 5'11.5", 170 lbs. Deb: 6/29/31 MC																								
1931	NY-A	1	0	0	0	0	0	0	0	0	0	—	—	—	—	0	0	0	0	0	0	1.000	-0	/S	0.0
1934	NY-A	89	279	54	80	13	2	0	18	26	16	.287	.348	.348	86	-8	-5	34	2	3	-1	.944	4	S3	0.1
1935	NY-A	149	639	108	192	33	9	5	67	57	39	.300	.361	.404	103	-2	3	95	7	3	0	**.964**	-7	*3S	0.3
1936	*NY-A	135	568	116	181	39	**15**	10	70	68	38	.319	.392	.493	121	15	18	113	3	0	1	**.957**	3	*3	2.3
1937	*NY-A★	154	648	143	179	34	10	4	62	90	53	.276	.365	.378	87	-11	-11	94	4	2	0	.962	5	*3	-0.2
1938	*NY-A☆	151	631	132	196	36	8	10	80	74	44	.311	.386	.441	107	7	8	113	13	1	3	.959	-7	*3	0.6
1939	*NY-A★	152	648	**139**	**213**	**46**	10	14	80	81	41	.329	.404	.495	131	29	30	134	7	6	-2	.958	-15	*3	1.5
1940	NY-A†	139	588	102	147	26	6	10	53	50	48	.250	.311	.366	78	-23	-19	71	4	2	0	.949	-1	*3	-1.6
1941	*NY-A	136	561	106	148	22	5	8	42	57	38	.264	.332	.364	85	-13	-12	73	3	2	-0	.946	-10	*3	-1.8
1942	*NY-A	69	265	42	58	8	2	8	25	23	18	.219	.281	.355	80	-9	-8	28	1	1	-0	.959	5	3	-0.3
Total	10	1175	4827	942	1394	257	67	69	497	526	335	.289	.360	.413	100	-15	3	756	44	20	1	.956	-22	*3/S	0.9
■ **RAY ROLLING**	Rolling, Raymond Copeland b: 9/8/1886, Martinsburg, Mo. d: 8/25/66, St.Paul, Minn. BR/TR, 5'10.5", 160 lbs. Deb: 9/06/12																								
1912	StL-N	5	15	0	3	0	0	0	0	0	5	.200	.200	.200	10	-2	-2	1	0			.947	-0	/2	-0.2
■ **RED ROLLINGS**	Rollings, William Russell b: 3/21/04, Mobile, Ala. d: 12/31/64, Mobile, Ala. BL/TR, 5'11", 167 lbs. Deb: 4/17/27																								
1927	Bos-A	82	184	19	49	4	1	0	9	12	10	.266	.325	.299	64	-10	-9	18	3	1	0	.938	-5	31/2	-1.2
1928	Bos-A	50	48	7	11	3	1	0	9	6	8	.229	.315	.333	72	-2	-2	5	0	0	0	1.000	-2	/12O3	-0.4
1930	Bos-N	52	123	10	29	6	0	0	10	9	5	.236	.288	.285	40	-12	-11	10	2			.973	3	32	-0.6
Total	3	184	355	36	89	13	2	0	28	27	23	.251	.311	.299	57	-24	-23	34	5	1		.947	-5	/321O	-2.2
■ **RICH ROLLINS**	Rollins, Richard John "Red" b: 4/16/38, Mount Pleasant, Pa. BR/TR, 5'10", 185 lbs. Deb: 6/16/61																								
1961	Min-A	13	17	3	5	1	0	0	3	2	2	.294	.400	.353	98	0	0	3	0	0	0	1.000	1	/23	0.1
1962	Min-A★	159	624	96	186	23	5	16	96	75	61	.298	.379	.428	112	16	13	104	3	1	0	.943	-5	*3/S	1.0
1963	Min-A	136	531	75	163	23	1	16	61	36	59	.307	.360	.444	122	17	16	84	2	0	1	.935	-7	*3/2	1.0
1964	Min-A	148	596	87	161	25	**10**	12	68	53	80	.270	.335	.406	104	4	3	80	2	5	-2	.947	-2	*3	-0.3
1965	*Min-A	140	469	59	117	22	1	5	32	37	54	.249	.310	.333	79	-10	-13	48	4	0	1	.958	-4	*32	-1.8
1966	Min-A	90	269	30	66	7	1	10	40	13	34	.245	.290	.390	88	-3	-5	28	0	2	-1	.953	-4	3/2O	-1.2
1967	Min-A	109	339	31	83	11	2	6	39	27	58	.245	.306	.342	84	-4	-7	34	1	1	-0	.963	-10	3	-2.0
1968	Min-A	93	203	14	49	5	0	6	30	10	34	.241	.287	.355	89	-2	-3	20	3	1	0	.931	-2	3	-0.5
1969	Sea-A	58	187	15	42	7	0	4	21	7	19	.225	.271	.326	68	-9	-8	16	2	0	1	.948	3	3/S	-0.5
1970	Mil-A	14	25	3	5	1	0	0	5	3	4	.200	.286	.240	46	-2	-2	2	0	0	0	1.000	1	/3	-0.1
	Cle-A	42	43	6	10	0	0	2	4	3	5	.233	.283	.372	75	-1	-2	5	0	0	0	.600	-1	/3	-0.3
	Yr	56	68	9	15	1	0	2	9	6	9	.221	.284	.324	65	-3	-3	7	0	0	0	.900	-0	3	-0.4
Total	10	1002	3303	419	887	125	20	77	399	266	410	.269	.330	.388	98	6	-7	424	17	10	-1	.947	-30	3/2SO	-4.6
■ **ROLLINSON**	Rollinson Deb: 6/17/1884																								
1884	Was-U	1	3	0	0	0	0	0		0		.000	.000	.000	-99	-1	-1	0				.714	0	/C	0.0
■ **BILL ROMAN**	Roman, William Anthony b: 10/11/38, Detroit, Mich. BL/TL, 6'4", 190 lbs. Deb: 9/30/64																								
1964	Det-A	3	8	2	3	0	0	1	1	0	2	.375	.375	.750	201	1	1	2	0	0	0	1.000	0	/1	0.1
1965	Det-A	21	27	0	2	0	0	0	0	2	7	.074	.138	.074	-38	-5	-5	0	0	0	0	1.000	-0	/1	-0.6
Total	2	24	35	2	5	0	0	1	1	2	9	.143	.189	.229	17	-4	-4	3	0	0	0	1.000	-0	/1	-0.5
■ **JOHNNY ROMANO**	Romano, John Anthony "Honey" b: 8/23/34, Hoboken, N.J. BR/TR, 5'11", 205 lbs. Deb: 9/12/58																								
1958	Chi-A	4	7	1	2	0	0	0	1	1	0	.286	.375	.286	86	-0	-0	1	0	0	0	1.000	1	/C	0.1
1959	*Chi-A	53	126	20	37	5	1	5	25	23	18	.294	.407	.468	141	8	8	25	0	1	-1	.979	1	C	1.0
1960	Cle-A	108	316	40	86	12	2	16	52	37	50	.272	.354	.475	126	9	11	53	0	0	0	.988	-11	C	0.6
1961	Cle-A★	142	509	76	152	29	1	21	80	61	60	.299	.379	.483	132	21	23	95	0	0	0	.989	-9	*C	2.1
1962	Cle-A★	135	459	71	120	19	3	25	81	73	64	.261	.369	.479	130	18	20	82	0	1	-1	.990	-9	*C	1.5
1963	Cle-A	89	255	28	55	5	2	10	34	38	49	.216	.322	.369	94	-2	-2	32	4	3	-1	.993	-11	C/O	-1.1
1964	Cle-A	106	352	46	85	18	1	19	47	51	83	.241	.349	.460	124	11	12	54	2	2	-1	.991	-5	C/1	1.1
1965	Chi-A	122	356	39	86	11	0	18	48	59	74	.242	.357	.424	129	11	14	54	0	2	-1	.992	4	*C/O1	2.3
1966	Chi-A	122	329	33	76	12	0	15	47	58	72	.231	.348	.404	124	8	11	50	0	0	0	.993	3	*C	2.1
1967	StL-N	24	58	1	7	1	0	0	2	13	15	.121	.282	.138	24	-5	-5	3	1	0	0	.983	-1	C	-0.5
Total	10	905	2767	355	706	112	10	129	417	414	485	.255	.358	.443	123	79	90	450	7	9	-3	.990	-36	C/O1	9.2
■ **TOM ROMANO**	Romano, Thomas Michael b: 10/25/58, Syracuse, N.Y. BR/TR, 5'10", 170 lbs. Deb: 9/01/87																								
1987	Mon-N	7	3	1	0	0	0	0	0	0	1	.000	.000	.000	-97	-1	-1	0	0	0	0	.000	-1	/O	-0.2
■ **ED ROMERO**	Romero, Edgardo Ralph (Rivera) b: 12/9/57, Santurce, P.R. BR/TR, 5'11", 175 lbs. Deb: 7/16/77																								
1977	Mil-A	10	25	4	7	1	0	0	2	4	3	.280	.379	.320	93	-0	-0	3	0	0	0	.971	0	S	0.1
1980	Mil-A	42	104	20	27	7	0	1	10	9	11	.260	.319	.356	87	-2	-2	12	2	0	1	.894	4	S2/3	0.6
1981	*Mil-A	44	91	6	18	3	0	1	10	4	9	.198	.232	.264	45	-7	-6	4	0	2	-1	.949	10	S2/3	0.5
1982	Mil-A	52	144	18	36	8	0	1	7	8	16	.250	.289	.326	73	-6	-5	13	0	0	0	.975	-1	2S/3O	-0.4
1983	Mil-A	59	145	17	46	7	0	1	18	8	8	.317	.353	.386	112	1	2	20	1	0	0	.962	-10	SO/32D	-0.6
1984	Mil-A	116	357	36	90	12	0	1	31	29	25	.252	.310	.294	71	-15	-13	31	3	3	-1	.943	2	3S2/1OD	-0.9
1985	Mil-A	88	251	24	63	11	1	0	21	26	20	.251	.321	.303	72	-9	-9	26	1	1	-0	.977	8	S2O/3	0.4
1986	*Bos-A	100	233	41	49	11	0	2	23	18	16	.210	.273	.283	51	-16	-16	19	2	0	1	.959	-8	S3/2O	-1.7
1987	Bos-A	88	235	23	64	5	0	0	14	18	22	.272	.324	.294	64	-11	-12	21	0	2	-1	.973	2	2S3/1	-0.8
1988	*Bos-A	31	75	3	18	3	0	0	5	3	8	.240	.278	.280	55	-4	-5	5	0	0	0	1.000	-1	3/S/21D	-0.5
1989	Bos-A	46	113	14	24	4	0	0	6	7	7	.212	.264	.248	42	-8	-9	7	0	2	-1	.983	13	23S	0.4
	Atl-N	7	19	1	5	1	0	1	1	0	0	.263	.263	.474	104	0	-0	2	0	0	0	.947	5	/2S3	0.5
	Mil-A	15	50	3	10	3	0	0	3	0	10	.200	.200	.260	29	-5	-5	2	0	0	0	1.000	0	2/3SD	-0.4
1990	Det-A	32	70	8	16	3	0	0	4	6	4	.229	.289	.271	57	-4	-4	6	0	0	0	.982	6	3/D	0.2
Total	12	730	1912	218	473	79	1	8	155	140	159	.247	.300	.302	67	-86	-83	172	9	10	-3	.958	31	S23/O1D	-2.6
■ **KEVIN ROMINE**	Romine, Kevin Andrew b: 5/23/61, Exeter, N.H. BR/TR, 5'11", 185 lbs. Deb: 9/05/85																								
1985	Bos-A	24	28	3	6	2	0	0	1	1	4	.214	.241	.286	42	-2	-2	2	1	0	0	1.000	-5	O/D	-0.8
1986	Bos-A	35	35	6	9	2	0	0	2	3	9	.257	.316	.314	72	-1	-1	4	2	0	1	1.000	-6	O	-0.7
1987	Bos-A	9	24	5	7	2	0	0	2	2	6	.292	.346	.375	89	-0	-0	3	0	0	0	1.000	-0	/OD	-0.1
1988	*Bos-A	57	78	17	15	2	1	1	6	7	15	.192	.259	.282	49	-5	-5	6	2	0	1	.957	-13	O/D	-1.9
1989	Bos-A	92	274	30	75	13	0	1	23	21	53	.274	.330	.332	82	-4	-6	28	1	1	-0	.982	-2	O/D	-1.1
1990	Bos-A	70	136	21	37	7	0	2	14	12	27	.272	.336	.368	92	-1	-1	16	4	0	1	.976	-11	O/D	-1.2
1991	Bos-A	44	55	7	9	2	0	1	7	3	10	.164	.207	.255	26	-6	-6	3	1	1	-0	.964	-4	OD	-1.1
Total	7	331	630	89	158	30	1	5	55	49	124	.251	.308	.325	73	-19	-23	62	11	2	2	.980	-41	O/D	-6.9

YEAR	TM/L	G	AB	R	H	2B	3B	HR	RBI	BB	SO	AVG	OBP	SLG	PRO+	BR	/A	RC	SB	CS	SBR	FA	FR	POS	TPR

■ HENRI RONDEAU Rondeau, Henri Joseph b: 5/5/1887, Danielson, Conn. d: 5/28/43, Woonsocket, R.I. BR/TR, 5'10.5", 175 lbs. Deb: 4/11/13

1913	Det-A	35	70	5	13	2	0	0	5	14	16	.186	.321	.214	58	-3	-3	5	1			1.000	-2	C/1	-0.4
1915	Was-A	14	40	3	7	0	0	0	4	4	3	.175	.250	.175	27	-3	-4	2	1	2	-1	1.000	3	O	-0.3
1916	Was-A	50	162	20	36	5	3	1	28	18	18	.222	.311	.309	87	-3	-2	18	7			.958	3	O	-0.1
Total	3	99	272	28	56	7	3	1	37	36	37	.206	.305	.265	71	-9	-9	25	9	2		.967	4	/OC1	-0.8

■ GENE ROOF Roof, Eugene Lawrence b: 1/13/58, Paducah, Ky. BB/TR, 6'2", 180 lbs. Deb: 9/03/81 F

1981	StL-N	23	60	11	18	6	0	0	3	12	16	.300	.417	.400	129	3	3	11	5	1	1	.950	-2	O	0.2
1982	StL-N	11	15	3	4	0	0	0	2	1	4	.267	.313	.267	63	-1	-1	1	2	0	1	1.000	-0	/O	0.2
1983	StL-N	6	3	1	0	0	0	0	0	0	0	.000	.000	.000	-99	-1	-1	0	0	0	0	.000	0	/O	-0.1
	Mon-N	8	12	2	2	2	0	0	1	1	3	.167	.231	.333	55	-1	-1	1	0	0	0	1.000	-1	/O	-0.1
	Yr	14	15	3	2	2	0	0	1	1	3	.133	.188	.267	25	-2	-2	1	0	0	0	1.000	-1	/O	-0.2
Total	3	48	90	17	24	8	0	0	6	14	23	.267	.365	.356	102	1	1	14	7	1	2	.958	-3	/O	0.0

■ PHIL ROOF Roof, Phillip Anthony b: 3/5/41, Paducah, Ky. BR/TR, 6'3", 210 lbs. Deb: 4/29/61 FC

1961	Mil-N	1	0	0	0	0	0	0	0	0	0	—	—	—	—	0	0	0	0	0	0	1.000	0	/C	0.0
1964	Mil-N	1	2	0	0	0	0	0	0	0	0	.000	.000	.000	-99	-1	-1	0	0	0	0	1.000	0	/C	0.1
1965	Cal-A	9	22	1	3	0	0	0	0	0	6	.136	.136	.136	-23	-3	-3	0	0	0	0	.983	6	/C	0.3
	Cle-A	43	52	3	9	1	0	0	3	5	13	.173	.259	.192	30	-5	-5	3	0	0	0	.994	13	C	1.0
	Yr	52	74	4	12	1	0	0	3	5	19	.162	.225	.176	15	-8	-8	3	0	0	0	.992	19	C	1.3
1966	KC-A	127	369	33	77	14	3	7	44	37	95	.209	.286	.320	76	-12	-11	31	2	5	-2	.985	-1	*C/1	-0.7
1967	KC-A	114	327	23	67	14	5	6	24	23	85	.205	.268	.333	79	-10	-9	30	4	1	1	.991	-1	*C	-0.4
1968	Oak-A	34	64	5	12	0	0	1	2	2	15	.188	.212	.234	37	-5	-5	3	1	0	0	.968	-1	C	-0.5
1969	Oak-A	106	247	19	58	6	1	2	19	33	55	.235	.337	.291	81	-6	-5	25	1	0	0	.983	-1	*C	-0.1
1970	Mil-A	110	321	39	73	7	1	13	37	32	72	.227	.307	.377	87	-6	-6	36	3	2	-0	.988	8	*C/1	0.6
1971	Mil-A	41	114	6	22	2	1	1	10	8	28	.193	.252	.254	44	-8	-8	7	0	0	0	.975	3	C	-0.4
	Min-A	31	87	6	21	4	0	0	6	8	18	.241	.305	.287	67	-3	-4	6	0	1	-1	.985	8	C	0.5
	Yr	72	201	12	43	6	1	1	16	16	46	.214	.275	.269	54	-12	-12	13	0	1	-1	.980	11	C	0.1
1972	Min-A	61	146	16	30	11	1	3	12	6	27	.205	.237	.356	71	-5	-6	12	0	1	-1	.978	-2	C	-0.8
1973	Min-A	47	117	10	23	4	1	1	15	13	27	.197	.277	.274	53	-7	-7	9	0	0	0	.992	6	C	0.0
1974	Min-A	44	97	10	19	1	0	2	13	6	24	.196	.257	.268	49	-6	-7	6	0	0	0	1.000	8	C	0.2
1975	Min-A	63	126	18	38	2	0	7	21	9	28	.302	.353	.484	132	5	5	22	0	0	0	.989	7	C	1.3
1976	Min-A	18	46	1	10	3	0	0	4	2	6	.217	.250	.283	54	-3	-3	3	0	0	0	.962	5	C/D	0.3
	Chi-A	4	9	0	1	0	0	0	0	0	3	.111	.111	.111	-35	-2	-2	0	0	0	0	1.000	-0	/C	-0.2
	Yr	22	55	1	11	3	0	0	4	2	9	.200	.228	.255	40	-4	-4	3	0	0	0	.967	5	C/D	0.1
1977	Tor-A	3	5	0	0	0	0	0	0	1	1	.000	.000	.000	-99	-1	-1	0	0	0	0	1.000	1	/C	0.0
Total	15	857	2151	190	463	69	13	43	210	184	504	.215	.284	.319	73	-79	-77	193	11	10	-3	.986	58	C/1D	1.2

■ GEORGE ROOKS Rooks, George Brinton McClellan (b: George Brinton Mc Clellan Ruckser) b: 10/21/1863, Chicago, Ill. d: 3/11/35, Chicago, Ill. BR/TR, 5'11", 170 lbs. Deb: 5/12/1891 F

| 1891 | Bos-N | 5 | 16 | 1 | 2 | 0 | 0 | 0 | 4 | 1 | | .125 | .300 | .125 | 24 | -1 | -2 | 1 | 0 | | | 1.000 | 1 | /O | -0.1 |

■ ROLANDO ROOMES Roomes, Rolando Audley b: 2/15/62, Kingston, Jamaica BR/TR, 6'3", 180 lbs. Deb: 4/12/88

1988	Chi-N	17	16	3	3	0	0	0	0	0	4	.188	.188	.188	8	-2	-2	0	0	1	-1	.833	-1	/O	-0.4
1989	Cin-N	107	315	36	83	18	5	7	34	13	100	.263	.299	.419	100	0	-1	38	12	8	-1	.981	-3	*O	-0.7
1990	Cin-N	30	61	5	13	0	0	2	7	0	20	.213	.213	.311	41	-5	-5	3	0	0	0	1.000	-0	O	-0.6
	Mon-N	16	14	1	4	0	1	0	1	1	6	.286	.333	.429	112	0	0	1	0	2	-1	1.000	-1	/O	-0.3
	Yr	46	75	6	17	0	1	2	8	1	26	.227	.237	.333	54	-5	-5	5	0	2	-1	1.000	-2	O	-0.9
Total	3	170	406	45	103	18	6	9	42	14	130	.254	.284	.394	88	-7	-8	43	12	11	-3	.980	-5	O	-2.0

■ FRANK ROONEY Rooney, Frank (b: Frank Rovny) b: 10/12/1884, Podebrady, Bohemia (Austria-Hungary) d: 4/6/77, Bessemer, Mich. Deb: 4/18/14

| 1914 | Ind-F | 12 | 35 | 1 | 7 | 0 | 1 | 1 | 8 | 1 | 0 | .200 | .222 | .343 | 54 | -2 | -3 | 3 | 2 | | | .980 | -1 | /1 | -0.4 |

■ PAT ROONEY Rooney, Patrick Eugene b: 11/28/57, Chicago, Ill. BR/TR, 6'1", 190 lbs. Deb: 9/09/81

| 1981 | Mon-N | 4 | 5 | 0 | 0 | 0 | 0 | 0 | 0 | 0 | 3 | .000 | .000 | .000 | -99 | -1 | -1 | 0 | 0 | 0 | 0 | 1.000 | -0 | /O | -0.2 |

■ JORGE ROQUE Roque, Jorge (Vargas) b: 4/28/50, Ponce, P.R. BR/TR, 5'10", 158 lbs. Deb: 9/04/70

1970	StL-N	5	1	2	0	0	0	0	0	0	1	.000	.500	.000	45	0	0	0	0	0	0	.000	0	/O	0.0
1971	StL-N	3	10	2	3	0	0	0	1	0	3	.300	.300	.300	68	-0	-0	1	0	0	0	1.000	0	/O	0.0
1972	StL-N	32	67	3	7	2	1	1	5	6	19	.104	.178	.209	10	-8	-8	2	1	1	-0	.980	2	O	-0.8
1973	Mon-N	25	61	7	9	2	0	1	6	4	17	.148	.212	.230	22	-7	-7	2	2	2	-1	.878	2	O	-0.7
Total	4	65	139	14	19	4	1	2	12	10	40	.137	.205	.223	20	-15	-15	6	4	3	-1	.934	4	/O	-1.5

■ LUIS ROSADO Rosado, Luis (Robles) b: 12/6/55, Santurce, P.R. BR/TR, 6', 180 lbs. Deb: 9/08/77

1977	NY-N	9	24	1	5	1	0	0	3	1	3	.208	.269	.250	42	-2	-2	2	0	0	0	.980	-0	/1C	-0.2
1980	NY-N	2	4	0	0	0	0	0	0	0	1	.000	.000	.000	-99	-1	-1	0	0	0	0	1.000	-0	/1	-0.1
Total	2	11	28	1	5	1	0	0	3	1	4	.179	.233	.214	23	-3	-3	2	0	0	0	.983	-0	/1C	-0.3

■ BUDDY ROSAR Rosar, Warren Vincent b: 7/3/14, Buffalo, N.Y. BR/TR, 5'9", 190 lbs. Deb: 4/29/39

1939	NY-A	43	105	18	29	5	1	0	12	13	10	.276	.356	.343	81	-3	-3	14	4	0	1	.980	4	C	0.4
1940	NY-A	73	228	34	68	11	3	4	37	19	11	.298	.357	.425	106	1	2	36	7	1	2	.983	1	C	0.8
1941	*NY-A	67	209	25	60	17	2	1	36	22	10	.287	.355	.402	101	-0	0	29	0	0	0	.996	0	C	0.5
1942	*NY-A☆	69	209	18	48	10	0	2	34	17	20	.230	.288	.306	68	-9	-9	17	1	2	-1	.996	4	C	-0.2
1943	Cle-A☆	115	382	53	108	17	1	1	41	33	12	.283	.340	.340	106	-0	-4	44	0	4	-2	.983	7	*C	1.5
1944	Cle-A	99	331	29	87	9	3	0	30	34	17	.263	.339	.308	89	-5	-4	37	1	2	-1	**.989**	4	C	0.5
1945	Phi-A	92	300	23	63	12	1	1	25	20	16	.210	.262	.267	54	-18	-18	20	2	1	0	.987	-0	C	-1.5
1946	Phi-A★	121	424	34	120	22	2	2	47	36	17	.283	.339	.358	96	-3	-3	48	1	3	-2	**1.000**	7	*C	1.0
1947	Phi-A★	102	359	40	93	20	2	1	33	40	13	.259	.335	.334	85	-6	-7	41	1	3	-2	**.996**	13	*C	1.1
1948	Phi-A★	90	302	30	77	13	0	4	41	39	12	.255	.344	.338	82	-7	-7	38	0	2	-1	**.997**	-3	C	-0.5
1949	Phi-A	32	95	7	19	2	0	0	6	16	5	.200	.315	.221	45	-7	-7	8	0	0	0	.992	-2	C	-0.7
1950	Bos-A	27	84	13	25	7	0	1	12	7	4	.298	.352	.357	75	-2	-3	10	0	0	0	.991	-1	C	-0.3
1951	Bos-A	58	170	11	39	7	1	1	13	19	14	.229	.307	.288	56	-9	-11	16	0	0	0	.996	0	C	-0.9
Total	13	988	3198	335	836	147	15	18	367	315	161	.261	.330	.334	84	-70	-67	358	17	18	-6	.992	33	C	1.7

■ JIMMY ROSARIO Rosario, Angel Ramon (Ferrer) b: 5/5/45, Bayamon, P.R. BB/TR, 5'10", 155 lbs. Deb: 4/08/71

1971	*SF-N	92	192	26	43	6	1	0	13	33	35	.224	.341	.266	75	-5	-5	20	7	4	-0	1.000	8	O	0.1
1972	SF-N	7	2	1	0	0	0	0	0	0	0	.000	.000	.000	-99	-1	-1	0	0	1	-1	.000	0	/O	-0.1
1976	Mil-A	15	37	4	7	0	0	1	5	3	8	.189	.250	.270	53	-2	-2	2	1	3	-2	1.000	-2	O/D	-0.7
Total	3	114	231	31	50	6	1	1	18	36	43	.216	.325	.264	70	-8	-8	22	8	8	-2	1.000	6	/OD	-0.7

■ SANTIAGO ROSARIO Rosario, Santiago b: 7/25/39, Guayanilla, P.R. BL/TL, 5'11", 165 lbs. Deb: 6/23/65

| 1965 | KC-A | 81 | 85 | 8 | 20 | 3 | 0 | 2 | 8 | 6 | 16 | .235 | .293 | .341 | 81 | -2 | -2 | 8 | 0 | 0 | 0 | .991 | -1 | 1/O | -0.4 |

■ VICTOR ROSARIO Rosario, Victor Manuel (Rivera) b: 8/28/66, Hato Mayor Del Rey, D.R. BR/TR, 5'11", 155 lbs. Deb: 9/06/90

| 1990 | Atl-N | 9 | 7 | 3 | 1 | 0 | 0 | 0 | 0 | 1 | 1 | .143 | .250 | .143 | 10 | -1 | -1 | 0 | 0 | 0 | 0 | 1.000 | 1 | /S2 | 0.0 |

YEAR	TM/L	G	AB	R	H	2B	3B	HR	RBI	BB	SO	AVG	OBP	SLG	PRO+	BR	/A	RC	SB	CS	SBR	FA	FR	POS	TPR
■ **PETE ROSE**	Rose, Peter Edward "Charlie Hustle" b: 4/14/41, Cincinnati, Ohio BB/TR, 5'11", 200 lbs. Deb: 4/08/63 M																								
1963	Cin-N	157	623	101	170	25	9	6	41	55	72	.273	.337	.371	101	4	1	77	13	15	-5	.971	-23	*2/O	-1.2
1964	Cin-N	136	516	64	139	13	2	4	34	36	51	.269	.319	.326	79	-12	-14	53	4	10	-5	.979	-14	*2	-2.4
1965	Cin-N★	162	670	117	**209**	35	11	11	81	69	76	.312	.383	.446	124	31	25	118	8	3	1	.975	-18	*2	2.3
1966	Cin-N	156	654	97	205	38	5	16	70	37	61	.313	.351	.460	113	20	13	100	4	9	-4	.981	-8	*23	1.1
1967	Cin-N★	148	585	86	176	32	8	12	76	56	66	.301	.365	.444	117	23	16	95	11	6	-0	.982	-9	*O2	0.3
1968	Cin-N†	149	626	94	**210**	42	6	10	49	56	76	**.335**	**.394**	.470	149	45	40	**113**	3	7	-3	.990	9	*O/21	4.3
1969	Cin-N★	156	627	**120**	218	33	11	16	82	88	65	**.348**	.432	.512	155	56	52	138	7	10	-4	.988	7	*O/2	4.8
1970	*Cin-N★	159	649	120	**205**	37	9	15	52	73	64	.316	.387	.470	128	27	26	121	12	7	-1	**.997**	2	*O	1.9
1971	Cin-N★	160	632	86	192	27	4	13	44	68	50	.304	.374	.421	127	22	23	100	13	9	-2	.994	2	*O	1.6
1972	*Cin-N	154	645	107	**198**	31	11	6	57	73	46	.307	.383	.417	135	25	29	109	10	3	1	.994	12	*O	3.7
1973	*Cin-N★	160	680	115	**230**	36	8	5	64	65	42	**.338**	.401	.437	139	31	35	119	10	7	-1	.992	9	*O	3.7
1974	Cin-N★	163	652	**110**	185	**45**	7	3	51	106	54	.284	.388	.388	119	19	21	104	2	4	-2	**.997**	12	*O	2.4
1975	*Cin-N★	162	662	**112**	210	**47**	4	7	74	89	50	.317	.407	.432	130	33	31	120	0	1	-1	.963	-35	*3O	-0.6
1976	*Cin-N★	162	665	**130**	**215**	**42**	6	10	63	86	54	.323	.406	.450	139	40	38	123	9	5	-0	**.969**	-12	*3/O	2.6
1977	Cin-N★	162	655	95	204	38	7	9	64	66	42	.311	.379	.432	115	17	15	111	16	4	2	.958	-24	*3	-0.8
1978	Cin-N★	159	655	103	198	**51**	3	7	52	62	30	.302	.365	.421	119	17	17	102	13	9	-2	.961	-24	*3/O1	-1.1
1979	Phi-N★	163	628	90	208	40	5	4	59	95	32	.331	.421	.430	128	33	30	116	20	11	-1	.995	-5	*1/32	1.6
1980	*Phi-N★	162	655	95	185	**42**	1	1	64	66	33	.282	.354	.354	93	0	-4	83	12	8	-1	**.997**	9	*1	-0.6
1981	*Phi-N★	107	431	73	**140**	18	5	0	33	46	26	.325	.394	.390	118	15	12	67	4	4	-1	.996	9	*1	1.5
1982	Phi-N★	162	634	80	172	25	4	3	54	66	32	.271	.347	.338	90	-5	-6	75	8	8	-2	.995	6	*1	-1.3
1983	*Phi-N	151	493	52	121	14	3	0	45	52	28	.245	.320	.286	70	-19	-18	46	7	7	-2	.990	0	*1O	-2.8
1984	Mon-N	95	278	34	72	6	2	0	23	31	20	.259	.335	.295	82	-7	-5	27	1	1	-0	.988	8	1O	-0.1
	Cin-N	26	96	9	35	9	0	0	11	9	7	.365	.430	.458	143	7	6	20	0	0	0	.990	-3	1/M	0.2
	Yr	121	374	43	107	15	2	0	34	40	27	.286	.360	.337	99	-0	1	46	1	1	-0	.989	5	1O	0.1
1985	Cin-N★	119	405	60	107	12	2	2	46	86	35	.264	.398	.319	98	7	4	59	8	1	2	.995	0	*1/M	0.0
1986	Cin-N	72	237	15	52	8	2	0	25	30	31	.219	.317	.270	61	-11	-12	23	3	0	1	.990	-1	1/M	-1.7
Total	24	3562	14053	2165	4256	746	135	160	1314	1566	1143	.303	.377	.409	117	416	378	2220	198	149	-30	.991	-90	*O132	19.4
■ **BOBBY ROSE**	Rose, Robert Richard b: 3/15/67, Covina, Cal. BR/TR, 5'11", 170 lbs. Deb: 8/12/89																								
1989	Cal-A	14	38	4	8	1	2	1	3	2	10	.211	.268	.421	93	-1	-1	4	0	0	0	.920	-1	3/2	-0.1
1990	Cal-A	7	13	5	5	0	0	1	2	2	1	.385	.467	.615	204	2	2	4	0	0	0	1.000	-1	/23	0.1
1991	Cal-A	22	65	5	18	5	1	1	8	3	13	.277	.309	.431	102	-0	-0	8	0	0	0	1.000	-1	/2O31	-0.1
1992	Cal-A	30	84	10	18	5	0	2	10	8	9	.214	.298	.345	81	-2	-2	9	1	1	-0	.953	8	2/1	0.6
Total	4	73	200	24	49	11	3	5	23	15	33	.245	.307	.405	98	-1	-1	25	1	1	-0	.965	6	/23O1	0.5
■ **JOHNNY ROSEBORO**	Roseboro, John Junior b: 5/13/33, Ashland, Ohio BL/TR, 5'11.5", 190 lbs. Deb: 6/14/57 C																								
1957	Bro-N	35	69	6	10	2	0	2	6	10	20	.145	.253	.261	35	-6	-7	5	0	0	0	.972	3	C/1	-0.4
1958	LA-N☆	114	384	52	104	11	9	14	43	36	56	.271	.336	.456	104	3	2	58	11	8	-2	.987	-16	*C/O	-1.0
1959	*LA-N	118	397	39	92	14	7	10	38	52	69	.232	.325	.378	81	-7	-11	50	7	5	-1	.991	6	*C	0.1
1960	LA-N	103	287	22	61	15	3	8	42	44	53	.213	.325	.369	84	-4	-6	37	7	6	-2	.993	3	C/13	0.1
1961	LA-N★	128	394	59	99	16	6	18	59	56	62	.251	.350	.459	104	7	3	67	6	4	-1	.986	7	*C	1.5
1962	LA-N★	128	389	45	97	16	7	7	55	50	60	.249	.345	.380	101	-2	1	54	12	3	2	.985	-2	*C	0.6
1963	*LA-N	135	470	50	111	13	7	9	49	36	50	.236	.295	.351	91	-9	-6	48	7	6	-2	.992	-10	*C	-1.3
1964	LA-N	134	414	42	119	24	1	3	45	44	61	.287	.361	.372	115	5	9	57	3	3	-1	.993	1	*C	1.5
1965	*LA-N	136	437	42	102	10	0	8	57	34	51	.233	.292	.311	75	-17	-14	39	1	6	-3	.994	-2	*C/3	-1.4
1966	*LA-N	142	445	47	123	23	2	9	53	44	51	.276	.346	.398	115	4	9	60	3	2	-0	.993	6	*C	2.4
1967	LA-N	116	334	37	91	18	2	4	24	38	33	.272	.350	.374	117	4	7	43	2	4	-2	.984	-11	*C	0.0
1968	Min-A	135	380	31	82	12	0	8	39	46	57	.216	.304	.311	82	-6	-8	37	2	3	-1	.991	-5	*C	-0.7
1969	*Min-A★	115	361	33	95	12	0	3	32	39	44	.263	.335	.321	83	-7	-8	39	5	5	-2	.980	0	*C	-0.4
1970	Was-A	46	86	7	20	4	0	1	6	18	10	.233	.365	.314	94	-1	0	11	1	1	-0	1.000	-3	C	-0.2
Total	14	1585	4847	512	1206	190	44	104	548	547	677	.249	.329	.371	95	-34	-28	604	67	56	-14	.989	-22	*C/1O3	0.8
■ **BOB ROSELLI**	Roselli, Robert Edward b: 12/10/31, San Francisco, Cal. BR/TR, 5'11", 185 lbs. Deb: 8/16/55																								
1955	Mil-N	6	9	1	2	1	0	0	0	1	4	.222	.364	.333	91	-0	-0	1	0	0	0	.917	0	/C	0.0
1956	Mil-N	4	2	1	1	0	0	1	1	0	1	.500	.500	2.000	564	1	1	2	0	0	0	1.000	2	/C	0.3
1958	Mil-N	1	1	0	0	0	0	0	0	0	0	.000	.000	.000	-99	-0	-0	0	0	0	0	.000	0	H	0.0
1961	Chi-A	22	38	2	10	3	0	0	4	0	11	.263	.263	.342	61	-2	-2	3	0	0	0	1.000	-1	C	-0.3
1962	Chi-A	35	64	4	12	3	1	1	5	11	15	.188	.316	.313	70	-3	-3	7	1	0	0	.988	-1	C	-0.3
Total	5	68	114	8	25	7	1	2	10	12	31	.219	.305	.351	76	-4	-4	13	1	0	0	.986	-1	/C	-0.3
■ **DAVE ROSELLO**	Rosello, David (Rodriguez) b: 6/26/50, Mayaguez, P.R. BR/TR, 5'11", 160 lbs. Deb: 9/10/72																								
1972	Chi-N	5	12	2	3	0	0	1	3	3	2	.250	.400	.500	139	1	1	3	0	0	0	.846	1	/S	0.2
1973	Chi-N	16	38	4	10	2	0	0	2	2	4	.263	.300	.316	66	-2	-2	2	2	2	-1	.964	3	2/S	0.1
1974	Chi-N	62	148	9	30	7	0	0	10	10	28	.203	.253	.250	39	-12	-12	10	1	1	-0	.972	3	2S	-0.7
1975	Chi-N	19	58	7	15	2	0	1	8	9	8	.259	.358	.345	92	-0	-0	7	0	1	-1	.952	1	S	0.2
1976	Chi-N	91	227	27	55	5	1	1	11	41	33	.242	.361	.286	78	-2	-5	25	1	2	-1	.966	-7	S/2	-0.4
1977	Chi-N	56	82	18	18	2	1	1	9	12	12	.220	.319	.305	62	-3	-5	9	0	0	0	.938	-3	3S/2	-0.7
1979	Cle-A	59	107	20	26	6	1	3	14	15	27	.243	.336	.402	98	-0	-0	16	1	0	0	.976	-5	23S	-0.3
1980	Cle-A	71	117	16	29	3	0	2	12	9	19	.248	.302	.325	71	-5	-5	12	0	0	0	.980	3	23/SD	0.0
1981	Cle-A	43	84	11	20	4	0	1	7	7	12	.238	.297	.321	79	-2	-2	8	0	1	-1	.979	3	2/3SD	0.1
Total	9	422	873	114	206	31	3	10	76	108	145	.236	.321	.313	73	-25	-30	92	5	7	-3	.975	0	2S/3D	-1.5
■ **CHIEF ROSEMAN**	Roseman, James John b: 1856, New York, N.Y. d: 7/4/38, Brooklyn, N.Y. BR/TR, 5'7", 167 lbs. Deb: 5/01/1882 M																								
1882	Tro-N	82	331	41	78	21	6	1	29	3	41	.236	.243	.344	90	-5	-3	28				.853	-3	*O	-0.6
1883	NY-a	93	398	48	100	13	6	0		11		.251	.271	.314	85	-5	-8	35				.855	-3	*O/1	-1.0
1884	*NY-a	107	436	97	130	16	11	4		21		.298	.339	.413	152	22	24	63				.885	-2	*O	1.8
1885	NY-a	101	410	72	114	13	14	4		25		.278	.335	.407	148	17	22	57				.865	-7	*O/P	1.2
1886	NY-a	134	559	90	127	19	10	5		24		.227	.269	.324	91	-9	-6	52	6			.891	-3	*O/P	-1.0
1887	Phi-a	21	73	16	16	2	1	0		10		.219	.352	.274	78	-1	-1	8	3			.821	-0	O	-0.2
	NY-a	60	241	30	55	10	1	1		9		.228	.265	.290	59	-14	-12	20	3			.868	-8	O/1P	-1.7
	Bro-a	1	3	2	1	0	0	0		0		.333	.500	.333	136	0	0	1	0			1.000	-3	/O	-0.3
	Yr	82	317	48	72	12	2	1		19		.227	.290	.287	65	-15	-13	29	6			.856	-11	O/1P	-2.2
1890	StL-a	80	302	47	103	26	0	2		30		.341	.449	.447	147	28	21	65	7			.819	-8	O1M	0.8
	Lou-a	2	8	0	2	0	0	0		0		.250	.250	.250	50	-1	-0	1	0			.864	-1	/1	-0.1
	Yr	82	310	47	105	26	0	2		30		.339	.444	.442	145	28	20	66	7			.819	-9	O1	0.7
Total	7	681	2761	443	726	120	49	17	29	133	41	.263	.312	.360	111	31	37	329	19			.866	-38	O/1P	-1.1
■ **AL ROSEN**	Rosen, Albert Leonard "Flip" b: 2/29/24, Spartanburg, S.C. BR/TR, 5'10.5", 180 lbs. Deb: 9/10/47																								
1947	Cle-A	7	9	1	1	0	0	0	0	0	3	.111	.111	.111	-39	-2	-2	0	0	0	0	.000	1	/3O	-0.1
1948	*Cle-A	5	5	0	1	0	0	0	0	0	2	.200	.200	.200	7	-1	-1	0	0	0	0	1.000	0	/3	0.0
1949	Cle-A	23	44	3	7	2	0	0	5	7	4	.159	.275	.205	28	-5	-4	3	0	1	-1	1.000	-1	3	-0.6
1950	Cle-A	155	554	100	159	23	4	**37**	116	100	72	.287	.405	.543	146	34	37	120	5	7	-3	.969	1	*3	3.0
1951	Cle-A	154	573	82	152	30	1	24	102	85	71	.265	.362	.447	125	14	18	96	7	5	-1	.958	-15	*3	0.1

YEAR	TM/L	G	AB	R	H	2B	3B	HR	RBI	BB	SO	AVG	OBP	SLG	PRO+	BR	/A	RC	SB	CS	SBR	FA	FR	POS	TPR
1952	Cle-A★	148	567	101	171	32	5	28	**105**	75	54	.302	.387	.524	162	39	43	115	8	6	-1	.958	-20	*3/1S	2.0
1953	Cle-A★	155	599	**115**	201	27	5	**43**	**145**	85	48	.336	.422	**.613**	**181**	**63**	**65**	**155**	8	7	-2	.964	1	*3/1S	**6.0**
1954	*Cle-A★	137	466	76	140	20	2	24	102	85	43	.300	.412	.506	148	34	33	100	6	2	1	.959	-14	31/2S	1.6
1955	Cle-A★	139	492	61	120	13	1	21	81	92	44	.244	.367	.402	103	7	4	76	4	2	0	.963	3	*31	0.4
1956	Cle-A	121	416	64	111	18	2	15	61	58	44	.267	.357	.428	104	4	2	62	1	3	-2	.945	-8	*3	-0.5
Total	10	1044	3725	603	1063	165	20	192	717	587	385	.285	.386	.495	138	188	197	729	39	33	-8	.961	-52	3/1S20	11.9

■ GOODY ROSEN
Rosen, Goodwin George b: 8/28/12, Toronto, Ont., Can. BL/TL, 5'10", 155 lbs. Deb: 9/14/37

YEAR	TM/L	G	AB	R	H	2B	3B	HR	RBI	BB	SO	AVG	OBP	SLG	PRO+	BR	/A	RC	SB	CS	SBR	FA	FR	POS	TPR
1937	Bro-N	22	77	10	24	5	1	0	6	6	6	.312	.361	.403	106	1	1	12	2			.981	1	O	0.1
1938	Bro-N	138	473	75	133	17	11	4	51	65	43	.281	.368	.389	106	7	6	74	0			**.989**	13	*O	1.5
1939	Bro-N	54	183	22	46	6	4	1	12	23	21	.251	.335	.344	80	-4	-5	23	4			1.000	-3	O	-1.0
1944	Bro-N	89	264	38	69	8	3	0	23	26	27	.261	.330	.314	83	-6	-5	29	0			.991	12	O	0.4
1945	Bro-N†	145	606	126	197	24	11	12	75	50	36	.325	.379	.460	134	26	26	110	4			.993	2	*O	2.1
1946	Bro-N	3	3	0	1	0	0	0	0	0	1	.333	.333	.333	89	-0	-0	0	0			.000	-1	/O	-0.1
	NY-N	100	310	39	87	11	4	5	30	48	32	.281	.377	.390	117	9	8	47	2			.976	4	O	0.8
	Yr	103	313	39	88	11	4	5	30	48	33	.281	.377	.390	117	8	8	47	2			.976	3	O	0.7
Total	6	551	1916	310	557	71	34	22	197	218	166	.291	.364	.398	111	32	31	295	12			.989	28	O	3.8

■ HARRY ROSENBERG
Rosenberg, Harry b: 6/22/09, San Francisco, Cal. BR/TR, 5'9.5", 160 lbs. Deb: 7/15/30 F

YEAR	TM/L	G	AB	R	H	2B	3B	HR	RBI	BB	SO	AVG	OBP	SLG	PRO+	BR	/A	RC	SB	CS	SBR	FA	FR	POS	TPR
1930	NY-N	9	5	1	0	0	0	0	0	1	4	.000	.167	.000	-56	-1	-1	0	0			1.000	-1	/O	-0.2

■ LOU ROSENBERG
Rosenberg, Louis b: 3/5/04, San Francisco, Cal. d: 9/8/91, Daly City, Cal. BR/TR, 5'7", 155 lbs. Deb: 5/22/23 F

YEAR	TM/L	G	AB	R	H	2B	3B	HR	RBI	BB	SO	AVG	OBP	SLG	PRO+	BR	/A	RC	SB	CS	SBR	FA	FR	POS	TPR
1923	Chi-A	3	4	0	1	0	0	0	0	0	1	.250	.250	.250	32	-0	-0	0	0	1	-1	1.000	-1	/2	-0.2

■ MAX ROSENFELD
Rosenfeld, Max b: 12/23/02, New York, N.Y. d: 3/10/69, Miami, Fla. BR/TR, 5'8", 175 lbs. Deb: 4/21/31

YEAR	TM/L	G	AB	R	H	2B	3B	HR	RBI	BB	SO	AVG	OBP	SLG	PRO+	BR	/A	RC	SB	CS	SBR	FA	FR	POS	TPR
1931	Bro-N	3	9	0	2	1	0	0	0	1	1	.222	.300	.333	70	-0	-0	1	0			1.000	-1	/O	-0.1
1932	Bro-N	34	39	8	14	3	0	2	7	0	10	.359	.359	.590	153	2	3	8	2			.970	-9	O	-0.7
1933	Bro-N	5	9	0	1	0	0	0	0	1	1	.111	.200	.111	-10	-1	-1	0	0			1.000	0	/O	-0.1
Total	3	42	57	8	17	4	0	2	7	2	12	.298	.322	.474	115	1	1	9	2			.978	-9	/O	-0.9

■ LARRY ROSENTHAL
Rosenthal, Lawrence John b: 5/21/10, St.Paul, Minn. d: 3/4/92, Woodbury, Minn. BL/TL, 6'0.5", 190 lbs. Deb: 6/20/36

YEAR	TM/L	G	AB	R	H	2B	3B	HR	RBI	BB	SO	AVG	OBP	SLG	PRO+	BR	/A	RC	SB	CS	SBR	FA	FR	POS	TPR
1936	Chi-A	85	317	71	89	15	8	3	46	59	37	.281	.394	.407	95	1	-1	55	2	0	1	.977	6	O	0.2
1937	Chi-A	58	97	20	28	5	3	0	9	9	20	.289	.355	.402	90	-1	-1	14	1	0	0	.980	-3	O	-0.4
1938	Chi-A	61	105	14	30	5	1	1	12	12	13	.286	.359	.381	83	-2	-3	15	0	1	-1	.959	-3	O	-0.6
1939	Chi-A	107	324	50	86	21	5	10	51	53	46	.265	.369	.454	106	5	3	58	6	4	-1	.990	-3	O	-0.3
1940	Chi-A	107	276	46	83	14	5	6	42	64	32	.301	.432	.453	128	15	15	61	2	3	-1	.977	-3	O	0.7
1941	Chi-A	20	59	9	14	4	0	0	1	12	5	.237	.366	.305	80	-1	-1	7	0	0	0	.938	-1	O	-0.3
	Cle-A	45	75	10	14	3	1	1	8	9	10	.187	.274	.293	53	-6	-5	7	1	0	0	1.000	0	O/1	-0.5
	Yr	65	134	19	28	7	1	1	9	21	15	.209	.316	.299	66	-7	-6	14	1	0	0	.971	-1	O/1	-0.8
1944	NY-A	36	101	9	20	3	0	0	9	19	15	.198	.325	.228	57	-5	-5	9	1	0	0	.986	3	O	-0.4
	Phi-A	32	54	5	11	2	0	1	6	5	9	.204	.271	.296	63	-3	-3	5	0	0	0	.960	-4	O	-0.8
	Yr	68	155	14	31	5	0	1	15	24	24	.200	.307	.252	60	-7	-7	14	1	0	0	.979	-2	O	-1.2
1945	Phi-A	28	75	6	15	3	2	0	5	9	8	.200	.286	.293	68	-3	-3	7	0	1	-1	1.000	-2	O	-0.8
Total	8	579	1483	240	390	75	25	22	189	251	195	.263	.370	.392	96	-0	-4	237	13	9	-2	.979	-11	O/1	-3.2

■ SI ROSENTHAL
Rosenthal, Simon b: 11/13/03, Boston, Mass. d: 4/7/69, Boston, Mass. BL/TL, 5'9", 165 lbs. Deb: 9/08/25

YEAR	TM/L	G	AB	R	H	2B	3B	HR	RBI	BB	SO	AVG	OBP	SLG	PRO+	BR	/A	RC	SB	CS	SBR	FA	FR	POS	TPR
1925	Bos-A	19	72	6	19	5	2	0	8	7	3	.264	.329	.389	82	-2	-2	10	1	0	0	.919	0	O	-0.3
1926	Bos-A	104	285	34	76	12	3	4	34	19	18	.267	.317	.372	82	-9	-8	34	4	1	1	.962	-13	O	-2.4
Total	2	123	357	40	95	17	5	4	42	26	21	.266	.319	.375	82	-12	-10	44	5	1	1	.950	-13	/O	-2.7

■ BUNNY ROSER
Roser, John William Joseph "Jack" b: 11/15/01, St.Louis, Mo. d: 5/6/79, Rocky Hill, Conn. BL/TL, 5'11", 175 lbs. Deb: 8/24/22

YEAR	TM/L	G	AB	R	H	2B	3B	HR	RBI	BB	SO	AVG	OBP	SLG	PRO+	BR	/A	RC	SB	CS	SBR	FA	FR	POS	TPR
1922	Bos-N	32	113	13	27	3	4	0	16	10	19	.239	.306	.336	69	-6	-5	12	2	1	0	.915	-2	O	-0.9

■ CHET ROSS
Ross, Chester James b: 4/1/17, Buffalo, N.Y. d: 2/21/89, Buffalo, N.Y. BR/TR, 6'1", 195 lbs. Deb: 9/15/39

YEAR	TM/L	G	AB	R	H	2B	3B	HR	RBI	BB	SO	AVG	OBP	SLG	PRO+	BR	/A	RC	SB	CS	SBR	FA	FR	POS	TPR
1939	Bos-N	11	31	4	10	1	1	0	0	2	10	.323	.364	.419	118	0	1	5	0			1.000	1	/O	0.1
1940	Bos-N	149	569	84	160	23	14	17	89	59	127	.281	.352	.460	130	17	21	96	4			.962	7	*O	2.0
1941	Bos-N	29	50	1	6	1	0	0	4	9	17	.120	.254	.140	14	-6	-5	2	0			1.000	-1	O	-0.7
1942	Bos-N	76	220	20	43	7	2	5	19	16	37	.195	.250	.314	66	-11	-10	17	0			.992	-1	O	-1.5
1943	Bos-N	94	285	27	62	12	2	7	32	26	67	.218	.285	.347	84	-7	-7	28	1			.977	3	O	-0.8
1944	Bos-N	54	154	20	35	9	2	5	26	12	23	.227	.287	.409	91	-2	-3	18	1			1.000	3	O	-0.2
Total	6	413	1309	156	316	53	21	34	170	124	281	.241	.309	.392	100	-8	-4	166	6			.976	11	O	-1.1

■ DON ROSS
Ross, Donald Raymond b: 7/16/14, Pasadena, Cal. BR/TR, 6'1", 185 lbs. Deb: 4/19/38

YEAR	TM/L	G	AB	R	H	2B	3B	HR	RBI	BB	SO	AVG	OBP	SLG	PRO+	BR	/A	RC	SB	CS	SBR	FA	FR	POS	TPR
1938	Det-A	77	265	22	69	7	1	1	30	29	11	.260	.333	.306	58	-15	-18	29	1	0	0	.946	4	3	-1.1
1940	Bro-N	10	38	4	11	2	0	1	8	3	3	.289	.341	.421	103	0	0	6	1			.879	-0	3	0.0
1942	Det-A	87	226	29	62	10	2	3	30	36	16	.274	.379	.376	104	5	3	34	2	1	0	.964	-3	O3	-0.3
1943	Det-A	89	247	19	66	13	0	0	18	20	3	.267	.325	.320	82	-3	-6	27	2	0	1	.985	-8	OS/23	-1.4
1944	Det-A	66	167	14	35	5	0	2	15	14	9	.210	.275	.275	54	-9	-10	13	2	1	0	.958	-1	O/S1	-1.4
1945	Det-A	8	29	3	11	4	0	0	4	5	1	.379	.471	.517	175	3	3	8	2	0	1	.960	-0	/3	0.4
	Cle-A	106	363	26	95	15	1	2	43	42	15	.262	.340	.325	97	-2	-0	41	0	4	-2	.958	-13	*3	-1.5
	Yr	114	392	29	106	19	1	2	47	47	16	.270	.350	.339	104	1	3	48	2	4	-2	.958	-14	*3	-1.1
1946	Cle-A	55	153	12	41	7	0	3	14	17	12	.268	.341	.373	106	-0	1	20	0	0	0	.944	-12	3/O	-1.1
Total	7	498	1488	129	390	63	4	12	162	166	70	.262	.338	.334	86	-22	-27	177	10	6		.946	-33	3O/S21	-6.4

■ JOE ROSSI
Rossi, Joseph Anthony b: 3/13/23, Oakland, Cal. BR/TR, 6'1", 205 lbs. Deb: 4/20/52

YEAR	TM/L	G	AB	R	H	2B	3B	HR	RBI	BB	SO	AVG	OBP	SLG	PRO+	BR	/A	RC	SB	CS	SBR	FA	FR	POS	TPR
1952	Cin-N	55	145	14	32	0	1	1	6	20	20	.221	.319	.255	61	-7	-7	13	1	0	0	.982	2	C	-0.3

■ CLAUDE ROSSMAN
Rossman, Claude R. b: 6/17/1881, Philmont, N.Y. d: 1/16/28, Poughkeepsie, N.Y. BL/TL, 6', Deb: 9/16/04

YEAR	TM/L	G	AB	R	H	2B	3B	HR	RBI	BB	SO	AVG	OBP	SLG	PRO+	BR	/A	RC	SB	CS	SBR	FA	FR	POS	TPR
1904	Cle-A	18	62	5	13	5	0	0	6	0		.210	.210	.290	58	-3	-3	4	0			.933	-4	O	-0.9
1906	Cle-A	118	396	49	122	13	2	1	53	17		.308	.338	.359	120	8	8	55	11			.984	-8	*1/O	-0.3
1907	*Det-A	153	571	60	158	21	8	0	69	33		.277	.317	.342	106	6	3	73	20			.981	-14	*1	-1.6
1908	*Det-A	138	524	45	154	33	13	2	71	27		.294	.330	.418	137	22	20	74	8			.981	6	*1	2.6
1909	Det-A	82	287	16	75	8	3	0	39	13		.261	.293	.310	87	-4	-5	29	10			.981	-6	1	-1.3
	StL-A	2	8	0	1	0	0	0	0	0		.125	.125	.125	-23	-1	-1	0	0			1.000	-0	/O	-0.2
	Yr	84	295	16	76	8	3	0	39	13		.258	.289	.305	84	-5	-6	29	10			.981	-6	1/O	-1.5
Total	5	511	1848	175	523	80	26	3	238	90		.283	.317	.359	113	27	22	236	49			.982	-26	1/O	-1.7

■ RICO ROSSY
Rossy, Elam Jose (Ramos) b: 2/16/64, San Juan, P.R. BR/TR, 5'10", 175 lbs. Deb: 9/11/91

YEAR	TM/L	G	AB	R	H	2B	3B	HR	RBI	BB	SO	AVG	OBP	SLG	PRO+	BR	/A	RC	SB	CS	SBR	FA	FR	POS	TPR
1991	Atl-N	5	1	0	0	0	0	0	0	0	1	.000	.000	.000	-94	-0	-0	0	0	0	0	.000	0	/S	0.0
1992	KC-A	59	149	21	32	8	1	1	12	20	20	.215	.312	.302	72	-5	-5	13	0	3	-2	.961	5	S/32	0.1
Total	2	64	150	21	32	8	1	1	12	20	21	.213	.310	.300	71	-5	-6	13	0	3	-2	.961	5	/S32	0.1

■ FRANK ROTH
Roth, Francis Charles b: 10/11/1878, Chicago, Ill. d: 3/27/55, Burlington, Wis. BR/TR, 5'10", 160 lbs. Deb: 4/18/03 FC

YEAR	TM/L	G	AB	R	H	2B	3B	HR	RBI	BB	SO	AVG	OBP	SLG	PRO+	BR	/A	RC	SB	CS	SBR	FA	FR	POS	TPR
1903	Phi-N	68	220	27	60	11	4	0	22	9		.273	.304	.359	92	-4	-3	26	3			.935	-7	C/3	-0.3
1904	Phi-N	81	229	28	59	8	1	1	20	12		.258	.298	.314	93	-3	-2	25	8			.958	-11	C/12	-0.6
1905	StL-A	35	107	9	25	3	0	0	7	6		.234	.274	.262	74	-4	-3	8	1			.962	-7	C	-0.7

YEAR	TM/L	G	AB	R	H	2B	3B	HR	RBI	BB	SO	AVG	OBP	SLG	PRO+	BR	/A	RC	SB	CS	SBR	FA	FR	POS	TPR
1906	Chi-A	16	51	4	10	1	1	0	7	3		.196	.241	.255	57	-3	-2	4	1			.990	3	C	0.2
1909	Cin-N	56	147	12	35	7	2	0	16	6		.238	.287	.313	87	-3	-3	14	5			.967	-3	C	-0.2
1910	Cin-N	26	29	3	7	2	0	0	3	0	2	.241	.267	.310	71	-1	-1	3	1			.938	-0	/CO	-0.1
Total	6	282	783	83	196	32	8	1	75	36	2	.250	.289	.315	86	-17	-14	80	19			.956	-24	C/O213	-1.7

■ BRAGGO ROTH Roth, Robert Frank b: 8/28/1892, Burlington, Wis. d: 9/11/36, Chicago, Ill. BR/TR, 5'7.5", 170 lbs. Deb: 9/01/14 F

YEAR	TM/L	G	AB	R	H	2B	3B	HR	RBI	BB	SO	AVG	OBP	SLG	PRO+	BR	/A	RC	SB	CS	SBR	FA	FR	POS	TPR
1914	Chi-A	34	126	14	37	4	6	1	10	8	25	.294	.355	.444	142	6	6	20	3	3	-1	.924	2	O	0.5
1915	Chi-A	70	240	44	60	6	10	3	35	29	50	.250	.338	.396	116	5	4	34	12	6	0	.837	-15	3O	-1.2
	Cle-A	39	144	23	43	4	7	4	20	22	22	.299	.399	.507	168	12	12	32	14	4	2	.878	-6	O	0.6
	Yr	109	384	67	103	10	17	**7**	55	51	72	.268	.361	.438	135	18	16	66	26	10	2	.906	-21	O3	-0.6
1916	Cle-A	125	409	50	117	19	7	4	72	38	48	.286	.350	.396	117	11	8	62	29	14	0	.954	3	*O	0.7
1917	Cle-A	145	495	69	141	30	9	1	72	52	73	.285	.355	.388	118	15	11	82	51			.957	-0	*O	0.5
1918	Cle-A	106	375	53	106	21	12	1	59	53	41	.283	.383	.411	127	19	15	69	35			.936	-3	*O	0.6
1919	Phi-A	48	195	33	63	13	8	5	29	15	21	.323	.377	.549	156	14	14	42	11			.975	-5	O	0.6
	Bos-A	63	227	32	58	9	4	0	23	24	32	.256	.337	.330	93	-3	-1	27	9			.943	-4	O	-1.0
	Yr	111	422	65	121	22	12	5	52	39	53	.287	.355	.431	124	11	12	68	20			.955	-9	*O	-0.4
1920	Was-A	138	468	80	136	23	8	9	92	75	57	.291	.395	.432	122	15	17	85	24	12	0	.952	-10	*O	-0.2
1921	NY-A	43	152	29	43	9	2	2	10	19	20	.283	.370	.408	96	-0	-1	24	1	2	-1	.923	-3	O	-0.7
Total	8	811	2831	427	804	138	73	30	422	335	389	.284	.367	.416	122	94	85	477	189	41		.944	-42	O/3	0.4

■ BOB ROTHEL Rothel, Robert Burton b: 9/17/23, Columbia Station Ohio d: 3/21/84, Huron, Ohio BR/TR, 5'10.5", 170 lbs. Deb: 4/22/45

YEAR	TM/L	G	AB	R	H	2B	3B	HR	RBI	BB	SO	AVG	OBP	SLG	PRO+	BR	/A	RC	SB	CS	SBR	FA	FR	POS	TPR
1945	Cle-A	4	10	0	2	0	0	0	0	3	1	.200	.385	.200	75	-0	-0	1	0	0	0	.875	-1	/3	-0.1

■ BOBBY ROTHERMEL Rothermel, Edward Hill b: 12/18/1870, Fleetwood, Pa. d: 2/11/27, Detroit, Mich. Deb: 6/18/1899

YEAR	TM/L	G	AB	R	H	2B	3B	HR	RBI	BB	SO	AVG	OBP	SLG	PRO+	BR	/A	RC	SB	CS	SBR	FA	FR	POS	TPR
1899	Bal-N	10	21	1	2	0	0	0	3	1		.095	.136	.095	-34	-4	-4	0	0			.867	-2	/23S	-0.6

■ JACK ROTHFUSS Rothfuss, John Albert b: 4/18/1872, Newark, N.J. d: 4/20/47, Basking Ridge, N.J BR/TR, 5'11.5", 195 lbs. Deb: 8/02/1897

YEAR	TM/L	G	AB	R	H	2B	3B	HR	RBI	BB	SO	AVG	OBP	SLG	PRO+	BR	/A	RC	SB	CS	SBR	FA	FR	POS	TPR
1897	Pit-N	35	115	20	36	3	1	2	18	5		.313	.352	.409	104	-0	1	18	3			.984	-1	1	0.0

■ CLAUDE ROTHGEB Rothgeb, Claude James b: 1/1/1880, Milford, Ill. d: 7/6/44, Manitowoc, Wis. BB, 6'0.5", 200 lbs. Deb: 6/17/05

YEAR	TM/L	G	AB	R	H	2B	3B	HR	RBI	BB	SO	AVG	OBP	SLG	PRO+	BR	/A	RC	SB	CS	SBR	FA	FR	POS	TPR
1905	Was-A	7	16	2	2	0	0	0	0	0		.125	.125	.125	-21	-2	-2	0	1			1.000	0	/O	-0.2

■ JACK ROTHROCK Rothrock, John Houston b: 3/14/05, Long Beach, Cal. d: 2/2/80, San Bernardino, Cal BB/TR, 5'11.5", 165 lbs. Deb: 7/28/25

YEAR	TM/L	G	AB	R	H	2B	3B	HR	RBI	BB	SO	AVG	OBP	SLG	PRO+	BR	/A	RC	SB	CS	SBR	FA	FR	POS	TPR
1925	Bos-A	22	55	6	19	3	3	0	7	3	7	.345	.379	.509	124	2	2	10	0	0	0	.893	-4	S	0.0
1926	Bos-A	15	17	3	5	1	0	0	2	3	1	.294	.400	.353	101	0	0	3	0	0	0	.692	-2	/S	-0.1
1927	Bos-A	117	428	61	111	24	8	1	36	24	46	.259	.302	.360	73	-19	-18	44	5	5	-2	.953	4	S231	-1.0
1928	Bos-A	117	344	52	92	9	4	3	22	33	40	.267	.333	.343	79	-11	-10	41	12	6	0	.979	-17	O31S/2PC	-2.9
1929	Bos-A	143	473	70	142	19	7	6	59	43	47	.300	.361	.408	100	-1	0	70	23	13	-1	.970	2	*O	-0.7
1930	Bos-A	45	65	4	18	3	1	0	4	2	9	.277	.299	.354	67	-4	-3	6	0	2	-1	.947	1	/O3	-0.4
1931	Bos-A	133	475	81	132	32	3	4	42	47	48	.278	.343	.383	96	-6	-3	64	13	7	-0	.982	-1	O2/13S	-0.8
1932	Bos-A	12	48	3	10	1	0	0	0	5	5	.208	.283	.229	35	-5	-4	4	3	0	1	.973	2	O	-0.2
	Chi-A	39	64	8	12	2	1	0	6	5	9	.188	.246	.250	31	-7	-6	4	1	0	0	.929	-9	O/31	-1.3
	Yr	51	112	11	22	3	1	0	6	10	14	.196	.262	.241	33	-11	-10	8	4	0	1	.961	-7	O/31	-1.5
1934	*StL-N	154	647	106	184	35	3	11	72	49	56	.284	.336	.399	90	-4	-10	91	10			.975	5	*O/2	-1.1
1935	StL-N	129	502	76	137	18	5	3	56	57	29	.273	.347	.347	84	-8	-10	66	7			.980	1	*O	-1.4
1937	Phi-A	88	232	28	62	15	0	0	21	28	15	.267	.346	.332	73	-9	-9	28	1	0	0	.992	-6	O/2	-1.5
Total	11	1014	3350	498	924	162	35	28	327	299	312	.276	.336	.370	85	-72	-71	431	75	33		.976	-24	O/S231CP	-11.4

■ EDD ROUSH Roush, Edd J b: 5/8/1893, Oakland City, Ind. d: 3/21/88, Bradenton, Fla. BL/TL, 5'11", 170 lbs. Deb: 8/20/13 CH

YEAR	TM/L	G	AB	R	H	2B	3B	HR	RBI	BB	SO	AVG	OBP	SLG	PRO+	BR	/A	RC	SB	CS	SBR	FA	FR	POS	TPR
1913	Chi-A	9	10	2	1	0	0	0	0	0	2	.100	.100	.100	-42	-2	-2	0	0			1.000	-0	/O	-0.2
1914	Ind-F	74	166	26	54	8	4	1	30	6	20	.325	.353	.440	112	5	2	32	12			.989	2	O/1	0.2
1915	New-F	145	551	73	164	20	11	3	60	38	25	.298	.350	.390	124	11	15	89	28			.972	4	*O	1.3
1916	NY-N	39	69	4	13	0	1	0	5	1	4	.188	.200	.217	30	-6	-6	4	4			.952	-1	O	-0.9
	Cin-N	69	272	34	78	7	14	0	15	13	19	.287	.336	.415	133	9	10	43	15			.971	6	O	1.4
	Yr	108	341	38	91	7	15	0	20	14	23	.267	.309	.375	114	3	4	46	19			.969	5	O	0.5
1917	Cin-N	136	522	82	178	19	14	4	67	27	24	**.341**	.379	.454	162	32	35	94	21			.962	2	*O	3.3
1918	Cin-N	113	435	61	145	18	10	5	62	22	10	.333	.368	**.455**	**153**	24	25	80	24			.960	8	*O	3.0
1919	*Cin-N	133	504	73	162	19	12	4	71	42	19	**.321**	.380	.431	147	27	28	88	20			.989	10	*O	3.2
1920	Cin-N	149	579	81	196	22	16	4	90	42	22	.339	.386	.453	142	30	31	98	36	24	-4	.975	16	*O1/2	3.4
1921	Cin-N	112	418	68	147	27	12	4	71	31	8	.352	.403	.502	145	23	26	80	19	17	-5	.980	2	*O	1.5
1922	Cin-N	49	165	29	58	7	4	1	24	19	5	.352	.428	.461	132	8	9	33	5	3	-0	.990	1	O	0.5
1923	Cin-N	138	527	88	185	**41**	18	6	88	46	16	.351	.406	.531	149	34	35	109	10	15	-6	.970	-4	*O	1.6
1924	Cin-N	121	483	67	168	23	**21**	3	72	22	11	.348	.376	.501	135	21	22	86	17	13	-3	.959	-5	*O	0.7
1925	Cin-N	134	540	91	183	28	16	8	83	35	14	.339	.383	.494	125	18	19	97	22	20	-5	.978	1	*O	0.6
1926	Cin-N	144	563	95	182	37	10	7	79	38	17	.323	.366	.462	125	16	18	92	8			.955	-12	*O/1	-0.4
1927	NY-N	140	570	83	173	27	4	7	58	26	15	.304	.335	.402	97	-4	-4	74	18			.975	-4	*O	-1.6
1928	NY-N	46	163	20	41	5	3	2	13	14	8	.252	.315	.356	75	-6	-6	18	1			.955	2	O	-0.7
1929	NY-N	115	450	76	146	19	7	8	52	45	16	.324	.390	.451	108	6	6	78	6			.982	-1	*O	-0.2
1931	Cin-N	101	376	46	102	12	5	1	41	17	5	.271	.308	.338	78	-14	-11	40	2			.981	-4	O	-2.2
Total	18	1967	7363	1099	2376	339	182	68	981	484	260	.323	.369	.446	127	232	252	1236	268	92		.972	23	*O/12	14.5

■ PHIL ROUTCLIFFE Routcliffe, Philip John "Chicken" b: 10/24/1870, Oswego, N.Y. d: 10/4/18, Oswego, N.Y. BR/TR, 6', 175 lbs. Deb: 4/21/1890

YEAR	TM/L	G	AB	R	H	2B	3B	HR	RBI	BB	SO	AVG	OBP	SLG	PRO+	BR	/A	RC	SB	CS	SBR	FA	FR	POS	TPR
1890	Pit-N	1	4	1	1	0	0	0	1	0	0	.250	.400	.250	105	0	0	1	1			1.000	0	/O	0.0

■ DAVE ROWAN Rowan, David (b: David Drohan) b: 12/6/1882, Elora, Ont., Canada d: 7/30/55, Toronto, Ont., Can BL/TL, 5'11", 175 lbs. Deb: 5/27/11

YEAR	TM/L	G	AB	R	H	2B	3B	HR	RBI	BB	SO	AVG	OBP	SLG	PRO+	BR	/A	RC	SB	CS	SBR	FA	FR	POS	TPR
1911	StL-A	18	65	7	25	1	1	0	11	4		.385	.420	.431	143	3	4	12	0			.945	-2	1	0.2

■ WADE ROWDON Rowdon, Wade Lee b: 9/7/60, Riverhead, N.Y. BR/TR, 6'2", 180 lbs. Deb: 9/08/84

YEAR	TM/L	G	AB	R	H	2B	3B	HR	RBI	BB	SO	AVG	OBP	SLG	PRO+	BR	/A	RC	SB	CS	SBR	FA	FR	POS	TPR
1984	Cin-N	4	7	0	2	0	0	0	0	0	1	.286	.286	.286	58	-0	-0	1	0	0	0	1.000	1	/S3	0.1
1985	Cin-N	5	9	2	2	0	0	0	2	2	1	.222	.364	.222	64	-0	-0	1	0	0	0	.667	-1	/3	-0.2
1986	Cin-N	38	80	9	20	5	1	0	10	9	17	.250	.333	.338	82	-1	-2	10	2	0	1	.889	-7	/3SO2	-0.8
1987	Chi-N	11	31	2	7	1	1	1	4	3	10	.226	.294	.419	83	-1	-1	3	0	2	-1	.818	-1	/3	-0.4
1988	Bal-A	20	30	1	3	0	0	0	0	0	6	.100	.100	.100	-45	-6	-6	-0	1	1	-0	.947	1	/3OD	-0.5
Total	5	78	157	14	34	6	2	1	16	14	35	.217	.285	.299	59	-8	-9	15	3	3	-1	.866	-7	/3OSD2	-1.8

■ DAVE ROWE Rowe, David E. b: 2/1856, Jacksonville, Ill. BR/TR, 5'9", 180 lbs. Deb: 5/30/1877 FM

YEAR	TM/L	G	AB	R	H	2B	3B	HR	RBI	BB	SO	AVG	OBP	SLG	PRO+	BR	/A	RC	SB	CS	SBR	FA	FR	POS	TPR
1877	Chi-N	2	7	0	2	0	0	0	0	0	3	.286	.286	.286	72	-0	-0	1				.667	-1	/OP	-0.1
1882	Cle-N	24	97	13	25	4	3	1	17	4	9	.258	.287	.392	119	2	2	11				.837	-3	O/P	-0.1
1883	Bal-a	59	256	40	80	11	6	0		2		.313	.318	.402	127	8	7	34				.798	-9	O/S1P	-0.2
1884	StL-U	109	485	95	142	32	11	4		10		.293	.307	.429	141	22	19	65				**.947**	-2	*OS/21P	1.4
1885	StL-N	16	62	8	10	3	0	0	3	5	8	.161	.224	.210	44	-4	-3	3				.906	-2	O	-0.5
1886	KC-N	105	429	53	103	24	8	3	57	15	43	.240	.266	.354	82	-7	-12	42	2			.851	-5	*OS/2M	-1.6
1888	KC-a	32	122	14	21	3	4	0	13	6		.172	.217	.262	52	-6	-7	8	2			.914	2	OM	-0.6
Total	7	347	1458	223	383	77	32	8	90	42	63	.263	.284	.376	107	14	6	163	4			.878	-19	O/S21P	-1.7

YEAR	TM/L	G	AB	R	H	2B	3B	HR	RBI	BB	SO	AVG	OBP	SLG	PRO+	BR	/A	RC	SB	CS	SBR	FA	FR	POS	TPR

■ HARLAND ROWE   Rowe, Harland Stimson "Hypie" b: 4/20/1896, Springvale, Me. d: 5/26/69, Springvale, Maine BL/TR, 6'1", 170 lbs. Deb: 6/23/16

| 1916 | Phi-A | 17 | 36 | 2 | 5 | 1 | 0 | 0 | 3 | 2 | 8 | .139 | .184 | .167 | 6 | -4 | -4 | 1 | | 0 | | .842 | -3 | /3O | -0.7 |

■ JACK ROWE   Rowe, John Charles b: 12/8/1856, Harrisburg, Pa. d: 4/25/11, St.Louis, Mo. BL/TR, 5'8", 170 lbs. Deb: 9/06/1879 FM

1879	Buf-N	8	34	8	12	1	0	0	8	0	1	.353	.353	.382	139	1	1	5				.905	2	/CO	0.3
1880	Buf-N	79	326	43	82	10	6	1	36	6	17	.252	.265	.328	98	-0	-1	29				.897	-19	*CO/3	-2.0
1881	Buf-N	64	246	30	82	11	11	1	43	1	12	.333	.336	.480	156	14	14	41				.900	-7	C/S3O	0.9
1882	Buf-N	75	308	43	82	14	5	1	42	12	0	.266	.294	.354	105	2	1	33				.950	-13	CS/3O	-0.9
1883	Buf-N	87	374	65	104	18	7	1	38	15	14	.278	.306	.372	102	2	1	44				.899	-17	COS/3	-1.2
1884	Buf-N	93	400	85	126	14	14	4	61	23	14	.315	.352	.450	146	23	20	65				.943	-10	CO/S	1.4
1885	Buf-N	98	421	62	122	28	8	2	51	13	19	.290	.311	.409	127	13	11	55				.834	-14	SCO	-1.2
1886	Det-N	111	468	97	142	21	9	6	87	26	27	.303	.340	.425	128	17	15	74	12			.880	-20	*S/C	-0.4
1887	*Det-N	124	537	135	171	30	10	6	96	39	11	.318	.368	.445	123	19	16	98	22			.907	-27	*S	-0.8
1888	Det-N	105	451	62	125	19	8	2	74	19	28	.277	.311	.368	118	9	9	56	10			.861	-9	*S	0.2
1889	Pit-N	75	317	57	82	14	3	2	32	22	16	.259	.313	.341	93	-7	-2	36	5			.896	-10	S	-0.6
1890	Buf-P	125	504	77	126	22	7	2	76	48	18	.250	.324	.333	84	-16	-8	59	10			.901	-2	*SM	-0.2
Total	12	1044	4386	764	1256	202	88	28	644	224	177	.286	.323	.392	116	77	78	594	59			.882	-147	SCO/3	-3.3

■ SCHOOLBOY ROWE   Rowe, Lynwood Thomas b: 1/11/10, Waco, Tex. d: 1/8/61, ElDorado, Ark. BR/TR, 6'4.5", 210 lbs. Deb: 4/15/33 C

1933	Det-A	21	50	6	11	1	0	0	6	1	4	.220	.235	.240	26	-5	-5	3	0	0	0	1.000	2	P	0.0
1934	*Det-A	51	109	15	33	8	1	2	22	6	20	.303	.339	.450	102	-0	-0	17	0	0	0	1.000	-0	P	0.0
1935	*Det-A☆	45	109	19	34	3	2	3	28	12	12	.312	.380	.459	120	3	3	19	0	0	0	.981	-2	P	0.0
1936	Det-A★	45	90	16	23	2	1	1	13	13	15	.256	.356	.333	71	-4	-4	12	0	0	0	.984	2	P	0.0
1937	Det-A	10	10	2	2	0	0	1	1	1		.200	.273	.200	21	-1	-1	1	0	0	0	1.000	0	P	0.0
1938	Det-A	4	6	1	1	1	0	0	0	0	1	.167	.167	.333	21	-1	-1	0	0	0	0	.889	1	/P	0.0
1939	Det-A	31	61	7	15	1	1	1	12	5	7	.246	.303	.328	57	-4	-4	5	1	1	-0	.947	0	P	0.0
1940	*Det-A	27	67	7	18	6	1	1	18	5	13	.269	.319	.433	85	-1	-2	9	1	1	-0	1.000	-0	P	0.0
1941	Det-A	32	55	10	15	0	3	1	12	5	8	.273	.333	.436	93	-0	-1	8	0	0	0	.927	1	P	0.0
1942	Det-A	2	4	0	0	0	0	0	0	0	0	.000	.000	.000	-93	-1	-1	0	0	0	0	1.000	0	/P	0.0
	Bro-N	14	19	2	4	0	0	0	2	1	4	.211	.250	.211	35	-2	-2	1	0			1.000	0	/P	0.0
1943	Phi-N	82	120	14	36	7	0	4	18	15	21	.300	.382	.458	148	7	7	20	0			.981	0	P	0.0
1946	Phi-N	30	61	4	11	5	0	1	6	3	16	.180	.219	.311	51	-4	-4	4	0			1.000	-2	P	0.0
1947	Phi-N★	43	79	9	22	2	0	2	11	13	18	.278	.380	.380	106	1	1	12	0			.974	-1	P	0.0
1948	Phi-N	31	52	3	10	1	0	0	1	2	14	.192	.250	.250	36	-5	-5	4	1			.976	1	P	0.0
1949	Phi-N	23	17	1	4	1	0	1	1	2	4	.235	.316	.471	111	0	0	3	0			.870	1	P	0.0
Total	15	491	909	116	239	36	9	18	153	86	157	.263	.328	.382	87	-17	-18	119	3	2		.974	2	P	0.0

■ BAMA ROWELL   Rowell, Carvel William b: 1/13/16, Citronelle, Ala. BL/TR, 5'11", 185 lbs. Deb: 9/04/39

1939	Bos-N	21	59	5	11	2	2	0	6	1	4	.186	.200	.288	32	-6	-5	3	0			.853	-2	O	-0.8
1940	Bos-N	130	486	46	148	19	8	3	58	18	22	.305	.331	.395	105	-1	2	64	12			.953	-3	*2/O	0.6
1941	Bos-N	138	483	49	129	23	6	7	60	39	36	.267	.322	.383	102	-2	-0	61	11			.935	-10	*2O/3	-0.3
1946	Bos-N	95	293	37	82	12	6	3	31	29	15	.280	.345	.392	108	3	3	41	5			.978	-0	O	-0.1
1947	Bos-N	113	384	48	106	23	2	5	40	18	14	.276	.310	.385	86	-10	-9	47	7			.945	-8	*O/23	-2.1
1948	Phi-N	77	196	15	47	16	2	1	22	8	14	.240	.270	.357	70	-9	-9	18	2			.821	-12	3O2	-2.1
Total	6	574	1901	200	523	95	26	19	217	113	105	.275	.316	.382	95	-26	-19	233	37			.945	-35	2O/3	-4.8

■ ED ROWEN   Rowen, W. Edward b: 10/22/1857, Bridgeport, Conn. d: 2/22/1892, Bridgeport, Conn. 6'1", 170 lbs. Deb: 5/01/1882

1882	Bos-N	83	327	36	81	7	4	1	43	19	18	.248	.289	.303	90	-3	-3	29				.885	-12	OC/S3	-1.3
1883	Phi-a	49	196	28	43	10	1	0		10		.219	.257	.281	67	-6	-8	15				.855	-2	C/O32	-0.7
1884	Phi-a	4	15	4	6	1	0	0		1		.400	.471	.467	198	2	2	3				.806	-3	/C	-0.1
Total	3	136	538	68	130	18	5	1	43	30	18	.242	.283	.299	85	-7	-10	47				.866	-17	/COS32	-2.1

■ CHUCK ROWLAND   Rowland, Charles Leland b: 7/23/1899, Warrenton, N.C. BR/TR, 6'1", 185 lbs. Deb: 5/11/23

| 1923 | Phi-A | 5 | 6 | 0 | 0 | 0 | 0 | 0 | 0 | 0 | 2 | .000 | .000 | .000 | -99 | -2 | -2 | 0 | 0 | 0 | 0 | 1.000 | 0 | /C | -0.1 |

■ RICH ROWLAND   Rowland, Richard Garnet b: 2/25/67, Cloverdale, Cal. BR/TR, 6'1", 210 lbs. Deb: 9/07/90

1990	Det-A	7	19	3	3	1	0	0	2	0	4	.158	.238	.211	26	-2	-2	1	0	0	0	.967	-0	/CD	-0.2
1991	Det-A	4	4	0	1	0	0	0	1	1	2	.250	.400	.250	83	-0	-0	1	0	0	0	1.000	0	/CD	0.0
1992	Det-A	6	14	2	3	0	0	0	3	3	3	.214	.353	.214	61	-1	-1	1	0	0	0	1.000	0	/C13D	-0.1
Total	3	17	37	5	7	1	0	0	6	9	.189	.302	.216	47	-2	-2	3	0	0	0	.974	0	/CD31	-0.3

■ JIM ROXBURGH   Roxburgh, James A. b: 1/17/1858, San Francisco, Cal d: 2/21/34, San Francisco, Csl BR/TR, Deb: 5/30/1884

1884	Bal-a	2	4	1	2	0	0	0		1		.500	.667	.500	281	1	1	1				.824	-0	/C	0.1
1887	Phi-a	2	8	0	1	0	0	0		0		.125	.125	.125	-29	-1	-1	0	0			.875	-2	/C2	-0.2
Total	2	4	12	1	3	0	0	0		1		.250	.357	.250	83	-0	-0	1	0			.840	-2	/C2	-0.1

■ STAN ROYER   Royer, Stanley Dean b: 8/31/67, Olney, Ill. BR/TR, 6'3", 195 lbs. Deb: 9/11/91

1991	StL-N	9	21	1	6	1	0	0	1	1	2	.286	.318	.333	83	-0	-0	2	0	0	0	1.000	0	/3	-0.2
1992	StL-N	13	31	6	10	2	0	2	9	1	4	.323	.344	.581	160	2	2	6	0	0	0	.900	-0	/31	0.0
Total	2	22	52	7	16	3	0	2	10	2	6	.308	.333	.481	128	2	2	9	0	0	0	.947	-2	/31	0.0

■ JERRY ROYSTER   Royster, Jeron Kennis b: 10/18/52, Sacramento, Cal. BR/TR, 6', 165 lbs. Deb: 8/14/73

1973	LA-N	10	19	1	4	0	0	0	2	0	5	.211	.211	.211	18	-2	-2	1	1	0	0	.842	2	/32	0.0
1974	LA-N	6	0	2	0	0	0	0	0	0	0	—	—	—	—	0	0	0	0	0	0	1.000	2	/23O	0.2
1975	LA-N	13	36	2	9	2	1	0	1	1	3	.250	.270	.361	77	-1	-1	3	1	0	0	1.000	-1	/O23S	-0.2
1976	Atl-N	149	533	65	132	13	1	5	45	52	53	.248	.316	.304	72	-16	-20	52	24	13	-1	.962	17	*3/S	-0.5
1977	Atl-N	140	445	64	96	10	2	6	28	38	67	.216	.279	.288	47	-30	-37	36	28	10	2	.953	-28	3S2/O	-5.8
1978	Atl-N	140	529	67	137	17	8	2	35	56	49	.259	.333	.332	78	-8	-15	60	27	17	-2	.974	-13	2S/3	-1.8
1979	Atl-N	154	601	103	164	25	6	3	51	62	59	.273	.341	.349	83	-8	-14	78	35	8	6	.948	13	32	1.0
1980	Atl-N	123	392	42	95	17	5	1	20	37	48	.242	.309	.319	73	-12	-14	39	22	13	-1	.948	-15	23O	-3.1
1981	Atl-N	64	93	13	19	4	1	0	9	7	14	.204	.260	.269	49	-6	-6	6	7	5	-1	.950	3	32	-0.4
1982	*Atl-N	108	261	43	77	13	2	2	25	22	36	.295	.354	.383	102	2	1	37	14	6	1	.943	-2	3O2S	0.0
1983	Atl-N	91	268	32	63	10	3	3	30	28	35	.235	.307	.328	71	-9	-11	25	11	7	-1	.940	8	32OS	-0.3
1984	Atl-N	81	227	22	47	13	1	2	21	15	41	.207	.259	.295	52	-14	-16	16	6	4	-1	.973	5	23SO	-1.0
1985	SD-N	90	249	31	70	13	2	5	31	32	31	.281	.365	.410	118	6	7	37	6	5	-1	.975	2	23/SO	1.0
1986	SD-N	118	257	31	66	12	0	5	26	32	45	.257	.339	.362	95	-2	-1	31	3	5	-2	.931	-4	3S2/O	-0.6
1987	Chi-A	55	154	25	37	11	0	7	23	19	28	.240	.328	.448	101	0	-0	23	2	1	0	.969	-8	3O/2D	-0.8
	NY-A	18	42	1	15	2	0	0	4	4	4	.357	.413	.405	120	1	1	7	2	1	0	.909	2	3/2SO	0.3
	Yr	73	196	26	52	13	0	7	27	23	32	.265	.345	.439	104	1	1	30	4	2	0	.954	-5	30/2S	-0.5
1988	Atl-N	68	102	8	18	3	0	1	6	6	16	.176	.222	.206	22	-10	-11	5	4	0	0	1.000	-5	O3/2S	-1.4
Total	16	1428	4208	552	1049	165	33	40	352	411	534	.249	.318	.333	76	-108	-138	456	189	95	-0	.951	-19	32SO/D	-13.4

■ WILLIE ROYSTER   Royster, Willie Arthur b: 4/11/54, Clarksville, Va. BR/TR, 5'11", 180 lbs. Deb: 9/03/81

| 1981 | Bal-A | 4 | 4 | 0 | 0 | 0 | 0 | 0 | 0 | 0 | 2 | .000 | .000 | .000 | -99 | -1 | -1 | 0 | 0 | 0 | 0 | 1.000 | -0 | /C | -0.1 |

YEAR	TM/L	G	AB	R	H	2B	3B	HR	RBI	BB	SO	AVG	OBP	SLG	PRO+	BR	/A	RC	SB	CS	SBR	FA	FR	POS	TPR
■ **VIC ROZNOVSKY** Roznovsky, Victor Joseph b: 10/19/38, Shiner, Tex. BL/TR, 6'1", 180 lbs. Deb: 6/28/64																									
1964	Chi-N	35	76	2	15	1	0	0	2	5	18	.197	.247	.211	29	-7	-7	4	0	1	-1	.976	-6	C	-1.4
1965	Chi-N	71	172	9	38	4	1	3	15	16	30	.221	.298	.308	70	-6	-7	17	1	0	0	.984	2	C	-0.2
1966	Bal-A	41	97	4	23	5	0	1	10	9	11	.237	.308	.320	82	-2	-2	10	0	0	0	.995	-3	C	-0.3
1967	Bal-A	45	97	7	20	5	0	0	10	1	20	.206	.214	.258	39	-7	-7	4	0	0	0	.993	-2	C	-0.9
1969	Phi-N	13	13	0	3	0	0	0	1	1	4	.231	.286	.231	47	-1	-1	1	0	0	0	1.000	0	/C	-0.1
Total	5	205	455	22	99	15	1	4	38	32	83	.218	.275	.281	59	-24	-24	36	1	1	-0	.988	-9	C	-2.9
■ **AL RUBELING** Rubeling, Albert William b: 5/10/13, Baltimore, Md. d: 1/28/88, Baltimore, Md. BR/TR, 6', 185 lbs. Deb: 4/16/40																									
1940	Phi-A	108	376	49	92	16	6	4	38	48	58	.245	.330	.351	78	-13	-11	45	4	5	-2	.933	-7	32	-1.7
1941	Phi-A	6	19	0	5	0	0	0	2	2	1	.263	.333	.263	61	-1	-1	2	0	0	0	.833	-2	/3	-0.2
1943	Pit-N	47	168	23	44	8	4	0	9	8	17	.262	.295	.357	85	-3	-4	17	0			.974	-0	2/3	-0.2
1944	Pit-N	92	184	22	45	7	2	4	30	19	19	.245	.322	.370	90	-1	-2	23	4			1.000	-1	O23	-0.3
Total	4	253	747	94	186	31	12	8	79	77	95	.249	.321	.355	82	-18	-19	87	8	5		.939	-10	3/2O	-2.4
■ **SONNY RUBERTO** Ruberto, John Edward b: 1/2/46, Staten Island, N.Y. BR/TR, 5'11", 175 lbs. Deb: 5/25/69 C																									
1969	SD-N	19	21	3	3	0	0	0	0	1	7	.143	.182	.143	-8	-3	-3	1	0	0	0	1.000	4	C	0.2
1972	Cin-N	2	3	0	0	0	0	0	0	0	1	.000	.250	.000	-25	-0	-0	0	0	0	0	1.000	-0	/C	-0.1
Total	2	21	24	3	3	0	0	0	0	1	8	.125	.192	.125	-10	-3	-3	1	0	0	0	1.000	4	/C	0.1
■ **ART RUBLE** Ruble, William Arthur "Speedy" b: 3/11/03, Knoxville, Tenn. d: 11/1/83, Maryville, Tenn. BL/TR, 5'10.5", 168 lbs. Deb: 4/18/27																									
1927	Det-A	56	91	16	15	4	2	0	11	14	15	.165	.283	.253	39	-8	-8	7	2	2	-1	.970	-7	O	-1.7
1934	Phi-N	19	54	7	15	4	0	0	8	7	3	.278	.361	.352	81	-0	-1	7	0			.839	-2	O	-0.3
Total	2	75	145	23	30	8	2	0	19	21	18	.207	.311	.290	55	-9	-10	14	2	2		.929	-9	/O	-2.0
■ **JOHNNY RUCKER** Rucker, John Joel b: 1/15/17, Crabapple, Ga. d: 8/7/85, Moultrie, Ga. BL/TR, 6'2", 175 lbs. Deb: 4/16/40																									
1940	NY-N	86	277	38	82	7	5	4	23	7	32	.296	.313	.401	95	-2	-3	34	4			.954	-3	O	-0.9
1941	NY-N	143	622	95	179	38	9	1	42	29	61	.288	.320	.383	95	-4	-6	76	8			.967	5	*O	-0.9
1943	NY-N	132	505	56	138	19	4	2	46	22	44	.273	.304	.339	85	-11	-11	53	4			.969	2	*O	-1.6
1944	NY-N	144	587	79	143	14	8	6	39	24	48	.244	.275	.325	69	-26	-26	54	8			.985	-6	*O	-4.1
1945	NY-N	105	429	58	117	19	11	7	51	20	36	.273	.305	.417	98	-3	-3	55	7			.978	-1	O	-1.0
1946	NY-N	95	197	28	52	8	2	1	13	7	27	.264	.300	.340	81	-5	-6	20	4			.948	-10	O	-1.8
Total	6	705	2617	354	711	105	39	21	214	109	248	.272	.302	.366	87	-51	-54	293	35			.971	-13	O	-10.3
■ **JOHN RUDDERHAM** Rudderham, John Edmund b: 8/30/1863, Quincy, Mass. d: 4/3/42, Randolph, Mass. BR/TR, 5'8", 170 lbs. Deb: 9/18/1884																									
1884	Bos-U	1	4	0	1	0	0	0		0		.250	.250	.250	71	-0	-0	0				.000	-1	/O	-0.1
■ **JOE RUDI** Rudi, Joseph Oden b: 9/7/46, Modesto, Cal. BR/TR, 6'2", 200 lbs. Deb: 4/11/67 C																									
1967	KC-A	19	43	4	8	2	0	0	1	3	7	.186	.239	.233	41	-3	-3	2	0	0	0	.984	-2	/1O	-0.6
1968	Oak-A	68	181	10	32	5	1	1	12	12	32	.177	.236	.232	44	-13	-12	10	1	1	-0	.987	-3	O	-2.1
1969	Oak-A	35	122	10	23	3	1	2	6	5	16	.189	.220	.279	41	-10	-10	7	1	1	-0	1.000	2	O1	-1.0
1970	Oak-A	106	350	40	108	23	2	11	42	16	61	.309	.342	.480	129	10	12	54	3	1	0	.982	-2	O1	0.4
1971	*Oak-A	127	513	62	137	23	4	10	52	28	62	.267	.306	.386	97	-5	-4	57	3	2	-0	.996	7	*O/1	-0.4
1972	*Oak-A★	147	593	94	**181**	32	**9**	19	75	37	62	.305	.348	.486	154	31	34	95	3	4	-2	.992	-1	*O/3	2.8
1973	*Oak-A	120	437	53	118	25	1	12	66	30	72	.270	.320	.414	111	2	5	55	0	0	0	.992	4	*O/1D	0.3
1974	*Oak-A★	158	593	73	174	**39**	4	22	99	34	92	.293	.337	.484	143	23	28	94	2	3	-1	.984	-7	*O1/D	1.3
1975	*Oak-A★	126	468	66	130	26	6	21	75	40	56	.278	.339	.494	136	18	19	76	2	1	0	.991	-12	1O/D	0.0
1976	Oak-A	130	500	54	135	32	3	13	94	41	71	.270	.329	.424	124	11	13	68	6	1	1	.989	-1	*O/1D	0.8
1977	Cal-A	64	242	48	64	13	2	13	53	22	48	.264	.336	.496	128	7	8	42	1	0	0	1.000	5	O/D	1.1
1978	Cal-A	133	497	58	127	27	1	17	79	28	82	.256	.298	.416	103	-3	-0	60	2	1	0	.992	7	*OD1	0.1
1979	Cal-A	90	330	35	80	11	3	11	61	24	61	.242	.296	.394	87	-8	-7	38	0	0	0	.989	6	O/1D	-0.4
1980	Cal-A	104	372	42	88	17	1	16	53	17	84	.237	.279	.417	90	-8	-6	41	1	0	0	.991	8	O/1D	-0.1
1981	Bos-A	49	122	14	22	3	0	6	24	8	29	.180	.242	.352	66	-5	-6	10	0	0	0	1.000	-1	D/1O	-0.8
1982	Oak-A	71	193	21	41	6	1	5	18	24	35	.212	.303	.332	77	-7	-6	21	0	0	0	.991	-7	1O/D	-1.5
Total	16	1547	5556	684	1468	287	39	179	810	369	870	.264	.314	.427	112	41	66	730	25	15	-1	.991	3	*O1/D3	-0.1
■ **DUTCH RUDOLPH** Rudolph, John Herman b: 7/10/1882, Natrona, Pa. d: 4/17/67, Natrona, Pa. BL/TL, 5'10", 160 lbs. Deb: 7/03/03																									
1903	Phi-N	1	1	0	0	0	0	0	0	0		.000	.000	.000	-99	-0	-0	0	0			.000	0	H	0.0
1904	Chi-N	2	3	0	1	0	0	0	0	0		.333	.333	.333	106	0	0	0	0			1.000	-1	/O	-0.1
Total	2	3	4	0	1	0	0	0	0	0		.250	.250	.250	52	-0	-0	0	0				-1	/O	-0.1
■ **KEN RUDOLPH** Rudolph, Kenneth Victor b: 12/29/46, Rockford, Ill. BR/TR, 6'1", 185 lbs. Deb: 4/20/69																									
1969	Chi-N	27	34	7	7	1	0	1	6	6	11	.206	.325	.324	73	-1	-1	4	0	0	0	.977	1	C/O	-0.1
1970	Chi-N	20	40	1	4	1	0	0	2	1	12	.100	.122	.125	-30	-8	-8	1	0	0	0	1.000	1	C	-0.6
1971	Chi-N	25	76	5	15	3	0	0	7	6	20	.197	.265	.237	38	-6	-7	5	0	0	0	1.000	7	C	0.1
1972	Chi-N	42	106	10	25	1	1	2	9	6	14	.236	.283	.321	64	-4	-5	8	1	2	-1	.966	5	C	0.0
1973	Chi-N	64	170	12	35	8	1	2	17	7	25	.206	.242	.300	46	-12	-13	10	1	4	-2	.970	-3	C	-1.7
1974	SF-N	57	158	11	41	3	0	0	10	21	15	.259	.350	.278	74	-4	-5	15	0	0	0	.996	3	C	0.0
1975	StL-N	44	80	5	16	2	0	1	6	3	10	.200	.229	.262	35	-7	-7	4	0	0	0	.972	2	C	-0.5
1976	StL-N	27	50	1	8	3	0	0	5	1	7	.160	.176	.220	12	-6	-6	2	0	0	0	.940	2	C	-0.4
1977	SF-N	11	15	1	3	0	0	0	0	1	3	.200	.250	.200	22	-2	-2	1	0	0	0	.946	3	C	0.1
	Bal-A	11	14	2	4	1	0	0	2	0	4	.286	.286	.357	79	-1	-0	1	0	0	0	1.000	5	C	0.4
Total	9	328	743	55	158	23	2	6	64	52	121	.213	.268	.273	48	-49	-55	51	2	6	-3	.980	25	C/O	-2.7
■ **MUDDY RUEL** Ruel, Herold Dominic b: 2/20/1896, St.Louis, Mo. d: 11/13/63, Palo Alto, Cal. BR/TR, 5'9", 150 lbs. Deb: 5/29/15 MC																									
1915	StL-A	10	14	0	0	0	0	0	1	5	5	.000	.263	.000	-22	-2	-2	0	0			.958	-1	/C	-0.3
1917	NY-A	6	17	1	2	0	0	0	1	2	2	.118	.211	.118	0	-2	-2	1	1			1.000	-1	/C	-0.3
1918	NY-A	3	6	0	2	0	0	0	0	2	1	.333	.500	.333	148	1	1	1	1			1.000	0	/C	0.1
1919	NY-A	79	233	18	56	6	0	0	31	34	26	.240	.340	.266	71	-7	-8	22	4			.975	2	C	0.1
1920	NY-A	82	261	30	70	14	1	1	15	15	18	.268	.310	.341	70	-11	-12	28	4	2	0	.984	1	C	-0.6
1921	Bos-A	113	358	41	99	21	1	1	45	41	15	.277	.352	.349	82	-10	-9	45	2	7	-4	.977	-10	*C	-1.5
1922	Bos-A	116	361	34	92	15	1	0	28	41	26	.255	.333	.302	67	-17	-16	39	4	2	0	.978	-2	*C	-1.2
1923	Was-A	136	449	63	142	24	3	0	54	55	21	.316	.394	.383	111	6	9	70	4	6	-2	.980	19	*C	3.0
1924	*Was-A	149	501	50	142	20	2	0	57	62	20	.283	.370	.331	84	-11	-9	65	7	11	-5	.980	14	*C	0.9
1925	*Was-A	127	393	55	122	9	2	0	54	63	16	.310	.411	.344	95	-0	1	60	4	5	-2	.982	12	*C/1	1.6
1926	Was-A	117	368	42	110	22	4	1	53	61	14	.299	.401	.389	109	6	8	61	7	6	-2	**.989**	2	*C	1.4
1927	Was-A	131	428	61	132	16	5	1	52	63	18	.308	.403	.376	104	5	6	65	9	6	-1	.988	-3	*C	1.1
1928	Was-A	108	350	31	90	18	2	0	55	44	14	.257	.342	.320	75	-12	-11	40	12	10	-2	**.989**	7	*C/1	0.1
1929	Was-A	69	188	16	46	4	2	0	20	31	7	.245	.352	.287	66	-8	-9	20	0	4	-2	.990	9	C	0.3
1930	Was-A	66	198	18	50	3	4	0	26	24	13	.253	.342	.308	66	-9	-10	23	1	0	0	.986	4	C	0.0
1931	Bos-A	33	83	6	25	5	0	0	6	9	6	.301	.370	.361	98	-1	0	12	0	0	0	.945	1	C	0.3
	Det-A	14	50	1	6	1	0	0	3	5	1	.120	.200	.140	-9	-8	-8	2	0	0	0	.975	3	C	-0.4
	Yr	47	133	7	31	6	0	0	9	14	7	.233	.306	.278	56	-9	-8	12	0	0	0	.958	4	C	-0.1
1932	Det-A	51	136	10	32	4	2	0	18	17	6	.235	.320	.294	58	-8	-9	14	1	0	0	.989	-2	C	-0.7
1933	StL-A	36	63	13	12	2	0	0	8	24	4	.190	.414	.222	68	-1	-1	8	0	0	0	1.000	3	C	0.2

YEAR	TM/L	G	AB	R	H	2B	3B	HR	RBI	BB	SO	AVG	OBP	SLG	PRO+	BR	/A	RC	SB	CS	SBR	FA	FR	POS	TPR
1934	Chi-A	22	57	4	12	3	0	0	7	8	5	.211	.308	.263	47	-4	-5	5	0	0	0	.976	-2	C	-0.5
Total	19	1468	4514	494	1242	187	29	4	534	606	238	.275	.365	.332	83	-93	-85	581	61	59		.982	53	*C/1	3.6

■ DUTCH RUETHER Ruether, Walter Henry b: 9/13/1893, Alameda, Cal. d: 5/16/70, Phoenix, Ariz. BL/TL, 6′1.5″, 180 lbs. Deb: 4/13/17

YEAR	TM/L	G	AB	R	H	2B	3B	HR	RBI	BB	SO	AVG	OBP	SLG	PRO+	BR	/A	RC	SB	CS	SBR	FA	FR	POS	TPR
1917	Chi-N	31	44	3	12	1	3	0	11	8	11	.273	.385	.432	139	3	2	7	0			1.000	1	P/1	0.1
	Cin-N	19	24	1	5	2	0	0	1	3	6	.208	.296	.292	84	-0	-0	2	1			.833	-0	/P	0.0
	Yr	50	68	4	17	3	3	0	12	11	17	.250	.354	.382	122	2	2	9	1			.920	0	P/1	0.1
1918	Cin-N	2	3	0	0	0	0	0	0	0	2	.000	.000	.000	-99	-1	-1	0	0			1.000	-0	/P	0.0
1919	*Cin-N	42	92	8	24	2	3	0	6	4	18	.261	.292	.348	94	-1	-1	9	1			.971	-3	P	0.0
1920	Cin-N	45	104	3	20	4	0	0	10	5	24	.192	.229	.231	33	-9	-9	6	0	0	0	.952	0	P/1	0.0
1921	Bro-N	49	97	12	34	5	2	2	13	4	9	.351	.376	.505	127	4	4	18	1	0	0	.966	-1	P	0.0
1922	Bro-N	67	125	12	26	6	1	2	20	12	11	.208	.283	.320	56	-9	-8	12	0	0	0	1.000	-0	P	0.0
1923	Bro-N	49	117	6	32	1	0	0	10	12	12	.274	.341	.282	68	-5	-5	12	0	0	0	.968	-2	P/1	0.0
1924	Bro-N	34	62	5	15	1	1	0	4	5	2	.242	.299	.290	60	-4	-3	6	0	0	0	.981	1	P	0.0
1925	*Was-A	55	108	18	36	3	2	1	15	10	8	.333	.390	.426	109	1	2	18	0	1	-1	.962	-3	P/1	0.0
1926	Was-A	47	92	6	23	2	0	1	11	6	10	.250	.296	.304	58	-6	-6	9	0	0	0	.974	-2	P	0.0
	*NY-A	13	21	2	2	0	0	0	0	0	1	.095	.136	.095	-39	-4	-4	0	0	0	0	.875	-1	/P	0.0
	Yr	60	113	8	25	2	0	1	11	6	11	.221	.267	.265	40	-10	-10	8	0	0	0	.957	-3	P	0.0
1927	NY-A	35	80	7	21	3	0	1	10	8	15	.262	.330	.338	76	-3	-3	9	0	0	0	1.000	0	P	0.0
Total	11	488	969	83	250	30	12	7	111	77	129	.258	.314	.335	76	-34	-32	108	3	1		.970	-9	P/1	0.1

■ RUDY RUFER Rufer, Rudolph Joseph b: 10/28/26, Ridgewood, N.Y. BR/TR, 6′0.5″, 165 lbs. Deb: 9/22/49

YEAR	TM/L	G	AB	R	H	2B	3B	HR	RBI	BB	SO	AVG	OBP	SLG	PRO+	BR	/A	RC	SB	CS	SBR	FA	FR	POS	TPR
1949	NY-N	7	15	1	1	0	0	0	2	2	0	.067	.176	.067	-32	-3	-3	0	0			.957	-1	/S	-0.3
1950	NY-N	15	11	1	1	0	0	0	0	0	1	.091	.091	.091	-52	-2	-2	0	1			.889	1	/S	-0.1
Total	2	22	26	2	2	0	0	0	2	2	1	.077	.143	.077	-40	-5	-5	0	1			.938	1	/S	-0.4

■ RED RUFFING Ruffing, Charles Herbert b: 5/3/04, Granville, Ill. d: 2/17/86, Mayfield Hts., O. BR/TR, 6′1.5″, 205 lbs. Deb: 5/31/24 CH

YEAR	TM/L	G	AB	R	H	2B	3B	HR	RBI	BB	SO	AVG	OBP	SLG	PRO+	BR	/A	RC	SB	CS	SBR	FA	FR	POS	TPR
1924	Bos-A	8	7	0	1	0	1	0	0	0	1	.143	.143	.429	44	-1	-1	0	0	0	0	1.000	-1	/P	0.0
1925	Bos-A	37	79	6	17	4	2	0	11	1	22	.215	.235	.316	39	-8	-8	6	0	0	0	.983	-1	P	0.0
1926	Bos-A	37	51	8	10	1	0	1	5	2	12	.196	.226	.275	31	-5	-5	3	0	1	-1	.978	-1	P	0.0
1927	Bos-A	29	55	5	14	3	1	0	4	0	6	.255	.268	.345	59	-4	-3	5	0	0	0	.978	0	P	0.0
1928	Bos-A	60	121	12	38	13	1	2	19	3	12	.314	.331	.488	115	1	2	19	0	0	0	.951	-3	P	0.0
1929	Bos-A	60	114	9	35	9	0	2	17	2	13	.307	.325	.439	97	-1	-1	16	0	0	0	.946	-2	P/O	-0.1
1930	Bos-A	6	11	2	3	2	0	0	1	0	1	.273	.273	.455	84	-0	-0	1	0	0	0	.667	-1	/P	0.0
	NY-A	52	99	15	37	6	2	4	21	7	7	.374	.415	.596	160	8	8	24	0	0	0	.938	-2	P	0.0
	Yr	58	110	17	40	8	2	4	22	7	8	.364	.402	.582	153	7	8	25	0	0	0	.914	-3	P	0.0
1931	NY-A	48	109	14	36	8	1	3	12	1	13	.330	.336	.505	125	2	3	18	0	0	0	1.000	-3	P/O	0.0
1932	*NY-A	55	124	20	38	6	1	3	19	6	10	.306	.338	.444	106	-0	1	18	0	0	0	.955	-2	P	0.0
1933	NY-A	55	115	10	29	3	1	2	13	7	15	.252	.295	.348	74	-5	-4	12	0	0	0	.964	-0	P	0.0
1934	NY-A★	45	113	11	28	3	0	2	13	3	17	.248	.274	.327	58	-8	-7	10	0	0	0	.933	-3	P	0.0
1935	NY-A	50	109	13	37	10	0	2	18	3	9	.339	.363	.486	125	2	3	19	0	0	0	1.000	-2	P	0.0
1936	*NY-A	53	127	14	37	5	0	5	22	11	12	.291	.348	.449	99	-1	-1	20	0	0	0	.986	2	P	0.0
1937	*NY-A	54	129	11	26	3	0	1	10	13	24	.202	.275	.248	32	-13	-13	9	0	0	0	.974	-4	P	0.0
1938	*NY-A☆	45	107	12	24	4	1	3	17	17	21	.224	.331	.364	74	-4	-4	14	0	0	0	1.000	-2	P	0.0
1939	*NY-A★	44	114	12	35	1	0	1	20	7	18	.307	.347	.342	78	-4	-4	14	1	0	0	.952	-2	P	0.0
1940	NY-A★	33	89	8	11	4	0	1	7	3	9	.124	.152	.202	-9	-15	-14	2	0	0	0	.947	-3	P	0.0
1941	*NY-A☆	38	89	10	27	8	1	2	22	4	12	.303	.333	.483	115	1	1	14	0	0	0	1.000	-3	P	0.0
1942	*NY-A☆	30	80	8	20	4	0	1	13	5	13	.250	.302	.338	81	-2	-2	8	0	0	0	.974	-2	P	0.0
1945	NY-A	21	46	4	10	0	1	1	5	0	8	.217	.217	.326	54	-3	-3	3	0	0	0	.929	-2	P	0.0
1946	NY-A	8	25	1	3	1	0	0	1	1	8	.120	.154	.160	-12	-4	-4	1	0	0	0	1.000	-1	/P	0.0
1947	Chi-A	14	24	2	5	0	0	0	3	1	3	.208	.240	.208	26	-2	-2	1	0	0	0	1.000	-0	/P	0.0
Total	22	882	1937	207	521	98	13	36	273	97	266	.269	.306	.389	81	-67	-59	238	1	1	-0	.968	-35	P/O	-0.1

■ CHICO RUIZ Ruiz, Hiraldo (Sablon) b: 12/5/38, Santo Domingo, Cuba d: 2/9/72, San Diego, Cal. BB/TR, 6′, 173 lbs. Deb: 4/13/64

YEAR	TM/L	G	AB	R	H	2B	3B	HR	RBI	BB	SO	AVG	OBP	SLG	PRO+	BR	/A	RC	SB	CS	SBR	FA	FR	POS	TPR
1964	Cin-N	77	311	33	76	13	2	2	16	7	41	.244	.270	.318	63	-15	-16	28	11	3	2	.942	-10	32	-2.4
1965	Cin-N	29	18	7	2	1	0	0	1	0	5	.111	.111	.167	-21	-3	-3	-0	1	2	-1	.875	4	/3S	0.0
1966	Cin-N	82	110	13	28	2	1	0	5	5	14	.255	.287	.291	56	-6	-7	9	1	2	-1	.927	1	3/OS	-0.7
1967	Cin-N	105	250	32	55	12	4	0	13	11	35	.220	.259	.300	53	-13	-16	18	9	4	0	.969	2	23S/O	-1.1
1968	Cin-N	85	139	15	36	2	1	0	9	12	18	.259	.318	.288	78	-3	-3	13	4	3	-1	.979	8	21/3S	0.5
1969	Cin-N	88	196	19	48	4	1	0	13	14	28	.245	.295	.276	58	-10	-11	17	4	2	0	.949	-6	2S/31O	-1.3
1970	Cal-A	68	107	10	26	3	1	0	12	7	16	.243	.296	.290	64	-5	-5	9	3	0	1	.985	0	3/2S1C	-0.4
1971	Cal-A	31	19	4	5	0	0	0	0	2	7	.263	.333	.263	76	-1	-0	2	1	0	0	1.000	3	/32	0.3
Total	8	565	1150	133	276	37	10	2	69	58	164	.240	.281	.295	60	-55	-62	96	34	16	1	.966	0	23/S1OC	-5.1

■ CHICO RUIZ Ruiz, Manuel (Cruz) b: 11/1/51, Santurce, P.R. BR/TR, 5′11.5″, 170 lbs. Deb: 7/29/78

YEAR	TM/L	G	AB	R	H	2B	3B	HR	RBI	BB	SO	AVG	OBP	SLG	PRO+	BR	/A	RC	SB	CS	SBR	FA	FR	POS	TPR
1978	Atl-N	18	46	3	13	3	0	0	2	2	4	.283	.313	.348	76	-1	-2	5	0	0	0	.984	1	2/3	0.1
1980	Atl-N	25	26	3	8	2	1	0	2	3	7	.308	.379	.462	129	1	1	4	0	1	-1	.875	2	3/S2	0.2
Total	2	43	72	6	21	5	1	0	4	5	11	.292	.338	.389	95	0	-0	9	0	1	-1	.880	3	/32S	0.3

■ JOE RULLO Rullo, Joseph Vincent b: 6/16/16, New York, N.Y. d: 10/28/69, Philadelphia, Pa. BR/TR, 5′11″, 168 lbs. Deb: 9/22/43

YEAR	TM/L	G	AB	R	H	2B	3B	HR	RBI	BB	SO	AVG	OBP	SLG	PRO+	BR	/A	RC	SB	CS	SBR	FA	FR	POS	TPR
1943	Phi-A	16	55	2	16	3	0	0	6	8	7	.291	.381	.345	114	1	1	8	0	0	0	.963	-1	2	0.2
1944	Phi-A	35	96	5	16	0	0	0	5	6	19	.167	.223	.167	12	-11	-11	4	1	0	0	.954	3	2/1O	-0.6
Total	2	51	151	7	32	3	0	0	11	14	26	.212	.283	.232	50	-10	-9	12	1	0	0	.957	2	/2O1	-0.4

■ WILLIAM RUMLER Rumler, William George b: 3/27/1891, Milford, Neb. d: 5/26/66, Lincoln, Neb. BR/TR, 6′1″, 190 lbs. Deb: 5/04/14

YEAR	TM/L	G	AB	R	H	2B	3B	HR	RBI	BB	SO	AVG	OBP	SLG	PRO+	BR	/A	RC	SB	CS	SBR	FA	FR	POS	TPR
1914	StL-A	34	46	2	8	1	0	0	6	3	12	.174	.240	.196	32	-4	-4	3	2	2	-1	1.000	-3	C/O	-0.8
1916	StL-A	27	37	6	12	3	0	0	10	3	7	.324	.375	.405	141	1	2	6	0			.971	0	/C	0.3
1917	StL-A	78	88	7	23	3	4	1	16	8	9	.261	.323	.420	132	2	3	12	2			.938	-0	/O	0.2
Total	3	139	171	15	43	7	4	1	32	14	28	.251	.312	.357	107	-0	1	20	4	2		.986	-3	/CO	-0.3

■ PAUL RUNGE Runge, Paul William b: 5/21/58, Kingston, N.Y. BR/TR, 6′, 175 lbs. Deb: 9/25/81

YEAR	TM/L	G	AB	R	H	2B	3B	HR	RBI	BB	SO	AVG	OBP	SLG	PRO+	BR	/A	RC	SB	CS	SBR	FA	FR	POS	TPR
1981	Atl-N	10	27	2	7	1	0	0	2	4	4	.259	.355	.296	84	-0	-0	3	0	0	0	.911	-1	S	-0.1
1982	Atl-N	4	2	0	0	0	0	0	0	0	0	.000	.000	.000	-96	-1	-1	0	0	0	0	.000	0	/H	-0.1
1983	Atl-N	5	8	0	2	0	0	0	1	1	4	.250	.333	.250	59	-0	-0	1	0	0	0	1.000	-1	/2	-0.1
1984	Atl-N	28	90	5	24	3	1	0	3	10	14	.267	.340	.322	81	-1	-2	10	5	3	-0	.970	10	2/S3	0.8
1985	Atl-N	50	87	15	19	3	0	1	5	18	18	.218	.352	.287	76	-1	-2	10	0	1	-1	.929	4	3/S2	0.1
1986	Atl-N	7	8	1	2	0	0	0	0	2	4	.250	.400	.250	79	-0	-0	1	0	0	0	1.000	2	/2	0.2
1987	Atl-N	27	47	9	10	1	0	3	8	5	10	.213	.288	.426	82	-1	-1	5	0	1	-1	.923	1	3/S2	-0.1
1988	Atl-N	52	76	11	16	5	0	0	7	14	21	.211	.333	.276	73	-2	-2	7	0	0	0	1.000	-1	3/2S	-0.4
Total	8	183	345	43	80	13	1	4	26	54	75	.232	.336	.310	77	-7	-9	37	5	5	-2	.941	13	/32S	0.3

■ TOM RUNNELLS Runnells, Thomas William b: 4/17/55, Greeley, Colo. BB/TR, 6′, 175 lbs. Deb: 8/09/85 MC

YEAR	TM/L	G	AB	R	H	2B	3B	HR	RBI	BB	SO	AVG	OBP	SLG	PRO+	BR	/A	RC	SB	CS	SBR	FA	FR	POS	TPR
1985	Cin-N	28	35	3	7	1	0	0	0	3	4	.200	.263	.229	37	-3	-3	2	0	0	0	1.000	1	S/2	-0.2
1986	Cin-N	12	11	1	1	1	0	0	0	0	2	.091	.091	.182	-26	-2	-2	0	0	0	0	1.000	1	/23	-0.1
Total	2	40	46	4	8	2	0	0	0	3	6	.174	.224	.217	23	-5	-5	2	0	0	0	1.000	2	/S23	-0.3

YEAR	TM/L	G	AB	R	H	2B	3B	HR	RBI	BB	SO	AVG	OBP	SLG	PRO+	BR	/A	RC	SB	CS	SBR	FA	FR	POS	TPR
■ **PETE RUNNELS**	Runnels, James Edward (b: James Edward Runnells) b: 1/28/28, Lufkin, Tex. d: 5/20/91, Pasadena, Tex. BL/TR, 6', 170 lbs. Deb: 7/01/51 MC																								
1951	Was-A	78	273	31	76	12	2	0	25	31	24	.278	.354	.337	89	-4	-3	34	0	3	-2	.949	-21	S	-2.1
1952	Was-A	152	555	70	158	18	3	1	64	72	55	.285	.368	.333	99	-0	2	69	0	10	-6	.966	-15	*S/2	-0.8
1953	Was-A	137	486	64	125	15	5	2	50	64	36	.257	.347	.321	83	-11	-9	55	3	4	-2	.958	-33	*S2	-3.5
1954	Was-A	139	488	75	131	17	15	3	56	78	60	.268	.369	.383	112	6	9	72	2	3	-1	.953	-19	*S2/O	0.0
1955	Was-A	134	503	66	143	16	4	2	49	55	51	.284	.356	.344	94	-7	-3	60	3	9	-5	.976	-3	*2/S	0.0
1956	Was-A	147	578	72	179	29	9	8	76	58	64	.310	.375	.433	113	11	11	91	5	5	-2	.995	0	12/S	1.0
1957	Was-A	134	473	53	109	18	4	2	35	55	51	.230	.313	.298	69	-20	-19	46	2	3	-1	.995	2	132	-2.2
1958	Bos-A	147	568	103	183	32	5	8	59	87	49	.322	.418	.438	127	32	27	107	1	2	-1	.985	8	*21	4.0
1959	Bos-A★	147	560	95	176	33	6	6	57	95	48	.314	.415	.427	126	29	25	102	6	5	-1	.982	6	*21/S	3.5
1960	Bos-A★	143	528	80	169	29	2	2	35	71	51	**.320**	.403	.394	112	15	13	86	5	2	0	**.986**	9	*21/3	3.2
1961	Bos-A	143	360	49	114	20	3	3	38	46	32	.317	.399	.414	115	11	10	60	5	1	1	**.995**	1	*13/2S	0.5
1962	Bos-A★	152	562	80	183	33	5	10	60	79	57	**.326**	.411	.456	129	29	27	110	3	4	-2	.993	-1	*1	1.4
1963	Hou-N	124	388	35	98	9	1	2	23	45	42	.253	.335	.296	89	-7	-4	38	2	0	1	.993	-10	12/3	-1.5
1964	Hou-N	22	51	3	10	1	0	0	3	8	7	.196	.305	.216	53	-3	-3	3	0	0	0	.986	-2	1	-0.6
Total	14	1799	6373	876	1854	282	64	49	630	844	627	.291	.376	.378	106	81	82	934	37	51	-20	.994	-78	12S/30	2.9
■ **JOHN RUSS**	Russ, John b: Louisville, Ky. Deb: 7/04/1882																								
1882	Bal-a	1	3	0	1	0	0	0		0		.333	.333	.333	136	0	0	0				.000	-1	/OP	0.0
■ **REB RUSSELL**	Russell, Ewell Albert b: 4/12/1889, Jackson, Miss. d: 9/30/73, Indianapolis, Ind BL/TL, 5'11", 185 lbs. Deb: 4/18/13																								
1913	Chi-A	52	106	9	20	5	3	1	7	1	29	.189	.204	.321	54	-7	-7	7	0			.952	-5	P	0.0
1914	Chi-A	46	64	6	17	1	1	0	7	1	14	.266	.277	.313	78	-2	-2	6	0			.946	0	P	0.0
1915	Chi-A	45	86	11	21	2	3	0	7	4	14	.244	.293	.337	86	-2	-2	9	1			.971	-2	P	0.0
1916	Chi-A	56	91	9	13	2	0	0	6	0	18	.143	.152	.165	-5	-12	-12	3	1			.974	-2	P	0.0
1917	*Chi-A	39	68	5	19	3	3	0	9	2	10	.279	.300	.412	115	1	1	8	0			.984	-1	P/O	0.0
1918	Chi-A	27	50	2	7	3	0	0	3	0	6	.140	.157	.200	8	-6	-6	2	0			1.000	-2	P/O	0.0
1919	Chi-A	1	0	0	0	0	0	0	0	0	0	—	—	—	—	0	0	0	0			.000	0	/P	0.0
1922	Pit-N	60	220	51	81	14	8	12	75	14	18	.368	.423	.668	175	24	24	61	4	2	0	.968	-2	O	1.7
1923	Pit-N	94	291	49	84	18	7	9	58	20	21	.289	.341	.491	115	6	5	49	3	1	0	.970	-2	O	-0.2
Total	9	420	976	142	262	48	25	22	172	42	130	.268	.309	.436	104	2	1	144	9	3		.968	-15	PO	1.5
■ **RIP RUSSELL**	Russell, Glen David b: 1/26/15, Los Angeles, Cal. d: 9/26/76, Los Alamitos, Cal BR/TR, 6'1", 180 lbs. Deb: 5/05/39																								
1939	Chi-N	143	542	55	148	24	5	9	79	36	56	.273	.318	.386	87	-10	-11	66	2			.988	-5	*1	-3.2
1940	Chi-N	68	215	15	53	7	2	5	33	8	23	.247	.277	.367	78	-8	-7	20	1			.982	-6	1/3	-1.8
1941	Chi-N	6	17	1	5	1	0	0	1	1	5	.294	.333	.353	97	-0	-0	2	0			.975	0	/1	0.0
1942	Chi-N	102	302	32	73	9	0	8	41	17	21	.242	.282	.351	88	-7	-6	29	0			.974	-12	123/O	-2.0
1946	*Bos-A	80	274	22	57	10	1	6	35	13	30	.208	.247	.318	54	-17	-19	19	1	1	-0	.942	-1	3/2	-2.0
1947	Bos-A	26	52	8	8	1	0	1	3	8	7	.154	.267	.231	36	-4	-5	3	0	0	0	.923	1	3	-0.4
Total	6	425	1402	133	344	52	8	29	192	83	142	.245	.289	.356	77	-46	-47	140	4	1		.984	-22	1/32O	-9.4
■ **HARVEY RUSSELL**	Russell, Harvey Holmes b: 1/10/1887, Marshall, Va. d: 1/8/80, Alexnadria, Va. BL/TR, 5'9.5", 163 lbs. Deb: 4/17/14																								
1914	Bal-F	81	168	18	39	3	2	0	13	18	17	.232	.310	.274	65	-7	-8	16	2			.956	-17	C/SO	-2.2
1915	Bal-F	53	73	5	19	1	2	0	11	14	5	.260	.407	.329	114	3	2	11	1			.989	-4	C	0.0
Total	2	134	241	23	58	4	4	0	24	32	22	.241	.342	.290	80	-4	-5	27	3			.965	-22	/COS	-2.2
■ **JIM RUSSELL**	Russell, James William b: 10/1/18, Fayette City, Pa. d: 11/24/87, Pittsburgh, Pa. BB/TR, 6'1", 181 lbs. Deb: 9/12/42																								
1942	Pit-N	5	14	2	1	0	0	0	0	1	4	.071	.133	.071	-38	-2	-2	0	0			1.000	1	/O	-0.2
1943	Pit-N	146	533	79	138	19	11	4	44	77	67	.259	.354	.358	102	6	4	70	12			.990	3	*O/1	-0.1
1944	Pit-N	152	580	109	181	34	14	8	66	79	63	.312	.399	.460	136	34	31	112	6			.986	13	*O	3.6
1945	Pit-N	146	510	88	145	24	8	12	77	71	40	.284	.377	.433	120	18	15	88	15			.973	3	*O	1.2
1946	Pit-N	146	516	68	143	29	6	8	50	67	54	.277	.362	.403	114	12	11	78	11			.966	-2	*O/1	0.1
1947	Pit-N	128	478	68	121	21	8	8	51	63	58	.253	.343	.381	89	-5	-7	64	7			.980	11	*O	-0.3
1948	Bos-N	89	322	44	85	18	1	9	54	46	31	.264	.361	.410	110	4	5	49	4			.992	6	O	0.6
1949	Bos-N	130	415	57	96	22	1	8	54	64	68	.231	.337	.347	88	-9	-5	52	3			.975	-9	*O	-2.0
1950	Bro-N	77	214	37	49	8	2	10	32	31	36	.229	.329	.425	95	-1	-2	30	1			.993	4	O	0.0
1951	Bro-N	16	13	2	0	0	0	0	0	4	6	.000	.278	.000	-18	-2	-2	0	0	0	0	1.000	-1	/O	-0.3
Total	10	1035	3595	554	959	175	51	67	428	503	427	.267	.360	.400	108	55	46	544	59	0		.981	27	O/1	2.6
■ **JOHN RUSSELL**	Russell, John William b: 1/5/61, Oklahoma City, Okla. BR/TR, 6', 200 lbs. Deb: 6/22/84																								
1984	Phi-N	39	99	11	28	8	1	2	11	12	33	.283	.360	.444	123	3	3	16	0	1	-1	1.000	-1	O/C	0.1
1985	Phi-N	81	216	22	47	12	0	9	23	18	72	.218	.278	.398	85	-5	-5	24	2	0	1	1.000	-6	O1	-1.4
1986	Phi-N	93	315	35	76	21	2	13	60	25	103	.241	.303	.444	100	0	-1	42	0	1	-1	.976	-5	C	-0.1
1987	Phi-N	24	62	5	9	1	0	3	8	3	17	.145	.185	.306	26	-7	-7	2	0	1	-1	.955	0	O/C	-0.8
1988	Phi-N	22	49	5	12	1	0	2	4	3	15	.245	.302	.388	95	-0	-0	5	0	0	0	.945	3	C	0.3
1989	Atl-N	74	159	14	29	2	0	2	9	8	53	.182	.226	.233	31	-14	-15	8	0	0	0	.990	-7	CO/13P	-2.1
1990	Tex-A	68	128	16	35	4	0	2	8	11	41	.273	.331	.352	91	-1	-1	15	1	0	0	.980	2	CD/O13	0.2
1991	Tex-A	22	27	3	3	0	0	0	1	1	7	.111	.143	.111	-29	-5	-5	1	0	0	0	1.000	-0	/OCD	-0.5
1992	Tex-A	7	10	1	1	0	0	0	2	1	4	.100	.250	.100	2	-1	-1	0	0	0	0	1.000	1	/COD	0.0
Total	9	430	1065	112	240	49	3	33	126	82	345	.225	.284	.370	79	-30	-33	112	3	3	-1	1.000	-14	CO/D13P	-4.3
■ **LLOYD RUSSELL**	Russell, Lloyd Opal b: 4/10/13, Atoka, Okla. d: 5/24/68, Waco, Tex. BR/TR, 5'11", 166 lbs. Deb: 4/26/38																								
1938	Cle-A	2	0	0	0	0	0	0	0	0	0	—	—	—	—	0	0	0	0	0	0	.000	0	R	0.0
■ **PAUL RUSSELL**	Russell, Paul A. b: 1870, Reading, Pa. d: Pottstown, Pa. Deb: 7/29/1894																								
1894	StL-N	3	10	1	1	0	0	0	0	0	2	.100	.100	.100	-51	-2	-2	0	0			1.000	0	/O32	-0.2
■ **BILL RUSSELL**	Russell, William Ellis b: 10/21/48, Pittsburg, Kan. BR/TR, 6', 175 lbs. Deb: 4/07/69 C																								
1969	LA-N	98	212	35	48	6	2	5	15	22	45	.226	.302	.344	87	-6	-4	23	4	1	1	.978	7	O	0.1
1970	LA-N	81	278	30	72	11	9	0	28	16	28	.259	.306	.363	82	-9	-7	32	9	1	2	.983	6	O/S	-0.2
1971	LA-N	91	211	29	48	7	4	2	15	11	39	.227	.266	.327	71	-10	-8	18	6	3	0	.964	4	2O/S	-0.2
1972	LA-N	129	434	47	118	19	5	4	34	34	64	.272	.328	.366	99	-2	-1	53	14	7	0	.949	17	*S/O	3.4
1973	LA-N★	162	615	55	163	26	3	4	56	34	63	.265	.305	.337	81	-19	-16	62	15	7	0	.963	9	*S	1.5
1974	*LA-N	160	553	61	149	18	6	5	65	53	53	.269	.338	.351	97	-5	-2	64	14	5	1	.946	-19	*S/O	0.1
1975	LA-N	84	252	24	52	9	2	0	14	23	28	.206	.278	.258	52	-17	-16	19	5	0	2	.967	-21	S	-2.9
1976	LA-N★	149	554	53	152	17	3	5	65	21	46	.274	.304	.343	85	-13	-12	55	15	5	2	.963	-14	*S	-0.6
1977	*LA-N	153	634	84	176	28	6	4	51	24	43	.278	.306	.360	78	-20	-20	64	16	7	1	.963	10	*S	0.8
1978	*LA-N	155	625	72	179	32	4	3	46	30	34	.286	.321	.365	92	-8	-8	69	10	6	-1	.962	12	*S	2.5
1979	LA-N	153	627	72	170	26	4	7	56	24	43	.271	.299	.359	80	-19	-18	60	6	9	-4	.957	-27	*S	-3.3
1980	LA-N★	130	466	38	123	23	2	3	34	18	44	.264	.296	.341	79	-15	-14	48	13	2	3	.968	-22	*S	-1.9
1981	*LA-N	82	262	20	61	9	2	0	22	19	20	.233	.287	.282	64	-13	-12	19	2	1	0	.965	10	S	0.6
1982	LA-N	153	497	64	136	20	2	3	46	63	30	.274	.360	.340	99	0	2	63	10	2	2	.961	-4	*S	1.4
1983	*LA-N	131	451	47	111	13	1	1	30	33	31	.246	.303	.286	64	-21	-21	40	13	9	-2	.964	1	*S	-1.0
1984	LA-N	89	262	25	70	12	1	0	19	25	24	.267	.331	.321	85	-5	-5	28	4	4	-1	.965	-4	SO/2	-0.6
1985	LA-N	76	169	19	44	6	1	0	13	18	9	.260	.335	.308	83	-4	-3	19	4	0	1	.919	-7	SO/23	-0.7

YEAR	TM/L	G	AB	R	H	2B	3B	HR	RBI	BB	SO	AVG	OBP	SLG	PRO+	BR	/A	RC	SB	CS	SBR	FA	FR	POS	TPR
1986	LA-N	105	216	21	54	11	0	0	18	15	23	.250	.305	.301	73	-9	-7	21	7	0	2	1.000	-7	OS/23	-1.1
Total	18	2181	7318	796	1926	293	57	46	627	483	667	.263	.312	.338	83	-195	-172	759	167	69	9	.960	-49	*SO/23	-2.1

■ HANK RUSZKOWSKI Ruszkowski, Henry Alexander b: 11/10/25, Cleveland, Ohio BR/TR, 6', 190 lbs. Deb: 9/26/44

YEAR	TM/L	G	AB	R	H	2B	3B	HR	RBI	BB	SO	AVG	OBP	SLG	PRO+	BR	/A	RC	SB	CS	SBR	FA	FR	POS	TPR
1944	Cle-A	3	8	1	3	0	0	0	1	0	1	.375	.375	.375	119	0	0	1	0	0	0	1.000	-0	/C	0.0
1945	Cle-A	14	49	2	10	0	0	0	5	4	9	.204	.264	.204	38	-4	-4	3	0	0	0	.975	3	C	0.0
1947	Cle-A	23	27	5	7	2	0	3	4	2	6	.259	.310	.667	172	2	2	6	0	0	0	1.000	-2	C	0.1
Total	3	40	84	8	20	2	0	3	10	6	16	.238	.289	.369	91	-2	-1	9	0	0	0	.981	1	/C	0.1

■ BABE RUTH Ruth, George Herman "The Bambino" or "The Sultan Of Swat"
b: 2/6/1895, Baltimore, Md. d: 8/16/48, New York, N.Y. BL/TL, 6'2", 215 lbs. Deb: 7/11/14 CH

YEAR	TM/L	G	AB	R	H	2B	3B	HR	RBI	BB	SO	AVG	OBP	SLG	PRO+	BR	/A	RC	SB	CS	SBR	FA	FR	POS	TPR
1914	Bos-A	5	10	1	2	1	0	0	2	0	4	.200	.200	.300	50	-1	-1	1	0			1.000	-0	/P	0.0
1915	*Bos-A	42	92	16	29	10	1	4	21	9	23	.315	.376	.576	191	9	9	20	0			.976	1	P	0.0
1916	*Bos-A	67	136	18	37	5	3	3	15	10	23	.272	.322	.419	122	3	3	19	0			.973	0	P	0.0
1917	Bos-A	52	123	14	40	6	3	2	12	12	18	.325	.385	.472	163	9	9	22	0			.984	2	P	0.0
1918	*Bos-A	95	317	50	95	26	11	**11**	66	57	58	.300	.410	.555	194	35	35	72	6			.949	3	OP1	2.6
1919	Bos-A	130	432	**103**	139	34	12	**29**	**114**	101	58	.322	**.456**	**.657**	**224**	**67**	**70**	**128**	7			**.996**	5	*OP/1	**6.0**
1920	NY-A	142	458	**158**	172	36	9	**54**	**137**	**148**	80	.376	**.530**	**.847**	**252**	**113**	**110**	**211**	14	14	-4	.936	0	*O/1P	**8.9**
1921	*NY-A	152	540	**177**	204	44	16	**59**	**171**	**144**	81	.378	**.512**	**.846**	**236**	**119**	**117**	**238**	17	13	-3	.966	4	*O/P1	**9.6**
1922	*NY-A	110	406	94	128	24	8	35	99	84	80	.315	.434	**.672**	**181**	51	49	120	2	6	-3	.964	1	*O/1	3.7
1923	*NY-A	152	522	**151**	205	45	13	**41**	**131**	**170**	93	.393	**.545**	**.764**	**238**	**119**	**118**	**223**	17	21	-8	.973	16	*O/1	**10.8**
1924	NY-A	153	529	**143**	200	39	7	**46**	121	**142**	81	**.378**	**.513**	**.739**	**221**	**101**	**101**	**205**	9	13	-5	.962	7	*O	**8.5**
1925	NY-A	98	359	61	104	12	2	25	66	59	68	.290	.393	.543	138	19	20	78	2	4	-2	.974	9	O	1.8
1926	*NY-A	152	495	**139**	184	30	5	**47**	**146**	**144**	76	.372	**.516**	**.737**	**228**	**97**	**99**	**196**	11	9	-2	.979	1	*O/1	**8.2**
1927	*NY-A	151	540	**158**	192	29	8	**60**	164	**138**	89	.356	**.487**	**.772**	**229**	101	103	200	7	6	-2	.963	5	*O	**8.9**
1928	*NY-A	154	536	**163**	173	29	8	**54**	**142**	**135**	87	.323	.461	**.709**	**210**	**84**	**87**	**182**	4	5	-2	.975	-3	*O	**6.8**
1929	NY-A	135	499	121	172	26	6	**46**	154	72	60	.345	.430	**.697**	**199**	62	**67**	150	5	3	-0	.984	-9	*O	4.5
1930	NY-A	145	518	150	186	28	9	**49**	153	**136**	61	.359	**.493**	**.732**	**216**	**90**	**94**	191	10	10	-3	.965	-0	*O/P	**7.0**
1931	NY-A	145	534	149	199	31	3	**46**	163	**128**	51	.373	**.495**	**.700**	**223**	**92**	**96**	**192**	5	4	-1	.972	-12	*O/1	**6.8**
1932	*NY-A	133	457	120	156	13	5	41	137	**130**	62	.341	**.489**	.661	**206**	71	75	157	2	2	-1	.961	-7	*O/1	5.4
1933	NY-A★	137	459	97	138	21	3	34	103	**114**	90	.301	.442	.582	180	50	54	124	4	5	-2	.970	-7	*O/P1	3.6
1934	NY-A★	125	365	78	105	17	4	22	84	103	63	.288	.447	.537	164	33	37	95	1	3	-2	.962	-6	*O	2.3
1935	Bos-N	28	72	13	13	0	0	6	12	20	24	.181	.359	.431	121	2	2	12	0			.952	-4	O	-0.2
Total	22	2503	8399	2174	2873	506	136	714	2213	2056	1330	.342	.474	.690	209	1322	1355	2838	123	118		.968	5	*OP/1	105.2

■ JIM RUTHERFORD Rutherford, James Hollis b: 9/26/1886, Stillwater, Minn. d: 9/18/56, Cleveland, Ohio BL/TR, 6'1", 180 lbs. Deb: 7/12/10

YEAR	TM/L	G	AB	R	H	2B	3B	HR	RBI	BB	SO	AVG	OBP	SLG	PRO+	BR	/A	RC	SB	CS	SBR	FA	FR	POS	TPR
1910	Cle-A	1	2	0	1	0	0	0	0	0		.500	.500	.500	210	0	0	0	0			1.000	-0	/O	0.0

■ MICKEY RUTNER Rutner, Milton b: 3/18/20, Hempstead, N.Y. BR/TR, 5'11", 190 lbs. Deb: 9/11/47

YEAR	TM/L	G	AB	R	H	2B	3B	HR	RBI	BB	SO	AVG	OBP	SLG	PRO+	BR	/A	RC	SB	CS	SBR	FA	FR	POS	TPR
1947	Phi-A	12	48	4	12	1	0	1	4	3	2	.250	.294	.333	73	-2	-2	4	0	0	0	.885	-3	3	-0.5

■ MARK RYAL Ryal, Mark Dwayne b: 4/28/60, Henryetta, Okla. BL/TL, 6'1", 185 lbs. Deb: 9/07/82

YEAR	TM/L	G	AB	R	H	2B	3B	HR	RBI	BB	SO	AVG	OBP	SLG	PRO+	BR	/A	RC	SB	CS	SBR	FA	FR	POS	TPR
1982	KC-A	6	13	0	1	0	0	0	0	1	3	.077	.143	.077	-38	-2	-2	0	0	0	0	.900	-1	/O	-0.3
1985	Chi-A	12	33	4	5	3	0	0	3	3	3	.152	.222	.242	26	-3	-4	2	0	0	0	1.000	-1	O	-0.5
1986	Cal-A	13	32	6	12	0	0	2	5	2	4	.375	.412	.563	164	3	3	7	1	0	0	.900	-1	/O1D	0.2
1987	Cal-A	58	100	7	20	6	0	5	18	3	15	.200	.223	.410	65	-6	-5	8	0	0	0	.955	-6	O/1D	-1.1
1989	Phi-N	29	33	2	8	2	0	0	5	1	6	.242	.265	.303	62	-2	-2	3	0	0	0	1.000	-1	/1O	-0.3
1990	Pit-N	9	12	0	1	0	0	0	0	0	3	.083	.083	.083	-56	-2	-2	0	0	0	0	1.000	-1	/O	-0.4
Total	6	127	223	19	47	11	0	7	31	10	34	.211	.245	.354	61	-13	-13	19	1	0	0	.957	-11	/O1D	-2.4

■ CONNIE RYAN Ryan, Cornelius Joseph b: 2/27/20, New Orleans, La. BR/TR, 5'11", 175 lbs. Deb: 4/14/42 MC

YEAR	TM/L	G	AB	R	H	2B	3B	HR	RBI	BB	SO	AVG	OBP	SLG	PRO+	BR	/A	RC	SB	CS	SBR	FA	FR	POS	TPR
1942	NY-N	11	27	4	5	0	0	0	2	4	3	.185	.290	.185	40	-2	-2	2	1			.944	7	2	0.5
1943	Bos-N	132	457	52	97	10	2	1	24	58	56	.212	.301	.249	61	-22	-21	38	7			.962	-20	*23	-3.8
1944	Bos-N★	88	332	56	98	18	5	4	25	36	40	.295	.364	.416	114	9	7	50	13			.974	13	23	2.4
1946	Bos-N	143	502	55	121	28	8	1	48	55	63	.241	.317	.335	84	-10	-11	56	7			.968	-2	*23	-0.5
1947	Bos-N	150	544	60	144	33	5	5	69	71	60	.265	.351	.371	94	-5	-4	74	5			.973	-7	*2/S	0.0
1948	*Bos-N	51	122	14	26	3	0	0	10	21	16	.213	.333	.238	58	-6	-6	11	0			.966	4	2/3	0.0
1949	Bos-N	85	208	28	52	13	1	6	20	21	30	.250	.319	.409	99	-2	-1	27	1			.973	6	3S2/1	0.6
1950	Bos-N	20	72	12	14	2	0	3	6	12	9	.194	.326	.347	82	-2	-2	8	0			1.000	1	2	0.0
	Cin-N	106	367	45	95	18	5	3	43	52	46	.259	.352	.360	87	-5	-6	48	4			.973	11	*2	0.9
	Yr	126	439	57	109	20	5	6	49	64	55	.248	.348	.358	87	-8	-7	57	4			.978	12	*2	0.9
1951	Cin-N	136	473	75	112	17	4	16	53	79	72	.237	.350	.391	97	1	-0	69	11	6	-0	.970	-3	*2/31O	0.2
1952	Phi-N	154	577	81	139	24	6	12	49	69	72	.241	.327	.366	93	-6	-5	73	13	5	1	.972	-5	*2	-0.1
1953	Phi-N	90	247	47	73	14	6	5	26	30	35	.296	.372	.462	116	6	6	45	5	1	1	.958	-5	2/1	0.5
	Chi-A	17	54	6	12	1	0	0	6	9	12	.222	.333	.241	55	-3	-3	5	2	0	1	.927	-1	3	-0.4
1954	Cin-N	1	0	0	0	0	0	0	0	1	0	—	1.000	—	182	0	0	0	0	0	0	.000	0	H	0.0
Total	12	1184	3982	535	988	181	42	56	381	518	514	.248	.337	.357	90	-49	-47	506	69	12		.970	-1	23/S1O	0.3

■ CYCLONE RYAN Ryan, Daniel R. b: 1866, Capperwhite, Ireland d: 1/30/17, Medfield, Mass. TR , 6', Deb: 8/08/1887

YEAR	TM/L	G	AB	R	H	2B	3B	HR	RBI	BB	SO	AVG	OBP	SLG	PRO+	BR	/A	RC	SB	CS	SBR	FA	FR	POS	TPR
1887	NY-a	8	32	4	7	1	0	0		3		.219	.286	.250	54	-2	-2	3	1			.938	-0	/1P	-0.2
1891	Bos-N	1	1	0	0	0	0	0	0	0	0	.000	.000	.000	-89	-0	-0	0	0			1.000	0	/P	0.0
Total	2	9	33	4	7	1	0	0	0	3	0	.212	.278	.242	50	-2	-2	3	1			1.000	0	/1P	-0.2

■ MIKE RYAN Ryan, J. b: St.Louis, Mo. Deb: 7/25/1895

YEAR	TM/L	G	AB	R	H	2B	3B	HR	RBI	BB	SO	AVG	OBP	SLG	PRO+	BR	/A	RC	SB	CS	SBR	FA	FR	POS	TPR
1895	StL-N	2	2	0	0	0	0	0	0	0	0	.000	.000	.000	-99	-1	-1	0	0			.000	-1	/3	-0.1

■ JIMMY RYAN Ryan, James Edward "Pony" b: 2/11/1863, Clinton, Mass. d: 10/26/23, Chicago, Ill. BR/TL, 5'9", 162 lbs. Deb: 10/08/1885

YEAR	TM/L	G	AB	R	H	2B	3B	HR	RBI	BB	SO	AVG	OBP	SLG	PRO+	BR	/A	RC	SB	CS	SBR	FA	FR	POS	TPR
1885	Chi-N	3	13	2	6	1	0	0	2	1	1	.462	.500	.538	205	2	2	4				.737	1	/SO	0.2
1886	*Chi-N	84	327	58	100	17	6	4	53	12	28	.306	.330	.431	113	11	3	51	10			.828	1	O/S32P	0.2
1887	Chi-N	126	508	117	145	23	10	11	74	53	19	.285	.360	.435	108	15	4	100	50			.857	-2	*O/P2	-0.2
1888	Chi-N	129	549	115	**182**	**33**	10	**16**	64	35	50	.332	.377	**.515**	172	**51**	45	**133**	60			.878	4	*O/P	4.3
1889	Chi-N	135	576	140	177	31	14	17	72	70	62	.307	.388	.498	141	37	32	**132**	45			.926	6	*OS	3.2
1890	Chi-P	118	486	99	165	32	5	6	89	60	36	.340	.416	.463	131	27	23	109	30			.919	2	*O	1.7
1891	Chi-N	118	505	110	140	22	15	9	66	53	38	.277	.355	.434	131	19	19	90	27			.905	5	*O/SP	1.8
1892	Chi-N	128	505	105	148	21	11	10	65	61	41	.293	.375	.438	146	29	28	95	27			.921	5	*O/S	2.6
1893	Chi-N	83	341	82	102	21	7	3	30	59	25	.299	.407	.428	126	14	15	64	8			.908	-1	OS/P	0.8
1894	Chi-N	108	474	132	171	37	7	3	62	50	23	.361	.425	.487	115	18	12	106	11			.910	9	*O	1.1
1895	Chi-N	108	438	83	139	22	8	6	49	48	22	.317	.392	.445	111	12	7	86	18			.937	2	*O	0.0
1896	Chi-N	128	489	83	149	24	10	3	86	46	16	.305	.369	.413	104	6	3	89	29			.912	-0	*O	-0.7
1897	Chi-N	136	520	103	156	33	17	5	85	50		.300	.369	.458	113	12	9	101	27			.945	7	*O	0.5
1898	Chi-N	144	572	122	185	32	13	4	79	73		.323	.405	.446	144	34	34	119	29			.914	-7	*O	1.6
1899	Chi-N	125	525	91	158	20	10	3	68	43		.301	.357	.394	109	4	6	80	9			.956	-1	*O	-0.4
1900	Chi-N	105	415	66	115	25	4	5	59	29		.277	.329	.393	102	-2	0	62	19			.913	-11	*O	-1.7
1902	Was-A	120	484	92	155	32	6	6	44	43		.320	.385	.448	129	20	20	90	10			.949	3	*O	1.4
1903	Was-A	114	437	42	109	25	4	7	46	17		.249	.290	.373	96	-2	-3	52	9			.970	3	*O	-0.7

YEAR	TM/L	G	AB	R	H	2B	3B	HR	RBI	BB	SO	AVG	OBP	SLG	PRO+	BR	/A	RC	SB	CS	SBR	FA	FR	POS	TPR
Total	18	2012	8164	1642	2502	451	157	118	1093	803	361	.306	.374	.444	124	306	259	1562	418			.918	26	*O/SP23	15.7

■ JOHN RYAN Ryan, John A. (Played 1 Game Under Real Name Of Daniel Sheehan) b: Birmingham, Mich. Deb: 6/11/1884

YEAR	TM/L	G	AB	R	H	2B	3B	HR	RBI	BB	SO	AVG	OBP	SLG	PRO+	BR	/A	RC	SB	CS	SBR	FA	FR	POS	TPR
1884	Was-U	7	28	2	4	0	1	0		1		.143	.172	.214	31	-2	-2	1				.667	-1	/O3	-0.3
	Wil-U	2	6	0	1	0	0	0		1		.167	.286	.167	55	-0	-0	0				.800	-0	/O	0.0
	Yr	9	34	2	5	0	1	0		2		.147	.194	.206	36	-2	-2	1				.706	-1	/O3	-0.3

■ JACK RYAN Ryan, John Bernard b: 11/12/1868, Haverhill, Mass. d: 8/21/52, Boston, Mass. BR/TR, 5'10.5", 165 lbs. Deb: 9/02/1889 C

YEAR	TM/L	G	AB	R	H	2B	3B	HR	RBI	BB	SO	AVG	OBP	SLG	PRO+	BR	/A	RC	SB	CS	SBR	FA	FR	POS	TPR
1889	Lou-a	21	79	8	14	1	0	0	2	3	17	.177	.207	.190	15	-9	-8	4	2			.864	-6	C/O3	-1.2
1890	*Lou-a	93	337	43	73	16	4	0		12		.217	.244	.288	60	-19	-17	26	6			.932	5	C/OS1	-0.5
1891	Lou-a	75	253	24	57	5	4	2	25	15	40	.225	.271	.300	67	-12	-11	22	3			.930	-1	C1/3O2	-0.7
1894	Bos-N	53	201	39	54	12	7	1	29	13	16	.269	.316	.413	70	-9	-12	28	3			.911	-0	C/1	-0.6
1895	Bos-N	49	189	22	55	7	0	0	18	6	6	.291	.313	.328	62	-9	-12	22	3			.951	3	C/2O	-0.4
1896	Bos-N	8	32	2	3	1	0	0	0	0	1	.094	.094	.125	-40	-6	-7	0	0			.911	2	/C	-0.3
1898	Bro-N	87	301	39	57	11	4	0	24	15		.189	.233	.252	39	-25	-24	20	5			.960	3	C/31	-1.3
1899	Bal-N	2	4	0	2	1	0	0	1	0		.500	.500	.750	229	1	1	2	1			1.000	1	/C	0.2
1901	StL-N	83	300	27	59	6	5	0	31	7		.197	.218	.250	37	-25	-23	19	5			.982	4	C/21O	-1.2
1902	StL-N	76	267	23	48	4	4	0	14	4		.180	.195	.225	31	-23	-21	14	2			.966	-8	C/132S	-2.3
1903	StL-N	67	227	18	54	5	1	1	10	10		.238	.270	.282	60	-13	-12	19	2			.971	-9	C1/S	-1.6
1912	Was-A	1	1	0	0	0	0	0	0	0		.000	.000	.000	-99	-0	-0	0	0			1.000	0	/3	0.0
1913	Was-A	1	1	0	0	0	0	0	0	0	0	.000	.000	.000	-98	-0	-0	0	0			1.000	0	/C	0.0
Total	13	616	2192	245	476	69	29	4	154	85	80	.217	.248	.281	50	-148	-148	175	32			.947	-6	C/123OS	-9.9

■ BUDDY RYAN Ryan, John Budd b: 10/6/1885, Denver, Colo. d: 7/9/56, Sacramento, Cal. BL/TR, 5'9.5", 172 lbs. Deb: 4/11/12

YEAR	TM/L	G	AB	R	H	2B	3B	HR	RBI	BB	SO	AVG	OBP	SLG	PRO+	BR	/A	RC	SB	CS	SBR	FA	FR	POS	TPR
1912	Cle-A	93	328	53	89	12	9	1	31	30		.271	.343	.372	101	2	0	46	12			.963	5	O	0.0
1913	Cle-A	73	243	26	72	6	1	0	32	11	13	.296	.332	.329	91	-2	-3	29	9			.986	-2	O/1	-0.8
Total	2	166	571	79	161	18	10	1	63	41	13	.282	.339	.354	97	-1	-3	75	21			.973	3	O/1	-0.8

■ BLONDY RYAN Ryan, John Collins b: 1/4/06, Lynn, Mass d: 11/28/59, Swampscott, Mass. BR/TR, 6'1", 178 lbs. Deb: 7/13/30

YEAR	TM/L	G	AB	R	H	2B	3B	HR	RBI	BB	SO	AVG	OBP	SLG	PRO+	BR	/A	RC	SB	CS	SBR	FA	FR	POS	TPR
1930	Chi-A	28	87	9	18	0	4	1	10	6	13	.207	.258	.333	50	-7	-7	8	2	0	1	.875	-1	3/S2	-0.5
1933	*NY-N	146	525	47	125	10	5	3	48	15	62	.238	.259	.293	58	-29	-28	38	0			.950	17	*S	-0.1
1934	NY-N	110	385	35	93	19	0	2	41	19	68	.242	.277	.306	57	-24	-23	31	3			.953	12	3S2	-0.6
1935	Phi-N	39	129	13	34	3	0	1	10	7	20	.264	.312	.310	61	-6	-7	12	1			.912	2	S/23	-0.3
	NY-A	30	105	12	25	1	3	0	11	3	10	.238	.259	.305	48	-9	-8	8	0	0	0	.908	-4	S	-1.0
1937	*NY-N	21	75	10	18	3	1	1	13	6	8	.240	.296	.347	73	-3	-3	7	0			.941	1	S/23	-0.1
1938	NY-N	12	24	1	5	0	0	0	0	1	3	.208	.240	.208	24	-2	-2	1	0			1.000	-1	/23S	-0.3
Total	6	386	1330	127	318	36	13	8	133	57	184	.239	.271	.304	57	-80	-78	105	6	0		.936	26	S/32	-2.9

■ JACK RYAN Ryan, John Francis b: 5/5/05, Mineral, Minn. d: 9/2/67, Rochester, Minn. BR/TR, 6', 185 lbs. Deb: 6/18/29

YEAR	TM/L	G	AB	R	H	2B	3B	HR	RBI	BB	SO	AVG	OBP	SLG	PRO+	BR	/A	RC	SB	CS	SBR	FA	FR	POS	TPR
1929	Bos-A	2	3	0	0	0	0	0	0	0	0	.000	.000	.000	-99	-1	-1	0	0	0	0	1.000	-1	/O	-0.2

■ JOHNNY RYAN Ryan, John Joseph b: 10/1853, Philadelphia, Pa. d: 3/22/02, Philadelphia, Pa. 5'7.5", 150 lbs. Deb: 8/19/1873

YEAR	TM/L	G	AB	R	H	2B	3B	HR	RBI	BB	SO	AVG	OBP	SLG	PRO+	BR	/A	RC	SB	CS	SBR	FA	FR	POS	TPR
1873	Phi-n	2	8	1	2	0	0	0	1	0	0	.250	.250	.250	46	-1	-1	1						/1O	0.0
1874	Bal-n	47	184	29	33	7	1	0		5		.179	.201	.228	37	-13	-12	9						*O/P	-0.9
1875	NH-n	37	146	17	23	2	1	0		3		.158	.174	.185	28	-11	-8	5						O/PS3	-0.4
1876	Lou-N	64	241	32	61	5	1	1	18	6	23	.253	.271	.295	75	-3	-9	20				.886	-7	*O/P	-1.5
1877	Cin-N	6	26	2	4	0	1	0	2	1	5	.154	.185	.231	34	-2	-2	1				.769	-1	/O	-0.3
Total	3 n	86	338	47	58	9	2	0	1	8		.172	.191	.210	34	-24	-21	14						/OP3S1	-1.3
Total	2	70	267	34	65	5	2	1	20	7	28	.243	.263	.288	72	-5	-11	21				.877	-9	/OP	-1.8

■ MIKE RYAN Ryan, Michael James b: 11/25/41, Haverhill, Mass. BR/TR, 6'2", 205 lbs. Deb: 10/03/64 C

YEAR	TM/L	G	AB	R	H	2B	3B	HR	RBI	BB	SO	AVG	OBP	SLG	PRO+	BR	/A	RC	SB	CS	SBR	FA	FR	POS	TPR
1964	Bos-A	1	3	0	1	0	0	0	2	1	0	.333	.500	.333	131	0	0	1	0	0	0	1.000	-1	/C	0.0
1965	Bos-A	33	107	7	17	0	1	3	9	5	19	.159	.196	.262	27	-10	-11	4	0	0	0	.981	0	C	-1.0
1966	Bos-A	116	369	27	79	15	3	2	32	29	68	.214	.271	.287	55	-19	-23	28	1	0	0	.992	1	*C	-1.6
1967	*Bos-A	79	226	21	45	4	2	2	27	26	42	.199	.285	.261	58	-10	-12	17	2	0	1	.988	1	C	-0.7
1968	Phi-N	96	296	12	53	6	1	1	15	15	59	.179	.219	.216	31	-25	-25	12	0	3	-2	.991	-4	C	-2.8
1969	Phi-N	133	446	41	91	17	2	12	44	30	66	.204	.257	.332	66	-23	-21	36	1	1	-0	.991	2	*C	-1.3
1970	Phi-N	46	134	14	24	8	0	2	11	16	24	.179	.267	.284	49	-10	-10	9	0	0	0	.992	-13	C	-2.0
1971	Phi-N	43	134	9	22	5	1	3	6	10	32	.164	.222	.284	42	-10	-10	8	0	0	0	1.000	12	C	0.3
1972	Phi-N	46	106	6	19	4	0	2	10	10	25	.179	.256	.274	49	-7	-7	7	0	0	0	.992	6	C	0.0
1973	Phi-N	28	69	7	16	1	2	1	5	6	19	.232	.293	.348	75	-2	-2	6	0	0	0	.992	1	C	-0.1
1974	Pit-N	15	30	2	3	0	0	0	0	4	16	.100	.206	.100	-13	-4	-4	1	0	0	0	1.000	3	C	-0.1
Total	11	636	1920	146	370	60	12	28	161	152	370	.193	.253	.280	51	-120	-126	128	4	4	-1	.991	10	C	-9.3

■ TOM RYDER Ryder, Thomas BL , Deb: 7/22/1884

YEAR	TM/L	G	AB	R	H	2B	3B	HR	RBI	BB	SO	AVG	OBP	SLG	PRO+	BR	/A	RC	SB	CS	SBR	FA	FR	POS	TPR
1884	StL-U	8	28	4	7	1	0	0		2		.250	.300	.286	96	0	-0	2				.650	-0	/O	0.0

■ GENE RYE Rye, Eugene Rudolph "Half-Pint" (b: Eugene Rudolph Mercantelli)
b: 11/15/06, Chicago, Ill. d: 1/21/80, Park Ridge, Ill. BL/TR, 5'6", 165 lbs. Deb: 4/22/31

YEAR	TM/L	G	AB	R	H	2B	3B	HR	RBI	BB	SO	AVG	OBP	SLG	PRO+	BR	/A	RC	SB	CS	SBR	FA	FR	POS	TPR
1931	Bos-A	17	39	3	7	0	0	0	1	2	5	.179	.220	.179	6	-5	-5	2	0	0	0	.944	-1	O	-0.7

■ ALEX SABO Sabo, Alexander "Giz" (b: Alexander Szabo) b: 2/14/10, New Brunswick, N.J BR/TR, 6', 192 lbs. Deb: 8/01/36

YEAR	TM/L	G	AB	R	H	2B	3B	HR	RBI	BB	SO	AVG	OBP	SLG	PRO+	BR	/A	RC	SB	CS	SBR	FA	FR	POS	TPR
1936	Was-A	4	8	1	3	0	0	0	1	0	2	.375	.375	.375	91	-0	-0	1	0	0	0	.923	1	/C	0.1
1937	Was-A	1	0	0	0	0	0	0	0	0	0	—	—	—	—	0	0	0	0	0	0	1.000	-0	/C	0.0
Total	2	5	8	1	3	0	0	0	1	0	2	.375	.375	.375	91	-0	-0	1	0	0	0	.929	1	/C	0.1

■ CHRIS SABO Sabo, Christopher Andrew b: 1/19/62, Detroit, Mich. BR/TR, 5'11", 185 lbs. Deb: 4/04/88

YEAR	TM/L	G	AB	R	H	2B	3B	HR	RBI	BB	SO	AVG	OBP	SLG	PRO+	BR	/A	RC	SB	CS	SBR	FA	FR	POS	TPR
1988	Cin-N★	137	538	74	146	40	2	11	44	29	52	.271	.316	.414	104	4	2	69	46	14	5	**.966**	19	*3/S	2.7
1989	Cin-N	82	304	40	79	21	1	6	29	25	33	.260	.318	.395	99	1	-1	38	14	9	-1	.943	-3	3	-0.5
1990	*Cin-N★	148	567	95	153	38	2	25	71	61	58	.270	.345	.476	118	17	14	94	25	10	2	**.966**	-6	*3	1.1
1991	Cin-N★	153	582	91	175	35	3	26	88	44	79	.301	.356	.505	134	29	26	103	19	6	2	.966	-15	*3	1.4
1992	Cin-N	96	344	42	84	19	3	12	43	30	54	.244	.307	.422	99	1	-1	41	4	5	-2	.961	-1	3	-0.3
Total	5	616	2335	342	637	153	11	80	275	189	276	.273	.332	.451	114	52	41	346	108	44	6	.962	-6	3/S	4.4

■ FRANK SACKA Sacka, Frank b: 8/30/24, Romulus, Mich. BR/TR, 6', 195 lbs. Deb: 4/29/51

YEAR	TM/L	G	AB	R	H	2B	3B	HR	RBI	BB	SO	AVG	OBP	SLG	PRO+	BR	/A	RC	SB	CS	SBR	FA	FR	POS	TPR
1951	Was-A	7	16	1	4	0	0	0	3	0	5	.250	.250	.250	36	-1	-1	1	0	0	0	.962	2	/C	0.0
1953	Was-A	7	18	2	5	0	0	0	3	3	1	.278	.381	.278	82	-0	-0	2	0	0	0	1.000	2	/C	0.2
Total	2	14	34	3	9	0	0	0	6	3	6	.265	.324	.265	62	-2	-2	3	0	0	0	.982	3	/C	0.2

■ MIKE SADEK Sadek, Michael George b: 5/30/46, Minneapolis, Minn. BR/TR, 5'9", 165 lbs. Deb: 4/13/73

YEAR	TM/L	G	AB	R	H	2B	3B	HR	RBI	BB	SO	AVG	OBP	SLG	PRO+	BR	/A	RC	SB	CS	SBR	FA	FR	POS	TPR
1973	SF-N	39	66	6	11	1	1	0	4	11	8	.167	.286	.212	38	-5	-5	5	1	0	0	.981	7	C	0.3
1975	SF-N	42	106	14	25	5	2	0	9	14	14	.236	.325	.321	76	-3	-3	10	1	0	0	.995	7	C	0.5
1976	SF-N	55	93	8	19	2	0	0	7	11	10	.204	.295	.226	48	-6	-6	7	0	0	0	.985	8	C	0.2
1977	SF-N	61	126	12	29	7	0	1	15	12	5	.230	.297	.310	63	-7	-6	12	2	1	0	.992	10	C	0.4
1978	SF-N	40	109	15	26	3	0	2	9	10	11	.239	.303	.321	77	-4	-3	11	1	0	0	.975	2	C	-0.1
1979	SF-N	63	126	14	30	5	0	1	11	15	24	.238	.324	.302	77	-5	-3	12	1	0	0	.993	1	C/O	0.0

YEAR	TM/L	G	AB	R	H	2B	3B	HR	RBI	BB	SO	AVG	OBP	SLG	PRO+	BR	/A	RC	SB	CS	SBR	FA	FR	POS	TPR
1980	SF-N	64	151	14	38	4	1	1	16	27	18	.252	.365	.311	93	-1	-0	19	0	0	0	.974	4	C	0.6
1981	SF-N	19	36	5	6	3	0	0	3	8	7	.167	.318	.250	64	-2	-1	4	0	0	0	.979	7	C	0.6
Total	8	383	813	88	184	30	4	5	74	108	97	.226	.319	.292	70	-31	-30	80	6	1	1	.985	45	C/O	2.5

■ ED SADOWSKI Sadowski, Edward Roman b: 1/19/32, Pittsburgh, Pa. BR/TR, 5'11", 175 lbs. Deb: 4/20/60 F

YEAR	TM/L	G	AB	R	H	2B	3B	HR	RBI	BB	SO	AVG	OBP	SLG	PRO+	BR	/A	RC	SB	CS	SBR	FA	FR	POS	TPR
1960	Bos-A	38	93	10	20	2	0	3	8	8	13	.215	.284	.333	64	-5	-5	8	0	0	0	.995	6	C	0.2
1961	LA-A	69	164	16	38	13	0	4	12	11	33	.232	.280	.384	68	-6	-9	16	2	3	-1	.987	8	C	0.0
1962	LA-A	27	55	4	11	4	0	1	3	2	14	.200	.228	.327	49	-4	-4	4	1	0	0	.968	3	C	0.0
1963	LA-A	80	174	24	30	1	1	4	15	17	33	.172	.246	.259	44	-14	-12	11	2	1	0	.997	20	C	1.0
1966	Atl-N	3	9	1	1	0	0	0	1	1	1	.111	.200	.111	-10	-1	-1	0	0	0	0	1.000	1	/C	-0.1
Total	5	217	495	55	100	20	1	12	39	39	94	.202	.262	.319	56	-30	-31	39	5	4	-1	.991	37	C	1.1

■ BOB SADOWSKI Sadowski, Robert Frank "Sid" b: 1/15/37, St.Louis, Mo. BL/TR, 6', 175 lbs. Deb: 9/16/60

YEAR	TM/L	G	AB	R	H	2B	3B	HR	RBI	BB	SO	AVG	OBP	SLG	PRO+	BR	/A	RC	SB	CS	SBR	FA	FR	POS	TPR
1960	StL-N	1	1	0	0	0	0	0	0	1	0	.000	.500	.000	47	0	0	0	0	0	0	.000	-1	/2	-0.1
1961	Phi-N	16	54	4	7	0	0	0	0	4	7	.130	.203	.130	-9	-8	-8	1	1	0	0	.971	-1	3	-0.9
1962	Chi-A	79	130	22	30	3	3	6	24	13	22	.231	.301	.438	97	-1	-1	17	0	0	0	.955	5	32	0.5
1963	LA-A	88	144	12	36	6	0	1	22	15	34	.250	.321	.313	83	-4	-3	15	2	1	0	1.000	-3	O/32	-0.7
Total	4	184	329	38	73	9	3	7	46	33	63	.222	.295	.331	73	-13	-12	34	3	1	0	.965	-0	/3O2	-1.2

■ TOM SAFFELL Saffell, Thomas Judson b: 7/26/21, Etowah, Tenn. BL/TR, 5'11", 170 lbs. Deb: 7/02/49

YEAR	TM/L	G	AB	R	H	2B	3B	HR	RBI	BB	SO	AVG	OBP	SLG	PRO+	BR	/A	RC	SB	CS	SBR	FA	FR	POS	TPR
1949	Pit-N	73	205	36	66	7	1	2	25	21	27	.322	.385	.395	107	3	3	32	5			.992	-3	O	-0.3
1950	Pit-N	67	182	18	37	7	0	2	6	14	34	.203	.264	.275	41	-15	-16	14	1			.993	6	O	-1.2
1951	Pit-N	49	65	11	13	0	0	1	5	5	18	.200	.257	.246	35	-6	-6	4	1	1	-0	.929	-4	O	-1.1
1955	Pit-N	73	113	21	19	1	0	1	3	15	22	.168	.266	.204	27	-12	-11	7	1	0	0	.964	-7	O	-2.0
	KC-A	9	37	5	8	0	0	0	1	4	7	.216	.293	.216	38	-3	-3	3	1	0	0	.962	-0	/O	-0.3
Total	4	271	602	91	143	15	1	6	40	59	108	.238	.307	.296	60	-33	-34	61	9	1		.980	-8	O	-4.9

■ HARRY SAGE Sage, Harry "Doc" b: 3/16/1864, Rock Island, Ill. d: 5/27/47, Rock Island, Ill. BR/TR, 5'10", 185 lbs. Deb: 4/17/1890

YEAR	TM/L	G	AB	R	H	2B	3B	HR	RBI	BB	SO	AVG	OBP	SLG	PRO+	BR	/A	RC	SB	CS	SBR	FA	FR	POS	TPR
1890	Tol-a	81	275	40	41	8	4	2		29		.149	.235	.229	38	-21	-22	18	10			.948	8	C/O	-0.7

■ PONY SAGER Sager, Samuel B. b: 1847, Marshalltown, Iowa 140 lbs. Deb: 5/06/1871

YEAR	TM/L	G	AB	R	H	2B	3B	HR	RBI	BB	SO	AVG	OBP	SLG	PRO+	BR	/A	RC	SB	CS	SBR	FA	FR	POS	TPR
1871	Rok-n	8	39	9	11	0	0	0	5	2	2	.282	.317	.282	77	-1	-1	5	5					/SO	0.0

■ VIC SAIER Saier, Victor Sylvester b: 5/4/1891, Lansing, Mich. d: 5/14/67, E.Lansing, Mich. BL/TR, 5'11", 185 lbs. Deb: 5/03/11

YEAR	TM/L	G	AB	R	H	2B	3B	HR	RBI	BB	SO	AVG	OBP	SLG	PRO+	BR	/A	RC	SB	CS	SBR	FA	FR	POS	TPR
1911	Chi-N	86	259	42	67	15	1	1	37	25	37	.259	.340	.336	89	-3	-3	34	11			.980	-4	1	-0.8
1912	Chi-N	122	451	74	130	25	14	2	61	34	65	.288	.340	.419	107	3	3	67	11			.992	-5	*1	-0.4
1913	Chi-N	149	519	94	150	15	**21**	14	92	62	62	.289	.370	.480	141	28	27	97	26			.983	-5	*1	2.1
1914	Chi-N	153	537	87	129	24	8	18	72	94	61	.240	.357	.415	130	21	21	85	19			.986	-11	*1	0.8
1915	Chi-N	144	497	74	131	35	11	11	64	64	62	.264	.350	.445	140	24	23	83	29	9	3	.985	-5	*1	2.0
1916	Chi-N	147	498	60	126	25	3	7	50	79	68	.253	.356	.357	108	14	8	66	20	17	-4	.984	-0	*1	-0.2
1917	Chi-N	6	21	5	5	1	0	0	2	2	1	.238	.304	.286	75	-0	-1	2	0			1.000	2	/1	0.1
1919	Pit-N	58	166	19	37	3	3	2	17	18	13	.223	.306	.313	83	-2	-3	17	5			.985	-5	1	-1.0
Total	8	865	2948	455	775	143	61	55	395	378	369	.263	.351	.409	119	83	76	450	121	26		.986	-33	1	2.6

■ EBBA ST.CLAIRE St.Claire, Edward Joseph b: 8/5/21, Whitehall, N.Y. d: 8/22/82, Whitehall, N.Y. BB/TR, 6'1", 219 lbs. Deb: 4/17/51 F

YEAR	TM/L	G	AB	R	H	2B	3B	HR	RBI	BB	SO	AVG	OBP	SLG	PRO+	BR	/A	RC	SB	CS	SBR	FA	FR	POS	TPR
1951	Bos-N	72	220	22	62	17	2	1	25	12	24	.282	.322	.391	98	-3	-1	29	2	0	1	.977	3	C	0.4
1952	Bos-N	39	108	5	23	2	0	2	4	8	12	.213	.267	.287	56	-7	-6	8	0	1	-1	.972	4	C	-0.2
1953	Mil-N	33	80	7	16	3	0	2	5	3	9	.200	.229	.313	42	-7	-7	6	0	0	0	.992	3	C	-0.3
1954	NY-N	20	42	5	11	1	0	2	6	12	7	.262	.436	.429	126	2	2	9	0	0	0	.975	2	C	0.5
Total	4	164	450	39	112	23	2	7	40	35	52	.249	.306	.356	81	-15	-12	52	2	1	0	.978	12	C	0.4

■ LENN SAKATA Sakata, Lenn Haruki b: 6/8/54, Honolulu, Hawaii BR/TR, 5'9", 160 lbs. Deb: 7/21/77

YEAR	TM/L	G	AB	R	H	2B	3B	HR	RBI	BB	SO	AVG	OBP	SLG	PRO+	BR	/A	RC	SB	CS	SBR	FA	FR	POS	TPR
1977	Mil-A	53	154	13	25	2	0	2	12	9	22	.162	.209	.214	16	-18	-18	7	1	3	-2	.985	17	2	0.1
1978	Mil-A	30	78	8	15	4	0	0	3	8	11	.192	.267	.244	44	-6	-6	5	1	0	0	.975	0	2	-0.4
1979	Mil-A	4	14	1	7	2	0	0	1	0	1	.500	.500	.643	206	2	2	5	0	0	0	1.000	2	/2	0.4
1980	Bal-A	43	83	12	16	3	2	1	9	6	10	.193	.247	.313	53	-6	-5	6	2	1	0	.984	6	2/SD	0.2
1981	Bal-A	61	150	19	34	4	0	5	15	11	18	.227	.284	.353	83	-4	-4	15	4	0	1	.963	2	S2	0.4
1982	Bal-A	136	343	40	89	18	1	6	31	30	39	.259	.326	.370	91	-4	-4	42	7	4	-0	.977	-6	2S	-0.3
1983	*Bal-A	66	134	23	34	7	0	3	12	16	17	.254	.338	.373	97	-1	-0	17	8	4	0	.990	4	2/CD	0.6
1984	Bal-A	81	157	23	30	1	0	3	11	6	15	.191	.221	.255	32	-15	-14	8	4	1	1	.988	5	2/O	-0.7
1985	Bal-A	55	97	15	22	3	0	3	6	6	15	.227	.279	.351	73	-4	-4	9	3	2	-0	.960	-1	2/D	-0.4
1986	Oak-A	17	34	4	12	2	0	0	5	3	6	.353	.405	.412	133	1	2	5	0	1	-1	.984	5	2/D	0.6
1987	NY-A	19	45	5	12	0	1	2	4	2	4	.267	.313	.444	99	-0	-0	5	0	1	-1	.929	1	3/2	0.0
Total	11	565	1289	163	296	46	4	25	109	97	158	.230	.288	.330	71	-53	-51	123	30	17	-1	.982	36	2S/3DOC	0.5

■ MARK SALAS Salas, Mark Bruce b: 3/8/61, Montebello, Cal. BL/TR, 6', 205 lbs. Deb: 6/19/84

YEAR	TM/L	G	AB	R	H	2B	3B	HR	RBI	BB	SO	AVG	OBP	SLG	PRO+	BR	/A	RC	SB	CS	SBR	FA	FR	POS	TPR
1984	StL-N	14	20	1	2	1	0	0	1	0	3	.100	.100	.150	-31	-3	-3	0	0	0	0	1.000	-1	/CO	-0.4
1985	Min-A	120	360	51	108	20	5	9	41	18	37	.300	.335	.458	108	6	4	53	0	1	-1	.991	2	*C/D	1.0
1986	Min-A	91	258	28	60	7	4	8	33	18	32	.233	.285	.384	78	-8	-9	27	3	1	0	.980	-6	C/D	-1.0
1987	Min-A	22	45	8	17	2	0	3	9	5	6	.378	.440	.622	171	5	5	12	0	1	-1	.989	1	C	0.5
	NY-A	50	115	13	23	4	0	3	12	10	17	.200	.281	.313	58	-7	-7	11	0	0	0	1.000	-3	C/OD	-0.7
	Yr	72	160	21	40	6	0	6	21	15	23	.250	.326	.400	91	-2	-2	21	0	1	-1	.996	-2	C/DO	-0.2
1988	Chi-A	75	196	17	49	7	0	3	9	12	17	.250	.303	.332	78	-6	-6	20	0	0	0	.979	0	C/D	-0.2
1989	Cle-A	30	77	4	17	4	1	2	7	5	13	.221	.277	.377	81	-2	-2	8	0	0	0	1.000	-0	D/C	-0.2
1990	Det-A	74	164	18	38	3	0	9	24	21	28	.232	.323	.415	104	1	1	22	0	0	0	.988	-4	C/3D	-0.1
1991	Det-A	33	57	2	5	1	0	1	7	0	10	.088	.119	.158	-24	-10	-10	1	0	0	0	1.000	0	C/1D	-1.0
Total	8	509	1292	142	319	49	10	38	143	89	163	.247	.302	.389	86	-23	-27	154	3	3	-1	.987	-11	C/D1O3	-2.1

■ ANGEL SALAZAR Salazar, Argenis Antonio (Yepez) b: 11/4/61, ElTigre, Venez. BR/TR, 6', 173 lbs. Deb: 8/10/83

YEAR	TM/L	G	AB	R	H	2B	3B	HR	RBI	BB	SO	AVG	OBP	SLG	PRO+	BR	/A	RC	SB	CS	SBR	FA	FR	POS	TPR
1983	Mon-N	36	37	5	8	1	1	0	1	1	8	.216	.237	.297	47	-3	-3	2	0	0	0	.966	2	S	0.1
1984	Mon-N	80	174	12	27	4	2	0	12	4	38	.155	.179	.201	7	-22	-21	6	1	1	-0	.960	-3	S	-2.0
1986	KC-A	117	298	24	73	20	2	0	24	7	47	.245	.267	.326	59	-17	-17	26	1	1	-0	.978	-5	*S/2	-1.3
1987	KC-A	116	317	24	65	7	0	2	21	6	46	.205	.220	.246	23	-35	-36	16	4	4	-1	.981	22	*S	-0.7
1988	Chi-N	34	60	4	15	1	1	0	1	1	11	.250	.262	.300	58	-3	-3	5	0	0	0	.966	7	S/23	0.5
Total	5	383	886	69	188	33	6	2	59	19	150	.212	.231	.270	36	-79	-80	55	6	6	-2	.974	23	S/23	-3.4

■ LUIS SALAZAR Salazar, Luis Ernesto (Garcia) b: 5/19/56, Barcelona, Venez. BR/TR, 5'9", 180 lbs. Deb: 8/15/80

YEAR	TM/L	G	AB	R	H	2B	3B	HR	RBI	BB	SO	AVG	OBP	SLG	PRO+	BR	/A	RC	SB	CS	SBR	FA	FR	POS	TPR
1980	SD-N	44	169	28	57	4	7	1	25	9	25	.337	.374	.462	140	7	8	29	11	2	2	.944	-3	3/O	0.7
1981	SD-N	109	400	37	121	19	6	3	38	16	72	.303	.331	.403	116	3	6	51	11	8	-2	.955	1	3O	0.3
1982	SD-N	145	524	55	127	15	5	8	62	23	80	.242	.277	.336	75	-22	-18	48	32	9	4	.938	16	*3S/O	0.0
1983	SD-N	134	481	52	124	16	2	14	45	17	80	.258	.286	.387	88	-12	-10	53	24	9	2	.949	10	*3S	0.2
1984	*SD-N	93	228	20	55	7	2	3	17	6	38	.241	.261	.329	65	-11	-11	17	11	7	-1	.970	5	3O/S	-0.9
1985	Chi-A	122	327	39	80	18	2	10	45	12	60	.245	.271	.404	79	-9	-11	35	14	4	2	.968	-19	O3/1D	-3.1
1986	Chi-A	4	7	1	1	0	0	0	0	1	3	.143	.250	.143	10	-1	-1	0	0	0	0	.000	0	/D	-0.1
1987	SD-N	84	189	13	48	5	0	3	17	14	30	.254	.305	.328	70	-9	-8	19	3	3	-1	.957	-9	3SO/P1	-1.7

YEAR	TM/L	G	AB	R	H	2B	3B	HR	RBI	BB	SO	AVG	OBP	SLG	PRO+	BR	/A	RC	SB	CS	SBR	FA	FR	POS	TPR
1988	Det-A	130	452	61	122	14	1	12	62	21	70	.270	.307	.385	96	-5	-3	52	6	0	2	.992	-10	OS3/21	-1.1
1989	SD-N	95	246	27	66	7	2	8	22	11	44	.268	.302	.411	102	-0	-0	29	1	3	-2	.968	7	3O/S1	0.6
	*Chi-N	26	80	7	26	5	0	1	12	4	13	.325	.357	.425	114	2	2	11	0	1	-1	.921	-6	3/O	-0.5
	Yr	121	326	34	92	12	2	9	34	15	57	.282	.316	.414	105	2	1	40	1	4	-2	.959	1	3O/S1	0.1
1990	Chi-N	115	410	44	104	13	3	12	47	19	59	.254	.293	.388	80	-9	-13	47	3	1	0	.950	-20	3O	-3.4
1991	Chi-N	103	333	34	86	14	1	14	38	15	45	.258	.292	.432	97	-1	-3	39	0	3	-2	.956	-7	3/1O	-1.2
1992	Chi-N	98	255	20	53	7	2	5	25	11	34	.208	.241	.310	54	-16	-16	17	1	1	-0	.926	3	3OS/1	-1.5
Total	13	1302	4101	438	1070	144	33	94	455	179	653	.261	.294	.381	88	-83	-78	446	117	51	5	.950	-31	3OS/1D2P	-11.7

■ **ED SALES** Sales, Edward A. b: 1861, Harrisburg, Pa. d: 8/10/12, New Haven, Conn. TR , Deb: 7/15/1890

YEAR	TM/L	G	AB	R	H	2B	3B	HR	RBI	BB	SO	AVG	OBP	SLG	PRO+	BR	/A	RC	SB	CS	SBR	FA	FR	POS	TPR
1890	Pit-N	51	189	19	43	7	3	1	23	16	15	.228	.298	.312	90	-5	-1	19	3			.871	-14	S	-1.1

■ **BILL SALKELD** Salkeld, William Franklin b: 3/8/17, Pocatello, Idaho d: 4/22/67, Los Angeles, Cal. BL/TR, 5'10", 190 lbs. Deb: 4/18/45

YEAR	TM/L	G	AB	R	H	2B	3B	HR	RBI	BB	SO	AVG	OBP	SLG	PRO+	BR	/A	RC	SB	CS	SBR	FA	FR	POS	TPR
1945	Pit-N	95	267	45	83	16	1	15	52	50	16	.311	.420	.547	161	25	24	63	2			.973	-9	C	1.9
1946	Pit-N	69	160	18	47	8	0	3	19	39	16	.294	.432	.400	133	10	10	32	2			.972	-1	C	1.2
1947	Pit-N	47	61	5	13	2	0	0	8	6	8	.213	.284	.246	41	-5	-5	4	0			.971	-3	C	-0.7
1948	*Bos-N	78	198	26	48	8	1	8	28	42	37	.242	.378	.414	116	5	6	34	1			.990	5	C	1.5
1949	Bos-N	66	161	17	41	5	0	5	25	44	24	.255	.417	.379	121	6	7	29	1			.980	-4	C	0.6
1950	Chi-A	1	3	0	0	0	0	0	0	1	0	.000	.250	.000	-33	-1	-1	0	0	0	0	1.000	-0	/C	-0.1
Total	6	356	850	111	232	39	2	31	132	182	101	.273	.402	.433	129	41	40	162	6	0		.979	-11	C	4.4

■ **CHICO SALMON** Salmon, Ruthford Eduardo b: 12/3/40, Colon, Panama BR/TR, 5'10", 170 lbs. Deb: 6/28/64

YEAR	TM/L	G	AB	R	H	2B	3B	HR	RBI	BB	SO	AVG	OBP	SLG	PRO+	BR	/A	RC	SB	CS	SBR	FA	FR	POS	TPR
1964	Cle-A	86	283	43	87	17	2	4	25	13	37	.307	.342	.424	113	4	4	41	10	6	-1	1.000	-8	O21	-0.5
1965	Cle-A	79	120	20	29	8	0	3	12	5	19	.242	.283	.383	87	-2	-2	12	7	4	-0	.985	-6	1O/23	-1.0
1966	Cle-A	126	422	46	108	13	2	7	40	21	41	.256	.291	.346	82	-10	-10	44	10	1	2	.958	-18	S21O/3	-2.2
1967	Cle-A	90	203	19	46	13	1	2	19	17	29	.227	.290	.330	82	-4	-5	20	10	4	1	1.000	1	O12S/3	-0.2
1968	Cle-A	103	276	24	59	8	1	3	12	12	30	.214	.254	.283	63	-13	-12	19	7	7	-2	.971	-15	23SO1	-3.1
1969	*Bal-A	52	91	18	27	5	0	3	12	10	22	.297	.379	.451	130	4	4	16	0	0	0	1.000	-5	1/2S3O	-0.1
1970	Bal-A	63	172	19	43	4	0	7	22	8	30	.250	.287	.395	85	-4	-4	19	2	2	-1	.946	-20	S23/1	-2.3
1971	Bal-A	42	84	11	15	1	0	2	7	3	21	.179	.207	.262	32	-8	-8	4	0	0	0	1.000	-3	/123S	-1.1
1972	Bal-A	17	16	2	1	1	0	0	0	0	4	.063	.063	.125	-44	-3	-3	0	0	0	0	1.000	0	/13	-0.3
Total	9	658	1667	202	415	70	6	31	149	89	233	.249	.291	.354	84	-36	-36	174	46	24	-1	.959	-75	2S1O/3	-10.8

■ **TIM SALMON** Salmon, Timothy James b: 8/24/68, Long Beach, Cal. BR/TR, 6'3", 200 lbs. Deb: 8/21/92

YEAR	TM/L	G	AB	R	H	2B	3B	HR	RBI	BB	SO	AVG	OBP	SLG	PRO+	BR	/A	RC	SB	CS	SBR	FA	FR	POS	TPR
1992	Cal-A	23	79	8	14	1	0	2	6	11	23	.177	.286	.266	56	-5	-4	6	1	1	-0	.953	-0	O	-0.6

■ **JACK SALTZGAVER** Saltzgaver, Otto Hamlin b: 1/23/03, Croton, Iowa d: 2/1/78, Keokuk, Iowa BL/TR, 5'11", 165 lbs. Deb: 4/12/32

YEAR	TM/L	G	AB	R	H	2B	3B	HR	RBI	BB	SO	AVG	OBP	SLG	PRO+	BR	/A	RC	SB	CS	SBR	FA	FR	POS	TPR
1932	NY-A	20	47	10	6	2	1	0	5	10	10	.128	.281	.213	31	-5	-4	4	1	1	-0	.958	-3	2	-0.7
1934	NY-A	94	350	64	95	8	1	6	36	48	28	.271	.359	.351	90	-7	-4	48	8	1	2	.953	-16	3/1	-1.3
1935	NY-A	61	149	17	39	6	0	3	18	23	12	.262	.368	.362	95	-2	-0	21	0	2	-1	.937	-13	23/1	-1.2
1936	NY-A	34	90	14	19	5	0	1	13	13	18	.211	.311	.300	53	-7	-6	9	0	0	0	.972	-5	3/21	-0.9
1937	NY-A	17	11	6	2	0	0	0	0	3	4	.182	.357	.182	40	-1	-1	1	0	0	0	1.000	0	/1	-0.1
1945	Pit-N	52	117	20	38	5	3	0	10	8	8	.325	.368	.419	114	3	2	18	0			.963	-4	2/3	0.0
Total	6	278	764	131	199	26	5	10	82	105	80	.260	.351	.347	85	-19	-14	101	9	4		.957	-40	3/21	-4.2

■ **ED SAMCOFF** Samcoff, Edward William b: 9/1/24, Sacramento, Cal. BR/TR, 5'10", 165 lbs. Deb: 4/21/51

YEAR	TM/L	G	AB	R	H	2B	3B	HR	RBI	BB	SO	AVG	OBP	SLG	PRO+	BR	/A	RC	SB	CS	SBR	FA	FR	POS	TPR
1951	Phi-A	4	11	0	0	0	0	0	0	1	2	.000	.083	.000	-75	-3	-3	0	0	0	0	1.000	-2	/2	-0.4

■ **RON SAMFORD** Samford, Ronald Edward b: 2/28/30, Dallas, Tex. BR/TR, 5'11", 156 lbs. Deb: 4/15/54

YEAR	TM/L	G	AB	R	H	2B	3B	HR	RBI	BB	SO	AVG	OBP	SLG	PRO+	BR	/A	RC	SB	CS	SBR	FA	FR	POS	TPR
1954	NY-N	12	5	2	0	0	0	0	0	0	1	.000	.000	.000	-99	-1	-1	0	0	1	-1	1.000	3	/2	0.1
1955	Det-A	1	1	0	0	0	0	0	0	0	1	.000	.000	.000	-99	-0	-0	0	0	0	0	1.000	0	/S	0.0
1957	Det-A	54	91	6	20	1	2	0	5	6	15	.220	.276	.275	49	-6	-6	7	1	0	0	.964	13	S2/3	0.9
1959	Was-A	91	237	23	53	13	0	5	22	11	29	.224	.264	.342	65	-12	-12	19	1	0	0	.947	0	S2	-0.6
Total	4	158	334	31	73	14	2	5	27	17	46	.219	.263	.317	58	-20	-20	27	2	1	0	.952	17	S/23	0.4

■ **BILL SAMPLE** Sample, William Amos b: 4/2/55, Roanoke, Va. BR/TR, 5'9", 175 lbs. Deb: 9/02/78

YEAR	TM/L	G	AB	R	H	2B	3B	HR	RBI	BB	SO	AVG	OBP	SLG	PRO+	BR	/A	RC	SB	CS	SBR	FA	FR	POS	TPR
1978	Tex-A	8	15	2	7	2	0	0	3	0	3	.467	.467	.600	197	2	2	4	0	0	0	.000	-1	/OD	0.1
1979	Tex-A	128	325	60	95	21	2	5	35	37	28	.292	.368	.415	112	6	6	50	8	6	-1	1.000	-4	*O/D	-0.2
1980	Tex-A	99	204	29	53	10	0	4	19	18	15	.260	.338	.368	96	-2	-1	26	8	5	-1	.973	-9	O/D	-1.2
1981	Tex-A	66	230	36	65	16	0	3	25	17	21	.283	.350	.391	120	4	6	33	4	1	1	.993	-1	O	0.3
1982	Tex-A	97	360	56	94	14	2	10	29	27	35	.261	.318	.394	99	-3	-1	47	10	2	2	.981	2	O/D	0.0
1983	Tex-A	147	554	80	152	28	3	12	57	44	46	.274	.333	.401	103	1	2	79	44	8	8	.988	6	*O	1.2
1984	Tex-A	130	489	67	121	20	2	5	33	29	46	.247	.290	.327	68	-20	-22	46	18	6	2	.986	0	*O/D	-2.4
1985	NY-A	59	139	18	40	5	0	1	15	9	10	.288	.340	.345	90	-2	-2	17	2	1	0	.989	-4	O	-0.7
1986	Atl-N	92	200	23	57	11	0	6	14	14	26	.285	.341	.430	105	3	1	31	4	2	0	.986	-8	O/2	-0.8
Total	9	826	2516	371	684	127	9	46	230	195	230	.272	.331	.384	98	-11	-8	334	98	31	11	.987	-19	O/D2	-3.7

■ **AMADO SAMUEL** Samuel, Amado Ruperto b: 12/6/38, San Pedro De Macoris, D.R. BR/TR, 6'1", 170 lbs. Deb: 4/10/62

YEAR	TM/L	G	AB	R	H	2B	3B	HR	RBI	BB	SO	AVG	OBP	SLG	PRO+	BR	/A	RC	SB	CS	SBR	FA	FR	POS	TPR
1962	Mil-N	76	209	16	43	10	0	3	20	12	54	.206	.249	.297	47	-16	-16	15	0	2	-1	.958	-4	S2/3	-1.6
1963	Mil-N	15	17	0	3	1	0	0	0	0	4	.176	.176	.235	18	-2	-2	1	0	1	-1	.786	2	/S2	0.0
1964	NY-N	53	142	7	33	7	0	0	5	4	24	.232	.264	.282	55	-9	-8	10	0	1	-1	.945	7	S3/2	-0.1
Total	3	144	368	23	79	18	0	3	25	16	82	.215	.251	.288	49	-27	-26	26	0	4	-2	.942	4	/S23	-1.7

■ **JUAN SAMUEL** Samuel, Juan Milton b: 12/9/60, San Pedro De Macoris, , D.R. BR/TR, 5'11", 170 lbs. Deb: 8/24/83

YEAR	TM/L	G	AB	R	H	2B	3B	HR	RBI	BB	SO	AVG	OBP	SLG	PRO+	BR	/A	RC	SB	CS	SBR	FA	FR	POS	TPR
1983	*Phi-N	18	65	14	18	1	2	2	5	4	16	.277	.329	.446	114	1	1	9	3	2	-0	.916	3	2	0.5
1984	Phi-N☆	160	701	105	191	36	**19**	15	69	28	168	.272	.307	.442	107	5	3	99	72	15	13	.962	-22	*2	0.0
1985	Phi-N	161	663	101	175	31	13	19	74	33	141	.264	.305	.436	102	2	-0	87	53	19	5	.983	-2	*2	0.8
1986	Phi-N	145	591	90	157	36	12	16	78	26	142	.266	.306	.448	102	2	-1	80	42	14	4	.967	-9	*2	0.0
1987	Phi-N★	160	655	113	178	37	**15**	28	100	60	162	.272	.338	.502	115	16	13	109	35	15	2	.978	-19	*2	0.3
1988	Phi-N	157	629	68	153	32	9	12	67	39	151	.243	.300	.380	92	-6	-7	73	33	10	4	.978	-26	*2/O3	-2.5
1989	Phi-N	51	199	32	49	3	1	8	20	18	45	.246	.312	.392	100	-0	-0	26	11	3	2	.993	5	O	0.5
	NY-N	86	333	37	76	13	1	3	28	24	75	.228	.300	.300	76	-12	-10	33	31	9	4	.986	7	O	-0.2
	Yr	137	532	69	125	16	2	11	48	42	120	.235	.304	.335	85	-12	-10	58	42	12	5	.989	11	*O	0.3
1990	LA-N	143	492	62	119	24	3	13	52	51	126	.242	.319	.382	95	-5	-4	60	38	20	-1	.972	-5	*2O	-0.8
1991	LA-N★	153	594	74	161	22	6	12	58	49	133	.271	.330	.389	104	1	2	78	23	8	2	.978	4	*2	1.2
1992	LA-N	47	122	7	32	3	1	0	15	7	22	.262	.308	.303	75	-4	-4	12	2	2	-1	.974	-2	2/O	-0.6
	KC-A	29	102	15	29	5	3	0	8	7	27	.284	.336	.392	102	0	0	14	6	1	1	.903	-3	O2	-0.2
Total	10	1310	5146	718	1338	243	85	128	574	346	1208	.260	.314	.415	101	-2	-7	679	349	118	34	.973	-70	*2O/3	-1.0

■ **IKE SAMULS** Samuls, Samuel Earl b: 2/20/1876, Chicago, Ill. d: 1/1/42, Los Angeles, Cal. BR/TR, Deb: 8/03/1895

YEAR	TM/L	G	AB	R	H	2B	3B	HR	RBI	BB	SO	AVG	OBP	SLG	PRO+	BR	/A	RC	SB	CS	SBR	FA	FR	POS	TPR
1895	StL-N	24	74	5	17	2	0	0	5	5	7	.230	.278	.257	41	-6	-6	7	5			.750	-3	3/S	-0.7

■ **GUS SANBERG** Sanberg, Gustave E. b: 2/23/1896, Long Island City, N.Y. d: 2/3/30, Los Angeles, Cal. BR/TR, 6'1", 189 lbs. Deb: 5/11/23

YEAR	TM/L	G	AB	R	H	2B	3B	HR	RBI	BB	SO	AVG	OBP	SLG	PRO+	BR	/A	RC	SB	CS	SBR	FA	FR	POS	TPR
1923	Cin-N	7	17	1	3	1	0	0	1	1	1	.176	.222	.235	21	-2	-2	1	0	0	0	1.000	-1	/C	-0.2
1924	Cin-N	24	52	1	9	0	0	0	3	2	7	.173	.204	.173	2	-7	-7	2	0	0	0	1.000	0	C	-0.6
Total	2	31	69	2	12	1	0	0	4	3	8	.174	.208	.188	7	-9	-9	3	0	0	0	1.000	-1	/C	-0.8

YEAR	TM/L	G	AB	R	H	2B	3B	HR	RBI	BB	SO	AVG	OBP	SLG	PRO+	BR	/A	RC	SB	CS	SBR	FA	FR	POS	TPR

■ ALEJANDRO SANCHEZ Sanchez, Alejandro (Pimentel) b: 2/14/59, San Pedro, D.R. BR/TR, 6', 185 lbs. Deb: 9/06/82

1982	Phi-N	7	14	3	4	1	0	2	4	0	4	.286	.286	.786	186	1	1	3	0	0	0	1.000	0	/O	0.2
1983	Phi-N	8	7	2	2	0	0	0	2	0	2	.286	.286	.286	59	-0	-0	1	0	0	0	.500	-0	/O	-0.1
1984	SF-N	13	41	3	8	0	1	0	2	0	12	.195	.195	.244	23	-4	-4	1	2	3	-1	.952	-0	/O	-0.6
1985	Det-A	71	133	19	33	6	2	6	12	0	39	.248	.248	.459	89	-3	-3	13	2	2	-1	.923	-6	OD	-0.9
1986	Min-A	8	16	1	2	0	0	0	1	1	8	.125	.176	.125	-16	-3	-3	0	0	0	0	.000	-0	/OD	-0.3
1987	Oak-A	2	3	0	0	0	0	0	0	0	1	.000	.000	.000	-99	-1	-1	0	0	0	0	1.000	-0	/OD	-0.1
Total	6	109	214	28	49	7	3	8	21	1	66	.229	.233	.402	71	-9	-9	18	4	5	-2	.929	-6	OD	-1.8

■ CELERINO SANCHEZ Sanchez, Celerino (Perez) b: 2/3/44, Veracruz, Mexico d: 5/1/92, Leon, Mexico BR/TR, 5'11", 160 lbs. Deb: 6/13/72

1972	NY-A	71	250	18	62	8	3	0	22	12	30	.248	.293	.304	81	-7	-6	21	0	0	0	.939	4	3	-0.3
1973	NY-A	34	64	12	14	3	0	1	9	2	12	.219	.242	.313	57	-4	-4	5	1	1	-0	1.000	1	3D/SO	-0.3
Total	2	105	314	30	76	11	3	1	31	14	42	.242	.283	.306	76	-11	-10	26	1	1	-0	.943	5	/3DOS	-0.6

■ ORLANDO SANCHEZ Sanchez, Orlando (Marquez) b: 9/7/56, Canovanas, P.R. BL/TR, 6'1", 195 lbs. Deb: 5/06/81

1981	StL-N	27	49	5	14	2	1	0	6	2	6	.286	.314	.367	90	-1	-1	5	1	0	0	.926	-2	C	-0.2
1982	StL-N	26	37	6	7	0	1	0	3	5	5	.189	.286	.243	49	-2	-2	3	0	0	0	1.000	-1	C	-0.3
1983	StL-N	6	6	0	0	0	0	0	0	0	4	.000	.000	.000	-99	-2	-2	0	0	0	0	1.000	-0	/C	-0.2
1984	KC-A	10	10	0	1	1	0	0	2	0	2	.100	.100	.200	-19	-2	-2	0	0	0	0	1.000	-0	/C	-0.2
	Bal-A	4	8	0	2	0	0	0	1	0	2	.250	.250	.250	40	-1	-1	1	0	0	0	1.000	-0	/C	-0.1
	Yr	14	18	0	3	1	0	0	3	0	4	.167	.167	.222	7	-2	-2	0	0	0	0	1.000	-0	/C	-0.3
Total	4	73	110	11	24	3	2	0	12	7	19	.218	.265	.282	53	-7	-7	9	1	0	0	.962	-3	/C	-1.0

■ REY SANCHEZ Sanchez, Rey Francisco (Guadalupe) b: 10/5/67, Rio Piedras, P.R. BR/TR, 5'10", 180 lbs. Deb: 9/08/91

1991	Chi-N	13	23	1	6	0	0	0	2	4	3	.261	.370	.261	77	-0	-1	3	0	0	0	1.000	2	S/2	0.2
1992	Chi-N	74	255	24	64	14	3	1	19	10	17	.251	.287	.341	75	-8	-9	24	2	1	0	.974	14	S/2	1.1
Total	2	87	278	25	70	14	3	1	21	14	20	.252	.295	.335	76	-8	-8	26	2	1	0	.976	16	/S2	1.3

■ HEINIE SAND Sand, John Henry b: 7/3/1897, San Francisco, Cal d: 11/3/58, San Francisco, Cal. BR/TR, 5'8", 160 lbs. Deb: 4/17/23

1923	Phi-N	132	470	85	107	16	5	4	32	82	56	.228	.347	.309	67	-15	-23	57	7	3	0	.934	-2	*S3	-1.2
1924	Phi-N	137	539	79	132	21	6	6	40	52	57	.245	.316	.340	67	-18	-27	60	5	4	-1	.959	2	*S	-1.1
1925	Phi-N	148	496	69	138	30	7	3	55	64	65	.278	.364	.385	84	-5	-11	73	1	1	-0	.928	-6	*S	-0.3
1926	Phi-N	149	567	99	154	30	5	4	37	66	56	.272	.350	.363	88	-5	-9	73	2			.939	-3	*S	0.3
1927	Phi-N	141	535	87	160	22	8	1	49	58	59	.299	.369	.376	98	1	1	75	5			.949	-15	S3	-0.3
1928	Phi-N	141	426	38	90	26	1	0	38	60	47	.211	.310	.277	53	-27	-29	40	1			.951	-1	*S	-1.5
Total	6	848	3033	457	781	145	32	18	251	382	340	.258	.343	.344	77	-69	-99	378	21	8		.943	-25	S/3	-4.1

■ RYNE SANDBERG Sandberg, Ryne Dee b: 9/18/59, Spokane, Wash. BR/TR, 6'2", 180 lbs. Deb: 9/02/81

1981	Phi-N	13	6	2	1	0	0	0	0	0	1	.167	.167	.167	-5	-1	-1	0	0	0	0	1.000	4	/S2	0.4
1982	Chi-N	156	635	103	172	33	5	7	54	36	90	.271	.314	.372	89	-8	-10	75	32	12	6	.970	5	*32	-0.6
1983	Chi-N	158	633	94	165	25	4	8	48	51	79	.261	.319	.351	81	-13	-16	75	37	11	5	.986	41	*2/S	3.8
1984	*Chi-N★	156	636	114	200	36	19	19	84	52	101	.314	.369	.520	135	38	31	126	32	7	5	.993	23	*2	6.7
1985	Chi-N★	153	609	113	186	31	6	26	83	57	97	.305	.364	.504	127	32	24	117	54	11	10	.986	8	*2/S	4.9
1986	Chi-N★	154	627	68	178	28	5	14	76	46	79	.284	.333	.411	97	-2	-3	86	34	11	4	.994	5	*2	1.2
1987	Chi-N★	132	523	81	154	25	2	16	59	59	79	.294	.368	.442	109	11	8	89	21	2	5	.985	1	*2	2.1
1988	Chi-N★	155	618	77	163	23	8	19	69	54	91	.264	.324	.419	107	8	5	82	25	10	2	.987	11	*2	2.6
1989	*Chi-N★	157	606	104	176	25	5	30	76	59	85	.290	.357	.497	132	32	26	109	15	5	2	.992	1	*2	3.6
1990	Chi-N★	155	615	116	188	30	3	40	100	50	84	.306	.359	.559	138	38	32	124	25	7	3	.989	7	*2	4.6
1991	Chi-N★	158	585	104	170	32	2	26	100	87	89	.291	.384	.485	137	35	31	114	22	8	2	.995	11	*2	4.9
1992	Chi-N★	158	612	100	186	32	8	26	87	68	73	.304	.374	.510	145	38	36	117	17	6	2	.990	14	*2	5.8
Total	12	1705	6705	1076	1939	320	67	231	836	619	948	.289	.351	.460	118	212	164	1114	314	90	40	.990	131	*23/S	40.0

■ BEN SANDERS Sanders, Alexander Bennett b: 2/16/1865, Catharpen, Va. d: 8/29/30, Memphis, Tenn. BR/TR, 6', 210 lbs. Deb: 6/06/1888

1888	Phi-N	57	236	26	58	11	2	1	25	8	12	.246	.276	.322	88	-2	-4	25	13			.929	3	PO/3	-0.3
1889	Phi-N	44	169	21	47	8	2	0	21	6	11	.278	.307	.349	78	-4	-6	20	4			.879	-3	P/O	-0.1
1890	Phi-P	52	189	31	59	6	6	0	30	10	10	.312	.347	.407	101	0	-1	28	2			.924	1	PO	-0.1
1891	Phi-a	40	156	24	39	6	4	1	19	7	12	.250	.291	.359	86	-3	-4	17	2			.839	-6	OP	-0.7
1892	Lou-N	54	198	30	54	12	2	3	18	16	17	.273	.330	.399	133	5	7	29	6			.930	-3	P1/O	0.0
Total	5	247	948	132	257	43	16	5	113	47	62	.271	.310	.366	96	-4	-7	119	27			.916	-8	P/O13	-1.2

■ DEION SANDERS Sanders, Deion Luwynn b: 8/9/67, Ft.Myers, Fla. BL/TL, 6'1", 195 lbs. Deb: 6/01/89

1989	NY-A	14	47	7	11	2	0	2	7	3	8	.234	.280	.404	92	-1	-1	6	1	0	0	.969	-0	O	-0.1
1990	NY-A	57	133	24	21	2	2	3	9	13	27	.158	.238	.271	42	-11	-11	9	8	2	1	.973	-4	O/D	-1.5
1991	Atl-N	54	110	16	21	1	2	4	13	12	23	.191	.270	.345	68	-4	-5	11	11	3	2	.952	-5	O	-1.0
1992	*Atl-N	97	303	54	92	6	14	8	28	18	52	.304	.347	.495	125	13	10	51	26	9	2	.983	-1	O	1.1
Total	4	222	593	101	145	11	18	17	57	46	110	.245	.302	.410	94	-3	-6	77	46	14	5	.974	-10	O/D	-1.5

■ JOHN SANDERS Sanders, John Frank b: 11/20/45, Grand Island, Neb. BR/TR, 6'2", 200 lbs. Deb: 4/13/65

| 1965 | KC-A | 1 | 0 | 0 | 0 | 0 | 0 | 0 | 0 | 0 | 0 | — | — | — | | 0 | 0 | 0 | 0 | 0 | 0 | .000 | 0 | R | 0.0 |

■ RAY SANDERS Sanders, Raymond Floyd b: 12/4/16, Bonne Terre, Mo. d: 10/28/83, Washington, Mo. BL/TR, 6'2", 185 lbs. Deb: 4/14/42

1942	*StL-N	95	282	37	71	17	2	5	39	42	31	.252	.351	.379	106	6	3	39	2			.991	-4	1	-0.5
1943	*StL-N	144	478	69	134	21	5	11	73	77	33	.280	.381	.414	124	20	14	80	1			.995	-7	*1	0.3
1944	*StL-N	154	601	87	177	34	9	12	102	71	50	.295	.371	.441	126	23	21	101	2			.994	-13	*1	0.1
1945	StL-N	143	537	85	148	29	3	8	78	83	55	.276	.375	.385	109	11	9	84	3			.986	-5	*1	-0.5
1946	Bos-N	80	259	43	63	12	6	6	35	50	38	.243	.368	.359	105	4	4	38	0			.988	4	1	0.3
1948	*Bos-N	5	4	0	1	0	0	0	2	1	0	.250	.400	.250	81	-0	-0	0	0			.000	0	H	0.0
1949	Bos-N	9	21	0	3	1	0	0	0	4	9	.143	.280	.190	30	-2	-2	1	0			.984	2	/1	0.0
Total	7	630	2182	321	597	114	19	42	329	328	216	.274	.370	.401	115	61	52	344	8			.991	-21	1	-0.3

■ REGGIE SANDERS Sanders, Reginald Jerome b: 9/9/49, Birmingham, Ala. BR/TR, 6'2", 205 lbs. Deb: 9/01/74

| 1974 | Det-A | 26 | 99 | 12 | 27 | 7 | 0 | 3 | 16 | 2 | 14 | .273 | .284 | .434 | 108 | 1 | 1 | 13 | 1 | 0 | 0 | .987 | 1 | 1/D | 0.0 |

■ REGGIE SANDERS Sanders, Reginald Lavern b: 12/1/67, Florence, S.C. BR/TR, 6'1", 180 lbs. Deb: 8/22/91

1991	Cin-N	9	40	6	8	0	0	1	3	0	9	.200	.200	.275	31	-4	-4	2	1	1	-0	1.000	1	/O	-0.4
1992	Cin-N	116	385	62	104	26	6	12	36	48	98	.270	.357	.462	124	15	13	65	16	7	1	.978	5	*O	1.8
Total	2	125	425	68	112	26	6	13	39	48	107	.264	.344	.445	116	12	9	67	17	8	0	.802	5	O	1.4

■ MIKE SANDLOCK Sandlock, Michael Joseph b: 10/17/15, Old Greenwich, Conn. BB/TR, 6'1", 185 lbs. Deb: 9/19/42

1942	Bos-N	2	1	1	1	0	0	0	0	0	0	1.000	1.000	1.000	496	0	0	1	0			.000	0	/S	0.0
1944	Bos-N	30	30	1	3	0	0	0	0	0	6	.100	.250	.100	1	-4	-4	1	0			.956	7	3/S	0.3
1945	Bro-N	80	195	21	55	14	2	2	17	18	19	.282	.346	.405	109	2	2	28	2			.991	6	CS/23	0.6
1946	Bro-N	19	34	1	5	0	0	0	3	3	4	.147	.216	.147	4	-4	-4	1	0			.973	6	C/3	0.2
1953	Pit-N	64	186	10	43	5	0	2	12	19	16	.231	.281	.258	42	-16	-15	14	0			.991	16	C	0.3
Total	5	195	446	34	107	19	2	4	31	38	45	.240	.304	.305	66	-21	-21	46	2	0		.989	30	C/S32	1.4

■ CHARLIE SANDS Sands, Charles Duane b: 12/17/47, Newport News, Va. BL/TR, 6'2", 215 lbs. Deb: 6/21/67

YEAR	TM/L	G	AB	R	H	2B	3B	HR	RBI	BB	SO	AVG	OBP	SLG	PRO+	BR	/A	RC	SB	CS	SBR	FA	FR	POS	TPR
1967	NY-A	1	1	0	0	0	0	0	0	0	1	.000	.000	.000	-99	-0	-0	0	0	0	0	.000	0	H	0.0
1971	*Pit-N	28	25	4	5	2	0	1	5	7	6	.200	.375	.400	120	1	1	4	0	0	0	1.000	0	/C	0.1
1972	Pit-N	1	1	0	0	0	0	0	0	0	0	.000	.000	.000	-99	-0	-0	0	0	0	0	.000	0	H	0.0
1973	Cal-A	17	33	5	9	2	1	1	5	5	10	.273	.368	.485	150	2	2	6	0	0	0	.917	-8	C	-0.5
1974	Cal-A	43	83	6	16	2	0	4	13	23	17	.193	.374	.361	119	2	3	12	0	0	0	1.000	-1	D/C	0.3
1975	Oak-A	3	2	0	1	0	0	0	0	1	1	.500	.667	.500	239	1	1	1	0	0	0	.000	0	/D	0.1
Total	6	93	145	15	31	6	1	6	23	36	35	.214	.374	.393	125	5	6	24	0	0	0	.955	-8	/DC	0.0

■ TOMMY SANDT Sandt, Thomas James b: 12/22/50, Brooklyn, N.Y. BR/TR, 5'11", 175 lbs. Deb: 6/29/75 C

YEAR	TM/L	G	AB	R	H	2B	3B	HR	RBI	BB	SO	AVG	OBP	SLG	PRO+	BR	/A	RC	SB	CS	SBR	FA	FR	POS	TPR
1975	Oak-A	1	0	0	0	0	0	0	0	0	0	—	—	—	—	0	0	0	0	0	0	.000	0	/2	0.0
1976	Oak-A	41	67	6	14	1	0	0	3	7	9	.209	.284	.224	52	-4	-4	5	0	0	0	.966	3	S/23	0.2
Total	2	42	67	6	14	1	0	0	3	7	9	.209	.284	.224	52	-4	-4	5	0	0	0	1.000	3	/S23	0.2

■ JACK SANFORD Sanford, John Doward b: 6/23/17, Chatham, Va. BR/TR, 6'3", 195 lbs. Deb: 8/24/40

YEAR	TM/L	G	AB	R	H	2B	3B	HR	RBI	BB	SO	AVG	OBP	SLG	PRO+	BR	/A	RC	SB	CS	SBR	FA	FR	POS	TPR
1940	Was-A	34	122	5	24	4	2	0	10	6	17	.197	.234	.262	30	-13	-12	8	0	0	0	.993	-2	1	-1.6
1941	Was-A	3	5	1	2	0	1	0	0	1	1	.400	.500	.800	251	1	1	2	0	0	0	1.000	-0	/1	0.1
1946	Was-A	10	26	7	6	0	1	0	1	2	6	.231	.286	.308	70	-1	-1	2	0	0	0	.971	-2	/1	-0.3
Total	3	47	153	13	32	4	4	0	11	9	24	.209	.253	.288	44	-13	-12	12	0	0	0	.989	-4	/1	-1.8

■ MANNY SANGUILLEN Sanguillen, Manuel De Jesus (Magan) b: 3/21/44, Colon, Panama BR/TR, 6', 193 lbs. Deb: 7/23/67

YEAR	TM/L	G	AB	R	H	2B	3B	HR	RBI	BB	SO	AVG	OBP	SLG	PRO+	BR	/A	RC	SB	CS	SBR	FA	FR	POS	TPR
1967	Pit-N	30	96	6	26	4	0	0	8	4	12	.271	.300	.313	75	-3	-3	8	0	1	-1	.986	-5	C	-0.8
1969	Pit-N	129	459	62	139	21	6	5	57	12	48	.303	.325	.407	106	1	2	56	8	4	0	.981	4	*C	1.3
1970	*Pit-N	128	486	63	158	19	9	7	61	17	45	.325	.348	.444	113	6	7	69	2	3	-1	.988	1	*C	1.3
1971	*Pit-N☆	138	533	60	170	26	5	7	81	19	32	.319	.346	.426	118	11	11	70	6	4	-1	.994	5	*C	2.2
1972	*Pit-N★	136	520	55	155	18	8	7	71	21	38	.298	.325	.404	108	3	4	65	1	2	-1	.988	-3	*C/O	0.6
1973	Pit-N	149	589	64	166	26	7	12	65	17	29	.282	.305	.411	99	-5	-3	67	2	5	-2	.983	0	CO	-0.4
1974	*Pit-N	151	596	77	171	21	4	7	68	21	27	.287	.317	.371	95	-8	-6	65	2	2	-1	.985	-6	*C	-0.6
1975	*Pit-N☆	133	481	60	158	24	4	9	58	48	31	.328	.393	.451	135	22	23	83	5	4	-1	.987	-5	*C	2.3
1976	Pit-N	114	389	52	113	16	6	2	36	28	18	.290	.341	.378	103	2	1	46	2	4	-2	.978	-7	*C	-0.4
1977	Oak-A	152	571	42	157	17	5	6	58	22	35	.275	.304	.354	80	-17	-16	57	2	5	-2	.985	-8	CD/O1	-2.5
1978	Pit-N	85	220	15	58	5	1	3	16	9	10	.264	.299	.336	74	-7	-8	21	2	2	-1	1.000	-2	1C	-1.4
1979	*Pit-N	56	74	8	17	5	2	0	4	2	5	.230	.250	.351	59	-4	-4	6	0	0	0	.947	0	/C1	-0.5
1980	Pit-N	47	48	2	12	3	0	0	2	3	1	.250	.294	.313	68	-2	-2	4	3	2	-0	.956	0	/1	-0.2
Total	13	1448	5062	566	1500	205	57	65	585	223	331	.296	.329	.398	103	-2	6	616	35	38	-12	.986	-27	*C/OD1	0.9

■ ED SANICKI Sanicki, Edward Robert "Butch" b: 7/7/23, Wallington, N.J. BR/TR, 5'9", 175 lbs. Deb: 9/14/49

YEAR	TM/L	G	AB	R	H	2B	3B	HR	RBI	BB	SO	AVG	OBP	SLG	PRO+	BR	/A	RC	SB	CS	SBR	FA	FR	POS	TPR
1949	Phi-N	7	13	4	3	0	0	3	7	1	4	.231	.286	.923	217	2	2	3	0			1.000	-1	/O	0.1
1951	Phi-N	13	4	1	2	1	0	0	1	1	1	.500	.600	.750	265	1	1	2	1	0	0	1.000	-4	O	-0.3
Total	2	20	17	5	5	1	0	3	8	2	5	.294	.368	.882	231	3	3	6	1	0		1.000	-5	/O	-0.2

■ BEN SANKEY Sankey, Benjamin Turner b: 9/2/07, Nauvoo, Ala. BR/TR, 5'10", 155 lbs. Deb: 10/05/29

YEAR	TM/L	G	AB	R	H	2B	3B	HR	RBI	BB	SO	AVG	OBP	SLG	PRO+	BR	/A	RC	SB	CS	SBR	FA	FR	POS	TPR
1929	Pit-N	2	7	1	1	0	0	0	0	0	1	.143	.143	.143	-28	-1	-1	0	0			.909	-0	/S	-0.2
1930	Pit-N	13	30	6	5	0	0	0	0	2	3	.167	.219	.167	-5	-5	-5	1	0			.871	-0	/S2	-0.4
1931	Pit-N	57	132	14	30	2	5	0	14	14	10	.227	.301	.318	67	-6	-6	14	0			.920	-9	S/23	-1.1
Total	3	72	169	21	36	2	5	0	14	16	14	.213	.281	.284	49	-13	-13	15	0			.914	-10	/S23	-1.7

■ ANDRES SANTANA Santana, Andres Confesor (Belonis) b: 2/5/68, San Pedro De Macoris, D.R. BB/TR, 5'11", 160 lbs. Deb: 9/16/90

YEAR	TM/L	G	AB	R	H	2B	3B	HR	RBI	BB	SO	AVG	OBP	SLG	PRO+	BR	/A	RC	SB	CS	SBR	FA	FR	POS	TPR
1990	SF-N	6	2	0	0	0	0	0	1	0	0	.000	.000	.000	-99	-1	-1	0	0	0	0	1.000	1	/S	0.1

■ RAFAEL SANTANA Santana, Rafael Francisco (De La Cruz) b: 1/31/58, LaRomana, D.R. BR/TR, 6'1", 165 lbs. Deb: 4/05/83

YEAR	TM/L	G	AB	R	H	2B	3B	HR	RBI	BB	SO	AVG	OBP	SLG	PRO+	BR	/A	RC	SB	CS	SBR	FA	FR	POS	TPR
1983	StL-N	30	14	1	3	0	0	0	2	2	2	.214	.353	.214	61	-1	-1	1	0	1	-1	.857	2	/2S3	0.1
1984	NY-N	51	152	14	42	11	1	1	12	9	17	.276	.317	.382	97	-1	-1	17	0	3	-2	.970	-3	S	-0.1
1985	NY-N	154	529	41	136	19	1	1	29	29	54	.257	.296	.302	69	-23	-21	45	1	0	0	.965	-11	*S	-1.9
1986	*NY-N	139	394	38	86	11	0	1	28	36	43	.218	.287	.254	52	-26	-25	27	0	0	0	.973	17	*S/2	0.3
1987	NY-N	139	439	41	112	21	2	5	44	29	57	.255	.303	.346	75	-18	-15	44	1	1	-0	.973	15	*S	1.0
1988	NY-A	148	480	50	115	12	1	4	38	33	61	.240	.290	.294	64	-23	-22	38	1	2	-1	.966	-9	*S	-2.1
1990	Cle-A	7	13	3	3	0	0	1	3	0	0	.231	.231	.462	89	-0	-0	1	0	0	0	1.000	-2	/S	-0.2
Total	7	668	2021	188	497	74	5	13	156	138	234	.246	.296	.307	68	-92	-85	173	3	7	-3	.969	9	S/23	-2.9

■ BENITO SANTIAGO Santiago, Benito (Rivera) b: 3/9/65, Ponce, P.R. BR/TR, 6'1", 185 lbs. Deb: 9/14/86

YEAR	TM/L	G	AB	R	H	2B	3B	HR	RBI	BB	SO	AVG	OBP	SLG	PRO+	BR	/A	RC	SB	CS	SBR	FA	FR	POS	TPR
1986	SD-N	17	62	10	18	2	0	3	6	2	12	.290	.313	.468	115	1	1	9	0	1	-1	.946	-6	C	-0.5
1987	SD-N	146	546	64	164	33	2	18	79	16	112	.300	.326	.467	111	4	6	77	21	12	-1	.976	-7	*C	0.8
1988	SD-N	139	492	49	122	22	2	10	46	24	82	.248	.284	.362	86	-11	-10	46	15	7	0	.985	-5	*C	-0.5
1989	SD-N★	129	462	50	109	16	3	16	62	26	89	.236	.278	.387	88	-9	-9	47	11	6	-0	.975	-6	*C	-0.8
1990	SD-N†	100	344	42	93	8	5	11	53	27	55	.270	.329	.419	103	1	1	47	5	5	-2	.980	-5	C	0.1
1991	SD-N★	152	580	60	155	22	3	17	87	23	114	.267	.300	.403	93	-5	-7	61	8	10	-4	.985	-1	*C/O	-0.2
1992	SD-N★	106	386	37	97	21	0	10	42	21	52	.251	.290	.383	86	-7	-8	38	2	5	-2	.982	-10	*C	-1.6
Total	7	789	2872	312	758	124	15	85	375	139	516	.264	.301	.406	95	-25	-26	324	62	46	-9	.980	-38	C/O	-2.7

■ RON SANTO Santo, Ronald Edward b: 2/25/40, Seattle, Wash. BR/TR, 6', 190 lbs. Deb: 6/26/60

YEAR	TM/L	G	AB	R	H	2B	3B	HR	RBI	BB	SO	AVG	OBP	SLG	PRO+	BR	/A	RC	SB	CS	SBR	FA	FR	POS	TPR
1960	Chi-N	95	347	44	87	24	2	9	44	31	44	.251	.312	.409	97	-3	-2	42	0	3	-2	.945	-19	3	-2.4
1961	Chi-N	154	578	84	164	32	6	23	83	73	77	.284	.364	.479	120	18	17	95	2	3	-1	.937	5	*3	2.2
1962	Chi-N	162	604	44	137	20	4	17	83	65	94	.227	.304	.358	74	-20	-23	65	4	1	1	.955	11	*3/S	-0.9
1963	Chi-N★	162	630	79	187	29	6	25	99	42	92	.297	.345	.481	128	27	23	99	6	4	-1	.951	13	*3	3.8
1964	Chi-N☆	161	592	94	185	33	**13**	30	114	**86**	96	.313	**.401**	.564	162	55	52	135	3	4	-2	.963	17	*3	**6.7**
1965	Chi-N★	164	608	88	173	30	4	33	101	88	109	.285	.379	.510	144	40	38	121	3	1	0	.957	19	*3	5.5
1966	Chi-N★	155	561	93	175	21	8	30	94	**95**	78	.312	**.417**	.538	161	51	50	127	4	5	-2	.956	29	*3/S	**7.6**
1967	Chi-N	161	586	107	176	23	4	31	98	**96**	103	.300	.401	.512	153	48	45	120	1	5	-3	.957	**31**	*3	**7.5**
1968	Chi-N★	162	577	86	142	17	3	26	98	**96**	106	.246	.357	.421	124	25	21	87	3	4	-2	**.971**	17	*3	4.2
1969	Chi-N★	160	575	97	166	18	4	29	123	96	97	.289	.392	.485	128	36	27	108	1	3	-2	.947	6	*3	3.3
1970	Chi-N	154	555	83	148	30	4	26	114	92	108	.267	.372	.476	112	21	11	100	2	0	1	.945	13	*3/O	2.4
1971	Chi-N★	154	555	77	148	22	1	21	88	79	95	.267	.358	.423	105	16	6	84	4	0	1	.958	-3	*3/O	0.3
1972	Chi-N★	133	464	68	140	25	5	17	74	69	75	.302	.397	.487	135	32	26	89	1	4	-2	.948	6	*3/2SO	3.1
1973	Chi-N★	149	536	65	143	29	2	20	77	63	97	.267	.348	.440	109	12	7	76	1	2	-1	.950	-12	*3	-0.7
1974	Chi-A	117	375	29	83	12	1	5	41	37	72	.221	.295	.299	69	-14	-15	31	0	2	-1	.970	6	D23/1S	-0.9
Total	15	2243	8143	1138	2254	365	67	342	1331	1108	1343	.277	.366	.464	123	345	284	1379	35	41	-14	.954	137	*3/D2SO1	41.7

■ RAFAEL SANTO DOMINGO Santo Domingo, Rafael (Molina) b: 11/24/55, Orocovis, P.R. BB/TR, 6', 160 lbs. Deb: 9/07/79

YEAR	TM/L	G	AB	R	H	2B	3B	HR	RBI	BB	SO	AVG	OBP	SLG	PRO+	BR	/A	RC	SB	CS	SBR	FA	FR	POS	TPR
1979	Cin-N	7	6	0	1	0	0	0	0	1	3	.167	.286	.167	26	-1	-1	0	0	0	0	.000	0	/H	-0.1

■ NELSON SANTOVENIA Santovenia, Nelson Gil (Mayol) b: 7/27/61, Pinar Del Rio, Cuba BR/TR, 6'3", 215 lbs. Deb: 9/16/87

YEAR	TM/L	G	AB	R	H	2B	3B	HR	RBI	BB	SO	AVG	OBP	SLG	PRO+	BR	/A	RC	SB	CS	SBR	FA	FR	POS	TPR
1987	Mon-N	2	1	0	0	0	0	0	0	0	0	.000	.000	.000	-97	-0	-0	0	0	0	0	1.000	-0	/C	0.0
1988	Mon-N	92	309	26	73	20	2	8	41	24	77	.236	.298	.392	92	-2	-4	36	2	3	-1	.983	2	C/1	0.4
1989	Mon-N	97	304	30	76	14	1	5	31	24	37	.250	.311	.352	88	-4	-5	31	2	1	0	.981	12	C/1	1.3

YEAR	TM/L	G	AB	R	H	2B	3B	HR	RBI	BB	SO	AVG	OBP	SLG	PRO+	BR	/A	RC	SB	CS	SBR	FA	FR	POS	TPR
1990	Mon-N	59	163	13	31	3	1	6	28	8	31	.190	.228	.331	54	-11	-11	10	0	3	-2	.980	2	C	-0.8
1991	Mon-N	41	96	7	24	5	0	2	14	2	18	.250	.265	.365	76	-3	-3	8	0	0	0	.976	-4	C/1	-0.6
1992	Chi-A	2	3	1	1	0	0	1	2	0	0	.333	.333	1.333	355	1	1	1	0	0	0	1.000	-0	/C	0.1
Total	6	293	876	77	205	42	4	22	116	58	163	.234	.286	.366	83	-21	-22	87	4	7	-3	.981	12	C/1	0.4

■ **EDWARD SANTRY** Santry, Edward b: Chicago, Ill. d: 3/6/1899, Chicago, Ill. Deb: 8/07/1884

YEAR	TM/L	G	AB	R	H	2B	3B	HR	RBI	BB	SO	AVG	OBP	SLG	PRO+	BR	/A	RC	SB	CS	SBR	FA	FR	POS	TPR
1884	Det-N	6	22	1	4	0	0	0	0	1	2	.182	.217	.182	29	-2	-2	1				.821	-0	/S2	-0.2

■ **JOE SARGENT** Sargent, Joseph Alexander "Horse Belly" b: 9/24/1893, Rochester, N.Y. d: 7/5/50, Rochester, N.Y. BR/TR, 5'10", 165 lbs. Deb: 4/27/21

YEAR	TM/L	G	AB	R	H	2B	3B	HR	RBI	BB	SO	AVG	OBP	SLG	PRO+	BR	/A	RC	SB	CS	SBR	FA	FR	POS	TPR
1921	Det-A	66	178	21	45	8	5	2	22	24	26	.253	.342	.388	87	-4	-4	24	2	3	-1	.927	3	23S	0.1

■ **BILL SARNI** Sarni, William Florine b: 9/19/27, Los Angeles, Cal. d: 4/15/83, Creve Coeur, Mo. BR/TR, 5'11", 187 lbs. Deb: 5/09/51

YEAR	TM/L	G	AB	R	H	2B	3B	HR	RBI	BB	SO	AVG	OBP	SLG	PRO+	BR	/A	RC	SB	CS	SBR	FA	FR	POS	TPR
1951	StL-N	36	86	7	15	1	0	0	2	9	13	.174	.253	.186	20	-10	-10	4	1	0	0	.984	0	C	-0.8
1952	StL-N	3	5	0	1	0	0	0	0	0	1	.200	.200	.200	11	-1	-1	0	0	0	0	1.000	2	/C	0.2
1954	StL-N	123	380	40	114	18	4	9	70	25	42	.300	.343	.439	101	1	0	55	3	3	-1	**.996**	-13	*C	-0.8
1955	StL-N	107	325	32	83	15	2	3	34	27	33	.255	.314	.342	74	-12	-12	33	1	1	-0	.987	-6	C	-1.5
1956	StL-N	43	148	12	43	7	2	5	22	8	15	.291	.331	.466	111	2	2	22	1	0	0	.992	3	C	0.7
	NY-N	78	238	16	55	9	3	5	23	20	31	.231	.293	.357	74	-9	-9	25	0	1	-1	.993	-6	C	-1.3
	Yr	121	386	28	98	16	5	10	45	28	46	.254	.308	.399	88	-7	-7	47	1	1	-0	.992	-3	*C	-0.6
Total	5	390	1182	107	311	50	11	22	151	89	135	.263	.316	.380	84	-28	-29	139	6	5	-1	.991	-19	C	-3.5

■ **MACKEY SASSER** Sasser, Mack Daniel b: 8/3/62, Fort Gaines, Ga. BL/TR, 6'1", 210 lbs. Deb: 7/17/87

YEAR	TM/L	G	AB	R	H	2B	3B	HR	RBI	BB	SO	AVG	OBP	SLG	PRO+	BR	/A	RC	SB	CS	SBR	FA	FR	POS	TPR
1987	SF-N	2	4	0	0	0	0	0	0	0	0	.000	.000	.000	-99	-1	-1	0	0	0	0	1.000	0	/C	-0.1
	Pit-N	12	23	2	5	0	0	0	2	0	2	.217	.217	.217	16	-3	-3	1	0	0	0	1.000	-1	/C	-0.4
	Yr	14	27	2	5	0	0	0	2	0	2	.185	.185	.185	-2	-4	-4	1	0	0	0	1.000	-1	/C	-0.5
1988	*NY-N	60	123	9	35	10	1	1	17	6	9	.285	.318	.407	112	1	1	15	0	0	0	.977	9	C/3O	1.3
1989	NY-N	72	182	17	53	14	2	1	22	7	15	.291	.317	.407	111	1	2	22	0	1	-1	.992	0	C/3	0.4
1990	NY-N	100	270	31	83	14	0	6	41	15	19	.307	.346	.426	111	4	4	38	0	0	0	.975	-9	C/1	0.0
1991	NY-N	96	228	18	62	14	2	5	35	9	19	.272	.303	.417	101	-1	-1	26	0	2	-1	.994	-9	CO1	-1.0
1992	NY-N	92	141	7	34	6	0	2	18	3	10	.241	.257	.326	65	-7	-7	11	0	0	0	.989	-11	C1/O	-1.8
Total	6	434	971	84	272	58	5	15	135	40	74	.280	.310	.396	99	-6	-4	113	0	3	-2	.983	-21	C/O13	-1.6

■ **TOM SATRIANO** Satriano, Thomas Victor Nicholas b: 8/28/40, Pittsburgh, Pa. BL/TR, 6'1", 190 lbs. Deb: 7/23/61

YEAR	TM/L	G	AB	R	H	2B	3B	HR	RBI	BB	SO	AVG	OBP	SLG	PRO+	BR	/A	RC	SB	CS	SBR	FA	FR	POS	TPR
1961	LA-A	35	96	15	19	5	1	1	8	12	16	.198	.294	.302	53	-5	-7	10	2	0	1	.915	0	32/S	-0.6
1962	LA-A	10	19	4	8	2	0	2	6	0	1	.421	.421	.842	238	3	3	6	0	0	0	.833	-0	/3	0.3
1963	LA-A	23	50	1	9	1	0	0	2	9	10	.180	.305	.200	48	-3	-3	4	0	0	0	.952	3	3/C1	0.0
1964	LA-A	108	255	18	51	9	0	1	17	30	37	.200	.284	.247	55	-17	-14	17	0	2	-1	.917	-2	31C/S2	-1.8
1965	Cal-A	47	79	8	13	2	0	1	4	10	10	.165	.258	.228	40	-6	-6	5	1	1	-0	1.000	0	3C2/1	-0.5
1966	Cal-A	103	226	16	54	5	3	0	24	27	32	.239	.320	.288	78	-6	-6	21	3	3	-1	.991	-9	C13/2	-1.5
1967	Cal-A	90	201	13	45	7	0	4	21	28	25	.224	.319	.318	92	-2	-1	21	1	0	0	.962	-7	3C2/1	-0.8
1968	Cal-A	111	297	20	75	9	0	8	35	37	44	.253	.337	.364	117	5	6	37	0	0	0	.989	-9	C23/1	0.3
1969	Cal-A	41	108	5	28	2	0	1	16	18	15	.259	.370	.306	95	-0	0	13	0	2	-1	1.000	-1	C/12	0.0
	Bos-A	47	127	9	24	2	0	0	11	22	12	.189	.318	.205	46	-8	-9	9	0	0	0	.978	-2	C	-0.9
	Yr	88	235	14	52	4	0	1	27	40	27	.221	.342	.251	68	-8	-8	21	0	2	-1	.987	-2	C/12	-0.9
1970	Bos-A	59	165	21	39	9	1	3	13	21	23	.236	.326	.358	83	-2	-4	19	0	0	0	.985	0	C	-0.1
Total	10	674	1623	130	365	53	5	21	157	214	225	.225	.317	.303	79	-43	-39	160	7	8	-3	.987	-26	C3/12S	-5.6

■ **FRANK SAUCIER** Saucier, Francis Field b: 5/28/26, Leslie, Mo. BL/TR, 6'1", 180 lbs. Deb: 7/21/51

YEAR	TM/L	G	AB	R	H	2B	3B	HR	RBI	BB	SO	AVG	OBP	SLG	PRO+	BR	/A	RC	SB	CS	SBR	FA	FR	POS	TPR
1951	StL-A	18	14	4	1	1	0	0	1	3	4	.071	.278	.143	16	-2	-2	1	0	0	0	.714	-1	/O	-0.2

■ **ED SAUER** Sauer, Edward "Horn" b: 1/3/20, Pittsburgh, Pa. d: 7/1/88, Thousand Oaks, Cal BR/TR, 6'1", 188 lbs. Deb: 9/17/43 F

YEAR	TM/L	G	AB	R	H	2B	3B	HR	RBI	BB	SO	AVG	OBP	SLG	PRO+	BR	/A	RC	SB	CS	SBR	FA	FR	POS	TPR
1943	Chi-N	14	55	3	15	3	0	0	9	3	6	.273	.322	.327	89	-1	-1	6	1			1.000	2	O	0.1
1944	Chi-N	23	50	3	11	4	0	0	5	2	6	.220	.250	.300	55	-3	-3	4	0			.960	-0	O	-0.4
1945	*Chi-N	49	93	8	24	4	1	2	11	8	23	.258	.317	.387	97	-1	-1	12	2			1.000	-2	O	-0.4
1949	StL-N	24	45	5	10	2	1	0	1	3	8	.222	.271	.311	53	-3	-3	4	0			1.000	-2	O	-0.5
	Bos-N	79	214	26	57	12	0	3	31	17	34	.266	.323	.364	89	-5	-3	25	0			.972	-7	O	-1.3
	Yr	103	259	31	67	14	1	3	32	20	42	.259	.314	.355	82	-8	-7	29	0			.974	-9	O	-1.8
Total	4	189	457	45	117	25	2	5	57	33	77	.256	.309	.352	83	-13	-11	50	3			.981	-10	O	-2.5

■ **HANK SAUER** Sauer, Henry John b: 3/17/17, Pittsburgh, Pa. BR/TR, 6'4", 199 lbs. Deb: 9/09/41 FC

YEAR	TM/L	G	AB	R	H	2B	3B	HR	RBI	BB	SO	AVG	OBP	SLG	PRO+	BR	/A	RC	SB	CS	SBR	FA	FR	POS	TPR
1941	Cin-N	9	33	4	10	4	0	0	5	1	4	.303	.324	.424	109	0	0	4	0			.957	1	/O	0.1
1942	Cin-N	7	20	4	5	0	0	2	4	2	2	.250	.318	.550	152	1	1	4	0			.976	0	/1	0.1
1945	Cin-N	31	116	18	34	1	0	5	20	6	16	.293	.328	.431	112	1	1	17	2			.972	1	O/1	0.1
1948	Cin-N	145	530	78	138	22	1	35	97	60	85	.260	.340	.504	130	17	19	92	2			.973	4	*O1	1.6
1949	Cin-N	42	152	22	36	6	0	4	16	18	19	.237	.318	.355	79	-4	-4	16	0			.956	5	O/1	-0.1
	Chi-N	96	357	59	104	17	1	27	83	37	47	.291	.363	.571	151	22	23	75	0			.981	2	O	2.0
	Yr	138	509	81	140	23	1	31	99	55	66	.275	.349	.507	129	17	18	89	0			.972	7	*O/1	1.9
1950	Chi-N★	145	540	85	148	32	2	32	103	60	67	.274	.350	.519	127	18	19	96	1			.965	-1	*O1	1.1
1951	Chi-N	141	525	77	138	19	4	30	89	45	77	.263	.325	.486	113	9	7	84	2	1	0	.981	10	*O	1.3
1952	Chi-N★	151	567	89	153	31	3	**37**	**121**	77	92	.270	.361	.531	143	33	32	111	1	2	-1	.983	17	*O	4.2
1953	Chi-N	108	395	61	104	16	5	19	60	50	56	.263	.349	.473	109	7	5	66	0	0	0	.970	3	*O	0.4
1954	Chi-N	142	520	98	150	18	1	41	103	70	68	.288	.379	.563	140	31	30	114	2	1	0	.963	-2	*O	2.2
1955	Chi-N	79	261	29	55	8	1	12	28	26	47	.211	.287	.387	77	-9	-9	28	0	0	0	.984	-1	O	-1.4
1956	StL-N	75	151	11	45	4	0	5	24	25	31	.298	.408	.424	124	6	6	27	0	0	0	1.000	-1	O	0.3
1957	NY-N	127	378	46	98	14	0	26	76	49	59	.259	.344	.508	126	13	13	67	1	0	0	.992	-12	O	-0.4
1958	SF-N	88	236	27	59	8	0	12	46	35	37	.250	.356	.436	111	3	4	39	0	0	0	.950	-4	O	-0.3
1959	SF-N	13	15	1	1	0	0	1	1	0	7	.067	.067	.267	-17	-3	-2	0	0	0	0	.000	-0	/O	-0.3
Total	15	1399	4796	709	1278	200	19	288	876	561	714	.266	.347	.496	123	144	145	840	11	4		.974	22	*O/1	10.9

■ **RUSTY SAUNDERS** Saunders, Russell Collier b: 3/12/06, Trenton, N.J. d: 11/24/67, Trenton, N.J. BR/TR, 6'2", 205 lbs. Deb: 9/24/27

YEAR	TM/L	G	AB	R	H	2B	3B	HR	RBI	BB	SO	AVG	OBP	SLG	PRO+	BR	/A	RC	SB	CS	SBR	FA	FR	POS	TPR
1927	Phi-A	5	15	2	2	1	0	0	2	3	2	.133	.278	.200	24	-2	-2	1	0	0	0	.818	0	/O	-0.2

■ **AL SAUTERS** Sauters, Al b: Philadelphia, Pa. Deb: 9/08/1890

YEAR	TM/L	G	AB	R	H	2B	3B	HR	RBI	BB	SO	AVG	OBP	SLG	PRO+	BR	/A	RC	SB	CS	SBR	FA	FR	POS	TPR
1890	Phi-a	14	41	1	4	0	0	0		11		.098	.288	.098	17	-4	-4	1	0			.850	-4	3/O2	-0.6

■ **DON SAVAGE** Savage, Donald Anthony b: 3/5/19, Bloomfield, N.J. d: 12/25/61, Montclair, N.J. BR/TR, 6', 180 lbs. Deb: 4/18/44

YEAR	TM/L	G	AB	R	H	2B	3B	HR	RBI	BB	SO	AVG	OBP	SLG	PRO+	BR	/A	RC	SB	CS	SBR	FA	FR	POS	TPR
1944	NY-A	71	239	31	63	7	5	4	24	20	41	.264	.323	.385	98	0	-1	29	1	1	-0	.946	-10	3	-1.2
1945	NY-A	34	58	5	13	1	0	0	3	3	14	.224	.262	.241	44	-4	-4	4	1	0	0	.891	1	3/O	-0.3
Total	2	105	297	36	76	8	5	4	27	23	55	.256	.312	.357	88	-4	-5	33	2	1	0	.935	-10	/3O	-1.5

■ **JIMMIE SAVAGE** Savage, James Harold b: 8/29/1883, Southington, Conn. d: 6/26/40, New Castle, Pa. BB/TR, 5'5", 150 lbs. Deb: 9/03/12

YEAR	TM/L	G	AB	R	H	2B	3B	HR	RBI	BB	SO	AVG	OBP	SLG	PRO+	BR	/A	RC	SB	CS	SBR	FA	FR	POS	TPR
1912	Phi-N	2	3	1	0	0	0	0	0	1	0	.000	.250	.000	-27	-1	-1	0	0			.750	-0	/2	-0.1
1914	Pit-F	132	479	81	136	9	9	1	26	67	32	.284	.372	.347	106	6	6	71	17			.963	-9	O3S/2	-0.5
1915	Pit-F	14	21	0	3	0	0	0	0	1	0	.143	.182	.143	-4	-3	-3	1	0			1.000	-1	/O3	-0.4
Total	3	148	503	82	139	9	9	1	26	69	32	.276	.364	.336	101	2	3	72	17			.964	-10	/O3S2	-1.0

YEAR	TM/L	G	AB	R	H	2B	3B	HR	RBI	BB	SO	AVG	OBP	SLG	PRO+	BR	/A	RC	SB	CS	SBR	FA	FR	POS	TPR

■ TED SAVAGE　Savage, Theodore Edmund (b: Ephesian Savage)　b: 2/21/36, Venice, Ill.　BR/TR, 6'1", 185 lbs.　Deb: 4/09/62

1962	Phi-N	127	335	54	89	11	2	7	39	40	66	.266	.347	.373	96	-2	-1	46	16	5	2	.974	-3	*O	-0.7
1963	Pit-N	85	149	22	29	2	1	5	14	14	31	.195	.268	.322	69	-6	-6	11	4	3	-1	.943	-2	O	-1.1
1965	StL-N	30	63	7	10	3	0	1	4	6	9	.159	.232	.254	34	-5	-6	3	1	1	-0	.938	0	O	-0.7
1966	StL-N	16	29	4	5	2	1	0	3	4	7	.172	.273	.310	61	-1	-2	3	4	0	1	1.000	-1	/O	-0.1
1967	StL-N	9	8	1	1	0	0	0	0	1	3	.125	.222	.125	2	-1	-1	0	0	0	0	.000	0	H	-0.1
	Chi-N	96	225	40	49	10	1	5	33	40	54	.218	.348	.338	93	1	-1	27	7	6	-2	.979	-4	O/3	-1.0
	Yr	105	233	41	50	10	1	5	33	41	57	.215	.344	.330	90	-0	-1	27	7	6	-2	.979	-4	O/3	-1.1
1968	Chi-N	3	8	0	2	0	0	0	0	0	1	.250	.250	.250	47	-0	-1	0	0	1	-1	1.000	-0	/O	-0.2
	LA-N	61	126	7	26	6	1	2	7	10	20	.206	.270	.317	82	-4	-3	9	1	2	-1	.985	4	O	-0.2
	Yr	64	134	7	28	6	1	2	7	10	21	.209	.269	.313	80	-4	-3	9	1	3	-2	.986	3	O	-0.4
1969	Cin-N	68	110	20	25	7	0	2	11	20	27	.227	.346	.345	90	-0	-1	15	3	0	1	.983	3	O/2	-0.2
1970	Mil-A	114	276	43	77	10	5	12	50	57	44	.279	.406	.482	143	19	18	57	10	6	-1	.953	-10	O/1	0.4
1971	Mil-A	14	17	2	3	0	0	0	1	5	4	.176	.364	.176	58	-1	-1	2	1	0	0	1.000	-2	/O	-0.3
	KC-A	19	29	2	5	0	0	0	1	3	6	.172	.250	.172	22	-3	-3	1	2	0	1	1.000	-0	/O	-0.4
	Yr	33	46	4	8	0	0	0	2	8	10	.174	.296	.174	36	-4	-4	3	3	0	1	1.000	-3	O	-0.7
Total	9	642	1375	202	321	51	11	34	163	200	272	.233	.335	.361	94	-5	-6	175	49	24	0	.970	-16	O/123	-4.2

■ BOB SAVERINE　Saverine, Robert Paul "Rabbit"　b: 6/2/41, Norwalk, Conn.　BB/TR, 5'9", 165 lbs.　Deb: 9/12/59

1959	Bal-A	1	0	1	0	0	0	0	0	0	0	—	—	—	—	0	0	0	0	0	0	.000	0	R	0.0
1962	Bal-A	8	21	2	5	2	0	0	3	1	3	.238	.273	.333	65	-1	-1	1	0	2	-1	1.000	2	/2	0.0
1963	Bal-A	115	167	21	39	1	2	1	12	25	44	.234	.333	.281	76	-5	-4	17	8	3	1	.976	-9	O2S	-1.2
1964	Bal-A	46	34	14	5	1	0	0	0	3	6	.147	.216	.176	11	-4	-4	1	3	1	0	1.000	5	S/O	0.1
1966	Was-A	120	406	54	102	10	4	5	24	27	62	.251	.301	.333	83	-10	-9	41	4	3	-1	.972	-19	23S/O	-2.5
1967	Was-A	89	233	22	55	13	0	0	8	17	34	.236	.288	.292	75	-8	-7	20	8	0	2	.957	-20	2S/3O	-2.3
Total	6	379	861	114	206	27	6	6	47	73	149	.239	.300	.305	76	-28	-26	81	23	9	2	.971	-40	2/OS3	-5.9

■ CARL SAWATSKI　Sawatski, Carl Ernest "Swats"　b: 11/4/27, Shickshinny, Pa.　d: 11/24/91, Little Rock, Ark.　BL/TR, 5'10", 210 lbs.　Deb: 9/29/48

1948	Chi-N	2	2	0	0	0	0	0	0	0	0	.000	.000	.000	-99	-1	-1	0	0			.000	0	H	-0.1
1950	Chi-N	38	103	4	18	1	0	1	7	11	19	.175	.254	.214	25	-11	-11	6	0			.983	-1	C	-1.1
1953	Chi-N	43	59	5	13	3	0	1	5	7	7	.220	.303	.322	62	-3	-3	6	0	0	0	.943	-1	C	-0.3
1954	Chi-A	43	109	6	20	3	3	1	12	15	20	.183	.282	.294	56	-6	-7	9	0	0	0	.987	0	C	-0.6
1957	*Mil-N	58	105	13	25	4	0	6	17	10	15	.238	.316	.448	110	0	1	15	0	0	0	.986	6	C	0.8
1958	Mil-N	10	10	1	1	0	0	0	1	2	5	.100	.250	.100	-3	-1	-1	0	0	0	0	1.000	1	/C	-0.1
	Phi-N	60	183	12	42	4	1	5	12	16	42	.230	.302	.344	72	-8	-7	19	0	0	0	.986	-3	C	-0.9
	Yr	70	193	13	43	4	1	5	13	18	47	.223	.299	.332	68	-9	-9	19	0	0	0	.987	-3	C	-0.9
1959	Phi-N	74	198	15	58	10	0	9	43	32	36	.293	.394	.480	129	10	9	38	0	0	0	.979	-14	C	-0.1
1960	StL-N	78	179	16	41	4	0	6	27	22	24	.229	.313	.352	75	-4	-6	19	0	0	0	.993	-7	C	-1.1
1961	StL-N	86	174	23	52	8	0	10	33	25	17	.299	.387	.517	125	10	7	35	0	0	0	.996	-7	C/O	0.3
1962	StL-N	85	222	26	56	9	1	13	42	36	38	.252	.357	.477	111	7	4	39	0	0	0	.997	-1	C	0.5
1963	StL-N	50	105	12	25	0	0	6	14	15	28	.238	.333	.410	103	2	1	15	2	0	1	.986	-5	C	-0.3
Total	11	633	1449	133	351	46	5	58	213	191	251	.242	.333	.401	92	-7	-15	202	2	0		.988	-32	C/O	-2.9

■ CARL SAWYER　Sawyer, Carl Everett "Huck"　b: 10/19/1890, Seattle, Wash.　d: 1/17/57, Los Angeles, Cal.　BR/TR, 5'11", 160 lbs.　Deb: 9/11/15

1915	Was-A	10	32	8	8	1	0	0	3	4	5	.250	.351	.281	88	-0	-0	4	2			.964	-2	/2S	-0.2
1916	Was-A	16	31	3	6	1	0	0	2	4	4	.194	.306	.226	60	-1	-1	3	3			.963	2	/2S3	0.1
Total	2	26	63	11	14	2	0	0	5	8	9	.222	.329	.254	74	-2	-2	7	5			.964	-1	/2S3	-0.1

■ DAVE SAX　Sax, David John　b: 9/22/58, Sacramento, Cal.　BR/TR, 6', 185 lbs.　Deb: 9/01/82　F

1982	LA-N	2	2	0	0	0	0	0	0	0	0	.000	.000	.000	-99	-1	-1	0	0	0	0	1.000	0	/O	0.0
1983	LA-N	7	8	0	0	0	0	0	1	0	0	.000	.000	.000	-99	-2	-2	0	0	0	0	.917	-0	/C	-0.2
1985	Bos-A	22	36	2	11	3	0	0	6	3	3	.306	.359	.389	101	0	0	5	0	1	-1	.985	-2	C/O	-0.2
1986	Bos-A	4	11	1	5	1	0	1	1	0	1	.455	.455	.818	237	2	2	4	0	0	0	1.000	-1	/C1	0.1
1987	Bos-A	2	3	0	0	0	0	0	0	0	1	.000	.000	.000	-97	-1	-1	0	0	0	0	1.000	1	/C	0.0
Total	5	37	60	3	16	4	0	1	8	3	5	.267	.302	.383	84	-1	-1	9	0	1	-1	.980	-1	/CO1	-0.3

■ OLLIE SAX　Sax, Erik Oliver　b: 11/5/04, Branford, Conn.　d: 3/21/82, Newark, N.J.　BR/TR, 5'8", 164 lbs.　Deb: 4/13/28

| 1928 | StL-A | 16 | 17 | 4 | 3 | 0 | 0 | 0 | 0 | 5 | 3 | .176 | .364 | .176 | 45 | -1 | -1 | 2 | 0 | 0 | 0 | .955 | 3 | /3 | 0.2 |

■ STEVE SAX　Sax, Stephen Louis　b: 1/29/60, Sacramento, Cal.　BR/TR, 5'11", 185 lbs.　Deb: 8/18/81　F

1981	*LA-N	31	119	15	33	2	0	2	9	7	14	.277	.317	.345	91	-2	-2	12	5	7	-3	.975	2	2	-0.1
1982	LA-N★	150	638	88	180	23	7	4	47	49	53	.282	.335	.359	97	-5	-3	79	49	19	3	.977	-9	*2	0.0
1983	LA-N★	155	623	94	175	18	5	5	41	58	73	.281	.343	.350	93	-5	-5	76	56	30	-1	.961	-30	*2	-3.0
1984	LA-N	145	569	70	138	24	4	1	35	47	53	.243	.301	.304	71	-22	-21	51	34	19	-1	.973	12	*2	-0.5
1985	*LA-N	136	488	62	136	8	4	1	42	54	43	.279	.354	.318	92	-5	-3	56	27	11	2	.969	-9	*2/3	-0.6
1986	LA-N★	157	633	91	210	43	4	6	56	59	58	.332	.391	.441	139	26	31	110	40	17	2	.980	-5	*2	3.6
1987	LA-N	157	610	84	171	22	7	6	46	44	61	.280	.332	.369	88	-13	-10	76	37	11	5	.982	1	*2/3O	0.3
1988	*LA-N	160	632	70	175	19	4	5	57	45	51	.277	.326	.343	95	-6	-4	73	42	12	5	.981	-19	*2	-1.2
1989	NY-A★	158	651	88	205	26	3	5	63	52	44	.315	.366	.387	114	12	13	91	43	17	3	.987	-10	*2	1.1
1990	NY-A★	155	615	70	160	24	2	4	42	49	46	.260	.319	.325	80	-15	-16	68	43	9	8	.987	-13	*2	-1.9
1991	NY-A	158	652	85	198	38	2	10	56	41	38	.304	.348	.414	110	8	8	92	31	11	3	.990	-7	*2/3D	0.7
1992	Chi-A	143	567	74	134	26	4	4	47	43	42	.236	.292	.317	73	-22	-21	51	30	12	2	.972	-28	*2	-4.5
Total	12	1705	6797	891	1915	273	46	53	541	548	576	.282	.337	.359	96	-49	-32	835	437	175	26	.978	-114	*2/3DO	-6.1

■ JIMMY SAY　Say, James I.　b: 1862, Baltimore, Md.　d: 6/23/1894, Baltimore, Md.　Deb: 7/22/1882　F

1882	Lou-a	1	4	1	1	0	0	0		0		.250	.250	.250	73	-0	-0					.333	-1	/3	-0.1
	Phi-a	22	82	12	17	2	0	1		1		.207	.217	.268	56	-3	-4	5				.884	1	S	-0.2
	Yr	23	86	13	18	2	0	1		1		.209	.218	.267	57	-3	-5	5				.884	0	S/3	-0.3
1884	Wil-U	16	59	3	13	1	2	0		1		.220	.233	.305	79	-1	-1	4				.733	-3	3	-0.4
	KC-U	2	8	0	2	0	0	0		0		.250	.250	.250	80	-0	-0	1				.200	-2	/3	-0.2
	Yr	18	67	3	15	1	2	0		1		.224	.235	.299	79	-1	-2	5				.680	-5	3	-0.6
1887	Cle-a	16	64	9	24	5	3	0		1		.375	.385	.547	165	5	5	14	0			.714	-4	3	0.1
Total	3	57	217	25	57	8	5	1		3		.263	.273	.359	97	-0	-1	24	0			.690	-9	/3S	-0.8

■ LOU SAY　Say, Louis I.　b: 2/4/1854, Baltimore, Md.　d: 6/5/30, Fallston, Md.　BR/TR, 5'7", 145 lbs.　Deb: 4/14/1873　F

1873	Mar-n	3	12	1	2	0	0	0	2	0	0	.167	.167	.167	-2	-1	-1	0						/SO	-0.1
1874	Bal-n	18	67	4	14	3	0	0		0		.209	.209	.254	47	-4	-4	4						S	-0.3
1875	Was-n	11	39	4	10	0	0	0		0		.256	.256	.256	81	-1	-1	3						/S2O	-0.1
1880	Cin-N	48	191	14	38	8	1	0	15	4	31	.199	.215	.251	58	-8	-8	11				.832	1	S	-0.4
1882	Phi-a	49	199	35	45	4	3	1		8		.226	.256	.291	75	-3	-6	15				.867	6	S	0.2
1883	Bal-a	74	324	52	83	13	2	1		10		.256	.278	.318	89	-3	-5	29				.794	7	*S	0.4
1884	Bal-U	78	339	65	81	14	2	2		11		.239	.263	.310	84	-2	-8	28				.795	2	*S	-0.5
	KC-U	17	70	6	14	2	0	1		2		.200	.222	.271	76	-2	-1	4				.860	9	S/2	0.7
	Yr	95	409	71	95	16	2	3		13		.232	.256	.303	83	-5	-9	33				.808	10	S/2	0.2

YEAR	TM/L	G	AB	R	H	2B	3B	HR	RBI	BB	SO	AVG	OBP	SLG	PRO+	BR	/A	RC	SB	CS	SBR	FA	FR	POS	TPR
Total	3 n	32	118	9	26	3	0	0	2	0		.220	.220	.246	53	-6	-5	7						/SO2	-0.5
Total	4	266	1123	172	261	41	8	5	15	35	31	.232	.256	.297	79	-19	-28	88				.820	24	S/2	0.4
■ JERRY SCALA Scala, Gerard Daniel b: 9/27/26, Bayonne, N.J. BL/TR, 5'11", 178 lbs. Deb: 4/22/48																									
1948	Chi-A	3	6	1	0	0	0	0	0	0	3	.000	.000	.000	-99	-2	-2	0	0	0	0	1.000	-0	/O	-0.2
1949	Chi-A	37	120	17	30	7	1	1	13	17	19	.250	.348	.350	88	-3	-2	16	3	3	-1	.988	-3	O	-0.8
1950	Chi-A	40	67	8	13	2	1	0	6	10	10	.194	.299	.254	44	-6	-5	5	0	0	0	1.000	-4	O	-0.9
Total	3	80	193	26	43	9	2	1	19	27	32	.223	.321	.306	67	-10	-9	22	3	3	-1	.993	-7	/O	-1.9
■ SKEETER SCALZI Scalzi, Frank John b: 6/16/13, Lafferty, Ohio d: 8/25/84, Pittsburgh, Pa. BR/TR, 5'6", 160 lbs. Deb: 7/21/39																									
1939	NY-N	11	18	3	6	0	0	0	0	3	2	.333	.429	.333	106	0	0	2	1			.875	2	/S3	0.3
■ JOHNNY SCALZI Scalzi, John Anthony b: 3/22/07, Stamford, Conn. d: 9/27/62, Port Chester, N.Y BR/TR, 5'7", 170 lbs. Deb: 6/19/31																									
1931	Bos-N	2	1	0	0	0	0	0	0	0	1	.000	.000	.000	-99	-0	-0	0	0			.000	0	H	0.0
■ MORT SCANLAN Scanlan, Mortimer J. b: 3/18/1861, Chicago, Ill. d: 12/29/28, Chicago, Ill. 6'1", 186 lbs. Deb: 4/21/1890																									
1890	NY-N	3	10	0	0	0	0	0	0	2	5	.000	.167	.000	-49	-2	-2	0	1			1.000	-0	/1	-0.2
■ PATRICK SCANLAN Scanlan, Patrick J. b: 3/25/1861, Novs Scotia d: 7/17/13, Springfield, Mass. Deb: 7/04/1884																									
1884	Bos-U	6	24	2	7	1	0	0		0		.292	.292	.333	113	0	0	2				.800	0	/O	0.0
■ PAT SCANLON Scanlon, James Patrick b: 9/23/52, Minneapolis, Minn. BL/TR, 6', 180 lbs. Deb: 9/27/74																									
1974	Mon-N	2	4	1	1	0	0	0	0	0	1	.250	.250	.250	38	-0	-0	0	0	0	0	1.000	1	/3	0.0
1975	Mon-N	60	109	5	20	3	1	2	15	17	25	.183	.294	.284	58	-6	-6	9	0	1	-1	.957	2	3/1	-0.5
1976	Mon-N	11	27	2	5	1	0	1	2	2	5	.185	.241	.333	59	-1	-2	2	0	0	0	.842	-1	/31	-0.3
1977	SD-N	47	79	9	15	3	0	1	11	12	20	.190	.297	.266	58	-5	-4	6	0	0	0	.957	-5	23/O	-0.8
Total	4	120	219	17	41	7	1	4	28	31	51	.187	.288	.283	58	-13	-12	17	0	1	-1	.938	-3	/321O	-1.6
■ RUSS SCARRITT Scarritt, Russell Mallory b: 1/14/03, Pensacola, Fla. BL/TR, 5'10.5", 165 lbs. Deb: 4/18/29																									
1929	Bos-A	151	540	69	159	26	17	1	71	34	38	.294	.337	.411	94	-8	-6	73	13	11	-3	.944	1	*O	-1.6
1930	Bos-A	113	447	48	129	17	8	2	48	12	49	.289	.312	.376	76	-19	-16	50	4	7	-3	.967	4	*O	-2.1
1931	Bos-A	10	39	2	6	1	0	0	1	2	2	.154	.195	.179	-1	-6	-5	1	0	0	0	1.000	1	/O	-0.5
1932	Phi-N	11	11	0	2	0	0	0	0	1	2	.182	.250	.182	16	-1	-1	1	0			1.000	-0	/O	-0.2
Total	4	285	1037	119	296	44	25	3	120	49	91	.285	.320	.385	82	-33	-29	125	17	18		.956	6	O	-4.4
■ LES SCARSELLA Scarsella, Leslie George b: 11/23/13, Santa Cruz, Cal. d: 12/17/58, San Francisco, Cal BL/TL, 5'11", 185 lbs. Deb: 9/15/35																									
1935	Cin-N	6	10	4	2	1	0	0	0	3	1	.200	.385	.300	89	-0	0	1	0			1.000	1	/1	0.0
1936	Cin-N	115	485	63	152	21	9	3	65	14	36	.313	.335	.412	107	-1	3	66	6			.989	2	*1	-0.7
1937	Cin-N	110	329	35	81	11	4	3	34	17	26	.246	.285	.331	70	-15	-13	30	5			.984	-5	1O	-2.6
1939	Cin-N	16	14	0	2	0	0	0	2	0	2	.143	.143	.143	-23	-2	-2	0	0			.000	0	H	-0.2
1940	Bos-N	18	60	7	18	1	3	0	8	3	5	.300	.344	.417	115	1	1	9	2			.986	-1	1	-0.1
Total	5	265	898	109	255	34	16	6	109	37	70	.284	.315	.378	92	-18	-12	107	13			.988	-4	1/O	-3.6
■ STEVE SCARSONE Scarsone, Steven b: 4/11/66, Anaheim, Cal. BR/TR, 6'2", 170 lbs. Deb: 5/15/92																									
1992	Phi-N	7	13	1	2	0	0	0	0	1	6	.154	.214	.154	6	-2	-2	0	0	0	0	1.000	-2	/2	-0.4
	Bal-A	11	17	2	3	0	0	0	0	1	6	.176	.222	.176	13	-2	-2	1	0	0	0	.875	-1	/23S	-0.3
Total	1	18	30	3	5	0	0	0	0	2	12	.167	.219	.167	10	-4	-4	1	0	0	0	.929	-3	/23S	-0.7
■ PAUL SCHAAL Schaal, Paul b: 3/3/43, Pittsburgh, Pa. BR/TR, 5'11", 180 lbs. Deb: 9/03/64																									
1964	LA-A	17	32	3	4	0	0	0	0	2	5	.125	.176	.125	-16	-5	-5	1	0	1	-1	1.000	-1	/23	-0.6
1965	Cal-A	155	483	48	108	12	2	9	45	61	88	.224	.312	.313	80	-13	-12	50	6	3	0	.970	-10	*3/2	-2.7
1966	Cal-A	138	386	59	94	15	7	6	24	68	56	.244	.364	.365	113	8	9	55	6	4	-1	.948	-2	*3	0.4
1967	Cal-A	99	272	31	51	9	1	6	20	38	39	.188	.289	.294	76	-9	-7	25	2	2	-1	.970	-2	3/S2	-1.2
1968	Cal-A	60	219	22	46	7	1	2	16	29	25	.210	.308	.279	82	-5	-4	19	5	7	-3	.958	9	3	0.3
1969	KC-A	61	205	22	54	6	0	1	13	25	27	.263	.349	.307	84	-3	-3	24	2	1	0	.897	-19	3/2S	-2.2
1970	KC-A	124	380	50	102	12	3	5	35	43	39	.268	.344	.355	93	-3	-3	47	7	4	-0	.938	-16	3S/2	-2.0
1971	KC-A	161	548	80	150	31	6	11	63	103	51	.274	.391	.412	129	24	24	95	7	5	-1	.940	-12	*3	1.1
1972	KC-A	127	435	47	99	19	3	6	41	61	59	.228	.325	.326	95	-2	-1	46	1	3	-2	.947	-16	*3/S	-2.3
1973	KC-A	121	396	61	114	14	3	8	42	63	45	.288	.392	.399	114	15	11	63	5	6	-2	.913	-12	*3	-0.4
1974	KC-A	12	34	3	6	2	0	1	4	5	5	.176	.300	.324	75	-1	-1	3	0	0	0	.949	1	3	-0.1
	Cal-A	53	165	10	41	5	0	2	20	18	27	.248	.322	.315	89	-3	-2	16	2	2	-1	.903	-10	3	-1.3
	Yr	65	199	13	47	7	0	3	24	23	32	.236	.318	.317	86	-4	-3	19	2	2	-1	.914	-9	3	-1.4
Total	11	1128	3555	436	869	132	26	57	323	516	466	.244	.344	.344	98	4	6	444	43	38	-10	.943	-91	*3/2S	-11.0
■ GERMANY SCHAEFER Schaefer, Herman A. b: 2/4/1877, Chicago, Ill. d: 5/16/19, Saranac Lake, N.Y. BR/TR, 5'9", 175 lbs. Deb: 10/05/01																									
1901	Chi-N	2	5	0	3	1	0	0	0	2		.600	.714	.800	352	2	2	3	0			1.000	1	/23	0.2
1902	Chi-N	81	291	32	57	2	3	0	14	19		.196	.250	.223	48	-18	-17	21	12			.864	-8	3/1OS	-2.7
1905	Det-A	153	554	64	135	17	9	2	47	45		.244	.302	.318	96	-2	-3	64	19			.955	7	*2/S	0.6
1906	Det-A	124	446	48	106	14	3	2	42	32		.238	.289	.296	81	-8	-10	50	31			.948	9	*2/S	0.0
1907	*Det-A	109	372	45	96	12	3	1	32	30		.258	.313	.315	97	0	-1	46	21			.961	-6	2S3/O	-0.7
1908	*Det-A	153	584	96	151	20	10	3	52	37		.259	.304	.342	106	5	3	74	40			.918	2	S23	0.8
1909	Det-A	87	280	26	70	12	0	0	22	14		.250	.286	.293	79	-6	-7	27	12			.966	14	2/O	0.5
	Was-A	37	128	13	31	5	1	1	4	6		.242	.281	.320	94	-2	-1	12	2			.941	0	2/3	-0.2
	Yr	124	408	39	101	17	1	1	26	20		.248	.284	.301	84	-8	-9	39	14			.960	14	*2/O3	0.3
1910	Was-A	74	229	27	63	6	5	0	14	25		.275	.352	.345	124	5	7	34	17			.953	-0	2O/3	0.5
1911	Was-A	125	440	74	147	14	7	0	45	57		.334	.412	.398	129	18	19	82	22			.980	0	*1/O	1.8
1912	Was-A	60	166	21	41	7	3	0	19	23		.247	.342	.325	90	-1	-2	22	11			.900	-11	O12/P	-1.4
1913	Was-A	54	100	17	32	1	1	0	7	15	12	.320	.419	.350	123	4	4	17	6			.926	-2	2/13PO	0.1
1914	Was-A	30	29	6	7	1	0	0	2	3	5	.241	.313	.276	74	-1	-1	3	4	1	1	1.000	0	/2O	0.0
1915	New-F	59	154	26	33	5	3	0	8	25	11	.214	.328	.286	86	-3	-2	16	3			.952	-1	O1/32	-0.4
1916	NY-A	1	1	0	0	0	0	0	0	0	0	.000	.000	.000	-98	-0	-0	0	0			.000	0	/O	0.0
1918	Cle-A	1	5	2	0	0	0	0	0	0	0	.000	.000	.000	-91	-1	-1	-0	1			1.000	-0	/2	-0.2
Total	15	1150	3784	497	972	117	48	9	308	333	28	.257	.319	.320	97	-8	-11	472	201	1		.954	3	213/SOP	-1.1
■ JEFF SCHAEFER Schaefer, Jeffrey Scott b: 5/31/60, Patchogue, N.Y. BR/TR, 5'10", 170 lbs. Deb: 4/07/89																									
1989	Chi-A	15	10	2	1	0	0	0	0	0	2	.100	.100	.100	-45	-2	-2	0	1	1	-0	.900	1	/S23D	-0.1
1990	Sea-A	55	107	11	22	3	0	0	6	3	11	.206	.241	.234	33	-9	-10	7	4	1	1	.933	12	3S/2	0.4
1991	Sea-A	84	164	19	41	7	1	1	11	5	25	.250	.272	.323	64	-8	-8	13	3	1	0	.968	2	S32/D	-0.4
1992	Sea-A	65	70	5	8	2	0	1	3	2	10	.114	.139	.186	-10	-10	-10	1	0	1	-1	.922	14	S3/2	0.5
Total	4	219	351	37	72	12	1	2	20	10	48	.205	.231	.262	37	-30	-30	21	8	4	0	.957	29	S/32D	0.4
■ HARRY SCHAFER Schafer, Harry C. "Silk Stocking" b: 8/14/1846, Philadelphia, Pa. d: 2/28/35, Philadelphia, Pa. BR/TR, 5'9.5", 143 lbs. Deb: 5/05/1871																									
1871	Bos-n	31	149	38	42	7	5	0	28	3	1	.282	.296	.396	94	-1	-2	22	13					*3/2	-0.3
1872	Bos-n	48	226	50	66	12	5	1	37	0	8	.292	.292	.403	106	3	0	28						*3/O	-0.2
1873	Bos-n	60	295	65	79	8	3	2	43	3	1	.268	.275	.336	73	-8	-13	27						*3O	-1.1
1874	Bos-n	71	325	69	84	13	3	1		0		.258	.258	.326	80	-5	-9	28						*3	-0.7

YEAR	TM/L	G	AB	R	H	2B	3B	HR	RBI	BB	SO	AVG	OBP	SLG	PRO+	BR	/A	RC	SB	CS	SBR	FA	FR	POS	TPR
1875	Bos-n	51	216	47	62	9	0	0		0		.287	.287	.329	108	2	1	21						*3/O	0.1
1876	Bos-N	70	286	47	72	11	0	0	35	4	11	.252	.262	.290	82	-5	-5	22				.810	3	*3	-0.1
1877	Bos-N	33	141	20	39	5	2	0	13	0	7	.277	.277	.340	90	-1	-2	14				.621	-12	O/3S	-1.3
1878	Bos-N	2	8	0	1	0	0	0	0	0	1	.125	.125	.125	-16	-1	-1	0				1.000	-1	/O	-0.2
Total	5 n	261	1211	269	333	49	16	4	108	6	10	.275	.279	.352	89	-9	-22	126						3/O2	-2.2
Total	3	105	435	67	112	16	2	0	48	4	19	.257	.264	.303	83	-7	-8	36				.810	-9	/3OS	-1.6

■ **JIMMIE SCHAFFER** Schaffer, Jimmie Ronald b: 4/5/36, Limeport, Pa. BR/TR, 5'9", 185 lbs. Deb: 5/20/61 C

YEAR	TM/L	G	AB	R	H	2B	3B	HR	RBI	BB	SO	AVG	OBP	SLG	PRO+	BR	/A	RC	SB	CS	SBR	FA	FR	POS	TPR
1961	StL-N	68	153	15	39	7	0	1	16	9	29	.255	.301	.320	59	-8	-10	14	0	0	0	.996	4	C	-0.4
1962	StL-N	70	66	7	16	2	1	0	6	6	16	.242	.306	.303	58	-3	-4	6	1	0	0	.993	7	C	0.4
1963	Chi-N	57	142	17	34	7	0	7	19	11	35	.239	.294	.437	102	1	0	16	0	0	0	.996	1	C	0.3
1964	Chi-N	54	122	9	25	6	1	2	9	17	17	.205	.307	.320	74	-3	-4	10	2	4	-2	.970	-8	C	-1.3
1965	Chi-A	17	31	2	6	3	1	0	1	3	4	.194	.265	.355	79	-1	-1	2	0	0	0	1.000	3	C	0.2
	NY-N	24	37	0	5	2	0	0	0	1	15	.135	.158	.189	-3	-5	-5	1	0	0	0	.968	-1	C	-0.5
1966	Phi-N	8	15	2	2	1	0	1	4	1	7	.133	.188	.400	58	-1	-1	1	0	0	0	.952	-1	/C	-0.1
1967	Phi-N	2	2	1	0	0	0	0	0	1	1	.000	.333	.000	3	-0	-0	0	0	0	0	1.000	0	/C	0.0
1968	Cin-N	4	6	0	1	0	0	0	1	0	3	.167	.167	.167	0	-1	-1	0	0	0	0	1.000	-1	/C	-0.2
Total	8	304	574	53	128	28	3	11	56	49	127	.223	.286	.340	69	-21	-25	51	3	4	-2	.989	5	C	-1.6

■ **JOHNNY SCHAIVE** Schaive, John Edward b: 2/25/34, Springfield, Ill. BR/TR, 5'8", 175 lbs. Deb: 9/19/58

YEAR	TM/L	G	AB	R	H	2B	3B	HR	RBI	BB	SO	AVG	OBP	SLG	PRO+	BR	/A	RC	SB	CS	SBR	FA	FR	POS	TPR
1958	Was-A	7	24	1	6	0	0	0	1	1	4	.250	.280	.250	48	-2	-2	1	0	0	0	1.000	-1	/2	-0.2
1959	Was-A	16	59	3	9	2	0	0	2	0	7	.153	.167	.186	-3	-8	-8	2	0	0	0	.977	4	2	-0.3
1960	Was-A	6	12	1	3	1	0	0	0	0	3	.250	.250	.333	57	-1	-1	1	0	0	0	.917	-0	/2	-0.1
1962	Was-A	82	225	20	57	15	1	6	29	6	25	.253	.273	.409	81	-7	-7	21	0	1	-1	.967	4	3/2	-0.3
1963	Was-A	3	3	0	0	0	0	0	0	0	1	.000	.000	.000	-99	-1	-1	0	0	0	0	.000	0	H	-0.1
Total	5	114	323	25	75	18	1	6	32	7	40	.232	.251	.350	61	-19	-18	24	0	1	-1	.980	7	/32	-1.0

■ **ROY SCHALK** Schalk, Le Roy John b: 11/9/08, Chicago, Ill. BR/TR, 5'10", 168 lbs. Deb: 9/17/32

YEAR	TM/L	G	AB	R	H	2B	3B	HR	RBI	BB	SO	AVG	OBP	SLG	PRO+	BR	/A	RC	SB	CS	SBR	FA	FR	POS	TPR
1932	NY-A	3	12	3	3	1	0	0	0	2	2	.250	.357	.333	84	-0	-0	2	0	0	0	.867	-2	/2	-0.1
1944	Chi-A	146	587	47	129	14	4	1	44	45	52	.220	.276	.262	55	-35	-34	43	5	4	-1	.964	-14	*2/S	-4.3
1945	Chi-A	133	513	50	127	23	1	1	65	32	41	.248	.293	.302	75	-18	-17	45	3	6	-3	.977	6	*2	-0.5
Total	3	282	1112	100	259	38	5	2	109	79	95	.233	.285	.281	64	-53	-51	90	8	10	-4	.970	-9	2/S	-4.9

■ **RAY SCHALK** Schalk, Raymond William "Cracker" b: 8/12/1892, Harvey, Ill. d: 5/19/70, Chicago, Ill. BR/TR, 5'9", 165 lbs. Deb: 8/11/12 MCH

YEAR	TM/L	G	AB	R	H	2B	3B	HR	RBI	BB	SO	AVG	OBP	SLG	PRO+	BR	/A	RC	SB	CS	SBR	FA	FR	POS	TPR
1912	Chi-A	23	63	7	18	2	0	0	8	3		.286	.357	.317	96	-0	-0	8	2			.917	4	C	0.6
1913	Chi-A	129	401	38	98	15	5	1	38	27	36	.244	.297	.314	80	-12	-11	40	14			.980	-0	*C	0.0
1914	Chi-A	136	392	30	106	13	2	0	36	38	24	.270	.347	.314	100	1	1	50	24	11	1	.974	6	*C	2.0
1915	Chi-A	135	413	46	110	14	4	1	54	62	21	.266	.366	.327	104	6	4	51	15	18	-6	**.984**	-3	*C	0.6
1916	Chi-A	129	410	36	95	12	9	0	41	41	31	.232	.311	.305	84	-7	-8	45	30	13	1	**.988**	9	*C	1.3
1917	*Chi-A	140	424	48	96	12	5	2	51	59	27	.226	.331	.292	88	-3	-4	47	19			.981	5	*C	1.4
1918	Chi-A	108	333	35	73	6	3	0	22	36	22	.219	.301	.255	67	-12	-13	29	12			.978	-4	*C	-0.9
1919	*Chi-A	131	394	57	111	9	3	0	34	51	25	.282	.367	.320	93	-1	-1	50	11			.981	1	*C	1.0
1920	Chi-A	151	485	64	131	25	5	1	61	68	19	.270	.362	.348	89	-6	-6	67	10	4	1	**.986**	-1	*C	0.5
1921	Chi-A	128	416	32	105	24	4	0	47	40	36	.252	.328	.329	69	-20	-19	47	3	4	-2	**.985**	8	*C	-0.5
1922	Chi-A	142	442	57	124	22	3	4	60	67	36	.281	.379	.371	97	-0	0	68	12	4	1	**.989**	20	*C	2.8
1923	Chi-A	123	382	42	87	12	2	1	44	39	28	.228	.306	.277	55	-25	-24	35	6	4	-1	.983	5	*C	-1.3
1924	Chi-A	57	153	15	30	4	2	1	11	21	10	.196	.301	.268	49	-12	-11	13	1	5	-3	.959	6	C	-0.4
1925	Chi-A	125	343	44	94	18	1	0	52	57	27	.274	.382	.332	87	-7	-4	49	11	5	0	.983	3	*C	0.6
1926	Chi-A	82	226	26	60	9	1	0	32	27	11	.265	.349	.314	77	-8	-7	27	5	1	1	.977	-6	C	-0.7
1927	Chi-A	16	26	2	6	2	0	0	2	2	1	.231	.286	.308	55	-2	-2	2	0	0	0	1.000	1	CM	0.0
1928	Chi-A	2	1	0	1	0	0	0	1	0	0	1.000	1.000	1.000	433	0	0	1	1	0	0	1.000	1	/CM	0.1
1929	NY-N	5	2	0	0	0	0	0	0	0	1	.000	.000	.000	-99	-1	-1	0	0			1.000	1	/C	0.0
Total	18	1762	5306	579	1345	199	49	11	594	638	355	.253	.340	.316	83	-108	-104	630	176	69		.981	55	*C	7.1

■ **BIFF SCHALLER** Schaller, Walter b: 9/23/1889, Chicago, Ill. d: 10/9/39, Emeryville, Cal. BL/TR, 5'11", 168 lbs. Deb: 4/30/11

YEAR	TM/L	G	AB	R	H	2B	3B	HR	RBI	BB	SO	AVG	OBP	SLG	PRO+	BR	/A	RC	SB	CS	SBR	FA	FR	POS	TPR
1911	Det-A	40	60	8	8	0	1	1	7	4		.133	.200	.217	15	-7	-7	3	1			1.000	-1	O/1	-0.8
1913	Chi-A	36	96	12	21	3	0	0	4	20	16	.219	.353	.250	78	-2	-2	10	5			.918	-6	O	-1.0
Total	2	76	156	20	29	3	1	1	11	24	16	.186	.298	.237	54	-9	-9	13	6			.949	-7	/O1	-1.8

■ **BOBBY SCHANG** Schang, Robert Martin b: 12/7/1886, Wales Center, N.Y. d: 8/29/66, Sacramento, Cal. BR/TR, 5'7", 165 lbs. Deb: 9/23/14 F

YEAR	TM/L	G	AB	R	H	2B	3B	HR	RBI	BB	SO	AVG	OBP	SLG	PRO+	BR	/A	RC	SB	CS	SBR	FA	FR	POS	TPR
1914	Pit-N	11	35	0	8	1	1	0	1	0	10	.229	.229	.314	64	-2	-2	2	0			.964	-2	C	-0.3
1915	Pit-N	56	125	13	23	6	3	0	4	14	32	.184	.271	.280	68	-5	-5	10	2	2	-1	.974	-7	C	-1.0
	NY-N	12	21	1	3	0	0	0	1	4	5	.143	.280	.143	31	-2	-1	1	1			.875	-3	/C	-0.4
	Yr	68	146	14	26	6	3	0	5	18	37	.178	.273	.260	63	-6	-6	12	3	2	-0	.960	-9	C	-1.4
1927	StL-N	3	5	0	1	0	0	0	0	0	0	.200	.200	.200	7	-1	-1	0	0			1.000	-0	/C	-0.1
Total	3	82	186	14	35	7	4	0	6	18	47	.188	.263	.269	62	-9	-9	14	3	2		.962	-11	/C	-1.8

■ **WALLY SCHANG** Schang, Walter Henry b: 8/22/1889, S.Wales, N.Y. d: 3/6/65, St.Louis, Mo. BB/TR, 5'10", 180 lbs. Deb: 5/01/13 FC

YEAR	TM/L	G	AB	R	H	2B	3B	HR	RBI	BB	SO	AVG	OBP	SLG	PRO+	BR	/A	RC	SB	CS	SBR	FA	FR	POS	TPR
1913	*Phi-A	79	207	32	55	16	3	3	30	34	44	.266	.392	.415	140	11	11	34	4			.967	-5	C	1.4
1914	*Phi-A	107	307	44	88	11	8	3	45	32	33	.287	.371	.404	138	13	14	47	7	7	-2	.956	1	*C	2.3
1915	Phi-A	116	359	64	89	9	11	1	44	66	47	.248	.385	.343	122	12	13	55	18	3	4	.890	-1	3OC	1.9
1916	Phi-A	110	338	41	90	15	8	7	38	38	44	.266	.358	.420	140	14	15	57	14			.966	5	OC	2.2
1917	Phi-A	118	316	41	90	14	9	3	36	29	24	.285	.362	.415	139	14	14	49	6			.956	-10	C3/O	1.2
1918	*Bos-A	88	225	36	55	7	1	0	20	46	35	.244	.377	.284	101	3	3	26	4			.962	-13	CO/3S	-0.7
1919	Bos-A	113	330	43	101	16	3	0	55	71	42	.306	.436	.373	136	18	20	58	15			.972	-4	*C	2.6
1920	Bos-A	122	387	58	118	30	7	4	51	64	37	.305	.413	.450	134	18	21	75	7	7	-2	.958	-3	CO	1.7
1921	*NY-A	134	424	77	134	30	5	6	55	78	35	.316	.428	.453	122	20	18	88	7	4	-0	.969	-6	*C	1.8
1922	*NY-A	124	408	46	130	21	7	1	53	53	36	.319	.405	.412	111	10	9	72	12	6	0	.976	0	*C	1.5
1923	*NY-A	84	272	39	75	8	2	2	29	27	17	.276	.360	.342	84	-5	-5	36	5	2	0	.970	-8	C	-0.9
1924	NY-A	114	356	46	104	19	7	5	52	48	43	.292	.382	.427	109	5	5	59	2	6	-3	.972	-2	*C	0.7
1925	NY-A	73	167	17	40	8	1	2	24	17	9	.240	.310	.335	65	-10	-9	18	3	1	0	.974	2	C	-0.3
1926	StL-A	103	285	36	94	19	5	8	50	32	20	.330	.405	.516	133	16	14	59	5	5	-2	.968	-1	C/O	1.6
1927	StL-A	97	264	40	84	15	2	5	42	41	33	.318	.414	.447	119	11	9	49	3	2	-0	.976	-9	C	0.5
1928	StL-A	91	245	41	70	10	5	3	39	68	26	.286	.448	.404	121	14	13	52	8	2	1	.984	-12	C	0.8
1929	StL-A	94	249	43	59	10	5	5	36	74	22	.237	.424	.378	104	7	6	46	1	4	-2	**.988**	-6	C	0.5
1930	Phi-A	45	92	16	16	4	1	1	9	17	15	.174	.309	.272	47	-7	-8	9	0	0	0	.973	2	C	-0.3
1931	Det-A	30	76	9	14	2	0	0	2	14	11	.184	.311	.211	38	-6	-7	6	1	0	0	.965	-0	C	-0.4
Total	19	1842	5307	769	1506	264	90	59	710	849	573	.284	.393	.401	117	156	158	896	122	49		.967	-68	*CO/3S	18.1

■ **ART SCHAREIN** Scharein, Arthur Otto "Scoop" b: 6/30/05, Decatur, Ill. d: 7/2/69, San Antonio, Tex. BR/TR, 5'11", 155 lbs. Deb: 7/06/32 F

YEAR	TM/L	G	AB	R	H	2B	3B	HR	RBI	BB	SO	AVG	OBP	SLG	PRO+	BR	/A	RC	SB	CS	SBR	FA	FR	POS	TPR
1932	StL-A	81	303	43	92	19	2	0	42	25	10	.304	.363	.380	87	-3	-5	41	4	8	-4	.965	18	3/S2	1.4
1933	StL-A	123	471	49	96	13	3	0	26	41	21	.204	.269	.244	35	-43	-47	32	7	9	-3	.949	14	3S/2	-2.7
1934	StL-A	1	2	0	1	0	0	0	2	0	0	.500	.500	.500	146	0	0	0	0	0	0	.000	0	H	0.0
Total	3	205	776	92	189	32	5	0	70	66	31	.244	.306	.298	56	-45	-52	73	11	17	-7	.956	32	3/S2	-1.3

YEAR	TM/L	G	AB	R	H	2B	3B	HR	RBI	BB	SO	AVG	OBP	SLG	PRO+	BR	/A	RC	SB	CS	SBR	FA	FR	POS	TPR

■ GEORGE SCHAREIN   Scharein, George Albert "Tom" b: 11/21/14, Decatur, Ill. d: 12/23/81, Decatur, Ill. BR/TR, 6'1", 174 lbs. Deb: 4/19/37 F

1937	Phi-N	146	511	44	123	20	1	0	57	36	47	.241	.293	.284	53	-30	-35	44	13			.947	10	*S	-1.5
1938	Phi-N	117	390	47	93	16	4	1	29	16	33	.238	.268	.308	60	-23	-21	32	11			.921	-2	S2/3	-1.6
1939	Phi-N	118	399	35	95	17	1	1	33	13	40	.238	.262	.293	50	-29	-28	31	4			.958	-9	*S	-2.8
1940	Phi-N	7	17	0	5	0	0	0	0	0	3	.294	.294	.294	65	-1	-1	1	0			.839	-1	/S	-0.1
Total	4	388	1317	126	316	53	6	2	119	65	123	.240	.277	.294	54	-82	-85	108	28			.943	-2	S/23	-6.0

■ NICK SCHARF   Scharf, Edward T. b: 7/1858, Baltimore, Md. d: 5/12/37, Baltimore, Md. TR , Deb: 5/18/1882

1882	Bal-a	10	39	4	8	1	1	1			0	.205	.205	.359	94	-1	-0	3				.727	-2	/O3	-0.2
1883	Bal-a	3	13	1	2	1	0	0			1	.154	.214	.231	42	-1	-1	1				.643	-3	/S	-0.3
Total	2	13	52	5	10	2	1	1			1	.192	.208	.327	79	-1	-1	4				.992	-4	/OS3	-0.5

■ AL SCHEER   Scheer, Allan G. b: 10/21/1888, Dayton, Ohio d: 5/6/59, Logansport, Ind. BL/TR, 5'9", 165 lbs. Deb: 8/02/13

1913	Bro-N	6	22	3	5	0	0	0	2	4		.227	.292	.227	48	-1	-1	2	1			.800	-1	/O	-0.3
1914	Ind-F	120	363	63	111	23	6	3	45	49	39	.306	.396	.427	121	18	12	68	9			.926	-5	*O/2S	0.3
1915	New-F	155	546	75	146	25	14	2	60	65	38	.267	.353	.375	121	11	15	87	31			.971	-2	*O	0.5
Total	3	281	931	141	262	48	20	5	105	116	81	.281	.368	.392	119	27	26	156	41			.953	-9	O/2S	0.5

■ HEINIE SCHEER   Scheer, Henry b: 7/31/1900, New York, N.Y. d: 3/21/76, New Haven, Conn. BR/TR, 5'8", 146 lbs. Deb: 4/20/22

1922	Phi-A	51	135	10	23	3	0	4	12	3	25	.170	.188	.281	21	-16	-17	7	1	0	0	.976	9	23	-0.6
1923	Phi-A	69	210	26	50	8	1	2	21	17	41	.238	.301	.314	61	-12	-12	21	3	4	-2	.971	-8	2	-2.1
Total	2	120	345	36	73	11	1	6	33	20	66	.212	.259	.301	46	-28	-29	28	4	4	-1	.973	0	/23	-2.7

■ FRITZ SCHEEREN   Scheeren, Frederick "Dutch" b: 9/8/1891, Kokomo, Ind. d: 6/17/73, Oil City, Pa. BR/TR, 6', 180 lbs. Deb: 9/14/14

1914	Pit-N	11	31	4	9	0	1	1	2	1	6	.290	.313	.452	132	1	1	4	1			.824	-3	O	-0.3
1915	Pit-N	4	3	0	0	0	0	0	0	0	0	.000	.000	.000	-99	-1	-1	0	0			.000	-1	/O	-0.1
Total	2	15	34	4	9	0	1	1	2	1	6	.265	.286	.412	111	0	0	4	1			.824	-4	/O	-0.4

■ BOB SCHEFFING   Scheffing, Robert Boden b: 8/11/13, Overland, Mo. d: 10/26/85, Phoenix, Ariz. BR/TR, 6'2", 189 lbs. Deb: 4/27/41 MC

1941	Chi-N	51	132	9	32	8	0	1	20	5	19	.242	.270	.326	70	-6	-6	10	2			.966	-3	C	-0.6
1942	Chi-N	44	102	7	20	3	0	2	12	7	11	.196	.248	.284	58	-6	-6	7	2			.986	4	C	0.0
1946	Chi-N	63	115	8	32	4	1	0	18	12	18	.278	.346	.330	94	-1	-1	13	0			1.000	-7	C	-0.6
1947	Chi-N	110	363	33	96	11	5	5	50	25	25	.264	.312	.364	82	-12	-10	39	2			.984	-6	C	-0.9
1948	Chi-N	102	293	23	88	18	2	5	45	22	27	.300	.351	.427	114	3	5	44	0			.989	-5	C	0.6
1949	Chi-N	55	149	12	40	6	1	3	19	9	9	.268	.314	.383	88	-3	-3	16	0			.977	-3	C	-0.4
1950	Chi-N	12	16	0	3	1	0	0	1	0	2	.188	.188	.250	14	-2	-2	1	0			.917	0	/C	-0.2
	Cin-N	21	47	4	13	0	0	2	6	4	2	.277	.333	.404	93	-1	-1	5	0			1.000	-4	C	-0.4
	Yr	33	63	4	16	1	0	2	7	4	4	.254	.299	.365	74	-3	-3	6	0			.982	-3	C	-0.6
1951	Cin-N	47	122	9	31	2	0	2	14	16	9	.254	.345	.320	79	-3	-3	15	0	0	0	.976	-4	C	-0.5
	StL-N	12	18	0	2	0	0	0	2	3	5	.111	.238	.111	-3	-3	-3	1	0	0	0	1.000	1	C	-0.1
	Yr	59	140	9	33	2	0	2	16	19	14	.236	.331	.293	68	-5	-6	15	0	0	0	.980	-2	C	-0.6
Total	8	517	1357	105	357	53	9	20	187	103	127	.263	.316	.360	86	-32	-27	150	6	0		.984	-25	C	-3.1

■ TED SCHEFFLER   Scheffler, Theodore J. b: 4/5/1864, New York, N.Y. d: 2/24/49, Jamaica, N.Y. BR/TR, 5'10", 160 lbs. Deb: 8/07/1888

1888	Det-N	27	94	17	19	3	1	0	4	9	9	.202	.286	.255	76	-2	-2	8	4			.847	-4	O	-0.7
1890	Roc-a	119	445	111	109	12	6	3		78		.245	.374	.319	116	9	14	84	77			.911	9	*O/C	1.7
Total	2	146	539	128	128	15	7	3	4	87	9	.237	.360	.308	109	6	12	92	81			.899	5	O/C	1.0

■ FRANK SCHEIBECK   Scheibeck, Frank S. b: 6/28/1865, Detroit, Mich. d: 10/22/56, Detroit, Mich. BR/TR, 5'7", 145 lbs. Deb: 5/09/1887

1887	Cle-a	3	9	2	2	0	0	0			2	.222	.364	.222	70	-0	-0	1	0			.500	-2	/S3P	-0.1
1888	Det-N	1	4	0	0	0	0	0	0	0	0	.000	.000	.000	-99	-1	-1	0	0			.500	-1	/S	-0.3
1890	Tol-a	134	485	72	117	13	5	1			76	.241	.350	.295	90	-1	-3	72	57			.883	1	*S	0.4
1894	Pit-N	28	102	20	36	2	3	1	10	11	9	.353	.416	.461	114	2	3	23	7			.891	-8	S/O32	-0.4
	Was-N	52	196	49	45	2	4	0	17	45	24	.230	.384	.281	66	-9	-8	26	11			.876	5	S	0.0
	Yr	80	298	69	81	4	7	1	27	56	33	.272	.394	.342	83	-7	-5	49	18			.878	-3	S/O32	-0.4
1895	Was-N	48	167	17	31	5	2	0	25	17	21	.186	.265	.240	32	-17	-16	13	5			.888	-2	S/32	-1.3
1899	Was-N	27	94	19	27	4	1	0	9	11		.287	.368	.351	99	0	0	15	5			.877	-10	S	-0.7
1901	Cle-A	93	329	33	70	11	3	0	38	18		.213	.258	.264	47	-24	-22	25	3			.897	-14	S	-2.6
1906	Det-A	3	10	1	1	0	0	0	0	0		.100	.250	.100	11	-1	-1	0	0			.889	-1	/2	-0.2
Total	8	389	1396	213	329	37	18	2	99	182	54	.236	.329	.292	71	-51	-49	175	88			.884	-32	S/O23P	-5.2

■ RICHIE SCHEINBLUM   Scheinblum, Richard Alan b: 11/5/42, New York, N.Y. BB/TR, 6'1", 180 lbs. Deb: 9/01/65

1965	Cle-A	4	1	1	0	0	0	0	0	0	0	.000	.000	.000	-99	-0	-0	0	0	0	0	.000	0	H	0.0
1967	Cle-A	18	66	8	21	4	2	0	6	5	10	.318	.366	.439	136	3	3	10	0	2	-1	.943	-0	O	0.1
1968	Cle-A	19	55	3	12	5	0	0	5	5	8	.218	.295	.309	84	-1	-1	5	0	0	0	1.000	1	O	-0.1
1969	Cle-A	102	199	13	37	5	1	1	13	19	30	.186	.257	.236	37	-16	-17	11	0	2	-1	.974	-1	O	-2.3
1971	Was-A	27	49	5	7	3	0	0	4	8	5	.143	.263	.204	36	-4	-4	3	0	0	0	.933	3	O	-0.1
1972	KC-A★	134	450	60	135	21	4	8	66	58	40	.300	.385	.418	139	23	23	71	0	1	-1	.965	-3	*O	1.7
1973	Cin-N	29	54	5	12	2	0	1	8	10	4	.222	.344	.315	88	-1	-1	6	0	0	0	.960	-1	O	-0.2
	Cal-A	77	229	28	75	10	2	3	21	35	27	.328	.419	.428	150	13	16	42	0	0	0	.969	-0	O/D	1.3
1974	Cal-A	10	26	1	4	0	0	0	2	1	2	.154	.185	.154	-2	-3	-3	0	0	0	0	.929	-1	/OD	-0.5
	KC-A	36	83	7	15	2	0	0	2	8	8	.181	.253	.205	31	-7	-8	4	0	1	-1	.000	0	D/O	-1.0
	Yr	46	109	8	19	2	0	0	4	9	10	.174	.237	.193	24	-10	-11	4	0	1	-1	.929	-2	DO	-1.5
	StL-N	6	6	0	2	0	0	0	0	0	1	.333	.333	.333	88	-0	-0	1	0	0	0	.000	0	H	0.0
Total	8	462	1218	131	320	52	9	13	127	149	135	.263	.346	.352	104	6	8	153	0	6	-4	.965	-3	O/D	-1.1

■ DANNY SCHELL   Schell, Clyde Daniel b: 12/26/27, Fostoria, Mich. d: 5/11/72, Mayville, Mich. BR/TR, 6'1", 195 lbs. Deb: 4/13/54

1954	Phi-N	92	272	25	77	14	3	7	33	17	31	.283	.330	.434	97	-2	-2	34	0	3	-2	.974	1	O	-0.6
1955	Phi-N	2	2	0	0	0	0	0	0	0	1	.000	.000	.000	-99	-1	-1	0	0	0	0	.000	0	H	-0.1
Total	2	94	274	25	77	14	3	7	33	17	32	.281	.328	.431	96	-2	-2	34	0	3	-2	1.000	1	/O	-0.7

■ AL SCHELLHASE   Schellhase, Albert Herman "Schelley" b: 9/13/1864, Evansville, Ind. d: 1/3/19, Evansville, Ind. BR/TR, 5'8", 148 lbs. Deb: 5/07/1890

1890	Bos-N	9	29	1	4	0	0	0	1	1	10	.138	.167	.138	-9	-4	-4	1	0			.778	-1	/OCS3	-0.5
1891	Lou-a	7	20	4	3	0	0	0	1	1	2	.150	.190	.150	-1	-3	-3	1	3			.943	0	/C	-0.1
Total	2	16	49	5	7	0	0	0	2	2	12	.143	.176	.143	-6	-7	-7	2	3			.922	-1	/CO3S	-0.6

■ FRED SCHEMANSKE   Schemanske, Frederick George "Buck" b: 4/28/03, Detroit, Mich. d: 2/18/60, Detroit, Mich. BR/TR, 6'2", 190 lbs. Deb: 9/15/23

| 1923 | Was-A | 2 | 2 | 0 | 2 | 0 | 0 | 0 | 2 | 1 | 0 | 1.000 | 1.000 | 1.000 | 450 | 2 | 2 | 2 | 0 | 0 | 0 | .000 | -0 | /P | 0.0 |

■ MIKE SCHEMER   Schemer, Michael "Lefty" b: 11/20/17, Baltimore, Md. d: 4/22/83, Miami, Fla. BL/TL, 6', 180 lbs. Deb: 8/08/45

1945	NY-N	31	108	10	36	3	1	1	10	6	1	.333	.368	.407	114	2	2	14	2			.993	4	1	0.4
1946	NY-N	1	1	0	0	0	0	0	0	0	0	.000	.000	.000	-99	-0	-0	0	0			.000	0	H	0.0
Total	2	32	109	10	36	3	1	1	10	6	1	.330	.365	.404	112	2	2	14	2				4	/1	0.4

YEAR	TM/L	G	AB	R	H	2B	3B	HR	RBI	BB	SO	AVG	OBP	SLG	PRO+	BR	/A	RC	SB	CS	SBR	FA	FR	POS	TPR

■ BILL SCHENCK   Schenck, William G.   b: Brooklyn, N.Y.   5'7″, 171 lbs.   Deb: 5/29/1882

1882	Lou-a	60	231	37	60	11	3	0		8		.260	.285	.333	114	2	4	22				.814	-7	*3/SP	-0.1
1884	Ric-a	42	151	14	31	4	0	3		1		.205	.216	.291	67	-5	-5	10				.836	-5	S/2	-0.9
1885	Bro-a	1	4	0	0	0	0	0		0		.000	.000	.000	-99	-1	-1	0				1.000	0	/3	-0.1
Total	3	103	386	51	91	15	3	3		9		.236	.255	.313	93	-5	-2	32				.817	-12	/3S2P	-1.1

■ HANK SCHENZ   Schenz, Henry Leonard   b: 4/11/19, New Richmond, Ohio   d: 5/12/88, Cincinnati, Ohio   BR/TR, 5'9.5″, 175 lbs.   Deb: 9/18/46

1946	Chi-N	6	11	0	2	0	0	0	1	0	0	.182	.182	.182	3	-1	-1	0		1		1.000	0	/3	-0.1
1947	Chi-N	7	14	2	1	0	0	0	0	2	1	.071	.235	.071	-16	-2	-2	1	0			.917	0	/3	-0.2
1948	Chi-N	96	337	43	88	17	1	1	14	18	15	.261	.306	.326	74	-14	-12	34	3			.974	-5	2/3	-1.3
1949	Chi-N	7	14	2	6	0	0	0	1	1	0	.429	.467	.429	146	1	1	3	2			1.000	1	/3	0.2
1950	Pit-N	58	101	17	23	4	2	1	5	6	7	.228	.271	.337	57	-6	-7	8	0			.987	3	23/S	-0.3
1951	Pit-N	25	61	5	13	1	0	0	3	0	2	.213	.226	.230	22	-7	-7	3	0	2	-1	.961	-3	2/3	-1.0
	*NY-N	8	0	1	0	0	0	0	0	0	0	—	—	—	—	0	0	0	0	0	0	.000	0	R	0.0
	Yr	33	61	6	13	1	0	0	3	0	2	.213	.226	.230	22	-7	-7	3	0	2	-1	.961	-3	2/3	-1.0
Total	6	207	538	70	133	22	3	2	24	27	25	.247	.291	.310	63	-29	-28	49	6	2		.974	-5	2/3S	-2.7

■ JOE SCHEPNER   Schepner, Joseph Maurice "Gentleman Joe"   b: 8/10/1895, Aliquippa, Pa.   d: 7/25/59, Mobile, Ala.   BR/TR, 5'10″, 160 lbs.   Deb: 9/11/19

| 1919 | StL-A | 14 | 48 | 2 | 10 | 4 | 0 | 0 | 6 | 1 | 5 | .208 | .224 | .292 | 43 | -4 | -4 | 3 | 0 | | | .947 | -1 | 3 | -0.5 |

■ BOB SCHERBARTH   Scherbarth, Robert Elmer   b: 1/18/26, Milwaukee, Wis.   BR/TR, 6', 180 lbs.   Deb: 4/23/50

| 1950 | Bos-A | 1 | 0 | 0 | 0 | 0 | 0 | 0 | 0 | 0 | 0 | — | — | — | — | 0 | 0 | 0 | 0 | 0 | 0 | .000 | 0 | /C | 0.0 |

■ HARRY SCHERER   Scherer, Harry   Deb: 7/24/1889

| 1889 | Lou-a | 1 | 3 | 0 | 1 | 0 | 0 | 0 | 0 | 0 | 0 | .333 | .333 | .333 | 94 | -0 | -0 | 0 | 0 | | | .500 | -1 | /O | -0.1 |

■ LOU SCHIAPPACASSE   Schiappacasse, Louis Joseph   b: 3/29/1881, Ann Arbor, Mich.   d: 9/20/10, Ann Arbor, Mich.   BR/TR,   Deb: 9/07/02

| 1902 | Det-A | 2 | 5 | 0 | 0 | 0 | 0 | 0 | 1 | 1 | | .000 | .167 | .000 | -50 | -1 | -1 | 0 | 0 | | | .000 | -1 | /O | -0.2 |

■ MORRIE SCHICK   Schick, Maurice Francis   b: 4/17/1892, Chicago, Ill.   d: 10/25/79, Hazel Crest, Ill.   BR/TR, 5'11″, 170 lbs.   Deb: 4/15/17

| 1917 | Chi-N | 14 | 34 | 3 | 5 | 0 | 0 | 0 | 3 | 3 | 10 | .147 | .216 | .147 | 11 | -3 | -4 | 1 | 0 | | | .960 | 0 | O | -0.5 |

■ CHUCK SCHILLING   Schilling, Charles Thomas   b: 10/25/37, Brooklyn, N.Y.   BR/TR, 5'11″, 170 lbs.   Deb: 4/11/61

1961	Bos-A	158	646	87	167	25	2	5	62	78	77	.259	.340	.327	77	-17	-19	76	7	6	-2	**.991**	15	*2	1.2
1962	Bos-A	119	413	48	95	17	1	7	35	29	48	.230	.287	.327	63	-21	-22	38	1	0		.985	13	*2	0.3
1963	Bos-A	146	576	63	135	25	0	8	33	41	72	.234	.291	.319	69	-22	-24	54	3	2	-0	.985	-14	*2	-2.7
1964	Bos-A	47	163	18	32	6	0	0	7	15	22	.196	.264	.233	38	-13	-14	11	0	1	-1	.974	-0	2	-1.2
1965	Bos-A	71	171	14	41	3	2	3	9	13	17	.240	.293	.333	73	-5	-6	15	0	1	-1	.976	10	2	0.7
Total	5	541	1969	230	470	76	5	23	146	176	236	.239	.305	.317	68	-78	-86	193	11	10	-3	.985	24	2	-1.7

■ BILL SCHINDLER   Schindler, William Gibbons   b: 7/10/1896, Perryville, Mo.   d: 2/6/79, Perryville, Mo.   BR/TR, 5'11″, 160 lbs.   Deb: 9/03/20

| 1920 | StL-N | 1 | 2 | 0 | 0 | 0 | 0 | 0 | 0 | 0 | 1 | .000 | .000 | .000 | -99 | -1 | -0 | 0 | 0 | 0 | 0 | 1.000 | -0 | /C | -0.1 |

■ DUTCH SCHIRICK   Schirick, Harry Ernest   b: 6/15/1890, Ruby, N.Y.   d: 11/12/68, Kingston, N.Y.   BR/TR, 5'8″, 160 lbs.   Deb: 9/17/14

| 1914 | StL-A | 1 | 0 | 0 | 0 | 0 | 0 | 0 | 1 | 0 | | — | 1.000 | — | 211 | 0 | 0 | 2 | 2 | | | .000 | 0 | H | 0.1 |

■ LARRY SCHLAFLY   Schlafly, Harry Linton   b: 9/20/1878, Port Washington, Ohio   d: 6/27/19, Canton, Ohio   BR/TR, 5'11″, 182 lbs.   Deb: 9/18/02   M

1902	Chi-N	10	31	5	10	0	3	0	5	6		.323	.432	.516	198	4	4	8	2			1.000	-4	/O23	0.0
1906	Was-A	123	426	60	105	13	8	2	30	50		.246	.334	.329	113	6	8	60	29			.961	14	*2	2.5
1907	Was-A	24	74	10	10	0	0	1	4	22		.135	.347	.176	73	-1	-0	8	7			.928	-9	2	-1.1
1914	Buf-F	51	127	16	33	7	1	2	19	12	22	.260	.338	.378	101	1	0	18	3			.951	2	2/1C30M	0.2
Total	4	208	658	91	158	20	12	5	58	90	22	.240	.341	.330	111	9	12	94	41			.954	3	2/103C	1.6

■ ADMIRAL SCHLEI   Schlei, George Henry   b: 1/12/1878, Cincinnati, Ohio   d: 1/24/58, Huntington, W.Va.   BR/TR, 5'8.5″, 179 lbs.   Deb: 4/24/04

1904	Cin-N	97	291	25	69	8	3	0	32	17		.237	.279	.285	69	-9	-12	26	7			.977	10	C	0.8
1905	Cin-N	99	314	32	71	8	3	1	36	22		.226	.283	.280	62	-12	-16	29	9			.962	16	C/1	0.8
1906	Cin-N	116	388	44	95	13	8	4	54	29		.245	.304	.351	100	1	-1	46	7			.961	9	C1	1.8
1907	Cin-N	84	246	28	67	3	2	0	27	28		.272	.347	.301	99	2	1	29	5			.980	5	C/1O	1.6
1908	Cin-N	92	300	31	66	6	4	1	22	22		.220	.278	.277	79	-8	-7	24	2			.962	-8	C	-0.7
1909	NY-N	92	279	25	68	12	0	0	30	40		.244	.343	.287	94	0	-0	30	4			.963	3	C	1.2
1910	NY-N	55	99	10	19	2	1	0	8	14	10	.192	.304	.232	57	-5	-5	9	4			.986	0	C	-0.2
1911	NY-N	1	1	0	0	0	0	0	0	0	1	.000	.000	.000	-97	-0	-0	0	0			.000	0	H	0.0
Total	8	636	1918	195	455	52	21	6	209	172	11	.237	.304	.296	82	-31	-41	193	38			.968	37	C/1O	5.3

■ RUDY SCHLESINGER   Schlesinger, William Cordes   b: 11/5/41, Cincinnati, Ohio   BR/TR, 6'2″, 175 lbs.   Deb: 5/04/65

| 1965 | Bos-A | 1 | 1 | 0 | 0 | 0 | 0 | 0 | 0 | 0 | 0 | .000 | .000 | .000 | -94 | -0 | -0 | 0 | 0 | 0 | 0 | .000 | 0 | H | 0.0 |

■ DUTCH SCHLIEBNER   Schliebner, Frederick Paul   b: 5/19/1891, Charlottenburg, Germany   d: 4/15/75, Toledo, Ohio   BR/TR, 5'10″, 180 lbs.   Deb: 4/17/23

1923	Bro-N	19	76	11	19	4	0	0	4	5	7	.250	.296	.303	60	-5	-4	7	1	0	0	.981	3	1	-0.2
	StL-A	127	444	50	122	19	6	4	52	39	60	.275	.339	.372	82	-9	-12	58	3	2	-0	.989	-0	*1	-1.9
Total	1	146	520	61	141	23	6	4	56	44	67	.271	.333	.362	79	-13	-16	65	4	2	0	.988	2	1	-2.1

■ JAY SCHLUETER   Schlueter, Jay D   b: 7/31/49, Phoenix, Ariz.   BR/TR, 6', 182 lbs.   Deb: 6/18/71

| 1971 | Hou-N | 7 | 3 | 1 | 1 | 0 | 0 | 0 | 0 | 0 | 1 | .333 | .333 | .333 | 92 | -0 | -0 | 0 | 0 | 0 | 0 | 1.000 | 1 | /O | 0.1 |

■ NORM SCHLUETER   Schlueter, Norman John "Duke"   b: 9/25/16, Belleville, Ill.   BR/TR, 5'10″, 175 lbs.   Deb: 5/28/38

1938	Chi-A	35	118	11	27	5	1	0	7	4	15	.229	.254	.288	35	-12	-12	9	1	0	0	.952	-3	C	-1.3
1939	Chi-A	34	56	5	13	2	1	0	8	1	11	.232	.246	.304	39	-5	-5	3	2	0	1	.988	1	C	-0.3
1944	Cle-A	49	122	2	15	4	0	0	11	12	22	.123	.201	.156	3	-15	-15	4	0	2	-1	.985	-8	C	-2.3
Total	3	118	296	18	55	11	2	0	26	17	48	.186	.230	.236	24	-33	-33	16	3	2	-0	.974	-10	C	-3.9

■ RAY SCHMANDT   Schmandt, Raymond Henry   b: 1/25/1896, St.Louis, Mo.   d: 2/2/69, St.Louis, Mo.   BR/TR, 6'1″, 175 lbs.   Deb: 6/24/15

1915	StL-A	3	4	0	0	0	0	0	0	0	1	.000	.000	.000	-99	-1	-1	0	0			1.000	-0	/1	-0.1
1918	Bro-N	34	114	11	35	5	4	0	18	7	7	.307	.347	.421	134	4	4	16	1			.934	-4	2	0.3
1919	Bro-N	47	127	8	21	4	0	0	10	4	13	.165	.191	.197	16	-13	-13	4	0			.911	0	21/3	-1.4
1920	*Bro-N	28	63	7	15	2	1	0	7	3	4	.238	.273	.302	63	-3	-3	5	1	1	-0	.995	3	1	0.0
1921	Bro-N	95	350	42	107	8	5	1	43	11	22	.306	.329	.366	81	-8	-10	41	3	4	-2	.989	0	1	-1.3
1922	Bro-N	110	396	54	106	17	3	2	44	21	28	.268	.306	.341	67	-20	-19	41	6	6	-2	.989	5	*1	-2.0
Total	6	317	1054	122	284	36	13	3	122	46	75	.269	.301	.337	72	-41	-42	108	11	11		.990	5	1/23	-4.5

■ GEORGE SCHMEES   Schmees, George Edward "Rocky"   b: 9/6/24, Cincinnati, Ohio   BL/TL, 6', 190 lbs.   Deb: 4/15/52

1952	StL-A	34	61	9	8	1	1	0	3	2	18	.131	.159	.180	-6	-9	-9	2	0	0	0	.932	-1	O/1	-1.0
	Bos-A	42	64	8	13	3	0	0	3	10	11	.203	.311	.250	53	-3	-4	5	0	1	-1	1.000	-7	O/P1	-1.4
	Yr	76	125	17	21	4	1	0	6	12	29	.168	.241	.216	26	-12	-13	7	0	1	-1	.960	-8	O/1P	-2.4

■ BOSS SCHMIDT   Schmidt, Charles   b: 9/12/1880, Coal Hill, Ark.   d: 11/14/32, Clarksville, Ark.   BB/TR, 5'11″, 200 lbs.   Deb: 4/30/06   F

| 1906 | Det-A | 68 | 216 | 13 | 47 | 4 | 3 | 0 | 10 | 6 | | .218 | .242 | .264 | 57 | -11 | -11 | 15 | 1 | | | .958 | 7 | C | 0.3 |

YEAR	TM/L	G	AB	R	H	2B	3B	HR	RBI	BB	SO	AVG	OBP	SLG	PRO+	BR	/A	RC	SB	CS	SBR	FA	FR	POS	TPR
1907	*Det-A	104	349	32	85	6	6	0	23	5		.244	.265	.295	76	-9	-11	31	8			.944	3	*C	0.2
1908	*Det-A	122	419	45	111	14	3	1	38	16		.265	.297	.320	96	-1	-3	41	5			.951	9	*C	1.9
1909	*Det-A	84	253	21	53	8	2	1	28	7		.209	.240	.269	58	-12	-13	19	7			.955	-6	C/O	-1.4
1910	Det-A	71	197	22	51	7	7	1	23	2		.259	.277	.381	99	-0	-2	21	2			.973	-7	C	-0.3
1911	Det-A	28	46	4	13	2	1	0	2	0		.283	.298	.370	82	-1	-1	5	0			1.000	-2	/CO	-0.3
Total	6	477	1480	137	360	41	22	3	124	36		.243	.269	.307	79	-34	-41	132	23			.955	4	C/O	0.4

■ BUTCH SCHMIDT
Schmidt, Charles John "Butcher Boy" b: 7/19/1886, Baltimore, Md. d: 9/4/52, Baltimore, Md. BL/TL, 6'1.5", 200 lbs. Deb: 5/11/09

YEAR	TM/L	G	AB	R	H	2B	3B	HR	RBI	BB	SO	AVG	OBP	SLG	PRO+	BR	/A	RC	SB	CS	SBR	FA	FR	POS	TPR
1909	NY-A	1	2	0	0	0	0	0	0	0		.000	.000	.000	-99	-0	-0	0	0			.500	-0	/P	0.0
1913	Bos-N	22	78	6	24	2	2	1	14	2	5	.308	.333	.423	113	1	1	11	1			.983	1	1	0.2
1914	*Bos-N	147	537	67	153	17	9	1	71	43	55	.285	.350	.356	111	7	8	71	14			.990	3	*1	0.7
1915	Bos-N	127	458	46	115	26	7	2	60	36	59	.251	.318	.352	107	1	4	52	3	10	-5	.987	-4	*1	-1.0
Total	4	297	1075	119	292	45	18	4	145	81	119	.272	.335	.358	109	9	12	134	18	10		.988	-1	1/P	-0.1

■ DAVE SCHMIDT
Schmidt, David Frederick b: 12/22/56, Mesa, Ariz. BR/TR, 6'1", 190 lbs. Deb: 4/28/81

YEAR	TM/L	G	AB	R	H	2B	3B	HR	RBI	BB	SO	AVG	OBP	SLG	PRO+	BR	/A	RC	SB	CS	SBR	FA	FR	POS	TPR
1981	Bos-A	15	42	6	10	1	0	2	3	7	17	.238	.347	.405	109	1	1	6	0	0	0	1.000	-4	C	-0.3

■ MIKE SCHMIDT
Schmidt, Michael Jack b: 9/27/49, Dayton, Ohio BR/TR, 6'2", 203 lbs. Deb: 9/12/72

YEAR	TM/L	G	AB	R	H	2B	3B	HR	RBI	BB	SO	AVG	OBP	SLG	PRO+	BR	/A	RC	SB	CS	SBR	FA	FR	POS	TPR
1972	Phi-N	13	34	2	7	0	0	1	3	5	15	.206	.325	.294	75	-1	-1	4	0	0	0	.964	2	3/2	0.1
1973	Phi-N	132	367	43	72	11	0	18	52	62	136	.196	.326	.373	91	-2	-4	48	8	2	1	.954	**21**	*3/21S	1.9
1974	Phi-N★	162	568	108	160	28	7	**36**	116	106	138	.282	.398	**.546**	156	**48**	45	**130**	23	12	-0	.954	26	*3	**7.1**
1975	Phi-N	158	562	93	140	34	3	**38**	95	101	180	.249	.367	.523	139	34	31	113	29	12	2	.954	**24**	*3S	5.8
1976	*Phi-N★	160	584	112	153	31	4	**38**	107	100	149	.262	.380	.524	150	43	40	121	14	9	-1	.961	**25**	*3	**6.5**
1977	*Phi-N★	154	544	114	149	27	11	38	101	104	122	.274	.399	.574	151	46	42	129	15	8	-0	.964	29	*3/S2	**6.8**
1978	*Phi-N	145	513	93	129	27	2	21	78	91	103	.251	.368	.435	122	18	18	90	19	6	2	.963	10	*3/S	2.9
1979	Phi-N★	160	541	109	137	25	4	45	114	**120**	115	.253	.392	.564	153	45	42	123	9	5	-0	.954	18	*3/S	**6.0**
1980	*Phi-N†	150	548	104	157	25	8	**48**	**121**	89	119	.286	.388	**.624**	**169**	**56**	**53**	**137**	12	5	1	.946	23	*3	**7.6**
1981	*Phi-N★	102	354	**78**	112	19	2	**31**	**91**	**73**	71	.316	**.439**	**.644**	**195**	**50**	**48**	**102**	12	4	1	.956	23	*3	**7.2**
1982	Phi-N★	148	514	108	144	26	3	35	87	**107**	131	.280	**.407**	**.547**	**161**	**47**	**46**	118	14	7	0	.950	19	*3	**6.2**
1983	*Phi-N★	154	534	104	136	16	4	**40**	109	**128**	148	.255	**.402**	.524	**156**	43	**44**	117	7	8	-3	.959	23	*3/S	**6.4**
1984	Phi-N★	151	528	93	146	23	3	**36**	**106**	92	116	.277	.388	.536	**155**	41	**40**	108	5	7	-3	.941	12	*3/1S	4.9
1985	Phi-N	158	549	89	152	31	5	33	93	87	117	.277	.379	.532	148	39	37	113	1	3	-2	.993	5	*13/S	3.4
1986	Phi-N★	160	552	97	160	29	1	**37**	**119**	89	84	.290	.395	**.547**	**152**	**44**	**41**	122	1	2	-1	**.980**	-7	*31	3.0
1987	Phi-N★	147	522	88	153	28	0	35	113	83	80	.293	.392	.548	141	35	33	111	2	1	0	.971	13	*3/1S	4.2
1988	Phi-N	108	390	52	97	21	2	12	62	49	42	.249	.342	.405	111	7	7	55	3	0	1	.939	3	*3/1	1.1
1989	Phi-N†	42	148	19	30	7	0	6	28	21	17	.203	.302	.372	91	-2	-2	16	0	1	-1	.918	-5	3	-0.8
Total	18	2404	8352	1506	2234	408	59	548	1595	1507	1883	.267	.384	.527	147	592	561	1757	174	92	-3	.955	265	*31/S2	80.3

■ BOB SCHMIDT
Schmidt, Robert Benjamin b: 4/22/33, St.Louis, Mo. BR/TR, 6'2", 205 lbs. Deb: 4/16/58

YEAR	TM/L	G	AB	R	H	2B	3B	HR	RBI	BB	SO	AVG	OBP	SLG	PRO+	BR	/A	RC	SB	CS	SBR	FA	FR	POS	TPR
1958	SF-N☆	127	393	46	96	20	2	14	54	33	59	.244	.308	.412	90	-7	-6	44	0	1	-1	.982	-3	*C	-0.3
1959	SF-N	71	181	17	44	7	1	5	20	13	24	.243	.297	.376	80	-6	-5	19	0	2	-1	1.000	-0	C	-0.4
1960	SF-N	110	344	31	92	12	1	8	37	26	51	.267	.319	.378	96	-5	-2	39	0	3	-2	.981	-3	*C	-0.1
1961	SF-N	2	6	0	1	0	0	0	1	0	1	.167	.167	.167	-12	-1	-1	0	0	0	0	1.000	1	/C	0.0
	Cin-N	27	70	4	9	0	0	1	4	8	14	.129	.218	.171	5	-10	-10	2	0	0	0	.993	1	C	-0.7
	Yr	29	76	4	10	0	0	1	5	8	15	.132	.214	.171	4	-11	-11	2	0	0	0	.994	3	C	-0.7
1962	Was-A	88	256	28	62	14	0	10	31	14	37	.242	.284	.414	86	-6	-6	30	0	0	0	**.997**	-2	C	-0.5
1963	Was-A	9	15	3	3	1	0	0	0	3	5	.200	.333	.267	71	-0	-0	1	0	0	0	1.000	-1	/C	-0.2
1965	NY-A	20	40	4	10	1	0	1	3	3	8	.250	.302	.350	85	-1	-1	4	0	0	0	.990	2	C	0.2
Total	7	454	1305	133	317	55	4	39	150	100	199	.243	.299	.381	84	-36	-32	141	0	6	-4	.988	-5	C	-2.0

■ WALTER SCHMIDT
Schmidt, Walter Joseph b: 3/20/1887, Coal Hill, Ark. d: 7/4/73, Modesto, Cal. BR/TR, 5'9", 159 lbs. Deb: 4/13/16 F

YEAR	TM/L	G	AB	R	H	2B	3B	HR	RBI	BB	SO	AVG	OBP	SLG	PRO+	BR	/A	RC	SB	CS	SBR	FA	FR	POS	TPR
1916	Pit-N	64	184	16	35	1	2	2	15	10	13	.190	.236	.250	49	-11	-11	12	3			.976	0	C	-0.8
1917	Pit-N	72	183	9	45	7	0	0	17	11	11	.246	.296	.284	76	-5	-5	16	4			.978	8	C	0.8
1918	Pit-N	105	323	31	77	6	3	0	27	17	19	.238	.281	.276	67	-12	-13	27	7			.981	16	*C	1.2
1919	Pit-N	85	267	23	67	9	2	0	29	23	9	.251	.310	.300	81	-5	-6	26	5			.982	1	C	0.3
1920	Pit-N	94	310	22	86	8	4	0	20	24	15	.277	.337	.329	89	-3	-4	36	9	3	1	.971	-5	C	-0.1
1921	Pit-N	114	393	30	111	9	3	0	38	12	13	.282	.307	.321	65	-19	-20	38	10	6	-1	**.986**	7	*C	-0.8
1922	Pit-N	40	152	21	50	11	1	0	22	1	5	.329	.333	.414	91	-2	-2	20	2	1	0	.995	-5	C	-0.5
1923	Pit-N	97	335	39	83	7	2	0	37	22	12	.248	.300	.281	53	-22	-23	29	10	5	0	.981	-9	C	-2.6
1924	Pit-N	58	177	16	43	3	2	1	20	13	5	.243	.295	.299	59	-10	-10	17	6	1	1	.986	2	C	-0.4
1925	StL-N	37	87	9	22	2	1	0	9	4	3	.253	.293	.299	51	-6	-7	8	1	0	0	.967	6	C	0.1
Total	10	766	2411	216	619	63	20	3	234	137	105	.257	.301	.303	68	-94	-101	231	57	16		.980	21	C	-2.8

■ HANK SCHMULBACH
Schmulbach, Henry Alrives b: 1/17/25, E.St.Louis, Ill. BL/TR, 5'11", 165 lbs. Deb: 9/27/43

YEAR	TM/L	G	AB	R	H	2B	3B	HR	RBI	BB	SO	AVG	OBP	SLG	PRO+	BR	/A	RC	SB	CS	SBR	FA	FR	POS	TPR
1943	StL-A	1	0	1	0	0	0	0	0	0	0	—	—	—	—	0	0	0	0	0	0	.000	0	R	0.0

■ DAVE SCHNECK
Schneck, David Lee b: 6/18/49, Allentown, Pa. BL/TL, 5'10", 200 lbs. Deb: 7/14/72

YEAR	TM/L	G	AB	R	H	2B	3B	HR	RBI	BB	SO	AVG	OBP	SLG	PRO+	BR	/A	RC	SB	CS	SBR	FA	FR	POS	TPR
1972	NY-N	37	123	7	23	3	2	3	10	10	26	.187	.254	.317	63	-7	-6	10	0	1	-1	.985	-0	O	-0.9
1973	NY-N	13	36	2	7	0	1	0	0	1	4	.194	.216	.250	29	-3	-3	1	0	0	0	1.000	2	O	-0.2
1974	NY-N	93	254	23	52	11	1	5	25	16	43	.205	.255	.315	60	-15	-14	21	4	1	1	.974	11	O	-0.6
Total	3	143	413	32	82	14	4	8	35	27	73	.199	.251	.310	58	-25	-24	32	4	2	0	.979	12	O	-1.7

■ RED SCHOENDIENST
Schoendienst, Albert Fred b: 2/2/23, Germantown, Ill. BB/TR, 6', 170 lbs. Deb: 4/17/45 MCH

YEAR	TM/L	G	AB	R	H	2B	3B	HR	RBI	BB	SO	AVG	OBP	SLG	PRO+	BR	/A	RC	SB	CS	SBR	FA	FR	POS	TPR
1945	StL-N	137	565	89	157	22	6	1	47	21	17	.278	.305	.343	78	-17	-18	59	**26**			.983	3	*OS/2	-2.1
1946	*StL-N★	142	606	94	170	28	5	0	34	37	27	.281	.322	.343	85	-10	-13	67	12			**.984**	-1	*23/S	-0.4
1947	StL-N	151	659	91	167	25	9	3	48	48	27	.253	.304	.332	66	-30	-34	65	6			.976	-2	*2/3O	-2.5
1948	StL-N★	119	408	64	111	21	4	4	36	28	16	.272	.319	.373	82	-8	-11	49	1			.980	1	2	-0.5
1949	StL-N★	151	640	102	190	25	2	3	54	51	18	.297	.351	.356	86	-8	-12	82	8			**.987**	24	*2S/3O	1.9
1950	StL-N★	153	642	81	177	**43**	9	7	63	33	32	.276	.313	.403	83	-14	-18	79	3			.985	8	*2S/3	-0.3
1951	StL-N★	135	553	88	160	32	7	6	54	35	23	.289	.335	.405	98	-2	-3	75	0	1	-1	.990	16	*2/S	1.9
1952	StL-N☆	152	620	91	188	40	7	7	67	42	30	.303	.347	.424	113	10	10	89	9	6	-1	.977	**33**	*23/S	4.9
1953	StL-N★	146	564	107	193	35	5	15	79	60	23	.342	.405	.502	135	30	30	114	3	3	-1	**.983**	25	*2	**5.8**
1954	StL-N★	148	610	98	192	38	8	5	79	54	22	.315	.371	.428	107	7	7	96	4	2	0	.980	**33**	*2	4.8
1955	StL-N★	145	553	68	148	21	3	11	51	54	28	.268	.337	.376	89	-8	-8	70	7	7	-2	**.985**	-15	*2	-1.4
1956	StL-N	40	153	22	48	9	0	0	15	13	5	.314	.367	.373	100	0	0	21	0	1	-1	.995	-2	2	0.1
	NY-N	92	334	39	99	12	3	2	14	28	10	.296	.354	.368	95	-2	-1	42	1	2	-1	.993	-11	2	-0.6
	Yr	132	487	61	147	21	3	2	29	41	15	.302	.358	.370	97	-1	-1	63	1	3	-2	**.993**	-12	*2	-0.5
1957	NY-N	57	254	35	78	8	4	9	33	10	8	.307	.338	.476	116	5	5	40	2	1	0	.984	-2	2	0.8
	*Mil-N	93	394	56	122	23	4	6	32	23	7	.310	.349	.434	117	5	8	59	2	3	-1	.987	4	2/O	1.9
	Yr	150	648	91	**200**	31	8	15	65	33	15	.309	.345	.451	117	10	13	99	4	4	-1	.986	3	*2/O	2.7
1958	*Mil-N	106	427	47	112	23	1	1	24	31	21	.262	.314	.328	77	-18	-13	44	3	1	0	**.987**	1	*2	-0.5
1959	Mil-N	5	3	0	0	0	0	0	0	0	0	.000	.000	.000	-99	-1	-1	0	0	0	0	.667	-0	/2	-0.1
1960	Mil-N	68	226	21	58	9	1	1	19	17	13	.257	.311	.319	79	-8	-6	23	1	0	0	.964	-17	2	-1.8
1961	StL-N	72	120	9	36	9	0	1	12	12	6	.300	.364	.400	93	1	-1	18	1	0	0	.955	-11	2	-0.9
1962	StL-N	98	143	21	43	4	0	2	12	9	12	.301	.346	.371	84	-1	-3	17	0	0	0	.986	-0	2/3	-0.2

YEAR	TM/L	G	AB	R	H	2B	3B	HR	RBI	BB	SO	AVG	OBP	SLG	PRO+	BR	/A	RC	SB	CS	SBR	FA	FR	POS	TPR
1963	StL-N	6	5	0	0	0	0	0	0	0	1	.000	.000	.000	-91	-1	-1	0	0	0	0	.000	0	H	-0.1
Total	19	2216	8479	1223	2449	427	78	84	773	606	346	.289	.338	.387	93	-70	-83	1109	89	27		.983	88	*2O/S3	10.7
■ **JUMBO SCHOENECK**	Schoeneck, Louis N. b: 3/3/1862, Chicago, Ill. d: 1/20/30, Chicago, Ill. BR/TR, 6'3", 223 lbs. Deb: 4/20/1884																								
1884	CP-U	90	366	56	116	22	2	2		8		.317	.332	.404	149	17	17	50				.956	0	*1	0.7
	Bal-U	16	60	5	15	2	0	0		0		.250	.250	.283	72	-1	-2	4				.962	2	1	-0.2
	Yr	106	426	61	131	24	2	2		8		.308	.320	.387	137	16	15	54				**.957**	2	*1	0.5
1888	Ind-N	48	169	15	40	4	0	0	20	9	24	.237	.283	.260	75	-4	-5	16	11			.974	-1	1/P	-1.0
1889	Ind-N	16	62	3	15	2	2	0	8	3	3	.242	.299	.339	78	-2	-2	7	1			.978	2	1	-0.1
Total	3	170	657	79	186	30	4	2	28	20	27	.283	.308	.350	114	10	9	77	12			.964	3	1/P	-0.6
■ **DICK SCHOFIELD**	Schofield, John Richard "Ducky" b: 1/7/35, Springfield, Ill. BB/TR, 5'9", 165 lbs. Deb: 7/03/53 F																								
1953	StL-N	33	39	9	7	0	0	2	4	2	11	.179	.220	.333	42	-3	-3	3	0	0	0	.917	10	S	0.6
1954	StL-N	43	7	17	1	0	1	0	1	0	3	.143	.143	.429	42	-1	-1	-1	1	1	-0	1.000	14	S	1.2
1955	StL-N	12	4	3	0	0	0	0	0	0	1	.000	.000	.000	-99	-1	-1	0	0	0	0	1.000	3	/S	0.2
1956	StL-N	16	30	3	3	2	0	0	1	0	6	.100	.100	.167	-30	-5	-5	0	0	0	0	.923	-1	/S	-0.6
1957	StL-N	65	56	10	9	0	0	0	1	7	13	.161	.254	.161	14	-7	-7	2	1	3	-2	.948	10	S	0.2
1958	StL-N	39	108	16	23	4	0	1	8	23	15	.213	.351	.278	67	-4	-5	12	0	2	-1	.932	-5	S	-0.8
	Pit-N	26	27	4	4	0	1	0	2	3	6	.148	.233	.222	22	-3	-3	1	0	1	-1	1.000	0	/S3	-0.3
	Yr	65	135	20	27	4	1	1	10	26	21	.200	.329	.267	59	-7	-7	13	0	3	-2	.943	-5	S/3	-1.1
1959	Pit-N	81	145	21	34	10	1	1	9	16	22	.234	.311	.338	73	-6	-5	16	1	1	-0	.980	10	2/SO	0.7
1960	*Pit-N	65	102	9	34	4	1	0	10	16	20	.333	.429	.392	126	5	5	18	0	1	-1	.947	8	S2/3	1.4
1961	Pit-N	60	78	16	15	2	1	0	2	10	19	.192	.284	.244	42	-6	-6	6	0	1	-1	.923	10	3/S2O	0.4
1962	Pit-N	54	104	19	30	3	0	2	10	17	22	.288	.388	.375	106	2	2	17	0	1	-1	.933	-6	3/2S	-0.4
1963	Pit-N	138	541	54	133	18	2	3	32	69	83	.246	.334	.303	84	-8	-8	58	2	4	-2	.966	10	*S2/3	1.1
1964	Pit-N	121	398	50	98	22	5	3	36	54	60	.246	.346	.349	97	0	0	52	1	2	-1	.950	2	*S	0.9
1965	Pit-N	31	109	13	25	5	0	0	6	15	19	.229	.323	.275	70	-4	-4	11	1	0	0	.974	4	S	0.3
	SF-N	101	379	39	77	10	1	2	19	33	50	.203	.272	.251	47	-25	-27	26	2	4	-2	.984	-6	S	-3.0
	Yr	132	488	52	102	15	1	2	25	48	69	.209	.284	.256	52	-29	-30	37	3	4	-2	**.981**	-2	*S	-2.7
1966	SF-N	11	16	4	1	0	0	0	0	2	2	.063	.167	.063	-32	-3	-3	0	0	0	0	1.000	2	/S	-0.1
	NY-A	25	58	5	9	2	0	0	2	9	8	.155	.269	.190	36	-5	-4	4	0	0	0	.909	5	S	0.2
	LA-N	20	70	10	18	2	0	0	4	8	8	.257	.350	.257	78	-2	-1	7	1	1	-0	.923	-3	3/S	-0.5
1967	LA-N	84	232	23	50	10	1	2	15	31	40	.216	.308	.293	79	-7	-5	20	1	2	-1	.976	-0	S/23	0.0
1968	*StL-N	69	127	14	28	7	1	1	8	13	31	.220	.303	.315	87	-2	-2	12	1	2	-1	.973	9	S2	1.0
1969	Bos-A	94	226	30	58	9	3	2	20	29	44	.257	.351	.350	92	-0	-2	29	0	2	-1	.981	2	2S/3O	0.3
1970	Bos-A	76	139	16	26	1	2	1	14	21	26	.187	.298	.245	48	-9	-10	10	0	1	-1	.969	-4	23/S	-1.5
1971	Mil-A	23	28	2	3	2	0	0	1	2	8	.107	.194	.179	6	-4	-3	1	0	0	0	1.000	-2	3/S2	-0.5
	StL-N	34	60	7	13	2	0	1	6	10	9	.217	.347	.300	82	-1	-1	7	0	0	0	.935	2	S2/3	0.3
Total	19	1321	3083	394	699	113	20	21	211	390	526	.227	.319	.297	73	-100	-101	311	12	29	-14	.961	73	S2/3O	1.1
■ **DICK SCHOFIELD**	Schofield, Richard Craig b: 11/21/62, Springfield, Ill. BR/TR, 5'10", 176 lbs. Deb: 9/08/83 F																								
1983	Cal-A	21	54	4	11	2	0	3	4	6	8	.204	.295	.407	92	-1	-1	6	0	0	0	.929	5	S	0.5
1984	Cal-A	140	400	39	77	10	3	4	21	33	79	.192	.264	.262	47	-29	-29	29	5	2	0	**.982**	3	*S	-1.2
1985	Cal-A	147	438	50	96	19	3	8	41	35	70	.219	.289	.331	70	-19	-18	43	11	4	1	.963	1	*S	-0.3
1986	*Cal-A	139	458	67	114	17	6	13	57	48	55	.249	.327	.397	97	-3	-2	63	23	5	4	.972	15	*S	2.9
1987	Cal-A	134	479	52	120	17	3	9	46	37	63	.251	.307	.355	78	-17	-15	56	19	3	4	**.984**	-18	*S/2D	-1.7
1988	Cal-A	155	527	61	126	11	6	6	34	40	57	.239	.304	.317	76	-18	-16	55	20	5	3	**.983**	23	*S	2.3
1989	Cal-A	91	302	42	69	11	2	4	26	28	47	.228	.300	.318	76	-10	-9	31	9	3	1	.983	-8	S	-0.9
1990	Cal-A	99	310	41	79	8	1	1	18	52	61	.255	.365	.297	89	-3	-2	38	3	4	-2	.966	12	S	1.7
1991	Cal-A	134	427	44	96	9	3	0	31	50	69	.225	.310	.260	60	-22	-22	39	8	4	0	.975	12	*S	0.0
1992	Cal-A	1	3	0	1	0	0	0	0	1	0	.333	.500	.333	139	0	0	1	0	0	0	1.000	-1	/S	0.0
	NY-N	142	420	52	86	18	2	4	36	60	82	.205	.311	.286	71	-15	-15	41	11	4	1	**.988**	13	*S	1.0
Total	10	1203	3818	452	875	122	29	52	314	390	591	.229	.308	.317	74	-135	-128	403	109	34	12	.977	58	*S/2D	4.3
■ **OTTO SCHOMBERG**	Schomberg, Otto H. (b: Otto H. Shambrick) b: 11/14/1864, Milwaukee, Wis. d: 5/3/27, Ottawa, Kan. BL/TL, Deb: 7/07/1886																								
1886	Pit-a	72	246	53	67	6	6	1		57		.272	.417	.358	147	17	17	41	7			.966	-7	1	0.2
1887	Ind-N	112	419	91	129	18	16	5	83	56	32	.308	.397	.463	145	24	27	88	21			.958	-10	*1/O	0.5
1888	Ind-N	30	112	11	24	5	1	1	10	10	12	.214	.290	.304	90	-1	-1	12	6			.857	-5	O1	-0.7
Total	3	214	777	155	220	29	23	7	93	123	44	.283	.389	.407	139	41	44	140	34			.961	-22	1/O	0.0
■ **JERRY SCHOONMAKER**	Schoonmaker, Jerald Lee b: 12/14/33, Seymour, Mo. BR/TR, 5'11", 190 lbs. Deb: 6/11/55																								
1955	Was-A	20	46	5	7	0	1	1	4	5	11	.152	.235	.261	35	-4	-4	3	1	0	0	.960	-1	O	-0.5
1957	Was-A	30	23	5	2	1	0	0	0	2	11	.087	.160	.130	-20	-4	-4	1	0	0	0	1.000	-3	O	-0.7
Total	2	50	69	10	9	1	1	1	4	7	22	.130	.211	.217	16	-8	-8	4	1	0	0	.975	-4	/O	-1.2
■ **GENE SCHOTT**	Schott, Eugene Arthur b: 7/14/13, Batavia, Ohio BR/TR, 6'2", 185 lbs. Deb: 4/16/35																								
1935	Cin-N	36	60	6	12	2	0	0	2	3	13	.200	.238	.233	28	-6	-6	3	0			.965	3	P	0.0
1936	Cin-N	39	60	10	18	3	1	1	8	5	18	.300	.354	.433	118	1	1	10	0			.947	1	P	0.0
1937	Cin-N	50	49	5	7	2	0	0	4	1	14	.143	.160	.184	-7	-7	-7	1	0			.961	1	P	0.0
1938	Cin-N	31	24	3	3	0	0	0	0	1	4	.125	.160	.125	-21	-4	-4	0	0			1.000	1	P	0.0
1939	Phi-N	8	6	3	2	0	1	0	0	0	0	.333	.333	.667	168	0	0	1	0			.500	-1	/P	0.0
	Bro-N	1	0	0	0	0	0	0	0	0	0	—	—	—	—	0	0	0	0			.000	0	R	0.0
	Yr	9	6	3	2	0	1	0	0	0	0	.333	.333	.667	166	0	0	1	0			.500	-1	/P	0.0
Total	5	165	199	27	42	7	2	1	14	10	49	.211	.249	.281	45	-16	-15	16	0			.959	6	P	0.0
■ **PAUL SCHRAMKA**	Schramka, Paul Edward b: 3/22/28, Milwaukee, Wis. BL/TL, 6', 185 lbs. Deb: 4/14/53																								
1953	Chi-N	2	0	0	0	0	0	0	0	0	0	—	—	—	—	0	0	0	0	0	0	.000	-0	/O	0.0
■ **OSSEE SCHRECKENGOST**	Schreckengost, Ossee Freeman (a.k.a. Of Ossee Schreck) b: 4/11/1875, New Bethlehem, Pa. d: 7/9/14, Philadelphia, Pa. BR/TR, 5'10", 180 lbs. Deb: 9/08/1897																								
1897	Lou-N	1	3	0	0	0	0	0	0	0		.000	.000	.000	-99	-1	-1	0	0			1.000	-0	/C	-0.1
1898	Cle-N	10	35	5	11	2	3	0	10	0		.314	.314	.543	146	2	2	6	1			.860	-0	/C	0.2
1899	StL-N	6	8	0	0	0	0	0	0	1		.000	.111	.000	-67	-2	-2	0	0			1.000	-1	/1O	-0.2
	Cle-N	43	150	15	47	8	3	0	10	6		.313	.348	.407	115	1	3	23	4			.911	-6	C/1SO	0.0
	StL-N	66	269	42	77	12	2	2	37	14		.286	.324	.368	88	-5	-5	38	14			.963	-3	1C/2	-0.6
	Yr	115	427	57	124	20	5	2	47	21		.290	.328	.375	94	-5	-5	60	18			.927	-10	C1/OS2	-0.8
1901	Bos-A	86	280	37	85	13	5	0	38	19		.304	.356	.386	108	2	3	42	6			.926	2	C/1	1.1
1902	Cle-A	18	74	5	25	0	0	0	9	0		.338	.338	.338	91	-1	-1	9	2			.967	-1	1	-0.2
	Phi-A	79	284	45	92	17	2	2	43	9		.324	.347	.419	107	4	2	44	3			.960	23	C/1O	3.0
	Yr	97	358	50	117	17	2	2	52	9		.327	.345	.402	104	2	1	54	5			.960	21	C1/O	2.8
1903	Phi-A	92	306	26	78	13	4	3	30	11		.255	.285	.353	87	-4	-6	32	0			.975	18	C1	2.1
1904	Phi-A	95	311	23	58	9	1	1	21	5		.186	.199	.232	34	-23	-24	16	3			.979	5	C/1	-1.1
1905	*Phi-A	123	420	30	114	19	6	0	45	3		.271	.278	.345	96	-3	-4	44	9			**.984**	12	*C/1	2.1
1906	Phi-A	98	338	29	96	20	1	1	41	10		.284	.305	.358	104	2	1	40	5			.971	8	C/1	1.9
1907	Phi-A	101	356	30	97	16	3	0	38	17		.272	.306	.334	102	1	-0	39	4			**.985**	16	C/1	2.8

YEAR	TM/L	G	AB	R	H	2B	3B	HR	RBI	BB	SO	AVG	OBP	SLG	PRO+	BR	/A	RC	SB	CS	SBR	FA	FR	POS	TPR
1908	Phi-A	71	207	16	46	7	1	0	16	6		.222	.248	.266	63	-8	-9	14	1			.978	9	C/1	0.6
	Chi-A	6	16	1	3	0	0	0	0	1		.188	.235	.188	38	-1	-1	1	0			.982	4	/C	0.4
	Yr	77	223	17	49	7	1	0	16	7		.220	.247	.260	61	-9	-10	15	1			.978	13	C/1	1.0
Total	11	895	3057	304	829	136	31	9	338	102		.271	.297	.345	90	-36	-43	349	52			.970	86	C/1O2S	12.0

■ HANK SCHREIBER Schreiber, Henry Walter b: 7/12/1891, Cleveland, Ohio d: 2/23/68, Indianapolis, Ind. BR/TR, 5'11", 165 lbs. Deb: 4/14/14

YEAR	TM/L	G	AB	R	H	2B	3B	HR	RBI	BB	SO	AVG	OBP	SLG	PRO+	BR	/A	RC	SB	CS	SBR	FA	FR	POS	TPR
1914	Chi-A	1	2	0	0	0	0	0	0	0	1	.000	.000	.000	-99	-0	-0	0	0			.000	-1	/O	-0.1
1917	Bos-N	2	7	1	2	0	0	0	0	0	1	.286	.286	.286	80	-0	-0	1	0			1.000	-1	/S3	-0.1
1919	Cin-N	19	58	5	13	4	0	0	4	0	12	.224	.224	.293	56	-3	-3	4	0			.984	7	3/S	0.4
1921	NY-N	4	6	2	2	0	0	0	2	1	1	.333	.429	.333	104	0	0	1	0	0	0	.500	-0	/2S3	0.0
1926	Chi-N	10	18	2	1	1	0	0	0	0	1	.056	.056	.111	-55	-4	-4	0	0			1.000	1	/S32	-0.3
Total	5	36	91	10	18	5	0	0	6	1	16	.198	.207	.253	34	-8	-8	5	0	0		.986	6	/3S2O	-0.1

■ TED SCHREIBER Schreiber, Theodore Henry b: 7/11/38, Brooklyn, N.Y. BR/TR, 5'11", 175 lbs. Deb: 4/14/63

YEAR	TM/L	G	AB	R	H	2B	3B	HR	RBI	BB	SO	AVG	OBP	SLG	PRO+	BR	/A	RC	SB	CS	SBR	FA	FR	POS	TPR
1963	NY-N	39	50	1	8	0	0	0	2	4	14	.160	.236	.160	16	-5	-5	2	0	1	-1	.977	8	3/S2	0.2

■ POP SCHRIVER Schriver, William Frederick b: 7/11/1865, Brooklyn, N.Y. d: 12/27/32, Brooklyn, N.Y. BR/TR, 5'9.5", 172 lbs. Deb: 4/29/1886

YEAR	TM/L	G	AB	R	H	2B	3B	HR	RBI	BB	SO	AVG	OBP	SLG	PRO+	BR	/A	RC	SB	CS	SBR	FA	FR	POS	TPR
1886	Bro-a	8	21	2	1	0	0	0		2		.048	.130	.048	-42	-3	-3	0	0			.667	0	/OC	-0.3
1888	Phi-N	40	134	15	26	5	2	1	23	7	21	.194	.250	.284	68	-4	-5	10	2			.870	-3	C/S3O	-0.6
1889	Phi-N	55	211	24	56	10	0	1	19	16	8	.265	.323	.327	77	-5	-8	25	5			.920	3	C/23	0.0
1890	Phi-N	57	223	37	61	9	6	0	35	22	15	.274	.339	.368	105	2	1	32	9			.916	-1	C1/32O	0.3
1891	Chi-N	27	90	15	30	1	4	1	21	10	9	.333	.412	.467	158	7	7	18	1			.964	2	C/1	1.0
1892	Chi-N	92	326	40	73	10	6	1	34	27	25	.224	.297	.301	82	-7	-7	31	4			.929	-9	CO	-1.0
1893	Chi-N	64	229	49	65	8	3	4	34	14	9	.284	.336	.397	98	-2	-1	33	4			.926	2	C/O	0.4
1894	Chi-N	96	349	55	96	12	3	3	47	29	21	.275	.341	.352	65	-17	-21	47	9			.923	-1	*C/S31	-1.0
1895	NY-N	24	92	16	29	2	1	1	16	9	10	.315	.382	.391	104	1	1	15	3			.898	-3	C/1	0.0
1897	Cin-N	61	178	29	54	12	4	1	30	19		.303	.374	.433	105	3	1	31	3			.959	-4	C	0.2
1898	Pit-N	95	315	25	72	15	3	0	32	23		.229	.285	.295	68	-14	-13	28	0			.957	-4	C/1	-0.8
1899	Pit-N	91	301	31	85	19	5	1	49	23		.282	.341	.389	100	-0	-0	44	4			.958	6	C/1	1.0
1900	*Pit-N	37	92	12	27	7	0	1	12	10		.293	.381	.402	115	2	2	14	0			.959	-5	C/1	0.0
1901	StL-N	53	166	17	45	7	3	1	23	12		.271	.335	.367	109	1	2	23	2			.971	4	C1	0.8
Total	14	800	2727	367	720	117	40	16	375	223	118	.264	.329	.354	89	-37	-45	351	46			.934	-15	C/1O32S	0.0

■ BOB SCHRODER Schroder, Robert James b: 12/30/44, Ridgefield, N.J. BL/TR, 6', 175 lbs. Deb: 4/20/65

YEAR	TM/L	G	AB	R	H	2B	3B	HR	RBI	BB	SO	AVG	OBP	SLG	PRO+	BR	/A	RC	SB	CS	SBR	FA	FR	POS	TPR
1965	SF-N	31	9	4	2	0	0	0	1	1	1	.222	.300	.222	48	-1	-1	1	0	0	0	1.000	10	/23	0.9
1966	SF-N	10	33	0	8	0	0	0	2	0	2	.242	.242	.242	34	-3	-3	2	0	0	0	.963	-5	/S	-0.8
1967	SF-N	62	135	20	31	4	0	0	7	15	15	.230	.307	.259	64	-6	-6	12	1	0	0	.993	-10	2/3	-1.5
1968	SF-N	35	44	5	7	1	1	0	2	7	3	.159	.288	.227	56	-2	-2	3	0	0	0	.960	-3	2/S3	-0.6
Total	4	138	221	29	48	5	1	0	12	23	21	.217	.294	.249	58	-11	-11	18	1	0	0	.989	-9	/2S3	-2.0

■ BILL SCHROEDER Schroeder, Alfred William b: 9/7/58, Baltimore, Md. BR/TR, 6'2", 200 lbs. Deb: 7/13/83

YEAR	TM/L	G	AB	R	H	2B	3B	HR	RBI	BB	SO	AVG	OBP	SLG	PRO+	BR	/A	RC	SB	CS	SBR	FA	FR	POS	TPR
1983	Mil-A	23	73	7	13	2	1	3	7	3	23	.178	.221	.356	60	-5	-4	6	0	1	-1	.980	-3	C	-0.7
1984	Mil-A	61	210	29	54	6	0	14	25	8	54	.257	.291	.486	115	2	3	27	0	1	-1	.987	-5	C/1D	0.0
1985	Mil-A	53	194	18	47	8	0	8	25	12	61	.242	.293	.407	90	-3	-3	22	0	1	-1	.987	-7	C/1D	-0.9
1986	Mil-A	64	217	32	46	14	0	7	19	9	59	.212	.263	.373	69	-9	-10	22	1	0	0	.995	-4	C1D	-1.2
1987	Mil-A	75	250	35	83	12	0	14	42	16	56	.332	.379	.548	138	15	14	52	5	2	0	.995	-6	C/1D	1.1
1988	Mil-A	41	122	9	19	2	0	5	10	6	36	.156	.208	.295	39	-10	-10	6	0	0	0	1.000	5	C1/D	-0.4
1989	Cal-A	41	138	16	28	2	0	6	15	3	44	.203	.220	.348	59	-8	-8	10	0	0	0	.991	10	C/1	0.3
1990	Cal-A	18	58	7	13	3	0	4	9	1	10	.224	.237	.483	98	-1	-1	5	0	0	0	1.000	2	C/1	0.2
Total	8	376	1262	153	303	49	1	61	152	58	343	.240	.282	.426	91	-20	-20	149	6	5	-1	.992	-8	C/1D	-1.6

■ RICK SCHU Schu, Rick Spencer b: 1/26/62, Philadelphia, Pa. BR/TR, 6', 170 lbs. Deb: 9/01/84

YEAR	TM/L	G	AB	R	H	2B	3B	HR	RBI	BB	SO	AVG	OBP	SLG	PRO+	BR	/A	RC	SB	CS	SBR	FA	FR	POS	TPR
1984	Phi-N	17	29	12	8	2	1	2	5	6	6	.276	.400	.621	180	3	3	8	0	0	0	.952	-0	3	0.3
1985	Phi-N	112	416	54	105	21	4	7	24	38	78	.252	.318	.373	90	-4	-6	49	8	6	-1	.933	-10	*3	-2.0
1986	Phi-N	92	208	32	57	10	1	8	25	18	44	.274	.338	.447	111	4	3	32	2	2	-1	.913	1	3	0.3
1987	Phi-N	92	196	24	46	6	3	7	23	20	36	.235	.312	.403	85	-4	-5	25	0	2	-1	.905	-1	31	-0.9
1988	Bal-A	89	270	22	69	9	4	4	20	21	49	.256	.316	.363	92	-4	-3	30	6	4	-1	.937	-12	3/1D	-1.6
1989	Bal-A	1	0	0	0	0	0	0	0	0	0	—	—	—	—	0	0	0	0	0	0	1.000	-0	/2	0.0
	Det-A	98	266	25	57	11	0	7	21	24	37	.214	.279	.335	74	-10	-9	24	1	2	-1	.934	-2	3/21SD	-1.2
	Yr	99	266	25	57	11	0	7	21	24	37	.214	.279	.335	74	-10	-9	24	1	2	-1	.934	-2	3/D21S	-1.2
1990	Cal-A	61	157	19	42	8	0	6	14	11	25	.268	.315	.433	110	1	1	21	0	0	0	.918	0	31/O2	0.1
1991	Phi-N	17	22	1	2	0	0	0	2	1	7	.091	.130	.091	-37	-4	-4	0	0	0	0	.667	-1	/31	-0.5
Total	8	579	1564	189	386	67	13	41	134	139	282	.247	.312	.385	92	-18	-19	189	17	16	-5	.927	-25	3/1D2OS	-5.5

■ HEINIE SCHUBLE Schuble, Henry George b: 11/1/06, Houston, Tex. BR/TR, 5'9", 152 lbs. Deb: 7/08/27

YEAR	TM/L	G	AB	R	H	2B	3B	HR	RBI	BB	SO	AVG	OBP	SLG	PRO+	BR	/A	RC	SB	CS	SBR	FA	FR	POS	TPR
1927	StL-N	65	218	29	56	6	2	4	28	7	27	.257	.283	.358	69	-10	-10	21	0			.915	-7	S	-1.1
1929	Det-A	92	258	35	60	11	7	2	28	19	23	.233	.288	.353	64	-15	-15	27	3	2	-0	.886	-10	S/3	-1.5
1932	Det-A	102	340	58	92	20	6	5	52	24	37	.271	.319	.409	84	-7	-9	45	14	5	1	.941	8	3S	0.6
1933	Det-A	49	96	12	21	4	1	0	6	5	17	.219	.257	.281	42	-8	-8	7	2	0	1	.951	1	3/S2	-0.5
1934	Det-A	11	15	2	4	2	0	0	2	1	4	.267	.313	.400	83	-0	-0	2	0	0	0	1.000	0	/S32	0.0
1935	Det-A	11	8	3	2	0	0	0	0	1	0	.250	.333	.250	55	-1	-0	1	0	0	0	.714	1	/32	0.1
1936	StL-N	2	0	0	0	0	0	0	0	0	0	—	—	—	—	0	0	0	0			.000	0	/3	0.0
Total	7	332	935	139	235	43	16	11	116	57	108	.251	.296	.367	70	-41	-44	103	19	7		.906	-6	S3/2	-2.4

■ WES SCHULMERICH Schulmerich, Edward Wesley b: 8/21/01, Hillsboro, Ore. d: 6/26/85, Corvallis, Ore. BR/TR, 5'11", 210 lbs. Deb: 5/01/31

YEAR	TM/L	G	AB	R	H	2B	3B	HR	RBI	BB	SO	AVG	OBP	SLG	PRO+	BR	/A	RC	SB	CS	SBR	FA	FR	POS	TPR
1931	Bos-N	95	327	36	101	17	7	2	43	28	30	.309	.363	.422	115	5	6	51	0			.966	-4	O	-0.4
1932	Bos-N	119	404	47	105	22	5	11	57	27	61	.260	.314	.421	99	-3	-1	55	5			.968	3	*O	-0.5
1933	Bos-N	29	85	10	21	6	1	1	13	5	10	.247	.289	.376	97	-1	-1	10	0			.980	1	O	-0.1
	Phi-N	97	365	53	122	19	4	8	59	32	45	.334	.394	.474	130	23	17	69	1			.977	-2	O	1.1
	Yr	126	450	63	143	25	5	9	72	37	55	.318	.375	.456	126	21	17	78	1			.978	-1	*O	1.0
1934	Phi-N	15	52	2	13	1	0	0	1	4	8	.250	.316	.269	51	-3	-4	4	0			.963	-1	O	-0.5
	Cin-N	74	209	21	55	8	3	5	19	22	43	.263	.333	.402	98	-1	-1	28	1			.976	-2	O	-0.5
	Yr	89	261	23	68	9	3	5	20	26	51	.261	.330	.375	88	-4	-4	33	1			.974	-3	O	-1.0
Total	4	429	1442	169	417	73	20	27	192	118	197	.289	.347	.424	109	19	17	217	7			.971	-6	O	-0.9

■ ART SCHULT Schult, Arthur William "Dutch" b: 6/20/28, Brooklyn, N.Y. BR/TR, 6'4", 220 lbs. Deb: 5/17/53

YEAR	TM/L	G	AB	R	H	2B	3B	HR	RBI	BB	SO	AVG	OBP	SLG	PRO+	BR	/A	RC	SB	CS	SBR	FA	FR	POS	TPR
1953	NY-A	7	0	3	0	0	0	0	0	0	0	—	—	—	—	0	0	0	0	0	0	.000	0	R	0.0
1956	Cin-N	5	7	3	3	0	0	0	2	1	1	.429	.500	.429	144	1	1	2	0	0	0	.000	-0	/O	0.0
1957	Cin-N	21	34	4	9	2	0	0	4	0	2	.265	.286	.324	59	-2	-2	3	0	0	0	1.000	1	/O	-0.2
	Was-A	77	247	30	65	14	0	4	35	14	30	.263	.305	.368	84	-6	-6	26	0	1	-1	.987	-1	1O	-1.1
1959	Chi-N	42	118	17	32	7	0	2	14	7	14	.271	.323	.381	88	-2	-2	13	0	0	0	.985	-4	1O	-0.8
1960	Chi-N	12	15	1	2	1	0	0	1	1	3	.133	.188	.200	6	-2	-2	1	0	0	0	1.000	-1	/O1	-0.3
Total	5	164	421	58	111	24	0	6	56	23	50	.264	.308	.363	81	-12	-11	44	0	1	-1	.987	-5	/1O	-2.4

■ FRANK SCHULTE Schulte, Frank M. "Wildfire" b: 9/17/1882, Cohocton, N.Y. d: 10/2/49, Oakland, Cal. BL/TR, 5'11", 170 lbs. Deb: 9/21/04

YEAR	TM/L	G	AB	R	H	2B	3B	HR	RBI	BB	SO	AVG	OBP	SLG	PRO+	BR	/A	RC	SB	CS	SBR	FA	FR	POS	TPR
1904	Chi-N	20	84	16	24	4	3	2	13	2		.286	.310	.476	142	3	3	13	1			.949	0	O	0.3
1905	Chi-N	123	493	67	135	15	14	1	47	32		.274	.326	.367	103	3	1	68	16			.981	-7	*O	-1.2
1906	*Chi-N	146	563	77	158	18	**13**	7	60	31		.281	.324	.396	118	13	10	85	25			.975	0	*O	0.3
1907	*Chi-N	97	342	44	98	14	7	2	32	22		.287	.339	.386	120	10	7	51	7			.973	-3	O	0.1
1908	*Chi-N	102	386	42	91	20	2	1	43	29		.236	.294	.306	88	-4	-5	40	15			.994	-6	*O	-1.9
1909	Chi-N	140	538	57	142	16	11	4	60	24		.264	.298	.357	101	-1	-2	64	23			.968	-13	*O	-2.4
1910	*Chi-N	151	559	93	168	29	15	**10**	68	39	57	.301	.349	.460	137	22	22	97	22			.968	-6	*O	0.9
1911	Chi-N	154	577	105	173	30	21	**21**	**107**	76	71	.300	.384	**.534**	**155**	**41**	**40**	**127**	23			.971	-5	*O	2.7
1912	Chi-N	139	553	90	146	27	11	12	64	53	70	.264	.336	.418	106	2	3	83	17			.952	-4	*O	-0.8
1913	Chi-N	132	497	85	138	28	6	9	68	39	68	.278	.336	.412	113	7	7	73	21			.956	-8	*O	-0.7
1914	Chi-N	137	465	54	112	22	7	5	61	39	55	.241	.306	.351	95	-4	-3	53	16			.954	-10	*O	-2.0
1915	Chi-N	151	550	66	137	20	6	12	62	49	68	.249	.313	.373	107	4	4	66	19	17	-5	.962	4	*O	-0.4
1916	Chi-N	72	230	31	68	11	1	5	27	20	35	.296	.352	.417	123	9	7	37	9			.951	-3	O	0.1
	Pit-N	55	177	12	45	5	3	0	14	17	19	.254	.323	.316	96	-0	-0	20	5			.968	-2	O	-0.5
	Yr	127	407	43	113	16	4	5	41	37	54	.278	.339	.373	111	9	6	56	14			.958	-5	*O	-0.4
1917	Pit-N	30	103	11	22	5	1	0	7	10	14	.214	.283	.282	71	-3	-3	9	5			.963	-0	O	-0.6
	Phi-N	64	149	21	32	10	0	1	15	16	22	.215	.299	.302	81	-2	-3	14	4			.923	-10	O	-1.7
	Yr	94	252	32	54	15	1	1	22	26	36	.214	.293	.294	77	-6	-7	23	9			.943	-10	O	-2.3
1918	Was-A	93	267	35	77	14	3	0	44	47	36	.288	.406	.363	135	13	14	41	5			.969	1	O	1.2
Total	15	1806	6533	906	1766	288	124	92	792	545	515	.270	.332	.395	114	115	100	942	233	17		.966	-70	*O	-6.6

■ FRED SCHULTE Schulte, Fred William "Fritz" (b: Fred William Schult) b: 1/13/01, Belvidere, Ill. d: 5/20/83, Belvidere, Ill. BR/TR, 6'1", 183 lbs. Deb: 4/15/27

YEAR	TM/L	G	AB	R	H	2B	3B	HR	RBI	BB	SO	AVG	OBP	SLG	PRO+	BR	/A	RC	SB	CS	SBR	FA	FR	POS	TPR
1927	StL-A	60	189	32	60	16	5	3	34	20	14	.317	.383	.503	124	7	6	34	5	3	-0	.916	-3	O	0.1
1928	StL-A	146	556	90	159	44	6	7	85	51	60	.286	.347	.424	99	1	-2	83	6	5	-1	.973	17	*O	0.5
1929	StL-A	121	446	63	137	24	5	3	71	59	44	.307	.389	.404	101	5	2	74	8	3	1	**.989**	13	*O	0.7
1930	StL-A	113	392	59	109	23	5	5	62	41	44	.278	.348	.401	86	-6	-8	55	12	8	-1	.966	-2	O/1	-1.7
1931	StL-A	134	553	100	168	32	7	9	65	56	49	.304	.369	.436	107	9	6	89	6	8	-3	.971	6	*O	-0.1
1932	StL-A	146	565	106	166	35	6	9	73	71	44	.294	.373	.425	100	6	1	90	5	9	-4	.986	0	*O/1	-1.0
1933	*Was-A	144	550	98	162	30	7	5	87	61	27	.295	.366	.402	104	3	4	81	10	12	-4	.980	16	*O	0.8
1934	Was-A	136	524	72	156	32	6	3	73	53	34	.298	.363	.399	100	-2	1	76	3	7	-3	.986	-1	*O	-0.8
1935	Was-A	76	226	33	60	6	4	2	23	26	22	.265	.344	.354	83	-6	-5	28	0	3	-2	.980	-8	O	-1.5
1936	Pit-N	74	238	28	62	7	3	1	17	20	20	.261	.320	.328	73	-8	-9	26	1			.977	-3	O	-1.4
1937	Pit-N	29	20	5	2	0	0	0	3	4	3	.100	.280	.100	7	-2	-2	1	0			.800	-1	/O	-0.4
Total	11	1179	4259	686	1241	249	54	47	593	462	361	.291	.362	.408	98	6	-6	637	56	58		.976	35	*O/1	-4.8

■ HAM SCHULTE Schulte, Herman Joseph (b: Herman Joseph Schultehenrich) b: 9/1/12, St.Charles, Mo. BR/TR, 5'8.5", 158 lbs. Deb: 4/16/40 F

YEAR	TM/L	G	AB	R	H	2B	3B	HR	RBI	BB	SO	AVG	OBP	SLG	PRO+	BR	/A	RC	SB	CS	SBR	FA	FR	POS	TPR
1940	Phi-N	120	436	44	103	18	2	1	21	32	30	.236	.288	.294	63	-23	-21	40	3			**.980**	-10	*2/S	-2.4

■ JOHNNY SCHULTE Schulte, John Clement b: 9/8/1896, Fredericktown, Mo. d: 6/28/78, St.Louis, Mo. BL/TR, 5'11", 190 lbs. Deb: 4/18/23 C

YEAR	TM/L	G	AB	R	H	2B	3B	HR	RBI	BB	SO	AVG	OBP	SLG	PRO+	BR	/A	RC	SB	CS	SBR	FA	FR	POS	TPR
1923	StL-A	7	3	1	0	0	0	0	1	4	0	.000	.571	.000	56	0	0	1	0	0	0	1.000	1	/C1	0.1
1927	StL-N	64	156	35	45	8	2	9	32	47	19	.288	.456	.538	160	17	16	41	1			.956	3	C	2.2
1928	Phi-N	65	113	14	28	2	2	4	17	15	12	.248	.336	.407	90	-1	-2	16	0			.949	-5	C	-0.5
1929	Chi-N	31	69	6	18	3	0	0	9	7	11	.261	.329	.304	58	-4	-4	7	0			.978	-0	C	-0.2
1932	StL-A	15	24	2	5	2	0	0	3	1	6	.208	.240	.292	35	-2	-2	2	0	0	0	.864	-1	/C	-0.3
	Bos-N	10	9	1	2	0	0	1	2	2	1	.222	.364	.556	149	1	1	2	0			1.000	1	C	0.1
Total	5	192	374	59	98	15	4	14	64	76	49	.262	.388	.436	112	10	9	68	1	0		.957	-2	C/1	1.4

■ JACK SCHULTE Schulte, John Herman Frank b: 11/15/1881, Cincinnati, Ohio d: 8/17/75, Roseville, Mich. BR/TR, 5'9", 180 lbs. Deb: 8/19/06

YEAR	TM/L	G	AB	R	H	2B	3B	HR	RBI	BB	SO	AVG	OBP	SLG	PRO+	BR	/A	RC	SB	CS	SBR	FA	FR	POS	TPR
1906	Bos-N	2	7	0	0	0	0	0	0	0		.000	.000	.000	-99	-2	-2	0	0			1.000	-1	/S	-0.3

■ LEN SCHULTE Schulte, Leonard Bernard (b: Leonard Bernard Schultehenrich) b: 12/5/16, St.Charles, Mo. d: 5/6/86, Orlando, Fla. BR/TR, 5'10", 160 lbs. Deb: 9/27/44 F

YEAR	TM/L	G	AB	R	H	2B	3B	HR	RBI	BB	SO	AVG	OBP	SLG	PRO+	BR	/A	RC	SB	CS	SBR	FA	FR	POS	TPR
1944	StL-A	1	0	0	0	0	0	0	0	1	0	—	1.000	—	188	0	0	0	0	0	0	.000	0	H	0.0
1945	StL-A	119	430	37	106	16	1	0	36	24	35	.247	.286	.288	64	-19	-21	36	0	3	-2	.961	-8	32S	-2.9
1946	StL-A	4	5	1	2	0	0	0	2	0	0	.400	.400	.400	118	0	0	0	0	0	0	1.000	1	/23	0.1
Total	3	124	435	38	108	16	1	0	38	25	35	.248	.289	.290	65	-18	-21	37	0	3	-2	.962	-7	/32S	-2.8

■ HOWIE SCHULTZ Schultz, Howard Henry "Stretch" or "Steeple" b: 7/3/22, St.Paul, Minn. BR/TR, 6'6", 200 lbs. Deb: 8/16/43

YEAR	TM/L	G	AB	R	H	2B	3B	HR	RBI	BB	SO	AVG	OBP	SLG	PRO+	BR	/A	RC	SB	CS	SBR	FA	FR	POS	TPR
1943	Bro-N	45	182	20	49	12	0	1	34	6	24	.269	.300	.352	88	-3	-3	18	3			.986	2	1	-0.5
1944	Bro-N	138	526	59	134	32	3	11	83	24	67	.255	.290	.390	92	-9	-8	55	6			.988	-0	*1	-1.5
1945	Bro-N	39	142	18	34	8	2	1	19	10	14	.239	.294	.345	78	-5	-5	14	2			.984	3	1	-0.4
1946	Bro-N	90	249	27	63	14	1	3	27	16	34	.253	.298	.353	84	-6	-6	26	2			.989	5	1	-0.5
1947	Bro-N	2	1	0	0	0	0	0	0	0	0	.000	.000	.000	-96	-0	-0	0	0			1.000	-0	/1	0.0
	Phi-N	114	403	30	90	19	1	6	35	21	70	.223	.264	.320	56	-27	-26	33	0			.993	-1	*1	-3.0
	Yr	116	404	30	90	19	1	6	35	21	70	.223	.263	.319	56	-28	-26	32	0			.993	-1	*1	-3.0
1948	Phi-N	6	13	0	1	0	0	0	1	1	2	.077	.143	.077	-40	-3	-2	0	0			1.000	0	/1	-0.2
	Cin-N	36	72	9	12	0	0	2	9	4	7	.167	.211	.250	25	-8	-7	4	2			.982	-3	1	-1.1
	Yr	42	85	9	13	0	0	2	10	5	9	.153	.200	.224	15	-10	-10	4	2			.984	-3	1	-1.3
Total	6	470	1588	163	383	85	7	24	208	82	218	.241	.281	.349	75	-61	-58	150	15			.989	6	1	-7.2

■ JOHN SCHULTZ Schultz, John b: St.Louis, Mo. Deb: 8/07/1891

YEAR	TM/L	G	AB	R	H	2B	3B	HR	RBI	BB	SO	AVG	OBP	SLG	PRO+	BR	/A	RC	SB	CS	SBR	FA	FR	POS	TPR
1891	StL-a	1	2	0	0	0	0	0	0	0	0	.000	.000	.000	-87	-1	-1	0	0			1.000	0	/C	0.0

■ JOE SCHULTZ Schultz, Joseph Charles Jr. "Dode" b: 8/29/18, Chicago, Ill. BL/TR, 5'11", 184 lbs. Deb: 9/27/39 FMC

YEAR	TM/L	G	AB	R	H	2B	3B	HR	RBI	BB	SO	AVG	OBP	SLG	PRO+	BR	/A	RC	SB	CS	SBR	FA	FR	POS	TPR
1939	Pit-N	4	14	3	4	2	0	0	2	2	0	.286	.375	.429	117	0	0	2	0			1.000	1	/C	0.1
1940	Pit-N	16	36	2	7	0	1	0	4	2	1	.194	.237	.250	35	-3	-3	2	0			.917	-3	C	-0.6
1941	Pit-N	2	2	1	1	0	0	0	0	0	0	.500	.500	.500	183	0	0	1	0			.000	0	/C	0.0
1943	StL-A	46	92	6	22	5	0	0	8	9	8	.239	.307	.293	74	-3	-3	8	0	1	-1	.979	-5	C	-0.8
1944	StL-A	3	8	1	2	0	0	0	0	0	1	.250	.250	.250	41	-1	-1	1	0	0	0	.818	-1	/C	-0.1
1945	StL-A	41	44	1	13	2	0	0	8	3	1	.295	.340	.341	93	-0	-0	5	0	0	0	.941	0	/C	0.0
1946	StL-A	42	57	1	22	4	0	0	14	11	2	.386	.485	.456	156	6	5	14	0	0	0	1.000	-5	C	0.2
1947	StL-A	43	38	3	7	0	0	1	1	4	5	.184	.262	.263	45	-3	-3	3	0	0	0	.000	0	H	-0.3
1948	StL-A	43	37	0	7	0	0	0	9	6	3	.189	.302	.189	32	-3	-4	2	0	0	0	.000	0	H	-0.3
Total	9	240	328	18	85	13	1	1	46	37	21	.259	.334	.314	81	-7	-8	38	0	1		.964	-12	/C	-1.8

■ JOE SCHULTZ Schultz, Joseph Charles Sr. "Germany" b: 7/24/1893, Pittsburgh, Pa. d: 4/13/41, Columbia, S.C. BR/TR, 5'11.5", 172 lbs. Deb: 9/28/12 F

YEAR	TM/L	G	AB	R	H	2B	3B	HR	RBI	BB	SO	AVG	OBP	SLG	PRO+	BR	/A	RC	SB	CS	SBR	FA	FR	POS	TPR
1912	Bos-N	4	12	1	3	1	0	0	4	0	2	.250	.250	.333	58	-1	-1	1	0			.824	-0	/2	-0.1
1913	Bos-N	9	18	2	4	0	0	0	1	2	7	.222	.333	.222	59	-1	-1	2	0			1.000	0	/O2	-0.1
1915	Bro-N	56	120	13	35	3	2	0	4	10	18	.292	.346	.350	109	2	1	14	3	4	-2	.894	-4	3/S	-0.3
	Chi-N	7	8	1	2	0	0	0	3	0	2	.250	.250	.250	51	-0	-0	1	0			.857	0	/2	0.0
	Yr	63	128	14	37	3	2	0	7	10	20	.289	.341	.344	106	1	1	15	3	4	-2	.894	-3	3/2S	-0.3
1916	Pit-N	77	204	18	53	8	2	0	22	7	14	.260	.298	.319	88	-3	-3	22	6			.840	-15	23/OS	-1.9
1919	StL-N	88	229	24	58	9	1	2	21	11	7	.253	.287	.328	90	-5	-3	22	4			1.000	-7	O/23	-1.4

YEAR	TM/L	G	AB	R	H	2B	3B	HR	RBI	BB	SO	AVG	OBP	SLG	PRO+	BR	/A	RC	SB	CS	SBR	FA	FR	POS	TPR
1920	StL-N	99	320	38	84	5	5	0	32	21	11	.262	.308	.309	81	-9	-8	31	5	4	-1	.945	-4	O	-1.9
1921	StL-N	92	275	37	85	20	3	6	45	15	11	.309	.347	.469	116	5	6	44	4	3	-1	.977	-2	O/31	-0.1
1922	StL-N	112	344	50	108	13	4	2	64	19	10	.314	.350	.392	96	-5	-2	48	3	1	0	.976	2	O	-0.6
1923	StL-N	2	7	0	2	0	0	0	1	1	0	.286	.375	.286	78	-0	-0	1	0	0	0	1.000	0	/O	0.0
1924	StL-N	12	12	0	2	0	0	0	2	3	0	.167	.333	.167	39	-1	-1	1	0	0	0	1.000	-1	/O	-0.2
	Phi-N	88	284	35	80	15	1	5	29	20	18	.282	.329	.394	83	-3	-8	37	6	2	1	.960	-6	O	-1.8
	Yr	100	296	35	82	15	1	5	31	23	18	.277	.329	.385	82	-4	-8	38	6	2	1	.960	-7	O	-2.0
1925	Phi-N	24	64	10	22	6	0	0	8	4	1	.344	.382	.438	100	1	0	10	1	1	-0	.923	-2	O	-0.3
	Cin-N	33	62	6	20	3	1	0	13	3	1	.323	.354	.403	95	-1	-0	9	3	1	0	.950	-4	O/2	-0.5
	Yr	57	126	16	42	9	1	0	21	7	2	.333	.368	.421	99	0	-0	19	4	2	0	.932	-6	O/2	-0.8
Total	11	703	1959	235	558	83	19	15	249	116	102	.285	.327	.370	93	-21	-20	242	35	16		.966	-43	O/321S	-9.2

■ JEFF SCHULZ Schulz, Jeffrey Alan b: 6/2/61, Evansville, Ind. BL/TR, 6'1", 190 lbs. Deb: 9/02/89

YEAR	TM/L	G	AB	R	H	2B	3B	HR	RBI	BB	SO	AVG	OBP	SLG	PRO+	BR	/A	RC	SB	CS	SBR	FA	FR	POS	TPR
1989	KC-A	7	9	0	2	0	0	0	1	0	2	.222	.222	.222	26	-1	-1	0	0	0	0	1.000	-0	/O	-0.1
1990	KC-A	30	66	5	17	5	1	0	6	6	13	.258	.319	.364	92	-1	-1	7	0	0	0	.943	-3	O/D	-0.4
1991	Pit-N	3	3	0	0	0	0	0	0	0	2	.000	.000	.000	-99	-1	-1	0	0	0	0	.000	0	/H	-0.1
Total	3	40	78	5	19	5	1	0	7	6	17	.244	.298	.333	77	-3	-2	8	0	0	0	.951	-4	/OD	-0.6

■ BILL SCHUSTER Schuster, William Charles "Broadway Bill" b: 8/4/12, Buffalo, N.Y. d: 6/28/87, ElMonte, Cal. BR/TR, 5'9", 164 lbs. Deb: 9/29/37

YEAR	TM/L	G	AB	R	H	2B	3B	HR	RBI	BB	SO	AVG	OBP	SLG	PRO+	BR	/A	RC	SB	CS	SBR	FA	FR	POS	TPR
1937	Pit-N	3	6	2	3	0	0	0	1	1	0	.500	.571	.500	193	1	1	2	0			1.000	1	/S	0.2
1939	Bos-N	2	3	0	0	0	0	0	0	0	1	.000	.000	.000	-99	-1	-1	0	0			.833	-0	/S3	-0.1
1943	Chi-N	13	51	3	15	2	1	0	0	3	2	.294	.333	.373	105	0	0	6	0			.977	7	S	0.8
1944	Chi-N	60	154	14	34	7	1	1	14	12	16	.221	.277	.299	62	-8	-8	12	4			.946	-4	S/2	-1.0
1945	*Chi-N	45	47	8	9	2	1	0	2	7	4	.191	.296	.277	61	-2	-2	4	2			.949	8	S/23	0.7
Total	5	123	261	27	61	11	3	1	17	23	23	.234	.296	.310	72	-10	-10	23	6			.954	11	/S23	0.6

■ RANDY SCHWARTZ Schwartz, Douglas Randall b: 2/9/44, Los Angeles, Cal. BL/TL, 6'3", 230 lbs. Deb: 9/08/65

YEAR	TM/L	G	AB	R	H	2B	3B	HR	RBI	BB	SO	AVG	OBP	SLG	PRO+	BR	/A	RC	SB	CS	SBR	FA	FR	POS	TPR
1965	KC-A	6	7	0	2	0	0	0	1	0	4	.286	.286	.286	64	-0	-0	1	0	0	0	1.000	1	/1	0.0
1966	KC-A	10	11	0	1	0	0	0	1	1	3	.091	.167	.091	-24	-2	-2	0	0	0	0	1.000	-0	/1	-0.2
Total	2	16	18	0	3	0	0	0	2	1	7	.167	.211	.167	10	-2	-2	1	0	0	0	1.000	0	/1	-0.2

■ BILL SCHWARTZ Schwartz, William August "Pop" or "Scooper Bill" b: 4/3/1864, Jamestown, Ky. d: 12/22/40, Newport, Ky. BR/TR, 6'1", 195 lbs. Deb: 5/03/1883

YEAR	TM/L	G	AB	R	H	2B	3B	HR	RBI	BB	SO	AVG	OBP	SLG	PRO+	BR	/A	RC	SB	CS	SBR	FA	FR	POS	TPR
1883	Col-a	2	4	0	1	0	0	0		0		.250	.250	.250	67	-0	-0	0				.600	-1	/1C	-0.1
1884	Cin-U	29	106	14	25	4	0	1		3		.236	.257	.302	82	-1	-3	8				.837	-4	C/O3	-0.4
Total	2	31	110	14	26	4	0	1		3		.236	.257	.300	81	-1	-3	9				.828	-6	/CO31	-0.5

■ BILL SCHWARTZ Schwartz, William Charles "Blab" b: 4/22/1884, Cleveland, Ohio d: 8/29/61, Nashville, Tenn. BR/TR, 6'2", 185 lbs. Deb: 5/02/04

YEAR	TM/L	G	AB	R	H	2B	3B	HR	RBI	BB	SO	AVG	OBP	SLG	PRO+	BR	/A	RC	SB	CS	SBR	FA	FR	POS	TPR
1904	Cle-A	24	86	5	13	2	0	0	0	0		.151	.151	.174	3	-9	-9	3	4			.980	-4	1/3	-1.6

■ BILL SCHWARZ Schwarz, William De Witt b: 1/30/1891, Birmingham, Ala. d: 6/24/49, Jacksonville, Fla TR , Deb: 8/20/14

YEAR	TM/L	G	AB	R	H	2B	3B	HR	RBI	BB	SO	AVG	OBP	SLG	PRO+	BR	/A	RC	SB	CS	SBR	FA	FR	POS	TPR
1914	NY-A	1	1	0	0	0	0	0	0	0	1	.000	.000	.000	-99	-0	-0	0	0			1.000	0	/C	0.0

■ AL SCHWEITZER Schweitzer, Albert Caspar "Cheese" b: 12/23/1882, Cleveland, Ohio d: 1/27/69, Newark, Ohio BR/TR, 5'6", 170 lbs. Deb: 4/30/08

YEAR	TM/L	G	AB	R	H	2B	3B	HR	RBI	BB	SO	AVG	OBP	SLG	PRO+	BR	/A	RC	SB	CS	SBR	FA	FR	POS	TPR
1908	StL-A	64	182	22	53	4	2	1	14	20		.291	.374	.352	135	8	8	27	6			.952	5	O	1.2
1909	StL-A	27	76	7	17	2	0	0	2	5		.224	.298	.250	79	-2	-2	6	3			.933	-3	O	-0.6
1910	StL-A	113	379	37	87	11	2	2	37	36		.230	.303	.285	90	-6	-4	40	26			.937	-4	*O	-1.5
1911	StL-A	76	237	31	51	11	4	0	34	43		.215	.338	.295	80	-6	-5	28	12			.934	-1	O	-0.9
Total	4	280	874	97	208	28	8	3	87	104		.238	.327	.299	95	-6	-2	101	47			.940	-3	O	-1.8

■ PI SCHWERT Schwert, Pius Louis b: 11/22/1892, Angola, N.Y. d: 3/11/41, Washington, D.C. BR/TR, 5'10.5", 160 lbs. Deb: 10/06/14

YEAR	TM/L	G	AB	R	H	2B	3B	HR	RBI	BB	SO	AVG	OBP	SLG	PRO+	BR	/A	RC	SB	CS	SBR	FA	FR	POS	TPR
1914	NY-A	2	5	0	0	0	0	0	0	2	2	.000	.286	.000	-13	-1	-1	0	0			.909	1	/C	0.0
1915	NY-A	9	18	6	5	3	0	0	6	1	6	.278	.316	.444	128	0	0	3	0			.972	0	/C	0.1
Total	2	11	23	6	5	3	0	0	6	3	8	.217	.308	.348	97	-0	-0	3	0			.957	1	/C	0.1

■ ART SCHWIND Schwind, Arthur Edwin b: 11/4/1889, Ft.Wayne, Ind. d: 1/13/68, Sullivan, Ill. BB/TR, 5'8", 150 lbs. Deb: 10/03/12

YEAR	TM/L	G	AB	R	H	2B	3B	HR	RBI	BB	SO	AVG	OBP	SLG	PRO+	BR	/A	RC	SB	CS	SBR	FA	FR	POS	TPR
1912	Bos-N	1	2	0	1	0	0	0	0	0	0	.500	.500	.500	171	0	0	0	0			.000	0	/3	0.0

■ JERRY SCHYPINSKI Schypinski, Gerald Albert b: 9/16/31, Detroit, Mich. BL/TR, 5'10", 170 lbs. Deb: 8/31/55

YEAR	TM/L	G	AB	R	H	2B	3B	HR	RBI	BB	SO	AVG	OBP	SLG	PRO+	BR	/A	RC	SB	CS	SBR	FA	FR	POS	TPR
1955	KC-A	22	69	7	15	2	0	0	5	1	6	.217	.229	.246	27	-7	-7	4	0	0	0	.932	-2	S/2	-0.8

■ MIKE SCIOSCIA Scioscia, Michael Lorri b: 11/27/58, Upper Darby, Pa. BL/TR, 6'2", 220 lbs. Deb: 4/20/80

YEAR	TM/L	G	AB	R	H	2B	3B	HR	RBI	BB	SO	AVG	OBP	SLG	PRO+	BR	/A	RC	SB	CS	SBR	FA	FR	POS	TPR
1980	LA-N	54	134	8	34	5	1	1	8	12	9	.254	.315	.328	81	-4	-3	15	1	0	0	.992	3	C	0.2
1981	*LA-N	93	290	27	80	10	0	2	29	36	18	.276	.358	.331	100	-0	1	34	0	2	-1	.987	-3	C	0.0
1982	LA-N	129	365	31	80	11	1	5	38	44	31	.219	.305	.296	70	-15	-13	34	2	0	1	.986	-7	*C	-1.6
1983	LA-N	12	35	3	11	3	0	1	7	5	2	.314	.400	.486	145	2	2	7	0	0	0	1.000	-3	C	0.0
1984	LA-N	114	341	29	93	18	0	5	38	52	26	.273	.371	.370	110	6	6	48	2	1	0	.985	14	*C	2.6
1985	*LA-N	141	429	47	127	26	3	7	53	77	21	.296	.409	.420	136	22	24	78	3	3	-1	.986	2	*C	3.3
1986	LA-N	122	374	36	94	18	1	5	26	62	23	.251	.362	.345	103	0	4	49	3	3	-1	.982	-1	*C	0.9
1987	LA-N	142	461	44	122	26	1	6	38	55	23	.265	.344	.364	90	-7	-5	58	7	4	-0	.989	11	*C	1.4
1988	*LA-N	130	408	29	105	18	0	3	35	38	31	.257	.321	.324	88	-7	-6	40	0	3	-2	.991	8	*C	1.0
1989	LA-N★	133	408	40	102	16	0	10	44	52	29	.250	.339	.363	102	1	2	52	0	2	-1	.988	18	*C	2.7
1990	LA-N★	135	435	46	115	25	0	12	66	55	31	.264	.351	.405	110	5	7	62	4	1	1	.989	5	*C	2.1
1991	LA-N	119	345	39	91	16	2	8	40	47	32	.264	.357	.391	113	6	7	51	4	3	-1	.990	9	*C	2.1
1992	LA-N	117	348	19	77	6	3	3	24	32	31	.221	.289	.282	63	-17	-16	28	3	2	-0	.988	11	*C	0.0
Total	13	1441	4373	398	1131	198	12	68	446	567	307	.259	.347	.356	99	-7	9	555	29	24	-6	.988	67	*C	14.7

■ LOU SCOFFIC Scoffic, Louis "Weaser" b: 5/20/13, Herrin, Ill. BR/TR, 5'10", 182 lbs. Deb: 4/16/36

YEAR	TM/L	G	AB	R	H	2B	3B	HR	RBI	BB	SO	AVG	OBP	SLG	PRO+	BR	/A	RC	SB	CS	SBR	FA	FR	POS	TPR
1936	StL-N	4	7	2	3	0	0	0	2	1	2	.429	.500	.429	153	1	1	2	0			.875	-0	/O	0.0

■ DARYL SCONIERS Sconiers, Daryl Anthony b: 10/3/58, San Bernardino, Cal. BL/TL, 6'2", 195 lbs. Deb: 9/13/81

YEAR	TM/L	G	AB	R	H	2B	3B	HR	RBI	BB	SO	AVG	OBP	SLG	PRO+	BR	/A	RC	SB	CS	SBR	FA	FR	POS	TPR
1981	Cal-A	15	52	6	14	1	1	1	7	1	10	.269	.283	.385	91	-1	-1	6	0	0	0	1.000	1	1/D	-0.1
1982	Cal-A	12	13	0	2	0	0	0	2	2	1	.154	.267	.154	19	-1	-1	0	0	0	0	1.000	0	/1D	-0.1
1983	Cal-A	106	314	49	86	19	3	8	46	17	41	.274	.311	.430	102	-0	0	39	4	2	0	.986	-5	1D/O	-0.7
1984	Cal-A	57	160	14	39	4	0	4	17	13	17	.244	.301	.344	78	-5	-5	15	1	2	-1	.990	-1	1/D	-0.9
1985	Cal-A	44	98	14	28	6	1	2	12	15	18	.286	.381	.429	122	3	3	17	2	1	0	.973	-1	D/1	0.2
Total	5	234	637	83	169	30	5	15	84	48	87	.265	.317	.399	97	-4	-3	77	7	5	-1	.989	-6	1/DO	-1.6

■ SCOTT Scott Deb: 7/16/1884

YEAR	TM/L	G	AB	R	H	2B	3B	HR	RBI	BB	SO	AVG	OBP	SLG	PRO+	BR	/A	RC	SB	CS	SBR	FA	FR	POS	TPR
1884	Bal-U	13	53	10	12	1	1	1		2		.226	.255	.340	90	-0	-1	5				.909	-2	O/3	-0.3

■ TONY SCOTT Scott, Anthony b: 9/18/51, Cincinnati, Ohio BB/TR, 6', 175 lbs. Deb: 9/01/73

YEAR	TM/L	G	AB	R	H	2B	3B	HR	RBI	BB	SO	AVG	OBP	SLG	PRO+	BR	/A	RC	SB	CS	SBR	FA	FR	POS	TPR
1973	Mon-N	11	1	2	0	0	0	0	0	0	1	.000	.000	.000	-97	-0	-0	0	0	0	0	.000	1	/O	0.0
1974	Mon-N	19	7	2	2	0	0	0	1	1	3	.286	.375	.286	82	-0	-0	1	1	1	-0	1.000	1	O	0.0
1975	Mon-N	92	143	19	26	4	2	0	11	12	38	.182	.259	.238	37	-12	-13	8	5	6	-2	.962	7	O	-1.0
1977	StL-N	95	292	38	85	16	3	3	41	33	48	.291	.369	.397	107	3	4	42	13	10	-2	.996	9	O	0.8
1978	StL-N	96	219	28	50	5	2	1	14	14	41	.228	.281	.283	59	-12	-12	16	5	6	-2	.946	-2	O	-1.9

YEAR	TM/L	G	AB	R	H	2B	3B	HR	RBI	BB	SO	AVG	OBP	SLG	PRO+	BR	/A	RC	SB	CS	SBR	FA	FR	POS	TPR
1979	StL-N	153	587	69	152	22	10	6	68	34	92	.259	.305	.361	80	-16	-17	62	37	17	1	.984	10	*O	-1.2
1980	StL-N	143	415	51	104	19	3	0	28	35	68	.251	.310	.311	72	-14	-16	40	22	10	1	**.997**	-8	*O	-2.9
1981	StL-N	45	176	21	40	5	2	2	17	5	22	.227	.253	.313	58	-10	-10	12	10	7	-1	1.000	4	O	-0.9
	*Hou-N	55	225	28	66	13	2	2	22	15	32	.293	.338	.396	113	2	3	31	8	3	1	.985	-1	O	0.1
	Yr	100	401	49	106	18	4	4	39	20	54	.264	.301	.359	88	-8	-7	43	18	10	-1	.992	3	O	-0.8
1982	Hou-N	132	460	43	110	16	3	1	29	15	56	.239	.265	.293	61	-27	-23	35	18	4	3	.982	-9	*O	-3.5
1983	Hou-N	80	186	20	42	6	1	2	17	11	39	.226	.269	.301	62	-11	-9	16	5	4	-1	1.000	-1	O	-1.3
1984	Hou-N	25	21	2	4	1	0	0	0	4	3	.190	.320	.238	63	-1	-1	2	0	0	0	1.000	-1	/O	-0.2
	Mon-N	45	71	8	18	4	0	0	5	7	21	.254	.321	.310	81	-2	-2	7	1	1	-0	1.000	-2	O	-0.4
	Yr	70	92	10	22	5	0	0	5	11	24	.239	.320	.293	78	-3	-2	9	1	1	-0	1.000	-3	O	-0.6
Total	11	991	2803	331	699	111	28	17	253	186	464	.249	.300	.327	75	-100	-96	272	125	69	-4	.986	9	O	-12.4

■ DONNIE SCOTT Scott, Donald Malcolm b: 8/16/61, Dunedin, Fla. BB/TR, 5'11", 185 lbs. Deb: 9/30/83

YEAR	TM/L	G	AB	R	H	2B	3B	HR	RBI	BB	SO	AVG	OBP	SLG	PRO+	BR	/A	RC	SB	CS	SBR	FA	FR	POS	TPR
1983	Tex-A	2	4	0	0	0	0	0	0	0	0	.000	.000	.000	-99	-1	-1	0	0	0	0	1.000	1	/C	0.0
1984	Tex-A	81	235	16	52	9	0	3	20	20	44	.221	.282	.298	59	-12	-13	20	0	1	-1	.974	4	C	-0.6
1985	Sea-A	80	185	18	41	13	0	4	23	15	41	.222	.280	.357	72	-7	-7	19	1	1	-0	.981	-7	C	-1.2
1991	Cin-N	10	19	0	3	0	0	0	0	0	2	.158	.158	.158	-11	-3	-3	0	0	0	0	1.000	-3	/C	-0.6
Total	4	173	443	34	96	22	0	7	43	35	87	.217	.274	.314	60	-23	-25	39	1	2	-1	.977	-5	C	-2.4

■ PETE SCOTT Scott, Floyd John b: 12/21/1898, Woodland, Cal. d: 5/3/53, Daly City, Cal. BR/TR, 5'11.5", 175 lbs. Deb: 4/13/26

YEAR	TM/L	G	AB	R	H	2B	3B	HR	RBI	BB	SO	AVG	OBP	SLG	PRO+	BR	/A	RC	SB	CS	SBR	FA	FR	POS	TPR
1926	Chi-N	77	189	34	54	13	1	3	34	22	31	.286	.363	.413	107	3	2	29	3			.968	-1	O/3	-0.2
1927	Chi-N	71	156	28	49	18	1	0	21	19	18	.314	.392	.442	123	6	6	27	1			.986	-2	O	0.1
1928	Pit-N	60	177	33	55	10	4	5	33	18	14	.311	.378	.497	122	7	6	33	1			.979	2	O/1	0.5
Total	3	208	522	95	158	41	6	8	88	59	63	.303	.377	.450	117	15	13	88	5			.976	-1	O/13	0.4

■ GARY SCOTT Scott, Gary Thomas b: 8/22/68, New Rochelle, N.Y. BR/TR, 6', 175 lbs. Deb: 4/09/91

YEAR	TM/L	G	AB	R	H	2B	3B	HR	RBI	BB	SO	AVG	OBP	SLG	PRO+	BR	/A	RC	SB	CS	SBR	FA	FR	POS	TPR
1991	Chi-N	31	79	8	13	3	0	1	5	13	14	.165	.305	.241	53	-4	-5	6	0	1	-1	.969	2	3	-0.4
1992	Chi-N	36	96	8	15	2	0	2	11	5	14	.156	.198	.240	23	-10	-10	4	0	1	-1	.937	-2	3/S	-1.3
Total	2	67	175	16	28	5	0	3	16	18	28	.160	.250	.240	38	-14	-15	10	0	2	-1	.953	0	/3S	-1.7

■ GEORGE SCOTT Scott, George Charles "Boomer" b: 3/23/44, Greenville, Miss. BR/TR, 6'2", 215 lbs. Deb: 4/12/66

YEAR	TM/L	G	AB	R	H	2B	3B	HR	RBI	BB	SO	AVG	OBP	SLG	PRO+	BR	/A	RC	SB	CS	SBR	FA	FR	POS	TPR
1966	Bos-A★	162	601	73	147	18	7	27	90	65	152	.245	.326	.433	105	12	5	81	4	0	1	.991	3	*1/3	-0.2
1967	*Bos-A	159	565	74	171	21	7	19	82	63	119	.303	.377	.465	136	34	29	97	10	8	-2	.987	-5	*1/3	1.4
1968	Bos-A	124	350	23	60	14	0	3	25	26	88	.171	.239	.237	42	-23	-26	18	3	5	-2	.987	1	*1/3	-3.9
1969	Bos-A	152	549	63	139	14	5	16	52	61	74	.253	.332	.384	95	-0	-4	69	4	3	-1	.954	-6	*31	-1.4
1970	Bos-A	127	480	50	142	24	5	16	63	44	95	.296	.357	.467	117	16	12	74	4	11	-5	.934	-8	31	-0.7
1971	Bos-A	146	537	72	141	16	4	24	78	41	102	.263	.321	.441	106	8	4	69	0	3	-2	.992	-7	*1	-2.0
1972	Mil-A	152	578	71	154	24	4	20	88	43	130	.266	.322	.426	123	13	14	76	16	4	2	.992	-5	*13	0.0
1973	Mil-A	158	604	98	185	30	4	24	107	61	94	.306	.372	.488	144	32	33	106	9	5	-0	.994	7	*1/D	2.7
1974	Mil-A	158	604	74	170	36	2	17	82	59	90	.281	.348	.432	124	18	18	84	9	9	-3	**.992**	8	*1/D	1.3
1975	Mil-A★	158	617	86	176	26	4	**36**	**109**	51	97	.285	.343	.515	139	29	29	99	6	5	-1	.989	3	*1D/3	2.1
1976	Mil-A	156	606	73	166	21	5	18	77	53	118	.274	.337	.414	122	14	15	82	0	1	-1	.991	-2	*1	0.2
1977	Bos-A★	157	584	103	157	26	5	33	95	57	112	.269	.340	.500	112	19	10	93	1	1	-0	.985	0	*1	0.1
1978	Bos-A	120	412	51	96	16	4	12	54	44	86	.233	.307	.379	83	-5	-10	44	1	1	-0	.991	-8	*1/D	-2.7
1979	Bos-A	45	156	18	35	9	1	4	23	17	22	.224	.301	.372	76	-5	-6	14	0	0	0	.986	-2	1	-1.0
	KC-A	44	146	19	39	8	2	1	20	12	32	.267	.331	.370	87	-2	-3	15	1	1	-0	.989	-3	1/3D	-0.8
	NY-A	16	44	9	14	3	1	1	6	2	7	.318	.348	.500	128	1	2	8	1	0	0	1.000	-0	D/1	0.2
	Yr	105	346	46	88	20	4	6	49	31	61	.254	.319	.387	87	-5	-7	37	2	1	0	.987	-5	1D/3	-1.6
Total	14	2034	7433	957	1992	306	60	271	1051	699	1418	.268	.335	.435	113	161	123	1027	69	57	-14	.990	-25	*13/D	-4.7

■ JIM SCOTT Scott, James Walter b: 9/22/1888, Shenandoah, Pa. d: 5/12/72, S.Pasadena, Fla. BR/TR, 5'9.5", 165 lbs. Deb: 4/22/14

YEAR	TM/L	G	AB	R	H	2B	3B	HR	RBI	BB	SO	AVG	OBP	SLG	PRO+	BR	/A	RC	SB	CS	SBR	FA	FR	POS	TPR
1914	Pit-F	8	24	2	6	1	0	0	1	5	0	.250	.379	.292	93	0	0	3	1			.800	-3	/S	-0.2

■ JOHN SCOTT Scott, John Henry b: 1/24/52, Jackson, Miss. BR/TR, 6'2", 165 lbs. Deb: 9/07/74

YEAR	TM/L	G	AB	R	H	2B	3B	HR	RBI	BB	SO	AVG	OBP	SLG	PRO+	BR	/A	RC	SB	CS	SBR	FA	FR	POS	TPR
1974	SD-N	14	15	3	1	0	0	0	0	0	4	.067	.067	.067	-65	-3	-3	0	1	0	0	1.000	1	/O	-0.2
1975	SD-N	25	9	6	0	0	0	0	0	0	2	.000	.000	.000	-99	-2	-2	0	2	0	1	.000	0	/O	-0.2
1977	Tor-A	79	233	26	56	9	0	2	15	8	39	.240	.266	.305	54	-15	-15	17	10	8	-2	.963	-5	O/D	-2.4
Total	3	118	257	35	57	9	0	2	15	8	45	.222	.245	.280	43	-20	-21	17	13	8	-1	.965	-3	/OD	-2.8

■ LE GRANT SCOTT Scott, Le Grant Edward b: 7/25/10, Cleveland, Ohio BL/TL, 5'8.5", 170 lbs. Deb: 4/19/39

YEAR	TM/L	G	AB	R	H	2B	3B	HR	RBI	BB	SO	AVG	OBP	SLG	PRO+	BR	/A	RC	SB	CS	SBR	FA	FR	POS	TPR
1939	Phi-N	76	232	31	65	15	1	1	26	22	14	.280	.343	.366	93	-3	-2	29	5			.959	1	O	-0.3

■ EVERETT SCOTT Scott, Lewis Everett "Deacon" b: 11/19/1892, Bluffton, Ind. d: 11/2/60, Fort Wayne, Ind. BR/TR, 5'8", 148 lbs. Deb: 4/14/14

YEAR	TM/L	G	AB	R	H	2B	3B	HR	RBI	BB	SO	AVG	OBP	SLG	PRO+	BR	/A	RC	SB	CS	SBR	FA	FR	POS	TPR
1914	Bos-A	144	539	66	129	15	6	2	37	32	43	.239	.286	.301	76	-17	-17	48	9	14	-6	.949	-11	*S	-2.4
1915	*Bos-A	100	359	25	72	11	0	0	28	17	21	.201	.237	.231	41	-27	-26	22	4	7	-3	.961	4	*S	-1.9
1916	*Bos-A	123	366	37	85	19	2	0	27	23	24	.232	.283	.295	73	-13	-13	37	8			**.967**	7	*S/23	0.0
1917	Bos-A	157	528	40	127	24	7	0	50	20	46	.241	.268	.313	78	-17	-16	49	12			**.953**	8	*S	-0.1
1918	*Bos-A	126	443	40	98	11	5	0	43	12	16	.221	.242	.269	55	-26	-26	32	11			**.976**	18	*S	-0.3
1919	Bos-A	138	507	41	141	19	0	0	38	19	26	.278	.306	.316	79	-18	-14	50	8			**.976**	7	*S	0.1
1920	Bos-A	154	569	41	153	21	12	4	61	21	15	.269	.300	.369	80	-21	-18	60	4	11	-5	**.973**	17	*S	0.7
1921	Bos-A	154	576	65	151	21	9	1	62	27	21	.262	.295	.335	62	-35	-33	55	5	9	-4	**.972**	**38**	*S	1.5
1922	*NY-A	154	557	64	150	23	5	3	45	23	22	.269	.304	.345	67	-26	-28	59	2	3	-1	**.966**	19	*S	0.6
1923	*NY-A	152	533	48	131	16	4	6	60	13	19	.246	.266	.325	54	-37	-38	45	1	3	-2	**.961**	-11	*S	-3.5
1924	NY-A	153	548	56	137	12	6	4	64	21	15	.250	.278	.316	53	-40	-40	47	3	7	-3	.966	10	*S	-1.6
1925	NY-A	22	60	3	13	0	0	0	4	2	2	.217	.242	.217	17	-8	-7	3	0	1	-1	.988	3	S	-0.3
	Was-A	33	103	10	28	6	1	0	18	4	4	.272	.299	.350	65	-6	-6	10	1	2	-1	.932	3	S/3	-0.1
	Yr	55	163	13	41	6	1	0	22	6	6	.252	.278	.301	48	-13	-13	13	1	3	-2	.952	6	S/3	-0.4
1926	Chi-A	40	143	15	36	10	1	0	13	9	8	.252	.296	.336	67	-8	-7	14	1	3	-2	.955	5	S	0.0
	Cin-N	4	6	1	4	0	0	0	1	0	0	.667	.667	.667	267	1	1	2	0			.875	0	/S	0.2
Total	13	1654	5837	552	1455	208	58	20	551	243	282	.249	.281	.315	65	-297	-287	532	69	60		.965	117	*S/32	-7.1

■ MILT SCOTT Scott, Milton Parker "Mikado Milt" b: 1/17/1866, Chicago, Ill. d: 11/3/38, Baltimore, Md. 5'9", 160 lbs. Deb: 9/30/1882

YEAR	TM/L	G	AB	R	H	2B	3B	HR	RBI	BB	SO	AVG	OBP	SLG	PRO+	BR	/A	RC	SB	CS	SBR	FA	FR	POS	TPR
1882	Chi-N	1	5	1	2	0	0	0	0	0	0	.400	.400	.400	151	0	0	1				1.000	0	/1	0.0
1884	Det-N	110	438	29	108	17	5	3	50	9	62	.247	.262	.329	90	-8	-4	39				.968	-1	*1	-1.6
1885	Det-N	38	148	14	39	7	0	0	12	4	16	.264	.283	.311	92	-1	-2	13				.967	2	1	-0.4
	Pit-a	55	210	15	52	7	1	0		5		.248	.272	.290	81	-5	-4	17				.986	3	1	-0.7
1886	Bal-a	137	484	48	92	11	4	2		22		.190	.239	.242	53	-26	-24	31	11			.974	8	*1/P	-2.8
Total	4	341	1285	107	293	42	10	5	62	40	78	.228	.257	.288	75	-40	-34	101	11			.973	12	1/P	-5.5

■ DICK SCOTT Scott, Richard Edward b: 7/19/62, Ellsworth, Maine BR/TR, 6'1", 170 lbs. Deb: 5/19/89

YEAR	TM/L	G	AB	R	H	2B	3B	HR	RBI	BB	SO	AVG	OBP	SLG	PRO+	BR	/A	RC	SB	CS	SBR	FA	FR	POS	TPR
1989	Oak-A	3	2	0	0	0	0	0	1	0	0	.000	.000	.000	-99	-1	-1	0	0	0	0	.000	0	/S	-0.1

■ RODNEY SCOTT Scott, Rodney Darrell b: 10/16/53, Indianapolis, Ind. BB/TR, 6', 160 lbs. Deb: 4/11/75

YEAR	TM/L	G	AB	R	H	2B	3B	HR	RBI	BB	SO	AVG	OBP	SLG	PRO+	BR	/A	RC	SB	CS	SBR	FA	FR	POS	TPR
1975	KC-A	48	15	13	1	0	0	0	0	1	3	.067	.125	.067	-43	-3	-3	0	4	2	0	1.000	6	D/2SR	0.3
1976	Mon-N	7	10	3	4	0	0	0	0	1	1	.400	.455	.400	138	1	1	2	2	0	1	1.000	-0	/2S	0.1

YEAR	TM/L	G	AB	R	H	2B	3B	HR	RBI	BB	SO	AVG	OBP	SLG	PRO+	BR	/A	RC	SB	CS	SBR	FA	FR	POS	TPR
1977	Oak-A	133	364	56	95	4	4	0	20	43	50	.261	.344	.294	77	-10	-10	41	33	18	-1	.963	-30	2S/3OD	-3.2
1978	Chi-N	78	227	41	64	5	1	0	15	43	41	.282	.403	.313	91	4	0	35	27	10	2	.929	-8	3O/2S	-0.7
1979	Mon-N	151	562	69	134	12	5	3	42	66	82	.238	.321	.294	69	-23	-22	61	39	12	5	.980	-15	*2S	-2.1
1980	Mon-N	154	567	84	127	13	**13**	0	46	70	75	.224	.310	.293	69	-22	-22	60	63	13	11	.982	-16	*2S	-1.7
1981	*Mon-N	95	336	43	69	9	3	0	26	50	35	.205	.310	.250	60	-16	-16	32	30	7	5	.983	-15	2	-2.3
1982	Mon-N	14	25	2	5	0	0	0	1	3	2	.200	.286	.200	37	-2	-2	2	5	0	2	.971	-1	2	-0.2
	NY-A	10	26	5	5	0	0	0	0	4	2	.192	.300	.192	39	-2	-2	2	2	0	1	.963	1	/S2	0.0
Total	8	690	2132	316	504	43	26	3	150	281	291	.236	.328	.285	71	-73	-76	235	205	62	24	.979	-80	2S/3DO	-9.8

■ JIM SCRANTON Scranton, James Dean b: 4/5/60, Torrance, Cal. BR/TR, 6', 175 lbs. Deb: 9/05/84

YEAR	TM/L	G	AB	R	H	2B	3B	HR	RBI	BB	SO	AVG	OBP	SLG	PRO+	BR	/A	RC	SB	CS	SBR	FA	FR	POS	TPR
1984	KC-A	2	2	0	0	0	0	0	0	0	0	.000	.000	.000	-99	-1	-1	0	0	0	0	1.000	-1	/S3	-0.1
1985	KC-A	6	4	1	0	0	0	0	0	0	0	.000	.000	.000	-99	-1	-1	0	0	0	0	1.000	2	/S	0.1
Total	2	8	6	1	0	0	0	0	0	0	0	.000	.000	.000	-99	-2	-2	0	0	0	0	1.000	2	/S3	0.0

■ CHUCK SCRIVENER Scrivener, Wayne Allison b: 10/3/47, Alexandria, Va. BR/TR, 5'9", 170 lbs. Deb: 9/18/75

YEAR	TM/L	G	AB	R	H	2B	3B	HR	RBI	BB	SO	AVG	OBP	SLG	PRO+	BR	/A	RC	SB	CS	SBR	FA	FR	POS	TPR
1975	Det-A	4	16	0	4	1	0	0	0	0	1	.250	.250	.313	56	-1	-1	1	1	0	0	1.000	-2	/3S	-0.3
1976	Det-A	80	222	28	49	7	1	2	16	19	34	.221	.282	.288	65	-9	-10	19	1	0	0	.976	7	2S/3	0.3
1977	Det-A	61	72	10	6	0	0	0	2	5	9	.083	.143	.083	-35	-14	-14	1	0	0	0	.981	10	S/23	-0.2
Total	3	145	310	38	59	8	1	2	18	24	44	.190	.249	.242	40	-24	-25	22	2	0	1	.970	15	/S23	-0.2

■ TONY SCRUGGS Scruggs, Anthony Raymond b: 3/19/66, Riverside, Cal. BR/TR, 6'1", 210 lbs. Deb: 4/08/91

YEAR	TM/L	G	AB	R	H	2B	3B	HR	RBI	BB	SO	AVG	OBP	SLG	PRO+	BR	/A	RC	SB	CS	SBR	FA	FR	POS	TPR
1991	Tex-A	5	6	1	0	0	0	0	0	0	1	.000	.000	.000	-99	-2	-2	0	0	0	0	1.000	-1	/O	-0.3

■ KEN SEARS Sears, Kenneth Eugene "Ziggy" b: 7/6/17, Streator, Ill. d: 7/17/68, Bridgeport, Tex. BL/TR, 6'1", 200 lbs. Deb: 5/02/43

YEAR	TM/L	G	AB	R	H	2B	3B	HR	RBI	BB	SO	AVG	OBP	SLG	PRO+	BR	/A	RC	SB	CS	SBR	FA	FR	POS	TPR
1943	NY-A	60	187	22	52	7	0	2	22	11	18	.278	.328	.348	97	-1	-1	21	1	3	-2	.974	1	C	0.2
1946	StL-A	7	15	1	5	0	0	0	1	3	0	.333	.444	.333	114	1	1	2	0	0	0	1.000	-3	/C	-0.2
Total	2	67	202	23	57	7	0	2	23	14	18	.282	.338	.347	99	-0	-0	23	1	3	-2	.975	-2	/C	0.0

■ JIMMY SEBRING Sebring, James Dennison b: 3/22/1882, Liberty, Pa. d: 12/22/09, Williamsport, Pa. BL/TR, 6', 180 lbs. Deb: 9/08/02

YEAR	TM/L	G	AB	R	H	2B	3B	HR	RBI	BB	SO	AVG	OBP	SLG	PRO+	BR	/A	RC	SB	CS	SBR	FA	FR	POS	TPR
1902	Pit-N	19	80	15	26	4	4	0	15	5		.325	.365	.475	153	5	5	15	2			.974	4	O	0.7
1903	*Pit-N	124	506	71	140	16	13	4	64	32		.277	.325	.383	99	-0	-2	72	20			.927	7	*O	-0.3
1904	Pit-N	80	305	28	82	11	7	0	32	17		.269	.307	.351	101	1	-0	36	8			.959	9	O	0.4
	Cin-N	56	222	22	50	9	2	0	24	14		.225	.271	.284	66	-7	-10	20	8			1.000	4	O	-1.0
	Yr	136	527	50	132	20	9	0	56	31		.250	.292	.323	86	-7	-10	56	16			.974	12	*O	-0.6
1905	Cin-N	58	217	31	62	10	5	2	28	14		.286	.329	.406	107	4	1	34	11			.885	-6	O	-0.8
1909	Bro-N	25	81	11	8	1	1	0	5	11		.099	.207	.136	7	-9	-8	3	3			.951	-2	O	-1.3
	Was-A	1	0	0	0	0	0	0	0	0		—	—	—	—	0	0	0	0			.000	-1	/O	-0.1
Total	5	363	1411	178	368	51	32	6	168	93		.261	.308	.355	94	-7	-15	180	52			.945	14	O	-2.4

■ FRANK SECORY Secory, Frank Edward b: 8/24/12, Mason City, Iowa BR/TR, 6'1", 200 lbs. Deb: 4/28/40 U

YEAR	TM/L	G	AB	R	H	2B	3B	HR	RBI	BB	SO	AVG	OBP	SLG	PRO+	BR	/A	RC	SB	CS	SBR	FA	FR	POS	TPR
1940	Det-A	1	1	0	0	0	0	0	0	0	1	.000	.000	.000	-91	-0	-0	0	0	0	0	.000	0	H	0.0
1942	Cin-N	2	5	1	0	0	0	0	1	3	2	.000	.375	.000	14	-0	-0	0	0			.857	0	/O	0.0
1944	Chi-N	22	56	10	18	1	0	4	17	6	8	.321	.387	.554	163	4	4	13	1			1.000	0	O	0.4
1945	*Chi-N	35	57	4	9	1	0	0	6	2	7	.158	.186	.175	1	-8	-7	2	0			1.000	-1	O	-1.0
1946	Chi-N	33	43	6	10	3	0	3	12	6	6	.233	.327	.512	139	2	2	7	0			.833	-3	/O	-0.1
Total	5	93	162	21	37	5	0	7	36	17	24	.228	.302	.389	95	-2	-2	22	1	0		.964	-4	/O	-0.7

■ CHARLIE SEE See, Charles Henry "Chad" b: 10/13/1896, Pleasantville, N.Y d: 7/19/48, Bridgeport, Conn. BL/TR, 5'10.5", 175 lbs. Deb: 8/06/19

YEAR	TM/L	G	AB	R	H	2B	3B	HR	RBI	BB	SO	AVG	OBP	SLG	PRO+	BR	/A	RC	SB	CS	SBR	FA	FR	POS	TPR
1919	Cin-N	8	14	1	4	0	0	0	1	1	0	.286	.333	.286	89	-0	-0	1	0			.833	-1	/O	-0.2
1920	Cin-N	47	82	9	25	4	0	0	15	1	7	.305	.329	.354	97	-0	-0	9	2	4	-2	1.000	3	O/P	-0.1
1921	Cin-N	37	106	11	26	5	1	1	7	7	5	.245	.298	.340	72	-5	-4	11	3	2	-0	.954	-0	O	-0.7
Total	3	92	202	21	55	9	1	1	23	9	12	.272	.313	.342	83	-6	-5	21	5	6		.967	1	/OP	-1.0

■ LARRY SEE See, Ralph Laurence b: 6/20/60, Norwalk, Cal. BR/TR, 6'1", 195 lbs. Deb: 9/03/86

YEAR	TM/L	G	AB	R	H	2B	3B	HR	RBI	BB	SO	AVG	OBP	SLG	PRO+	BR	/A	RC	SB	CS	SBR	FA	FR	POS	TPR
1986	LA-N	13	20	1	5	2	0	0	2	2	7	.250	.318	.350	90	-0	-0	2	0	0	0	.979	1	/1	0.1
1988	Tex-A	13	23	0	3	0	0	0	0	1	8	.130	.167	.130	-15	-4	-4	1	0	0	0	1.000	-0	/C1/3D	-0.4
Total	2	26	43	1	8	2	0	0	2	3	15	.186	.239	.233	32	-4	-4	3	0	0	0	.967	1	/1DC3	-0.3

■ BOB SEEDS Seeds, Robert Ira "Suitcase Bob" b: 2/24/07, Ringgold, Tex. BR/TR, 6', 180 lbs. Deb: 4/19/30

YEAR	TM/L	G	AB	R	H	2B	3B	HR	RBI	BB	SO	AVG	OBP	SLG	PRO+	BR	/A	RC	SB	CS	SBR	FA	FR	POS	TPR
1930	Cle-A	85	277	37	79	11	3	3	32	12	22	.285	.315	.379	72	-11	-12	32	1	3	-2	.953	2	O	-1.5
1931	Cle-A	48	134	26	41	4	1	1	10	11	11	.306	.359	.373	88	-1	-2	18	1	0	0	.966	-2	O/1	-0.6
1932	Cle-A	2	4	0	0	0	0	0	0	0	0	.000	.000	.000	-94	-1	-1	0	0	0	0	.000	-0	/O	-0.2
	Chi-A	116	434	53	126	18	6	2	45	31	37	.290	.342	.373	91	-9	-5	55	5	7	-3	.964	-9	*O	-2.2
	Yr	118	438	53	126	18	6	2	45	31	37	.288	.339	.370	89	-11	-7	54	5	7	-3	.964	-9	*O	-2.4
1933	Bos-A	82	230	26	56	13	4	0	23	21	20	.243	.310	.335	71	-10	-9	24	1	3	-2	.985	-5	1O	-2.0
1934	Bos-A	8	6	0	1	0	0	0	1	0	1	.167	.167	.167	-13	-1	-1	0	0	0	0	.000	-0	/O	-0.1
	Cle-A	61	186	28	46	8	1	0	18	21	13	.247	.327	.301	62	-10	-10	20	2	1	0	.977	-4	O	-1.5
	Yr	69	192	28	47	8	1	0	19	21	14	.245	.322	.297	59	-11	-12	20	2	1	0	.977	-4	O	-1.6
1936	*NY-A	13	42	12	11	1	0	4	10	5	3	.262	.340	.571	126	1	1	8	3	1	0	1.000	1	/O3	0.2
1938	NY-N	81	296	35	86	12	3	9	52	20	33	.291	.338	.443	112	4	4	44	0			.987	-5	O	-0.3
1939	NY-N	63	173	33	46	5	1	5	26	22	31	.266	.352	.393	99	0	0	25	1			.975	-8	O	-0.9
1940	NY-N	56	155	18	45	5	2	4	16	17	19	.290	.371	.426	118	4	4	25	0			.985	-4	O	-0.2
Total	9	615	1937	268	537	77	21	28	233	160	190	.277	.336	.382	89	-33	-32	251	14	15		.970	-35	O/13	-9.3

■ PAT SEEREY Seerey, James Patrick b: 3/17/23, Wilburton, Okla. d: 4/28/86, Jennings, Mo. BR/TR, 5'10", 200 lbs. Deb: 6/09/43

YEAR	TM/L	G	AB	R	H	2B	3B	HR	RBI	BB	SO	AVG	OBP	SLG	PRO+	BR	/A	RC	SB	CS	SBR	FA	FR	POS	TPR
1943	Cle-A	26	72	8	16	3	0	1	5	4	19	.222	.263	.306	70	-3	-3	5	0	0	0	.974	1	O	-0.3
1944	Cle-A	101	342	39	80	16	0	15	39	19	99	.234	.276	.412	99	-4	-3	36	0	2	-1	.986	1	O	-0.8
1945	Cle-A	126	414	56	98	22	2	14	56	66	97	.237	.342	.401	120	8	10	60	1	2	-1	.975	-15	*O	-1.2
1946	Cle-A	117	404	57	91	17	2	26	62	65	101	.225	.334	.470	131	11	15	64	2	3	-1	.981	-5	*O	0.4
1947	Cle-A	82	216	24	37	4	1	11	29	34	66	.171	.284	.352	78	-8	-7	22	0	1	-1	.957	-8	O	-1.9
1948	Cle-A	10	23	7	6	0	0	1	6	7	8	.261	.433	.391	123	1	1	4	0	0	0	1.000	-2	/O	-0.1
	Chi-A	95	340	44	78	11	0	18	64	61	94	.229	.347	.421	107	1	3	53	0	0	0	.981	-0	O	-0.2
	Yr	105	363	51	84	11	0	19	70	68	102	.231	.353	.419	108	2	4	57	0	0	0	.982	-2	*O	-0.3
1949	Chi-A	4	4	1	0	0	0	0	0	3	1	.000	.429	.000	19	-0	-0	0	0	0	0	1.000	-1	/O	-0.1
Total	7	561	1815	236	406	73	5	86	261	259	485	.224	.321	.412	109	6	16	246	3	8	-4	.978	-27	O	-4.2

■ EMMETT SEERY Seery, John Emmett b: 2/13/1861, Princeville, Ill. BL/TR, Deb: 4/17/1884

YEAR	TM/L	G	AB	R	H	2B	3B	HR	RBI	BB	SO	AVG	OBP	SLG	PRO+	BR	/A	RC	SB	CS	SBR	FA	FR	POS	TPR
1884	Bal-U	105	463	113	144	25	7	2		20		.311	.340	.408	137	24	17	66				.828	7	*O/C3	1.9
	KC-U	1	4	2	2	1	0	0		1		.500	.600	.750	407	1	1	2				.000	-0	/O	0.1
	Yr	106	467	115	146	26	7	2		21		.313	.342	.411	139	25	18	67				.828	6	*O/C3	2.0
1885	StL-N	59	216	20	35	7	0	1	14	16	37	.162	.220	.208	42	-14	-12	10				.874	5	O/3	-0.8
1886	StL-N	126	453	73	108	22	6	2	48	57	82	.238	.324	.327	105	1	5	57	24			.883	-5	*O/P	-0.2
1887	Ind-N	122	465	104	104	18	15	4	28	71	68	.224	.331	.353	95	-3	-0	72	48			.891	7	*O/S	0.4
1888	Ind-N	133	500	87	110	20	10	5	50	64	73	.220	.316	.330	106	7	6	79	80			.939	9	*O/S	1.0
1889	Ind-N	127	526	123	165	26	12	8	59	67	59	.314	.401	.454	138	30	28	106	19			.909	1	*O	2.3

YEAR	TM/L	G	AB	R	H	2B	3B	HR	RBI	BB	SO	AVG	OBP	SLG	PRO+	BR	/A	RC	SB	CS	SBR	FA	FR	POS	TPR
1890	Bro-P	104	394	78	88	12	7	1	50	70	36	.223	.348	.297	70	-12	-16	57	44			.894	7	*O	-1.0
1891	Cin-a	97	372	77	106	15	10	4	36	81	52	.285	.423	.411	131	25	19	75	19			.898	3	*O	1.6
1892	Lou-N	42	154	18	31	6	1	0	15	24	19	.201	.309	.253	78	-4	-2	14	6			.961	3	O	-0.1
Total	9	916	3547	695	893	152	68	27	300	471	426	.252	.345	.356	108	55	45	538	240			.896	36	O/3CSP	5.2
■ **KAL SEGRIST** Segrist, Kal Hill b: 4/14/31, Greenville, Tex. BR/TR, 6', 180 lbs. Deb: 7/16/52																									
1952	NY-A	13	23	3	1	0	0	0	1	3	1	.043	.154	.043	-46	-4	-4	0	0	0	0	.971	0	2/3	-0.4
1955	Bal-A	7	9	1	3	0	0	0	0	2	0	.333	.455	.333	123	0	0	1	0	0	0	1.000	0	/312	0.1
Total	2	20	32	4	4	0	0	0	1	5	1	.125	.243	.125	4	-4	-4	2	0	0	0	.971	1	/231	-0.3
■ **DAVID SEGUI** Segui, David Vincent b: 7/19/66, Kansas City, Kan. BB/TL, 6'1", 170 lbs. Deb: 5/08/90 F																									
1990	Bal-A	40	123	14	30	7	0	2	15	11	15	.244	.311	.350	87	-3	-2	10	0	0	0	.990	1	1/D	-0.3
1991	Bal-A	86	212	15	59	7	0	2	22	12	19	.278	.317	.340	85	-5	-4	21	1	1	-0	.996	1	1O/D	-0.5
1992	Bal-A	115	189	21	44	9	0	1	17	20	23	.233	.306	.296	70	-7	-7	18	1	0	0	.998	2	1O	-0.8
Total	3	241	524	50	133	23	0	5	54	43	57	.254	.312	.326	80	-15	-14	49	2	1	0	.995	5	1/OD	-1.6
■ **KURT SEIBERT** Seibert, Kurt Elliott b: 10/16/55, Cheverly, Md. BB/TR, 6', 165 lbs. Deb: 9/03/79																									
1979	Chi-N	7	2	2	0	0	0	0	0	0	1	.000	.000	.000	-91	-1	-1	0	0	0	0	1.000	2	/2	0.2
■ **SOCKS SEIBOLD** Seibold, Harry b: 4/3/1896, Philadelphia, Pa. d: 9/21/65, Philadelphia, Pa. BR/TR, 5'8.5", 162 lbs. Deb: 9/18/15																									
1915	Phi-A	10	26	3	3	1	0	0	2	4	4	.115	.233	.154	16	-3	-3	1	0			.714	-4	/S	-0.7
1916	Phi-A	5	12	0	2	1	0	0	1	0	4	.167	.167	.250	26	-1	-1	1	0			1.000	2	/PO	0.0
1917	Phi-A	36	59	6	13	1	1	0	5	4	8	.220	.281	.271	70	-2	-2	5	1			.978	-2	P/O	-0.1
1919	Phi-A	15	13	1	2	0	0	0	1	0	4	.154	.154	.154	-13	-2	-2	0	0			.941	0	P	0.0
1929	Bos-N	33	70	6	20	2	0	0	9	6	6	.286	.342	.314	67	-4	-3	8	0			1.000	-1	P	0.0
1930	Bos-N	36	90	6	19	2	0	1	5	6	6	.211	.260	.267	29	-11	-10	6	0			.941	-3	P	0.0
1931	Bos-N	33	70	3	9	0	0	0	2	1	9	.129	.141	.129	-28	-12	-12	2	0			1.000	0	P	0.0
1932	Bos-N	28	46	2	7	0	0	0	2	2	0	.152	.188	.152	-8	-7	-7	1	0			1.000	2	P	0.0
1933	Bos-N	11	9	0	1	0	0	0	0	2	2	.111	.273	.111	14	-1	-1	0	0			1.000	0	P	0.0
Total	9	207	395	27	76	7	1	1	27	25	43	.192	.242	.223	25	-43	-41	24	1			.982	-5	P/SO	-0.8
■ **RICKY SEILHEIMER** Seilheimer, Ricky Allen b: 8/30/60, Brenham, Tex. BL/TR, 5'11", 185 lbs. Deb: 7/05/80																									
1980	Chi-A	21	52	4	11	3	1	1	3	4	15	.212	.268	.365	72	-2	-2	5	1	0	0	.946	-3	C	-0.4
■ **KEVIN SEITZER** Seitzer, Kevin Lee b: 3/26/62, Springfield, Ill. BR/TR, 5'11", 180 lbs. Deb: 9/03/86																									
1986	KC-A	28	96	16	31	4	1	2	11	19	14	.323	.440	.448	140	7	7	21	0	0	0	.987	1	1/O3	0.6
1987	KC-A★	161	641	105	**207**	33	8	15	83	80	85	.323	.400	.470	126	29	27	120	12	7	-1	.947	8	*31/OD	2.9
1988	KC-A	149	559	90	170	32	5	5	60	72	64	.304	.389	.406	122	20	19	89	10	8	-2	.938	3	*3/OD	1.9
1989	KC-A	160	597	78	168	17	2	4	48	102	76	.281	.391	.337	107	11	11	85	17	8	0	.950	-10	*3/SO1	0.3
1990	KC-A	158	622	91	171	31	5	6	38	67	66	.275	.347	.370	102	2	3	82	7	5	-1	.953	-9	*32	-0.6
1991	KC-A	85	234	28	62	11	3	1	25	29	21	.265	.351	.350	94	-1	-1	30	4	1	1	.940	0	3/D	0.0
1992	Mil-A	148	540	74	146	35	1	5	71	57	44	.270	.342	.367	101	-0	1	66	13	11	-3	**.969**	-13	*3/21	-1.4
Total	7	889	3289	482	955	163	25	38	336	426	370	.290	.375	.390	112	68	68	493	63	40	-5	.950	-20	3/12OSD	3.7
■ **KIP SELBACH** Selbach, Albert Karl b: 3/24/1872, Columbus, Ohio d: 2/17/56, Columbus, Ohio BR/TR, 5'7", 190 lbs. Deb: 4/24/1894																									
1894	Was-N	97	372	69	114	21	17	7	71	51	20	.306	.390	.511	121	10	12	85	21			.915	-9	OS	-0.1
1895	Was-N	129	516	115	166	21	**22**	6	55	69	28	.322	.403	.483	132	23	25	116	31			.912	16	*O/S2	2.6
1896	Was-N	127	487	100	148	17	13	5	100	76	28	.304	.405	.423	121	18	18	107	49			.946	7	*O	1.2
1897	Was-N	124	486	113	152	25	16	5	59	80		.313	.414	.461	131	24	24	115	46			.955	13	*O	2.4
1898	Was-N	132	515	88	156	28	11	3	60	64		.303	.383	.417	130	20	21	95	25			.948	20	*O/S	2.9
1899	Cin-N	140	521	104	154	27	11	3	87	70		.296	.384	.407	115	14	12	101	38			.953	17	*O	1.7
1900	NY-N	141	523	98	176	29	12	4	68	72		.337	.425	.461	151	34	38	121	36			.951	10	*O	3.4
1901	NY-N	125	502	89	145	29	6	1	56	45		.289	.349	.376	115	7	10	71	8			.942	-10	*O	-0.9
1902	Bal-A	128	503	86	161	27	9	3	60	58		.320	.394	.427	122	20	17	97	22			.941	9	*O	1.7
1903	Was-A	140	533	68	134	23	12	3	49	41		.251	.305	.356	96	-1	-3	67	20			.956	-3	*O/3	-1.5
1904	Was-A	48	178	15	49	8	4	0	14	24		.275	.361	.365	132	7	7	28	9			.931	3	O	0.8
	Bos-A	98	376	50	97	19	8	0	30	48		.258	.347	.351	115	11	8	52	10			.961	1	O	0.4
	Yr	146	554	65	146	27	12	0	44	72		.264	.351	.356	120	18	16	79	19			.950	4	*O	1.2
1905	Bos-A	121	418	54	103	16	6	4	47	67		.246	.355	.342	120	13	12	58	12			.928	-1	*O	0.6
1906	Bos-A	60	228	15	48	9	2	0	23	18		.211	.274	.268	70	-8	-8	19	7			.966	1	O	-1.1
Total	13	1610	6158	1064	1803	299	149	44	779	783	76	.293	.376	.411	121	192	194	1132	334			.944	75	*O/S23	14.1
■ **GEORGE SELKIRK** Selkirk, George Alexander "Twinkletoes" b: 1/4/08, Huntsville, Ont., Canada d: 1/19/87, Ft.Lauderdale, Fla BL/TR, 6'1", 182 lbs. Deb: 8/12/34																									
1934	NY-A	46	176	23	55	7	1	5	38	15	17	.313	.370	.449	118	2	4	29	1	1	-0	.989	-2	O	0.0
1935	NY-A	128	491	64	153	29	12	11	94	44	36	.312	.372	.487	128	14	17	87	2	7	-4	.975	6	*O	1.4
1936	*NY-A★	137	493	93	152	28	9	18	107	94	60	.308	.420	.511	133	24	27	111	13	7	-0	.974	3	*O	2.1
1937	*NY-A	78	256	49	84	13	5	18	68	34	24	.328	.411	.629	157	22	22	68	8	2	1	.987	5	O	2.3
1938	*NY-A	99	335	58	85	12	5	10	62	68	52	.254	.384	.409	99	1	1	58	9	4	0	.973	-3	O	-0.4
1939	*NY-A★	128	418	103	128	17	4	21	101	103	49	.306	.452	.517	149	35	36	110	12	5	1	**.989**	-4	*O	2.6
1940	NY-A	118	379	68	102	17	5	19	71	84	43	.269	.406	.491	137	20	22	83	3	6	-3	.962	-3	*O	1.1
1941	*NY-A	70	164	30	36	5	0	6	25	28	30	.220	.340	.360	86	-3	-3	22	1	0	0	.967	-2	O	-0.7
1942	*NY-A	42	78	15	15	3	0	0	10	16	8	.192	.330	.231	60	-4	-3	7	0	0	0	1.000	-1	O	-0.6
Total	9	846	2790	503	810	131	41	108	576	486	319	.290	.400	.483	128	111	124	575	49	32	-5	.977	-1	O	7.8
■ **RUBE SELLERS** Sellers, Oliver b: 3/7/1881, Duquesne, Pa. d: 1/14/52, Pittsburgh, Pa. BR/TR, 5'10", 180 lbs. Deb: 8/12/10																									
1910	Bos-N	12	32	3	5	0	0	0	2	6	5	.156	.289	.156	29	-3	-3	2	1			1.000	-2	/O	-0.6
■ **FRANK SELMAN** Selman, Frank C. (a.k.a. Frank C. Williams 1871-75) b: Baltimore, Md. Deb: 5/04/1871																									
1871	Kek-n	14	65	14	15	3	0	1	10	4	0	.231	.275	.323	70	-2	-3	6	1					3/CS	-0.2
1872	Oly-n	9	41	3	10	3	0	0	1	0	0	.244	.244	.317	75	-1	-1	3						/C3	-0.2
1873	Mar-n	1	3	1	1	0	0	0	0	0	0	.333	.333	.333	126	-0	0	0						/P	0.0
1874	Bal-n	12	54	9	16	4	1	0		0		.296	.296	.407	122	1	1	7						/SCO	0.1
1875	Was-n	1	3	0	1	0	0	0		0		.333	.333	.333	136	0	0	0						/1	0.0
Total	5 n	37	166	27	43	10	1	1		4		.259	.276	.349	89	-2	-2	16						/3CS1OP	-0.3
■ **CAREY SELPH** Selph, Carey Isom b: 12/5/01, Donaldson, Ark. d: 2/24/76, Houston, Tex. BR/TR, 5'9.5", 175 lbs. Deb: 5/25/29																									
1929	StL-N	25	51	8	12	1	1	0	7	6	4	.235	.316	.294	52	-4	-4	5	1			.981	-5	2	-0.7
1932	Chi-A	116	396	50	112	19	8	0	51	31	9	.283	.341	.371	90	-9	-5	50	7	6	-2	.910	-6	32	-0.6
Total	2	141	447	58	124	20	9	0	58	37	13	.277	.338	.362	85	-13	-9	55	8	6		.955	-11	/32	-1.3
■ **MIKE SEMBER** Sember, Michael David b: 2/24/53, Hammond, Ind. BR/TR, 6', 185 lbs. Deb: 8/18/77																									
1977	Chi-N	3	4	0	1	0	0	0	0	0	2	.250	.250	.250	31	-0	-0	0	0	0	0	1.000	1	/2	0.0
1978	Chi-N	9	3	2	1	0	0	0	0	1	1	.333	.500	.333	122	0	0	1	0	0	0	.667	1	/3S	0.1
Total	2	12	7	2	2	0	0	0	0	1	3	.286	.375	.286	74	-0	-0	1	0	0	0	.978	1	/3S2	0.1

YEAR	TM/L	G	AB	R	H	2B	3B	HR	RBI	BB	SO	AVG	OBP	SLG	PRO+	BR	/A	RC	SB	CS	SBR	FA	FR	POS	TPR

■ ANDY SEMINICK   Seminick, Andrew Wasil b: 9/12/20, Pierce, W.Va.   BR/TR, 5'11", 187 lbs.   Deb: 9/14/43 C

1943	Phi-N	22	72	9	13	2	0	2	5	7	22	.181	.253	.292	60	-4	-4	5	0			.930	1	C/O	-0.2
1944	Phi-N	22	63	9	14	2	1	0	4	6	17	.222	.300	.286	68	-3	-3	5	2			.963	1	C/O	-0.2
1945	Phi-N	80	188	18	45	7	2	6	26	18	38	.239	.313	.394	98	-2	-1	23	3			.979	-0	C/3O	0.2
1946	Phi-N	124	406	55	107	15	5	12	52	39	86	.264	.334	.414	115	5	6	52	2			.974	-6	*C	0.7
1947	Phi-N	111	337	48	85	16	2	13	50	58	69	.252	.370	.427	115	6	8	56	4			.978	7	*C	2.1
1948	Phi-N	125	391	49	88	11	3	13	44	58	68	.225	.328	.368	90	-6	-5	49	4			.965	6	*C	0.9
1949	Phi-N★	109	334	52	81	11	2	24	68	69	74	.243	.380	.503	138	17	19	67	0			.975	7	C	3.0
1950	*Phi-N	130	393	55	113	15	3	24	68	68	50	.288	.400	.524	143	25	26	84	0			.976	4	*C	3.4
1951	Phi-N	101	291	42	66	8	1	11	37	63	67	.227	.370	.375	102	2	3	46	1	0	0	.979	-3	C	0.4
1952	Cin-N	108	336	38	86	16	1	14	50	35	65	.256	.330	.435	111	4	4	48	1	3	-2	.973	-4	C	0.4
1953	Cin-N	119	387	46	91	12	0	19	64	49	82	.235	.323	.413	90	-6	-6	53	2	2	-1	.982	-5	*C	-0.6
1954	Cin-N	86	247	25	58	9	4	7	30	48	39	.235	.364	.389	93	-0	-1	37	0	0	0	.989	3	C	0.6
1955	Cin-N	6	15	1	2	0	0	1	1	0	3	.133	.133	.333	18	-2	-2	1	0	0	0	1.000	2	/C	0.0
	Phi-N	93	289	32	71	12	1	11	34	32	59	.246	.333	.408	97	-2	-1	39	1	2	-1	.994	10	C	1.1
	Yr	99	304	33	73	12	1	12	35	32	62	.240	.325	.405	93	-4	-3	39	1	2	-1	.994	12	C	1.1
1956	Phi-N	60	161	16	32	3	1	7	23	31	38	.199	.332	.360	88	-3	-2	19	3	0	1	.976	-8	C	-0.7
1957	Phi-N	8	11	0	1	0	0	0	1	3		.091	.167	.091	-29	-2	-2	0	0	0	0	1.000	1	/C	-0.1
Total	15	1304	3921	495	953	139	26	164	556	582	780	.243	.347	.417	107	31	39	584	23	7		.977	15	*C/O3	11.0

■ SONNY SENERCHIA   Senerchia, Emanuel Robert b: 4/6/31, Newark, N.J.   BR/TR, 6'1", 195 lbs.   Deb: 8/22/52

| 1952 | Pit-N | 29 | 100 | 5 | 22 | 5 | 0 | 3 | 11 | 4 | 21 | .220 | .250 | .360 | 66 | -5 | -5 | 8 | 0 | 3 | -2 | .953 | -8 | 3 | -1.7 |

■ COUNT SENSENDERFER   Sensenderfer, John Phillips Jenkins b: 12/28/1847, Philadelphia, Pa. d: 5/3/03, Philadelphia, Pa.   5'9", 170 lbs.   Deb: 5/20/1871

1871	Ath-n	25	127	38	41	5	2	0	23	0	1	.323	.323	.394	106	1	1	18	5					*O	0.1
1872	Ath-n	1	5	2	2	0	0	0	1	0	0	.400	.400	.400	146	0	0	0						/O	0.0
1873	Ath-n	20	86	12	24	1	0	0	8	0	2	.279	.279	.291	63	-3	-5	7						O/1	-0.4
1874	Ath-n	5	16	3	3	0	0	0		0	1	.188	.188	.188	18	-1	-2	1						/O	-0.1
Total	4 n	51	234	55	70	6	2	0		0		.299	.299	.342	84	-4	-5	26						/O1	-0.4

■ PAUL SENTELL   Sentell, Leopold Theodore b: 8/27/1879, New Orleans, La. d: 4/27/23, Cincinnati, Ohio   BR/TR, 5'9", 176 lbs.   Deb: 4/12/06 U

1906	Phi-N	63	192	19	44	5	1	1	14	14		.229	.292	.281	79	-5	-5	22	15			.887	-9	32/OS	-1.4
1907	Phi-N	3	3	0	0	0	0	0	0	1		.000	.250	.000	-21	-0	-0	0	0			1.000	-2	/SO	-0.3
Total	2	66	195	19	44	5	1	1	14	15		.226	.291	.277	77	-5	-5	22	15			1.000	-11	/32SO	-1.7

■ TED SEPKOWSKI   Sepkowski, Theodore Walter (b: Theodore Walter Sczepkowski) b: 11/9/23, Baltimore, Md.   BL/TR, 5'11", 190 lbs.   Deb: 9/09/42

1942	Cle-A	5	10	0	1	0	0	0	0	0	3	.100	.100	.100	-46	-2	-2	0	0	0	0	.824	1	/2	-0.1
1946	Cle-A	2	8	2	4	1	0	0	1	0	0	.500	.500	.625	228	1	1	3	0	0	0	.833	-1	/3	0.1
1947	Cle-A	10	8	0	1	1	0	0	0	1	1	.125	.222	.250	32	-1	-1	1	0	0	0	.000	-0	/O	-0.1
	NY-A	2	0	1	0	0	0	0	0	0	0	—	—	—	—	0	0	0	0	1	-1	.000	0	R	-0.1
	Yr	12	8	1	1	1	0	0	0	1	1	.125	.222	.250	32	-1	-1	1	0	1	-1	.000	-0	/O	-0.2
Total	3	19	26	3	6	2	0	0	1	1	4	.231	.259	.308	61	-2	-1	3	0	1	-1	.946	-1	/32O	-0.2

■ BILL SERENA   Serena, William Robert b: 10/2/24, Alameda, Cal.   BR/TR, 5'9.5", 175 lbs.   Deb: 9/16/49

1949	Chi-N	12	37	3	8	3	0	1	7	7	9	.216	.341	.378	95	-0	-0	5	0			.923	-4	3	-0.5
1950	Chi-N	127	435	56	104	20	4	17	61	65	75	.239	.339	.421	100	-1	-0	64	1			.945	-2	*3	-0.4
1951	Chi-N	13	39	8	13	3	1	1	4	11	4	.333	.490	.538	173	5	5	11	0	2	-1	.941	-4	3	0.0
1952	Chi-N	122	390	49	107	21	5	15	61	39	83	.274	.345	.469	122	12	11	62	1	0	0	.971	-1	32	1.2
1953	Chi-N	93	275	30	69	10	5	10	52	41	46	.251	.350	.433	100	1	0	43	0	0	0	.983	-15	23	-1.2
1954	Chi-N	41	63	8	10	0	1	4	13	14	18	.159	.331	.381	81	-2	-2	8	0	0	0	.933	-3	3/2	-0.5
Total	6	408	1239	154	311	57	16	48	198	177	235	.251	.348	.439	108	15	14	193	2	2		.951	-30	32	-1.4

■ PAUL SERNA   Serna, Paul David b: 11/16/58, ElCentro, Cal.   BR/TR, 5'8", 170 lbs.   Deb: 9/01/81

1981	Sea-A	30	94	11	24	2	0	4	9	3	11	.255	.293	.404	95	-0	-1	11	2	3	-1	.954	-3	S/2	-0.2
1982	Sea-A	65	169	15	38	3	0	3	8	4	13	.225	.247	.296	47	-12	-13	10	0	5	-3	.936	3	S23/D	-1.0
Total	2	95	263	26	62	5	0	7	17	7	24	.236	.264	.335	64	-13	-14	21	2	8	-4	.945	1	/S23D	-1.2

■ SCOTT SERVAIS   Servais, Scott Daniel b: 6/4/67, LaCrosse, Wis.   BR/TR, 6'2", 195 lbs.   Deb: 7/12/91

1991	Hou-N	16	37	0	6	3	0	0	6	4	8	.162	.244	.243	40	-3	-3	3	0	0	0	.988	2	C	0.0
1992	Hou-N	77	205	12	49	9	0	0	15	11	25	.239	.294	.283	68	-9	-8	17	0	0	0	.995	-2	C	-0.7
Total	2	93	242	12	55	12	0	0	21	15	33	.227	.286	.277	64	-13	-11	19	0	0	0	.994	0	/C	-0.7

■ WALTER SESSI   Sessi, Walter Anthony "Watsie" b: 7/23/18, Finleyville, Pa.   BL/TL, 6'3", 225 lbs.   Deb: 9/18/41

1941	StL-N	5	13	2	0	0	0	1	2			.000	.071	.000	-74	-3	-3	0	0			.750	-1	/O	-0.5
1946	StL-N	15	14	2	2	0	0	1	2	1	4	.143	.200	.357	54	-1	-1	1	0			.000	0	H	-0.1
Total	2	20	27	4	2	0	0	2	2		6	.074	.138	.185	-9	-4	-4	1	0			.924	-1	/O	-0.6

■ JOHN SEVCIK   Sevcik, John Joseph b: 7/11/42, Oak Park, Ill.   BR/TR, 6'2", 205 lbs.   Deb: 4/24/65

| 1965 | Min-A | 12 | 16 | 1 | 1 | 1 | 0 | 0 | 1 | 0 | 5 | .063 | .118 | .125 | -30 | -3 | -3 | 0 | 0 | 0 | 0 | 1.000 | 3 | C | 0.0 |

■ HANK SEVEREID   Severeid, Henry Levai b: 6/1/1891, Story City, Iowa d: 12/17/68, San Antonio, Tex.   BR/TR, 6', 175 lbs.   Deb: 5/15/11

1911	Cin-N	37	56	5	17	6	1	0	10	3	6	.304	.350	.446	127	1	2	8	0			.913	-3	C	0.0
1912	Cin-N	50	114	10	27	0	3	0	13	8	11	.237	.287	.289	60	-7	-6	10	0			.943	-9	C/1O	-1.3
1913	Cin-N	8	6	0	0	0	0	0	0	1	1	.000	.143	.000	-58	-1	-1	0	0			1.000	-1	/CO	-0.2
1915	StL-A	80	203	22	45	6	1	1	22	16	25	.222	.279	.276	68	-9	-8	16	2	1	0	.966	-10	C	-1.4
1916	StL-A	100	293	23	80	8	2	0	34	26	17	.273	.341	.314	102	-1	1	33	3			.976	-16	C/13	-1.0
1917	StL-A	143	501	45	133	23	4	1	57	28	20	.265	.306	.333	99	-5	-3	51	6			.966	-19	*C/1	-1.1
1918	StL-A	51	133	8	34	4	0	0	11	18	4	.256	.337	.286	97	-0	0	14	4			.946	-5	C	-0.2
1919	StL-A	112	351	16	87	12	2	0	36	21	13	.248	.298	.293	65	-16	-17	30	2			.983	-5	*C	-1.3
1920	StL-A	123	422	46	117	14	5	2	49	33	11	.277	.336	.348	79	-11	-13	51	5	3	-0	.983	3	*C	-0.2
1921	StL-A	143	472	66	153	23	7	2	78	42	9	.324	.379	.415	97	-2	-2	76	7	2	1	.972	-3	*C	0.3
1922	StL-A	137	517	49	166	32	7	3	78	28	12	.321	.356	.427	100	2	-1	77	1	4	-2	.993	9	*C	1.1
1923	StL-A	122	432	50	133	27	6	3	51	31	11	.308	.356	.419	98	1	-2	66	3	0	1	.993	9	*C	1.3
1924	StL-A	137	432	37	133	23	2	4	48	36	15	.308	.362	.398	90	-3	-7	62	1	6	-3	.989	-2	*C	-0.4
1925	StL-A	34	109	15	40	9	0	1	21	11	2	.367	.425	.477	122	5	4	22	0	2	-1	.993	-0	C	0.4
	*Was-A	50	110	11	39	8	1	0	14	13	6	.355	.423	.445	123	4	4	21	0	0	0	.986	2	C	0.7
	Yr	84	219	26	79	17	1	1	35	24	8	.361	.424	.461	123	9	9	43	0	2	-1	.990	1	C	1.1
1926	Was-A	22	34	2	7	1	0	0	4	3	2	.206	.270	.235	33	-3	-3	2	0	0	0	.977	0	C	-0.2
	*NY-A	41	127	13	34	8	1	0	13	13	4	.268	.336	.346	79	-4	-4	15	1	1	-0	.988	-3	C	-0.5
	Yr	63	161	15	41	9	1	0	17	16	6	.255	.322	.323	70	-7	-7	17	1	1	-0	.985	-3	C	-0.7
Total	15	1390	4312	408	1245	204	42	17	539	331	169	.289	.342	.367	91	-44	-55	556	35	19		.978	-55	*C/1O3	-4.0

■ RICH SEVERSON   Severson, Richard Allen b: 1/18/45, Artesia, Cal.   BR/TR, 6', 174 lbs.   Deb: 4/10/70

| 1970 | KC-A | 77 | 240 | 22 | 60 | 11 | 1 | 1 | 22 | 16 | 33 | .250 | .300 | .317 | 70 | -10 | -10 | 23 | 0 | 0 | 0 | .962 | 1 | S2 | -0.2 |
| 1971 | KC-A | 16 | 30 | 4 | 9 | 0 | 2 | 0 | 1 | 3 | 5 | .300 | .364 | .433 | 126 | 1 | 1 | 5 | 0 | 0 | 0 | 1.000 | 6 | /2S3 | 0.8 |

YEAR	TM/L	G	AB	R	H	2B	3B	HR	RBI	BB	SO	AVG	OBP	SLG	PRO+	BR	/A	RC	SB	CS	SBR	FA	FR	POS	TPR
Total	2	93	270	26	69	11	3	1	23	19	38	.256	.307	.330	76	-9	-9	28	0	0	0	.958	7	/S23	0.6

■ ED SEWARD
Seward, Edward William (b: Edward William Sourhardt) b: 6/29/1867, Cleveland, Ohio d: 7/30/47, Cleveland, Ohio TR , 5'7", 175 lbs. Deb: 9/30/1885 U

YEAR	TM/L	G	AB	R	H	2B	3B	HR	RBI	BB	SO	AVG	OBP	SLG	PRO+	BR	/A	RC	SB	CS	SBR	FA	FR	POS	TPR
1885	Pro-N	1	3	0	0	0	0	0	0	0	2	.000	.000	.000	-99	-1	-1	0				1.000	1	/P	0.0
1887	Phi-a	74	266	31	50	10	0	5		16		.188	.239	.282	47	-19	-19	22	14			.901	-3	PO	-0.5
1888	Phi-a	64	225	27	32	3	3	2	14	18		.142	.215	.209	39	-15	-15	13	12			.887	4	P/O	-0.1
1889	Phi-a	46	143	22	31	5	3	2	17	22	19	.217	.333	.336	94	-1	-0	18	6			.885	-4	P/O2	-0.2
1890	Phi-a	26	72	7	10	4	0	0		8		.139	.244	.194	32	-6	-6	4	3			.811	-2	P/O	-0.2
1891	Cle-N	7	19	2	4	2	0	0	1	3	4	.211	.318	.316	83	-0	-0	2	0			1.000	-2	/OP1	-0.2
Total	6	218	728	89	127	24	6	9	32	67	25	.174	.253	.261	53	-42	-41	60	35			.882	-7	P/O12	-1.2

■ GEORGE SEWARD
Seward, George E. b: St.Louis, Mo. 5'7.5", 145 lbs. Deb: 5/19/1875

YEAR	TM/L	G	AB	R	H	2B	3B	HR	RBI	BB	SO	AVG	OBP	SLG	PRO+	BR	/A	RC	SB	CS	SBR	FA	FR	POS	TPR
1875	StL-n	25	97	13	24	2	0	0		1		.247	.255	.268	89	-2	-0	7						C/O2	0.0
1876	NY-N	1	3	0	0	0	0	0	0	0	0	.000	.000	.000	-99	-1	-1	0				1.000	1	/2	0.0
1882	StL-a	38	144	23	31	1	1	0		12		.215	.276	.236	71	-3	-4	10				.776	-0	O/C	-0.4
Total	2	39	147	23	31	1	1	0	0	12	0	.211	.270	.231	68	-4	-5	10				.942	0	/OC2	-0.4

■ LUKE SEWELL
Sewell, James Luther b: 1/5/01, Titus, Ala. d: 5/14/87, Akron, Ohio BR/TR, 5'9", 160 lbs. Deb: 6/30/21 FMC

YEAR	TM/L	G	AB	R	H	2B	3B	HR	RBI	BB	SO	AVG	OBP	SLG	PRO+	BR	/A	RC	SB	CS	SBR	FA	FR	POS	TPR
1921	Cle-A	3	6	0	0	0	0	0	1	0	3	.000	.000	.000	-99	-2	-2	0	0	0	0	1.000	1	/C	-0.1
1922	Cle-A	41	87	14	23	5	0	0	10	5	8	.264	.312	.322	65	-4	-4	9	1	1	-0	.963	0	C	-0.3
1923	Cle-A	10	10	2	2	0	1	0	1	1	0	.200	.273	.400	76	-0	-0	1	0	0	0	.833	0	/C	0.0
1924	Cle-A	63	165	27	48	9	1	0	17	22	13	.291	.387	.358	92	-1	-1	25	1	0	0	.959	5	C	0.7
1925	Cle-A	74	220	30	51	10	2	0	18	33	18	.232	.337	.295	61	-12	-12	25	6	2	1	.971	7	C/O	-0.2
1926	Cle-A	126	433	41	103	16	4	0	46	36	27	.238	.302	.293	55	-28	-29	42	9	3	1	.983	2	*C	-1.7
1927	Cle-A	128	470	52	138	27	6	0	53	20	23	.294	.328	.377	82	-13	-13	54	4	8	-4	.963	-2	*C	-0.9
1928	Cle-A	122	411	52	111	16	9	3	52	26	27	.270	.318	.375	81	-12	-12	49	3	4	-2	.972	13	*C	0.9
1929	Cle-A	124	406	41	96	16	3	1	39	29	26	.236	.287	.298	49	-30	-32	36	6	6	-2	.966	4	*C	-1.7
1930	Cle-A	76	292	40	75	21	2	1	43	14	9	.257	.293	.353	61	-17	-19	30	5	2	0	.974	-2	C	-1.2
1931	Cle-A	108	375	45	103	30	4	1	53	36	17	.275	.341	.384	86	-5	-8	51	1	1	-0	.980	-8	*C	-0.8
1932	Cle-A	87	300	36	76	20	2	2	52	38	24	.253	.337	.353	74	-9	-12	37	4	5	-2	.978	4	C	-0.5
1933	*Was-A	141	474	65	125	30	4	2	61	48	24	.264	.335	.357	84	-11	-10	60	7	2	1	.990	-6	*C	-0.7
1934	Was-A	72	207	21	49	7	3	2	21	22	10	.237	.313	.329	68	-11	-10	22	0	1	-1	.994	-1	C/O123	-0.9
1935	Chi-A	118	421	52	120	19	3	2	67	32	18	.285	.336	.359	78	-13	-14	51	3	2	-0	.988	6	*C	-0.2
1936	Chi-A	128	451	59	113	20	5	5	73	54	16	.251	.332	.350	66	-23	-25	56	11	2	2	.984	12	*C	-0.4
1937	Chi-A☆	122	412	51	111	21	6	1	61	46	18	.269	.343	.357	77	-14	-14	51	4	5	-2	.985	6	*C	-0.3
1938	Chi-A	65	211	23	45	4	1	0	27	20	20	.213	.284	.242	32	-22	-22	16	0	0	0	.985	7	C	-1.1
1939	Cle-A	16	20	1	3	1	0	0	1	3	1	.150	.261	.200	20	-2	-2	1	0	0	0	.966	-1	C/1	-0.2
1942	StL-A	6	12	1	1	0	0	0	0	1	5	.083	.154	.083	-32	-2	-2	0	0	0	0	.944	1	/CM	-0.1
Total	20	1630	5383	653	1393	272	56	20	696	486	307	.259	.323	.341	70	-231	-246	616	65	44	-7	.978	48	*C/O132	-9.7

■ JOE SEWELL
Sewell, Joseph Wheeler b: 10/9/1898, Titus, Ala. d: 3/6/90, Mobile, Ala. BL/TR, 5'6.5", 155 lbs. Deb: 9/10/20 FCH

YEAR	TM/L	G	AB	R	H	2B	3B	HR	RBI	BB	SO	AVG	OBP	SLG	PRO+	BR	/A	RC	SB	CS	SBR	FA	FR	POS	TPR
1920	*Cle-A	22	70	14	23	4	1	0	12	9	4	.329	.412	.414	116	2	2	13	1	0	0	.884	3	S	0.7
1921	Cle-A	154	572	101	182	36	12	4	93	80	17	.318	.412	.444	117	19	18	109	7	6	-2	.944	-3	*S	2.6
1922	Cle-A	153	558	80	167	28	7	2	83	73	20	.299	.386	.385	101	4	3	86	10	12	-4	.939	15	*S2	2.8
1923	Cle-A	153	553	98	195	41	10	3	109	98	12	.353	.456	.479	147	43	43	128	9	6	-1	.930	5	*S	5.9
1924	Cle-A	153	594	99	188	**45**	5	4	106	67	13	.316	.388	.429	109	10	9	102	3	2	-0	.960	**21**	*S	4.4
1925	Cle-A	155	608	78	204	37	7	1	98	64	4	.336	.402	.424	109	11	10	106	7	6	-2	**.967**	16	*S/2	3.8
1926	Cle-A	154	578	91	187	41	5	4	85	65	6	.324	.399	.433	116	16	15	104	17	7	1	.955	3	*S	3.4
1927	Cle-A	153	569	83	180	48	5	1	92	51	7	.316	.382	.424	108	8	7	85	3	16	-9	**.962**	6	*S	1.9
1928	Cle-A	155	588	79	190	40	2	4	70	58	9	.323	.391	.418	111	12	12	100	7	1	2	**.963**	27	*S3	5.5
1929	Cle-A	152	578	90	182	38	3	7	73	48	4	.315	.372	.427	102	5	2	93	6	6	-2	.975	15	*3	2.0
1930	Cle-A	109	353	44	102	17	6	0	48	41	3	.289	.374	.371	86	-4	-6	51	1	4	-2	.950	0	3	-0.3
1931	NY-A	130	484	102	146	22	1	6	64	61	8	.302	.390	.388	111	6	10	78	1	1	-0	.952	-2	*3/2	1.5
1932	*NY-A	125	503	95	137	21	3	11	68	56	3	.272	.349	.392	96	-6	-2	71	0	2	-1	.974	2	*3	0.6
1933	NY-A	135	524	87	143	18	1	2	54	71	4	.273	.361	.323	87	-11	-6	65	2	2	-1	.964	3	*3	0.4
Total	14	1903	7132	1141	2226	436	68	49	1055	842	114	.312	.391	.413	109	116	117	1193	74	71	-20	.951	109	*S3/2	35.2

■ TOMMY SEWELL
Sewell, Thomas Wesley b: 4/16/06, Titus, Ala. d: 7/30/56, Montgomery, Ala. BL/TR, 5'7.5", 155 lbs. Deb: 6/21/27 F

YEAR	TM/L	G	AB	R	H	2B	3B	HR	RBI	BB	SO	AVG	OBP	SLG	PRO+	BR	/A	RC	SB	CS	SBR	FA	FR	POS	TPR
1927	Chi-N	1	1	0	0	0	0	0	0	0	0	.000	.000	.000	-99	-0	-0	0	0			.000	0	H	0.0

■ JIMMY SEXTON
Sexton, Jimmy Dale b: 12/15/51, Mobile, Ala. BR/TR, 5'10", 175 lbs. Deb: 9/02/77

YEAR	TM/L	G	AB	R	H	2B	3B	HR	RBI	BB	SO	AVG	OBP	SLG	PRO+	BR	/A	RC	SB	CS	SBR	FA	FR	POS	TPR
1977	Sea-A	14	37	5	8	1	1	1	3	2	6	.216	.256	.378	71	-2	-2	3	1	1	-0	.929	3	S	0.2
1978	Hou-N	88	141	17	29	3	2	2	6	13	28	.206	.273	.298	64	-8	-7	14	16	2	4	.981	-3	S/32	-0.1
1979	Hou-N	52	43	8	9	0	0	0	1	7	7	.209	.320	.209	50	-3	-3	3	1	3	-2	.943	7	S/32	0.3
1981	Oak-A	7	3	3	0	0	0	0	0	0	2	.000	.000	.000	-99	-1	-1	0	2	0	1	1.000	1	/3D	0.1
1982	Oak-A	69	139	19	34	4	0	2	14	9	24	.245	.295	.317	71	-6	-5	16	16	0	5	.957	-3	S/3D	-0.1
1983	StL-N	6	9	1	1	1	0	0	0	1	4	.111	.200	.222	17	-1	-1	0	0	0	0	1.000	1	/S3	0.0
Total	6	236	372	53	81	9	3	5	24	32	71	.218	.281	.298	64	-20	-18	37	36	6	7	.962	6	S/3D2	0.4

■ TOM SEXTON
Sexton, Thomas William b: 3/14/1865, Rock Island, Ill. d: 2/8/34, Rock Island, Ill. Deb: 9/27/1884

YEAR	TM/L	G	AB	R	H	2B	3B	HR	RBI	BB	SO	AVG	OBP	SLG	PRO+	BR	/A	RC	SB	CS	SBR	FA	FR	POS	TPR
1884	Mil-U	12	47	9	11	2	0	0		4		.234	.294	.277	173	-0	3	4				.853	-1	S	0.2

■ SOCKS SEYBOLD
Seybold, Ralph Orlando b: 11/23/1870, Washingtonville, O d: 12/22/21, Greensburg, Pa. BR/TR, 5'11", 175 lbs. Deb: 8/20/1899

YEAR	TM/L	G	AB	R	H	2B	3B	HR	RBI	BB	SO	AVG	OBP	SLG	PRO+	BR	/A	RC	SB	CS	SBR	FA	FR	POS	TPR
1899	Cin-N	22	85	13	19	5	1	0	8	6		.224	.275	.306	58	-5	-5	8	2			.917	1	O	-0.6
1901	Phi-A	114	449	74	150	24	14	8	90	40		.334	.397	.503	142	29	26	99	15			.954	-6	*O1	1.1
1902	Phi-A	137	522	91	165	27	12	**16**	97	43		.316	.375	.506	137	28	25	105	6			.963	2	*O	1.7
1903	Phi-A	137	522	76	156	**45**	8	8	84	38		.299	.353	.462	137	27	24	89	5			.964	-2	*O1	1.5
1904	Phi-A	143	510	56	149	26	9	3	64	42		.292	.351	.396	130	21	18	79	12			.975	1	*O1	1.3
1905	*Phi-A	133	492	64	135	37	4	6	59	42		.274	.340	.402	133	19	18	73	5			.983	9	*O	2.3
1906	Phi-A	116	411	41	130	23	2	5	59	30		.316	.366	.418	141	21	20	70	9			.925	-5	*O	1.0
1907	Phi-A	147	564	58	153	29	4	5	92	40		.271	.324	.363	117	11	10	75	10			.973	1	*O	0.5
1908	Phi-A	48	130	5	28	2	0	0	3	12		.215	.287	.231	64	-4	-5	9	2			.921	-4	O	-1.1
Total	9	997	3685	478	1085	218	54	51	556	293		.294	.352	.424	129	148	131	606	66			.961	-4	O/1	7.7

■ CY SEYMOUR
Seymour, James Bentley b: 12/9/1872, Albany, N.Y. d: 9/20/19, New York, N.Y. BL/TL, 6', 200 lbs. Deb: 4/22/1896

YEAR	TM/L	G	AB	R	H	2B	3B	HR	RBI	BB	SO	AVG	OBP	SLG	PRO+	BR	/A	RC	SB	CS	SBR	FA	FR	POS	TPR
1896	NY-N	12	32	2	7	0	0	0	0	0	7	.219	.219	.219	17	-4	-4	2	0			.857	0	P/O	-0.1
1897	NY-N	44	137	13	33	5	1	2	14	4		.241	.262	.336	59	-9	-8	13	3			.850	7	P/O	-0.2
1898	NY-N	80	297	41	82	5	2	4	23	9		.276	.300	.347	88	-7	-6	34	8			.887	7	PO/2	-0.6
1899	NY-N	50	159	25	52	3	2	2	27	4		.327	.344	.409	110	1	1	24	2			.839	3	P/O13	-0.2
1900	NY-N	23	40	9	12	0	0	0	2	3		.300	.349	.300	84	-1	-1	4	0			.828	-0	P/O1	-0.2
1901	Bal-A	134	547	84	166	19	8	1	77	28		.303	.337	.373	93	-3	-6	85	38			.945	14	*O/1	-0.3
1902	Bal-A	72	280	38	75	8	8	3	41	18		.268	.314	.386	89	-3	-5	40	12			.956	1	O	-0.8
	Cin-N	62	244	27	83	8	2	2	37	12		.340	.376	.414	131	12	9	42	8			.920	4	O/P3	1.0
1903	Cin-N	135	558	85	191	25	15	7	72	33		.342	.382	.478	131	30	22	116	25			.902	5	*O	1.7
1904	Cin-N	131	531	71	166	26	13	5	58	29		.313	.348	.439	131	24	19	88	11			.951	13	*O	2.5

YEAR	TM/L	G	AB	R	H	2B	3B	HR	RBI	BB	SO	AVG	OBP	SLG	PRO+	BR	/A	RC	SB	CS	SBR	FA	FR	POS	TPR
1905	Cin-N	149	581	95	**219**	**40**	**21**	8	**121**	51		**.377**	.428	**.559**	**175**	**65**	**57**	**153**	21			.947	12	*O	6.3
1906	Cin-N	79	307	35	79	7	2	4	38	24		.257	.315	.332	98	0	-1	36	9			.968	10	O	0.6
	NY-N	72	269	35	86	12	3	4	42	18		.320	.365	.431	145	14	13	51	20			.978	-2	O	0.9
	Yr	151	576	70	165	19	5	8	80	42		.286	.338	.378	120	14	12	87	29			.972	8	*O	1.5
1907	NY-N	131	473	46	139	25	8	3	75	36		.294	.349	.400	131	18	16	77	21			.975	3	*O	1.7
1908	NY-N	156	587	60	157	23	2	5	92	30		.267	.306	.339	101	3	-0	67	18			.949	11	*O	0.5
1909	NY-N	80	280	37	87	12	5	1	30	25		.311	.369	.400	137	12	12	46	14			.968	0	O	1.0
1910	NY-N	79	287	32	76	9	4	1	40	23	18	.265	.324	.334	92	-3	-3	34	10			.936	-6	O	-1.4
1913	Bos-N	39	73	2	13	2	0	0	10	7	7	.178	.259	.205	33	-6	-6	4	2			.950	0	O	-0.7
Total	16	1528	5682	737	1723	229	96	52	799	354	32	.303	.346	.405	117	143	108	917	222			.945	81	*OP/132	11.7

■ TILLIE SHAFER
Shafer, Arthur Joseph b: 3/22/1889, Los Angeles, Cal. d: 1/10/62, Los Angeles, Cal. BB/TR, 5'10", 165 lbs. Deb: 4/24/09

YEAR	TM/L	G	AB	R	H	2B	3B	HR	RBI	BB	SO	AVG	OBP	SLG	PRO+	BR	/A	RC	SB	CS	SBR	FA	FR	POS	TPR
1909	NY-N	38	84	11	15	2	1	0	7	14		.179	.296	.226	61	-3	-3	8	6			.750	-0	32/O	-0.4
1910	NY-N	29	21	5	4	1	0	0	1	0	6	.190	.190	.238	25	-2	-2	1	0			.889	5	/32S	0.3
1912	*NY-N	78	163	48	47	4	1	0	23	30	19	.288	.408	.325	99	3	2	31	22			.879	-7	S32	-0.3
1913	*NY-N	138	508	74	146	17	12	5	52	61	55	.287	.369	.398	118	14	13	82	32			.923	-9	32SO	0.7
Total	4	283	776	138	212	24	14	5	83	105	80	.273	.366	.360	106	11	10	122	60			.903	-12	3/2SO	0.3

■ RALPH SHAFER
Shafer, Ralph Newton b: 3/17/1894, Cincinnati, Ohio d: 2/5/50, Akron, Ohio 5'11", Deb: 7/25/14

YEAR	TM/L	G	AB	R	H	2B	3B	HR	RBI	BB	SO	AVG	OBP	SLG	PRO+	BR	/A	RC	SB	CS	SBR	FA	FR	POS	TPR
1914	Pit-N	1	0	0	0	0	0	0	0	0	0	—	—	—	—	0	0	0	0			.000	0	H	0.0

■ SHAFFER
Shaffer Deb: 9/15/1875

YEAR	TM/L	G	AB	R	H	2B	3B	HR	RBI	BB	SO	AVG	OBP	SLG	PRO+	BR	/A	RC	SB	CS	SBR	FA	FR	POS	TPR
1875	Atl-n	1	4	0	0	0	0	0		0		.000	.000	.000	-99	-1	-1	0						/O	-0.1

■ FRANK SHAFFER
Shaffer, Frank Deb: 4/24/1884

YEAR	TM/L	G	AB	R	H	2B	3B	HR	RBI	BB	SO	AVG	OBP	SLG	PRO+	BR	/A	RC	SB	CS	SBR	FA	FR	POS	TPR
1884	Alt-U	19	74	11	21	2	0	0		3		.284	.312	.311	110	1	1	7				.889	-3	O/C3	-0.2
	KC-U	44	164	18	28	3	2	0		15		.171	.240	.213	63	-7	-4	9				.768	-3	O/C2S3	-0.6
	Bal-U	3	13	1	1	0	0	0		0		.077	.077	.077	-43	-2	-2	0				.750	-1	/O	-0.2
	Yr	66	251	30	50	5	2	0		18		.199	.253	.235	71	-8	-5	15				.796	-6	O/C32S	-1.0

■ ORATOR SHAFFER
Shaffer, George b: 1852, Philadelphia, Pa. BL/TR, 5'9", 165 lbs. Deb: 5/23/1874 F

YEAR	TM/L	G	AB	R	H	2B	3B	HR	RBI	BB	SO	AVG	OBP	SLG	PRO+	BR	/A	RC	SB	CS	SBR	FA	FR	POS	TPR
1874	Har-n	9	34	6	8	0	0	1		0		.235	.235	.324	72	-1	-1	3						/O	-0.1
	Mut-n	1	5	1	1	0	0	0		0		.200	.200	.200	27	-0	-0	0						/O	0.0
	Yr	10	39	7	9	0	0	1		0		.231	.231	.308	67	-1	-2	3						O	-0.1
1875	Phi-n	19	70	10	17	2	1	0		0		.243	.243	.300	83	-1	-1	5						O/31	-0.1
1877	Lou-N	61	260	38	74	9	5	3	34	9	17	.285	.309	.392	101	6	-1	32				.835	14	*O/1	0.8
1878	Ind-N	63	266	48	90	19	6	0	30	13	20	.338	.369	.455	**196**	20	**25**	46				.842	8	*O	2.7
1879	Chi-N	73	316	53	96	13	0	0	35	6	28	.304	.317	.345	111	6	3	35				.801	20	*O/3	1.8
1880	Cle-N	83	338	62	90	14	9	0	21	17	36	.266	.301	.361	126	8	9	38				.901	17	*O	2.3
1881	Cle-N	85	343	48	88	13	6	1	34	23	20	.257	.303	.338	107	1	4	36				.880	2	*O	0.4
1882	Cle-N	84	313	37	67	14	2	3	28	27	27	.214	.276	.300	88	-4	-3	27				.805	-9	*O	-1.1
1883	Buf-N	95	401	67	117	11	3	0	41	27	39	.292	.336	.334	103	3	2	46				.861	20	*O	1.8
1884	StL-U	106	467	130	168	**40**	10	2		30		.360	.398	.501	195	49	46	96				.870	-3	*O/21	3.6
1885	StL-N	69	257	30	50	11	2	0	18	19	31	.195	.250	.253	67	-10	-8	17				.918	11	O	0.1
	Phi-a	2	9	1	2	0	1	0		1		.222	.300	.444	128	0	0	1				1.000	-1	/O	0.0
1886	Phi-a	21	82	15	22	3	3	0		8		.268	.333	.378	123	2	2	12	3			.815	0	O	0.2
1890	Phi-a	100	390	55	110	15	5	1		47		.282	.367	.354	118	9	10	63	29			**.958**	2	*O/1	0.7
Total	2 n	29	109	17	26	2	1	1		0		.239	.239	.303	77	-2	-3	8	0					/O31	-0.2
Total	11	842	3442	584	974	162	52	10	241	227	218	.283	.328	.369	123	89	89	448	32			.865	82	O/213	13.3

■ TAYLOR SHAFFER
Shaffer, Taylor b: 7/1870, Philadelphia, Pa. Deb: 4/17/1890 F

YEAR	TM/L	G	AB	R	H	2B	3B	HR	RBI	BB	SO	AVG	OBP	SLG	PRO+	BR	/A	RC	SB	CS	SBR	FA	FR	POS	TPR
1890	Phi-a	69	261	28	45	3	4	0		28		.172	.258	.215	42	-19	-18	20	19			.921	4	2	-0.9

■ ART SHAMSKY
Shamsky, Arthur Louis b: 10/14/41, St.Louis, Mo. BL/TL, 6'1", 175 lbs. Deb: 4/17/65

YEAR	TM/L	G	AB	R	H	2B	3B	HR	RBI	BB	SO	AVG	OBP	SLG	PRO+	BR	/A	RC	SB	CS	SBR	FA	FR	POS	TPR
1965	Cin-N	64	96	13	25	4	3	2	10	10	29	.260	.330	.427	104	1	1	15	1	0	0	.966	1	O/1	0.2
1966	Cin-N	96	234	41	54	5	0	21	47	32	45	.231	.323	.521	120	9	6	39	0	2	-1	.973	-2	O	0.0
1967	Cin-N	76	147	6	29	3	1	3	13	15	34	.197	.276	.293	56	-7	-9	12	0	1	-1	.984	0	O	-1.2
1968	NY-N	116	345	30	82	14	4	12	48	21	58	.238	.295	.406	108	3	3	41	1	0	0	.993	-3	O1	-0.6
1969	*NY-N	100	303	42	91	9	3	14	47	36	32	.300	.380	.488	139	17	16	57	1	2	-1	.992	-6	O/1	0.4
1970	NY-N	122	403	48	118	19	2	11	49	49	33	.293	.374	.432	115	9	9	64	1	1	-0	1.000	1	O1	0.2
1971	NY-N	68	135	13	25	6	2	5	18	21	18	.185	.299	.370	90	-2	-2	14	1	1	-0	.984	3	O/1	-0.1
1972	Chi-N	15	16	1	2	0	0	0	1	3	3	.125	.263	.125	12	-2	-2	1	0	0	0	1.000	0	/1	-0.2
	Oak-A	8	7	0	0	0	0	0	0	1	2	.000	.125	.000	-64	-1	-1	0	0	0	0	.000	0	H	-0.2
Total	8	665	1686	194	426	60	15	68	233	188	254	.253	.333	.427	109	27	21	243	5	7	-3	.987	-6	O/1	-1.5

■ JIM SHANDLEY
Shandley, James J. b: New York d: 11/4/04, Brooklyn, N.Y. Deb: 5/03/1876

YEAR	TM/L	G	AB	R	H	2B	3B	HR	RBI	BB	SO	AVG	OBP	SLG	PRO+	BR	/A	RC	SB	CS	SBR	FA	FR	POS	TPR
1876	NY-N	2	8	0	1	0	0	0	0	0	0	.125	.125	.125	-19	-1	-1	0				.600	-1	/O	-0.1

■ WALLY SHANER
Shaner, Walter Dedaker "Skinny" b: 5/24/1900, Lynchburg, Va. BR/TR, 6'2", 195 lbs. Deb: 5/04/23

YEAR	TM/L	G	AB	R	H	2B	3B	HR	RBI	BB	SO	AVG	OBP	SLG	PRO+	BR	/A	RC	SB	CS	SBR	FA	FR	POS	TPR
1923	Cle-A	3	4	1	1	0	0	0	0	1	1	.250	.400	.250	74	-0	-0	0	0	0	0	1.000	-1	/O3	-0.1
1926	Bos-A	69	191	20	54	12	2	0	21	17	13	.283	.348	.366	89	-4	-3	25	1	0	0	.965	0	O	-0.6
1927	Bos-A	122	406	54	111	33	6	3	49	21	35	.273	.311	.406	87	-11	-10	48	11	4	1	.955	-8	*O/1	-2.2
1929	Cin-N	13	28	5	9	0	0	1	4	4	5	.321	.406	.429	112	0	1	5	1			1.000	-1	/1O	-0.1
Total	4	207	629	80	175	45	8	4	74	43	54	.278	.327	.394	89	-14	-12	79	13	4		.959	-9	O/13	-3.0

■ HOWIE SHANKS
Shanks, Howard Samuel "Hank" b: 7/21/1890, Chicago, Ill. d: 7/30/41, Monaca, Pa. BR/TR, 5'11", 170 lbs. Deb: 5/09/12 C

YEAR	TM/L	G	AB	R	H	2B	3B	HR	RBI	BB	SO	AVG	OBP	SLG	PRO+	BR	/A	RC	SB	CS	SBR	FA	FR	POS	TPR
1912	Was-A	116	399	52	92	14	7	1	48	40		.231	.305	.308	75	-13	-13	45	21			.962	-2	*O	-2.1
1913	Was-A	109	390	38	99	11	5	1	37	15	40	.254	.287	.315	75	-13	-14	39	24			.978	3	*O	-1.6
1914	Was-A	143	500	44	112	22	10	4	64	29	51	.224	.269	.332	78	-14	-17	47	18	16	-4	.954	-1	*O	-3.0
1915	Was-A	141	492	52	123	19	8	0	47	30	42	.250	.297	.321	83	-11	-12	48	12	14	-5	.982	7	O32	-1.2
1916	Was-A	140	471	51	119	15	7	1	48	41	34	.253	.317	.321	92	-5	-5	54	23	12	-0	.987	10	O3/S1	0.2
1917	Was-A	126	430	45	87	15	5	0	28	33	37	.202	.269	.260	62	-20	-20	35	15			.929	13	SO/1	-0.4
1918	Was-A	120	436	42	112	19	4	1	56	31	21	.257	.312	.326	94	-5	-4	50	23			.957	1	O2/3	-0.4
1919	Was-A	135	491	33	122	8	7	1	54	25	48	.248	.289	.299	66	-23	-23	47	13			.922	-11	S2/O	-2.8
1920	Was-A	128	444	56	119	16	7	4	37	29	43	.268	.316	.363	82	-14	-12	51	11	6	-0	.951	-6	3O1/2S	-1.8
1921	Was-A	154	562	81	170	24	**18**	7	69	57	38	.302	.370	.447	113	6	10	93	11	10	-3	**.960**	5	*3/2	2.1
1922	Was-A	84	272	35	77	10	9	1	32	25	25	.283	.352	.397	100	-2	-0	41	6	0	2	.920	7	3O	1.0
1923	Bos-A	131	464	38	118	19	5	3	57	19	37	.254	.285	.336	63	-26	-27	44	6	6	-2	.939	-19	32/OS	-3.9
1924	Bos-A	72	193	22	50	16	3	0	25	21	12	.259	.332	.373	81	-6	-6	25	1	0	0	.972	7	S3/O12	0.6
1925	NY-A	66	155	15	40	3	1	1	18	20	15	.258	.343	.310	68	-7	-7	18	1	0	0	.938	-6	32/O	-1.0
Total	14	1665	5699	604	1440	211	96	25	620	415	443	.253	.308	.337	82	-154	-148	637	185	64		.971	10	O3S2/1	-14.3

■ DOC SHANLEY
Shanley, Harry Root b: 1890, Granbury, Tex. d: 12/13/34, St.Petersburg, Fla BR/TR, 6', 174 lbs. Deb: 9/15/12

YEAR	TM/L	G	AB	R	H	2B	3B	HR	RBI	BB	SO	AVG	OBP	SLG	PRO+	BR	/A	RC	SB	CS	SBR	FA	FR	POS	TPR
1912	StL-A	5	8	1	0	0	0	0	1	2		.000	.200	.000	-43	-1	-1	0	0			.833	-2	/S	-0.3

YEAR	TM/L	G	AB	R	H	2B	3B	HR	RBI	BB	SO	AVG	OBP	SLG	PRO+	BR	/A	RC	SB	CS SBR	FA	FR	POS	TPR

■ WARREN SHANNABROOK Shannabrook, Warren H. b: 11/30/1880, Massillon, Ohio d: 3/10/64, N.Canton, Ohio BR/TR, 6', 170 lbs. Deb: 8/13/06

| 1906 | Was-A | 1 | 2 | 0 | 0 | 0 | 0 | 0 | 0 | 0 | 0 | .000 | .000 | .000 | -99 | -0 | -0 | 0 | 0 | | 1.000 | -1 | /3 | -0.1 |

■ DAN SHANNON Shannon, Daniel W. b: 3/23/1865, Bridgeport, Conn. d: 10/25/13, Bridgeport, Conn. 175 lbs. Deb: 4/17/1889 M

1889	Lou-a	121	498	90	128	22	12	4	48	42	52	.257	.315	.373	99	-3	-1	68	26		.910	7	*2M	1.0
1890	Phi-P	19	75	15	18	5	1	1	16	4	12	.240	.278	.373	73	-3	-3	9	4		.926	-4	2	-0.5
	NY-P	83	324	59	70	7	8	3	44	25	34	.216	.274	.315	54	-20	-25	35	21		.908	1	2/S	-1.5
	Yr	102	399	74	88	12	9	4	60	29	46	.221	.275	.326	57	-23	-28	44	25		.911	-3	2/S	-2.0
1891	Was-a	19	67	7	9	2	0	0	3	6	9	.134	.205	.164	8	-8	-7	3	3		.878	1	S/2M	-0.5
Total	3	242	964	171	225	36	21	8	111	77	107	.233	.291	.339	75	-33	-37	115	54		.911	5	2/S	-1.5

■ FRANK SHANNON Shannon, John Francis b: 12/3/1873, San Francisco, Cal. d: 2/27/34, Boston, Mass. 5'3", 155 lbs. Deb: 10/01/1892

1892	Was-N	1	4	0	1	0	0	0	2	0	2	.250	.250	.250	54	-1	-0	0	0		.625	-1	/S	-0.1
1896	Lou-N	31	115	14	18	1	1	1	15	13	15	.157	.248	.209	23	-13	-12	7	3		.830	-13	S/3	-2.0
Total	2	32	119	14	19	1	1	1	17	13	17	.160	.248	.210	24	-13	-12	8	3		.820	-13	S/S3	-2.1

■ JOE SHANNON Shannon, Joseph Aloysius b: 2/11/1897, Jersey City, N.J. d: 7/28/55, Jersey City, N.J. BR/TR, 5'11", 170 lbs. Deb: 7/07/15 F

| 1915 | Bos-N | 5 | 10 | 3 | 2 | 0 | 0 | 0 | 1 | 0 | 3 | .200 | .200 | .200 | 22 | -1 | -1 | 1 | 0 | | .750 | -1 | /O2 | -0.2 |

■ RED SHANNON Shannon, Maurice Joseph b: 2/11/1897, Jersey City, N.J. d: 4/12/70, Jersey City, N.J. BB/TR, 5'11", 170 lbs. Deb: 10/07/15 F

1915	Bos-N	1	3	0	0	0	0	0	0	0	0	.000	.000	.000	-99	-1	-0	0	0		.857	0	/2	-0.1
1917	Phi-A	11	35	8	10	0	0	0	7	6	9	.286	.390	.286	108	1	1	4	2		.875	-0	S	0.1
1918	Phi-A	72	225	23	54	6	5	0	16	42	52	.240	.367	.311	103	3	3	28	5		.898	-4	S2	0.3
1919	Phi-A	39	155	14	42	7	2	0	14	12	28	.271	.331	.342	88	-2	-2	18	4		.948	-5	2	-0.6
	Bos-A	80	290	36	75	11	7	0	17	17	42	.259	.313	.345	90	-6	-4	32	7		.973	-4	2	-0.5
	Yr	119	445	50	117	18	9	0	31	29	70	.263	.320	.344	89	-9	-7	50	11		.965	-9	*2	-1.1
1920	Was-A	63	222	30	64	8	7	0	30	22	32	.288	.352	.387	99	-1	-0	30	2 5 -2		.919	-19	S23	-1.8
	Phi-A	24	88	4	15	1	1	0	3	4	12	.170	.207	.205	9	-12	-12	4	1 1 -0		.945	-1	S	-1.1
	Yr	87	310	34	79	9	8	0	33	26	44	.255	.313	.335	73	-13	-12	32	3 6 -3		.931	-21	S23	-2.9
1921	Phi-A	1	1	0	0	0	0	0	0	0	0	.000	.000	.000	-99	-0	-0	0	0		.000	0	H	0.0
1926	Chi-N	19	51	9	17	5	0	0	4	6	3	.333	.414	.431	126	2	2	9	0		.957	-2	S	0.2
Total	7	310	1070	124	277	38	22	0	91	109	178	.259	.334	.336	89	-16	-14	125	21	6	.957	-36	2S/3	-3.5

■ MIKE SHANNON Shannon, Thomas Michael "Moonman" b: 7/5/39, St.Louis, Mo. BR/TR, 6'3", 195 lbs. Deb: 9/11/62

1962	StL-N	10	15	3	2	0	0	0	0	1	3	.133	.188	.133	-11	-2	-3	0	0 0 0		1.000	1	/O	-0.2
1963	StL-N	32	26	3	8	0	0	1	2	0	6	.308	.333	.423	106	0	0	3	0 1 -1		.944	2	O	0.2
1964	*StL-N	88	253	30	66	8	2	9	43	19	54	.261	.313	.415	95	1	-2	32	4 0 1		.983	-7	O	-1.1
1965	StL-N	124	244	32	54	17	3	3	25	28	46	.221	.307	.352	78	-5	-7	26	2 1 0		.994	-1	*O/C	-1.1
1966	StL-N	137	459	61	132	20	6	16	64	37	106	.288	.341	.462	120	12	12	70	8 4 0		.985	7	*O/C	1.4
1967	*StL-N	130	482	53	118	18	3	12	77	37	89	.245	.304	.369	93	-6	-5	52	2 4 -2		.919	-10	3/O	-2.0
1968	*StL-N	156	576	62	153	29	2	15	79	37	114	.266	.312	.401	114	8	8	70	1 2 -1		.952	-7	*3	0.1
1969	StL-N	150	551	51	140	15	5	12	55	49	87	.254	.316	.365	90	-8	-8	63	1 4 -2		.945	-19	*3	-3.0
1970	StL-N	55	137	18	37	9	2	0	22	16	20	.213	.292	.287	51	-12	-12	14	1 1 -0		.919	-13	3	-2.7
Total	9	882	2780	313	710	116	23	68	367	224	525	.255	.313	.387	96	-11	-16	331	19 17 -5		.938	-46	3O/C	-8.4

■ OWEN SHANNON Shannon, Owen Dennis Ignatius b: 12/22/1885, Omaha, Neb. d: 4/10/18, Omaha, Neb. BR/TR, Deb: 9/06/03

1903	StL-A	9	28	1	6	2	0	0	3	1		.214	.241	.286	59	-1	-1	2	0		.957	-0	/C1	-0.1
1907	Was-A	4	7	0	1	0	0	0	0	0		.143	.143	.143	-9	-1	-1	0	0		1.000	3	/C	0.2
Total	2	13	35	1	7	2	0	0	3	1		.200	.222	.257	47	-2	-2	2	0		.970	2	/C1	0.1

■ WALLY SHANNON Shannon, Walter Charles b: 1/23/33, Cleveland, Ohio d: 2/8/92, Creve Coeur, Mo. BL/TR, 6', 178 lbs. Deb: 7/09/59

1959	StL-N	47	95	5	27	5	0	0	5	0	12	.284	.292	.337	63	-5	-5	9	0 0 0		1.000	-11	S2	-1.4
1960	StL-N	18	23	2	4	0	0	0	1	3	6	.174	.296	.174	30	-2	-2	1	0 0 0		1.000	2	2/S	0.0
Total	2	65	118	7	31	5	0	0	6	3	18	.263	.293	.305	56	-7	-8	11	0 0 0		.955	-9	/2S	-1.4

■ SPIKE SHANNON Shannon, William Porter b: 2/7/1878, Pittsburgh, Pa. d: 5/16/40, Minneapolis, Minn. BB/TR, 5'11", 180 lbs. Deb: 4/15/04 U

1904	StL-N	134	500	84	140	10	3	1	26	50		.280	.349	.318	112	6	9	73	34		.978	9	*O	1.0
1905	StL-N	140	544	73	146	16	3	0	41	47		.268	.327	.309	93	-4	-4	68	27		.984	0	*O	-1.1
1906	StL-N	80	302	36	78	4	0	0	25	36		.258	.337	.272	94	-2	-0	35	15		.972	6	O	0.2
	NY-N	76	287	42	73	5	1	0	25	34		.254	.340	.279	91	-1	-1	35	18		.958	-7	O	-1.4
	Yr	156	589	78	151	9	1	0	50	70		.256	.338	.275	93	-3	-2	71	33		.966	-1	*O	-1.2
1907	NY-N	155	585	104	155	12	5	1	33	82		.265	.361	.308	106	11	8	80	33		.977	2	*O	0.5
1908	NY-N	77	268	34	60	2	1	1	21	28		.224	.314	.250	77	-4	-6	26	13		.976	-3	O	-1.4
	Pit-N	32	127	10	25	0	2	0	12	9		.197	.250	.228	53	-7	-7	8	5		.947	1	O	-0.8
	Yr	109	395	44	85	2	3	1	33	37		.215	.294	.243	70	-11	-13	34	18		.964	-2	*O	-2.2
Total	5	694	2613	383	677	49	15	3	183	286		.259	.337	.293	96	-3	-1	326	145		.974	8	O	-3.0

■ BILLY SHANTZ Shantz, Wilmer Ebert b: 7/31/27, Pottstown, Pa. BR/TR, 6'1", 160 lbs. Deb: 4/13/54 F

1954	Phi-A	51	164	13	42	9	3	1	17	17	23	.256	.326	.366	89	-3	-3	19	0 0 0		.975	-13	C	-1.4
1955	KC-A	79	217	18	56	4	1	1	12	11	14	.258	.294	.300	59	-12	-13	18	0 0 0		.990	-10	C	-2.1
1960	NY-A	1	0	0	0	0	0	0	0	0	0	—	—	—		0	0	0	0 0 0		1.000	-0	/C	0.0
Total	3	131	381	31	98	13	4	2	29	28	37	.257	.308	.328	72	-15	-15	38	0 0 0		.984	-23	C	-3.5

■ RALPH SHARMAN Sharman, Ralph Edward "Bally" b: 4/11/1895, Cleveland, Ohio d: 5/24/18, Camp Sheridan, Ala BR/TR, 5'11", 176 lbs. Deb: 9/10/17

| 1917 | Phi-A | 13 | 37 | 2 | 11 | 2 | 1 | 0 | 2 | 3 | 2 | .297 | .366 | .405 | 137 | 2 | 2 | 6 | 1 | | .941 | -1 | O | 0.0 |

■ DICK SHARON Sharon, Richard Louis b: 4/15/50, San Mateo, Cal. BR/TR, 6'2", 195 lbs. Deb: 5/13/73

1973	Det-A	91	178	20	43	9	0	7	16	10	31	.242	.287	.410	87	-3	-4	20	2 0 1		.970	-10	O	-1.6
1974	Det-A	60	129	12	28	4	0	2	10	14	29	.217	.294	.295	67	-5	-5	11	4 4 -1		.989	-5	O	-1.4
1975	SD-N	91	160	14	31	7	0	4	20	26	35	.194	.306	.313	77	-6	-5	15	0 2 -1		.948	-0	O	-0.8
Total	3	242	467	46	102	20	0	13	46	50	95	.218	.294	.345	79	-13	-14	46	6 6 -2		.969	-15	O	-3.8

■ BILL SHARP Sharp, William Howard b: 1/18/50, Lima, Ohio BL/TL, 5'10", 178 lbs. Deb: 5/26/73

1973	Chi-A	77	196	23	54	8	3	4	22	19	28	.276	.349	.408	109	3	2	28	2 3 -1		.981	2	O/D	0.1
1974	Chi-A	100	320	45	81	13	2	4	24	25	37	.253	.311	.344	86	-5	-6	33	0 3 -2		.986	-1	O	-1.3
1975	Chi-A	18	35	1	7	0	0	0	4	2	3	.200	.243	.200	26	-3	-3	2	0 0 0		.941	-3	O	-0.7
	Mil-A	125	373	37	95	27	3	1	34	19	26	.255	.293	.351	81	-10	-10	36	0 3 -0		.994	-3	*O	-2.0
	Yr	143	408	38	102	27	3	1	38	21	29	.250	.288	.338	76	-13	-14	38	0 3 -2		.991	-6	O	-2.7
1976	Mil-A	78	180	16	44	4	0	0	11	10	15	.244	.288	.267	64	-8	-8	13	1 3 -2		.975	0	O/D	-1.2
Total	4	398	1104	122	281	52	8	9	95	75	109	.255	.306	.341	83	-23	-25	113	3 12 -6		.985	-5	O/D	-5.1

■ BUD SHARPE Sharpe, Bayard Heston b: 8/6/1881, West Chester, Pa. d: 5/31/16, Haddock, Ga. BL/TR, Deb: 4/14/05

1905	Bos-N	46	170	8	31	3	2	0	11	7		.182	.215	.224	31	-15	-14	9	0		.904	2	O/C1	-1.5
1910	Bos-N	115	439	30	105	14	3	0	29	14	31	.239	.264	.285	58	-24	-26	34	4		.987	7	*1	-2.0
	Pit-N	4	16	2	3	0	1	0	1	0	2	.188	.188	.313	43	-1	-1	1	0		1.000	0	/1	-0.1

YEAR	TM/L	G	AB	R	H	2B	3B	HR	RBI	BB	SO	AVG	OBP	SLG	PRO+	BR	/A	RC	SB	CS	SBR	FA	FR	POS	TPR
	Yr	119	455	32	108	14	4	0	30	14	33	.237	.262	.286	57	-25	-27	35	4			.987	8	*1	-2.1
Total	2	165	625	40	139	17	6	0	41	21	33	.222	.249	.269	51	-39	-41	44	4			.987	9	1/OC	-3.6

■ MIKE SHARPERSON Sharperson, Michael Tyrone b: 10/4/61, Orangeburg, S.C. BR/TR, 6'3", 190 lbs. Deb: 4/06/87

YEAR	TM/L	G	AB	R	H	2B	3B	HR	RBI	BB	SO	AVG	OBP	SLG	PRO+	BR	/A	RC	SB	CS	SBR	FA	FR	POS	TPR
1987	Tor-A	32	96	4	20	4	1	0	9	7	15	.208	.269	.271	43	-8	-8	7	2	1	0	.971	-5	2	-1.1
	LA-N	10	33	7	9	2	0	0	1	4	5	.273	.351	.333	85	-1	-1	4	0	0	0	1.000	2	/32	0.1
1988	*LA-N	46	59	8	16	1	0	0	4	1	12	.271	.295	.288	70	-2	-2	5	0	1	-1	.949	-0	2/3S	-0.3
1989	LA-N	27	28	2	7	3	0	0	5	4	7	.250	.344	.357	102	0	0	3	0	1	-1	1.000	-0	/213S	0.0
1990	LA-N	129	357	42	106	14	2	3	36	46	39	.297	.379	.373	111	5	7	54	15	6	1	.949	6	*3S/21	1.4
1991	LA-N	105	216	24	60	11	2	2	20	25	24	.278	.355	.375	108	2	3	30	1	3	-2	.981	-5	3S1/2	-0.3
1992	LA-N★	128	317	48	95	21	0	3	36	47	33	.300	.390	.394	124	11	12	50	2	2	-1	.979	1	23/S	1.4
Total	6	477	1106	135	313	56	5	8	111	134	135	.283	.363	.364	105	8	11	153	20	14	-2	.953	-2	32/S1	1.2

■ JACK SHARROTT Sharrott, John Henry b: 8/13/1869, Bangor, Me. d: 12/31/27, Los Angeles, Cal. BR/TR, 5'9", 165 lbs. Deb: 4/22/1890

YEAR	TM/L	G	AB	R	H	2B	3B	HR	RBI	BB	SO	AVG	OBP	SLG	PRO+	BR	/A	RC	SB	CS	SBR	FA	FR	POS	TPR
1890	NY-N	32	109	16	22	3	2	0	14	0	14	.202	.202	.266	37	-9	-9	7	6			.932	-2	P/O	-0.5
1891	NY-N	10	30	5	10	2	0	1	7	1	2	.333	.355	.500	156	2	2	7	3			.950	1	P	0.0
1892	NY-N	4	8	1	1	0	0	0	0	0	1	.125	.125	.125	-24	-1	-1	0	0			.333	-1	/OP	-0.2
1893	Phi-N	50	152	25	38	4	3	1	22	8	14	.250	.287	.336	67	-8	-8	17	6			.824	-8	OP	-1.2
Total	4	96	299	47	71	9	5	2	43	9	31	.237	.260	.321	63	-16	-16	31	15			.927	-10	/PO	-1.9

■ SHAG SHAUGHNESSY Shaughnessy, Francis Joseph b: 4/8/1883, Amboy, Ill. d: 5/15/69, Montreal, Que., Can BR/TR, 6'1.5", 185 lbs. Deb: 4/17/05 C

YEAR	TM/L	G	AB	R	H	2B	3B	HR	RBI	BB	SO	AVG	OBP	SLG	PRO+	BR	/A	RC	SB	CS	SBR	FA	FR	POS	TPR
1905	Was-A	1	3	0	0	0	0	0	0	0		.000	.000	.000	-99	-1	-1	0	0			.667	-0	/O	-0.1
1908	Phi-A	8	29	2	9	0	0	0	1	2		.310	.355	.310	109	1	0	4	3			1.000	-1	/O	-0.1
Total	2	9	32	2	9	0	0	0	1	2		.281	.324	.281	91	-0	-0	4	3			.938	-1	/O	-0.2

■ AL SHAW Shaw, Albert Simpson b: 3/1/1881, Toledo, Ill. d: 12/30/74, Danville, Ill. BL/TR, 5'8.5", 165 lbs. Deb: 9/28/07

YEAR	TM/L	G	AB	R	H	2B	3B	HR	RBI	BB	SO	AVG	OBP	SLG	PRO+	BR	/A	RC	SB	CS	SBR	FA	FR	POS	TPR
1907	StL-N	9	25	2	7	0	0	0	1	3		.280	.379	.280	111	0	1	4	1			.947	-1	/O	0.0
1908	StL-N	107	367	40	97	13	4	1	19	25		.264	.311	.330	110	1	3	40	9			.931	7	O/S3	0.7
1909	StL-N	114	331	45	82	12	7	2	34	55		.248	.355	.344	125	8	11	45	15			.940	-1	O	0.7
1914	Bro-F	112	376	81	122	27	7	5	49	44	59	.324	.395	.473	148	23	23	83	24			.955	1	*O	2.0
1915	KC-F	132	448	67	126	22	10	6	67	46	45	.281	.348	.415	129	13	15	73	15			.942	-14	*O	-0.5
Total	5	474	1547	235	434	74	28	14	170	173	104	.281	.353	.392	129	46	53	244	64			.942	-8	O/S3	2.9

■ AL SHAW Shaw, Alfred "Shoddy" b: 10/3/1874, Burslem, England d: 3/25/58, Uhrichsville, Ohio BR/TR, 5'8", 170 lbs. Deb: 6/08/01

YEAR	TM/L	G	AB	R	H	2B	3B	HR	RBI	BB	SO	AVG	OBP	SLG	PRO+	BR	/A	RC	SB	CS	SBR	FA	FR	POS	TPR
1901	Det-A	55	171	20	46	7	0	1	23	10		.269	.321	.327	77	-4	-6	20	2			.938	-0	C/13S	-0.2
1907	Bos-A	76	198	10	38	1	3	0	7	18		.192	.269	.227	59	-9	-8	14	4			.971	15	C/1	1.4
1908	Chi-A	32	49	0	4	1	0	0	2	2		.082	.118	.102	-29	-7	-7	1	0			.953	2	C	-0.4
1909	Bos-N	18	41	1	4	0	0	0	0	5		.098	.213	.098	-3	-5	-5	1	0			.975	4	C	0.0
Total	4	181	459	31	92	9	3	1	32	35		.200	.267	.240	53	-25	-26	35	6			.961	21	C/13S	0.8

■ BEN SHAW Shaw, Benajmin Nathaniel b: 6/18/1893, LaCenter, Ky. d: 3/16/59, Aurora, Ohio BR/TR, 5'11.5", 190 lbs. Deb: 4/11/17

YEAR	TM/L	G	AB	R	H	2B	3B	HR	RBI	BB	SO	AVG	OBP	SLG	PRO+	BR	/A	RC	SB	CS	SBR	FA	FR	POS	TPR
1917	Pit-N	2	2	0	0	0	0	0	0	0	0	.000	.000	.000	-97	-0	-0	0	0			.000	0	H	-0.1
1918	Pit-N	21	36	5	7	1	0	0	2	2	2	.194	.275	.222	50	-2	-2	2	0			.981	-2	/1C	-0.4
Total	2	23	38	5	7	1	0	0	2	2	2	.184	.262	.211	43	-2	-3	2	0				-2	/1C	-0.5

■ HUNKY SHAW Shaw, Royal N b: 9/29/1884, Yakima, Wash. d: 7/3/69, Yakima, Wash. BB/TR, 5'8", 165 lbs. Deb: 5/16/08

YEAR	TM/L	G	AB	R	H	2B	3B	HR	RBI	BB	SO	AVG	OBP	SLG	PRO+	BR	/A	RC	SB	CS	SBR	FA	FR	POS	TPR
1908	Pit-N	1	1	0	0	0	0	0	0	0		.000	.000	.000	-99	-0	-0	0	0			.000	0	H	0.0

■ MARTY SHAY Shay, Arthur Joseph b: 4/25/1896, Boston, Mass. d: 2/20/51, Worcester, Mass. BR/TR, 5'7.5", 148 lbs. Deb: 9/16/16

YEAR	TM/L	G	AB	R	H	2B	3B	HR	RBI	BB	SO	AVG	OBP	SLG	PRO+	BR	/A	RC	SB	CS	SBR	FA	FR	POS	TPR
1916	Chi-N	2	7	0	2	0	0	0	0	0	1	.286	.286	.286	68	-0	-0	1	0			.917	0	/S	0.0
1924	Bos-N	19	68	4	16	3	1	0	2	5	5	.235	.297	.309	65	-4	-3	6	2	1	0	.950	-12	2/S	-1.5
Total	2	21	75	4	18	3	1	0	2	5	6	.240	.296	.307	66	-4	-3	7	2	1		.929	-12	/2S	-1.5

■ DANNY SHAY Shay, Daniel C. b: 11/8/1876, Springfield, Ohio d: 12/1/27, Kansas City, Mo. TR, 5'10", Deb: 4/30/01

YEAR	TM/L	G	AB	R	H	2B	3B	HR	RBI	BB	SO	AVG	OBP	SLG	PRO+	BR	/A	RC	SB	CS	SBR	FA	FR	POS	TPR
1901	Cle-A	19	75	4	17	2	2	0	10	2		.227	.266	.307	61	-4	-4	6	0			.901	-4	S	-0.5
1904	StL-N	99	340	45	87	11	1	1	18	39		.256	.338	.303	103	1	3	49	36			.911	-7	S/2	-0.1
1905	StL-N	78	281	30	67	12	1	0	28	35		.238	.329	.288	87	-4	-3	32	11			.953	-13	2S	-1.6
1907	NY-N	35	79	10	15	1	1	1	6	12		.190	.304	.266	76	-2	-2	8	5			.931	-7	2/SO	-1.1
Total	4	231	775	89	186	26	5	2	62	88		.240	.325	.294	90	-9	-6	95	52			.902	-31	S/2O	-3.3

■ GERRY SHEA Shea, Gerald J. b: 7/26/1881, St.Louis, Mo. d: 5/3/64, Berkeley, Mo. TR, 5'7", 160 lbs. Deb: 10/01/05

YEAR	TM/L	G	AB	R	H	2B	3B	HR	RBI	BB	SO	AVG	OBP	SLG	PRO+	BR	/A	RC	SB	CS	SBR	FA	FR	POS	TPR
1905	StL-N	2	6	0	2	0	0	0	0	0		.333	.333	.333	102	-0	-0	1	0			.917	1	/C	0.1

■ NAP SHEA Shea, John Edward "Napoleon" b: 5/23/1874, Ware, Mass. d: 7/8/68, Bloomfield Hills, Mich. BR/TR, 5'5", 155 lbs. Deb: 9/11/02

YEAR	TM/L	G	AB	R	H	2B	3B	HR	RBI	BB	SO	AVG	OBP	SLG	PRO+	BR	/A	RC	SB	CS	SBR	FA	FR	POS	TPR
1902	Phi-N	3	8	1	1	0	0	0	0	1		.125	.300	.125	32	-1	-1	0	0			1.000	0	/C	0.0

■ MERV SHEA Shea, Mervyn David John b: 9/5/1900, San Francisco, Cal d: 1/27/53, Sacramento, Cal. BR/TR, 5'11", 175 lbs. Deb: 4/23/27 C

YEAR	TM/L	G	AB	R	H	2B	3B	HR	RBI	BB	SO	AVG	OBP	SLG	PRO+	BR	/A	RC	SB	CS	SBR	FA	FR	POS	TPR
1927	Det-A	34	85	5	15	6	3	0	9	7	15	.176	.239	.318	43	-8	-8	6	0	0	0	.949	-1	C	-0.6
1928	Det-A	39	85	8	20	2	3	0	9	9	11	.235	.316	.329	69	-4	-4	9	2	2	-1	.951	4	C	0.1
1929	Det-A	50	162	23	47	6	0	3	24	19	18	.290	.365	.383	92	-1	-1	23	2	1	0	.964	-6	C	-0.3
1933	Bos-A	16	56	1	8	3	0	0	8	4	7	.143	.200	.196	5	-8	-8	2	0	0	0	1.000	-2	C	-0.8
	StL-A	94	279	26	73	11	1	1	27	43	26	.262	.360	.319	76	-6	-9	35	2	0	1	.995	9	C	0.5
	Yr	110	335	27	81	14	1	1	35	47	33	.242	.335	.299	65	-14	-16	37	2	0	1	**.996**	7	*C	-0.3
1934	Chi-A	62	176	8	28	3	0	0	5	24	19	.159	.260	.176	14	-22	-23	9	0	1	-1	.972	1	C	-1.9
1935	Chi-A	46	122	8	28	2	0	0	13	30	9	.230	.382	.246	64	-5	-5	14	0	0	0	.990	8	C	0.5
1936	Chi-A	14	24	3	3	0	0	0	2	6	5	.125	.300	.125	8	-3	-4	1	0	0	0	1.000	1	C	-0.2
1937	Chi-A	25	71	7	15	1	0	0	5	15	10	.211	.349	.225	48	-5	-5	7	1	0	0	.966	3	C	-0.1
1938	Bro-N	48	120	14	22	5	0	0	12	28	20	.183	.338	.225	56	-6	-6	11	1			.977	-1	C	-0.5
1939	Det-A	4	2	0	0	0	0	0	0	0	1	.000	.000	.000	-93	-1	-1	0	0	0	0	.500	-1	/C	-0.1
1944	Phi-N	7	15	2	4	0	0	1	1	4	4	.267	.421	.467	155	1	1	3	0			.952	-0	/C	0.1
Total	11	439	1197	105	263	39	7	5	115	189	145	.220	.327	.277	58	-67	-72	122	8	4		.976	16	C	-3.3

■ DANNY SHEAFFER Sheaffer, Danny Todd b: 8/2/61, Jacksonville, Fla. BR/TR, 6' ", 185 lbs. Deb: 4/09/87

YEAR	TM/L	G	AB	R	H	2B	3B	HR	RBI	BB	SO	AVG	OBP	SLG	PRO+	BR	/A	RC	SB	CS	SBR	FA	FR	POS	TPR
1987	Bos-A	25	66	5	8	1	0	1	5	0	14	.121	.121	.182	-21	-11	-12	1	0	0	0	.977	-3	C	-1.3
1989	Cle-A	7	16	1	1	0	0	0	0	2	2	.063	.167	.063	-32	-3	-3	0	0	0	0	.000	0	/3OD	-0.3
Total	2	32	82	6	9	1	0	1	5	2	16	.110	.131	.159	-22	-14	-14	1	0	0	0	.984	-2	/CD3O	-1.6

■ DAVE SHEAN Shean, David William b: 7/9/1883, Arlington, Mass. d: 5/22/63, Boston, Mass. BR/TR, 5'11", 175 lbs. Deb: 9/10/06

YEAR	TM/L	G	AB	R	H	2B	3B	HR	RBI	BB	SO	AVG	OBP	SLG	PRO+	BR	/A	RC	SB	CS	SBR	FA	FR	POS	TPR
1906	Phi-A	22	75	7	16	3	2	0	3	5		.213	.280	.307	82	-1	-2	9	6			.980	-2	2	-0.4
1908	Phi-N	14	48	4	7	2	0	0	2	1		.146	.180	.188	17	-4	-5	2	1			.871	-6	S	-1.3
1909	Phi-N	36	112	14	26	2	2	0	4	14		.232	.323	.286	88	-1	-1	11	3			.982	-2	21/OS	-0.4
	Bos-N	75	267	32	66	11	4	1	29	17		.247	.297	.330	90	-2	-4	31	14			.956	8	2	0.3
	Yr	111	379	46	92	13	6	1	33	31		.243	.305	.317	90	-4	-5	42	17			.960	6	21/OS	-0.1
1910	Bos-N	150	543	52	130	12	7	3	36	42	45	.239	.294	.304	71	-19	-22	53	16			.953	**43**	*2	1.9
1911	Chi-N	54	145	17	28	4	0	0	15	8	15	.193	.240	.221	29	-14	-14	9	4			.947	1	2S/3	-1.2
1912	Bos-N	4	10	1	3	0	0	0	0	1	2	.300	.417	.300	96	0	0	1	0			.917	-1	/S	-0.1

YEAR	TM/L	G	AB	R	H	2B	3B	HR	RBI	BB	SO	AVG	OBP	SLG	PRO+	BR	/A	RC	SB	CS	SBR	FA	FR	POS	TPR
1917	Cin-N	131	442	36	93	9	5	2	35	22	39	.210	.249	.267	61	-22	-20	31	10			.961	19	*2	0.5
1918	*Bos-A	115	425	58	112	16	3	0	34	40	25	.264	.331	.315	97	-2	-1	51	11			.967	-9	*2	-0.3
1919	Bos-A	29	100	4	14	0	0	0	8	5	7	.140	.189	.140	-7	-14	-13	3	1			.981	4	2	-0.8
Total	9	630	2167	225	495	59	23	6	166	155	133	.228	.284	.285	70	-80	-82	200	66			.961	55	2/S1O3	-1.8
■ **RAY SHEARER** Shearer, Ray Solomon b: 9/19/29, Jacobus, Pa. d: 2/21/82, York, Pa. BR/TR, 6', 200 lbs. Deb: 9/18/57																									
1957	Mil-N	2	2	1	1	0	0	0	0	1	1	.500	.667	.500	237	1	1	1	0	0	0	.000	-0	/O	0.0
■ **JOHN SHEARON** Shearon, John M. b: 1870, Pittsburgh, Pa. d: 2/1/23, Bradford, Pa. Deb: 7/28/1891																									
1891	Cle-N	30	124	10	30	1	1	0	13	1	15	.242	.248	.266	49	-8	-9	10	6			.814	-4	O/P	-1.1
1896	Cle-N	16	64	6	11	0	1	0	3	4	6	.172	.221	.203	13	-8	-9	4	3			.818	-4	O	-1.2
Total	2	46	188	16	41	1	2	0	16	5	21	.218	.238	.245	36	-16	-17	14	9			.815	-9	/OP	-2.3
■ **JIMMY SHECKARD** Sheckard, Samuel James Tilden b: 11/23/1878, Upper Chanceford, Pa. d: 1/15/47, Lancaster, Pa. BL/TR, 5'9", 175 lbs. Deb: 9/14/1897																									
1897	Bro-N	13	49	12	14	3	2	3	14	6		.286	.364	.612	164	3	4	13	5			.753	-4	S/O	0.0
1898	Bro-N	105	408	51	113	17	9	4	64	37		.277	.349	.392	113	6	6	61	8			.926	-4	*O/3	-0.5
1899	Bal-N	147	536	104	158	18	10	3	75	56		.295	.380	.382	104	9	5	111	**77**			.943	21	*O/1	1.3
1900	Bro-N	85	273	74	82	19	10	1	39	42		.300	.412	.454	131	16	14	66	30			.925	2	O	0.9
1901	Bro-N	133	554	116	196	29	**19**	11	104	47		.354	.409	**.534**	168	50	48	139	35			.944	7	*O3	4.4
1902	Bal-A	4	15	3	4	1	0	0	0	1		.267	.313	.333	76	-0	-1	2	2			1.000	-1	/O	-0.2
	Bro-N	123	486	86	129	20	10	4	37	57		.265	.351	.372	122	14	14	74	23			.964	8	*O	1.5
1903	Bro-N	139	515	99	171	29	9	**9**	75	75		.332	.422	.476	161	40	**42**	**137**	**67**			.951	23	*O	5.3
1904	Bro-N	143	507	70	121	23	6	1	46	56		.239	.316	.314	97	-2	-0	61	21			.956	7	*O/2	-0.1
1905	Bro-N	130	480	58	140	20	11	3	41	61		.292	.376	.398	142	20	25	84	23			.967	15	*O	3.4
1906	*Chi-N	149	549	90	144	27	10	1	45	67		.262	.349	.353	113	14	10	85	30			.986	0	*O	0.3
1907	*Chi-N	143	484	76	129	23	1	1	36	76		.267	.373	.324	112	14	11	77	31			.975	-10	*O	-0.5
1908	*Chi-N	115	403	54	93	18	3	2	22	62		.231	.336	.305	101	5	3	49	18			.955	-2	*O	-0.4
1909	Chi-N	148	525	81	134	29	5	1	43	72		.255	.346	.335	109	9	7	70	15			.967	-3	*O	-0.2
1910	*Chi-N	144	507	82	130	27	6	5	51	83	53	.256	.366	.363	114	11	11	78	22			.976	7	*O	1.2
1911	Chi-N	156	539	**121**	149	26	11	4	50	**147**	58	.276	**.434**	.388	130	32	32	106	32			.963	15	*O	3.8
1912	Chi-N	146	523	85	128	22	10	3	47	**122**	81	.245	.392	.342	102	8	8	76	15			.962	8	*O	0.8
1913	StL-N	52	136	18	27	2	1	0	17	41	25	.199	.388	.228	79	-1	-1	14	5			.953	-3	O	-0.6
	Cin-N	47	116	16	22	1	3	0	7	27	16	.190	.343	.250	71	-3	-3	12	6			.969	-3	O	-0.8
	Yr	99	252	34	49	3	4	0	24	68	41	.194	.368	.238	76	-4	-4	26	11			.960	-6	O	-1.4
Total	17	2122	7605	1296	2084	354	136	56	813	1135	233	.274	.375	.378	120	244	233	1314	465			.958	83	*O/3S21	19.6
■ **JIM SHEEHAN** Sheehan, James Thomas "Big Jim" b: 6/3/13, New Haven, Conn. BR/TR, 6'2", 196 lbs. Deb: 9/26/36																									
1936	NY-N	1	4	0	0	0	0	0	0	0	2	.000	.000	.000	-99	-1	-1	0	0			.833	-0	/C	-0.1
■ **JACK SHEEHAN** Sheehan, John Thomas b: 4/15/1893, Chicago, Ill. d: 5/29/87, W.Palm Beach, Fla. BB/TR, 5'8.5", 165 lbs. Deb: 9/11/20																									
1920	*Bro-N	3	5	0	2	1	0	0	0	1	0	.400	.500	.600	208	1	1	2	0	0	0	.875	0	/S3	0.1
1921	Bro-N	5	12	2	0	0	0	0	0	0	1	.000	.000	.000	-97	-3	-3	0	0	0	0	.900	-0	/2S3	-0.4
Total	2	8	17	2	2	1	0	0	0	1	1	.118	.167	.176	-7	-3	-3	2	0	0	0	.909	0	/S23	-0.3
■ **TOMMY SHEEHAN** Sheehan, Thomas H. b: 11/6/1877, Sacramento, Cal. d: 5/22/59, Panama City, Pan. BR/TR, 5'8", 160 lbs. Deb: 8/02/00																									
1900	NY-N	1	2	0	0	0	0	0	0	0		.000	.000	.000	-99	-1	-1	0	0			.000	0	/S	0.0
1906	Pit-N	95	315	28	76	6	3	1	34	18		.241	.284	.289	76	-8	-10	32	13			.947	-5	3	-1.3
1907	Pit-N	75	226	23	62	2	3	0	25	23		.274	.341	.310	103	2	1	30	10			.941	-1	3S	0.3
1908	Bro-N	146	468	45	100	18	2	0	29	53		.214	.300	.261	83	-9	-7	41	9			.930	-6	*3	-0.9
Total	4	317	1011	96	238	26	8	1	88	94		.235	.304	.280	85	-16	-16	104	32			.938	-12	3/S	-1.9
■ **BIFF SHEEHAN** Sheehan, Timothy James b: 2/13/1868, Hartford, Conn. d: 10/21/23, Hartford, Conn. TR, 5'9", 165 lbs. Deb: 7/22/1895																									
1895	StL-N	52	180	24	57	3	6	1	18	20	6	.317	.394	.417	113	4	4	34	7			.940	-2	O1	-0.1
1896	StL-N	6	19	0	3	0	0	0	1	4	0	.158	.304	.158	27	-2	-2	1	0			1.000	-1	/O	-0.2
Total	2	58	199	24	60	3	6	1	19	24	6	.302	.385	.392	105	2	2	35	7			.948	-3	/O1	-0.3
■ **EARL SHEELY** Sheely, Earl Homer "Whitey" b: 2/12/1893, Bushnell, Ill. d: 9/16/52, Seattle, Wash. BR/TR, 6'3.5", 195 lbs. Deb: 4/14/21 F																									
1921	Chi-A	154	563	68	171	25	6	11	95	57	34	.304	.375	.428	106	4	5	90	4	9	-4	.988	5	*1	0.2
1922	Chi-A	149	526	72	167	37	4	6	80	60	27	.317	.393	.437	117	14	14	92	4	6	-2	.993	2	*1	0.7
1923	Chi-A	156	570	74	169	25	3	4	88	79	30	.296	.387	.372	102	3	4	87	5	5	-2	.992	-1	*1	-0.6
1924	Chi-A	146	535	84	171	34	3	3	103	95	28	.320	.426	.411	120	18	21	102	7	4	-0	.991	-10	*1	0.2
1925	Chi-A	153	600	93	189	43	3	9	111	68	23	.315	.389	.442	117	10	15	106	3	3	-1	.988	-5	*1	0.1
1926	Chi-A	145	525	77	157	40	2	6	89	75	13	.299	.394	.417	116	11	14	92	3	1	0	**.995**	0	*1	0.5
1927	Chi-A	45	129	11	27	3	0	2	16	20	5	.209	.320	.279	58	-8	-7	12	1	3	-2	.982	-4	1	-1.5
1929	Pit-N	139	485	63	142	22	4	6	88	75	24	.293	.392	.392	93	-1	-3	77	6			**.996**	-0	*1	-1.6
1931	Bos-N	147	538	30	147	15	2	1	77	34	21	.273	.319	.314	73	-21	-19	56	0			.992	-3	*1	-3.5
Total	9	1234	4471	572	1340	244	27	48	747	563	205	.300	.383	.399	104	30	44	715	33	31		.991	-14	*1	-5.5
■ **BUD SHEELY** Sheely, Hollis Kimball b: 11/26/20, Spokane, Wash. d: 10/17/85, Sacramento, Cal. BL/TR, 6'1", 200 lbs. Deb: 7/26/51 F																									
1951	Chi-A	34	89	2	16	2	0	0	7	6	7	.180	.240	.202	21	-10	-10	5	0	0	0	.986	3	C	-0.5
1952	Chi-A	36	75	1	18	2	0	0	3	12	7	.240	.352	.267	73	-2	-2	8	0	1	-1	.992	-2	C	-0.3
1953	Chi-A	31	46	4	10	1	0	0	2	9	8	.217	.345	.239	58	-2	-2	5	0	0	0	1.000	0	C	-0.1
Total	3	101	210	7	44	5	0	0	12	27	22	.210	.305	.233	49	-14	-14	17	0	1	-1	.991	2	/C	-0.9
■ **CHUCK SHEERIN** Sheerin, Charles Joseph b: 4/17/09, Brooklyn, N.Y. d: 9/27/86, Valley Stream, N.Y. BR/TR, 5'11.5", 198 lbs. Deb: 4/21/36																									
1936	Phi-N	39	72	4	19	4	0	0	4	7	18	.264	.329	.319	68	-2	-3	8	0			.942	-3	23/S	-0.5
■ **LARRY SHEETS** Sheets, Larry Kent b: 12/6/59, Staunton, Va. BL/TR, 6'3", 225 lbs. Deb: 9/18/84																									
1984	Bal-A	8	16	3	7	1	0	1	2	1	3	.438	.471	.688	221	2	2	5	0	0	0	1.000	0	/O	0.2
1985	Bal-A	113	328	43	86	8	0	17	50	28	52	.262	.324	.442	110	3	4	43	0	1	-1	.875	-2	D/O1	0.1
1986	Bal-A	112	338	42	92	17	1	18	60	21	56	.272	.319	.488	117	6	7	47	2	0	1	.984	-0	DO/C13	0.6
1987	Bal-A	135	469	74	148	23	0	31	94	31	67	.316	.362	.563	144	25	27	90	1	1	-0	.975	-4	*O/1D	1.8
1988	Bal-A	136	452	38	104	19	1	10	47	42	72	.230	.304	.343	83	-11	-10	45	1	6	-3	.974	1	OD/1	-1.5
1989	Bal-A	102	304	33	74	12	1	7	33	26	58	.243	.309	.359	90	-5	-4	34	1	1	-0	.000	0	D	-0.4
1990	Det-A	131	360	40	94	17	2	10	52	24	42	.261	.311	.403	97	-2	-2	41	1	3	-2	.981	-7	OD	-1.3
Total	7	737	2267	273	605	97	5	94	338	173	350	.267	.324	.438	109	18	24	305	6	12	-5	.976	-12	DO/1C3	-0.5
■ **GARY SHEFFIELD** Sheffield, Gary Antonian b: 11/18/68, Tampa, Fla. BR/TR, 5'11", 190 lbs. Deb: 9/03/88																									
1988	Mil-A	24	80	12	19	1	0	4	12	7	7	.237	.299	.400	93	-1	-1	8	3	1	0	.967	-10	S	-0.9
1989	Mil-A	95	368	34	91	18	0	5	32	27	33	.247	.306	.337	82	-9	-9	39	10	6	-1	.959	-17	S3/D	-2.2
1990	Mil-A	125	487	67	143	30	1	10	67	44	41	.294	.356	.421	117	11	11	73	25	10	2	.934	-4	*3	0.9
1991	Mil-A	50	175	25	34	12	2	2	22	19	15	.194	.284	.320	69	-8	-7	16	5	5	-2	.922	-11	3/D	-2.0
1992	SD-N★	146	557	87	184	34	3	33	100	48	40	**.330**	.390	.580	166	50	48	118	5	6	-2	.961	9	*3	5.9
Total	5	440	1667	225	471	95	6	54	233	145	136	.283	.346	.444	120	43	42	254	48	28	-2	.945	-34	3/SD	1.7

YEAR	TM/L	G	AB	R	H	2B	3B	HR	RBI	BB	SO	AVG	OBP	SLG	PRO+	BR	/A	RC	SB	CS	SBR	FA	FR	POS	TPR

■ JOHN SHELBY Shelby, John T. b: 2/23/58, Lexington, Ky. BB/TR, 6'1", 175 lbs. Deb: 9/15/81

1981	Bal-A	7	2	2	0	0	0	0	0	0	1	.000	.000	.000	-99	-1	-1	0	2	0	1	1.000	-2	/O	-0.2
1982	Bal-A	26	35	8	11	3	0	1	2	0	5	.314	.314	.486	116	1	1	5	0	1	-1	1.000	-8	O	-0.8
1983	*Bal-A	126	325	52	84	15	2	5	27	18	64	.258	.297	.363	82	-9	-8	37	15	2	3	.981	-14	*O/D	-2.2
1984	Bal-A	128	383	44	80	12	5	6	30	20	71	.209	.248	.313	55	-24	-23	31	12	4	1	.993	-10	*O	-3.6
1985	Bal-A	69	205	28	58	6	2	7	27	7	44	.283	.307	.434	103	-1	0	26	5	1	1	.981	0	O/2D	0.0
1986	Bal-A	135	404	54	92	14	4	11	49	18	75	.228	.264	.364	70	-18	-18	39	18	6	2	.978	-12	O/D	-3.1
1987	Bal-A	21	32	4	6	0	0	1	3	1	13	.188	.212	.281	30	-3	-3	2	0	1	-1	1.000	-3	O/D	-0.7
	LA-N	120	476	61	132	26	0	21	69	31	97	.277	.323	.464	108	2	4	70	16	6	1	.972	11	*O	1.2
1988	*LA-N	140	494	65	130	23	6	10	64	44	128	.263	.323	.395	109	3	5	62	16	5	2	.982	7	*O	0.9
1989	LA-N	108	345	28	63	11	1	1	12	25	92	.183	.238	.229	35	-29	-29	18	10	7	-1	.991	0	O	-3.5
1990	LA-N	25	24	2	6	1	0	0	2	0	7	.250	.250	.292	50	-2	-2	2	1	0	0	1.000	-3	O	-0.5
	Det-A	78	222	22	55	9	3	4	20	10	51	.248	.280	.369	80	-7	-7	20	3	5	-2	.973	-1	O/D	-1.1
1991	Det-A	53	143	19	22	8	1	3	8	1	23	.204	.204	.287	34	-13	-13	7	0	2	-1	.982	-1	O/D	-1.7
Total	11	1036	3090	389	739	128	24	70	313	182	671	.239	.282	.364	79	-101	-94	320	98	40	5	.982	-36	O/D2	-15.3

■ BOB SHELDON Sheldon, Bob Mitchell b: 11/27/50, Montebello, Cal. BL/TR, 6', 170 lbs. Deb: 4/10/74

1974	Mil-A	10	17	4	2	1	1	0	4	2	.118	.286	.294	67	-1	-1	2	0	1	-1	1.000	-1	/2D	-0.2
1975	Mil-A	53	181	17	52	3	3	0	14	13	14	.287	.342	.337	92	-2	-2	20	0	3	-2	.977	-8	2/D	-1.0
1977	Mil-A	31	64	9	13	4	1	0	3	6	9	.203	.271	.297	55	-4	-4	6	0	0	0	1.000	1	D/2	-0.3
Total	3	94	262	30	67	8	5	0	17	23	25	.256	.321	.324	81	-6	-6	27	0	4	-2	.979	-9	/2DB	-1.5

■ HUGH SHELLEY Shelley, Hubert Leneirre b: 10/26/10, Rogers, Tex. d: 6/16/78, Beaumont, Tex. BR/TR, 6', 170 lbs. Deb: 6/25/35

| 1935 | Det-A | 7 | 8 | 1 | 2 | 0 | 0 | 0 | 1 | 2 | 1 | .250 | .400 | .250 | 74 | -0 | -0 | 1 | 0 | 0 | 0 | 1.000 | -1 | /O | -0.2 |

■ SKEETER SHELTON Shelton, Andrew Kemper b: 6/29/1888, Huntington, W.Va. d: 1/9/54, Huntington, W.Va. BR/TR, 5'11", 175 lbs. Deb: 8/25/15

| 1915 | NY-A | 10 | 40 | 1 | 1 | 0 | 0 | 0 | 2 | 10 | .025 | .071 | .025 | -71 | -8 | -8 | 0 | 0 | 1.000 | 0 | O | -1.0 |

■ STEVE SHEMO Shemo, Stephen Michael b: 4/9/15, Swoyersville, Pa. BR/TR, 5'11", 175 lbs. Deb: 4/18/44

1944	Bos-N	18	31	3	9	2	0	1	1	3	.290	.313	.355	84	-1	-1	4	0	.966	3	2/3	0.3
1945	Bos-N	17	46	4	11	1	0	0	7	1	3	.239	.255	.261	43	-4	-4	3	0	.921	-6	2/3S	-0.9
Total	2	35	77	7	20	3	0	0	8	2	6	.260	.278	.299	60	-4	-4	7	0	.948	-3	/23S	-0.6

■ JACK SHEPARD Shepard, Jack Leroy b: 5/13/32, Clovis, Cal. BR/TR, 6'2", 195 lbs. Deb: 6/19/53

1953	Pit-N	2	4	0	1	0	0	0	0	2	.250	.250	.250	31	-0	-0	0	0	0	0	.750	-0	/C	-0.1
1954	Pit-N	82	227	24	69	8	2	3	22	26	33	.304	.375	.396	103	1	2	33	0	0	0	.977	2	C	0.6
1955	Pit-N	94	264	24	63	10	2	2	23	33	25	.239	.323	.314	71	-11	-10	27	1	0	0	.982	-10	C	-1.8
1956	Pit-N	100	256	24	62	11	2	7	30	25	37	.242	.310	.383	87	-6	-5	29	1	1	-0	.990	1	C/1	-0.1
Total	4	278	751	72	195	29	6	12	75	84	97	.260	.334	.362	86	-16	-14	90	2	1	0	.982	-8	C/1	-1.4

■ RAY SHEPARDSON Shepardson, Raymond Francis b: 5/3/1897, Little Falls, N.Y. d: 11/8/75, Little Falls, N.Y. BR/TR, 5'11.5", 170 lbs. Deb: 9/19/24

| 1924 | StL-N | 3 | 6 | 1 | 0 | 0 | 0 | 0 | 0 | 3 | .000 | .000 | .000 | -99 | -2 | -2 | 0 | 0 | 0 | 0 | 1.000 | 0 | /C | -0.2 |

■ RON SHEPHERD Shepherd, Ronald Wayne b: 10/27/60, Longview, Tex. BR/TR, 6'4", 175 lbs. Deb: 9/05/84

1984	Tor-A	12	4	0	0	0	0	0	0	3	.000	.000	.000	-97	-1	-1	0	0	1	-1	1.000	-1	/OD	-0.3
1985	Tor-A	38	35	7	4	2	0	0	1	2	12	.114	.162	.171	-8	-5	-5	1	3	0	1	1.000	-4	OD	-0.8
1986	Tor-A	65	69	16	14	4	0	2	4	3	22	.203	.236	.348	55	-4	-5	6	0	0	0	1.000	-8	OD	-1.3
Total	3	115	108	23	18	6	0	2	5	5	37	.167	.204	.278	29	-11	-11	7	3	1	0	1.000	-13	/OD	-2.4

■ JOHN SHEPPARD Sheppard, John b: Baltimore, Md. Deb: 6/27/1873

| 1873 | Mar-n | 3 | 11 | 1 | 0 | 0 | 0 | 0 | 0 | 0 | .000 | .000 | .000 | -99 | -3 | -2 | 0 | | | | | | /OC | -0.1 |

■ SHERIDAN Sheridan Deb: 10/09/1875

| 1875 | Atl-n | 1 | 4 | 0 | 0 | 0 | 0 | 0 | 0 | .000 | .000 | .000 | -99 | -1 | -1 | 0 | | | | | | /O | -0.1 |

■ RED SHERIDAN Sheridan, Eugene Anthony b: 11/14/1896, Brooklyn, N.Y. d: 11/25/75, Queens Village, N.Y. BR/TR, 5'10.5", 160 lbs. Deb: 7/03/18

1918	Bro-N	2	4	0	1	0	0	0	0	1	.250	.400	.250	100	0	0	1	1	1.000	-1	/2	-0.1
1920	Bro-N	3	2	0	0	0	0	0	0	0	.000	.000	.000	-97	-1	-1	0	0	0	0	1.000	1	/S	0.1
Total	2	5	6	0	1	0	0	0	0	1	1	.167	.286	.167	37	-0	-0	1	1	0	.957	1	/S2	0.0

■ NEILL SHERIDAN Sheridan, Neill Rawlins "Wild Horse" b: 11/20/21, Sacramento, Cal. BR/TR, 6'1.5", 195 lbs. Deb: 9/19/48

| 1948 | Bos-A | 2 | 1 | 0 | 0 | 0 | 0 | 0 | 0 | 0 | 1 | .000 | .000 | .000 | -95 | -0 | -0 | 0 | 0 | 0 | 0 | .000 | 0 | H | 0.0 |

■ PAT SHERIDAN Sheridan, Patrick Arthur b: 12/4/57, Ann Arbor, Mich. BL/TR, 6'3", 175 lbs. Deb: 9/16/81

1981	KC-A	3	1	0	0	0	0	0	0	0	1	.000	.000	.000	-99	-0	-0	0	0	0	0	1.000	-1	/O	-0.1
1983	KC-A	109	333	43	90	12	2	7	36	20	64	.270	.312	.381	89	-5	-5	41	12	3	2	.988	-2	*O	-0.8
1984	*KC-A	138	481	64	136	24	4	8	53	41	91	.283	.340	.399	103	3	2	68	19	6	2	.986	-3	*O	-0.3
1985	*KC-A	78	206	18	47	9	2	3	17	23	38	.228	.309	.335	76	-7	-7	23	11	3	2	.983	-4	O/D	-1.1
1986	Det-A	98	236	41	56	9	1	6	19	21	57	.237	.302	.360	80	-7	-7	27	9	2	2	.977	-10	O/D	-1.7
1987	*Det-A	141	421	57	109	19	3	6	49	44	90	.259	.330	.361	87	-10	-7	50	18	13	-2	.976	-12	*O	-2.4
1988	Det-A	127	347	47	88	9	5	11	47	44	64	.254	.341	.403	112	4	6	48	8	6	-1	.981	-6	*O/D	-0.5
1989	Det-A	50	120	16	29	3	0	3	15	17	21	.242	.336	.342	93	-1	-1	15	4	0	1	.982	-3	O/D	-0.4
	*SF-N	70	161	20	33	3	4	3	14	13	45	.205	.264	.329	71	-7	-6	15	4	1	1	.983	-4	O	-1.2
1991	NY-A	62	113	13	23	3	0	4	7	13	30	.204	.286	.336	71	-4	-5	10	1	1	0	1.000	-3	O/D	-0.8
Total	9	876	2419	319	611	91	21	51	257	236	501	.253	.321	.371	91	-34	-29	296	86	35	5	.983	-48	O/D	-9.3

■ ED SHERLING Sherling, Edward Creech "Shine" b: 7/17/1897, Coalsburg, Pa. d: 11/16/65, Enterprise, Cal. BR/TR, 6'1", 185 lbs. Deb: 8/13/24

| 1924 | Phi-A | 4 | 2 | 2 | 1 | 1 | 0 | 0 | 0 | 0 | 0 | .500 | .500 | 1.000 | 278 | 0 | 0 | 1 | 0 | 0 | 0 | .000 | 0 | H | 0.0 |

■ MONK SHERLOCK Sherlock, John Clinton b: 10/26/04, Buffalo, N.Y. d: 11/26/85, Buffalo, N.Y. BR/TR, 5'10", 175 lbs. Deb: 4/20/30 F

| 1930 | Phi-N | 92 | 299 | 51 | 97 | 18 | 2 | 0 | 38 | 27 | 28 | .324 | .380 | .398 | 83 | -5 | -8 | 45 | 0 | .990 | 4 | 1/2O | -0.9 |

■ VINCE SHERLOCK Sherlock, Vincent Thomas "Baldy" b: 3/27/09, Buffalo, N.Y. BR/TR, 6', 180 lbs. Deb: 9/18/35 F

| 1935 | Bro-N | 9 | 26 | 4 | 12 | 1 | 0 | 0 | 6 | 1 | 2 | .462 | .481 | .500 | 168 | 2 | 2 | 7 | 1 | .907 | -1 | /2 | 0.2 |

■ DENNIS SHERRILL Sherrill, Dennis Lee b: 3/3/56, Miami, Fla. BR/TR, 6', 165 lbs. Deb: 9/04/78

1978	NY-A	2	1	1	0	0	0	0	0	0	1	.000	.000	.000	-99	-0	-0	0	0	0	0	.000	-0	/3D	-0.1
1980	NY-A	3	4	0	1	0	0	0	0	0	1	.250	.250	.250	38	-0	-0	0	0	0	0	1.000	-0	/S2	-0.1
Total	2	5	5	1	1	0	0	0	0	0	2	.200	.200	.200	11	-1	-1	0	0	0	0	.964	-1	/S2D3	-0.2

■ NORM SHERRY Sherry, Norman Burt b: 7/16/31, New York, N.Y. BR/TR, 5'11", 181 lbs. Deb: 4/12/59 FMC

1959	LA-N	2	3	0	1	0	0	0	0	0	0	.333	.500	.333	119	0	0	0	0	0	0	1.000	-1	/C	-0.1
1960	LA-N	47	138	22	39	4	1	8	19	12	29	.283	.353	.500	122	6	4	25	0	0	0	.993	-4	C	0.3
1961	LA-N	47	121	10	31	2	0	5	21	9	36	.256	.308	.397	78	-3	-4	13	0	0	0	.993	-4	C	0.1
1962	LA-N	35	88	7	16	2	0	3	16	6	17	.182	.242	.307	49	-7	-6	6	0	0	0	.992	9	C	0.3
1963	NY-N	63	147	6	20	1	0	2	11	10	26	.136	.206	.184	13	-16	-17	5	1	0	0	.980	3	C	-1.3

YEAR	TM/L	G	AB	R	H	2B	3B	HR	RBI	BB	SO	AVG	OBP	SLG	PRO+	BR	/A	RC	SB	CS	SBR	FA	FR	POS	TPR
Total	5	194	497	45	107	9	1	18	69	37	102	.215	.280	.346	69	-20	-22	49	1	0	0	.989	11	C	-0.7

■ BARRY SHETRONE Shetrone, Barry Stevan b: 7/6/38, Baltimore, Md. BL/TR, 6'2", 190 lbs. Deb: 7/27/59

YEAR	TM/L	G	AB	R	H	2B	3B	HR	RBI	BB	SO	AVG	OBP	SLG	PRO+	BR	/A	RC	SB	CS	SBR	FA	FR	POS	TPR
1959	Bal-A	33	79	8	16	1	1	0	5	5	9	.203	.250	.241	36	-7	-7	6	3	0	1	.947	-4	O	-1.1
1960	Bal-A	1	0	1	0	0	0	0	0	0	0	—	—	—	—	0	0	0	0	0	0	.000	0	R	0.0
1961	Bal-A	3	7	0	1	0	0	0	1	0	2	.143	.143	.143	-24	-1	-1	0	0	0	0	1.000	-0	/O	-0.2
1962	Bal-A	21	24	3	6	1	0	1	1	0	5	.250	.250	.417	80	-1	-1	3	0	0	0	1.000	-0	/O	-0.1
1963	Was-A	2	2	0	0	0	0	0	0	0	0	.000	.000	.000	-99	-1	-1	0	0	0	0	.000	0	H	-0.1
Total	5	60	112	12	23	2	1	1	7	5	16	.205	.239	.268	39	-10	-9	8	3	0	1	.962	-5	/O	-1.5

■ JOHN SHETZLINE Shetzline, John Henry b: 1850, Philadelphia, Pa. d: 12/15/1892, Philadelphia, Pa. 5'11.5", 190 lbs. Deb: 5/02/1882

YEAR	TM/L	G	AB	R	H	2B	3B	HR	RBI	BB	SO	AVG	OBP	SLG	PRO+	BR	/A	RC	SB	CS	SBR	FA	FR	POS	TPR
1882	Bal-a	73	282	23	62	8	3	0		5		.220	.233	.270	75	-9	-6	18				.800	3	32/OS	-0.1

■ JIMMY SHEVLIN Shevlin, James Cornelius b: 7/9/09, Cincinnati, Ohio d: 10/30/74, Ft.Lauderdale, Fla BL/TL, 5'10.5", 155 lbs. Deb: 6/29/30

YEAR	TM/L	G	AB	R	H	2B	3B	HR	RBI	BB	SO	AVG	OBP	SLG	PRO+	BR	/A	RC	SB	CS	SBR	FA	FR	POS	TPR
1930	Det-A	28	14	4	2	0	0	0	2	2	3	.143	.250	.143	2	-2	-2	1	0	0	0	1.000	1	1	-0.2
1932	Cin-N	7	24	3	5	2	0	0	4	4	0	.208	.345	.292	76	-1	-1	3	4			.985	-0	/1	-0.2
1934	Cin-N	18	39	6	12	2	0	0	6	6	5	.308	.400	.359	107	1	1	6	0			1.000	0	1	0.0
Total	3	53	77	13	19	4	0	0	12	12	8	.247	.356	.299	77	-2	-2	9	4	0		.995	1	/1	-0.4

■ PETE SHIELDS Shields, Francis Leroy b: 9/21/1891, Swiftwater, Miss. d: 2/11/61, Jackson, Miss. BR/TR, 6', 175 lbs. Deb: 4/14/15

YEAR	TM/L	G	AB	R	H	2B	3B	HR	RBI	BB	SO	AVG	OBP	SLG	PRO+	BR	/A	RC	SB	CS	SBR	FA	FR	POS	TPR
1915	Cle-A	23	72	4	15	6	0	0	6	4	14	.208	.250	.292	61	-4	-4	5	3	3	-1	.974	0	1	-0.6

■ TOMMY SHIELDS Shields, Thomas Charles b: 8/14/64, Fairfax, Va. BL/TR, 6', 180 lbs. Deb: 7/25/92

YEAR	TM/L	G	AB	R	H	2B	3B	HR	RBI	BB	SO	AVG	OBP	SLG	PRO+	BR	/A	RC	SB	CS	SBR	FA	FR	POS	TPR
1992	Bal-A	2	0	0	0	0	0	0	0	0	0	—	—	—	—	0	0	0	0	0	0	.000	0	/R	0.0

■ JIM SHILLING Shilling, James Robert b: 5/14/14, Tulsa, Okla. d: 9/12/86, Tulsa, Okla. BR/TR, 5'11", 175 lbs. Deb: 4/21/39

YEAR	TM/L	G	AB	R	H	2B	3B	HR	RBI	BB	SO	AVG	OBP	SLG	PRO+	BR	/A	RC	SB	CS	SBR	FA	FR	POS	TPR
1939	Cle-A	31	98	8	27	7	2	0	12	7	9	.276	.324	.388	84	-3	-2	12	1	0	0	.935	4	2/S	0.3
	Phi-N	11	33	3	10	1	3	0	4	1	4	.303	.324	.515	126	1	1	5	0			.944	-2	/2S3O	0.0
Total	1	42	131	11	37	8	5	0	16	8	13	.282	.324	.420	94	-2	-2	17	1	0		.936	2	/2S3O	0.3

■ GINGER SHINAULT Shinault, Enoch Erskine b: 9/7/1892, Benton, Ark. d: 12/29/30, Denver, Colo. BR/TR, 5'11", 170 lbs. Deb: 7/04/21

YEAR	TM/L	G	AB	R	H	2B	3B	HR	RBI	BB	SO	AVG	OBP	SLG	PRO+	BR	/A	RC	SB	CS	SBR	FA	FR	POS	TPR
1921	Cle-A	22	29	5	11	1	0	0	4	6	5	.379	.486	.414	129	2	2	7	1	0	0	.917	2	C	0.4
1922	Cle-A	13	15	1	2	1	0	0	0	0	2	.133	.133	.200	-14	-3	-3	0	0	0	0	.400	-4	C	-0.6
Total	2	35	44	6	13	2	0	0	4	6	7	.295	.380	.341	85	-1	-1	7	1	0	0	.868	-2	/C	-0.2

■ BILLY SHINDLE Shindle, William b: 12/5/1860, Gloucester, N.J. d: 6/3/36, Lakeland, N.J. BR/TR, 5'8.5", 155 lbs. Deb: 10/04/1886

YEAR	TM/L	G	AB	R	H	2B	3B	HR	RBI	BB	SO	AVG	OBP	SLG	PRO+	BR	/A	RC	SB	CS	SBR	FA	FR	POS	TPR
1886	Det-N	7	26	4	7	0	0	0	4	0	5	.269	.269	.269	62	-1	-1	2	2			.900	1	/S	0.0
1887	Det-N	22	84	17	24	3	2	0	12	7	10	.286	.341	.369	96	-0	-0	15	13			.818	-5	3/O	-0.4
1888	Bal-a	135	514	61	107	14	8	1	53	20		.208	.249	.272	71	-17	-15	49	52			**.922**	**37**	*3	2.2
1889	Bal-a	138	567	122	178	24	7	3	64	42	37	.314	.369	.397	118	15	13	106	56			.862	20	*3	3.2
1890	Phi-P	132	584	127	188	21	21	10	90	40	30	.322	.369	.481	125	21	18	126	51			.856	8	*S/3	2.7
1891	Phi-N	103	415	68	87	13	1	0	38	33	39	.210	.278	.246	53	-23	-25	34	17			.874	6	*3/S	-1.2
1892	Bal-N	143	619	100	156	20	18	3	50	35	34	.252	.301	.357	98	-2	-4	75	24			.882	36	*3/S	3.4
1893	Bal-N	125	521	100	136	22	11	1	75	66	17	.261	.353	.351	88	-7	-8	72	17			.885	8	*3	0.2
1894	Bro-N	116	476	94	141	22	9	4	96	29	20	.296	.344	.405	88	-15	-8	77	19			.897	1	*3	-0.5
1895	Bro-N	116	477	91	133	21	2	3	69	47	28	.279	.357	.350	92	-9	-2	68	17			.897	0	*3	0.0
1896	Bro-N	131	516	75	144	24	9	1	61	24	20	.279	.316	.366	86	-15	-10	71	24			.912	-12	*3	-1.6
1897	Bro-N	134	542	83	154	32	6	4	105	35		.284	.336	.387	96	-9	-4	82	23			.904	-12	*3	-1.0
1898	Bro-N	120	466	50	105	10	3	1	41	10		.225	.249	.266	48	-33	-32	34	3			.911	7	*3	-2.3
Total	13	1422	5807	992	1560	226	97	31	758	388	240	.269	.323	.357	90	-94	-78	813	318			.892	95	*3S/O	4.7

■ RAY SHINES Shines, Anthony Raymond b: 7/18/56, Durham, N.C. BB/TR, 6'1", 210 lbs. Deb: 9/09/83

YEAR	TM/L	G	AB	R	H	2B	3B	HR	RBI	BB	SO	AVG	OBP	SLG	PRO+	BR	/A	RC	SB	CS	SBR	FA	FR	POS	TPR
1983	Mon-N	3	2	0	1	0	0	0	0	0	0	.500	.500	.500	179	0	0	1	0	0	0	.000	0	/O	0.0
1984	Mon-N	12	20	0	6	1	0	0	2	0	3	.300	.300	.350	86	-1	-0	2	0	0	0	1.000	-1	/13	-0.2
1985	Mon-N	47	50	0	6	0	0	0	3	4	9	.120	.185	.120	-14	-7	-7	1	0	1	-1	.950	0	/1P	-0.8
1987	Mon-N	6	9	0	2	0	0	0	0	1	0	.222	.364	.222	58	-0	-0	1	1	0	0	1.000	-0	/1	0.0
Total	4	68	81	0	15	1	0	0	5	5	12	.185	.241	.198	24	-8	-8	4	1	1	-0	.975	-1	/1P3O	-1.0

■ RALPH SHINNERS Shinners, Ralph Peter b: 10/4/1895, Monches, Wis. d: 7/23/62, Milwaukee, Wis. BR/TR, 6', 180 lbs. Deb: 4/12/22

YEAR	TM/L	G	AB	R	H	2B	3B	HR	RBI	BB	SO	AVG	OBP	SLG	PRO+	BR	/A	RC	SB	CS	SBR	FA	FR	POS	TPR
1922	NY-N	56	135	16	34	4	2	0	15	5	22	.252	.308	.311	60	-8	-8	12	3	5	-2	.915	-4	O	-1.5
1923	NY-N	33	13	5	2	1	0	0	0	2	1	.154	.267	.231	33	-1	-1	1	0	0	0	1.000	-1	/O	-0.2
1925	StL-N	74	251	39	74	9	2	7	36	12	19	.295	.330	.430	90	-3	-4	35	8	5	-1	.982	-3	O	-1.1
Total	3	163	399	60	110	14	4	7	51	19	42	.276	.320	.383	78	-13	-14	48	11	10	-3	.959	-8	O	-2.8

■ TIM SHINNICK Shinnick, Timothy James "Dandy" or "Good Eye" b: 11/6/1867, Exeter, N.H. d: 5/18/44, Exeter, N.H. BB/TR, 5'9", 150 lbs. Deb: 4/19/1890

YEAR	TM/L	G	AB	R	H	2B	3B	HR	RBI	BB	SO	AVG	OBP	SLG	PRO+	BR	/A	RC	SB	CS	SBR	FA	FR	POS	TPR
1890	*Lou-a	133	493	87	126	16	11	1		62		.256	.348	.339	107	5	7	82	62			.925	-25	*2/3	-0.9
1891	Lou-a	128	443	79	98	10	11	1	54	54	47	.221	.314	.300	79	-11	-10	54	36			.915	-21	*2/3S	-2.2
Total	2	261	936	166	224	26	22	2	54	116	47	.239	.332	.321	94	-7	-4	136	98			.920	-45	2/3S	-3.1

■ BILL SHIPKE Shipke, William Martin "Skipper Bill" or "Muskrat Bill" (b: William Martin Shipkrethaver)
b: 11/18/1882, St.Louis, Mo. d: 9/10/40, Omaha, Neb. BR/TR, 5'7", 145 lbs. Deb: 4/23/06

YEAR	TM/L	G	AB	R	H	2B	3B	HR	RBI	BB	SO	AVG	OBP	SLG	PRO+	BR	/A	RC	SB	CS	SBR	FA	FR	POS	TPR
1906	Cle-A	2	6	0	0	0	0	0	0	0		.000	.000	.000	-99	-1	-1	0	0			.933	2	/2	0.0
1907	Was-A	64	189	17	37	3	2	1	9	15		.196	.255	.249	66	-8	-7	14	6			.944	7	3	0.3
1908	Was-A	111	341	40	71	7	8	0	20	38		.208	.297	.276	94	-4	-1	34	15			.932	-6	*3/2	-0.4
1909	Was-A	9	16	2	2	1	0	0	0	2		.125	.222	.188	31	-1	-1	1	0			.905	2	/3S	0.1
Total	4	186	552	59	110	11	10	1	29	55		.199	.278	.261	80	-15	-10	49	21			.935	5	3/2S	0.0

■ CRAIG SHIPLEY Shipley, Craig Barry b: 1/7/63, Parramatta, Australia BR/TR, 6'1", 175 lbs. Deb: 6/22/86

YEAR	TM/L	G	AB	R	H	2B	3B	HR	RBI	BB	SO	AVG	OBP	SLG	PRO+	BR	/A	RC	SB	CS	SBR	FA	FR	POS	TPR
1986	LA-N	12	27	3	3	1	0	0	4	2	5	.111	.200	.148	-3	-4	-4	1	0	0	0	.914	-1	S/23	-0.4
1987	LA-N	26	35	3	9	1	0	0	2	0	6	.257	.257	.286	45	-3	-3	2	0	0	0	.949	3	S/3	0.0
1989	NY-N	4	7	3	1	0	0	0	0	0	1	.143	.143	.143	-19	-1	-1	0	0	0	0	1.000	-0	/S3	-0.1
1991	SD-N	37	91	6	25	3	0	1	6	2	14	.275	.298	.341	77	-3	-3	9	0	1	-1	.902	-1	S2	-0.3
1992	SD-N	52	105	7	26	6	0	0	7	2	21	.248	.262	.305	58	-6	-6	8	1	1	-0	.986	10	S2/3	0.5
Total	5	131	265	22	64	11	0	1	19	6	47	.242	.264	.294	55	-16	-16	20	1	2	-1	.942	11	/S23	-0.3

■ ART SHIRES Shires, Charles Arthur "Art The Great" b: 8/13/07, Italy, Tex. d: 7/13/67, Italy, Tex. BL/TR, 6'1", 195 lbs. Deb: 8/20/28

YEAR	TM/L	G	AB	R	H	2B	3B	HR	RBI	BB	SO	AVG	OBP	SLG	PRO+	BR	/A	RC	SB	CS	SBR	FA	FR	POS	TPR
1928	Chi-A	33	123	20	42	6	1	1	11	13	10	.341	.409	.431	122	4	4	21	0	3	-2	.990	3	1	0.3
1929	Chi-A	100	353	41	110	20	7	3	41	32	20	.312	.370	.433	108	3	4	56	4	5	-2	.991	0	1/2	-0.6
1930	Chi-A	37	128	14	33	5	1	1	18	6	6	.258	.291	.336	61	-8	-8	13	2	0	1	.979	-2	1	-1.2
	Was-A	38	84	11	31	5	0	1	19	5	5	.369	.404	.464	119	3	3	15	1	3	-2	.982	0	1	0.0
	Yr	75	212	25	64	10	1	2	37	11	11	.302	.336	.387	84	-6	-5	27	3	3	-1	.980	-2	1	-1.2
1932	Bos-N	82	298	32	71	9	3	5	30	25	21	.238	.299	.339	74	-12	-10	32	1			.988	-2	1	-1.9
Total	4	290	986	118	287	45	12	11	119	81	62	.291	.347	.395	95	-10	-7	137	8	11		.988	-1	1/2	-3.4

■ BART SHIRLEY Shirley, Barton Arvin b: 1/4/40, Corpus Christi, Tex. BR/TR, 5'10", 183 lbs. Deb: 9/14/64

YEAR	TM/L	G	AB	R	H	2B	3B	HR	RBI	BB	SO	AVG	OBP	SLG	PRO+	BR	/A	RC	SB	CS	SBR	FA	FR	POS	TPR
1964	LA-N	18	62	6	17	1	1	0	7	4	8	.274	.318	.323	87	-1	-1	5	0	0	0	.900	1	3/S	0.0

YEAR	TM/L	G	AB	R	H	2B	3B	HR	RBI	BB	SO	AVG	OBP	SLG	PRO+	BR	/A	RC	SB	CS	SBR	FA	FR	POS	TPR
1966	LA-N	12	5	2	1	0	0	0	0	0	2	.200	.200	.200	13	-1	-1	0	0	0	0	1.000	3	/S	0.2
1967	NY-N	6	12	1	0	0	0	0	0	0	5	.000	.000	.000	-99	-3	-3	0	0	0	0	.917	0	/2	-0.3
1968	LA-N	39	83	6	15	3	0	0	4	10	13	.181	.269	.217	51	-5	-4	4	0	1	-1	.903	3	S2	-0.1
Total	4	75	162	15	33	4	1	0	11	14	28	.204	.267	.241	53	-10	-9	10	0	1	-1	.936	6	/S23	-0.2

■ **MULE SHIRLEY** Shirley, Ernest Raeford b: 5/24/01, Snow Hill, N.C. d: 8/4/55, Goldsboro, N.C. BL/TL, 5′11″, 180 lbs. Deb: 5/06/24

YEAR	TM/L	G	AB	R	H	2B	3B	HR	RBI	BB	SO	AVG	OBP	SLG	PRO+	BR	/A	RC	SB	CS	SBR	FA	FR	POS	TPR
1924	*Was-A	30	77	12	18	2	2	0	16	3	7	.234	.262	.312	49	-6	-6	7	0	0	0	.984	0	1	-0.7
1925	Was-A	14	23	2	3	1	0	0	2	1	7	.130	.167	.174	-14	-4	-4	1	0	0	0	1.000	0	/1	-0.4
Total	2	44	100	14	21	3	2	0	18	4	14	.210	.240	.280	34	-10	-10	7	0	0	0	.988	0	/1	-1.1

■ **IVEY SHIVER** Shiver, Ivey Merwin "Chick" b: 1/22/07, Sylvester, Ga. d: 8/31/72, Savannah, Ga. BR/TR, 6′1.5″, 190 lbs. Deb: 4/14/31

YEAR	TM/L	G	AB	R	H	2B	3B	HR	RBI	BB	SO	AVG	OBP	SLG	PRO+	BR	/A	RC	SB	CS	SBR	FA	FR	POS	TPR
1931	Det-A	2	9	2	1	0	0	0	0	0	3	.111	.111	.111	-40	-2	-2	0	0	0	0	1.000	-1	/O	-0.3
1934	Cin-N	19	59	6	12	1	0	2	6	3	15	.203	.242	.322	51	-4	-4	5	1			1.000	-2	O	-0.7
Total	2	21	68	8	13	1	0	2	6	3	18	.191	.225	.294	38	-6	-6	5	1	0		1.000	-3	/O	-1.0

■ **GEORGE SHOCH** Shoch, George Quintus b: 1/6/1859, Philadelphia, Pa. d: 9/30/37, Philadelphia, Pa. BR/TR, 5′6″, 158 lbs. Deb: 9/10/1886

YEAR	TM/L	G	AB	R	H	2B	3B	HR	RBI	BB	SO	AVG	OBP	SLG	PRO+	BR	/A	RC	SB	CS	SBR	FA	FR	POS	TPR
1886	Was-N	26	95	11	28	2	1	1	18	2	13	.295	.309	.368	112	0	1	12	2			.882	-5	O/S	-0.4
1887	Was-N	70	264	47	63	9	1	1	18	21	16	.239	.304	.292	72	-11	-8	33	29			.897	7	O/S2	-0.2
1888	Was-N	90	317	46	58	6	3	2	24	25	22	.183	.262	.240	66	-12	-10	27	23			.900	4	SO/2P	-0.5
1889	Was-N	30	109	12	26	2	0	0	11	20	5	.239	.385	.257	88	-1	0	15	9			.905	3	O/S	0.2
1891	Mil-a	34	127	29	40	7	1	1	16	18	5	.315	.435	.409	121	9	4	29	12			.932	3	S/3	0.8
1892	Bal-N	76	308	42	85	15	3	1	50	24	19	.276	.340	.354	109	4	3	43	14			.872	0	SO/3	0.5
1893	Bro-N	94	327	53	86	17	1	2	54	48	13	.263	.366	.339	94	-3	-0	45	9			.892	-3	O3S/2	-0.4
1894	Bro-N	64	239	47	77	6	5	1	37	26	6	.322	.400	.402	103	-1	3	47	16			.926	-1	O3/2S	0.0
1895	Bro-N	61	216	49	56	9	7	0	29	32	6	.259	.368	.366	99	-2	2	33	7			.952	-6	O2/S3	-0.6
1896	Bro-N	76	250	36	73	7	4	1	28	33	10	.292	.381	.364	105	1	4	41	11			.941	-12	2O/3S	-0.4
1897	Bro-N	85	284	42	79	9	2	0	38	49		.278	.393	.324	96	-1	2	42	6			.941	4	2S/O	0.8
Total	11	706	2536	414	671	89	28	10	323	298	115	.265	.355	.334	95	-15	1	365	138			.912	-7	OS2/3P	-0.2

■ **COSTEN SHOCKLEY** Shockley, John Costen b: 2/8/42, Georgetown, Del. BL/TL, 6′2″, 200 lbs. Deb: 7/17/64

YEAR	TM/L	G	AB	R	H	2B	3B	HR	RBI	BB	SO	AVG	OBP	SLG	PRO+	BR	/A	RC	SB	CS	SBR	FA	FR	POS	TPR
1964	Phi-N	11	35	4	8	0	0	1	2	2	8	.229	.270	.314	65	-2	-2	3	0	0	0	.968	-1	/1	-0.3
1965	Cal-A	40	107	5	20	2	0	2	17	9	16	.187	.256	.262	49	-7	-7	7	0	0	0	.996	0	1/O	-0.9
Total	2	51	142	9	28	2	0	3	19	11	24	.197	.260	.275	53	-9	-9	10	0	0	0	.991	-1	/1O	-1.2

■ **CHARLIE SHOEMAKER** Shoemaker, Charles Landis b: 8/10/39, Los Angeles, Cal. d: 5/31/90, Mount Penn, Pa. BL/TR, 5′10″, 155 lbs. Deb: 9/09/61

YEAR	TM/L	G	AB	R	H	2B	3B	HR	RBI	BB	SO	AVG	OBP	SLG	PRO+	BR	/A	RC	SB	CS	SBR	FA	FR	POS	TPR
1961	KC-A	7	26	5	10	2	0	0	1	2	2	.385	.429	.462	138	1	1	5	0	0	0	1.000	0	/2	0.2
1962	KC-A	5	11	1	2	0	0	0	0	0	2	.182	.182	.182	-2	-2	-2	0	0	0	0	1.000	1	/2	0.0
1964	KC-A	16	52	6	11	2	2	0	3	0	9	.212	.212	.327	46	-4	-4	4	0	0	0	.964	-5	2	-0.8
Total	3	28	89	12	23	4	2	0	4	2	13	.258	.275	.348	68	-4	-4	9	0	0	0	.981	-3	/2	-0.6

■ **STRICK SHOFNER** Shofner, Frank Strickland b: 7/23/19, Crawford, Tex. BL/TR, 5′10.5″, 187 lbs. Deb: 4/19/47

YEAR	TM/L	G	AB	R	H	2B	3B	HR	RBI	BB	SO	AVG	OBP	SLG	PRO+	BR	/A	RC	SB	CS	SBR	FA	FR	POS	TPR
1947	Bos-A	5	13	1	2	0	1	0	0	0	3	.154	.154	.308	25	-1	-1	1	0	0	0	1.000	1	/3	-0.1

■ **EDDIE SHOKES** Shokes, Edward Christopher b: 1/27/20, Charleston, S.C. BL/TL, 6′, 170 lbs. Deb: 6/09/41

YEAR	TM/L	G	AB	R	H	2B	3B	HR	RBI	BB	SO	AVG	OBP	SLG	PRO+	BR	/A	RC	SB	CS	SBR	FA	FR	POS	TPR
1941	Cin-N	1	1	0	0	0	0	0	0	0	1	.000	.000	.000	-99	-0	-0	0	0			.000	0	H	0.0
1946	Cin-N	31	83	3	10	1	0	0	5	18	21	.120	.277	.133	19	-8	-8	4	1			.996	-1	1	-1.2
Total	2	32	84	3	10	1	0	0	5	18	22	.119	.275	.131	18	-9	-8	4	1				-1	/1	-1.2

■ **RAY SHOOK** Shook, Raymond Curtis b: 11/18/1889, Perry, Ohio d: 9/16/70, South Bend, Ind. BR/TR, 5′7.5″, 155 lbs. Deb: 4/16/16

YEAR	TM/L	G	AB	R	H	2B	3B	HR	RBI	BB	SO	AVG	OBP	SLG	PRO+	BR	/A	RC	SB	CS	SBR	FA	FR	POS	TPR
1916	Chi-A	1	0	0	0	0	0	0	0	0	0	—	—	—	—	0	0	0	0			.000	0	R	0.0

■ **RON SHOOP** Shoop, Ronald Lee b: 9/19/31, Rural Valley, Pa. BR/TR, 5′11″, 180 lbs. Deb: 8/22/59

YEAR	TM/L	G	AB	R	H	2B	3B	HR	RBI	BB	SO	AVG	OBP	SLG	PRO+	BR	/A	RC	SB	CS	SBR	FA	FR	POS	TPR
1959	Det-A	3	7	1	1	0	0	0	1	0	1	.143	.143	.143	-20	-1	-1	0	0	0	0	1.000	-1	/C	-0.2

■ **TOM SHOPAY** Shopay, Thomas Michael b: 2/21/45, Bristol, Conn. BL/TR, 5′9.5″, 160 lbs. Deb: 9/17/67

YEAR	TM/L	G	AB	R	H	2B	3B	HR	RBI	BB	SO	AVG	OBP	SLG	PRO+	BR	/A	RC	SB	CS	SBR	FA	FR	POS	TPR
1967	NY-A	8	27	2	8	1	0	2	6	1	5	.296	.321	.556	161	2	2	5	2	0	1	.917	1	/O	0.3
1969	NY-A	28	48	2	4	0	1	0	0	2	10	.083	.120	.125	-33	-8	-8	1	0	1	-1	1.000	1	O	-0.9
1971	*Bal-A	47	74	10	19	2	0	0	5	3	7	.257	.286	.284	62	-4	-4	6	2	1	0	1.000	-1	O	-0.5
1972	Bal-A	49	40	3	9	0	0	0	2	5	12	.225	.311	.225	60	-2	-2	3	0	0	0	1.000	-0	/O	-0.2
1975	Bal-A	40	31	4	5	1	0	0	2	4	7	.161	.257	.194	31	-3	-3	2	3	0	1	1.000	-3	O/CD	-0.4
1976	Bal-A	14	20	4	4	0	0	0	1	3	3	.200	.304	.200	53	-1	-1	2	1	0	0	1.000	-4	O/C	-0.5
1977	Bal-A	67	69	15	13	3	0	1	4	8	7	.188	.273	.275	53	-5	-4	5	3	3	-1	1.000	-18	O/D	-2.4
Total	7	253	309	40	62	7	1	3	20	26	51	.201	.263	.259	50	-21	-20	23	11	5	0	.993	-24	O/DC	-4.6

■ **DAVE SHORT** Short, David Orvis b: 5/11/17, Magnolia, Ark. d: 11/22/83, Shreveport, La. BL/TR, 5′11.5″, 162 lbs. Deb: 9/16/40

YEAR	TM/L	G	AB	R	H	2B	3B	HR	RBI	BB	SO	AVG	OBP	SLG	PRO+	BR	/A	RC	SB	CS	SBR	FA	FR	POS	TPR
1940	Chi-A	4	3	1	1	0	0	0	0	1	2	.333	.500	.333	119	0	0	1	0	0	0	.000	0	H	0.0
1941	Chi-A	3	8	0	0	0	0	0	0	2	1	.000	.200	.000	-44	-2	-2	0	0	0	0	.800	-0	/O	-0.2
Total	2	7	11	1	1	0	0	0	0	3	3	.091	.286	.091	3	-1	-1	1	0	0	0		-0	/O	-0.2

■ **CHICK SHORTEN** Shorten, Charles Henry b: 4/19/1892, Scranton, Pa. d: 10/23/65, Scranton, Pa. BL/TL, 6′, 175 lbs. Deb: 9/22/15

YEAR	TM/L	G	AB	R	H	2B	3B	HR	RBI	BB	SO	AVG	OBP	SLG	PRO+	BR	/A	RC	SB	CS	SBR	FA	FR	POS	TPR
1915	Bos-A	6	14	1	3	1	0	0	0	0	2	.214	.214	.286	51	-1	-1	1	0			1.000	-1	/O	-0.2
1916	*Bos-A	53	112	14	33	2	1	0	11	10	8	.295	.352	.330	105	1	1	14	1			1.000	-8	O	-0.9
1917	Bos-A	69	168	12	30	4	2	0	16	10	10	.179	.229	.226	39	-13	-12	9	2			.977	-5	O	-2.2
1919	Det-A	95	270	37	85	9	3	0	22	22	13	.315	.366	.370	110	3	4	40	5			.973	-6	O	-0.8
1920	Det-A	116	364	35	105	9	6	1	40	28	14	.288	.339	.354	86	-8	-7	44	2	4	-2	.989	-1	O	-1.7
1921	Det-A	92	217	33	59	11	3	0	23	20	11	.272	.333	.350	75	-8	-8	26	2	3	-1	.981	-4	O	-1.6
1922	StL-A	55	131	22	36	12	5	2	16	16	8	.275	.354	.489	114	3	2	23	0	1	-1	1.000	-2	O	-0.3
1924	Cin-N	41	69	7	19	3	0	0	6	4	2	.275	.315	.319	71	-3	-3	7	0	0	0	1.000	-4	O	-0.7
Total	8	527	1345	161	370	51	20	3	134	110	68	.275	.330	.349	87	-26	-24	163	12	8		.985	-31	O	-8.4

■ **BURT SHOTTON** Shotton, Burton Edwin "Barney" b: 10/18/1884, Brownhelm, Ohio d: 7/29/62, Lake Wales, Fla. BL/TR, 5′11″, 175 lbs. Deb: 9/13/09 MC

YEAR	TM/L	G	AB	R	H	2B	3B	HR	RBI	BB	SO	AVG	OBP	SLG	PRO+	BR	/A	RC	SB	CS	SBR	FA	FR	POS	TPR
1909	StL-A	17	61	5	16	0	1	0	0	5		.262	.328	.295	104	-0	0	7	3			.915	1	O	0.1
1911	StL-A	139	572	84	146	11	8	0	36	51		.255	.317	.302	76	-20	-17	62	26			.950	7	*O	-1.8
1912	StL-A	154	580	87	168	15	8	2	40	86		.290	.390	.353	117	14	17	92	35			.941	7	*O	1.5
1913	StL-A	147	549	105	163	23	8	1	28	**99**	63	.297	.405	.373	132	24	26	95	43			.951	13	*O	3.4
1914	StL-A	154	579	82	156	19	9	0	38	64	66	.269	.344	.333	108	3	6	69	40	29	-5	.940	2	*O	-0.5
1915	StL-A	156	559	93	158	18	11	1	30	118	62	.283	.409	.360	135	27	30	87	43	32	-6	.931	-3	*O	1.5
1916	StL-A	157	618	97	174	23	6	1	36	**111**	67	.282	.391	.343	127	21	24	88	41	28	-5	.950	10	*O	2.4
1917	StL-A	118	398	47	89	9	1	1	20	62	47	.224	.330	.259	83	-7	-5	38	16			.923	-12	*O	-2.6
1918	Was-A	126	505	68	132	16	7	0	21	67	28	.261	.349	.321	104	3	4	61	25			.942	6	*O	0.3
1919	StL-N	85	270	35	77	13	5	1	20	22	25	.285	.341	.381	125	6	7	39	16			.927	-5	O	-0.2
1920	StL-N	62	180	28	41	5	0	1	12	18	14	.228	.305	.272	69	-7	-6	17	5	1	1	.959	1	O	-0.9
1921	StL-N	38	48	9	12	1	1	1	7	7	4	.250	.357	.375	96	-0	-0	6	0	2	-1	.958	-0	O	-0.2
1922	StL-N	34	30	5	6	1	0	0	2	4	6	.200	.294	.233	39	-3	-3	2	0	1	-1	1.000	-1	/O	-0.4
1923	StL-N	1	0	1	0	0	0	0	0	0	0	—	—	—	—	0	0	0	0	0	0	.000	0	R	0.0
Total	14	1388	4949	746	1338	154	65	9	290	714	382	.270	.365	.333	110	61	84	663	293	93		.942	25	*O	2.6

YEAR	TM/L	G	AB	R	H	2B	3B	HR	RBI	BB	SO	AVG	OBP	SLG	PRO+	BR	/A	RC	SB	CS	SBR	FA	FR	POS	TPR
■ JOHN SHOUPE	Shoupe, John F. b: 9/30/1851, Cincinnati, Ohio d: 2/13/20, Cincinnati, Ohio BL/TL, 5'7", 140 lbs. Deb: 5/03/1879																								
1879	Tro-N	11	44	5	4	0	0	0	1	0	3	.091	.091	.091	-43	-6	-6	0				.820	-3	S/2	-0.8
1882	StL-a	2	7	1	0	0	0	0		0		.000	.000	.000	-96	-1	-1	0				1.000	1	/2	0.0
1884	Was-U	1	4	1	3	0	0	0		0		.750	.750	.750	423	1	1	2				.857	2	/O	0.3
Total	3	14	55	7	7	0	0	0	1	0	3	.127	.127	.127	-16	-7	-6	3				.857	-0	/S2O	-0.5
■ JOHN SHOVLIN	Shovlin, John Joseph "Brode" b: 1/14/1891, Drifton, Pa. d: 2/16/76, Bethesda, Md. BR/TR, 5'7", 163 lbs. Deb: 6/21/11																								
1911	Pit-N	2	1	1	0	0	0	0	0	0	1	.000	.000	.000	-96	-0	-0	0	0			.000	0	H	0.0
1919	StL-A	9	35	4	7	0	0	0	1	5	2	.200	.300	.200	41	-3	-3	2	0			.936	-2	/2	-0.4
1920	StL-A	7	7	2	2	0	0	0	2	0	0	.286	.286	.286	50	-0	-1	1	0	0	0	1.000	1	/S	0.0
Total	3	18	43	7	9	0	0	0	3	5	3	.209	.292	.209	39	-3	-3	3	0	0		.983	-1	/2S	-0.4
■ GEORGE SHUBA	Shuba, George Thomas "Shotgun" b: 12/13/24, Youngstown, Ohio BL/TR, 5'11", 180 lbs. Deb: 7/02/48																								
1948	Bro-N	63	161	21	43	6	0	4	32	34	31	.267	.395	.379	107	4	3	27	1			.936	-10	O	-0.9
1949	Bro-N	1	1	0	0	0	0	0	0	0	0	.000	.000	.000	-96	-0	-0	0	0			.000	0	H	0.0
1950	Bro-N	34	111	15	23	8	2	3	12	13	22	.207	.302	.396	80	-3	-4	14	2			.984	3	O	-0.2
1952	*Bro-N	94	256	40	78	12	1	9	40	38	29	.305	.395	.465	136	14	13	47	1	3	-2	.992	-2	O	0.7
1953	*Bro-N	74	169	19	43	12	1	5	23	17	20	.254	.326	.426	92	-2	-2	23	1	2	-1	.984	-5	O	-1.0
1954	Bro-N	45	65	3	10	5	0	2	10	7	10	.154	.247	.323	46	-5	-6	5	0	0	0	.913	-1	O	-0.7
1955	*Bro-N	44	51	8	14	2	0	1	8	11	10	.275	.422	.373	110	2	2	9	0	0	0	.909	-2	/O	-0.1
Total	7	355	814	106	211	45	4	24	125	120	122	.259	.359	.413	104	9	6	125	5	5		.967	-18	O	-2.2
■ FRANK SHUGART	Shugart, Frank Harry (b: Frank Harry Shugarts) b: 12/10/1866, Luthersburg, Pa. d: 9/9/44, Clearfield, Pa. BL/TR, 5'8", 170 lbs. Deb: 8/23/1890																								
1890	Chi-P	29	106	8	20	5	5	0	15	5	13	.189	.232	.330	49	-8	-9	10	5			.881	-5	S/O	-1.0
1891	Pit-N	75	320	57	88	19	8	3	33	20	26	.275	.324	.412	119	5	6	51	21			.902	4	S	1.3
1892	Pit-N	137	554	94	148	19	14	0	62	47	48	.267	.329	.352	107	5	5	75	28			.886	9	*S/CO	1.7
1893	Pit-N	52	210	37	55	7	3	1	32	19	15	.262	.332	.338	81	-6	-5	28	12			.882	-3	S	-0.5
	StL-N	59	246	41	69	10	4	0	28	22	10	.280	.354	.354	90	-3	-3	36	13			.907	-3	OS/3	-0.5
	Yr	111	456	78	124	17	7	1	60	41	25	.272	.344	.346	86	-9	-8	65	25			.868	-6	SO/3	-1.0
1894	StL-N	133	527	103	154	19	18	7	72	38	37	.292	.349	.436	90	-10	-10	91	21			.912	-3	*O/S3	-1.7
1895	Lou-N	113	473	61	125	14	13	4	70	31	25	.264	.315	.374	84	-16	-10	62	14			.874	-17	*SO	-2.1
1897	Phi-N	40	163	20	41	8	2	5	25	8		.252	.287	.417	87	-5	-4	22	5			.872	-5	S	-0.7
1901	Chi-A	107	415	62	104	9	12	2	47	28		.251	.301	.345	81	-12	-11	49	12			.885	-8	*S	-0.9
Total	8	745	3014	483	804	110	79	22	384	218	174	.267	.323	.378	91	-50	-42	424	131			.883	-32	SO/3C	-4.4
■ TERRY SHUMPERT	Shumpert, Terrance Darnell b: 8/16/66, Paducah, Ky. BR/TR, 5'11", 190 lbs. Deb: 5/01/90																								
1990	KC-A	32	91	7	25	6	1	0	8	2	17	.275	.298	.363	85	-2	-2	8	3	3	-1	.977	-0	2/D	-0.3
1991	KC-A	144	369	45	80	16	4	5	34	30	75	.217	.285	.322	67	-16	-17	32	17	11	-2	.975	3	*2	-1.3
1992	KC-A	36	94	6	14	5	1	1	11	3	17	.149	.175	.255	19	-10	-10	4	2	2	-1	.969	1	2/SD	-1.0
Total	3	212	554	58	119	27	6	6	53	35	109	.215	.269	.318	62	-29	-29	44	22	16	-3	.974	3	2/DS	-2.6
■ VINCE SHUPE	Shupe, Vincent William b: 9/5/21, E.Canton, Ohio d: 4/5/62, Canton, Ohio BL/TL, 5'11", 180 lbs. Deb: 7/07/45																								
1945	Bos-N	78	283	22	76	8	0	0	15	17	16	.269	.312	.297	69	-11	-11	26	3			.989	1	1	-1.5
■ ED SICKING	Sicking, Edward Joseph b: 3/30/1897, St.Bernard, Ohio d: 8/30/78, Cincinnati, Ohio BR/TR, 5'9.5", 165 lbs. Deb: 8/26/16																								
1916	Chi-N	1	1	0	0	0	0	0	0	0	0	.000	.000	.000	-90	-0	-0	0	0			.000	0	H	0.0
1918	NY-N	46	132	9	33	4	0	0	12	6	11	.250	.283	.280	73	-4	-4	10	2			.917	-8	32/S	-1.3
1919	NY-N	6	15	2	5	0	0	0	3	1	0	.333	.412	.333	127	1	1	2	0			.971	3	/S	0.4
	Phi-N	61	185	16	40	2	1	0	15	8	17	.216	.253	.238	45	-12	-13	12	4			.925	5	S2	-0.6
	Yr	67	200	18	45	2	1	0	18	9	17	.225	.265	.245	51	-11	-12	14	4			.933	8	S2	-0.2
1920	NY-N	46	134	11	23	3	1	0	9	10	10	.172	.234	.209	28	-12	-12	7	6	2	1	.915	4	32/S	-0.7
	Cin-N	37	123	12	33	3	0	0	17	13	5	.268	.338	.293	83	-2	-2	12	2	3	-1	.955	1	2/S3	-0.1
	Yr	83	257	23	56	6	1	0	26	23	15	.218	.285	.249	55	-15	-14	19	8	5	-1	.952	4	23S	-0.8
1927	Pit-N	6	7	1	1	1	0	0	3	1	0	.143	.250	.286	40	-1	-1	1	0			1.000	2	/2	0.1
Total	5	203	597	51	135	13	2	0	59	39	43	.226	.277	.255	57	-31	-32	45	14	5		.965	5	/2S3	-2.2
■ NORM SIEBERN	Siebern, Norman Leroy b: 7/26/33, St.Louis, Mo. BL/TR, 6'3", 205 lbs. Deb: 6/15/56																								
1956	*NY-A	54	162	27	33	1	4	4	21	19	38	.204	.287	.333	66	-9	-8	16	1	1	-0	.971	0	O	-1.0
1958	*NY-A	134	460	79	138	19	5	14	55	66	87	.300	.389	.454	136	21	23	82	5	8	-3	.982	5	*O	1.9
1959	NY-A	120	380	52	103	17	0	11	53	41	71	.271	.345	.403	108	3	4	56	3	1	0	.989	-2	O/1	-0.2
1960	KC-A	144	520	69	145	31	6	19	69	72	68	.279	.369	.471	125	19	18	93	0	0	0	.987	-1	O1	0.9
1961	KC-A	153	560	68	166	36	5	18	98	82	91	.296	.387	.475	129	24	24	108	2	4	-2	.989	-1	*1O	1.0
1962	KC-A★	162	600	114	185	25	6	25	117	110	88	.308	.416	.495	140	41	39	**129**	3	1	0	.994	5	*1	3.2
1963	KC-A☆	152	556	80	151	25	2	16	83	79	82	.272	.362	.410	111	14	11	85	1	4	-2	.991	4	*1O	0.6
1964	Bal-A★	150	478	92	117	24	2	12	56	**106**	87	.245	.384	.379	114	13	13	78	2	3	-1	.995	4	*1	1.0
1965	Bal-A	106	297	44	76	13	4	8	32	50	49	.256	.365	.407	117	9	8	47	1	2	-1	.991	1	1	0.4
1966	Cal-A	125	336	29	83	14	1	5	41	63	61	.247	.366	.339	107	4	5	45	0	1	-1	.992	1	1	0.0
1967	SF-N	46	58	6	9	1	1	0	4	14	13	.155	.319	.207	54	-3	-3	5	0	0	0	1.000	0	1/O	-0.4
	*Bos-A	33	44	2	9	0	2	0	7	6	8	.205	.300	.295	71	-1	-2	4	0	0	0	.981	1	1/O	-0.2
1968	Bos-A	27	30	0	2	0	0	0	0	0	5	.067	.067	.067	-56	-6	-6	0	0	0	0	1.000	-1	/1O	-0.8
Total	12	1406	4481	662	1217	206	38	132	636	708	748	.272	.372	.423	118	129	128	749	18	25	-10	.992	17	1O	6.4
■ DICK SIEBERT	Siebert, Richard Walther b: 2/19/12, Fall River, Mass. d: 12/9/78, Minneapolis, Minn. BL/TL, 6', 170 lbs. Deb: 9/07/32 F																								
1932	Bro-N	6	7	1	2	0	0	0	0	2	2	.286	.444	.286	104	0	0	1	0			1.000	-0	/1	0.0
1936	Bro-N	2	2	0	0	0	0	0	0	0	0	.000	.000	.000	-99	-1	-1	0	0			1.000	0	/O	0.0
1937	StL-N	22	38	3	7	2	0	0	2	4	8	.184	.279	.237	41	-3	-3	3	1			.979	-1	/1	-0.5
1938	StL-N	1	1	0	1	0	0	0	0	0	0	1.000	1.000	1.000	427	0	0	1	0			.000	0	H	0.0
	Phi-A	48	194	24	55	8	3	0	28	10	9	.284	.329	.356	73	-9	-8	22	2	3	-1	1.000	5	1	-0.8
1939	Phi-A	101	402	58	118	28	3	6	47	21	22	.294	.329	.423	93	-7	-6	56	4	1	1	.991	5	1	-1.0
1940	Phi-A	154	595	69	170	31	6	5	77	33	34	.286	.325	.383	85	-16	-14	74	8	6	-1	.985	8	*1	-2.1
1941	Phi-A	123	467	63	156	28	8	5	79	37	22	.334	.385	.460	126	15	17	82	1	3	-2	.990	6	*1	1.2
1942	Phi-A	153	612	57	159	25	7	2	74	24	17	.260	.291	.333	76	-22	-21	59	4	5	-2	.989	-2	*1	-3.5
1943	Phi-A★	146	558	50	140	26	7	1	72	33	21	.251	.295	.328	83	-14	-14	50	6	7	-2	.990	4	*1	-2.2
1944	Phi-A	132	468	52	143	27	5	6	52	62	17	.306	.387	.423	133	20	21	83	2	0	1	.993	-4	1O	1.2
1945	Phi-A†	147	573	62	153	29	1	7	51	50	33	.267	.328	.358	99	-1	-1	69	2	7	-4	.991	10	*1	-0.5
Total	11	1035	3917	439	1104	204	40	32	482	276	185	.282	.332	.379	96	-36	-29	500	30	32		.990	31	1/O	-8.2
■ FRED SIEFKE	Siefke, Frederick Edwin b: 3/27/1870, New York, N.Y. d: 4/18/1893, New York, N.Y. Deb: 5/02/1890																								
1890	Bro-a	16	58	1	8	2	0	0		5		.138	.206	.172	14	-6	-6	3	2			.811	0	3	-0.5
■ JOHN SIEGEL	Siegel, John b: York, Pa. Deb: 6/09/1884																								
1884	Phi-U	8	31	4	7	2	0	0		1		.226	.250	.290	89	-1	-0	2				.533	-5	/3	-0.4

YEAR	TM/L	G	AB	R	H	2B	3B	HR	RBI	BB	SO	AVG	OBP	SLG	PRO+	BR	/A	RC	SB	CS	SBR	FA	FR	POS	TPR
■ **JOHNNY SIEGLE**	Siegle, John Herbert b: 7/8/1874, Urbana, Ohio d: 2/12/68, Urbana, Ohio BR/TR, 5'10", 165 lbs. Deb: 9/15/05																								
1905	Cin-N	17	56	9	17	1	2	1	8	7		.304	.381	.446	132	3	2	10	0			.960	-1	O	0.1
1906	Cin-N	22	68	4	8	2	2	0	7	3		.118	.167	.206	16	-7	-7	3	0			.959	0	O	-0.9
Total	2	39	124	13	25	3	4	1	15	10		.202	.267	.315	72	-4	-5	13	0			.959	-1	/O	-0.8
■ **OSCAR SIEMER**	Siemer, Oscar Sylvester "Cotton" b: 8/14/01, St.Louis, Mo. d: 12/5/59, St.Louis, Mo. BR/TR, 5'9", 162 lbs. Deb: 5/20/25																								
1925	Bos-N	16	46	5	14	0	1	1	6	1	0	.304	.319	.413	94	-1	-1	6	0	0	0	.900	-2	C	-0.1
1926	Bos-N	31	73	3	15	1	0	0	5	2	7	.205	.227	.219	22	-8	-7	4	0			.920	-2	C	-0.8
Total	2	47	119	8	29	1	1	1	11	3	7	.244	.262	.294	51	-9	-8	10	0	0		.913	-4	/C	-0.9
■ **RUBEN SIERRA**	Sierra, Ruben Angel (Garcia) b: 10/6/65, Rio Piedras, P.R. BB/TR, 6'1", 175 lbs. Deb: 6/01/86																								
1986	Tex-A	113	382	50	101	13	10	16	55	22	65	.264	.306	.476	106	3	2	51	7	8	-3	.972	-10	*O/D	-1.4
1987	Tex-A	158	643	97	169	35	4	30	109	39	114	.263	.307	.470	102	-0	-0	85	16	11	-2	.963	5	*O	-0.2
1988	Tex-A	156	615	77	156	32	2	23	91	44	91	.254	.305	.424	99	-0	-2	77	18	4	3	.979	6	*O/D	0.2
1989	Tex-A★	162	634	101	194	35	**14**	29	**119**	43	82	.306	.352	**.543**	146	37	36	122	8	2	1	.973	6	*O	3.9
1990	Tex-A	159	608	70	170	37	2	16	96	49	86	.280	.334	.426	111	8	8	85	9	0	3	.967	0	*O/D	0.7
1991	Tex-A★	161	661	110	203	44	5	25	116	56	91	.307	.361	.502	139	31	32	117	16	4	2	.979	5	*O	3.6
1992	Tex-A★	124	500	66	139	30	6	14	70	31	59	.278	.320	.446	116	6	8	70	12	4	1	.970	0	*O/D	0.7
	*Oak-A	27	101	17	28	4	1	3	17	14	9	.277	.365	.426	126	3	4	16	2	0	1	1.000	1	O/D	0.5
	Yr	151	601	83	167	34	7	17	87	45	68	.278	.328	.443	118	9	12	87	14	4	2	.976	1	*O/D	1.2
Total	7	1060	4144	588	1160	230	44	156	673	298	597	.280	.329	.470	118	88	88	623	88	33	7	.973	15	*O/D	8.0
■ **ROY SIEVERS**	Sievers, Roy Edward "Squirrel" b: 11/18/26, St.Louis, Mo. BR/TR, 6'1", 195 lbs. Deb: 4/21/49 C																								
1949	StL-A	140	471	84	144	28	1	16	91	70	75	.306	.398	.471	124	20	17	89	1	5	-3	.973	6	*O/3	1.4
1950	StL-A	113	370	46	88	20	4	10	57	34	42	.238	.305	.395	75	-14	-16	43	1	3	-2	.983	6	O3	-1.4
1951	StL-A	31	89	10	20	2	1	1	11	9	21	.225	.303	.303	62	-4	-5	8	0	0	0	.985	-2	O	-0.7
1952	StL-A	11	30	3	6	3	0	0	5	1	4	.200	.226	.300	44	-2	-2	2	0	0	0	.968	-1	/1	-0.4
1953	StL-A	92	285	37	77	15	0	8	35	32	47	.270	.344	.407	100	1	-0	40	0	1	-1	.992	-6	1	-1.0
1954	Was-A	145	514	75	119	26	6	24	102	80	77	.232	.337	.446	120	8	12	78	2	1	0	.971	9	*O/1	1.5
1955	Was-A	144	509	74	138	20	8	25	106	73	66	.271	.367	.489	136	20	23	90	1	2	-1	.988	-1	*O1/3	1.5
1956	Was-A★	152	550	92	139	27	2	29	95	100	88	.253	.373	.467	121	17	17	100	0	0	0	.987	2	O1	0.9
1957	Was-A☆	152	572	99	172	23	5	**42**	**114**	76	55	.301	.389	.579	163	47	48	131	1	1	-0	.985	4	*O1	4.3
1958	Was-A	148	550	85	162	18	1	39	108	53	63	.295	.361	.544	148	32	33	106	3	1	0	.991	5	*O1	3.1
1959	Was-A★	115	385	55	93	19	0	21	49	53	62	.242	.336	.455	116	8	8	59	1	1	-0	.989	5	1O	0.5
1960	Chi-A	127	444	87	131	22	0	28	93	74	69	.295	.399	.534	152	32	33	95	1	1	-0	.993	-7	*1/O	1.6
1961	Chi-A★	141	492	76	145	26	6	27	92	61	62	.295	.379	.537	144	29	30	101	1	0	0	.993	0	*1	1.9
1962	Phi-N	144	477	61	125	19	5	21	80	56	80	.262	.348	.455	117	9	11	78	2	1	0	.991	4	*1/O	0.6
1963	Phi-N	138	450	46	108	19	2	19	82	43	72	.240	.313	.418	110	4	5	60	0	2	-1	.989	-1	*1	-0.2
1964	Phi-N	49	120	7	22	3	1	4	16	13	20	.183	.269	.325	67	-5	-5	10	0	0	0	.992	-1	1	-0.8
	Was-A	33	58	5	10	1	0	4	11	9	14	.172	.284	.397	87	-1	-1	7	0	0	0	1.000	1	1	0.0
1965	Was-A	12	21	3	4	1	0	0	0	4	3	.190	.320	.238	62	-1	-1	2	0	0	0	1.000	-1	/1	-0.2
Total	17	1887	6387	945	1703	292	42	318	1147	841	920	.267	.357	.475	124	198	206	1097	14	19	-7	.991	21	1O/3	12.6
■ **FRANK SIFFELL**	Siffell, Frank b: 1860, Germany d: 10/26/09, Philadelphia, Pa. Deb: 6/14/1884																								
1884	Phi-a	7	17	3	3	1	0	0		0		.176	.222	.235	48	-1	-1	1				.875	-3	/C	-0.3
1885	Phi-a	3	10	0	1	0	0	0		0		.100	.100	.100	-34	-1	-2	0				.750	-3	/CO	-0.4
Total	2	10	27	3	4	1	0	0		0		.148	.179	.185	18	-2	-3	1				.841	-6	/CO	-0.7
■ **FRANK SIGAFOOS**	Sigafoos, Francis Leonard b: 3/21/04, Easton, Pa. d: 4/12/68, Indianapolis, Ind. BR/TR, 5'9", 170 lbs. Deb: 9/03/26																								
1926	Phi-A	13	43	4	11	0	0	0	2	0	3	.256	.256	.256	32	-4	-4	3	0	0	0	.915	-3	S	-0.6
1929	Det-A	14	23	3	4	1	0	0	2	5	4	.174	.321	.217	41	-2	-2	2	0	2	-1	.909	-2	/3S	-0.4
	Chi-A	7	3	1	1	0	0	0	1	2	1	.333	.600	.333	148	0	1	1	0	0	0	1.000	1	/2	0.2
	Yr	21	26	4	5	1	0	0	3	7	5	.192	.364	.231	56	-1	-1	2	0	2	-1	.909	-1	/32S	-0.2
1931	Cin-N	21	65	6	11	2	0	0	8	0	6	.169	.182	.200	3	-9	-8	3	0			.881	-3	3/S	-1.1
Total	3	55	134	14	27	3	0	0	13	7	14	.201	.246	.224	25	-14	-14	8	0	2		.887	-7	/3S2	-1.9
■ **PADDY SIGLIN**	Siglin, Wesley Peter b: 9/24/1891, Aurelia, Iowa d: 8/5/56, Oakland, Cal. BR/TR, 5'10", 160 lbs. Deb: 9/12/14																								
1914	Pit-N	14	39	4	6	0	0	0	2	4	6	.154	.233	.154	16	-4	-4	2	1			.911	-6	2	-1.1
1915	Pit-N	6	7	1	2	0	0	0	0	1	2	.286	.375	.286	103	0	0	1	1			.800	-0	/2	0.0
1916	Pit-N	3	4	0	1	0	0	0	0	0	2	.250	.250	.250	53	-0	-0	0	0			.857	0	/2	0.0
Total	3	23	50	5	9	0	0	0	2	5	10	.180	.255	.180	32	-4	-4	3	2			.895	-5	/2	-1.1
■ **TRIPP SIGMAN**	Sigman, Wesley Triplett b: 1/17/1899, Mooresville, N.C. d: 3/8/71, Augusta, Ga. BL/TR, 6', 180 lbs. Deb: 9/18/29																								
1929	Phi-N	10	29	8	15	1	0	2	9	3	1	.517	.563	.759	210	6	5	12	0			.944	-2	O	0.3
1930	Phi-N	52	100	15	27	4	1	4	6	6	9	.270	.324	.450	79	-3	-4	14	1			.932	-1	O	-0.6
Total	2	62	129	23	42	5	1	6	15	9	10	.326	.379	.519	108	3	2	26	1			.935	-3	/O	-0.3
■ **EDDIE SILBER**	Silber, Edward James b: 6/6/14, Philadelphia, Pa. d: 10/26/76, Dunedin, Fla. BR/TR, 5'11", 170 lbs. Deb: 9/03/37																								
1937	StL-A	22	83	10	26	2	0	0	4	5	13	.313	.352	.337	74	-3	-3	9	0	2	-1	.871	-7	O	-1.1
1939	StL-A	1	1	0	0	0	0	0	0	0	1	.000	.000	.000	-98	-0	-0	0	0	0	0	.000	0	H	0.0
Total	2	23	84	10	26	2	0	0	4	5	14	.310	.348	.333	72	-3	-3	9	0	2	-1	1.000	-7	/O	-1.1
■ **ED SILCH**	Silch, Edward "Baldy" b: 2/22/1865, St.Louis, Mo. d: 1/15/1895, St.Louis, Mo. TR, Deb: 4/29/1888																								
1888	Bro-a	14	48	5	13	4	0	0	3	4		.271	.327	.354	122	1	1	7	4			.870	-2	O	-0.1
■ **DANNY SILVA**	Silva, Daniel James b: 10/5/1896, Everett, Mass. d: 4/4/74, Hyannis, Mass. BR/TR, 6', 170 lbs. Deb: 8/11/19																								
1919	Was-A	1	4	0	1	0	0	0	0	0	0	.250	.250	.250	41	-0	-0	0	0			1.000	1	/3	0.0
■ **AL SILVERA**	Silvera, Aaron Albert b: 8/26/35, San Diego, Cal. BR/TR, 6', 180 lbs. Deb: 6/12/55																								
1955	Cin-N	13	7	3	1	0	0	0	2	0	1	.143	.143	.143	-23	-1	-1	0	0	0	0	.000	-0	/O	-0.2
1956	Cin-N	1	0	0	0	0	0	0	0	0	0	—	—	—	—	0	0	0	0	0	0	.000	0	R	0.0
Total	2	14	7	3	1	0	0	0	2	0	1	.143	.143	.143	-23	-1	-1	0	0	0	0	1.000	-0	/O	-0.2
■ **CHARLIE SILVERA**	Silvera, Charles Anthony Ryan "Swede" b: 10/13/24, San Francisco, Cal BR/TR, 5'10", 175 lbs. Deb: 9/29/48 C																								
1948	NY-A	4	14	1	8	0	1	0	1	0	1	.571	.571	.714	243	3	3	6	0	0	0	1.000	0	/C	0.3
1949	*NY-A	58	130	8	41	2	0	0	13	18	5	.315	.403	.331	95	0	0	18	2	1	0	.985	4	C	0.6
1950	NY-A	18	25	2	4	0	0	0	1	1	2	.160	.192	.160	-9	-4	-4	1	0	0	0	.959	3	C	-0.1
1951	NY-A	18	51	5	14	3	0	1	7	5	3	.275	.339	.392	101	-0	-0	5	0	0	0	1.000	0	C	0.1
1952	NY-A	20	55	4	18	3	0	0	11	5	2	.327	.383	.382	121	1	1	7	0	3	-2	1.000	-3	C	-0.2
1953	NY-A	42	82	11	23	3	1	0	12	9	5	.280	.352	.341	91	-1	-1	11	0	1	-1	.992	6	C/3	0.6
1954	NY-A	20	37	1	10	1	0	0	4	3	2	.270	.341	.297	79	-1	-1	3	0	1	-1	.962	5	C	0.4
1955	NY-A	14	26	1	5	0	0	0	1	6	4	.192	.344	.192	48	-2	-2	2	0	0	0	1.000	3	C	0.2
1956	NY-A	7	9	0	2	0	0	0	0	2	3	.222	.364	.222	60	-0	-0	1	0	0	0	.909	-1	/C	-0.1
1957	Chi-N	26	53	1	11	3	0	0	2	4	5	.208	.263	.264	43	-4	-4	3	0	0	0	.982	3	C	-0.1
Total	10	227	482	34	136	15	2	1	52	53	32	.282	.356	.328	86	-9	-8	58	2	6	-3	.985	21	C/3	1.7

YEAR	TM/L	G	AB	R	H	2B	3B	HR	RBI	BB	SO	AVG	OBP	SLG	PRO+	BR	/A	RC	SB	CS	SBR	FA	FR	POS	TPR
■ LUIS SILVERIO Silverio, Luis Pascual (Delmonte) b: 10/23/56, Villa Gonzalez, D.R BR/TR, 5'11", 165 lbs. Deb: 9/09/78																									
1978	KC-A	8	11	7	6	2	1	0	3	2	3	.545	.615	.909	315	3	3	6	1	1	-0	.833	-2	/OD	0.1
■ TOM SILVERIO Silverio, Tomas Roberto (Veloz) b: 10/14/45, Santiago, D.R. BL/TL, 5'10", 170 lbs. Deb: 4/30/70																									
1970	Cal-A	15	15	1	0	0	0	0	0	2	4	.000	.118	.000	-67	-3	-3	0	0	1	-1	1.000	-2	/O1	-0.7
1971	Cal-A	3	3	0	1	0	0	0	0	0	0	.333	.333	.333	96	-0	-0	0	0	0	0	.000	-1	/O	-0.1
1972	Cal-A	13	12	1	2	0	0	0	0	0	5	.167	.167	.167	-1	-1	-1	0	0	0	0	1.000	-1	/O	-0.3
Total	3	31	30	2	3	0	0	0	0	2	9	.100	.156	.100	-27	-5	-5	1	0	1	-1	1.000	-4	/O1	-1.1
■ DAVE SILVESTRI Silvestri, David Joseph b: 9/29/67, St.Louis, Mo. BR/TR, 6', 180 lbs. Deb: 4/27/92																									
1992	NY-A	7	13	3	4	0	2	0	1	0	3	.308	.308	.615	150	1	1	2	0	0	0	.889	1	/S	0.2
■ KEN SILVESTRI Silvestri, Kenneth Joseph "Hawk" b: 5/3/16, Chicago, Ill. d: 3/31/92, Tallahassee, Fla. BB/TR, 6'1", 200 lbs. Deb: 4/18/39 MC																									
1939	Chi-A	22	75	6	13	3	0	2	5	6	13	.173	.244	.293	36	-7	-8	6	0	1	-1	.947	-0	C	-0.7
1940	Chi-A	28	24	5	6	2	0	2	10	4	7	.250	.357	.583	138	1	1	4	0	0	0	1.000	-0	/C	0.1
1941	NY-A	17	40	6	10	5	0	1	4	7	6	.250	.362	.450	115	1	1	7	0	0	0	1.000	0	C	0.2
1946	NY-A	13	21	4	6	1	0	0	1	3	7	.286	.375	.333	98	0	0	3	0	0	0	.977	2	C	0.3
1947	NY-A	3	10	0	2	0	0	0	0	2	2	.200	.333	.200	51	-1	-1	1	0	0	0	1.000	-2	/C	-0.2
1949	Phi-N	4	4	1	0	0	0	0	0	2	1	.000	.333	.000	-3	-0	-0	0	0			1.000	0	/C2S	0.0
1950	*Phi-N	11	20	2	5	0	1	0	4	4	3	.250	.400	.350	101	0	0	3	0			1.000	-1	/C	-0.1
1951	Phi-N	4	9	2	2	0	0	0	1	3	2	.222	.417	.222	78	-0	-0	1	0	0	0	1.000	-3	/C2	-0.3
Total	8	102	203	26	44	11	1	5	25	31	41	.217	.326	.355	78	-6	-6	25	0	1		.974	-3	/C2S	-0.7
■ AL SIMMONS Simmons, Aloysius Harry "Bucketfoot Al" (b: Aloys Szymanski) b: 5/22/02, Milwaukee, Wis. d: 5/26/56, Milwaukee, Wis. BR/TR, 5'11", 190 lbs. Deb: 4/15/24 CH																									
1924	Phi-A	152	594	69	183	31	9	8	102	30	60	.308	.343	.431	98	-4	-4	84	16	15	-4	.976	6	*O	-1.2
1925	Phi-A	153	654	122	**253**	43	12	24	129	35	41	.387	.419	**.599**	146	51	45	**155**	7	14	-6	.966	5	*O	3.1
1926	Phi-A	147	583	90	199	53	10	19	109	48	49	.341	.392	.564	139	37	33	129	10	3	1	.975	-4	*O	1.9
1927	Phi-A	106	406	86	159	36	11	15	108	31	30	.392	.436	.645	168	44	41	107	10	2	2	.985	3	*O	3.6
1928	Phi-A	119	464	78	163	33	9	15	107	31	30	.351	.396	.558	144	30	29	100	1	4	-2	.988	2	*O	2.0
1929	*Phi-A	143	581	114	212	41	9	34	**157**	31	38	.365	.398	.642	158	50	47	145	4	2	0	.989	17	*O	**5.1**
1930	*Phi-A	138	554	**152**	211	41	16	36	165	39	34	**.381**	.423	.708	173	64	60	163	9	2	2	**.990**	6	*O	5.1
1931	*Phi-A	128	513	105	200	37	13	22	128	47	45	**.390**	.444	.641	172	60	55	145	3	3	-1	.987	8	*O	4.9
1932	Phi-A	154	670	144	**216**	28	9	35	151	47	76	.322	.368	.548	129	30	27	134	4	2	0	.980	-5	*O	1.1
1933	Chi-A★	146	605	85	200	29	10	14	119	39	49	.331	.373	.481	130	20	23	109	5	1	1	.990	14	*O	2.9
1934	Chi-A★	138	558	102	192	36	7	18	104	53	58	.344	.403	.530	135	31	29	120	3	2	-0	.987	5	*O	2.6
1935	Chi-A★	128	525	68	140	22	7	16	79	33	43	.267	.313	.427	87	-11	-13	68	4	6	-2	.981	1	*O	-1.8
1936	Det-A	143	568	96	186	38	6	13	112	49	35	.327	.383	.484	112	10	10	105	6	4	-1	**.986**	-4	*O/1	0.0
1937	Was-A	103	419	60	117	21	10	8	84	27	35	.279	.329	.434	95	-8	-5	60	3	2	-0	.984	5	*O	-0.3
1938	Was-A	125	470	79	142	23	6	21	95	38	40	.302	.357	.511	123	8	13	86	2	1	0	.983	-8	*O	0.1
1939	Bos-N	93	330	39	93	17	5	7	43	22	40	.282	.331	.427	110	0	3	43	0			.982	-0	O	0.0
	*Cin-N	9	21	0	3	0	0	0	1	2	3	.143	.217	.143	-1	-3	-3	1	0			.938	1	/O	-0.2
	Yr	102	351	39	96	17	5	7	44	24	43	.274	.324	.410	103	-3	0	44	0			.978	1	O	-0.2
1940	Phi-A	37	81	7	25	4	0	1	19	4	8	.309	.341	.395	92	-1	-1	10	0	0	0	.963	2	O	0.0
1941	Phi-A	9	24	1	3	1	0	0	1	1	2	.125	.160	.167	-14	-4	-4	0	0	0	0	1.000	1	/O	-0.3
1943	Bos-A	40	133	9	27	5	0	1	12	8	21	.203	.248	.263	49	-9	-9	8	0	1	-1	.986	-2	O	-1.4
1944	Phi-A	4	6	1	3	0	0	0	2	0	0	.500	.500	.500	189	1	1	1	0	0	0	1.000	-0	/O	0.0
Total	20	2215	8759	1507	2927	539	149	307	1827	615	737	.334	.380	.535	132	399	378	1771	87	64		.982	52	*O/1	27.2
■ HACK SIMMONS Simmons, George Washington b: 1/29/1885, Brooklyn, N.Y. d: 4/26/42, Arverne, N.Y. BR/TR, 5'8", 179 lbs. Deb: 4/15/10																									
1910	Det-A	42	110	12	25	3	1	0	9	10		.227	.303	.273	75	-2	-3	10	1			.984	-0	1/3O	-0.4
1912	NY-A	110	401	45	96	17	2	0	41	33		.239	.308	.292	68	-14	-18	41	19			.946	-28	21/S	-4.9
1914	Bal-F	114	352	50	95	16	5	1	38	32	26	.270	.341	.352	94	-1	-2	47	7			.894	-8	O2/1S3	-1.4
1915	Bal-F	39	88	8	18	7	1	1	14	10	9	.205	.293	.341	83	-2	-2	10	1			1.000	-3	2O	-0.6
Total	4	305	951	115	234	43	9	2	102	85	35	.246	.318	.317	80	-19	-25	108	28			.953	-40	2/O13S	-7.3
■ JOHN SIMMONS Simmons, John Earl b: 7/7/24, Birmingham, Ala. BR/TR, 6'1.5", 192 lbs. Deb: 4/22/49																									
1949	Was-A	62	93	12	20	0	0	0	5	11	6	.215	.298	.215	38	-8	-8	6	0	0	0	1.000	-5	O	-1.3
■ JOE SIMMONS Simmons, Joseph S. b: 6/13/1845, New York, N.Y. 5'9", 166 lbs. Deb: 5/08/1871 M																									
1871	Chi-n	27	129	29	28	6	1	0	17	1	0	.217	.223	.279	39	-9	-13	9	4					*O/1	-0.8
1872	Cle-n	18	89	11	23	5	1	0	9	1	2	.258	.267	.337	90	-2	-1	8						1/O	0.0
1875	Wes-n	13	53	5	9	1	0	0		0		.170	.170	.189	23	-4	-4	2						O/1M	-0.4
Total	3 n	58	271	45	60	12	2	0		2		.221	.227	.280	51	-15	-17	19						/O1	-1.2
■ NELSON SIMMONS Simmons, Nelson Bernard b: 6/27/63, Washington, D.C. BB/TR, 6'1", 185 lbs. Deb: 9/04/84																									
1984	Det-A	9	30	4	13	2	0	0	3	2	5	.433	.469	.500	169	3	3	6	1	0	0	1.000	-1	/OD	0.2
1985	Det-A	75	251	31	60	11	0	10	33	26	41	.239	.310	.402	94	-3	-2	32	1	0	0	.945	-1	OD	-0.4
1987	Bal-A	16	49	3	13	1	1	1	4	3	8	.265	.308	.388	85	-1	-1	5	0	1	-1	1.000	1	O/D	-0.1
Total	3	100	330	38	86	14	1	11	40	31	54	.261	.324	.409	99	-1	-1	43	2	1	0	.963	-1	/OD	-0.3
■ TED SIMMONS Simmons, Ted Lyle b: 8/9/49, Highland Park, Mich. BB/TR, 6', 200 lbs. Deb: 9/21/68																									
1968	StL-N	2	3	0	1	0	0	0	0	1	1	.333	.500	.333	156	0	0	1	0	0	0	1.000	-1	/C	0.0
1969	StL-N	5	14	0	3	0	1	0	3	1	1	.214	.267	.357	73	-1	-1	1	0	0	0	.957	-1	/C	-0.2
1970	StL-N	82	284	29	69	8	2	3	24	37	37	.243	.334	.317	74	-9	-10	31	2	2	-1	.990	-3	C	-0.9
1971	StL-N	133	510	64	155	32	4	7	77	36	50	.304	.353	.424	115	12	10	71	1	3	-2	.989	-13	*C	0.0
1972	StL-N☆	152	594	70	180	36	6	16	96	29	57	.303	.338	.465	127	18	18	86	1	3	-2	.991	6	*C1	2.9
1973	StL-N★	161	619	62	192	36	2	13	91	61	47	.310	.374	.438	124	21	21	94	2	2	-1	.987	10	*C/1O	3.7
1974	StL-N☆	152	599	66	163	33	6	20	103	47	35	.272	.331	.447	117	11	11	83	0	0	0	.986	-4	*C1	1.3
1975	StL-N	157	581	80	193	32	3	18	100	63	35	.332	.398	.491	141	36	33	108	1	3	-2	.983	-6	*C/1O	3.3
1976	StL-N	150	546	60	159	35	3	5	75	73	35	.291	.375	.394	117	15	14	80	0	7	-4	.993	-9	*C1/O3	0.3
1977	StL-N★	150	516	82	164	25	3	21	95	79	37	.318	.410	.500	145	33	35	100	2	6	-3	.987	-14	*C/O	2.2
1978	StL-N★	152	516	71	148	40	5	22	80	77	39	.287	.383	.512	150	33	34	98	1	1	-0	.988	-5	*CO	3.3
1979	StL-N†	123	448	68	127	22	0	26	87	61	34	.283	.374	.507	137	24	23	84	0	1	-1	.985	-5	*C	2.2
1980	StL-N	145	495	84	150	33	2	21	98	59	45	.303	.379	.505	140	30	28	94	1	0	0	.985	-9	*C/O	2.4
1981	*Mil-A★	100	380	45	82	13	3	14	61	23	32	.216	.266	.376	88	-9	-7	36	0	1	-1	.980	-9	CD/1	-1.5
1982	*Mil-A	137	539	73	145	29	0	23	97	32	40	.269	.312	.451	114	3	7	70	0	0	0	**.995**	-1	*CD	1.1
1983	Mil-A★	153	600	76	185	39	3	13	108	41	51	.308	.355	.448	129	15	21	89	4	2	0	.975	-4	CD	2.1
1984	Mil-A	132	497	44	110	23	2	4	52	30	40	.221	.270	.300	60	-29	-26	36	3	0	1	.995	-1	D13	-3.0
1985	Mil-A	143	528	60	144	28	2	12	76	57	32	.273	.345	.402	104	3	4	71	1	1	-0	.992	-3	D1C/3	-0.1
1986	Atl-N	76	127	14	32	5	0	4	25	12	14	.252	.321	.386	89	-1	-2	16	1	0	0	.964	-3	1C/3	-0.6
1987	Atl-N	73	177	20	49	8	0	4	30	21	23	.277	.354	.390	92	-0	-2	24	1	1	-0	.984	-1	1C/3	-0.4
1988	Atl-N	78	107	6	21	6	0	2	11	15	9	.196	.295	.308	70	-4	-4	10	0	0	0	.993	-1	1C	-0.6
Total	21	2456	8680	1074	2472	483	47	248	1389	855	694	.285	.352	.437	118	201	209	1284	21	33	-14	.987	-78	*CD1/O3	17.5

YEAR	TM/L	G	AB	R	H	2B	3B	HR	RBI	BB	SO	AVG	OBP	SLG	PRO+	BR	/A	RC	SB	CS	SBR	FA	FR	POS	TPR
■ **MIKE SIMMS**		Simms, Michael Howard b: 1/12/67, Orange, Cal. BR/TR, 6'4", 185 lbs. Deb: 9/05/90																							
1990	Hou-N	12	13	3	4	1	0	1	2	0	4	.308	.308	.615	152	1	1	2	0	0	0	1.000	-0	/1	0.1
1991	Hou-N	49	123	18	25	5	0	3	16	18	38	.203	.305	.317	80	-4	-3	13	1	0	0	.889	-5	O	-0.9
1992	Hou-N	15	24	1	6	1	0	1	3	2	9	.250	.333	.417	118	0	1	3	0	0	0	1.000	-1	/O1	-0.1
Total	3	76	160	22	35	7	0	5	21	20	51	.219	.309	.356	92	-3	-2	18	1	0	0	.903	-6	/O1	-0.9
■ **HANK SIMON**		Simon, Henry Joseph b: 8/25/1862, Hawkinsville, N.Y. d: 1/1/25, Albany, N.Y. BR/TR, Deb: 10/07/1887																							
1887	Cle-a	3	10	1	1	0	0	0		0		.100	.100	.100	-45	-2	-2	0	0			1.000	-1	/O	-0.2
1890	Bro-a	89	373	66	96	17	11	0		34		.257	.323	.362	108	1	3	52	23			.951	6	O	0.6
	Syr-a	38	156	33	47	5	3	2		17		.301	.370	.410	148	6	9	29	12			.941	-3	O	0.4
	Yr	127	529	99	143	22	14	2		51		.270	.337	.376	119	7	12	81	35			.948	3	*O	1.0
Total	2	130	539	100	144	22	14	2		51		.267	.333	.371	116	6	10	81	35			.949	3	O	0.8
■ **MIKE SIMON**		Simon, Michael Edward b: 4/13/1883, Hayden, Ind. d: 6/10/63, Los Angeles, Cal. BR/TR, 5'11", 188 lbs. Deb: 6/27/09																							
1909	Pit-N	12	18	2	3	0	0	0	2	1		.167	.211	.167	16	-2	-2	1	0			.917	0	/C	-0.1
1910	Pit-N	22	50	3	10	0	1	0	5	1	2	.200	.216	.240	31	-4	-5	3	1			1.000	-4	C	-0.8
1911	Pit-N	71	215	19	49	4	3	0	22	10	14	.228	.275	.274	52	-14	-15	16	1			.968	0	C	-0.8
1912	Pit-N	42	113	10	34	2	1	0	11	5	9	.301	.331	.336	84	-3	-3	12	1			.991	3	C	0.4
1913	Pit-N	92	255	23	63	6	2	1	17	10	15	.247	.281	.298	68	-12	-10	21	3			.975	22	C	1.9
1914	StL-F	93	276	21	57	11	2	0	21	18	21	.207	.263	.261	47	-18	-20	21	2			.984	12	C	-0.2
1915	Bro-F	47	142	7	25	5	1	0	12	9	12	.176	.225	.225	33	-12	-12	8	1			.992	-0	C	-0.9
Total	7	379	1069	85	241	28	10	1	90	54	73	.225	.269	.273	54	-65	-66	82	9			.979	34	C	-0.5
■ **SYL SIMON**		Simon, Sylvester Adam "Sammy" b: 12/14/1897, Evansville, Ind. d: 2/28/73, Chandler, Ind. BR/TR, 5'10.5", 170 lbs. Deb: 10/01/23																							
1923	StL-A	1	1	0	0	0	0	0	0	0	0	.000	.000	.000	-95	-0	-0	0	0	0	0	.000	0	H	0.0
1924	StL-A	23	32	5	8	1	1	0	6	3	5	.250	.314	.344	66	-2	-2	4	0	0	0	.889	-0	/3S	-0.1
Total	2	24	33	5	8	1	1	0	6	3	5	.242	.306	.333	61	-2	-2	4	0	0	0	.987	-0	/3S	-0.1
■ **MEL SIMONS**		Simons, Melbern Ellis "Butch" b: 7/1/1900, Carlyle, Ill. d: 11/10/74, Paducah, Ky. BL/TR, 5'10", 175 lbs. Deb: 4/14/31																							
1931	Chi-A	68	189	24	52	9	0	0	12	12	17	.275	.318	.323	73	-8	-7	20	1	1	-0	.950	-9	O	-1.8
1932	Chi-A	7	5	0	0	0	0	0	0	0	1	.000	.000	.000	-99	-1	-1	0	0	0	0	1.000	-3	/O	-0.4
Total	2	75	194	24	52	9	0	0	12	12	18	.268	.311	.314	69	-10	-8	20	1	1	-0	.951	-12	/O	-2.2
■ **HARRY SIMPSON**		Simpson, Harry Leon "Suitcase" or "Goody" b: 12/3/25, Atlanta, Ga. d: 4/3/79, Akron, Ohio BL/TR, 6'1", 180 lbs. Deb: 4/21/51																							
1951	Cle-A	122	332	51	76	7	0	7	24	45	48	.229	.325	.313	77	-12	-9	36	6	4	-1	.971	-4	O1	-1.8
1952	Cle-A	146	545	66	145	21	10	10	65	56	82	.266	.337	.396	111	2	6	75	5	3	-0	.988	-4	*O1	-0.4
1953	Cle-A	82	242	25	55	3	1	7	22	18	27	.227	.284	.335	68	-12	-11	23	0	0	0	.968	-6	O/1	-1.9
1955	Cle-A	3	1	1	0	0	0	0	0	2	0	.000	.667	.000	88	0	0	0	0	0	0	.000	0	H	0.0
	KC-A	112	396	42	119	16	7	5	52	34	61	.301	.359	.414	106	4	3	57	3	5	-2	.978	1	*O/1	-0.2
	Yr	115	397	43	119	16	7	5	52	36	61	.300	.361	.413	106	4	4	57	3	5	-2	.978	1	*O/1	-0.2
1956	KC-A★	141	543	76	159	22	**11**	21	105	47	82	.293	.350	.490	119	13	13	87	2	3	-1	.965	-15	*O1	-1.1
1957	KC-A	50	179	24	53	9	6	6	24	12	28	.296	.340	.514	128	7	6	28	0	1	-1	.996	1	1O	0.3
	*NY-A	75	224	27	56	7	3	7	39	19	36	.250	.309	.402	94	-3	-2	27	1	0	0	.952	-2	O1	-0.8
	Yr	125	403	51	109	16	**9**	13	63	31	64	.270	.323	.452	110	4	4	55	1	1	-0	.957	-2	O1	-0.5
1958	NY-A	24	51	1	11	2	1	0	6	6	12	.216	.310	.294	70	-2	-2	5	0	0	0	1.000	-3	O	-0.5
	KC-A	78	212	21	56	7	1	7	27	26	33	.264	.345	.406	104	2	1	31	0	2	-1	.990	-3	1O	-0.6
	Yr	102	263	22	67	9	2	7	33	32	45	.255	.338	.384	98	-0	-0	35	0	2	-1	.990	-5	1O	-1.1
1959	KC-A	8	14	1	4	0	0	1	2	2	4	.286	.412	.500	146	1	1	3	0	0	0	1.000	0	/1	0.1
	Chi-A	38	75	5	14	5	1	2	13	4	14	.187	.228	.360	59	-5	-4	6	0	0	0	.947	-2	O/1	-0.7
	Yr	46	89	6	18	5	1	3	15	6	18	.202	.260	.382	75	-4	-3	9	0	0	0	.947	-2	O/1	-0.6
	Pit-N	9	15	3	4	2	0	0	2	0	2	.267	.267	.400	75	-1	-1	2	0	0	0	1.000	-0	/O	-0.1
Total	8	888	2829	343	752	101	41	73	381	271	429	.266	.332	.408	102	-6	1	380	17	18	-6	.974	-37	O1	-7.7
■ **JOE SIMPSON**		Simpson, Joe Allen b: 12/31/51, Purcell, Okla. BL/TL, 6'3", 175 lbs. Deb: 9/02/75																							
1975	LA-N	9	6	3	2	0	0	0	0	0	2	.333	.333	.333	89	-0	-0	1	0	0	0	1.000	1	/O	0.1
1976	LA-N	23	30	2	4	1	0	0	0	1	6	.133	.161	.167	-7	-4	-4	1	0	1	-1	1.000	1	O	-0.4
1977	LA-N	29	23	2	4	0	0	0	1	2	6	.174	.240	.174	13	-3	-3	1	1	1	-0	.957	3	O/1	-0.1
1978	LA-N	10	5	1	2	0	0	0	1	0	2	.400	.400	.400	125	0	0	1	0	0	0	1.000	1	O	0.1
1979	Sea-A	120	265	29	75	11	0	2	27	11	21	.283	.314	.347	77	-8	-9	28	6	3	0	.966	-5	*O	-1.6
1980	Sea-A	129	365	42	91	15	3	3	34	28	43	.249	.305	.332	74	-13	-13	39	17	4	3	.977	-8	*O/1	-2.3
1981	Sea-A	91	288	32	64	11	3	2	30	15	41	.222	.263	.302	60	-14	-16	24	12	3	2	.978	-0	O	-1.7
1982	Sea-A	105	296	39	76	14	4	2	23	22	48	.257	.313	.351	80	-7	-8	30	8	14	-6	.984	-7	O	-2.3
1983	KC-A	91	119	16	20	2	2	0	8	11	21	.168	.250	.218	30	-11	-11	7	1	1	-0	.995	-0	1O/PD	-1.3
Total	9	607	1397	166	338	54	12	9	124	90	190	.242	.291	.317	67	-61	-64	132	45	27	-3	.978	-14	O/1PD	-9.5
■ **MARTY SIMPSON**		Simpson, Martin b: Baltimore, Md. Deb: 5/14/1873																							
1873	Mar-n	4	15	4	2	0	0	0	1	0	0	.133	.133	.133	-28	-2	-1	0						/2C	-0.1
■ **DICK SIMPSON**		Simpson, Richard Charles b: 7/28/43, Washington, D.C. BR/TR, 6'4", 176 lbs. Deb: 9/21/62																							
1962	LA-A	6	8	1	2	1	0	0	1	2	3	.250	.400	.375	114	0	0	1	0	0	0	1.000	-1	/O	0.0
1964	LA-A	21	50	11	7	1	0	2	4	8	15	.140	.259	.280	55	-3	-3	4	2	2	-1	1.000	-2	O	-0.6
1965	Cal-A	8	27	2	6	1	0	0	3	2	8	.222	.276	.259	54	-2	-2	2	1	0	0	.875	-1	/O	-0.3
1966	Cin-N	92	84	26	20	2	0	4	14	10	32	.238	.333	.405	96	1	-0	12	0	1	-1	.921	-1	O	-0.3
1967	Cin-N	44	54	8	14	3	0	1	6	7	11	.259	.344	.370	94	0	-0	7	0	1	-1	.973	4	O	0.3
1968	StL-N	26	56	11	13	0	0	3	8	8	21	.232	.328	.393	117	1	1	7	0	1	-1	1.000	-0	O	-0.1
	Hou-N	59	177	25	33	7	2	3	11	20	61	.186	.284	.299	77	-5	-5	15	4	4	-1	.970	-6	O	-1.7
	Yr	85	233	36	46	7	2	6	19	28	82	.197	.294	.322	86	-4	-3	23	4	5	-2	.979	-6	O	-1.8
1969	NY-A	6	11	2	3	2	0	0	4	3	6	.273	.429	.455	153	1	1	2	0	0	0	1.000	-1	/O	0.0
	Sea-A	26	51	8	9	2	0	2	5	4	17	.176	.236	.333	59	-3	-3	4	3	1	0	1.000	-3	O	-0.7
	Yr	32	62	10	12	4	0	2	9	7	23	.194	.275	.355	77	-2	-2	6	3	1	0	1.000	-4	O	-0.7
Total	7	288	518	94	107	19	2	15	56	64	174	.207	.301	.338	84	-10	-10	54	10	10	-3	.967	-10	O	-3.4
■ **DUKE SIMS**		Sims, Duane B b: 6/5/41, Salt Lake City, Ut. BL/TR, 6'2", 205 lbs. Deb: 9/22/64																							
1964	Cle-A	2	6	0	0	0	0	0	0	0	2	.000	.000	.000	-99	-2	-2	0	0	0	0	1.000	1	/C	-0.1
1965	Cle-A	48	118	9	21	0	0	6	15	15	33	.178	.271	.331	69	-5	-5	11	0	0	0	.980	-2	C	-0.5
1966	Cle-A	52	133	12	35	2	2	6	19	11	31	.263	.338	.444	122	4	4	19	0	1	-1	.975	-5	C	0.1
1967	Cle-A	88	272	25	55	8	2	12	37	30	64	.202	.295	.379	97	-1	-1	30	3	3	-1	.989	-3	C	0.0
1968	Cle-A	122	361	48	90	21	0	11	44	62	68	.249	.367	.399	134	16	17	54	1	3	-2	.983	-1	C1/O	2.0
1969	Cle-A	114	326	40	77	8	0	18	45	66	80	.236	.374	.426	120	12	11	57	1	2	-1	.991	-4	*C/O1	1.2
1970	Cle-A	110	345	46	91	12	0	23	56	46	59	.264	.360	.499	128	16	14	63	0	4	-2	.993	-2	CO1	0.8
1971	LA-N	90	230	23	63	7	2	6	25	30	39	.274	.360	.400	122	5	7	34	0	1	-1	.992	0	C	0.9
1972	LA-N	51	151	7	29	7	0	2	11	17	23	.192	.278	.278	60	-8	-8	11	0	1	-1	.989	-1	C	-0.8
	*Det-A	38	98	11	31	4	0	4	19	19	18	.316	.432	.480	166	10	9	22	0	0	0	.994	-3	C/O	0.8
1973	Det-A	80	252	31	61	10	0	8	30	30	36	.242	.327	.377	92	-1	-3	32	1	2	-1	.979	2	C/O	0.1
	NY-A	4	9	3	3	0	0	1	1	3	1	.333	.500	.667	234	2	2	3	0	0	0	1.000	1	/CD	0.2

YEAR	TM/L	G	AB	R	H	2B	3B	HR	RBI	BB	SO	AVG	OBP	SLG	PRO+	BR	/A	RC	SB	CS	SBR	FA	FR	POS	TPR
	Yr	84	261	34	64	10	0	9	31	33	37	.245	.334	.387	97	1	-1	35	1	2	-1	.979	2	C/OD	0.3
1974	NY-A	5	15	1	2	1	0	0	2	1	5	.133	.188	.200	12	-2	-2	1	0	0	0	1.000	-0	/CD	-0.2
	Tex-A	39	106	7	22	0	0	3	6	8	24	.208	.282	.292	67	-5	-4	9	0	0	0	.970	-3	C/OD	-0.6
	Yr	44	121	8	24	1	0	3	8	9	29	.198	.271	.281	60	-6	-6	9	0	0	0	.971	-3	C/DO	-0.8
Total	11	843	2422	263	580	80	6	100	310	338	483	.239	.341	.401	111	42	39	346	6	16	-8	.986	-20	C/1OD	3.9
■ GREG SIMS Sims, Gregory Emmett b: 6/28/46, San Francisco, Cal BB/TR, 6', 190 lbs. Deb: 4/15/66																									
1966	Hou-N	7	6	1	1	0	0	0	0	1	3	.167	.286	.167	32	-1	-0	0	0	0	0	.500	-0	/O	-0.1
■ MATT SINATRO Sinatro, Matthew Stephen b: 3/22/60, Hartford, Conn. BR/TR, 5'9", 175 lbs. Deb: 9/22/81																									
1981	Atl-N	12	32	4	9	1	1	0	4	5	4	.281	.378	.375	111	1	1	5	1	0	0	1.000	4	C	0.6
1982	Atl-N	37	81	10	11	2	0	1	4	4	9	.136	.176	.198	4	-10	-11	2	0	1	-1	1.000	4	C	-0.7
1983	Atl-N	7	12	0	2	0	0	0	2	2	1	.167	.286	.167	26	-1	-1	1	0	0	0	.967	2	/C	0.0
1984	Atl-N	2	4	0	0	0	0	0	0	0	0	.000	.000	.000	-93	-1	-1	0	0	0	0	1.000	-0	/C	-0.2
1987	Oak-A	6	3	0	0	0	0	0	0	0	1	.000	.000	.000	-99	-1	-1	0	0	0	0	1.000	-0	/C	-0.1
1988	Oak-A	10	9	1	3	2	0	0	5	0	1	.333	.333	.556	149	0	1	1	0	0	0	1.000	2	/C	0.3
1989	Det-A	13	25	2	3	0	0	0	1	1	3	.120	.185	.120	-13	-4	-4	1	0	0	0	1.000	0	C	-0.3
1990	Sea-A	30	50	2	15	1	0	0	4	4	10	.300	.352	.320	88	-1	-1	5	1	0	0	.992	7	C	0.7
1991	Sea-A	5	8	1	2	0	0	0	1	1	1	.250	.333	.250	64	-0	-0	1	0	0	0	1.000	1	/C	0.1
1992	Sea-A	18	28	0	3	0	0	0	0	0	5	.107	.107	.107	-40	-5	-5	0	0	0	0	1.000	0	C	-0.5
Total	10	140	252	20	48	6	1	1	21	17	35	.190	.244	.234	34	-22	-22	16	2	1	0	.996	19	C	-0.1
■ HOSEA SINER Siner, Hosea John b: 3/20/1885, Shelburn, Ind. d: 6/10/48, Sullivan, Ind. BR/TR, 5'10.5", 185 lbs. Deb: 7/28/09																									
1909	Bos-N	10	23	1	3	0	0	0	1	2		.130	.200	.130	3	-3	-3	1	0			.909	-1	/32S	-0.5
■ KEN SINGLETON Singleton, Kenneth Wayne b: 6/10/47, New York, N.Y. BB/TR, 6'4", 213 lbs. Deb: 6/24/70																									
1970	NY-N	69	198	22	52	8	0	5	26	30	48	.263	.362	.379	99	0	0	28	1	1	-0	.968	-3	O	-0.5
1971	NY-N	115	298	34	73	5	0	13	46	61	64	.245	.377	.393	120	9	10	45	0	1	-1	.974	-7	O	-0.1
1972	Mon-N	142	507	77	139	23	2	14	50	70	99	.274	.364	.410	118	15	13	75	5	10	-5	.972	-2	*O	0.0
1973	Mon-N	162	560	100	169	26	2	23	103	123	91	.302	**.429**	.479	146	45	42	113	2	8	-4	.983	2	*O	3.4
1974	Mon-N	148	511	68	141	20	2	9	74	93	84	.276	.387	.376	108	13	10	77	5	2	0	.955	-10	*O	-0.6
1975	Bal-A	155	586	88	176	37	4	15	55	118	82	.300	.418	.454	156	41	46	118	3	5	-2	.990	-6	*O	3.2
1976	Bal-A	154	544	62	151	25	2	13	70	79	76	.278	.369	.403	134	20	24	82	2	2	-1	.983	-3	*OD	1.5
1977	Bal-A★	152	536	90	176	24	0	24	99	107	101	.328	.442	.507	168	49	53	124	0	1	-1	.986	1	*O/D	4.6
1978	Bal-A	149	502	67	147	21	2	20	81	98	94	.293	.410	.462	**154**	34	38	100	0	0	0	.976	-13	*O/D	2.0
1979	*Bal-A★	159	570	93	168	29	1	35	111	109	118	.295	.409	.533	158	44	47	127	3	1	0	.981	-6	*OD	3.5
1980	Bal-A	156	583	85	177	28	3	24	104	92	94	.304	.399	.485	143	35	36	113	0	2	-1	.984	-10	*O/D	1.8
1981	Bal-A★	103	363	48	101	16	1	13	49	61	59	.278	.382	.435	135	18	18	57	0	0	0	**1.000**	-3	OD	1.3
1982	Bal-A	156	561	71	141	27	2	14	77	86	93	.251	.353	.381	102	3	4	75	0	1	-1	1.000	-0	*D/O	0.3
1983	*Bal-A	151	507	52	140	21	3	18	84	99	83	.276	.395	.436	131	24	25	86	0	2	-1	.000	0	*D	2.4
1984	Bal-A	111	363	28	78	7	1	6	36	37	60	.215	.287	.289	61	-19	-18	27	0	0	0	.000	0	*D	-1.8
Total	15	2082	7189	985	2029	317	25	246	1065	1263	1246	.282	.391	.436	132	332	350	1247	21	36	-15	.980	-60	*OD	21.0
■ FRED SINGTON Sington, Frederic William b: 2/24/10, Brimingham, Ala. BR/TR, 6'2", 215 lbs. Deb: 9/23/34																									
1934	Was-A	9	35	2	10	2	0	0	6	4	3	.286	.359	.343	85	-1	-1	4	0	1	-1	.933	-1	/O	-0.2
1935	Was-A	20	22	1	4	0	0	0	3	5	1	.182	.333	.182	38	-2	-2	2	0	0	0	.889	0	/O	-0.2
1936	Was-A	25	94	13	30	8	0	1	28	15	9	.319	.413	.436	116	2	3	18	0	0	0	.946	-1	O	0.1
1937	Was-A	78	228	27	54	15	4	3	36	37	33	.237	.348	.377	87	-6	-4	32	1	1	-0	.961	-3	O	-0.9
1938	Bro-N	17	53	10	19	6	1	2	5	13	5	.358	.493	.623	200	8	8	18	1			1.000	-2	O	0.6
1939	Bro-N	32	84	13	23	5	0	1	7	15	15	.274	.384	.369	100	1	1	11	0			.978	-1	O	-0.1
Total	6	181	516	66	140	36	5	7	85	89	66	.271	.382	.401	104	3	5	85	2	2		.961	-7	O	-0.7
■ DICK SIPEK Sipek, Richard Francis b: 1/16/23, Chicago, Ill. BL/TR, 5'9", 170 lbs. Deb: 4/28/45																									
1945	Cin-N	82	156	14	38	6	2	0	13	9	15	.244	.302	.308	71	-6	-6	14	0			.972	-0	O	-0.8
■ JOHN SIPIN Sipin, John White b: 8/29/46, Watsonville, Cal. BR/TR, 6'1.5", 175 lbs. Deb: 5/24/69																									
1969	SD-N	68	229	22	51	12	2	2	9	8	44	.223	.252	.319	61	-13	-12	18	2	0	1	.976	-2	2	-0.9
■ GEORGE SISLER Sisler, George Harold "Georgeous George" b: 3/24/1893, Manchester, Ohio d: 3/26/73, Richmond Heights, Mo. BL/TL, 5'11", 170 lbs. Deb: 6/28/15 FMCH																									
1915	StL-A	81	274	28	78	10	2	3	29	7	27	.285	.307	.369	106	-1	0	32	10	9	-2	.989	-3	1OP	-0.8
1916	StL-A	151	580	83	177	21	11	4	76	40	37	.305	.355	.400	133	17	20	84	34	26	-5	.985	-2	*1/PO3	0.7
1917	StL-A	135	539	60	190	30	9	2	52	30	19	.353	.390	.453	163	34	36	104	37			.985	4	*1/2	3.8
1918	StL-A	114	452	69	154	21	9	2	41	40	17	.341	.400	.440	159	29	30	92	**45**			.990	9	*1/P	3.7
1919	StL-A	132	511	96	180	31	15	10	83	27	20	.352	.390	.530	153	36	34	112	28			.991	13	*1	4.4
1920	StL-A	154	631	137	**257**	49	18	19	122	46	19	**.407**	.449	.632	179	73	71	176	42	17	**2**	.990	15	*1/P	8.0
1921	StL-A	138	582	125	216	38	**18**	12	104	34	27	.371	.411	.560	137	38	33	133	**35**	11	**4**	.993	8	*1	3.8
1922	StL-A	142	586	**134**	**246**	42	**18**	8	105	49	14	**.420**	.467	.594	169	**64**	**62**	**162**	**51**	19	**4**	.988	12	*1	**6.8**
1924	StL-A	151	636	94	194	27	10	9	74	31	29	.305	.340	.421	90	-7	-12	87	19	17	-5	.984	1	*1M	-2.4
1925	StL-A	150	649	100	224	21	15	12	105	27	24	.345	.371	.479	109	12	7	110	11	12	-4	.983	11	*1/PM	0.4
1926	StL-A	150	613	78	178	21	12	7	71	30	30	.290	.327	.398	84	-13	-16	79	12	8	-1	.987	-4	*1/PM	-3.0
1927	StL-A	149	614	87	201	32	8	5	97	24	15	.327	.357	.430	100	2	-1	87	**27**	7	**4**	.984	11	*1	0.3
1928	Was-A	20	49	1	12	1	0	0	2	1	2	.245	.260	.265	39	-4	-4	3	0	1	-1	1.000	-2	/1O	-0.8
	Bos-N	118	491	71	167	26	4	4	68	30	15	.340	.380	.434	119	9	12	78	11			.988	7	*1/P	0.9
1929	Bos-N	154	629	67	205	40	8	2	79	33	17	.326	.363	.424	98	-5	-2	94	6			.982	3	*1	-1.3
1930	Bos-N	116	431	54	133	15	7	3	67	23	15	.309	.346	.397	82	-14	-12	58	7			.987	5	*1	-1.5
Total	15	2055	8267	1284	2812	425	164	102	1175	472	327	.340	.379	.468	124	269	258	1490	375	127		.987	88	*1/OP23	23.0
■ DICK SISLER Sisler, Richard Allan b: 11/2/20, St.Louis, Mo. BL/TR, 6'2", 205 lbs. Deb: 4/16/46 FMC																									
1946	*StL-N	83	235	17	61	11	2	3	42	14	28	.260	.307	.362	86	-4	-5	26	0			.988	-2	1O	-1.1
1947	StL-N	46	74	4	15	2	1	0	9	3	8	.203	.234	.257	29	-7	-8	5	0			.976	-0	1/O	-0.9
1948	Phi-N	121	446	60	122	21	3	11	56	47	46	.274	.344	.408	105	2	3	66	1			.983	-4	*1	-0.2
1949	Phi-N	121	412	42	119	19	6	7	50	25	38	.289	.333	.415	102	-1	0	57	0			.987	-9	1	-0.9
1950	*Phi-N★	141	523	79	155	29	4	13	83	64	50	.296	.373	.442	115	11	12	88	1			.987	2	*O	0.8
1951	Phi-N	125	428	46	123	20	5	8	52	40	39	.287	.351	.414	107	3	4	63	1	0	0	.968	0	*O	0.1
1952	Cin-N	11	27	3	5	1	1	0	4	3	5	.185	.267	.296	56	-2	-2	2	0	0	0	1.000	-1	/O	-0.3
	StL-N	119	418	48	109	14	5	13	60	29	35	.261	.312	.411	99	-2	-2	53	3	3	-1	.985	2	*1	-0.5
	Yr	130	445	51	114	15	6	13	64	32	40	.256	.309	.404	96	-3	-4	56	3	3	-1	.985	1	*1/O	-0.8
1953	StL-N	32	43	3	11	1	1	0	4	1	4	.256	.273	.326	55	-3	-3	4	0	0	0	1.000	1	1	-0.2
Total	8	799	2606	302	720	118	28	55	360	226	253	.276	.336	.406	101	-4	-1	365	6	3		.985	-10	1O	-3.2
■ SIBBY SISTI Sisti, Sebastian Daniel b: 7/26/20, Buffalo, N.Y. BR/TR, 5'11", 175 lbs. Deb: 7/21/39 C																									
1939	Bos-N	63	215	19	49	7	1	1	11	12	38	.228	.269	.284	52	-16	-14	16	4			.994	0	23S	-1.1
1940	Bos-N	123	459	73	115	19	5	6	34	36	64	.251	.311	.353	87	-11	-8	53	4			.936	-2	*32	-0.7
1941	Bos-N	140	541	72	140	24	3	1	45	38	76	.259	.309	.320	81	-17	-14	54	7			.916	-8	*3/2S	-1.9

YEAR	TM/L	G	AB	R	H	2B	3B	HR	RBI	BB	SO	AVG	OBP	SLG	PRO+	BR	/A	RC	SB	CS	SBR	FA	FR	POS	TPR
1942	Bos-N	129	407	50	86	11	4	4	35	45	55	.211	.296	.287	73	-14	-13	36	5			.970	-4	*2/O	-1.1
1946	Bos-N	1	0	0	0	0	0	0	0	0	0	—	—	—	—	0	0	0	0			.000	0	/3	0.0
1947	Bos-N	56	153	22	43	8	0	2	15	20	17	.281	.371	.373	100	0	1	22	2			.947	-9	S/2	-0.6
1948	*Bos-N	83	221	30	54	6	2	0	21	31	34	.244	.340	.290	73	-8	-7	24	0			.972	-5	2S	-0.9
1949	Bos-N	101	268	39	69	12	0	5	22	34	42	.257	.343	.358	93	-4	-2	33	1			.989	-13	O2S/3	-1.5
1950	Bos-N	69	105	21	18	3	1	2	11	16	19	.171	.287	.276	52	-8	-7	9	1			.931	0	S23/10	-0.6
1951	Bos-N	114	362	46	101	20	2	2	38	32	50	.279	.341	.362	96	-5	-2	46	4	5	-2	.944	-23	S2/310	-2.1
1952	Bos-N	90	245	19	52	10	1	4	24	14	43	.212	.255	.310	58	-15	-14	19	2	0	1	.966	-12	2OS/3	-2.5
1953	Mil-N	38	23	8	5	1	0	0	4	5	2	.217	.357	.261	69	-1	-1	2	0	0	0	1.000	4	2/S3	0.4
1954	Mil-N	9	0	2	0	0	0	0	0	0	0	—	—	—	—	0	0	0	0	0	0	.000	0	R	0.0
Total	13	1016	2999	401	732	121	19	27	260	283	440	.244	.313	.324	79	-98	-81	315	30	5		.973	-72	23S/O1	-12.6

■ ED SIXSMITH
Sixsmith, Edward b: 2/26/1863, Philadelphia, Pa. d: 12/12/26, Philadelphia, Pa. BR/TR, Deb: 9/11/1884

YEAR	TM/L	G	AB	R	H	2B	3B	HR	RBI	BB	SO	AVG	OBP	SLG	PRO+	BR	/A	RC	SB	CS	SBR	FA	FR	POS	TPR
1884	Phi-N	1	2	0	0	0	0	0	0	0	0	.000	.000	.000	-99	-0	-0	0				1.000	-1	/C	-0.1

■ TED SIZEMORE
Sizemore, Theodore Crawford b: 4/15/45, Gadsden, Ala. BR/TR, 5'10", 165 lbs. Deb: 4/07/69

YEAR	TM/L	G	AB	R	H	2B	3B	HR	RBI	BB	SO	AVG	OBP	SLG	PRO+	BR	/A	RC	SB	CS	SBR	FA	FR	POS	TPR
1969	LA-N	159	590	69	160	20	5	4	46	45	40	.271	.328	.342	95	-9	-4	66	5	5	-2	.979	-6	*2S/O	0.3
1970	LA-N	96	340	40	104	10	1	1	34	34	19	.306	.369	.350	98	-2	0	42	5	1	1	.984	-6	2/OS	0.2
1971	StL-N	135	478	53	126	14	5	3	42	42	26	.264	.324	.333	83	-8	-10	50	4	6	-2	.976	-1	2SO/3	-0.2
1972	StL-N	120	439	53	116	17	4	2	38	37	36	.264	.327	.335	90	-6	-5	49	8	3	1	.976	0	*2	0.2
1973	StL-N	142	521	69	147	22	1	1	54	68	34	.282	.367	.334	96	-0	-0	69	6	4	-1	.981	9	*2/3	1.8
1974	StL-N	129	504	68	126	17	0	2	47	70	37	.250	.341	.296	80	-12	-11	55	8	4	0	.980	13	*2/SO	0.9
1975	StL-N	153	562	56	135	23	1	3	49	45	37	.240	.299	.301	64	-25	-28	51	1	5	-3	.972	-25	*2	-5.0
1976	LA-N	84	266	18	64	8	1	0	18	15	22	.241	.281	.278	60	-14	-14	21	2	3	-1	.986	2	2/3C	-0.9
1977	*Phi-N	152	519	64	146	20	3	4	47	52	40	.281	.348	.355	85	-7	-10	56	8	11	-4	.986	9	*2	0.6
1978	*Phi-N	108	351	38	77	12	0	0	25	25	29	.219	.273	.254	48	-24	-24	23	8	1	2	.978	4	*2	-1.2
1979	Chi-N	98	330	36	82	17	0	2	24	32	25	.248	.321	.318	68	-11	-15	34	3	3	-1	.973	15	2	0.7
	Bos-A	26	88	12	23	7	0	1	6	4	5	.261	.301	.375	77	-2	-3	8	1	0	0	.993	9	2/C	0.7
1980	Bos-A	9	23	1	5	1	0	0	0	0	0	.217	.217	.261	29	-2	-2	1	0	0	0	.927	3	/2	0.1
Total	12	1411	5011	577	1311	188	21	23	430	469	350	.262	.327	.321	80	-123	-126	526	59	46	-10	.979	28	*2/SO3C	-1.8

■ FRANK SKAFF
Skaff, Francis Michael b: 9/30/13, LaCrosse, Wis. d: 4/12/88, Towson, Md. BR/TR, 5'10", 185 lbs. Deb: 9/11/35 MC

YEAR	TM/L	G	AB	R	H	2B	3B	HR	RBI	BB	SO	AVG	OBP	SLG	PRO+	BR	/A	RC	SB	CS	SBR	FA	FR	POS	TPR
1935	Bro-N	6	11	4	6	1	1	0	3	0	2	.545	.545	.818	267	2	2	4	0			.857	-0	/3	0.2
1943	Phi-A	32	64	8	18	2	1	1	8	6	11	.281	.343	.391	115	1	1	9	0	0	0	.976	1	1/3S	0.2
Total	2	38	75	12	24	3	2	1	11	6	13	.320	.370	.453	138	3	3	14	0	0		.900	1	/13S	0.4

■ DAVE SKAGGS
Skaggs, David Lindsey b: 6/12/51, Santa Monica, Cal. BR/TR, 6'2", 200 lbs. Deb: 4/17/77

YEAR	TM/L	G	AB	R	H	2B	3B	HR	RBI	BB	SO	AVG	OBP	SLG	PRO+	BR	/A	RC	SB	CS	SBR	FA	FR	POS	TPR
1977	Bal-A	80	216	22	62	9	1	1	24	20	34	.287	.347	.352	97	-2	-0	28	0	0	0	.995	-1	C	0.1
1978	Bal-A	36	86	6	13	1	1	0	2	9	14	.151	.232	.186	20	-9	-9	4	0	1	-1	.988	5	C	-0.4
1979	*Bal-A	63	137	9	34	8	0	1	14	13	14	.248	.313	.328	76	-5	-4	13	0	0	0	.984	2	C	0.0
1980	Bal-A	2	5	0	1	0	0	0	0	0	1	.200	.200	.200	10	-1	-1	0	0	0	0	1.000	1	/C	0.0
	Cal-A	24	66	7	13	0	0	1	9	9	13	.197	.293	.242	50	-4	-4	5	0	0	0	.968	-10	C	-1.4
	Yr	26	71	7	14	0	0	1	9	9	14	.197	.287	.239	47	-5	-5	5	0	0	0	.971	-9	C	-1.4
Total	4	205	510	44	123	18	2	3	49	51	76	.241	.310	.302	72	-21	-18	50	0	1	-1	.988	-3	C	-1.7

■ BUD SKETCHLEY
Sketchley, Harry Clement b: 3/30/19, Virden, Man., Can. d: 12/19/79, Los Angeles, Cal. BL/TL, 5'10", 180 lbs. Deb: 4/14/42

YEAR	TM/L	G	AB	R	H	2B	3B	HR	RBI	BB	SO	AVG	OBP	SLG	PRO+	BR	/A	RC	SB	CS	SBR	FA	FR	POS	TPR
1942	Chi-A	13	36	1	7	1	0	0	3	7	4	.194	.326	.222	57	-2	-2	3	0	1	-1	.952	-1	O	-0.4

■ ROE SKIDMORE
Skidmore, Robert Roe b: 10/30/45, Decatur, Ill. BR/TR, 6'3", 188 lbs. Deb: 9/17/70

YEAR	TM/L	G	AB	R	H	2B	3B	HR	RBI	BB	SO	AVG	OBP	SLG	PRO+	BR	/A	RC	SB	CS	SBR	FA	FR	POS	TPR
1970	Chi-N	1	1	0	1	0	0	0	0	0	0	1.000	1.000	1.000	390	0	0	1	0	0	0	.000	0	H	0.0

■ BILL SKIFF
Skiff, William Franklin b: 10/16/1895, New Rochelle, N.Y. d: 12/25/76, Bronxville, N.Y. BR/TR, 5'10", 170 lbs. Deb: 5/17/21

YEAR	TM/L	G	AB	R	H	2B	3B	HR	RBI	BB	SO	AVG	OBP	SLG	PRO+	BR	/A	RC	SB	CS	SBR	FA	FR	POS	TPR
1921	Pit-N	16	45	7	13	2	0	0	11	0	4	.289	.289	.333	63	-2	-2	4	1	1	-0	.982	-2	C	-0.4
1926	NY-A	6	11	0	1	0	0	0	0	0	1	.091	.091	.091	-53	-2	-2	0	0	0	0	1.000	-1	/C	-0.3
Total	2	22	56	7	14	2	0	0	11	0	5	.250	.250	.286	40	-5	-5	4	1	1	-0	.984	-3	/C	-0.7

■ ALEXANDER SKINNER
Skinner, Alexander b: 8/14/1856, Chicago, Ill. d: 3/5/01, Washington, Mass. Deb: 7/12/1884

YEAR	TM/L	G	AB	R	H	2B	3B	HR	RBI	BB	SO	AVG	OBP	SLG	PRO+	BR	/A	RC	SB	CS	SBR	FA	FR	POS	TPR
1884	Bal-U	1	3	0	1	0	0	0		0		.333	.333	.333	114	0	0	0				1.000	0	/O	0.0
	CP-U	1	3	1	1	0	0	0		0		.333	.333	.333	127	0	0	0				.000	-0	/O	0.0
	Yr	2	6	1	2	0	0	0		0		.333	.333	.333	120	0	0	1				1.000	-0	/O	0.0

■ CAMP SKINNER
Skinner, Elisha Harrison b: 6/25/1897, Douglasville, Ga. d: 8/4/44, Douglasville, Ga. BL/TR, 5'11", 165 lbs. Deb: 5/02/22

YEAR	TM/L	G	AB	R	H	2B	3B	HR	RBI	BB	SO	AVG	OBP	SLG	PRO+	BR	/A	RC	SB	CS	SBR	FA	FR	POS	TPR
1922	NY-A	27	33	1	6	0	0	0	2	0	4	.182	.206	.182	2	-5	-5	1	1	0	0	1.000	-0	/O	-0.5
1923	Bos-A	7	13	1	3	2	0	0	1	0	0	.231	.231	.385	60	-1	-1	1	0	0	0	.000	-1	/O	-0.2
Total	2	34	46	2	9	2	0	0	3	0	4	.196	.213	.239	18	-6	-6	2	1	0	0	1.000	-2	/O	-0.7

■ JOEL SKINNER
Skinner, Joel Patrick b: 2/21/61, LaJolla, Cal. BR/TR, 6'4", 204 lbs. Deb: 6/12/83 F

YEAR	TM/L	G	AB	R	H	2B	3B	HR	RBI	BB	SO	AVG	OBP	SLG	PRO+	BR	/A	RC	SB	CS	SBR	FA	FR	POS	TPR
1983	Chi-A	6	11	2	3	0	0	0	1	0	1	.273	.273	.273	49	-1	-1	0	0	0	0	.960	2	/C	0.2
1984	Chi-A	43	80	4	17	2	0	0	3	7	19	.213	.276	.237	42	-6	-6	5	1	0	0	.989	10	C	0.5
1985	Chi-A	22	44	9	15	4	1	1	5	5	13	.341	.408	.545	153	4	3	9	0	0	0	.971	4	C	0.8
1986	Chi-A	60	149	17	30	5	1	4	20	9	43	.201	.252	.329	55	-9	-10	13	1	0	0	.988	-7	C	-1.3
	NY-A	54	166	6	43	4	0	1	17	7	40	.259	.289	.301	62	-9	-9	13	0	4	-2	.981	6	C	-0.2
	Yr	114	315	23	73	9	1	5	37	16	83	.232	.271	.314	58	-18	-19	25	1	4	-2	.984	-1	*C	-1.5
1987	NY-A	64	139	9	19	4	0	3	14	8	46	.137	.189	.230	11	-18	-18	5	0	0	0	.984	-3	C	-1.7
1988	NY-A	88	251	23	57	15	0	4	23	14	72	.227	.268	.335	68	-11	-11	22	0	0	0	.990	-7	C/O1	-1.3
1989	Cle-A	79	178	10	41	10	0	1	13	9	42	.230	.271	.303	61	-9	-10	14	1	1	-0	.990	-4	C	-1.1
1990	Cle-A	49	139	16	35	4	1	2	16	7	44	.252	.288	.338	75	-5	-5	13	0	0	0	.996	0	C	-0.2
1991	Cle-A	99	284	23	69	14	0	1	24	14	67	.243	.281	.303	61	-15	-15	23	0	2	-1	.991	0	C	-1.1
Total	9	564	1441	119	329	62	3	17	136	80	387	.228	.271	.311	60	-80	-81	117	3	7	-3	.988	2	C/O1	-5.4

■ BOB SKINNER
Skinner, Robert Ralph b: 10/3/31, LaJolla, Cal. BL/TR, 6'4", 190 lbs. Deb: 4/13/54 FMC

YEAR	TM/L	G	AB	R	H	2B	3B	HR	RBI	BB	SO	AVG	OBP	SLG	PRO+	BR	/A	RC	SB	CS	SBR	FA	FR	POS	TPR
1954	Pit-N	132	470	67	117	15	9	8	46	47	59	.249	.317	.370	80	-15	-14	56	4	0	1	.986	-3	*1/O	-2.2
1956	Pit-N	113	233	29	47	8	3	5	29	26	50	.202	.285	.326	65	-12	-11	22	1	1	-0	.977	-9	O1/3	-2.5
1957	Pit-N	126	387	58	118	12	6	13	45	38	50	.305	.370	.468	127	13	14	70	10	4	1	.963	3	O/13	1.2
1958	Pit-N★	144	529	93	170	33	9	13	70	58	55	.321	.390	.491	135	25	27	102	12	4	1	.977	9	*O	2.9
1959	Pit-N	143	547	78	153	18	4	13	61	67	65	.280	.358	.399	102	2	3	81	10	7	-1	.964	6	*O/1	0.0
1960	*Pit-N★	145	571	83	156	33	6	15	86	59	86	.273	.342	.431	109	8	7	82	11	8	-2	.981	7	*O	0.6
1961	Pit-N	119	381	61	102	20	3	3	42	51	49	.268	.360	.360	91	-3	-3	51	3	5	-2	.973	-2	O	-1.2
1962	Pit-N	144	510	87	154	29	7	20	75	76	89	.302	.397	.504	140	30	30	106	10	4	1	.960	-9	*O	1.3
1963	Pit-N	34	122	18	33	5	5	0	8	13	22	.270	.341	.393	110	2	2	16	4	1	1	.983	-2	O	-0.1
	Cin-N	72	194	25	49	10	2	3	17	21	42	.253	.332	.371	99	1	0	23	1	2	-1	1.000	-2	O	-0.6
	Yr	106	316	43	82	15	7	3	25	34	64	.259	.335	.380	103	3	2	39	5	3	-0	.993	-4	O	-0.7
1964	Cin-N	25	59	6	13	3	0	3	5	4	12	.220	.270	.424	89	-1	-1	7	0	0	0	.913	-0	O	-0.2
	*StL-N	55	118	10	32	5	0	1	16	11	20	.271	.333	.339	83	-1	-3	14	0	0	0	.938	-0	O	-0.4
	Yr	80	177	16	45	8	0	4	21	15	32	.254	.313	.367	85	-2	-4	21	0	0	0	.930	-1	O	-0.6

YEAR	TM/L	G	AB	R	H	2B	3B	HR	RBI	BB	SO	AVG	OBP	SLG	PRO+	BR	/A	RC	SB	CS	SBR	FA	FR	POS	TPR
1965	StL-N	80	152	25	47	5	4	5	26	12	30	.309	.360	.493	126	7	6	26	1	0	0	.935	-4	O	0.0
1966	StL-N	49	45	2	7	1	0	1	5	2	17	.156	.208	.244	25	-5	-5	2	0	0	0	.000	0	H	-0.5
Total	12	1381	4318	642	1198	197	58	103	531	485	646	.277	.353	.421	108	51	52	656	67	36	-2	.969	-7	O1/3	-1.7

■ LOU SKIZAS

Skizas, Louis Peter "The Nervous Greek" b: 6/2/32, Chicago, Ill. BR/TR, 5'11", 175 lbs. Deb: 4/19/56

YEAR	TM/L	G	AB	R	H	2B	3B	HR	RBI	BB	SO	AVG	OBP	SLG	PRO+	BR	/A	RC	SB	CS	SBR	FA	FR	POS	TPR
1956	NY-A	6	6	0	1	0	0	0	1	0	2	.167	.167	.167	-12	-1	-1	0	0	0	0	.000	0	H	-0.1
	KC-A	83	297	39	94	11	3	11	39	15	17	.316	.349	.485	118	6	6	45	3	1	0	.975	5	O	0.8
	Yr	89	303	39	95	11	3	11	40	15	19	.314	.346	.479	116	5	5	45	3	1	0	.975	5	O	0.7
1957	KC-A	119	376	34	92	14	1	18	44	27	15	.245	.299	.431	95	-3	-4	47	5	2	0	.976	-9	O3	-1.7
1958	Det-A	23	33	4	8	2	0	1	2	5	1	.242	.342	.394	95	0	-0	4	0	0	0	.750	-3	/O3	-0.3
1959	Chi-A	8	13	3	1	0	0	0	0	3	2	.077	.250	.077	-6	-2	-2	0	0	0	0	1.000	-0	/O	-0.2
Total	4	239	725	80	196	27	4	30	86	50	37	.270	.319	.443	102	0	-1	97	8	3	1	.973	-7	O/3	-1.5

■ BILL SKOWRON

Skowron, William Joseph "Moose" b: 12/18/30, Chicago, Ill. BR/TR, 5'11", 195 lbs. Deb: 4/13/54

YEAR	TM/L	G	AB	R	H	2B	3B	HR	RBI	BB	SO	AVG	OBP	SLG	PRO+	BR	/A	RC	SB	CS	SBR	FA	FR	POS	TPR
1954	NY-A	87	215	37	73	12	9	7	41	19	18	.340	.396	.577	170	18	19	47	2	1	0	.986	-1	1/32	1.6
1955	*NY-A	108	288	46	92	17	3	12	61	21	32	.319	.372	.524	141	14	15	52	1	1	-0	.989	-3	1/3	0.8
1956	*NY-A	134	464	78	143	21	6	23	90	50	60	.308	.383	.528	143	24	26	90	4	4	-1	.993	3	*1/3	2.0
1957	*NY-A★	122	457	54	139	15	5	17	88	31	60	.304	.352	.470	125	13	14	70	3	2	-0	.992	6	*1	1.3
1958	*NY-A★	126	465	61	127	22	3	14	73	28	69	.273	.320	.424	107	1	3	59	1	1	-0	**.993**	-2	*1/3	-0.8
1959	NY-A★	74	282	39	84	13	5	15	59	20	47	.298	.351	.539	145	14	16	50	1	0	0	.991	0	1	1.1
1960	*NY-A★	146	538	63	166	34	3	26	91	38	95	.309	.356	.528	144	25	28	95	2	3	-1	.991	9	*1	2.4
1961	*NY-A☆	150	561	76	150	23	4	28	89	35	108	.267	.320	.472	115	4	8	78	0	0	0	.993	-1	*1	-0.6
1962	*NY-A	140	478	63	129	16	6	23	80	36	99	.270	.328	.473	116	7	9	71	0	1	-1	.991	-5	*1	-0.5
1963	*LA-N	89	237	19	48	8	0	4	19	13	49	.203	.253	.287	59	-14	-12	15	0	1	-1	.991	-1	1/3	-1.8
1964	Was-A	73	262	28	71	10	0	13	41	11	56	.271	.308	.458	110	2	3	35	0	0	0	.994	-2	1	-0.2
	Chi-A	73	273	19	80	11	3	4	38	19	36	.293	.341	.399	108	2	3	36	0	0	0	.998	-1	1	-0.1
	Yr	146	535	47	151	21	3	17	79	30	92	.282	.325	.428	109	4	5	71	0	0	0	.996	-3	*1	-0.3
1965	Chi-A†	146	559	63	153	24	3	18	78	32	77	.274	.319	.424	116	5	9	68	1	3	-2	.994	-6	*1	-0.6
1966	Chi-A	120	337	27	84	15	2	6	29	26	45	.249	.309	.359	98	-4	-1	35	1	1	-0	.991	1	1	-0.6
1967	Chi-A	8	8	0	0	0	0	0	1	0	1	.000	.000	.000	-99	-2	-2	0	0	0	0	.000	0	H	-0.2
	Cal-A	62	123	8	27	2	1	1	10	4	18	.220	.267	.276	63	-6	-6	8	0	0	0	.988	-1	1	-0.9
	Yr	70	131	8	27	2	1	1	11	4	19	.206	.252	.260	53	-8	-7	7	0	0	0	.988	-1	1	-1.1
Total	14	1658	5547	681	1566	243	53	211	888	383	870	.282	.335	.459	121	104	131	810	16	18	-6	.992	-3	*1/32	2.9

■ BOB SKUBE

Skube, Robert Jacob b: 10/8/57, Northridge, Cal. BL/TL, 6', 180 lbs. Deb: 9/17/82

YEAR	TM/L	G	AB	R	H	2B	3B	HR	RBI	BB	SO	AVG	OBP	SLG	PRO+	BR	/A	RC	SB	CS	SBR	FA	FR	POS	TPR
1982	Mil-A	4	3	0	2	0	0	0	0	0	0	.667	.667	.667	285	1	1	1	0	0	0	.000	-1	/OD	0.0
1983	Mil-A	12	25	2	5	1	1	0	9	4	7	.200	.310	.320	80	-1	-1	2	0	0	0	1.000	-1	/O1D	-0.1
Total	2	16	28	2	7	1	1	0	9	4	7	.250	.344	.357	101	-0	0	4	0	0	0	1.000	-1	/OD1	-0.1

■ GORDON SLADE

Slade, Gordon Leigh "Oskie" b: 10/9/04, Salt Lake City, Utah d: 1/2/74, Long Beach, Cal. BR/TR, 5'10.5", 160 lbs. Deb: 4/21/30

YEAR	TM/L	G	AB	R	H	2B	3B	HR	RBI	BB	SO	AVG	OBP	SLG	PRO+	BR	/A	RC	SB	CS	SBR	FA	FR	POS	TPR
1930	Bro-N	25	37	8	8	2	0	1	2	3	5	.216	.275	.351	51	-3	-3	4	0			.938	10	S	0.7
1931	Bro-N	85	272	27	65	13	2	1	29	23	28	.239	.310	.313	68	-12	-12	28	2			.947	11	S/3	0.7
1932	Bro-N	79	250	23	60	15	1	1	23	11	26	.240	.280	.320	62	-14	-13	23	3			.943	11	S3	0.3
1933	StL-N	39	62	6	7	1	0	0	3	6	7	.113	.191	.129	-7	-9	-9	2	1			.941	3	S/2	-0.5
1934	Cin-N	138	555	61	158	19	8	4	52	25	34	.285	.320	.369	86	-13	-11	66	6			.952	2	S2	-0.1
1935	Cin-N	71	196	22	55	10	0	1	14	16	16	.281	.341	.347	88	-4	-3	24	0			.927	-12	S2/O3	-1.2
Total	6	437	1372	147	353	60	11	8	123	84	116	.257	.307	.335	73	-54	-50	146	12			.945	25	S/23O	-0.1

■ ART SLADEN

Sladen, Arthur b: 10/28/1860, Dracut, Mass. d: 2/28/14, Dracut, Mass. Deb: 4/17/1884

YEAR	TM/L	G	AB	R	H	2B	3B	HR	RBI	BB	SO	AVG	OBP	SLG	PRO+	BR	/A	RC	SB	CS	SBR	FA	FR	POS	TPR
1884	Bos-U	2	7	0	0	0	0	0		0		.000	.000	.000	-99	-1	-1	0				1.000	-1	/O	-0.2

■ JIMMY SLAGLE

Slagle, James Franklin "Rabbit" or "Shorty" b: 7/11/1873, Worthville, Pa. d: 5/10/56, Chicago, Ill. BL/TR, 5'7", 144 lbs. Deb: 4/17/1899

YEAR	TM/L	G	AB	R	H	2B	3B	HR	RBI	BB	SO	AVG	OBP	SLG	PRO+	BR	/A	RC	SB	CS	SBR	FA	FR	POS	TPR
1899	Was-N	147	599	92	163	15	8	0	41	55		.272	.338	.324	83	-14	-13	76	22			.953	20	*O	-0.3
1900	Phi-N	141	574	115	165	16	9	0	45	60		.287	.358	.347	96	-2	-2	89	34			.922	1	*O	-1.1
1901	Phi-N	48	183	20	37	6	2	1	20	16		.202	.277	.273	59	-9	-10	17	5			.930	6	O	-0.7
	Bos-N	66	255	35	69	7	0	0	7	34		.271	.359	.298	84	-1	-4	34	14			.935	-2	O	-1.1
	Yr	114	438	55	106	13	2	1	27	50		.242	.325	.288	74	-10	-14	50	19			.932	4	*O	-1.8
1902	Chi-N	115	454	64	143	11	4	0	28	53		.315	.387	.357	133	18	19	81	40			.965	7	*O	2.0
1903	Chi-N	139	543	104	162	20	6	0	44	81		.298	.393	.357	118	15	17	94	33			.936	2	*O	0.9
1904	Chi-N	120	481	73	125	12	10	1	31	41		.260	.322	.333	103	2	2	63	28			.921	-3	*O	-0.8
1905	Chi-N	155	568	96	153	19	4	0	37	97		.269	.379	.317	104	11	8	82	27			.962	3	*O	0.4
1906	Chi-N	127	498	71	119	8	6	0	33	63		.239	.324	.279	84	-5	-8	56	25			.976	2	*O	-1.3
1907	*Chi-N	136	489	71	126	6	6	0	32	76		.258	.359	.294	99	7	3	65	28			.962	-10	*O	-1.4
1908	Chi-N	104	352	38	78	4	1	0	26	43		.222	.306	.239	72	-8	-10	33	17			.976	-6	*O	-2.3
Total	10	1298	4996	779	1340	124	56	2	344	619		.268	.352	.317	97	13	4	689	273			.950	22	*O	-5.7

■ JACK SLATTERY

Slattery, John Terrence b: 1/6/1878, S.Boston, Mass. d: 7/17/49, Boston, Mass. BR/TR, 6'2", 191 lbs. Deb: 9/28/01 MC

YEAR	TM/L	G	AB	R	H	2B	3B	HR	RBI	BB	SO	AVG	OBP	SLG	PRO+	BR	/A	RC	SB	CS	SBR	FA	FR	POS	TPR
1901	Bos-A	1	3	1	1	0	0	0	1	1		.333	.500	.333	137	0	0	1	0			1.000	0	/C	0.0
1903	Cle-A	4	11	1	0	0	0	0	0	0		.000	.000	.000	-99	-3	-3	0	0			.885	-1	/1	-0.4
	Chi-A	63	211	8	46	3	2	0	20	2		.218	.233	.251	47	-14	-13	13	2			.974	-8	C/1	-1.6
	Yr	67	222	9	46	3	2	0	20	2		.207	.221	.239	40	-17	-16	13	2			.974	-9	C/1	-2.0
1906	StL-N	3	7	0	2	0	0	0	0	1		.286	.375	.286	111	0	0	1	0			1.000	-1	/C	0.0
1909	Was-A	32	56	4	12	2	0	0	6	2		.214	.254	.250	62	-3	-2	4	1			.953	-1	1/C	-0.3
Total	4	103	288	14	61	5	2	0	27	6		.212	.236	.243	47	-19	-18	19	3			.974	-10	/C1	-2.3

■ MIKE SLATTERY

Slattery, Michael J. b: 11/26/1866, Boston, Mass. d: 10/16/04, Boston, Mass. BL/TL, 6'2", 210 lbs. Deb: 4/19/1884

YEAR	TM/L	G	AB	R	H	2B	3B	HR	RBI	BB	SO	AVG	OBP	SLG	PRO+	BR	/A	RC	SB	CS	SBR	FA	FR	POS	TPR
1884	Bos-U	106	413	60	86	6	2	0		4		.208	.216	.232	52	-20	-19	21				.802	6	*O1	-1.4
1888	*NY-N	103	391	50	96	12	6	1	35	13	28	.246	.272	.315	89	-5	-5	41	26			.919	0	*O	-0.7
1889	*NY-N	12	48	7	14	2	0	1	12	4	3	.292	.346	.396	108	0	0	7	2			.852	-1	O	0.0
1890	NY-P	97	411	80	126	20	11	5	67	27	25	.307	.352	.445	105	7	-0	73	18			.905	-14	*O	-1.4
1891	Cin-N	41	158	24	33	3	2	1	16	10	10	.209	.256	.272	55	-9	-9	12	1			.941	-0	O	-1.0
	Was-a	15	60	8	17	1	0	0	5	4	5	.283	.358	.300	96	-0	0	9	6			.862	-2	O	-0.2
Total	5	374	1481	229	372	44	21	8	135	62	71	.251	.284	.325	83	-28	-33	163	53			.883	-11	O/1	-4.7

■ DON SLAUGHT

Slaught, Donald Martin b: 9/11/58, Long Beach, Cal. BR/TR, 6'1", 190 lbs. Deb: 7/06/82

YEAR	TM/L	G	AB	R	H	2B	3B	HR	RBI	BB	SO	AVG	OBP	SLG	PRO+	BR	/A	RC	SB	CS	SBR	FA	FR	POS	TPR
1982	KC-A	43	115	14	32	6	0	3	8	9	12	.278	.331	.409	102	0	0	15	0	0	0	.994	2	C	0.4
1983	KC-A	83	276	21	86	13	4	0	28	11	27	.312	.338	.388	99	-1	-1	34	3	1	0	.964	-7	C/D	-0.4
1984	*KC-A	124	409	48	108	27	4	4	42	20	55	.264	.302	.379	86	-8	-8	46	0	0	0	.982	-10	*C/D	-1.2
1985	Tex-A	102	343	34	96	17	4	8	35	20	41	.280	.331	.423	103	2	1	46	5	4	-1	.990	-11	*C	-0.6
1986	Tex-A	95	314	39	83	17	1	13	46	16	59	.264	.310	.449	101	1	-0	42	3	2	-0	.993	-6	C/D	-0.1
1987	Tex-A	95	237	25	53	15	2	8	16	24	51	.224	.298	.405	84	-6	-6	27	0	3	-2	.985	-0	C/D	-0.4
1988	NY-A	97	322	33	91	25	1	9	43	24	54	.283	.338	.450	120	7	8	47	1	0	0	.979	-12	C/D	0.3
1989	NY-A	117	350	34	88	21	3	5	38	30	57	.251	.319	.371	95	-3	-2	41	1	1	-0	.991	-5	*C/D	-0.2
1990	*Pit-N	84	230	27	69	18	3	4	29	27	27	.300	.381	.457	134	10	11	42	0	1	-1	.979	-3	C	1.1
1991	*Pit-N	77	220	19	65	17	1	1	29	21	32	.295	.365	.395	116	4	5	32	1	0	0	.987	-5	C/3	0.4

YEAR	TM/L	G	AB	R	H	2B	3B	HR	RBI	BB	SO	AVG	OBP	SLG	PRO+	BR	/A	RC	SB	CS	SBR	FA	FR	POS	TPR
1992	*Pit-N	87	255	26	88	17	3	4	37	17	23	.345	.391	.482	148	15	15	46	2	2	-1	.988	-4	C	1.6
Total	11	1004	3071	320	859	193	26	59	351	219	438	.280	.334	.417	106	22	23	418	16	14	-4	.985	-62	C/D3	0.9

■ ENOS SLAUGHTER Slaughter, Enos Bradsher "Country" b: 4/27/16, Roxboro, N.C. BL/TR, 5'9", 192 lbs. Deb: 4/19/38 H

YEAR	TM/L	G	AB	R	H	2B	3B	HR	RBI	BB	SO	AVG	OBP	SLG	PRO+	BR	/A	RC	SB	CS	SBR	FA	FR	POS	TPR
1938	StL-N	112	395	59	109	20	10	8	58	32	38	.276	.330	.438	104	4	1	57	1			.970	-2	O	-0.4
1939	StL-N	149	604	95	193	**52**	5	12	86	44	53	.320	.371	.482	120	22	17	108	2			.968	**16**	*O	2.8
1940	StL-N	140	516	96	158	25	13	17	73	50	35	.306	.370	.504	131	26	23	99	8			.989	3	*O	1.9
1941	StL-N★	113	425	71	132	22	9	13	76	53	28	.311	.390	.496	139	27	24	86	4			.947	-8	*O	0.9
1942	*StL-N★	152	591	100	**188**	31	**17**	13	98	88	30	**.318**	.412	.494	153	**50**	45	**128**	9			.987	4	*O	4.3
1946	*StL-N★	156	609	100	183	30	8	18	**130**	69	41	.300	.374	.465	131	29	26	110	9			.981	6	*O	2.5
1947	StL-N★	147	551	100	162	31	13	10	86	59	27	.294	.366	.452	111	12	9	93	4			.982	9	*O	1.0
1948	StL-N★	146	549	91	176	27	11	11	90	81	29	.321	.409	.470	130	31	27	110	4			.971	6	*O	2.4
1949	StL-N★	151	568	92	191	34	**13**	13	96	79	37	.336	.418	.511	141	40	37	127	3			.983	1	*O	3.0
1950	StL-N★	148	556	82	161	26	7	10	101	66	33	.290	.367	.415	100	5	2	87	3			.978	-1	*O	-0.6
1951	StL-N★	123	409	48	115	17	8	4	64	67	25	.281	.386	.391	109	8	8	67	7	2	1	.995	-0	*O	0.5
1952	StL-N★	140	510	73	153	17	12	11	101	70	25	.300	.386	.445	130	22	22	93	6	1	1	.989	2	*O	2.0
1953	StL-N★	143	492	64	143	34	9	6	89	80	28	.291	.395	.433	116	14	14	90	4	4	-1	**.996**	-6	*O	0.2
1954	NY-A	69	125	19	31	4	2	1	19	28	8	.248	.386	.336	102	1	2	18	0	2	-1	.974	-6	O	-0.7
1955	NY-A	10	9	1	1	0	0	0	1	1	1	.111	.200	.111	-15	-1	-1	0	0	0	0	.000	0	H	-0.1
	KC-A	108	267	49	86	12	4	5	34	40	17	.322	.414	.453	132	14	13	50	2	3	-1	.985	-4	O	0.5
	Yr	118	276	50	87	12	4	5	35	41	18	.315	.408	.442	127	12	12	50	2	3	-1	.985	-4	O	0.4
1956	KC-A	91	223	37	62	14	3	2	23	29	20	.278	.364	.395	100	0	0	33	1	0	0	.981	-3	O	-0.5
	*NY-A	24	83	15	24	4	2	0	4	5	6	.289	.330	.386	91	-2	-1	11	1	1	-0	1.000	-2	O	-0.4
	Yr	115	306	52	86	18	5	2	27	34	26	.281	.355	.392	97	-1	-1	44	2	1	0	.985	-5	O	-0.9
1957	*NY-A	96	209	24	53	7	1	5	34	40	19	.254	.373	.368	105	2	3	30	0	2	-1	1.000	-3	O	-0.5
1958	*NY-A	77	138	21	42	4	1	4	19	21	16	.304	.396	.435	133	6	7	25	2	0	1	.957	-5	O	0.1
1959	NY-A	74	99	10	17	2	0	6	21	13	19	.172	.268	.374	77	-4	-3	10	1	0	0	.964	-5	O	-0.9
	Mil-N	11	18	0	3	0	0	0	1	3	3	.167	.286	.167	27	-2	-2	1	0	0	0	1.000	-1	/O	-0.3
Total	19	2380	7946	1247	2383	413	148	169	1304	1018	538	.300	.382	.453	122	306	270	1432	71	15		.980	-0	*O	17.7

■ SCOTTIE SLAYBACK Slayback, Elbert b: 10/5/01, Paducah, Ky. d: 11/30/79, Cincinnati, Ohio BR/TR, 5'8", 165 lbs. Deb: 9/26/26

YEAR	TM/L	G	AB	R	H	2B	3B	HR	RBI	BB	SO	AVG	OBP	SLG	PRO+	BR	/A	RC	SB	CS	SBR	FA	FR	POS	TPR
1926	NY-N	2	8	0	0	0	0	0	0	0	0	.000	.000	.000	-99	-2	-2	0	0			.889	-1	/2	-0.4

■ BRUCE SLOAN Sloan, Bruce Adams "Fatso" b: 10/4/14, McAlester, Okla. d: 9/24/73, Oklahoma City, Okla. BL/TL, 5'9", 195 lbs. Deb: 4/29/44

YEAR	TM/L	G	AB	R	H	2B	3B	HR	RBI	BB	SO	AVG	OBP	SLG	PRO+	BR	/A	RC	SB	CS	SBR	FA	FR	POS	TPR
1944	NY-N	59	104	7	28	4	1	1	9	13	8	.269	.350	.356	99	0	0	13	0			.935	-4	O	-0.5

■ TOD SLOAN Sloan, Yale Yeastman b: 12/24/1890, Madisonville, Tenn d: 9/12/56, Akron, Ohio BL/TR, 6', 175 lbs. Deb: 9/22/13

YEAR	TM/L	G	AB	R	H	2B	3B	HR	RBI	BB	SO	AVG	OBP	SLG	PRO+	BR	/A	RC	SB	CS	SBR	FA	FR	POS	TPR
1913	StL-A	7	26	2	7	1	0	0	2	1	9	.269	.321	.308	87	-1	-0	3	1			.950	2	/O	0.1
1917	StL-A	109	313	32	72	6	2	2	25	28	34	.230	.307	.281	83	-7	-6	28	8			.963	-3	O	-1.4
1919	StL-A	27	63	9	15	1	3	0	6	12	3	.238	.368	.349	99	1	0	8	0			.933	-1	O	-0.1
Total	3	143	402	43	94	8	5	2	33	41	46	.234	.319	.294	86	-7	-6	39	9			.957	-1	O	-1.4

■ RON SLOCUM Slocum, Ronald Reece b: 7/2/45, Modesto, Cal. BR/TR, 6'2", 185 lbs. Deb: 9/08/69

YEAR	TM/L	G	AB	R	H	2B	3B	HR	RBI	BB	SO	AVG	OBP	SLG	PRO+	BR	/A	RC	SB	CS	SBR	FA	FR	POS	TPR
1969	SD-N	13	24	6	7	1	0	1	5	0	5	.292	.292	.458	112	0	0	3	0	0	0	.938	-1	/23S	-0.1
1970	SD-N	60	71	8	10	2	2	1	11	8	24	.141	.237	.268	37	-7	-6	4	0	1	-1	.978	13	CS3/2	0.6
1971	SD-N	7	18	1	0	0	0	0	0	0	8	.000	.053	.000	-90	-4	-4	0	0	0	0	.905	1	/3	-0.3
Total	3	80	113	15	17	3	2	2	16	8	37	.150	.220	.265	33	-11	-10	8	0	1	-1	.887	13	/3CS2	0.2

■ CRAIG SMAJSTRLA Smajstrla, Craig Lee b: 6/19/62, Houston, Tex. BB/TR, 5'9", 165 lbs. Deb: 9/06/88

YEAR	TM/L	G	AB	R	H	2B	3B	HR	RBI	BB	SO	AVG	OBP	SLG	PRO+	BR	/A	RC	SB	CS	SBR	FA	FR	POS	TPR
1988	Hou-N	8	3	2	0	0	0	0	0	0	1	.000	.000	.000	-99	-1	-1	0	0	0	0	1.000	1	/2	0.1

■ CHARLIE SMALL Small, Charles Albert b: 10/24/05, Auburn, Me. d: 1/14/53, Auburn, Me. BL/TR, 5'11", 180 lbs. Deb: 7/07/30

YEAR	TM/L	G	AB	R	H	2B	3B	HR	RBI	BB	SO	AVG	OBP	SLG	PRO+	BR	/A	RC	SB	CS	SBR	FA	FR	POS	TPR
1930	Bos-A	25	18	1	3	1	0	0	0	2	5	.167	.250	.222	22	-2	-2	1	1	0	0	1.000	-0	/O	-0.2

■ HANK SMALL Small, George Henry b: 7/31/53, Atlanta, Ga. BR/TR, 6'3", 205 lbs. Deb: 9/27/78

YEAR	TM/L	G	AB	R	H	2B	3B	HR	RBI	BB	SO	AVG	OBP	SLG	PRO+	BR	/A	RC	SB	CS	SBR	FA	FR	POS	TPR
1978	Atl-N	1	4	0	0	0	0	0	0	0	0	.000	.000	.000	-90	-1	-1	0	0	0	0	1.000	0	/1	-0.1

■ JIM SMALL Small, James Arthur b: 3/8/37, Portland, Ore. BL/TL, 6'1.5", 180 lbs. Deb: 6/22/55

YEAR	TM/L	G	AB	R	H	2B	3B	HR	RBI	BB	SO	AVG	OBP	SLG	PRO+	BR	/A	RC	SB	CS	SBR	FA	FR	POS	TPR
1955	Det-A	12	4	2	0	0	0	0	0	1	1	.000	.200	.000	-44	-1	-1	0	0	0	0	1.000	-1	/O	-0.1
1956	Det-A	58	91	13	29	4	2	0	10	6	10	.319	.361	.407	102	0	0	14	0	0	0	.940	-3	O	-0.3
1957	Det-A	36	42	7	9	2	0	0	0	2	11	.214	.250	.262	39	-3	-4	2	0	2	-1	1.000	-3	O	-0.8
1958	KC-A	2	4	0	0	0	0	0	0	1	0	.000	.200	.000	-39	-1	-1	0	0	0	0	1.000	0	/O	-0.1
Total	4	108	141	22	38	6	2	0	10	10	22	.270	.318	.340	75	-5	-5	16	0	2	-1	.957	-6	/O	-1.3

■ ROY SMALLEY Smalley, Roy Frederick Jr. b: 10/25/52, Los Angeles, Cal. BB/TR, 6'1", 185 lbs. Deb: 4/30/75 F

YEAR	TM/L	G	AB	R	H	2B	3B	HR	RBI	BB	SO	AVG	OBP	SLG	PRO+	BR	/A	RC	SB	CS	SBR	FA	FR	POS	TPR
1975	Tex-A	78	250	22	57	8	0	3	33	30	42	.228	.311	.296	73	-9	-8	25	4	0	1	.941	4	S2/C	0.3
1976	Tex-A	41	129	15	29	2	0	1	8	29	27	.225	.367	.264	85	-1	-1	15	2	0	1	.963	-6	2/S	-0.3
	Min-A	103	384	46	104	16	3	2	36	47	79	.271	.353	.344	102	4	2	49	0	4	-2	.967	5	*S	1.8
	Yr	144	513	61	133	18	3	3	44	76	106	.259	.357	.324	98	3	1	64	2	4	-2	.966	-1	*S2	1.5
1977	Min-A	150	584	93	135	21	5	6	56	74	89	.231	.319	.315	75	-20	-19	62	5	5	-2	.958	19	*S	1.5
1978	Min-A	158	586	80	160	31	3	19	77	85	70	.273	.366	.433	122	20	19	92	2	8	-4	.970	18	*S	5.3
1979	Min-A★	162	621	94	168	28	3	24	95	80	80	.271	.357	.441	110	13	10	101	2	3	-1	.968	**33**	*S/1	**5.7**
1980	Min-A	133	486	64	135	24	1	12	63	65	63	.278	.365	.405	103	9	4	72	3	3	-1	.975	21	*S/1D	3.8
1981	Min-A	56	167	24	44	7	1	7	22	31	24	.263	.379	.443	128	9	7	27	0	0	0	.946	-17	SD/1	-0.7
1982	Min-A	4	13	2	2	1	0	0	0	3	4	.154	.313	.231	51	-1	-1	1	0	0	0	1.000	1	/S	0.0
	NY-A	142	486	55	125	14	2	20	67	68	100	.257	.348	.418	111	7	8	75	0	1	-1	.977	-19	S3/2D	-0.4
	Yr	146	499	57	127	15	2	20	67	71	104	.255	.347	.413	109	6	7	76	0	1	-1	.979	-18	S3/D2	-0.4
1983	NY-A	130	451	70	124	24	1	18	62	58	68	.275	.360	.452	127	14	16	75	3	3	-1	.959	-16	S31	0.6
1984	NY-A	67	209	17	50	8	1	7	26	15	35	.239	.290	.388	89	-5	-3	23	2	1	0	.905	0	3S/1D	-0.3
	Chi-A	47	135	15	23	4	0	4	13	22	30	.170	.287	.289	57	-7	-8	12	1	1	-0	.947	-8	3/S1D	-1.7
	Yr	114	344	32	73	12	1	11	39	37	65	.212	.289	.349	76	-12	-11	35	3	2	-0	.923	-7	3S/D1	-2.0
1985	Min-A	129	388	57	100	20	0	12	45	60	65	.258	.359	.402	102	6	3	58	0	2	-1	.987	-15	DS3/1	-0.9
1986	Min-A	143	459	59	113	20	4	20	57	68	80	.246	.343	.438	108	7	6	70	1	3	-2	.963	-4	*DS/3	0.1
1987	*Min-A	110	309	32	85	16	1	8	34	36	52	.275	.353	.411	98	1	-0	46	2	0	1	.850	-3	D3/S	-0.3
Total	13	1653	5657	745	1454	244	25	163	694	771	908	.257	.348	.395	103	48	34	801	27	34	-12	.966	14	*SD3/21C	14.5

■ ROY SMALLEY Smalley, Roy Frederick Sr. b: 6/9/26, Springfield, Mo. BR/TR, 6'3", 190 lbs. Deb: 4/20/48 F

YEAR	TM/L	G	AB	R	H	2B	3B	HR	RBI	BB	SO	AVG	OBP	SLG	PRO+	BR	/A	RC	SB	CS	SBR	FA	FR	POS	TPR
1948	Chi-N	124	361	25	78	11	4	4	36	23	76	.216	.265	.302	55	-24	-22	27	0			.941	9	*S	-0.7
1949	Chi-N	135	477	57	117	21	10	8	35	36	77	.245	.304	.382	85	-13	-11	54	2			.947	14	*S	1.2
1950	Chi-N	154	557	58	128	21	9	21	85	49	114	.230	.297	.413	85	-15	-14	68	2			.945	**21**	*S	1.9
1951	Chi-N	79	238	24	55	7	4	8	31	25	53	.231	.304	.395	85	-5	-6	29	0	0	0	.953	-13	S	-1.3
1952	Chi-N	87	261	36	58	14	1	5	30	29	58	.222	.305	.341	78	-8	-8	29	0	0	0	.952	-11	S	-1.4
1953	Chi-N	82	253	20	63	9	0	6	25	28	57	.249	.329	.356	77	-8	-8	32	0	0	0	.932	-6	S	-0.9
1954	Mil-N	25	36	5	8	0	0	1	7	4	9	.222	.317	.306	67	-2	-2	3	0	0	0	.950	4	/S21	0.3
1955	Phi-N	92	260	33	51	11	1	7	39	39	58	.196	.306	.327	69	-12	-11	26	0	0	0	.974	-16	S/23	-2.0

YEAR	TM/L	G	AB	R	H	2B	3B	HR	RBI	BB	SO	AVG	OBP	SLG	PRO+	BR	/A	RC	SB	CS	SBR	FA	FR	POS	TPR
1956	Phi-N	65	168	14	38	9	3	0	16	23	29	.226	.323	.315	74	-6	-6	18	0	0	0	.949	-1	S	-0.3
1957	Phi-N	28	31	5	5	0	1	1	1	1	9	.161	.212	.323	42	-3	-3	2	0	0	0	.941	1	S	-0.1
1958	Phi-N	1	2	0	0	0	0	0	0	0	1	.000	.000	.000	-99	-1	-1	0	0	0	0	.714	0	/S	0.0
Total	11	872	2644	277	601	103	33	61	305	257	541	.227	.300	.360	77	-95	-91	288	4	0		.947	3	S/213	-3.3
■ WILL SMALLEY	Smalley, William Darwin "Deacon" b: 6/27/1871, Oakland, Cal. d: 10/11/1891, Bay City, Mich. BR/TR, Deb: 4/19/1890																								
1890	Cle-N	136	502	62	107	11	1	0	42	60	44	.213	.303	.239	62	-23	-21	40	10			.895	17	*3	0.0
1891	Was-a	11	38	5	6	0	1	0	3	5	2	.158	.256	.211	37	-3	-3	2	0			.762	-2	/32	-0.4
Total	2	147	540	67	113	11	2	0	45	65	46	.209	.300	.237	60	-26	-24	43	10			.887	15	3/2	-0.4
■ JOE SMAZA	Smaza, Joseph Paul b: 7/7/23, Detroit, Mich. d: 5/30/79, Royal Oak, Mich. BL/TL, 5'11", 175 lbs. Deb: 9/18/46																								
1946	Chi-A	2	5	2	1	0	0	0	0	0	0	.200	.200	.200	12	-1	-1	0	0	0	0	.000	-1	/O	-0.1
■ BILL SMILEY	Smiley, William B. b: 1856, Baltimore, Md. d: 7/11/1884, Baltimore, Md. Deb: 10/13/1874																								
1874	Bal-n	2	7	0	0	0	0	0		0		.000	.000	.000	-99	-2	-1	0						/3	-0.1
1882	StL-a	59	240	30	51	4	2	0		6		.213	.232	.246	59	-9	-11	14				.885	-7	*2/O	-1.5
	Bal-a	16	61	3	9	0	0	0		0		.148	.148	.148	-0	-6	-6	1				.843	2	2/S	-0.3
	Yr	75	301	33	60	4	2	0		6		.199	.215	.226	48	-16	-16	15				.874	-5	2/OS	-1.8
■ EDGAR SMITH	Smith, Albert Edgar b: 10/15/1860, North Haven, Conn. TR , 6', 200 lbs. Deb: 7/06/1883																								
1883	Bos-N	30	115	10	25	5	3	0	16	5	11	.217	.250	.313	68	-4	-4	9				.905	-0	O/C	-0.4
■ ALECK SMITH	Smith, Alexander Benjamin "Broadway Aleck" b: 1871, New York, N.Y. d: 7/9/19, New York, N.Y. TR , Deb: 4/23/1897																								
1897	Bro-N	66	237	36	71	13	1	1	39	4		.300	.317	.376	87	-7	-5	33	12			.903	-6	CO/1	-0.6
1898	Bro-N	52	199	25	52	6	5	0	23	3		.261	.276	.342	77	-7	-7	22	7			.909	-10	OC/321	-1.5
1899	Bro-N	17	61	6	11	0	1	0	6	2		.180	.206	.213	15	-7	-7	3	0			.917	-3	C	-0.9
	Bal-N	41	120	17	46	6	4	0	25	4		.383	.417	.500	144	8	7	29	7			.951	-4	C/O1	0.5
	Yr	58	181	23	57	6	5	0	31	6		.315	.347	.403	101	1	-0	29	7			.939	-7	C/O1	-0.4
1900	Bro-N	7	25	2	6	0	0	0	3	1		.240	.269	.240	39	-2	-2	2	2			.875	-2	/3C	-0.4
1901	NY-N	26	78	5	11	0	0	0	6	0		.141	.141	.141	-19	-12	-11	2	2			.962	-2	C	-1.1
1902	Bal-A	41	145	10	34	3	0	0	21	8		.234	.275	.255	45	-10	-11	12	5			.947	-6	C/1O23	-1.4
1903	Bos-A	11	33	4	10	1	0	0	4	0		.303	.303	.333	86	-0	-1	3	0			.932	0	C	0.0
1904	Chi-N	10	29	2	6	1	0	0	1	3		.207	.281	.241	62	-1	-1	2	1			.778	-2	/OC3	-0.3
1906	NY-N	16	28	0	5	0	0	0	2	1		.179	.207	.179	20	-3	-3	1	1			1.000	-1	/C1O	-0.3
Total	9	287	955	107	252	30	11	1	130	26		.264	.288	.321	69	-41	-41	111	37			.933	-35	C/O132	-6.0
■ AL SMITH	Smith, Alphonse Eugene "Fuzzy" b: 2/7/28, Kirkwood, Mo. BR/TR, 6'1", 191 lbs. Deb: 7/10/53																								
1953	Cle-A	47	150	28	36	9	0	3	14	20	25	.240	.341	.360	92	-2	-1	21	2	0	1	.920	-3	O/3	-0.6
1954	*Cle-A	131	481	101	135	29	6	11	50	88	65	.281	.399	.435	126	22	21	90	2	9	-5	.984	-3	*O3/S	0.8
1955	Cle-A★	154	607	**123**	186	27	4	22	77	93	77	.306	.411	.473	132	35	32	128	11	6	-0	.977	-17	*O3/S2	0.9
1956	Cle-A	141	526	87	144	26	5	16	71	84	72	.274	.382	.433	112	13	11	90	6	3	0	.981	-7	*O3/2	-0.1
1957	Cle-A	135	507	78	125	23	5	11	49	79	70	.247	.353	.377	100	1	2	73	12	6	0	.913	-16	3O	-1.6
1958	Chi-A	139	480	61	121	23	5	12	58	48	77	.252	.326	.396	100	-2	-0	59	3	3	-1	.970	-1	*O/3	-1.0
1959	*Chi-A	129	472	65	112	16	4	17	55	46	74	.237	.312	.396	94	-5	-5	58	7	5	-1	.980	10	*O/3	-0.2
1960	Chi-A★	142	536	80	169	31	3	12	72	50	65	.315	.377	.451	124	17	18	89	8	3	1	.966	-5	*O	0.6
1961	Chi-A	147	532	88	148	29	4	28	93	56	67	.278	.352	.506	128	18	20	91	4	4	-1	.948	-11	3O	0.5
1962	Chi-A	142	511	62	149	23	8	16	82	57	60	.292	.366	.462	122	15	16	83	3	3	-1	.935	-23	*3O	-0.8
1963	Bal-A	120	368	45	100	17	1	10	39	32	74	.272	.335	.405	109	3	4	49	9	0	3	.971	-4	O	-0.2
1964	Cle-A	61	136	15	22	1	1	4	9	8	32	.162	.214	.272	34	-12	-12	7	0	1	-1	1.000	-3	O/3	-1.8
	Bos-A	29	51	10	11	4	0	2	7	13	10	.216	.385	.412	116	2	2	9	0	0	0	.917	-2	3/O	0.0
	Yr	90	187	25	33	5	1	6	16	21	42	.176	.267	.310	59	-10	-10	15	0	1	-1	.987	-4	O3	-1.8
Total	12	1517	5357	843	1458	258	46	164	676	674	768	.272	.360	.429	113	106	106	846	67	43	-6	.961	-84	*O3/S2	-3.5
■ TONY SMITH	Smith, Anthony b: 5/14/1884, Chicago, Ill. d: 2/27/64, Galveston, Tex. BR/TR, 5'9", 150 lbs. Deb: 8/12/07																								
1907	Was-A	51	139	12	26	1	1	0	8	18		.187	.285	.209	63	-6	-4	11	3			.920	-9	S	-1.4
1910	Bro-N	106	321	31	58	10	1	1	16	69	53	.181	.329	.227	65	-12	-11	30	9			.941	12	*S/3	0.6
1911	Bro-N	13	40	3	6	1	0	0	2	8	7	.150	.292	.175	33	-3	-3	2	1			.870	0	S/2	-0.2
Total	3	170	500	46	90	12	2	1	26	95	60	.180	.314	.218	62	-21	-18	43	13			.931	4	S/32	-1.0
■ KLONDIKE SMITH	Smith, Armstrong Frederick b: 1/4/1887, London, England d: 11/15/59, Springfield, Mass. BL/TL, 5'9", 160 lbs. Deb: 9/28/12																								
1912	NY-A	7	27	0	5	1	0	0	0	0		.185	.185	.222	15	-3	-3	1	1			1.000	-1	/O	-0.5
■ BILLY SMITH	Smith, Billy Edward b: 7/14/53, Jonesboro, La. BB/TR, 6'2.5", 185 lbs. Deb: 4/13/75																								
1975	Cal-A	59	143	10	29	5	1	0	14	12	27	.203	.265	.252	50	-10	-9	10	1	3	-2	.932	-9	S/13D	-1.5
1976	Cal-A	13	8	0	3	0	0	0	0	0	2	.375	.375	.375	128	0	0	1	0	0	0	.625	-1	S/D	0.0
1977	Bal-A	109	367	44	79	12	2	5	29	33	71	.215	.282	.300	62	-21	-18	33	3	2	-0	.991	4	*2/S13	-0.7
1978	Bal-A	85	250	29	65	12	2	5	30	27	40	.260	.335	.384	108	1	3	34	3	0	1	.986	-1	2/S	0.8
1979	*Bal-A	68	189	18	47	9	4	6	33	15	33	.249	.311	.434	102	-1	0	27	1	0	0	.980	-8	2/S	-0.4
1981	SF-N	36	61	6	11	0	0	1	5	9	16	.180	.286	.230	48	-4	-4	5	0	0	0	.971	-0	S/23	-0.3
Total	6	370	1018	107	234	38	9	17	111	96	189	.230	.299	.335	79	-35	-28	110	8	5	-1	.987	-15	2/S13D	-2.1
■ BOBBY GENE SMITH	Smith, Bobby Gene b: 5/28/34, Hood River, Ore. BR/TR, 5'11", 185 lbs. Deb: 4/16/57																								
1957	StL-N	93	185	24	39	7	1	3	18	13	35	.211	.263	.308	52	-12	-13	14	1	1	-0	.973	-8	O	-2.5
1958	StL-N	28	88	8	25	3	0	2	5	2	18	.284	.308	.386	79	-2	-3	11	1	0	0	1.000	-1	O	-0.5
1959	StL-N	43	60	11	13	1	1	1	7	1	9	.217	.230	.317	41	-5	-5	4	0	0	0	.971	-4	O	-1.0
1960	Phi-N	98	217	24	62	5	2	4	27	10	28	.286	.317	.382	90	-3	-3	24	2	3	-1	1.000	1	O/3	-0.6
1961	Phi-N	79	174	16	44	7	0	2	18	15	32	.253	.316	.328	72	-7	-7	17	0	1	-1	.971	7	O	-0.3
1962	NY-N	8	22	1	3	0	1	0	2	3	2	.136	.240	.227	26	-2	-2	1	0	1	-1	1.000	-0	/O	-0.3
	Chi-N	13	29	3	5	0	0	1	2	2	6	.172	.226	.276	33	-3	-3	2	0	1	-1	1.000	-0	/O	-0.4
	StL-N	91	130	13	30	9	0	0	12	7	14	.231	.270	.300	48	-9	-10	9	1	1	-0	1.000	3	O	-1.0
	Yr	112	181	17	38	9	1	1	16	12	22	.210	.259	.287	43	-14	-16	12	1	3	-2	1.000	2	O	-1.7
1965	Cal-A	23	57	1	13	3	0	0	5	2	10	.228	.267	.281	57	-3	-3	4	0	1	-1	1.000	-0	O	-0.5
Total	7	476	962	101	234	35	5	13	96	55	154	.243	.286	.331	64	-47	-50	86	5	9	-4	.986	-4	O/3	-7.1
■ BRICK SMITH	Smith, Brick Dudley b: 5/2/59, Charlotte, N.C. BR/TR, 6'4", 225 lbs. Deb: 9/13/87																								
1987	Sea-A	5	8	1	1	0	0	0	0	2	4	.125	.300	.125	18	-1	-1	0	0	0	0	.963	0	/1D	-0.1
1988	Sea-A	4	10	1	1	0	0	0	1	0	1	.100	.100	.100	-42	-2	-2	0	0	0	0	1.000	1	/1	-0.1
Total	2	9	18	2	2	0	0	0	1	2	5	.111	.200	.111	-12	-3	-3	1	0	0	0	.983	1	/1D	-0.2
■ BERNIE SMITH	Smith, Calvin Bernard b: 9/4/41, Ponchatoula, La. BR/TR, 5'9", 164 lbs. Deb: 7/31/70																								
1970	Mil-A	44	76	8	21	3	1	1	6	11	12	.276	.382	.382	110	2	2	11	1	3	-2	.979	-7	O	-0.8
1971	Mil-A	15	36	1	5	1	0	1	3	0	5	.139	.162	.250	15	-4	-4	1	0	0	0	.923	-3	O	-0.8
Total	2	59	112	9	26	4	1	2	9	11	17	.232	.317	.339	83	-2	-2	12	1	3	-2	.967	-9	/O	-1.6
■ REGGIE SMITH	Smith, Carl Reginald b: 4/2/45, Shreveport, La. BB/TR, 6', 195 lbs. Deb: 9/18/66																								
1966	Bos-A	6	26	1	4	1	0	0	0	0	5	.154	.154	.192	-1	-3	-4	1	0	0	0	.944	1	/O	-0.4

YEAR	TM/L	G	AB	R	H	2B	3B	HR	RBI	BB	SO	AVG	OBP	SLG	PRO+	BR	/A	RC	SB	CS	SBR	FA	FR	POS	TPR
1967	*Bos-A	158	565	78	139	24	6	15	61	57	95	.246	.316	.389	99	5	-0	71	16	6	1	.983	17	*O/2	1.2
1968	Bos-A	155	558	78	148	**37**	5	15	69	64	77	.265	.345	.430	125	23	19	80	22	18	-4	.985	10	*O	1.9
1969	Bos-A★	143	543	87	168	29	7	25	93	54	67	.309	.373	.527	142	34	30	99	7	13	-6	.959	6	*O	2.4
1970	Bos-A	147	580	109	176	32	7	22	74	51	60	.303	.364	.497	126	26	21	102	10	7	-1	.977	16	*O	2.9
1971	Bos-A	159	618	85	175	**33**	2	30	96	63	82	.283	.354	.489	128	28	23	106	11	3	2	.966	16	*O	3.4
1972	Bos-A★	131	467	75	126	25	4	21	74	68	63	.270	.367	.475	142	29	26	85	15	4	2	.981	5	*O	3.0
1973	Bos-A	115	423	79	128	23	2	21	69	68	49	.303	.400	.515	148	33	29	88	3	2	-0	.983	7	*O/1D	3.1
1974	StL-N★	143	517	79	160	26	9	23	100	71	70	.309	.394	.528	158	38	39	105	4	3	-1	.976	5	*O/1	3.9
1975	StL-N★	135	477	67	144	26	3	19	76	63	59	.302	.387	.488	137	27	25	87	9	7	-2	.963	-7	O1/3	1.0
1976	StL-N	47	170	20	37	7	1	8	23	14	28	.218	.281	.412	94	-2	-2	18	1	2	-1	.986	6	1O3	0.1
	LA-N	65	225	35	63	8	4	10	26	18	42	.280	.336	.484	133	8	8	36	2	0	1	.985	2	O/3	1.0
	Yr	112	395	55	100	15	5	18	49	32	70	.253	.312	.453	116	6	6	54	3	2	-0	.989	9	O13	1.1
1977	*LA-N★	148	488	104	150	27	4	32	87	104	76	.307	**.432**	.576	**168**	50	51	129	7	5	-1	.980	-8	*O	3.6
1978	*LA-N★	128	447	82	132	27	2	29	93	70	90	.295	.392	.559	**164**	38	38	102	12	5	1	.950	-6	*O	2.8
1979	LA-N	68	234	41	64	13	1	10	32	31	50	.274	.363	.466	126	8	9	39	6	5	-1	.988	4	O	0.9
1980	LA-N★	92	311	47	100	13	0	15	55	41	63	.322	.402	.508	155	22	23	64	5	6	-2	.994	6	O	2.5
1981	*LA-N	41	35	5	7	1	0	1	8	7	8	.200	.333	.314	88	-1	-0	3	0	0	0	1.000	0	/1	0.0
1982	SF-N	106	349	51	99	11	0	18	56	46	46	.284	.367	.470	133	15	15	61	7	0	2	.982	2	1	1.5
Total	17	1987	7033	1123	2020	363	57	314	1092	890	1030	.287	.370	.489	136	379	351	1277	137	86	-11	.976	81	*O1/3D2	34.8

■ CHARLIE SMITH Smith, Charles J. b: 12/11/1840, Brooklyn, N.Y. d: 11/15/1897, Great Neck, N.Y. 5'10.5", 150 lbs. Deb: 5/18/1871

YEAR	TM/L	G	AB	R	H	2B	3B	HR	RBI	BB	SO	AVG	OBP	SLG	PRO+	BR	/A	RC	SB	CS	SBR	FA	FR	POS	TPR
1871	Mut-n	14	72	15	19	2	1	0	5	1	1	.264	.274	.319	77	-3	-1	8	6					3/2	-0.1

■ POP SMITH Smith, Charles Marvin b: 10/12/1856, Digby, N.S., Canada d: 4/18/27, Boston, Mass. BR/TR, 5'11", 170 lbs. Deb: 5/01/1880

YEAR	TM/L	G	AB	R	H	2B	3B	HR	RBI	BB	SO	AVG	OBP	SLG	PRO+	BR	/A	RC	SB	CS	SBR	FA	FR	POS	TPR
1880	Cin-N	83	334	35	69	10	9	0	27	6	36	.207	.221	.290	72	-10	-9	22				.855	-11	*2	-1.6
1881	Cle-N	10	34	1	4	0	0	0	3	0	8	.118	.118	.118	-27	-5	-4	0				.838	-2	3	-0.6
	Wor-N	11	41	1	3	0	0	0	2	3	5	.073	.136	.073	-31	-6	-6	0				.955	2	/O2	-0.4
	Buf-N	3	11	3	0	0	0	0	1	3	5	.000	.214	.000	-27	-1	-1	0				.840	-1	/2	-0.2
	Yr	24	86	5	7	0	0	0	6	6	18	.081	.141	.081	-28	-12	-12	1				.838	-1	3/O2	-1.2
1882	Bal-a	1	3	0	0	0	0	0		0		.000	.000	.000	-99	-1	-1	0				1.000	-0	/O	-0.1
	Lou-a	3	11	1	2	0	0	0		0		.182	.182	.182	24	-1	-1	0				.778	-0	/S	-0.1
	Yr	4	14	1	2	0	0	0		0		.143	.143	.143	-4	-1	-1	0				.778	-0	/SO	-0.2
1883	Col-a	97	405	82	106	14	**17**	4		22		.262	.300	.410	137	12	17	51				.889	18	*23/P	3.1
1884	Col-a	108	445	78	106	18	10	6		20		.238	.289	.364	124	7	13	48				.905	29	*2	4.0
1885	Pit-a	106	453	85	113	11	13	0		25		.249	.293	.331	101	-0	1	45				.922	33	*2	3.4
1886	Pit-a	126	483	75	105	20	9	2		42		.217	.288	.308	89	-6	-6	55	38			**.895**	21	*S2/C	1.5
1887	Pit-N	122	456	69	98	12	7	2	54	30	48	.215	.283	.285	63	-24	-19	46	30			.914	-6	*2S	-1.9
1888	Pit-N	131	481	61	99	15	2	4	52	22	78	.206	.248	.270	72	-17	-12	42	37			.901	-2	S2	-1.0
1889	Pit-N	72	258	26	54	10	2	5	27	24	38	.209	.292	.322	80	-10	-5	28	12			.897	0	S/23O	-0.2
	Bos-N	59	208	21	54	13	4	0	32	23	30	.260	.345	.361	93	0	-2	30	11			.890	-0	S	0.1
	Yr	131	466	47	108	23	6	5	59	47	68	.232	.315	.339	87	-10	-7	59	23			.894	-0	*S/23O	-0.1
1890	Bos-N	134	463	82	106	16	12	1	53	80	81	.229	.353	.322	92	3	-3	68	39			.918	-20	*2/S	-1.4
1891	Was-a	27	90	13	16	2	2	0	13	13	16	.178	.295	.244	60	-5	-4	7	2			.919	7	2/S3	0.4
Total	12	1093	4176	633	935	141	87	24	264	313	345	.224	.288	.317	89	-63	-44	445	169			.904	68	2S/3OPC	5.0

■ CHARLEY SMITH Smith, Charles William b: 9/15/37, Charleston, S.C. BR/TR, 6', 177 lbs. Deb: 9/08/60

YEAR	TM/L	G	AB	R	H	2B	3B	HR	RBI	BB	SO	AVG	OBP	SLG	PRO+	BR	/A	RC	SB	CS	SBR	FA	FR	POS	TPR
1960	LA-N	18	60	2	10	1	1	0	5	1	15	.167	.180	.217	8	-8	-8	3	0	0	0	.953	0	3	-0.8
1961	LA-N	9	24	4	6	1	0	2	3	1	6	.250	.280	.542	103	0	-0	4	0	0	0	1.000	-0	/3S	0.0
	Phi-N	112	411	43	102	13	4	9	47	23	76	.248	.296	.365	75	-16	-15	43	3	4	-2	.924	-2	3S	-1.7
	Yr	121	435	47	108	14	4	11	50	24	82	.248	.295	.375	77	-15	-15	47	3	4	-2	.926	-3	3S	-1.7
1962	Chi-A	65	145	11	30	4	0	2	17	9	32	.207	.258	.276	44	-12	-11	9	0	1	-1	.944	2	3	-1.0
1963	Chi-A	4	7	0	2	0	1	0	1	0	2	.286	.286	.571	136	0	0	1	0	0	0	1.000	2	/S	0.2
1964	Chi-A	2	7	1	1	0	1	0	0	1	1	.143	.250	.429	87	-0	-0	0	0	0	0	1.000	3	/3	0.3
	NY-N	127	443	44	106	12	0	20	58	19	101	.239	.275	.402	90	-8	-7	47	2	2	-1	.917	-13	3SO	-2.1
1965	NY-N	135	499	49	122	20	3	16	62	17	123	.244	.275	.393	89	-11	-9	50	2	1	0	.957	10	*3/S2	-0.1
1966	StL-N	116	391	34	104	13	4	10	43	22	81	.266	.305	.396	93	-4	-4	45	0	2	-1	.964	-1	*3/S	-0.9
1967	NY-A	135	425	38	95	15	3	9	38	32	110	.224	.279	.336	84	-10	-9	37	0	2	-1	.947	11	*3	0.0
1968	NY-A	46	70	2	16	4	1	1	7	5	18	.229	.280	.357	95	-1	-1	7	0	0	0	.961	4	3	0.3
1969	Chi-N	2	2	0	0	0	0	0	0	0	0	.000	.000	.000	-89	-1	-1	0	0	0	0	.000	0	H	-0.1
Total	10	771	2484	228	594	83	18	69	281	130	565	.239	.281	.370	82	-70	-65	246	7	12	-5	.945	14	3/SO2	-5.9

■ CHRIS SMITH Smith, Christopher William b: 7/18/57, Torrance, Cal. BB/TR, 6', 185 lbs. Deb: 5/14/81

YEAR	TM/L	G	AB	R	H	2B	3B	HR	RBI	BB	SO	AVG	OBP	SLG	PRO+	BR	/A	RC	SB	CS	SBR	FA	FR	POS	TPR
1981	Mon-N	7	7	0	0	0	0	0	0	0	2	.000	.000	.000	-99	-2	-2	0	0	0	0	1.000	0	/2	-0.2
1982	Mon-N	2	2	0	0	0	0	0	0	0	1	.000	.000	.000	-98	-1	-1	0	0	0	0	.000	0	/H	-0.1
1983	SF-N	22	67	13	22	6	1	1	11	7	12	.328	.408	.493	153	5	5	14	0	0	0	.976	-2	1/O3	0.2
Total	3	31	76	13	22	6	1	1	11	7	15	.289	.365	.434	124	2	2	14	0	0	0	.903	-2	/1O32	-0.1

■ EARL SMITH Smith, Earl Calvin b: 3/14/28, Sunnyside, Wash. BR/TR, 6', 185 lbs. Deb: 4/14/55

YEAR	TM/L	G	AB	R	H	2B	3B	HR	RBI	BB	SO	AVG	OBP	SLG	PRO+	BR	/A	RC	SB	CS	SBR	FA	FR	POS	TPR
1955	Pit-N	5	16	1	1	0	0	0	0	4	2	.063	.286	.063	-1	-2	-2	1	0	0	0	1.000	-0	/O	-0.3

■ EARL SMITH Smith, Earl Leonard "Sheriff" b: 1/20/1891, Oak Hill, Ohio d: 3/14/43, Portsmouth, Ohio BB/TR, 5'11", 170 lbs. Deb: 9/12/16

YEAR	TM/L	G	AB	R	H	2B	3B	HR	RBI	BB	SO	AVG	OBP	SLG	PRO+	BR	/A	RC	SB	CS	SBR	FA	FR	POS	TPR
1916	Chi-N	14	27	2	7	1	1	0	4	2	5	.259	.310	.370	98	0	-0	4	1			.800	-3	/O	-0.3
1917	StL-A	52	199	31	56	7	7	0	10	15	21	.281	.332	.387	124	4	5	27	5			.977	6	O	0.8
1918	StL-A	89	286	28	77	10	5	0	32	13	16	.269	.303	.339	97	-3	-2	33	13			.952	1	O	-0.6
1919	StL-A	88	252	21	63	12	5	1	36	18	27	.250	.300	.349	80	-7	-7	27	1			.971	10	O	-0.2
1920	StL-A	103	353	45	108	21	8	3	55	13	18	.306	.336	.436	100	0	-1	51	11	4	1	.916	-5	3O	-0.3
1921	StL-A	25	78	7	26	4	2	2	14	3	4	.333	.366	.513	115	2	2	14	0	0	0	.878	-3	3/O	-0.1
	Was-A	59	180	20	39	5	2	2	12	10	19	.217	.266	.300	46	-16	-14	15	1	0	0	.949	4	O/3	-1.3
	Yr	84	258	27	65	9	4	4	26	13	23	.252	.296	.364	69	-13	-13	28	1	0	0	.944	0	O3	-1.4
1922	Was-A	65	205	22	53	12	2	1	23	8	17	.259	.293	.351	71	-10	-9	20	4	4	-1	.917	1	O/3	-1.2
Total	7	495	1580	176	429	72	32	9	186	82	127	.272	.311	.375	90	-30	-28	191	36	8			11	O/3	-3.2

■ EARL SMITH Smith, Earl Sutton "Oil" b: 2/14/1897, Hot Springs, Ark. d: 6/8/63, Little Rock, Ark. BL/TR, 5'10.5", 180 lbs. Deb: 4/24/19

YEAR	TM/L	G	AB	R	H	2B	3B	HR	RBI	BB	SO	AVG	OBP	SLG	PRO+	BR	/A	RC	SB	CS	SBR	FA	FR	POS	TPR
1919	NY-N	21	36	5	9	2	1	0	8	3	3	.250	.308	.361	102	-0	0	4	1			.973	-3	C/2	-0.2
1920	NY-N	91	262	20	77	7	1	1	30	18	16	.294	.344	.340	98	-1	-0	31	5	2	0	.976	-5	C	0.0
1921	*NY-N	89	229	35	77	8	4	10	51	27	8	.336	.409	.537	148	16	16	50	4	3	-1	.965	-10	C	0.9
1922	*NY-N	90	234	29	65	11	4	9	39	37	12	.278	.383	.474	119	7	7	44	1	1	-0	.978	-2	C	0.8
1923	NY-N	24	34	2	7	1	1	1	4	4	1	.206	.289	.382	77	-1	-1	4	0	0	0	.975	2	C	0.1
	Bos-N	72	191	22	55	15	1	3	19	22	10	.288	.364	.424	112	2	3	30	0	1	-1	.975	-4	C	0.2
	Yr	96	225	24	62	16	2	4	23	26	11	.276	.353	.418	106	1	2	34	0	1	-1	.975	-2	C	0.3
1924	Bos-N	33	59	1	16	3	0	0	8	6	3	.271	.338	.322	81	-2	-1	6	0	1	-1	.946	-1	C	-0.2
	Pit-N	39	111	12	41	10	1	4	21	13	4	.369	.435	.586	168	11	11	29	2	0	1	.974	0	C	1.4
	Yr	72	170	13	57	13	1	4	29	19	7	.335	.402	.494	140	10	10	34	2	1	0	.967	-1	C	1.2
1925	*Pit-N	109	329	34	103	22	3	8	64	31	13	.313	.374	.471	107	7	4	59	4	1	1	.968	11	C	1.9

YEAR	TM/L	G	AB	R	H	2B	3B	HR	RBI	BB	SO	AVG	OBP	SLG	PRO+	BR	/A	RC	SB	CS	SBR	FA	FR	POS	TPR
1926	Pit-N	105	292	29	101	17	2	2	46	28	7	.346	.407	.438	121	12	10	52	1			.964	4	C	1.9
1927	*Pit-N	66	189	16	51	3	1	5	25	21	11	.270	.346	.376	87	-2	-3	25	0			.986	-4	C	-0.4
1928	Pit-N	32	85	8	21	6	0	2	11	11	7	.247	.333	.388	85	-2	-2	11	0			.967	-4	C	-0.4
	*StL-N	24	58	3	13	2	0	0	7	5	4	.224	.286	.259	42	-5	-5	4	0			1.000	-1	C	-0.4
	Yr	56	143	11	34	8	0	2	18	16	11	.238	.314	.336	68	-6	-7	15	0			.980	-5	C	-0.8
1929	StL-N	57	145	9	50	8	0	1	22	18	6	.345	.417	.421	107	3	3	26	0			.962	-5	C	0.1
1930	StL-N	8	10	0	0	0	0	0	0	3	1	.000	.231	.000	-36	-2	-2	0	0			.913	1	/C	-0.1
Total	12	860	2264	225	686	115	19	46	355	247	106	.303	.374	.432	111	45	38	377	18	9		.952	-20	C/2	5.6

■ EDGAR SMITH	Smith, Edgar Eugene b: 6/12/1862, Providence, R.I. d: 11/3/1892, Providence, R.I. BR/TR, 5'10", 160 lbs. Deb: 5/25/1883																								
1883	Pro-N	2	9	2	2	1	0	0	1	0	2	.222	.222	.333	64	-0	-0	1				1.000	-0	/1O	-0.1
	Phi-N	1	4	1	3	0	0	0	1	0	0	.750	.750	.750	393	1	1	2				.000	-1	/PO	0.0
	Yr	3	13	3	5	1	0	0	2	0	2	.385	.385	.462	158	1	1	2				1.000	-1	/O1P	-0.1
1884	Was-a	14	57	5	5	0	1	0		1		.088	.103	.123	-29	-7	-6	1				.794	5	O/P	-0.1
1885	Pro-N	1	4	0	1	0	0	0	0	0	0	.250	.250	.250	65	-0	-0	0				.750	0	/P	0.0
1890	Cle-N	8	24	2	7	0	1	0	4	4	1	.292	.393	.375	129	1	1	4	0			.900	1	/PO	0.0
Total	4	26	98	10	18	1	2	0	6	5	3	.184	.223	.235	49	-6	-5	8	0			.821	5	/OP1	-0.2

■ MAYO SMITH	Smith, Edward Mayo b: 1/17/15, New London, Mo. d: 11/24/77, Boynton Beach, Fla BL/TR, 6', 183 lbs. Deb: 6/24/45 M																								
1945	Phi-A	73	203	18	43	5	0	0	11	36	13	.212	.333	.236	67	-7	-7	19	0	1	-1	.976	-8	O	-2.0

■ ELMER SMITH	Smith, Elmer Ellsworth b: 3/23/1868, Pittsburgh, Pa. d: 11/3/45, Pittsburgh, Pa. BL/TL, 5'11", 178 lbs. Deb: 5/31/1886																								
1886	Cin-a	10	32	7	9	1	1	0		9		.281	.439	.375	153	3	3	5	0			.667	-3	P/O	0.0
1887	Cin-a	52	186	26	47	10	6	0		11		.253	.298	.371	86	-3	-4	23	5			.851	-6	P/O	-0.1
1888	Cin-a	40	129	15	29	4	1	0	9	20		.225	.329	.271	92	0	-1	12	2			.838	-6	P/O	-0.1
1889	Cin-a	29	83	12	23	3	1	2	17	7	18	.277	.348	.410	114	2	1	12	1			.821	-4	P	0.0
1892	Pit-N	138	511	86	140	16	14	4	63	82	43	.274	.375	.384	131	22	22	84	22			.885	-5	*OP	0.9
1893	Pit-N	128	518	121	179	26	23	7	103	77	23	.346	.435	.525	160	43	45	133	26			.921	3	*O	3.4
1894	Pit-N	125	489	128	174	33	19	6	72	65	12	.356	.436	.538	137	29	30	133	33			.933	4	*O/P	2.0
1895	Pit-N	124	480	88	145	14	12	1	81	55	25	.302	.381	.387	106	2	7	86	34			.896	-3	*O	-0.5
1896	Pit-N	122	484	121	175	21	14	6	94	74	18	.362	.454	.500	160	41	45	129	33			.946	9	*O	3.6
1897	Pit-N	123	467	99	145	19	17	6	54	70		.310	.408	.463	135	22	25	102	25			.904	3	*O	1.6
1898	Cin-N	123	486	79	166	21	10	1	66	69		.342	.425	.432	136	32	27	101	20			.949	4	*O/P	2.0
1899	Cin-N	87	339	65	101	13	6	1	24	47		.298	.385	.381	108	6	5	56	10			.922	-1	O	-0.2
1900	Cin-N	29	111	14	31	4	4	1	18	18		.279	.389	.414	125	4	4	20	5			.930	0	O	0.2
	NY-N	85	312	47	81	9	7	2	34	24		.260	.315	.353	88	-7	-5	41	14			.953	-8	O	-1.8
	Yr	114	423	61	112	13	11	3	52	42		.265	.335	.369	98	-3	-1	61	19			.944	-8	*O	-1.6
1901	Pit-N	4	4	0	0	0	0	0	0	2		.000	.333	.000	1	-0	-0	0	0			1.000	-0	/O	-0.1
	Bos-N	16	57	5	10	2	1	0	3	6		.175	.254	.246	42	-4	-5	4	2			.833	-3	O	-0.9
	Yr	20	61	5	10	2	1	0	3	8		.164	.261	.230	40	-4	-5	4	2			.846	-3	O	-1.0
Total	14	1235	4688	913	1455	196	136	37	638	636	139	.310	.397	.434	128	191	199	942	232			.921	-18	*OP	10.0

■ ELMER SMITH	Smith, Elmer John b: 9/21/1892, Sandusky, Ohio d: 8/3/84, Columbia, Ky. BL/TR, 5'10", 165 lbs. Deb: 9/20/14																								
1914	Cle-A	13	53	5	17	3	0	0	8	2	11	.321	.345	.377	113	1	1	7	1	1	-0	1.000	1	O	0.1
1915	Cle-A	144	476	37	118	23	12	3	67	36	75	.248	.301	.366	97	-3	-4	53	10	11	-4	.923	0	*O	-1.4
1916	Cle-A	79	213	25	59	15	3	3	40	18	35	.277	.336	.418	119	6	4	32	3			.966	-2	O	0.0
	Was-A	45	168	12	36	10	3	2	27	18	28	.214	.298	.345	94	-2	-2	19	4			.988	1	O	-0.3
	Yr	124	381	37	95	25	6	5	67	36	63	.249	.319	.386	108	4	2	51	7			.976	-1	*O	-0.3
1917	Was-A	35	117	8	26	4	3	0	17	5	14	.222	.260	.308	74	-4	-4	10	1			.901	-0	O	-0.7
	Cle-A	64	161	21	42	5	1	3	22	13	18	.261	.316	.360	99	1	-1	20	6			.986	-1	O	-0.4
	Yr	99	278	29	68	9	4	3	39	18	32	.245	.293	.338	89	-4	-5	29	7			.943	-1	O	-1.1
1919	Cle-A	114	395	60	110	24	6	9	54	41	30	.278	.354	.438	115	11	8	64	15			.957	-6	*O	-0.6
1920	*Cle-A	129	456	82	144	37	10	12	103	53	35	.316	.391	.520	135	25	23	93	5	4	-1	.970	-8	*O	0.6
1921	Cle-A	129	431	98	125	28	9	16	85	56	46	.290	.374	.508	121	14	13	83	0	2	-1	.971	-8	*O	-0.4
1922	Bos-A	73	231	43	66	13	6	6	32	25	21	.286	.358	.472	116	4	5	39	0	3	-2	.947	2	O	0.1
	*NY-A	21	27	1	5	0	0	1	5	3	5	.185	.267	.296	46	-2	-2	2	0	0	0	.933	-2	O	-0.4
	Yr	94	258	44	71	13	6	7	37	28	26	.275	.348	.453	108	2	2	41	0	3	-2	.945	1	O	-0.3
1923	NY-A	70	183	30	56	6	2	7	35	21	21	.306	.377	.475	121	6	5	34	3	1	0	.948	-2	O	0.1
1925	Cin-N	96	284	47	77	13	7	8	46	28	20	.271	.339	.451	102	-1	0	43	6	5	-1	.967	-5	O	-1.0
Total	10	1012	3195	469	881	181	62	70	541	319	359	.276	.344	.437	112	55	46	499	54	27		.957	-29	O	-4.3

■ MIKE SMITH	Smith, Elwood Hope b: 11/16/04, Norfolk, Va. d: 5/31/81, Chesapeake, Va. BL/TR, 5'11.5", 170 lbs. Deb: 9/04/26																								
1926	NY-N	4	7	0	1	0	0	0	0	0	2	.143	.143	.143	-23	-1	-1	0	0			1.000	0	/O	-0.1

■ CARR SMITH	Smith, Emanuel Carr b: 4/8/01, Kernersville, N.C. d: 4/14/89, Miami, Fla. BR/TR, 6'1", 175 lbs. Deb: 9/23/23																								
1923	Was-A	5	9	0	1	1	0	0	1	0	0	.111	.111	.222	-14	-2	-1	0	0	0	0	1.000	-1	/O	-0.3
1924	Was-A	5	10	1	2	0	0	0	0	0	3	.200	.200	.200	3	-1	-1	0	0	0	0	1.000	-1	/O	-0.3
Total	2	10	19	1	3	1	0	0	1	0	3	.158	.158	.211	-5	-3	-3	1	0	0	0	1.000	-3	/O	-0.6

■ ERNIE SMITH	Smith, Ernest Henry "Kansas City Kid" b: 10/11/1899, Totowa, N.J. d: 4/6/73, Brooklyn, N.Y. BR/TR, 5'8", 155 lbs. Deb: 4/17/30																								
1930	Chi-A	24	79	5	19	3	0	0	3	5	6	.241	.286	.278	45	-7	-6	7	2	0	1	.920	0	S	-0.3

■ FRANK SMITH	Smith, Frank L. b: 11/24/1857, Canada d: 10/11/28, Canandaigua, N.Y. Deb: 8/06/1884																								
1884	Pit-a	10	36	3	9	0	1	0		0		.250	.250	.306	81	-1	-1	3				.930	-3	/CO	-0.3

■ FRED SMITH	Smith, Fred Vincent b: 7/29/1886, Cleveland, Ohio d: 5/28/61, Cleveland, Ohio BR/TR, 5'11.5", 185 lbs. Deb: 4/17/13 F																								
1913	Bos-N	92	285	35	65	9	3	0	27	29	55	.228	.302	.281	65	-12	-13	26	7			.920	-15	32S/O	-2.8
1914	Buf-F	145	473	48	104	12	10	2	45	49	78	.220	.297	.300	69	-18	-20	52	24			.930	-0	*3S/1	-1.4
1915	Buf-F	35	114	8	27	2	4	0	11	13	15	.237	.320	.325	88	-1	-2	13	2			.920	3	S/3	0.4
	Bro-F	110	385	41	95	16	6	5	58	25	49	.247	.298	.358	93	-5	-4	50	21			.920	1	S3	0.5
	Yr	145	499	49	122	18	10	5	69	38	64	.244	.303	.351	92	-6	-6	63	23			.920	4	*S3	0.9
1917	StL-N	56	165	11	30	0	2	1	17	17	22	.182	.262	.224	51	-9	-9	10	4			.950	7	3/2S	-0.1
Total	4	438	1422	143	321	39	25	8	158	133	219	.226	.296	.305	74	-46	-47	152	58			.932	-4	3S/201	-3.4

■ GEORGE SMITH	Smith, George Cornelius b: 7/7/37, St.Petersburg, Fla. d: 6/15/87, St.Petersburg, Fla. BR/TR, 5'10", 170 lbs. Deb: 8/04/63																								
1963	Det-A	52	171	16	37	8	2	0	17	18	34	.216	.298	.287	63	-8	-8	16	4	0	1	.982	11	2	0.9
1964	Det-A	5	7	1	2	0	0	0	2	1	4	.286	.375	.286	86	-0	-0	1	1	0	0	1.000	1	/2	0.1
1965	Det-A	32	53	6	5	0	0	1	1	3	18	.094	.143	.151	-16	-8	-8	1	0	0	0	.984	3	2/S3	-0.5
1966	Bos-A	128	403	41	86	19	4	8	37	37	86	.213	.284	.340	71	-11	-16	39	4	0	1	.969	16	*2S	1.0
Total	4	217	634	64	130	27	6	9	57	59	142	.205	.278	.309	62	-27	-33	57	9	0	3	.944	30	2/S3	1.5

■ HEINIE SMITH	Smith, George Henry b: 10/24/1871, Pittsburgh, Pa. d: 6/25/39, Buffalo, N.Y. BR/TR, 5'9.5", 160 lbs. Deb: 9/08/1897 M																								
1897	Lou-N	21	76	7	20	3	0	1	7	3		.263	.300	.342	72	-4	-3	8	1			.928	-2	2	-0.4
1898	Lou-N	35	121	14	23	4	0	0	13	6		.190	.240	.223	34	-11	-10	9	6			.910	-6	2	-1.4
1899	Pit-N	15	53	9	15	3	1	0	12	5		.283	.345	.377	98	-0	-0	8	2			.851	-4	2/S	-0.3

YEAR	TM/L	G	AB	R	H	2B	3B	HR	RBI	BB	SO	AVG	OBP	SLG	PRO+	BR	/A	RC	SB	CS	SBR	FA	FR	POS	TPR
1901	NY-N	9	29	5	6	2	1	1	4	1		.207	.233	.448	99	-0	-0	3	1			.969	-1	/2P	-0.1
1902	NY-N	138	511	46	129	19	2	0	33	17		.252	.279	.297	79	-14	-14	53	32			.953	4	*2M	-0.6
1903	Det-A	93	336	36	75	11	3	1	22	19		.223	.271	.283	68	-14	-12	32	12			.928	-2	2	-1.1
Total	6	311	1126	117	268	42	7	3	91	51		.238	.276	.296	71	-43	-40	113	54			.934	-11	2/PS	-3.9

■ GERMANY SMITH
Smith, George J. b: 4/21/1863, Pittsburgh, Pa. d: 12/1/27, Altoona, Pa. BR/TR, 6', 175 lbs. Deb: 4/17/1884

YEAR	TM/L	G	AB	R	H	2B	3B	HR	RBI	BB	SO	AVG	OBP	SLG	PRO+	BR	/A	RC	SB	CS	SBR	FA	FR	POS	TPR
1884	Alt-U	25	108	9	34	8	1	0		1		.315	.321	.407	143	5	4	14				.871	6	S/P	0.9
	Cle-N	72	291	31	74	14	4	4	26	2	45	.254	.259	.371	93	-2	-3	29				.879	9	2S	0.7
1885	Bro-a	108	419	63	108	17	11	4		10		.258	.275	.379	107	3	2	45				.884	**40**	*S	3.9
1886	Bro-a	105	426	66	105	17	6	2		19		.246	.279	.329	91	-5	-6	46	22			.860	13	*S/OC	0.7
1887	Bro-a	103	435	79	128	19	16	4		13		.294	.316	.439	110	4	3	70	26			**.886**	**32**	*S/3	2.9
1888	Bro-a	103	402	47	86	10	7	3	61	22		.214	.255	.296	79	-10	-9	38	27			.844	6	*S/2	-0.1
1889	*Bro-a	121	446	89	103	22	3	3	53	40	42	.231	.296	.314	75	-14	-14	53	35			.899	-4	*S/O	-1.0
1890	*Bro-N	129	481	76	92	6	5	1	47	42	23	.191	.260	.231	45	-33	-33	36	24			.904	4	*S	-2.0
1891	Cin-N	138	512	50	103	11	5	3	53	38	32	.201	.258	.260	52	-31	-31	39	16			.909	11	*S	-1.1
1892	Cin-N	139	506	58	121	13	6	8	63	42	52	.239	.297	.336	94	-5	-4	58	19			.920	25	*S	2.4
1893	Cin-N	130	500	63	118	18	6	4	56	38	20	.236	.293	.320	63	-26	-29	52	14			**.934**	20	*S	-0.3
1894	Cin-N	127	482	73	127	33	5	3	76	41	28	.263	.324	.371	66	-25	-29	65	15			.911	20	*S	-0.2
1895	Cin-N	127	503	75	151	23	6	4	74	34	24	.300	.345	.394	88	-7	-10	75	13			.923	2	*S	-0.2
1896	Cin-N	120	456	65	131	21	9	3	71	28	22	.287	.330	.393	86	-6	-11	69	22			.926	-10	*S	-1.5
1897	Bro-N	112	428	47	86	17	3	0	29	14		.201	.233	.255	30	-45	-41	27	1			.908	-11	*S	-4.3
1898	StL-N	51	157	16	25	2	1	1	9	24		.159	.275	.204	37	-12	-13	10	1			.904	-7	S	-1.6
Total	15	1710	6552	907	1592	251	94	47	618	408	288	.243	.289	.332	76	-210	-224	726	235			.902	155	*S/23OCP	-0.8

■ GREG SMITH
Smith, Gregory Allen b: 4/5/67, Baltimore, Md. BB/TR, 5'11", 170 lbs. Deb: 9/02/89

YEAR	TM/L	G	AB	R	H	2B	3B	HR	RBI	BB	SO	AVG	OBP	SLG	PRO+	BR	/A	RC	SB	CS	SBR	FA	FR	POS	TPR
1989	Chi-N	4	5	1	2	0	0	0	2	0	0	.400	.500	.400	149	0	0	1	0	0	0	.778	0	/2	0.1
1990	Chi-N	18	44	4	9	2	1	0	5	2	5	.205	.239	.295	43	-3	-4	3	1	0	0	1.000	4	/2S	0.1
1991	LA-N	5	3	1	0	0	0	0	0	0	2	.000	.000	.000	-99	-1	-1	0	0	0	0	.000	0	/2	-0.1
Total	3	27	52	6	11	2	1	0	7	2	7	.212	.255	.288	47	-4	-4	4	1	0	0	.944	4	/2S	0.1

■ HAL SMITH
Smith, Harold Raymond "Cura" b: 6/1/31, Barling, Ark. BR/TR, 5'11", 189 lbs. Deb: 5/02/56 C

YEAR	TM/L	G	AB	R	H	2B	3B	HR	RBI	BB	SO	AVG	OBP	SLG	PRO+	BR	/A	RC	SB	CS	SBR	FA	FR	POS	TPR
1956	StL-N	75	227	27	64	12	0	5	23	15	22	.282	.326	.401	94	-2	-2	28	1	0	0	.982	-2	C	-0.1
1957	StL-N☆	100	333	25	93	12	3	2	37	18	18	.279	.316	.351	78	-10	-11	35	2	2	-1	.990	-1	C	-0.8
1958	StL-N	77	220	13	50	4	1	1	24	14	14	.227	.274	.268	42	-17	-19	16	0	0	0	.989	-1	C	-1.6
1959	StL-N★	142	452	35	122	15	3	13	50	15	28	.270	.295	.403	78	-12	-15	47	2	6	-3	.989	5	*C	-0.6
1960	StL-N	127	337	20	77	16	0	2	28	29	33	.228	.292	.294	56	-18	-21	27	1	0	0	.990	18	*C	0.3
1961	StL-N	45	125	6	31	4	1	0	10	11	12	.248	.314	.296	57	-6	-8	12	0	0	0	.993	17	C	1.1
1965	Pit-N	4	3	0	0	0	0	0	0	0	1	.000	.000	.000	-99	-1	-1	0	0	0	0	1.000	2	/C	0.1
Total	7	570	1697	126	437	63	8	23	172	102	128	.258	.301	.345	69	-66	-77	165	6	8	-3	.933	38	C	-1.6

■ HAL SMITH
Smith, Harold Wayne b: 12/7/30, W.Frankfort, Ill. BR/TR, 6', 195 lbs. Deb: 4/11/55

YEAR	TM/L	G	AB	R	H	2B	3B	HR	RBI	BB	SO	AVG	OBP	SLG	PRO+	BR	/A	RC	SB	CS	SBR	FA	FR	POS	TPR
1955	Bal-A	135	424	41	115	23	4	4	52	30	21	.271	.322	.373	93	-9	-5	47	1	3	-2	.986	-3	*C	-0.5
1956	Bal-A	77	229	16	60	14	0	3	18	17	22	.262	.316	.362	85	-7	-5	22	1	0	0	.994	3	C	0.1
	KC-A	37	142	15	39	9	2	2	24	3	12	.275	.290	.408	82	-4	-4	16	1	1	-0	.986	1	C	-0.2
	Yr	114	371	31	99	23	2	5	42	20	34	.267	.306	.380	85	-12	-9	38	2	1	0	.991	5	*C	-0.1
1957	KC-A	107	360	41	109	26	0	13	41	14	44	.303	.331	.483	118	8	7	52	2	2	-1	.983	-1	*C	1.0
1958	KC-A	99	315	32	86	19	2	5	46	25	47	.273	.330	.394	97	-1	-2	41	0	0	0	.949	-1	3C1	-0.1
1959	KC-A	108	292	36	84	12	0	5	31	34	39	.288	.368	.380	104	3	3	42	0	3	-2	.953	7	3C	0.9
1960	*Pit-N	77	258	37	76	18	2	11	45	22	48	.295	.355	.508	132	11	11	45	1	1	-0	.985	-6	C	0.9
1961	Pit-N	67	193	12	43	10	0	3	26	11	38	.223	.268	.321	55	-12	-13	16	0	0	0	.990	-1	C	-1.0
1962	Hou-N	109	345	32	81	14	0	12	35	24	55	.235	.288	.380	84	-12	-8	35	0	0	0	.986	2	C/31	-0.3
1963	Hou-N	31	58	1	14	2	0	0	2	4	15	.241	.290	.276	68	-3	-2	4	0	0	0	.985	-3	C	-0.5
1964	Cin-N	32	66	6	8	1	0	0	3	12	20	.121	.256	.136	14	-7	-8	2	1	0	0	.983	-3	C	-1.0
Total	10	879	2682	269	715	148	10	58	323	196	361	.267	.320	.394	94	-33	-26	323	7	10	-4	.989	-3	C3/1	-0.7

■ HARRY SMITH
Smith, Harry Thomas b: 10/31/1874, Yorkshire, England d: 2/17/33, Salem, N.J. BR/TR, Deb: 7/11/01 M

YEAR	TM/L	G	AB	R	H	2B	3B	HR	RBI	BB	SO	AVG	OBP	SLG	PRO+	BR	/A	RC	SB	CS	SBR	FA	FR	POS	TPR
1901	Phi-A	11	34	3	11	1	0	0	3	2		.324	.378	.353	99	0	0	5	1			.969	-2	/CO	-0.2
1902	Pit-N	50	185	14	35	4	1	0	12	4		.189	.211	.222	32	-15	-15	10	4			.972	-2	C	-1.3
1903	*Pit-N	61	212	15	37	3	2	0	19	12		.175	.219	.208	21	-22	-23	11	2			.974	-4	C/O	-2.0
1904	Pit-N	47	141	17	35	3	1	0	18	16		.248	.346	.284	93	0	-0	16	5			.964	-3	C/O	0.1
1905	Pit-N	1	3	0	0	0	0	0	1	0		.000	.000	.000	-98	-1	-1	0	1			1.000	0	/C	-0.1
1906	Pit-N	1	1	0	0	0	0	0	0	0		.000	.000	.000	-96	-0	-0	0	0			.800	0	/C	0.0
1907	Pit-N	18	38	4	10	1	0	0	1	4		.263	.364	.289	104	1	0	4	0			.939	-3	C	-0.1
1908	Bos-N	41	130	13	32	2	2	1	16	7		.246	.295	.315	97	-1	-1	13	2			.975	0	C	0.3
1909	Bos-N	43	113	9	19	4	1	0	4	5		.168	.203	.221	30	-9	-10	5	3			.972	2	CM	-0.6
1910	Bos-N	70	147	8	35	4	0	1	15	5	14	.238	.263	.286	57	-8	-9	12	5			.949	3	C	-0.3
Total	10	343	1004	83	214	22	7	2	89	55	14	.213	.262	.255	54	-54	-58	78	23				-9	C/O	-4.2

■ HARRY SMITH
Smith, Harry W. b: 2/5/1856, N.Vernon, Ind. d: 6/4/1898, N.Vernon, Ind. BR/TR, 6', 175 lbs. Deb: 5/08/1877

YEAR	TM/L	G	AB	R	H	2B	3B	HR	RBI	BB	SO	AVG	OBP	SLG	PRO+	BR	/A	RC	SB	CS	SBR	FA	FR	POS	TPR
1877	Chi-N	24	94	7	19	1	0	0	3	4	6	.202	.235	.213	37	-6	-8	5				.853	-7	2O	-1.4
	Cin-N	10	36	4	9	2	1	0	3	1	5	.250	.270	.361	109	-0	0	4				.879	1	/C2O	0.1
	Yr	34	130	11	28	3	1	0	6	5	11	.215	.244	.254	54	-6	-7	8				.837	-7	2O/C	-1.3
1889	Lou-a	1	2	0	1	0	0	0	1	0	1	.500	.500	.500	192	0	0	1	0			.000	-2	/OC	-0.1
Total	2	35	132	11	29	3	1	0	7	5	12	.220	.248	.258	56	-6	-7	9	0			.967	-8	/2OC	-1.4

■ HARVEY SMITH
Smith, Harvey Fetterhoff b: 7/24/1871, Union Deposit, Pa d: 11/12/62, Harrisburg, Pa. BL/TR, 5'8", 160 lbs. Deb: 8/19/1896

YEAR	TM/L	G	AB	R	H	2B	3B	HR	RBI	BB	SO	AVG	OBP	SLG	PRO+	BR	/A	RC	SB	CS	SBR	FA	FR	POS	TPR
1896	Was-N	36	131	21	36	7	2	0	17	12	7	.275	.345	.359	88	-2	-2	20	9			.861	3	3	0.1

■ HAPPY SMITH
Smith, Henry Joseph b: 7/14/1883, Coquille, Ore. d: 2/26/61, San Jose, Cal. BL/TR, 6', 185 lbs. Deb: 4/15/10

YEAR	TM/L	G	AB	R	H	2B	3B	HR	RBI	BB	SO	AVG	OBP	SLG	PRO+	BR	/A	RC	SB	CS	SBR	FA	FR	POS	TPR
1910	Bro-N	35	76	6	18	2	0	0	5	4	14	.237	.275	.263	59	-4	-4	6	4			.974	2	O	-0.2

■ JACK SMITH
Smith, Jack b: 6/23/1895, Chicago, Ill. d: 5/2/72, Westchester, Ill. BL/TL, 5'8", 165 lbs. Deb: 9/30/15

YEAR	TM/L	G	AB	R	H	2B	3B	HR	RBI	BB	SO	AVG	OBP	SLG	PRO+	BR	/A	RC	SB	CS	SBR	FA	FR	POS	TPR
1915	StL-N	4	16	2	3	0	1	0	0	1	5	.188	.235	.313	65	-1	-1	1	0			1.000	-1	/O	-0.2
1916	StL-N	130	357	43	87	6	5	6	34	20	50	.244	.291	.339	94	-3	-3	37	24	16	-2	.949	-11	*O	-2.5
1917	StL-N	137	462	64	137	16	11	3	34	38	65	.297	.351	.398	133	16	17	70	25			.961	-10	*O	0.1
1918	StL-N	42	166	24	35	2	1	0	4	7	21	.211	.260	.235	53	-9	-9	11	5			.941	1	O	-1.2
1919	StL-N	119	408	47	91	16	3	0	15	26	29	.223	.271	.277	69	-17	-15	37	30			.960	-0	*O	-2.5
1920	StL-N	91	313	53	104	22	5	1	28	25	23	.332	.385	.444	143	15	17	53	14	9	-1	.963	-10	O	0.0
1921	StL-N	116	411	86	135	22	9	7	33	21	24	.328	.361	.477	122	11	12	69	11	6	-0	.955	-6	*O	-0.2
1922	StL-N	143	510	117	158	23	12	8	46	50	30	.310	.375	.449	117	9	12	88	18	7	1	.951	-8	*O	-0.4
1923	StL-N	124	407	98	126	16	6	5	41	27	20	.310	.356	.415	105	1	3	61	32	11	3	.974	4	*O	0.3
1924	StL-N	124	459	91	130	18	6	2	33	33	27	.283	.333	.362	88	-9	-8	54	24	16	-2	.968	10	*O	-0.8
1925	StL-N	80	243	53	61	11	4	4	31	19	13	.251	.308	.379	73	-10	-11	31	20	2	5	.958	-3	O	-1.2
1926	StL-N	1	1	0	0	0	0	0	0	0	1	.000	.000	.000	-96	-0	-0	0	0			.000	0	H	0.0
	Bos-N	96	322	46	100	15	2	2	25	28	12	.311	.369	.388	114	2	6	46	11			.973	2	O	0.2

YEAR	TM/L	G	AB	R	H	2B	3B	HR	RBI	BB	SO	AVG	OBP	SLG	PRO+	BR	/A	RC	SB	CS	SBR	FA	FR	POS	TPR
	Yr	97	323	46	100	15	2	2	25	28	13	.310	.368	.387	113	2	6	46	11			.973	2	O	0.2
1927	Bos-N	84	183	27	58	6	4	1	24	16	12	.317	.375	.410	119	3	5	28	8			.950	-0	O	0.2
1928	Bos-N	96	254	30	71	9	2	1	32	21	14	.280	.335	.343	82	-8	-6	29	6			.988	1	O	-1.0
1929	Bos-N	19	20	2	5	0	0	0	2	2	2	.250	.318	.250	45	-2	-2	2	0			.833	-3	/O	-0.5
Total	15	1406	4532	783	1301	182	71	40	382	334	348	.287	.339	.385	103	-2	18	618	228	67		.961	-36	*O	-9.7
■ STUB SMITH	Smith, James A. b: 11/26/1876, Elmwood, Ill. BL/TR, 145 lbs. Deb: 9/10/1898																								
1898	Bos-N	3	10	1	1	0	0	0	0	0		.100	.100	.100	-41	-2	-2	0	0			.933	0	/S	-0.1
■ RED SMITH	Smith, James Carlisle b: 4/6/1890, Greenville, S.C. d: 10/11/66, Atlanta, Ga. BR/TR, 5'11", 165 lbs. Deb: 9/05/11																								
1911	Bro-N	28	111	10	29	6	1	0	19	5	13	.261	.299	.333	80	-4	-3	12	5			.900	-2	3	-0.5
1912	Bro-N	128	486	75	139	28	6	4	57	54	51	.286	.362	.393	111	5	7	77	22			.938	5	*3	1.3
1913	Bro-N	151	540	70	160	**40**	10	6	76	45	67	.296	.358	.441	124	18	16	90	22			.933	-3	*3	1.6
1914	Bro-N	90	330	39	81	10	8	4	48	30	26	.245	.310	.361	97	-1	-2	39	11			.937	12	3	1.5
	Bos-N	60	207	30	65	17	1	3	37	28	24	.314	.401	.449	153	14	14	39	4			.937	10	3	2.8
	Yr	150	537	69	146	27	9	7	85	58	50	.272	.346	.395	119	13	12	78	15			.937	23	*3	4.3
1915	Bos-N	157	549	66	145	34	4	2	65	67	49	.264	.345	.352	116	9	12	71	10	5	0	.947	-6	*3	1.4
1916	Bos-N	150	509	48	132	16	10	3	60	53	55	.259	.333	.348	114	6	9	66	13			.928	-4	*3	1.1
1917	Bos-N	147	505	60	149	31	6	2	62	53	61	.295	.369	.392	142	21	24	78	16			.925	-21	*3	0.7
1918	Bos-N	119	429	55	128	20	3	2	65	45	47	.298	.373	.373	133	16	18	63	8			.922	4	*3	2.7
1919	Bos-N	87	241	24	59	6	0	1	25	40	22	.245	.359	.282	98	1	2	27	6			.981	-0	O3	0.0
Total	9	1117	3907	477	1087	208	49	27	514	420	415	.278	.353	.377	120	85	97	562	117	5		.932	-5	*3/O	12.6
■ HARRY SMITH	Smith, James Harry b: 5/15/1890, Baltimore, Md. d: 4/1/22, Charlotte, N.C. BR/TR, 5'10", 180 lbs. Deb: 9/21/14																								
1914	NY-N	5	7	0	3	0	0	0	2	3	1	.429	.600	.429	215	1	1	2	1			1.000	2	/C	0.3
1915	NY-N	21	32	1	4	0	1	0	3	6	12	.125	.263	.188	40	-2	-2	1	0	1	-1	.967	-3	C	-0.5
	Bro-F	28	65	5	13	0	0	1	4	7	16	.200	.278	.246	55	-4	-4	5	2			.967	-5	C/O	-0.8
1917	Cin-N	8	17	0	2	0	0	0	1	2	7	.118	.211	.118	2	-2	-2	1	0			.978	4	/C	0.3
1918	Cin-N	13	27	4	5	1	2	0	4	3	6	.185	.267	.370	95	-0	-0	3	1			1.000	-2	/CO	-0.2
Total	4	75	148	10	27	1	3	1	14	21	42	.182	.284	.250	62	-7	-6	12	4	1		.975	-4	/CO	-0.9
■ JIMMY SMITH	Smith, James Lawrence "Greenfield Jimmy" b: 5/15/1895, Pittsburgh, Pa. d: 1/1/74, Pittsburgh, Pa. BB/TR, 5'9", 152 lbs. Deb: 9/26/14																								
1914	Chi-F	3	6	1	3	1	0	0	1	0	0	.500	.500	.667	245	1	1	2	0			1.000	1	/S	0.2
1915	Chi-F	95	318	32	69	11	4	4	30	14	65	.217	.250	.314	70	-15	-13	27	4			.904	-13	S/2	-2.1
	Bal-F	33	108	9	19	1	1	1	11	11	23	.176	.258	.231	43	-7	-8	8	3			.883	-4	S	-1.0
	Yr	128	426	41	88	12	5	5	41	25	88	.207	.252	.293	62	-22	-21	35	7			.898	-17	*S/2	-3.1
1916	Pit-N	36	96	4	18	1	1	0	5	6	22	.188	.257	.219	46	-6	-6	6	0			.929	1	S/3	-0.4
1917	NY-N	36	96	12	22	5	1	0	9	9	18	.229	.295	.302	86	-2	-1	10	6			.971	-2	2/S	-0.3
1918	Bos-N	34	102	8	23	3	4	1	14	3	13	.225	.255	.363	91	-2	-2	10	1			1.000	-1	2/SO3	-0.2
1919	*Cin-N	28	40	9	11	1	3	1	10	4	8	.275	.341	.525	163	3	3	7	1			1.000	-2	/3S2O	0.2
1921	Phi-N	67	247	31	57	8	1	4	22	11	28	.231	.266	.320	50	-16	-19	19	2	8	-4	.971	8	2	-1.4
1922	Phi-N	38	114	13	25	1	0	1	6	5	9	.219	.258	.254	30	-11	-13	7	1	3	-2	.952	-3	S2/3	-1.5
Total	8	370	1127	119	247	32	15	12	108	63	186	.219	.265	.306	63	-56	-58	96	18	11		.910	-15	S2/3O	-6.5
■ JIM SMITH	Smith, James Lorne b: 9/8/54, Santa Monica, Cal. BR/TR, 6'3", 185 lbs. Deb: 4/12/82																								
1982	Pit-N	42	42	5	10	2	1	0	4	5	7	.238	.319	.333	80	-1	-1	5	0	1	-1	.929	8	S/23	0.8
■ JOHN SMITH	Smith, John b: Baltimore, Md. Deb: 4/14/1873																								
1873	Mar-n	5	19	2	2	0	0	0	1	0	0	.105	.105	.105	-49	-3	-2	0						/SO	-0.2
1874	Bal-n	6	20	1	3	1	0	0		0		.150	.150	.200	10	-2	-2	1						/SO	-0.2
1875	NH-n	1	3	0	0	0	0	0		1		.000	.250	.000	-6	-0	-0	0						/S	0.0
Total	3 n	12	42	3	5	1	0	0		1		.119	.140	.143	-14	-5	-4	1						/SO	-0.4
■ DWIGHT SMITH	Smith, John Dwight b: 11/8/63, Tallahassee, Fla. BL/TR, 5'11", 175 lbs. Deb: 5/01/89																								
1989	*Chi-N	109	343	52	111	19	6	9	52	31	51	.324	.383	.493	138	21	18	66	9	4	0	.975	1	*O	1.8
1990	Chi-N	117	290	34	76	15	0	6	27	28	46	.262	.331	.376	88	-2	-5	36	11	6	-0	.986	-4	O	-1.1
1991	Chi-N	90	167	16	38	7	2	3	21	11	32	.228	.279	.347	72	-6	-7	16	2	3	-1	.962	-3	O	-1.2
1992	Chi-N	109	217	28	60	10	3	3	24	13	40	.276	.320	.392	98	-0	-1	26	9	8	-2	.979	-11	O	-1.6
Total	4	425	1017	130	285	51	11	21	124	83	169	.280	.338	.414	104	13	6	143	31	21	-3	.977	-16	O	-2.1
■ JOHN SMITH	Smith, John J. b: San Francisco, Cal. 5'11", 210 lbs. Deb: 5/01/1882																								
1882	Tro-N	35	149	27	36	4	3	0	14	3	24	.242	.257	.309	84	-3	-2	12				.960	-0	1	-0.6
	Wor-N	19	70	10	17	3	2	0	5	5	10	.243	.293	.343	101	0	0	7				.939	1	1	-0.1
	Yr	54	219	37	53	7	5	0	19	8	34	.242	.269	.320	90	-3	-2	19				.952	1	1	-0.7
■ JACK SMITH	Smith, John Joseph (b: John Joseph Coffey) b: 8/8/1893, Oswayo, Pa. d: 12/4/62, New York, N.Y. TR, 5'9", Deb: 5/18/12																								
1912	Det-A	1	0	0	0	0	0	0	0	0		—	—	—	—	0	0	0	0			1.000	1	/3	0.1
■ JOHN SMITH	Smith, John Marshall b: 9/27/06, Washington, D.C. d: 5/9/82, Silver Spring, Md. BB/TR, 6'1", 180 lbs. Deb: 9/17/31																								
1931	Bos-A	4	15	2	2	0	0	0	1	2	1	.133	.235	.133	-1	-2	-2	1	1	0	0	1.000	-1	/1	-0.3
■ JUD SMITH	Smith, Judson Grant b: 1/13/1869, Green Oak, Mich. d: 12/7/47, Los Angeles, Cal. BR/TR, Deb: 5/21/1893																								
1893	Cin-N	17	43	7	10	1	0	1	5	9	5	.233	.365	.326	84	-1	-1	6	1			.750	-2	/O3S	-0.2
	StL-N	4	13	1	1	0	0	0	0	1	2	.077	.200	.077	-24	-2	-2	0	0			.889	1	/3	-0.1
	Yr	21	56	8	11	1	0	1	5	10	7	.196	.328	.268	60	-3	-3	5	1			.844	-1	3/OS	-0.3
1896	Pit-N	10	35	6	12	2	1	0	4	2	2	.343	.395	.457	132	1	2	8	3			.909	2	3	0.3
1898	Was-N	66	234	33	71	7	5	3	28	22		.303	.378	.415	127	8	8	42	11			.903	-9	3S/12	0.0
1901	Pit-N	6	21	1	3	1	0	0	0	3		.143	.250	.190	28	-2	-2	1	0			.947	0	/3	-0.2
Total	4	103	346	48	97	11	6	4	37	37	9	.280	.363	.382	110	5	5	57	15			.900	-9	/3SO12	-0.2
■ KEITH SMITH	Smith, Keith Lavarne b: 5/3/53, Palmetto, Fla. BR/TR, 5'9", 178 lbs. Deb: 8/02/77																								
1977	Tex-A	23	67	13	16	4	0	2	6	4	7	.239	.301	.388	85	-1	-1	9	2	0	1	.975	-1	O	-0.2
1979	StL-N	6	13	1	3	0	0	0	0	0	1	.231	.231	.231	26	-1	-1	0	0	1	-1	1.000	2	/O	0.0
1980	StL-N	24	31	3	4	1	0	0	2	2	2	.129	.182	.161	-3	-4	-4	1	0	0	0	1.000	0	/O	-0.5
Total	3	53	111	17	23	5	0	2	8	6	10	.207	.261	.306	54	-7	-7	10	2	1	0	.985	2	/O	-0.7
■ KEN SMITH	Smith, Kenneth Earl b: 2/12/58, Youngstown, Ohio BL/TR, 6'1", 195 lbs. Deb: 9/22/81																								
1981	Atl-N	5	3	0	1	1	0	0	0	0	1	.333	.333	.667	174	0	0	1	0	0	0	1.000	0	/1	0.1
1982	Atl-N	48	41	6	12	1	0	0	3	6	13	.293	.383	.317	94	0	-0	6	0	0	0	1.000	-0	/1O	0.0
1983	Atl-N	30	12	2	2	0	0	1	2	1	5	.167	.231	.417	71	-0	-1	1	1	0	0	1.000	3	1	0.3
Total	3	83	56	8	15	2	0	1	5	7	19	.268	.349	.357	93	-0	-0	8	1	0	0	1.000	3	/1O	0.4
■ PADDY SMITH	Smith, Lawrence Patrick b: 5/16/1894, Pelham, N.Y. d: 12/2/90, New Rochelle, N.Y. BL/TR, 6', 195 lbs. Deb: 7/06/20																								
1920	Bos-A	2	2	0	0	0	0	0	0	0	1	.000	.000	.000	-99	-1	-1	0	0	0	0	.000	0	/C	-0.1

YEAR	TM/L	G	AB	R	H	2B	3B	HR	RBI	BB	SO	AVG	OBP	SLG	PRO+	BR	/A	RC	SB	CS	SBR	FA	FR	POS	TPR
■ BULL SMITH	Smith, Lewis Oscar b: 8/20/1880, Plum, W.Va. d: 5/1/28, Charleston, W.Va. BR/TR, 6', 180 lbs. Deb: 8/30/04																								
1904	Pit-N	13	42	2	6	0	1	0	0	1		.143	.163	.190	9	-4	-5	1	0			.857	-0	O	-0.6
1906	Chi-N	1	1	0	0	0	0	0	0	0		.000	.000	.000	-95	-0	-0	0	0			.000	0	H	0.0
1911	Was-A	1	0	0	0	0	0	0	0	0		—	—	—	—	0	0	0	0			.000	0	R	0.0
Total	3	15	43	2	6	0	1	0	0	1		.140	.159	.186	6	-5	-5	1	0			.852	-0	/O	-0.6
■ LEO SMITH	Smith, Lionel H. b: 5/13/1859, Brooklyn, N.Y. d: 8/30/35, Brooklyn, N.Y. 5'6", 142 lbs. Deb: 8/28/1890																								
1890	Roc-a	35	112	11	21	1	3	0		14		.188	.283	.250	64	-5	-4	8	1			.948	8	S	0.5
■ LONNIE SMITH	Smith, Lonnie b: 12/22/55, Chicago, Ill. BR/TR, 5'9", 170 lbs. Deb: 9/02/78																								
1978	Phi-N	17	4	6	0	0	0	0	0	4	3	.000	.500	.000	50	0	0	2	4	0	1	1.000	2	O	0.3
1979	Phi-N	17	30	4	5	2	0	0	3	1	7	.167	.194	.233	15	-4	-4	1	2	1	0	1.000	2	O	-0.2
1980	*Phi-N	100	298	69	101	14	4	3	20	26	48	.339	.399	.443	128	15	13	54	33	13	2	.969	-11	O	0.1
1981	*Phi-N	62	176	40	57	14	3	2	11	18	14	.324	.402	.472	141	11	10	35	21	10	0	.971	3	O	1.3
1982	*StL-N★	156	592	**120**	182	35	8	8	69	64	74	.307	.383	.434	127	24	23	102	68	26	5	.970	6	*O	3.1
1983	StL-N	130	492	83	158	31	5	8	45	41	55	.321	.384	.453	131	21	21	85	43	18	2	.941	-2	*O	1.8
1984	StL-N	145	504	77	126	20	4	6	49	70	90	.250	.352	.341	98	-1	1	70	50	13	7	.948	-3	*O	0.1
1985	StL-N	28	96	15	25	2	2	0	7	15	20	.260	.377	.323	98	1	1	13	12	6	0	1.000	-1	O	-0.2
	*KC-A	120	448	77	115	23	4	6	41	41	69	.257	.325	.366	88	-7	-7	60	40	7	8	.958	-3	*O	-0.6
1986	KC-A	134	508	80	146	25	7	8	44	46	78	.287	.358	.411	107	7	6	77	26	9	2	.965	4	*OD	0.8
1987	KC-A	48	167	26	42	7	1	3	8	24	31	.251	.359	.359	89	-1	-2	24	9	4	0	.915	-2	OD	-0.4
1988	Atl-N	43	114	14	27	3	0	3	9	10	25	.237	.298	.342	79	-2	-3	12	4	2	0	.968	-1	O	-0.6
1989	Atl-N	134	482	89	152	34	4	21	79	76	95	.315	**.420**	.533	166	47	45	113	25	12	0	.993	9	*O	5.3
1990	Atl-N	135	466	72	142	27	9	9	42	58	69	.305	.389	.459	125	22	18	86	10	10	-3	.956	5	*O	1.8
1991	*Atl-N	122	353	58	97	19	1	7	44	50	64	.275	.379	.394	111	10	8	57	9	5	-0	.965	-8	O	-0.3
1992	*Atl-N	84	158	23	39	8	2	6	33	17	37	.247	.331	.437	107	3	2	25	4	0	1	.954	0	O	0.2
Total	15	1475	4888	853	1414	264	54	90	504	561	779	.289	.372	.421	118	146	132	816	360	136	26	.963	1	*O/D	12.5
■ RED SMITH	Smith, Marvin Harold b: 7/17/1900, Ashley, Ill. d: 2/19/61, Los Angeles, Cal. BL/TR, 5'7", 165 lbs. Deb: 4/14/25																								
1925	Phi-A	20	14	1	4	0	0	0	1	2	5	.286	.375	.286	65	-1	-1	2	0	0	0	.864	1	S/3	0.1
■ MILT SMITH	Smith, Milton b: 3/27/29, Columbus, Ga. BR/TR, 5'10", 165 lbs. Deb: 7/21/55																								
1955	Cin-N	36	102	15	20	3	1	3	8	13	24	.196	.293	.333	62	-5	-6	10	2	2	-1	.915	-2	3/2	-0.8
■ NATE SMITH	Smith, Nathaniel Beverly b: 4/26/35, Chicago, Ill. BR/TR, 5'11", 170 lbs. Deb: 9/19/62																								
1962	Bal-A	5	9	3	2	1	0	0	0	1	4	.222	.364	.333	94	-0	-0	1	0	0	0	1.000	1	/C	0.1
■ OLLIE SMITH	Smith, Oliver H. b: 1868, Mt.Vernon, Ohio BL/TL, Deb: 7/11/1894																								
1894	Lou-N	38	134	26	40	6	1	3	20	27	15	.299	.427	.425	116	3	5	31	13			.883	-2	O	0.0
■ OZZIE SMITH	Smith, Osborne Earl b: 12/26/54, Mobile, Ala. BB/TR, 5'11", 150 lbs. Deb: 4/07/78																								
1978	SD-N	159	590	69	152	17	6	1	46	47	43	.258	.312	.312	81	-19	-14	61	40	12	5	.970	26	*S	3.8
1979	SD-N	156	587	77	124	18	6	0	27	37	37	.211	.260	.262	46	-46	-42	42	28	7	4	.976	20	*S	0.0
1980	SD-N	158	609	67	140	18	5	0	35	71	49	.230	.315	.276	70	-25	-21	62	57	15	8	.974	**41**	*S	4.8
1981	SD-N★	110	450	53	100	11	2	0	21	41	37	.222	.294	.256	62	-24	-20	36	22	12	-1	**.976**	**26**	*S	1.7
1982	*StL-N★	140	488	58	121	24	1	2	43	68	32	.248	.342	.314	84	-8	-8	58	25	5	5	**.984**	**33**	*S	4.4
1983	StL-N★	159	552	69	134	30	6	3	50	64	36	.243	.323	.335	82	-12	-12	65	34	7	6	.975	18	*S	2.7
1984	StL-N★	124	412	53	106	20	5	1	44	56	17	.257	.349	.337	96	-2	-0	55	35	7	6	**.982**	**26**	*S	4.5
1985	*StL-N★	158	537	70	148	22	3	6	54	65	27	.276	.356	.361	102	3	3	73	31	8	5	**.983**	16	*S	4.0
1986	StL-N★	153	514	67	144	19	4	0	54	79	27	.280	.378	.333	99	2	3	73	31	7	5	**.978**	-9	*S	1.3
1987	*StL-N★	158	600	104	182	40	4	0	75	89	36	.303	.394	.383	105	10	8	102	43	9	8	**.987**	19	*S	4.7
1988	StL-N★	153	575	80	155	27	1	3	51	74	43	.270	.354	.336	98	2	1	80	57	9	**12**	.972	**23**	*S	**5.1**
1989	StL-N★	155	593	82	162	30	8	2	50	55	37	.273	.337	.361	96	0	-2	76	29	7	5	.976	6	*S	2.2
1990	StL-N★	143	512	61	130	21	1	1	50	61	33	.254	.336	.305	77	-14	-14	60	32	6	6	.980	-13	*S	-1.0
1991	StL-N★	150	550	96	157	30	3	3	50	83	36	.285	.380	.367	110	11	11	86	35	9	5	**.987**	-21	*S	0.6
1992	StL-N★	132	518	73	153	20	2	0	31	59	34	.295	.367	.342	103	4	4	72	43	9	8	.985	8	*S	3.3
Total	15	2208	8087	1079	2108	347	57	22	681	949	524	.261	.340	.326	88	-119	-104	1000	542	129	85	.979	219	*S	42.1
■ KEITH SMITH	Smith, Patrick Keith b: 10/20/61, Los Angeles, Cal. BB/TR, 6'1", 175 lbs. Deb: 4/12/84																								
1984	NY-A	2	4	0	0	0	0	0	0	0	2	.000	.200	.000	-41	-1	-1	0	0	0	0	.923	2	/S	0.2
1985	NY-A	4	0	1	0	0	0	0	0	0	0	—	—	—	—	0	0	0	0	0	0	1.000	1	/S	0.1
Total	2	6	4	1	0	0	0	0	0	0	2	.000	.200	.000	-41	-1	-1	0	0	0	0	.929	3	/S	0.3
■ PAUL SMITH	Smith, Paul Leslie b: 3/19/31, New Castle, Pa. BL/TL, 5'8", 165 lbs. Deb: 4/14/53																								
1953	Pit-N	118	389	41	110	12	7	4	44	24	23	.283	.329	.380	85	-9	-9	50	3	0	1	.985	-2	1O	-1.3
1957	Pit-N	81	150	12	38	4	0	3	11	12	17	.253	.313	.340	78	-5	-5	15	0	2	-1	1.000	-3	O/1	-1.1
1958	Pit-N	6	3	0	1	0	0	0	0	3	0	.333	.667	.333	180	1	1	1	0	0	0	.000	0	H	0.1
	Chi-N	18	20	1	3	0	0	0	1	3	4	.150	.261	.150	13	-2	-2	1	0	0	0	.941	0	/1	-0.3
	Yr	24	23	1	4	0	0	0	1	6	4	.174	.345	.174	44	-2	-2	2	0	0	0	.941	0	/1	-0.2
Total	3	223	562	54	152	16	7	7	56	42	44	.270	.326	.361	81	-16	-15	67	3	2	-0	.984	-5	/1O	-2.6
■ PAUL SMITH	Smith, Paul Stoner b: 5/7/1888, Mt.Zion, Ill. d: 7/3/58, Decatur, Ill. BL/TR, 6'1", 190 lbs. Deb: 9/19/16																								
1916	Cin-N	10	44	5	10	0	1	0	1	1	8	.227	.244	.273	60	-2	-2	4	3			1.000	-1	O	-0.4
■ RAY SMITH	Smith, Raymond Edward b: 9/18/55, Glendale, Cal. BR/TR, 6'1", 185 lbs. Deb: 4/09/81																								
1981	Min-A	15	40	4	8	1	0	1	1	0	3	.200	.200	.300	40	-3	-3	2	0	0	0	1.000	1	C	-0.2
1982	Min-A	9	23	1	5	0	1	0	1	1	3	.217	.250	.304	50	-2	-2	2	0	0	0	1.000	1	/C	0.0
1983	Min-A	59	152	11	34	5	0	0	8	10	12	.224	.276	.257	46	-11	-11	11	1	0	0	.984	11	C	0.2
Total	3	83	215	16	47	6	1	1	10	11	18	.219	.260	.270	45	-15	-16	15	1	0	0	.988	14	/C	0.0
■ DICK SMITH	Smith, Richard Arthur b: 5/17/39, Lebanon, Ore. BR/TR, 6'2", 205 lbs. Deb: 7/20/63																								
1963	NY-N	20	42	4	10	0	1	0	3	5	10	.238	.319	.286	74	-1	-1	4	3	2	-0	1.000	-1	O/1	-0.3
1964	NY-N	46	94	14	21	6	1	0	3	1	29	.223	.247	.309	57	-6	-5	7	6	2	1	.987	-0	1O	-0.6
1965	LA-N	10	6	0	0	0	0	0	1	0	3	.000	.000	.000	-99	-2	-2	0	0	0	0	1.000	-0	/O	-0.2
Total	3	76	142	18	31	6	2	0	7	6	42	.218	.260	.289	56	-8	-8	11	9	4	0	1.000	-2	/O1	-1.1
■ DICK SMITH	Smith, Richard Harrison b: 7/21/27, Blandburg, Pa. BR/TR, 5'8", 160 lbs. Deb: 9/14/51																								
1951	Pit-N	12	46	2	8	0	0	0	4	8	8	.174	.296	.174	29	-4	-4	3	0	2	-1	.936	2	3	-0.4
1952	Pit-N	29	66	8	7	1	0	0	5	9	3	.106	.213	.121	-5	-9	-10	2	0	0	0	.958	5	3/2S	-0.5
1953	Pit-N	13	43	4	7	0	1	0	2	6	6	.163	.265	.209	26	-5	-5	2	0	1	-1	.961	5	S	0.1
1954	Pit-N	12	31	2	3	1	1	0	0	6	5	.097	.243	.194	16	-4	-4	2	0	0	0	.933	2	/3	-0.2
1955	Pit-N	4	0	1	0	0	0	0	0	1	0	—	1.000	—	198	0	0	0	0	0	0	.000	0	/S	0.0
Total	5	70	186	17	25	2	2	0	11	30	22	.134	.255	.167	15	-22	-22	9	0	3	-2	.944	14	/3S2	-1.0
■ DICK SMITH	Smith, Richard Kelly b: 8/25/44, Lincolnton, N.C. BR/TR, 6'5", 200 lbs. Deb: 8/20/69																								
1969	Was-A	21	28	2	3	0	0	0	0	4	7	.107	.242	.107	1	-4	-3	1	0	0	0	.909	-2	/O	-0.6

YEAR	TM/L	G	AB	R	H	2B	3B	HR	RBI	BB	SO	AVG	OBP	SLG	PRO+	BR	/A	RC	SB	CS	SBR	FA	FR	POS	TPR
■ RED SMITH	Smith, Richard Paul b: 5/18/04, Brokaw, Wis. d: 3/8/78, Toledo, Ohio BR/TR, 5'10", 185 lbs. Deb: 5/31/27 C																								
1927	NY-N	1	0	0	0	0	0	0	0	0	0	—	—	—	—	0	0	0	0			1.000	-0	/C	0.0
■ BOB SMITH	Smith, Robert Eldridge b: 4/22/1895, Rogersville, Tenn. d: 7/19/87, Waycross, Ga. BR/TR, 5'10", 175 lbs. Deb: 4/19/23																								
1923	Bos-N	115	375	30	94	16	3	0	40	17	35	.251	.285	.309	59	-24	-22	32	4	9	-4	.944	14	*S/2	-0.2
1924	Bos-N	106	347	32	79	12	3	2	38	15	26	.228	.260	.297	51	-25	-24	27	5	2	0	.958	8	S3	-0.5
1925	Bos-N	58	174	17	49	9	4	0	23	5	6	.282	.302	.379	80	-7	-5	19	2	2	-1	.906	3	S2P/O	0.0
1926	Bos-N	40	84	10	25	6	2	0	13	2	4	.298	.314	.417	105	-1	0	10	0			.972	2	P	0.0
1927	Bos-N	54	109	10	27	3	1	1	10	2	4	.248	.261	.321	60	-7	-6	9	0			.966	2	P	0.0
1928	Bos-N	39	92	11	23	2	0	1	8	1	6	.250	.258	.304	49	-7	-7	7	2			.965	3	P	0.0
1929	Bos-N	39	99	12	17	4	2	1	8	2	8	.172	.188	.283	16	-14	-13	5	1			.986	4	P/S	0.2
1930	Bos-N	39	81	7	19	2	0	0	4	0	5	.235	.235	.259	20	-10	-10	5	0			.984	2	P	0.0
1931	Chi-N	36	87	7	19	2	0	0	4	5	2	.218	.261	.241	35	-8	-8	6	0			1.000	1	P	0.0
1932	*Chi-N	36	42	5	10	4	1	0	4	0	2	.238	.238	.381	64	-2	-2	4	1			1.000	3	P/2	0.2
1933	Cin-N	23	25	2	5	1	0	0	1	1	0	.200	.231	.240	35	-2	-2	1	1			.882	-1	P/S	0.0
	Bos-N	14	20	1	4	0	1	0	2	0	1	.200	.200	.300	45	-2	-1	1	0			1.000	1	P	0.0
	Yr	37	45	3	9	1	1	0	3	1	1	.200	.217	.267	39	-4	-3	3	1			.946	0	P/S	0.0
1934	Bos-N	42	36	5	9	1	0	0	3	0	1	.250	.250	.278	44	-3	-3	3	0			1.000	1	P	0.0
1935	Bos-N	47	63	3	17	0	0	0	4	1	5	.270	.281	.270	53	-4	-4	4	0			.980	-1	P	0.0
1936	Bos-N	35	45	1	10	2	0	0	4	0	4	.222	.222	.267	33	-4	-4	3	0			1.000	1	P	0.0
1937	Bos-N	19	10	1	2	0	0	0	0	1	1	.200	.273	.200	33	-1	-1	1	0			1.000	-1	P	0.0
Total	15	742	1689	154	409	64	17	5	166	52	110	.242	.265	.309	53	-122	-111	136	16	13		.941	42	PS/230	-0.3
■ JOE SMITH	Smith, Salvatore (b: Salvatore Persico) b: 12/29/1893, New York, N.Y. d: 1/12/74, Yonkers, N.Y. BR/TR, 5'7", 170 lbs. Deb: 7/07/13																								
1913	NY-A	14	32	1	5	0	0	0	2	1	14	.156	.182	.156	-1	-4	-4	1	1			.952	0	C	-0.3
■ SKYROCKET SMITH	Smith, Samuel J. b: 3/19/1868, St.Louis, Mo. d: 4/26/16, St.Louis, Mo. BR , 6'2", 170 lbs. Deb: 4/18/1888																								
1888	Lou-a	58	206	27	49	9	4	1	31	24		.238	.349	.335	126	7	7	26	5			.970	-0	1	0.2
■ SYD SMITH	Smith, Sydney E. b: 8/31/1883, Smithville, S.C. d: 6/5/61, Orangeburg, S.C. BR/TR, 5'10", 190 lbs. Deb: 4/14/08																								
1908	Phi-A	46	128	8	26	8	0	1	10	4		.203	.233	.289	65	-5	-6	8	0			.975	-0	C/1O	-0.4
	StL-A	27	76	6	14	4	0	0	5	4		.184	.225	.237	50	-4	-4	4	2			.977	8	C	0.7
	Yr	73	204	14	40	12	0	1	15	8		.196	.230	.270	60	-9	-10	13	2			.976	8	C/1O	0.3
1910	Cle-A	9	27	1	9	1	0	0	3	3		.333	.400	.370	140	1	1	4	0			.958	0	/C	0.2
1911	Cle-A	58	154	8	46	8	1	1	21	11		.299	.353	.383	104	1	1	21	0			.979	9	C/13	1.3
1914	Pit-N	5	11	1	3	0	0	0	1	0	1	.273	.273	.273	65	-1	-0	1	0			1.000	-0	/C	0.0
1915	Pit-N	1	1	0	0	0	0	0	0	0	0	.000	.000	.000	-99	-0	-0	0	0			.000	0	H	0.0
Total	5	146	397	24	98	21	1	2	40	22	1	.247	.291	.320	83	-7	-8	38	2			.977	16	C/13O	1.8
■ TOM SMITH	Smith, Thomas N. b: 1851, Guelph, Ontario, Canada d: 3/28/1889, Detroit, Mich. Deb: 9/15/1875																								
1875	Atl-n	3	12	0	1	0	0	0		0		.083	.083	.083	-48	-2	-1	0						/2	-0.1
1882	Phi-a	20	65	10	6	0	0	0		12		.092	.234	.092	12	-5	-7	1				.732	2	3/SO2	-0.4
■ TOMMY SMITH	Smith, Tommy Alexander b: 8/1/48, Albermarle, N.C. BL/TR, 6'3", 215 lbs. Deb: 9/06/73																								
1973	Cle-A	14	41	6	10	2	0	2	3	1	2	.244	.262	.439	93	-1	-1	4	1	0	0	1.000	-1	O	-0.2
1974	Cle-A	23	31	4	3	1	0	0	0	2	7	.097	.176	.129	-11	-4	-4	1	0	0	0	.938	-2	O/D	-0.7
1975	Cle-A	8	8	0	1	0	0	0	2	0	1	.125	.125	.125	-29	-1	-1	0	0	0	0	1.000	-1	/OD	-0.2
1976	Cle-A	55	164	17	42	3	1	2	12	8	8	.256	.291	.323	80	-4	-4	16	8	0	2	.979	-0	O/D	-0.4
1977	Sea-A	21	27	1	7	1	1	0	4	0	6	.259	.259	.370	70	-1	-1	2	0	1	-1	1.000	-2	O	-0.3
Total	5	121	271	28	63	7	2	4	21	11	24	.232	.265	.317	68	-12	-12	23	9	1	2	.977	-5	/OD	-1.8
■ VINNIE SMITH	Smith, Vincent Ambrose b: 12/7/15, Richmond, Va. d: 12/14/79, Virginia Beach, Va BR/TR, 6'1", 176 lbs. Deb: 9/10/41 U																								
1941	Pit-N	9	33	3	10	1	0	0	5	1	5	.303	.324	.333	86	-1	-1	3	0			.941	-2	/C	-0.2
1946	Pit-N	7	21	2	4	0	0	0	0	1	5	.190	.227	.190	19	-2	-2	1	0			.967	1	/C	-0.1
Total	2	16	54	5	14	1	0	0	5	2	10	.259	.286	.278	59	-3	-3	3	0			.953	-1	/C	-0.3
■ WALLY SMITH	Smith, Wallace H. b: 3/13/1889, Philadelphia, Pa. d: 6/10/30, Florence, Ariz. BR/TR, 5'11.5", 180 lbs. Deb: 4/17/11																								
1911	StL-N	81	194	23	42	6	5	2	19	21	33	.216	.303	.330	79	-6	-6	21	5			.936	2	3S/2O	-0.2
1912	StL-N	75	219	22	56	5	5	0	26	29	27	.256	.351	.324	87	-4	-3	26	4			.949	-1	3S/1	-0.2
1914	Was-A	45	97	11	19	4	1	0	8	3	12	.196	.235	.258	46	-6	-7	6	3	4	-2	.955	-4	2/1S3O	-1.3
Total	3	201	510	56	117	15	11	2	53	53	72	.229	.312	.314	77	-16	-15	53	12	4		.947	-3	/3S21O	-1.7
■ WIB SMITH	Smith, Wilbur Floyd b: 8/30/1886, Evart, Mich. d: 11/18/59, Fargo, N.D. BL/TR, 5'10.5", 165 lbs. Deb: 5/31/09																								
1909	StL-A	17	42	3	8	0	0	0	2	0		.190	.190	.190	22	-4	-4	2	0			.836	-9	C/1	-1.4
■ RED SMITH	Smith, Willard Jehu b: 4/11/1892, Logansport, Ind. d: 7/17/72, Noblesville, Ind. BR/TR, 5'8", 165 lbs. Deb: 9/17/17																								
1917	Pit-N	11	21	1	3	1	0	0	2	3	4	.143	.250	.190	35	-2	-2	1	1			1.000	2	/C	0.0
1918	Pit-N	15	24	1	4	1	0	0	3	3	0	.167	.259	.208	42	-2	-2	1	0			.939	-1	C	-0.2
Total	2	26	45	2	7	2	0	0	5	6	4	.156	.255	.200	38	-3	-3	2	1			.969	1	/C	-0.2
■ BILL SMITH	Smith, William E. b: Cleveland, Ohio d: 8/9/1886, Toronto, Ont., Can. 5'11", 178 lbs. Deb: 9/17/1884																								
1884	Cle-N	1	3	0	0	0	0	0	0	0	2	.000	.000	.000	-97	-1	-1	0				.000	-0	/O	-0.1
■ BILL SMITH	Smith, William J. b: Baltimore, Md. d: 8/9/1886, Deb: 4/14/1873 M																								
1873	Mar-n	6	23	2	4	0	0	0	1	0	0	.174	.174	.174	4	-3	-2	1						/OC2M	-0.1
■ WILLIE SMITH	Smith, Willie b: 2/11/39, Anniston, Ala. BL/TL, 6', 190 lbs. Deb: 6/18/63																								
1963	Det-A	17	8	2	1	0	0	0	0	0	1	.125	.125	.125	-29	-1	-1	0	0	0	0	1.000	0	P	0.0
1964	LA-A	118	359	46	108	14	6	11	51	8	39	.301	.320	.465	128	6	10	49	7	5	-1	.977	-6	OP	-0.1
1965	Cal-A	136	459	52	120	14	9	14	57	32	60	.261	.311	.423	109	3	4	58	9	8	-2	.980	-0	*O/1	-0.4
1966	Cal-A	90	195	18	36	3	2	1	20	12	37	.185	.243	.236	39	-15	-15	12	1	0	0	.974	-3	O	-2.1
1967	Cle-A	21	32	0	7	2	0	0	2	1	10	.219	.242	.281	54	-2	-2	1	0	2	-1	.800	-1	/O1	-0.5
1968	Cle-A	33	42	1	6	2	0	0	3	3	14	.143	.217	.190	25	-4	-4	2	0	0	0	1.000	-0	/1PO	-0.5
	Chi-N	55	142	13	39	8	2	5	25	12	33	.275	.335	.465	129	6	5	23	0	0	0	1.000	-6	O/1P	-0.4
1969	Chi-N	103	195	21	48	9	1	9	25	25	49	.246	.332	.441	102	4	0	29	1	0	0	.929	-6	O1	-0.9
1970	Chi-N	87	167	15	36	9	1	5	24	11	32	.216	.268	.371	62	-8	-10	17	2	1	0	.994	-5	1/O	-1.8
1971	Cin-N	31	55	3	9	2	0	1	4	3	9	.164	.207	.255	31	-5	-5	2	0	0	0	1.000	1	1	-0.5
Total	9	691	1654	171	410	63	21	46	211	107	284	.248	.297	.395	94	-17	-18	194	20	16	-4	.975	-26	O/1P	-7.2
■ HOMER SMOOT	Smoot, Homer Vernon "Doc" b: 3/23/1878, Galestown, Md. d: 3/25/28, Salisbury, Md. BL/TR, 5'10", 180 lbs. Deb: 4/17/02																								
1902	StL-N	129	518	58	161	19	4	3	48	23		.311	.351	.380	131	14	17	80	20			.931	-1	*O	0.8
1903	StL-N	129	500	67	148	22	8	4	49	32		.296	.341	.396	114	5	8	77	17			.942	-7	*O	-0.7
1904	StL-N	137	520	58	146	23	6	3	66	37		.281	.331	.365	121	9	12	74	23			.966	2	*O	0.6
1905	StL-N	139	534	73	166	21	16	4	58	33		.311	.358	.433	140	22	24	94	21			.975	1	*O	1.8
1906	StL-N	86	343	41	85	9	10	0	31	11		.248	.287	.332	98	-4	-2	36	3			.953	2	O	-0.6
	Cin-N	60	220	11	57	8	1	1	17	13		.259	.303	.318	90	-2	-3	22	0			.944	1	O	-0.6

YEAR	TM/L	G	AB	R	H	2B	3B	HR	RBI	BB	SO	AVG	OBP	SLG	PRO+	BR	/A	RC	SB	CS	SBR	FA	FR	POS	TPR
	Yr	146	563	52	142	17	11	1	48	24		.252	.294	.327	94	-6	-5	58	3			.950	2	*O	-1.2
Total	5	680	2635	308	763	102	45	15	269	149		.290	.334	.380	120	44	54	382	84			.953	-2	O	1.3

■ HENRY SMOYER Smoyer, Henry Neitz "Hennie" (b: Henry Neitz Smowery) b: 4/24/1890, Fredricksburg, Pa. d: 2/28/58, Dubois, Pa. BR/TR, 5'6", Deb: 8/14/12

YEAR	TM/L	G	AB	R	H	2B	3B	HR	RBI	BB	SO	AVG	OBP	SLG	PRO+	BR	/A	RC	SB	CS	SBR	FA	FR	POS	TPR
1912	StL-A	6	14	1	3	0	0	0	0	2		.214	.313	.214	53	-1	-1	1	0			1.000	-0	/S3	-0.1

■ FRANK SMYKAL Smykal, Frank John (b: Frank John Smejkal) b: 10/13/1889, Chicago, Ill. d: 8/11/50, Chicago, Ill. BR/TR, 5'7", 150 lbs. Deb: 8/30/16

YEAR	TM/L	G	AB	R	H	2B	3B	HR	RBI	BB	SO	AVG	OBP	SLG	PRO+	BR	/A	RC	SB	CS	SBR	FA	FR	POS	TPR
1916	Pit-N	6	10	1	3	0	0	0	2	3	1	.300	.500	.300	147	1	1	2	1			.842	-1	/S3	0.1

■ CLANCY SMYRES Smyres, Clarence Melvin b: 5/24/22, Culver City, Cal. BB/TR, 5'11.5", 175 lbs. Deb: 4/18/44

YEAR	TM/L	G	AB	R	H	2B	3B	HR	RBI	BB	SO	AVG	OBP	SLG	PRO+	BR	/A	RC	SB	CS	SBR	FA	FR	POS	TPR
1944	Bro-N	5	2	1	0	0	0	0	0	0	0	.000	.000	.000	-99	-1	-1	0	0			.000	0	H	-0.1

■ RED SMYTH Smyth, James Daniel b: 1/30/1893, Holly Springs, Miss. d: 4/14/58, Inglewood, Cal. BL/TR, 5'9", 152 lbs. Deb: 8/11/15

YEAR	TM/L	G	AB	R	H	2B	3B	HR	RBI	BB	SO	AVG	OBP	SLG	PRO+	BR	/A	RC	SB	CS	SBR	FA	FR	POS	TPR
1915	Bro-N	19	22	3	3	1	0	0	3	4	2	.136	.269	.182	37	-2	-2	1	1	2	-1	1.000	-1	/O	-0.4
1916	Bro-N	2	5	0	0	0	0	0	0	0	3	.000	.000	.000	-97	-1	-1	0	0			1.000	-0	/2	-0.2
1917	Bro-N	29	24	5	3	0	0	0	1	4	6	.125	.250	.125	16	-2	-2	1	0			.667	-1	/3O	-0.3
	StL-N	38	72	5	15	0	2	0	4	4	9	.208	.269	.264	66	-3	-3	5	3			.889	-5	O	-1.0
	Yr	67	96	10	18	0	2	0	5	8	15	.188	.264	.229	52	-5	-5	6	3			.871	-6	O/3	-1.3
1918	StL-N	40	113	19	24	1	2	0	4	16	11	.212	.315	.257	78	-3	-2	10	3			.956	-0	O2	-0.4
Total	4	128	236	32	45	2	4	0	12	28	31	.191	.285	.233	60	-11	-10	17	7	2		.934	-7	/O23	-2.3

■ JOHN SNEED Sneed, Jonathon L. b: Columbus, Ohio d: 1/4/1899, Memphis, Tenn. Deb: 5/01/1884

YEAR	TM/L	G	AB	R	H	2B	3B	HR	RBI	BB	SO	AVG	OBP	SLG	PRO+	BR	/A	RC	SB	CS	SBR	FA	FR	POS	TPR
1884	Ind-a	27	102	14	22	4	0	1		6		.216	.259	.284	82	-2	-2	8				.817	-0	O	-0.2
1890	Tol-a	9	30	3	6	0	0	0		8		.200	.368	.200	69	-1	-1	4	5			.889	2	/O	0.1
	Col-a	128	484	114	141	13	15	2		63		.291	.383	.393	141	21	26	90	39			.883	-8	*O/S	1.3
	Yr	137	514	117	147	13	15	2		71		.286	.382	.381	136	20	26	94	44			.883	-5	*O/S	1.4
1891	Col-a	99	366	66	94	9	6	1	61	55	29	.257	.366	.322	106	3	6	53	24			.894	-4	*O	-0.1
Total	3	263	982	197	263	26	21	4	61	132	29	.268	.364	.349	120	21	30	155	68			.879	-10	O/S	1.1

■ CHARLIE SNELL Snell, Charles Anthony (b: Charles Anthony Schnell)
b: 11/29/1893, Hampstead, Md. d: 4/4/88, Reading, Pa. BR/TR, 5'11", 160 lbs. Deb: 7/19/12

YEAR	TM/L	G	AB	R	H	2B	3B	HR	RBI	BB	SO	AVG	OBP	SLG	PRO+	BR	/A	RC	SB	CS	SBR	FA	FR	POS	TPR
1912	StL-A	8	19	0	4	1	0	0	0	3		.211	.348	.263	78	-0	-0	2	0			.941	2	/C	0.2

■ WALLY SNELL Snell, Walter Henry "Doc" b: 5/19/1889, W.Bridgewater, Mass. d: 7/23/80, Providence, R.I. BR/TR, 5'10", 170 lbs. Deb: 8/01/13

YEAR	TM/L	G	AB	R	H	2B	3B	HR	RBI	BB	SO	AVG	OBP	SLG	PRO+	BR	/A	RC	SB	CS	SBR	FA	FR	POS	TPR
1913	Bos-A	5	8	1	3	0	0	0	0	0	0	.375	.375	.375	117	0	0	1	1			1.000	0	/C	0.1

■ DUKE SNIDER Snider, Edwin Donald "The Silver Fox" b: 9/19/26, Los Angeles, Cal. BL/TR, 6', 190 lbs. Deb: 4/17/47 H

YEAR	TM/L	G	AB	R	H	2B	3B	HR	RBI	BB	SO	AVG	OBP	SLG	PRO+	BR	/A	RC	SB	CS	SBR	FA	FR	POS	TPR
1947	Bro-N	40	83	6	20	3	1	0	5	3	24	.241	.276	.301	51	-6	-6	7	2			.980	-2	O	-0.9
1948	Bro-N	53	160	22	39	6	6	5	21	12	27	.244	.297	.450	96	-1	-2	21	4			.989	-3	O	-0.7
1949	*Bro-N	146	552	100	161	28	7	23	92	56	92	.292	.361	.493	122	20	17	100	12			.984	4	*O	1.3
1950	Bro-N★	152	620	109	**199**	31	10	31	107	58	79	.321	.379	.553	139	36	34	131	16			.983	9	*O	3.5
1951	Bro-N★	150	606	96	168	26	6	29	101	62	97	.277	.344	.483	118	15	14	96	14	10	-2	.987	3	*O	0.9
1952	*Bro-N☆	144	534	80	162	25	7	21	92	55	77	.303	.368	.494	136	26	25	96	7	4	-0	.992	1	*O	2.1
1953	*Bro-N★	153	590	**132**	198	38	4	42	126	82	90	.336	.419	**.627**	165	59	57	161	16	7	1	.987	-3	*O	4.7
1954	Bro-N★	149	584	**120**	199	39	10	40	130	84	96	.341	.427	.647	170	**65**	**62**	**161**	6	6	-2	.981	-5	*O	4.8
1955	*Bro-N★	148	538	**126**	166	34	6	42	**136**	104	87	.309	.421	.628	169	59	57	145	9	7	-2	.989	1	*O	4.8
1956	*Bro-N★	151	542	112	158	33	2	**43**	101	**99**	101	.292	**.402**	**.598**	152	**50**	**45**	**128**	3	3	-1	.984	-0	*O	3.6
1957	Bro-N	139	508	91	139	25	7	40	92	77	104	.274	.370	.587	139	37	30	106	3	4	-2	.990	-6	*O	1.4
1958	LA-N	106	327	45	102	12	3	15	58	32	49	.312	.375	.505	126	14	13	59	2	2	-1	.987	-13	O	-0.6
1959	*LA-N	126	370	59	114	11	2	23	88	58	71	.308	.402	.535	137	26	22	78	1	5	-3	.975	-17	*O	-0.2
1960	LA-N	101	235	38	57	13	5	14	36	46	54	.243	.369	.519	131	13	11	46	1	0	0	.965	-12	O	-0.3
1961	LA-N	85	233	35	69	8	3	16	56	29	43	.296	.376	.562	133	15	12	48	1	1	-0	.975	3	O	1.1
1962	LA-N	80	158	28	44	11	3	5	30	36	32	.278	.418	.481	150	11	12	34	2	0	1	.967	-2	O	0.8
1963	NY-N★	129	354	44	86	8	3	14	45	56	74	.243	.348	.401	113	8	7	53	0	1	-1	.986	-11	*O	-1.0
1964	SF-N	91	167	16	35	7	0	4	17	22	40	.210	.302	.323	74	-5	-5	17	0	0	0	.979	-4	O	-1.1
Total	18	2143	7161	1259	2116	358	85	407	1333	971	1237	.295	.381	.540	138	441	405	1487	99	50		.985	-58	*O	24.2

■ VAN SNIDER Snider, Van Voorhees b: 8/11/63, Birmingham, Ala. BL/TR, 6'3", 185 lbs. Deb: 9/02/88

YEAR	TM/L	G	AB	R	H	2B	3B	HR	RBI	BB	SO	AVG	OBP	SLG	PRO+	BR	/A	RC	SB	CS	SBR	FA	FR	POS	TPR
1988	Cin-N	11	28	4	6	1	0	1	6	0	13	.214	.214	.357	59	-2	-2	2	0	1	-1	1.000	-1	/O	-0.3
1989	Cin-N	8	7	1	1	0	0	0	0	0	5	.143	.143	.143	-17	-1	-1	0	0	0	0	1.000	-2	/O	-0.3
Total	2	19	35	5	7	1	0	1	6	0	18	.200	.200	.314	44	-3	-3	2	0	1	-1	1.000	-2	/O	-0.6

■ ROXY SNIPES Snipes, Wyatt Eure "Rock" b: 10/28/1896, Marion, S.C. d: 5/1/41, Fayetteville, N.C. BL/TR, 6', 185 lbs. Deb: 7/15/23

YEAR	TM/L	G	AB	R	H	2B	3B	HR	RBI	BB	SO	AVG	OBP	SLG	PRO+	BR	/A	RC	SB	CS	SBR	FA	FR	POS	TPR
1923	Chi-A	1	1	0	0	0	0	0	0	0	0	.000	.000	.000	-99	-0	-0	0	0	0	0	.000	0	H	0.0

■ CHAPPIE SNODGRASS Snodgrass, Amzie Beal b: 3/18/1870, Springfield, Ohio d: 9/9/51, New York, N.Y. BR/TR, 5'10", 165 lbs. Deb: 5/15/01

YEAR	TM/L	G	AB	R	H	2B	3B	HR	RBI	BB	SO	AVG	OBP	SLG	PRO+	BR	/A	RC	SB	CS	SBR	FA	FR	POS	TPR
1901	Bal-A	3	10	0	1	0	0	0	1	0		.100	.100	.100	-43	-2	-2	0	0			.500	-1	/O	-0.3

■ FRED SNODGRASS Snodgrass, Frederick Carlisle "Snow" b: 10/19/1887, Ventura, Cal. d: 4/5/74, Ventura, Cal. BR/TR, 5'11.5", 175 lbs. Deb: 6/04/08

YEAR	TM/L	G	AB	R	H	2B	3B	HR	RBI	BB	SO	AVG	OBP	SLG	PRO+	BR	/A	RC	SB	CS	SBR	FA	FR	POS	TPR
1908	NY-N	6	4	2	1	0	0	0	1	0		.250	.250	.250	57	-0	-0	0	1			1.000	1	/C	0.1
1909	NY-N	28	70	10	21	5	0	1	6	7		.300	.387	.414	146	4	4	15	10			.921	-1	O/C1	0.3
1910	NY-N	123	396	69	127	22	8	2	44	71	52	.321	.440	.432	154	32	32	90	33			.970	-8	*O/1C3	2.0
1911	*NY-N	151	534	83	157	27	10	1	77	72	59	.294	.393	.388	115	16	14	102	51			.973	9	*O/13	1.5
1912	*NY-N	146	535	91	144	24	9	3	69	70	65	.269	.362	.364	96	1	-1	87	43			.948	-3	*O1/2	-1.1
1913	*NY-N	141	457	65	133	21	6	3	49	53	44	.291	.373	.383	115	11	11	72	27			.968	6	*O/12	1.1
1914	NY-N	113	392	54	103	20	4	0	44	37	43	.263	.336	.334	103	0	2	50	25			.977	5	O1/23	0.2
1915	NY-N	80	252	36	49	9	0	0	20	35	33	.194	.307	.230	68	-9	-8	19	11	12	-4	.935	4	O	-1.2
	Bos-N	23	79	10	22	2	0	0	9	7	9	.278	.352	.304	104	0	1	8	0	4	-2	.938	-2	O/1	-0.5
	Yr	103	331	46	71	11	0	0	29	42	42	.215	.318	.248	76	-9	-7	27	11	16	-6	.935	2	O/1	-1.7
1916	Bos-N	112	382	33	95	13	5	1	32	34	54	.249	.318	.317	100	-1	0	45	14			.983	13	*O	0.9
Total	9	923	3101	453	852	143	42	11	351	386	359	.275	.367	.359	110	54	54	488	215	16		.965	24	O/1C23	3.3

■ CHARLIE SNOW Snow, Charles M. b: 8/3/1849, Lowell, Mass. Deb: 10/01/1874

YEAR	TM/L	G	AB	R	H	2B	3B	HR	RBI	BB	SO	AVG	OBP	SLG	PRO+	BR	/A	RC	SB	CS	SBR	FA	FR	POS	TPR
1874	Atl-n	1	2	0	1	0	0	0		0		.500	.500	.500	248	0	0	1						/O	0.0

■ J. T. SNOW Snow, Jack Thomas b: 2/26/68, Long Beach, Cal. BB/TL, 6'2", 200 lbs. Deb: 9/20/92

YEAR	TM/L	G	AB	R	H	2B	3B	HR	RBI	BB	SO	AVG	OBP	SLG	PRO+	BR	/A	RC	SB	CS	SBR	FA	FR	POS	TPR
1992	NY-A	7	14	1	2	1	0	0	2	5	5	.143	.368	.214	66	-0	-0	1	0	0	0	1.000	-0	/1D	-0.1

■ BERNIE SNYDER Snyder, Bernard Austin b: 8/25/13, Philadelphia, Pa. BR/TR, 6', 165 lbs. Deb: 9/15/35

YEAR	TM/L	G	AB	R	H	2B	3B	HR	RBI	BB	SO	AVG	OBP	SLG	PRO+	BR	/A	RC	SB	CS	SBR	FA	FR	POS	TPR
1935	Phi-A	10	32	5	11	1	0	0	3	1	2	.344	.364	.375	92	-0	-0	4	0	0	0	.880	-3	/2S	-0.2

■ CHARLES SNYDER Snyder, Charles b: Camden, N.J. d: 3/3/01, Philadelphia, Pa. BR/TR, Deb: 9/19/1890

YEAR	TM/L	G	AB	R	H	2B	3B	HR	RBI	BB	SO	AVG	OBP	SLG	PRO+	BR	/A	RC	SB	CS	SBR	FA	FR	POS	TPR
1890	Phi-a	9	33	5	9	1	0	0		2		.273	.314	.303	86	-1	-1	3	0			.583	-3	/OC	-0.3

■ POP SNYDER Snyder, Charles N. b: 10/6/1854, Washington, D.C. d: 10/29/24, Washington, D.C. BR/TR, 5'11.5", 184 lbs. Deb: 6/16/1873 MU

YEAR	TM/L	G	AB	R	H	2B	3B	HR	RBI	BB	SO	AVG	OBP	SLG	PRO+	BR	/A	RC	SB	CS	SBR	FA	FR	POS	TPR
1873	Was-n	28	108	16	21	2	0	0	3	3	3	.194	.216	.213	28	-9	-9	5						C/O	-0.7
1874	Bal-n	39	152	24	33	4	2	1		2		.217	.227	.289	64	-6	-6	10						C	-0.4

YEAR	TM/L	G	AB	R	H	2B	3B	HR	RBI	BB	SO	AVG	OBP	SLG	PRO+	BR	/A	RC	SB	CS	SBR	FA	FR	POS	TPR
1875	Phi-n	66	263	37	64	7	2	1		4		.243	.255	.297	87	-2	-4	20						*C/O	-0.1
1876	Lou-N	56	224	21	44	4	1	1	9	2	7	.196	.204	.237	39	-12	-18	11				.833	11	*C/O	-0.5
1877	Lou-N	61	248	23	64	7	2	2	28	3	14	.258	.267	.327	73	-4	-11	22				**.910**	15	*C/OS	0.6
1878	Bos-N	60	226	21	48	5	0	0	14	1	19	.212	.216	.235	44	-12	-15	12				**.912**	5	*C/O	-0.8
1879	Bos-N	81	329	42	78	16	3	2	35	5	31	.237	.249	.322	85	-5	-6	27				**.925**	**24**	*C/O	1.9
1881	Bos-N	62	219	14	50	8	0	0	16	3	23	.228	.239	.265	61	-10	-9	14				.897	3	*C/OS2	-0.4
1882	Cin-a	72	309	49	90	12	2	1		9		.291	.311	.353	117	7	5	35				.916	19	*C/1OM	2.3
1883	Cin-a	58	250	38	64	14	6	0		8		.256	.279	.360	99	1	-1	26				.919	14	C/SM	1.4
1884	Cin-a	67	268	32	69	9	9	0		7		.257	.276	.358	103	2	0	27				.922	27	C/1OM	3.0
1885	Cin-a	39	152	13	36	4	3	1		6		.237	.270	.322	87	-2	-2	14				.880	3	C/1	0.4
1886	Cin-a	60	220	33	41	8	3	0		13		.186	.242	.250	54	-11	-12	16	11			.874	-5	C1/O	-1.3
1887	Cle-a	74	282	33	72	12	6	0		9		.255	.281	.340	77	-10	-9	29	5			.905	19	C1	1.2
1888	Cle-a	64	237	22	51	7	3	0	14	6		.215	.238	.270	67	-9	-8	18	9			.901	8	C/1O	0.4
1889	Cle-N	22	83	5	16	3	0	0	12	2	12	.193	.221	.229	27	-8	-8	5	4			.907	2	C	-0.3
1890	Cle-P	13	48	5	9	1	0	0	12	1	9	.188	.220	.208	17	-6	-5	2	1			.958	3	C	-0.1
1891	Was-a	8	27	4	5	0	1	0	2	0	3	.185	.241	.259	47	-2	-2	2	0			1.000	0	/1COM	-0.1
Total	3 n	133	523	77	118	13	4	2	3	9	3	.226	.239	.277	67	-18	-19	35	0					C/OD	-1.2
Total	15	797	3122	355	737	110	39	7	142	75	118	.236	.256	.303	74	-82	-101	260	30			.904	147	C/1OS2	7.7

■ REDLEG SNYDER

Snyder, Emanuel Sebastian (b: Emanuel Sebastian Schneider)
b: 12/12/1854, Camden, N.J. d: 11/24/32, Camden, N.J. BR/TR, 5'10", 175 lbs. Deb: 4/25/1876

YEAR	TM/L	G	AB	R	H	2B	3B	HR	RBI	BB	SO	AVG	OBP	SLG	PRO+	BR	/A	RC	SB	CS	SBR	FA	FR	POS	TPR
1876	Cin-N	55	205	10	31	3	1	0	12	1	19	.151	.155	.176	12	-19	-14	6				.825	5	*O	-0.9
1884	Wil-U	17	52	4	10	0	0	0		1		.192	.208	.192	35	-3	-4	2				.976	1	1/O	-0.4
Total	2	72	257	14	41	3	1	0	12	2	19	.160	.166	.179	17	-22	-18	8				.825	5	/O1	-1.3

■ COONEY SNYDER

Snyder, Frank C. b: Toronto, Ontario, Canada d: 3/9/17, Toronto, Ont., Can. Deb: 5/19/1898

YEAR	TM/L	G	AB	R	H	2B	3B	HR	RBI	BB	SO	AVG	OBP	SLG	PRO+	BR	/A	RC	SB	CS	SBR	FA	FR	POS	TPR
1898	Lou-N	17	61	4	10	0	0	0	6	3		.164	.215	.164	9	-7	-7	3	0			.935	-6	C	-1.1

■ FRANK SNYDER

Snyder, Frank Elton "Pancho" b: 5/27/1893, San Antonio, Tex. d: 1/5/62, San Antonio, Tex. BR/TR, 6'2", 185 lbs. Deb: 8/25/12 C

YEAR	TM/L	G	AB	R	H	2B	3B	HR	RBI	BB	SO	AVG	OBP	SLG	PRO+	BR	/A	RC	SB	CS	SBR	FA	FR	POS	TPR
1912	StL-N	11	18	2	2	0	0	0	0	2	7	.111	.200	.111	-14	-3	-3	1	1			.919	0	C	-0.2
1913	StL-N	7	21	1	4	0	1	0	2	0	4	.190	.190	.286	35	-2	-2	1	0			.956	2	/C	0.1
1914	StL-N	100	326	19	75	15	4	1	25	13	28	.230	.262	.310	71	-13	-13	27	1			**.979**	5	C	0.0
1915	StL-N	144	473	41	141	22	7	2	55	39	49	.298	.353	.387	124	13	13	65	3	6	-3	.983	7	*C	3.1
1916	StL-N	132	406	23	105	12	4	0	39	18	31	.259	.290	.308	84	-8	-8	39	7			.973	9	C1/S	0.5
1917	StL-N	115	313	18	74	9	2	1	33	27	43	.236	.301	.288	83	-7	-6	27	4			.975	0	C/2	0.2
1918	StL-N	39	112	5	28	7	1	0	10	6	13	.250	.288	.330	92	-2	-1	11	4			.959	2	C/1	0.3
1919	StL-N	50	154	7	28	4	2	0	14	5	13	.182	.213	.234	36	-12	-11	8	2			.983	5	C/1	-0.3
	NY-N	32	92	7	21	6	0	0	11	8	9	.228	.297	.293	79	-2	-2	8	1			.983	-4	C	-0.4
	Yr	82	246	14	49	10	2	0	25	13	22	.199	.245	.256	53	-15	-14	16	3			.983	1	C/1	-0.7
1920	NY-N	87	264	26	66	13	4	3	27	17	18	.250	.295	.364	89	-4	-4	29	2	2	-1	.978	1	C	0.2
1921	*NY-N	108	309	36	99	13	2	8	45	27	24	.320	.382	.453	120	9	9	53	3	4	-2	.985	5	*C	1.7
1922	*NY-N	104	318	34	109	21	5	5	51	23	25	.343	.387	.487	123	11	11	58	1	5	-3	.980	-3	C	0.9
1923	*NY-N	120	402	37	103	13	6	5	63	24	29	.256	.298	.356	73	-17	-16	43	5	3	-0	**.990**	3	*C	-0.8
1924	*NY-N	118	354	37	107	18	3	5	53	30	43	.302	.357	.412	109	3	4	53	3	0	1	.987	-16	*C	-0.4
1925	NY-N	107	325	21	78	9	1	11	51	20	49	.240	.286	.375	70	-17	-15	35	0	0	0	**.985**	3	C	-0.7
1926	NY-N	55	148	10	32	3	2	5	16	13	13	.216	.280	.365	73	-6	-6	15	0			.981	-0	C	-0.3
1927	StL-N	63	194	7	50	5	0	1	30	9	18	.258	.291	.299	56	-11	-12	17	0			.981	0	C	-0.8
Total	16	1392	4229	331	1122	170	44	47	525	281	416	.265	.313	.360	90	-69	-63	489	37	20		.981	17	*C/12S	3.1

■ JERRY SNYDER

Snyder, Gerald George b: 7/21/29, Jenks, Okla. BR/TR, 6', 170 lbs. Deb: 5/08/52

YEAR	TM/L	G	AB	R	H	2B	3B	HR	RBI	BB	SO	AVG	OBP	SLG	PRO+	BR	/A	RC	SB	CS	SBR	FA	FR	POS	TPR
1952	Was-A	36	57	5	9	2	0	0	2	5	8	.158	.226	.193	18	-6	-6	3	1	0	0	.965	7	2/S	0.2
1953	Was-A	29	62	10	21	4	0	0	4	5	8	.339	.388	.403	117	1	1	9	1	1	-0	.988	7	S/2	0.9
1954	Was-A	64	154	17	36	3	1	0	17	15	18	.234	.302	.266	60	-9	-8	13	3	0	1	.978	9	S/2	0.6
1955	Was-A	46	107	7	24	5	0	0	5	6	6	.224	.265	.271	47	-8	-8	7	1	1	-0	.977	1	2S	-0.5
1956	Was-A	43	148	14	40	3	1	2	14	10	9	.270	.321	.345	76	-5	-5	15	1	0	0	.968	-5	S/2	-0.6
1957	Was-A	42	93	6	14	1	0	1	4	4	9	.151	.186	.194	4	-12	-12	3	0	1	-1	.966	1	S2/3	-1.1
1958	Was-A	6	9	1	1	0	0	0	1	1	1	.111	.200	.111	-12	-1	-1	0	0	0	0	1.000	-1	/2S	-0.2
Total	7	266	630	60	145	18	2	3	47	46	59	.230	.284	.279	54	-42	-39	51	7	3	0	.971	20	S/23	-0.7

■ JIM SNYDER

Snyder, James C. A. b: 9/15/1847, Brooklyn, N.Y. d: 12/1/22, Rockaway Beach, N.Y 5'7", 130 lbs. Deb: 5/07/1872

YEAR	TM/L	G	AB	R	H	2B	3B	HR	RBI	BB	SO	AVG	OBP	SLG	PRO+	BR	/A	RC	SB	CS	SBR	FA	FR	POS	TPR
1872	Eck-n	26	106	16	27	2	3	0	10	0	1	.255	.255	.330	93	-3	1	9						S/OC	0.1

■ CORY SNYDER

Snyder, James Cory b: 11/11/62, Inglewood, Cal. BR/TR, 6'3", 185 lbs. Deb: 6/13/86

YEAR	TM/L	G	AB	R	H	2B	3B	HR	RBI	BB	SO	AVG	OBP	SLG	PRO+	BR	/A	RC	SB	CS	SBR	FA	FR	POS	TPR
1986	Cle-A	103	416	58	113	21	1	24	69	16	123	.272	.299	.500	115	5	6	58	2	3	-1	.987	-7	OS3/D	-0.2
1987	Cle-A	157	577	74	136	24	2	33	82	31	166	.236	.276	.456	89	-11	-12	74	5	1	1	.971	2	*OS	-1.2
1988	Cle-A	142	511	71	139	24	3	26	75	42	101	.272	.329	.483	121	15	13	79	5	1	1	.985	14	*O/D	2.3
1989	Cle-A	132	489	49	105	17	0	18	59	23	134	.215	.253	.360	70	-21	-22	41	6	5	-1	**.997**	19	*O/SD	-0.7
1990	Cle-A	123	438	46	102	27	3	14	55	21	118	.233	.271	.404	87	-10	-10	44	1	4	-2	.975	2	*O/S	-1.3
1991	Chi-A	50	117	10	22	4	0	3	11	6	41	.188	.228	.299	46	-9	-9	7	0	0	0	.981	-2	O1	-1.2
	Tor-A	21	49	4	7	0	1	0	6	3	19	.143	.192	.184	4	-6	-7	2	0	0	0	1.000	-2	O/13D	-0.9
	Yr	71	166	14	29	4	1	3	17	9	60	.175	.217	.265	33	-15	-15	9	0	0	0	.985	-4	O1/3D	-2.1
1992	SF-N	124	390	48	105	22	2	14	57	23	96	.269	.313	.444	118	5	7	51	4	4	-1	.992	-5	O13/2S	-0.2
Total	7	852	2987	360	729	139	12	132	414	165	798	.244	.285	.431	95	-33	-32	355	23	18	-4	.984	19	O/S13D2	-3.4

■ JIM SNYDER

Snyder, James Robert b: 8/15/32, Dearbon, Mich. BR/TR, 6'1", 185 lbs. Deb: 9/15/61 MC

YEAR	TM/L	G	AB	R	H	2B	3B	HR	RBI	BB	SO	AVG	OBP	SLG	PRO+	BR	/A	RC	SB	CS	SBR	FA	FR	POS	TPR
1961	Min-A	3	5	0	0	0	0	0	0	0	1	.000	.000	.000	-95	-1	-1	0	0	0	0	1.000	0	/2	-0.1
1962	Min-A	12	10	1	1	0	0	0	1	0	0	.100	.100	.100	-44	-2	-2	0	0	1	-1	.941	-6	/21	-0.8
1964	Min-A	26	71	3	11	2	0	1	9	4	11	.155	.211	.225	21	-8	-8	3	0	0	0	.990	-4	2	-1.0
Total	3	41	86	4	12	2	0	1	10	4	12	.140	.187	.198	6	-11	-11	3	0	1	-1	.984	-10	/21	-1.9

■ JACK SNYDER

Snyder, John William b: 10/6/1886, Lincoln Township, Pa. d: 12/13/81, Brownsville, Pa. BR/TR, 5'9", 168 lbs. Deb: 6/13/14

YEAR	TM/L	G	AB	R	H	2B	3B	HR	RBI	BB	SO	AVG	OBP	SLG	PRO+	BR	/A	RC	SB	CS	SBR	FA	FR	POS	TPR
1914	Buf-F	1	0	0	0	0	0	0	0	1	0	—	1.000	—	193	0	0	0	0			.000	0	/C	0.0
1917	Bro-N	7	11	1	3	0	0	0	1	0	2	.273	.273	.273	66	-0	-0	1	0			1.000	0	/C	0.0
Total	2	8	11	1	3	0	0	0	1	1	2	.273	.333	.273	84	-0	-0	1	0			1.000	0	/C	0.0

■ JOSH SNYDER

Snyder, Joshua M. b: 3/1844, Brooklyn, N.Y. d: 4/21/1881, Brooklyn, N.Y. Deb: 5/18/1872

YEAR	TM/L	G	AB	R	H	2B	3B	HR	RBI	BB	SO	AVG	OBP	SLG	PRO+	BR	/A	RC	SB	CS	SBR	FA	FR	POS	TPR
1872	Eck-n	9	42	3	6	2	0	0	1	1	1	.143	.163	.190	10	-4	-3	1						/O	-0.2

■ RUSS SNYDER

Snyder, Russell Henry b: 6/22/34, Oak, Neb. BL/TR, 6'1", 190 lbs. Deb: 4/18/59

YEAR	TM/L	G	AB	R	H	2B	3B	HR	RBI	BB	SO	AVG	OBP	SLG	PRO+	BR	/A	RC	SB	CS	SBR	FA	FR	POS	TPR
1959	KC-A	73	243	41	76	13	2	3	21	19	29	.313	.367	.420	113	5	5	38	6	2	1	.986	3	O	0.5
1960	KC-A	125	304	45	79	10	5	4	26	20	28	.260	.308	.365	81	-8	-9	34	7	3	0	.986	-10	O	-2.2
1961	Bal-A	115	312	46	91	13	5	1	13	20	32	.292	.334	.375	91	-5	-4	39	5	3	-0	.966	-16	*O	-2.5
1962	Bal-A	139	416	47	127	19	4	9	40	17	46	.305	.336	.435	111	2	5	58	7	4	-0	.974	-3	*O	-0.4
1963	Bal-A	148	429	51	110	21	2	7	36	40	48	.256	.323	.364	94	-4	-3	53	18	5	2	.988	-18	*O	-2.6
1964	Bal-A	56	93	11	27	3	0	1	7	11	22	.290	.365	.355	102	1	1	12	0	2	-1	.971	-9	O	-1.1

YEAR	TM/L	G	AB	R	H	2B	3B	HR	RBI	BB	SO	AVG	OBP	SLG	PRO+	BR	/A	RC	SB	CS	SBR	FA	FR	POS	TPR
1965	Bal-A	132	345	49	93	11	2	1	29	27	38	.270	.324	.322	83	-7	-7	36	3	4	-2	1.000	-7	*O	-2.2
1966	*Bal-A	117	373	66	114	21	5	3	41	38	37	.306	.370	.413	127	12	13	57	2	1	0	.986	-13	*O	-0.5
1967	Bal-A	108	275	40	65	8	2	4	23	32	48	.236	.318	.324	91	-3	-3	31	5	2	0	.985	-1	O	-0.8
1968	Chi-A	38	82	2	11	2	0	1	5	4	16	.134	.174	.195	12	-9	-9	3	0	0	0	1.000	-5	O	-1.8
	Cle-A	68	217	30	61	8	2	2	23	25	21	.281	.355	.364	120	5	6	29	1	1	-0	.991	4	O/1	0.7
	Yr	106	299	32	72	10	2	3	28	29	37	.241	.308	.318	90	-3	-3	30	1	1	-0	.992	-1	O/1	-1.1
1969	Cle-A	122	266	26	66	10	0	2	24	25	33	.248	.313	.308	72	-9	-10	26	3	2	-0	.961	-4	O	-1.8
1970	Mil-A	124	276	34	64	11	0	4	31	16	40	.232	.274	.315	62	-15	-15	23	1	3	-2	.966	-16	*O	-3.7
Total	12	1365	3631	488	984	150	29	42	319	294	438	.271	.327	.363	94	-33	-31	441	58	32	-2	.981	-96	*O/1	-18.4

■ CHIEF SOCKALEXIS

Sockalexis, Louis M. b: 10/24/1871, Old Town, Maine d: 12/24/13, Burlington, Maine BL/TR, 5'11", 185 lbs. Deb: 4/22/1897

YEAR	TM/L	G	AB	R	H	2B	3B	HR	RBI	BB	SO	AVG	OBP	SLG	PRO+	BR	/A	RC	SB	CS	SBR	FA	FR	POS	TPR
1897	Cle-N	66	278	43	94	9	8	3	42	18		.338	.385	.460	116	8	6	57	16			.888	1	O	0.2
1898	Cle-N	21	67	11	15	2	0	0	10	1		.224	.246	.254	44	-5	-5	4	0			.964	2	O	-0.4
1899	Cle-N	7	22	0	6	1	0	0	3	1		.273	.304	.318	76	-1	-1	2	0			.818	1	/O	0.0
Total	3	94	367	54	115	12	8	3	55	20		.313	.355	.414	103	2	0	64	16			.896	4	/O	-0.2

■ BILL SODD

Sodd, William b: 9/18/14, Ft.Worth, Tex. BR/TR, 6'2", 210 lbs. Deb: 9/27/37

YEAR	TM/L	G	AB	R	H	2B	3B	HR	RBI	BB	SO	AVG	OBP	SLG	PRO+	BR	/A	RC	SB	CS	SBR	FA	FR	POS	TPR
1937	Cle-A	1	1	0	0	0	0	0	0	0	1	.000	.000	.000	-99	-0	-0	0	0	0	0	.000	0	H	0.0

■ ERIC SODERHOLM

Soderholm, Eric Thane b: 9/24/48, Cortland, N.Y. BR/TR, 5'11", 187 lbs. Deb: 9/03/71

YEAR	TM/L	G	AB	R	H	2B	3B	HR	RBI	BB	SO	AVG	OBP	SLG	PRO+	BR	/A	RC	SB	CS	SBR	FA	FR	POS	TPR
1971	Min-A	21	64	9	10	4	0	1	4	10	17	.156	.299	.266	59	-3	-3	6	0	1	-1	.942	3	3	-0.1
1972	Min-A	93	287	28	54	10	0	13	39	19	48	.188	.246	.359	75	-9	-10	24	3	3	-1	.942	2	3	-1.2
1973	Min-A	35	111	22	33	7	2	1	9	21	16	.297	.414	.423	131	6	6	20	1	2	-1	.921	0	3/S	0.5
1974	Min-A	141	464	63	128	18	3	10	51	48	68	.276	.350	.392	109	8	6	63	7	3	0	.956	-4	*3/S	0.2
1975	Min-A	117	419	62	120	17	2	11	58	53	66	.286	.367	.415	118	12	11	62	3	5	-2	.969	12	*3/D	2.1
1977	Chi-A	130	460	77	129	20	3	25	67	47	47	.280	.352	.500	129	18	18	77	2	4	-2	**.978**	0	*3/D	1.5
1978	Chi-A	143	457	57	118	17	1	20	67	39	44	.258	.322	.431	109	5	4	61	2	2	-1	.964	0	*3D/2	0.2
1979	Chi-A	56	210	31	53	8	2	6	34	19	19	.252	.314	.395	90	-3	-3	24	0	1	-1	.986	15	3	1.0
	Tex-A	63	147	15	40	6	0	4	19	12	9	.272	.331	.395	96	-1	-1	19	0	0	0	.944	1	3D/1	0.0
	Yr	119	357	46	93	14	2	10	53	31	28	.261	.321	.395	93	-4	-4	42	0	1	-1	.975	16	3D/1	1.0
1980	*NY-A	95	275	38	79	13	1	11	35	27	25	.287	.353	.462	123	8	8	43	0	0	0	.952	-1	D3	0.7
Total	9	894	2894	402	764	120	14	102	383	295	359	.264	.337	.421	109	41	36	398	18	21	-7	.962	28	3/D1S2	4.9

■ RICK SOFIELD

Sofield, Richard Michael b: 12/16/56, Cheyenne, Wyo. BL/TR, 6'1", 195 lbs. Deb: 4/06/79

YEAR	TM/L	G	AB	R	H	2B	3B	HR	RBI	BB	SO	AVG	OBP	SLG	PRO+	BR	/A	RC	SB	CS	SBR	FA	FR	POS	TPR
1979	Min-A	35	93	8	28	5	0	0	12	12	27	.301	.381	.355	96	1	0	12	2	3	-1	.954	-3	O	-0.5
1980	Min-A	131	417	52	103	18	4	9	49	24	92	.247	.291	.374	75	-12	-16	46	4	5	-2	.979	-5	*O/D	-2.7
1981	Min-A	41	102	9	18	2	0	0	5	8	22	.176	.236	.196	24	-10	-10	4	3	2	-0	.983	-1	O	-1.3
Total	3	207	612	69	149	25	4	9	66	44	141	.243	.296	.342	71	-21	-26	62	9	10	-3	.975	-8	O/D	-4.5

■ LUIS SOJO

Sojo, Luis Beltran (Sojo) b: 1/3/66, Caracas, Venez. BR/TR, 5'11", 170 lbs. Deb: 7/14/90

YEAR	TM/L	G	AB	R	H	2B	3B	HR	RBI	BB	SO	AVG	OBP	SLG	PRO+	BR	/A	RC	SB	CS	SBR	FA	FR	POS	TPR
1990	Tor-A	33	80	14	18	3	0	1	9	5	5	.225	.271	.300	58	-4	-5	6	1	1	-0	.969	-3	2/SO3D	-0.8
1991	Cal-A	113	364	38	94	14	1	3	20	14	26	.258	.295	.327	72	-14	-14	33	4	2	0	.981	20	*2/S3OD	0.8
1992	Cal-A	106	368	37	100	12	3	7	43	14	24	.272	.300	.378	90	-7	-6	35	7	11	-5	.985	2	2/3S	-0.6
Total	3	252	812	89	212	29	4	11	72	33	55	.261	.295	.347	79	-25	-25	75	12	14	-5	.982	19	2/3SOD	-0.6

■ TONY SOLAITA

Solaita, Tolia b: 1/15/47, Nuuyli, Amer.Somoa d: 2/10/90, Tafuna, Amer.Somoa BL/TL, 6', 215 lbs. Deb: 9/16/68

YEAR	TM/L	G	AB	R	H	2B	3B	HR	RBI	BB	SO	AVG	OBP	SLG	PRO+	BR	/A	RC	SB	CS	SBR	FA	FR	POS	TPR
1968	NY-A	1	1	0	0	0	0	0	0	0	1	.000	.000	.000	-99	-0	-0	0	0	0	0	1.000	-0	/1	0.0
1974	KC-A	96	239	31	64	12	0	7	30	35	70	.268	.364	.406	115	7	6	36	0	3	-2	.991	3	1D/O	0.3
1975	KC-A	93	231	35	60	11	0	16	44	39	79	.260	.371	.515	145	15	14	45	0	1	-1	.994	3	D1	1.5
1976	KC-A	31	68	4	16	4	0	0	9	6	17	.235	.297	.294	73	-2	-2	7	0	0	0	.974	0	D/1	-0.3
	Cal-A	63	215	25	58	9	0	9	33	34	44	.270	.369	.437	145	10	12	36	1	1	-0	.998	8	1/D	1.7
	Yr	94	283	29	74	13	0	9	42	40	61	.261	.353	.403	126	8	9	42	1	1	-0	.996	8	1D	1.4
1977	Cal-A	116	324	40	78	15	0	14	53	56	77	.241	.353	.417	113	5	7	49	1	3	-2	.990	1	1/D	0.1
1978	Cal-A	60	94	10	21	3	0	1	14	16	25	.223	.336	.287	80	-2	-2	10	0	0	0	1.000	1	D1	-0.1
1979	Mon-N	29	42	5	12	4	0	1	7	11	16	.286	.434	.452	143	3	3	9	0	0	0	.989	0	1	0.3
	Tor-A	36	102	14	27	8	1	2	13	17	16	.265	.370	.422	112	2	2	17	0	0	0	1.000	1	D/1	0.2
Total	7	525	1316	164	336	66	1	50	203	214	345	.255	.361	.421	120	38	39	209	2	8	-4	.993	17	1D/O	3.7

■ MOSE SOLOMON

Solomon, Morris Hirsch "The Rabbi Of Swat" b: 12/8/1900, New York, N.Y. d: 6/25/66, Miami, Fla. BL/TL, 5'9.5", 180 lbs. Deb: 9/30/23

YEAR	TM/L	G	AB	R	H	2B	3B	HR	RBI	BB	SO	AVG	OBP	SLG	PRO+	BR	/A	RC	SB	CS	SBR	FA	FR	POS	TPR
1923	NY-N	2	8	0	3	1	0	0	1	0	1	.375	.375	.500	131	0	0	1	0	0	0	.833	-0	/O	0.0

■ MOOSE SOLTERS

Solters, Julius Joseph (b: Julius Joseph Soltesz) b: 3/22/06, Pittsburgh, Pa. d: 9/28/75, Pittsburgh, Pa. BR/TR, 6', 190 lbs. Deb: 4/17/34

YEAR	TM/L	G	AB	R	H	2B	3B	HR	RBI	BB	SO	AVG	OBP	SLG	PRO+	BR	/A	RC	SB	CS	SBR	FA	FR	POS	TPR
1934	Bos-A	101	365	61	109	25	4	7	58	18	50	.299	.333	.447	93	-2	-5	54	9	4	0	.933	2	O	-0.7
1935	Bos-A	24	79	15	19	6	1	0	8	2	7	.241	.268	.342	53	-5	-6	7	1	1	-0	.966	3	O	-0.4
	StL-A	127	552	79	182	39	6	18	104	34	35	.330	.369	.520	122	20	16	106	10	1	2	.989	16	*O	2.8
	Yr	151	631	94	201	45	7	18	112	36	42	.319	.356	.498	113	14	10	112	11	2	2	.985	19	*O	2.4
1936	StL-A	152	628	100	183	45	7	17	134	41	76	.291	.336	.467	93	-7	-10	99	3	0	1	.956	12	*O	-0.3
1937	Cle-A	152	589	90	190	42	11	20	109	42	56	.323	.372	.533	125	20	20	113	6	9	-4	.953	2	*O	1.2
1938	Cle-A	67	199	30	40	6	3	2	22	13	28	.201	.250	.291	36	-21	-20	15	4	1	1	.969	1	O	-1.8
1939	Cle-A	41	102	19	28	7	2	2	19	9	15	.275	.333	.441	100	-1	-0	15	2	1	0	.915	-3	O	-0.4
	StL-A	40	131	14	27	6	1	0	14	10	20	.206	.262	.267	35	-13	-13	9	1	0	0	.935	0	O	-1.3
	Yr	81	233	33	55	13	3	2	33	19	35	.236	.294	.343	63	-14	-14	24	3	1	0	.927	-3	O	-1.7
1940	Chi-A	116	428	65	132	28	3	12	80	27	54	.308	.351	.472	110	6	5	70	3	3	-1	.971	5	*O	0.4
1941	Chi-A	76	251	24	65	9	4	4	43	18	31	.259	.311	.375	82	-8	-7	28	3	2	-0	.966	1	O	-1.0
1943	Chi-A	42	97	6	15	0	0	1	8	7	5	.155	.212	.186	17	-10	-10	3	0	1	-1	.941	-3	O	-1.7
Total	9	938	3421	503	990	213	42	83	599	221	377	.289	.334	.449	96	-21	-32	519	42	23	-1	.960	36	O	-3.2

■ JOCK SOMERLOTT

Somerlott, John Wesley b: 10/26/1882, Flint, Ind. d: 4/21/65, Butler, Ind. BR/TR, 6', 160 lbs. Deb: 9/19/10

YEAR	TM/L	G	AB	R	H	2B	3B	HR	RBI	BB	SO	AVG	OBP	SLG	PRO+	BR	/A	RC	SB	CS	SBR	FA	FR	POS	TPR
1910	Was-A	16	63	6	14	0	0	0	2	3		.222	.258	.222	53	-4	-3	4	2			.994	0	1	-0.4
1911	Was-A	13	40	2	7	0	0	0	2	0		.175	.195	.175	4	-5	-5	2	2			.992	2	1	-0.3
Total	2	29	103	8	21	0	0	0	4	3		.204	.234	.204	32	-9	-8	6	4			.993	2	/1	-0.7

■ ED SOMERVILLE

Somerville, Edward b: 3/1/1853, Philadelphia, Pa. d: 10/1/1877, London, Ont., Canada BR/TR, Deb: 4/30/1875

YEAR	TM/L	G	AB	R	H	2B	3B	HR	RBI	BB	SO	AVG	OBP	SLG	PRO+	BR	/A	RC	SB	CS	SBR	FA	FR	POS	TPR
1875	Cen-n	14	55	6	13	3	0	0		2		.236	.263	.291	100	-0	0	4						2	0.0
	NH-n	33	134	14	29	4	0	0		1		.216	.222	.246	71	-5	-2	8						2/1S3	-0.2
	Yr	47	189	20	42	7	0	0		3		.222	.234	.259	80	-5	-2	12						2/1S3	-0.2
1876	Lou-N	64	256	29	48	5	1	0	14	1	6	.188	.191	.215	30	-17	-24	11				.870	**30**	*2	0.5

■ JOE SOMMER

Sommer, Joseph John b: 11/20/1858, Covington, Ky. d: 1/16/38, Cincinnati, Ohio BR/TR, Deb: 7/08/1880

YEAR	TM/L	G	AB	R	H	2B	3B	HR	RBI	BB	SO	AVG	OBP	SLG	PRO+	BR	/A	RC	SB	CS	SBR	FA	FR	POS	TPR
1880	Cin-N	24	88	10	16	1	0	0	6	0	2	.182	.182	.193	28	-6	-6	3				.913	-1	O/S3C	-0.7
1882	Cin-a	80	354	82	102	12	6	1		24		.288	.333	.364	128	13	10	44				**.925**	4	*O	1.3
1883	Cin-a	97	413	79	115	5	7	3		20		.278	.312	.346	106	5	2	46				.854	-1	*O/3P	0.0
1884	Bal-a	107	479	96	129	11	10	4		8		.269	.293	.359	110	7	4	52				.841	6	*3/O2	1.0
1885	Bal-a	110	471	84	118	23	6	1		24		.251	.291	.331	100	-0	1	47				.921	12	*O/S3P1	0.9
1886	Bal-a	139	560	79	117	18	4	1		24		.209	.245	.261	61	-26	-24	45	31			.900	13	*O23/SP	-1.0

YEAR	TM/L	G	AB	R	H	2B	3B	HR	RBI	BB	SO	AVG	OBP	SLG	PRO+	BR	/A	RC	SB	CS	SBR	FA	FR	POS	TPR
1887	Bal-a	131	463	88	123	11	5	0		63		.266	.358	.311	95	-3	2	64	29			.902	0	*O23/SP	0.1
1888	Bal-a	79	297	31	65	10	0	0	35	18		.219	.266	.253	71	-10	-9	24	13			.871	-4	OS/21	-1.2
1889	Bal-a	106	386	51	85	13	2	1	36	42	49	.220	.298	.272	64	-17	-18	38	18			.929	9	*O/S	-0.9
1890	Cle-N	9	35	4	8	1	0	0	0	2	2	.229	.270	.257	57	-2	-2	2	0			.789	-2	/OP	-0.4
	Bal-a	38	129	13	33	4	2	0		13		.256	.324	.318	88	-1	-2	17	10			.892	1	O	-0.2
Total	10	920	3675	617	911	109	42	11	77	238	53	.248	.297	.309	90	-40	-41	380	101			.901	38	O3/2SP1C	-1.1
■ **PETE SOMMERS**	Sommers, Joseph Andrews b: 10/26/1866, Cleveland, Ohio d: 7/22/08, Cleveland, Ohio BR/TR, 5'11.5", 181 lbs. Deb: 4/27/1887																								
1887	NY-a	33	116	9	21	3	0	1		7		.181	.234	.233	33	-10	-10	8	6			.830	-8	C/O1	-1.3
1888	Bos-N	4	13	1	3	1	0	0	0	0	3	.231	.231	.308	71	-0	-0	1	0			.880	-0	/C	-0.1
1889	Chi-N	12	45	5	10	5	0	0	8	2	8	.222	.271	.333	66	-2	-2	4	0			.836	-5	C/O	-0.6
	Ind-N	23	84	12	21	2	2	2	14	1	16	.250	.267	.393	83	-2	-2	10	2			.905	-2	C/O	-0.3
	Yr	35	129	17	31	7	2	2	22	3	24	.240	.269	.372	77	-4	-5	14	2			.882	-7	C/O	-0.9
1890	NY-N	17	47	4	5	1	1	0	1	4	13	.106	.192	.170	7	-5	-6	2	0			.837	1	C/1O	-0.4
	Cle-N	9	34	4	7	1	1	0	1	2	3	.206	.250	.294	61	-2	-2	3	0			.906	1	/CO	0.0
	Yr	26	81	8	12	2	2	0	2	6	16	.148	.216	.222	29	-7	-7	4	0			.865	1	C/1O	-0.4
Total	4	98	339	35	67	13	4	3	24	16	43	.198	.242	.286	51	-22	-22	27	8			.860	-15	/CO1	-2.7
■ **BILL SOMMERS**	Sommers, William Dunn b: 2/17/23, Brooklyn, N.Y. BR/TR, 6', 180 lbs. Deb: 4/25/50																								
1950	StL-A	65	137	24	35	5	1	0	14	25	14	.255	.370	.307	72	-4	-5	17	0	1	-1	.917	-9	32	-1.4
■ **BILL SORRELL**	Sorrell, William b: 10/14/40, Morehead, Ky. BL/TR, 6', 190 lbs. Deb: 9/02/65																								
1965	Phi-N	10	13	2	5	0	0	1	2	2	1	.385	.467	.615	206	2	2	4	0	0	0	.000	0	/3	0.2
1967	SF-N	18	17	1	3	1	0	0	1	3	2	.176	.300	.235	56	-1	-1	2	0	0	0	1.000	-1	/O	-0.2
1970	KC-A	57	135	12	36	2	0	4	14	10	13	.267	.317	.370	89	-2	-2	15	1	0	0	.873	-6	3/O1	-0.9
Total	3	85	165	15	44	3	0	5	17	15	16	.267	.328	.376	95	-1	-1	20	1	0	0	.873	-7	/3O1	-0.9
■ **CHICK SORRELLS**	Sorrells, Raymond Edwin b: 7/31/1896, Stringtown, Okla. d: 7/20/83, Terrell, Tex. BR/TR, 5'9", 155 lbs. Deb: 9/18/22																								
1922	Cle-A	2	1	0	0	0	0	0	0	0	0	.000	.000	.000	-99	-0	-0	0	0	0	0	1.000	0	/S	0.0
■ **PAUL SORRENTO**	Sorrento, Paul Anthony b: 11/17/65, Somerville, Mass. BL/TR, 6'2", 195 lbs. Deb: 9/08/89																								
1989	Min-A	14	21	2	5	0	0	0	1	5	4	.238	.385	.238	74	-0	-0	2	0	0	0	1.000	-0	/1D	-0.1
1990	Min-A	41	121	11	25	4	1	5	13	12	31	.207	.284	.380	79	-3	-4	13	1	1	-0	.992	-1	D1	-0.6
1991	*Min-A	26	47	6	12	2	0	4	13	4	11	.255	.314	.553	129	2	2	7	0	0	0	1.000	1	1/D	0.2
1992	Cle-A	140	458	52	123	24	1	18	60	51	89	.269	.343	.443	117	11	10	67	0	3	-2	.993	-1	*1D	0.0
Total	4	221	647	71	165	30	2	27	87	72	135	.255	.331	.433	109	10	8	89	1	4	-2	.993	-2	1/D	-0.5
■ **SAMMY SOSA**	Sosa, Samuel Peralta b: 11/10/68, San Pedro De Macoris, D.R. BR/TR, 6', 165 lbs. Deb: 6/16/89																								
1989	Tex-A	25	84	8	20	3	0	1	3	0	20	.238	.238	.310	52	-5	-6	5	0	2	-1	.944	-2	O	-0.9
	Chi-A	33	99	19	27	5	0	3	10	11	27	.273	.357	.414	120	2	3	15	7	3	0	.969	-5	O/D	-0.2
	Yr	58	183	27	47	8	0	4	13	11	47	.257	.306	.366	89	-3	-3	19	7	5	-1	.960	-7	O/D	-1.1
1990	Chi-A	153	532	72	124	26	10	15	70	33	150	.233	.285	.404	93	-9	-7	58	32	16	0	.962	9	*O	-0.1
1991	Chi-A	116	316	39	64	10	1	10	33	14	98	.203	.241	.335	59	-19	-18	24	13	6	0	.973	-3	*O/D	-2.3
1992	Chi-N	67	262	41	68	7	2	8	25	19	63	.260	.319	.393	98	-0	-1	33	15	7	0	.961	-3	O	-0.6
Total	4	394	1293	179	303	51	13	37	141	77	358	.234	.285	.380	85	-31	-29	135	67	34	-0	.965	-4	O/D	-4.1
■ **DENNY SOTHERN**	Sothern, Dennis Elwood b: 1/20/04, Washington, D.C. d: 12/7/77, Durham, N.C. BR/TR, 5'11", 175 lbs. Deb: 9/10/26																								
1926	Phi-N	14	53	5	13	1	0	3	10	4	10	.245	.310	.434	94	-0	-1	7	0			.975	2	O	0.0
1928	Phi-N	141	579	82	165	27	5	5	38	34	53	.285	.327	.375	80	-15	-18	69	17			.964	8	*O	-1.8
1929	Phi-N	76	294	52	90	21	3	5	27	16	24	.306	.346	.449	90	-3	-6	44	13			.967	3	O	-0.7
1930	Phi-N	90	347	66	97	26	1	5	36	22	37	.280	.326	.403	70	-14	-18	45	6			.967	8	O	-1.4
	Pit-N	17	51	4	9	4	0	1	4	3	4	.176	.222	.314	28	-6	-6	3	2			.971	-1	O	-0.7
	Yr	107	398	70	106	30	1	6	40	25	41	.266	.313	.392	65	-21	-24	48	8			.967	8	O	-2.1
1931	Bro-N	19	31	10	5	1	0	0	0	4	8	.161	.257	.194	23	-3	-3	2	0			.958	-1	O	-0.5
Total	5	357	1355	219	379	80	9	19	115	83	136	.280	.325	.394	77	-42	-52	170	38			.966	20	O	-5.1
■ **BUD SOUCHOCK**	Souchock, Stephen b: 3/3/19, Yatesboro, Pa. BR/TR, 6'2.5", 203 lbs. Deb: 5/25/46																								
1946	NY-A	47	86	15	26	3	3	2	10	7	13	.302	.362	.477	131	4	3	15	0	3	-2	.964	-2	1	-0.1
1948	NY-A	44	118	11	24	3	1	3	11	7	13	.203	.248	.322	51	-9	-9	9	3	0	1	.988	-2	1	-1.0
1949	Chi-A	84	252	29	59	13	5	7	37	25	38	.234	.303	.409	90	-6	-5	32	5	2	0	.951	2	O1	-0.5
1951	Det-A	91	188	33	46	10	3	11	28	18	27	.245	.314	.505	118	3	3	27	0	2	-1	.941	-6	O/312	-0.6
1952	Det-A	92	265	40	66	16	4	13	45	21	28	.249	.304	.487	117	4	4	34	1	0	0	.964	1	O3/1	0.2
1953	Det-A	89	278	29	84	13	3	11	46	8	35	.302	.326	.489	119	5	5	42	5	1	1	.962	-1	O/1	0.2
1954	Det-A	25	39	6	7	0	1	3	8	2	10	.179	.220	.462	84	-1	-1	3	1	1	-0	1.000	-1	/O3	-0.3
1955	Det-A	1	1	0	1	0	0	0	1	0	0	1.000	1.000	1.000	449	0	0	1	0	0	0	.000	0	H	0.0
Total	8	473	1227	163	313	58	20	50	186	88	164	.255	.307	.457	106	-0	1	163	15	9	-1	.957	-10	O/132	-2.1
■ **CLYDE SOUTHWICK**	Southwick, Clyde Aubra b: 11/3/1886, Maxwell, Iowa d: 10/14/61, Freeport, Ill. BL/TR, 6', 180 lbs. Deb: 8/22/11																								
1911	StL-A	4	12	3	3	0	0	0	0	1		.250	.308	.250	58	-1	-1	1	0			.938	-1	/C	-0.1
■ **BILL SOUTHWORTH**	Southworth, William Frederick b: 11/10/45, Madison, Wis. BR/TR, 6'2", 205 lbs. Deb: 10/02/64																								
1964	Mil-N	3	7	2	2	0	0	1	2	0	3	.286	.444	.714	219	1	1	2	0	0	0	1.000	-1	/3	0.0
■ **BILLY SOUTHWORTH**	Southworth, William Harrison b: 3/9/1893, Harvard, Neb. d: 11/15/69, Columbus, Ohio BL/TR, 5'9", 170 lbs. Deb: 8/04/13 MC																								
1913	Cle-A	1	0	0	0	0	0	0	0	0	0	—	—	—	—	0	0	0	0			.000	0	/O	0.0
1915	Cle-A	60	177	25	39	2	5	0	8	36	12	.220	.352	.288	90	-0	-1	18	2	4	-2	.942	1	O	-0.4
1918	Pit-N	64	246	37	84	5	7	2	43	26	9	.341	.409	.443	154	18	17	49	19			.980	9	O	2.4
1919	Pit-N	121	453	56	127	14	**14**	4	61	32	22	.280	.329	.400	114	9	7	64	23			.968	5	*O	0.5
1920	Pit-N	146	546	64	155	17	13	2	53	52	20	.284	.348	.374	104	6	4	68	23	25	-8	**.991**	10	*O	-0.5
1921	Bos-N	141	569	86	175	25	15	7	79	36	13	.308	.351	.441	115	6	10	84	22	20	-5	.975	9	*O	0.3
1922	Bos-N	43	158	27	51	4	4	4	18	18	1	.323	.392	.475	128	5	6	30	4	1	1	.955	5	O	0.8
1923	Bos-N	153	611	95	195	29	16	6	78	61	23	.319	.383	.448	124	17	21	103	14	16	-5	.943	6	*O/2	1.0
1924	NY-N	94	281	40	72	13	0	3	36	32	16	.256	.332	.335	81	-8	-7	32	1	6	-3	.935	-3	O	-1.7
1925	NY-N	123	473	79	138	19	5	6	44	51	11	.292	.363	.391	97	-4	-1	66	6	13	-6	.964	-7	*O	-2.1
1926	NY-N	36	116	23	38	6	1	5	30	7	1	.328	.366	.526	139	6	6	21	1			.970	-2	O	0.2
	StL-N	99	391	76	124	22	6	11	69	26	9	.317	.364	.488	123	14	12	67	13			.971	-3	O	0.3
	Yr	135	507	99	162	28	7	16	99	33	10	.320	.365	.497	127	19	18	88	14			.971	-5	*O	0.5
1927	StL-N	92	306	52	92	15	5	2	39	23	7	.301	.350	.402	98	0	-1	42	10			.970	-7	O	-1.3
1929	StL-N	19	32	1	6	2	0	0	3	2	4	.188	.235	.250	20	-4	-4	2	0			1.000	-0	/OM	-0.4
Total	13	1192	4359	661	1296	173	91	52	561	402	148	.297	.359	.415	111	65	70	647	138	85		.965	23	*O/2	-0.9
■ **JOHN SOWDERS**	Sowders, John b: 12/10/1866, Louisville, Ky. d: 7/29/08, Indianapolis, Ind BR/TL, 6', Deb: 6/28/1887 F																								
1887	Ind-N	1	2	0	0	0	0	0	0	0	1	.000	.000	.000	-99	-1	-1	0	1			1.000	-1	/OP	0.0
1889	KC-a	28	87	11	19	3	0	0	6	4	20	.218	.269	.253	48	-5	-6	6	1			.842	-3	P/O	-0.1
1890	Bro-P	40	132	14	25	3	0	1	20	10	12	.189	.246	.235	28	-13	-15	8	0			.921	-2	P/O	-0.1
Total	3	69	221	25	44	6	0	1	26	14	33	.199	.253	.240	35	-19	-21	14	1			.884	-6	/PO	-0.2

YEAR	TM/L	G	AB	R	H	2B	3B	HR	RBI	BB	SO	AVG	OBP	SLG	PRO+	BR	/A	RC	SB	CS	SBR	FA	FR	POS	TPR
■ **LEN SOWDERS** Sowders, Leonard b: 6/29/1861, Louisville, Ky. d: 11/19/1888, Indianapolis, Ind. Deb: 9/10/1886 F																									
1886	Bal-a	23	76	10	20	3	1	0		12		.263	.364	.329	123	2	3	12	6			.889	-1	O/1	0.1
■ **AL SPALDING** Spalding, Albert Goodwill b: 9/2/1850, Byron, Ill. d: 9/9/15, San Diego, Cal. BR/TR, 6'1", 170 lbs. Deb: 5/05/1871 MH																									
1871	Bos-n	31	144	43	39	10	1	1	31	8	1	.271	.309	.375	92	-1	-2	18	2					*P/O	0.3
1872	Bos-n	48	244	60	87	13	5	0	48	3	1	.357	.364	.451	142	14	11	42						*P/O	0.6
1873	Bos-n	60	322	83	106	13	2	1	59	3	1	.329	.335	.391	104	5	-1	44						*PO	0.8
1874	Bos-n	71	359	80	119	15	1	0		3		.331	.337	.379	121	11	7	47						*P	0.0
1875	Bos-n	74	343	68	107	12	3	0		4		.312	.320	.364	131	12	10	41						*PO/1	0.8
1876	Chi-N	66	292	54	91	14	2	0	44	6	3	.312	.326	.373	118	10	4	36				.951	1	*PO/1M	-0.2
1877	Chi-N	60	254	29	65	7	6	0	35	3	16	.256	.265	.331	77	-4	-8	23				.959	6	*12/P3M	-0.2
1878	Chi-N	1	4	0	2	0	0	0	0	0	0	.500	.500	.500	215	1	0	1				.429	-2	/2	-0.1
Total	5 n	284	1412	334	458	63	12	2	138	21	3	.324	.334	.390	120	40	25	192						P/O1	2.5
Total	3	127	550	83	158	21	8	0	79	9	19	.287	.299	.355	99	6	-4	60				.948	5	/P1203	-0.5
■ **DICK SPALDING** Spalding, Charles Harry b: 10/13/1893, Philadelphia, Pa. d: 2/3/50, Philadelphia, Pa. BL/TL, 5'11", 185 lbs. Deb: 4/18/27 C																									
1927	Phi-N	115	442	68	131	16	3	0	25	38	40	.296	.352	.346	86	-7	-7	54	5			**.992**	3	*O	-1.2
1928	Was-A	16	23	1	8	0	0	0	0	0	4	.348	.348	.348	84	-1	-1	2	0	2	-1	1.000	-3	O	-0.5
Total	2	131	465	69	139	16	3	0	25	38	44	.299	.352	.346	86	-7	-8	56	5	2		.993	-0	O	-1.7
■ **AL SPANGLER** Spangler, Albert Donald b: 7/8/33, Philadelphia, Pa. BL/TL, 6', 175 lbs. Deb: 9/16/59 C																									
1959	Mil-N	6	12	3	5	0	1	0	0	1	1	.417	.462	.583	192	1	1	4	1	0	0	1.000	-1	/O	0.1
1960	Mil-N	101	105	26	28	5	2	0	6	14	17	.267	.358	.352	103	-0	1	15	6	2	1	.989	-14	O	-1.4
1961	Mil-N	68	97	23	26	2	0	0	6	28	9	.268	.432	.289	102	1	2	15	4	2	0	1.000	1	O	0.2
1962	Hou-N	129	418	51	119	10	9	5	35	70	46	.285	.391	.388	119	9	13	69	7	6	-2	.960	-5	*O	0.1
1963	Hou-N	120	430	52	121	25	4	4	27	50	38	.281	.358	.386	122	9	12	60	5	8	-3	.987	2	*O	0.5
1964	Hou-N	135	449	51	110	18	5	4	38	41	43	.245	.314	.334	88	-10	-7	48	7	8	-3	.964	-11	*O	-2.8
1965	Hou-N	38	112	18	24	1	1	1	7	14	8	.214	.302	.268	66	-5	-4	10	1	1	-0	.956	-3	O	-0.9
	Cal-A	51	96	17	25	1	0	0	1	8	9	.260	.317	.271	70	-4	-3	10	4	0	1	.973	-4	O	-0.7
1966	Cal-A	6	9	2	6	0	0	0	0	2	2	.667	.727	.667	312	3	3	5	0	0	0	1.000	-1	/O	0.2
1967	Chi-N	62	130	18	33	7	0	0	13	23	17	.254	.366	.308	91	0	-1	16	2	2	-1	.986	-1	O	-0.4
1968	Chi-N	88	177	21	48	9	3	2	18	20	24	.271	.348	.390	114	5	4	24	0	1	-1	.973	-3	O	-0.3
1969	Chi-N	82	213	23	45	8	1	4	23	21	16	.211	.285	.315	60	-9	-13	20	0	2	-1	.950	-8	O	-2.7
1970	Chi-N	21	14	2	2	1	0	1	1	3	3	.143	.294	.429	81	-0	-0	2	0	0	0	1.000	1	/O	0.0
1971	Chi-N	5	5	0	2	0	0	0	0	0	1	.400	.400	.400	111	0	0	1	0	0	0	.000	0	H	0.0
Total	13	912	2267	307	594	87	26	21	175	295	234	.262	.350	.351	100	0	8	298	37	32	-8	.973	-45	O	-8.1
■ **BOB SPEAKE** Speake, Robert Charles "Spook" b: 8/22/30, Springfield, Mo. BL/TL, 6'1", 178 lbs. Deb: 4/16/55																									
1955	Chi-N	95	261	36	57	9	5	12	43	28	71	.218	.301	.429	91	-4	-4	34	3	4	-2	.959	-3	O/1	-1.2
1957	Chi-N	129	418	65	97	14	5	16	50	38	68	.232	.301	.404	89	-8	-7	51	5	6	-2	.974	6	O1	-1.0
1958	SF-N	66	71	9	15	3	0	3	10	13	15	.211	.333	.380	90	-1	-1	9	0	1	-1	.938	0	O	-0.1
1959	SF-N	15	11	0	1	0	0	0	1	1	4	.091	.167	.091	-30	-2	-2	0	0	0	0	.000	0	H	-0.2
Total	4	305	761	110	170	26	10	31	104	80	158	.223	.302	.406	88	-15	-14	95	8	11	-4	.966	3	O/1	-2.5
■ **TRIS SPEAKER** Speaker, Tristram E "The Grey Eagle" b: 4/4/1888, Hubbard, Tex. d: 12/8/58, Lake Whitney, Tex. BL/TL, 5'11.5", 193 lbs. Deb: 9/14/07 MH																									
1907	Bos-A	7	19	0	3	0	0	0	1	1		.158	.200	.158	15	-2	-2	1	0			1.000	1	/O	-0.1
1908	Bos-A	31	116	12	26	2	2	0	9	4		.224	.262	.276	73	-3	-4	9	3			1.000	4	O	-0.1
1909	Bos-A	143	544	73	168	26	13	7	77	38		.309	.362	.443	151	32	30	99	35			.973	**23**	*O	5.3
1910	Bos-A	141	538	92	183	20	14	7	65	52		.340	.404	.468	169	45	43	115	35			.957	15	*O	5.6
1911	Bos-A	141	500	88	167	34	13	8	70	59		.334	.418	.502	158	38	39	115	25			.956	6	*O	3.7
1912	*Bos-A	153	580	136	222	**53**	12	**10**	90	82		.383	**.464**	.567	185	**73**	69	**175**	52			.958	22	*O	**8.0**
1913	Bos-A	141	520	94	189	35	22	3	71	65	22	.363	.441	.533	180	56	54	136	46			.942	24	*O	**7.4**
1914	Bos-A	158	571	101	**193**	**46**	18	4	90	77	25	.338	.423	**.503**	178	**55**	**55**	**124**	42	29	-5	.968	28	*O/P1	**7.6**
1915	*Bos-A	150	547	108	176	25	12	0	69	81	14	.322	.416	.411	152	35	37	97	29	25	-6	.976	13	*O	3.9
1916	Cle-A	151	546	102	**211**	**41**	8	2	79	82	20	**.386**	**.470**	**.502**	**181**	**65**	**61**	132	35	27	-6	.975	9	*O	**6.1**
1917	Cle-A	142	523	90	184	42	11	2	60	67	14	.352	.432	.486	168	51	47	118	30			.980	8	*O	5.1
1918	Cle-A	127	471	73	150	**33**	11	0	61	64	9	.318	.403	.435	140	31	26	90	27			.973	11	*O	3.3
1919	Cle-A	134	494	83	146	38	12	2	63	73	12	.296	.395	.433	125	23	19	89	15			.983	19	*OM	3.0
1920	*Cle-A	150	552	137	214	**50**	11	8	107	97	13	.388	.483	.562	171	66	63	152	10	13	-5	.977	10	*OM	5.4
1921	Cle-A	132	506	107	183	**52**	14	3	75	68	12	.362	.439	.538	146	38	37	121	2	4	-2	**.984**	10	*OM	3.3
1922	Cle-A	131	426	85	161	**48**	8	11	71	77	11	.378	**.474**	.606	178	53	52	127	8	3	1	**.983**	8	*OM	5.1
1923	Cle-A	150	574	133	218	**59**	11	17	130	93	15	.380	.469	.610	183	71	71	166	10	9	-2	.968	10	*OM	6.5
1924	Cle-A	135	486	94	167	36	9	9	65	72	13	.344	.432	.510	141	32	31	109	5	7	-3	.963	5	*OM	2.3
1925	Cle-A	117	429	79	167	35	5	12	87	70	12	.389	**.479**	.578	166	47	46	123	5	2	0	.967	10	*OM	**4.5**
1926	Cle-A	150	539	96	164	52	8	7	86	94	15	.304	.408	.469	127	24	24	110	6	1	1	.981	10	*OM	2.4
1927	Was-A	141	523	71	171	43	6	2	73	55	8	.327	.395	.444	119	14	15	88	9	8	-2	.967	1	*O1	0.6
1928	Phi-A	64	191	28	51	22	2	3	30	10	5	.267	.310	.450	95	-2	-2	27	5	1	1	.975	1	O	-0.4
Total	22	2789	10195	1882	3514	792	222	117	1529	1381	220	.345	.428	.500	156	843	813	2321	434	129		.970	247	*O/1P	88.5
■ **HORACE SPEED** Speed, Horace Arthur b: 10/4/51, Los Angeles, Cal. BR/TR, 6'1", 180 lbs. Deb: 4/10/75																									
1975	SF-N	17	15	2	2	1	0	0	1	1	8	.133	.235	.200	21	-2	-2	1	0	0	0	.900	1	/O	-0.1
1978	Cle-A	70	106	13	24	4	1	0	4	14	31	.226	.322	.283	72	-4	-3	9	2	4	-2	.977	-12	O/D	-1.9
1979	Cle-A	26	14	6	2	0	0	0	1	5	7	.143	.368	.143	44	-1	-1	1	2	1	0	.875	-5	O	-0.5
Total	3	113	135	21	28	5	1	0	6	20	46	.207	.318	.259	63	-6	-6	11	4	5	-2	.956	-16	/OD	-2.5
■ **TIM SPEHR** Spehr, Timothy Joseph b: 7/2/66, Excelsior Springs, Mo. BR/TR, 6'2", 205 lbs. Deb: 7/18/91																									
1991	KC-A	37	74	7	14	5	0	3	14	9	18	.189	.286	.378	82	-2	-2	8	1	0	0	.986	12	C	1.1
■ **CHRIS SPEIER** Speier, Chris Edward b: 6/28/50, Alameda, Cal. BR/TR, 6'1", 182 lbs. Deb: 4/07/71																									
1971	*SF-N	157	601	74	141	17	6	8	46	56	90	.235	.307	.323	80	-16	-15	58	4	7	-3	.958	-12	*S	-1.1
1972	SF-N★	150	562	74	151	25	2	15	71	82	92	.269	.365	.400	116	15	14	87	9	4	0	.974	-5	*S	3.3
1973	SF-N★	153	542	58	135	17	4	11	71	66	69	.249	.333	.356	87	-6	-9	63	4	5	-2	.956	-10	*S/2	0.0
1974	SF-N☆	141	501	55	125	19	5	9	53	62	64	.250	.337	.361	91	-3	-5	64	3	2	-0	.969	3	*S/2	1.5
1975	SF-N	141	487	60	132	30	5	10	69	70	50	.271	.364	.415	111	11	9	73	4	5	-2	**.982**	1	*S/3	2.3
1976	SF-N	145	495	51	112	18	4	3	40	60	52	.226	.315	.297	72	-15	-17	47	2	2	-1	.974	-1	*S/231	-0.2
1977	SF-N	6	17	1	3	1	0	0	0	0	3	.176	.176	.235	9	-2	-2	1	0	0	0	.920	2	/S	0.0
	Mon-N	139	531	58	125	30	6	5	38	67	78	.235	.322	.343	81	-15	-13	59	1	2	-1	.970	-12	*S	-1.0
	Yr	145	548	59	128	31	6	5	38	67	81	.234	.318	.339	79	-18	-16	60	1	2	-1	.968	-10	*S	-1.0
1978	Mon-N	150	501	47	126	18	3	5	51	60	75	.251	.333	.329	87	-8	-8	56	1	0	0	.975	1	*S	1.3
1979	Mon-N	113	344	31	78	13	1	7	26	43	45	.227	.318	.331	78	-10	-10	35	0	0	0	.970	4	*S	0.6
1980	Mon-N	128	388	35	103	14	4	1	32	52	38	.265	.352	.330	91	-3	-3	45	0	3	-2	.965	-0	*S/3	0.9
1981	*Mon-N	96	307	33	69	10	2	2	25	38	29	.225	.310	.290	70	-11	-11	27	1	2	-1	.964	-11	S	-1.4
1982	Mon-N	156	530	41	136	26	4	7	60	47	67	.257	.318	.360	88	-7	-9	58	1	6	-3	.982	-21	*S	-1.9
1983	Mon-N	88	261	31	67	12	2	2	22	29	37	.257	.336	.341	88	-4	-4	31	2	1	0	.962	-11	S3/2	-0.8

YEAR	TM/L	G	AB	R	H	2B	3B	HR	RBI	BB	SO	AVG	OBP	SLG	PRO+	BR	/A	RC	SB	CS	SBR	FA	FR	POS	TPR
1984	Mon-N	25	40	1	6	0	0	0	1	1	8	.150	.171	.150	-10	-6	-6	1	0	0	0	.960	-2	S/3	-0.7
	StL-N	38	118	9	21	7	1	3	8	9	19	.178	.242	.331	61	-7	-6	9	0	0	0	.983	10	S/3	0.6
	Yr	63	158	10	27	7	1	3	9	10	27	.171	.225	.285	44	-12	-12	9	0	0	0	.980	8	S/3	-0.1
	Min-A	12	33	2	7	0	0	0	1	3	7	.212	.278	.212	36	-3	-3	2	0	0	0	.977	-3	S	-0.5
1985	Chi-N	106	218	16	53	11	0	4	24	17	34	.243	.298	.349	72	-6	-9	21	1	3	-2	.964	2	S32	-0.5
1986	Chi-N	95	155	21	44	8	0	6	23	15	32	.284	.351	.452	111	4	2	24	2	2	-1	.984	9	3S/2	1.2
1987	*SF-N	111	317	39	79	13	0	11	39	42	51	.249	.343	.394	99	-2	0	43	4	7	-3	.989	2	23S	0.1
1988	SF-N	82	171	26	37	9	1	3	18	23	39	.216	.313	.333	89	-3	-2	17	3	3	-1	.985	3	23S	0.2
1989	SF-N	28	37	7	9	4	0	0	2	5	9	.243	.333	.351	99	-0	0	4	0	0	0	1.000	-2	/3S21	-0.2
Total	19	2260	7156	770	1759	302	50	112	720	847	988	.246	.329	.349	88	-97	-106	826	42	54	-20	.970	-52	*S32/1	3.7
■ BOB SPENCE	Spence, John Robert b: 2/10/46, San Diego, Cal. BL/TR, 6'4", 215 lbs. Deb: 9/05/69																								
1969	Chi-A	12	26	0	4	1	0	0	3	0	9	.154	.154	.192	-4	-4	-4	1	0	0	0	1.000	-0	/1	-0.5
1970	Chi-A	46	130	11	29	4	1	4	15	11	32	.223	.289	.362	75	-4	-5	14	0	0	0	.994	3	1	-0.5
1971	Chi-A	14	27	2	4	0	0	0	1	5	6	.148	.281	.148	24	-3	-3	1	0	0	0	.986	-1	/1	-0.4
Total	3	72	183	13	37	5	1	4	19	16	47	.202	.270	.306	57	-10	-11	16	0	0	0	.993	2	/1	-1.4
■ STAN SPENCE	Spence, Stanley Orville b: 3/20/15, S.Portsmouth, Ky. d: 1/9/83, Kinston, N.C. BL/TL, 5'10.5", 180 lbs. Deb: 6/08/40																								
1940	Bos-A	51	68	5	19	2	1	2	13	4	9	.279	.319	.426	88	-1	-1	9	0	1	-1	1.000	-4	O	-0.6
1941	Bos-A	86	203	22	47	10	3	2	28	18	14	.232	.304	.340	68	-9	-10	22	1	0	0	1.000	-1	O/1	-1.3
1942	Was-A☆	149	629	94	203	27	**15**	4	79	62	16	.323	.384	.432	131	25	25	111	5	2	0	.973	-3	*O	1.5
1943	Was-A	149	570	72	152	23	10	12	88	84	39	.267	.366	.405	130	20	22	93	8	1	2	.983	3	*O	2.0
1944	Was-A★	153	592	83	187	31	8	18	100	69	28	.316	.391	.486	157	38	41	118	3	7	-3	.989	19	*O/1	5.0
1946	Was-A★	152	578	83	169	50	10	16	87	62	31	.292	.365	.497	148	28	33	104	1	7	-4	.982	8	*O	3.1
1947	Was-A★	147	506	62	141	22	6	16	73	81	41	.279	.378	.441	131	19	21	89	2	2	-1	.984	8	*O	2.1
1948	Bos-A	114	391	71	92	17	4	12	61	82	33	.235	.368	.391	97	2	-0	62	0	2	-1	.977	-1	O1	-0.7
1949	Bos-A	7	20	3	3	1	0	0	1	6	1	.150	.346	.200	43	-1	-2	2	0	0	0	1.000	1	/O	-0.1
	StL-A	104	314	46	77	13	3	13	45	52	36	.245	.356	.430	103	3	1	50	1	1	-0	.995	3	O/1	-0.1
	Yr	111	334	49	80	14	3	13	46	58	37	.240	.355	.416	99	1	-1	52	1	1	-0	.996	4	O/1	-0.2
Total	9	1112	3871	541	1090	196	60	95	575	520	248	.282	.369	.437	126	124	130	660	21	23	-8	.984	34	O/1	10.9
■ SPENCER	Spencer Deb: 6/03/1872																								
1872	Nat-n	1	4	1	0	0	0	0	0	0	0	.000	.000	.000	-86	-1	-1	0						/S	-0.1
■ CHET SPENCER	Spencer, Chester Arthur b: 3/4/1883, S.Webster, Ohio d: 11/10/38, Portsmouth, Ohio BL/TR, 6', 180 lbs. Deb: 8/22/06																								
1906	Bos-N	8	27	1	4	1	0	0	0	0		.148	.148	.185	4	-3	-3	1	0			.875	-1	/O	-0.5
■ DARYL SPENCER	Spencer, Daryl Dean "Big Dee" b: 7/13/29, Wichita, Kan. BR/TR, 6'2", 190 lbs. Deb: 9/17/52																								
1952	NY-N	7	17	0	5	0	1	0	3	1	4	.294	.333	.412	105	0	0	2	0	0	0	1.000	1	/S3	0.2
1953	NY-N	118	408	55	85	18	5	20	56	42	74	.208	.287	.424	81	-12	-13	49	0	1	-1	.927	-10	S32	-1.8
1956	NY-N	146	489	46	108	13	2	14	42	35	65	.221	.277	.342	66	-25	-24	45	1	3	-2	.974	-2	2S3	-1.8
1957	NY-N	148	534	65	133	31	2	11	50	50	50	.249	.315	.376	85	-12	-11	62	3	1	0	.950	14	*S2/3	1.6
1958	SF-N	148	539	71	138	20	5	17	74	73	60	.256	.348	.406	101	0	2	77	1	0	0	.955	-1	*S2	1.4
1959	SF-N	152	555	59	147	20	1	12	62	58	67	.265	.334	.369	89	-9	-8	69	5	0	2	.970	-4	*2/S	0.1
1960	StL-N	148	507	70	131	20	3	16	58	81	74	.258	.366	.404	102	10	4	77	1	1	-0	.946	-24	*S2	-0.9
1961	StL-N	37	130	19	33	4	0	4	21	23	17	.254	.366	.377	89	0	-2	17	1	0	0	.956	-1	S	0.1
	LA-N	60	189	27	46	7	0	8	27	20	35	.243	.329	.407	86	-2	-4	25	0	1	-1	.964	5	3/S	0.1
	Yr	97	319	46	79	11	0	12	48	43	52	.248	.344	.395	88	-1	-5	43	1	1	-0	.964	4	3S	0.2
1962	LA-N	77	157	24	37	5	1	2	12	32	31	.236	.365	.318	91	-2	-1	19	0	0	0	.925	7	3S	0.7
1963	LA-N	7	9	0	1	0	0	0	0	3	2	.111	.333	.111	37	-1	-1	1	0	0	0	1.000	-0	/3	-0.1
	Cin-N	50	155	21	37	7	0	1	23	31	37	.239	.369	.303	93	1	0	21	1	0	0	.979	3	3	0.3
	Yr	57	164	21	38	7	0	1	23	34	39	.232	.367	.293	91	0	-0	21	1	0	0	.979	2	3	0.2
Total	10	1098	3689	457	901	145	20	105	428	449	516	.244	.329	.380	88	-51	-57	465	13	7	-0	.953	-13	S23	-0.1
■ TUBBY SPENCER	Spencer, Edward Russell b: 1/26/1884, Oil City, Pa. d: 2/1/45, San Francisco, Cal. BR/TR, 5'10", 215 lbs. Deb: 7/23/05																								
1905	StL-A	35	115	6	27	1	2	0	11	7		.235	.285	.278	83	-3	-2	10	2			.962	-6	C	-0.5
1906	StL-A	58	188	15	33	6	1	0	17	7		.176	.205	.218	34	-15	-14	10	4			.935	-5	C	-1.5
1907	StL-A	71	230	27	61	11	1	1	25	7		.265	.296	.335	102	-0	-0	24	1			.957	-2	C	0.4
1908	StL-A	91	286	19	60	6	1	0	28	17		.210	.254	.238	60	-12	-13	17	1			.983	-1	C	-0.7
1909	Bos-A	28	74	6	12	1	0	0	9	6		.162	.225	.176	26	-6	-6	3	2			.992	-4	C	-1.0
1911	Phi-N	11	32	2	5	1	0	1	3	3	7	.156	.229	.281	42	-3	-3	2	0			.925	-1	C	-0.3
1916	Det-A	19	54	7	20	1	1	1	10	6	6	.370	.443	.481	172	5	5	13	2			.988	-7	C	0.0
1917	Det-A	70	192	13	46	8	3	0	22	15	15	.240	.324	.313	95	-1	-1	19	0			.978	-2	C	0.1
1918	Det-A	66	155	11	34	8	1	0	8	19	18	.219	.313	.284	83	-3	-3	14	1			.966	-12	C/1	-1.3
Total	9	449	1326	106	298	43	10	3	133	87	46	.225	.281	.279	76	-38	-36	112	13			.966	-40	C/1	-4.8
■ TOM SPENCER	Spencer, Hubert Thomas b: 2/28/51, Gallipolis, Ohio BR/TR, 6', 170 lbs. Deb: 7/17/78 C																								
1978	Chi-A	29	65	3	12	1	0	0	4	2	9	.185	.209	.200	15	-7	-7	2	0	1	-1	1.000	-1	O/D	-1.0
■ JIM SPENCER	Spencer, James Lloyd b: 7/30/47, Hanover, Pa. BL/TL, 6'2", 195 lbs. Deb: 9/07/68 F																								
1968	Cal-A	19	68	2	13	1	0	0	5	3	10	.191	.236	.206	36	-5	-5	3	0	0	0	.994	3	1	-0.4
1969	Cal-A	113	386	39	98	14	3	10	31	26	53	.254	.304	.383	96	-6	-3	45	1	0	0	.991	-1	*1	-1.3
1970	Cal-A	146	511	61	140	20	4	12	68	28	61	.274	.312	.399	98	-5	-3	61	0	2	-1	**.995**	-1	*1	-1.8
1971	Cal-A	148	510	50	121	21	2	18	59	48	63	.237	.307	.392	104	-3	1	59	0	1	-1	**.996**	2	*1	-1.1
1972	Cal-A	82	212	13	47	5	0	1	14	12	25	.222	.263	.259	59	-12	-10	13	0	1	-1	.990	-2	1O	-2.0
1973	Cal-A	29	87	10	21	4	2	2	11	9	9	.241	.320	.402	111	0	1	11	0	0	0	1.000	-2	1/D	-0.3
	Tex-A	102	352	35	94	12	3	4	43	34	41	.267	.333	.352	97	-3	-1	40	0	3	-2	.999	5	1/D	-0.5
	Yr	131	439	45	115	16	5	6	54	43	50	.262	.331	.362	100	-3	0	51	0	3	-2	**.999**	3	*1/D	-0.8
1974	Tex-A	118	352	36	98	11	4	7	44	22	27	.278	.326	.392	109	2	3	44	1	2	-1	.998	1	1D	0.1
1975	Tex-A	132	403	50	107	18	1	11	47	35	43	.266	.327	.397	105	1	2	51	0	1	-1	.995	5	1D	0.1
1976	Chi-A	150	518	53	131	13	2	14	70	49	52	.253	.319	.367	100	-0	-0	60	6	4	-1	**.998**	8	*1/D	-0.3
1977	Chi-A	128	470	56	116	16	1	18	69	36	50	.247	.303	.400	90	-7	-7	55	1	2	-1	.991	2	*1	-1.3
1978	*NY-A	71	150	12	34	9	1	7	24	15	32	.227	.297	.440	107	0	1	18	0	1	-1	1.000	1	D1	0.0
1979	NY-A	106	295	60	85	15	3	23	53	38	25	.288	.369	.593	158	22	23	60	0	2	-1	.992	0	D1	1.9
1980	*NY-A	97	259	38	61	9	0	13	43	30	44	.236	.317	.421	102	-0	0	34	1	0	0	.990	2	1D	-0.1
1981	NY-A	25	63	6	9	2	0	2	4	9	7	.143	.250	.270	50	-4	-4	4	0	0	0	1.000	2	1	-0.3
	*Oak-A	54	171	14	35	6	0	2	9	10	20	.205	.249	.275	53	-11	-10	11	1	0	0	.997	2	1	-1.1
	Yr	79	234	20	44	8	0	4	13	19	27	.188	.249	.274	52	-15	-14	15	1	0	0	.998	5	1	-1.4
1982	Oak-A	33	101	6	17	3	1	2	5	3	20	.168	.192	.277	28	-10	-10	5	0	0	0	.992	2	1	-0.9
Total	15	1553	4908	541	1227	179	27	146	599	407	582	.250	.310	.387	98	-41	-24	574	11	19	-8	.995	30	*1D/O	-9.3
■ BEN SPENCER	Spencer, Lloyd Benjamin b: 5/15/1890, Patapsco, Md. d: 9/1/70, Finksburg, Md. BL/TL, 5'8", 160 lbs. Deb: 9/08/13 F																								
1913	Was-A	8	21	2	6	1	1	0	2	2	4	.286	.348	.429	124	1	1	3	0			.917	-1	/O	-0.1

YEAR	TM/L	G	AB	R	H	2B	3B	HR	RBI	BB	SO	AVG	OBP	SLG	PRO+	BR	/A	RC	SB	CS	SBR	FA	FR	POS	TPR

■ ROY SPENCER Spencer, Roy Hampton b: 2/22/1900, Scranton, N.C. d: 2/8/73, Port Charlotte, Fla BR/TR, 5'10", 168 lbs. Deb: 4/19/25

1925	Pit-N	14	28	1	6	1	0	0	2	1	3	.214	.241	.250	24	-3	-3	2	1	0	0	.905	-2	C	-0.5
1926	Pit-N	28	43	5	17	3	0	0	4	1	0	.395	.409	.465	128	2	2	8	0			.970	-1	C	0.2
1927	*Pit-N	38	92	9	26	3	1	0	13	3	3	.283	.305	.337	67	-4	-5	9	0			.974	2	C	-0.1
1929	Was-A	50	116	18	18	4	0	1	9	8	15	.155	.222	.216	13	-15	-15	6	0	0	0	.967	-2	C	-1.3
1930	Was-A	93	321	32	82	11	4	0	36	18	27	.255	.303	.315	57	-21	-21	32	3	0	1	.989	5	C	-0.7
1931	Was-A	145	483	48	133	16	3	1	60	35	21	.275	.327	.327	72	-19	-19	53	0	0	0	.985	7	*C	-0.3
1932	Was-A	102	317	28	78	9	0	1	41	24	17	.246	.301	.284	53	-22	-21	28	0	1	-1	.978	-10	C	-2.4
1933	Cle-A	75	227	26	46	5	2	0	23	23	17	.203	.282	.242	38	-19	-21	17	0	0	0	.990	5	C	-1.1
1934	Cle-A	5	7	0	1	1	0	0	2	0	1	.143	.143	.286	8	-1	-1	0	0	0	0	1.000	1	/C	0.0
1936	NY-N	19	18	3	5	1	0	0	3	2	3	.278	.350	.333	86	-0	-0	2				1.000	1	C	0.1
1937	Bro-N	51	117	5	24	2	2	0	4	8	17	.205	.256	.256	39	-10	-10	8	0			1.000	9	C	0.1
1938	Bro-N	16	45	2	12	1	1	0	6	5	6	.267	.340	.333	84	-1	-1	5	0			.968	-0	C	-0.1
Total	12	636	1814	177	448	57	13	3	203	128	130	.247	.301	.298	56	-113	-116	171	4	1		.984	16	C	-6.1

■ VERN SPENCER Spencer, Vernon Murray b: 2/23/1896, Wixom, Mich. d: 6/3/71, Wixon, Mich. BL/TR, 5'7", 165 lbs. Deb: 7/04/20

| 1920 | NY-N | 45 | 140 | 15 | 28 | 2 | 3 | 0 | 19 | 11 | 17 | .200 | .258 | .257 | 49 | -9 | -9 | 9 | 4 | 3 | -1 | .932 | -1 | O | -1.4 |

■ PAUL SPERAW Speraw, Paul Bachman "Polly" or "Birdie" b: 10/5/1893, Annville, Pa. d: 2/22/62, Cedar Rapids, Iowa BR/TR, 5'8.5", 145 lbs. Deb: 9/15/20

| 1920 | StL-A | 1 | 2 | 0 | 0 | 0 | 0 | 0 | 0 | 0 | 0 | .000 | .000 | .000 | -97 | -1 | -1 | 0 | 0 | 0 | 0 | 1.000 | 0 | /3 | 0.0 |

■ ED SPERBER Sperber, Edwin George b: 1/21/1895, Cincinnati, Ohio d: 1/5/76, Cincinnati, Ohio BL/TL, 5'11", 175 lbs. Deb: 4/16/24

1924	Bos-N	24	59	8	17	2	0	1	12	10	9	.288	.400	.373	113	1	2	10	3	1	0	.897	-3	O	-0.2
1925	Bos-N	2	2	0	0	0	0	0	0	0	0	.000	.000	.000	-99	-1	-1	0	0	0	0	.000	0	H	-0.1
Total	2	26	61	8	17	2	0	1	12	10	9	.279	.389	.361	106	1	1	10	3	1	0	.978	-3	/O	-0.3

■ ROB SPERRING Sperring, Robert Walter b: 10/10/49, San Francisco, Cal. BR/TR, 6'1", 185 lbs. Deb: 8/11/74

1974	Chi-N	42	107	9	22	3	0	1	5	9	28	.206	.267	.262	46	-7	-8	8	1	2	-1	.952	5	2/S	-0.3
1975	Chi-N	65	144	25	30	4	1	1	9	16	31	.208	.292	.271	54	-8	-9	11	0	2	-1	.946	13	32S/O	0.4
1976	Chi-N	43	93	8	24	3	0	0	7	9	25	.258	.324	.290	69	-3	-4	9	0	2	-1	.955	-9	3S/2O	-1.4
1977	Hou-N	58	129	6	24	3	0	1	9	12	23	.186	.255	.233	35	-12	-11	8	0	0	0	.940	-2	S23	-1.1
Total	4	208	473	48	100	13	1	3	30	46	107	.211	.283	.262	51	-31	-32	35	1	6	-3	.964	6	/2S3O	-2.4

■ STAN SPERRY Sperry, Stanley Kenneth b: 2/19/14, Evansville, Wis. d: 9/27/62, Evansville, Wis. BL/TR, 5'10.5", 164 lbs. Deb: 7/28/36

1936	Phi-N	20	37	2	5	3	0	0	4	3	5	.135	.200	.216	11	-5	-5	2	0			.900	-4	2	-0.9
1938	Phi-A	60	253	28	69	6	3	0	27	15	9	.273	.313	.320	61	-16	-15	25	1	2	-1	.959	-8	2	-1.9
Total	2	80	290	30	74	9	3	0	31	18	14	.255	.299	.307	54	-21	-20	27	1	2		.951	-12	/2	-2.8

■ BILL SPIERS Spiers, William James b: 6/5/66, Orangeburg, S.C. BL/TR, 6'2", 190 lbs. Deb: 4/07/89

1989	Mil-A	114	345	44	88	9	3	4	33	21	63	.255	.300	.333	79	-10	-10	37	10	2	2	.962	14	S3/21D	1.2
1990	Mil-A	112	363	44	88	15	3	2	36	16	45	.242	.276	.317	66	-17	-17	29	11	6	-0	.976	-6	*S	-1.4
1991	Mil-A	133	414	71	117	13	6	8	54	34	55	.283	.340	.401	107	2	4	56	14	8	-1	.970	-12	*S/OD	0.1
1992	Mil-A	12	16	2	5	2	0	0	2	1	4	.313	.353	.438	123	0	0	2	1	1	-0	1.000	-2	/S23D	-0.3
Total	4	371	1138	161	298	39	12	14	125	72	167	.262	.308	.354	86	-25	-23	124	36	17	1	.970	-5	S/32D1O	-0.3

■ HARRY SPIES Spies, Henry b: 6/12/1866, New Orleans, La. d: 7/8/42, Los Angeles, Cal. BR/TR, 5'11.5", 170 lbs. Deb: 4/20/1895

1895	Cin-N	14	50	2	11	0	1	0	5	3	2	.220	.264	.260	35	-5	-5	4	0			.867	2	C/1	-0.2
	Lou-N	72	276	42	74	14	7	2	35	11	19	.268	.313	.391	88	-8	-5	36	4			.981	-3	1C/S	-0.4
	Yr	86	326	44	85	14	8	2	40	14	21	.261	.305	.371	79	-13	-10	39	4			.979	-1	1C/S	-0.6

■ ED SPIEZIO Spiezio, Edward Wayne b: 10/31/41, Joliet, Ill. BR/TR, 5'11", 180 lbs. Deb: 7/23/64

1964	StL-N	12	12	0	4	0	0	0	0	0	1	.333	.333	.333	81	-0	-0	1	0	0	0	.000	0	H	0.0
1965	StL-N	10	18	0	3	0	0	0	5	1	4	.167	.250	.167	18	-2	-2	1	0	0	0	1.000	0	/3	-0.2
1966	StL-N	26	73	4	16	5	1	2	10	5	11	.219	.269	.397	82	-2	-2	6	1	0	0	.885	-4	3	-0.6
1967	*StL-N	55	105	9	22	2	0	3	10	7	18	.210	.265	.314	66	-5	-5	8	2	1	0	.962	1	3/O	-0.4
1968	*StL-N	29	51	1	8	0	0	2	5	6	6	.157	.232	.157	19	-5	-5	2	1	1	-0	1.000	1	O/3	-0.5
1969	SD-N	121	355	29	83	9	0	13	43	38	64	.234	.315	.369	95	-4	-3	41	1	2	-1	.939	1	3/O	-0.2
1970	SD-N	110	316	45	90	18	1	12	42	43	42	.285	.377	.462	122	11	12	57	4	0	1	.953	2	3	1.5
1971	SD-N	97	308	16	71	10	1	7	36	22	50	.231	.290	.338	83	-9	-7	29	6	5	-1	.962	1	3/O	-0.9
1972	SD-N	20	29	2	4	2	0	0	4	1	6	.138	.167	.207	6	-4	-3	1	1	0	0	1.000	-2	/3	-0.5
	Chi-A	74	277	20	66	10	1	2	22	13	43	.238	.277	.303	71	-10	-10	22	0	1	-1	.952	7	3	-0.6
Total	9	554	1544	126	367	56	4	39	174	135	245	.238	.306	.355	88	-30	-24	168	16	10	-1	.949	8	3/O	-2.4

■ CHARLIE SPIKES Spikes, Leslie Charles b: 1/23/51, Bogalusa, La. BR/TR, 6'3", 220 lbs. Deb: 9/01/72

1972	NY-A	14	34	2	5	1	0	0	3	1	13	.147	.171	.176	4	-4	-4	1	0	1	-1	1.000	0	/O	-0.6
1973	Cle-A	140	506	68	120	12	3	23	73	45	103	.237	.306	.409	98	-2	-3	62	5	3	-0	.964	5	*OD	-0.3
1974	Cle-A	155	568	63	154	23	1	22	80	34	100	.271	.320	.431	116	9	9	74	10	7	-1	.968	0	*O	0.2
1975	Cle-A	111	345	41	79	13	3	11	33	30	51	.229	.291	.380	88	-6	-6	35	7	6	-2	.974	1	*O/D	-1.1
1976	Cle-A	101	334	34	79	11	5	4	31	23	50	.237	.296	.326	83	-8	-7	32	5	6	-2	.985	-1	O/D	-1.3
1977	Cle-A	32	95	13	22	2	0	3	11	11	17	.232	.324	.347	86	-2	-2	10	0	2	-1	.972	-3	O/D	-0.7
1978	Det-A	10	28	1	7	1	0	0	2	2	6	.250	.344	.286	77	-1	-1	3	0	0	0	.909	-1	/O	-0.3
1979	Atl-N	66	93	12	26	8	0	3	21	5	30	.280	.316	.462	102	1	1	13	0	0	0	.842	-3	O	-0.4
1980	Atl-N	41	36	6	10	1	0	0	2	3	18	.278	.350	.306	82	-1	-1	4	0	0	0	1.000	0	O	-0.1
Total	9	670	2039	240	502	72	12	65	256	154	388	.246	.306	.389	96	-13	-14	233	27	25	-7	.969	-0	O/D	-4.6

■ HARRY SPILMAN Spilman, William Harry b: 7/18/54, Albany, Ga. BL/TR, 6'1", 190 lbs. Deb: 9/11/78

1978	Cin-N	4	4	1	1	0	0	0	0	0	1	.250	.250	.250	40	-0	-0	0	0	0	0	.000	0	H	0.0
1979	*Cin-N	43	56	7	12	3	0	0	5	7	5	.214	.323	.268	63	-3	-3	5	0	0	0	1.000	0	1/3	-0.3
1980	Cin-N	65	101	14	27	4	0	4	19	9	19	.267	.333	.426	110	1	1	14	0	0	0	.986	1	1/OC3	0.1
1981	Cin-N	23	24	4	4	1	0	0	3	3	1	.167	.259	.208	33	-2	-2	1	0	0	0	1.000	0	/31	-0.2
	*Hou-N	28	34	5	10	0	0	0	1	2	3	.294	.333	.294	83	-1	-1	3	0	1	-1	1.000	-0	1	-0.2
	Yr	51	58	9	14	1	0	0	4	5	10	.241	.302	.259	61	-3	-3	4	0	1	-1	.984	0	1/3	-0.4
1982	Hou-N	38	61	7	17	2	0	3	11	5	10	.279	.333	.459	129	1	2	9	0	0	0	.989	-1	1	0.1
1983	Hou-N	42	78	7	13	3	0	1	9	5	12	.167	.217	.244	29	-8	-7	4	0	0	0	1.000	-2	1/C	-1.0
1984	Hou-N	32	72	14	19	2	0	2	15	12	10	.264	.369	.375	118	1	2	11	0	0	0	.978	-3	1/C	-0.3
1985	Hou-N	44	66	3	9	1	0	1	4	3	7	.136	.174	.197	4	-9	-8	2	0	0	0	1.000	-1	1/C	-1.1
1986	Det-A	24	49	6	12	2	0	3	8	3	8	.245	.288	.469	102	-0	-0	6	0	0	0	1.000	0	D/3C1	0.0
	SF-N	58	94	12	27	7	0	2	22	12	13	.287	.368	.426	124	2	3	16	0	0	0	.994	0	1/3C2O	0.2
1987	*SF-N	83	90	5	24	5	0	1	14	9	20	.267	.333	.356	87	-2	-2	10	1	1	0	.875	-2	3/1C	-0.5
1988	SF-N	40	40	4	7	1	1	0	3	4	6	.175	.250	.325	67	-2	-2	3	0	0	0	1.000	1	/1CO	-0.2
	Hou-N	7	5	0	0	0	0	0	0	0	3	.000	.000	.000	-99	-1	-1	0	0	0	0	1.000	0	/1	-0.1
	Yr	47	45	4	7	1	1	0	3	4	9	.156	.224	.289	48	-3	-3	3	0	0	0	1.000	1	/1CO	-0.3
1989	Hou-N	32	36	7	10	3	0	0	3	7	2	.278	.395	.361	122	1	1	5	0	0	0	1.000	0	/1C	0.1
Total	12	563	810	96	192	34	1	18	117	81	126	.237	.309	.348	85	-20	-16	92	1	2	-1	.991	-8	1/3CDO2	-3.3

HAL SPINDEL Spindel, Harold Stewart b: 5/27/13, Chandler, Okla. BR/TR, 6', 185 lbs. Deb: 4/23/39

YEAR	TM/L	G	AB	R	H	2B	3B	HR	RBI	BB	SO	AVG	OBP	SLG	PRO+	BR	/A	RC	SB	CS	SBR	FA	FR	POS	TPR
1939	StL-A	48	119	13	32	3	1	0	11	8	7	.269	.315	.311	59	-7	-7	11	0	2	-1	.993	-0	C	-0.7
1945	Phi-N	36	87	7	20	3	0	0	8	6	7	.230	.280	.264	53	-6	-5	7	0			.964	0	C	-0.3
1946	Phi-N	1	3	0	1	0	0	0	1	0	0	.333	.333	.333	92	-0	-0	0	0			1.000	-0	/C	0.0
Total	3	85	209	20	53	6	1	0	20	14	14	.254	.300	.292	57	-13	-13	17	0	2		.980	0	/C	-1.0

ANDY SPOGNARDI Spognardi, Andrea Ettore b: 10/18/08, Boston, Mass. BR/TR, 5'9.5", 160 lbs. Deb: 9/02/32

YEAR	TM/L	G	AB	R	H	2B	3B	HR	RBI	BB	SO	AVG	OBP	SLG	PRO+	BR	/A	RC	SB	CS	SBR	FA	FR	POS	TPR
1932	Bos-A	17	34	9	10	1	0	0	1	6	6	.294	.400	.324	92	-0	-0	5	0	0	0	.979	3	/2S3	0.3

AL SPOHRER Spohrer, Alfred Ray b: 12/3/02, Philadelphia, Pa. d: 7/17/72, Plymouth, N.H. BR/TR, 5'10.5", 175 lbs. Deb: 4/13/28

YEAR	TM/L	G	AB	R	H	2B	3B	HR	RBI	BB	SO	AVG	OBP	SLG	PRO+	BR	/A	RC	SB	CS	SBR	FA	FR	POS	TPR
1928	NY-N	2	2	0	0	0	0	0	0	0	0	.000	.000	.000	-99	-1	-1	0	0			1.000	0	/C	-0.1
	Bos-N	51	124	15	27	3	0	0	9	5	11	.218	.254	.242	32	-13	-12	7	1			.976	-5	C	-1.4
	Yr	53	126	15	27	3	0	0	9	5	11	.214	.250	.238	30	-13	-12	7	1			.977	-5	C	-1.5
1929	Bos-N	114	342	42	93	21	8	2	48	26	35	.272	.327	.398	82	-12	-10	44	1			.954	-10	*C	-0.9
1930	Bos-N	112	356	44	113	22	8	2	37	22	24	.317	.361	.441	96	-4	-2	55	3			.957	-18	*C	-1.0
1931	Bos-N	114	350	23	84	17	5	0	27	22	27	.240	.285	.317	64	-19	-18	32	2			.982	-0	*C	-1.0
1932	Bos-N	104	335	31	90	12	2	0	33	15	26	.269	.300	.316	69	-16	-14	32	2			.991	10	*C	0.1
1933	Bos-N	67	184	11	46	6	1	1	12	11	13	.250	.292	.310	78	-7	-5	17	3			.972	-6	C	-0.8
1934	Bos-N	100	265	25	59	15	0	0	17	14	18	.223	.262	.279	49	-21	-18	19	1			.977	0	C	-1.4
1935	Bos-N	92	260	22	63	7	1	1	16	9	12	.242	.273	.288	55	-18	-15	20	0			.958	-10	C	-2.1
Total	8	756	2218	213	575	103	25	6	199	124	166	.259	.301	.336	70	-110	-95	226	13			.972	-39	C	-8.6

JIM SPOTTS Spotts, James Russell b: 4/10/09, Honey Brook, Pa. d: 6/15/64, Medford, N.J. BR/TR, 5'10.5", 175 lbs. Deb: 4/23/30

YEAR	TM/L	G	AB	R	H	2B	3B	HR	RBI	BB	SO	AVG	OBP	SLG	PRO+	BR	/A	RC	SB	CS	SBR	FA	FR	POS	TPR
1930	Phi-N	3	2	1	0	0	0	0	0	0	1	.000	.000	.000	-93	-1	-1	0	0			1.000	0	/C	-0.1

CHARLIE SPRAGUE Sprague, Charles Wellington b: 10/10/1864, Cleveland, Ohio d: 12/31/12, Des Moines, Iowa BL/TL, 5'11", 150 lbs. Deb: 9/17/1887

YEAR	TM/L	G	AB	R	H	2B	3B	HR	RBI	BB	SO	AVG	OBP	SLG	PRO+	BR	/A	RC	SB	CS	SBR	FA	FR	POS	TPR
1887	Chi-N	3	13	0	2	0	0	0	0	0	2	.154	.154	.154	-12	-2	-2	0	0			.667	-1	/PO	-0.1
1889	Cle-N	2	7	2	1	0	0	0	1	1	0	.143	.250	.143	12	-1	-1	1	1			.857	1	/P	0.0
1890	Tol-a	55	199	25	47	5	6	1		16		.236	.303	.337	88	-3	-4	24	10			.892	-6	OP	-0.7
Total	3	60	219	27	50	5	6	1	1	17	2	.228	.293	.320	79	-5	-7	25	11			.892	-6	/OP	-0.8

ED SPRAGUE Sprague, Edward Nelson Jr. b: 7/25/67, Castro Valley, Cal. BR/TR, 6'2", 215 lbs. Deb: 5/08/91 F

YEAR	TM/L	G	AB	R	H	2B	3B	HR	RBI	BB	SO	AVG	OBP	SLG	PRO+	BR	/A	RC	SB	CS	SBR	FA	FR	POS	TPR
1991	Tor-A	61	160	17	44	7	0	4	20	19	43	.275	.363	.394	105	2	2	23	0	3	-2	.870	-1	31/CD	-0.2
1992	*Tor-A	22	47	6	11	2	0	1	7	3	7	.234	.280	.340	70	-2	-2	5	0	0	0	.985	1	C/13D	-0.1
Total	2	83	207	23	55	9	0	5	27	22	50	.266	.345	.382	97	1	-0	28	0	3	-2	.870	0	/31CD	-0.3

HARRY SPRATT Spratt, Henry Lee b: 7/10/1887, Broadford, Va. d: 7/3/69, Washington, D.C. BL/TR, 5'8.5", 175 lbs. Deb: 4/13/11

YEAR	TM/L	G	AB	R	H	2B	3B	HR	RBI	BB	SO	AVG	OBP	SLG	PRO+	BR	/A	RC	SB	CS	SBR	FA	FR	POS	TPR
1911	Bos-N	62	154	22	37	4	4	2	13	13	25	.240	.299	.357	77	-4	-6	17	1			.892	-8	S/23O	-1.3
1912	Bos-N	27	89	6	23	3	2	3	15	7	11	.258	.313	.438	102	-0	-0	12	2			.842	-13	S	-1.2
Total	2	89	243	28	60	7	6	5	28	20	36	.247	.304	.387	86	-4	-6	29	3			.871	-22	/S2O3	-2.5

GEORGE SPRIGGS Spriggs, George Herman b: 5/22/41, Newell, Md. BL/TR, 5'11", 175 lbs. Deb: 9/15/65

YEAR	TM/L	G	AB	R	H	2B	3B	HR	RBI	BB	SO	AVG	OBP	SLG	PRO+	BR	/A	RC	SB	CS	SBR	FA	FR	POS	TPR
1965	Pit-N	9	2	5	1	0	0	0	0	0	0	.500	.500	.500	182	0	0	1	2	0	1	.000	0	/O	0.1
1966	Pit-N	9	7	0	1	0	0	0	0	0	3	.143	.143	.143	-20	-1	-1	0	0	0	0	.000	0	H	-0.1
1967	Pit-N	38	57	14	10	1	1	0	5	6	20	.175	.254	.228	39	-4	-4	4	3	0	1	1.000	-1	O	-0.6
1969	KC-A	23	29	4	4	2	1	0	0	3	8	.138	.242	.276	44	-2	-2	2	0	0	0	1.000	-1	/O	-0.4
1970	KC-A	51	130	12	27	2	3	1	7	14	32	.208	.285	.292	59	-7	-7	12	4	3	-1	.953	1	O	-0.9
Total	5	130	225	35	43	5	5	1	12	23	63	.191	.269	.271	51	-15	-15	19	9	3	1	.965	-1	/O	-1.9

STEVE SPRINGER Springer, Steven Michael b: 2/11/61, Long Beach, Cal. BR/TR, 6', 190 lbs. Deb: 5/22/90

YEAR	TM/L	G	AB	R	H	2B	3B	HR	RBI	BB	SO	AVG	OBP	SLG	PRO+	BR	/A	RC	SB	CS	SBR	FA	FR	POS	TPR
1990	Cle-A	4	12	1	2	0	0	0	1	0	6	.167	.167	.167	-7	-2	-2	0	0	0	0	1.000	-1	/3D	-0.2
1992	NY-N	4	5	0	2	1	0	0	0	0	1	.400	.400	.600	181	0	0	1	0	0	0	1.000	-0	/23	0.0
Total	2	8	17	1	4	1	0	0	1	0	7	.235	.235	.294	48	-1	-1	2	0	0	0	1.000	-1	/32D	-0.2

JOE SPRINZ Sprinz, Joseph Conrad "Mule" b: 8/3/02, St.Louis, Mo. BR/TR, 5'11", 185 lbs. Deb: 7/16/30

YEAR	TM/L	G	AB	R	H	2B	3B	HR	RBI	BB	SO	AVG	OBP	SLG	PRO+	BR	/A	RC	SB	CS	SBR	FA	FR	POS	TPR
1930	Cle-A	17	45	5	8	1	0	0	2	4	4	.178	.245	.200	14	-6	-6	2	0	0	0	1.000	6	C	0.1
1931	Cle-A	1	3	0	0	0	0	0	0	0	0	.000	.000	.000	-95	-1	-1	0	0	0	0	1.000	0	/C	-0.1
1933	StL-N	3	5	1	1	0	0	0	0	1	1	.200	.333	.200	53	-0	-0	0	0			1.000	2	/C	0.2
Total	3	21	53	6	9	1	0	0	2	5	5	.170	.241	.189	12	-7	-7	3	0	0		1.000	8	/C	0.2

FREDDY SPURGEON Spurgeon, Fred b: 10/9/1900, Wabash, Ind. d: 11/5/70, Kalamazoo, Mich. BR/TR, 5'11.5", 160 lbs. Deb: 9/19/24

YEAR	TM/L	G	AB	R	H	2B	3B	HR	RBI	BB	SO	AVG	OBP	SLG	PRO+	BR	/A	RC	SB	CS	SBR	FA	FR	POS	TPR
1924	Cle-A	3	7	0	1	1	0	0	0	0	0	.143	.250	.286	37	-1	-1	1	0	0	0	.882	1	/2	0.0
1925	Cle-A	107	376	50	108	9	3	0	32	15	21	.287	.315	.327	62	-21	-22	39	8	5	-1	.927	-4	32/S	-2.0
1926	Cle-A	149	614	101	181	31	3	0	49	27	36	.295	.327	.355	77	-21	-22	73	7	2	1	.962	-8	*2	-2.3
1927	Cle-A	57	179	30	45	6	1	1	19	18	14	.251	.323	.313	65	-9	-9	19	8	1	2	.938	-8	2	-1.3
Total	4	316	1176	181	335	47	7	1	100	60	71	.285	.322	.339	70	-52	-53	131	23	8	2	.958	-19	2/3S	-5.6

ED SPURNEY Spurney, Edward Frederick b: 1/19/1872, Cleveland, Ohio d: 10/12/32, Cleveland, Ohio Deb: 6/26/1891

YEAR	TM/L	G	AB	R	H	2B	3B	HR	RBI	BB	SO	AVG	OBP	SLG	PRO+	BR	/A	RC	SB	CS	SBR	FA	FR	POS	TPR
1891	Pit-N	3	7	2	2	1	0	0	0	2	1	.286	.444	.429	161	1	1	1	0			.889	-1	/S	0.0

MIKE SQUIRES Squires, Michael Lynn b: 3/5/52, Kalamazoo, Mich. BL/TL, 5'11", 185 lbs. Deb: 9/01/75 C

YEAR	TM/L	G	AB	R	H	2B	3B	HR	RBI	BB	SO	AVG	OBP	SLG	PRO+	BR	/A	RC	SB	CS	SBR	FA	FR	POS	TPR
1975	Chi-A	20	65	5	15	0	0	0	4	8	5	.231	.315	.231	55	-3	-4	5	3	0	1	.988	0	1	-0.4
1977	Chi-A	3	3	0	0	0	0	0	0	0	1	.000	.000	.000	-99	-1	-1	0	0	0	0	1.000	0	/1	0.0
1978	Chi-A	46	150	25	42	9	2	0	19	16	21	.280	.349	.367	101	1	0	20	4	4	-1	.997	-2	1	-0.6
1979	Chi-A	122	295	44	78	10	1	2	22	22	9	.264	.320	.325	74	-10	-10	30	15	5	2	.995	4	*1/O	-0.9
1980	Chi-A	131	343	38	97	11	3	2	33	33	24	.283	.347	.350	92	-3	-3	41	8	9	-3	.995	4	*1/C	-0.7
1981	Chi-A	92	294	35	78	9	0	0	25	22	17	.265	.316	.296	79	-8	-7	29	7	2	1	.992	2	1/O	-0.9
1982	Chi-A	116	195	33	52	9	3	1	21	14	13	.267	.316	.359	85	-4	-4	21	3	3	-1	.995	7	*1	-0.1
1983	*Chi-A	143	153	21	34	4	1	1	11	22	11	.222	.328	.281	67	-6	-6	15	3	3	-1	**.996**	6	*1/3D	-0.4
1984	Chi-A	104	82	9	15	1	0	0	6	6	7	.183	.239	.195	21	-9	-9	4	2	2	-1	1.000	4	13/OP	-0.7
1985	Chi-A	2	0	1	0	0	0	0	0	0	0	—	—	—	—	0	0	0	0	0	0	.000	0	/R	0.0
Total	10	779	1580	211	411	53	10	6	141	143	108	.260	.323	.318	78	-43	-44	166	45	28	-3	.995	25	1/3DOCP	-4.7

MARV STAEHLE Staehle, Marvin Gustave b: 3/13/42, Oak Park, Ill. BL/TR, 5'10", 172 lbs. Deb: 9/15/64

YEAR	TM/L	G	AB	R	H	2B	3B	HR	RBI	BB	SO	AVG	OBP	SLG	PRO+	BR	/A	RC	SB	CS	SBR	FA	FR	POS	TPR
1964	Chi-A	6	5	0	2	0	0	0	2	0	0	.400	.400	.400	127	0	0	1	1	0	0	.000	0	H	0.0
1965	Chi-A	7	7	0	3	0	0	0	2	0	0	.429	.429	.429	154	0	0	1	0	0	0	.000	0	H	0.0
1966	Chi-A	8	15	2	2	0	0	0	0	4	2	.133	.316	.133	37	-1	-1	1	1	0	0	1.000	1	/2	0.0
1967	Chi-A	32	54	1	6	1	0	0	1	4	8	.111	.172	.130	-10	-7	-7	1	1	1	-0	1.000	1	2/S	-0.7
1969	Mon-N	6	17	4	7	2	0	1	1	2	0	.412	.474	.706	226	3	3	6	0	0	0	.944	-1	/2	0.3
1970	Mon-N	104	321	41	70	9	1	0	26	39	21	.218	.309	.252	52	-21	-21	27	1	3	-2	.963	-13	2/S	-2.9
1971	Atl-N	22	36	5	4	0	0	0	1	5	4	.111	.238	.111	2	-5	-5	1	0	0	0	1.000	4	/23	-0.1
Total	7	185	455	53	94	12	1	1	33	54	35	.207	.296	.244	50	-30	-30	38	4	4	-1	.971	-8	2/S3	-3.4

HEINIE STAFFORD Stafford, Henry Alexander b: 11/1/1891, Orleans, Vt. d: 1/29/72, Lake Worth, Fla. BR/TR, 5'7", 160 lbs. Deb: 10/05/16

YEAR	TM/L	G	AB	R	H	2B	3B	HR	RBI	BB	SO	AVG	OBP	SLG	PRO+	BR	/A	RC	SB	CS	SBR	FA	FR	POS	TPR
1916	NY-N	1	1	0	0	0	0	0	0	0	0	.000	.000	.000	-99	-0	-0	0	0			.000	0	H	0.0

YEAR	TM/L	G	AB	R	H	2B	3B	HR	RBI	BB	SO	AVG	OBP	SLG	PRO+	BR	/A	RC	SB	CS	SBR	FA	FR	POS	TPR

■ **GENERAL STAFFORD**   Stafford, James Joseph "Jamsey"   b: 7/9/1868, Webster, Mass.   d: 9/18/23, Worcester, Mass.   BR/TR, 5'8", 165 lbs.   Deb: 8/27/1890   F

1890	Buf-P	15	49	11	7	1	0	0	3	7	8	.143	.250	.163	14	-6	-5	3	2			.893	-2	P/O	-0.2
1893	NY-N	67	281	58	79	7	4	5	27	25	31	.281	.344	.388	96	-2	-2	45	19			.901	-7	O	-1.0
1894	NY-N	14	46	10	10	1	1	0	4	10	7	.217	.368	.283	61	-3	-2	6	2			.750	-3	/3O21	-0.5
1895	NY-N	123	463	79	129	12	5	3	73	40	32	.279	.344	.346	82	-13	-11	71	42			.911	-8	*2O/3	-1.2
1896	NY-N	59	230	28	66	9	1	0	40	13	18	.287	.333	.335	80	-7	-6	32	15			.897	-5	O/S	-1.2
1897	NY-N	7	23	0	2	0	0	0	3	3		.087	.192	.087	-26	-4	-4	0	0			1.000	-3	/OS	-0.7
	Lou-N	111	432	68	120	16	5	7	53	31		.278	.330	.387	92	-8	-6	63	14			.887	-12	*S/O3	-1.3
	Yr	118	455	68	122	16	5	7	56	34		.268	.323	.371	86	-12	-10	62	14			.882	-15	*SO/3	-2.0
1898	Lou-N	49	181	26	54	3	0	1	25	19		.298	.365	.331	102	1	1	26	7			.901	-8	2O/3	-0.6
	Bos-N	37	123	21	32	2	0	1	8	4		.260	.289	.301	66	-5	-6	12	3			.909	-3	O/1	-1.1
	Yr	86	304	47	86	5	0	2	33	23		.283	.335	.319	87	-5	-5	38	10			.924	-12	O2/31	-1.7
1899	Bos-N	55	182	29	55	4	2	3	40	7		.302	.328	.396	90	-1	-4	28	9			.956	-8	O/2S	-1.3
	Was-N	31	118	11	29	5	1	1	14	5		.246	.276	.331	67	-6	-6	12	4			.951	-5	2S/3	-0.8
	Yr	86	300	40	84	9	3	4	54	12		.280	.308	.370	81	-7	-10	41	13			.956	-13	O2S/3	-2.1
Total	8	568	2128	341	583	60	19	21	290	164	96	.274	.331	.350	83	-54	-51	298	117			.911	-66	O2S/3P1	-9.9

■ **BOB STAFFORD**   Stafford, Robert M.   b: 6/26/1872, Oak Ridge, N.C.   d: 8/21/16, Moore's Springs, N.C.   Deb: 10/12/1890

| 1890 | Phi-a | 1 | 2 | 0 | 0 | 0 | 0 | 0 | | 0 | | .000 | .000 | .000 | -99 | -0 | -0 | 0 | 0 | | | 1.000 | 1 | /O | 0.0 |

■ **STEVE STAGGS**   Staggs, Stephen Robert   b: 5/6/51, Anchorage, Alaska   BR/TR, 5'9", 150 lbs.   Deb: 7/01/77

1977	Tor-A	72	290	37	75	11	6	2	28	36	38	.259	.340	.359	90	-3	-4	36	5	9	-4	.965	-14	2	-1.6
1978	Oak-A	47	78	10	19	2	2	0	19	17	.244	.392	.321	108	1	2	11	2	3	-1	.976	-3	2/S3D	0.0
Total	2	119	368	47	94	13	8	2	28	55	55	.255	.352	.351	94	-2	-2	47	7	12	-5	.968	-17	2/D3S	-1.6

■ **CHICK STAHL**   Stahl, Charles Sylvester   b: 1/10/1873, Avila, Ind.   d: 3/28/07, W.Baden, Ind.   BL/TL, 5'10", 160 lbs.   Deb: 4/19/1897   M

1897	*Bos-N	114	469	112	166	30	13	4	97	38		.354	.406	.499	130	25	20	105	18			.928	-3	*O	0.8
1898	Bos-N	125	467	72	144	21	8	3	52	46		.308	.375	.407	118	15	11	77	6			.968	-2	*O	0.1
1899	Bos-N	148	576	122	202	23	19	7	52	72		.351	.426	.493	139	42	34	139	33			.969	6	*O/P	2.6
1900	Bos-N	136	553	88	163	23	16	5	82	34		.295	.336	.421	96	4	-6	90	27			**.968**	9	*O	-0.7
1901	Bos-A	131	515	105	156	20	16	6	72	54		.303	.376	.439	128	18	20	100	29			.957	-1	*O	0.8
1902	Bos-A	127	508	92	164	22	11	2	58	37		.323	.373	.421	117	14	12	93	24			.953	-5	*O	-0.1
1903	*Bos-A	77	299	60	82	12	4	2	44	28		.274	.338	.375	108	5	4	43	10			.961	-2	O	-0.3
1904	Bos-A	157	587	83	170	27	19	3	67	64		.290	.356	.416	139	33	29	99	11			.961	-15	*O	0.6
1905	Bos-A	134	500	61	129	17	4	0	47	50		.258	.332	.308	102	3	3	60	18			.977	-5	*O	-1.0
1906	Bos-A	155	595	63	170	24	6	4	51	47		.286	.345	.366	123	16	16	84	13			.961	10	*OM	2.0
Total	10	1304	5069	858	1546	219	118	36	622	470		.305	.369	.416	121	175	142	891	189			.961	-7	*O/P	4.8

■ **JAKE STAHL**   Stahl, Garland   b: 4/13/1879, Elkhart, Ill.   d: 9/18/22, Monrovia, Cal.   BR/TR, 6'2", 195 lbs.   Deb: 4/20/03   M

1903	Bos-A	40	92	14	22	3	5	2	8	4		.239	.286	.446	111	2	1	12	1			.956	-2	C/O	0.1
1904	Was-A	142	520	54	136	29	12	3	50	21		.262	.309	.381	120	10	10	72	25			.978	6	*1O	1.3
1905	Was-A	141	501	66	125	22	12	5	66	28		.250	.311	.371	121	9	11	74	41			.986	2	*1M	0.9
1906	Was-A	137	482	38	107	9	8	0	51	21		.222	.262	.274	71	-18	-16	45	30			.983	-2	*1M	-2.4
1908	NY-A	75	274	34	70	18	5	2	42	11		.255	.299	.380	119	5	5	36	17			.933	4	O/1	0.7
	Bos-A	78	262	29	64	9	11	0	23	20		.244	.333	.363	123	8	7	36	13			.984	-2	1	0.4
	Yr	153	536	63	134	27	16	2	65	31		.250	.316	.371	121	13	12	72	30			.984	2	1O	1.1
1909	Bos-A	127	435	62	128	19	12	6	60	43		.294	.377	.434	133	28	27	77	16			.986	-11	*1	1.7
1910	Bos-A	144	531	68	144	19	16	10	77	42		.271	.334	.424	134	21	19	82	22			.985	-7	*1	1.3
1912	*Bos-A	95	326	40	98	21	6	3	60	31		.301	.372	.429	123	12	10	57	13			.980	-2	1M	0.7
1913	Bos-A	2	2	0	0	0	0	0	0	0	1	.000	.000	.000	-98	-0	-1	0	0			.000	0	HM	-0.1
Total	9	981	3425	405	894	149	87	31	437	221	1	.261	.322	.382	120	75	74	490	178			.983	-14	1/OC	4.6

■ **LARRY STAHL**   Stahl, Larry Floyd   b: 6/29/41, Belleville, Ill.   BL/TL, 6'1", 185 lbs.   Deb: 9/11/64

1964	KC-A	15	46	7	12	1	0	3	6	1	10	.261	.277	.478	102	0	-0	6	0	0	0	.955	1	O	0.0
1965	KC-A	28	81	9	16	2	1	4	14	5	16	.198	.253	.395	82	-2	-2	8	1	0	0	1.000	1	O	-0.2
1966	KC-A	119	312	37	78	11	5	5	34	17	63	.250	.291	.365	90	-6	-5	34	5	3	-0	.980	-4	O	-1.3
1967	NY-N	71	155	9	37	5	0	1	18	8	25	.239	.285	.290	66	-7	-0	12	2	2	-1	.969	6	O	-0.3
1968	NY-N	53	183	15	43	7	2	3	10	21	38	.235	.314	.344	97	-0	-0	22	3	0	1	.983	6	O/1	0.5
1969	SD-N	95	162	10	32	6	2	3	10	17	31	.198	.278	.315	68	-8	-7	13	3	3	-1	.981	4	O1	-0.7
1970	SD-N	52	66	5	12	2	0	0	3	2	14	.182	.206	.212	13	-8	-8	3	2	2	-1	1.000	0	O	-0.9
1971	SD-N	114	308	27	78	13	4	8	36	26	59	.253	.311	.399	107	-1	2	37	4	3	-1	.987	5	O/1	-0.3
1972	SD-N	107	297	31	67	9	3	7	20	31	67	.226	.299	.347	89	-7	-4	31	1	3	-2	.986	-2	O/1	-1.3
1973	*Cin-N	76	112	17	25	2	2	2	12	14	34	.225	.317	.333	85	-3	-2	13	1	0	0	1.000	-1	O/1	-0.4
Total	10	730	1721	167	400	58	19	36	163	142	357	.232	.293	.351	86	-41	-33	180	22	16	-3	.983	16	O/1	-4.4

■ **ROY STAIGER**   Staiger, Roy Joseph   b: 1/6/50, Tulsa, Okla.   BR/TR, 6', 195 lbs.   Deb: 9/12/75

1975	NY-N	13	19	2	3	1	0	0	4	0	5	.158	.158	.211	2	-3	-2	0	0	0	0	1.000	1	3	-0.1
1976	NY-N	95	304	23	67	8	1	2	26	25	35	.220	.282	.273	62	-17	-15	23	3	3	-1	.967	19	3/S	0.4
1977	NY-N	40	123	16	31	9	2	0	11	4	20	.252	.276	.374	76	-5	-4	12	1	0	0	.934	6	3/S	0.1
1979	NY-A	4	11	1	3	1	0	0	1	1	0	.273	.333	.364	90	-0	-0	1	0	0	0	1.000	0	/3	0.0
Total	4	152	457	42	104	19	3	4	38	30	59	.228	.277	.300	64	-24	-22	36	4	3	-1	.960	26	3/S	0.4

■ **TUCK STAINBACK**   Stainback, George Tucker   b: 8/4/10, Los Angeles, Cal.   BR/TR, 5'11.5", 175 lbs.   Deb: 4/17/34

1934	Chi-N	104	359	47	110	14	3	2	46	8	42	.306	.327	.379	90	-6	-5	45	7			.955	-6	O/3	-1.5
1935	Chi-N	47	94	16	24	4	0	3	11	0	13	.255	.271	.394	76	-3	-4	9	1			.932	-5	O	-0.9
1936	Chi-N	44	75	13	13	3	0	1	5	6	14	.173	.235	.253	31	-7	-8	5	1			1.000	-4	O	-1.2
1937	Chi-N	72	160	18	37	7	1	0	14	7	16	.231	.268	.287	49	-11	-12	12	3			.981	-2	O	-1.5
1938	StL-N	6	10	2	0	0	0	0	0	0	3	.000	.000	.000	-95	-3	-3	0	0			1.000	1	/O	-0.2
	Phi-N	30	81	9	21	3	0	1	11	3		.259	.294	.333	74	-3	-3	4	1			.980	-2	O	-0.6
	Bro-N	35	104	15	34	6	3	0	20	2	4	.327	.346	.442	113	2	2	16	1			.981	-1	O	0.0
	Yr	71	195	26	55	9	3	1	31	5	10	.282	.307	.374	86	-4	-4	23	2			.982	-3	O	-0.8
1939	Bro-N	68	201	22	54	7	0	3	19	4	23	.269	.290	.348	68	-9	-10	21	0			.938	-5	O	-1.7
1940	Det-A	15	40	4	9	2	0	1	1	1	9	.225	.262	.275	36	-4	-4	3	0	0	0	.968	-4	/O	-0.1
1941	Det-A	94	200	19	49	8	1	2	10	3	21	.245	.260	.325	49	-14	-16	18	6	3	0	.948	-15	O	-3.4
1942	*NY-A	15	10	0	2	0	0	0	0	0	2	.200	.200	.200	13	-1	-1	0	0	0	0	1.000	-0	/O	-0.1
1943	*NY-A	71	231	31	60	11	7	0	10	7	16	.260	.285	.325	77	-7	-7	21	3	3	-1	.993	-1	O	-1.3
1944	NY-A	30	78	13	17	3	0	0	5	3	7	.218	.247	.256	42	-6	-6	6	1	0	0	.957	-3	O	-1.0
1945	NY-A	95	327	40	84	12	5	2	32	13	20	.257	.289	.352	82	-7	-9	33	0	4	-2	.968	9	O	-0.7
1946	Phi-A	91	291	35	71	10	2	0	20	7	20	.244	.264	.292	56	-18	-18	23	3	2	-0	.963	3	O	-2.0
Total	13	817	2261	284	585	90	14	17	204	64	213	.259	.284	.333	68	-97	-104	219	27	12		.965	-29	O/3	-16.2

■ **MATT STAIRS**   Stairs, Matthew Wade   b: 2/27/69, St.John, N.B., Canada   BR/TR, 5'9", 175 lbs.   Deb: 5/29/92

| 1992 | Mon-N | 13 | 30 | 2 | 5 | 2 | 0 | 0 | 5 | 7 | 7 | .167 | .324 | .233 | 61 | -1 | -1 | 3 | 0 | 0 | 0 | .933 | -1 | O | -0.3 |

YEAR	TM/L	G	AB	R	H	2B	3B	HR	RBI	BB	SO	AVG	OBP	SLG	PRO+	BR	/A	RC	SB	CS	SBR	FA	FR	POS	TPR

■ GALE STALEY
Staley, George Gaylord b: 5/2/1899, DePere, Wis. d: 4/19/89, Walnut Creek, Cal. BL/TR, 5'8.5", 167 lbs. Deb: 9/16/25

| 1925 | Chi-N | 7 | 26 | 2 | 11 | 2 | 0 | 0 | 3 | 2 | 1 | .423 | .464 | .500 | 144 | 2 | 2 | 6 | 0 | 1 | -1 | .979 | 4 | /2 | 0.5 |

■ VIRGIL STALLCUP
Stallcup, Thomas Virgil "Red" b: 1/3/22, Ravensford, N.C. d: 5/2/89, Greenville, S.C. BR/TR, 6'3", 185 lbs. Deb: 4/18/47

1947	Cin-N	8	1	1	0	0	0	0	0	0	1	.000	.000	.000	-99	-0	-0	0	0			.000	0	/S	0.0
1948	Cin-N	149	539	40	123	30	4	3	65	18	52	.228	.253	.315	55	-37	-34	40	2			.956	-0	*S	-2.7
1949	Cin-N	141	575	49	146	28	5	3	45	9	44	.254	.268	.336	60	-33	-34	49	1			.962	-0	*S	-3.3
1950	Cin-N	136	483	44	121	23	2	6	54	17	39	.251	.276	.356	65	-26	-26	44	4			**.973**	-5	*S	-2.1
1951	Cin-N	121	428	33	103	17	2	8	49	6	40	.241	.251	.346	58	-26	-27	34	2	4	-2	**.969**	-8	*S	-2.9
1952	Cin-N	2	1	0	0	0	0	0	0	0	0	.000	.000	.000	-99	-0	-0	0	0	0	0	.000	0	/S	0.0
	StL-N	29	31	4	4	1	0	0	1	1	5	.129	.156	.161	-12	-5	-5	0	0	0	0	1.000	2	S	-0.3
	Yr	31	32	4	4	1	0	0	1	1	5	.125	.152	.156	-15	-5	-5	1	0	0	0	1.000	2	S	-0.3
1953	StL-N	1	1	0	0	0	0	0	0	0	0	.000	.000	.000	-99	-0	-0	0	0	0	0	.000	0	H	0.0
Total	7	587	2059	171	497	99	13	22	214	51	181	.241	.260	.334	58	-127	-126	168	9	4		.965	-21	S	-11.3

■ GEORGE STALLER
Staller, George Walborn "Stopper" b: 4/1/16, Rutherford Heights, Pa. d: 7/3/92, Harrisburg, Pa. BL/TL, 5'11", 190 lbs. Deb: 9/14/43 C

| 1943 | Phi-A | 21 | 85 | 14 | 23 | 1 | 3 | 3 | 12 | 5 | 6 | .271 | .326 | .459 | 129 | 3 | 3 | 13 | 1 | 0 | 0 | .977 | -1 | O | 0.1 |

■ GEORGE STALLINGS
Stallings, George Tweedy "Gentleman George" b: 11/17/1867, Augusta, Ga. d: 5/13/29, Haddock, Ga. BR/TR, 6'1", 187 lbs. Deb: 5/22/1890 M

1890	Bro-N	4	11	1	0	0	0	0	0	0	3	.000	.154	.000	-53	-2	-2	0	0			.933	-1	/C	-0.3
1897	Phi-N	2	9	1	2	0	0	0	0	0		.222	.222	.333	47	-1	-1	1	0			1.000	1	/O1M	0.0
1898	Phi-N	1	0	1	0	0	0	0	0	0		—	—	—	—	0	0	0	0			.000	0	/HM	0.0
Total	3	7	20	3	2	1	0	0	0	1	3	.100	.182	.150	-7	-3	-3	1	0			.986	-1	/C1O	-0.3

■ OSCAR STANAGE
Stanage, Oscar Harland b: 3/17/1883, Tulare, Cal. d: 11/11/64, Detroit, Mich. BR/TR, 5'11", 190 lbs. Deb: 5/19/06 C

1906	Cin-N	1	1	0	0	0	0	0	0	0		.000	.000	.000	-96	-0	-0	0	0			1.000	-0	/C	0.0
1909	*Det-A	77	252	17	66	8	6	0	21	11		.262	.298	.341	98	-0	-1	26	2			.964	-8	C	-0.3
1910	Det-A	88	275	24	57	7	4	2	25	20		.207	.266	.280	68	-9	-11	21	1			.952	-2	C	-0.6
1911	Det-A	141	503	45	133	13	7	3	51	20		.264	.297	.336	73	-18	-21	51	3			.952	-13	*C	-1.9
1912	Det-A	121	394	35	103	9	4	0	41	34		.261	.326	.305	83	-9	-8	40	3			.950	-28	*C	-2.4
1913	Det-A	80	241	19	54	13	2	0	21	21	35	.224	.292	.295	73	-9	-8	22	5			.960	-8	C	-1.1
1914	Det-A	122	400	16	77	8	4	0	25	24	58	.192	.242	.233	41	-29	-30	25	2	1	0	.960	-6	*C	-2.8
1915	Det-A	100	300	27	67	9	2	1	31	19	41	.223	.274	.277	62	-14	-15	25	5	1	1	.964	-9	*C	-1.8
1916	Det-A	94	291	16	69	17	3	0	30	17	48	.237	.286	.316	78	-8	-9	28	3			.969	-9	C	-1.2
1917	Det-A	99	297	19	61	14	1	0	30	20	35	.205	.262	.259	59	-15	-15	21	3			.977	-4	C	-1.3
1918	Det-A	54	186	9	47	4	0	1	14	11	18	.253	.294	.290	80	-6	-5	16	2			.980	-8	C/1S	-1.1
1919	Det-A	38	120	9	29	4	1	1	15	7	12	.242	.295	.317	73	-5	-4	11	1			.974	1	C/1	-0.1
1920	Det-A	78	238	12	55	17	0	0	17	14	21	.231	.277	.303	55	-16	-16	21	0			.958	-10	C	-2.0
1925	Det-A	3	5	0	1	0	0	0	0	0	0	.200	.200	.200	2	-1	-1	0	0	0	0	1.000	-1	/C	-0.1
Total	14	1096	3503	248	819	123	34	8	321	219	268	.234	.284	.295	69	-138	-144	305	30	2		.961	-105	*C/1S	-16.7

■ JERRY STANDAERT
Standaert, Jerome John b: 11/2/01, Chicago, Ill. d: 8/4/64, Chicago, Ill. BR/TR, 5'10", 168 lbs. Deb: 4/16/25

1925	Bro-N	1	1	0	0	0	0	0	0	0	1	.000	.000	.000	-99	-0	-0	0	0	0	0	.000	0	H	0.0
1926	Bro-N	66	113	13	39	8	2	0	14	5	7	.345	.378	.451	124	3	4	19	0			.918	-11	23/S	-0.6
1929	Bos-A	19	18	1	3	2	0	0	4	3	2	.167	.286	.278	47	-1	-1	2	0			.958	-0	1	-0.2
Total	3	86	132	14	42	10	2	0	18	8	10	.318	.362	.424	111	2	2	20	0	0		.966	-11	/231S	-0.8

■ PETE STANICEK
Stanicek, Peter Louis b: 4/18/63, Harvey, Ill. BB/TR, 5'11", 175 lbs. Deb: 9/01/87 F

1987	Bal-A	30	113	9	31	3	0	0	9	8	19	.274	.333	.301	72	-5	-4	13	8	1	2	.975	-6	2D/3	-0.7
1988	Bal-A	83	261	29	60	7	1	4	17	28	45	.230	.314	.310	78	-8	-7	25	12	6	0	.985	-5	O2/D	-1.3
Total	2	113	374	38	91	10	1	4	26	36	64	.243	.320	.307	76	-12	-11	38	20	7	2	.967	-10	/O2D3	-2.0

■ STEVE STANICEK
Stanicek, Stephen Blair b: 6/19/61, Lake Forest, Ill. BR/TR, 6'1", 190 lbs. Deb: 9/16/87 F

1987	Mil-A	4	7	2	2	0	0	0	0	0	2	.286	.286	.286	51	-0	-0	1	0	0	0	.000	0	/D	0.0
1989	Phi-N	9	9	0	1	0	0	0	1	0	3	.111	.111	.111	-36	-2	-2	0	0	0	0	.000	0	H	-0.2
Total	2	13	16	2	3	0	0	0	1	0	5	.188	.188	.188	4	-2	-2	1	0	0			0	/D	-0.2

■ TOM STANKARD
Stankard, Thomas Francis b: 3/20/1882, Waltham, Mass. d: 6/13/58, Waltham, Mass. BR/TR, 6', 190 lbs. Deb: 7/02/04

| 1904 | Pit-N | 2 | 2 | 0 | 0 | 0 | 0 | 0 | 0 | 0 | 0 | .000 | .000 | .000 | -97 | -0 | -0 | 0 | 0 | | | 1.000 | -1 | /S3 | -0.1 |

■ ANDY STANKIEWICZ
Stankiewicz, Andrew Neal b: 8/10/64, Inglewood, Cal. BR/TR, 5'9", 165 lbs. Deb: 4/11/92

| 1992 | NY-A | 116 | 400 | 52 | 107 | 22 | 2 | 2 | 25 | 38 | 42 | .268 | .339 | .348 | 91 | -3 | -4 | 47 | 9 | 5 | -0 | .973 | 6 | S2/D | 0.8 |

■ EDDIE STANKY
Stanky, Edward Raymond "The Brat" or "Muggsy" b: 9/3/16, Philadelphia, Pa. BR/TR, 5'8", 170 lbs. Deb: 4/21/43 MC

1943	Chi-N	142	510	92	125	15	1	0	47	92	42	.245	.363	.278	88	-4	-3	58	4			.966	12	*2S/3	1.8
1944	Chi-N	13	25	4	6	0	1	0	2	2	2	.240	.296	.320	74	-1	-1	2	1			.875	2	/2S3	-0.1
	Bro-N	89	261	32	72	9	2	0	16	44	13	.276	.382	.326	102	3	3	37	3			.961	3	2S/3	-1.0
	Yr	102	286	36	78	9	3	0	16	46	15	.273	.375	.325	100	2	2	39	4			.958	-16	2S/3	-0.9
1945	Bro-N	153	555	**128**	143	29	5	1	39	**148**	42	.258	.417	.333	111	18	18	93	6			.962	9	*2/S	3.6
1946	Bro-N	144	483	98	132	24	7	0	36	**137**	56	.273	**.436**	.352	124	26	25	90	3			.977	-5	*2	3.1
1947	*Bro-N★	146	559	97	141	24	5	3	53	103	39	.252	.373	.329	85	-5	-8	78	3			**.985**	7	*2	0.8
1948	*Bos-N†	67	247	49	79	14	2	2	29	61	13	.320	.455	.417	140	17	18	52	3			.981	5	2	2.6
1949	Bos-N	138	506	90	144	24	5	1	42	113	41	.285	.417	.358	116	14	18	86	3			.979	-9	*2	1.5
1950	NY-N☆	152	527	115	158	25	5	8	51	**144**	50	.300	**.460**	.412	131	35	35	116	9			.976	2	*2	4.2
1951	*NY-N	145	515	88	127	17	2	14	43	127	63	.247	.401	.369	108	13	12	90	8	5	-1	.977	-1	*2	1.8
1952	StL-N	53	83	13	19	4	0	1	7	19	9	.229	.373	.277	83	-1	-1	11	0	0	0	1.000	-1	2M	-0.1
1953	StL-N	17	30	5	8	0	0	0	1	6	4	.267	.405	.267	80	-0	-0	4	0	0	0	1.000	1	/2M	0.1
Total	11	1259	4301	811	1154	185	35	29	364	996	374	.268	.410	.348	109	114	116	717	48	5		.975	3	*2/S3	18.5

■ FRED STANLEY
Stanley, Frederick Blair b: 8/13/47, Farnhamville, Iowa BR/TR, 5'10", 167 lbs. Deb: 9/11/69 C

1969	Sea-A	17	43	2	12	2	1	0	4	3	8	.279	.326	.372	96	-0	-0	6	1	0	0	.962	-4	S/2	-0.3
1970	Mil-A	6	0	1	0	0	0	0	0	0	0	—	—	—	—	0	0	0	0	0	0	1.000	2	/2	0.2
1971	Cle-A	60	129	14	29	4	0	2	12	27	25	.225	.363	.302	83	-0	-2	16	1	0	0	.971	7	S/2	1.1
1972	Cle-A	6	12	1	2	0	0	0	2	3	2	.167	.286	.250	58	-1	-1	0	0	0	0	.917	-3	/S2	-0.4
	SD-N	39	85	15	17	2	0	0	2	12	19	.200	.306	.224	57	-5	-4	7	1	0	0	.989	3	2S/3	0.1
1973	NY-A	26	66	6	14	0	1	1	5	7	16	.212	.288	.288	65	-3	-3	6	0	0	0	.981	3	S2	0.3
1974	NY-A	33	38	2	7	0	0	0	3	3	2	.184	.244	.184	25	-4	-3	1	1	2	-1	.973	12	S2	0.9
1975	NY-A	117	252	34	56	5	1	0	15	21	27	.222	.285	.250	54	-15	-15	18	3	1	0	.977	4	S2/3	-0.3
1976	*NY-A	110	260	32	62	2	2	1	20	34	29	.238	.329	.273	78	-6	-6	26	1	0	0	**.983**	-24	S2/3	-1.9
1977	*NY-A	48	46	6	12	1	0	0	7	8	6	.261	.370	.326	93	-0	-0	6	0	0	0	.958	3	S/32	0.4
1978	*NY-A	81	160	14	35	7	0	1	9	25	31	.219	.324	.281	73	-5	-5	14	0	0	0	.959	-5	S2/3	-0.3
1979	NY-A	57	100	9	20	1	0	2	14	5	19	.200	.238	.270	38	-9	-9	6	0	0	0	.978	13	S3/210	0.5
1980	NY-A	49	86	13	18	3	0	0	7	15	22	.209	.269	.244	42	-7	-7	6	2	0	0	.923	7	S23	0.2
1981	*Oak-A	66	145	15	28	3	0	0	7	15	23	.193	.269	.221	44	-10	-10	11	2	0	0	.986	-17	S/2	-2.2

YEAR	TM/L	G	AB	R	H	2B	3B	HR	RBI	BB	SO	AVG	OBP	SLG	PRO+	BR	/A	RC	SB	CS	SBR	FA	FR	POS	TPR
1982	Oak-A	101	228	33	44	7	0	2	17	29	32	.193	.287	.250	51	-15	-14	17	0	1	-1	.963	-20	S/2	-2.7
Total	14	816	1650	197	356	38	5	10	120	196	243	.216	.302	.263	62	-81	-77	144	11	6	-0	.971	-18	S2/3O1	-4.4

■ JIM STANLEY
Stanley, James F. b: 1889, BB/TR, 5'6", 148 lbs. Deb: 4/19/14

YEAR	TM/L	G	AB	R	H	2B	3B	HR	RBI	BB	SO	AVG	OBP	SLG	PRO+	BR	/A	RC	SB	CS	SBR	FA	FR	POS	TPR
1914	Chi-F	54	98	13	19	3	0	0	4	19	14	.194	.347	.224	68	-3	-3	9	2			.878	-10	S/32O	-1.1

■ JOE STANLEY
Stanley, Joseph b: New Jersey Deb: 4/24/1884

YEAR	TM/L	G	AB	R	H	2B	3B	HR	RBI	BB	SO	AVG	OBP	SLG	PRO+	BR	/A	RC	SB	CS	SBR	FA	FR	POS	TPR
1884	Bal-U	6	21	3	5	1	0	0		0		.238	.238	.286	69	-1	-1	1				.444	-2	/O	-0.3

■ JOE STANLEY
Stanley, Joseph Bernard b: 4/2/1881, Washington, D.C. d: 9/13/67, Detroit, Mich. BB/TR, 5'9.5", 150 lbs. Deb: 9/11/1897 F

YEAR	TM/L	G	AB	R	H	2B	3B	HR	RBI	BB	SO	AVG	OBP	SLG	PRO+	BR	/A	RC	SB	CS	SBR	FA	FR	POS	TPR
1897	Was-N	1	1	0	0	0	0	0	0	0		.000	.000	.000	-99	-0	-0	0	0			.000	-0	/P	0.0
1902	Was-A	3	12	2	4	0	0	0	1	0		.333	.333	.333	84	-0	-0	1	0			.833	-1	/O	-0.1
1903	Bos-N	86	308	40	77	12	5	1	47	18		.250	.306	.331	85	-8	-6	36	10			.902	3	O/PS	-0.7
1904	Bos-N	3	8	0	0	0	0	0	0	0		.000	.000	.000	-99	-2	-2	0	0			.800	1	/O	-0.1
1905	Was-A	28	92	13	24	2	1	1	17	7		.261	.313	.337	111	1	1	12	4			.944	0	O	0.0
1906	Was-A	73	221	18	36	0	4	0	9	20		.163	.236	.199	39	-16	-14	14	6			.934	-5	O/P	-2.5
1909	Chi-N	22	52	4	7	1	0	0	2	6		.135	.224	.154	17	-5	-5	2	0			.947	-4	O	-1.1
Total	7	216	694	77	148	15	10	2	76	51		.213	.275	.272	67	-30	-27	65	20			.988	-6	O/PS	-4.5

■ MICKEY STANLEY
Stanley, Mitchell Jack b: 7/20/42, Grand Rapids, Mich BR/TR, 6'1", 195 lbs. Deb: 9/13/64

YEAR	TM/L	G	AB	R	H	2B	3B	HR	RBI	BB	SO	AVG	OBP	SLG	PRO+	BR	/A	RC	SB	CS	SBR	FA	FR	POS	TPR
1964	Det-A	4	11	3	3	0	0	0	1	0	1	.273	.273	.273	52	-1	-1	1	0	0	0	1.000	-1	/O	-0.2
1965	Det-A	30	117	14	28	6	0	3	13	3	12	.239	.258	.368	75	-4	-4	11	1	0	0	.986	3	O	-0.3
1966	Det-A	92	235	28	68	15	4	3	19	17	20	.289	.337	.426	115	5	4	33	2	1	0	1.000	2	O	0.4
1967	Det-A	145	333	38	70	7	3	7	24	29	46	.210	.273	.312	71	-12	-13	30	9	2	2	.982	-8	*O/1	-2.6
1968	*Det-A	153	583	88	151	16	6	11	60	42	57	.259	.313	.364	102	3	1	62	4	3	-1	**1.000**	3	*O1/S2	-0.4
1969	Det-A	149	592	73	139	28	1	16	70	52	56	.235	.299	.367	82	-13	-16	64	8	4	0	.985	-19	*OS/1	-3.6
1970	Det-A	142	568	83	143	21	11	13	47	45	56	.252	.307	.396	92	-7	-8	67	10	1	2	**1.000**	6	*O/1	-0.7
1971	Det-A	139	401	43	117	14	5	7	41	24	44	.292	.332	.404	103	3	1	52	1	3	-2	.988	6	*O	0.1
1972	*Det-A	142	435	45	102	16	6	14	55	29	49	.234	.282	.395	97	-2	-3	45	1	0	0	.994	6	*O	-0.3
1973	Det-A	157	602	81	147	23	5	17	57	48	65	.244	.300	.384	86	-8	-13	68	0	4	-2	.993	13	*O	-1.1
1974	Det-A	99	394	40	87	13	2	8	34	26	63	.221	.271	.325	68	-16	-17	32	5	3	-0	.992	6	O1/2	-1.7
1975	Det-A	52	164	26	42	7	3	3	19	15	27	.256	.322	.390	96	-0	-1	21	1	1	-0	.983	-1	O1/3D	-0.5
1976	Det-A	84	214	34	55	17	1	4	29	14	19	.257	.303	.402	101	1	-0	25	2	0	1	.969	-2	O13/S2D	-0.4
1977	Det-A	75	222	30	51	9	1	8	23	18	30	.230	.287	.387	78	-6	-8	24	0	0	0	.972	-6	O/1SD	-1.6
1978	Det-A	53	151	15	40	9	0	3	8	9	19	.265	.306	.384	90	-2	-2	17	0	1	-1	.960	-6	O1	-1.1
Total	15	1516	5022	641	1243	201	48	117	500	371	564	.248	.300	.377	89	-59	-80	549	44	23	-1	.991	2	*O/1S3D2	-14.0

■ MIKE STANLEY
Stanley, Robert Michael b: 6/25/63, Ft.Lauderdale, Fla BR/TR, 6'1", 185 lbs. Deb: 6/24/86

YEAR	TM/L	G	AB	R	H	2B	3B	HR	RBI	BB	SO	AVG	OBP	SLG	PRO+	BR	/A	RC	SB	CS	SBR	FA	FR	POS	TPR
1986	Tex-A	15	30	4	10	3	0	1	1	3	7	.333	.394	.533	146	2	2	7	1	0	0	.857	-1	/3COD	0.1
1987	Tex-A	78	216	34	59	8	1	6	37	31	48	.273	.367	.403	104	2	2	33	3	0	1	.980	-11	C1/OD	-0.5
1988	Tex-A	94	249	21	57	8	0	3	27	37	62	.229	.329	.297	75	-7	-7	26	0	0	0	.991	-3	CD/13	-0.7
1989	Tex-A	67	122	9	30	3	1	1	11	12	29	.246	.324	.311	78	-3	-3	12	1	0	0	.978	-4	CD/13	-0.6
1990	Tex-A	103	189	21	47	8	1	2	19	30	25	.249	.352	.333	92	-1	-1	24	1	0	0	.985	-3	CD/31	-0.1
1991	Tex-A	95	181	25	45	13	1	3	25	34	44	.249	.373	.381	111	4	4	29	0	0	0	.980	-10	C1/3OD	-0.4
1992	NY-A	68	173	24	43	7	0	8	27	33	45	.249	.372	.428	121	6	6	28	0	0	0	.980	5	C/1D	1.3
Total	7	520	1160	138	291	50	4	24	147	180	260	.251	.354	.363	98	3	2	160	6	0	2	.983	-26	C/D13O	-0.9

■ JACK STANSBURY
Stansbury, John James b: 12/6/1885, Phillipsburg, N.J. d: 12/26/70, Easton, Pa. BR/TR, 5'9", 165 lbs. Deb: 6/30/18

YEAR	TM/L	G	AB	R	H	2B	3B	HR	RBI	BB	SO	AVG	OBP	SLG	PRO+	BR	/A	RC	SB	CS	SBR	FA	FR	POS	TPR
1918	Bos-A	20	47	3	6	1	0	0	2	6	3	.128	.241	.149	18	-5	-4	2	0			.980	2	3/O	-0.2

■ BUCK STANTON
Stanton, George Washington b: 6/19/06, Stantonsburg, N.C d: 1/1/92, San Antonio, Tex. BL/TL, 5'10", 150 lbs. Deb: 9/05/31

YEAR	TM/L	G	AB	R	H	2B	3B	HR	RBI	BB	SO	AVG	OBP	SLG	PRO+	BR	/A	RC	SB	CS	SBR	FA	FR	POS	TPR
1931	StL-A	13	15	3	3	2	0	0	0	0	6	.200	.200	.333	37	-1	-1	1	0	0	0	.750	-0	/O	-0.2

■ HARRY STANTON
Stanton, Harry Andrew b: St.Louis, Mo. TR , Deb: 10/14/00

YEAR	TM/L	G	AB	R	H	2B	3B	HR	RBI	BB	SO	AVG	OBP	SLG	PRO+	BR	/A	RC	SB	CS	SBR	FA	FR	POS	TPR
1900	StL-N	1	0	0	0	0	0	0	0	0		—	—	—	—	0	0	0	0			.000	0	/C	0.0

■ LEROY STANTON
Stanton, Leroy Bobby b: 4/10/46, Latta, S.C. BR/TR, 6'1", 195 lbs. Deb: 9/10/70

YEAR	TM/L	G	AB	R	H	2B	3B	HR	RBI	BB	SO	AVG	OBP	SLG	PRO+	BR	/A	RC	SB	CS	SBR	FA	FR	POS	TPR
1970	NY-N	4	4	0	1	0	1	0	0	0	0	.250	.250	.750	157	0	0	0	0	0	0	1.000	0	/O	0.0
1971	NY-N	5	21	2	4	1	0	0	2	2	4	.190	.261	.238	43	-2	-2	1	0	0	0	1.000	-1	/O	-0.3
1972	Cal-A	127	402	44	101	15	3	12	39	22	100	.251	.297	.393	110	1	3	42	2	3	-1	.983	2	*O	-0.2
1973	Cal-A	119	306	41	72	9	2	8	34	27	88	.235	.301	.356	92	-7	-4	31	3	3	-1	.965	-7	*O	-1.5
1974	Cal-A	118	415	48	111	21	2	11	62	33	107	.267	.329	.407	117	5	8	54	10	8	-2	.975	4	*O	0.6
1975	Cal-A	137	440	67	115	20	3	14	82	52	85	.261	.347	.416	124	9	13	66	18	6	2	.961	2	*O/D	1.2
1976	Cal-A	93	231	12	44	13	1	2	25	24	57	.190	.270	.281	66	-11	-9	16	2	6	-3	.985	-15	O/D	-3.2
1977	Sea-A	133	454	56	125	24	1	27	90	42	115	.275	.343	.511	131	17	18	79	0	1	-1	.953	5	OD	1.8
1978	Sea-A	93	302	24	55	11	0	3	24	34	80	.182	.267	.248	46	-21	-21	21	1	0	0	1.000	-0	DO	-2.3
Total	9	829	2575	294	628	114	13	77	358	236	636	.244	.313	.388	103	-9	6	310	36	27	-5	.972	-9	O/D	-3.9

■ TOM STANTON
Stanton, Thomas Patrick b: 10/25/1874, St.Louis, Mo. d: 1/17/57, St.Louis, Mo. BB/TR, 5'10", 175 lbs. Deb: 4/19/04

YEAR	TM/L	G	AB	R	H	2B	3B	HR	RBI	BB	SO	AVG	OBP	SLG	PRO+	BR	/A	RC	SB	CS	SBR	FA	FR	POS	TPR
1904	Chi-N	1	3	0	0	0	0	0	0	0		.000	.000	.000	-99	-1	-1	0	0			1.000	-0	/C	-0.1

■ JOE STAPLES
Staples, Joseph F. b: Buffalo, N.Y. Deb: 9/19/1885

YEAR	TM/L	G	AB	R	H	2B	3B	HR	RBI	BB	SO	AVG	OBP	SLG	PRO+	BR	/A	RC	SB	CS	SBR	FA	FR	POS	TPR
1885	Buf-N	7	22	0	1	0	0	0	0	0	9	.045	.045	.045	-68	-4	-4	0				.545	-3	/O2	-0.8

■ DAVE STAPLETON
Stapleton, David Leslie b: 1/16/54, Fairhope, Ala. BR/TR, 6'1", 178 lbs. Deb: 5/30/80

YEAR	TM/L	G	AB	R	H	2B	3B	HR	RBI	BB	SO	AVG	OBP	SLG	PRO+	BR	/A	RC	SB	CS	SBR	FA	FR	POS	TPR
1980	Bos-A	106	449	61	144	33	5	7	45	13	32	.321	.341	.463	112	10	7	67	3	2	-0	.979	10	2/1O3D	2.2
1981	Bos-A	93	355	45	101	17	1	10	42	21	22	.285	.326	.423	108	6	3	45	0	4	-2	.948	-7	S321/D	-0.3
1982	Bos-A	150	538	66	142	28	1	14	65	31	40	.264	.308	.398	87	-7	-11	58	2	4	-2	.991	2	*1S/23OD	-1.4
1983	Bos-A	151	542	54	134	31	1	10	66	40	44	.247	.301	.363	76	-14	-19	56	1	1	-0	.993	-2	*1/2	-3.0
1984	Bos-A	13	39	4	9	2	0	0	1	3	3	.231	.286	.282	55	-2	-2	3	0	0	0	1.000	1	1/D	-0.2
1985	Bos-A	30	66	4	15	6	0	0	2	4	11	.227	.271	.318	58	-4	-4	6	0	0	0	1.000	1	2/1D	-0.2
1986	*Bos-A	39	39	4	5	1	0	0	3	2	10	.128	.171	.154	-11	-6	-6	1	0	0	0	1.000	3	1/23	-0.4
Total	7	582	2028	238	550	118	8	41	224	114	162	.271	.312	.398	90	-17	-32	236	6	11	-5	1.000	7	12/S3DO	-3.3

■ WILLIE STARGELL
Stargell, Wilver Dornel b: 3/6/40, Earlsboro, Okla. BL/TL, 6'2.5", 225 lbs. Deb: 9/16/62 CH

YEAR	TM/L	G	AB	R	H	2B	3B	HR	RBI	BB	SO	AVG	OBP	SLG	PRO+	BR	/A	RC	SB	CS	SBR	FA	FR	POS	TPR
1962	Pit-N	10	31	1	9	3	1	0	4	3	10	.290	.353	.452	114	1	1	5	0	1	-1	.929	-1	/O	-0.1
1963	Pit-N	108	304	34	74	11	6	11	47	19	85	.243	.292	.428	104	1	1	36	0	2	-1	.953	-10	O1	-1.5
1964	Pit-N★	117	421	53	115	19	7	21	78	17	92	.273	.305	.501	123	10	11	62	1	1	-0	.900	-10	O1	-0.5
1965	Pit-N★	144	533	68	145	25	8	27	107	39	127	.272	.330	.501	130	20	19	87	1	1	-0	.965	-6	*O/1	0.8
1966	Pit-N★	140	485	84	153	30	0	33	102	48	109	.315	.384	.581	164	41	41	107	2	3	-1	.945	-10	*O1	2.5
1967	Pit-N	134	462	54	125	18	6	20	73	67	103	.271	.367	.465	136	23	23	78	1	0	0	.938	-6	O1	1.1
1968	Pit-N	128	435	57	103	15	1	24	67	47	105	.237	.320	.441	129	14	14	61	5	0	2	.945	-11	*O1	-0.1
1969	Pit-N	145	522	89	160	31	6	29	92	61	120	.307	.385	.556	164	41	43	112	1	0	0	.970	-10	*O1	2.5
1970	*Pit-N	136	474	70	125	18	3	31	85	44	119	.264	.333	.511	125	13	14	77	0	1	-1	.976	-1	*O/1	0.6
1971	*Pit-N★	141	511	104	151	26	0	**48**	125	83	154	.295	.401	.628	188	59	59	131	0	0	0	.984	-6	*O	**4.9**
1972	*Pit-N★	138	495	75	145	28	2	33	112	65	129	.293	.377	.558	166	40	41	105	1	1	-0	.984	-12	*1O	2.0

YEAR	TM/L	G	AB	R	H	2B	3B	HR	RBI	BB	SO	AVG	OBP	SLG	PRO+	BR	/A	RC	SB	CS	SBR	FA	FR	POS	TPR
1973	Pit-N★	148	522	106	156	**43**	3	**44**	**119**	80	129	.299	.395	**.646**	**189**	**58**	**59**	136	0	0	0	.975	1	*O	5.5
1974	*Pit-N	140	508	90	153	37	4	25	96	87	106	.301	.409	.537	**169**	44	**47**	115	0	2	-1	.967	-3	*O/1	3.8
1975	*Pit-N	124	461	71	136	32	2	22	90	58	109	.295	.377	.516	147	28	28	91	0	0	0	.992	-10	*1	1.1
1976	Pit-N	117	428	54	110	20	3	20	65	50	101	.257	.342	.458	124	13	13	70	2	0	1	.988	-10	*1	-0.5
1977	Pit-N	63	186	29	51	12	0	13	35	31	55	.274	.386	.548	144	13	12	39	0	1	-1	.986	-1	1	0.7
1978	Pit-N★	122	390	60	115	18	2	28	97	50	93	.295	.385	.567	156	32	30	85	3	2	-0	.994	-2	*1	2.3
1979	*Pit-N	126	424	60	119	19	0	32	82	47	105	.281	.357	.552	138	24	22	81	0	1	-1	**.997**	-6	*1	0.9
1980	Pit-N	67	202	28	53	10	1	11	38	26	52	.262	.352	.485	129	8	8	35	0	0	0	.992	0	1	0.5
1981	Pit-N	38	60	2	17	4	0	0	9	5	9	.283	.338	.350	93	-0	-1	8	0	0	0	1.000	-2	/1	-0.4
1982	Pit-N	74	73	6	17	4	0	3	17	10	24	.233	.325	.411	102	0	0	10	0	0	0	1.000	0	/1	0.0
Total	21	2360	7927	1195	2232	423	55	475	1540	937	1936	.282	.363	.529	147	483	485	1531	17	16	-5	.961	-115	*O1	26.1

■ MATT STARK
Stark, Matthew Scott b: 1/21/65, Whittier, Cal. BR/TR, 6'4", 225 lbs. Deb: 4/08/87

YEAR	TM/L	G	AB	R	H	2B	3B	HR	RBI	BB	SO	AVG	OBP	SLG	PRO+	BR	/A	RC	SB	CS	SBR	FA	FR	POS	TPR
1987	Tor-A	5	12	0	1	0	0	0	0	0	0	.083	.083	.083	-55	-3	-3	-0	0	0	0	1.000	1	/C	-0.2
1990	Chi-A	8	16	0	4	1	0	0	3	1	6	.250	.294	.313	71	-1	-1	1	0	0	0	.000	0	/D	-0.1
Total	2	13	28	0	5	1	0	0	3	1	6	.179	.207	.214	15	-3	-3	1	0	0	0	.932	1	/DC	-0.3

■ DOLLY STARK
Stark, Monroe Randolph b: 1/19/1885, Ripley, Miss. d: 12/1/24, Memphis, Tenn. BR/TR, 5'9", 160 lbs. Deb: 9/12/09

YEAR	TM/L	G	AB	R	H	2B	3B	HR	RBI	BB	SO	AVG	OBP	SLG	PRO+	BR	/A	RC	SB	CS	SBR	FA	FR	POS	TPR
1909	Cle-A	19	60	4	12	0	0	0	1	6		.200	.273	.200	48	-3	-3	4	4			.875	-10	S	-1.5
1910	Bro-N	30	103	7	17	3	0	0	8	7	19	.165	.225	.194	23	-10	-10	5	2			.893	-1	S	-1.1
1911	Bro-N	70	193	25	57	4	1	0	19	20	24	.295	.370	.326	100	-0	1	26	6			.910	-3	S2/3	-0.1
1912	Bro-N	8	22	2	4	0	0	0	2	1	3	.182	.217	.182	10	-3	-3	1	2			.892	0	/S	-0.2
Total	4	127	378	38	90	7	1	0	30	34	<u>46</u>	.238	.308	.262	66	-16	-15	37	14			.896	-14	/S23	-2.9

■ GEORGE STARNAGLE
Starnagle, George Henry (b: George Henry Steuernagel)
b: 10/6/1873, Belleville, Ill. d: 2/15/46, Belleville, Ill. BR/TR, 5'11", 175 lbs. Deb: 9/14/02

YEAR	TM/L	G	AB	R	H	2B	3B	HR	RBI	BB	SO	AVG	OBP	SLG	PRO+	BR	/A	RC	SB	CS	SBR	FA	FR	POS	TPR
1902	Cle-A	1	3	0	0	0	0	0	0	0		.000	.000	.000	-99	-1	-1	0	0			.667	-1	/C	-0.1

■ CHARLIE STARR
Starr, Charles Watkin b: 8/30/1878, Pike Co., Ohio d: 10/18/37, Pasadena, Cal. TR , Deb: 4/29/05

YEAR	TM/L	G	AB	R	H	2B	3B	HR	RBI	BB	SO	AVG	OBP	SLG	PRO+	BR	/A	RC	SB	CS	SBR	FA	FR	POS	TPR
1905	StL-A	26	97	9	20	0	0	0	6	7		.206	.260	.206	51	-5	-5	6	0			.940	-4	2/3	-0.9
1908	Pit-N	20	59	8	11	2	0	0	8	13		.186	.342	.220	81	-0	-0	7	6			.926	-5	2/S3	-0.7
1909	Bos-N	61	216	16	48	2	3	0	6	31		.222	.333	.259	80	-2	-4	22	7			.931	-9	2/S3	-1.5
	Phi-N	3	3	0	0	0	0	0	0	0		.000	.000	.000	-99	-1	-1	0	0			.000	0	H	-0.1
	Yr	64	219	16	48	2	3	0	6	31		.219	.329	.256	78	-3	-4	21	7			.931	-9	2/S3	-1.6
Total	3	110	375	33	79	4	3	0	20	51		.211	.315	.237	72	-9	-10	34	13			.932	-18	/2S3	-3.2

■ CHICK STARR
Starr, William b: 2/26/11, Brooklyn, N.Y. d: 8/12/91, LaJolla, Cal. BR/TR, 6'1", 175 lbs. Deb: 8/23/35

YEAR	TM/L	G	AB	R	H	2B	3B	HR	RBI	BB	SO	AVG	OBP	SLG	PRO+	BR	/A	RC	SB	CS	SBR	FA	FR	POS	TPR
1935	Was-A	12	24	1	5	0	0	0	1	0	1	.208	.208	.208	8	-3	-3	1	0	0	0	.971	2	C	-0.1
1936	Was-A	1	0	0	0	0	0	0	0	0	0	—	—	—	—	0	0	0	0	0	0	.000	0	/C	0.0
Total	2	13	24	1	5	0	0	0	1	0	1	.208	.208	.208	8	-3	-3	1	0	0	0	.971	2	/C	-0.1

■ JOE START
Start, Joseph "Old Reliable" or "Rocks" b: 10/14/1842, New York, N.Y. d: 3/27/27, Providence, R.I. BL/TL, 5'9", 165 lbs. Deb: 5/18/1871 M

YEAR	TM/L	G	AB	R	H	2B	3B	HR	RBI	BB	SO	AVG	OBP	SLG	PRO+	BR	/A	RC	SB	CS	SBR	FA	FR	POS	TPR
1871	Mut-n	33	161	35	58	5	1	1	34	3	0	.360	.372	.422	140	6	9	27	4					*1	0.7
1872	Mut-n	55	280	62	74	6	0	0	49	0	0	.264	.264	.286	74	-10	-6	22						*1	-0.2
1873	Mut-n	53	251	42	67	11	3	1	28	4	0	.267	.278	.347	83	-5	-5	25						*1/OM	-0.1
1874	Mut-n	63	306	67	94	14	4	2		4		.307	.316	.399	122	9	7	40						*1	0.5
1875	Mut-n	68	309	56	87	9	5	4		3		.282	.288	.382	123	9	6	35						*1	0.5
1876	NY-N	56	264	40	73	6	0	0	21	1	2	.277	.279	.299	107	-2	3	23				**.964**	3	*1	0.4
1877	Har-N	60	271	55	90	3	6	1	21	6	2	.332	.347	.399	150	10	14	38				**.964**	-2	*1	1.1
1878	Chi-N	61	285	58	**100**	12	5	1	27	2	3	.351	.355	.439	150	17	15	46				.957	-2	*1	1.0
1879	Pro-N	66	317	70	101	11	5	2	37	7	4	.319	.333	.404	144	14	14	44				**.973**	0	*1/O	1.1
1880	Pro-N	82	345	53	96	14	6	0	27	13	20	.278	.304	.354	126	8	9	38				.971	-3	*1	-0.1
1881	Pro-N	79	348	56	114	12	6	0	29	9	7	.328	.345	.397	135	12	13	49				.963	-4	*1	0.1
1882	Pro-N	82	356	58	117	8	10	0	48	11	7	.329	.349	.407	142	16	16	52				.974	2	*1	0.8
1883	Pro-N	87	370	63	105	16	7	1	57	22	16	.284	.324	.373	108	5	4	46				.957	-1	*1	-0.5
1884	*Pro-N	93	381	80	105	10	5	2	32	35	25	.276	.337	.344	117	7	9	45				**.980**	1	*1	-0.1
1885	Pro-N	101	374	47	103	11	4	0	41	39	10	.275	.344	.326	122	9	11	43				.972	1	*1	0.0
1886	Was-N	31	122	10	27	4	1	0	17	5	13	.221	.252	.270	63	-6	-5	10	4			.973	-2	1	-1.0
Total	5 n	272	1307	262	380	45	13	8	<u>111</u>	14		.291	.298	.363	106	8	11	149	8					1/O	1.4
Total	11	798	3433	590	1031	107	55	7	357	150	109	.300	.330	.370	127	90	103	432	4			.968	-7	1/O	2.8

■ JOE STATON
Staton, Joseph b: 3/8/48, Seattle, Wash. BL/TL, 6'3", 175 lbs. Deb: 9/05/72

YEAR	TM/L	G	AB	R	H	2B	3B	HR	RBI	BB	SO	AVG	OBP	SLG	PRO+	BR	/A	RC	SB	CS	SBR	FA	FR	POS	TPR
1972	Det-A	6	2	1	0	0	0	0	0	0	1	.000	.000	.000	-97	-0	-0	0	0	1	-1	1.000	0	/1	-0.1
1973	Det-A	9	17	2	4	0	0	0	3	0	3	.235	.235	.235	31	-2	-2	1	1	0	0	.969	2	/1	0.0
Total	2	15	19	3	4	0	0	0	3	0	4	.211	.211	.211	18	-2	-2	1	1	1	-0	.973	2	/1	-0.1

■ JIGGER STATZ
Statz, Arnold John b: 10/20/1897, Waukegan, Ill. d: 3/16/88, Corona Del Mar, Cal. BR/TR, 5'7.5", 150 lbs. Deb: 7/30/19

YEAR	TM/L	G	AB	R	H	2B	3B	HR	RBI	BB	SO	AVG	OBP	SLG	PRO+	BR	/A	RC	SB	CS	SBR	FA	FR	POS	TPR
1919	NY-N	21	60	7	18	2	1	0	6	3	8	.300	.333	.367	112	1	1	7	2			.977	-1	O/2	-0.1
1920	NY-N	16	30	0	4	0	1	0	5	2	9	.133	.188	.200	11	-3	-3	1	0	1	-1	.944	-3	O	-0.8
	Bos-A	2	3	0	0	0	0	0	0	0	0	.000	.000	.000	-99	-1	-1	0	0	0	0	1.000	-1	/O	-0.2
1922	Chi-N	110	462	77	137	19	5	1	34	41	31	.297	.355	.366	85	-9	-10	60	16	13	-3	.959	9	*O	-1.1
1923	Chi-N	154	655	110	209	33	8	10	70	56	42	.319	.375	.440	114	14	14	105	29	23	-5	.975	18	*O	1.5
1924	Chi-N	135	549	69	152	22	5	3	49	37	50	.277	.325	.352	80	-14	-15	63	13	9	-2	.961	15	*O/2	-1.1
1925	Chi-N	38	148	21	38	6	3	2	14	11	16	.257	.317	.378	76	-5	-6	19	4	0	1	.943	2	O	-0.5
1927	Bro-N	130	507	64	139	24	7	1	21	26	43	.274	.310	.355	77	-17	-17	54	10			.990	15	*O/2	-0.9
1928	Bro-N	77	171	28	40	8	1	0	16	18	12	.234	.311	.292	59	-10	-10	16	3			.965	-6	O/2	-1.8
Total	8	683	2585	376	737	114	31	17	215	194	211	.285	.337	.373	87	-45	-47	325	77	<u>46</u>		.969	48	O/2	-5.0

■ RUSTY STAUB
Staub, Daniel Joseph b: 4/1/44, New Orleans, La. BL/TR, 6'2", 200 lbs. Deb: 4/09/63 C

YEAR	TM/L	G	AB	R	H	2B	3B	HR	RBI	BB	SO	AVG	OBP	SLG	PRO+	BR	/A	RC	SB	CS	SBR	FA	FR	POS	TPR
1963	Hou-N	150	513	43	115	17	4	6	45	59	58	.224	.310	.308	84	-13	-9	51	0	0	0	.989	-0	*1O	-1.7
1964	Hou-N	89	292	26	63	10	2	8	35	21	31	.216	.275	.346	78	-10	-9	27	1	1	-0	.992	-1	1O	-1.5
1965	Hou-N	131	410	43	105	20	1	14	63	52	57	.256	.343	.412	120	7	10	56	3	0	1	.951	4	*O/1	1.1
1966	Hou-N	153	554	60	155	28	3	13	81	58	61	.280	.349	.412	119	9	13	79	2	1	0	.962	11	*O/1	1.8
1967	Hou-N★	149	546	71	182	**44**	1	10	74	60	47	.333	.402	.473	155	36	38	100	0	4	-2	.962	6	*O	3.7
1968	Hou-N★	161	591	54	172	37	1	6	72	73	57	.291	.376	.387	132	24	25	88	2	0	1	.992	-1	*1O	1.4
1969	Mon-N☆	158	549	89	166	26	5	29	79	110	61	.302	.427	.526	165	53	52	128	3	4	-2	.966	5	*O	4.8
1970	Mon-N★	160	569	98	156	23	7	30	94	112	93	.274	.396	.497	138	33	33	117	12	11	-3	.985	8	*O	2.9
1971	Mon-N☆	162	599	94	186	34	6	19	97	74	42	.311	.394	.482	147	39	38	111	9	5	-0	.945	2	*O	3.4
1972	NY-N	66	239	32	70	11	0	9	38	31	13	.293	.379	.452	139	11	12	41	0	1	-1	.982	-4	O	0.5
1973	*NY-N	152	585	77	163	36	1	15	76	74	52	.279	.363	.421	118	14	15	89	1	1	-0	.978	9	*O	1.8
1974	NY-N	151	561	65	145	22	2	19	78	77	39	.258	.351	.406	113	9	10	78	2	1	0	.983	8	*O	1.2
1975	NY-N	155	574	93	162	30	4	19	105	77	55	.282	.376	.448	134	22	26	97	2	0	1	.986	3	*O	2.4
1976	Det-A★	161	589	73	176	28	3	15	96	83	49	.299	.392	.433	136	33	30	99	3	1	0	.970	-6	*OD	2.1
1977	Det-A	158	623	84	173	34	3	22	101	59	47	.278	.341	.448	107	11	6	89	1	1	-0	.000	0	*D	0.6
1978	Det-A	162	642	75	175	30	1	24	121	76	35	.273	.352	.435	117	17	15	96	3	1	0	.000	0	*D	1.6

YEAR	TM/L	G	AB	R	H	2B	3B	HR	RBI	BB	SO	AVG	OBP	SLG	PRO+	BR	/A	RC	SB	CS	SBR	FA	FR	POS	TPR
1979	Det-A	68	246	32	58	12	1	9	40	32	18	.236	.336	.402	95	-0	-2	33	1	0	0	.000	0	D	-0.1
	Mon-N	38	86	9	23	3	0	3	14	14	10	.267	.370	.407	113	2	2	13	0	0	0	.994	-2	1/O	-0.2
1980	Tex-A	109	340	42	102	23	2	9	55	39	18	.300	.375	.459	131	13	15	55	1	1	-0	.977	-2	D1O	1.0
1981	NY-N	70	161	9	51	9	0	5	21	22	12	.317	.402	.466	148	10	10	30	1	0	0	.989	-2	1	0.7
1982	NY-N	112	219	11	53	9	0	3	27	24	10	.242	.317	.324	80	-6	-5	22	0	0	0	.959	0	O1	-0.7
1983	NY-N	104	115	5	34	6	0	3	28	14	10	.296	.377	.426	123	4	4	18	0	0	0	.976	-1	/1O	0.3
1984	NY-N	78	72	2	19	4	0	1	18	4	9	.264	.303	.361	87	-1	-1	8	0	0	0	1.000	-0	/1	-0.2
1985	NY-N	54	45	2	12	3	0	1	8	10	4	.267	.400	.400	128	2	2	8	0	0	0	1.000	-0	/O	0.2
Total	23	2951	9720	1189	2716	499	47	292	1466	1255	888	.279	.366	.431	125	318	333	1534	47	33	-6	.969	37	*OD1	27.1

■ **ECKY STEARNS** Stearns, Daniel Eckford b: 10/17/1861, Buffalo, N.Y. d: 6/28/44, Glendale, Cal. BL/TR, 6'1", 185 lbs. Deb: 8/17/1880

1880	Buf-N	28	104	8	19	6	1	0	13	3	23	.183	.206	.260	55	-5	-5	6				.774	-9	O/C3S	-1.4
1881	Det-N	3	11	1	1	1	0	0	0	0	2	.091	.091	.182	-16	-1	-1	0				.714	-1	/S	-0.2
1882	Cin-a	49	214	28	55	10	2	0		6		.257	.277	.322	96	0	-1	20				.931	-2	1O/2S	-0.7
1883	Bal-a	93	382	54	94	10	9	1		**34**		.246	.308	.327	102	3	1	39				.947	3	*1/O	-0.5
1884	Bal-a	100	396	61	94	12	3	3		28		.237	.298	.306	96	1	-1	37				.949	4	*1/2	-0.8
1885	Bal-a	67	253	40	47	3	8	1		38		.186	.306	.273	88	-2	-1	22				.973	1	1/OC	-0.6
	Buf-N	30	105	7	21	6	1	0	9	8	23	.200	.257	.276	70	-3	-4	8				.821	-7	S1/C	-1.1
1889	KC-a	139	560	96	160	24	12	3	87	56	69	.286	.351	.387	106	9	3	102	67			.967	0	*1/3	-0.4
Total	7	509	2025	295	491	72	36	8	109	173	117	.242	.306	.325	96	2	-9	233	67			.956	-10	1/OSC32	-5.7

■ **JOHN STEARNS** Stearns, John Hardin b: 8/21/51, Denver, Col. BR/TR, 6', 185 lbs. Deb: 9/22/74 C

1974	Phi-N	1	2	0	1	0	0	0	0	0	0	.500	.500	.500	173	0	0	1	0	0	0	1.000	-1	/C	0.0
1975	NY-N	59	169	25	32	5	1	3	10	17	15	.189	.271	.284	57	-11	-10	13	4	1	1	.994	6	C	-0.1
1976	NY-N	32	103	13	27	6	0	2	10	16	11	.262	.367	.379	119	2	3	14	1	2	-1	.987	3	C	0.7
1977	NY-N★	139	431	52	108	25	1	12	55	77	76	.251	.373	.397	112	7	9	64	9	8	-2	.982	4	*C/1	1.5
1978	NY-N	143	477	65	126	24	1	15	73	70	57	.264	.368	.413	122	13	15	75	25	13	-0	.985	-3	*C/3	1.7
1979	NY-N☆	155	538	58	131	29	2	9	66	52	57	.243	.315	.355	86	-13	-11	54	15	15	-5	.983	5	*C13/O	-0.7
1980	NY-N★	91	319	42	91	25	1	0	45	33	24	.285	.354	.370	105	2	3	44	7	3	0	.985	5	C1/3	1.0
1981	NY-N	80	273	25	74	12	1	1	24	24	17	.271	.330	.333	90	-4	-3	30	12	2	2	.983	-2	C/13	-0.1
1982	NY-N★	98	352	46	103	25	3	4	28	30	35	.293	.352	.415	114	6	7	51	17	7	1	.987	-7	C3	0.4
1983	NY-N	4	0	2	0	0	0	0	0	0	0	—	—	—	—	0	0	0	0	0	0	.000	0	/R	0.0
1984	NY-N	8	17	6	3	1	0	0	1	4	2	.176	.333	.235	63	-1	-1	2	1	0	0	1.000	-1	/C1	-0.1
Total	11	810	2681	334	696	152	10	46	312	323	294	.260	.345	.375	102	2	13	347	91	51	-3	.985	11	C/13O	4.3

■ **JOHN STEDRONSKY** Stedronsky, John b: Troy, N.Y. Deb: 9/25/1879

1879	Chi-N	4	12	0	1	0	0	0	0	0	3	.083	.083	.083	-42	-2	-2	0				.789	1	/3	0.0

■ **FARMER STEELMAN** Steelman, Morris James b: 6/29/1875, Millville, N.J. d: 9/16/44, Merchantville, N.J. TR , Deb: 9/15/1899

1899	Lou-N	4	15	2	1	0	1	0	2	2		.067	.176	.200	3	-2	-2	1	0			.929	-2	/C	-0.3
1900	Bro-N	1	4	0	0	0	0	0	0	0		.000	.000	.000	-94	-1	-1	0	0			1.000	0	/C	-0.1
1901	Bro-N	1	3	0	1	0	0	0	0	0		.333	.333	.333	91	-0	-0	0	0			.875	1	/C	0.1
	Phi-A	27	88	5	23	2	0	0	7	10		.261	.350	.284	74	-2	-3	11	4			1.000	2	CO	0.0
1902	Phi-A	10	32	1	6	1	0	0	6	2		.188	.235	.219	25	-3	-3	2	2			1.000	1	/CO	-0.2
Total	4	43	142	8	31	3	1	0	15	14		.218	.297	.254	52	-9	-9	14	6			.985	2	/CO	-0.5

■ **JIM STEELS** Steels, James Earl b: 5/30/61, Jackson, Miss. BL/TL, 5'10", 185 lbs. Deb: 4/06/87

1987	SD-N	62	68	9	13	1	1	0	6	11	14	.191	.304	.235	47	-5	-5	5	3	2	-0	.960	-6	O	-1.2
1988	Tex-A	36	53	4	10	1	0	0	5	0	15	.189	.189	.208	11	-6	-6	2	2	0	1	1.000	-5	O/1D	-1.1
1989	SF-N	13	12	0	1	0	0	0	0	2	4	.083	.214	.083	-12	-2	-2	0	0	0	0	1.000	0	/1O	-0.1
Total	3	111	133	13	24	2	1	0	11	13	33	.180	.253	.211	28	-13	-13	8	5	2	0	.973	-11	/O1D	-2.4

■ **GENE STEERE** Steere, Frederick Eugene b: 8/16/1872, S.Scituate, R.I. d: 3/13/42, San Francisco, Cal Deb: 8/29/1894

1894	Pit-N	10	39	3	8	0	0	0	4	2	1	.205	.244	.205	10	-6	-6	3	2			.896	-3	S	-0.6

■ **JOHN STEFERO** Stefero, John Robert b: 9/22/59, Sumter, S.C. BL/TR, 5'8", 185 lbs. Deb: 6/24/83

1983	Bal-A	9	11	2	5	1	0	0	4	3	2	.455	.571	.545	213	2	2	4	0	0	0	.920	0	/C	0.2
1986	Bal-A	52	120	14	28	2	0	2	13	16	25	.233	.324	.300	72	-4	-4	12	0	1	-1	.984	-2	C/2	-0.4
1987	Mon-N	18	56	4	11	0	0	1	3	3	17	.196	.237	.250	28	-6	-6	3	0	0	0	.981	-0	C	-0.5
Total	3	79	187	20	44	3	0	3	20	22	44	.235	.316	.299	67	-8	-8	19	0	1	-1	.979	-2	/C2	-0.7

■ **DAVE STEGMAN** Stegman, David William b: 1/30/54, Inglewood, Cal. BR/TR, 5'11", 190 lbs. Deb: 9/04/78

1978	Det-A	8	14	3	4	2	0	1	3	1	2	.286	.333	.643	164	1	1	2	0	0	0	1.000	-2	/O	-0.1
1979	Det-A	12	31	6	6	0	0	3	5	2	3	.194	.242	.484	88	-1	-1	3	1	1	-0	1.000	1	O	-0.1
1980	Det-A	65	130	12	23	5	0	2	9	14	23	.177	.257	.262	41	-10	-11	10	1	1	-0	.988	-13	O/D	-2.6
1982	NY-A	2	0	0	0	0	0	0	0	0	0	—	—	—	—	0	0	0	0	0	0	.000	0	/D	0.0
1983	Chi-A	30	53	5	9	2	0	0	4	10	9	.170	.302	.208	42	-4	-4	4	0	1	-1	1.000	-7	O	-1.2
1984	Chi-A	55	92	13	24	1	2	2	11	4	18	.261	.306	.380	85	-2	-2	11	3	0	1	.985	-9	O/D	-1.1
Total	6	172	320	39	66	10	2	8	32	31	55	.206	.280	.325	64	-15	-17	31	5	3	-0	.991	-31	O/D	-5.1

■ **JUSTIN STEIN** Stein, Justin Marion "Ott" b: 8/9/11, St.Louis, Mo. d: 5/1/92, Creve Coeur, Mo. BR/TR, 5'11", 180 lbs. Deb: 5/28/38

1938	Phi-N	11	39	6	10	0	1	0	2	2	4	.256	.293	.308	67	-2	-2	4	0			.880	0	/32	-0.2
	Cin-N	11	18	3	6	1	0	0	1	0	1	.333	.333	.389	101	-0	-0	2	0			.857	1	/S2	0.1
	Yr	22	57	9	16	1	1	0	3	2	5	.281	.305	.333	78	-2	-2	6	0			.857	1	/3S2	-0.1

■ **BILL STEIN** Stein, William Allen b: 1/21/47, Battle Creek, Mich. BR/TR, 5'10", 170 lbs. Deb: 9/06/72

1972	StL-N	14	35	2	11	0	1	2	3	0	7	.314	.314	.543	141	1	2	6	1	0	0	1.000	-3	/3O	-0.1
1973	StL-N	32	55	4	12	2	0	0	2	7	18	.218	.306	.255	57	-3	-3	5	0	0	0	1.000	-1	O/13	-0.5
1974	Chi-A	13	43	5	12	1	0	0	5	7	8	.279	.380	.302	96	0	0	5	0	0	0	.871	-2	3/D	-0.2
1975	Chi-A	76	226	23	61	7	1	3	21	18	32	.270	.327	.350	90	-3	-3	25	2	2	-1	.974	3	23D/O	0.1
1976	Chi-A	117	392	32	105	15	2	4	36	22	67	.268	.310	.347	92	-4	-5	41	4	2	0	.960	-11	23/1SOD	-1.3
1977	Sea-A	151	556	53	144	26	5	13	67	29	79	.259	.302	.394	89	-10	-10	62	3	4	-2	.964	-11	*3/SD	-2.4
1978	Sea-A	114	403	41	105	24	4	4	37	37	56	.261	.323	.370	95	-3	-3	48	1	0	0	.929	-6	*3/D	-1.0
1979	Sea-A	88	250	28	62	9	2	7	27	17	28	.248	.301	.384	82	-6	-7	26	1	2	-1	.959	11	32/S	0.3
1980	Sea-A	67	198	16	53	5	1	5	27	16	25	.268	.326	.379	92	-2	-2	24	1	2	-1	.972	5	32/1D	0.3
1981	Tex-A	53	115	21	38	6	0	2	22	7	15	.330	.369	.435	138	4	5	16	1	2	-1	1.000	1	1/O32S	0.4
1982	Tex-A	85	184	14	44	8	0	1	16	12	23	.239	.293	.299	66	-9	-8	16	0	0	0	.957	3	23/S1OD	-0.4
1983	Tex-A	78	232	21	72	15	1	2	33	8	31	.310	.333	.409	105	1	1	30	2	3	-1	.975	0	213/D	0.0
1984	Tex-A	27	43	3	12	1	0	0	3	5	9	.279	.354	.302	81	-1	-1	5	0	0	0	.967	-3	2/13D	-0.3
1985	Tex-A	44	79	5	20	3	1	1	12	1	15	.253	.272	.354	69	-3	-4	7	0	0	0	.952	1	3/12OD	-0.3
Total	14	959	2811	268	751	122	18	44	311	186	413	.267	.316	.370	91	-38	-37	315	16	16	-5	.950	-13	32/1DOS	-5.4

■ **TERRY STEINBACH** Steinbach, Terry Lee b: 3/2/62, New Ulm, Minn. BR/TR, 6'1", 195 lbs. Deb: 9/12/86

1986	Oak-A	6	15	3	5	0	0	2	4	1	0	.333	.375	.733	208	2	2	4	0	0	0	.962	-0	/C	0.2
1987	Oak-A	122	391	66	111	16	3	16	56	32	66	.284	.352	.463	122	8	11	62	1	2	-1	.986	-12	*C3/1D	0.5

YEAR	TM/L	G	AB	R	H	2B	3B	HR	RBI	BB	SO	AVG	OBP	SLG	PRO+	BR	/A	RC	SB	CS	SBR	FA	FR	POS	TPR
1988	*Oak-A★	104	351	42	93	19	1	9	51	33	47	.265	.338	.402	110	3	5	47	3	0	1	.983	5	C/31OD	1.6
1989	*Oak-A★	130	454	37	124	13	1	7	42	30	66	.273	.321	.352	93	-6	-4	49	1	2	-1	.985	-7	*CO1/3D	-0.7
1990	*Oak-A	114	379	32	95	15	2	9	57	19	66	.251	.294	.372	89	-9	-7	39	0	1	-1	.988	-4	CD/1	-0.6
1991	Oak-A	129	456	50	125	31	1	6	67	22	70	.274	.318	.386	99	-5	-1	52	2	2	-1	.980	-24	*C/1D	-2.0
1992	*Oak-A	128	438	48	122	20	1	12	53	45	58	.279	.347	.411	116	7	9	58	2	3	-1	.985	-4	*C/1D	1.1
Total	7	733	2484	278	675	114	9	61	330	182	373	.272	.329	.399	105	-0	15	311	9	10	-3	.984	-46	C/D13O	0.1

■ **HANK STEINBACHER** Steinbacher, Henry John b: 3/22/13, Sacramento, Cal. d: 4/3/77, Sacramento, Cal. BL/TR, 5'11", 180 lbs. Deb: 4/21/37

YEAR	TM/L	G	AB	R	H	2B	3B	HR	RBI	BB	SO	AVG	OBP	SLG	PRO+	BR	/A	RC	SB	CS	SBR	FA	FR	POS	TPR
1937	Chi-A	26	73	13	19	4	1	1	9	4	7	.260	.299	.384	71	-4	-4	9	2	0	1	.960	-2	O	-0.5
1938	Chi-A	106	399	59	132	23	8	4	61	41	19	.331	.393	.459	110	8	7	72	1	3	-2	.963	-4	*O	-0.2
1939	Chi-A	71	111	16	19	2	1	1	15	21	8	.171	.303	.234	38	-10	-10	9	0	0	0	1.000	-2	O	-1.2
Total	3	203	583	88	170	29	10	6	85	66	34	.292	.364	.407	92	-5	-7	90	3	3	-1	.968	-8	O	-1.9

■ **GENE STEINBRENNER** Steinbrenner, Eugene Gass b: 11/17/1892, Pittsburgh, Pa. d: 4/25/70, Pittsburgh, Pa. BR/TR, 5'8.5", 155 lbs. Deb: 4/25/12

YEAR	TM/L	G	AB	R	H	2B	3B	HR	RBI	BB	SO	AVG	OBP	SLG	PRO+	BR	/A	RC	SB	CS	SBR	FA	FR	POS	TPR
1912	Phi-N	3	9	0	2	1	0	0	1	0	3	.222	.222	.333	48	-1	-1	1	0			.900	-1	/2	-0.2

■ **BILL STEINECKE** Steinecke, William Robert b: 2/7/07, Cincinnati, Ohio d: 7/20/86, St.Augustine, Fla BR/TR, 5'8.5", 175 lbs. Deb: 9/16/31

YEAR	TM/L	G	AB	R	H	2B	3B	HR	RBI	BB	SO	AVG	OBP	SLG	PRO+	BR	/A	RC	SB	CS	SBR	FA	FR	POS	TPR
1931	Pit-N	4	4	0	0	0	0	0	0	0	1	.000	.000	.000	-99	-1	-1	0	0			.000	0	/C	-0.1

■ **BEN STEINER** Steiner, Benjamin Saunders b: 7/28/21, Alexandria, Va. d: 10/27/88, Venice, Fla. BL/TR, 5'11", 165 lbs. Deb: 4/17/45

YEAR	TM/L	G	AB	R	H	2B	3B	HR	RBI	BB	SO	AVG	OBP	SLG	PRO+	BR	/A	RC	SB	CS	SBR	FA	FR	POS	TPR
1945	Bos-A	78	304	39	78	8	3	3	20	31	29	.257	.327	.332	89	-3	-4	35	10	6	-1	.967	-4	2	-0.4
1946	Bos-A	3	4	1	1	0	0	0	0	0	0	.250	.250	.250	38	-0	-0	0	0	0	0	.750	0	/3	0.0
1947	Det-A	1	0	1	0	0	0	0	0	0	0	—	—	—	—	0	0	0	0	0	0	.000	0	R	0.0
Total	3	82	308	41	79	8	3	3	20	31	29	.256	.326	.331	89	-3	-4	35	10	6	-1	.866	-4	/23	-0.4

■ **RED STEINER** Steiner, James Harry b: 1/7/15, Los Angeles, Cal. BL/TR, 6', 185 lbs. Deb: 5/11/45

YEAR	TM/L	G	AB	R	H	2B	3B	HR	RBI	BB	SO	AVG	OBP	SLG	PRO+	BR	/A	RC	SB	CS	SBR	FA	FR	POS	TPR
1945	Cle-A	12	20	0	3	0	0	0	2	1	4	.150	.190	.150	-1	-3	-2	0	0	0	0	1.000	1	/C	-0.2
	Bos-A	26	59	6	12	1	0	0	4	14	2	.203	.356	.220	67	-2	-2	6	0	0	0	.986	-5	C	-0.6
	Yr	38	79	6	15	1	0	0	6	15	6	.190	.319	.203	52	-4	-4	6	0	0	0	.989	-4	C	-0.8

■ **HARRY STEINFELDT** Steinfeldt, Harry M. b: 9/29/1877, St.Louis, Mo. d: 8/17/14, Bellevue, Ky. BR/TR, 5'9.5", 180 lbs. Deb: 4/22/1898

YEAR	TM/L	G	AB	R	H	2B	3B	HR	RBI	BB	SO	AVG	OBP	SLG	PRO+	BR	/A	RC	SB	CS	SBR	FA	FR	POS	TPR
1898	Cin-N	88	308	47	91	18	6	0	43	27		.295	.354	.393	107	5	2	49	9			.917	-0	2O3/S1	0.2
1899	Cin-N	107	386	62	94	16	8	0	43	40		.244	.323	.326	77	-11	-12	49	19			.885	-6	32/SO	-1.4
1900	Cin-N	134	510	57	125	29	7	2	66	27		.245	.290	.341	76	-20	-18	58	14			.922	**36**	32/OS	2.0
1901	Cin-N	105	382	40	95	18	7	6	47	28		.249	.302	.380	104	-2	1	49	10			.886	10	32	1.3
1902	Cin-N	129	479	53	133	20	7	1	49	24		.278	.320	.355	99	4	-2	61	12			.912	21	*3/O	2.1
1903	Cin-N	118	439	71	137	**32**	12	6	83	47		.312	.386	.481	132	26	19	87	6			.937	7	*3S	2.7
1904	Cin-N	99	349	35	85	11	6	1	52	29		.244	.309	.318	86	-2	-6	42	16			.887	-7	3	-1.1
1905	Cin-N	114	384	49	104	16	9	1	39	30		.271	.327	.367	96	3	-2	54	15			.919	14	*3/12O	1.6
1906	*Chi-N	151	539	81	**176**	27	10	3	**83**	47		.327	.395	.430	149	36	33	109	29			**.954**	-17	*3/2	2.3
1907	*Chi-N	152	542	52	144	25	5	1	70	37		.266	.323	.336	100	4	-0	70	19			**.967**	-5	*3	0.0
1908	*Chi-N	150	539	63	130	20	6	1	62	36		.241	.294	.306	88	-5	-8	54	12			.940	-12	*3	-1.6
1909	Chi-N	151	528	73	133	27	6	2	59	57		.252	.331	.337	105	5	3	68	22			.940	10	*3	2.0
1910	*Chi-N	129	448	70	113	21	1	2	58	36	29	.252	.323	.317	88	-7	-7	51	10			**.946**	0	*3	-0.3
1911	Bos-N	19	63	5	16	4	0	1	8	6	3	.254	.338	.365	89	-0	-1	8	1			.810	-5	3	-0.6
Total	14	1646	5896	758	1576	284	90	27	762	471	32	.267	.329	.360	101	34	2	808	194			.926	47	*32/OS1	9.2

■ **BILL STELLBAUER** Stellbauer, William Jennings b: 3/20/1894, Bremond, Tex. d: 2/16/74, New Braunfels, Tex BR/TR, 5'10", 175 lbs. Deb: 4/12/16

YEAR	TM/L	G	AB	R	H	2B	3B	HR	RBI	BB	SO	AVG	OBP	SLG	PRO+	BR	/A	RC	SB	CS	SBR	FA	FR	POS	TPR
1916	Phi-A	25	48	2	13	2	1	0	5	6	7	.271	.352	.354	118	1	1	7	2			.857	-4	O	-0.3

■ **RICK STELMASZEK** Stelmaszek, Richard Francis b: 10/8/48, Chicago, Ill. BL/TR, 6'1", 195 lbs. Deb: 6/25/71 C

YEAR	TM/L	G	AB	R	H	2B	3B	HR	RBI	BB	SO	AVG	OBP	SLG	PRO+	BR	/A	RC	SB	CS	SBR	FA	FR	POS	TPR
1971	Was-A	6	9	0	0	0	0	0	0	0	3	.000	.000	.000	-99	-2	-2	0	0	0	0	1.000	-1	/C	-0.3
1973	Tex-A	7	9	0	1	0	0	0	0	1	2	.111	.200	.111	-11	-1	-1	0	0	0	0	1.000	-0	/C	-0.1
	Cal-A	22	26	2	4	1	0	0	3	6	7	.154	.313	.192	49	-2	-1	2	0	0	0	1.000	-2	C	-0.3
	Yr	29	35	2	5	1	0	0	3	7	9	.143	.286	.171	34	-3	-3	2	0	0	0	1.000	-2	C	-0.4
1974	Chi-N	25	44	2	10	2	0	1	7	10	6	.227	.370	.341	96	0	0	6	0	0	0	.983	-6	C	-0.5
Total	3	60	88	4	15	3	0	1	10	17	18	.170	.305	.239	55	-5	-5	8	0	0	0	.993	-9	/C	-1.2

■ **FRED STEM** Stem, Frederick Boothe b: 9/22/1885, Oxford, N.C. d: 9/5/64, Darlington, S.C. BL/TR, 6'2", 160 lbs. Deb: 9/15/08

YEAR	TM/L	G	AB	R	H	2B	3B	HR	RBI	BB	SO	AVG	OBP	SLG	PRO+	BR	/A	RC	SB	CS	SBR	FA	FR	POS	TPR
1908	Bos-N	20	72	9	20	0	1	0	3	2		.278	.297	.306	94	-1	-1	7	1			.995	-1	1	-0.2
1909	Bos-N	73	245	13	51	2	3	0	11	12		.208	.254	.241	51	-14	-15	17	5			.989	10	1	-0.6
Total	2	93	317	22	71	2	4	0	14	14		.224	.263	.256	60	-14	-15	24	6			.990	10	/1	-0.8

■ **CASEY STENGEL** Stengel, Charles Dillon "The Old Professor"
b: 7/30/1890, Kansas City, Mo. d: 9/29/75, Glendale, Cal. BL/TL, 5'11", 175 lbs. Deb: 9/17/12 MCH

YEAR	TM/L	G	AB	R	H	2B	3B	HR	RBI	BB	SO	AVG	OBP	SLG	PRO+	BR	/A	RC	SB	CS	SBR	FA	FR	POS	TPR
1912	Bro-N	17	57	9	18	1	0	1	13	15	9	.316	.466	.386	140	4	4	13	5			.902	-2	O	0.1
1913	Bro-N	124	438	60	119	16	8	7	43	56	58	.272	.356	.393	110	8	7	65	19			.960	2	*O	0.4
1914	Bro-N	126	412	55	130	13	10	4	60	56	55	.316	**.404**	.425	143	26	24	76	19			.964	-8	*O	1.2
1915	Bro-N	132	459	52	109	20	12	3	50	34	46	.237	.294	.353	94	-3	-4	48	5	10	-5	.959	0	*O	-1.6
1916	*Bro-N	127	462	66	129	27	8	8	53	33	51	.279	.329	.424	127	15	14	70	11			.965	3	*O	1.2
1917	Bro-N	150	549	69	141	23	12	6	73	60	62	.257	.336	.375	115	12	11	72	18			.969	13	*O	1.7
1918	Pit-N	39	122	18	30	4	1	1	12	16	14	.246	.343	.320	99	1	1	16	11			.973	2	O	0.1
1919	Pit-N	89	321	38	94	10	10	4	43	35	35	.293	.364	.424	131	15	13	53	12			.957	3	O	1.1
1920	Phi-N	129	445	53	130	25	6	9	50	38	35	.292	.356	.436	121	15	13	66	7	13	-6	.954	-3	*O	-0.5
1921	Phi-N	24	59	7	18	3	1	0	4	6	7	.305	.369	.390	94	0	-0	9	1	1	-0	.969	2	O	0.1
	NY-N	18	22	4	5	1	0	0	2	1	5	.227	.261	.273	41	-2	-2	1	0	1	-1	.875	-3	/O	-0.6
	Yr	42	81	11	23	4	1	0	6	7	12	.284	.341	.358	81	-2	-2	10	1	2	-1	.950	-0	O	-0.5
1922	*NY-N	84	250	48	92	8	10	7	48	21	17	.368	.436	.564	155	21	21	62	4	2	0	.969	-4	O	1.2
1923	*NY-N	75	218	39	74	11	5	5	43	20	18	.339	.400	.505	139	12	12	45	6	2	1	.983	-7	O	0.2
1924	Bos-N	131	461	57	129	20	6	5	39	45	39	.280	.348	.382	100	-2	0	61	13	13	-4	.978	-7	*O	-1.9
1925	Bos-N	12	13	0	1	0	0	0	2	1	2	.077	.143	.077	-46	-3	-3	0	0	1	-1	1.000	-0	/O	-0.3
Total	14	1277	4288	575	1219	182	89	60	535	437	453	.284	.356	.410	119	118	110	654	131	43		.964	-9	*O	2.4

■ **MIKE STENHOUSE** Stenhouse, Michael Steven b: 5/29/58, Pueblo, Colo. BL/TR, 6'1", 195 lbs. Deb: 10/03/82 F

YEAR	TM/L	G	AB	R	H	2B	3B	HR	RBI	BB	SO	AVG	OBP	SLG	PRO+	BR	/A	RC	SB	CS	SBR	FA	FR	POS	TPR
1982	Mon-N	1	1	0	0	0	0	0	0	0	1	.000	.000	.000	-98	-0	-0	0	0	0	0	.000	0	/H	0.0
1983	Mon-N	24	40	2	5	1	0	0	2	4	10	.125	.205	.150	-0	-5	-5	1	0	0	0	1.000	-1	/O1	-0.7
1984	Mon-N	80	175	14	32	8	0	4	16	26	32	.183	.292	.297	69	-8	-7	16	0	0	0	.986	-3	O1	-1.2
1985	Min-A	81	179	23	40	5	0	5	21	29	18	.223	.332	.335	79	-3	-5	22	1	0	0	.929	0	DO/1	-0.5
1986	Bos-A	21	21	1	2	1	0	0	1	12	5	.095	.424	.143	63	-0	-0	3	0	0	0	1.000	-0	/O1	-0.1
Total	5	207	416	40	79	15	0	9	40	71	66	.190	.309	.291	67	-17	-17	41	1	0	0	.973	-4	/O1D	-2.5

■ **RENNIE STENNETT** Stennett, Renaldo Antonio (Porte) b: 4/5/51, Colon, Panama BR/TR, 5'11", 175 lbs. Deb: 7/10/71

YEAR	TM/L	G	AB	R	H	2B	3B	HR	RBI	BB	SO	AVG	OBP	SLG	PRO+	BR	/A	RC	SB	CS	SBR	FA	FR	POS	TPR
1971	Pit-N	50	153	24	54	5	4	1	15	7	9	.353	.381	.458	137	7	7	26	1	1	-0	.954	2	2	1.2
1972	*Pit-N	109	370	43	106	14	5	3	30	9	43	.286	.307	.376	95	-4	-4	37	4	3	-1	.977	10	2O/S	0.8
1973	Pit-N	128	466	45	113	18	3	10	55	16	63	.242	.268	.358	74	-19	-18	42	2	3	-1	.981	1	2S/O	-0.9
1974	*Pit-N	157	673	84	196	29	3	7	56	32	51	.291	.325	.374	99	-6	-3	77	8	9	-3	.980	13	*2/O	1.5

YEAR	TM/L	G	AB	R	H	2B	3B	HR	RBI	BB	SO	AVG	OBP	SLG	PRO+	BR	/A	RC	SB	CS	SBR	FA	FR	POS	TPR
1975	*Pit-N	148	616	89	176	25	7	7	62	33	42	.286	.326	.383	97	-4	-4	74	5	4	-1	.979	13	*2	1.6
1976	Pit-N	157	654	59	168	31	9	2	60	19	32	.257	.279	.341	75	-23	-24	59	18	6	2	.981	17	*2/S	0.6
1977	Pit-N	116	453	53	152	20	4	5	51	29	24	.336	.378	.430	113	11	9	71	28	18	-2	.982	-7	*2	0.8
1978	Pit-N	106	333	30	81	9	2	3	35	13	22	.243	.276	.309	60	-17	-18	26	2	1	0	.971	-12	2/3	-2.6
1979	*Pit-N	108	319	31	76	13	2	0	24	24	25	.238	.292	.292	57	-18	-19	25	1	4	-2	.974	6	*2	-1.0
1980	SF-N	120	397	34	97	13	2	2	37	22	31	.244	.287	.302	66	-19	-18	32	4	4	-1	.973	-13	*2	-2.7
1981	SF-N	38	87	8	20	0	0	1	7	3	6	.230	.264	.264	51	-6	-6	6	2	1	0	1.000	-2	2	-0.7
Total	11	1237	4521	500	1239	177	41	41	432	207	348	.274	.308	.359	85	-98	-96	475	75	54	-10	.978	28	*2/SO3	-1.4

■ JAKE STENZEL

Stenzel, Jacob Charles (b: Jacob Charles Stelzle)
b: 6/24/1867, Cincinnati, Ohio d: 1/6/19, Cincinnati, Ohio BR/TR, 5'10", 168 lbs. Deb: 6/16/1890

YEAR	TM/L	G	AB	R	H	2B	3B	HR	RBI	BB	SO	AVG	OBP	SLG	PRO+	BR	/A	RC	SB	CS	SBR	FA	FR	POS	TPR
1890	Chi-N	11	41	3	11	1	0	0	3	1	0	.268	.286	.293	68	-2	-2	4	0			.857	-4	/OC	-0.4
1892	Pit-N	3	9	0	0	0	0	0	0	1	3	.000	.100	.000	-68	-2	-2	0	1			1.000	0	/OC	-0.1
1893	Pit-N	60	224	57	81	13	4	4	37	24	17	.362	.423	.509	152	16	16	56	16			.905	-9	OC/S2	0.5
1894	Pit-N	131	522	148	185	39	20	13	121	75	13	.354	.441	.580	148	40	41	165	61			.925	-1	*O	2.3
1895	Pit-N	129	514	114	192	38	13	7	97	57	25	.374	.447	.539	165	44	49	152	53			.912	-5	*O	2.7
1896	Pit-N	114	479	104	173	26	14	2	82	32	13	.361	.409	.486	143	26	29	122	57			.922	-3	*O/1	1.4
1897	*Bal-N	131	536	113	189	**43**	7	4	116	36		.353	.404	.481	133	25	25	136	69			.932	-11	*O	0.4
1898	Bal-N	35	138	33	35	5	2	0	22	12		.254	.340	.319	87	-2	-2	17	4			.926	-2	O	-0.6
	StL-N	108	404	64	114	15	11	1	33	41		.282	.367	.381	112	8	7	67	21			.943	0	*O	-0.1
	Yr	143	542	97	149	20	13	1	55	53		.275	.360	.365	106	7	5	84	25			.940	-2	*O	-0.7
1899	StL-N	35	128	21	35	9	0	1	19	16		.273	.367	.367	99	1	0	21	8			.949	-1	O	-0.3
	Cin-N	9	29	5	9	1	0	0	3	4		.310	.412	.345	107	1	1	5	2			1.000	-1	/O	-0.1
	Yr	44	157	26	44	10	0	1	22	20		.280	.376	.363	101	1	1	26	10			.957	-2	O	-0.4
Total	9	766	3024	662	1024	190	71	32	533	299	71	.339	.408	.480	136	155	162	744	292			.927	-36	O/C12S	5.7

■ RAY STEPHENS

Stephens, Carl Ray b: 9/22/62, Houston, Tex. BR/TR, 6', 190 lbs. Deb: 9/20/90

YEAR	TM/L	G	AB	R	H	2B	3B	HR	RBI	BB	SO	AVG	OBP	SLG	PRO+	BR	/A	RC	SB	CS	SBR	FA	FR	POS	TPR
1990	StL-N	5	15	2	2	1	0	1	1	0	3	.133	.133	.400	41	-1	-1	0	0	0	0	1.000	2	/C	0.1
1991	StL-N	6	7	0	2	0	0	0	0	1	3	.286	.375	.286	88	-0	-0	1	0	0	0	1.000	1	/C	0.1
1992	Tex-A	8	13	0	2	0	0	0	0	0	5	.154	.154	.154	-14	-2	-2	0	0	0	0	1.000	-0	/CD	-0.2
Total	3	19	35	2	6	1	0	1	1	1	11	.171	.194	.286	32	-3	-3	1	0	0	0	1.000	3	/CD	0.0

■ GENE STEPHENS

Stephens, Glen Eugene b: 1/20/33, Gravette, Ark. BL/TR, 6'3.5", 175 lbs. Deb: 4/16/52

YEAR	TM/L	G	AB	R	H	2B	3B	HR	RBI	BB	SO	AVG	OBP	SLG	PRO+	BR	/A	RC	SB	CS	SBR	FA	FR	POS	TPR
1952	Bos-A	21	53	10	12	5	0	0	5	3	8	.226	.268	.321	59	-3	-3	4	4	2	0	.962	0	O	-0.4
1953	Bos-A	78	221	30	45	6	2	3	18	29	56	.204	.302	.290	57	-12	-14	22	3	3	-1	.966	-7	O	-2.4
1955	Bos-A	109	157	25	46	9	4	3	18	20	34	.293	.380	.459	114	6	4	29	0	0	0	.947	-11	O	-0.9
1956	Bos-A	104	63	22	17	2	0	1	7	12	12	.270	.387	.349	85	0	-1	9	0	1	-1	.983	-17	O	-1.8
1957	Bos-A	120	173	25	46	6	4	3	26	26	20	.266	.362	.399	102	2	1	26	0	2	-1	.987	-19	O	-2.2
1958	Bos-A	134	270	38	59	10	1	9	25	22	46	.219	.280	.363	71	-10	-12	27	1	2	-1	.975	-16	*O	-3.3
1959	Bos-A	92	270	34	75	13	1	3	39	29	33	.278	.356	.367	95	0	-1	38	5	2	0	.981	1	O	-0.3
1960	Bos-A	35	109	9	25	4	0	2	11	14	22	.229	.317	.321	71	-4	-4	13	5	1	1	.951	-1	O	-0.6
	Bal-A	84	193	38	46	11	0	5	11	25	25	.238	.329	.373	91	-3	-2	26	4	2	0	.992	-10	O	-1.5
	Yr	119	302	47	71	15	0	7	22	39	47	.235	.325	.354	83	-7	-7	39	9	3	1	.979	-11	*O	-2.1
1961	Bal-A	32	58	4	11	2	0	0	2	14	7	.190	.347	.224	57	-3	-3	6	1	1	-0	1.000	-6	O	-1.0
	KC-A	62	183	22	38	6	1	4	26	16	27	.208	.279	.317	59	-11	-11	17	3	2	-0	.968	1	O	-1.3
	Yr	94	241	26	49	8	1	4	28	30	34	.203	.297	.295	59	-14	-14	23	4	3	-1	.975	-5	O	-2.3
1962	KC-A	5	4	0	0	0	0	0	0	1	1	.000	.200	.000	-40	-1	-1	0	0	0	0	.000	0	H	-0.1
1963	Chi-A	6	18	5	7	0	0	1	2	1	3	.389	.421	.556	174	2	2	4	0	0	0	.909	1	/O	0.3
1964	Chi-A	82	141	21	33	4	2	3	17	21	28	.234	.341	.355	97	-1	-0	18	1	2	-1	.969	-5	O	-0.9
Total	12	964	1913	283	460	78	15	37	207	233	322	.240	.327	.355	82	-37	-46	239	27	20	-4	.973	-87	O	-16.4

■ JIM STEPHENS

Stephens, James Walter "Little Nemo" b: 12/10/1883, Salineville, Ohio d: 1/2/65, Oxford, Ala. BR/TR, 5'6.5", 157 lbs. Deb: 4/11/07

YEAR	TM/L	G	AB	R	H	2B	3B	HR	RBI	BB	SO	AVG	OBP	SLG	PRO+	BR	/A	RC	SB	CS	SBR	FA	FR	POS	TPR
1907	StL-A	58	173	15	35	6	3	0	11	15		.202	.270	.272	73	-5	-5	14	3			.967	-3	C	-0.4
1908	StL-A	47	150	14	30	4	1	0	6	9		.200	.255	.240	61	-6	-6	9	0			.960	-0	C	-0.3
1909	StL-A	79	223	18	49	5	0	3	18	13		.220	.278	.283	83	-6	-4	18	5			.980	3	C	0.6
1910	StL-A	99	289	24	62	3	7	0	23	16		.215	.261	.273	72	-11	-9	22	2			.971	3	C	0.3
1911	StL-A	70	212	11	49	5	5	0	17	17		.231	.300	.302	71	-9	-8	19	1			.949	-2	C	-0.4
1912	StL-A	75	205	13	51	7	5	0	22	7		.249	.274	.332	76	-8	-7	19	3			.954	4	C	0.2
Total	6	428	1252	95	276	30	21	3	97	77		.220	.273	.285	73	-46	-40	102	14			.965	5	C	-0.0

■ VERN STEPHENS

Stephens, Vernon Decatur "Junior" or "Buster"
b: 10/23/20, McAlister, N.Mex. d: 11/3/68, Long Beach, Cal. BR/TR, 5'10", 185 lbs. Deb: 9/13/41

YEAR	TM/L	G	AB	R	H	2B	3B	HR	RBI	BB	SO	AVG	OBP	SLG	PRO+	BR	/A	RC	SB	CS	SBR	FA	FR	POS	TPR
1941	StL-A	3	2	0	1	0	0	0	0	0	0	.500	.500	.500	160	0	0	1	0	0	0	.500	-0	/S	0.0
1942	StL-A	145	575	84	169	26	6	14	92	41	53	.294	.341	.433	115	10	9	83	1	3	-2	.944	-10	*S	0.7
1943	StL-A★	137	512	75	148	27	3	22	91	54	73	.289	.357	.482	142	26	25	90	3	2	-0	.943	-25	*SO	0.9
1944	*StL-A★	145	559	91	164	32	1	20	**109**	62	54	.293	.365	.462	128	25	21	101	2	2	-1	.954	-4	*S	2.9
1945	StL-A†	149	571	90	165	27	3	**24**	89	55	70	.289	.352	.473	132	25	22	98	2	1	0	**.961**	-17	*S/3	1.8
1946	StL-A★	115	450	67	138	19	4	14	64	35	49	.307	.357	.460	121	15	12	73	0	1	-1	.950	0	*S	1.9
1947	StL-A	150	562	74	157	18	4	15	83	70	61	.279	.359	.406	110	9	8	88	8	4	0	.970	12	*S	2.9
1948	Bos-A★	155	635	114	171	25	8	29	137	77	56	.269	.350	.471	112	12	8	103	1	0	0	.971	10	*S	2.6
1949	Bos-A★	155	610	113	177	31	2	39	**159**	101	73	.290	.391	.539	135	37	31	132	2	2	-1	.966	4	*S	4.3
1950	Bos-A☆	149	628	125	185	34	6	30	**144**	65	43	.295	.361	.511	110	16	8	114	1	0	0	.981	-0	*S	1.8
1951	Bos-A★	109	377	62	113	21	2	17	78	38	33	.300	.364	.501	120	15	11	62	1	2	-1	.978	14	3/S	2.2
1952	Bos-A	92	295	35	75	13	2	7	44	39	31	.254	.343	.383	95	1	-2	40	2	2	-1	.957	4	S3	0.5
1953	Chi-A	44	129	14	24	6	0	1	14	13	18	.186	.261	.256	39	-11	-11	9	2	0	1	.990	-3	3/S	-1.4
	StL-A	46	165	16	53	8	0	4	17	18	24	.321	.388	.442	121	6	5	28	0	0	0	.954	-2	3	0.2
	Yr	90	294	30	77	14	0	5	31	31	42	.262	.332	.361	85	-5	-6	36	2	0	1	.968	-5	3/S	-1.2
1954	Bal-A	101	365	31	104	17	1	8	46	17	36	.285	.317	.403	104	-3	-0	46	0	3	-2	.966	-6	3	-1.1
1955	Bal-A	3	6	0	1	0	0	0	0	0	0	.167	.286	.167	26	-1	-1	0	0	0	0	1.000	-1	/3	-0.1
	Chi-A	22	56	10	14	3	0	3	7	7	11	.250	.333	.464	110	1	1	9	0	0	0	1.000	4	3	0.5
	Yr	25	62	10	15	3	0	3	7	7	11	.242	.329	.435	102	0	0	9	0	0	0	1.000	4	3	0.4
Total	15	1720	6497	1001	1859	307	42	247	1174	692	685	.286	.355	.460	118	185	147	1076	25	22	-6	.960	-20	*S3/O	20.6

■ RIGGS STEPHENSON

Stephenson, Jackson Riggs "Old Hoss" b: 1/5/1898, Akron, Ala. d: 11/15/85, Tuscaloosa, Ala. BR/TR, 5'10", 185 lbs. Deb: 4/13/21

YEAR	TM/L	G	AB	R	H	2B	3B	HR	RBI	BB	SO	AVG	OBP	SLG	PRO+	BR	/A	RC	SB	CS	SBR	FA	FR	POS	TPR
1921	Cle-A	65	206	45	68	17	2	2	34	23	15	.330	.408	.461	119	7	7	40	4	1	1	.942	-1	2/3	0.7
1922	Cle-A	86	233	47	79	24	5	2	32	27	18	.339	.421	.511	141	15	15	52	3	0	1	.952	-5	32/O	1.3
1923	Cle-A	91	301	48	96	20	6	5	65	15	25	.319	.357	.475	118	6	6	50	6	5	-1	.970	9	2/O3	1.4
1924	Cle-A	71	240	33	89	20	0	4	44	27	10	.371	.439	.504	141	16	15	53	1	2	-1	.961	-13	2/O	0.1
1925	Cle-A	19	54	8	16	3	1	1	9	7	3	.296	.387	.444	110	1	1	10	1	1	-0	.946	1	O	0.1
1926	Chi-N	82	281	40	95	18	3	3	44	31	16	.338	.404	.456	129	13	12	51	2			.950	-4	O	0.4
1927	Chi-N	152	579	101	199	**46**	9	7	82	65	28	.344	.415	.491	142	36	36	117	8			.975	4	*O/3	3.0
1928	Chi-N	137	512	75	166	36	9	8	90	68	29	.324	.407	.477	132	24	25	99	8			.982	0	*O	1.6
1929	*Chi-N	136	495	91	179	36	6	17	110	67	21	.362	.445	.562	147	39	39	123	10			.984	-0	*O	2.7
1930	Chi-N	109	341	56	125	21	1	5	68	32	20	.367	.421	.478	116	11	10	67	2			.958	-5	O	0.0

YEAR	TM/L	G	AB	R	H	2B	3B	HR	RBI	BB	SO	AVG	OBP	SLG	PRO+	BR	/A	RC	SB	CS	SBR	FA	FR	POS	TPR
1931	Chi-N	80	263	34	84	14	4	1	52	37	14	.319	.405	.414	119	9	9	47	1			.985	-2	O	0.2
1932	*Chi-N	147	583	86	189	49	4	4	85	54	27	.324	.383	.443	123	19	20	102	3			.984	-5	*O	0.5
1933	Chi-N	97	346	45	114	17	4	4	51	34	16	.329	.397	.436	138	18	18	60	5			.985	-2	O	1.2
1934	Chi-N	38	74	5	16	0	0	0	7	7	5	.216	.293	.216	39	-6	-6	5	0			1.000	1	O	-0.5
Total	14	1310	4508	714	1515	321	54	63	773	494	247	.336	.407	.473	130	208	207	876	54	9		.978	-22	O2/3	12.7

■ JOHN STEPHENSON

Stephenson, John Herman b: 4/13/41, S.Portsmouth, Ky. BL/TR, 5'11", 180 lbs. Deb: 4/14/64

YEAR	TM/L	G	AB	R	H	2B	3B	HR	RBI	BB	SO	AVG	OBP	SLG	PRO+	BR	/A	RC	SB	CS	SBR	FA	FR	POS	TPR
1964	NY-N	37	57	2	9	0	0	1	2	4	18	.158	.226	.211	24	-6	-6	3	0	0	0	.800	-2	3/O	-0.8
1965	NY-N	62	121	9	26	5	0	4	15	8	19	.215	.264	.355	75	-5	-4	9	0	1	-1	.981	-8	C/O	-1.2
1966	NY-N	63	143	17	28	1	1	1	11	8	28	.196	.248	.238	37	-12	-12	7	0	0	0	.973	-1	C/O	-1.1
1967	Chi-N	18	49	3	11	3	1	0	5	1	6	.224	.255	.327	62	-2	-3	4	0	0	0	1.000	1	C	-0.1
1968	Chi-N	2	2	0	0	0	0	0	0	0	0	.000	.000	.000	-94	-0	-0	0	0	0	0	.000	0	H	-0.1
1969	SF-N	22	27	2	6	2	0	0	3	0	4	.222	.222	.296	45	-2	-2	1	0	0	0	.941	-3	/C3	-0.5
1970	SF-N	23	43	3	3	1	0	0	6	2	7	.070	.111	.093	-45	-9	-9	0	0	0	0	1.000	3	/CO	-0.6
1971	Cal-A	98	279	24	61	17	0	3	25	22	21	.219	.283	.312	74	-12	-10	24	0	0	0	.992	-9	C	-1.6
1972	Cal-A	66	146	14	40	3	1	2	17	11	8	.274	.342	.349	112	1	2	16	0	0	0	.993	-7	C	-0.4
1973	Cal-A	60	122	9	30	5	0	1	9	7	7	.246	.292	.311	76	-5	-4	11	0	0	0	.980	-8	C	-1.1
Total	10	451	989	83	214	37	3	12	93	63	118	.216	.272	.296	64	-52	-46	75	0	1	-1	.986	-34	C/3O	-7.5

■ JOE STEPHENSON

Stephenson, Joseph Chester b: 6/30/21, Detroit, Mich. BR/TR, 6'2", 185 lbs. Deb: 9/19/43 F

YEAR	TM/L	G	AB	R	H	2B	3B	HR	RBI	BB	SO	AVG	OBP	SLG	PRO+	BR	/A	RC	SB	CS	SBR	FA	FR	POS	TPR
1943	NY-N	9	24	4	6	1	0	0	1	0	5	.250	.250	.292	56	-1	-1	2	0			.973	2	/C	0.1
1944	Chi-N	4	8	1	1	0	0	0	0	1	3	.125	.222	.125	-1	-1	-1	0	1			1.000	1	/C	0.0
1947	Chi-A	16	35	3	5	0	0	0	3	1	7	.143	.211	.143	-1	-5	-5	1	0	0	0	.959	0	C	-0.4
Total	3	29	67	8	12	1	0	0	4	2	15	.179	.225	.194	19	-7	-7	3	1	0		.970	3	/C	-0.3

■ PHIL STEPHENSON

Stephenson, Phillip Raymond b: 9/19/60, Guthrie, Okla. BL/TL, 6'1", 195 lbs. Deb: 4/05/89

YEAR	TM/L	G	AB	R	H	2B	3B	HR	RBI	BB	SO	AVG	OBP	SLG	PRO+	BR	/A	RC	SB	CS	SBR	FA	FR	POS	TPR
1989	Chi-N	17	21	0	3	0	0	0	0	2	3	.143	.217	.143	5	-3	-3	1	1	0	0	1.000	-1	/O	-0.3
	SD-N	10	17	4	6	0	0	2	2	3	2	.353	.450	.706	225	3	3	6	0	0	0	.977	0	/1	0.3
	Yr	27	38	4	9	0	0	2	2	5	5	.237	.326	.395	100	0	0	6	1	0	0	.977	-0	/1O	0.0
1990	SD-N	103	182	26	38	9	1	4	19	30	43	.209	.321	.335	80	-4	-5	21	2	1	0	.997	3	1	-0.5
1991	SD-N	11	7	0	2	0	0	0	0	2	3	.286	.444	.286	106	0	0	1	0	0	0	.000	0	/H	0.0
1992	SD-N	53	71	5	11	2	1	0	8	10	11	.155	.259	.211	34	-6	-6	5	0	0	0	1.000	-3	O/1	-1.0
Total	4	194	298	35	60	11	2	6	29	47	62	.201	.310	.312	72	-10	-10	34	3	1	0	.993	-1	/1O	-1.5

■ DUMMY STEPHENSON

Stephenson, Reuben Crandol b: 9/22/1869, Petersburg, N.J. d: 12/1/24, Trenton, N.J. BR/TR, 5'11.5", 180 lbs. Deb: 9/09/1892

YEAR	TM/L	G	AB	R	H	2B	3B	HR	RBI	BB	SO	AVG	OBP	SLG	PRO+	BR	/A	RC	SB	CS	SBR	FA	FR	POS	TPR
1892	Phi-N	8	37	4	10	3	0	0	5	0	2	.270	.289	.351	95	-0	-0	4	0			.800	-2	/O	-0.2

■ BOB STEPHENSON

Stephenson, Robert Lloyd b: 8/11/28, Blair, Okla. BR/TR, 6', 165 lbs. Deb: 4/14/55

YEAR	TM/L	G	AB	R	H	2B	3B	HR	RBI	BB	SO	AVG	OBP	SLG	PRO+	BR	/A	RC	SB	CS	SBR	FA	FR	POS	TPR
1955	StL-N	67	111	19	27	3	0	0	6	5	18	.243	.276	.270	46	-9	-9	8	2	1	0	.938	-1	S/23	-0.7

■ WALTER STEPHENSON

Stephenson, Walter McQueen "Tarzan" b: 3/27/11, Saluda, N.C. BR/TR, 6', 180 lbs. Deb: 4/29/35

YEAR	TM/L	G	AB	R	H	2B	3B	HR	RBI	BB	SO	AVG	OBP	SLG	PRO+	BR	/A	RC	SB	CS	SBR	FA	FR	POS	TPR
1935	*Chi-N	16	26	2	10	1	1	0	2	1	5	.385	.407	.500	142	2	1	6	0			1.000	2	/C	0.3
1936	Chi-N	6	12	0	1	0	0	0	1	0	5	.083	.083	.083	-54	-3	-3	0	0			1.000	-0	/C	-0.3
1937	Phi-N	10	23	1	6	0	0	0	2	2	3	.261	.320	.261	55	-1	-1	2	0			.967	0	/C	-0.1
Total	3	32	61	3	17	1	1	0	5	3	13	.279	.313	.328	70	-2	-3	7	0			.984	2	/C	-0.1

■ DUTCH STERRETT

Sterrett, Charles Hurlbut b: 10/1/1889, Milroy, Pa. d: 12/9/65, Baltimore, Md. BR/TR, 5'11.5", 165 lbs. Deb: 6/20/12

YEAR	TM/L	G	AB	R	H	2B	3B	HR	RBI	BB	SO	AVG	OBP	SLG	PRO+	BR	/A	RC	SB	CS	SBR	FA	FR	POS	TPR
1912	NY-A	66	230	30	61	4	7	1	32	11		.265	.310	.357	85	-4	-5	28	8			.972	-9	O1C/2	-1.7
1913	NY-A	21	35	0	6	0	0	0	3	1	5	.171	.216	.171	14	-4	-4	1	1			1.000	-1	/1C	-0.5
Total	2	87	265	30	67	4	7	1	35	12	5	.253	.298	.332	77	-7	-9	29	9			.986	-10	/O1C2	-2.2

■ CHUCK STEVENS

Stevens, Charles Augustus b: 7/10/18, Van Houten, N.Mex BB/TL, 6'1", 180 lbs. Deb: 9/16/41

YEAR	TM/L	G	AB	R	H	2B	3B	HR	RBI	BB	SO	AVG	OBP	SLG	PRO+	BR	/A	RC	SB	CS	SBR	FA	FR	POS	TPR
1941	StL-A	4	13	2	2	0	0	0	2	0	1	.154	.154	.154	-18	-2	-2	0	0	0	0	.966	-1	/1	-0.3
1946	StL-A	122	432	53	107	17	4	3	27	47	62	.248	.324	.326	78	-10	-12	46	4	6	-2	**.995**	3	*1	-1.9
1948	StL-A	85	287	34	75	12	4	1	26	41	26	.261	.354	.341	83	-5	-6	39	2	2	-1	.991	1	1	-0.7
Total	3	211	732	89	184	29	8	4	55	88	89	.251	.333	.329	79	-17	-21	86	6	8	-3	.993	3	1	-2.9

■ STEVENS

Stevens Deb: 5/04/1875

YEAR	TM/L	G	AB	R	H	2B	3B	HR	RBI	BB	SO	AVG	OBP	SLG	PRO+	BR	/A	RC	SB	CS	SBR	FA	FR	POS	TPR
1875	Was-n	1	4	0	1	0	0	0		0		.250	.250	.250	76	-0	-0	0						/O	0.0

■ LEE STEVENS

Stevens, De Wain Lee b: 7/10/67, Kansas City, Mo. BL/TL, 6'4", 205 lbs. Deb: 7/16/90

YEAR	TM/L	G	AB	R	H	2B	3B	HR	RBI	BB	SO	AVG	OBP	SLG	PRO+	BR	/A	RC	SB	CS	SBR	FA	FR	POS	TPR
1990	Cal-A	67	248	28	53	10	0	7	32	22	75	.214	.278	.339	73	-10	-9	22	1	1	-0	.994	-4	1	-1.9
1991	Cal-A	18	58	8	17	7	0	0	9	6	12	.293	.359	.414	113	1	1	8	1	2	-1	.989	-1	1/O	-0.1
1992	Cal-A	106	312	25	69	19	0	7	37	29	64	.221	.289	.349	79	-10	-9	31	1	4	-2	.995	-4	1/D	-2.1
Total	3	191	618	61	139	36	0	14	78	57	151	.225	.291	.351	80	-18	-17	62	3	7	-3	.994	-8	1/OD	-4.1

■ ED STEVENS

Stevens, Edward Lee "Big Ed" b: 1/12/25, Galveston, Tex. BL/TL, 6'1", 190 lbs. Deb: 8/09/45 C

YEAR	TM/L	G	AB	R	H	2B	3B	HR	RBI	BB	SO	AVG	OBP	SLG	PRO+	BR	/A	RC	SB	CS	SBR	FA	FR	POS	TPR
1945	Bro-N	55	201	29	55	14	3	4	29	32	20	.274	.376	.433	125	7	7	35	0			.987	0	1	0.4
1946	Bro-N	103	310	34	75	13	7	10	60	27	44	.242	.303	.426	104	0	0	40	2			.986	-4	1	-0.9
1947	Bro-N	5	13	0	2	1	0	0	0	1	5	.154	.214	.231	18	-2	-2	1	0			.971	1	/1	-0.1
1948	Pit-N	128	429	47	109	19	6	10	69	35	53	.254	.313	.396	89	-7	-8	54	4			**.996**	5	*1	-0.3
1949	Pit-N	67	221	22	58	10	1	4	32	22	24	.262	.332	.371	86	-4	-4	29	1			.995	10	1	0.5
1950	Pit-N	17	46	2	9	2	0	0	3	4	5	.196	.260	.239	31	-5	-5	3	0			1.000	1	1	-0.4
Total	6	375	1220	134	308	59	17	28	193	121	151	.252	.322	.398	95	-9	-11	162	7			.992	13	1	-0.8

■ R C STEVENS

Stevens, R C b: 7/22/34, Moultrie, Ga. BL/TR, 6'5", 219 lbs. Deb: 4/15/58

YEAR	TM/L	G	AB	R	H	2B	3B	HR	RBI	BB	SO	AVG	OBP	SLG	PRO+	BR	/A	RC	SB	CS	SBR	FA	FR	POS	TPR
1958	Pit-N	59	90	16	24	3	1	7	18	5	25	.267	.320	.556	129	3	3	17	0	0	0	.991	3	1	0.4
1959	Pit-N	3	7	2	2	0	0	1	1	0	0	.286	.286	.714	157	0	0	1	0	0	0	1.000	0	/1	0.0
1960	Pit-N	9	3	1	0	0	0	0	0	0	1	.000	.000	.000	-99	-1	-1	0	0	0	0	1.000	1	/1	0.0
1961	Was-A	33	62	2	8	1	0	0	2	7	15	.129	.217	.145	-1	-9	-9	2	1	0	0	1.000	4	1	-0.6
Total	4	104	162	21	34	4	1	8	21	12	41	.210	.273	.395	77	-6	-6	20	1	0	0	.995	7	/1	-0.2

■ BOBBY STEVENS

Stevens, Robert Jordan b: 4/17/07, Chevy Chase, Md. BL/TR, 5'8", 149 lbs. Deb: 7/03/31

YEAR	TM/L	G	AB	R	H	2B	3B	HR	RBI	BB	SO	AVG	OBP	SLG	PRO+	BR	/A	RC	SB	CS	SBR	FA	FR	POS	TPR
1931	Phi-N	12	35	3	12	0	0	0	4	2	2	.343	.410	.343	97	1	0	5	0			.870	-5	S	-0.4

■ ACE STEWART

Stewart, Asa b: 2/14/1869, Terre Haute, Ind. d: 4/17/12, Terre Haute, Ind. BR/TR, 5'10", 176 lbs. Deb: 4/18/1895

YEAR	TM/L	G	AB	R	H	2B	3B	HR	RBI	BB	SO	AVG	OBP	SLG	PRO+	BR	/A	RC	SB	CS	SBR	FA	FR	POS	TPR
1895	Chi-N	97	365	52	88	8	10	8	76	39	40	.241	.314	.384	76	-11	-15	50	14			.911	-8	*2	-1.5

■ TUFFY STEWART

Stewart, Charles Eugene b: 7/31/1883, Chicago, Ill. d: 11/18/34, Chicago, Ill. BL/TL, 5'10", 167 lbs. Deb: 8/08/13

YEAR	TM/L	G	AB	R	H	2B	3B	HR	RBI	BB	SO	AVG	OBP	SLG	PRO+	BR	/A	RC	SB	CS	SBR	FA	FR	POS	TPR
1913	Chi-N	9	8	1	1	1	0	0	2	2	5	.125	.300	.250	58	-0	-0	1	1			1.000	0	/O	0.0
1914	Chi-N	2	1	0	0	0	0	0	0	0	0	.000	.000	.000	-99	-0	-0	0	0			.000	0	H	0.0
Total	2	11	9	1	1	1	0	0	2	2	5	.111	.273	.222	43	-1	-1	1	1			.982	0	/O	0.0

■ BUD STEWART

Stewart, Edward Perry b: 6/15/16, Sacramento, Cal. BL/TR, 5'11", 170 lbs. Deb: 4/19/41

YEAR	TM/L	G	AB	R	H	2B	3B	HR	RBI	BB	SO	AVG	OBP	SLG	PRO+	BR	/A	RC	SB	CS	SBR	FA	FR	POS	TPR
1941	Pit-N	73	172	27	46	7	0	0	10	12	17	.267	.315	.308	76	-5	-5	18	3			.962	-2	O	-0.9
1942	Pit-N	82	183	21	40	8	4	0	20	22	16	.219	.302	.306	76	-5	-5	18	2			1.000	-4	O3/2	-1.2

YEAR	TM/L	G	AB	R	H	2B	3B	HR	RBI	BB	SO	AVG	OBP	SLG	PRO+	BR	/A	RC	SB	CS	SBR	FA	FR	POS	TPR
1948	NY-A	6	5	1	1	1	0	0	0	0	0	.200	.200	.400	58	-0	-0	0	0	0	0	.000	0	H	0.0
	Was-A	118	401	56	112	17	13	7	69	49	27	.279	.361	.439	115	6	8	66	8	9	-3	.975	-4	*O	-0.5
	Yr	124	406	57	113	18	13	7	69	49	27	.278	.359	.438	115	6	7	66	8	9	-3	.975	-4	*O	-0.5
1949	Was-A	118	388	58	110	23	4	8	43	49	33	.284	.368	.425	112	5	6	65	6	4	-1	.982	-7	*O	-0.6
1950	Was-A	118	378	46	101	15	6	4	35	46	33	.267	.348	.370	88	-9	-6	53	5	4	-1	.991	-3	*O	-1.4
1951	Chi-A	95	217	40	60	13	5	6	40	29	9	.276	.367	.465	127	7	8	36	1	6	-3	.983	-7	O	-0.4
1952	Chi-A	92	225	23	60	10	0	5	30	28	17	.267	.350	.378	102	1	1	34	3	0	1	.982	-4	O	-0.5
1953	Chi-A	53	59	16	16	2	0	2	13	14	3	.271	.411	.407	118	2	2	11	1	0	0	1.000	-4	O	-0.2
1954	Chi-A	18	13	0	1	0	0	0	0	3	2	.077	.250	.077	-7	-2	-2	0	0	0	0	1.000	-0	/O	-0.2
Total	9	773	2041	288	547	96	32	32	260	252	157	.268	.351	.393	102	-0	5	301	29	23		.982	-35	O/32	-5.9
■ GLEN STEWART	Stewart, Glen Weldon "Gabby" b: 9/29/12, Tullahoma, Tenn. BR/TR, 6', 175 lbs. Deb: 6/26/40																								
1940	NY-N	15	29	1	4	1	0	0	0	1	2	.138	.167	.172	-6	-4	-4	1	0			.875	1	/3S	-0.3
1943	Phi-N	110	336	23	71	10	1	2	24	32	41	.211	.284	.265	61	-17	-16	26	1			.947	-9	S2/1C	-2.0
1944	Phi-N	118	377	32	83	11	5	0	29	28	40	.220	.274	.276	57	-22	-21	27	0			.963	5	3S/2	-1.4
Total	3	243	742	56	158	22	6	2	53	61	83	.213	.275	.267	56	-44	-41	54	1			.953	-4	S/321C	-3.7
■ JIMMY STEWART	Stewart, James Franklin b: 6/11/39, Opelika, Ala. BB/TR, 6', 165 lbs. Deb: 9/03/63																								
1963	Chi-N	13	37	1	11	2	0	0	1	1	7	.297	.316	.351	87	-0	-1	4	1	1	-0	.973	1	/S2	0.0
1964	Chi-N	132	415	59	105	17	0	3	33	49	61	.253	.335	.316	81	-7	-9	47	10	8	-2	.981	-6	2S/O3	-1.0
1965	Chi-N	116	282	26	63	9	4	0	19	30	53	.223	.303	.284	65	-12	-13	27	13	3	2	.955	-14	OS	-2.7
1966	Chi-N	57	90	4	16	4	1	0	4	7	12	.178	.253	.244	38	-7	-7	6	1	1	-0	1.000	-1	O/2S3	-1.0
1967	Chi-N	6	6	1	1	0	0	0	1	0	0	.167	.167	.167	-4	-1	-1	0	0	0	0	.000	0	H	-0.1
	Chi-A	24	18	5	3	0	0	0	1	1	6	.167	.211	.167	13	-2	-2	1	1	0	0	1.000	0	/O2S	-0.1
1969	Cin-N	119	221	26	56	3	4	4	24	19	33	.253	.313	.357	83	-4	-5	25	4	2	0	.973	-1	O2/3S	-0.8
1970	*Cin-N	101	105	15	28	3	1	1	8	8	13	.267	.325	.343	79	-3	-3	12	5	3	-0	1.000	3	O2/3C1	0.0
1971	Cin-N	80	82	7	19	2	2	0	9	9	12	.232	.308	.305	76	-3	-2	8	3	1	0	1.000	-3	O/32	-0.5
1972	Hou-N	68	96	14	21	5	2	0	9	6	9	.219	.265	.313	65	-5	-5	8	0	1	-1	1.000	-2	O/123	-0.8
1973	Hou-N	61	68	6	13	0	0	0	3	9	12	.191	.295	.191	37	-5	-5	5	0	0	0	1.000	1	/3O2	-0.5
Total	10	777	1420	164	336	45	14	8	112	139	218	.237	.308	.305	71	-49	-53	142	38	20	-1	.969	-22	O2S/31C	-7.5
■ STUFFY STEWART	Stewart, John Franklin b: 1/31/1894, Jasper, Fla. d: 12/30/80, Lake City, Fla. BR/TR, 5'9.5", 160 lbs. Deb: 9/03/16																								
1916	StL-N	9	17	0	3	0	0	0	1	0	3	.176	.176	.176	9	-2	-2	1	0			.833	-2	/2	-0.4
1917	StL-N	13	9	4	0	0	0	0	0	0	4	.000	.000	.000	-99	-2	-2	0	0			1.000	-3	/O2	-0.5
1922	Pit-N	3	13	3	2	0	0	0	0	0	1	.154	.154	.154	-20	-2	-2	0	0	0	0	.875	-1	/2	-0.3
1923	Bro-N	4	11	3	4	1	0	1	1	1	1	.364	.417	.727	202	1	1	3	0	0	0	.786	-1	/2	0.0
1925	Was-A	7	17	3	6	1	0	0	3	1	2	.353	.389	.412	105	0	0	3	1	0	0	.929	1	/32	0.1
1926	Was-A	62	63	27	17	6	1	0	9	6	6	.270	.333	.397	92	-1	-1	8	8	4	0	.975	7	2/3	0.6
1927	Was-A	56	129	24	31	6	2	0	4	8	15	.240	.285	.318	57	-9	-8	11	12	2	2	.939	1	2/3	-0.4
1929	Was-A	22	6	10	0	0	0	0	0	1	0	.000	.143	.000	-60	-1	-1	0	0	1	-1	1.000	8	/2	0.6
Total	8	176	265	74	63	14	3	1	18	17	32	.238	.284	.325	61	-16	-15	26	21	7		.932	10	/23O	-0.3
■ MARK STEWART	Stewart, Mark "Big Slick" b: 10/11/1889, Whitlock, Tenn. d: 1/17/32, Memphis, Tenn. BL/TR, 6'1", 180 lbs. Deb: 10/04/13																								
1913	Cin-N	1	1	0	0	0	0	0	0	0	0	.000	.000	.000	-99	-0	-0	0	0			.000	0	/C	0.0
■ NEB STEWART	Stewart, Walter Nesbitt b: 5/21/18, S.Charleston, Ohio BR/TR, 6'1", 195 lbs. Deb: 9/08/40																								
1940	Phi-N	10	31	3	4	0	0	0	0	1	5	.129	.156	.129	-21	-5	-5	1	0			.944	0	/O	-0.5
■ BILL STEWART	Stewart, William Wayne b: 4/15/28, Bay City, Mich. BR/TR, 5'11", 200 lbs. Deb: 4/17/55																								
1955	KC-A	11	18	2	2	1	0	0	0	1	6	.111	.158	.167	-13	-3	-3	1	0	0	0	1.000	-0	/O	-0.3
■ ROYLE STILLMAN	Stillman, Royle Eldon b: 1/2/51, Santa Monica, Cal. BL/TL, 5'11", 180 lbs. Deb: 6/22/75																								
1975	Bal-A	13	14	1	6	0	0	0	1	1	3	.429	.467	.429	165	1	1	3	0	0	0	1.000	-0	/O	0.1
1976	Bal-A	20	22	0	2	0	0	0	1	3	4	.091	.200	.091	-14	-3	-3	1	0	0	0	1.000	-0	/1D	-0.3
1977	Chi-A	56	119	18	25	7	1	3	13	17	21	.210	.309	.361	82	-3	-3	14	2	1	0	.977	-3	OD/1	-0.6
Total	3	89	155	19	33	7	1	3	15	21	28	.213	.307	.329	77	-5	-5	18	2	1	0	.978	-3	/OD1	-0.8
■ KURT STILLWELL	Stillwell, Kurt Andrew b: 6/4/65, Glendale, Cal. BB/TR, 5'11", 175 lbs. Deb: 4/13/86 F																								
1986	Cin-N	104	279	31	64	6	1	0	26	30	47	.229	.309	.258	56	-15	-17	24	6	2	1	.951	-2	S	-1.3
1987	Cin-N	131	395	54	102	20	7	4	33	32	50	.258	.317	.375	79	-10	-12	46	4	6	-2	.914	-21	S23	-3.1
1988	KC-A★	128	459	63	115	28	5	10	53	47	76	.251	.324	.399	100	1	0	60	6	5	-1	.976	-18	*S	-0.8
1989	KC-A	130	463	52	121	20	7	7	54	42	64	.261	.327	.380	99	-1	-1	60	9	6	-1	.970	-32	*S	-2.3
1990	KC-A	144	506	60	126	35	4	3	51	39	60	.249	.308	.352	85	-11	-10	54	0	2	-1	.957	-20	*S	-2.1
1991	KC-A	122	385	44	102	17	1	6	51	33	56	.265	.325	.361	89	-5	-6	44	3	4	-2	.959	-25	*S	-2.4
1992	SD-N	114	379	35	86	15	3	2	24	26	58	.227	.278	.298	61	-18	-20	32	4	1	1	.970	-14	*2	-3.4
Total	7	873	2866	339	716	141	28	32	292	249	411	.250	.313	.352	83	-60	-65	321	32	26	-6	.960	-133	S2/3	-15.4
■ RON STILLWELL	Stillwell, Ronald Roy b: 12/3/39, Los Angeles, Cal. BR/TR, 5'11", 165 lbs. Deb: 7/03/61 F																								
1961	Was-A	8	16	3	2	1	0	0	1	1	4	.125	.176	.188	-3	-2	-2	1	0	0	0	.929	-1	/S	-0.3
1962	Was-A	6	22	5	6	0	0	0	2	2	2	.273	.333	.273	66	-1	-1	2	0	0	0	1.000	-2	/2S	-0.3
Total	2	14	38	8	8	1	0	0	3	3	6	.211	.268	.237	37	-3	-3	3	0	0	0	.929	-3	/2S	-0.6
■ CRAIG STIMAC	Stimac, Craig Steven b: 11/18/54, Oak Park, Ill. BR/TR, 6'2", 185 lbs. Deb: 8/12/80																								
1980	SD-N	20	50	5	11	2	0	0	7	1	6	.220	.235	.260	40	-4	-4	3	0	0	0	.982	4	C/3	0.1
1981	SD-N	9	9	0	1	0	0	0	0	0	3	.111	.111	.111	-40	-2	-2	0	0	0	0	.000	0	/H	-0.2
Total	2	29	59	5	12	2	0	0	7	1	9	.203	.217	.237	29	-6	-5	4	0	0	0	.955	4	/C3	-0.1
■ BOB STINSON	Stinson, Gorrell Robert b: 10/11/45, Elkin, N.C. BB/TR, 5'11.5", 185 lbs. Deb: 9/23/69																								
1969	LA-N	4	8	1	3	0	0	0	2	0	2	.375	.375	.375	119	0	0	0	0	1	-1	.952	1	/C	0.0
1970	LA-N	4	3	1	0	0	0	0	0	0	1	.000	.000	.000	-99	-1	-1	0	0	0	0	1.000	-0	/C	-0.1
1971	StL-N	17	19	3	4	1	0	0	1	1	7	.211	.250	.263	44	-1	-1	1	0	0	0	.971	3	/CO	0.2
1972	Hou-N	27	35	3	6	1	0	0	2	1	6	.171	.216	.200	19	-4	-4	2	0	0	0	.964	-4	C/O	-0.8
1973	Mon-N	48	111	12	29	6	1	3	12	17	15	.261	.374	.414	114	3	3	18	0	1	-1	.979	-3	C/3	0.0
1974	Mon-N	38	87	4	15	2	0	1	6	15	16	.172	.294	.230	45	-6	-6	6	1	1	-0	1.000	1	C	-0.5
1975	KC-A	63	147	18	39	9	1	1	9	18	29	.265	.349	.361	98	1	0	20	1	0	0	.993	7	C/12OD	1.0
1976	*KC-A	79	209	26	55	7	1	2	25	25	29	.263	.345	.335	99	1	0	25	3	1	0	.979	-6	C	-0.4
1977	Sea-A	105	297	27	80	11	1	8	32	37	50	.269	.362	.394	107	3	4	41	0	3	-2	.984	-7	C/D	-0.2
1978	Sea-A	124	364	46	94	14	3	11	55	45	42	.258	.349	.404	112	6	6	52	2	1	0	.987	-18	*C/D	-0.9
1979	Sea-A	95	247	19	60	8	0	6	28	33	38	.243	.342	.348	85	-4	-4	30	1	2	-1	.978	-7	C	-0.9
1980	Sea-A	48	107	6	23	2	0	1	8	9	19	.215	.282	.262	50	-7	-7	8	0	0	0	.979	-9	C	-1.5
Total	12	652	1634	166	408	61	7	33	180	201	254	.250	.340	.356	93	-9	-10	205	8	10	-4	.984	-42	C/OD213	-4.1
■ GAT STIRES	Stires, Garrett b: 10/13/1849, Hunterdon Co., N.J d: 6/13/33, Byron, Ill. BL/TR, 5'8", 180 lbs. Deb: 5/06/1871																								
1871	Rok-n	25	110	23	30	4	6	2	24	7	5	.273	.316	.473	129	3	4	18	3					*O	0.3

■ SNUFFY STIRNWEISS
Stirnweiss, George Henry b: 10/26/18, New York, N.Y. d: 9/15/58, Newark Bay, N.J. BR/TR, 5'8.5", 175 lbs. Deb: 4/22/43

YEAR	TM/L	G	AB	R	H	2B	3B	HR	RBI	BB	SO	AVG	OBP	SLG	PRO+	BR	/A	RC	SB	CS	SBR	FA	FR	POS	TPR
1943	*NY-A	83	274	34	60	8	4	1	25	47	37	.219	.333	.288	82	-5	-5	28	11	9	-2	.938	-6	S/2	-0.9
1944	NY-A	154	643	**125**	**205**	35	**16**	8	43	73	87	.319	.389	.460	137	35	33	**128**	**55**	11	**10**	**.982**	19	*2	7.2
1945	NY-A†	152	632	**107**	**195**	32	**22**	10	64	78	62	**.309**	.385	**.476**	**143**	**39**	**36**	**121**	**33**	17	-0	.970	26	*2	**7.4**
1946	NY-A★	129	487	75	122	19	7	0	37	66	58	.251	.340	.318	83	-8	-9	57	18	6	**2**	.991	-6	32/S	-0.9
1947	*NY-A	148	571	102	146	18	8	5	41	89	47	.256	.358	.342	96	-1	-1	76	5	3	-0	.983	-11	*2	-0.1
1948	NY-A	141	515	90	130	20	7	3	32	86	62	.252	.360	.336	87	-8	-8	68	5	4	-1	**.993**	-11	*2	-1.1
1949	*NY-A	70	157	29	41	8	2	0	11	29	20	.261	.380	.338	90	-1	-1	23	3	2	-0	.974	4	2/3	0.4
1950	NY-A	7	2	0	0	0	0	0	0	0	0	.000	.000	.000	-99	-1	-1	0	0	0	0	1.000	1	/2	0.1
	StL-A	93	326	32	71	16	2	1	24	51	49	.218	.324	.288	56	-20	-22	33	3	3	-1	.975	-24	23/S	-4.3
	Yr	100	328	32	71	16	2	1	24	51	49	.216	.322	.287	55	-21	-22	33	3	3	-1	.975	-23	23/S	-4.2
1951	Cle-A	50	88	10	19	1	0	1	4	22	25	.216	.373	.261	78	-2	-1	11	1	0	0	.992	7	2/3	0.7
1952	Cle-A	1	0	0	0	0	0	0	0	0	0	—	—	—	—	0	0	0	0	0	0	.000	0	/3	0.0
Total	10	1028	3695	604	989	157	68	29	281	541	447	.268	.362	.371	102	28	21	545	134	55	7	.980	-0	23/S	8.5

■ JACK STIVETTS
Stivetts, John Elmer "Happy Jack" b: 3/31/1868, Ashland, Pa. d: 4/18/30, Ashland, Pa. BR/TR, 6'2", 185 lbs. Deb: 6/26/1889

YEAR	TM/L	G	AB	R	H	2B	3B	HR	RBI	BB	SO	AVG	OBP	SLG	PRO+	BR	/A	RC	SB	CS	SBR	FA	FR	POS	TPR
1889	StL-a	27	79	12	18	2	2	0	7	3	13	.228	.265	.304	56	-4	-6	7	0			.896	-1	P/O	-0.1
1890	StL-a	67	226	36	65	15	6	7		16		.288	.337	.500	131	12	7	40	2			.894	4	PO/1	0.1
1891	StL-a	85	302	45	92	10	2	7	54	10	32	.305	.331	.421	102	5	-2	44	4			.898	3	PO	-0.2
1892	*Bos-N	71	240	40	71	14	2	3	36	27	28	.296	.369	.408	126	11	8	40	8			.904	-0	PO/1	0.0
1893	Bos-N	50	172	32	51	5	6	3	25	12	14	.297	.342	.448	103	2	-1	29	6			.955	-4	P/O3	-0.2
1894	Bos-N	68	244	55	80	12	7	8	64	16	21	.328	.369	.533	108	5	1	51	3			.943	-4	PO/1	-0.1
1895	Bos-N	46	158	20	30	6	4	0	24	6	18	.190	.220	.278	27	-17	-19	10	1			.961	-1	P/1O	-0.3
1896	Bos-N	67	221	42	76	9	6	3	49	12	10	.344	.380	.480	121	8	6	43	4			.946	-6	PO/13	-0.2
1897	*Bos-N	61	199	41	73	9	9	2	37	15		.367	.417	.533	141	14	12	46	2			.926	-3	OP/21	0.1
1898	Bos-N	41	111	16	28	1	1	2	16	10		.252	.314	.333	81	-2	-3	13	1			.909	-5	O1/S2P	-0.9
1899	Cle-N	18	39	8	8	1	1	0	2	6		.205	.326	.282	73	-2	-1	4	0			1.000	1	/OPS3	-0.2
Total	11	601	1991	347	592	84	46	35	314	133	136	.297	.344	.438	105	31	1	327	31			.924	-18	PO/1S32	-2.0

■ MILT STOCK
Stock, Milton Joseph b: 7/11/1893, Chicago, Ill. d: 7/16/77, Montrose, Ala. BR/TR, 5'8", 154 lbs. Deb: 9/29/13 C

YEAR	TM/L	G	AB	R	H	2B	3B	HR	RBI	BB	SO	AVG	OBP	SLG	PRO+	BR	/A	RC	SB	CS	SBR	FA	FR	POS	TPR
1913	NY-N	7	17	2	3	1	0	0	1	2	1	.176	.263	.235	43	-1	-1	1	2			.838	3	/S	0.2
1914	NY-N	115	365	52	96	17	1	3	41	34	21	.263	.333	.340	103	0	2	44	11			.939	15	*3/S	2.2
1915	*Phi-N	69	227	37	59	7	3	1	15	22	26	.260	.325	.330	98	-0	-0	26	6	2	1	.971	2	3/S	0.5
1916	Phi-N	132	509	61	143	25	6	1	43	27	33	.281	.320	.360	105	4	2	56	21	26	-9	.955	-6	*3S	-1.0
1917	Phi-N	150	564	76	149	27	6	3	53	51	34	.264	.326	.349	103	5	2	71	25			.942	-9	*3S	-0.3
1918	Phi-N	123	481	62	132	14	1	1	42	35	22	.274	.325	.314	89	-2	-6	54	20			.946	-5	*3	-0.9
1919	StL-N	135	492	56	151	16	4	0	52	49	21	.307	.371	.356	127	13	16	70	17			.966	17	23	4.3
1920	StL-N	155	639	85	204	28	6	0	76	40	27	.319	.360	.382	117	11	14	86	15	17	-6	.939	-8	*3	0.9
1921	StL-N	149	587	96	180	27	6	3	84	48	26	.307	.360	.388	100	-1	1	85	11	3	2	.940	-22	*3	-0.9
1922	StL-N	151	581	85	177	33	9	5	79	42	29	.305	.352	.418	103	-2	1	83	7	12	-5	.950	-9	*3/S	-0.1
1923	StL-N	151	603	63	174	33	3	2	96	40	21	.289	.334	.363	86	-14	-12	74	9	6	-1	.955	-14	*3/2	-1.3
1924	Bro-N	142	561	66	136	14	4	2	52	26	32	.242	.277	.292	54	-37	-35	45	3	8	-4	.931	-23	*3	-5.1
1925	Bro-N	146	615	98	202	28	9	1	62	38	28	.328	.368	.408	101	-1	1	93	8	1	2	.978	1	*2/3	0.6
1926	Bro-N	3	8	0	0	0	0	0	0	1	0	.000	.111	.000	-69	-2	-2	0	0			.923	-1	/2	-0.2
Total	14	1628	6249	839	1806	270	58	22	696	455	321	.289	.339	.361	98	-28	-17	789	155	75		.945	-59	*32/S	-1.1

■ LEN STOCKWELL
Stockwell, Leonard Clark b: 8/25/1859, Cordova, Ill. d: 1/28/05, Niles, Cal. TR , 5'11", 165 lbs. Deb: 5/17/1879

YEAR	TM/L	G	AB	R	H	2B	3B	HR	RBI	BB	SO	AVG	OBP	SLG	PRO+	BR	/A	RC	SB	CS	SBR	FA	FR	POS	TPR
1879	Cle-N	2	6	0	0	0	0	0	0	0	2	.000	.000	.000	-99	-1	-1	0				1.000	1	/O	0.0
1884	Lou-a	2	9	0	1	0	0	0		0		.111	.111	.111	-27	-1	-1	0				.667	-1	/OC	-0.2
1890	Cle-N	2	7	2	2	1	0	0	0	0	3	.286	.286	.429	111	0	0	1	0			1.000	0	/O1	0.0
Total	3	6	22	2	3	1	0	0	0	0	5	.136	.136	.182	0	-2	-2	1	0			.900	1	/O1C	-0.2

■ STODDARD
Stoddard Deb: 9/25/1875

YEAR	TM/L	G	AB	R	H	2B	3B	HR	RBI	BB	SO	AVG	OBP	SLG	PRO+	BR	/A	RC	SB	CS	SBR	FA	FR	POS	TPR
1875	Atl-n	2	9	1	1	1	0	0		0		.111	.111	.222	14	-1	-1	0						/O	0.0

■ AL STOKES
Stokes, Albert John (b: Albert John Stocek) b: 1/1/1900, Chicago, Ill. d: 12/19/86, Grantham, N.H. BR/TR, 5'9", 175 lbs. Deb: 5/10/25

YEAR	TM/L	G	AB	R	H	2B	3B	HR	RBI	BB	SO	AVG	OBP	SLG	PRO+	BR	/A	RC	SB	CS	SBR	FA	FR	POS	TPR
1925	Bos-A	17	52	7	11	0	1	0	1	4	8	.212	.268	.250	32	-5	-5	4	0	0	0	.969	3	C	-0.2
1926	Bos-A	30	86	7	14	3	3	0	6	8	28	.163	.234	.267	32	-9	-9	6	0	0	0	.931	-4	C	-1.0
Total	2	47	138	14	25	3	4	0	7	12	36	.181	.247	.261	32	-15	-14	9	0	0	0	.946	-1	/C	-1.2

■ GENE STONE
Stone, Eugene Daniel b: 1/16/44, Burbank, Cal. BL/TL, 5'11", 190 lbs. Deb: 5/13/69

YEAR	TM/L	G	AB	R	H	2B	3B	HR	RBI	BB	SO	AVG	OBP	SLG	PRO+	BR	/A	RC	SB	CS	SBR	FA	FR	POS	TPR
1969	Phi-N	18	28	4	6	0	1	0	0	4	9	.214	.313	.286	70	-1	-1	3	0	0	0	1.000	-1	/1	-0.2

■ GEORGE STONE
Stone, George Robert b: 9/3/1877, Lost Nation, Iowa d: 1/3/45, Clinton, Iowa BL/TL, 5'9", 175 lbs. Deb: 4/20/03

YEAR	TM/L	G	AB	R	H	2B	3B	HR	RBI	BB	SO	AVG	OBP	SLG	PRO+	BR	/A	RC	SB	CS	SBR	FA	FR	POS	TPR
1903	Bos-A	2	2	0	0	0	0	0	0	0		.000	.000	.000	-95	-0	-0	0	0			.000	0	H	-0.1
1905	StL-A	154	632	76	**187**	25	13	7	52	44		.296	.347	.410	148	27	31	102	26			.954	1	*O	2.7
1906	StL-A	154	581	91	208	25	20	6	71	52		**.358**	**.416**	**.501**	**195**	**58**	**61**	**141**	35			.968	-1	*O	5.6
1907	StL-A	155	596	77	191	13	11	4	59	59		.320	.387	.399	152	36	36	105	23			.970	-3	*O	2.9
1908	StL-A	148	588	89	165	21	8	5	31	55		.281	.345	.369	131	21	21	81	20			.947	-0	*O	1.6
1909	StL-A	83	310	33	89	5	4	1	15	24		.287	.340	.339	123	5	8	39	8			.928	2	O	0.7
1910	StL-A	152	562	60	144	17	12	0	40	48		.256	.315	.329	108	1	5	65	20			.972	-2	*O	-0.5
Total	7	848	3271	426	984	106	68	23	268	282		.301	.360	.396	145	147	160	533	132			.966	-4	O	12.9

■ RON STONE
Stone, Harry Ronald b: 9/9/42, Corning, Cal. BL/TL, 6'2", 195 lbs. Deb: 4/13/66

YEAR	TM/L	G	AB	R	H	2B	3B	HR	RBI	BB	SO	AVG	OBP	SLG	PRO+	BR	/A	RC	SB	CS	SBR	FA	FR	POS	TPR
1966	KC-A	26	22	2	6	1	0	0	0	0	2	.273	.273	.318	71	-1	-1	2	1	1	-0	1.000	-1	/O1	-0.3
1969	Phi-N	103	222	22	53	7	1	1	24	29	28	.239	.335	.293	79	-6	-5	21	3	1	0	.978	-3	O	-1.1
1970	Phi-N	123	321	30	84	12	5	3	39	38	45	.262	.342	.358	90	-5	-4	40	5	6	-2	.968	-4	O/1	-1.4
1971	Phi-N	95	185	16	42	8	1	2	23	25	36	.227	.319	.314	80	-4	-4	19	2	2	-1	.964	-1	O/1	-0.8
1972	Phi-N	41	54	3	9	0	1	0	3	9	11	.167	.286	.204	40	-4	-4	3	0	0	0	1.000	3	O	-0.2
Total	5	388	804	73	194	28	8	6	89	101	122	.241	.329	.318	81	-20	-18	85	11	10	-3	.973	-6	O/1	-3.8

■ JEFF STONE
Stone, Jeffrey Glen b: 12/26/60, Kennett, Mo. BL/TR, 6', 175 lbs. Deb: 9/09/83

YEAR	TM/L	G	AB	R	H	2B	3B	HR	RBI	BB	SO	AVG	OBP	SLG	PRO+	BR	/A	RC	SB	CS	SBR	FA	FR	POS	TPR
1983	Phi-N	9	4	2	3	0	2	0	3	0	1	.750	.750	1.750	580	2	2	7	4	0	1	.000	0	/O	0.4
1984	Phi-N	51	185	27	67	4	6	1	15	9	26	.362	.398	.465	139	10	10	37	27	5	5	.916	-2	O	1.2
1985	Phi-N	88	264	36	70	4	3	3	11	15	50	.265	.307	.337	78	-7	-8	28	15	5	2	.966	-6	O	-1.5
1986	Phi-N	82	249	32	69	6	4	6	19	20	52	.277	.341	.406	101	2	1	36	19	6	2	.982	2	O	0.3
1987	Phi-N	66	125	19	32	7	1	1	16	8	38	.256	.316	.352	74	-4	-5	14	3	1	0	1.000	-1	O	-0.6
1988	Bal-A	26	61	4	10	1	0	0	1	4	11	.164	.215	.180	12	-7	-7	2	4	1	1	.963	-2	O/D	-0.9
1989	Tex-A	22	36	5	6	1	2	0	5	3	5	.167	.250	.306	55	-2	-2	2	2	1	0	.000	-1	D/O	-0.4
	Bos-A	18	15	3	3	0	0	0	1	1	2	.200	.250	.200	27	-1	-2	1	1	0	0	1.000	-3	O/D	-0.5
	Yr	40	51	8	9	1	2	0	6	4	7	.176	.250	.275	46	-4	-4	3	3	1	0	1.000	-5	DO	-0.9
1990	Bos-A	10	2	1	1	0	0	0	1	0	1	.500	.500	.500	173	0	0	0	0	1	-1	.000	0	/D	0.0
Total	8	372	941	129	261	23	18	11	72	60	186	.277	.328	.375	92	-8	-10	128	75	20	11	.963	-14	O/D	-2.0

YEAR	TM/L	G	AB	R	H	2B	3B	HR	RBI	BB	SO	AVG	OBP	SLG	PRO+	BR	/A	RC	SB	CS	SBR	FA	FR	POS	TPR

■ JOHN STONE
Stone, John Thomas "Rocky" b: 10/10/05, Lynchburg, Tenn. d: 11/30/55, Shelbyville, Tenn. BL/TR, 6'1", 178 lbs. Deb: 8/31/28

1928	Det-A	26	113	20	40	10	3	2	21	5	8	.354	.387	.549	141	6	6	24	1	0	0	.962	-1	O	0.3
1929	Det-A	51	150	23	39	11	2	2	15	11	13	.260	.311	.400	81	-5	-5	19	1	1	-0	.986	-1	O	-0.8
1930	Det-A	127	425	60	132	29	11	3	56	32	49	.311	.360	.452	102	2	1	67	6	9	-4	.966	1	*O	-0.8
1931	Det-A	147	584	86	191	28	11	10	76	56	48	.327	.388	.464	119	20	17	103	13	13	-4	.959	4	*O	0.6
1932	Det-A	145	582	106	173	35	12	17	108	58	64	.297	.361	.486	113	13	10	103	2	1	0	.961	3	*O	0.4
1933	Det-A	148	574	86	161	33	11	11	80	54	37	.280	.341	.434	103	3	1	86	1	4	-2	.970	1	*O	-0.7
1934	Was-A	113	419	77	132	28	7	7	67	52	26	.315	.395	.465	126	14	16	79	1	2	-1	.966	7	*O	1.6
1935	Was-A	125	455	78	143	27	18	1	78	39	29	.314	.372	.459	118	9	11	77	4	5	-2	.955	0	*O	0.5
1936	Was-A	123	437	95	149	22	11	15	90	60	26	.341	.421	.545	145	25	29	104	8	0	2	.967	7	*O	2.9
1937	Was-A	139	542	84	179	33	15	6	88	66	36	.330	.403	.480	127	19	22	107	6	4	-1	.984	7	*O	2.2
1938	Was-A	56	213	24	52	12	4	3	28	30	16	.244	.337	.380	85	-7	-5	29	2	1	0	.974	-2	O	-0.7
Total	11	1200	4494	739	1391	268	105	77	707	463	352	.310	.376	.467	116	100	105	797	45	40	-10	.967	25	*O	5.5

■ TIGE STONE
Stone, William Arthur b: 9/18/01, Macon, Ga. d: 1/1/60, Jacksonville, Fla. BR/TR, 5'8", 145 lbs. Deb: 8/23/23

| 1923 | StL-N | 5 | 1 | 0 | 1 | 0 | 0 | 0 | 0 | 2 | 0 | 1.000 | 1.000 | 1.000 | 438 | 1 | 1 | 1 | 0 | 0 | 0 | .000 | -2 | /OP | -0.2 |

■ JOHN STONEHAM
Stoneham, John Andrew b: 11/8/08, Wood River, Ill. BL/TR, 5'9.5", 168 lbs. Deb: 9/18/33

| 1933 | Chi-A | 10 | 25 | 4 | 3 | 0 | 0 | 1 | 3 | 2 | 2 | .120 | .185 | .240 | 12 | -3 | -3 | 1 | 0 | 0 | 0 | 1.000 | -2 | /O | -0.5 |

■ HOWIE STORIE
Storie, Howard Edward "Sponge" b: 5/15/11, Pittsfield, Mass. d: 7/27/68, Pittsfield, Mass. BR/TR, 5'10", 175 lbs. Deb: 9/07/31

1931	Bos-A	6	17	2	2	0	0	0	0	3	2	.118	.250	.118	-1	-2	-2	1	0	0	0	1.000	0	/C	-0.2
1932	Bos-A	6	8	0	3	0	0	0	0	0	0	.375	.375	.375	98	-0	-0	1	0	0	0	1.000	0	/C	0.0
Total	2	12	25	2	5	0	0	0	0	3	2	.200	.286	.200	31	-2	-2	2	0	0	0	1.000	1	/C	-0.2

■ ALAN STORKE
Storke, Alan Marshall b: 9/27/1884, Auburn, N.Y. d: 3/18/10, Newton, Mass. BR/TR, Deb: 9/24/06

1906	Pit-N	5	12	1	3	1	0	0	1	1	1	.250	.308	.333	96	-0	-0	2	1			1.000	0	/3S	0.0
1907	Pit-N	112	357	24	92	6	6	1	39	16		.258	.293	.317	90	-5	-5	37	6			.925	-13	31/2S	-1.9
1908	Pit-N	64	202	20	51	5	3	1	12	9		.252	.284	.322	94	-2	-2	20	4			.988	-6	1/32	-1.0
1909	Pit-N	37	118	12	30	5	2	0	12	7		.254	.302	.331	89	-1	-2	12	1			.994	-1	13	-0.2
	StL-N	48	174	11	49	5	0	0	10	12		.282	.328	.310	105	-0	1	19	5			.958	-1	S/21	-0.2
	Yr	85	292	23	79	10	2	0	22	19		.271	.317	.318	97	-1	-1	32	6			.958	-2	S13/2	-0.2
Total	4	266	863	68	225	22	11	2	74	45		.261	.300	.319	94	-8	-8	90	17			.990	-20	/13S2	-3.1

■ LIN STORTI
Storti, Lindo Ivan b: 12/5/06, Santa Monica, Cal. d: 7/24/82, Ontario, Cal. BB/TR, 5'11", 165 lbs. Deb: 9/18/30

1930	StL-A	7	28	6	9	1	0	2	2	2	6	.321	.367	.429	98	-0	-0	4	0	0	0	.975	1	/2	0.1
1931	StL-A	86	273	32	60	15	4	3	26	15	50	.220	.263	.337	55	-18	-19	24	0	2	-1	.926	9	3/2	-0.7
1932	StL-A	53	193	19	50	11	2	3	26	5	20	.259	.278	.383	66	-9	-11	20	1	0	0	.956	-4	3	-1.1
1933	StL-A	70	210	26	41	7	4	3	21	25	31	.195	.281	.310	53	-14	-15	19	2	2	-1	.934	-2	32	-1.4
Total	4	216	704	83	160	34	11	9	75	47	107	.227	.277	.345	59	-41	-46	68	3	4	-2	.936	4	3/2	-3.1

■ TOM STOUCH
Stouch, Thomas Carl b: 12/2/1870, Perryville, Ohio d: 10/7/56, Lancaster, Pa. BR/TR, 6'2", 165 lbs. Deb: 7/07/1898

| 1898 | Lou-N | 4 | 16 | 4 | 5 | 1 | 0 | 0 | 6 | 1 | | .313 | .353 | .375 | 110 | 0 | 0 | 2 | 0 | | | .850 | -2 | /2 | -0.2 |

■ GEORGE STOVALL
Stovall, George Thomas "Firebrand" b: 11/23/1878, Independence, Mo. d: 11/5/51, Burlington, Iowa BR/TR, 6'2", 180 lbs. Deb: 7/04/04 FM

1904	Cle-A	52	181	18	54	10	1	1	31	2		.298	.317	.381	121	4	4	24	3			.978	-2	1/2O3	0.1
1905	Cle-A	112	423	41	115	31	1	1	47	13		.272	.295	.357	105	1	1	50	13			.975	-5	12/O	-0.6
1906	Cle-A	116	443	54	121	19	5	0	37	8		.273	.288	.339	97	-4	-3	50	15			.985	-5	132	-0.9
1907	Cle-A	124	466	38	110	17	6	1	36	18		.236	.267	.305	82	-10	-11	44	13			.983	-4	*1/3	-2.0
1908	Cle-A	138	534	71	156	29	6	2	45	17		.292	.316	.380	126	13	13	69	14			.990	3	*1/OS	1.5
1909	Cle-A	145	565	60	139	17	10	2	49	6		.246	.259	.322	80	-13	-16	53	25			.988	10	*1	-0.8
1910	Cle-A	142	521	49	136	19	4	0	52	14		.261	.284	.313	86	-10	-10	52	16			.988	7	*1/2	-0.4
1911	Cle-A	126	458	48	124	17	7	0	79	21		.271	.306	.338	79	-14	-14	50	11			.986	7	*1/2M	-0.8
1912	StL-A	116	398	35	101	17	5	0	45	14		.254	.286	.322	76	-15	-13	39	11			.983	5	1M	-1.0
1913	StL-A	89	303	34	87	14	3	1	24	7	23	.287	.305	.363	98	-3	-2	34	7			.988	8	1M	0.5
1914	KC-F	124	450	51	128	20	5	7	75	23	35	.284	.325	.398	109	1	4	63	6			.989	4	*1/3M	0.6
1915	KC-F	130	480	48	111	21	3	0	44	29	36	.231	.283	.287	71	-20	-17	44	8			.987	5	*1M	-1.7
Total	12	1414	5222	547	1382	231	56	15	564	172	94	.265	.292	.339	92	-69	-66	571	142			.986	33	*1/230S	-5.5

■ HARRY STOVEY
Stovey, Harry Duffield (b: Harry Duffield Stowe)
b: 12/20/1856, Philadelphia, Pa. d: 9/20/37, New Bedford, Mass BR/TR, 5'11.5", 175 lbs. Deb: 5/01/1880 M

1880	Wor-N	83	355	76	94	21	14	6	28	12	46	.265	.289	.454	136	17	13	48				.860	-5	O1/P	0.3
1881	Wor-N	75	341	57	92	25	7	2	30	12	23	.270	.295	.402	111	6	3	41				.955	-5	*1OM	-0.6
1882	Wor-N	84	360	90	104	13	10	5	26	22	34	.289	.330	.422	136	16	14	51				.956	4	1O	1.2
1883	Phi-a	94	421	110	127	31	6	14		26		.302	.342	.504	156	31	26	74				.965	0	*1/OP	1.5
1884	Phi-a	104	448	124	146	22	23	10		26		.326	.368	.545	185	46	42	92				.960	-1	*1	2.6
1885	Phi-a	112	486	130	153	27	9	13		39		.315	.371	.488	163	39	35	90				.967	4	*1OM	2.5
1886	Phi-a	123	489	115	144	28	11	7		64		.294	.377	.440	156	33	33	109	68			.870	3	O1/P	2.3
1887	Phi-a	124	497	125	142	31	12	4		56		.286	.366	.421	121	15	15	106	74			.902	12	O1	1.7
1888	Phi-a	130	530	127	152	25	20	9	65	62		.287	.365	.460	168	40	40	124	87			.943	4	*O1	3.6
1889	Phi-a	137	556	152	171	38	13	19	119	77	68	.308	.393	.525	165	45	46	143	63			.897	18	*O/1	5.0
1890	Bos-P	118	481	142	143	25	11	12	85	81	38	.297	.404	.470	127	26	19	134	97			.921	2	*O/1	1.4
1891	Bos-N	134	544	118	152	31	20	16	95	78	69	.279	.372	.498	138	37	26	125	57			.910	9	*O/1	2.7
1892	Bos-N	38	146	21	24	8	1	0	12	14	19	.164	.252	.233	44	-9	-11	14	20			.901	0	O	-1.1
	Bal-N	74	283	58	77	14	11	4	55	40	32	.272	.364	.442	142	16	14	54	20			.913	-3	O1	0.7
	Yr	112	429	79	101	22	12	4	67	54	51	.235	.326	.371	107	7	3	67	40			.908	-3	*O1	-0.4
1893	Bal-N	8	26	4	4	2	0	0	5	8	3	.154	.353	.231	57	-1	-1	3	1			.864	0	/O	-0.1
	Bro-N	48	175	43	44	6	6	1	29	44	19	.251	.402	.371	113	4	6	36	22			.901	-3	O	0.1
	Yr	56	201	47	48	8	6	1	34	52	14	.239	.395	.353	105	3	4	38	23			.895	-2	O	0.0
Total	14	1486	6138	1492	1769	347	174	122	549	661	343	.288	.360	.461	143	360	320	1244	509			.896	40	O1/P	23.8

■ RAY STOVIAK
Stoviak, Raymond Thomas b: 6/6/15, Scottdale, Pa. BL/TL, 6'1", 195 lbs. Deb: 6/05/38

| 1938 | Phi-N | 10 | 10 | 1 | 0 | 0 | 0 | 0 | 0 | 0 | 3 | .000 | .000 | .000 | -99 | -3 | -3 | 0 | 0 | | | 1.000 | -1 | /O | -0.4 |

■ JOE STRAIN
Strain, Joseph Allan b: 4/30/54, Denver, Colo. BR/TR, 5'10", 169 lbs. Deb: 6/28/79

1979	SF-N	67	257	27	62	8	1	1	12	13	21	.241	.286	.292	62	-15	-13	22	8	4	0	.982	-1	2/3	-1.0
1980	SF-N	77	189	26	54	6	0	0	16	10	10	.286	.322	.317	81	-5	-5	18	1	2	-1	.989	-11	2/3S	-1.5
1981	Chi-N	25	74	7	14	1	0	0	1	5	7	.189	.250	.203	28	-7	-7	4	0	0	0	.975	7	2	0.2
Total	3	169	520	60	130	15	1	1	29	28	38	.250	.293	.288	64	-27	-24	43	9	6	-1	.983	-5	2/3S	-2.3

■ PAUL STRAND
Strand, Paul Edward b: 12/19/1893, Carbonado, Wash. d: 7/2/74, Salt Lake City, Utah BR/TL, 6'0.5", 190 lbs. Deb: 5/15/13

1913	Bos-N	7	6	0	1	0	0	0	0	0	0	.167	.167	.167	-5	-1	-1	0	0			.875	0	/P	0.0
1914	Bos-N	18	24	2	8	2	0	0	3	0	0	.333	.333	.417	123	0	1	3	0			.813	-0	P	0.0
1915	Bos-N	24	22	3	2	0	0	0	1	1	0	.091	.091	.091	-47	-4	-4	0	0			.750	-1	/PO	-0.2
1924	Phi-A	47	167	15	38	9	4	0	13	4	9	.228	.254	.329	49	-13	-14	13	3	3	-1	.988	-6	O	-2.3

YEAR	TM/L	G	AB	R	H	2B	3B	HR	RBI	BB	SO	AVG	OBP	SLG	PRO+	BR	/A	RC	SB	CS	SBR	FA	FR	POS	TPR
Total	4	96	219	20	49	11	4	0	18	4	15	.224	.244	.311	47	-17	-18	17	3	3		.989	-7	/OP	-2.5
■ **LARRY STRANDS**	Strands, John Lawrence b: 12/5/1885, Chicago, Ill. d: 1/19/57, Forest Park, Ill. BR/TR, 5′10.5″, 165 lbs. Deb: 4/25/15																								
1915	New-F	35	75	7	14	3	1	1	11	6	11	.187	.247	.293	62	-4	-4	6	1			.852	-7	3/2O	-1.1
■ **SAMMY STRANG**	Strang, Samuel Nicklin "The Dixie Thrush" (b: Samuel Strang Nicklin) b: 12/16/1876, Chattanooga, Tenn. d: 3/13/32, Chattanooga, Tenn. BB/TR, 5′8″, 160 lbs. Deb: 7/10/1896																								
1896	Lou-N	14	46	6	12	0	0	0	7	6	6	.261	.346	.261	66	-2	-2	6	4			.803	-8	S	-0.8
1900	Chi-N	27	102	15	29	3	0	0	9	8		.284	.348	.314	87	-2	-1	12	1			.887	-11	3/S2	-1.1
1901	NY-N	135	493	55	139	14	6	1	34	59		.282	.362	.341	109	5	8	80	40			.877	2	32/OS	1.2
1902	Chi-A	137	536	108	158	18	5	3	46	76		.295	.387	.364	114	10	14	94	38			.890	5	*3	1.9
	Chi-N	3	11	1	4	0	0	0	0	0		.364	.364	.364	128	0	0	2	1			1.000	-1	/23	0.0
1903	Bro-N	135	508	101	138	21	5	0	38	75		.272	.372	.333	105	5	7	83	46			.914	-7	*3/O2	0.1
1904	Bro-N	77	271	28	52	11	0	1	9	45		.192	.313	.244	75	-6	-6	27	16			.910	-32	23/S	-3.9
1905	*NY-N	111	294	51	76	9	4	3	29	58		.259	.389	.347	118	11	10	52	23			.915	-18	2O/S13	-0.9
1906	NY-N	113	313	50	100	16	4	4	49	54		.319	.423	.435	164	27	26	69	21			.944	3	2O/S31	3.1
1907	NY-N	123	306	56	77	20	4	4	30	60		.252	.388	.382	137	18	17	55	21			.947	-1	O2/31S	1.5
1908	NY-N	28	53	8	5	0	0	0	2	23		.094	.385	.094	52	-0	-1	4	5			.863	-3	2/OS	-0.5
Total	10	903	2933	479	790	112	28	16	253	464	6	.269	.376	.343	113	65	72	484	216			.891	-71	32O/S1	0.6
■ **ALAN STRANGE**	Strange, Alan Cochrane "Inky" b: 11/7/09, Philadelphia, Pa. BR/TR, 5′9″, 162 lbs. Deb: 4/17/34																								
1934	StL-A	127	430	39	100	17	2	1	45	48	28	.233	.310	.288	51	-28	-34	41	3	1	0	.955	4	*S	-2.1
1935	StL-A	49	147	8	34	6	1	0	17	17	7	.231	.311	.286	53	-10	-11	14	0	0	0	.960	2	S	-0.6
	Was-A	20	54	3	10	2	1	0	5	4	1	.185	.241	.259	30	-6	-6	4	0	0	0	.974	3	S	-0.2
	Yr	69	201	11	44	8	2	0	22	21	8	.219	.293	.279	47	-15	-16	18	0	0	0	.963	5	S	-0.8
1940	StL-A	54	167	26	31	8	3	0	6	22	12	.186	.284	.269	43	-14	-14	14	2	1	0	.962	3	S/2	-0.8
1941	StL-A	45	112	14	26	4	0	0	11	15	5	.232	.323	.268	56	-6	-7	10	1	0	0	.973	2	S/13	-0.3
1942	StL-A	19	37	3	10	2	0	0	5	3	1	.270	.325	.324	82	-1	-1	4	0	1	-1	.935	5	3/S2	0.3
Total	5	314	947	93	211	39	7	1	89	109	54	.223	.304	.282	50	-65	-72	86	6	3	0	.959	18	S/321	-3.7
■ **DOUG STRANGE**	Strange, Joseph Douglas b: 4/13/64, Greenville, S.C. BB/TR, 6′2″, 170 lbs. Deb: 7/13/89																								
1989	Det-A	64	196	16	42	4	1	1	14	17	36	.214	.280	.260	54	-12	-11	14	3	3	-1	.878	1	3/2SD	-1.1
1991	Chi-N	3	9	0	4	1	0	0	1	0	1	.444	.500	.556	188	1	1	3	1	0	0	.800	-1	/3	0.0
1992	Chi-N	52	94	7	15	1	0	1	5	10	15	.160	.240	.202	26	-9	-9	5	1	0	0	.900	-0	32	-1.0
Total	3	119	299	23	61	6	1	2	20	27	52	.204	.274	.251	49	-20	-19	22	5	3	-0	.882	-1	/32SD	-2.1
■ **ASA STRATTON**	Stratton, Asa Evans b: 2/10/1853, Grafton, Mass. d: 8/14/25, Fitchburg, Mass. Deb: 6/17/1881																								
1881	Wor-N	1	4	0	1	0	0	0	0	0	2	.250	.250	.250	55	-0	-0	0				.333	-1	/S	-0.2
■ **SCOTT STRATTON**	Stratton, C. Scott b: 10/2/1869, Campbellsburg, Ky. d: 3/8/39, Louisville, Ky. BL/TR, 6′, 180 lbs. Deb: 4/21/1888																								
1888	Lou-a	67	249	35	64	8	1	1	29	12		.257	.310	.309	104	1	2	28	10			.821	-5	OP	-0.4
1889	Lou-a	62	229	30	66	7	5	4	34	13	36	.288	.332	.415	116	3	4	36	10			.915	5	OP1	0.4
1890	*Lou-a	55	189	29	61	3	5	0		16		.323	.385	.392	135	8	8	32	8			.977	5	P/O	0.0
1891	Pit-N	2	8	1	1	0	0	0	0	0	3	.125	.125	.125	-27	-1	-1	0	0			.900	1	/P	0.0
	Lou-a	34	115	9	27	2	0	0	8	11	13	.235	.307	.252	64	-5	-5	12	8			.939	2	P/1O	-0.3
1892	Lou-N	63	219	22	56	2	9	0	23	17	21	.256	.318	.347	112	1	3	28	9			.915	1	PO/1	-0.1
1893	Lou-N	60	217	34	49	8	5	0	16	25	15	.226	.309	.309	71	-11	-7	23	6			.975	5	PO/1	-0.3
1894	Lou-N	13	37	9	12	1	2	0	4	4	2	.324	.390	.459	114	0	1	7	1			.929	2	/PO	0.1
	Chi-N	23	96	29	36	5	4	3	23	6	1	.375	.417	.604	138	7	6	26	3			.933	-1	P/O1	0.0
	Yr	36	133	38	48	6	6	3	27	10	3	.361	.410	.564	133	7	7	33	4			.932	1	PO/1	0.1
1895	Chi-N	10	24	3	7	1	1	0	2	4	2	.292	.393	.417	104	1	0	5	1			.833	-1	/PO	-0.1
Total	8	389	1383	201	379	37	32	8	139	108	93	.274	.335	.364	105	3	10	196	56			.938	14	PO/1	-0.7
■ **JOE STRAUB**	Straub, Joseph b: 1/19/1858, Germany d: 2/13/29, Pueblo, Colo. BR/TR, 5′10″, 160 lbs. Deb: 6/24/1880																								
1880	Tro-N	3	12	1	3	0	0	0	3	1	3	.250	.308	.250	87	-0	-0	1				.815	0	/C	0.0
1882	Phi-a	8	32	2	6	2	0	0		1		.188	.212	.250	50	-1	-2	2				.830	-1	/CO	-0.2
1883	Col-a	27	100	4	13	0	0	0		4		.130	.163	.130	-5	-11	-10	2				.860	-3	C1/O	-1.2
Total	3	38	144	7	22	2	0	0	3	6	3	.153	.187	.167	17	-13	-12	5				.843	-4	/C1O	-1.4
■ **JOE STRAUSS**	Strauss, Joseph "Dutch" or "The Socker" (b: Joseph Strasser) b: 11/16/1858, Cincinnati, Ohio d: 6/24/06, Cincinnati, Ohio BR/TR, Deb: 7/27/1884																								
1884	KC-U	16	60	4	12	3	0	0		1		.200	.213	.250	64	-3	-1	3				.833	-1	O/C23	-0.2
1885	Lou-a	2	6	0	1	0	0	0		0		.167	.167	.167	7	-1	-1	0				.000	-2	/OC	-0.2
1886	Lou-a	74	297	36	64	5	6	1		8		.215	.239	.283	61	-13	-15	27	25			.857	4	O/PC	-1.1
	Bro-a	9	36	6	9	1	1	0		1		.250	.270	.333	89	-1	-1	4	4			1.000	1	/OC	0.0
	Yr	83	333	42	73	6	7	1		9		.219	.242	.288	64	-13	-16	31	29			.866	5	O/CP	-1.1
Total	3	101	399	46	86	9	7	1		10		.216	.237	.281	63	-16	-18	35	29			.861	2	/OCP23	-1.5
■ **DARRYL STRAWBERRY**	Strawberry, Darryl Eugene b: 3/12/62, Los Angeles, Cal. BL/TL, 6′6″, 190 lbs. Deb: 5/06/83																								
1983	NY-N	122	420	63	108	15	7	26	74	47	128	.257	.338	.512	134	17	17	74	19	6	2	.984	1	*O	1.7
1984	NY-N★	147	522	75	131	27	4	26	97	75	131	.251	.345	.467	128	18	19	87	27	8	3	.980	4	*O	2.3
1985	NY-N★	111	393	78	109	15	4	29	79	73	96	.277	.392	.557	167	34	35	87	26	11	1	.991	-4	*O	2.9
1986	*NY-N★	136	475	76	123	27	5	27	93	72	141	.259	.363	.507	142	24	26	92	28	12	1	.975	2	*O	2.6
1987	NY-N★	154	532	108	151	32	5	39	104	97	122	.284	.401	.583	165	45	49	132	36	12	4	.972	1	*O	4.8
1988	*NY-N★	153	543	101	146	27	3	**39**	101	85	127	.269	.371	**.545**	**168**	42	45	111	29	14	0	.971	7	*O	5.0
1989	NY-N†	134	476	69	107	26	1	29	77	61	105	.225	.314	.466	126	11	14	72	11	4	1	.972	9	*O	2.2
1990	NY-N★	152	542	92	150	18	1	37	108	70	110	.277	.364	.518	140	29	29	104	15	8	-0	.989	6	*O	3.2
1991	LA-N†	139	505	86	134	22	4	28	99	75	125	.265	.364	.491	141	26	27	92	10	8	-2	.978	-2	*O	2.1
1992	LA-N	43	156	20	37	8	0	5	25	19	34	.237	.324	.385	101	0	0	20	3	1	0	.986	-1	O	-0.1
Total	10	1291	4564	768	1196	217	34	285	857	674	1119	.262	.361	.512	144	245	262	871	204	84	11	.979	23	*O	26.7
■ **GABBY STREET**	Street, Charles Evard "Old Sarge" b: 9/30/1882, Huntsville, Ala. d: 2/6/51, Joplin, Mo. BR/TR, 5′11″, 180 lbs. Deb: 9/13/04 MC																								
1904	Cin-N	11	33	1	4	1	0	0	0	1		.121	.147	.152	-7	-4	-4	1	2			.973	4	C	0.1
1905	Cin-N	2	2	0	0	0	0	0	0	2		.000	.500	.000	48	0	0	0	0			1.000	1	/C	0.1
	Bos-N	3	12	0	2	0	0	0	0	0		.167	.167	.167	-0	-1	-1	1	1			.778	-2	/C	-0.3
	Cin-N	29	91	8	23	5	1	0	8	6		.253	.306	.330	81	-1	-2	10	1			.975	3	C	0.3
	Yr	34	105	8	25	5	1	0	8	8		.238	.298	.305	73	-3	-4	10	2			.957	2	C	0.1
1908	Was-A	131	394	31	81	12	7	1	32	40		.206	.289	.279	92	-6	-2	33	5			.973	-1	*C	0.9
1909	Was-A	137	407	25	86	12	1	0	29	26		.211	.262	.246	63	-18	-16	27	2			.981	11	*C	0.8
1910	Was-A	89	257	13	52	6	0	1	16	23		.202	.273	.237	63	-11	-10	17	1			**.978**	10	C	0.9
1911	Was-A	72	216	16	48	7	1	0	14	14		.222	.279	.264	53	-14	-13	17	4			.973	7	C	0.0
1912	NY-A	29	88	4	16	1	1	0	6	7		.182	.258	.216	34	-7	-8	5	1			.958	-4	C	-0.9
1931	StL-N	1	1	0	0	0	0	0	0	0	0	.000	.000	.000	-96	-0	-0	0	0			1.000	0	/CM	0.0
Total	8	504	1501	98	312	44	11	2	105	119	0	.208	.273	.256	66	-64	-58	111	17			.974	29	C	1.9

■ **WALT STREULI** Streuli, Walter Herbert b: 9/26/35, Memphis, Tenn. BR/TR, 6'2", 195 lbs. Deb: 9/25/54

YEAR	TM/L	G	AB	R	H	2B	3B	HR	RBI	BB	SO	AVG	OBP	SLG	PRO+	BR	/A	RC	SB	CS	SBR	FA	FR	POS	TPR
1954	Det-A	1	0	0	0	0	0	0	0	1	0	—	1.000	—	195	0	0	0	0	0	0	1.000	-0	/C	0.0
1955	Det-A	2	4	1	1	1	0	0	1	0	0	.250	.250	.500	100	-0	-0	1	0	0	0	1.000	0	/C	0.0
1956	Det-A	3	8	0	2	1	0	0	1	1	2	.250	.333	.375	87	-0	-0	1	0	0	0	.933	0	/C	0.0
Total	3	6	12	1	3	2	0	0	2	2	2	.250	.357	.417	106	0	0	2	0	0	0	.957	0	/C	0.0

■ **JOHN STRICK** Strick, John Quincy Adams Deb: 5/18/1882

YEAR	TM/L	G	AB	R	H	2B	3B	HR	RBI	BB	SO	AVG	OBP	SLG	PRO+	BR	/A	RC	SB	CS	SBR	FA	FR	POS	TPR
1882	Lou-a	32	110	17	18	6	1	0		9		.164	.227	.236	60	-5	-4	6				.898	-0	C/O2S1	-0.3

■ **CUB STRICKER** Stricker, John A. (b: John A. Streaker) b: 2/15/1860, Philadelphia, Pa. d: 11/19/37, Philadelphia, Pa. BR/TR, 5'3", 138 lbs. Deb: 5/02/1882 M

YEAR	TM/L	G	AB	R	H	2B	3B	HR	RBI	BB	SO	AVG	OBP	SLG	PRO+	BR	/A	RC	SB	CS	SBR	FA	FR	POS	TPR
1882	Phi-a	72	272	34	59	6	1	0		15		.217	.258	.246	63	-8	-12	18				.904	**23**	*2/PO	1.1
1883	Phi-a	89	330	67	90	8	0	1		19		.273	.312	.306	92	0	-4	32				.837	-20	*2/C	-2.0
1884	Phi-a	107	399	59	92	16	11	1		19		.231	.267	.333	91	-1	-5	36				.870	-34	*2/OCP	-3.4
1885	Phi-a	106	398	71	93	9	3	1		21		.234	.284	.279	76	-8	-11	32				.879	-13	*2	-1.9
1887	Cle-a	131	534	122	141	19	4	2		53		.264	.334	.326	89	-8	-5	89	86			.912	10	*2/SP	0.7
1888	Cle-a	127	493	80	115	13	6	1	33	50		.233	.311	.290	99	-0	2	65	60			.929	23	*2/OP	2.7
1889	Cle-N	136	566	83	142	10	4	1	47	58	18	.251	.323	.288	74	-19	-17	64	32			.932	7	*2/S	-0.2
1890	Cle-P	127	544	93	133	19	8	2	65	54	16	.244	.318	.320	79	-21	-13	65	24			.905	5	*2S	0.0
1891	Bos-a	139	514	96	111	15	4	0	46	63	34	.216	.309	.261	67	-21	-20	59	54			.942	**24**	*2	0.9
1892	StL-N	28	98	12	20	1	0	0	11	10	7	.204	.297	.214	60	-5	-4	8	5			.939	-4	2/SM	-0.7
	Bal-N	75	269	45	71	5	5	3	37	32	18	.264	.344	.353	110	5	4	38	13			.918	3	2	0.7
	Yr	103	367	57	91	6	5	3	48	42	25	.248	.332	.316	97	0	-0	46	18			.923	-2	*2/S	0.0
1893	Was-N	59	218	28	40	7	1	0	20	20	12	.183	.252	.225	29	-22	-21	14	4			.903	7	2O/S3	-1.2
Total	11	1196	4635	790	1107	128	47	12	259	414	105	.239	.306	.294	80	-107	-107	521	278			.907	30	*2/SOP3C	-3.3

■ **GEORGE STRICKLAND** Strickland, George Bevan "Bo" b: 1/10/26, New Orleans, La. BR/TR, 6'1", 180 lbs. Deb: 5/07/50 MC

YEAR	TM/L	G	AB	R	H	2B	3B	HR	RBI	BB	SO	AVG	OBP	SLG	PRO+	BR	/A	RC	SB	CS	SBR	FA	FR	POS	TPR
1950	Pit-N	23	27	0	3	0	0	0	2	3	8	.111	.226	.111	-8	-4	-4	1	0			.978	3	S/3	-0.1
1951	Pit-N	138	454	59	98	12	7	9	47	65	83	.216	.318	.333	73	-15	-17	52	4	2	0	.943	12	*S2	0.4
1952	Pit-N	76	232	17	41	6	2	5	22	21	45	.177	.248	.284	46	-17	-18	17	4	2	0	.953	15	2S/13	0.1
	Cle-A	31	88	8	19	4	0	1	8	14	15	.216	.324	.295	78	-3	-2	10	0	0	0	.964	10	S/2	1.0
1953	Cle-A	123	419	43	119	17	4	5	47	51	52	.284	.362	.379	103	1	3	63	0	0	0	.974	16	*S/1	2.7
1954	*Cle-A	112	361	42	77	12	3	6	37	55	62	.213	.319	.313	72	-12	-13	39	2	1	0	.961	-12	*S	-1.6
1955	Cle-A	130	388	34	81	9	5	2	34	49	60	.209	.302	.273	54	-24	-26	35	1	0	0	**.976**	8	*S	-0.7
1956	Cle-A	85	171	22	36	1	2	3	17	22	27	.211	.301	.292	56	-11	-11	15	0	1	-1	.986	16	2S3	0.7
1957	Cle-A	89	201	21	47	8	2	1	19	26	29	.234	.325	.308	75	-7	-6	20	0	3	-2	.980	15	2S3	1.1
1959	Cle-A	132	441	55	105	15	2	3	48	51	64	.238	.317	.302	74	-17	-15	45	1	1	-0	.971	-9	3S/2	-1.9
1960	Cle-A	32	42	4	7	0	0	1	3	4	8	.167	.255	.238	35	-4	-4	3	0	0	0	.962	1	S3/2	-0.3
Total	10	971	2824	305	633	84	27	36	284	361	453	.224	.314	.311	70	-112	-113	299	12	10		.963	74	S23/1	1.4

■ **GEORGE STRIEF** Strief, George Andrew b: 10/16/1856, Cincinnati, Ohio d: 4/1/46, Cleveland, Ohio BR/TR, 5'7", 172 lbs. Deb: 5/01/1879 U

YEAR	TM/L	G	AB	R	H	2B	3B	HR	RBI	BB	SO	AVG	OBP	SLG	PRO+	BR	/A	RC	SB	CS	SBR	FA	FR	POS	TPR
1879	Cle-N	71	264	24	46	7	1	0	15	10	23	.174	.204	.208	37	-17	-17	12				.918	-9	O2	-2.6
1882	Pit-a	79	297	45	58	9	6	2		13		.195	.229	.286	76	-8	-6	20				.917	0	*2/S	-0.4
1883	StL-a	82	302	22	68	9	0	1		12		.225	.255	.265	64	-10	-13	21				.899	6	*2O	-0.5
1884	StL-a	48	184	22	37	5	2	2		13		.201	.254	.283	75	-4	-5	14				.848	-3	O/21	-0.8
	KC-U	15	56	5	6	5	0	0		4		.107	.167	.196	26	-4	-3	2				.900	8	2	0.5
	CP-U	15	53	6	11	5	0	0		3		.208	.250	.302	86	-1	-1	4				.905	-2	2	-0.2
	Yr	30	109	11	17	10	0	0		7		.156	.207	.248	57	-5	-4	6				.902	7	2	0.3
	Cle-N	8	29	2	7	2	0	0	0	0	5	.241	.241	.310	70	-1	-1	2				1.000	-0	/O3	-0.1
1885	Phi-a	44	175	19	48	8	5	0		9		.274	.310	.377	112	4	2	21				.828	-2	3S/O2	0.0
Total	5	362	1360	145	281	50	14	5	15	64	28	.207	.242	.275	69	-43	-44	95				.899	-1	2O/3S1	-4.1

■ **LOU STRINGER** Stringer, Louis Bernard b: 5/13/17, Grand Rapids, Mich BR/TR, 5'11", 173 lbs. Deb: 4/15/41

YEAR	TM/L	G	AB	R	H	2B	3B	HR	RBI	BB	SO	AVG	OBP	SLG	PRO+	BR	/A	RC	SB	CS	SBR	FA	FR	POS	TPR
1941	Chi-N	145	512	59	126	31	4	5	53	59	86	.246	.324	.352	94	-6	-4	62	3			.960	20	*2/S	2.6
1942	Chi-N	121	406	45	96	10	5	9	41	31	55	.236	.292	.352	92	-7	-5	42	3			.955	2	*2/3	0.3
1946	Chi-N	80	209	26	51	3	1	3	19	26	34	.244	.328	.311	83	-5	-4	22	0			.956	-5	2/S3	-0.5
1948	Bos-A	4	11	1	1	0	0	1	1	0	3	.091	.091	.364	17	-1	-2	0	0	0	0	.947	2	/2	0.1
1949	Bos-A	35	41	10	11	4	0	1	6	5	10	.268	.348	.439	100	0	-0	6	0	0	0	.978	3	/2	0.3
1950	Bos-A	24	17	7	5	1	0	0	2	0	4	.294	.294	.353	59	-1	-1	2	1	0	0	.778	3	/32S	0.2
Total	6	409	1196	148	290	49	10	19	122	121	192	.242	.313	.348	90	-20	-17	135	7	0		.958	26	2/S3	3.0

■ **JOE STRIPP** Stripp, Joseph Valentine "Jersey Joe" b: 2/3/03, Harrison, N.J. d: 6/10/89, Orlando, Fla. BR/TR, 5'11.5", 175 lbs. Deb: 7/02/28

YEAR	TM/L	G	AB	R	H	2B	3B	HR	RBI	BB	SO	AVG	OBP	SLG	PRO+	BR	/A	RC	SB	CS	SBR	FA	FR	POS	TPR
1928	Cin-N	42	139	18	40	7	3	1	17	8	8	.288	.340	.403	95	-1	-1	19	0			.931	-7	O3/S	-0.8
1929	Cin-N	64	187	24	40	3	2	3	20	24	15	.214	.313	.299	55	-14	-12	19	2			.960	8	3/2	-0.2
1930	Cin-N	130	464	74	142	37	6	3	64	51	37	.306	.377	.431	100	-3	1	75	15			.996	0	13	-0.3
1931	Cin-N	105	426	71	138	26	2	3	42	21	31	.324	.359	.415	114	4	7	64	5			.957	4	3/1	1.6
1932	Bro-N	138	534	94	162	36	9	6	64	36	30	.303	.350	.438	113	7	9	84	14			.954	16	31	2.7
1933	Bro-N	141	537	69	149	20	7	1	51	26	23	.277	.312	.346	92	-9	-6	59	5			.967	5	*3	0.7
1934	Bro-N	104	384	50	121	19	6	1	40	22	20	.315	.354	.404	108	1	4	55	2			.941	-6	3/1S	0.1
1935	Bro-N	109	373	44	114	13	5	3	43	22	15	.306	.344	.391	99	-1	-0	49	2			.962	7	31/O	0.8
1936	Bro-N	110	439	51	139	31	1	1	60	22	12	.317	.351	.399	100	1	0	62	2			**.968**	8	*3	1.1
1937	Bro-N	90	300	37	73	10	2	1	26	20	18	.243	.291	.300	60	-16	-17	25	1			.971	-6	31/S	-2.3
1938	StL-N	54	199	24	57	7	0	0	18	18	10	.286	.349	.322	81	-3	-5	23	0			.977	-8	3	-1.2
	Bos-N	59	229	19	63	10	0	1	19	10	7	.275	.305	.332	84	-8	-5	24	2			.966	1	3	-0.3
	Yr	113	428	43	120	17	0	1	37	28	17	.280	.326	.327	82	-11	-10	46	2			**.971**	-7	*3	-1.5
Total	11	1146	4211	575	1238	219	43	24	464	280	226	.294	.340	.384	96	-42	-26	555	50			.961	21	31/OS2	1.9

■ **ALLIE STROBEL** Strobel, Albert Irving b: 6/11/1884, Boston, Mass. d: 2/10/55, Hollywood, Fla. BR/TR, 6', 160 lbs. Deb: 8/29/05

YEAR	TM/L	G	AB	R	H	2B	3B	HR	RBI	BB	SO	AVG	OBP	SLG	PRO+	BR	/A	RC	SB	CS	SBR	FA	FR	POS	TPR
1905	Bos-N	5	19	1	2	0	0	0	2	0		.105	.105	.105	-38	-3	-3	0	0			1.000	-0	/3O	-0.4
1906	Bos-N	100	317	28	64	10	3	1	24	29		.202	.273	.262	69	-12	-11	25	2			.946	-6	2/SO	-1.8
Total	2	105	336	29	66	10	3	1	26	29		.196	.264	.253	63	-15	-14	26	2			1.000	-6	/2S3O	-2.2

■ **JIM STRONER** Stroner, James M. b: 9/26/1892, Chicago, Ill. d: 11/16/71, Chicago, Ill. BR/TR, 5'10", 175 lbs. Deb: 5/01/29

YEAR	TM/L	G	AB	R	H	2B	3B	HR	RBI	BB	SO	AVG	OBP	SLG	PRO+	BR	/A	RC	SB	CS	SBR	FA	FR	POS	TPR
1929	Pit-N	6	8	0	3	1	0	0	0	1	0	.375	.444	.500	130	0	0	2	0			.571	-0	/3	0.0

■ **ED STROUD** Stroud, Edwin Marvin b: 10/31/39, Lapine, Ala. BL/TR, 5'11", 180 lbs. Deb: 9/11/66

YEAR	TM/L	G	AB	R	H	2B	3B	HR	RBI	BB	SO	AVG	OBP	SLG	PRO+	BR	/A	RC	SB	CS	SBR	FA	FR	POS	TPR
1966	Chi-A	12	36	3	6	2	0	0	1	2	8	.167	.231	.222	33	-3	-3	2	3	0	1	1.000	-0	O	-0.3
1967	Chi-A	20	27	6	8	0	1	0	3	1	5	.296	.345	.370	116	0	0	3	7	2	1	1.000	-1	O	0.0
	Was-A	87	204	36	41	5	3	1	10	25	29	.201	.291	.270	69	-8	-7	17	8	6	-1	.983	-13	O	-2.6
	Yr	107	231	42	49	5	4	1	13	26	34	.212	.297	.281	75	-8	-7	20	15	8	-0	.985	-14	O	-2.6
1968	Was-A	105	306	41	73	10	10	4	23	20	50	.239	.285	.376	102	-1	-0	30	9	3	1	.979	-4	O	-0.9
1969	Was-A	123	206	35	52	5	6	4	29	30	33	.252	.353	.393	114	3	4	31	12	2	2	.982	-11	O	-0.8
1970	Was-A	129	433	69	115	11	5	5	32	40	79	.266	.332	.349	92	-7	-4	51	29	8	4	.993	2	*O	-0.4
1971	Chi-A	53	141	19	25	4	3	0	2	11	20	.177	.237	.248	36	-12	-12	7	4	5	-2	1.000	-11	O	-2.9
Total	6	529	1353	209	320	37	28	14	100	129	224	.237	.307	.336	87	-28	-22	141	72	26	6	.988	-38	O	-7.9

YEAR	TM/L	G	AB	R	H	2B	3B	HR	RBI	BB	SO	AVG	OBP	SLG	PRO+	BR	/A	RC	SB	CS	SBR	FA	FR	POS	TPR

■ **STEVE STROUGHTER** Stroughter, Stephen Lewis b: 3/15/52, Visalia, Cal. BL/TR, 6'2", 190 lbs. Deb: 4/07/82

| 1982 | Sea-A | 26 | 47 | 4 | 8 | 1 | 0 | 1 | 3 | 3 | 9 | .170 | .235 | .255 | 34 | -4 | -4 | 3 | 0 | 0 | 0 | 1.000 | 1 | /OD | -0.4 |

■ **AMOS STRUNK** Strunk, Amos Aaron b: 1/22/1889, Philadelphia, Pa. d: 7/22/79, Llanerch, Pa. BL/TL, 5'11.5", 175 lbs. Deb: 9/24/08

1908	Phi-A	12	34	4	8	1	0	0	0	0	4	.235	.316	.265	83	-0	-1	3	0			.903	1	O	0.0
1909	Phi-A	11	35	1	4	0	0	0	2	1	1	.114	.139	.114	-20	-5	-5	1	2			1.000	-1	O	-0.7
1910	*Phi-A	16	48	9	16	0	1	0	2	3		.333	.373	.375	135	2	2	8	4			1.000	1	O	0.2
1911	*Phi-A	74	215	42	55	7	2	1	21	21	35	.256	.363	.321	93	-1	-1	31	13			.958	1	O/1	-0.2
1912	Phi-A	122	412	58	119	13	12	3	63	47		.289	.366	.400	124	10	13	72	29			.990	11	*O	1.8
1913	Phi-A	94	292	30	89	11	12	0	46	29	23	.305	.368	.425	135	11	12	49	14			.962	-2	O	0.7
1914	*Phi-A	122	404	58	111	15	3	2	45	57	38	.275	.364	.342	117	8	10	53	25	22	-6	.987	9	*O	0.8
1915	Phi-A	132	485	76	144	28	16	1	45	56	45	.297	.371	.427	144	22	24	78	17	19	-6	.980	12	*O1	2.5
1916	Phi-A	150	544	71	172	30	9	3	49	66	59	.316	.393	.421	152	30	33	91	21	23	-8	.978	2	*O/1	2.2
1917	Phi-A	148	540	83	152	26	7	1	45	68	37	.281	.363	.361	123	15	16	76	16			.986	-2	*O	0.6
1918	*Bos-A	114	413	50	106	18	9	0	35	36	13	.257	.316	.344	101	-1	-1	50	20			.988	-5	*O	-1.3
1919	Bos-A	48	184	27	50	11	3	0	17	13	13	.272	.323	.364	98	-2	-1	22	3			.968	-1	O	-0.6
	Phi-A	60	194	15	41	6	4	0	13	23	15	.211	.298	.284	63	-9	-9	17	3			.981	1	O	-1.3
	Yr	108	378	42	91	17	7	0	30	36	28	.241	.310	.323	79	-11	-10	39	6			.974	-1	*O	-1.9
1920	Phi-A	58	202	23	60	9	3	0	20	21	9	.297	.363	.371	94	-1	-1	26	0	6	-4	.990	-4	*O	-1.3
	Chi-A	53	188	33	45	8	1	1	16	28	15	.239	.338	.399	72	-7	-7	21	1	0	0	.981	-1	O	-1.0
	Yr	111	390	56	105	17	4	1	36	49	24	.269	.351	.341	83	-8	-8	48	1	6	-3	.985	-5	*O	-2.3
1921	Chi-A	121	401	68	133	19	10	3	69	38	27	.332	.391	.451	116	9	10	69	7	10	-4	.970	-8	*O	-0.9
1922	Chi-A	92	311	36	90	11	4	0	33	33	28	.289	.358	.350	85	-6	-6	40	9	6	-1	.989	2	O/1	-1.0
1923	Chi-A	54	54	7	17	0	0	0	8	8	5	.315	.403	.315	92	-0	-0	8	1	0	0	1.000	-0	/O1	0.0
1924	Chi-A	1	1	0	0	0	0	0	0	0	0	.000	.000	.000	-99	-0	-0	0	0	0	0	.000	0	/H	0.0
	Phi-A	30	42	5	6	0	0	0	1	7	4	.143	.265	.143	7	-6	-6	2	0	0	0	1.000	-3	/O	-0.8
	Yr	31	43	5	6	0	0	0	1	7	4	.140	.260	.140	5	-6	-6	2	0	0	0	1.000	-3	/O	-0.8
Total	17	1512	4999	696	1418	213	96	15	530	573	331	.284	.359	.374	112	68	82	720	185	86		.980	13	*O/1	-0.3

■ **AL STRUVE** Struve, Al b: St.Louis, Mo. Deb: 6/22/1884

| 1884 | StL-a | 2 | 7 | 2 | 2 | 0 | 0 | 0 | | | | .286 | .286 | .286 | 87 | -0 | -0 | 1 | | | | .000 | 1 | /OC | 0.1 |

■ **LUKE STUART** Stuart, Luther Lane b: 5/23/1892, Alamance Co., N.C. d: 6/15/47, Winston-Salem, N.C. BR/TR, 5'8", 165 lbs. Deb: 7/28/21

| 1921 | StL-A | 3 | 3 | 2 | 1 | 0 | 0 | 1 | 2 | 0 | 1 | .333 | .333 | 1.333 | 291 | 1 | 1 | 1 | 0 | 0 | 0 | 1.000 | -1 | /2 | 0.0 |

■ **DICK STUART** Stuart, Richard Lee "Dr. Strangeglove" b: 11/7/32, San Francisco, Cal. BR/TR, 6'4", 212 lbs. Deb: 7/10/58

1958	Pit-N	67	254	38	68	12	5	16	48	11	75	.268	.311	.543	124	6	7	41	0	0	0	.973	0	1	0.3
1959	Pit-N	118	397	64	118	15	2	27	78	42	86	.297	.367	.549	141	22	22	78	1	1	-0	.976	1	*1/O	1.6
1960	*Pit-N	122	438	48	114	17	5	23	83	39	107	.260	.321	.479	115	8	8	63	0	0	0	.986	-1	*1	-0.3
1961	Pit-N★	138	532	83	160	28	8	35	117	34	121	.301	.347	.581	140	28	28	97	0	3	-2	.983	-1	*1/O	1.4
1962	Pit-N	114	394	52	90	11	4	16	64	32	94	.228	.290	.398	83	-11	-11	44	0	1	-1	.982	2	*1	-1.7
1963	Bos-A	157	612	81	160	25	4	42	118	44	144	.261	.312	.521	125	20	18	91	0	0	0	.979	8	*1	2.0
1964	Bos-A	156	603	73	168	27	1	33	114	37	130	.279	.323	.491	117	16	13	93	0	0	0	.981	1	*1	0.7
1965	Phi-N	149	538	53	126	19	1	28	95	39	136	.234	.290	.429	101	-2	-1	66	1	0	0	.986	3	*1/3	-0.5
1966	NY-N	31	87	7	19	0	0	4	13	9	26	.218	.292	.356	81	-2	-2	8	0	1	-1	.974	-1	1	-0.6
	*LA-N	38	91	4	24	1	0	3	9	11	17	.264	.356	.374	112	1	2	12	0	1	-1	.991	3	1	0.3
	Yr	69	178	11	43	1	0	7	22	20	43	.242	.325	.365	97	-2	-1	19	0	2	-1	.982	2	1	-0.3
1969	Cal-A	22	51	3	8	2	0	1	4	3	21	.157	.204	.255	29	-5	-5	2	0	0	0	.991	-1	1	-0.8
Total	10	1112	3997	506	1055	157	30	228	743	301	957	.264	.319	.489	117	81	79	595	2	7	-4	.982	13	*1/O3	2.4

■ **BILL STUART** Stuart, William Alexander "Chauncey" b: 8/28/1873, Boalsburg, Pa. d: 10/14/28, Fort Worth, Tex. 5'11", 170 lbs. Deb: 8/15/1895

1895	Pit-N	19	77	5	19	3	0	0	10	2	6	.247	.275	.286	49	-6	-5	7	2			.913	-1	S/2	-0.5
1899	NY-N	1	3	0	0	0	0	0	0	0		.000	.000	.000	-99	-1	-1	0	0			1.000	-0	/2	-0.1
Total	2	20	80	5	19	3	0	0	10	2	6	.237	.265	.275	43	-7	-6	7	2			.909	-1	/S2	-0.6

■ **FRANKLIN STUBBS** Stubbs, Franklin Lee b: 10/21/60, Richland, N.C. BL/TL, 6'2", 215 lbs. Deb: 4/28/84

1984	LA-N	87	217	22	42	2	3	8	17	24	63	.194	.274	.341	73	-9	-8	22	2	2	-1	.993	-1	1O	-1.3
1985	LA-N	10	9	0	2	0	0	0	2	0	3	.222	.222	.222	25	-1	-1	0	0	0	0	1.000	-0	/1	-0.1
1986	LA-N	132	420	55	95	11	1	23	58	37	107	.226	.292	.421	101	-5	-1	51	7	1	2	.969	-4	*O1	-0.8
1987	LA-N	129	386	48	90	16	3	16	52	31	85	.233	.292	.415	87	-10	-9	47	8	1	2	.994	7	*1O	-0.7
1988	*LA-N	115	242	30	54	13	0	8	34	23	61	.223	.293	.376	94	-3	-2	28	11	3	2	.978	2	1O	-0.4
1989	LA-N	69	103	11	30	6	0	4	15	16	27	.291	.387	.466	145	6	6	18	3	2	-0	.948	1	O/1	0.7
1990	Hou-N	146	448	59	117	23	2	23	71	48	114	.261	.335	.475	124	11	13	74	19	6	2	.991	-9	1O	0.0
1991	Mil-A	103	362	48	77	16	2	11	38	35	71	.213	.286	.359	79	-12	-11	39	13	4	2	.991	5	1/OD	-1.0
1992	Mil-A	92	288	37	66	11	1	9	42	27	68	.229	.297	.368	87	-6	-5	32	11	8	-2	.987	6	1D/O	-0.6
Total	9	883	2475	310	573	98	12	102	329	241	599	.232	.302	.404	97	-28	-18	310	74	27	6	.990	7	1O/D	-4.2

■ **MOOSE STUBING** Stubing, Lawrence George b: 3/31/38, Bronx, N.Y. BL/TL, 6'3", 220 lbs. Deb: 4/14/67 MC

| 1967 | Cal-A | 5 | 5 | 0 | 0 | 0 | 0 | 0 | 0 | 0 | 4 | .000 | .000 | .000 | -99 | -1 | -1 | 0 | 0 | 0 | 0 | .000 | 0 | H | -0.1 |

■ **SEEM STUDLEY** Studley, Seymour L. "Warhorse" b: Washington, D.C. d: 1874, Washington, D.C. Deb: 4/20/1872

| 1872 | Nat-n | 5 | 21 | 3 | 2 | 0 | 0 | 0 | 2 | 0 | 0 | .095 | .095 | .095 | -35 | -3 | -4 | 0 | | | | | | /O | -0.3 |

■ **GEORGE STUMPF** Stumpf, George Frederick b: 12/15/10, New Orleans, La. BL/TL, 5'8", 155 lbs. Deb: 9/19/31

1931	Bos-A	7	28	2	7	1	1	0	4	1	2	.250	.276	.357	69	-2	-1	3	0	0	0	1.000	-1	/O	-0.3
1932	Bos-A	79	169	18	34	2	2	1	18	18	21	.201	.278	.254	40	-15	-15	13	1	1	-0	.952	-7	O	-2.3
1933	Bos-A	22	41	8	14	3	0	0	5	4	2	.341	.400	.415	117	1	1	8	4	0	1	1.000	-3	O	-0.1
1936	Chi-A	10	22	3	6	1	0	0	5	2	1	.273	.333	.318	59	-1	-1	2	0	0	0	1.000	0	/O	-0.1
Total	4	118	260	31	61	7	3	1	32	25	26	.235	.302	.296	57	-17	-16	26	5	1	1	.969	-11	/O	-2.8

■ **BILL STUMPF** Stumpf, William Frederick b: 3/21/1892, Baltimore, Md. d: 2/14/66, Crownsville, Md. BR/TR, 6'0.5", 175 lbs. Deb: 5/11/12

1912	NY-A	42	129	8	31	0	0	0	10	6		.240	.279	.240	46	-8	-8	9	5			.892	-14	S/2310	-2.2
1913	NY-A	12	29	5	6	1	0	0	1	3	3	.207	.281	.241	53	-2	-2	2	0			.818	-3	/S2O	-0.5
Total	2	54	158	13	37	1	0	0	11	9	3	.234	.280	.241	47	-10	-11	12	5			.877	-18	/S2301	-2.7

■ **GUY STURDY** Sturdy, Guy R. b: 8/7/1899, Sherman, Tex. d: 5/4/65, Marshall, Tex. BL/TL, 6'0.5", 180 lbs. Deb: 9/30/27

1927	StL-A	5	21	5	9	1	0	0	5	1	4	.429	.455	.476	137	1	1	4	2	0	1	.974	-1	/1	0.1
1928	StL-A	54	45	3	10	1	0	1	8	8	4	.222	.340	.311	70	-2	-2	5	1	0	0	1.000	-0	/1	-0.2
Total	2	59	66	8	19	2	0	1	13	9	4	.288	.373	.364	91	-0	-1	10	3	0	1	.975	-1	/1	-0.1

■ **BOBBY STURGEON** Sturgeon, Robert Howard b: 8/6/19, Clinton, Ind. BR/TR, 6', 175 lbs. Deb: 4/16/40

1940	Chi-N	7	21	1	4	1	0	0	2	0	1	.190	.190	.238	18	-2	-2	1	0			.848	2	/S	0.0
1941	Chi-N	129	433	45	106	15	3	0	25	9	30	.245	.260	.293	58	-26	-24	31	5			.956	-4	*S/23	-2.0
1942	Chi-N	63	162	8	40	7	1	0	7	4	13	.247	.269	.302	70	-7	-6	13	2			.988	21	2S/3	1.8
1946	Chi-N	100	294	26	87	12	2	1	21	10	18	.296	.319	.361	94	-4	-3	33	0			.934	-13	S2	-1.3

YEAR	TM/L	G	AB	R	H	2B	3B	HR	RBI	BB	SO	AVG	OBP	SLG	PRO+	BR	/A	RC	SB	CS	SBR	FA	FR	POS	TPR
1947	Chi-N	87	232	16	59	10	5	0	21	7	12	.254	.276	.341	66	-13	-12	19	0			.975	13	S2/3	0.5
1948	Bos-N	34	78	10	17	3	1	0	4	4	5	.218	.256	.282	46	-6	-6	5	0			.938	-3	2/S3	-0.8
Total	6	420	1220	106	313	48	12	1	80	34	79	.257	.277	.318	68	-58	-54	103	7			.951	14	S2/3	-1.8

■ DEAN STURGIS Sturgis, Dean Donnell b: 12/1/1892, Beloit, Kan. d: 6/4/50, Uniontown, Pa. BR/TR, 6'1", 180 lbs. Deb: 5/01/14

YEAR	TM/L	G	AB	R	H	2B	3B	HR	RBI	BB	SO	AVG	OBP	SLG	PRO+	BR	/A	RC	SB	CS	SBR	FA	FR	POS	TPR
1914	Phi-A	4	4	1	1	0	0	0	0	1	2	.250	.400	.250	100	0	0	0	0			1.000	0	/C	0.0

■ JOHNNY STURM Sturm, John Peter Joseph b: 1/23/16, St.Louis, Mo. BL/TL, 6'1", 185 lbs. Deb: 4/15/41

YEAR	TM/L	G	AB	R	H	2B	3B	HR	RBI	BB	SO	AVG	OBP	SLG	PRO+	BR	/A	RC	SB	CS	SBR	FA	FR	POS	TPR
1941	*NY-A	124	524	58	125	17	3	3	36	37	50	.239	.293	.300	58	-33	-32	46	3	5	-2	.990	-2	*1	-4.5

■ GEORGE STUTZ Stutz, George "Kid" or "Satan" b: 2/12/1893, Philadelphia, Pa. d: 12/29/30, Philadelphia, Pa. BL/TR, 5'5", 150 lbs. Deb: 8/17/26

YEAR	TM/L	G	AB	R	H	2B	3B	HR	RBI	BB	SO	AVG	OBP	SLG	PRO+	BR	/A	RC	SB	CS	SBR	FA	FR	POS	TPR
1926	Phi-N	6	9	0	0	0	0	0	0	0	2	.000	.000	.000	-95	-2	-3	0	0			.938	1	/S	-0.1

■ LENA STYLES Styles, William Graves b: 11/27/1899, Gurley, Ala. d: 3/14/56, Gurley, Ala. BR/TR, 6'1", 185 lbs. Deb: 9/10/19

YEAR	TM/L	G	AB	R	H	2B	3B	HR	RBI	BB	SO	AVG	OBP	SLG	PRO+	BR	/A	RC	SB	CS	SBR	FA	FR	POS	TPR
1919	Phi-A	8	22	0	6	1	0	0	5	1	6	.273	.304	.318	74	-1	-1	2	0			.974	0	/C	0.0
1920	Phi-A	24	50	5	13	3	1	0	5	6	7	.260	.339	.360	84	-1	-1	7	1	0	0	.966	2	/C1	0.1
1921	Phi-A	4	5	0	1	0	0	0	0	0	2	.200	.200	.200	2	-1	-1	0	0	0	0	.333	-1	/C	-0.2
1930	Cin-N	7	12	2	3	0	1	0	1	1	2	.250	.357	.417	91	-0	-0	2	0			.875	0	/C1	0.0
1931	Cin-N	34	87	7	21	3	0	0	5	8	7	.241	.313	.276	63	-5	-4	8	0			.949	-7	C	-0.9
Total	5	77	176	14	44	7	2	0	16	16	24	.250	.320	.313	71	-7	-7	19	1	0		.929	-6	/C1	-1.0

■ NEIL STYNES Stynes, Cornelius William b: 12/10/1868, Arlington, Mass. d: 3/26/44, Somerville, Mass. BR/TR, 6', 165 lbs. Deb: 9/08/1890

YEAR	TM/L	G	AB	R	H	2B	3B	HR	RBI	BB	SO	AVG	OBP	SLG	PRO+	BR	/A	RC	SB	CS	SBR	FA	FR	POS	TPR
1890	Cle-P	2	8	0	0	0	0	0	0	0	0	.000	.000	.000	-99	-2	-2	0	0			.846	-0	/C	-0.2

■ KEN SUAREZ Suarez, Kenneth Raymond b: 4/12/43, Tampa, Fla. BR/TR, 5'9", 175 lbs. Deb: 4/14/66

YEAR	TM/L	G	AB	R	H	2B	3B	HR	RBI	BB	SO	AVG	OBP	SLG	PRO+	BR	/A	RC	SB	CS	SBR	FA	FR	POS	TPR
1966	KC-A	35	69	5	10	0	1	0	2	15	26	.145	.298	.174	41	-5	-5	5	2	0	1	.954	5	C	0.3
1967	KC-A	39	63	7	15	5	0	2	9	16	21	.238	.392	.413	143	4	4	12	1	0	0	.979	7	C	1.3
1968	Cle-A	17	10	1	1	0	0	0	0	1	3	.100	.182	.100	-13	-1	-1	0	0	0	0	1.000	1	C/23O	0.0
1969	Cle-A	36	85	7	25	5	0	1	9	15	12	.294	.400	.388	117	3	3	13	1	0	0	.991	6	C	1.0
1971	Cle-A	50	123	10	25	7	0	1	9	18	15	.203	.315	.285	65	-4	-6	12	0	1	-1	.993	9	C	0.4
1972	Tex-A	25	33	2	5	1	0	0	4	1	4	.152	.176	.182	7	-4	-4	1	0	0	0	.965	1	C	-0.3
1973	Tex-A	93	278	25	69	11	0	1	27	33	16	.248	.339	.299	84	-6	-4	29	1	2	-1	.989	3	C	0.1
Total	7	295	661	57	150	29	1	5	60	99	97	.227	.334	.297	81	-13	-13	71	5	3	-0	.984	31	C/O32	2.8

■ LUIS SUAREZ Suarez, Luis Abelardo b: 8/24/16, Alto Songo, Cuba d: 6/5/91, Havana, Cuba BR/TR, 5'11", 170 lbs. Deb: 5/28/44

YEAR	TM/L	G	AB	R	H	2B	3B	HR	RBI	BB	SO	AVG	OBP	SLG	PRO+	BR	/A	RC	SB	CS	SBR	FA	FR	POS	TPR
1944	Was-A	1	2	0	0	0	0	0	0	0	0	.000	.000	.000	-99	-1	-1	0	0	0	0	1.000	0	/3	0.0

■ TONY SUCK Suck, Anthony (b: Charles Anthony Zuck) b: 6/11/1858, Chicago.Ill. d: 1/29/1895, Chicago, Ill. 5'9", 164 lbs. Deb: 8/09/1883

YEAR	TM/L	G	AB	R	H	2B	3B	HR	RBI	BB	SO	AVG	OBP	SLG	PRO+	BR	/A	RC	SB	CS	SBR	FA	FR	POS	TPR
1883	Buf-N	2	7	1	0	0	0	0	0	1	4	.000	.125	.000	-56	-1	-1	0				.000	-2	/OC	-0.3
1884	CP-U	53	188	18	28	2	0	0		13		.149	.204	.160	25	-14	-14	6				.904	-3	CSO/3	-1.3
	Bal-U	3	10	2	3	0	0	0		0		.300	.300	.300	94	0	-0	1				.882	2	/C	0.1
	Yr	56	198	20	31	2	0	0		13		.157	.209	.167	28	-14	-14	7				.901	-2	CSO/3	-1.2
Total	2	58	205	21	31	2	0	0	0	14	4	.151	.205	.161	25	-15	-15	7				.894	-4	/CSO3	-1.5

■ BILL SUDAKIS Sudakis, William Paul "Suds" b: 3/27/46, Joliet, Ill. BB/TR, 6'1", 190 lbs. Deb: 9/03/68

YEAR	TM/L	G	AB	R	H	2B	3B	HR	RBI	BB	SO	AVG	OBP	SLG	PRO+	BR	/A	RC	SB	CS	SBR	FA	FR	POS	TPR
1968	LA-N	24	87	11	24	4	2	3	12	15	14	.276	.382	.471	168	6	7	15	1	0	0	.953	4	3	1.3
1969	LA-N	132	462	50	108	17	5	14	53	40	94	.234	.296	.383	96	-8	-4	52	3	2	-0	.946	11	*3	0.8
1970	LA-N	94	269	37	71	11	0	14	44	35	46	.264	.355	.461	122	6	8	45	4	0	1	.983	-5	C3/O1	0.5
1971	LA-N	41	83	10	16	3	0	3	7	12	22	.193	.302	.337	86	-2	-1	8	0	1	-1	1.000	1	C/31O	-0.1
1972	NY-N	18	49	3	7	0	0	1	7	6	14	.143	.236	.204	27	-5	-5	3	0	0	0	.967	1	/1C	-0.5
1973	Tex-A	82	235	32	60	11	0	15	43	23	53	.255	.322	.494	132	7	8	36	0	1	-1	.962	-4	31/COD	0.2
1974	NY-A	89	259	26	60	8	0	7	39	25	48	.232	.302	.344	88	-5	-4	29	0	0	0	.990	2	D1/3C	-0.5
1975	Cal-A	30	58	4	7	2	0	1	6	12	15	.121	.282	.207	43	-4	-4	4	1	1	-0	.941	-1	D/C1	-0.5
	Cle-A	20	46	4	9	0	0	1	3	4	7	.196	.260	.261	48	-3	-3	3	0	1	-1	1.000	-1	1/C	-0.5
	Yr	50	104	8	16	2	0	2	9	16	22	.154	.273	.231	45	-8	-7	7	1	2	-1	1.000	-2	1DC	-1.0
Total	8	530	1548	177	362	56	7	59	214	172	313	.234	.313	.393	103	-8	2	194	9	6	-1	.942	7	3/C1DO	0.7

■ PETE SUDER Suder, Peter "Pecky" b: 4/16/16, Aliquippa, Pa. BR/TR, 6', 175 lbs. Deb: 4/15/41

YEAR	TM/L	G	AB	R	H	2B	3B	HR	RBI	BB	SO	AVG	OBP	SLG	PRO+	BR	/A	RC	SB	CS	SBR	FA	FR	POS	TPR
1941	Phi-A	139	531	45	130	20	9	4	52	19	47	.245	.271	.339	62	-32	-30	43	1	3	-2	.957	-7	*3/S	-3.5
1942	Phi-A	128	476	46	122	20	4	4	54	24	39	.256	.293	.340	78	-15	-15	43	4	4	-1	.954	3	S32	-0.8
1943	Phi-A	131	475	30	105	14	5	3	41	14	40	.221	.243	.291	56	-28	-28	31	1	1	-0	.971	-8	23/S	-3.3
1946	Phi-A	128	455	38	128	20	3	2	50	18	37	.281	.309	.352	85	-11	-10	48	1	1	-0	.959	1	S32/1O	-0.5
1947	Phi-A	145	528	45	127	28	4	5	60	35	44	.241	.290	.337	73	-20	-21	51	0	3	-2	**.986**	-17	*2/S3	-3.1
1948	Phi-A	148	519	64	125	23	5	7	60	60	60	.241	.321	.345	77	-18	-18	60	1	3	-2	.988	-1	*2	-1.2
1949	Phi-A	118	445	44	119	24	6	10	75	23	35	.267	.306	.416	93	-10	-8	52	0	1	-1	.975	7	23/S	0.2
1950	Phi-A	77	248	34	61	10	0	8	35	23	31	.246	.310	.383	78	-10	-9	29	2	2	-1	.979	1	23S/1	-0.7
1951	Phi-A	123	440	46	108	18	1	1	42	30	42	.245	.295	.298	59	-24	-26	37	5	5	-2	**.987**	10	*2S/3	-1.1
1952	Phi-A	74	228	22	55	7	2	1	20	16	17	.241	.291	.303	61	-11	-13	21	1	1	-0	.991	3	2S3	-0.8
1953	Phi-A	115	454	44	130	11	3	4	35	17	35	.286	.312	.350	76	-14	-16	48	3	3	-1	.974	4	32/S	-1.2
1954	Phi-A	69	205	8	41	11	1	0	16	7	16	.200	.226	.263	34	-19	-19	11	0	0	0	.961	9	23/S	-1.0
1955	KC-A	26	81	3	17	4	1	0	1	2	13	.210	.229	.284	37	-7	-7	5	0	1	-1	.990	-3	2	-1.0
Total	13	1421	5085	469	1268	210	44	49	541	288	456	.249	.291	.337	71	-219	-221	478	19	28	-11	.982	2	23S/1O	-18.0

■ WILLIAM SUERO Suero, Williams Urban b: 11/7/65, Santo Domingo, D.R. BR/TR, 5'9", 175 lbs. Deb: 4/09/92

YEAR	TM/L	G	AB	R	H	2B	3B	HR	RBI	BB	SO	AVG	OBP	SLG	PRO+	BR	/A	RC	SB	CS	SBR	FA	FR	POS	TPR
1992	Mil-A	18	16	4	3	1	0	0	0	2	1	.188	.316	.250	62	-1	-1	1	1	1	-0	.971	4	2/SD	0.3

■ JOE SUGDEN Sugden, Joseph b: 7/31/1870, Philadelphia, Pa. d: 6/28/59, Philadelphia, Pa. BB/TR, 5'10", 180 lbs. Deb: 7/20/1893 C

YEAR	TM/L	G	AB	R	H	2B	3B	HR	RBI	BB	SO	AVG	OBP	SLG	PRO+	BR	/A	RC	SB	CS	SBR	FA	FR	POS	TPR
1893	Pit-N	27	92	20	24	4	3	0	12	10	11	.261	.340	.370	92	-1	-1	12	1			.956	-0	C	0.1
1894	Pit-N	39	139	23	46	13	2	2	23	14	2	.331	.404	.496	119	4	4	30	3			.910	-5	C/3SO	0.2
1895	Pit-N	49	155	28	48	4	1	1	17	16	12	.310	.385	.368	102	0	2	25	4			.903	3	C	0.8
1896	Pit-N	80	301	42	89	5	7	0	36	19	9	.296	.348	.359	92	-5	-3	42	5			.952	2	C/1O	0.6
1897	Pit-N	84	288	31	64	6	4	0	38	18		.222	.275	.271	46	-23	-22	26	9			.941	-4	C/1	-1.4
1898	StL-N	89	289	29	73	7	1	0	34	23		.253	.314	.284	70	-10	-11	29	5			.937	-0	CO/1	-0.6
1899	Cle-N	76	250	19	69	5	1	0	14	11		.276	.307	.304	73	-11	-8	25	2			.935	1	C/O13	-0.2
1901	Chi-A	48	153	21	42	7	1	0	19	13		.275	.339	.333	89	-2	-2	20	4			.970	4	C/1	0.6
1902	StL-A	68	200	25	50	7	2	0	15	20		.250	.327	.305	77	-6	-5	22	2			.956	-2	C/1P	-0.1
1903	StL-A	79	241	18	51	4	0	0	22	25		.212	.288	.228	58	-12	-11	19	4			.983	6	C/1	0.2
1904	StL-A	105	348	25	93	6	3	0	30	28		.267	.331	.302	107	1	4	39	6			**.989**	-1	C1	1.3
1905	StL-A	90	266	21	46	4	0	0	23	23		.173	.247	.188	41	-18	-16	15	3			.983	21	C/1	1.3
1912	Det-A	1	4	1	1	0	0	0	0	0		.250	.250	.250	44	-0	-0	0	0			.941	1	/1	0.0
Total	13	835	2726	303	696	72	25	3	283	220	34	.255	.318	.303	78	-83	-70	305	48			.957	27	C/1O3SP	2.8

■ GUS SUHR Suhr, August Richard b: 1/3/06, San Francisco, Cal. BL/TR, 6', 180 lbs. Deb: 4/15/30

YEAR	TM/L	G	AB	R	H	2B	3B	HR	RBI	BB	SO	AVG	OBP	SLG	PRO+	BR	/A	RC	SB	CS	SBR	FA	FR	POS	TPR
1930	Pit-N	151	542	93	155	26	14	17	107	80	56	.286	.380	.480	106	6	5	99	11			.992	-7	*1	-1.5
1931	Pit-N	87	270	26	57	13	4	4	32	38	25	.211	.308	.333	73	-10	-10	30	4			.993	0	1	-1.6
1932	Pit-N	154	581	78	153	31	16	5	81	63	39	.263	.337	.398	99	-2	-1	82	7			.988	-10	*1	-2.3

YEAR	TM/L	G	AB	R	H	2B	3B	HR	RBI	BB	SO	AVG	OBP	SLG	PRO+	BR	/A	RC	SB	CS	SBR	FA	FR	POS	TPR
1933	Pit-N	154	566	72	151	31	11	10	75	72	52	.267	.350	.413	117	14	14	87	2			.991	-4	*1	-0.5
1934	Pit-N	151	573	67	162	36	13	13	103	66	52	.283	.360	.459	115	14	13	98	4			.994	-5	*1	-0.6
1935	Pit-N	153	529	68	144	33	12	10	81	70	54	.272	.357	.437	109	10	7	89	6			.989	-7	*1/O	-1.4
1936	Pit-N☆	156	583	111	182	33	12	11	118	95	34	.312	.410	.467	133	33	31	119	8			**.993**	-4	*1	1.1
1937	Pit-N	151	575	69	160	28	14	5	97	83	42	.278	.369	.402	109	9	9	92	2			.993	-4	*1	-1.2
1938	Pit-N	145	530	82	156	35	14	3	64	87	37	.294	.394	.430	126	22	22	97	4			.993	-8	*1	-0.4
1939	Pit-N	63	204	23	59	10	2	1	31	25	23	.289	.367	.373	101	0	1	31	4			.993	-4	1	-0.9
	Phi-N	60	198	21	63	12	2	3	24	34	14	.318	.421	.444	137	11	11	40	1			.995	1	1	0.6
	Yr	123	402	44	122	22	4	4	55	59	37	.303	.394	.408	118	11	12	71	5			.994	-4	*1	-0.3
1940	Phi-N	10	25	4	4	0	0	2	5	5	5	.160	.300	.400	95	-0	-0	3	0			.967	-2	/1	-0.2
Total	11	1435	5176	714	1446	288	114	84	818	718	433	.279	.368	.428	112	106	102	867	53			.992	-53	*1/O	-8.9

■ CLYDE SUKEFORTH Sukeforth, Clyde Leroy "Sukey" b: 11/30/01, Washington, Me. BL/TR, 5'10", 155 lbs. Deb: 5/23/26 MC

YEAR	TM/L	G	AB	R	H	2B	3B	HR	RBI	BB	SO	AVG	OBP	SLG	PRO+	BR	/A	RC	SB	CS	SBR	FA	FR	POS	TPR
1926	Cin-N	1	1	0	0	0	0	0	0	0	1	.000	.000	.000	-99	-0	-0	0	0			.000	0	H	0.0
1927	Cin-N	38	58	12	11	2	0	0	2	7	2	.190	.277	.224	37	-5	-5	4	2			.970	1	C	-0.3
1928	Cin-N	33	53	5	7	2	1	0	3	3	5	.132	.179	.208	1	-8	-8	2	0			.966	1	C	-0.6
1929	Cin-N	84	237	31	84	16	2	1	33	17	6	.354	.398	.451	115	4	6	41	8			.981	-8	C	0.4
1930	Cin-N	94	296	30	84	9	3	1	19	17	12	.284	.325	.345	65	-18	-16	33	1			.976	-3	C	-1.0
1931	Cin-N	112	351	22	90	15	4	0	25	38	13	.256	.334	.322	82	-10	-7	40	0			.965	-8	*C	-0.8
1932	Bro-N	59	111	14	26	4	4	0	12	6	10	.234	.280	.342	68	-5	-5	11	1			.991	-3	C	-0.7
1933	Bro-N	20	36	1	2	0	0	0	0	2	1	.056	.105	.056	-55	-7	-7	0	0			.983	3	C	-0.4
1934	Bro-N	27	43	5	7	1	0	0	1	1	6	.163	.182	.186	-1	-6	-6	1	0			1.000	-1	C	-0.6
1945	Bro-N	18	51	2	15	1	0	0	1	4	1	.294	.345	.314	85	-1	-1	6	0			.947	-3	C	-0.3
Total	10	486	1237	122	326	50	14	2	96	95	57	.264	.319	.331	71	-57	-49	138	12			.974	-20	C	-4.3

■ GUY SULARZ Sularz, Guy Patrick b: 11/7/55, Minneapolis, Minn. BR/TR, 5'11", 165 lbs. Deb: 9/02/80

YEAR	TM/L	G	AB	R	H	2B	3B	HR	RBI	BB	SO	AVG	OBP	SLG	PRO+	BR	/A	RC	SB	CS	SBR	FA	FR	POS	TPR
1980	SF-N	25	65	3	16	1	1	0	3	9	6	.246	.338	.292	79	-2	-1	7	1	0	0	.975	12	2/3	1.2
1981	SF-N	10	20	0	4	0	0	0	2	2	4	.200	.304	.200	46	-1	-1	1	0	1	-1	1.000	4	/23	0.3
1982	SF-N	63	101	15	23	3	0	1	7	9	11	.228	.291	.287	62	-5	-5	9	3	0	1	.961	10	S3/2	0.9
1983	SF-N	10	20	3	2	0	0	0	0	3	2	.100	.217	.100	-10	-3	-3	0	0	0	0	.917	3	/S3	0.0
Total	4	108	206	21	45	4	1	1	12	23	23	.218	.300	.262	59	-11	-11	18	4	1	1	.954	29	/S23	2.4

■ ERNIE SULIK Sulik, Ernest Richard "Dave" b: 7/7/10, San Francisco, Cal. d: 5/31/63, Oakland, Cal. BL/TL, 5'10", 178 lbs. Deb: 4/15/36

YEAR	TM/L	G	AB	R	H	2B	3B	HR	RBI	BB	SO	AVG	OBP	SLG	PRO+	BR	/A	RC	SB	CS	SBR	FA	FR	POS	TPR
1936	Phi-N	122	404	69	116	14	4	6	36	40	22	.287	.353	.386	90	-0	-6	57	4			.971	-6	*O	-1.5

■ SULLIVAN Sullivan b: Bristol, R.I. Deb: 5/14/1875

YEAR	TM/L	G	AB	R	H	2B	3B	HR	RBI	BB	SO	AVG	OBP	SLG	PRO+	BR	/A	RC	SB	CS	SBR	FA	FR	POS	TPR
1875	NH-n	2	8	3	3	0	0	0		0		.375	.375	.375	184	0	1	1						/O	0.1

■ ANDY SULLIVAN Sullivan, Andrew R. b: 8/30/1884, Southborough, Mass d: 2/14/20, Framingham, Mass. TR , Deb: 9/13/04

YEAR	TM/L	G	AB	R	H	2B	3B	HR	RBI	BB	SO	AVG	OBP	SLG	PRO+	BR	/A	RC	SB	CS	SBR	FA	FR	POS	TPR
1904	Bos-N	1	1	0	0	0	0	0	0	1		.000	.500	.000	62	0	0	0	0			1.000	-0	/S	0.0

■ JACKIE SULLIVAN Sullivan, Carl Mancel b: 2/22/18, Princeton, Tex. BR/TR, 5'11", 172 lbs. Deb: 7/06/44

YEAR	TM/L	G	AB	R	H	2B	3B	HR	RBI	BB	SO	AVG	OBP	SLG	PRO+	BR	/A	RC	SB	CS	SBR	FA	FR	POS	TPR
1944	Det-A	1	1	0	0	0	0	0	0	0	0	.000	.000	.000	-95	-0	-0	0	0	0	0	1.000	-0	/2	0.0

■ DAN SULLIVAN Sullivan, Daniel C. "Link" b: 5/9/1857, Providence, R.I. d: 10/26/1893, Providence, R.I. TR , 5'11", 194 lbs. Deb: 5/02/1882

YEAR	TM/L	G	AB	R	H	2B	3B	HR	RBI	BB	SO	AVG	OBP	SLG	PRO+	BR	/A	RC	SB	CS	SBR	FA	FR	POS	TPR
1882	Lou-a	67	286	44	78	8	2	0		9		.273	.295	.315	112	2	4	27				.878	7	*C3/OS	1.2
1883	Lou-a	37	147	8	31	5	2	0		3		.211	.227	.272	65	-6	-5	9				.897	-7	C/O3S	-0.9
1884	Lou-a	63	247	27	59	8	6	0		9		.239	.268	.320	98	-2	-0	22				.930	-15	C/O	-0.8
1885	Lou-a	13	44	3	8	1	0	0		2		.182	.234	.205	42	-3	-3	2				.948	-3	C	-0.4
	StL-a	17	60	4	7	2	0	0		6		.117	.197	.150	12	-6	-6	2				.956	1	C/1	-0.4
	Yr	30	104	7	15	3	0	0		8		.144	.212	.173	24	-8	-9	4				.952	-2	C/1	-0.8
1886	Pit-a	1	4	0	0	0	0	0		0		.000	.000	.000	-99	-1	-1	0	0			.600	-1	/C	-0.2
Total	5	198	788	86	183	24	10	0		29		.232	.261	.288	85	-16	-11	62	0			.908	-18	C/301S	-1.5

■ DENNY SULLIVAN Sullivan, Dennis J. b: 6/26/1858, Boston, Mass. d: 12/31/25, Boston, Mass. TR , Deb: 8/25/1879

YEAR	TM/L	G	AB	R	H	2B	3B	HR	RBI	BB	SO	AVG	OBP	SLG	PRO+	BR	/A	RC	SB	CS	SBR	FA	FR	POS	TPR
1879	Pro-N	5	19	5	5	2	0	0	2	1	1	.263	.300	.368	121	0	0	2				.429	-4	/3O	-0.3
1880	Bos-N	1	4	1	1	0	0	0	1	0	1	.250	.250	.250	72	-0	-0	0				.857	-1	/C	-0.1
Total	2	6	23	6	6	2	0	0	3	1	2	.261	.292	.348	113	0	0	2					-4	/3CO	-0.4

■ DENNY SULLIVAN Sullivan, Dennis William b: 9/28/1882, Hillsboro, Wis. d: 6/2/56, W.Los Angeles, Cal BL/TR, Deb: 4/22/05

YEAR	TM/L	G	AB	R	H	2B	3B	HR	RBI	BB	SO	AVG	OBP	SLG	PRO+	BR	/A	RC	SB	CS	SBR	FA	FR	POS	TPR
1905	Was-A	3	11	0	0	0	0	0	0	1		.000	.083	.000	-76	-2	-2	0	0			1.000	-1	/O	-0.3
1907	Bos-A	144	551	73	135	18	0	1	26	44		.245	.314	.283	92	-4	-4	59	16			.975	1	*O	-0.9
1908	Bos-A	101	355	33	85	7	8	0	25	14		.239	.276	.304	86	-5	-6	34	14			.981	8	O	-0.2
	Cle-A	4	6	0	0	0	0	0	0	0		.000	.000	.000	-99	-1	-1	0	0			1.000	-0	/O	-0.2
	Yr	105	361	33	85	7	8	0	25	14		.235	.272	.299	83	-6	-7	33	14			.982	8	O	-0.4
1909	Cle-A	3	2	0	1	0	0	0	0	0		.500	.500	.500	207	0	0	0	0			.000	-1	/O	-0.1
Total	4	255	925	106	221	25	8	1	51	59		.239	.295	.286	87	-13	-13	93	30			.978	7	O	-1.7

■ HAYWOOD SULLIVAN Sullivan, Haywood Cooper b: 12/15/30, Donalsonville, Ga. BR/TR, 6'4", 215 lbs. Deb: 9/20/55 FM

YEAR	TM/L	G	AB	R	H	2B	3B	HR	RBI	BB	SO	AVG	OBP	SLG	PRO+	BR	/A	RC	SB	CS	SBR	FA	FR	POS	TPR
1955	Bos-A	2	6	1	0	0	0	0	0	0	1	.000	.000	.000	-92	-2	-2	0	0	0	0	1.000	1	/C	-0.1
1957	Bos-A	2	1	0	0	0	0	0	0	0	0	.000	.000	.000	-95	-0	-0	0	0	0	0	1.000	0	/C	0.0
1959	Bos-A	4	2	0	0	0	0	0	0	1	1	.000	.333	.000	-0	-0	-0	0	0	0	0	1.000	1	/C	0.0
1960	Bos-A	52	124	9	20	1	0	3	10	16	24	.161	.257	.242	35	-11	-12	8	0	0	0	.992	6	C	-0.4
1961	KC-A	117	331	42	80	16	2	6	40	46	45	.242	.334	.356	84	-7	-7	41	1	0	0	.984	-6	C1/O	-0.9
1962	KC-A	95	274	33	68	7	2	4	29	31	54	.248	.327	.332	75	-8	-9	31	1	0	0	.980	-9	C/1	-1.5
1963	KC-A	40	113	9	24	6	1	0	8	15	15	.212	.305	.283	63	-5	-5	9	0	0	0	.992	7	C	0.3
Total	7	312	851	94	192	30	5	13	87	109	140	.226	.314	.318	70	-33	-35	89	2	0	1	.985	-0	C/1O	-2.6

■ JOHN SULLIVAN Sullivan, John Eugene b: 2/16/1873, Illinois d: 6/5/24, St.Paul, Minn. BR/TR, 5'10", 170 lbs. Deb: 4/19/05

YEAR	TM/L	G	AB	R	H	2B	3B	HR	RBI	BB	SO	AVG	OBP	SLG	PRO+	BR	/A	RC	SB	CS	SBR	FA	FR	POS	TPR
1905	Det-A	13	32	4	5	0	0	0	4	4		.156	.250	.156	30	-2	-2	2	0			.964	4	C	0.3
1908	Pit-N	1	1	0	0	0	0	0	0	0		.000	.000	.000	-99	-0	-0	0	0			1.000	0	/C	0.0
Total	2	14	33	4	5	0	0	0	4	4		.152	.243	.152	26	-3	-3	2	0			.965	4	/C	0.3

■ CHUB SULLIVAN Sullivan, John Frank b: 1/12/1856, Boston, Mass. d: 9/12/1881, Boston, Mass. BR/TR, 6', 164 lbs. Deb: 9/24/1877

YEAR	TM/L	G	AB	R	H	2B	3B	HR	RBI	BB	SO	AVG	OBP	SLG	PRO+	BR	/A	RC	SB	CS	SBR	FA	FR	POS	TPR
1877	Cin-N	8	32	4	8	0	0	0	4	1	0	.250	.273	.250	74	-1	-1	2				.944	-1	/1	-0.1
1878	Cin-N	61	244	29	63	4	2	0	20	2	9	.258	.264	.291	91	-5	-1	19				**.975**	5	*1	0.2
1880	Wor-N	43	166	22	43	6	3	0	0	4	6	.259	.276	.331	97	1	-1	16				.983	3	1	-0.2
Total	3	112	442	55	114	10	5	0	24	7	15	.258	.269	.303	92	-5	-3	37				.976	7	1	-0.1

■ JOHN SULLIVAN Sullivan, John Lawrence b: 3/21/1890, Williamsport, Pa. d: 4/1/66, Milton, Pa. BR/TR, 5'11", 180 lbs. Deb: 4/18/20

YEAR	TM/L	G	AB	R	H	2B	3B	HR	RBI	BB	SO	AVG	OBP	SLG	PRO+	BR	/A	RC	SB	CS	SBR	FA	FR	POS	TPR
1920	Bos-N	81	250	36	74	14	4	1	28	29	29	.296	.374	.396	126	8	9	39	3	2	-0	.977	-2	O/1	0.2
1921	Bos-N	5	5	0	0	0	0	0	0	0	0	.000	.000	.000	-99	-1	-1	0	0	0	0	.000	0	H	-0.1
	Chi-N	76	240	28	79	14	4	4	41	19	26	.329	.381	.471	124	8	8	42	3	5	-2	.962	-7	O	-0.5
	Yr	81	245	28	79	14	4	4	41	19	26	.322	.374	.461	120	7	7	41	3	5	-2	.962	-7	O	-0.6
Total	2	162	495	64	153	28	8	5	69	48	55	.309	.374	.428	123	15	16	80	6	7	-2	.953	-9	O/1	-0.4

YEAR	TM/L	G	AB	R	H	2B	3B	HR	RBI	BB	SO	AVG	OBP	SLG	PRO+	BR	/A	RC	SB	CS	SBR	FA	FR	POS	TPR

■ JOHN SULLIVAN Sullivan, John Paul b: 11/2/20, Chicago, Ill. BR/TR, 5'10", 170 lbs. Deb: 6/07/42 C

1942	Was-A	94	357	38	84	16	1	0	42	25	30	.235	.285	.286	61	-19	-18	31	2	0	1	.936	-11	S	-2.4
1943	Was-A	134	456	49	95	12	2	1	55	57	59	.208	.298	.250	63	-21	-19	39	6	2	1	.946	11	*S	0.2
1944	Was-A	138	471	49	118	12	1	0	30	52	43	.251	.325	.280	77	-14	-12	46	3	3	-1	.934	-14	*S	-1.6
1947	Was-A	49	133	13	34	0	1	0	5	22	14	.256	.361	.271	79	-3	-3	15	0	2	-1	.963	8	S/2	0.6
1948	Was-A	85	173	25	36	4	1	0	12	22	25	.208	.297	.243	46	-13	-13	14	2	2	-1	.951	2	S/2	-0.8
1949	StL-A	105	243	29	55	8	3	0	18	38	35	.226	.331	.284	61	-12	-14	25	5	2	0	.942	-9	S3/2	-1.9
Total	6	605	1833	203	422	52	9	1	162	216	206	.230	.312	.270	66	-83	-78	169	18	11	-1	.969	-13	S/32	-5.9

■ JOHN SULLIVAN Sullivan, John Peter b: 1/3/41, Somerville, N.J. BL/TR, 6', 195 lbs. Deb: 9/20/63

1963	Det-A	3	5	0	0	0	0	0	0	2	1	.000	.286	.000	-11	-1	-1	0	0	0	0	1.000	0	/C	0.0
1964	Det-A	2	3	0	0	0	0	0	0	0	1	.000	.000	.000	-99	-1	-1	0	0	0	0	1.000	0	/C	-0.1
1965	Det-A	34	86	5	23	0	0	2	11	9	13	.267	.344	.337	93	-0	-1	11	0	0	0	.994	1	C	0.2
1967	NY-N	65	147	4	32	5	0	0	6	6	26	.218	.248	.252	44	-11	-10	9	0	2	-1	.991	-11	C	-2.2
1968	Phi-N	12	18	0	4	0	0	0	1	2	4	.222	.300	.222	59	-1	-1	1	0	0	0	.967	-0	/C	-0.1
Total	5	116	259	9	59	5	0	2	18	19	45	.228	.283	.270	59	-13	-13	21	0	2	-1	.942	-10	/C	-2.2

■ JOE SULLIVAN Sullivan, Joseph Daniel b: 1/6/1870, Charlestown, Mass. d: 11/2/1897, Charlestown, Mass. 5'10", 178 lbs. Deb: 4/27/1893

1893	Was-N	128	508	72	135	16	13	2	64	36	24	.266	.324	.360	86	-13	-10	63	7			.860	-29	*S	-2.8
1894	Was-N	17	60	7	15	3	0	0	5	6	2	.250	.357	.300	63	-3	-3	8	3			.900	-3	/2S3O	-0.4
	Phi-N	75	304	63	107	10	8	3	63	23	10	.352	.407	.467	115	6	8	64	10			.887	-16	S	-0.3
	Yr	92	364	70	122	13	8	3	68	29	12	.335	.398	.440	106	3	5	71	13			.884	-19	S/23O	-0.7
1895	Phi-N	94	373	75	126	7	3	2	50	24	20	.338	.395	.389	104	4	4	66	15			.879	-18	*S/O	-0.9
1896	Phi-N	48	191	45	48	5	3	2	24	18	12	.251	.347	.340	84	-4	-3	26	9			.962	-4	O/S3	-0.9
	StL-N	51	212	25	62	4	2	2	21	9	12	.292	.351	.358	93	-3	-2	30	5			.955	-6	O/2	-0.9
	Yr	99	403	70	110	9	5	4	45	27	24	.273	.349	.350	89	-7	-5	56	14			.959	-10	O/2S3	-1.8
Total	4	413	1648	287	493	45	29	11	227	116	80	.299	.363	.382	96	-13	-7	257	49			.948	-75	S/O23	-6.2

■ MARC SULLIVAN Sullivan, Marc Cooper b: 7/25/58, Quincy, Mass. BR/TR, 6'4", 205 lbs. Deb: 10/01/82 F

1982	Bos-A	2	6	0	2	0	0	0	0	0	2	.333	.333	.333	79	-0	-0	1	0	0	0	1.000	1	/C	0.1
1984	Bos-A	2	6	1	3	0	0	0	1	1	0	.500	.571	.500	191	1	1	2	0	0	0	.950	1	/C	0.1
1985	Bos-A	32	69	10	12	2	0	2	3	6	15	.174	.240	.290	43	-5	-6	5	0	0	0	.993	4	C	-0.1
1986	Bos-A	41	119	15	23	4	0	1	14	7	32	.193	.262	.252	40	-10	-10	6	0	0	0	.986	-5	C	-1.2
1987	Bos-A	60	160	11	27	5	0	2	10	4	43	.169	.199	.237	15	-20	-20	7	0	0	0	.994	0	C	-1.6
Total	5	137	360	37	67	11	0	5	28	18	92	.186	.237	.258	33	-34	-35	23	0	0	0	.990	1	C	-2.6

■ MARTY SULLIVAN Sullivan, Martin C. b: 10/20/1862, Lowell, Mass. d: 1/6/1894, Lowell, Mass. BR/TR, Deb: 4/30/1887

1887	Chi-N	115	472	98	134	13	16	7	77	36	53	.284	.340	.424	100	8	-3	82	35			.847	-7	*O/P	-1.0
1888	Chi-N	75	314	40	74	12	6	7	39	15	32	.236	.273	.379	101	2	-1	36	9			.927	3	O	0.0
1889	Ind-N	69	256	45	73	11	3	4	35	50	31	.285	.404	.398	124	11	10	48	15			.910	-5	O/1	0.3
1890	Bos-N	121	505	82	144	19	7	6	61	56	48	.285	.357	.386	110	12	6	83	33			.951	4	*O/3	0.5
1891	Bos-N	17	67	15	15	1	0	2	7	5	3	.224	.288	.328	72	-2	-3	9	7			.926	-2	O	-0.5
	Cle-N	1	4	0	1	0	0	0	1	0	1	.250	.250	.250	45	-0	-0	0	0			.000	-0	/O	-0.1
	Yr	18	71	15	16	1	0	2	8	5	4	.225	.286	.324	71	-2	-3	9	7			.926	-3	O	-0.6
Total	5	398	1618	280	441	56	32	26	220	162	168	.273	.341	.395	106	32	10	258	99			.909	-7	O/13P	-0.8

■ MIKE SULLIVAN Sullivan, Michael Joseph b: 6/10/1860, Webster, Mass. d: 6/16/29, Webster, Mass. BR/TR, 5'8.5", 165 lbs. Deb: 4/26/1888

| 1888 | Phi-a | 28 | 112 | 20 | 31 | 5 | 6 | 1 | 19 | 3 | | .277 | .296 | .455 | 143 | 5 | 5 | 18 | 10 | | | .742 | -6 | O3 | -0.2 |

■ PAT SULLIVAN Sullivan, Patrick J. b: 12/22/1862, Milwaukee, Wis. TR, 5'11", 165 lbs. Deb: 8/30/1884

| 1884 | KC-U | 31 | 114 | 15 | 22 | 3 | 1 | 0 | | 4 | | .193 | .220 | .237 | 63 | -5 | -3 | 6 | | | | .767 | 1 | 3/OCP | -0.1 |

■ RUSS SULLIVAN Sullivan, Russell Guy b: 2/19/23, Fredericksburg, Va BL/TR, 6', 196 lbs. Deb: 9/08/51

1951	Det-A	7	26	2	5	1	0	1	1	2	1	.192	.250	.346	60	-2	-2	2	0	0	0	.938	0	/O	-0.2
1952	Det-A	15	52	7	17	2	1	3	5	3	5	.327	.375	.577	161	4	4	12	1	0	0	.826	-2	O	0.2
1953	Det-A	23	72	7	18	5	1	1	6	13	5	.250	.379	.389	109	1	1	11	0	0	0	.958	3	O	0.4
Total	3	45	150	16	40	8	2	5	12	18	11	.267	.357	.447	118	4	4	25	1	0	0	.920	1	/O	0.4

■ SUTER SULLIVAN Sullivan, Suter G. b: 10/14/1872, Baltimore, Md. d: 4/19/25, Baltimore, Md. Deb: 7/24/1898

1898	StL-N	42	144	10	32	3	0	0	12	13		.222	.300	.243	55	-8	-8	11	1			.875	-13	SO/21P	-1.9
1899	Cle-N	127	473	37	116	16	3	0	55	25		.245	.297	.292	67	-25	-20	48	16			.938	5	*3O/S12	-1.3
Total	2	169	617	47	148	19	3	0	67	38		.240	.298	.280	64	-33	-28	59	17			.889	-8	3/OS21P	-3.2

■ TOM SULLIVAN Sullivan, Thomas Brandon b: 12/19/06, Nome, Alaska d: 8/16/44, Seattle, Wash. BR/TR, 6', 190 lbs. Deb: 6/14/25

| 1925 | Cin-N | 1 | 1 | 0 | 0 | 0 | 0 | 0 | 0 | 0 | 0 | .000 | .000 | .000 | -99 | -0 | -0 | 0 | 0 | 0 | 0 | 1.000 | -0 | /C | 0.0 |

■ SLEEPER SULLIVAN Sullivan, Thomas Jefferson "Old Iron Hands" b: St.Louis, Mo. d: 9/25/1899, Camden, N.J. BR/TR, 175 lbs. Deb: 5/03/1881

1881	Buf-N	35	121	13	23	4	0	0	15	1	21	.190	.197	.223	32	-9	-9	5				.853	-12	C/O	-2.0
1882	StL-a	51	188	24	34	3	3	0		3		.181	.194	.229	40	-11	-12	9				.840	-17	C	-2.6
1883	StL-a	8	27	2	6	0	1	0		0		.222	.222	.296	62	-1	-1	2				.939	5	CO	0.3
1884	StL-U	2	9	0	1	0	0	0		0		.111	.111	.111	-24	-1	-1	0				.000	-1	/OCP	-0.2
Total	4	96	345	39	64	7	4	0	15	4	21	.186	.195	.229	38	-22	-24	16				.852	-26	/COP	-4.5

■ TED SULLIVAN Sullivan, Timothy Paul b: 1851, County Clare, Ireland d: 7/5/29, Washington, D.C. Deb: 9/09/1884 MU

| 1884 | KC-U | 3 | 9 | 0 | 3 | 0 | 0 | 0 | | 1 | | .333 | .400 | .333 | 173 | 1 | 1 | 1 | | | | 1.000 | -2 | /OSM | -0.1 |

■ BILL SULLIVAN Sullivan, William b: 7/4/1853, Holyoke, Mass. d: 11/13/1884, Holyoke, Mass. Deb: 8/09/1878

| 1878 | Chi-N | 2 | 6 | 1 | 1 | 0 | 0 | 0 | 0 | 0 | 0 | .167 | .167 | .167 | 9 | -1 | -1 | 0 | | | | 1.000 | -1 | /O | -0.1 |

■ BILLY SULLIVAN Sullivan, William Joseph Jr. b: 10/23/10, Chicago, Ill. BL/TR, 6', 170 lbs. Deb: 6/09/31 F

1931	Chi-A	92	363	48	100	16	5	2	33	20	14	.275	.315	.364	83	-12	-9	41	4	4	-1	.912	-9	3/O1	-1.3
1932	Chi-A	93	307	31	97	16	1	1	45	20	9	.316	.358	.384	99	-3	-0	41	1	3	-2	.990	-3	13/CO	-0.7
1933	Chi-A	54	125	9	24	0	1	0	13	10	5	.192	.252	.208	24	-14	-13	7	0	0	0	.982	-3	1/C	-1.7
1935	Cin-N	85	241	29	64	9	4	2	36	19	16	.266	.324	.361	87	-5	-4	29	4			.992	-2	13/2	-0.5
1936	Cle-A	93	319	39	112	32	6	2	48	16	9	.351	.382	.508	117	8	7	61	5	2	0	.968	-2	C/31O	0.8
1937	Cle-A	72	168	26	48	12	3	3	22	17	7	.286	.355	.446	100	-0	-0	26	1	4	-2	.949	-6	C/13	-0.6
1938	StL-A	111	375	35	104	16	1	7	49	20	10	.277	.316	.381	74	-16	-16	45	8	5	-1	.990	-1	C/1	-1.2
1939	StL-A	118	332	53	96	17	5	5	50	34	18	.289	.362	.416	96	-1	-2	49	3	3	-1	.954	4	OC/1	0.0
1940	*Det-A	78	220	36	68	14	4	3	41	31	11	.309	.399	.450	109	7	4	44	2	0	1	.976	1	C/3	1.0
1941	Det-A	85	234	29	66	15	1	3	29	35	11	.282	.375	.393	94	2	-1	36	0	3	-2	.976	5	C	0.7
1942	Bro-N	43	101	11	27	2	1	0	14	12	6	.267	.345	.337	98	0	0	13	1			.962	-0	C	0.2
1947	Pit-N	38	55	1	14	3	0	0	8	6	3	.255	.328	.309	68	-2	-2	6	1			1.000	1	C	-0.1
Total	12	962	2840	347	820	152	32	29	388	240	119	.289	.346	.395	91	-36	-37	397	30	24		.972	-11	C13/O2	-3.4

■ BILLY SULLIVAN Sullivan, William Joseph Sr. b: 2/1/1875, Oakland, Wis. d: 1/28/65, Newberg.Ore. BR/TR, 5'9", 155 lbs. Deb: 9/13/1899 FM

| 1899 | Bos-N | 22 | 74 | 10 | 20 | 2 | 0 | 2 | 12 | 1 | | .270 | .308 | .378 | 80 | -2 | -3 | 9 | 2 | | | .952 | 5 | C | 0.4 |

YEAR	TM/L	G	AB	R	H	2B	3B	HR	RBI	BB	SO	AVG	OBP	SLG	PRO+	BR	/A	RC	SB	CS	SBR	FA	FR	POS	TPR
1900	Bos-N	72	238	36	65	6	0	8	41	9		.273	.302	.399	83	-4	-8	31	4			.974	-1	C/S2	-0.2
1901	Chi-A	98	367	54	90	15	6	4	56	10		.245	.271	.351	74	-15	-14	40	12			**.967**	-1	C/3	-0.4
1902	Chi-A	76	263	36	64	12	3	1	26	6		.243	.266	.323	65	-14	-12	27	11			.967	-3	C/1O	-0.7
1903	Chi-A	32	111	10	21	4	0	1	7	5		.189	.224	.252	45	-8	-7	7	3			.988	-2	C	-0.7
1904	Chi-A	108	371	29	85	18	4	1	44	12		.229	.255	.307	81	-10	-9	34	11			.964	2	*C	0.6
1905	Chi-A	98	323	25	65	10	3	2	26	13		.201	.239	.269	64	-15	-13	26	14			.974	-4	C/13	-0.9
1906	*Chi-A	118	387	37	83	18	4	2	33	22		.214	.262	.297	77	-12	-10	36	10			**.974**	-4	*C	-0.4
1907	Chi-A	112	329	30	59	8	4	0	36	21		.179	.235	.228	50	-19	-18	21	6			.983	-1	*C/2	-1.1
1908	Chi-A	137	430	40	82	8	4	0	29	22		.191	.235	.228	51	-23	-23	27	15			**.985**	-20	*C	-3.5
1909	Chi-A	97	265	11	43	3	0	0	16	17		.162	.226	.174	28	-22	-20	13	9			.983	5	CM	-0.8
1910	Chi-A	45	142	10	26	4	1	0	6	7		.183	.227	.225	43	-10	-9	7	0			.976	13	C	0.9
1911	Chi-A	89	256	26	55	9	3	0	31	16		.215	.266	.273	52	-17	-16	19	1			**.986**	1	C	-0.7
1912	Chi-A	41	91	9	19	2	1	0	15	9		.209	.287	.253	57	-5	-5	7	0			.975	1	C	-0.1
1914	Chi-A	1	0	0	0	0	0	0	0	0	0	—	—	—	—	0	0	0	0			1.000	-0	/C	0.0
1916	Det-A	1	0	0	0	0	0	0	0	0	0	—	—	—	—	0	0	0	0			.000	0	/C	0.0
Total	16	1147	3647	363	777	119	33	21	378	170	0	.213	.254	.281	63	-175	-167	305	98			.976	-8	*C/1O32S	-7.6

■ HOMER SUMMA

Summa, Homer Wayne b: 11/3/1898, Gentry, Mo. d: 1/29/66, Los Angeles, Cal. BL/TR, 5'10.5", 170 lbs. Deb: 9/13/20

YEAR	TM/L	G	AB	R	H	2B	3B	HR	RBI	BB	SO	AVG	OBP	SLG	PRO+	BR	/A	RC	SB	CS	SBR	FA	FR	POS	TPR
1920	Pit-N	10	22	1	7	1	1	0	1	3	1	.318	.400	.455	141	1	1	4	1	0	0	.950	1	/O	0.2
1922	Cle-A	12	46	9	16	3	3	1	6	1	1	.348	.400	.609	159	4	4	10	1	2	-1	1.000	0	O	0.2
1923	Cle-A	137	525	92	172	27	6	3	69	33	20	.328	.374	.419	109	6	6	80	9	13	-5	.951	-13	*O	-1.9
1924	Cle-A	111	390	55	113	21	6	2	38	11	16	.290	.311	.390	79	-13	-14	46	4	2	0	.941	-6	O	-2.4
1925	Cle-A	75	224	28	74	10	1	0	25	13	6	.330	.375	.384	92	-2	-2	33	3	2	-0	.966	-9	O/3	-1.3
1926	Cle-A	154	581	74	179	31	6	4	76	47	9	.308	.368	.403	100	1	0	88	15	8	-0	.975	7	*O	-0.3
1927	Cle-A	145	574	73	164	41	7	4	74	32	18	.286	.331	.402	89	-10	-11	73	6	5	-1	.955	-8	*O	-2.9
1928	Cle-A	134	504	60	143	26	3	3	57	20	15	.284	.319	.365	78	-16	-16	59	4	2	0	.971	-4	*O	-2.9
1929	*Phi-A	37	81	12	22	4	0	0	10	2	1	.272	.298	.321	57	-5	-5	8	1	1	-0	.980	-5	O	-1.1
1930	Phi-A	25	54	10	15	2	1	1	5	4	1	.278	.339	.407	85	-1	-1	8	0	0	0	.938	0	O	-0.2
Total	10	840	3001	414	905	166	34	18	361	166	88	.302	.346	.398	92	-35	-39	409	44	35	-8	.961	-36	O/3	-12.6

■ CHAMP SUMMERS

Summers, John Junior b: 6/15/46, Bremerton, Wash. BL/TR, 6'2", 205 lbs. Deb: 5/04/74 C

YEAR	TM/L	G	AB	R	H	2B	3B	HR	RBI	BB	SO	AVG	OBP	SLG	PRO+	BR	/A	RC	SB	CS	SBR	FA	FR	POS	TPR
1974	Oak-A	20	24	2	3	1	0	0	3	1	5	.125	.160	.167	-6	-3	-3	1	0	0	0	1.000	-4	O/D	-0.7
1975	Chi-N	76	91	14	21	5	1	1	16	10	13	.231	.314	.341	78	-2	-3	10	0	0	0	.889	-2	O	-0.6
1976	Chi-N	83	126	11	26	2	0	3	13	13	31	.206	.286	.294	59	-6	-7	11	1	0	0	.964	-2	O1/C	-1.0
1977	Cin-N	59	76	11	13	4	0	3	6	6	16	.171	.241	.342	53	-5	-5	6	0	0	0	1.000	1	O/3	-0.5
1978	Cin-N	13	35	4	9	2	0	1	3	7	4	.257	.381	.400	118	1	1	5	2	1	0	.933	-2	O	-0.2
1979	Cin-N	27	60	10	12	2	1	1	11	13	15	.200	.351	.317	83	-1	-1	7	0	1	-1	.941	-1	O/1	-0.3
	Det-A	90	246	47	77	12	1	20	51	40	33	.313	.415	.614	168	26	25	63	7	6	-2	.989	-10	OD/1	1.1
1980	Det-A	120	347	61	103	19	1	17	60	52	52	.297	.396	.504	142	23	21	69	4	3	-1	.953	-8	DO/1	1.2
1981	Det-A	64	165	16	42	8	0	3	21	19	35	.255	.342	.358	98	1	0	22	1	1	-0	.964	-2	DO	-0.2
1982	SF-N	70	125	15	31	5	0	4	19	16	17	.248	.347	.384	105	1	1	17	0	1	-1	.913	-3	O/1	-0.4
1983	SF-N	29	22	3	3	0	0	0	3	7	8	.136	.345	.136	39	-1	-1	1	0	0	0	1.000	0	/O	-0.1
1984	*SD-N	47	54	5	10	3	0	1	12	4	15	.185	.254	.296	54	-3	-3	4	0	0	0	1.000	-1	/1	-0.5
Total	11	698	1371	199	350	63	4	54	218	188	244	.255	.353	.425	111	29	25	215	15	13	-3	.959	-33	OD/13C	-2.2

■ KID SUMMERS

Summers, William b: Toronto, Ont., Canada d: 10/16/1895, Toronto, Ont., Can. TR , Deb: 8/05/1893

YEAR	TM/L	G	AB	R	H	2B	3B	HR	RBI	BB	SO	AVG	OBP	SLG	PRO+	BR	/A	RC	SB	CS	SBR	FA	FR	POS	TPR
1893	StL-N	2	1	1	0	0	0	0	0	0	0	.000	.500	.000	40	0	0	0	0			.500	-0	/OC	0.0

■ CARL SUMNER

Sumner, Carl Ringdahl "Lefty" b: 9/28/08, Cambridge, Mass. BL/TL, 5'8", 170 lbs. Deb: 7/28/28

YEAR	TM/L	G	AB	R	H	2B	3B	HR	RBI	BB	SO	AVG	OBP	SLG	PRO+	BR	/A	RC	SB	CS	SBR	FA	FR	POS	TPR
1928	Bos-A	16	29	6	8	1	1	0	3	5	6	.276	.382	.379	103	0	0	5	0	0	0	.923	-3	O	-0.3

■ ART SUNDAY

Sunday, Arthur (b: August Wacher) b: 1/21/1862, Springfield, Ohio BL/TL, 5'9", 193 lbs. Deb: 5/05/1890

YEAR	TM/L	G	AB	R	H	2B	3B	HR	RBI	BB	SO	AVG	OBP	SLG	PRO+	BR	/A	RC	SB	CS	SBR	FA	FR	POS	TPR
1890	Bro-P	24	83	26	22	5	1	0	13	15	9	.265	.419	.349	102	2	1	12	0			.909	-5	O	-0.4

■ BILLY SUNDAY

Sunday, William Ashley "Parson" or "The Evangelist" b: 11/19/1862, Ames, Iowa d: 11/6/35, Chicago, Ill. BL/TR, 5'10", 160 lbs. Deb: 5/22/1883

YEAR	TM/L	G	AB	R	H	2B	3B	HR	RBI	BB	SO	AVG	OBP	SLG	PRO+	BR	/A	RC	SB	CS	SBR	FA	FR	POS	TPR
1883	Chi-N	14	54	6	13	4	0	0	5	1	18	.241	.255	.315	68	-2	-2	4				.647	-5	O	-0.6
1884	Chi-N	43	176	25	39	4	1	4	28	4	36	.222	.239	.324	70	-5	-7	14				.663	-9	O	-1.6
1885	*Chi-N	46	172	36	44	3	3	2	20	12	33	.256	.304	.343	95	2	-2	18				.825	-9	O	-1.1
1886	Chi-N	28	103	16	25	2	2	0	6	7	26	.243	.291	.301	70	-2	-5	12	10			.914	-0	O	-0.5
1887	Chi-N	50	199	41	58	6	6	3	32	21	20	.291	.362	.427	106	6	1	44	34			.766	-8	O	-0.6
1888	Pit-N	120	505	69	119	14	3	0	15	12	36	.236	.256	.275	77	-16	-11	55	71			.939	17	*O	0.2
1889	Pit-N	81	321	62	77	10	6	2	25	27	33	.240	.307	.327	87	-9	-4	48	47			.946	8	O	0.2
1890	Pit-N	86	358	58	92	9	2	1	33	32	20	.257	.327	.302	97	-6	1	55	56			.883	11	O/P	0.8
	Phi-N	31	119	26	31	3	1	0	6	18	7	.261	.367	.303	96	1	0	24	28			.950	3	O	0.2
	Yr	117	477	84	123	12	3	1	39	50	27	.258	.337	.302	96	-5	1	79	84			.900	15	*O/P	1.0
Total	8	499	2007	339	498	55	24	12	170	134	229	.248	.300	.317	87	-32	-29	275	246			.883	9	O/P	-3.0

■ JIM SUNDBERG

Sundberg, James Howard b: 5/18/51, Galesburg, Ill. BR/TR, 6', 195 lbs. Deb: 4/04/74

YEAR	TM/L	G	AB	R	H	2B	3B	HR	RBI	BB	SO	AVG	OBP	SLG	PRO+	BR	/A	RC	SB	CS	SBR	FA	FR	POS	TPR
1974	Tex-A☆	132	368	45	91	13	3	3	36	62	61	.247	.356	.323	99	1	2	43	2	4	-2	.990	6	*C	1.2
1975	Tex-A	155	472	45	94	9	0	6	36	51	77	.199	.283	.256	54	-28	-28	35	3	1	0	.981	5	*C	-1.6
1976	Tex-A	140	448	33	102	24	2	3	34	37	61	.228	.287	.310	73	-14	-16	39	0	0	0	**.991**	17	*C	0.6
1977	Tex-A	149	453	61	132	20	3	6	65	53	77	.291	.368	.389	105	6	5	67	2	3	-1	**.994**	23	*C	3.0
1978	Tex-A★	149	518	54	144	23	6	6	58	64	70	.278	.361	.380	108	7	7	69	2	5	-2	**.997**	16	*C/D	2.5
1979	Tex-A	150	495	50	136	23	4	5	64	51	51	.275	.348	.368	94	-3	-3	62	3	3	-1	**.995**	10	*C	1.2
1980	Tex-A	151	505	59	138	24	1	10	63	64	67	.273	.356	.384	106	3	5	69	2	2	-1	.993	6	*C	1.6
1981	Tex-A	102	339	42	94	17	2	3	28	50	48	.277	.372	.366	120	8	10	48	2	5	-2	.996	-3	C/O	0.8
1982	Tex-A	139	470	37	118	22	5	10	47	49	57	.251	.323	.383	98	-4	-1	57	2	6	-3	.991	-2	*C/O	-0.1
1983	Tex-A	131	378	30	76	14	0	2	28	35	64	.201	.272	.254	47	-27	-26	26	0	4	-2	.993	5	*C	-1.9
1984	Mil-A★	110	348	43	91	19	4	7	43	38	63	.261	.334	.399	106	1	3	48	1	1	-0	**.995**	7	*C	1.4
1985	*KC-A	115	367	38	90	12	4	10	35	33	67	.245	.309	.381	88	-6	-6	42	0	2	-1	.992	1	*C	-0.1
1986	KC-A	140	429	41	91	9	1	12	42	57	91	.212	.305	.322	69	-17	-18	44	1	1	-0	**.995**	-1	*C	-1.1
1987	Chi-N	61	139	9	28	2	0	4	15	19	40	.201	.306	.302	60	-7	-8	13	0	0	0	.994	9	C	0.3
1988	Chi-N	24	54	8	13	1	0	2	9	8	15	.241	.339	.370	99	0	0	7	0	0	0	1.000	-1	C	0.0
	Tex-A	38	91	13	26	4	0	4	13	5	17	.286	.323	.462	114	2	1	13	0	0	0	1.000	0	C	0.3
1989	Tex-A	76	147	13	29	7	1	2	8	23	37	.197	.306	.299	70	-5	-6	15	0	0	0	.992	1	C/D	-0.2
Total	16	1962	6021	621	1493	243	36	95	624	699	963	.248	.328	.348	89	-86	-78	698	20	37	-16	.993	97	*C/OD	7.9

■ B.J. SURHOFF

Surhoff, William James b: 8/4/64, Bronx, N.Y. BL/TR, 6'1", 190 lbs. Deb: 4/08/87 F

YEAR	TM/L	G	AB	R	H	2B	3B	HR	RBI	BB	SO	AVG	OBP	SLG	PRO+	BR	/A	RC	SB	CS	SBR	FA	FR	POS	TPR
1987	Mil-A	115	395	50	118	22	3	7	68	36	30	.299	.357	.423	103	4	2	56	11	10	-3	.984	6	C3/1D	1.1
1988	Mil-A	139	493	47	121	21	0	5	38	31	49	.245	.294	.318	71	-19	-19	46	21	6	3	.990	-8	*C3/1SO	-1.7
1989	Mil-A	126	436	42	108	17	4	5	55	25	29	.248	.293	.339	79	-13	-13	41	14	12	-3	.985	-5	*CD/3	-1.5
1990	Mil-A	135	474	55	131	21	4	6	59	41	37	.276	.335	.376	99	-1	-0	61	18	7	1	.985	-6	*C3	0.3
1991	Mil-A	143	505	57	146	19	4	5	68	26	33	.289	.324	.372	94	-6	-4	54	5	8	-3	.995	-2	*C/3O2D	-0.2
1992	Mil-A	139	480	63	121	19	1	4	62	46	41	.252	.320	.321	82	-12	-11	50	14	8	-1	.990	6	*C1/O3D	0.0
Total	6	797	2783	314	745	119	16	32	350	205	219	.268	.320	.356	88	-47	-45	308	83	51	-6	.988	-9	C/3D1O2S	-2.0

■ GEORGE SUSCE
Susce, George Cyril Methodius "Good Kid" b: 8/13/08, Pittsburgh, Pa. d: 2/25/86, Sarasota, Fla. BR/TR, 5'11.5", 200 lbs. Deb: 4/23/29 FC

YEAR	TM/L	G	AB	R	H	2B	3B	HR	RBI	BB	SO	AVG	OBP	SLG	PRO+	BR	/A	RC	SB	CS	SBR	FA	FR	POS	TPR
1929	Phi-N	17	17	5	5	3	0	1	1	1	2	.294	.368	.647	137	1	1	4	0			.900	-2	C	-0.1
1932	Det-A	2	0	0	0	0	0	0	0	0	0	—	—	—	—	0	0	0	0	0	0	1.000	-0	/C	0.0
1939	Pit-N	31	75	8	17	3	1	1	4	12	5	.227	.333	.333	81	-2	-2	8	0			.984	2	C	0.2
1940	StL-A	61	113	6	24	4	0	0	13	9	9	.212	.282	.248	38	-10	-10	7	1	0	0	.984	6	C	-0.1
1941	Cle-A	1	0	0	0	0	0	0	0	0	0	—	—	—	—	0	0	0	0	0	0	1.000	-0	/C	0.0
1942	Cle-A	2	1	1	1	0	0	0	0	1	0	1.000	1.000	1.000	492	1	1	1	0	0	0	1.000	-0	/C	0.1
1943	Cle-A	3	1	0	0	0	0	0	0	0	0	.000	.000	.000	-99	-0	-0	0	0	0	0	1.000	1	/C	0.0
1944	Cle-A	29	61	3	14	1	0	0	4	2	5	.230	.254	.246	45	-5	-4	4	0	0	0	.948	1	C	-0.2
Total	8	146	268	23	61	11	1	2	22	25	21	.228	.301	.299	60	-15	-15	24	1	0		.974	8	C	-0.1

■ PETE SUSKO
Susko, Peter Jonathan b: 7/2/04, Laura, Ohio d: 5/22/78, Jacksonville, Fla. BL/TL, 5'11", 172 lbs. Deb: 8/01/34

YEAR	TM/L	G	AB	R	H	2B	3B	HR	RBI	BB	SO	AVG	OBP	SLG	PRO+	BR	/A	RC	SB	CS	SBR	FA	FR	POS	TPR
1934	Was-A	58	224	25	64	5	3	2	25	18	10	.286	.342	.362	85	-6	-5	28	3	4	-2	.988	3	1	-0.8

■ BUTCH SUTCLIFFE
Sutcliffe, Charles Inigo b: 7/22/15, Fall River, Mass. BR/TR, 5'8.5", 165 lbs. Deb: 8/28/38

YEAR	TM/L	G	AB	R	H	2B	3B	HR	RBI	BB	SO	AVG	OBP	SLG	PRO+	BR	/A	RC	SB	CS	SBR	FA	FR	POS	TPR
1938	Bos-N	4	4	1	1	0	0	0	2	2	1	.250	.500	.250	124	0	0	1	0			.800	0	/C	0.1

■ SY SUTCLIFFE
Sutcliffe, Elmer Ellsworth b: 4/15/1862, Wheaton, Ill. d: 2/13/1893, Wheaton, Ill. BL, 6'2", 170 lbs. Deb: 10/02/1884

YEAR	TM/L	G	AB	R	H	2B	3B	HR	RBI	BB	SO	AVG	OBP	SLG	PRO+	BR	/A	RC	SB	CS	SBR	FA	FR	POS	TPR
1884	Chi-N	4	15	4	3	1	0	0	2	2	4	.200	.294	.267	72	-0	-1	1				.976	2	/C	0.2
1885	Chi-N	11	43	5	8	1	1	0	4	2	5	.186	.222	.256	47	-2	-3	3				.838	-5	C/O	-0.7
	StL-N	16	49	2	6	1	0	0	4	5	10	.122	.204	.143	15	-4	-4	1				.881	-2	C/O	-0.5
	Yr	27	92	7	14	2	1	0	8	7	15	.152	.212	.196	32	-7	-7	4				.862	-7	C/O	-1.2
1888	Det-N	49	191	17	49	5	3	0	23	5	14	.257	.276	.314	90	-2	-2	19	6			.901	7	SC/102	0.6
1889	Cle-N	46	161	17	40	3	2	1	21	14	6	.248	.309	.311	76	-5	-5	17	5			.892	9	C/1O	0.6
1890	Cle-P	99	386	62	127	14	8	2	60	33	16	.329	.382	.422	127	9	15	68	10			.883	-5	CO/S3	1.3
1891	Was-a	53	201	29	71	8	3	2	33	17	17	.353	.409	.453	157	13	14	42	8			.918	-4	OC/S3	0.9
1892	Bal-N	66	276	41	77	10	7	1	27	14	15	.279	.316	.377	108	3	2	38	12			.958	-7	1	-0.8
Total	7	344	1322	177	381	43	24	6	174	92	87	.288	.336	.371	109	10	16	188	41			.887	-5	C/1OS32	1.6

■ GARY SUTHERLAND
Sutherland, Gary Lynn b: 9/27/44, Glendale, Cal. BR/TR, 6', 185 lbs. Deb: 9/17/66 F

YEAR	TM/L	G	AB	R	H	2B	3B	HR	RBI	BB	SO	AVG	OBP	SLG	PRO+	BR	/A	RC	SB	CS	SBR	FA	FR	POS	TPR
1966	Phi-N	3	3	0	0	0	0	0	0	0	0	.000	.000	.000	-99	-1	-1	0	0	0	0	1.000	1	/S	0.0
1967	Phi-N	103	231	23	57	12	1	1	19	17	22	.247	.298	.320	76	-7	-7	20	0	3	-2	.928	-14	SO	-2.1
1968	Phi-N	67	138	16	38	7	0	0	15	8	15	.275	.315	.326	93	-1	-1	14	0	0	0	.968	-2	2S3/O	-0.2
1969	Mon-N	141	544	63	130	26	1	3	35	37	31	.239	.290	.307	67	-24	-24	46	5	7	-3	.971	10	*2S/O	-0.5
1970	Mon-N	116	359	37	74	10	0	3	26	31	22	.206	.273	.259	43	-29	-29	26	2	2	-1	.975	3	2S/3	-1.8
1971	Mon-N	111	304	25	78	7	2	4	26	18	12	.257	.302	.332	79	-8	-8	28	3	4	-2	.963	0	2S/O3	-0.2
1972	Hou-N	5	8	0	1	0	0	0	1	0	0	.125	.125	.125	-29	-1	-1	0	0	0	0	.000	-1	/23	-0.2
1973	Hou-N	16	54	8	14	5	0	0	3	3	5	.259	.298	.352	80	-2	-2	5	0	0	0	.971	-4	2/S	-0.5
1974	Det-A	149	619	60	157	20	1	5	49	26	37	.254	.284	.313	69	-23	-26	51	1	3	-2	.976	-23	*2S/3	-4.5
1975	Det-A	129	503	51	130	12	3	6	39	45	41	.258	.323	.330	81	-10	-12	53	0	2	-1	.968	-7	*2	-1.4
1976	Det-A	42	117	10	24	5	2	0	6	7	12	.205	.250	.282	53	-7	-7	7	0	1	-1	.984	1	2	-0.4
	Mil-A	59	115	9	25	2	0	1	9	8	7	.217	.274	.261	58	-6	-6	7	0	2	-1	.955	-0	2/1D	-0.6
	Yr	101	232	19	49	7	2	1	15	15	19	.211	.262	.272	56	-13	-13	14	0	3	-2	.970	1	2/D1	-1.0
1977	SD-N	80	103	5	25	3	0	1	11	7	15	.243	.291	.301	66	-6	-5	9	0	0	0	.943	-4	23/1	-0.8
1978	StL-N	10	6	1	1	0	0	0	0	0	0	.167	.167	.167	-7	-1	-1	0	0	0	0	1.000	2	/2	0.1
Total	13	1031	3104	308	754	109	10	24	239	207	219	.243	.292	.308	69	-125	-130	267	11	24	-11	.971	-38	2S/3OD1	-13.1

■ LEO SUTHERLAND
Sutherland, Leonardo (Cantin) b: 4/6/58, Santiago, Cuba BL/TL, 5'10", 165 lbs. Deb: 8/11/80

YEAR	TM/L	G	AB	R	H	2B	3B	HR	RBI	BB	SO	AVG	OBP	SLG	PRO+	BR	/A	RC	SB	CS	SBR	FA	FR	POS	TPR
1980	Chi-A	34	89	9	23	3	0	0	5	1	11	.258	.267	.292	53	-6	-6	7	4	1	1	.943	-1	O	-0.7
1981	Chi-A	11	12	6	2	0	0	0	0	3	1	.167	.333	.167	49	-1	-1	1	2	1	0	1.000	-3	/O	-0.4
Total	2	45	101	15	25	3	0	0	5	4	12	.248	.276	.277	53	-6	-6	8	6	2	1	.949	-4	/O	-1.1

■ GLENN SUTKO
Sutko, Glenn Edward b: 5/9/68, Atlanta, Ga. BR/TR, 6'3", 225 lbs. Deb: 10/03/90

YEAR	TM/L	G	AB	R	H	2B	3B	HR	RBI	BB	SO	AVG	OBP	SLG	PRO+	BR	/A	RC	SB	CS	SBR	FA	FR	POS	TPR
1990	Cin-N	1	1	0	0	0	0	0	0	0	1	.000	.000	.000	-96	-0	-0	0	0	0	0	1.000	0	/C	0.0
1991	Cin-N	10	10	0	1	0	0	0	1	2	6	.100	.250	.100	2	-1	-1	0	0	0	0	.875	0	/C	-0.1
Total	2	11	11	0	1	0	0	0	1	2	7	.091	.231	.091	-6	-2	-2	0	0	0	0	.889	0	/C	-0.1

■ EZRA SUTTON
Sutton, Ezra Ballou b: 9/17/1850, Palmyra, N.Y. d: 6/20/07, Braintree, Mass. BR/TR, 5'8.5", 153 lbs. Deb: 5/04/1871

YEAR	TM/L	G	AB	R	H	2B	3B	HR	RBI	BB	SO	AVG	OBP	SLG	PRO+	BR	/A	RC	SB	CS	SBR	FA	FR	POS	TPR
1871	Cle-n	29	128	35	45	3	7	3	23	1	0	.352	.357	.555	166	9	10	27	3					*3	0.5
1872	Cle-n	22	108	30	30	8	1	0	10	1	1	.278	.284	.370	106	-0	1	12						3	0.0
1873	Ath-n	51	242	51	81	7	7	0	32	2	2	.335	.340	.421	114	7	3	35						*3/S2	-0.1
1874	Ath-n	55	244	54	72	10	2	0		0		.295	.295	.352	97	1	-3	26						3S	-0.3
1875	Ath-n	75	358	83	116	11	7	2		1		.324	.326	.411	138	18	12	49						*3/P1O	1.0
1876	Phi-N	54	236	45	70	12	7	1	31	3	2	.297	.305	.419	141	9	10	31				.915	-4	12/3O	0.5
1877	Bos-N	58	253	43	74	10	6	0	39	4	10	.292	.304	.379	110	4	2	30				.882	-9	S3	-0.4
1878	Bos-N	60	239	31	54	9	3	1	29	2	14	.226	.232	.301	69	-7	-9	17				.888	-1	*3/S	-0.7
1879	Bos-N	84	339	54	84	13	4	0	34	2	18	.248	.252	.310	82	-6	-7	27				.884	-12	S3	-1.4
1880	Bos-N	76	288	41	72	9	2	0	25	7	7	.250	.268	.295	94	-3	-2	23				.896	4	S3	0.6
1881	Bos-N	83	333	43	97	12	4	0	31	13	9	.291	.318	.351	116	4	6	38				.877	-3	*3/S	0.4
1882	Bos-N	81	319	44	80	8	1	2	38	24	25	.251	.303	.301	94	-1	-1	30				.856	-5	*3/S	-0.3
1883	Bos-N	94	414	101	134	28	15	3	73	17	12	.324	.350	.486	147	24	23	72				.866	-1	*3/OS	1.9
1884	Bos-N	110	468	102	**162**	28	7	3	61	29	22	.346	.384	.455	164	33	34	84				**.908**	-4	*3	2.7
1885	Bos-N	110	457	78	143	23	8	4	47	17	25	.313	.338	.425	151	21	24	67				.875	-0	*3S/21	2.4
1886	Bos-N	116	499	83	138	21	6	3	48	26	21	.277	.312	.361	108	2	5	63	18			.859	-5	OS32	0.0
1887	Bos-N	77	326	58	99	14	9	3	46	13	6	.304	.342	.429	115	6	6	55	17			.875	15	SO23	1.8
1888	Bos-N	28	110	16	24	3	1	1	16	7	3	.218	.277	.291	82	-2	-2	12	10			.859	-5	3/S	-0.7
Total	5 n	232	1080	253	344	39	24	5	65	5	3	.319	.322	.413	123	35	24	149	5					3/SP2O1	1.1
Total	13	1031	4281	739	1231	190	73	21	518	164	174	.288	.315	.381	119	86	88	550	45			.871	-30	3S/O21	6.8

■ DALE SVEUM
Sveum, Dale Curtis b: 11/23/63, Richmond, Cal. BB/TR, 6'2", 185 lbs. Deb: 5/12/86

YEAR	TM/L	G	AB	R	H	2B	3B	HR	RBI	BB	SO	AVG	OBP	SLG	PRO+	BR	/A	RC	SB	CS	SBR	FA	FR	POS	TPR
1986	Mil-A	91	317	35	78	13	2	7	35	32	63	.246	.317	.366	83	-6	-8	37	4	3	-1	.865	-8	32S	-1.6
1987	Mil-A	153	535	86	135	27	3	25	95	40	133	.252	.306	.454	95	-3	-5	70	2	6	-3	.965	-13	*S2	-0.8
1988	Mil-A	129	467	41	113	14	4	9	51	21	122	.242	.276	.347	73	-17	-18	45	1	0	0	.955	-6	*S/2D	-1.3
1990	Mil-A	48	117	15	23	7	0	1	12	12	30	.197	.282	.282	59	-6	-6	10	0	1	-1	.918	-5	32/1S	-1.2
1991	Mil-A	90	266	33	64	19	1	4	43	32	78	.241	.324	.365	93	-3	-2	31	2	4	-2	.968	-6	S3/2D	-0.7
1992	Phi-N	54	135	13	24	4	0	2	16	16	39	.178	.265	.252	47	-9	-9	9	0	0	0	.948	2	S/31	-0.6
	Chi-A	40	114	15	25	9	0	2	12	12	29	.219	.294	.351	82	-3	-3	12	1	1	-0	.944	-10	S/13	-1.1
Total	6	605	1951	238	462	93	10	50	264	165	494	.237	.298	.372	82	-49	-52	213	10	15	-6	.958	-47	S3/21D	-7.3

■ HARRY SWACINA
Swacina, Harry Joseph "Swats" b: 8/22/1881, St.Louis, Mo. d: 6/21/44, Birmingham, Ala. BR/TR, 6'2", 190 lbs. Deb: 9/13/07

YEAR	TM/L	G	AB	R	H	2B	3B	HR	RBI	BB	SO	AVG	OBP	SLG	PRO+	BR	/A	RC	SB	CS	SBR	FA	FR	POS	TPR
1907	Pit-N	26	95	9	19	1	1	0	10	4		.200	.240	.232	47	-6	-6	6	1			.996	-1	1	-0.9
1908	Pit-N	53	176	7	38	6	1	0	13	5		.216	.238	.261	59	-8	-8	12	4			.983	-5	1	-1.7
1914	Bal-F	158	617	70	173	26	8	0	90	14	23	.280	.297	.348	81	-15	-18	72	15			.985	10	*1	-1.2
1915	Bal-F	85	301	24	74	13	1	1	38	9	11	.246	.268	.306	66	-13	-14	29	9			.986	6	1/2	-1.1
Total	4	322	1189	110	304	46	11	1	151	32	34	.256	.276	.315	72	-42	-46	118	29			.986	10	1/2	-4.9

YEAR	TM/L	G	AB	R	H	2B	3B	HR	RBI	BB	SO	AVG	OBP	SLG	PRO+	BR	/A	RC	SB	CS	SBR	FA	FR	POS	TPR

■ ANDY SWAN Swan, Andrew J. Deb: 7/23/1884

1884	Was-a	5	21	3	3	1	0	0		0		.143	.143	.190	10	-2	-2	1				.824	-3	/13	-0.5
	Ric-a	3	10	2	5	0	0	0		0		.500	.500	.500	235	1	1	3				1.000	-0	/1	0.1
	Yr	8	31	5	8	1	0	0		0		.258	.258	.290	88	-1	-0	2				.902	-3	/13	-0.4

■ MARTY SWANDELL Swandell, John Martin (b: Martin Schwendel) b: 1845, Brooklyn, N.Y. d: 10/25/06, Brooklyn, N.Y. TL, 5'10.5", 146 lbs. Deb: 5/07/1872 U

1872	Eck-n	14	55	8	11	0	0	0	4	2	1	.200	.228	.200	39	-4	-2	3						/3O12	-0.2
1873	Res-n	2	9	1	1	0	0	0	1	0	0	.111	.111	.111	-37	-1	-1	0						/1	-0.1
Total	2 n	16	64	9	12	0	0	0	5	2	1	.188	.212	.188	27	-6	-4	3						/3O12	-0.3

■ PINKY SWANDER Swander, Edward O. b: 7/4/1880, Portsmouth, Ohio d: 10/24/44, Springfield, Mass. BL/TL, 5'9", 180 lbs. Deb: 9/18/03

1903	StL-A	14	51	9	14	2	2	0	6	10		.275	.413	.392	146	3	4	8	0			.833	-2	O	0.1
1904	StL-A	1	1	0	0	0	0	0	0	0		.000	.000	.000	-99	-0	-0	0	0			.000	0	H	0.0
Total	2	15	52	9	14	2	2	0	6	10		.269	.406	.385	142	3	3	8	0				-2	/O	0.1

■ EVAR SWANSON Swanson, Ernest Evar b: 10/15/02, DeKalb, Ill. d: 7/17/73, Galesburg, Ill. BR/TR, 5'9", 170 lbs. Deb: 4/18/29

1929	Cin-N	148	574	100	172	35	12	4	43	41	47	.300	.353	.423	96	-8	-4	84	33			.970	-3	*O	-1.6
1930	Cin-N	95	301	43	93	15	3	2	22	11	17	.309	.335	.399	81	-11	-9	39	4			.963	0	O	-1.2
1932	Chi-A	14	52	9	16	3	1	0	8	8	3	.308	.400	.404	116	1	2	9	3	1	0	.960	-2	O	-0.1
1933	Chi-A	144	539	102	165	25	7	1	63	93	35	.306	.411	.384	117	14	17	92	19	11	-1	.973	-5	O	0.4
1934	Chi-A	117	426	71	127	9	5	0	34	59	31	.298	.385	.343	86	-4	-6	61	10	3	1	.980	-3	*O	-1.2
Total	5	518	1892	325	573	87	28	7	170	212	133	.303	.376	.390	98	-9	-0	285	69	15		.971	-14	O	-3.7

■ KARL SWANSON Swanson, Karl Edward b: 12/17/03, N.Henderson, Ill. BL/TR, 5'10", 155 lbs. Deb: 8/12/28

1928	Chi-A	22	64	2	9	1	0	0	6	4	7	.141	.191	.156	-8	-10	-10	3	3	0	1	.943	1	2	-0.7
1929	Chi-A	2	1	0	0	0	0	0	0	0	0	.000	.000	.000	-99	-0	-0	0	0	0	0	.000	0	H	0.0
Total	2	24	65	2	9	1	0	0	6	4	7	.138	.188	.154	-9	-10	-10	3	3	0	1	.918	1	/2	-0.7

■ STAN SWANSON Swanson, Stanley Lawrence b: 5/19/44, Yuba City, Cal. BR/TR, 5'11", 168 lbs. Deb: 6/23/71

| 1971 | Mon-N | 49 | 106 | 14 | 26 | 3 | 0 | 2 | 11 | 10 | 13 | .245 | .310 | .330 | 81 | -3 | -3 | 11 | 1 | 3 | -2 | 1.000 | -1 | O | -0.7 |

■ BILL SWANSON Swanson, William Andrew b: 10/12/1888, New York, N.Y. d: 10/14/54, New York, N.Y. BB/TR, 5'6", 156 lbs. Deb: 9/02/14

| 1914 | Bos-A | 11 | 20 | 0 | 4 | 2 | 0 | 0 | 0 | 3 | 4 | .200 | .304 | .300 | 82 | -0 | -0 | 2 | 0 | 1 | -1 | .875 | -3 | /23S | -0.5 |

■ ED SWARTWOOD Swartwood, Cyrus Edward b: 1/12/1859, Rockford, Ill. d: 5/15/24, Pittsburgh, Pa. BL/TR, 198 lbs. Deb: 8/11/1881 U

1881	Buf-N	1	3	0	1	0	0	0		1	0	.333	.500	.333	170	0	0	1				.500	-1	/O	0.0
1882	Pit-a	76	325	**86**	107	**18**	11	4		21		.329	.370	.489	197	29	32	60				.788	-8	*O/1	2.0
1883	Pit-a	94	413	86	**147**	24	8	3		24		**.356**	**.391**	.475	**186**	35	38	79				.936	2	1O/C	2.9
1884	Pit-a	102	399	74	115	19	6	0		33		.288	.365	.366	140	20	19	55				.804	-3	*O1/3P	1.1
1885	Bro-a	99	399	80	106	8	9	0		36		.266	.334	.331	113	7	7	45				.851	-10	*O/1SC	-0.5
1886	Bro-a	122	471	95	132	13	10	3		**70**		.280	.377	.369	135	23	22	82	37			.884	7	*O/C	2.3
1887	Bro-a	91	363	72	92	14	8	1		46		.253	.342	.344	93	-2	-3	54	29			.835	2	O	-0.2
1890	Tol-a	126	462	106	151	23	11	3		80		.327	.444	.444	160	42	40	117	53			.925	8	*O/P	3.8
1892	Pit-N	13	42	8	10	1	0	0	4	13	11	.238	.418	.262	109	2	2	5	1			.933	4	O	0.5
Total	9	724	2877	607	861	120	63	14	4	324	11	.299	.379	.399	144	157	157	497	120			.856	0	0/1CPS3	11.9

■ CHARLIE SWEASY Sweasy, Charles James (b: Charles James Swasey) b: 11/2/1847, Newark, N.J. d: 3/30/08, Newark, N.J. BR/TR, 5'9", 172 lbs. Deb: 5/19/1871 M

1871	Oly-n	5	19	5	4	1	0	0	4	1	0	.211	.250	.263	50	-1	-1	1	0					/2	-0.1
1872	Cle-n	12	52	8	16	0	0	0	6	2	1	.308	.333	.308	104	-0	1	6						2/O	0.0
1873	Bos-n	1	4	0	1	0	0	0	0	0	0	.250	.250	.250	44	-0	-0	0						/2	0.0
1874	Bal-n	8	33	2	8	0	0	0		2		.242	.286	.242	70	-1	-1	2						/2O	-0.1
	Atl-n	10	44	4	5	1	0	0		2		.114	.114	.136	-24	-6	-5	1						2	-0.4
	Yr	18	77	6	13	1	0	0		2		.169	.190	.182	20	-7	-6	3						2/O	-0.5
1875	RS-n	19	76	7	13	0	0	0		4		.171	.213	.171	38	-5	-4	3						2M	-0.3
1876	Cin-N	56	225	18	46	5	2	0	10	2	5	.204	.211	.244	60	-11	-6	12				.864	2	*2/O	-0.3
1878	Pro-N	55	212	23	37	3	0	0	8	7	23	.175	.201	.189	29	-16	-16	8				.846	-9	*2	-1.9
Total	5 n	55	228	26	47	2	0	0	10	9	1	.206	.236	.215	49	-13	-10	13						/2O	-0.9
Total	2	111	437	41	83	8	2	0	18	9	28	.190	.206	.217	44	-27	-22	20				.855	-6	2/O	-2.2

■ BUCK SWEENEY Sweeney, Charles Francis b: 4/15/1890, Pittsburgh, Pa. d: 3/13/55, Pittsburgh, Pa. Deb: 9/28/14

| 1914 | Phi-A | 1 | 1 | 0 | 0 | 0 | 0 | 0 | 0 | 0 | 1 | .000 | .000 | .000 | -99 | -0 | -0 | 0 | 0 | | | 1.000 | -0 | /O | -0.1 |

■ CHARLIE SWEENEY Sweeney, Charles J. b: 4/13/1863, San Francisco, Cal d: 4/4/02, San Francisco, Cal. BR/TR, 5'10.5", 181 lbs. Deb: 5/11/1882

1882	Pro-N	4	4	0	0	0	0	0	0	0	1	.000	.000	.000	-99	-1	-1	0				.500	1	/O	-0.1
1883	Pro-N	22	87	9	19	3	0	0	15	2	10	.218	.236	.253	47	-5	-6	5				.863	3	P/O	0.0
1884	Pro-N	41	168	24	50	9	0	1	19	11	17	.298	.341	.369	126	5	5	22				.940	-2	PO/1	-0.2
	StL-U	45	171	31	54	14	2	1		10		.316	.354	.439	161	12	11	27				.943	4	PO/1	0.1
1885	StL-N	71	267	27	55	7	1	0	24	12	33	.206	.240	.240	59	-13	-10	16				.827	-3	OP	-1.0
1886	StL-N	17	64	4	16	2	0	0	7	3	10	.250	.284	.281	77	-2	-1	5	0			.929	-3	P/OS	-0.1
1887	Cle-a	36	133	22	30	4	4	0		21		.226	.331	.316	85	-2	-2	18	11			.936	-4	10/PS3	-0.6
Total	6	233	894	117	224	39	7	2	65	59	71	.251	.297	.317	95	-7	-4	93	11			.909	-3	P/O1S3	-1.9

■ DAN SWEENEY Sweeney, Daniel J. b: 1/28/1868, Philadelphia, Pa. d: 7/13/13, Louisville, Ky. 5'5", 160 lbs. Deb: 4/18/1895

| 1895 | Lou-N | 22 | 90 | 18 | 24 | 5 | 0 | 1 | 16 | 17 | 2 | .267 | .389 | .356 | 101 | 0 | 1 | 14 | 2 | | | .794 | -4 | O | -0.4 |

■ JEFF SWEENEY Sweeney, Edward Francis "Ed" b: 7/19/1888, Chicago, Ill. d: 7/4/47, Chicago, Ill. BR/TR, 6'1", 200 lbs. Deb: 5/16/08

1908	NY-A	32	82	4	12	2	0	0	2	5		.146	.195	.171	19	-7	-7	3	0			.955	-0	C/1O	-0.6
1909	NY-A	67	176	19	47	3	0	0	21	16		.267	.328	.284	93	-1	-1	18	3			.947	3	C/1	0.8
1910	NY-A	78	215	25	43	4	4	0	13	17		.200	.271	.256	62	-9	-10	18	12			.974	6	C	0.3
1911	NY-A	83	229	17	53	6	5	0	18	14		.231	.290	.301	63	-10	-12	24	8			.964	-3	C	-0.8
1912	NY-A	110	351	37	94	12	1	0	30	27		.268	.325	.308	77	-8	-11	37	6			.955	-10	*C	-1.0
1913	NY-A	117	351	35	93	10	2	2	40	37	41	.265	.348	.322	96	-0	-1	42	11			.964	9	*C/1O	1.9
1914	NY-A	87	258	25	55	8	1	1	22	35	30	.213	.316	.264	75	-7	-7	26	19	6	2	.980	2	C	0.5
1915	NY-A	53	137	12	26	2	0	0	5	25	12	.190	.319	.204	57	-6	-6	11	3	3	-1	.975	-6	C	-0.8
1919	Pit-N	17	42	0	4	1	0	0	5	5	5	.095	.191	.119	-5	-5	-5	1	1			.944	-3	C	-0.8
Total	9	644	1841	174	427	48	13	3	151	181	89	.232	.310	.277	73	-54	-60	180	63	9		.964	-2	C/1O	-0.6

■ HANK SWEENEY Sweeney, Henry Leon b: 12/28/15, Franklin, Tenn. d: 5/6/80, Columbia, Tenn. BL/TL, 6', 185 lbs. Deb: 10/01/44

| 1944 | Pit-N | 1 | 2 | 0 | 0 | 0 | 0 | 0 | 0 | 0 | 1 | .000 | .000 | .000 | -96 | -1 | -1 | 0 | 0 | | | 1.000 | 0 | /1 | 0.0 |

■ JERRY SWEENEY Sweeney, Jeremiah H. b: 1860, Boston, Mass. d: 8/25/1891, Boston, Mass. 5'9.5", 157 lbs. Deb: 8/22/1884

| 1884 | KC-U | 31 | 129 | 16 | 34 | 3 | 0 | 0 | | 4 | | .264 | .286 | .287 | 108 | -1 | 2 | 11 | | | | .958 | 3 | 1 | 0.1 |

■ ROONEY SWEENEY Sweeney, John J. b: 1860, d: 6/1/1889, New York, N.Y. 5'8", 155 lbs. Deb: 7/25/1883

| 1883 | Bal-a | 25 | 101 | 13 | 21 | 5 | 2 | 0 | | 4 | | .208 | .238 | .297 | 69 | -3 | -4 | 7 | | | | .878 | -1 | C/O | -0.3 |
| 1884 | Bal-U | 48 | 186 | 37 | 42 | 7 | 1 | 0 | | 15 | | .226 | .284 | .274 | 81 | -2 | -5 | 15 | | | | .917 | -9 | CO/3 | -0.9 |

YEAR	TM/L	G	AB	R	H	2B	3B	HR	RBI	BB	SO	AVG	OBP	SLG	PRO+	BR	/A	RC	SB	CS	SBR	FA	FR	POS	TPR
1885	StL-N	3	11	1	1	0	0	0	0	0	4	.091	.091	.091	-44	-2	-2	0				.750	-0	/OC	-0.2
Total	3	76	298	51	64	12	3	0	0	19	4	.215	.262	.275	73	-6	-10	22				.905	-10	/CO3	-1.4

■ PETE SWEENEY

Sweeney, Peter Jay b: 12/31/1863, California d: 8/22/01, San Francisco, Cal BR/TR, Deb: 9/28/1888

YEAR	TM/L	G	AB	R	H	2B	3B	HR	RBI	BB	SO	AVG	OBP	SLG	PRO+	BR	/A	RC	SB	CS	SBR	FA	FR	POS	TPR
1888	Was-N	11	44	3	8	0	1	0	5	0	4	.182	.182	.227	33	-3	-3	2	0			.784	-0	/3O	-0.3
1889	Was-N	49	193	13	44	7	3	1	23	11	26	.228	.284	.311	72	-9	-7	20	8			.802	-10	3/2O	-1.4
	StL-a	9	38	8	14	2	0	0	8	1	5	.368	.415	.421	125	2	1	8	2			.780	-1	/3O	0.0
1890	StL-a	49	190	23	34	3	2	0		17		.179	.271	.216	40	-12	-17	14	8			.880	-5	23/1O	-1.8
	Lou-a	2	7	1	1	1	0	0		1		.143	.250	.286	61	-0	-0	1	1			.889	-1	/S	-0.1
	Phi-a	14	49	5	8	1	1	0		7		.163	.281	.224	52	-3	-3	3	0			.915	-6	/2O3	-0.7
	Yr	65	246	29	43	5	3	0		25		.175	.272	.220	43	-15	-19	18	9			.889	-12	23/O1S	-2.6
Total	3	134	521	53	109	14	7	1	36	37	35	.209	.280	.269	59	-25	-28	47	19			.799	-24	/32O1S	-4.3

■ BILL SWEENEY

Sweeney, William John b: 3/6/1886, Covington, Ky. d: 5/26/48, Cambridge, Mass. BR/TR, 5'11", 175 lbs. Deb: 6/14/07

YEAR	TM/L	G	AB	R	H	2B	3B	HR	RBI	BB	SO	AVG	OBP	SLG	PRO+	BR	/A	RC	SB	CS	SBR	FA	FR	POS	TPR
1907	Chi-N	3	10	1	1	0	0	0	1	1		.100	.182	.100	-11	-1	-1	0	1			.571	-4	/S	-0.6
	Bos-N	58	191	24	50	2	0	0	18	15		.262	.316	.272	85	-3	-3	19	8			.871	0	3SO/21	-0.3
	Yr	61	201	25	51	2	0	0	19	16		.254	.309	.264	80	-4	-4	20	9			.871	-3	3SO/21	-0.9
1908	Bos-N	127	418	44	102	15	3	0	40	45		.244	.317	.294	97	-1	-0	45	17			.930	12	*3/S2	1.8
1909	Bos-N	138	493	44	120	19	3	1	36	37		.243	.296	.300	81	-9	-12	50	25			.903	7	*3S	-0.1
1910	Bos-N	150	499	43	133	22	4	5	46	61	28	.267	.349	.357	101	4	1	71	25			.903	-1	*S31	0.5
1911	Bos-N	137	523	92	164	33	6	3	63	77	26	.314	.404	.417	120	23	17	101	33			.944	11	*2	2.6
1912	Bos-N	153	593	84	204	31	13	1	100	68	34	.344	.416	.445	133	31	30	123	27			.959	**27**	*2	5.1
1913	Bos-N	139	502	65	129	17	6	0	47	66	50	.257	.347	.315	88	-4	-6	59	18			.939	1	*2	-0.7
1914	Chi-N	134	463	45	101	14	5	1	38	53	15	.218	.298	.276	71	-16	-15	44	18			.954	15	*2	-0.2
Total	8	1039	3692	442	1004	153	40	11	389	423	153	.272	.349	.344	100	24	10	513	172			.845	67	23S/1O	8.1

■ BILL SWEENEY

Sweeney, William Joseph b: 12/29/04, Cleveland, Ohio d: 4/18/57, San Diego, Cal. BR/TR, 5'11", 180 lbs. Deb: 4/13/28

YEAR	TM/L	G	AB	R	H	2B	3B	HR	RBI	BB	SO	AVG	OBP	SLG	PRO+	BR	/A	RC	SB	CS	SBR	FA	FR	POS	TPR
1928	Det-A	89	309	47	78	15	5	0	19	15	28	.252	.287	.333	62	-17	-18	28	12	9	-2	.993	4	1/O	-2.2
1930	Bos-A	88	243	32	75	13	0	4	30	9	15	.309	.333	.412	91	-5	-4	32	5	3	-0	.997	-1	1/3	-0.9
1931	Bos-A	131	498	48	147	30	3	1	58	20	30	.295	.322	.373	87	-13	-10	56	5	12	-6	**.993**	10	*1	-1.6
Total	3	308	1050	127	300	58	8	5	107	44	73	.286	.314	.370	80	-36	-31	117	22	24	-8	.949	13	1/O3	-4.7

■ RICK SWEET

Sweet, Ricky Joe b: 9/7/52, Longview, Wash. BB/TR, 6'1", 200 lbs. Deb: 4/08/78 C

YEAR	TM/L	G	AB	R	H	2B	3B	HR	RBI	BB	SO	AVG	OBP	SLG	PRO+	BR	/A	RC	SB	CS	SBR	FA	FR	POS	TPR
1978	SD-N	88	226	15	50	8	0	1	11	27	22	.221	.307	.270	68	-11	-9	19	1	4	-2	.984	3	C	-0.7
1982	NY-N	3	3	0	1	0	0	0	0	0	1	.333	.333	.333	88	-0	-0	0	0	0	0	.000	0	/H	0.0
	Sea-A	88	258	29	66	6	1	4	24	20	24	.256	.314	.333	76	-8	-8	29	3	0	1	.993	-6	C	-1.1
1983	Sea-A	93	249	18	55	9	0	1	22	13	26	.221	.260	.269	44	-18	-19	15	2	2	-1	.987	-3	C	-1.9
Total	3	272	736	62	172	23	1	6	57	60	73	.234	.294	.292	63	-37	-37	63	6	6	-2	.988	-7	C	-3.7

■ HAM SWEIGERT

Sweigert, Hampton Deb: 10/12/1890

YEAR	TM/L	G	AB	R	H	2B	3B	HR	RBI	BB	SO	AVG	OBP	SLG	PRO+	BR	/A	RC	SB	CS	SBR	FA	FR	POS	TPR
1890	Phi-a	1	1	0	0	0	0	0		1		.000	.500	.000	53	0	0	1	1			.000	-0	/O	0.0

■ AUGIE SWENTOR

Swentor, August William b: 11/21/1899, Seymour, Conn. d: 11/10/69, Waterbury, Conn. BR/TR, 6', 185 lbs. Deb: 9/12/22

YEAR	TM/L	G	AB	R	H	2B	3B	HR	RBI	BB	SO	AVG	OBP	SLG	PRO+	BR	/A	RC	SB	CS	SBR	FA	FR	POS	TPR
1922	Chi-A	1	1	0	0	0	0	0	0	0	1	.000	.000	.000	-99	-0	-0	0	0	0	0	.000	0	H	0.0

■ STEVE SWETONIC

Swetonic, Stephen Albert b: 8/13/03, Mt.Pleasant, Pa. d: 4/22/74, Canonsburg, Pa. BR/TR, 5'11", 185 lbs. Deb: 4/17/29

YEAR	TM/L	G	AB	R	H	2B	3B	HR	RBI	BB	SO	AVG	OBP	SLG	PRO+	BR	/A	RC	SB	CS	SBR	FA	FR	POS	TPR
1929	Pit-N	42	48	11	13	3	1	0	2	2	6	.271	.314	.375	68	-2	-3	6	0			.960	2	P	0.0
1930	Pit-N	23	36	2	4	2	0	0	2	1	5	.111	.135	.167	-27	-8	-8	1	0			1.000	-1	P	0.0
1931	Pit-N	14	7	0	1	0	0	0	0	1	3	.143	.250	.143	8	-1	-1	0	0			1.000	-0	P	0.0
1932	Pit-N	24	54	1	5	1	0	0	2	2	7	.093	.125	.111	-37	-10	-10	1	0			1.000	-1	P	0.0
1933	Pit-N	31	55	3	11	0	2	0	4	1	7	.200	.214	.273	38	-4	-4	3	0			.950	-1	P	0.0
1935	Pit-N	1	0	1	0	0	0	0	0	0	0	—	—	—	—	0	0	0	0			.000	0	R	0.0
Total	6	135	200	18	34	6	3	0	10	7	28	.170	.202	.230	13	-25	-26	11	0			.973	-2	P	0.0

■ POP SWETT

Swett, William E. b: 4/16/1870, San Francisco, Cal d: 11/22/37, San Francisco, Cal Deb: 5/03/1890

YEAR	TM/L	G	AB	R	H	2B	3B	HR	RBI	BB	SO	AVG	OBP	SLG	PRO+	BR	/A	RC	SB	CS	SBR	FA	FR	POS	TPR
1890	Bos-P	37	94	16	18	4	3	1	12	16	26	.191	.321	.330	71	-3	-4	12	4			.820	-8	C/O	-0.8

■ BOB SWIFT

Swift, Robert Virgil b: 3/6/15, Salina, Kan. d: 10/17/66, Detroit, Mich. BR/TR, 5'11.5", 180 lbs. Deb: 4/16/40 MC

YEAR	TM/L	G	AB	R	H	2B	3B	HR	RBI	BB	SO	AVG	OBP	SLG	PRO+	BR	/A	RC	SB	CS	SBR	FA	FR	POS	TPR
1940	StL-A	130	398	37	97	20	1	0	39	28	39	.244	.295	.299	53	-27	-28	36	1	0	0	.980	-20	*C	-3.7
1941	StL-A	63	170	13	44	7	0	0	21	22	11	.259	.344	.300	69	-6	-7	19	2	0	1	.985	-4	C	-0.6
1942	StL-A	29	76	3	15	4	0	1	8	3	5	.197	.228	.289	44	-6	-6	5	0	2	-1	1.000	-1	C	-0.7
	Phi-A	60	192	9	44	3	0	0	15	13	17	.229	.278	.245	48	-13	-13	13	1	2	-1	.970	2	C	-0.8
	Yr	89	268	12	59	7	0	1	23	16	22	.220	.264	.257	47	-19	-19	18	1	4	-2	.977	1	C	-1.5
1943	Phi-A	77	224	16	43	5	1	1	11	35	16	.192	.301	.237	58	-11	-11	17	0	0	0	.976	-3	C	-0.9
1944	Det-A	80	247	15	63	11	1	1	19	27	27	.255	.331	.320	82	-4	-6	27	2	0	1	.982	1	C	0.1
1945	*Det-A	95	279	19	65	5	0	0	24	26	22	.233	.298	.251	56	-14	-16	22	1	0	0	.988	1	C	-0.9
1946	Det-A	42	107	13	25	2	0	2	10	14	7	.234	.322	.308	72	-3	-4	11	0	0	0	.980	-4	C	-0.7
1947	Det-A	97	279	23	70	11	0	1	21	33	16	.251	.330	.301	74	-8	-9	29	2	2	-1	.989	-0	C	-0.4
1948	Det-A	113	292	23	65	6	0	4	33	51	29	.223	.338	.284	65	-13	-14	32	1	0	0	.991	6	*C	-0.1
1949	Det-A	74	189	16	45	6	0	2	18	26	20	.238	.330	.302	68	-9	-9	21	0	0	0	.989	1	C	-0.5
1950	Det-A	67	132	14	30	4	0	2	9	25	6	.227	.350	.303	66	-6	-6	15	0	0	0	.995	8	C	0.3
1951	Det-A	44	104	8	20	0	0	0	5	12	10	.192	.276	.192	28	-10	-10	7	0	0	0	.982	2	C	-0.7
1952	Det-A	28	58	3	8	1	0	0	4	7	7	.138	.242	.155	12	-7	-7	2	0	0	0	.977	6	C	0.0
1953	Det-A	2	3	0	1	1	0	0	1	2	1	.333	.600	.667	245	1	1	2	0	0	0	1.000	1	/C	0.2
Total	14	1001	2750	212	635	86	3	14	238	324	233	.231	.313	.280	61	-135	-144	256	10	6	-1	.985	-5	C	-9.4

■ JOSH SWINDELL

Swindell, Joshua Ernest b: 7/5/1883, Rose Hill, Kan. d: 3/19/69, Fruita, Colo. BR/TR, 6', 180 lbs. Deb: 9/16/11

YEAR	TM/L	G	AB	R	H	2B	3B	HR	RBI	BB	SO	AVG	OBP	SLG	PRO+	BR	/A	RC	SB	CS	SBR	FA	FR	POS	TPR
1911	Cle-A	4	4	0	1	0	0	0	0	0		.250	.250	.250	39	-0	-0	0	0			.800	-0	/P	0.0
1913	Cle-A	1	0	0	0	0	0	0	0	0	0	—	—	—	—	0	0	0	0			.000	0	H	0.0
Total	2	5	4	0	1	0	0	0	0	0	0	.250	.250	.250	39	-0	-0	0	0			.977	-0	/P	0.0

■ CHARLIE SWINDELLS

Swindells, Charles Jay "Swin" b: 10/26/1878, Rockford, Ill. d: 7/22/40, Portland, Ore. BR/TR, 5'11.5", 180 lbs. Deb: 9/07/04

YEAR	TM/L	G	AB	R	H	2B	3B	HR	RBI	BB	SO	AVG	OBP	SLG	PRO+	BR	/A	RC	SB	CS	SBR	FA	FR	POS	TPR
1904	StL-N	3	8	0	1	0	0	0	0	0		.125	.125	.125	-24	-1	-1	0	0			1.000	-0	/C	-0.1

■ STEVE SWISHER

Swisher, Steven Eugene b: 8/9/51, Parkersburg, W.Va. BR/TR, 6'2", 205 lbs. Deb: 6/14/74

YEAR	TM/L	G	AB	R	H	2B	3B	HR	RBI	BB	SO	AVG	OBP	SLG	PRO+	BR	/A	RC	SB	CS	SBR	FA	FR	POS	TPR
1974	Chi-N	90	280	21	60	5	0	5	27	37	63	.214	.310	.286	65	-11	-13	25	0	3	-2	.987	-1	C	-1.2
1975	Chi-N	93	254	20	54	16	2	1	22	30	57	.213	.306	.303	66	-10	-12	22	1	0	0	.979	-8	C	-1.6
1976	Chi-N☆	109	377	25	89	13	3	5	42	20	82	.236	.278	.326	65	-15	-19	33	2	1	0	.983	-3	*C	-2.0
1977	Chi-N	74	205	21	39	7	0	5	15	9	47	.190	.231	.298	37	-18	-20	14	0	0	0	.976	-3	C	-2.2
1978	StL-N	45	115	11	32	5	1	1	10	8	14	.278	.331	.365	96	-1	-1	13	1	0	0	.991	6	C	0.7
1979	StL-N	38	73	4	11	1	1	1	3	6	17	.151	.215	.233	22	-8	-8	4	0	0	0	.974	1	C	-0.6
1980	StL-N	18	24	2	6	1	0	0	2	1	7	.250	.280	.292	58	-1	-1	1	0	0	0	.957	0	/C	-0.1
1981	SD-N	16	28	2	4	0	0	0	0	2	11	.143	.200	.143	-2	-4	-3	1	0	0	0	.971	-0	C	-0.4
1982	SD-N	26	58	2	10	1	0	2	3	5	24	.172	.238	.293	50	-4	-4	4	0	0	0	.981	1	C	-0.2
Total	9	509	1414	108	305	49	7	20	124	118	322	.216	.281	.303	59	-72	-81	117	4	4	-1	.982	-5	C	-7.6

YEAR	TM/L	G	AB	R	H	2B	3B	HR	RBI	BB	SO	AVG	OBP	SLG	PRO+	BR	/A	RC	SB	CS	SBR	FA	FR	POS	TPR

■ RON SWOBODA   Swoboda, Ronald Alan "Rocky"   b: 6/30/44, Baltimore, Md.   BR/TR, 6'2", 205 lbs.   Deb: 4/12/65

1965	NY-N	135	399	52	91	15	3	19	50	33	102	.228	.292	.424	102	-2	-0	47	2	3	-1	.947	-2	*O	-0.9
1966	NY-N	112	342	34	76	9	4	8	50	31	76	.222	.296	.342	79	-11	-10	34	4	2	0	.987	-4	O	-1.9
1967	NY-N	134	449	47	126	17	3	13	53	41	96	.281	.342	.419	119	10	10	65	3	1	0	.957	3	*O1	0.8
1968	NY-N	132	450	46	109	14	6	11	59	52	113	.242	.326	.373	109	6	6	55	8	1	2	.975	4	*O	0.6
1969	*NY-N	109	327	38	77	10	2	9	52	43	90	.235	.328	.361	91	-3	-4	39	1	1	-0	.988	-2	O	-1.1
1970	NY-N	115	245	29	57	8	2	9	40	40	72	.233	.343	.392	96	-1	-1	33	2	4	-2	.984	-14	*O	-2.0
1971	Mon-N	39	75	7	19	4	3	0	6	11	16	.253	.364	.387	112	2	2	10	0	1	-1	.977	2	O	0.2
	NY-A	54	138	17	36	2	1	2	20	27	35	.261	.393	.333	114	3	4	20	0	0	0	.965	-3	O	-0.1
1972	NY-A	63	113	9	28	8	0	1	12	17	29	.248	.346	.345	110	1	2	14	0	1	-1	.983	-5	O/1	-0.5
1973	NY-A	35	43	6	5	0	0	1	2	4	18	.116	.191	.186	7	-5	-5	2	0	0	0	1.000	-4	O/D	-1.0
Total	9	928	2581	285	624	87	24	73	344	299	647	.242	.325	.379	101	0	4	320	20	14	-2	.972	-25	O/1D	-5.9

■ LOU SYLVESTER   Sylvester, Louis J.   b: 2/14/1855, Springfield, Ill.   BR/TR, 5'3", 165 lbs.   Deb: 4/18/1884

1884	Cin-U	82	333	67	89	13	8	2		18		.267	.305	.372	119	10	5	39				.792	0	*O/PS	0.4
1886	Lou-a	45	154	41	35	5	3	0	29			.227	.350	.299	100	2	1	18	3			.913	-0	O	0.0
	Cin-a	17	55	10	10	0	0	3	7			.182	.286	.345	96	-0	-0	6	2			.909	1	O	0.0
	Yr	62	209	51	45	5	3	3	36			.215	.333	.311	99	2	1	24	5			.912	1	O	0.0
1887	StL-a	29	112	20	25	4	3	1	13			.223	.310	.339	75	-2	-5	16	13			.923	2	O/2	-0.2
Total	3	173	654	138	159	22	14	6		67		.243	.315	.347	104	10	1	79	18			.854	3	O/PS2	0.2

■ JOE SZEKELY   Szekely, Joseph   b: 2/2/25, Cleveland, Ohio   BR/TR, 5'11", 180 lbs.   Deb: 9/13/53

| 1953 | Cin-N | 5 | 13 | 0 | 1 | 0 | 0 | 0 | 0 | 0 | 3 | .077 | .077 | .077 | -59 | -3 | -3 | 0 | 0 | 0 | 0 | 1.000 | 1 | /O | -0.2 |

■ KEN SZOTKIEWICZ   Szotkiewicz, Kenneth John   b: 2/25/47, Wilmington, Del.   BL/TR, 6', 165 lbs.   Deb: 4/07/70

| 1970 | Det-A | 47 | 84 | 9 | 9 | 1 | 0 | 3 | 9 | 12 | 29 | .107 | .219 | .226 | 23 | -9 | -9 | 5 | 0 | 0 | 0 | .971 | 9 | S | 0.3 |

■ JERRY TABB   Tabb, Jerry Lynn   b: 3/17/52, Altus, Okla.   BL/TR, 6'2", 195 lbs.   Deb: 9/08/76

1976	Chi-N	11	24	2	7	0	0	0	0	3	2	.292	.370	.292	82	-0	-0	3	0	0	0	1.000	-1	/1	-0.1
1977	Oak-A	51	144	8	32	3	0	6	19	10	26	.222	.273	.368	74	-6	-5	13	0	1	-1	.993	-2	1/D	-1.0
1978	Oak-A	12	9	0	1	0	0	0	1	2	5	.111	.273	.111	12	-1	-1	0	0	0	0	1.000	-0	/1D	-0.1
Total	3	74	177	10	40	3	0	6	20	15	33	.226	.286	.345	72	-7	-7	16	0	1	-1	.994	-3	/1D	-1.2

■ PAT TABLER   Tabler, Patrick Sean   b: 2/2/58, Hamilton, Ohio   BR/TR, 6'2", 200 lbs.   Deb: 8/21/81

1981	Chi-N	35	101	11	19	3	1	1	5	13	26	.188	.281	.267	54	-6	-6	7	0	1	-1	.982	1	2	-0.5
1982	Chi-N	25	85	9	20	4	2	1	7	6	20	.235	.293	.365	81	-2	-2	9	0	0	0	.949	-3	3	-0.8
1983	Cle-A	124	430	56	125	23	5	6	65	66	63	.291	.374	.409	111	11	8	63	2	4	-2	.948	-3	O3/2D	-1.1
1984	Cle-A	144	473	66	137	21	3	10	68	47	62	.290	.358	.410	110	8	7	68	3	1	0	.998	-13	103/2D	-1.1
1985	Cle-A	117	404	47	111	18	3	5	59	27	55	.275	.323	.371	90	-6	-5	43	0	6	-4	.983	1	1D/32	-1.4
1986	Cle-A	130	473	61	154	29	2	6	48	29	75	.326	.368	.433	119	11	12	74	3	1	0	.990	1	*1D	0.6
1987	Cle-A★	151	553	66	170	34	3	11	86	51	84	.307	.372	.439	113	12	12	93	5	2	0	.984	5	1D	1.1
1988	Cle-A	41	143	16	32	5	1	1	17	23	27	.224	.335	.294	76	-3	-4	15	1	0	0	1.000	-1	D1	-0.5
	KC-A	89	301	37	93	17	2	1	49	23	41	.309	.362	.389	109	4	4	42	2	3	-1	.986	-2	DO/13	0.0
	Yr	130	444	53	125	22	3	2	66	46	68	.282	.353	.358	98	1	0	57	3	3	-1	.986	-2	DO1/3	-0.5
1989	KC-A	123	390	36	101	11	1	2	42	37	42	.259	.326	.308	80	-10	-9	39	0	0	0	.970	2	OD1/23	-1.0
1990	KC-A	75	195	12	53	14	0	1	19	20	21	.272	.343	.359	98	-1	-0	22	0	2	-1	.986	-0	OD/31	-0.3
	NY-N	17	43	6	12	1	1	1	10	3	8	.279	.340	.419	108	0	0	6	0	0	0	1.000	1	O	0.1
1991	*Tor-A	82	185	20	40	5	1	1	21	29	21	.216	.326	.270	64	-7	-8	18	0	0	0	.985	0	D1/O	-1.0
1992	*Tor-A	49	135	11	34	5	0	0	16	11	14	.252	.308	.289	65	-6	-6	11	0	0	0	1.000	-1	1/O3D	-1.0
Total	12	1202	3911	454	1101	190	25	47	512	375	559	.282	.348	.379	99	7	2	511	16	20	-7	.988	-14	1DO/32	-5.8

■ GREG TABOR   Tabor, Gregory Steven   b: 5/21/61, Castro Valley, Cal.   BR/TR, 6' ", 165 lbs.   Deb: 9/10/87

| 1987 | Tex-A | 9 | 9 | 4 | 1 | 0 | 0 | 0 | 0 | 0 | 4 | .111 | .111 | .222 | -15 | -1 | -1 | 0 | 0 | 0 | 0 | .938 | 4 | /2D | 0.2 |

■ JIM TABOR   Tabor, James Reubin "Rawhide"   b: 11/5/16, New Hope, Ala.   d: 8/22/53, Sacramento, Cal.   BR/TR, 6'2", 175 lbs.   Deb: 8/02/38

1938	Bos-A	19	57	8	18	3	2	1	8	1	6	.316	.328	.491	98	-0	-1	8	0	1	-1	.889	1	3/S	0.0
1939	Bos-A	149	577	76	167	33	8	14	95	40	54	.289	.337	.447	95	-3	-6	82	16	10	-1	.923	7	*3	0.1
1940	Bos-A	120	459	73	131	28	6	21	81	42	58	.285	.345	.510	114	11	8	81	14	10	-2	.926	5	*3	1.3
1941	Bos-A	126	498	65	139	29	3	16	101	36	48	.279	.328	.446	100	-0	-2	69	17	9	-0	.930	2	*3	0.3
1942	Bos-A	139	508	56	128	18	2	12	75	37	47	.252	.303	.366	85	-10	-12	53	6	13	-6	.924	-9	*3	-2.6
1943	Bos-A	137	537	57	130	26	3	13	85	43	54	.242	.299	.374	95	-4	-5	59	7	7	-2	.938	-8	*3/O	-1.6
1944	Bos-A	116	438	54	125	25	3	13	72	31	38	.285	.340	.445	123	10	11	63	4	4	-1	.950	3	*3	1.5
1946	Phi-N	124	463	53	124	15	2	10	50	36	51	.268	.322	.374	100	-3	-1	56	3			.954	-3	*3	-0.3
1947	Phi-N	75	251	27	59	14	0	4	31	20	21	.235	.297	.339	71	-12	-11	25	2			.916	-17	3	-2.8
Total	9	1005	3788	473	1021	191	29	104	598	286	377	.270	.322	.418	99	-12	-19	496	69	54		.933	-19	3/OS	-4.1

■ JEFF TACKETT   Tackett, Jeffrey Wilson   b: 12/1/65, Fresno, Cal.   BR/TR, 6'2", 200 lbs.   Deb: 9/11/91

1991	Bal-A	6	8	1	1	0	0	0	0	2	1	.125	.300	.125	23	-1	-1	1	0	0	0	1.000	0	/C	0.0
1992	Bal-A	66	179	21	43	8	1	5	24	17	28	.240	.313	.380	94	-2	-2	19	0	0	0	.997	5	C/3	0.7
Total	2	72	187	22	44	8	1	5	24	19	30	.235	.313	.369	91	-3	-2	20	0	0	0	.997	6	/C3	0.7

■ DOUG TAITT   Taitt, Douglas John "Poco"   b: 8/3/02, Bay City, Mich.   d: 12/12/70, Portland, Ore.   BL/TR, 6', 176 lbs.   Deb: 4/10/28

1928	Bos-A	143	482	51	144	28	14	3	61	36	32	.299	.350	.434	107	2	4	74	13	6	0	.975	5	*O/P	0.0
1929	Bos-A	26	65	6	18	4	0	0	8	5	8	.277	.365	.338	84	-1	-1	8	0	1	-1	.955	-0	O	-0.3
	Chi-A	47	124	11	21	7	0	0	12	8	13	.169	.220	.226	15	-16	-16	7	0	0	0	.966	0	O	-1.7
	Yr	73	189	17	39	11	0	0	18	16	18	.206	.272	.265	39	-17	-17	14	0	1	-1	.961	0	O	-2.0
1931	Phi-N	38	151	13	34	4	2	1	15	7	14	.225	.245	.298	42	-12	-13	11	0			.990	5	O	-1.1
1932	Phi-N	4	2	0	0	0	0	0	1	2	0	.000	.500	.000	43	0	0	0	0			.000	H	0.02
Total	4	258	824	81	217	43	16	4	95	58	64	.263	.314	.369	79	-27	-26	100	13	7		.975	10	O/P	-3.1

■ BOB TALBOT   Talbot, Robert Dale   b: 6/6/27, Visalia, Cal.   BR/TR, 6', 170 lbs.   Deb: 9/16/53

1953	Chi-N	8	30	5	10	0	0	0	0	4		.333	.333	.400	88	-0	-1	3	1	0	0	1.000	3	/O	0.2
1954	Chi-N	114	403	45	97	15	4	1	19	16	25	.241	.275	.305	50	-29	-30	32	3	6	-3	.985	-6	*O	-4.4
Total	2	122	433	50	107	15	5	1	19	16	29	.247	.279	.312	53	-30	-30	36	4	6	-2	.986	-4	O	-4.2

■ TIM TALTON   Talton, Marion Lee   b: 1/14/39, Pikeville, N.C.   BL/TR, 6'3", 200 lbs.   Deb: 7/08/66

1966	KC-A	37	53	8	18	3	1	2	6	1	5	.340	.364	.547	163	4	4	10	0	1	-1	1.000	-1	C/1	-0.2
1967	KC-A	46	59	7	15	3	1	0	5	7	13	.254	.333	.339	102	0	0	6	0	0	0	.971	-5	C/1	-0.4
Total	2	83	112	15	33	6	2	2	11	8	18	.295	.347	.438	131	4	4	16	0	1	-1	.980	-6	/C1	-0.5

■ JOHN TAMARGO   Tamargo, John Felix   b: 11/7/51, Tampa, Fla.   BB/TR, 5'10", 180 lbs.   Deb: 9/03/76

1976	StL-N	10	10	2	3	0	0	0	0	3	0	.300	.462	.300	118	1	1	2	0	0	0	1.000	-1	/C	0.0
1977	StL-N	4	4	0	0	0	0	0	0	0	0	.000	.000	.000	-99	-1	-1	0	0	0	0	1.000	-0	/C	-0.1
1978	StL-N	6	6	0	0	0	0	0	0	0	3	.000	.000	.000	-99	-2	-2	0	0	0	0	.000	0	/C	-0.2
	SF-N	36	92	6	22	4	1	1	8	18	7	.239	.364	.337	101	0	1	12	1	1	-0	.965	-2	C	-0.1

YEAR	TM/L	G	AB	R	H	2B	3B	HR	RBI	BB	SO	AVG	OBP	SLG	PRO+	BR	/A	RC	SB	CS	SBR	FA	FR	POS	TPR
	Yr	42	98	6	22	4	1	1	8	18	9	.224	.345	.316	89	-1	-1	12	1	1	-0	.965	-2	C	-0.3
1979	SF-N	30	60	7	12	3	0	2	6	4	8	.200	.250	.350	66	-3	-3	6	0	0	0	.985	-6	C	-0.8
	Mon-N	12	21	0	8	2	0	0	5	3	3	.381	.458	.476	157	2	2	5	0	0	0	1.000	-1	/C	0.1
	Yr	42	81	7	20	5	0	2	11	7	11	.247	.307	.383	92	-2	-1	10	0	0	0	.989	-7	C	-0.7
1980	Mon-N	37	51	4	14	3	0	1	13	6	5	.275	.351	.392	107	1	1	8	0	0	0	.975	-2	C	-0.1
Total	5	135	244	19	59	12	1	4	33	34	27	.242	.335	.348	92	-3	-2	32	1	1	-0	.974	-12	/C	-1.2

■ LEO TANKERSLEY

Tankersley, Lawrence William b: 6/8/01, Terrell, Tex. d: 9/18/80, Dallas, Tex. BR/TR, 6′, 176 lbs. Deb: 7/02/25

YEAR	TM/L	G	AB	R	H	2B	3B	HR	RBI	BB	SO	AVG	OBP	SLG	PRO+	BR	/A	RC	SB	CS	SBR	FA	FR	POS	TPR
1925	Chi-A	1	3	0	0	0	0	0	0	0	0	.000	.000	.000	-99	-1	-1	0	0	0	0	1.000	-1	/C	-0.1

■ JESSE TANNEHILL

Tannehill, Jesse Niles "Powder" b: 7/14/1874, Dayton, Ky. d: 9/22/56, Dayton, Ky. BB/TL, 5′8″, 150 lbs. Deb: 6/17/1894 FC

YEAR	TM/L	G	AB	R	H	2B	3B	HR	RBI	BB	SO	AVG	OBP	SLG	PRO+	BR	/A	RC	SB	CS	SBR	FA	FR	POS	TPR
1894	Cin-N	5	11	0	0	0	0	0	1	1	2	.000	.083	.000	-75	-3	-3	0	0			.600	-1	/P	0.0
1897	Pit-N	56	184	22	49	8	2	0	22	18		.266	.338	.332	80	-6	-5	23	4			.900	7	OP	-0.1
1898	Pit-N	60	152	25	44	9	3	1	17	7		.289	.321	.408	111	1	1	22	4			.956	4	P/O	0.0
1899	Pit-N	47	132	17	34	5	3	0	10	8		.258	.310	.341	79	-4	-4	15	2			.954	3	P/O	-0.1
1900	Pit-N	34	110	19	37	7	0	0	17	5		.336	.365	.400	110	1	1	18	2			.924	1	P/O	0.0
1901	Pit-N	42	135	19	33	3	3	1	12	6		.244	.277	.333	74	-4	-5	13	0			.917	-2	PO	-0.1
1902	Pit-N	44	148	27	43	6	1	1	17	12		.291	.352	.365	117	4	3	21	3			.969	-3	PO	-0.2
1903	NY-A	40	111	18	26	6	2	1	13	8		.234	.292	.351	87	-1	-2	12	1			.969	1	P/O	-0.2
1904	Bos-A	45	122	14	24	2	6	0	6	9		.197	.252	.311	74	-3	-4	10	1			.991	2	P/O	-0.1
1905	Bos-A	37	93	11	21	2	0	1	12	16		.226	.339	.280	96	0	0	10	1			.946	2	P	0.0
1906	Bos-A	31	79	12	22	2	2	0	4	6		.278	.329	.354	115	1	1	10	1			.948	0	P	0.0
1907	Bos-A	21	51	2	10	3	1	0	6	2		.196	.241	.294	71	-2	-2	4	0			.981	0	P	0.0
1908	Bos-A	1	2	0	1	0	0	0	0	0		.500	.500	.500	219	0	0	0	0			1.000	0	/P	0.0
	Was-A	26	43	1	11	1	0	0	3	2		.256	.289	.279	92	-1	-0	3	0			.897	1	P	0.0
	Yr	27	45	1	12	1	0	0	3	2		.267	.298	.289	99	-0	-0	4	0			.907	2	P	0.0
1909	Was-A	16	36	2	6	1	0	0	1	5		.167	.286	.194	55	-2	-2	2	0			1.000	-0	/OP	-0.3
1911	Cin-N	1	1	0	0	0	0	0	0	0	1	.000	.000	.000	-99	-0	-0	0	0			1.000	0	/P	0.0
Total	15	506	1410	189	361	55	23	5	141	105	3	.256	.312	.338	90	-18	-19	163	19			.953	16	P/O	-1.1

■ LEE TANNEHILL

Tannehill, Lee Ford b: 10/26/1880, Dayton, Ky. d: 2/16/38, Live Oak, Fla. BR/TR, 5′11″, 170 lbs. Deb: 4/22/03 F

YEAR	TM/L	G	AB	R	H	2B	3B	HR	RBI	BB	SO	AVG	OBP	SLG	PRO+	BR	/A	RC	SB	CS	SBR	FA	FR	POS	TPR
1903	Chi-A	138	503	48	113	14	3	2	50	25		.225	.263	.276	65	-23	-20	42	10			.908	-4	*S	-2.0
1904	Chi-A	153	547	50	125	31	5	0	61	20		.229	.260	.303	81	-15	-12	50	14			.947	**28**	*3	2.2
1905	Chi-A	142	480	38	96	17	2	0	39	45		.200	.274	.244	68	-18	-16	38	8			.931	28	*3	1.9
1906	*Chi-A	116	378	26	69	8	3	0	33	31		.183	.254	.220	50	-21	-20	25	7			.951	**40**	3S	2.5
1907	Chi-A	33	108	9	26	2	0	0	11	8		.241	.293	.259	79	-3	-2	10	3			.912	5	3/S	0.4
1908	Chi-A	141	482	44	104	15	3	0	35	25		.216	.257	.259	69	-17	-16	34	6			.935	18	*3/S	0.8
1909	Chi-A	155	531	39	118	21	5	0	47	31		.222	.269	.281	77	-17	-14	44	12			.941	7	3S	-0.4
1910	Chi-A	67	230	17	51	10	0	1	21	11		.222	.263	.278	73	-9	-7	18	3			.947	3	S1/3	-0.3
1911	Chi-A	141	516	60	131	17	6	0	49	32		.254	.300	.310	73	-21	-19	49	0			.957	**43**	*S2/31	2.9
1912	Chi-A	4	3	0	0	0	0	0	0	1		.000	.400	.000	18	-0	-0	0	0			.667	-1	/3S	-0.1
Total	10	1090	3778	331	833	135	27	3	346	229		.220	.269	.273	70	-143	-128	310	63			.938	166	3S/12	7.9

■ CHUCK TANNER

Tanner, Charles William b: 7/4/29, New Castle, Pa. BL/TL, 6′, 185 lbs. Deb: 4/12/55 FM

YEAR	TM/L	G	AB	R	H	2B	3B	HR	RBI	BB	SO	AVG	OBP	SLG	PRO+	BR	/A	RC	SB	CS	SBR	FA	FR	POS	TPR
1955	Mil-N	97	243	27	60	9	3	6	27	27	32	.247	.322	.383	91	-5	-3	28	0	0	0	.981	-4	O	-1.0
1956	Mil-N	60	63	6	15	2	0	1	4	10	10	.238	.342	.317	84	-2	-1	7	0	0	0	.800	-3	/O	-0.4
1957	Mil-N	22	69	5	17	3	0	2	6	5	4	.246	.297	.377	86	-2	-1	8	0	0	0	1.000	-0	O	-0.3
	Chi-N	95	318	42	91	16	2	7	42	23	20	.286	.338	.415	103	0	1	44	0	2	-1	.988	-1	O	-0.6
	Yr	117	387	47	108	19	2	9	48	28	24	.279	.331	.408	100	-2	-0	51	0	2	-1	.990	-1	*O	-0.9
1958	Chi-N	73	103	10	27	6	0	4	17	9	10	.262	.321	.437	100	-0	-0	14	1	0	0	.955	-2	O	-0.3
1959	Cle-A	14	48	6	12	2	0	1	5	2	9	.250	.280	.354	76	-2	-2	4	0	0	0	1.000	-1	O	-0.3
1960	Cle-A	21	25	2	7	1	0	0	4	4	6	.280	.379	.320	94	-0	-0	3	1	0	0	1.000	-1	/O	0.0
1961	LA-A	7	8	0	1	0	0	0	0	2	2	.125	.300	.125	16	-1	-1	0	0	0	0	.000	-0	/O	-0.1
1962	LA-A	7	8	0	1	0	0	0	0	0	0	.125	.125	.125	-34	-1	-1	0	0	0	0	.000	-1	/O	-0.2
Total	8	396	885	98	231	39	5	21	105	82	93	.261	.325	.388	93	-13	-9	109	2	2	-1	.983	-13	O	-3.2

■ WALTER TAPPAN

Tappan, Walter Van Dorn "Tap" b: 10/8/1890, Carlinville, Ill. d: 12/19/67, Lynwood, Cal. BR/TR, 5′8″, 158 lbs. Deb: 4/16/14

YEAR	TM/L	G	AB	R	H	2B	3B	HR	RBI	BB	SO	AVG	OBP	SLG	PRO+	BR	/A	RC	SB	CS	SBR	FA	FR	POS	TPR
1914	KC-F	18	39	1	8	1	0	1	3	1	0	.205	.225	.308	53	-3	-2	3	1			.875	-2	/S32	-0.4

■ EL TAPPE

Tappe, Elvin Walter b: 5/21/27, Quincy, Ill. BR/TR, 5′11″, 180 lbs. Deb: 4/24/54 MC

YEAR	TM/L	G	AB	R	H	2B	3B	HR	RBI	BB	SO	AVG	OBP	SLG	PRO+	BR	/A	RC	SB	CS	SBR	FA	FR	POS	TPR
1954	Chi-N	46	119	5	22	3	0	0	4	10	9	.185	.248	.210	21	-14	-14	7	0	0	0	.986	6	C	-0.6
1955	Chi-N	2	0	0	0	0	0	0	0	0	0	—	—	—	—	0	0	0	0	0	0	1.000	1	/C	0.1
1956	Chi-N	3	1	0	0	0	0	0	0	1	0	.000	.500	.000	51	0	0	0	0	0	0	1.000	0	/C	0.0
1958	Chi-N	17	28	2	6	0	0	0	4	3	1	.214	.290	.214	37	-2	-2	1	0	0	0	.962	-1	C	-0.3
1960	Chi-N	51	103	11	24	7	0	0	3	11	12	.233	.313	.301	70	-4	-4	10	0	1	-1	.992	9	C	0.6
1962	Chi-N	26	53	3	11	0	0	0	6	4	3	.208	.288	.208	34	-5	-5	3	0	0	0	1.000	4	CM	0.0
Total	6	145	304	21	63	10	0	0	17	29	25	.207	.283	.240	41	-25	-25	22	0	1	-1	.989	19	C	-0.2

■ TED TAPPE

Tappe, Theodore Nash b: 2/2/31, Seattle, Wash. BL/TR, 6′3″, 185 lbs. Deb: 9/14/50

YEAR	TM/L	G	AB	R	H	2B	3B	HR	RBI	BB	SO	AVG	OBP	SLG	PRO+	BR	/A	RC	SB	CS	SBR	FA	FR	POS	TPR
1950	Cin-N	7	5	1	1	0	0	1	1	1	1	.200	.333	.800	187	1	1	1	0			.000	0	H	0.1
1951	Cin-N	4	3	0	1	0	0	0	0	0	0	.333	.333	.333	79	-0	-0	0	0	0	0	.000	0	H	0.0
1955	Chi-N	23	50	12	13	2	0	4	10	11	11	.260	.413	.540	151	4	4	12	0	0	0	1.000	-2	O	0.1
Total	3	34	58	13	15	2	0	5	11	12	12	.259	.403	.552	151	5	5	14	0	0			-2	/O	0.2

■ ARLIE TARBERT

Tarbert, Wilbur Arlington b: 9/10/04, Cleveland, Ohio d: 11/27/46, Cleveland, Ohio BR/TR, 6′, 160 lbs. Deb: 6/18/27

YEAR	TM/L	G	AB	R	H	2B	3B	HR	RBI	BB	SO	AVG	OBP	SLG	PRO+	BR	/A	RC	SB	CS	SBR	FA	FR	POS	TPR
1927	Bos-A	33	69	5	13	1	0	0	5	3	12	.188	.253	.203	20	-8	-8	4	0	0	0	.944	-4	O	-1.3
1928	Bos-A	6	17	1	3	1	0	0	2	1	1	.176	.222	.235	21	-2	-2	1	1	0	0	.900	-0	/O	-0.2
Total	2	39	86	6	16	2	0	0	7	4	13	.186	.247	.209	20	-10	-10	5	1	0	0	.935	-5	/O	-1.5

■ DANNY TARTABULL

Tartabull, Danilo (Mora) b: 10/30/62, San Juan, P.R. BR/TR, 6′1″, 205 lbs. Deb: 9/07/84 F

YEAR	TM/L	G	AB	R	H	2B	3B	HR	RBI	BB	SO	AVG	OBP	SLG	PRO+	BR	/A	RC	SB	CS	SBR	FA	FR	POS	TPR
1984	Sea-A	10	20	3	6	1	0	2	7	2	3	.300	.391	.650	185	2	2	5	0	0	0	.931	2	/S2	0.4
1985	Sea-A	19	61	8	20	7	1	1	7	8	14	.328	.406	.525	152	5	4	14	1	0	0	.940	-3	S/3	0.4
1986	Sea-A	137	511	76	138	25	6	25	96	61	157	.270	.349	.489	124	17	17	85	4	8	-4	.953	1	*O2/3D	1.2
1987	KC-A	158	582	95	180	27	3	34	101	79	136	.309	.393	.541	141	38	36	124	9	4	0	.976	-6	*O/D	2.3
1988	KC-A	146	507	80	139	38	3	26	102	76	119	.274	.373	.515	145	32	31	99	8	5	-1	.963	-4	*OD	2.3
1989	KC-A	133	441	54	118	22	0	18	62	69	123	.268	.370	.440	128	17	18	74	4	2	0	.982	-7	OD	0.9
1990	KC-A	88	313	41	84	19	0	15	60	36	93	.268	.344	.473	128	10	11	50	1	1	-0	.965	-4	OD	0.6
1991	KC-A★	132	484	78	153	35	3	31	100	65	121	.316	.400	**.593**	170	46	46	116	6	3	0	.965	-10	*O/D	3.3
1992	NY-A	123	421	72	112	19	0	25	85	103	115	.266	.410	.489	148	33	31	91	2	2	-1	.980	1	OD	3.0
Total	9	946	3340	507	950	193	16	177	620	499	881	.284	.380	.511	142	200	197	657	35	25	-5	.969	-31	OD/2S3	14.4

■ JOSE TARTABULL

Tartabull, Jose Milages (Guzman) b: 11/27/38, Cienfuegos, Cuba BL/TL, 5′11″, 165 lbs. Deb: 4/10/62 F

YEAR	TM/L	G	AB	R	H	2B	3B	HR	RBI	BB	SO	AVG	OBP	SLG	PRO+	BR	/A	RC	SB	CS	SBR	FA	FR	POS	TPR
1962	KC-A	107	310	49	86	6	5	0	22	20	19	.277	.323	.329	74	-10	-11	36	19	5	3	.974	4	O	-1.0
1963	KC-A	79	242	27	58	8	5	1	19	17	17	.240	.290	.326	69	-9	-10	26	16	1	4	.986	-3	O	-1.3
1964	KC-A	104	100	9	20	2	0	0	3	5	12	.200	.238	.220	28	-10	-10	6	4	0	1	.978	-12	O	-2.3

YEAR	TM/L	G	AB	R	H	2B	3B	HR	RBI	BB	SO	AVG	OBP	SLG	PRO+	BR	/A	RC	SB	CS	SBR	FA	FR	POS	TPR
1965	KC-A	68	218	28	68	11	4	1	19	18	20	.312	.364	.413	122	6	6	33	11	5	0	.986	7	O	1.1
1966	KC-A	37	127	13	30	2	3	0	4	11	13	.236	.297	.299	74	-4	-4	13	8	1	2	1.000	0	O	-0.4
	Bos-A	68	195	28	54	7	4	0	11	6	11	.277	.299	.354	79	-4	-6	20	11	3	2	.989	-2	O	-0.9
	Yr	105	322	41	84	9	7	0	15	17	24	.261	.298	.332	77	-8	-10	34	19	4	3	.994	-2	O	-1.3
1967	*Bos-A	115	247	36	55	1	2	0	10	23	26	.223	.289	.243	54	-12	-14	18	6	6	-2	.989	-12	O	-3.5
1968	Bos-A	72	139	24	39	6	0	0	6	6	5	.281	.310	.324	87	-1	-2	14	2	3	-1	.984	-4	O	-1.0
1969	Oak-A	75	266	28	71	11	1	0	11	9	11	.267	.291	.316	73	-11	-10	24	3	4	-2	.993	1	O	-1.5
1970	Oak-A	24	13	5	3	2	0	0	2	0	2	.231	.231	.385	69	-1	-1	1	1	0	0	1.000	-2	/O	-0.2
Total	9	749	1857	247	484	56	24	2	107	115	136	.261	.304	.320	75	-56	-62	192	81	28	8	.986	-24	O	-11.0
■ LA SCHELLE TARVER	Tarver, La Schelle b: 1/30/59, Modesto, Cal. BL/TL, 5'11", 165 lbs. Deb: 7/12/86																								
1986	Bos-A	13	25	3	3	0	0	0	1	1	4	.120	.154	.120	-24	-4	-4	0	0	1	-1	1.000	-1	/O	-0.7
■ WILLIE TASBY	Tasby, Willie b: 1/8/33, Shreveport, La. BR/TR, 5'11", 175 lbs. Deb: 9/09/58																								
1958	Bal-A	18	50	6	10	3	0	1	1	7	15	.200	.310	.320	78	-2	-1	5	1	1	-0	1.000	-4	O	-0.7
1959	Bal-A	142	505	69	126	16	5	13	48	34	80	.250	.305	.378	88	-10	-9	57	3	5	-2	.968	3	*O	-1.4
1960	Bal-A	39	85	9	18	2	1	0	3	9	12	.212	.295	.259	52	-6	-6	7	1	0	0	.980	-8	O	-1.4
	Bos-A	105	385	68	108	17	1	7	37	51	54	.281	.372	.384	101	4	2	58	3	1	0	.979	3	*O	0.0
	Yr	144	470	77	126	19	2	7	40	60	66	.268	.358	.362	93	-1	-3	64	4	1	1	.979	-5	*O	-1.4
1961	Was-A	141	494	54	124	13	2	17	63	58	94	.251	.332	.389	93	-6	-5	60	4	10	-5	.985	2	*O	-1.5
1962	Was-A	11	34	4	7	0	0	0	0	2	6	.206	.250	.206	24	-4	-4	2	0	0	0	.933	-2	O	-0.6
	Cle-A	75	199	25	48	7	0	4	17	25	41	.241	.326	.337	81	-6	-5	22	0	2	-1	1.000	-12	O/3	-2.2
	Yr	86	233	29	55	7	0	4	17	27	47	.236	.315	.318	73	-9	-8	23	0	2	-1	.992	-14	O/3	-2.8
1963	Cle-A	52	116	11	26	3	1	4	5	15	25	.224	.318	.371	93	-1	-1	13	0	1	-1	.981	-5	O/2	-0.8
Total	6	583	1868	246	467	61	10	46	174	201	327	.250	.328	.367	89	-29	-27	224	12	20	-8	.980	-22	O/23	-8.6
■ POP TATE	Tate, Edward Christopher "Dimples" b: 12/22/1860, Richmond, Va. d: 6/25/32, Richmond, Va. BR/TL, 5'10", 178 lbs. Deb: 9/26/1885																								
1885	Bos-N	4	13	1	2	0	0	0	2	1	3	.154	.214	.154	21	-1	-1	0				.865	1	/C	0.1
1886	Bos-N	31	106	13	24	3	1	0	3	7	17	.226	.274	.274	70	-4	-3	8	0			.885	-4	C	-0.3
1887	Bos-N	60	231	34	60	5	3	0	27	8	9	.260	.296	.307	69	-9	-9	24	7			.924	13	C/O	0.7
1888	Bos-N	41	148	18	34	7	1	1	6	8	7	.230	.278	.311	88	-2	-2	14	3			.854	-3	C/O	-0.1
1889	Bal-a	72	253	28	46	6	3	1	27	13	37	.182	.236	.241	37	-21	-21	16	4			.938	-3	C1	-1.6
1890	Bal-a	19	71	7	13	1	1	0		4		.183	.284	.225	50	-4	-4	6	3			.923	-2	C/1	-0.5
Total	6	227	822	101	179	22	9	2	65	41	73	.218	.269	.274	60	-40	-41	68	17			.905	3	C/1O	-1.7
■ BENNIE TATE	Tate, Henry Bennett b: 12/3/01, Whitwell, Tenn. d: 10/27/73, W.Frankfort, Ill. BL/TR, 5'8", 165 lbs. Deb: 4/29/24																								
1924	*Was-A	21	43	2	13	2	0	0	7	1	2	.302	.318	.349	74	-2	-2	5	0	0	0	.841	-3	C	-0.4
1925	Was-A	16	27	0	13	3	0	0	7	2	2	.481	.517	.593	185	3	3	8	0	1	-1	.955	2	C	0.5
1926	Was-A	59	142	17	38	5	2	1	13	15	1	.268	.338	.352	82	-4	-4	18	0	0	0	.960	-5	C	-0.6
1927	Was-A	61	131	12	41	5	1	1	24	8	4	.313	.357	.389	95	-1	-1	17	0	3	-2	.977	4	C	0.4
1928	Was-A	57	122	10	30	6	0	0	15	10	4	.246	.303	.295	58	-7	-7	10	0	4	-2	.985	2	C	-0.5
1929	Was-A	81	265	26	78	12	3	0	30	16	8	.294	.335	.362	79	-8	-8	31	2	5	-2	.971	-2	C	-0.6
1930	Was-A	14	20	1	5	0	0	0	2	0	1	.250	.250	.250	27	-2	-2	1	0	0	0	.933	-1	/C	-0.2
	Chi-A	72	230	26	73	11	2	0	27	18	10	.317	.367	.383	94	-3	-2	33	2	1	0	.981	-10	C	-0.5
	Yr	86	250	27	78	11	2	0	29	18	11	.312	.358	.372	88	-5	-4	34	2	1	0	.978	-11	C	-0.7
1931	Chi-A	89	273	27	73	12	3	0	22	26	10	.267	.331	.333	80	-10	-7	31	1	1	-0	.987	7	C	0.4
1932	Chi-A	4	10	1	1	0	0	0	0	1	0	.100	.182	.100	-27	-2	-2	0	0	0	0	1.000	0	/C	-0.1
	Bos-A	81	273	21	67	12	5	2	26	20	6	.245	.297	.348	68	-14	-13	28	0	1	-1	.974	-5	C	-1.3
	Yr	85	283	22	68	12	5	2	26	21	6	.240	.293	.339	65	-16	-15	28	0	1	-1	.975	-5	C	-1.4
1934	Chi-N	11	24	1	3	0	0	0	0	1	3	.125	.160	.125	-23	-4	-4	0	0			1.000	-3	/C	-0.7
Total	10	566	1560	144	435	68	16	4	173	118	51	.279	.330	.351	78	-54	-48	182	5	16		.974	-14	C	-3.6
■ HUGHIE TATE	Tate, Hugh Henry b: 5/19/1880, Everett, Pa. d: 8/7/56, Greenville, Pa. BR/TR, 5'11", 190 lbs. Deb: 9/21/05																								
1905	Was-A	4	13	1	4	0	1	0	2	0		.308	.308	.462	149	1	1	2	1			1.000	0	/O	0.1
■ LEE TATE	Tate, Lee Willie "Skeeter" b: 3/18/32, Black Rock, Ark. BR/TR, 5'10", 165 lbs. Deb: 9/12/58																								
1958	StL-N	10	35	4	7	2	0	0	1	4	3	.200	.282	.257	42	-3	-3	3	0	0	0	.950	-4	/S	-0.7
1959	StL-N	41	50	5	7	1	1	1	4	5	7	.140	.232	.260	29	-5	-5	3	0	0	0	.927	1	S/23	-0.4
Total	2	51	85	9	14	3	1	1	5	9	10	.165	.253	.259	34	-8	-8	5	0	0	0	.934	-4	/S32	-1.1
■ JIM TATUM	Tatum, James Ray b: 10/9/67, Grossmont, Cal. BR/TR, 6'2", 200 lbs. Deb: 9/18/92																								
1992	Mil-A	5	8	0	1	0	0	0	0	1	2	.125	.222	.125	-0	-1	-1	0	0	0	0	1.000	-0	/3	-0.1
■ JARVIS TATUM	Tatum, Jarvis b: 10/11/46, Fresno, Cal. BR/TR, 6', 185 lbs. Deb: 9/07/68																								
1968	Cal-A	17	51	7	9	1	0	0	2	0	9	.176	.176	.196	13	-5	-5	2	0	0	0	1.000	-0	O	-0.7
1969	Cal-A	10	22	2	7	0	0	0	0	0	6	.318	.318	.318	83	-1	-1	2	0	1	-1	.857	-1	/O	-0.2
1970	Cal-A	75	181	28	43	7	0	0	6	17	35	.238	.303	.276	63	-9	-9	15	1	0	0	.982	-5	O	-1.6
Total	3	102	254	37	59	8	0	0	8	17	50	.232	.280	.264	56	-15	-14	18	1	1	-0	.979	-6	/O	-2.5
■ TOMMY TATUM	Tatum, V T b: 7/16/19, Decatur, Tex. d: 11/7/89, Oklahoma City, Okla BR/TR, 6', 185 lbs. Deb: 8/01/41																								
1941	Bro-N	8	12	1	2	1	0	0	1	1	3	.167	.231	.250	34	-1	-1	1	0			1.000	-1	/O	-0.3
1947	Bro-N	4	6	0	0	0	0	0	0	0	1	.000	.000	.000	-96	-2	-2	0	0			1.000	-1	/O	-0.3
	Cin-N	69	176	19	48	5	2	1	16	16	16	.273	.333	.341	80	-5	-5	21	7			1.000	4	O/2	-0.3
	Yr	73	182	19	48	5	2	1	16	16	17	.264	.323	.330	74	-7	-7	20	7			1.000	3	O/2	-0.6
Total	2	81	194	20	50	6	2	1	17	17	20	.258	.318	.325	72	-8	-8	22	7			1.000	2	/O2	-0.9
■ EDDIE TAUBENSEE	Taubensee, Edward Kenneth b: 10/31/68, Beeville, Tex. BL/TR, 6'3", 205 lbs. Deb: 5/18/91																								
1991	Cle-A	26	66	5	16	2	1	0	8	5	16	.242	.296	.303	66	-3	-3	6	0	0	0	.979	-8	C	-0.9
1992	Hou-N	104	297	23	66	15	0	5	28	31	78	.222	.300	.323	81	-9	-7	30	2	1	0	.992	3	*C	0.2
Total	2	130	363	28	82	17	1	5	36	36	94	.226	.299	.320	78	-12	-10	36	2	1	0	.990	-4	C	-0.7
■ FRED TAUBY	Tauby, Fred Joseph (b: Fred Joseph Taubensee) b: 3/27/06, Canton, Ohio d: 11/23/55, Concordia, Cal. BR/TR, 5'9.5", 168 lbs. Deb: 9/01/35																								
1935	Chi-A	13	32	5	4	1	0	0	2	2	3	.125	.176	.156	-13	-5	-6	1	0	0	0	1.000	2	/O	-0.4
1937	Phi-N	11	20	2	0	0	0	0	3	0	5	.000	.000	.000	-93	-5	-6	0	1			1.000	-2	/O	-0.8
Total	2	24	52	7	4	1	0	0	5	2	8	.077	.111	.096	-43	-11	-11	1	1	0		1.000	-0	/O	-1.2
■ DON TAUSSIG	Taussig, Donald Franklin b: 2/19/32, New York, N.Y. BR/TR, 6', 180 lbs. Deb: 4/23/58																								
1958	SF-N	39	50	10	10	0	0	1	4	3	8	.200	.245	.260	35	-5	-5	3	0	0	0	1.000	-9	O	-1.4
1961	StL-N	98	188	27	54	14	5	2	25	16	34	.287	.343	.447	98	2	-1	28	2	2	-1	.992	8	O	0.4
1962	Hou-N	16	25	1	5	0	0	1	1	2	11	.200	.259	.320	59	-2	-1	2	0	0	0	1.000	1	/O	-0.1
Total	3	153	263	38	69	14	5	4	30	21	53	.262	.317	.399	84	-5	-7	33	2	2	-1	.994	-0	O	-1.1
■ JACKIE TAVENER	Tavener, John Adam "Rabbit" b: 12/27/1897, Celina, Ohio d: 9/14/69, Fort Worth, Tex. BL/TR, 5'5", 138 lbs. Deb: 9/24/21																								
1921	Det-A	2	4	0	0	0	0	0	0	0	1	.000	.000	.000	-99	-1	-1	0	0	0	0	1.000	1	/S	0.0
1925	Det-A	134	453	45	111	11	11	0	47	39	60	.245	.309	.318	60	-28	-27	47	5	4	-1	.963	7	*S	-0.8
1926	Det-A	156	532	65	141	22	14	1	58	52	53	.265	.332	.365	80	-15	-16	66	8	7	-2	.952	9	*S	0.7

YEAR	TM/L	G	AB	R	H	2B	3B	HR	RBI	BB	SO	AVG	OBP	SLG	PRO+	BR	/A	RC	SB	CS	SBR	FA	FR	POS	TPR
1927	Det-A	116	419	60	115	22	9	5	59	36	38	.274	.333	.406	90	-7	-7	53	20	8	1	.948	4	*S	0.9
1928	Det-A	132	473	59	123	24	15	5	52	33	51	.260	.314	.406	86	-10	-11	60	13	8	-1	.944	14	*S	1.7
1929	Cle-A	92	250	25	53	9	4	2	27	26	28	.212	.289	.304	51	-18	-19	23	1	4	-2	.945	23	S	1.0
Total	6	632	2131	254	543	88	53	13	243	186	231	.255	.318	.364	75	-79	-82	249	47	31	-5	.951	58	S	3.5

■ **ALEX TAVERAS** Taveras, Alejandro Antonio (Betances) b: 10/9/55, Santiago, D.R. BR/TR, 5'10", 155 lbs. Deb: 9/09/76

YEAR	TM/L	G	AB	R	H	2B	3B	HR	RBI	BB	SO	AVG	OBP	SLG	PRO+	BR	/A	RC	SB	CS	SBR	FA	FR	POS	TPR
1976	Hou-N	14	46	3	10	0	0	0	2	2	1	.217	.250	.217	37	-4	-4	2	1	2	-1	.923	1	/2S	-0.2
1982	LA-N	11	3	1	1	1	0	0	2	0	1	.333	.333	.667	178	0	0	1	0	0	0	1.000	4	/23S	0.4
1983	LA-N	10	4	0	0	0	0	0	0	0	1	.000	.000	.000	-99	-1	-1	0	0	0	0	.000	2	/S23	0.1
Total	3	35	53	4	11	1	0	0	4	2	3	.208	.236	.226	34	-5	-4	3	1	2	-1	.938	7	/2S3	0.3

■ **FRANK TAVERAS** Taveras, Franklin Crisostomo (Fabian) b: 12/24/49, Las Matas De Santa Cruz, D.R. BR/TR, 6', 168 lbs. Deb: 9/25/71

YEAR	TM/L	G	AB	R	H	2B	3B	HR	RBI	BB	SO	AVG	OBP	SLG	PRO+	BR	/A	RC	SB	CS	SBR	FA	FR	POS	TPR
1971	Pit-N	1	0	0	0	0	0	0	0	0	0	—	—	—	—	0	0	0	0	0	0	.000	0	R	0.0
1972	Pit-N	4	3	0	0	0	0	0	0	1	1	.000	.250	.000	-24	-0	-0	0	0	0	0	1.000	-1	/S	-0.1
1974	*Pit-N	126	333	33	82	4	2	0	26	25	41	.246	.303	.270	63	-17	-15	29	13	4	2	.941	-17	*S	-1.8
1975	*Pit-N	134	378	44	80	9	4	0	23	37	42	.212	.285	.257	52	-24	-24	32	17	6	2	.953	-15	*S	-2.5
1976	Pit-N	144	519	76	134	8	6	0	24	44	79	.258	.321	.297	75	-15	-16	56	58	11	11	.952	-5	*S	0.8
1977	Pit-N	147	544	72	137	20	10	1	29	38	71	.252	.308	.331	69	-22	-24	61	**70**	18	**10**	.962	-22	*S	-2.1
1978	Pit-N	157	654	81	182	31	9	0	38	29	60	.278	.314	.353	82	-13	-16	72	46	25	-1	.946	-29	*S	-2.9
1979	Pit-N	11	45	4	11	3	0	0	1	0	2	.244	.244	.311	48	-3	-3	3	2	1	0	.935	-4	S	-0.7
	NY-N	153	635	89	167	26	9	1	33	33	72	.263	.301	.337	77	-23	-20	63	42	19	1	.966	-22	*S	-2.5
	Yr	164	680	93	178	29	9	1	34	33	74	.262	.298	.335	75	-26	-24	66	44	20	1	.964	-26	*S	-3.2
1980	NY-N	141	562	65	157	27	0	0	25	23	64	.279	.309	.327	80	-17	-15	53	32	18	-1	.959	-39	*S	-4.2
1981	NY-N	84	283	30	65	11	3	0	11	12	36	.230	.266	.290	58	-16	-16	23	16	4	2	.931	-22	S	-3.0
1982	Mon-N	48	87	9	14	5	1	0	4	7	6	.161	.223	.241	29	-8	-8	5	4	0	1	.947	-1	S2	-0.7
Total	11	1150	4043	503	1029	144	44	2	214	249	474	.255	.302	.313	71	-159	-158	395	300	106	26	.953	-176	*S/2	-19.7

■ **TAYLOR** Taylor Deb: 9/10/1874

YEAR	TM/L	G	AB	R	H	2B	3B	HR	RBI	BB	SO	AVG	OBP	SLG	PRO+	BR	/A	RC	SB	CS	SBR	FA	FR	POS	TPR
1874	Bal-n	13	48	3	13	1	0	0		0		.271	.271	.292	80	-1	-1	4						1	-0.1

■ **TONY TAYLOR** Taylor, Antonio Nemesio (Sanchez) b: 12/19/35, Central Alara, Cuba BR/TR, 5'9", 179 lbs. Deb: 4/15/58 C

YEAR	TM/L	G	AB	R	H	2B	3B	HR	RBI	BB	SO	AVG	OBP	SLG	PRO+	BR	/A	RC	SB	CS	SBR	FA	FR	POS	TPR
1958	Chi-N	140	497	63	117	15	3	6	27	40	93	.235	.301	.314	64	-26	-25	50	21	6	3	.968	9	*2/3	-0.4
1959	Chi-N	150	624	96	175	30	8	8	38	45	86	.280	.335	.393	94	-6	-5	84	23	9	2	.970	10	*2/S	1.8
1960	Chi-N	19	76	14	20	3	3	1	9	8	12	.263	.341	.421	108	1	1	12	2	0	1	.977	-2	2	0.1
	Phi-N	127	505	66	145	22	4	4	35	33	86	.287	.333	.370	92	-5	-5	62	24	11	1	.968	-6	*2/3	0.2
	Yr	146	581	80	165	25	7	5	44	41	98	.284	.334	.377	94	-4	-4	73	26	11	1	.969	-8	*2/3	0.3
1961	Phi-N	106	400	47	100	17	3	2	26	29	59	.250	.304	.322	67	-19	-18	38	11	5	0	.980	0	2/3	-0.8
1962	Phi-N	152	625	87	162	21	5	7	43	68	82	.259	.337	.342	85	-14	-11	76	20	9	1	.972	-15	*2/S	-1.0
1963	Phi-N	157	640	102	180	20	10	5	49	42	99	.281	.332	.367	102	1	2	79	23	9	2	**.986**	-9	*23	1.0
1964	Phi-N	154	570	62	143	13	6	4	46	46	74	.251	.321	.316	81	-14	-13	60	13	7	-0	.977	-21	*2	-2.2
1965	Phi-N	106	323	41	74	14	3	3	27	22	58	.229	.303	.319	77	-10	-10	32	5	4	-1	.958	-2	2/3	-0.6
1966	Phi-N	125	434	47	105	14	8	5	40	31	56	.242	.294	.346	77	-13	-14	42	8	4	0	.988	4	23	-0.6
1967	Phi-N	132	462	55	110	16	6	2	34	42	74	.238	.308	.312	77	-12	-13	42	10	9	-2	.991	-8	132/S	-2.7
1968	Phi-N	145	547	59	137	20	2	3	38	39	60	.250	.304	.311	85	-10	-10	54	22	5	4	.966	16	*3/21	1.2
1969	Phi-N	138	557	68	146	24	5	3	30	42	62	.262	.318	.339	87	-12	-10	60	19	10	-0	.967	-2	321	-0.9
1970	Phi-N	124	439	74	132	26	9	9	55	50	67	.301	.376	.462	127	15	16	71	9	11	-4	.996	-0	23O/S	1.6
1971	Phi-N	36	107	9	25	2	1	1	5	9	10	.234	.293	.299	68	-4	-4	9	2	2	-1	1.000	5	23/1	0.0
	Det-A	55	181	27	52	10	2	3	19	12	11	.287	.335	.414	107	2	1	25	5	1	1	.995	1	2/3	0.8
1972	*Det-A	78	228	33	69	12	4	1	20	14	34	.303	.348	.404	119	6	5	31	5	1	1	.966	-8	2/31	0.2
1973	Det-A	84	275	35	63	9	3	5	24	17	29	.229	.276	.338	68	-11	-13	24	9	5	-0	.987	-14	2/13OD	-2.4
1974	Phi-N	62	64	5	21	4	0	2	13	6	6	.328	.394	.484	139	4	3	12	0	0	0	1.000	-1	/132	0.3
1975	Phi-N	79	103	13	25	5	1	1	17	17	18	.243	.355	.340	90	-0	-1	12	3	3	-1	.913	1	3/12	-0.1
1976	Phi-N	26	23	2	6	1	0	0	3	1	7	.261	.320	.304	76	-1	-1	2	0	0	0	.000	-0	/23	-0.1
Total	19	2195	7680	1005	2007	298	86	75	598	613	1083	.261	.322	.352	88	-128	-122	876	234	111	4	.976	-41	*23/1OSD	-4.6

■ **BEN TAYLOR** Taylor, Benjamin Eugene b: 9/30/27, Metropolis, Ill. BL/TL, 6', 175 lbs. Deb: 7/29/51

YEAR	TM/L	G	AB	R	H	2B	3B	HR	RBI	BB	SO	AVG	OBP	SLG	PRO+	BR	/A	RC	SB	CS	SBR	FA	FR	POS	TPR
1951	StL-A	33	93	14	24	2	1	3	6	9	22	.258	.337	.398	95	-0	-1	12	1	1	-0	.972	-2	1	-0.4
1952	Det-A	7	18	0	3	0	0	0	0	0	5	.167	.167	.167	-7	-3	-3	0	0	0	0	1.000	-0	/1	-0.3
1955	Mil-N	12	10	2	1	0	0	0	0	2	4	.100	.250	.100	-3	-1	-1	0	0	0	0	1.000	-0	/1	-0.1
Total	3	52	121	16	28	2	1	3	6	11	31	.231	.306	.339	73	-4	-5	13	1	1	-0	.976	-2	/1	-0.8

■ **CHINK TAYLOR** Taylor, C L b: 2/9/1898, Burnet, Tex. d: 7/7/80, Temple, Tex. BR/TR, 5'9", 160 lbs. Deb: 4/18/25

YEAR	TM/L	G	AB	R	H	2B	3B	HR	RBI	BB	SO	AVG	OBP	SLG	PRO+	BR	/A	RC	SB	CS	SBR	FA	FR	POS	TPR
1925	Chi-N	8	6	2	0	0	0	0	0	0	0	.000	.000	.000	-99	-2	-2	0	0	0	0	1.000	-1	/O	-0.2

■ **CARL TAYLOR** Taylor, Carl Means b: 1/20/44, Sarasota, Fla. BR/TR, 6'2", 207 lbs. Deb: 4/11/68

YEAR	TM/L	G	AB	R	H	2B	3B	HR	RBI	BB	SO	AVG	OBP	SLG	PRO+	BR	/A	RC	SB	CS	SBR	FA	FR	POS	TPR
1968	Pit-N	44	71	5	15	1	0	0	7	10	10	.211	.309	.225	63	-3	-3	5	1	0	0	.979	-5	C/O	-0.7
1969	Pit-N	104	221	30	77	10	1	4	33	31	36	.348	.435	.457	153	16	17	45	0	1	-1	.914	0	O1	1.4
1970	StL-N	104	245	39	61	12	2	6	45	41	30	.249	.359	.388	98	1	0	34	5	2	0	.986	-3	O1/3	-0.5
1971	Pit-N	7	12	1	2	0	1	0	0	0	5	.167	.167	.333	39	-1	-1	0	0	0	0	1.000	-0	/O	-0.2
	KC-A	20	39	3	7	0	0	0	3	5	13	.179	.273	.179	30	-3	-3	2	0	1	-1	.964	1	O	-0.4
1972	KC-A	63	113	17	30	2	1	0	11	17	16	.265	.366	.301	101	1	1	14	4	1	1	.982	-5	C/O13	-0.4
1973	KC-A	69	145	18	33	6	1	0	16	32	20	.228	.367	.283	79	-1	-3	17	2	2	-1	.980	2	C/1D	0.0
Total	6	411	846	113	225	31	6	10	115	136	130	.266	.371	.352	103	10	8	117	12	7	-1	.980	-11	CO/13D	-0.8

■ **DANNY TAYLOR** Taylor, Daniel Turney b: 12/23/1900, Lash, Pa. d: 10/11/72, Latrobe, Pa. BR/TR, 5'10", 190 lbs. Deb: 6/30/26

YEAR	TM/L	G	AB	R	H	2B	3B	HR	RBI	BB	SO	AVG	OBP	SLG	PRO+	BR	/A	RC	SB	CS	SBR	FA	FR	POS	TPR
1926	Was-A	21	50	10	15	0	1	1	5	5	7	.300	.364	.400	102	-0	0	7	1	2	-1	1.000	-1	O	-0.3
1929	Chi-N	2	3	0	0	0	0	0	0	1	1	.000	.250	.000	-32	-1	-1	0	0			1.000	-0	/O	-0.1
1930	Chi-N	74	219	43	62	14	3	2	37	27	34	.283	.364	.402	84	-5	-5	32	6			.971	-1	O	-0.9
1931	Chi-N	88	270	48	81	13	6	5	41	31	46	.300	.372	.448	117	8	7	47	4			.989	4	O	0.7
1932	Chi-N	6	22	3	5	2	0	0	3	3	1	.227	.320	.318	73	-1	-1	2	1			.900	-0	/O	-0.1
	Bro-N	105	395	84	128	22	7	11	48	33	41	.324	.378	.499	136	18	19	76	13			.989	4	O	1.7
	Yr	111	417	87	133	24	7	11	51	36	42	.319	.374	.489	133	18	19	78	14			.983	4	*O	1.6
1933	Bro-N	103	358	75	102	21	9	9	40	47	45	.285	.368	.469	144	18	20	64	11			.977	2	O	1.7
1934	Bro-N	120	405	62	121	24	6	7	57	63	47	.299	.396	.440	130	16	19	74	12			.975	-8	*O	0.6
1935	Bro-N	112	352	51	102	19	5	7	59	46	32	.290	.372	.432	118	8	10	60	6			.970	-6	O	0.0
1936	Bro-N	43	116	12	34	6	0	2	15	11	14	.293	.359	.397	102	1	1	16	2			.981	-3	O	-0.3
Total	9	674	2190	388	650	121	37	44	305	267	268	.297	.374	.446	121	62	68	379	56	2		.979	-10	O	3.0

■ **DWIGHT TAYLOR** Taylor, Dwight Bernard b: 3/24/60, Los Angeles, Cal. BL/TL, 5'9", 166 lbs. Deb: 4/14/86

YEAR	TM/L	G	AB	R	H	2B	3B	HR	RBI	BB	SO	AVG	OBP	SLG	PRO+	BR	/A	RC	SB	CS	SBR	FA	FR	POS	TPR
1986	KC-A	4	2	1	0	0	0	0	0	0	0	.000	.000	.000	-98	-1	-1	0	0	0	0	.000	-1	/OD	-0.1

■ **ED TAYLOR** Taylor, Edward James b: 11/17/01, Chicago, Ill. d: 1/30/92, Chula Vista, Cal. BR/TR, 5'6.5", 160 lbs. Deb: 4/14/26

YEAR	TM/L	G	AB	R	H	2B	3B	HR	RBI	BB	SO	AVG	OBP	SLG	PRO+	BR	/A	RC	SB	CS	SBR	FA	FR	POS	TPR
1926	Bos-N	92	272	37	73	8	2	0	33	38	26	.268	.368	.313	93	-4	-0	34	4			.945	-1	3S	0.5

YEAR	TM/L	G	AB	R	H	2B	3B	HR	RBI	BB	SO	AVG	OBP	SLG	PRO+	BR	/A	RC	SB	CS	SBR	FA	FR	POS	TPR

■ LIVE OAK TAYLOR   Taylor, Edward S.   Deb: 8/21/1877

1877	Har-N	2	8	0	3	0	0	0	0	0	2	.375	.375	.375	153	0	0	1				1.000	-1	/O	0.0
1884	Pit-a	41	152	22	32	4	1	0		6		.211	.255	.250	67	-5	-5	10				.798	-1	O	-0.6
Total	2	43	160	22	35	4	1	0	0	6	2	.219	.260	.256	70	-5	-5	11				.802	-1	/O	-0.6

■ FRED TAYLOR   Taylor, Frederick Rankin   b: 12/3/24, Zanesville, Ohio   BL/TR, 6'3", 201 lbs.   Deb: 9/12/50

1950	Was-A	6	16	1	2	0	0	0	0	1	2	.125	.176	.125	-23	-3	-3	0	0	0	0	.968	0	/1	-0.3
1951	Was-A	6	12	1	2	1	0	0	0	0	4	.167	.167	.250	12	-2	-1	1	0	0	0	.962	-0	/1	-0.2
1952	Was-A	10	19	3	5	1	0	0	4	3	2	.263	.364	.316	93	-0	-0	3	0	0	0	1.000	1	/1	0.1
Total	3	22	47	5	9	2	0	0	4	4	8	.191	.255	.234	33	-5	-4	3	0	0	0	.979	1	/1	-0.4

■ HARRY TAYLOR   Taylor, Harry Leonard   b: 4/4/1866, Halsey Valley, N.Y.   d: 7/12/55, Buffalo, N.Y.   BL , 6'2", 160 lbs.   Deb: 4/18/1890

1890	*Lou-a	134	553	115	169	7	7	0		68		.306	.383	.344	120	14	16	92	45			.982	5	*1S/2C	1.5
1891	Lou-a	93	356	81	105	7	4	2	37	55	33	.295	.397	.354	120	11	12	57	15			.979	3	1/32C	0.9
1892	Lou-N	125	493	66	128	7	1	0	34	58	23	.260	.342	.278	98	-3	3	56	24			.923	-8	O12/3S	-0.9
1893	Bal-N	88	360	50	102	9	1	1	54	32	11	.283	.347	.322	79	-9	-10	50	24			.976	-3	*1	-1.2
Total	4	440	1762	312	504	30	13	3	125	213	67	.286	.367	.323	105	13	21	256	108				-2	1/O2S3C	0.3

■ HARRY TAYLOR   Taylor, Harry Warren   b: 12/26/07, McKeesport, Pa.   d: 4/27/69, Toledo, Ohio   BL/TL, 6'1.5", 185 lbs.   Deb: 4/14/32

| 1932 | Chi-N | 10 | 8 | 1 | 1 | 0 | 0 | 0 | 1 | 1 | 1 | .125 | .222 | .125 | -4 | -1 | -1 | 0 | 0 | | | 1.000 | -0 | /1 | -0.1 |

■ SANDY TAYLOR   Taylor, James B.   5'10.5", 175 lbs.   Deb: 8/11/1879

| 1879 | Tro-N | 24 | 97 | 10 | 21 | 4 | 0 | 0 | 8 | 1 | 8 | .216 | .224 | .258 | 63 | -4 | -3 | 6 | | | | .765 | -3 | O | -0.7 |

■ ZACK TAYLOR   Taylor, James Wren   b: 7/27/1898, Yulee, Fla.   d: 9/19/74, Orlando, Fla.   BR/TR, 5'11.5", 180 lbs.   Deb: 6/15/20   MC

1920	Bro-N	9	13	3	5	2	0	0	5	0	2	.385	.385	.538	158	1	1	2	0	1	-1	.882	-1	/C	-0.1
1921	Bro-N	30	102	6	20	0	2	0	8	1	8	.196	.212	.235	17	-12	-12	5	2	0	1	.965	0	C	-1.0
1922	Bro-N	7	14	0	3	0	0	0	2	1	1	.214	.267	.214	26	-2	-2	1	0	0	0	.950	-1	/C	-0.2
1923	Bro-N	96	337	29	97	11	6	0	46	9	13	.288	.312	.356	78	-12	-11	36	2	5	-2	.967	14	C	0.5
1924	Bro-N	99	345	36	100	9	4	1	39	14	14	.290	.319	.348	81	-10	-9	38	0	1	-1	.988	-8	C	-1.2
1925	Bro-N	109	352	33	109	16	4	3	44	17	19	.310	.343	.403	92	-5	-4	48	0	0	0	.959	-9	C	-0.8
1926	Bos-N	125	432	36	110	22	3	0	42	28	27	.255	.303	.319	74	-20	-15	41	1			.985	2	*C	-0.5
1927	Bos-N	30	96	8	23	2	1	1	14	8	5	.240	.298	.313	69	-5	-4	9	0			.988	12	C	0.9
	NY-N	83	258	18	60	7	3	0	21	17	20	.233	.283	.283	52	-17	-17	21	2			.972	-4	C	-1.6
	Yr	113	354	26	83	9	4	1	35	25	25	.234	.287	.291	56	-22	-21	30	2			.978	8	*C	-0.7
1928	Bos-N	125	399	36	100	15	1	2	30	33	29	.251	.313	.308	66	-21	-18	39	2			.985	-12	*C	-2.0
1929	Bos-N	34	101	8	25	7	0	0	10	7	9	.248	.303	.317	56	-7	-7	10	0			.965	6	C	0.2
	*Chi-N	64	215	29	59	16	3	1	31	19	18	.274	.336	.391	79	-7	-7	28	0			.979	-1	C	-0.2
	Yr	98	316	37	84	23	3	1	41	26	27	.266	.326	.367	72	-14	-14	38	0			.974	5	C	0.0
1930	Chi-N	32	95	12	22	2	1	0	11	2	12	.232	.255	.305	34	-10	-10	7	0			1.000	-1	C	-0.8
1931	Chi-N	8	4	0	1	0	0	0	0	2	1	.250	.500	.250	106	0	0	1	0			1.000	1	/C	0.1
1932	Chi-N	21	30	2	6	1	0	0	3	1	4	.200	.226	.233	24	-3	-3	2	0			1.000	3	C	0.0
1933	Chi-N	16	11	0	0	0	0	0	0	0	1	.000	.000	.000	-99	-3	-3	0	0			1.000	-0	C	-0.3
1934	NY-A	4	7	0	1	0	0	0	0	0	1	.143	.143	.143	-28	-1	-1	0	0	0	0	1.000	-0	/C	-0.1
1935	Bro-N	26	54	2	7	3	0	0	5	2	8	.130	.175	.185	-3	-8	-8	1	0			.970	0	C	-0.7
Total	16	918	2865	258	748	113	28	9	311	161	192	.261	.304	.329	68	-143	-130	289	9	7		.977	1	C	-7.8

■ JOE TAYLOR   Taylor, Joe Cephus   b: 3/2/26, Chapman, Ala.   BR/TR, 6'1", 185 lbs.   Deb: 8/26/54

1954	Phi-A	18	58	5	13	1	1	1	8	2	9	.224	.250	.328	57	-4	-4	4	0	1	-1	.943	-0	O	-0.6
1957	Cin-N	33	107	14	28	7	0	4	9	6	24	.262	.301	.439	89	-1	-2	13	0	1	-1	.971	4	O	0.0
1958	StL-N	18	23	2	7	3	0	1	3	2	4	.304	.360	.565	135	1	1	5	0	0	0	1.000	-0	/O	0.1
	Bal-A	36	77	11	21	4	0	2	9	7	19	.273	.333	.403	107	0	1	9	0	0	0	.972	-2	O	-0.2
1959	Bal-A	14	32	2	5	1	0	1	2	11	5	.156	.372	.281	84	-0	-0	4	0	0	0	1.000	-3	O	-0.3
Total	4	119	297	34	74	16	1	9	31	28	61	.249	.314	.401	92	-4	-4	35	0	2	-1	.969	-1	/O	-1.0

■ LEO TAYLOR   Taylor, Leo Thomas "Chink"   b: 5/13/01, Walla Walla, Wash.   d: 5/20/82, Seattle, Wash.   BR/TR, 5'10.5", 150 lbs.   Deb: 5/03/23

| 1923 | Chi-A | 1 | 0 | 0 | 0 | 0 | 0 | 0 | 0 | 0 | 0 | — | — | — | 0 | 0 | 0 | 0 | 0 | 0 | 0 | .000 | 0 | R | 0.0 |

■ HAWK TAYLOR   Taylor, Robert Dale   b: 4/3/39, Metropolis, Ill.   BR/TR, 6'2", 190 lbs.   Deb: 6/09/57

1957	Mil-N	7	1	2	0	0	0	0	0	0	0	.000	.000	.000	-99	-0	-0	0	0	0	0	.000	0	/C	0.0
1958	Mil-N	4	8	1	1	1	0	0	0	0	3	.125	.125	.250	-4	-1	-1	0	0	0	0	1.000	-0	/O	-0.2
1961	Mil-N	20	26	1	5	0	0	1	3	1	11	.192	.276	.308	58	-2	-2	2	0	1	-1	1.000	0	/OC	-0.2
1962	Mil-N	20	47	3	12	0	0	0	2	2	10	.255	.286	.255	48	-3	-3	3	0	1	-1	.960	1	O	-0.4
1963	Mil-N	16	29	1	2	0	0	0	0	1	12	.069	.100	.069	-51	-6	-6	0	0	0	0	1.000	1	/O	-0.6
1964	NY-N	92	225	20	54	8	0	4	23	8	33	.240	.272	.329	70	-10	-9	19	0	0	0	.981	-0	CO	-0.8
1965	NY-N	25	46	5	7	0	0	4	10	1	9	.152	.170	.413	61	-3	-3	2	0	0	0	.962	-2	C/1	-0.5
1966	NY-N	53	109	5	19	2	0	3	12	3	19	.174	.204	.275	32	-10	-10	4	0	1	-1	1.000	-4	C1	-1.4
1967	NY-N	13	37	3	9	3	0	0	4	2	8	.243	.282	.324	74	-1	-1	3	0	0	0	.955	5	C	0.4
	Cal-A	23	52	5	16	3	0	1	3	4	8	.308	.357	.423	135	2	2	8	0	0	0	1.000	2	C	0.5
1969	KC-A	64	89	7	24	5	0	3	21	6	18	.270	.316	.427	105	0	0	11	0	0	0	.909	-4	O/C	-0.4
1970	KC-A	57	55	3	9	3	0	0	6	6	16	.164	.258	.218	33	-5	-5	3	0	0	0	1.000	0	/C1	-0.5
Total	11	394	724	56	158	25	0	16	82	36	146	.218	.259	.319	62	-39	-37	57	0	3	-2	.984	-1	C/O1	-4.1

■ BOB TAYLOR   Taylor, Robert Lee   b: 3/20/44, Leland, Miss.   BL/TR, 5'9", 170 lbs.   Deb: 4/09/70

| 1970 | SF-N | 63 | 84 | 12 | 16 | 0 | 0 | 2 | 10 | 12 | 13 | .190 | .320 | .262 | 58 | -5 | -4 | 8 | 0 | 0 | 0 | 1.000 | -0 | O/C | -0.5 |

■ SAMMY TAYLOR   Taylor, Samuel Douglas   b: 2/27/33, Woodruff, S.C.   BL/TR, 6'2", 185 lbs.   Deb: 4/27/58

1958	Chi-N	96	301	30	78	12	2	6	36	27	46	.259	.320	.372	84	-8	-7	35	2	1	0	.988	-11	C	-1.3
1959	Chi-N	110	353	41	95	13	2	13	43	35	47	.269	.337	.428	103	1	1	51	1	0	0	.982	-15	*C	-0.8
1960	Chi-N	74	150	14	31	9	0	3	17	6	18	.207	.242	.327	55	-10	-10	10	0	1	-1	.978	-9	C	-1.8
1961	Chi-N	89	235	26	56	8	2	8	23	23	39	.238	.317	.391	86	-5	-5	29	0	0	0	.989	-8	C	-1.0
1962	Chi-N	7	15	0	2	1	0	0	1	3	3	.133	.278	.200	30	-1	-2	1	0	0	0	1.000	-1	/C	-0.3
	NY-N	68	158	12	35	4	2	3	20	23	17	.222	.328	.329	76	-5	-5	18	0	0	0	.991	-9	C	-1.2
	Yr	75	173	12	37	5	2	3	21	26	20	.214	.323	.318	72	-6	-7	19	0	0	0	.992	-10	C	-1.5
1963	NY-N	22	35	3	9	0	1	0	6	5	7	.257	.350	.314	91	-0	-0	3	0	0	0	1.000	0	C	-0.3
	Cin-N	3	6	0	0	0	0	0	0	0	2	.000	.000	.000	-97	-2	-2	0	0	0	0	.833	-1	/C	-0.3
	Yr	25	41	3	9	0	1	0	6	5	9	.220	.304	.268	65	-2	-2	3	0	0	0	.984	-1	C	-0.3
	Cle-A	4	10	1	3	0	0	0	1	0	2	.300	.300	.300	69	-0	-0	1	0	0	0	1.000	-1	C	-0.1
Total	6	473	1263	127	309	47	9	33	147	122	181	.245	.315	.375	84	-29	-29	147	3	2	-0	.986	-55	C	-6.8

■ TOMMY TAYLOR   Taylor, Thomas Livingstone Carlton   b: 9/17/1892, Mexia, Tex.   d: 4/5/56, Greenville, Miss.   BR/TR, 5'8.5", 160 lbs.   Deb: 7/09/24

| 1924 | *Was-A | 26 | 73 | 11 | 19 | 3 | 1 | 0 | 10 | 2 | 8 | .260 | .289 | .329 | 61 | -5 | -4 | 7 | 2 | 0 | 1 | .923 | -5 | 3/2O | -0.7 |

■ BILLY TAYLOR   Taylor, William H.   b: 1872, Butler, Ky.   d: 9/12/05, Cincinnati, Ohio   Deb: 9/19/1898

| 1898 | Lou-N | 9 | 24 | 2 | 6 | 1 | 0 | 0 | 2 | 1 | | .250 | .308 | .292 | 73 | -1 | -1 | 3 | 1 | | | .909 | -1 | /32 | -0.2 |

■ BILLY TAYLOR

Taylor, William Henry "Bollicky Bill" b: 1855, Washington, D.C. d: 5/14/1900, Jacksonville, Fla. BR/TR, 5'11.5", 204 lbs. Deb: 5/21/1881

YEAR	TM/L	G	AB	R	H	2B	3B	HR	RBI	BB	SO	AVG	OBP	SLG	PRO+	BR	/A	RC	SB	CS	SBR	FA	FR	POS	TPR
1881	Wor-N	6	28	3	3	1	0	0	2	0	2	.107	.107	.143	-21	-4	-4	0				.882	1	/OP	-0.2
	Det-N	1	4	0	2	2	0	0	1	0	0	.500	.500	1.000	346	1	1	2				.750	-0	/3	0.1
	Cle-N	24	103	6	25	1	0	0	12	0	8	.243	.243	.252	59	-5	-4	6				.859	-1	O/P3	-0.5
	Yr	31	135	9	30	4	0	0	15	0	10	.222	.222	.252	50	-8	-7	8				.864	-0	O/P3	-0.6
1882	Pit-a	70	299	40	84	16	13	3		7		.281	.297	.452	157	14	16	41				.862	-11	C13/OP	0.4
1883	Pit-a	83	369	43	96	13	7	2		9		.260	.278	.350	106	-0	3	37				.747	-15	OCP/1	-0.9
1884	StL-U	43	186	44	68	23	1	3		7		.366	.389	.548	206	21	20	41				.872	1	P1/O	0.6
	Phi-a	30	111	8	28	6	2	0		2		.252	.272	.342	95	0	-1	11				.784	2	P	0.0
1885	Phi-a	6	21	0	4	0	0	0		0		.190	.190	.190	21	-2	-2	1				.556	-1	/P	0.0
1886	Bal-a	10	39	4	12	0	1	0		1		.308	.325	.359	119	1	1	5	1			.800	-1	/P1C	0.0
1887	Phi-a	1	4	0	1	0	0	0		0		.250	.250	.250	41	-0	-0	0	0			1.000	-0	/P	0.0
Total	7	274	1164	148	323	62	24	8	15	26	10	.277	.294	.393	125	26	29	144	1				-26	P/OC13	-0.5

■ BILL TAYLOR

Taylor, William Michael b: 12/30/29, Alhambra, Cal. BL/TR, 6'3", 212 lbs. Deb: 4/14/54

YEAR	TM/L	G	AB	R	H	2B	3B	HR	RBI	BB	SO	AVG	OBP	SLG	PRO+	BR	/A	RC	SB	CS	SBR	FA	FR	POS	TPR
1954	NY-N	55	65	4	12	1	0	2	10	3	15	.185	.243	.292	38	-6	-6	5	0	0	0	1.000	-3	/O	-0.9
1955	NY-N	65	64	9	17	4	0	4	12	1	16	.266	.277	.516	104	0	-0	8	0	0	0	.000	-1	/O	-0.1
1956	NY-N	1	4	0	1	1	0	0	0	0	1	.250	.250	.500	96	-0	-0	1	0	0	0	1.000	-0	/O	0.0
1957	NY-N	11	9	0	0	0	0	0	0	1	2	.000	.100	.000	-70	-2	-2	0	0	0	0	.000	0	H	-0.2
	Det-A	9	23	4	8	2	0	1	3	0	3	.348	.348	.565	142	1	1	5	0	0	0	1.000	-1	/O	0.0
1958	Det-A	8	8	0	3	0	0	0	1	0	2	.375	.375	.375	100	0	0	1	0	0	0	1.000	-0	/O	0.0
Total	5	149	173	17	41	8	0	7	26	5	39	.237	.267	.405	74	-7	-7	19	0	0	0	1.000	-5	/O	-1.2

■ BIRDIE TEBBETTS

Tebbetts, George Robert b: 11/10/12, Burlington, Vt. BR/TR, 5'11.5", 170 lbs. Deb: 9/16/36 M

YEAR	TM/L	G	AB	R	H	2B	3B	HR	RBI	BB	SO	AVG	OBP	SLG	PRO+	BR	/A	RC	SB	CS	SBR	FA	FR	POS	TPR
1936	Det-A	10	33	7	10	1	2	1	4	5	3	.303	.395	.545	129	1	1	7	0	0	0	.982	2	C	0.4
1937	Det-A	50	162	15	31	4	3	2	16	10	13	.191	.238	.290	32	-17	-18	12	0	0	0	.963	-4	C	-1.8
1938	Det-A	53	143	16	42	6	2	1	25	12	13	.294	.348	.385	79	-4	-5	19	1	2	-1	.985	-5	C	-0.8
1939	Det-A	106	341	37	89	22	2	4	53	25	20	.261	.315	.372	70	-13	-17	40	2	1	0	.970	15	*C	0.2
1940	*Det-A	111	379	46	112	24	4	4	46	35	14	.296	.357	.412	90	-1	-6	55	4	5	-2	.975	18	*C	1.8
1941	Det-A☆	110	359	28	102	19	4	2	47	38	29	.284	.354	.376	85	-3	-8	50	1	2	-1	.977	7	C	0.6
1942	Det-A★	99	308	24	76	11	0	1	27	39	17	.247	.335	.292	71	-8	-11	33	4	0	1	.977	7	C	0.5
1946	Det-A	87	280	20	68	11	2	1	34	28	23	.243	.312	.307	69	-10	-12	26	1	3	-2	.982	-1	C	-1.1
1947	Det-A	20	53	1	5	1	0	0	2	3	3	.094	.143	.113	-27	-9	-9	1	0	1	-1	1.000	8	C	-0.1
	Bos-A	90	291	22	87	10	0	1	28	21	30	.299	.346	.344	86	-3	-6	34	2	4	-2	.974	-3	C	-0.5
	Yr	110	344	23	92	11	0	1	30	24	33	.267	.315	.308	69	-12	-15	32	2	5	-2	.980	5	*C	-0.6
1948	Bos-A★	128	446	54	125	26	2	5	68	62	32	.280	.371	.381	95	1	-2	63	5	2	0	.981	-9	*C	-0.2
1949	Bos-A★	122	403	42	109	14	0	5	48	62	22	.270	.369	.342	83	-5	-9	55	8	1	**2**	.980	-6	*C	-0.6
1950	Bos-A	79	268	33	83	10	1	8	45	29	26	.310	.377	.444	100	4	-0	43	1	1	-0	.988	-6	C	-0.3
1951	Cle-A	55	137	8	36	6	0	2	18	8	7	.263	.308	.350	82	-5	-4	14	0	0	0	.977	-1	C	-0.3
1952	Cle-A	42	101	4	25	4	0	1	8	12	9	.248	.339	.317	89	-2	-1	11	0	1	-1	.986	-4	C	-0.4
Total	14	1162	3704	357	1000	169	22	38	469	389	261	.270	.341	.358	81	-73	-106	461	29	23	-5	.978	19	*C	-2.6

■ PUSSY TEBEAU

Tebeau, Charles Alston b: 2/22/1870, Worcester, Mass. d: 3/25/50, Pittsfield, Mass. BR/TR, 5'10", 175 lbs. Deb: 7/22/1895

YEAR	TM/L	G	AB	R	H	2B	3B	HR	RBI	BB	SO	AVG	OBP	SLG	PRO+	BR	/A	RC	SB	CS	SBR	FA	FR	POS	TPR
1895	Cle-N	2	6	3	3	0	0	0	1	2	1	.500	.625	.500	185	1	1	3	1			1.000	1	/O	0.1

■ GEORGE TEBEAU

Tebeau, George E. "White Wings" b: 12/26/1861, St.Louis, Mo. d: 2/4/23, Denver, Colo. BR/TR, 5'9", 175 lbs. Deb: 4/16/1887 F

YEAR	TM/L	G	AB	R	H	2B	3B	HR	RBI	BB	SO	AVG	OBP	SLG	PRO+	BR	/A	RC	SB	CS	SBR	FA	FR	POS	TPR
1887	Cin-a	85	318	57	94	12	5	4		31		.296	.364	.403	113	7	6	62	37			.887	4	O/P	0.6
1888	Cin-a	121	411	72	94	12	12	3	51	61		.229	.338	.338	114	12	8	61	37			.911	4	*O	0.8
1889	Cin-a	135	496	110	125	21	11	7	70	69	62	.252	.350	.381	107	8	5	90	61			.887	-5	*O/1	-0.3
1890	Tol-a	94	381	71	102	16	10	1		51		.268	.359	.370	114	9	7	72	55			.951	3	*O/P	0.6
1894	Was-N	61	222	41	50	10	6	0	28	37	20	.225	.341	.324	65	-13	-12	32	17			.857	-9	O	-1.9
	Cle-N	40	150	32	47	9	4	0	25	25	18	.313	.411	.427	100	2	1	31	9			.928	-5	O1/3	-0.5
	Yr	101	372	73	97	19	10	0	53	62	38	.261	.369	.366	80	-11	-11	63	26			.880	-14	O1/3	-2.4
1895	Cle-N	91	337	57	110	16	6	0	68	50	28	.326	.415	.409	109	10	6	64	12			.873	-9	O1	-0.4
Total	6	627	2315	440	622	96	54	15	242	324	128	.269	.364	.376	105	35	22	411	228			.900	-19	O/1P3	-1.1

■ PATSY TEBEAU

Tebeau, Oliver Wendell b: 12/5/1864, St.Louis, Mo. d: 5/15/18, St.Louis, Mo. BR/TR, 5'8", 163 lbs. Deb: 9/20/1887 FM

YEAR	TM/L	G	AB	R	H	2B	3B	HR	RBI	BB	SO	AVG	OBP	SLG	PRO+	BR	/A	RC	SB	CS	SBR	FA	FR	POS	TPR
1887	Chi-N	20	68	8	11	3	0	0	10	4	4	.162	.208	.206	15	-8	-9	5	8			.855	-3	3	-1.0
1889	Cle-N	136	521	72	147	20	6	8	76	37	41	.282	.332	.390	105	1	3	78	26			.897	0	*3	0.6
1890	Cle-P	110	450	86	135	26	6	5	74	34	20	.300	.353	.418	117	4	10	73	14			**.872**	13	*3M	2.2
1891	Cle-N	61	249	38	65	8	3	1	41	16	13	.261	.313	.329	86	-4	-5	30	12			.884	6	3/OM	0.3
1892	*Cle-N	86	340	47	83	13	3	2	49	23	34	.244	.307	.318	87	-4	-6	36	6			.911	-2	3/21SM	-0.5
1893	Cle-N	116	486	90	160	32	8	2	102	32	11	.329	.375	.440	112	11	6	90	19			.980	6	13/2M	1.0
1894	Cle-N	125	523	82	158	23	7	3	89	35	35	.302	.347	.390	76	-18	-22	84	30			.977	-4	*12/3SM	-1.9
1895	*Cle-N	63	264	50	84	13	2	2	52	16	18	.318	.362	.405	94	-0	-3	43	8			.992	6	1/23M	0.4
1896	*Cle-N	132	543	56	146	22	6	2	94	21	22	.269	.300	.343	67	-24	-29	65	20			.985	7	*1/32SPM	-1.7
1897	Cle-N	109	412	62	110	15	9	0	59	30		.267	.323	.347	73	-14	-18	52	11			**.994**	0	*12/3SM	-1.4
1898	Cle-N	131	477	53	123	11	4	1	63	53		.258	.341	.304	86	-7	-7	54	5			.984	3	12/S3M	-0.2
1899	StL-N	77	281	27	69	10	3	1	26	18		.246	.303	.313	67	-12	-13	29	5			.980	-3	1S/32M	-1.4
1900	StL-N	1	4	0	0	0	0	0	0	0		.000	.000	.000	-99	-1	-1	0	0			.700	-1	/SM	-0.1
Total	13	1167	4618	671	1291	196	57	27	735	319	198	.280	.332	.364	87	-76	-93	638	164			.984	29	13/2SPO	-3.7

■ DICK TEED

Teed, Richard Leroy b: 3/8/26, Springfield, Mass. BB/TR, 5'11", 180 lbs. Deb: 7/24/53

YEAR	TM/L	G	AB	R	H	2B	3B	HR	RBI	BB	SO	AVG	OBP	SLG	PRO+	BR	/A	RC	SB	CS	SBR	FA	FR	POS	TPR
1953	Bro-N	1	1	0	0	0	0	0	0	0	1	.000	.000	.000	-98	-0	-0	0	0	0	0	.000	0	H	0.0

■ WILFREDO TEJADA

Tejada, Wilfredo Aristides (Andujar) b: 11/12/62, Santo Domingo, D.R. BR/TR, 6', 175 lbs. Deb: 9/09/86

YEAR	TM/L	G	AB	R	H	2B	3B	HR	RBI	BB	SO	AVG	OBP	SLG	PRO+	BR	/A	RC	SB	CS	SBR	FA	FR	POS	TPR
1986	Mon-N	10	25	1	6	1	0	0	2	2	8	.240	.296	.280	60	-1	-1	2	0	0	0	1.000	-1	C	-0.1
1988	Mon-N	8	15	1	4	2	0	0	2	0	4	.267	.267	.400	85	-0	-0	2	0	0	0	1.000	3	/C	0.3
Total	2	18	40	2	10	3	0	0	4	2	12	.250	.286	.325	70	-2	-2	4	0	0	0	1.000	2	/C	0.2

■ JOHNNY TEMPLE

Temple, John Ellis b: 8/8/28, Lexington, N.C. BR/TR, 5'11", 175 lbs. Deb: 4/15/52 C

YEAR	TM/L	G	AB	R	H	2B	3B	HR	RBI	BB	SO	AVG	OBP	SLG	PRO+	BR	/A	RC	SB	CS	SBR	FA	FR	POS	TPR
1952	Cin-N	30	97	8	19	3	0	1	5	5	1	.196	.235	.258	37	-8	-8	5	2	1	0	.984	-1	2	-0.8
1953	Cin-N	63	110	14	29	4	0	1	9	7	12	.264	.314	.327	67	-5	-5	12	1	0	0	.964	10	2	0.6
1954	Cin-N	146	505	60	155	14	8	0	44	62	24	.307	.385	.366	94	0	-1	77	21	7	2	.973	-10	*2	0.0
1955	Cin-N	150	588	94	165	20	3	0	50	80	32	.281	.368	.325	81	-9	-13	79	19	4	3	.971	-3	*2/S	-0.1
1956	Cin-N★	154	632	88	180	18	3	2	41	58	40	.285	.346	.332	78	-13	-18	76	14	4	2	.981	-7	*2/O	-1.0
1957	Cin-N★	145	557	85	158	24	4	0	37	**94**	34	.284	.391	.341	92	4	-1	86	19	5	**3**	.974	-21	*2	-0.8
1958	Cin-N	141	542	82	166	31	6	3	47	91	41	.306	.406	.402	109	16	12	96	15	8	-0	.979	-19	*2/1	0.3
1959	Cin-N★	149	598	102	186	35	6	8	67	72	40	.311	.387	.430	114	17	14	104	14	3	2	.974	-26	*2	0.3
1960	Cle-A	98	381	50	102	13	1	2	19	32	20	.268	.326	.323	79	-12	-11	41	11	5	0	.974	-30	23	-3.4
1961	Cle-A★	129	518	73	143	22	3	3	30	61	36	.276	.352	.347	90	-7	-6	65	9	5	-0	.969	-30	*2	-2.2
1962	Bal-A	78	270	28	71	8	1	1	17	36	22	.263	.352	.311	84	-6	-4	33	7	4	-0	.981	-19	2	-1.6
	Hou-N	31	95	14	25	4	0	0	12	7	11	.263	.314	.305	72	-4	-3	10	1	0	0	.941	-8	2/3	-0.9
1963	Hou-N	100	322	22	85	12	1	1	17	41	24	.264	.347	.317	99	-2	1	40	7	2	1	.970	-20	23	-1.4

YEAR	TM/L	G	AB	R	H	2B	3B	HR	RBI	BB	SO	AVG	OBP	SLG	PRO+	BR	/A	RC	SB	CS	SBR	FA	FR	POS	TPR
1964	Cin-N	6	3	0	0	0	0	0	0	2	1	.000	.400	.000	23	-0	-0	0	0	0	0	.000	0	H	0.0
Total	13	1420	5218	720	1484	208	36	22	395	648	338	.284	.365	.351	91	-30	-45	725	140	48	13	.974	-183	*2/31OS	-11.0

■ GARRY TEMPLETON Templeton, Garry Lewis b: 3/24/56, Lockney, Tex. BB/TR, 5′11″, 190 lbs. Deb: 8/09/76

YEAR	TM/L	G	AB	R	H	2B	3B	HR	RBI	BB	SO	AVG	OBP	SLG	PRO+	BR	/A	RC	SB	CS	SBR	FA	FR	POS	TPR
1976	StL-N	53	213	32	62	8	2	1	17	7	33	.291	.317	.362	91	-3	-3	24	11	7	-1	.922	1	S	0.4
1977	StL-N★	153	621	94	200	19	**18**	8	79	15	70	.322	.339	.449	111	6	8	85	28	24	-6	.958	-3	*S	1.5
1978	StL-N	155	647	82	181	31	**13**	2	47	22	87	.280	.304	.377	91	-11	-10	74	34	11	4	.953	23	*S	3.8
1979	StL-N†	154	672	105	**211**	32	**19**	9	62	18	91	.314	.333	.458	113	10	9	100	26	10	2	.960	18	*S	4.6
1980	StL-N	118	504	83	161	19	9	4	43	18	43	.319	.343	.417	108	6	4	66	31	15	0	.959	28	*S	4.7
1981	StL-N	80	333	47	96	16	8	1	33	14	55	.288	.317	.393	98	-1	-2	37	8	12	-5	.960	5	S	0.7
1982	SD-N	141	563	76	139	25	8	6	64	26	82	.247	.281	.352	80	-19	-16	49	27	16	-2	.961	-24	*S	-3.0
1983	SD-N	126	460	39	121	20	2	3	40	21	57	.263	.295	.335	77	-17	-15	42	16	6	1	.960	-14	*S	-1.7
1984	*SD-N	148	493	40	127	19	3	2	35	39	81	.258	.313	.320	79	-14	-14	48	8	3	1	.960	-23	*S	-2.4
1985	SD-N★	148	546	63	154	30	2	6	55	41	88	.282	.333	.377	100	-1	-0	69	16	6	1	.968	-7	*S	0.9
1986	SD-N	147	510	42	126	21	2	2	44	35	86	.247	.297	.308	68	-23	-22	44	10	5	0	.966	-28	*S	-3.9
1987	SD-N	148	510	42	113	13	5	5	48	42	92	.222	.282	.296	55	-34	-32	42	14	3	2	.972	9	*S	-0.8
1988	SD-N	110	362	35	90	15	7	3	36	20	50	.249	.288	.354	85	-8	-8	36	8	2	1	.968	15	*S/3	1.8
1989	SD-N	142	506	43	129	26	3	6	40	23	80	.255	.287	.354	82	-13	-13	47	1	3	-2	.970	13	*S	1.0
1990	SD-N	144	505	45	125	25	3	9	59	24	59	.248	.282	.362	75	-18	-18	46	1	4	-2	.957	-9	*S	-1.9
1991	SD-N	32	57	5	11	1	1	1	6	1	9	.193	.207	.298	39	-5	-5	2	0	1	-1	.950	-3	3/S	-0.8
	NY-N	80	219	20	50	9	1	2	20	9	29	.228	.259	.306	59	-12	-12	16	3	1	0	.963	5	S1/3O	-0.6
	Yr	112	276	25	61	10	2	3	26	10	38	.221	.248	.304	54	-17	-17	18	3	2	-0	.963	3	S13/O	-1.4
Total	16	2079	7721	893	2096	329	106	70	728	375	1092	.271	.306	.369	87	-156	-147	829	242	129	-5	.961	6	*S/13O	4.3

■ GENE TENACE Tenace, Fury Gene (b: Fiore Gino Tennaci) b: 10/10/46, Russellton, Pa. BR/TR, 6′, 190 lbs. Deb: 5/29/69 MC

YEAR	TM/L	G	AB	R	H	2B	3B	HR	RBI	BB	SO	AVG	OBP	SLG	PRO+	BR	/A	RC	SB	CS	SBR	FA	FR	POS	TPR
1969	Oak-A	16	38	1	6	0	0	1	2	1	15	.158	.200	.237	23	-4	-4	2	0	0	0	1.000	-0	C	-0.4
1970	Oak-A	38	105	19	32	6	0	7	20	23	30	.305	.430	.562	178	11	11	26	0	2	-1	.990	4	C	1.6
1971	*Oak-A	65	179	26	49	7	0	7	25	29	34	.274	.381	.430	132	8	8	31	2	1	0	.994	-6	C/O	0.4
1972	*Oak-A	82	227	22	51	5	3	5	32	24	42	.225	.307	.339	97	-2	-1	24	0	0	0	.979	-8	C/O123	-0.9
1973	*Oak-A	160	510	83	132	18	2	24	84	101	94	.259	.391	.443	142	27	31	94	2	2	-1	.989	-11	*1C/2D	1.0
1974	*Oak-A	158	484	71	102	17	1	26	73	**110**	105	.211	.370	.411	133	19	24	78	2	9	-5	.995	-9	*1C/2	0.7
1975	*Oak-A★	158	498	83	127	17	0	29	87	106	127	.255	.398	.464	146	32	34	100	7	4	-0	.984	-16	*C1/D	2.1
1976	Oak-A	128	417	64	104	19	1	22	66	81	91	.249	.376	.458	150	25	27	76	5	4	-1	.995	-20	1C/D	0.4
1977	SD-N	147	437	66	102	24	4	15	61	**125**	119	.233	.417	.410	137	21	28	87	5	3	-0	.980	-7	C13	2.2
1978	SD-N	142	401	60	90	18	4	16	61	101	98	.224	.394	.409	135	18	22	73	6	5	-1	.993	-3	1C/3	1.6
1979	SD-N	151	463	61	122	16	4	20	67	105	106	.263	.407	.445	141	25	29	91	2	6	-3	**.998**	-3	C1	2.4
1980	SD-N	133	316	46	70	11	1	17	50	92	63	.222	.403	.424	139	18	20	58	4	4	-1	.979	-7	*C1	1.6
1981	StL-N	58	129	26	30	7	0	5	22	38	26	.233	.421	.403	131	8	8	26	0	0	0	.980	-6	C/1	0.3
1982	*StL-N	66	124	18	32	9	0	7	18	36	31	.258	.439	.500	160	13	12	31	1	1	-0	.994	1	C/1	1.5
1983	Pit-N	53	62	7	11	5	0	0	6	12	17	.177	.346	.258	68	-2	-2	7	0	1	-1	.989	-1	1/CO	-0.5
Total	15	1555	4390	653	1060	179	20	201	674	984	998	.241	.391	.429	137	219	249	805	36	42	-14	.986	-92	C1/3OD2	14.0

■ JOHN TENER Tener, John Kinley b: 7/25/1863, County Tyrone, Ireland d: 5/19/46, Pittsburgh, Pa. BR/TR, 6′4″, 180 lbs. Deb: 6/08/1885

YEAR	TM/L	G	AB	R	H	2B	3B	HR	RBI	BB	SO	AVG	OBP	SLG	PRO+	BR	/A	RC	SB	CS	SBR	FA	FR	POS	TPR
1885	Bal-a	1	4	0	0	0	0	0		0		.000	.000	.000	-99	-1	-1	0				.000	-1	/O	-0.2
1888	Chi-N	12	46	4	9	1	0	0	1	1	15	.196	.229	.217	42	-3	-3	3	1			.892	0	P/O	0.0
1889	Chi-N	42	150	18	41	4	2	1	19	7	22	.273	.306	.347	79	-4	-5	17	2			.929	3	P/O1	-0.1
1890	Pit-P	18	63	7	12	0	0	2	5	7	10	.190	.301	.286	64	-4	-3	6	1			.966	2	P/O3	-0.2
Total	4	73	263	29	62	5	2	3	25	15	47	.236	.287	.304	67	-11	-11	25	4			.933	4	/PO31	-0.5

■ TOM TENNANT Tennant, Thomas Francis b: 7/3/1882, Monroe, Wis. d: 2/15/55, San Carlos, Cal. BL/TL, 5′11″, 165 lbs. Deb: 4/18/12

YEAR	TM/L	G	AB	R	H	2B	3B	HR	RBI	BB	SO	AVG	OBP	SLG	PRO+	BR	/A	RC	SB	CS	SBR	FA	FR	POS	TPR
1912	StL-A	2	2	1	0	0	0	0	0	0		.000	.000	.000	-99	-1	-1	0	0			.000	0	H	-0.1

■ FRED TENNEY Tenney, Fred Clay b: 7/9/1859, Marlborough, N.H. d: 6/15/19, Fall River, Mass. Deb: 4/28/1884

YEAR	TM/L	G	AB	R	H	2B	3B	HR	RBI	BB	SO	AVG	OBP	SLG	PRO+	BR	/A	RC	SB	CS	SBR	FA	FR	POS	TPR
1884	Was-U	32	119	17	28	3	1	0		6		.235	.272	.277	89	-2	-1	9				.867	-1	O/1	-0.2
	Bos-U	4	17	1	2	0	0	0		0		.118	.118	.118	-21	-2	-2	0				.750	-1	/P	0.0
	Wil-U	1	3	0	0	0	0	0		0		.000	.000	.000	-97	-1	-1	0				1.000	0	/P	0.0
	Yr	37	139	18	30	3	1	0		6		.216	.248	.252	72	-4	-4	9				.867	-1	O/1P	-0.2

■ FRED TENNEY Tenney, Frederick b: 11/26/1871, Georgetown, Mass. d: 7/3/52, Boston, Mass. BL/TL, 5′9″, 155 lbs. Deb: 6/16/1894 M

YEAR	TM/L	G	AB	R	H	2B	3B	HR	RBI	BB	SO	AVG	OBP	SLG	PRO+	BR	/A	RC	SB	CS	SBR	FA	FR	POS	TPR
1894	Bos-N	27	86	23	34	7	1	2	21	12	9	.395	.469	.570	140	8	6	27	6			.893	-0	C/O1	0.6
1895	Bos-N	49	173	35	47	9	1	1	21	24	5	.272	.360	.353	80	-3	-5	25	6			.885	-4	OC	-0.7
1896	Bos-N	88	348	64	117	14	3	2	49	36	12	.336	.400	.411	110	9	6	69	18			.957	1	OC	0.4
1897	*Bos-N	132	566	125	180	24	3	1	85	49		.318	.376	.376	93	0	-6	99	34			.988	5	*1/O	0.0
1898	Bos-N	117	488	106	160	25	5	0	62	33		.328	.370	.400	115	12	9	85	23			.980	5	*1/C	1.2
1899	Bos-N	150	603	115	209	19	17	1	67	63		.347	.411	.439	122	29	20	126	28			.978	10	*1	2.8
1900	Bos-N	112	437	77	122	13	5	1	56	39		.279	.346	.339	80	-5	-14	60	17			.981	9	*1	-0.5
1901	Bos-N	115	451	66	127	13	1	1	22	37		.282	.340	.322	85	-3	-9	58	15			.976	7	*1/C	-0.3
1902	Bos-N	134	489	88	154	18	3	2	30	73		.315	.410	.376	141	29	28	90	21			**.985**	13	*1	4.0
1903	Bos-N	122	447	79	140	22	3	3	41	70		.313	.415	.396	137	23	25	87	21			.974	8	*1	3.0
1904	Bos-N	147	533	76	144	17	9	1	37	57		.270	.351	.341	119	11	13	75	17			.986	8	*1/O	1.9
1905	Bos-N	149	549	84	158	18	3	0	28	67		.288	.368	.332	112	9	11	77	17			.982	22	*1/PM	2.9
1906	Bos-N	143	544	61	154	12	8	1	28	58		.283	.357	.340	121	13	14	76	17			.983	10	*1M	2.2
1907	Bos-N	150	554	83	151	18	8	0	26	82		.273	.370	.334	121	17	17	79	15			.989	9	*1M	2.4
1908	NY-N	156	583	**101**	149	20	1	2	49	72		.256	.343	.304	102	8	5	68	17			.990	10	*1	1.4
1909	NY-N	101	375	43	88	8	2	3	30	52		.235	.333	.291	92	-1	-2	39	8			.986	8	1	0.6
1911	Bos-N	102	369	52	97	13	4	1	36	50	17	.263	.352	.328	84	-3	-7	45	5			.985	2	1/OM	-0.5
Total	17	1994	7595	1278	2231	270	77	22	688	874	43	.294	.371	.358	109	152	112	1184	285				124	*1O/CP	21.4

■ FRANK TEPEDINO Tepedino, Frank Ronald b: 11/23/47, Brooklyn, N.Y. BL/TL, 5′11″, 192 lbs. Deb: 5/12/67

YEAR	TM/L	G	AB	R	H	2B	3B	HR	RBI	BB	SO	AVG	OBP	SLG	PRO+	BR	/A	RC	SB	CS	SBR	FA	FR	POS	TPR
1967	NY-A	9	5	0	2	0	0	0	0	1	1	.400	.500	.400	175	1	1	1	0	0	0	1.000	0	/1	0.1
1969	NY-A	13	39	6	9	0	0	0	4	4	4	.231	.302	.231	53	-2	-2	3	1	0	0	.950	-1	O	-0.4
1970	NY-A	16	19	2	6	2	0	0	2	1	2	.316	.350	.421	118	0	0	2	0	1	-1	1.000	-1	/1O	-0.1
1971	NY-A	6	6	0	0	0	0	0	0	0	0	.000	.000	.000	-99	-2	-2	0	0	0	0	1.000	-0	/O	-0.2
	Mil-A	53	106	11	21	1	0	2	7	4	17	.198	.234	.264	41	-8	-8	6	2	2	-1	.986	3	1	-0.8
	Yr	59	112	11	21	1	0	2	7	4	17	.188	.222	.250	34	-10	-10	6	2	2	-1	.986	3	1/O	-1.0
1972	NY-A	8	8	0	0	0	0	0	0	0	1	.000	.000	.000	-99	-2	-2	0	0	0	0	.000	0	H	-0.2
1973	Atl-N	74	148	20	45	5	0	4	29	13	21	.304	.360	.419	107	3	2	21	0	0	0	.992	2	1	0.1
1974	Atl-N	78	169	11	39	5	1	0	16	9	13	.231	.274	.272	51	-11	-11	11	1	2	-1	.988	1	1	-1.5
1975	Atl-N	8	7	0	0	0	0	0	0	1	2	.000	.125	.000	-61	-2	-2	0	0	0	0	.000	0	H	-0.2
Total	8	265	507	50	122	13	1	6	58	33	61	.241	.290	.306	65	-23	-24	44	4	5	-2	.989	4	1/O	-3.2

■ JOE TEPSIC Tepsic, Joseph John b: 9/18/23, Slovan, Pa. BR/TR, 5′9″, 170 lbs. Deb: 7/12/46

YEAR	TM/L	G	AB	R	H	2B	3B	HR	RBI	BB	SO	AVG	OBP	SLG	PRO+	BR	/A	RC	SB	CS	SBR	FA	FR	POS	TPR
1946	Bro-N	15	5	2	0	0	0	0	0	1	1	.000	.167	.000	-50	-1	-1	0	0			1.000	-0	/O	-0.1

■ JERRY TERRELL Terrell, Jerry Wayne b: 7/13/46, Waseca, Minn. BR/TR, 6', 170 lbs. Deb: 4/14/73

YEAR	TM/L	G	AB	R	H	2B	3B	HR	RBI	BB	SO	AVG	OBP	SLG	PRO+	BR	/A	RC	SB	CS	SBR	FA	FR	POS	TPR
1973	Min-A	124	438	43	116	15	2	1	32	21	56	.265	.300	.315	71	-16	-18	42	13	7	-0	.962	-14	S32/OD	-2.2
1974	Min-A	116	229	43	56	4	6	0	19	11	27	.245	.279	.314	68	-9	-10	19	3	2	-0	.960	**23**	S23D/O1	1.7
1975	Min-A	108	385	48	110	16	2	1	36	19	27	.286	.324	.345	87	-6	-7	41	4	4	-1	.947	-3	S213/OD	-0.6
1976	Min-A	89	171	29	42	3	1	0	8	9	15	.246	.287	.275	63	-7	-8	14	11	2	2	.988	7	23SD/O	0.3
1977	Min-A	93	214	32	48	6	0	1	20	11	21	.224	.265	.266	46	-16	-16	13	10	4	1	.953	5	32/S1OD	-1.0
1978	KC-A	73	133	14	27	1	0	0	8	4	13	.203	.226	.211	23	-13	-14	6	8	4	0	1.000	6	23S/1	-0.7
1979	KC-A	31	40	5	12	3	0	1	2	1	1	.300	.317	.450	102	0	-0	5	1	0	0	.963	2	3/2PS	0.2
1980	KC-A	23	16	4	1	0	0	0	0	0	0	.063	.063	.063	-65	-4	-4	0	0	0	0	1.000	2	/O12PD	-0.2
Total	8	657	1626	218	412	48	11	4	125	76	160	.253	.289	.304	66	-71	-75	141	50	23	1	.961	27	3S2/D1OP	-2.5

■ TOM TERRELL Terrell, John Thomas b: 6/19/1867, Louisville, Ky. d: 7/9/1893, Louisville, Ky. Deb: 10/05/1886

YEAR	TM/L	G	AB	R	H	2B	3B	HR	RBI	BB	SO	AVG	OBP	SLG	PRO+	BR	/A	RC	SB	CS	SBR	FA	FR	POS	TPR
1886	Lou-a	1	4	0	1	0	0	0		0		.250	.250	.250	55	-0	-0	0	0			.000	-2	/OC	-0.2

■ TERRY Terry Deb: 4/26/1875

YEAR	TM/L	G	AB	R	H	2B	3B	HR	RBI	BB	SO	AVG	OBP	SLG	PRO+	BR	/A	RC	SB	CS	SBR	FA	FR	POS	TPR
1875	Was-n	6	22	0	4	0	1	0		0		.182	.182	.273	57	-1	-1	1						/O1	-0.1

■ ADONIS TERRY Terry, William H b: 8/7/1864, Westfield, Mass. d: 2/24/15, Milwaukee, Wis. BR/TR, 5'11.5", 168 lbs. Deb: 5/01/1884 U

YEAR	TM/L	G	AB	R	H	2B	3B	HR	RBI	BB	SO	AVG	OBP	SLG	PRO+	BR	/A	RC	SB	CS	SBR	FA	FR	POS	TPR
1884	Bro-a	67	236	15	55	10	3	0		8		.233	.258	.301	84	-4	-4	19				.764	-1	PO	0.1
1885	Bro-a	71	264	23	45	1	3	1		10		.170	.201	.208	31	-20	-20	11				.883	2	OP/3	-1.2
1886	Bro-a	75	299	34	71	8	9	2		10		.237	.265	.344	91	-4	-4	33	17			.934	4	POS	-0.3
1887	Bro-a	86	352	56	103	6	10	3		16		.293	.323	.392	100	-0	-1	55	27			.895	3	OP/S	-0.3
1888	Bro-a	30	115	13	29	6	0	0	8	5		.252	.283	.304	91	-1	-1	12	7			.909	1	P/O1	0.0
1889	*Bro-a	49	160	29	48	6	6	2	26	14	14	.300	.356	.450	131	6	6	29	8			.963	5	P1	0.0
1890	*Bro-N	99	363	63	101	17	9	4	59	40	34	.278	.356	.408	124	11	11	66	32			.930	-1	OP/1	0.2
1891	Bro-N	30	91	10	19	7	1	0	6	9	26	.209	.301	.308	80	-2	-2	10	4			.957	-2	P/O	-0.1
1892	Bal-N	1	4	0	0	0	0	0	0	0	1	.000	.000	.000	-97	-1	-1	0	0			1.000	0	/P	0.0
	Pit-N	31	100	10	16	0	4	2	11	10	11	.160	.236	.300	63	-5	-5	8	2			.938	-0	P/O	-0.1
	Yr	32	104	10	16	0	4	2	11	10	12	.154	.228	.288	57	-6	-6	7	2			.940	-0	P/O	-0.1
1893	Pit-N	26	71	9	18	4	3	0	11	3	11	.254	.293	.394	85	-2	-2	9	1			.920	0	P	0.0
1894	Pit-N	1	0	0	0	0	0	0	0	0	0	—	—	—	—	0	0	0	0			.000	0	/P	0.0
	Chi-N	30	95	19	33	4	2	0	17	11	12	.347	.415	.432	101	1	0	19	3			.875	-2	P/O1	-0.1
	Yr	31	95	19	33	4	2	0	17	11	12	.347	.415	.432	101	1	0	19	3			.875	-2	P/O1	-0.1
1895	Chi-N	40	137	18	30	3	2	1	10	2	17	.219	.236	.292	35	-13	-15	10	1			.895	2	P/OS	-0.1
1896	Chi-N	30	99	14	26	4	2	0	15	8	12	.263	.324	.343	75	-3	-4	13	4			.968	-2	P	0.0
1897	Chi-N	1	3	1	0	0	0	0	0	0		.000	.000	.000	-96	-1	-1	0	0			.750	0	/P	0.0
Total	14	667	2389	314	594	76	54	15	163	146	138	.249	.295	.344	87	-38	-43	293	106			.903	10	PO/S13	-1.9

■ BILL TERRY Terry, William Harold "Memphis Bill" b: 10/30/1898, Atlanta, Ga. d: 1/9/89, Jacksonville, Fla. BL/TL, 6'1", 200 lbs. Deb: 9/24/23 MH

YEAR	TM/L	G	AB	R	H	2B	3B	HR	RBI	BB	SO	AVG	OBP	SLG	PRO+	BR	/A	RC	SB	CS	SBR	FA	FR	POS	TPR
1923	NY-N	3	7	1	1	0	0	0	0	2	2	.143	.333	.143	30	-1	-1	0	0	0	0	1.000	0	/1	-0.1
1924	*NY-N	77	163	26	39	7	2	5	24	17	18	.239	.311	.399	91	-3	-2	21	1	1	-0	.988	-2	1	-0.6
1925	NY-N	133	489	75	156	31	6	11	70	42	52	.319	.374	.474	120	11	14	86	4	5	-2	.990	4	*1	0.8
1926	NY-N	98	225	26	65	12	5	5	43	22	17	.289	.352	.453	117	4	5	35	3			.979	4	1O	0.5
1927	NY-N	150	580	101	189	32	13	20	121	46	53	.326	.377	.529	141	31	31	112	1			.993	5	*1	2.6
1928	NY-N	149	568	100	185	36	11	17	101	64	36	.326	.394	.518	136	30	29	114	7			.993	-2	*1	1.4
1929	NY-N	150	607	103	226	39	5	14	117	48	35	.372	.418	.522	132	30	31	128	10			.994	7	*1/O	2.0
1930	NY-N	154	633	139	**254**	39	15	23	129	57	33	**.401**	.452	.619	159	58	60	170	8			.990	13	*1	4.9
1931	NY-N	153	611	**121**	213	43	**20**	9	112	47	36	.349	.397	.529	150	39	41	130	8			.990	9	*1	3.5
1932	NY-N	154	643	124	225	42	11	28	117	32	23	.350	.382	.580	158	46	48	142	4			.991	14	*1M	4.8
1933	*NY-N★	123	475	68	153	20	5	6	58	40	23	.322	.375	.423	129	17	18	77	3			.992	1	*1M	0.8
1934	NY-N★	153	602	109	213	30	6	8	83	60	47	.354	.414	.463	138	31	33	122	0			**.994**	6	*1M	2.5
1935	NY-N★	145	596	91	203	32	8	6	64	41	55	.341	.383	.451	126	20	21	104	7			**.996**	6	*1M	1.2
1936	*NY-N	79	229	36	71	10	5	2	39	19	19	.310	.363	.424	112	4	4	35	0			.996	3	1M	0.1
Total	14	1721	6428	1120	2193	373	112	154	1078	537	449	.341	.393	.506	137	318	332	1275	56	6		.992	67	*1/O	24.4

■ ZEB TERRY Terry, Zebulon Alexander b: 6/17/1891, Denison, Tex. d: 3/14/88, Los Angeles, Cal. BR/TR, 5'8", 129 lbs. Deb: 4/12/16

YEAR	TM/L	G	AB	R	H	2B	3B	HR	RBI	BB	SO	AVG	OBP	SLG	PRO+	BR	/A	RC	SB	CS	SBR	FA	FR	POS	TPR
1916	Chi-A	94	269	20	51	8	4	0	17	33	36	.190	.292	.249	62	-12	-12	23	4			.935	-10	S	-1.9
1917	Chi-A	2	1	0	0	0	0	0	0	2	0	.000	.667	.000	102	0	0	0	0			1.000	-1	/S	0.0
1918	Bos-N	28	105	17	32	2	2	0	8	8	14	.305	.360	.362	125	3	3	14	1			.977	8	S	1.3
1919	Pit-N	129	472	46	107	12	6	0	27	31	26	.227	.280	.278	65	-18	-20	39	12			**.960**	-31	*S	-4.9
1920	Chi-N	133	496	56	139	26	9	0	52	44	22	.280	.341	.369	102	3	2	61	12	16	-6	.962	14	S2	1.9
1921	Chi-N	123	488	59	134	18	1	2	45	27	19	.275	.318	.328	71	-20	-20	49	1	13	-8	.972	6	*2	-1.9
1922	Chi-N	131	496	56	142	24	2	0	67	34	16	.286	.335	.343	74	-18	-19	56	2	11	-6	.964	9	*2/S3	-1.2
Total	7	640	2327	254	605	90	24	2	216	179	133	.260	.318	.322	78	-61	-66	243	32	40		.956	-5	S2/3	-6.7

■ WAYNE TERWILLIGER Terwilliger, Willard Wayne "Twig" b: 6/27/25, Clare, Mich. BR/TR, 5'11", 170 lbs. Deb: 8/06/49 C

YEAR	TM/L	G	AB	R	H	2B	3B	HR	RBI	BB	SO	AVG	OBP	SLG	PRO+	BR	/A	RC	SB	CS	SBR	FA	FR	POS	TPR
1949	Chi-N	36	112	11	25	2	1	2	10	16	22	.223	.326	.313	74	-4	-4	13	0			.978	4	2	0.2
1950	Chi-N	133	480	63	116	22	3	10	32	43	63	.242	.311	.363	77	-17	-16	56	13			.967	-9	*2/13O	-1.9
1951	Chi-N	50	192	26	41	6	0	0	10	29	21	.214	.317	.245	52	-12	-12	17	3	1	0	.969	-4	2	-1.4
	Bro-N	37	50	11	14	1	0	0	4	8	7	.280	.390	.300	87	-0	-0	7	1	0	0	.949	6	2/3	0.7
	Yr	87	242	37	55	7	0	0	14	37	28	.227	.332	.256	59	-12	-13	23	4	1	1	.964	3	2/3	-0.7
1953	Was-A	134	464	62	117	24	4	4	46	64	65	.252	.343	.347	89	-8	-6	58	7	4	-0	.982	5	*2	0.6
1954	Was-A	106	337	42	70	10	1	3	24	32	40	.208	.282	.270	55	-22	-20	27	3	3	-1	.972	13	23/S	-0.3
1955	NY-N	80	257	29	66	16	1	1	18	36	42	.257	.350	.339	84	-5	-5	30	2	4	-2	.985	26	2/S3	2.4
1956	NY-N	14	18	0	4	1	0	0	0	0	5	.222	.222	.278	34	-2	-2	1	0	0	0	.958	2	/2	0.1
1959	KC-A	74	180	27	48	11	0	2	18	19	31	.267	.337	.361	90	-2	-2	23	2	2	-1	.972	20	2/S3	2.0
1960	KC-A	2	1	0	0	0	0	0	0	0	0	.000	.000	.000	-99	-0	-0	0	0	0	0	1.000	0	/2	0.0
Total	9	666	2091	271	501	93	10	22	162	247	296	.240	.323	.325	76	-72	-68	230	31	14		.974	64	2/3SO1	2.4

■ AL TESCH Tesch, Albert John "Tiny" b: 1/27/1891, Jersey City, N.J. d: 8/3/47, Jersey City, N.J. BB/TR, 5'10", 155 lbs. Deb: 8/21/15

YEAR	TM/L	G	AB	R	H	2B	3B	HR	RBI	BB	SO	AVG	OBP	SLG	PRO+	BR	/A	RC	SB	CS	SBR	FA	FR	POS	TPR
1915	Bro-F	8	7	2	2	1	0	0	2	0	0	.286	.286	.429	110	0	0	1	0			.867	3	/2	0.3

■ NICK TESTA Testa, Nicholas b: 6/29/28, New York, N.Y. BR/TR, 5'8", 180 lbs. Deb: 4/23/58 C

YEAR	TM/L	G	AB	R	H	2B	3B	HR	RBI	BB	SO	AVG	OBP	SLG	PRO+	BR	/A	RC	SB	CS	SBR	FA	FR	POS	TPR
1958	SF-N	1	0	0	0	0	0	0	0	0	0	—	—	—	—	0	0	0	0	0	0	.000	-1	/C	0.0

■ DICK TETTELBACH Tettelbach, Richard Morley "Tut" b: 6/26/29, New Haven, Conn. BR/TR, 6', 195 lbs. Deb: 9/25/55

YEAR	TM/L	G	AB	R	H	2B	3B	HR	RBI	BB	SO	AVG	OBP	SLG	PRO+	BR	/A	RC	SB	CS	SBR	FA	FR	POS	TPR
1955	NY-A	2	5	0	0	0	0	0	0	0	0	.000	.000	.000	-99	-1	-1	0	0	0	0	1.000	0	/O	-0.2
1956	Was-A	18	64	10	10	1	2	1	9	14	15	.156	.308	.281	56	-4	-4	7	0	1	-1	1.000	2	O	-0.4
1957	Was-A	9	11	2	2	0	0	0	1	4	2	.182	.400	.182	65	-0	-0	1	0	0	0	.900	-0	/O	-0.1
Total	3	29	80	12	12	1	2	1	10	18	17	.150	.306	.250	49	-6	-6	8	0	1	-1	.980	2	/O	-0.7

■ MICKEY TETTLETON Tettleton, Mickey Lee b: 9/16/60, Oklahoma City, Okla. BB/TR, 6'2", 200 lbs. Deb: 6/30/84

YEAR	TM/L	G	AB	R	H	2B	3B	HR	RBI	BB	SO	AVG	OBP	SLG	PRO+	BR	/A	RC	SB	CS	SBR	FA	FR	POS	TPR
1984	Oak-A	33	76	10	20	2	1	1	5	11	21	.263	.356	.355	105	0	1	10	0	0	0	.992	0	C	0.2
1985	Oak-A	78	211	23	53	12	0	3	15	28	59	.251	.344	.351	98	-2	0	26	2	2	-1	.989	-1	C/D	0.2
1986	Oak-A	90	211	26	43	9	0	10	35	39	51	.204	.331	.389	103	-1	1	31	7	1	2	.984	-2	C	0.5

YEAR	TM/L	G	AB	R	H	2B	3B	HR	RBI	BB	SO	AVG	OBP	SLG	PRO+	BR	/A	RC	SB	CS	SBR	FA	FR	POS	TPR
1987	Oak-A	82	211	19	41	3	0	8	26	30	65	.194	.295	.322	68	-11	-9	22	1	1	-0	.987	4	C/1D	-0.1
1988	Bal-A	86	283	31	74	11	1	11	37	28	70	.261	.332	.424	113	4	5	38	0	1	-1	.992	-10	C	0.1
1989	Bal-A★	117	411	72	106	21	2	26	65	73	117	.258	.371	.509	150	26	27	80	3	2	-0	.994	-7	CD	2.4
1990	Bal-A	135	444	68	99	21	2	15	51	106	160	.223	.378	.381	117	12	14	71	2	4	-2	.991	-13	CD/1O	0.5
1991	Det-A	154	501	85	132	17	2	31	89	101	131	.263	.389	.491	140	31	30	99	3	3	-1	.990	-15	*CD/O1	2.2
1992	Det-A	157	525	82	125	25	0	32	83	**122**	137	.238	.383	.469	135	30	29	100	0	6	-4	**.996**	-18	*CD/1O	1.4
Total	9	932	2873	416	693	121	8	137	406	538	811	.241	.364	.432	123	88	98	477	18	20	-7	.991	-62	CD/1O	7.4

■ **TIM TEUFEL** Teufel, Timothy Shawn b: 7/7/58, Greenwich, Conn. BR/TR, 6', 175 lbs. Deb: 9/03/83

1983	Min-A	21	78	11	24	7	1	3	6	2	8	.308	.325	.538	128	3	3	13	0	0	0	.990	-1	2/SD	0.2
1984	Min-A	157	568	76	149	30	3	14	61	76	73	.262	.351	.400	103	7	4	79	1	3	-2	.984	-12	*2	-0.4
1985	Min-A	138	434	58	113	24	3	10	50	48	70	.260	.338	.399	95	1	-2	58	4	2	0	.980	-33	*2/D	-3.1
1986	*NY-N	93	279	35	69	20	1	4	31	32	42	.247	.327	.369	94	-3	-2	34	1	2	-1	.971	-18	2/13	-1.9
1987	NY-N	97	299	55	92	29	0	14	61	44	53	.308	.400	.545	155	21	23	66	3	2	-0	.972	-11	2/1	1.5
1988	*NY-N	90	273	35	64	20	0	4	31	29	41	.234	.310	.352	94	-4	-2	30	0	1	-1	.981	12	2/1	1.3
1989	NY-N	83	219	27	56	7	2	2	15	32	50	.256	.353	.333	102	0	2	27	1	3	-2	.960	-1	21	-0.2
1990	NY-N	80	175	28	43	11	0	10	24	15	33	.246	.305	.480	113	2	2	24	0	0	0	.991	-4	123	-0.3
1991	NY-N	20	34	2	4	0	0	1	2	2	8	.118	.167	.206	4	-4	-4	1	1	1	-0	1.000	0	/132	-0.5
	SD-N	97	307	39	70	16	0	11	42	49	69	.228	.336	.388	100	2	1	42	8	2	1	.987	-14	23	-1.1
	Yr	117	341	41	74	16	0	12	44	51	77	.217	.321	.370	91	-3	-4	42	9	3	1	.987	-14	23/1	-1.6
1992	SD-N	101	246	23	55	10	0	6	25	31	45	.224	.313	.337	81	-5	-6	26	2	1	0	.987	-4	23/1	-1.0
Total	10	977	2912	389	739	174	10	79	348	360	492	.254	.338	.402	104	21	17	400	21	17	-4	.980	-86	2/31DS	-5.5

■ **GEORGE TEXTOR** Textor, George Bernhardt b: 12/27/1888, Newport, Ky. d: 3/10/54, Massillon, Ohio BB/TR, 5'10.5", 174 lbs. Deb: 4/19/14

1914	Ind-F	22	57	2	10	0	0	0	4	2	9	.175	.230	.175	14	-6	-7	2	0			.955	2	C	-0.4
1915	New-F	3	6	1	2	0	0	0	0	0	0	.333	.333	.333	102	-0	-0	1	0			1.000	-1	/C	-0.1
Total	2	25	63	3	12	0	0	0	4	2	9	.190	.239	.190	21	-6	-7	3	0			.957	1	/C	-0.5

■ **MOE THACKER** Thacker, Morris Benton b: 5/21/34, Louisville, Ky. BR/TR, 6'3", 210 lbs. Deb: 4/20/58

1958	Chi-N	11	24	4	6	1	0	2	3	1	7	.250	.280	.542	113	0	0	3	0	0	0	.952	1	/C	0.1
1960	Chi-N	54	90	5	14	1	0	0	6	14	20	.156	.269	.167	23	-9	-9	4	1	1	-0	.980	5	C	-0.3
1961	Chi-N	25	35	3	6	0	0	0	2	11	11	.171	.383	.171	53	-2	-2	3	0	0	0	.973	-1	C	-0.2
1962	Chi-N	65	107	8	20	5	0	0	9	14	40	.187	.287	.234	40	-9	-9	8	0	1	-1	.996	13	C	0.5
1963	StL-N	3	4	0	0	0	0	0	0	0	3	.000	.000	.000	-91	-1	-1	0	0	0	0	1.000	1	/C	0.0
Total	5	158	260	20	46	7	0	2	20	40	81	.177	.291	.227	41	-20	-21	18	1	2	-1	.984	18	C	0.1

■ **AL THAKE** Thake, Albert b: 9/21/1849, Wymondham, England d: 9/1/1872, Hamilton, N.Y. 6', Deb: 6/13/1872

1872	Atl-n	18	80	14	23	2	2	0	16	0	1	.287	.287	.363	84	-0	-3	9						O/2	-0.1

■ **RON THEOBALD** Theobald, Ronald Merrill b: 7/28/43, Oakland, Cal. BR/TR, 5'8", 165 lbs. Deb: 4/12/71

1971	Mil-A	126	388	50	107	12	2	1	23	38	39	.276	.345	.325	92	-4	-3	46	11	8	-2	.973	1	*2/S3	0.6
1972	Mil-A	125	391	45	86	11	0	1	19	68	38	.220	.343	.256	81	-6	-5	37	0	7	-4	.988	-13	*2	-1.9
Total	2	251	779	95	193	23	2	2	42	106	77	.248	.344	.290	87	-10	-9	83	11	15	-6	.980	-12	2/3S	-1.3

■ **GEORGE THEODORE** Theodore, George Basil b: 11/13/47, Salt Lake City, Ut. BR/TR, 6'4", 190 lbs. Deb: 4/14/73

1973	*NY-N	45	116	14	30	4	0	1	15	10	13	.259	.323	.319	80	-3	-3	11	1	0	0	.984	2	O/1	-0.3
1974	NY-N	60	76	7	12	1	0	1	1	8	14	.158	.247	.211	29	-7	-7	3	0	0	0	.990	-2	1O	-1.0
Total	2	105	192	21	42	5	0	2	16	18	27	.219	.292	.276	60	-10	-10	14	1	0	0	.958	-0	/O1	-1.3

■ **TOMMY THEVENOW** Thevenow, Thomas Joseph b: 9/6/03, Madison, Ind. d: 7/29/57, Madison, Ind. BR/TR, 5'10", 155 lbs. Deb: 9/04/24

1924	StL-N	23	89	4	18	4	1	0	7	1	6	.202	.211	.270	28	-9	-9	4	1	3	-2	.951	8	S	0.0
1925	StL-N	50	175	17	47	7	2	0	17	7	12	.269	.301	.331	60	-10	-11	18	3	0	1	.950	3	S	-0.2
1926	*StL-N	156	563	64	144	15	5	2	63	27	26	.256	.291	.311	60	-30	-33	50	8			.956	18	*S	0.2
1927	StL-N	59	191	23	37	6	1	0	4	14	8	.194	.249	.236	29	-19	-20	11	2			.945	7	S	-0.7
1928	*StL-N	69	171	11	35	8	3	0	13	20	12	.205	.288	.287	50	-12	-13	15	0			.931	-4	S/31	-1.1
1929	Phi-N	90	317	30	72	11	0	0	35	25	25	.227	.288	.262	35	-31	-34	25	3			.953	3	S	-1.9
1930	Phi-N	156	573	57	164	21	1	0	78	23	26	.286	.316	.326	52	-40	-47	58	1			.941	-2	*S	-2.8
1931	Pit-N	120	404	35	86	12	1	0	38	28	22	.213	.266	.248	39	-34	-34	28	0			.964	9	*S	-1.4
1932	Pit-N	59	194	12	46	3	3	0	26	7	12	.237	.264	.284	48	-14	-14	15	0			.918	-1	S3	-1.1
1933	Pit-N	73	253	20	79	5	1	0	34	3	5	.312	.320	.340	89	-4	-4	25	2			.975	-13	2/S3	-1.4
1934	Pit-N	122	446	37	121	16	2	0	54	20	20	.271	.306	.316	65	-21	-22	41	0			.969	-18	23/S	-3.4
1935	Pit-N	110	408	38	97	9	9	0	47	12	23	.238	.261	.304	50	-28	-30	30	1			.951	4	3S/2	-2.1
1936	Cin-N	106	321	25	75	7	2	0	36	15	23	.234	.268	.268	48	-25	-22	21	2			.945	-9	S23	-2.5
1937	Bos-N	21	34	5	4	0	1	0	2	4	2	.118	.211	.176	7	-4	-4	2	0			.969	1	S/32	-0.2
1938	Pit-N	15	25	2	5	0	0	0	2	4	0	.200	.333	.200	49	-1	-2	2	0			1.000	3	/2S3	0.2
Total	15	1229	4164	380	1030	124	32	2	456	210	222	.247	.285	.294	52	-284	-297	346	23	3		.950	9	S23/1	-18.4

■ **HENRY THIELMAN** Thielman, Henry Joseph b: 10/3/1880, St.Cloud, Minn. d: 9/2/42, New York, N.Y. BR/TR, 5'11", 175 lbs. Deb: 4/17/02 F

1902	NY-N	6	9	0	1	0	0	0	0	2		.111	.273	.111	19	-1	-1	1	1			.800	1	/PO	-0.1
	Cin-N	28	91	6	12	0	2	0	4	5		.132	.186	.176	11	-9	-10	3	0			.910	-2	P/O	-0.2
	Yr	34	100	6	13	0	2	0	4	7		.130	.194	.170	12	-10	-11	4	1			.903	-1	P/O	-0.3
1903	Bro-N	9	23	3	5	1	0	1	2	5		.217	.357	.391	117	1	1	3	0			.750	-0	/OP	-0.1
Total	2	43	123	9	18	1	2	1	6	12		.146	.228	.211	32	-10	-11	7	1			.918	-1	/PO	-0.4

■ **ANDRES THOMAS** Thomas, Andres Perez (b: Andres Perez (Thomas)) b: 11/10/63, Boca Chica, D.R. BR/TR, 6'1", 185 lbs. Deb: 9/03/85

1985	Atl-N	15	18	6	5	0	0	0	2	0	2	.278	.278	.278	53	-1	-1	1	0	0	0	.920	3	S	0.2
1986	Atl-N	102	323	26	81	17	2	6	32	8	49	.251	.269	.372	71	-12	-14	26	4	6	-2	.958	26	S	1.7
1987	Atl-N	82	324	29	75	11	0	5	39	14	50	.231	.268	.312	50	-22	-24	25	6	5	-1	.953	9	S	-0.9
1988	Atl-N	153	606	54	153	22	2	13	68	14	95	.252	.271	.360	76	-18	-21	54	7	3	0	.959	-8	*S	-1.8
1989	Atl-N	141	554	41	118	18	0	13	57	12	62	.213	.230	.316	53	-34	-36	35	3	3	-1	.956	6	*S	-2.1
1990	Atl-N	84	278	26	61	8	0	5	30	11	43	.219	.249	.302	48	-19	-21	18	2	1	0	.967	3	S/3	-1.3
Total	6	577	2103	182	493	76	4	42	228	59	301	.234	.256	.334	61	-106	-117	159	22	18	-4	.958	38	S/3	-4.2

■ **PINCH THOMAS** Thomas, Chester David b: 1/24/1888, Camp Point, Ill. d: 12/24/53, Modesto, Cal. BL/TR, 5'9.5", 173 lbs. Deb: 4/24/12

1912	Bos-A	13	30	0	6	0	0	0	5	2		.200	.250	.200	28	-3	-3	2	1			.966	2	/C	0.0
1913	Bos-A	38	91	6	26	1	2	1	15	2	11	.286	.309	.374	97	-1	-1	10	1			.983	1	C	0.3
1914	Bos-A	66	130	9	25	1	0	0	5	18	17	.192	.291	.200	48	-8	-8	8	1			.966	-2	C/1	-0.6
1915	*Bos-A	86	203	21	48	4	4	0	21	13	20	.236	.286	.296	76	-7	-6	18	3	2	-0	.969	5	C	0.3
1916	*Bos-A	99	216	21	57	10	1	1	21	33	13	.264	.364	.333	109	4	4	30	4			.981	-8	C	0.2
1917	Bos-A	83	202	24	48	7	0	0	24	27	9	.238	.333	.272	86	-3	-2	19	2			**.986**	3	C	0.7
1918	Cle-A	32	73	2	18	0	1	0	5	6	6	.247	.304	.274	68	-2	-3	6	0			.948	1	C	-0.1
1919	Cle-A	34	46	2	5	0	0	0	2	4	3	.109	.180	.109	-17	-7	-8	1	0			.980	-2	C	-0.9
1920	*Cle-A	9	9	2	3	1	0	0	0	3	1	.333	.500	.444	147	1	1	2	0	0	0	1.000	1	/C	0.2
1921	Cle-A	21	35	1	9	3	0	0	4	10	2	.257	.422	.343	96	0	0	6	0	0	0	.882	-6	C	-0.5
Total	10	481	1035	88	245	27	8	2	102	118	82	.237	.318	.284	78	-25	-26	104	12	2		.973	-5	C/1	-0.4

YEAR	TM/L	G	AB	R	H	2B	3B	HR	RBI	BB	SO	AVG	OBP	SLG	PRO+	BR	/A	RC	SB	CS	SBR	FA	FR	POS	TPR

■ DAN THOMAS Thomas, Danny Lee b: 5/9/51, Birmingham, Ala. d: 6/12/80, Mobile, Ala. BR/TR, 6'2", 190 lbs. Deb: 9/02/76

1976	Mil-A	32	105	13	29	5	1	4	15	14	28	.276	.372	.457	145	6	6	18	1	2	-1	.955	-0	O	0.4
1977	Mil-A	22	70	11	19	3	2	2	11	8	11	.271	.354	.457	119	2	2	11	0	2	-1	1.000	1	/OD	0.1
Total	2	54	175	24	48	8	3	6	26	22	39	.274	.365	.457	134	8	8	29	1	4	-2	.966	0	/OD	0.5

■ DERREL THOMAS Thomas, Derrel Osbon b: 1/14/51, Los Angeles, Cal. BB/TR, 6', 160 lbs. Deb: 9/14/71

1971	Hou-N	5	5	0	0	0	0	0	0	0	2	.000	.000	.000	-99	-1	-1	-0	0	1	-1	1.000	1	/2	-0.1
1972	SD-N	130	500	48	115	15	5	5	36	41	73	.230	.291	.310	76	-19	-15	45	9	9	-3	.967	-18	2S/O	-2.6
1973	SD-N	113	404	41	96	7	1	0	22	34	52	.238	.300	.260	61	-23	-19	35	15	5	2	.914	-14	S2	-2.1
1974	SD-N	141	523	48	129	24	6	3	41	51	58	.247	.315	.333	85	-13	-10	54	7	8	-3	.976	6	*23O/S	-0.3
1975	SF-N	144	540	99	149	21	9	6	48	57	56	.276	.348	.381	98	2	-1	75	28	13	1	.974	-7	*2/O	0.1
1976	SF-N	81	272	38	63	5	4	2	19	29	26	.232	.315	.301	73	-8	-9	26	10	11	-4	.964	2	2/OS3	-0.7
1977	SF-N	148	506	75	135	13	10	8	44	46	70	.267	.330	.379	90	-7	-7	63	15	13	-3	.991	5	O2S/31	-0.4
1978	SD-N	128	352	36	80	10	2	3	26	35	37	.227	.300	.293	73	-15	-12	34	11	6	-0	.991	22	O231	1.0
1979	LA-N	141	406	47	104	15	4	5	44	41	49	.256	.332	.350	87	-7	-6	49	18	5	2	.996	-3	*03/2S1	-1.2
1980	LA-N	117	297	32	79	18	3	1	22	26	48	.266	.327	.357	93	-3	-3	33	7	9	-3	.987	10	OS2/C3	-0.4
1981	*LA-N	80	218	25	54	4	0	4	24	25	23	.248	.325	.321	87	-4	-3	25	7	2	1	.986	-5	2SO3	-0.4
1982	LA-N	66	98	13	26	2	1	0	2	10	12	.265	.333	.306	82	-2	-2	10	2	3	-1	1.000	2	O23/S	-0.1
1983	*LA-N	118	192	38	48	6	6	2	8	27	36	.250	.348	.375	101	1	1	27	9	3	1	.990	7	OS/23	0.9
1984	Mon-N	108	243	26	62	12	2	0	20	20	33	.255	.312	.321	82	-7	-6	23	0	4	-2	.963	-38	SO2/31	-4.4
	Cal-A	14	29	3	4	0	1	0	2	3	4	.138	.219	.207	19	-3	-3	1	0	0	0	.889	-5	/OS3	-0.8
1985	Phi-N	63	92	16	19	2	0	4	12	11	14	.207	.291	.359	79	-2	-3	10	2	0	1	.906	-8	SOC23	-0.9
Total	15	1597	4677	585	1163	154	54	43	370	456	593	.249	.319	.332	83	-114	-99	509	140	92	-13	.970	-43	2OS3/1C	-11.2

■ FRANK THOMAS Thomas, Frank Edward b: 5/27/68, Columbus, Ga. BR/TR, 6'5", 240 lbs. Deb: 8/02/90

1990	Chi-A	60	191	39	63	11	3	7	31	44	54	.330	.460	.529	180	22	23	49	0	1	-1	.989	-5	1/D	1.4
1991	Chi-A	158	559	104	178	31	2	32	109	**138**	112	.318	**.454**	.553	**181**	**66**	**68**	**145**	1	2	-1	.996	-4	*D1	5.8
1992	Chi-A	160	573	108	185	**46**	2	24	115	**122**	88	.323	**.446**	.536	178	62	64	142	6	3	0	.992	-10	*1/D	4.4
Total	3	378	1323	251	426	88	7	63	255	304	254	.322	.451	.542	180	150	155	335	7	6	-2	.992	-19	1D	11.6

■ FRANK THOMAS Thomas, Frank Joseph b: 6/11/29, Pittsburgh, Pa. BR/TR, 6'3", 205 lbs. Deb: 8/17/51

1951	Pit-N	39	148	21	39	9	2	2	16	9	15	.264	.306	.392	84	-3	-4	16	0	2	-1	1.000	1	O	-0.5
1952	Pit-N	6	21	1	2	0	0	0	0	1	1	.095	.136	.095	-34	-4	-4	0	0	0	0	1.000	-0	/O	-0.5
1953	Pit-N	128	455	68	116	22	1	30	102	50	93	.255	.331	.505	115	8	8	76	1	2	-1	.976	10	*O	1.2
1954	Pit-N★	153	577	81	172	32	7	23	94	51	74	.298	.365	.497	124	18	19	106	3	2	-0	.989	12	*O	2.3
1955	Pit-N★	142	510	72	125	16	2	25	72	60	76	.245	.327	.431	101	-1	-0	72	2	0	1	.984	-0	*O	-0.6
1956	Pit-N	157	588	69	166	24	3	25	80	36	61	.282	.329	.461	112	7	8	80	0	5	-3	.942	-8	*3O/2	-0.4
1957	Pit-N	151	594	72	172	30	1	23	89	44	66	.290	.342	.460	116	10	12	90	3	1	0	.977	-1	1O3	0.4
1958	Pit-N★	149	562	89	158	26	4	35	109	42	79	.281	.339	.528	129	18	20	95	0	1	-1	.926	-32	*3/O1	-1.1
1959	Cin-N	108	374	41	84	18	2	12	47	27	56	.225	.282	.380	72	-15	-16	37	0	2	-1	.927	-13	3O1	-3.3
1960	Chi-N	135	479	54	114	12	1	21	64	28	74	.238	.280	.399	84	-12	-12	51	1	0	0	.983	-10	1O3	-2.8
1961	Chi-N	15	50	7	13	2	0	2	6	2	8	.260	.288	.420	84	-1	-1	5	0	0	0	1.000	-1	O/1	-0.3
	Mil-N	124	423	58	120	13	3	25	67	29	70	.284	.338	.506	128	11	14	66	2	4	-2	.954	-5	*O1	0.1
	Yr	139	473	65	133	15	3	27	73	31	78	.281	.333	.497	123	10	13	70	2	4	-2	.956	-6	*O1	-0.2
1962	NY-N	156	571	69	152	23	3	34	94	48	95	.266	.332	.496	117	13	12	91	2	1	0	.962	-2	*O13	0.2
1963	NY-N	126	420	34	109	9	1	15	60	33	48	.260	.318	.393	102	2	1	46	0	0	0	.988	-1	O1/3	-0.7
1964	NY-N	60	197	19	50	6	1	3	19	10	29	.254	.297	.340	81	-6	-5	19	1	1	0	1.000	1	O1/3	-0.8
	Phi-N	39	143	20	42	11	0	7	26	5	12	.294	.318	.517	132	5	5	22	0	1	-1	.976	1	O	0.4
	Yr	99	340	39	92	17	1	10	45	15	41	.271	.305	.415	103	-1	-0	41	1	2	-1	.982	2	1O/3	-0.4
1965	Phi-N	35	77	7	20	4	0	1	7	4	10	.260	.296	.351	83	-2	-2	7	0	0	0	1.000	-1	O1/3	-0.4
	Hou-N	23	58	7	10	2	0	3	9	3	15	.172	.213	.362	63	-3	-3	5	0	0	0	.984	-2	1/3O	-0.6
	Mil-N	15	33	3	7	3	0	0	1	2	11	.212	.257	.303	57	-2	-2	3	0	0	0	.979	-1	/1O	-0.3
	Yr	73	168	17	37	9	0	4	17	9	36	.220	.260	.345	71	-7	-7	15	0	0	0	.985	-3	1O/3	-1.3
1966	Chi-N	5	5	0	0	0	0	0	0	0	0	.000	.000	.000	-99	-1	-1	-0	0	0	0	.000	0	H	-0.1
Total	16	1766	6285	792	1671	262	31	286	962	484	894	.266	.323	.454	108	40	50	886	15	22	-9	.978	-52	*O31/2	-7.8

■ FRED THOMAS Thomas, Frederick Harvey "Tommy" b: 12/19/1892, Milwaukee, Wis. d: 1/15/86, Rice Lake, Wis. BR/TR, 5'10", 160 lbs. Deb: 4/22/18

1918	*Bos-A	44	144	19	37	2	1	1	11	15	20	.257	.331	.306	94	-1	-1	16	4			.968	5	3/S	0.6
1919	Phi-A	124	453	42	96	11	10	2	23	43	52	.212	.283	.294	61	-23	-24	41	12			.945	-5	*3	-2.5
1920	Phi-A	76	255	27	59	6	3	1	11	26	17	.231	.307	.290	58	-15	-15	25	8	4	0	.960	1	3S	-1.0
	Was-A	3	7	0	1	0	0	0	0	0	1	.143	.143	.143	-25	-1	-1	0	0	1	-1	1.000	2	/3	0.0
	Yr	79	262	27	60	6	3	1	11	26	18	.229	.303	.286	56	-16	-16	24	8	5	-1	.962	3	3S	-1.0
Total	3	247	859	88	193	19	14	4	45	84	90	.225	.297	.293	65	-40	-41	81	24	5		.954	3	3/S	-2.9

■ GEORGE THOMAS Thomas, George Edward b: 11/29/37, Minneapolis, Minn. BR/TR, 6'3.5", 190 lbs. Deb: 9/11/57 C

1957	Det-A	1	1	0	0	0	0	0	0	0	1	.000	.000	.000	-97	-0	-0	0	0	0	0	.000	-0	/3	-0.1
1958	Det-A	1	0	0	0	0	0	0	0	0	0	—	—	—	—	0	0	0	0	0	0	.000	-0	/O	0.0
1961	Det-A	17	6	2	0	0	0	0	0	0	4	.000	.000	.000	-97	-2	-2	0	0	0	0	.000	4	/OS	0.2
	LA-A	79	282	39	79	12	1	13	59	21	66	.280	.337	.468	101	4	0	43	3	6	-3	.986	-11	O3	-1.5
	Yr	96	288	41	79	12	1	13	59	21	70	.274	.330	.458	99	2	-1	42	3	6	-3	.986	-7	O3/S	-1.3
1962	LA-A	56	181	13	43	10	2	4	12	21	37	.238	.320	.381	91	-3	-2	23	0	0	0	.957	1	O	-0.4
1963	LA-A	53	167	14	35	7	1	4	15	9	32	.210	.254	.335	68	-8	-7	14	0	0	0	.941	-2	O3/1	-1.2
	Det-A	49	109	13	26	4	1	1	11	11	22	.239	.314	.321	76	-3	-3	12	2	1	0	1.000	-2	O/2	-0.7
	Yr	102	276	27	61	11	2	5	26	20	54	.221	.279	.330	71	-11	-9	25	2	1	0	.974	-4	O3/12	-1.9
1964	Det-A	105	308	39	88	15	2	12	44	18	53	.286	.331	.464	117	7	6	47	4	1	1	.988	-2	O3	0.1
1965	Det-A	79	169	19	36	5	1	3	10	12	39	.213	.273	.308	64	-8	-8	13	2	3	-1	.948	-3	O/2	-1.5
1966	Bos-A	69	173	25	41	4	0	5	20	23	33	.237	.333	.347	87	-0	-3	20	1	0	0	1.000	1	O/3C1	-0.4
1967	*Bos-A	65	89	10	19	2	0	1	6	3	23	.213	.255	.270	51	-5	-6	6	0	1	-1	.973	-8	O/1C	-1.7
1968	Bos-A	12	10	3	2	0	0	1	1	1	3	.200	.273	.500	122	-0	-0	2	1	0	0	1.000	-2	/O	-0.1
1969	Bos-A	29	51	9	18	3	1	0	8	3	11	.353	.400	.451	131	6	3	10	0	0	0	1.000	-4	O1/C3	-0.2
1970	Bos-A	38	99	13	34	8	0	2	13	11	12	.343	.420	.485	139	7	6	20	0	0	0	.972	-5	O/3	0.0
1971	Bos-A	9	13	0	1	0	0	0	1	1	4	.077	.143	.077	-34	-2	-2	0	0	0	0	1.000	-2	/O	-0.1
	Min-A	23	30	4	8	1	0	0	2	4	3	.267	.353	.300	84	-0	-0	4	0	0	0	1.000	-4	O/13	-0.5
	Yr	32	43	4	9	1	0	0	3	5	7	.209	.292	.233	48	-3	-3	4	0	0	0	1.000	-5	O/13	-1.0
Total	13	685	1688	203	430	71	9	46	202	138	343	.255	.320	.389	77	-12	-19	213	13	12	-2	.976	-39	O/31C2S	-8.5

■ HERB THOMAS Thomas, Herbert Mark b: 5/26/02, Sampson City, Fla. d: 12/4/91, Starke, Fla. BR/TR, 5'4.5", 157 lbs. Deb: 8/28/24

1924	Bos-N	32	127	12	28	1	1	1	8	9	8	.220	.288	.291	58	-8	-7	11	5	2	0	.983	8	O	-0.1
1925	Bos-N	5	17	2	4	0	1	0	0	2	0	.235	.350	.353	88	-0	-0	2	0	1	-1	.963	-1	/2	-0.2
1927	Bos-N	24	74	11	17	6	1	0	6	3	9	.230	.269	.338	67	-4	-3	7	2			.972	-11	2/S	-1.4
	NY-N	13	17	2	3	1	0	1	1	1	1	.176	.263	.353	64	-1	-1	0	0			.900	-0	/OS	-0.1
	Yr	37	91	13	20	7	1	1	7	4	10	.220	.268	.341	65	-5	-5	8	2			.972	-11	2/SO	-1.5
Total	3	74	235	27	52	11	4	2	15	15	18	.221	.285	.315	63	-14	-12	21	7	3		.976	-4	/O2S	-1.8

■ IRA THOMAS
Thomas, Ira Felix b: 1/22/1881, Ballston Spa, N.Y. d: 10/11/58, Philadelphia, Pa. BR/TR, 6'2", 200 lbs. Deb: 5/18/06 C

YEAR	TM/L	G	AB	R	H	2B	3B	HR	RBI	BB	SO	AVG	OBP	SLG	PRO+	BR	/A	RC	SB	CS	SBR	FA	FR	POS	TPR
1906	NY-A	44	115	12	23	1	2	0	15	8		.200	.252	.243	50	-6	-7	8	2			.938	-5	C	-0.9
1907	NY-A	80	208	20	40	5	4	1	24	10		.192	.236	.269	57	-9	-11	15	5			.953	8	C/1	0.2
1908	*Det-A	40	101	6	31	1	0	0	8	5		.307	.346	.317	111	2	1	11	0			.972	-5	C	-0.2
1909	Phi-A	84	256	22	57	9	3	0	31	18		.223	.292	.281	79	-5	-6	22	4			**.985**	12	C	1.5
1910	*Phi-A	60	180	14	50	8	2	1	19	6		.278	.301	.361	108	1	1	20	2			.967	9	C	1.6
1911	*Phi-A	103	297	33	81	14	3	0	39	23		.273	.341	.340	92	-4	-3	36	4			.974	6	*C	1.2
1912	Phi-A	48	139	14	30	4	2	1	13	8		.216	.268	.295	63	-7	-7	12	3			.971	-1	C	-0.4
1913	Phi-A	22	53	3	15	4	1	0	6	4	8	.283	.333	.396	116	1	1	7	0			.983	3	C	0.5
1914	Phi-A	2	3	0	0	0	0	0	0	0	0	.000	.000	.000	-99	-1	-1	0	0			1.000	0	/C	0.0
1915	Phi-A	1	0	0	0	0	0	0	0	0	0	—	—	—	—	0	0	0	0			1.000	0	/C	0.0
Total	10	484	1352	124	327	46	17	3	155	82	8	.242	.295	.308	81	-29	-31	130	20			.970	27	C/1	3.5

■ GORMAN THOMAS
Thomas, James Gorman b: 12/12/50, Charleston, S.C. BR/TR, 6'2", 210 lbs. Deb: 4/06/73

YEAR	TM/L	G	AB	R	H	2B	3B	HR	RBI	BB	SO	AVG	OBP	SLG	PRO+	BR	/A	RC	SB	CS	SBR	FA	FR	POS	TPR
1973	Mil-A	59	155	16	29	7	1	2	11	14	61	.187	.254	.284	53	-10	-10	11	5	5	-2	.957	-4	O/3D	-1.7
1974	Mil-A	17	46	10	12	4	0	2	11	8	15	.261	.370	.478	143	3	3	9	4	0	1	1.000	-1	O/D	0.3
1975	Mil-A	121	240	34	43	12	2	10	28	31	84	.179	.273	.371	80	-7	-7	25	4	2	0	.961	-13	*O/D	-2.4
1976	Mil-A	99	227	27	45	9	2	8	36	31	67	.198	.297	.361	94	-2	-2	24	2	3	-1	.986	-5	O/3D	-1.1
1978	Mil-A	137	452	70	111	24	1	32	86	73	133	.246	.353	.515	141	24	24	85	3	4	-2	.983	-4	*O	1.4
1979	Mil-A	156	557	97	136	29	0	**45**	123	98	175	.244	.359	.539	138	30	30	110	1	5	-3	.991	4	*O/D	2.3
1980	Mil-A	162	628	78	150	26	3	38	105	58	170	.239	.305	.471	113	5	8	91	8	5	-1	.985	3	*O/D	0.4
1981	*Mil-A★	103	363	54	94	22	0	21	65	50	85	.259	.352	.493	149	19	21	63	4	5	-2	.979	3	O/D	2.0
1982	*Mil-A	158	567	96	139	29	1	**39**	112	84	143	.245	.347	.506	139	24	28	100	3	7	-3	.991	10	*O	3.1
1983	Mil-A	46	164	21	30	6	1	5	18	23	50	.183	.287	.323	73	-7	-5	15	2	1	0	.992	-0	O	-0.7
	Cle-A	106	371	51	82	17	0	17	51	57	98	.221	.326	.404	96	0	-2	51	8	3	1	.982	12	*O	0.7
	Yr	152	535	72	112	23	1	22	69	80	148	.209	.314	.379	90	-7	-7	66	10	4	1	.985	11	*O	0.0
1984	Sea-A	35	108	6	17	3	0	1	13	28	27	.157	.336	.213	56	-5	-5	9	0	3	-2	1.000	-3	O/D	-1.1
1985	Sea-A	135	484	76	104	16	1	32	87	84	126	.215	.332	.450	111	8	8	74	3	2	-0	.000	0	*D	0.7
1986	Sea-A	57	170	24	33	4	0	10	26	27	55	.194	.308	.394	89	-3	-3	21	1	2	-1	.000	0	D	-0.4
	Mil-A	44	145	21	26	4	1	6	10	31	50	.179	.324	.345	80	-3	-4	17	2	2	-1	.980	-1	D/1	-0.6
	Yr	101	315	45	59	8	1	16	36	58	105	.187	.316	.371	85	-6	-6	39	3	4	-2	.980	-1	D/1	-1.0
Total	13	1435	4677	681	1051	212	13	268	782	697	1339	.225	.328	.448	114	75	84	706	50	49	-14	.984	1	*OD/13	2.9

■ LEE THOMAS
Thomas, James Leroy b: 2/5/36, Peoria, Ill. BL/TR, 6'2", 198 lbs. Deb: 4/22/61 C

YEAR	TM/L	G	AB	R	H	2B	3B	HR	RBI	BB	SO	AVG	OBP	SLG	PRO+	BR	/A	RC	SB	CS	SBR	FA	FR	POS	TPR
1961	NY-A	2	2	0	1	0	0	0	0	0	0	.500	.500	.500	177	0	0	1	0	0	0	.000	0	H	0.0
	LA-A	130	450	77	128	11	5	24	70	47	74	.284	.355	.491	111	14	7	75	0	5	-3	.966	-3	O1	-0.6
	Yr	132	452	77	129	11	5	24	70	47	74	.285	.355	.491	111	14	8	75	0	5	-3	.966	-3	O1	-0.6
1962	LA-A★	160	583	88	169	21	2	26	104	55	74	.290	.357	.467	124	16	18	96	6	1	1	.982	-10	1O	-0.1
1963	LA-A	149	528	52	116	12	6	9	55	53	82	.220	.302	.316	78	-18	-14	52	6	0	2	.996	3	*1O	-1.7
1964	LA-A	47	172	14	47	8	1	2	24	18	22	.273	.342	.366	108	-0	2	23	1	0	0	.949	-1	O/1	-0.1
	Bos-A	107	401	44	103	19	2	13	42	34	29	.257	.321	.411	97	1	-2	50	2	1	0	.995	3	*O/1	-0.4
	Yr	154	573	58	150	27	3	15	66	52	51	.262	.328	.398	100	0	0	73	3	1	0	.981	3	*O/1	-0.5
1965	Bos-A	151	521	74	141	27	4	22	75	72	42	.271	.362	.464	126	23	20	87	6	2	1	.984	5	*1O	1.9
1966	Atl-N	39	126	11	25	1	1	6	15	10	15	.198	.263	.365	71	-5	-5	13	1	1	-0	.987	2	1	-0.6
	Chi-N	75	149	15	36	4	0	1	9	14	15	.242	.319	.289	70	-5	-6	14	0	0	0	.992	-2	1O	-0.9
	Yr	114	275	26	61	5	1	7	24	24	30	.222	.294	.324	71	-10	-11	27	1	1	-0	.989	0	1O	-1.5
1967	Chi-N	77	191	16	42	4	1	2	23	15	22	.220	.287	.283	61	-9	-10	16	1	0	0	.969	-4	O1	-1.8
1968	Hou-N	90	201	14	39	4	0	1	11	14	22	.194	.250	.229	45	-13	-13	11	2	1	0	.973	-0	O/1	-1.8
Total	8	1027	3324	405	847	111	22	106	428	332	397	.255	.328	.397	99	3	-2	438	25	11	1	.975	-6	O1	-6.1

■ BUD THOMAS
Thomas, John Tillman b: 3/10/29, Sedalia, Mo. BR/TR, 6', 180 lbs. Deb: 9/02/51

YEAR	TM/L	G	AB	R	H	2B	3B	HR	RBI	BB	SO	AVG	OBP	SLG	PRO+	BR	/A	RC	SB	CS	SBR	FA	FR	POS	TPR
1951	StL-A	14	20	3	7	0	0	1	1	0	3	.350	.350	.500	124	1	1	4	2	0	1	1.000	1	S	0.3

■ KITE THOMAS
Thomas, Keith Marshall b: 4/27/24, Kansas City, Kan. BR/TR, 6'1.5", 195 lbs. Deb: 4/19/52

YEAR	TM/L	G	AB	R	H	2B	3B	HR	RBI	BB	SO	AVG	OBP	SLG	PRO+	BR	/A	RC	SB	CS	SBR	FA	FR	POS	TPR
1952	Phi-A	75	116	24	29	6	1	6	18	20	27	.250	.365	.474	124	5	4	20	0	1	-1	.957	-3	O	0.0
1953	Phi-A	24	49	1	6	0	0	0	2	3	6	.122	.173	.122	-18	-8	-8	1	0	0	0	1.000	-0	O	-0.9
	Was-A	38	58	10	17	3	2	1	12	11	7	.293	.414	.466	141	3	4	11	0	0	0	1.000	-2	/OC	0.2
	Yr	62	107	11	23	3	2	1	14	14	13	.215	.311	.308	68	-5	-5	10	0	0	0	1.000	-2	O/C	-0.7
Total	2	137	223	35	52	9	3	7	32	34	40	.233	.340	.395	98	0	-1	32	0	1	-1	.978	-5	/OC	-0.7

■ LEO THOMAS
Thomas, Leo Raymond "Tommy" b: 7/26/23, Turlock, Cal. BR/TR, 5'11.5", 178 lbs. Deb: 4/29/50

YEAR	TM/L	G	AB	R	H	2B	3B	HR	RBI	BB	SO	AVG	OBP	SLG	PRO+	BR	/A	RC	SB	CS	SBR	FA	FR	POS	TPR
1950	StL-A	35	121	19	24	6	0	1	9	20	14	.198	.312	.273	49	-9	-10	11	0	1	-1	.964	-4	3	-1.4
1952	StL-A	41	124	12	29	5	1	0	12	17	7	.234	.336	.290	73	-4	-4	13	2	0	1	.934	4	3/S2	0.0
	Chi-A	19	24	1	4	0	0	0	6	6	4	.167	.333	.167	42	-2	-2	2	0	0	0	.952	0	/3	-0.1
	Yr	60	148	13	33	5	1	0	18	23	11	.223	.335	.270	68	-5	-6	15	2	0	1	.936	4	3/S2	-0.1
Total	2	95	269	32	57	11	1	1	27	43	25	.212	.325	.271	59	-14	-15	27	2	1	0	.948	1	/3S2	-1.5

■ RAY THOMAS
Thomas, Raymond Joseph b: 7/9/10, Dover, N.H. BR/TR, 5'10.5", 175 lbs. Deb: 7/21/38

YEAR	TM/L	G	AB	R	H	2B	3B	HR	RBI	BB	SO	AVG	OBP	SLG	PRO+	BR	/A	RC	SB	CS	SBR	FA	FR	POS	TPR
1938	Bro-N	1	3	1	1	0	0	0	0	0	0	.333	.333	.333	82	-0	-0	0	0			1.000	0	/C	0.0

■ RED THOMAS
Thomas, Robert William b: 4/25/1898, Hargrove, Ala. d: 3/29/62, Fremont, Ohio BR/TR, 5'11", 165 lbs. Deb: 9/13/21

YEAR	TM/L	G	AB	R	H	2B	3B	HR	RBI	BB	SO	AVG	OBP	SLG	PRO+	BR	/A	RC	SB	CS	SBR	FA	FR	POS	TPR
1921	Chi-N	8	30	5	8	3	0	1	5	4	5	.267	.371	.467	120	1	1	5	0	1	-1	.962	1	/O	0.1

■ ROY THOMAS
Thomas, Roy Allen b: 3/24/1874, Norristown, Pa. d: 11/20/59, Norristown, Pa. BL/TL, 5'11", 150 lbs. Deb: 4/14/1899 FC

YEAR	TM/L	G	AB	R	H	2B	3B	HR	RBI	BB	SO	AVG	OBP	SLG	PRO+	BR	/A	RC	SB	CS	SBR	FA	FR	POS	TPR
1899	Phi-N	150	547	137	178	12	4	0	47	115		.325	.457	.362	130	30	34	116	42			.952	4	*O1	2.5
1900	Phi-N	140	531	**132**	168	4	3	0	33	**115**		.316	.451	.335	119	25	25	102	37			.958	-2	*O/P	1.2
1901	Phi-N	129	479	102	148	5	2	1	28	**100**		.309	.437	.334	123	24	23	86	27			.967	-2	*O	1.1
1902	Phi-N	138	500	89	143	4	7	0	24	**107**		.286	**.415**	.322	128	25	25	79	17			.974	5	*O	2.2
1903	Phi-N	130	477	88	156	11	2	1	27	**107**		.327	**.453**	.365	139	31	33	92	17			.963	14	*O	3.7
1904	Phi-N	139	496	92	144	6	6	3	29	**102**		.290	.415	.345	141	28	31	86	28			.974	15	*O	3.9
1905	Phi-N	147	562	118	178	11	6	0	31	93		.317	.417	.358	137	28	31	98	23			.983	19	*O	4.4
1906	Phi-N	142	493	81	125	10	7	0	16	**107**		.254	.392	.302	117	17	17	71	22			**.986**	10	*O	2.2
1907	Phi-N	121	419	70	102	15	3	1	23	**83**		.243	.375	.301	114	11	12	55	11			.980	5	*O	1.4
1908	Phi-N	6	24	2	4	0	0	0	0	2		.167	.231	.167	26	-2	-2	1	0			1.000	-1	/O	-0.3
	Pit-N	102	386	52	99	11	10	1	24	49		.256	.348	.345	121	11	11	50	11			.975	5	*O	1.3
	Yr	108	410	54	103	11	10	1	24	51		.251	.341	.334	116	9	9	50	11			.976	4	*O	1.0
1909	Bos-N	82	281	36	74	9	1	0	11	47		.263	.369	.302	104	5	4	34	5			.976	-2	O	-0.1
1910	Phi-N	23	71	7	13	0	2	0	4	7	5	.183	.266	.239	46	-5	-5	6	4			.952	-2	O	-0.8
1911	Phi-N	21	30	5	5	2	0	0	2	8	6	.167	.342	.233	61	-1	-1	3	0			1.000	1	O	-0.1
Total	13	1470	5296	1011	1537	100	53	7	299	1042	11	.290	.413	.333	124	228	237	880	244			.972	71	*O/1P	22.6

■ VALMY THOMAS
Thomas, Valmy b: 10/21/28, Santurce, P.R. BR/TR, 5'9", 165 lbs. Deb: 4/16/57

YEAR	TM/L	G	AB	R	H	2B	3B	HR	RBI	BB	SO	AVG	OBP	SLG	PRO+	BR	/A	RC	SB	CS	SBR	FA	FR	POS	TPR
1957	NY-N	88	241	30	60	10	3	6	31	16	29	.249	.298	.390	83	-6	-6	28	0	0	0	.991	2	C	-0.1
1958	SF-N	63	143	14	37	5	0	3	16	13	24	.259	.325	.357	82	-4	-4	17	1	0	0	.992	2	C	0.1
1959	Phi-N	66	140	5	28	2	0	1	7	9	19	.200	.253	.236	31	-14	-14	7	1	0	0	.980	15	C/3	0.4

YEAR	TM/L	G	AB	R	H	2B	3B	HR	RBI	BB	SO	AVG	OBP	SLG	PRO+	BR	/A	RC	SB	CS	SBR	FA	FR	POS	TPR
1960	Bal-A	8	16	0	1	0	0	0	0	1	0	.063	.118	.063	-51	-3	-3	-0	0	1	-1	1.000	1	/C	-0.3
1961	Cle-A	27	86	7	18	3	0	2	6	6	7	.209	.261	.314	54	-6	-6	5	0	0	0	.988	9	C	0.4
Total	5	252	626	56	144	20	3	12	60	45	79	.230	.285	.329	64	-33	-32	57	2	1	0	.988	29	C/3	0.5
■ **BILL THOMAS**	Thomas, William Miskey b: 12/8/1877, Norristown, Pa. d: 1/14/50, Evansburg, Pa. BR/TR, 5'10", 190 lbs. Deb: 5/01/02 F																								
1902	Phi-N	6	17	1	2	0	0	0	0	1		.118	.167	.118	-12	-2	-2	0	0			.500	-1	/O12	-0.4
■ **WALT THOMAS**	Thomas, William Walter "Tommy" b: 4/28/1884, Foot-Of-Ten, Pa. d: 6/6/50, Altoona, Pa. BR/TR, 5'8", Deb: 9/18/08																								
1908	Bos-N	5	13	2	2	0	0	0	1	3		.154	.313	.154	51	-1	-1	1	2			.864	-1	/S	-0.2
■ **ART THOMASON**	Thomason, Arthur Wilson b: 2/12/1889, Liberty, Mo. d: 5/2/44, Kansas City, Mo. BL/TL, 5'8", 150 lbs. Deb: 8/10/10																								
1910	Cle-A	20	70	4	12	0	1	0	2	5		.171	.227	.200	33	-5	-5	4	3			.944	2	O	-0.5
■ **GARY THOMASSON**	Thomasson, Gary Leah b: 7/29/51, San Diego, Cal. BL/TL, 6'1", 180 lbs. Deb: 9/05/72																								
1972	SF-N	10	27	5	9	1	1	0	1	1	7	.333	.357	.444	125	1	1	4	0	0	0	1.000	-1	/1O	-0.1
1973	SF-N	112	235	35	67	10	4	4	30	22	43	.285	.346	.413	105	3	2	36	2	0	1	.992	-0	1O	-0.1
1974	SF-N	120	315	41	77	14	3	2	29	38	56	.244	.326	.327	79	-7	-8	35	7	1	2	.981	3	O1	-0.8
1975	SF-N	114	326	44	74	12	3	7	32	37	48	.227	.308	.347	78	-8	-10	38	9	3	1	.978	9	O1	-0.4
1976	SF-N	103	328	45	85	20	5	8	38	30	45	.259	.323	.424	107	4	3	45	8	3	1	.959	-4	O1	-0.6
1977	SF-N	145	446	63	114	24	6	17	71	75	102	.256	.364	.451	118	12	12	78	16	4	2	.959	1	*O1	1.0
1978	Oak-A	47	154	17	31	4	1	5	16	15	44	.201	.272	.338	74	-6	-5	14	4	1	1	.969	2	O/1	-0.5
	*NY-A	55	116	20	32	4	1	3	20	13	22	.276	.349	.405	114	2	2	17	0	2	-1	.972	0	O/D	0.0
	Yr	102	270	37	63	8	2	8	36	28	66	.233	.305	.367	92	-4	-3	31	4	3	-1	.971	2	O/1D	-0.5
1979	LA-N	115	315	39	78	11	1	14	45	43	70	.248	.340	.422	108	3	4	47	4	2	0	.980	-1	*O/1	-0.1
1980	LA-N	80	111	6	24	3	0	1	12	17	26	.216	.326	.270	69	-4	-4	10	0	0	0	.974	-1	O/1	-0.6
Total	9	901	2373	315	591	103	25	61	294	291	463	.249	.332	.391	98	-2	-5	324	50	16	5	.970	7	O1/D	-2.2
■ **JIM THOME**	Thome, James Howard b: 8/27/70, Peoria, Ill. BL/TR, 6'3", 190 lbs. Deb: 9/04/91																								
1991	Cle-A	27	98	7	25	4	2	1	9	5	16	.255	.298	.367	82	-2	-2	9	1	1	-0	.900	1	3	-0.2
1992	Cle-A	40	117	8	24	3	1	2	12	10	34	.205	.279	.299	61	-6	-6	10	2	0	1	.882	-6	3	-1.2
Total	2	67	215	15	49	7	3	3	21	15	50	.228	.288	.330	71	-8	-9	19	3	1	0	.890	-5	/3	-1.4
■ **ANDREW THOMPSON**	Thompson, Andrew M. b: 1845, Illinois Deb: 4/26/1875 M																								
1875	Was-n	11	41	3	4	0	1	0		0		.098	.098	.146	-17	-5	-4	1						C/O	-0.3
■ **BOBBY THOMPSON**	Thompson, Bobby La Rue b: 11/3/53, Charlotte, N.C. BB/TR, 5'11", 175 lbs. Deb: 4/16/78																								
1978	Tex-A	64	120	23	27	3	3	2	12	9	26	.225	.290	.350	79	-3	-3	13	7	2	1	.982	-5	O/D	-0.9
■ **TIM THOMPSON**	Thompson, Charles Lemoine b: 3/1/24, Coalport, Pa. BL/TR, 5'11", 190 lbs. Deb: 4/28/54 C																								
1954	Bro-N	10	13	2	2	1	0	0	1	1	1	.154	.214	.231	15	-2	-2	1	0	0	0	.909	-1	/CO	-0.2
1956	KC-A	92	268	21	73	13	2	1	27	17	23	.272	.321	.347	76	-9	-9	29	2	4	-2	.981	2	C	-0.6
1957	KC-A	81	230	25	47	10	0	7	19	18	26	.204	.262	.339	62	-12	-13	20	0	0	0	.993	-3	C	-1.4
1958	Det-A	4	6	1	1	0	0	0	0	3	2	.167	.444	.167	70	0	-0	1	0	0	0	1.000	-1	/C	-0.1
Total	4	187	517	49	123	24	2	8	47	39	52	.238	.294	.338	68	-23	-24	51	2	4	-2	.986	-3	C/O	-2.3
■ **DANNY THOMPSON**	Thompson, Danny Leon b: 2/1/47, Wichita, Kan. d: 12/10/76, Rochester, Minn. BR/TR, 6', 183 lbs. Deb: 6/25/70																								
1970	*Min-A	96	302	25	66	9	0	0	22	7	39	.219	.236	.248	33	-27	-28	17	0	0	0	.986	-12	23/S	-3.5
1971	Min-A	48	57	10	15	2	0	0	7	7	12	.263	.344	.298	81	-1	-1	5	0	0	0	.897	1	3/2S	0.0
1972	Min-A	144	573	54	158	22	6	4	48	34	57	.276	.319	.356	96	-0	-3	63	3	4	-2	.957	-9	*S	0.8
1973	Min-A	99	347	29	78	13	2	1	36	16	41	.225	.263	.282	52	-22	-23	24	1	0	0	.950	7	S/3D	-0.5
1974	Min-A	97	264	25	66	6	1	4	25	22	29	.250	.313	.326	81	-5	-7	24	1	1	-0	.963	-21	S/3D	-1.9
1975	Min-A	112	355	25	96	11	2	5	37	18	30	.270	.306	.355	84	-7	-8	37	0	3	-2	.941	-17	*S/32D	-1.8
1976	Min-A	34	124	9	29	4	0	0	6	3	8	.234	.258	.266	52	-7	-8	9	1	1	-0	.988	-1	S	-0.5
	Tex-A	64	196	12	42	3	0	1	13	13	19	.214	.267	.245	49	-12	-13	13	2	2	-1	.976	-7	32S/D	-2.0
	Yr	98	320	21	71	7	0	1	19	16	27	.222	.263	.253	50	-19	-20	21	3	3	-1	.981	-9	S32/D	-2.5
Total	7	694	2218	189	550	70	11	15	194	120	235	.248	.289	.310	70	-82	-90	192	8	11	-4	.956	-60	S3/2D	-9.4
■ **DON THOMPSON**	Thompson, Donald Newlin b: 12/28/23, Swepsonville, N.C. BL/TL, 6', 185 lbs. Deb: 4/24/49																								
1949	Bos-N	7	11	0	2	0	0	0	0	0	2	.182	.182	.182	-2	-2	-2	0	0			.800	-0	/O	-0.2
1951	Bro-N	80	118	25	27	3	0	0	6	12	12	.229	.305	.254	51	-8	-8	8	2	8	-4	.987	-11	O	-2.5
1953	*Bro-N	96	153	25	37	5	0	1	12	14	13	.242	.310	.294	57	-9	-10	13	2	3	-1	.989	-14	O	-2.6
1954	Bro-N	34	25	2	1	0	0	0	1	5	5	.040	.226	.040	-25	-5	-5	1	0	0	0	1.000	-9	O	-1.4
Total	4	217	307	52	67	8	0	1	19	31	32	.218	.296	.254	46	-23	-24	22	4	11		.984	-35	O	-6.7
■ **FRANK THOMPSON**	Thompson, Frank Deb: 9/11/1875																								
1875	Atl-n	1	5	1	2	0	0	0		0		.400	.400	.400	204	0	0	1						O	0.0
■ **FRANK THOMPSON**	Thompson, Frank E b: 7/2/1895, Springfield, Mo. d: 6/27/40, Jasper Co., Mo. BR/TR, 5'8", 155 lbs. Deb: 5/06/20																								
1920	StL-A	22	53	7	9	0	0	0	5	13	10	.170	.343	.170	38	-4	-4	4	1	1	-0	.878	-4	3/2	-0.8
■ **HANK THOMPSON**	Thompson, Henry Curtis b: 12/8/25, Oklahoma City, Okla d: 9/30/69, Fresno, Cal. BL/TR, 5'9", 174 lbs. Deb: 7/17/47																								
1947	StL-A	27	78	10	20	1	1	0	5	10	7	.256	.341	.295	76	-2	-2	8	2	1	0	.957	1	2	0.0
1949	NY-N	75	275	51	77	10	4	9	34	42	30	.280	.377	.444	120	8	8	50	5			.961	-8	2/3	0.4
1950	NY-N	148	512	82	148	17	6	20	91	83	60	.289	.391	.463	123	20	19	97	8			.944	5	*3O	2.1
1951	*NY-N	87	264	37	62	8	4	8	33	43	23	.235	.342	.386	95	-1	-1	36	1	2	-1	.925	-14	3	-1.8
1952	NY-N	128	423	67	110	13	9	17	67	50	38	.260	.344	.454	119	11	10	68	4	4	-1	.979	9	O3/2	1.4
1953	NY-N	114	388	80	117	15	8	24	74	60	39	.302	.400	.567	146	28	27	93	6	5	-1	.956	-3	*3/O2	2.0
1954	*NY-N	136	448	76	118	18	1	26	86	90	58	.263	.392	.482	126	20	19	92	3	0	1	.945	-4	*3/2O	1.3
1955	NY-N	135	432	65	106	13	1	17	63	84	56	.245	.373	.398	105	6	5	71	2	2	-1	.943	2	*3/2S	0.7
1956	NY-N	83	183	24	43	9	0	8	29	31	26	.235	.349	.415	105	2	2	29	2	1	0	.908	0	3O/S	0.2
Total	9	933	3003	492	801	104	34	129	482	493	337	.267	.374	.453	118	90	88	545	33	15		.941	-13	3O2/S	6.3
■ **HOMER THOMPSON**	Thompson, Homer Thomas b: 6/1/1891, Spring City, Tenn. d: 9/12/57, Atlanta, Ga. BR/TR, 5'9", 160 lbs. Deb: 10/05/12 F																								
1912	NY-A	1	0	0	0	0	0	0	0	0		—	—	—	—	0	0	0	0			.500	-1	/C	0.0
■ **SHAG THOMPSON**	Thompson, James Alfred b: 4/29/1893, Haw River, N.C. d: 1/7/90, Black Mountain, N.C BL/TR, 5'8.5", 165 lbs. Deb: 6/08/14																								
1914	Phi-A	16	29	3	5	0	1	0	2	7	8	.172	.351	.241	82	-0	-0	3	1			.941	1	/O	0.1
1915	Phi-A	17	33	5	11	2	0	0	2	4	6	.333	.405	.394	144	2	2	5	0	1	-1	1.000	0	/O	0.1
1916	Phi-A	15	17	4	0	0	0	0	0	7	6	.000	.292	.000	-12	-2	-2	0	1			1.000	-1	/O	-0.3
Total	3	48	79	12	16	2	1	0	4	18	20	.203	.357	.253	87	-1	-0	8	2	1		.978	1	/O	-0.1
■ **JASON THOMPSON**	Thompson, Jason Dolph b: 7/6/54, Hollywood, Cal. BL/TL, 6'3", 210 lbs. Deb: 4/23/76																								
1976	Det-A	123	412	45	90	12	1	17	54	68	72	.218	.331	.376	103	4	2	53	2	4	-2	.994	2	*1	-0.7
1977	Det-A☆	158	585	87	158	24	5	31	105	73	91	.270	.352	.487	120	21	16	100	0	1	-1	.991	-7	*1	-0.1
1978	Det-A★	153	589	79	169	25	3	26	96	74	96	.287	.367	.472	130	27	25	104	0	0	0	.993	-5	*1	1.0
1979	Det-A	145	492	58	121	16	1	20	79	70	90	.246	.341	.404	97	1	-1	68	2	0	1	.994	0	*1	-0.9

YEAR	TM/L	G	AB	R	H	2B	3B	HR	RBI	BB	SO	AVG	OBP	SLG	PRO+	BR	/A	RC	SB	CS	SBR	FA	FR	POS	TPR
1980	Det-A	36	126	10	27	5	0	4	20	13	26	.214	.293	.349	73	-4	-5	12	0	1	-1	1.000	4	1	-0.4
	Cal-A	102	312	59	99	14	0	17	70	70	60	.317	.442	.526	168	31	32	76	2	0	1	1.000	-3	1D	2.7
	Yr	138	438	69	126	19	0	21	90	83	86	.288	.402	.475	141	27	27	86	2	1	0	1.000	1	1D	2.3
1981	Pit-N	86	223	36	54	13	0	15	42	59	49	.242	.401	.502	150	18	17	48	0	0	0	.989	-1	1	1.3
1982	Pit-N★	156	550	87	156	32	0	31	101	101	107	.284	.397	.511	148	41	39	117	1	0	0	.993	-1	*1	3.0
1983	Pit-N	152	517	70	134	20	1	18	76	99	128	.259	.379	.406	115	16	14	84	1	0	0	.993	-6	*1	0.0
1984	Pit-N	154	543	61	138	22	0	17	74	87	73	.254	.359	.389	110	9	9	78	0	0	0	.990	-10	*1	-1.1
1985	Pit-N	123	402	42	97	17	1	12	61	84	58	.241	.372	.378	111	9	9	61	0	0	0	.992	2	*1	0.5
1986	Mon-N	30	51	6	10	4	0	0	4	18	12	.196	.406	.275	92	1	1	7	0	1	-1	.962	-3	1	-0.4
Total	11	1418	4802	640	1253	204	12	208	782	816	862	.261	.369	.438	121	172	158	809	8	7	-2	.992	-29	*1/D	4.9

■ TUG THOMPSON Thompson, John P. b: London, Ontario, Canada BL , 160 lbs. Deb: 8/31/1882

YEAR	TM/L	G	AB	R	H	2B	3B	HR	RBI	BB	SO	AVG	OBP	SLG	PRO+	BR	/A	RC	SB	CS	SBR	FA	FR	POS	TPR
1882	Cin-a	1	5	0	1	0	0	0		0		.200	.200	.200	33	-0	-0	0				.000	-1	/O	-0.1
1884	Ind-a	24	97	10	20	3	0	0		2		.206	.222	.237	53	-5	-5	5				.429	-11	OC	-1.3
Total	2	25	102	10	21	3	0	0		2		.206	.221	.235	52	-5	-5	5				.409	-11	/OC	-1.4

■ FRESCO THOMPSON Thompson, Lafayette Fresco "Tommy" b: 6/6/02, Centerville, Ala. d: 11/20/68, Fullerton, Cal. BR/TR, 5'8", 150 lbs. Deb: 9/05/25

YEAR	TM/L	G	AB	R	H	2B	3B	HR	RBI	BB	SO	AVG	OBP	SLG	PRO+	BR	/A	RC	SB	CS	SBR	FA	FR	POS	TPR
1925	Pit-N	14	37	4	9	2	1	0	8	4	1	.243	.317	.351	66	-2	-2	4	2	1	0	.977	-2	2	-0.4
1926	NY-N	2	8	1	5	0	0	0	1	2	0	.625	.700	.625	262	2	2	4	1			1.000	-1	/2	0.1
1927	Phi-N	153	597	78	181	32	14	1	70	34	36	.303	.343	.409	99	-0	-1	81	19			.963	-5	*2	-0.1
1928	Phi-N	152	634	99	182	34	11	3	50	42	27	.287	.332	.390	85	-12	-15	80	19			.966	9	*2	-0.2
1929	Phi-N	148	623	115	202	41	3	4	53	75	34	.324	.398	.419	96	5	-1	104	16			.965	12	*2	1.6
1930	Phi-N	122	478	77	135	34	4	4	46	35	29	.282	.331	.395	70	-20	-25	61	7			.955	1	*2	-1.7
1931	Bro-N	74	181	26	48	6	1	1	21	23	16	.265	.351	.326	84	-3	-3	22	5			.946	-3	2S/3	-0.4
1932	Bro-N	3	1	0	0	0	0	0	0	0	0	.000	.000	.000	-99	-0	-0	0	0			.000	0	H	0.0
1934	NY-N	1	1	0	0	0	0	0	0	0	0	.000	.000	.000	-99	-0	-0	0	0			.000	0	H	0.0
Total	9	669	2560	400	762	149	34	13	249	215	143	.298	.353	.398	88	-30	-46	357	69	1		.962	10	2/S3	-1.1

■ MILT THOMPSON Thompson, Milton Bernard b: 1/5/59, Washington, D.C. BL/TR, 5'11", 170 lbs. Deb: 9/04/84

YEAR	TM/L	G	AB	R	H	2B	3B	HR	RBI	BB	SO	AVG	OBP	SLG	PRO+	BR	/A	RC	SB	CS	SBR	FA	FR	POS	TPR
1984	Atl-N	25	99	16	30	1	0	2	4	11	11	.303	.373	.374	103	2	1	16	14	2	3	.956	3	O	0.6
1985	Atl-N	73	182	17	55	7	2	0	6	7	36	.302	.339	.363	91	-1	-2	23	9	4	0	.964	-5	O	-0.9
1986	Phi-N	96	299	38	75	7	1	6	23	26	62	.251	.313	.341	78	-8	-9	34	19	4	3	.991	4	O	-0.5
1987	Phi-N	150	527	86	159	26	9	7	43	42	87	.302	.353	.425	102	4	2	85	46	10	8	.989	9	*O	1.3
1988	Phi-N	122	378	53	109	16	2	2	33	39	59	.288	.356	.357	103	4	3	48	17	9	-0	.983	5	*O	0.4
1989	StL-N	155	545	60	158	28	8	4	68	39	91	.290	.342	.393	106	6	4	73	27	8	3	.978	2	*O	0.7
1990	StL-N	135	418	42	91	14	7	6	30	39	60	.218	.292	.328	70	-17	-17	44	25	5	5	.971	-4	*O	-2.0
1991	StL-N	115	326	55	100	16	5	6	34	32	53	.307	.369	.442	126	12	11	53	16	9	-1	.991	9	O	1.9
1992	StL-N	109	208	31	61	9	1	4	17	16	39	.293	.350	.404	114	3	4	30	18	6	2	.974	-3	O	0.2
Total	9	980	2982	398	838	124	35	37	258	251	498	.281	.340	.383	99	5	-4	407	191	57	23	.981	19	O	1.7

■ ROBBY THOMPSON Thompson, Robert Randall b: 5/10/62, W.Palm Beach, Fla. BR/TR, 5'11", 170 lbs. Deb: 4/08/86

YEAR	TM/L	G	AB	R	H	2B	3B	HR	RBI	BB	SO	AVG	OBP	SLG	PRO+	BR	/A	RC	SB	CS	SBR	FA	FR	POS	TPR
1986	SF-N	149	549	73	149	27	3	7	47	42	112	.271	.329	.370	97	-6	-2	64	12	15	-5	.976	1	*2/S	-0.1
1987	*SF-N	132	420	62	110	26	5	10	44	40	91	.262	.338	.419	104	-1	2	58	16	11	-2	.972	6	*2	1.2
1988	SF-N†	138	477	66	126	24	6	7	48	40	111	.264	.326	.384	108	2	4	62	14	5	1	.978	-9	*2	0.1
1989	*SF-N	148	547	91	132	26	**11**	13	50	51	133	.241	.321	.400	108	3	5	75	12	2	2	.989	5	*2	1.8
1990	SF-N	144	498	67	122	22	3	15	56	34	96	.245	.301	.392	92	-9	-6	59	14	4	2	.989	**28**	*2	2.6
1991	SF-N	144	492	74	129	24	5	19	48	63	95	.262	.353	.447	128	16	18	81	14	7	0	.985	10	*2	3.2
1992	SF-N	128	443	54	115	25	1	14	49	43	75	.260	.336	.415	118	7	9	61	5	9	-4	.978	20	*2	3.0
Total	7	983	3426	487	883	174	34	85	342	313	713	.258	.329	.403	107	12	30	460	87	53	-6	.981	60	2/S	11.8

■ TOMMY THOMPSON Thompson, Rupert Lockhart b: 5/19/10, Elkhart, Ill. d: 5/24/71, Auburn, Cal. BL/TR, 5'9.5", 155 lbs. Deb: 9/03/33

YEAR	TM/L	G	AB	R	H	2B	3B	HR	RBI	BB	SO	AVG	OBP	SLG	PRO+	BR	/A	RC	SB	CS	SBR	FA	FR	POS	TPR
1933	Bos-N	24	97	6	18	1	0	0	6	4	6	.186	.218	.196	21	-10	-9	4	0			1.000	2	O	-0.9
1934	Bos-N	105	343	40	91	12	3	0	37	13	19	.265	.300	.318	71	-17	-13	34	2			.964	10	O	-0.7
1935	Bos-N	112	297	34	81	7	1	4	30	36	17	.273	.353	.343	96	-4	-0	36	2			.965	1	O	-0.2
1936	Bos-N	106	266	37	76	9	0	4	36	31	12	.286	.362	.365	103	-0	2	38	3			1.000	0	O1	-0.2
1938	Chi-A	19	18	2	2	0	0	0	2	1	2	.111	.158	.111	-31	-4	-4	0	0	0	0	1.000	-0	/1	-0.3
1939	Chi-A	1	0	0	0	0	0	0	1	0	0	—	—	—	—	0	-0	0	0	0	0	.000	0	H	0.0
	StL-A	30	86	23	26	5	0	1	7	23	7	.302	.455	.395	117	4	4	18	0	0	0	.977	-0	O	0.3
	Yr	31	86	23	26	5	0	1	8	23	7	.302	.455	.395	117	4	4	19	0	0	0	.977	-0	O	0.3
Total	6	397	1107	142	294	34	4	9	119	108	63	.266	.335	.328	84	-30	-21	130	7	0		.975	13	O/1	-2.0

■ RYAN THOMPSON Thompson, Ryan Orlando b: 11/4/67, Chestertown, Md. BR/TR, 6'3", 200 lbs. Deb: 9/01/92

YEAR	TM/L	G	AB	R	H	2B	3B	HR	RBI	BB	SO	AVG	OBP	SLG	PRO+	BR	/A	RC	SB	CS	SBR	FA	FR	POS	TPR
1992	NY-N	30	108	15	24	7	1	3	10	8	24	.222	.276	.389	87	-2	-2	11	2	2	-1	.988	0	O	-0.3

■ SAM THOMPSON Thompson, Samuel Luther "Big Sam" b: 3/5/1860, Danville, Ind. d: 11/7/22, Detroit, Mich. BL/TL, 6'2", 207 lbs. Deb: 7/02/1885 H

YEAR	TM/L	G	AB	R	H	2B	3B	HR	RBI	BB	SO	AVG	OBP	SLG	PRO+	BR	/A	RC	SB	CS	SBR	FA	FR	POS	TPR
1885	Det-N	63	254	58	77	11	9	7	44	16	22	.303	.344	.500	170	19	19	45				.885	7	O/3	2.2
1886	Det-N	122	503	101	156	18	13	8	89	35	31	.310	.355	.445	138	25	22	86	13			.945	10	*O	2.7
1887	*Det-N	127	545	118	**203**	29	**23**	11	**166**	32	19	**.372**	.416	**.571**	168	**53**	**50**	**142**	22			.909	7	*O	**4.5**
1888	Det-N	56	238	51	67	10	8	6	40	23	10	.282	.352	.466	162	17	17	42	5			.882	-7	O	0.8
1889	Phi-N	128	533	103	158	36	4	**20**	111	36	22	.296	.348	.492	124	22	14	102	24			.901	-7	*O	0.3
1890	Phi-N	132	549	116	**172**	**41**	9	4	102	42	29	.313	.371	.443	136	26	23	102	25			.939	2	*O	1.9
1891	Phi-N	133	554	108	163	23	10	7	90	52	20	.294	.363	.410	124	19	17	95	29			.937	19	*O	2.8
1892	Phi-N	153	609	109	186	28	11	9	104	59	19	.305	.377	.432	147	34	34	112	28			.937	4	*O	2.9
1893	Phi-N	131	600	130	**222**	**37**	13	11	126	50	17	.370	.424	.530	155	45	46	146	18			.931	-11	*O/1	2.3
1894	Phi-N	99	437	108	178	29	27	13	141	40	13	.407	.458	.686	179	51	53	152	24			**.977**	-4	*O	3.2
1895	Phi-N	119	538	131	211	45	21	**18**	**165**	31	11	.392	.430	**.654**	179	59	58	167	27			.943	12	*O	4.9
1896	Phi-N	119	517	103	154	28	7	12	100	28	13	.298	.341	.449	110	5	6	86	12			**.974**	18	*O	1.2
1897	Phi-N	3	13	2	3	0	1	0	3	1		.231	.286	.385	78	-1	-0	1	0			.833	0	/O	-0.1
1898	Phi-N	14	63	14	22	5	3	1	15	4		.349	.388	.571	182	5	6	15	2			1.000	2	O	0.6
1906	Det-A	8	31	4	7	0	1	0	3	1		.226	.250	.290	67	-1	-1	2	0			1.000	-0	/O	-0.2
Total	15	1407	5984	1256	1979	340	160	127	1299	450	226	.331	.384	.505	148	376	362	1297	229			.935	53	*O/13	30.0

■ SCOT THOMPSON Thompson, Vernon Scot b: 12/7/55, Grove City, Pa. BL/TL, 6'3", 195 lbs. Deb: 9/03/78

YEAR	TM/L	G	AB	R	H	2B	3B	HR	RBI	BB	SO	AVG	OBP	SLG	PRO+	BR	/A	RC	SB	CS	SBR	FA	FR	POS	TPR
1978	Chi-N	19	36	7	15	3	0	0	2	2	4	.417	.447	.500	147	3	3	8	0	0	0	1.000	-1	/O1	0.1
1979	Chi-N	128	346	36	100	13	5	2	29	17	37	.289	.324	.373	82	-5	-9	40	4	3	-1	.971	-4	*O	-1.8
1980	Chi-N	102	226	26	48	10	1	2	13	28	31	.212	.302	.292	62	-10	-12	19	6	6	-2	.963	-2	O1	-1.9
1981	Chi-N	57	115	8	19	5	0	0	8	7	8	.165	.213	.209	19	-12	-13	6	2	0	1	.980	-2	O/1	-1.6
1982	Chi-N	49	74	11	27	5	1	0	7	5	4	.365	.405	.459	138	4	4	13	0	1	-1	1.000	3	O/1	0.6
1983	Chi-N	53	88	4	17	3	1	0	10	3	14	.193	.220	.250	28	-8	-9	4	0	0	0	1.000	-2	O/1	-1.2
1984	SF-N	120	245	30	75	7	1	1	31	30	26	.306	.382	.355	112	4	5	32	5	3	-0	.998	-1	1/O	0.0
1985	SF-N	64	111	8	23	5	0	0	6	2	10	.207	.221	.252	34	-10	-10	5	0	0	0	.995	2	1	-1.0
	Mon-N	34	32	2	9	1	0	0	4	3	7	.281	.343	.313	90	-1	-0	3	0	0	0	1.000	-0	/1O	-0.1
	Yr	98	143	10	32	6	0	0	10	5	17	.224	.250	.266	47	-11	-10	8	0	0	0	.995	2	1/O	-1.1
Total	8	626	1273	132	333	52	9	5	110	97	141	.262	.315	.328	76	-35	-41	131	17	13	-3	.973	-8	O1	-6.9

■ BOBBY THOMSON

Thomson, Robert Brown "The Staten Island Scot" b: 10/25/23, Glasgow, Scotland BR/TR, 6'2", 185 lbs. Deb: 9/09/46

YEAR	TM/L	G	AB	R	H	2B	3B	HR	RBI	BB	SO	AVG	OBP	SLG	PRO+	BR	/A	RC	SB	CS	SBR	FA	FR	POS	TPR
1946	NY-N	18	54	8	17	4	1	2	9	4	5	.315	.362	.537	152	3	3	10	0			.935	0	3	0.4
1947	NY-N	138	545	105	154	26	5	29	85	40	78	.283	.336	.508	121	13	13	92	1			.980	9	*O/2	1.5
1948	NY-N★	138	471	75	117	20	2	16	63	30	77	.248	.296	.401	87	-10	-11	53	2			.970	6	*O	-1.1
1949	NY-N★	156	641	99	198	35	9	27	109	44	45	.309	.355	.518	132	25	25	115	10			.982	20	*O	3.6
1950	NY-N	149	563	79	142	22	7	25	85	55	45	.252	.324	.449	101	-1	-1	81	3			.978	10	*O	0.3
1951	*NY-N	148	518	89	152	27	8	32	101	73	57	.293	.385	.562	150	37	36	113	5	5	-2	.966	-11	O3	2.0
1952	NY-N★	153	608	89	164	29	**14**	24	108	52	74	.270	.331	.482	122	16	16	97	5	2	0	.940	-7	3O	0.5
1953	NY-N	154	608	80	175	22	6	26	106	43	57	.288	.338	.472	106	6	4	95	4	2	0	.983	3	*O	0.2
1954	Mil-N	43	99	7	23	3	0	2	15	12	29	.232	.315	.323	71	-5	-4	10	0	0	0	.980	1	O	-0.4
1955	Mil-N	101	343	40	88	12	3	12	56	34	52	.257	.324	.414	99	-3	-1	45	2	1	0	.969	0	O	-0.5
1956	Mil-N	142	451	59	106	10	4	20	74	43	75	.235	.304	.408	95	-8	-4	55	2	4	-2	.974	-4	*O/3	-1.6
1957	Mil-N	41	148	15	35	5	3	4	23	8	27	.236	.285	.392	86	-5	-3	17	2	1	0	.988	-1	O	-0.7
	NY-N	81	215	24	52	7	4	8	38	19	39	.242	.303	.423	93	-3	-3	26	1	2	-1	.992	-4	O/3	-1.1
	Yr	122	363	39	87	12	7	12	61	27	66	.240	.296	.410	90	-7	-6	43	3	3	-1	.990	-5	*O/3	-1.8
1958	Chi-N	152	547	67	155	27	5	21	82	56	76	.283	.354	.466	117	11	13	87	0	2	-1	.989	4	*O/3	0.7
1959	Chi-N	122	374	55	97	15	2	11	52	35	50	.259	.326	.398	93	-5	-4	48	1	0	0	.987	-7	*O	-1.6
1960	Bos-A	40	114	12	30	3	1	5	20	11	15	.263	.328	.439	102	1	0	15	0	1	-1	.971	2	O/1	0.0
	Bal-A	3	6	0	0	0	0	0	0	0	3	.000	.000	.000	-99	-2	-2	0	0	0	0	.000	-1	/O	-0.3
	Yr	43	120	12	30	3	1	5	20	11	18	.250	.313	.417	93	-1	-2	14	0	1	-1	.971	1	O/1	-0.3
Total	15	1779	6305	903	1705	267	74	264	1026	559	804	.270	.333	.462	111	73	79	958	38	20		.980	20	*O3/21	1.9

■ DICKIE THON

Thon, Richard William b: 6/20/58, South Bend, Ind. BR/TR, 5'11", 175 lbs. Deb: 5/22/79

YEAR	TM/L	G	AB	R	H	2B	3B	HR	RBI	BB	SO	AVG	OBP	SLG	PRO+	BR	/A	RC	SB	CS	SBR	FA	FR	POS	TPR
1979	*Cal-A	35	56	6	19	3	0	0	8	5	10	.339	.393	.393	117	1	1	8	0	0	0	.923	1	2/S3	0.4
1980	Cal-A	80	267	32	68	12	2	0	15	10	28	.255	.284	.315	65	-13	-13	23	7	5	-1	.928	-12	S2D3/1	-2.2
1981	*Hou-N	49	95	13	26	6	0	0	3	9	13	.274	.337	.337	96	-1	-0	11	6	1	1	.950	-5	2S/3	-0.3
1982	Hou-N	136	496	73	137	31	**10**	3	36	37	48	.276	.328	.397	110	1	5	69	37	8	6	.975	5	*S/32	2.8
1983	Hou-N★	154	619	81	177	28	9	20	79	54	73	.286	.345	.457	128	16	20	95	34	16	1	.966	21	*S	5.8
1984	Hou-N	5	17	3	6	0	1	0	1	0	4	.353	.389	.471	151	1	1	2	0	1	-1	1.000	-0	/S	0.1
1985	Hou-N	84	251	26	63	6	1	6	29	18	50	.251	.301	.355	85	-6	-5	27	8	3	1	.967	7	S	0.9
1986	*Hou-N	106	278	24	69	13	1	3	21	29	49	.248	.319	.335	83	-7	-6	28	6	5	-1	.972	-2	*S	-0.2
1987	Hou-N	32	66	6	14	1	0	1	3	16	13	.212	.366	.273	75	-2	-2	8	3	0	1	.925	-8	S	-0.6
1988	SD-N	95	258	36	68	12	2	1	18	33	49	.264	.349	.337	100	0	1	34	19	4	3	.954	-20	S/23	-1.1
1989	Phi-N	136	435	45	118	18	4	15	60	33	81	.271	.323	.434	115	7	7	61	6	3	0	.972	16	*S	3.4
1990	Phi-N	149	552	54	141	20	4	8	48	37	77	.255	.306	.350	80	-16	-15	57	12	5	1	.964	3	*S	0.0
1991	Phi-N	146	539	44	136	18	4	9	44	25	84	.252	.285	.351	79	-17	-16	52	11	5	0	.969	-8	*S	-1.4
1992	Tex-A	95	275	30	68	15	3	4	37	20	40	.247	.298	.367	88	-6	-5	32	12	2	2	.958	0	S	0.4
Total	14	1302	4204	473	1110	183	41	70	402	326	619	.264	.318	.377	96	-42	-26	509	161	58	14	.965	-3	*S/23D1	8.0

■ JACK THONEY

Thoney, John "Bullet Jack" (b: John Thoeny) b: 12/8/1879, Ft.Thomas, Ky. d: 10/24/48, Covington, Ky. BR/TR, 5'10", 175 lbs. Deb: 4/26/02

YEAR	TM/L	G	AB	R	H	2B	3B	HR	RBI	BB	SO	AVG	OBP	SLG	PRO+	BR	/A	RC	SB	CS	SBR	FA	FR	POS	TPR
1902	Cle-A	28	105	14	30	7	1	0	11	9		.286	.342	.371	102	-0	0	15	4			.891	-15	2S/O	-1.3
	Bal-A	3	11	1	0	0	0	0	0	1		.000	.083	.000	-72	-3	-3	0	1			.778	-2	/3	-0.4
	Yr	31	116	15	30	7	1	0	11	10		.259	.317	.336	84	-3	-2	14	5			.891	-17	2S/3O	-1.7
1903	Cle-A	32	122	10	25	3	0	1	9	2		.205	.218	.254	42	-9	-8	8	7			.889	1	O/23	-0.9
1904	Was-A	17	70	6	21	3	0	0	6	1		.300	.310	.343	108	0	0	8	2			.860	2	O	0.1
	NY-A	36	128	17	24	4	2	0	12	8		.188	.241	.250	53	-6	-7	10	9			.826	1	3O	-0.7
	Yr	53	198	23	45	7	2	0	18	9		.227	.264	.283	71	-6	-7	18	11			.886	3	O3	-0.6
1908	Bos-A	109	416	58	106	5	9	2	30	13		.255	.282	.325	95	-3	-4	42	16			.948	8	*O	0.0
1909	Bos-A	13	40	1	5	1	0	0	3	2		.125	.167	.150	0	-5	-5	1	2			.960	1	O	-0.5
1911	Bos-A	26	20	5	5	0	0	0	2	0		.250	.250	.250	40	-2	-2	1	1			.000	0	H	-0.2
Total	6	264	912	112	216	23	12	3	73	36		.237	.269	.298	75	-27	-28	87	42			.929	-4	O/32S	-3.9

■ ANDY THORNTON

Thornton, Andre b: 8/13/49, Tuskegee, Ala. BR/TR, 6'2", 205 lbs. Deb: 7/28/73

YEAR	TM/L	G	AB	R	H	2B	3B	HR	RBI	BB	SO	AVG	OBP	SLG	PRO+	BR	/A	RC	SB	CS	SBR	FA	FR	POS	TPR
1973	Chi-N	17	35	3	7	3	0	0	2	7	9	.200	.333	.286	68	-1	-1	4	0	0	0	.989	2	/1	0.0
1974	Chi-N	107	303	41	79	16	4	10	46	48	50	.261	.369	.439	120	11	9	51	2	1	0	.992	8	1/3	1.2
1975	Chi-N	120	372	70	109	21	4	18	60	88	63	.293	.433	.516	156	35	33	89	3	2	-0	.988	3	*1/3	2.9
1976	Chi-N	27	85	8	17	6	0	2	14	20	14	.200	.364	.341	93	1	-0	13	2	0	1	.987	1	1	0.0
	Mon-N	69	183	20	35	5	2	9	24	28	32	.191	.308	.388	93	-1	-2	24	2	1	0	.994	0	1O	-0.5
	Yr	96	268	28	52	11	2	11	38	48	46	.194	.327	.373	93	0	-2	37	4	1	1	.991	1	1O	-0.5
1977	Cle-A	131	433	77	114	20	5	28	70	70	82	.263	.379	.527	149	27	29	89	3	4	-2	.995	-3	*1/D	1.8
1978	Cle-A	145	508	97	133	22	4	33	105	93	72	.262	.382	.516	152	36	36	99	4	7	-3	.995	5	*1	3.0
1979	Cle-A	143	515	89	120	31	1	26	93	90	93	.233	.351	.449	114	11	11	86	5	4	-1	.994	-3	*1D	-0.1
1981	Cle-A	69	226	22	54	12	0	6	30	23	37	.239	.309	.372	97	-1	-1	23	3	1	0	.986	-1	D1	-0.2
1982	Cle-A★	161	589	90	161	26	1	32	116	109	81	.273	.389	.484	139	34	34	109	6	7	-2	1.000	0	*D/1	3.1
1983	Cle-A	141	508	78	143	27	1	17	77	87	72	.281	.389	.439	123	22	19	90	4	2	0	.991	2	*D1	1.9
1984	Cle-A★	155	587	91	159	26	0	33	99	91	79	.271	.371	.484	132	29	27	108	6	5	-1	.979	0	*D1	2.5
1985	Cle-A	124	461	49	109	13	0	22	88	47	75	.236	.307	.408	94	-5	-4	56	3	2	-0	.000	0	*D	-0.4
1986	Cle-A	120	401	49	92	14	0	17	66	65	67	.229	.338	.392	100	-0	1	55	4	1	1	.000	0	*D	0.1
1987	Cle-A	36	85	8	10	2	0	0	5	10	25	.118	.211	.141	-4	-13	-13	3	1	0	0	.000	0	D	-1.2
Total	14	1565	5291	792	1342	244	22	253	895	876	851	.254	.364	.452	123	184	179	900	48	37	-8	.992	14	D1/O3	14.1

■ JOHN THORNTON

Thornton, John b: 1870, Washington, D.C. 5'10.5", 175 lbs. Deb: 8/14/1889

YEAR	TM/L	G	AB	R	H	2B	3B	HR	RBI	BB	SO	AVG	OBP	SLG	PRO+	BR	/A	RC	SB	CS	SBR	FA	FR	POS	TPR
1889	Was-N	1	4	0	0	0	0	0	1	0	1	.000	.000	.000	-99	-1	-1	0	0			1.000	-0	/P	0.0
1891	Phi-N	39	123	7	17	3	0	0	6	2	10	.138	.152	.163	-7	-17	-17	3	1			.881	-0	P/O	-0.2
1892	Phi-N	5	13	1	5	0	0	0	2	0	0	.385	.385	.385	135	0	0	2	0			.857	-1	/PO	-0.1
	StL-N	1	3	0	0	0	0	0	0	0	2	.000	.000	.000	-99	-1	-1	0	0			.000	-0	/O	-0.1
	Yr	6	16	1	5	0	0	0	2	0	2	.313	.313	.313	92	-0	-0	2	0			.500	-1	/PO	-0.2
Total	3	46	143	8	22	3	0	0	9	2	13	.154	.166	.175	0	-18	-18	5	1			.881	-1	/PO	-0.4

■ LOU THORNTON

Thornton, Louis b: 4/26/63, Montgomery, Ala. BL/TR, 6'2", 185 lbs. Deb: 4/08/85

YEAR	TM/L	G	AB	R	H	2B	3B	HR	RBI	BB	SO	AVG	OBP	SLG	PRO+	BR	/A	RC	SB	CS	SBR	FA	FR	POS	TPR
1985	*Tor-A	56	72	18	17	1	1	1	8	2	24	.236	.267	.319	58	-4	-4	6	1	0	0	.957	-7	OD	-1.1
1987	Tor-A	12	2	5	1	0	0	0	0	1	0	.500	.667	.500	212	0	0	0	0	1	-1	.000	-2	/OD	-0.2
1988	Tor-A	11	2	1	0	0	0	0	0	0	1	.000	.000	.000	-99	-1	-1	0	0	0	0	1.000	-4	O/D	-0.5
1989	NY-N	13	13	5	4	1	0	0	1	0	1	.308	.308	.385	102	-0	-0	2	2	0	1	1.000	-1	/O	0.0
1990	NY-N	3	0	0	0	0	0	0	0	0	0	—	—	—	—	0	0	0	0	0	0	1.000	-1	/O	-0.1
Total	5	95	89	29	22	2	1	1	9	3	25	.247	.280	.326	65	-4	-4	8	3	1	0	.965	-13	/OD	-1.9

■ OTIS THORNTON

Thornton, Otis Benjamin b: 6/30/45, Docena, Ala. BR/TR, 6'1", 186 lbs. Deb: 7/06/73

YEAR	TM/L	G	AB	R	H	2B	3B	HR	RBI	BB	SO	AVG	OBP	SLG	PRO+	BR	/A	RC	SB	CS	SBR	FA	FR	POS	TPR
1973	Hou-N	2	3	0	0	0	0	0	1	0	2	.000	.000	.000	-99	-1	-1	0	0	0	0	1.000	0	/C	-0.1

■ WALTER THORNTON

Thornton, Walter Miller b: 2/18/1875, Lewiston, Maine d: 7/14/60, Los Angeles, Cal. TL, 6'1", 180 lbs. Deb: 7/01/1895

YEAR	TM/L	G	AB	R	H	2B	3B	HR	RBI	BB	SO	AVG	OBP	SLG	PRO+	BR	/A	RC	SB	CS	SBR	FA	FR	POS	TPR
1895	Chi-N	8	22	4	7	1	0	1	7	3	1	.318	.400	.500	125	1	1	5	0			.900	-1	/P1	0.0
1896	Chi-N	9	22	6	8	0	1	0	1	5	2	.364	.481	.455	144	2	2	6	2			.800	-1	/PO	0.0
1897	Chi-N	75	265	39	85	9	6	0	55	30		.321	.402	.400	108	6	4	50	13			.781	-11	OP	-1.0

YEAR	TM/L	G	AB	R	H	2B	3B	HR	RBI	BB	SO	AVG	OBP	SLG	PRO+	BR	/A	RC	SB	CS	SBR	FA	FR	POS	TPR
1898	Chi-N	62	210	34	62	5	2	0	14	22		.295	.362	.338	101	1	1	30	8			.877	-3	OP	-0.3
Total	4	154	519	83	162	15	9	1	77	60	3	.312	.390	.382	108	10	8	90	23			.821	-15	/OP1	-1.3

■ **BOB THORPE** Thorpe, Benjamin Robert b: 11/19/26, Caryville, Fla. BR/TR, 6'1.5", 190 lbs. Deb: 4/19/51

YEAR	TM/L	G	AB	R	H	2B	3B	HR	RBI	BB	SO	AVG	OBP	SLG	PRO+	BR	/A	RC	SB	CS	SBR	FA	FR	POS	TPR
1951	Bos-N	2	2	1	1	0	1	0	1	0	0	.500	.500	1.500	448	1	1	2	0	0	0	.000	0	H	0.1
1952	Bos-N	81	292	20	76	8	2	3	26	5	42	.260	.275	.332	70	-13	-12	26	3	1	0	.972	0	O	-1.5
1953	Mil-N	27	37	1	6	1	0	0	5	1	6	.162	.184	.189	-3	-6	-5	1	0	1	-1	1.000	-5	O	-1.1
Total	3	110	331	22	83	9	3	3	32	6	48	.251	.266	.323	64	-18	-17	28	3	2	-0	.975	-5	/O	-2.5

■ **JIM THORPE** Thorpe, James Francis b: 5/28/1887, Prague, Okla. d: 3/28/53, Long Beach, Cal. BR/TR, 6'1", 185 lbs. Deb: 4/14/13

YEAR	TM/L	G	AB	R	H	2B	3B	HR	RBI	BB	SO	AVG	OBP	SLG	PRO+	BR	/A	RC	SB	CS	SBR	FA	FR	POS	TPR
1913	NY-N	19	35	6	5	0	0	1	2	1	9	.143	.167	.229	12	-4	-4	1	2			.944	-1	/O	-0.5
1914	NY-N	30	31	5	6	1	0	0	2	0	4	.194	.194	.226	25	-3	-3	1	1			.750	-2	/O	-0.5
1915	NY-N	17	52	8	12	3	1	0	1	2	16	.231	.259	.327	82	-2	-1	5	4	2	0	.933	-2	O	-0.4
1917	Cin-N	77	251	29	62	2	8	4	36	6	35	.247	.267	.367	98	-3	-2	26	11			.962	2	O	-0.5
	*NY-N	26	57	12	11	3	2	0	4	8	10	.193	.303	.316	93	-1	-0	6	1			.939	-3	O	-0.5
	Yr	103	308	41	73	5	10	4	40	14	45	.237	.275	.357	97	-4	-2	32	12			.958	-1	O	-1.0
1918	NY-N	58	113	15	28	4	4	1	11	4	18	.248	.286	.381	105	-0	0	12	3			.983	-12	O	-1.5
1919	NY-N	2	3	0	1	0	0	0	1	0	0	.333	.333	.333	102	-0	-0	0	0			1.000	-1	/O	-0.1
	Bos-N	60	156	16	51	7	3	1	25	6	30	.327	.360	.429	143	7	7	25	7			.926	-7	O/1	-0.2
	Yr	62	159	16	52	7	3	1	26	6	30	.327	.359	.428	142	6	7	26	7			.928	-7	O/1	-0.3
Total	6	289	698	91	176	20	18	7	82	27	122	.252	.286	.362	99	-6	-3	77	29	2		.951	-25	O/1	-4.2

■ **BUCK THRASHER** Thrasher, Frank Edward b: 8/6/1889, Watkinsville, Ga. d: 6/12/38, Cleveland, Ohio BL/TR, 5'11", 182 lbs. Deb: 9/27/16

YEAR	TM/L	G	AB	R	H	2B	3B	HR	RBI	BB	SO	AVG	OBP	SLG	PRO+	BR	/A	RC	SB	CS	SBR	FA	FR	POS	TPR
1916	Phi-A	7	29	4	9	2	1	0	4	2	1	.310	.355	.448	148	1	1	5	0			1.000	-1	/O	0.0
1917	Phi-A	23	77	5	18	2	1	0	2	3	12	.234	.272	.286	71	-3	-3	6	0			.938	-3	O	-0.8
Total	2	30	106	9	27	4	2	0	6	5	13	.255	.295	.330	92	-2	-1	11	0			.951	-4	/O	-0.8

■ **MARV THRONEBERRY** Throneberry, Marvin Eugene "Marvelous Marv" b: 9/2/33, Collierville, Tenn. BL/TL, 6', 197 lbs. Deb: 9/25/55 F

YEAR	TM/L	G	AB	R	H	2B	3B	HR	RBI	BB	SO	AVG	OBP	SLG	PRO+	BR	/A	RC	SB	CS	SBR	FA	FR	POS	TPR
1955	NY-A	1	2	1	2	1	0	0	3	0	0	1.000	1.000	1.500	574	1	1	3	1	0	0	1.000	0	/1	0.2
1958	*NY-A	60	150	30	34	5	2	7	19	19	40	.227	.318	.427	107	0	1	21	1	1	-0	.991	-1	1/O	-0.3
1959	NY-A	80	192	27	46	5	0	8	22	18	51	.240	.305	.391	93	-3	-2	24	0	0	0	.989	-1	1O	-0.6
1960	KC-A	104	236	29	59	9	2	11	41	23	60	.250	.317	.445	103	0	0	32	0	0	0	.991	1	1	-0.4
1961	KC-A	40	130	17	31	2	1	6	24	19	30	.238	.336	.408	97	-0	-0	18	0	0	0	.996	1	1O	-0.2
	Bal-A	56	96	9	20	3	0	5	11	12	20	.208	.296	.396	85	-3	-2	11	0	0	0	.923	-3	O1	-0.6
	Yr	96	226	26	51	5	1	11	35	31	50	.226	.319	.403	93	-3	-3	29	0	0	0	.991	-2	1O	-0.8
1962	Bal-A	9	9	1	0	0	0	0	0	4	6	.000	.308	.000	-9	-1	-1	0	0	0	0	1.000	-0	/O	-0.1
	NY-N	116	357	29	87	11	3	16	49	34	83	.244	.309	.426	94	-3	-4	46	1	3	-2	.981	4	1	-0.8
1963	NY-N	14	14	0	2	1	0	0	1	1	5	.143	.200	.214	19	-1	-1	1	0	0	0	1.000	-0	/1	-0.2
Total	7	480	1186	143	281	37	8	53	170	130	295	.237	.313	.416	96	-10	-9	155	3	4	-2	.987	1	1/O	-3.0

■ **FAYE THRONEBERRY** Throneberry, Maynard Faye b: 6/22/31, Fisherville, Tenn. BL/TR, 6', 190 lbs. Deb: 4/15/52 F

YEAR	TM/L	G	AB	R	H	2B	3B	HR	RBI	BB	SO	AVG	OBP	SLG	PRO+	BR	/A	RC	SB	CS	SBR	FA	FR	POS	TPR
1952	Bos-A	98	310	38	80	11	3	5	23	33	67	.258	.331	.361	86	-3	-6	41	16	7	1	.955	-0	O	-0.9
1955	Bos-A	60	144	20	37	7	3	6	27	14	31	.257	.327	.472	104	2	0	23	0	0	0	.960	1	O	0.0
1956	Bos-A	24	50	6	11	2	0	1	3	3	16	.220	.264	.320	48	-4	-4	4	0	0	0	.909	-2	O	-0.7
1957	Bos-A	1	1	0	0	0	0	0	0	0	1	.000	.000	.000	-95	-0	-0	0	0	0	0	.000	0	H	0.0
	Was-A	68	195	21	36	8	2	2	12	17	37	.185	.254	.277	45	-15	-15	14	0	1	-1	.983	-6	O	-2.5
	Yr	69	196	21	36	8	2	2	12	17	38	.184	.252	.276	45	-15	-15	14	0	1	-1	.983	-6	O	-2.5
1958	Was-A	44	87	12	16	1	1	4	7	4	28	.184	.245	.356	64	-5	-5	8	0	1	-1	1.000	-3	O	-1.0
1959	Was-A	117	327	36	82	11	2	10	42	33	61	.251	.325	.388	95	-2	-2	42	6	4	-1	.953	-2	O	-0.8
1960	Was-A	85	157	18	39	7	1	1	23	18	33	.248	.330	.325	78	-5	-4	17	1	1	-0	.947	-3	O	-1.0
1961	LA-A	24	31	1	6	1	0	0	0	5	10	.194	.306	.226	40	-2	-3	2	0	0	0	1.000	1	/O	-0.3
Total	8	521	1302	152	307	48	12	29	137	127	284	.236	.309	.358	79	-34	-39	151	23	14	-2	.962	-15	O	-7.2

■ **GARY THURMAN** Thurman, Gary Montez b: 11/12/64, Indianapolis, Ind. BR/TR, 5'10", 175 lbs. Deb: 8/30/87

YEAR	TM/L	G	AB	R	H	2B	3B	HR	RBI	BB	SO	AVG	OBP	SLG	PRO+	BR	/A	RC	SB	CS	SBR	FA	FR	POS	TPR
1987	KC-A	27	81	12	24	2	0	0	5	8	20	.296	.360	.321	81	-2	-2	10	7	2	1	.971	4	O	0.2
1988	KC-A	35	66	6	11	1	0	0	2	4	20	.167	.214	.182	12	-8	-8	3	5	1	1	.949	-7	O/D	-1.5
1989	KC-A	72	87	24	17	2	1	0	5	15	26	.195	.314	.241	59	-4	-4	11	16	0	5	.949	-17	O/D	-1.8
1990	KC-A	23	60	5	14	3	0	0	3	2	12	.233	.258	.283	52	-4	-4	4	1	1	-0	1.000	-2	O	-0.7
1991	KC-A	80	184	24	51	9	0	2	13	11	42	.277	.321	.359	87	-3	-3	21	15	5	2	.970	-5	O	-0.7
1992	KC-A	88	200	25	49	6	3	0	20	9	34	.245	.281	.305	63	-10	-10	17	9	6	-1	.986	2	O/D	-1.0
Total	6	325	678	96	166	23	4	2	48	49	154	.245	.298	.299	66	-30	-31	66	53	15	7	.973	-25	O/D	-5.5

■ **BOB THURMAN** Thurman, Robert Burns b: 5/14/17, Wichita, Kan. BL/TL, 6'1", 205 lbs. Deb: 4/14/55

YEAR	TM/L	G	AB	R	H	2B	3B	HR	RBI	BB	SO	AVG	OBP	SLG	PRO+	BR	/A	RC	SB	CS	SBR	FA	FR	POS	TPR
1955	Cin-N	82	152	19	33	2	3	7	22	17	26	.217	.296	.408	80	-4	-5	16	0	2	-1	.949	-4	O	-1.1
1956	Cin-N	80	139	25	41	5	2	8	22	10	14	.295	.342	.532	123	5	4	25	0	0	0	.953	-3	O	0.0
1957	Cin-N	74	190	38	47	4	2	16	40	15	33	.247	.306	.542	114	5	3	31	0	0	0	.987	-0	O	0.0
1958	Cin-N	94	178	23	41	7	4	4	20	20	38	.230	.322	.382	81	-4	-5	21	1	2	-1	.976	2	O	-0.6
1959	Cin-N	4	4	1	1	0	0	0	2	0	1	.250	.250	.250	33	-0	-0	0	0	0	0	.000	0	H	0.0
Total	5	334	663	106	163	18	11	35	106	62	112	.246	.315	.465	99	2	-3	94	1	4	-2	.970	-5	O	-1.7

■ **EDDIE TIEMEYER** Tiemeyer, Edward Carl b: 5/9/1885, Cincinnati, Ohio d: 9/27/46, Cincinnati, Ohio BR/TR, 5'11.5", 185 lbs. Deb: 8/19/06

YEAR	TM/L	G	AB	R	H	2B	3B	HR	RBI	BB	SO	AVG	OBP	SLG	PRO+	BR	/A	RC	SB	CS	SBR	FA	FR	POS	TPR
1906	Cin-N	5	11	3	2	0	0	0	0	1		.182	.250	.182	34	-1	-1	1	0			1.000	0	/3P	0.0
1907	Cin-N	1	0	1	0	0	0	0	0	1		—	1.000	—	207	0	0	0	0			.000	0	H	0.0
1909	NY-A	3	8	1	3	1	0	0	0	1		.375	.444	.500	197	1	1	2	0			.962	-1	/1	0.0
Total	3	9	19	5	5	1	0	0	0	3		.263	.364	.316	110	0	0	2	0				-0	/13P	0.0

■ **MIKE TIERNAN** Tiernan, Michael Joseph "Silent Mike" b: 1/21/1867, Trenton, N.J. d: 11/9/18, New York, N.Y. BL/TL, 5'11", 165 lbs. Deb: 4/30/1887

YEAR	TM/L	G	AB	R	H	2B	3B	HR	RBI	BB	SO	AVG	OBP	SLG	PRO+	BR	/A	RC	SB	CS	SBR	FA	FR	POS	TPR
1887	NY-N	103	407	82	117	13	12	10	62	32	31	.287	.344	.452	127	11	14	75	28			.865	-9	*O/P	0.3
1888	*NY-N	113	443	75	130	16	8	9	52	42	42	.293	.364	.427	156	28	28	90	52			**.960**	-0	*O	2.4
1889	*NY-N	122	499	**147**	167	23	14	10	73	**96**	32	.335	.447	.497	165	48	**48**	129	33			.896	-3	*O	3.6
1890	NY-N	133	553	132	168	25	21	**13**	59	68	53	.304	.385	**.495**	**158**	**40**	**40**	130	56			.896	-15	*O	1.8
1891	NY-N	134	542	111	166	30	12	**16**	73	69	32	.306	.388	.494	**165**	39	43	128	53			.901	-9	*O	2.7
1892	NY-N	116	450	79	129	16	10	5	66	57	46	.287	.369	.400	137	20	21	76	20			.899	-3	*O	1.1
1893	NY-N	125	511	114	158	19	12	14	102	72	24	.309	.399	.476	134	25	25	110	26			.927	-9	*O	0.8
1894	*NY-N	112	424	84	117	19	13	5	77	54	21	.276	.359	.417	89	-8	-8	76	28			.922	-11	*O	-2.0
1895	NY-N	120	476	127	165	23	21	7	70	66	19	.347	.427	.527	151	34	37	126	36			.946	-5	*O	1.8
1896	NY-N	133	521	132	192	24	16	7	89	77	18	.369	.452	.516	162	46	48	141	35			.970	-2	*O	3.0
1897	NY-N	127	528	123	174	29	10	5	72	61		.330	.400	.451	128	19	22	114	40			.931	-11	*O	0.1
1898	NY-N	103	415	90	116	15	11	5	49	43		.280	.357	.405	122	10	12	70	19			.973	-12	*O	-0.7
1899	NY-N	35	137	17	35	4	2	0	7	10		.255	.306	.314	73	-6	-5	14	2			.938	-4	O	-1.1
Total	13	1476	5906	1313	1834	256	162	106	851	747	318	.311	.392	.463	140	305	324	1278	428			.924	-92	*O/P	13.8

■ **COTTON TIERNEY** Tierney, James Arthur b: 2/10/1894, Kansas City, Kan. d: 4/18/53, Kansas City, Mo. BR/TR, 5'8", 175 lbs. Deb: 9/23/20

YEAR	TM/L	G	AB	R	H	2B	3B	HR	RBI	BB	SO	AVG	OBP	SLG	PRO+	BR	/A	RC	SB	CS	SBR	FA	FR	POS	TPR
1920	Pit-N	12	46	4	11	5	0	0	8	3	4	.239	.286	.348	79	-1	-1	5	1	1	-0	.964	-2	2/S	-0.3
1921	Pit-N	117	442	49	132	22	8	3	52	24	31	.299	.338	.405	93	-3	-5	59	4	6	-2	.965	-27	23/OS	-3.0

YEAR	TM/L	G	AB	R	H	2B	3B	HR	RBI	BB	SO	AVG	OBP	SLG	PRO+	BR	/A	RC	SB	CS	SBR	FA	FR	POS	TPR
1922	Pit-N	122	441	58	152	26	14	7	86	22	40	.345	.378	.515	127	17	16	82	7	8	-3	.964	-35	*2/OS3	-1.8
1923	Pit-N	29	120	22	35	5	2	2	23	2	10	.292	.309	.417	88	-2	-3	15	2	1	0	.941	-3	2	-0.5
	Phi-N	121	480	68	152	31	1	11	65	24	42	.317	.352	.454	100	6	-1	75	3	4	-2	.975	18	*2/O3	1.6
	Yr	150	600	90	187	36	3	13	88	26	52	.312	.343	.447	97	4	-4	90	5	5	-2	.968	15	*2/O3	1.1
1924	Bos-N	136	505	38	131	16	1	6	58	22	37	.259	.296	.331	71	-23	-21	49	11	8	-2	.964	-1	*23	-2.0
1925	Bro-N	93	265	27	68	14	4	2	39	12	23	.257	.294	.362	68	-14	-13	27	0	3	-2	.963	-1	3/12	-1.1
Total	6	630	2299	266	681	119	30	31	331	109	187	.296	.332	.415	93	-20	-27	312	28	31	-10	.966	-50	23/OS1	-7.1

■ BILL TIERNEY Tierney, William J. b: 5/14/1858, Boston, Mass. d: 9/21/1898, Boston, Mass. Deb: 5/02/1882

YEAR	TM/L	G	AB	R	H	2B	3B	HR	RBI	BB	SO	AVG	OBP	SLG	PRO+	BR	/A	RC	SB	CS	SBR	FA	FR	POS	TPR
1882	Cin-a	1	5	1	0	0	0	0		0		.000	.000	.000	-95	-1	-1	0				.917	0	/1	-0.1
1884	Bal-U	1	3	0	1	0	0	0		1		.333	.500	.333	169	0	0	1				1.000	-0	/O	0.0
Total	2	2	8	1	1	0	0	0		1		.125	.222	.125	19	-1	-1	1					0	/O1	-0.1

■ JOHN TILLEY Tilley, John C. b: 1856, New York, N.Y. Deb: 8/23/1882

YEAR	TM/L	G	AB	R	H	2B	3B	HR	RBI	BB	SO	AVG	OBP	SLG	PRO+	BR	/A	RC	SB	CS	SBR	FA	FR	POS	TPR
1882	Cle-N	15	56	2	5	1	1	0	4	2	11	.089	.121	.143	-16	-7	-7	1				.857	2	O	-0.5
1884	Tol-a	17	56	5	10	2	0	0		4		.179	.246	.214	52	-3	-3	3				.632	-4	O	-0.7
	StP-U	9	26	2	4	1	0	0		3		.154	.241	.192	89	-1	1	1				.938	0	/O	0.1
Total	2	41	138	9	19	4	1	0	4	9	11	.138	.196	.181	27	-11	-9	5				.818	-2	/O	-1.1

■ BOB TILLMAN Tillman, John Robert b: 3/24/37, Nashville, Tenn. BR/TR, 6'4", 205 lbs. Deb: 4/15/62

YEAR	TM/L	G	AB	R	H	2B	3B	HR	RBI	BB	SO	AVG	OBP	SLG	PRO+	BR	/A	RC	SB	CS	SBR	FA	FR	POS	TPR
1962	Bos-A	81	249	28	57	6	4	14	38	19	65	.229	.286	.454	93	-3	-4	31	0	0	0	.983	-4	C	-0.5
1963	Bos-A	96	307	24	69	10	2	8	32	34	64	.225	.304	.349	80	-7	-8	33	0	0	0	.992	1	C	-0.4
1964	Bos-A	131	425	43	118	18	1	17	61	49	74	.278	.352	.445	114	12	9	65	0	0	0	.989	-8	*C	0.7
1965	Bos-A	111	368	20	79	10	3	6	35	40	69	.215	.292	.307	66	-14	-17	32	0	0	0	.988	-7	*C	-1.9
1966	Bos-A	78	204	12	47	8	0	3	24	22	35	.230	.305	.314	71	-5	-8	20	0	0	0	.990	-3	C	-0.8
1967	Bos-A	30	64	4	12	1	0	1	4	3	18	.188	.224	.250	37	-5	-5	3	0	0	0	.977	2	C	-0.3
	NY-A	22	63	5	16	1	0	2	9	7	17	.254	.329	.365	109	0	1	7	0	0	0	.970	0	C	0.2
	Yr	52	127	9	28	2	0	3	13	10	35	.220	.277	.307	70	-4	-5	10	0	0	0	.974	2	C	-0.1
1968	Atl-N	86	236	16	52	4	0	5	20	16	55	.220	.278	.301	74	-7	-8	19	1	0	0	.990	-1	C	-0.4
1969	*Atl-N	69	190	18	37	5	0	12	29	18	47	.195	.264	.411	86	-4	-5	19	0	0	0	.988	-10	C	-1.2
1970	Atl-N	71	223	19	53	5	0	11	30	20	66	.238	.300	.408	83	-5	-6	28	0	0	0	.988	-2	C	-0.5
Total	9	775	2329	189	540	68	10	79	282	228	510	.232	.302	.371	85	-39	-50	258	1	0	0	.988	-31	C	-5.1

■ RUSTY TILLMAN Tillman, Kerry Jerome b: 8/29/60, Jacksonville, Fla. BR/TR, 6', 185 lbs. Deb: 6/06/82

YEAR	TM/L	G	AB	R	H	2B	3B	HR	RBI	BB	SO	AVG	OBP	SLG	PRO+	BR	/A	RC	SB	CS	SBR	FA	FR	POS	TPR
1982	NY-N	12	13	4	2	1	0	0	0	0	4	.154	.154	.231	6	-2	-2	1	1	0	0	1.000	0	/O	-0.1
1986	Oak-A	22	39	6	10	1	0	1	6	3	11	.256	.310	.359	88	-1	-1	5	2	0	1	.952	-3	O	-0.4
1988	SF-N	4	4	1	1	0	0	1	3	2	1	.250	.500	1.000	335	1	1	2	0	0	0	1.000	-0	/O	0.1
Total	3	38	56	11	13	2	0	2	9	5	16	.232	.295	.375	88	-1	-1	8	3	0	1	.958	-4	/O	-0.4

■ BEN TINCUP Tincup, Austin Ben b: 12/14/1890, Adair, Okla. d: 7/5/80, Claremore, Okla. BL/TR, 6'1", 180 lbs. Deb: 5/22/14 C

YEAR	TM/L	G	AB	R	H	2B	3B	HR	RBI	BB	SO	AVG	OBP	SLG	PRO+	BR	/A	RC	SB	CS	SBR	FA	FR	POS	TPR
1914	Phi-N	31	53	3	9	1	1	0	1	0	18	.170	.170	.226	16	-6	-6	2	0			.926	1	P	0.0
1915	Phi-N	11	9	1	0	0	0	0	0	0	3	.000	.000	.000	-99	-2	-2	0	0			1.000	0	P	0.0
1916	Phi-N	1	1	0	0	0	0	0	0	0	0	.000	.000	.000	-97	-0	-0	0	0			.000	0	H	0.0
1918	Phi-N	11	8	0	1	1	0	0	0	0	4	.125	.125	.250	13	-1	-1	0	0			.800	1	/PO	0.0
1928	Chi-N	2	3	0	0	0	0	0	0	0	0	.000	.000	.000	-99	-1	-1	0	0			1.000	0	/P	0.0
Total	5	56	74	4	10	2	1	0	1	0	25	.135	.135	.189	-4	-10	-10	2	0			.917	2	/PO	0.0

■ RON TINGLEY Tingley, Ronald Irvin b: 5/27/59, Presque Isle, Maine BR/TR, 6'2", 180 lbs. Deb: 9/25/82

YEAR	TM/L	G	AB	R	H	2B	3B	HR	RBI	BB	SO	AVG	OBP	SLG	PRO+	BR	/A	RC	SB	CS	SBR	FA	FR	POS	TPR
1982	SD-N	8	20	0	2	0	0	0	0	0	7	.100	.100	.100	-46	-4	-4	0	0	0	0	.957	3	/C	-0.1
1988	Cle-A	9	24	1	4	0	0	1	2	2	8	.167	.231	.292	44	-2	-2	1	0	0	0	1.000	3	/C	0.2
1989	Cal-A	4	3	0	1	0	0	0	0	1	0	.333	.500	.333	142	0	0	1	0	0	0	.889	0	/C	0.1
1990	Cal-A	5	3	0	0	0	0	0	0	1	1	.000	.250	.000	-25	-0	-0	0	0	0	0	1.000	1	/C	0.0
1991	Cal-A	45	115	11	23	7	0	1	13	8	34	.200	.258	.287	51	-8	-8	9	1	1	-0	.988	10	C	0.4
1992	Cal-A	71	127	15	25	2	1	3	8	13	35	.197	.282	.299	64	-6	-6	11	0	1	-1	.987	11	C	0.7
Total	6	142	292	27	55	9	1	5	23	25	85	.188	.259	.277	50	-20	-20	22	1	2	-1	.985	28	C	1.3

■ JOE TINKER Tinker, Joseph Bert b: 7/27/1880, Muscotah, Kan. d: 7/27/48, Orlando, Fla. BR/TR, 5'9", 175 lbs. Deb: 4/17/02 MH

YEAR	TM/L	G	AB	R	H	2B	3B	HR	RBI	BB	SO	AVG	OBP	SLG	PRO+	BR	/A	RC	SB	CS	SBR	FA	FR	POS	TPR
1902	Chi-N	131	494	55	129	19	5	2	54	26		.261	.298	.332	97	-5	-3	60	27			.906	4	*S/3	0.9
1903	Chi-N	124	460	67	134	21	7	2	70	37		.291	.345	.380	110	4	6	73	27			.906	0	*S3	1.0
1904	Chi-N	141	488	55	108	12	13	3	41	29		.221	.268	.318	81	-12	-12	55	41			.925	19	*S/O	1.2
1905	Chi-N	149	547	70	135	18	8	2	66	34		.247	.292	.320	79	-13	-15	65	31			.940	17	*S	0.5
1906	*Chi-N	148	523	75	122	18	4	1	64	43		.233	.293	.289	77	-11	-15	59	30			**.944**	4	*S/3	-0.6
1907	*Chi-N	117	402	36	89	11	3	1	36	25		.221	.269	.271	65	-15	-17	37	20			.939	16	*S	0.1
1908	*Chi-N	157	548	67	146	22	14	6	68	32		.266	.307	.391	118	11	9	75	30			**.958**	30	*S	4.9
1909	Chi-N	143	516	56	132	26	11	4	57	17		.256	.280	.372	100	-2	-4	59	23			**.940**	16	*S	1.6
1910	*Chi-N	134	473	48	136	25	9	3	69	24	35	.288	.322	.397	110	3	3	66	20			.942	16	*S	2.5
1911	Chi-N	144	536	61	149	24	12	4	69	39	31	.278	.327	.390	100	-2	-2	77	30			**.937**	**23**	*S	3.1
1912	Chi-N	142	550	80	155	24	7	0	75	38	21	.282	.331	.351	87	-11	-11	73	25			.943	25	*S	2.6
1913	Cin-N	110	382	47	121	20	13	1	57	20	26	.317	.352	.445	127	12	12	61	10			.968	17	*S/3M	**3.9**
1914	Chi-F	126	438	50	112	21	7	2	46	38	30	.256	.317	.349	95	-7	-3	58	19			.947	19	*SM	2.7
1915	Chi-F	31	67	7	18	2	1	0	9	13	5	.269	.387	.328	118	2	2	10	3			.914	-2	S/23M	0.1
1916	Chi-N	7	10	0	1	0	0	0	1	1	1	.100	.182	.100	-11	-1	-1	0	0			.909	-0	/S3M	-0.2
Total	15	1804	6434	774	1687	263	114	31	782	416	149	.262	.308	.353	95	-46	-51	830	336			.938	204	*S/32O	24.3

■ JIM TIPPER Tipper, James b: 6/18/1849, Middletown, Conn. d: 4/21/1895, New Haven, Conn. 5'5.5", 148 lbs. Deb: 4/26/1872

YEAR	TM/L	G	AB	R	H	2B	3B	HR	RBI	BB	SO	AVG	OBP	SLG	PRO+	BR	/A	RC	SB	CS	SBR	FA	FR	POS	TPR
1872	Man-n	24	113	23	33	2	0	0	21	0	0	.292	.292	.310	91	-2	-1	10						O/3	0.0
1874	Har-n	45	197	35	60	10	0	0		0		.305	.305	.355	104	2	0	22						*O	0.1
1875	NH-n	41	158	10	25	0	0	0		0		.158	.158	.158	11	-14	-11	4						O	-0.9
Total	3 n	110	468	68	118	12	0	0		0		.252	.252	.278	74	-14	-11	36						O/3	-0.8

■ ERIC TIPTON Tipton, Eric Gordon "Dukie" or "Blue Devil" b: 4/20/15, Petersburg, Va. BR/TR, 5'11", 190 lbs. Deb: 6/09/39

YEAR	TM/L	G	AB	R	H	2B	3B	HR	RBI	BB	SO	AVG	OBP	SLG	PRO+	BR	/A	RC	SB	CS	SBR	FA	FR	POS	TPR
1939	Phi-A	47	104	12	24	4	2	1	14	13	7	.231	.316	.337	68	-5	-5	11	2	0	1	.942	-5	O	-0.9
1940	Phi-A	2	8	2	1	0	1	0	0	1	1	.125	.222	.375	53	-1	-1	1	0	0	0	1.000	-0	/O	-0.1
1941	Phi-A	1	4	0	2	0	0	0	0	0	0	.500	.500	.500	169	0	0	1	0	0	0	1.000	-0	/O	0.0
1942	Cin-N	63	207	22	46	5	5	4	18	25	14	.222	.309	.353	94	-2	-2	22	1			.977	-1	O	-0.6
1943	Cin-N	140	493	82	142	26	7	9	49	85	36	.288	.395	.424	138	26	27	88	1			.984	-1	*O	1.9
1944	Cin-N	140	479	62	144	28	3	3	36	59	32	.301	.380	.390	121	13	15	71	5			.983	3	*O	1.1
1945	Cin-N	108	331	32	80	17	1	5	34	40	37	.242	.327	.344	89	-6	-5	40	11			.970	-1	O	-1.0
Total	7	501	1626	212	439	80	19	22	151	223	127	.270	.360	.383	112	25	30	234	20	0		.977	-6	O	0.4

■ JOE TIPTON Tipton, Joe Hicks b: 2/18/23, McCaysville, Ga. BR/TR, 5'11", 185 lbs. Deb: 5/02/48

YEAR	TM/L	G	AB	R	H	2B	3B	HR	RBI	BB	SO	AVG	OBP	SLG	PRO+	BR	/A	RC	SB	CS	SBR	FA	FR	POS	TPR
1948	*Cle-A	47	90	11	26	3	0	1	13	4	10	.289	.333	.356	85	-2	-2	12	0	0	0	.971	0	C	0.0
1949	Chi-A	67	191	20	39	5	3	3	19	27	17	.204	.306	.309	65	-11	-10	19	1	1	-0	.992	2	C	-0.5
1950	Phi-A	64	184	15	49	5	1	6	20	19	16	.266	.335	.402	90	-4	-3	26	0	0	0	.987	-4	C	-0.5
1951	Phi-A	72	213	23	51	9	0	3	20	51	25	.239	.389	.324	92	1	0	32	1	1	-0	.969	2	C	0.5

YEAR	TM/L	G	AB	R	H	2B	3B	HR	RBI	BB	SO	AVG	OBP	SLG	PRO+	BR	/A	RC	SB	CS	SBR	FA	FR	POS	TPR
1952	Phi-A	23	68	6	13	4	0	3	8	15	10	.191	.337	.382	94	0	-0	10	0	0	0	.990	-2	C	-0.2
	Cle-A	43	105	15	26	2	0	6	22	21	21	.248	.383	.438	137	5	5	19	1	0	0	.971	-8	C	-0.1
	Yr	66	173	21	39	6	0	9	30	36	31	.225	.365	.416	119	5	5	29	1	0	0	.979	-11	C	-0.3
1953	Cle-A	47	109	17	25	2	0	6	13	19	13	.229	.359	.413	111	2	2	16	0	0	0	1.000	-7	C	-0.4
1954	Was-A	54	157	9	35	6	1	1	10	30	30	.223	.354	.293	83	-3	-2	18	0	1	-1	.992	3	C	0.3
Total	7	417	1117	116	264	36	5	29	125	186	142	.236	.351	.355	91	-13	-10	152	3	3	-1	.984	-14	C	-0.9
■ TOM TISCHINSKI	Tischinski, Thomas Arthur b: 7/12/44, Kansas City, Mo. BR/TR, 5'10", 190 lbs. Deb: 4/11/69																								
1969	Min-A	37	47	2	9	0	0	0	2	8	8	.191	.309	.191	42	-3	-3	4	0	0	0	1.000	0	C	-0.3
1970	Min-A	24	46	6	9	0	0	1	2	9	6	.196	.327	.261	63	-2	-2	4	0	0	0	.990	1	C	0.0
1971	Min-A	21	23	0	3	2	0	0	2	1	4	.130	.200	.217	18	-3	-3	1	0	0	0	.982	3	C	0.1
Total	3	82	116	8	21	2	0	1	6	18	18	.181	.296	.224	46	-8	-8	9	0	0	0	.992	4	/C	-0.2
■ JOHN TITUS	Titus, John Franklin "Silent John" b: 2/21/1876, St.Clair, Pa. d: 1/8/43, St.Clair, Pa. BL/TL, 5'9", 156 lbs. Deb: 6/08/03																								
1903	Phi-N	72	280	38	80	15	6	2	34	19		.286	.340	.404	116	4	5	42	5			.952	3	O	0.3
1904	Phi-N	146	504	60	148	25	5	4	55	46		.294	.361	.387	136	19	21	79	15			.952	8	*O	2.2
1905	Phi-N	147	548	99	169	36	14	2	89	69		.308	.396	.436	154	34	37	102	11			.962	9	*O	3.9
1906	Phi-N	145	484	67	129	22	5	1	57	78		.267	.377	.339	124	17	17	71	12			.974	7	*O	1.9
1907	Phi-N	145	523	72	144	23	12	3	63	47		.275	.344	.382	130	16	17	75	9			.928	-5	*O	0.8
1908	Phi-N	149	539	75	154	24	5	2	48	53		.286	.364	.360	127	21	19	82	27			.963	-3	*O	1.1
1909	Phi-N	151	540	69	146	22	6	3	46	66		.270	.367	.350	121	17	16	79	23			.971	5	*O	1.7
1910	Phi-N	143	535	91	129	26	5	3	35	93	44	.241	.358	.325	96	3	0	70	20			.976	1	*O	-0.6
1911	Phi-N	76	236	35	67	14	1	8	26	32	16	.284	.372	.453	129	9	9	40	3			.979	-1	O	0.5
1912	Phi-N	45	157	43	43	9	5	3	22	33	14	.274	.403	.452	125	8	7	31	6			.917	-7	O	-0.2
	Bos-N	96	345	56	112	23	6	2	48	49	20	.325	.422	.443	134	20	19	67	5			.965	-5	O	0.9
	Yr	141	502	99	155	32	11	5	70	82	34	.309	.416	.446	131	28	26	98	11			.952	-12	*O	0.7
1913	Bos-N	87	269	33	80	14	2	5	38	35	22	.297	.392	.420	129	12	12	45	4			.919	-7	O	0.2
Total	11	1402	4960	738	1401	253	72	38	561	620	116	.282	.372	.385	127	181	180	783	140			.959	7	*O	12.7
■ JIM TOBIN	Tobin, James Anthony "Abba Dabba" b: 12/27/12, Oakland, Cal. d: 5/19/69, Oakland, Cal. BR/TR, 6', 185 lbs. Deb: 4/30/37 F																								
1937	Pit-N	21	34	7	15	4	0	0	6	4	3	.441	.500	.559	187	4	4	9	0			.938	-2	P	0.0
1938	Pit-N	56	103	8	25	6	1	0	11	9	12	.243	.310	.320	73	-4	-4	11	0			1.000	-2	P	0.0
1939	Pit-N	43	74	9	18	3	1	2	11	2	12	.243	.263	.392	75	-3	-3	8	0			1.000	-1	P	0.0
1940	Bos-N	20	43	5	12	3	0	0	3	1	10	.279	.295	.349	82	-1	-1	4	0			.957	-1	P	0.0
1941	Bos-N	43	103	6	19	5	0	0	9	10	31	.184	.257	.233	40	-8	-8	6	1			.966	4	P	0.0
1942	Bos-N	47	114	14	28	2	0	6	15	16	23	.246	.344	.421	126	3	4	17	0			.947	6	P	0.0
1943	Bos-N	46	107	8	30	4	0	2	12	6	16	.280	.319	.374	101	-0	-0	12	0			.927	2	P/1	0.0
1944	Bos-N★	62	116	13	22	5	1	2	18	16	28	.190	.288	.302	63	-5	-6	11	0			.972	7	P	0.0
1945	Bos-N	41	77	9	11	3	0	3	12	15	22	.143	.290	.299	64	-4	-4	7	0			1.000	2	P	0.0
	*Det-A	17	25	2	3	0	0	2	5	1	5	.120	.154	.360	44	-2	-2	1	0	0	0	.950	1	P	0.0
Total	9	396	796	81	183	35	3	17	102	80	162	.230	.303	.345	82	-20	-20	85	1	0		.965	17	P/1	0.0
■ JOHNNY TOBIN	Tobin, John Martin "Tip" b: 9/15/06, Jamaica Plain, Mass. BR/TR, 6'3", 187 lbs. Deb: 9/22/32																								
1932	NY-N	1	1	0	0	0	0	0	0	0	0	.000	.000	.000	-99	-0	-0	0	0			.000	0	H	0.0
■ JOHNNY TOBIN	Tobin, John Patrick "Jackie" b: 1/8/21, Oakland, Cal. d: 1/18/82, Oakland, Cal. BL/TR, 6', 165 lbs. Deb: 4/20/45 F																								
1945	Bos-A	84	278	25	70	6	2	0	21	26	24	.252	.320	.288	75	-8	-8	26	2	6	-3	.951	9	3/2O	0.0
■ JACK TOBIN	Tobin, John Thomas b: 5/4/1892, St.Louis, Mo. d: 12/10/69, St.Louis, Mo. BL/TL, 5'8", 142 lbs. Deb: 4/16/14 C																								
1914	StL-F	139	529	81	143	24	10	7	35	51	53	.270	.340	.393	103	5	2	81	20			.952	5	*O	0.1
1915	StL-F	158	625	92	**184**	26	13	6	51	68	42	.294	.366	.406	121	21	18	109	31			.965	3	*O	1.4
1916	StL-A	77	150	16	32	4	1	0	10	12	13	.213	.272	.253	61	-8	-7	13	7			.842	-9	O	-1.9
1918	StL-A	122	480	59	133	19	5	0	36	48	26	.277	.349	.338	111	5	6	60	13			.971	-1	*O	-0.2
1919	StL-A	127	486	54	159	22	7	6	57	36	24	.327	.376	.438	125	17	16	82	8			.953	2	*O	1.0
1920	StL-A	147	593	94	202	34	10	4	62	39	23	.341	.383	.452	117	17	14	101	21	13	-2	.960	4	*O	0.6
1921	StL-A	150	671	132	236	31	**18**	8	59	45	22	.352	.395	.487	117	23	18	125	7	12	-5	.956	8	*O	0.9
1922	StL-A	146	625	122	207	34	8	13	66	56	22	.331	.388	.474	119	21	18	113	7	9	-3	.940	-8	*O	-0.4
1923	StL-A	151	637	91	202	32	15	13	73	42	13	.317	.363	.476	113	15	10	108	8	7	-2	.969	-9	*O	-1.0
1924	StL-A	136	569	87	170	30	8	2	48	50	12	.299	.357	.390	87	-6	-11	79	6	10	-4	.957	2	*O	-2.1
1925	StL-A	77	193	25	58	11	0	2	27	9	5	.301	.335	.389	79	-5	-7	26	8	2	1	1.000	-5	O/1	-1.3
1926	Was-A	27	33	5	7	0	1	0	3	0	0	.212	.212	.273	26	-4	-4	2	0	0	0	1.000	-2	/O	-0.5
	Bos-A	51	209	26	57	9	0	1	14	16	3	.273	.324	.330	73	-9	-8	22	6	5	-1	.966	-3	O	-1.6
	Yr	78	242	31	64	9	1	1	17	16	3	.264	.310	.322	67	-13	-12	24	6	5	-1	.970	-5	O	-2.1
1927	Bos-A	111	374	52	116	18	3	2	40	36	9	.310	.371	.390	100	-1	0	52	5	4	-1	.947	-5	O	-1.1
Total	13	1619	6174	936	1906	294	99	64	581	508	267	.309	.364	.420	108	92	66	973	147	62		.957	-16	*O/1	-6.1
■ BILL TOBIN	Tobin, William F. b: 10/10/1854, Hartford, Conn. d: 10/10/12, Hartford, Conn. BL, Deb: 7/21/1880																								
1880	Wor-N	5	16	1	2	0	0	0	3	0	5	.125	.125	.125	-14	-2	-2	0				1.000	-0	/1	-0.2
	Tro-N	33	136	14	22	1	1	0	8	4	20	.162	.186	.184	24	-10	-11	5				.950	-1	1	-1.4
	Yr	38	152	15	24	1	1	0	11	4	25	.158	.179	.178	20	-12	-13	5				.958	-1	1	-1.6
■ AL TODD	Todd, Alfred Chester b: 1/7/02, Troy, N.Y. d: 3/8/85, Elmira, N.Y. BR/TR, 6'1", 198 lbs. Deb: 4/25/32																								
1932	Phi-N	33	70	8	16	5	0	0	9	1	9	.229	.260	.300	45	-5	-6	6	1			.899	-4	C	-0.9
1933	Phi-N	73	136	13	28	4	0	0	10	4	18	.206	.239	.235	32	-11	-13	8	1			.983	5	C/O	-0.7
1934	Phi-N	91	302	33	96	22	2	4	41	10	39	.318	.344	.444	96	3	-2	44	3			.976	-2	C	0.0
1935	Phi-N	107	328	40	95	18	3	3	42	19	35	.290	.334	.390	85	-3	-7	42	3			.968	-12	C	-1.5
1936	Pit-N	76	267	28	73	10	5	2	28	11	24	.273	.307	.371	80	-7	-8	31	4			.976	1	C	-0.3
1937	Pit-N	133	514	51	158	18	10	8	86	16	36	.307	.330	.428	104	1	1	69	2			.972	-2	*C	0.7
1938	Pit-N	133	491	52	130	19	7	7	75	18	31	.265	.296	.375	83	-12	-13	48	2			.985	10	*C	0.4
1939	Bro-N	86	245	28	68	10	0	5	32	13	16	.278	.317	.380	83	-5	-6	28	1			.985	8	C	0.5
1940	Chi-N	104	381	31	97	13	2	6	42	11	29	.255	.283	.346	74	-15	-14	36	1			.984	-6	*C	-1.2
1941	Chi-N	6	6	1	1	0	0	0	0	0	1	.167	.167	.167	-6	-1	-1	0	0			.000	0	H	-0.1
1943	Chi-N	21	45	1	6	0	0	0	1	1	5	.133	.152	.133	-17	-7	-7	1	0			.986	4	C	-0.2
Total	11	863	2785	286	768	119	29	35	366	104	243	.276	.307	.377	82	-62	-75	312	18			.977	1	C/O	-3.3
■ PHIL TODT	Todt, Philip Julius "Hook" b: 8/9/01, St.Louis, Mo. d: 11/15/73, St.Louis, Mo. BL/TL, 6', 175 lbs. Deb: 4/25/24																								
1924	Bos-A	52	103	17	27	8	2	1	14	6	9	.262	.309	.408	84	-3	-3	13	0	1	-1	.983	-3	1/O	-0.7
1925	Bos-A	141	544	62	151	29	13	11	75	44	29	.278	.343	.439	97	-4	-4	83	3	2	-0	.991	3	*1	-0.9
1926	Bos-A	154	599	56	153	19	12	7	69	40	38	.255	.306	.362	76	-25	-22	68	3	2	-0	.988	10	*1	-2.1
1927	Bos-A	140	516	55	122	22	6	6	52	28	23	.236	.280	.337	61	-33	-31	47	6	2	1	.991	9	*1	-3.0
1928	Bos-A	144	539	61	136	31	8	12	73	26	47	.252	.290	.406	83	-17	-16	63	6	5	-1	**.997**	3	*1	-2.6
1929	Bos-A	153	534	49	140	38	10	4	64	31	28	.262	.305	.393	80	-19	-17	63	6	7	-2	.991	3	*1	-3.0
1930	Bos-A	111	383	49	103	22	5	11	62	24	33	.269	.312	.439	92	-9	-6	53	4	1	1	.993	3	*1	-1.2
1931	*Phi-A	62	197	23	48	14	2	5	44	8	22	.244	.273	.411	73	-8	-9	22	1	1	-0	.995	-4	1	-1.7
Total	8	957	3415	372	880	183	58	57	453	207	229	.258	.305	.395	81	-117	-109	411	29	21	-4	.992	24	1/O	-15.2

■ BOBBY TOLAN
Tolan, Robert b: 11/19/45, Los Angeles, Cal. BL/TL, 5'11", 170 lbs. Deb: 9/03/65 C

YEAR	TM/L	G	AB	R	H	2B	3B	HR	RBI	BB	SO	AVG	OBP	SLG	PRO+	BR	/A	RC	SB	CS	SBR	FA	FR	POS	TPR
1965	StL-N	17	69	8	13	2	0	0	6	0	4	.188	.200	.217	16	-7	-8	3	2	1	0	.970	-1	O	-1.1
1966	StL-N	43	93	10	16	5	1	1	6	6	15	.172	.238	.280	43	-7	-7	6	1	2	-1	.952	-1	O/1	-1.1
1967	*StL-N	110	265	35	67	7	3	6	32	19	43	.253	.313	.370	96	-2	-2	30	12	7	-1	.992	4	O1	-0.2
1968	*StL-N	92	278	28	64	12	1	5	17	13	42	.230	.272	.335	82	-7	-6	23	9	5	-0	.967	1	O/1	-1.1
1969	Cin-N	152	637	104	194	25	10	21	93	27	92	.305	.348	.474	122	22	18	103	26	12	1	.974	1	*O	1.1
1970	*Cin-N	152	589	112	186	34	6	16	80	62	94	.316	.388	.475	130	26	26	113	**57**	20	5	.978	3	*O	2.5
1972	*Cin-N	149	604	88	171	28	5	8	82	44	88	.283	.338	.386	112	4	8	78	42	15	4	.990	6	*O	1.1
1973	Cin-N	129	457	42	94	14	2	9	51	27	68	.206	.255	.304	57	-29	-26	33	15	10	-2	.966	-1	*O	-3.7
1974	SD-N	95	357	45	95	16	1	8	40	20	41	.266	.321	.384	101	-2	-1	42	7	9	-3	.971	-1	O	-0.9
1975	SD-N	147	506	58	129	19	4	5	43	28	45	.255	.307	.338	84	-15	-11	48	11	13	-5	.971	-1	*O1	-2.3
1976	*Phi-N	110	272	32	71	7	0	5	35	7	39	.261	.290	.342	76	-8	-9	25	10	5	0	.992	-7	1O	-2.1
1977	Phi-N	15	16	1	2	0	0	0	1	1	4	.125	.176	.125	-17	-3	-3	0	0	0	0	.944	-0	/1	-0.3
	Pit-N	49	74	7	15	4	0	2	9	4	10	.203	.244	.338	53	-5	-5	6	1	1	-0	1.000	0	1/O	-0.6
	Yr	64	90	8	17	4	0	2	10	5	14	.189	.232	.300	40	-8	-8	6	1	1	-0	.992	-0	1/O	-0.9
1979	SD-N	22	21	2	4	0	1	0	2	0	2	.190	.190	.286	30	-2	-2	1	0	0	0	1.000	0	/1O	-0.2
Total	13	1282	4238	572	1121	173	34	86	497	258	587	.265	.317	.382	96	-37	-30	511	193	100	-2	.976	3	*O1	-8.9

■ JOSE TOLENTINO
Tolentino, Jose (Franco) b: 6/3/61, Mexico City, Mexico BL/TL, 6'1", 195 lbs. Deb: 7/28/91

YEAR	TM/L	G	AB	R	H	2B	3B	HR	RBI	BB	SO	AVG	OBP	SLG	PRO+	BR	/A	RC	SB	CS	SBR	FA	FR	POS	TPR
1991	Hou-N	44	54	6	14	4	0	1	6	4	9	.259	.310	.389	101	-0	-0	6	0	0	0	.982	1	1/O	0.1

■ WAYNE TOLLESON
Tolleson, Jimmy Wayne b: 11/22/55, Spartanburg, S.C. BB/TR, 5'9", 160 lbs. Deb: 9/01/81

YEAR	TM/L	G	AB	R	H	2B	3B	HR	RBI	BB	SO	AVG	OBP	SLG	PRO+	BR	/A	RC	SB	CS	SBR	FA	FR	POS	TPR
1981	Tex-A	14	24	6	4	0	0	0	1	1	5	.167	.200	.167	7	-3	-3	1	2	0	1	1.000	-1	/3S	-0.3
1982	Tex-A	38	70	6	8	1	0	0	2	5	14	.114	.173	.129	-16	-11	-11	2	1	1	-0	.958	5	S/32	-0.4
1983	Tex-A	134	470	64	122	13	2	3	20	40	68	.260	.320	.315	77	-15	-14	51	33	10	4	.972	-10	*2S/D	-1.3
1984	Tex-A	118	338	35	72	9	2	0	9	27	47	.213	.277	.251	46	-24	-25	25	22	4	4	.979	-7	*2/S3OD	-2.4
1985	Tex-A	123	323	45	101	9	5	1	18	21	46	.313	.355	.381	100	1	0	43	21	12	-1	.972	-4	S23/D	0.3
1986	Chi-A	81	260	39	65	7	3	3	29	38	43	.250	.346	.335	84	-4	-5	33	13	6	0	.955	-10	3S/OD	-1.5
	NY-A	60	215	22	61	9	2	0	14	14	33	.284	.333	.344	86	-4	-4	25	4	4	-1	.981	6	S/32	0.6
	Yr	141	475	61	126	16	5	3	43	52	76	.265	.340	.339	85	-8	-9	58	17	10	-1	.981	-4	S3/2OD	-0.9
1987	NY-A	121	349	48	77	4	0	1	22	43	72	.221	.306	.241	48	-25	-24	29	5	3	-0	.970	-3	*S/3	-1.7
1988	NY-A	21	59	8	15	2	0	0	5	8	12	.254	.343	.288	79	-1	-1	7	1	0	0	.981	6	23/S	0.5
1989	NY-A	80	140	16	23	5	2	1	9	16	23	.164	.255	.250	43	-11	-10	10	5	1	1	.912	10	3S2D	0.2
1990	NY-A	73	74	12	11	1	1	0	4	6	21	.149	.213	.189	13	-9	-9	4	1	0	0	.983	15	S2/3D	0.8
Total	10	863	2322	301	559	60	17	9	133	219	384	.241	.308	.293	66	-105	-105	228	108	41	8	.974	7	S23/DO	-5.2

■ TIM TOLMAN
Tolman, Timothy Lee b: 4/20/56, Santa Monica, Cal. BR/TR, 6', 195 lbs. Deb: 9/09/81

YEAR	TM/L	G	AB	R	H	2B	3B	HR	RBI	BB	SO	AVG	OBP	SLG	PRO+	BR	/A	RC	SB	CS	SBR	FA	FR	POS	TPR
1981	Hou-N	4	8	0	1	0	0	0	0	0	0	.125	.125	.125	-30	-1	-1	0	0	0	0	1.000	-0	/O	-0.2
1982	Hou-N	15	26	4	5	2	0	1	3	4	3	.192	.300	.385	98	-0	-0	3	0	0	0	1.000	-0	/O1	-0.1
1983	Hou-N	43	56	4	11	4	0	2	10	6	9	.196	.274	.375	83	-2	-1	5	0	1	-1	1.000	-1	/1O	-0.4
1984	Hou-N	14	17	2	3	1	0	0	0	0	3	.176	.176	.235	16	-2	-2	1	0	0	0	1.000	-0	/O1	-0.2
1985	Hou-N	31	43	4	6	1	0	2	8	1	10	.140	.178	.302	33	-4	-4	2	0	1	-1	1.000	-1	/O1	-0.6
1986	Det-A	16	34	4	6	1	0	0	2	6	4	.176	.300	.206	41	-3	-3	3	1	1	-0	1.000	-1	/O1D	-0.4
1987	Det-A	9	12	3	1	1	0	0	1	7	2	.083	.450	.167	77	0	0	2	0	0	0	1.000	-1	/OD	-0.1
Total	7	132	196	21	33	10	0	5	24	24	31	.168	.266	.296	58	-12	-11	16	1	3	-2	1.000	-4	/O1D	-2.0

■ CHICK TOLSON
Tolson, Charles Julius "Toby" b: 11/6/1898, Washington, D.C. d: 4/16/65, Washington, D.C. BR/TR, 6', 185 lbs. Deb: 7/03/25

YEAR	TM/L	G	AB	R	H	2B	3B	HR	RBI	BB	SO	AVG	OBP	SLG	PRO+	BR	/A	RC	SB	CS	SBR	FA	FR	POS	TPR
1925	Cle-A	3	12	0	3	0	0	0	0	2	1	.250	.357	.250	56	-1	-1	1	0	0	0	1.000	0	/1	-0.1
1926	Chi-N	57	80	4	25	6	1	1	8	5	8	.313	.353	.450	113	1	1	12	0			.991	0	1	0.1
1927	Chi-N	39	54	6	16	4	0	2	17	4	9	.296	.345	.481	119	1	1	9	0			1.000	0	/1	0.1
1929	*Chi-N	32	109	13	28	5	0	1	19	9	16	.257	.325	.330	63	-6	-6	12	0			.978	-2	1	-1.0
1930	Chi-N	13	20	0	6	1	0	0	1	6	5	.300	.462	.350	99	0	0	4	1			.979	1	/1	0.0
Total	5	144	275	23	78	16	1	4	45	26	39	.284	.350	.393	90	-4	-4	38	1	0		.985	-1	/1	-0.9

■ GEORGE TOMER
Tomer, George Clarence b: 11/26/1895, Perry, Iowa d: 12/15/84, Perry, Iowa BL/TR, 6', 180 lbs. Deb: 9/17/13

YEAR	TM/L	G	AB	R	H	2B	3B	HR	RBI	BB	SO	AVG	OBP	SLG	PRO+	BR	/A	RC	SB	CS	SBR	FA	FR	POS	TPR
1913	StL-A	1	1	0	0	0	0	0	0	0	1	.000	.000	.000	-99	-0	-0	0	0			.000	0	H	0.0

■ PHIL TOMNEY
Tomney, Philip Howard "Buster" b: 7/17/1863, Reading, Pa. d: 3/18/1892, Reading, Pa. BR/TR, 5'7", 155 lbs. Deb: 9/07/1888

YEAR	TM/L	G	AB	R	H	2B	3B	HR	RBI	BB	SO	AVG	OBP	SLG	PRO+	BR	/A	RC	SB	CS	SBR	FA	FR	POS	TPR
1888	Lou-a	34	120	15	18	3	0	0	4	7		.150	.197	.175	22	-10	-10	6	11			.882	6	S	-0.3
1889	Lou-a	112	376	61	80	8	5	4	38	46	47	.213	.304	.293	73	-13	-12	42	26			.857	27	*S	1.8
1890	*Lou-a	108	386	72	107	21	7	1		43		.277	.357	.376	121	9	11	63	27			**.902**	18	*S	3.0
Total	3	254	882	148	205	32	12	5	42	96	47	.232	.313	.313	88	-14	-11	112	64			.878	50	S	4.5

■ TONY TONNEMAN
Tonneman, Charles Richard b: 9/10/1881, Chicago, Ill. d: 8/7/51, Prescott, Ariz. BR/TR, 5'10.5", 175 lbs. Deb: 9/19/11

YEAR	TM/L	G	AB	R	H	2B	3B	HR	RBI	BB	SO	AVG	OBP	SLG	PRO+	BR	/A	RC	SB	CS	SBR	FA	FR	POS	TPR
1911	Bos-A	2	5	0	1	1	0	0	3	1		.200	.333	.400	105	0	0	1	0			.900	1	/C	0.1

■ BERT TOOLEY
Tooley, Albert R. b: 8/30/1886, Howell, Mich. d: 8/17/76, Marshall, Mich. BR/TR, 5'10", 155 lbs. Deb: 4/12/11

YEAR	TM/L	G	AB	R	H	2B	3B	HR	RBI	BB	SO	AVG	OBP	SLG	PRO+	BR	/A	RC	SB	CS	SBR	FA	FR	POS	TPR
1911	Bro-N	119	433	55	89	11	3	1	29	53	63	.206	.295	.252	56	-26	-24	37	18			.925	-8	*S	-2.5
1912	Bro-N	77	265	34	62	6	5	2	37	19	21	.234	.285	.317	67	-14	-12	28	12			.885	-15	S	-2.1
Total	2	196	698	89	151	17	8	3	66	72	84	.216	.291	.277	60	-40	-36	64	30			.909	-24	S	-4.6

■ SPECS TOPORCER
Toporcer, George b: 2/9/1899, New York, N.Y. d: 5/17/89, Huntington Station, N.Y. BL/TR, 5'10.5", 165 lbs. Deb: 4/13/21

YEAR	TM/L	G	AB	R	H	2B	3B	HR	RBI	BB	SO	AVG	OBP	SLG	PRO+	BR	/A	RC	SB	CS	SBR	FA	FR	POS	TPR
1921	StL-N	22	53	4	14	1	0	0	2	3	4	.264	.304	.283	57	-3	-3	5	1	0	0	.938	0	2/S	-0.2
1922	StL-N	116	352	56	114	25	6	3	36	24	18	.324	.370	.455	117	6	8	60	2	1	0	.939	-23	S/32O	-0.6
1923	StL-N	97	303	45	77	11	3	3	35	41	14	.254	.349	.340	84	-7	-6	38	4	3	-1	.945	-13	2S/13	-1.5
1924	StL-N	70	198	30	62	10	3	1	24	11	14	.313	.362	.409	108	2	2	29	2	3	-1	.974	-16	3S/2	-1.0
1925	StL-N	83	268	38	76	13	4	2	26	36	15	.284	.373	.384	92	-1	-2	41	7	2	1	.960	-3	S/2	0.2
1926	*StL-N	64	88	13	22	3	2	0	9	8	9	.250	.327	.330	74	-3	-3	10	1			.983	-9	2/S3	-1.2
1927	StL-N	86	290	37	72	13	4	0	19	27	16	.248	.314	.321	68	-12	-13	30	5			.980	-11	3S/21	-1.9
1928	StL-N	8	14	0	0	0	0	0	0	0	3	.000	.000	.000	-98	-4	-4	0	0			1.000	0	/12	-0.4
Total	8	546	1566	223	437	76	22	9	151	150	93	.279	.347	.373	90	-22	-21	212	22	9		.946	-74	S2/310	-6.6

■ JEFF TORBORG
Torborg, Jeffrey Allen b: 11/26/41, Plainfield, N.J. BR/TR, 6'0.5", 195 lbs. Deb: 5/10/64 MC

YEAR	TM/L	G	AB	R	H	2B	3B	HR	RBI	BB	SO	AVG	OBP	SLG	PRO+	BR	/A	RC	SB	CS	SBR	FA	FR	POS	TPR
1964	LA-N	28	43	4	10	1	1	0	4	3	8	.233	.298	.302	75	-2	-1	4	0	0	0	.977	-2	C	-0.3
1965	LA-N	56	150	8	36	5	1	3	13	10	26	.240	.292	.347	85	-4	-3	14	0	0	0	.991	4	C	0.3
1966	LA-N	46	120	4	27	3	0	1	13	10	23	.225	.285	.275	61	-7	-6	9	0	0	0	.986	6	C	0.3
1967	LA-N	76	196	11	42	4	1	2	12	13	31	.214	.267	.276	60	-11	-9	13	1	3	-2	.989	12	C	0.4
1968	LA-N	37	93	2	15	2	0	0	4	6	10	.161	.212	.183	21	-9	-8	4	0	0	0	.991	10	C	0.4
1969	LA-N	51	124	7	23	4	0	0	7	9	17	.185	.241	.218	31	-12	-11	7	1	0	0	.996	11	C	0.2
1970	LA-N	64	134	11	31	8	0	1	17	14	15	.231	.304	.313	69	-6	-6	13	1	1	-0	.983	10	C	0.6
1971	Cal-A	55	123	6	25	5	0	0	5	3	6	.203	.222	.244	34	-11	-10	6	0	0	0	.987	5	C	-0.5
1972	Cal-A	59	153	5	32	3	0	0	8	14	21	.209	.280	.229	56	-9	-8	9	0	0	0	.998	16	C	1.1
1973	Cal-A	102	255	20	56	7	0	1	18	21	32	.220	.279	.259	57	-16	-13	18	0	2	-1	.991	8	*C	-0.3
Total	10	574	1391	78	297	42	3	8	101	103	189	.214	.270	.265	56	-87	-75	97	3	6	-3	.990	79	C	2.2

YEAR	TM/L	G	AB	R	H	2B	3B	HR	RBI	BB	SO	AVG	OBP	SLG	PRO+	BR	/A	RC	SB	CS	SBR	FA	FR	POS	TPR
■ EARL TORGESON	Torgeson, Clifford Earl "The Earl Of Snohomish" b: 1/1/24, Snohomish, Wash. d: 11/8/90, Everett, Wash. BL/TL, 6'3", 180 lbs. Deb: 4/15/47																								
1947	Bos-N	128	399	73	112	20	6	16	78	82	59	.281	.403	.481	137	22	23	83	11			.984	-1	*1	1.8
1948	*Bos-N	134	438	70	111	23	5	10	67	81	54	.253	.372	.397	110	7	8	71	19			.993	1	*1	0.9
1949	Bos-N	25	100	17	26	5	1	4	19	13	4	.260	.345	.450	118	2	2	15	4			.988	-3	1	-0.1
1950	Bos-N	156	576	**120**	167	30	3	23	87	119	69	.290	.412	.472	141	31	37	121	15			.986	-0	*1	3.2
1951	Bos-N	155	581	99	153	21	4	24	92	102	70	.263	.375	.437	127	17	22	99	20	11	-1	.988	-1	*1	1.4
1952	Bos-N	122	382	49	88	17	0	5	34	81	38	.230	.366	.314	94	-2	0	51	11	7	-1	.989	-1	*1/O	-0.6
1953	Phi-N	111	379	58	104	25	8	11	64	53	57	.274	.366	.470	117	9	10	70	7	1	2	.987	-3	*1	0.4
1954	Phi-N	135	490	63	133	22	6	5	54	75	52	.271	.368	.371	93	-3	-3	71	7	1	2	.990	-10	*1	-1.8
1955	Phi-N	47	150	29	40	5	3	1	17	32	20	.267	.396	.360	104	2	2	22	2	3	-1	.995	-1	1	-0.3
	Det-A	89	300	58	85	10	1	9	50	61	29	.283	.404	.413	123	11	12	56	9	0	**3**	.992	-0	1	0.9
1956	Det-A	117	318	61	84	9	3	12	42	78	47	.264	.409	.425	120	13	12	61	6	4	-1	.992	-7	1	0.0
1957	Det-A	30	50	5	12	2	1	1	5	12	10	.240	.387	.380	108	1	1	8	0	0	0	1.000	0	1	0.1
	Chi-A	86	251	53	74	11	2	7	46	49	44	.295	.410	.438	131	13	13	47	7	3	0	.998	-5	1/O	0.4
	Yr	116	301	58	86	13	3	8	51	61	54	.286	.406	.429	127	14	14	56	7	3	0	.999	-5	1/O	0.5
1958	Chi-A	96	188	37	50	8	0	10	30	48	29	.266	.415	.468	146	13	14	39	7	2	1	.978	-2	1	1.0
1959	*Chi-A	127	277	40	61	5	3	9	45	62	55	.220	.363	.357	100	1	2	39	7	6	-2	.983	-6	*1	-1.1
1960	Chi-A	68	57	12	15	2	0	2	9	21	8	.263	.462	.404	137	4	5	13	1	0	0	.983	0	1	0.5
1961	Chi-A	20	15	1	1	0	0	0	1	3	5	.067	.222	.067	-19	-3	-2	0	0	0	0	1.000	-0	/1	-0.3
	NY-A	22	18	3	2	0	0	0	0	8	3	.111	.385	.111	42	-1	-1	1	0	1	-1	.969	-0	/1	-0.2
	Yr	42	33	4	3	0	0	0	1	11	8	.091	.318	.091	16	-4	-3	2	0	1	-1	.970	-0	/1	-0.5
Total	15	1668	4969	848	1318	215	46	149	740	980	653	.265	.387	.417	118	139	157	870	133	39		.989	-39	*1/O	6.2
■ RED TORPHY	Torphy, Walter Anthony b: 11/6/1891, Fall River, Mass. d: 2/11/80, Fall River, Mass. BR/TR, 5'11", 169 lbs. Deb: 9/25/20																								
1920	Bos-N	3	15	1	3	2	0	0	2	0	1	.200	.200	.333	54	-1	-1	1	0	0	0	.969	-1	/1	-0.2
■ FRANK TORRE	Torre, Frank Joseph b: 12/30/31, Brooklyn, N.Y. BL/TL, 6'3", 205 lbs. Deb: 4/20/56 F																								
1956	Mil-N	111	159	17	41	6	0	0	16	11	4	.258	.306	.296	67	-8	-7	14	1	0	0	.993	6	1	-0.4
1957	*Mil-N	129	364	46	99	19	5	5	40	29	19	.272	.341	.393	104	-1	2	49	0	0	0	**.996**	1	*1	-0.2
1958	*Mil-N	138	372	41	115	22	5	6	55	42	14	.309	.390	.444	131	12	16	63	2	0	1	**.994**	6	*1	1.7
1959	Mil-N	115	263	23	60	15	1	1	33	35	12	.228	.326	.304	75	-11	-8	28	0	0	0	.994	-0	1	-1.3
1960	Mil-N	21	44	2	9	1	0	0	5	3	2	.205	.255	.227	36	-4	-4	3	0	0	0	1.000	-1	1	-0.6
1962	Phi-N	108	168	13	52	8	2	0	20	24	6	.310	.408	.381	117	5	5	26	1	1	-0	.980	3	1	0.6
1963	Phi-N	92	112	8	28	7	2	1	10	11	7	.250	.333	.375	105	1	1	15	0	0	0	.989	5	1	0.5
Total	7	714	1482	150	404	78	15	13	179	155	64	.273	.352	.372	101	-7	6	197	4	1	1	.993	19	1	0.3
■ JOE TORRE	Torre, Joseph Paul b: 7/18/40, Brooklyn, N.Y. BR/TR, 6'2", 212 lbs. Deb: 9/25/60 FM																								
1960	Mil-N	2	2	0	1	0	0	0	0	0	1	.500	.500	.500	189	0	0	1	0	0	0	.000	0	H	0.0
1961	Mil-N	113	406	40	113	21	4	10	42	28	60	.278	.331	.424	105	-1	2	54	3	5	-2	.982	-8	*C	-0.2
1962	Mil-N	80	220	23	62	8	1	5	26	24	24	.282	.358	.395	105	1	2	31	1	0	0	.986	6	C	1.0
1963	Mil-N☆	142	501	57	147	19	4	14	71	42	79	.293	.354	.431	126	16	17	71	1	5	-3	.994	-6	*C1/O	1.1
1964	Mil-N★	154	601	87	193	36	5	20	109	36	67	.321	.366	.498	140	31	31	99	2	4	-2	**.995**	-8	C1	2.4
1965	Mil-N★	148	523	68	152	21	1	27	80	61	79	.291	.373	.489	140	29	29	91	0	1	-1	.991	-6	*C1	2.6
1966	Atl-N★	148	546	83	172	20	3	36	101	60	61	.315	.385	.560	157	43	42	112	0	4	-2	.984	-3	*C1	4.3
1967	Atl-N★	135	477	67	132	18	1	20	68	49	75	.277	.348	.444	127	15	16	68	2	2	-1	.991	-5	*C1	1.6
1968	Atl-N	115	424	45	115	11	2	10	55	34	72	.271	.333	.377	112	7	7	51	1	0	0	**.996**	-11	C1	0.1
1969	StL-N	159	602	72	174	29	6	18	101	66	85	.289	.364	.447	126	21	21	99	0	0	0	.996	-3	*1C	0.7
1970	StL-N★	161	624	89	203	27	9	21	100	70	91	.325	.399	.498	136	35	34	120	2	2	-1	.987	-8	C3/1	2.8
1971	StL-N★	161	634	97	**230**	34	8	24	**137**	63	70	**.363**	.424	.555	169	62	60	**145**	4	1	1	.951	-17	*3	4.4
1972	StL-N★	149	544	71	157	26	6	11	81	54	64	.289	.361	.419	123	16	16	80	3	0	1	.963	-15	*31	-0.1
1973	StL-N★	141	519	67	149	17	2	13	69	65	78	.287	.377	.403	116	13	14	78	2	0	1	.993	-12	*13	-0.6
1974	StL-N	147	529	59	149	28	1	11	70	69	88	.282	.373	.401	117	13	14	80	1	2	-1	.992	3	*13	0.8
1975	NY-N	114	361	33	89	16	3	6	35	35	55	.247	.317	.357	91	-7	-5	36	0	0	0	.950	-1	31	-0.7
1976	NY-N	114	310	36	95	10	3	5	31	21	35	.306	.360	.406	124	7	9	41	1	3	-2	.989	3	1/3	0.6
1977	NY-N	26	51	2	9	3	0	1	9	2	10	.176	.208	.294	34	-5	-5	2	0	0	0	.988	-1	1/3M	-0.7
Total	18	2209	7874	996	2342	344	59	252	1185	779	1094	.297	.367	.452	129	298	302	1258	23	29	-11	.990	-93	C13/O	20.1
■ GIL TORRES	Torres, Don Gilberto (Nunez) b: 8/23/15, Regla, Cuba d: 1/10/83, Regla, Cuba BR/TR, 6', 155 lbs. Deb: 4/25/40 F																								
1940	Was-A	2	0	0	0	0	0	0	0	0	0	—	—	—	—	0	0	0	0	0	0	1.000	0	/P	0.0
1944	Was-A	134	524	42	140	20	6	0	58	21	24	.267	.297	.328	82	-16	-13	47	10	7	-1	.952	9	*32/1	-0.4
1945	Was-A	147	562	39	133	12	5	0	48	21	29	.237	.264	.276	62	-32	-27	40	7	4	-0	.953	-21	*S/3	-4.0
1946	Was-A	63	185	18	47	8	0	0	13	11	12	.254	.296	.297	70	-8	-7	16	3	2	-0	.939	2	S3/2P	-0.4
Total	4	346	1271	99	320	40	11	0	119	53	65	.252	.282	.301	72	-56	-47	102	20	13	-2	.951	-11	S3/2P1	-4.8
■ FELIX TORRES	Torres, Felix (Sanchez) b: 5/1/32, Ponce, P.R. BR/TR, 5'11", 165 lbs. Deb: 4/10/62																								
1962	LA-A	127	451	44	117	19	4	11	74	28	73	.259	.308	.392	90	-9	-7	50	0	0	0	.938	-3	*3	-0.9
1963	LA-A	138	463	40	121	32	1	4	51	30	73	.261	.310	.361	93	-8	-5	48	1	0	0	.939	-4	*3/1	-0.9
1964	LA-A	100	277	25	64	10	0	12	28	13	56	.231	.268	.397	91	-8	-4	25	1	3	-2	.970	-0	3/1	-0.7
Total	3	365	1191	109	302	61	5	27	153	71	202	.254	.300	.381	91	-24	-16	123	2	3	-1	.945	-8	3/1	-2.5
■ HECTOR TORRES	Torres, Hector Epitacio (Marroquin) b: 9/16/45, Monterrey, Mexico BR/TR, 6', 175 lbs. Deb: 4/10/68 C																								
1968	Hou-N	128	466	44	104	11	1	1	24	18	64	.223	.252	.258	54	-27	-26	29	2	3	-1	.958	-4	*S/2	-2.1
1969	Hou-N	34	69	5	11	1	0	1	8	2	12	.159	.183	.217	12	-8	-8	2	0	0	0	.944	0	S	-0.7
1970	Hou-N	31	65	6	16	1	2	0	5	6	8	.246	.310	.323	73	-3	-2	6	0	0	0	.947	1	S/2	0.1
1971	Chi-N	31	58	4	13	3	0	0	2	4	10	.224	.274	.276	49	-3	-4	4	0	0	0	.962	1	S/2	-0.2
1972	Mon-N	83	181	14	28	4	1	2	7	13	26	.155	.215	.221	24	-18	-18	8	0	2	-1	.965	15	2S/OP3	-0.2
1973	Hou-N	38	66	3	6	1	0	0	2	7	13	.091	.189	.106	-16	-10	-10	1	0	1	-1	.952	7	S2	-0.2
1975	SD-N	112	352	31	91	12	0	5	26	22	32	.259	.302	.335	82	-12	-9	34	2	3	-1	.971	11	S32	0.9
1976	SD-N	74	215	8	42	6	0	4	15	16	31	.195	.254	.279	56	-14	-12	14	2	1	0	.949	-16	S/32	-2.3
1977	Tor-A	91	266	33	64	7	3	5	26	16	33	.241	.286	.346	70	-11	-11	24	1	1	-0	.980	-2	S2/3	-0.6
Total	9	622	1738	148	375	46	7	18	115	104	229	.216	.262	.281	55	-106	-101	123	7	11	-5	.962	12	S2/3OP	-5.3
■ RICARDO TORRES	Torres, Ricardo J. (Martinez) b: 4/16/1891, Regla, Cuba d: 4/17/60, Regla, Cuba BR/TR, 5'11", 160 lbs. Deb: 5/18/20 F																								
1920	Was-A	16	30	8	10	1	0	0	3	1	4	.333	.355	.367	94	-0	-0	4	0	0	0	1.000	-1	/1C	-0.1
1921	Was-A	2	3	1	1	0	0	0	0	1	1	.333	.500	.333	122	0	0	1	0	0	0	.750	-1	/C	-0.1
1922	Was-A	4	4	0	0	0	0	0	0	0	1	.000	.000	.000	-99	-1	-1	0	0	0	0	1.000	1	/C	0.0
Total	3	22	37	9	11	1	0	0	3	2	6	.297	.333	.324	76	-1	-1	4	0	0	0	.955	-1	/C1	-0.2
■ RUSTY TORRES	Torres, Rosendo (Hernandez) b: 9/30/48, Aquadilla, P.R. BB/TR, 5'10", 180 lbs. Deb: 9/20/71																								
1971	NY-A	9	26	5	10	3	0	2	3	0	8	.385	.385	.731	223	3	4	7	0	1	-1	1.000	0	/O	0.3
1972	NY-A	80	199	15	42	7	0	3	13	18	44	.211	.280	.291	73	-7	-7	16	0	4	-2	.978	-6	O	-2.0
1973	Cle-A	122	312	31	64	8	1	7	28	50	62	.205	.321	.304	76	-8	-9	32	6	5	-1	.976	-5	*O	-2.0
1974	Cle-A	108	150	19	28	2	0	3	12	13	24	.187	.252	.260	48	-10	-10	10	2	1	0	.959	-19	O/D	-3.3
1976	Cal-A	120	264	37	54	16	3	6	27	36	39	.205	.300	.356	98	-3	-1	29	4	4	-1	.990	-11	*O/3D	-1.7

YEAR	TM/L	G	AB	R	H	2B	3B	HR	RBI	BB	SO	AVG	OBP	SLG	PRO+	BR	/A	RC	SB	CS	SBR	FA	FR	POS	TPR
1977	Cal-A	58	77	9	12	1	1	3	10	10	18	.156	.253	.312	55	-5	-5	6	0	1	-1	.984	-12	O	-1.8
1978	Chi-A	16	44	7	14	3	0	3	6	6	7	.318	.400	.591	174	4	4	10	0	1	-1	.964	-2	O	0.1
1979	Chi-A	90	170	26	43	5	0	8	24	23	37	.253	.349	.424	107	2	2	26	0	0	0	.976	-13	O	-1.3
1980	KC-A	51	72	10	12	0	0	0	3	8	7	.167	.250	.167	16	-8	-8	3	1	3	-2	.973	-4	O/D	-1.4
Total	9	654	1314	159	279	45	5	35	126	164	246	.212	.303	.334	82	-32	-30	139	13	20	-8	.977	-73	O/D3	-13.1

■ KELVIN TORVE

Torve, Kelvin Curtis b: 1/10/60, Rapid City, S.Dak. BL/TR, 6'3", 205 lbs. Deb: 6/25/88

YEAR	TM/L	G	AB	R	H	2B	3B	HR	RBI	BB	SO	AVG	OBP	SLG	PRO+	BR	/A	RC	SB	CS	SBR	FA	FR	POS	TPR
1988	Min-A	12	16	1	3	0	0	1	2	1	2	.188	.235	.375	66	-1	-1	1	0	1	-1	1.000	0	/1D	-0.2
1990	NY-N	20	38	0	11	4	0	0	2	4	9	.289	.386	.395	116	1	1	6	0	0	0	1.000	-2	/1O	-0.2
1991	NY-N	10	8	0	0	0	0	0	0	0	1	.000	.000	.000	-99	-2	-2	0	0	0	0	1.000	1	/1	-0.1
Total	3	42	62	1	14	4	0	1	4	5	12	.226	.304	.339	78	-2	-2	7	0	1	-1	1.000	-2	/1OD	-0.5

■ CESAR TOVAR

Tovar, Cesar Leonardo "Pepito" (b: Cesar Leonard Perez (Tovar)) b: 7/3/40, Caracas, Venez. BR/TR, 5'9", 155 lbs. Deb: 4/12/65

YEAR	TM/L	G	AB	R	H	2B	3B	HR	RBI	BB	SO	AVG	OBP	SLG	PRO+	BR	/A	RC	SB	CS	SBR	FA	FR	POS	TPR
1965	Min-A	18	25	3	5	1	0	0	2	2	3	.200	.259	.240	41	-2	-2	2	2	0	1	.800	1	/23OS	-0.1
1966	Min-A	134	465	57	121	19	5	2	41	44	50	.260	.329	.335	86	-4	-8	54	16	6	1	.978	-8	2SO	-0.8
1967	Min-A	164	649	98	173	32	7	6	47	46	51	.267	.328	.365	97	4	-2	80	19	11	-1	.994	-4	O32/S	-1.0
1968	Min-A	157	613	89	167	31	6	6	47	34	41	.272	.328	.372	106	8	5	80	35	13	3	.966	-2	O3S2/PC1	0.6
1969	*Min-A	158	535	99	154	25	5	11	52	37	37	.288	.344	.415	109	7	6	80	45	12	6	.983	9	*O23	2.0
1970	*Min-A	161	650	120	195	**36**	**13**	10	54	52	47	.300	.359	.442	118	17	16	103	30	15	0	.977	0	*O/23	0.8
1971	Min-A	157	657	94	**204**	29	3	1	45	45	39	.311	.357	.368	103	5	3	87	18	14	-3	.986	4	*O/32	-0.4
1972	Min-A	141	548	86	145	20	6	2	31	39	39	.265	.329	.334	93	-1	-4	63	21	10	0	.983	7	*O	-0.4
1973	Phi-N	97	328	49	88	18	4	1	21	29	35	.268	.337	.357	90	-3	-4	41	6	4	-1	.928	-16	3O2	-2.2
1974	Tex-A	138	562	78	164	24	6	4	58	47	33	.292	.356	.377	114	9	11	79	13	9	-2	.980	-1	*O/D	0.3
1975	Tex-A	102	427	53	110	16	0	3	28	27	25	.258	.306	.316	77	-13	-13	40	16	11	-2	.919	-3	DO/2	-2.0
	*Oak-A	19	26	5	6	1	0	0	3	3	3	.231	.310	.269	66	-1	-1	3	4	0	1	1.000	-0	/23SD	0.0
	Yr	121	453	58	116	17	0	3	31	30	28	.256	.307	.313	76	-15	-14	43	20	11	-1	.919	-3	DO/23S	-2.0
1976	Oak-A	29	45	1	8	0	0	0	4	4	4	.178	.275	.178	36	-4	-3	2	1	2	-1	.958	-5	O/D	-1.0
	NY-A	13	39	2	6	1	0	0	2	4	3	.154	.250	.179	27	-3	-3	2	0	1	-1	1.000	1	D/2	-0.3
	Yr	42	84	3	14	1	0	0	6	8	7	.167	.263	.179	32	-7	-7	4	1	3	-2	.958	-4	OD/2	-1.3
Total	12	1488	5569	834	1546	253	55	46	435	413	410	.278	.337	.368	99	19	1	717	226	108	3	.980	-18	O32/DS1C	-4.5

■ BABE TOWNE

Towne, Jay King b: 3/12/1880, Coon Rapid, Iowa d: 10/29/38, Des Moines, Iowa BL/TR, 5'10", 180 lbs. Deb: 8/01/06

YEAR	TM/L	G	AB	R	H	2B	3B	HR	RBI	BB	SO	AVG	OBP	SLG	PRO+	BR	/A	RC	SB	CS	SBR	FA	FR	POS	TPR
1906	*Chi-A	14	36	3	10	0	0	0	6	7		.278	.395	.278	115	1	1	4	0			.923	-4	C	-0.2

■ GEORGE TOWNSEND

Townsend, George Hodgson "Sleepy" b: 6/4/1867, Hartsdale, N.Y. d: 3/15/30, New Haven, Conn. BR/TR, 5'7.5", 180 lbs. Deb: 6/25/1887

YEAR	TM/L	G	AB	R	H	2B	3B	HR	RBI	BB	SO	AVG	OBP	SLG	PRO+	BR	/A	RC	SB	CS	SBR	FA	FR	POS	TPR
1887	Phi-a	31	109	12	21	3	0	0		3		.193	.214	.220	23	-11	-11	7	8			.865	-7	C/O	-1.3
1888	Phi-a	42	161	13	25	6	0	0	12	4		.155	.181	.193	22	-14	-14	6	2			.912	-2	C	-1.1
1890	Bal-a	18	67	6	16	4	1	0		4		.239	.282	.328	78	-2	-2	7	3			.930	2	C	0.1
1891	Bal-a	61	204	29	39	5	4	0	18	20	21	.191	.279	.255	55	-11	-12	16	3			.909	-11	C/O	-1.5
Total	4	152	541	60	101	18	5	0	30	31	21	.187	.239	.238	42	-38	-39	36	16			.905	-17	C/O	-3.8

■ JIM TOY

Toy, James Madison b: 2/20/1858, Beaver Falls, Pa. d: 3/13/19, Beaver Falls, Pa. 5'6", 160 lbs. Deb: 4/20/1887

YEAR	TM/L	G	AB	R	H	2B	3B	HR	RBI	BB	SO	AVG	OBP	SLG	PRO+	BR	/A	RC	SB	CS	SBR	FA	FR	POS	TPR
1887	Cle-a	109	423	56	94	20	5	1		17		.222	.256	.300	58	-25	-23	35	8			.975	3	1OC/3S	-2.2
1890	Bro-a	44	160	11	29	3	0	0		11		.181	.238	.200	32	-13	-13	8	2			.867	-1	C	-0.8
Total	2	153	583	67	123	23	5	1		28		.211	.251	.273	51	-39	-36	44	10			.859	3	/1CO3S	-3.0

■ JIM TRABER

Traber, James Joseph b: 12/26/61, Columbus, Ohio BL/TL, 6', 194 lbs. Deb: 9/21/84

YEAR	TM/L	G	AB	R	H	2B	3B	HR	RBI	BB	SO	AVG	OBP	SLG	PRO+	BR	/A	RC	SB	CS	SBR	FA	FR	POS	TPR
1984	Bal-A	10	21	3	5	0	0	0	2	2	4	.238	.304	.238	54	-1	-1	2	0	0	0	.000	0	/D	-0.1
1986	Bal-A	65	212	28	54	7	0	13	44	18	31	.255	.328	.472	116	4	4	32	0	0	0	.988	1	1D/O	0.3
1988	Bal-A	103	352	25	78	6	0	10	45	19	42	.222	.263	.324	65	-18	-16	28	1	2	-1	.990	8	1DO	-1.4
1989	Bal-A	86	234	14	49	8	0	4	26	19	41	.209	.269	.295	61	-13	-12	18	4	3	-1	.998	6	1/D	-1.2
Total	4	264	819	70	186	21	0	27	117	58	118	.227	.283	.352	77	-28	-25	79	5	5	-2	.993	15	1/DO	-2.4

■ DICK TRACEWSKI

Tracewski, Richard Joseph b: 2/3/35, Eynon, Pa. BR/TR, 5'11", 167 lbs. Deb: 4/12/62 MC

YEAR	TM/L	G	AB	R	H	2B	3B	HR	RBI	BB	SO	AVG	OBP	SLG	PRO+	BR	/A	RC	SB	CS	SBR	FA	FR	POS	TPR
1962	LA-N	15	2	3	0	0	0	0	0	2	0	.000	.500	.000	50	0	0	0	0	0	0	1.000	4	/S	0.4
1963	*LA-N	104	217	23	49	2	1	1	10	19	39	.226	.288	.258	63	-11	-9	16	2	3	-1	.957	19	S2	1.4
1964	LA-N	106	304	31	75	13	4	1	26	31	61	.247	.316	.326	88	-7	-4	33	3	3	-1	.970	-0	23S	-0.1
1965	*LA-N	78	186	17	40	6	0	1	20	25	30	.215	.315	.263	69	-8	-6	15	2	6	-3	.950	8	32/S	-0.1
1966	Det-A	81	124	15	24	1	1	0	7	10	32	.194	.254	.218	36	-10	-10	7	1	1	-0	.947	11	2/S	0.2
1967	Det-A	74	107	19	30	4	2	1	9	8	20	.280	.330	.383	107	1	1	14	1	1	-0	.965	9	S23	1.3
1968	*Det-A	90	212	30	33	3	1	4	15	24	51	.156	.242	.236	44	-14	-15	13	3	0	1	.982	-5	S32	-1.6
1969	Det-A	66	79	10	11	2	0	0	4	15	20	.139	.277	.165	25	-7	-8	5	3	0	1	.957	16	S2/3	1.1
Total	8	614	1231	148	262	31	9	8	91	134	253	.213	.291	.272	65	-56	-52	104	15	14	-4	.958	62	S23	2.6

■ JIM TRACY

Tracy, James Edwin b: 12/31/55, Hamilton, Ohio BL/TR, 6', 185 lbs. Deb: 7/20/80

YEAR	TM/L	G	AB	R	H	2B	3B	HR	RBI	BB	SO	AVG	OBP	SLG	PRO+	BR	/A	RC	SB	CS	SBR	FA	FR	POS	TPR
1980	Chi-N	42	122	12	31	3	3	3	9	13	37	.254	.326	.402	95	0	-1	16	2	2	-1	.950	-7	O/1	-1.1
1981	Chi-N	45	63	6	15	2	1	0	5	12	14	.238	.360	.302	85	-0	-1	8	1	0	0	1.000	-2	O	-0.3
Total	2	87	185	18	46	5	4	3	14	25	51	.249	.338	.368	92	-0	-2	24	3	2	-0	.964	-9	/O1	-1.4

■ JOHN TRAFFLEY

Traffley, John M. b: 1862, Chicago, Ill. d: 5/15/1900, Baltimore, Md. 5'9", 180 lbs. Deb: 6/15/1889 F

YEAR	TM/L	G	AB	R	H	2B	3B	HR	RBI	BB	SO	AVG	OBP	SLG	PRO+	BR	/A	RC	SB	CS	SBR	FA	FR	POS	TPR
1889	Lou-a	1	2	0	1	0	0	0	0	0	0	.500	.500	.500	192	0	0	1	0			.000	-1	/O	0.0

■ BILL TRAFFLEY

Traffley, William F. b: 12/21/1859, Staten Island, N.Y d: 6/24/08, Denver, Colo. BR/TR, 5'11.5", 185 lbs. Deb: 7/27/1878 F

YEAR	TM/L	G	AB	R	H	2B	3B	HR	RBI	BB	SO	AVG	OBP	SLG	PRO+	BR	/A	RC	SB	CS	SBR	FA	FR	POS	TPR
1878	Chi-N	2	9	1	1	0	0	0	1	0	1	.111	.111	.111	-25	-1	-1	0				1.000	-1	/C	-0.2
1883	Cin-a	30	105	17	21	5	0	0		4		.200	.229	.248	51	-5	-6	6				.851	2	C/S	-0.3
1884	Bal-a	53	210	25	37	4	6	0		3		.176	.192	.252	44	-12	-13	10				.926	-8	C/O1	-1.6
1885	Bal-a	69	254	27	39	4	5	1		17		.154	.215	.220	40	-17	-16	12				**.943**	2	CO/2	-0.8
1886	Bal-a	25	85	15	18	0	1	0		10		.212	.295	.235	70	-3	-2	8	8			.952	-3	C	-0.2
Total	5	179	663	85	116	13	12	1	1	34	1	.175	.220	.235	46	-38	-39	37	8			.927	-8	C/O2S1	-3.1

■ WALT TRAGESSER

Tragesser, Walter Joseph b: 6/14/1887, Lafayette, Ind. d: 12/14/70, Lafayette, Ind. BR/TR, 6', 175 lbs. Deb: 7/30/13

YEAR	TM/L	G	AB	R	H	2B	3B	HR	RBI	BB	SO	AVG	OBP	SLG	PRO+	BR	/A	RC	SB	CS	SBR	FA	FR	POS	TPR
1913	Bos-N	2	0	0	0	0	0	0	0	0	0	—	—	—	—	0	0	0	0			1.000	-0	/C	0.0
1915	Bos-N	7	7	1	0	0	0	0	0	0	2	.000	.000	.000	-99	-2	-2	0	0			.944	1	/C	-0.1
1916	Bos-N	41	54	3	11	1	0	0	4	5	10	.204	.283	.222	59	-3	-2	4	0			.971	4	C	0.3
1917	Bos-N	98	297	23	66	10	2	0	25	15	36	.222	.264	.269	68	-13	-11	22	5			.971	-2	C	-0.6
1918	Bos-N	7	1	0	0	0	0	0	0	0	0	.000	.000	.000	-99	-0	-0	0	0			.833	1	/C	0.0
1919	Bos-N	20	40	3	7	2	0	0	3	2	10	.175	.233	.225	39	-3	-3	2	1			.959	-0	C	-0.2
	Phi-N	35	114	7	27	7	0	0	8	9	31	.237	.298	.298	74	-3	-4	10	4			.953	4	C	0.3
	Yr	55	154	10	34	9	0	0	11	11	41	.221	.281	.279	67	-6	-6	13	5			.954	4	C	0.1
1920	Phi-N	62	176	17	37	11	1	6	26	4	36	.210	.236	.386	73	-6	-7	16	4	0	1	.944	-13	C	-1.7
Total	7	272	689	54	148	31	3	6	66	35	125	.215	.260	.295	67	-29	-29	54	14	0		.961	-6	C	-2.0

■ RED TRAMBACK

Tramback, Stephen Joseph b: 11/1/15, Iselin, Pa. d: 12/28/79, Buffalo, N.Y. BL/TL, 6', 175 lbs. Deb: 9/15/40

YEAR	TM/L	G	AB	R	H	2B	3B	HR	RBI	BB	SO	AVG	OBP	SLG	PRO+	BR	/A	RC	SB	CS	SBR	FA	FR	POS	TPR
1940	NY-N	2	4	0	1	0	0	0	0	1	1	.250	.400	.250	82	-0	-0	1	1			.667	-0	/O	0.0

YEAR	TM/L	G	AB	R	H	2B	3B	HR	RBI	BB	SO	AVG	OBP	SLG	PRO+	BR	/A	RC	SB	CS	SBR	FA	FR	POS	TPR
■ **ALAN TRAMMELL** Trammell, Alan Stuart b: 2/21/58, Garden Grove, Cal. BR/TR, 6', 175 lbs. Deb: 9/09/77																									
1977	Det-A	19	43	6	8	0	0	0	0	4	12	.186	.255	.186	21	-5	-5	2	0	0	0	.961	-7	S	-1.0
1978	Det-A	139	448	49	120	14	6	2	34	45	56	.268	.337	.339	88	-5	-6	52	3	1	0	.979	6	*S	1.7
1979	Det-A	142	460	68	127	11	4	6	50	43	55	.276	.338	.357	85	-7	-9	56	17	14	-3	.961	-13	*S	-1.0
1980	Det-A★	146	560	107	168	21	5	9	65	69	63	.300	.380	.404	112	14	12	87	12	12	-4	.980	-27	*S	-0.2
1981	Det-A	105	392	52	101	15	3	2	31	49	31	.258	.345	.327	91	-1	-3	47	10	3	1	.983	6	*S	1.5
1982	Det-A	157	489	66	126	34	3	9	57	52	47	.258	.329	.395	97	-1	-2	67	19	8	1	.978	-8	*S	0.6
1983	Det-A	142	505	83	161	31	2	14	66	57	64	.319	.388	.471	139	25	27	96	30	10	3	.979	-18	*S	2.6
1984	*Det-A†	139	555	85	174	34	5	14	69	60	63	.314	.383	.468	135	27	27	100	19	13	-2	.980	-12	*SD	2.4
1985	Det-A★	149	605	79	156	21	7	13	57	50	71	.258	.317	.380	90	-9	-8	76	14	5	1	.977	-16	*S	-0.8
1986	Det-A	151	574	107	159	33	7	21	75	59	57	.277	.350	.469	121	16	16	95	25	12	0	.969	6	*S/D	3.5
1987	*Det-A★	151	597	109	205	34	3	28	105	60	47	.343	.406	.551	157	44	47	137	21	2	5	.971	-10	*S	5.2
1988	Det-A†	128	466	73	145	24	1	15	69	46	46	.311	.378	.464	140	22	24	79	7	4	-0	.980	-7	*S	2.7
1989	Det-A	121	449	54	109	20	3	5	43	45	45	.243	.317	.334	86	-9	-8	50	10	2	2	.985	12	*S/D	1.6
1990	Det-A★	146	559	71	170	37	1	14	89	68	55	.304	.381	.449	130	24	24	95	12	10	-2	.979	1	*S/D	3.4
1991	Det-A	101	375	57	93	20	0	9	55	37	39	.248	.320	.373	90	-4	-5	47	11	2	2	.979	4	S/D	0.8
1992	Det-A	29	102	11	28	7	1	1	11	15	4	.275	.373	.392	113	2	2	14	2	2	-1	.977	-1	S	0.3
Total	16	1965	7179	1077	2050	356	51	162	876	759	755	.286	.357	.417	113	132	133	1100	212	100	4	.977	-83	*S/D	23.3
■ **CECIL TRAVIS** Travis, Cecil Howell b: 8/8/13, Riverdale, Ga. BL/TR, 6'1.5", 185 lbs. Deb: 5/16/33																									
1933	Was-A	18	43	7	13	1	0	0	2	2	5	.302	.348	.326	80	-1	-1	5	0	0	0	.974	4	3	0.3
1934	Was-A	109	392	48	125	22	4	1	53	24	37	.319	.361	.403	101	-2	0	56	1	5	-3	.937	3	3	0.4
1935	Was-A	138	534	85	170	27	8	0	61	41	28	.318	.377	.399	104	1	4	82	4	2	0	.963	21	*3O	2.7
1936	Was-A	138	517	77	164	34	10	2	92	39	21	.317	.366	.433	102	-3	1	82	4	4	-1	.938	-13	SO/23	-0.8
1937	Was-A	135	526	72	181	27	7	3	66	39	34	.344	.395	.439	115	9	12	92	3	2	-0	.965	-11	*S	0.9
1938	Was-A☆	146	567	96	190	30	5	5	67	58	22	.335	.401	.432	117	9	15	100	6	5	-1	.950	3	*S	2.5
1939	Was-A	130	476	55	139	20	9	5	63	34	25	.292	.342	.403	97	-8	-3	65	0	3	-2	.958	-4	*S	0.2
1940	Was-A★	136	528	60	170	37	11	2	76	48	23	.322	.381	.445	121	11	16	94	0	1	-1	.934	16	*3S	3.3
1941	Was-A★	152	608	106	**218**	39	19	7	101	52	25	.359	.410	.520	152	38	42	131	2	2	-1	.964	2	*S3	5.1
1945	Was-A	15	54	4	13	2	1	0	10	4	5	.241	.293	.315	83	-2	-1	4	0	1	-1	.920	0	3	-0.1
1946	Was-A	137	465	45	117	22	3	1	56	45	47	.252	.323	.318	85	-12	-9	47	2	4	-2	.959	-19	S3	-2.6
1947	Was-A	74	204	10	44	4	1	1	10	16	19	.216	.273	.260	50	-14	-14	14	1	3	-2	.932	-2	3S	-1.7
Total	12	1328	4914	665	1544	265	78	27	657	402	291	.314	.370	.416	109	26	63	772	23	32	-12	.955	0	S3/O2	10.2
■ **BRIAN TRAXLER** Traxler, Brian Lee b: 9/26/67, Waukegan, Ill. BL/TL, 5'10", 200 lbs. Deb: 4/24/90																									
1990	LA-N	9	11	0	1	1	0	0	0	0	4	.091	.091	.182	-28	-2	-2	0	0	0	0	1.000	1	/1	-0.2
■ **JIM TRAY** Tray, James b: 2/14/1860, Jackson, Mich. d: 7/28/05, Jackson, Mich. 5'8", 144 lbs. Deb: 9/06/1884																									
1884	Ind-a	6	21	2	6	0	0	0		2		.286	.348	.286	115	0	0	2				.857	-2	/C1	-0.1
■ **PIE TRAYNOR** Traynor, Harold Joseph b: 11/11/1899, Framingham, Mass. d: 3/16/72, Pittsburgh, Pa. BR/TR, 6', 170 lbs. Deb: 9/15/20 MH																									
1920	Pit-N	17	52	6	11	3	1	0	2	3	6	.212	.268	.308	63	-2	-3	4	1	3	-2	.860	-6	S	-1.0
1921	Pit-N	7	19	0	5	0	0	0	2	1	2	.263	.300	.263	49	-1	-1	2	0	0	0	.917	1	/3S	-0.1
1922	Pit-N	142	571	89	161	17	12	4	81	27	28	.282	.319	.375	77	-19	-20	70	17	3	3	.945	-4	*3S	-0.9
1923	Pit-N	153	616	108	208	19	**19**	12	101	34	19	.338	.377	.489	124	22	20	112	28	13	1	.950	8	*3/S	4.1
1924	Pit-N	142	545	86	160	26	13	5	82	37	26	.294	.340	.417	100	1	-1	74	24	18	-4	.968	9	*3	1.5
1925	*Pit-N	150	591	114	189	39	14	6	106	52	19	.320	.377	.464	106	12	6	103	15	9	-1	**.957**	23	*3/S	3.6
1926	Pit-N	152	574	83	182	25	17	3	92	38	14	.317	.361	.436	108	10	6	88	8			.952	7	*3/S	2.2
1927	*Pit-N	149	573	93	196	32	9	5	106	22	11	.342	.370	.455	112	15	9	92	11			.962	13	*3/S	2.9
1928	Pit-N	144	569	91	192	38	12	3	124	28	10	.337	.370	.462	112	12	9	93	12			.946	4	*3	2.0
1929	Pit-N	130	540	94	192	27	12	4	108	30	7	.356	.393	.472	111	11	9	96	13			.951	-1	*3	1.2
1930	Pit-N	130	497	90	182	22	11	9	119	48	19	.366	.423	.509	124	21	21	104	7			.941	5	*3	2.9
1931	Pit-N	155	615	81	183	37	15	2	103	54	28	.298	.354	.416	107	6	6	93	6			.925	-9	*3	0.6
1932	Pit-N	135	513	74	169	27	10	2	68	32	20	.329	.373	.433	118	12	13	84	6			.936	-3	*3	1.9
1933	Pit-N★	154	624	85	190	27	6	1	82	35	24	.304	.342	.372	104	3	3	80	5			.946	-1	*3	1.3
1934	Pit-N★	119	444	62	137	22	10	1	61	21	27	.309	.341	.410	98	-0	-2	56	3			.954	-10	*3M	-0.7
1935	Pit-N	57	204	24	57	10	3	1	36	10	17	.279	.323	.373	84	-4	-5	23	2			.888	-3	3/1M	-0.6
1937	Pit-N	5	12	3	2	0	0	0	0	0	1	.167	.167	.167	-9	-2	-2	0	0			1.000	1	/3M	0.0
Total	17	1941	7559	1183	2416	371	164	58	1273	472	278	.320	.362	.435	107	96	71	1174	158	46		.947	34	*3/S1	20.9
■ **FRED TREACEY** Treacey, Frederick S. b: 1847, Brooklyn, N.Y. 5'9.5", 145 lbs. Deb: 5/16/1871 F																									
1871	Chi-n	25	124	39	42	7	5	**4**	33	2	5	.339	.349	.573	144	9	6	30	13					*O	0.4
1872	Ath-n	47	236	53	64	7	2	2	29	5	10	.271	.286	.343	93	-2	-2	24						*O	-0.1
1873	Phi-n	51	243	49	62	7	2	1	32	5	6	.255	.270	.313	68	-8	-10	21						*O	-0.7
1874	Chi-n	35	146	18	28	6	0	0		3		.192	.208	.233	40	-9	-10	7						O	-0.7
1875	Cen-n	11	46	9	12	2	0	0		2		.261	.292	.304	116	0	1	4						O	0.1
	Phi-n	43	179	24	38	3	3	0		1		.212	.217	.263	62	-6	-7	10						O	-0.6
	Yr	54	225	33	50	5	3	0		3		.222	.232	.271	73	-6	-6	15						O	-0.5
1876	NY-N	57	256	47	54	5	1	0	18	1	5	.211	.214	.238	58	-13	-8	13				.844	12	*O	0.3
Total	5 n	212	974	192	246	32	12	7	94	18	21	.253	.266	.332	82	-17	-23	97						O	-1.6
■ **PETE TREACEY** Treacey, Peter b: 1852, Brooklyn, N.Y. Deb: 8/05/1876 F																									
1876	NY-N	2	5	1	0	0	0	0	0	1	0	.000	.167	.000	-46	-1	-1	0				.750	-1	/S	-0.2
■ **RAY TREADAWAY** Treadaway, Edgar Raymond b: 10/31/07, Ragland, Ala. d: 10/12/35, Chattanooga, Tenn. BL/TR, 5'7", 150 lbs. Deb: 9/17/30																									
1930	Was-A	6	19	1	4	2	0	0	1	0	3	.211	.211	.316	31	-2	-2	1	0	0	0	.833	-1	/3	-0.3
■ **GEORGE TREADWAY** Treadway, George B. BL , 6', 185 lbs. Deb: 4/27/1893																									
1893	Bal-N	115	458	78	119	16	17	1	67	57	50	.260	.347	.376	92	-4	-5	70	24			.901	8	*O	-0.2
1894	Bro-N	123	479	124	157	27	26	4	102	72	43	.328	.418	.518	136	21	28	119	27			.892	1	*O/1	1.6
1895	Bro-N	86	339	54	87	14	3	7	54	33	22	.257	.326	.378	90	-9	-4	46	9			.886	-9	O	-1.6
1896	Lou-N	2	7	0	1	0	0	0	1	1	0	.143	.250	.143	7	-1	-1	0	0			.500	-1	/O1	-0.2
Total	4	326	1283	256	364	57	46	12	224	163	115	.284	.368	.428	108	7	18	235	60			.891	-1	O/1	-0.4
■ **JEFF TREADWAY** Treadway, Hugh Jeffery b: 1/22/63, Columbus, Ga. BL/TR, 5'10", 170 lbs. Deb: 9/04/87																									
1987	Cin-N	23	84	9	28	4	0	2	4	2	6	.333	.356	.452	108	1	1	14	1	0	0	.958	-7	2	-0.5
1988	Cin-N	103	301	30	76	19	4	2	23	27	30	.252	.320	.362	92	-2	-3	36	2	0	1	.984	3	2/3	0.4
1989	Atl-N	134	473	58	131	18	3	8	40	30	38	.277	.320	.378	96	-1	-3	56	3	2	-0	.981	3	*2/3	0.5
1990	Atl-N	128	474	56	134	20	2	11	59	25	42	.283	.323	.403	93	-2	-5	59	3	4	-2	.976	10	*2	0.6
1991	*Atl-N	106	306	41	98	17	2	3	32	23	19	.320	.372	.418	115	9	7	46	2	2	-1	.960	-8	2	0.0
1992	*Atl-N	61	126	5	28	6	1	0	5	9	16	.222	.274	.286	54	-7	-8	9	1	2	-1	.993	0	2/3	-0.9
Total	6	555	1764	199	495	84	12	26	163	116	151	.281	.328	.386	95	-1	-11	221	12	10	-2	.976	0	2/3	0.1
■ **RED TREADWAY** Treadway, Thadford Leon b: 4/28/20, Athalone, N.C. BL/TR, 5'10", 175 lbs. Deb: 7/25/44																									
1944	NY-N	50	170	23	51	5	2	0	5	13	11	.300	.350	.353	98	-0	-0	22	2			.957	1	O	-0.1

YEAR	TM/L	G	AB	R	H	2B	3B	HR	RBI	BB	SO	AVG	OBP	SLG	PRO+	BR	/A	RC	SB	CS	SBR	FA	FR	POS	TPR
1945	NY-N	88	224	31	54	4	2	4	23	20	13	.241	.303	.330	75	-7	-8	24	3			.940	-9	O	-2.0
Total	2	138	394	54	105	9	4	4	28	33	24	.266	.323	.340	85	-8	-8	46	5			.948	-8	/O	-2.1

■ FRANK TRECHOCK

Trechock, Frank Adam b: 12/24/15, Windber, Pa. d: 1/16/89, Minneapolis, Minn. BR/TR, 5'10", 175 lbs. Deb: 9/19/37

YEAR	TM/L	G	AB	R	H	2B	3B	HR	RBI	BB	SO	AVG	OBP	SLG	PRO+	BR	/A	RC	SB	CS	SBR	FA	FR	POS	TPR
1937	Was-A	1	4	0	2	0	0	0	0	0	1	.500	.500	.500	160	0	0	1	0	0	0	.750	0	/S	0.1

■ NICK TREMARK

Tremark, Nicholas Joseph b: 10/15/12, Yonkers, N.Y. BL/TL, 5'5", 150 lbs. Deb: 8/09/34

YEAR	TM/L	G	AB	R	H	2B	3B	HR	RBI	BB	SO	AVG	OBP	SLG	PRO+	BR	/A	RC	SB	CS	SBR	FA	FR	POS	TPR
1934	Bro-N	17	28	3	7	1	0	0	6	2	2	.250	.300	.286	61	-2	-1	2	0			1.000	-1	/O	-0.3
1935	Bro-N	10	13	1	3	1	0	0	3	1	1	.231	.286	.308	61	-1	-1	1	0			1.000	-1	/O	-0.1
1936	Bro-N	8	32	6	8	2	0	0	1	3	2	.250	.333	.313	74	-1	-1	3	0			1.000	1	/O	0.0
Total	3	35	73	10	18	4	0	0	10	6	5	.247	.313	.301	67	-3	-3	7	0			1.000	-0	/O	-0.4

■ OVERTON TREMPER

Tremper, Carlton Overton b: 3/22/06, Brooklyn, N.Y. BR/TR, 5'10", 163 lbs. Deb: 6/16/27

YEAR	TM/L	G	AB	R	H	2B	3B	HR	RBI	BB	SO	AVG	OBP	SLG	PRO+	BR	/A	RC	SB	CS	SBR	FA	FR	POS	TPR
1927	Bro-N	26	60	4	14	0	0	0	4	0	2	.233	.246	.233	29	-6	-6	3	0			1.000	-4	O	-1.1
1928	Bro-N	10	31	1	6	2	1	0	1	0	1	.194	.194	.323	33	-3	-3	2	0			1.000	-0	/O	-0.4
Total	2	36	91	5	20	2	1	0	5	0	3	.220	.228	.264	30	-9	-9	5	0			1.000	-4	/O	-1.5

■ GEORGE TRENWITH

Trenwith, George b: Philadelphia, Pa. d: 2/1/1890, Philadelphia, Pa. Deb: 4/30/1875

YEAR	TM/L	G	AB	R	H	2B	3B	HR	RBI	BB	SO	AVG	OBP	SLG	PRO+	BR	/A	RC	SB	CS	SBR	FA	FR	POS	TPR
1875	Cen-n	10	45	5	8	0	0	0		1		.178	.196	.178	33	-3	-2	2						3	-0.2
	NH-n	6	25	1	6	2	0	0		0		.240	.240	.320	105	-0	0	2						/3	0.0
	Yr	16	70	6	14	2	0	0		1		.200	.211	.229	58	-3	-2	3						3	-0.2

■ MIKE TRESH

Tresh, Michael b: 2/23/14, Hazleton, Pa. d: 10/4/66, Detroit, Mich. BR/TR, 5'11", 170 lbs. Deb: 9/04/38 F

YEAR	TM/L	G	AB	R	H	2B	3B	HR	RBI	BB	SO	AVG	OBP	SLG	PRO+	BR	/A	RC	SB	CS	SBR	FA	FR	POS	TPR
1938	Chi-A	10	29	3	7	2	0	0	2	8	4	.241	.405	.310	80	-0	-1	4	0	0	0	.978	2	C	0.1
1939	Chi-A	119	352	49	91	5	2	0	38	64	30	.259	.377	.284	70	-12	-13	43	3	2	-0	.985	2	*C	-0.5
1940	Chi-A	135	480	62	135	15	5	1	64	49	40	.281	.349	.340	78	-13	-14	56	3	10	-5	.983	7	*C	-0.1
1941	Chi-A	115	390	38	98	10	1	0	33	38	27	.251	.319	.282	61	-21	-21	36	1	0	0	.981	10	*C	0.0
1942	Chi-A	72	233	21	54	8	1	0	15	28	24	.232	.314	.275	68	-10	-9	22	2	0	1	.977	-6	C	-0.9
1943	Chi-A	86	279	20	60	3	0	0	20	37	20	.215	.307	.226	57	-14	-14	22	2	1	0	.982	-1	C	-0.9
1944	Chi-A	93	312	22	81	8	1	0	25	37	15	.260	.342	.292	83	-6	-5	32	0	3	-2	.981	-3	C	-0.4
1945	Chi-A†	150	458	50	114	12	0	0	47	65	37	.249	.342	.275	82	-9	-8	48	6	3	0	.984	-2	*C	-0.1
1946	Chi-A	80	217	28	47	5	2	0	21	36	24	.217	.336	.258	70	-8	-7	21	0	2	-1	.995	14	C	1.0
1947	Chi-A	90	274	19	66	6	2	0	20	26	26	.241	.311	.277	67	-13	-11	24	2	0	1	.975	-7	C	-1.3
1948	Chi-A	39	108	10	27	1	0	1	11	9	9	.250	.308	.287	61	-6	-6	10	0	0	0	.983	-1	C	-0.5
1949	Cle-A	38	37	4	8	0	0	0	1	5	7	.216	.310	.216	41	-3	-3	3	0	0	0	1.000	6	C	0.3
Total	12	1027	3169	326	788	75	14	2	297	402	263	.249	.335	.283	71	-115	-112	322	19	21	-7	.983	22	*C	-3.3

■ TOM TRESH

Tresh, Thomas Michael b: 9/20/37, Detroit, Mich. BB/TR, 6', 191 lbs. Deb: 9/03/61 F

YEAR	TM/L	G	AB	R	H	2B	3B	HR	RBI	BB	SO	AVG	OBP	SLG	PRO+	BR	/A	RC	SB	CS	SBR	FA	FR	POS	TPR
1961	NY-A	9	8	1	2	0	0	0	0	0	1	.250	.250	.250	36	-1	-1	0	0	0	0	1.000	3	/S	0.2
1962	*NY-A★	157	622	94	178	26	5	20	93	67	74	.286	.363	.441	119	14	16	103	4	8	-4	.970	-11	*SO	0.9
1963	*NY-A★	145	520	91	140	28	5	25	71	83	79	.269	.374	.487	140	29	29	100	3	3	-1	.981	2	*O	2.4
1964	*NY-A	153	533	75	131	25	5	16	73	73	110	.246	.344	.402	105	6	5	78	13	0	4	**.996**	-14	*O	-1.3
1965	NY-A	156	602	94	168	29	6	26	74	59	92	.279	.348	.477	133	24	25	101	5	2	0	.970	-21	*O	-0.3
1966	NY-A	151	537	76	125	12	4	27	68	86	89	.233	.345	.421	123	15	17	81	5	4	-1	.985	28	O3	4.1
1967	NY-A	130	448	45	98	23	3	14	53	50	86	.219	.303	.377	104	-0	2	51	1	0	0	.972	4	*O	-0.1
1968	NY-A	152	507	60	99	18	3	11	52	76	97	.195	.305	.308	89	-7	-5	51	10	5	0	.951	9	*SO	1.7
1969	NY-A	45	143	13	26	5	2	1	9	17	23	.182	.269	.266	52	-10	-9	11	2	1	0	.980	0	S	-0.5
	Det-A	94	331	46	74	13	1	13	37	39	47	.224	.309	.387	90	-3	-5	41	2	2	-1	.965	-18	SO/3	-1.7
	Yr	139	474	59	100	18	3	14	46	56	70	.211	.297	.350	79	-13	-14	51	4	3	-1	.971	-18	*SO/3	-2.2
Total	9	1192	4251	595	1041	179	34	153	530	550	698	.245	.337	.411	113	66	74	618	45	25	-2	.979	-19	OS/3	5.4

■ ALEX TREVINO

Trevino, Alejandro (Castro) b: 8/26/57, Monterrey, Mex. BR/TR, 5'11", 170 lbs. Deb: 9/11/78 F

YEAR	TM/L	G	AB	R	H	2B	3B	HR	RBI	BB	SO	AVG	OBP	SLG	PRO+	BR	/A	RC	SB	CS	SBR	FA	FR	POS	TPR
1978	NY-N	6	12	3	3	0	0	0	0	1	2	.250	.308	.250	60	-1	-1	1	0	0	0	1.000	0	/C3	-0.1
1979	NY-N	79	207	24	56	11	1	0	20	20	27	.271	.338	.333	87	-4	-3	22	2	2	-1	.976	10	C3/2	0.8
1980	NY-N	106	355	26	91	11	2	0	37	13	41	.256	.285	.299	65	-18	-17	27	0	3	-2	.977	-5	C3/2	-2.2
1981	NY-N	56	149	17	39	2	0	0	10	13	19	.262	.325	.275	73	-5	-5	14	3	0	1	.963	3	C/2O3	0.0
1982	Cin-N	120	355	24	89	10	3	1	33	34	34	.251	.321	.304	74	-11	-11	33	3	1	0	.979	4	*C/3	-0.3
1983	Cin-N	74	167	14	36	8	1	1	13	17	20	.216	.288	.293	59	-9	-9	14	0	0	0	.987	11	C/32	0.4
1984	Cin-N	6	6	0	1	0	0	0	0	0	2	.167	.167	.167	-6	-1	-1	0	0	0	0	1.000	-0	/C	-0.1
	Atl-N	79	266	36	65	16	0	3	28	16	27	.244	.290	.338	71	-9	-11	26	5	2	0	.989	7	C	-0.1
	Yr	85	272	36	66	16	0	3	28	16	29	.243	.287	.335	69	-10	-12	26	5	2	0	.989	6	C	-0.2
1985	SF-N	57	157	17	34	10	1	6	19	20	24	.217	.305	.408	103	-1	0	19	0	0	0	.978	-0	C/3	0.2
1986	LA-N	89	202	31	53	13	0	4	26	27	35	.262	.352	.386	111	1	3	28	0	0	0	.969	-4	C/1	0.3
1987	LA-N	72	144	16	32	7	1	3	16	6	28	.222	.273	.347	65	-8	-7	12	1	0	0	.987	-3	C/O3	-0.8
1988	Hou-N	78	193	19	48	17	0	2	13	24	29	.249	.341	.368	108	1	2	24	5	2	0	.977	-9	C/O	-0.2
1989	Hou-N	59	131	15	38	7	1	2	16	7	18	.290	.331	.405	113	1	2	17	0	0	0	.989	-3	C/13	0.0
1990	Hou-N	42	69	3	13	3	0	1	10	6	11	.188	.273	.275	53	-5	-4	5	0	1	-1	.992	6	C/1	0.2
	NY-N	9	10	0	3	1	0	0	2	1	0	.300	.364	.400	110	0	0	2	0	0	0	.929	0	/C	0.1
	Cin-N	7	7	0	3	1	0	0	1	0	0	.429	.500	.571	186	1	1	2	0	0	0	1.000	1	/C	0.2
	Yr	58	86	3	19	5	0	1	13	7	11	.221	.302	.314	71	-3	-3	8	0	1	-1	.982	7	C/1	0.5
Total	13	939	2430	245	604	117	10	23	244	205	317	.249	.312	.333	81	-65	-61	247	19	11	-1	.979	17	C/3201	-1.6

■ BOBBY TREVINO

Trevino, Carlos (Castro) b: 8/15/43, Monterrey, Mexico BR/TR, 6'2", 185 lbs. Deb: 5/22/68 F

YEAR	TM/L	G	AB	R	H	2B	3B	HR	RBI	BB	SO	AVG	OBP	SLG	PRO+	BR	/A	RC	SB	CS	SBR	FA	FR	POS	TPR
1968	Cal-A	17	40	1	9	1	0	0	1	2	9	.225	.262	.250	58	-2	-2	3	0	1	-1	.962	-0	O	-0.4

■ GUS TRIANDOS

Triandos, Gus b: 7/30/30, San Francisco, Cal BR/TR, 6'3", 215 lbs. Deb: 8/13/53

YEAR	TM/L	G	AB	R	H	2B	3B	HR	RBI	BB	SO	AVG	OBP	SLG	PRO+	BR	/A	RC	SB	CS	SBR	FA	FR	POS	TPR
1953	NY-A	18	51	5	8	2	0	1	6	3	9	.157	.204	.255	24	-6	-5	3	0	0	0	.991	0	1/C	-0.6
1954	NY-A	2	1	0	0	0	0	0	0	0	1	.000	.000	.000	-99	-0	-0	0	0	0	0	.000	0	/C	0.0
1955	Bal-A	140	481	47	133	17	3	12	65	40	55	.277	.335	.399	104	-3	1	64	0	0	0	.989	0	*1C/3	-0.3
1956	Bal-A	131	452	47	126	18	1	21	88	48	73	.279	.351	.462	122	7	12	68	0	0	0	.989	10	C1	2.1
1957	Bal-A☆	129	418	44	106	21	1	19	72	38	73	.254	.320	.445	114	3	6	58	0	0	0	.992	-2	*C	0.9
1958	Bal-A★	137	474	59	116	10	0	30	79	60	65	.245	.331	.456	120	8	12	67	1	0	0	.987	1	*C	2.1
1959	Bal-A★	126	393	43	85	7	1	25	73	65	56	.216	.332	.430	110	4	5	57	0	0	0	.981	2	*C	1.4
1960	Bal-A	109	364	36	98	18	0	12	54	41	62	.269	.345	.418	107	3	3	52	0	0	0	.989	-7	*C	0.2
1961	Bal-A	115	397	35	97	21	0	17	63	44	60	.244	.321	.426	100	-2	-1	52	0	0	0	.989	5	*C	0.9
1962	Bal-A	66	207	20	33	7	0	6	23	29	43	.159	.263	.280	48	-16	-15	15	0	0	0	.985	-1	C	-1.4
1963	Det-A	106	327	28	78	13	0	14	41	32	67	.239	.318	.407	98	1	-1	41	0	0	0	**.998**	-6	C	-0.3
1964	Phi-N	73	188	17	47	9	0	8	33	26	41	.250	.344	.426	117	4	4	27	0	0	0	.985	2	C/1	1.0
1965	Phi-N	30	82	3	14	2	0	0	4	9	17	.171	.253	.195	29	-8	-7	4	0	0	0	.975	-5	C	-1.3
	Hou-N	24	72	5	13	2	0	2	7	5	14	.181	.244	.292	54	-5	-4	5	0	0	0	.970	-2	C	-0.5
	Yr	54	154	8	27	4	0	2	11	14	31	.175	.249	.240	40	-12	-12	9	0	0	0	.973	-7	C	-1.8
Total	13	1206	3907	389	954	147	6	167	608	440	636	.244	.324	.413	103	-10	9	514	1	0	0	.987	-2	C1/3	4.2

■ MANNY TRILLO

Trillo, Jesus Manuel Marcano (b: Jesus Manuel Marcano (Trillo)) b: 12/25/50, Caripito, Ven. BR/TR, 6'1", 164 lbs. Deb: 6/28/73

YEAR	TM/L	G	AB	R	H	2B	3B	HR	RBI	BB	SO	AVG	OBP	SLG	PRO+	BR	/A	RC	SB	CS	SBR	FA	FR	POS	TPR
1973	Oak-A	17	12	0	3	2	0	0	3	0	4	.250	.250	.417	90	-0	-0	1	0	0	0	.941	5	2	0.5

YEAR	TM/L	G	AB	R	H	2B	3B	HR	RBI	BB	SO	AVG	OBP	SLG	PRO+	BR	/A	RC	SB	CS	SBR	FA	FR	POS	TPR
1974	*Oak-A	21	33	3	5	0	0	0	2	2	8	.152	.222	.152	10	-4	-4	1	0	0	0	.949	6	2	0.3
1975	Chi-N	154	545	55	135	12	2	7	70	45	78	.248	.309	.316	70	-19	-22	53	1	7	-4	.967	16	*2/S	-0.2
1976	Chi-N	158	582	42	139	24	3	4	59	53	70	.239	.306	.311	69	-18	-25	55	17	6	2	.981	18	*2/S	0.6
1977	Chi-N★	152	504	51	141	18	5	7	57	44	58	.280	.344	.377	84	-4	-11	62	3	5	-2	.970	30	*2	2.7
1978	Chi-N	152	552	53	144	17	5	4	55	50	67	.261	.325	.332	75	-11	-19	59	0	7	-4	.978	**29**	*2	1.7
1979	Phi-N	118	431	40	112	22	1	6	42	20	59	.260	.299	.357	76	-14	-15	42	4	7	-3	.985	6	*2	-0.5
1980	*Phi-N	141	531	68	155	25	9	7	43	32	46	.292	.336	.412	102	5	1	70	8	3	1	.987	19	*2	3.1
1981	*Phi-N★	94	349	37	100	14	3	6	36	26	37	.287	.341	.395	104	4	2	48	10	4	1	.987	11	2	2.0
1982	Phi-N★	149	549	52	149	24	1	0	39	33	53	.271	.316	.319	76	-16	-17	52	8	10	-4	**.994**	5	*2	-0.8
1983	Cle-A★	88	320	33	87	13	1	1	29	21	46	.272	.317	.328	75	-9	-11	30	1	3	-2	.989	3	2	-0.5
	Mon-N	31	121	16	32	8	0	2	16	10	18	.264	.331	.380	97	-1	-0	16	0	0	0	.979	-6	2	-0.5
1984	SF-N	98	401	45	102	21	1	4	36	25	55	.254	.303	.342	84	-11	-9	41	0	0	0	.988	-8	2/3	-1.4
1985	SF-N	125	451	36	101	16	2	3	25	40	44	.224	.289	.288	65	-23	-20	40	2	0	1	.981	4	*2/3	-1.2
1986	Chi-N	81	152	22	45	10	0	1	19	16	21	.296	.363	.382	98	1	0	21	0	2	-1	.949	-0	31/2	-0.2
1987	Chi-N	108	214	27	63	8	0	8	26	25	37	.294	.368	.444	110	5	3	34	0	3	-2	.994	-4	132/S	-0.5
1988	Chi-N	76	164	15	41	5	0	1	14	8	32	.250	.285	.299	65	-7	-8	15	2	0	1	.994	1	132/S	-0.7
1989	Cin-N	17	39	3	8	0	0	0	0	2	9	.205	.262	.205	34	-3	-3	2	0	0	0	1.000	-4	2/1S	-0.8
Total	17	1780	5950	598	1562	239	33	61	571	452	742	.263	.318	.345	80	-126	-159	641	56	57	-17	.981	129	*23/1S	3.6

■ **COAKER TRIPLETT** Triplett, Herman Coaker b: 12/18/11, Boone, N.C. d: 1/30/92, Boone, N.C. BR/TR, 5′11″, 185 lbs. Deb: 4/19/38

YEAR	TM/L	G	AB	R	H	2B	3B	HR	RBI	BB	SO	AVG	OBP	SLG	PRO+	BR	/A	RC	SB	CS	SBR	FA	FR	POS	TPR
1938	Chi-N	12	36	4	9	2	1	0	2	0	1	.250	.250	.361	65	-2	-2	3	0			1.000	-1	/O	-0.3
1941	StL-N	76	185	29	53	6	3	3	21	18	27	.286	.350	.400	104	3	1	25	0			.965	-3	O	-0.4
1942	StL-N	64	154	18	42	7	4	1	23	17	15	.273	.345	.390	107	3	2	20	1			.966	-3	O	-0.4
1943	StL-N	9	25	1	2	0	0	1	4	1	6	.080	.115	.200	-9	-4	-4	0	0			1.000	-0	/O	-0.5
	Phi-N	105	360	45	98	16	4	14	52	28	28	.272	.325	.456	129	9	11	52	2			.970	1	O	0.8
	Yr	114	385	46	100	16	4	15	56	29	34	.260	.312	.439	120	5	7	51	2			.972	1	O	0.3
1944	Phi-N	84	184	15	43	5	1	1	25	19	10	.234	.305	.288	70	-8	-7	15	1			.989	-1	O	-1.0
1945	Phi-N	120	363	36	87	11	1	7	46	40	27	.240	.315	.333	83	-10	-8	39	6			.945	-3	O	-1.6
Total	6	470	1307	148	334	47	14	27	173	123	114	.256	.320	.375	97	-8	-8	155	10			.965	-9	O	-3.4

■ **HAL TROSKY** Trosky, Harold Arthur Sr. (b: Harold Arthur Troyavesky Sr.)
b: 11/11/12, Norway, Iowa d: 6/18/79, Cedar Rapids, Ia. BL/TR, 6′2″, 207 lbs. Deb: 9/11/33 F

YEAR	TM/L	G	AB	R	H	2B	3B	HR	RBI	BB	SO	AVG	OBP	SLG	PRO+	BR	/A	RC	SB	CS	SBR	FA	FR	POS	TPR
1933	Cle-A	11	44	6	13	1	2	1	8	2	12	.295	.340	.477	110	1	0	7	0	0	0	.990	-1	1	-0.1
1934	Cle-A	154	625	117	206	45	9	35	142	58	49	.330	.388	.598	149	44	42	145	2	2	-1	.986	0	*1	2.6
1935	Cle-A	154	632	84	171	33	7	26	113	46	60	.271	.321	.468	100	-2	-4	94	1	2	-1	.993	1	*1	-1.9
1936	Cle-A	151	629	124	216	45	9	42	**162**	36	58	.343	.382	.644	148	42	41	150	6	5	-1	.985	1	*1/2	2.3
1937	Cle-A	153	601	104	179	36	9	32	128	65	60	.298	.367	.547	127	22	22	122	3	1	0	.993	-2	*1	0.2
1938	Cle-A	150	554	106	185	40	9	19	110	67	40	.334	.407	.542	138	30	31	125	5	1	1	.993	4	*1	1.8
1939	Cle-A	122	448	89	150	31	4	25	104	52	28	.335	.405	.589	157	33	35	108	2	3	-1	.992	11	*1	3.0
1940	Cle-A	140	522	85	154	39	4	25	93	79	45	.295	.392	.529	140	28	31	116	1	2	-1	.991	-7	*1	0.9
1941	Cle-A	89	310	43	91	17	0	11	51	44	21	.294	.383	.455	127	10	12	57	1	2	-1	.989	-3	1	0.2
1944	Chi-A	135	497	55	120	32	2	10	70	62	30	.241	.327	.374	101	-0	1	62	3	2	-0	.993	-9	*1	-1.7
1946	Chi-A	88	299	22	76	12	3	2	31	34	37	.254	.330	.334	89	-5	-4	33	4	3	-1	.991	-8	1	-1.8
Total	11	1347	5161	835	1561	331	58	228	1012	545	440	.302	.371	.522	130	202	208	1018	28	23	-5		-12	*1/2	5.5

■ **MIKE TROST** Trost, Michael J. b: 1866, Philadelphia, Pa. d: 3/24/01, Philadelphia, Pa. TR, 6′0.5″, 180 lbs. Deb: 8/21/1890

YEAR	TM/L	G	AB	R	H	2B	3B	HR	RBI	BB	SO	AVG	OBP	SLG	PRO+	BR	/A	RC	SB	CS	SBR	FA	FR	POS	TPR
1890	StL-a	17	51	10	13	2	0	1		6		.255	.345	.353	95	1	-1	8	4			.890	1	C/O	0.0
1895	Lou-N	3	12	1	1	0	0	0	1	0	1	.083	.083	.083	-60	-3	-3	0	1			1.000	-1	/1	-0.3
Total	2	20	63	11	14	2	0	1	1	6	1	.222	.300	.302	68	-2	-3	8	5				0	/CO1	-0.3

■ **SAM TROTT** Trott, Samuel W. b: 3/1859, Maryland d: 6/5/25, Catonsville, Md. BL/TL, 5′9″, 190 lbs. Deb: 5/29/1880 M

YEAR	TM/L	G	AB	R	H	2B	3B	HR	RBI	BB	SO	AVG	OBP	SLG	PRO+	BR	/A	RC	SB	CS	SBR	FA	FR	POS	TPR
1880	Bos-N	39	125	14	26	4	1	0	9	3	5	.208	.227	.256	65	-5	-4	7				.893	6	C/O	0.3
1881	Det-N	6	25	3	5	2	1	0	2	1	3	.200	.231	.360	80	-1	-1	2				.868	-2	/C	-0.3
1882	Det-N	32	129	11	31	7	1	0	12	0	13	.240	.240	.310	75	-4	-4	10				.890	7	C/S2103	0.3
1883	Det-N	75	295	27	72	14	1	0	29	10	23	.244	.269	.298	76	-10	-7	24				.882	-17	2C/O1	-1.9
1884	Bal-a	71	284	36	73	17	9	3		4		.257	.272	.412	118	6	5	33				.931	16	C/2O	2.4
1885	Bal-a	21	88	12	24	2	2	0		5		.273	.312	.341	110	1	1	10				.882	-5	C/O2S	-0.2
1887	Bal-a	85	300	44	77	16	3	0		27		.257	.322	.330	89	-6	-3	35	8			.915	5	C2/O1S	0.7
1888	Bal-a	31	108	19	30	11	4	0	22	4		.278	.304	.454	148	5	5	16	1			.908	-4	C/O21	0.3
Total	8	360	1354	166	338	73	22	3	74	54	44	.250	.280	.343	95	-12	-7	137	9			.906	6	C/2O1S3	1.6

■ **QUINCY TROUPPE** Trouppe, Quincy Thomas b: 12/25/12, Dublin, Ga. BB/TR, 6′2.5″, 225 lbs. Deb: 4/30/52

YEAR	TM/L	G	AB	R	H	2B	3B	HR	RBI	BB	SO	AVG	OBP	SLG	PRO+	BR	/A	RC	SB	CS	SBR	FA	FR	POS	TPR
1952	Cle-A	6	10	1	1	0	0	0	0	1	3	.100	.182	.100	-22	-2	-2	0	0	0	0	1.000	2	/C	0.1

■ **DASHER TROY** Troy, John Joseph b: 5/8/1856, New York, N.Y. d: 3/30/38, Ozone Park, N.Y. BR/TR, Deb: 8/23/1881

YEAR	TM/L	G	AB	R	H	2B	3B	HR	RBI	BB	SO	AVG	OBP	SLG	PRO+	BR	/A	RC	SB	CS	SBR	FA	FR	POS	TPR
1881	Det-N	11	44	2	15	3	0	0	4	3	8	.341	.383	.409	143	3	2	7				.792	-4	/32	-0.1
1882	Det-N	40	152	22	37	7	2	0	14	5	10	.243	.268	.316	86	-2	-2	13				.847	-19	2S	-1.9
	Pro-N	4	17	1	4	0	0	0	1	0	1	.235	.235	.235	52	-1	-1	1				.750	-1	/S	-0.2
	Yr	44	169	23	41	7	2	0	15	5	11	.243	.264	.308	83	-3	-3	14				.847	-21	2S	-2.1
1883	NY-N	85	316	37	68	7	5	0	20	9	33	.215	.237	.269	54	-17	-17	21				.879	-14	*2S	-2.6
1884	*NY-a	107	421	80	111	22	10	2		19		.264	.300	.378	126	10	12	49				.879	-21	*2	-0.6
1885	NY-a	45	177	24	39	3	3	2		5		.220	.258	.305	86	-4	-2	14				.866	-13	2/OS	-1.2
Total	5	292	1127	166	274	42	20	4	39	41	52	.243	.274	.327	93	-12	-8	105				.873	-72	2/S3O	-6.6

■ **FRED TRUAX** Truax, Frederick W. b: 1868, d: 12/18/1899, Omaha, Neb. Deb: 8/18/1890

YEAR	TM/L	G	AB	R	H	2B	3B	HR	RBI	BB	SO	AVG	OBP	SLG	PRO+	BR	/A	RC	SB	CS	SBR	FA	FR	POS	TPR
1890	Pit-N	1	3	0	1	0	0	0	1	1	1	.333	.500	.333	167	0	0	1	0			1.000	0	/O	0.0

■ **HARRY TRUBY** Truby, Harry Garvin "Bird Eye" b: 5/12/1870, Ironton, Ohio d: 3/21/53, Ironton, Ohio TR, 5′11″, 185 lbs. Deb: 8/21/1895 U

YEAR	TM/L	G	AB	R	H	2B	3B	HR	RBI	BB	SO	AVG	OBP	SLG	PRO+	BR	/A	RC	SB	CS	SBR	FA	FR	POS	TPR
1895	Chi-N	33	119	17	40	3	0	0	16	10	7	.336	.402	.361	94	1	-1	21	7			.950	0	2	0.1
1896	Chi-N	29	109	13	28	2	2	2	31	6	5	.257	.314	.367	78	-3	-4	14	4			.935	0	2	-0.2
	Pit-N	8	32	1	5	0	0	0	3	2	4	.156	.206	.156	-3	-5	-4	1	1			.949	-3	/2	-0.6
	Yr	37	141	14	33	2	2	2	34	8	9	.234	.289	.319	61	-8	-8	15	5			.938	-3	2	-0.8
Total	2	70	260	31	73	5	2	2	50	18	16	.281	.342	.338	76	-7	-9	37	12			.944	-3	/2	-0.7

■ **FRANK TRUESDALE** Truesdale, Frank Day b: 3/31/1884, St.Louis, Mo. d: 8/27/43, Albuquerque, N.M. BB/TR, 5′8″, 145 lbs. Deb: 4/27/10

YEAR	TM/L	G	AB	R	H	2B	3B	HR	RBI	BB	SO	AVG	OBP	SLG	PRO+	BR	/A	RC	SB	CS	SBR	FA	FR	POS	TPR
1910	StL-A	123	415	39	91	7	2	1	25	48		.219	.303	.253	79	-11	-8	40	29			.914	-8	*2	-2.0
1911	StL-A	1	0	1	0	0	0	0	0	0		—	—	—	—	0	0	0	0			.000	0	R	0.0
1914	NY-A	77	217	22	46	4	0	0	13	39	35	.212	.340	.230	72	-5	-5	18	11	11	-3	.947	-2	2/3	-1.2
1918	Bos-A	15	36	6	10	1	0	0	2	4	5	.278	.350	.306	100	0	0	4	1			.913	-1	2	0.0
Total	4	216	668	68	147	12	2	1	40	91	40	.220	.318	.249	78	-16	-13	63	41	11		.924	-11	2/3	-3.2

■ **ED TRUMBULL** Trumbull, Edward J. (b: Edward J. Trembly) b: 11/3/1860, Chicopee, Mass. d: 1/14/37, Kingston, Pa. Deb: 5/10/1884

YEAR	TM/L	G	AB	R	H	2B	3B	HR	RBI	BB	SO	AVG	OBP	SLG	PRO+	BR	/A	RC	SB	CS	SBR	FA	FR	POS	TPR
1884	Was-a	25	86	5	10	2	0	0		2		.116	.136	.140	-10	-10	-8	2				.828	-0	OP	-0.4

YEAR	TM/L	G	AB	R	H	2B	3B	HR	RBI	BB	SO	AVG	OBP	SLG	PRO+	BR	/A	RC	SB	CS	SBR	FA	FR	POS	TPR

■ EDDIE TUCKER Tucker, Eddie Jack "Scooter" b: 11/18/66, Greenville, Miss. BR/TR, 6'2", 205 lbs. Deb: 6/14/92

| 1992 | Hou-N | 20 | 50 | 5 | 6 | 1 | 0 | 0 | 3 | 3 | 13 | .120 | .200 | .140 | -2 | -7 | -6 | 1 | 1 | 1 | -0 | .976 | -6 | C | -1.3 |

■ OLLIE TUCKER Tucker, Oliver Dinwiddie b: 1/27/02, Radiant, Va. d: 7/13/40, Radiant, Va. BL/TR, 5'11", 180 lbs. Deb: 4/17/27

1927	Was-A	20	24	1	5	2	0	0	8	4	2	.208	.321	.292	61	-1	-1	3	0	0	0	1.000	-0	/O	-0.2
1928	Cle-A	14	47	5	6	0	0	1	2	7	3	.128	.255	.191	19	-6	-6	2	0	2	-1	1.000	-0	O	-0.8
Total	2	34	71	6	11	2	0	1	10	11	5	.155	.277	.225	33	-7	-7	5	0	2	-1	1.000	-1	/O	-1.0

■ TOMMY TUCKER Tucker, Thomas Joseph "Foghorn" b: 10/28/1863, Holyoke, Mass. d: 10/22/35, Montague, Mass. BB/TR, 5'11", 165 lbs. Deb: 4/16/1887

1887	Bal-a	136	524	114	144	15	9	6		29		.275	.347	.372	109	3	9	100	85			.976	4	*1	-0.1
1888	Bal-a	136	520	74	149	17	12	6	61	16		.287	.330	.400	141	20	22	85	43			.975	4	*1/OP	1.3
1889	Bal-a	134	527	103	196	22	11	5	99	42	26	.372	.450	.484	166	50	48	147	63			.964	-1	*1O	3.3
1890	Bos-N	132	539	104	159	17	8	1	62	56	22	.295	.387	.362	112	18	10	94	43			.979	-2	*1	0.2
1891	Bos-N	140	548	103	148	16	5	2	69	37	30	.270	.349	.328	89	2	-9	74	26			.976	-3	*1/P	-1.6
1892	*Bos-N	149	542	85	153	15	7	1	62	45	35	.282	.365	.341	106	13	5	78	22			.972	-12	*1	-1.2
1893	Bos-N	121	486	83	138	13	2	7	91	27	31	.284	.347	.362	84	-7	-13	65	8			.980	-11	*1	-2.3
1894	Bos-N	123	500	112	165	24	6	3	100	53	21	.330	.412	.420	95	5	-3	97	18			.985	2	*1/O	0.0
1895	Bos-N	125	462	87	115	19	6	3	73	61	29	.249	.360	.335	76	-10	-17	64	15			.978	6	*1	-0.7
1896	Bos-N	122	474	74	144	27	5	2	72	30	29	.304	.363	.395	96	1	-3	73	6			.985	3	*1	0.1
1897	Bos-N	4	14	0	3	2	0	0	4	2		.214	.313	.357	72	-1	-1	2	0			.957	1	/1	0.0
	Was-N	93	352	52	119	18	5	5	61	27		.338	.403	.460	128	14	14	75	18			.984	-3	*1	1.0
	Yr	97	366	52	122	20	5	5	65	29		.333	.399	.456	126	14	14	76	18			.982	-3	1	1.0
1898	Bro-N	73	283	35	79	9	4	1	34	12		.279	.325	.350	94	-3	-3	34	1			.991	7	1	0.4
	StL-N	72	252	18	60	7	2	0	20	18		.238	.319	.282	71	-8	-9	24	1			.973	-0	1	-0.9
	Yr	145	535	53	139	16	6	1	54	30		.260	.322	.318	83	-11	-12	58	2			.982	7	*1	-0.5
1899	Cle-N	127	456	40	110	19	3	0	40	24		.241	.297	.296	68	-23	-18	43	3			.977	-1	*1	-1.7
Total	13	1687	6479	1084	1882	240	85	42	848	479	223	.290	.364	.373	103	74	33	1053	352			.978	-8	*1/OP	-2.2

■ THURMAN TUCKER Tucker, Thurman Lowell "Joe E." b: 9/26/17, Gordon, Tex. BL/TR, 5'11", 170 lbs. Deb: 4/14/42

1942	Chi-A	7	24	2	3	0	1	0	1	0	4	.125	.125	.208	-7	-3	-3	1	0	0	0	.900	-1	/O	-0.5
1943	Chi-A	139	528	81	124	15	6	3	39	79	72	.235	.336	.303	87	-6	-6	60	29	17	-2	.988	15	*O	0.0
1944	Chi-A★	124	446	59	128	15	6	2	46	57	40	.287	.368	.361	110	7	7	63	13	12	-3	.991	18	*O	1.6
1946	Chi-A	121	438	62	126	20	3	1	36	54	54	.288	.367	.354	106	3	5	61	9	10	-3	.990	2	*O	-0.2
1947	Chi-A	89	254	28	60	9	4	1	17	38	25	.236	.336	.315	85	-6	-4	31	10	4	1	.978	-1	O	-0.8
1948	*Cle-A	83	242	52	63	13	2	1	19	31	17	.260	.347	.343	86	-5	-4	33	11	2	2	1.000	-1	O	-0.6
1949	Cle-A	80	197	28	48	5	2	0	14	18	19	.244	.307	.289	59	-12	-11	19	4	2	0	.984	2	O	-1.1
1950	Cle-A	57	101	13	18	2	0	1	7	14	14	.178	.284	.228	34	-10	-10	8	1	0	0	.968	-5	O	-1.5
1951	Cle-A	1	1	0	0	0	0	0	0	0	1	.000	.000	.000	-99	-0	-0	0	0	0	0	.000	0	H	0.0
Total	9	701	2231	325	570	79	24	9	179	291	237	.255	.342	.325	89	-33	-28	275	77	47	-5	.988	29	O	-3.1

■ JERRY TURBIDY Turbidy, Jeremiah b: 7/4/1852, Dudley, Mass. d: 9/5/20, Webster, Mass. 5'8", 165 lbs. Deb: 7/27/1884

| 1884 | KC-U | 13 | 49 | 5 | 11 | 4 | 0 | 0 | | 3 | | .224 | .269 | .306 | 108 | -0 | 1 | 4 | | | | .830 | 6 | S | 0.6 |

■ EDDIE TURCHIN Turchin, Edward Lawrence "Smiley" b: 2/10/17, New York, N.Y. d: 2/8/82, Brookhaven, N.Y. BR/TR, 5'10", 165 lbs. Deb: 5/09/43

| 1943 | Cle-A | 11 | 13 | 4 | 3 | 0 | 0 | 0 | 1 | 3 | 1 | .231 | .375 | .231 | 84 | -0 | -0 | 1 | 0 | 0 | 0 | 1.000 | 1 | /3S | 0.2 |

■ PETE TURGEON Turgeon, Eugene Joseph b: 1/3/1897, Minneapolis, Minn. d: 1/24/77, Wichita Falls, Tex BR/TR, 5'6", 145 lbs. Deb: 9/20/23

| 1923 | Chi-N | 3 | 6 | 1 | 1 | 0 | 0 | 0 | 0 | 0 | 0 | .167 | .167 | .167 | -12 | -1 | -1 | 0 | 0 | 0 | 0 | .875 | 0 | /S | -0.1 |

■ EARL TURNER Turner, Earl Edwin b: 5/6/23, Pittsfield, Mass. BR/TR, 5'9", 170 lbs. Deb: 9/25/48

1948	Pit-N	2	1	0	0	0	0	0	0	0	0	.000	.000	.000	-98	-0	-0	0	0			.000	0	/C	0.0
1950	Pit-N	40	74	10	18	0	0	3	5	4	13	.243	.282	.365	66	-4	-4	7	1			.974	2	C	-0.1
Total	2	42	75	10	18	0	0	3	5	4	13	.240	.278	.360	64	-4	-4	7	1			.974	2	/C	-0.1

■ TUCK TURNER Turner, George A. b: 2/13/1873, W.New Brighton, N.Y. d: 7/16/45, Staten Island, N.Y. BB/TL, 5'6.5", 155 lbs. Deb: 8/18/1893

1893	Phi-N	36	155	32	50	4	3	1	13	9	19	.323	.364	.406	107	1	1	26	7			.933	-2	O	-0.2
1894	Phi-N	80	339	91	141	21	9	1	82	23	15	.416	.456	.540	145	23	25	91	11			.916	0	O/P	0.8
1895	Phi-N	59	210	51	81	8	6	2	43	25	11	.386	.453	.510	150	17	16	57	14			.847	-8	O	0.4
1896	Phi-N	13	32	12	7	2	0	0	0	8	5	.219	.375	.281	77	-1	-1	6	6			.905	2	/O	0.0
	StL-N	51	203	30	50	7	8	1	27	14	21	.246	.298	.374	82	-7	-6	25	6			.961	-5	O	-1.3
	Yr	64	235	42	57	9	8	1	27	22	26	.243	.310	.362	81	-8	-6	31	12			.948	-4	O	-1.3
1897	StL-N	103	416	58	121	17	12	2	41	35		.291	.350	.404	101	-2	-0	64	8			.945	-7	*O	-1.3
1898	StL-N	35	141	20	28	8	0	0	7	14		.199	.280	.255	53	-8	-9	11	1			.929	-3	O	-1.4
Total	6	377	1496	294	478	67	38	7	213	128	69	.320	.377	.429	112	23	27	280	53			.920	-32	O/P	-3.0

■ JERRY TURNER Turner, John Webber b: 1/17/54, Texarkana, Ark. BL/TL, 5'9", 180 lbs. Deb: 9/02/74

1974	SD-N	17	48	4	14	1	0	0	2	3	5	.292	.333	.313	85	-1	-1	5	2	1	0	1.000	-2	O	-0.3
1975	SD-N	11	22	1	6	0	0	0	0	2	1	.273	.333	.273	74	-1	-1	2	0	0	0	.909	-0	/O	-0.1
1976	SD-N	105	281	41	75	16	5	5	37	32	38	.267	.342	.413	123	5	8	41	12	6	0	.960	-8	O	-0.3
1977	SD-N	118	289	43	71	16	1	10	48	31	43	.246	.319	.412	105	-3	-1	38	12	4	1	.947	-1	O	-0.1
1978	SD-N	106	225	28	63	9	1	8	37	21	32	.280	.349	.436	128	5	7	34	6	4	-1	.970	-1	O	0.4
1979	SD-N	138	448	55	111	23	2	9	61	34	58	.248	.304	.368	88	-11	-8	50	4	2	0	.958	-7	*O	-2.0
1980	SD-N	85	153	22	44	5	0	3	18	10	18	.288	.339	.379	106	0	1	20	8	3	1	1.000	-3	O	-0.3
1981	SD-N	33	31	5	7	0	0	2	6	4	3	.226	.314	.419	115	0	0	4	0	1	-1	.833	-0	/O	0.0
	Chi-A	10	12	1	2	0	0	0	2	1	7	.167	.231	.167	16	-1	-1	1	0	0	0	1.000	-0	/O	-0.1
1982	Det-A	85	210	21	52	3	0	8	27	20	37	.248	.313	.376	88	-3	-4	25	1	3	-2	.909	-4	DO	-1.0
1983	SD-N	25	23	1	3	0	0	1	8	1	6	.130	.167	.130	-17	-4	-4	0	0	0	0	.000	0	/O	-0.4
Total	10	733	1742	222	448	73	9	45	238	159	245	.257	.322	.387	101	-14	-10	220	45	24	-1	.959	-25	O/D	-4.2

■ SHANE TURNER Turner, Shane Lee b: 1/8/63, Los Angeles, Cal. BL/TR, 5'10", 180 lbs. Deb: 8/19/88

1988	Phi-N	18	35	1	6	0	0	0	1	5	9	.171	.275	.171	30	-3	-3	2	0	0	0	.941	-2	/3S	-0.6
1991	Bal-A	4	1	0	0	0	0	0	0	0	0	.000	.000	.000	-99	-0	-0	0	0	0	0	1.000	0	/2D	0.0
1992	Sea-A	34	74	8	20	5	0	0	5	9	15	.270	.349	.338	93	-0	-0	8	2	1	0	.881	-5	3O	-0.6
Total	3	56	110	9	26	5	0	0	6	14	24	.236	.323	.282	71	-4	-4	10	2	1	0	.898	-7	/3OSD2	-1.2

■ TERRY TURNER Turner, Terrence Lamont "Cotton Top" b: 2/28/1881, Sandy Lake, Pa. d: 7/18/60, Cleveland, Ohio BR/TR, 5'8", 149 lbs. Deb: 8/25/01 C

1901	Pit-N	2	7	0	3	0	0	1	0	0		.429	.429	.429	145	0	0	1	0			.833	1	/3	0.2
1904	Cle-A	111	404	41	95	9	6	1	45	11		.235	.255	.295	74	-13	-12	35	5			.940	3	*S	-0.7
1905	Cle-A	155	586	49	155	16	14	4	72	14		.265	.289	.360	104	1	0	69	17			.945	-25	*S	-2.3
1906	Cle-A	147	584	85	170	27	7	2	62	35		.291	.338	.372	124	14	15	87	27			.960	24	*S	4.7
1907	Cle-A	140	524	57	127	20	7	0	46	19		.242	.272	.307	84	-10	-11	54	27			.950	-3	*S	-1.1
1908	Cle-A	60	201	21	48	11	1	0	19	15		.239	.298	.303	95	-1	-1	23	18			.952	-4	OS	-0.7
1909	Cle-A	53	208	25	52	7	4	0	16	19		.250	.304	.322	94	-1	-2	24	14			.969	10	2S	0.9
1910	Cle-A	150	574	71	132	14	3	6	33	53		.230	.301	.275	79	-12	-13	57	31			.973	2	S3/2	-0.7
1911	Cle-A	117	417	59	105	16	3	0	28	34		.252	.310	.333	78	-12	-13	52	29			.970	2	32S	-1.0

YEAR	TM/L	G	AB	R	H	2B	3B	HR	RBI	BB	SO	AVG	OBP	SLG	PRO+	BR	/A	RC	SB	CS	SBR	FA	FR	POS	TPR
1912	Cle-A	103	370	54	114	14	4	0	33	31		.308	.363	.368	106	5	3	57	19			**.951**	-3	*3	0.1
1913	Cle-A	120	388	60	96	13	4	0	44	55	35	.247	.348	.302	88	-3	-4	48	13			.954	16	32S	1.5
1914	Cle-A	121	428	43	105	14	9	1	33	44	36	.245	.319	.327	91	-3	-5	50	17	13	-3	**.963**	21	*32	1.8
1915	Cle-A	75	262	35	66	14	1	0	14	29	13	.252	.329	.313	90	-2	-3	29	12	11	-3	.965	-9	23	-1.4
1916	Cle-A	124	428	52	112	15	3	0	38	40	29	.262	.325	.311	86	-5	-8	52	15			.963	5	32	0.2
1917	Cle-A	69	180	16	37	7	0	0	15	14	19	.206	.263	.244	51	-10	-11	13	4			.980	-2	32/S	-1.4
1918	Cle-A	74	233	24	58	7	2	0	23	22	15	.249	.316	.296	77	-4	-7	24	6			.969	-4	32/S	-0.9
1919	Phi-A	38	127	7	24	3	0	0	6	5	9	.189	.220	.213	21	-13	-13	6	2			.946	1	S2/3	-1.1
Total	17	1659	5921	699	1499	207	77	8	528	435	156	.253	.308	.318	89	-69	-84	681	256	24		.952	37	S32/O	-1.9

■ TOM TURNER Turner, Thomas Richard b: 9/8/16, Custer Co., Okla. d: 5/14/86, Kennewick, Wash. BR/TR, 6'2", 195 lbs. Deb: 4/25/40

YEAR	TM/L	G	AB	R	H	2B	3B	HR	RBI	BB	SO	AVG	OBP	SLG	PRO+	BR	/A	RC	SB	CS	SBR	FA	FR	POS	TPR
1940	Chi-A	37	96	11	20	1	2	0	6	3	12	.208	.240	.260	29	-10	-10	6	1	0	0	.969	2	C	-0.6
1941	Chi-A	38	126	7	30	5	0	0	8	9	15	.238	.289	.278	51	-9	-9	10	2	0	1	.979	5	C	0.0
1942	Chi-A	56	182	18	44	9	1	3	21	19	15	.242	.313	.352	89	-3	-3	21	0	1	-1	.971	-1	C	0.0
1943	Chi-A	51	154	16	37	7	1	2	11	13	21	.240	.299	.338	86	-3	-3	15	1	0	0	.978	4	C	0.5
1944	Chi-A	36	113	9	26	6	0	2	13	5	16	.230	.263	.336	71	-5	-5	8	0	1	-1	.958	-2	C	-0.6
	*StL-A	15	25	2	8	1	0	0	4	2	5	.320	.370	.360	103	0	0	3	0	0	0	.969	-1	C	0.0
	Yr	51	138	11	34	7	0	2	17	7	21	.246	.283	.341	77	-4	-5	11	0	1	-1	.960	-3	C	-0.6
Total	5	233	696	63	165	29	4	7	63	51	84	.237	.290	.320	70	-30	-29	63	4	2	0	.972	7	C	-0.7

■ BILL TUTTLE Tuttle, William Robert b: 7/4/29, Elwood, Ill. BR/TR, 6', 190 lbs. Deb: 9/10/52

YEAR	TM/L	G	AB	R	H	2B	3B	HR	RBI	BB	SO	AVG	OBP	SLG	PRO+	BR	/A	RC	SB	CS	SBR	FA	FR	POS	TPR
1952	Det-A	7	25	2	6	0	0	0	2	0	1	.240	.240	.240	34	-2	-2	1	0	0	0	1.000	1	/O	-0.2
1954	Det-A	147	530	64	141	20	11	7	58	62	60	.266	.345	.385	102	-0	1	69	5	8	-3	.985	4	*O	-0.5
1955	Det-A	154	603	102	168	23	4	14	78	76	54	.279	.360	.400	107	4	6	85	6	3	0	.985	15	*O	1.4
1956	Det-A	140	546	61	138	22	4	9	65	38	48	.253	.303	.357	73	-22	-22	55	5	4	-1	.976	10	*O	-2.0
1957	Det-A	133	451	49	113	12	4	5	47	44	41	.251	.319	.328	75	-14	-15	45	2	6	-3	.982	4	*O	-2.2
1958	KC-A	148	511	77	118	14	9	11	51	74	58	.231	.329	.358	88	-7	-8	59	7	9	-3	.988	1	*O	-1.8
1959	KC-A	126	463	74	139	19	6	7	43	48	38	.300	.371	.413	113	10	9	71	10	6	-1	.984	12	*O	1.4
1960	KC-A	151	559	75	143	21	3	8	40	66	52	.256	.337	.347	85	-10	-11	64	1	5	-3	.988	17	*O	-0.4
1961	KC-A	25	84	15	22	2	2	0	8	9	9	.262	.333	.333	79	-2	-2	10	0	0	0	.951	-1	O	-0.5
	Min-A	113	370	38	91	12	3	5	38	43	41	.246	.324	.335	73	-12	-15	39	1	3	-2	.943	-13	3O/2	-3.0
	Yr	138	454	53	113	14	5	5	46	52	50	.249	.326	.335	74	-14	-17	49	1	3	-2	.970	-14	O3/2	-3.5
1962	Min-A	110	123	21	26	4	1	1	13	19	14	.211	.322	.285	62	-6	-6	12	1	0	0	.973	-16	*O	-2.5
1963	Min-A	16	3	0	0	0	0	0	0	1	0	.000	.250	.000	-22	-0	-0	0	0	0	0	1.000	-4	O	-0.5
Total	11	1270	4268	578	1105	149	47	67	443	480	416	.259	.336	.363	88	-61	-66	509	38	44	-15	.983	29	*O/32	-10.8

■ GUY TUTWILER Tutwiler, Guy Isbell "King Tut" b: 7/17/1889, Coalburg, Ala. d: 8/15/30, Birmingham, Ala. BL/TR, 6', 175 lbs. Deb: 8/29/11

YEAR	TM/L	G	AB	R	H	2B	3B	HR	RBI	BB	SO	AVG	OBP	SLG	PRO+	BR	/A	RC	SB	CS	SBR	FA	FR	POS	TPR
1911	Det-A	13	32	3	6	2	0	0	3	2		.188	.235	.250	34	-3	-3	2	0			.778	-4	/2O	-0.8
1913	Det-A	14	47	4	10	0	1	0	7	4	12	.213	.275	.255	56	-3	-3	4	2			.987	1	1	-0.2
Total	2	27	79	7	16	2	1	0	10	6	12	.203	.259	.253	47	-6	-6	5	2				-3	/12O	-1.0

■ ART TWINEHAM Twineham, Arthur W. "Old Hoss" b: 11/26/1866, Galesburg, Ill. BL/TL, 6'1.5", 190 lbs. Deb: 9/11/1893

YEAR	TM/L	G	AB	R	H	2B	3B	HR	RBI	BB	SO	AVG	OBP	SLG	PRO+	BR	/A	RC	SB	CS	SBR	FA	FR	POS	TPR
1893	StL-N	14	48	8	15	2	0	0	11	1	2	.313	.340	.354	86	-1	-1	6	0			.928	2	C	0.2
1894	StL-N	38	127	22	40	4	1	1	16	9	11	.315	.387	.386	89	-2	-2	20	2			.939	4	C	0.4
Total	2	52	175	30	55	6	1	1	27	10	13	.314	.375	.377	88	-3	-3	26	2			.936	6	/C	0.6

■ LARRY TWITCHELL Twitchell, Lawrence Grant b: 2/18/1864, Cleveland, Ohio d: 8/23/30, Cleveland, Ohio BR/TR, 6', 185 lbs. Deb: 4/30/1886

YEAR	TM/L	G	AB	R	H	2B	3B	HR	RBI	BB	SO	AVG	OBP	SLG	PRO+	BR	/A	RC	SB	CS	SBR	FA	FR	POS	TPR
1886	Det-N	4	16	0	1	0	0	0	0	0	2	.063	.063	.063	-60	-3	-3	0	0			1.000	0	/PO	-0.1
1887	*Det-N	65	264	44	88	14	6	0	51	8	19	.333	.358	.432	116	7	5	46	12			.871	-6	OP	-0.1
1888	Det-N	131	524	71	128	19	4	5	67	28	45	.244	.286	.324	97	-2	-2	54	14			.885	-9	*O/P	-1.4
1889	Cle-N	134	549	73	151	16	11	4	95	29	37	.275	.315	.366	93	-7	-6	70	17			.916	-10	*O/P	-1.6
1890	Cle-P	56	233	33	52	6	3	2	36	17	17	.223	.279	.300	61	-15	-11	21	4			.821	-9	O	-1.8
	Buf-P	44	172	24	38	3	1	2	17	23	12	.221	.316	.285	68	-9	-6	17	4			.918	-1	OP/1	-0.7
	Yr	100	405	57	90	9	4	4	53	40	29	.222	.295	.294	64	-23	-17	38	8			.857	-10	OP/1	-2.5
1891	Col-a	57	224	32	62	9	4	2	35	20	28	.277	.341	.379	116	2	4	33	10			.887	-10	O/P	-0.6
1892	Was-N	51	192	20	42	9	5	0	20	11	31	.219	.275	.318	83	-5	-4	19	8			.897	-5	O/S3	-1.1
1893	Lou-N	45	187	37	58	11	3	2	31	17	20	.310	.377	.433	127	4	7	34	7			.874	-2	O	0.2
1894	Lou-N	52	210	28	56	16	3	2	32	15	20	.267	.316	.400	78	-10	-7	31	8			.908	6	O/P	-0.4
Total	9	639	2571	362	676	103	40	19	384	168	231	.263	.313	.356	93	-37	-23	326	84			.890	-45	O/PS13	-7.6

■ BABE TWOMBLY Twombly, Clarence Edward b: 1/18/1896, Jamaica Plain, Mass. d: 11/23/74, San Clemente, Cal. BL/TR, 5'10", 165 lbs. Deb: 4/14/20 F

YEAR	TM/L	G	AB	R	H	2B	3B	HR	RBI	BB	SO	AVG	OBP	SLG	PRO+	BR	/A	RC	SB	CS	SBR	FA	FR	POS	TPR
1920	Chi-N	78	183	25	43	1	1	2	14	17	20	.235	.303	.284	68	-7	-7	15	5	9	-4	.970	0	O/2	-1.5
1921	Chi-N	87	175	22	66	8	1	1	18	11	10	.377	.414	.451	129	8	8	31	4	6	-2	.968	0	O	0.3
Total	2	165	358	47	109	9	2	3	32	28	30	.304	.357	.366	98	1	0	46	9	15	-6	.969	1	/O2	-1.2

■ GEORGE TWOMBLY Twombly, George Frederick "Silent George" b: 6/4/1892, Boston, Mass. d: 2/17/75, Lexington, Mass. BR/TR, 5'9", 165 lbs. Deb: 7/09/14 F

YEAR	TM/L	G	AB	R	H	2B	3B	HR	RBI	BB	SO	AVG	OBP	SLG	PRO+	BR	/A	RC	SB	CS	SBR	FA	FR	POS	TPR
1914	Cin-N	68	240	22	56	0	5	0	19	14	27	.233	.284	.275	64	-10	-11	21	12			.968	1	O	-1.4
1915	Cin-N	46	66	5	13	0	1	0	5	8	8	.197	.293	.227	57	-3	-3	5	5	3	-0	1.000	-4	O	-0.9
1916	Cin-N	3	5	0	0	0	0	0	0	1	1	.000	.167	.000	-48	-1	-1	0	0			1.000	-0	/O	-0.1
1917	Bos-N	32	102	8	19	1	1	0	9	18	5	.186	.314	.216	68	-3	-3	9	4			.943	-5	O/1	-1.1
1919	Was-A	1	4	0	0	0	0	0	0	0	0	.000	.000	.000	-99	-1	-1	0	0			.000	-1	/O	-0.2
Total	5	150	417	35	88	1	7	0	33	41	41	.211	.289	.247	62	-18	-19	35	21	3		.967	-9	O/1	-3.7

■ JIM TYACK Tyack, James Frederick b: 1/9/11, Florence, Mont. BL/TR, 6'2", 195 lbs. Deb: 4/20/43

YEAR	TM/L	G	AB	R	H	2B	3B	HR	RBI	BB	SO	AVG	OBP	SLG	PRO+	BR	/A	RC	SB	CS	SBR	FA	FR	POS	TPR
1943	Phi-A	54	155	11	40	8	1	0	23	14	9	.258	.320	.323	88	-2	-2	17	1	1	-0	.977	1	O	-0.4

■ FRED TYLER Tyler, Frederick Franklin "Clancy" b: 12/16/1891, Derry, N.H. d: 10/14/45, E.Derry, N.H. BR/TR, 5'10.5", 180 lbs. Deb: 4/14/14 F

YEAR	TM/L	G	AB	R	H	2B	3B	HR	RBI	BB	SO	AVG	OBP	SLG	PRO+	BR	/A	RC	SB	CS	SBR	FA	FR	POS	TPR
1914	Bos-N	6	19	2	2	0	0	0	2	1	5	.105	.150	.105	-24	-3	-3	0	0			1.000	-1	/C	-0.3

■ JOHNNIE TYLER Tyler, John Anthony "Ty Ty" or "Katz" (b: John Tylka)
b: 7/30/06, Mt.Pleasant, Pa. d: 7/11/72, Mt.Pleasant, Pa. BB/TR, 6', 175 lbs. Deb: 9/16/34

YEAR	TM/L	G	AB	R	H	2B	3B	HR	RBI	BB	SO	AVG	OBP	SLG	PRO+	BR	/A	RC	SB	CS	SBR	FA	FR	POS	TPR
1934	Bos-N	3	6	0	1	0	0	0	1	0	3	.167	.167	.167	-11	-1	-1	0	0			1.000	1	/O	0.0
1935	Bos-N	13	47	7	16	2	1	2	11	4	3	.340	.404	.553	168	4	4	11	0			.893	-0	O	0.3
Total	2	16	53	7	17	2	1	2	12	4	6	.321	.379	.509	148	3	3	11	0			.906	1	/O	0.3

■ EARL TYREE Tyree, Earl Carlton "Ty" b: 3/4/1890, Huntsville, Ill. d: 5/17/54, Rushville, Ill. BR/TR, 5'8", 160 lbs. Deb: 10/05/14

YEAR	TM/L	G	AB	R	H	2B	3B	HR	RBI	BB	SO	AVG	OBP	SLG	PRO+	BR	/A	RC	SB	CS	SBR	FA	FR	POS	TPR
1914	Chi-N	1	4	1	0	0	0	0	0	0	0	.000	.000	.000	-99	-1	-1	0	0			1.000	-1	/C	-0.2

■ JIM TYRONE Tyrone, James Vernon b: 1/29/49, Alice, Tex. BR/TR, 6'1", 185 lbs. Deb: 8/27/72 F

YEAR	TM/L	G	AB	R	H	2B	3B	HR	RBI	BB	SO	AVG	OBP	SLG	PRO+	BR	/A	RC	SB	CS	SBR	FA	FR	POS	TPR
1972	Chi-N	13	8	1	0	0	0	0	0	0	3	.000	.000	.000	-90	-2	-2	0	1	0	0	1.000	2	/O	0.0
1974	Chi-N	57	81	19	15	0	1	3	3	6	8	.185	.241	.321	54	-5	-5	6	1	1	-0	.962	-1	O/3	-0.8
1975	Chi-N	11	22	0	5	0	1	0	3	1	4	.227	.261	.318	58	-1	-1	2	1	1	-0	1.000	-0	/O	-0.2
1977	Oak-A	96	294	32	72	11	1	5	26	25	62	.245	.304	.340	76	-10	-9	31	3	1	0	.950	1	O/1SD	-1.1
Total	4	177	405	52	92	11	3	8	32	32	77	.227	.284	.328	67	-18	-18	39	6	3	0	.955	2	O/DS13	-2.1

YEAR	TM/L	G	AB	R	H	2B	3B	HR	RBI	BB	SO	AVG	OBP	SLG	PRO+	BR	/A	RC	SB	CS	SBR	FA	FR	POS	TPR
■ **WAYNE TYRONE** Tyrone, Oscar Wayne b: 8/1/50, Alice, Tex. BR/TR, 6'1", 185 lbs. Deb: 7/15/76 F																									
1976	Chi-N	30	57	3	13	1	0	1	8	3	21	.228	.267	.298	55	-3	-4	5	0	0	0	1.000	-1	/O13	-0.6
■ **TY TYSON** Tyson, Albert Thomas b: 6/1/1892, Wilkes-Barre, Pa. d: 8/16/53, Buffalo, N.Y. BR/TR, 5'11", 169 lbs. Deb: 4/13/26																									
1926	NY-N	97	335	40	98	16	1	3	35	15	28	.293	.329	.373	90	-6	-5	40	6			.980	3	O	-0.8
1927	NY-N	43	159	24	42	7	2	1	17	10	19	.264	.308	.352	76	-5	-5	17	5			.929	-3	O	-1.1
1928	Bro-N	59	210	25	57	11	1	1	21	10	14	.271	.317	.348	75	-8	-8	23	3			.965	0	O	-1.1
Total	3	199	704	89	197	34	4	5	73	35	61	.280	.320	.361	82	-19	-18	79	14			.966	0	O	-3.0
■ **TURKEY TYSON** Tyson, Cecil Washington "Slim" b: 12/6/14, Elm City, N.C. BL/TR, 6'5.5", 225 lbs. Deb: 4/23/44																									
1944	Phi-N	1	1	0	0	0	0	0	0	0	0	.000	.000	.000	-99	-0	-0	0	0			.000	0	H	0.0
■ **MIKE TYSON** Tyson, Michael Ray b: 1/13/50, Rocky Mount, N.C. BR/TR, 5'9", 170 lbs. Deb: 9/05/72																									
1972	StL-N	13	37	1	7	1	0	0	0	1	9	.189	.211	.216	22	-4	-4	2	0	1	-1	.981	4	2/S	0.0
1973	StL-N	144	469	48	114	15	4	1	33	23	66	.243	.281	.299	61	-25	-25	37	2	5	-2	.944	-19	*S2	-3.0
1974	StL-N	151	422	35	94	14	5	1	37	22	70	.223	.266	.287	55	-26	-26	29	4	2	0	.955	15	*S2	0.6
1975	StL-N	122	368	45	98	16	3	2	37	24	39	.266	.316	.342	80	-9	-10	40	5	2	0	.971	-12	S2/3	-1.3
1976	StL-N	76	245	26	70	12	9	3	28	16	34	.286	.330	.445	117	5	5	34	3	1	0	.971	8	2	1.8
1977	StL-N	138	418	42	103	15	2	7	57	30	48	.246	.300	.342	73	-17	-16	41	3	4	-2	.979	22	*2	1.4
1978	StL-N	125	377	26	88	16	0	3	26	24	41	.233	.279	.300	63	-19	-19	29	2	0	1	.977	0	*2	-1.1
1979	StL-N	75	190	18	42	8	2	5	20	13	28	.221	.275	.363	72	-8	-8	18	2	1	0	.975	8	2	0.4
1980	Chi-N	123	341	34	81	19	3	3	23	15	61	.238	.274	.337	65	-15	-17	31	1	2	-1	.968	9	*2	-0.3
1981	Chi-N	50	92	6	17	2	0	2	8	7	15	.185	.250	.272	46	-6	-7	7	1	0	0	.940	0	2/S	-0.5
Total	10	1017	2959	281	714	118	28	27	269	175	411	.241	.287	.327	69	-124	-127	268	23	18	-4	.973	36	2S/3	-2.0
■ **BOB UECKER** Uecker, Robert George b: 1/26/35, Milwaukee, Wis. BR/TR, 6'1", 190 lbs. Deb: 4/13/62																									
1962	Mil-N	33	64	5	16	2	0	1	8	7	15	.250	.324	.328	78	-2	-2	6	0	0	0	.982	4	C	0.3
1963	Mil-N	13	16	3	4	2	0	0	0	2	5	.250	.333	.375	105	0	0	2	0	0	0	.958	1	/C	0.1
1964	StL-N	40	106	8	21	1	0	1	6	17	24	.198	.315	.236	53	-5	-6	9	0	1	-1	.987	5	C	-0.1
1965	StL-N	53	145	17	33	7	0	2	10	24	27	.228	.345	.317	80	-1	-3	18	0	1	-1	.985	-1	C	-0.3
1966	Phi-N	78	207	15	43	6	0	7	30	22	36	.208	.284	.338	72	-8	-8	19	0	0	0	.985	1	C	-0.3
1967	Phi-N	18	35	3	6	2	0	0	7	5	9	.171	.275	.229	45	-2	-2	2	0	0	0	.973	0	C	-0.2
	Atl-N	62	158	14	23	2	0	3	13	19	51	.146	.237	.215	31	-14	-14	8	0	1	-1	.972	5	C	-0.8
	Yr	80	193	17	29	4	0	3	20	24	60	.150	.244	.218	33	-16	-16	11	0	1	-1	.972	5	C	-1.0
Total	6	297	731	65	146	22	0	14	74	96	167	.200	.295	.287	63	-33	-35	64	0	3	-2	.981	14	C	-1.3
■ **FRENCHY UHALT** Uhalt, Bernard Bartholomew b: 4/27/10, Bakersfield, Cal. BL/TR, 5'10", 180 lbs. Deb: 4/17/34																									
1934	Chi-A	57	165	28	40	5	1	0	16	29	12	.242	.359	.285	66	-7	-7	19	6	5	-1	.935	-1	O	-1.1
■ **TED UHLAENDER** Uhlaender, Theodore Otto b: 10/21/40, Chicago, Heights, Ill. BL/TR, 6'2", 190 lbs. Deb: 9/04/65																									
1965	Min-A	13	22	1	4	0	0	0	1	0	2	.182	.182	.182	3	-3	-3	1	1	0	0	1.000	1	/O	-0.2
1966	Min-A	105	367	39	83	12	2	2	22	27	33	.226	.281	.286	60	-17	-20	32	10	2	2	.985	12	*O	-1.1
1967	Min-A	133	415	41	107	19	7	6	49	13	45	.258	.285	.381	88	-4	-7	44	4	4	-1	**.996**	7	*O	-0.7
1968	Min-A	140	488	52	138	21	5	7	52	28	46	.283	.326	.389	110	8	6	63	16	7	1	.986	-2	*O	-0.2
1969	*Min-A	152	554	93	151	18	2	8	62	44	52	.273	.331	.356	90	-6	-7	68	15	9	-1	.997	-6	*O	-2.3
1970	Cle-A	141	473	56	127	21	2	11	46	39	44	.268	.326	.391	92	-3	-5	60	3	6	-3	.991	-14	*O	-3.0
1971	Cle-A	141	500	52	144	20	3	2	47	38	44	.288	.338	.352	88	-3	-8	59	3	6	-3	.992	1	*O	-1.7
1972	*Cin-N	73	113	9	18	3	0	0	6	13	11	.159	.246	.186	26	-11	-10	5	0	1	-1	.976	0	O	-1.3
Total	8	898	2932	343	772	114	21	36	285	202	277	.263	.313	.353	86	-38	-55	330	52	35	-5	.991	-1	O	-10.5
■ **GEORGE UHLE** Uhle, George Ernest "The Bull" b: 9/18/1898, Cleveland, Ohio d: 2/26/85, Lakewood, Ohio BR/TR, 6', 190 lbs. Deb: 4/30/19 C																									
1919	Cle-A	26	43	7	13	2	1	0	6	1	5	.302	.318	.395	94	-0	-1	5	0			.915	0	P	0.0
1920	*Cle-A	27	32	4	11	0	0	0	2	2	2	.344	.382	.344	91	-0	-0	4	1	0	0	1.000	0	P	0.0
1921	Cle-A	48	94	21	23	2	3	1	18	6	9	.245	.290	.362	64	-5	-5	10	0	0	0	.938	-3	P	0.0
1922	Cle-A	56	109	21	29	8	2	0	14	13	6	.266	.350	.376	88	-2	-2	15	1	2	-1	.932	-3	P	0.0
1923	Cle-A	58	144	23	52	10	3	0	22	7	10	.361	.391	.472	127	5	5	26	2	1	0	.982	0	P	0.0
1924	Cle-A	59	107	10	33	6	1	1	19	4	8	.308	.339	.411	92	-2	-2	14	0	1	-1	1.000	1	P	0.0
1925	Cle-A	55	101	10	29	3	3	0	13	7	7	.287	.339	.376	81	-3	-3	13	0	0	0	.943	-3	P	0.0
1926	Cle-A	50	132	16	30	3	0	1	11	10	12	.227	.287	.273	46	-10	-11	11	2	2	-1	.933	-0	P	0.0
1927	Cle-A	43	79	4	21	7	1	0	14	5	12	.266	.310	.380	78	-3	-3	9	0	1	-1	.974	-1	P	0.0
1928	Cle-A	55	98	9	28	3	2	1	17	8	4	.286	.340	.388	90	-1	-2	13	0	0	0	.972	3	P	0.0
1929	Det-A	40	108	18	37	1	1	0	13	6	6	.343	.377	.370	93	-1	-1	15	0	0	0	.929	-3	P	0.0
1930	Det-A	59	117	15	36	4	2	2	21	8	13	.308	.352	.427	95	-1	-1	18	0	0	0	.975	-3	P	0.0
1931	Det-A	53	90	8	22	6	0	2	7	8	8	.244	.306	.378	76	-3	-3	10	0	1	-1	1.000	-1	P	0.0
1932	Det-A	38	55	2	10	3	1	0	4	6	5	.182	.262	.273	37	-5	-5	4	0	0	0	1.000	-1	P	0.0
1933	Det-A	1	0	0	0	0	0	0	0	0	0	—	—	—	—	0	0	0	0	0	0	.000	0	/P	0.0
	NY-N	8	5	1	0	0	0	0	0	1	3	.000	.167	.000	-50	-1	-1	0	0			1.000	0	/P	0.0
	NY-A	12	20	1	8	1	0	0	1	4	2	.400	.500	.450	163	2	2	5	0	0	0	1.000	-1	P	0.0
1934	NY-A	10	5	1	3	0	1	0	1	0	0	.600	.600	1.000	329	1	1	3	0	0	0	1.000	-0	P	0.0
1936	Cle-A	24	21	1	8	1	0	1	4	2	0	.381	.435	.571	145	2	1	5	0	0	0	.000	-1	/P	0.0
Total	17	722	1360	172	393	60	21	9	187	98	112	.289	.339	.384	86	-27	-29	181	6	8		.960	-15	P	0.0
■ **MAURY UHLER** Uhler, Maurice William b: 12/14/1886, Pikesville, Md. d: 5/4/18, Baltimore, Md. BR/TR, 5'11", 165 lbs. Deb: 4/14/14																									
1914	Cin-N	46	56	12	12	2	0	0	3	5	11	.214	.279	.250	56	-3	-3	5	4			.932	-8	O	-1.3
■ **CHARLIE UHLIR** Uhlir, Charles Karel b: 7/30/12, Chicago, Ill. d: 7/9/84, Spirit Lake, Iowa BL/TL, 5'7.5", 150 lbs. Deb: 8/03/34																									
1934	Chi-A	14	27	3	4	0	0	0	3	2	6	.148	.207	.148	-7	-4	-4	1	0	0	0	1.000	-1	/O	-0.5
■ **MIKE ULISNEY** Ulisney, Michael Edward "Slugs" b: 9/28/17, Greenwald, Pa. BR/TR, 5'9", 165 lbs. Deb: 5/05/45																									
1945	Bos-N	11	18	4	7	1	0	1	4	1	0	.389	.421	.611	184	2	2	5	0			.714	-2	/C	0.0
■ **SCOTT ULLGER** Ullger, Scott Matthew b: 6/10/56, New York, N.Y. BR/TR, 6'2", 186 lbs. Deb: 4/17/83																									
1983	Min-A	35	79	8	15	4	0	0	5	5	21	.190	.247	.241	34	-7	-7	3	0	2	-1	.990	-2	1/3D	-1.1
■ **GEORGE ULRICH** Ulrich, George T. b: 6/5/1869, Philadelphia, Pa. Deb: 5/01/1892																									
1892	Was-N	6	24	1	7	1	0	0	0	0	4	.292	.292	.333	93	-0	-0	3	2			.889	-1	/3SC	-0.1
1893	Cin-N	1	3	0	0	0	0	0	0	0	0	.000	.250	.000	-29	-1	-1	0	1			1.000	-0	/O	-0.1
1896	NY-N	14	45	4	8	1	0	0	1	1	1	.178	.229	.200	15	-5	-5	2	0			.920	0	O/3	-0.5
Total	3	21	72	5	15	2	0	0	1	1	5	.208	.250	.236	36	-6	-6	6	3			.923	-1	/O3CS	-0.7
■ **TOM UMPHLETT** Umphlett, Thomas Mullen b: 5/12/30, Scotland Neck, N.C BR/TR, 6'2", 180 lbs. Deb: 4/16/53																									
1953	Bos-A	137	495	53	140	27	5	3	59	34	30	.283	.331	.376	86	-7	-10	62	4	2	0	.983	6	*O	-1.0
1954	Was-A	114	342	21	75	8	3	1	33	17	42	.219	.256	.269	46	-27	-25	21	1	2	-1	.989	0	*O	-3.0
1955	Was-A	110	323	34	70	10	0	2	19	24	35	.217	.271	.266	47	-25	-23	24	2	1	0	.988	4	*O	-2.3
Total	3	361	1160	108	285	45	8	6	111	75	107	.246	.293	.314	65	-59	-58	107	7	5	-1	.986	10	O	-6.3

YEAR	TM/L	G	AB	R	H	2B	3B	HR	RBI	BB	SO	AVG	OBP	SLG	PRO+	BR	/A	RC	SB	CS	SBR	FA	FR	POS	TPR
■ **BOB UNGLAUB**	Unglaub, Robert Alexander b: 7/31/1881, Baltimore, Md. d: 11/29/16, Baltimore, Md. BR/TR, 5'11", 178 lbs. Deb: 4/15/04 M																								
1904	NY-A	6	19	2	4	0	0	0	2	0		.211	.211	.211	32	-1	-2	1	0			.786	-1	/3S	-0.3
	Bos-A	9	13	1	2	1	0	0	2	1		.154	.214	.231	39	-1	-1	1	0			.625	-2	/23S	-0.3
	Yr	15	32	3	6	1	0	0	4	1		.188	.212	.219	35	-2	-2	2	0			.842	-3	/32S	-0.6
1905	Bos-A	43	121	18	27	5	1	0	11	6		.223	.260	.281	71	-4	-4	10	2			.928	1	3/21	-0.3
1907	Bos-A	139	544	49	138	17	13	1	62	23		.254	.284	.338	99	-3	-2	59	14			.986	-1	*1M	-0.8
1908	Bos-A	72	266	23	70	11	3	1	25	7		.263	.287	.338	100	-0	-1	27	6			.980	2	1	-0.1
	Was-A	72	276	23	85	10	5	0	29	8		.308	.327	.380	142	8	10	36	8			.928	11	32/1	2.5
	Yr	144	542	46	155	21	8	1	54	15		.286	.308	.360	120	8	9	63	14			.981	13	132	2.4
1909	Was-A	130	480	43	127	14	9	3	41	22		.265	.301	.350	111	1	4	54	15			.992	1	1O2/3	0.3
1910	Was-A	124	431	29	101	9	4	0	44	21		.234	.270	.274	74	-16	-13	37	21			.985	6	*1	-0.9
Total	6	595	2150	188	554	67	35	5	216	88		.258	.288	.328	99	-16	-9	226	66			.986	16	1/32OS	0.1
■ **AL UNSER**	Unser, Albert Bernard b: 10/12/12, Morrisonville, Ill BR/TR, 6'1", 175 lbs. Deb: 9/14/42 F																								
1942	Det-A	4	8	2	3	0	0	0	0	0	2	.375	.375	.375	103	0	0	1	0	0	0	1.000	1	/C	0.1
1943	Det-A	38	101	14	25	5	0	0	4	15	15	.248	.350	.297	84	-1	-2	11	0	1	-1	.982	-3	C	-0.3
1944	Det-A	11	25	2	3	0	1	1	5	3	2	.120	.214	.320	49	-2	-2	2	0	0	0	.864	-4	/2C	-0.6
1945	Cin-N	67	204	23	54	10	3	3	21	14	24	.265	.318	.387	98	-2	-1	25	0			.956	0	C	0.2
Total	4	120	338	41	85	15	4	4	30	32	43	.251	.322	.355	90	-4	-5	39	0	1		.967	-7	C/2	-0.6
■ **DEL UNSER**	Unser, Delbert Bernard b: 12/9/44, Decatur, Ill. BL/TL, 6'1", 180 lbs. Deb: 4/10/68 FC																								
1968	Was-A	156	635	66	146	13	7	1	30	46	66	.230	.284	.277	73	-22	-20	52	11	6	-0	.988	19	*O/1	-1.2
1969	Was-A	153	581	69	166	19	**8**	7	57	58	54	.286	.351	.382	111	4	8	79	8	10	-4	.972	6	*O	0.1
1970	Was-A	119	322	37	83	5	1	5	30	30	29	.258	.321	.326	83	-9	-7	35	1	1	-0	.984	-3	*O	-1.5
1971	Was-A	153	581	63	148	19	6	9	41	59	68	.255	.326	.355	98	-5	-2	70	11	6	-0	.981	3	*O	-0.7
1972	Cle-A	132	383	29	91	12	0	1	17	28	46	.238	.291	.277	67	-14	-15	31	5	9	-4	.989	2	*O	-2.5
1973	Phi-N	136	440	64	127	20	4	11	52	47	55	.289	.359	.427	114	10	9	68	5	8	-3	.988	12	*O	1.3
1974	Phi-N	142	454	72	120	18	5	11	61	50	62	.264	.339	.399	101	3	1	62	6	4	-1	.981	-3	*O	-0.8
1975	NY-N	147	531	65	156	18	2	10	53	37	76	.294	.340	.392	107	1	4	70	4	3	-1	.987	8	*O	0.6
1976	NY-N	77	276	28	63	13	2	5	25	18	40	.228	.278	.344	80	-9	-8	26	4	4	-1	.995	0	O	-1.3
	Mon-N	69	220	29	50	6	2	7	15	11	44	.227	.264	.368	75	-7	-8	21	3	3	-1	.983	-3	O	-1.6
	Yr	146	496	57	113	19	4	12	40	29	84	.228	.272	.355	78	-17	-16	47	7	7	-2	.990	-3	*O	-2.9
1977	Mon-N	113	289	33	79	14	1	12	40	33	41	.273	.348	.453	116	5	6	45	2	5	-2	.976	-2	O1	-0.2
1978	Mon-N	130	179	16	35	5	0	2	15	24	29	.196	.294	.257	56	-10	-10	15	2	0	1	.994	3	1O	-0.9
1979	Phi-N	95	141	26	42	8	0	6	29	14	33	.298	.361	.482	124	5	5	24	2	0	1	.978	-1	O1	0.3
1980	*Phi-N	96	110	15	29	6	4	0	10	10	21	.264	.325	.391	94	-0	-1	14	0	1	-1	1.000	7	1O	0.5
1981	Phi-N	62	59	5	9	3	0	0	6	13	9	.153	.306	.203	45	-4	-4	4	0	0	0	1.000	2	1O	-0.3
1982	Phi-N	19	14	0	0	0	0	0	0	3	2	.000	.176	.000	-46	-3	-3	0	0	0	0	1.000	0	/1O	-0.3
Total	15	1799	5215	617	1344	179	42	87	481	481	675	.258	.321	.358	93	-56	-46	616	64	60	-17	.984	49	*O1	-8.5
■ **JOHN UPHAM**	Upham, John Leslie b: 12/29/41, Windsor, Ont., Can. BL/TL, 6', 180 lbs. Deb: 4/16/67																								
1967	Chi-N	8	3	1	2	0	0	0	0	0	0	.667	.667	.667	270	1	1	1	0	0	0	.000	0	/P	0.0
1968	Chi-N	13	10	0	2	0	0	0	0	0	3	.200	.200	.200	19	-1	-1	0	0	0	0	1.000	0	/PO	0.0
Total	2	21	13	1	4	0	0	0	0	0	3	.308	.308	.308	78	-0	-0	2	0	0	0	1.000	0	/PO	0.0
■ **DIXIE UPRIGHT**	Upright, R T b: 5/30/26, Kannapolis, N.C. d: 11/13/86, Concord, N.C. BL/TL, 6', 175 lbs. Deb: 4/18/53																								
1953	StL-A	9	8	3	2	0	0	1	1	1	3	.250	.333	.625	151	1	0	2	0	0	0	.000	0	H	0.0
■ **WILLIE UPSHAW**	Upshaw, Willie Clay b: 4/27/57, Blanco, Tex. BL/TL, 6', 185 lbs. Deb: 4/09/78																								
1978	Tor-A	95	224	26	53	8	2	1	17	21	35	.237	.302	.304	69	-8	-9	20	4	6	-2	.943	-6	OD1	-2.0
1980	Tor-A	34	61	10	13	3	1	1	5	6	14	.213	.284	.344	68	-2	-3	7	1	0	0	.983	1	1D/O	-0.2
1981	Tor-A	61	111	15	19	3	1	4	10	11	16	.171	.252	.324	61	-5	-6	9	2	1	0	1.000	-2	D1O	-0.9
1982	Tor-A	160	580	77	155	25	7	21	75	52	91	.267	.329	.443	100	7	-0	82	8	8	-2	.989	-1	*1/D	-1.3
1983	Tor-A	160	579	99	177	26	7	27	104	61	98	.306	.377	.515	134	34	29	113	10	7	-1	.985	3	*1/D	2.1
1984	Tor-A	152	569	79	158	31	9	19	84	55	86	.278	.347	.464	118	16	14	92	10	4	1	.990	-3	*1/D	0.2
1985	*Tor-A	148	501	79	138	31	5	15	65	48	71	.275	.344	.447	112	10	8	76	8	8	-2	.992	1	*1/D	-0.1
1986	Tor-A	155	573	85	144	28	6	9	60	78	87	.251	.343	.368	91	-4	-5	80	23	5	4	.992	5	*1/D	-0.8
1987	Tor-A	150	512	68	125	22	4	15	58	58	78	.244	.325	.391	87	-8	-10	65	10	11	-4	.993	12	*1	-1.2
1988	Cle-A	149	493	58	121	22	3	11	50	62	66	.245	.332	.369	94	-2	-3	61	12	9	-2	.991	1	*1	-1.6
Total	10	1264	4203	596	1103	199	45	123	528	452	642	.262	.337	.419	102	37	14	605	88	59	-9	.990	11	*1/OD	-5.8
■ **TOM UPTON**	Upton, Thomas Herbert "Muscles" b: 12/29/26, Ester, Mo. BR/TR, 6', 160 lbs. Deb: 4/19/50 F																								
1950	StL-A	124	389	50	92	5	6	2	30	52	45	.237	.328	.296	58	-22	-25	42	7	2	1	.946	-10	*S/23	-2.4
1951	StL-A	52	131	9	26	4	3	0	12	12	22	.198	.271	.275	46	-10	-10	10	1	1	-0	.949	-4	S	-1.2
1952	Was-A	5	5	1	0	0	0	0	0	1	0	.000	.167	.000	-53	-1	-1	0	0	0	0	1.000	2	/S	0.1
Total	3	181	525	60	118	9	9	2	42	65	67	.225	.313	.288	55	-33	-36	51	8	3	1	.948	-13	S/23	-3.5
■ **LUKE URBAN**	Urban, Louis John b: 3/22/1898, Fall River, Mass. d: 12/7/80, Somerset, Mass. BR/TR, 5'8", 168 lbs. Deb: 7/19/27																								
1927	Bos-N	35	111	11	32	5	0	0	10	3	6	.288	.313	.333	79	-4	-3	11	1			.947	-8	C	-0.9
1928	Bos-N	15	17	0	3	0	0	0	2	0	1	.176	.222	.176	6	-2	-2	1	0			1.000	1	C	-0.1
Total	2	50	128	11	35	5	0	0	12	3	7	.273	.301	.313	69	-7	-5	12	1			.955	-7	/C	-1.0
■ **BILLY URBANSKI**	Urbanski, William Michael b: 6/5/03, Linoleumville, N.Y d: 7/12/73, Perth Amboy, N.J. BR/TR, 5'8", 165 lbs. Deb: 7/04/31																								
1931	Bos-N	82	303	22	72	13	4	0	17	10	32	.238	.274	.307	58	-19	-18	27	3			.961	11	3S	-0.2
1932	Bos-N	136	563	80	153	25	8	8	46	28	60	.272	.307	.387	89	-12	-9	68	8			.946	1	*S	0.4
1933	Bos-N	144	566	65	142	21	4	0	35	33	48	.251	.298	.302	78	-20	-15	52	4			.953	-4	*S	-0.9
1934	Bos-N	146	605	104	177	30	6	7	53	56	37	.293	.357	.397	110	2	9	90	4			**.961**	-10	*S	0.7
1935	Bos-N	132	514	53	118	17	0	4	30	40	32	.230	.286	.286	59	-32	-27	42	3			.939	-27	*S	-4.7
1936	Bos-N	122	494	55	129	17	5	0	26	31	42	.261	.310	.316	74	-21	-17	48	2			.937	-18	S3	-2.8
1937	Bos-N	1	1	0	0	0	0	0	0	0	1	.000	.000	.000	-99	-0	-0	0	0			.000	0	H	0.0
Total	7	763	3046	379	791	123	27	19	207	198	252	.260	.309	.337	81	-103	-78	327	24			.949	-47	S3	-7.5
■ **JOSE URIBE**	Uribe, Jose Altagracia (Played Under Real Name Of Jose Altagracia Gonzalez (Uribe) In 1984) b: 1/21/59, San Cristobal, D.R. BB/TR, 5'10", 165 lbs. Deb: 9/13/84																								
1984	StL-N	8	19	4	4	0	0	0	3	0	2	.211	.211	.211	19	-2	-2	1	1	0	0	.955	0	/S2	-0.1
1985	SF-N	147	476	46	113	20	4	3	26	30	57	.237	.285	.315	71	-21	-18	44	8	2	1	.961	-2	*S/2	-0.6
1986	SF-N	157	453	46	101	15	1	3	43	61	76	.223	.315	.280	69	-20	-17	43	22	11	0	.977	12	*S	0.9
1987	*SF-N	95	309	44	90	16	5	5	30	24	35	.291	.344	.424	107	1	3	48	12	2	2	.971	11	S	2.3
1988	SF-N	141	493	47	124	10	7	3	35	36	69	.252	.302	.318	82	-14	-11	48	14	10	-2	.970	-3	*S	-0.5
1989	*SF-N	151	453	34	100	12	6	1	30	34	74	.221	.275	.280	61	-24	-22	34	6	6	-2	.973	8	*S	-0.5
1990	SF-N	138	415	35	103	8	6	1	24	29	49	.248	.297	.304	68	-19	-17	35	5	9	-4	.965	16	*S	0.3
1991	SF-N	90	231	23	51	8	4	1	12	20	33	.221	.283	.303	67	-11	-10	20	3	4	-2	.966	6	S	-0.1
1992	SF-N	66	162	24	39	9	1	2	13	14	25	.241	.301	.346	87	-4	-3	17	2	2	-1	.971	9	S	0.9
Total	9	993	3011	303	725	98	34	19	216	248	420	.241	.299	.315	75	-113	-98	289	73	46	-6	.970	56	S/2	2.6

YEAR	TM/L	G	AB	R	H	2B	3B	HR	RBI	BB	SO	AVG	OBP	SLG	PRO+	BR	/A	RC	SB	CS	SBR	FA	FR	POS	TPR

■ **LON URY**   Ury, Louis Newton "Old Sleep"   b: 1877, Ft.Scott, Kan.   d: 3/4/18, Kansas City, Mo.   TR , 6',   Deb: 9/09/03

| 1903 | StL-N | 2 | 7 | 0 | 1 | 0 | 0 | 0 | 0 | 0 | 0 | .143 | .143 | .143 | -19 | -1 | -1 | 0 | 0 | | | 1.000 | 0 | /1 | -0.1 |

■ **BOB USHER**   Usher, Robert Royce   b: 3/1/25, San Diego, Cal.   BR/TR, 6'1.5", 180 lbs.   Deb: 4/16/46

1946	Cin-N	92	152	16	31	5	1	5	14	13	27	.204	.271	.270	56	-9	-9	12	2			.982	-12	O/3	-2.5
1947	Cin-N	9	22	2	4	0	0	1	1	2	2	.182	.250	.318	50	-2	-2	2	0			1.000	0	/O	-0.2
1950	Cin-N	106	321	51	83	17	0	6	35	27	38	.259	.316	.368	79	-10	-10	37	3			.985	-5	O	-1.8
1951	Cin-N	114	303	27	63	12	2	5	25	19	36	.208	.257	.310	51	-21	-22	23	4	5	-2	.974	-3	O	-3.0
1952	Chi-N	1	0	0	0	0	0	0	0	1	0	—	1.000	—	197	0	0	0	0	0	0	.000	0	H	0.0
1957	Cle-A	1	8	1	1	0	0	0	1	0	3	.125	.222	.125	-3	-1	-1	0	0	0	0	1.000	-2	/O3	-0.3
	Was-A	96	295	36	77	7	1	5	27	27	30	.261	.327	.342	84	-7	-6	34	0	0	0	.979	3	O	-0.8
	Yr	106	303	37	78	7	1	5	27	28	33	.257	.324	.337	82	-8	-7	34	0	0	0	.979	2	O/3	-1.1
Total	6	428	1101	133	259	41	4	18	102	90	136	.235	.295	.329	69	-49	-49	107	9	5		.980	-19	O/3	-8.6

■ **DUTCH USSAT**   Ussat, William August   b: 4/11/04, Dayton, Ohio   d: 5/29/59, Dayton, Ohio   BR/TR, 6'1", 170 lbs.   Deb: 9/13/25

1925	Cle-A	1	1	0	0	0	0	0	0	0	0	.000	.000	.000	-99	-0	-0	0	0	0	0	1.000	0	/2	0.0
1927	Cle-A	4	16	4	3	0	1	0	2	0	1	.188	.278	.313	53	-1	-1	1	0	0	0	1.000	-1	/3	-0.2
Total	2	5	17	4	3	0	1	0	2	0	1	.176	.263	.294	44	-1	-1	1	0	0	0		-1	/32	-0.2

■ **TEX VACHE**   Vache, Ernest Lewis   b: 11/17/1894, Santa Monica, Cal.   d: 6/11/53, Los Angeles, Cal.   BR/TR, 6'1", 200 lbs.   Deb: 4/16/25

| 1925 | Bos-A | 110 | 252 | 41 | 79 | 15 | 7 | 3 | 48 | 21 | 33 | .313 | .382 | .464 | 114 | 5 | 5 | 45 | 2 | 2 | -1 | .908 | -12 | O | -1.0 |

■ **GENE VADEBONCOEUR**   Vadeboncoeur, Onesime Eugene   b: 7/15/1858, Louiseville, Que.   d: 10/16/35, Haverhill, Mass.   BR/TR, 5'6", 150 lbs.   Deb: 7/11/1884

| 1884 | Phi-N | 4 | 14 | 1 | 3 | 0 | 0 | 0 | 3 | 1 | 2 | .214 | .267 | .214 | 56 | -1 | -1 | 1 | | | | .846 | -1 | /C | -0.1 |

■ **HARRY VAHRENHORST**   Vahrenhorst, Harry Henry "Van"   b: 2/13/1885, St.Louis, Mo.   d: 10/10/43, St.Louis, Mo.   BR/TR, 6'1", 175 lbs.   Deb: 9/21/04

| 1904 | StL-A | 1 | 1 | 0 | 0 | 0 | 0 | 0 | 0 | 0 | 0 | .000 | .000 | .000 | -99 | -0 | -0 | 0 | 0 | | | .000 | 0 | H | 0.0 |

■ **MIKE VAIL**   Vail, Michael Lewis   b: 11/10/51, San Francisco, Cal.   BR/TR, 6', 185 lbs.   Deb: 8/18/75

1975	NY-N	38	162	17	49	8	1	3	17	9	37	.302	.339	.420	115	2	2	23	0	0	0	.971	8	O	0.9
1976	NY-N	53	143	8	31	5	1	0	9	6	19	.217	.248	.266	49	-10	-9	9	0	1	-1	.941	-2	O	-1.5
1977	NY-N	108	279	29	73	12	1	8	35	19	58	.262	.313	.398	94	-5	-3	30	0	7	-4	.965	-0	O	-1.1
1978	Cle-A	14	34	2	8	2	1	0	2	1	9	.235	.257	.353	71	-1	-1	3	1	1	-0	1.000	-0	/OD	-0.2
	Chi-N	74	180	15	60	6	2	4	33	3	24	.333	.344	.456	109	4	2	25	0	1	-1	.981	-8	O/3	-0.8
1979	Chi-N	87	179	28	60	8	2	7	35	14	27	.335	.383	.520	131	10	8	34	0	2	-1	.964	-5	O/3	0.1
1980	Chi-N	114	312	30	93	17	2	6	47	14	77	.298	.330	.423	101	3	0	40	2	5	-2	.963	-6	O	-1.1
1981	Cin-N	31	31	1	5	1	0	0	3	0	9	.161	.161	.161	-8	-4	-4	1	0	0	0	1.000	0	/O	-0.5
1982	Cin-N	78	189	9	48	10	1	4	29	6	33	.254	.277	.381	81	-5	-6	18	0	0	0	.988	1	O	-0.6
1983	SF-N	18	26	1	4	1	0	0	3	0	7	.154	.185	.192	5	-3	-3	1	0	0	0	1.000	-1	/1O	-0.5
	Mon-N	34	53	5	15	2	0	2	4	8	10	.283	.387	.434	128	2	2	9	0	0	0	.958	2	O/13	0.4
	Yr	52	79	6	19	3	0	2	7	8	17	.241	.326	.354	90	-1	-1	10	0	0	0	.960	1	O/13	-0.1
1984	LA-N	16	16	1	1	0	0	0	2	1	7	.063	.118	.063	-49	-3	-3	0	0	0	0	.000	-0	/O	-0.4
Total	10	665	1604	146	447	71	11	34	219	81	317	.279	.315	.400	95	-11	-15	192	3	17	-9	.968	-10	O/13D	-5.3

■ **ROY VALDES**   Valdes, Rogelio Lazaro (Rojas)   b: 2/20/20, Havana, Cuba   BR/TR, 5'11", 185 lbs.   Deb: 5/03/44

| 1944 | Was-A | 1 | 1 | 0 | 0 | 0 | 0 | 0 | 0 | 0 | 0 | .000 | .000 | .000 | -99 | -0 | -0 | 0 | 0 | 0 | 0 | .000 | 0 | H | 0.0 |

■ **SANDY VALDESPINO**   Valdespino, Hilario (Borroto)   b: 1/14/39, San Jose De Las Lajas, Cuba   BL/TL, 5'8", 170 lbs.   Deb: 4/12/65

1965	*Min-A	108	245	38	64	8	2	1	22	20	28	.261	.322	.322	80	-5	-6	26	7	4	-0	.990	0	O	-0.9
1966	Min-A	52	108	11	19	1	1	2	9	4	24	.176	.212	.259	33	-9	-10	5	2	2	-1	1.000	-1	O	-1.4
1967	Min-A	99	97	9	16	2	0	1	3	5	22	.165	.206	.216	23	-9	-10	4	3	1	0	.977	-11	O	-2.4
1968	Atl-N	36	86	8	20	1	0	1	4	10	20	.233	.320	.279	81	-2	-2	8	0	0	0	.976	-1	O	-0.4
1969	Hou-N	41	119	17	29	4	0	2	12	15	19	.244	.328	.277	73	-4	-4	12	2	2	-1	.976	-2	O	-0.9
	Sea-A	20	38	3	8	1	0	0	2	1	7	.211	.250	.237	37	-3	-3	2	0	1	-1	.889	2	/O	-0.2
1970	Mil-A	8	9	0	0	0	0	0	0	0	4	.000	.000	.000	-99	-2	-2	0	0	0	0	.000	-0	/O	-0.3
1971	KC-A	18	63	10	20	6	0	2	15	2	5	.317	.338	.508	138	3	3	10	0	0	0	.950	-2	O	0.0
Total	7	382	765	96	176	23	3	7	67	57	129	.230	.288	.295	66	-32	-34	67	14	10	-2	.974	-15	O	-6.5

■ **JULIO VALDEZ**   Valdez, Julio Julian (b: Julio Julian Castillo (Valdez)   b: 6/3/56, San Cristobal, D.R.   BB/TR, 6'2", 160 lbs.   Deb: 9/02/80

1980	Bos-A	8	19	4	5	1	0	1	4	0	5	.263	.300	.474	103	0	-0	3	2	0	1	.935	7	/S	0.8
1981	Bos-A	17	23	1	5	0	0	0	3	0	2	.217	.217	.217	24	-2	-2	1	0	1	-1	.955	3	S	0.1
1982	Bos-A	28	20	3	5	1	0	0	1	0	7	.250	.250	.300	48	-1	-2	1	1	0	0	.976	7	S/D	0.6
1983	Bos-A	12	25	3	3	0	0	0	1	1	4	.120	.185	.120	-13	-4	-4	1	0	0	0	.939	-1	/2SD	-0.5
Total	4	65	87	11	18	2	0	1	8	1	18	.207	.233	.264	36	-7	-8	6	3	1	0	.955	16	/S2D	1.0

■ **JOSE VALDIVIELSO**   Valdivielso, Jose (Lopez) (b: Jose Martinez De Valdivielso (Lopez))   b: 5/22/34, Matanzas, Cuba   BR/TR, 6'1", 175 lbs.   Deb: 6/21/55

1955	Was-A	94	294	32	65	12	5	2	28	21	38	.221	.280	.316	63	-17	-15	26	1	2	-1	.956	9	S	0.1
1956	Was-A	90	246	18	58	8	4	2	29	29	36	.236	.319	.333	72	-10	-10	26	3	1	0	.947	16	S	1.3
1959	Was-A	24	14	1	4	0	0	0	0	1	3	.286	.333	.286	72	-1	-0	1	0	0	0	1.000	5	S	0.5
1960	Was-A	117	268	23	57	11	1	2	19	20	36	.213	.277	.246	43	-21	-21	19	1	2	-1	.954	9	*S/3	-0.6
1961	Min-A	76	149	15	29	5	0	1	9	8	19	.195	.236	.248	28	-15	-16	8	1	1	-0	.971	-2	S23	-1.5
Total	5	401	971	89	213	26	8	9	85	79	132	.219	.284	.290	55	-64	-62	80	6	6	-2	.955	37	S/23	-0.2

■ **JOHN VALENTIN**   Valentin, John William   b: 2/18/67, Mineola, N.Y.   BR/TR, 6', 170 lbs.   Deb: 7/26/92

| 1992 | Bos-A | 58 | 185 | 21 | 51 | 13 | 0 | 5 | 25 | 20 | 17 | .276 | .353 | .427 | 112 | 4 | 3 | 28 | 1 | 0 | 0 | .963 | 4 | S | 1.2 |

■ **JOSE VALENTIN**   Valentin, Jose Antonio   b: 10/12/69, Manati, P.R.   BB/TR, 5'10", 175 lbs.   Deb: 9/17/92

| 1992 | Mil-A | 4 | 3 | 1 | 0 | 0 | 0 | 0 | 0 | 1 | 0 | .000 | .000 | .000 | -99 | -1 | -1 | 0 | 0 | 0 | 0 | .667 | -1 | /2S | -0.2 |

■ **ELLIS VALENTINE**   Valentine, Ellis Clarence   b: 7/30/54, Helena, Ark.   BR/TR, 6'4", 207 lbs.   Deb: 9/03/75

1975	Mon-N	12	33	2	12	4	0	1	3	2	4	.364	.400	.576	161	3	3	7	0	0	0	.867	-1	O	0.1
1976	Mon-N	94	305	36	85	15	2	7	39	30	51	.279	.343	.410	108	5	3	46	14	1	4	.972	4	O	0.8
1977	Mon-N★	127	508	63	149	28	2	25	76	30	58	.293	.333	.504	124	13	14	78	13	5	1	.972	-3	O	0.7
1978	Mon-N	151	570	75	165	35	2	25	76	35	88	.289	.333	.489	129	18	19	90	13	8	-1	.970	12	*O	2.4
1979	Mon-N	146	548	73	151	29	3	21	82	22	74	.276	.305	.454	105	1	1	65	11	9	-2	.983	1	*O	-0.6
1980	Mon-N	86	311	40	98	22	2	13	67	24	44	.315	.362	.524	147	19	19	60	5	5	-2	.970	-2	O	1.3
1981	Mon-N	22	76	8	16	3	0	3	15	6	11	.211	.268	.368	78	-2	-2	7	0	1	-1	1.000	-2	O	-0.6
	NY-N	48	169	15	35	8	1	5	21	5	38	.207	.230	.355	65	-9	-8	12	0	3	-2	.957	-0	O	-1.3
	Yr	70	245	23	51	11	1	8	36	11	49	.208	.242	.359	69	-11	-11	19	0	4	-2	.969	-2	O	-1.9
1982	NY-N	111	337	33	97	14	1	8	48	15	38	.288	.300	.407	97	-3	-3	36	1	3	-2	.983	-2	O	-0.9
1983	Cal-A	86	271	30	65	10	2	13	43	18	48	.240	.287	.435	97	-3	-3	33	2	1	0	.963	-7	O	-1.2
1985	Tex-A	11	38	5	8	2	0	1	4	2	8	.211	.250	.395	72	-2	-2	3	0	1	-1	1.000	-1	/OD	-0.4
Total	10	894	3166	380	881	169	15	123	474	180	462	.278	.324	.458	113	39	42	437	59	37	-5	.972	-3	O/D	0.3

■ **FRED VALENTINE**   Valentine, Fred Lee "Squeaky"   b: 1/19/35, Clarksdale, Miss.   BB/TR, 6'1", 190 lbs.   Deb: 9/07/59

| 1959 | Bal-A | 12 | 19 | 0 | 6 | 0 | 1 | 0 | 1 | 3 | 4 | .316 | .409 | .316 | 104 | 0 | 0 | 2 | 0 | 1 | -1 | .889 | -2 | /O | -0.2 |

YEAR	TM/L	G	AB	R	H	2B	3B	HR	RBI	BB	SO	AVG	OBP	SLG	PRO+	BR	/A	RC	SB	CS	SBR	FA	FR	POS	TPR
1963	Bal-A	26	41	5	11	1	0	0	1	8	5	.268	.388	.293	96	0	0	5	0	0	0	1.000	-1	O	-0.2
1964	Was-A	102	212	20	48	5	0	4	20	21	44	.226	.305	.307	71	-8	-8	20	4	2	0	.978	-4	O	-1.5
1965	Was-A	12	29	6	7	0	0	0	1	4	5	.241	.353	.241	73	-1	-1	3	3	0	1	1.000	-0	O	0.0
1966	Was-A	146	508	77	140	29	7	16	59	51	63	.276	.353	.455	132	20	21	81	22	10	1	.980	-4	*O/1	1.1
1967	Was-A	151	457	52	107	16	1	11	44	56	76	.234	.331	.346	104	1	3	58	17	3	3	.989	-6	*O	-0.6
1968	Was-A	37	101	11	24	2	0	3	7	6	11	.238	.294	.347	96	-1	-1	9	1	0	0	1.000	-1	O	-0.3
	Bal-A	47	91	9	17	3	2	2	5	7	20	.187	.253	.330	75	-3	-3	8	0	0	0	.972	-1	O	-0.6
	Yr	84	192	20	41	5	2	5	12	13	31	.214	.274	.339	86	-4	-4	17	1	0	0	.986	-3	O	-0.9
Total	7	533	1458	180	360	56	10	36	138	156	228	.247	.331	.373	106	9	13	187	47	16	5	.983	-20	O/1	-2.3

■ **BOB VALENTINE** Valentine, Robert Deb: 5/20/1876

YEAR	TM/L	G	AB	R	H	2B	3B	HR	RBI	BB	SO	AVG	OBP	SLG	PRO+	BR	/A	RC	SB	CS	SBR	FA	FR	POS	TPR
1876	NY-N	1	3	0	0	0	0	0	0	0	0	.000	.000	.000	-99	-1	-1	0				.400	-0	/C	-0.1

■ **BOBBY VALENTINE** Valentine, Robert John b: 5/13/50, Stamford, Conn. BR/TR, 5'10", 189 lbs. Deb: 9/02/69 MC

YEAR	TM/L	G	AB	R	H	2B	3B	HR	RBI	BB	SO	AVG	OBP	SLG	PRO+	BR	/A	RC	SB	CS	SBR	FA	FR	POS	TPR
1969	LA-N	5	0	3	0	0	0	0	0	0	0	—	—	—	—	0	0	0	0	0	0	.000	0	R	0.0
1971	LA-N	101	281	32	70	10	2	1	25	15	20	.249	.292	.310	75	-11	-9	24	5	3	-0	.961	1	S32O	-0.5
1972	LA-N	119	391	42	107	11	2	3	32	27	33	.274	.324	.335	90	-6	-5	41	5	5	-2	.976	3	23OS	-0.1
1973	Cal-A	32	126	12	38	5	2	1	13	5	9	.302	.328	.397	112	0	1	17	6	1	1	.948	0	S/O	0.6
1974	Cal-A	117	371	39	97	10	3	3	39	25	25	.261	.313	.329	90	-7	-5	39	8	5	-1	.950	-8	OS3/2D	-1.2
1975	Cal-A	26	57	5	16	2	0	0	5	4	3	.281	.339	.316	92	-1	-0	6	0	2	-1	.958	-2	D/13O	-0.4
	SD-N	7	15	1	2	0	0	1	1	4	0	.133	.316	.333	86	-0	-0	2	1	0	0	1.000	-1	/O	-0.1
1976	SD-N	15	49	3	18	4	0	0	4	6	2	.367	.436	.449	165	4	4	9	0	1	-1	1.000	1	O/1	0.4
1977	SD-N	44	67	5	12	3	0	1	10	7	10	.179	.257	.269	46	-6	-5	4	0	0	0	.962	-1	S3/1	-0.6
	NY-N	42	83	8	11	1	0	1	3	6	9	.133	.191	.181	0	-12	-11	2	0	0	0	1.000	-1	1S/3	-1.2
	Yr	86	150	13	23	4	0	2	13	13	19	.153	.221	.220	20	-17	-16	7	0	0	0	.969	-2	S13	-1.8
1978	NY-N	69	160	17	43	7	0	1	18	19	18	.269	.350	.331	95	-1	-1	18	1	1	-0	.977	-9	2/3	-0.8
1979	Sea-A	62	98	9	27	6	0	0	7	22	5	.276	.408	.337	102	2	2	14	1	2	-1	.971	-7	SO/23C	-0.6
Total	10	639	1698	176	441	59	9	12	157	140	134	.260	.319	.326	86	-39	-29	177	27	20	-4	.957	-24	SO23/1DC	-4.5

■ **BENNY VALENZUELA** Valenzuela, Benjamin Beltran "Papelero" b: 6/2/33, Los Mochis, Mexico BR/TR, 5'10", 175 lbs. Deb: 4/27/58

YEAR	TM/L	G	AB	R	H	2B	3B	HR	RBI	BB	SO	AVG	OBP	SLG	PRO+	BR	/A	RC	SB	CS	SBR	FA	FR	POS	TPR
1958	StL-N	10	14	0	3	1	0	0	0	1	0	.214	.267	.286	45	-1	-1	1	0	0	0	.875	0	/3	-0.1

■ **DAVE VALLE** Valle, David b: 10/30/60, Bayside, N.Y. BR/TR, 6'2", 200 lbs. Deb: 9/07/84

YEAR	TM/L	G	AB	R	H	2B	3B	HR	RBI	BB	SO	AVG	OBP	SLG	PRO+	BR	/A	RC	SB	CS	SBR	FA	FR	POS	TPR
1984	Sea-A	13	27	4	8	1	0	1	4	1	5	.296	.321	.444	111	0	0	4	0	0	0	1.000	2	C	0.3
1985	Sea-A	31	70	2	11	1	0	0	4	1	17	.157	.181	.171	-3	-10	-10	2	0	0	0	.976	-1	C	-1.0
1986	Sea-A	22	53	10	18	3	0	5	15	7	7	.340	.417	.679	191	7	7	14	0	0	0	.982	-4	C/1	0.3
1987	Sea-A	95	324	40	83	16	3	12	53	15	46	.256	.295	.435	86	-5	-8	38	2	0	1	.989	1	CD/1O	-0.1
1988	Sea-A	93	290	29	67	15	2	10	50	18	38	.231	.297	.400	89	-3	-5	31	0	1	-1	.989	6	C/1D	0.6
1989	Sea-A	94	316	32	75	10	3	7	34	29	32	.237	.313	.354	85	-5	-6	34	0	0	0	.993	-3	C	-0.4
1990	Sea-A	107	308	37	66	15	0	7	33	45	48	.214	.328	.331	84	-5	-6	34	1	2	-1	**.997**	-0	*C/1	-0.1
1991	Sea-A	132	324	38	63	8	1	8	32	34	49	.194	.289	.299	63	-16	-16	26	0	2	-1	.992	9	*C/1	-0.2
1992	Sea-A	124	367	39	88	16	1	9	30	27	58	.240	.306	.362	86	-7	-7	41	0	0	0	.990	-4	*C	-0.5
Total	9	711	2079	231	479	85	10	59	255	177	300	.230	.304	.366	83	-45	-51	224	3	5	-2	.991	6	C/D1O	-1.1

■ **HECTOR VALLE** Valle, Hector Jose b: 10/27/40, Vega Baja, P.R. BR/TR, 5'9", 180 lbs. Deb: 6/06/65

YEAR	TM/L	G	AB	R	H	2B	3B	HR	RBI	BB	SO	AVG	OBP	SLG	PRO+	BR	/A	RC	SB	CS	SBR	FA	FR	POS	TPR
1965	LA-N	9	13	1	4	0	0	0	2	2	3	.308	.400	.308	110	0	0	2	0	0	0	1.000	-0	/C	0.0

■ **ELMER VALO** Valo, Elmer William b: 3/5/21, Ribnik, Czech. BL/TR, 5'11", 190 lbs. Deb: 9/22/40 C

YEAR	TM/L	G	AB	R	H	2B	3B	HR	RBI	BB	SO	AVG	OBP	SLG	PRO+	BR	/A	RC	SB	CS	SBR	FA	FR	POS	TPR
1940	Phi-A	6	23	6	8	0	0	0	0	3	0	.348	.423	.348	104	0	0	4	2	0	1	1.000	1	/O	0.1
1941	Phi-A	15	50	13	21	0	1	2	6	4	2	.420	.463	.580	179	5	5	14	0	0	0	1.000	-1	O	0.4
1942	Phi-A	133	459	64	115	13	10	2	40	70	21	.251	.355	.336	95	-1	-1	58	13	8	-1	.964	1	*O	-0.8
1943	Phi-A	77	249	31	55	6	2	3	18	35	13	.221	.319	.297	81	-5	-5	24	2	6	-3	.986	-1	O	-1.3
1946	Phi-A	108	348	59	107	21	6	1	31	60	18	.307	.411	.411	131	17	17	64	9	8	-2	.974	1	O	1.2
1947	Phi-A	112	370	60	111	12	6	5	36	64	21	.300	.406	.405	123	16	15	69	11	3	2	.973	-1	*O	1.0
1948	Phi-A	113	383	72	117	17	4	3	46	81	13	.305	.432	.394	120	16	16	72	10	6	-1	.983	-1	*O	0.9
1949	Phi-A	150	547	86	155	27	12	5	85	119	32	.283	.413	.404	121	18	21	101	14	11	-2	.981	10	*O	2.0
1950	Phi-A	129	446	62	125	16	5	10	46	82	22	.280	.400	.406	109	7	9	81	12	7	-1	.982	4	*O	0.6
1951	Phi-A	123	444	75	134	27	8	7	55	75	20	.302	.412	.446	129	23	21	87	11	6	-0	.981	-0	*O	1.6
1952	Phi-A	129	388	69	109	26	4	5	47	101	16	.281	.432	.407	126	24	21	76	12	11	-3	.962	-3	*O	1.1
1953	Phi-A	50	85	15	19	3	0	0	9	22	7	.224	.383	.259	73	-2	-2	10	0	1	-1	1.000	-1	O	-0.4
1954	Phi-A	95	224	28	48	11	6	1	33	51	18	.214	.360	.330	90	-1	-1	31	2	1	0	.965	2	O	-0.3
1955	KC-A	112	283	50	103	17	4	3	37	52	18	.364	.463	.484	153	25	24	67	5	3	-0	.987	2	O	2.2
1956	KC-A	9	9	1	2	0	0	0	2	1	1	.222	.300	.222	40	-1	-1	1	0	0	0	.000	-0	/O	-0.1
	Phi-N	98	291	40	84	13	3	5	37	48	21	.289	.395	.405	118	9	9	48	7	6	-2	.966	-0	O	0.3
1957	Bro-N	81	161	14	44	10	1	4	26	25	16	.273	.374	.422	104	4	2	24	0	1	-1	1.000	-4	O	-0.5
1958	LA-N	65	101	9	25	2	1	1	14	12	11	.248	.327	.317	69	-4	-4	11	0	1	-1	1.000	-6	O	-1.2
1959	Cle-A	34	24	3	7	0	0	0	5	7	0	.292	.452	.292	113	1	1	3	0	0	0	1.000	-1	/O	0.0
1960	NY-A	8	5	1	0	0	0	0	0	2	1	.000	.286	.000	-17	-1	-1	0	0	0	0	.000	-1	/O	-0.2
	Was-A	76	64	6	18	3	0	0	16	17	4	.281	.439	.328	112	2	2	11	0	0	0	1.000	-1	/O	0.2
	Yr	84	69	7	18	3	0	0	16	19	5	.261	.427	.304	103	2	2	11	0	0	0	1.000	-1	/O	0.0
1961	Min-A	33	32	0	5	2	0	0	4	3	3	.156	.250	.219	25	-3	-4	2	0	0	0	1.000	0	/O	-0.4
	Phi-N	50	43	4	8	2	0	1	8	8	6	.186	.327	.302	69	-2	-2	5	0	0	0	.000	0	/O	-0.2
Total	20	1806	5029	768	1420	228	73	58	601	942	284	.282	.399	.391	114	147	143	864	110	79	-14	.977	2	*O	6.2

■ **DEACON Van BUREN** Van Buren, Edward Eugene b: 12/14/1870, LaSalle Co., Ill. d: 6/29/57, Portland, Ore. BL/TR, 5'10", 175 lbs. Deb: 4/21/04

YEAR	TM/L	G	AB	R	H	2B	3B	HR	RBI	BB	SO	AVG	OBP	SLG	PRO+	BR	/A	RC	SB	CS	SBR	FA	FR	POS	TPR
1904	Bro-N	1	1	0	1	0	0	0	0	0		1.000	1.000	1.000	533	0	0	1	0			.000	0	H	0.0
	Phi-N	12	43	2	10	2	0	0	3	3		.233	.283	.279	77	-1	-1	4	2			.962	1	O	-0.1
	Yr	13	44	2	11	2	0	0	3	3		.250	.298	.295	87	-1	-1	5	2			.962	1	O	-0.1

■ **AL Van CAMP** Van Camp, Albert Joseph b: 9/7/03, Moline, Ill. d: 2/2/81, Davenport, Iowa BR/TR, 5'11.5", 175 lbs. Deb: 9/11/28

YEAR	TM/L	G	AB	R	H	2B	3B	HR	RBI	BB	SO	AVG	OBP	SLG	PRO+	BR	/A	RC	SB	CS	SBR	FA	FR	POS	TPR
1928	Cle-A	5	17	0	4	1	0	0	2	0	1	.235	.235	.294	38	-2	-2	1	1	0	0	.980	-1	/1	-0.2
1931	Bos-A	101	324	34	89	15	4	0	33	20	24	.275	.319	.346	79	-12	-10	36	3	2	-0	.973	-5	O1	-2.0
1932	Bos-A	34	103	10	23	4	2	0	6	4	17	.223	.252	.301	44	-9	-9	8	0	0	0	.985	1	1	-0.9
Total	3	140	444	44	116	20	6	0	41	24	42	.261	.301	.333	69	-23	-20	45	4	2	0	.991	-5	/O1	-3.1

■ **CARL VANDAGRIFT** Vandagrift, Carl William b: 4/22/1883, Cantrall, Ill. d: 10/9/20, Fort Wayne, Ind. BR/TR, 5'8", 155 lbs. Deb: 5/19/14

YEAR	TM/L	G	AB	R	H	2B	3B	HR	RBI	BB	SO	AVG	OBP	SLG	PRO+	BR	/A	RC	SB	CS	SBR	FA	FR	POS	TPR
1914	Ind-F	43	136	25	34	4	0	0	9	9	15	.250	.301	.279	59	-6	-8	16	7			.925	-7	23/S	-1.5

■ **JOHN VANDERWAL** Vanderwal, John Henry b: 4/29/66, Grand Rapids, Mich. BL/TL, 6'1", 180 lbs. Deb: 9/06/91

YEAR	TM/L	G	AB	R	H	2B	3B	HR	RBI	BB	SO	AVG	OBP	SLG	PRO+	BR	/A	RC	SB	CS	SBR	FA	FR	POS	TPR
1991	Mon-N	21	61	4	13	4	1	1	8	1	18	.213	.226	.361	63	-3	-3	4	0	0	0	1.000	-1	O	-0.5
1992	Mon-N	105	213	21	51	8	2	4	24	24	36	.239	.316	.352	90	-3	-3	25	3	0	1	.981	0	O/1	-0.3
Total	2	126	274	25	64	12	3	5	28	25	54	.234	.298	.354	84	-6	-6	30	3	0	1	.985	-1	/O1	-0.8

■ **FRED Van DUSEN** Van Dusen, Frederick William b: 7/31/37, Jackson Heights, N.Y. BL/TL, 6'3", 180 lbs. Deb: 9/11/55

YEAR	TM/L	G	AB	R	H	2B	3B	HR	RBI	BB	SO	AVG	OBP	SLG	PRO+	BR	/A	RC	SB	CS	SBR	FA	FR	POS	TPR
1955	Phi-N	1	0	0	0	0	0	0	0	0	0	—	1.000	—	199	0	0	0	0	0	0	.000	0	H	0.0

YEAR	TM/L	G	AB	R	H	2B	3B	HR	RBI	BB	SO	AVG	OBP	SLG	PRO+	BR	/A	RC	SB	CS	SBR	FA	FR	POS	TPR

■ BILL Van DYKE — Van Dyke, William Jennings b: 12/15/1863, Paris, Ill. d: 5/5/33, ElPaso, Tex. BR/TR, 5'8", 170 lbs. Deb: 4/17/1890

1890	Tol-a	129	502	74	129	14	11	2		25		.257	.296	.341	87	-8	-10	74	73			.924	-7	*O3/2C	-1.8
1892	StL-N	4	16	2	2	0	0	0	1	0	1	.125	.125	.125	-25	-2	-2	0	0			.875	-1	/O	-0.3
1893	Bos-N	3	12	2	3	1	0	0	1	0	1	.250	.250	.333	52	-1	-1	1	1			1.000	-1	/O	-0.2
Total	3	136	530	78	134	15	11	2	2	25	2	.253	.290	.334	83	-11	-13	76	74			.924	-8	O/32C	-2.3

■ DAVE Van GORDER — Van Gorder, David Thomas b: 3/27/57, Los Angeles, Cal. BR/TR, 6'2", 205 lbs. Deb: 6/15/82

1982	Cin-N	51	137	4	25	3	1	0	7	14	19	.182	.263	.219	35	-11	-12	8	1	0	0	.986	-2	C	-1.2
1984	Cin-N	38	101	10	23	2	0	0	6	12	17	.228	.310	.248	56	-5	-6	8	0	0	0	1.000	2	C/1	-0.3
1985	Cin-N	73	151	12	36	7	0	2	24	9	19	.238	.286	.325	67	-6	-7	13	0	0	0	.989	-3	C	-0.9
1986	Cin-N	9	10	0	0	0	0	0	0	1	2	.000	.091	.000	-70	-2	-2	0	0	0	0	1.000	1	/C	-0.2
1987	Bal-A	12	21	4	5	0	0	1	1	3	6	.238	.333	.381	91	-0	-0	3	0	0	0	.978	1	C	0.1
Total	5	183	420	30	89	12	1	3	38	39	63	.212	.282	.267	52	-25	-27	32	1	0	0	.990	-2	C/1	-2.5

■ GEORGE Van HALTREN — Van Haltren, George Edward Martin "Rip" b: 3/30/1866, St.Louis, Mo. d: 9/29/45, Oakland, Cal. BL/TL, 5'11", 170 lbs. Deb: 6/27/1887 M

1887	Chi-N	45	172	30	35	4	0	3	17	15	15	.203	.271	.279	48	-10	-14	17	12			.927	-3	OP	-1.0
1888	Chi-N	81	318	46	90	9	14	4	34	22	34	.283	.329	.437	135	16	12	54	21			.872	-2	OP	0.3
1889	Chi-N	134	543	126	168	20	10	9	81	82	41	.309	.405	.433	129	29	24	109	28			.898	-3	*O/S2	1.6
1890	Bro-P	92	376	84	126	8	9	5	54	41	23	.335	.405	.444	121	16	12	84	35			.896	5	OP/S	0.6
1891	Bal-a	139	566	136	180	14	15	9	83	71	46	.318	.398	.443	142	33	31	133	75			.882	-12	OS/P2	1.7
1892	Bal-N	135	556	105	168	20	12	7	57	70	34	.302	.382	.419	141	31	28	110	49			.850	0	*O/P31SM	2.1
	Pit-N	13	55	10	11	2	2	0	5	6	0	.200	.279	.309	79	-1	-1	7	6			.905	-2	O	-0.1
	Yr	148	611	115	179	22	14	7	62	76	34	.293	.373	.409	135	29	27	117	55			.854	-2	*O/P31S	1.7
1893	Pit-N	124	529	129	179	14	11	3	79	75	25	.338	.422	.423	130	24	25	113	37			.869	-6	*OS/2	1.1
1894	*NY-N	137	519	109	172	22	4	7	104	55	22	.331	.400	.430	103	3	4	110	43			.914	-2	*O	-0.6
1895	NY-N	131	521	113	177	23	19	8	103	57	29	.340	.408	.503	140	28	30	123	32			.914	-3	*O/P	1.3
1896	NY-N	133	562	136	197	18	**21**	5	74	55	36	.351	.410	.484	141	30	33	131	39			.952	4	*O/P	2.2
1897	NY-N	129	564	117	186	22	9	3	64	40		.330	.375	.417	112	7	9	110	50			.937	9	*O	0.7
1898	NY-N	156	654	129	204	28	16	2	68	59		.312	.372	.413	129	21	24	117	36			.917	-2	*O	0.9
1899	NY-N	151	604	117	182	21	3	2	58	74		.301	.378	.356	106	4	8	96	31			.932	3	*O	-0.1
1900	NY-N	141	571	114	180	30	7	1	51	50		.315	.371	.398	118	10	14	105	**45**			.939	10	*O/P	1.2
1901	NY-N	135	543	82	182	23	6	1	47	51		.335	.396	.405	138	24	27	100	24			.941	4	*O/P	2.0
1902	NY-N	24	88	14	23	1	2	0	7	17		.261	.381	.318	117	3	3	13	6			.925	2	O	0.3
1903	NY-N	84	280	42	72	6	1	0	28	28		.257	.325	.286	72	-8	-10	32	14			.959	-6	O	-1.9
Total	17	1984	8021	1639	2532	285	161	69	1014	868	305	.316	.385	.417	123	257	259	1566	583			.915	-6	*O/PS231	12.0

■ JOHN VANN — Vann, John Silas b: 6/7/1893, Fairland, Okla. d: 6/10/58, Shreveport, La. BR/TR, Deb: 6/11/13

| 1913 | StL-N | 1 | 1 | 0 | 0 | 0 | 0 | 0 | 0 | 0 | 1 | .000 | .000 | .000 | -99 | -0 | -0 | 0 | 0 | | | .000 | 0 | H | 0.0 |

■ JAY Van NOY — Van Noy, Jay Lowell b: 11/4/28, Garland, Utah BL/TR, 6'1", 200 lbs. Deb: 6/18/51

| 1951 | StL-N | 6 | 7 | 1 | 0 | 0 | 0 | 0 | 0 | 1 | 6 | .000 | .125 | .000 | -63 | -2 | -2 | 0 | 0 | 0 | 0 | 1.000 | -0 | /O | -0.2 |

■ MAURICE Van ROBAYS — Van Robays, Maurice Rene "Bomber" b: 11/15/14, Detroit, Mich. d: 3/1/65, Detroit, Mich. BR/TR, 6'0.5", 190 lbs. Deb: 9/07/39

1939	Pit-N	27	105	13	33	9	0	2	16	6	10	.314	.351	.457	118	2	2	16	0			.919	-4	O/3	-0.2
1940	Pit-N	145	572	82	156	27	4	11	116	33	58	.273	.316	.402	98	-4	-3	69	2			.963	-4	*O/1	-1.5
1941	Pit-N	129	457	62	129	23	5	4	78	41	29	.282	.343	.381	104	2	2	57	0			.974	7	*O	0.2
1942	Pit-N	100	328	29	76	13	5	1	46	30	24	.232	.298	.311	76	-9	-10	30	0			.986	5	O	-1.0
1943	Pit-N	69	236	32	68	17	7	1	35	18	19	.288	.344	.432	119	6	5	34	0			.940	-3	O	-1.0
1946	Pit-N	59	146	14	31	5	3	1	12	11	15	.212	.272	.308	63	-7	-8	11	0			.955	-5	O/1	-1.5
Total	6	529	1844	232	493	94	27	20	303	139	155	.267	.321	.380	97	-10	-11	218	2			.966	-3	O/13	-4.0

■ ANDY Van SLYKE — Van Slyke, Andrew James b: 12/21/60, Utica, N.Y. BL/TR, 6'2", 192 lbs. Deb: 6/17/83

1983	StL-N	101	309	51	81	15	5	8	38	46	64	.262	.360	.421	115	7	7	50	21	7	2	.974	-2	O3/1	0.5
1984	StL-N	137	361	45	88	16	4	7	50	63	71	.244	.356	.368	107	4	5	54	28	5	5	1.000	-12	O31	-0.5
1985	*StL-N	146	424	61	110	25	6	13	55	47	54	.259	.336	.439	116	8	9	66	34	6	7	.996	-2	*O/1	1.0
1986	StL-N	137	418	48	113	23	7	13	61	47	85	.270	.345	.452	119	10	10	68	21	8	2	.969	3	*O1	1.1
1987	Pit-N	157	564	93	165	36	11	21	82	56	122	.293	.361	.507	126	21	20	108	34	15	8	.988	10	*O/1	3.0
1988	Pit-N★	154	587	101	169	23	**15**	25	100	57	126	.288	.352	.506	146	31	32	107	30	9	4	.991	17	*O	5.1
1989	Pit-N	130	476	64	113	18	9	9	53	47	100	.237	.310	.370	97	-4	-2	55	16	4	2	.989	14	*O/1	1.1
1990	*Pit-N	136	493	67	140	26	6	17	77	66	89	.284	.370	.465	133	19	22	89	14	4	2	.976	3	*O	2.4
1991	*Pit-N	138	491	87	130	24	7	17	83	71	85	.265	.362	.446	128	18	19	85	10	3	1	.996	1	*O	1.9
1992	*Pit-N★	154	614	103	**199**	**45**	12	14	89	58	99	.324	.386	.505	152	40	41	122	12	3	2	.989	11	*O	5.3
Total	10	1390	4737	720	1308	251	82	144	688	558	895	.276	.355	.455	126	154	163	804	220	57	32	.987	43	*O/13	20.9

■ IKE Van ZANDT — Van Zandt, Charles Isaac b: 1877, Brooklyn, N.Y. d: 9/14/08, Nashua, N.H. BL, Deb: 8/05/01

1901	NY-N	3	6	1	1	0	0	0	0	0		.167	.167	.167	-3	-1	-1	0	0			.333	-2	/PO	-0.1
1904	Chi-N	3	11	0	0	0	0	0	0	0		.000	.000	.000	-99	-3	-3	0	0			1.000	0	/O	-0.3
1905	StL-A	94	322	31	75	15	1	1	20	7		.233	.252	.295	77	-11	-9	27	7			.878	-11	O/P1	-2.6
Total	3	100	339	32	76	15	1	1	20	7		.224	.242	.283	70	-14	-12	27	7			.872	-13	/OP1	-3.0

■ DICK Van ZANT — Van Zant, Richard "Foghorn Dick" b: 11/1864, Indiana d: 8/6/12, Wayne Co., Ind. Deb: 10/04/1888

| 1888 | Cle-a | 10 | 31 | 1 | 8 | 1 | 0 | 0 | 1 | 1 | | .258 | .303 | .290 | 96 | -0 | -0 | 3 | 1 | | | .784 | 0 | 3 | 0.0 |

■ EDDIE VARGAS — Vargas, Hediberto (Rodriguez) b: 2/23/59, Guanica, P.R. BR/TR, 6'4", 205 lbs. Deb: 9/08/82

1982	Pit-N	8	8	1	3	1	0	0	3	0	2	.375	.375	.500	139	0	0	2	0	0	0	1.000	0	/1	0.0
1984	Pit-N	18	31	3	7	2	0	0	2	3	5	.226	.294	.290	65	-1	-1	3	0	0	0	.982	-0	1	-0.2
Total	2	26	39	4	10	3	0	0	5	3	7	.256	.310	.333	80	-1	-1	4	0	0	0	.986	-0	/1	-0.2

■ BUCK VARNER — Varner, Glen Gann b: 8/17/30, Hixson, Tenn. BL/TR, 5'10", 170 lbs. Deb: 9/19/52

| 1952 | Was-A | 2 | 4 | 0 | 0 | 0 | 0 | 0 | 0 | 0 | 1 | .000 | .200 | .000 | -43 | -1 | -1 | 0 | 0 | 0 | 0 | 1.000 | -0 | /O | -0.1 |

■ PETE VARNEY — Varney, Richard Fred b: 4/10/49, Roxbury, Mass. BR/TR, 6'3", 235 lbs. Deb: 8/26/73

1973	Chi-A	5	4	0	0	0	0	0	0	1	0	.000	.200	.000	-38	-1	-1	0	0	0	0	1.000	0	/C	0.0
1974	Chi-A	9	28	1	7	0	0	0	2	1	8	.250	.276	.250	51	-2	-2	2	0	0	0	.981	1	/C	0.0
1975	Chi-A	36	107	12	29	5	1	2	8	6	28	.271	.316	.393	98	-0	-1	14	2	0	1	.988	-1	C/D	0.0
1976	Chi-A	14	41	5	10	2	0	3	5	2	9	.244	.279	.512	128	1	1	5	0	0	0	.988	1	C	0.3
	Atl-N	5	10	0	1	0	0	0	0	0	2	.100	.100	.100	-41	-2	-2	0	0	0	0	1.000	0	/C	-0.3
Total	4	69	190	18	47	7	1	5	15	10	47	.247	.289	.374	86	-4	-4	21	2	0	1	.988	1	/CD	0.0

■ GARY VARSHO — Varsho, Gary Andrew b: 6/20/61, Marshfield, Wis. BL/TR, 5'11", 190 lbs. Deb: 7/06/88

1988	Chi-N	46	73	6	20	3	0	0	5	1	6	.274	.284	.315	69	-3	-3	7	5	0	2	.906	-2	O	-0.4
1989	Chi-N	61	87	10	16	4	0	4	13	4	13	.184	.220	.276	38	-7	-8	6	3	0	1	.929	-3	O	-1.1
1990	Chi-N	46	48	10	12	4	0	1	6	3	6	.250	.265	.333	59	-2	-3	4	2	0	1	1.000	-1	/O	-0.3
1991	*Pit-N	99	187	23	51	11	2	4	23	19	34	.273	.346	.417	115	3	4	29	9	2	2	.989	-4	O/1	

YEAR	TM/L	G	AB	R	H	2B	3B	HR	RBI	BB	SO	AVG	OBP	SLG	PRO+	BR	/A	RC	SB	CS	SBR	FA	FR	POS	TPR
1992	*Pit-N	103	162	22	36	6	3	4	22	10	32	.222	.267	.370	80	-5	-5	16	5	2	0	.984	-5	O	-1.1
Total	5	355	557	71	135	28	7	8	57	35	91	.242	.290	.361	82	-14	-14	62	24	4	5	.967	-14	O/1	-2.9

■ **JIM VATCHER** Vatcher, James Ernest b: 5/27/66, Santa Monica, Cal. BR/TR, 5'9", 165 lbs. Deb: 5/30/90

YEAR	TM/L	G	AB	R	H	2B	3B	HR	RBI	BB	SO	AVG	OBP	SLG	PRO+	BR	/A	RC	SB	CS	SBR	FA	FR	POS	TPR
1990	Phi-N	36	46	5	12	1	0	1	4	4	6	.261	.320	.348	84	-1	-1	5	0	0	0	1.000	-6	O	-0.8
	Atl-N	21	27	2	7	1	1	0	3	1	9	.259	.286	.370	75	-1	-1	3	0	0	0	1.000	-1	/O	-0.2
	Yr	57	73	7	19	2	1	1	7	5	15	.260	.308	.356	80	-2	-2	8	0	0	0	1.000	-7	O	-1.0
1991	SD-N	17	20	3	4	0	0	0	2	4	6	.200	.333	.200	52	-1	-1	2	1	0	0	.900	-2	O	-0.3
1992	SD-N	13	16	1	4	1	0	0	2	3	6	.250	.368	.313	91	0	-0	2	0	0	0	1.000	-2	O	-0.2
Total	3	87	109	11	27	3	1	1	11	12	27	.248	.322	.321	77	-3	-3	12	1	0	0	.980	-11	/O	-1.5

■ **GLENN VAUGHAN** Vaughan, Glenn Edward "Sparky" b: 2/15/44, Compton, Cal. BB/TR, 5'11", 170 lbs. Deb: 9/20/63

YEAR	TM/L	G	AB	R	H	2B	3B	HR	RBI	BB	SO	AVG	OBP	SLG	PRO+	BR	/A	RC	SB	CS	SBR	FA	FR	POS	TPR
1963	Hou-N	9	30	1	5	0	0	0	0	2	5	.167	.219	.167	14	-3	-3	1	1	0	0	.914	-3	/S3	-0.6

■ **ARKY VAUGHAN** Vaughan, Joseph Floyd b: 3/9/12, Clifty, Ark. d: 8/30/52, Eagleville, Cal. BL/TR, 5'10.5", 175 lbs. Deb: 4/17/32 H

YEAR	TM/L	G	AB	R	H	2B	3B	HR	RBI	BB	SO	AVG	OBP	SLG	PRO+	BR	/A	RC	SB	CS	SBR	FA	FR	POS	TPR
1932	Pit-N	129	497	71	158	15	10	4	61	39	26	.318	.375	.412	113	9	10	79	10			.934	-20	*S	0.1
1933	Pit-N	152	573	85	180	29	**19**	9	97	64	23	.314	.388	.478	146	35	35	112	3			.945	-9	*S	3.8
1934	Pit-N★	149	558	115	186	41	11	12	94	**94**	38	.333	**.431**	.511	148	44	42	135	10			.952	3	*S	**5.2**
1935	Pit-N★	137	499	108	192	34	10	19	99	**97**	18	**.385**	**.491**	**.607**	**187**	**72**	**70**	**163**	4			.950	-11	*S	**6.3**
1936	Pit-N☆	156	568	**122**	190	30	11	9	78	**118**	21	.335	**.453**	.474	146	47	45	137	6			.945	-11	*S	4.2
1937	Pit-N★	126	469	71	151	17	**17**	5	72	54	22	.322	.394	.463	132	22	22	91	7			.956	0	*SO	2.8
1938	Pit-N☆	148	541	88	174	35	5	7	68	104	21	.322	.433	.444	140	36	36	115	14			.961	18	*S	**6.5**
1939	Pit-N★	152	595	94	182	30	11	6	62	70	20	.306	.385	.424	119	16	17	103	12			.962	9	*S	3.9
1940	Pit-N★	156	594	**113**	178	40	**15**	7	95	88	25	.300	.393	.453	134	29	29	113	12			.942	8	*S/3	**5.0**
1941	Pit-N★	106	374	69	118	20	7	6	38	50	13	.316	.399	.455	141	21	21	72	8			.958	-12	S/3	1.7
1942	Bro-N★	128	495	82	137	18	4	2	49	51	17	.277	.348	.341	100	2	1	63	8			.959	-10	*3/S2	-0.7
1943	Bro-N	149	610	**112**	186	39	6	5	66	60	13	.305	.370	.413	126	20	20	96	**20**			.965	-24	S3	0.4
1947	*Bro-N	64	126	24	41	5	2	2	25	27	11	.325	.444	.444	132	8	8	27	4			1.000	1	O3	0.7
1948	Bro-N	65	123	19	30	3	0	3	22	21	8	.244	.354	.341	86	-1	-2	15	0			1.000	1	O/3	-0.2
Total	14	1817	6622	1173	2103	356	128	96	926	937	276	.318	.406	.453	136	361	356	1323	118			.951	-59	*S3/O2	39.7

■ **FRED VAUGHN** Vaughn, Frederick Thomas "Muscles" b: 10/18/18, Coalinga, Cal. d: 3/2/64, Near Lake Wales, Fla. BR/TR, 5'10", 185 lbs. Deb: 8/20/44

YEAR	TM/L	G	AB	R	H	2B	3B	HR	RBI	BB	SO	AVG	OBP	SLG	PRO+	BR	/A	RC	SB	CS	SBR	FA	FR	POS	TPR
1944	Was-A	30	109	10	28	2	1	1	21	9	24	.257	.319	.321	87	-2	-2	11	2	2	-1	.942	-2	2/3	-0.3
1945	Was-A	80	268	28	63	7	4	1	25	23	48	.235	.298	.302	81	-9	-6	25	0	3	-2	.946	-5	2/S	-0.9
Total	2	110	377	38	91	9	5	2	46	32	72	.241	.304	.308	83	-11	-8	36	2	5	-2	.945	-6	2/3S	-1.2

■ **GREG VAUGHN** Vaughn, Gregory Lamont b: 7/3/65, Sacramento, Cal. BR/TR, 6', 195 lbs. Deb: 8/10/89

YEAR	TM/L	G	AB	R	H	2B	3B	HR	RBI	BB	SO	AVG	OBP	SLG	PRO+	BR	/A	RC	SB	CS	SBR	FA	FR	POS	TPR
1989	Mil-A	38	113	18	30	3	0	5	23	13	23	.265	.341	.425	116	2	2	18	4	1	1	.943	-3	OD	0.0
1990	Mil-A	120	382	51	84	26	2	17	61	33	91	.220	.284	.432	98	-3	-3	44	7	4	-0	.967	-1	*O/D	-0.6
1991	Mil-A	145	542	81	132	24	5	27	98	62	125	.244	.322	.456	116	8	10	82	2	2	-1	.994	13	*OD	1.9
1992	Mil-A	141	501	77	114	18	2	23	78	60	123	.228	.316	.409	104	1	2	63	15	15	-5	.990	3	*O/D	-0.2
Total	4	444	1538	227	360	71	9	72	260	168	362	.234	.312	.432	108	8	11	208	28	22	-5	.984	13	O/D	1.1

■ **FARMER VAUGHN** Vaughn, Harry Francis b: 3/1/1864, Rural Dale, Ohio d: 2/21/14, Cincinnati, Ohio BR/TR, 6'3", 177 lbs. Deb: 10/07/1886

YEAR	TM/L	G	AB	R	H	2B	3B	HR	RBI	BB	SO	AVG	OBP	SLG	PRO+	BR	/A	RC	SB	CS	SBR	FA	FR	POS	TPR
1886	Cin-a	1	3	0	0	0	0	0		0		.000	.250	.000	-17	-0	-0	0	0			.917	1	/C	0.0
1888	Lou-a	51	189	15	37	4	2	1	21	4		.196	.216	.254	54	-10	-9	12	4			.863	-2	OC	-0.9
1889	Lou-a	90	360	39	86	11	5	3	45	7	41	.239	.253	.322	66	-17	-16	34	13			.900	3	CO1/3	-0.9
1890	NY-P	44	166	27	44	7	0	1	22	10	9	.265	.307	.325	65	-7	-10	19	6			.877	-12	CO/32	-1.6
1891	Cin-a	51	175	21	45	7	1	1	14	14	15	.257	.316	.326	79	-3	-6	21	7			.923	7	C/O13P	0.4
	Mil-a	25	99	13	33	7	0	0	9	4	5	.333	.359	.404	101	2	-1	15	1			.924	2	C/1O	0.3
	Yr	76	274	34	78	14	1	1	23	18	20	.285	.331	.354	88	-1	-7	36	8			.923	9	C/O13P	0.7
1892	Cin-N	91	346	45	88	10	5	2	50	16	13	.254	.295	.329	92	-5	-4	38	10			.929	-13	C1O/3	-1.2
1893	Cin-N	121	483	68	135	17	12	1	108	35	17	.280	.332	.371	86	-9	-11	66	16			**.969**	1	CO1	-0.4
1894	Cin-N	72	284	50	88	15	5	8	64	12	11	.310	.338	.482	94	-3	-5	49	5			.918	-1	C1/OS	-0.2
1895	Cin-N	92	334	60	102	23	5	1	48	17	10	.305	.339	.413	91	-3	-6	54	15			.934	10	C1/32	1.0
1896	Cin-N	114	433	71	127	20	9	2	66	16	7	.293	.320	.395	84	-8	-12	59	7			.984	3	1C	-0.2
1897	Cin-N	54	199	21	58	13	5	0	30	2		.291	.299	.407	80	-5	-8	26	2			.986	0	1C	-0.5
1898	Cin-N	78	275	35	84	12	4	1	46	11		.305	.334	.389	100	1	-1	39	4			.979	-3	1C	-0.1
1899	Cin-N	31	108	9	19	1	0	0	2	3		.176	.198	.185	5	-14	-14	5	2			.982	3	1/CO	-0.9
Total	13	915	3454	474	946	147	53	21	525	151	128	.274	.307	.365	82	-82	-104	435	92			.926	-1	C1O/3S2P	-5.2

■ **MO VAUGHN** Vaughn, Maurice Samuel b: 12/15/67, Norwalk, Conn. BL/TR, 6'1", 225 lbs. Deb: 6/27/91

YEAR	TM/L	G	AB	R	H	2B	3B	HR	RBI	BB	SO	AVG	OBP	SLG	PRO+	BR	/A	RC	SB	CS	SBR	FA	FR	POS	TPR
1991	Bos-A	74	219	21	57	12	0	4	32	26	43	.260	.344	.370	93	-0	-2	28	2	1	0	.985	-2	1D	-0.6
1992	Bos-A	113	355	42	83	16	2	13	57	47	67	.234	.328	.400	98	2	-1	46	3	3	-1	.982	-2	1D	-0.9
Total	2	187	574	63	140	28	2	17	89	73	110	.244	.334	.389	96	1	-2	74	5	4	-1	.983	-4	1/D	-1.5

■ **BOBBY VAUGHN** Vaughn, Robert b: 6/4/1885, Stamford, N.Y. d: 4/11/65, Seattle, Wash. BR/TR, 5'9", 150 lbs. Deb: 6/12/09

YEAR	TM/L	G	AB	R	H	2B	3B	HR	RBI	BB	SO	AVG	OBP	SLG	PRO+	BR	/A	RC	SB	CS	SBR	FA	FR	POS	TPR
1909	NY-A	5	14	1	2	0	0	0	0	1		.143	.200	.143	8	-1	-1	1	1			.882	-3	/2S	-0.5
1915	StL-F	144	521	69	146	19	9	0	32	58	38	.280	.356	.351	103	7	3	81	24			.953	-8	*2S/3	-0.3
Total	2	149	535	70	148	19	9	0	32	59	38	.277	.352	.346	101	5	2	81	25			.951	-11	2/S3	-0.8

■ **BOBBY VEACH** Veach, Robert Hayes b: 6/29/1888, Island, Ky. d: 8/7/45, Detroit, Mich. BL/TR, 5'11", 160 lbs. Deb: 8/06/12

YEAR	TM/L	G	AB	R	H	2B	3B	HR	RBI	BB	SO	AVG	OBP	SLG	PRO+	BR	/A	RC	SB	CS	SBR	FA	FR	POS	TPR
1912	Det-A	23	79	8	27	5	1	0	15	5		.342	.388	.430	138	3	4	14	2			.927	2	O	0.4
1913	Det-A	137	491	54	132	22	10	0	64	53	31	.269	.346	.354	107	4	4	66	22			.917	-5	*O	-0.7
1914	Det-A	149	531	56	146	19	14	1	72	50	29	.275	.341	.369	110	8	6	68	20	20	-6	.965	3	*O	-0.3
1915	Det-A	152	569	81	178	**40**	10	3	**112**	68	43	.313	.390	.434	140	32	29	97	16	19	-7	.975	2	*O	1.8
1916	Det-A	150	566	92	173	33	15	3	91	52	41	.306	.367	.433	135	26	24	94	24	15	-2	.967	4	*O	2.0
1917	Det-A	154	571	79	182	31	12	8	**103**	61	44	.319	.393	.457	160	40	40	108	21			.956	4	*O	3.9
1918	Det-A	127	499	59	139	21	13	3	**78**	35	23	.279	.331	.391	123	8	11	69	21			.977	3	*O/P	0.7
1919	Det-A	139	538	87	**191**	**45**	**17**	3	101	33	33	.355	.398	.519	160	38	39	115	19			.967	11	*O	4.2
1920	Det-A	154	612	92	188	39	15	11	113	36	22	.307	.353	.474	121	13	15	101	11	7	-1	.967	15	*O	1.6
1921	Det-A	150	612	110	207	43	13	16	128	48	31	.338	.387	.529	133	27	28	123	14	10	-2	.974	15	*O	2.8
1922	Det-A	155	618	96	202	34	13	9	126	42	27	.327	.377	.468	123	16	19	111	9	1	2	.982	8	*O	1.7
1923	Det-A	114	293	45	94	13	3	2	39	29	21	.321	.388	.406	111	5	5	49	10	3	1	.943	-14	O	-1.2
1924	Bos-A	142	519	77	153	35	9	5	99	47	18	.295	.359	.426	102	0	0	81	5	5	-2	.956	-1	*O	-1.0
1925	Bos-A	1	5	0	1	0	0	0	2	1	1	.200	.333	.200	38	-0	-0	0	0	0	0	1.000	0	/O	0.0
	NY-A	56	116	13	41	10	2	0	15	8	0	.353	.400	.474	123	4	4	20	1	4	-2	.957	-7	O	-0.6
	*Was-A	18	37	4	9	3	0	0	8	3	3	.243	.300	.324	60	-2	-2	4	0	0	0	.923	-3	O	-0.5
	Yr	75	158	17	51	13	2	0	25	12	4	.323	.374	.430	106	1	1	24	1	4	-2	.952	-10	O	-1.1
Total	14	1821	6656	953	2063	393	147	64	1166	571	367	.310	.370	.442	127	221	225	1120	195	84		.964	38	*O/P	14.8

■ **PEEK-A-BOO VEACH** Veach, William Walter b: 6/15/1862, Indianapolis, Ind d: 11/12/37, Indianapolis, Ind. Deb: 8/24/1884

YEAR	TM/L	G	AB	R	H	2B	3B	HR	RBI	BB	SO	AVG	OBP	SLG	PRO+	BR	/A	RC	SB	CS	SBR	FA	FR	POS	TPR
1884	KC-U	27	82	9	11	1	0	1		9		.134	.220	.183	43	-5	-3	3				.833	-1	OP/21	-0.3
1887	Lou-a	1	3	0	0	0	0	0		1		.000	.250	.000	-25	-0	-0	0	0			.750	-0	/P	0.0
1890	Cle-N	64	238	24	56	10	5	0	32	33	28	.235	.336	.319	95	-1	-0	29	9			.971	6	1	0.3

YEAR	TM/L	G	AB	R	H	2B	3B	HR	RBI	BB	SO	AVG	OBP	SLG	PRO+	BR	/A	RC	SB	CS	SBR	FA	FR	POS	TPR
	Pit-N	8	30	6	9	1	1	2	5	8	3	.300	.447	.600	235	4	5	8	0			.968	0	/1	0.4
	Yr	72	268	30	65	11	6	2	37	41	31	.243	.349	.351	110	3	5	37	9			.971	7	1	0.7
Total	3	100	353	39	76	12	6	3	37	51	31	.215	.319	.309	96	-2	1	41	9			.971	6	/1OP2	0.4
■ **COOT VEAL**	Veal, Orville Inman b: 7/9/32, Sandersville, Ga. BR/TR, 6'1", 165 lbs. Deb: 7/30/58																								
1958	Det-A	58	207	29	53	10	2	0	16	14	21	.256	.306	.324	69	-7	-9	19	1	1	-0	.981	-8	S	-1.3
1959	Det-A	77	89	12	18	1	0	1	15	8	7	.202	.276	.247	42	-7	-7	7	0	0	0	.962	10	S	0.5
1960	Det-A	27	64	8	19	5	1	0	8	11	7	.297	.400	.406	115	2	2	11	0	0	0	.988	-2	S/32	0.1
1961	Was-A	69	218	21	44	10	0	0	8	19	29	.202	.275	.248	41	-18	-18	15	1	8	-5	.974	0	S	-1.7
1962	Pit-N	1	1	0	0	0	0	0	0	0	1	.000	.000	.000	-99	-0	-0	0	0	0	0	.000	0	H	0.0
1963	Det-A	15	32	5	7	0	0	0	4	4	4	.219	.306	.219	48	-2	-2	2	0	0	0	.980	4	S	0.2
Total	6	247	611	75	141	26	3	1	51	56	69	.231	.301	.288	59	-32	-35	53	2	9	-5	.976	4	S/32	-2.2
■ **JESUS VEGA**	Vega, Jesus Anthony (Morales) b: 10/14/55, Bayamon, P.R. BR/TR, 6'1", 176 lbs. Deb: 9/05/79																								
1979	Min-A	4	7	0	0	0	0	0	0	0	2	.000	.000	.000	-96	-2	-2	0	0	0	0	.000	0	/H	-0.2
1980	Min-A	12	30	3	5	0	0	0	4	3	7	.167	.242	.167	13	-3	-4	1	1	0	0	1.000	0	/1D	-0.3
1982	Min-A	71	199	23	53	6	0	5	29	8	19	.266	.295	.372	80	-5	-6	21	6	1	1	.974	-1	D1/O	-0.7
Total	3	87	236	26	58	6	0	5	33	11	28	.246	.279	.335	65	-11	-12	23	7	1	2	.975	-1	/D1O	-1.2
■ **RANDY VELARDE**	Velarde, Randy Lee b: 11/24/62, Midland, Tex. BR/TR, 6', 185 lbs. Deb: 8/20/87																								
1987	NY-A	8	22	1	4	0	0	0	1	0	6	.182	.182	.182	-3	-3	-3	1	0	0	0	.933	0	/S	-0.2
1988	NY-A	48	115	18	20	6	0	5	12	8	24	.174	.240	.357	65	-6	-6	9	1	1	-0	.967	8	2S3	0.4
1989	NY-A	33	100	12	34	4	2	2	11	7	14	.340	.389	.480	145	6	6	18	0	3	-2	.954	2	3/S	0.6
1990	NY-A	95	229	21	48	6	2	5	19	20	53	.210	.276	.319	66	-11	-11	19	0	3	-2	.945	9	3S/O2D	-0.2
1991	NY-A	80	184	19	45	11	1	1	15	18	43	.245	.322	.332	81	-4	-4	20	3	1	0	.935	7	3S/O	0.4
1992	NY-A	121	412	57	112	24	1	7	46	38	78	.272	.336	.386	100	1	-0	53	7	2	1	.974	-8	S3O/2	-0.2
Total	6	385	1062	128	263	51	6	20	104	91	218	.248	.312	.363	87	-17	-18	119	11	10	-3	.935	19	3S/O2D	0.8
■ **GUILLERMO VELASQUEZ**	Velasquez, Guillermo b: 4/23/68, Mexicali, Mexico BL/TR, 6'3", 220 lbs. Deb: 9/14/92																								
1992	SD-N	15	23	1	7	0	0	1	5	1	7	.304	.333	.435	112	0	0	3	0	0	0	.933	-1	/1O	-0.1
■ **FREDDIE VELAZQUEZ**	Velazquez, Federico Antonio (Velasquez) b: 12/6/37, Santo Domingo, D.R. BR/TR, 6'1", 185 lbs. Deb: 4/20/69																								
1969	Sea-A	6	16	1	2	2	0	0	2	1	3	.125	.176	.250	18	-2	-2	0	0	0	0	1.000	-1	/C	-0.2
1973	Atl-N	15	23	2	8	1	0	0	3	1	3	.348	.375	.391	105	0	0	3	0	0	0	.975	2	C	0.2
Total	2	21	39	3	10	3	0	0	5	2	6	.256	.293	.333	71	-1	-2	4	0	0	0	.985	1	/C	0.0
■ **OTTO VELEZ**	Velez, Otoniel (Franceschi) b: 11/29/50, Ponce, P.R. BR/TR, 6', 195 lbs. Deb: 9/04/73																								
1973	NY-A	23	77	9	15	4	0	2	7	15	24	.195	.326	.325	87	-1	-1	9	0	1	-1	.959	1	O	-0.2
1974	NY-A	27	67	9	14	1	1	2	10	15	24	.209	.354	.343	104	1	1	9	0	0	0	.986	-4	1/O3	-0.4
1975	NY-A	6	8	0	2	0	0	0	1	2	0	.250	.400	.250	90	0	0	1	0	0	0	1.000	-0	/1D	0.0
1976	*NY-A	49	94	11	25	6	0	2	10	23	26	.266	.410	.394	137	6	6	17	0	0	0	.979	-3	O/13D	0.2
1977	Tor-A	120	360	50	92	19	3	16	62	65	87	.256	.371	.458	123	14	13	64	4	2	0	.973	0	OD	1.0
1978	Tor-A	91	248	29	66	14	2	9	38	45	41	.266	.383	.448	130	12	11	43	1	3	-2	.982	7	O/1D	1.4
1979	Tor-A	99	274	45	79	21	0	15	48	46	45	.288	.396	.529	145	19	19	58	0	1	-1	.971	-5	O/1D	1.0
1980	Tor-A	104	357	54	96	12	3	20	62	54	86	.269	.368	.487	126	16	14	65	0	0	0	.975	0	D/1	1.4
1981	Tor-A	80	240	32	51	9	2	11	28	55	60	.213	.366	.404	114	9	7	38	0	3	-2	1.000	-0	D/1	0.5
1982	Tor-A	28	52	4	10	1	0	1	5	13	15	.192	.354	.269	68	-1	-2	6	1	0	0	.000	0	D	-0.2
1983	Cle-A	10	25	1	2	0	0	0	1	3	6	.080	.179	.080	-25	-4	-4	0	0	0	0	.000	0	/D	-0.5
Total	11	637	1802	244	452	87	11	78	272	336	414	.251	.372	.441	122	69	63	311	6	10	-4	.973	-4	OD/13	4.2
■ **PAT VELTMAN**	Veltman, Arthur Patrick b: 3/24/06, Mobile, Ala. d: 10/1/80, San Antonio, Tex. BR/TR, 6', 175 lbs. Deb: 4/17/26																								
1926	Chi-A	5	4	1	1	0	0	0	0	1	1	.250	.400	.250	75	-0	-0	0	0	0	0	1.000	0	/S	0.0
1928	NY-N	1	3	1	1	0	1	0	0	1	0	.333	.500	1.000	282	1	1	2	0			1.000	0	/O	0.1
1929	NY-N	2	1	1	0	0	0	0	0	2	0	.000	.667	.000	81	0	0	0	0			1.000	-0	/C	0.0
1931	Bos-N	1	1	0	0	0	0	0	0	0	0	.000	.000	.000	-99	-0	-0	0	0			.000	0	H	0.0
1932	NY-N	2	1	0	0	0	0	0	0	0	1	.000	.000	.000	-99	-0	-0	0	0			.000	0	H	0.0
1934	Pit-N	12	28	1	3	0	0	0	2	0	1	.107	.107	.107	-41	-6	-6	0	0			1.000	-2	C	-0.7
Total	6	23	38	4	5	0	1	0	2	4	3	.132	.214	.184	7	-5	-5	3	0	0		1.000	-2	/COS	-0.6
■ **MAX VENABLE**	Venable, William McKinley b: 6/6/57, Phoenix, Ariz. BL/TR, 5'10", 185 lbs. Deb: 4/08/79																								
1979	SF-N	55	85	12	14	1	1	0	3	10	18	.165	.260	.200	29	-8	-8	5	3	3	-1	.914	-1	O	-1.0
1980	SF-N	64	138	13	37	5	0	0	10	15	22	.268	.340	.304	83	-3	-3	16	8	2	1	1.000	-3	O	-0.6
1981	SF-N	18	32	2	6	0	2	0	1	4	3	.188	.278	.313	68	-1	-1	3	3	1	0	1.000	-0	/O	-0.2
1982	SF-N	71	125	17	28	2	1	1	7	7	16	.224	.265	.280	53	-8	-8	9	9	3	1	.986	5	O	-0.3
1983	SF-N	94	228	28	50	7	4	6	27	22	34	.219	.296	.364	85	-6	-5	27	15	2	3	.993	6	O	0.3
1984	Mon-N	38	71	7	17	2	0	2	7	3	7	.239	.280	.352	80	-2	-2	7	1	0	0	1.000	-4	O	-0.7
1985	Cin-N	77	135	21	39	12	3	0	10	6	17	.289	.319	.422	101	1	-0	18	11	3	2	1.000	-1	O	-0.1
1986	Cin-N	108	147	17	31	7	1	2	15	17	24	.211	.293	.313	64	-7	-7	15	7	2	1	.969	-10	O	-1.9
1987	Cin-N	7	7	2	1	0	0	0	2	0	0	.143	.143	.143	-23	-1	-1	0	0	0	0	1.000	-1	/O	-0.2
1989	Cal-A	20	53	7	19	4	0	0	4	1	16	.358	.370	.434	128	2	2	9	0	0	0	1.000	-3	O	-0.1
1990	Cal-A	93	189	26	49	9	3	4	21	24	31	.259	.343	.402	110	2	3	28	5	1	1	.975	-12	O/D	-1.0
1991	Cal-A	82	187	24	46	8	2	3	21	11	30	.246	.295	.358	80	-5	-5	19	2	1	0	.967	-11	O/D	-1.8
Total	12	727	1397	176	337	57	17	18	128	120	218	.241	.304	.345	81	-38	-36	157	64	18	8	.982	-35	O/D	-7.6
■ **ROBIN VENTURA**	Ventura, Robin Mark b: 7/14/67, Santa Maria, Cal. BL/TR, 6'1", 185 lbs. Deb: 9/12/89																								
1989	Chi-A	16	45	5	8	3	0	0	7	8	6	.178	.315	.244	61	-2	-2	4	0	0	0	.962	2	3	0.0
1990	Chi-A	150	493	48	123	17	1	5	54	55	53	.249	.326	.318	83	-11	-10	54	1	4	-2	.939	-0	*3/1	-1.2
1991	Chi-A	157	606	92	172	25	1	23	100	80	67	.284	.371	.442	127	21	23	97	2	4	-2	.959	1	*31	2.2
1992	Chi-A★	157	592	85	167	38	1	16	93	93	71	.282	.380	.431	130	23	25	99	2	4	-2	.957	24	*3/1	4.8
Total	4	480	1736	230	470	83	3	44	254	236	197	.271	.360	.398	114	31	36	254	5	12	-6	.953	27	3/1	5.8
■ **VINCE VENTURA**	Ventura, Vincent b: 4/18/17, New York, N.Y. BR/TR, 6'1.5", 190 lbs. Deb: 5/08/45																								
1945	Was-A	18	58	4	12	0	0	0	2	4	4	.207	.258	.207	39	-5	-4	3	0	0	0	.886	-1	O	-0.7
■ **EMIL VERBAN**	Verban, Emil Matthew "Dutch" or "Antelope" b: 8/27/15, Lincoln, Ill. d: 6/8/89, Quincy, Ill. BR/TR, 5'11", 165 lbs. Deb: 4/18/44																								
1944	*StL-N	146	498	51	128	14	2	0	43	19	14	.257	.287	.293	62	-24	-25	43	0			.968	-6	*2	-2.4
1945	StL-N†	155	597	59	166	22	8	0	72	19	15	.278	.304	.342	77	-18	-20	61	4			**.978**	-19	*2	-2.9
1946	StL-N	1	1	0	0	0	0	0	0	0	0	.000	.000	.000	-96	-0	-0	0	0			.000	0	H	0.0
	Phi-N	138	473	44	130	17	5	0	34	21	18	.275	.306	.332	83	-13	-11	48	5			.963	-3	*2	-0.5
	Yr	139	474	44	130	17	5	0	34	21	18	.274	.305	.331	83	-13	-12	48	5			.963	-3	*2	-0.5
1947	Phi-N★	155	540	50	154	14	8	0	42	23	8	.285	.316	.341	77	-20	-18	56	5			.982	17	*2	1.0
1948	Phi-N	55	169	14	39	5	1	0	11	11	5	.231	.282	.272	51	-12	-11	14	0			.975	-4	2	-1.3
	Chi-N	56	248	37	73	15	1	1	16	4	7	.294	.308	.375	88	-6	-5	28	4			.964	6	2	0.4
	Yr	111	417	51	112	20	2	1	27	15	12	.269	.297	.333	72	-18	-16	41	4			.969	2	*2	-0.9
1949	Chi-N	98	343	38	99	11	1	0	22	8	2	.289	.309	.327	72	-14	-13	34	3			.965	3	2	-0.7

YEAR	TM/L	G	AB	R	H	2B	3B	HR	RBI	BB	SO	AVG	OBP	SLG	PRO+	BR	/A	RC	SB	CS	SBR	FA	FR	POS	TPR
1950	Chi-N	45	37	7	4	1	0	0	1	3	5	.108	.175	.135	-17	-6	-6	1	0			.966	6	/2S3O	-0.1
	Bos-N	4	5	1	0	0	0	0	0	0	0	.000	.000	.000	-99	-1	-1	0	0			.833	1	/2	0.0
	Yr	49	42	8	4	1	0	0	1	3	5	.095	.156	.119	-27	-8	-8	1	0			.927	7	2/S3O	-0.1
Total	7	853	2911	301	793	99	26	1	241	108	74	.272	.301	.325	73	-116	-112	286	21			.971	1	2/SO3	-6.5

■ GENE VERBLE
Verble, Gene Kermit "Satchel" b: 6/29/28, Concord, N.C. BR/TR, 5'10", 163 lbs. Deb: 4/17/51

YEAR	TM/L	G	AB	R	H	2B	3B	HR	RBI	BB	SO	AVG	OBP	SLG	PRO+	BR	/A	RC	SB	CS	SBR	FA	FR	POS	TPR
1951	Was-A	68	177	16	36	3	2	0	15	18	10	.203	.277	.243	42	-14	-14	12	1	1	-0	.978	-2	S2/3	-1.3
1953	Was-A	13	21	4	4	0	0	0	2	2	1	.190	.261	.190	24	-2	-2	1	0	0	0	1.000	2	/S	0.0
Total	2	81	198	20	40	3	2	0	17	20	11	.202	.275	.237	40	-17	-16	13	1	1	-0	.981	1	/S23	-1.3

■ FRANK VERDI
Verdi, Frank Michael b: 6/2/26, Brooklyn, N.Y. BR/TR, 5'10.5", 170 lbs. Deb: 5/10/53

YEAR	TM/L	G	AB	R	H	2B	3B	HR	RBI	BB	SO	AVG	OBP	SLG	PRO+	BR	/A	RC	SB	CS	SBR	FA	FR	POS	TPR
1953	NY-A	1	0	0	0	0	0	0	0	0	0	—	—	—	—	0	0	0	0	0	0	.000	0	/S	0.0

■ JOHNNY VERGEZ
Vergez, John Louis b: 7/9/06, Oakland, Cal. d: 7/15/91, Davis, Cal. BR/TR, 5'8", 165 lbs. Deb: 4/14/31

YEAR	TM/L	G	AB	R	H	2B	3B	HR	RBI	BB	SO	AVG	OBP	SLG	PRO+	BR	/A	RC	SB	CS	SBR	FA	FR	POS	TPR
1931	NY-N	152	565	67	157	24	2	13	81	29	65	.278	.320	.396	94	-8	-6	73	11			.932	-3	*3	0.0
1932	NY-N	118	376	42	98	21	3	6	43	25	36	.261	.310	.380	86	-8	-7	45	1			.935	5	*3/S	0.5
1933	NY-N	123	458	57	124	21	6	16	72	39	66	.271	.332	.448	123	12	12	66	1			.928	-14	*3	0.7
1934	NY-N	108	320	31	64	18	1	7	27	28	55	.200	.269	.328	60	-19	-18	29	1			.943	10	*3	-0.4
1935	Phi-N	148	546	56	136	27	4	9	63	46	67	.249	.312	.363	73	-15	-22	64	8			**.953**	-7	*3/S	-2.3
1936	Phi-N	15	40	4	11	2	0	1	5	3	11	.275	.326	.400	86	-0	-1	6	0			.964	0	3	0.0
	StL-N	8	18	1	3	1	0	0	1	1	3	.167	.211	.222	17	-2	-2	1	0			.929	0	/3	-0.2
	Yr	23	58	5	14	3	0	1	6	4	14	.241	.290	.345	66	-2	-3	6	0			.952	0	3	-0.2
Total	6	672	2323	258	593	114	16	52	292	171	303	.255	.311	.385	87	-41	-44	285	22			.939	-8	3/S	-1.7

■ MICKEY VERNON
Vernon, James Barton b: 4/22/18, Marcus Hook, Pa. BL/TL, 6'2", 180 lbs. Deb: 7/08/39 MC

YEAR	TM/L	G	AB	R	H	2B	3B	HR	RBI	BB	SO	AVG	OBP	SLG	PRO+	BR	/A	RC	SB	CS	SBR	FA	FR	POS	TPR
1939	Was-A	76	276	23	71	15	4	1	30	24	28	.257	.317	.351	76	-12	-9	31	1	1	-0	.985	-3	1	-1.9
1940	Was-A	5	19	0	3	0	0	0	0	0	3	.158	.158	.158	-19	-3	-3	0	0	0	0	1.000	-0	/1	-0.4
1941	Was-A	138	531	73	159	27	11	9	93	43	51	.299	.352	.443	114	6	9	84	9	3	1	.992	-6	*1	-0.6
1942	Was-A	151	621	76	168	34	6	9	86	59	63	.271	.337	.388	104	2	3	87	25	6	4	.982	-8	*1	-1.1
1943	Was-A	145	553	89	148	29	8	7	70	67	55	.268	.357	.387	122	13	16	83	24	8	2	.990	-11	*1	-0.1
1946	Was-A★	148	587	88	207	**51**	8	8	85	49	64	**.353**	.403	.508	163	40	44	120	14	10	-2	.990	-1	*1	3.4
1947	Was-A	154	600	77	159	29	12	7	85	49	42	.265	.320	.388	99	-5	-3	73	12	12	-4	.987	-4	*1	-1.6
1948	Was-A★	150	558	78	135	27	7	3	48	54	43	.242	.310	.332	73	-24	-22	56	15	11	-2	.989	5	*1	-2.0
1949	Cle-A	153	584	72	170	27	4	18	83	58	51	.291	.357	.443	113	7	8	96	9	7	-2	.991	19	*1	2.4
1950	Cle-A	28	90	8	17	0	0	0	10	12	10	.189	.284	.189	24	-10	-10	6	2	0	1	.996	1	1	-0.8
	Was-A	90	327	47	100	17	3	9	65	50	29	.306	.404	.459	127	11	13	67	6	1	1	.990	1	*1	1.3
	Yr	118	417	55	117	17	3	9	75	62	39	.281	.379	.400	104	1	4	72	8	1	2	**.991**	3	*1	0.5
1951	Was-A	141	546	69	160	30	7	9	87	53	45	.293	.358	.423	112	7	9	84	7	6	-2	**.994**	-4	*1	-0.3
1952	Was-A	154	569	71	143	33	9	10	80	89	66	.251	.353	.394	111	7	9	84	7	7	-2	**.993**	1	*1	0.2
1953	Was-A★	152	608	101	205	**43**	11	15	115	63	57	**.337**	.403	.518	151	40	42	127	4	6	-2	.992	-3	*1	3.0
1954	Was-A★	151	597	90	173	**33**	14	20	97	61	61	.290	.360	.492	140	24	28	106	1	4	-2	**.992**	-9	*1	1.0
1955	Was-A★	150	538	74	162	23	8	14	85	74	50	.301	.389	.452	133	20	24	93	0	4	-2	.994	-8	*1	0.5
1956	Bos-A★	119	403	67	125	28	4	15	84	57	40	.310	.405	.511	125	24	17	84	1	0	0	.989	-3	*1	0.8
1957	Bos-A	102	270	36	65	18	1	7	38	41	35	.241	.351	.393	97	2	-0	38	0	0	0	.992	4	1	-0.1
1958	Cle-A★	119	355	49	104	22	3	8	55	44	56	.293	.374	.439	126	12	13	58	0	4	-2	.987	-2	1	0.3
1959	Mil-N	74	91	8	20	4	0	3	14	7	20	.220	.283	.363	77	-4	-3	9	0	0	0	.983	1	1/O	-0.3
1960	Pit-N	9	8	0	1	0	0	0	1	1	0	.125	.222	.125	-2	-1	-1	0	0	0	0	.000	0	H	-0.1
Total	20	2409	8731	1196	2495	490	120	172	1311	955	869	.286	.359	.428	116	155	183	1387	137	90	-13	.990	-32	*1/O	3.6

■ ZOILO VERSALLES
Versalles, Zoilo Casanova (Rodriguez) "Zorro" b: 12/18/39, Veldado, Cuba BR/TR, 5'10", 150 lbs. Deb: 8/01/59

YEAR	TM/L	G	AB	R	H	2B	3B	HR	RBI	BB	SO	AVG	OBP	SLG	PRO+	BR	/A	RC	SB	CS	SBR	FA	FR	POS	TPR
1959	Was-A	29	59	4	9	0	0	1	1	4	15	.153	.219	.203	17	-7	-7	3	1	0	0	.943	3	S	-0.2
1960	Was-A	15	45	2	6	2	2	0	4	2	5	.133	.170	.267	16	-5	-5	2	0	0	0	.935	-1	S	-0.5
1961	Min-A	129	510	65	143	25	5	7	53	25	61	.280	.315	.390	83	-10	-14	61	16	9	-1	.952	-2	*S	-0.5
1962	Min-A	160	568	69	137	18	3	17	67	37	71	.241	.290	.373	74	-20	-22	59	5	5	-2	.970	32	*S	2.2
1963	Min-A★	159	621	74	162	31	**13**	10	54	33	66	.261	.303	.401	94	-5	-6	74	7	4	-0	.961	-2	*S	0.3
1964	Min-A	160	659	94	171	33	**10**	20	64	42	88	.259	.312	.431	103	2	2	91	14	4	2	.957	-17	*S	-0.2
1965	*Min-A★	160	666	**126**	182	**45**	**12**	19	77	41	122	.273	.322	.462	115	15	12	102	27	5	**5**	.950	2	*S	3.1
1966	Min-A	137	543	73	135	20	6	7	36	40	85	.249	.308	.346	82	-8	-12	55	10	12	-4	.942	-17	*S	-2.3
1967	Min-A	160	581	63	116	16	7	6	50	33	113	.200	.250	.282	53	-32	-37	39	5	3	-0	.958	2	*S	-2.2
1968	LA-N	122	403	29	79	16	3	2	24	26	84	.196	.245	.266	57	-23	-20	26	6	4	-1	.954	8	*S	-0.1
1969	Cle-A	72	217	21	49	11	1	1	13	21	47	.226	.300	.300	66	-9	-10	19	3	1	0	.975	-11	23/S	-1.9
	Was-A	31	75	9	20	2	1	0	6	3	13	.267	.304	.320	79	-3	-2	7	1	0	0	.935	-1	S/23	-0.2
	Yr	103	292	30	69	13	2	1	19	24	60	.236	.301	.305	69	-12	-12	27	4	1	1	.978	-13	23S	-2.1
1971	Atl-N	66	194	21	37	11	0	5	22	11	40	.191	.234	.325	53	-12	-13	13	2	1	0	.902	-14	3S/2	-2.7
Total	12	1400	5141	650	1246	230	63	95	471	318	810	.242	.292	.367	82	-116	-135	552	97	48	0	.956	-20	*S/32	-5.2

■ TOM VERYZER
Veryzer, Thomas Martin b: 2/11/53, Port Jefferson, N.Y BR/TR, 6'1", 185 lbs. Deb: 8/14/73

YEAR	TM/L	G	AB	R	H	2B	3B	HR	RBI	BB	SO	AVG	OBP	SLG	PRO+	BR	/A	RC	SB	CS	SBR	FA	FR	POS	TPR
1973	Det-A	18	20	1	6	0	1	0	2	2	4	.300	.364	.400	108	0	0	3	0	0	0	.857	-5	S	-0.4
1974	Det-A	22	55	4	13	2	0	2	9	5	8	.236	.300	.382	92	-0	-1	7	1	0	0	.927	-10	S	-0.9
1975	Det-A	128	404	37	102	13	1	5	48	23	76	.252	.301	.327	74	-12	-14	38	2	6	-3	.960	-4	*S	-0.8
1976	Det-A	97	354	31	83	8	2	1	25	21	44	.234	.289	.277	64	-15	-16	27	1	4	-2	.966	-1	S	-0.8
1977	Det-A	125	350	31	69	12	1	2	28	16	44	.197	.232	.254	31	-33	-35	21	0	1	-1	.969	10	*S	-1.3
1978	Cle-A	130	421	48	114	18	4	1	32	13	36	.271	.301	.340	81	-12	-11	42	1	2	-1	.963	-4	*S	-0.1
1979	Cle-A	149	449	41	99	9	3	0	34	34	54	.220	.281	.254	45	-34	-34	32	2	5	-2	.974	4	*S	-1.6
1980	Cle-A	109	358	28	97	12	0	2	28	10	25	.271	.306	.321	72	-14	-14	32	0	5	-3	.971	-1	*S	-0.5
1981	Cle-A	75	221	13	54	4	0	0	14	10	10	.244	.280	.262	58	-12	-12	16	1	0	0	.970	-7	S	-1.1
1982	NY-N	40	54	6	18	2	0	0	4	3	4	.333	.368	.370	108	1	1	7	1	0	0	.962	-2	2S	0.0
1983	Chi-N	59	88	5	18	3	0	1	3	3	13	.205	.231	.273	37	-7	-8	5	0	0	0	.978	7	S3	0.0
1984	*Chi-N	44	74	5	14	1	0	0	4	3	11	.189	.259	.203	29	-7	-7	4	0	0	0	.966	-2	S/32	-0.8
Total	12	996	2848	250	687	84	12	14	231	143	329	.241	.285	.294	61	-144	-152	235	9	23	-11	.966	-14	S/23	-8.3

■ ERNIE VICK
Vick, Henry Arthur b: 7/2/1900, Toledo, Ohio d: 7/16/80, Ann Arbor, Mich. BR/TR, 5'9.5", 185 lbs. Deb: 6/29/22

YEAR	TM/L	G	AB	R	H	2B	3B	HR	RBI	BB	SO	AVG	OBP	SLG	PRO+	BR	/A	RC	SB	CS	SBR	FA	FR	POS	TPR
1922	StL-N	3	6	1	2	2	0	0	0	0	0	.333	.333	.667	159	0	0	1	0	0	0	.875	-0	/C	0.0
1924	StL-N	16	23	2	8	1	0	0	0	3	3	.348	.423	.391	122	1	1	4	0	0	0	.974	3	C	0.4
1925	StL-N	14	32	3	6	2	1	0	3	3	1	.188	.257	.313	44	-3	-3	3	0	0	0	.929	0	/C	-0.2
1926	StL-N	24	51	6	10	2	0	0	4	3	4	.196	.241	.235	27	-5	-5	3	0			.944	-1	C	-0.5
Total	4	57	112	12	26	7	1	0	7	9	8	.232	.289	.313	58	-7	-7	11	0	0		.944	2	/C	-0.3

■ SAMMY VICK
Vick, Samuel Bruce b: 4/12/1895, Batesville, Miss. d: 8/17/86, Memphis, Tenn. BR/TR, 5'10.5", 163 lbs. Deb: 9/20/17

YEAR	TM/L	G	AB	R	H	2B	3B	HR	RBI	BB	SO	AVG	OBP	SLG	PRO+	BR	/A	RC	SB	CS	SBR	FA	FR	POS	TPR
1917	NY-A	10	36	4	10	3	0	0	2	1	6	.278	.297	.361	100	-0	-0	4	2			.882	-1	O	-0.2
1918	NY-A	2	3	1	2	0	0	0	1	0	0	.667	.667	.667	296	1	1	1	0			.000	-1	/O	0.0
1919	NY-A	106	407	59	101	15	9	2	27	35	55	.248	.308	.344	82	-10	-10	44	9			.952	-4	*O	-2.3
1920	NY-A	51	118	21	26	7	1	0	11	14	20	.220	.313	.297	60	-6	-7	12	1	1	-0	.949	-4	O	-1.3
1921	Bos-A	44	77	5	20	3	1	0	9	1	10	.260	.269	.325	52	-6	-6	6	0	1	-1	1.000	-1	O	-0.8
Total	5	213	641	90	159	28	11	2	50	51	91	.248	.305	.335	76	-22	-22	67	12	2		.951	-11	O	-4.6

YEAR	TM/L	G	AB	R	H	2B	3B	HR	RBI	BB	SO	AVG	OBP	SLG	PRO+	BR	/A	RC	SB	CS	SBR	FA	FR	POS	TPR
■ SAM VICO	Vico, George Steve b: 8/9/23, San Fernando, Cal. BL/TR, 6'4", 200 lbs. Deb: 4/20/48																								
1948	Det-A	144	521	50	139	23	9	8	58	39	39	.267	.326	.392	88	-9	-11	63	2	2	-1	.988	-3	*1	-1.5
1949	Det-A	67	142	15	27	5	2	4	18	21	17	.190	.311	.338	72	-6	-6	16	0	0	0	.985	2	1	-0.4
Total	2	211	663	65	166	28	11	12	76	60	56	.250	.323	.380	85	-15	-17	79	2	2	-1	.987	-1	1	-1.9
■ JOSE VIDAL	Vidal, Jose (Nicolas) "Papito" b: 4/3/40, Batey Lechugas, D.R. BR/TR, 6', 190 lbs. Deb: 9/05/66																								
1966	Cle-A	17	32	4	6	1	1	0	3	5	11	.188	.297	.281	67	-1	-1	3	0	1	-1	1.000	-1	O	-0.3
1967	Cle-A	16	34	4	4	0	0	0	0	7	12	.118	.268	.118	17	-3	-3	1	0	1	-1	1.000	-1	O	-0.6
1968	Cle-A	37	54	5	9	0	0	2	5	2	15	.167	.196	.278	43	-4	-4	3	3	0	1	1.000	-5	O/1	-1.0
1969	Sea-A	18	26	7	5	0	1	1	2	4	8	.192	.323	.385	99	-0	-0	3	1	1	-0	.917	-0	/O	-0.1
Total	4	88	146	20	24	1	2	3	10	18	46	.164	.261	.260	53	-8	-8	11	4	3	-1	.985	-7	/O1	-2.0
■ HECTOR VILLANUEVA	Villanueva, Hector (Balasquide) b: 10/2/64, Rio Piedras, P.R. BR/TR, 6'1", 220 lbs. Deb: 6/01/90																								
1990	Chi-N	52	114	14	31	4	1	7	18	4	27	.272	.308	.509	112	3	2	17	1	0	0	.991	-4	C1	-0.2
1991	Chi-N	71	192	23	53	10	1	13	32	21	30	.276	.347	.542	140	11	10	36	0	0	0	.979	-9	C/1	0.4
1992	Chi-N	51	112	9	17	6	0	2	13	11	24	.152	.228	.259	37	-9	-10	6	0	0	0	.978	6	C/1	-0.2
Total	3	174	418	46	101	20	2	22	63	36	81	.242	.305	.457	105	4	2	59	1	0	0	.981	-7	C/1	0.0
■ CHARLIE VINSON	Vinson, Charles Anthony "Chuck" b: 1/5/44, Washington, D.C. BL/TL, 6'3", 207 lbs. Deb: 9/19/66																								
1966	Cal-A	13	22	3	4	2	0	1	6	5	9	.182	.357	.409	123	1	1	4	0	0	0	1.000	-1	1	0.0
■ RUBE VINSON	Vinson, Ernest Augustus b: 3/20/1879, Dover, Del. d: 10/12/51, Chester, Pa. 5'9", 168 lbs. Deb: 9/27/04																								
1904	Cle-A	15	49	12	15	1	0	0	2	10		.306	.433	.327	143	3	3	8	2			1.000	3	O	0.6
1905	Cle-A	39	134	12	26	3	1	0	9	7		.194	.245	.231	51	-7	-8	9	4			.930	-3	O	-1.4
1906	Chi-A	10	24	2	6	0	0	0	3	2		.250	.308	.250	77	-1	-1	2	1			.600	-3	/O	-0.4
Total	3	64	207	26	47	4	1	0	14	19		.227	.301	.256	77	-5	-5	20	7			.919	-3	/O	-1.2
■ JIM VIOX	Viox, James Harry b: 12/30/1890, Lockland, Ohio d: 1/6/69, Erlanger, Ky. BR/TR, 5'7", 150 lbs. Deb: 5/09/12																								
1912	Pit-N	33	70	8	13	2	3	1	7	3	9	.186	.219	.343	53	-5	-5	6	2			.957	-4	3/SO2	-0.9
1913	Pit-N	137	492	86	156	32	8	2	65	64	28	.317	.399	.427	142	25	28	88	14			.959	-43	*2S	-1.7
1914	Pit-N	143	506	52	134	18	5	1	57	63	33	.265	.351	.326	106	3	6	60	9			.939	-25	*2/SO	-2.2
1915	Pit-N	150	503	56	129	17	8	2	45	75	31	.256	.357	.334	111	9	10	63	12	8	-1	.954	-23	*23/O	-1.4
1916	Pit-N	43	132	12	33	7	0	1	17	17	11	.250	.340	.326	104	1	1	16	2			.937	-16	23	-1.6
Total	5	506	1703	214	465	76	24	7	191	222	112	.273	.361	.358	116	33	39	233	39	8		.949	-111	2/3SO	-7.8
■ BILL VIRDON	Virdon, William Charles b: 6/9/31, Hazel Park, Mich. BL/TR, 6', 175 lbs. Deb: 4/12/55 MC																								
1955	StL-N	144	534	58	150	18	6	17	68	36	64	.281	.327	.433	100	-1	-1	73	2	4	-2	.966	-0	*O	-1.0
1956	StL-N	24	71	10	15	2	0	2	9	5	8	.211	.273	.324	60	-4	-4	6	0	1	-1	.982	-1	O	-0.7
	Pit-N	133	509	67	170	21	10	8	37	33	63	.334	.376	.462	126	17	18	84	6	6	-2	.989	4	*O	1.4
	Yr	157	580	77	185	23	10	10	46	38	71	.319	.363	.445	118	13	14	90	6	7	-2	.988	3	*O	0.7
1957	Pit-N	144	561	59	141	28	11	8	50	33	69	.251	.293	.383	82	-17	-15	62	3	3	-1	.986	12	*O	-1.2
1958	Pit-N	144	604	75	161	24	11	9	46	52	70	.267	.326	.387	90	-11	-9	78	5	3	-0	.993	11	*O	-0.6
1959	Pit-N	144	519	67	132	24	2	8	41	55	65	.254	.328	.355	83	-13	-12	62	7	4	-0	.979	**24**	*O	0.4
1960	*Pit-N	120	409	60	108	16	9	8	40	40	44	.264	.330	.406	99	-0	-0	57	8	2	1	.983	7	*O	0.3
1961	Pit-N	146	599	81	156	22	8	9	58	49	45	.260	.316	.369	81	-16	-17	71	5	8	-3	.985	5	*O	-2.3
1962	Pit-N	156	663	82	164	27	**10**	6	47	36	65	.247	.287	.345	69	-30	-30	62	5	13	-6	.976	-1	*O	-4.8
1963	Pit-N	142	554	58	149	22	6	8	53	43	55	.269	.322	.374	99	-0	-1	68	1	2	-1	.988	1	*O	-0.9
1964	Pit-N	145	473	59	115	11	3	3	27	30	48	.243	.288	.298	66	-21	-21	38	1	5	-3	.976	-12	*O	-4.4
1965	Pit-N	135	481	58	134	22	5	4	24	30	49	.279	.322	.370	94	-4	-4	58	4	3	-1	.970	-8	*O	-1.9
1968	Pit-N	6	3	1	1	0	0	1	2	0	2	.333	.333	1.333	388	1	1	1	0	0	0	1.000	0	/O	0.1
Total	12	1583	5980	735	1596	237	81	91	502	442	647	.267	.318	.379	89	-100	-95	721	47	54	-18	.982	41	*O	-15.6
■ OZZIE VIRGIL	Virgil, Osvaldo Jose Jr. b: 12/7/56, Mayaguez, P.R. BR/TR, 6'1", 205 lbs. Deb: 10/05/80 F																								
1980	Phi-N	1	5	1	1	1	0	0	0	0	1	.200	.200	.400	60	-0	-0	0	0	0	0	1.000	-1	/C	-0.1
1981	Phi-N	6	6	0	0	0	0	0	0	0	2	.000	.000	.000	-96	-2	-2	0	0	0	0	1.000	0	/C	-0.2
1982	Phi-N	49	101	11	24	6	0	3	8	10	26	.238	.306	.386	91	-1	-1	11	0	1	-1	.964	4	C	0.3
1983	*Phi-N	55	140	11	30	7	0	6	23	8	34	.214	.272	.393	83	-4	-4	12	0	2	-1	.966	-5	C	-0.8
1984	Phi-N	141	456	61	119	21	2	18	68	45	91	.261	.334	.434	113	8	7	62	1	1	-0	.992	-3	*C	1.0
1985	Phi-N★	131	426	47	105	16	3	19	55	49	85	.246	.331	.432	109	6	5	59	0	0	0	**.994**	-4	*C	0.7
1986	Atl-N	114	359	45	80	9	0	15	48	63	73	.223	.345	.373	93	0	-2	49	1	0	0	.984	14	*C	2.0
1987	Atl-N★	123	429	57	106	13	1	27	72	47	81	.247	.331	.471	104	5	2	63	0	1	-1	.989	-2	*C	0.8
1988	Atl-N	107	320	23	82	10	0	9	31	22	54	.256	.314	.372	92	-2	-4	36	2	0	1	.990	-11	C	-0.8
1989	Tor-A	9	11	2	2	1	0	1	2	4	3	.182	.400	.545	167	1	1	3	0	0	0	1.000	-0	/CD	0.1
1990	Tor-A	3	5	0	0	0	0	0	0	0	3	.000	.000	.000	-98	-1	-1	0	0	0	0	1.000	-0	/CD	-0.1
Total	11	739	2258	258	549	84	6	98	307	248	453	.243	.326	.416	101	11	1	296	4	5	-2	.987	-8	C/D	2.9
■ OZZIE VIRGIL	Virgil, Osvaldo Jose Sr. (Pichardo) b: 5/17/33, Montecristi, D.R. BR/TR, 6', 175 lbs. Deb: 9/23/56 FC																								
1956	NY-N	3	12	2	5	1	1	0	2	0	0	.417	.417	.667	186	1	1	4	1	0	0	.800	-2	/3	0.0
1957	NY-N	96	226	26	53	0	2	4	24	14	27	.235	.279	.305	57	-14	-14	17	2	3	-1	.926	9	3O/S	-0.6
1958	Det-A	49	193	19	47	10	2	3	19	8	20	.244	.274	.363	69	-7	-9	18	1	0	0	.981	3	3	-0.6
1960	Det-A	62	132	16	30	4	2	3	13	4	14	.227	.250	.356	60	-7	-8	11	1	1	-0	.974	8	3/2SC	0.1
1961	Det-A	20	30	1	4	0	0	1	1	1	5	.133	.161	.233	4	-4	-4	1	0	0	0	.938	-1	/3C2S	-0.5
	KC-A	11	21	1	3	0	0	0	0	0	3	.143	.143	.143	-23	-4	-4	-0	0	0	0	.818	0	/3C	-0.3
	Yr	31	51	2	7	0	0	1	1	1	8	.137	.154	.196	-7	-8	-8	0	0	0	0	.889	-1	3/C2S	-0.8
1962	Bal-A	1	0	0	0	0	0	0	0	1	0	—	1.000	—	206	0	0	0	0	0	0	.000	0	H	0.0
1965	Pit-N	39	49	3	13	2	0	1	5	2	10	.265	.294	.367	85	-1	-1	5	0	0	0	1.000	2	C/32	0.1
1966	SF-N	42	89	7	19	2	0	2	9	4	12	.213	.247	.303	51	-6	-6	6	1	1	-0	.984	1	C3/12O	-0.6
1969	SF-N	1	1	0	0	0	0	0	0	0	0	.000	.000	.000	-99	-0	-0	0	0	0	0	.000	0	H	0.0
Total	9	324	753	75	174	19	7	14	73	34	91	.231	.264	.331	59	-42	-44	61	6	5	-1	.951	19	3/CO2S1	-2.4
■ JAKE VIRTUE	Virtue, Jacob Kitchline "Guesses" b: 3/2/1865, Philadelphia, Pa. d: 2/3/43, Camden, N.J. BB/TR, 5'9.5", 165 lbs. Deb: 7/21/1890																								
1890	Cle-N	62	223	39	68	6	5	2	25	49	15	.305	.432	.404	150	16	17	44	9			.982	0	1	1.2
1891	Cle-N	139	517	82	135	19	14	2	72	75	40	.261	.363	.364	110	12	8	76	15			.972	-10	*1	-0.7
1892	*Cle-N	147	557	98	157	15	20	2	89	84	68	.282	.380	.391	130	26	23	90	14			.984	-4	*1	1.1
1893	Cle-N	97	378	87	100	16	10	1	60	54	14	.265	.358	.368	89	-2	-6	55	11			.975	1	1O/S3P	-0.6
1894	Cle-N	29	89	15	23	4	1	0	10	13	3	.258	.359	.326	65	-4	-5	11	1			.885	-2	O/21P	-0.6
Total	5	474	1764	321	483	60	50	7	256	275	140	.274	.376	.376	113	48	37	276	50			.978	-15	1/O3S2P	0.4
■ JOE VISNER	Visner, Joseph Paul (b: Joseph Paul Vezina) b: 9/27/1859, Minneapolis, Minn. d: 6/17/45, Fosston, Minn. BL/TR, 5'11", 180 lbs. Deb: 7/04/1885																								
1885	Bal-a	4	13	2	3	0	0	0		2		.231	.333	.231	85	-0	-0	1				.750	-1	/O	-0.1
1889	*Bro-a	80	295	56	76	12	10	8	68	36	36	.258	.346	.447	127	10	10	51	13			.871	-16	CO	-0.2
1890	Pit-P	127	521	110	138	15	**22**	3	71	76	44	.265	.367	.395	115	5	14	84	18			.893	-6	*O	0.3
1891	Was-a	18	68	13	19	2	3	1	7	8	7	.279	.355	.441	137	2	3	12	2			.806	-2	O/C3	0.0
	StL-a	6	27	2	4	0	1	0	1	0	3	.148	.148	.222	6	-3	-4	1	0			1.000	0	/O	-0.4
	Yr	24	95	15	23	2	4	1	8	8	10	.242	.301	.379	96	-1	-1	12	2			.846	-2	O/C3	-0.4

YEAR	TM/L	G	AB	R	H	2B	3B	HR	RBI	BB	SO	AVG	OBP	SLG	PRO+	BR	/A	RC	SB	CS	SBR	FA	FR	POS	TPR
Total	4	235	924	183	240	29	36	12	147	122	90	.260	.353	.408	116	14	23	149	33			.892	-25	O/C3	-0.4
■ JOE VITELLI Vitelli, Antonio Joseph b: 4/12/08, Mckees Rocks, Pa. d: 2/7/67, Pittsburgh, Pa. BR/TR, 6'1", 195 lbs. Deb: 5/30/44																									
1944	Pit-N	4	3	0	0	0	0	0	0	0	0	.000	.000	.000	-96	-1	-1	0	0			.750	0	/P	0.0
1945	Pit-N	1	0	1	0	0	0	0	0	0	0	—	—	—	—	0	0	0	0			.000	0	R	0.0
Total	2	5	3	1	0	0	0	0	0	0	0	.000	.000	.000	-96	-1	-1	0	0				0	/P	0.0
■ OSSIE VITT Vitt, Oscar Joseph b: 1/4/1890, San Francisco, Cal. d: 1/31/63, Oakland, Cal. BR/TR, 5'10", 150 lbs. Deb: 4/11/12 M																									
1912	Det-A	76	273	39	67	4	4	0	19	18		.245	.297	.289	70	-12	-10	28	17			.929	0	O32	-1.2
1913	Det-A	99	359	45	86	11	3	2	33	31	18	.240	.304	.304	79	-10	-10	36	5			.960	5	23/O	-0.6
1914	Det-A	66	195	35	49	7	0	0	8	31	8	.251	.354	.287	90	-0	-1	24	10	8	-2	.964	2	23/OS	-0.1
1915	Det-A	152	560	116	140	18	13	1	48	80	22	.250	.348	.334	99	4	1	74	26	18	-3	**.964**	14	*3/2	2.0
1916	Det-A	153	597	88	135	17	12	0	42	75	28	.226	.314	.295	80	-12	-14	65	18			**.964**	28	*3/S	2.1
1917	Det-A	140	512	65	130	13	6	0	47	56	15	.254	.329	.303	93	-4	-3	58	18			.940	-17	*3	-2.0
1918	Det-A	81	267	29	64	5	2	0	17	32	6	.240	.321	.273	83	-6	-5	27	5			.953	4	3/2O	0.1
1919	Bos-A	133	469	64	114	10	3	0	40	44	11	.243	.309	.277	69	-21	-17	47	9			**.970**	14	*3	0.2
1920	Bos-A	87	296	50	65	10	4	1	28	43	10	.220	.321	.291	66	-15	-13	31	5	4	-1	.986	-6	32	-1.6
1921	Bos-A	78	232	29	44	11	1	0	13	45	13	.190	.321	.246	48	-18	-17	22	1	2	-1	.962	-4	3/O1	-1.6
Total	10	1065	3760	560	894	106	48	4	295	455	131	.238	.322	.295	80	-93	-90	412	114	32		.960	40	32/OS1	-2.7
■ JOSE VIZCAINO Vizcaino, Jose Luis (Pimental) b: 3/26/68, San Cristobal, D.R. BB/TR, 6'1", 150 lbs. Deb: 9/10/89																									
1989	LA-N	7	10	2	2	0	0	0	0	0	1	.200	.200	.200	15	-1	-1	0	0	0	0	.882	2	/S	0.1
1990	LA-N	37	51	3	14	1	1	0	2	4	8	.275	.327	.333	85	-1	-1	5	1	1	-0	.956	3	S/2	0.2
1991	Chi-N	93	145	7	38	5	0	0	10	5	18	.262	.287	.297	61	-7	-8	13	2	1	0	.947	7	3S/2	0.1
1992	Chi-N	86	285	25	64	10	4	1	17	14	35	.225	.261	.298	57	-16	-17	23	3	0	1	.969	2	S3/2	-1.1
Total	4	223	491	37	118	16	5	1	29	23	62	.240	.274	.299	60	-25	-27	41	6	2	1	.964	13	/S32	-0.7
■ OMAR VIZQUEL Vizquel, Omar Enrique (Gonzalez) b: 4/24/67, Caracas, Venez. BB/TR, 5'9", 155 lbs. Deb: 4/03/89																									
1989	Sea-A	143	387	45	85	7	3	1	20	28	40	.220	.274	.261	50	-24	-26	28	1	4	-2	.971	11	*S	-0.8
1990	Sea-A	81	255	19	63	3	2	2	18	18	22	.247	.297	.298	66	-11	-12	23	4	1	1	.980	-2	S	-0.7
1991	Sea-A	142	426	42	98	16	4	1	41	45	37	.230	.304	.293	66	-19	-19	40	7	2	1	.980	24	*S/2	1.6
1992	Sea-A	136	483	49	142	20	4	0	21	32	38	.294	.340	.352	93	-3	-4	54	15	13	-3	**.989**	0	*S	0.4
Total	4	502	1551	155	388	46	13	4	100	123	137	.250	.306	.304	70	-58	-61	146	27	20	-4	.980	33	S/2	0.5
■ OTTO VOGEL Vogel, Otto Henry b: 10/26/1899, Mendota, Ill. d: 7/19/69, Iowa City, Iowa BR/TR, 6', 195 lbs. Deb: 6/05/23																									
1923	Chi-N	41	81	10	17	0	1	1	6	7	11	.210	.297	.272	51	-6	-6	7	2	3	-1	.929	-2	O/3	-1.0
1924	Chi-N	70	172	28	46	11	2	1	24	10	26	.267	.319	.372	84	-4	-4	20	4	4	-1	.956	1	O/3	-0.7
Total	2	111	253	38	63	11	3	2	30	17	37	.249	.312	.340	73	-9	-10	27	6	7	-2	.948	-1	/O3	-1.7
■ JACK VOIGT Voigt, John David b: 5/17/66, Sarasota, Fla. BR/TR, 6'1", 175 lbs. Deb: 8/03/92																									
1992	Bal-A	1	0	0	0	0	0	0	0	0	0	—	—	—	—	0	0	0	0	0	0	.000	0	/R	0.0
■ CLYDE VOLLMER Vollmer, Clyde Frederick b: 9/24/21, Cincinnati, Ohio BR/TR, 6'1", 190 lbs. Deb: 5/31/42																									
1942	Cin-N	12	43	2	4	0	0	1	4	1	5	.093	.114	.163	-20	-7	-7	1	0			1.000	1	O	-0.6
1946	Cin-N	9	22	1	4	0	0	0	1	1	3	.182	.217	.182	14	-2	-2	1	2			1.000	-3	/O	-0.6
1947	Cin-N	78	155	19	34	10	0	1	13	9	18	.219	.267	.303	51	-11	-11	13	0			.984	-7	O	-2.0
1948	Cin-N	7	9	0	1	0	0	0	0	1	1	.111	.200	.111	-14	-1	-1	0	0			.000	-1	/O	-0.2
	Was-A	1	5	1	2	0	0	0	0	0	1	.400	.400	.400	116	0	0	1	0	0	0	1.000	0	/O	0.0
1949	Was-A	129	443	58	112	17	1	14	59	53	62	.253	.335	.391	94	-7	-5	59	1	2	-1	.982	4	*O	-0.7
1950	Was-A	6	14	4	4	0	0	0	1	2	3	.286	.375	.286	75	-1	-0	2	1	0	0	1.000	0	/O	0.0
	Bos-A	57	169	35	48	10	0	7	37	21	35	.284	.363	.467	102	2	0	29	1	0	0	.954	-2	O	-0.3
	Yr	63	183	39	52	10	0	7	38	23	38	.284	.364	.454	100	2	-0	31	2	0	1	.957	-1	O	-0.3
1951	Bos-A	115	386	66	97	9	2	22	85	55	66	.251	.346	.456	105	7	2	59	0	0	0	.986	0	*O	-0.1
1952	Bos-A	90	250	35	66	12	4	11	50	39	47	.264	.370	.476	124	12	9	42	2	2	-1	1.000	-1	O	0.5
1953	Bos-A	1	0	0	0	0	0	0	0	1	0	—	1.000	—	180	0	0	0	0	0	0	.000	0	H	0.0
	Was-A	118	408	54	106	15	3	11	74	48	59	.260	.342	.392	100	-1	0	58	0	2	-1	.979	7	*O	0.2
	Yr	119	408	54	106	15	3	11	74	49	59	.260	.343	.392	101	-1	0	58	0	2	-1	.979	7	*O	0.2
1954	Was-A	62	117	8	30	4	0	2	15	12	28	.256	.331	.342	89	-2	-2	13	0	0	0	1.000	-3	O	-0.6
Total	10	685	2021	283	508	77	10	69	339	243	328	.251	.335	.402	95	-11	-17	278	7	6		.984	-3	O	-4.4
■ FRITZ Von KOLNITZ Von Kolnitz, Alfred Holmes b: 5/20/1893, Charleston, S.C. d: 3/18/48, Mount Pleasant, S.C. BR/TR, 5'10.5", 175 lbs. Deb: 4/18/14																									
1914	Cin-N	41	104	8	23	2	0	0	6	6	16	.221	.270	.240	51	-6	-6	7	4			.914	-4	3O/C1	-1.1
1915	Cin-N	50	78	6	15	4	1	0	6	7	11	.192	.259	.269	59	-4	-4	5	1	3	-2	.933	-6	3/S1CO	-1.2
1916	Chi-A	24	44	1	10	3	0	0	7	2	6	.227	.261	.295	66	-2	-2	3	0			.909	-5	3	-0.7
Total	3	115	226	15	48	9	1	0	19	15	33	.212	.264	.261	56	-12	-12	16	5	3		.918	-15	/3OS1C	-3.0
■ JOE VOSMIK Vosmik, Joseph Franklin b: 4/4/10, Cleveland, Ohio d: 1/27/62, Cleveland, Ohio BR/TR, 6', 185 lbs. Deb: 9/13/30																									
1930	Cle-A	9	26	1	6	2	0	0	4	1	1	.231	.259	.308	42	-2	-2	2	0	0	0	.933	1	/O	-0.2
1931	Cle-A	149	591	80	189	36	14	7	117	38	30	.320	.363	.464	110	12	7	97	7	7	-2	.970	6	*O	0.1
1932	Cle-A	153	621	106	194	39	12	10	97	58	42	.312	.376	.462	109	14	8	109	2	3	-1	**.989**	24	*O	2.0
1933	Cle-A	119	438	53	115	20	10	4	56	42	13	.263	.331	.381	84	-8	-10	56	0	2	-1	.985	6	*O	-1.1
1934	Cle-A	104	405	71	138	33	2	6	78	35	10	.341	.393	.477	122	14	13	76	1	1	-0	.976	-2	*O	0.6
1935	Cle-A★	152	620	93	**216**	**47**	**20**	10	110	59	30	.348	.408	.537	140	38	37	137	2	1	0	.986	1	*O	3.0
1936	Cle-A	138	506	76	145	29	7	7	94	79	21	.287	.383	.413	96	-1	-2	85	5	1	1	.978	-1	*O	-0.6
1937	StL-A	144	594	81	193	47	9	4	93	49	38	.325	.377	.455	108	8	7	102	2	3	-1	.972	8	*O	0.8
1938	Bos-A	146	621	121	**201**	37	6	9	86	59	26	.324	.384	.446	103	7	3	107	0	3	-2	.978	3	*O	0.0
1939	Bos-A	145	554	89	153	29	6	7	84	66	33	.276	.356	.388	87	-7	-11	73	4	3	-1	.974	-4	*O	-1.9
1940	Bro-N	116	404	45	114	14	6	1	42	22	21	.282	.321	.354	81	-8	-11	45	0			.976	0	O	-1.6
1941	Bro-N	25	56	0	11	0	0	0	4	4	4	.196	.250	.196	26	-5	-6	3	0			1.000	-5	O	-1.2
1944	Was-A	14	36	2	7	2	0	0	9	2	3	.194	.237	.250	41	-3	-3	2	0	0	0	1.000	-2	O	-0.6
Total	13	1414	5472	818	1682	335	92	65	874	514	272	.307	.369	.438	104	58	30	895	23	24		.979	34	*O	-0.7
■ ALEX VOSS Voss, Alexander b: 5/1855, Roswell, Ga. d: 8/31/06, Cincinnati, Ohio BR/TR, 6'1", 180 lbs. Deb: 4/17/1884																									
1884	Was-U	63	245	33	47	9	0	0		5		.192	.208	.229	49	-13	-12	12				.848	4	P31O/S	-0.7
	KC-U	14	45	1	4	0	0	0		0		.089	.089	.089	-46	-6	-5	0				.867	1	/OP	-0.2
	Yr	77	290	34	51	9	0	0		5		.176	.190	.207	36	-19	-17	12				.859	5	PO31/S	-0.9
■ BILL VOSS Voss, William Edward b: 10/31/43, Glendale, Cal. BL/TL, 6'2", 160 lbs. Deb: 9/14/65																									
1965	Chi-A	11	33	4	6	0	1	1	3	3	5	.182	.250	.333	68	-2	-1	3	0	0	0	1.000	-1	O	-0.3
1966	Chi-A	2	2	0	0	0	0	0	0	0	2	.000	.000	.000	-99	-1	-0	0	0	0	0	1.000	-0	/O	-0.1
1967	Chi-A	13	22	4	2	0	0	0	0	0	1	.091	.091	.091	-48	-4	-4	0	1	1	-0	1.000	-2	O	-0.7
1968	Chi-A	61	167	14	26	2	1	2	15	16	34	.156	.238	.216	38	-12	-12	9	5	3	-0	.963	-4	O	-2.2
1969	Cal-A	133	349	33	91	11	4	2	40	35	40	.261	.328	.332	90	-7	-4	38	5	3	-0	.995	1	*O/1	-0.9
1970	Cal-A	80	181	21	44	4	3	3	30	23	18	.243	.335	.348	92	-2	-2	22	2	1	0	.979	2	O	-0.2
1971	Mil-A	97	275	31	69	4	0	10	30	24	45	.251	.313	.375	95	-3	-2	33	2	2	-1	.987	-4	O	-1.1

YEAR	TM/L	G	AB	R	H	2B	3B	HR	RBI	BB	SO	AVG	OBP	SLG	PRO+	BR	/A	RC	SB	CS	SBR	FA	FR	POS	TPR
1972	Mil-A	27	36	1	3	1	0	0	1	5	4	.083	.195	.111	-7	-5	-5	1	0	1	-1	.929	-3	O	-0.9
	Oak-A	40	97	10	22	5	1	1	5	9	16	.227	.299	.330	92	-2	-1	10	0	0	0	1.000	-1	O	-0.4
	Yr	67	133	11	25	6	1	1	6	14	20	.188	.270	.271	64	-6	-6	9	0	1	-1	.987	-4	O	-1.3
	StL-N	11	15	1	4	2	0	0	3	2	2	.267	.353	.400	115	0	0	2	0	0	0	1.000	-0	/O	0.0
Total	8	475	1177	119	267	29	10	19	127	117	167	.227	.300	.317	78	-36	-32	117	15	11	-2	.986	-11	O/1	-6.8

■ PHIL VOYLES Voyles, Philip Vance b: 5/12/1900, Murphy, N.C. d: 11/3/72, Marlboro, Mass. BL/TR, 5'11.5", 175 lbs. Deb: 9/04/29

YEAR	TM/L	G	AB	R	H	2B	3B	HR	RBI	BB	SO	AVG	OBP	SLG	PRO+	BR	/A	RC	SB	CS	SBR	FA	FR	POS	TPR
1929	Bos-N	20	68	9	16	0	2	0	14	6	8	.235	.297	.294	49	-6	-5	6	0			.922	-2	O	-0.8

■ GEORGE VUKOVICH Vukovich, George Stephen b: 6/24/56, Chicago, Ill. BL/TR, 6', 198 lbs. Deb: 4/13/80

YEAR	TM/L	G	AB	R	H	2B	3B	HR	RBI	BB	SO	AVG	OBP	SLG	PRO+	BR	/A	RC	SB	CS	SBR	FA	FR	POS	TPR
1980	*Phi-N	78	58	6	13	1	1	0	8	6	9	.224	.297	.276	58	-3	-3	5	0	0	0	.933	1	O	-0.3
1981	*Phi-N	20	26	5	10	0	0	1	4	1	0	.385	.407	.500	150	2	2	6	1	0	0	1.000	0	/O	0.2
1982	Phi-N	123	335	41	91	18	2	6	42	32	47	.272	.335	.391	100	1	0	41	2	9	-5	.977	-1	*O	-0.8
1983	Cle-A	124	312	31	77	13	2	3	44	24	37	.247	.305	.330	72	-11	-12	30	3	4	-2	.986	-13	*O	-2.9
1984	Cle-A	134	437	38	133	22	5	9	60	34	61	.304	.356	.439	117	11	10	66	1	4	-2	.994	14	*O	1.8
1985	Cle-A	149	434	43	106	22	0	8	45	30	75	.244	.295	.350	76	-15	-14	43	2	2	-1	.988	-7	*O	-2.6
Total	6	628	1602	164	430	76	10	27	203	127	229	.268	.324	.379	92	-15	-18	191	9	19	-9	.987	-6	O	-4.6

■ JOHN VUKOVICH Vukovich, John Christopher b: 7/31/47, Sacramento, Cal. BR/TR, 6'1", 190 lbs. Deb: 9/11/70 MC

YEAR	TM/L	G	AB	R	H	2B	3B	HR	RBI	BB	SO	AVG	OBP	SLG	PRO+	BR	/A	RC	SB	CS	SBR	FA	FR	POS	TPR
1970	Phi-N	3	8	1	1	0	0	0	0	1	0	.125	.222	.125	-5	-1	-1	0	0	0	0	.778	1	/S3	0.0
1971	Phi-N	74	217	11	36	5	0	0	14	12	34	.166	.213	.189	15	-24	-24	9	2	1	0	.956	10	3	-1.6
1973	Mil-A	55	128	10	16	3	0	2	9	9	40	.125	.182	.195	7	-16	-16	5	0	2	-1	.948	-4	31/S	-2.2
1974	Mil-A	38	80	5	15	1	0	3	11	1	16	.188	.198	.313	45	-6	-6	4	2	1	0	.945	2	S32/1	-0.2
1975	Cin-N	31	38	4	8	3	0	0	2	4	5	.211	.286	.289	59	-2	-2	4	0	0	0	.925	7	3	0.5
1976	Phi-N	4	8	2	1	0	0	1	2	0	2	.125	.125	.500	69	-0	-0	1	0	0	0	1.000	-0	/31	-0.1
1977	Phi-N	2	2	0	0	0	0	0	0	0	1	.000	.000	.000	-96	-1	-1	0	0	0	0	.000	0	H	-0.1
1979	Phi-N	10	15	0	3	1	0	0	1	0	3	.200	.200	.267	25	-2	-2	1	0	0	0	1.000	2	/32	0.0
1980	Phi-N	49	62	4	10	1	1	0	5	2	7	.161	.200	.210	14	-7	-8	2	0	1	-1	.958	0	3/2S1	-0.8
1981	Phi-N	11	1	0	0	0	0	0	0	0	1	.000	.000	.000	-96	-0	-0	0	0	0	0	.800	1	/312	0.0
Total	10	277	559	37	90	14	1	6	44	29	109	.161	.205	.222	20	-59	-59	25	4	5	-2	.951	18	3/21S	-4.5

■ FRANK WADDEY Waddey, Frank Orum b: 8/21/05, Memphis, Tenn. d: 10/21/90, Knoxville, Tenn. BL/TL, 5'10.5", 185 lbs. Deb: 4/16/31

YEAR	TM/L	G	AB	R	H	2B	3B	HR	RBI	BB	SO	AVG	OBP	SLG	PRO+	BR	/A	RC	SB	CS	SBR	FA	FR	POS	TPR
1931	StL-A	14	22	3	6	1	0	0	2	2	3	.273	.333	.318	70	-1	-1	2	0	0	0	1.000	-3	/O	-0.4

■ HAM WADE Wade, Abraham Lincoln b: 12/20/1880, Spring City, Pa. d: 7/21/68, Riverside, N.J. BR/TR, 5'8", 155 lbs. Deb: 9/09/07

YEAR	TM/L	G	AB	R	H	2B	3B	HR	RBI	BB	SO	AVG	OBP	SLG	PRO+	BR	/A	RC	SB	CS	SBR	FA	FR	POS	TPR
1907	NY-N	1	0	0	0	0	0	0	0	0		—	—	—	—	0	0	0	0			1.000	0	/O	0.0

■ GALE WADE Wade, Galeard Lee b: 1/20/29, Hollister, Mo. BL/TR, 6'1.5", 185 lbs. Deb: 4/11/55

YEAR	TM/L	G	AB	R	H	2B	3B	HR	RBI	BB	SO	AVG	OBP	SLG	PRO+	BR	/A	RC	SB	CS	SBR	FA	FR	POS	TPR
1955	Chi-N	9	33	5	6	1	0	1	1	4	3	.182	.270	.303	52	-2	-2	3	0	0	0	.867	-2	/O	-0.5
1956	Chi-N	10	12	0	0	0	0	0	0	1	0	.000	.077	.000	-78	-3	-3	-0	0	0	0	.875	-0	/O	-0.4
Total	2	19	45	5	6	1	0	1	1	5	3	.133	.220	.222	18	-5	-5	3	0	0	0	.870	-2	/O	-0.9

■ RIP WADE Wade, Richard Frank b: 1/12/1898, Duluth, Minn. d: 6/16/57, Sandstone, Minn. BL/TR, 5'11", 174 lbs. Deb: 4/19/23

YEAR	TM/L	G	AB	R	H	2B	3B	HR	RBI	BB	SO	AVG	OBP	SLG	PRO+	BR	/A	RC	SB	CS	SBR	FA	FR	POS	TPR
1923	Was-A	33	69	8	16	2	2	2	14	5	10	.232	.284	.406	84	-2	-2	8	0	0	0	.967	-2	O	-0.5

■ WOODY WAGENHORST Wagenhorst, Elwood Otto b: 6/3/1863, Kutztown, Pa. d: 2/12/46, Deb: 6/25/1888

YEAR	TM/L	G	AB	R	H	2B	3B	HR	RBI	BB	SO	AVG	OBP	SLG	PRO+	BR	/A	RC	SB	CS	SBR	FA	FR	POS	TPR
1888	Phi-N	2	8	2	1	0	0	0	0	0	1	.125	.125	.125	-18	-1	-1	0	0			.800	-1	/3	-0.2

■ BUTTS WAGNER Wagner, Albert b: 9/17/1869, Mansfield, Pa. d: 11/26/28, Pittsburgh, Pa. BR/TR, 5'10", 170 lbs. Deb: 4/27/1898 F

YEAR	TM/L	G	AB	R	H	2B	3B	HR	RBI	BB	SO	AVG	OBP	SLG	PRO+	BR	/A	RC	SB	CS	SBR	FA	FR	POS	TPR
1898	Was-N	63	223	20	50	11	2	1	31	14		.224	.279	.305	68	-10	-10	21	4			.833	-10	3O/S2	-1.9
	Bro-N	11	38	2	9	1	1	0	3	2		.237	.275	.316	69	-2	-2	4	0			.813	-3	3	-0.4
	Yr	74	261	22	59	12	3	1	34	16		.226	.279	.307	68	-12	-11	24	4			.828	-13	3O/S2	-2.3

■ HEINIE WAGNER Wagner, Charles F. b: 9/23/1880, New York, N.Y. d: 3/20/43, New Rochelle, N.Y. BR/TR, 5'9", 183 lbs. Deb: 7/01/02 MC

YEAR	TM/L	G	AB	R	H	2B	3B	HR	RBI	BB	SO	AVG	OBP	SLG	PRO+	BR	/A	RC	SB	CS	SBR	FA	FR	POS	TPR
1902	NY-N	17	56	4	12	1	0	0	2	0		.214	.214	.232	38	-4	-4	4	3			.862	-3	S	-0.6
1906	Bos-A	9	32	1	9	0	0	0	4	1		.281	.303	.281	84	-1	-1	4	2			.943	1	/2	0.1
1907	Bos-A	111	385	29	82	10	4	2	21	31		.213	.275	.275	76	-10	-10	37	20			.931	5	*S/23	-0.2
1908	Bos-A	153	526	62	130	11	5	1	46	27		.247	.288	.293	86	-7	-9	50	20			.939	32	*S	3.0
1909	Bos-A	124	430	53	110	16	7	1	49	35		.256	.316	.333	103	2	1	50	18			.933	14	*S/2	2.0
1910	Bos-A	142	491	61	134	26	7	1	52	44		.273	.335	.360	115	10	8	68	26			.927	-12	*S	0.2
1911	Bos-A	80	261	34	67	13	8	1	38	29		.257	.340	.379	101	0	0	38	15			.946	-4	2S	-0.2
1912	*Bos-A	144	504	75	138	25	6	2	68	62		.274	.358	.359	100	5	1	72	21			.922	-13	*S	0.0
1913	Bos-A	110	365	43	83	14	8	2	34	40	29	.227	.316	.326	86	-6	-7	38	9			.938	4	*S/2	0.7
1915	Bos-A	84	267	38	64	11	2	0	29	37	34	.240	.339	.296	93	-2	-1	30	8	4	0	.927	-16	2/3O	-1.7
1916	Bos-A	6	8	2	4	1	0	0	0	3	0	.500	.636	.625	278	2	2	4	2			1.000	2	/32S	0.5
1918	Bos-A	3	8	0	1	0	0	0	0	1	0	.125	.222	.125	5	-1	-1	0	0			.900	-0	/23	-0.1
Total	12	983	3333	402	834	128	47	10	343	310	63	.250	.319	.326	95	-12	-19	396	144	4		.928	11	S2/3O	3.7

■ HAL WAGNER Wagner, Harold Edward b: 7/2/15, E.Riverton, N.J. d: 8/7/79, Riverside, N.J. BL/TR, 6', 165 lbs. Deb: 10/03/37

YEAR	TM/L	G	AB	R	H	2B	3B	HR	RBI	BB	SO	AVG	OBP	SLG	PRO+	BR	/A	RC	SB	CS	SBR	FA	FR	POS	TPR
1937	Phi-A	1	0	0	0	0	0	0	0	0	0	—	—	—	—	0	0	0	0	0	0	1.000	0	/C	0.0
1938	Phi-A	33	88	10	20	2	1	0	8	8	9	.227	.299	.273	45	-8	-7	8	0	0	0	.972	-1	C	-0.7
1939	Phi-A	5	8	0	1	0	0	0	0	0	3	.125	.125	.125	-37	-2	-2	0	0	0	0	1.000	2	/C	0.0
1940	Phi-A	34	75	9	19	5	1	0	10	11	6	.253	.356	.347	85	-2	-1	10	0	0	0	.964	3	C	0.3
1941	Phi-A	46	131	18	29	8	2	1	15	19	9	.221	.320	.336	75	-5	-4	16	1	0	0	.976	2	C	0.1
1942	Phi-A☆	104	288	26	68	17	1	1	30	24	29	.236	.304	.313	74	-10	-10	28	1	0	0	.986	-2	C	-0.6
1943	Phi-A	111	289	22	69	17	1	1	26	36	17	.239	.327	.315	89	-4	-3	31	3	3	-1	.980	-8	C	-0.7
1944	Phi-A	5	4	0	1	0	0	0	0	0	0	.250	.250	.250	44	-0	-0	0	0	0	0	1.000	0	/C	0.0
	Bos-A	66	223	21	74	13	4	1	38	29	14	.332	.418	.439	147	14	15	45	1	1	-0	.970	0	C	1.9
	Yr	71	227	21	75	13	4	1	38	29	14	.330	.415	.436	145	14	14	45	1	1	-0	.971	0	C	1.9
1946	*Bos-A★	117	370	39	85	12	2	6	52	69	32	.230	.354	.322	85	-3	-5	48	3	1	0	.983	-7	*C	-0.6
1947	Bos-A	21	65	5	15	3	0	0	6	9	5	.231	.324	.277	63	-3	-3	7	0	0	0	.978	-1	C	-0.3
	Det-A	71	191	19	55	10	0	5	33	28	16	.288	.382	.419	119	6	6	33	0	1	-1	.990	-4	C	0.5
	Yr	92	256	24	70	13	0	5	39	37	21	.273	.367	.383	105	4	2	39	0	1	-1	.987	-5	C	0.2
1948	Det-A	54	109	10	22	3	0	0	10	20	11	.202	.326	.229	48	-7	-8	10	1	0	0	.989	-4	C	-0.8
	Phi-N	3	4	0	0	0	0	0	0	0	0	.000	.000	.000	-99	-1	-1	0	0			1.000	1	/C	0.0
1949	Phi-N	1	4	0	0	0	0	0	0	0	1	.000	.000	.000	-99	-1	-1	0	0			.750	-1	/C	-0.2
Total	12	672	1849	179	458	90	12	15	228	253	152	.248	.343	.334	87	-24	-27	235	10	6		.981	-21	C	-1.1

■ HONUS WAGNER Wagner, John Peter "The Flying Dutchman" b: 2/24/1874, Mansfield, Pa. d: 12/6/55, Carnegie, Pa. BR/TR, 5'11", 200 lbs. Deb: 7/19/1897 FMCH

YEAR	TM/L	G	AB	R	H	2B	3B	HR	RBI	BB	SO	AVG	OBP	SLG	PRO+	BR	/A	RC	SB	CS	SBR	FA	FR	POS	TPR
1897	Lou-N	61	237	37	80	17	4	2	39	15		.338	.379	.468	127	7	8	51	19			.908	3	O/2	0.7
1898	Lou-N	151	588	80	176	29	3	10	105	31		.299	.340	.410	117	9	10	94	27			.972	-5	132	0.6
1899	Lou-N	147	571	98	192	43	13	7	113	40		.336	.391	.494	142	31	31	128	37			.928	2	3O/21	2.6
1900	*Pit-N	135	527	107	201	**45**	**22**	4	100	41		**.381**	.434	**.573**	**175**	53	53	**152**	38			.965	-7	*O/321P	3.4
1901	Pit-N	140	549	101	194	37	11	6	**126**	53		.353	.416	.494	159	45	43	137	**49**			.918	9	SO3/2	5.2
1902	Pit-N	136	534	**105**	176	**30**	16	3	**91**	43		.330	.391	**.463**	158	**39**	**37**	**117**	**42**			1.000	8	OS1/P2	4.4
1903	*Pit-N	129	512	97	182	30	**19**	5	101	44		**.355**	.414	.518	160	42	40	133	46			.933	25	*SO/1	**6.4**

YEAR	TM/L	G	AB	R	H	2B	3B	HR	RBI	BB	SO	AVG	OBP	SLG	PRO+	BR	/A	RC	SB	CS	SBR	FA	FR	POS	TPR
1904	Pit-N	132	490	97	171	**44**	14	4	75	59		**.349**	**.423**	**.520**	**186**	**53**	**51**	**134**	**53**			.929	-6	*S/O12	**5.0**
1905	Pit-N	147	548	114	199	32	14	6	101	54		.363	.424	.505	173	52	50	146	57			.935	20	*S/O	**7.4**
1906	Pit-N	142	516	**103**	175	**38**	9	2	71	58		**.339**	.411	.459	165	**43**	41	**123**	53			.941	24	*S/O3	**7.4**
1907	Pit-N	142	515	98	180	**38**	14	6	82	46		**.350**	**.407**	**.513**	**186**	**50**	**50**	**137**	**61**			.938	4	*S/1	**6.3**
1908	Pit-N	151	568	100	**201**	**39**	**19**	10	**109**	54		**.354**	**.415**	**.542**	**205**	**65**	**65**	**148**	**53**			.943	-7	*S	**7.0**
1909	*Pit-N	137	495	92	168	**39**	10	5	**100**	66		**.339**	**.420**	**.489**	**168**	**48**	**43**	**117**	35			.940	6	*S/O	**5.6**
1910	Pit-N	150	556	90	**178**	34	8	4	81	59	47	.320	.390	.432	132	28	24	103	24			.935	3	*S1/2	3.4
1911	Pit-N	130	473	87	158	23	16	9	89	67	34	**.334**	.423	.507	154	39	36	109	20			.932	4	*S1/O	**4.6**
1912	Pit-N	145	558	91	181	35	20	7	**102**	59	38	.324	.395	.496	145	32	33	118	26			**.962**	23	*S	**6.6**
1913	Pit-N	114	413	51	124	18	4	3	56	26	40	.300	.349	.385	114	5	7	60	21			**.962**	13	*S	3.1
1914	Pit-N	150	552	60	139	15	9	1	50	51	51	.252	.317	.317	93	-7	-5	60	23			**.950**	7	*S3/1	1.5
1915	Pit-N	156	566	68	155	32	17	6	78	39	64	.274	.325	.422	127	15	16	79	22	15	-2	**.948**	-5	*S21	2.0
1916	Pit-N	123	432	45	124	15	9	1	39	34	36	.287	.350	.370	120	11	11	61	11			.942	-15	S1/2	0.1
1917	Pit-N	74	230	15	61	7	1	0	24	24	17	.265	.337	.304	94	0	-1	25	5			.985	-4	13/2SM	-0.7
Total	21	2792	10430	1736	3415	640	252	101	1732	963	327	.327	.390	.466	150	661	644	2231	722	15		.940	101	*SO13/2P	82.6
■ JOE WAGNER Wagner, Joseph Bernard b: 4/24/1889, New York, N.Y. d: 11/15/48, Bronx, N.Y. BR/TR, 5'11", 165 lbs. Deb: 4/25/15																									
1915	Cin-N	75	197	17	35	5	2	0	13	8	35	.178	.210	.223	31	-17	-17	9	4	6	-2	.961	6	2S/3	-1.4
■ LEON WAGNER Wagner, Leon Lamar b: 5/13/34, Chattanooga, Tenn. BL/TR, 6'1", 195 lbs. Deb: 6/22/58																									
1958	SF-N	74	221	31	70	9	0	13	35	18	34	.317	.371	.534	139	11	12	45	1	0	0	.949	-0	O	0.9
1959	SF-N	87	129	20	29	4	3	5	22	25	24	.225	.363	.419	110	2	2	20	0	0	0	.941	-2	O	0.0
1960	StL-N	39	98	12	21	2	0	4	11	17	17	.214	.336	.357	83	-1	-2	12	0	1	-1	.963	1	O	-0.4
1961	LA-A	133	453	74	127	19	2	28	79	48	65	.280	.353	.517	116	17	11	85	5	1	1	.971	2	*O	0.7
1962	LA-A★	160	612	96	164	21	5	37	107	50	87	.268	.328	.500	123	14	17	101	7	5	-1	.972	-7	*O	0.0
1963	LA-A★	149	550	73	160	11	1	26	90	49	73	.291	.356	.456	134	19	23	90	5	7	-3	.960	-2	*O	1.1
1964	Cle-A	163	641	94	162	19	2	31	100	56	121	.253	.319	.434	108	5	6	89	14	2	3	.959	-1	*O	0.0
1965	Cle-A	144	517	91	152	18	1	28	79	60	52	.294	.371	.495	143	30	29	99	12	2	2	.957	-9	*O	1.7
1966	Cle-A	150	549	70	153	20	0	23	66	46	69	.279	.336	.441	121	14	14	80	5	2	0	.990	-8	*O	0.0
1967	Cle-A	135	433	56	105	15	1	15	54	37	76	.242	.320	.386	107	4	4	55	3	3	-1	.980	-7	*O	-1.1
1968	Cle-A	38	49	5	9	4	0	0	6	6	6	.184	.273	.265	65	-2	-2	3	0	0	0	.500	-3	O	-0.7
	Chi-A	69	162	14	46	8	0	1	18	21	31	.284	.366	.352	117	4	4	22	2	1	0	.941	-8	O	-0.7
	Yr	107	211	19	55	12	0	1	24	27	37	.261	.345	.332	106	2	2	25	2	1	0	.895	-11	O	-1.4
1969	SF-N	11	12	0	4	0	0	0	2	2	1	.333	.467	.333	130	1	1	2	0	0	0	1.000	0	/O	0.1
Total	12	1352	4426	636	1202	150	15	211	669	435	656	.272	.343	.455	121	118	117	703	54	24	2	.964	-44	*O	1.6
■ MARK WAGNER Wagner, Mark Duane b: 3/4/54, Conneaut, Ohio BR/TR, 6'1", 175 lbs. Deb: 8/20/76																									
1976	Det-A	39	115	9	30	2	3	0	12	6	18	.261	.298	.330	81	-3	-3	11	0	2	-1	.947	10	S	1.0
1977	Det-A	22	48	4	7	0	1	1	3	4	12	.146	.226	.250	28	-5	-5	3	0	1	-1	.923	-1	S/2	-0.5
1978	Det-A	39	109	10	26	1	2	0	6	3	11	.239	.272	.284	55	-6	-7	8	1	0	0	.964	-6	S/2	-0.9
1979	Det-A	75	146	16	40	3	0	1	13	16	25	.274	.346	.315	77	-4	-4	17	3	2	-0	.974	7	S2/3	0.6
1980	Det-A	45	72	5	17	1	0	0	3	7	11	.236	.304	.250	52	-4	-5	6	0	1	-1	.935	2	S/32	-0.1
1981	Tex-A	50	85	15	22	4	1	1	14	8	13	.259	.323	.365	103	-0	0	10	1	1	-0	.964	2	S/23	0.5
1982	Tex-A	60	179	14	43	4	1	0	8	10	28	.240	.280	.274	56	-11	-10	13	1	0	0	.955	-0	S	-0.5
1983	Tex-A	2	2	0	0	0	0	0	0	0	1	.000	.000	.000	-99	-1	-1	0	0	0	0	1.000	1	/S	0.1
1984	Oak-A	82	87	8	20	5	1	0	12	7	11	.230	.287	.310	70	-4	-3	7	2	0	1	.951	12	S3/2PD	1.1
Total	9	414	843	81	205	20	9	3	71	61	130	.243	.297	.299	66	-38	-37	76	8	7	-2	.953	25	S/23DP	1.3
■ BILL WAGNER Wagner, William Joseph b: 1/2/1894, Jessup, Iowa d: 1/11/51, Waterloo, Iowa BR/TR, 6', 187 lbs. Deb: 7/16/14																									
1914	Pit-N	3	1	0	0	0	0	0	0	0	0	.000	.000	.000	-99	-0	-0	0	0			1.000	0	/C	0.0
1915	Pit-N	5	5	0	0	0	0	0	0	1	2	.000	.167	.000	-48	-1	-1	0	0			1.000	2	/C	0.1
1916	Pit-N	19	38	2	9	0	2	0	2	5	8	.237	.326	.342	104	0	0	4	0			.936	2	C	0.3
1917	Pit-N	53	151	15	31	7	2	0	9	11	22	.205	.264	.278	64	-6	-7	11	1			.958	-4	C1	-0.9
1918	Bos-N	13	47	2	10	0	0	1	7	4	5	.213	.275	.277	71	-2	-2	3	0			.917	-5	C	-0.6
Total	5	93	242	19	50	7	4	1	18	21	37	.207	.273	.281	69	-9	-9	19	1			.947	-5	/C1	-1.1
■ KERMIT WAHL Wahl, Kermit Emerson b: 11/18/22, Columbia, S.Dak. d: 9/16/87, Tucson, Ariz. BR/TR, 5'11", 170 lbs. Deb: 6/23/44																									
1944	Cin-N	4	1	0	0	0	0	0	0	0	0	.000	.000	.000	-99	-0	-0	0	0			.000	0	/3	0.0
1945	Cin-N	71	194	18	39	8	2	0	10	23	22	.201	.286	.263	54	-12	-12	16	2			.948	5	2S/3	-0.3
1947	Cin-N	39	81	8	14	0	0	1	4	6	12	.173	.239	.210	20	-9	-9	4	0			.964	6	3/S2	-0.3
1950	Phi-A	89	280	26	72	12	3	2	27	30	30	.257	.331	.343	74	-12	-11	32	1	1	-0	.946	11	3S/2	0.0
1951	Phi-A	20	59	4	11	2	0	0	6	9	5	.186	.294	.220	40	-5	-5	4	0	0	0	.967	2	3	-0.3
	StL-A	8	27	2	9	1	1	0	3	0	3	.333	.333	.444	106	0	0	4	0	0	0	.950	1	/3	0.0
	Yr	28	86	6	20	3	1	0	9	9	8	.233	.305	.291	60	-5	-5	8	0	0	0	.962	3	3	-0.3
Total	5	231	642	58	145	23	6	3	50	68	72	.226	.302	.294	60	-38	-37	60	3	1		.949	25	3/S2	-0.9
■ EDDIE WAITKUS Waitkus, Edward Stephen b: 9/4/19, Cambridge, Mass. d: 9/15/72, Jamaica Plain, Mass. BL/TL, 6'1", 175 lbs. Deb: 4/15/41																									
1941	Chi-N	12	28	1	5	0	0	0	0	0	3	.179	.207	.179	10	-3	-3	1	0			.949	-1	/1	-0.5
1946	Chi-N	113	441	50	134	24	5	4	55	23	14	.304	.340	.408	114	5	6	60	3			.996	4	*1	0.4
1947	Chi-N	130	514	60	150	28	6	2	35	32	17	.292	.336	.381	94	-8	-5	66	3			.994	8	*1	-0.1
1948	Chi-N★	139	562	87	166	27	10	7	44	43	19	.295	.348	.416	110	4	7	81	11			.992	7	*1O	1.1
1949	Phi-N†	54	209	41	64	16	3	1	28	33	12	.306	.403	.426	126	8	9	38	3			.994	1	1	0.9
1950	*Phi-N	154	641	102	182	32	5	2	44	55	29	.284	.341	.359	86	-14	-12	79	3			.993	-2	*1	-1.8
1951	Phi-N	145	610	65	157	27	4	1	46	53	22	.257	.317	.320	73	-24	-23	64	0	3	-2	.992	-2	*1	-3.3
1952	Phi-N	146	499	51	144	29	4	2	49	64	23	.289	.371	.375	108	7	7	75	2	2	-1	.991	-2	*1	0.0
1953	Phi-N	81	247	24	72	9	2	1	16	13	23	.291	.330	.356	79	-8	-7	30	1	1	-0	.989	-1	1	-1.1
1954	Bal-A	95	311	35	88	17	4	2	33	28	25	.283	.344	.383	107	-1	2	41	0	1	-1	1.000	1	1	-0.1
1955	Bal-A	38	85	2	22	1	1	0	9	11	10	.259	.344	.294	78	-3	-2	9	2	0	1	.974	-2	1	-0.5
	Phi-N	33	107	10	30	5	0	2	14	17	7	.280	.379	.383	105	1	1	15	0	1	-1	.996	0	1	-0.1
Total	11	1140	4254	528	1214	215	44	24	373	372	204	.285	.344	.374	96	-35	-20	560	28	8		.993	10	*1/O	-5.1
■ CHARLIE WAITT Waitt, Charles C. b: 10/14/1853, Hallowell, Me. d: 10/21/12, San Francisco, Cal. 5'11", 165 lbs. Deb: 5/25/1875																									
1875	StL-n	31	118	14	25	9	0	0		2		.212	.225	.288	84	-3	-1	8						O/1	-0.1
1877	Chi-N	10	41	2	4	0	0	0	2	0	3	.098	.098	.098	-34	-6	-7	0				.793	2	O	-0.5
1882	Bal-a	72	250	19	39	4	0	0		13		.156	.198	.172	28	-19	-16	9				.874	0	*O	-1.5
1883	Phi-N	1	3	0	1	0	0	0	0	0	1	.333	.333	.333	114	0	0	0				.333	-1	/O	-0.1
Total	3	83	294	21	44	4	0	0	2	13	4	.150	.186	.163	18	-25	-23	9				.855	1	/O	-2.1
■ DON WAKAMATSU Wakamatsu, Wilbur Donald b: 2/22/63, Hood River, Ore. BR/TR, 6'2", 200 lbs. Deb: 5/22/91																									
1991	Chi-A	18	31	2	7	0	0	0	0	1	6	.226	.250	.226	33	-3	-3	2	0	0	0	1.000	-0	C	-0.3
■ HOWARD WAKEFIELD Wakefield, Howard John b: 4/2/1884, Bucyrus, Ohio d: 4/16/41, Chicago, Ill. BR/TR, 6'1", 205 lbs. Deb: 9/18/05 F																									
1905	Cle-A	10	26	3	4	0	0	0	1	0		.154	.185	.154	8	-3	-3	1	0			.926	-3	/C	-0.6
1906	Was-A	77	211	17	59	9	2	1	21	7		.280	.303	.355	111	1	2	25	6			.946	-15	C	-0.8
1907	Cle-A	26	37	4	5	2	0	0	3	3		.135	.200	.189	24	-3	-3	1	0			.930	-0	C	-0.3

YEAR	TM/L	G	AB	R	H	2B	3B	HR	RBI	BB	SO	AVG	OBP	SLG	PRO+	BR	/A	RC	SB	CS	SBR	FA	FR	POS	TPR
Total	3	113	274	24	68	11	2	1	25	10		.248	.277	.314	89	-5	-4	28	6			.943	-18	/C	-1.7

■ DICK WAKEFIELD
Wakefield, Richard Cummings b: 5/6/21, Chicago, Ill. d: 8/26/85, Wayne Co., Mich. BL/TR, 6'4", 210 lbs. Deb: 6/26/41 F

YEAR	TM/L	G	AB	R	H	2B	3B	HR	RBI	BB	SO	AVG	OBP	SLG	PRO+	BR	/A	RC	SB	CS	SBR	FA	FR	POS	TPR
1941	Det-A	7	7	0	1	0	0	0	0	0	1	.143	.143	.143	-22	-1	-1	0	0	0	0	1.000	-0	/O	-0.2
1943	Det-A★	155	633	91	**200**	**38**	8	7	79	62	60	.316	.377	.434	127	29	23	101	4	5	-2	.959	-6	*O	0.8
1944	Det-A	78	276	53	98	15	5	12	53	55	29	.355	.464	.576	186	37	35	79	2	2	-1	.963	-4	O	2.7
1946	Det-A	111	396	64	106	11	5	12	59	59	55	.268	.364	.412	110	10	7	63	3	5	-2	.964	0	*O	-0.1
1947	Det-A	112	368	59	104	15	5	8	51	80	44	.283	.412	.416	127	19	17	69	1	4	-2	.950	-2	*O	0.8
1948	Det-A	110	322	50	89	20	5	11	53	70	55	.276	.406	.472	129	17	15	67	0	1	-1	.948	0	O	1.0
1949	Det-A	59	126	17	26	3	1	6	19	32	24	.206	.367	.389	100	0	0	20	0	0	0	1.000	2	O	0.0
1950	NY-A	3	2	0	1	0	0	0	1	1	1	.500	.667	.500	208	0	0	1	0	0	0	.000	0	H	0.0
1952	NY-N	3	2	0	0	0	0	0	0	1	1	.000	.333	.000	-0	-0	-0	0	0	0	0	.000	0	H	0.0
Total	9	638	2132	334	625	102	29	56	315	360	270	.293	.396	.447	130	110	97	401	10	17	-7	.959	-11	O	5.0

■ ED WALCZAK
Walczak, Edwin Joseph "Husky" b: 9/21/18, Artic, R.I. BR/TR, 5'11", 180 lbs. Deb: 9/03/45

YEAR	TM/L	G	AB	R	H	2B	3B	HR	RBI	BB	SO	AVG	OBP	SLG	PRO+	BR	/A	RC	SB	CS	SBR	FA	FR	POS	TPR
1945	Phi-N	20	57	6	12	3	0	0	2	6	9	.211	.286	.263	55	-4	-3	4	0			.966	1	2/S	-0.2

■ FRED WALDEN
Walden, Thomas Fred b: 6/25/1890, Fayette, Mo. d: 9/27/55, Jefferson Barracks, Mo. BR/TR, Deb: 6/03/12

YEAR	TM/L	G	AB	R	H	2B	3B	HR	RBI	BB	SO	AVG	OBP	SLG	PRO+	BR	/A	RC	SB	CS	SBR	FA	FR	POS	TPR
1912	StL-A	1	0	0	0	0	0	0	0	0		—	—	—	—	0	0	0	0			.000	-1	/C	-0.1

■ IRV WALDRON
Waldron, Irving J. b: 1/21/1876, Hillside, N.Y. d: 7/22/44, Worcester, Mass. BR/TR, Deb: 4/25/01

YEAR	TM/L	G	AB	R	H	2B	3B	HR	RBI	BB	SO	AVG	OBP	SLG	PRO+	BR	/A	RC	SB	CS	SBR	FA	FR	POS	TPR
1901	Mil-A	62	266	48	79	8	6	0	29	16		.297	.342	.372	103	-1	1	39	12			.883	-2	O	-0.5
	Was-A	79	332	54	107	14	3	0	23	22		.322	.368	.383	110	4	5	52	8			.955	-5	O	-0.5
	Yr	141	598	102	186	22	9	0	52	38		.311	.356	.378	107	3	6	91	20			.923	-7	*O	-1.0

■ JIM WALEWANDER
Walewander, James b: 5/2/62, Chicago, Ill. BB/TR, 5'10", 160 lbs. Deb: 5/31/87

YEAR	TM/L	G	AB	R	H	2B	3B	HR	RBI	BB	SO	AVG	OBP	SLG	PRO+	BR	/A	RC	SB	CS	SBR	FA	FR	POS	TPR
1987	Det-A	53	54	24	13	3	1	1	4	7	6	.241	.328	.389	93	-1	-0	7	2	1	0	1.000	15	23/SD	1.4
1988	Det-A	88	175	23	37	5	0	0	6	12	26	.211	.262	.240	43	-13	-13	13	11	4	1	.977	14	2/S3D	0.4
1990	NY-A	9	5	1	1	1	0	0	1	0	0	.200	.200	.400	64	-0	-0	0	1	1	-0	1.000	1	/23SD	0.1
Total	3	150	234	48	51	9	1	1	11	19	32	.218	.277	.278	56	-15	-13	19	14	6	1	.981	31	/23DS	1.9

■ RUBE WALKER
Walker, Albert Bluford b: 5/16/26, Lenoir, N.C. BL/TR, 6'1", 185 lbs. Deb: 4/20/48 C

YEAR	TM/L	G	AB	R	H	2B	3B	HR	RBI	BB	SO	AVG	OBP	SLG	PRO+	BR	/A	RC	SB	CS	SBR	FA	FR	POS	TPR
1948	Chi-N	79	171	17	47	8	0	5	26	24	17	.275	.371	.409	115	3	4	25	0			.980	-3	C	0.3
1949	Chi-N	56	172	11	42	4	1	3	22	9	18	.244	.282	.331	66	-9	-9	15	0			.964	-5	C	-1.1
1950	Chi-N	74	213	19	49	7	1	6	16	18	34	.230	.290	.357	70	-10	-10	22	0			.975	1	C	-0.6
1951	Chi-N	37	107	9	25	4	0	2	5	12	13	.234	.311	.327	71	-4	-4	11	0	0	0	.969	-4	C	-0.7
	Bro-N	36	74	6	18	4	0	2	9	6	14	.243	.300	.378	80	-2	-2	8	0	0	0	.972	-5	C	-0.6
	Yr	73	181	15	43	8	0	4	14	18	27	.238	.307	.348	74	-6	-7	19	0	0	0	.970	-8	C	-1.3
1952	Bro-N	46	139	9	36	8	0	1	19	8	17	.259	.304	.338	77	-4	-4	14	0	0	0	.987	5	C	0.3
1953	Bro-N	43	95	5	23	6	0	3	9	7	11	.242	.301	.400	79	-3	-3	12	0	0	0	.978	1	C	-0.1
1954	Bro-N	50	155	12	28	7	0	5	23	24	17	.181	.294	.323	59	-9	-10	15	0	0	0	.996	1	C	-0.6
1955	Bro-N	48	103	6	26	5	0	2	13	15	11	.252	.347	.359	86	-1	-2	11	1	0	0	.987	2	C	0.1
1956	*Bro-N	54	146	5	31	6	1	3	20	7	18	.212	.248	.329	50	-10	-11	11	0	1	-1	.986	-1	C	-1.2
1957	Bro-N	60	166	12	30	8	0	2	23	15	33	.181	.249	.265	35	-15	-17	10	2	0	1	.992	-6	C	-2.0
1958	LA-N	25	44	3	5	2	0	1	7	5	10	.114	.204	.227	14	-6	-6	2	0	0	0	.985	-2	C	-0.7
Total	11	608	1585	114	360	69	3	35	192	150	213	.227	.296	.341	68	-70	-74	158	3	1		.982	-15	C	-6.9

■ TONY WALKER
Walker, Anthony Bruce b: 7/1/59, San Diego, Cal. BR/TR, 6'2", 205 lbs. Deb: 4/08/86

YEAR	TM/L	G	AB	R	H	2B	3B	HR	RBI	BB	SO	AVG	OBP	SLG	PRO+	BR	/A	RC	SB	CS	SBR	FA	FR	POS	TPR
1986	Hou-N	84	90	19	20	7	0	2	10	11	15	.222	.307	.367	87	-2	-2	10	11	3	2	.986	-14	O	-1.5

■ FRANK WALKER
Walker, Charles Franklin b: 9/22/1894, Enoree, S.C. d: 9/16/74, Bristol, Tenn. BR/TR, 5'11", 165 lbs. Deb: 9/06/17

YEAR	TM/L	G	AB	R	H	2B	3B	HR	RBI	BB	SO	AVG	OBP	SLG	PRO+	BR	/A	RC	SB	CS	SBR	FA	FR	POS	TPR
1917	Det-A	2	2	0	0	0	0	0	0	0	1	.000	.000	.000	-99	-0	-0	0	0			.000	0	H	-0.1
1918	Det-A	55	167	10	33	10	3	1	20	7	29	.198	.234	.311	67	-8	-8	12	3			.922	-2	O	-1.3
1920	Phi-A	24	91	10	21	2	2	0	10	5	14	.231	.286	.297	54	-6	-6	7	0	2	-1	.983	-1	O	-1.0
1921	Phi-A	19	66	6	15	3	0	1	6	8	11	.227	.311	.318	60	-4	-4	7	1	0	0	.961	1	O	-0.4
1925	NY-N	39	81	12	18	1	0	1	5	9	11	.222	.308	.272	51	-6	-6	7	1	1	-0	.960	-1	O	-0.8
Total	5	139	407	38	87	16	5	3	41	29	66	.214	.273	.300	58	-25	-24	34	5	3		.949	-4	O	-3.6

■ TILLY WALKER
Walker, Clarence William b: 9/4/1887, Telford, Tenn. d: 9/20/59, Chattanooga, Tenn BR/TR, 5'11", 165 lbs. Deb: 4/12/11

YEAR	TM/L	G	AB	R	H	2B	3B	HR	RBI	BB	SO	AVG	OBP	SLG	PRO+	BR	/A	RC	SB	CS	SBR	FA	FR	POS	TPR
1911	Was-A	95	356	44	99	6	4	2	39	15		.278	.311	.334	82	-10	-9	41	12			.917	-1	O	-1.5
1912	Was-A	39	110	22	30	2	1	0	9	8		.273	.333	.309	83	-2	-2	15	11			.837	-3	O/2	-0.6
1913	StL-A	23	85	7	25	4	1	0	11	2	9	.294	.310	.365	100	-1	-0	11	5			.911	-0	O	-0.2
1914	StL-A	151	517	67	154	24	16	6	78	51	72	.298	.365	.441	148	25	27	87	29	17	-2	.972	16	*O	3.8
1915	StL-A	144	510	53	137	20	7	5	49	36	77	.269	.323	.365	110	2	4	62	20	17	-4	.940	15	*O	0.8
1916	*Bos-A	128	467	68	124	29	11	3	46	23	45	.266	.303	.394	109	2	2	61	14			.959	-4	*O	-0.9
1917	Bos-A	106	337	41	83	18	7	2	37	25	38	.246	.300	.359	102	-1	-1	38	6			.972	6	O	0.0
1918	Phi-A	114	414	56	122	20	0	**11**	48	41	44	.295	.360	.423	135	17	16	64	8			.953	5	*O	1.6
1919	Phi-A	125	456	47	133	30	6	10	64	26	41	.292	.330	.450	116	8	7	68	8			.933	-4	*O	-0.4
1920	Phi-A	149	585	79	157	23	7	17	82	41	59	.268	.321	.419	94	-7	-8	80	8	3	1	.940	6	*O	-1.2
1921	Phi-A	142	556	89	169	32	5	23	101	73	41	.304	.389	.504	125	21	21	111	3	4	-2	.955	9	*O	1.7
1922	Phi-A	153	565	111	160	31	4	37	99	61	64	.283	.357	.549	130	24	22	110	4	6	-2	.956	-2	*O	0.7
1923	Phi-A	52	109	12	30	5	2	2	16	14	11	.275	.368	.413	104	1	1	17	1	2	-1	1.000	-2	O	-0.3
Total	13	1421	5067	696	1423	244	71	118	679	416	501	.281	.339	.427	115	79	80	762	129	49		.949	41	*O/2	3.5

■ CHICO WALKER
Walker, Cleotha b: 11/25/57, Jackson, Miss. BB/TR, 5'9", 179 lbs. Deb: 9/02/80

YEAR	TM/L	G	AB	R	H	2B	3B	HR	RBI	BB	SO	AVG	OBP	SLG	PRO+	BR	/A	RC	SB	CS	SBR	FA	FR	POS	TPR
1980	Bos-A	19	57	3	12	0	0	1	5	6	10	.211	.297	.263	52	-3	-4	5	3	2	-0	.958	1	2/D	-0.3
1981	Bos-A	6	17	3	6	0	0	0	2	1	2	.353	.389	.353	108	0	0	2	0	2	-1	1.000	-2	/2	-0.3
1983	Bos-A	4	5	2	2	0	2	0	1	0	0	.400	.400	1.200	299	1	1	2	0	0	0	1.000	0	/O	0.2
1984	Bos-A	3	2	0	0	0	0	0	1	0	1	.000	.000	.000	-96	-1	-1	0	0	0	0	1.000	0	/2	-0.1
1985	Chi-N	21	12	3	1	0	0	0	0	0	5	.083	.083	.083	-48	-2	-3	0	1	0	0	1.000	-2	/O2	-0.4
1986	Chi-N	28	101	21	28	3	2	1	7	10	20	.277	.342	.376	91	-0	-1	14	15	4	2	.956	-5	O	-0.5
1987	Chi-N	47	105	15	21	4	0	0	7	12	23	.200	.282	.238	38	-9	-9	8	11	4	1	.974	-5	O/3	-1.5
1988	Cal-A	33	78	8	12	1	0	0	2	6	15	.154	.214	.167	8	-9	-9	3	2	1	0	.933	-2	O/23	-1.2
1991	Chi-N	124	374	51	96	10	1	6	34	33	57	.257	.317	.337	80	-8	-10	42	13	5	1	.929	-23	3O/2	-3.4
1992	Chi-N	19	26	2	3	0	0	0	2	3	4	.115	.207	.115	-6	-4	-4	1	1	0	0	1.000	0	/O23	-0.4
	NY-N	107	227	24	70	12	1	4	36	24	46	.308	.375	.423	126	8	8	37	14	1	4	.971	-7	32O	0.5
	Yr	126	253	26	73	12	1	4	38	27	50	.289	.357	.391	112	4	4	37	15	1	4	.960	-7	3O2	0.1
Total	10	411	1004	132	251	30	6	12	97	95	183	.250	.315	.328	77	-27	-31	113	60	19	7	.970	-45	O/32D	-7.4

■ DUANE WALKER
Walker, Duane Allen b: 3/13/57, Pasadena, Tex. BL/TL, 6', 185 lbs. Deb: 5/25/82

YEAR	TM/L	G	AB	R	H	2B	3B	HR	RBI	BB	SO	AVG	OBP	SLG	PRO+	BR	/A	RC	SB	CS	SBR	FA	FR	POS	TPR
1982	Cin-N	86	239	26	52	10	0	5	22	27	58	.218	.302	.322	73	-8	-8	26	9	3	1	.992	-1	O	-1.1
1983	Cin-N	109	225	14	53	12	1	2	29	20	43	.236	.298	.324	70	-8	-9	23	6	3	0	.956	2	O	-1.0
1984	Cin-N	83	195	35	57	10	3	10	28	33	35	.292	.395	.528	150	15	14	43	7	3	0	.950	-5	O	0.8
1985	Cin-N	37	48	5	8	2	1	2	6	6	18	.167	.259	.375	72	-2	-2	5	1	0	0	.882	-1	O	-0.3
	Tex-A	53	132	14	23	2	0	5	11	15	29	.174	.264	.303	54	-8	-9	11	2	1	0	1.000	1	OD	-0.8

YEAR	TM/L	G	AB	R	H	2B	3B	HR	RBI	BB	SO	AVG	OBP	SLG	PRO+	BR	/A	RC	SB	CS	SBR	FA	FR	POS	TPR
1988	StL-N	24	22	1	4	1	0	0	3	2	7	.182	.250	.227	38	-2	-2	1	0	0	0	.000	-2	/O1	-0.4
Total	5	392	861	95	197	37	5	24	99	103	190	.229	.313	.367	86	-13	-16	109	25	10	2	.967	-6	O/D1	-2.8

■ ERNIE WALKER

Walker, Ernest Robert b: 9/17/1890, Blossburg, Ala. d: 4/1/65, Pell City, Ala. BL/TR, 6', 165 lbs. Deb: 4/13/13 F

YEAR	TM/L	G	AB	R	H	2B	3B	HR	RBI	BB	SO	AVG	OBP	SLG	PRO+	BR	/A	RC	SB	CS	SBR	FA	FR	POS	TPR
1913	StL-A	7	14	0	3	0	0	0	2	0	5	.214	.214	.214	26	-1	-1	1	0			1.000	-0	/O	-0.2
1914	StL-A	74	131	19	39	5	3	1	14	13	26	.298	.366	.405	137	5	5	20	6	4	-1	.960	-6	O	-0.3
1915	StL-A	50	109	15	23	4	2	0	9	23	32	.211	.348	.284	93	-0	0	10	5	8	-3	.881	-6	O	-1.1
Total	3	131	254	34	65	9	5	1	25	36	63	.256	.351	.343	112	3	4	31	11	12		.928	-12	/O	-1.6

■ DIXIE WALKER

Walker, Fred "The People's Cherce" b: 9/24/10, Villa Rica, Ga. d: 5/17/82, Birmingham, Ala. BL/TR, 6'1", 175 lbs. Deb: 4/28/31 FC

YEAR	TM/L	G	AB	R	H	2B	3B	HR	RBI	BB	SO	AVG	OBP	SLG	PRO+	BR	/A	RC	SB	CS	SBR	FA	FR	POS	TPR
1931	NY-A	2	10	1	3	2	0	0	1	0	4	.300	.300	.500	113	0	0	1	0	0	0	1.000	-0	/O	0.0
1933	NY-A	98	328	68	90	15	7	15	51	26	28	.274	.330	.500	125	6	9	54	2	2	-1	.962	5	O	0.9
1934	NY-A	17	17	2	2	0	0	0	0	1	3	.118	.167	.118	-27	-3	-3	0	0	0	0	1.000	-0	/O	-0.3
1935	NY-A	8	13	1	2	1	0	0	1	0	1	.154	.154	.231	-2	-2	-2	0	0	0	0	.750	-1	/O	-0.2
1936	NY-A	6	20	3	7	0	2	1	5	1	3	.350	.381	.700	167	2	2	5	1	1	-0	1.000	-1	/O	0.0
	Chi-A	26	70	12	19	2	0	0	11	14	6	.271	.400	.300	73	-2	-2	10	1	0	0	1.000	1	O	-0.2
	Yr	32	90	15	26	2	2	1	16	15	9	.289	.396	.389	92	-0	-1	15	2	1	0	1.000	-0	O	-0.2
1937	Chi-A	154	593	105	179	28	**16**	9	95	78	26	.302	.383	.449	109	9	9	105	1	2	-1	.952	-10	*O	-0.6
1938	Det-A	127	454	84	140	27	6	6	43	65	32	.308	.396	.434	102	7	3	81	5	4	-1	.979	-9	*O	-0.9
1939	Det-A	43	154	30	47	4	5	4	19	15	8	.305	.367	.474	106	3	1	26	4	1	1	.970	4	O	0.4
	Bro-N	61	225	27	63	6	4	2	38	20	10	.280	.339	.369	87	-3	-4	28	1			.968	2	O	-0.4
1940	Bro-N	143	556	75	171	37	8	6	66	42	21	.308	.357	.435	111	13	8	88	3			.973	2	*O	0.4
1941	*Bro-N	148	531	88	165	32	8	9	71	70	18	.311	.391	.452	131	27	24	99	4			.976	11	*O	2.8
1942	Bro-N	118	393	57	114	28	1	6	54	47	15	.290	.367	.412	126	14	13	64	1			.986	-1	*O	0.7
1943	Bro-N★	138	540	83	163	32	6	5	71	49	24	.302	.363	.411	123	16	16	82	3			.969	3	*O	1.2
1944	Bro-N★	147	535	77	191	37	8	13	91	72	27	**.357**	.434	.529	173	51	52	128	6			.962	-3	*O	4.3
1945	Bro-N	154	607	102	182	42	9	8	**124**	75	16	.300	.381	.438	128	23	24	105	6			.992	12	*O	2.8
1946	Bro-N★	150	576	80	184	29	9	9	116	67	28	.319	.391	.448	136	29	28	104	14			.969	-8	*O	1.4
1947	*Bro-N★	148	529	77	162	31	3	9	94	97	26	.306	.415	.427	119	22	20	101	6			.964	-8	*O	0.4
1948	Pit-N	129	408	39	129	19	3	2	54	52	18	.316	.393	.392	111	9	8	66	1			.977	-12	*O	-0.9
1949	Pit-N	88	181	26	51	4	1	1	18	26	11	.282	.372	.331	88	-1	-2	24	0			.984	-4	O/1	-0.8
Total	18	1905	6740	1037	2064	376	96	105	1023	817	325	.306	.383	.437	121	220	204	1171	59	10		.906	-16	*O/1	11.0

■ GEE WALKER

Walker, Gerald Holmes b: 3/19/08, Gulfport, Miss. d: 3/20/81, Whitfield, Miss. BR/TR, 5'11", 188 lbs. Deb: 4/14/31 FC

YEAR	TM/L	G	AB	R	H	2B	3B	HR	RBI	BB	SO	AVG	OBP	SLG	PRO+	BR	/A	RC	SB	CS	SBR	FA	FR	POS	TPR
1931	Det-A	59	189	20	56	17	2	1	28	14	21	.296	.345	.423	98	-0	-1	26	10	7	-1	.953	-3	O	-0.8
1932	Det-A	127	480	71	155	32	6	8	78	13	38	.323	.345	.465	104	4	1	78	30	6	**5**	.949	4	*O	0.3
1933	Det-A	127	483	68	135	29	7	9	64	15	49	.280	.304	.424	90	-9	-10	61	26	9	**2**	.942	-1	*O	-1.3
1934	*Det-A	98	347	54	104	19	2	6	39	19	20	.300	.340	.418	94	-4	-4	49	20	9	1	.947	2	O	-0.4
1935	*Det-A	98	362	52	109	22	6	7	53	15	21	.301	.329	.453	104	-2	0	52	6	4	-1	.954	-3	O	-0.6
1936	Det-A	134	550	105	194	55	5	12	93	23	30	.353	.387	.536	125	20	20	112	17	8	0	.948	5	*O	1.7
1937	Det-A†	151	635	105	213	42	4	18	113	41	74	.335	.380	.499	117	18	16	121	23	7	3	.956	-6	*O	0.7
1938	Chi-A	120	442	69	135	23	6	16	87	38	32	.305	.360	.493	109	6	5	79	9	4	0	.958	-5	*O	-0.3
1939	Chi-A	149	598	95	174	30	11	13	111	28	43	.291	.330	.443	94	-6	-8	84	17	6	2	.967	9	*O	-0.3
1940	Was-A	140	595	87	175	29	7	13	96	24	58	.294	.325	.432	101	-7	-2	84	21	4	4	.967	-2	*O	-0.6
1941	Cle-A	121	445	56	126	26	11	6	48	18	46	.283	.313	.431	100	-5	-3	56	12	6	0	.982	8	*O	-0.1
1942	Cin-N	119	422	40	97	20	2	5	50	31	44	.230	.290	.322	79	-12	-12	40	11			.973	4	*O	-1.4
1943	Cin-N	114	429	48	105	23	2	3	54	12	38	.245	.270	.329	74	-17	-16	35	6			.980	-6	*O	-2.9
1944	Cin-N	121	478	56	133	21	3	5	62	23	48	.278	.318	.366	96	-6	-4	53	7			.967	-7	*O	-1.8
1945	Cin-N	106	316	28	80	11	2	2	21	16	38	.253	.289	.320	71	-14	-13	29	8			.962	-7	O/3	-2.4
Total	15	1784	6771	954	1991	399	76	124	997	330	600	.294	.331	.430	99	-33	-30	959	223	70		.961	-7	*O/3	-10.2

■ GREG WALKER

Walker, Gregory Lee b: 10/6/59, Douglas, Ga. BL/TR, 6'3", 210 lbs. Deb: 9/18/82

YEAR	TM/L	G	AB	R	H	2B	3B	HR	RBI	BB	SO	AVG	OBP	SLG	PRO+	BR	/A	RC	SB	CS	SBR	FA	FR	POS	TPR
1982	Chi-A	11	17	3	7	2	1	2	7	2	3	.412	.474	1.000	292	4	4	8	0	0	0	.000	0	/D	0.4
1983	*Chi-A	118	307	32	83	16	3	10	55	28	57	.270	.335	.440	107	4	3	46	2	1	0	.985	-7	1D	-0.7
1984	Chi-A	136	442	62	130	29	2	24	75	35	66	.294	.349	.532	134	22	20	79	8	5	-1	.995	-5	*1D	0.9
1985	Chi-A	163	601	77	155	38	4	24	92	44	100	.258	.311	.454	102	3	1	81	5	2	0	.994	-3	*1/D	-1.1
1986	Chi-A	78	282	37	78	10	6	13	51	29	44	.277	.348	.493	122	10	8	48	1	2	-1	.993	-1	1/D	0.1
1987	Chi-A	157	566	85	145	33	2	27	94	75	112	.256	.348	.465	110	11	9	93	2	1	0	.994	-14	*1/D	-1.6
1988	Chi-A	99	377	45	93	22	1	8	42	29	77	.247	.306	.374	90	-6	-6	43	0	1	-1	.993	-14	1	-2.9
1989	Chi-A	77	233	25	49	14	0	5	26	23	50	.210	.290	.335	77	-8	-7	22	0	0	0	.987	-6	1D	-1.6
1990	Chi-A	2	5	0	1	0	0	0	0	0	2	.200	.200	.200	12	-1	-1	0	0	0	0	1.000	0	/1D	0.0
	Bal-A	14	34	2	5	0	0	0	2	3	9	.147	.237	.147	10	-4	-4	1	1	0	0	.000	0	D	-0.4
	Yr	16	39	2	6	0	0	0	2	3	11	.154	.233	.154	10	-5	-4	1	1	0	0	1.000	0	D/1	-0.4
Total	9	855	2864	368	746	164	19	113	444	268	520	.260	.328	.449	108	37	28	422	19	12	-2	.993	-49	1/D	-6.9

■ HARRY WALKER

Walker, Harry William "Harry The Hat" b: 10/22/16, Pascagoula, Miss. BL/TR, 6'2", 190 lbs. Deb: 9/25/40 FMC

YEAR	TM/L	G	AB	R	H	2B	3B	HR	RBI	BB	SO	AVG	OBP	SLG	PRO+	BR	/A	RC	SB	CS	SBR	FA	FR	POS	TPR
1940	StL-N	7	27	2	5	2	0	0	6	0	2	.185	.185	.259	20	-3	-3	1	0			1.000	2	/O	-0.2
1941	StL-N	7	15	3	4	1	0	0	1	2	1	.267	.353	.333	88	-0	-0	2	0			.875	-1	/O	-0.2
1942	*StL-N	74	191	38	60	12	2	0	16	11	14	.314	.355	.398	112	4	3	28	2			.968	-1	O/2	-0.1
1943	*StL-N★	148	564	76	166	28	6	2	53	40	24	.294	.341	.376	102	4	1	76	5			.965	-6	*O/2	-1.3
1946	*StL-N	112	346	53	82	14	6	3	27	30	29	.237	.300	.338	77	-9	-11	37	12			.974	5	O/1	-1.1
1947	StL-N	10	25	2	5	1	0	0	0	4	2	.200	.310	.240	46	-2	-2	2	0			.938	-2	O	-0.4
	Phi-N	130	488	79	181	28	16	1	41	59	37	.371	.443	.500	156	37	40	111	13			.966	14	*O/1	4.5
	Yr	140	513	81	186	29	**16**	1	41	63	39	**.363**	.436	.487	150	35	38	112	13			.964	12	*O/1	4.1
1948	Phi-N	112	332	34	97	11	2	2	23	33	30	.292	.358	.355	95	-2	-1	44	4			.981	2	O/13	-0.4
1949	Chi-N	42	159	20	42	6	3	1	14	11	6	.264	.312	.358	81	-5	-4	18	2			.947	-3	O	-0.9
	Cin-N	86	314	53	100	15	2	1	23	34	17	.318	.385	.389	107	5	4	48	4			.963	2	O/1	0.2
	Yr	128	473	73	142	21	5	2	37	45	23	.300	.361	.378	99	-0	-0	66	6			.959	-2	*O/1	-0.7
1950	StL-N	60	150	17	31	5	0	0	7	18	12	.207	.292	.240	40	-12	-13	11	0			.969	-1	O/1	-1.6
1951	StL-N	8	26	6	8	1	0	0	2	2	1	.308	.357	.346	90	-0	-0	3	0	0	0	1.000	-1	/O1	-0.2
1955	StL-N	11	14	2	5	2	0	0	1	1	0	.357	.400	.500	137	1	1	3	0	0	0	1.000	1	/OM	0.2
Total	11	807	2651	385	786	126	37	10	214	245	175	.296	.358	.383	103	17	13	386	42	0		.968	10	O/123	-1.5

■ HUB WALKER

Walker, Harvey Willos b: 8/17/06, Gulfport, Miss. d: 11/26/82, San Jose, Cal. BL/TR, 5'10.5", 175 lbs. Deb: 4/15/31 F

YEAR	TM/L	G	AB	R	H	2B	3B	HR	RBI	BB	SO	AVG	OBP	SLG	PRO+	BR	/A	RC	SB	CS	SBR	FA	FR	POS	TPR
1931	Det-A	90	252	27	72	13	1	0	16	23	25	.286	.355	.345	82	-5	-6	34	10	1	2	.961	-0	O	-0.8
1935	Det-A	9	25	4	4	3	0	0	1	3	4	.160	.250	.280	38	-2	-2	2	0	0	0	1.000	-0	/O	-0.3
1936	Cin-N	92	258	49	71	18	1	4	23	35	32	.275	.366	.399	113	3	5	41	8			.970	-4	O/C1	-0.2
1937	Cin-N	78	221	33	55	9	4	1	19	34	24	.249	.349	.339	92	-3	-1	28	7			.993	4	O/2	0.0
1945	*Det-A	28	23	4	3	0	0	0	1	9	4	.130	.375	.130	46	-1	-1	2	1	0	0	1.000	-2	/O	-0.3
Total	5	297	779	117	205	43	6	5	60	104	89	.263	.354	.353	92	-8	-6	106	26	1		.975	-4	O/21C	-1.6

■ JOHNNY WALKER

Walker, John Miles b: 12/11/1896, Toulon, Ill. d: 8/19/76, Hollywood, Fla. BR/TR, 6', 175 lbs. Deb: 9/19/19

YEAR	TM/L	G	AB	R	H	2B	3B	HR	RBI	BB	SO	AVG	OBP	SLG	PRO+	BR	/A	RC	SB	CS	SBR	FA	FR	POS	TPR
1919	Phi-A	3	9	0	0	0	0	0	0	0	2	.000	.000	.000	-99	-2	-2	0	0			.941	-0	/C	-0.2
1920	Phi-A	9	22	0	5	1	0	0	5	0	1	.227	.227	.273	32	-2	-2	1	0	0	0	.960	-1	/C	-0.2

YEAR	TM/L	G	AB	R	H	2B	3B	HR	RBI	BB	SO	AVG	OBP	SLG	PRO+	BR	/A	RC	SB	CS	SBR	FA	FR	POS	TPR
1921	Phi-A	113	423	41	109	14	5	2	46	9	29	.258	.278	.329	54	-30	-30	39	5	0	2	.989	-6	1/C	-3.5
Total	3	125	454	41	114	15	5	2	51	9	32	.251	.270	.319	50	-35	-35	40	5	0		.968	-7	/1C	-3.9
■ SPEED WALKER	Walker, Joseph Richard b: 1/23/1898, Munhall, Pa. d: 6/20/59, W.Mifflin, Pa. BR/TR, 6', 170 lbs. Deb: 9/15/23																								
1923	StL-N	2	7	1	2	0	0	0	0	0	1	.286	.286	.286	52	-0	-0	1	0	0	0	1.000	-0	/1	-0.1
■ LARRY WALKER	Walker, Larry Kenneth Robert b: 12/1/66, Maple River, B.C., Canada BL/TR, 6'2", 185 lbs. Deb: 8/16/89																								
1989	Mon-N	20	47	4	8	0	0	0	4	5	13	.170	.264	.170	26	-4	-4	3	1	1	-0	1.000	0	O	-0.5
1990	Mon-N	133	419	59	101	18	3	19	51	49	112	.241	.328	.434	112	4	6	61	21	7	2	.985	9	*O	1.5
1991	Mon-N	137	487	59	141	30	2	16	64	42	102	.290	.352	.458	128	16	17	78	14	9	-1	.991	9	*O1	2.0
1992	Mon-N★	143	528	85	159	31	4	23	93	41	97	.301	.358	.506	143	28	28	95	18	6	2	.993	14	*O	4.2
Total	4	433	1481	207	409	79	9	58	212	137	324	.276	.344	.459	125	43	47	237	54	23	2	.990	31	O/1	7.2
■ FLEET WALKER	Walker, Moses Fleetwood b: 10/7/1856, Mt.Pleasant, Ohio d: 5/11/24, Cleveland, Ohio BR/TR, Deb: 5/01/1884 F																								
1884	Tol-a	42	152	23	40	2	3	0		8		.263	.325	.316	109	3	2	16				.887	-6	C/O	-0.1
■ OSCAR WALKER	Walker, Oscar b: 3/18/1854, Brooklyn, N.Y. d: 5/20/1889, Brooklyn, N.Y. BL/TL, 5'10", 166 lbs. Deb: 9/17/1875																								
1875	Atl-n	1	2	0	0	0	0	0		1		.000	.333	.000	30	-0	-0	0						/O	0.0
1879	Buf-N	72	287	35	79	15	6	1	35	8	38	.275	.295	.380	118	6	5	33				.946	3	*1	0.5
1880	Buf-N	34	126	12	29	4	2	1	15	6	18	.230	.265	.317	95	-0	-1	11				.917	-2	1O	-0.4
1882	StL-a	76	318	48	76	15	7	**7**		10		.239	.262	.396	115	6	4	34				.846	8	*O/21	1.1
1884	Bro-a	95	382	59	103	12	8	2		9		.270	.292	.359	113	5	5	41				.868	0	O1	0.0
1885	Bal-a	4	13	1	0	0	0	0		0		.000	.000	.000	-99	-3	-3	0				.667	-1	/O	-0.4
Total	5	281	1126	155	287	46	23	11	50	33	56	.255	.278	.366	110	14	11	119				.850	8	O1/2	0.8
■ WALT WALKER	Walker, Walter S. b: 1860, Ionia, Mich. d: 2/28/22, Pontiac, Mich. Deb: 5/08/1884																								
1884	Det-N	1	4	1	1	0	0	0	0	0	0	.250	.250	.250	61	-0	-0	0				.750	-1	C	-0.1
■ WELDAY WALKER	Walker, Welday Wilberforce b: 6/1859, Steubenville, Ohio d: 11/23/37, Steubenville, Ohio Deb: 7/15/1884 F																								
1884	Tol-a	5	18	1	4	1	0	0		0		.222	.222	.278	62	-1	-1	1				.667	-1	/O	-0.2
■ CURT WALKER	Walker, William Curtis b: 7/3/1896, Beeville, Tex. d: 12/9/55, Beeville, Tex. BL/TR, 5'9.5", 170 lbs. Deb: 9/17/19																								
1919	NY-A	1	1	0	0	0	0	0	0	0	0	.000	.000	.000	-99	-0	-0	0	0			.000	0	H	0.0
1920	NY-N	8	14	0	1	0	0	0	0	1	3	.071	.133	.071	-41	-3	-2	0	0	0	0	1.000	-1	/O	-0.4
1921	NY-N	64	192	30	55	13	5	3	35	15	8	.286	.338	.453	107	2	2	29	4	3	-1	.978	1	O	-0.2
	Phi-N	21	77	11	26	2	1	0	8	5	5	.338	.378	.390	96	1	-0	11	0	2	-1	.970	-5	O	-0.8
	Yr	85	269	41	81	15	6	3	43	20	13	.301	.349	.435	104	2	1	40	4	5	-2	.976	-4	O	-1.0
1922	Phi-N	148	581	102	196	36	11	12	89	56	46	.337	.399	.499	119	26	18	118	11	4	1	.955	5	*O	1.3
1923	Phi-N	140	527	66	148	26	5	5	66	45	31	.281	.337	.378	79	-9	-17	66	12	12	-4	.947	5	*O/1	-2.4
1924	Phi-N	24	71	11	21	6	1	1	8	7	4	.296	.359	.451	103	2	0	11	0	1	-1	.900	-4	O	-0.5
	Cin-N	109	397	55	119	21	10	4	46	44	15	.300	.371	.433	117	9	10	65	7	5	-1	.978	0	*O	0.2
	Yr	133	468	66	140	27	11	5	54	51	19	.299	.369	.436	114	10	10	76	7	6	-2	.969	-4	*O	-0.3
1925	Cin-N	145	509	86	162	22	16	6	71	57	31	.318	.387	.460	118	13	14	91	14	11	-2	**.983**	1	*O	0.4
1926	Cin-N	155	571	83	175	24	20	6	78	60	31	.306	.372	.450	124	16	18	95	3			.961	4	*O	1.2
1927	Cin-N	146	527	60	154	16	10	6	80	47	19	.292	.350	.395	102	-0	2	72	5			.957	3	*O	-0.5
1928	Cin-N	123	427	64	119	15	12	6	73	49	14	.279	.354	.412	101	-0	1	63	19			.955	4	*O	-0.3
1929	Cin-N	141	492	76	154	28	15	7	83	85	17	.313	.416	.474	126	18	22	99	17			.969	-6	*O	0.6
1930	Cin-N	134	472	74	145	26	11	8	51	64	30	.307	.391	.460	110	5	9	85	4			.965	-6	*O	-0.5
Total	12	1359	4858	718	1475	235	117	64	688	535	254	.304	.374	.440	110	79	76	805	96	38		.963	2	*O/1	-1.9
■ HOWARD WALL	Wall, Howard Deb: 9/13/1873																								
1873	Was-n	1	4	1	1	0	0	0	0	0	0	.250	.250	.250	49	-0	-0	0						/S	0.0
■ JOE WALL	Wall, Joseph Francis "Gummy" b: 7/24/1873, Brooklyn, N.Y. d: 7/17/36, Brooklyn, N.Y. BL/TL, Deb: 9/22/01																								
1901	NY-N	4	8	0	4	0	0	0	1	0		.500	.500	.500	198	1	1	2	0			1.000	-3	/CO	-0.1
1902	NY-N	6	14	2	5	2	0	0	0	2		.357	.438	.500	191	2	2	3	0			1.000	-0	/O	0.1
	Bro-N	5	18	0	3	0	0	0	0	3		.167	.318	.167	50	-1	-1	1	0			.893	-3	/C	-0.4
	Yr	11	32	2	8	2	0	0	0	5		.250	.368	.313	110	1	1	4	0			.893	-3	/CO	-0.3
Total	2	15	40	2	12	2	0	0	1	5		.300	.391	.350	127	2	2	6	0			.903	-6	/CO	-0.4
■ JACK WALLACE	Wallace, Clarence Eugene b: 8/6/1890, Winnfield, La. d: 10/15/60, Winnfield, La. BR/TR, 5'10.5", 175 lbs. Deb: 9/27/15																								
1915	Chi-N	2	7	1	2	0	0	0	1	0	2	.286	.375	.286	101	0	0	1	0			1.000	2	/C	0.2
■ DON WALLACE	Wallace, Donald Allen b: 8/25/40, Sapulpa, Okla. BL/TR, 5'8", 165 lbs. Deb: 4/12/67																								
1967	Cal-A	23	6	2	0	0	0	0	0	3	2	.000	.333	.000	6	-1	-0	0	0	1	-1	1.000	5	/213	0.4
■ DOC WALLACE	Wallace, Frederick Renshaw "Jesse" b: 9/30/1893, Church Hill, Md. d: 12/31/64, Haverford, Pa. BR/TR, 5'6.5", 135 lbs. Deb: 5/02/19																								
1919	Phi-N	2	4	0	1	0	0	0	0	0	1	.250	.250	.250	47	-0	-0	0	0			.875	0	/S	0.0
■ JIM WALLACE	Wallace, James L. b: 11/14/1881, Boston, Mass. d: 5/16/53, Revere, Mass. BL/TL, 5'9", 150 lbs. Deb: 8/24/05																								
1905	Pit-N	7	29	3	6	1	0	0	3	3		.207	.281	.241	55	-1	-2	3	2			.929	1	/O	-0.1
■ BOBBY WALLACE	Wallace, Roderick John b: 11/4/1873, Pittsburgh, Pa. d: 11/3/60, Torrance, Cal. BR/TR, 5'8", 170 lbs. Deb: 9/15/1894 MUCH																								
1894	Cle-N	4	13	0	2	1	0	0	1	0	1	.154	.154	.231	-7	-2	-2	0	0			1.000	1	/P	0.0
1895	Cle-N	30	98	16	21	2	3	0	10	6	17	.214	.274	.296	46	-8	-9	9	0			.910	3	P	0.0
1896	*Cle-N	45	149	19	35	6	3	1	17	11	21	.235	.287	.336	62	-8	-9	16	2			.950	-2	OP/1	-0.8
1897	Cle-N	130	516	99	173	33	21	4	112	48		.335	.394	.504	129	25	21	112	14			.928	4	*3/O	2.3
1898	Cle-N	154	593	81	160	25	13	3	99	63		.270	.343	.371	106	3	5	81	7			.936	17	*32	2.2
1899	StL-N	151	577	91	170	28	14	12	108	54		.295	.357	.454	119	15	13	103	17			.919	38	*S3	5.3
1900	StL-N	126	485	70	130	25	9	4	70	40		.268	.328	.381	96	-4	-3	65	7			.934	3	*S/3	0.8
1901	StL-N	134	550	69	178	34	15	2	91	20		.324	.350	.451	138	19	23	95	15			.929	**30**	*S	**6.1**
1902	StL-A	133	494	71	141	32	9	1	63	45		.285	.350	.393	107	4	5	77	18			.948	11	*S/PO	2.2
1903	StL-A	135	511	63	136	21	7	1	54	28		.266	.309	.341	98	-3	-1	59	10			.924	18	*S	2.3
1904	StL-A	139	541	57	149	29	4	2	69	42		.275	.330	.355	124	10	14	73	20			**.947**	8	*S	2.9
1905	StL-A	156	587	67	159	25	9	1	59	45		.271	.324	.349	120	9	12	73	13			.935	19	*S	3.7
1906	StL-A	139	476	64	123	21	7	2	67	58		.258	.344	.345	121	11	13	68	24			.949	3	*S	2.2
1907	StL-A	147	538	56	138	20	7	0	70	54		.257	.328	.320	107	5	5	64	16			.941	8	*S	1.9
1908	StL-A	137	487	59	123	24	4	1	60	52		.253	.327	.324	111	7	7	54	5			**.951**	18	*S	3.1
1909	StL-A	116	403	36	96	12	2	0	35	38		.238	.310	.278	92	-5	-2	36	7			.946	11	S3	1.3
1910	StL-A	138	508	47	131	19	7	0	37	49		.258	.324	.323	110	2	6	57	12			.948	22	S3	3.6
1911	StL-A	125	410	35	95	12	2	0	31	46		.232	.312	.271	66	-19	-17	37	8			.943	2	*S/2M	-0.7
1912	StL-A	100	323	39	78	14	5	0	31	43		.241	.332	.316	89	-5	-4	35	3			.942	8	S3/2M	1.2
1913	StL-A	55	147	11	31	5	0	0	21	14	16	.211	.293	.245	59	-8	-7	11	1			.931	-5	S/3	-1.0
1914	StL-A	26	73	3	16	2	1	0	5	5	13	.219	.269	.274	66	-3	-3	6	1	1	-0	.889	-11	S/3	-1.5
1915	StL-A	9	13	1	3	0	1	0	4	5	0	.231	.444	.385	154	1	1	2	0	1	-1	.848	1	/S	0.2
1916	StL-A	14	18	0	5	0	0	0	1	2	1	.278	.350	.278	93	-0	-0	2	0			.958	5	/3S	0.6

YEAR	TM/L	G	AB	R	H	2B	3B	HR	RBI	BB	SO	AVG	OBP	SLG	PRO+	BR	/A	RC	SB	CS	SBR	FA	FR	POS	TPR
1917	StL-N	8	10	0	1	0	0	0	2	0	1	.100	.100	.100	-40	-2	-2	0	0			1.000	-1	/3S	-0.3
1918	StL-N	32	98	3	15	1	0	0	4	6	9	.153	.202	.163	12	-10	-10	4	1			.959	2	2S/3	-0.8
Total	25	2383	8618	1057	2309	391	143	34	1121	774	79	.268	.331	.358	106	35	55	1139	201	2		.938	212	*S3/P2O1	36.8

■ **TIM WALLACH** Wallach, Timothy Charles b: 9/14/57, Huntington Park, Cal. BR/TR, 6'3", 200 lbs. Deb: 9/06/80

YEAR	TM/L	G	AB	R	H	2B	3B	HR	RBI	BB	SO	AVG	OBP	SLG	PRO+	BR	/A	RC	SB	CS	SBR	FA	FR	POS	TPR
1980	Mon-N	5	11	1	2	0	0	1	2	1	5	.182	.250	.455	93	-0	-0	1	0	0	0	1.000	-1	/O1	-0.1
1981	*Mon-N	71	212	19	50	9	1	4	13	15	37	.236	.299	.344	81	-5	-5	22	0	1	-1	1.000	-3	O13	-1.2
1982	Mon-N	158	596	89	160	31	3	28	97	36	81	.268	.314	.471	115	11	9	84	6	4	-1	.948	-5	*3/O1	0.0
1983	Mon-N	156	581	54	156	33	3	19	70	55	97	.269	.338	.434	113	9	9	85	0	3	-2	.956	-7	*3	-0.2
1984	Mon-N★	160	582	55	143	25	4	18	72	50	101	.246	.313	.395	102	-3	0	70	3	7	-3	.959	16	*3/S	1.2
1985	Mon-N★	155	569	70	148	36	3	22	81	38	79	.260	.312	.450	117	6	10	73	9	9	-3	.967	37	*3	4.3
1986	Mon-N	134	480	50	112	22	1	18	71	44	72	.233	.311	.396	94	-5	-4	57	8	4	0	.958	15	*3	0.8
1987	Mon-N★	153	593	89	177	**42**	4	26	123	37	98	.298	.347	.514	121	19	17	105	9	5	-0	.952	-0	*3/P	1.4
1988	Mon-N	159	592	52	152	32	5	12	69	38	88	.257	.305	.389	93	-3	-6	64	2	6	-3	.962	12	*3/2	0.2
1989	Mon-N★	154	573	76	159	**42**	0	13	77	58	81	.277	.345	.419	116	13	12	77	3	7	-3	.958	6	*3/P	1.7
1990	Mon-N★	161	626	69	185	37	5	21	98	42	80	.296	.343	.471	126	17	19	96	6	9	-4	.954	4	*3	2.2
1991	Mon-N	151	577	60	130	22	1	13	73	50	100	.225	.294	.334	77	-18	-17	56	2	4	-2	**.968**	6	*3	-1.3
1992	Mon-N	150	537	53	120	29	1	9	59	50	90	.223	.299	.331	79	-15	-15	54	2	2	-1	.964	19	31	-0.1
Total	13	1767	6529	737	1694	360	31	204	905	514	1009	.259	.320	.418	105	24	29	843	50	61	-22	.959	99	*3/1OP2S	8.9

■ **JACK WALLAESA** Wallaesa, John b: 8/31/19, Easton, Pa. d: 12/27/86, Easton, Pa. BB/TR, 6'3", 191 lbs. Deb: 9/22/40

YEAR	TM/L	G	AB	R	H	2B	3B	HR	RBI	BB	SO	AVG	OBP	SLG	PRO+	BR	/A	RC	SB	CS	SBR	FA	FR	POS	TPR
1940	Phi-A	6	20	0	3	0	0	0	2	0	2	.150	.150	.150	-22	-4	-4	0	0	0	0	.903	1	/S	-0.2
1942	Phi-A	36	117	13	30	4	1	2	13	8	26	.256	.315	.359	90	-2	-2	14	0	1	-1	.920	-7	S	-0.8
1946	Phi-A	63	194	16	38	4	2	5	11	14	47	.196	.250	.314	57	-12	-12	16	1	0	0	.916	-16	S	-2.6
1947	Chi-A	81	205	25	40	9	1	7	32	23	51	.195	.279	.351	78	-8	-7	20	2	2	-1	.968	13	SO/3	0.6
1948	Chi-A	33	48	2	9	0	0	1	3	1	12	.188	.204	.250	21	-6	-5	2	0	0	0	1.000	-0	/SO	-0.5
Total	5	219	584	56	120	17	4	15	61	46	138	.205	.267	.325	65	-31	-29	52	3	3	-1	.933	-10	S/O3	-3.5

■ **NORM WALLEN** Wallen, Norman Edward (b: Norman Edward Walentoski) b: 2/13/17, Milwaukee, Wis. BR/TR, 5'11.5", 175 lbs. Deb: 4/20/45

YEAR	TM/L	G	AB	R	H	2B	3B	HR	RBI	BB	SO	AVG	OBP	SLG	PRO+	BR	/A	RC	SB	CS	SBR	FA	FR	POS	TPR
1945	Bos-N	4	15	1	2	0	1	0	1	1	1	.133	.188	.267	25	-2	-2	1	0			.800	-2	/3	-0.3

■ **TY WALLER** Waller, Elliott Tyrone b: 3/14/57, Fresno, Cal. BR/TR, 6', 180 lbs. Deb: 9/06/80

YEAR	TM/L	G	AB	R	H	2B	3B	HR	RBI	BB	SO	AVG	OBP	SLG	PRO+	BR	/A	RC	SB	CS	SBR	FA	FR	POS	TPR
1980	StL-N	5	12	3	1	0	0	0	0	1	5	.083	.154	.083	-31	-2	-2	0	0	0	0	1.000	-2	/3	-0.5
1981	Chi-N	30	71	10	19	2	1	3	13	4	18	.268	.307	.451	108	1	0	10	2	0	1	.978	-1	3/2O	0.0
1982	Chi-N	17	21	4	5	0	0	0	1	2	5	.238	.304	.238	52	-1	-1	2	0	0	0	1.000	0	/O3	-0.1
1987	Hou-N	11	6	1	1	1	0	0	0	0	3	.167	.167	.333	30	-1	-1	0	0	0	0	1.000	-1	/O	-0.1
Total	4	63	110	18	26	3	1	3	14	7	31	.236	.282	.364	78	-3	-4	13	2	0	1	.961	-4	/3O2	-0.7

■ **DENNY WALLING** Walling, Dennis Martin b: 4/17/54, Neptune, N.J. BL/TR, 6'1", 185 lbs. Deb: 9/07/75

YEAR	TM/L	G	AB	R	H	2B	3B	HR	RBI	BB	SO	AVG	OBP	SLG	PRO+	BR	/A	RC	SB	CS	SBR	FA	FR	POS	TPR
1975	Oak-A	6	8	0	1	1	0	0	2	0	4	.125	.125	.250	4	-1	-1	0	0	0	0	1.000	-1	/O	-0.2
1976	Oak-A	3	11	1	3	0	0	0	0	0	3	.273	.273	.273	63	-1	-1	1	0	0	0	.889	-1	/O	-0.1
1977	Hou-N	6	21	1	6	0	1	0	6	2	4	.286	.348	.381	105	-0	0	3	0	1	-1	1.000	0	/O	0.0
1978	Hou-N	120	247	30	62	11	3	3	36	30	24	.251	.335	.356	101	-2	0	32	9	2	2	.980	3	O	0.2
1979	Hou-N	82	147	21	48	8	4	3	31	17	21	.327	.396	.497	151	9	10	29	3	2	-0	.985	-0	O	0.8
1980	*Hou-N	100	284	30	85	6	5	3	29	35	26	.299	.376	.387	123	6	9	43	4	3	-1	.989	-4	1O	0.0
1981	*Hou-N	65	158	23	37	6	0	5	23	28	17	.234	.349	.367	109	1	2	22	2	1	0	.990	-4	1O	-0.4
1982	Hou-N	85	146	22	30	4	1	1	14	23	19	.205	.314	.267	69	-6	-5	12	4	2	0	1.000	0	O1	-0.7
1983	Hou-N	100	135	24	40	5	3	3	19	15	16	.296	.367	.444	132	4	5	22	2	2	-1	.992	-2	13O	0.2
1984	Hou-N	87	249	37	70	11	5	3	31	16	28	.281	.327	.402	112	1	3	33	7	1	2	.956	-1	31/O	0.2
1985	Hou-N	119	345	44	93	20	1	7	45	25	26	.270	.319	.394	101	-1	-0	42	5	2	0	.938	-2	31O	-0.5
1986	*Hou-N	130	382	54	119	23	1	13	58	36	31	.312	.371	.479	136	16	18	67	1	1	-0	.960	2	*3O/1	1.8
1987	Hou-N	110	325	45	92	21	4	5	33	39	37	.283	.360	.418	110	3	5	50	5	1	1	.948	-4	31/O	-0.1
1988	Hou-N	65	176	19	43	10	2	1	20	15	18	.244	.304	.341	88	-3	-3	19	1	0	0	.950	9	3/1O	0.6
	StL-N	19	58	3	13	3	0	0	1	2	7	.224	.250	.276	50	-4	-4	4	1	0	0	1.000	-2	O/31	-0.7
	Yr	84	234	22	56	13	2	1	21	17	25	.239	.291	.325	79	-7	-6	23	2	0	1	.941	6	3O/1	-0.1
1989	StL-N	69	79	9	24	7	0	1	11	14	12	.304	.409	.430	136	5	4	15	0	0	0	.969	-2	1/3O	0.2
1990	StL-N	78	127	7	28	5	0	1	19	8	15	.220	.267	.283	51	-8	-9	9	0	0	0	1.000	1	13/O	-0.9
1991	Tex-A	24	44	1	4	1	0	0	2	3	8	.091	.184	.114	-16	-7	-7	1	0	0	0	.950	-3	3/O	-1.0
1992	Hou-N	3	3	1	1	0	0	0	0	0	0	.333	.333	.333	95	-0	-0	0	0	0	0	.000	0	/H	0.0
Total	18	1271	2945	372	799	142	30	49	380	308	316	.271	.341	.390	107	12	28	405	44	18	2	.947	-11	3O1	-0.6

■ **JOE WALLIS** Wallis, Harold Joseph b: 1/9/52, E.St.Louis, Ill. BB/TR, 5'10", 195 lbs. Deb: 9/02/75

YEAR	TM/L	G	AB	R	H	2B	3B	HR	RBI	BB	SO	AVG	OBP	SLG	PRO+	BR	/A	RC	SB	CS	SBR	FA	FR	POS	TPR
1975	Chi-N	16	56	9	16	2	2	1	4	5	14	.286	.344	.446	113	1	1	9	2	0	1	1.000	0	O	0.1
1976	Chi-N	121	338	51	86	11	5	5	21	33	62	.254	.323	.361	86	-3	-6	39	3	9	-5	.976	7	O	-0.7
1977	Chi-N	56	80	14	20	3	0	2	8	16	25	.250	.375	.363	89	0	-1	12	0	1	-1	.974	0	O	-0.2
1978	Chi-N	28	55	7	17	2	1	1	6	5	13	.309	.367	.436	110	2	1	8	0	2	-1	1.000	2	O	0.1
	Oak-A	85	279	28	66	16	1	6	26	26	42	.237	.302	.366	91	-5	-3	31	1	4	-2	.980	3	O/D	-0.7
1979	Oak-A	23	78	6	11	2	0	1	3	10	18	.141	.247	.205	25	-8	-8	5	1	0	0	1.000	-1	O	-1.0
Total	5	329	886	115	216	36	9	16	68	95	174	.244	.318	.359	86	-13	-16	104	7	16	-8	.982	11	O/D	-2.4

■ **LEE WALLS** Walls, Ray Lee b: 1/6/33, San Diego, Cal. BR/TR, 6'3", 205 lbs. Deb: 4/21/52 C

YEAR	TM/L	G	AB	R	H	2B	3B	HR	RBI	BB	SO	AVG	OBP	SLG	PRO+	BR	/A	RC	SB	CS	SBR	FA	FR	POS	TPR
1952	Pit-N	32	80	6	15	0	1	2	5	8	22	.188	.261	.287	51	-5	-6	6	0	0	0	1.000	0	O	-0.7
1956	Pit-N	143	474	72	130	20	11	11	54	50	83	.274	.346	.432	110	5	7	70	3	5	-2	.967	6	*O/3	0.4
1957	Pit-N	8	22	3	4	1	0	0	0	2	5	.182	.250	.227	30	-2	-2	2	1	0	0	1.000	1	/O	-0.2
	Chi-N	117	366	42	88	10	5	6	33	27	67	.240	.294	.344	72	-15	-14	36	5	3	-0	.984	-5	O/3	-2.5
	Yr	125	388	45	92	11	5	6	33	29	72	.237	.292	.338	70	-17	-17	38	6	3	0	.985	-4	*O/3	-2.7
1958	Chi-N★	136	513	80	156	19	3	24	72	47	62	.304	.371	.493	128	19	20	94	4	4	-1	.992	5	*O	1.7
1959	Chi-N	120	354	43	91	18	3	8	33	42	73	.257	.344	.393	97	-2	-1	49	0	2	-1	.967	-8	*O	-1.5
1960	Cin-N	29	84	12	23	3	2	1	7	17	20	.274	.396	.393	115	3	3	14	2	0	1	.960	1	O/1	0.3
	Phi-N	65	181	19	36	6	1	3	19	14	32	.199	.256	.293	50	-13	-13	13	3	2	-0	.947	-9	3O/1	-2.4
	Yr	94	265	31	59	9	3	4	26	31	52	.223	.304	.325	72	-10	-10	26	5	2	0	.958	-8	O3/1	-2.1
1961	Phi-N	91	261	32	73	6	4	8	30	19	48	.280	.329	.425	99	-1	-1	34	2	2	-1	.987	-4	13O	-0.8
1962	LA-N	60	109	9	29	3	1	0	17	10	21	.266	.328	.312	77	-4	-3	12	1	0	0	.929	-1	O1/3	-0.5
1963	LA-N	64	86	12	20	1	0	3	11	7	25	.233	.290	.349	89	-2	-1	8	0	0	0	1.000	2	O/13	0.0
1964	LA-N	37	28	1	5	1	0	0	3	2	12	.179	.233	.214	29	-3	-2	1	0	0	0	1.000	-0	/OC	-0.3
Total	10	902	2558	331	670	88	31	66	284	245	470	.262	.330	.398	96	-19	-14	338	21	18	-5	.977	-13	O/31C	-6.5

■ **AUSTIN WALSH** Walsh, Austin Edward b: 9/1/1891, Cambridge, Mass. d: 1/26/55, Glendale, Cal. BL/TL, 5'11", 175 lbs. Deb: 4/19/14

YEAR	TM/L	G	AB	R	H	2B	3B	HR	RBI	BB	SO	AVG	OBP	SLG	PRO+	BR	/A	RC	SB	CS	SBR	FA	FR	POS	TPR
1914	Chi-F	57	121	14	29	6	1	1	10	4	25	.240	.264	.331	73	-5	-5	11	0			1.000	-3	O	-0.9

■ **JIMMY WALSH** Walsh, James Charles b: 9/22/1885, Kallila, Ireland d: 7/3/62, Syracuse, N.Y. BL/TR, 5'10.5", 170 lbs. Deb: 8/26/12

YEAR	TM/L	G	AB	R	H	2B	3B	HR	RBI	BB	SO	AVG	OBP	SLG	PRO+	BR	/A	RC	SB	CS	SBR	FA	FR	POS	TPR
1912	Phi-A	31	107	11	27	8	2	0	15	12		.252	.328	.364	102	-0	0	15	7			.947	0	O	-0.1
1913	Phi-A	97	303	56	77	16	5	0	27	38	40	.254	.341	.340	102	0	1	39	15			.961	1	O	-0.2
1914	NY-A	43	136	13	26	1	3	1	11	29	21	.191	.333	.265	80	-2	-2	12	6	9	-4	.977	-1	O	-0.9
	*Phi-A	68	216	35	51	11	6	3	36	30	27	.236	.340	.384	123	5	6	29	6	12	-5	.966	-0	O/13S	-0.2

YEAR	TM/L	G	AB	R	H	2B	3B	HR	RBI	BB	SO	AVG	OBP	SLG	PRO+	BR	/A	RC	SB	CS	SBR	FA	FR	POS	TPR
	Yr	111	352	48	77	12	9	4	47	59	48	.219	.337	.338	106	3	4	41	12	21	-9	.971	-1	O/13S	-1.1
1915	Phi-A	117	417	48	86	15	6	1	20	57	64	.206	.306	.278	78	-12	-10	40	22	12	-1	.976	7	*O/31	-0.9
1916	Phi-A	114	390	42	91	13	6	1	27	54	36	.233	.330	.305	95	-3	-1	45	27	14	-0	.939	-0	*O/1	-0.9
	*Bos-A	14	17	5	3	1	0	0	2	4	2	.176	.333	.235	71	-0	-0	2	3	2	-0	1.000	-3	/O3	-0.4
	Yr	128	407	47	94	14	6	1	29	58	38	.231	.330	.302	94	-4	-2	47	30	16	-1	.940	-3	*O/31	-1.3
1917	Bos-A	57	185	25	49	6	3	0	12	25	14	.265	.352	.330	109	2	3	22	6			.982	-0	O	0.0
Total	6	541	1771	235	410	71	31	6	150	249	204	.232	.330	.317	96	-11	-4	203	92	49		.964	4	O/31S	-3.6

■ **JOHN WALSH** Walsh, John Gabriel b: 3/25/1879, Wilkes-Barre, Pa. d: 4/25/47, Jamaica, N.Y. BR/TR, 5'8.5", 162 lbs. Deb: 6/22/03

YEAR	TM/L	G	AB	R	H	2B	3B	HR	RBI	BB	SO	AVG	OBP	SLG	PRO+	BR	/A	RC	SB	CS	SBR	FA	FR	POS	TPR
1903	Phi-N	1	3	0	0	0	0	0	0	0		.000	.000	.000	-99	-1	-1	0	0			1.000	-0	/3	-0.1

■ **JOE WALSH** Walsh, Joseph Francis b: 10/14/1886, Minersville, Pa. d: 1/6/67, Buffalo, N.Y. BR/TR, 6'2", 170 lbs. Deb: 10/08/10

YEAR	TM/L	G	AB	R	H	2B	3B	HR	RBI	BB	SO	AVG	OBP	SLG	PRO+	BR	/A	RC	SB	CS	SBR	FA	FR	POS	TPR
1910	NY-A	1	4	0	2	1	0	0	2	0		.500	.500	.750	275	1	1	1	0			1.000	-1	/C	0.0
1911	NY-A	4	9	2	2	1	0	0	0	0		.222	.222	.333	51	-1	-1	1	0			1.000	-3	/C	-0.3
Total	2	5	13	2	4	2	0	0	2	0		.308	.308	.462	114	0	0	2	0			1.000	-4	/C	-0.3

■ **JOE WALSH** Walsh, Joseph Patrick "Tweet" b: 3/13/17, Roxbury, Mass. BR/TR, 5'10", 155 lbs. Deb: 7/01/38

YEAR	TM/L	G	AB	R	H	2B	3B	HR	RBI	BB	SO	AVG	OBP	SLG	PRO+	BR	/A	RC	SB	CS	SBR	FA	FR	POS	TPR
1938	Bos-N	4	8	0	0	0	0	0	0	0	2	.000	.000	.000	-99	-2	-2	0	0			.900	-2	/S	-0.4

■ **JOE WALSH** Walsh, Joseph R. "Reddy" b: 11/5/1864, Chicago, Ill. d: 8/8/11, Omaha, Neb. BL/TR, Deb: 9/03/1891

YEAR	TM/L	G	AB	R	H	2B	3B	HR	RBI	BB	SO	AVG	OBP	SLG	PRO+	BR	/A	RC	SB	CS	SBR	FA	FR	POS	TPR
1891	Bal-a	26	100	14	21	0	1	1	10	6	18	.210	.255	.260	49	-7	-7	8	4			.865	6	S2	0.1

■ **DEE WALSH** Walsh, Leo Thomas b: 3/28/1890, St.Louis, Mo. d: 7/14/71, St.Louis, Mo. BB/TR, 5'9.5", 165 lbs. Deb: 4/10/13

YEAR	TM/L	G	AB	R	H	2B	3B	HR	RBI	BB	SO	AVG	OBP	SLG	PRO+	BR	/A	RC	SB	CS	SBR	FA	FR	POS	TPR
1913	StL-A	23	53	8	9	0	1	0	5	6	11	.170	.302	.208	51	-3	-3	4	3			.933	2	S/3	0.1
1914	StL-A	7	23	1	2	0	0	0	1	2	4	.087	.160	.087	-27	-3	-3	0	1	1	-0	.919	-1	/S	-0.4
1915	StL-A	59	150	13	33	5	0	0	6	14	25	.220	.308	.253	71	-5	-5	12	6	6	-2	.951	1	O/3P2S	-0.8
Total	3	89	226	22	44	5	1	0	12	22	40	.195	.292	.226	56	-12	-11	17	10	7		.924	3	/OS32P	-1.1

■ **JIMMY WALSH** Walsh, Michael Timothy "Runt" b: 3/25/1886, Lima, Ohio d: 1/21/47, Baltimore, Md. BR/TR, 5'9", 174 lbs. Deb: 4/25/10

YEAR	TM/L	G	AB	R	H	2B	3B	HR	RBI	BB	SO	AVG	OBP	SLG	PRO+	BR	/A	RC	SB	CS	SBR	FA	FR	POS	TPR
1910	Phi-N	88	242	28	60	8	3	3	31	25	38	.248	.323	.343	91	-2	-3	29	5			.947	-2	2O/S3	-0.6
1911	Phi-N	94	289	29	78	20	3	1	31	21	30	.270	.324	.370	93	-3	-4	36	5			.962	-6	O2/S3CP1	-1.1
1912	Phi-N	51	150	16	40	6	3	2	19	8	20	.267	.304	.387	83	-3	-4	18	3			.944	0	23/C	-0.5
1913	Phi-N	26	30	3	10	4	0	0	5	1	5	.333	.355	.467	128	1	1	5	1			1.000	-1	/2S3O	0.0
1914	Bal-F	120	428	54	132	25	4	10	65	22	56	.308	.345	.456	123	13	11	76	18			.932	3	*3/2SO	1.8
1915	Bal-F	106	401	43	121	20	1	9	60	21	44	.302	.340	.424	120	10	9	65	12			.936	-9	*3	0.5
	StL-F	17	31	5	6	1	0	0	1	3	4	.194	.306	.226	54	-1	-2	3	1			.913	-1	/3	-0.2
	Yr	123	432	48	127	21	1	9	61	24	48	.294	.337	.410	115	9	7	67	13			.934	-10	*3	0.3
Total	6	502	1571	178	447	84	14	25	212	101	197	.285	.332	.404	106	14	8	232	45			.925	-15	3/2OSC1P	-0.1

■ **TOM WALSH** Walsh, Thomas Joseph b: 2/28/1885, Davenport, Iowa d: 3/16/63, Naples, Fla. BR/TR, 5'11", 170 lbs. Deb: 8/15/06

YEAR	TM/L	G	AB	R	H	2B	3B	HR	RBI	BB	SO	AVG	OBP	SLG	PRO+	BR	/A	RC	SB	CS	SBR	FA	FR	POS	TPR
1906	Chi-N	2	1	0	0	0	0	0	0	0		.000	.000	.000	-95	-0	-0	0	0			1.000	0	/C	0.0

■ **WALT WALSH** Walsh, Walter William b: 4/30/1897, Newark, N.J. d: 1/15/66, Avon By The Sea, N.J. BR/TR, 5'11", 170 lbs. Deb: 5/04/20

YEAR	TM/L	G	AB	R	H	2B	3B	HR	RBI	BB	SO	AVG	OBP	SLG	PRO+	BR	/A	RC	SB	CS	SBR	FA	FR	POS	TPR
1920	Phi-N	2	0	0	0	0	0	0	0	0	0	—	—	—	—	0	0	0	0	0	0	.000	0	R	0.0

■ **ROXY WALTERS** Walters, Alfred John b: 11/5/1892, San Francisco, Cal. d: 6/3/56, Almeda, Cal. BR/TR, 5'8.5", 160 lbs. Deb: 9/16/15

YEAR	TM/L	G	AB	R	H	2B	3B	HR	RBI	BB	SO	AVG	OBP	SLG	PRO+	BR	/A	RC	SB	CS	SBR	FA	FR	POS	TPR
1915	NY-A	2	3	0	1	0	0	0	0	0	0	.333	.333	.333	100	-0	-0	0	0			1.000	2	/C	0.2
1916	NY-A	66	203	13	54	9	3	0	23	14	42	.266	.320	.340	96	-1	-1	24	2			.974	17	C	2.2
1917	NY-A	61	171	16	45	2	0	0	14	9	22	.263	.304	.275	76	-5	-5	15	2			.968	11	C	1.1
1918	NY-A	64	191	18	38	5	1	0	12	9	18	.199	.239	.236	42	-14	-14	11	3			.953	-5	C/O	-1.8
1919	Bos-A	48	135	7	26	2	0	0	9	7	15	.193	.259	.207	33	-12	-11	8	1			.982	5	C	-0.3
1920	Bos-A	88	258	25	51	11	1	0	28	30	21	.198	.303	.248	49	-19	-17	22	2	2	-1	.980	8	C/1	-0.4
1921	Bos-A	54	169	17	34	4	1	0	14	10	11	.201	.254	.237	27	-19	-18	11	3	0	1	.990	15	C	0.1
1922	Bos-A	38	98	4	19	2	0	0	6	6	8	.194	.240	.214	19	-12	-11	6	0	0	0	.967	6	C	-0.4
1923	Bos-A	40	104	9	26	4	0	0	5	2	6	.250	.264	.288	45	-8	-8	8	0	2	-1	.974	7	C/2	-0.2
1924	Cle-A	32	74	10	19	2	0	0	5	10	6	.257	.345	.284	63	-4	-4	8	0	1	-1	.979	6	C/2	0.2
1925	Cle-A	5	20	0	4	0	0	0	0	0	2	.200	.200	.200	2	-3	-3	1	0	0	0	1.000	-0	/C	-0.3
Total	11	498	1426	119	317	41	6	0	116	97	151	.222	.281	.259	51	-96	-94	113	13	5		.975	71	C/O21	0.4

■ **DAN WALTERS** Walters, Daniel Gene b: 8/15/66, Brunswick, Maine BR/TR, 6'4", 225 lbs. Deb: 6/01/92

YEAR	TM/L	G	AB	R	H	2B	3B	HR	RBI	BB	SO	AVG	OBP	SLG	PRO+	BR	/A	RC	SB	CS	SBR	FA	FR	POS	TPR
1992	SD-N	57	179	14	45	11	1	4	22	10	28	.251	.298	.391	91	-2	-3	21	1	0	0	.992	7	C	0.8

■ **FRED WALTERS** Walters, Fred James "Whale" b: 9/4/12, Laurel, Miss. d: 2/1/80, Laurel, Miss. BR/TR, 6'1", 210 lbs. Deb: 4/17/45

YEAR	TM/L	G	AB	R	H	2B	3B	HR	RBI	BB	SO	AVG	OBP	SLG	PRO+	BR	/A	RC	SB	CS	SBR	FA	FR	POS	TPR
1945	Bos-A	40	93	2	16	2	0	0	5	10	9	.172	.252	.194	29	-8	-8	4	1	1	-0	.993	6	C	-0.1

■ **KEN WALTERS** Walters, Kenneth Rogers b: 11/11/33, Fresno, Cal. BR/TR, 6'1", 180 lbs. Deb: 4/12/60

YEAR	TM/L	G	AB	R	H	2B	3B	HR	RBI	BB	SO	AVG	OBP	SLG	PRO+	BR	/A	RC	SB	CS	SBR	FA	FR	POS	TPR
1960	Phi-N	124	426	42	102	10	0	8	37	16	50	.239	.269	.319	60	-24	-24	34	4	3	-1	.988	6	*O	-2.5
1961	Phi-N	86	180	23	41	8	2	2	14	5	25	.228	.253	.328	53	-12	-12	13	2	2	-1	.975	1	O/13	-1.4
1963	Cin-N	49	75	6	14	2	0	1	7	4	14	.187	.237	.253	40	-6	-6	4	0	2	-1	.889	-2	O/1	-1.1
Total	3	259	681	71	157	20	2	11	58	25	89	.231	.261	.314	56	-42	-42	51	6	7	-2	.979	4	O/13	-5.0

■ **BUCKY WALTERS** Walters, William Henry b: 4/19/09, Philadelphia, Pa. d: 4/20/91, Abington, Pa. BR/TR, 6'1", 180 lbs. Deb: 9/18/31 MC

YEAR	TM/L	G	AB	R	H	2B	3B	HR	RBI	BB	SO	AVG	OBP	SLG	PRO+	BR	/A	RC	SB	CS	SBR	FA	FR	POS	TPR
1931	Bos-N	9	38	2	8	2	0	0	0	0	3	.211	.211	.263	28	-4	-4	2	0			.947	0	/32	-0.3
1932	Bos-N	22	75	8	14	3	1	0	4	2	18	.187	.208	.253	24	-8	-8	4	0			.910	2	3	-0.4
1933	Bos-A	52	195	27	50	8	3	4	28	19	24	.256	.326	.390	90	-3	-3	26	1	1	-0	.940	1	3/2	0.1
1934	Bos-A	23	88	10	19	4	4	4	18	3	12	.216	.242	.489	79	-3	-4	10	0	0	0	.906	6	3	0.2
	Phi-N	83	300	36	78	20	3	4	38	19	54	.260	.308	.387	75	-7	-12	34	1			.950	-7	3/2P	-1.5
1935	Phi-N	49	96	14	24	2	1	0	6	9	12	.250	.314	.292	58	-5	-6	9	0			1.000	1	P/O23	-0.2
1936	Phi-N	64	121	12	29	10	1	1	16	7	15	.240	.281	.364	66	-5	-7	12	0			.974	9	P/23	0.0
1937	Phi-N★	56	137	15	38	6	0	1	16	5	16	.277	.303	.343	69	-5	-6	14	1			.988	5	P/3	-0.1
1938	Phi-N	15	35	6	10	2	0	1	3	1	5	.286	.306	.429	103	-0	-0	4	1			.955	0	P	0.0
	Cin-N	36	64	10	9	1	0	0	5	7	18	.141	.236	.156	10	-8	-8	3	0			.981	2	P	0.0
	Yr	51	99	16	19	3	0	1	8	8	23	.192	.259	.253	42	-8	-8	7	1			.973	3	P	0.0
1939	*Cin-N☆	40	120	16	39	8	1	1	16	5	12	.325	.357	.433	111	2	2	18	1			.979	4	P	0.0
1940	*Cin-N★	37	117	11	24	3	0	1	18	4	14	.205	.231	.256	34	-11	-11	7	2			.945	-1	P	0.0
1941	Cin-N★	39	106	6	20	6	0	0	9	7	13	.189	.239	.245	36	-9	-9	6	0			.977	2	P	0.0
1942	Cin-N★	40	99	13	24	6	1	2	13	3	13	.242	.265	.384	89	-2	-2	10	0			.961	1	P/O	-0.1
1943	Cin-N	37	90	11	24	7	1	1	12	6	15	.267	.313	.400	107	0	0	12	1			.971	1	P	0.0
1944	Cin-N★	37	107	9	30	4	0	0	13	8	18	.280	.330	.318	86	-2	-2	12	0			1.000	1	P	0.0
1945	Cin-N	24	61	11	14	3	0	3	8	3	14	.230	.266	.426	93	-1	-1	6	2			.975	-0	P	0.0
1946	Cin-N	24	55	6	7	2	0	0	5	4	12	.127	.186	.164	-0	-7	-7	2	2			.940	2	P	0.0
1947	Cin-N	20	45	3	12	2	0	0	4	2	13	.267	.298	.311	62	-2	-2	4	0			.962	-1	P	0.0
1948	Cin-N	7	15	1	4	0	0	0	2	0	2	.267	.267	.267	46	-1	-1	1	0			1.000	1	/PM	0.0
1950	Bos-N	1	2	0	0	0	0	0	0	0	0	.000	.000	.000	-99	-1	-1	0	0			1.000	-0	/P	0.0
Total	19	715	1966	227	477	99	16	23	234	114	303	.243	.286	.344	69	-83	-91	198	12	1		.974	28	P3/2O	-2.3

YEAR	TM/L	G	AB	R	H	2B	3B	HR	RBI	BB	SO	AVG	OBP	SLG	PRO+	BR	/A	RC	SB	CS	SBR	FA	FR	POS	TPR
■ **DANNY WALTON**	Walton, Daniel James "Mickey" b: 7/14/47, Los Angeles, Cal. BR/TR, 6', 200 lbs. Deb: 4/20/68																								
1968	Hou-N	2	2	0	0	0	0	0	0	0	1	.000	.000	.000	-99	-0	-0	0	0	0	0	.000	0	H	-0.1
1969	Sea-A	23	92	12	20	1	2	3	10	5	26	.217	.280	.370	82	-3	-3	9	2	0	1	.976	-1	O	-0.4
1970	Mil-A	117	397	32	102	20	1	17	66	51	126	.257	.350	.441	116	9	9	63	2	3	-1	.965	-6	*O	-0.4
1971	Mil-A	30	69	5	14	3	0	2	9	7	22	.203	.286	.333	76	-2	-2	6	0	0	0	.923	-4	O/3	-0.7
	NY-A	5	14	1	2	0	0	1	2	0	7	.143	.143	.357	40	-1	-1	1	0	0	0	1.000	-1	/O	-0.2
	Yr	35	83	6	16	3	0	3	11	7	29	.193	.264	.337	71	-4	-3	7	0	0	0	.933	-4	O/3	-0.9
1973	Min-A	37	96	13	17	1	1	4	8	17	28	.177	.301	.333	75	-3	-3	10	0	0	0	1.000	-3	OD/3	-0.7
1975	Min-A	42	63	4	11	2	0	1	8	4	18	.175	.224	.254	34	-6	-6	3	0	0	0	.962	-1	/1CD	-0.7
1976	LA-N	18	15	0	2	0	0	0	2	1	2	.133	.188	.133	-8	-2	-2	0	0	0	0	.000	0	H	-0.2
1977	Hou-N	13	21	0	4	0	0	0	1	0	5	.190	.190	.190	3	-3	-3	1	0	0	0	.956	-0	/1	-0.3
1980	Tex-A	10	10	2	2	0	0	0	1	3	5	.200	.385	.200	67	-0	-0	1	0	0	0	.000	0	/D	0.0
Total	9	297	779	69	174	27	4	28	107	88	240	.223	.310	.376	90	-11	-11	94	4	3	-1	.966	-15	O/D1C3	-3.7
■ **JEROME WALTON**	Walton, Jerome O'Terrell b: 7/8/65, Newnan, Ga. BR/TR, 6'1", 175 lbs. Deb: 4/04/89																								
1989	*Chi-N	116	475	64	139	23	3	5	46	27	77	.293	.339	.385	99	4	-0	64	24	7	3	.990	4	*O	0.4
1990	Chi-N	101	392	63	103	16	2	2	21	50	70	.263	.352	.329	82	-4	-8	49	14	7	0	.977	3	O	-0.8
1991	Chi-N	123	270	42	59	13	1	5	17	19	55	.219	.277	.330	67	-11	-13	24	7	3	0	.983	-10	*O	-2.5
1992	Chi-N	30	55	7	7	0	1	0	1	9	13	.127	.273	.164	26	-5	-5	3	1	2	-1	.944	-3	O	-1.0
Total	4	370	1192	176	308	52	7	12	85	105	215	.258	.326	.344	83	-17	-26	141	46	19	2	.982	-6	O	-3.9
■ **REGGIE WALTON**	Walton, Reginald Sherard b: 10/24/52, Kansas City, Mo. BR/TR, 6'3", 205 lbs. Deb: 6/13/80																								
1980	Sea-A	31	83	8	23	6	0	2	9	3	10	.277	.310	.422	98	-0	-1	10	2	2	-1	.929	-2	OD	-0.4
1981	Sea-A	12	6	1	0	0	0	0	0	1	2	.000	.143	.000	-54	-1	-1	0	0	0	0	.000	-2	/OD	-0.3
1982	Pit-N	13	15	1	3	1	0	0	0	1	1	.200	.294	.267	56	-1	-1	1	0	0	0	.000	0	/O	-0.1
Total	3	56	104	10	26	7	0	2	9	5	13	.250	.297	.375	83	-2	-3	12	2	2	-1	.929	-4	/OD	-0.8
■ **BILL WAMBSGANSS**	Wambsganss, William Adolph b: 3/19/1894, Cleveland, Ohio d: 12/8/85, Lakewood, Ohio BR/TR, 5'11", 175 lbs. Deb: 8/04/14																								
1914	Cle-A	43	143	12	31	6	2	0	12	8	24	.217	.277	.287	67	-6	-6	10	2	7	-4	.921	-1	S/2	-0.9
1915	Cle-A	121	375	30	73	4	4	0	21	36	50	.195	.272	.227	48	-23	-24	24	8	9	-3	.938	7	23	-1.9
1916	Cle-A	136	475	57	117	14	4	0	45	41	40	.246	.313	.293	77	-10	-14	52	13			.925	-8	*S2/3	-1.7
1917	Cle-A	141	499	52	127	17	6	0	43	37	42	.255	.315	.313	85	-5	-10	54	16			.951	15	*2/1	1.4
1918	Cle-A	87	315	34	93	15	2	0	40	21	21	.295	.345	.356	102	4	0	44	16			.952	-2	2	0.4
1919	Cle-A	139	526	60	146	17	6	2	60	32	24	.278	.323	.344	82	-9	-13	63	18			.963	11	*2	0.4
1920	*Cle-A	153	565	83	138	16	11	1	55	54	26	.244	.316	.317	66	-26	-28	57	9	18	-8	.960	8	*2	-2.2
1921	Cle-A	107	410	80	117	28	5	2	47	44	27	.285	.359	.393	90	-5	-6	61	13	7	-0	.963	-18	*2/3	-2.0
1922	Cle-A	142	538	89	141	22	6	0	47	60	26	.262	.341	.325	74	-19	-19	64	17	11	-2	.961	-27	*2S	-4.2
1923	Cle-A	101	345	59	100	20	4	1	59	43	15	.290	.373	.380	99	0	0	51	12	9	-2	.963	5	2/3S	0.4
1924	Bos-A	156	632	93	174	41	5	0	49	54	33	.275	.336	.356	79	-20	-21	79	14	8	-1	.963	14	*2	-0.5
1925	Bos-A	111	360	50	83	12	4	1	41	52	21	.231	.329	.294	59	-22	-21	38	3	5	-2	.957	4	*2/1	-1.7
1926	Phi-A	54	54	11	19	3	0	0	1	8	8	.352	.444	.407	116	2	2	10	1	1	-0	.923	0	S/2	0.3
Total	13	1491	5237	710	1359	215	59	7	520	490	357	.259	.328	.327	78	-139	-159	608	142	75		.958	8	*2S/31	-12.2
■ **LLOYD WANER**	Waner, Lloyd James "Little Poison" b: 3/16/06, Harrah, Okla. d: 7/22/82, Oklahoma City, Okla. BL/TR, 5'9", 150 lbs. Deb: 4/12/27 FH																								
1927	*Pit-N	150	629	**133**	223	17	6	2	27	37	23	.355	.396	.410	108	16	10	99	14			.976	-1	*O/2	-0.1
1928	Pit-N	152	659	121	221	22	14	5	61	40	13	.335	.377	.434	107	11	7	104	8			.980	7	*O	0.4
1929	Pit-N	151	662	134	234	28	**20**	5	74	37	20	.353	.395	.479	113	16	14	121	6			.987	16	*O	1.7
1930	Pit-N	68	260	32	94	8	3	1	36	5	5	.362	.376	.427	93	-2	-2	39	3			.983	2	O	-0.5
1931	Pit-N	154	681	90	**214**	25	13	4	57	39	16	.314	.352	.407	104	3	4	99	7			.979	**18**	*O/2	1.2
1932	Pit-N	134	565	90	188	27	11	2	38	31	11	.333	.367	.430	116	11	12	90	6			.986	12	*O	1.6
1933	Pit-N	121	500	59	138	14	5	0	26	22	8	.276	.307	.324	80	-13	-13	52	3			.982	1	*O	-1.9
1934	Pit-N	140	611	95	173	27	6	1	48	38	12	.283	.326	.352	80	-16	-17	73	6			.979	12	*O	-1.1
1935	Pit-N	122	537	83	166	22	14	0	46	22	10	.309	.336	.402	95	-2	-5	73	1			.989	6	*O	-0.3
1936	Pit-N	106	414	67	133	13	8	1	31	31	5	.321	.369	.399	104	4	3	62	1			.984	1	O	0.0
1937	Pit-N	129	537	80	177	23	4	1	45	34	12	.330	.370	.393	107	6	6	81	3			.988	6	*O	0.8
1938	Pit-N☆	147	619	79	194	25	7	5	57	28	11	.313	.343	.401	103	2	2	85	5			.986	2	*O	-0.1
1939	Pit-N	112	379	49	108	15	3	0	24	17	13	.285	.321	.340	79	-12	-11	42	0			.992	6	O/3	-0.8
1940	Pit-N	72	166	30	43	3	0	0	3	5	5	.259	.285	.277	56	-10	-10	13	2			.989	-1	O	-1.3
1941	Pit-N	3	4	2	1	0	0	0	1	2	0	.250	.500	.250	116	0	0	1	0			1.000	0	/O	0.1
	Bos-N	19	51	7	21	1	0	0	4	2	0	.412	.434	.431	151	3	3	10	1			.969	-1	O	0.2
	Cin-N	55	164	17	42	4	1	0	6	8	0	.256	.291	.293	64	-8	-8	14	0			.986	-3	O	-1.4
	Yr	77	219	26	64	5	1	0	11	12	0	.292	.329	.324	85	-4	-4	24	1			.981	-4	O	-1.1
1942	Phi-N	101	287	23	75	7	3	0	10	16	6	.261	.300	.307	82	-8	-7	27	1			.967	-1	O	-1.2
1944	Bro-N	15	14	3	4	0	0	0	1	3	0	.286	.412	.286	101	0	0	2	0			1.000	-2	/O	-0.2
	Pit-N	19	14	2	5	0	0	0	2	2	0	.357	.438	.357	120	1	1	2	0			1.000	-2	/O	-0.2
	Yr	34	28	5	9	0	0	0	3	5	0	.321	.424	.321	110	1	1	4	0			1.000	-4	O	-0.4
1945	Pit-N	23	19	5	5	0	0	0	1	1	3	.263	.300	.263	55	-1	-1	2	0			1.000	-0	/O	-0.1
Total	18	1993	7772	1201	2459	281	118	27	598	420	173	.316	.353	.393	99	1	-12	1092	67			.983	76	*O/23	-3.2
■ **PAUL WANER**	Waner, Paul Glee "Big Poison" b: 4/16/03, Harrah, Okla. d: 8/29/65, Sarasota, Fla. BL/TL, 5'8.5", 153 lbs. Deb: 4/13/26 FCH																								
1926	Pit-N	144	536	101	180	35	**22**	8	79	66	19	**.336**	**.413**	.528	144	**39**	36	**115**	11			.976	8	*O	**3.3**
1927	*Pit-N	155	623	114	**237**	42	**18**	9	**131**	60	14	**.380**	.437	.549	152	56	50	145	5			.980	8	*O1	4.6
1928	Pit-N	152	602	**142**	223	**50**	19	6	86	77	16	.370	.446	.547	152	53	50	145	6			.975	5	*O1	4.2
1929	Pit-N	151	596	131	200	43	15	15	100	89	24	.336	.424	.534	133	35	33	135	15			.986	2	*O/1	2.2
1930	Pit-N	145	589	117	217	32	18	8	77	57	18	.368	.428	.525	128	29	29	129	18			.959	-3	*O	1.4
1931	Pit-N	150	559	88	180	35	10	6	70	73	21	.322	.404	.453	131	26	27	108	6			.976	15	*O1	3.1
1932	Pit-N	154	630	107	215	**62**	10	8	82	56	24	.341	.397	.510	144	37	39	130	13			.974	3	*O	3.1
1933	Pit-N★	154	618	101	191	38	16	7	70	60	20	.309	.372	.456	136	29	29	109	3			.981	5	*O	2.6
1934	Pit-N★	146	599	**122**	**217**	32	16	14	90	68	24	**.362**	.429	.539	154	50	48	142	8			.985	7	*O	4.7
1935	Pit-N★	139	549	98	176	29	12	11	78	61	22	.321	.392	.477	128	26	24	105	2			.983	3	*O	2.1
1936	Pit-N	148	585	107	218	53	9	5	94	74	29	**.373**	.446	.520	156	51	50	140	7			.960	9	*O	5.0
1937	Pit-N★	154	619	94	219	30	9	2	74	63	34	.354	.413	.441	132	30	30	118	4			.970	1	*O/1	2.5
1938	Pit-N	148	625	77	175	31	6	6	69	47	28	.280	.331	.378	94	-5	-6	79	2			.977	-3	*O	-1.3
1939	Pit-N	125	461	62	151	30	6	3	45	35	18	.328	.375	.438	120	11	12	74	0			.978	2	*O	1.0
1940	Pit-N	89	238	32	69	16	1	1	32	23	14	.290	.352	.378	102	1	1	32	0			.985	-5	O/1	-0.7
1941	Bro-N	11	35	5	6	0	0	0	4	8	0	.171	.326	.171	41	-2	-2	2	0			.923	-2	/O	-0.5
	Bos-N	95	294	40	82	10	2	2	46	47	14	.279	.378	.347	110	4	6	41	1			.965	-4	O/1	-0.3
	Yr	106	329	45	88	10	2	2	50	55	14	.267	.372	.328	102	2	3	42	1			.961	-6	O/1	-0.8
1942	Bos-N	114	333	43	86	17	1	1	39	62	20	.258	.376	.324	108	6	6	45	2			.969	-8	O	-0.7
1943	Bro-N	82	225	29	70	16	0	1	26	35	9	.311	.406	.396	132	11	11	37	0			.960	-1	O	0.7
1944	Bro-N	83	136	16	39	4	1	0	16	27	7	.287	.405	.331	111	3	4	20	0			.983	-2	O	0.0
	NY-A	9	7	1	1	0	0	0	1	2	1	.143	.333	.143	37	-0	-0	1	1	0	0	.000	0	H	0.0
1945	NY-A	1	0	0	0	0	0	0	0	1	0	—	1.000	—	191	0	0	0	0	0	0	.000	0	H	0.0
Total	20	2549	9459	1627	3152	605	191	113	1309	1091	376	.333	.404	.473	133	491	474	1853	104	0		.975	40	*O/1	37.0

YEAR	TM/L	G	AB	R	H	2B	3B	HR	RBI	BB	SO	AVG	OBP	SLG	PRO+	BR	/A	RC	SB	CS	SBR	FA	FR	POS	TPR

■ JACK WANNER
Wanner, Clarence Curtis "Johnny"   b: 11/29/1885, Geneseo, Ill.   d: 5/28/19, Geneseo, Ill.   BR/TR, 5'11.5", 190 lbs.   Deb: 9/28/09

| 1909 | NY-A | 3 | 8 | 0 | 1 | 0 | 0 | 0 | 0 | 0 | 2 | .125 | .300 | .125 | 35 | -0 | -0 | 1 | 1 | | | .600 | -2 | /S | -0.3 |

■ PEE-WEE WANNINGER
Wanninger, Paul Louis   b: 12/12/02, Birmingham, Ala.   d: 3/7/81, N.Augusta, S.C.   BL/TR, 5'7", 150 lbs.   Deb: 4/22/25

1925	NY-A	117	403	35	95	13	6	1	22	11	34	.236	.256	.305	43	-37	-36	30	3	5	-2	.944	-6	*S/32	-3.0
1927	Bos-A	18	60	4	12	0	0	0	1	6	2	.200	.284	.200	28	-6	-6	3	2	4	-2	.890	-1	S	-0.7
	Cin-N	28	93	14	23	2	2	0	8	6	7	.247	.293	.312	64	-5	-5	9	0			.953	6	S	0.4
Total	2	163	556	53	130	15	8	1	31	23	43	.234	.266	.295	45	-48	-47	42	5	9		.941	-1	S/32	-3.3

■ AARON WARD
Ward, Aaron Lee   b: 8/28/1896, Booneville, Ark.   d: 1/30/61, New Orleans, La.   BR/TR, 5'10.5", 160 lbs.   Deb: 8/14/17

1917	NY-A	8	26	0	3	0	0	0	1	1	5	.115	.148	.115	-19	-4	-4	0	0			.926	-2	/S	-0.7
1918	NY-A	20	32	2	4	1	0	0	1	2	7	.125	.176	.156	0	-4	-4	1	1			.941	4	S/O2	0.0
1919	NY-A	27	34	5	7	2	0	0	2	5	6	.206	.308	.265	61	-2	-2	3	0			1.000	3	/13S2	0.0
1920	NY-A	127	496	62	127	18	7	11	54	33	84	.256	.304	.387	79	-15	-17	58	7	5	-1	.965	22	*3S	1.0
1921	*NY-A	153	556	77	170	30	10	5	75	42	68	.306	.363	.423	98	-0	-2	85	6	8	-3	.961	19	*23	1.8
1922	*NY-A	154	558	69	149	19	5	7	68	45	64	.267	.328	.357	77	-18	-19	68	7	4	-0	.974	3	*2/3	-1.3
1923	*NY-A	152	567	79	161	26	11	10	82	56	65	.284	.351	.422	101	-1	-0	84	8	8	-2	.980	14	*2	1.2
1924	NY-A	120	400	42	101	13	10	8	66	40	45	.253	.324	.395	85	-11	-11	52	4	4	-2	.973	8	*2/S	-0.4
1925	NY-A	125	439	41	108	22	3	4	38	49	49	.246	.326	.337	70	-21	-20	50	1	4	-2	.966	-11	*23	-2.9
1926	NY-A	22	31	5	10	2	0	0	3	2	6	.323	.364	.387	97	-0	-0	4	0	0	0	1.000	-4	/23	-0.4
1927	Chi-A	145	463	75	125	25	8	5	56	63	56	.270	.360	.391	97	-3	-1	65	6	5	-1	.963	-19	*2/3	-1.6
1928	Cle-A	6	9	0	1	0	0	0	0	1	2	.111	.200	.111	-16	-2	-2	0	0	0	0	.818	2	/3S2	0.1
Total	12	1059	3611	457	966	158	54	50	446	339	457	.268	.335	.383	85	-77	-82	472	37	38		.970	36	23/S10	-3.2

■ CHUCK WARD
Ward, Charles William   b: 7/30/1894, St.Louis, Mo.   d: 4/4/69, Indian Rocks, Fla.   BR/TR, 5'11.5", 170 lbs.   Deb: 4/11/17

1917	Pit-N	125	423	25	100	12	3	0	43	32	43	.236	.302	.279	76	-10	-11	38	5			.912	-27	*S/23	-3.7
1918	Bro-N	2	6	0	2	0	0	0	3	0	0	.333	.333	.333	104	-0	0	1	0			1.000	1	/3	-0.1
1919	Bro-N	45	150	7	35	1	2	0	8	7	11	.233	.277	.267	62	-6	-7	11	0			.920	-6	3	-1.3
1920	Bro-N	19	71	7	11	1	0	0	4	3	3	.155	.200	.169	6	-8	-9	3	1	0	0	.928	-9	S	-1.7
1921	Bro-N	12	28	1	2	1	0	0	0	4	2	.071	.188	.107	-19	-5	-5	1	0	0	0	.937	4	S	0.0
1922	Bro-N	33	91	12	25	5	1	0	14	5	8	.275	.320	.352	74	-4	-4	10	1	1	-0	.934	-3	S/3	-0.4
Total	6	236	769	52	175	20	6	0	72	51	67	.228	.286	.269	63	-33	-35	64	7	1		.919	-41	S/32	-7.2

■ CHRIS WARD
Ward, Chris Gilbert   b: 5/18/49, Oakland, Cal.   BL/TL, 6', 180 lbs.   Deb: 9/10/72

1972	Chi-N	1	1	0	0	0	0	0	0	0	0	.000	.000	.000	-90	-0	-0	0	0	0	0	.000	0	H	0.0
1974	Chi-N	92	137	8	28	4	0	1	15	18	13	.204	.297	.255	53	-8	-9	10	0	2	-1	.977	2	O/1	-0.9
Total	2	93	138	8	28	4	0	1	15	18	13	.203	.295	.254	52	-8	-9	10	0	2	-1		2	/O1	-0.9

■ PIGGY WARD
Ward, Frank Gray   b: 4/16/1867, Chambersburg, Pa.   d: 10/24/12, Altoona, Pa.   5'9.5", 196 lbs.   Deb: 6/12/1883

1883	Phi-N	1	5	0	0	0	0	0	0	0	2	.000	.000	.000	-99	-1	-1	0				1.000	-1	/3	-0.2
1889	Phi-N	7	25	0	4	1	0	0	4	0	7	.160	.160	.200	1	-3	-4	1	1			.848	-2	/2O	-0.5
1891	Pit-N	6	18	3	6	0	0	0	2	3	3	.333	.455	.333	137	1	1	4	3			.833	-1	/O	0.0
1892	Bal-N	56	186	28	54	6	5	1	33	31	18	.290	.403	.392	139	11	10	34	10			.892	1	O/2SC	0.9
1893	Bal-N	11	49	11	12	1	3	0	5	5	2	.245	.327	.388	90	-1	-1	8	4			.846	-1	/O1	-0.2
	Cin-N	42	150	44	42	4	1	0	10	37	10	.280	.440	.320	103	5	4	34	27			.827	-2	O/1	0.0
	Yr	53	199	55	54	5	4	0	15	42	12	.271	.415	.337	101	4	3	42	31			.832	-3	O/1	-0.2
1894	Was-N	98	347	86	105	11	7	0	36	80	31	.303	.447	.375	105	7	10	79	41			.900	-22	2O/S3	-0.8
Total	6	221	780	172	223	23	16	1	90	156	73	.286	.419	.360	108	19	20	160	86			.852	-28	0/2S13C	-0.8

■ GARY WARD
Ward, Gary Lamell   b: 12/6/53, Los Angeles, Cal.   BR/TR, 6'2", 202 lbs.   Deb: 9/03/79

1979	Min-A	10	14	2	4	0	0	0	1	3	3	.286	.412	.286	89	0	-0	2	0	1	-1	1.000	-1	/O	-0.1
1980	Min-A	13	41	11	19	6	2	1	10	3	6	.463	.500	.732	228	8	8	16	0	0	0	1.000	-1	/O	0.5
1981	Min-A	85	295	42	78	7	6	3	29	28	48	.264	.328	.359	92	-1	-3	34	5	2	0	.975	6	O/D	-0.1
1982	Min-A	152	570	85	165	33	7	28	91	37	105	.289	.334	.519	127	21	19	95	13	1	3	.989	13	*O/D	3.1
1983	Min-A★	157	623	76	173	34	5	19	88	44	98	.278	.328	.440	105	7	4	85	8	1	2	.978	26	*O/D	2.6
1984	Tex-A	155	602	97	171	21	7	21	79	55	95	.284	.344	.447	113	13	11	87	7	5	-1	.987	12	*O/D	1.8
1985	Tex-A★	154	593	77	170	28	7	15	70	39	97	.287	.332	.433	106	5	5	82	26	7	4	.969	2	*O/D	0.5
1986	Tex-A	105	380	54	120	15	5	5	51	31	72	.316	.373	.405	109	7	6	56	12	8	-1	.996	13	*O/D	1.4
1987	NY-A	146	529	65	131	22	1	16	78	51	101	.248	.293	.384	74	-18	-17	55	9	1	2	.985	-4	OD1	-2.2
1988	NY-A	91	231	26	52	8	0	4	24	24	41	.225	.304	.312	73	-8	-8	21	0	1	-1	.992	-4	O1/3D	-1.5
1989	NY-A	8	17	3	5	1	0	0	1	3	5	.294	.400	.353	115	0	1	2	0	0	0	1.000	-1	/OD	-0.1
	Det-A	105	275	24	69	10	2	9	29	21	54	.251	.304	.400	99	-2	-1	30	1	3	-2	.990	0	O1D	-0.5
	Yr	113	292	27	74	11	2	9	30	24	59	.253	.310	.397	100	-1	-1	33	1	3	-2	.991	-1	OD1	-0.6
1990	Det-A	106	309	32	79	11	2	9	46	30	50	.256	.324	.392	98	-1	-1	38	2	0	1	.988	-4	OD/1	-0.7
Total	12	1287	4479	594	1236	196	41	130	597	351	775	.276	.330	.425	104	33	22	602	83	30	7	.984	55	*O/D13	4.8

■ JIM WARD
Ward, James H.   b: 3/1855, Boston, Mass.   d: 6/4/1886, Boston, Mass.   Deb: 8/03/1876

| 1876 | Phi-N | 1 | 4 | 1 | 2 | 0 | 0 | 0 | 1 | 0 | 1 | .500 | .500 | .500 | 236 | 1 | 1 | 1 | | | | .750 | -0 | /C | 0.0 |

■ RUBE WARD
Ward, John Andrew   b: 2/6/1879, New Lexington, Ohio   d: 1/17/45, Akron, Ohio   Deb: 4/28/02

| 1902 | Bro-N | 13 | 31 | 4 | 9 | 1 | 0 | 0 | 2 | 2 | | .290 | .333 | .323 | 102 | 0 | 0 | 3 | 0 | | | .850 | -1 | O | -0.2 |

■ JOHN WARD
Ward, John E.   b: Washington, D.C.   Deb: 5/23/1884

| 1884 | Was-U | 1 | 4 | 0 | 1 | 0 | 0 | 0 | | 0 | | .250 | .250 | .250 | 72 | -0 | -0 | 0 | | | | .000 | -1 | /O | -0.1 |

■ JAY WARD
Ward, John Francis   b: 9/9/38, Brookfield, Mo.   BR/TR, 6'1", 185 lbs.   Deb: 5/06/63   C

1963	Min-A	9	15	0	1	1	0	0	2	1	5	.067	.125	.133	-27	-3	-3	0	0	0	0	1.000	-1	/3O	-0.3
1964	Min-A	12	31	4	7	2	0	0	2	6	13	.226	.351	.290	80	-1	-1	4	0	0	0	.977	2	/2O	0.0
1970	Cin-N	6	3	0	0	0	0	0	0	2	1	.000	.400	.000	17	-0	-0	0	0	0	0	1.000	-0	/312	0.0
Total	3	27	49	4	8	3	0	0	4	9	19	.163	.293	.224	46	-3	-3	4	0	0	0	.977	-1	/23O1	-0.3

■ JOHN WARD
Ward, John Montgomery   b: 3/3/1860, Bellefonte, Pa.   d: 3/4/25, Augusta, Ga.   BL/TR, 5'9", 165 lbs.   Deb: 7/15/1878   MH

1878	Pro-N	37	138	14	27	5	4	1	15	2	13	.196	.207	.312	69	-5	-5	9				.866	2	P	0.0
1879	Pro-N	83	364	71	104	9	4	2	41	7	14	.286	.299	.349	115	5	6	39				.938	3	*P3/O	0.1
1880	Pro-N	86	356	53	81	12	2	0	27	6	16	.228	.240	.272	76	-10	-8	24				.983	14	*P3/OM	0.7
1881	Pro-N	85	357	56	87	18	6	0	53	5	10	.244	.254	.328	83	-8	-7	30				.887	6	OPS	-0.3
1882	Pro-N	83	355	58	87	10	3	1	39	13	22	.245	.272	.299	83	-7	-6	30				.824	10	OP/S	0.1
1883	NY-N	88	380	76	97	18	7	7	54	8	25	.255	.271	.395	100	-1	-0	42				.859	19	OP/3S2	1.3
1884	NY-N	113	482	98	122	11	8	2	51	28	47	.253	.294	.322	91	-3	-5	47				.847	8	O2/PM	0.2
1885	NY-N	111	446	72	101	8	9	0	37	17	39	.226	.255	.285	75	-13	-12	33				.904	6	*S	-0.3
1886	NY-N	122	491	82	134	17	5	2	81	19	46	.273	.300	.340	93	-4	-5	44	36			.870	-3	*S	-0.5
1887	NY-N	129	545	114	184	16	5	1	53	29	12	.338	.375	.391	121	12	16	125	111			.919	30	*S	3.9
1888	*NY-N	122	510	70	128	14	5	2	49	9	13	.251	.265	.310	86	-9	-8	53	38			.857	-4	*S	-0.9
1889	*NY-N	114	479	87	143	13	4	1	67	27	7	.299	.339	.349	94	-4	-4	79	62			.890	5	*S/2	0.6
1890	Bro-P	128	561	134	189	15	12	4	60	51	22	.337	.394	.428	115	18	11	122	63			.878	21	*SM	3.1

YEAR	TM/L	G	AB	R	H	2B	3B	HR	RBI	BB	SO	AVG	OBP	SLG	PRO+	BR	/A	RC	SB	CS	SBR	FA	FR	POS	TPR
1891	Bro-N	105	441	85	122	13	5	0	39	36	10	.277	.335	.329	96	-2	-1	69	57			.878	-0	S2M	0.4
1892	Bro-N	148	614	109	163	13	3	1	47	82	19	.265	.355	.301	105	4	8	99	**88**			.920	3	*2M	1.2
1893	NY-N	135	588	129	193	27	9	2	77	47	5	.328	.379	.415	112	10	10	113	46			.918	7	*2M	1.6
1894	*NY-N	136	540	100	143	12	5	0	77	34	6	.265	.310	.306	50	-43	-42	67	39			.924	5	*2M	-2.5
Total	17	1825	7647	1408	2105	231	96	26	867	420	326	.275	.314	.341	94	-59	-54	1044	540			.885	132	S2PO/3	8.6

■ JOE WARD Ward, Joseph A. b: 9/2/1884, Philadelphia, Pa. d: 8/11/34, Philadelphia, Pa. TR, Deb: 4/24/06

YEAR	TM/L	G	AB	R	H	2B	3B	HR	RBI	BB	SO	AVG	OBP	SLG	PRO+	BR	/A	RC	SB	CS	SBR	FA	FR	POS	TPR
1906	Phi-N	35	129	12	38	8	6	0	11	5		.295	.321	.450	140	5	5	20	2			.929	-6	3/2S	0.0
1909	NY-A	9	28	3	5	0	0	0	0	1		.179	.233	.179	30	-2	-2	2	2			.846	-5	/21	-0.9
	Phi-N	74	184	21	49	8	2	0	23	9		.266	.304	.332	96	-1	-1	21	7			.944	-10	2/S1O	-1.3
1910	Phi-N	48	124	11	18	2	1	0	13	3	11	.145	.178	.177	4	-15	-16	5	1			.975	2	1/S3	-1.5
Total	3	166	465	47	110	18	9	0	47	18	11	.237	.271	.314	78	-14	-14	47	12			.929	-20	/213SO	-3.7

■ HAP WARD Ward, Joseph Nichols b: 11/15/1885, Leesburg, N.J. d: 9/13/79, Elmer, N.J. Deb: 5/18/12

YEAR	TM/L	G	AB	R	H	2B	3B	HR	RBI	BB	SO	AVG	OBP	SLG	PRO+	BR	/A	RC	SB	CS	SBR	FA	FR	POS	TPR
1912	Det-A	1	2	0	0	0	0	0	0	0		.000	.000	.000	-99	-1	-1	0	0			1.000	0	/O	0.0

■ KEVIN WARD Ward, Kevin Michael b: 9/28/61, Lansdale, Pa. BR/TR, 6'1", 195 lbs. Deb: 5/10/91

YEAR	TM/L	G	AB	R	H	2B	3B	HR	RBI	BB	SO	AVG	OBP	SLG	PRO+	BR	/A	RC	SB	CS	SBR	FA	FR	POS	TPR
1991	SD-N	44	107	13	26	7	2	2	8	9	27	.243	.308	.402	95	-1	-1	11	1	4	-2	.982	-2	O	-0.6
1992	SD-N	81	147	12	29	5	0	3	12	14	38	.197	.276	.293	59	-7	-8	10	2	3	-1	.946	-6	O	-1.8
Total	2	125	254	25	55	12	2	5	20	23	65	.217	.289	.339	74	-8	-9	22	3	7	-3	.961	-9	/O	-2.4

■ PETE WARD Ward, Peter Thomas b: 7/26/39, Montreal, Que., Can BL/TR, 6'1", 200 lbs. Deb: 9/21/62 C

YEAR	TM/L	G	AB	R	H	2B	3B	HR	RBI	BB	SO	AVG	OBP	SLG	PRO+	BR	/A	RC	SB	CS	SBR	FA	FR	POS	TPR
1962	Bal-A	8	21	1	3	2	0	0	2	4	5	.143	.280	.238	43	-2	-2	2	0	0	0	1.000	-0	/O	-0.2
1963	Chi-A	157	600	80	177	34	6	22	84	52	77	.295	.356	.482	135	25	26	104	7	6	-2	.923	-5	*3/2S	2.1
1964	Chi-A	144	539	61	152	28	3	23	94	56	76	.282	.352	.473	131	19	21	91	1	1	-0	.958	13	*3	3.3
1965	Chi-A	138	507	62	125	25	3	10	57	56	83	.247	.329	.367	104	-1	3	61	2	4	-2	.952	9	*3/2	0.7
1966	Chi-A	84	251	22	55	7	1	3	28	24	49	.219	.295	.291	74	-10	-8	23	3	1	0	.989	-2	O3/1	-1.3
1967	Chi-A	146	467	49	109	16	2	18	62	61	109	.233	.336	.392	119	9	11	65	3	2	-0	.991	-17	O13	-1.3
1968	Chi-A	125	399	43	86	15	0	15	50	76	85	.216	.355	.366	117	12	12	58	4	3	-1	.946	-9	31O	-0.1
1969	Chi-A	105	199	22	49	7	0	6	32	33	38	.246	.362	.372	101	2	1	30	0	0	0	.994	-2	13/O	-0.2
1970	NY-A	66	77	5	20	2	2	1	18	9	17	.260	.337	.377	102	-0	0	10	0	0	0	1.000	-1	1	-0.1
Total	9	973	3060	345	776	136	17	98	427	371	539	.254	.342	.405	116	56	65	443	20	17	-4	.945	-14	3O1/2S	2.9

■ PRESTON WARD Ward, Preston Meyer b: 7/24/27, Columbia, Mo. BL/TR, 6'3", 198 lbs. Deb: 4/20/48

YEAR	TM/L	G	AB	R	H	2B	3B	HR	RBI	BB	SO	AVG	OBP	SLG	PRO+	BR	/A	RC	SB	CS	SBR	FA	FR	POS	TPR
1948	Bro-N	42	146	9	38	9	2	1	21	15	23	.260	.329	.370	86	-2	-3	19	0			.990	-2	1	-0.5
1950	Chi-N	80	285	31	72	11	2	6	33	27	42	.253	.317	.368	81	-9	-8	34	3			.995	10	1	0.0
1953	Chi-N	33	100	10	23	5	0	4	12	18	21	.230	.347	.400	92	-1	-1	15	3	1	0	.961	-7	O/1	-0.8
	Pit-N	88	281	35	59	7	1	8	27	44	39	.210	.319	.327	69	-12	-12	31	1	3	-2	.991	4	1	-1.2
	Yr	121	381	45	82	12	1	12	39	62	60	.215	.327	.346	76	-13	-13	46	4	4	-1	.991	-2	1O	-2.0
1954	Pit-N	117	360	37	97	16	2	7	48	39	61	.269	.341	.383	90	-6	-5	49	0	0	0	.984	5	1O3	-0.4
1955	Pit-N	84	179	16	38	7	4	5	25	22	28	.212	.299	.380	80	-6	-5	21	0	0	0	.998	2	1/O	-0.6
1956	Pit-N	16	30	3	10	0	1	1	11	6	4	.333	.444	.500	157	3	3	7	0	0	0	1.000	-5	/3O	-0.2
	Cle-A	87	150	18	38	10	0	6	21	16	20	.253	.325	.440	98	-1	-1	23	0	0	0	.988	2	1O	-0.1
1957	Cle-A	10	11	2	2	1	0	0	0	0	2	.182	.182	.273	23	-1	-1	1	0	0	0	1.000	-0	/1	-0.1
1958	Cle-A	48	148	22	50	3	1	4	21	10	27	.338	.384	.453	133	6	6	26	0	1	-1	.957	-3	31	0.1
	KC-A	81	268	28	68	10	1	6	24	27	36	.254	.322	.366	87	-4	-5	33	0	1	-1	.989	-7	13/O	-1.5
	Yr	129	416	50	118	13	2	10	45	37	63	.284	.344	.397	103	2	2	58	0	2	-1	.992	-10	13/O	-1.4
1959	KC-A	58	109	8	27	4	1	2	19	7	12	.248	.293	.358	76	-4	-4	11	0	0	0	.982	-3	1/O	-0.8
Total	9	744	2067	219	522	83	15	50	262	231	315	.253	.328	.380	88	-36	-36	269	7	6		.992	-3	1/O3	-6.1

■ TURNER WARD Ward, Turner Max b: 4/11/65, Orlando, Fla. BB/TR, 6'2", 200 lbs. Deb: 9/10/90

YEAR	TM/L	G	AB	R	H	2B	3B	HR	RBI	BB	SO	AVG	OBP	SLG	PRO+	BR	/A	RC	SB	CS	SBR	FA	FR	POS	TPR
1990	Cle-A	14	46	10	16	2	1	1	10	3	8	.348	.388	.500	147	3	3	9	3	0	1	.957	0	O/D	0.4
1991	Cle-A	40	100	11	23	7	0	0	5	10	16	.230	.300	.300	66	-4	-5	10	0	0	0	1.000	-2	O	-0.7
	Tor-A	8	13	1	4	0	0	0	2	1	2	.308	.357	.308	83	-0	-0	1	0	0	0	1.000	-1	/O	-0.2
	Yr	48	113	12	27	7	0	0	7	11	18	.239	.306	.301	68	-5	-5	11	0	0	0	1.000	-3	O	-0.9
1992	Tor-A	18	29	7	10	3	0	1	3	4	4	.345	.424	.552	164	3	3	6	0	1	-1	1.000	-1	O	0.1
Total	3	80	188	29	53	12	1	2	20	18	30	.282	.345	.388	102	1	1	26	3	1	0	.991	-4	/OD	-0.4

■ BUZZY WARES Wares, Clyde Ellsworth b: 5/23/1886, Vandalia, Mich. d: 5/26/64, South Bend, Ind. BR/TR, 5'10", 150 lbs. Deb: 9/15/13 C

YEAR	TM/L	G	AB	R	H	2B	3B	HR	RBI	BB	SO	AVG	OBP	SLG	PRO+	BR	/A	RC	SB	CS	SBR	FA	FR	POS	TPR
1913	StL-A	11	35	5	10	2	0	0	1	1	3	.286	.306	.343	92	-1	-0	4	2			.973	-4	/2	-0.5
1914	StL-A	81	215	20	45	10	1	0	23	28	35	.209	.300	.265	73	-7	-6	19	10	10	-3	.903	-2	S/2	-0.7
Total	2	92	250	25	55	12	1	0	24	29	38	.220	.301	.276	76	-8	-7	23	12	10		.973	-6	/S2	-1.2

■ FRED WARNER Warner, Frederick John Rodney b: 1855, Philadelphia, Pa. d: 2/13/1886, Philadelphia, Pa. 5'7", 155 lbs. Deb: 4/30/1875

YEAR	TM/L	G	AB	R	H	2B	3B	HR	RBI	BB	SO	AVG	OBP	SLG	PRO+	BR	/A	RC	SB	CS	SBR	FA	FR	POS	TPR
1875	Cen-n	14	57	11	14	1	0	0		1		.246	.259	.263	88	-1	-0	4						O	0.0
1876	Phi-N	1	3	0	0	0	0	0	0	0	0	.000	.000	.000	-99	-1	-1	0				.600	-0	/O	-0.1
1878	Ind-N	43	165	19	41	4	0	0	10	2	15	.248	.257	.273	86	-4	-1	12				.907	-3	*S/O	-0.2
1879	Cle-N	76	316	32	77	11	4	0	22	2	20	.244	.248	.304	82	-6	-6	24				.827	0	3O/1	-0.5
1883	Phi-N	39	141	13	32	6	1	0	13	5	21	.227	.253	.284	69	-6	-4	10				.775	-9	3/O	-1.2
1884	Bro-a	84	352	40	78	4	0	1		17		.222	.259	.241	66	-12	-12	23				.824	-6	*3	-1.6
Total	5	243	977	104	228	25	5	1	45	26	56	.233	.254	.272	74	-30	-24	69				.815	-18	3/SO1	-3.6

■ HOOKS WARNER Warner, Hoke Hayden b: 5/22/1894, Del Rio, Tex. d: 2/19/47, San Francisco, Cal BL/TR, 5'10.5", 170 lbs. Deb: 8/21/16

YEAR	TM/L	G	AB	R	H	2B	3B	HR	RBI	BB	SO	AVG	OBP	SLG	PRO+	BR	/A	RC	SB	CS	SBR	FA	FR	POS	TPR
1916	Pit-N	44	168	12	40	1	1	2	14	6	19	.238	.264	.292	70	-6	-6	15	6			.899	-11	3/2	-1.9
1917	Pit-N	3	5	0	1	0	0	0	0	0	1	.200	.200	.200	22	-0	-0	0	0			1.000	1	/3	0.1
1919	Pit-N	6	8	0	1	0	0	0	2	3	1	.125	.364	.125	48	-0	-0	0	0			.818	1	/3	0.0
1921	Chi-N	14	38	4	8	1	0	0	3	2	1	.211	.268	.237	35	-3	-4	2	1	1	-0	.957	-1	3	-0.4
Total	4	67	219	16	50	2	1	2	19	11	22	.228	.268	.274	61	-10	-11	18	7	1		.906	-10	/32	-2.2

■ JOHN WARNER Warner, John Joseph b: 8/15/1872, New York, N.Y. d: 12/21/43, Far Rockaway, N.Y. BL/TR, 5'11", 165 lbs. Deb: 4/23/1895

YEAR	TM/L	G	AB	R	H	2B	3B	HR	RBI	BB	SO	AVG	OBP	SLG	PRO+	BR	/A	RC	SB	CS	SBR	FA	FR	POS	TPR
1895	Bos-N	3	7	2	1	0	0	0	1	1	0	.143	.333	.143	25	-1	-1	0	0			.917	1	/C	0.0
	Lou-N	67	232	20	62	4	2	1	20	11	16	.267	.320	.315	70	-11	-9	28	10			.931	-11	C/12	-1.1
	Yr	70	239	22	63	4	2	1	21	12	16	.264	.320	.310	69	-12	-10	28	10			.930	-10	C/12	-1.1
1896	Lou-N	33	110	9	25	1	1	0	10	10	10	.227	.303	.255	52	-8	-7	10	3			.939	9	C/1	0.5
	NY-N	19	54	9	14	1	0	0	3	3	7	.259	.310	.278	59	-3	-3	6	1			.922	1	C	0.0
	Yr	52	164	18	39	2	1	0	13	13	17	.238	.306	.262	54	-11	-10	16	4			.934	10	C/1	0.5
1897	NY-N	110	397	50	109	6	3	2	51	26		.275	.344	.320	78	-13	-11	48	8			.952	17	*C	1.5
1898	NY-N	110	373	40	96	14	5	0	42	22		.257	.316	.322	86	-8	-7	42	9			.968	15	*C/O	1.7
1899	NY-N	88	293	38	78	8	1	0	19	15		.266	.313	.300	71	-12	-11	33	15			.952	12	C/1	0.6
1900	NY-N	34	108	15	27	4	0	0	13	8		.250	.314	.287	69	-5	-4	11	1			.948	3	C	0.2
1901	NY-N	87	291	19	70	6	1	0	20	3		.241	.266	.268	57	-17	-15	22	3			.967	-3	C	-1.0
1902	Bos-A	65	222	19	52	5	7	0	12	13		.234	.283	.320	65	-10	-11	21	0			.979	5	C	0.0
1903	NY-N	89	285	38	81	8	5	0	34	7		.284	.318	.347	86	-4	-6	35	5			**.986**	12	C	1.4
1904	NY-N	86	287	29	57	5	1	1	15	14		.199	.241	.233	45	-18	-19	19	7			**.982**	2	C	-0.9
1905	StL-N	41	137	9	35	2	2	1	12	6		.255	.301	.321	88	-3	-2	14	2			.958	3	C	0.5

YEAR	TM/L	G	AB	R	H	2B	3B	HR	RBI	BB	SO	AVG	OBP	SLG	PRO+	BR	/A	RC	SB	CS	SBR	FA	FR	POS	TPR
	Det-A	36	119	12	24	2	3	0	7	8		.202	.252	.269	65	-5	-5	9	2			.974	1	C	0.0
1906	Det-A	50	153	15	37	4	2	0	10	12		.242	.326	.294	92	-0	-1	17	4			.978	9	C	1.3
	Was-A	32	103	5	21	4	1	1	9	2		.204	.226	.291	65	-5	-4	8	3			.968	9	C	0.8
	Yr	82	256	20	58	8	3	1	19	14		.227	.288	.293	82	-5	-5	25	7			.974	18	C	2.1
1907	Was-A	72	207	11	53	5	0	0	17	12		.256	.306	.280	95	-3	-1	19	3			.971	-8	C	-0.4
1908	Was-A	51	116	8	28	2	1	0	8	8		.241	.313	.276	100	-1	0	12	7			.982	1	C/1	0.5
Total	14	1073	3494	348	870	81	35	6	303	181	33	.249	.301	.297	73	-126	-116	355	83			.966	77	*C/1O2	5.6

■ **JACKIE WARNER** Warner, John Joseph b: 8/1/43, Monrovia, Cal. BR/TR, 6', 180 lbs. Deb: 4/12/66

YEAR	TM/L	G	AB	R	H	2B	3B	HR	RBI	BB	SO	AVG	OBP	SLG	PRO+	BR	/A	RC	SB	CS	SBR	FA	FR	POS	TPR
1966	Cal-A	45	123	22	26	4	1	7	16	9	55	.211	.265	.431	99	-1	-1	14	0	0	0	.984	-2	O	-0.4

■ **JACK WARNER** Warner, John Ralph b: 8/29/03, Evansville, Ind. d: 3/13/86, Mt.Vernon, Ill. BR/TR, 5'9.5", 165 lbs. Deb: 9/24/25

YEAR	TM/L	G	AB	R	H	2B	3B	HR	RBI	BB	SO	AVG	OBP	SLG	PRO+	BR	/A	RC	SB	CS	SBR	FA	FR	POS	TPR
1925	Det-A	10	39	7	13	0	0	0	2	3	6	.333	.381	.333	84	-1	-1	5	0	0	0	1.000	-2	3	-0.2
1926	Det-A	100	311	41	78	8	6	0	34	38	24	.251	.342	.315	71	-12	-12	37	8	4	0	.956	-4	3/S	-1.0
1927	Det-A	139	559	78	149	22	9	1	45	47	45	.267	.330	.343	74	-21	-22	63	15	4	2	.947	-5	*3	-1.7
1928	Det-A	75	206	33	44	4	4	0	13	16	15	.214	.274	.272	43	-17	-17	16	4	4	-1	.944	6	3/S	-1.0
1929	Bro-N	17	62	3	17	2	0	0	4	7	6	.274	.348	.306	65	-3	-3	7	3			.945	-2	S	-0.3
1930	Bro-N	21	25	4	8	1	0	0	0	2	7	.320	.370	.360	79	-1	-1	3	1			1.000	2	/3	0.1
1931	Bro-N	9	4	2	2	0	0	0	0	1	1	.500	.600	.500	200	1	1	1	0			1.000	3	/S3	0.3
1933	Phi-N	107	340	31	76	15	1	0	22	28	33	.224	.285	.274	53	-17	-22	26	1			.973	3	23/S	-1.4
Total	8	478	1546	199	387	52	20	1	120	142	137	.250	.319	.312	65	-71	-77	158	32	12		.950	0	3/2S	-5.2

■ **HAL WARNOCK** Warnock, Harold Charles b: 1/6/12, New York, N.Y. BL/TR, 6'2", 180 lbs. Deb: 9/02/35

YEAR	TM/L	G	AB	R	H	2B	3B	HR	RBI	BB	SO	AVG	OBP	SLG	PRO+	BR	/A	RC	SB	CS	SBR	FA	FR	POS	TPR
1935	StL-A	6	7	1	2	2	0	0	0	0	3	.286	.286	.571	112	0	0	1	0	0	0	1.000	-1	/O	-0.1

■ **BENNIE WARREN** Warren, Bennie Louis b: 3/2/12, Elk City, Okla. BR/TR, 6'1", 184 lbs. Deb: 9/13/39

YEAR	TM/L	G	AB	R	H	2B	3B	HR	RBI	BB	SO	AVG	OBP	SLG	PRO+	BR	/A	RC	SB	CS	SBR	FA	FR	POS	TPR
1939	Phi-N	18	56	4	13	0	0	1	7	7	7	.232	.317	.286	65	-3	-3	6	0			.958	-4	C	-0.5
1940	Phi-N	106	289	33	71	6	1	12	34	40	46	.246	.339	.398	107	1	3	39	1			.975	-4	C/1	0.6
1941	Phi-N	121	345	34	74	13	2	9	35	44	66	.214	.309	.342	86	-8	-6	36	0			.973	-4	*C	-0.1
1942	Phi-N	90	225	19	47	6	3	7	20	24	36	.209	.288	.356	92	-4	-3	22	0			.972	-2	C/1	0.1
1946	NY-N	39	69	7	11	1	1	4	8	14	21	.159	.301	.377	91	-1	-1	9	0			.965	1	C	0.2
1947	NY-N	3	5	0	1	0	0	0	0	0	1	.200	.200	.200	6	-1	-1	0	0			1.000	-1	/C	-0.1
Total	6	377	989	97	217	26	7	33	104	129	177	.219	.313	.360	92	-15	-10	111	1			.972	-13	C/1	0.2

■ **BILL WARREN** Warren, William Hackney "Hack" b: 2/11/1883, Missouri d: 1/28/60, Whiteville, Tenn. BR/TR, 5'8", 165 lbs. Deb: 4/30/14

YEAR	TM/L	G	AB	R	H	2B	3B	HR	RBI	BB	SO	AVG	OBP	SLG	PRO+	BR	/A	RC	SB	CS	SBR	FA	FR	POS	TPR
1914	Ind-F	26	50	5	12	2	0	0	5	5	7	.240	.309	.280	61	-2	-3	5	2			.931	-5	C	-0.7
1915	New-F	5	3	0	1	0	0	0	1	0	0	.333	.333	.333	102	-0	-0	0	0			1.000	-0	/C1	0.0
Total	2	31	53	5	13	2	0	0	6	5	7	.245	.310	.283	63	-2	-3	6	2			.932	-5	/C1	-0.7

■ **RABBIT WARSTLER** Warstler, Harold Burton b: 9/13/03, N.Canton, Ohio d: 5/31/64, N.Canton, Ohio BR/TR, 5'7.5", 150 lbs. Deb: 7/24/30

YEAR	TM/L	G	AB	R	H	2B	3B	HR	RBI	BB	SO	AVG	OBP	SLG	PRO+	BR	/A	RC	SB	CS	SBR	FA	FR	POS	TPR
1930	Bos-A	54	162	16	30	2	3	1	13	20	21	.185	.275	.253	36	-16	-15	12	0	2	-1	.947	-3	S	-1.3
1931	Bos-A	66	181	20	44	5	3	0	10	15	27	.243	.308	.304	65	-10	-9	17	2	3	-1	.933	1	2S/3	-0.5
1932	Bos-A	115	388	26	82	15	5	0	34	22	43	.211	.259	.276	40	-36	-34	28	9	6	-1	.939	**28**	*S	0.2
1933	Bos-A	92	322	44	70	13	1	1	17	42	36	.217	.308	.273	55	-20	-20	29	2	4	-2	.951	1	S	-1.4
1934	Phi-A	117	419	56	99	19	3	1	36	51	30	.236	.321	.303	64	-23	-21	45	9	3	1	.969	16	*2/S	0.2
1935	Phi-A	138	496	62	124	20	7	3	59	56	53	.250	.326	.337	72	-21	-20	58	8	4	0	.959	2	*2/3	-0.7
1936	Phi-A	66	236	27	59	8	6	1	24	36	16	.250	.354	.347	75	-9	-8	32	0	0	0	.973	11	2	0.6
	Bos-N	74	304	27	64	6	0	0	17	22	33	.211	.266	.230	37	-27	-25	19	2			.948	13	S	-0.7
1937	Bos-N	149	555	57	124	20	0	3	36	51	62	.223	.291	.276	60	-34	-27	48	4			.942	-11	*S	-2.8
1938	Bos-N	142	467	37	108	10	4	0	40	48	38	.231	.303	.270	65	-25	-19	39	3			.937	-7	*S/2	-1.6
1939	Bos-N	114	342	34	83	11	3	0	24	24	31	.243	.292	.292	62	-20	-17	29	2			.953	1	S23	-1.0
1940	Bos-N	33	57	6	12	0	0	0	4	10	5	.211	.328	.211	54	-3	-3	4	0			.974	-1	2/3S	-0.3
	Chi-N	45	159	19	36	4	1	1	18	8	19	.226	.263	.283	52	-11	-10	12	1			.939	-1	S2	-0.8
	Yr	78	216	25	48	4	1	1	22	18	24	.222	.282	.264	53	-14	-13	16	1			.960	-2	2S/3	-1.1
Total	11	1205	4088	431	935	133	36	11	332	405	414	.229	.300	.287	59	-256	-229	372	42	22		.942	49	S2/3	-10.1

■ **CARL WARWICK** Warwick, Carl Wayne b: 2/27/37, Dallas, Tex. BR/TL, 5'10", 170 lbs. Deb: 4/11/61

YEAR	TM/L	G	AB	R	H	2B	3B	HR	RBI	BB	SO	AVG	OBP	SLG	PRO+	BR	/A	RC	SB	CS	SBR	FA	FR	POS	TPR
1961	LA-N	19	11	2	1	0	0	0	1	2	3	.091	.231	.091	-9	-2	-2	0	0	0	0	1.000	-0	O	-0.2
	StL-N	55	152	27	38	6	2	4	16	18	33	.250	.329	.395	83	-2	-4	21	3	0	1	.970	1	O	-0.4
	Yr	74	163	29	39	6	2	4	17	20	36	.239	.322	.374	77	-4	-6	21	3	0	1	.970	1	O	-0.6
1962	StL-N	13	23	4	8	0	0	1	4	2	2	.348	.400	.478	123	1	1	4	2	0	1	1.000	0	O	0.1
	Hou-N	130	477	63	124	17	1	16	60	38	77	.260	.315	.400	98	-7	-3	59	2	3	-1	.986	-3	*O	-1.4
	Yr	143	500	67	132	17	1	17	64	40	79	.264	.319	.404	98	-6	-2	63	4	3	-1	.986	-2	*O	-1.3
1963	Hou-N	150	528	49	134	19	5	7	47	49	70	.254	.320	.348	98	-5	-1	58	3	3	-1	.988	-2	*O/1	-1.2
1964	*StL-N	88	158	14	41	7	1	3	15	11	30	.259	.308	.373	83	-2	-4	19	2	0	1	.933	-1	O	-0.6
1965	StL-N	50	77	3	12	2	1	0	6	4	18	.156	.198	.208	13	-9	-10	3	1	0	0	.960	-0	O/1	-1.1
	Bal-A	9	14	3	0	0	0	0	0	3	2	.000	.176	.000	-44	-3	-3	0	0	0	0	1.000	-1	/O	-0.4
1966	Chi-N	16	22	3	5	0	0	0	0	0	6	.227	.227	.227	27	-2	-2	1	0	0	0	1.000	1	O	-0.2
Total	6	530	1462	168	363	51	10	31	149	127	241	.248	.309	.360	87	-30	-27	165	13	6	0	.980	-4	O/1	-5.4

■ **BILL WARWICK** Warwick, Firmin Newton b: 11/26/1897, Philadelphia, Pa. d: 12/19/84, San Antonio, Tex. BR/TR, 6'0.5", 180 lbs. Deb: 7/18/21

YEAR	TM/L	G	AB	R	H	2B	3B	HR	RBI	BB	SO	AVG	OBP	SLG	PRO+	BR	/A	RC	SB	CS	SBR	FA	FR	POS	TPR
1921	Pit-N	1	1	0	0	0	0	0	0	0	0	.000	.000	.000	-97	-0	-0	0	0	0	0	.500	-0	/C	0.0
1925	StL-N	13	41	8	12	1	2	1	6	5	5	.293	.370	.488	114	1	1	7	0	1	-1	1.000	-4	C	-0.3
1926	StL-N	9	14	0	5	0	0	0	2	0	2	.357	.357	.357	89	-0	-0	2	0			.923	2	/C	0.2
Total	3	23	56	8	17	1	2	1	8	5	7	.304	.361	.446	105	1	0	9	0	1		.954	-2	/C	-0.1

■ **JIMMY WASDELL** Wasdell, James Charles b: 5/15/14, Cleveland, Ohio d: 8/6/83, New Port Richey, Fla. BL/TL, 5'11", 185 lbs. Deb: 9/03/37

YEAR	TM/L	G	AB	R	H	2B	3B	HR	RBI	BB	SO	AVG	OBP	SLG	PRO+	BR	/A	RC	SB	CS	SBR	FA	FR	POS	TPR
1937	Was-A	32	110	13	28	4	4	2	12	7	13	.255	.299	.418	82	-4	-3	13	0	1	-1	.995	-0	1/O	-0.6
1938	Was-A	53	140	19	33	2	1	2	16	12	12	.236	.296	.307	55	-11	-9	13	5	2	0	.996	-1	1/O	-1.2
1939	Was-A	29	109	12	33	5	1	0	13	9	16	.303	.361	.367	94	-2	-1	15	3	1	0	.964	-2	1	-0.5
1940	Was-A	10	35	3	3	1	0	0	0	2	7	.086	.135	.114	-37	-7	-7	1	0	0	0	1.000	-1	/1	-0.9
	Bro-N	77	230	35	64	14	4	3	37	18	24	.278	.333	.413	99	1	-1	32	4			.947	-7	O1	-1.1
1941	*Bro-N	94	265	39	79	14	3	4	48	16	15	.298	.345	.419	110	4	3	40	2			.956	-6	O1	-0.7
1942	Pit-N	122	409	44	106	11	2	3	38	47	22	.259	.337	.318	90	-3	-4	46	1			.957	-3	O/1	-1.4
1943	Pit-N	4	2	0	1	0	0	0	1	2	0	.500	.750	.500	256	1	1	1	0			.000	0	H	0.1
	Phi-N	141	522	54	136	19	6	4	67	46	22	.261	.323	.343	96	-5	-3	58	6			.988	-8	1O	-1.9
	Yr	145	524	54	137	19	6	4	68	48	22	.261	.326	.344	97	-4	-2	59	6			.988	-8	1O	-1.8
1944	Phi-N	133	451	47	125	20	3	3	40	45	17	.277	.344	.355	100	-1	1	55	0			.980	-9	*O/1	-1.5
1945	Phi-N	134	500	65	150	19	8	7	60	32	11	.300	.346	.412	113	6	7	72	7			.967	-2	O1	-0.3
1946	Phi-N	26	51	7	13	0	2	1	5	3	2	.255	.309	.392	101	-0	-0	6	0			.923	-2	O/1	-0.3
	Cle-A	32	41	1	11	0	0	0	4	4	4	.268	.333	.268	74	-2	-1	4	1	0	0	.939	-2	/1O	-0.3
1947	Cle-A	1	1	0	0	0	0	0	0	0	0	.000	.000	.000	-99	-0	-0	0	0	0	0	.000	0	H	0.0
Total	11	888	2866	339	782	109	34	29	341	243	165	.273	.332	.365	96	-23	-18	355	29	4		.966	-45	O1	-10.6

■ LINK WASEM
Wasem, Lincoln William b: 1/30/11, Birmingham, Ohio d: 3/6/79, S.Laguna, Cal. BR/TR, 5'9.5", 180 lbs. Deb: 5/05/37

YEAR	TM/L	G	AB	R	H	2B	3B	HR	RBI	BB	SO	AVG	OBP	SLG	PRO+	BR	/A	RC	SB	CS	SBR	FA	FR	POS	TPR
1937	Bos-N	2	1	0	0	0	0	0	0	0	0	.000	.000	.000	-99	-0	-0	0	0			1.000	0	/C	0.0

■ LIBE WASHBURN
Washburn, Libeus b: 6/16/1874, Lyme, N.H. d: 3/22/40, Malone, N.Y. BB/TL, 5'10", 180 lbs. Deb: 5/30/02

YEAR	TM/L	G	AB	R	H	2B	3B	HR	RBI	BB	SO	AVG	OBP	SLG	PRO+	BR	/A	RC	SB	CS	SBR	FA	FR	POS	TPR
1902	NY-N	6	9	1	4	0	0	0	0	2		.444	.615	.444	229	2	2	3	1			1.000	-1	/O	0.1
1903	Phi-N	8	18	1	3	0	0	0	1	1		.167	.211	.167	8	-2	-2	1	0			1.000	-1	/PO	0.0
Total	2	14	27	2	7	0	0	0	1	3		.259	.375	.259	89	-0	-0	4	1			1.000	-1	/OP	0.1

■ CLAUDELL WASHINGTON
Washington, Claudell b: 8/31/54, Los Angeles, Cal. BL/TL, 6', 190 lbs. Deb: 7/05/74

YEAR	TM/L	G	AB	R	H	2B	3B	HR	RBI	BB	SO	AVG	OBP	SLG	PRO+	BR	/A	RC	SB	CS	SBR	FA	FR	POS	TPR
1974	*Oak-A	73	221	16	63	10	5	0	19	13	44	.285	.328	.376	109	0	2	24	6	8	-3	.985	-1	DO	-0.4
1975	*Oak-A★	148	590	86	182	24	7	10	77	32	80	.308	.349	.424	120	12	14	85	40	15	3	.978	-3	*O	0.8
1976	Oak-A	134	490	65	126	20	6	5	53	30	90	.257	.304	.353	96	-6	-3	49	37	20	-1	.963	-2	*O/D	-1.3
1977	Tex-A	129	521	63	148	31	2	12	68	25	112	.284	.321	.420	99	-1	-2	68	21	8	2	.978	-1	*O/D	-0.7
1978	Tex-A	12	42	1	7	0	0	0	2	1	12	.167	.186	.167	-0	-6	-6	1	0	1	-1	.917	-1	/OD	-0.8
	Chi-A	86	314	33	83	16	5	6	31	12	57	.264	.294	.404	94	-3	-4	34	5	5	-2	.959	-2	O/D	-1.1
	Yr	98	356	34	90	16	5	6	33	13	69	.253	.281	.376	83	-9	-9	34	5	6	-2	.957	-3	O/D	-1.9
1979	Chi-A	131	471	79	132	33	5	13	66	28	93	.280	.325	.454	108	4	4	65	19	11	-1	.974	4	*O	0.1
1980	Chi-A	32	90	15	26	4	2	1	12	5	19	.289	.333	.411	103	0	0	11	4	2	0	.933	-2	O/D	-0.2
	NY-N	79	284	38	78	16	4	10	42	20	63	.275	.325	.465	121	6	7	42	17	5	2	.978	0	O	0.7
1981	Atl-N	85	320	37	93	22	3	5	37	15	47	.291	.330	.425	110	4	4	44	12	6	0	.993	-4	O	-0.3
1982	*Atl-N	150	563	94	150	24	6	16	80	50	107	.266	.333	.416	104	6	3	80	33	10	4	.950	-10	*O	-0.7
1983	Atl-N	134	496	75	138	24	8	9	44	35	103	.278	.326	.413	96	1	-3	67	31	9	4	.974	-4	*O	-0.7
1984	Atl-N★	120	416	62	119	21	2	17	61	59	77	.286	.376	.469	127	21	17	73	21	9	1	.967	-5	*O	1.0
1985	Atl-N	122	398	62	110	14	6	15	43	40	66	.276	.344	.455	115	11	8	61	14	4	2	.962	-14	O	-0.7
1986	Atl-N	40	137	17	37	11	0	5	14	14	26	.270	.338	.460	112	3	2	18	4	7	-3	.957	-5	O	-0.8
	NY-A	54	135	19	32	5	0	6	16	7	33	.237	.285	.407	87	-3	-3	16	6	1	1	.985	-6	O	-0.8
1987	NY-A	102	312	42	87	17	0	9	44	27	54	.279	.336	.420	100	-1	-0	46	10	1	2	.988	0	OD	0.1
1988	NY-A	126	455	62	140	22	3	11	64	24	74	.308	.345	.442	120	10	11	68	15	6	1	.984	2	*O	1.0
1989	Cal-A	110	418	53	114	18	4	13	42	27	84	.273	.320	.428	111	4	5	57	13	5	1	.975	-3	*O/D	0.0
1990	Cal-A	12	34	3	6	1	0	1	3	2	8	.176	.222	.294	44	-3	-3	2	1	0	0	1.000	1	/O	-0.2
	NY-A	33	80	4	13	1	1	0	6	2	17	.162	.183	.200	7	-10	-10	3	3	1	0	1.000	1	O/D	-1.0
	Yr	45	114	7	19	2	1	1	9	4	25	.167	.195	.228	18	-13	-13	5	4	1	1	1.000	2	O/D	-1.2
Total	17	1912	6787	926	1884	334	69	164	824	468	1266	.278	.328	.420	106	50	42	914	312	134	13	.973	-55	*O/D	-6.0

■ HERB WASHINGTON
Washington, Herbert Lee b: 11/16/51, Belzonia, Miss. BR/TR, 6', 170 lbs. Deb: 4/04/74

YEAR	TM/L	G	AB	R	H	2B	3B	HR	RBI	BB	SO	AVG	OBP	SLG	PRO+	BR	/A	RC	SB	CS	SBR	FA	FR	POS	TPR
1974	*Oak-A	92	0	29	0	0	0	0	0	0	0	—	—	—	—	0	0	0	29	16	-1	.000	0	R	-0.1
1975	Oak-A	13	0	4	0	0	0	0	0	0	0	—	—	—	—	0	0	0	2	1	0	.000	0	R	0.0
Total	2	105	0	33	0	0	0	0	0	0	0	—	—	—	—	0	0	0	31	17	-1		0		-0.1

■ LA RUE WASHINGTON
Washington, La Rue b: 9/7/53, Long Beach, Cal. BR/TR, 6', 170 lbs. Deb: 9/07/78

YEAR	TM/L	G	AB	R	H	2B	3B	HR	RBI	BB	SO	AVG	OBP	SLG	PRO+	BR	/A	RC	SB	CS	SBR	FA	FR	POS	TPR
1978	Tex-A	3	3	0	0	0	0	0	0	0	1	.000	.000	.000	-99	-1	-1	0	0	0	0	1.000	2	/2D	0.1
1979	Tex-A	25	18	5	5	0	0	0	2	4	0	.278	.409	.278	90	0	0	3	2	1	0	1.000	-3	O/3	-0.3
Total	2	28	21	5	5	0	0	0	2	4	1	.238	.360	.238	67	-1	-1	3	2	1	0		-1	/O23D	-0.2

■ RON WASHINGTON
Washington, Ronald b: 4/29/52, New Orleans, La. BR/TR, 5'11", 163 lbs. Deb: 9/10/77

YEAR	TM/L	G	AB	R	H	2B	3B	HR	RBI	BB	SO	AVG	OBP	SLG	PRO+	BR	/A	RC	SB	CS	SBR	FA	FR	POS	TPR
1977	LA-N	10	19	4	7	0	0	0	1	0	2	.368	.400	.368	108	0	0	2	1	1	-0	.857	-2	S	-0.1
1981	Min-A	28	84	8	19	3	1	0	5	4	14	.226	.270	.286	56	-4	-5	7	4	1	1	.951	6	S/O	0.4
1982	Min-A	119	451	48	122	17	6	5	39	14	79	.271	.292	.368	78	-13	-15	45	3	3	-1	.972	-44	S2/3	-5.1
1983	Min-A	99	317	28	78	7	3	4	26	22	50	.246	.297	.325	69	-12	-14	30	10	5	0	.962	-17	S2/3D	-2.3
1984	Min-A	88	197	25	58	11	5	3	23	4	31	.294	.312	.447	102	1	0	26	1	1	-0	.978	-16	S/23D	-1.2
1985	Min-A	70	135	24	37	6	4	1	14	8	15	.274	.315	.400	89	-1	-2	17	5	1	1	.951	-4	S2/31D	-0.3
1986	Min-A	48	74	15	19	3	0	4	11	3	21	.257	.286	.459	96	-0	-1	9	1	2	-1	.917	0	2D/S3	-0.1
1987	Bal-A	26	79	7	16	3	1	1	6	1	15	.203	.213	.304	36	-7	-7	4	0	1	-1	1.000	2	3/2OSD	-0.6
1988	Cle-A	69	223	30	57	14	2	2	21	9	35	.256	.300	.363	82	-5	-6	24	3	3	-1	.933	-14	S/32D	-1.6
1989	Hou-N	7	7	1	1	1	0	0	0	0	4	.143	.143	.286	20	-1	-1	0	0	0	0	.000	-0	/23	-0.1
Total	10	564	1586	190	414	65	22	20	146	65	266	.261	.294	.368	79	-43	-50	165	28	18	-2	.958	-88	S2/3DO1	-11.0

■ GEORGE WASHINGTON
Washington, Sloan Vernon "Vern" b: 6/4/07, Linden, Tex. d: 2/17/85, Linden, Tex. BL/TR, 5'11.5", 190 lbs. Deb: 4/17/35

YEAR	TM/L	G	AB	R	H	2B	3B	HR	RBI	BB	SO	AVG	OBP	SLG	PRO+	BR	/A	RC	SB	CS	SBR	FA	FR	POS	TPR
1935	Chi-A	108	339	40	96	22	3	8	47	10	18	.283	.310	.437	89	-6	-7	45	1	0	0	.974	0	O	-0.9
1936	Chi-A	20	49	6	8	2	0	1	5	1	4	.163	.180	.265	8	-7	-8	2	0	0	0	.938	-2	O	-0.9
Total	2	128	388	46	104	24	3	9	52	11	22	.268	.294	.415	78	-14	-15	48	1	0	0	.970	-2	/O	-1.8

■ U L WASHINGTON
Washington, U L b: 10/27/53, Stringtown, Okla. BB/TR, 5'11", 175 lbs. Deb: 9/06/77

YEAR	TM/L	G	AB	R	H	2B	3B	HR	RBI	BB	SO	AVG	OBP	SLG	PRO+	BR	/A	RC	SB	CS	SBR	FA	FR	POS	TPR
1977	KC-A	10	20	0	4	1	1	0	1	5	4	.200	.360	.350	94	0	-0	3	1	0	0	.872	0	/S	0.1
1978	KC-A	69	129	10	34	2	1	0	9	10	20	.264	.317	.295	71	-4	-5	12	12	6	0	.927	-11	S2/D	-1.2
1979	KC-A	101	268	32	68	12	5	2	25	20	44	.254	.306	.358	77	-8	-9	30	10	7	-1	.970	1	S2/3	-0.2
1980	*KC-A	153	549	79	150	16	11	6	53	53	78	.273	.337	.375	94	-3	-4	70	20	7	2	.957	-26	*S	-1.1
1981	KC-A	98	339	40	77	19	1	2	29	41	43	.227	.311	.307	79	-9	-8	32	10	10	-3	.973	-21	S	-2.4
1982	KC-A	119	437	64	125	19	3	10	60	38	48	.286	.343	.412	106	4	4	65	23	7	3	.961	-11	*S/D	0.7
1983	KC-A	144	547	76	129	19	6	5	41	48	78	.236	.299	.320	70	-22	-22	59	40	7	8	.947	-10	*S/D	-1.1
1984	*KC-A	63	170	18	38	6	0	1	10	14	31	.224	.283	.276	55	-10	-10	13	4	6	-2	.961	0	S	-0.7
1985	Mon-N	68	193	24	48	9	4	1	17	15	33	.249	.303	.352	88	-5	-3	21	6	3	0	.978	-10	2/S3	-1.1
1986	Pit-N	72	135	14	27	0	4	0	10	15	27	.200	.280	.259	49	-9	-9	12	6	0	2	.947	-8	S/2	-1.3
1987	Pit-N	10	10	1	3	0	0	0	0	2	3	.300	.417	.300	93	0	0	2	0	0	0	.833	-0	/S3	0.0
Total	11	907	2797	358	703	103	36	27	255	261	409	.251	.315	.343	82	-67	-67	320	132	53	8	.956	-95	S2/3D	-8.3

■ MARK WASINGER
Wasinger, Mark Thomas b: 8/4/61, Monterey, Cal. BR/TR, 6', 165 lbs. Deb: 5/27/86

YEAR	TM/L	G	AB	R	H	2B	3B	HR	RBI	BB	SO	AVG	OBP	SLG	PRO+	BR	/A	RC	SB	CS	SBR	FA	FR	POS	TPR
1986	SD-N	3	8	0	0	0	0	0	1	0	2	.000	.000	.000	-99	-2	-2	0	0	0	0	.500	-1	/32	-0.4
1987	SF-N	44	80	16	22	3	0	1	3	8	14	.275	.341	.350	88	-2	-1	10	2	0	1	.973	3	32/S	0.3
1988	SF-N	3	2	1	0	0	0	0	0	0	0	.000	.000	.000	-99	-1	-0	0	0	0	0	.000	0	/3	-0.1
Total	3	50	90	17	22	3	0	1	4	8	16	.244	.306	.311	68	-4	-4	10	2	0	1	.907	2	/32S	-0.2

■ FRED WATERMAN
Waterman, Frederick A. b: 12/1845, New York, N.Y. d: 12/16/1899, Cincinnati, Ohio 5'7.5", 148 lbs. Deb: 5/05/1871

YEAR	TM/L	G	AB	R	H	2B	3B	HR	RBI	BB	SO	AVG	OBP	SLG	PRO+	BR	/A	RC	SB	CS	SBR	FA	FR	POS	TPR
1871	Oly-n	32	158	46	50	7	4	0	17	10	0	.316	.357	.411	127	4	6	28	11					*3/C	0.3
1872	Oly-n	9	44	13	18	1	1	0	6	0	0	.409	.409	.477	181	4	4	9						/3C	0.2
1873	Was-n	15	80	20	28	3	3	0	10	1	1	.350	.358	.463	144	4	4	14						/SO3	0.3
1875	Chi-n	5	20	2	6	0	0	0		0		.300	.300	.300	107	0	0	2						/32	0.0
Total	4 n	61	302	81	102	11	8	0		11		.338	.361	.427	137	12	15	52						/3SCO2	0.8

■ JOHN WATHAN
Wathan, John David b: 10/4/49, Cedar Rapids, Iowa BR/TR, 6'2", 205 lbs. Deb: 5/26/76 MC

YEAR	TM/L	G	AB	R	H	2B	3B	HR	RBI	BB	SO	AVG	OBP	SLG	PRO+	BR	/A	RC	SB	CS	SBR	FA	FR	POS	TPR
1976	*KC-A	27	42	5	12	1	0	0	5	2	5	.286	.333	.310	88	-1	-1	4	0	2	-1	.984	-1	C/1	-0.2
1977	*KC-A	55	119	18	39	5	3	2	21	5	8	.328	.355	.471	122	3	3	20	2	0	1	.993	-2	C/1D	0.2
1978	*KC-A	67	190	19	57	10	1	2	28	3	12	.300	.325	.395	99	-0	-1	23	2	1	0	1.000	1	1C	-0.2
1979	KC-A	90	199	26	41	7	3	2	28	7	24	.206	.233	.302	42	-16	-17	13	2	1	0	.993	-2	1CD/O	-2.0
1980	*KC-A	126	453	57	138	14	7	6	58	50	42	.305	.377	.406	114	11	10	69	17	3	3	.982	-11	CO1	0.4

YEAR	TM/L	G	AB	R	H	2B	3B	HR	RBI	BB	SO	AVG	OBP	SLG	PRO+	BR	/A	RC	SB	CS	SBR	FA	FR	POS	TPR
1981	*KC-A	89	301	24	76	9	3	1	19	19	23	.252	.301	.312	78	-9	-9	27	11	6	-0	.979	-11	CO/1	-1.8
1982	KC-A	121	448	79	121	11	3	3	51	48	46	.270	.343	.328	85	-7	-7	49	36	9	5	.980	-17	*C/1	-1.5
1983	KC-A	128	437	49	107	18	3	2	32	27	56	.245	.290	.314	66	-20	-20	40	28	7	4	.985	-4	C1/O	-1.8
1984	*KC-A	97	171	17	31	7	1	2	10	21	34	.181	.271	.269	50	-11	-12	12	6	6	-2	.975	5	C1/OD	-0.7
1985	*KC-A	60	145	11	34	8	1	1	9	17	15	.234	.319	.324	76	-4	-4	15	1	1	-0	.986	12	C/1D	0.9
Total	10	860	2505	305	656	90	25	21	261	199	265	.262	.320	.343	83	-55	-57	271	105	36	10	.982	-31	C1/OD	-6.7

■ **DAVE WATKINS** Watkins, David Roger b: 3/15/44, Owensboro, Ky. BR/TR, 5'10", 185 lbs. Deb: 4/09/69

YEAR	TM/L	G	AB	R	H	2B	3B	HR	RBI	BB	SO	AVG	OBP	SLG	PRO+	BR	/A	RC	SB	CS	SBR	FA	FR	POS	TPR
1969	Phi-N	69	148	17	26	2	1	4	12	22	53	.176	.291	.284	63	-7	-7	13	2	3	-1	.981	-4	C/O3	-1.1

■ **GEORGE WATKINS** Watkins, George Archibald b: 6/4/1900, Freesrone Co., Tex d: 6/1/70, Houston, Tex. BL/TR, 6', 175 lbs. Deb: 4/15/30

YEAR	TM/L	G	AB	R	H	2B	3B	HR	RBI	BB	SO	AVG	OBP	SLG	PRO+	BR	/A	RC	SB	CS	SBR	FA	FR	POS	TPR
1930	*StL-N	119	391	85	146	32	7	17	87	24	49	.373	.415	.621	141	28	26	96	5			.956	-6	O1/2	1.2
1931	*StL-N	131	503	93	145	30	13	13	51	31	66	.288	.336	.477	112	9	7	81	15			.958	-6	*O	-0.7
1932	StL-N	127	458	67	143	35	3	9	63	45	46	.312	.384	.461	122	18	16	84	18			.949	3	*O	1.1
1933	StL-N	138	525	66	146	24	5	5	62	39	62	.278	.342	.371	98	3	0	71	11			.953	1	*O	-0.7
1934	NY-N	105	296	38	73	18	3	6	33	24	34	.247	.316	.389	90	-5	-5	40	2			.944	-10	O	-1.7
1935	Phi-N	150	600	80	162	25	5	17	76	40	78	.270	.320	.413	87	-5	-13	82	3			.958	5	*O	-1.3
1936	Phi-N	19	70	7	17	4	0	2	5	5	13	.243	.293	.386	74	-2	-3	8	2			.889	-3	O	-0.6
	Bro-N	105	364	54	93	24	6	4	43	38	34	.255	.334	.387	93	-3	-4	51	5			.969	-4	O	-1.2
	Yr	124	434	61	110	28	6	6	48	43	47	.253	.328	.387	90	-5	-7	59	7			.959	-7	*O	-1.8
Total	7	894	3207	490	925	192	42	73	420	246	382	.288	.347	.443	105	43	25	513	61			.954	-20	O/12	-3.9

■ **ED WATKINS** Watkins, James Edward b: 6/21/1877, Philadelphia, Pa. d: 3/29/33, Kelvin, Ariz. Deb: 9/06/02

YEAR	TM/L	G	AB	R	H	2B	3B	HR	RBI	BB	SO	AVG	OBP	SLG	PRO+	BR	/A	RC	SB	CS	SBR	FA	FR	POS	TPR
1902	Phi-N	1	3	0	0	0	0	0	0	1		.000	.250	.000	-22	-0	-0	0	0			1.000	-0	/O	-0.1

■ **BILL WATKINS** Watkins, William Henry b: 5/5/1858, Brantford, Ont., Can d: 6/9/37, Port Huron, Mich. 5'10", 156 lbs. Deb: 8/01/1884 M

YEAR	TM/L	G	AB	R	H	2B	3B	HR	RBI	BB	SO	AVG	OBP	SLG	PRO+	BR	/A	RC	SB	CS	SBR	FA	FR	POS	TPR
1884	Ind-a	34	127	16	26	4	0	0		5		.205	.241	.236	60	-5	-5	7				.845	-6	3/2SM	-1.0

■ **NEAL WATLINGTON** Watlington, Julius Neal b: 12/25/22, Yanceyville, N.C. BL/TR, 6', 195 lbs. Deb: 7/10/53

YEAR	TM/L	G	AB	R	H	2B	3B	HR	RBI	BB	SO	AVG	OBP	SLG	PRO+	BR	/A	RC	SB	CS	SBR	FA	FR	POS	TPR
1953	Phi-A	21	44	4	7	1	0	0	3	3	8	.159	.213	.182	7	-6	-6	2	0	1	-1	.978	0	/C	-0.6

■ **ART WATSON** Watson, Arthur Stanhope "Watty" b: 1/11/1884, Jeffersonville, Ind. d: 5/9/50, Buffalo, N.Y. BL/TR, 5'10", 175 lbs. Deb: 5/19/14

YEAR	TM/L	G	AB	R	H	2B	3B	HR	RBI	BB	SO	AVG	OBP	SLG	PRO+	BR	/A	RC	SB	CS	SBR	FA	FR	POS	TPR
1914	Bro-F	22	46	7	13	4	1	1	3	1	6	.283	.298	.478	120	1	1	7	0			.977	2	C	0.4
1915	Bro-F	9	19	4	5	0	3	0	1	3	4	.263	.364	.579	177	2	2	4	0			.957	-3	/C	-0.1
	Buf-F	22	30	6	14	1	0	1	13	0	4	.467	.467	.600	208	4	4	9	0			.778	-4	/CO	0.0
	Yr	31	49	10	19	1	3	1	14	3	8	.388	.423	.592	195	6	5	13	0			.878	-7	C/O	-0.1
Total	2	53	95	17	32	5	4	2	17	4	14	.337	.364	.537	159	6	6	19	0			.946	-5	/CO	0.3

■ **JOHNNY WATSON** Watson, John Thomas b: 1/16/08, Tazewell, Va. d: 4/29/65, Huntington, W.Va. BL/TR, 6', 175 lbs. Deb: 9/26/30

YEAR	TM/L	G	AB	R	H	2B	3B	HR	RBI	BB	SO	AVG	OBP	SLG	PRO+	BR	/A	RC	SB	CS	SBR	FA	FR	POS	TPR
1930	Det-A	4	12	1	3	2	0	0	3	1	2	.250	.308	.417	80	-0	-0	2	0	0	0	.933	-1	/S	-0.1

■ **BOB WATSON** Watson, Robert Jose "Bull" b: 4/10/46, Los Angeles, Cal. BR/TR, 6'2", 205 lbs. Deb: 9/09/66 C

YEAR	TM/L	G	AB	R	H	2B	3B	HR	RBI	BB	SO	AVG	OBP	SLG	PRO+	BR	/A	RC	SB	CS	SBR	FA	FR	POS	TPR
1966	Hou-N	1	1	0	0	0	0	0	0	0	0	.000	.000	.000	-99	-0	-0	0	0	0	0	.000	0	H	0.0
1967	Hou-N	6	14	1	3	0	0	1	2	0	3	.214	.214	.429	82	-0	-0	1	0	0	0	.958	0	/1	-0.1
1968	Hou-N	45	140	13	32	7	0	2	8	13	32	.229	.299	.321	88	-2	-2	13	1	0	0	.885	-8	O	-1.3
1969	Hou-N	20	40	3	11	3	0	0	3	6	5	.275	.396	.350	113	1	1	6	0	0	0	1.000	-1	/O1C	0.0
1970	Hou-N	97	327	48	89	19	2	11	61	24	59	.272	.330	.443	110	1	3	46	1	1	-0	.992	-8	1/CO	-1.2
1971	Hou-N	129	468	49	135	17	3	9	67	41	56	.288	.348	.395	113	6	8	62	0	3	-2	.985	-14	O1	-1.7
1972	Hou-N	147	548	74	171	27	4	16	86	53	83	.312	.381	.464	142	28	29	100	1	1	-0	.978	-10	*O/1	1.4
1973	Hou-N★	158	573	97	179	24	3	16	94	85	73	.312	.405	.449	137	31	31	104	1	4	-2	.969	-7	*O1/C	1.5
1974	Hou-N	150	524	69	156	19	4	11	67	60	61	.298	.373	.412	125	14	17	80	3	4	-2	.981	-15	*O1	-0.5
1975	Hou-N★	132	485	67	157	27	1	18	85	40	50	.324	.379	.495	152	25	30	87	3	5	-2	.993	-1	*1/O	2.0
1976	Hou-N	157	585	76	183	31	3	16	102	62	64	.313	.382	.458	151	29	35	102	3	3	-1	.990	-2	*1	2.3
1977	Hou-N	151	554	77	160	38	6	22	110	57	69	.289	.362	.498	141	21	28	102	5	0	2	.994	12	*1	3.3
1978	Hou-N	139	461	51	133	25	4	14	79	51	57	.289	.364	.451	137	17	21	72	3	1	0	.992	10	*1	2.5
1979	Hou-N	49	163	15	39	4	0	3	18	16	23	.239	.307	.319	75	-6	-5	16	0	0	0	.993	3	1	-0.5
	Bos-A	84	312	48	105	19	4	13	53	29	33	.337	.402	.548	145	23	21	66	3	2	-0	.988	2	1D	1.9
1980	*NY-A	130	469	62	144	25	3	13	68	48	56	.307	.373	.456	128	17	18	75	2	1	0	.990	-2	*1D	1.0
1981	*NY-A	59	156	15	33	3	3	6	12	24	17	.212	.317	.385	103	0	1	17	0	0	0	.997	-1	1/D	-0.3
1982	NY-A	7	17	3	4	3	0	0	3	3	0	.235	.350	.412	110	0	0	2	0	0	0	1.000	-1	/1D	-0.1
	Atl-N	57	114	16	28	3	1	5	22	14	20	.246	.328	.421	104	1	1	15	1	1	-0	1.000	-3	1/O	-0.5
1983	Atl-N	65	149	14	46	9	0	6	37	18	23	.309	.383	.490	131	8	7	26	0	2	-1	.984	-3	1	0.1
1984	Atl-N	49	85	4	18	4	0	2	12	9	12	.212	.287	.329	68	-3	-4	8	0	0	0	.983	1	1	-0.4
Total	19	1832	6185	802	1826	307	41	184	989	653	796	.295	.367	.447	130	213	239	1001	27	28	-9	.991	-46	*1O/DC	9.4

■ **ALLIE WATT** Watt, Albert Bailey b: 12/12/1899, Philadelphia, Pa. d: 3/15/68, Norfolk, Va. BR/TR, 5'8", 154 lbs. Deb: 10/03/20 F

YEAR	TM/L	G	AB	R	H	2B	3B	HR	RBI	BB	SO	AVG	OBP	SLG	PRO+	BR	/A	RC	SB	CS	SBR	FA	FR	POS	TPR
1920	Was-A	1	1	0	1	1	0	0	1	0	0	1.000	1.000	2.000	700	1	1	2	0	0	0	1.000	0	/2	0.1

■ **JOHNNY WATWOOD** Watwood, John Clifford "Lefty" b: 8/17/05, Alexander City, Ala. d: 3/1/80, Goodwater, Ala. BL/TL, 6'1", 186 lbs. Deb: 4/16/29

YEAR	TM/L	G	AB	R	H	2B	3B	HR	RBI	BB	SO	AVG	OBP	SLG	PRO+	BR	/A	RC	SB	CS	SBR	FA	FR	POS	TPR
1929	Chi-A	85	278	33	84	12	6	2	28	22	21	.302	.355	.410	98	-1	-1	41	6	3	0	.942	-2	O	-0.7
1930	Chi-A	133	427	75	129	25	4	2	51	52	35	.302	.382	.393	100	-0	2	66	5	7	-3	.989	3	1O	-0.7
1931	Chi-A	128	367	51	104	16	6	1	47	56	30	.283	.380	.368	103	1	4	56	9	3	1	.944	3	*O/1	0.2
1932	Chi-A	13	49	5	15	2	0	0	0	1	3	.306	.333	.347	82	-2	-1	6	0	0	0	.960	-2	O	-0.4
	Bos-A	95	266	26	66	11	0	0	30	20	11	.248	.301	.289	55	-18	-17	24	7	4	-0	.945	-1	O1	-2.1
	Yr	108	315	31	81	13	0	0	30	21	14	.257	.306	.298	59	-20	-18	30	7	4	-0	.948	-4	O1	-2.5
1933	Bos-A	13	30	2	4	0	0	0	2	3	3	.133	.212	.133	-7	-5	-5	1	0	0	0	.950	-1	/O	-0.5
1939	Phi-N	2	6	0	1	0	0	0	0	0	0	.167	.167	.167	-11	-1	-1	0	0			.933	-1	/1	-0.2
Total	6	469	1423	192	403	66	16	5	158	154	103	.283	.356	.363	89	-26	-19	193	27	17		.948	-0	O/1	-4.4

■ **BOB WAY** Way, Robert Clinton b: 4/2/06, Emlenton, Pa. d: 6/20/74, Pittsburgh, Pa. BR/TR, 5'10.5", 168 lbs. Deb: 4/12/27

YEAR	TM/L	G	AB	R	H	2B	3B	HR	RBI	BB	SO	AVG	OBP	SLG	PRO+	BR	/A	RC	SB	CS	SBR	FA	FR	POS	TPR
1927	Chi-A	5	3	3	1	0	0	0	1	0	0	.333	.333	.333	75	-0	-0	0	0	0	0	1.000	1	/2	0.0

■ **ROY WEATHERLY** Weatherly, Cyril Roy "Stormy" b: 2/25/15, Warren, Tex. d: 1/19/91, Woodville, Tex. BL/TR, 5'6.5", 170 lbs. Deb: 6/27/36

YEAR	TM/L	G	AB	R	H	2B	3B	HR	RBI	BB	SO	AVG	OBP	SLG	PRO+	BR	/A	RC	SB	CS	SBR	FA	FR	POS	TPR
1936	Cle-A	84	349	64	117	28	6	8	53	16	29	.335	.364	.519	115	7	6	61	3	8	-4	.973	4	O	0.3
1937	Cle-A	53	134	19	27	4	0	5	13	6	14	.201	.246	.343	47	-12	-12	11	1	1	-0	.964	-3	O/3	-1.5
1938	Cle-A	83	210	32	55	14	3	2	18	14	14	.262	.308	.386	74	-10	-9	24	8	5	-1	.975	-1	O	-1.1
1939	Cle-A	95	323	43	100	16	6	1	32	19	23	.310	.348	.406	95	-4	-3	47	7	2	1	.961	-8	O	-1.1
1940	Cle-A	135	578	90	175	35	11	12	59	27	26	.303	.335	.464	108	2	4	88	9	8	-2	.969	6	*O	0.1
1941	Cle-A	102	363	59	105	21	5	3	37	32	20	.289	.350	.399	103	-1	1	52	2	5	-2	.968	-8	O	-1.4
1942	Cle-A	128	473	61	122	23	7	5	39	35	25	.258	.310	.368	96	-7	-4	54	8	13	-5	.991	2	*O	-1.4
1943	*NY-A	77	280	37	74	8	3	7	28	18	9	.264	.311	.389	104	0	0	34	4	7	-3	.983	-2	O	-0.9
1946	NY-A	2	2	0	1	0	0	0	0	0	0	.500	.500	.500	178	0	0	1	0	0	0	.000	0	H	0.0
1950	NY-N	52	69	10	18	3	3	0	11	13	10	.261	.378	.391	102	1	1	10	0			1.000	-1	O	-0.1
Total	10	811	2781	415	794	152	44	43	290	180	170	.286	.331	.418	99	-25	-15	382	42	49		.975	-10	O/3	-7.1

YEAR	TM/L	G	AB	R	H	2B	3B	HR	RBI	BB	SO	AVG	OBP	SLG	PRO+	BR	/A	RC	SB	CS	SBR	FA	FR	POS	TPR
■ ART WEAVER	Weaver, Arthur Coggshall "Six O'Clock" b: 4/7/1879, Wichita, Kan. d: 3/23/17, Denver, Colo. TR , 6'1", 160 lbs. Deb: 9/14/02																								
1902	StL-N	11	33	2	6	2	0	0	3	1		.182	.206	.242	40	-2	-2	2	0			.983	1	C	0.0
1903	StL-N	16	49	4	12	0	0	0	5	4		.245	.302	.245	59	-3	-2	4	1			.969	3	C	0.2
	Pit-N	16	48	8	11	0	1	0	3	2		.229	.260	.271	50	-3	-3	3	0			.978	-1	C/1	-0.3
	Yr	32	97	12	23	0	1	0	8	6		.237	.282	.258	54	-6	-6	8	1			.972	2	C/1	-0.1
1905	StL-A	28	92	5	11	2	1	0	3	1		.120	.129	.163	-8	-11	-11	2	0			.962	5	C	-0.3
1908	Chi-A	15	35	1	7	1	0	0	1	1		.200	.222	.229	47	-2	-2	2	0			.953	-5	C	-0.7
Total	4	86	257	20	47	5	2	0	15	9		.183	.211	.218	31	-21	-21	13	1			.967	4	/C1	-1.1
■ BUCK WEAVER	Weaver, George Daniel b: 8/18/1890, Pottstown, Pa. d: 1/31/56, Chicago, Ill. BR/TR, 5'11", 170 lbs. Deb: 4/11/12																								
1912	Chi-A	147	523	55	117	21	8	1	43	9		.224	.245	.300	58	-32	-30	41	12			.915	-6	*S	-2.4
1913	Chi-A	151	533	51	145	17	8	4	52	15	60	.272	.302	.356	94	-8	-7	61	20			.929	**34**	*S	4.2
1914	Chi-A	136	541	64	133	20	9	2	28	20	40	.246	.279	.327	83	-14	-13	47	14	20	-8	.928	5	*S	-0.5
1915	Chi-A	148	563	83	151	18	11	3	49	32	58	.268	.316	.355	98	-2	-4	68	24	20	-5	.939	1	*S	0.4
1916	Chi-A	151	582	78	132	27	6	3	38	30	48	.227	.280	.309	76	-18	-19	57	22	13	-1	.941	7	3S	-0.8
1917	*Chi-A	118	447	64	127	16	5	3	32	27	29	.284	.332	.362	110	5	4	61	19			**.949**	9	*3S	1.7
1918	Chi-A	112	420	37	126	12	5	0	29	11	24	.300	.323	.352	103	-0	-1	53	20			.941	-0	S3/2	0.4
1919	*Chi-A	140	571	89	169	33	9	3	75	11	21	.296	.315	.401	100	-3	-3	77	22			.963	0	3S	0.4
1920	Chi-A	151	629	102	208	34	8	2	74	28	23	.331	.365	.420	107	6	6	93	19	17	-5	.933	-10	*3S	-0.1
Total	9	1254	4809	623	1308	198	69	21	420	183	303	.272	.307	.355	92	-66	-67	557	172	70		.935	39	S3/2	3.3
■ JIM WEAVER	Weaver, James Francis b: 10/10/59, Kingston, N.Y. BL/TL, 6'3", 190 lbs. Deb: 4/10/85																								
1985	Det-A	12	7	2	1	1	0	0	0	1	4	.143	.250	.286	47	-1	-1	0	0	1	-1	1.000	-2	/OD	-0.3
1987	Sea-A	7	4	2	0	0	0	0	0	2	3	.000	.333	.000	-1	-1	-1	0	1	1	-0	1.000	-1	/O	-0.1
1989	SF-N	12	20	2	4	3	0	0	2	0	7	.200	.200	.350	56	-1	-1	2	1	0	0	1.000	-2	/O	-0.3
Total	3	31	31	6	5	4	0	0	2	3	14	.161	.235	.290	47	-2	-2	2	2	2	-1	.947	-4	/OD	-0.7
■ FARMER WEAVER	Weaver, William B. b: 3/23/1865, Parkersburg, W.Va. d: 1/23/43, Akron, Ohio BL , Deb: 9/16/1888																								
1888	Lou-a	26	112	12	28	1	1	0	8	3		.250	.276	.277	82	-2	-2	12	12			.878	-2	O	-0.4
1889	Lou-a	124	499	62	145	17	6	0	60	40	22	.291	.352	.349	104	2	4	70	21			.918	-1	*O/C32	0.0
1890	*Lou-a	130	557	101	161	27	9	3		29		.289	.333	.386	117	8	10	89	45			.933	-1	*O/S3	0.4
1891	Lou-a	135	565	76	160	25	7	1	55	33	23	.283	.335	.358	102	-0	1	80	30			**.956**	17	*O/C	1.2
1892	Lou-N	138	551	58	140	15	4	0	57	40	17	.254	.315	.296	94	-8	-2	62	30			.902	-11	*OC/1	-1.6
1893	Lou-N	106	439	79	128	17	7	2	49	27	12	.292	.348	.376	102	-4	2	65	17			.913	-1	OC	-0.1
1894	Lou-N	64	244	19	54	5	2	3	24	7	11	.221	.249	.295	34	-28	-24	20	3			.958	-0	OC1/2	-2.0
	Pit-N	30	115	16	40	7	2	0	24	6	1	.348	.405	.443	107	1	2	23	4			.943	-10	CS/3O	-0.5
	Yr	94	359	35	94	12	4	3	48	13	12	.262	.301	.343	59	-26	-23	41	7			.947	-10	OCS1/32	-2.5
Total	7	753	3082	423	856	114	38	9	277	185	86	.278	.330	.348	97	-31	-10	421	162			.927	-9	O/CS132	-3.0
■ SKEETER WEBB	Webb, James Laverne b: 11/4/09, Meridian, Miss. d: 7/8/86, Meridian, Miss. BR/TR, 5'9.5", 150 lbs. Deb: 7/20/32																								
1932	StL-N	1	0	0	0	0	0	0	0	0	0	—	—	—	—	0	0	0	0			.000	0	/S	0.0
1938	Cle-A	20	58	11	16	2	0	0	2	8	7	.276	.364	.310	72	-2	-2	7	1	0	0	.964	-2	S/32	-0.3
1939	Cle-A	81	269	28	71	14	1	2	26	15	24	.264	.305	.346	68	-14	-13	28	1	1	-0	.932	-9	S	-1.4
1940	Chi-A	84	334	33	79	11	2	1	29	30	33	.237	.299	.290	53	-23	-23	30	3	6	-3	.969	-10	2/S3	-2.9
1941	Chi-A	29	84	7	16	2	0	0	6	3	9	.190	.227	.214	18	-10	-10	4	1	0	0	.940	6	2/S3	-0.3
1942	Chi-A	32	94	5	16	2	1	0	4	4	13	.170	.204	.213	18	-10	-10	4	1	2	-1	.961	2	2	-0.8
1943	Chi-A	58	213	15	50	5	2	0	22	6	19	.235	.256	.277	56	-12	-12	14	5	4	-1	.953	-3	2	-1.4
1944	Chi-A	139	513	44	108	19	6	0	30	20	39	.211	.242	.271	47	-37	-36	33	7	3	0	.944	-5	*S/2	-3.1
1945	*Det-A	118	407	43	81	12	2	0	21	30	35	.199	.254	.238	41	-30	-33	25	8	7	-2	.957	23	*S2	-0.3
1946	Det-A	64	169	12	37	1	1	0	17	9	18	.219	.258	.237	37	-14	-15	10	3	3	-1	.972	15	2/S	0.2
1947	Det-A	50	79	13	16	3	0	0	6	7	9	.203	.267	.241	41	-6	-6	6	3	0	1	.992	12	2/S	0.8
1948	Phi-A	23	54	5	8	2	0	0	3	0	9	.148	.148	.185	-12	-9	-9	1	0	0	0	1.000	3	/2S	-0.5
Total	12	699	2274	216	498	73	15	3	166	132	215	.219	.263	.268	46	-167	-169	163	33	26		.946	32	S2/3	-10.0
■ EARL WEBB	Webb, William Earl b: 9/17/1898, Bon Air, Tenn. d: 5/23/65, Jamestown, Tenn. BL/TR, 6'1", 185 lbs. Deb: 8/13/25																								
1925	NY-N	4	3	0	0	0	0	0	0	1	1	.000	.250	.000	-31	-1	-1	0	0	0	0	.000	0	H	-0.1
1927	Chi-N	102	332	58	100	18	4	14	52	48	31	.301	.391	.506	138	18	18	66	3			.959	2	O	1.4
1928	Chi-N	62	140	22	35	7	3	3	23	14	17	.250	.318	.407	90	-3	-3	18	0			.986	2	O	-0.3
1930	Bos-A	127	449	61	145	30	6	16	66	44	56	.323	.385	.523	133	18	21	91	2	1	0	.959	-5	*O	0.7
1931	Bos-A	151	589	96	196	**67**	3	14	103	70	51	.333	.404	.528	151	37	41	127	2	2	-1	.948	-2	*O	2.6
1932	Bos-A	52	192	23	54	9	1	5	27	25	15	.281	.364	.417	105	1	2	30	0	0	0	.964	-3	O/1	-0.4
	Det-A	88	338	49	97	19	8	3	51	39	18	.287	.361	.417	97	1	-1	52	1	1	-0	.955	0	O	-0.6
	Yr	140	530	72	151	28	9	8	78	64	33	.285	.362	.417	100	1	0	82	1	1	-0	.958	-2	*O/1	-1.0
1933	Det-A	6	11	1	3	0	0	0	3	3	0	.273	.429	.273	87	0	0	2	0	0	0	1.000	-1	/O	-0.1
	Chi-A	58	107	16	31	5	0	1	8	16	13	.290	.382	.364	103	0	1	16	0	0	0	1.000	-4	O1	-0.4
	Yr	64	118	17	34	5	0	1	11	19	13	.288	.387	.356	102	0	1	18	0	0	0	1.000	-5	O1	-0.5
Total	7	650	2161	326	661	155	25	56	333	260	202	.306	.381	.478	125	72	79	402	8	4		.958	-11	O/1	2.8
■ BILL WEBB	Webb, William Joseph b: 6/25/1895, Chicago, Ill. d: 1/12/43, Chicago, Ill. BR/TR, 5'10", 161 lbs. Deb: 9/17/17 C																								
1917	Pit-N	5	15	1	3	0	0	0	0	2	3	.200	.294	.200	51	-1	-1	1	0			1.000	1	/2S	0.0
■ HARRY WEBER	Weber, Harry b: Indianapolis, Ind. Deb: 5/30/1884																								
1884	Det-N	2	8	0	0	0	0	0	0	0	2	.000	.000	.000	-99	-2	-2	0				.750	0	/O	-0.1
■ JOE WEBER	Weber, Joseph Edward b: 1861, Hamilton, Ont., Canada d: 12/15/21, Hamilton, Ont., Can Deb: 7/22/1884																								
1884	Ind-a	3	8	0	0	0	0	0		0		.000	.111	.000	-61	-1	-1	0				.794	1	/C	0.0
■ LENNY WEBSTER	Webster, Leonard Irell b: 2/10/65, New Orleans, La. BR/TR, 5'9", 185 lbs. Deb: 9/01/89																								
1989	Min-A	14	20	3	6	2	0	0	1	3	2	.300	.391	.400	116	1	1	3	0	0	0	1.000	-2	C	-0.1
1990	Min-A	2	6	1	2	1	0	0	0	1	1	.333	.429	.500	149	1	0	1	0	0	0	1.000	-1	/C	0.0
1991	Min-A	18	34	7	10	1	0	3	8	6	10	.294	.400	.588	162	3	3	8	0	0	0	.986	4	C	0.7
1992	Min-A	53	118	10	33	10	1	1	13	9	11	.280	.331	.407	102	1	0	15	0	2	-1	.995	1	C	0.2
Total	4	87	178	21	51	14	1	4	22	19	24	.287	.355	.444	117	5	4	27	0	2	-1	.994	3	/C	0.8
■ MITCH WEBSTER	Webster, Mitchell Dean b: 5/16/59, Larned, Kan. BB/TL, 6', 185 lbs. Deb: 9/02/83																								
1983	Tor-A	11	11	2	2	0	0	0	0	1	1	.182	.250	.182	20	-1	-1	1	0	0	0	1.000	-3	/OD	-0.4
1984	Tor-A	26	22	9	5	2	1	0	4	1	7	.227	.261	.409	79	-1	-1	2	0	0	0	.875	-3	O/1D	-0.4
1985	Tor-A	4	1	0	0	0	0	0	0	0	0	.000	.000	.000	-98	-0	-0	0	0	1	-1	.000	-1	/OD	-0.2
	Mon-N	74	212	32	58	8	2	11	30	20	33	.274	.336	.486	135	7	8	33	15	9	-1	.993	-5	O	0.1
1986	Mon-N	151	576	89	167	31	**13**	8	49	57	78	.290	.358	.431	117	13	14	90	36	15	2	.977	4	*O	1.5
1987	Mon-N	156	588	101	165	30	8	15	63	70	95	.281	.363	.435	107	10	7	99	33	10	4	.982	1	*O	0.7
1988	Mon-N	81	259	33	66	5	2	2	13	36	37	.255	.357	.313	90	-0	-2	31	12	10	-2	.994	-3	O	-1.0
	Chi-N	70	264	36	70	11	6	4	26	19	50	.265	.322	.398	101	2	0	35	10	4	1	.971	2	O	0.1
	Yr	151	523	69	136	16	8	6	39	55	87	.260	.340	.356	95	1	-2	66	22	14	-2	.982	-1	*O	-0.9
1989	*Chi-N	98	272	40	70	12	4	3	19	30	55	.257	.333	.364	92	0	-2	36	14	2	3	.965	-1	O	-0.3

YEAR	TM/L	G	AB	R	H	2B	3B	HR	RBI	BB	SO	AVG	OBP	SLG	PRO+	BR	/A	RC	SB	CS	SBR	FA	FR	POS	TPR
1990	Cle-A	128	437	58	110	20	6	12	55	20	61	.252	.289	.407	93	-6	-6	52	22	6	3	.991	9	*O/1D	0.4
1991	Cle-A	13	32	2	4	0	0	0	0	3	9	.125	.200	.125	-8	-5	-5	1	2	2	-1	1.000	-1	O	-0.6
	Pit-N	36	97	9	17	3	4	1	9	9	31	.175	.245	.320	59	-6	-6	7	0	0	0	.963	-2	O	-0.8
	LA-N	58	74	12	21	5	1	1	10	9	21	.284	.361	.419	122	2	2	12	0	1	-1	1.000	-8	O/1	-0.8
	Yr	94	171	21	38	8	5	2	19	18	52	.222	.296	.363	86	-4	-3	18	0	1	-1	.978	-10	O/1	-1.6
1992	LA-N	135	262	33	70	12	5	6	35	27	49	.267	.340	.420	116	5	5	40	11	5	0	.977	-12	O	-0.9
Total	10	1041	3107	456	825	139	52	63	313	302	527	.266	.335	.405	103	19	15	438	155	65	8	.981	-22	O/D1	-2.6
■ RAY WEBSTER Webster, Ramon Alberto b: 8/31/42, Colon, Panama BL/TL, 6', 185 lbs. Deb: 4/11/67																									
1967	KC-A	122	360	41	92	15	4	11	51	32	44	.256	.320	.411	118	6	7	46	5	3	-0	.989	-3	1O	-0.1
1968	Oak-A	66	196	17	42	11	1	3	23	12	24	.214	.260	.327	81	-6	-5	16	3	0	1	.988	-1	1	-1.0
1969	Oak-A	64	77	5	20	0	1	1	13	12	8	.260	.367	.325	99	-0	0	9	0	0	0	1.000	1	1	0.1
1970	SD-N	95	116	12	30	3	0	2	11	11	12	.259	.323	.336	80	-4	-3	13	1	1	-0	.981	-1	1/O	-0.5
1971	SD-N	10	8	0	1	0	0	0	0	2	1	.125	.300	.125	26	-1	-1	0	0	0	0	.000	0	H	-0.1
	Oak-A	7	5	0	0	0	0	0	0	0	2	.000	.000	.000	-99	-1	-1	0	0	0	0	1.000	0	/1	-0.1
	Chi-N	16	16	1	5	2	0	0	0	1	3	.313	.353	.438	107	0	0	3	0	0	0	1.000	0	/1	0.0
Total	5	380	778	76	190	31	6	17	98	70	94	.244	.309	.365	99	-5	-2	87	9	4	0	.989	-3	1/O	-1.7
■ RAY WEBSTER Webster, Raymond George b: 11/15/37, Grass Valley, Cal. BR/TR, 6', 175 lbs. Deb: 4/17/59																									
1959	Cle-A	40	74	10	15	2	1	2	10	5	7	.203	.253	.338	63	-4	-4	6	1	0	0	.929	0	2/3	-0.2
1960	Bos-A	7	3	1	0	0	0	0	1	1	0	.000	.250	.000	-25	-1	-1	0	0	0	0	1.000	1	/2	0.1
Total	2	47	77	11	15	2	1	2	11	6	7	.195	.253	.325	59	-5	-4	6	1	0	0	.931	2	/23	-0.1
■ PETE WECKBECKER Weckbecker, Peter b: 8/30/1864, Butler, Pa. d: 5/16/35, Hampton, Va. 5'7", 150 lbs. Deb: 10/05/1889																									
1889	Ind-N	1	1	0	0	0	0	0	2	0	0	.000	.000	.000	-98	-0	-0	0	0			1.000	0	/C	0.0
1890	*Lou-a	32	101	17	24	1	0	0		8		.238	.300	.248	65	-4	-4	10	7			.941	1	C	0.0
Total	2	33	102	17	24	1	0	0	2	8	0	.235	.297	.245	63	-5	-4	10	7			.941	1	/C	0.0
■ ERIC WEDGE Wedge, Eric Michael b: 1/27/68, Fort Wayne, Ind. BR/TR, 6'3", 215 lbs. Deb: 10/05/91																									
1991	Bos-A	1	1	0	1	0	0	0	0	0	0	1.000	1.000	1.000	434	0	0	1	0	0	0	.000	0	/D	0.0
1992	Bos-A	27	68	11	17	2	0	5	11	13	18	.250	.370	.500	135	4	3	14	0	0	0	1.000	-0	D/C	0.4
Total	2	28	69	11	18	2	0	5	11	13	18	.261	.378	.507	139	4	4	15	0	0	0		-0	/DC	0.4
■ BERT WEEDEN Weeden, Charles Albert b: 12/21/1882, Northwood, N.H. d: 1/7/39, Northwood, N.H. BL/TL, 6', 200 lbs. Deb: 6/04/11																									
1911	Bos-N	1	1	0	0	0	0	0	0	0	0	.000	.000	.000	-93	-0	-0	0	0			.000	0	H	0.0
■ JOHNNY WEEKLY Weekly, Johnny b: 6/14/37, Waterproof, La. d: 11/24/74, Walnut Creek, Cal. BR/TR, 6' ", 200 lbs. Deb: 4/13/62																									
1962	Hou-N	13	26	3	5	1	0	2	2	7	4	.192	.364	.462	129	1	1	5	0	0	0	1.000	-1	/O	0.0
1963	Hou-N	34	80	4	18	3	0	3	14	7	14	.225	.295	.375	98	-1	-0	9	0	0	0	1.000	1	O	-0.1
1964	Hou-N	6	15	0	2	0	0	0	3	1	3	.133	.188	.133	-8	-2	-2	0	0	0	0	1.000	1	/O	-0.1
Total	3	53	121	7	25	4	0	5	19	15	21	.207	.299	.364	92	-2	-1	14	0	0	0	1.000	0	/O	-0.2
■ JOHN WEHNER Wehner, John Paul b: 6/29/67, Pittsburgh, Pa. BR/TR, 6'3", 204 lbs. Deb: 7/17/91																									
1991	Pit-N	37	106	15	36	7	0	0	7	7	17	.340	.381	.406	123	3	3	18	3	0	1	.936	7	3	1.2
1992	*Pit-N	55	123	11	22	6	0	0	4	12	22	.179	.252	.228	37	-10	-10	7	3	0	1	.960	5	31/2	-0.5
Total	2	92	229	26	58	13	0	0	11	19	39	.253	.310	.310	77	-7	-7	25	6	0	2	.947	12	/312	0.7
■ STUMP WEIDMAN Weidman, George E. b: 2/17/1861, Rochester, N.Y. d: 3/2/05, New York, N.Y. BR/TR, Deb: 8/26/1880 U																									
1880	Buf-N	23	78	8	8	1	0	0	3	2	11	.103	.125	.115	-18	-9	-9	1				.893	-3	PO	-0.5
1881	Det-N	13	47	8	12	1	0	0	5	2	2	.255	.286	.277	75	-1	-1	4				1.000	-2	P	0.0
1882	Det-N	50	193	20	42	7	1	0	20	2	19	.218	.226	.264	57	-9	-9	12				.906	0	P/OS	0.0
1883	Det-N	79	313	34	58	6	1	1	24	4	38	.185	.196	.220	27	-27	-25	14				.909	-2	PO/2	-1.2
1884	Det-N	81	300	24	49	6	0	0	26	13	41	.163	.198	.183	22	-27	-24	11				.846	-2	OP/S2	-1.8
1885	Det-N	44	153	7	24	2	1	1	14	8	32	.157	.199	.203	30	-12	-12	6				.869	-5	P/O2	-0.3
1886	KC-N	51	179	13	30	2	0	0	7	5	46	.168	.190	.179	12	-18	-20	7	3			.936	3	P/O	-0.1
1887	Det-N	21	82	12	17	2	0	0	11	3	3	.207	.235	.232	30	-7	-8	6	6			.837	-1	P/O	-0.1
	NY-a	14	46	5	7	1	1	0		4		.152	.220	.217	25	-5	-4	3	2			.882	2	P/O	0.0
	NY-N	1	3	0	1	0	0	0	0	0	0	.333	.333	.333	92	-0	-0	0	0			.500	-0	/P	0.0
1888	NY-N	2	7	1	0	0	0	0	1	2	1	.000	.222	.000	-23	-1	-1	0	0			.714	-0	/P	0.0
Total	9	379	1401	132	248	28	4	2	111	45	193	.177	.203	.207	28	-116	-113	64	11			.885	-10	PO/2S	-4.0
■ RALPH WEIGEL Weigel, Ralph Richard "Wig" b: 10/2/21, Coldwater, Ohio d: 4/15/92, Memphis, Tenn. BR/TR, 6'1", 180 lbs. Deb: 9/18/46																									
1946	Cle-A	6	12	0	2	0	0	0	0	0	2	.167	.167	.167	-7	-2	-2	0	1	0	0	1.000	-1	/C	-0.3
1948	Chi-A	66	163	8	38	7	3	0	26	13	18	.233	.294	.313	64	-9	-9	14	1	2	-1	.969	-7	C/O	-1.4
1949	Was-A	34	60	4	14	2	0	0	4	8	6	.233	.324	.267	58	-4	-3	5	0	1	-1	.985	1	C	-0.3
Total	3	106	235	12	54	9	3	0	30	21	26	.230	.296	.294	59	-15	-14	20	2	3	-1	.976	-8	/CO	-2.0
■ PODGE WEIHE Weihe, John Garibaldi b: 11/13/1862, Cincinnati, Ohio d: 4/15/14, Cincinnati, Ohio BR/TR, 5'11", 175 lbs. Deb: 8/06/1883																									
1883	Cin-a	1	4	1	1	0	0	0		0		.250	.250	.250	58	-0	-0	0				1.000	0	/O	0.0
1884	Ind-a	63	256	29	65	13	2	4		9		.254	.279	.367	115	3	4	27				.860	-0	O/21	0.2
Total	2	64	260	30	66	13	2	4		9		.254	.279	.365	114	3	4	27				.864	0	/O21	0.2
■ DICK WEIK Weik, Richard Henry "Legs" b: 11/17/27, Waterloo, Iowa d: 4/21/91, Harvey, Ill. BR/TR, 6'3.5", 184 lbs. Deb: 9/08/48																									
1948	Was-A	3	4	1	3	0	1	0	0	0	0	.750	.750	1.250	439	2	2	4	0	0	0	1.000	-0	/P	0.0
1949	Was-A	28	28	3	5	0	0	0	2	1	8	.179	.207	.179	2	-4	-4	1	0	0	0	.964	1	P	0.0
1950	Was-A	14	13	0	2	0	0	0	0	0	3	.154	.154	.154	-22	-2	-2	0	0	0	0	1.000	-1	P	0.0
	Cle-A	11	5	0	1	1	0	0	0	0	4	.200	.200	.400	52	-0	-0	0	0	0	0	1.000	0	P	0.0
	Yr	25	18	0	3	1	0	0	0	0	7	.167	.167	.222	-1	-3	-3	1	0	0	0	1.000	-1	P	0.0
1953	Cle-A	1	0	1	0	0	0	0	0	0	0	—	—	—	—	0	0	0	0	0	0	.000	0	R	0.0
	Det-A	12	2	1	1	1	0	0	1	0	1	.500	.500	1.000	300	1	1	1	0	0	0	1.000	0	P	0.0
	Yr	13	2	2	1	1	0	0	1	0	1	.500	.500	1.000	301	1	1	1	0	0	0	1.000	0	P	0.0
1954	Det-A	9	1	0	0	0	0	0	0	0	0	.000	.000	.000	-99	-0	-0	0	0	0	0	.500	-1	/P	0.0
Total	5	78	53	6	12	2	1	0	3	1	16	.226	.241	.302	43	-5	-5	6	0	0	0	.958	0	/P	0.0
■ ELMER WEINGARTNER Weingartner, Elmer William "Dutch" b: 8/13/18, Cleveland, Ohio BR/TR, 5'11", 178 lbs. Deb: 4/19/45																									
1945	Cle-A	20	39	5	9	1	0	0	1	4	11	.231	.302	.256	66	-2	-2	3	0	0	0	.871	-3	S	-0.3
■ PHIL WEINTRAUB Weintraub, Philip "Mickey" b: 10/12/07, Chicago, Ill. d: 6/21/87, Palm Springs, Cal BL/TL, 6'1", 195 lbs. Deb: 9/05/33																									
1933	NY-N	8	15	3	3	0	0	1	1	3	2	.200	.333	.400	110	0	0	2	0			.667	-3	/O	-0.3
1934	NY-N	31	74	13	26	2	0	0	15	15	10	.351	.461	.378	130	4	4	15	0			.944	-4	O	0.0
1935	NY-N	64	112	18	27	3	3	1	6	17	13	.241	.341	.348	87	-2	-2	14	0			.975	-3	1/O	-0.6
1937	Cin-N	49	177	27	48	10	4	3	20	19	25	.271	.345	.424	113	2	3	25	1			.976	-3	O	-0.1
	NY-N	6	9	3	3	2	0	0	1	1	1	.333	.400	.556	155	1	1	2	0			1.000	-0	/O	0.0
	Yr	55	186	30	51	12	4	3	21	20	26	.274	.348	.430	115	3	4	27	1			.976	-3	O	-0.1
1938	Phi-N	100	351	51	109	23	2	4	45	64	43	.311	.422	.422	137	19	21	68	1			.988	2	1	1.2
1944	NY-N	104	361	55	114	18	9	13	77	59	59	.316	.412	.524	162	31	31	82	0			.992	3	1	2.9

YEAR	TM/L	G	AB	R	H	2B	3B	HR	RBI	BB	SO	AVG	OBP	SLG	PRO+	BR	/A	RC	SB	CS	SBR	FA	FR	POS	TPR
1945	NY-N	82	283	45	77	9	1	10	42	54	29	.272	.389	.417	122	11	10	48	2			.993	3	1	0.8
Total	7	444	1382	215	407	67	19	32	207	232	182	.295	.398	.440	133	66	68	256	4			.990	-4	1/O	3.9
■ AL WEIS	Weis, Albert John b: 4/2/38, Franklin Square, N.Y BB/TR, 6', 170 lbs. Deb: 9/15/62																								
1962	Chi-A	7	12	2	1	0	0	0	0	2	3	.083	.267	.083	-1	-2	-2	1	1	0	0	.882	-1	/S23	-0.2
1963	Chi-A	99	210	41	57	9	0	0	18	18	37	.271	.335	.314	85	-4	-4	26	15	1	4	.990	14	2S/3	1.9
1964	Chi-A	133	328	36	81	4	4	2	23	22	41	.247	.300	.302	70	-14	-13	32	22	7	2	.966	12	*2/SO	1.0
1965	Chi-A	103	135	29	40	4	3	1	12	12	22	.296	.362	.393	122	3	4	20	4	1	1	.975	25	2/S3O	3.4
1966	Chi-A	129	187	20	29	4	1	0	9	17	50	.155	.233	.187	24	-18	-17	8	3	5	-2	.987	**37**	2S	2.3
1967	Chi-A	50	53	9	13	2	0	0	4	1	7	.245	.273	.283	67	-2	-2	3	3	3	-1	.986	11	2S	1.0
1968	NY-N	90	274	15	47	6	0	1	14	21	63	.172	.236	.204	33	-22	-22	14	3	1	0	.958	7	S2/3	-1.0
1969	*NY-N	103	247	20	53	9	2	2	23	15	51	.215	.260	.291	53	-15	-16	19	3	3	-1	.960	13	S2/3	0.2
1970	NY-N	75	121	20	25	7	1	1	11	7	21	.207	.256	.306	50	-9	-9	8	1	1	-0	.952	2	2S	-0.4
1971	NY-N	11	11	3	0	0	0	0	1	2	4	.000	.154	.000	-54	-2	-2	0	0	0	0	1.000	1	/23	-0.2
Total	10	800	1578	195	346	45	11	7	115	117	299	.219	.279	.275	59	-86	-83	132	55	22	3	.975	121	2S/3O	8.0
■ BUTCH WEIS	Weis, Arthur John b: 3/2/03, St.Louis, Mo. BL/TL, 5'11", 180 lbs. Deb: 4/15/22																								
1922	Chi-N	2	2	2	1	0	0	0	0	0	0	.500	.500	.500	156	0	0	0	0	0	0	.000	0	H	0.0
1923	Chi-N	22	26	2	6	1	0	0	2	5	8	.231	.355	.269	67	-1	-1	3	0	1	-1	1.000	-1	/O	-0.3
1924	Chi-N	37	133	19	37	8	1	0	23	15	14	.278	.356	.353	90	-1	-1	17	4	5	-2	.978	6	O	0.0
1925	Chi-N	67	180	16	48	5	3	2	25	23	22	.267	.350	.361	81	-4	-5	23	2	4	-2	.964	-5	O	-1.3
Total	4	128	341	39	92	14	4	2	50	43	44	.270	.353	.352	84	-7	-7	43	6	10	-4	.973	0	/O	-1.6
■ BUD WEISER	Weiser, Harry Budson b: 1/8/1891, Shamokin, Pa. d: 7/31/61, Shamokin, Pa. BR/TR, 5'11", 165 lbs. Deb: 4/29/15																								
1915	Phi-N	37	64	6	9	2	0	0	8	7	12	.141	.236	.172	24	-6	-6	3	2	2	-1	.897	-5	O	-1.4
1916	Phi-N	4	10	1	3	1	0	0	1	0	3	.300	.300	.400	110	0	0	1	0			1.000	-1	/O	-0.1
Total	2	41	74	7	12	3	0	0	9	7	15	.162	.244	.203	36	-6	-6	5	2	2		.912	-6	/O	-1.5
■ GARY WEISS	Weiss, Gary Lee b: 12/27/55, Brenham, Tex. BB/TR, 5'10", 170 lbs. Deb: 9/13/80																								
1980	LA-N	8	0	2	0	0	0	0	0	0	0	—	—	—	—	0	0	0	0	0	0	.000	0	/R	0.0
1981	LA-N	14	19	2	2	0	0	0	1	1	4	.105	.150	.105	-28	-3	-3	0	0	0	0	.920	-1	S	-0.4
Total	2	22	19	4	2	0	0	0	1	1	4	.105	.150	.105	-28	-3	-3	0	0	0	0		-1	/S	-0.4
■ JOE WEISS	Weiss, Joseph Harold b: 1/27/1894, Chicago, Ill. d: 7/7/67, Cedar Rapids, Iowa BR/TR, 6', 165 lbs. Deb: 8/29/15																								
1915	Chi-F	29	85	6	19	1	2	0	11	3	24	.224	.250	.282	60	-5	-4	6	0			.992	-1	1	-0.6
■ WALT WEISS	Weiss, Walter William b: 11/28/63, Tuxedo, N.Y. BB/TR, 6', 175 lbs. Deb: 7/12/87																								
1987	Oak-A	16	26	3	12	4	0	0	1	2	2	.462	.500	.615	208	4	4	7	1	2	-1	.974	5	S/D	0.7
1988	*Oak-A	147	452	44	113	17	3	3	39	35	56	.250	.317	.321	82	-12	-10	47	4	4	-1	.979	10	*S	1.1
1989	*Oak-A	84	236	30	55	11	0	3	21	21	39	.233	.298	.318	76	-8	-7	23	6	1	1	.953	-14	S	-1.4
1990	*Oak-A	138	445	50	118	17	1	2	35	46	53	.265	.339	.321	89	-7	-5	51	9	3	1	.979	-26	*S	-1.9
1991	Oak-A	40	133	15	30	6	1	0	13	12	14	.226	.290	.286	63	-7	-6	12	6	0	2	.970	-10	S	-1.2
1992	*Oak-A	103	316	36	67	5	2	0	21	43	39	.212	.308	.241	58	-17	-16	26	6	3	0	.956	-16	*S	-2.5
Total	6	528	1608	178	395	60	7	8	130	159	203	.246	.319	.307	79	-48	-40	167	32	13	2	.970	-51	S/D	-5.2
■ JOHNNY WELAJ	Welaj, John Ludwig b: 5/27/14, Moss Creek, Pa. BR/TR, 6', 164 lbs. Deb: 5/02/39																								
1939	Was-A	63	201	23	55	11	2	1	33	13	20	.274	.318	.363	80	-8	-6	25	13	2	3	.975	-4	O	-0.8
1940	Was-A	88	215	31	55	9	0	3	21	19	20	.256	.322	.340	77	-9	-7	23	8	7	-2	.978	-1	O	-1.1
1941	Was-A	49	96	16	20	4	0	0	5	6	16	.208	.255	.250	36	-9	-9	6	3	1	0	.979	-0	O	-0.9
1943	Phi-A	93	281	45	68	16	1	0	15	15	17	.242	.280	.306	72	-11	-11	24	12	5	1	.960	0	O	-1.5
Total	4	293	793	115	198	40	3	4	74	53	73	.250	.298	.323	71	-37	-32	79	36	15	2	.970	-5	O	-4.3
■ CURT WELCH	Welch, Curtis Benton b: 2/11/1862, E.Liverpool, Ohio d: 8/29/1896, E.Liverpool, Ohio BR/TR, 5'10", 175 lbs. Deb: 5/01/1884																								
1884	Tol-a	109	425	61	95	24	5	0		10		.224	.248	.304	79	-8	-11	33				.888	16	*O/2C1	0.3
1885	*StL-a	112	432	84	117	18	8	3		23		.271	.318	.370	114	10	7	52				**.946**	14	*O	1.6
1886	*StL-a	138	563	114	158	31	13	2		29		.281	.332	.393	123	17	13	95	59			**.952**	14	*O/2	2.1
1887	*StL-a	131	544	98	151	32	7	3		25		.278	.322	.379	88	-3	-13	97	89			.941	19	*O/21	0.3
1888	Phi-a	136	549	125	155	22	8	1	61	33		.282	.355	.357	133	21	22	106	95			.952	4	*O/2	2.1
1889	Phi-a	125	516	134	140	**39**	6	0	39	67	30	.271	.375	.370	116	13	14	99	66			.923	8	*O	1.6
1890	Phi-a	103	396	100	106	21	4	2		49		.268	.392	.356	126	15	17	82	64			.919	14	*O/P	2.4
	Bal-a	19	68	16	9	4	0	0		9		.132	.253	.191	31	-5	-6	5	8			.974	2	O/1	-0.4
	Yr	122	464	116	115	25	4	2		58		.248	.372	.332	112	10	11	86	72			.926	16	*O/1P	2.0
1891	Bal-a	132	514	122	138	22	10	3	55	77	42	.268	.400	.368	122	21	20	98	50			.946	19	*O2/S	3.1
1892	Bal-N	63	237	42	56	1	3	1	22	36	9	.236	.363	.278	94	2	1	30	14			.905	-4	O	-0.6
	Cin-N	25	94	14	19	0	2	1	7	7	8	.202	.299	.277	77	-2	-2	10	7			.925	-0	O	-0.3
	Yr	88	331	56	75	1	5	2	29	43	17	.227	.345	.278	89	-1	-2	40	21			.911	-4	O	-0.9
1893	Lou-N	14	47	5	8	1	0	0	2	16	4	.170	.400	.191	66	-1	-0	4	1			.912	-0	O	-0.1
Total	10	1107	4385	915	1152	215	66	16	186	381	93	.263	.345	.353	110	79	61	712	453			.933	107	*O/21SCP	12.1
■ FRANK WELCH	Welch, Frank Tiguer "Bugger" b: 8/10/1897, Birmingham, Ala. d: 7/25/57, Birmingham, Ala. BR/TR, 5'9", 175 lbs. Deb: 9/09/19																								
1919	Phi-A	15	54	5	9	1	1	2	7	7	10	.167	.262	.333	66	-3	-3	5	0			.909	0	O	-0.4
1920	Phi-A	100	360	43	93	17	5	4	40	26	41	.258	.312	.367	78	-12	-12	39	2	9	-5	.937	-6	O	-2.9
1921	Phi-A	115	403	48	115	18	6	7	45	34	43	.285	.347	.412	92	-5	-5	60	6	0	2	.943	3	*O	-0.8
1922	Phi-A	114	375	43	97	17	3	11	49	40	40	.259	.335	.408	90	-5	-6	52	3	4	-2	.949	-0	*O	-1.5
1923	Phi-A	125	421	56	125	19	9	4	55	48	40	.297	.374	.413	106	5	4	67	1	4	-2	.967	3	*O	-0.2
1924	Phi-A	94	293	47	85	13	2	5	31	35	27	.290	.372	.399	98	-0	-1	45	2	3	-1	.985	1	O	-0.5
1925	Phi-A	85	202	40	56	5	4	4	41	29	14	.277	.373	.401	90	-1	-3	33	2	1	0	.968	-3	O	-0.8
1926	Phi-A	75	174	26	49	8	1	4	23	26	9	.282	.381	.408	100	2	1	28	2	5	-2	.975	-5	O	-1.0
1927	Bos-A	15	28	2	5	2	0	0	4	5	1	.179	.303	.250	46	-2	-2	2	0	2	-1	1.000	2	/O	-0.2
Total	9	738	2310	310	634	100	31	41	295	250	225	.274	.350	.398	92	-20	-27	330	18	28		.955	-5	O	-8.3
■ HERB WELCH	Welch, Herbert M. "Dutch" b: 10/19/1898, RoEllen, Tenn. d: 4/13/67, Memphis, Tenn. BL/TR, 5'6", 154 lbs. Deb: 9/15/25																								
1925	Bos-A	13	38	2	11	0	1	0	2	0	6	.289	.289	.342	60	-2	-2	4	0	0	0	.893	5	S	0.4
■ TUB WELCH	Welch, James T. b: 7/3/1866, St.Louis, Mo. TR, 5'11", 230 lbs. Deb: 6/12/1890																								
1890	Tol-a	35	108	15	31	3	1	1		8		.287	.358	.361	112	2	2	17	7			.930	0	C1	0.3
1895	Lou-N	47	153	18	37	4	1	1	8	13	7	.242	.310	.301	63	-9	-7	15	2			.888	-1	C1	-0.4
Total	2	82	261	33	68	7	2	2	8	21	7	.261	.330	.326	83	-7	-6	32	9			.911	-1	/C1	-0.1
■ MILT WELCH	Welch, Milton Edward b: 7/26/24, Farmersville, Ill BR/TR, 5'10", 175 lbs. Deb: 6/05/45																								
1945	Det-A	1	2	0	0	0	0	0	0	0	1	.000	.000	.000	-94	-1	-1	0	0	0	0	1.000	1	/C	0.0
■ HARRY WELCHONCE	Welchonce, Harry Monroe "Welch" b: 11/20/1883, North Point, Pa. d: 2/26/77, Arcadia, Cal. BL/TR, 6', 170 lbs. Deb: 4/17/11																								
1911	Phi-N	26	66	9	14	4	0	0	6	7	8	.212	.288	.273	56	-4	-4	5	0			.929	-3	O	-0.8

YEAR	TM/L	G	AB	R	H	2B	3B	HR	RBI	BB	SO	AVG	OBP	SLG	PRO+	BR	/A	RC	SB	CS	SBR	FA	FR	POS	TPR

■ MIKE WELDAY   Welday, Lyndon Earl   b: 12/19/1879, Conway, Iowa   d: 5/28/42, Leavenworth, Kan.   BL/TL,   Deb: 4/21/07

1907	Chi-A	24	35	2	8	1	1	0	0	0	6	.229	.341	.314	113	1	1	4	0			.938	-3	O	-0.2
1909	Chi-A	29	74	3	14	0	0	0	5	4		.189	.231	.189	34	-6	-5	4	2			.886	1	O	-0.6
Total	2	53	109	5	22	1	1	0	5	10		.202	.269	.229	60	-5	-4	8	2			.900	-2	/O	-0.8

■ OLLIE WELF   Welf, Oliver Henry   b: 1/17/1889, Cleveland, Ohio   d: 6/15/67, Cleveland, Ohio   BR/TL, 5'9", 160 lbs.   Deb: 8/30/16

| 1916 | Cle-A | 1 | 0 | 0 | 0 | 0 | 0 | 0 | 0 | 0 | 0 | — | — | — | — | 0 | 0 | 0 | 0 | | | .000 | 0 | R | 0.0 |

■ BRAD WELLMAN   Wellman, Brad Eugene   b: 8/17/59, Lodi, Cal.   BR/TR, 6', 170 lbs.   Deb: 9/04/82

1982	SF-N	6	4	1	1	0	0	0	0	1		.250	.250	.250	40	-0	-0	0	0	0	0	1.000	0	/2	0.0
1983	SF-N	82	182	15	39	3	0	1	16	22	39	.214	.299	.247	55	-11	-10	14	5	3	-0	.965	2	2/S	-0.7
1984	SF-N	93	265	23	60	9	1	2	25	19	41	.226	.278	.291	62	-14	-13	21	10	5	0	.977	16	2S/3	0.7
1985	SF-N	71	174	16	41	11	1	0	16	4	33	.236	.269	.310	65	-9	-8	14	5	2	0	.983	-2	23/S	-1.0
1986	SF-N	12	13	0	2	0	0	0	1	1	2	.154	.214	.154	3	-2	-2	0	0	0	0	1.000	-0	/S23	-0.2
1987	LA-N	3	4	1	1	0	0	0	1	0	1	.250	.250	.250	34	-0	-0	0	0	0	0	1.000	1	/2S3	0.1
1988	KC-A	71	107	11	29	3	0	1	6	6	23	.271	.322	.327	81	-2	-3	11	1	2	-1	.972	15	2S/3D	1.3
1989	KC-A	103	178	30	41	4	0	2	12	7	36	.230	.283	.287	55	-11	-11	12	5	3	-0	.995	19	2S/3D	1.1
Total	8	441	927	97	214	30	2	6	77	59	176	.231	.282	.287	61	-50	-47	73	26	15	-1	.978	50	2/S3D	1.3

■ BOB WELLMAN   Wellman, Robert Joseph   b: 7/15/25, Norwood, Ohio   BR/TR, 6'4", 210 lbs.   Deb: 9/23/48

1948	Phi-A	4	10	1	2	0	1	0	3	2		.200	.385	.400	109	-0	0	2	0	0	0	1.000	0	/1O	0.0
1950	Phi-A	11	15	1	5	0	0	1	1	0	3	.333	.333	.533	121	0	0	3	0	0	0	1.000	-0	/O	0.0
Total	2	15	25	2	7	0	1	1	1	3	5	.280	.357	.480	117	0	1	5	0	0	0	.889	0	/O1	0.0

■ GREG WELLS   Wells, Gregory De Wayne   b: 4/25/54, McIntosh, Ala.   BR/TR, 6'5", 218 lbs.   Deb: 8/10/81

1981	Tor-A	32	73	7	18	5	0	0	5	5	12	.247	.295	.315	71	-2	-3	6	0	2	-1	.994	-0	1/D	-0.5
1982	Min-A	15	54	5	11	1	2	0	3	1	8	.204	.218	.296	39	-5	-5	4	0	0	0	.962	-2	1/D	-0.8
Total	2	47	127	12	29	6	2	0	8	6	20	.228	.263	.307	58	-7	-8	10	0	2	-1	.983	-2	1/D	-1.3

■ JAKE WELLS   Wells, Jacob   b: 8/9/1863, Memphis, Tenn.   d: 3/16/27, Hendersonville, N.C.   BR/TR,   Deb: 8/10/1888

1888	Det-N	16	57	5	9	1	0	0		0	5	.158	.158	.175	7	-6	-6	2	0			.917	5	C	0.0
1890	StL-a	30	105	17	25	3	0	0		10		.238	.333	.267	70	-2	-5	10	1			.941	2	C/O	0.0
Total	2	46	162	22	34	4	0	0	2	10	5	.210	.277	.235	52	-8	-10	12	1			.932	6	/CO	0.0

■ LEO WELLS   Wells, Leo Donald   b: 7/18/17, Kansas City, Kan.   BR/TR, 5'9", 170 lbs.   Deb: 4/16/42

1942	Chi-A	35	62	8	12	2	0	1	4	4	5	.194	.242	.274	46	-5	-5	4	1	0	0	1.000	11	S/3	0.7
1946	Chi-A	45	127	11	24	4	1	1	11	12	34	.189	.259	.260	47	-9	-9	8	3	4	-2	.942	8	3/S	-0.2
Total	2	80	189	19	36	6	1	2	15	16	39	.190	.254	.265	47	-14	-13	13	4	4	-1	.938	19	/3S	0.5

■ JIMMY WELSH   Welsh, James Daniel   b: 10/9/02, Denver, Colo.   d: 10/30/70, Oakland, Cal.   BL/TR, 6'1", 174 lbs.   Deb: 4/14/25

1925	Bos-N	122	484	69	151	25	8	7	63	20	24	.312	.350	.440	110	-0	5	74	7	4	-0	.960	6	*O/2	0.4
1926	Bos-N	134	490	69	136	18	11	3	57	33	28	.278	.333	.378	100	-6	-0	62	6			.965	10	*O	0.0
1927	Bos-N	131	497	72	143	26	7	9	54	23	27	.288	.330	.423	109	-1	4	67	11			.969	13	*O/1	0.9
1928	NY-N	124	476	77	146	22	5	9	54	29	30	.307	.357	.431	104	3	3	71	4			.981	-0	*O	-0.5
1929	NY-N	38	129	25	32	7	0	2	8	9	3	.248	.331	.349	69	-6	-6	15	3			.940	-6	O	-1.4
	Bos-N	53	186	24	54	8	7	2	16	13	9	.290	.350	.441	98	-2	-1	28	1			.979	9	O	0.4
	Yr	91	315	49	86	15	7	4	24	22	12	.273	.342	.403	86	-8	-7	43	4			.970	2	O	-1.0
1930	Bos-N	113	422	51	116	21	9	3	36	29	23	.275	.327	.389	75	-19	-17	53	5			.980	11	*O	-1.2
Total	6	715	2684	387	778	127	47	35	288	156	144	.290	.340	.411	98	-33	-12	370	37	4		.971	42	O/21	-1.4

■ LEW WENDELL   Wendell, Lewis Charles   b: 3/22/1892, New York, N.Y.   d: 7/11/53, Brooklyn, N.Y.   BR/TR, 5'11", 178 lbs.   Deb: 6/10/15

1915	NY-N	20	36	0	8	1	1	0	5	2	7	.222	.263	.306	76	-1	-1	3	0			.920	-5	C	-0.6
1916	NY-N	2	2	0	0	0	0	0	0	0	2	.000	.000	.000	-99	-0	-0	0	0			.000	0	H	-0.1
1924	Phi-N	21	32	3	8	1	0	0	2	3	5	.250	.314	.281	54	-2	-2	3	0	0	0	1.000	-1	C	-0.3
1925	Phi-N	18	26	0	2	0	0	0	3	1	3	.077	.111	.077	-47	-6	-6	0	0	0	0	.909	-1	/C	-0.6
1926	Phi-N	1	4	0	0	0	0	0	0	0	0	.000	.000	.000	-95	-1	-1	0	0			.333	-1	/C	-0.2
Total	5	62	100	3	18	2	1	0	10	6	17	.180	.226	.220	23	-10	-11	6	0	0		.925	-8	/C	-1.8

■ JACK WENTZ   Wentz, John George (b: John George Wernz)   b: 3/4/1863, Louisville, Ky.   d: 9/14/07, Louisville, Ky.   BR/TR, 5'10.5", 175 lbs.   Deb: 4/15/1891

| 1891 | Lou-a | 1 | 4 | 0 | 1 | 0 | 0 | 0 | 0 | 0 | 0 | .250 | .250 | .250 | 46 | -0 | -0 | 0 | 0 | | | .667 | -1 | /2 | -0.1 |

■ STAN WENTZEL   Wentzel, Stanley Aaron   b: 1/13/17, Lorane, Pa.   BR/TR, 6'1", 200 lbs.   Deb: 9/23/45

| 1945 | Bos-N | 4 | 19 | 3 | 4 | 0 | 1 | 0 | 6 | 0 | 3 | .211 | .211 | .316 | 45 | -1 | -2 | 1 | 1 | | | 1.000 | -1 | /O | -0.3 |

■ JULIE WERA   Wera, Julian Valentine   b: 2/9/02, Winona, Minn.   d: 12/12/75, Rochester, Minn.   BR/TR, 5'8", 164 lbs.   Deb: 4/14/27

1927	NY-A	38	42	7	10	3	0	1	8	1	5	.238	.273	.381	70	-2	-2	4	0	0	0	1.000	3	3	0.1
1929	NY-A	5	12	1	5	0	0	0	2	1	1	.417	.462	.417	137	1	1	2	0	0	0	1.000	-1	/3	0.0
Total	2	43	54	8	15	3	0	1	10	2	6	.278	.316	.389	85	-2	-1	7	0	0	0	1.000	2	/3	0.1

■ BILLY WERBER   Werber, William Murray   b: 6/20/08, Berwyn, Md.   BR/TR, 5'10", 170 lbs.   Deb: 6/25/30

1930	NY-A	4	14	5	4	0	0	0	2	3	1	.286	.412	.286	84	-0	-0	2	0	0	0	.955	1	/S3	0.1
1933	NY-A	3	2	0	0	0	0	0	0	0	0	.000	.000	.000	-99	-1	-1	0	0	0	0	.000	0	/3	-0.1
	Bos-A	108	425	64	110	30	6	3	39	33	39	.259	.312	.379	83	-12	-11	52	15	5	2	.910	-17	S3/2	-1.8
	Yr	111	427	64	110	30	6	3	39	33	39	.258	.311	.377	82	-12	-12	52	15	5	2	.910	-17	S3/2	-1.9
1934	Bos-A	152	623	129	200	41	10	11	67	77	37	.321	.397	.472	115	22	16	121	40	15	3	.941	20	*3S	4.2
1935	Bos-A	124	462	84	118	30	3	14	61	69	41	.255	.357	.424	95	1	-4	76	29	7	5	.942	17	*3	2.1
1936	Bos-A	145	535	89	147	29	6	10	67	89	37	.275	.382	.407	90	-2	-8	89	23	13	-1	.935	-12	*3O/2	-1.7
1937	Phi-A	128	493	85	144	31	4	7	70	74	39	.292	.386	.414	103	3	4	84	35	13	2	.958	0	*3/O	1.0
1938	Phi-A	134	499	92	129	22	7	11	69	93	37	.259	.377	.397	96	-3	-1	79	19	15	-3	.935	13	*3	-0.2
1939	*Cin-N	147	599	115	173	35	5	5	57	91	46	.289	.388	.390	109	12	11	96	15			.933	13	*3	2.5
1940	*Cin-N	143	584	105	162	35	5	12	48	68	40	.277	.361	.416	113	12	11	92	16			.962	3	*3	1.7
1941	Cin-N	109	418	56	100	9	2	4	46	53	24	.239	.328	.299	77	-11	-11	43	14			.959	13	*3	0.4
1942	NY-N	98	370	51	76	9	2	1	51	52	22	.205	.308	.249	64	-15	-15	30	9			.927	10	3	-0.4
Total	11	1295	5024	875	1363	271	50	78	539	701	363	.271	.364	.392	97	5	-9	765	215	68		.944	49	*3/SO2	7.8

■ PERRY WERDEN   Werden, Percival Wheritt   b: 7/21/1865, St.Louis, Mo.   d: 1/9/34, Minneapolis, Minn.   BR/TR, 6'2", 220 lbs.   Deb: 4/24/1884

1884	StL-U	18	76	7	18	2	0	0		2		.237	.256	.263	73	-2	-2	5				.893	-1	P/O	-0.2
1888	Was-N	3	10	0	3	0	0	0	2	1	4	.300	.364	.300	123	0	0	1	0			.857	-0	/O	0.0
1890	Tol-a	128	498	113	147	22	20	6			78	.295	.404	.456	152	37	35	118	59			.972	6	*1/O	3.0
1891	Bal-a	139	552	102	160	20	18	6	104	52	59	.290	.348	.424	126	19	18	104	46			.980	1	*1	1.1
1892	StL-N	149	598	73	154	22	6	3	84	59	52	.258	.328	.355	114	6	10	78	20			.982	12	*1	1.4
1893	StL-N	125	500	73	138	22	29	1	94	49	25	.276	.349	.442	111	6	6	83	11			.968	3	*1/O	0.5
1897	Lou-N	131	506	76	153	21	14	5	83	40		.302	.366	.429	113	6	9	87	14			.984	18	*1	2.3
Total	7	693	2740	444	773	109	87	26	367	281	140	.282	.359	.414	122	73	76	477	150			.978	38	1/PO	8.1

YEAR	TM/L	G	AB	R	H	2B	3B	HR	RBI	BB	SO	AVG	OBP	SLG	PRO+	BR	/A	RC	SB	CS	SBR	FA	FR	POS	TPR
■ JOHNNY WERHAS Werhas, John Charles "Peaches" b: 2/7/38, Highland Park, Mich. BR/TR, 6'2", 200 lbs. Deb: 4/14/64																									
1964	LA-N	29	83	6	16	2	1	0	8	13	12	.193	.302	.241	59	-5	-4	6	0	0	0	.952	4	3	0.0
1965	LA-N	4	3	1	0	0	0	0	0	1	2	.000	.250	.000	-24	-0	-0	0	0	0	0	1.000	-0	/1	-0.1
1967	LA-N	7	7	0	1	0	0	0	0	0	3	.143	.143	.143	-20	-1	-1	0	0	0	0	.000	0	H	-0.1
	Cal-A	49	75	8	12	1	1	2	6	10	22	.160	.267	.280	64	-3	-3	5	0	0	0	.963	1	3/1O	-0.3
Total	3	89	168	15	29	3	2	2	14	24	39	.173	.280	.250	57	-10	-8	12	0	0	0	.956	4	/31O	-0.5
■ DON WERNER Werner, Donald Paul b: 3/8/53, Appleton, Wis. BR/TR, 6'1", 185 lbs. Deb: 9/02/75																									
1975	Cin-N	7	8	0	1	0	0	0	0	0	0	.125	.222	.125	-2	-1	-1	0	0	0	0	.923	0	/C	-0.1
1976	Cin-N	3	4	0	2	1	0	0	1	1	1	.500	.600	.750	275	1	1	2	0	0	0	1.000	1	/C	0.2
1977	Cin-N	10	23	3	4	0	0	2	4	2	3	.174	.240	.435	75	-1	-1	2	0	1	-1	1.000	1	C	0.0
1978	Cin-N	50	113	7	17	2	1	0	11	14	30	.150	.250	.186	23	-11	-11	6	1	0	0	.987	5	C	-0.6
1980	Cin-N	24	64	2	11	2	0	0	5	7	10	.172	.264	.203	32	-6	-6	4	1	0	0	.962	1	C	-0.4
1981	Tex-A	2	8	1	2	0	0	0	0	0	2	.250	.250	.250	47	-1	-1	0	0	1	-1	.000	0	/D	-0.1
1982	Tex-A	22	59	4	12	2	0	0	3	3	7	.203	.242	.237	34	-5	-5	4	0	0	0	.980	1	C	-0.3
Total	7	118	279	17	49	7	1	2	24	27	53	.176	.256	.229	36	-24	-24	18	2	2	-1	.979	9	C/D	-1.3
■ JOE WERRICK Werrick, Joseph Abraham b: 10/25/1861, St.Paul, Minn. d: 5/10/43, St.Peter, Minn. BR/TR, 5'9", 151 lbs. Deb: 9/27/1884																									
1884	StP-U	9	27	3	2	0	0	0		1		.074	.107	.074	-70	-4	-2	0				.756	-0	/S	-0.2
1886	Lou-a	136	561	75	140	20	14	3		33		.250	.294	.351	98	1	-4	65	19			.853	-1	*3	-0.2
1887	Lou-a	136	533	90	152	21	13	7		38		.285	.336	.413	108	6	4	93	49			.831	-0	*3	0.5
1888	Lou-a	111	413	49	89	12	7	0	51	30		.215	.274	.278	81	-9	-7	36	15			.811	-13	3S/2O	-1.7
Total	4	392	1534	217	383	53	34	10	51	102		.250	.300	.348	96	-5	-9	194	83			.834	-14	3/S2O	-1.6
■ DON WERT Wert, Donald Ralph b: 7/29/38, Strasburg, Pa. BR/TR, 5'9", 165 lbs. Deb: 5/11/63																									
1963	Det-A	78	251	31	65	6	2	7	25	24	51	.259	.329	.382	95	-0	-1	31	3	3	-1	.957	3	32/S	0.4
1964	Det-A	148	525	63	135	18	5	9	55	50	74	.257	.329	.362	91	-5	-6	63	3	4	-2	.965	0	*3/S	-0.9
1965	Det-A	162	609	81	159	22	2	12	54	73	71	.261	.343	.363	100	2	1	76	5	6	-2	**.976**	5	*3/S2	0.0
1966	Det-A	150	559	56	150	20	2	11	70	64	69	.268	.346	.370	103	5	4	71	6	3	0	.972	-18	*3	-1.9
1967	Det-A	142	534	60	137	23	2	6	40	44	59	.257	.321	.341	93	-2	-4	58	1	1	-0	.978	-5	*3/S	-1.1
1968	*Det-A★	150	536	44	107	15	1	12	37	37	79	.200	.258	.299	66	-21	-23	40	0	3	-2	.966	-6	*3/S	-3.6
1969	Det-A	132	423	46	95	11	1	14	50	49	60	.225	.307	.355	81	-9	-11	45	3	1	0	.966	-0	*3	-1.2
1970	Det-A	128	363	34	79	13	0	6	33	44	56	.218	.309	.303	69	-14	-15	33	1	3	-2	.953	-2	*3/2	-2.0
1971	Was-A	20	40	2	2	1	0	0	2	4	10	.050	.156	.075	-35	-7	-7	0	0	0	0	1.000	-4	/S32	-1.1
Total	9	1110	3840	417	929	129	15	77	366	389	529	.242	.317	.343	87	-52	-62	417	22	24	-8	.968	-27	*3/S2	-11.4
■ DENNIS WERTH Werth, Dennis Dean b: 12/29/52, Lincoln, Ill. BR/TR, 6'1", 200 lbs. Deb: 9/17/79																									
1979	NY-A	3	4	1	1	0	0	0	0	0	0	.250	.250	.250	36	-0	-0	0	0	0	0	1.000	0	/1	0.0
1980	NY-A	39	65	15	20	3	0	3	12	12	19	.308	.416	.492	150	5	5	13	0	1	-1	1.000	-2	1/OC3D	0.2
1981	NY-A	34	55	7	6	1	0	0	1	12	12	.109	.269	.127	18	-5	-5	2	1	0	0	1.000	0	1/OCD	-0.6
1982	KC-A	41	15	5	2	0	0	0	2	4	2	.133	.316	.133	29	-1	-1	1	0	0	0	.990	2	1/C	0.1
Total	4	117	139	28	29	4	0	3	15	28	33	.209	.341	.302	82	-2	-2	16	1	1	-0	.996	1	/1ODC3	-0.3
■ DEL WERTZ Wertz, Dwight Lyman Moody b: 10/11/1888, Canton, Ohio d: 5/26/58, Sarasota, Fla. BR/TR, 5'10", 160 lbs. Deb: 5/23/14																									
1914	Buf-F	3	0	1	0	0	0	0	0	0	0	—	—	—	—	0	0	0	0			1.000	1	/S	0.1
■ VIC WERTZ Wertz, Victor Woodrow b: 2/9/25, York, Pa. d: 7/7/83, Detroit, Mich. BL/TR, 6', 186 lbs. Deb: 4/15/47																									
1947	Det-A	102	333	60	96	22	4	6	44	47	66	.288	.376	.432	121	11	10	56	2	0	1	.965	-2	O	0.4
1948	Det-A	119	391	49	97	19	9	7	67	48	70	.248	.335	.396	92	-4	-6	56	0	0	0	.954	1	O	-1.0
1949	Det-A★	155	608	96	185	26	6	20	133	80	61	.304	.385	.465	124	20	20	110	2	3	-1	.981	2	*O	1.3
1950	Det-A	149	559	99	172	37	4	27	123	91	55	.308	.408	.533	135	33	31	128	0	1	-1	.967	-8	*O	1.4
1951	Det-A★	138	501	86	143	24	4	27	94	78	61	.285	.383	.511	139	28	27	101	0	3	-2	.989	3	*O	2.3
1952	Det-A☆	85	285	46	70	15	3	17	51	46	44	.246	.352	.498	134	13	12	53	1	0	0	.986	3	O	1.3
	StL-A	37	130	22	45	5	0	6	19	23	20	.346	.444	.523	164	13	12	33	0	0	0	.955	-3	O	0.9
	Yr	122	415	68	115	20	3	23	70	69	64	.277	.381	.506	143	25	25	85	1	0	0	.976	0	*O	2.2
1953	StL-A	128	440	61	118	18	6	19	70	72	44	.268	.376	.466	124	17	16	79	1	4	-2	.974	7	*O	1.6
1954	Bal-A	29	94	5	19	1	0	1	13	11	17	.202	.286	.245	50	-7	-6	7	0	0	0	.963	2	O	-0.5
	*Cle-A	94	295	33	81	14	2	14	48	34	40	.275	.350	.478	123	9	8	50	0	2	-1	.989	2	1/O	0.5
	Yr	123	389	38	100	15	2	15	61	45	57	.257	.334	.422	106	2	2	56	0	2	-1	.989	4	1O	0.0
1955	Cle-A	74	257	30	65	11	2	14	55	32	33	.253	.338	.475	112	5	4	41	1	1	-0	.984	-3	1/O	-0.4
1956	Cle-A	136	481	65	127	22	0	32	106	75	87	.264	.369	.509	127	20	18	93	0	0	0	.991	1	*1	1.0
1957	Cle-A★	144	515	84	145	21	0	28	105	78	88	.282	.378	.485	136	25	26	97	2	3	-1	.988	-2	*1	1.5
1958	Cle-A	25	43	5	12	1	0	3	12	5	7	.279	.354	.512	139	2	2	7	0	0	0	.980	0	/1	0.2
1959	Bos-A	94	247	38	68	13	0	7	49	22	32	.275	.339	.413	101	2	0	34	0	0	0	.992	2	1	-0.2
1960	Bos-A	131	443	45	125	22	0	19	103	37	54	.282	.339	.460	110	7	6	66	0	2	-1	.987	3	*1	-0.1
1961	Bos-A	99	317	33	83	16	2	11	60	38	43	.262	.345	.429	103	2	1	46	0	0	0	.991	3	1	-0.2
	Det-A	8	6	0	1	0	0	0	1	0	1	.167	.167	.167	-10	-1	-1	0	0	0	0	.000	0	H	-0.1
	Yr	107	323	33	84	16	2	11	61	38	44	.260	.342	.424	101	1	0	46	0	0	0	.991	3	1	-0.3
1962	Det-A	74	105	7	34	2	0	5	18	5	13	.324	.360	.486	121	3	3	18	0	0	0	.988	0	1	0.2
1963	Det-A	6	5	0	0	0	0	0	0	0	1	.000	.000	.000	-97	-1	-1	0	0	0	0	.000	0	H	-0.1
	Min-A	35	44	3	6	0	0	3	7	6	5	.136	.240	.341	59	-2	-3	4	0	0	0	1.000	1	/1	-0.2
	Yr	41	49	3	6	0	0	3	7	6	6	.122	.218	.306	44	-4	-4	3	0	0	0	1.000	1	/1	-0.3
Total	17	1862	6099	867	1692	289	42	266	1178	828	842	.277	.366	.469	121	195	180	1079	9	19	-9	.973	12	O1	9.8
■ JIM WESSINGER Wessinger, James Michael b: 9/25/55, Utica, N.Y. BR/TR, 5'10", 165 lbs. Deb: 8/04/79																									
1979	Atl-N	10	7	2	0	0	0	0	0	1	4	.000	.125	.000	-59	-2	-2	0	0	0	0	.833	1	/2	-0.1
■ MAX WEST West, Max Edward b: 11/28/16, Dexter, Mo. BL/TR, 6'1.5", 182 lbs. Deb: 4/19/38																									
1938	Bos-N	123	418	47	98	16	5	10	63	38	38	.234	.300	.368	92	-11	-5	46	5			.986	-9	*O/1	-1.8
1939	Bos-N	130	449	67	128	26	6	19	82	51	55	.285	.364	.497	139	18	22	82	1			.974	-7	*O	1.1
1940	Bos-N★	139	524	72	137	27	5	7	72	65	54	.261	.344	.372	103	-1	3	72	2			.975	1	*O1	-0.5
1941	Bos-N	138	484	63	134	28	4	12	68	72	68	.277	.373	.426	130	17	20	80	5			.981	6	*O	1.8
1942	Bos-N	134	452	54	115	22	0	16	56	68	59	.254	.354	.409	126	14	15	71	4			.991	-1	1O	0.7
1946	Bos-N	1	1	0	0	0	0	0	0	0	1	.000	.000	.000	-99	-0	-0	0	0			1.000	-0	/1	0.0
	Cin-N	72	202	16	43	13	0	5	18	32	36	.213	.323	.351	95	-2	-1	24	1			.952	-1	O	-0.5
	Yr	73	203	16	43	13	0	5	18	32	37	.212	.322	.350	94	-2	-1	24	1			.952	-1	O/1	-0.5
1948	Pit-N	87	146	19	26	4	0	8	21	27	29	.178	.310	.370	82	-3	-4	18	1			.991	-4	1O	-0.8
Total	7	824	2676	338	681	136	20	77	380	353	340	.254	.344	.407	114	31	49	392	19			.975	-15	O1	-0.0
■ BUCK WEST West, Milton Douglas b: 8/29/1860, Spring Mill, Ohio d: 1/13/29, Mansfield, Ohio BL/TR, 5'10", 200 lbs. Deb: 8/24/1884																									
1884	Cin-a	33	131	20	32	2	8	1		2		.244	.256	.405	109	2	1	14				.825	-6	O	-0.5
1890	Cle-N	37	151	20	37	6	1	2	29	7	11	.245	.283	.338	84	-4	-3	16	4			.831	-1	O	-0.5
Total	2	70	282	40	69	8	9	3	29	9	11	.245	.271	.369	96	-2	-2	30	4			.828	-7	/O	-1.0

YEAR	TM/L	G	AB	R	H	2B	3B	HR	RBI	BB	SO	AVG	OBP	SLG	PRO+	BR	/A	RC	SB	CS	SBR	FA	FR	POS	TPR
■ DICK WEST	West, Richard Thomas b: 11/24/15, Louisville, Ky. BR/TR, 6'2", 180 lbs. Deb: 9/28/38																								
1938	Cin-N	1	1	0	0	0	0	0	0	0	0	.000	.000	.000	-99	-0	-0	0	0			.000	0	H	0.0
1939	Cin-N	8	19	1	4	0	0	0	4	1	4	.211	.250	.211	25	-2	-2	1	0			1.000	-1	/OC	-0.3
1940	Cin-N	7	28	4	11	2	0	1	6	0	2	.393	.393	.571	161	2	2	6	1			1.000	-3	/C	0.0
1941	Cin-N	67	172	15	37	5	2	1	17	6	23	.215	.246	.285	49	-12	-12	12	4			.970	-3	C	-1.2
1942	Cin-N	33	79	9	14	3	0	1	8	5	13	.177	.226	.253	40	-6	-6	5	1			.989	3	C/O	-0.3
1943	Cin-N	3	0	1	0	0	0	0	0	0	0	—	—	—	—	0	0	0	0			.000	0	R	0.0
Total	6	119	299	30	66	10	2	3	35	12	42	.221	.253	.298	55	-18	-18	24	6			.977	-4	/CO	-1.8
■ SAM WEST	West, Samuel Filmore b: 10/5/04, Longview, Tex. d: 11/23/85, Lubbock, Tex. BL/TL, 5'11", 165 lbs. Deb: 4/17/27 C																								
1927	Was-A	38	67	9	16	4	1	0	6	8	8	.239	.320	.328	69	-3	-3	7	1	0	0	.939	-1	O	-0.5
1928	Was-A	125	378	59	114	30	7	3	40	20	23	.302	.338	.442	104	1	1	54	5	6	-2	**.996**	-10	*O	-1.7
1929	Was-A	142	510	60	136	16	8	3	75	45	41	.267	.326	.347	73	-20	-21	59	9	8	-2	.978	15	*O	-1.6
1930	Was-A	120	411	75	135	22	10	6	67	37	34	.328	.385	.474	116	11	10	75	5	5	-2	.972	3	*O	0.4
1931	Was-A	132	526	77	175	43	13	3	91	30	37	.333	.369	.481	121	15	15	90	6	8	-3	.990	21	*O	2.2
1932	Was-A	146	554	88	159	27	12	6	83	48	57	.287	.345	.412	96	-5	-3	79	4	5	-2	.979	19	*O	0.5
1933	StL-A★	133	517	93	155	25	12	11	48	59	49	.300	.373	.458	112	14	9	89	10	8	-2	.988	8	*O	0.9
1934	StL-A★	122	482	90	157	22	10	9	55	62	55	.326	.403	.469	115	18	12	92	3	5	-2	.972	7	*O	1.1
1935	StL-A☆	138	527	93	158	37	4	10	70	75	46	.300	.388	.442	109	12	9	92	1	6	-3	**.989**	17	*O	1.6
1936	StL-A	152	533	78	148	26	4	7	70	94	70	.278	.386	.381	87	-6	-8	85	2	0	1	.983	9	*O	-0.4
1937	StL-A★	122	457	68	150	37	4	7	58	46	28	.328	.390	.473	115	11	11	85	1	1	-0	.987	12	*O	1.7
1938	StL-A	44	165	17	51	8	2	1	27	14	9	.309	.363	.400	91	-2	-2	25	1	0	0	.971	-3	O	-0.5
	Was-A	92	344	51	104	19	5	5	47	33	21	.302	.363	.430	105	-1	2	55	1	1	-0	.983	-3	O	-0.3
	Yr	136	509	68	155	27	7	6	74	47	30	.305	.363	.420	100	-4	0	79	2	1	0	.979	-6	*O	-0.8
1939	Was-A	115	390	52	110	20	8	3	52	67	29	.282	.387	.397	109	3	7	65	1	1	-0	.992	3	O1	0.4
1940	Was-A	57	99	7	25	6	1	1	18	16	13	.253	.357	.364	93	-2	-1	14	0	2	-1	.990	-1	1/O	-0.4
1941	Was-A	26	37	3	10	0	0	0	6	11	2	.270	.438	.270	95	0	1	6	1	0	0	1.000	-0	/O	0.0
1942	Chi-A	49	151	14	35	5	0	0	25	31	18	.232	.363	.265	80	-3	-2	18	2	0	1	.983	-3	O	-0.7
Total	16	1753	6148	934	1838	347	101	75	838	696	540	.299	.371	.425	103	44	37	991	53	56	-18	.983	93	*O/1	2.7
■ MAX WEST	West, Walter Maxwell b: 7/14/04, Sunset, Tex. d: 4/25/71, Houston, Tex. BR/TR, 5'11", 165 lbs. Deb: 9/18/28																								
1928	Bro-N	7	21	4	6	1	1	0	1	4	1	.286	.400	.429	118	1	1	4	0			.882	1	/O	0.2
1929	Bro-N	5	8	1	2	1	0	0	1	1	0	.250	.333	.375	77	-0	-0	1	0			1.000	-1	/O	-0.1
Total	2	12	29	5	8	2	1	0	2	5	1	.276	.382	.414	107	0	0	5	0			.895	1	/O	0.1
■ BILLY WEST	West, William Nelson b: 8/21/1840, Philadelphia, Pa. Deb: 5/22/1874																								
1874	Atl-n	9	35	4	7	1	0	0		1		.200	.222	.229	50	-2	-1	2						2	-0.1
1876	NY-N	1	4	0	0	0	0	0	0	0	0	.000	.000	.000	-99	-1	-1	0				1.000	-0	/2	-0.1
■ OSCAR WESTERBERG	Westerberg, Oscar William b: 7/8/1882, Alameda, Cal. d: 4/17/09, Alameda, Cal. BB/TR, Deb: 9/05/07																								
1907	Bos-N	2	6	0	2	0	0	0	1	1		.333	.429	.333	140	0	0	1	0			1.000	-1	/S	0.0
■ JIM WESTLAKE	Westlake, James Patrick b: 7/3/30, Sacramento, Cal. BL/TL, 6'1", 190 lbs. Deb: 4/16/55 F																								
1955	Phi-N	1	1	0	0	0	0	0	0	0	1	.000	.000	.000	-99	-0	-0	0	0	0	0	.000	0	H	0.0
■ WALLY WESTLAKE	Westlake, Waldon Thomas b: 11/8/20, Gridley, Cal. BR/TR, 6', 186 lbs. Deb: 4/15/47 F																								
1947	Pit-N	112	407	59	111	17	4	17	69	27	63	.273	.324	.459	103	2	0	56	5			.988	4	*O	-0.2
1948	Pit-N	132	428	78	122	10	6	17	65	46	40	.285	.360	.456	117	11	10	71	2			.976	-0	*O	0.4
1949	Pit-N	147	525	77	148	24	8	23	104	45	69	.282	.345	.490	118	14	12	86	6			.982	5	*O	1.1
1950	Pit-N	139	477	69	136	15	6	24	95	48	78	.285	.359	.493	118	14	12	83	1			**.991**	4	*O	1.0
1951	Pit-N	50	181	28	51	4	0	16	45	9	26	.282	.323	.569	131	7	7	32	0	1	-1	.908	5	3O	1.0
	StL-N	73	267	36	68	8	5	6	39	24	42	.255	.325	.390	91	-3	-4	34	1	2	-1	.982	2	O	-0.5
	Yr	123	448	64	119	12	5	22	84	33	68	.266	.324	.462	107	4	3	66	1	3	-2	.984	7	O3	0.5
1952	StL-N	21	74	7	16	3	0	0	10	8	11	.216	.293	.257	53	-4	-5	5	1	1	-0	1.000	6	O	0.1
	Cin-N	59	183	29	37	4	0	3	14	31	29	.202	.324	.273	67	-7	-7	16	0	2	-1	.992	-2	O	-1.2
	Yr	80	257	36	53	7	0	3	24	39	40	.206	.315	.268	63	-12	-12	22	1	3	-2	.995	5	O	-1.1
	Cle-A	29	69	11	16	4	1	1	9	8	16	.232	.312	.362	93	-1	-1	8	1	0	0	1.000	-3	O	-0.5
1953	Cle-A	82	218	42	72	7	1	9	46	35	29	.330	.427	.495	153	16	17	49	2	0	1	.963	-11	O	0.4
1954	*Cle-A	85	240	36	63	9	2	11	42	26	37	.262	.340	.454	114	4	4	36	0	1	-1	.964	-7	O	-0.6
1955	Cle-A	16	20	2	5	1	0	0	1	3	5	.250	.348	.300	73	-1	-1	2	0	0	0	1.000	-0	/O	-0.1
	Bal-A	8	24	0	3	1	0	0	0	6	5	.125	.300	.167	30	-2	-2	1	0	0	0	1.000	-1	/O	-0.4
	Yr	24	44	2	8	2	0	0	1	9	10	.182	.321	.227	49	-3	-3	3	0	0	0	1.000	-2	O	-0.5
1956	Phi-N	5	4	0	0	0	0	0	0	1	3	.000	.200	.000	-41	-1	-1	0	0	0	0	.000	0	H	-0.1
Total	10	958	3117	474	848	107	33	127	539	317	453	.272	.346	.450	111	49	42	480	19	7		.983	1	O/3	0.4
■ AL WESTON	Weston, Alfred John b: 12/11/05, Lynn, Mass. BR/TR, 6', 195 lbs. Deb: 7/07/29																								
1929	Bos-N	3	3	0	0	0	0	0	0	0	2	.000	.000	.000	-99	-1	-1	0	0			.000	0	H	-0.1
■ WES WESTRUM	Westrum, Wesley Noreen b: 11/28/22, Clearbrook, Minn. BR/TR, 5'11", 185 lbs. Deb: 9/17/47 MC																								
1947	NY-N	6	12	1	5	1	0	0	2	0	2	.417	.417	.500	142	1	1	3	0			1.000	0	/C	0.1
1948	NY-N	66	125	14	20	3	1	4	16	20	36	.160	.276	.296	54	-8	-8	11	3			.981	8	C	0.3
1949	NY-N	64	169	23	41	4	1	7	28	37	39	.243	.385	.402	111	4	4	28	1			.980	-0	C	0.7
1950	NY-N	140	437	68	103	13	3	23	71	92	73	.236	.371	.437	111	9	9	74	2			**.999**	10	*C	2.5
1951	*NY-N	124	361	59	79	12	0	20	70	104	93	.219	.400	.418	119	15	15	70	1	0	0	.987	8	*C	2.8
1952	NY-N☆	114	322	47	71	11	0	14	43	76	68	.220	.374	.385	110	8	7	53	1	2	-1	.978	-4	*C	0.8
1953	NY-N☆	107	290	40	65	5	0	12	30	56	73	.224	.352	.366	86	-4	-5	41	2	0	1	.982	4	*C/3	0.4
1954	*NY-N	98	246	25	46	3	1	8	27	45	60	.187	.320	.305	63	-13	-13	27	0	1	-1	.985	12	C	0.3
1955	NY-N	69	137	11	29	1	0	4	18	24	18	.212	.333	.307	71	-5	-5	14	0	1	-1	.987	10	C	0.6
1956	NY-N	68	132	10	29	5	2	3	8	25	28	.220	.348	.356	91	-1	-1	16	0	0	0	.982	13	C	1.4
1957	NY-N	63	91	4	15	1	0	1	2	10	24	.165	.255	.209	27	-9	-9	5	0	1	-1	.966	2	C	-0.7
Total	11	919	2322	302	503	59	8	96	315	489	514	.217	.357	.373	95	-4	-6	342	10	5		.985	64	C/3	9.2
■ JEFF WETHERBY	Wetherby, Jeffrey Barrett b: 10/18/63, Granada Hills, Cal. BL/TL, 6'2", 195 lbs. Deb: 6/07/89																								
1989	Atl-N	52	48	5	10	2	1	1	7	4	6	.208	.269	.354	75	-2	-2	4	1	0	0	1.000	-2	/O	-0.4
■ DUTCH WETZEL	Wetzel, Franklin Burton b: 7/7/1893, Columbus, Ind. d: 3/5/42, Hollywood, Cal. BR/TR, 5'9.5", 177 lbs. Deb: 9/15/20																								
1920	StL-A	7	21	5	9	1	1	0	5	4	1	.429	.520	.571	183	3	3	6	0	1	-1	.875	0	/O	0.2
1921	StL-A	61	119	16	25	2	0	2	10	9	20	.210	.271	.277	38	-11	-12	9	0	0	0	.981	-2	O	-1.5
Total	2	68	140	21	34	3	1	2	15	13	21	.243	.312	.321	59	-8	-9	15	0	1	-1	.957	-2	/O	-1.3
■ BILL WHALEY	Whaley, William Carl b: 2/10/1899, Indianapolis, Ind. d: 3/3/43, Indianapolis, Ind. BR/TR, 5'11", 178 lbs. Deb: 4/18/23																								
1923	StL-A	23	50	5	12	2	1	0	1	4	2	.240	.309	.320	62	-3	-3	5	0	0	0	1.000	-0	O	-0.4
■ BERT WHALING	Whaling, Albert James b: 6/22/1888, Los Angeles, Cal. d: 1/21/65, Sawtelle, Cal. BR/TR, 6', 185 lbs. Deb: 4/22/13																								
1913	Bos-N	79	211	22	51	8	2	0	25	10	32	.242	.283	.299	65	-10	-10	19	3			**.990**	3	C	-0.1

YEAR	TM/L	G	AB	R	H	2B	3B	HR	RBI	BB	SO	AVG	OBP	SLG	PRO+	BR	/A	RC	SB	CS	SBR	FA	FR	POS	TPR
1914	Bos-N	60	172	18	36	7	0	0	12	21	28	.209	.303	.250	65	-7	-7	13	2			.981	12	C	1.0
1915	Bos-N	72	190	10	42	6	2	0	13	8	38	.221	.264	.274	66	-9	-8	14	0	1	-1	.986	1	C	-0.3
Total	3	211	573	50	129	21	4	0	50	39	98	.225	.283	.276	65	-25	-24	46	5	1		.986	16	C	0.6

■ **MACK WHEAT** Wheat, McKinley Davis b: 6/9/1893, Polo, Mo. d: 8/14/79, Los Banos, Cal. BR/TR, 5′11.5″, 167 lbs. Deb: 4/14/15 F

YEAR	TM/L	G	AB	R	H	2B	3B	HR	RBI	BB	SO	AVG	OBP	SLG	PRO+	BR	/A	RC	SB	CS	SBR	FA	FR	POS	TPR
1915	Bro-N	8	14	0	1	0	0	0	0	0	5	.071	.071	.071	-56	-3	-3	0	0			.957	-0	/C	-0.3
1916	Bro-N	2	2	0	0	0	0	0	0	0	1	.000	.000	.000	-97	-0	-0	0	0			1.000	0	/C	0.0
1917	Bro-N	29	60	2	8	1	0	0	0	1	12	.133	.161	.150	-4	-7	-7	1	1			.968	1	C/O	-0.7
1918	Bro-N	57	157	11	34	7	1	1	3	8	24	.217	.255	.293	67	-7	-6	12	2			.966	-1	C/O	-0.6
1919	Bro-N	41	112	5	23	3	0	0	8	2	22	.205	.246	.232	43	-8	-8	7	1			.944	-4	C	-0.9
1920	Phi-N	78	230	15	52	10	3	3	20	8	35	.226	.261	.335	67	-9	-11	20	3	1	0	.961	9	C	0.3
1921	Phi-N	10	27	1	5	2	1	0	4	0	3	.185	.241	.333	47	-2	-2	2	0	0	0	.980	5	/C	0.3
Total	7	225	602	34	123	23	5	4	35	19	102	.204	.241	.279	52	-36	-38	42	7	1		.961	9	C/O	-1.9

■ **ZACK WHEAT** Wheat, Zachary Davis "Buck" b: 5/23/1888, Hamilton, Mo. d: 3/11/72, Sedalia, Mo. BL/TR, 5′10″, 170 lbs. Deb: 9/11/09 FH

YEAR	TM/L	G	AB	R	H	2B	3B	HR	RBI	BB	SO	AVG	OBP	SLG	PRO+	BR	/A	RC	SB	CS	SBR	FA	FR	POS	TPR
1909	Bro-N	26	102	15	31	7	3	0	4	6		.304	.343	.431	145	4	5	15	1			.952	2	O	0.6
1910	Bro-N	156	606	78	172	36	15	2	55	47	80	.284	.341	.403	120	11	13	87	16			.962	6	*O	1.2
1911	Bro-N	140	534	55	153	26	13	5	76	29	58	.287	.332	.412	112	3	6	79	21			.955	-3	*O	-0.4
1912	Bro-N	123	453	70	138	28	7	8	65	39	40	.305	.367	.450	128	13	16	79	16			.968	3	*O	1.2
1913	Bro-N	138	535	64	161	28	10	7	58	25	45	.301	.335	.430	114	10	8	79	19			.978	9	*O	1.2
1914	Bro-N	145	533	66	170	26	9	9	89	47	50	.319	.377	.452	143	29	28	95	20			.962	18	*O	4.2
1915	Bro-N	146	528	64	136	15	12	5	66	52	42	.258	.330	.360	107	6	5	65	21	14	-2	.953	10	*O	0.7
1916	*Bro-N	149	568	76	177	32	13	9	73	43	49	.312	.366	**.461**	149	**34**	**33**	**103**	19			.975	9	*O	3.9
1917	Bro-N	109	362	38	113	15	11	1	41	20	18	.312	.352	.423	133	15	14	53	5			.979	6	O	1.7
1918	Bro-N	105	409	39	137	15	3	0	51	16	17	**.335**	.369	.386	131	14	14	59	9			.979	4	*O	1.4
1919	Bro-N	137	536	70	159	23	11	5	62	33	27	.297	.344	.409	123	16	15	76	15			.971	-1	*O	0.5
1920	*Bro-N	148	583	89	191	26	13	9	73	48	21	.328	.385	.463	138	32	30	102	8	10	-4	.971	-4	*O	1.2
1921	Bro-N	148	568	91	182	31	10	14	85	44	19	.320	.372	.484	121	20	17	101	11	8	-2	.965	-4	*O	0.0
1922	Bro-N	152	600	92	201	29	12	16	112	45	22	.335	.388	.503	129	24	25	116	9	6	-1	**.991**	2	*O	1.4
1923	Bro-N	98	349	63	131	13	5	8	65	23	12	.375	.417	.510	148	22	23	73	3	3	-1	.908	-11	O	0.5
1924	Bro-N	141	566	92	212	41	8	14	97	49	18	.375	.428	.549	165	48	51	132	3	4	-2	.965	5	*O	4.3
1925	Bro-N	150	616	125	221	42	14	14	103	45	22	.359	.403	.541	143	35	37	134	3	1	0	.962	0	*O	2.6
1926	Bro-N	111	411	68	119	31	2	5	35	21	14	.290	.326	.411	99	-3	-2	53	4			.955	2	*O	-0.7
1927	Phi-A	88	247	34	80	12	1	1	38	18	5	.324	.379	.393	95	1	-1	35	2	3	-1	.983	-3	O	-0.8
Total	19	2410	9106	1289	2884	476	172	132	1248	650	559	.317	.367	.450	129	334	335	1539	205	49		.966	50	*O	24.7

■ **WOODY WHEATON** Wheaton, Elwood Pierce b: 10/3/14, Philadelphia, Pa. BL/TL, 5′8.5″, 160 lbs. Deb: 9/28/43

YEAR	TM/L	G	AB	R	H	2B	3B	HR	RBI	BB	SO	AVG	OBP	SLG	PRO+	BR	/A	RC	SB	CS	SBR	FA	FR	POS	TPR
1943	Phi-A	7	30	2	6	2	0	0	2	3	2	.200	.294	.267	65	-1	-1	2	0	0	0	1.000	1	/O	-0.1
1944	Phi-A	30	59	1	11	2	0	0	5	5	3	.186	.250	.220	35	-5	-5	3	1	2	-1	1.000	2	P/O	-0.2
Total	2	37	89	3	17	4	0	0	7	8	5	.191	.265	.236	45	-6	-6	5	1	2	-1	.981	3	/OP	-0.3

■ **DON WHEELER** Wheeler, Donald Wesley "Scott" b: 9/29/22, Minneapolis, Minn BR/TR, 5′10″, 175 lbs. Deb: 4/23/49

YEAR	TM/L	G	AB	R	H	2B	3B	HR	RBI	BB	SO	AVG	OBP	SLG	PRO+	BR	/A	RC	SB	CS	SBR	FA	FR	POS	TPR
1949	Chi-A	67	192	17	46	9	2	1	22	27	19	.240	.333	.323	76	-7	-6	22	2	0	1	.976	3	C	0.0

■ **ED WHEELER** Wheeler, Edward b: 6/15/1878, Sherman, Mich. d: 8/15/60, Ft.Worth, Tex. BB/TR, 5′10″, 160 lbs. Deb: 5/10/02

YEAR	TM/L	G	AB	R	H	2B	3B	HR	RBI	BB	SO	AVG	OBP	SLG	PRO+	BR	/A	RC	SB	CS	SBR	FA	FR	POS	TPR
1902	Bro-N	30	96	4	12	0	0	0	5	3		.125	.152	.125	-14	-13	-13	2	1			.863	-3	32/S	-1.7

■ **ED WHEELER** Wheeler, Edward Raymond b: 5/24/15, Los Angeles, Cal. d: 8/4/83, Centralia, Wash. BR/TR, 5′9″, 160 lbs. Deb: 4/19/45

YEAR	TM/L	G	AB	R	H	2B	3B	HR	RBI	BB	SO	AVG	OBP	SLG	PRO+	BR	/A	RC	SB	CS	SBR	FA	FR	POS	TPR
1945	Cle-A	46	72	12	14	2	0	0	1	8	13	.194	.275	.222	47	-5	-5	5	1	1	-0	.912	-6	3S/2	-1.1

■ **GEORGE WHEELER** Wheeler, George Harrison "Heavy" b: 11/10/1881, Shelburn, Ind. d: 6/14/18, Clinton, Ind. BL/TR, 5′9.5″, 180 lbs. Deb: 7/27/10

YEAR	TM/L	G	AB	R	H	2B	3B	HR	RBI	BB	SO	AVG	OBP	SLG	PRO+	BR	/A	RC	SB	CS	SBR	FA	FR	POS	TPR
1910	Cin-N	3	3	0	0	0	0	0	0	0	2	.000	.000	.000	-99	-1	-1	0	0			.000	0	H	-0.1

■ **HARRY WHEELER** Wheeler, Harry Eugene b: 3/3/1858, Versailles, Ind. d: 10/9/1900, Cincinnati, Ohio BR/TR, 5′11″, 165 lbs. Deb: 6/19/1878 M

YEAR	TM/L	G	AB	R	H	2B	3B	HR	RBI	BB	SO	AVG	OBP	SLG	PRO+	BR	/A	RC	SB	CS	SBR	FA	FR	POS	TPR
1878	Pro-N	7	27	7	4	0	0	0	1	2	15	.148	.207	.148	18	-2	-2	1				.875	-2	/P	0.0
1879	Cin-N	1	3	0	0	0	0	0	0	0	2	.000	.000	.000	-99	-1	-1	0				1.000	-0	/OP	-0.1
1880	Cle-N	1	4	0	1	0	0	0	0	0	0	.250	.250	.250	72	-0	-0	0				1.000	-0	/O	0.0
	Cin-N	17	65	1	6	2	0	0	2	0	15	.092	.092	.123	-28	-8	-8	1				.750	1	O	-0.7
	Yr	18	69	1	7	2	0	0	2	0	15	.101	.101	.130	-22	-8	-8	1				.759	1	O	-0.7
1882	Cin-a	76	344	59	86	11	11	1		7		.250	.265	.355	102	2	-1	33				.808	-5	*O1/P	-0.7
1883	Col-a	82	371	42	84	6	7	0		6		.226	.239	.280	72	-14	-9	25				.803	-2	*O/2P	-1.0
1884	StL-a	5	19	0	5	2	0	0		1		.263	.300	.368	116	0	0	2				.600	-1	/O	-0.1
	KC-U	14	62	11	16	1	0	0		3		.258	.292	.274	106	-0	1	5				.769	0	O/PM	0.0
	CP-U	37	158	29	36	5	3	1		4		.228	.247	.316	90	-2	-2	13				.774	-5	O	-0.6
	Bal-U	17	69	3	18	2	0	0		0		.261	.261	.290	78	-1	-2	5				.815	-1	O	-0.3
	Yr	68	289	43	70	8	3	1		7		.242	.260	.301	90	-3	-3	23				.781	-5	O/P	-0.9
Total	6	257	1122	152	256	29	21	2	3	23	32	.228	.244	.297	80	-26	-23	86				.791	-14	O/P12	-3.5

■ **DICK WHEELER** Wheeler, Richard (b: Richard Wheeler Maynard) b: 1/14/1898, Keene, N.H. d: 2/12/62, Lexington, Mass. BR/TR, 5′11″, 185 lbs. Deb: 6/17/18

YEAR	TM/L	G	AB	R	H	2B	3B	HR	RBI	BB	SO	AVG	OBP	SLG	PRO+	BR	/A	RC	SB	CS	SBR	FA	FR	POS	TPR
1918	StL-N	3	6	0	0	0	0	0	0	0	3	.000	.000	.000	-99	-1	-1	0	0			.000	-1	/O	-0.3

■ **BOBBY WHEELOCK** Wheelock, Warren H. b: 8/6/1864, Charlestown, Mass. d: 3/13/28, Boston, Mass. BR/TR, 5′8″, 160 lbs. Deb: 5/19/1887

YEAR	TM/L	G	AB	R	H	2B	3B	HR	RBI	BB	SO	AVG	OBP	SLG	PRO+	BR	/A	RC	SB	CS	SBR	FA	FR	POS	TPR
1887	Bos-N	48	166	32	42	4	2	2	15	15	15	.253	.315	.337	83	-4	-4	25	20			.878	-7	OS/2	-0.9
1890	Col-a	52	190	24	45	6	1	1		25		.237	.326	.295	92	-3	-1	30	34			.885	-1	S	0.1
1891	Col-a	136	498	82	114	15	1	0	39	78	55	.229	.336	.263	79	-13	-8	63	52			.899	19	*S	1.5
Total	3	236	854	138	201	25	4	3	54	118	70	.235	.330	.285	83	-20	-12	118	106			.894	11	S/O2	0.7

■ **JIMMY WHELAN** Whelan, James Francis b: 5/11/1890, Kansas City, Mo. d: 11/29/29, Dayton, Ohio BR/TR, 5′8.5″, 165 lbs. Deb: 4/24/13

YEAR	TM/L	G	AB	R	H	2B	3B	HR	RBI	BB	SO	AVG	OBP	SLG	PRO+	BR	/A	RC	SB	CS	SBR	FA	FR	POS	TPR
1913	StL-N	1	1	0	0	0	0	0	0	0	0	.000	.000	.000	-99	-0	-0	0	0			.000	0	H	0.0

■ **TOM WHELAN** Whelan, Thomas Joseph b: 1/3/1894, Lynn, Mass. d: 6/26/57, Boston, Mass. BR/TR, 5′11″, 175 lbs. Deb: 8/13/20

YEAR	TM/L	G	AB	R	H	2B	3B	HR	RBI	BB	SO	AVG	OBP	SLG	PRO+	BR	/A	RC	SB	CS	SBR	FA	FR	POS	TPR
1920	Bos-N	1	1	0	0	0	0	0	0	1	1	.000	.500	.000	54	0	0	0	0	0	0	1.000	0	/1	0.0

■ **PETE WHISENANT** Whisenant, Thomas Peter b: 12/14/29, Asheville, N.C. BR/TR, 6′2″, 200 lbs. Deb: 4/16/52 C

YEAR	TM/L	G	AB	R	H	2B	3B	HR	RBI	BB	SO	AVG	OBP	SLG	PRO+	BR	/A	RC	SB	CS	SBR	FA	FR	POS	TPR
1952	Bos-N	24	52	3	10	2	0	0	7	4	13	.192	.250	.231	35	-5	-4	3	1	1	-0	.973	2	O	-0.3
1955	StL-N	58	115	10	22	5	1	2	9	5	29	.191	.225	.304	39	-10	-10	8	2	0	1	.964	-1	O	-1.2
1956	Chi-N	103	314	37	75	16	3	11	46	24	53	.239	.295	.414	89	-6	-5	38	8	2	1	.992	6	O	-0.3
1957	Cin-N	67	90	18	19	3	2	5	11	5	24	.211	.253	.456	80	-2	-3	10	0	1	-1	.982	-9	O	-1.4
1958	Cin-N	85	203	33	48	9	2	11	40	18	37	.236	.299	.463	93	-1	-3	28	3	0	1	1.000	-1	O/2	-0.6
1959	Cin-N	36	71	13	17	2	0	5	11	8	18	.239	.316	.479	105	1	0	11	0	0	0	.966	-2	O	-0.3
1960	Cin-N	1	1	0	0	0	0	0	0	0	0	.000	.000	.000	-98	-0	-0	0	0	0	0	.000	0	H	0.0
	Cle-A	7	6	0	1	0	0	0	0	0	2	.167	.167	.167	-10	-1	-1	0	0	0	0	1.000	-1	/O	-0.2
	Was-A	58	115	19	26	9	0	3	9	19	14	.226	.336	.383	95	-1	-1	15	2	1	0	1.000	-9	O	-1.2
	Yr	65	121	19	27	9	0	3	9	19	16	.223	.329	.372	90	-2	-2	15	2	1	0	1.000	-10	O	-1.4
1961	Min-A	10	6	1	0	0	0	0	0	1	2	.000	.143	.000	-55	-1	-1	0	0	0	0	1.000	-2	/O	-0.3
	Cin-N	26	15	6	3	0	0	0	1	2	4	.200	.294	.200	34	-1	-1	1	1	0	0	1.000	1	O/C3	-0.1

YEAR	TM/L	G	AB	R	H	2B	3B	HR	RBI	BB	SO	AVG	OBP	SLG	PRO+	BR	/A	RC	SB	CS	SBR	FA	FR	POS	TPR
Total	8	475	988	140	221	46	8	37	134	86	196	.224	.287	.399	80	-29	-30	114	17	5	2	.988	-16	O/3C2	-5.9

■ **LARRY WHISENTON** Whisenton, Larry b: 7/3/56, St.Louis, Mo. BL/TL, 6'1", 190 lbs. Deb: 9/17/77

YEAR	TM/L	G	AB	R	H	2B	3B	HR	RBI	BB	SO	AVG	OBP	SLG	PRO+	BR	/A	RC	SB	CS	SBR	FA	FR	POS	TPR
1977	Atl-N	4	4	1	1	0	0	0	1	0	3	.250	.250	.250	31	-0	-0	0	0	0	0	.000	0	H	0.0
1978	Atl-N	6	16	1	3	1	0	0	2	1	2	.188	.235	.250	32	-1	-2	1	0	0	0	1.000	-1	/O	-0.3
1979	Atl-N	13	37	3	9	2	1	0	1	3	3	.243	.300	.351	72	-1	-2	4	1	0	0	1.000	3	O	0.2
1981	Atl-N	9	5	1	1	0	0	0	0	2	1	.200	.429	.200	81	0	0	1	0	0	0	.000	-0	/O	0.0
1982	*Atl-N	84	143	21	34	7	2	4	17	23	33	.238	.343	.399	103	2	1	20	2	2	-1	.964	-3	O	-0.3
Total	5	116	205	27	48	10	3	4	21	29	42	.234	.329	.371	90	-1	-3	26	3	2	-0	.968	-0	/O	-0.4

■ **LEW WHISTLER** Whistler, Lewis (b: Lewis Wissler) b: 3/10/1868, St.Louis, Mo. d: 12/30/59, St.Louis, Mo. TR , Deb: 8/07/1890

YEAR	TM/L	G	AB	R	H	2B	3B	HR	RBI	BB	SO	AVG	OBP	SLG	PRO+	BR	/A	RC	SB	CS	SBR	FA	FR	POS	TPR
1890	NY-N	45	170	27	49	9	7	2	29	20	37	.288	.366	.459	142	9	9	32	8			.982	-2	1	0.4
1891	NY-N	72	265	39	65	8	7	3	38	24	45	.245	.315	.362	103	-1	1	32	4			.852	-16	SO/123	-1.2
1892	Bal-N	52	209	32	47	6	6	2	21	18	22	.225	.296	.340	91	-2	-3	25	12			.973	-1	1/O	-0.6
	Lou-N	80	285	42	67	4	7	5	34	30	45	.235	.312	.351	111	1	4	36	14			.978	-2	12	-0.1
	Yr	132	494	74	114	10	13	7	55	48	67	.231	.305	.346	102	-1	1	62	26			.976	-3	*12/O	-0.7
1893	Lou-N	13	47	5	10	1	1	0	9	5	5	.213	.302	.277	60	-3	-2	4	1			.946	-0	1	-0.2
	StL-N	10	38	5	9	1	0	0	2	3	2	.237	.293	.263	50	-3	-3	3	0			.923	-1	/O1	-0.4
	Yr	23	85	10	19	2	1	0	11	8	7	.224	.298	.271	55	-6	-5	7	1			.949	-2	1/O	-0.6
Total	4	272	1014	150	247	29	28	12	133	100	156	.244	.318	.363	105	1	6	134	39			.976	-22	1/SO23	-2.1

■ **LOU WHITAKER** Whitaker, Louis Rodman b: 5/12/57, Brooklyn, N.Y. BL/TR, 5'11", 160 lbs. Deb: 9/09/77

YEAR	TM/L	G	AB	R	H	2B	3B	HR	RBI	BB	SO	AVG	OBP	SLG	PRO+	BR	/A	RC	SB	CS	SBR	FA	FR	POS	TPR
1977	Det-A	11	32	5	8	1	0	0	2	4	6	.250	.333	.281	66	-1	-1	3	2	2	-1	1.000	-3	/2	-0.5
1978	Det-A	139	484	71	138	12	7	3	58	61	65	.285	.366	.357	101	5	3	66	7	7	-2	.978	12	*2/D	2.3
1979	Det-A	127	423	75	121	14	8	3	42	78	66	.286	.398	.378	107	10	8	69	20	10	0	.986	2	*2	1.8
1980	Det-A	145	477	68	111	19	1	1	45	73	79	.233	.335	.283	69	-16	-18	50	8	4	0	.985	-3	*2	-1.2
1981	Det-A	109	335	48	88	14	4	5	36	40	42	.263	.343	.373	103	3	2	45	5	3	-0	.985	6	*2	1.4
1982	Det-A	152	560	76	160	22	8	15	65	48	58	.286	.343	.434	111	9	8	85	11	3	2	**.988**	12	*2/D	3.0
1983	Det-A★	161	643	94	206	40	6	12	72	67	70	.320	.385	.457	134	28	30	114	17	10	-1	.983	-13	*2	2.3
1984	*Det-A★	143	558	90	161	25	1	13	56	62	63	.289	.360	.407	112	10	10	83	6	5	-1	.979	-11	*2	0.3
1985	Det-A★	152	609	102	170	29	8	21	73	80	56	.279	.365	.456	124	20	21	107	6	4	-1	.985	-16	*2	1.0
1986	Det-A★	144	584	95	157	26	6	20	73	63	70	.269	.340	.437	110	7	8	82	13	8	-1	.984	-1	*2	1.1
1987	*Det-A†	149	604	110	160	38	6	16	59	71	108	.265	.343	.427	107	3	6	93	13	5	1	.976	-14	*2	0.0
1988	Det-A	115	403	54	111	18	2	12	55	66	61	.275	.377	.419	128	14	16	67	2	0	1	.984	-23	*2	-0.2
1989	Det-A	148	509	77	128	21	1	28	85	89	59	.251	.366	.462	135	23	25	91	6	3	0	.985	-1	*2/D	2.8
1990	Det-A	132	472	75	112	22	2	18	60	74	71	.237	.341	.407	107	6	5	68	8	2	1	.991	12	*2/D	2.1
1991	Det-A	138	470	94	131	26	2	23	78	90	45	.279	.397	.489	142	30	30	99	4	2	0	**.994**	-11	*2/D	2.1
1992	Det-A	130	453	77	126	26	0	19	71	81	46	.278	.389	.461	135	25	24	85	6	4	-1	.984	-14	*2D	1.2
Total	16	2095	7616	1211	2088	353	62	209	930	1047	965	.274	.363	.419	115	176	177	1208	134	72	-3	.984	-68	*2/D	19.5

■ **STEVE WHITAKER** Whitaker, Stephen Edward b: 5/7/43, Tacoma, Wash. BL/TR, 6'1", 187 lbs. Deb: 8/23/66

YEAR	TM/L	G	AB	R	H	2B	3B	HR	RBI	BB	SO	AVG	OBP	SLG	PRO+	BR	/A	RC	SB	CS	SBR	FA	FR	POS	TPR
1966	NY-A	31	114	15	28	3	2	7	15	9	24	.246	.306	.491	130	3	4	18	0	0	0	.955	-0	O	0.2
1967	NY-A	122	441	37	107	12	3	11	50	23	89	.243	.285	.358	92	-7	-5	43	2	5	-2	.982	6	*O	-0.8
1968	NY-A	28	60	3	7	2	0	0	3	8	18	.117	.221	.150	14	-6	-6	2	0	1	-1	.917	-1	O	-1.0
1969	Sea-A	69	116	15	29	2	1	6	13	12	29	.250	.326	.440	114	2	2	18	2	0	1	.962	-2	O	-0.1
1970	SF-N	16	27	3	3	1	0	0	4	2	14	.111	.172	.148	-13	-4	-4	1	0	0	0	.857	-1	/O	-0.6
Total	5	266	758	73	174	20	6	24	85	54	174	.230	.285	.367	92	-13	-10	82	4	6	-2	.967	1	O	-2.3

■ **FUZZ WHITE** White, Albert Eugene b: 6/27/18, Springfield, Mo. BL/TR, 6', 175 lbs. Deb: 9/17/40

YEAR	TM/L	G	AB	R	H	2B	3B	HR	RBI	BB	SO	AVG	OBP	SLG	PRO+	BR	/A	RC	SB	CS	SBR	FA	FR	POS	TPR
1940	StL-A	2	2	0	0	0	0	0	0	0	0	.000	.000	.000	-98	-1	-1	0	0	0	0	.000	0	H	-0.1
1947	NY-N	7	13	3	3	0	0	0	0	0	0	.231	.231	.231	23	-1	-1	0	0			1.000	0	/O	-0.2
Total	2	9	15	3	3	0	0	0	0	0	0	.200	.200	.200	6	-2	-2	0	0	0			0	/O	-0.3

■ **C. B. WHITE** White, C. B. b: Wakeman, Ohio Deb: 6/01/1883

YEAR	TM/L	G	AB	R	H	2B	3B	HR	RBI	BB	SO	AVG	OBP	SLG	PRO+	BR	/A	RC	SB	CS	SBR	FA	FR	POS	TPR
1883	Phi-N	1	1	0	0	0	0	0	0	0	0	.000	.000	.000	-99	-0	-0	0				.667	0	/S3	0.0

■ **CHARLIE WHITE** White, Charles b: 8/12/28, Kinston, N.C. BL/TR, 5'11", 192 lbs. Deb: 4/18/54

YEAR	TM/L	G	AB	R	H	2B	3B	HR	RBI	BB	SO	AVG	OBP	SLG	PRO+	BR	/A	RC	SB	CS	SBR	FA	FR	POS	TPR
1954	Mil-N	50	93	14	22	4	0	1	8	9	8	.237	.304	.312	65	-5	-5	8	0	0	0	.981	-2	C	-0.6
1955	Mil-N	12	30	3	7	1	0	0	4	5	7	.233	.361	.267	74	-1	-1	3	0	0	0	1.000	-2	C	-0.2
Total	2	62	123	17	29	5	0	1	12	14	15	.236	.319	.301	67	-6	-5	11	0	0	0	.986	-4	/C	-0.8

■ **DEVON WHITE** White, Devon Markes b: 12/29/62, Kingston, Jamaica BB/TR, 6'2", 180 lbs. Deb: 9/02/85

YEAR	TM/L	G	AB	R	H	2B	3B	HR	RBI	BB	SO	AVG	OBP	SLG	PRO+	BR	/A	RC	SB	CS	SBR	FA	FR	POS	TPR
1985	Cal-A	21	7	7	1	0	0	0	0	1	3	.143	.333	.143	37	-1	-1	1	3	1	0	1.000	-5	O	-0.5
1986	*Cal-A	29	51	8	12	1	1	1	3	6	8	.235	.316	.353	83	-1	-1	7	6	0	2	.961	-3	O	-0.3
1987	Cal-A	159	639	103	168	33	5	24	87	39	135	.263	.307	.443	99	-6	-3	87	32	11	3	.980	14	*O	0.8
1988	Cal-A	122	455	76	118	22	2	11	51	23	84	.259	.298	.389	93	-7	-5	52	17	8	0	.976	15	*O	0.7
1989	Cal-A★	156	636	86	156	18	13	12	56	31	129	.245	.283	.371	84	-16	-15	64	44	16	4	.989	15	*O/D	0.0
1990	Cal-A	125	443	57	96	17	3	11	44	44	116	.217	.292	.343	79	-14	-13	47	21	6	3	.972	8	*O	-0.5
1991	*Tor-A	156	642	110	181	40	10	17	60	55	135	.282	.345	.455	115	16	13	105	33	10	4	**.998**	17	*O	3.0
1992	*Tor-A	153	641	98	159	26	7	17	60	47	133	.248	.304	.390	89	-7	-11	81	37	4	9	.985	15	*O/D	0.9
Total	8	921	3514	545	891	157	41	93	361	246	743	.254	.306	.401	94	-36	-35	444	193	56	24	.984	77	O/D	4.1

■ **DON WHITE** White, Donald William b: 1/8/19, Everett, Wash. d: 6/15/87, Carlsbad, Cal. BR/TR, 6'1", 195 lbs. Deb: 4/19/48

YEAR	TM/L	G	AB	R	H	2B	3B	HR	RBI	BB	SO	AVG	OBP	SLG	PRO+	BR	/A	RC	SB	CS	SBR	FA	FR	POS	TPR
1948	Phi-A	86	253	29	62	14	2	1	28	19	16	.245	.303	.328	68	-12	-12	25	0	1	-1	.957	-4	O3	-1.9
1949	Phi-A	57	169	12	36	6	0	0	10	14	12	.213	.273	.249	40	-15	-14	12	2	0	1	.989	-2	O/3	-1.8
Total	2	143	422	41	98	20	2	1	38	33	28	.232	.291	.296	57	-27	-27	38	2	1	0	.971	-6	O/3	-3.7

■ **ED WHITE** White, Edward Perry b: 4/6/26, Anniston, Ala. d: 9/28/82, Lakeland, Fla. BR/TR, 6'2", 200 lbs. Deb: 9/16/55

YEAR	TM/L	G	AB	R	H	2B	3B	HR	RBI	BB	SO	AVG	OBP	SLG	PRO+	BR	/A	RC	SB	CS	SBR	FA	FR	POS	TPR
1955	Chi-A	3	4	0	2	0	0	0	0	1	1	.500	.600	.500	193	1	1	1	0	0	0	1.000	-0	/O	0.0

■ **ELDER WHITE** White, Elder Lafayette b: 12/23/34, Colerain, N.C. BR/TR, 5'11", 165 lbs. Deb: 4/10/62

YEAR	TM/L	G	AB	R	H	2B	3B	HR	RBI	BB	SO	AVG	OBP	SLG	PRO+	BR	/A	RC	SB	CS	SBR	FA	FR	POS	TPR
1962	Chi-N	23	53	4	8	2	0	0	1	8	11	.151	.274	.189	26	-5	-6	4	3	0	1	.986	0	S/3	-0.3

■ **ELMER WHITE** White, Elmer b: 5/23/1850, Caton, N.Y. d: 3/17/1872, Caton, N.Y. Deb: 5/04/1871

YEAR	TM/L	G	AB	R	H	2B	3B	HR	RBI	BB	SO	AVG	OBP	SLG	PRO+	BR	/A	RC	SB	CS	SBR	FA	FR	POS	TPR
1871	Cle-n	15	70	13	18	2	0	0	9	1	6	.257	.268	.286	63	-4	-3	5	0					O/C	-0.1

■ **FRANK WHITE** White, Frank b: 9/4/50, Greenville, Miss. BR/TR, 5'11", 170 lbs. Deb: 6/12/73

YEAR	TM/L	G	AB	R	H	2B	3B	HR	RBI	BB	SO	AVG	OBP	SLG	PRO+	BR	/A	RC	SB	CS	SBR	FA	FR	POS	TPR
1973	KC-A	51	139	20	31	6	1	0	5	8	23	.223	.265	.281	50	-9	-10	11	3	1	0	.937	7	S2	0.1
1974	KC-A	99	204	19	45	6	3	1	18	5	33	.221	.239	.294	50	-13	-14	13	3	4	-2	.962	25	2S3/D	1.3
1975	KC-A	111	304	43	76	10	2	7	36	20	39	.250	.298	.365	84	-6	-7	34	11	3	2	.987	15	2S/3CD	1.6
1976	*KC-A	152	446	39	102	17	6	2	46	19	42	.229	.265	.307	67	-19	-20	37	20	11	-1	.973	**21**	*2S	1.2
1977	*KC-A	152	474	59	116	21	5	5	50	25	67	.245	.285	.342	70	-20	-21	49	23	5	4	**.989**	-3	*2/S	-0.9
1978	*KC-A★	143	461	66	127	24	6	7	50	26	59	.275	.318	.399	98	-1	-2	59	13	10	-2	.978	-17	*2	-1.1
1979	KC-A★	127	467	73	124	26	4	10	48	25	54	.266	.304	.403	87	-8	-10	56	28	8	4	.982	-22	*2	-1.9
1980	*KC-A	154	560	70	148	23	4	7	60	19	69	.264	.291	.357	76	-19	-19	57	19	6	2	.988	-7	*2	-1.5
1981	*KC-A★	94	364	35	91	17	1	9	38	19	50	.250	.287	.376	91	-6	-5	37	4	2	0	.988	-16	2	-1.7

YEAR	TM/L	G	AB	R	H	2B	3B	HR	RBI	BB	SO	AVG	OBP	SLG	PRO+	BR	/A	RC	SB	CS	SBR	FA	FR	POS	TPR
1982	KC-A★	145	524	71	156	45	6	11	56	16	65	.298	.321	.469	114	8	8	73	10	7	-1	.978	-15	*2	0.0
1983	KC-A	146	549	52	143	35	6	11	77	20	51	.260	.286	.406	88	-10	-11	58	13	5	1	**.990**	9	*2	0.6
1984	*KC-A	129	479	58	130	22	5	17	56	27	72	.271	.313	.445	106	3	3	63	5	5	-2	.985	13	*2	1.9
1985	*KC-A	149	563	62	140	25	1	22	69	28	86	.249	.285	.414	88	-10	-11	65	10	4	1	.980	14	*2	1.0
1986	KC-A★	151	566	76	154	37	3	22	84	43	88	.272	.326	.465	110	8	7	84	4	4	-1	.987	-0	*2/S3	1.1
1987	KC-A	154	563	67	138	32	2	17	78	51	86	.245	.310	.400	84	-12	-14	67	1	3	-2	.987	8	*2/D	0.0
1988	KC-A	150	537	48	126	25	1	8	58	21	67	.235	.269	.330	66	-25	-25	44	7	3	0	**.994**	7	*2/D	-1.2
1989	KC-A	135	418	34	107	22	1	2	36	30	52	.256	.309	.328	80	-11	-11	43	3	2	-0	.985	7	*2/O	0.0
1990	KC-A	82	241	20	52	14	1	2	21	10	32	.216	.256	.307	58	-14	-14	18	1	0	0	.978	2	2/O	-1.0
Total	18	2324	7859	912	2006	407	58	160	886	412	1035	.255	.295	.383	85	-164	-176	866	178	83	4	.984	48	*2S/3DOC	-0.5

■ DOC WHITE White, Guy Harris b: 4/9/1879, Washington, D.C. d: 2/19/69, Silver Spring, Md. BL/TL, 6′1″, 150 lbs. Deb: 4/22/01

YEAR	TM/L	G	AB	R	H	2B	3B	HR	RBI	BB	SO	AVG	OBP	SLG	PRO+	BR	/A	RC	SB	CS	SBR	FA	FR	POS	TPR
1901	Phi-N	31	98	15	27	3	1	1	10	2		.276	.297	.357	88	-2	-2	12	1			.951	2	P/O	0.0
1902	Phi-N	61	179	17	47	3	1	1	15	11		.263	.305	.307	89	-2	-2	20	5			.931	-2	PO	-0.6
1903	Chi-A	38	99	10	20	3	0	0	5	19		.202	.331	.232	75	-2	-2	8	1			.969	3	P/O	0.0
1904	Chi-A	33	76	7	12	2	0	0	2	10		.158	.256	.184	42	-5	-4	5	3			.951	1	P/O	-0.1
1905	Chi-A	37	90	7	15	4	1	0	7	4		.167	.202	.233	40	-6	-6	5	3			.960	1	P/O	0.1
1906	*Chi-A	29	65	11	12	1	1	0	3	13		.185	.321	.231	76	-1	-1	7	3			.922	2	P/O	0.0
1907	Chi-A	48	90	12	20	1	0	0	2	12		.222	.314	.233	78	-2	-2	9	2			.986	4	P/O2	-0.1
1908	Chi-A	51	109	12	25	1	0	0	10	12		.229	.306	.239	79	-2	-2	10	4			.986	6	P/O	-0.1
1909	Chi-A	72	192	24	45	1	5	0	7	33		.234	.347	.292	106	2	3	23	7			.926	-4	OP	-0.3
1910	Chi-A	56	126	14	25	1	2	0	8	14		.198	.279	.238	65	-5	-5	10	2			.972	1	PO	-0.3
1911	Chi-A	39	78	12	20	1	1	0	6	7		.256	.318	.295	74	-3	-3	8	1			.919	-1	P/1O	0.0
1912	Chi-A	32	56	5	7	1	1	0	0	7		.125	.222	.179	15	-6	-6	2	0			1.000	-1	P	0.0
1913	Chi-A	20	25	1	3	0	0	0	0	3	1	.120	.214	.120	-2	-3	-3	1	0			.959	2	P/1	0.0
Total	13	547	1283	147	278	22	13	2	75	147	1	.217	.298	.259	74	-39	-35	121	32			.960	14	P/O12	-1.4

■ DEACON WHITE White, James Laurie b: 12/7/1847, Caton, N.Y. d: 7/7/39, Aurora, Ill. BL/TR, 5′11″, 175 lbs. Deb: 5/04/1871 FM

YEAR	TM/L	G	AB	R	H	2B	3B	HR	RBI	BB	SO	AVG	OBP	SLG	PRO+	BR	/A	RC	SB	CS	SBR	FA	FR	POS	TPR
1871	Cle-n	29	146	40	47	6	5	1	21	4	1	.322	.340	.452	132	5	6	24	2					*C/2	0.4
1872	Cle-n	22	108	21	37	3	2	0	22	4	1	.343	.366	.407	146	5	6	17						C/2OM	0.4
1873	Bos-n	60	310	79	121	20	8	0	**64**	0	2	.390	.390	.506	149	23	17	64						*C/O	1.3
1874	Bos-n	70	350	75	106	4	7	3		4		.303	.311	.380	112	7	3	42						*CO/12	0.4
1875	Bos-n	80	372	77	136	20	4	1		2		**.366**	.369	.449	175	29	27	63						*C/O1	2.5
1876	Chi-N	66	303	66	104	18	1	1	**60**	7	3	.343	.358	.419	141	18	13	47				.844	7	*C/O13P	1.9
1877	Bos-N	59	266	51	**103**	14	**11**	2	**49**	8	3	**.387**	.405	**.545**	**190**	**28**	**27**	**60**				.963	1	1O/C	2.4
1878	Cin-N	61	258	41	81	4	1	0	29	10	5	.314	.340	.337	136	6	10	30				.909	-4	*CO/3	0.6
1879	Cin-N	78	333	55	110	16	6	1	52	6	9	.330	.342	.423	159	17	20	49				.901	2	*CO/1M	2.1
1880	Cin-N	35	141	21	42	4	2	0	7	9	7	.298	.340	.355	137	5	6	17				.738	-3	O/12	0.1
1881	Buf-N	78	319	58	99	24	4	0	53	9	8	.310	.329	.411	133	11	11	44				.943	-9	12O/3C	0.1
1882	Buf-N	83	337	51	95	17	0	1	33	15	16	.282	.313	.341	108	4	3	37				.837	-10	*3C	-0.4
1883	Buf-N	94	391	62	114	14	5	0	47	23	18	.292	.331	.353	106	4	3	47				.797	-10	*3C	-0.5
1884	Buf-N	110	452	82	147	16	11	5	74	32	13	.325	.370	.442	149	28	26	76				.825	-7	*3/C	1.8
1885	Buf-N	98	404	54	118	6	6	0	57	12	11	.292	.313	.337	106	4	2	44				.888	1	*3	0.4
1886	Det-N	124	491	65	142	19	5	1	76	31	35	.289	.331	.354	106	5	3	62	9			.847	-8	*3	-0.2
1887	*Det-N	111	449	71	136	20	11	3	75	26	15	.303	.353	.416	111	9	7	75	20			.848	-0	*3/O1	0.7
1888	Det-N	125	527	75	157	22	5	4	71	21	24	.298	.336	.381	131	18	18	73	12			.857	-3	*3	1.7
1889	Pit-N	55	225	35	57	10	1	0	26	16	18	.253	.314	.307	83	-7	-4	23	2			.872	-10	3/1	-1.0
1890	Buf-P	122	439	62	114	13	4	0	47	67	30	.260	.381	.308	95	-4	4	54	3			.905	19	31/SP	1.8
Total	5 n	261	1286	292	447	53	26	5	107	14	4	.348	.355	.441	144	68	60	210	8					C/O21	5.0
Total	15	1299	5335	849	1619	217	73	18	756	292	215	.303	.344	.382	123	147	146	738	46			.853	-33	3C1O/2PS	11.5

■ JERRY WHITE White, Jerome Cardell b: 8/23/52, Shirley, Mass. BB/TR, 5′11″, 165 lbs. Deb: 9/16/74

YEAR	TM/L	G	AB	R	H	2B	3B	HR	RBI	BB	SO	AVG	OBP	SLG	PRO+	BR	/A	RC	SB	CS	SBR	FA	FR	POS	TPR
1974	Mon-N	9	10	0	4	1	1	0	2	0	0	.400	.400	.700	193	1	1	3	3	0	1	1.000	0	/O	0.2
1975	Mon-N	39	97	14	29	4	1	2	7	10	7	.299	.364	.423	113	2	2	16	5	2	0	.976	6	O	0.7
1976	Mon-N	114	278	32	68	11	1	2	21	27	31	.245	.316	.313	76	-7	-9	29	15	7	0	.982	-6	O	-1.9
1977	Mon-N	16	21	4	4	0	0	0	1	1	3	.190	.227	.190	14	-3	-2	1	1	0	0	1.000	-1	/O	-0.3
1978	Mon-N	18	10	2	2	0	0	0	0	1	3	.200	.273	.200	34	-1	-1	1	1	0	0	.000	0	/O	-0.1
	Chi-N	59	136	22	37	6	0	1	10	23	16	.272	.377	.338	90	1	-1	18	4	3	-1	.981	6	O	0.3
	Yr	77	146	24	39	6	0	1	10	24	19	.267	.371	.329	89	0	-1	19	5	3	-0	.981	6	O	0.2
1979	Mon-N	88	138	30	41	7	1	3	18	21	23	.297	.394	.428	125	5	5	25	8	4	0	.983	-1	O	0.3
1980	Mon-N	110	214	22	56	9	3	7	23	30	37	.262	.355	.430	118	6	5	34	8	7	-2	.946	-2	O	-0.1
1981	*Mon-N	59	119	11	26	5	1	3	11	13	17	.218	.295	.353	82	-3	-3	14	5	2	0	.952	-1	O	-0.5
1982	Mon-N	69	115	13	28	6	1	2	13	8	26	.243	.304	.365	85	-2	-2	12	3	3	-1	1.000	-1	O	-0.5
1983	Mon-N	40	34	4	5	1	0	0	0	12	8	.147	.383	.176	60	-1	-1	4	4	0	1	1.000	0	O	0.0
1986	StL-N	25	24	1	3	0	0	1	3	2	3	.125	.192	.250	21	-3	-3	1	0	0	0	1.000	-1	/O	-0.4
Total	11	646	1196	155	303	50	9	21	109	148	174	.253	.339	.363	94	-4	-8	158	57	28	0	.974	-2	O	-2.3

■ JACK WHITE White, John Peter b: 8/31/05, New York, N.Y. d: 6/19/71, Flushing, N.Y. BB/TR, 5′7.5″, 150 lbs. Deb: 6/22/27

YEAR	TM/L	G	AB	R	H	2B	3B	HR	RBI	BB	SO	AVG	OBP	SLG	PRO+	BR	/A	RC	SB	CS	SBR	FA	FR	POS	TPR
1927	Cin-N	5	4	1	0	0	0	0	0	0	0	.000	.000	.000	-99	-1	-1	0	0			1.000	0	/2S	-0.1
1928	Cin-N	1	3	0	0	0	0	0	0	0	1	.000	.000	.000	-99	-1	-1	0	0			.833	-1	/2	-0.1
Total	2	6	7	1	0	0	0	0	0	0	1	.000	.000	.000	-99	-2	-2	0	0			.929	-0	/2S	-0.2

■ JACK WHITE White, John Wallace b: 1/19/1878, Indianapolis, Ind. d: 9/30/63, Indianapolis, Ind BR/TR, 5′6″, Deb: 6/26/04

YEAR	TM/L	G	AB	R	H	2B	3B	HR	RBI	BB	SO	AVG	OBP	SLG	PRO+	BR	/A	RC	SB	CS	SBR	FA	FR	POS	TPR
1904	Bos-N	1	5	1	0	0	0	0	0	0		.000	.000	.000	-99	-1	-1	0	0			1.000	1	/O	0.0

■ JO-JO WHITE White, Joyner Clifford b: 6/1/09, Red Oak, Ga. d: 10/9/86, Tacoma, Wash. BL/TR, 5′11″, 165 lbs. Deb: 4/15/32 FMC

YEAR	TM/L	G	AB	R	H	2B	3B	HR	RBI	BB	SO	AVG	OBP	SLG	PRO+	BR	/A	RC	SB	CS	SBR	FA	FR	POS	TPR
1932	Det-A	80	208	25	54	6	3	2	21	22	19	.260	.330	.346	73	-7	-9	23	6	8	-3	.962	-0	O	-1.4
1933	Det-A	91	234	43	59	9	5	2	34	27	26	.252	.337	.359	83	-5	-6	29	5	5	-2	.977	0	O	-0.9
1934	*Det-A	115	384	97	120	18	5	0	44	69	39	.313	.419	.385	108	9	9	71	28	6	**5**	.959	-0	*O	0.8
1935	*Det-A	114	412	82	99	13	12	2	32	68	42	.240	.348	.345	83	-11	-9	53	19	10	-0	.962	-2	O	-1.4
1936	Det-A	58	51	11	14	3	0	0	6	9	10	.275	.383	.333	78	-1	-1	7	2	0	1	.938	-7	O	-0.7
1937	Det-A	94	305	50	75	5	7	0	21	50	40	.246	.354	.308	67	-13	-14	37	12	7	-1	.973	-3	O	-1.9
1938	Det-A	78	206	40	54	6	1	0	15	30	15	.262	.359	.301	63	-9	-11	24	3	4	-2	.967	0	O	-1.3
1943	Phi-A	139	500	69	124	17	7	1	30	61	51	.248	.335	.316	91	-5	-4	59	12	4	1	.966	-4	*O	-1.5
1944	Phi-A	85	267	30	59	4	2	1	21	40	27	.221	.329	.262	71	-9	-8	27	5	4	-1	.949	-1	O/S	-1.5
	Cin-N	24	85	9	20	2	0	0	5	10	7	.235	.316	.259	65	-4	-3	8	0			1.000	1	O	-0.4
Total	9	878	2652	456	678	83	42	8	229	386	276	.256	.353	.328	82	-56	-58	337	92	48		.965	-16	O/S	-10.2

■ MIKE WHITE White, Joyner Michael b: 12/18/38, Detroit, Mich. BR/TR, 5′8″, 160 lbs. Deb: 9/21/63 F

YEAR	TM/L	G	AB	R	H	2B	3B	HR	RBI	BB	SO	AVG	OBP	SLG	PRO+	BR	/A	RC	SB	CS	SBR	FA	FR	POS	TPR
1963	Hou-N	3	7	0	2	0	0	0	0	0	0	.286	.286	.286	69	-0	-0	1	0	0	0	1.000	1	/2	0.1
1964	Hou-N	89	280	30	76	11	3	0	27	20	47	.271	.320	.332	89	-6	-4	28	1	1	-0	.978	6	O2/3	0.0
1965	Hou-N	8	9	0	0	0	0	0	0	1	2	.000	.100	.000	-74	-2	-2	0	0	0	0	1.000	-0	/3	-0.2
Total	3	100	296	30	78	11	3	0	27	21	49	.264	.312	.321	84	-8	-6	29	1	1	-0	.985	7	/O23	-0.1

YEAR	TM/L	G	AB	R	H	2B	3B	HR	RBI	BB	SO	AVG	OBP	SLG	PRO+	BR	/A	RC	SB	CS	SBR	FA	FR	POS	TPR

■ MYRON WHITE White, Myron Alan b: 8/1/57, Long Beach, Cal. BL/TL, 5'11", 180 lbs. Deb: 9/04/78

| 1978 | LA-N | 7 | 4 | 1 | 2 | 0 | 0 | 0 | 1 | 0 | 1 | .500 | .500 | .500 | 181 | 0 | 0 | 1 | 0 | 1 | -1 | 1.000 | 0 | /O | 0.0 |

■ ROY WHITE White, Roy Hilton b: 12/27/43, Los Angeles, Cal. BB/TR, 5'10", 172 lbs. Deb: 9/07/65 C

1965	NY-A	14	42	7	14	2	0	0	3	4	7	.333	.404	.381	125	2	2	7	2	1	0	1.000	-1	O/2	0.1
1966	NY-A	115	316	39	71	13	2	7	20	37	43	.225	.308	.345	91	-5	-3	35	14	7	0	.957	0	O/2	-0.7
1967	NY-A	70	214	22	48	8	0	2	18	19	25	.224	.291	.290	75	-7	-6	20	10	4	1	.968	-6	O3	-1.6
1968	NY-A	159	577	89	154	20	7	17	62	73	50	.267	.352	.414	136	23	25	86	20	11	-1	.997	10	*O	2.9
1969	NY-A★	130	448	55	130	30	5	7	74	81	51	.290	.400	.426	136	22	24	81	18	10	-1	.989	11	*O	2.8
1970	NY-A☆	162	609	109	180	30	6	22	94	95	66	.296	.391	.473	144	33	37	116	24	10	1	.994	7	*O	3.7
1971	NY-A	147	524	86	153	22	7	19	84	86	66	.292	.399	.469	134	34	38	103	14	7	0	1.000	10	*O	4.3
1972	NY-A	155	556	76	150	29	0	10	54	99	59	.270	.385	.376	131	23	25	88	23	7	3	.994	9	*O	3.3
1973	NY-A	162	639	88	157	22	3	18	60	78	81	.246	.330	.374	101	-1	1	80	16	9	-1	.977	4	*O	-0.3
1974	NY-A	136	473	68	130	19	8	7	43	67	44	.275	.369	.393	123	14	16	73	15	6	1	.993	3	OD	1.7
1975	NY-A	148	556	81	161	32	5	12	59	72	50	.290	.373	.430	130	20	22	91	16	15	-4	.984	11	*O/1D	2.3
1976	*NY-A	156	626	**104**	179	29	3	14	65	83	52	.286	.370	.409	129	23	24	98	31	13	2	.987	6	*O	2.6
1977	*NY-A	143	519	72	139	25	2	14	52	75	58	.268	.360	.405	109	7	8	77	18	11	-1	.981	10	*O/D	1.1
1978	*NY-A	103	346	44	93	13	3	8	43	42	35	.269	.351	.393	112	5	6	48	10	4	1	.992	-4	OD	-0.1
1979	NY-A	81	205	24	44	6	0	3	27	23	21	.215	.294	.288	59	-12	-11	17	2	2	-1	1.000	0	DO	-1.3
Total	15	1881	6650	964	1803	300	51	160	758	934	708	.271	.363	.404	122	180	206	1020	233	117	-0	.988	71	*OD/312	20.8

■ SAMMY WHITE White, Samuel Charles b: 7/7/28, Wenatchee, Wash. d: 8/5/91, Princeville, Hawaii BR/TR, 6'3", 195 lbs. Deb: 9/26/51

1951	Bos-A	4	11	0	2	0	0	0	0	0	3	.182	.182	.182	-1	-2	-2	0	0	0	0	1.000	1	/C	-0.1
1952	Bos-A	115	381	35	107	20	2	10	49	16	43	.281	.310	.423	95	-1	-4	46	2	3	-1	.983	-2	*C	-0.2
1953	Bos-A☆	136	476	59	130	34	2	13	64	29	48	.273	.318	.435	96	-1	-4	63	3	2	-0	.986	9	*C	1.0
1954	Bos-A	137	493	46	139	25	2	14	75	21	50	.282	.311	.426	90	-7	-9	60	1	3	-2	.979	13	*C	0.9
1955	Bos-A	143	544	65	142	30	4	11	64	44	58	.261	.324	.392	84	-8	-14	64	1	2	-1	.984	-0	*C	-1.0
1956	Bos-A	114	392	28	96	15	2	5	44	35	40	.245	.307	.332	61	-18	-24	37	2	1	0	.984	7	*C	-1.2
1957	Bos-A	111	340	24	73	10	1	3	31	25	38	.215	.268	.276	46	-24	-26	22	0	1	-1	.985	-4	*C	-2.8
1958	Bos-A	102	328	25	85	15	3	6	35	21	37	.259	.306	.378	81	-6	-9	37	1	1	-0	.988	-2	*C	-0.7
1959	Bos-A	119	377	34	107	13	4	1	42	23	39	.284	.327	.347	81	-8	-10	40	4	2	0	.990	1	*C	-0.3
1961	Mil-N	21	63	1	14	1	0	1	5	2	9	.222	.246	.286	43	-5	-5	4	0	0	0	.974	4	C	-0.1
1962	Phi-N	41	97	7	21	4	0	2	12	2	16	.216	.240	.320	50	-7	-7	6	0	0	0	.975	5	C	-0.1
Total	11	1043	3502	324	916	167	20	66	421	218	381	.262	.307	.377	79	-82	-114	379	14	15	-5	.984	30	*C	-4.5

■ SAM WHITE White, Samuel Lambeth b: 8/23/1892, Greater Preston, Yorkshire, England d: 11/11/29, Philadelphia, Pa. BL/TR, 6', 185 lbs. Deb: 9/08/19

| 1919 | Bos-N | 1 | 1 | 0 | 0 | 0 | 0 | 0 | 0 | 0 | 0 | .000 | .000 | .000 | -99 | -0 | -0 | 0 | 0 | | | 1.000 | 2 | /C | 0.1 |

■ BARNEY WHITE White, William Barney "Bear" b: 6/25/23, Paris, Tex. BR/TR, 5'11", 186 lbs. Deb: 6/05/45

| 1945 | Bro-N | 4 | 1 | 2 | 0 | 0 | 0 | 0 | 0 | 1 | 1 | .000 | .500 | .000 | 46 | 0 | 0 | 0 | 0 | | | 1.000 | 0 | /S3 | 0.0 |

■ BILL WHITE White, William De Kova b: 1/28/34, Lakewood, Fla. BL/TL, 6', 195 lbs. Deb: 5/07/56

1956	NY-N	138	508	63	130	23	7	22	59	47	72	.256	.324	.459	108	4	5	76	15	8	-0	.989	2	*1/O	-0.3
1958	SF-N	26	29	5	7	1	0	1	4	7	5	.241	.389	.379	107	0	1	5	1	0	0	1.000	-1	/1O	0.0
1959	StL-N☆	138	517	77	156	33	9	12	72	34	61	.302	.347	.470	108	10	6	83	15	10	-2	.962	-2	O1	-0.5
1960	StL-N★	144	554	81	157	27	10	16	79	42	83	.283	.336	.455	105	10	4	84	12	6	0	.990	-6	*1O	-1.3
1961	StL-N★	153	591	89	169	28	11	20	90	64	84	.286	.357	.472	107	15	7	96	8	1	-4	.989	-2	*1	-1.2
1962	StL-N	159	614	93	199	31	3	20	102	58	69	.324	.388	.482	120	28	20	114	9	7	-2	.993	1	*1O	1.0
1963	StL-N★	162	658	106	200	26	8	27	109	59	100	.304	.361	.491	131	35	28	117	10	9	-2	.991	-2	*1	1.8
1964	*StL-N★	160	631	92	191	37	4	21	102	52	103	.303	.357	.474	121	26	19	107	7	6	-2	**.996**	-1	*1	1.0
1965	StL-N	148	543	82	157	26	3	24	73	63	86	.289	.367	.481	125	27	21	97	3	3	-1	.992	6	*1	1.8
1966	Phi-N	159	577	85	159	23	6	22	103	68	109	.276	.355	.451	122	18	18	96	16	6	1	**.994**	7	*1	1.6
1967	Phi-N	110	308	29	77	6	2	8	33	52	61	.250	.364	.360	107	5	5	44	6	1	1	.993	0	1	0.1
1968	Phi-N	127	385	34	92	16	2	9	40	39	79	.239	.312	.361	102	1	1	44	0	1	-1	.994	4	*1	-0.4
1969	StL-N	49	57	7	12	1	0	0	4	11	15	.211	.338	.228	61	-2	-2	5	1	0	0	1.000	1	1	-0.2
Total	13	1673	5972	843	1706	278	65	202	870	596	927	.286	.353	.455	115	177	132	968	103	68	-10	.992	8	*1O	3.4

■ BILL WHITE White, William Dighton b: 5/1/1860, Bridgeport, Ohio d: 12/29/24, Bellaire, Ohio TR , Deb: 5/03/1884

1884	Pit-a	74	291	25	66	7	10	0		13		.227	.262	.320	90	-3	-3	25				.807	-11	S3/O	-1.3
1886	Lou-a	135	557	96	143	17	10	1		37		.257	.304	.329	95	-0	-5	61	14			.871	17	*S/P	1.1
1887	Lou-a	132	512	85	129	7	9	2		47		.252	.315	.313	76	-15	-17	65	41			.869	22	*S	0.5
1888	Lou-a	49	198	35	55	6	5	1	30	7		.278	.313	.374	125	4	5	29	15			.816	-3	S3	0.3
	*StL-a	76	275	31	48	2	3	2	30	21		.175	.238	.225	46	-14	-19	17	6			.892	-3	S/2	-1.9
	Yr	125	473	66	103	8	8	3	60	28		.218	.269	.288	77	-10	-14	43	21			.864	-6	*S3/2	-1.6
Total	4	466	1833	272	441	39	37	6	60	125		.241	.292	.312	84	-27	-39	196	76			.860	22	S/302P	-1.3

■ BILL WHITE White, William Edward b: Milner, Ga. Deb: 6/21/1879

| 1879 | Pro-N | 1 | 4 | 1 | 1 | 0 | 0 | 0 | 0 | 0 | 1 | .250 | .250 | .250 | 67 | -0 | -0 | 0 | | | | 1.000 | 0 | /1 | 0.0 |

■ WARREN WHITE White, William Warren (a.k.a. William Warren) d: 3/3/1898, 5'10.5", 170 lbs. Deb: 6/17/1871 M

1871	Oly-n	1	4	0	0	0	0	0	0	0	0	.000	.000	.000	-99	-1	-1	0	0					/2	-0.1
1872	Nat-n	10	45	7	12	0	0	0	3	0	0	.267	.267	.267	55	-2	-3	3						3S	-0.3
1873	Was-n	39	160	29	43	3	5	0	18	0	1	.269	.269	.350	83	-4	-3	15						*3/S	-0.3
1874	Bal-n	45	212	20	56	1	0	0		1		.264	.268	.269	72	-7	-6	16						*3M	-0.5
1875	Chi-n	69	285	37	71	9	0	0		0		.249	.249	.281	82	-5	-5	20						*3/SO2	-0.5
1884	Was-U	4	18	2	1	0	0	0		0		.056	.056	.056	-64	-3	-3	0				.692	-1	/3S2	-0.3
Total	5 n	164	706	93	182	13	5	0	21	1	1	.258	.259	.290	76	-18	-19	55						3/SO2	-1.7

■ ED WHITED Whited, Edward Morris b: 2/9/64, Bristol, Pa. BR/TR, 6'3", 195 lbs. Deb: 7/05/89

| 1989 | Atl-N | 36 | 74 | 5 | 12 | 3 | 0 | 1 | 4 | 6 | 15 | .162 | .225 | .243 | 33 | -6 | -7 | 4 | 1 | 0 | 0 | .914 | -0 | 3/1 | -0.7 |

■ BURGESS WHITEHEAD Whitehead, Burgess Urquhart "Whitey" b: 6/29/10, Tarboro, N.C. BR/TR, 5'10.5", 160 lbs. Deb: 4/30/33

1933	StL-N	12	7	2	2	0	0	0	0	0	1	.286	.286	.286	60	-0	-0	0	0			1.000	0	/S2	0.0
1934	*StL-N	100	332	55	92	13	5	1	24	12	19	.277	.310	.355	73	-11	-13	38	5			.962	-1	2S3	-0.9
1935	StL-N★	107	338	45	89	10	2	0	33	11	14	.263	.289	.305	57	-19	-21	30	5			.980	5	2/3S	-1.0
1936	*NY-N	154	632	99	176	31	3	4	47	29	32	.278	.317	.356	82	-17	-16	70	14			.969	29	*2	2.3
1937	*NY-N★	152	574	64	164	15	6	5	52	28	20	.286	.323	.359	84	-12	-13	67	7			**.974**	26	*2	2.3
1939	NY-N	95	335	31	80	6	3	2	24	24	19	.239	.299	.293	59	-19	-19	28	1			.970	21	2/S3	0.7
1940	NY-N	133	568	68	160	9	6	4	36	26	17	.282	.319	.340	81	-14	-15	59	9			.947	13	32/S	-2.0
1941	NY-N	116	403	41	92	15	4	1	23	14	10	.228	.258	.293	54	-25	-26	27	7			.970	-0	2/3	-2.0
1946	Pit-N	55	127	10	28	1	2	0	5	6	6	.220	.261	.260	47	-9	-9	8	3			.963	-6	2/3S	-1.4
Total	9	924	3316	415	883	100	31	17	245	150	138	.266	.304	.331	72	-126	-132	328	51			.972	86	23/S	0.3

■ MILT WHITEHEAD Whitehead, Milton P. b: 1862, Canada d: 8/15/01, Highland, Cal. Deb: 4/20/1884

| 1884 | StL-U | 99 | 393 | 61 | 83 | 15 | 1 | 1 | | 8 | | .211 | .227 | .262 | 63 | -14 | -16 | 24 | | | | .803 | -11 | *S/OP23 | -2.3 |

YEAR	TM/L	G	AB	R	H	2B	3B	HR	RBI	BB	SO	AVG	OBP	SLG	PRO+	BR	/A	RC	SB	CS	SBR	FA	FR	POS	TPR
	KC-U	5	22	2	3	0	0	0		0		.136	.136	.136	-9	-2	-2	0				.857	-1	/2CS3	-0.3
	Yr	104	415	63	86	15	1	1		8		.207	.222	.255	59	-16	-18	24				.804	-12	S/2O3PC	-2.6
■ GIL WHITEHOUSE	Whitehouse, Gilbert Arthur b: 10/15/1893, Somerville, Mass. d: 2/14/26, Brewer, Me. BB/TR, 5'10", 170 lbs. Deb: 6/20/12																								
1912	Bos-N	2	3	0	0	0	0	0	0	0	3	.000	.000	.000	-98	-1	-1	0	0			.667	-1	/C	-0.2
1915	New-F	35	120	16	27	6	2	0	9	6	16	.225	.268	.308	73	-5	-4	11	3			.949	-1	O/PC	-0.7
Total	2	37	123	16	27	6	2	0	9	6	19	.220	.262	.301	69	-6	-5	11	3			.846	-2	/OCP	-0.9
■ GURDON WHITELEY	Whiteley, Gurdon W. b: 10/5/1859, Ashaway, R.I. d: 11/24/24, Cranston, R.I. 5'11", 190 lbs. Deb: 8/07/1884																								
1884	Cle-N	8	34	4	5	0	0	0	0	1	8	.147	.171	.147	1	-4	-4	1				.800	1	/O	-0.3
1885	Bos-N	33	135	14	25	2	2	1	7	1	25	.185	.191	.252	44	-9	-8	7				.781	-2	O/C	-1.0
Total	2	41	169	18	30	2	2	1	7	2	33	.178	.187	.231	34	-12	-12	8				.785	-1	/OC	-1.3
■ GEORGE WHITEMAN	Whiteman, George "Lucky" b: 12/23/1882, Peoria, Ill. d: 2/10/47, Houston, Tex. BR/TR, 5'7", 160 lbs. Deb: 9/13/07																								
1907	Bos-A	4	12	0	2	0	0	0	1	0		.167	.167	.167	7	-1	-1	0	0			1.000	-1	/O	-0.2
1913	NY-A	11	32	8	11	3	1	0	2	7	2	.344	.462	.500	181	4	4	8	2			.938	1	O	0.5
1918	*Bos-A	71	214	24	57	14	0	1	28	20	9	.266	.335	.346	107	1	2	28	9			.935	-11	O	-1.5
Total	3	86	258	32	70	17	1	1	31	27	11	.271	.345	.357	113	4	4	36	11			.936	-11	/O	-1.2
■ MARK WHITEN	Whiten, Mark Anthony b: 11/25/66, Pensacola, Fla. BB/TR, 6'3", 210 lbs. Deb: 7/12/90																								
1990	Tor-A	33	88	12	24	1	1	2	7	7	14	.273	.326	.375	94	-1	-1	11	2	0	1	1.000	2	O/D	0.1
1991	Tor-A	46	149	12	33	4	3	2	19	11	35	.221	.280	.329	65	-7	-7	13	0	1	-1	1.000	3	O	-0.7
	Cle-A	70	258	34	66	14	4	7	26	19	50	.256	.312	.422	100	-0	-0	32	4	2	0	.962	11	O/D	0.9
	Yr	116	407	46	99	18	7	9	45	30	85	.243	.300	.388	87	-7	-8	45	4	3	-1	.975	14	*O/D	0.2
1992	Cle-A	148	508	73	129	19	4	9	43	72	102	.254	.349	.360	98	1	0	64	16	12	-2	.980	13	*O/D	0.8
Total	3	297	1003	131	252	38	12	20	95	109	201	.251	.328	.373	93	-7	-8	120	22	15	-2	.979	28	O/D	1.1
■ FRED WHITFIELD	Whitfield, Fred Dwight b: 1/7/38, Vandiver, Ala. BL/TL, 6'1", 190 lbs. Deb: 5/27/62																								
1962	StL-N	73	158	20	42	7	1	8	34	7	30	.266	.301	.475	95	0	-2	21	1	0	0	.987	1	1	-0.2
1963	Cle-A	109	346	44	87	17	3	21	54	24	61	.251	.307	.500	123	9	9	54	0	1	-1	.987	-3	1	0.1
1964	Cle-A	101	293	29	79	13	1	10	29	12	58	.270	.303	.423	100	-1	-1	34	0	5	-3	.992	-2	1	-0.9
1965	Cle-A	132	468	49	137	23	1	26	90	16	42	.293	.319	.513	131	17	17	71	2	2	-1	.993	4	*1	1.5
1966	Cle-A	137	502	59	121	15	2	27	78	27	76	.241	.285	.440	105	1	1	61	1	2	-1	.991	-4	*1	-1.3
1967	Cle-A	100	257	24	56	10	0	9	31	25	45	.218	.290	.362	91	-3	-3	26	3	3	-1	.993	4	1	-0.5
1968	Cin-N	87	171	15	44	8	0	6	32	9	29	.257	.302	.409	105	2	1	20	0	3	-2	.981	-1	1	-0.4
1969	Cin-N	74	74	2	11	0	0	1	8	18	27	.149	.315	.189	42	-5	-5	6	0	0	0	.985	1	1	-0.5
1970	Mon-N	4	15	0	1	0	0	0	0	1	3	.067	.125	.067	-47	-3	-3	0	0	0	0	.976	2	/1	-0.2
Total	9	817	2284	242	578	93	8	108	356	139	371	.253	.301	.443	107	17	14	293	7	16	-8	.990	3	1	-2.4
■ TERRY WHITFIELD	Whitfield, Terry Bertland b: 1/12/53, Blythe, Cal. BL/TR, 6'1", 197 lbs. Deb: 9/29/74																								
1974	NY-A	2	5	0	1	0	0	0	0	0	1	.200	.200	.200	16	-1	-1	0	0	0	0	.000	-1	/O	-0.1
1975	NY-A	28	81	9	22	1	1	0	7	1	17	.272	.280	.309	68	-4	-3	7	1	0	0	.978	0	O/D	-0.4
1976	NY-A	1	0	0	0	0	0	0	0	0	0	—	—	—	—	0	0	0	0	0	0	.000	-1	/O	-0.1
1977	SF-N	114	326	41	93	21	3	7	36	20	46	.285	.330	.433	103	1	1	46	2	3	-1	.972	-0	O	-0.4
1978	SF-N	149	488	70	141	20	2	10	32	33	69	.289	.337	.400	109	3	5	62	5	11	-5	.988	-6	*O	-1.3
1979	SF-N	133	394	52	113	20	4	5	44	36	47	.287	.353	.396	111	3	6	52	5	4	-1	.957	-7	*O	-0.6
1980	SF-N	118	321	38	95	16	2	4	26	20	44	.296	.339	.396	107	2	2	42	4	2	0	.987	-0	O	-0.1
1984	LA-N	87	180	15	44	8	0	4	18	17	35	.244	.313	.356	88	-3	-3	18	1	4	-2	.988	-5	O	-1.1
1985	*LA-N	79	104	8	27	7	0	3	16	6	27	.260	.300	.413	101	-1	-0	12	0	0	0	.926	-5	O	-0.6
1986	LA-N	19	14	0	1	0	0	0	0	5	2	.071	.316	.071	14	-1	-1	0	0	0	0	1.000	-0	/O	-0.2
Total	10	730	1913	233	537	93	12	33	179	138	288	.281	.332	.394	103	-2	6	241	18	24	-9	.976	-24	O/D	-4.9
■ ED WHITING	Whiting, Edward C. (a.k.a. Harry Zieber) b: 1860, Philadelphia, Pa. BL/TR, 188 lbs. Deb: 5/02/1882																								
1882	Bal-a	74	308	43	80	14	5	0		7		.260	.276	.338	115	2	5	29				.834	-8	*C/1O	-0.1
1883	Lou-a	58	240	35	70	16	4	2		9		.292	.317	.417	145	9	12	33				.884	-8	C/O231	0.6
1884	Lou-a	42	157	16	35	7	3	0		9		.223	.274	.306	96	-1	-0	13				.891	-2	C/O1	0.1
1886	Was-N	6	21	0	0	0	0	0	0	1	12	.000	.045	.000	-90	-5	-4	0	0			.919	-3	/C	-0.6
Total	4	180	726	94	185	37	12	2	0	26	12	.255	.282	.347	114	5	12	75	0			.866	-20	C/O123	0.0
■ DICK WHITMAN	Whitman, Dick Corwin b: 11/9/20, Woodburn, Ore. BL/TR, 5'11", 170 lbs. Deb: 4/16/46																								
1946	Bro-N	104	265	39	69	15	3	2	31	22	19	.260	.317	.362	92	-3	-3	30	5			1.000	-2	O	-0.9
1947	Bro-N	4	10	1	4	0	0	0	2	1	0	.400	.455	.400	124	0	0	2	0			1.000	0	/O	0.0
1948	Bro-N	60	165	24	48	13	0	0	20	14	12	.291	.346	.370	91	-1	-2	22	4			.990	-1	O	-0.6
1949	*Bro-N	23	49	8	9	2	0	0	2	4	4	.184	.245	.224	26	-5	-5	2	0			.952	-1	O	-0.7
1950	*Phi-N	75	132	21	33	7	0	0	12	10	10	.250	.317	.303	65	-7	-6	13	1			.983	-4	O	-1.1
1951	Phi-N	19	17	0	2	0	0	0	0	0	1	.118	.118	.118	-37	-3	-3	0	0	0	0	.000	-3	/O	-0.6
Total	6	285	638	93	165	37	3	2	67	51	46	.259	.316	.335	78	-19	-20	69	10	0		.992	-11	O	-3.9
■ FRANK WHITMAN	Whitman, Walter Franklin "Hooker" b: 8/15/24, Marengo, Ind. BR/TR, 6'2", 175 lbs. Deb: 6/30/46																								
1946	Chi-A	17	16	7	1	0	0	0	1	2	6	.063	.211	.063	-22	-3	-2	0	0	1	-1	1.000	4	/S12	0.1
1948	Chi-A	3	6	0	0	0	0	0	0	0	3	.000	.000	.000	-99	-2	-2	0	0	0	0	.500	-1	/S	-0.3
Total	2	20	22	7	1	0	0	0	1	2	9	.045	.160	.045	-43	-4	-4	0	0	1	-1	.885	3	/S21	-0.2
■ DAN WHITMER	Whitmer, Daniel Charles b: 11/23/55, Redlands, Cal. BR/TR, 6'3", 195 lbs. Deb: 7/20/80																								
1980	Cal-A	48	87	8	21	3	0	0	7	4	21	.241	.275	.276	53	-6	-5	7	1	0	0	1.000	4	C	0.0
1981	Tor-A	7	9	0	1	1	0	0	0	1	2	.111	.200	.222	20	-1	-1	0	0	0	0	1.000	1	/C	0.0
Total	2	55	96	8	22	4	0	0	7	5	23	.229	.267	.271	49	-7	-6	7	1	0	0	1.000	5	/C	0.0
■ PINKY WHITNEY	Whitney, Arthur Carter b: 1/2/05, San Antonio, Tex. d: 9/1/87, Center, Tex. BR/TR, 5'10", 165 lbs. Deb: 4/11/28																								
1928	Phi-N	151	585	73	176	35	4	10	103	36	30	.301	.342	.426	96	-2	-4	83	3			.955	3	*3	0.7
1929	Phi-N	154	612	89	200	43	14	8	115	61	35	.327	.390	.482	108	14	8	113	7			.967	**21**	*3	3.2
1930	Phi-N	149	606	87	207	41	5	8	117	40	41	.342	.383	.465	97	4	-3	104	3			.965	20	*3	2.3
1931	Phi-N	130	501	64	144	36	5	9	74	30	38	.287	.331	.433	96	2	-3	73	6			.948	-6	*3	-0.2
1932	Phi-N	154	624	93	186	33	11	13	124	35	66	.298	.335	.449	97	6	-3	95	6			**.960**	5	*3/2	1.3
1933	Phi-N	31	121	12	32	4	0	3	19	8	8	.264	.310	.372	83	-1	-3	12	1			.963	-4	3	-0.6
	Bos-N	100	382	42	94	17	2	8	49	25	23	.246	.296	.364	95	-7	-3	40	2			.971	1	32	0.4
	Yr	131	503	54	126	21	2	11	68	33	31	.250	.299	.366	92	-8	-6	52	3			.969	-4	*32	-0.2
1934	Bos-N	146	563	58	146	26	2	12	79	25	54	.259	.294	.377	85	-18	-13	61	7			**.968**	3	*32/S	-0.3
1935	Bos-N	126	458	41	125	23	4	4	60	24	36	.273	.312	.367	89	-12	-7	51	2			.958	6	32	0.5
1936	Bos-N	10	40	1	7	0	0	0	5	2	4	.175	.233	.175	12	-5	-5	1	0			.971	1	3	-0.3
	Phi-N	114	411	44	121	17	3	6	59	37	33	.294	.354	.394	92	1	-5	58	2			.955	10	*3/2	0.9
	Yr	124	451	45	128	17	3	6	64	39	37	.284	.343	.375	86	-4	-9	59	2			.956	11	*3/2	0.6
1937	Phi-N	138	487	56	166	19	4	8	79	43	44	.341	.395	.446	118	20	15	84	6			**.982**	4	*3	2.1
1938	Phi-N	102	300	27	83	9	1	3	38	27	22	.277	.336	.343	90	-5	-4	34	0			.934	-2	3/12	-0.5
1939	Phi-N	34	75	9	14	0	1	1	6	7	4	.187	.256	.253	38	-7	-6	5	0			.991	1	1/23	-0.7

YEAR	TM/L	G	AB	R	H	2B	3B	HR	RBI	BB	SO	AVG	OBP	SLG	PRO+	BR	/A	RC	SB	CS	SBR	FA	FR	POS	TPR
Total	12	1539	5765	696	1701	303	56	93	927	400	438	.295	.343	.415	96	-9	-36	815	45			.961	63	*32/1S	8.8

■ ART WHITNEY Whitney, Arthur Wilson b: 1/16/1858, Brockton, Mass. d: 8/15/43, Lowell, Mass. BR/TR, 5'8", 155 lbs. Deb: 5/01/1880 F

YEAR	TM/L	G	AB	R	H	2B	3B	HR	RBI	BB	SO	AVG	OBP	SLG	PRO+	BR	/A	RC	SB	CS	SBR	FA	FR	POS	TPR
1880	Wor-N	76	302	38	67	13	5	1	36	9	15	.222	.244	.308	79	-4	-8	23				.860	-1	*3	-0.6
1881	Det-N	58	214	23	39	7	5	0	9	7	15	.182	.208	.262	45	-13	-14	12				.849	7	*3	-0.5
1882	Pro-N	11	40	2	3	0	0	0	1	2	11	.075	.119	.075	-36	-6	-6	0				.784	-2	S	-0.7
	Det-N	31	115	10	21	0	0	0	4	1	12	.183	.190	.183	20	-10	-10	4				.854	1	3/SP	-0.6
	Yr	42	155	12	24	0	0	0	5	3	23	.155	.171	.155	5	-16	-16	4				.854	-1	3S/P	-1.3
1884	Pit-a	23	94	10	28	4	0	0		1		.298	.305	.340	111	1	1	10				.916	4	3/OS	0.4
1885	Pit-a	90	373	53	87	10	4	0		16		.233	.267	.282	77	-10	-9	29				**.918**	-14	*S/32O	-2.0
1886	Pit-a	136	511	70	122	13	4	0		51		.239	.315	.280	89	-5	-4	51	15			**.906**	11	*3S/P	0.9
1887	Pit-N	119	431	57	112	11	4	0	51	55	18	.260	.346	.304	89	-7	-2	50	10			**.924**	-4	*3	-0.4
1888	*NY-N	90	328	28	72	1	4	1	28	8	22	.220	.240	.256	61	-14	-14	22	7			.887	7	3	-0.6
1889	*NY-N	129	473	71	103	12	2	1	59	56	39	.218	.303	.258	59	-24	-24	44	19			.882	-0	*3/P	-1.8
1890	NY-P	119	442	71	97	12	3	0	45	64	19	.219	.322	.260	53	-24	-32	41	8			.865	-12	3S	-3.1
1891	Cin-a	93	347	42	69	6	1	3	33	31	20	.199	.270	.248	46	-22	-27	26	8			.903	-5	3	-2.4
	StL-a	3	11	0	0	0	0	0	0	1	2	.000	.083	.000	-65	-2	-3	0	0			.867	2	/3	-0.1
	Yr	96	358	42	69	6	1	3	33	32	22	.193	.265	.240	43	-24	-30	25	8			**.902**	-3	3	-2.5
Total	11	978	3681	475	820	89	32	6	266	302	173	.223	.285	.269	66	-140	-152	312	67			.888	-7	3S/P2O	-11.5

■ FRANK WHITNEY Whitney, Frank Thomas "Jumbo" b: 2/18/1856, Brockton, Mass. d: 10/30/43, Baltimore, Md. BR/TR, 5'7.5", 152 lbs. Deb: 5/17/1876 F

YEAR	TM/L	G	AB	R	H	2B	3B	HR	RBI	BB	SO	AVG	OBP	SLG	PRO+	BR	/A	RC	SB	CS	SBR	FA	FR	POS	TPR
1876	Bos-N	34	139	27	33	7	1	0	15	1	3	.237	.243	.302	79	-3	-3	10				.818	3	O/2	-0.1

■ JIM WHITNEY Whitney, James Evans "Grasshopper Jim" b: 11/10/1857, Conklin, N.Y. d: 5/21/1891, Binghamton, N.Y. BL/TR, 6'2", 172 lbs. Deb: 5/02/1881

YEAR	TM/L	G	AB	R	H	2B	3B	HR	RBI	BB	SO	AVG	OBP	SLG	PRO+	BR	/A	RC	SB	CS	SBR	FA	FR	POS	TPR
1881	Bos-N	75	282	37	72	17	3	0	32	19	18	.255	.302	.337	106	1	3	29				.808	-9	*PO/1	-0.5
1882	Bos-N	61	251	49	81	18	7	5	48	24	13	.323	.382	.510	183	24	24	50				.886	-3	P/O1	-0.1
1883	Bos-N	96	409	78	115	27	10	5	57	25	29	.281	.323	.433	124	13	12	59				.921	-4	PO/1	0.1
1884	Bos-N	66	270	41	70	17	5	3	40	16	38	.259	.301	.393	117	5	5	33				1.000	-1	PO1/3	-0.4
1885	Bos-N	72	290	35	68	8	4	0	36	17	24	.234	.277	.290	86	-5	-4	24				.901	5	PO/1	-0.3
1886	KC-N	67	247	25	59	13	3	2	23	29	39	.239	.319	.340	94	1	-2	29	5			.927	6	PO/3	-0.1
1887	Was-N	54	201	29	53	9	6	2	22	18	24	.264	.324	.398	107	0	2	30	10			.905	2	P/O	-0.2
1888	Was-N	42	141	13	24	0	0	1	17	7	20	.170	.209	.191	32	-11	-10	6	3			.882	-2	P/O1	-0.2
1889	Ind-N	10	32	6	12	4	1	0	4	5	6	.375	.474	.563	188	4	4	10	2			1.000	-1	/PO	0.0
1890	Phi-a	7	21	3	5	0	0	0		1		.238	.273	.238	54	-1	-1	1	0			.900	-1	/PO	0.0
Total	10	550	2144	316	559	113	39	18	279	161	211	.261	.313	.375	112	31	33	271	20			.900	-9	PO/13	-1.7

■ ERNIE WHITT Whitt, Leo Ernest b: 6/13/52, Detroit, Mich. BL/TR, 6'2", 200 lbs. Deb: 9/12/76

YEAR	TM/L	G	AB	R	H	2B	3B	HR	RBI	BB	SO	AVG	OBP	SLG	PRO+	BR	/A	RC	SB	CS	SBR	FA	FR	POS	TPR
1976	Bos-A	8	18	4	4	2	0	1	3	2	2	.222	.300	.500	117	1	0	3	0	0	0	1.000	-1	/C	0.0
1977	Tor-A	23	41	4	7	3	0	0	6	2	12	.171	.209	.244	23	-4	-4	2	0	0	0	1.000	1	C	-0.3
1978	Tor-A	2	4	0	0	0	0	0	0	1	1	.000	.200	.000	-38	-1	-1	0	0	0	0	1.000	0	/C	0.0
1980	Tor-A	106	295	23	70	12	2	6	34	22	30	.237	.290	.353	72	-10	-12	27	1	3	-2	.986	6	*C	-0.4
1981	Tor-A	74	195	16	46	9	0	1	16	20	30	.236	.307	.297	70	-6	-7	19	5	2	0	.991	9	C	0.4
1982	Tor-A	105	284	28	74	14	2	11	42	26	34	.261	.323	.440	98	2	-1	40	3	1	0	.982	1	C/D	0.3
1983	Tor-A	123	344	53	88	15	2	17	56	50	55	.256	.350	.459	114	10	7	55	1	1	-0	.992	6	*C	1.7
1984	Tor-A	124	315	35	75	12	1	15	46	43	49	.238	.331	.425	104	3	2	44	0	3	-2	.994	12	*C	1.7
1985	*Tor-A★	139	412	55	101	21	2	19	64	47	59	.245	.324	.444	105	4	3	58	3	6	-3	.988	6	*C	1.2
1986	Tor-A	131	395	48	106	19	2	16	56	35	39	.268	.328	.448	106	4	3	56	0	1	-1	.991	-4	*C	0.6
1987	Tor-A	135	446	57	120	24	1	19	75	44	50	.269	.336	.455	105	4	3	64	0	1	-1	.994	6	*C	1.6
1988	Tor-A	127	398	63	100	11	2	16	70	61	38	.251	.352	.410	112	8	8	59	4	2	0	.994	-6	*C	1.1
1989	*Tor-A	129	385	42	101	24	1	11	53	52	53	.262	.350	.416	117	8	9	56	5	4	-1	.992	-2	*C/D	1.2
1990	Atl-N	67	180	14	31	8	0	2	10	23	27	.172	.266	.250	40	-14	-15	12	0	2	-1	.991	2	C	-1.2
1991	Bal-A	35	62	5	15	2	0	0	3	8	12	.242	.329	.274	71	-2	-2	5	0	0	0	1.000	-1	C/D	-0.2
Total	15	1328	3774	447	938	176	15	134	534	436	491	.249	.327	.410	98	6	-9	501	22	26	-9	.991	36	*C/D	7.7

■ POSSUM WHITTED Whitted, George Bostic b: 2/4/1890, Durham, N.C. d: 10/16/62, Wilmington, N.C. BR/TR, 5'8.5", 168 lbs. Deb: 9/16/12

YEAR	TM/L	G	AB	R	H	2B	3B	HR	RBI	BB	SO	AVG	OBP	SLG	PRO+	BR	/A	RC	SB	CS	SBR	FA	FR	POS	TPR
1912	StL-N	12	46	7	12	3	0	0	7	3	5	.261	.306	.326	75	-2	-2	5	1			.857	-3	3	-0.5
1913	StL-N	123	404	44	89	10	5	0	38	31	44	.220	.282	.270	59	-22	-21	32	9			.989	23	OS3/21	0.4
1914	StL-N	20	31	3	4	1	0	0	1	0	3	.129	.129	.161	-14	-4	-4	1	1			.889	-3	/3O2	-0.8
	*Bos-N	66	218	36	57	11	4	2	31	18	18	.261	.326	.376	109	2	2	30	10			.967	4	O2/13S	0.5
	Yr	86	249	39	61	12	4	2	32	18	21	.245	.304	.349	95	-2	-2	30	11			.957	1	O2/31S	-0.3
1915	*Phi-N	128	448	46	126	17	3	1	43	29	47	.281	.328	.339	101	1	0	55	24	15	-2	.978	4	*O/1	-0.4
1916	Phi-N	147	526	68	148	20	12	6	68	19	46	.281	.309	.399	113	8	6	69	29	17	-2	.964	5	*O1	0.2
1917	Phi-N	149	553	69	155	24	9	3	70	30	56	.280	.317	.373	107	6	3	68	10			.977	4	*O1/32	0.0
1918	Phi-N	24	86	7	21	4	0	0	3	4	10	.244	.278	.291	69	-3	-3	7	4			.982	2	O/1	-0.3
1919	Phi-N	78	289	32	72	14	1	3	32	14	20	.249	.284	.336	80	-6	-8	28	5			.955	0	O2/1	-1.1
	Pit-N	35	131	15	51	7	7	0	21	6	4	.389	.420	.550	183	14	13	32	7			.988	3	1/3O	1.6
	Yr	113	420	47	123	21	8	3	53	20	24	.293	.327	.402	112	8	5	57	12			.955	3	O12/3	0.5
1920	Pit-N	134	494	53	129	11	12	1	74	35	36	.261	.314	.338	85	-8	-10	52	11	11	-3	.961	-3	*31/O	-1.1
1921	Pit-N	108	403	60	114	23	7	7	63	26	21	.283	.328	.427	96	-2	-3	54	5	10	-5	.988	9	*O/1	-0.6
1922	Bro-N	1	1	0	0	0	0	0	0	0	0	.000	.000	.000	-99	-0	-0	0	0	0	0	.000	0	H	0.0
Total	11	1025	3630	440	978	145	60	23	451	215	310	.269	.313	.361	95	-16	-26	433	116	53		.975	44	O3/12S	-2.1

■ FLOYD WICKER Wicker, Floyd Euliss b: 9/12/43, Burlington, N.C. BL/TR, 6'2", 175 lbs. Deb: 6/23/68

YEAR	TM/L	G	AB	R	H	2B	3B	HR	RBI	BB	SO	AVG	OBP	SLG	PRO+	BR	/A	RC	SB	CS	SBR	FA	FR	POS	TPR
1968	StL-N	5	4	2	2	0	0	0	0	0	0	.500	.500	.500	204	0	0	1	0	0	0	.000	0	H	0.1
1969	Mon-N	41	39	2	4	0	0	0	2	2	20	.103	.146	.103	-29	-7	-7	1	0	0	0	1.000	1	O	-0.6
1970	Mil-A	15	41	3	8	1	0	1	3	1	8	.195	.214	.293	38	-4	-4	2	0	0	0	1.000	-1	O	-0.5
1971	Mil-A	11	8	0	1	0	0	0	0	2	0	.125	.300	.125	24	-1	-1	0	0	0	0	.000	0	H	-0.1
	SF-N	9	21	3	3	0	0	0	1	2	5	.143	.250	.143	14	-2	-2	1	0	0	0	1.000	1	/O	-0.2
Total	4	81	113	10	18	1	0	1	6	7	33	.159	.215	.195	15	-13	-13	5	0	0	0	1.000	1	/O	-1.3

■ AL WICKLAND Wickland, Albert b: 1/27/1888, Chicago, Ill. d: 3/14/80, Port Washington, Wis. BL/TL, 5'7", 155 lbs. Deb: 8/21/13

YEAR	TM/L	G	AB	R	H	2B	3B	HR	RBI	BB	SO	AVG	OBP	SLG	PRO+	BR	/A	RC	SB	CS	SBR	FA	FR	POS	TPR
1913	Cin-N	26	79	7	17	5	5	0	8	6	19	.215	.279	.405	94	-1	-1	9	3			.983	1	O	-0.1
1914	Chi-F	157	536	74	148	31	10	6	68	**81**	58	.276	.375	.405	129	17	22	94	17			.962	-1	*O	1.4
1915	Chi-F	30	86	11	21	2	2	1	5	13	11	.244	.343	.349	110	1	1	12	3			.946	-2	O	-0.2
	Pit-F	110	389	63	117	12	8	1	30	52	47	.301	.386	.380	127	14	15	72	23			.968	4	*O	1.4
	Yr	140	475	74	138	14	10	2	35	65	58	.291	.378	.375	124	15	16	83	26			.966	2	*O	1.2
1918	Bos-N	95	332	55	87	7	13	4	32	53	39	.262	.367	.398	139	15	16	52	12			.975	3	O	1.5
1919	NY-A	26	46	2	7	1	0	0	1	2	10	.152	.188	.174	2	-6	-6	1	0			1.000	-4	O	-1.1
Total	5	444	1468	212	397	58	38	12	144	207	184	.270	.364	.386	124	40	47	239	58			.968	-1	O	2.9

■ TOM WIEDENBAUER Wiedenbauer, Thomas John b: 11/5/58, Menomonie, Wis. BR/TR, 6'1", 180 lbs. Deb: 9/14/79

YEAR	TM/L	G	AB	R	H	2B	3B	HR	RBI	BB	SO	AVG	OBP	SLG	PRO+	BR	/A	RC	SB	CS	SBR	FA	FR	POS	TPR
1979	Hou-N	4	6	0	4	1	0	0	2	0	2	.667	.667	.833	326	2	2	3	0	0	0	1.000	0	/O	0.2

■ TOM WIEGHAUS Wieghaus, Thomas Robert b: 2/1/57, Chicago Heights, Ill BR/TR, 6', 195 lbs. Deb: 10/04/81

YEAR	TM/L	G	AB	R	H	2B	3B	HR	RBI	BB	SO	AVG	OBP	SLG	PRO+	BR	/A	RC	SB	CS	SBR	FA	FR	POS	TPR
1981	Mon-N	1	1	0	0	0	0	0	0	0	0	.000	.000	.000	-99	-0	-0	0	0	0	0	1.000	1	/C	0.1

YEAR	TM/L	G	AB	R	H	2B	3B	HR	RBI	BB	SO	AVG	OBP	SLG	PRO+	BR	/A	RC	SB	CS	SBR	FA	FR	POS	TPR
1983	Mon-N	1	0	0	0	0	0	0	0	0	0	—	—	—	—	0	0	0	0	0	0	1.000	-0	/C	0.0
1984	Hou-N	6	10	0	0	0	0	0	1	1	3	.000	.091	.000	-78	-2	-2	0	0	0	0	1.000	2	/C	0.0
Total	3	8	11	0	0	0	0	0	1	1	3	.000	.083	.000	-80	-3	-2	0	0	0	0	1.000	3	/C	0.1
■ **WHITEY WIETELMANN** Wietelmann, William Frederick b: 3/15/19, Zanesville, Ohio BB/TR, 6', 170 lbs. Deb: 9/06/39 C																									
1939	Bos-N	23	69	2	14	1	0	0	5	2	9	.203	.225	.217	21	-8	-7	3	1			.953	2	S/2	-0.4
1940	Bos-N	35	41	3	8	1	0	0	1	5	5	.195	.283	.220	43	-3	-3	3	0			.962	3	2/3S	0.0
1941	Bos-N	16	33	1	3	0	0	0	0	1	2	.091	.118	.091	-43	-6	-6	0	0			1.000	3	2/S3	-0.3
1942	Bos-N	13	34	4	7	2	0	0	0	4	5	.206	.289	.265	64	-2	-1	2	0			.941	-1	S/2	-0.1
1943	Bos-N	153	534	33	115	14	1	0	39	46	40	.215	.281	.245	53	-32	-31	39	9			.957	20	*S	0.1
1944	Bos-N	125	417	46	100	18	1	2	32	33	25	.240	.300	.302	67	-16	-19	40	0			.954	-6	*S2/3	-1.6
1945	Bos-N	123	428	53	116	15	3	4	33	39	27	.271	.335	.348	89	-6	-6	53	4			.972	3	2S/3P	0.4
1946	Bos-N	44	78	7	16	0	0	0	5	14	8	.205	.326	.205	52	-4	-4	6	0			.915	-6	S/32P	-0.9
1947	Pit-N	48	128	21	30	4	1	1	7	12	10	.234	.300	.305	59	-7	-8	11	0			.885	-13	S2/31	-1.9
Total	9	580	1762	170	409	55	6	7	122	156	131	.232	.298	.282	63	-84	-85	157	14			.952	4	S2/3P1	-4.7
■ **ALAN WIGGINS** Wiggins, Alan Anthony b: 2/17/58, Los Angeles, Cal. d: 1/6/91, Los Angeles, Cal. BB/TR, 6'2", 160 lbs. Deb: 9/04/81																									
1981	SD-N	15	14	4	5	0	0	0	0	1	0	.357	.400	.357	125	0	0	3	2	0	1	.750	0	/O	0.1
1982	SD-N	72	254	40	65	3	3	1	15	13	19	.256	.295	.303	71	-11	-9	25	33	6	6	.967	2	O/2	-0.3
1983	SD-N	144	503	83	139	20	2	0	22	65	43	.276	.360	.324	94	-4	-1	72	66	13	12	.992	8	*O1	1.4
1984	*SD-N	158	596	106	154	19	7	3	34	75	57	.258	.344	.329	90	-6	-6	79	70	21	8	.962	-29	*2	-2.2
1985	SD-N	10	37	3	2	1	0	0	0	2	4	.054	.103	.081	-49	-7	-7	0	0	1	-1	1.000	-3	/2	-1.2
	Bal-A	76	298	43	85	11	4	0	21	29	16	.285	.353	.349	96	-2	-1	39	30	13	1	.960	-24	2	-2.1
1986	Bal-A	71	239	30	60	3	1	0	11	22	20	.251	.314	.272	62	-12	-12	24	21	7	2	.978	-19	2/D	-2.6
1987	Bal-A	85	306	37	71	4	2	1	15	28	34	.232	.299	.268	53	-21	-19	26	20	7	2	.983	-0	D2/O	-1.6
Total	7	631	2247	346	581	61	19	5	118	235	193	.259	.331	.309	80	-62	-55	269	242	68	32	.967	-66	2O/D1	-8.5
■ **DEL WILBER** Wilber, Delbert Quentin "Babe" b: 2/24/19, Lincoln Park, Mich BR/TR, 6'3", 200 lbs. Deb: 4/21/46 MC																									
1946	StL-N	4	4	0	0	0	0	0	0	1	0	.000	.200	.000	-39	-1	-1	0	0			1.000	1	/C	0.0
1947	StL-N	51	99	7	23	8	1	0	12	5	13	.232	.269	.333	57	-6	-7	8	0			.983	1	C	-0.4
1948	StL-N	27	58	5	11	2	0	0	10	4	9	.190	.242	.224	25	-6	-6	3	0			.949	-3	C	-0.9
1949	StL-N	2	4	0	1	0	0	0	0	0	0	.250	.250	.250	33	-0	-0	0	0			1.000	0	/C	0.0
1951	Phi-N	84	245	30	68	7	3	8	34	17	26	.278	.324	.429	102	-0	0	33	0	1	-1	.978	4	C	0.6
1952	Phi-N	2	2	0	0	0	0	0	0	0	1	.000	.000	.000	-99	-1	-1	0	0	0	0	.000	0	H	-0.1
	Bos-A	47	135	7	36	10	1	3	23	7	20	.267	.308	.422	94	-0	-2	17	1	0	0	.995	1	C	0.1
1953	Bos-A	58	112	16	27	6	1	7	29	6	21	.241	.286	.500	103	0	-0	14	0	0	0	.980	-3	C/1	-0.2
1954	Bos-A	24	61	2	8	2	1	1	7	4	6	.131	.185	.246	15	-7	-8	3	0	0	0	.950	-5	C	-1.4
Total	8	299	720	67	174	35	7	19	115	44	96	.242	.287	.389	79	-21	-25	78	1	1		.978	-4	C/1	-2.3
■ **CLAUDE WILBORN** Wilborn, Claude Edward b: 9/1/12, Woodsdale, N.C. BL/TR, 6'1", 180 lbs. Deb: 9/08/40																									
1940	Bos-N	5	7	0	0	0	0	0	0	0	1	.000	.000	.000	-99	-2	-2	0	0			.500	-1	/O	-0.3
■ **TED WILBORN** Wilborn, Thaddeaus Iglehart b: 12/16/58, Waco, Tex. BB/TR, 6', 165 lbs. Deb: 4/05/79																									
1979	Tor-A	22	12	3	0	0	0	0	0	1	7	.000	.077	.000	-76	-3	-3	0	0	1	-1	.875	-2	/O	-0.5
1980	NY-A	8	8	2	2	0	0	0	1	0	1	.250	.250	.250	38	-1	-1	1	0	0	0	1.000	1	/O	0.0
Total	2	30	20	5	2	0	0	0	1	1	8	.100	.143	.100	-33	-4	-4	1	0	1	-1	.933	-1	/O	-0.5
■ **WILEY** Wiley Deb: 6/23/1884																									
1884	Was-U	1	4	0	0	0	0	0		0		.000	.000	.000	-99	-1	-1	0				.333	-1	/3	-0.1
■ **ROB WILFONG** Wilfong, Robert Donald b: 9/1/53, Pasadena, Cal. BL/TR, 6'1", 185 lbs. Deb: 4/10/77																									
1977	Min-A	73	171	22	42	1	1	1	13	17	26	.246	.321	.281	67	-8	-7	17	10	4	1	.959	4	2/D	0.1
1978	Min-A	92	199	23	53	8	0	1	11	19	27	.266	.336	.322	84	-3	-4	24	8	4	0	.986	6	2/D	0.7
1979	Min-A	140	419	71	131	22	6	9	59	29	54	.313	.360	.458	115	11	8	72	11	4	1	.979	21	*2/O	3.6
1980	Min-A	131	416	55	103	16	5	8	45	34	61	.248	.309	.368	79	-9	-13	47	10	6	-1	**.995**	-4	*2/O	-1.1
1981	Min-A	93	305	32	75	11	3	3	19	29	43	.246	.311	.331	80	-6	-8	33	2	4	-2	.980	4	2	-0.1
1982	Min-A	25	81	7	13	1	0	0	5	7	13	.160	.236	.173	14	-9	-10	3	0	2	-1	.980	-0	2	-1.0
	*Cal-A	55	102	17	25	4	2	1	11	7	17	.245	.294	.353	77	-3	-3	11	4	0	1	.982	9	2/3OSD	0.7
	Yr	80	183	24	38	5	2	1	16	14	30	.208	.268	.273	49	-13	-13	13	4	2	0	.981	9	2/3OSD	-0.3
1983	Cal-A	65	177	17	45	7	1	2	17	10	25	.254	.294	.339	74	-6	-6	17	0	2	-1	.995	12	23/SD	0.6
1984	Cal-A	108	307	31	76	13	2	6	33	20	53	.248	.298	.362	82	-8	-8	34	3	2	-0	.975	3	2/SD	-0.2
1985	Cal-A	83	217	16	41	3	0	4	13	16	32	.189	.245	.258	38	-19	-18	15	4	1	1	.986	21	2/D	0.5
1986	*Cal-A	92	288	25	63	11	3	3	33	16	34	.219	.265	.309	56	-18	-18	23	1	4	-2	.982	9	2	-0.8
1987	SF-N	2	8	2	1	0	0	1	2	1	2	.125	.222	.500	89	-0	-0	1	1	0	0	.833	-2	/2	-0.2
Total	11	959	2690	318	668	97	23	39	261	205	387	.248	.305	.345	77	-79	-87	297	54	33	-4	.982	80	2/3OSD	2.8
■ **SPIDER WILHELM** Wilhelm, Charles Ernest b: 5/23/29, Baltimore, Md. BR/TR, 5'9", 170 lbs. Deb: 9/06/53																									
1953	Phi-A	7	7	1	2	1	0	0	0	0	3	.286	.286	.429	87	-0	-0	1	0	0	0	.875	-0	/S	0.0
■ **JIM WILHELM** Wilhelm, James Webster b: 9/20/52, San Rafael, Cal. BR/TR, 6'3", 190 lbs. Deb: 9/04/78																									
1978	SD-N	10	19	2	7	2	0	0	4	0	2	.368	.400	.474	155	1	1	4	1	0	0	1.000	-1	O	0.1
1979	SD-N	39	103	8	25	4	3	0	8	2	12	.243	.257	.340	65	-6	-5	9	1	1	-0	.985	4	O	-0.3
Total	2	49	122	10	32	6	3	0	12	2	14	.262	.280	.361	79	-5	-4	13	2	1	0	.987	3	/O	-0.2
■ **JOE WILHOIT** Wilhoit, Joseph William b: 12/20/1885, Hiawatha, Kan. d: 9/25/30, Santa Barbara, Cal. BL/TR, 6'2", 175 lbs. Deb: 4/12/16																									
1916	Bos-N	116	383	44	88	13	4	2	38	27	45	.230	.282	.300	82	-10	-8	39	18			.979	2	*O	-1.3
1917	Bos-N	54	186	20	51	5	0	1	10	17	15	.274	.335	.317	107	1	2	21	5			.928	-3	O	-0.4
	Pit-N	9	10	0	2	0	0	0	0	1	1	.200	.273	.200	44	-1	-1	1	0			1.000	-0	/O1	-0.1
	*NY-N	34	50	9	17	2	2	0	8	8	5	.340	.431	.460	179	5	5	10	0			1.000	-2	O	0.3
	Yr	97	246	29	70	7	2	1	18	26	21	.285	.353	.341	118	5	6	31	5			.941	-5	O/1	-0.2
1918	NY-N	64	135	13	37	3	3	0	15	17	14	.274	.355	.341	115	3	3	17	4			.975	-8	O	-0.7
1919	Bos-A	6	18	7	6	0	0	0	2	5	2	.333	.478	.333	138	1	1	3	1			1.000	-1	/O	0.0
Total	4	283	782	93	201	23	9	3	73	75	82	.257	.323	.321	101	-1	2	91	28			.969	-11	O/1	-2.2
■ **DENNEY WILIE** Wilie, Dennis Ernest b: 9/22/1890, Mt.Calm, Tex. d: 6/20/66, Hayward, Cal. BL/TL, 5'8", 155 lbs. Deb: 7/27/11																									
1911	StL-N	28	51	10	12	3	1	0	3	8	11	.235	.361	.333	97	-0	0	7	3			1.000	-3	O	-0.3
1912	StL-N	30	48	2	11	0	1	0	6	7	9	.229	.351	.271	73	-2	-1	5	0			.917	-3	O	-0.5
1915	Cle-A	45	131	14	33	4	1	2	10	26	18	.252	.384	.344	115	4	4	17	2	6	-3	.910	-2	O	-0.4
Total	3	103	230	26	56	7	3	2	19	41	38	.243	.372	.326	102	3	3	28	5	6		.925	-8	/O	-1.2
■ **HARRY WILKE** Wilke, Henry Joseph b: 12/14/1900, Cincinnati, Ohio d: 6/21/91, Hamilton, Ohio BR/TR, 5'10.5", 171 lbs. Deb: 5/12/27																									
1927	Chi-N	3	9	0	0	0	0	0	0	0	1	.000	.000	.000	-99	-3	-3	0	0			1.000	0	/3	-0.2
■ **CURTIS WILKERSON** Wilkerson, Curtis Vernon b: 4/26/61, Petersburgh, Va. BB/TR, 5'9", 158 lbs. Deb: 9/10/83																									
1983	Tex-A	16	35	7	6	0	1	0	1	2	5	.171	.216	.229	23	-4	-4	2	3	0	1	1.000	2	/S23	0.0
1984	Tex-A	153	484	47	120	12	0	1	26	22	72	.248	.283	.279	55	-28	-30	38	12	10	-2	.944	-28	*S2	-5.0

YEAR	TM/L	G	AB	R	H	2B	3B	HR	RBI	BB	SO	AVG	OBP	SLG	PRO+	BR	/A	RC	SB	CS	SBR	FA	FR	POS	TPR
1985	Tex-A	129	360	35	88	11	6	0	22	22	63	.244	.295	.308	65	-17	-17	33	14	7	0	.957	3	*S2/D	-0.5
1986	Tex-A	110	236	27	56	10	3	0	15	11	42	.237	.274	.305	56	-14	-15	19	9	7	-2	.968	15	2S/D	0.2
1987	Tex-A	85	138	28	37	5	3	2	14	6	16	.268	.308	.391	84	-3	-3	16	6	3	0	.946	11	S23/D	0.9
1988	Tex-A	117	338	41	99	12	5	0	28	26	43	.293	.347	.358	95	-0	-2	42	9	4	0	.970	10	2S3/D	1.3
1989	Chi-N	77	160	18	39	4	2	1	10	8	33	.244	.280	.313	64	-7	-8	14	4	2	0	.881	4	32/SO	-0.4
1990	Chi-N	77	186	21	41	5	1	0	16	7	36	.220	.249	.258	37	-15	-17	11	2	2	-1	.888	-4	32/SO	-2.2
1991	*Pit-N	85	191	20	36	9	1	2	18	15	40	.188	.248	.277	48	-14	-13	14	2	1	0	.992	3	2S3	-0.9
1992	KC-A	111	296	27	74	10	1	2	29	18	47	.250	.295	.311	69	-12	-12	28	18	7	1	.968	-4	S2/3D	-1.0
Total	10	960	2424	271	596	78	23	8	179	137	397	.246	.290	.307	64	-114	-121	217	79	43	-2	.956	12	S23/DO	-7.6

■ RICK WILKINS

Wilkins, Richard David b: 6/4/67, Jacksonville, Fla. BL/TR, 6'2", 210 lbs. Deb: 6/06/91

YEAR	TM/L	G	AB	R	H	2B	3B	HR	RBI	BB	SO	AVG	OBP	SLG	PRO+	BR	/A	RC	SB	CS	SBR	FA	FR	POS	TPR
1991	Chi-N	86	203	21	45	9	0	6	22	19	56	.222	.307	.355	82	-4	-5	23	3	3	-1	.993	9	C	0.7
1992	Chi-N	83	244	20	66	9	1	8	22	28	53	.270	.346	.414	112	5	4	34	0	2	-1	.993	10	C	1.8
Total	2	169	447	41	111	18	1	14	44	47	109	.248	.328	.387	98	1	-1	56	3	5	-2	.993	20	C	2.5

■ BOBBY WILKINS

Wilkins, Robert Linwood b: 8/11/22, Denton, N.C. BR/TR, 5'9", 165 lbs. Deb: 4/18/44

YEAR	TM/L	G	AB	R	H	2B	3B	HR	RBI	BB	SO	AVG	OBP	SLG	PRO+	BR	/A	RC	SB	CS	SBR	FA	FR	POS	TPR
1944	Phi-A	24	25	7	6	0	0	0	3	1	4	.240	.296	.240	55	-1	-1	2	0	0	0	.943	5	/S	0.4
1945	Phi-A	62	154	22	40	6	0	0	4	10	17	.260	.305	.299	76	-5	-5	13	2	4	-2	.923	0	S/O	-0.4
Total	2	86	179	29	46	6	0	0	7	11	21	.257	.304	.291	73	-6	-6	15	2	4	-2	.926	5	/SO	0.0

■ ED WILKINSON

Wilkinson, Edward Henry b: 6/20/1890, Jacksonville, Ore d: 4/9/18, Tucson, Ariz. BR/TR, 6', 170 lbs. Deb: 7/04/11

YEAR	TM/L	G	AB	R	H	2B	3B	HR	RBI	BB	SO	AVG	OBP	SLG	PRO+	BR	/A	RC	SB	CS	SBR	FA	FR	POS	TPR
1911	NY-A	10	13	2	3	0	0	0	1	0		.231	.231	.231	27	-1	-1	1	0			.800	-1	/O2	-0.2

■ BOB WILL

Will, Robert Lee "Butch" b: 7/15/31, Berwyn, Ill. BL/TL, 5'10.5", 175 lbs. Deb: 4/16/57

YEAR	TM/L	G	AB	R	H	2B	3B	HR	RBI	BB	SO	AVG	OBP	SLG	PRO+	BR	/A	RC	SB	CS	SBR	FA	FR	POS	TPR
1957	Chi-N	70	112	13	25	3	0	1	10	5	21	.223	.256	.277	44	-9	-9	8	1	0	0	.963	-5	O	-1.5
1958	Chi-N	6	4	1	1	0	0	0	0	2	0	.250	.500	.250	108	0	0	1	0	0	0	.000	0	/O	0.0
1960	Chi-N	138	475	58	121	20	9	6	53	47	54	.255	.323	.373	91	-6	-6	56	1	5	-3	.992	2	*O	-1.3
1961	Chi-N	86	113	9	29	9	0	0	8	15	19	.257	.344	.336	80	-3	-3	14	0	1	-1	1.000	-2	O/1	-0.6
1962	Chi-N	87	92	6	22	3	0	2	15	13	22	.239	.333	.337	78	-2	-3	11	0	0	0	1.000	-0	/O	-0.4
1963	Chi-N	23	23	0	4	0	0	0	1	1	3	.174	.208	.174	11	-3	-3	1	0	0	0	1.000	-0	/1	-0.3
Total	6	410	819	87	202	35	9	9	87	83	119	.247	.317	.344	80	-23	-22	91	2	6	-3	.988	-6	O/1	-4.1

■ JERRY WILLARD

Willard, Gerald Duane b: 3/14/60, Oxnard, Cal. BL/TR, 6'2", 195 lbs. Deb: 4/11/84

YEAR	TM/L	G	AB	R	H	2B	3B	HR	RBI	BB	SO	AVG	OBP	SLG	PRO+	BR	/A	RC	SB	CS	SBR	FA	FR	POS	TPR
1984	Cle-A	87	246	21	55	8	1	10	37	26	55	.224	.298	.386	86	-4	-5	28	1	0	0	.981	-1	C/D	-0.2
1985	Cle-A	104	300	39	81	13	0	7	36	28	59	.270	.334	.383	97	-1	-1	40	0	0	0	.990	0	C/D	0.4
1986	Oak-A	75	161	17	43	7	0	4	26	22	28	.267	.362	.385	112	1	3	23	0	1	-1	.994	-11	C/D	-0.5
1987	Oak-A	7	6	1	1	0	0	0	0	2	1	.167	.375	.167	55	-0	-0	1	0	0	0	1.000	-0	/13D	-0.1
1990	Chi-A	3	3	0	0	0	0	0	0	0	2	.000	.000	.000	-99	-1	-1	0	0	0	0	.000	0	/C	-0.1
1991	*Atl-N	17	14	1	3	0	0	1	4	2	5	.214	.313	.429	100	0	-0	2	0	0	0	1.000	0	/C	0.0
1992	Atl-N	26	23	2	8	1	0	2	7	1	3	.348	.375	.652	171	2	2	4	0	0	0	1.000	0	/C	0.3
	Mon-N	21	25	0	3	0	0	0	1	1	7	.120	.154	.120	-22	-4	-4	0	0	0	0	.952	0	/1	-0.4
	Yr	47	48	2	11	1	0	2	8	2	10	.229	.260	.375	75	-2	-2	3	0	0	0	.952	1	/1C	-0.1
Total	7	340	778	81	194	29	1	24	111	82	160	.249	.323	.382	94	-7	-6	98	1	1	-0	.988	-11	C/1D3	-0.6

■ RIP WILLIAMS

Williams, Alva Mitchel "Buff" b: 1/31/1882, Carthage, Ill. d: 7/23/33, Keokuk, Iowa BR/TR, 5'11.5", 187 lbs. Deb: 4/12/11

YEAR	TM/L	G	AB	R	H	2B	3B	HR	RBI	BB	SO	AVG	OBP	SLG	PRO+	BR	/A	RC	SB	CS	SBR	FA	FR	POS	TPR
1911	Bos-A	95	284	36	68	8	5	0	31	24		.239	.314	.303	73	-10	-10	31	9			.975	1	1C	-0.6
1912	Was-A	61	157	14	50	11	4	0	22	7		.318	.352	.439	125	4	4	24	2			.978	4	C	1.2
1913	Was-A	66	106	9	30	6	2	1	12	9	16	.283	.339	.406	115	2	2	15	3			.985	-4	C/1O	-0.1
1914	Was-A	81	169	17	47	6	4	1	22	13	19	.278	.341	.379	112	3	2	22	2	2	-1	.975	-5	C/1O	0.0
1915	Was-A	91	197	14	48	8	4	0	31	18	20	.244	.320	.325	91	-2	-2	23	4	3	-1	.967	8	C1/3	0.8
1916	Was-A	76	202	16	54	10	2	0	20	15	19	.267	.324	.337	100	-1	-0	25	5			.982	-9	1C/3	-0.9
1918	Cle-A	28	71	5	17	2	2	0	7	9	6	.239	.325	.324	87	-0	-1	9	2			.980	-2	1/C	-0.4
Total	7	498	1186	111	314	51	23	2	145	95	80	.265	.328	.352	97	-4	-6	149	27	5		.977	-6	C1/O3	-0.0

■ ART WILLIAMS

Williams, Arthur Franklin b: 8/26/1877, Somerville, Mass. d: 5/16/41, Arlington, Va. TR , Deb: 5/07/02

YEAR	TM/L	G	AB	R	H	2B	3B	HR	RBI	BB	SO	AVG	OBP	SLG	PRO+	BR	/A	RC	SB	CS	SBR	FA	FR	POS	TPR
1902	Chi-N	47	160	17	37	3	0	0	14	15		.231	.305	.250	74	-5	-4	16	9			.917	-3	O1	-0.9

■ GUS WILLIAMS

Williams, August Joseph "Gloomy Gus" b: 5/7/1888, Omaha, Neb. d: 4/16/64, Sterling, Ill. BL/TL, 6', 185 lbs. Deb: 4/12/11 F

YEAR	TM/L	G	AB	R	H	2B	3B	HR	RBI	BB	SO	AVG	OBP	SLG	PRO+	BR	/A	RC	SB	CS	SBR	FA	FR	POS	TPR
1911	StL-A	9	26	1	7	3	0	0	4	0		.269	.296	.385	93	-1	-0	3	0			.867	-1	/O	-0.2
1912	StL-A	64	216	32	63	13	7	2	32	27		.292	.370	.444	138	9	10	41	18			.930	2	O	0.8
1913	StL-A	148	538	72	147	21	16	5	53	57	87	.273	.346	.400	121	11	13	80	31			.951	4	*O	1.1
1914	StL-A	144	499	51	126	19	6	4	47	36	120	.253	.308	.339	98	-5	-3	56	35	20	-2	.933	2	*O	-0.9
1915	StL-A	45	119	15	24	2	2	1	11	6	16	.202	.246	.277	59	-7	-6	10	11	1	3	.949	-5	O	-1.1
Total	5	410	1398	171	367	58	31	12	147	126	223	.263	.327	.374	110	8	14	191	95	21		.939	1	O	-0.3

■ BERNIE WILLIAMS

Williams, Bernabe (Figueroa) b: 9/13/68, San Juan, P.R. BB/TR, 6'2", 180 lbs. Deb: 7/07/91

YEAR	TM/L	G	AB	R	H	2B	3B	HR	RBI	BB	SO	AVG	OBP	SLG	PRO+	BR	/A	RC	SB	CS	SBR	FA	FR	POS	TPR
1991	NY-A	85	320	43	76	19	4	3	34	48	57	.237	.339	.350	91	-3	-3	41	10	5	0	.979	6	O	0.0
1992	NY-A	62	261	39	73	14	2	5	26	29	36	.280	.354	.406	110	5	4	37	7	6	-2	.995	8	O	0.9
Total	2	147	581	82	149	33	6	8	60	77	93	.256	.345	.375	99	2	1	78	17	11	-2	.986	14	O	0.9

■ BERNIE WILLIAMS

Williams, Bernard b: 10/8/48, Alameda, Cal. BR/TR, 6'1", 175 lbs. Deb: 9/07/70

YEAR	TM/L	G	AB	R	H	2B	3B	HR	RBI	BB	SO	AVG	OBP	SLG	PRO+	BR	/A	RC	SB	CS	SBR	FA	FR	POS	TPR
1970	SF-N	7	16	2	5	2	0	0	1	2	1	.313	.389	.438	122	1	1	2	1	1	-0	1.000	1	/O	0.1
1971	SF-N	35	73	8	13	1	0	1	5	12	24	.178	.294	.233	52	-4	-4	6	1	1	-0	.933	-3	O	-1.0
1972	SF-N	46	68	12	13	3	1	3	9	7	22	.191	.267	.397	85	-2	-2	7	0	0	0	1.000	3	O	0.0
1974	SD-N	14	15	1	2	0	0	0	0	0	6	.133	.133	.133	-26	-2	-2	0	0	0	0	1.000	0	/O	-0.3
Total	4	102	172	23	33	6	1	4	15	21	53	.192	.280	.308	66	-8	-8	15	2	2	-1	.974	0	/O	-1.2

■ BILLY WILLIAMS

Williams, Billy Leo b: 6/15/38, Whistler, Ala. BL/TR, 6'1", 175 lbs. Deb: 8/06/59 CH

YEAR	TM/L	G	AB	R	H	2B	3B	HR	RBI	BB	SO	AVG	OBP	SLG	PRO+	BR	/A	RC	SB	CS	SBR	FA	FR	POS	TPR
1959	Chi-N	18	33	0	5	0	1	0	2	1	7	.152	.176	.212	3	-5	-5	1	0	0	0	1.000	-0	O	-0.5
1960	Chi-N	12	47	4	13	0	2	2	7	5	12	.277	.346	.489	127	2	2	8	0	0	0	.962	0	O	0.1
1961	Chi-N	146	529	75	147	20	7	25	86	45	70	.278	.340	.484	114	11	10	87	6	0	2	.954	-6	*O	-0.2
1962	Chi-N★	159	618	94	184	22	8	22	91	70	72	.298	.373	.466	119	21	18	107	9	9	-3	.967	4	*O	1.0
1963	Chi-N	161	612	87	175	36	9	25	95	68	78	.286	.359	.497	136	34	30	108	7	6	-2	.987	5	*O	2.7
1964	Chi-N★	162	645	100	201	39	2	33	98	59	84	.312	.371	.532	145	42	39	125	10	7	-1	.950	-10	*O	2.1
1965	Chi-N★	164	645	115	203	39	6	34	108	65	76	.315	.380	.552	155	49	48	132	10	1	2	.968	-0	*O	4.4
1966	Chi-N	162	648	100	179	23	5	29	91	69	61	.276	.350	.461	122	20	19	104	6	3	0	.976	8	*O	2.0
1967	Chi-N	162	634	92	176	21	12	28	84	68	67	.278	.349	.481	129	28	25	106	6	3	0	.989	-9	*O	0.9
1968	Chi-N★	163	642	91	185	30	8	30	98	48	53	.288	.340	.500	140	36	32	107	4	1	1	.967	-12	*O	1.3
1969	Chi-N	163	642	103	188	33	10	21	95	59	70	.293	.356	.474	116	25	15	106	3	2	-0	.957	-1	*O	0.5
1970	Chi-N	161	636	**137**	**205**	34	4	42	129	72	65	.322	.393	.586	142	51	41	**147**	7	1	2	.989	-1	*O	3.2
1971	Chi-N	157	594	86	179	27	5	28	93	77	44	.301	.384	.505	131	39	29	112	7	5	-1	.977	-3	*O	1.9
1972	Chi-N★	150	574	95	191	34	6	37	122	62	59	**.333**	.403	**.606**	166	**61**	**54**	**137**	3	1	0	.984	-6	*O/1	4.3
1973	Chi-N★	156	576	72	166	22	2	20	86	76	72	.288	.372	.438	115	19	14	94	4	3	-1	.985	6	*O1	1.2
1974	Chi-N	117	404	55	113	22	0	16	68	67	44	.280	.383	.453	128	19	17	71	4	5	-2	.986	1	1O	1.1
1975	*Oak-A	155	520	68	127	20	1	23	81	76	68	.244	.343	.419	117	10	12	78	0	0	0	.971	-0	*D/1	1.1

YEAR	TM/L	G	AB	R	H	2B	3B	HR	RBI	BB	SO	AVG	OBP	SLG	PRO+	BR	/A	RC	SB	CS	SBR	FA	FR	POS	TPR
1976	Oak-A	120	351	36	74	12	0	11	41	58	44	.211	.323	.339	98	-2	0	41	4	2	0	.000	-0	*D/O	0.0
Total	18	2488	9350	1410	2711	434	88	426	1475	1045	1046	.290	.364	.492	131	463	401	1671	90	49	-2	.973	-25	*OD/1	27.1

■ DALLAS WILLIAMS Williams, Dallas McKinley b: 2/28/58, Brooklyn, N.Y. BL/TL, 5'11", 165 lbs. Deb: 9/19/81

YEAR	TM/L	G	AB	R	H	2B	3B	HR	RBI	BB	SO	AVG	OBP	SLG	PRO+	BR	/A	RC	SB	CS	SBR	FA	FR	POS	TPR
1981	Bal-A	2	2	0	1	0	0	0	0	0	0	.500	.500	.500	189	0	0	1	0	0	0	1.000	-0	/O	0.0
1983	Cin-N	18	36	2	2	0	0	0	1	3	6	.056	.128	.056	-46	-7	-7	0	0	0	0	1.000	-0	O	-0.8
Total	2	20	38	2	3	0	0	0	1	3	6	.079	.146	.079	-35	-7	-7	1	0	0	0	1.000	-1	/O	-0.8

■ DANA WILLIAMS Williams, Dana Lamont b: 3/20/63, Weirton, W.Va. BR/TR, 5'10", 170 lbs. Deb: 6/21/89

YEAR	TM/L	G	AB	R	H	2B	3B	HR	RBI	BB	SO	AVG	OBP	SLG	PRO+	BR	/A	RC	SB	CS	SBR	FA	FR	POS	TPR
1989	Bos-A	8	5	1	1	1	0	0	0	0	1	.200	.333	.400	100	0	0	1	0	0	0	1.000	0	/OD	0.0

■ DAVEY WILLIAMS Williams, David Carlous b: 11/2/27, Dallas, Tex. BR/TR, 5'10", 160 lbs. Deb: 9/16/49 C

YEAR	TM/L	G	AB	R	H	2B	3B	HR	RBI	BB	SO	AVG	OBP	SLG	PRO+	BR	/A	RC	SB	CS	SBR	FA	FR	POS	TPR
1949	NY-N	13	50	7	12	1	1	1	5	7	4	.240	.333	.360	86	-1	-1	7	0			.953	-10	2	-1.1
1951	*NY-N	30	64	17	17	1	0	2	8	5	8	.266	.319	.375	85	-1	-1	7	1	1	-0	1.000	2	2	0.1
1952	NY-N	138	540	70	137	26	3	13	55	48	63	.254	.324	.385	95	-3	-4	71	2	3	-1	.973	-15	*2	-1.4
1953	NY-N★	112	340	51	101	11	2	3	34	44	19	.297	.382	.368	95	0	-1	50	2	5	-2	.982	0	2	0.2
1954	*NY-N	142	544	65	121	18	3	9	46	43	33	.222	.285	.316	56	-35	-36	48	1	1	-0	**.982**	-7	*2	-3.3
1955	NY-N	82	247	25	62	4	1	4	15	17	17	.251	.305	.324	67	-12	-12	24	0	2	-1	.968	-8	2	-1.6
Total	6	517	1785	235	450	61	10	32	163	164	144	.252	.321	.351	79	-52	-54	207	6	12		.978	-38	2	-7.1

■ DEWEY WILLIAMS Williams, Dewey Edgar "Dee" b: 2/5/16, Durham, N.C. BR/TR, 6', 160 lbs. Deb: 6/28/44

YEAR	TM/L	G	AB	R	H	2B	3B	HR	RBI	BB	SO	AVG	OBP	SLG	PRO+	BR	/A	RC	SB	CS	SBR	FA	FR	POS	TPR
1944	Chi-N	79	262	23	63	7	2	0	27	23	18	.240	.302	.282	65	-12	-12	22	2			.981	4	C	-0.3
1945	*Chi-N	59	100	16	28	2	2	2	5	13	13	.280	.363	.400	114	2	2	14	0			.978	2	C	0.6
1946	Chi-N	4	5	0	1	0	0	0	0	0	2	.200	.200	.200	14	-1	-1	0	0			1.000	0	/C	0.0
1947	Chi-N	3	2	0	0	0	0	0	0	0	1	.000	.000	.000	-99	-1	-1	0	0			.000	0	/C	-0.1
1948	Cin-N	48	95	9	16	2	0	1	5	10	18	.168	.248	.221	29	-10	-9	6	0			.961	-3	C	-1.0
Total	5	193	464	48	108	11	4	3	37	46	52	.233	.302	.293	67	-21	-20	41	2			.976	3	C	-0.8

■ EARL WILLIAMS Williams, Earl Baxter b: 1/27/03, Cumberland Gap, Tenn. d: 3/10/58, Knoxville, Tnnn. BR/TR, 6'0.5", 185 lbs. Deb: 5/27/28

YEAR	TM/L	G	AB	R	H	2B	3B	HR	RBI	BB	SO	AVG	OBP	SLG	PRO+	BR	/A	RC	SB	CS	SBR	FA	FR	POS	TPR
1928	Bos-N	3	2	0	0	0	0	0	0	0	1	.000	.000	.000	-99	-1	-1	0	0			1.000	0	/C	0.0

■ EARL WILLIAMS Williams, Earl Craig b: 7/14/48, Newark, N.J. BR/TR, 6'3", 220 lbs. Deb: 9/13/70

YEAR	TM/L	G	AB	R	H	2B	3B	HR	RBI	BB	SO	AVG	OBP	SLG	PRO+	BR	/A	RC	SB	CS	SBR	FA	FR	POS	TPR
1970	Atl-N	10	19	4	7	4	0	0	5	3	4	.368	.455	.579	165	2	2	5	0	0	0	1.000	1	/13	0.3
1971	Atl-N	145	497	64	129	14	1	33	87	42	80	.260	.326	.491	121	17	13	78	0	1	-1	.981	-8	C31	0.5
1972	Atl-N	151	565	72	146	24	2	28	87	62	118	.258	.338	.457	113	17	11	85	0	0	0	.980	-19	*C31	-0.5
1973	*Bal-A	132	459	58	109	18	1	22	83	66	107	.237	.337	.425	114	8	9	65	0	2	-1	.987	-9	C1/D	0.0
1974	*Bal-A	118	413	47	105	16	0	14	52	40	79	.254	.330	.395	111	4	6	54	0	2	-1	.983	-14	C1/D	-0.9
1975	Atl-N	111	383	42	92	13	0	11	50	34	63	.240	.307	.360	82	-9	-10	40	0	0	0	.989	-5	1C	-2.1
1976	Atl-N	61	184	18	39	3	0	9	26	19	33	.212	.289	.375	82	-4	-5	19	0	0	0	.995	-9	C1	-1.4
	Mon-N	61	190	17	45	10	2	8	29	14	32	.237	.289	.437	100	-0	-1	22	0	0	0	.981	6	1C	0.3
	Yr	122	374	35	84	13	2	17	55	33	65	.225	.289	.406	91	-4	-6	40	0	0	0	.986	-2	1C	-1.1
1977	Oak-A	100	348	39	84	13	0	13	38	18	58	.241	.288	.391	84	-9	-8	34	2	0	1	.989	-4	DC1	-1.2
Total	8	889	3058	361	756	115	6	138	457	298	574	.247	.321	.424	105	27	16	401	2	5	-2		-60	C1/3D	-5.0

■ EDDIE WILLIAMS Williams, Edward Laquan b: 11/1/64, Shreveport, La. BR/TR, 6', 175 lbs. Deb: 4/18/86

YEAR	TM/L	G	AB	R	H	2B	3B	HR	RBI	BB	SO	AVG	OBP	SLG	PRO+	BR	/A	RC	SB	CS	SBR	FA	FR	POS	TPR
1986	Cle-A	5	7	2	1	0	0	0	1	0	3	.143	.143	.143	-22	-1	-1	0	0	0	0	.000	-2	/O	-0.3
1987	Cle-A	22	64	9	11	4	0	1	4	9	19	.172	.284	.281	50	-5	-5	5	0	0	0	.982	2	3	-0.3
1988	Cle-A	10	21	3	4	0	0	0	1	0	3	.190	.227	.190	18	-2	-2	1	0	0	0	1.000	3	3	0.0
1989	Chi-A	66	201	25	55	8	0	3	10	18	31	.274	.345	.358	101	0	1	25	1	2	-1	.909	1	3	0.1
1990	SD-N	14	42	5	12	3	0	3	4	5	6	.286	.362	.571	151	3	3	8	0	1	-1	.897	-1	3	0.1
Total	5	117	335	44	83	15	0	7	20	32	62	.248	.324	.355	89	-5	-5	39	1	3	-2	.929	3	3/O	-0.4

■ DIB WILLIAMS Williams, Edwin Dibrell b: 1/19/10, Greenbrier, Ark. d: 4/2/92, Searcy, Ark. BR/TR, 5'11.5", 175 lbs. Deb: 4/27/30

YEAR	TM/L	G	AB	R	H	2B	3B	HR	RBI	BB	SO	AVG	OBP	SLG	PRO+	BR	/A	RC	SB	CS	SBR	FA	FR	POS	TPR
1930	Phi-A	67	191	24	50	10	3	3	22	15	19	.262	.322	.393	77	-6	-7	25	2	1	0	.951	4	2S/3	0.0
1931	*Phi-A	86	294	41	79	12	2	6	40	19	21	.269	.313	.384	78	-8	-11	36	2	0	1	.931	7	S2/O	0.4
1932	Phi-A	62	215	30	54	10	1	4	24	22	23	.251	.329	.363	76	-7	-8	26	0	1	-1	.952	7	2/S	0.1
1933	Phi-A	115	408	52	118	20	5	11	73	32	35	.289	.342	.444	106	3	2	63	1	0	0	.921	-9	S2/1	0.0
1934	Phi-A	66	205	25	56	10	1	2	17	21	18	.273	.341	.361	84	-6	-5	26	0	1	-1	.956	-0	2/S	-0.2
1935	Phi-A	4	10	0	1	0	0	0	0	0	1	.100	.100	.100	-49	-2	-2	0	0	0	0	1.000	-2	/2	-0.4
	Bos-A	75	251	26	63	12	0	3	25	24	23	.251	.319	.335	65	-12	-14	28	2	0	1	.952	-5	32S/1	-1.4
	Yr	79	261	26	64	12	0	3	25	24	24	.245	.311	.326	61	-14	-16	28	2	0	1	.973	-7	23S/1	-1.8
Total	6	475	1574	198	421	74	12	29	201	133	140	.267	.327	.385	82	-37	-44	204	7	3	0	.955	1	2S/310	-1.5

■ DENNY WILLIAMS Williams, Evon Daniel b: 12/13/1899, Portland, Ore. d: 3/23/29, San Clemente, Cal. BL/TR, 5'8.5", 150 lbs. Deb: 4/15/21

YEAR	TM/L	G	AB	R	H	2B	3B	HR	RBI	BB	SO	AVG	OBP	SLG	PRO+	BR	/A	RC	SB	CS	SBR	FA	FR	POS	TPR
1921	Cin-N	10	7	0	0	0	0	0	0	0	2	.000	.000	.000	-99	-2	-2	0	0	1	-1	1.000	-0	/O	-0.3
1924	Bos-A	25	85	17	31	3	0	0	4	10	5	.365	.438	.400	117	3	3	15	3	3	-1	.972	-2	O	-0.1
1925	Bos-A	69	218	28	50	1	3	0	13	17	11	.229	.285	.261	39	-20	-20	16	2	6	-3	.953	-2	O	-2.7
1928	Bos-A	16	18	1	4	0	0	0	1	1	1	.222	.263	.222	29	-2	-2	1	0	0	0	1.000	-2	/O	-0.4
Total	4	120	328	46	85	4	3	0	18	28	19	.259	.319	.290	56	-21	-21	32	5	10	-5	.959	-7	/O	-3.5

■ CY WILLIAMS Williams, Fred b: 12/21/1887, Wadena, Ind. d: 4/23/74, Eagle River, Wis. BL/TL, 6'2", 180 lbs. Deb: 7/18/12

YEAR	TM/L	G	AB	R	H	2B	3B	HR	RBI	BB	SO	AVG	OBP	SLG	PRO+	BR	/A	RC	SB	CS	SBR	FA	FR	POS	TPR
1912	Chi-N	28	62	3	15	1	1	0	1	6	14	.242	.309	.290	65	-3	-3	6	2			1.000	-2	O	-0.6
1913	Chi-N	49	156	17	35	3	3	4	32	5	26	.224	.262	.359	76	-6	-6	15	5			.976	-5	O	-1.2
1914	Chi-N	55	94	12	19	2	2	0	5	13	13	.202	.312	.266	73	-3	-3	8	2			.941	-3	O	-0.7
1915	Chi-N	151	518	59	133	22	6	13	64	26	49	.257	.305	.398	112	5	5	64	15	10	-2	.968	4	*O	0.2
1916	Chi-N	118	405	55	113	19	9	**12**	66	51	64	.279	.372	.459	140	27	22	74	6			.989	-4	*O	1.4
1917	Chi-N	138	468	53	113	22	4	5	42	38	78	.241	.308	.338	91	-1	-5	52	8			.960	12	*O	0.0
1918	Phi-N	94	351	49	97	14	1	6	39	27	30	.276	.337	.373	109	7	4	47	10			.968	0	O	-0.1
1919	Phi-N	109	435	54	121	21	1	9	39	30	43	.278	.335	.393	111	9	6	58	9			.970	4	*O	0.3
1920	Phi-N	148	590	88	192	36	10	**15**	72	32	45	.325	.364	.497	139	32	29	103	18	12	-2	.972	10	*O	2.8
1921	Phi-N	146	562	67	180	28	6	18	75	30	32	.320	.357	.488	112	15	10	91	5	15	-8	.979	16	*O	0.7
1922	Phi-N	151	584	98	180	30	6	26	92	74	49	.308	.392	.514	120	27	19	116	11	14	-5	.973	2	*O	0.5
1923	Phi-N	136	535	98	157	22	3	**41**	114	59	57	.293	.371	.576	131	33	25	112	11	10	-3	.981	-3	*O	1.0
1924	Phi-N	148	558	101	183	31	11	24	93	67	49	.328	.403	.552	137	42	33	121	7	12	-5	.962	-3	*O	1.5
1925	Phi-N	107	314	78	104	11	5	13	60	53	34	.331	.435	.522	132	23	19	72	4	9	-4	.989	-5	O	0.4
1926	Phi-N	107	336	63	116	13	4	18	53	38	35	.345	.418	.568	155	30	27	78	2			.963	-8	O	1.4
1927	Phi-N	131	492	86	135	18	2	**30**	98	61	57	.274	.365	.502	128	20	19	90	0			.970	1	*O	1.2
1928	Phi-N	99	238	31	61	9	0	12	37	54	34	.256	.400	.445	117	9	8	45	0			1.000	-2	O	0.1
1929	Phi-N	66	65	11	19	2	0	5	21	22	9	.292	.471	.554	144	7	6	18	0			.966	-0	O	0.5
1930	Phi-N	21	17	1	8	2	0	0	2	4	3	.471	.571	.588	169	3	2	6	0			1.000	-1	/O	0.1
Total	19	2002	6780	1024	1981	306	74	251	1005	690	721	.292	.365	.470	123	278	218	1177	115	82		.973	15	*O	9.5

■ PAPA WILLIAMS Williams, Fred b: 7/17/13, Meridian, Miss. BR/TR, 6'1", 200 lbs. Deb: 4/19/45

YEAR	TM/L	G	AB	R	H	2B	3B	HR	RBI	BB	SO	AVG	OBP	SLG	PRO+	BR	/A	RC	SB	CS	SBR	FA	FR	POS	TPR
1945	Cle-A	16	19	0	4	0	0	0	0	1	2	.211	.250	.211	36	-2	-1	1	0	0	0	1.000	0	/1	-0.1

YEAR	TM/L	G	AB	R	H	2B	3B	HR	RBI	BB	SO	AVG	OBP	SLG	PRO+	BR	/A	RC	SB	CS	SBR	FA	FR	POS	TPR
■ GEORGE WILLIAMS	Williams, George b: 10/23/39, Detroit, Mich. BR/TR, 5'11", 165 lbs. Deb: 7/16/61																								
1961	Phi-N	17	36	4	9	0	0	0	1	4	4	.250	.325	.250	56	-2	-2	3	0	0	0	.967	2	2	0.1
1962	Hou-N	5	8	1	3	1	0	0	2	0	1	.375	.375	.500	143	0	0	2	0	0	0	1.000	0	/2	0.1
1964	KC-A	37	91	10	19	6	0	0	2	6	12	.209	.265	.275	49	-6	-6	7	0	0	0	.970	-3	2/S3O	-0.8
Total	3	59	135	15	31	7	0	0	5	10	17	.230	.288	.281	56	-8	-8	11	0	0	0	.970	-1	/2O3S	-0.6
■ GERALD WILLIAMS	Williams, Gerald Floyd b: 8/10/66, New Orleans, La. BR/TR, 6'2", 190 lbs. Deb: 9/15/92																								
1992	NY-A	15	27	7	8	2	0	3	6	0	3	.296	.296	.704	169	2	2	6	2	0	1	.913	-1	O	0.2
■ HARRY WILLIAMS	Williams, Harry Peter b: 6/23/1890, Omaha, Neb. d: 12/21/63, Huntington Park, Cal. BR/TR, 6'1.5", 200 lbs. Deb: 8/07/13 F																								
1913	NY-A	27	82	18	21	3	1	1	12	15	10	.256	.378	.354	114	2	2	13	6			.981	-2	1	0.0
1914	NY-A	59	178	9	29	5	2	1	17	26	26	.163	.287	.230	56	-9	-9	12	3	6	-3	.976	-5	1	-2.1
Total	2	86	260	27	50	8	3	2	29	41	36	.192	.316	.269	75	-7	-7	25	9	6		.977	-7	/1	-2.1
■ JIM WILLIAMS	Williams, James Alfred b: 4/29/47, Zachary, La. BR/TR, 6'2", 190 lbs. Deb: 9/08/69																								
1969	SD-N	13	25	4	7	1	0	0	2	3	11	.280	.357	.320	95	-0	-0	3	0	0	0	.900	-1	/O	-0.1
1970	SD-N	11	14	4	4	0	0	0	0	1	3	.286	.333	.286	70	-1	-1	2	1	0	0	1.000	0	/O	0.0
Total	2	24	39	8	11	1	0	0	2	4	14	.282	.349	.308	86	-1	-1	5	1	0	0	.938	-1	/O	-0.1
■ JIMY WILLIAMS	Williams, James Francis b: 10/4/43, Santa Maria, Cal. BR/TR, 5'10", 170 lbs. Deb: 4/26/66 MC																								
1966	StL-N	13	11	1	3	0	0	0	1	1	5	.273	.333	.273	71	-0	-0	1	0	0	0	1.000	-2	/S2	-0.2
1967	StL-N	1	2	0	0	0	0	0	0	0	1	.000	.000	.000	-99	-1	-1	0	0	0	0	1.000	1	/S	0.0
Total	2	14	13	1	3	0	0	0	1	1	6	.231	.286	.231	46	-1	-1	1	0	0	0	1.000	-1	/S2	-0.2
■ JIMMY WILLIAMS	Williams, James Thomas b: 12/20/1876, St.Louis, Mo. d: 1/16/65, St.Petersburg, Fla BR/TR, 5'9", 175 lbs. Deb: 4/15/1899																								
1899	Pit-N	152	617	126	219	28	**27**	9	116	60		.355	.416	.532	160	49	49	152	26			.902	7	*3	5.1
1900	*Pit-N	106	416	73	110	15	11	5	68	32		.264	.323	.389	95	-3	-4	60	18			.889	6	*3/S	0.2
1901	Bal-A	130	501	113	159	26	**21**	7	96	56		.317	.388	.495	138	29	26	108	21			.935	-2	*2	2.6
1902	Bal-A	125	498	83	156	27	**21**	8	83	36		.313	.364	.500	132	23	20	99	14			.945	4	*23/1	2.6
1903	NY-A	132	502	60	134	30	12	3	82	39		.267	.326	.392	108	9	5	70	9			**.957**	16	*2	2.6
1904	NY-A	146	559	62	147	31	7	2	74	38		.263	.313	.354	106	7	4	69	14			.951	17	*2	2.7
1905	NY-A	129	470	54	107	20	8	6	62	50		.228	.305	.343	94	3	-3	56	14			**.964**	5	*2	0.3
1906	NY-A	139	501	62	139	25	7	3	77	44		.277	.338	.373	112	13	7	70	8			.958	11	*2	2.1
1907	NY-A	139	504	53	136	17	11	2	63	35		.270	.319	.359	108	8	4	65	14			.966	-1	*2	0.2
1908	StL-A	148	539	63	127	20	7	4	53	55		.236	.310	.321	105	4	3	57	7			.963	5	*2	0.8
1909	StL-A	110	374	32	73	3	6	0	22	29		.195	.257	.235	60	-19	-16	24	6			.962	-6	*2	-2.7
Total	11	1456	5481	781	1507	242	138	49	796	474		.275	.336	.396	114	123	96	830	151			.955	61	*23/S1	16.5
■ KEN WILLIAMS	Williams, Kenneth Roy b: 6/28/1890, Grants Pass, Ore. d: 1/22/59, Grants Pass, Ore. BL/TR, 6', 170 lbs. Deb: 7/14/15																								
1915	Cin-N	71	219	22	53	10	4	0	16	15	20	.242	.297	.324	86	-3	-4	22	4	3	-1	.948	2	O	-0.6
1916	Cin-N	10	27	1	3	0	0	0	1	2	5	.111	.172	.111	-12	-4	-3	1	1			.955	1	O	-0.3
1918	StL-A	2	1	0	0	0	0	0	0	1	0	.000	.500	.000	53	0	0	0	0			.000	0	H	0.0
1919	StL-A	65	227	32	68	10	5	6	35	26	25	.300	.376	.467	133	11	10	42	7			.937	4	O	1.0
1920	StL-A	141	521	90	160	34	13	10	72	41	26	.307	.362	.480	118	14	12	91	18	8	1	.961	8	*O	1.0
1921	StL-A	146	547	115	190	31	7	24	117	74	42	.347	.429	.561	142	42	38	130	20	17	-4	.932	7	*O	2.7
1922	StL-A	153	585	128	194	34	11	**39**	**155**	74	31	.332	.413	.627	162	56	53	150	37	19	-0	.970	7	*O	4.6
1923	StL-A	147	555	106	198	37	12	29	91	79	32	.357	.439	.623	168	61	57	148	18	17	-5	.967	11	*O	5.0
1924	StL-A	114	398	78	129	21	4	18	84	69	17	.324	.425	.533	137	28	24	93	20	11	-1	.968	6	*O	2.1
1925	StL-A	102	411	83	136	31	5	25	105	37	14	.331	.390	.613	144	29	26	97	10	5	0	.955	5	*O	2.1
1926	StL-A	108	347	55	97	15	7	17	74	39	23	.280	.354	.510	118	10	8	63	5	4	-1	.948	1	O/2	0.1
1927	StL-A	131	423	70	136	23	6	17	74	57	30	.322	.403	.525	135	24	22	86	9	7	-2	.965	6	*O	1.9
1928	Bos-A	133	462	59	140	25	1	8	67	37	15	.303	.356	.413	104	1	2	66	4	9	-4	.971	-3	*O	-1.3
1929	Bos-A	74	139	21	48	14	2	3	21	15	7	.345	.409	.540	146	9	9	29	1	5	-3	.963	-5	O/1	0.0
Total	14	1397	4862	860	1552	285	77	196	913	566	287	.319	.393	.530	136	278	253	1016	154	105		.958	48	*O/12	18.3
■ KENNY WILLIAMS	Williams, Kenneth Royal b: 4/6/64, Berkeley, Cal. BR/TR, 6'2", 187 lbs. Deb: 9/02/86																								
1986	Chi-A	15	31	2	4	0	0	1	1	1	11	.129	.182	.226	10	-4	-4	1	1	1	-0	1.000	0	O/D	-0.4
1987	Chi-A	116	391	48	110	18	2	11	50	10	83	.281	.315	.422	91	-5	-6	50	21	10	0	.981	6	*O	-0.3
1988	Chi-A	73	220	18	35	4	2	8	28	10	64	.159	.223	.305	46	-16	-16	15	6	5	-1	.959	-4	O3/D	-2.3
1989	Det-A	94	258	29	53	5	1	6	23	18	63	.205	.270	.302	63	-13	-13	21	9	4	0	.979	4	O/1D	-1.1
1990	Det-A	57	83	10	11	2	0	0	5	3	24	.133	.172	.157	-7	-12	-12	2	2	2	-1	1.000	-3	O/D	-1.7
	Tor-A	49	72	13	14	6	1	0	8	7	18	.194	.275	.306	61	-4	-4	7	7	2	1	1.000	-7	O/D	-1.0
	Yr	106	155	23	25	8	1	0	13	10	42	.161	.222	.226	25	-16	-16	8	9	4	0	1.000	-10	OD	-2.7
1991	Tor-A	13	29	5	6	2	0	1	3	4	5	.207	.324	.379	90	-0	-0	4	1	0	0	1.000	-0	/OD	0.0
	Mon-N	34	70	11	19	5	2	0	1	3	22	.271	.311	.400	100	-0	-0	9	2	1	0	.957	1	O	0.0
Total	6	451	1154	136	252	42	8	27	119	56	290	.218	.271	.339	66	-55	-55	108	49	25	-0	.981	-3	O/3D1	-6.8
■ MARK WILLIAMS	Williams, Mark Westley b: 7/28/53, Elmira, N.Y. BL/TL, 6', 180 lbs. Deb: 5/20/77																								
1977	Oak-A	3	2	0	0	0	0	0	1	1	1	.000	.333	.000	0	-0	-0	0	0	0	0	1.000	-0	/O	0.0
■ MATT WILLIAMS	Williams, Matthew Derrick b: 11/28/65, Bishop, Cal. BR/TR, 6'2", 205 lbs. Deb: 4/11/87																								
1987	SF-N	84	245	28	46	9	2	8	21	16	68	.188	.240	.339	54	-18	-16	19	4	3	-1	.975	20	S3	0.8
1988	SF-N	52	156	17	32	6	1	8	19	8	41	.205	.253	.410	91	-3	-3	14	0	1	-1	.967	10	3S	0.7
1989	*SF-N	84	292	31	59	18	1	18	50	14	72	.202	.244	.455	98	-4	-3	30	1	2	-1	.961	6	3S	0.4
1990	SF-N★	159	617	87	171	27	2	33	**122**	33	138	.277	.321	.488	124	13	16	92	7	4	-0	.959	4	*3	2.1
1991	SF-N	157	589	72	158	24	5	34	98	33	128	.268	.314	.499	129	16	19	88	5	5	-2	.964	9	*3/S	2.8
1992	SF-N	146	529	58	120	13	5	20	66	39	109	.227	.287	.384	93	-9	-6	54	7	7	-2	.945	7	*3	-0.1
Total	6	682	2428	293	586	97	16	121	376	143	556	.241	.290	.444	106	-5	7	297	24	22	-6	.958	56	3S	6.7
■ OTTO WILLIAMS	Williams, Otto George b: 11/2/1877, Newark, N.J. d: 3/19/37, Omaha, Neb. BR/TR, 5'8", 165 lbs. Deb: 10/05/02 C																								
1902	StL-N	2	5	0	2	0	0	0	2	1		.400	.500	.400	185	1	1	2	1			.813	1	/S	0.2
1903	StL-N	53	187	10	38	4	2	0	9	9		.203	.240	.246	40	-15	-14	13	6			.885	-5	S/2	-1.7
	Chi-N	38	130	14	29	5	0	0	13	4		.223	.246	.262	46	-10	-9	11	8			.937	5	S/213	-0.3
	Yr	91	317	24	67	9	2	0	22	13		.211	.242	.252	43	-25	-23	24	14			.904	0	S/213	-2.0
1904	Chi-N	57	185	21	37	4	1	0	8	13		.200	.256	.232	52	-10	-10	14	9			.973	-0	O1S/23	-1.2
1906	Was-A	20	51	3	7	0	0	0	2	2		.137	.185	.137	2	-6	-5	2	0			.897	0	/S213	-0.5
Total	4	170	558	48	113	13	3	0	34	29		.203	.244	.237	43	-40	-38	42	24			.905	1	/SO213	-3.5
■ REGGIE WILLIAMS	Williams, Reginald Bernard b: 5/5/66, Laurens, S.C. BB/TR, 6'1", 180 lbs. Deb: 9/08/92																								
1992	Cal-A	14	26	5	6	1	1	0	2	1	10	.231	.259	.346	69	-1	-1	2	0	2	-1	1.000	-1	O/D	-0.4
■ REGGIE WILLIAMS	Williams, Reginald Dewayne b: 8/29/60, Memphis, Tenn. BR/TR, 5'11", 185 lbs. Deb: 9/02/85																								
1985	LA-N	22	9	4	3	0	0	0	0	0	4	.333	.333	.333	90	-0	-0	1	1	0	0	.900	-3	O	-0.3
1986	LA-N	128	303	35	84	14	2	4	32	23	57	.277	.332	.376	102	-2	0	37	9	3	1	.984	-16	*O	-1.8
1987	LA-N	39	36	6	4	0	0	0	4	5	9	.111	.220	.111	-9	-6	-5	1	1	1	-0	.913	-8	O	-1.4

YEAR	TM/L	G	AB	R	H	2B	3B	HR	RBI	BB	SO	AVG	OBP	SLG	PRO+	BR	/A	RC	SB	CS	SBR	FA	FR	POS	TPR
1988	Cle-A	11	31	7	7	2	0	1	3	0	6	.226	.226	.387	66	-1	-2	2	0	0	0	1.000	-2	O	-0.4
Total	4	200	379	52	98	16	2	5	39	28	76	.259	.313	.351	87	-9	-7	41	11	4	1		-29	O	-3.9

■ **DICK WILLIAMS** Williams, Richard Hirschfeld b: 5/7/28, St.Louis, Mo. BR/TR, 6', 190 lbs. Deb: 6/10/51 MC

YEAR	TM/L	G	AB	R	H	2B	3B	HR	RBI	BB	SO	AVG	OBP	SLG	PRO+	BR	/A	RC	SB	CS	SBR	FA	FR	POS	TPR
1951	Bro-N	23	60	5	12	3	1	1	5	4	10	.200	.250	.333	54	-4	-4	5	0	0	0	1.000	-2	O	-0.6
1952	Bro-N	36	68	13	21	4	1	0	11	2	10	.309	.329	.397	99	-0	-0	8	0	0	0	1.000	-2	O/13	-0.2
1953	*Bro-N	30	55	4	12	2	0	2	5	3	10	.218	.271	.364	62	-3	-3	6	0	0	0	.923	-7	O	-1.1
1954	Bro-N	16	34	5	5	0	0	1	2	2	7	.147	.194	.235	11	-5	-5	1	0	0	0	1.000	-4	O	-0.9
1956	Bro-N	7	7	0	2	0	0	0	0	0	1	.286	.286	.286	50	-0	-1	1	0	0	0	.000	0	H	-0.1
	Bal-A	87	353	45	101	18	4	11	37	30	40	.286	.342	.453	117	3	7	52	5	5	-2	.990	-3	O12/3	-0.2
1957	Bal-A	47	167	16	39	10	2	1	17	14	21	.234	.293	.335	76	-7	-6	15	0	1	-1	1.000	0	O31	-0.8
	Cle-A	67	205	33	58	7	0	6	17	12	19	.283	.326	.405	99	-1	-1	24	3	4	-2	.973	-3	O3	-0.7
	Yr	114	372	49	97	17	2	7	34	26	40	.261	.311	.374	89	-8	-6	39	3	5	-2	.984	-2	O31	-1.5
1958	Bal-A	128	409	36	113	17	0	4	32	37	47	.276	.339	.347	94	-5	-3	44	0	6	-4	1.000	-9	O31/2	-2.0
1959	KC-A	130	488	72	130	33	1	16	75	28	60	.266	.313	.436	102	1	-0	64	4	1	1	.957	-8	31O/2	-1.1
1960	KC-A	127	420	47	121	31	0	12	65	39	68	.288	.350	.448	113	8	7	62	0	0	0	.951	5	31O	0.9
1961	Bal-A	103	310	37	64	15	2	8	24	20	38	.206	.255	.345	60	-19	-18	25	0	4	-2	.968	-10	O1/3	-3.6
1962	Bal-A	82	178	20	44	7	1	1	18	14	26	.247	.306	.315	71	-8	-7	16	0	0	0	1.000	-2	O1/3	-1.2
1963	Bos-A	79	136	15	35	8	0	2	12	15	25	.257	.331	.360	91	-1	-1	17	0	0	0	.976	-6	31/O	-0.9
1964	Bos-A	61	69	10	11	2	0	5	11	7	10	.159	.247	.406	74	-2	-3	6	0	0	0	1.000	5	13/O	0.2
Total	13	1023	2959	358	768	157	12	70	331	227	392	.260	.315	.392	92	-44	-38	346	12	21	-9	.989	-46	O31/2	-12.3

■ **RINALDO WILLIAMS** Williams, Rinaldo Lewis b: 12/18/1893, Santa Cruz, Cal. d: 4/24/66, Cottonwood, Ariz. BL/TR, Deb: 10/08/14

YEAR	TM/L	G	AB	R	H	2B	3B	HR	RBI	BB	SO	AVG	OBP	SLG	PRO+	BR	/A	RC	SB	CS	SBR	FA	FR	POS	TPR
1914	Bro-F	4	15	1	4	2	0	0	0	0	0	.267	.267	.400	89	-0	-0	2	0			.923	0	/3	0.0

■ **BOB WILLIAMS** Williams, Robert Elias b: 4/27/1884, Monday, Ohio d: 8/6/62, Nelsonville, Ohio BR/TR, 6', 190 lbs. Deb: 7/03/11

YEAR	TM/L	G	AB	R	H	2B	3B	HR	RBI	BB	SO	AVG	OBP	SLG	PRO+	BR	/A	RC	SB	CS	SBR	FA	FR	POS	TPR
1911	NY-A	20	47	3	9	2	0	0	8	5		.191	.269	.234	38	-4	-4	3	1			.942	-1	C	-0.3
1912	NY-A	20	44	7	6	1	0	0	3	9		.136	.283	.159	26	-4	-4	2	0			.930	-4	C	-0.7
1913	NY-A	6	19	0	3	0	0	0	0	1	3	.158	.200	.158	5	-2	-2	1	0			.971	0	/C	-0.2
Total	3	46	110	10	18	3	0	0	11	15	3	.164	.264	.191	28	-10	-11	6	1			.941	-4	/C	-1.2

■ **TED WILLIAMS** Williams, Theodore Samuel "The Kid", "The Thumper" or "The Splendid Splinter"
b: 8/30/18, San Diego, Cal. BL/TR, 6'3", 205 lbs. Deb: 4/20/39 MH

YEAR	TM/L	G	AB	R	H	2B	3B	HR	RBI	BB	SO	AVG	OBP	SLG	PRO+	BR	/A	RC	SB	CS	SBR	FA	FR	POS	TPR
1939	Bos-A	149	565	131	185	44	11	31	**145**	107	64	.327	.436	.609	158	56	53	**157**	2	1	0	.945	2	*O	4.5
1940	Bos-A★	144	561	**134**	193	43	14	23	113	96	54	.344	**.442**	.594	159	57	54	154	4	4	-1	.960	1	*O/P	4.2
1941	Bos-A★	143	456	**135**	185	33	3	**37**	120	**145**	27	**.406**	**.551**	**.735**	**232**	**102**	**100**	**202**	2	4	-2	.961	-5	*O	**8.1**
1942	Bos-A★	150	522	**141**	186	34	5	**36**	**137**	**145**	51	**.356**	**.499**	**.648**	**214**	**93**	**90**	**185**	3	2	-0	.988	3	*O	**8.4**
1946	*Bos-A★	150	514	**142**	176	37	8	38	123	**156**	44	.342	**.497**	**.667**	**211**	**94**	**90**	**188**	0	0	0	.971	-0	*O	**8.4**
1947	Bos-A★	156	528	**125**	181	40	9	**32**	**114**	**162**	47	**.343**	**.499**	**.634**	**199**	**91**	**86**	**186**	0	1	-1	.975	1	*O	**7.8**
1948	Bos-A★	137	509	124	188	**44**	3	25	127	**126**	41	**.369**	**.497**	**.615**	**185**	**76**	**72**	**172**	4	0	1	.983	0	*O	6.2
1949	Bos-A★	155	566	**150**	194	**39**	3	**43**	**159**	**162**	48	.343	**.490**	**.650**	**187**	**89**	**83**	**193**	1	1	-0	.983	3	*O	**7.3**
1950	Bos-A★	89	334	82	106	24	1	28	97	82	21	.317	.452	.647	163	41	36	103	3	0	1	.956	-4	O	2.7
1951	Bos-A★	148	531	109	169	28	4	30	126	**144**	45	.318	**.464**	**.556**	159	**63**	**55**	**152**	1	1	-0	.988	3	*O	**5.1**
1952	Bos-A	6	10	2	4	0	1	1	3	2	2	.400	.500	.900	264	2	2	5	0	0	0	1.000	-0	/O	0.2
1953	Bos-A†	37	91	17	37	6	0	13	34	19	10	.407	.509	.901	261	22	22	44	0	1	-1	.970	-4	O	1.6
1954	Bos-A★	117	386	93	133	23	1	29	89	**136**	32	**.345**	**.516**	**.635**	**193**	**71**	**65**	**139**	0	0	0	.982	-3	*O	**5.7**
1955	Bos-A★	98	320	77	114	21	3	28	83	91	24	.356	.501	.703	203	**59**	55	118	2	0	1	.989	-1	O	4.9
1956	Bos-A★	136	400	71	138	28	2	24	82	102	39	.345	**.479**	.605	164	54	47	121	0	0	0	.973	-4	*O	3.6
1957	Bos-A★	132	420	96	163	28	1	38	87	119	43	**.388**	**.528**	**.731**	**227**	**90**	86	167	0	1	-1	.995	-3	*O	7.5
1958	Bos-A★	129	411	81	135	23	2	26	85	98	49	**.328**	**.462**	.584	174	54	50	112	1	0	0	.957	-12	*O	3.2
1959	Bos-A★	103	272	32	69	15	0	10	43	52	27	.254	.377	.419	113	8	7	45	0	0	0	.970	-8	O	-0.5
1960	Bos-A★	113	310	56	98	15	0	29	72	75	41	.316	.454	.645	187	43	42	95	1	1	-0	.993	-2	O	3.5
Total	19	2292	7706	1798	2654	525	71	521	1839	2019	709	.344	.483	.634	186	1166	1093	2538	24	17	-3	.974	-34	*O/P	92.4

■ **WALT WILLIAMS** Williams, Walter Allen "No-Neck" b: 12/19/43, Brownwood, Tex. BR/TR, 5'6", 185 lbs. Deb: 4/21/64 C

YEAR	TM/L	G	AB	R	H	2B	3B	HR	RBI	BB	SO	AVG	OBP	SLG	PRO+	BR	/A	RC	SB	CS	SBR	FA	FR	POS	TPR
1964	Hou-N	10	9	1	0	0	0	0	0	0	2	.000	.000	.000	-99	-2	-2	0	1	0	0	1.000	0	/O	-0.2
1967	Chi-A	104	275	35	66	16	3	3	15	17	20	.240	.289	.353	92	-4	-3	27	3	2	-0	.983	-2	O	-1.0
1968	Chi-A	63	133	6	32	6	0	1	8	4	17	.241	.273	.308	75	-4	-4	10	0	1	-1	1.000	-2	O	-1.0
1969	Chi-A	135	471	59	143	22	1	3	32	26	33	.304	.344	.374	96	0	-3	62	6	2	1	.985	2	*O	-0.6
1970	Chi-A	110	315	43	79	18	1	3	15	19	30	.251	.298	.343	73	-11	-12	32	3	3	-1	.949	2	O	-1.6
1971	Chi-A	114	361	43	106	17	3	8	35	24	27	.294	.346	.424	114	7	6	52	5	5	-2	1.000	-2	O/3	-0.2
1972	Chi-A	77	221	22	55	7	1	2	11	13	20	.249	.291	.317	79	-6	-6	21	6	1	1	.990	1	O/3	-0.7
1973	Cle-A	104	350	43	101	15	1	8	38	14	29	.289	.318	.406	101	0	-1	43	9	4	0	.970	5	OD	0.2
1974	NY-A	43	53	5	6	0	0	0	3	1	10	.113	.130	.113	-31	-9	-9	1	1	0	0	.955	-6	O/D	-1.6
1975	NY-A	82	185	27	52	5	1	5	16	8	23	.281	.321	.400	106	0	1	23	0	1	-1	.982	-3	OD/2	-0.4
Total	10	842	2373	284	640	106	11	33	173	126	211	.270	.311	.365	91	-28	-32	270	34	19	-1	.981	-5	O/D23	-7.1

■ **WASH WILLIAMS** Williams, Washington J. b: Philadelphia, Pa. d: 1/1890, Philadelphia, Pa. 5'11", 180 lbs. Deb: 8/05/1884

YEAR	TM/L	G	AB	R	H	2B	3B	HR	RBI	BB	SO	AVG	OBP	SLG	PRO+	BR	/A	RC	SB	CS	SBR	FA	FR	POS	TPR
1884	Ric-a	2	8	0	2	0	0	0		0		.250	.250	.250	67	-0	-0	1				.500	-1	/O	-0.1
1885	Chi-N	1	4	0	1	0	0	0	0	0	0	.250	.250	.250	54	-0	-0	0				.500	-0	/OP	-0.1
Total	2	3	12	0	3	0	0	0	0	0	0	.250	.250	.250	62	-0	-1	1				.500	-1	/OP	-0.2

■ **BILLY WILLIAMS** Williams, William b: 6/13/33, Newberry, S.C. BL/TR, 6'3", 195 lbs. Deb: 8/15/69

YEAR	TM/L	G	AB	R	H	2B	3B	HR	RBI	BB	SO	AVG	OBP	SLG	PRO+	BR	/A	RC	SB	CS	SBR	FA	FR	POS	TPR
1969	Sea-A	4	10	1	0	0	0	0	0	1	3	.000	.167	.000	-51	-2	-2	0	0	0	0	1.000	1	/O	-0.2

■ **WOODY WILLIAMS** Williams, Woodrow Wilson b: 8/22/12, Pamplin, Va. BR/TR, 5'11", 175 lbs. Deb: 9/05/38

YEAR	TM/L	G	AB	R	H	2B	3B	HR	RBI	BB	SO	AVG	OBP	SLG	PRO+	BR	/A	RC	SB	CS	SBR	FA	FR	POS	TPR
1938	Bro-N	20	51	6	17	1	1	0	6	4	1	.333	.382	.392	111	1	1	8	1			.931	-7	S/3	-0.5
1943	Cin-N	30	69	8	26	2	1	0	11	1	3	.377	.386	.435	139	3	3	11	0			.986	1	2/3S	0.5
1944	Cin-N	155	653	73	157	23	3	1	35	44	24	.240	.290	.289	66	-31	-28	56	7			**.971**	15	*2	-0.5
1945	Cin-N	133	482	46	114	14	0	0	27	39	24	.237	.296	.266	58	-27	-26	40	6			.969	-10	*2	-2.8
Total	4	338	1255	133	314	40	5	1	79	88	52	.250	.301	.292	69	-55	-51	115	14			.971	-1	2/S3	-3.3

■ **NED WILLIAMSON** Williamson, Edward Nagle b: 10/24/1857, Philadelphia, Pa. d: 3/3/1894, Willow Springs, Ark BR/TR, 5'11", 170 lbs. Deb: 5/01/1878

YEAR	TM/L	G	AB	R	H	2B	3B	HR	RBI	BB	SO	AVG	OBP	SLG	PRO+	BR	/A	RC	SB	CS	SBR	FA	FR	POS	TPR
1878	Ind-N	63	250	31	58	10	2	1	19	5	15	.232	.247	.300	91	-6	-1	19				.867	-4	*3	-0.2
1879	Chi-N	80	320	66	94	20	13	1	36	24	31	.294	.343	.447	149	20	18	50				**.871**	17	*3/1C	3.3
1880	Chi-N	75	311	65	78	20	2	0	31	15	26	.251	.285	.328	101	3	0	30				**.893**	12	*3C/2	1.4
1881	Chi-N	82	343	56	92	12	6	1	48	19	19	.268	.307	.347	100	2	-0	37				**.909**	22	*3/2PSC	2.2
1882	Chi-N	83	348	66	98	27	4	3	60	27	21	.282	.333	.408	130	15	12	49				**.881**	16	*3/P	2.7
1883	Chi-N	98	402	83	111	**49**	5	2	59	22	48	.276	.314	.438	118	12	8	57				.807	18	*3/CP	2.2
1884	Chi-N	107	417	84	116	18	8	**27**	84	42	56	.278	.344	.554	164	37	31	82				.861	24	*3C/P	4.9
1885	*Chi-N	113	407	87	97	16	5	3	65	**75**	60	.238	.357	.324	106	14	4	48				**.892**	12	*3/PC	1.7
1886	*Chi-N	121	430	69	93	17	8	6	58	80	71	.216	.339	.335	92	6	-5	55	13			.869	-2	*S/CP	-0.6
1887	Chi-N	127	439	77	117	20	14	9	78	73	57	.267	.377	.437	113	19	8	92	45			.890	-31	*S/P	-1.9
1888	Chi-N	132	452	75	113	9	14	8	73	65	71	.250	.352	.385	128	21	17	72	25			.884	-12	*S	0.8
1889	Chi-N	47	173	16	41	3	1	1	30	23	22	.237	.340	.283	73	-4	-6	18	2			.844	-24	S	-2.4

YEAR	TM/L	G	AB	R	H	2B	3B	HR	RBI	BB	SO	AVG	OBP	SLG	PRO+	BR	/A	RC	SB	CS	SBR	FA	FR	POS	TPR
1890	Chi-P	73	261	34	51	7	3	2	26	36	35	.195	.311	.268	55	-15	-17	23	3			.809	-20	3S	-2.7
Total	13	1201	4553	809	1159	228	85	64	667	506	532	.255	.332	.384	113	123	69	630	88			.866	29	3S/CP21	11.4

■ HOWIE WILLIAMSON

Williamson, Nathaniel Howard b: 12/23/04, Little Rock, Ark. d: 8/15/69, Texarkana, Ark. BL/TL, 6', 170 lbs. Deb: 7/07/28

YEAR	TM/L	G	AB	R	H	2B	3B	HR	RBI	BB	SO	AVG	OBP	SLG	PRO+	BR	/A	RC	SB	CS	SBR	FA	FR	POS	TPR
1928	StL-N	10	9	0	2	0	0	0	0	1	4	.222	.300	.222	38	-1	-1	1	0			.000	0	H	-0.1

■ JULIUS WILLIGROD

Willigrod, Julius b: Iowa d: 11/27/06, San Francisco, Cal BL , Deb: 7/15/1882

YEAR	TM/L	G	AB	R	H	2B	3B	HR	RBI	BB	SO	AVG	OBP	SLG	PRO+	BR	/A	RC	SB	CS	SBR	FA	FR	POS	TPR
1882	Det-N	1	3	0	1	0	0	0	1	0	1	.333	.333	.333	115	0	0	0				1.000	-1	/S	0.0
	Cle-N	9	36	5	5	1	1	0	2	3	7	.139	.205	.222	38	-2	-2	2				.813	-3	/O	-0.5
	Yr	10	39	5	6	1	1	0	3	3	8	.154	.214	.231	44	-2	-2	2				.813	-3	/OS	-0.5

■ HUGH WILLINGHAM

Willingham, Thomas Hugh b: 5/30/06, Dalhart, Tex. d: 6/15/88, ElReno, Okla. BR/TR, 6', 180 lbs. Deb: 9/13/30

YEAR	TM/L	G	AB	R	H	2B	3B	HR	RBI	BB	SO	AVG	OBP	SLG	PRO+	BR	/A	RC	SB	CS	SBR	FA	FR	POS	TPR
1930	Chi-A	3	4	2	1	0	0	0	0	2	1	.250	.500	.250	100	0	0	1	0	0	0	1.000	-0	/2	0.0
1931	Phi-N	23	35	5	9	2	1	1	3	2	9	.257	.297	.457	93	-0	-1	5	0			.875	0	/S3O	0.0
1932	Phi-N	4	2	0	0	0	0	0	0	0	0	.000	.000	.000	-89	-1	-1	0	0			.000	0	H	-0.1
1933	Phi-N	1	1	0	0	0	0	0	0	0	0	.000	.000	.000	-89	-0	-0	0	0			.000	0	H	0.0
Total	4	31	42	7	10	2	1	1	3	4	10	.238	.304	.405	82	-1	-1	6	0	0			-0	/S3O2	-0.1

■ WILLS

Wills Deb: 5/14/1884

YEAR	TM/L	G	AB	R	H	2B	3B	HR	RBI	BB	SO	AVG	OBP	SLG	PRO+	BR	/A	RC	SB	CS	SBR	FA	FR	POS	TPR
1884	Was-a	4	15	1	2	2	0	0		0		.133	.133	.267	32	-1	-1	1				.889	2	/O	0.1
	KC-U	5	21	2	3	1	0	0		0		.143	.143	.190	14	-2	-1	1				1.000	1	/O	-0.1
Total	1	9	36	3	5	3	0	0		0		.139	.139	.222	22	-3	-2	1				.938	2	/O	0.0

■ DAVE WILLS

Wills, Davis Bowles b: 1/26/1877, Charlottesville, Va. d: 10/12/59, Washington, D.C. BL/TL, Deb: 6/08/1899

YEAR	TM/L	G	AB	R	H	2B	3B	HR	RBI	BB	SO	AVG	OBP	SLG	PRO+	BR	/A	RC	SB	CS	SBR	FA	FR	POS	TPR
1899	Lou-N	24	94	15	21	3	1	0	12	2		.223	.240	.277	41	-8	-8	7	1			.957	-3	1	-1.0

■ BUMP WILLS

Wills, Elliott Taylor b: 7/27/52, Washington, D.C. BB/TR, 5'9", 177 lbs. Deb: 4/07/77 F

YEAR	TM/L	G	AB	R	H	2B	3B	HR	RBI	BB	SO	AVG	OBP	SLG	PRO+	BR	/A	RC	SB	CS	SBR	FA	FR	POS	TPR
1977	Tex-A	152	541	87	155	28	6	9	62	65	96	.287	.363	.410	109	9	8	83	28	12	1	.982	3	*2/S1D	2.3
1978	Tex-A	157	539	78	135	17	4	9	57	63	91	.250	.333	.347	91	-5	-5	68	52	14	7	.981	21	*2	3.5
1979	Tex-A	146	543	90	148	21	3	5	46	53	58	.273	.342	.350	88	-9	-8	68	35	11	4	.976	7	*2	1.3
1980	Tex-A	146	578	102	152	31	5	5	58	51	71	.263	.326	.360	90	-9	-7	73	34	9	5	.984	19	*2	2.6
1981	Tex-A	102	410	51	103	13	2	2	41	32	49	.251	.307	.307	82	-12	-9	38	12	9	-2	.983	9	*2/D	0.4
1982	Chi-N	128	419	64	114	18	4	6	38	46	76	.272	.351	.377	101	3	2	61	35	10	5	.963	-18	*2	-0.7
Total	6	831	3030	472	807	128	24	36	302	310	441	.266	.338	.360	94	-22	-19	390	196	65	20	.979	40	2/DS1	9.4

■ MAURY WILLS

Wills, Maurice Morning b: 10/2/32, Washington, D.C. BB/TR, 5'11", 170 lbs. Deb: 6/06/59 FM

YEAR	TM/L	G	AB	R	H	2B	3B	HR	RBI	BB	SO	AVG	OBP	SLG	PRO+	BR	/A	RC	SB	CS	SBR	FA	FR	POS	TPR
1959	*LA-N	83	242	27	63	5	2	0	7	13	27	.260	.298	.298	55	-14	-16	22	7	3	0	.966	2	S	-0.8
1960	LA-N	148	516	75	152	15	2	0	27	35	47	.295	.343	.331	80	-9	-13	62	**50**	12	**8**	.945	21	*S	2.7
1961	LA-N★	148	613	105	173	12	10	1	31	59	50	.282	.346	.339	76	-13	-20	77	**35**	15	2	.959	12	*S	0.5
1962	LA-N★	165	695	130	208	13	**10**	6	48	51	57	.299	.349	.373	100	-5	0	106	**104**	13	**23**	.956	-5	*S	3.4
1963	*LA-N☆	134	527	83	159	19	3	0	34	44	48	.302	.357	.349	112	4	8	69	**40**	19	1	.959	-5	*S3	1.2
1964	LA-N	158	630	81	173	15	5	2	34	41	73	.275	.319	.324	88	-15	-9	70	**53**	17	**6**	.963	-8	*S/3	-0.1
1965	*LA-N★	158	650	92	186	14	7	0	33	40	64	.286	.331	.329	93	-11	-6	77	**94**	31	10	.970	21	*S	3.8
1966	*LA-N★	143	594	60	162	14	2	1	39	34	60	.273	.314	.308	80	-20	-15	57	38	24	-3	.967	9	*S/3	0.5
1967	Pit-N	149	616	92	186	12	9	3	45	31	44	.302	.336	.365	100	0	0	78	29	10	3	.948	9	*3/S	1.2
1968	Pit-N	153	627	76	174	12	6	0	31	45	57	.278	.327	.316	95	-4	-3	67	52	21	3	.957	-9	*3S	-0.9
1969	Mon-N	47	189	23	42	3	0	0	8	20	21	.222	.297	.238	51	-12	-12	15	15	6	1	.950	-3	S/2	-0.9
	LA-N	104	434	57	129	7	8	4	39	39	40	.297	.357	.378	114	4	8	59	25	15	-1	.969	7	*S	2.6
	Yr	151	623	80	171	10	8	4	47	59	61	.274	.338	.335	94	-8	-4	73	40	21	-1	.963	4	*S/2	1.7
1970	LA-N	132	522	77	141	19	3	0	34	50	34	.270	.334	.318	79	-17	-14	57	28	13	1	.959	-19	*S/3	-1.8
1971	LA-N	149	601	73	169	14	3	3	44	40	44	.281	.326	.329	92	-11	-7	66	15	8	-0	.978	1	*S/3	1.4
1972	LA-N	71	132	16	17	3	1	0	4	10	18	.129	.190	.167	2	-17	-17	5	1	1	-0	.984	-4	S3	-1.8
Total	14	1942	7588	1067	2134	177	71	20	458	552	684	.281	.331	.331	88	-139	-115	885	586	208	51	.963	30	*S3/2	11.0

■ KID WILLSON

Willson, Frank Hoxie b: 11/3/1895, Bloomington, Neb. d: 4/17/64, Union Gap, Wash. BL/TL, 6'1", 190 lbs. Deb: 7/02/18

YEAR	TM/L	G	AB	R	H	2B	3B	HR	RBI	BB	SO	AVG	OBP	SLG	PRO+	BR	/A	RC	SB	CS	SBR	FA	FR	POS	TPR
1918	Chi-A	4	1	2	0	0	0	0	0	1	1	.000	.500	.000	50	0	0	0	0			.000	0	H	0.0
1927	Chi-A	7	10	1	1	0	0	0	1	0	2	.100	.100	.100	-49	-2	-2	0	0	0	0	1.000	0	/O	-0.2
Total	2	11	11	3	1	0	0	0	1	1	3	.091	.167	.091	-31	-2	-2	0	0	0			0	/O	-0.2

■ WALT WILMOT

Wilmot, Walter Robert b: 10/18/1863, Plover, Wis. d: 2/1/29, Chicago, Ill. BB/TR, Deb: 4/20/1888

YEAR	TM/L	G	AB	R	H	2B	3B	HR	RBI	BB	SO	AVG	OBP	SLG	PRO+	BR	/A	RC	SB	CS	SBR	FA	FR	POS	TPR
1888	Was-N	119	473	61	106	16	9	4	43	23	55	.224	.263	.321	93	-7	-3	53	46			.872	11	*O	0.5
1889	Was-N	108	432	88	125	19	**19**	9	57	51	32	.289	.367	.484	147	21	26	94	40			.927	15	*O	3.2
1890	Chi-N	139	571	114	159	15	12	**13**	99	64	44	.278	.353	.415	121	18	14	113	76			.938	13	*O	2.0
1891	Chi-N	121	498	102	139	14	10	11	71	55	21	.279	.357	.414	126	16	16	91	42			.922	-5	*O	0.7
1892	Chi-N	92	380	47	82	7	7	2	35	40	20	.216	.297	.287	78	-9	-10	43	31			.903	2	O	-1.1
1893	Chi-N	94	392	69	118	14	14	3	61	40	8	.301	.367	.431	115	7	8	78	39			.873	-0	*O	0.3
1894	Chi-N	133	597	134	197	45	12	5	130	35	23	.330	.368	.471	97	1	-6	135	74			.872	-7	*O	-1.6
1895	Chi-N	108	466	86	132	16	6	8	72	30	19	.283	.327	.395	82	-10	-15	72	28			.914	4	*O	-1.7
1897	NY-N	11	34	8	9	2	0	1	4	2		.265	.306	.412	91	-1	-1	5	1			.938	0	/O	-0.1
1898	NY-N	35	138	16	33	4	2	2	22	9		.239	.286	.341	82	-4	-4	15	4			.886	-5	O	-1.0
Total	10	960	3981	725	1100	152	91	58	594	349	222	.276	.337	.404	107	32	26	699	381			.903	28	O	1.2

■ ARCHIE WILSON

Wilson, Archie Clifton b: 11/25/23, Los Angeles, Cal. BR/TR, 5'11", 175 lbs. Deb: 9/18/51

YEAR	TM/L	G	AB	R	H	2B	3B	HR	RBI	BB	SO	AVG	OBP	SLG	PRO+	BR	/A	RC	SB	CS	SBR	FA	FR	POS	TPR
1951	NY-A	4	4	0	0	0	0	0	0	0	0	.000	.200	.000	-44	-1	-1	0	0	0	0	1.000	-0	/O	-0.1
1952	NY-A	3	2	0	1	0	0	0	1	0	0	.500	.500	.500	190	0	0	1	0	0	0	.000	0	H	0.0
	Was-A	26	96	8	20	2	3	0	14	5	11	.208	.255	.292	54	-6	-6	5	0	0	0	.971	1	O	-0.7
	Bos-A	18	38	1	10	3	0	0	2	2	3	.263	.300	.342	73	-1	-2	4	0	0	0	.944	-2	O	-0.4
	Yr	47	136	9	31	5	3	0	17	7	14	.228	.271	.309	61	-7	-8	9	0	0	0	.966	-1	O	-1.1
Total	2	51	140	9	31	5	3	0	17	7	14	.221	.268	.300	58	-8	-8	9	0	0	0	.967	-1	/O	-1.2

■ ART WILSON

Wilson, Arthur Earl "Dutch" b: 12/11/1885, Macon, Ill. d: 6/12/60, Chicago, Ill. BR/TR, 5'8", 170 lbs. Deb: 9/29/08

YEAR	TM/L	G	AB	R	H	2B	3B	HR	RBI	BB	SO	AVG	OBP	SLG	PRO+	BR	/A	RC	SB	CS	SBR	FA	FR	POS	TPR
1908	NY-N	1	0	0	0	0	0	0	0	0		—	—	—	—	0	0	0	0			.000	0	R	0.0
1909	NY-N	19	42	4	10	2	1	0	5	4		.238	.304	.333	96	-0	-0	4	0			.985	-4	C	-0.4
1910	NY-N	26	52	10	14	4	1	0	5	9	6	.269	.387	.385	125	2	2	9	2			.975	-1	C/1	0.3
1911	*NY-N	66	109	17	33	9	1	1	17	19	12	.303	.411	.431	132	6	5	22	6			.963	-6	C	0.3
1912	*NY-N	65	121	17	35	6	0	3	19	13	14	.289	.358	.413	107	2	1	19	2			.960	1	C	0.5
1913	*NY-N	54	79	5	15	0	1	0	8	11	11	.190	.289	.215	45	-5	-5	5	1			.965	8	C	0.4
1914	Chi-F	137	440	78	128	31	8	10	64	70	80	.291	.394	.466	153	27	30	90	13			.974	13	*C	5.6
1915	Chi-F	96	269	44	82	11	2	7	31	65	38	.305	.442	.439	169	24	26	60	8			.980	-8	C	2.6
1916	Pit-N	53	128	11	33	5	2	1	12	13	27	.258	.331	.352	109	2	2	17	4			.981	-9	C	-0.5
	Chi-N	36	114	5	22	3	1	0	5	6	14	.193	.233	.237	40	-7	-9	7	1			.953	-4	C	-1.1
	Yr	89	242	16	55	8	3	1	17	19	41	.227	.286	.298	76	-6	-7	23	5			.967	-13	C	-1.6
1917	Chi-N	81	211	17	45	9	2	2	25	32	36	.213	.322	.303	86	-1	-3	22	6			.968	7	C	1.1
1918	Bos-N	89	280	15	69	8	2	0	19	24	31	.246	.310	.289	87	-5	-4	26	5			.977	-10	C	-0.8
1919	Bos-N	71	191	14	49	8	1	0	16	25	19	.257	.346	.309	102	1	1	22	2			.977	-2	C/1	0.5

YEAR	TM/L	G	AB	R	H	2B	3B	HR	RBI	BB	SO	AVG	OBP	SLG	PRO+	BR	/A	RC	SB	CS	SBR	FA	FR	POS	TPR
1920	Bos-N	16	19	0	1	0	0	0	0	1	1	.053	.143	.053	-44	-3	-3	0	0	0	0	1.000	-2	/3C	-0.5
1921	Cle-A	2	1	0	0	0	0	0	0	0	0	.000	.000	.000	-99	-0	-0	0	0	0	0	1.000	0	/C	0.0
Total	14	812	2056	237	536	96	22	24	226	292	289	.261	.357	.364	114	40	44	302	50	0		.972	-16	C/31	8.0

■ ARTIE WILSON
Wilson, Arthur Lee b: 10/28/20, Springfield, Ala. BL/TR, 5'10", 162 lbs. Deb: 4/18/51

YEAR	TM/L	G	AB	R	H	2B	3B	HR	RBI	BB	SO	AVG	OBP	SLG	PRO+	BR	/A	RC	SB	CS	SBR	FA	FR	POS	TPR
1951	NY-N	19	22	2	4	0	0	0	1	2	1	.182	.250	.182	18	-2	-3	1	2	0	1	1.000	3	/2S1	0.1

■ CHARLIE WILSON
Wilson, Charles Woodrow "Swamp Baby" b: 1/13/05, Clinton, S.C. d: 12/19/70, Rochester, N.Y. BB/TR, 5'10.5", 178 lbs. Deb: 4/14/31

YEAR	TM/L	G	AB	R	H	2B	3B	HR	RBI	BB	SO	AVG	OBP	SLG	PRO+	BR	/A	RC	SB	CS	SBR	FA	FR	POS	TPR
1931	Bos-N	16	58	7	11	4	0	1	11	3	5	.190	.230	.310	45	-5	-5	4	0			.917	-2	3	-0.6
1932	StL-N	24	96	7	19	3	3	1	2	3	8	.198	.222	.323	43	-8	-8	7	0			.935	-7	S	-1.3
1933	StL-N	1	1	0	0	0	0	0	0	0	1	.000	.000	.000	-95	-0	-0	0	0			.000	0	/S	0.0
1935	StL-N	16	31	1	10	0	0	0	1	2	2	.323	.364	.323	83	-0	-1	3	0			.933	-1	/3	-0.1
Total	4	57	186	15	40	7	3	2	14	8	16	.215	.247	.317	50	-13	-13	14	0			.935	-10	/S3	-2.0

■ CRAIG WILSON
Wilson, Craig b: 11/28/64, Annapolis, Md. BR/TR, 5'11", 175 lbs. Deb: 9/06/89

YEAR	TM/L	G	AB	R	H	2B	3B	HR	RBI	BB	SO	AVG	OBP	SLG	PRO+	BR	/A	RC	SB	CS	SBR	FA	FR	POS	TPR
1989	StL-N	6	4	1	1	0	0	0	1	1	2	.250	.400	.250	87	0	-0	1	0	0	0	.500	-0	/3	0.0
1990	StL-N	55	121	13	30	2	0	0	7	8	14	.248	.295	.264	55	-7	-7	8	0	2	-1	.971	0	3O/21	-0.9
1991	StL-N	60	82	5	14	2	0	0	13	6	10	.171	.227	.195	20	-9	-9	4	0	0	0	.905	-1	3/O12	-1.1
1992	StL-N	61	106	6	33	6	0	0	13	10	18	.311	.371	.368	111	2	2	13	1	2	-1	.970	-3	32/O	-0.2
Total	4	182	313	25	78	10	0	0	34	25	44	.249	.305	.281	65	-14	-14	25	1	4	-2	.944	-5	/32O1	-2.2

■ DAN WILSON
Wilson, Daniel Allen b: 3/25/69, Arlington Heights, Ill. BR/TR, 6'3", 190 lbs. Deb: 9/07/92

YEAR	TM/L	G	AB	R	H	2B	3B	HR	RBI	BB	SO	AVG	OBP	SLG	PRO+	BR	/A	RC	SB	CS	SBR	FA	FR	POS	TPR
1992	Cin-N	12	25	2	9	1	0	0	3	3	8	.360	.429	.400	130	1	1	4	0	0	0	1.000	0	/C	0.2

■ EDDIE WILSON
Wilson, Edward Francis b: 9/7/09, Hamden, Conn. d: 4/11/79, Hamden, Conn. BL/TL, 5'11", 165 lbs. Deb: 6/21/36

YEAR	TM/L	G	AB	R	H	2B	3B	HR	RBI	BB	SO	AVG	OBP	SLG	PRO+	BR	/A	RC	SB	CS	SBR	FA	FR	POS	TPR
1936	Bro-N	52	173	28	60	8	1	3	25	14	25	.347	.402	.457	129	8	8	34	3			.926	-5	O	0.0
1937	Bro-N	36	54	11	12	4	1	1	8	17	14	.222	.408	.389	116	2	2	11	1			.966	-3	O	-0.2
Total	2	88	227	39	72	12	2	4	33	31	39	.317	.404	.441	126	10	10	44	4			.936	-9	/O	-0.2

■ FRANK WILSON
Wilson, Francis Edward "Squash" b: 4/20/01, Malden, Mass. d: 11/25/74, Leicester, Mass. BL/TR, 6', 185 lbs. Deb: 6/20/24

YEAR	TM/L	G	AB	R	H	2B	3B	HR	RBI	BB	SO	AVG	OBP	SLG	PRO+	BR	/A	RC	SB	CS	SBR	FA	FR	POS	TPR
1924	Bos-N	61	215	20	51	7	0	1	15	23	22	.237	.311	.284	63	-11	-10	20	3	4	-2	.973	3	O	-1.2
1925	Bos-N	12	31	3	13	1	1	0	0	4	1	.419	.486	.516	171	3	3	8	2	1	0	1.000	1	O	0.3
1926	Bos-N	87	236	22	56	11	3	0	23	20	21	.237	.300	.309	70	-12	-9	22	3			.934	1	O	-1.2
1928	Cle-A	2	1	0	0	0	0	0	0	1	0	.000	.500	.000	41	0	0	0	0	0	0	.000	0	H	0.0
	StL-A	6	5	1	0	0	0	0	0	0	0	.000	.000	.000	-97	-1	-1	0	0	0	0	.000	-0	/O	-0.2
	Yr	8	6	1	0	0	0	0	0	1	0	.000	.143	.000	-58	-1	-1	0	0	0	0	.000	-0	/O	-0.2
Total	4	168	488	46	120	19	4	1	38	48	44	.246	.315	.307	72	-22	-17	50	8	5		.958	4	O	-2.3

■ TUG WILSON
Wilson, George Archer b: 1860, Brooklyn, N.Y. d: 11/28/14, New York, N.Y. Deb: 5/09/1884

YEAR	TM/L	G	AB	R	H	2B	3B	HR	RBI	BB	SO	AVG	OBP	SLG	PRO+	BR	/A	RC	SB	CS	SBR	FA	FR	POS	TPR
1884	Bro-a	24	82	13	19	4	0	0		5		.232	.276	.280	84	-1	-1	7				.826	-3	OC/12	-0.4

■ SQUANTO WILSON
Wilson, George Francis b: 3/29/1889, Old Town, Me. d: 3/26/67, Winthrop, Maine BB/TR, 5'9.5", 170 lbs. Deb: 10/02/11

YEAR	TM/L	G	AB	R	H	2B	3B	HR	RBI	BB	SO	AVG	OBP	SLG	PRO+	BR	/A	RC	SB	CS	SBR	FA	FR	POS	TPR
1911	Det-A	5	16	2	3	0	0	0	0	2		.188	.278	.188	29	-1	-2	1	0			.900	-1	/C	-0.2
1914	Bos-A	1	0	0	0	0	0	0	0	0	0	—	—	—	—	0	0	0	0			.000	0	/1	0.0
Total	2	6	16	2	3	0	0	0	0	2	0	.188	.278	.188	29	-1	-2	1	0				-1	/C1	-0.2

■ ICEHOUSE WILSON
Wilson, George Peacock b: 9/14/12, Maricopa, Cal. d: 10/13/73, Moraga, Cal. BR/TR, 6', 186 lbs. Deb: 5/31/34

YEAR	TM/L	G	AB	R	H	2B	3B	HR	RBI	BB	SO	AVG	OBP	SLG	PRO+	BR	/A	RC	SB	CS	SBR	FA	FR	POS	TPR
1934	Det-A	1	1	0	0	0	0	0	0	0	0	.000	.000	.000	-99	-0	-0	0	0	0	0	.000	0	H	0.0

■ GEORGE WILSON
Wilson, George Washington "Teddy" b: 8/30/25, Cherryville, N.C. d: 10/29/74, Gastonia, N.C. BL/TR, 6'1.5", 185 lbs. Deb: 4/15/52

YEAR	TM/L	G	AB	R	H	2B	3B	HR	RBI	BB	SO	AVG	OBP	SLG	PRO+	BR	/A	RC	SB	CS	SBR	FA	FR	POS	TPR
1952	Chi-A	8	9	0	1	0	0	0	1	1	2	.111	.200	.111	-12	-1	-1	0	0	0	0	1.000	0	/O	-0.1
	NY-N	62	112	9	27	7	0	2	16	3	14	.241	.261	.357	69	-5	-5	11	0	0	0	.923	-3	O/1	-0.9
1953	NY-N	11	8	0	1	0	0	0	0	2	2	.125	.364	.125	34	-1	-1	1	0	0	0	.000	0	H	-0.1
1956	NY-N	53	68	5	9	1	0	1	2	5	14	.132	.192	.191	3	-9	-9	3	0	0	0	1.000	0	/O	-1.0
	*NY-A	11	12	1	2	0	0	0	0	3	0	.167	.333	.167	37	-1	-1	1	0	0	0	.750	-2	/O	-0.3
Total	3	145	209	15	40	8	0	3	19	14	32	.191	.246	.273	41	-17	-17	15	0	0	0	.932	-5	/O1	-2.4

■ GLENN WILSON
Wilson, Glenn Dwight b: 12/22/58, Baytown, Tex. BR/TR, 6'1", 190 lbs. Deb: 4/15/82

YEAR	TM/L	G	AB	R	H	2B	3B	HR	RBI	BB	SO	AVG	OBP	SLG	PRO+	BR	/A	RC	SB	CS	SBR	FA	FR	POS	TPR
1982	Det-A	84	322	39	94	15	1	12	34	15	51	.292	.323	.457	111	4	4	44	2	3	-1	.987	7	O/D	0.8
1983	Det-A	144	503	55	135	25	6	11	65	25	79	.268	.307	.408	97	-5	-3	61	1	1	-0	.988	-7	*O	-1.5
1984	Phi-N	132	341	28	82	21	3	6	31	17	56	.240	.279	.372	80	-9	-10	33	7	1	2	.968	-12	*O/3	-2.4
1985	Phi-N★	161	608	73	167	39	5	14	102	35	117	.275	.314	.424	102	2	-0	73	7	4	-0	.968	20	*O	1.6
1986	Phi-N	155	584	70	158	30	4	15	84	42	91	.271	.324	.413	98	0	-2	76	5	1	1	.989	21	*O	1.5
1987	Phi-N	154	569	55	150	21	2	14	54	38	82	.264	.311	.381	80	-15	-17	62	3	6	-3	.968	15	*O/P	-1.0
1988	Sea-A	78	284	28	71	10	1	3	17	15	52	.250	.288	.324	68	-11	-13	23	1	1	-0	.980	1	O/D	-1.5
	Pit-N	37	126	11	34	8	0	2	15	3	18	.270	.292	.381	93	-2	-2	13	0	0	0	.985	-1	O	-0.4
1989	Pit-N	100	330	42	93	20	4	9	49	32	39	.282	.347	.448	130	11	12	49	1	4	-2	.977	1	O1	0.9
	Hou-N	28	102	8	22	6	0	2	15	5	14	.216	.252	.333	68	-5	-4	8	0	1	-1	.966	5	O	-0.1
	Yr	128	432	50	115	26	4	11	64	37	53	.266	.326	.421	116	6	8	56	1	5	-3	.974	6	*O1	0.8
1990	Hou-N	118	368	42	90	14	0	10	55	26	64	.245	.296	.364	83	-10	-9	35	0	3	-2	.975	7	*O/1	-0.6
Total	9	1191	4137	451	1096	209	26	98	521	253	663	.265	.309	.399	94	-41	-45	479	27	25	-7	.977	57	*O/1D3P	-2.7

■ GRADY WILSON
Wilson, Grady Herbert b: 11/23/22, Columbus, Ga. BR/TR, 6'0.5", 170 lbs. Deb: 5/15/48

YEAR	TM/L	G	AB	R	H	2B	3B	HR	RBI	BB	SO	AVG	OBP	SLG	PRO+	BR	/A	RC	SB	CS	SBR	FA	FR	POS	TPR
1948	Pit-N	12	10	1	1	1	0	0	1	0	3	.100	.100	.200	-20	-2	-2	0	0			.846	1	/S	-0.1

■ HENRY WILSON
Wilson, Henry C. b: Baltimore, Md. Deb: 10/12/1898

YEAR	TM/L	G	AB	R	H	2B	3B	HR	RBI	BB	SO	AVG	OBP	SLG	PRO+	BR	/A	RC	SB	CS	SBR	FA	FR	POS	TPR
1898	Bal-N	1	2	0	0	0	0	0	0	1		.000	.333	.000	-2	-0	-0	0	0			1.000	0	/C	0.0

■ JIMMIE WILSON
Wilson, James "Ace" b: 7/23/1900, Philadelphia, Pa. d: 5/31/47, Bradenton, Fla. BR/TR, 6'1.5", 200 lbs. Deb: 4/17/23 MC

YEAR	TM/L	G	AB	R	H	2B	3B	HR	RBI	BB	SO	AVG	OBP	SLG	PRO+	BR	/A	RC	SB	CS	SBR	FA	FR	POS	TPR
1923	Phi-N	85	252	27	66	9	0	1	25	4	17	.262	.276	.310	49	-17	-21	21	4	2	0	.960	-3	C/O	-2.0
1924	Phi-N	95	280	32	78	16	3	6	39	17	12	.279	.322	.421	87	-2	-6	37	5	4	-1	.968	5	C/1O	0.3
1925	Phi-N	108	335	42	110	19	3	3	54	32	25	.328	.390	.430	100	6	1	57	5	3	-0	.982	-9	C/O	-0.3
1926	Phi-N	90	279	40	85	10	2	4	32	25	20	.305	.362	.398	99	2	0	40	3			.950	0	C	0.5
1927	Phi-N	128	443	50	122	15	2	2	45	34	15	.275	.330	.332	77	-13	-14	48	13			.975	-19	*C	-2.4
1928	Phi-N	21	70	11	21	4	1	0	13	9	8	.300	.380	.386	97	0	0	10	3			.990	2	C	0.3
	*StL-N	120	411	45	106	26	2	2	50	45	24	.258	.333	.345	76	-13	-14	48	9			.983	1	*C	-0.3
	Yr	141	481	56	127	30	3	2	63	54	32	.264	.340	.351	79	-13	-14	58	12			.985	2	*C	0.0
1929	StL-N	120	394	59	128	27	8	4	71	43	19	.325	.394	.464	111	8	7	71	4			.972	5	*C	2.0
1930	*StL-N	107	362	54	115	25	7	1	58	28	17	.318	.368	.434	90	-4	-6	57	8			.987	10	C	1.2
1931	*StL-N	115	383	45	105	20	2	0	51	28	15	.274	.332	.337	77	-10	-12	45	5			.985	11	*C	0.6
1932	StL-N	92	274	36	68	16	2	2	28	15	18	.248	.290	.343	67	-12	-13	28	9			.982	2	C/12	-0.7
1933	StL-N★	113	369	34	94	17	0	1	45	23	33	.255	.300	.309	71	-12	-14	34	6			.982	2	*C	-0.6
1934	Phi-N	91	277	25	81	11	0	3	35	14	10	.292	.326	.365	75	-6	-11	31	1			.987	2	C/12M	-0.5
1935	Phi-N★	93	290	38	81	20	0	1	37	19	19	.279	.326	.359	76	-6	-10	35	4			.982	8	C/2M	0.1
1936	Phi-N	85	230	25	64	12	0	1	27	12	21	.278	.314	.343	70	-7	-10	24	5			.960	-6	C/1M	-1.4
1937	Phi-N	39	87	15	24	3	0	1	8	6	4	.276	.323	.345	75	-2	-3	9	1			.978	-1	C/1M	-0.4

YEAR	TM/L	G	AB	R	H	2B	3B	HR	RBI	BB	SO	AVG	OBP	SLG	PRO+	BR	/A	RC	SB	CS	SBR	FA	FR	POS	TPR
1938	Phi-N	3	2	0	0	0	0	0	0	0	1	.000	.000	.000	-99	-1	-1	0	0			1.000	0	/CM	0.0
1939	Cin-N	4	3	0	1	0	0	0	0	0	1	.333	.333	.333	79	-0	-0	0	0			.000	-0	/C	0.0
1940	*Cin-N	16	37	2	9	2	0	0	3	2	1	.243	.282	.297	59	-2	-2	3	1			.982	3	C	0.2
Total	18	1525	4778	580	1358	252	32	32	621	356	280	.284	.336	.370	82	-92	-128	600	86	9		.977	11	*C/1O2	-3.4

■ GARY WILSON Wilson, James Garrett b: 1/12/1877, Baltimore, Md. d: 5/1/69, Randallstown, Md. BR/TR, 5'7", 168 lbs. Deb: 9/27/02

YEAR	TM/L	G	AB	R	H	2B	3B	HR	RBI	BB	SO	AVG	OBP	SLG	PRO+	BR	/A	RC	SB	CS	SBR	FA	FR	POS	TPR
1902	Bos-A	2	8	0	1	0	0	0	1	0		.125	.125	.125	-30	-1	-1	0	0			.800	0	/2	-0.1

■ JIM WILSON Wilson, James George b: 12/29/60, Corvallis, Ore. BR/TR, 6'3", 230 lbs. Deb: 9/13/85

YEAR	TM/L	G	AB	R	H	2B	3B	HR	RBI	BB	SO	AVG	OBP	SLG	PRO+	BR	/A	RC	SB	CS	SBR	FA	FR	POS	TPR
1985	Cle-A	4	14	2	5	0	0	0	4	1	3	.357	.400	.357	110	0	0	2	0	0	0	1.000	-1	/1D	-0.1
1989	Sea-A	5	8	0	0	0	0	0	0	0	3	.000	.000	.000	-97	-2	-2	0	0	0	0	.000	0	/D	-0.2
Total	2	9	22	2	5	0	0	0	4	1	6	.227	.261	.227	36	-2	-2	2	0	0	0	.988	-1	/D1	-0.3

■ CHIEF WILSON Wilson, John Owen b: 8/21/1883, Austin, Tex. d: 2/22/54, Bertram, Tex. BL/TR, 6'2", 185 lbs. Deb: 4/15/08

YEAR	TM/L	G	AB	R	H	2B	3B	HR	RBI	BB	SO	AVG	OBP	SLG	PRO+	BR	/A	RC	SB	CS	SBR	FA	FR	POS	TPR
1908	Pit-N	144	529	47	120	8	7	3	43	22		.227	.260	.285	74	-16	-16	42	12			.955	1	*O	-2.5
1909	*Pit-N	154	569	64	155	22	12	4	59	19		.272	.303	.374	102	3	-2	69	17			.957	6	*O	-0.2
1910	Pit-N	146	536	59	148	14	13	4	50	21	68	.276	.312	.373	94	-3	-7	64	8			.972	3	*O	-1.1
1911	Pit-N	148	544	72	163	34	12	12	**107**	41	55	.300	.353	.472	125	19	16	93	10			.977	7	*O	1.5
1912	Pit-N	152	583	80	175	19	**36**	11	95	35	67	.300	.342	.513	134	21	22	106	16			.961	1	*O	1.5
1913	Pit-N	155	580	71	154	12	14	10	73	32	62	.266	.307	.386	102	-4	-1	68	9			.969	6	*O	-0.2
1914	StL-N	154	580	64	150	27	12	9	73	32	66	.259	.302	.393	107	1	2	69	14			**.983**	17	*O	1.4
1915	StL-N	107	348	33	96	13	6	3	39	19	43	.276	.321	.374	110	3	3	41	8	15	-7	**.984**	12	*O	0.5
1916	StL-N	120	355	30	85	8	2	3	32	20	46	.239	.289	.299	81	-8	-8	33	4			.955	-11	*O	-2.7
Total	9	1280	4624	520	1246	157	114	59	571	241	407	.269	.311	.391	105	16	10	585	98	15		.968	42	*O	-1.8

■ LES WILSON Wilson, Lester Wilbur "Tug" b: 7/15/1885, Gratiot County, Mich. d: 4/4/69, Edmonds, Wash. BL/TR, 5'11", 170 lbs. Deb: 7/15/11

YEAR	TM/L	G	AB	R	H	2B	3B	HR	RBI	BB	SO	AVG	OBP	SLG	PRO+	BR	/A	RC	SB	CS	SBR	FA	FR	POS	TPR
1911	Bos-A	5	7	0	0	0	0	0	0	2		.000	.222	.000	-36	-1	-1	0	0			1.000	-1	/O	-0.2

■ HACK WILSON Wilson, Lewis Robert b: 4/26/1900, Ellwood City, Pa. d: 11/23/48, Baltimore, Md. BR/TR, 5'6", 190 lbs. Deb: 9/29/23 H

YEAR	TM/L	G	AB	R	H	2B	3B	HR	RBI	BB	SO	AVG	OBP	SLG	PRO+	BR	/A	RC	SB	CS	SBR	FA	FR	POS	TPR
1923	NY-N	3	10	0	2	0	0	0	0	0	1	.200	.200	.200	6	-1	-1	0	0	0	0	.857	-1	/O	-0.2
1924	*NY-N	107	383	62	113	19	12	10	57	44	46	.295	.369	.486	131	14	16	70	4	3	-1	.967	-7	*O	0.2
1925	NY-N	62	180	28	43	7	4	6	30	21	33	.239	.322	.422	92	-4	-3	25	5	2	0	.975	-11	O	-1.5
1926	Chi-N	142	529	97	170	36	8	**21**	109	**69**	61	.321	.406	**.539**	**150**	39	**38**	115	10			.973	2	*O	3.0
1927	Chi-N	146	551	119	175	30	12	**30**	129	71	70	.318	.401	.579	160	46	46	126	13			.967	-1	*O	3.5
1928	Chi-N	145	520	89	163	32	9	**31**	120	77	94	.313	.404	.588	159	42	43	122	4			.960	-10	*O	2.3
1929	*Chi-N	150	574	135	198	30	5	39	**159**	78	83	.345	.425	.618	155	49	49	148	3			.970	-3	*O	3.3
1930	Chi-N	155	585	146	208	35	6	**56**	**190**	**105**	84	.356	.454	**.723**	**177**	**75**	**75**	**189**	3			.951	-7	*O	4.9
1931	Chi-N	112	395	66	103	22	4	13	61	63	69	.261	.362	.435	112	8	7	66	1			.978	-5	*O	-0.5
1932	Bro-N	135	481	77	143	37	5	23	123	51	85	.297	.366	.538	142	26	27	97	2			.955	-9	*O	1.0
1933	Bro-N	117	360	41	96	13	2	9	54	52	50	.267	.359	.389	119	8	10	53	7			.963	-7	O/2	-0.2
1934	Bro-N	67	172	24	45	5	0	6	27	40	33	.262	.401	.395	120	5	7	30	0			.974	-3	O	0.2
	Phi-N	7	20	0	2	0	0	0	3	3	4	.100	.217	.100	-11	-3	-4	0	0			1.000	-1	/O	-0.4
	Yr	74	192	24	47	5	0	6	30	43	37	.245	.383	.365	105	2	3	29	0			.977	-4	O	-0.2
Total	12	1348	4760	884	1461	266	67	244	1062	674	713	.307	.395	.545	145	305	310	1042	52	5		.965	-62	*O/2	15.6

■ TACK WILSON Wilson, Michael b: 5/16/55, Shreveport, La. BR/TR, 5'10", 185 lbs. Deb: 4/09/83

YEAR	TM/L	G	AB	R	H	2B	3B	HR	RBI	BB	SO	AVG	OBP	SLG	PRO+	BR	/A	RC	SB	CS	SBR	FA	FR	POS	TPR
1983	Min-A	5	4	4	1	1	0	0	1	0	0	.250	.250	.500	97	-0	-0	1	0	0	0	1.000	-0	/OD	0.0
1987	Cal-A	7	2	5	1	0	0	0	0	1	0	.500	.667	.500	224	0	1	1	0	0	0	1.000	-1	/OD	-0.1
Total	2	12	6	9	2	1	0	0	1	1	0	.333	.429	.500	150	0	0	1	0	0	0	1.000	-2	/OD	-0.1

■ PARKE WILSON Wilson, Parke Asel b: 10/26/1867, Keithsburg, Ill. d: 12/20/34, Hermosa Beach, Cal BR/TR, 5'11", 166 lbs. Deb: 7/19/1893

YEAR	TM/L	G	AB	R	H	2B	3B	HR	RBI	BB	SO	AVG	OBP	SLG	PRO+	BR	/A	RC	SB	CS	SBR	FA	FR	POS	TPR
1893	NY-N	31	114	16	28	4	1	2	21	7	9	.246	.289	.351	71	-5	-5	13	5			.969	-7	C	-0.8
1894	NY-N	49	175	35	58	5	5	1	32	14	5	.331	.387	.434	100	0	0	34	8			.841	-9	C1	-0.4
1895	NY-N	67	238	32	56	9	0	0	30	14	16	.235	.281	.273	46	-19	-18	22	11			.938	3	C1/3	-0.9
1896	NY-N	75	253	33	60	2	0	0	23	13	14	.237	.277	.245	41	-21	-20	21	9			.936	-4	C/1	-1.4
1897	NY-N	46	154	29	46	9	3	0	22	15		.299	.365	.396	104	0	1	25	5			.929	-2	C1/O2	0.2
1898	NY-N	1	4	0	0	0	0	0	0	0		.000	.000	.000	-99	-1	-1	0	0			1.000	0	/O	-0.1
1899	NY-N	97	328	49	88	8	6	0	42	43		.268	.360	.329	93	-3	-1	47	16			.925	-8	C1S3/O	-0.5
Total	7	366	1266	194	336	37	15	3	170	106	44	.265	.327	.325	74	-50	-45	162	54			.926	-27	C/1S3O2	-3.9

■ BOB WILSON Wilson, Robert b: 2/22/25, Dallas, Tex. d: 4/23/85, Dallas, Tex. BR/TR, 5'11", 197 lbs. Deb: 5/17/58

YEAR	TM/L	G	AB	R	H	2B	3B	HR	RBI	BB	SO	AVG	OBP	SLG	PRO+	BR	/A	RC	SB	CS	SBR	FA	FR	POS	TPR
1958	LA-N	3	5	0	1	0	0	0	0	0	1	.200	.200	.200	6	-1	-1	0	0	0	0	1.000	-0	/O	-0.1

■ RED WILSON Wilson, Robert James b: 3/7/29, Milwaukee, Wis. BR/TR, 6', 200 lbs. Deb: 9/22/51

YEAR	TM/L	G	AB	R	H	2B	3B	HR	RBI	BB	SO	AVG	OBP	SLG	PRO+	BR	/A	RC	SB	CS	SBR	FA	FR	POS	TPR
1951	Chi-A	4	11	1	3	1	0	0	0	1	2	.273	.333	.364	90	-0	-0	1	0	0	0	1.000	-1	/C	-0.1
1952	Chi-A	2	3	0	0	0	0	0	0	0	1	.000	.000	.000	-99	-1	-1	0	0	0	0	1.000	1	/C	0.0
1953	Chi-A	71	164	21	41	6	1	0	10	26	12	.250	.353	.299	75	-4	-5	17	2	3	-1	.981	10	C	0.6
1954	Chi-A	8	20	2	4	0	0	1	1	1	2	.200	.238	.350	58	-1	-1	2	0	0	0	1.000	4	/C	0.3
	Det-A	54	170	22	48	11	1	2	22	27	12	.282	.381	.394	115	4	4	26	3	1	0	.996	2	C	0.9
	Yr	62	190	24	52	11	1	3	23	28	14	.274	.367	.389	108	2	3	27	3	1	0	.997	6	C	1.2
1955	Det-A	78	241	26	53	9	0	2	17	26	23	.220	.296	.282	57	-15	-14	18	1	2	-1	.984	-6	C	-1.9
1956	Det-A	78	228	32	66	12	2	7	38	42	18	.289	.400	.452	124	9	9	43	2	1	0	.991	3	C	1.5
1957	Det-A	60	180	21	43	8	1	3	13	25	19	.239	.341	.344	86	-2	-3	22	2	3	-1	1.000	1	C	-0.1
1958	Det-A	103	298	31	89	13	1	3	29	35	30	.299	.376	.379	101	5	2	45	10	0	3	.992	7	*C	1.8
1959	Det-A	67	228	28	60	17	2	4	35	10	23	.263	.300	.408	88	-3	-5	25	2	2	-1	.988	2	C	0.0
1960	Det-A	45	134	17	29	4	0	1	14	16	14	.216	.300	.269	54	-8	-9	12	3	0	1	.980	-0	C	-0.6
	Cle-A	32	88	5	19	3	0	1	10	6	7	.216	.274	.284	53	-6	-6	7	0	0	0	.989	7	C	0.3
	Yr	77	222	22	48	7	0	2	24	22	21	.216	.290	.275	53	-14	-14	19	3	0	1	.984	7	C	-0.3
Total	10	602	1765	206	455	84	8	24	189	215	163	.258	.341	.355	87	-24	-28	217	25	12	0	.990	31	C	2.7

■ MIKE WILSON Wilson, Samuel Marshall b: 12/2/1896, Edge Hill, Pa. d: 5/16/78, Boynton Beach, Fla BR/TR, 5'10.5", 160 lbs. Deb: 6/04/21

YEAR	TM/L	G	AB	R	H	2B	3B	HR	RBI	BB	SO	AVG	OBP	SLG	PRO+	BR	/A	RC	SB	CS	SBR	FA	FR	POS	TPR
1921	Pit-N	5	4	0	0	0	0	0	0	0	0	.000	.000	.000	-97	-1	-1	0	0	0	0	.833	0	/C	-0.1

■ NEIL WILSON Wilson, Samuel O'Neil b: 6/14/35, Lexington, Tenn. BL/TR, 6'1", 175 lbs. Deb: 4/17/60

YEAR	TM/L	G	AB	R	H	2B	3B	HR	RBI	BB	SO	AVG	OBP	SLG	PRO+	BR	/A	RC	SB	CS	SBR	FA	FR	POS	TPR
1960	SF-N	6	10	0	0	0	0	0	0	1	2	.000	.091	.000	-77	-2	-2	0	0	0	0	.958	0	/C	-0.2

■ TOM WILSON Wilson, Thomas G. "Slats" b: 6/3/1890, Fleming, Kan. d: 3/7/53, San Pedro, Cal. BB/TR, 6'1.5", 160 lbs. Deb: 9/08/14

YEAR	TM/L	G	AB	R	H	2B	3B	HR	RBI	BB	SO	AVG	OBP	SLG	PRO+	BR	/A	RC	SB	CS	SBR	FA	FR	POS	TPR
1914	Was-A	1	1	0	0	0	0	0	0	0	0	.000	.000	.000	-96	-0	-0	0	0			.000	0	/C	0.0

■ BILL WILSON Wilson, William Donald b: 11/6/28, Central City, Neb. BR/TR, 6'2", 200 lbs. Deb: 9/24/50

YEAR	TM/L	G	AB	R	H	2B	3B	HR	RBI	BB	SO	AVG	OBP	SLG	PRO+	BR	/A	RC	SB	CS	SBR	FA	FR	POS	TPR
1950	Chi-A	3	6	0	0	0	0	0	0	2	2	.000	.250	.000	-33	-1	-1	0	0	0	0	1.000	-1	/O	-0.2
1953	Chi-A	9	17	1	1	0	0	0	1	0	7	.059	.111	.059	-51	-4	-4	0	0	0	0	1.000	0	/O	-0.4
1954	Chi-A	20	35	4	6	1	0	2	5	7	5	.171	.310	.371	83	-1	-1	3	0	1	-1	.943	-2	O	-0.4
	Phi-A	94	323	43	77	10	1	15	33	39	59	.238	.335	.415	104	2	1	47	1	2	-1	.989	8	O	0.5
	Yr	114	358	47	83	11	1	17	38	46	64	.232	.333	.411	102	1	0	50	1	3	-2	.984	6	*O	0.1
1955	KC-A	98	273	39	61	12	0	15	38	24	63	.223	.289	.432	91	-5	-5	32	1	1	-0	.969	-3	O/P	-1.2

YEAR	TM/L	G	AB	R	H	2B	3B	HR	RBI	BB	SO	AVG	OBP	SLG	PRO+	BR	/A	RC	SB	CS	SBR	FA	FR	POS	TPR
Total	4	224	654	87	145	23	1	32	77	72	136	.222	.308	.407	92	-9	-10	83	2	4	-2	.979	3	O/P	-1.7

■ BILL WILSON
Wilson, William G. b: 10/28/1867, Hannibal, Mo. d: 5/9/24, St.Paul, Minn. TR , Deb: 4/30/1890

YEAR	TM/L	G	AB	R	H	2B	3B	HR	RBI	BB	SO	AVG	OBP	SLG	PRO+	BR	/A	RC	SB	CS	SBR	FA	FR	POS	TPR
1890	Pit-N	83	304	30	65	11	3	0	21	22	50	.214	.271	.270	67	-16	-10	24	5			.874	2	CO1/S	-0.5
1897	Lou-N	105	381	43	81	12	4	1	41	18		.213	.257	.273	41	-34	-32	31	9			.940	-1	*C/3	-1.8
1898	Lou-N	29	102	5	17	1	2	1	13	5		.167	.213	.245	32	-9	-9	6	3			.895	-4	C/1	-1.0
Total	3	217	787	78	163	24	9	2	75	45	50	.207	.257	.268	49	-59	-51	62	17			.912	-3	C/O13S	-3.3

■ MOOKIE WILSON
Wilson, William Hayward b: 2/9/56, Bamberg, S.C. BB/TR, 5'10", 170 lbs. Deb: 9/02/80

YEAR	TM/L	G	AB	R	H	2B	3B	HR	RBI	BB	SO	AVG	OBP	SLG	PRO+	BR	/A	RC	SB	CS	SBR	FA	FR	POS	TPR
1980	NY-N	27	105	16	26	5	3	0	4	12	19	.248	.325	.352	91	-1	-1	12	7	7	-2	.973	2	O	-0.2
1981	NY-N	92	328	49	89	8	8	3	14	20	59	.271	.317	.372	96	-3	-2	38	24	12	0	.983	3	O	-0.3
1982	NY-N	159	639	90	178	25	9	5	55	32	102	.279	.315	.369	91	-9	-8	78	58	16	8	.988	9	*O	0.5
1983	NY-N	152	638	91	176	25	6	7	51	18	103	.276	.300	.367	85	-15	-15	71	54	16	7	.984	5	*O	-0.8
1984	NY-N	154	587	88	162	28	10	10	54	26	90	.276	.309	.409	102	-2	-1	78	46	9	8	.990	17	*O	2.1
1985	NY-N	93	337	56	93	16	8	6	26	28	52	.276	.332	.424	113	4	5	46	24	9	2	.964	2	O	0.6
1986	*NY-N	123	381	61	110	17	5	9	45	32	72	.289	.345	.430	116	6	7	58	25	7	3	.979	-6	*O	0.2
1987	NY-N	124	385	58	115	19	7	9	34	35	85	.299	.360	.455	120	8	10	66	21	6	3	.963	-8	*O	0.2
1988	*NY-N	112	378	61	112	17	5	8	41	27	63	.296	.346	.431	128	10	12	55	15	4	2	.976	-7	*O	0.5
1989	NY-N	80	249	22	51	10	1	3	18	10	47	.205	.238	.289	53	-17	-15	17	7	4	-0	.975	-3	O	-2.1
	*Tor-A	54	238	32	71	9	1	2	17	3	37	.298	.313	.370	93	-3	-3	28	12	1	3	.991	-3	O	-0.5
1990	Tor-A	147	588	81	156	36	4	3	51	31	102	.265	.302	.355	82	-14	-15	64	23	4	5	.992	8	*O/D	-0.6
1991	*Tor-A	86	241	26	58	12	4	2	28	8	35	.241	.280	.349	70	-9	-11	24	11	3	2	.973	-1	OD	-1.1
Total	12	1403	5094	731	1397	227	71	67	438	282	866	.274	.315	.386	96	-45	-36	634	327	98	39	.982	19	*O/D	-1.5

■ WILLIE WILSON
Wilson, Willie James b: 7/9/55, Montgomery, Ala. BB/TR, 6'3", 195 lbs. Deb: 9/04/76

YEAR	TM/L	G	AB	R	H	2B	3B	HR	RBI	BB	SO	AVG	OBP	SLG	PRO+	BR	/A	RC	SB	CS	SBR	FA	FR	POS	TPR
1976	KC-A	12	6	0	1	0	0	0	0	0	2	.167	.167	.167	-2	-1	-1	0	2	1	0	.875	-2	/O	-0.2
1977	KC-A	13	34	10	11	2	0	0	1	1	8	.324	.343	.382	97	-0	-0	4	6	3	0	.960	0	/OD	0.0
1978	*KC-A	127	198	43	43	8	2	0	16	16	33	.217	.282	.278	57	-11	-11	18	46	12	7	.978	-14	*O/D	-2.2
1979	KC-A	154	588	113	185	18	13	6	49	28	92	.315	.353	.420	106	6	4	99	**83**	12	**18**	.985	15	*O	2.9
1980	*KC-A	161	705	**133**	**230**	28	**15**	3	49	28	81	.326	.357	.421	112	11	11	117	79	10	**18**	.988	22	*O	4.3
1981	*KC-A	102	439	54	133	10	7	1	32	18	42	.303	.336	.364	103	1	1	56	34	8	5	.987	22	*O	2.6
1982	KC-A★	136	585	87	194	19	**15**	3	46	26	81	**.332**	.366	.431	118	14	14	96	37	11	5	.987	15	*O	2.9
1983	KC-A★	137	576	90	159	22	8	2	33	33	75	.276	.316	.352	84	-13	-13	72	59	8	13	.975	1	*O	-0.3
1984	*KC-A	128	541	81	163	24	9	2	44	39	56	.301	.352	.390	104	4	3	82	47	5	**11**	.990	10	*O	2.1
1985	*KC-A	141	605	87	168	25	**21**	4	43	29	94	.278	.316	.408	96	-4	-4	80	43	11	6	.995	3	*O	0.0
1986	KC-A	156	631	77	170	20	7	9	44	31	97	.269	.313	.366	82	-14	-16	76	34	8	5	.993	5	*O	-1.0
1987	KC-A	146	610	97	170	18	**15**	4	30	32	88	.279	.321	.377	82	-14	-16	78	59	11	**11**	**.997**	3	*O/D	-0.7
1988	KC-A	147	591	81	155	17	**11**	1	37	22	106	.262	.291	.333	74	-21	-21	61	35	7	6	.989	-0	*O	-2.0
1989	KC-A	112	383	58	97	17	7	3	43	27	78	.253	.304	.358	86	-8	-7	43	24	6	4	.977	-3	*O/D	-1.0
1990	KC-A	115	307	49	89	13	3	2	42	30	57	.290	.357	.371	106	2	3	44	24	6	4	1.000	-6	*O/D	-0.1
1991	Oak-A	113	294	38	70	14	4	0	28	18	43	.238	.291	.313	71	-13	-11	26	20	5	3	.983	-4	O/D	-1.3
1992	*Oak-A	132	396	38	107	15	5	0	37	35	65	.270	.331	.333	90	-7	-5	45	28	8	4	.981	7	*O/D	0.3
Total	17	2032	7489	1136	2145	270	142	40	574	413	1098	.286	.329	.376	94	-66	-69	997	660	132	119	.987	74	*O/D	6.3

■ ED WINCENIAK
Winceniak, Edward Joseph b: 4/16/29, Chicago, Ill. BR/TR, 5'9", 165 lbs. Deb: 4/25/56

YEAR	TM/L	G	AB	R	H	2B	3B	HR	RBI	BB	SO	AVG	OBP	SLG	PRO+	BR	/A	RC	SB	CS	SBR	FA	FR	POS	TPR
1956	Chi-N	15	17	1	2	0	0	0	0	1	3	.118	.167	.118	-22	-3	-3	0	0	0	0	.889	-0	/32	-0.3
1957	Chi-N	17	50	5	12	3	0	1	8	2	9	.240	.269	.360	68	-2	-2	4	0	0	0	1.000	-3	/S32	-0.5
Total	2	32	67	6	14	3	0	1	8	3	12	.209	.243	.299	45	-5	-5	5	0	0	0	.955	-3	/3S2	-0.8

■ GORDIE WINDHORN
Windhorn, Gordon Ray b: 12/19/33, Watseka, Ill. BR/TR, 6'1", 185 lbs. Deb: 9/10/59

YEAR	TM/L	G	AB	R	H	2B	3B	HR	RBI	BB	SO	AVG	OBP	SLG	PRO+	BR	/A	RC	SB	CS	SBR	FA	FR	POS	TPR
1959	NY-A	7	11	0	0	0	0	0	0	0	3	.000	.000	.000	-99	-3	-3	0	0	0	0	1.000	-1	/O	-0.4
1961	LA-N	34	33	10	8	2	1	2	6	4	3	.242	.324	.545	115	1	1	5	0	1	-1	.944	2	O	0.2
1962	KC-A	14	19	1	3	1	0	0	1	0	3	.158	.158	.211	-2	-3	-3	1	0	0	0	1.000	-2	/O	-0.5
	LA-A	40	45	9	8	6	0	0	1	7	10	.178	.288	.311	63	-2	-2	4	1	1	-0	1.000	-7	O	-1.0
	Yr	54	64	10	11	7	0	0	2	7	13	.172	.254	.281	44	-5	-5	5	1	1	-0	1.000	-9	O	-1.5
Total	3	95	108	20	19	9	1	2	8	11	19	.176	.252	.333	55	-7	-7	10	1	2	-1	.981	-8	/O	-1.7

■ BILL WINDLE
Windle, Willis Brewer b: 12/13/04, Galena, Kan. d: 12/8/81, Corpus Christi, Tex BL/TL, 5'11.5", 170 lbs. Deb: 9/27/28

YEAR	TM/L	G	AB	R	H	2B	3B	HR	RBI	BB	SO	AVG	OBP	SLG	PRO+	BR	/A	RC	SB	CS	SBR	FA	FR	POS	TPR
1928	Pit-N	1	1	1	1	1	0	0	0	0	0	1.000	1.000	2.000	641	1	1	2	0			1.000	0	/1	0.1
1929	Pit-N	2	1	0	0	0	0	0	0	0	1	.000	.000	.000	-98	-0	-0	0	0			1.000	-0	/1	0.0
Total	2	3	2	1	1	1	0	0	0	0	1	.500	.500	1.000	264	0	0	2	0			1.000	-0	/1	0.1

■ ROBBIE WINE
Wine, Robert Paul Jr. b: 7/13/62, Norristown, Pa. BR/TR, 6'2", 190 lbs. Deb: 9/02/86 F

YEAR	TM/L	G	AB	R	H	2B	3B	HR	RBI	BB	SO	AVG	OBP	SLG	PRO+	BR	/A	RC	SB	CS	SBR	FA	FR	POS	TPR
1986	Hou-N	9	12	2	3	1	0	0	0	1	4	.250	.308	.333	79	-0	-0	1	0	0	0	1.000	3	/C	0.3
1987	Hou-N	14	29	1	3	1	0	0	0	1	10	.103	.133	.138	-29	-5	-5	1	0	0	0	.979	-1	C	-0.6
Total	2	23	41	3	6	2	0	0	0	2	14	.146	.186	.195	2	-6	-6	2	0	0	0	.988	2	/C	-0.3

■ BOBBY WINE
Wine, Robert Paul Sr. b: 9/17/38, New York, N.Y. BR/TR, 6'1", 187 lbs. Deb: 9/20/60 FMC

YEAR	TM/L	G	AB	R	H	2B	3B	HR	RBI	BB	SO	AVG	OBP	SLG	PRO+	BR	/A	RC	SB	CS	SBR	FA	FR	POS	TPR
1960	Phi-N	4	14	1	2	0	0	0	0	0	2	.143	.143	.143	-22	-2	-2	0	0	0	0	1.000	0	/S	-0.2
1962	Phi-N	112	311	30	76	15	0	4	25	11	49	.244	.270	.331	62	-18	-17	23	2	0	1	.979	7	S3	-0.3
1963	Phi-N	142	418	29	90	14	3	6	44	14	83	.215	.242	.306	58	-24	-23	28	1	3	-2	.971	15	*S/3	-0.2
1964	Phi-N	126	283	28	60	8	3	4	34	25	37	.212	.276	.304	64	-14	-13	23	1	0	0	.965	7	*S3	0.0
1965	Phi-N	139	394	31	90	8	1	5	33	31	69	.228	.285	.292	64	-19	-18	30	0	0	0	.967	22	*S/1	1.2
1966	Phi-N	46	89	8	21	5	0	0	5	6	13	.236	.292	.292	63	-4	-4	7	0	1	-1	.974	13	S/O	1.0
1967	Phi-N	135	363	27	69	12	5	2	28	29	77	.190	.250	.267	48	-24	-25	23	3	2	-0	**.980**	29	*S/1	1.5
1968	Phi-N	27	71	5	12	3	0	2	7	6	17	.169	.234	.296	58	-4	-4	4	0	0	0	.972	3	S/3	0.2
1969	Mon-N	121	370	23	74	8	1	3	25	28	49	.200	.256	.251	43	-28	-28	23	0	0	0	.949	17	*S/13	0.1
1970	Mon-N	159	501	40	116	21	3	3	51	39	94	.232	.288	.303	59	-29	-29	44	0	1	-1	.976	20	*S	0.7
1971	Mon-N	119	340	25	68	9	0	1	16	25	46	.200	.255	.235	39	-27	-27	20	0	0	0	.982	2	*S	-1.2
1972	Mon-N	34	18	2	4	1	0	0	0	0	2	.222	.222	.278	41	-1	-1	1	0	0	0	1.000	5	3/S2	0.4
Total	12	1164	3172	249	682	104	16	30	268	214	538	.215	.265	.286	54	-195	-193	227	7	7	-2	.971	138	*S/3102	3.2

■ RALPH WINEGARNER
Winegarner, Ralph Lee b: 10/29/09, Benton, Kan. d: 88, Benton, Kan. BR/TR, 6', 182 lbs. Deb: 9/20/30 C

YEAR	TM/L	G	AB	R	H	2B	3B	HR	RBI	BB	SO	AVG	OBP	SLG	PRO+	BR	/A	RC	SB	CS	SBR	FA	FR	POS	TPR
1930	Cle-A	5	22	5	10	1	0	0	2	1	7	.455	.478	.500	143	2	2	5	0	0	0	.857	1	/3	0.2
1932	Cle-A	7	7	1	1	0	0	0	0	0	5	.143	.143	.143	-24	-1	-1	0	0	0	0	.750	-0	/P	0.0
1934	Cle-A	32	51	9	10	2	0	1	5	3	11	.196	.241	.294	37	-5	-5	4	0	0	0	1.000	1	P/O	0.0
1935	Cle-A	65	84	11	26	4	1	3	17	9	12	.310	.376	.488	120	3	2	15	1	1	-0	.944	2	P/O31	0.2
1936	Cle-A	18	16	0	2	0	0	0	2	1	6	.125	.176	.125	-24	-3	-3	0	0	0	0	1.000	-0	/P	0.0
1949	StL-A	9	5	2	2	0	0	1	2	1	2	.400	.500	1.000	280	1	1	3	0	0	0	1.000	-0	/P	0.0
Total	6	136	185	28	51	7	1	5	28	15	43	.276	.330	.405	86	-4	-4	27	1	1	-0	.952	2	/P3O1	0.4

■ DAVE WINFIELD
Winfield, David Mark b: 10/3/51, St.Paul, Minn. BR/TR, 6'6", 220 lbs. Deb: 6/19/73

YEAR	TM/L	G	AB	R	H	2B	3B	HR	RBI	BB	SO	AVG	OBP	SLG	PRO+	BR	/A	RC	SB	CS	SBR	FA	FR	POS	TPR
1973	SD-N	56	141	9	39	4	1	3	12	12	19	.277	.333	.383	107	-0	1	17	0	0	0	.956	-2	O/1	-0.3
1974	SD-N	145	498	57	132	18	4	20	75	40	96	.265	.321	.438	116	5	7	66	9	7	-2	.960	9	*O	1.0
1975	SD-N	143	509	74	136	20	2	15	76	69	82	.267	.358	.403	118	8	12	77	23	4	5	.972	6	*O	1.8

YEAR	TM/L	G	AB	R	H	2B	3B	HR	RBI	BB	SO	AVG	OBP	SLG	PRO+	BR	/A	RC	SB	CS	SBR	FA	FR	POS	TPR
1976	SD-N	137	492	81	139	26	4	13	69	65	78	.283	.370	.431	138	18	23	80	26	7	4	.982	12	*O	3.5
1977	SD-N★	157	615	104	169	29	7	25	92	58	75	.275	.337	.467	126	10	18	95	16	7	1	.972	16	*O	2.8
1978	SD-N★	158	587	88	181	30	5	24	97	55	81	.308	.370	.499	153	31	36	105	21	9	1	.979	-12	*O/1	1.9
1979	SD-N★	159	597	97	184	27	10	34	**118**	85	71	.308	.396	.558	**167**	**47**	**52**	132	15	9	-1	.986	11	*O	5.6
1980	SD-N★	162	558	89	154	25	6	20	87	79	83	.276	.368	.450	135	21	25	94	23	7	3	.987	-2	*O	2.1
1981	*NY-A★	105	388	52	114	25	1	13	68	43	41	.294	.366	.464	140	19	19	66	11	1	3	.985	-6	*O/D	1.3
1982	NY-A★	140	539	84	151	24	8	37	106	45	64	.280	.336	.560	143	28	29	93	5	3	-0	.974	12	*O/D	3.6
1983	NY-A★	152	598	99	169	26	8	32	116	58	77	.283	.348	.513	139	26	29	97	15	6	1	.978	-11	*O	1.4
1984	NY-A★	141	567	106	193	34	4	19	100	53	71	.340	.397	.515	156	38	41	113	6	4	-1	.994	2	*O	3.8
1985	NY-A★	155	633	105	174	34	6	26	114	52	96	.275	.330	.471	119	13	15	94	19	7	2	.991	12	*O/D	2.2
1986	NY-A★	154	565	90	148	31	5	24	104	77	106	.262	.352	.462	121	16	17	89	6	5	-1	.984	5	*O/3D	1.5
1987	NY-A★	156	575	83	158	22	1	27	97	76	96	.275	.359	.457	116	13	14	91	5	6	-2	.989	-4	*O/D	0.2
1988	NY-A★	149	559	96	180	37	2	25	107	69	88	.322	.398	.530	159	43	44	115	9	4	0	.989	-3	*O/D	3.7
1990	NY-A	20	61	7	13	3	0	2	6	4	13	.213	.273	.361	75	-2	-2	6	0	0	0	1.000	-3	O/D	-0.5
	Cal-A	112	414	63	114	18	2	19	72	48	68	.275	.352	.466	130	15	16	65	0	1	-1	.989	-6	*O/D	0.7
	Yr	132	475	70	127	21	2	21	78	52	81	.267	.342	.453	122	12	13	71	0	1	-1	.989	-8	*OD	0.2
1991	Cal-A	150	568	75	149	27	4	28	86	56	109	.262	.330	.472	119	13	13	84	7	2	1	.990	-1	*OD	1.1
1992	*Tor-A	156	583	92	169	33	3	26	108	82	89	.290	.378	.491	136	33	30	110	2	3	-1	1.000	1	*DO	2.9
Total	19	2707	10047	1551	2866	493	83	432	1710	1126	1503	.285	.359	.480	134	393	438	1689	218	92	10	.982	35	*OD/13	40.3

■ AL WINGO

Wingo, Absalom Holbrook "Red" b: 5/6/1898, Norcross, Ga. d: 10/9/64, Detroit, Mich. BL/TR, 5'11", 180 lbs. Deb: 9/09/19 F

YEAR	TM/L	G	AB	R	H	2B	3B	HR	RBI	BB	SO	AVG	OBP	SLG	PRO+	BR	/A	RC	SB	CS	SBR	FA	FR	POS	TPR
1919	Phi-A	15	59	9	18	1	3	0	2	4	12	.305	.349	.424	115	1	1	8	0			.815	-3	O	-0.3
1924	Det-A	78	150	21	43	12	2	1	26	21	13	.287	.374	.413	105	1	1	23	2	5	-2	.925	-8	O	-1.1
1925	Det-A	130	440	104	163	34	10	5	68	69	31	.370	.456	.527	151	35	36	106	14	13	-4	.971	8	*O	3.0
1926	Det-A	108	298	45	84	19	0	1	45	52	32	.282	.389	.356	94	-0	-1	45	4	2	0	.923	4	O/3	-0.2
1927	Det-A	75	137	15	32	8	2	0	20	25	14	.234	.352	.321	74	-4	-5	17	1	0	0	.891	-3	O	-0.9
1928	Det-A	87	242	30	69	13	2	2	30	40	17	.285	.389	.380	101	3	2	38	2	2	-1	.968	-3	O	-0.6
Total	6	493	1326	224	409	87	19	9	191	211	119	.308	.404	.423	114	35	35	237	23	22		.944	-6	O/3	-0.1

■ ED WINGO

Wingo, Edmond Armand (b: Edmond Armand La Riviere)
b: 10/8/1895, St.Anne De Bellevue, Que., Canada d: 12/5/64, Lachine, Que., Can. BR/TR, 5'6", 145 lbs. Deb: 10/02/20

YEAR	TM/L	G	AB	R	H	2B	3B	HR	RBI	BB	SO	AVG	OBP	SLG	PRO+	BR	/A	RC	SB	CS	SBR	FA	FR	POS	TPR
1920	Phi-A	1	4	0	1	0	0	0	1	0	0	.250	.250	.250	32	-0	-0	0	0	0	0	1.000	1	/C	0.0

■ IVEY WINGO

Wingo, Ivey Brown b: 7/8/1890, Gainesville, Ga. d: 3/1/41, Waycross, Ga.. BL/TR, 5'10", 160 lbs. Deb: 4/20/11 FMC

YEAR	TM/L	G	AB	R	H	2B	3B	HR	RBI	BB	SO	AVG	OBP	SLG	PRO+	BR	/A	RC	SB	CS	SBR	FA	FR	POS	TPR
1911	StL-N	25	57	4	12	2	0	0	3	3	7	.211	.250	.246	40	-5	-5	3	0			.916	0	C	-0.3
1912	StL-N	100	310	38	82	18	8	2	44	23	45	.265	.317	.394	96	-4	-3	40	8			.957	4	C	0.9
1913	StL-N	112	307	25	78	5	8	2	35	17	41	.254	.295	.342	83	-8	-7	34	18			.945	0	C/1O	0.0
1914	StL-N	80	237	24	71	8	5	4	26	18	17	.300	.352	.426	132	8	9	38	15			.958	-3	C/O	1.2
1915	Cin-N	119	339	26	75	11	6	3	29	13	33	.221	.250	.316	69	-13	-14	27	10	11	-4	.966	3	C/O	-0.8
1916	Cin-N	119	347	30	85	8	11	2	40	25	27	.245	.298	.349	100	-1	-0	40	4			.958	7	*CM	1.6
1917	Cin-N	121	399	37	106	16	11	2	39	25	13	.266	.311	.376	115	4	6	47	9			.967	-5	*C	1.2
1918	Cin-N	100	323	35	82	15	6	0	31	19	18	.254	.297	.337	95	-3	-3	33	6			.973	-6	C/O	-0.1
1919	*Cin-N	76	245	30	67	12	6	0	27	23	19	.273	.336	.371	115	4	5	30	4			.969	3	C	1.5
1920	Cin-N	108	364	32	96	11	5	2	38	19	13	.264	.300	.338	84	-8	-8	37	6	4	-1	.958	-10	*C/2	-1.2
1921	Cin-N	97	295	20	79	7	6	3	38	21	14	.268	.319	.363	84	-9	-7	35	3	2	-0	.959	5	C/O	0.3
1922	Cin-N	80	260	24	74	13	3	3	45	23	11	.285	.343	.392	91	-4	-4	34	1	4	-2	.964	4	C	0.2
1923	Cin-N	61	171	10	45	9	2	1	24	9	11	.263	.304	.357	75	-7	-6	18	1	1	-0	.969	3	C	-0.1
1924	Cin-N	66	192	21	55	5	4	1	23	14	8	.286	.338	.370	91	-3	-2	24	1	1	-0	.989	5	C/1	0.5
1925	Cin-N	55	146	6	30	7	0	0	12	11	8	.205	.261	.253	33	-15	-14	10	1	2	-1	.965	3	C	-0.9
1926	Cin-N	7	10	0	2	0	0	0	1	1	0	.200	.333	.200	48	-1	-1	1	0			1.000	-0	/C	-0.1
1929	Cin-N	1	1	0	0	0	0	0	0	0	0	.000	.000	.000	-99	-0	-0	0	0			.000	0	/C	0.0
Total	17	1327	4003	362	1039	147	81	25	455	264	285	.260	.307	.355	91	-65	-55	452	87	25		.962	14	*C/O12	3.9

■ GEORGE WINKELMAN

Winkelman, George Edward b: 2/18/1865, Washington, D.C. d: 5/19/60, Washington, D.C. BL/TL, Deb: 8/04/1883

YEAR	TM/L	G	AB	R	H	2B	3B	HR	RBI	BB	SO	AVG	OBP	SLG	PRO+	BR	/A	RC	SB	CS	SBR	FA	FR	POS	TPR
1883	Lou-a	4	13	2	0	0	0	0		1		.000	.071	.000	-81	-2	-2	0				.625	0	/O	-0.2
1886	Was-N	1	5	0	1	0	0	0	0	0	1	.200	.200	.200	23	-0	-0	0	0			.000	-1	/OP	0.0
Total	2	5	18	2	1	0	0	0	0	1	1	.056	.105	.056	-51	-3	-3	0	0			.625	-0	/OP	-0.2

■ HERM WINNINGHAM

Winningham, Herman Son b: 12/1/61, Orangeburg, S.C. BL/TR, 5'11", 185 lbs. Deb: 9/01/84

YEAR	TM/L	G	AB	R	H	2B	3B	HR	RBI	BB	SO	AVG	OBP	SLG	PRO+	BR	/A	RC	SB	CS	SBR	FA	FR	POS	TPR
1984	NY-N	14	27	5	11	1	1	0	5	1	7	.407	.429	.519	167	2	2	6	2	1	0	1.000	-4	O	-0.2
1985	Mon-N	125	312	30	74	6	5	3	21	28	72	.237	.300	.317	77	-11	-9	32	20	9	1	.983	-4	*O	-1.6
1986	Mon-N	90	185	23	40	6	3	4	11	18	51	.216	.286	.346	74	-7	-7	17	12	7	-1	.980	-7	O/S	-1.7
1987	Mon-N	137	347	34	83	20	3	4	41	34	68	.239	.307	.349	71	-13	-15	37	29	10	3	.975	-8	*O	-2.3
1988	Mon-N	47	90	10	21	2	1	0	6	12	18	.233	.324	.278	71	-3	-3	8	4	5	-2	.982	-3	O	-0.9
	Cin-N	53	113	6	26	1	3	0	15	5	27	.230	.263	.292	57	-6	-7	9	8	3	1	1.000	-3	O	-1.1
	Yr	100	203	16	47	3	4	0	21	17	45	.232	.291	.286	63	-9	-10	17	12	8	-1	.992	-7	O	-2.0
1989	Cin-N	115	251	40	63	11	3	3	13	24	50	.251	.316	.355	88	-3	-4	29	14	5	1	.980	-7	O	-1.1
1990	*Cin-N	84	160	20	41	8	5	3	17	14	31	.256	.316	.425	98	0	-1	22	6	4	-1	1.000	-9	O	-1.2
1991	Cin-N	98	169	17	38	6	1	1	4	11	40	.225	.272	.290	56	-9	-10	13	4	4	-1	.953	-8	O	-2.1
1992	Bos-A	105	234	27	55	8	1	1	14	10	53	.235	.266	.291	53	-14	-15	17	6	5	-1	.975	-4	O/D	-2.3
Total	9	868	1888	212	452	69	26	19	147	157	417	.239	.298	.334	74	-64	-68	189	105	53	-0	.980	-58	O/DS	-14.5

■ TOM WINSETT

Winsett, John Thomas "Long Tom" b: 11/24/09, McKenzie, Tenn. BL/TR, 6'2", 190 lbs. Deb: 4/20/30

YEAR	TM/L	G	AB	R	H	2B	3B	HR	RBI	BB	SO	AVG	OBP	SLG	PRO+	BR	/A	RC	SB	CS	SBR	FA	FR	POS	TPR
1930	Bos-A	1	1	0	0	0	0	0	0	0	1	.000	.000	.000	-99	-0	-0	0	0	0	0	.000	0	H	0.0
1931	Bos-A	64	76	6	15	1	0	1	7	4	21	.197	.247	.250	33	-8	-7	5	0	0	0	1.000	-0	/O	-0.7
1933	Bos-A	6	12	1	1	0	0	0	0	1	6	.083	.154	.083	-36	-2	-2	0	0	0	0	1.000	-2	/O	-0.4
1935	StL-N	7	12	2	6	1	0	0	2	2	3	.500	.571	.583	203	2	2	4	0			.000	-1	/O	0.1
1936	Bro-N	22	85	13	20	7	0	1	18	11	14	.235	.330	.353	83	-2	-2	10	0			1.000	1	O	-0.1
1937	Bro-N	118	350	32	83	15	5	5	42	45	64	.237	.329	.351	84	-7	-7	44	3			.960	1	*O/P	-0.9
1938	Bro-N	12	30	6	9	1	0	1	7	6	4	.300	.417	.433	131	2	2	6	0			.882	-2	/O	0.0
Total	7	230	566	60	134	25	5	8	76	69	113	.237	.325	.341	79	-15	-15	69	3	0		.963	-2	O/P	-2.0

■ MATT WINTERS

Winters, Matthew Littleton b: 3/18/60, Buffalo, N.Y. BL/TR, 6'3", 215 lbs. Deb: 5/30/89

YEAR	TM/L	G	AB	R	H	2B	3B	HR	RBI	BB	SO	AVG	OBP	SLG	PRO+	BR	/A	RC	SB	CS	SBR	FA	FR	POS	TPR
1989	KC-A	42	107	14	25	6	0	2	9	14	23	.234	.322	.346	89	-1	-1	12	0	0	0	.939	-4	O/D	-0.6

■ KETTLE WIRTS

Wirts, Elwood Vernon b: 10/31/1897, Consumnes, Cal. d: 7/12/68, Sacramento, Cal. BR/TR, 5'11", 170 lbs. Deb: 7/20/21

YEAR	TM/L	G	AB	R	H	2B	3B	HR	RBI	BB	SO	AVG	OBP	SLG	PRO+	BR	/A	RC	SB	CS	SBR	FA	FR	POS	TPR
1921	Chi-N	7	11	0	2	0	0	0	1	0	3	.182	.182	.182	-3	-2	-2	0	0	0	0	1.000	1	/C	-0.1
1922	Chi-N	31	58	7	10	2	0	1	6	12	15	.172	.314	.259	48	-4	-4	5	0	0	0	.968	-5	C	-0.8
1923	Chi-N	5	5	2	1	0	0	0	1	2	0	.200	.429	.200	71	-0	-0	1	0	0	0	1.000	1	/C	0.1
1924	Chi-A	6	12	0	1	0	0	0	0	2	2	.083	.214	.083	-22	-2	-2	0	0	0	0	1.000	1	/C	-0.1
Total	4	49	86	9	14	2	0	1	8	16	20	.163	.294	.221	35	-8	-8	7	0	0	0	.981	-3	/C	-0.9

■ HUGHIE WISE

Wise, Hugh Edward b: 3/9/06, Campbellsville, Ky. d: 7/21/87, Plantation, Fla. BB/TR, 6', 178 lbs. Deb: 9/26/30

YEAR	TM/L	G	AB	R	H	2B	3B	HR	RBI	BB	SO	AVG	OBP	SLG	PRO+	BR	/A	RC	SB	CS	SBR	FA	FR	POS	TPR
1930	Det-A	2	6	0	2	0	0	0	0	0	0	.333	.333	.333	68	-0	-0	1	0	0	0	1.000	1	/C	0.1

YEAR	TM/L	G	AB	R	H	2B	3B	HR	RBI	BB	SO	AVG	OBP	SLG	PRO+	BR	/A	RC	SB	CS	SBR	FA	FR	POS	TPR

■ CASEY WISE   Wise, Kendall Cole   b: 9/8/32, Lafayette, Ind.   BB/TR, 6′, 170 lbs.   Deb: 4/16/57

1957	Chi-N	43	106	12	19	3	1	0	7	11	14	.179	.256	.226	32	-10	-10	6	0	0	0	.940	3	2/S	-0.5
1958	*Mil-N	31	71	8	14	1	0	0	0	4	8	.197	.240	.211	23	-8	-7	3	1	1	-0	1.000	0	2/S3	-0.6
1959	Mil-N	22	76	11	13	2	0	1	5	10	5	.171	.267	.237	39	-7	-6	5	0	0	0	.989	-7	2/S	-1.2
1960	Det-A	30	68	6	10	0	2	2	5	4	9	.147	.194	.294	29	-7	-7	3	1	0	0	.983	3	2S/3	-0.3
Total	4	126	321	37	56	6	3	3	17	29	36	.174	.243	.240	31	-32	-30	17	2	1	0	.968	-2	/2S3	-2.6

■ NICK WISE   Wise, Nicholas Joseph   b: 6/15/1866, Boston, Mass.   d: 1/15/23, Boston, Mass.   BR/TR, 5′11″, 194 lbs.   Deb: 6/20/1888

| 1888 | Bos-N | 1 | 3 | 0 | 0 | 0 | 0 | 0 | 0 | 0 | 0 | .000 | .000 | .000 | -98 | -1 | -1 | 0 | | | | .000 | -0 | /OC | -0.1 |

■ SAM WISE   Wise, Samuel Washington "Modoc"   b: 8/18/1857, Akron, Ohio   d: 1/22/10, Akron, Ohio   BL/TR, 5′10.5″, 170 lbs.   Deb: 7/30/1881

1881	Det-N	1	4	0	2	0	0	0	0	0	2	.500	.500	.500	207	0	0	1				.571	-0	/3	0.0
1882	Bos-N	78	298	44	66	11	4	4	34	5	45	.221	.234	.326	77	-8	-8	23				.852	-13	*S/3	-1.5
1883	Bos-N	96	406	73	110	25	7	4	58	13	74	.271	.294	.397	105	3	2	48				.823	-2	*S	0.2
1884	Bos-N	114	426	60	91	15	9	4	41	25	104	.214	.257	.319	81	-10	-9	36				.884	6	*S/2	-0.2
1885	Bos-N	107	424	71	120	20	10	4	46	25	61	.283	.320	.406	139	15	18	57				.858	13	*S2/O	3.0
1886	Bos-N	96	387	71	112	19	12	6	72	33	61	.289	.345	.432	140	16	18	70	31			.956	-24	12S/O	-1.0
1887	Bos-N	113	467	103	156	27	17	9	92	36	44	.334	.390	.522	153	33	33	115	43			.869	-6	SO2	2.3
1888	Bos-N	105	417	66	100	19	12	4	40	34	61	.240	.306	.372	115	9	8	59	33			.888	10	S/3102	1.9
1889	Was-N	121	472	79	118	15	8	4	62	61	62	.250	.331	.341	98	-3	1	65	24			.916	-23	2S3O	-1.4
1890	Buf-P	119	505	95	148	29	11	6	102	46	45	.293	.359	.430	122	8	16	87	19			.906	5	*2	2.2
1891	Bal-a	103	388	70	96	14	5	1	48	62	52	.247	.364	.317	97	2	1	58	33			.888	-13	*2S	-0.6
1893	Was-N	122	521	102	162	27	17	5	77	49	27	.311	.375	.457	126	15	18	99	20			.924	14	*23	2.8
Total	12	1175	4715	834	1281	221	112	49	672	389	643	.272	.332	.397	116	81	98	718	203			.859	-33	S2/130	7.7

■ PHIL WISNER   Wisner, Philip N.   b: 7/1869, Washington, D.C.   d: 7/5/36, Washington, D.C.   TR ,   Deb: 8/30/1895

| 1895 | Was-N | 1 | 0 | 0 | 0 | 0 | 0 | 0 | 0 | 0 | 0 | — | — | — | — | 0 | 0 | 0 | | | | .250 | -1 | /S | 0.0 |

■ DAVE WISSMAN   Wissman, David Alvin   b: 2/17/41, Greenfield, Mass.   BL/TR, 6′2″, 178 lbs.   Deb: 9/15/64

| 1964 | Pit-N | 16 | 27 | 2 | 4 | 0 | 0 | 0 | 1 | 9 | | .148 | .179 | .148 | -7 | -4 | -4 | 1 | 0 | 0 | 0 | 1.000 | 0 | O | -0.4 |

■ TEX WISTERZIL   Wisterzil, George John   b: 3/7/1891, Detroit, Mich.   d: 6/27/64, San Antonio, Tex.   BR/TR, 5′9.5″, 150 lbs.   Deb: 4/14/14

1914	Bro-F	149	534	54	137	18	10	0	66	34	47	.257	.314	.328	83	-12	-12	64	17			.956	15	*3	0.9
1915	Bro-F	36	106	13	33	3	3	0	21	21	7	.311	.438	.396	147	8	8	23	8			.949	3	3	1.3
	Chi-F	7	20	3	4	1	0	0	3	2	2	.200	.304	.250	68	-1	-1	2	0			.955	1	/3	0.0
	StL-F	8	24	1	5	1	0	0	4	2	2	.208	.296	.250	58	-1	-1	2	2			.939	2	/3	0.1
	Chi-F	42	144	12	36	3	1	0	14	5	10	.250	.280	.285	70	-6	-5	14	2			.968	9	3	0.6
	Yr	93	294	29	78	8	4	0	39	31	21	.265	.345	.320	99	-0	1	40	12			.958	15	3	2.0
Total	2	242	828	83	215	26	14	0	105	65	68	.260	.326	.325	89	-13	-11	105	29			.957	30	3	2.9

■ MICKEY WITEK   Witek, Nicholas Joseph   b: 12/19/15, Luzerne, Pa.   d: 8/24/90, Kingston, Pa.   BR/TR, 5′10″, 170 lbs.   Deb: 4/16/40

1940	NY-N	119	433	34	111	7	0	3	31	24	17	.256	.295	.293	62	-22	-22	34	2			.958	19	S2	0.6
1941	NY-N	26	94	11	34	5	1	1	16	4	2	.362	.388	.447	132	4	4	16	0			.933	2	2	0.7
1942	NY-N	148	553	72	144	19	6	5	48	36	20	.260	.306	.344	89	-8	-9	54	2			.978	-1	*2	-0.1
1943	NY-N	153	622	68	195	17	0	6	55	41	23	.314	.356	.370	109	7	7	78	1			.967	16	*2	3.3
1946	NY-N	82	284	32	75	13	2	4	29	28	10	.264	.330	.366	97	-1	-1	34	1			.962	-12	23	-1.1
1947	NY-N	51	160	22	35	4	1	3	17	15	12	.219	.286	.313	58	-10	-10	15	1			.983	11	2/3	0.4
1949	NY-A	1	1	0	1	0	0	0	0	0	0	1.000	1.000	1.000	430	0	0	1	0	0	0	.000	0	H	0.0
Total	7	580	2147	239	595	65	9	22	196	148	84	.277	.324	.347	90	-29	-31	235	7	0		.969	34	2/S3	3.8

■ FRANK WITHROW   Withrow, Frank Blaine "Kid"   b: 6/14/1891, Greenwood, Mo.   d: 9/5/66, Omaha, Neb.   BR/TR, 5′11.5″, 187 lbs.   Deb: 4/15/20

1920	Phi-N	48	132	8	24	4	1	0	12	8	26	.182	.239	.227	33	-11	-12	9	0	0	0	.973	3	C	-0.6
1922	Phi-N	10	21	3	7	2	0	0	3	3	5	.333	.417	.429	108	1	1	4	0	0	0	.909	1	/C	0.2
Total	2	58	153	11	31	6	1	0	15	11	31	.203	.265	.255	45	-10	-11	12	0	0	0	.965	4	/C	-0.4

■ CORKY WITHROW   Withrow, Raymond Wallace   b: 11/28/37, High Coal, W.Va.   BR/TR, 6′3.5″, 197 lbs.   Deb: 9/06/63

| 1963 | StL-N | 6 | 9 | 0 | 0 | 0 | 0 | 0 | 1 | 0 | 2 | .000 | .000 | .000 | -91 | -2 | -2 | 0 | 0 | 0 | 0 | 1.000 | 0 | /O | -0.3 |

■ RON WITMEYER   Witmeyer, Ronald Herman   b: 6/28/67, West Islip, N.Y.   BL/TL, 6′3″, 215 lbs.   Deb: 8/25/91

| 1991 | Oak-A | 11 | 19 | 0 | 1 | 0 | 0 | 0 | 0 | 0 | 5 | .053 | .053 | .053 | -75 | -4 | -4 | 0 | 0 | 0 | 0 | 1.000 | 0 | /1 | -0.4 |

■ WHITEY WITT   Witt, Lawton Walter (b: Ladislaw Waldemar Wittkowski)   b: 9/28/1895, Orange, Mass.   d: 7/14/88, Salem Co., N.J.   BL/TR, 5′7″, 150 lbs.   Deb: 4/12/16

1916	Phi-A	143	563	64	138	16	15	2	36	55	71	.245	.315	.337	101	-4	-1	66	19			.902	-1	*S	0.7
1917	Phi-A	128	452	62	114	13	4	0	28	65	45	.252	.346	.299	98	1	1	50	12			.935	5	*S/O3	1.2
1919	Phi-A	122	460	56	123	15	6	0	33	46	26	.267	.334	.326	85	-8	-9	52	11			.972	-3	O2/3	-1.4
1920	Phi-A	65	218	29	70	11	3	1	25	27	16	.321	.396	.413	113	5	7	36	2	3	-1	.960	-2	*O2/S	-0.8
1921	Phi-A	154	629	100	198	31	11	4	45	77	52	.315	.390	.418	106	8	7	104	16	15	-4	.959	-2	*O	-1.0
1922	*NY-A	140	528	98	157	11	6	4	40	**89**	29	.297	.400	.364	98	5	3	81	5	8	-3	.976	-5	*O	-1.5
1923	*NY-A	146	596	113	187	18	10	6	56	67	42	.314	.386	.408	107	9	8	95	2	7	-4	**.979**	2	*O	-0.3
1924	NY-A	147	600	88	178	26	5	1	36	45	20	.297	.346	.362	83	-16	-15	76	9	7	-2	.976	-1	*O	-2.6
1925	NY-A	31	40	9	8	2	1	0	6	2	2	.200	.304	.300	55	-3	-3	4	1	1	-0	1.000	-1	O	-0.4
1926	Bro-N	63	85	13	22	1	1	0	3	12	6	.259	.351	.294	76	-2	-2	9	1			.920	-2	O	-0.5
Total	10	1139	4171	632	1195	144	62	18	302	489	309	.287	.362	.364	97	-5	-6	574	78	41		.971	-15	OS/23	-6.6

■ JERRY WITTE   Witte, Jerome Charles   b: 7/30/15, St.Louis, Mo.   BR/TR, 6′1″, 190 lbs.   Deb: 9/10/46

1946	StL-A	18	73	7	14	2	0	2	4	0	18	.192	.192	.301	35	-7	-7	4	0	0	0	.967	-2	1	-1.1
1947	StL-A	34	99	4	14	2	1	2	12	11	22	.141	.227	.242	30	-10	-10	6	0	0	0	.983	-1	1	-1.3
Total	2	52	172	11	28	4	1	4	16	11	40	.163	.213	.267	32	-16	-17	10	0	0	0	.977	-4	/1	-2.4

■ JOHN WOCKENFUSS   Wockenfuss, Johnny Bilton   b: 2/27/49, Welch, W.Va.   BR/TR, 6′, 190 lbs.   Deb: 8/11/74

1974	Det-A	13	29	1	4	1	0	0	2	3	2	.138	.219	.172	13	-3	-3	1	0	0	0	.932	-1	C	-0.4
1975	Det-A	35	118	15	27	6	3	4	13	10	15	.229	.289	.432	97	-0	-1	13	0	0	0	.982	4	C	0.4
1976	Det-A	60	144	18	32	7	2	3	10	17	14	.222	.309	.361	92	-1	-1	15	0	3	-2	.941	-4	C	-1.0
1977	Det-A	53	164	26	45	8	1	9	25	14	18	.274	.331	.500	117	5	4	28	0	0	0	.985	-7	C/OD	-0.2
1978	Det-A	71	187	28	53	5	0	7	22	21	14	.283	.359	.422	116	5	4	27	0	1	-1	.978	-8	O/D	-0.6
1979	Det-A	87	231	27	61	9	1	15	46	18	40	.264	.326	.506	116	5	4	34	2	2	-1	.996	0	1CD/O	0.4
1980	Det-A	126	372	56	102	13	2	16	65	68	64	.274	.391	.449	126	17	16	68	1	4	-2	.983	0	1DCO	1.2
1981	Det-A	70	172	20	37	4	0	9	25	28	22	.215	.325	.395	103	2	1	23	0	0	0	.984	-3	D1/CO	-0.3
1982	Det-A	70	193	28	58	9	0	8	32	29	21	.301	.382	.472	135	10	10	37	1	0	0	.981	-6	1C1D/0	0.7
1983	Det-A	92	245	32	66	8	1	9	44	31	37	.269	.351	.420	114	4	5	37	1	1	-0	1.000	4	DC1/30	0.9
1984	Phi-N	86	180	20	52	3	1	6	24	30	24	.289	.390	.417	125	7	7	31	0	1	0	.996	-7	1C/3	0.0
1985	Phi-N	32	37	1	6	0	0	0	2	8	7	.162	.311	.162	35	-3	-3	2	0	0	0	1.000	-2	/1C	-0.4
Total	12	795	2072	267	543	73	11	86	310	277	278	.262	.351	.432	114	49	43	316	5	11	-5	.972	-27	C1DO/3	0.7

YEAR	TM/L	G	AB	R	H	2B	3B	HR	RBI	BB	SO	AVG	OBP	SLG	PRO+	BR	/A	RC	SB	CS	SBR	FA	FR	POS	TPR

■ ANDY WOEHR Woehr, Andrew Emil b: 2/4/1896, Fort Wayne, Ind. d: 7/24/90, Fort Wayne, Ind. BR/TR, 5'11", 165 lbs. Deb: 9/15/23

1923	Phi-N	13	41	3	14	2	0	0	3	1	1	.341	.357	.390	87	-0	-1	6	0	0	0	.975	3	3	0.3
1924	Phi-N	50	152	11	33	4	5	0	17	5	8	.217	.252	.309	44	-11	-13	12	2	2	-1	.920	-5	3/2	-1.6
Total	2	63	193	14	47	6	5	0	20	6	9	.244	.274	.326	53	-11	-14	17	2	2	-1	.935	-2	/32	-1.3

■ JOE WOERLIN Woerlin, Joseph b: 10/9/1864, France d: 6/22/19, St.Louis, Mo. Deb: 7/21/1895

| 1895 | Was-N | 1 | 3 | 1 | 1 | 0 | 0 | 0 | 0 | 0 | | .333 | .333 | .333 | 75 | -0 | -0 | 0 | 0 | | | 1.000 | -0 | /S | 0.0 |

■ JIM WOHLFORD Wohlford, James Eugene b: 2/28/51, Visalia, Cal. BR/TR, 5'11", 175 lbs. Deb: 9/01/72

1972	KC-A	15	25	3	6	1	0	0	2	2	6	.240	.321	.280	80	-1	-1	3	0	0	0	.950	-2	/2	-0.3
1973	KC-A	45	109	21	29	1	3	2	10	11	12	.266	.333	.385	95	0	-1	14	1	1	-0	1.000	3	DO	0.1
1974	KC-A	143	501	55	136	16	7	2	44	39	74	.271	.328	.343	88	-4	-7	55	16	13	-3	.982	1	*O/D	-1.6
1975	KC-A	116	353	45	90	10	5	0	30	34	37	.255	.322	.312	78	-9	-10	38	12	7	-1	.953	-6	*O/D	-2.1
1976	*KC-A	107	293	47	73	10	2	1	24	29	24	.249	.319	.307	83	-5	-6	27	22	16	-3	.975	-1	O/2D	-1.3
1977	Mil-A	129	391	41	97	16	3	2	36	21	49	.248	.288	.320	65	-19	-19	32	17	16	-5	.981	-2	*O/2D	-2.9
1978	Mil-A	46	118	16	35	7	2	1	19	6	10	.297	.331	.415	108	1	1	16	3	2	-0	.982	-5	O/D	-0.5
1979	Mil-A	63	175	19	46	13	1	1	17	9	28	.263	.295	.366	77	-6	-6	19	6	2	1	.969	-2	O/D	-0.9
1980	SF-N	91	193	17	54	6	4	1	24	13	23	.280	.329	.368	96	-2	-1	22	1	4	-2	.989	-0	O/3	-0.5
1981	SF-N	50	68	4	11	3	0	1	7	4	9	.162	.208	.250	30	-6	-6	3	0	0	0	1.000	-3	O	-1.0
1982	SF-N	97	250	37	64	12	1	2	25	30	36	.256	.336	.336	89	-3	-3	28	8	3	1	.992	-2	O	-0.7
1983	Mon-N	83	141	7	39	8	0	1	14	5	14	.277	.301	.355	82	-4	-4	14	0	0	0	.988	3	O	-0.2
1984	Mon-N	95	213	20	64	13	2	5	29	14	19	.300	.344	.451	127	5	7	34	3	0	1	.989	-2	O/3	0.4
1985	Mon-N	70	125	7	24	5	1	1	15	16	18	.192	.280	.272	60	-7	-6	10	0	2	-1	1.000	-5	O	-1.4
1986	Mon-N	70	94	10	25	4	2	1	11	9	17	.266	.330	.383	97	-1	-0	11	0	2	-1	1.000	3	O/3	-0.5
Total	15	1220	3049	349	793	125	33	21	305	241	376	.260	.316	.343	85	-59	-62	325	89	68	-14	.980	-26	O/D23	-13.4

■ JOHN WOJCIK Wojcik, John Joseph b: 4/6/42, Olean, N.Y. BL/TR, 6' ", 175 lbs. Deb: 9/09/62

1962	KC-A	16	43	8	13	4	0	0	9	13	4	.302	.474	.395	133	3	3	11	3	0	1	1.000	-1	O	0.3
1963	KC-A	19	59	7	11	0	0	0	2	8	8	.186	.284	.186	34	-5	-5	4	2	0	1	1.000	0	O	-0.5
1964	KC-A	6	22	1	3	0	0	0	0	2	8	.136	.208	.136	-2	-3	-3	1	0	0	0	1.000	0	/O	-0.4
Total	3	41	124	16	27	4	0	0	11	23	20	.218	.345	.250	65	-4	-5	15	5	0	2	1.000	-1	/O	-0.6

■ RAY WOLF Wolf, Raymond Bernard "Grandpa" b: 7/15/04, Chicago, Ill. d: 10/6/79, Fort Worth, Tex. BR/TR, 5'11", 175 lbs. Deb: 7/27/27

| 1927 | Cin-N | 1 | 1 | 0 | 0 | 0 | 0 | 0 | 0 | 0 | 0 | .000 | .000 | .000 | -99 | -0 | -0 | 0 | 0 | | | 1.000 | -0 | /1 | 0.0 |

■ JIMMY WOLF Wolf, William Van Winkle "Chicken" b: 5/12/1862, Louisville, Ky. d: 5/16/03, Louisville, Ky. BR/TR, 5'9", 190 lbs. Deb: 5/02/1882 M

1882	Lou-a	78	318	46	95	11	8	0		9		.299	.318	.384	144	11	14	40				.902	-2	*O/S1P	1.1
1883	Lou-a	98	389	59	102	17	9	1		5		.262	.272	.360	110	0	4	39				.890	17	*OC/S2	1.9
1884	Lou-a	110	486	79	146	24	11	3		4		.300	.310	.414	144	18	21	64				.884	0	*OC/S31	1.8
1885	Lou-a	112	483	79	141	23	17	1		11		.292	.309	.416	130	15	15	64				.917	-0	*O/C3P	1.1
1886	Lou-a	130	545	93	148	17	12	3		27		.272	.310	.363	106	6	1	70	23			.934	9	*O/1C2P	0.6
1887	Lou-a	137	569	103	160	27	13	2		34		.281	.331	.385	99	0	-2	89	45			.940	8	*O1	0.3
1888	Lou-a	128	538	80	154	28	11	0	67	25		.286	.320	.379	130	15	16	80	41			.886	7	OS/3C1	2.0
1889	Lou-a	130	546	72	159	20	9	3	57	29	34	.291	.333	.377	106	2	4	76	18			.946	-1	O12S/3M	0.1
1890	*Lou-a	134	543	100	197	29	11	4		43		**.363**	.421	.479	172	45	47	132	46			.939	-2	*O3	3.6
1891	Lou-a	138	537	67	136	17	8	1	82	42	36	.253	.317	.320	86	-11	-9	60	13			.918	5	*O/13	-0.7
1892	StL-N	3	14	1	2	0	0	0	1	0	1	.143	.143	.143	-13	-2	-2	0	0			1.000	-1	/O	-0.3
Total	11	1198	4968	779	1440	213	109	18	207	229	71	.290	.327	.387	120	100	110	715	186			.918	41	*O/S1C32P	11.5

■ HARRY WOLFE Wolfe, Harold "Whitey" b: 11/24/1890, Massachusetts d: 7/28/71, Fort Wayne, Ind. BR/TR, 5'8", 160 lbs. Deb: 4/15/17

1917	Chi-N	9	5	1	2	0	0	0	1	1	1	.400	.500	.400	164	1	1	1	0			1.000	0	/OS	0.1
	Pit-N	3	5	0	0	0	0	0	0	1	4	.000	.167	.000	-45	-1	-1	0	0			.875	1	/2S	0.0
	Yr	12	10	1	2	0	0	0	1	2	5	.200	.333	.200	61	-0	-0	1	0			1.000	1	/OS2	0.1

■ LARRY WOLFE Wolfe, Laurence Marcy b: 3/2/53, Melbourne, Fla. BR/TR, 5'11", 170 lbs. Deb: 9/16/77

1977	Min-A	8	25	3	6	1	0	0	6	1	0	.240	.269	.280	51	-2	-2	2	0	0	0	1.000	0	/3	-0.2
1978	Min-A	88	235	25	55	10	1	3	25	36	27	.234	.336	.323	85	-3	-4	26	0	1	-1	.953	6	3/S	0.1
1979	Bos-A	47	78	12	19	4	0	3	15	17	21	.244	.385	.410	109	2	2	14	0	0	0	.963	6	2/3SC1	0.8
1980	Bos-A	18	23	3	3	1	0	1	4	0	5	.130	.130	.304	15	-3	-3	1	0	0	0	1.000	1	3/D	-0.2
Total	4	161	361	43	83	16	1	7	50	54	53	.230	.332	.338	84	-6	-7	43	0	1	-1	.957	13	3/2SD1C	0.5

■ POLLY WOLFE Wolfe, Roy Chamberlain b: 9/1/1888, Knoxville, Ill. d: 11/21/38, Morris, Ill. BL/TR, 5'10", 170 lbs. Deb: 9/22/12

1912	Chi-A	1	1	0	0	0	0	0	0	0	0	.000	.000	.000	-99	-0	-0	0	0			.000	0	H	0.0
1914	Chi-A	8	28	0	6	0	0	0	0	3	6	.214	.290	.214	53	-2	-1	2	1	1	-0	.875	-1	/O	-0.4
Total	2	9	29	0	6	0	0	0	0	3	6	.207	.281	.207	47	-2	-2	2	1	1			-1	/O	-0.4

■ ABE WOLSTENHOLME Wolstenholme, Abraham Lincoln b: 3/4/1861, Philadelphia, Pa. d: 3/4/16, Philadelphia, Pa. Deb: 6/04/1883

| 1883 | Phi-N | 3 | 11 | 0 | 1 | 1 | 0 | 0 | 0 | 0 | | .091 | .091 | .182 | -22 | -2 | -1 | 0 | | | | .727 | -3 | /CO | -0.3 |

■ HARRY WOLTER Wolter, Harry Meigs b: 7/11/1884, Monterey, Cal. d: 7/7/70, Palo Alto, Cal. BL/TL, 5'10", 175 lbs. Deb: 5/14/07

1907	Cin-N	4	15	1	2	0	0	0	1	0		.133	.133	.133	-16	-2	-2	0	0			1.000	-0	/O	-0.3
	Pit-N	1	1	0	0	0	0	0	0	0		.000	.000	.000	-99	-0	-0	0	0			.000	-0	/P	0.0
	StL-N	16	47	4	16	0	0	0	6	3		.340	.380	.340	130	1	2	7	1			.962	3	O/P	0.5
	Yr	21	63	5	18	0	0	0	7	3		.286	.318	.286	91	-1	-1	6	1			.969	3	O/P	0.2
1909	Bos-A	54	122	14	30	2	4	2	10	9		.246	.298	.377	110	1	1	14	2			.978	-1	1P/O	0.1
1910	NY-A	135	479	84	128	15	9	4	42	66		.267	.364	.361	120	17	14	78	39			.940	-3	*O/1	0.5
1911	NY-A	122	434	78	132	17	15	4	36	62		.304	.396	.440	120	21	16	86	28			.951	4	*O/1	1.4
1912	NY-A	12	32	8	11	2	1	0	1	10		.344	.512	.469	171	4	4	10	5			.923	-1	/O	0.2
1913	NY-A	127	425	53	108	18	6	2	43	80	50	.254	.377	.339	109	9	9	58	13			.946	-7	*O	-0.4
1917	Chi-N	117	353	44	88	15	7	0	28	38	40	.249	.324	.331	94	1	-2	39	7			.942	-4	O/1	-1.2
Total	7	588	1908	286	515	69	42	12	167	268	90	.270	.365	.369	114	53	42	292	95			.941	-10	O/1P	0.8

■ HARRY WOLVERTON Wolverton, Harry Sterling "Fighting Harry"
b: 12/6/1873, Mt.Vernon, Ohio d: 2/4/37, Oakland, Cal. BL/TR, 5'11", 205 lbs. Deb: 9/25/1898 M

1898	Chi-N	13	49	4	16	1	0	0	2	1		.327	.353	.347	101	-0	0	7	1			.848	3	3	0.3
1899	Chi-N	99	389	50	111	14	11	1	49	30		.285	.350	.386	105	1	2	61	14			.860	-6	3/S	-0.2
1900	Chi-N	3	11	2	2	0	0	0	0	2		.182	.308	.182	38	-1	-1	1	1			.875	-2	/3	-0.3
	Phi-N	101	383	42	108	10	8	3	58	20		.282	.323	.373	92	-5	-5	50	4			.881	-9	*3	-1.2
	Yr	104	394	44	110	10	8	3	58	22		.279	.322	.368	91	-6	-6	51	5			.881	-11	*3	-1.5
1901	Phi-N	93	379	42	117	15	4	0	43	22		.309	.356	.369	109	5	4	57	13			**.921**	3	3	0.8
1902	Was-A	59	249	35	62	8	3	1	23	13		.249	.294	.317	69	-10	-11	26	8			.904	3	3	-0.7
	Phi-N	34	136	12	40	3	2	0	16	9		.294	.347	.346	114	2	2	18	3			.931	9	3	1.2
1903	Phi-N	123	494	72	152	13	12	0	53	18		.308	.341	.383	110	3	5	72	10			**.941**	1	*3	0.7
1904	Phi-N	102	398	43	106	15	5	0	49	26		.266	.319	.329	105	0	2	50	10			.925	1	*3	0.7
1905	Bos-N	122	463	38	104	15	7	2	55	23		.225	.276	.300	74	-17	-15	43	10			.934	4	*3	-0.7

YEAR	TM/L	G	AB	R	H	2B	3B	HR	RBI	BB	SO	AVG	OBP	SLG	PRO+	BR	/A	RC	SB	CS	SBR	FA	FR	POS	TPR
1912	NY-A	34	50	6	15	1	1	0	4	2		.300	.340	.360	94	-0	-0	6	1			.821	-2	/3M	-0.2
Total	9	783	3001	346	833	95	53	7	352	166		.278	.325	.352	97	-21	-16	391	83			.909	6	3/S	0.4

■ SID WOMACK Womack, Sidney Kirk "Tex" b: 10/2/1896, Greensburg, La. d: 8/28/58, Jackson, Miss. BR/TR, 5'10.5", 185 lbs. Deb: 8/15/26

YEAR	TM/L	G	AB	R	H	2B	3B	HR	RBI	BB	SO	AVG	OBP	SLG	PRO+	BR	/A	RC	SB	CS	SBR	FA	FR	POS	TPR
1926	Bos-N	1	3	0	0	0	0	0	1	0	0	.000	.000	.000	-99	-1	-1	0	0			1.000	0	/C	-0.1

■ WOOD Wood Deb: 9/30/1874

YEAR	TM/L	G	AB	R	H	2B	3B	HR	RBI	BB	SO	AVG	OBP	SLG	PRO+	BR	/A	RC	SB	CS	SBR	FA	FR	POS	TPR
1874	Bal-n	1	6	0	0	0	0	0		0		.000	.000	.000	-99	-1	-1	0						/2	-0.1

■ DOC WOOD Wood, Charles Spencer b: 2/28/1900, Batesville, Miss. d: 11/3/74, New Orleans, La. BR/TR, 5'10", 150 lbs. Deb: 7/21/23

YEAR	TM/L	G	AB	R	H	2B	3B	HR	RBI	BB	SO	AVG	OBP	SLG	PRO+	BR	/A	RC	SB	CS	SBR	FA	FR	POS	TPR
1923	Phi-A	3	3	0	1	0	0	0	0	0	0	.333	.333	.333	75	-0	-0	0	0	0	0	.833	1	/S	0.1

■ TED WOOD Wood, Edward Robert b: 1/4/67, Mansfield, Ohio BL/TL, 6'2", 178 lbs. Deb: 9/04/91

YEAR	TM/L	G	AB	R	H	2B	3B	HR	RBI	BB	SO	AVG	OBP	SLG	PRO+	BR	/A	RC	SB	CS	SBR	FA	FR	POS	TPR
1991	SF-N	10	25	0	3	0	0	0	1	2	11	.120	.185	.120	-13	-4	-4	1	0	0	0	.909	-1	/O	-0.5
1992	SF-N	24	58	5	12	2	0	1	3	6	15	.207	.292	.293	70	-2	-2	4	0	0	0	.972	1	O	-0.2
Total	2	34	83	5	15	2	0	1	4	8	26	.181	.261	.241	45	-6	-6	5	0	0	0	.957	-1	/O	-0.7

■ FRED WOOD Wood, Fred S. b: 1863, Hamilton, Ont., Canada d: 8/23/33, New York, N.Y. 5'5", 160 lbs. Deb: 5/14/1884 F

YEAR	TM/L	G	AB	R	H	2B	3B	HR	RBI	BB	SO	AVG	OBP	SLG	PRO+	BR	/A	RC	SB	CS	SBR	FA	FR	POS	TPR
1884	Det-N	12	42	4	2	0	0	0	1	3	18	.048	.111	.048	-51	-7	-7	0				.889	-1	/COS	-0.7
1885	Buf-N	1	4	0	1	0	0	0	0	0	0	.250	.250	.250	60	-0	-0	0				.833	-0	/C	0.0
Total	2	13	46	4	3	0	0	0	1	3	18	.065	.122	.065	-41	-7	-7	0				.883	-2	/COS	-0.7

■ GEORGE WOOD Wood, George A. "Dandy" b: 11/9/1858, Boston, Mass. d: 4/4/24, Harrisburg, Pa. BL/TR, 5'10.5", 175 lbs. Deb: 5/01/1880 MU

YEAR	TM/L	G	AB	R	H	2B	3B	HR	RBI	BB	SO	AVG	OBP	SLG	PRO+	BR	/A	RC	SB	CS	SBR	FA	FR	POS	TPR
1880	Wor-N	81	327	37	80	16	5	0	28	10	37	.245	.267	.324	91	-0	-4	29				.887	-7	*O/31	-1.3
1881	Det-N	80	337	54	100	18	9	2	32	19	32	.297	.334	.421	131	14	12	49				.862	-2	*O	0.8
1882	Det-N	84	375	69	101	12	12	**7**	29	14	30	.269	.296	.421	127	11	11	48				.884	2	*O	1.1
1883	Det-N	99	441	81	133	26	11	5	47	25	37	.302	.339	.444	142	19	22	68				.876	9	*O/P	2.6
1884	Det-N	114	473	79	119	16	10	8	29	39	75	.252	.309	.378	122	8	13	57				.896	3	*O/3	1.2
1885	Det-N	82	362	62	105	19	8	5	28	13	19	.290	.315	.428	138	14	14	50				.885	0	O3/SP	1.2
1886	Phi-N	106	450	81	123	18	15	4	50	23	75	.273	.309	.407	115	8	7	61	9			.904	-5	*O/S3	0.0
1887	Phi-N	113	491	118	142	22	19	14	66	40	51	.289	.350	.497	127	22	17	94	19			.873	-10	*O/S32	0.5
1888	Phi-N	106	433	67	99	19	6	6	51	39	44	.229	.303	.342	102	5	1	52	20			.905	0	*O/3P	-0.1
1889	Phi-N	97	422	77	106	21	4	5	53	53	33	.251	.336	.355	87	-2	-8	58	17			.915	-4	O/SP	-1.2
	Bal-a	3	10	1	2	0	0	0	1	0	2	.200	.200	.200	15	-1	-1	1	1			1.000	-0	/O	-0.1
1890	Phi-P	132	539	115	156	20	14	9	102	51	35	.289	.360	.429	109	8	6	92	20			.895	14	*O/3	1.2
1891	Phi-a	132	528	105	163	18	14	3	61	72	52	.309	.399	.413	132	26	23	98	22			.939	7	*O/3SM	2.3
1892	Bal-N	21	76	9	17	1	1	0	10	10	8	.224	.330	.263	79	-1	-1	7	1			.911	2	O	0.0
	Cin-N	30	107	10	21	2	4	0	14	10	17	.196	.271	.290	72	-4	-4	10	4			.863	-2	O	-0.6
	Yr	51	183	19	38	3	5	0	24	20	25	.208	.296	.279	75	-5	-5	17	5			.885	1	O	-0.6
Total	13	1280	5371	965	1467	228	132	68	601	418	547	.273	.329	.403	117	125	107	773	113			.895	10	*O/3SP21	7.6

■ HARRY WOOD Wood, Harold Austin b: 2/10/1881, Waterville, Maine d: 5/18/55, Bethesda, Md. BL/TR, 5'10", 155 lbs. Deb: 4/19/03

YEAR	TM/L	G	AB	R	H	2B	3B	HR	RBI	BB	SO	AVG	OBP	SLG	PRO+	BR	/A	RC	SB	CS	SBR	FA	FR	POS	TPR
1903	Cin-N	2	3	0	0	0	0	0	0	1		.000	.250	.000	-24	-0	-1	0	0			.000	-1	/O	-0.1

■ JAKE WOOD Wood, Jacob b: 6/22/37, Elizabeth, N.J. BR/TR, 6'1", 170 lbs. Deb: 4/11/61

YEAR	TM/L	G	AB	R	H	2B	3B	HR	RBI	BB	SO	AVG	OBP	SLG	PRO+	BR	/A	RC	SB	CS	SBR	FA	FR	POS	TPR
1961	Det-A	162	663	96	171	17	**14**	11	69	58	141	.258	.321	.376	83	-14	-16	84	30	9	4	.969	-27	*2	-2.2
1962	Det-A	111	367	68	83	10	5	8	30	33	59	.226	.292	.346	68	-15	-17	40	24	3	**5**	.950	-31	2	-3.4
1963	Det-A	85	351	50	95	11	2	11	27	24	61	.271	.330	.407	102	2	1	50	18	5	2	.958	-11	2/3	0.0
1964	Det-A	64	125	11	29	2	2	1	7	4	24	.232	.256	.304	54	-8	-8	10	0	0	0	.989	-1	12/3O	-1.0
1965	Det-A	58	104	12	30	3	0	2	7	10	19	.288	.357	.375	107	1	1	12	3	3	-1	.977	-2	2/1S3	0.0
1966	Det-A	98	230	39	58	9	3	2	27	28	48	.252	.336	.343	94	-1	-1	27	4	3	-1	.968	-13	2/31	-1.2
1967	Det-A	14	20	2	1	1	0	0	0	1	7	.050	.095	.100	-41	-4	-4	0	0	0	0	1.000	-0	/12	-0.4
	Cin-N	16	17	1	2	0	0	0	1	1	3	.118	.167	.118	-15	-3	-3	0	0	0	0	1.000	0	/O	-0.3
Total	7	608	1877	279	469	53	26	35	168	159	362	.250	.313	.362	82	-40	-47	223	79	23	10	.963	-85	2/13OS	-8.5

■ JIMMY WOOD Wood, James Leon b: 12/1/1844, Brooklyn, N.Y. d: 11/30/1886, TR, 5'8.5", 150 lbs. Deb: 5/08/1871 M

YEAR	TM/L	G	AB	R	H	2B	3B	HR	RBI	BB	SO	AVG	OBP	SLG	PRO+	BR	/A	RC	SB	CS	SBR	FA	FR	POS	TPR
1871	Chi-n	28	135	45	51	10	6	1	29	11	3	.378	.425	.563	163	14	10	41	18					*2M	0.5
1872	Tro-n	25	116	40	38	9	3	2	27	2	1	.328	.339	.509	155	7	7	22						2M	0.4
	Eck-n	7	30	10	6	1	1	0	0	4	1	.200	.294	.300	98	-0	1	3						2M	0.0
	Yr	32	146	50	44	10	4	2	27	6	2	.301	.329	.466	145	7	8	24						2	0.4
1873	Phi-n	42	209	67	67	11	1	0	27	8	1	.321	.346	.383	110	4	2	30						*2M	0.0
Total	3 n	102	490	162	162	31	11	3	83	25	6	.331	.363	.457	136	25	20	95						2	0.9

■ JOE WOOD Wood, Joseph "Smokey Joe" (b: Howard Ellsworth Wood)
b: 10/25/1889, Kansas City, Mo. d: 7/27/85, West Haven, Conn. BR/TR, 5'11", 180 lbs. Deb: 8/24/08 F

YEAR	TM/L	G	AB	R	H	2B	3B	HR	RBI	BB	SO	AVG	OBP	SLG	PRO+	BR	/A	RC	SB	CS	SBR	FA	FR	POS	TPR
1908	Bos-A	6	7	1	0	0	0	0	0	0		.000	.000	.000	-97	-1	-2	0	0			.889	-0	/P	0.0
1909	Bos-A	24	55	4	9	0	1	0	3	2		.164	.207	.200	28	-4	-5	2	0			.971	-4	P	0.0
1910	Bos-A	35	69	9	18	2	1	1	5	5		.261	.311	.362	108	1	0	8	0			.975	2	P	0.0
1911	Bos-A	44	88	15	23	4	2	2	11	10		.261	.343	.420	114	1	1	13	1			.947	2	P	0.0
1912	*Bos-A	43	124	16	36	13	1	1	13	11		.290	.348	.435	118	3	2	19	0			.974	8	P	0.0
1913	Bos-A	24	56	10	15	5	0	0	10	4	7	.268	.317	.357	95	-0	-1	6	1			.955	4	P	0.0
1914	Bos-A	21	43	2	6	1	0	0	1	3	14	.140	.213	.163	13	-5	-5	2	1			1.000	1	P	0.0
1915	Bos-A	29	54	6	14	1	1	1	7	5	10	.259	.322	.370	111	0	0	7	1	1	-0	.982	1	P	0.0
1917	Cle-A	10	6	1	0	0	0	0	0	0	3	.000	.000	.000	-93	-1	-1	0	0			1.000	0	/P	0.0
1918	Cle-A	119	422	41	125	22	4	5	66	36	38	.296	.356	.403	118	14	9	63	8			.962	0	O2/1	0.6
1919	Cle-A	72	192	30	49	10	5	1	27	32	21	.255	.367	.375	102	3	2	28	3			.932	-8	O/P	-1.1
1920	*Cle-A	61	137	25	37	11	2	1	30	25	16	.270	.390	.401	107	3	2	24	1	1	-0	.987	-6	O/P	-0.7
1921	Cle-A	66	194	32	71	16	5	4	60	25	17	.366	.438	.562	151	16	15	49	2	0	1	.973	-13	O	-0.1
1922	Cle-A	142	505	74	150	33	8	8	92	50	63	.297	.367	.442	109	7	7	85	5	1	1	.960	2	*O	0.0
Total	14	696	1952	266	553	118	30	24	325	208	189	.283	.357	.411	110	36	27	305	23	3		.962	-11	OP/21	-1.3

■ JOE WOOD Wood, Joseph Perry "J.P." or "Little Joe" b: 10/3/19, Houston, Tex. d: 3/25/85, Houston, Tex. BR/TR, 5'9.5", 160 lbs. Deb: 5/02/43

YEAR	TM/L	G	AB	R	H	2B	3B	HR	RBI	BB	SO	AVG	OBP	SLG	PRO+	BR	/A	RC	SB	CS	SBR	FA	FR	POS	TPR
1943	Det-A	60	164	22	53	4	4	1	17	6	13	.323	.347	.415	114	4	2	21	2	2	-1	.896	-16	23	-1.4

■ KEN WOOD Wood, Kenneth Lanier b: 7/1/24, Lincolnton, N.C. BR/TR, 6', 200 lbs. Deb: 4/28/48

YEAR	TM/L	G	AB	R	H	2B	3B	HR	RBI	BB	SO	AVG	OBP	SLG	PRO+	BR	/A	RC	SB	CS	SBR	FA	FR	POS	TPR
1948	StL-A	10	24	2	2	0	1	0	2	1	4	.083	.120	.167	-24	-4	-4	0	0	0	0	1.000	1	/O	-0.4
1949	StL-A	7	6	0	0	0	0	0	0	1	2	.000	.143	.000	-58	-1	-1	0	0	0	0	.000	-1	/O	-0.3
1950	StL-A	128	369	42	83	24	0	13	62	38	58	.225	.299	.396	74	-15	-17	40	0	4	-2	.952	-2	O	-2.4
1951	StL-A	109	333	40	79	19	0	15	44	27	49	.237	.296	.429	92	-5	-6	40	1	2	-1	.959	-4	*O	-1.4
1952	Bos-A	15	20	0	2	0	0	0	0	3	4	.100	.217	.100	-9	-3	-3	1	0	0	0	.889	-4	O	-0.8
	Was-A	61	210	26	50	8	6	6	32	30	21	.238	.333	.419	112	2	3	30	0	1	-1	.954	8	O	0.9
	Yr	76	230	26	52	8	6	6	32	33	25	.226	.323	.391	99	-1	-1	30	0	1	-1	.951	5	O	0.1
1953	Was-A	12	33	0	7	1	0	0	3	2	3	.212	.257	.242	36	-3	-3	2	0	0	0	1.000	1	/O	-0.2
Total	6	342	995	110	223	52	7	34	143	102	141	.224	.298	.393	81	-30	-32	113	1	7	-4	.956	-1	O	-4.6

■ BOB WOOD
Wood, Robert Lynn b: 7/28/1865, Thorn Hill, Ohio d: 5/22/43, Churchill, Ohio BR/TR, Deb: 5/02/1898

YEAR	TM/L	G	AB	R	H	2B	3B	HR	RBI	BB	SO	AVG	OBP	SLG	PRO+	BR	/A	RC	SB	CS	SBR	FA	FR	POS	TPR
1898	Cin-N	39	109	14	30	6	0	0	16	9		.275	.331	.330	84	-1	-3	13	1			.943	1	C/O1	0.1
1899	Cin-N	62	194	34	61	11	7	0	24	25		.314	.401	.443	129	9	8	37	3			.937	-11	C/O31	0.2
1900	Cin-N	45	139	17	37	8	1	0	22	10		.266	.315	.338	82	-4	-3	16	3			.967	-7	C3/O	-0.8
1901	Cle-A	98	346	45	101	23	3	1	49	12		.292	.327	.384	101	-2	-0	47	6			.952	-1	C/3O12S	0.7
1902	Cle-A	81	258	23	76	18	2	0	40	27		.295	.377	.380	115	5	6	39	1			.940	-7	C1/O23	0.4
1904	Det-A	49	175	15	43	6	2	1	17	5		.246	.271	.320	89	-3	-2	16	1			.974	10	C	1.4
1905	Det-A	8	24	1	2	1	0	0	0	1		.083	.120	.125	-22	-3	-3	0	0			.886	-0	/C	-0.3
Total	7	382	1245	149	350	73	15	2	168	89		.281	.338	.369	101	-0	3	168	15			.951	-16	C/31O2S	1.7

■ ROY WOOD
Wood, Roy Winton "Woody" b: 8/29/1892, Monticello, Ark. d: 4/6/74, Fayetteville, Ark. BR/TR, 6', 175 lbs. Deb: 6/16/13

YEAR	TM/L	G	AB	R	H	2B	3B	HR	RBI	BB	SO	AVG	OBP	SLG	PRO+	BR	/A	RC	SB	CS	SBR	FA	FR	POS	TPR
1913	Pit-N	14	35	4	10	4	0	0	2	1	8	.286	.306	.400	105	-0	0	4	0			.895	1	/O1	0.1
1914	Cle-A	72	220	24	52	6	3	1	15	13	26	.236	.300	.305	79	-5	-6	19	6	9	-4	.946	-1	O1	-1.4
1915	Cle-A	33	78	5	15	2	1	0	3	2	13	.192	.232	.244	41	-6	-6	4	1	2	-1	.990	-2	1/O	-1.0
Total	3	119	333	33	77	12	4	1	20	16	47	.231	.285	.300	73	-11	-12	27	7	11		.936	-1	/O1	-2.3

■ LARRY WOODALL
Woodall, Charles Lawrence b: 7/26/1894, Staunton, Va. d: 5/16/63, Cambridge, Mass. BR/TR, 5'9", 165 lbs. Deb: 5/20/20 C

YEAR	TM/L	G	AB	R	H	2B	3B	HR	RBI	BB	SO	AVG	OBP	SLG	PRO+	BR	/A	RC	SB	CS	SBR	FA	FR	POS	TPR
1920	Det-A	18	49	4	12	1	0	0	5	2	6	.245	.275	.265	45	-4	-4	4	0	0	0	.988	2	C	0.0
1921	Det-A	46	80	10	29	4	1	0	14	6	7	.363	.407	.438	117	2	2	15	1	0	0	.966	-7	C	-0.4
1922	Det-A	50	125	19	43	2	2	0	18	8	11	.344	.388	.392	107	1	2	19	0	1	-1	.977	-10	C	-0.7
1923	Det-A	71	148	20	41	12	2	1	19	22	9	.277	.371	.405	106	1	2	24	2	1	0	.983	-5	C	-0.1
1924	Det-A	67	165	23	51	9	2	0	25	21	5	.309	.387	.388	102	1	1	26	0	0	0	.986	0	C	0.4
1925	Det-A	75	171	20	35	4	1	0	13	24	8	.205	.303	.240	39	-16	-15	14	1	0	0	.967	-7	C	-1.8
1926	Det-A	67	146	18	34	5	0	0	15	15	2	.233	.304	.267	49	-11	-11	13	0	0	0	.979	-4	C	-1.1
1927	Det-A	88	246	28	69	8	6	0	39	37	9	.280	.375	.362	90	-2	-2	34	9	1	2	**.997**	4	C	0.8
1928	Det-A	65	186	19	39	7	1	0	13	24	10	.210	.300	.258	47	-14	-14	16	3	1	0	.992	4	C	-0.5
1929	Det-A	1	1	0	0	0	0	0	0	0	0	.000	.000	.000	-99	-0	-0	0	0	0	0	.000	0	H	0.0
Total	10	548	1317	161	353	52	15	1	161	159	67	.268	.347	.333	77	-41	-40	164	16	4	2	.984	-22	C	-3.4

■ DARRELL WOODARD
Woodard, Darrell Lee b: 12/10/56, Wilma, Ark. BR/TR, 5'11", 160 lbs. Deb: 8/06/78

YEAR	TM/L	G	AB	R	H	2B	3B	HR	RBI	BB	SO	AVG	OBP	SLG	PRO+	BR	/A	RC	SB	CS	SBR	FA	FR	POS	TPR
1978	Oak-A	33	9	10	0	0	0	0	0	1	1	.000	.100	.000	-73	-2	-2	-1	3	4	-2	.964	12	2/3D	0.8

■ MIKE WOODARD
Woodard, Michael Cary b: 3/2/60, Melrose Park, Ill. BL/TR, 5'9", 155 lbs. Deb: 9/11/85

YEAR	TM/L	G	AB	R	H	2B	3B	HR	RBI	BB	SO	AVG	OBP	SLG	PRO+	BR	/A	RC	SB	CS	SBR	FA	FR	POS	TPR
1985	SF-N	24	82	12	20	1	0	0	9	5	3	.244	.287	.256	56	-5	-5	7	6	1	1	.990	-5	2	-0.8
1986	SF-N	48	79	14	20	2	1	1	5	10	9	.253	.337	.342	92	-1	-1	11	7	2	1	.986	-2	2/S3	-0.1
1987	SF-N	10	19	0	4	1	0	0	1	0	1	.211	.211	.263	26	-2	-2	1	0	0	0	1.000	2	/2	0.0
1988	Chi-A	18	45	3	6	0	1	0	4	1	5	.133	.170	.178	-2	-6	-6	1	1	1	-0	.975	4	2/D	-0.2
Total	4	100	225	29	50	4	2	1	19	16	18	.222	.277	.271	55	-14	-13	20	14	4	2	.985	-1	/2D3S	-1.1

■ RED WOODHEAD
Woodhead, James b: 7/1851, Chelsea, Mass. d: 9/7/1881, Boston, Mass. 5'6", 160 lbs. Deb: 4/15/1873

YEAR	TM/L	G	AB	R	H	2B	3B	HR	RBI	BB	SO	AVG	OBP	SLG	PRO+	BR	/A	RC	SB	CS	SBR	FA	FR	POS	TPR
1873	Mar-n	1	5	1	0	0	0	0	0	0	0	.000	.000	.000	-99	-1	-1	0						/S	-0.1
1879	Syr-N	34	131	4	21	1	0	0	2	0	23	.160	.160	.168	9	-12	-10	4				.792	-7	3	-1.6

■ GENE WOODLING
Woodling, Eugene Richard b: 8/16/22, Akron, Ohio BL/TR, 5'9.5", 195 lbs. Deb: 9/23/43 C

YEAR	TM/L	G	AB	R	H	2B	3B	HR	RBI	BB	SO	AVG	OBP	SLG	PRO+	BR	/A	RC	SB	CS	SBR	FA	FR	POS	TPR
1943	Cle-A	8	25	5	8	2	1	1	5	1	5	.320	.346	.600	186	2	2	5	0	0	0	1.000	-1	/O	0.1
1946	Cle-A	61	133	8	25	1	4	0	9	16	13	.188	.280	.256	54	-9	-8	11	1	2	-1	1.000	-3	O	-1.3
1947	Pit-N	22	79	7	21	2	2	0	10	7	5	.266	.326	.342	75	-3	-3	9	0			.968	1	O	-0.2
1949	*NY-A	112	296	60	80	13	7	5	44	52	21	.270	.381	.412	110	5	5	50	2	2	-1	.982	-10	O	-1.0
1950	*NY-A	122	449	81	127	20	10	6	60	70	31	.283	.381	.412	106	3	5	75	5	3	-0	.993	10	*O	0.9
1951	*NY-A	120	420	65	118	15	8	15	71	62	37	.281	.373	.462	130	15	17	75	0	4	-2	.993	1	*O	1.1
1952	*NY-A	122	408	58	126	19	6	12	63	59	31	.309	.397	.473	151	24	27	81	1	4	-2	**.996**	6	*O	2.6
1953	*NY-A	125	395	64	121	26	4	10	58	82	29	.306	**.429**	.468	147	27	29	82	2	7	-4	**.996**	4	*O	2.5
1954	NY-A	97	304	33	76	12	5	3	40	53	35	.250	.361	.352	99	-0	1	42	3	4	-2	.983	-1	O	-0.5
1955	Bal-A	47	145	22	32	6	2	3	18	24	18	.221	.335	.352	91	-3	-1	18	1	1	-0	1.000	-8	O	-1.1
	Cle-A	79	259	33	72	15	1	5	35	36	15	.278	.372	.402	104	4	2	38	2	4	-2	.993	-3	O	-0.5
	Yr	126	404	55	104	21	3	8	53	60	33	.257	.359	.384	100	1	1	57	3	5	-2	.995	-11	*O	-1.6
1956	Cle-A	100	317	56	83	17	0	8	38	69	29	.262	.398	.391	107	7	6	53	2	6	-3	.981	-0	O	-0.2
1957	Cle-A	133	430	74	138	25	2	19	78	64	35	.321	.412	.521	155	33	34	94	0	5	-3	.992	11	*O	3.5
1958	Bal-A	133	413	57	114	16	1	15	65	66	49	.276	.378	.429	128	14	17	68	4	2	0	.974	-10	*O	0.1
1959	Bal-A★	140	440	63	132	22	2	14	77	78	35	.300	.405	.455	139	24	26	87	1	1	-0	.981	-13	*O	0.7
1960	Bal-A	140	435	68	123	18	3	11	62	84	40	.283	.403	.414	123	17	18	80	3	0	1	.995	-3	*O	1.0
1961	Was-A	110	342	39	107	16	4	10	57	50	24	.313	.404	.471	135	17	18	66	1	0	0	.988	-3	O	1.0
1962	Was-A	44	107	19	30	4	0	5	16	24	5	.280	.421	.458	138	7	7	23	1	0	0	.953	-4	O	0.1
	NY-N	81	190	18	52	8	1	5	24	24	22	.274	.358	.405	103	2	1	28	0	0	0	.986	-6	O	-0.8
Total	17	1796	5587	830	1585	257	63	147	830	921	479	.284	.388	.431	123	186	202	986	29	45		.989	-31	*O	8.0

■ SAM WOODRUFF
Woodruff, Orville Francis b: 12/27/1876, Chilo, Ohio d: 7/22/37, Cincinnati, Ohio BR/TR, 5'9", 160 lbs. Deb: 4/14/04

YEAR	TM/L	G	AB	R	H	2B	3B	HR	RBI	BB	SO	AVG	OBP	SLG	PRO+	BR	/A	RC	SB	CS	SBR	FA	FR	POS	TPR
1904	Cin-N	87	306	20	58	14	3	0	20	19		.190	.242	.255	49	-17	-20	23	9			.932	-4	32/SO	-2.3
1910	Cin-N	21	61	6	9	1	0	0	2	7	8	.148	.235	.164	18	-6	-6	3	2			.933	-1	3/2	-0.7
Total	2	108	367	26	67	15	3	0	22	26	8	.183	.241	.240	44	-23	-26	26	11			.932	-5	/32SO	-3.0

■ PETE WOODRUFF
Woodruff, Peter Frank b: Richmond, Va. BR/TR, Deb: 9/19/1899

YEAR	TM/L	G	AB	R	H	2B	3B	HR	RBI	BB	SO	AVG	OBP	SLG	PRO+	BR	/A	RC	SB	CS	SBR	FA	FR	POS	TPR
1899	NY-N	20	61	11	15	1	1	2	7	9		.246	.343	.393	105	0	0	9	3			1.000	-1	O/1	-0.2

■ AL WOODS
Woods, Alvis b: 8/8/53, Oakland, Cal. BL/TL, 6'3", 195 lbs. Deb: 4/07/77

YEAR	TM/L	G	AB	R	H	2B	3B	HR	RBI	BB	SO	AVG	OBP	SLG	PRO+	BR	/A	RC	SB	CS	SBR	FA	FR	POS	TPR
1977	Tor-A	122	440	58	125	17	4	6	35	36	38	.284	.338	.382	94	-2	-3	55	8	7	-2	.969	-2	*O/D	-1.2
1978	Tor-A	62	220	19	53	12	3	3	25	11	23	.241	.280	.364	78	-6	-7	21	1	2	-1	.978	3	O	-0.7
1979	Tor-A	132	436	57	121	24	4	5	36	40	28	.278	.340	.385	94	-3	-3	58	6	4	-1	.967	3	*O	-0.6
1980	Tor-A	109	373	54	112	18	2	15	47	37	35	.300	.365	.480	124	15	13	66	4	4	-1	.991	6	OD	1.4
1981	Tor-A	85	288	20	71	15	0	1	21	19	31	.247	.293	.309	69	-10	-12	25	3	4	-2	.973	3	O/D	-1.4
1982	Tor-A	85	201	20	47	11	1	3	24	21	20	.234	.306	.343	71	-6	-8	21	1	3	-2	.970	-7	OD	-1.8
1986	Min-A	23	28	5	9	1	0	2	8	3	5	.321	.387	.571	153	2	2	6	0	0	0	.000	0	/D	0.2
Total	7	618	1986	233	538	98	14	35	196	167	180	.271	.328	.387	93	-10	-19	252	23	24	-8	.974	6	O/D	-4.1

■ GARY WOODS
Woods, Gary Lee b: 7/20/54, Santa Barbara, Cal BR/TR, 6'2", 190 lbs. Deb: 9/14/76

YEAR	TM/L	G	AB	R	H	2B	3B	HR	RBI	BB	SO	AVG	OBP	SLG	PRO+	BR	/A	RC	SB	CS	SBR	FA	FR	POS	TPR
1976	Oak-A	6	8	0	1	0	0	0	0	0	3	.125	.125	.125	-28	-1	-1	0	0	0	0	1.000	-1	/OD	-0.2
1977	Tor-A	60	227	21	49	9	1	0	17	7	38	.216	.246	.264	38	-19	-19	14	5	4	-1	.994	3	O	-2.0
1978	Tor-A	8	19	1	3	1	0	0	0	1	1	.158	.200	.211	15	-2	-2	1	1	0	0	1.000	-0	/O	-0.2
1980	*Hou-N	19	53	8	20	5	0	2	15	2	9	.377	.400	.585	186	5	5	12	1	0	0	1.000	-1	O	0.4
1981	*Hou-N	54	110	10	23	4	1	0	12	11	22	.209	.281	.264	58	-6	-6	8	2	1	0	.984	0	O	-0.7
1982	Chi-N	117	245	28	66	15	1	4	30	21	48	.269	.327	.388	97	-0	-1	31	3	3	-1	1.000	-7	*O	-1.1
1983	Chi-N	93	190	25	46	9	0	4	22	15	27	.242	.298	.353	76	-6	-7	18	5	3	-0	.971	1	O/2	-0.8
1984	*Chi-N	87	98	13	23	4	1	3	10	15	21	.235	.336	.388	94	1	-1	13	2	1	0	1.000	-13	O/2	-1.5
1985	Chi-N	81	82	11	20	3	0	0	4	14	18	.244	.354	.280	72	-2	-3	9	0	1	-1	1.000	-13	O	-1.8
Total	9	525	1032	117	251	50	4	13	110	86	187	.243	.303	.337	76	-31	-35	106	19	13	-2	.992	-31	O/2D	-7.9

YEAR	TM/L	G	AB	R	H	2B	3B	HR	RBI	BB	SO	AVG	OBP	SLG	PRO+	BR	/A	RC	SB	CS	SBR	FA	FR	POS	TPR
■ JIM WOODS Woods, James Jerome "Woody" b: 9/17/39, Chicago, Ill. BR/TR, 6', 175 lbs. Deb: 9/27/57																									
1957	Chi-N	2	0	1	0	0	0	0	0	0	0	—	—	—	—	0	0	0	0	0	0	.000	0	R	0.0
1960	Phi-N	11	34	4	6	0	0	1	3	3	13	.176	.243	.265	39	-3	-3	2	0	0	0	.939	2	3	-0.1
1961	Phi-N	23	48	6	11	3	0	2	9	4	15	.229	.302	.417	89	-1	-1	5	0	0	0	.968	-1	3	-0.1
Total	3	36	82	11	17	3	0	3	12	7	28	.207	.278	.354	69	-4	-4	7	0	0	0	.953	1	/3	-0.2
■ RON WOODS Woods, Ronald Lawrence b: 2/1/43, Hamilton, Ohio BR/TR, 5'10", 173 lbs. Deb: 4/22/69																									
1969	Det-A	17	15	3	4	0	0	1	3	2	3	.267	.353	.467	122	1	0	3	0	0	0	1.000	-2	/O	-0.2
	NY-A	72	171	18	30	5	2	1	7	22	29	.175	.273	.246	48	-12	-11	13	2	0	1	1.000	-3	O	-1.7
	Yr	89	186	21	34	5	2	2	10	24	32	.183	.280	.263	54	-12	-11	15	2	0	1	1.000	-5	O	-1.9
1970	NY-A	95	225	30	51	5	3	8	27	33	35	.227	.326	.382	100	-2	-0	27	4	2	0	.974	-6	O	-1.0
1971	NY-A	25	32	4	8	1	0	1	2	4	2	.250	.333	.375	107	0	0	4	0	0	0	.929	-1	/O	-0.1
	Mon-N	51	138	26	41	7	3	1	17	19	18	.297	.382	.413	125	5	5	21	0	2	-1	.989	2	O	0.4
1972	Mon-N	97	221	21	57	5	1	10	31	22	33	.258	.325	.425	110	3	3	30	3	3	-1	.991	-2	O	-0.3
1973	Mon-N	135	318	45	73	11	3	3	31	56	34	.230	.345	.311	80	-5	-7	39	12	6	0	.977	-11	*O	-2.3
1974	Mon-N	90	127	15	26	0	0	1	12	17	17	.205	.303	.228	48	-8	-9	9	6	5	-1	.987	1	O	-1.1
Total	6	582	1247	162	290	34	12	26	130	175	171	.233	.328	.342	87	-18	-19	146	27	18	-3	.984	-22	O	-6.3
■ TRACY WOODSON Woodson, Tracy Michael b: 10/5/62, Richmond, Va. BR/TR, 6'3", 215 lbs. Deb: 4/07/87																									
1987	LA-N	53	136	14	31	8	1	1	11	9	21	.228	.286	.324	63	-8	-7	12	1	1	-0	.958	-1	3/1	-0.9
1988	*LA-N	65	173	15	43	4	1	3	15	7	32	.249	.282	.335	79	-6	-5	15	1	2	-1	.938	-5	31	-1.3
1989	LA-N	4	6	0	0	0	0	0	0	0	1	.000	.000	.000	-99	-2	-2	0	0	0	0	1.000	0	/3	-0.2
1992	StL-N	31	114	9	35	8	0	1	22	3	10	.307	.331	.404	108	1	1	15	0	0	0	.945	-6	3/1	-0.6
Total	4	153	429	38	109	20	2	5	48	19	64	.254	.292	.345	79	-14	-13	43	2	3	-1	.948	-12	3/1	-3.0
■ WOODY WOODWARD Woodward, William Frederick b: 9/23/42, Miami, Fla. BR/TR, 6'2", 185 lbs. Deb: 9/09/63																									
1963	Mil-N	10	2	1	0	0	0	0	0	0	0	.000	.000	.000	-99	-1	-1	0	0	0	0	1.000	4	/S	0.4
1964	Mil-N	77	115	18	24	2	1	0	11	6	28	.209	.260	.243	43	-9	-9	7	0	1	-1	.958	13	2S/31	0.6
1965	Mil-N	112	265	17	55	7	4	0	11	10	50	.208	.236	.264	41	-21	-21	16	2	2	-1	.977	11	*S/2	-0.6
1966	Atl-N	144	455	46	120	23	3	0	43	37	54	.264	.325	.327	81	-10	-11	49	2	2	-1	.973	-6	2S	-0.7
1967	Atl-N	136	429	30	97	15	2	0	25	37	51	.226	.289	.270	62	-21	-20	32	0	6	-4	**.982**	9	*2S	-0.7
1968	Atl-N	12	24	2	4	1	0	0	1	1	6	.167	.200	.208	23	-2	-2	1	1	0	0	.973	3	/S32	0.2
	Cin-N	56	119	13	29	2	0	0	10	7	23	.244	.297	.261	64	-4	-5	10	1	0	0	.968	-3	S/21	-0.6
	Yr	68	143	15	33	3	0	0	11	8	29	.231	.281	.252	58	-7	-7	10	2	0	1	.969	-1	S2/31	-0.4
1969	Cin-N	97	241	36	63	12	0	0	15	24	40	.261	.333	.311	77	-5	-7	25	3	2	-0	.966	-2	S/2	-0.1
1970	*Cin-N	100	264	23	59	8	3	1	14	20	21	.223	.283	.288	53	-17	-17	21	1	2	-1	.973	2	S32/1	-0.8
1971	Cin-N	136	273	22	66	9	1	0	18	27	28	.242	.310	.282	70	-11	-10	25	4	0	1	.987	-5	S3/2	-0.6
Total	9	880	2187	208	517	79	14	1	148	169	301	.236	.295	.287	64	-101	-103	186	14	15	-5	.974	24	S2/31	-2.9
■ JUNIOR WOOTEN Wooten, Earl Hazwell b: 1/16/24, Pelzer, S.C. BR/TL, 5'11", 160 lbs. Deb: 9/16/47																									
1947	Was-A	6	24	0	2	0	0	0	1	0	4	.083	.083	.083	-55	-5	-5	0	1	0	0	.905	-1	/O	-0.6
1948	Was-A	88	258	34	66	8	3	1	23	24	21	.256	.324	.322	74	-10	-9	29	2	1	0	.979	1	O/1P	-1.1
Total	2	94	282	34	68	8	3	1	24	24	25	.241	.305	.301	64	-15	-14	29	3	1	0	.972	1	/O1P	-1.7
■ FAVEL WORDSWORTH Wordsworth, Favel Perry b: 12/22/1850, New York, N.Y. d: 8/12/1888, New York, N.Y. Deb: 4/28/1873																									
1873	Res-n	12	42	5	10	1	0	0	3	2	1	.238	.273	.262	63	-2	-1	3						S/O	-0.1
■ CHUCK WORKMAN Workman, Charles Thomas b: 1/6/15, Leeton, Mo. d: 1/3/53, Kansas City, Mo. BL/TR, 6', 175 lbs. Deb: 9/18/38																									
1938	Cle-A	2	5	1	2	0	0	0	0	0	0	.400	.400	.400	103	0	0	1	0	0	0	.500	-0	/O	0.0
1941	Cle-A	9	4	2	0	0	0	0	0	1	1	.000	.200	.000	-45	-1	-1	0	0	0	0	.000	0	H	-0.1
1943	Bos-N	153	615	71	153	17	1	10	67	53	72	.249	.311	.328	86	-12	-11	66	12			.988	6	*O/13	-1.4
1944	Bos-N	140	418	46	87	18	3	11	53	42	41	.208	.287	.344	74	-14	-16	43	1			.983	-3	*O3	-2.3
1945	Bos-N	139	514	77	141	16	2	25	87	51	58	.274	.347	.459	122	14	14	84	9			.910	-17	*3O	-0.1
1946	Bos-N	25	48	5	8	2	0	2	7	3	11	.167	.231	.333	58	-3	-3	4	0			.920	-1	O	-0.5
	Pit-N	58	145	11	32	4	1	2	16	11	19	.221	.280	.303	64	-7	-7	13	2			1.000	6	O/3	-0.3
	Yr	83	193	16	40	6	1	4	23	14	30	.207	.268	.311	63	-10	-10	16	2			.986	5	O/3	-0.8
Total	6	526	1749	213	423	57	7	50	230	161	202	.242	.311	.368	91	-22	-24	209	24	0		.985	-8	O3/1	-4.7
■ HANK WORKMAN Workman, Henry Kilgariff b: 2/5/26, Los Angeles, Cal. BL/TR, 6'1", 185 lbs. Deb: 9/04/50																									
1950	NY-A	2	5	1	1	0	0	0	0	0	1	.200	.200	.200	3	-1	-1	0	0	0	0	1.000	-0	/1	-0.1
■ HERB WORTH Worth, Herbert b: 5/2/1847, Brooklyn, N.Y. d: 4/27/14, Brooklyn, N.Y. Deb: 7/29/1872																									
1872	Atl-n	1	6	1	1	1	0	0	1	0	0	.167	.167	.333	43	-0	-1	0						/O	0.0
■ CRAIG WORTHINGTON Worthington, Craig Richard b: 4/17/65, Los Angeles, Cal. BR/TR, 6', 200 lbs. Deb: 4/26/88																									
1988	Bal-A	26	81	5	15	2	0	2	4	9	24	.185	.267	.284	56	-5	-5	6	1	0	0	.961	1	3	-0.4
1989	Bal-A	145	497	57	123	23	0	15	70	61	114	.247	.335	.384	105	2	4	65	1	2	-1	.951	-10	*3	-0.6
1990	Bal-A	133	425	46	96	17	0	8	44	63	96	.226	.330	.322	86	-8	-6	47	1	2	-1	.945	-12	*3/D	-1.9
1991	Bal-A	31	102	11	23	3	0	4	12	12	14	.225	.313	.373	93	-2	-1	12	0	1	-1	.975	-3	3	-0.4
1992	Cle-A	9	24	0	4	0	0	0	2	2	4	.167	.231	.167	13	-3	-3	1	0	1	-1	.857	2	/3	-0.2
Total	5	344	1129	119	261	45	0	29	132	147	252	.231	.324	.348	91	-15	-11	131	3	6	-3	.949	-22	3/D	-3.5
■ RED WORTHINGTON Worthington, Robert Lee b: 4/24/06, Alhambra, Cal. d: 12/8/63, Sepulveda, Cal. BR/TR, 5'11", 170 lbs. Deb: 4/14/31																									
1931	Bos-N	128	491	47	143	25	10	4	44	26	38	.291	.328	.407	100	-3	-1	66	1			**.988**	-3	*O	-1.3
1932	Bos-N	105	435	62	132	35	8	8	61	15	24	.303	.330	.476	118	7	9	68	1			.987	-1	*O	0.1
1933	Bos-N	17	45	3	7	4	0	0	0	1	3	.156	.174	.244	20	-5	-4	1	0			.900	-1	O	-0.7
1934	Bos-N	41	65	6	16	5	0	0	6	6	5	.246	.319	.323	78	-2	-2	6	0			.920	-1	O	-0.3
	StL-N	1	1	0	0	0	0	0	0	0	1	.000	.000	.000	-94	-0	-0	0	0			.000	0	H	0.0
	Yr	42	66	6	16	5	0	0	6	6	6	.242	.315	.318	75	-3	-2	6	0			.920	-1	O	-0.3
Total	4	292	1037	118	298	69	18	12	111	48	71	.287	.321	.423	103	-4	1	142	2			.981	-7	O	-2.2
■ CHUCK WORTMAN Wortman, William Lewis b: 1/5/1892, Baltimore, Md. d: 8/19/77, Las Vegas, Nev. BR/TR, 5'7", 150 lbs. Deb: 7/20/16																									
1916	Chi-N	69	234	17	47	4	2	2	16	18	22	.201	.258	.261	54	-11	-14	17	4			.908	-21	S	-3.6
1917	Chi-N	75	190	24	33	4	1	0	9	18	23	.174	.245	.205	36	-13	-15	12	6			.918	-8	S/23	-2.4
1918	*Chi-N	17	17	4	2	0	0	1	3	1	2	.118	.167	.294	39	-1	-1	1	3			.864	2	/2S	0.1
Total	3	161	441	45	82	8	3	3	28	37	47	.186	.249	.238	46	-26	-30	30	13			.913	-27	S/23	-5.9
■ RON WOTUS Wotus, Ronald Allan b: 3/3/61, Colchester, Conn. BR/TR, 6'1", 164 lbs. Deb: 9/03/83																									
1983	Pit-N	5	3	0	0	0	0	0	0	0	1	.000	.000	.000	-98	-1	-1	0	0	0	0	1.000	1	/S2	0.0
1984	Pit-N	27	55	4	12	6	0	0	2	6	8	.218	.295	.327	75	-2	-2	5	0	0	0	.976	9	S/2	0.9
Total	2	32	58	4	12	6	0	0	2	6	9	.207	.281	.310	66	-3	-3	5	0	0	0	.976	10	/S2	0.9
■ JIMMY WOULFE Woulfe, James Joseph b: 11/25/1859, New Orleans, La. d: 12/20/24, New Orleans, La. TR , 5'11", Deb: 5/16/1884																									
1884	Cin-a	8	34	3	5	0	1	0		1		.147	.171	.206	23	-3	-3	1				.625	-3	/O3	-0.6
	Pit-a	15	53	7	6	1	0	0		0		.113	.113	.132	-19	-7	-7	1				.893	1	O	-0.6

YEAR	TM/L	G	AB	R	H	2B	3B	HR	RBI	BB	SO	AVG	OBP	SLG	PRO+	BR	/A	RC	SB	CS	SBR	FA	FR	POS	TPR
	Yr	23	87	10	11	1	1	0		1		.126	.136	.161	-2	-9	-10	2				.795	-2	O/3	-1.2

■ **AL WRIGHT** Wright, Albert Edgar "A-1" b: 11/11/12, San Francisco, Cal. BR/TR, 6'1.5", 170 lbs. Deb: 4/25/33

YEAR	TM/L	G	AB	R	H	2B	3B	HR	RBI	BB	SO	AVG	OBP	SLG	PRO+	BR	/A	RC	SB	CS	SBR	FA	FR	POS	TPR
1933	Bos-N	4	1	0	1	0	0	0	0	0	0	1.000	1.000	1.000	515	0	0	1	0			.500	-0	/2	0.0

■ **AB WRIGHT** Wright, Albert Owen b: 11/16/05, Terlton, Okla. BR/TR, 6'1.5", 190 lbs. Deb: 4/20/35

YEAR	TM/L	G	AB	R	H	2B	3B	HR	RBI	BB	SO	AVG	OBP	SLG	PRO+	BR	/A	RC	SB	CS	SBR	FA	FR	POS	TPR
1935	Cle-A	67	160	17	38	11	1	2	18	10	17	.237	.291	.356	65	-8	-9	17	2	1	0	.984	-8	O	-1.7
1944	Bos-N	71	195	20	50	9	0	7	35	18	31	.256	.326	.410	102	1	0	26	0			.968	-4	O	-0.6
Total	2	138	355	37	88	20	1	9	53	28	48	.248	.310	.386	85	-7	-9	43	2	1		.974	-11	/O	-2.3

■ **CY WRIGHT** Wright, Ceylon b: 8/16/1893, Minneapolis, Minn. d: 11/7/47, Hines, Ill. BL/TR, 5'9", 150 lbs. Deb: 6/30/16

YEAR	TM/L	G	AB	R	H	2B	3B	HR	RBI	BB	SO	AVG	OBP	SLG	PRO+	BR	/A	RC	SB	CS	SBR	FA	FR	POS	TPR
1916	Chi-A	8	18	0	0	0	0	0	0	1	7	.000	.053	.000	-83	-4	-4	0	0			.844	-1	/S	-0.5

■ **GLENN WRIGHT** Wright, Forest Glenn "Buckshot" b: 2/6/01, Archie, Mo. d: 4/6/84, Olathe, Kan. BR/TR, 5'11", 170 lbs. Deb: 4/15/24

YEAR	TM/L	G	AB	R	H	2B	3B	HR	RBI	BB	SO	AVG	OBP	SLG	PRO+	BR	/A	RC	SB	CS	SBR	FA	FR	POS	TPR
1924	Pit-N	153	616	80	177	28	18	7	111	27	52	.287	.318	.425	96	-4	-5	82	14	6	1	.946	11	*S	2.3
1925	*Pit-N	153	614	97	189	32	10	18	121	31	32	.308	.341	.480	100	4	-1	97	3	7	-3	.939	0	*S/3	1.1
1926	Pit-N	119	458	73	141	15	15	8	77	19	26	.308	.335	.459	106	6	3	67	6			.927	-13	*S	0.2
1927	*Pit-N	143	570	78	160	26	4	9	105	39	46	.281	.328	.388	85	-8	-13	71	4			.942	-17	*S	-1.5
1928	Pit-N	108	407	63	126	20	8	8	66	21	53	.310	.343	.457	103	3	1	61	3			.927	-24	*S/1O	-1.1
1929	Bro-N	24	25	4	5	0	0	1	6	3	6	.200	.286	.320	51	-2	-2	2	0			.667	-3	/S	-0.4
1930	Bro-N	135	532	83	171	28	12	22	126	32	70	.321	.360	.543	116	10	11	99	2			.964	-2	*S	2.2
1931	Bro-N	77	268	36	76	9	4	9	32	14	35	.284	.324	.448	106	1	1	39	1			.942	6	S	1.4
1932	Bro-N	127	446	50	122	31	5	11	60	12	57	.274	.293	.439	96	-5	-4	57	4			.939	8	*S/1	1.3
1933	Bro-N	71	192	19	49	13	0	1	18	11	24	.255	.299	.339	85	-5	-4	18	1			.936	-4	S/13	-0.6
1935	Chi-A	9	25	1	3	1	0	0	1	0	6	.120	.120	.160	-27	-5	-5	1	0	0	0	.943	0	/2	-0.4
Total	11	1119	4153	584	1219	203	76	94	723	209	407	.294	.328	.447	99	-5	-19	594	38	13		.941	-37	*S/1230	4.5

■ **GEORGE WRIGHT** Wright, George b: 1/28/1847, Yonkers, N.Y. d: 8/21/37, Boston, Mass. BR/TR, 5'9.5", 150 lbs. Deb: 5/05/1871 FMH

YEAR	TM/L	G	AB	R	H	2B	3B	HR	RBI	BB	SO	AVG	OBP	SLG	PRO+	BR	/A	RC	SB	CS	SBR	FA	FR	POS	TPR
1871	Bos-n	16	80	33	33	7	5	0	11	6	1	.412	.453	.625	200	11	10	27	9					S/1	0.7
1872	Bos-n	48	255	87	87	16	5	2	33	3	1	.341	.349	.467	141	14	11	45						*S	0.9
1873	Bos-n	59	325	99	126	13	7	3	48	8	2	.388	.402	.498	151	25	19	66						*S	1.1
1874	Bos-n	60	313	76	106	11	**15**	2		7		.339	.353	.489	156	22	19	55						*S	1.3
1875	Bos-n	79	406	105	135	18	7	1		2		.333	.336	.419	154	23	21	59						*S/P	1.5
1876	Bos-N	70	335	72	100	18	6	1	34	8	9	.299	.315	.397	134	12	11	43				.888	13	*S/2P	2.1
1877	Bos-N	61	290	58	80	15	1	0	35	9	15	.276	.298	.334	95	-0	-2	30				.878	9	*2/S	0.8
1878	Bos-N	59	267	35	60	5	1	0	12	6	22	.225	.242	.251	58	-11	-13	17				.947	11	*S	0.0
1879	Pro-N	85	388	79	107	15	10	1	42	13	20	.276	.299	.374	122	8	9	44				**.947**	11	*S	0.0
1880	Bos-N	1	4	2	1	0	0	0	0	0	0	.250	.250	.250	72	-0	-0	0				1.000	-0	/S	0.0
1881	Bos-N	7	25	4	5	0	0	0	0	3	1	.200	.286	.200	58	-1	-1	1				.963	-3	/S	-0.3
1882	Pro-N	46	185	14	30	1	2	0	9	4	36	.162	.180	.189	19	-16	-16	6				.873	-7	S	-2.0
Total	5 n	262	1379	400	487	65	39	8	92	26	4	.353	.365	.474	154	95	80	252						S/P1	5.5
Total	7	329	1494	264	383	54	20	2	132	43	103	.256	.277	.323	93	-8	-12	142				.911	43	S/2P	3.8

■ **GEORGE WRIGHT** Wright, George De Witt b: 12/22/58, Oklahoma City, Okla BB/TR, 5'11", 180 lbs. Deb: 4/10/82

YEAR	TM/L	G	AB	R	H	2B	3B	HR	RBI	BB	SO	AVG	OBP	SLG	PRO+	BR	/A	RC	SB	CS	SBR	FA	FR	POS	TPR
1982	Tex-A	150	557	69	147	20	5	11	50	30	78	.264	.305	.377	91	-11	-8	61	3	7	-3	.981	11	*O	-0.4
1983	Tex-A	162	634	79	175	28	6	18	80	41	82	.276	.322	.424	106	2	3	84	8	7	-2	.985	10	*O	0.7
1984	Tex-A	101	383	40	93	19	4	9	48	15	54	.243	.275	.384	78	-11	-13	39	0	2	-1	.983	-3	OD	-2.0
1985	Tex-A	109	363	21	69	13	0	2	18	25	49	.190	.242	.242	33	-33	-34	19	4	7	-3	.991	-1	*O/D	-4.1
1986	Tex-A	49	106	10	23	3	1	2	7	4	23	.217	.252	.321	53	-7	-7	7	3	5	-2	.969	-5	O	-1.5
	Mon-N	56	117	12	22	5	2	0	5	11	28	.188	.264	.265	47	-9	-8	8	1	1	-0	1.000	-2	O	-1.3
Total	5	627	2160	231	529	88	18	42	208	126	314	.245	.289	.361	78	-69	-67	218	19	29	-12	.984	10	O/D	-8.6

■ **JOE WRIGHT** Wright, Joseph b: 1873, Pittsburgh, Pa. BL/TL, 5'8", 175 lbs. Deb: 7/14/1895

YEAR	TM/L	G	AB	R	H	2B	3B	HR	RBI	BB	SO	AVG	OBP	SLG	PRO+	BR	/A	RC	SB	CS	SBR	FA	FR	POS	TPR
1895	Lou-N	60	228	30	63	10	4	1	30	12	28	.276	.315	.368	83	-8	-5	30	7			.963	-2	O	-1.0
1896	Lou-N	2	7	0	2	0	0	0	0	0	1	.286	.286	.286	55	-0	-0	1	0			1.000	-0	/O	-0.1
	Pit-N	15	52	5	16	2	1	0	6	1	2	.308	.321	.385	91	-1	-1	7	1			.958	-2	O/3	-0.3
	Yr	17	59	5	18	2	1	0	6	1	3	.305	.317	.373	87	-2	-1	7	1			.962	-2	O/3	-0.4
Total	2	77	287	35	81	12	5	1	36	13	31	.282	.316	.369	84	-10	-7	37	8			.963	-5	/O3	-1.4

■ **PAT WRIGHT** Wright, Patrick Francis b: 7/5/1865, Pottsville, Pa. d: 5/29/43, Springfield, Ill. BB/TR, 6'2", 190 lbs. Deb: 7/11/1890

YEAR	TM/L	G	AB	R	H	2B	3B	HR	RBI	BB	SO	AVG	OBP	SLG	PRO+	BR	/A	RC	SB	CS	SBR	FA	FR	POS	TPR
1890	Chi-N	1	2	0	0	0	0	0	0	1	0	.000	.333	.000	1	-0	-0	0	0			1.000	0	/2	0.0

■ **SAM WRIGHT** Wright, Samuel b: 11/25/1848, New York, N.Y. d: 5/6/28, Boston, Mass. BR/TR, 5'7.5", 146 lbs. Deb: 4/21/1875 F

YEAR	TM/L	G	AB	R	H	2B	3B	HR	RBI	BB	SO	AVG	OBP	SLG	PRO+	BR	/A	RC	SB	CS	SBR	FA	FR	POS	TPR
1875	NH-n	33	128	10	24	4	0	0		1		.188	.194	.219	49	-7	-5	6						S	-0.5
1876	Bos-N	2	8	0	1	0	0	0	0	0	0	.125	.125	.125	-16	-1	-1	0				.778	-0	/S	-0.1
1880	Cin-N	9	34	0	3	0	0	0	0	0	5	.088	.088	.088	-40	-5	-5	0				.889	-2	/S	-0.6
1881	Bos-N	1	4	0	1	0	0	0	0	0	0	.250	.250	.250	60	-0	-0	0				.667	-1	/S	-0.1
Total	3	12	46	0	5	0	0	0	0	0	5	.109	.109	.109	-27	-6	-6	1				.843	-3	/S	-0.8

■ **TAFFY WRIGHT** Wright, Taft Shedron b: 8/10/11, Tabor City, N.C. d: 10/22/81, Orlando, Fla. BL/TR, 5'10", 180 lbs. Deb: 4/18/38

YEAR	TM/L	G	AB	R	H	2B	3B	HR	RBI	BB	SO	AVG	OBP	SLG	PRO+	BR	/A	RC	SB	CS	SBR	FA	FR	POS	TPR
1938	Was-A	100	263	37	92	18	10	2	36	13	17	.350	.389	.517	134	9	12	52	1	2	-1	.982	-4	O	0.5
1939	Was-A	129	499	77	154	29	11	4	93	38	19	.309	.359	.435	110	1	6	78	1	2	-1	.950	-3	*O	-0.2
1940	Chi-A	147	581	79	196	31	9	5	88	43	25	.337	.385	.448	114	13	12	101	4	7	-3	.963	-4	*O	-0.2
1941	Chi-A	136	513	71	165	35	5	10	97	60	27	.322	.399	.468	130	22	23	101	5	4	-1	.973	-2	*O	1.1
1942	Chi-A	85	300	43	100	13	5	0	47	48	9	.333	.432	.410	141	18	19	55	1	8	-5	.968	-1	O	0.9
1946	Chi-A	115	422	46	116	19	4	7	52	42	17	.275	.342	.389	108	2	4	55	10	3	1	.991	-3	*O	-0.3
1947	Chi-A	124	401	48	130	13	0	4	54	48	17	.324	.398	.387	123	12	14	64	8	6	-1	.971	-4	*O	0.3
1948	Chi-A	134	455	50	127	15	6	4	61	38	18	.279	.341	.365	91	-8	-6	57	2	1	0	.987	1	*O	-1.2
1949	Phi-A	59	149	14	35	2	5	2	25	16	6	.235	.321	.356	82	-5	-4	16	0	0	0	.970	-0	O	-0.6
Total	9	1029	3583	465	1115	175	55	38	553	346	155	.311	.376	.423	116	64	79	580	32	33	-10	.972	-21	O	0.3

■ **TOM WRIGHT** Wright, Thomas Everette b: 9/22/23, Shelby, N.C. BL/TR, 5'11.5", 180 lbs. Deb: 9/15/48

YEAR	TM/L	G	AB	R	H	2B	3B	HR	RBI	BB	SO	AVG	OBP	SLG	PRO+	BR	/A	RC	SB	CS	SBR	FA	FR	POS	TPR
1948	Bos-A	3	2	1	1	0	1	0	0	0	0	.500	.500	1.500	400	1	1	2	0	0	0	.000	0	H	0.1
1949	Bos-A	5	4	1	1	1	0	0	1	1	1	.250	.400	.500	128	0	0	1	0	0	0	.000	0	H	0.0
1950	Bos-A	54	107	17	34	7	0	0	20	6	18	.318	.360	.383	82	-2	-3	15	0	0	0	.953	-2	O	-0.6
1951	Bos-A	28	63	8	14	1	1	1	9	11	8	.222	.347	.317	73	-1	-2	7	0	0	0	.950	-4	O	-0.7
1952	StL-A	29	66	6	16	0	0	1	6	12	20	.242	.359	.288	79	-1	-1	7	1	1	-0	.976	1	O	-0.2
	Chi-A	60	132	15	34	10	2	1	21	16	16	.258	.342	.386	102	0	0	19	1	0	0	.969	-2	O	-0.2
	Yr	89	198	21	50	10	2	2	27	28	36	.253	.348	.354	94	-1	-1	26	2	1	0	.971	-1	O	-0.4
1953	Chi-A	77	132	14	33	5	3	2	25	12	21	.250	.322	.379	86	-2	-3	17	0	0	0	.978	-5	O	-0.9
1954	Was-A	76	171	13	42	4	4	1	17	18	38	.246	.325	.333	85	-4	-3	20	0	0	0	1.000	-2	O	-0.7
1955	Was-A	7	7	0	0	0	0	0	0	0	1	.000	.000	.000	-99	-2	-2	0	0	0	0	.000	0	H	-0.2
1956	Was-A	2	1	0	0	0	0	0	0	0	0	.000	.000	.000	-99	-0	-0	0	0	0	0	.000	0	H	0.0
Total	9	341	685	75	175	28	11	6	99	76	123	.255	.336	.355	85	-12	-14	87	2	1	0	.977	-13	O	-3.4

YEAR	TM/L	G	AB	R	H	2B	3B	HR	RBI	BB	SO	AVG	OBP	SLG	PRO+	BR	/A	RC	SB	CS	SBR	FA	FR	POS	TPR

■ DICK WRIGHT   Wright, Willard James   b: 5/5/1890, Worcester, N.Y.   d: 1/24/52, Bethlehem, Pa.   BR/TR, 5'10", 170 lbs.   Deb: 6/30/15

| 1915 | Bro-F | 4 | 5 | 0 | 0 | 0 | 0 | 0 | 0 | 0 | 0 | .000 | .000 | .000 | -99 | -1 | -1 | 0 | 0 | | | .833 | -1 | /C | -0.2 |

■ BILL WRIGHT   Wright, William H.   Deb: 9/16/1887

| 1887 | Was-N | 1 | 3 | 0 | 2 | 0 | 0 | 0 | 0 | 0 | 0 | .667 | .667 | .667 | 290 | 1 | 1 | 1 | 0 | | | .778 | -0 | /C | 0.0 |

■ HARRY WRIGHT   Wright, William Henry   b: 1/10/1835, Sheffield, England   d: 10/3/1895, Atlantic City, N.J.   BR/TR, 5'9.5", 157 lbs.   Deb: 5/05/1871   FMH

1871	Bos-n	31	147	42	44	5	2	0	26	13	2	.299	.356	.361	103	2	1	22	7					*O/PSM	0.2
1872	Bos-n	48	208	39	54	6	0	0	22	9	2	.260	.290	.288	75	-5	-7	18						*O/PM	-0.3
1873	Bos-n	58	266	57	67	8	3	2	33	10	3	.252	.279	.327	72	-7	-12	25						*O/PM	-0.5
1874	Bos-n	40	184	44	56	9	2	2		4		.304	.319	.408	123	6	4	25						*O/PCM	0.5
1875	Bos-n	1	4	1	1	0	0	0		0		.250	.250	.250	71	-0	-0	0						/OM	0.0
1876	Bos-N	1	3	0	0	0	0	0	0	0	1	.000	.000	.000	-98	-1	-1	0				.000	-0	/OM	-0.1
1877	Bos-N	1	4	0	0	0	0	0	0	0	1	.000	.000	.000	-97	-1	-1	0				.667	1	/OM	0.0
Total	5 n	178	809	183	222	28	7	4	81	36	7	.274	.305	.341	89	-4	-14	89						O/PCS	-0.1
Total	2	2	7	0	0	0	0	0	0	0	2	.000	.000	.000	-97	-1	-2	0				.667	0	/O	-0.1

■ RASTY WRIGHT   Wright, William Smith   b: 1/31/1863, Birmingham, Mich.   d: 10/14/22, Duluth, Minn.   6'1", 258 lbs.   Deb: 4/17/1890

1890	Syr-a	88	348	82	106	10	6	0		69		.305	.428	.368	154	21	28	69	30			.907	4	O	2.5
	Cle-N	13	45	7	5	1	0	0	2	12	4	.111	.298	.133	29	-3	-3	3	3			.917	-1	O	-0.4
Total	1	101	393	89	111	11	6	0	2	81	4	.282	.412	.341	138	18	24	72	33			.908	3	O	2.1

■ RUSS WRIGHTSTONE   Wrightstone, Russell Guy   b: 3/18/1893, Bowmansdale, Pa.   d: 2/25/69, Harrisburg, Pa.   BL/TR, 5'10.5", 176 lbs.   Deb: 4/19/20

1920	Phi-N	76	206	23	54	6	1	3	17	10	25	.262	.303	.345	82	-4	-5	21	3	2	-0	.934	6	3/S2	0.3
1921	Phi-N	109	372	59	110	13	4	9	51	18	20	.296	.332	.425	92	-1	-5	51	4	4	-1	.922	4	3O/2	-0.1
1922	Phi-N	99	331	56	101	18	6	5	33	28	17	.305	.365	.441	98	3	-1	53	4	5	-2	.973	13	3S/1	1.5
1923	Phi-N	119	392	59	107	21	7	7	57	21	19	.273	.315	.416	82	-6	-12	51	5	2	0	.942	-4	3S/2	-0.7
1924	Phi-N	118	388	55	119	24	4	7	58	27	15	.307	.363	.443	102	8	2	62	5	4	-1	.944	-8	3/2SO	-0.6
1925	Phi-N	92	286	48	99	18	5	14	61	19	18	.346	.389	.591	135	19	15	63	0	3	-2	.937	-19	OS32/1	-0.6
1926	Phi-N	112	368	55	113	23	1	7	57	27	11	.307	.356	.432	106	5	3	55	5			.977	0	132/O	0.2
1927	Phi-N	141	533	62	163	24	5	6	75	48	20	.306	.365	.403	104	5	4	78	9			.989	1	*1/23	-0.4
1928	Phi-N	33	91	7	19	5	1	1	11	14	5	.209	.321	.319	65	-4	-5	10	0			.936	-4	O/1	-1.0
	NY-N	30	25	3	4	0	0	1	5	3	2	.160	.250	.280	38	-2	-2	2	0			1.000	-0	/1	-0.2
	Yr	63	116	10	23	5	1	2	16	17	7	.198	.306	.310	60	-6	-7	12	0			.936	-4	O/1	-1.2
Total	9	929	2992	427	889	152	34	60	425	215	152	.297	.349	.431	99	22	-7	447	35	20		.942	-12	310/S2	-1.0

■ ZEKE WRIGLEY   Wrigley, George Watson   b: 1/18/1874, Philadelphia, Pa.   d: 9/28/52, Philadelphia, Pa.   5'8.5", 150 lbs.   Deb: 8/31/1896

1896	Was-N	5	9	1	1	0	0	0	2	1	1	.111	.200	.111	-16	-1	-1	0	0			.909	3	/2S	0.1
1897	Was-N	104	388	65	110	14	8	3	64	21		.284	.320	.384	86	-10	-9	52	5			.885	-1	OS3/2	-0.9
1898	Was-N	111	400	50	98	9	10	2	39	20		.245	.283	.333	76	-14	-14	42	10			.895	10	S2/O3	0.1
1899	NY-N	4	15	1	3	0	0	0	1	1		.200	.250	.200	25	-2	-1	1	1			.818	-1	/3	-0.3
	Bro-N	15	49	4	10	2	2	0	11	3		.204	.250	.327	56	-3	-3	5	2			.870	-5	S/3	-0.7
	Yr	19	64	5	13	2	2	0	12	4		.203	.250	.297	49	-5	-5	6	3			.870	-6	S/3	-1.0
Total	4	239	861	121	222	25	20	5	117	46	1	.258	.296	.351	78	-30	-29	100	18			.892	5	S/O32	-1.7

■ RICK WRONA   Wrona, Richard James   b: 12/10/63, Tulsa, Okla.   BR/TR, 6'1", 185 lbs.   Deb: 9/03/88

1988	Chi-N	4	6	0	0	0	0	0	0	0	1	.000	.000	.000	-96	-2	-2	0	0	0	0	1.000	1	/C	0.0
1989	*Chi-N	38	92	11	26	2	1	2	14	2	21	.283	.305	.391	91	-1	-1	11	0	0	0	.983	2	C	0.2
1990	Chi-N	16	29	3	5	0	0	0	0	2	11	.172	.226	.172	10	-3	-4	1	1	0	0	.970	5	C	0.0
1992	Cin-N	11	23	0	4	0	0	0	0	0	3	.174	.174	.174	-1	-3	-3	0	0	0	0	.965	3	C/1	0.0
Total	4	69	150	14	35	2	1	2	14	4	36	.233	.258	.300	54	-9	-10	13	1	0	0	.977	9	/C1	0.2

■ YATS WUESTLING   Wuestling, George   b: 10/18/03, St.Louis, Mo.   d: 4/26/70, St.Louis, Mo.   BR/TR, 5'11", 167 lbs.   Deb: 6/15/29

1929	Det-A	54	150	13	30	4	1	0	16	9	24	.200	.250	.240	27	-16	-17	9	1	3	-2	.943	-2	S/23	-1.4
1930	Det-A	4	9	0	0	0	0	0	2	3		.000	.182	.000	-48	-2	-2	0	0	0	0	.842	1	/S	-0.1
	NY-A	25	58	5	11	0	1	0	3	4	14	.190	.242	.224	20	-7	-7	3	0	1	-1	.918	4	S/3	-0.2
	Yr	29	67	5	11	0	1	0	3	6	17	.164	.233	.194	10	-9	-9	3	0	1	-1	.904	5	S/3	-0.3
Total	2	83	217	18	41	4	2	0	19	15	41	.189	.245	.226	21	-26	-25	12	1	4	-2	.931	2	/S32	-1.7

■ JOE WYATT   Wyatt, Loral John   b: 4/6/1900, Petersburg, Ind.   d: 12/5/70, Oblong, Ill.   BR/TR, 6'1", 175 lbs.   Deb: 9/11/24

| 1924 | Cle-A | 4 | 12 | 1 | 2 | 0 | 0 | 0 | 1 | 2 | 1 | .167 | .286 | .167 | 18 | -1 | -1 | 1 | 0 | 0 | 0 | .833 | -1 | /O | -0.3 |

■ REN WYLIE   Wylie, James Renwick   b: 12/14/1861, Elizabeth, Pa.   d: 8/17/51, Wilkinsburg, Pa.   BR/TR, 5'11", 155 lbs.   Deb: 8/11/1882

| 1882 | Pit-a | 1 | 3 | 0 | 0 | 0 | 0 | 0 | | 0 | 0 | .000 | .000 | .000 | -99 | -1 | -1 | 0 | | | | 1.000 | 0 | /O | 0.0 |

■ FRANK WYMAN   Wyman, Frank H.   b: 5/10/1862, Haverhill, Mass.   d: 2/4/16, Everett, Mass.   Deb: 6/24/1884

1884	KC-U	30	124	16	27	4	0	0		3		.218	.236	.250	74	-4	-2	8				.743	5	O/P13	0.2
	CP-U	2	8	1	3	0	0	0		0		.375	.375	.375	155	0	0	1				.846	-0	/1	0.0
	Yr	32	132	17	30	4	0	0		3		.227	.244	.258	80	-4	-2	9				.743	4	O/1P3	0.2

■ BUTCH WYNEGAR   Wynegar, Harold Delano   b: 3/14/56, York, Pa.   BB/TR, 6', 194 lbs.   Deb: 4/09/76

1976	Min-A★	149	534	58	139	21	2	10	69	79	63	.260	.358	.363	108	10	8	72	0	0	0	.978	-10	*CD	0.3
1977	Min-A★	144	532	76	139	22	3	10	79	68	61	.261	.347	.370	97	-2	-1	70	2	3	-1	.993	-11	*C/3	-0.9
1978	Min-A	135	454	36	104	22	1	4	45	47	42	.229	.310	.295	73	-15	-16	46	1	0	0	.988	-3	*C/3	-1.6
1979	Min-A	149	504	74	136	20	0	7	57	74	36	.270	.366	.351	91	-1	-4	68	2	2	-1	.992	-4	*C	-0.4
1980	Min-A	146	486	61	124	18	3	5	57	63	36	.255	.343	.335	81	-7	-12	59	3	1	0	.988	-4	C/D	-0.3
1981	Min-A	47	150	11	37	5	0	0	10	17	9	.247	.327	.280	72	-4	-5	13	0	1	-1	.995	-1	C/D	-0.6
1982	Min-A	24	86	9	18	4	0	1	8	10	12	.209	.292	.291	59	-5	-5	7	0	0	0	.986	-2	C	-0.6
	NY-A	63	191	27	56	8	1	3	20	40	21	.293	.418	.393	126	9	9	33	0	1	-1	.993	-1	C	1.0
	Yr	87	277	36	74	12	1	4	28	50	33	.267	.381	.361	106	4	4	40	0	1	-1	.991	-2	C	0.4
1983	NY-A	94	301	40	89	18	2	6	42	52	29	.296	.401	.429	133	14	15	54	1	1	-0	.985	-13	C	0.6
1984	NY-A	129	442	48	118	13	1	6	45	65	35	.267	.361	.342	99	-0	2	53	1	4	-2	.993	-4	*C	0.3
1985	NY-A	102	309	27	69	15	0	5	32	64	43	.223	.357	.320	89	-3	-2	38	0	0	0	.990	-2	C	-0.3
1986	NY-A	61	194	19	40	4	1	7	29	30	21	.206	.313	.345	80	-5	-5	20	0	0	0	.994	-2	C	-0.3
1987	Cal-A	31	92	4	19	2	0	0	5	9	11	.207	.277	.228	37	-8	-8	6	0	0	0	.994	3	C/D	-0.3
1988	Cal-A	27	55	8	14	4	1	0	8	8	7	.255	.349	.418	117	1	1	8	0	0	0	.981	-0	C	0.2
Total	13	1301	4330	498	1102	176	15	65	506	626	428	.255	.351	.347	93	-17	-21	549	10	13	-5	.989	-43	*C/D3	-2.2

■ EARLY WYNN   Wynn, Early "Gus"   b: 1/6/20, Hartford, Ala.   BB/TR, 6', 200 lbs.   Deb: 9/13/39   CH

1939	Was-A	3	6	0	1	0	0	0	1	1	1	.167	.286	.167	20	-1	-1	0	0	0	0	1.000	-1	/P	0.0
1941	Was-A	5	15	1	2	1	0	0	0	0	5	.133	.133	.200	-14	-2	-2	0	0	0	0	.917	0	/P	0.0
1942	Was-A	30	69	4	15	2	0	0	7	3	13	.217	.250	.246	40	-6	-5	4	0	0	0	.953	-1	P	0.0
1943	Was-A	38	98	6	29	3	1	1	11	1	11	.296	.303	.378	102	-1	0	11	0	0	0	.947	-2	P	0.0
1944	Was-A	43	92	4	19	2	0	0	6	3	21	.207	.232	.261	42	-7	-7	5	0	0	0	.972	-2	P	0.0
1946	Was-A	25	47	4	15	2	0	1	9	5	7	.319	.385	.426	134	2	2	8	0	0	0	.962	-0	P	0.0

YEAR	TM/L	G	AB	R	H	2B	3B	HR	RBI	BB	SO	AVG	OBP	SLG	PRO+	BR	/A	RC	SB	CS	SBR	FA	FR	POS	TPR
1947	Was-A	54	120	6	33	6	0	2	13	1	19	.275	.281	.375	84	-4	-3	13	0	0	0	.980	-1	P	0.0
1948	Was-A	73	106	9	23	3	1	0	16	14	22	.217	.308	.264	55	-7	-7	9	0	0	0	.950	-1	P	0.0
1949	Cle-A	35	70	3	10	1	0	1	7	4	10	.143	.189	.200	3	-10	-10	2	0	0	0	1.000	1	P	0.0
1950	Cle-A	39	77	12	18	5	1	2	10	10	12	.234	.322	.403	87	-2	-2	11	0	0	0	.932	0	P	0.0
1951	Cle-A	41	108	8	20	8	1	1	13	7	9	.185	.235	.306	48	-9	-8	7	0	0	0	.982	-1	P	0.0
1952	Cle-A	44	99	5	22	2	0	0	10	9	15	.222	.287	.242	52	-7	-6	7	0	0	0	.943	-1	P	0.0
1953	Cle-A	37	91	11	25	2	0	3	10	7	17	.275	.327	.396	97	-1	-1	13	0	0	0	1.000	-1	P	0.0
1954	*Cle-A	40	93	10	17	3	0	0	4	7	13	.183	.240	.215	25	-10	-10	5	0	0	0	.957	-3	P	0.0
1955	Cle-A★	34	84	8	15	3	0	1	7	6	17	.179	.233	.250	29	-8	-9	5	0	0	0	.944	-3	P	0.0
1956	Cle-A★	38	101	5	23	5	0	1	15	7	22	.228	.278	.307	53	-7	-7	9	1	0	0	.955	1	P	0.0
1957	Cle-A★	40	86	4	10	0	0	0	4	11	23	.116	.216	.116	-7	-13	-12	3	0	0	0	1.000	-1	P	0.0
1958	Chi-A★	40	75	7	15	1	0	0	11	10	25	.200	.294	.213	43	-6	-5	5	0	0	0	1.000	-2	P	0.0
1959	*Chi-A★	37	90	11	22	7	0	2	8	9	18	.244	.320	.389	95	-1	-1	12	0	0	0	.957	-1	P	0.0
1960	Chi-A★	36	75	8	15	2	1	1	7	14	17	.200	.333	.293	72	-3	-3	9	0	0	0	.972	-2	P	0.0
1961	Chi-A	17	37	4	6	0	0	0	2	3	11	.162	.225	.162	5	-5	-5	1	0	0	0	1.000	-2	P	0.0
1962	Chi-A	27	54	5	7	1	0	0	2	7	17	.130	.230	.148	4	-7	-7	2	0	0	0	1.000	-2	P	0.0
1963	Cle-A	20	11	1	3	0	0	0	0	2	5	.273	.385	.273	89	-0	-0	1	0	0	0	1.000	-0	P	0.0
Total	23	796	1704	136	365	59	5	17	173	141	330	.214	.275	.285	54	-113	-109	145	1	0	0	.967	-25	P	0.0

■ JIM WYNN Wynn, James Sherman b: 3/12/42, Hamilton, Ohio BR/TR, 5'9", 170 lbs. Deb: 7/10/63

YEAR	TM/L	G	AB	R	H	2B	3B	HR	RBI	BB	SO	AVG	OBP	SLG	PRO+	BR	/A	RC	SB	CS	SBR	FA	FR	POS	TPR
1963	Hou-N	70	250	31	61	10	5	4	27	30	53	.244	.325	.372	107	0	2	32	4	2	0	.963	-7	OS/3	-0.7
1964	Hou-N	67	219	19	49	7	0	5	18	24	58	.224	.303	.324	81	-6	-5	21	5	5	-2	.958	1	O	-0.9
1965	Hou-N	157	564	90	155	30	7	22	73	84	126	.275	.374	.470	146	29	33	108	43	4	**11**	.978	14	*O	5.2
1966	Hou-N	105	418	62	107	21	1	18	62	41	81	.256	.324	.440	118	5	9	58	13	10	-2	.978	6	*O	0.8
1967	Hou-N★	158	594	102	148	29	3	37	107	74	137	.249	.334	.495	139	25	28	102	16	4	2	.968	6	*O	2.9
1968	Hou-N	156	542	85	146	23	5	26	67	90	131	.269	.378	.474	158	38	40	98	11	17	-7	.988	17	*O	4.6
1969	Hou-N	149	495	113	133	17	1	33	87	**148**	142	.269	.440	.507	168	51	52	126	23	7	3	.985	6	*O	5.3
1970	Hou-N	157	554	82	156	32	2	27	88	106	96	.282	.398	.493	143	32	35	114	24	5	4	.987	8	*O	3.9
1971	Hou-N	123	404	38	82	16	0	7	45	56	63	.203	.303	.295	72	-15	-14	36	10	5	0	.988	4	*O	-1.7
1972	Hou-N	145	542	117	148	29	3	24	90	103	99	.273	.391	.470	147	34	35	107	17	7	1	.983	5	*O	3.7
1973	Hou-N	139	481	90	106	14	5	20	55	91	102	.220	.349	.395	106	6	6	68	14	11	-2	.986	4	*O	0.1
1974	*LA-N★	150	535	104	145	17	4	32	108	108	104	.271	.393	.497	154	36	39	109	18	15	-4	.992	2	*O	3.2
1975	LA-N★	130	412	80	102	16	0	18	58	110	77	.248	.407	.417	135	21	24	79	7	3	0	.983	-3	*O	1.7
1976	Atl-N	148	449	75	93	19	1	17	66	**127**	111	.207	.382	.367	107	14	10	75	16	6	1	.971	10	*O	1.6
1977	NY-A	30	77	7	11	2	1	1	3	15	16	.143	.283	.234	43	-6	-6	6	1	0	0	1.000	2	D/O	-0.4
	Mil-A	36	117	10	23	3	1	0	10	17	31	.197	.299	.239	49	-8	-8	10	3	0	1	.967	-1	OD	-0.9
	Yr	66	194	17	34	5	2	1	13	32	47	.175	.292	.237	46	-14	-14	16	4	0	1	.981	1	DO	-1.3
Total	15	1920	6653	1105	1665	285	39	291	964	1224	1427	.250	.369	.436	129	256	281	1148	225	101	7	.981	72	*O/DS3	28.4

■ MARVELL WYNNE Wynne, Marvell b: 12/17/59, Chicago, Ill. BL/TL, 5'11", 185 lbs. Deb: 6/15/83

YEAR	TM/L	G	AB	R	H	2B	3B	HR	RBI	BB	SO	AVG	OBP	SLG	PRO+	BR	/A	RC	SB	CS	SBR	FA	FR	POS	TPR
1983	Pit-N	103	366	66	89	16	2	7	26	38	52	.243	.319	.355	85	-6	-8	43	12	10	-2	.983	-5	*O	-1.9
1984	Pit-N	154	653	77	174	24	11	0	39	42	81	.266	.311	.337	82	-16	-16	67	24	19	-4	.990	5	*O	-2.1
1985	Pit-N	103	337	21	69	6	3	2	18	18	48	.205	.247	.258	42	-26	-26	21	10	5	0	.987	6	O	-2.5
1986	SD-N	137	288	34	76	19	2	7	37	15	45	.264	.303	.417	98	-2	-2	32	11	11	-3	.986	-11	*O	-1.9
1987	SD-N	98	188	17	47	8	2	2	24	20	37	.250	.322	.346	80	-6	-5	21	11	6	-0	.981	-10	O	-1.7
1988	SD-N	128	333	37	88	13	4	11	42	31	62	.264	.327	.426	117	6	6	47	3	4	-2	.987	-11	*O	-1.0
1989	SD-N	105	294	19	74	11	1	6	35	12	41	.252	.283	.357	82	-8	-8	30	4	1	1	.971	-7	O	-1.7
	*Chi-N	20	48	8	9	2	1	1	4	1	7	.188	.220	.333	52	-3	-3	4	2	0	1	.944	-2	O	-0.6
	Yr	125	342	27	83	13	2	7	39	13	48	.243	.275	.354	77	-10	-11	34	6	1	1	.968	-10	*O	-2.3
1990	Chi-N	92	186	21	38	8	2	4	19	14	25	.204	.264	.333	59	-10	-11	16	3	2	-0	.991	-9	O	-2.3
Total	8	940	2693	300	664	107	28	40	244	191	398	.247	.298	.352	81	-72	-72	279	80	58	-11	.985	-46	O	-15.7

■ JOHNNY WYROSTEK Wyrostek, John Barney b: 7/12/19, Fairmont City, Ill. d: 12/12/86, St.Louis, Mo. BL/TR, 6'2", 180 lbs. Deb: 9/10/42

YEAR	TM/L	G	AB	R	H	2B	3B	HR	RBI	BB	SO	AVG	OBP	SLG	PRO+	BR	/A	RC	SB	CS	SBR	FA	FR	POS	TPR
1942	Pit-N	9	35	0	4	0	1	0	3	3	2	.114	.184	.171	4	-4	-4	1	0			1.000	1	/O	-0.4
1943	Pit-N	51	79	7	12	3	0	0	1	3	15	.152	.183	.190	7	-9	-10	3	0			.919	-5	O/312	-1.7
1946	Phi-N	145	545	73	153	30	4	6	45	70	42	.281	.366	.383	116	10	12	82	7			.981	17	*O	2.4
1947	Phi-N	128	454	68	124	24	7	5	51	61	45	.273	.364	.390	104	1	4	67	7			.971	1	*O	-0.2
1948	Cin-N	136	512	74	140	24	9	17	76	52	63	.273	.344	.455	119	9	11	83	7			.977	4	*O	0.8
1949	Cin-N	134	474	54	118	20	4	9	46	58	63	.249	.333	.365	86	-8	-9	60	7			.971	1	*O	-1.5
1950	Cin-N★	131	509	70	145	34	5	8	76	52	38	.285	.357	.418	103	3	2	76	1			.980	-2	*O/1	-0.4
1951	Cin-N★	142	537	52	167	31	3	2	61	54	54	.311	.376	.391	105	7	6	83	2	1	0	.970	-7	*O	-0.7
1952	Cin-N	30	106	12	25	1	3	1	10	18	7	.236	.347	.330	89	-1	-1	12	1	2	-1	1.000	2	O/1	-0.1
	Phi-N	98	321	45	88	16	3	1	37	44	26	.274	.363	.352	100	1	2	42	1	7	-4	.972	8	O	0.2
	Yr	128	427	57	113	17	6	2	47	62	33	.265	.359	.347	97	-0	0	54	2	9	-5	.980	10	*O/1	0.1
1953	Phi-N	125	409	42	111	14	2	6	47	38	43	.271	.339	.359	83	-10	-10	51	0	3	-2	.962	2	*O	-1.3
1954	Phi-N	92	259	28	62	12	4	3	28	29	39	.239	.318	.351	74	-10	-10	29	0	0	0	.990	-5	O1	-1.7
Total	11	1221	4240	525	1149	209	45	58	481	482	437	.271	.349	.383	98	-11	-6	589	33	13		.975	16	*O/132	-4.6

■ HENRY YAIK Yaik, Henry b: 3/1/1864, Detroit, Mich. d: 9/21/35, Detroit, Mich. 5'11", 185 lbs. Deb: 10/03/1888

YEAR	TM/L	G	AB	R	H	2B	3B	HR	RBI	BB	SO	AVG	OBP	SLG	PRO+	BR	/A	RC	SB	CS	SBR	FA	FR	POS	TPR
1888	Pit-N	2	6	0	2	0	0	0	1	1	0	.333	.429	.333	161	0	0	1	0			.625	2	/OC	0.2

■ AD YALE Yale, William M. b: 4/17/1870, Bristol, Conn. d: 4/27/48, Bridgeport, Conn. Deb: 9/18/05

YEAR	TM/L	G	AB	R	H	2B	3B	HR	RBI	BB	SO	AVG	OBP	SLG	PRO+	BR	/A	RC	SB	CS	SBR	FA	FR	POS	TPR
1905	Bro-N	4	13	1	1	0	0	0	1	1		.077	.143	.077	-37	-2	-2	0	0			1.000	-0	/1	-0.3

■ HUGH YANCY Yancy, Hugh b: 10/16/49, Sarasota, Fla. BR/TR, 5'11", 170 lbs. Deb: 7/05/72

YEAR	TM/L	G	AB	R	H	2B	3B	HR	RBI	BB	SO	AVG	OBP	SLG	PRO+	BR	/A	RC	SB	CS	SBR	FA	FR	POS	TPR
1972	Chi-A	3	9	0	1	0	0	0	0	0	0	.111	.111	.111	-33	-1	-1	-0	0	1	-1	1.000	0	/3	-0.2
1974	Chi-A	1	0	0	0	0	0	0	0	0	0	—	—	—	—	0	-0	0	0	0	0	.000	0	/D	0.0
1976	Chi-A	3	10	0	1	1	0	0	0	0	3	.100	.100	.200	-14	-1	-1	0	0	0	0	1.000	-1	/2	-0.2
Total	3	7	19	0	2	1	0	0	0	0	3	.105	.105	.158	-23	-3	-3	0	0	1	-1		-0	/23D	-0.4

■ GEORGE YANKOWSKI Yankowski, George Edward b: 11/19/22, Cambridge, Mass. BR/TR, 6', 180 lbs. Deb: 8/17/42

YEAR	TM/L	G	AB	R	H	2B	3B	HR	RBI	BB	SO	AVG	OBP	SLG	PRO+	BR	/A	RC	SB	CS	SBR	FA	FR	POS	TPR
1942	Phi-A	6	13	0	2	1	0	0	2	0	2	.154	.154	.231	7	-2	-2	0	0	0	0	1.000	0	/C	-0.1
1949	Chi-A	12	18	0	3	1	0	0	2	0	2	.167	.167	.222	3	-3	-3	0	0	0	0	1.000	1	/C	-0.1
Total	2	18	31	0	5	2	0	0	4	0	4	.161	.161	.226	5	-4	-4	0	0	0	0	1.000	1	/C	-0.2

■ GEORGE YANTZ Yantz, George Webb b: 7/27/1886, Louisville, Ky. d: 2/26/67, Louisville, Ky. BR/TR, 5'6.5", 168 lbs. Deb: 9/30/12

YEAR	TM/L	G	AB	R	H	2B	3B	HR	RBI	BB	SO	AVG	OBP	SLG	PRO+	BR	/A	RC	SB	CS	SBR	FA	FR	POS	TPR
1912	Chi-N	1	1	0	1	0	0	0	0	0	0	1.000	1.000	1.000	449	0	0	1	0			.000	0	/C	0.0

■ YAM YARYAN Yaryan, Clarence Everett b: 11/5/1892, Knowlton, Iowa d: 11/16/64, Birmingham, Ala. BR/TR, 5'10.5", 180 lbs. Deb: 4/23/21

YEAR	TM/L	G	AB	R	H	2B	3B	HR	RBI	BB	SO	AVG	OBP	SLG	PRO+	BR	/A	RC	SB	CS	SBR	FA	FR	POS	TPR
1921	Chi-A	45	102	11	31	8	2	0	15	9	16	.304	.366	.422	102	0	0	16	0	0	0	.933	-6	C	-0.4
1922	Chi-A	36	71	9	14	2	0	2	9	6	10	.197	.269	.310	51	-5	-5	6	1	0	0	.966	-1	C	-0.5
Total	2	81	173	20	45	10	2	2	24	15	26	.260	.326	.376	81	-5	-5	22	1	0	0	.948	-8	/C	-0.9

■ CARL YASTRZEMSKI Yastrzemski, Carl Michael "Yaz" b: 8/22/39, Southampton, N.Y. BL/TR, 5'11", 182 lbs. Deb: 4/11/61 H

YEAR	TM/L	G	AB	R	H	2B	3B	HR	RBI	BB	SO	AVG	OBP	SLG	PRO+	BR	/A	RC	SB	CS	SBR	FA	FR	POS	TPR
1961	Bos-A	148	583	71	155	31	6	11	80	50	96	.266	.327	.396	90	-7	-9	72	6	5	-1	.963	1	*O	-1.8

YEAR	TM/L	G	AB	R	H	2B	3B	HR	RBI	BB	SO	AVG	OBP	SLG	PRO+	BR	/A	RC	SB	CS	SBR	FA	FR	POS	TPR
1962	Bos-A	160	646	99	191	43	6	19	94	66	82	.296	.364	.469	118	20	17	103	7	4	-0	.969	16	*O	2.3
1963	Bos-A★	151	570	91	**183**	**40**	3	14	68	**95**	72	**.321**	**.419**	.475	145	**42**	**40**	**118**	8	5	-1	.980	13	*O	**4.6**
1964	Bos-A	151	567	77	164	29	9	15	67	75	90	.289	.374	.451	122	23	20	89	6	5	-1	.973	28	*O/3	4.0
1965	Bos-A†	133	494	78	154	**45**	3	20	72	70	58	.312	**.398**	**.536**	**154**	**42**	**38**	102	7	6	-2	.987	6	*O	**3.9**
1966	Bos-A☆	160	594	81	165	**39**	2	16	80	84	60	.278	.368	.431	117	24	17	92	8	9	-3	.985	17	*O	2.4
1967	*Bos-A★	161	579	**112**	**189**	31	4	**44**	**121**	91	69	**.326**	**.421**	**.622**	**189**	**76**	**71**	**155**	10	8	-2	.978	13	*O	**7.9**
1968	Bos-A★	157	539	90	162	32	2	23	74	**119**	90	**.301**	**.429**	.495	168	**58**	**53**	**121**	13	6	0	.991	17	*O/1	**7.0**
1969	Bos-A★	162	603	96	154	28	2	40	111	101	91	.255	.363	.507	134	33	29	113	15	7	0	.985	10	*O1	3.1
1970	Bos-A★	161	566	**125**	186	29	0	40	102	128	66	.329	**.453**	**.592**	**174**	**72**	**66**	**157**	23	13	-1	.990	2	1O	**5.6**
1971	Bos-A★	148	508	75	129	21	2	15	70	106	60	.254	.384	.392	112	18	13	80	8	7	-2	.993	14	*O	1.9
1972	Bos-A★	125	455	70	120	18	2	12	68	67	44	.264	.363	.391	118	16	13	66	5	4	-1	.974	8	O1	1.4
1973	Bos-A†	152	540	82	160	25	4	19	95	105	58	.296	.411	.463	138	37	32	103	9	7	-2	.994	-5	*13O	1.7
1974	Bos-A★	148	515	**93**	155	25	2	15	79	104	48	.301	.421	.445	139	38	33	102	12	7	-1	.997	-7	1O/D	1.8
1975	*Bos-A★	149	543	91	146	30	1	14	60	87	67	.269	.372	.405	110	16	10	84	8	4	0	.996	-1	*1/OD	0.0
1976	Bos-A★	155	546	71	146	23	2	21	102	80	67	.267	.362	.432	118	23	15	86	5	6	-2	.998	-8	1OD	-0.4
1977	Bos-A★	150	558	99	165	27	3	28	102	73	40	.296	.378	.505	124	30	21	110	11	1	3	**1.000**	14	*O/1D	3.1
1978	Bos-A†	144	523	70	145	21	2	17	81	76	44	.277	.372	.423	111	18	11	85	4	5	-2	.986	6	O1D	0.9
1979	Bos-A★	147	518	69	140	28	1	21	87	62	46	.270	.351	.450	108	10	6	81	3	3	-1	.996	6	D1O	0.6
1980	Bos-A	105	364	49	100	21	1	15	50	44	38	.275	.353	.462	115	11	8	58	0	2	-1	1.000	-3	DO1	0.2
1981	Bos-A	91	338	36	83	14	1	7	53	49	28	.246	.341	.355	95	1	-1	41	0	1	-1	.992	3	D1	-0.2
1982	Bos-A★	131	459	53	126	22	1	16	72	59	50	.275	.360	.431	110	11	7	72	0	1	-1	1.000	0	*D1/O	0.6
1983	Bos-A★	119	380	38	101	24	0	10	56	54	29	.266	.360	.408	103	7	3	55	0	0	0	1.000	-1	*D/1O	0.2
Total	23	3308	11988	1816	3419	646	59	452	1844	1845	1393	.285	.382	.462	128	617	515	2147	168	116	-19	.981	149	*O1D/3	50.8

■ AL YATES

Yates, Albert Arthur b: 5/26/45, Jersey City, N.J. BR/TR, 6'2", 210 lbs. Deb: 5/13/71

YEAR	TM/L	G	AB	R	H	2B	3B	HR	RBI	BB	SO	AVG	OBP	SLG	PRO+	BR	/A	RC	SB	CS	SBR	FA	FR	POS	TPR
1971	Mil-A	24	47	5	13	2	0	1	4	3	7	.277	.320	.383	100	-0	-0	5	1	0	0	1.000	1	O	0.0

■ BERT YEABSLEY

Yeabsley, Robert Watkins b: 12/17/1893, Philadelphia, Pa. d: 2/8/61, Philadelphia, Pa. BR/TR, 5'9.5", 175 lbs. Deb: 5/28/19

YEAR	TM/L	G	AB	R	H	2B	3B	HR	RBI	BB	SO	AVG	OBP	SLG	PRO+	BR	/A	RC	SB	CS	SBR	FA	FR	POS	TPR
1919	Phi-N	3	0	0	0	0	0	0	0	1	0	—	1.000	—	200	0	0	0	0			.000	0	H	0.0

■ GEORGE YEAGER

Yeager, George J. "Doc" b: 6/5/1874, Cincinnati, Ohio d: 7/5/40, Cincinnati, Ohio BR/TR, 5'10", 190 lbs. Deb: 9/25/1896

YEAR	TM/L	G	AB	R	H	2B	3B	HR	RBI	BB	SO	AVG	OBP	SLG	PRO+	BR	/A	RC	SB	CS	SBR	FA	FR	POS	TPR
1896	Bos-N	2	5	1	1	0	0	0	0	0	1	.200	.200	.200	6	-1	-1	0	0			1.000	-0	/1	-0.1
1897	*Bos-N	30	95	20	23	2	3	2	15	7		.242	.294	.389	75	-3	-4	12	2			.970	1	CO/23	-0.2
1898	Bos-N	68	221	37	59	13	1	3	24	16		.267	.328	.376	96	-0	-2	29	1			.951	-4	C1/OS	-0.2
1899	Bos-N	3	8	1	1	0	0	0	0	1		.125	.222	.125	-3	-1	-1	0	0			1.000	0	/OC	-0.1
1901	Cle-A	39	139	13	31	5	0	0	14	4		.223	.250	.259	43	-11	-10	10	2			.964	3	C/1O2	-0.4
	Pit-N	26	91	9	24	2	1	0	10	4		.264	.302	.308	75	-3	-3	9	1			.971	-2	C/31	-0.3
1902	NY-N	38	108	6	22	2	1	0	9	11		.204	.277	.241	60	-5	-5	8	1			.946	-1	C/1O	-0.3
	Bal-A	11	38	3	7	1	0	0	1	2		.184	.225	.211	20	-4	-4	2	0			.930	1	C	-0.2
Total	6	217	705	90	168	25	6	5	73	45	1	.238	.290	.312	69	-28	-30	71	7			.953	-2	C/1O23S	-1.8

■ JOE YEAGER

Yeager, Joseph F. "Little Joe" b: 8/28/1875, Philadelphia, Pa. d: 7/2/37, Detroit, Mich. BR/TR, Deb: 4/22/1898

YEAR	TM/L	G	AB	R	H	2B	3B	HR	RBI	BB	SO	AVG	OBP	SLG	PRO+	BR	/A	RC	SB	CS	SBR	FA	FR	POS	TPR
1898	Bro-N	43	134	12	23	5	1	0	15	7		.172	.218	.224	27	-13	-13	7	1			.908	5	P/OS2	-0.2
1899	Bro-N	23	47	12	9	0	1	0	4	6		.191	.333	.234	56	-2	-3	4	0			.914	3	SP/O3	0.1
1900	Bro-N	3	9	0	3	0	0	0	0	0		.333	.333	.333	79	-0	-0	1	0			1.000	-1	/P3	0.0
1901	Det-A	41	125	18	37	7	1	2	17	4		.296	.343	.416	105	1	1	20	3			.919	4	PS/2	0.3
1902	Det-A	50	161	17	39	6	5	1	23	5		.242	.282	.360	76	-5	-6	17	0			.957	-1	PO2/S3	-0.8
1903	Det-A	109	402	36	103	15	6	0	43	18		.256	.300	.323	90	-6	-5	44	9			.921	-9	*3/PS	-1.3
1905	NY-A	115	401	53	107	16	7	0	42	25		.267	.327	.342	101	6	1	50	8			.923	-0	3S	0.5
1906	NY-A	57	123	20	37	6	1	0	12	13		.301	.394	.366	126	6	5	20	3			.905	-1	S2/3	0.5
1907	StL-A	123	436	32	104	21	7	1	44	31		.239	.294	.326	98	-2	-1	47	11			.938	7	32S	0.9
1908	StL-A	10	15	3	5	1	0	0	1	1		.333	.474	.400	183	2	2	4	2			1.000	0	/2S	0.2
Total	10	574	1853	203	467	77	29	4	201	110		.252	.309	.331	91	-13	-20	214	37			.927	8	3/PS2O	0.2

■ STEVE YEAGER

Yeager, Stephen Wayne b: 11/24/48, Huntington, W.Va. BR/TR, 6', 190 lbs. Deb: 8/02/72

YEAR	TM/L	G	AB	R	H	2B	3B	HR	RBI	BB	SO	AVG	OBP	SLG	PRO+	BR	/A	RC	SB	CS	SBR	FA	FR	POS	TPR
1972	LA-N	35	106	18	29	0	1	4	15	16	26	.274	.374	.406	124	3	4	16	0	0	0	.984	9	C	1.4
1973	LA-N	54	134	18	34	5	0	2	10	15	33	.254	.342	.336	93	-2	-1	16	1	0	0	.981	5	C	0.6
1974	*LA-N	94	316	41	84	16	1	12	41	32	77	.266	.337	.437	120	6	7	46	2	2	-1	.992	13	C	2.4
1975	LA-N	135	452	34	103	16	1	12	54	40	75	.228	.302	.347	83	-13	-11	45	2	5	-2	.992	12	*C	0.5
1976	LA-N	117	359	42	77	11	3	11	35	30	84	.214	.288	.354	83	-10	-9	38	3	1	0	.985	9	*C	0.4
1977	*LA-N	125	387	53	99	21	2	16	55	43	84	.256	.336	.444	108	4	4	57	1	3	-2	.977	12	*C	1.8
1978	*LA-N	94	228	19	44	7	0	4	23	36	41	.193	.303	.276	63	-11	-11	20	0	0	0	.988	11	C	0.3
1979	LA-N	105	310	33	67	9	2	13	41	29	68	.216	.283	.384	81	-9	-9	31	1	0	0	.984	11	*C	0.6
1980	LA-N	96	227	20	48	8	0	2	20	20	54	.211	.275	.273	55	-14	-13	16	2	3	-1	.984	4	C	-0.9
1981	*LA-N	42	86	5	18	2	0	3	7	6	14	.209	.261	.337	71	-4	-3	7	0	0	0	.994	1	C	-0.1
1982	LA-N	82	196	13	48	5	2	2	18	13	28	.245	.295	.321	74	-7	-7	19	0	0	0	.990	7	C	0.3
1983	*LA-N	113	335	31	68	8	3	15	41	23	57	.203	.256	.379	74	-13	-13	28	1	1	-0	.985	-6	*C	-1.5
1984	LA-N	74	197	16	45	4	0	4	29	20	38	.228	.300	.310	72	-7	-7	19	1	2	-1	.994	-6	C	-1.2
1985	*LA-N	53	121	4	25	4	1	0	9	7	24	.207	.250	.256	43	-9	-9	7	0	1	-1	.992	9	C	0.1
1986	Sea-A	50	130	10	27	2	0	2	12	12	23	.208	.275	.269	48	-9	-9	9	0	0	0	1.000	-0	C	-0.7
Total	15	1269	3584	357	816	118	16	102	410	342	726	.228	.300	.355	83	-96	-87	375	14	18	-7	.987	90	*C	4.0

■ BILL YEATMAN

Yeatman, William Suter b: 1849, Alexandria, Va. d: 4/20/01, York, Pa. Deb: 4/20/1872

YEAR	TM/L	G	AB	R	H	2B	3B	HR	RBI	BB	SO	AVG	OBP	SLG	PRO+	BR	/A	RC	SB	CS	SBR	FA	FR	POS	TPR
1872	Nat-n	1	4	0	0	0	0	0	0	0	0	.000	.000	.000	-86	-1	-1	0						/O	-0.1

■ ERIC YELDING

Yelding, Eric Girard b: 2/22/65, Montrose, Ala. BR/TR, 5'11", 170 lbs. Deb: 4/09/89

YEAR	TM/L	G	AB	R	H	2B	3B	HR	RBI	BB	SO	AVG	OBP	SLG	PRO+	BR	/A	RC	SB	CS	SBR	FA	FR	POS	TPR
1989	Hou-N	70	90	19	21	2	0	0	9	7	19	.233	.296	.256	61	-5	-4	7	11	5	0	1.000	6	S2/O	0.3
1990	Hou-N	142	511	69	130	9	5	1	28	39	87	.254	.307	.297	69	-22	-20	48	64	25	4	.971	-6	OS2/3	-2.2
1991	Hou-N	78	276	19	67	11	1	1	20	13	46	.243	.277	.301	66	-14	-12	21	11	9	-2	.939	-14	S/O	-2.5
1992	Hou-N	9	8	1	2	0	0	0	0	0	3	.250	.250	.250	45	-1	-1	1	0	0	0	.000	-1	/SO	-0.2
Total	4	299	885	108	220	22	6	2	57	59	155	.249	.296	.294	67	-41	-37	76	86	39	2	.950	-15	SO/23	-4.6

■ ARCHIE YELLE

Yelle, Archie Joseph b: 6/11/1892, Saginaw, Mich. d: 5/2/83, Woodland, Cal. BR/TR, 5'10.5", 170 lbs. Deb: 5/12/17

YEAR	TM/L	G	AB	R	H	2B	3B	HR	RBI	BB	SO	AVG	OBP	SLG	PRO+	BR	/A	RC	SB	CS	SBR	FA	FR	POS	TPR
1917	Det-A	25	51	4	7	1	0	0	0	5	4	.137	.214	.157	13	-5	-5	2	2			.975	-1	C	-0.6
1918	Det-A	56	144	7	25	3	0	0	7	9	15	.174	.227	.194	28	-13	-12	6	0			.948	7	C	-0.2
1919	Det-A	6	4	1	0	0	0	0	0	1	0	.000	.200	.000	-42	-1	-1	0	0			.833	-1	/C	-0.1
Total	3	87	199	12	32	4	0	0	7	15	19	.161	.223	.181	23	-19	-18	8	2			.952	5	/C	-0.9

■ STEVE YERKES

Yerkes, Stephen Douglas b: 5/15/1888, Hatboro, Pa. d: 1/31/71, Lansdale, Pa. BR/TR, 5'9", 165 lbs. Deb: 9/29/09

YEAR	TM/L	G	AB	R	H	2B	3B	HR	RBI	BB	SO	AVG	OBP	SLG	PRO+	BR	/A	RC	SB	CS	SBR	FA	FR	POS	TPR
1909	Bos-A	5	7	0	2	0	0	0	0	0		.286	.286	.286	79	-0	-0	1	0			1.000	-1	/S	-0.1
1911	Bos-A	142	502	70	140	24	3	1	57	52		.279	.354	.345	96	-2	-2	68	14			.927	-20	*S23	-1.4
1912	*Bos-A	131	523	73	132	22	6	0	42	41		.252	.312	.317	76	-14	-18	54	4			.943	-15	*2	-3.6
1913	Bos-A	137	483	67	129	29	6	1	48	50	32	.267	.338	.358	101	2	1	62	11			.957	-18	*2	-2.1
1914	Bos-A	92	293	23	64	17	2	1	23	14	23	.218	.259	.300	68	-13	-13	24	5	6	-2	.972	4	2	-1.3
	Pit-F	39	142	18	48	9	5	1	25	11	13	.338	.386	.493	150	9	9	29	2			.974	8	S	2.0

YEAR	TM/L	G	AB	R	H	2B	3B	HR	RBI	BB	SO	AVG	OBP	SLG	PRO+	BR	/A	RC	SB	CS	SBR	FA	FR	POS	TPR
1915	Pit-F	121	434	44	125	17	8	1	49	30	27	.288	.337	.371	109	4	4	63	17			**.967**	-3	*2/S	0.3
1916	Chi-N	44	137	12	36	6	2	1	10	9	7	.263	.308	.358	94	0	-1	16	1			.919	1	2	0.2
Total	7	711	2521	307	676	124	32	6	254	207	102	.268	.328	.350	95	-14	-20	317	54	6		.956	-45	2S/3	-6.0

■ TOM YEWCIC Yewcic, Thomas J. "Kibby" b: 5/9/32, Conemaugh, Pa. BR/TR, 5'11", 180 lbs. Deb: 6/27/57

YEAR	TM/L	G	AB	R	H	2B	3B	HR	RBI	BB	SO	AVG	OBP	SLG	PRO+	BR	/A	RC	SB	CS	SBR	FA	FR	POS	TPR
1957	Det-A	1	1	0	0	0	0	0	0	0	0	.000	.000	.000	-97	-0	-0	0	0	0	0	.833	1	/C	0.0

■ ED YEWELL Yewell, Edwin Leonard b: 8/22/1862, Washington, D.C. d: 9/15/40, Washington, D.C. Deb: 5/12/1884

YEAR	TM/L	G	AB	R	H	2B	3B	HR	RBI	BB	SO	AVG	OBP	SLG	PRO+	BR	/A	RC	SB	CS	SBR	FA	FR	POS	TPR
1884	Was-a	27	93	14	23	3	1	0		1		.247	.263	.301	97	-1	0	8				.885	-3	2/O3S	-0.2
	Was-U	1	4	0	0	0	0	0		0		.000	.000	.000	-99	-1	-1	0				.571	-0	/3	-0.1
Total	1	28	97	14	23	3	1	0		1		.237	.253	.289	89	-2	-1	8				.773	-3	/23OS	-0.3

■ JOE YINGLING Yingling, Joseph Granville b: 7/23/1866, Westminster, Md. d: 10/24/46, Manchester, Md. BR/TL, 5'7.5", 145 lbs. Deb: 5/28/1886

YEAR	TM/L	G	AB	R	H	2B	3B	HR	RBI	BB	SO	AVG	OBP	SLG	PRO+	BR	/A	RC	SB	CS	SBR	FA	FR	POS	TPR
1886	Was-N	1	2	0	0	0	0	0	0	0	1	.000	.000	.000	-99	-0	-0	0	0			.500	0	/P	0.0
1894	Phi-N	1	4	0	1	0	0	0	0	0	1	.250	.250	.250	23	-0	-0	0	0			1.000	-1	/S	-0.1
Total	2	2	6	0	1	0	0	0	0	0	2	.167	.167	.167	-13	-1	-1	0	0				-1	/SP	-0.1

■ BILL YOHE Yohe, William Clyde b: 9/2/1878, Mt.Elere, Ill. d: 12/24/38, Bremerton, Wash. TR, 5'8", 180 lbs. Deb: 8/30/09

YEAR	TM/L	G	AB	R	H	2B	3B	HR	RBI	BB	SO	AVG	OBP	SLG	PRO+	BR	/A	RC	SB	CS	SBR	FA	FR	POS	TPR
1909	Was-A	21	72	6	15	2	0	0	4	3		.208	.240	.236	53	-4	-4	5	2			.921	3	3	0.0

■ TONY YORK York, Anthony Batton b: 11/27/12, Irene, Tex. d: 4/18/70, Hillsboro, Tex. BR/TR, 5'10", 165 lbs. Deb: 4/18/44

YEAR	TM/L	G	AB	R	H	2B	3B	HR	RBI	BB	SO	AVG	OBP	SLG	PRO+	BR	/A	RC	SB	CS	SBR	FA	FR	POS	TPR
1944	Chi-N	28	85	4	20	1	0	0	7	4	11	.235	.270	.247	46	-6	-6	6	0			.940	10	S3	0.5

■ RUDY YORK York, Preston Rudolph b: 8/17/13, Ragland, Ala. d: 2/5/70, Rome, Ga. BR/TR, 6'1", 209 lbs. Deb: 8/22/34 MC

YEAR	TM/L	G	AB	R	H	2B	3B	HR	RBI	BB	SO	AVG	OBP	SLG	PRO+	BR	/A	RC	SB	CS	SBR	FA	FR	POS	TPR
1934	Det-A	3	6	0	1	0	0	0	0	1	3	.167	.286	.167	19	-1	-1	0	0	0	0	1.000	-0	/C	-0.1
1937	Det-A	104	375	72	115	18	3	35	103	41	52	.307	.375	.651	150	27	26	91	3	2	-0	.960	-19	C3/1	1.0
1938	Det-A★	135	463	85	138	27	2	33	127	92	74	.298	.417	.579	139	34	30	116	1	2	-1	.990	-1	*CO/1	3.0
1939	Det-A	102	329	66	101	16	1	20	68	41	50	.307	.387	.544	126	17	13	70	5	0	2	.985	-8	C1	0.8
1940	*Det-A	155	588	105	186	46	6	33	134	89	88	.316	.410	.583	141	47	39	147	3	2	-0	.990	5	*1	2.6
1941	Det-A★	155	590	91	153	29	3	27	111	92	88	.259	.360	.456	104	12	4	101	3	1	0	.986	-1	*1	-0.8
1942	Det-A★	153	577	81	150	26	4	21	90	73	71	.260	.343	.428	107	11	5	86	3	3	-1	.988	15	*1	1.0
1943	Det-A★	155	571	90	155	22	11	**34**	**118**	84	88	.271	.366	**.527**	148	41	36	108	5	5	-2	.990	18	*1	4.6
1944	Det-A☆	151	583	77	161	27	7	18	98	68	73	.276	.353	.439	119	18	15	91	5	3	-0	.989	5	*1	1.2
1945	*Det-A	155	595	71	157	25	5	18	87	60	85	.264	.331	.413	109	10	6	78	6	6	-2	.988	-2	*1	-1.0
1946	*Bos-A★	154	579	78	160	30	6	17	119	86	93	.276	.371	.437	118	20	16	98	3	2	-0	.994	6	*1	1.3
1947	Bos-A	48	184	16	39	7	0	6	27	22	32	.212	.296	.348	73	-6	-7	18	0	0	0	.995	1	1	-0.9
	Chi-A	102	400	40	97	18	4	15	64	36	55	.243	.305	.420	104	-2	-0	51	1	0	0	.995	-1	*1	-0.5
	Yr	150	584	56	136	25	4	21	91	58	87	.233	.302	.397	94	-8	-8	68	1	0	0	**.995**	0	*1	-1.4
1948	Phi-A	31	51	4	8	0	0	0	6	7	15	.157	.259	.157	12	-6	-6	2	0	0	0	.988	-1	1	-0.7
Total	13	1603	5891	876	1621	291	52	277	1152	792	867	.275	.362	.483	121	223	175	1057	38	26	-4	.990	16	*1C/3O	11.5

■ TOM YORK York, Thomas J. b: 7/13/1851, Brooklyn, N.Y. d: 2/17/36, New York, N.Y. BL, 5'9", 165 lbs. Deb: 5/09/1871 MU

YEAR	TM/L	G	AB	R	H	2B	3B	HR	RBI	BB	SO	AVG	OBP	SLG	PRO+	BR	/A	RC	SB	CS	SBR	FA	FR	POS	TPR
1871	Tro-n	29	145	36	37	5	7	2	23	9	1	.255	.299	.428	104	1	0	20	2					*O	0.1
1872	Bal-n	51	249	65	64	8	4	1	42	4	1	.257	.269	.333	81	-5	-7	23						*O	-0.3
1873	Bal-n	57	277	70	84	10	5	2	49	3	3	.303	.311	.397	107	2	2	36						*O	0.3
1874	Phi-n	50	223	36	58	3	8	0		4		.260	.273	.345	92	-1	-2	22						*O	-0.1
1875	Har-n	86	376	68	112	12	7	0		4		.298	.305	.367	125	11	8	43						*O	0.8
1876	Har-N	67	263	47	68	12	7	1	39	10	4	.259	.286	.369	108	5	1	28				.899	2	*O	0.2
1877	Har-N	56	237	43	67	16	7	1	37	3	11	.283	.292	.422	137	5	9	30				.865	0	*O	0.6
1878	Pro-N	62	269	56	83	19	**10**	1	26	8	19	.309	.329	.465	159	16	16	42				.873	4	*OM	1.6
1879	Pro-N	81	342	69	106	25	5	1	50	19	28	.310	.346	.421	154	19	20	51				.898	-4	*O	1.0
1880	Pro-N	53	203	21	43	9	2	0	18	8	29	.212	.242	.276	77	-5	-4	14				.934	-3	O	-0.8
1881	Pro-N	85	316	57	96	23	5	2	47	29	26	.304	.362	.427	150	18	19	50				.859	-2	*OM	1.4
1882	Pro-N	81	321	48	86	23	7	1	40	19	14	.268	.309	.393	123	8	8	40				.873	-3	*O	0.5
1883	Cle-N	100	381	56	99	29	5	2	46	**37**	55	.260	.325	.378	114	7	8	48				.864	0	*O	0.6
1884	Bal-a	83	314	64	70	14	7	1		34		.223	.318	.322	108	6	4	33				.843	-5	*O	-0.2
1885	Bal-a	22	87	6	23	4	2	0		8		.264	.326	.356	120	2	2	10				.938	1	O	0.3
Total	5 n	273	1270	275	355	38	31	5	114	24	5	.280	.293	.370	104	9	2	143						O	0.8
Total	10	690	2733	467	741	174	57	10	303	175	186	.271	.317	.387	127	81	83	347				.878	-8	O	5.2

■ NED YOST Yost, Edgar Frederick b: 8/19/55, Eureka, Cal. BR/TR, 6'1", 190 lbs. Deb: 4/12/80

YEAR	TM/L	G	AB	R	H	2B	3B	HR	RBI	BB	SO	AVG	OBP	SLG	PRO+	BR	/A	RC	SB	CS	SBR	FA	FR	POS	TPR
1980	Mil-A	15	31	0	5	0	0	0	0	0	6	.161	.161	.161	-12	-5	-5	1	0	0	0	1.000	2	C	-0.2
1981	Mil-A	18	27	4	6	0	0	3	3	3	6	.222	.300	.556	150	1	1	5	0	0	0	.956	2	C	0.4
1982	*Mil-A	40	98	13	27	6	3	1	8	7	20	.276	.324	.429	111	0	1	14	3	1	0	.977	-2	C/D	0.1
1983	Mil-A	61	196	21	44	5	1	6	28	5	36	.224	.244	.352	67	-11	-9	15	1	0	0	.971	-6	C	-1.2
1984	Tex-A	80	242	15	44	4	0	6	25	6	47	.182	.202	.273	29	-23	-24	12	1	2	-1	.995	-5	C	-2.8
1985	Mon-N	5	11	1	2	0	0	0	0	0	2	.182	.182	.182	2	-1	-1	0	0	0	0	.962	1	/C	-0.1
Total	6	219	605	54	128	15	4	16	64	21	117	.212	.238	.329	56	-38	-36	47	5	3	-0	.982	-8	C/D	-3.8

■ EDDIE YOST Yost, Edward Frederick Joseph "The Walking Man" b: 10/13/26, Brooklyn, N.Y. BR/TR, 5'10", 170 lbs. Deb: 8/16/44 MC

YEAR	TM/L	G	AB	R	H	2B	3B	HR	RBI	BB	SO	AVG	OBP	SLG	PRO+	BR	/A	RC	SB	CS	SBR	FA	FR	POS	TPR
1944	Was-A	7	14	3	2	0	0	0	0	1	2	.143	.200	.143	-1	-2	-2	1	0	0	0	.917	-1	/3S	-0.2
1946	Was-A	8	25	2	2	1	0	0	1	5	5	.080	.233	.120	1	-3	-3	1	2	1	0	1.000	1	/3	-0.2
1947	Was-A	115	428	52	102	17	3	0	14	45	57	.238	.314	.292	71	-17	-16	41	3	5	-2	.958	-9	*3	-2.7
1948	Was-A	145	555	74	138	32	11	2	50	82	51	.249	.349	.357	91	-9	-6	73	4	3	-1	.966	-13	*3	-2.1
1949	Was-A	124	435	57	110	19	7	9	45	91	41	.253	.383	.391	107	5	7	71	3	3	-1	.954	-2	*3	0.1
1950	Was-A	155	573	114	169	26	2	11	58	**141**	63	.295	.440	.405	123	24	28	116	6	6	-2	.945	-2	*3	2.1
1951	Was-A	154	568	109	161	**36**	4	12	65	126	55	.283	.423	.424	132	30	32	117	6	4	-1	.954	-27	*3/O	0.3
1952	Was-A☆	157	587	92	137	32	3	12	49	**129**	73	.233	.378	.359	110	10	13	93	4	3	-1	.962	-35	*3	-2.7
1953	Was-A	152	577	107	157	30	7	9	45	**123**	59	.272	.403	.395	119	19	21	103	7	4	-0	.965	-13	*3	0.4
1954	Was-A	155	539	101	138	26	4	11	47	131	71	.256	.406	.380	123	19	23	97	7	3	0	.968	3	*3	2.4
1955	Was-A	122	375	64	91	17	5	7	48	95	54	.243	.410	.371	117	11	14	66	4	3	-1	.943	-6	*3	0.7
1956	Was-A	152	515	94	119	17	2	11	53	**151**	82	.231	.412	.336	100	9	9	86	8	5	-1	.963	11	*3/O	2.0
1957	Was-A	110	414	47	104	13	5	9	38	73	49	.251	.370	.372	104	4	5	58	1	11	-6	.952	-11	*3	-1.0
1958	Was-A	134	406	55	91	16	0	8	37	81	43	.224	.365	.323	93	-1	-0	52	3	6	-3	**.964**	-15	*3/O1	-1.8
1959	Det-A	148	521	**115**	145	19	0	21	61	**135**	77	.278	**.437**	.436	133	38	34	115	9	2	2	**.962**	-11	*3/2	2.5
1960	Det-A	143	497	78	129	23	2	14	47	**125**	69	.260	**.416**	.398	118	22	20	92	5	4	-1	.933	-27	*3	-0.9
1961	LA-A	76	213	29	43	4	0	3	15	50	48	.202	.358	.263	62	-7	-11	24	0	1	-1	.964	-10	3	-2.1
1962	LA-A	52	104	22	25	9	1	0	10	30	21	.240	.415	.346	111	3	3	17	0	2	-1	.950	-3	3/1	0.0
Total	18	2109	7346	1215	1863	337	56	139	683	1614	920	.254	.395	.371	109	154	170	1225	72	66	-18	.957	-169	*3/O1S2	-3.2

■ ELMER YOTER Yoter, Elmer Elsworth b: 6/26/1900, Plainfield, Pa. d: 7/26/66, Camp Hill, Pa. BR/TR, 5'7", 155 lbs. Deb: 9/09/21

YEAR	TM/L	G	AB	R	H	2B	3B	HR	RBI	BB	SO	AVG	OBP	SLG	PRO+	BR	/A	RC	SB	CS	SBR	FA	FR	POS	TPR
1921	Phi-A	3	3	0	0	0	0	0	0	0	0	.000	.000	.000	-99	-1	-1	0	0	0	0	.000	0	H	-0.1
1924	Cle-A	19	66	3	18	1	1	0	7	5	8	.273	.324	.318	65	-3	-3	7	0	0	0	.905	-2	3	-0.4
1927	Chi-N	13	27	2	6	1	1	0	5	4	4	.222	.323	.333	76	-1	-1	3	0			.947	-0	3	-0.1
1928	Chi-N	1	0	0	0	0	0	0	0	0	0	—	—	—	—	0	0	0	0			.000	0	/3	0.0

YEAR	TM/L	G	AB	R	H	2B	3B	HR	RBI	BB	SO	AVG	OBP	SLG	PRO+	BR	/A	RC	SB	CS	SBR	FA	FR	POS	TPR
Total	4	36	96	5	24	2	2	0	12	9	12	.250	.314	.313	63	-5	-5	10	0	0		.915	-2	/3	-0.6
■ DEL YOUNG Young, Delmer Edward b: 3/11/12, Cleveland, Ohio d: 12/8/79, San Francisco, Cal. BB/TR, 5'11", 168 lbs. Deb: 4/19/37 F																									
1937	Phi-N	109	360	36	70	9	2	0	24	18	55	.194	.235	.231	25	-36	-40	20	6			.950	11	*2	-2.3
1938	Phi-N	108	340	27	78	13	2	0	31	20	35	.229	.276	.279	55	-22	-20	27	0			.933	-2	S2	-1.6
1939	Phi-N	77	217	22	57	9	2	3	20	8	24	.263	.289	.364	77	-8	-8	22	1			.946	-18	S2	-2.1
1940	Phi-N	15	33	2	8	0	1	0	1	2	1	.242	.286	.303	65	-2	-2	3	0			.962	-0	/S2	-0.1
Total	4	309	950	87	213	31	7	3	76	48	115	.224	.264	.281	48	-68	-70	72	7			.938	-9	S2	-6.1
■ DEL YOUNG Young, Delmer John b: 10/24/1885, Macon City, Mo. d: 12/17/59, Cleveland, Ohio BL/TR, 5'11", 195 lbs. Deb: 9/24/09 F																									
1909	Cin-N	2	7	0	2	0	0	0	1	1		.286	.375	.286	106	0	0	1	0			1.000	0	/O	0.0
1914	Buf-F	80	174	17	48	5	5	4	22	3	13	.276	.288	.431	101	-1	-1	22	0			.944	-6	O	-0.9
1915	Buf-F	12	15	0	2	0	0	0	0	1	0	.133	.188	.133	-5	-2	-2	1	1			.667	-1	/O	-0.4
Total	3	94	196	17	52	5	5	4	23	5	13	.265	.284	.403	93	-2	-3	24	1			.933	-7	/O	-1.3
■ DON YOUNG Young, Donald Wayne b: 10/18/45, Houston, Tex. BR/TR, 6'2", 185 lbs. Deb: 9/09/65																									
1965	Chi-N	11	35	1	2	0	0	1	2	0	11	.057	.057	.143	-45	-7	-7	0	0	0	0	.933	-1	O	-0.9
1969	Chi-N	101	272	36	65	12	3	6	27	38	74	.239	.343	.371	89	1	-4	35	1	5	-3	.975	-7	*O	-1.9
Total	2	112	307	37	67	12	3	7	29	38	85	.218	.314	.345	76	-6	-10	36	1	5	-3	.972	-8	O	-2.8
■ ERIC YOUNG Young, Eric Orlando b: 11/26/66, Jacksonville, Fla. BR/TR, 5'9", 180 lbs. Deb: 7/30/92																									
1992	LA-N	49	132	9	34	1	0	1	11	8	9	.258	.300	.288	68	-6	-5	12	6	1	1	.957	11	2	0.8
■ GEORGE YOUNG Young, George Joseph b: 4/1/1890, Brooklyn, N.Y. d: 3/13/50, Brightwaters, N.Y. BL/TR, 6', 185 lbs. Deb: 8/10/13																									
1913	Cle-A	2	2	0	0	0	0	0	0	0	0	.000	.000	.000	-97	-0	-1	0	0			.000	0	H	-0.1
■ GERALD YOUNG Young, Gerald Anthony b: 10/22/64, Tele, Honduras BB/TR, 6'2", 185 lbs. Deb: 7/08/87																									
1987	Hou-N	71	274	44	88	9	2	1	15	26	27	.321	.382	.380	107	2	3	44	26	9	2	.980	5	O	0.8
1988	Hou-N	149	576	79	148	21	9	0	37	66	66	.257	.336	.325	94	-5	-3	67	65	27	3	.992	13	*O	1.0
1989	Hou-N	146	533	71	124	17	3	0	38	74	60	.233	.328	.276	77	-15	-13	51	34	25	-5	**.998**	26	*O	0.5
1990	Hou-N	57	154	15	27	4	1	1	4	20	23	.175	.270	.234	41	-12	-12	11	6	3	0	.990	-2	O	-1.5
1991	Hou-N	108	142	26	31	3	1	1	11	24	17	.218	.331	.275	77	-4	-3	15	16	5	2	1.000	-14	O	-1.7
1992	Hou-N	74	76	14	14	1	1	0	4	10	11	.184	.279	.224	47	-5	-5	6	6	2	1	.964	-15	O	-2.2
Total	6	605	1755	249	432	55	17	3	109	220	204	.246	.332	.302	83	-40	-32	193	153	71	3	.992	13	O	-3.1
■ HERMAN YOUNG Young, Herman John b: 4/14/1886, Boston, Mass. d: 12/13/66, Ipswich, Mass. BR/TR, 5'8", 155 lbs. Deb: 6/11/11																									
1911	Bos-N	9	25	2	6	0	0	0	0	0	3	.240	.269	.240	40	-2	-2	2	0			.905	4	/3S	0.1
■ JOHN YOUNG Young, John Thomas b: 2/9/49, Los Angeles, Cal. BL/TL, 6'3", 210 lbs. Deb: 9/09/71																									
1971	Det-A	2	4	1	2	1	0	0	1	0	0	.500	.500	.750	241	1	1	2	0	0	0	1.000	-0	/1	0.1
■ KEVIN YOUNG Young, Kevin Stacey b: 6/16/69, Alpena, Mich. BR/TR, 6'3", 210 lbs. Deb: 7/12/92																									
1992	Pit-N	10	7	2	4	0	0	0	4	2	0	.571	.667	.571	257	2	2	3	1	0	0	.750	-1	/31	0.1
■ PEP YOUNG Young, Lemuel Floyd b: 8/29/07, Jamestown, N.C. d: 1/14/62, Jamestown, N.C. BR/TR, 5'9", 162 lbs. Deb: 4/25/33																									
1933	Pit-N	25	20	3	6	1	1	0	0	0	5	.300	.300	.450	112	0	0	3	0			1.000	2	/2S	0.2
1934	Pit-N	19	17	3	4	0	0	0	2	0	6	.235	.235	.235	26	-2	-2	1	0			1.000	2	/2S	0.1
1935	Pit-N	128	494	60	131	25	10	7	82	21	59	.265	.298	.399	83	-11	-13	58	2			.952	-12	*2/3OS	-1.6
1936	Pit-N	125	475	47	118	23	10	6	77	29	52	.248	.293	.377	77	-15	-17	53	3			.966	-24	*2	-3.1
1937	Pit-N	113	408	43	106	20	3	9	54	26	63	.260	.306	.390	88	-8	-8	49	4			.942	18	S32	1.6
1938	Pit-N	149	562	58	156	36	5	4	79	40	64	.278	.329	.381	94	-5	-5	70	7			.973	**32**	*2	3.5
1939	Pit-N	84	293	34	81	14	3	3	29	23	29	.276	.333	.375	92	-4	-4	37	1			.967	3	2	0.4
1940	Pit-N	54	136	19	34	8	2	2	20	12	23	.250	.320	.382	94	-1	-1	18	1			.909	-5	2/S3	-0.4
1941	Cin-N	4	12	2	2	0	0	0	0	0	1	.167	.231	.167	13	-1	-1	1	0			.923	1	/3	-0.1
	StL-N	2	2	0	0	0	0	0	0	0	2	.000	.000	.000	-94	-1	-1	0	0			.000	0	H	-0.1
	Yr	6	14	2	2	0	0	0	0	0	3	.143	.200	.143	-2	-2	-2	0	0			.923	1	/3	-0.2
1945	StL-N	27	47	5	7	1	0	1	4	1	8	.149	.167	.234	10	-6	-6	2	0			.978	1	S/32	-0.5
Total	10	730	2466	274	645	128	34	32	347	152	312	.262	.308	.380	85	-54	-57	291	18			.964	18	2/S3O	0.0
■ MIKE YOUNG Young, Michael Darren b: 3/20/60, Oakland, Cal. BB/TR, 6'2", 195 lbs. Deb: 9/14/82																									
1982	Bal-A	6	2	2	0	0	0	0	0	0	1	.000	.000	.000	-99	-1	-1	0	0	0	0	1.000	-0	/OD	-0.1
1983	Bal-A	25	36	5	6	2	1	0	2	2	8	.167	.231	.278	40	-3	-3	2	1	0	0	.929	-4	O/D	-0.7
1984	Bal-A	123	401	59	101	17	2	17	52	58	110	.252	.356	.431	119	10	11	66	6	2	1	.982	-9	*O/D	-0.1
1985	Bal-A	139	450	72	123	22	1	28	81	48	104	.273	.349	.513	136	19	21	78	1	5	-3	.975	-0	OD	1.5
1986	Bal-A	117	369	43	93	15	1	9	42	49	90	.252	.344	.371	96	-2	-1	47	3	1	0	.962	2	OD	-0.1
1987	Bal-A	110	363	46	87	10	1	16	39	46	91	.240	.328	.405	96	-4	-2	48	10	7	-1	.975	-3	OD	-0.8
1988	Phi-N	75	146	13	33	14	0	1	14	26	43	.226	.347	.342	96	1	0	19	0	0	0	.938	-2	O	-0.3
	Mil-A	8	14	2	0	0	0	0	0	2	5	.000	.176	.000	-46	-3	-3	0	0	0	0	.000	-1	/OD	-0.4
1989	Cle-A	32	59	2	11	0	0	1	5	6	13	.186	.273	.237	44	-4	-4	4	1	2	-1	1.000	-0	D/O	-0.6
Total	8	635	1840	244	454	80	6	72	235	237	465	.247	.339	.414	107	14	19	266	22	17	-4	.969	-18	OD	-1.6
■ BABE YOUNG Young, Norman Robert b: 7/1/15, Astoria, N.Y. d: 12/25/83, Everett, Mass. BL/TL, 6'2.5", 185 lbs. Deb: 9/26/36																									
1936	NY-N	1	1	0	0	0	0	0	0	0	0	.000	.000	.000	-99	-0	-0	0	0			.000	0	H	0.0
1939	NY-N	22	75	8	23	4	0	3	14	5	6	.307	.373	.480	127	3	3	14	0			.982	-2	1	-0.1
1940	NY-N	149	556	75	159	27	4	17	101	69	28	.286	.367	.441	121	17	17	92	4			.992	-2	*1	0.0
1941	NY-N	152	574	90	152	28	5	25	104	66	39	.265	.346	.462	124	18	17	93	1			.986	-4	*1	0.2
1942	NY-N	101	287	37	80	17	1	11	59	34	22	.279	.365	.460	140	14	14	50	1			.972	-4	O1	0.7
1946	NY-N	104	291	30	81	11	0	7	33	30	21	.278	.346	.388	107	3	3	40	3			.988	-8	1O	-0.9
1947	NY-N	14	14	0	1	1	0	0	0	0	1	.071	.071	.143	-44	-3	-3	0	0			.000	0	H	-0.3
	Cin-N	95	364	55	103	21	3	14	79	35	26	.283	.349	.473	117	7	8	60	0			.990	-2	1	0.3
	Yr	109	378	55	104	22	3	14	79	35	27	.275	.340	.460	111	4	5	59	0			.990	-2	1	0.0
1948	Cin-N	49	130	11	30	7	2	1	12	19	12	.231	.329	.338	84	-3	-3	16	0			.993	0	1/O	-0.3
	StL-N	41	111	14	27	5	2	1	13	16	6	.243	.339	.351	82	-2	-3	14	0			.996	-4	1	-0.7
	Yr	90	241	25	57	12	4	2	25	35	18	.237	.333	.344	83	-5	-5	30	0			.995	-4	1/O	-1.0
Total	8	728	2403	320	656	121	17	79	415	274	161	.273	.352	.436	117	55	53	379	9			.989	-25	1/O	-1.1
■ RALPH YOUNG Young, Ralph Stuart b: 9/19/1889, Philadelphia, Pa. d: 1/24/65, Philadelphia, Pa. BB/TR, 5'5", 165 lbs. Deb: 4/10/13																									
1913	NY-A	7	15	2	1	0	0	0	0	3	3	.067	.222	.067	-15	-2	-2	1	2			.857	1	/S	0.0
1915	Det-A	123	378	44	92	6	5	0	31	53	31	.243	.339	.286	83	-4	-7	41	12	11	-3	.950	8	*2	-0.1
1916	Det-A	153	528	60	139	16	6	1	45	62	43	.263	.342	.322	96	1	-2	61	20	20	-6	.966	-1	*2/S3	-0.4
1917	Det-A	141	503	64	116	18	2	1	35	61	35	.231	.317	.280	83	-9	-9	49	8			.958	8	*2	0.7
1918	Det-A	91	298	31	56	7	1	0	21	54	17	.188	.313	.218	63	-12	-11	26	15			.939	-12	2	-1.9
1919	Det-A	125	456	63	96	13	5	1	25	53	32	.211	.294	.268	60	-25	-23	43	8			.970	17	*2/S	0.0
1920	Det-A	150	594	84	173	21	6	0	33	85	30	.291	.382	.347	96	-1	1	82	8	13	-5	.969	-11	*2	-1.0
1921	Det-A	107	401	70	120	8	3	0	29	69	23	.299	.406	.334	91	-1	-1	60	11	9	-2	.947	-23	*2	-2.2
1922	Phi-A	125	470	62	105	19	2	1	35	55	21	.223	.309	.279	53	-31	-33	43	8	6	-1	.960	-15	*2	-4.5

YEAR	TM/L	G	AB	R	H	2B	3B	HR	RBI	BB	SO	AVG	OBP	SLG	PRO+	BR	/A	RC	SB	CS	SBR	FA	FR	POS	TPR
Total	9	1022	3643	480	898	108	30	4	254	495	235	.247	.339	.296	79	-85	-86	406	92	59		.959	-28	2/S3	-9.4
■ **DICK YOUNG** Young, Richard Ennis b: 6/3/28, Seattle, Wash. BL/TR, 5'11", 175 lbs. Deb: 9/11/51																									
1951	Phi-N	15	68	7	16	5	0	0	2	3	6	.235	.268	.309	55	-4	-4	5	0	1	-1	.922	-9	2	-1.4
1952	Phi-N	5	9	3	2	1	0	0	0	1	3	.222	.300	.333	76	-0	-0	1	1	0	0	.900	-0	/2	0.0
Total	2	20	77	10	18	6	0	0	2	4	9	.234	.272	.312	58	-5	-5	6	1	1	-0	.919	-9	/2	-1.4
■ **BOBBY YOUNG** Young, Robert George b: 1/22/25, Granite, Md. d: 1/28/85, Baltimore, Md. BL/TR, 6'1", 175 lbs. Deb: 7/28/48																									
1948	StL-N	3	1	0	0	0	0	0	0	0	1	.000	.000	.000	-95	-0	-0	0	0			1.000	1	/3	0.0
1951	StL-A	147	611	75	159	13	9	1	31	44	51	.260	.310	.316	67	-26	-29	60	8	7	-2	.980	1	*2	-2.2
1952	StL-A	149	575	59	142	15	9	4	39	56	48	.247	.314	.325	76	-17	-19	62	3	3	-1	.984	-9	*2	-2.3
1953	StL-A	148	537	48	137	22	2	4	25	41	40	.255	.309	.326	70	-22	-23	56	2	1	0	.977	-17	*2	-3.2
1954	Bal-A	130	432	43	106	13	6	4	24	54	42	.245	.331	.331	88	-10	-6	49	4	4	-1	.976	-14	*2	-1.4
1955	Bal-A	59	186	5	37	3	0	1	8	11	23	.199	.244	.231	30	-19	-17	10	1	4	-2	.985	3	2	-1.3
	Cle-A	18	45	7	14	1	1	0	6	1	2	.311	.326	.378	86	-1	-1	6	0	0	0	.983	7	2/3	0.6
	Yr	77	231	12	51	4	1	1	14	12	25	.221	.259	.260	42	-20	-18	15	1	4	-2	.985	9	2/3	-0.7
1956	Cle-A	1	0	0	0	0	0	0	0	0	0	—	—	—	—	0	0	0	0	0	0	.000	0	R	0.0
1958	Phi-N	32	60	7	14	1	1	1	4	1	5	.233	.246	.333	52	-4	-4	4	0	0	0	.968	-2	2	-0.6
Total	8	687	2447	244	609	68	28	15	137	208	212	.249	.308	.318	71	-100	-100	247	18	19		.980	-32	2/3	-10.4
■ **RUSS YOUNG** Young, Russell Charles b: 9/15/02, Bryan, Ohio d: 5/13/84, Roseville, Cal. BB/TR, 6', 175 lbs. Deb: 4/16/31																									
1931	StL-A	16	34	2	4	0	0	1	2	2	4	.118	.167	.206	-3	-5	-5	1	0	0	0	1.000	2	C	-0.2
■ **JOEL YOUNGBLOOD** Youngblood, Joel Randolph b: 8/28/51, Houston, Tex. BR/TR, 6', 180 lbs. Deb: 4/13/76																									
1976	Cin-N	55	57	8	11	1	1	0	1	2	8	.193	.233	.246	35	-5	-5	3	1	0	0	.938	1	/O3C2	-0.4
1977	StL-N	25	27	1	5	2	0	0	1	3	5	.185	.267	.259	43	-2	-2	1	0	2	-1	1.000	-0	O/3	-0.4
	NY-N	70	182	16	46	11	1	0	11	13	40	.253	.303	.324	72	-8	-7	16	1	3	-2	.954	5	2O3	-0.3
	Yr	95	209	17	51	13	1	0	12	16	45	.244	.298	.316	67	-10	-9	17	1	5	-3	1.000	4	O23	-0.7
1978	NY-N	113	266	40	67	12	8	7	30	16	39	.252	.297	.436	106	-0	1	35	4	0	1	.989	9	O2/3S	1.1
1979	NY-N	158	590	90	162	37	5	16	60	60	84	.275	.349	.436	117	10	13	90	18	13	-2	.985	7	*O23	1.3
1980	NY-N	146	514	58	142	26	2	8	69	52	69	.276	.345	.381	105	2	4	67	14	11	-2	.984	19	*O3/2	1.7
1981	NY-N★	43	143	16	50	10	2	4	25	12	19	.350	.408	.531	167	12	12	28	2	5	-2	.962	-1	O	0.8
1982	NY-N	80	202	21	52	12	0	3	21	8	37	.257	.302	.361	85	-4	-4	20	0	4	-2	.969	-3	O/2S3	-1.1
	Mon-N	40	90	16	18	2	0	0	8	9	21	.200	.294	.222	45	-6	-6	6	2	1	0	1.000	-0	O	-0.8
	Yr	120	292	37	70	14	0	3	29	17	58	.240	.300	.318	73	-10	-11	27	2	5	-2	.979	-3	O/2S3	-1.9
1983	SF-N	124	373	59	109	20	3	17	53	33	59	.292	.358	.499	139	17	18	64	7	4	-0	.948	-29	23O	-1.0
1984	SF-N	134	469	50	119	17	1	10	51	48	86	.254	.328	.358	96	-4	-2	56	5	6	-2	.887	-26	*3O/2	-3.4
1985	SF-N	95	230	24	62	6	0	4	24	30	37	.270	.356	.348	103	0	2	29	3	2	-0	.955	-0	O/3	-0.1
1986	SF-N	97	184	20	47	12	0	5	28	18	34	.255	.325	.402	105	-0	1	25	1	1	-0	1.000	-6	O/132S	-0.7
1987	SF-N	69	91	9	23	3	0	3	11	5	13	.253	.299	.385	83	-3	-2	10	1	1	-0	1.000	-3	O/3	-0.5
1988	SF-N	83	123	12	31	4	0	0	16	10	17	.252	.313	.285	76	-4	-3	11	1	1	-0	.980	-11	O	-1.7
1989	Cin-N	76	118	13	25	5	0	3	13	13	21	.212	.301	.331	78	-3	-3	11	0	1	-1	.970	-10	O	-1.6
Total	14	1408	3659	453	969	180	23	80	422	332	589	.265	.332	.392	103	1	14	471	60	55	-15	.981	-49	O32/1SC	-7.1
■ **HENRY YOUNGMAN** Youngman, Henry b: 1865, Indiana, Pa. d: 1/24/36, Pittsburgh, Pa. TR , Deb: 4/19/1890																									
1890	Pit-N	13	47	6	6	1	1	0	4	6	9	.128	.226	.191	27	-4	-4	2	1			.750	-2	/32	-0.5
■ **ROSS YOUNGS** Youngs, Ross Middlebrook "Pep" (b: Royce Middlebrook Youngs) b: 4/10/1897, Shiner, Tex. d: 10/22/27, San Antonio, Tex. BL/TR, 5'8", 162 lbs. Deb: 9/25/17 H																									
1917	NY-N	7	26	5	9	2	3	0	1	1	5	.346	.370	.654	218	3	3	6	1			1.000	1	/O	0.4
1918	NY-N	121	474	70	143	16	8	1	25	44	49	.302	.368	.376	129	16	17	67	10			.950	-6	*O/2	0.5
1919	NY-N	130	489	73	152	**31**	7	2	43	51	47	.311	.384	.415	142	25	26	84	24			.942	2	*O	2.1
1920	NY-N	153	581	92	204	27	14	6	78	75	55	.351	.427	.477	161	47	48	118	18	18	-5	.935	3	*O	3.5
1921	*NY-N	141	504	90	165	24	16	3	102	71	47	.327	.411	.456	129	24	24	96	21	17	-4	.978	-4	*O	0.6
1922	*NY-N	149	559	105	185	34	10	7	86	55	50	.331	.398	.465	121	19	18	105	17	9	-0	.942	4	*O	1.1
1923	*NY-N	152	596	**121**	200	33	12	3	87	73	36	.336	.412	.446	128	26	27	108	13	19	-8	.959	1	*O	1.0
1924	*NY-N	133	526	112	187	33	12	10	74	77	31	.356	.441	.521	161	45	47	123	11	9	-2	.955	-1	*O/2	3.4
1925	NY-N	130	500	82	132	24	6	6	53	66	51	.264	.354	.372	89	-9	-6	69	17	11	-2	.952	-6	*O/2	-2.1
1926	NY-N	95	372	62	114	12	5	4	43	37	19	.306	.372	.398	109	5	5	55	21			.974	2	O	0.0
Total	10	1211	4627	812	1491	236	93	42	592	550	390	.322	.399	.441	131	201	210	831	153	83		.953	-4	*O/2	10.5
■ **EDDIE YOUNT** Yount, Floyd Edwin b: 12/19/16, Newton, N.C. d: 10/26/73, Newton, N.C. BR/TR, 6'1", 185 lbs. Deb: 9/09/37																									
1937	Phi-A	4	7	1	2	0	0	0	1	0	1	.286	.286	.286	45	-1	-1	1	0	0	0	1.000	-0	/O	-0.1
1939	Pit-N	2	2	0	0	0	0	0	0	0	2	.000	.000	.000	-99	-1	-1	0	0			.000	0	H	-0.1
Total	2	6	9	1	2	0	0	0	1	0	3	.222	.222	.222	14	-1	-1	1	0	0			-0	/O	-0.2
■ **ROBIN YOUNT** Yount, Robin R b: 9/16/55, Danville, Ill. BR/TR, 6', 170 lbs. Deb: 4/05/74 F																									
1974	Mil-A	107	344	48	86	14	5	3	26	12	46	.250	.277	.346	79	-10	-10	31	7	7	-2	.962	-11	*S	-1.1
1975	Mil-A	147	558	67	149	28	2	8	52	33	69	.267	.309	.367	90	-8	-8	64	12	4	1	.939	-23	*S	-1.5
1976	Mil-A	161	638	59	161	19	3	2	54	38	69	.252	.294	.301	76	-21	-19	55	16	11	-2	.963	-5	*S/O	-0.7
1977	Mil-A	154	605	66	174	34	4	4	49	41	80	.288	.335	.377	94	-5	-5	77	16	7	1	.964	-9	*S	0.4
1978	Mil-A	127	502	66	147	23	9	9	71	24	43	.293	.326	.428	110	5	5	71	16	5	2	.959	22	*S	4.5
1979	Mil-A	149	577	72	154	26	5	8	51	35	52	.267	.310	.371	83	-15	-15	63	11	8	-2	.969	5	*S	0.6
1980	Mil-A★	143	611	121	179	**49**	10	23	87	26	67	.293	.323	.519	131	19	21	101	20	5	3	.961	0	*S/D	3.9
1981	*Mil-A	96	377	50	103	15	5	10	49	22	37	.273	.317	.419	116	4	6	51	4	1	1	**.985**	28	S/D	4.5
1982	*Mil-A★	156	635	129	**210**	**46**	12	29	114	54	63	.331	.384	**.578**	**171**	**50**	**55**	**136**	14	3	2	.969	-4	*S/D	**6.7**
1983	Mil-A★	149	578	102	178	42	**10**	17	80	72	58	.308	.387	.503	155	35	41	115	12	5	1	.973	-5	*S/D	4.9
1984	Mil-A	160	624	105	186	27	7	16	80	67	67	.298	.367	.441	127	20	23	99	14	4	2	.971	15	*SD	5.0
1985	Mil-A	122	466	76	129	26	3	15	68	49	56	.277	.348	.442	115	9	10	73	10	4	1	.970	4	*OD/1	1.0
1986	Mil-A	140	522	82	163	31	7	9	46	62	73	.312	.389	.450	124	22	19	94	14	5	1	**.997**	12	*O/1D	2.7
1987	Mil-A	158	635	99	198	25	9	21	103	76	94	.312	.386	.479	124	26	24	120	19	9	0	.987	8	*O/D	2.6
1988	Mil-A	162	621	92	190	38	**11**	13	91	63	63	.306	.373	.465	132	28	27	106	22	4	4	.996	15	*O/D	4.2
1989	Mil-A	160	614	101	195	38	9	21	103	63	71	.318	.387	.511	153	41	42	**125**	19	3	4	.981	4	*OD	4.6
1990	Mil-A	158	587	98	145	17	5	17	77	78	89	.247	.341	.380	102	2	3	81	15	8	-0	.991	6	*O/D	0.5
1991	Mil-A	130	503	66	131	20	4	10	77	54	79	.260	.337	.376	99	-2	0	63	6	4	-1	.994	4	*OD	0.0
1992	Mil-A	150	557	71	147	40	3	8	77	53	81	.264	.331	.390	103	1	2	73	15	6	1	.995	2	*OD	0.2
Total	19	2729	10554	1570	3025	558	123	243	1355	922	1257	.287	.346	.432	116	202	222	1598	262	103	17	.964	67	*SOD/1	43.0
■ **JEFF YURAK** Yurak, Jeffrey Lynn b: 2/26/54, Pasadena, Cal. BB/TR, 6'3", 195 lbs. Deb: 9/15/78																									
1978	Mil-A	5	5	0	0	0	0	0	0	1	0	.000	.167	.000	-49	-1	-1	0	0	0	0	1.000	0	/O	-0.1
■ **SAL YVARS** Yvars, Salvador Anthony b: 2/20/24, New York, N.Y. BR/TR, 5'10", 187 lbs. Deb: 9/27/47																									
1947	NY-N	1	5	0	1	0	0	0	0	0	2	.200	.200	.200	6	-1	-1	0	0			1.000	-0	/C	-0.1
1948	NY-N	15	38	4	8	1	0	1	6	3	1	.211	.286	.316	62	-2	-2	3	0			1.000	3	C	0.1
1949	NY-N	3	8	0	0	0	0	0	0	1	1	.000	.111	.000	-68	-2	-2	0	0			1.000	1	/C	-0.1

YEAR	TM/L	G	AB	R	H	2B	3B	HR	RBI	BB	SO	AVG	OBP	SLG	PRO+	BR	/A	RC	SB	CS	SBR	FA	FR	POS	TPR
1950	NY-N	9	14	0	2	0	0	0	0	1	2	.143	.200	.143	-8	-2	-2	0	0			.963	2	/C	0.0
1951	*NY-N	25	41	9	13	2	0	2	3	5	7	.317	.417	.512	147	3	3	10	0	0	0	.942	-3	C	0.0
1952	NY-N	66	151	15	37	3	0	4	18	10	16	.245	.296	.344	77	-5	-5	14	0	0	0	.988	7	C	0.4
1953	NY-N	23	47	1	13	0	0	0	1	7	1	.277	.370	.277	71	-2	-2	5	0	0	0	1.000	1	C	0.0
	StL-N	30	57	4	14	2	0	1	6	4	6	.246	.306	.333	67	-3	-3	5	0	1	-1	.989	2	C	-0.1
	Yr	53	104	5	27	2	0	1	7	11	7	.260	.336	.308	69	-4	-4	10	0	1	-1	.994	3	C	-0.1
1954	StL-N	38	57	8	14	4	0	2	8	6	5	.246	.328	.421	93	-1	-1	8	1	0	0	1.000	-2	C	-0.2
Total	8	210	418	41	102	12	0	10	42	37	41	.244	.315	.344	76	-14	-14	46	1	1		.987	10	C	0.0
■ ELMER ZACHER	Zacher, Elmer Henry "Silver" b: 9/17/1883, Buffalo, N.Y. d: 12/20/44, Buffalo, N.Y. BR/TR, 5'9", 190 lbs. Deb: 4/30/10																								
1910	NY-N	1	0	0	0	0	0	0	0	0	0	—	—	—	—	0	0	0	0			1.000	-0	/O	0.0
	StL-N	47	132	7	28	5	1	0	10	10	19	.212	.278	.265	61	-7	-6	11	3			.966	3	O/2	-0.6
	Yr	48	132	7	28	5	1	0	10	10	19	.212	.278	.265	61	-7	-6	11	3			.966	2	O/2	-0.6
■ FRED ZAHNER	Zahner, Frederick Joseph b: 6/5/1870, Louisville, Ky. d: 7/24/1900, Louisville, Ky. Deb: 7/23/1894																								
1894	Lou-N	13	45	7	9	0	1	0	3	3	5	.200	.250	.244	22	-6	-5	3	2			.778	-5	C/O1	-0.8
1895	Lou-N	21	49	7	11	1	1	0	6	6	4	.224	.321	.286	63	-3	-2	5	0			.824	-6	C	-0.6
Total	2	34	94	14	20	1	2	0	9	9	9	.213	.288	.266	43	-9	-7	8	2			.805	-11	/CO1	-1.4
■ FRANKIE ZAK	Zak, Frank Thomas b: 2/22/22, Passaci, N.J. d: 2/6/72, Passaic, N.J. BR/TR, 5'10", 150 lbs. Deb: 4/21/44																								
1944	Pit-N☆	87	160	33	48	3	1	0	11	22	18	.300	.385	.331	99	2	1	22	6			.948	6	S	1.0
1945	Pit-N	15	28	2	4	2	0	0	3	3	5	.143	.226	.214	22	-3	-3	2	0			.971	1	S/2	-0.2
1946	Pit-N	21	20	8	4	0	0	0	0	1	0	.200	.238	.200	24	-2	-2	1	0			.929	9	S	0.7
Total	3	123	208	43	56	5	1	0	14	26	23	.269	.350	.303	82	-3	-4	25	6			.948	15	/S2	1.5
■ JACK ZALUSKY	Zalusky, John Francis b: 6/22/1879, Minneapolis, Minn d: 8/11/35, Minneapolis, Minn. BR/TR, 5'11.5", 172 lbs. Deb: 9/04/03																								
1903	NY-A	7	16	2	5	0	0	0	1	1		.313	.353	.313	95	0	-0	2	0			1.000	-1	/C1	-0.1
■ JOE ZAPUSTAS	Zapustas, Joseph John b: 7/25/07, Boston, Mass. BR/TR, 6'1", 185 lbs. Deb: 9/28/33																								
1933	Phi-A	2	5	0	1	0	0	0	0	0	0	.200	.200	.200	6	-1	-1	0	0	0	0	1.000	-1	/O	-0.1
■ JOSE ZARDON	Zardon, Jose Antonio (Sanchez) "Guineo" b: 5/20/23, Havana, Cuba BR/TR, 6', 150 lbs. Deb: 4/18/45																								
1945	Was-A	54	131	13	38	5	3	0	13	7	11	.290	.326	.374	112	0	1	15	3	1	0	.972	-1	O	-0.1
■ AL ZARILLA	Zarilla, Allen Lee "Zeke" b: 5/1/19, Los Angeles, Cal. BL/TR, 5'11", 180 lbs. Deb: 6/30/43 C																								
1943	StL-A	70	228	27	58	7	1	2	17	17	20	.254	.309	.320	82	-5	-5	23	1	1	-0	.962	-2	O	-1.1
1944	*StL-A	100	288	43	86	13	6	6	45	29	33	.299	.375	.448	127	13	11	52	1	1	-0	.977	-2	O	0.5
1946	StL-A	125	371	46	96	14	9	4	43	27	37	.259	.311	.377	87	-5	-7	43	3	5	-2	.973	3	*O	-1.1
1947	StL-A	127	380	34	85	15	6	3	38	40	45	.224	.303	.318	71	-14	-15	39	3	6	-3	.986	-10	*O	-3.5
1948	StL-A★	144	529	77	174	39	3	12	74	48	48	.329	.389	.482	128	22	20	103	11	6	-0	.962	-9	*O	0.4
1949	StL-A	15	56	10	14	1	0	1	6	8	2	.250	.354	.321	76	-1	-2	7	1	1	-0	1.000	-5	O	-0.8
	Bos-A	124	474	68	133	32	4	9	71	48	51	.281	.352	.422	97	1	-3	70	4	4	-1	.984	-2	*O	-1.2
	Yr	139	530	78	147	33	4	10	77	56	53	.277	.352	.411	95	-0	-5	77	5	5	-2	.985	-7	*O	-2.0
1950	Bos-A	130	471	92	153	32	10	9	74	76	47	.325	.423	.493	122	26	19	106	2	3	-1	.976	-4	*O	0.8
1951	Chi-A	120	382	56	98	21	2	10	60	60	57	.257	.363	.401	109	4	5	58	2	4	-2	.983	-12	*O	-1.2
1952	Chi-A	39	99	14	23	4	1	2	7	14	6	.232	.333	.354	90	-1	-1	13	1	0	0	.974	-6	O	-0.8
	StL-A	48	130	20	31	6	0	1	9	27	15	.238	.373	.308	88	-0	-1	17	2	1	0	.976	0	O	-0.2
	Bos-A	21	60	9	11	0	1	2	8	7	8	.183	.269	.317	58	-3	-4	6	2	0	1	.941	-1	O	-0.5
	Yr	108	289	43	65	10	2	5	24	48	29	.225	.339	.325	83	-5	-6	36	5	1	1	.968	-7	O	-1.5
1953	Bos-A	57	67	11	13	2	0	0	4	14	13	.194	.333	.224	50	-4	-4	5	0	1	-1	.947	-5	O	-1.1
Total	10	1120	3535	507	975	186	43	61	456	415	382	.276	.357	.405	102	32	12	543	33	33	-10	.974	-53	O	-9.8
■ NORM ZAUCHIN	Zauchin, Norbert Henry b: 11/17/29, Royal Oak, Mich. BR/TR, 6'4.5", 220 lbs. Deb: 9/23/51																								
1951	Bos-A	5	12	0	2	1	0	0	0	0	4	.167	.167	.250	11	-2	-2	0	0	1	-1	.957	-0	/1	-0.2
1955	Bos-A	130	477	65	114	10	0	27	93	69	105	.239	.339	.430	97	3	-3	73	3	0	1	**.995**	1	*1	-0.8
1956	Bos-A	44	84	12	18	2	0	2	11	14	22	.214	.333	.310	63	-3	-5	9	0	0	0	.990	-1	1	-0.7
1957	Bos-A	52	91	11	24	3	0	3	14	9	13	.264	.343	.396	96	0	-0	11	0	0	0	.972	0	1	-0.2
1958	Was-A	96	303	35	69	8	2	15	37	38	68	.228	.316	.416	101	-1	0	39	0	0	0	.995	2	1	-0.4
1959	Was-A	19	71	11	15	4	0	3	4	7	14	.211	.291	.394	87	-2	-1	7	2	0	1	.995	-2	1	-0.5
Total	6	346	1038	134	242	28	2	50	159	137	226	.233	.327	.408	93	-4	-11	139	5	1	1	.993	0	1	-2.8
■ ZAY	Zay Deb: 10/07/1886																								
1886	Bal-a	1	1	0	0	0	0	0		0		.000	.000	.000	-99	-0	-0	0	0			.000	-0	/OP	0.0
■ JOE ZDEB	Zdeb, Joseph Edmund b: 6/27/53, Compton, Ill. BR/TR, 5'11", 185 lbs. Deb: 4/07/77																								
1977	*KC-A	105	195	26	58	5	2	2	23	16	23	.297	.351	.374	97	-0	-1	24	6	5	-1	.970	-18	O/3D	-2.2
1978	KC-A	60	127	18	32	2	3	0	11	7	18	.252	.291	.315	69	-5	-5	12	3	0	1	.957	-9	O/23D	-1.6
1979	KC-A	15	23	3	4	1	1	0	0	2	4	.174	.240	.304	45	-2	-2	2	1	0	0	1.000	-1	/O	-0.3
Total	3	180	345	47	94	8	6	2	34	25	45	.272	.322	.348	83	-7	-8	38	10	5	0	.967	-29	O/D32	-4.1
■ DAVE ZEARFOSS	Zearfoss, David William Tilden b: 1/1/1868, Schenectady, N.Y. d: 9/12/45, Wilmington, Del. TR, 5'9", Deb: 4/17/1896																								
1896	NY-N	19	60	5	13	1	1	0	6	5	5	.217	.288	.267	50	-4	-4	5	2			.893	-4	C	-0.6
1897	NY-N	5	10	1	3	0	1	0	0	0		.300	.300	.500	112	0	0	2	0			.880	2	/C	0.2
1898	NY-N	1	1	0	1	0	0	0	0	0		1.000	1.000	1.000	489	0	0	1	0			1.000	1	/C	0.1
1904	StL-N	27	80	7	17	2	0	0	9	10		.213	.300	.237	70	-3	-2	6	0			.966	-2	C	-0.1
1905	StL-N	20	51	2	8	0	1	0	2	4		.157	.218	.196	25	-5	-5	2	0			.966	-0	C	-0.3
Total	5	72	202	15	42	3	3	0	17	19	5	.208	.279	.252	57	-11	-10	16	2			.943	-4	/C	-0.7
■ GEORGE ZEBER	Zeber, George William b: 8/29/50, Ellwood City, Pa. BB/TR, 5'11", 170 lbs. Deb: 5/07/77																								
1977	*NY-A	25	65	8	21	3	0	3	10	9	11	.323	.405	.508	149	4	5	14	0	0	0	.961	1	2/S3D	0.7
1978	NY-A	3	6	0	0	0	0	0	0	0	0	.000	.000	.000	-99	-2	-2	0	0	0	0	.750	-1	/2	-0.3
Total	2	28	71	8	21	3	0	3	10	9	11	.296	.375	.465	129	3	3	14	0	0	0	.953	-0	/23SD	0.4
■ ROLLIE ZEIDER	Zeider, Rollie Hubert "Bunions" b: 11/16/1883, Auburn, Ind. d: 9/12/67, Garrett, Ind. BR/TR, 5'10", 162 lbs. Deb: 4/14/10																								
1910	Chi-A	136	498	57	108	9	2	0	31	62		.217	.305	.243	75	-14	-12	52	49			.931	-1	2S/3	-1.4
1911	Chi-A	73	217	39	55	3	0	2	21	29		.253	.347	.295	82	-5	-4	32	28			.997	-5	1S3/2	-0.8
1912	Chi-A	130	420	57	103	12	10	1	42	50		.245	.330	.329	91	-6	-4	62	47			.979	6	13/S	0.1
1913	Chi-A	16	20	4	7	0	0	0	2	4	1	.350	.458	.350	139	1	1	4	3			1.000	2	/312	0.4
	NY-A	50	159	15	37	2	0	0	12	25	9	.233	.341	.245	72	-4	-4	14	3			.901	-14	S2/13	-1.8
	Yr	66	179	19	44	2	0	0	14	29	10	.246	.354	.257	79	-3	-3	18	6			.901	-11	S2/31	-1.4
1914	Chi-F	119	452	60	124	13	2	1	36	44	28	.274	.344	.319	95	-5	-2	65	35			.936	-0	*3/S	0.2
1915	Chi-F	129	494	65	112	22	2	0	34	43	24	.227	.297	.279	74	-18	-15	49	16			.941	0	23S	-1.2
1916	Chi-N	98	345	29	81	11	2	1	22	26	26	.235	.294	.287	71	-8	-12	32	9			.928	-8	32/OS1	-2.0
1917	Chi-N	108	354	36	86	14	2	0	27	28	30	.243	.302	.294	77	-7	-10	35	17			.901	-21	S32/1O	-3.0
1918	*Chi-N	82	251	31	56	3	2	0	26	23	20	.223	.288	.251	63	-10	-11	23	16			.956	-11	2/13	-1.9
Total	9	941	3210	393	769	89	22	5	253	334	138	.240	.315	.286	79	-76	-71	369	223			.945	-52	23S1/O	-11.4

■ TODD ZEILE
Zeile, Todd Edward b: 9/9/65, Van Nuys, Cal. BR/TR, 6'1", 190 lbs. Deb: 8/18/89

YEAR	TM/L	G	AB	R	H	2B	3B	HR	RBI	BB	SO	AVG	OBP	SLG	PRO+	BR	/A	RC	SB	CS	SBR	FA	FR	POS	TPR
1989	StL-N	28	82	7	21	3	1	1	8	9	14	.256	.330	.354	92	-0	-1	10	0	0	0	.971	-2	C	-0.1
1990	StL-N	144	495	62	121	25	3	15	57	67	77	.244	.337	.398	101	1	1	67	2	4	-2	.988	-11	*C31/O	-0.6
1991	StL-N	155	565	76	158	36	3	11	81	62	94	.280	.356	.412	115	12	12	82	17	11	-2	.943	-7	*3	0.5
1992	StL-N	126	439	51	113	18	4	7	48	68	70	.257	.357	.364	106	5	6	57	7	10	-4	.960	-7	*3	-0.5
Total	4	453	1581	196	413	82	11	34	194	206	255	.261	.349	.392	107	18	18	216	26	25	-7	.946	-26	3C/1O	-0.7

■ BART ZELLER
Zeller, Barton Wallace b: 7/22/41, Chicago Heights, Ill. BR/TR, 6'1", 185 lbs. Deb: 5/21/70 C

YEAR	TM/L	G	AB	R	H	2B	3B	HR	RBI	BB	SO	AVG	OBP	SLG	PRO+	BR	/A	RC	SB	CS	SBR	FA	FR	POS	TPR
1970	StL-N	1	0	0	0	0	0	0	0	0	0	—	—	—	—	0	0	0	0	0	0	1.000	-0	/C	0.0

■ GUS ZERNIAL
Zernial, Gus Edward "Ozark Ike" b: 6/27/23, Beaumont, Tex. BR/TR, 6'2.5", 210 lbs. Deb: 4/19/49

YEAR	TM/L	G	AB	R	H	2B	3B	HR	RBI	BB	SO	AVG	OBP	SLG	PRO+	BR	/A	RC	SB	CS	SBR	FA	FR	POS	TPR
1949	Chi-A	73	198	29	63	17	2	5	38	15	26	.318	.366	.500	132	7	7	37	0	1	-1	1.000	-5	O	0.0
1950	Chi-A	143	543	75	152	16	4	29	93	38	110	.280	.330	.484	110	1	3	84	0	2	-1	.969	2	*O	-0.2
1951	Chi-A	4	19	2	2	0	0	0	4	2	2	.105	.190	.105	-19	-3	-3	0	0	0	0	.933	1	/O	-0.2
	Phi-A	139	552	90	151	30	5	33	125	61	99	.274	.350	.525	132	23	22	102	2	2	-1	.974	10	*O	2.5
	Yr	143	571	92	153	30	5	**33**	**129**	63	101	.268	.345	.511	127	20	18	101	2	2	-1	.972	11	*O	2.3
1952	Phi-A	145	549	76	144	15	1	29	100	70	87	.262	.347	.452	114	14	10	89	5	1	1	.972	-1	*O	0.5
1953	Phi-A★	147	556	85	158	21	3	42	108	57	79	.284	.355	.559	138	30	28	113	4	0	1	.972	13	*O	3.6
1954	Phi-A	97	336	42	84	8	2	14	62	30	60	.250	.319	.411	98	-2	-2	44	0	0	0	.953	-1	O/1	-0.7
1955	KC-A	120	413	62	105	9	3	30	84	30	90	.254	.309	.508	116	6	6	59	1	0	0	.964	8	*O	1.0
1956	KC-A	109	272	36	61	12	0	16	44	33	66	.224	.317	.445	99	-2	-2	40	2	0	1	.984	2	O	-0.3
1957	KC-A	131	437	56	103	20	1	27	69	34	84	.236	.292	.471	104	1	-0	57	1	1	-0	.952	0	*O/1	-0.8
1958	Det-A	66	124	8	40	7	1	5	23	6	25	.323	.354	.516	127	6	5	22	0	0	0	.939	-2	O	0.1
1959	Det-A	60	132	11	30	4	0	7	26	7	27	.227	.266	.417	80	-3	-4	14	0	0	0	.972	-3	1/O	-1.0
Total	11	1234	4131	572	1093	159	22	237	776	383	755	.265	.331	.486	115	78	69	661	15	7	0	.968	24	*O/1	4.5

■ CHARLIE ZIEGLER
Ziegler, Charles W. b: 1/13/1875, Canton, Ohio d: 3/16/04, Canton, Ohio Deb: 9/23/1899

YEAR	TM/L	G	AB	R	H	2B	3B	HR	RBI	BB	SO	AVG	OBP	SLG	PRO+	BR	/A	RC	SB	CS	SBR	FA	FR	POS	TPR
1899	Cle-N	2	8	2	2	0	0	0	0	0		.250	.250	.250	40	-1	-1	1	0			.750	-1	/S2	-0.2
1900	Phi-N	3	11	0	3	0	0	0	1	0		.273	.273	.273	51	-1	-1	1	0			.889	-1	/3	-0.2
Total	2	5	19	2	5	0	0	0	1	0		.263	.263	.263	47	-1	-1	1	0				-2	/32S	-0.4

■ BENNY ZIENTARA
Zientara, Benedict Joseph b: 2/14/20, Chicago, Ill. d: 4/16/85, Lake Elsinore, Cal. BR/TR, 5'9", 165 lbs. Deb: 9/11/41

YEAR	TM/L	G	AB	R	H	2B	3B	HR	RBI	BB	SO	AVG	OBP	SLG	PRO+	BR	/A	RC	SB	CS	SBR	FA	FR	POS	TPR
1941	Cin-N	9	21	3	6	0	0	0	2	1	3	.286	.318	.286	71	-1	-1	2	0			.914	1	/2	0.1
1946	Cin-N	78	280	26	81	10	2	0	16	14	11	.289	.323	.339	91	-5	-4	30	3			.970	24	23	2.4
1947	Cin-N	117	418	60	108	18	1	2	24	23	23	.258	.297	.321	64	-22	-21	39	2			.976	-17	*23	-3.1
1948	Cin-N	74	187	17	35	1	2	0	7	12	11	.187	.236	.214	23	-20	-19	9	0			.990	12	2/3S	-0.4
Total	4	278	906	106	230	29	5	2	49	50	48	.254	.293	.304	64	-48	-45	80	5			.976	20	2/3S	-1.0

■ BILL ZIES
Zies, William BL , Deb: 8/09/1891

YEAR	TM/L	G	AB	R	H	2B	3B	HR	RBI	BB	SO	AVG	OBP	SLG	PRO+	BR	/A	RC	SB	CS	SBR	FA	FR	POS	TPR
1891	StL-a	2	3	0	1	0	0	0	0	0	0	.333	.333	.333	81	-0	-0	0	0			1.000	0	/C	0.0

■ CHIEF ZIMMER
Zimmer, Charles Louis b: 11/23/1860, Marietta, Ohio d: 8/22/49, Cleveland, Ohio BR/TR, 6', 190 lbs. Deb: 7/18/1884 MU

YEAR	TM/L	G	AB	R	H	2B	3B	HR	RBI	BB	SO	AVG	OBP	SLG	PRO+	BR	/A	RC	SB	CS	SBR	FA	FR	POS	TPR
1884	Det-N	8	29	0	2	1	0	0	0	1	14	.069	.100	.103	-38	-4	-4	0				.830	-2	/CO	-0.5
1886	NY-a	6	19	1	3	0	0	0		1		.158	.238	.158	28	-2	-1	1	0			.893	3	/C	0.2
1887	Cle-a	14	52	9	12	5	0	0		4		.231	.298	.327	78	-2	-1	6	1			.923	-4	C/1	-0.4
1888	Cle-a	65	212	27	51	11	4	0	22	18		.241	.312	.330	112	3	3	27	15			.917	7	C/O1S	1.4
1889	Cle-N	84	259	47	67	9	9	1	21	44	35	.259	.368	.375	112	5	5	42	14			.931	7	C/1	1.7
1890	Cle-N	125	444	54	95	16	6	2	57	46	54	.214	.303	.291	77	-13	-12	45	15			.937	12	*C	1.1
1891	Cle-N	116	440	55	112	21	4	3	69	33	49	.255	.312	.341	88	-5	-8	53	15			.936	18	*C/3	1.9
1892	*Cle-N	111	413	63	108	29	13	1	64	32	47	.262	.325	.402	117	9	7	61	18			.938	11	*C	2.4
1893	Cle-N	57	227	27	70	13	7	2	41	16	15	.308	.357	.454	110	4	2	39	4			.968	8	C/3	1.2
1894	Cle-N	90	341	55	97	20	5	4	65	17	31	.284	.328	.408	75	-13	-16	52	14			**.963**	10	*C	0.2
1895	*Cle-N	88	315	60	107	21	2	5	56	33	30	.340	.417	.467	123	15	12	69	14			.975	8	C/1	2.2
1896	*Cle-N	91	336	46	93	18	3	3	46	31	48	.277	.354	.375	89	-2	-6	48	4			**.972**	9	*C/3	1.1
1897	Cle-N	80	294	50	93	22	3	0	40	25		.316	.378	.412	103	4	1	51	8			.976	7	C	1.4
1898	Cle-N	20	63	5	15	2	0	0	4	5		.238	.304	.270	66	-3	-3	6	2			.970	5	C	0.3
1899	Cle-N	20	73	9	25	2	1	2	14	5		.342	.407	.479	154	4	5	15	1			.957	-1	C	0.5
	Lou-N	75	262	43	78	11	3	2	29	22		.298	.370	.385	107	3	3	43	9			.985	0	C1	0.8
	Yr	95	335	52	103	13	4	4	43	27		.307	.378	.406	117	7	8	58	10			**.978**	-1	C1	1.3
1900	*Pit-N	82	271	27	80	7	10	0	35	17		.295	.361	.395	108	3	3	42	4			.961	7	C/1	1.5
1901	Pit-N	69	236	17	52	7	3	0	21	20		.220	.290	.275	62	-10	-11	22	6			.975	-7	C	-1.1
1902	Pit-N	42	142	13	38	4	2	0	17	11		.268	.338	.324	101	1	0	18	4			.969	-0	C/1	0.5
1903	Phi-N	37	118	9	26	3	1	1	19	9		.220	.292	.288	68	-5	-5	11	3			.968	4	CM	0.3
Total	19	1280	4546	617	1224	222	76	26	620	390	323	.269	.339	.369	96	-8	-24	651	151			.952	103	*C/103S	16.7

■ DON ZIMMER
Zimmer, Donald William b: 1/17/31, Cincinnati, Ohio BR/TR, 5'9", 177 lbs. Deb: 7/02/54 MC

YEAR	TM/L	G	AB	R	H	2B	3B	HR	RBI	BB	SO	AVG	OBP	SLG	PRO+	BR	/A	RC	SB	CS	SBR	FA	FR	POS	TPR
1954	Bro-N	24	33	3	6	0	1	0	0	3	8	.182	.270	.242	34	-3	-3	2	2	0	1	.939	3	S	0.1
1955	*Bro-N	88	280	38	67	10	1	15	50	19	66	.239	.292	.443	89	-4	-5	34	5	3	-0	.976	9	2S/3	0.9
1956	Bro-N	17	20	4	6	1	0	0	2	0	7	.300	.333	.350	78	-0	-1	2	0	1	-1	.944	2	/S32	0.1
1957	Bro-N	84	269	23	59	9	1	6	19	16	63	.219	.263	.327	52	-16	-20	21	1	3	-2	.957	9	3S/2	-0.8
1958	LA-N	127	455	52	119	15	2	17	60	28	92	.262	.306	.415	86	-9	-10	55	14	2	3	.965	**33**	*S3/2O	3.5
1959	*LA-N	97	249	21	41	7	1	4	28	37	56	.165	.275	.249	38	-21	-23	18	3	1	0	.972	2	S/32	-1.5
1960	Chi-N	132	368	37	95	16	7	6	35	27	56	.258	.309	.389	90	-6	-5	42	8	6	-1	.980	6	23/SO	0.7
1961	Chi-N★	128	477	57	120	25	4	13	40	25	70	.252	.292	.403	81	-14	-14	52	5	1	1	.973	1	*2/3O	-0.1
1962	NY-N	14	52	3	4	1	0	0	1	3	10	.077	.127	.096	-38	-10	-10	1	0	1	-1	.961	5	3	-0.6
	Cin-N	63	192	16	48	11	2	2	16	14	30	.250	.304	.359	75	-6	-7	20	1	2	-1	.949	-1	32/S	-0.7
	Yr	77	244	19	52	12	2	2	17	17	40	.213	.267	.303	51	-16	-17	18	1	3	-2	.952	4	32/S	-1.3
1963	LA-N	22	23	4	5	1	0	1	2	3	10	.217	.308	.391	107	-0	0	3	0	0	0	.933	2	3/2S	0.2
	Was-A	83	298	37	74	12	1	13	44	18	57	.248	.296	.426	100	-1	-1	34	3	2	-0	.935	3	3/2	0.2
1964	Was-A	121	341	38	84	16	2	12	38	27	94	.246	.302	.411	96	-3	-2	40	1	3	-2	.955	-13	3/OC2	-1.9
1965	Was-A	95	226	20	45	6	0	2	17	26	59	.199	.287	.252	56	-13	-12	17	2	0	1	.966	-7	C32	-1.9
Total	12	1095	3283	353	773	130	22	91	352	246	678	.235	.291	.372	76	-106	-115	340	45	25	-2	.941	53	32S/CO	-1.8

■ EDDIE ZIMMERMAN
Zimmerman, Edward Desmond b: 1/4/1883, Oceanic, N.J. d: 5/6/45, Emmaus, Pa. BR/TR, 5'9", 160 lbs. Deb: 9/29/06

YEAR	TM/L	G	AB	R	H	2B	3B	HR	RBI	BB	SO	AVG	OBP	SLG	PRO+	BR	/A	RC	SB	CS	SBR	FA	FR	POS	TPR
1906	StL-N	5	14	0	3	0	0	0	0	1		.214	.214	.214	35	-1	-1	1	0			.929	-0	/3	-0.1
1911	Bro-N	122	417	31	77	10	7	3	36	34	37	.185	.249	.264	46	-33	-30	30	9			**.961**	3	*3	-2.6
Total	2	127	431	31	80	10	7	3	37	34	37	.186	.248	.262	45	-34	-31	31	9			.960	3	3	-2.7

■ JERRY ZIMMERMAN
Zimmerman, Gerald Robert b: 9/21/34, Omaha, Neb. BR/TR, 6'2", 185 lbs. Deb: 4/14/61 C

YEAR	TM/L	G	AB	R	H	2B	3B	HR	RBI	BB	SO	AVG	OBP	SLG	PRO+	BR	/A	RC	SB	CS	SBR	FA	FR	POS	TPR
1961	*Cin-N	76	204	8	42	5	0	0	10	11	21	.206	.253	.230	29	-20	-21	11	1	1	-0	.975	3	C	-1.5
1962	Min-A	34	62	8	17	4	0	0	7	3	5	.274	.318	.339	74	-2	-2	7	0	0	0	.992	2	C	0.1
1963	Min-A	39	56	3	13	1	0	0	3	2	8	.232	.259	.250	43	-4	-4	3	0	0	0	1.000	6	C	0.2
1964	Min-A	63	120	6	24	3	0	0	12	10	15	.200	.278	.225	42	-9	-9	7	0	0	0	.993	6	C	-0.2
1965	*Min-A	83	154	8	33	1	1	1	11	12	23	.214	.275	.253	49	-10	-10	10	0	0	0	**.997**	12	C	0.4
1966	Min-A	60	119	11	30	4	1	1	15	15	23	.252	.341	.328	88	-1	-2	13	0	0	0	.996	9	C	1.0

YEAR	TM/L	G	AB	R	H	2B	3B	HR	RBI	BB	SO	AVG	OBP	SLG	PRO+	BR	/A	RC	SB	CS	SBR	FA	FR	POS	TPR
1967	Min-A	104	234	13	39	3	0	1	12	22	49	.167	.244	.192	28	-20	-22	11	0	1	-1	.992	15	*C	-0.4
1968	Min-A	24	45	3	5	1	0	0	2	3	10	.111	.184	.133	-3	-6	-6	1	0	0	0	.991	5	C	0.0
Total	8	483	994	60	203	22	2	3	72	78	154	.204	.270	.239	43	-71	-76	64	1	2	-1	.991	58	C	-0.4

■ HEINIE ZIMMERMAN Zimmerman, Henry b: 2/9/1887, New York, N.Y. d: 3/14/69, New York, N.Y. BR/TR, 5′11.5″, 176 lbs. Deb: 9/08/07

YEAR	TM/L	G	AB	R	H	2B	3B	HR	RBI	BB	SO	AVG	OBP	SLG	PRO+	BR	/A	RC	SB	CS	SBR	FA	FR	POS	TPR
1907	*Chi-N	5	9	0	2	1	0	0	1	0		.222	.222	.333	70	-0	-0	1	0			.789	1	/2SO	0.1
1908	Chi-N	46	113	17	33	4	1	0	9	1		.292	.298	.345	101	0	-0	12	2			.923	-10	2/OS3	-1.2
1909	Chi-N	65	183	23	50	9	2	0	21	3		.273	.285	.344	93	-2	-3	19	7			.945	4	23S	0.2
1910	*Chi-N	99	335	35	95	16	6	3	38	20	36	.284	.326	.394	111	2	3	44	7			.948	-10	2S3/O1	-0.7
1911	Chi-N	143	535	80	164	22	17	9	85	25	50	.307	.343	.462	124	14	14	91	23			.946	-1	*231	1.1
1912	Chi-N	145	557	95	**207**	**41**	14	**14**	99	38	60	**.372**	.418	**.571**	**169**	**50**	**50**	**141**	23			.916	2	*31	5.1
1913	Chi-N	127	447	69	140	28	12	9	95	41	40	.313	.379	.490	147	26	26	87	18			.912	4	*3	3.2
1914	Chi-N	146	564	75	167	36	12	4	87	20	46	.296	.326	.424	123	12	12	79	17			.897	-21	*3S2	-0.3
1915	Chi-N	139	520	65	138	28	11	3	62	21	33	.265	.300	.379	105	1	1	61	19	13	-2	.943	-9	*23/S	-0.8
1916	Chi-N	107	398	54	116	25	5	6	64	16	33	.291	.324	.425	116	12	7	55	15	12	-3	.932	7	32/S	2.1
	NY-N	40	151	22	41	4	0	0	19	7	10	.272	.304	.298	90	-3	-2	14	9	8	-2	.943	-3	3/2	-0.4
	Yr	147	549	76	157	29	5	6	**83**	23	43	.286	.318	.390	110	9	6	68	24	20	-5	.935	4	*32/S	1.7
1917	*NY-N	150	585	61	174	22	9	5	**102**	16	43	.297	.317	.391	121	9	11	74	13			.947	13	*3/2	3.0
1918	NY-N	121	463	43	126	19	10	1	56	13	23	.272	.294	.363	102	-2	-1	51	14			.955	-4	*31	-0.5
1919	NY-N	123	444	56	113	20	6	4	58	21	30	.255	.296	.354	96	-4	-3	48	8			.940	-1	*3	0.1
Total	13	1456	5304	695	1566	275	105	58	796	242	404	.295	.331	.419	121	116	115	776	175	33		.928	-28	32/S10	11.0

■ ROY ZIMMERMAN Zimmerman, Roy Franklin b: 9/13/16, Pine Grove, Pa. BL/TL, 6′2″, 187 lbs. Deb: 9/02/45

YEAR	TM/L	G	AB	R	H	2B	3B	HR	RBI	BB	SO	AVG	OBP	SLG	PRO+	BR	/A	RC	SB	CS	SBR	FA	FR	POS	TPR
1945	NY-N	27	98	14	27	1	0	5	15	5	16	.276	.330	.439	111	1	1	14	1			.988	-2	1/O	-0.3

■ BILL ZIMMERMAN Zimmerman, William H. b: 1/20/1889, Kengen, Germany d: 10/4/52, Newark, N.J. BR/TR, 5′8.5″, 172 lbs. Deb: 4/14/15

YEAR	TM/L	G	AB	R	H	2B	3B	HR	RBI	BB	SO	AVG	OBP	SLG	PRO+	BR	/A	RC	SB	CS	SBR	FA	FR	POS	TPR
1915	Bro-N	22	57	3	16	2	0	0	7	4	8	.281	.328	.316	93	-0	-0	6	1			.864	-4	O	-0.6

■ FRANK ZINN Zinn, Frank b: 12/21/1865, Phoenixville, Pa. d: 5/12/36, Manayunk, Pa. 5′8″, 150 lbs. Deb: 4/18/1888

YEAR	TM/L	G	AB	R	H	2B	3B	HR	RBI	BB	SO	AVG	OBP	SLG	PRO+	BR	/A	RC	SB	CS	SBR	FA	FR	POS	TPR
1888	Phi-a	2	7	0	0	0	0	0	0	1		.000	.125	.000	-58	-1	-1	0	0			.938	-1	/C	-0.1

■ GUY ZINN Zinn, Guy b: 2/13/1887, Hallbrook, W.Va. d: 10/6/49, Clarksburg, W.Va. BL/TR, 5′10.5″, 170 lbs. Deb: 9/11/11

YEAR	TM/L	G	AB	R	H	2B	3B	HR	RBI	BB	SO	AVG	OBP	SLG	PRO+	BR	/A	RC	SB	CS	SBR	FA	FR	POS	TPR
1911	NY-A	9	27	5	4	0	2	0	1	4		.148	.281	.296	57	-1	-2	2	0			.923	-0	/O	-0.3
1912	NY-A	106	401	56	105	15	10	6	55	50		.262	.345	.394	105	6	2	60	17			.893	-12	*O	-1.5
1913	Bos-N	36	138	15	41	8	2	1	15	4	23	.297	.322	.406	105	1	0	18	3			.948	4	O	0.3
1914	Bal-F	61	225	30	63	10	6	3	25	16	26	.280	.336	.418	110	3	3	35	6			.935	-5	O	-0.5
1915	Bal-F	102	312	30	84	18	3	5	43	35	28	.269	.343	.394	113	6	5	45	2			.949	-5	O	-0.4
Total	5	314	1103	136	297	51	23	15	139	109	77	.269	.338	.398	107	14	8	160	28			.927	-17	O	-2.4

■ BUD ZIPFEL Zipfel, Marion Sylvester b: 11/18/38, Belleville, Ill. BL/TR, 6′3″, 200 lbs. Deb: 7/26/61

YEAR	TM/L	G	AB	R	H	2B	3B	HR	RBI	BB	SO	AVG	OBP	SLG	PRO+	BR	/A	RC	SB	CS	SBR	FA	FR	POS	TPR
1961	Was-A	50	170	17	34	7	5	4	18	15	49	.200	.265	.371	69	-8	-8	17	1	1	-0	.983	-4	1	-1.6
1962	Was-A	68	184	21	44	4	1	6	21	17	43	.239	.307	.370	82	-5	-5	21	1	2	-1	.976	-2	1O	-1.1
Total	2	118	354	38	78	11	6	10	39	32	92	.220	.287	.370	76	-14	-13	38	2	3	-1	.981	-7	/1O	-2.7

■ RICHIE ZISK Zisk, Richard Walter b: 2/6/49, Brooklyn, N.Y. BR/TR, 6′1″, 208 lbs. Deb: 9/08/71

YEAR	TM/L	G	AB	R	H	2B	3B	HR	RBI	BB	SO	AVG	OBP	SLG	PRO+	BR	/A	RC	SB	CS	SBR	FA	FR	POS	TPR
1971	Pit-N	7	15	2	3	1	0	1	2	4	7	.200	.368	.467	136	1	1	3	0	0	0	1.000	-1	/O	0.0
1972	Pit-N	17	37	4	7	3	0	0	4	7	10	.189	.318	.270	70	-1	-1	3	0	0	0	.938	-1	O	-0.3
1973	Pit-N	103	333	44	108	23	7	10	54	21	63	.324	.364	.526	148	18	19	62	0	0	0	.987	1	O	1.7
1974	*Pit-N	149	536	75	168	30	3	17	100	65	91	.313	.388	.476	146	29	32	99	1	1	-0	.985	9	*O	3.5
1975	*Pit-N	147	504	69	146	27	3	20	75	68	109	.290	.376	.474	136	24	24	90	0	1	-1	.975	-2	*O	1.7
1976	Pit-N	155	581	91	168	35	2	21	89	52	96	.289	.348	.465	128	20	20	90	1	0	0	.987	0	*O	1.5
1977	Chi-A★	141	531	78	154	17	6	30	101	55	98	.290	.360	.514	135	25	25	94	0	4	-2	.982	6	*OD	2.4
1978	Tex-A★	140	511	68	134	19	1	22	85	58	76	.262	.341	.432	116	11	11	74	3	3	-1	.988	-2	OD	0.4
1979	Tex-A	144	503	69	132	21	1	18	64	57	75	.262	.338	.416	103	1	2	69	1	1	-0	.972	-4	*O	-0.8
1980	Tex-A	135	448	48	130	17	1	19	77	39	72	.290	.347	.460	123	11	13	66	0	2	-1	.980	-3	DO	0.7
1981	Sea-A	94	357	42	111	12	1	16	43	28	63	.311	.366	.485	138	19	17	61	0	2	-1	.000	0	D	1.7
1982	Sea-A	131	503	61	147	28	1	21	62	49	89	.292	.356	.477	123	18	16	86	2	1	0	.000	0	*D	1.6
1983	Sea-A	90	285	30	69	12	0	12	36	30	61	.242	.314	.411	94	-1	-3	37	0	0	0	.000	0	D	-0.3
Total	13	1453	5144	681	1477	245	26	207	792	533	910	.287	.355	.466	126	174	176	834	8	15	-7	.981	3	OD	13.8

■ BILLY ZITZMANN Zitzmann, William Arthur b: 11/19/1895, Long Island City, N.Y. d: 5/29/85, Passaic, N.J. BR/TR, 5′10.5″, 175 lbs. Deb: 4/17/19

YEAR	TM/L	G	AB	R	H	2B	3B	HR	RBI	BB	SO	AVG	OBP	SLG	PRO+	BR	/A	RC	SB	CS	SBR	FA	FR	POS	TPR
1919	Pit-N	11	26	5	5	1	0	0	2	0	6	.192	.192	.231	26	-2	-2	1	2			.917	-2	/O	-0.5
	Cin-N	2	1	0	0	0	0	0	0	0	0	.000	.000	.000	-99	-0	-0	0	0			.000	-1	/O	-0.1
	Yr	13	27	5	5	1	0	0	2	0	6	.185	.185	.222	22	-3	-3	1	2			.917	-2	/O	-0.6
1925	Cin-N	104	301	53	76	13	3	0	21	35	22	.252	.342	.316	71	-13	-12	33	11	11	-3	.959	-14	O/S	-3.2
1926	Cin-N	53	94	21	23	2	1	0	3	6	7	.245	.304	.287	61	-5	-5	8	3			.965	-3	O	-0.9
1927	Cin-N	88	232	47	66	10	4	0	24	20	18	.284	.352	.362	94	-2	-1	30	9			.958	-9	O/S3	-1.2
1928	Cin-N	101	266	53	79	9	3	3	33	13	22	.297	.337	.387	90	-5	-4	34	13			.958	-6	O/3	-1.4
1929	Cin-N	47	84	18	19	3	0	0	6	9	10	.226	.309	.262	45	-7	-7	7	4			.940	-3	O/1	-1.0
Total	6	406	1004	197	268	38	11	3	89	83	85	.267	.333	.336	77	-35	-31	114	42	11		.956	-37	O/S13	-8.3

■ EDDIE ZOSKY Zosky, Edward James b: 2/10/68, Whittier, Cal. BR/TR, 6′, 175 lbs. Deb: 9/02/91

YEAR	TM/L	G	AB	R	H	2B	3B	HR	RBI	BB	SO	AVG	OBP	SLG	PRO+	BR	/A	RC	SB	CS	SBR	FA	FR	POS	TPR
1991	Tor-A	18	27	2	4	1	1	0	2	0	8	.148	.148	.259	10	-3	-3	1	0	0	0	1.000	1	S	-0.2
1992	Tor-A	8	7	1	2	0	1	0	1	0	2	.286	.286	.571	129	0	0	1	0	0	0	.923	1	/S	0.1
Total	2	26	34	3	6	1	2	0	3	0	10	.176	.176	.324	34	-3	-3	2	0	0	0	.980	2	/S	-0.1

■ BOB ZUPCIC Zupcic, Robert b: 8/18/66, Pittsburgh, Pa. BR/TR, 6′4″, 220 lbs. Deb: 9/07/91

YEAR	TM/L	G	AB	R	H	2B	3B	HR	RBI	BB	SO	AVG	OBP	SLG	PRO+	BR	/A	RC	SB	CS	SBR	FA	FR	POS	TPR
1991	Bos-A	18	25	3	4	0	0	1	3	1	6	.160	.192	.280	28	-2	-3	1	0	0	0	.875	-5	O	-0.7
1992	Bos-A	124	392	46	108	19	1	3	43	25	60	.276	.325	.352	85	-5	-8	45	2	2	-1	.977	-2	*O/D	-1.3
Total	2	142	417	49	112	19	1	4	46	26	66	.269	.318	.348	82	-8	-10	47	2	2	-1	.971	-6	O/D	-2.0

■ FRANK ZUPO Zupo, Frank Joseph "Noodles" b: 8/29/39, San Francisco, Cal BL/TR, 5′11″, 182 lbs. Deb: 7/01/57

YEAR	TM/L	G	AB	R	H	2B	3B	HR	RBI	BB	SO	AVG	OBP	SLG	PRO+	BR	/A	RC	SB	CS	SBR	FA	FR	POS	TPR
1957	Bal-A	10	12	2	1	0	0	0	0	1	4	.083	.154	.083	-36	-2	-2	0	0	0	0	.913	0	/C	-0.2
1958	Bal-A	1	2	0	0	0	0	0	0	0	1	.000	.000	.000	-99	-1	-1	0	0	0	0	1.000	0	/C	0.0
1961	Bal-A	5	4	1	2	1	0	0	0	1	1	.500	.600	.750	264	1	1	2	0	0	0	1.000	0	/C	0.1
Total	3	16	18	3	3	1	0	0	0	2	6	.167	.250	.222	31	-2	-2	2	0	0	0	.941	1	/C	-0.1

■ PAUL ZUVELLA Zuvella, Paul b: 10/31/58, San Mateo, Cal. BR/TR, 6′, 178 lbs. Deb: 9/04/82

YEAR	TM/L	G	AB	R	H	2B	3B	HR	RBI	BB	SO	AVG	OBP	SLG	PRO+	BR	/A	RC	SB	CS	SBR	FA	FR	POS	TPR
1982	Atl-N	2	1	0	0	0	0	0	0	0	0	.000	.000	.000	-96	-0	-0	0	0	0	0	.800	1	/S	0.1
1983	Atl-N	3	5	0	0	0	0	0	0	2	1	.000	.375	.000	11	-0	-0	0	0	0	0	.750	-2	/S	-0.2
1984	Atl-N	11	25	2	5	1	0	0	1	2	3	.200	.259	.240	38	-2	-2	2	0	0	0	1.000	1	/2S	-0.1
1985	Atl-N	81	190	16	48	8	1	0	4	16	14	.253	.311	.305	69	-7	-8	19	2	0	1	.986	9	2S/3	0.5
1986	NY-A	21	48	2	4	1	0	0	2	5	4	.083	.170	.104	-24	-8	-8	1	0	0	0	.966	4	S	-0.3
1987	NY-A	14	34	2	6	0	0	0	0	0	4	.176	.176	.176	-6	-5	-5	1	0	0	0	1.000	-1	/2S3	-0.6
1988	Cle-A	51	130	9	30	5	1	0	7	8	13	.231	.275	.285	56	-7	-8	10	0	0	0	.959	-3	S	-0.8
1989	Cle-A	24	58	10	16	2	0	2	6	1	11	.276	.300	.414	98	-0	-0	7	0	0	0	.963	-3	S/3D	-0.3

YEAR	TM/L	G	AB	R	H	2B	3B	HR	RBI	BB	SO	AVG	OBP	SLG	PRO+	BR	/A	RC	SB	CS	SBR	FA	FR	POS	TPR
1991	KC-A	2	0	0	0	0	0	0	0	0	0	—	—	—	—	0	0	0	0	0	0	.000	0	/3	0.0
Total	9	209	491	41	109	17	2	2	20	34	50	.222	.275	.277	52	-30	-32	41	2	0	1	.959	5	S/23D	-1.7

■ **DUTCH ZWILLING**   Zwilling, Edward Harrison b: 11/2/1888, St.Louis, Mo. d: 3/27/78, LaCrescenta, Cal. BL/TL, 5'6.5", 160 lbs. Deb: 8/14/10 C

YEAR	TM/L	G	AB	R	H	2B	3B	HR	RBI	BB	SO	AVG	OBP	SLG	PRO+	BR	/A	RC	SB	CS	SBR	FA	FR	POS	TPR
1910	Chi-A	27	87	7	16	5	0	0	5	11		.184	.283	.241	67	-3	-3	6	1			.940	-2	O	-0.7
1914	Chi-F	154	592	91	185	38	8	**16**	95	46	68	.313	.363	.485	149	28	33	116	21			.962	2	*O	2.9
1915	Chi-F	150	548	65	157	32	7	13	**94**	67	65	.286	.366	.442	146	25	29	102	24			.979	8	*O/1	3.2
1916	Chi-N	35	53	4	6	1	0	1	8	4	6	.113	.175	.189	11	-6	-6	2	0			1.000	-2	O	-1.0
Total	4	366	1280	167	364	76	15	30	202	128	139	.284	.351	.438	136	45	53	225	46			.969	6	O/1	4.4

The Pitcher Register

The Pitcher Register consists of the central pitching statistics of every man who has pitched in major league play since 1871, *without exception.* Pitcher batting is expressed in Batting Runs in the Pitcher Batting column, and in the newly added columns for base hits and batting average. Pitcher defense is expressed in Fielding Runs in the Pitcher Defense column.

The pitchers are listed alphabetically by surname and, when more than one pitcher bears the name, alphabetically by *given* name—not by "use name," by which we mean the name he may have had applied to him during his playing career. This is the standard method of alphabetizing used in other biographical reference works, and in the case of baseball it makes it easier to find a lesser-known player with a common surname like Smith or Johnson. This method also jibes with that employed in the Team Roster and Annual Record where, for example, Charles "Old Hoss" Radbourn is shown not as the puzzling O. Radbourn or H. Radbourn, as some reference books have it, but as C. Radbourn. On the whole, we have been conservative in ascribing nicknames, doing so only when the player was in fact known by that name during his playing days.

Each page of the Pitcher Register is topped at the corner by a finding aid: in capital letters, the surname of, first, the pitcher whose entry heads up the page and, second, the pitcher whose entry concludes it. Another finding aid is the use of boldface numerals indicating a league leading total in those categories in which a pitcher is truly attempting to excel. No boldface is given to the "leaders" in losses; in games started (innings pitched is the better category to highlight endurance); in hits allowed (the most would produce an absurd leader, while the fewest would tend to reward a man for pitching fewer innings—hits per nine innings is the better category in which to cite leaders); or (using the same reasoning as for hits allowed) in home runs allowed or bases on balls. Pitcher batting and pitcher defense, because the win-denominated numbers they produce are so small, are also not sorted for single-season leaders (although the all-time leaders in these categories, single season and lifetime, will be found in the separate section called "All-Time Leaders"). New to this edition are symbols denoting All Star Game selection and/or play; these appear to the right of the team/league column. Condensed type will appear occasionally throughout this section; it has no special significance but is designed to accommodate unusually wide figures, such as the 108.00 ERA of Harry Heitmann, who allowed four earned runs in his career of one-third of an inning's work.

The record of a man who pitched in more than one season is given in one line for each season, plus a career total line. If he pitched for more than one team in a given year, his totals for each team are given on separate lines; and if the teams for which he pitched in his "traded year" are in the same league, then his full record is stated in both separate and combined fashion. (In the odd case of a man playing for three or more clubs in one year, with some of these clubs being in the same league, the combined total line will reflect only his play in that one league.) A man who pitched in only one year has no additional career total line since it would be identical to his seasonal listing.

In *Total Baseball 1,* fractional innings were calculated for teams in the Annual Record but were rounded off to the nearest whole inning for individuals, in accordance with baseball scoring practice from 1976 through 1981 (for the previous century, fractional innings pitched were simply lopped off). In 1981, this rounding-off procedure cost Sammy Stewart of Baltimore an ERA title, as Oakland's Steve McCatty won the crown despite having a higher ERA when fractional innings were counted; this singular occurrence led to a change in baseball scoring practice. In the first edition our data base conformed to the 1976–1982 practice for all of pitching history, excepting those men who pitched only one-third of an inning in an entire season. In the second edition of *Total Baseball* we recalculated all fractional innings pitched: look for a superscript figure, either a one or a two, in the IP column to indicate thirds of innings.

Pitching records for the National Association are included in the Pitcher Register because the editors, like most baseball historians, regard it as a major league, inasmuch as it was the only professional league of its day and supplied the National League of 1876 with most of its personnel. In this edition of *Total Baseball,* we benefit from the SABR research project referred to in the Introduction to the Annual Record—which to date has produced games started, complete games, shutouts, saves, innings pitched, hits, and bases on balls and, for 1871–1873, strikeouts, earned runs and ERA. For the years 1874–1875 we have estimated ERA based on the teams' average of 40 percent of runs allowed being earned. For *Total Baseball 4* we expect to have full earned-run data, but for now this estimation produces reasonable results. Until Major League Baseball reverses the position it adopted in 1969 and restores the NA to official major league status, we will reluctantly continue the practice of carrying separate totals for the National Association rather than integrating them into the career marks of those pitchers whose major league tenures began before 1876 and concluded in that year or after it.

Gaps remain elsewhere in the official record of baseball and in the ongoing process of sabermetric reconstruction. The reader will note occasional blank elements in bio-

graphical lines; these are not typographical lapses but signs that the information does not exist or has not yet been found. However, unlike the case of batting records, there are no incomplete statistical columns for pitchers except in the National Association years of 1874–1875 and Pitcher Defense 1871–1875. Where official statistics did not exist or the raw data have not survived, as with batters facing pitchers before 1908 in the American League and before 1903 in the National, we have constructed figures from the available raw data. For example, to obtain a pitcher's BFP—Batters Facing Pitchers—for calculating Opponents' On Base Percentage or Batting Average, we have subtracted league base hits from league at-bats, divided by league innings pitched, multiplied by the pitcher's innings and added his hits and walks allowed

and hit-by-pitch, if available. Research in this area continues, and we hope one day to eliminate the need for inferential data all the way back to 1871. (In this edition, incidentally, we correct an error in Opponents' Batting Average and Opponents' On Base Percentage for pre-1909 pitchers in which the estimated at-bats mistakenly subtracted pitcher batting from league batting, resulting in a figure that was about 10 percent too high.)

For a key to the team and league abbreviations used in the Pitcher Register, flip to the last page of this volume. For a guide to the other procedures and abbreviations employed in the Pitcher Register, review the comments on the prodigiously extended pitching record below.

YEAR TM/L	W	L	PCT	G	GS	CG	SH	SV	IP	H	HR	BB	SO	RAT	ERA	ERA+	OAV	OOB	BH	AVG	PB	PR	/A	PD	TPI
● **RIP VAN WINKLE**				Van Winkle, Rip "Half Moon" (Also Played in 1874 as Geoffrey Crayon)																					
				b: 4/30/1820, Plattekill, N.Y.　d: 12/12/80, Hudson, N.Y.　BL/TL, 5'5", 145 lbs.　Deb: 5/7/1874 MUCHF ◆																					
1874 Bos-n	27	30	.474	57	57	56	1	0	498	502	5	18		9.4	3.90	104	.258	.270	40	.167	-3	5	3		-0.1
1875 Wes-n	29	22	.569	52	51	50	2	1	450	491	4	25		10.3	4.02	106	.260	.272	50	.200	1	7	7		0.5
1883 Bal-a	5	18	.217	27	23	19	0	1	196	207	7	76	77	13.0	3.44	101	.274	.340	18	.180	-0	-3	1	0	-0.1
1884 Was-U	0	1	.000	1	1	1	0	0	8	10	0	2	3	13.5	4.50	110	.309	.349	0	.000	-1	-0	-0	0	0.0
KC-U	5	2	.714	8	6	5	0	0	52	66	0	9	14	13.0	4.33	104	.312	.340	9	.250	2	3	1	0	0.1
Yr	5	3	.625	7	7	6	0	0	60	76	0	11	17	13.0	4.35	104	.311	.341	9	.225	2	3	1	0	0.1
1890 Cin-P	0	0	—	1	1	1	0	0	2	2	0	2	2	∞	∞	-97	1.000	1.000	1	.250	0	-2	-2	0	-0.2
1907 NY-N	16	13	.552	35	34	18	0	2	251	224	19	78	170	10.8	2.76	126	.236	.293	30	.250	1	17	20	2	2.2
1908 NY-N	16	12	.571	36	35	14	1	5	278	224	15	48	205	8.8	2.20	130	.215	.250	25	.200	1	24	20	-3	2.2
1909 NY-N	25	7	.781	36	35	18	0	5	273	202	24	82	208		2.21	164	.201	.261	20	.147	-1	42	43	1	4.2
1910 NY-N	18	12	.600	37	36	19	0	2	291	230	21	83	283	9.4	2.81	135	.211	.267	38	.277	4	40	32	1	3.6
1911 NY-N	20	10	.667	36	35	21	0	4	286	210	18	61	289	8.6	1.76	188	.202	.246	40	.296	4	54	49	-1	5.5
1912 NY-N	21	12	.636	35	35	13	0	3	262	215	23	77	249	10.0	2.92	116	.219	.275	34	.281	3	16	14	1	1.7
1913 NY-N	19	10	.655	36	36	18	0	3	290	219	23	64	251	8.8	2.08	184	.202	.247	31	.263	3	51	56	2	5.9
1914 Ind-F	11	11	.500	32	32	12	0	5	236	199	19	75	201	10.4	3.20	126	.226	.287	22	.227	-1	11	22	1	2.2
1915 NY-N	22	9	.710	36	36	15	0	5	280	217	11	88	243	9.8	2.38	155	.211	.274	33	.311	3	39	41	1	4.2
1936 NY-N☆	7	3	.700	13	13	5	0	3	96	79	7	28	72	10.0	3.00	140	.218	.274	11	.196	1	10	13	3	1.5
Bos-A	5	7	.417	16	16	1	0	0	104	114	8	29	72	12.4	3.81	112	.271	.318	20	.189	0	4	5	-2	0.7
1967 *Bos-A★	0	1	.000	1	1	0	0	0	⅓	5	2	1	1	180.0	108.00	1200	.833	.857	0	.000	0	-2	-2	0	-0.2
Total 2 n	56	52	.519	109	108	106	3	1	948	993	9	43		9.8	3.96	105	.259	.271	90	.184	-2	12	7		0.4
Total 14	190	128	.597	384	375	180	1	38	2903	2486	199	803	2338	10.2	2.76	134	.226	.285	294	.224	23	304	313	6	33.6

Looking at the biographical line for any pitcher, we see first his use name in full capitals, then his given name and nickname (and any other name he may have used or been born with, such as the matronymic of a Latin American player). His date and place of birth follow "b" and his date and place of death follow "d"; years through 1900 are expressed fully, in four digits, and years after 1900 are expressed in only their last two digits. Then come his manner of batting and throwing, abbreviated for a left-handed batter who throws right as BL/TR (a switch-hitter would be shown as BB for "bats both" and a switch thrower as TB for "throws both"). Next, and for most pitchers last, is the pitcher's debut date in the major leagues.

Some pitchers continue in major league baseball after their pitching days are through, as managers, coaches, or even umpires. A pitcher whose biographical line concludes with an M can also be located in the Manager Roster; one whose line bears a C will be listed in the Coach Roster; and one with a U occupies a place in the Umpire Roster. (In the last case we have placed a U on the biographical line only for those pitchers who umpired in at least six games in a year, for in the nineteenth century—and especially in the years of the National Association—there were literally hundreds of players who were pressed into service as umpires for a game or two; it would be misleading to accord such pitchers the same

code we give to Bob Emslie or Bill Dinneen.) The select few who have been enshrined in the Baseball Hall of Fame are noted with an H. They are also listed in the Hall of Fame Roster found toward the end of Bill Deane's "Awards and Honors" essay. New to this edition is an F in this line to denote family connection—father-son-grandson or brother.

A new feature is black diamond appears at the end of the biographical line for pitchers who also appear in the Player Register by virtue of their having played in 100 or more games at another position, including pinch hitter, or having played more than half of their total major league games at another position, or having played more games at a position other than pitcher in at least one year.

The explanations for the statistical column heads follow; for more technical information about formulas and calculations, see the Glossary. The vertical rules in the column-header line separate the stats into six logical groupings: year, team, league; wins and losses; game-related counting stats; inning-related counting stats; basic calculated averages; pitcher batting; sabermetric figures of more complex calculation; and run-denominated Linear Weights stats for pitching, fielding, and Total Pitcher Index. Note that the TPI (Total Pitcher Index) in this third edition may differ slightly from those in earlier volumes, because for players who were both batters and pitchers, the method of allocating Wins between TPI and

TPR (Total Player Rating) was improved. Previously, if a pitcher pitched in over half his games, all his batting was included with his pitcher rating (TPI); if he pitched in less than half his games, his Batting Wins were thrown over to his batter rating (TPR), with his TPI including only his Pitching Wins and Pitcher Defense. The new method prorates batting proportionally with the number of games pitched. In addition, fielding ratings at nonpitching positions for players who pitched in over half their games, previously omitted, are now part or the Total Baseball Ranking. In any case, the TPI/TPR values of batter-pitchers should remain about the same. Thus in 1918, Babe Ruth now has a batter rating or 2.6 Wins and a pitcher rating of 2.8 (total 5.4). In previous editions his marks used to be 4.1 and 1.0, respectively or 5.1 overall, with none of his batting counted in with his pitching record even though he pitched 20 of 95 games. The large jump in his pitcher rating is because now his pitcher batting is compared against average batting for pitchers.

Absent from the Pitcher Register in this edition are some statistics present in the original: Hits Per Game and Bases on Balls Per Game (still available in the Annual Record and Leaders sections, and now stated in combined fashion as Ratio); Strikeouts Per Game (still available in the Annual Record and Leaders sections and, in any event, fairly evident from a glance at the SO and IP columns); Park Factor for pitchers (still available from the Annual Record); Clutch Pitching Index, newly developed for *Total Baseball* but which we have judged to be of lesser interest and value than the more established sabermetric measures (still, it is present in the Annual Record and Leaders sections); and Wins Above Team, a stat that has so many cautions associated with it that we judged it to be of little value when applied to all 6,336 pitchers shown in the Register.

YEAR　Year in which a man pitched (When a space in the column is blank, this indicates that the man pitched for two or more clubs in the last year stated in the column; if those clubs were in the same league, then the man will also have a combined total line, beginning with the abbreviation "Yr" placed in the TM/L column.)

*　　　Denotes postseason play, World Series or League Championship Series.

Yr　　Year's totals for pitching with two or more clubs in same league (see comments for YEAR)

★　　Named to All Star Game, played

☆　　Named to All Star Game, did not play

†　　　Named to All Star Game, replaced because of injury

TM/L　Team and League (see comments for YEAR)

W　　Wins

L　　　Losses

PCT　Win Percentage (Wins divided by decisions)

G　　　Games pitched

GS　　Games Started

CG　　Complete Games

SH　　Shutouts (Complete-game shutouts only)

SV　　Saves (Employing definition in force at the time, and 1969 definition for years prior to 1969)

IP　　Innings Pitched (Fractional innings included, as discussed above)

H　　　Hits allowed

HR　　Home Runs allowed

BB　　Bases on Balls allowed

SO　　Strikeouts

RAT　Ratio (Hits allowed plus walks allowed per nine innings)

ERA　Earned Run Average (In a handful of cases, a pitcher will have faced one or more batters for his full season's work yet failed to retire any of them [thus having an innings-pitched figure of zero]; if any of the men he put on base came around to score earned runs, these runs produced an infinite ERA, expressed in the pitcher's record as ∞. (see Van Winkle's 1890 season)

ERA⁺　Adjusted Earned Run Average normalized to league average and adjusted for home-park factor. (See comments for /A.)

OAV　Opponents' Batting Average

OOB　Opponents' On Base Percentage

BH　　Base Hits (as a batter)

AVG　Batting Average

PB　　Pitcher Batting (Expressed in Batting Runs. Pitcher Batting is park-adjusted and weighted, for those who played primarily at other positions, by the ratio of games pitched to games played. For more technical data about Runs Per Win and Batting Run formulas, see Glossary.)

PR　　Pitching Runs (Linear Weights measure of runs saved *beyond* what a league-average pitcher might have saved, defined as zero. Occasionally the curious figure of −0 will appear in this column, or in the columns of other Linear Weights measures of batting, fielding, and the TPI. This "negative zero" figure signifies a run contribution that falls below the league average, but to so small a degree that it cannot be said to have cost the team a run. Also, this column and the Adjusted one to its right will each contain a pair of single-season leaders, the figures shown in boldface: the top mark in Starters' Runs and the top mark in Relievers' Runs. The former category is reserved for men who averaged more than three innings per game pitched, while the latter category is for those who averaged less than three innings per game pitched.)

/A   Adjusted (This signifies that the stat to the immediate left, in this instance Pitching Runs, is here normalized to league average and adjusted for home-park factor. A mark of 100 is a league-average performance, and superior marks exceed 100. An innovation for this edition is to use three-year averages for pitching park factors. If a team moved, or the park changed dramatically, then two-year averages are employed; if the park was used for only one year, then of course only that run-scoring data is used.)

PD   Pitcher Defense (Expressed in Fielding Runs. See comment above on PB and see Glossary.)

TPI   Total Pitcher Index (The sum, expressed in wins beyond league average, of a pitcher's Pitching Runs, Batting Runs [in the AL since 1973, 0], and Fielding Runs, all divided by the Runs Per Win factor for that year—generally around 10, historically in the 9–11 range; see Glossary.)

Total   For players whose careers include play in the National Association as well as other major leagues, two totals are given, as described above and as illustrated in Rip Van Winkle's record, where the record of his years in the National Association is shown alongside the notation "Total 2 n," where *2* stands for the number of years totaled and *n* stands for National Association. For players whose careers began in 1876 or later, the lifetime record is shown alongside the notation "Total x," where *x* stands for the number of post-1875 years totaled.

A New feature in this third edition of *Total Baseball* is the Relief Pitcher Register, which covers the exploits of all those who made notable contributions from the bullpen, including men who were principally starters, such as Three Finger Brown and Ed Walsh. This register focuses on a man's record in relief, breaking out his games, wins, losses, innings pitched, and Earned run average as a reliever. However, of interest for those who also started will be the columns for games started and innings pitched as a starter.

Here is a sample entry:

YEAR	TM/L	WR	LR	GR	SV	IPR	ERAR	RR	/A	RNK	GS	IPS
■ Dick Tidrow												
1972	Cle-A	1	0	5	0	14²	0.61	4	4	3	34	222²
1973	Cle-A	0	0	2	0	5	1.80	1	1	0	40	269²
1974	Cle-A										4	19
	NY-A	2	0	8	1	33	1.64	7	7	4	25	157²
	Yr	2	0	8	1	52	1.21	8	8	4	29	176²
1975	NY-A	6	3	37	5	69¹	3.12	5	4	5		
1976	NY-A	3	5	45	10	76²	2.70	7	6	8	2	15²
1977	NY-A	6	4	42	5	104¹	3.54	6	5	5	7	46²
1978	NY-A	0	1	6	0	30²	3.52	1	0	0	25	154²
1979	NY-A	2	1	14	2	22²	7.94	-9	-10	-14		
	Chi-N	11	5	63	4	102²	2.72	12	16	24		
1980	Chi-N	6	5	84	6	116	2.79	10	14	14		
1981	Chi-N	3	10	51	9	74²	5.06	-13	-11	-21		
1982	Chi-N	8	3	65	6	103²	3.39	2	4	4		
1983	Chi-A	2	4	49	7	88²	4.26	-2	-1	-1	1	3
1984	NY-N	0	0	11	0	15²	9.19	-10	-10	0		
Total	12	50	41	482	55	857²	3.50	22	30	31	138	889

TM/L   Team and league

WR   Wins in relief

LR   Losses in relief

SV   Saves

IPR   Innings pitched in relief

ERAR   Earned Run Average in relief

RR   Relief Runs (identical to Pitching Runs but confined to relievers)

/A   Adjusted Relief Runs

RNK   Relief Ranking (Adjusted Relief Runs, weighted for the greater value of a bullpen "closer" who limits his opponents' scoring in the late innings; see Glossary for formula. Relief Runs will tend to benefit long and middle relievers, who are effective over many innings, while Relief Ranking will tend to benefit relievers with perhaps fewer innings but more saves and decisions)

GS   Games started

IPS   Innings pitched as a starter

● **DON AASE** Aase, Donald William b: 9/8/54, Orange, Cal. BR/TR, 6'3", 210 lbs. Deb: 7/26/77

YEAR TM/L	W	L	PCT	G	GS	CG	SH	SV	IP	H	HR	BB	SO	RAT	ERA	ERA+	OAV	OOB	BH	AVG	PB	PR	/A	PD	TPI
1977 Bos-A	6	2	.750	13	13	4	2	0	92^1	85	6	19	49	10.2	3.12	144	.244	.285	0	—	0	10	14	-0	1.3
1978 Cal-A	11	8	.579	29	29	6	1	0	178^2	185	14	80	93	13.4	4.03	90	.270	.348	0	—	0	-5	-8	0	-0.7
1979 *Cal-A	9	10	.474	37	28	7	1	2	185^1	200	19	77	96	13.5	4.81	85	.277	.347	0	—	0	-12	-15	-2	-1.5
1980 Cal-A	8	13	.381	40	21	5	1	2	175	193	13	66	74	13.4	4.06	97	.287	.351	0	—	0	-1	-3	-1	-0.3
1981 Cal-A	4	4	.500	39	0	0	0	11	65^1	56	4	24	38	11.0	2.34	156	.234	.304	0	—	0	10	9	-0	1.0
1982 Cal-A	3	3	.500	24	0	0	0	4	52	45	5	23	40	11.8	3.46	117	.243	.327	0	—	0	4	3	-0	0.3
1984 Cal-A	4	1	.800	23	0	0	0	8	39	30	1	19	28	11.3	1.62	246	.221	.316	0	—	0	10	10	-0	1.1
1985 Bal-A	10	6	.625	54	0	0	0	14	88	83	6	35	67	12.2	3.78	106	.258	.332	0	—	0	4	2	0	0.2
1986 Bal-A★	6	7	.462	66	0	0	0	34	81^2	71	6	28	67	10.9	2.98	139	.234	.298	0	—	0	11	11	0	1.1
1987 Bal-A	1	0	1.000	7	0	0	0	2	8	8	1	4	3	13.5	2.25	195	.276	.364	0	—	0	2	2	-0	0.4
1988 Bal-A	0	0	—	35	0	0	0	0	46^2	40	4	37	28	14.9	4.05	96	.240	.377	0	—	0	-0	-1	-1	-0.1
1989 NY-N	1	5	.167	49	0	0	0	2	59^1	56	5	26	34	12.6	3.94	83	.245	.324	0	.000	-1	-3	-4	0	-0.5
1990 LA-N	3	1	.750	32	0	0	0	3	38	33	5	19	24	12.3	4.97	74	.232	.323	0	—	0	-5	-6	-1	-0.6
Total 13	66	60	.524	448	91	22	5	82	1109^1	1085	89	457	641	12.6	3.80	103	.259	.333	0	.000	-1	23	15	-5	1.7

● **BERT ABBEY** Abbey, Bert Wood b: 11/29/1869, Essex, Vt. d: 6/11/62, Essex Junction, Vt. BR/TR, 5'11", 175 lbs. Deb: 6/14/1892

YEAR TM/L	W	L	PCT	G	GS	CG	SH	SV	IP	H	HR	BB	SO	RAT	ERA	ERA+	OAV	OOB	BH	AVG	PB	PR	/A	PD	TPI
1892 Was-N	5	18	.217	27	23	19	0	1	195^2	207	7	76	77	13.3	3.45	94	.261	.330	9	.120	-3	-4	-4	2	-0.5
1893 Chi-N	2	4	.333	7	7	5	0	0	56	74	1	20	6	15.8	5.46	85	.309	.372	6	.231	-0	-5	-5	0	-0.4
1894 Chi-N	2	7	.222	11	11	10	0	0	92	119	3	37	24	15.6	5.18	108	.310	.375	5	.128	-5	1	4	-1	-0.2
1895 Chi-N	0	1	.000	1	1	1	0	0	8	10	0	2	3	14.6	4.50	113	.301	.359	1	.333	0	0	1	0	0.1
Bro-N	5	2	.714	8	6	5	0	0	52	66	0	9	14	13.5	4.33	102	.304	.341	5	.263	1	3	0	1	0.2
Yr	5	3	.625	9	7	6	0	0	60	76	0	11	17	13.5	4.35	103	.303	.340	6	.273	1	3	1	1	0.3
1896 Bro-N	8	8	.500	25	18	12	0	0	164^1	210	7	48	37	14.6	5.15	80	.308	.361	12	.190	-0	-14	-19	-2	-1.7
Total 5	22	40	.355	79	66	52	0	1	568	686	18	192	161	14.3	4.52	92	.292	.352	38	.169	-8	-19	-23	0	-2.5

● **CHARLIE ABBEY** Abbey, Charles S. b: 10/1868, Falls City, Neb. BL , 5'8.5", 169 lbs. Deb: 8/16/1893 ♦

YEAR TM/L	W	L	PCT	G	GS	CG	SH	SV	IP	H	HR	BB	SO	RAT	ERA	ERA+	OAV	OOB	BH	AVG	PB	PR	/A	PD	TPI
1896 Was-N	0	0	—	1	0	0	0	0	2	6	0	0	0	27.0	4.50	98	.511	.511	79	.262	0	-0	-0	-0	0.0

● **JIM ABBOTT** Abbott, James Anthony b: 9/19/67, Flint, Mich. BL/TL, 6'3", 200 lbs. Deb: 4/08/89

YEAR TM/L	W	L	PCT	G	GS	CG	SH	SV	IP	H	HR	BB	SO	RAT	ERA	ERA+	OAV	OOB	BH	AVG	PB	PR	/A	PD	TPI
1989 Cal-A	12	12	.500	29	29	4	2	0	181^1	190	13	74	115	13.3	3.92	97	.274	.347	0	—	0	-1	-2	-1	-0.2
1990 Cal-A	10	14	.417	33	33	4	1	0	211^2	246	16	72	105	13.7	4.51	85	.295	.355	0	—	0	-14	-16	1	-1.4
1991 Cal-A	18	11	.621	34	34	5	1	0	243	222	14	73	158	11.1	2.89	142	.244	.304	0	—	0	33	33	3	3.8
1992 Cal-A	7	15	.318	29	29	7	0	0	211	208	12	68	130	11.9	2.77	141	.263	.325	0	—	0	27	27	2	3.1
Total 4	47	52	.475	125	125	20	4	0	847	866	55	287	508	12.4	3.49	112	.268	.332	0	—	0	45	41	5	5.3

● **KYLE ABBOTT** Abbott, Lawrence Kyle b: 2/18/68, Newburyport, Mass. BL/TL, 6'4", 200 lbs. Deb: 9/10/91

YEAR TM/L	W	L	PCT	G	GS	CG	SH	SV	IP	H	HR	BB	SO	RAT	ERA	ERA+	OAV	OOB	BH	AVG	PB	PR	/A	PD	TPI
1991 Cal-A	1	2	.333	5	3	0	0	0	19^2	22	2	13	12	16.5	4.58	90	.301	.414	0	—	0	-1	-1	0	-0.1
1992 Phi-N	1	14	.067	31	19	0	0	0	133^1	147	20	45	88	13.0	5.13	68	.283	.341	2	.069	-1	-24	-24	-1	-2.7
Total 2	2	16	.111	36	22	0	0	0	153	169	22	58	100	13.5	5.06	71	.285	.351	2	.069	-1	-25	-25	-1	-2.8

● **DAN ABBOTT** Abbott, Leander Franklin "Big Dan" b: 3/16/1862, Portage, Ohio d: 2/13/30, Ottawa Lake, Mich. BR/TR, 5'11", 190 lbs. Deb: 4/19/1890

YEAR TM/L	W	L	PCT	G	GS	CG	SH	SV	IP	H	HR	BB	SO	RAT	ERA	ERA+	OAV	OOB	BH	AVG	PB	PR	/A	PD	TPI
1890 Tol-a	0	2	.000	3	1	1	0	1	13	19	0	8	1	19.4	6.23	63	.330	.421	1	.143	0	-3	-3	1	-0.2

● **PAUL ABBOTT** Abbott, Paul David b: 9/15/67, Van Nuys, Cal. BR/TR, 6'3", 185 lbs. Deb: 8/21/90

YEAR TM/L	W	L	PCT	G	GS	CG	SH	SV	IP	H	HR	BB	SO	RAT	ERA	ERA+	OAV	OOB	BH	AVG	PB	PR	/A	PD	TPI
1990 Min-A	0	5	.000	7	7	0	0	0	34^2	37	0	28	25	17.1	5.97	70	.282	.412	0	—	0	-8	-7	-1	-0.9
1991 Min-A	3	1	.750	15	3	0	0	0	47^1	38	5	36	43	14.1	4.75	90	.232	.370	0	—	0	-3	-3	-0	-0.3
1992 Min-A	0	0	—	6	0	0	0	0	11	12	1	5	13	14.7	3.27	123	.279	.367	0	—	0	1	1	1	0.0
Total 3	3	6	.333	28	10	0	0	0	93	87	6	69	81	15.3	5.03	83	.257	.386	0	—	0	-11	-9	-0	-1.2

● **GLENN ABBOTT** Abbott, William Glenn b: 2/16/51, Little Rock, Ark. BR/TR, 6'6", 200 lbs. Deb: 7/29/73

YEAR TM/L	W	L	PCT	G	GS	CG	SH	SV	IP	H	HR	BB	SO	RAT	ERA	ERA+	OAV	OOB	BH	AVG	PB	PR	/A	PD	TPI
1973 Oak-A	1	0	1.000	5	3	1	0	0	18^2	16	3	7	6	11.1	3.86	92	.225	.295	0	—	0	-0	-1	-0	0.0
1974 Oak-A	5	7	.417	19	17	3	0	0	96	89	4	34	38	11.8	3.00	111	.247	.317	0	—	0	7	3	-0	0.3
1975 *Oak-A	5	5	.500	30	15	3	1	0	114^1	109	12	50	51	12.7	4.25	85	.253	.333	0	—	0	-6	-8	-1	-0.7
1976 Oak-A	2	4	.333	19	10	0	0	0	62^1	87	6	16	27	15.0	5.49	61	.333	.374	0	—	0	-14	-15	0	-1.3
1977 Sea-A	12	13	.480	36	34	7	0	0	204^1	212	32	56	100	12.3	4.45	92	.270	.328	0	—	0	-9	-8	-0	-0.8
1978 Sea-A	7	15	.318	29	28	8	1	0	155^1	191	22	44	67	13.7	5.27	72	.303	.350	0	—	0	-26	-25	0	-2.5
1979 Sea-A	4	10	.286	23	19	3	0	0	116^2	138	19	38	25	13.8	5.17	84	.301	.358	0	—	0	-12	-11	-0	-1.1
1980 Sea-A	12	12	.500	31	31	7	2	0	215	228	27	49	78	11.7	4.10	101	.272	.315	0	—	0	-2	1	2	0.3
1981 Sea-A	4	9	.308	22	20	1	0	0	130^1	127	14	28	35	10.7	3.94	98	.258	.298	0	—	0	-4	-1	-0	-0.4
1983 Sea-A	5	3	.625	14	14	2	0	0	82^1	103	9	15	38	13.3	4.59	93	.311	.349	0	—	0	-5	-3	-1	-0.5
Det-A	2	1	.667	7	7	1	1	0	46^2	43	5	7	11	9.6	1.93	203	.244	.273	0	—	0	11	10	-1	1.2
Yr	7	4	.636	21	21	3	1	0	129	146	14	22	49	11.7	3.63	114	.285	.314	0	—	0	6	7	-1	0.7
1984 Det-A	3	4	.429	13	8	1	0	0	44	62	9	8	8	14.7	5.93	66	.326	.360	0	—	0	-9	-10	0	-0.9
Total 11	62	83	.428	248	206	37	5	0	1286	1405	162	352	484	12.5	4.39	89	.280	.331	0	—	0	-69	-67	-0	-6.4

● **AL ABER** Aber, Albert Julius "Lefty" b: 7/31/27, Cleveland, Ohio BL/TL, 6'2", 195 lbs. Deb: 9/15/50

YEAR TM/L	W	L	PCT	G	GS	CG	SH	SV	IP	H	HR	BB	SO	RAT	ERA	ERA+	OAV	OOB	BH	AVG	PB	PR	/A	PD	TPI
1950 Cle-A	1	0	1.000	1	1	1	0	0	9	5	0	4	4	9.0	2.00	217	.167	.265	0	.000	0	3	2	-0	0.2
1953 Cle-A	1	1	.500	6	0	0	0	0	6	6	0	9	4	22.5	7.50	50	.240	.441	0	—	1	-2	-2	0	-0.2
Det-A	4	3	.571	17	10	2	0	0	66^2	63	3	41	34	14.0	4.45	91	.260	.367	3	.130	-1	-3	-3	1	-0.3
Yr	5	4	.556	23	10	2	0	0	72^2	69	3	50	38	14.7	4.71	86	.258	.375	3	.130	-1	-6	-5	1	-0.5
1954 Det-A	5	11	.313	32	18	4	0	3	124^2	121	8	40	54	11.8	3.97	93	.257	.320	5	.128	-1	-3	-4	1	-0.5
1955 Det-A	6	3	.667	39	1	0	0	3	80	86	9	28	37	12.8	3.37	114	.275	.334	1	.059	-2	5	4	1	0.3
1956 Det-A	4	4	.500	42	0	0	0	7	63	65	1	25	21	13.1	3.43	120	.270	.343	3	.300	1	5	5	0	0.5
1957 Det-A	3	3	.500	28	0	0	0	1	37	46	6	11	15	14.1	6.81	57	.315	.367	1	.125	-0	-12	-12	1	-1.2
KC-A	0	0	—	3	0	0	0	0	3	6	2	2	0	24.0	12.00	33	.400	.471	1	1.000	0	-3	-3	0	-0.2
Yr	3	3	.500	31	0	0	0	1	40	52	8	13	15	14.6	7.20	54	.317	.367	2	.222	0	-15	-15	1	-1.4
Total 6	24	25	.490	168	30	7	0	14	389^1	398	29	160	169	13.0	4.18	93	.269	.342	14	.140	-3	-11	-13	3	-1.4

● **BILL ABERNATHIE** Abernathie, William Edward b: 1/30/29, Torrance, Cal. BR/TR, 5'10", 190 lbs. Deb: 9/27/52

YEAR TM/L	W	L	PCT	G	GS	CG	SH	SV	IP	H	HR	BB	SO	RAT	ERA	ERA+	OAV	OOB	BH	AVG	PB	PR	/A	PD	TPI
1952 Cle-A	0	0	—	1	0	0	0	1	2	4	1	1	0	22.5	13.50	25	.444	.500	0	.000	-0	-2	-2	-0	-0.2

● **TED ABERNATHY** Abernathy, Talmadge Lafayette b: 10/30/21, Bynum, N.C. BR/TL, 6'2", 210 lbs. Deb: 9/19/42

YEAR TM/L	W	L	PCT	G	GS	CG	SH	SV	IP	H	HR	BB	SO	RAT	ERA	ERA+	OAV	OOB	BH	AVG	PB	PR	/A	PD	TPI
1942 Phi-A	0	0	—	1	0	0	0	0	2^2	2	0	3	1	16.9	10.13	37	.222	.417	0	—	0	-2	-2	0	-0.1
1943 Phi-A	0	3	.000	5	2	1	0	0	14^2	24	0	13	10	22.7	12.89	26	.353	.457	1	.250	0	-16	-15	0	-1.4
1944 Phi-A	0	0	—	1	0	0	0	0	3	5	0	1	2	18.0	3.00	116	.417	.462	0	.000	-0	0	0	-0	0.0
Total 3	0	3	.000	7	2	1	0	0	20^1	31	0	17	13	21.2	11.07	31	.348	.453	1	.200	0	-17	-17	0	-1.5

● **TED ABERNATHY** Abernathy, Theodore Wade b: 3/6/33, Stanley, N.C. BR/TR, 6'4", 215 lbs. Deb: 4/13/55

YEAR TM/L	W	L	PCT	G	GS	CG	SH	SV	IP	H	HR	BB	SO	RAT	ERA	ERA+	OAV	OOB	BH	AVG	PB	PR	/A	PD	TPI
1955 Was-A	5	9	.357	40	14	3	2	0	119^1	136	9	67	79	15.8	5.96	64	.294	.392	4	.154	-1	-26	-28	1	-2.7
1956 Was-A	1	3	.250	5	4	2	0	0	30^1	35	2	10	18	13.6	4.15	104	.292	.351	2	.182	-0	0	1	2	0.2
1957 Was-A	2	10	.167	26	16	2	0	0	85	100	9	65	50	17.9	6.78	57	.314	.437	4	.167	0	-28	-27	1	-2.5
1960 Was-A	0	0	—	2	0	0	0	0	3	4	0	4	1	24.0	12.00	32	.308	.471	1	1.000	0	-3	-3	0	-0.2
1963 Cle-A	7	2	.778	43	0	0	0	12	59^1	54	3	29	47	12.6	2.88	126	.251	.340	2	.400	1	5	5	2	0.8
1964 Cle-A	2	6	.250	53	0	0	0	11	72^2	66	5	46	57	14.1	4.33	83	.247	.362	0	.000	-1	-6	-6	3	-0.4

YEAR	TM/L	W	L	PCT	G	GS	CG	SH	SV	IP	H	HR	BB	SO	RAT	ERA	ERA+	OAV	OOB	BH	AVG	PB	PR	/A	PD	TPI
1965	Chi-N	4	6	.400	**84**	0	0	0	**31**	136^1	113	7	56	104	11.5	2.57	143	.227	.311	3	.167	0	15	17	4	2.3
1966	Chi-N	1	3	.250	20	0	0	0	4	27^2	26	4	17	18	14.6	6.18	60	.255	.372	0	.000	-0	-8	-8	2	-0.7
	Atl-N	4	4	.500	38	0	0	0	4	65^1	58	5	36	42	12.9	3.86	94	.247	.347	2	.250	1	-2	-2	1	0.0
	Yr	5	7	.417	58	0	0	0	8	93	84	9	53	60	13.3	4.55	80	.248	.349	2	.167	0	-10	-9	2	-0.7
1967	Cin-N	6	3	.667	**70**	0	0	0	**28**	106^1	63	1	41	88	9.2	1.27	295	.170	.261	1	.059	-1	**25**	**29**	2	3.3
1968	Cin-N	10	7	.588	**78**	0	0	0	13	134^2	111	9	55	64	11.4	2.47	128	.228	.312	0	.000	-1	8	10	3	1.5
1969	Chi-N	4	3	.571	56	0	0	0	3	85^1	75	8	42	55	12.4	3.16	127	.234	.325	2	.250	0	4	8	2	1.1
1970	Chi-N	0	0	—	11	0	0	0	1	9	9	0	5	2	15.0	2.00	225	.281	.395	0	—	0	2	3	0	0.3
	StL-N	1	0	1.000	11	0	0	0	1	18^1	15	0	12	8	14.7	2.95	140	.246	.395	0	.000	-0	2	2	1	0.3
	Yr	1	0	1.000	22	0	0	0	2	27^1	24	0	17	10	14.5	2.63	161	.255	.386	0	.000	-0	4	5	1	0.6
	KC-A	9	3	.750	36	0	0	0	12	55^2	41	3	38	49	12.9	2.59	144	.209	.340	3	.214	0	7	7	0	0.8
1971	KC-A	4	6	.400	63	0	0	0	23	81	60	3	50	55	12.9	2.56	134	.210	.339	1	.077	-1	8	8	2	0.9
1972	KC-A	3	4	.429	45	0	0	0	5	58^1	44	2	19	28	10.2	1.70	179	.210	.284	0	.000	-1	9	9	1	1.0
Total	14	63	69	.477	681	34	7	2	148	1147^2	1010	70	592	765	12.9	3.46	106	.241	.341	25	.138	-4	12	26	27	6.0

● WOODY ABERNATHY

Abernathy, Virgil Woodrow b: 2/1/15, Forest City, N.C. BL/TL, 6', 170 lbs. Deb: 7/28/46

YEAR	TM/L	W	L	PCT	G	GS	CG	SH	SV	IP	H	HR	BB	SO	RAT	ERA	ERA+	OAV	OOB	BH	AVG	PB	PR	/A	PD	TPI
1946	NY-N	1	1	.500	15	1	0	0	1	40	32	5	10	6	9.4	3.37	102	.232	.284	0	.000	-1	0	0	-1	-0.1
1947	NY-N	0	0	—	1	0	0	0	0	2	4	0	1	0	22.5	9.00	45	.400	.455	0	—	0	-1	-1	-0	-0.1
Total	2	1	1	.500	16	1	0	0	1	42	36	5	11	6	10.1	3.64	95	.243	.296	0	.000	-1	-1	-1	-1	-0.2

● HARRY ABLES

Ables, Harry Terrell "Hans" b: 10/4/1884, Terrell, Tex. d: 2/8/51, San Antonio, Tex. BR/TL, 6'2.5", 200 lbs. Deb: 9/04/05

YEAR	TM/L	W	L	PCT	G	GS	CG	SH	SV	IP	H	HR	BB	SO	RAT	ERA	ERA+	OAV	OOB	BH	AVG	PB	PR	/A	PD	TPI
1905	StL-A	0	3	.000	6	3	1	0	0	30^2	37	0	13	11	14.7	3.82	67	.299	.366	0	.000	-1	-4	-4	-1	-0.7
1909	Cle-A	1	1	.500	5	3	3	0	0	29^2	26	1	10	24	11.2	2.12	120	.226	.294	0	.000	-2	1	1	-1	-0.1
1911	NY-A	0	1	.000	3	2	0	0	0	11	16	0	7	6	18.8	9.82	37	.333	.418	0	.000	-1	-8	-8	-0	-0.7
Total	3	1	5	.167	14	8	4	0	0	71^1	79	1	30	41	13.9	4.04	67	.276	.346	0	.000	-4	-11	-11	-2	-1.5

● GEORGE ABRAMS

Abrams, George Allen b: 11/9/1899, Seattle, Wash. d: 12/5/86, Clearwater, Fla. BR/TR, 5'9", 170 lbs. Deb: 4/19/23

YEAR	TM/L	W	L	PCT	G	GS	CG	SH	SV	IP	H	HR	BB	SO	RAT	ERA	ERA+	OAV	OOB	BH	AVG	PB	PR	/A	PD	TPI
1923	Cin-N	0	0	—	3	0	0	0	0	4^2	10	0	3	1	27.0	9.64	40	.500	.583	1	1.000	0	-3	-3	-0	-0.2

● JOHNNY ABREGO

Abrego, Johnny Ray b: 7/4/62, Corpus Christi, Tex BR/TR, 6', 185 lbs. Deb: 9/04/85

YEAR	TM/L	W	L	PCT	G	GS	CG	SH	SV	IP	H	HR	BB	SO	RAT	ERA	ERA+	OAV	OOB	BH	AVG	PB	PR	/A	PD	TPI
1985	Chi-N	1	1	.500	6	5	0	0	0	24	32	3	12	13	16.5	6.38	63	.352	.427	0	.000	-1	-7	-6	0	-0.7

● JIM ACKER

Acker, James Justin b: 9/24/58, Freer, Tex. BR/TR, 6'2", 212 lbs. Deb: 4/07/83

YEAR	TM/L	W	L	PCT	G	GS	CG	SH	SV	IP	H	HR	BB	SO	RAT	ERA	ERA+	OAV	OOB	BH	AVG	PB	PR	/A	PD	TPI
1983	Tor-A	5	1	.833	38	5	0	0	1	97^2	103	7	38	44	13.7	4.33	99	.273	.352	0	—	0	-3	-0	1	-0.2
1984	Tor-A	3	5	.375	32	3	0	0	1	72	79	3	25	33	13.8	4.38	94	.286	.358	0	—	0	-3	-2	-0	-0.5
1985	*Tor-A	7	2	.778	61	0	0	0	10	86^1	86	7	43	42	13.8	3.23	130	.268	.360	0	—	0	9	9	1	1.1
1986	Tor-A	2	4	.333	23	5	0	0	0	60	63	6	22	32	13.1	4.35	97	.281	.351	0	—	0	-1	-1	1	0.0
	Atl-N	3	8	.273	21	14	0	0	0	95	100	7	26	37	12.0	3.79	105	.274	.324	3	.107	-1	-1	2	1	0.1
1987	Atl-N	4	9	.308	68	0	0	0	14	114^2	109	11	51	68	12.9	4.16	104	.253	.338	3	.214	0	-1	2	1	0.4
1988	Atl-N	0	4	.000	21	1	0	0	0	42	45	6	14	25	12.9	4.71	78	.280	.341	2	.400	1	-6	-5	0	-0.4
1989	Atl-N	0	6	.000	59	0	0	0	2	97^2	84	5	20	68	9.7	2.67	137	.237	.280	1	.143	-0	9	11	1	1.2
	*Tor-A	2	1	.667	14	0	0	0	0	28^1	24	1	12	24	11.8	1.59	237	.235	.322	0	—	0	7	7	1	1.0
1990	Tor-A	4	4	.500	59	0	0	0	1	91^2	103	9	30	54	13.4	3.83	103	.281	.341	0	—	0	1	1	1	0.2
1991	*Tor-A	3	5	.375	54	4	0	0	1	88^1	77	16	36	44	11.7	5.20	81	.238	.318	0	—	0	-11	-10	0	-1.0
1992	Sea-A	0	0	—	17	0	0	0	0	30^2	45	4	12	11	16.7	5.28	76	.338	.393	0	—	0	-5	-4	-0	-0.5
Total	10	33	49	.402	467	32	0	0	30	904^1	918	82	329	482	12.7	3.97	103	.267	.337	9	.167	0	-5	10	8	1.4

● TOM ACKER

Acker, Thomas James b: 3/7/30, Paterson, N.J. BR/TR, 6'4", 215 lbs. Deb: 4/20/56

YEAR	TM/L	W	L	PCT	G	GS	CG	SH	SV	IP	H	HR	BB	SO	RAT	ERA	ERA+	OAV	OOB	BH	AVG	PB	PR	/A	PD	TPI
1956	Cin-N	4	3	.571	29	7	1	1	1	83^2	60	7	29	54	9.8	2.37	168	.201	.277	1	.053	-1	13	15	1	1.6
1957	Cin-N	10	5	.667	49	6	1	0	4	108^2	122	16	41	67	14.2	4.97	83	.293	.368	1	.053	-1	-13	-10	-0	-1.1
1958	Cin-N	4	3	.571	38	10	3	0	1	124^2	126	10	43	90	12.4	4.55	91	.266	.331	2	.067	-1	-8	-6	-2	-0.9
1959	Cin-N	1	2	.333	37	0	0	0	2	63^1	57	10	37	45	13.9	4.12	98	.246	.359	1	.111	-0	-1	-0	-1	-0.2
Total	4	19	13	.594	153	23	5	1	8	380^1	365	43	150	256	12.6	4.12	99	.257	.335	5	.065	-3	-10	-1	-2	-0.6

● FRITZ ACKLEY

Ackley, Florian Frederick b: 4/10/37, Hayward, Wis. BL/TR, 6'1.5", 202 lbs. Deb: 9/21/63

YEAR	TM/L	W	L	PCT	G	GS	CG	SH	SV	IP	H	HR	BB	SO	RAT	ERA	ERA+	OAV	OOB	BH	AVG	PB	PR	/A	PD	TPI
1963	Chi-A	1	0	1.000	2	2	0	0	0	13	7	2	7	11	9.7	2.08	169	.167	.286	1	.200	0	2	2	0	0.3
1964	Chi-A	0	0	—	3	2	0	0	0	6^1	10	2	4	6	19.9	8.53	41	.345	.424	1	1.000	1	-3	-4	0	-0.2
Total	2	1	0	1.000	5	4	0	0	0	19^1	17	4	11	17	13.0	4.19	83	.239	.341	2	.333	1	-1	-2	1	0.1

● CY ACOSTA

Acosta, Cecilio (Miranda) b: 11/22/46, Sabino, Mexico BR/TR, 5'10", 165 lbs. Deb: 6/04/72

YEAR	TM/L	W	L	PCT	G	GS	CG	SH	SV	IP	H	HR	BB	SO	RAT	ERA	ERA+	OAV	OOB	BH	AVG	PB	PR	/A	PD	TPI
1972	Chi-A	3	0	1.000	26	0	0	0	5	34^2	25	2	17	28	10.9	1.56	201	.210	.309	0	.000	-0	6	6	-1	0.6
1973	Chi-A	10	6	.625	48	0	0	0	18	97	66	8	39	60	10.4	2.23	178	.193	.289	0	.000	0	17	19	-1	1.8
1974	Chi-A	0	3	.000	27	0	0	0	3	45^2	43	3	18	19	13.0	3.74	100	.256	.346	0	.000	0	-1	-0	0	0.0
1975	Phi-N	0	0	—	6	0	0	0	1	8^2	9	2	3	2	12.5	6.23	60	.273	.333	0	—	0	-3	-2	-0	-0.3
Total	4	13	9	.591	107	0	0	0	27	186	143	15	77	109	11.2	2.66	140	.216	.309	0	.000	-0	20	22	-2	2.1

● ED ACOSTA

Acosta, Eduardo Elixbet b: 3/9/44, Boquete, Panama BB/TR, 6'5", 215 lbs. Deb: 9/07/70

YEAR	TM/L	W	L	PCT	G	GS	CG	SH	SV	IP	H	HR	BB	SO	RAT	ERA	ERA+	OAV	OOB	BH	AVG	PB	PR	/A	PD	TPI
1970	Pit-N	0	0	—	3	0	0	0	1	2^2	5	1	2	1	27.0	13.50	29	.417	.533	0	—	0	-3	-3	-0	-0.3
1971	SD-N	3	3	.500	8	6	3	1	0	46	43	4	7	16	9.8	2.74	120	.246	.275	0	.000	-2	4	3	-1	0.1
1972	SD-N	3	6	.333	46	2	0	0	0	89	105	7	30	53	14.0	4.45	74	.302	.362	1	.083	-0	-10	-11	-1	-1.3
Total	3	6	9	.400	57	8	3	1	1	137^2	153	12	39	70	12.8	4.05	81	.286	.339	1	.034	-2	-9	-11	-1	-1.5

● JOSE ACOSTA

Acosta, Jose "Acostica" b: 3/4/1891, Havana, Cuba d: 11/16/77, Havana, Cuba BR/TR, 5'6", 134 lbs. Deb: 7/28/20 F

YEAR	TM/L	W	L	PCT	G	GS	CG	SH	SV	IP	H	HR	BB	SO	RAT	ERA	ERA+	OAV	OOB	BH	AVG	PB	PR	/A	PD	TPI
1920	Was-A	5	4	.556	17	5	4	1	1	82^2	92	1	26	9	12.8	4.03	93	.290	.344	6	.240	1	-2	-3	-3	-0.4
1921	Was-A	5	4	.556	33	7	2	0	3	115^2	148	4	36	30	14.3	4.36	94	.317	.366	2	.067	-2	-1	-3	-1	-0.6
1922	Chi-A	0	2	.000	5	1	0	0	0	15	25	4	6	6	18.6	8.40	48	.417	.470	1	.200	0	-7	-7	-0	-0.7
Total	3	10	10	.500	55	13	6	1	4	213^1	265	9	68	45	14.0	4.51	88	.314	.365	9	.150	-1	-10	-13	-4	-1.7

● ACE ADAMS

Adams, Ace Townsend b: 3/2/12, Willows, Cal. BR/TR, 5'10.5", 182 lbs. Deb: 4/15/41

YEAR	TM/L	W	L	PCT	G	GS	CG	SH	SV	IP	H	HR	BB	SO	RAT	ERA	ERA+	OAV	OOB	BH	AVG	PB	PR	/A	PD	TPI
1941	NY-N	4	1	.800	38	0	0	0	1	71	84	3	35	18	15.2	4.82	77	.304	.385	1	.083	-1	-9	-9	-1	-1.1
1942	NY-N	7	4	.636	**61**	0	0	0	11	88	69	1	31	33	10.2	1.84	183	.223	.293	1	.100	-1	**14**	**15**	0	1.6
1943	NY-N☆	11	7	.611	**70**	3	1	0	9	140^1	121	5	55	46	11.4	2.82	122	.236	.311	4	.125	-1	9	10	-1	0.8
1944	NY-N	8	11	.421	**65**	4	1	0	**13**	137^2	149	8	58	32	13.8	4.25	86	.279	.354	3	.103	-2	-10	-9	-2	-1.2
1945	NY-N	11	9	.550	65	0	0	0	**15**	113	109	7	44	39	12.3	3.42	114	.252	.324	3	.188	0	5	6	1	0.7
1946	NY-N	0	1	.000	3	0	0	0	0	2^2	9	2	1	3	33.8	16.88	20	.500	.526	0	—	0	-4	-4	0	-0.4
Total	6	41	33	.554	302	7	2	0	49	552^2	541	26	224	171	12.6	3.47	104	.260	.334	12	.121	-5	5	9	-2	0.4

● BABE ADAMS

Adams, Charles Benjamin b: 5/18/1882, Tipton, Ind. d: 7/27/68, Silver Spring, Md BL/TR, 5'11.5", 185 lbs. Deb: 4/18/06

YEAR	TM/L	W	L	PCT	G	GS	CG	SH	SV	IP	H	HR	BB	SO	RAT	ERA	ERA+	OAV	OOB	BH	AVG	PB	PR	/A	PD	TPI
1906	StL-N	0	1	.000	1	1	0	0	0	4	9	0	2	0	24.8	13.50	19	.474	.524	0	.000	-0	-5	-5	0	-0.4
1907	Pit-N	0	2	.000	4	3	1	0	0	22	40	1	3	11	18.8	6.95	35	.408	.442	2	.286	0	-11	-11	0	-1.0
1909	*Pit-N	12	3	.800	25	12	7	3	2	130	88	0	23	65	7.9	1.11	246	.196	.240	2	.051	-3	22	23	-1	2.3
1910	Pit-N	18	9	.667	34	30	16	3	0	245	217	4	60	101	10.4	2.24	138	.240	.291	16	.193	1	22	23	-5	2.0
1911	Pit-N	22	12	.647	40	37	24	6	0	293^1	253	5	42	133	**9.3**	2.33	147	.237	**.271**	26	.252	4	35	36	-8	3.4
1912	Pit-N	11	8	.579	28	21	11	2	0	170^1	169	4	35	63	10.9	2.91	112	.262	.303	12	.226	4	10	7	-2	0.8
1913	Pit-N	21	10	.677	43	37	24	4	0	313^2	271	8	49	144	9.2	2.15	140	.235	.267	33	.289	8	37	30	-1	4.0
1914	Pit-N	13	16	.448	40	35	19	3	1	283	253	5	39	91	9.5	2.51	105	.244	**.276**	16	.165	1	9	4	-2	0.3

YEAR TM/L	W	L	PCT	G	GS	CG	SH	SV	IP	H	HR	BB	SO	RAT	ERA	ERA+	OAV	OOB	BH	AVG	PB	PR	/A	PD	TPI
1915 Pit-N	14	14	.500	40	30	17	2	2	245	229	6	34	62	9.7	2.87	95	.252	.280	12	.141	-2	-3	-4	-0	-0.7
1916 Pit-N	2	9	.182	16	10	4	1	0	72^1	91	2	12	22	13.2	5.72	47	.320	.355	6	.273	2	-25	-24	0	-2.3
1918 Pit-N	1	1	.500	3	3	2	0	0	22^2	15	0	4	6	7.5	1.19	241	.197	.237	3	.333	1	4	4	-1	0.6
1919 Pit-N	17	10	.630	34	29	23	6	1	263^1	213	1	23	92	**8.2**	1.98	152	.220	**.241**	17	.185	-0	27	30	-4	3.0
1920 Pit-N	17	13	.567	35	33	19	**8**	2	263	240	6	18	84	**8.9**	2.16	149	.244	**.259**	13	.146	-5	29	31	-2	2.7
1921 Pit-N	14	5	.737	25	20	11	2	0	160	155	4	18	55	**9.7**	2.64	**145**	.251	**.272**	16	.254	3	20	21	-2	2.4
1922 Pit-N	8	11	.421	27	19	12	4	0	171^1	191	1	15	39	11.0	3.57	114	.287	.307	16	.286	4	10	10	1	1.4
1923 Pit-N	13	7	.650	26	22	11	0	1	158^2	196	8	25	38	12.6	4.42	91	.309	.336	15	.273	5	-7	-7	-2	-0.6
1924 Pit-N	3	1	.750	9	3	2	0	0	39^2	31	1	3	5	7.7	1.13	338	.209	.225	2	.182	-0	12	12	-1	1.1
1925 *Pit-N	6	5	.545	33	10	3	0	3	101^1	129	7	17	18	13.2	5.42	82	.306	.338	7	.226	0	-13	-11	-2	-1.1
1926 Pit-N	2	3	.400	19	0	0	0	3	36^2	51	5	8	7	14.5	6.14	64	.347	.381	2	.222	-0	-9	-9	-1	-1.0
Total 19	194	140	.581	482	355	206	44	15	2995^1	2841	68	430	1036	10.0	2.76	118	.253	.284	216	.212	23	161	161	-32	16.9

● RED ADAMS Adams, Charles Dwight b: 10/7/21, Parlier, Cal. BR/TR, 6', 185 lbs. Deb: 5/05/46 C

1946 Chi-N	0	1	.000	8	0	0	0	0	12	18	1	7	8	18.8	8.25	40	.353	.431	0	.000	-0	-6	-7	1	-0.6

● DAN ADAMS Adams, Daniel Leslie "Rube" b: 6/19/1887, St.Louis, Mo. d: 10/6/64, St.Louis, Mo. BR/TR, 5'11.5", 165 lbs. Deb: 5/22/14

1914 KC-F	4	9	.308	36	14	6	0	3	136	141	3	52	38	13.2	3.51	88	.273	.347	7	.152	-1	-5	-6	-1	-0.8
1915 KC-F	0	2	.000	11	2	0	0	0	35	41	2	13	16	14.1	4.63	63	.301	.367	1	.111	-0	-6	-7	0	-0.7
Total 2	4	11	.267	47	16	6	0	3	171	182	5	65	54	13.4	3.74	82	.279	.351	8	.145	-1	-11	-13	-1	-1.5

● JOE ADAMS Adams, Joseph Edward b: 10/28/1877, Cowden, Ill. d: 10/8/52, Montgomery City, Mo BR/TL, 6', 190 lbs. Deb: 4/26/02

1902 StL-N	0	0	—	1	0	0	0	0	4	9	0	2	0	27.0	9.00	30	.442	.513	0	.000	-0	-3	-3	1	-0.2

● KARL ADAMS Adams, Karl Tutwiler "Rebel" b: 8/11/1891, Columbus, Ga. d: 9/17/67, Everett, Wash. BR/TR, 6'2", 170 lbs. Deb: 4/19/14

1914 Cin-N	0	0	—	4	0	0	0	0	8	14	0	5	5	21.4	9.00	33	.424	.500	1	.500	0	-6	-5	0	-0.5
1915 Chi-N	1	9	.100	26	12	3	0	0	107	105	5	43	57	12.6	4.71	59	.267	.342	0	.000	-4	-23	-23	0	-2.8
Total 2	1	9	.100	30	12	3	0	0	115	119	5	48	62	13.2	5.01	56	.279	.355	1	.031	-4	-29	-28	0	-3.3

● RICK ADAMS Adams, Reuben Alexander b: 12/23/1878, Paris, Tex. d: 3/10/55, Paris, Tex. BL/TL, 6', 165 lbs. Deb: 7/13/05

1905 Was-A	2	5	.286	11	6	3	1	0	62^2	63	1	24	25	13.5	3.59	74	.263	.347	4	.174	0	-6	-7	0	-0.6

● BOB ADAMS Adams, Robert Andrew b: 1/20/07, Birmingham, Ala. d: 3/6/70, Jacksonville, Fla. BR/TR, 6'0.5", 165 lbs. Deb: 9/27/31

1931 Phi-N	0	1	.000	1	1	0	0	0	6	14	0	1	3	22.5	9.00	47	.424	.441	0	.000	-0	-3	-3	-0	-0.3
1932 Phi-N	0	0	—	4	0	0	0	0	6	7	0	2	2	13.5	1.50	294	.318	.375	0	—	0	2	2	0	0.2
Total 2	0	1	.000	5	1	0	0	0	12	21	0	3	5	18.0	5.25	82	.382	.414	0	.000	-0	-2	-1	0	-0.1

● BOB ADAMS Adams, Robert Burdette b: 7/24/01, Holyoke, Mass. BR/TR, 5'11", 168 lbs. Deb: 9/22/25

1925 Bos-A	0	0	—	2	0	0	0	0	5^2	10	1	3	1	20.6	7.94	57	.417	.481	1	.333	0	-2	-2	1	-0.1

● WILLIE ADAMS Adams, William John Irvin b: 9/27/1890, Clearfield, Pa. d: 6/18/37, Albany, N.Y. BR/TR, 6'4", 180 lbs. Deb: 6/30/12

1912 StL-A	2	3	.400	13	5	0	0	0	46^1	50	0	19	16	13.8	3.88	85	.284	.360	0	.000	-2	-3	-3	-1	-0.6
1913 StL-A	0	0	—	4	0	0	0	0	9	12	1	4	5	19.0	10.00	29	.286	.388	0	.000	0	-7	-7	-0	-0.7
1914 Pit-F	1	1	.500	15	2	1	0	2	55^1	70	4	22	14	15.1	3.74	85	.326	.391	1	.067	-1	-3	-3	-1	-0.6
1918 Phi-A	5	12	.294	32	14	7	0	0	169	164	2	97	39	14.5	4.42	66	.272	.383	8	.140	-3	-31	-28	1	-3.2
1919 Phi-A	0	0	—	1	0	0	0	0	4^2	7	1	2	0	19.3	3.86	89	.389	.476	0	.000	-0	-0	-0	-0	-0.1
Total 5	8	16	.333	65	21	8	0	2	284^1	303	8	144	74	14.8	4.37	70	.287	.383	9	.102	-6	-44	-41	-2	-5.2

● MIKE ADAMSON Adamson, John Michael b: 9/13/47, San Diego, Cal. BR/TR, 6'2", 185 lbs. Deb: 7/01/67

1967 Bal-A	0	1	.000	3	2	0	0	0	9^2	9	1	12	8	19.6	8.38	38	.257	.447	1	.500	1	-6	-6	-0	-0.5
1968 Bal-A	0	2	.000	2	2	0	0	0	7^2	9	2	4	4	15.3	9.39	31	.281	.361	1	.333	0	-5	-6	-0	-0.5
1969 Bal-A	0	1	.000	6	0	0	0	0	8	10	0	6	2	18.0	4.50	79	.357	.471	0	.000	-0	-1	-1	1	-0.1
Total 3	0	4	.000	11	4	0	0	0	25^1	28	3	22	14	17.8	7.46	43	.295	.427	2	.333	1	-12	-12	-0	-1.1

● GRADY ADKINS Adkins, Grady Emmett "Butcher Boy" b: 6/29/1897, Jacksonville, Ark d: 3/31/66, Little Rock, Ark. BR/TR, 5'11", 175 lbs. Deb: 4/13/28

1928 Chi-A	10	16	.385	36	27	14	0	1	224^2	235	12	89	54	13.2	3.73	109	.278	.351	10	.143	-3	8	8	-1	0.4
1929 Chi-A	2	11	.154	31	15	5	0	0	138^1	168	12	67	24	15.4	5.33	80	.303	.379	11	.239	3	-17	-16	2	-1.1
Total 2	12	27	.308	67	42	19	0	1	363	403	24	156	78	14.0	4.34	95	.288	.363	21	.181	-1	-9	-8	1	-0.7

● DEWEY ADKINS Adkins, John Dewey b: 5/11/18, Norcatur, Kan. BR/TR, 6'2", 195 lbs. Deb: 9/19/42

1942 Was-A	0	0	—	1	1	0	0	0	6^1	7	0	6	3	18.5	9.95	37	.259	.394	1	.500	0	-4	-4	-0	-0.4
1943 Was-A	0	0	—	7	0	0	0	0	10^1	9	0	5	1	12.2	2.61	123	.250	.341	0	—	0	1	1	-1	0.0
1949 Chi-N	2	4	.333	30	5	1	0	0	82^1	98	10	39	43	15.0	5.68	71	.298	.372	4	.200	1	-15	-15	1	-1.2
Total 3	2	4	.333	38	6	1	0	0	99	114	10	50	47	14.9	5.64	70	.291	.371	5	.227	1	-19	-19	0	-1.6

● DOC ADKINS Adkins, Merle Theron b: 8/5/1872, Troy, Wis. d: 2/21/34, Durham, N.C. BR/TR, 5'10.5", 220 lbs. Deb: 6/24/02

1902 Bos-A	1	1	.500	4	2	1	0	0	20	30	2	7	3	16.6	4.05	88	.346	.395	2	.222	-0	-1	-1	0	-0.1
1903 NY-A	0	0	—	2	1	0	0	1	7	10	0	5	0	20.6	7.71	40	.334	.445	0	.000	-0	-4	-4	-1	-0.4
Total 2	1	1	.500	6	3	1	0	1	27	40	2	12	3	17.7	5.00	69	.343	.409	2	.167	-1	-5	-5	-0	-0.5

● STEVE ADKINS Adkins, Steven Thomas b: 10/26/64, Chicago, Ill. BR/TL, 6'6", 210 lbs. Deb: 9/12/90

1990 NY-A	1	2	.333	5	5	0	0	0	24	19	4	29	14	18.0	6.38	62	.226	.425	0	—	0	-7	-6	-0	-0.6

● JUAN AGOSTO Agosto, Juan Roberto (Gonzalez) b: 2/23/58, Rio Piedras, P.R. BL/TL, 6'2", 190 lbs. Deb: 9/07/81

1981 Chi-A	0	0	—	2	0	0	0	0	5^2	5	1	0	3	9.5	4.76	75	.238	.273	0	—	0	-1	-1	0	0.0
1982 Chi-A	0	0	—	1	0	0	0	0	2	7	0	0	1	31.5	18.00	22	.538	.538	0	—	0	-3	-3	0	-0.3
1983 *Chi-A	2	2	.500	39	0	0	0	7	41^2	41	2	11	29	11.4	4.10	102	.283	.338	0	—	0	-0	0	0	0.0
1984 Chi-A	2	1	.667	49	0	0	0	7	55^1	54	2	34	26	14.8	3.09	135	.270	.384	0	—	0	6	7	2	0.6
1985 Chi-A	4	3	.571	54	0	0	0	1	60^1	45	3	23	39	10.6	3.58	121	.210	.296	0	—	0	4	5	2	0.7
1986 Chi-A	0	2	.000	9	0	0	0	0	4^2	6	0	4	3	19.3	7.71	56	.300	.417	0	—	0	-2	-2	-0	-0.2
Min-A	1	2	.333	17	1	0	0	1	20^1	43	1	14	9	26.1	8.85	49	.443	.522	0	—	0	-11	-10	0	-1.0
Yr	1	4	.200	26	1	0	0	1	25	49	1	18	12	24.8	8.64	50	.419	.504	0	—	0	-12	-12	0	-1.2
1987 Hou-N	1	1	.500	27	0	0	0	2	27^1	26	1	10	6	11.9	2.63	149	.248	.313	0	.000	-0	4	4	1	0.5
1988 Hou-N	10	2	.833	75	0	0	0	4	91^2	74	6	30	33	10.2	2.26	147	.226	.291	0	.000	-0	12	11	4	1.6
1989 Hou-N	4	5	.444	71	0	0	0	1	83	81	3	32	46	12.5	2.93	116	.256	.329	1	.200	0	5	4	1	0.6
1990 Hou-N	9	8	.529	**82**	0	0	0	4	92^1	91	4	39	50	13.4	4.29	87	.261	.347	0	.000	-0	-5	-6	2	-0.5
1991 StL-N	5	3	.625	72	0	0	0	2	86	92	4	39	34	14.5	4.81	77	.291	.383	1	.333	1	-11	-10	1	-1.0
1992 StL-N	2	4	.333	22	0	0	0	0	31^2	39	2	9	13	14.5	6.25	55	.312	.372	0	.000	-0	-10	-10	1	-1.0
Sea-A	0	0	—	17	1	0	0	0	18^1	27	0	3	12	14.7	5.89	68	.346	.370	0	—	0	-4	-4	0	-0.4
Total 12	40	33	.548	537	2	0	0	29	620^1	631	29	248	304	13.2	3.99	94	.271	.349	2	.100	-1	-15	-16	15	-0.4

● RICK AGUILERA Aguilera, Richard Warren b: 12/31/61, San Gabriel, Cal. BR/TR, 6'5", 200 lbs. Deb: 6/12/85

1985 NY-N	10	7	.588	21	19	2	0	0	122^1	118	8	37	74	11.6	3.24	107	.258	.317	10	.278	3	5	3	-0	0.6
1986 *NY-N	10	7	.588	28	20	2	0	0	141^2	145	15	36	104	11.9	3.88	91	.263	.316	8	.157	2	-2	-5	2	-0.2
1987 NY-N	11	3	.786	18	17	1	0	0	115	124	12	33	77	12.5	3.60	105	.276	.330	9	.225	3	6	2	2	0.8
1988 *NY-N	0	4	.000	11	3	0	0	0	24^2	29	2	10	16	14.6	6.93	46	.296	.367	1	.250	0	-10	-10	0	-1.0

YEAR	TM/L	W	L	PCT	G	GS	CG	SH	SV	IP	H	HR	BB	SO	RAT	ERA	ERA+	OAV	OOB	BH	AVG	PB	PR	/A	PD	TPI
1989	NY-N	6	6	.500	36	0	0	0	7	69^1	59	3	21	80	10.6	2.34	140	.231	.295	0	.000	-0	9	7	-0	0.7
	Min-A	3	5	.375	11	11	3	0	0	75^2	71	5	17	57	10.6	3.21	129	.245	.289	0	—	0	6	8	1	0.8
1990	Min-A	5	3	.625	56	0	0	0	32	65^1	55	5	19	61	10.7	2.76	151	.224	.291	0	—	0	8	10	-1	0.9
1991	*Min-A★	4	5	.444	63	0	0	0	42	69	44	3	30	61	9.8	2.35	182	.183	.277	0	—	0	13	15	-0	1.5
1992	Min-A★	2	6	.250	64	0	0	0	41	66^2	60	7	17	52	10.5	2.84	142	.238	.289	0	—	0	8	9	-1	0.7
Total	8	51	46	.526	308	70	8	0	122	749^2	705	60	220	582	11.4	3.29	114	.249	.308	28	.203	8	43	38	2	4.8

● **HANK AGUIRRE** Aguirre, Henry John b: 1/31/32, Azusa, Cal. BR/TL, 6'4", 205 lbs. Deb: 9/10/55 C

YEAR	TM/L	W	L	PCT	G	GS	CG	SH	SV	IP	H	HR	BB	SO	RAT	ERA	ERA+	OAV	OOB	BH	AVG	PB	PR	/A	PD	TPI
1955	Cle-A	2	0	1.000	4	1	1	1	0	12^2	6	0	12	6	12.8	1.42	281	.143	.333	0	.000	-1	4	4	-0	0.3
1956	Cle-A	3	5	.375	16	9	2	1	1	65^1	63	7	27	31	12.5	3.72	113	.253	.329	2	.111	-2	3	4	-1	0.1
1957	Cle-A	1	1	.500	10	1	0	0	0	20^1	26	0	13	9	17.3	5.75	65	.317	.411	0	.000	-1	-4	-5	-0	-0.5
1958	Det-A	3	4	.429	44	3	0	0	5	69^2	67	5	27	38	12.3	3.75	108	.255	.326	3	.214	0	0	2	1	0.3
1959	Det-A	0	0	—	3	0	0	0	0	2^2	4	0	3	3	23.6	3.38	120	.364	.500	0	—	0	0	0	0	0.0
1960	Det-A	5	3	.625	37	6	1	0	10	94^2	75	7	30	80	10.3	2.85	139	.217	.286	1	.036	-3	11	12	-2	0.7
1961	Det-A	4	4	.500	45	0	0	0	8	55^1	44	5	38	32	13.7	3.25	126	.224	.356	0	.000	-1	5	5	-1	0.3
1962	Det-A★	16	8	.667	42	22	11	2	3	216	162	14	65	156	9.7	**2.21**	**184**	**.205**	**.269**	2	.027	-8	**42**	**45**	-3	3.5
1963	Det-A	14	15	.483	38	33	14	3	0	225^2	222	25	68	134	11.9	3.67	102	.256	.316	10	.132	-2	-1	2	-3	-0.3
1964	Det-A	5	10	.333	32	27	3	0	1	161^2	134	15	59	88	11.2	3.79	97	.223	.301	3	.057	-4	-3	-2	-3	-1.0
1965	Det-A	14	10	.583	32	32	10	2	0	208^1	185	24	60	141	11.0	3.59	97	.236	.298	6	.086	-3	-3	-3	-1	-0.7
1966	Det-A	3	9	.250	30	14	2	0	0	103^2	104	14	26	50	11.5	3.82	91	.260	.310	3	.120	0	-4	-4	-2	-0.6
1967	Det-A	0	1	.000	31	1	0	0	0	41^1	34	2	17	33	11.1	2.40	136	.219	.297	1	.500	1	4	4	0	0.6
1968	LA-N	1	2	.333	25	0	0	0	3	39^1	32	0	13	25	11.0	0.69	403	.227	.306	0	.000	-0	10	9	-1	0.9
1969	Chi-N	1	0	1.000	41	0	0	0	1	45	45	2	12	19	11.8	2.60	155	.269	.326	2	.400	1	5	7	1	0.9
1970	Chi-N	3	0	1.000	17	0	0	0	1	14	13	3	9	11	14.8	4.50	100	.250	.371	0	.000	-0	-1	0	-0	-0.1
Total	16	75	72	.510	447	149	44	9	33	1375^2	1216	123	479	856	11.4	3.24	116	.236	.307	33	.085	-21	67	79	-16	4.4

● **EDDIE AINSMITH** Ainsmith, Edward Wilbur "Dorf" b: 2/4/1892, Cambridge, Mass. d: 9/6/81, Ft.Lauderdale, Fla BR/TR, 5'11", 180 lbs. Deb: 8/09/10 ♦

YEAR	TM/L	W	L	PCT	G	GS	CG	SH	SV	IP	H	HR	BB	SO	RAT	ERA	ERA+	OAV	OOB	BH	AVG	PB	PR	/A	PD	TPI
1913	Was-A	0	0	—	1	0	0	0	0	0^1	2	0	0	0	54.0	54.00	5	.667	.667	49	.214	0	-2	-2	0	-0.2

● **RALEIGH AITCHISON** Aitchison, Raleigh Leonidas b: 12/5/1887, Tyndall, S.D. d: 9/26/58, Columbus, Kan. BR/TL, 5'11.5", 175 lbs. Deb: 4/19/11

YEAR	TM/L	W	L	PCT	G	GS	CG	SH	SV	IP	H	HR	BB	SO	RAT	ERA	ERA+	OAV	OOB	BH	AVG	PB	PR	/A	PD	TPI
1911	Bro-N	0	1	.000	1	0	0	0	0	1^1	1	0	1	0	13.5	0.00	—	.200	.333	0	—	0	1	0	-0	0.0
1914	Bro-N	12	7	.632	26	17	8	3	0	172^1	156	4	60	87	11.4	2.66	107	.244	.312	10	.196	1	2	4	-3	0.2
1915	Bro-N	0	4	.000	7	5	2	0	0	32^2	36	3	6	14	12.1	4.96	56	.267	.308	0	.000	-0	-8	-8	0	-0.8
Total	3	12	12	.500	34	22	10	3	0	206^1	193	7	67	101	11.6	3.01	95	.247	.311	10	.169	1	-5	-4	-3	-0.6

● **JACK AKER** Aker, Jackie Delane b: 7/13/40, Tulare, Cal. BR/TR, 6'2", 190 lbs. Deb: 5/03/64 C

YEAR	TM/L	W	L	PCT	G	GS	CG	SH	SV	IP	H	HR	BB	SO	RAT	ERA	ERA+	OAV	OOB	BH	AVG	PB	PR	/A	PD	TPI
1964	KC-A	0	1	.000	9	0	0	0	0	16^1	17	6	10	7	18.2	8.82	43	.266	.412	0	.000	-0	-9	-9	1	-0.9
1965	KC-A	4	3	.571	34	0	0	0	3	51^1	45	3	18	26	11.6	3.16	111	.242	.319	0	.000	-1	2	2	1	0.2
1966	KC-A	8	4	.667	66	0	0	0	**32**	113	81	7	28	68	8.9	1.99	171	.201	.258	2	.095	-1	**18**	**18**	3	2.2
1967	KC-A	3	8	.273	57	0	0	0	12	88	87	9	32	65	12.5	4.30	74	.264	.334	1	.125	-0	-10	-11	2	-1.0
1968	Oak-A	4	4	.500	54	0	0	0	11	74^2	72	6	33	44	13.4	4.10	69	.258	.349	1	.143	-0	-9	-11	0	-1.2
1969	Sea-A	0	2	.000	15	0	0	0	3	16^2	25	4	13	7	21.1	7.56	48	.357	.464	0	.000	0	-7	-7	1	-0.7
	NY-A	8	4	.667	38	0	0	0	11	65^2	51	4	22	40	10.6	2.06	169	.217	.295	1	.111	-0	11	10	2	1.3
	Yr	8	6	.571	53	0	0	0	14	82^1	76	8	35	47	12.6	3.17	111	.248	.333	1	.100	-0	4	3	2	0.6
1970	NY-A	4	2	.667	41	0	0	0	16	70	57	3	20	36	10.4	2.06	171	.226	.293	1	.063	-1	13	11	-0	1.1
1971	NY-A	4	4	.500	41	0	0	0	4	55^2	48	3	26	24	12.0	2.59	125	.238	.325	0	.000	-0	5	4	1	0.5
1972	NY-A	0	0	—	4	0	0	0	0	6	5	0	3	1	13.5	3.00	98	.238	.360	0	—	0	0	-0	1	0.1
	Chi-N	6	6	.500	48	0	0	0	17	67	65	4	23	36	12.5	2.96	129	.259	.333	0	.000	-0	4	6	2	0.8
1973	Chi-N	4	5	.444	47	0	0	0	12	63^2	76	8	23	25	14.3	4.10	96	.308	.371	0	.000	-1	-3	-1	2	0.0
1974	Atl-N	0	1	.000	17	0	0	0	0	16^2	17	3	9	7	14.0	3.78	100	.298	.394	0	.000	-0	-0	-0	0	0.0
	NY-N	2	1	.667	24	0	0	0	2	41^1	33	4	14	18	10.7	3.48	102	.213	.287	1	.500	1	1	0	-1	0.0
	Yr	2	2	.500	41	0	0	0	2	58	50	7	23	25	11.6	3.57	102	.234	.314	1	.333	1	0	0	-1	0.0
Total	11	47	45	.511	495	0	0	0	123	746	679	64	274	404	12.0	3.28	105	.247	.324	7	.076	-5	14	13	13	2.4

● **DARREL AKERFELDS** Akerfelds, Darrel Wayne b: 6/12/62, Denver, Colo. BR/TR, 6'2", 210 lbs. Deb: 8/01/86

YEAR	TM/L	W	L	PCT	G	GS	CG	SH	SV	IP	H	HR	BB	SO	RAT	ERA	ERA+	OAV	OOB	BH	AVG	PB	PR	/A	PD	TPI
1986	Oak-A	0	0	—	2	0	0	0	0	5^1	7	2	3	5	16.9	6.75	57	.304	.385	0	—	0	-2	-2	0	-0.1
1987	Cle-A	2	6	.250	16	13	1	0	0	74^2	84	18	38	42	15.5	6.75	67	.284	.378	0	—	0	-19	-18	-0	-1.7
1989	Tex-A	0	1	.000	6	0	0	0	0	11	11	1	5	9	13.1	3.27	121	.250	.327	0	—	0	1	1	0	0.1
1990	Phi-N	5	2	.714	71	0	0	0	3	93	65	10	54	42	11.8	3.77	101	.201	.320	1	.167	-0	0	0	-1	0.0
1991	Phi-N	2	1	.667	30	0	0	0	0	49^2	49	5	27	31	14.3	5.26	70	.257	.357	0	.000	-0	-9	-9	1	-0.9
Total	5	9	10	.474	125	13	1	0	3	233^2	216	36	127	129	13.7	5.08	79	.246	.350	1	.111	-0	-28	-28	0	-2.6

● **JERRY AKERS** Akers, Albert Earl b: 11/1/1887, Shelbyville, Ind. d: 5/15/79, Bay Pines, Fla. BR/TR, 5'11", 175 lbs. Deb: 5/04/12

YEAR	TM/L	W	L	PCT	G	GS	CG	SH	SV	IP	H	HR	BB	SO	RAT	ERA	ERA+	OAV	OOB	BH	AVG	PB	PR	/A	PD	TPI
1912	Was-A	1	1	.500	5	1	0	0	0	20^1	24	1	15	11	18.1	4.87	68	.300	.423	2	.333	0	-4	-3	-1	-0.4

● **GIBSON ALBA** Alba, Gibson Alberto (Rosado) b: 1/18/60, Santiago, D.R. BL/TL, 6'2", 160 lbs. Deb: 5/03/88

YEAR	TM/L	W	L	PCT	G	GS	CG	SH	SV	IP	H	HR	BB	SO	RAT	ERA	ERA+	OAV	OOB	BH	AVG	PB	PR	/A	PD	TPI
1988	StL-N	0	0	—	3	0	0	0	0	3^1	1	0	2	3	8.1	2.70	129	.091	.231	0	—	0	0	-0	-0	0.0

● **JOE ALBANESE** Albanese, Joseph Peter b: 6/26/33, New York, N.Y. BR/TR, 6'3", 215 lbs. Deb: 7/18/58

YEAR	TM/L	W	L	PCT	G	GS	CG	SH	SV	IP	H	HR	BB	SO	RAT	ERA	ERA+	OAV	OOB	BH	AVG	PB	PR	/A	PD	TPI
1958	Was-A	0	0	—	6	0	0	0	0	6	8	1	2	3	15.0	4.50	85	.348	.400	0	—	0	-0	-0	0	0.0

● **CY ALBERTS** Alberts, Frederick Joseph b: 1/14/1882, Grand Rapids, Mich d: 8/27/17, Fort Wayne, Ind. BR/TR, 6', 230 lbs. Deb: 9/17/10

YEAR	TM/L	W	L	PCT	G	GS	CG	SH	SV	IP	H	HR	BB	SO	RAT	ERA	ERA+	OAV	OOB	BH	AVG	PB	PR	/A	PD	TPI
1910	StL-N	1	2	.333	4	3	2	0	0	27^2	35	1	20	10	17.9	6.18	48	.330	.437	0	.000	-0	-10	-10	-1	-1.0

● **ED ALBOSTA** Albosta, Edward John "Rube" b: 10/27/18, Saginaw, Mich. BR/TR, 6'1", 175 lbs. Deb: 9/03/41

YEAR	TM/L	W	L	PCT	G	GS	CG	SH	SV	IP	H	HR	BB	SO	RAT	ERA	ERA+	OAV	OOB	BH	AVG	PB	PR	/A	PD	TPI
1941	Bro-N	0	2	.000	2	2	0	0	0	13	11	1	8	5	13.2	6.23	59	.239	.352	0	.000	-1	-4	-4	0	-0.4
1946	Pit-N	0	6	.000	17	6	0	0	0	39^2	41	3	35	19	17.5	6.13	58	.266	.405	1	.125	-1	-12	-11	0	-1.2
Total	2	0	8	.000	19	8	0	0	0	52^2	52	4	43	24	16.4	6.15	58	.260	.393	1	.083	-1	-16	-15	0	-1.6

● **ED ALBRECHT** Albrecht, Edward Arthur b: 2/28/29, Affton, Mo. d: 12/29/79, Cahokia, Ill. BR/TR, 5'10.5", 165 lbs. Deb: 10/02/49

YEAR	TM/L	W	L	PCT	G	GS	CG	SH	SV	IP	H	HR	BB	SO	RAT	ERA	ERA+	OAV	OOB	BH	AVG	PB	PR	/A	PD	TPI
1949	StL-A	1	0	1.000	1	1	1	0	0	5	1	0	4	1	9.0	5.40	84	.063	.250	0	.000	-0	-1	-0	0	0.0
1950	StL-A	0	1	.000	2	1	0	0	0	6^2	6	0	7	1	17.6	5.40	92	.250	.419	0	.000	-0	-1	-0	-0	-0.1
Total	2	1	1	.500	3	2	1	0	0	11^2	7	0	11	2	13.9	5.40	88	.175	.353	0	.000	-0	-1	-1	-0	-0.1

● **VIC ALBURY** Albury, Victor b: 5/12/47, Key West, Fla. BL/TL, 6', 190 lbs. Deb: 8/07/73

YEAR	TM/L	W	L	PCT	G	GS	CG	SH	SV	IP	H	HR	BB	SO	RAT	ERA	ERA+	OAV	OOB	BH	AVG	PB	PR	/A	PD	TPI
1973	Min-A	1	0	1.000	14	0	0	0	0	23^1	13	1	19	13	12.3	2.70	147	.169	.333	0	—	0	3	3	-1	0.2
1974	Min-A	8	9	.471	32	22	4	1	0	164	159	19	80	85	13.4	4.12	91	.259	.350	0	—	0	-9	-7	-1	-0.8
1975	Min-A	6	7	.462	32	15	2	0	1	135	115	16	97	72	14.4	4.53	85	.237	.368	0	.000	0	-11	-10	1	-1.0
1976	Min-A	3	1	.750	23	0	0	0	0	50^1	51	0	24	23	13.8	3.58	101	.271	.360	0	—	0	-0	0	-0	-0.1
Total	4	18	17	.514	101	37	6	1	1	372^2	338	36	220	193	13.8	4.11	92	.247	.357	0	.000	0	-18	-13	-1	-1.7

● **SANTO ALCALA** Alcala, Santo (b: Santo Anibal (Alcala)) b: 12/23/52, San Pedro De Macoris, D.R. BR/TR, 6'5", 195 lbs. Deb: 4/10/76

YEAR	TM/L	W	L	PCT	G	GS	CG	SH	SV	IP	H	HR	BB	SO	RAT	ERA	ERA+	OAV	OOB	BH	AVG	PB	PR	/A	PD	TPI
1976	Cin-N	11	4	.733	30	21	3	1	0	132	131	12	67	67	13.7	4.70	74	.261	.352	6	.140	-0	-18	-18	-1	-1.9
1977	Cin-N	1	1	.500	7	2	0	0	0	15^2	22	1	7	9	17.2	5.74	68	.349	.423	0	.000	-0	-3	-3	0	-0.3
	Mon-N	2	6	.250	31	10	0	0	2	101^2	104	12	47	64	13.5	4.69	81	.263	.344	2	.080	-1	-9	-10	-1	-1.2
	Yr	3	7	.300	38	12	0	0	2	117^1	126	13	54	73	14.0	4.83	79	.273	.352	2	.071	-1	-12	-13	-1	-1.5

YEAR TM/L	W	L	PCT	G	GS	CG	SH	SV	IP	H	HR	BB	SO	RAT	ERA	ERA+	OAV	OOB	BH	AVG	PB	PR	/A	PD	TPI
Total 2	14	11	.560	68	33	3	1	2	249^1	257	25	121	140	13.9	4.76	77	.268	.353	8	.113	-2	-30	-31	-2	-3.4
● DALE ALDERSON	Alderson, Dale Leonard b: 3/9/18, Belden, Neb. d: 2/12/82, Garden Grove, Cal. BR/TR, 5'10", 190 lbs. Deb: 9/18/43																								
1943 Chi-N	0	1	.000	4	2	0	0	0	14	21	2	3	4	15.4	6.43	52	.356	.387	0	.000	-0	-5	-5	0	-0.5
1944 Chi-N	0	0	—	12	1	0	0	0	21^2	31	2	9	7	16.6	6.65	53	.344	.404	0	.000	-1	-7	-7	1	-0.7
Total 2	0	1	.000	16	3	0	0	0	35^2	52	4	12	11	16.1	6.56	53	.349	.398	0	.000	-1	-12	-12	1	-1.2
● SCOTT ALDRED	Aldred, Scott Phillip b: 6/12/68, Flint, Mich. BL/TL, 6'4", 195 lbs. Deb: 9/09/90																								
1990 Det-A	1	2	.333	4	3	0	0	0	14^1	13	0	10	7	15.1	3.77	105	.265	.400	0	—	0	0	0	-0	0.0
1991 Det-A	2	4	.333	11	11	1	0	0	57^1	58	9	30	35	13.8	5.18	80	.266	.355	0	—	0	-7	-7	0	-0.6
1992 Det-A	3	8	.273	16	13	0	0	0	65	80	12	33	34	16.1	6.78	59	.307	.391	0	—	0	-21	-20	1	-1.9
Total 3	6	14	.300	31	27	1	0	0	136^2	151	21	73	76	15.0	5.80	70	.286	.377	0	—	0	-27	-26	0	-2.5
● JAY ALDRICH	Aldrich, Jay Robert b: 4/14/61, Alexandria, La. BR/TR, 6'3", 210 lbs. Deb: 6/05/87																								
1987 Mil-A	3	1	.750	31	0	0	0	0	58^1	71	8	13	22	13.3	4.94	93	.306	.348	0	—	0	-3	-2	-1	-0.5
1989 Mil-A	1	0	1.000	16	0	0	0	1	26	24	3	13	12	13.2	3.81	101	.253	.349	0	—	0	0	0	0	0.1
Atl-N	1	2	.333	8	0	0	0	0	12^1	7	0	6	7	9.5	2.19	167	.167	.271	0	.000	-0	2	2	-0	0.2
1990 Bal-A	1	2	.333	7	0	0	0	1	12	17	1	7	5	18.0	8.25	46	.327	.407	0	—	0	-6	-6	0	-0.6
Total 3	6	5	.545	62	0	0	0	2	108^2	119	12	39	46	13.3	4.72	89	.283	.348	0	.000	-0	-7	-6	-1	-0.8
● VIC ALDRIDGE	Aldridge, Victor Eddington b: 10/25/1893, Indian Springs, Ind d: 4/17/73, Terre Haute, Ind. BR/TR, 5'9.5", 175 lbs. Deb: 4/15/17																								
1917 Chi-N	6	6	.500	30	5	1	1	2	106^2	100	1	37	44	11.7	3.12	93	.252	.319	4	.138	-2	-5	-3	3	-0.2
1918 Chi-N	0	1	.000	3	0	0	0	0	12^1	11	0	6	10	12.4	1.46	191	.275	.370	1	.333	0	2	2	-0	0.2
1922 Chi-N	16	15	.516	36	34	20	2	0	258^1	287	14	56	66	12.4	3.52	119	.286	.332	26	.260	3	17	20	1	2.3
1923 Chi-N	16	9	.640	30	30	15	2	0	217	209	17	67	64	11.5	3.48	115	.251	.307	19	.268	3	12	12	-1	1.5
1924 Chi-N	15	12	.556	32	32	20	0	0	244^1	261	10	80	74	12.8	3.50	112	.279	.341	15	.176	-3	10	11	-0	0.7
1925 *Pit-N	15	7	.682	30	26	14	1	0	213^1	218	15	74	88	12.5	3.63	123	.269	.334	20	.233	-1	15	20	-3	1.5
1926 Pit-N	10	13	.435	30	26	12	1	1	190	204	7	73	61	13.3	4.07	97	.279	.348	16	.225	-1	-5	-3	-2	-0.5
1927 *Pit-N	15	10	.600	35	34	17	1	1	239^1	248	16	74	86	12.3	4.25	97	.270	.328	21	.219	-0	-9	-4	-3	-0.7
1928 NY-N	4	7	.364	22	17	3	0	2	119^1	133	7	45	33	13.7	4.83	81	.285	.352	11	.275	2	-11	-12	-1	-1.1
Total 9	97	80	.548	248	204	102	8	6	1600^2	1671	87	512	526	12.5	3.76	107	.273	.333	133	.229	2	26	44	-7	3.7
● DOYLE ALEXANDER	Alexander, Doyle Lafayette b: 9/4/50, Cordova, Ala. BR/TR, 6'3", 205 lbs. Deb: 6/26/71																								
1971 LA-N	6	6	.500	17	12	4	0	0	92^1	105	6	18	30	12.1	3.80	85	.282	.317	9	.273	3	-3	-6	-1	-0.4
1972 Bal-A	6	8	.429	35	9	2	2	2	106^1	78	5	30	49	9.2	2.45	125	.203	.262	2	.080	-1	7	7	2	0.9
1973 *Bal-A	12	8	.600	29	26	10	0	0	174^2	169	19	52	63	11.7	3.86	97	.258	.319	0	—	0	-1	-3	1	-0.1
1974 Bal-A	6	9	.400	30	12	2	0	0	114^1	127	7	43	40	13.7	4.01	86	.290	.359	0	—	0	-5	-7	3	-0.4
1975 Bal-A	8	8	.500	32	11	3	1	1	133^1	127	7	47	46	11.8	3.04	116	.251	.316	0	—	0	11	7	2	0.9
1976 Bal-A	3	4	.429	11	6	2	1	0	64^1	58	3	24	17	11.5	3.50	94	.247	.317	0	—	0	0	-2	1	0.2
*NY-A	10	5	.667	19	19	5	2	0	136^2	114	9	39	41	10.3	3.29	104	.229	.289	0	—	0	3	2	-2	0.0
Yr	13	9	.591	30	25	7	3	0	201	172	12	63	58	10.7	3.36	100	.234	.297	0	—	0	4	0	-1	0.2
1977 Tex-A	17	11	.607	34	34	12	1	0	237	221	24	82	82	11.6	3.65	112	.246	.311	0	—	0	11	11	1	1.3
1978 Tex-A	9	10	.474	31	28	7	1	0	191	198	18	71	81	12.7	3.86	97	.270	.336	0	—	0	-2	-3	2	-0.1
1979 Tex-A	5	7	.417	23	18	0	0	0	113^1	114	3	69	50	14.6	4.45	93	.268	.371	0	—	0	-3	-4	2	-0.1
1980 Atl-N	14	11	.560	35	35	7	1	0	231^2	227	20	74	114	11.8	4.20	89	.256	.316	15	.181	0	-15	-12	3	-0.9
1981 SF-N	11	7	.611	24	24	1	1	0	152^1	156	11	44	77	11.9	2.89	118	.263	.316	9	.176	1	10	9	-2	1.0
1982 NY-A	1	7	.125	16	11	0	0	0	66^2	81	14	14	26	12.8	6.08	66	.298	.332	0	—	0	-15	-15	-0	-1.4
1983 NY-A	0	2	.000	8	5	0	0	0	28^1	31	6	7	17	12.1	6.35	61	.277	.319	0	—	0	-7	-8	-0	-0.6
Tor-A	7	6	.538	17	15	5	0	0	116^2	126	14	26	46	11.8	3.93	109	.279	.319	0	—	0	2	5	0	0.2
Yr	7	8	.467	25	20	5	0	0	145	157	20	33	63	11.9	4.41	96	.278	.319	0	—	0	-6	-3	0	-0.4
1984 Tor-A	17	6	**.739**	36	35	11	2	0	261^2	238	21	59	139	10.3	3.13	131	.242	.287	0	—	0	25	28	-0	2.8
1985 *Tor-A	17	10	.630	36	36	6	1	0	260^2	268	28	67	142	11.8	3.45	122	.266	.315	0	—	0	20	22	0	2.3
1986 Tor-A	5	4	.556	17	17	3	0	0	111	120	18	20	65	11.7	4.46	95	.273	.310	0	—	0	-3	-3	-1	-0.4
Atl-N	6	6	.500	17	17	2	0	0	117^1	135	9	17	74	11.7	3.84	104	.287	.312	8	.211	1	-2	2	-1	0.2
1987 Atl-N	5	10	.333	16	16	3	0	0	117^2	115	21	27	64	11.0	4.13	105	.257	.302	1	.029	-3	-1	3	-2	-0.2
*Det-A	9	0	1.000	11	11	3	3	0	88^1	63	3	26	44	9.1	1.53	276	.201	.263	0	—	0	29	26	0	3.3
1988 Det-A☆	14	11	.560	34	34	5	1	0	229	260	30	46	126	12.2	4.32	88	.282	.320	0	—	0	-9	-13	-3	-1.5
1989 Det-A	6	18	.250	33	33	5	1	0	223	245	28	76	95	13.2	4.44	86	.280	.341	0	—	0	-14	-15	0	-1.5
Total 19	194	174	.527	561	464	98	18	3	3367^2	3376	324	978	1528	11.8	3.76	102	.261	.316	44	.166	1	38	32	7	5.5
● GERALD ALEXANDER	Alexander, Gerald Paul b: 3/26/68, Baton Rouge, La. BR/TR, 5'11", 190 lbs. Deb: 9/09/90																								
1990 Tex-A	0	0	—	3	2	0	0	0	7	14	0	5	8	25.7	7.71	51	.438	.526	0	—	0	-3	-3	0	-0.3
1991 Tex-A	5	3	.625	30	9	0	0	0	89^1	93	11	48	50	14.5	5.24	77	.272	.366	0	—	0	-11	-12	0	-1.1
1992 Tex-A	1	0	1.000	3	0	0	0	0	1^2	5	1	1	1	32.4	27.00	14	.500	.545	0	—	0	-4	-4	0	-0.3
Total 3	6	3	.667	36	11	0	0	0	98	112	12	54	59	15.6	5.79	69	.292	.385	0	—	0	-19	-19	0	-1.7
● PETE ALEXANDER	Alexander, Grover Cleveland b: 2/26/1887, Elba, Neb. d: 11/4/50, St.Paul, Neb. BR/TR, 6'1", 185 lbs. Deb: 4/15/11 H																								
1911 Phi-N	**28**	13	.683	48	37	**31**	**7**	3	**367**	285	5	129	227	10.3	2.57	134	**.219**	.293	24	.174	-2	34	35	1	3.5
1912 Phi-N	19	17	.528	46	34	25	3	3	**310^1**	289	11	105	**195**	11.6	2.81	129	.251	.317	19	.186	0	21	28	1	2.9
1913 Phi-N	22	8	.733	47	35	23	**9**	2	306^1	288	9	75	159	10.8	2.79	120	.254	.302	13	.126	-4	14	19	2	1.6
1914 Phi-N	**27**	15	.643	46	39	**32**	6	1	**355**	327	8	76	**214**	10.5	2.38	123	.244	.290	32	.234	2	16	22	4	3.2
1915 *Phi-N	**31**	10	**.756**	49	42	**36**	**12**	3	**376^1**	253	3	64	**241**	**7.8**	**1.22**	**225**	**.191**	**.234**	22	.169	0	**64**	**64**	7	**8.6**
1916 Phi-N	**33**	12	.733	48	45	**38**	**16**	3	**388^2**	323	6	50	**167**	8.9	**1.55**	**171**	.230	.262	33	.239	8	**46**	**48**	1	**7.0**
1917 Phi-N	**30**	13	.698	45	44	**34**	**8**	0	**387^2**	336	4	56	**200**	9.2	1.83	153	.234	.266	30	.216	4	**38**	**42**	2	**5.9**
1918 Chi-N	2	1	.667	3	3	3	0	0	26	19	0	3	15	8.0	1.73	161	.207	.240	1	.100	-1	3	3	0	0.3
1919 Chi-N	16	11	.593	30	27	20	**9**	1	235	180	3	38	121	8.3	**1.72**	**167**	**.211**	.245	12	.171	1	31	30	5	**4.3**
1920 Chi-N	**27**	14	.659	46	40	**33**	7	5	**363^1**	335	8	69	**173**	10.0	**1.91**	**168**	.248	.285	27	.229	4	**50**	**52**	2	**6.8**
1921 Chi-N	15	13	.536	31	29	21	**3**	1	252	286	10	33	77	11.4	3.39	113	.296	.320	29	.305	6	11	12	-1	1.7
1922 Chi-N	16	13	.552	33	31	20	1	1	245^2	283	8	34	48	11.7	3.63	116	.295	.321	15	.176	-2	13	16	3	1.6
1923 Chi-N	22	12	.647	39	36	26	3	2	305	308	17	30	72	**10.0**	3.19	126	.259	**.277**	24	.216	0	28	28	4	3.2
1924 Chi-N	12	5	.706	21	20	12	0	0	169^1	183	9	25	33	11.1	3.03	129	.272	.299	15	.231	1	16	16	2	1.9
1925 Chi-N	15	11	.577	32	30	20	1	0	236	270	14	29	63	11.5	3.39	127	.288	.312	19	.241	3	23	24	-2	2.4
1926 Chi-N	3	3	.500	7	7	4	0	0	52	55	0	7	12	10.7	3.46	111	.270	.294	7	.467	3	2	2	1	0.6
*StL-N	9	7	.563	23	16	11	2	2	148^1	136	8	24	35	9.8	2.91	134	.242	.276	6	.120	-4	15	16	-0	1.3
Yr	12	10	.545	30	23	15	2	2	200^1	191	8	31	47	**10.1**	3.05	127	.250	**.281**	13	.200	-1	17	19	1	1.9
1927 StL-N	21	10	.677	37	30	22	2	3	268	261	11	38	48	**10.1**	2.52	157	.258	**.286**	23	.245	3	**42**	**43**	1	**4.9**
1928 *StL-N	16	9	.640	34	31	18	1	2	243^2	262	15	37	59	11.1	3.36	119	.277	.306	25	.291	6	17	17	-1	2.2
1929 StL-N	9	8	.529	22	19	8	0	0	132	149	10	23	33	11.8	3.89	120	.285	.317	2	.049	-4	12	11	2	0.8
1930 Phi-N	0	3	.000	9	3	0	0	0	21^2	40	5	6	6	19.1	9.14	60	.396	.430	0	.000	-0	-10	-9	-1	-0.8
Total 20	373	208	.642	696	598	437	90	32	5189^1	4868	164	951	2198	10.2	2.56	135	.250	.288	378	.209	25	484	522	31	63.9
● BOB ALEXANDER	Alexander, Robert Somerville b: 8/7/22, Vancouver, B.C., Can BR/TR, 6'2.5", 205 lbs. Deb: 4/11/55																								
1955 Bal-A	1	0	1.000	4	0	0	0	0	4	8	0	2	1	24.8	13.50	28	.444	.524	0	—	0	-4	-4	-0	-0.4
1957 Cle-A	0	1	.000	5	0	0	0	0	7	10	0	5	1	20.6	9.00	41	.357	.471	0	.000	-0	-4	-4	-0	-0.4
Total 2	1	1	.500	9	0	0	0	0	11	18	0	7	2	22.1	10.64	35	.391	.491	0	.000	-0	-8	-8	-1	-0.8

YEAR TM/L	W	L	PCT	G	GS	CG	SH	SV	IP	H	HR	BB	SO	RAT	ERA	ERA+	OAV	OOB	BH	AVG	PB	PR	/A	PD	TPI
● **BRIAN ALLARD** Allard, Brian Marshall b: 1/3/58, Spring Valley, Ill. BR/TR, 6'1", 175 lbs. Deb: 8/08/79																									
1979 Tex-A	1	3	.250	7	4	2	0	0	33^1	36	4	13	14	13.2	4.32	96	.283	.350	0	—	0	-0	-1	0	0.0
1980 Tex-A	0	1	.000	5	2	0	0	0	14^1	13	0	10	10	15.1	5.65	69	.236	.364	0	—	0	-3	-3	-0	-0.2
1981 Sea-A	3	2	.600	7	7	1	0	0	48	48	5	8	20	10.5	3.75	103	.265	.296	0	—	0	-0	1	-0	-0.1
Total 3	4	6	.400	19	13	3	0	0	95^2	97	9	31	44	12.1	4.23	94	.267	.327	0	—	0	-3	-3	-1	-0.3
● **FRANK ALLEN** Allen, Frank Leon b: 8/26/1889, Newbern, Ala. d: 7/30/33, Gainesville, Ala. BR/TL, 5'9", 175 lbs. Deb: 5/18/12																									
1912 Bro-N	3	9	.250	20	15	5	1	0	109	119	1	57	58	14.6	3.63	92	.285	.373	6	.167	2	-3	-3	0	-0.2
1913 Bro-N	4	18	.182	34	25	11	0	2	174^2	144	6	81	82	12.1	2.83	116	.231	.329	7	.137	-1	7	9	-3	0.5
1914 Bro-N	8	14	.364	36	21	10	1	0	171^1	165	6	57	68	11.8	3.10	92	.265	.330	6	.128	0	-6	-5	-1	-0.6
Pit-F	1	0	1.000	1	1	1	0	0	7	9	0	0	3	11.6	5.14	62	.321	.321	1	.500	1	-2	-2	-0	-0.1
1915 Pit-F	23	13	.639	41	37	24	6	0	283^1	230	9	100	127	10.8	2.51	120	.227	.304	7	.079	-5	16	16	-1	1.2
1916 Bos-N	8	2	.800	19	14	7	2	1	113	102	1	31	63	10.9	2.07	120	.244	.302	7	.206	3	7	5	-1	0.8
1917 Bos-N	3	11	.214	29	14	2	0	0	112	124	3	47	56	14.2	3.94	65	.297	.376	5	.172	1	-15	-17	-2	-1.9
Total 6	50	67	.427	180	127	60	10	3	970^1	893	26	373	457	12.1	2.93	101	.252	.330	39	.135	2	5	3	-8	-0.3
● **JOHN ALLEN** Allen, John Marshall b: 10/27/1890, Berkeley Springs, W.Va. d: 9/24/67, Hagerstown, Md. BR/TR, 6'1", 170 lbs. Deb: 6/02/14																									
1914 Bal-F	0	0	—	1	0	0	0	0	2	2	0	2	2	22.5	18.00	19	.286	.500	0	—	0	-3	-3	0	-0.3
● **JOHNNY ALLEN** Allen, John Thomas b: 9/30/05, Lenoir, N.C. d: 3/29/59, St.Petersburg, Fla BR/TR, 6', 180 lbs. Deb: 4/19/32																									
1932 *NY-A	17	4	**.810**	33	21	13	3	4	192	162	10	76	109	11.4	3.70	110	.228	.306	9	.123	-1	17	8	-1	0.4
1933 NY-A	15	7	.682	25	24	10	1	1	184^2	171	9	87	119	12.8	4.39	89	.242	.328	13	.181	0	-2	-10	-1	-1.0
1934 NY-A	5	2	.714	13	10	4	0	0	71^2	62	3	32	54	12.1	2.89	141	.227	.313	5	.192	1	13	9	0	1.0
1935 NY-A	13	6	.684	23	23	12	2	0	167	149	11	58	113	11.4	3.61	112	**.238**	.307	15	.224	1	16	8	1	1.0
1936 Cle-A	20	10	.667	36	31	19	4	1	243	234	5	97	165	12.3	3.44	146	.256	.328	14	.161	-3	43	43	2	3.9
1937 Cle-A	15	1	**.938**	24	20	14	0	0	173	157	4	60	87	11.5	2.55	181	.244	.313	6	.090	-7	40	40	1	3.4
1938 Cle-A★	14	8	.636	30	27	13	0	0	200	189	15	81	112	12.3	4.18	111	.246	.321	20	.253	4	13	10	2	1.5
1939 Cle-A	9	7	.563	28	26	9	2	0	175	199	9	56	79	13.3	4.58	96	.291	.347	16	.225	1	1	-3	3	0.0
1940 Cle-A	9	8	.529	32	17	5	3	5	138^2	126	3	48	62	11.5	3.44	123	.243	.311	10	.208	0	15	12	-0	1.2
1941 StL-A	2	5	.286	20	9	2	0	1	67	89	4	29	27	16.1	6.58	65	.319	.387	3	.136	0	-18	-17	-0	-1.6
*Bro-N	3	0	1.000	11	4	1	0	0	57^1	38	6	12	21	7.8	2.51	146	.188	.234	1	.050	-2	7	7	-0	0.5
1942 Bro-N	10	6	.625	27	15	5	1	3	118	106	11	39	50	11.2	3.20	102	.238	.302	7	.179	-0	1	1	0	0.0
1943 Bro-N	5	1	.833	17	1	0	0	1	38	42	3	25	15	16.3	4.26	79	.280	.390	3	.429	2	-4	-4	-0	-0.2
NY-N	1	3	.250	15	0	0	0	2	41	37	4	14	24	11.2	3.07	112	.245	.309	0	.000	-2	1	2	1	0.1
Yr	6	4	.600	32	1	0	0	3	79	79	7	39	39	13.4	3.65	93	.261	.345	3	.143	-0	-2	-2	1	-0.1
1944 NY-N	4	7	.364	18	13	2	1	0	84	88	7	24	33	12.2	4.07	90	.260	.313	2	.083	-2	-4	-4	-1	-0.7
Total 13	142	75	.654	352	241	109	17	18	1950^1	1849	104	738	1070	12.1	3.75	113	.249	.321	124	.173	-8	138	102	6	9.5
● **LLOYD ALLEN** Allen, Lloyd Cecil b: 5/8/50, Merced, Cal. BR/TR, 6'1", 185 lbs. Deb: 9/01/69																									
1969 Cal-A	0	1	.000	4	1	0	0	0	10	5	1	10	5	13.5	5.40	65	.147	.341	1	.500	1	-2	-2	1	-0.1
1970 Cal-A	1	1	.500	8	2	0	0	0	24	23	0	11	12	13.1	2.63	138	.261	.350	0	.000	-0	3	3	-0	0.2
1971 Cal-A	4	6	.400	54	1	0	0	15	94	75	4	40	72	11.0	2.49	130	.221	.303	5	.294	2	10	8	0	1.1
1972 Cal-A	3	7	.300	42	6	0	0	5	85^1	76	7	55	53	14.1	3.48	84	.240	.357	2	.118	-1	-4	-5	-1	-0.7
1973 Cal-A	0	0	—	5	0	0	0	1	8^2	15	0	5	4	20.8	10.38	34	.417	.488	0	—	0	-6	-7	-0	-0.6
Tex-A	0	6	.000	23	5	0	0	1	41	58	3	39	25	22.4	9.22	40	.326	.459	0	—	0	-25	-25	1	-2.3
Yr	0	6	.000	28	5	0	0	2	49^2	73	3	44	29	22.1	9.42	39	.338	.460	0	—	0	-31	-32	1	-2.9
1974 Tex-A	0	1	.000	14	0	0	0	0	22	24	2	18	18	17.6	6.55	54	.276	.406	0	—	0	-7	-7	-1	-0.8
Chi-A	0	1	.000	6	2	0	0	0	7	7	0	12	3	25.7	10.29	36	.259	.500	0	—	0	-5	-5	-0	-0.5
Yr	0	2	.000	20	2	0	0	0	29	31	2	30	21	19.2	7.45	48	.265	.419	0	—	0	-12	-12	-1	-1.3
1975 Chi-A	0	2	.000	3	2	0	0	0	5^1	8	2	6	2	23.6	11.81	33	.348	.483	0	—	0	-5	-5	0	-0.4
Total 7	8	25	.242	159	19	0	0	22	297^1	291	19	196	194	15.1	4.69	70	.258	.373	8	.200	2	-41	-46	0	-4.1
● **MYRON ALLEN** Allen, Myron Smith "Zeke" b: 3/22/1854, Kingston, N.Y. d: 3/8/24, Kingston, N.Y. BR/TR, 5'8", 150 lbs. Deb: 7/19/1883 ♦																									
1883 NY-N	0	1	.000	1	1	1	0	0	8	8	0	3	0	12.4	1.13	275	.276	.344	0	.000	-1	2	2	-0	0.1
1887 Cle-a	1	0	1.000	2	0	0	0	0	9^2	9	0	3	1	12.1	0.93	466	.243	.317	128	.276	0	4	4	-0	0.3
1888 KC-a	0	2	.000	2	2	2	0	0	18	17	0	1	2	10.0	2.50	137	.240	.271	29	.213	0	1	2	1	0.3
Total 3	1	3	.250	5	3	3	0	0	35^2	34	0	7	3	11.1	1.77	205	.249	.300	157	.259	-0	7	7	0	0.7
● **NEIL ALLEN** Allen, Neil Patrick b: 1/24/58, Kansas City, Kan. BR/TR, 6'2", 190 lbs. Deb: 4/15/79																									
1979 NY-N	6	10	.375	50	5	0	0	8	99	100	4	47	65	13.4	3.55	103	.268	.350	0	.000	-2	2	1	0	0.0
1980 NY-N	7	10	.412	59	0	0	0	22	97^1	87	7	40	79	11.7	3.70	96	.244	.320	2	.143	-0	-1	-2	-1	-0.3
1981 NY-N	7	6	.538	43	0	0	0	18	66^2	64	4	26	50	12.2	2.97	117	.259	.330	1	.200	1	4	4	1	0.6
1982 NY-N	3	7	.300	50	0	0	0	19	64^2	65	5	30	59	13.4	3.06	119	.266	.349	1	.167	1	4	4	-0	0.4
1983 NY-N	2	7	.222	21	4	1	1	2	54	57	6	36	32	15.5	4.50	81	.278	.386	0	.000	-1	-5	-5	-0	-0.7
StL-N	10	6	.625	25	18	4	2	0	121^2	122	6	48	74	12.6	3.70	98	.265	.335	5	.128	-1	-1	-1	-0	-0.2
Yr	12	13	.480	46	22	5	3	2	175^2	179	12	84	106	13.5	3.94	92	.268	.351	5	.102	-2	-6	-6	-1	-0.9
1984 StL-N	9	6	.600	57	1	0	0	3	119	105	6	49	66	11.6	3.55	98	.239	.315	6	.240	1	0	-1	1	0.1
1985 StL-N	1	4	.200	23	1	0	0	2	29	32	3	17	10	15.5	5.59	63	.283	.382	0	.000	-0	-6	-7	-0	-0.7
NY-A	1	0	1.000	17	0	0	0	1	29^1	26	1	13	16	12.0	2.76	145	.234	.315	0	—	0	5	4	-0	0.4
1986 Chi-A	7	2	.778	22	17	2	2	0	113	101	8	38	57	11.2	3.82	113	.244	.311	0	—	0	4	6	-0	0.4
1987 Chi-A	0	7	.000	15	10	0	0	0	49^2	74	6	26	26	18.5	7.07	65	.365	.442	0	—	0	-14	-14	-0	-1.3
NY-A	0	1	.000	8	1	0	0	0	24^2	23	2	10	16	12.0	3.65	120	.242	.314	0	—	0	2	2	-0	0.2
Yr	0	8	.000	23	11	0	0	0	74^1	97	8	36	42	16.1	5.93	76	.321	.393	0	—	0	-12	-12	-1	-1.1
1988 NY-A	5	3	.625	41	2	0	1	0	117^1	121	14	37	61	12.3	3.84	103	.268	.326	0	—	0	2	1	-2	0.0
1989 Cle-A	0	1	.000	3	0	0	0	0	3	8	1	0	0	24.0	15.00	26	.500	.500	0	—	0	-4	-4	0	-0.4
Total 11	58	70	.453	434	59	7	6	75	988^1	985	73	417	611	12.8	3.88	97	.264	.339	15	.130	-1	-9	-11	-3	-1.5
● **BOB ALLEN** Allen, Robert Earl "Thin Man" b: 7/2/14, Smithville, Tenn. BR/TR, 6'1", 165 lbs. Deb: 9/19/37																									
1937 Phi-N	0	1	.000	3	1	0	0	0	12	18	2	8	8	19.5	6.75	64	.321	.406	1	.333	0	-4	-3	-1	-0.4
● **BOB ALLEN** Allen, Robert Gray b: 10/23/37, Tatum, Tex. BL/TL, 6'2", 185 lbs. Deb: 4/14/61																									
1961 Cle-A	3	2	.600	48	0	0	0	3	81^2	96	7	40	42	15.1	3.75	105	.294	.373	2	.167	0	3	2	-0	0.2
1962 Cle-A	1	1	.500	30	0	0	0	4	30^2	29	5	25	23	15.8	5.87	66	.250	.383	0	.000	-1	-6	-7	0	-0.7
1963 Cle-A	1	2	.333	43	0	0	0	2	56	58	5	29	51	14.1	4.66	78	.266	.355	1	.200	-0	-6	-6	0	-0.7
1966 Cle-A	2	2	.500	36	0	0	0	5	51^1	56	2	13	33	12.4	4.21	82	.273	.323	1	.111	-0	-4	-4	1	-0.4
1967 Cle-A	0	5	.000	47	0	0	0	5	54^1	49	4	25	50	12.4	2.98	110	.243	.329	0	—	0	2	2	1	0.3
Total 5	7	12	.368	204	0	0	0	19	274	288	23	132	199	14.0	4.11	89	.270	.353	4	.129	-1	-13	-14	2	-1.3
● **DANA ALLISON** Allison, Dana Eric b: 8/14/66, Front Royal, Va. BR/TL, 6'3", 215 lbs. Deb: 4/09/91																									
1991 Oak-A	1	1	.500	11	0	0	0	0	11	16	0	5	4	17.2	7.36	52	.381	.447	0	—	0	-4	-4	-0	-0.4
● **DOUG ALLISON** Allison, Douglas L. b: 7/1845, Philadelphia, Pa. d: 12/19/16, Washington, D.C. BR/TR, 5'10.5", 160 lbs. Deb: 5/05/1871 F♦																									
1878 Pro-N	0	0	—	1	0	0	0	0	5	11	0	1	0	21.6	1.80	123	.440	.462	22	.289	0	0	0	-0	0.0

YEAR	TM/L	W	L	PCT	G	GS	CG	SH	SV	IP	H	HR	BB	SO	RAT	ERA	ERA+	OAV	OOB	BH	AVG	PB	PR	/A	PD	TPI
● **MACK ALLISON**	Allison, Mack Pendleton b: 1/23/1887, Owensboro, Ky. d: 3/13/64, St.Joseph, Mo. BR/TR, 6'1", 185 lbs. Deb: 9/13/11																									
1911	StL-A	2	1	.667	3	3	3	0	0	26^1	24	0	5	2	10.6	2.05	165	.253	.304	2	.200	-0	4	4	-1	0.3
1912	StL-A	6	17	.261	31	20	11	1	1	169	171	4	49	43	12.0	3.62	92	.269	.327	7	.135	-3	-6	-6	-1	-1.0
1913	StL-A	1	3	.250	11	4	3	0	0	51^1	52	0	13	12	11.9	2.28	129	.287	.345	0	.000	-2	4	4	-2	0.0
Total	3	9	21	.300	45	27	17	1	1	246^2	247	4	67	57	11.9	3.17	102	.271	.328	9	.118	-6	2	2	-4	-0.7
● **LUIS ALOMA**	Aloma, Luis (Barba) "Witto" b: 7/23/23, Havana, Cuba BR/TR, 6'2", 195 lbs. Deb: 4/19/50																									
1950	Chi-A	7	2	.778	42	0	0	0	4	87^2	77	6	53	49	13.4	3.80	118	.234	.342	1	.067	-2	8	7	-0	0.4
1951	Chi-A	6	0	1.000	25	1	1	1	3	69^1	52	3	24	25	10.1	1.82	222	.215	.291	7	.350	2	18	17	-2	1.8
1952	Chi-A	3	1	.750	25	0	0	0	6	40	42	5	11	18	12.1	4.27	85	.278	.331	0	.000	-1	-3	-3	-0	-0.4
1953	Chi-A	2	0	1.000	24	0	0	0	2	38^1	41	7	23	23	15.0	4.70	86	.283	.381	0	.000	-1	-3	-3	0	-0.4
Total	4	18	3	.857	116	1	1	1	15	235^1	212	21	111	115	12.5	3.44	120	.245	.333	8	.167	-2	20	18	-2	1.4
● **MATTY ALOU**	Alou, Mateo Rojas (b: Mateo Rojas (Alou)) b: 12/22/38, Haina, D.R. BL/TL, 5'9", 160 lbs. Deb: 9/26/60 F♦																									
1965	SF-N	0	0	—	1	0	0	0	0	2	3	0	1	3	18.0	0.00	—	.333	.400	75	.231	0	1	1	-0	0.1
● **PORFI ALTAMIRANO**	Altamirano, Porfirio (Ramirez) b: 5/17/52, Darillo, Nic. BR/TR, 6', 175 lbs. Deb: 5/09/82																									
1982	Phi-N	5	1	.833	29	0	0	0	2	39	41	2	14	26	12.9	4.15	88	.281	.348	1	.250	0	-2	-2	0	-0.2
1983	Phi-N	2	3	.400	31	0	0	0	0	41^1	38	9	15	24	12.0	3.70	96	.255	.331	0	.000	-0	-0	-1	0	-0.1
1984	Chi-N	0	0	—	5	0	0	0	0	11^1	8	2	1	7	7.1	4.76	82	.195	.214	0	.000	-0	-1	-1	0	-0.1
Total	3	7	4	.636	65	0	0	0	2	91^2	87	13	30	57	11.8	4.03	91	.259	.325	1	.125	-0	-4	-4	1	-0.4
● **ERNIE ALTEN**	Alten, Ernest Matthias "Lefty" b: 12/1/1894, Avon, Ohio d: 9/9/81, Napa, Cal. BR/TL, 6', 175 lbs. Deb: 4/17/20																									
1920	Det-A	0	1	.000	14	1	0	0	0	23	40	2	9	4	19.6	9.00	41	.392	.446	0	.000	-1	-13	-13	0	-1.3
● **NICK ALTROCK**	Altrock, Nicholas b: 9/15/1876, Cincinnati, Ohio d: 1/20/65, Washington, D.C. BB/TL, 5'10", 197 lbs. Deb: 7/14/1898 C♦																									
1898	Lou-N	3	3	.500	11	7	6	0	0	70	89	2	21	13	14.5	4.50	79	.307	.360	7	.241	0	-7	-7	2	-0.4
1902	Bos-A	0	2	.000	3	2	1	0	1	18	19	0	7	5	13.0	2.00	179	.271	.338	0	.000	-1	3	3	1	0.2
1903	Bos-A	0	1	.000	1	1	1	0	0	8	13	0	4	3	19.1	9.00	34	.363	.427	2	.667	1	-5	-5	1	-0.3
	Chi-A	4	3	.571	12	8	6	1	0	71	59	4	19	19	10.4	2.15	130	.226	.288	9	.300	2	6	5	3	1.2
	Yr	4	4	.500	13	9	7	1	0	79	72	4	23	22	11.3	2.85	99	.242	.305	11	.333	3	1	-0	4	0.9
1904	Chi-A	19	14	.576	38	36	31	6	1	307	274	2	48	87	9.5	2.96	83	.240	.272	22	.198	0	-12	-17	4	-1.3
1905	Chi-A	23	12	.657	38	34	31	3	0	315^2	274	3	63	97	9.7	1.88	131	.235	.275	14	.125	-4	27	21	8	2.9
1906	*Chi-A	20	13	.606	38	30	25	4	0	287^2	269	0	42	99	9.8	2.06	123	.251	.280	16	.160	-1	20	15	4	2.0
1907	Chi-A	7	13	.350	30	21	15	1	2	213^2	210	3	31	61	10.2	2.57	93	.259	.288	13	.181	-0	-0	-4	5	0.1
1908	Chi-A	5	7	.417	23	13	8	1	2	136	127	2	18	21	9.7	2.71	85	.248	.276	10	.204	0	-5	-6	5	0.0
1909	Chi-A	0	1	.000	1	1	1	0	0	9	16	0	1	2	17.0	5.00	47	.485	.500	0	.000	-0	-3	-3	0	-0.3
	Was-A	1	3	.250	9	5	2	0	0	38	55	0	5	9	14.4	5.45	45	.333	.357	1	.053	-1	-13	-13	0	-1.4
	Yr	1	4	.200	10	6	3	0	0	47	71	0	6	11	14.9	5.36	45	.359	.380	1	.045	-1	-15	-15	1	-1.7
1912	Was-A	0	1	.000	1	0	0	0	0	1	1	0	2	0	27.0	18.00	19	.200	.429	0	.000	-0	-2	-2	-0	-0.2
1913	Was-A	0	0	—	4	0	0	0	0	9	7	0	4	2	12.0	5.00	59	.184	.279	0	.000	-0	-2	-2	0	-0.2
1914	Was-A	0	0	—	1	0	0	0	0	1	3	0	0	0	27.0	0.00	—	.750	.750	0	—	0	0	0	-0	0.0
1915	Was-A	0	0	—	1	0	0	0	1	3	7	0	1	2	24.0	9.00	33	.438	.471	0	.000	-0	-2	-2	-0	-0.2
1918	Was-A	1	2	.333	5	3	1	0	0	24	24	1	6	5	11.6	3.00	91	.279	.333	1	.125	0	-1	-1	0	0.0
1919	Was-A	0	0	—	1	0	0	0	0	0	4	0	0	0	—	∞	—	1.000	1.000	0	—	0	-4	-4	0	-0.3
1924	Was-A	0	0	—	1	0	0	0	0	2	4	0	0	0	18.0	0.00	—	.500	.500	1	1.000	1	1	1	0	0.2
Total	16	83	75	.525	218	161	128	16	7	1514	1455	17	272	425	10.4	2.67	95	.254	.291	97	.176	-2	3	-20	34	2.0
● **JOSE ALVAREZ**	Alvarez, Jose Lino b: 4/12/56, Tampa, Fla. BR/TR, 5'10", 170 lbs. Deb: 10/01/81																									
1981	Atl-N	0	0	—	1	0	0	0	0	2	0	0	0	2	0.0	0.00	—	.000	.000	0	—	0	1	1	-0	0.1
1982	Atl-N	0	0	—	7	0	0	0	0	7^2	8	1	2	6	11.7	4.70	79	.308	.357	0	—	0	-1	-1	0	-0.1
1988	Atl-N	5	6	.455	60	0	0	0	3	102^1	88	7	53	81	12.9	2.99	123	.240	.346	3	.375	1	5	8	1	1.1
1989	Atl-N	3	3	.500	30	0	0	0	2	50^1	44	4	24	45	12.3	2.86	128	.237	.327	0	.000	-0	4	4	1	0.5
Total	4	8	9	.471	98	0	0	0	5	162^1	140	12	79	134	12.5	2.99	123	.240	.337	3	.273	1	9	12	2	1.6
● **WILSON ALVAREZ**	Alvarez, Wilson Eduardo (Fuenmayor) b: 3/24/70, Maracaibo, Venez. BL/TL, 6'1", 175 lbs. Deb: 7/24/89																									
1989	Tex-A	0	1	.000	1	1	0	0	0	0	3	2	2	0	—	∞	—	1.000	1.000	0	—	0	-3	-3	0	-0.3
1991	Chi-A	3	2	.600	10	9	2	1	0	56^1	47	9	29	32	12.1	3.51	113	.230	.326	0	—	0	4	3	-0	0.3
1992	Chi-A	5	3	.625	34	9	0	0	1	100^1	103	12	65	66	15.4	5.20	73	.272	.384	0	—	0	-14	-15	-0	-1.5
Total	3	8	6	.571	45	19	2	1	1	156^2	153	23	96	98	14.5	4.77	81	.261	.369	0	—	0	-13	-16	-0	-1.5
● **RED AMES**	Ames, Leon Kessling b: 8/2/1882, Warren, Ohio d: 10/8/36, Warren, Ohio BB/TR, 5'10.5", 185 lbs. Deb: 9/14/03																									
1903	NY-N	2	0	1.000	2	2	2	1	0	14	5	0	8	14	8.4	1.29	260	.114	.250	0	.000	-1	3	3	-1	0.2
1904	NY-N	4	6	.400	16	13	11	1	3	115	94	2	38	93	10.6	2.27	120	.222	.291	5	.125	-1	6	6	-0	0.4
1905	*NY-N	22	8	.733	34	31	21	2	0	262^2	220	2	105	198	11.2	2.74	107	.230	.308	14	.144	-1	8	6	1	0.5
1906	NY-N	12	10	.545	31	25	15	1	1	203^1	166	1	93	156	11.6	2.66	98	.223	.312	4	.066	-3	-0	-1	3	-0.1
1907	NY-N	10	12	.455	39	26	17	2	1	233^1	184	4	108	146	11.6	2.16	115	.219	.315	12	.174	2	8	8	3	1.5
1908	NY-N	7	4	.636	18	15	5	0	1	114^1	96	0	27	81	9.8	1.81	133	.232	.281	7	.194	0	7	8	1	1.0
1909	NY-N	15	10	.600	34	26	20	2	1	244	217	3	81	156	11.1	2.69	95	.241	.306	6	.074	-5	-2	-4	7	-0.2
1910	NY-N	12	11	.522	33	23	13	3	0	190^1	161	3	63	94	10.9	2.22	133	.237	.308	11	.177	-1	17	16	4	2.0
1911	*NY-N	11	10	.524	34	23	13	1	2	205	170	0	54	118	10.0	2.68	126	.223	.277	6	.094	-3	16	16	3	1.5
1912	*NY-N	11	5	.688	33	22	9	2	2	179	194	3	35	83	11.7	2.46	137	.281	.320	13	.224	1	19	18	2	2.2
1913	NY-N	2	1	.667	8	5	2	0	1	41^2	35	0	8	30	9.5	2.16	144	.241	.286	2	.154	-1	5	4	2	0.6
	Cin-N	11	13	.458	31	24	12	1	2	187^1	185	7	70	80	12.5	2.88	113	.265	.336	6	.102	-4	7	8	0	0.3
	Yr	13	14	.481	39	29	14	1	3	229	220	7	78	110	11.9	2.75	117	.261	.327	8	.111	-5	12	12	2	0.9
1914	Cin-N	15	23	.395	47	36	18	3	**6**	297	274	8	94	128	11.3	2.64	111	.248	.311	12	.128	-4	5	10	4	1.1
1915	Cin-N	2	4	.333	17	7	4	1	1	68	82	2	24	26	14.0	4.50	64	.311	.368	1	.050	-1	-13	-12	1	-1.3
	StL-N	9	3	.750	15	14	8	2	1	113^1	93	1	32	48	9.9	2.46	113	.226	.282	4	.114	-2	4	4	2	0.4
	Yr	11	7	.611	32	21	12	3	2	181^1	175	3	56	74	11.5	3.23	87	.259	.316	5	.091	-3	-10	-8	2	-0.9
1916	StL-N	11	16	.407	45	22	10	2	**8**	228	225	3	57	98	11.3	2.64	100	.263	.313	12	.176	-0	-1	0	-2	-0.2
1917	StL-N	15	10	.600	43	19	10	2	3	209	189	2	57	62	10.7	2.71	99	.249	.304	12	.188	2	-0	-0	4	0.7
1918	StL-N	9	14	.391	27	25	17	0	1	206^2	192	1	52	68	10.8	2.31	117	.252	.304	10	.156	-1	10	9	-1	0.9
1919	StL-N	3	5	.375	23	7	1	0	1	70	88	1	25	19	14.7	4.89	57	.314	.373	4	.222	-0	-15	-16	-2	-1.9
	Phi-N	0	2	.000	3	2	1	0	1	16	26	0	3	4	16.3	6.19	52	.400	.426	2	.400	1	-6	-5	0	-0.4
	Yr	3	7	.300	26	9	2	0	2	86	114	1	28	23	14.9	5.13	56	.329	.380	6	.261	1	-21	-22	-2	-2.3
Total	17	183	167	.523	533	367	209	26	36	3198	2896	43	1034	1702	11.2	2.63	108	.245	.310	143	.141	-21	77	77	32	9.2
● **DOC AMOLE**	Amole, Morris George b: 7/5/1878, Coatesville, Pa. d: 3/7/12, Wilmington, Del. BR/TL, 5'9", 165 lbs. Deb: 8/19/1897																									
1897	Bal-N	4	4	.500	11	7	6	0	0	70	67	0	17	19	11.6	2.57	162	.250	.309	3	.107	-3	14	12	0	0.9
1898	Was-N	0	6	.000	7	5	4	0	0	49^1	83	0	22	11	20.3	7.84	47	.370	.440	2	.100	-2	-23	-23	1	-1.9
Total	2	4	10	.286	18	12	10	0	0	119^1	150	0	39	30	15.2	4.75	84	.305	.370	5	.104	-5	-10	-10	1	-1.0
● **VICENTE AMOR**	Amor, Vicente (Alvarez) b: 8/8/32, Havana, Cuba BR/TR, 6'3", 182 lbs. Deb: 4/16/55																									
1955	Chi-N	0	1	.000	4	0	0	0	0	6	11	0	3	3	21.0	4.50	91	.407	.467	0	—	0	-0	-0	1	0.0
1957	Cin-N	1	2	.333	9	4	1	0	0	27^1	39	2	10	9	16.8	5.93	69	.345	.408	1	.167	-0	-6	-6	-0	-0.6

YEAR	TM/L	W	L	PCT	G	GS	CG	SH	SV	IP	H	HR	BB	SO	RAT	ERA	ERA+	OAV	OOB	BH	AVG	PB	PR	/A	PD	TPI
Total	2	1	3	.250	13	4	1	0	0	33^1	50	2	13	12	17.6	5.67	72	.357	.419	1	.167	-0	-7	-6	0	-0.6

● WALTER ANCKER Ancker, Walter b: 4/10/1894, New York, N.Y. d: 2/13/54, Englewood, N.J. BR/TR, 6'1", 190 lbs. Deb: 9/03/15

YEAR	TM/L	W	L	PCT	G	GS	CG	SH	SV	IP	H	HR	BB	SO	RAT	ERA	ERA+	OAV	OOB	BH	AVG	PB	PR	/A	PD	TPI
1915	Phi-A	0	0	—	4	1	0	0	0	17^2	19	1	17	4	19.9	3.57	82	.279	.443	0	.000	-1	-1	-1	0	-0.2

● LARRY ANDERSEN Andersen, Larry Eugene b: 5/6/53, Portland, Ore. BR/TR, 6'3", 205 lbs. Deb: 9/05/75

YEAR	TM/L	W	L	PCT	G	GS	CG	SH	SV	IP	H	HR	BB	SO	RAT	ERA	ERA+	OAV	OOB	BH	AVG	PB	PR	/A	PD	TPI
1975	Cle-A	0	0	—	3	0	0	0	0	5^2	4	0	2	4	9.5	4.76	79	.200	.273	0	—	0	-1	-1	0	0.0
1977	Cle-A	0	1	.000	11	0	0	0	0	14^1	10	1	9	8	11.9	3.14	126	.200	.322	0	—	0	1	1	1	0.2
1979	Cle-A	0	0	—	8	0	0	0	0	16^2	25	3	4	7	15.7	7.56	56	.357	.392	0	—	0	-6	-6	0	-0.6
1981	Sea-A	3	3	.500	41	0	0	0	5	67^2	57	4	18	40	10.2	2.66	145	.228	.285	0	—	0	7	9	-0	0.8
1982	Sea-A	0	0	—	40	1	0	0	1	79^2	100	16	23	32	14.3	5.99	71	.311	.364	0	—	0	-17	-15	1	-1.5
1983	*Phi-N	1	0	1.000	17	0	0	0	0	26^1	19	0	9	14	9.6	2.39	149	.200	.269	0	.000	-0	4	3	0	0.4
1984	Phi-N	3	7	.300	64	0	0	0	4	90^2	85	5	25	54	10.9	2.38	152	.248	.299	0	.000	-0	12	13	0	1.3
1985	Phi-N	3	3	.500	57	0	0	0	3	73	78	5	26	50	13.2	4.32	85	.274	.341	0	.000	-0	-6	-5	2	-0.4
1986	Phi-N	0	0	—	10	0	0	0	0	12^2	19	0	3	9	15.6	4.26	90	.388	.423	0	—	0	-1	-1	0	0.0
	*Hou-N	2	1	.667	38	0	0	0	1	64^2	64	2	23	33	12.2	2.78	129	.276	.344	0	.000	-1	7	6	0	0.6
	Yr	2	1	.667	48	0	0	0	1	77^1	83	2	26	42	12.8	3.03	120	.294	.356	0	.000	-1	6	5	0	0.6
1987	Hou-N	9	5	.643	67	0	0	0	5	101^2	95	7	41	94	12.2	3.45	113	.246	.322	1	.167	0	7	5	-0	0.5
1988	Hou-N	2	4	.333	53	0	0	0	5	82^2	82	3	20	66	11.2	2.94	113	.254	.299	2	.333	1	5	3	-0	0.4
1989	Hou-N	4	4	.500	60	0	0	0	3	87^2	63	2	24	85	8.9	1.54	220	.198	.254	1	.333	0	**19**	18	1	2.0
1990	Hou-N	5	2	.714	50	0	0	0	6	73^2	61	2	24	68	10.5	1.95	190	.229	.296	0	.000	-0	15	14	1	1.6
	*Bos-A	0	0	—	15	0	0	0	1	22	18	0	3	25	9.0	1.23	332	.220	.256	0	—	0	7	7	-1	0.4
1991	SD-N	3	4	.429	38	0	0	0	13	47	39	0	13	40	10.0	2.30	165	.231	.286	0	.000	-0	7	8	0	0.8
1992	SD-N	1	1	.500	34	0	0	0	2	35	26	2	8	35	9.0	3.34	109	.202	.254	0	.000	0	1	1	0	0.2
Total	15	36	35	.507	606	1	0	0	49	901	845	52	275	664	11.3	3.12	120	.249	.309	4	.108	-1	61	61	6	6.7

● ALLAN ANDERSON Anderson, Allan Lee b: 1/7/64, Lancaster, Ohio BL/TL, 6', 186 lbs. Deb: 6/11/86

YEAR	TM/L	W	L	PCT	G	GS	CG	SH	SV	IP	H	HR	BB	SO	RAT	ERA	ERA+	OAV	OOB	BH	AVG	PB	PR	/A	PD	TPI
1986	Min-A	3	6	.333	21	10	1	0	0	84^1	106	11	30	51	14.6	5.55	78	.316	.374	0	—	0	-13	-12	0	-1.1
1987	Min-A	1	0	1.000	4	2	0	0	0	12^1	20	3	10	3	21.9	10.95	42	.392	.492	0	—	0	-9	-9	-0	-0.8
1988	Min-A	16	9	.640	30	30	3	1	0	202^1	199	14	37	83	10.8	**2.45**	**166**	.261	.301	0	—	0	34	36	1	4.1
1989	Min-A	17	10	.630	33	33	4	1	0	196^2	214	15	53	69	12.5	3.80	109	.275	.327	0	.000	0	2	7	-1	0.7
1990	Min-A	7	18	.280	31	31	5	1	0	188^2	214	20	39	82	12.3	4.53	92	.289	.329	0	—	0	-13	-8	2	-1.0
1991	Min-A	5	11	.313	29	22	2	0	0	134^1	148	24	42	51	13.1	4.96	86	.281	.340	0	—	0	-13	-10	-0	-1.0
Total	6	49	54	.476	148	128	15	3	0	818^2	901	87	211	339	12.5	4.11	101	.282	.331	0	.000	0	-12	5	2	0.9

● RED ANDERSON Anderson, Arnold Revola b: 6/19/12, Lawton, Iowa d: 8/7/72, Sioux City, Iowa BR/TR, 6'3", 210 lbs. Deb: 9/19/37

YEAR	TM/L	W	L	PCT	G	GS	CG	SH	SV	IP	H	HR	BB	SO	RAT	ERA	ERA+	OAV	OOB	BH	AVG	PB	PR	/A	PD	TPI
1937	Was-A	0	1	.000	2	1	0	0	0	10^2	11	0	11	3	19.4	6.75	66	.282	.451	0	.000	-0	-3	-3	0	-0.3
1940	Was-A	1	1	.500	2	2	2	0	0	14	12	0	5	3	10.9	3.86	108	.245	.315	3	.600	1	1	0	0	0.2
1941	Was-A	4	6	.400	32	6	1	0	0	112	127	7	53	34	14.7	4.18	97	.296	.377	8	.258	2	-0	-2	-1	0.0
Total	3	5	8	.385	36	9	3	0	0	136^2	150	7	69	40	14.7	4.35	94	.290	.378	11	.282	3	-2	-4	-1	-0.1

● DAVE ANDERSON Anderson, David S. b: 10/10/1868, Chester, Pa. d: 3/22/1897, Chester, Pa. TL , Deb: 8/24/1889

YEAR	TM/L	W	L	PCT	G	GS	CG	SH	SV	IP	H	HR	BB	SO	RAT	ERA	ERA+	OAV	OOB	BH	AVG	PB	PR	/A	PD	TPI
1889	Phi-N	0	1	.000	5	2	1	0	0	23	30	2	14	8	17.2	7.43	59	.306	.392	2	.182	-0	-9	-8	0	-0.6
1890	Phi-N	1	1	.500	3	2	1	0	0	19^1	31	0	11	7	20.0	7.45	49	.351	.429	1	.111	-1	-8	-8	0	-0.7
	Pit-N	2	11	.154	13	13	13	0	0	108	116	2	49	41	14.3	4.67	71	.266	.350	3	.071	-5	-13	-16	4	-1.4
	Yr	3	12	.200	16	15	14	0	0	127^1	147	2	60	48	15.1	5.09	66	.280	.361	4	.078	-6	-21	-25	4	-2.1
Total	2	3	13	.188	21	17	15	0	0	150^1	177	4	74	56	15.5	5.45	64	.284	.368	6	.097	-6	-30	-33	4	-2.7

● JOHN ANDERSON Anderson, John Charles b: 11/23/32, St.Paul, Minn. BR/TR, 6'1", 190 lbs. Deb: 8/17/58

YEAR	TM/L	W	L	PCT	G	GS	CG	SH	SV	IP	H	HR	BB	SO	RAT	ERA	ERA+	OAV	OOB	BH	AVG	PB	PR	/A	PD	TPI
1958	Phi-N	0	0	—	5	1	0	0	0	16	26	5	4	9	17.4	7.88	50	.361	.403	0	.000	-0	-7	-7	-0	-0.7
1960	Bal-A	0	0	—	4	0	0	0	0	4^2	8	0	4	1	23.1	13.50	28	.444	.545	0	—	0	-5	-5	0	-0.4
1962	StL-N	0	0	—	5	0	0	0	1	6^1	4	0	3	3	9.9	1.42	300	.182	.280	0	—	0	2	2	-0	0.2
	Hou-N	0	0	—	10	0	0	0	0	17^2	26	1	3	6	14.8	5.09	73	.338	.363	0	.000	-0	-2	-3	1	-0.2
	Yr	0	0	—	15	0	0	0	1	24	30	1	6	9	13.5	4.13	94	.300	.340	0	.000	-0	-0	-1	0	0.0
Total	3	0	0	—	24	1	0	0	1	44^2	64	6	14	19	15.9	6.45	60	.339	.387	0	.000	-0	-12	-13	0	-1.1

● FRED ANDERSON Anderson, John Frederick b: 12/11/1885, Calahan, N.C. d: 11/8/57, Winston-Salem, N.C. BR/TR, 6'2", 180 lbs. Deb: 9/25/09

YEAR	TM/L	W	L	PCT	G	GS	CG	SH	SV	IP	H	HR	BB	SO	RAT	ERA	ERA+	OAV	OOB	BH	AVG	PB	PR	/A	PD	TPI
1909	Bos-A	0	0	—	1	1	0	0	0	8	3	0	1	5	4.5	1.13	222	.115	.148	0	.000	-0	1	1	0	0.1
1913	Bos-A	0	6	.000	10	8	4	0	0	57^1	84	0	21	32	16.6	5.97	49	.350	.405	1	.050	-2	-19	-19	-0	-2.1
1914	Buf-F	13	15	.464	37	28	21	2	0	260^1	243	8	64	144	10.7	3.08	107	.249	.297	17	.189	-1	4	6	-1	0.4
1915	Buf-F	19	13	.594	36	28	14	5	0	240	192	5	72	142	10.0	2.51	124	.222	.285	12	.150	-4	14	16	-1	1.3
1916	NY-N	9	13	.409	38	27	13	2	2	188	206	7	38	98	11.9	3.40	72	.277	.316	8	.138	-0	-16	-20	-2	-2.5
1917	*NY-N	8	8	.500	38	18	8	1	3	162	122	1	34	69	**8.8**	**1.44**	**177**	.209	**.255**	3	.071	-3	23	20	-1	1.9
1918	NY-N	4	2	.667	18	4	2	1	**3**	70^2	62	1	17	24	10.3	2.67	98	.246	.299	0	.000	-3	1	-0	3	0.0
Total	7	53	57	.482	178	114	62	11	8	986^1	912	22	247	514	10.7	2.86	101	.248	.298	41	.131	-13	7	3	-2	-0.9

● BUD ANDERSON Anderson, Karl Adam b: 5/27/56, Westbury, N.Y. BR/TR, 6'3", 210 lbs. Deb: 6/11/82

YEAR	TM/L	W	L	PCT	G	GS	CG	SH	SV	IP	H	HR	BB	SO	RAT	ERA	ERA+	OAV	OOB	BH	AVG	PB	PR	/A	PD	TPI
1982	Cle-A	3	4	.429	25	5	1	0	0	80^2	84	4	30	44	12.8	3.35	122	.268	.334	0	—	0	7	7	-0	0.7
1983	Cle-A	1	6	.143	39	1	0	0	7	68^1	64	8	32	32	12.6	4.08	104	.255	.339	0	—	0	-0	1	-1	0.0
Total	2	4	10	.286	64	6	1	0	7	149	148	12	62	76	12.7	3.68	113	.262	.337	0	—	0	6	8	-1	0.7

● LARRY ANDERSON Anderson, Lawrence Dennis b: 12/3/52, Maywood, Cal. BR/TR, 6'3", 190 lbs. Deb: 9/25/74

YEAR	TM/L	W	L	PCT	G	GS	CG	SH	SV	IP	H	HR	BB	SO	RAT	ERA	ERA+	OAV	OOB	BH	AVG	PB	PR	/A	PD	TPI
1974	Mil-A	0	0	—	2	0	0	0	0	2^1	2	0	1	3	11.6	0.00	—	.250	.333	0	—	0	1	1	0	0.1
1975	Mil-A	1	0	1.000	8	1	1	1	0	30^1	36	3	6	13	12.5	5.04	76	.298	.331	0	—	0	-4	-4	0	-0.4
1977	Chi-A	1	3	.250	6	0	0	0	0	8^2	10	1	15	7	26.0	9.35	44	.286	.500	0	—	0	-5	-5	-0	-0.5
Total	3	2	3	.400	16	1	1	1	0	41^1	48	4	22	23	15.2	5.66	68	.293	.376	0	—	0	-8	-8	0	-0.8

● MIKE ANDERSON Anderson, Michael Allen b: 6/22/51, Florence, S.C. BR/TR, 6'2", 200 lbs. Deb: 9/02/71 F♦

YEAR	TM/L	W	L	PCT	G	GS	CG	SH	SV	IP	H	HR	BB	SO	RAT	ERA	ERA+	OAV	OOB	BH	AVG	PB	PR	/A	PD	TPI
1979	Phi-N	0	0	—	1	0	0	0	0	1	2	0	0	2	18.0	0.00	—	.400	.400	18	.231	0	0	0	0	0.0

● CRAIG ANDERSON Anderson, Norman Craig b: 7/1/38, Washington, D.C. BR/TR, 6'2", 205 lbs. Deb: 6/23/61

YEAR	TM/L	W	L	PCT	G	GS	CG	SH	SV	IP	H	HR	BB	SO	RAT	ERA	ERA+	OAV	OOB	BH	AVG	PB	PR	/A	PD	TPI
1961	StL-N	4	3	.571	25	0	0	0	1	38^2	38	3	12	21	11.9	3.26	135	.255	.315	3	.333	1	3	5	0	0.6
1962	NY-N	3	17	.150	50	14	2	0	4	131^1	150	18	63	62	14.9	5.35	78	.278	.359	3	.094	-2	-20	-17	3	-1.6
1963	NY-N	0	2	.000	3	2	0	0	0	9^1	17	0	3	6	19.3	8.68	40	.362	.400	1	.333	0	-6	-5	0	-0.5
1964	NY-N	0	1	.000	4	1	0	0	0	13	21	0	3	5	16.6	5.54	65	.382	.414	0	.000	-0	-3	-3	0	-0.3
Total	4	7	23	.233	82	17	2	0	5	192^1	226	21	81	94	14.6	5.10	81	.286	.357	7	.149	-1	-26	-20	3	-1.8

● RICK ANDERSON Anderson, Richard Arlen b: 11/29/56, Everett, Wash. BR/TR, 6', 175 lbs. Deb: 6/09/86

YEAR	TM/L	W	L	PCT	G	GS	CG	SH	SV	IP	H	HR	BB	SO	RAT	ERA	ERA+	OAV	OOB	BH	AVG	PB	PR	/A	PD	TPI
1986	NY-N	2	1	.667	15	5	0	0	1	49^2	45	3	11	21	10.1	2.72	130	.245	.287	1	.091	-1	6	5	-1	0.4
1987	KC-A	0	2	.000	6	2	0	0	0	13	26	3	9	12	25.6	13.85	33	.394	.481	0	—	0	-14	-13	0	-1.2
1988	KC-A	2	1	.667	7	3	0	0	0	34	41	3	9	9	13.5	4.24	94	.308	.357	0	—	0	-1	-1	-1	-0.2
Total	3	4	4	.500	28	10	0	0	1	96^2	112	9	29	42	13.4	4.75	81	.292	.347	1	.091	-1	-9	-10	-1	-1.0

● RICK ANDERSON Anderson, Richard Lee b: 12/25/53, Inglewood, Cal. d: 6/23/89, Wilmington, Cal. BR/TR, 6'2", 210 lbs. Deb: 9/18/79

YEAR	TM/L	W	L	PCT	G	GS	CG	SH	SV	IP	H	HR	BB	SO	RAT	ERA	ERA+	OAV	OOB	BH	AVG	PB	PR	/A	PD	TPI
1979	NY-A	0	0	—	1	0	0	0	0	2^1	1	0	4	0	19.3	3.86	106	.167	.500	0	—	0	0	0	1	0.1
1980	Sea-A	0	0	—	5	2	0	0	0	9^2	8	1	10	7	16.8	3.72	111	.229	.400	0	—	0	0	0	-0	0.0

YEAR	TM/L	W	L	PCT	G	GS	CG	SH	SV	IP	H	HR	BB	SO	RAT	ERA	ERA+	OAV	OOB	BH	AVG	PB	PR	/A	PD	TPI
Total	2	0	0	—	6	2	0	0	0	12	9	1	14	7	17.3	3.75	110	.220	.418	0	—	0	0	0	0	0.1
● **BOB ANDERSON**	Anderson, Robert Carl b: 9/29/35, E.Chicago, Ind. BR/TR, 6'4.5", 210 lbs. Deb: 7/31/57																									
1957	Chi-N	0	1	.000	8	0	0	0	0	16^1	20	2	8	7	16.0	7.71	50	.317	.403	0	.000	-1	-7	-7	0	-0.7
1958	Chi-N	3	3	.500	17	8	2	0	0	65^2	61	3	29	51	12.5	3.97	99	.255	.338	2	.118	-1	-0	-0	0	-0.1
1959	Chi-N	12	13	.480	37	36	7	1	0	235^1	245	21	77	113	12.5	4.13	96	.272	.333	6	.075	-4	-5	-5	1	-0.8
1960	Chi-N	9	11	.450	38	30	5	0	1	203^2	201	26	68	115	12.2	4.11	92	.255	.320	12	.169	0	-8	-8	1	-0.6
1961	Chi-N	7	10	.412	57	12	1	0	8	152	162	14	56	96	13.0	4.26	98	.275	.340	6	.143	0	-4	-1	4	0.2
1962	Chi-N	2	7	.222	57	4	0	0	4	107^2	111	9	60	82	14.7	5.02	83	.266	.364	3	.130	0	-13	-10	-0	-1.0
1963	Det-A	3	1	.750	32	3	0	0	0	60	58	5	21	38	12.8	3.30	113	.258	.337	4	.444	2	2	3	-0	0.4
Total	7	36	46	.439	246	93	15	1	13	840^2	858	80	319	502	12.9	4.26	93	.266	.337	33	.134	-4	-34	-29	5	-2.6
● **SCOTT ANDERSON**	Anderson, Scott Richard b: 8/1/62, Corvallis, Ore. BR/TR, 6'6", 190 lbs. Deb: 4/08/87																									
1987	Tex-A	0	1	.000	8	0	0	0	0	11^1	17	0	8	6	20.6	9.53	47	.347	.448	0	—	0	-6	-6	1	-0.5
1990	Mon-N	0	1	.000	4	3	0	0	0	18	12	1	5	16	8.5	3.00	122	.188	.246	0	.000	-0	2	1	-0	0.1
Total	2	0	2	.000	12	3	0	0	0	29^1	29	1	13	22	13.2	5.52	72	.257	.339	0	.000	-0	-5	-5	0	-0.4
● **VARNEY ANDERSON**	Anderson, Varney Samuel "Varn" b: 6/18/1866, Geneva, Ill. d: 11/5/41, Rockford, Ill. BR/TR, 5'10", 165 lbs. Deb: 8/01/1889																									
1889	Ind-N	0	1	.000	2	1	1	0	0	12	13	0	9	3	18.8	4.50	93	.268	.413	0	.000	-1	-1	-0	0	-0.1
1894	Was-N	0	2	.000	2	2	2	0	0	14	15	0	6	3	14.1	7.07	74	.271	.353	3	.429	1	-3	-3	-0	-0.2
1895	Was-N	9	16	.360	29	25	18	0	0	204^2	288	13	97	35	17.4	5.89	81	.327	.400	28	.289	3	-25	-25	1	-1.6
1896	Was-N	0	1	.000	2	2	1	0	0	9	23	0	3	0	26.0	13.00	34	.471	.502	3	.600	1	-9	-9	-1	-0.6
Total	4	9	20	.310	35	30	22	0	0	239^2	339	13	115	41	17.6	6.16	78	.328	.402	34	.298	4	-37	-37	0	-2.5
● **WALTER ANDERSON**	Anderson, Walter Carl "Lefty" b: 9/25/1897, Grand Rapids, Mich. d: 1/6/90, Battle Creek, Mich. BL/TL, 6'2", 160 lbs. Deb: 5/14/17																									
1917	Phi-A	0	0	—	14	2	0	0	0	38^2	32	0	21	10	12.6	3.03	91	.246	.355	3	.429	1	-2	-1	-0	0.0
1919	Phi-A	1	0	1.000	3	0	0	0	0	14	13	0	8	10	14.1	3.86	89	.245	.355	0	.000	-1	-1	-1	0	-0.1
Total	2	1	0	1.000	17	2	0	0	0	52^2	45	0	29	20	13.0	3.25	90	.246	.355	3	.273	0	-3	-2	-0	-0.1
● **BILL ANDERSON**	Anderson, William Edward "Lefty" b: 11/28/1895, Boston, Mass. d: 3/13/83, Medford, Mass. BR/TL, 6'1", 165 lbs. Deb: 9/10/25																									
1925	Bos-N	0	0	—	2	0	0	0	0	2^2	5	0	2	1	23.6	10.13	40	.500	.583	0	.000	-0	-2	-2	-0	-0.2
● **WINGO ANDERSON**	Anderson, Wingo Charlie b: 8/13/1886, Alvarado, Tex. d: 12/19/50, Fort Worth, Tex. BL/TL, 5'10.5", 150 lbs. Deb: 4/16/10																									
1910	Cin-N	0	0	—	7	2	0	0	0	17^1	16	0	17	11	17.7	4.67	62	.258	.425	1	.200	-0	-3	-3	-1	-0.4
● **JOHN ANDRE**	Andre, John Edward b: 1/3/23, Brockton, Mass. d: 11/25/76, Centerville, Mass. BL/TR, 6'4", 200 lbs. Deb: 4/16/55																									
1955	Chi-N	0	1	.000	22	3	0	0	1	45	45	7	28	19	14.8	5.80	70	.259	.365	1	.111	-1	-9	-9	-0	-0.9
● **ELBERT ANDREWS**	Andrews, Elbert De Vore b: 12/11/01, Greenwood, S.C. d: 11/25/79, Greenwood, S.C. BL/TR, 6', 175 lbs. Deb: 5/01/25																									
1925	Phi-A	0	0	—	6	0	0	0	0	8	12	0	11	0	25.9	10.13	46	.375	.535	0	—	0	-5	-5	-0	-0.4
● **HUB ANDREWS**	Andrews, Herbert Carl b: 8/31/22, Burbank, Okla. BR/TR, 6', 170 lbs. Deb: 4/20/47																									
1947	NY-N	0	0	—	7	0	0	0	0	8^2	14	1	4	2	18.7	6.23	65	.368	.429	0	—	0	-2	-2	0	-0.2
1948	NY-N	0	0	—	1	0	0	0	0	3	3	0	0	0	9.0	0.00	—	.300	.300	0	—	0	1	1	0	0.2
Total	2	0	0	—	8	0	0	0	0	11^2	17	1	4	2	16.2	4.63	87	.354	.404	0	—	0	-1	-1	0	0.0
● **IVY ANDREWS**	Andrews, Ivy Paul "Poison" b: 5/6/07, Dora, Ala. d: 11/24/70, Birmingham, Ala. BR/TR, 6'1", 200 lbs. Deb: 8/15/31																									
1931	NY-A	2	0	1.000	7	3	1	0	0	34^1	36	3	8	10	11.5	4.19	95	.273	.314	2	.182	0	1	-1	-0	-0.1
1932	NY-A	2	1	.667	4	1	1	0	0	24^2	20	0	9	7	10.6	1.82	223	.215	.284	2	.222	1	7	6	0	0.7
	Bos-A	8	6	.571	25	19	8	0	0	141^2	144	4	53	30	12.6	3.81	118	.262	.329	7	.137	-3	11	11	-1	0.7
	Yr	10	7	.588	29	20	9	0	0	166^1	164	4	62	37	12.3	3.52	126	.255	.322	9	.150	-2	18	17	-0	1.4
1933	Bos-A	7	13	.350	34	17	5	0	1	140	157	8	61	37	14.1	4.95	88	.279	.350	9	.214	-0	-10	-9	-1	-0.9
1934	StL-A	4	11	.267	43	13	2	0	3	139	166	7	65	51	15.0	4.66	107	.301	.375	14	.350	4	-3	5	-2	0.6
1935	StL-A	13	7	.650	50	20	10	0	1	213^1	231	10	53	43	12.0	3.54	135	.273	.317	9	.132	-6	22	30	-2	2.1
1936	StL-A	7	12	.368	36	25	11	0	1	191^1	221	19	50	33	12.7	4.84	111	.286	.330	10	.169	-1	4	11	-2	0.7
1937	Cle-A	3	4	.429	20	4	1	1	0	59^2	76	3	9	16	12.8	4.37	105	.311	.336	3	.250	1	2	2	-1	0.1
	*NY-A	3	2	.600	11	5	3	1	1	49	49	2	17	17	12.1	3.12	142	.259	.320	1	.067	-1	8	7	0	0.6
	Yr	6	6	.500	31	9	4	2	1	108^2	125	5	26	33	12.5	3.81	119	.289	.329	4	.148	-1	10	9	-0	0.7
1938	NY-A	1	3	.250	19	1	1	0	1	48	51	3	17	13	12.8	3.00	151	.268	.329	2	.167	-0	10	8	0	0.8
Total	8	50	59	.459	249	108	43	2	8	1041	1151	59	342	257	12.9	4.14	115	.279	.335	59	.185	-6	51	70	-9	5.3
● **JOHN ANDREWS**	Andrews, John Richard b: 2/9/49, Monterey Park, Cal. BL/TL, 5'10", 175 lbs. Deb: 4/08/73																									
1973	StL-N	1	1	.500	16	0	0	0	0	18^1	16	3	11	5	13.3	4.42	82	.235	.342	1	.500	0	-2	-2	-0	-0.2
● **NATE ANDREWS**	Andrews, Nathan Hardy b: 9/30/13, Pembroke, N.C. d: 4/26/91, Winston-Salem, N.C. BR/TR, 6', 195 lbs. Deb: 5/01/37																									
1937	StL-N	0	0	—	4	0	0	0	0	9	12	1	3	6	15.0	4.00	100	.324	.375	0	—	0	-0	-0	0	0.1
1939	StL-N	1	2	.333	11	1	0	0	0	16	24	0	12	6	20.3	6.75	61	.343	.439	0	.000	-0	-5	-5	0	-0.5
1940	Cle-A	0	1	.000	6	0	0	0	0	12	16	1	6	3	16.5	6.00	70	.327	.400	0	—	0	-2	-2	1	-0.1
1941	Cle-A	0	0	—	2	0	0	0	0	2^1	3	0	2	1	19.3	11.57	34	.300	.417	0	.000	-0	-2	-2	-0	-0.2
1943	Bos-N	14	20	.412	36	34	23	3	0	283^2	253	11	75	80	10.6	2.57	133	.238	.291	14	.156	-0	26	27	2	3.2
1944	Bos-N☆	16	15	.516	37	34	16	2	2	257^1	263	14	74	76	11.9	3.22	119	.261	.312	10	.114	-4	11	17	1	1.6
1945	Bos-N	7	12	.368	21	19	8	0	0	137^2	160	9	52	26	13.9	4.58	84	.295	.356	9	.209	0	-12	-11	-0	-1.1
1946	Cin-N	2	4	.333	7	7	3	0	0	43^1	50	2	8	13	12.3	3.95	85	.281	.316	1	.071	-1	-3	-3	-0	-0.4
	NY-N	1	0	1.000	3	2	0	0	0	12	17	2	4	5	15.8	6.00	57	.362	.412	1	.500	1	-3	-3	-0	-0.3
	Yr	3	4	.429	10	9	3	0	0	55^1	67	4	12	18	12.8	4.39	77	.296	.332	2	.125	0	-6	-6	-0	-0.7
Total	8	41	54	.432	127	97	50	5	2	773^1	798	40	236	216	12.1	3.46	106	.265	.321	35	.146	-4	10	17	4	2.3
● **FRED ANDRUS**	Andrus, Frederick Hotham b: 8/23/1850, Washington, Mich. d: 11/10/37, Detroit, Mich. BR/TR, 6'2", 185 lbs. Deb: 7/25/1876 ♦																									
1884	Chi-N	1	0	1.000	1	1	1	0	0	9	11	1	2	2	13.0	2.00	157	.297	.333	1	.200	0	1	1	0	0.1
● **JOAQUIN ANDUJAR**	Andujar, Joaquin b: 12/21/52, San Pedro De Macoris, D.R. BB/TR, 6', 180 lbs. Deb: 4/08/76																									
1976	Hou-N	9	10	.474	28	25	9	4	0	172^1	163	8	75	59	12.5	3.60	89	.255	.334	8	.140	-0	-2	-8	-1	-0.9
1977	Hou-N☆	11	8	.579	26	25	4	1	0	158^2	149	11	64	69	12.3	3.69	97	.251	.328	10	.189	1	4	-2	2	0.2
1978	Hou-N	5	7	.417	35	13	2	0	1	110^2	88	3	58	55	12.2	3.42	97	.224	.330	3	.130	-0	2	-1	2	0.1
1979	Hou-N★	12	12	.500	46	23	8	0	4	194	168	7	88	77	12.0	3.43	102	.233	.319	5	.088	-0	6	2	4	0.6
1980	*Hou-N	3	8	.273	35	14	0	0	2	122	132	8	43	75	12.9	3.91	84	.277	.337	5	.172	2	-4	-8	1	-0.5
1981	Hou-N	2	3	.400	9	3	0	0	0	23^2	29	2	12	18	15.6	4.94	67	.296	.373	0	.000	-0	-4	-4	-1	-0.5
	StL-N	6	1	.857	11	8	1	0	0	55^1	56	4	11	19	10.9	3.74	95	.265	.302	0	.000	-2	-2	-1	0	-0.3
	Yr	8	4	.667	20	11	1	0	0	79	85	6	23	37	12.3	4.10	85	.273	.323	0	.000	-2	-5	-5	-0	-0.8
1982	*StL-N	15	10	.600	38	37	9	5	0	265^2	237	11	50	137	10.0	2.47	146	.240	.282	15	.158	-1	33	34	2	3.8
1983	StL-N	6	16	.273	39	34	5	2	1	225	215	23	75	125	11.7	4.16	87	.253	.316	6	.082	-3	-13	-14	5	-1.2
1984	StL-N†	**20**	14	.588	36	36	12	**4**	0	**261^1**	218	20	70	147	10.2	3.34	104	.229	.286	11	.131	3	7	4	3	0.9
1985	*StL-N†	21	12	.636	38	38	10	2	0	269^2	265	15	82	112	11.9	3.40	104	.260	.322	10	.106	-2	6	4	-1	0.2
1986	Oak-A	12	7	.632	28	26	7	1	1	155^1	139	23	56	72	11.5	3.82	101	.239	.310	0	—	0	6	1	0	0.1
1987	Oak-A	3	5	.375	13	13	1	0	0	60^2	63	11	26	32	13.6	6.08	68	.269	.350	0	—	0	-11	-13	0	-1.1
1988	Hou-N	2	5	.286	23	10	0	0	0	78^2	94	9	21	35	13.7	4.00	83	.297	.350	4	.211	2	-5	-6	0	-0.4

YEAR TM/L	W	L	PCT	G	GS	CG	SH	SV	IP	H	HR	BB	SO	RAT	ERA	ERA+	OAV	OOB	BH	AVG	PB	PR	/A	PD	TPI
Total 13	127	118	.518	405	305	68	19	9	2153	2016	155	731	1032	11.7	3.58	98	.250	.316	77	.127	-1	24	-13	18	1.0
● NORM ANGELINI Angelini, Norman Stanley b: 9/24/47, San Francisco, Cal. BL/TL, 5′11″, 175 lbs. Deb: 7/22/72																									
1972 KC-A	2	1	.667	21	0	0	0	2	16	13	1	12	16	14.6	2.25	135	.228	.371	0	.000	-0	1	1	-0	0.1
1973 KC-A	0	0	—	7	0	0	0	1	3^2	2	0	7	3	22.1	4.91	84	.200	.529	0	—	0	-0	-0	-0	-0.1
Total 2	2	1	.667	28	0	0	0	3	19^2	15	1	19	19	16.0	2.75	117	.224	.402	0	.000	-0	1	1	-0	0.0
● CAP ANSON Anson, Adrian Constantine b: 4/11/1852, Marshalltown, Iowa d: 4/14/22, Chicago, Ill. BR/TR, 6′, 227 lbs. Deb: 5/06/1871 MH♦																									
1883 Chi-N	0	0	—	2	0	0	0	1	3	1	0	1	0	6.0	0.00	—	.091	.167	127	.308	1	1	1	0	0.1
1884 Chi-N	0	1	.000	1	0	0	0	0	1	3	2	1	1	36.0	18.00	17	.375	.444	159	.335	1	-2	-2	0	-0.1
Total 2	0	1	.000	3	0	0	0	1	4	4	2	2	1	13.5	4.50	71	.211	.286	2995	.329	1	-1	-1	0	0.0
● JOHNNY ANTONELLI Antonelli, John August b: 4/12/30, Rochester, N.Y. BL/TL, 6′, 190 lbs. Deb: 7/04/48																									
1948 Bos-N	0	0	—	4	0	0	0	1	4	2	0	3	0	11.3	2.25	170	.143	.294	0	—	0	1	1	0	0.1
1949 Bos-N	3	7	.300	22	10	3	1	0	96	99	6	42	48	13.4	3.56	106	.273	.351	3	.120	-1	5	2	-1	0.0
1950 Bos-N	2	3	.400	20	6	2	1	0	57^2	81	2	22	33	16.7	5.93	65	.335	.399	2	.125	-1	-11	-13	0	-1.3
1953 Mil-N	12	12	.500	31	26	11	2	1	175^1	167	15	71	131	12.3	3.18	123	.242	.314	11	.177	0	22	14	1	1.6
1954 *NY-N★	21	7	**.750**	39	37	18	**6**	2	258^2	209	22	94	152	10.7	**2.30**	**176**	**.219**	.293	16	.163	0	**51**	**50**	2	**5.5**
1955 NY-N	14	16	.467	38	34	14	2	1	235^1	206	24	82	143	11.4	3.33	121	.234	.307	17	.207	3	19	18	1	2.3
1956 NY-N★	20	13	.606	41	36	15	5	1	258^1	225	20	75	145	10.6	2.86	132	.234	.292	14	.157	1	26	27	1	3.1
1957 NY-N☆	12	18	.400	40	30	8	3	0	212^1	228	19	67	114	12.6	3.77	104	.276	.333	11	.153	3	3	4	-2	0.5
1958 SF-N☆	16	13	.552	41	34	13	0	3	241^2	216	31	87	143	11.4	3.28	116	.239	.308	19	.226	4	18	14	-3	1.6
1959 SF-N★	19	10	.655	40	38	17	**4**	1	282	247	29	76	165	10.4	3.10	123	.233	.286	16	.158	1	27	22	-1	2.4
1960 SF-N	6	7	.462	41	10	1	1	11	112^1	106	7	47	57	12.4	3.77	92	.253	.331	8	.235	2	-0	-4	-1	-0.2
1961 Cle-A	0	4	.000	11	7	0	0	0	48	68	8	18	23	16.3	6.56	60	.338	.395	4	.267	1	-14	-14	1	-1.2
Mil-N	1	0	1.000	9	0	0	0	0	10^2	16	2	3	8	16.0	7.59	49	.340	.380	0	.000	-0	-4	-5	-0	-0.5
Total 12	126	110	.534	377	268	102	25	21	1992^1	1870	185	687	1162	11.7	3.34	116	.247	.313	121	.178	15	141	118	-1	13.9
● BOB APODACA Apodaca, Robert John b: 1/31/50, Los Angeles, Cal. BR/TR, 5′11″, 170 lbs. Deb: 9/18/73																									
1973 NY-N	0	0	—	1	0	0	0	0	0	0	0	2	0	—	∞	—	—	1.000	0	—	0	-1	-1	0	-0.1
1974 NY-N	6	6	.500	35	8	1	0	3	103	92	7	42	54	11.9	3.50	102	.241	.319	3	.120	0	1	1	-1	0.1
1975 NY-N	3	4	.429	46	0	0	0	13	84^2	66	4	28	45	10.0	1.49	232	.222	.289	4	.364	1	20	18	2	2.4
1976 NY-N	3	7	.300	43	3	0	0	5	89^2	71	4	29	45	10.3	2.81	117	.223	.293	2	.125	0	7	5	1	0.6
1977 NY-N	4	8	.333	59	0	0	0	5	84	83	7	30	53	12.2	3.43	109	.255	.319	1	.167	-0	4	3	1	0.4
Total 5	16	25	.390	184	11	1	0	26	361^1	312	22	131	197	11.2	2.86	123	.236	.307	10	.172	2	32	26	4	3.4
● LUIS APONTE Aponte, Luis Eduardo (Yuripe) b: 6/14/53, ElTigre, Venez. BR/TR, 6′, 185 lbs. Deb: 9/04/80																									
1980 Bos-A	0	0	—	4	0	0	0	0	7	6	0	2	1	10.3	1.29	328	.250	.308	0	—	0	2	2	0	0.0
1981 Bos-A	1	0	1.000	7	0	0	0	1	15^2	11	0	3	11	8.0	0.57	674	.208	.250	0	—	0	5	6	1	0.6
1982 Bos-A	2	2	.500	40	0	0	0	3	85	78	5	25	44	10.9	3.18	136	.246	.301	0	—	0	8	11	2	1.0
1983 Bos-A	5	4	.556	34	0	0	0	3	62	74	7	23	32	14.4	3.63	120	.301	.365	0	—	0	3	5	1	0.5
1984 Cle-A	1	0	1.000	25	0	0	0	0	50^1	53	5	15	25	12.3	4.11	99	.269	.324	0	—	0	-1	-0	-1	-0.1
Total 5	9	6	.600	110	0	0	0	7	220	222	17	68	113	12.0	3.27	129	.265	.323	0	—	0	18	23	3	2.0
● KEVIN APPIER Appier, Robert Kevin b: 12/6/67, Lancaster, Cal. BR/TR, 6′2″, 180 lbs. Deb: 6/14/89																									
1989 KC-A	1	4	.200	6	5	0	0	0	21^2	34	3	12	10	19.1	9.14	42	.374	.447	0	—	0	-13	-13	-1	-1.2
1990 KC-A	12	8	.600	32	24	3	3	0	185^2	179	13	54	127	11.6	2.76	139	.252	.310	0	—	0	24	22	-0	2.4
1991 KC-A	13	10	.565	34	31	6	3	0	207^2	205	13	61	158	11.6	3.42	120	.255	.309	0	—	0	15	16	0	1.7
1992 KC-A	15	8	.652	30	30	3	0	0	208^1	167	10	68	150	10.2	2.46	162	.217	.282	0	—	0	34	35	0	3.8
Total 4	41	30	.577	102	90	12	6	0	623^1	585	39	195	445	11.4	3.10	128	.246	.306	0	—	0	61	61	-0	6.7
● FRED APPLEGATE Applegate, Frederick Romaine b: 5/9/1879, Williamsport, Pa. d: 4/21/68, Williamsport, Pa. BR/TR, 6′2″, 180 lbs. Deb: 9/30/04																									
1904 Phi-A	1	2	.333	3	3	3	0	0	21	29	0	8	12	16.3	6.43	42	.328	.390	2	.286	0	-9	-9	0	-0.8
● ED APPLETON Appleton, Edward Samuel "Whitey" b: 2/29/1892, Arlington, Tex. d: 1/27/32, Arlington, Tex. BR/TR, 6′0.5″, 173 lbs. Deb: 4/16/15																									
1915 Bro-N	4	10	.286	34	10	5	0	0	138^1	133	3	66	50	13.5	3.32	84	.263	.357	7	.159	-0	-9	-8	-1	-1.0
1916 Bro-N	1	2	.333	14	3	1	0	1	47	49	1	18	14	13.0	3.06	88	.278	.349	2	.167	-0	-2	-2	-1	-0.4
Total 2	5	12	.294	48	13	6	0	1	185^1	182	4	84	64	13.4	3.25	85	.267	.355	9	.161	-1	-11	-10	-2	-1.4
● PETE APPLETON Appleton, Peter William "Jake" (a.k.a. Jablonowski In 1927-33) b: 5/20/04, Terryville, Conn. d: 1/18/74, Trenton, N.J. BR/TR, 5′11″, 180 lbs. Deb: 9/14/27																									
1927 Cin-N	2	1	.667	6	2	2	1	0	29^2	29	0	17	3	14.0	1.82	208	.261	.359	6	.545	2	7	6	1	1.0
1928 Cin-N	3	4	.429	31	1	0	0	0	82^2	101	7	22	20	13.6	4.68	84	.311	.358	10	.323	3	-6	-7	2	-0.2
1930 Cle-A	8	7	.533	39	7	2	0	1	118^2	122	8	53	45	13.7	4.02	120	.274	.357	8	.200	-1	8	11	2	1.0
1931 Cle-A	4	4	.500	29	4	3	0	0	79^2	100	2	29	25	14.7	4.63	100	.293	.350	5	.208	0	-2	-0	-0	0.0
1932 Cle-A	0	0	—	4	0	0	0	0	5	11	1	3	1	25.2	16.20	29	.407	.467	0	—	0	-7	-6	0	-0.6
Bos-A	0	3	.000	11	3	0	0	0	46	49	2	26	15	15.1	4.11	109	.265	.362	3	.176	-0	2	2	2	0.4
Yr	0	3	.000	15	3	0	0	0	51	60	3	29	16	16.1	5.29	85	.283	.374	3	.176	-0	-5	-4	2	-0.2
1933 NY-A	0	0	—	1	0	0	0	0	2	3	0	1	0	18.0	0.00	—	.375	.444	0	—	0	1	1	0	0.1
1936 Was-A	14	9	.609	38	20	12	1	3	201^2	199	7	77	77	12.5	3.53	135	.254	.324	19	.250	2	34	28	1	2.8
1937 Was-A	8	15	.348	35	18	7	4	2	168	167	16	72	62	13.1	4.39	101	.260	.339	11	.186	-1	4	1	3	0.2
1938 Was-A	7	9	.438	43	10	5	0	5	164^1	175	12	61	62	13.0	4.60	98	.270	.333	15	.254	3	3	-2	-0	0.1
1939 Was-A	5	10	.333	40	4	2	0	6	102^2	104	7	48	50	13.7	4.56	95	.265	.351	4	.160	-1	1	-2	0	-0.3
1940 Chi-A	4	0	1.000	25	0	0	0	5	57^2	54	8	28	21	13.0	5.62	79	.248	.336	3	.176	-0	-8	-8	-0	-0.8
1941 Chi-A	0	3	.000	13	0	0	0	1	27^1	27	4	17	12	15.1	5.27	78	.257	.371	1	.250	0	-3	-4	0	-0.3
1942 Chi-A	0	0	—	4	0	0	0	0	4^2	2	0	3	2	9.6	3.86	93	.133	.278	0	—	0	-0	-0	0	0.0
StL-A	1	1	.500	14	0	0	0	2	27^1	25	1	11	12	11.9	2.96	125	.243	.316	1	.167	1	2	2	1	0.4
Yr	1	1	.500	18	0	0	0	2	32	27	1	14	14	11.5	3.09	119	.229	.311	1	.167	1	2	2	1	0.4
1945 StL-A	0	0	—	2	0	0	0	0	2^1	3	0	7	1	38.6	15.43	23	.273	.556	0	—	0	-3	-3	0	-0.3
Was-A	1	0	1.000	6	2	1	0	1	21^1	16	1	11	12	11.4	3.38	92	.211	.310	1	.200	-0	-0	-1	-0	-0.1
Yr	1	0	1.000	8	2	1	0	1	23^2	19	1	18	13	14.1	4.56	69	.218	.352	1	.200	-0	-3	-4	0	-0.4
Total 14	57	66	.463	341	71	34	6	26	1141	1187	76	486	420	13.4	4.30	104	.268	.343	87	.233	6	33	19	12	3.4
● LUIS AQUINO Aquino, Luis Antonio (Colon) b: 5/19/64, Santurce, P.R. BR/TR, 6′, 195 lbs. Deb: 8/08/86																									
1986 Tor-A	1	1	.500	7	0	0	0	0	11^1	14	2	3	5	13.5	6.35	66	.304	.347	0	—	0	-3	-3	-0	-0.3
1988 KC-A	1	0	1.000	7	5	1	1	0	29	33	1	17	11	15.8	2.79	143	.282	.378	0	—	0	4	4	-0	0.3
1989 KC-A	6	8	.429	34	16	2	1	0	141^1	148	6	35	68	11.9	3.50	110	.271	.320	0	—	0	6	5	1	0.7
1990 KC-A	4	1	.800	20	3	1	0	0	68^1	59	6	27	28	11.9	3.16	121	.237	.321	0	—	0	6	5	0	0.6
1991 KC-A	8	4	.667	38	18	1	1	3	157	152	10	47	80	11.6	3.44	120	.253	.311	0	—	0	11	12	0	1.2
1992 KC-A	3	6	.333	15	13	0	0	0	67^2	81	5	20	11	13.6	4.52	88	.303	.354	0	—	0	-4	-4	1	-0.4
Total 6	23	20	.535	121	55	5	3	3	474^2	487	30	149	203	12.3	3.60	110	.267	.327	0	—	0	20	19	2	2.1
● FRED ARCHER Archer, Frederick Marvin "Lefty" b: 3/7/10, Johnson City, Tenn. d: 10/31/81, Charlotte, N.C. BL/TL, 6′, 193 lbs. Deb: 9/05/36																									
1936 Phi-A	2	3	.400	6	5	2	0	0	36^2	41	3	15	9	14.5	6.38	80	.289	.369	4	.267	0	-5	-5	-0	-0.4
1937 Phi-A	0	0	—	1	0	0	0	0	3	4	0	0	2	12.0	6.00	79	.333	.333	0	—	0	-0	-0	0	0.0

YEAR	TM/L	W	L	PCT	G	GS	CG	SH	SV	IP	H	HR	BB	SO	RAT	ERA	ERA+	OAV	OOB	BH	AVG	PB	PR	/A	PD	TPI
Total	2	2	3	.400	7	5	2	0	0	39^2	45	3	15	11	14.3	6.35	80	.292	.366	4	.267	1	-6	-6	0	-0.4
● **JIM ARCHER** Archer, James William b: 5/25/32, Max Meadows, Va. BR/TL, 6', 190 lbs. Deb: 4/30/61																										
1961	KC-A	9	15	.375	39	27	9	2	5	205^1	204	11	60	110	11.8	3.20	129	.257	.313	4	.063	-5	19	21	-0	1.6
1962	KC-A	0	1	.000	18	1	0	0	0	27^2	40	8	10	12	16.3	9.43	44	.342	.394	1	1.000	0	-17	-16	-0	-1.6
Total	2	9	16	.360	57	28	9	2	5	233	244	19	70	122	12.3	3.94	105	.268	.323	5	.078	-4	2	5	-1	0.0
● **RUGGER ARDIZOIA** Ardizoia, Rinaldo Joseph b: 11/20/19, Oleggio, Italy BR/TR, 5'11", 180 lbs. Deb: 4/30/47																										
1947	NY-A	0	0	—	1	0	0	0	0	2	4	1	1	0	22.5	9.00	39	.500	.556	0	—	0	-1	-1	0	-0.1
● **FRANK ARELLANES** Arellanes, Frank Julian b: 1/28/1882, Santa Cruz, Cal. d: 12/13/18, San Jose, Cal. BR/TR, 6', 180 lbs. Deb: 7/28/08																										
1908	Bos-A	4	3	.571	11	8	6	1	0	79	60	1	18	33	9.2	1.82	135	.213	.267	5	.167	0	5	6	-1	0.5
1909	Bos-A	16	12	.571	45	28	17	1	**8**	230^2	192	3	43	82	9.4	2.18	114	.229	.270	13	.167	-1	8	8	0	0.7
1910	Bos-A	4	7	.364	18	13	2	0	0	100	106	1	24	33	12.0	2.88	89	.283	.332	6	.176	0	-4	-4	0	-0.4
Total	3	24	22	.522	74	49	25	2	8	409^2	358	5	85	148	10.0	2.28	110	.239	.285	24	.169	-1	9	10	-1	0.8
● **RUDY ARIAS** Arias, Rodolfo (Martinez) b: 6/6/31, Las Villas, Cuba BL/TL, 5'10", 165 lbs. Deb: 4/10/59																										
1959	Chi-A	2	0	1.000	34	0	0	0	2	44	49	7	20	28	14.3	4.09	92	.277	.354	0	.000	-1	-1	-2	1	-0.2
● **DON ARLICH** Arlich, Donald Louis b: 2/15/43, Wayne, Mich. BL/TL, 6'2", 185 lbs. Deb: 10/02/65																										
1965	Hou-N	0	0	—	1	1	0	0	0	6	5	0	1	0	9.0	3.00	112	.227	.261	0	.000	-0	0	0	-0	0.0
1966	Hou-N	0	1	.000	7	0	0	0	0	4	11	0	4	1	36.0	15.75	22	.478	.571	0	.000	-0	-5	-5	-0	-0.6
Total	2	0	1	.000	8	1	0	0	0	10	16	0	5	1	19.8	8.10	42	.356	.431	0	.000	-0	-5	-5	-0	-0.6
● **STEVE ARLIN** Arlin, Stephen Ralph b: 9/25/45, Seattle, Wash. BR/TR, 6'3.5", 195 lbs. Deb: 6/17/69																										
1969	SD-N	0	1	.000	4	1	0	0	0	10^2	13	2	9	9	18.6	9.28	38	.289	.407	0	.000	-0	-7	-7	-0	-0.7
1970	SD-N	1	0	1.000	2	2	1	1	0	12^2	11	0	8	3	13.5	2.84	140	.244	.358	0	.000	-1	2	2	0	0.1
1971	SD-N	9	19	.321	36	34	10	4	0	227^2	211	8	103	156	12.7	3.48	95	.244	.329	9	.123	-1	-0	-5	-1	-0.7
1972	SD-N	10	21	.323	38	37	12	3	0	250	217	19	122	159	12.5	3.60	91	.237	.332	11	.153	2	-4	-9	-0	-0.7
1973	SD-N	11	14	.440	34	27	7	3	0	180	196	26	72	98	13.4	5.10	68	.278	.346	10	.167	1	-29	-33	-1	-3.2
1974	SD-N	1	7	.125	16	12	1	0	1	64	85	5	37	18	17.4	5.91	60	.326	.413	2	.111	-1	-16	-17	-0	-1.7
	Cle-A	2	5	.286	11	10	1	0	0	43^2	59	1	22	20	16.7	6.60	55	.333	.407	0	—	0	-14	-14	-1	-1.5
Total	6	34	67	.337	141	123	32	11	1	788^2	792	61	373	463	13.5	4.33	78	.263	.348	32	.139	1	-69	-82	-3	-8.4
● **ORVILLE ARMBRUST** Armbrust, Orville Martin b: 3/2/10, Beirne, Ark. d: 10/2/67, Mobile, Ala. BR/TR, 5'10", 195 lbs. Deb: 9/18/34																										
1934	Was-A	1	0	1.000	3	2	0	0	0	12^2	10	1	3	3	9.2	2.13	203	.208	.255	0	.000	-1	3	3	1	0.3
● **HOWARD ARMSTRONG** Armstrong, Howard Elmer b: 12/2/1889, E.Claridon, Ohio d: 3/8/26, Canisteo, N.Y. BR/TR, 5'9", 165 lbs. Deb: 9/30/11																										
1911	Phi-A	0	1	.000	1	0	0	0	0	3	3	0	1	0	12.0	0.00	—	.273	.333	0	.000	-0	1	1	0	0.1
● **JACK ARMSTRONG** Armstrong, Jack William b: 3/7/65, Englewood, N.J. BR/TR, 6'5", 220 lbs. Deb: 6/21/88																										
1988	Cin-N	4	7	.364	14	13	0	0	0	65^1	63	8	38	45	13.9	5.79	62	.256	.356	2	.095	-1	-17	-16	1	-1.7
1989	Cin-N	2	3	.400	9	8	0	0	0	42^2	40	5	21	23	12.9	4.64	78	.245	.332	0	.000	-1	-5	-5	0	-0.5
1990	*Cin-N★	12	9	.571	29	27	2	1	0	166	151	9	59	110	11.7	3.42	115	.241	.313	5	.106	-2	7	10	0	0.9
1991	Cin-N	7	13	.350	27	24	1	0	0	139^2	158	25	54	93	13.8	5.48	69	.293	.359	4	.093	-2	-28	-26	-0	-2.8
1992	Cle-A	6	15	.286	35	23	1	0	0	166^2	176	23	67	114	13.3	4.64	87	.269	.340	0	—	0	-13	-11	1	-1.1
Total	5	31	47	.397	114	95	4	1	0	580^1	588	70	239	385	13.0	4.62	84	.264	.338	11	.092	-5	-56	-49	2	-5.2
● **MIKE ARMSTRONG** Armstrong, Michael Dennis b: 3/7/54, Glen Cove, N.Y. BR/TR, 6'3", 206 lbs. Deb: 8/12/80																										
1980	SD-N	0	0	—	11	0	0	0	0	14^1	16	3	13	14	18.2	5.65	61	.296	.433	0	.000	-0	-3	-4	-0	-0.4
1981	SD-N	0	2	.000	10	0	0	0	0	12	14	1	11	9	18.8	6.00	54	.311	.446	0	—	0	-3	-4	-0	-0.4
1982	KC-A	5	5	.500	52	0	0	0	6	112^2	88	9	43	75	10.7	3.20	128	.215	.295	0	—	0	11	11	-1	1.0
1983	KC-A	10	7	.588	58	0	0	0	3	102^2	86	11	45	52	11.7	3.86	106	.228	.315	0	—	0	2	2	-0	0.2
1984	NY-A	3	2	.600	36	0	0	0	1	54^1	47	6	26	43	12.1	3.48	109	.239	.327	0	—	0	3	2	-0	0.5
1985	NY-A	0	0	—	9	0	0	0	0	14^2	9	4	2	11	6.8	3.07	130	.173	.204	0	—	0	2	2	-0	0.3
1986	NY-A	0	1	.000	7	1	0	0	0	8^2	13	4	5	8	18.7	9.35	44	.351	.429	0	—	0	-5	-5	-0	-0.4
1987	Cle-A	1	0	1.000	14	0	0	0	1	18^2	27	4	10	9	17.8	8.68	52	.333	.407	0	—	0	-9	-9	-0	-0.8
Total	8	19	17	.528	197	1	0	0	11	338	300	42	155	221	12.3	4.10	97	.240	.326	0	.000	-0	-2	-4	-3	0.0
● **SCOTT ARNOLD** Arnold, Scott Gentry b: 8/18/62, Lexington, Ky. BR/TR, 6'2", 210 lbs. Deb: 4/07/88																										
1988	StL-N	0	0	—	6	0	0	0	0	6^2	9	0	4	8	17.6	5.40	64	.321	.406	0	—	0	-1	-1	0	-0.2
● **TONY ARNOLD** Arnold, Tony Dale b: 5/3/59, ElPaso, Tex. BR/TR, 5'11", 170 lbs. Deb: 8/09/86																										
1986	Bal-A	0	2	.000	11	0	0	0	0	25^1	25	0	11	7	12.8	3.55	116	.278	.356	0	—	0	2	2	1	0.4
1987	Bal-A	0	0	—	27	0	0	0	0	53	71	8	17	18	15.3	5.77	76	.330	.385	0	—	0	-8	-8	2	-0.5
Total	2	0	2	.000	38	0	0	0	0	78^1	96	8	28	25	14.5	5.06	85	.315	.376	0	—	0	-6	-6	3	-0.1
● **BRAD ARNSBERG** Arnsberg, Bradley James b: 8/20/63, Seattle, Wash. BR/TR, 6'4", 205 lbs. Deb: 9/06/86																										
1986	NY-A	0	0	—	2	1	0	0	0	8	13	1	1	3	15.8	3.38	121	.342	.359	0	—	0	1	1	-0	0.1
1987	NY-A	1	3	.250	6	2	0	0	0	19^1	22	5	13	14	16.3	5.59	78	.289	.393	0	—	0	-2	-3	1	-0.2
1989	Tex-A	2	1	.667	16	1	0	0	1	48	45	6	22	26	13.1	4.13	96	.247	.338	0	—	0	-1	-1	1	0.0
1990	Tex-A	6	1	.857	53	0	0	0	5	62^2	56	4	33	44	13.1	2.15	182	.235	.333	0	—	0	12	12	1	1.4
1991	Tex-A	0	1	.000	9	0	0	0	0	9^2	10	5	5	8	14.0	8.38	48	.256	.341	0	—	0	-5	-5	-0	-0.4
1992	Cle-A	0	0	—	8	0	0	0	0	10^2	13	6	11	5	21.9	11.81	34	.317	.481	0	—	0	-9	-9	-0	-1.0
Total	6	9	6	.600	94	4	0	0	6	158^1	159	27	85	100	14.3	4.26	94	.259	.356	0	—	0	-5	-4	2	-0.1
● **ORIE ARNTZEN** Arntzen, Orie Edgar "Old Folks" b: 10/18/09, Beverly, Ill. d: 1/28/70, Cedar Rapids, Iowa BR/TR, 6'1", 200 lbs. Deb: 4/20/43																										
1943	Phi-A	4	13	.235	32	20	9	0	0	164^1	172	5	69	66	13.5	4.22	81	.277	.354	8	.160	-1	-17	-15	-3	-2.0
● **GERRY ARRIGO** Arrigo, Gerald William b: 6/12/41, Chicago, Ill. BL/TL, 6'1", 195 lbs. Deb: 6/12/61																										
1961	Min-A	0	1	.000	7	2	0	0	0	9^2	9	0	10	6	19.6	10.24	41	.265	.457	1	.500	0	-7	-6	0	-0.6
1962	Min-A	0	0	—	1	0	0	0	0	1	3	0	1	1	36.0	18.00	23	.600	.667	0	—	0	-2	-2	0	-0.1
1963	Min-A	1	2	.333	5	1	0	0	0	15^2	12	2	4	13	9.2	2.87	127	.211	.262	0	.000	-0	1	1	0	0.1
1964	Min-A	7	4	.636	41	12	2	1	1	105^1	97	11	45	96	12.3	3.84	93	.244	.324	5	.172	0	-3	-3	0	-0.2
1965	Cin-N	2	4	.333	27	5	0	0	2	54	75	4	30	43	17.8	6.17	61	.342	.426	2	.167	1	-16	-15	-1	-1.5
1966	Cin-N	0	0	—	3	0	0	0	0	7^1	7	2	3	3	12.3	4.91	79	.250	.323	0	.000	-0	-1	-1	-0	-0.1
	NY-N	3	3	.500	17	5	0	0	0	43^1	47	5	16	28	13.1	3.74	97	.276	.339	5	.500	3	-1	-0	1	0.3
	Yr	3	3	.500	20	5	0	0	0	50^2	54	7	19	31	13.0	3.91	94	.273	.336	5	.455	3	-2	-1	0	0.2
1967	Cin-N	6	6	.500	32	5	1	1	1	74	61	6	35	56	12.2	3.16	119	.232	.331	4	.211	1	2	5	-2	0.4
1968	Cin-N	12	10	.545	36	31	5	1	0	205^1	181	13	77	140	11.5	3.33	95	.237	.310	5	.075	-2	-8	-4	1	-0.6
1969	Cin-N	4	7	.364	20	16	1	0	0	91	89	9	61	35	15.6	4.15	91	.256	.379	5	.161	-0	-6	-4	-2	-0.6
1970	Chi-A	0	3	.000	5	3	0	0	0	13^1	24	4	9	12	22.3	12.83	30	.393	.471	0	.000	-0	-13	-13	-0	-1.2
Total	10	35	40	.467	194	80	9	3	4	620	605	56	291	433	13.3	4.14	85	.258	.345	27	.151	2	-52	-42	-3	-4.1
● **FERNANDO ARROYO** Arroyo, Fernando b: 3/21/52, Sacramento, Cal. BR/TR, 6'3", 195 lbs. Deb: 6/28/75																										
1975	Det-A	2	1	.667	14	2	1	0	0	53^1	56	5	22	25	13.3	4.56	88	.272	.345	0	—	0	-5	-3	1	-0.2

YEAR TM/L	W	L	PCT	G	GS	CG	SH	SV	IP	H	HR	BB	SO	RAT	ERA	ERA+	OAV	OOB	BH	AVG	PB	PR	/A	PD	TPI
1977 Det-A	8	18	.308	38	28	8	1	0	209^1	227	23	52	60	12.0	4.17	103	.278	.321	0	—	0	-3	3	6	0.6
1978 Det-A	0	0	—	2	0	0	0	0	4^1	8	1	0	1	18.7	8.31	47	.400	.429	0	—	0	-2	-2	0	-0.3
1979 Det-A	1	1	.500	6	0	0	0	0	12	17	3	4	7	15.8	8.25	52	.340	.389	0	—	0	-5	-5	0	-0.6
1980 Min-A	6	6	.500	21	11	1	1	0	92^1	97	7	32	27	12.8	4.68	93	.273	.337	0	—	0	-7	-3	-1	-1.0
1981 Min-A	7	10	.412	23	19	2	0	0	128^1	144	11	34	39	12.8	3.93	100	.290	.342	0	—	0	-4	0	0	-0.3
1982 Min-A	0	1	.000	6	0	0	0	0	13^2	17	2	6	4	15.1	5.27	81	.321	.390	0	—	0	-2	-2	1	-0.2
Oak-A	0	0	—	10	0	0	0	0	22^1	23	4	7	9	12.5	5.24	75	.271	.333	0	—	0	-3	-3	0	0.0
Yr	0	1	.000	16	0	0	0	0	36	40	6	13	13	13.5	5.25	77	.288	.353	0	—	0	-5	-5	1	-0.2
1986 Oak-A	0	0	—	1	0	0	0	0	0	0	0	3	0	—	—	—	—	1.000	0	—	0	0	0	0	0.5
Total 8	24	37	.393	121	60	12	2	0	535^2	589	56	160	172	12.8	4.44	94	.283	.337	0	—	0	-30	-16	7	-1.5

● LUIS ARROYO Arroyo, Luis Enrique b: 2/18/27, Penuelas, P.R. BL/TL, 5'8", 190 lbs. Deb: 4/20/55

YEAR TM/L	W	L	PCT	G	GS	CG	SH	SV	IP	H	HR	BB	SO	RAT	ERA	ERA+	OAV	OOB	BH	AVG	PB	PR	/A	PD	TPI
1955 StL-N☆	11	8	.579	35	24	9	1	0	159	162	22	63	68	12.8	4.19	97	.261	.331	13	.232	1	-3	-2	-2	-0.4
1956 Pit-N	3	3	.500	18	2	1	0	0	28^2	36	5	12	17	15.1	4.71	80	.298	.361	2	.500	1	-3	-3	0	-0.2
1957 Pit-N	3	11	.214	54	10	0	0	1	130^2	151	19	31	101	13.0	4.68	81	.282	.329	5	.156	-1	-12	-13	-2	-1.6
1959 Cin-N	1	0	1.000	10	0	0	0	0	13^2	17	0	11	8	18.4	3.95	103	.321	.438	0	.000	-0	-0	0	0	0.0
1960 *NY-A	5	1	.833	29	0	0	0	7	40^2	30	2	22	29	11.5	2.88	125	.207	.311	0	.000	-0	5	3	0	0.3
1961 *NY-A☆	15	5	.750	**65**	0	0	0	**29**	119	83	5	49	87	10.2	2.19	169	.199	.288	7	.280	2	**24**	20	-1	2.1
1962 NY-A	1	3	.250	27	0	0	0	7	33^2	33	5	17	21	13.6	4.81	78	.262	.354	2	.500	1	-3	-4	-1	-0.4
1963 NY-A	1	1	.500	6	0	0	0	0	6	12	0	3	5	22.5	13.50	26	.444	.500	0	—	0	-7	-7	-0	-0.7
Total 8	40	32	.556	244	36	10	1	44	531^1	524	58	208	336	12.6	3.93	98	.256	.329	29	.227	3	2	-5	-5	-0.9

● RUDY ARROYO Arroyo, Rudolph b: 6/19/50, New York, N.Y. BL/TL, 6'2", 195 lbs. Deb: 6/01/71

YEAR TM/L	W	L	PCT	G	GS	CG	SH	SV	IP	H	HR	BB	SO	RAT	ERA	ERA+	OAV	OOB	BH	AVG	PB	PR	/A	PD	TPI
1971 StL-N	0	1	.000	9	0	0	0	0	11^2	18	2	5	5	17.7	5.40	67	.375	.434	0	.000	-0	-3	-2	-0	-0.3

● HARRY ARUNDEL Arundel, Harry b: 1854, Philadelphia, Pa. d: 3/25/04, Cleveland, Ohio Deb: 7/19/1875

YEAR TM/L	W	L	PCT	G	GS	CG	SH	SV	IP	H	HR	BB	SO	RAT	ERA	ERA+	OAV	OOB	BH	AVG	PB	PR	/A	PD	TPI
1875 Atl-n	0	1	.000	1	1	0	0	0	1^1	6	0	1		47.3	*13.50*	17	.429	.467	0	.000	-1	-2	-2		-0.1
1882 Pit-a	4	10	.286	14	14	13	0	0	120	155	3	23	47	13.4	4.65	56	.293	.323	10	.189	0	-26	-27	5	-1.9
1884 Pro-N	1	0	1.000	1	1	1	0	0	9	8	0	4	4	12.0	1.00	282	.250	.333	1	.333	0	2	2	-0	0.2
Total 2	5	10	.333	15	15	14	0	0	129	163	3	27	51	13.3	4.40	60	.291	.324	11	.196	0	-24	-25	5	-1.7

● KEN ASH Ash, Kenneth Lowther b: 9/16/01, Anmoore, W.Va. d: 11/15/79, Clakrsburg, W.Va. BR/TR, 5'11", 165 lbs. Deb: 4/17/25

YEAR TM/L	W	L	PCT	G	GS	CG	SH	SV	IP	H	HR	BB	SO	RAT	ERA	ERA+	OAV	OOB	BH	AVG	PB	PR	/A	PD	TPI
1925 Chi-A	0	0	—	2	0	0	0	0	4	7	2	0	0	15.8	9.00	46	.389	.389	0	—	0	-2	-2	-0	-0.2
1928 Cin-N	3	3	.500	8	5	2	0	0	36	43	1	13	6	14.3	6.50	61	.314	.377	1	.071	-1	-10	-10	0	-1.0
1929 Cin-N	1	5	.167	29	7	2	0	2	82	91	2	30	26	13.8	4.83	95	.292	.363	3	.143	-1	-1	-2	-0	-0.3
1930 Cin-N	2	0	1.000	16	1	1	0	0	39^1	37	1	16	15	12.1	3.43	141	.268	.344	2	.182	-1	7	6	1	0.6
Total 4	6	8	.429	55	13	5	0	2	161^1	178	6	59	47	13.6	4.96	90	.294	.363	6	.130	-3	-6	-9	1	-0.9

● ANDY ASHBY Ashby, Andrew Jason b: 7/11/67, Kansas City, Mo. BR/TR, 6'5", 180 lbs. Deb: 6/10/91

YEAR TM/L	W	L	PCT	G	GS	CG	SH	SV	IP	H	HR	BB	SO	RAT	ERA	ERA+	OAV	OOB	BH	AVG	PB	PR	/A	PD	TPI
1991 Phi-N	1	5	.167	8	8	0	0	0	42	41	5	19	26	13.5	6.00	61	.256	.346	1	.083	-1	-11	-11	0	-1.1
1992 Phi-N	1	3	.250	10	8	0	0	0	37	42	6	21	24	15.6	7.54	46	.290	.383	1	.091	-0	-17	-17	0	-1.6
Total 2	2	8	.200	18	16	0	0	0	79	83	11	40	50	14.5	6.72	53	.272	.364	2	.087	-1	-27	-28	0	-2.7

● PAUL ASSENMACHER Assenmacher, Paul Andre b: 12/10/60, Detroit, Mich. BL/TL, 6'3", 195 lbs. Deb: 4/12/86

YEAR TM/L	W	L	PCT	G	GS	CG	SH	SV	IP	H	HR	BB	SO	RAT	ERA	ERA+	OAV	OOB	BH	AVG	PB	PR	/A	PD	TPI
1986 Atl-N	7	3	.700	61	0	0	0	7	68^1	61	5	26	56	11.5	2.50	159	.241	.312	0	.000	-0	9	11	1	1.3
1987 Atl-N	1	1	.500	52	0	0	0	2	54^2	58	8	24	39	13.7	5.10	85	.260	.335	0	.000	-0	-6	-5	-1	-0.6
1988 Atl-N	8	7	.533	64	0	0	0	5	79^1	72	4	32	71	11.9	3.06	120	.251	.328	1	.333	1	3	5	0	0.7
1989 Atl-N	1	3	.250	49	0	0	0	0	57^2	55	2	16	64	11.2	3.59	102	.249	.303	0	.000	-0	-1	0	0	0.1
*Chi-N	2	1	.667	14	0	0	0	0	19	19	1	12	15	14.7	5.21	72	.275	.383	0	.000	-0	-4	-3	0	-0.3
Yr	3	4	.429	63	0	0	0	0	76^2	74	3	28	79	12.0	3.99	92	.253	.318	0	.000	-1	-4	-3	1	-0.2
1990 Chi-N	7	2	.778	74	1	0	0	10	103	90	10	36	95	11.1	2.80	146	.239	.308	0	.000	-1	11	15	1	1.5
1991 Chi-N	7	8	.467	75	0	0	0	15	102^2	85	10	31	117	10.4	3.24	120	.223	.287	1	.250	0	5	7	-1	0.8
1992 Chi-N	4	4	.500	70	0	0	0	8	68	72	6	26	67	13.4	4.10	88	.271	.342	0	.000	-0	-5	-4	-1	-0.5
Total 7	37	29	.561	459	1	0	0	47	552^2	512	46	203	524	11.8	3.44	113	.247	.317	2	.059	-1	14	27	1	3.0

● PEDRO ASTACIO Astacio, Pedro Julio b: 11/28/69, Hato Mayor, D.R. BR/TR, 6'2", 174 lbs. Deb: 7/03/92

YEAR TM/L	W	L	PCT	G	GS	CG	SH	SV	IP	H	HR	BB	SO	RAT	ERA	ERA+	OAV	OOB	BH	AVG	PB	PR	/A	PD	TPI
1992 LA-N	5	5	.500	11	11	4	4	0	82	80	1	20	43	11.2	1.98	175	.255	.304	3	.125	-1	14	13	-0	1.5

● KEITH ATHERTON Atherton, Keith Rowe b: 2/19/59, Mathews, Va. BR/TR, 6'4", 200 lbs. Deb: 7/14/83

YEAR TM/L	W	L	PCT	G	GS	CG	SH	SV	IP	H	HR	BB	SO	RAT	ERA	ERA+	OAV	OOB	BH	AVG	PB	PR	/A	PD	TPI
1983 Oak-A	2	5	.286	29	0	0	0	4	68^1	53	7	23	40	10.1	2.77	139	.215	.285	0	.000	0	10	8	-1	0.8
1984 Oak-A	7	6	.538	57	0	0	0	2	104	110	13	39	58	13.1	4.33	86	.274	.341	0	—	0	-4	-7	-2	-0.9
1985 Oak-A	4	7	.364	56	0	0	0	3	104^2	89	17	42	77	11.3	4.30	90	.231	.306	0	—	0	-2	-5	-2	-0.3
1986 Oak-A	1	2	.333	13	0	0	0	0	15^1	18	2	11	8	17.0	5.87	66	.295	.403	0	—	0	-3	-3	-0	0.0
Min-A	5	8	.385	47	0	0	0	10	81^2	82	9	35	59	13.0	3.75	115	.264	.340	0	—	0	4	5	-0	0.4
Yr	6	10	.375	60	0	0	0	10	97	100	11	46	67	13.6	4.08	104	.267	.349	0	—	0	1	2	-0	0.4
1987 *Min-A	7	5	.583	59	0	0	0	2	79^1	81	10	30	51	13.0	4.54	102	.262	.335	0	—	0	-1	1	-0	0.0
1988 Min-A	7	5	.583	49	0	0	0	3	74	65	10	22	43	10.8	3.41	119	.235	.296	0	—	0	5	5	-0	0.4
1989 Cle-A	0	3	.000	32	0	0	0	2	39	48	7	13	13	14.1	4.15	95	.293	.345	0	—	0	-1	-1	-1	-0.2
Total 7	33	41	.446	342	0	0	0	26	566^1	546	75	215	349	12.3	3.99	101	.253	.324	0	.000	0	8	3	-6	0.2

● TOMMY ATKINS Atkins, Francis Montgomery b: 12/9/1887, Ponca, Neb. d: 5/7/56, Cleveland, Ohio BL/TL, 5'10.5", 165 lbs. Deb: 10/02/09

YEAR TM/L	W	L	PCT	G	GS	CG	SH	SV	IP	H	HR	BB	SO	RAT	ERA	ERA+	OAV	OOB	BH	AVG	PB	PR	/A	PD	TPI
1909 Phi-A	0	0	—	1	1	0	0	0	6	6	0	5	4	16.5	4.50	53	.261	.393	0	.000	-0	-1	-1	0	-0.1
1910 Phi-A	3	2	.600	15	3	2	0	2	57	53	0	23	29	12.2	2.68	88	.254	.330	2	.118	-1	-1	-2	0	-0.4
Total 2	3	2	.600	16	4	2	0	2	63	59	0	28	33	12.6	2.86	83	.254	.337	2	.105	-1	-2	-3	0	-0.5

● JAMES ATKINS Atkins, James Curtis b: 3/10/21, Birmingham, Ala. BL/TR, 6'3", 205 lbs. Deb: 9/29/50

YEAR TM/L	W	L	PCT	G	GS	CG	SH	SV	IP	H	HR	BB	SO	RAT	ERA	ERA+	OAV	OOB	BH	AVG	PB	PR	/A	PD	TPI
1950 Bos-A	0	0	—	1	0	0	0	0	4^2	4	1	4	0	17.4	3.86	127	.235	.409	0	.000	-0	0	1	-0	0.0
1952 Bos-A	0	1	.000	3	1	0	0	0	10^1	11	0	7	2	15.7	3.48	113	.275	.383	2	.667	1	0	1	0	0.1
Total 2	0	1	.000	4	1	0	0	0	15	15	1	11	2	16.2	3.60	118	.263	.391	2	.400	0	1	1	0	0.1

● AL ATKINSON Atkinson, Albert Wright b: 3/9/1861, Clinton, Ill. d: 6/17/52, Elkhorn Township Mo. BR/TR, 5'11.5", 165 lbs. Deb: 5/01/1884

YEAR TM/L	W	L	PCT	G	GS	CG	SH	SV	IP	H	HR	BB	SO	RAT	ERA	ERA+	OAV	OOB	BH	AVG	PB	PR	/A	PD	TPI
1884 Phi-a	11	11	.500	22	22	20	1	0	184	186	3	21	93	10.6	4.21	81	.244	.274	16	.193	-1	-20	-17	0	-1.5
CP-U	6	10	.375	16	16	16	1	0	140	127	1	21	104	9.5	2.76	109	.226	.254	14	.206	-3	4	4	1	0.2
Bal-U	3	5	.375	8	8	8	0	0	69^2	60	4	12	50	9.3	2.33	143	.217	.249	4	.138	-2	5	8	0	0.5
Yr	9	15	.375	24	24	24	1	0	209^2	187	5	33	154	9.4	2.62	119	.223	.252	18	.186	-5	9	12	1	0.7
1886 Phi-a	25	17	.595	45	45	44	1	0	396^2	414	11	101	154	12.2	3.95	89	.256	.308	18	.122	-6	-22	-20	-2	-2.4
1887 Phi-a	6	8	.429	15	15	11	0	0	124^2	156	2	54	34	15.6	5.92	72	.292	.364	12	.203	-0	-22	-23	1	-1.7
Total 3	51	51	.500	106	106	99	3	0	915	943	21	209	435	11.7	3.96	88	.251	.297	64	.165	-12	-55	-47	-1	-4.9

● BILL ATKINSON Atkinson, William Cecil Glenn b: 10/4/54, Chatham, Ont., Can. BL/TR, 5'7", 165 lbs. Deb: 9/18/76

YEAR TM/L	W	L	PCT	G	GS	CG	SH	SV	IP	H	HR	BB	SO	RAT	ERA	ERA+	OAV	OOB	BH	AVG	PB	PR	/A	PD	TPI
1976 Mon-N	0	0	—	4	0	0	0	0	5	3	0	1	4	7.2	0.00	—	.176	.222	0	—	0	2	2	0	0.2
1977 Mon-N	7	2	.778	55	0	0	0	7	83^1	72	12	29	56	10.9	3.35	114	.234	.300	1	.200	-0	5	4	1	0.6
1978 Mon-N	2	2	.500	29	0	0	0	3	45^1	45	5	28	32	14.7	4.37	81	.268	.376	2	.500	1	-4	-4	0	-0.3
1979 Mon-N	2	0	1.000	10	0	0	0	1	13^2	9	0	4	7	8.6	1.98	186	.170	.228	0	.000	-0	3	3	-0	0.2
Total 4	11	4	.733	98	0	0	0	11	147^1	129	17	62	99	11.7	3.42	108	.236	.315	3	.300	1	6	5	1	0.7

YEAR	TM/L	W	L	PCT	G	GS	CG	SH	SV	IP	H	HR	BB	SO	RAT	ERA	ERA+	OAV	OOB	BH	AVG	PB	PR	/A	PD	TPI
● **DON AUGUST** August, Donald Glenn b: 7/3/63, Inglewood, Cal. BR/TR, 6'3", 190 lbs. Deb: 6/02/88																										
1988	Mil-A	13	7	.650	24	22	6	1	0	148^1	137	12	48	66	11.2	3.09	129	.245	.305	0	—	0	14	15	2	1.7
1989	Mil-A	12	12	.500	31	25	2	1	0	142^1	175	17	58	51	14.9	5.31	72	.302	.368	0	—	0	-23	-23	1	-2.2
1990	Mil-A	0	3	.000	5	0	0	0	0	11	13	0	5	2	14.7	6.55	59	.295	.367	0	—	0	-3	-3	0	-0.3
1991	Mil-A	9	8	.529	28	23	1	1	0	138^1	166	18	47	62	14.1	5.47	73	.301	.359	0	—	0	-21	-23	0	-2.1
Total	4	34	30	.531	88	70	9	3	0	440	491	47	158	181	13.4	4.64	85	.283	.345	0	—	0	-33	-35	4	-2.9
● **JERRY AUGUSTINE** Augustine, Gerald Lee b: 7/24/52, Kewaunee, Wis. BL/TL, 6', 185 lbs. Deb: 9/09/75																										
1975	Mil-A	2	0	1.000	5	3	1	0	0	26^2	26	2	12	8	13.2	3.04	126	.274	.361	0	—	0	2	2	-0	0.2
1976	Mil-A	9	12	.429	39	24	5	3	0	171^2	167	9	56	59	11.9	3.30	106	.261	.324	0	—	0	4	4	-2	0.2
1977	Mil-A	12	18	.400	33	33	10	1	0	209	222	23	72	68	12.8	4.48	91	.277	.339	0	—	0	-10	-10	0	-0.9
1978	Mil-A	13	12	.520	35	30	9	2	0	188^1	204	14	61	59	12.9	4.54	83	.280	.339	0	—	0	-16	-16	2	-1.4
1979	Mil-A	9	6	.600	43	2	0	0	5	85^2	95	6	30	41	13.2	3.47	120	.284	.344	0	—	0	7	7	-2	0.5
1980	Mil-A	4	3	.571	39	1	0	0	2	69^2	83	5	36	22	15.6	4.52	86	.301	.385	0	—	0	-4	-5	0	-0.5
1981	Mil-A	2	2	.500	27	2	0	0	2	61^1	75	4	18	26	13.8	4.26	80	.300	.349	0	—	0	-4	-6	0	-0.5
1982	Mil-A	1	3	.250	20	2	1	0	0	62	63	13	26	22	13.2	5.08	74	.267	.345	0	—	0	-7	-9	-1	-0.6
1983	Mil-A	3	3	.500	34	7	1	0	2	64^1	89	11	25	40	16.1	5.74	65	.328	.387	0	—	0	-12	-14	-0	-1.4
1984	Mil-A	0	0	—	4	0	0	0	0	5^1	4	0	4	3	15.2	0.00	—	.211	.375	0	—	0	2	2	0	0.3
Total	10	55	59	.482	279	104	27	6	11	944	1028	87	340	348	13.2	4.23	90	.281	.346	0	—	0	-37	-45	-3	-4.1
● **ELDON AUKER** Auker, Eldon Le Roy "Submarine" b: 9/21/10, Norcatur, Kan. BR/TR, 6'2", 194 lbs. Deb: 8/10/33																										
1933	Det-A	3	3	.500	15	6	2	1	0	55	63	3	25	17	14.7	5.24	82	.285	.363	2	.118	-1	-6	-6	-1	-0.7
1934	*Det-A	15	7	.682	43	18	10	2	1	205	234	9	56	86	12.9	3.42	128	.288	.336	11	.149	-2	24	22	3	2.2
1935	*Det-A	18	7	**.720**	36	25	13	2	0	195	213	13	61	63	13.1	3.83	109	.279	.340	16	.216	1	14	7	1	0.9
1936	Det-A	13	16	.448	35	31	14	2	0	215^1	263	11	83	66	14.6	4.89	101	.302	.365	24	.308	7	4	1	5	1.2
1937	Det-A	17	9	.654	39	32	19	1	1	252^2	250	13	97	73	12.6	3.88	120	.260	.331	18	.198	4	21	22	5	3.0
1938	Det-A	11	10	.524	27	24	12	1	0	160^2	184	14	56	46	13.7	5.27	95	.284	.346	5	.088	-4	-9	-5	3	-0.6
1939	Bos-A	9	10	.474	31	25	6	1	0	151	183	13	61	43	14.6	5.36	88	.294	.358	12	.226	2	-12	-11	2	-0.7
1940	StL-A	16	11	.593	38	35	20	2	0	263^2	299	17	96	78	13.6	3.96	116	.281	.342	19	.213	3	12	18	2	2.3
1941	StL-A	14	15	.483	34	31	13	0	0	216	268	20	85	60	14.8	5.50	78	.303	.365	10	.125	-3	-32	-29	1	-2.8
1942	StL-A	14	13	.519	35	34	17	2	0	249	273	16	86	62	13.1	4.08	91	.277	.337	14	.161	-1	-12	-11	1	-1.1
Total	10	130	101	.563	333	261	126	14	2	1963^1	2230	129	706	594	13.6	4.42	101	.285	.347	131	.187	5	3	11	21	3.7
● **DENNIS AUST** Aust, Dennis Kay b: 11/25/40, Tecumseh, Neb. BR/TR, 5'11", 180 lbs. Deb: 9/06/65																										
1965	StL-N	0	0	—	6	0	0	0	1	7^1	6	0	2	7	9.8	4.91	78	.214	.267	0	.000	-0	-1	-1	0	-0.1
1966	StL-N	0	1	.000	9	0	0	0	1	9^2	12	1	6	7	16.8	6.52	55	.308	.400	0	.000	-0	-3	-3	-0	-0.3
Total	2	0	1	.000	15	0	0	0	2	17	18	1	8	14	13.8	5.82	64	.269	.347	0	.000	-0	-4	-4	0	-0.4
● **JIM AUSTIN** Austin, James Parker b: 12/7/63, Farmville, Va. BR/TR, 6'2", 200 lbs. Deb: 7/04/91																										
1991	Mil-A	0	0	—	5	0	0	0	0	8^2	8	1	11	3	22.8	8.31	48	.276	.512	0	—	0	-4	-4	0	-0.3
1992	Mil-A	5	2	.714	47	0	0	0	0	58^1	38	2	32	30	11.1	1.85	206	.191	.309	0	—	0	14	13	-1	1.4
Total	2	5	2	.714	52	0	0	0	0	67	46	3	43	33	12.6	2.69	143	.202	.341	0	—	0	9	9	-1	1.1
● **RICK AUSTIN** Austin, Rick Gerald b: 10/27/46, Seattle, Was. BR/TL, 6'4", 190 lbs. Deb: 6/21/70																										
1970	Cle-A	2	5	.286	31	8	1	1	3	67^2	74	10	26	53	13.7	4.79	83	.281	.353	2	.111	0	-8	-6	1	-0.5
1971	Cle-A	0	0	—	23	0	0	0	1	23	25	3	20	20	18.8	5.09	75	.291	.440	0	.000	-0	-4	-3	0	-0.3
1975	Mil-A	2	3	.400	32	0	0	0	2	40	32	3	32	30	14.6	4.05	95	.222	.367	0	—	0	-1	-1	-1	-0.2
1976	Mil-A	0	0	—	3	0	0	0	0	5^1	10	1	0	3	18.6	5.06	69	.435	.458	0	—	0	-1	-1	0	-0.1
Total	4	4	8	.333	89	8	1	1	6	136	141	17	78	106	15.0	4.63	84	.273	.377	2	.105	0	-14	-11	1	-1.1
● **AL AUTRY** Autry, Albert b: 2/29/52, Modesto, Cal. BR/TR, 6'5", 225 lbs. Deb: 9/14/76																										
1976	Atl-N	1	0	1.000	1	1	0	0	0	5	4	2	3	3	12.6	5.40	70	.222	.333	0	.000	-0	-1	-1	-0	-0.1
● **STEVE AVERY** Avery, Steven Thomas b: 4/14/70, Trenton, Mich. BL/TL, 6'4", 180 lbs. Deb: 6/13/90																										
1990	Atl-N	3	11	.214	21	20	1	1	0	99	121	7	45	75	15.3	5.64	72	.302	.375	4	.133	-1	-20	-18	2	-1.7
1991	*Atl-N	18	8	.692	35	35	3	1	0	210^1	189	21	65	137	11.0	3.38	115	.240	.300	17	.215	3	7	12	-0	1.6
1992	*Atl-N	11	11	.500	35	35	2	2	0	233^2	216	14	71	129	11.1	3.20	117	.246	.302	13	.171	1	8	14	-0	1.6
Total	3	32	30	.516	91	90	6	4	0	543	526	42	181	341	11.8	3.71	104	.254	.316	34	.184	4	-5	8	1	1.5
● **JAY AVREA** Avrea, James Epherium b: 7/6/20, Cleburne, Tex. d: 6/26/87, Dallas, Tex. BR/TR, 6'1.5", 175 lbs. Deb: 4/22/50																										
1950	Cin-N	0	0	—	2	0	0	0	0	5^1	6	0	3	2	15.2	3.38	125	.273	.360	0	.000	-0	0	1	-0	0.0
● **BOBBY AYALA** Ayala, Robert Joseph b: 7/8/69, Ventura, Cal. BR/TR, 6'2", 190 lbs. Deb: 9/05/92																										
1992	Cin-N	2	1	.667	5	5	0	0	0	29	33	1	13	23	14.6	4.34	84	.297	.376	0	.000	-1	-3	-2	1	-0.2
● **JAKE AYDELOTT** Aydelott, Jacob Stuart b: 7/6/1861, N.Manchester, Ind. d: 10/22/26, Detroit, Mich. 6', 180 lbs. Deb: 5/15/1884																										
1884	Ind-a	5	7	.417	12	12	11	0	0	106	129	0	29	30	13.4	4.92	67	.282	.324	5	.114	-3	-20	-19	-2	-2.0
1886	Phi-a	0	2	.000	2	2	2	0	0	18	21	0	12	5	16.5	4.00	88	.304	.407	0	.000	-1	-1	-1	-0	-0.2
Total	2	5	9	.357	14	14	13	0	0	124	150	0	41	35	13.9	4.79	69	.285	.336	5	.100	-4	-21	-20	-2	-2.2
● **BILL AYERS** Ayers, William Oscar b: 9/27/19, Newnan, Ga. d: 9/24/80, Newnan, Ga. BR/TR, 6'3", 185 lbs. Deb: 4/17/47																										
1947	NY-N	0	3	.000	13	4	0	0	1	35^1	46	7	14	22	15.5	8.15	50	.322	.386	2	.250	0	-16	-16	1	-1.4
● **DOC AYERS** Ayers, Yancy Wyatt b: 5/20/1890, Fancy Gap, Va. d: 5/26/68, Pulaski, Va. BR/TR, 6'1", 185 lbs. Deb: 9/09/13																										
1913	Was-A	1	1	.500	4	2	1	1	1	17^2	12	0	4	17	8.7	1.53	193	.182	.239	0	.000	-1	3	3	1	0.3
1914	Was-A	12	15	.444	49	32	8	3	3	265^1	221	5	54	148	9.6	2.54	111	.238	.286	14	.169	-0	6	8	-2	0.6
1915	Was-A	14	9	.609	40	16	8	2	3	211^1	178	1	38	96	9.5	2.21	134	.234	.276	12	.190	-1	17	18	-4	1.2
1916	Was-A	5	9	.357	43	17	7	0	2	157	173	4	52	69	13.1	3.78	74	.285	.346	6	.140	-2	-17	-17	-4	-2.5
1917	Was-A	11	10	.524	40	15	12	3	1	207^2	192	3	59	78	11.2	2.17	121	.256	.317	13	.206	-0	11	11	-1	1.1
1918	Was-A	10	12	.455	40	24	11	4	3	219^2	215	2	63	67	11.7	2.83	96	.261	.319	10	.152	-2	-1	-2	-0	-0.5
1919	Was-A	0	6	.000	11	5	0	0	1	43^2	52	0	17	12	15.0	2.89	111	.317	.395	5	.417	2	2	2	1	0.4
	Det-A	5	3	.625	24	5	3	1	0	93^2	88	2	31	32	11.7	2.69	119	.254	.320	3	.125	-1	6	5	-0	0.4
	Yr	5	9	.357	35	10	3	1	1	137^1	140	2	48	44	12.5	2.75	116	.272	.337	8	.222	0	7	7	0	0.8
1920	Det-A	7	14	.333	46	23	8	3	1	208^2	217	6	62	103	12.4	3.88	96	.280	.340	9	.153	-2	-2	-4	-0	-0.6
1921	Det-A	0	0	—	2	1	0	0	0	4	9	0	2	0	24.8	9.00	47	.450	.500	0	—	0	-2	-2	-0	-0.2
Total	9	65	79	.451	299	140	58	17	15	1428^2	1357	23	382	622	11.3	2.84	105	.259	.315	72	.171	-8	22	21	-10	0.2
● **BOB AYRAULT** Ayrault, Robert Cunningham b: 4/27/66, Lake Tahoe, Cal. BR/TR, 6'4", 230 lbs. Deb: 6/07/92																										
1992	Phi-N	2	2	.500	30	0	0	0	0	43^1	32	0	17	27	10.4	3.12	112	.209	.292	0	—	0	2	2	0	0.2
● **BOB BABCOCK** Babcock, Robert Ernest b: 8/25/49, New Castle, Pa. BR/TR, 6'5", 210 lbs. Deb: 7/22/79																										
1979	Tex-A	0	0	—	4	0	0	0	0	5^1	7	1	7	6	23.6	10.13	41	.318	.483	0	—	0	-4	-4	0	-0.3
1980	Tex-A	1	2	.333	19	0	0	0	0	23^1	20	3	8	15	11.6	4.63	84	.238	.319	0	—	0	-2	-2	-0	-0.1
1981	Tex-A	1	1	.500	16	0	0	0	0	28^2	21	2	16	18	11.9	2.20	158	.219	.336	0	—	0	5	4	-0	0.5
Total	3	2	3	.400	39	0	0	0	0	57^1	48	6	31	39	12.9	3.92	94	.238	.347	0	—	0	-0	-1	-0	0.1

YEAR	TM/L	W	L	PCT	G	GS	CG	SH	SV	IP	H	HR	BB	SO	RAT	ERA	ERA+	OAV	OOB	BH	AVG	PB	PR	/A	PD	TPI
● **JOHNNY BABICH**	Babich, John Charles b: 5/14/13, Albion, Cal. BR/TR, 6'1.5", 185 lbs. Deb: 6/19/34																									
1934	Bro-N	7	11	.389	25	19	7	0	1	135	148	5	51	62	13.4	4.20	93	.281	.347	7	.140	-3	-2	-4	2	-0.5
1935	Bro-N	7	14	.333	37	24	7	2	0	143^1	191	7	52	55	15.4	6.66	60	.317	.373	9	.184	-0	-42	-43	0	-3.9
1936	Bos-N	0	0	—	3	0	0	0	0	6	11	1	6	1	27.0	10.50	37	.440	.563	0	.000	-0	-4	-4	0	-0.4
1940	Phi-A	14	13	.519	31	30	16	1	0	229^1	222	16	80	94	11.9	3.73	119	.248	.310	10	.116	-6	17	18	0	1.3
1941	Phi-A	2	7	.222	16	14	4	0	0	78^1	85	9	31	19	13.7	6.09	69	.281	.353	10	.400	4	-17	-17	1	-1.1
Total	5	30	45	.400	112	87	34	3	1	592	657	38	220	231	13.5	4.93	85	.279	.343	36	.171	-5	-49	-50	3	-4.6
● **LES BACKMAN**	Backman, Lester John b: 3/20/1888, Cleves, Ohio d: 11/8/75, Cincinnati, Ohio BR/TR, 6'0.5", 195 lbs. Deb: 7/03/09																									
1909	StL-N	3	11	.214	21	14	8	0	0	128^1	146	1	39	35	13.2	4.14	61	.302	.357	4	.103	-1	-22	-23	-0	-2.5
1910	StL-N	6	7	.462	26	11	4	0	2	116	117	4	53	41	13.3	3.03	98	.265	.346	4	.114	0	0	-1	-0	-0.1
Total	2	9	18	.333	47	25	12	0	2	244^1	263	5	92	76	13.3	3.61	76	.284	.352	8	.108	-1	-22	-24	-1	-2.6
● **EDDIE BACON**	Bacon, Edgar Suter b: 4/8/1895, Franklin Co., Ky. d: 10/2/63, Frankfurt, Ky. Deb: 8/13/17 ♦																									
1917	Phi-A	0	0	—	1	0	0	0	0	6	5	0	7	0	18.0	6.00	46	.238	.429	3	.500	1	-2	-2	1	0.0
● **MIKE BACSIK**	Bacsik, Michael James b: 4/1/52, Dallas, Tex. BR/TR, 6'1", 185 lbs. Deb: 6/15/75																									
1975	Tex-A	1	2	.333	7	3	0	0	0	26^2	28	1	9	13	12.8	3.71	101	.275	.339	0	—	0	0	0	-0	0.0
1976	Tex-A	3	2	.600	23	0	0	0	0	55	66	3	26	21	15.4	4.25	84	.308	.388	0	—	0	-4	-4	-1	-0.5
1977	Tex-A	0	0	—	2	0	0	0	0	2^1	9	1	0	1	34.7	19.29	21	.563	.563	0	—	0	-4	-4	0	-0.3
1979	Min-A	4	2	.667	31	0	0	0	0	65^2	61	6	29	33	12.3	4.39	100	.249	.328	0	—	0	-1	-0	-0	-0.1
1980	Min-A	0	0	—	10	0	0	0	0	23	26	1	11	9	14.5	4.30	101	.286	.363	0	—	0	-1	0	0	-0.1
Total	5	8	6	.571	73	3	0	0	0	172^2	190	12	75	77	14.0	4.43	91	.284	.359	0	—	0	-10	-8	-1	-1.0
● **FRED BACZEWSKI**	Baczewski, Frederic John "Lefty" b: 5/15/26, St.Paul, Minn. d: 11/14/76, Culver City, Cal. BL/TL, 6'2.5", 185 lbs. Deb: 4/26/53																									
1953	Chi-N	0	0	—	9	0	0	0	0	10	20	1	6	3	24.3	6.30	71	.435	.509	1	.500	0	-2	-2	-0	-0.2
	Cin-N	11	4	.733	24	18	10	1	1	138^1	125	13	52	58	11.6	3.45	126	.244	.315	8	.178	-0	13	14	-3	1.1
	Yr	11	4	.733	33	18	10	1	1	148^1	145	14	58	61	12.4	3.64	120	.259	.330	9	.191	0	11	12	-3	0.9
1954	Cin-N	6	6	.500	29	22	4	1	0	130	159	22	53	43	14.7	5.26	80	.305	.370	3	.071	-4	-17	-15	-1	-1.9
1955	Cin-N	0	0	—	1	0	0	0	0	1	2	2	0	0	18.0	18.00	24	.400	.400	0	—	0	-2	-2	-0	-0.1
Total	3	17	10	.630	63	40	14	2	1	279^1	306	38	111	104	13.5	4.45	96	.282	.351	12	.135	-3	-8	-5	-4	-1.1
● **LORE BADER**	Bader, Lore Verne "King" b: 4/27/1888, Bader, Ill. d: 6/2/73, LeRoy, Kan. BL/TR, 6', 175 lbs. Deb: 9/30/12 C																									
1912	NY-N	2	0	1.000	2	1	1	0	0	10	9	0	6	3	14.4	0.90	376	.250	.372	0	.000	-0	3	3	0	0.3
1917	Bos-A	2	0	1.000	15	1	0	0	1	38^1	48	1	18	14	15.7	2.35	110	.306	.381	3	.300	1	1	1	1	0.3
1918	Bos-A	1	3	.250	5	4	2	1	0	27	26	1	12	10	13.7	3.33	81	.271	.369	1	.111	-1	-2	-2	-1	-0.4
Total	3	5	3	.625	22	6	3	1	1	75^1	83	2	36	27	14.8	2.51	109	.287	.376	4	.182	-0	2	2	-0	0.2
● **ED BAECHT**	Baecht, Edward Joseph b: 5/15/07, Paden, Okla. d: 8/15/57, Grafton, Ill. BR/TR, 6'3", 195 lbs. Deb: 4/24/26																									
1926	Phi-N	2	0	1.000	28	1	1	0	0	56	73	4	28	14	16.4	6.11	68	.324	.402	2	.143	-1	-14	-12	2	-1.1
1927	Phi-N	0	1	.000	1	1	0	0	0	6	12	0	2	0	21.0	12.00	34	.429	.467	0	.000	-0	-5	-5	0	-0.4
1928	Phi-N	1	1	.500	9	1	0	0	0	24	37	1	9	10	17.3	6.00	71	.385	.438	1	.143	-0	-5	-5	0	-0.4
1931	Chi-N	2	4	.333	22	6	2	0	0	67	64	1	32	34	14.0	3.76	103	.250	.351	5	.278	1	1	1	1	0.2
1932	Chi-N	0	0	—	1	0	0	0	0	1	1	0	1	0	18.0	0.00	—	.333	.500	0	—	0	0	0	-0	0.0
1937	StL-A	0	0	—	3	0	0	0	0	6^1	13	3	6	3	29.8	12.79	38	.419	.538	0	.000	-0	-6	-6	0	-0.5
Total	6	5	6	.455	64	9	3	0	0	160^1	200	9	78	61	16.2	5.56	73	.313	.397	8	.190	-2	-29	-27	3	-2.2
● **JIM BAGBY**	Bagby, James Charles Jacob Jr. b: 9/8/16, Cleveland, Ohio d: 9/2/88, Marietta, Ga. BR/TR, 6'2", 170 lbs. Deb: 4/18/38 F																									
1938	Bos-A	15	11	.577	43	25	10	1	2	198^2	218	9	90	73	14.1	4.21	117	.283	.360	13	.191	-1	13	16	2	1.6
1939	Bos-A	5	5	.500	21	11	3	0	0	80	119	7	36	35	17.7	7.09	67	.347	.412	10	.294	3	-22	-21	-0	-1.7
1940	Bos-A	10	16	.385	36	21	6	1	2	182^2	217	15	83	57	14.8	4.73	95	.296	.368	15	.203	-0	-7	-5	0	-0.5
1941	Cle-A	9	15	.375	33	27	12	0	2	200^2	214	10	76	53	13.3	4.04	98	.273	.341	18	.243	2	2	-2	2	0.1
1942	Cle-A☆	17	9	.654	38	35	16	4	1	270^2	267	19	64	54	11.0	2.96	117	.258	.302	18	.189	1	21	15	0	1.7
1943	Cle-A☆	17	14	.548	36	33	16	3	1	**273**	248	15	80	70	10.9	3.10	100	.240	.296	30	.268	4	6	0	2	0.8
1944	Cle-A	4	5	.444	13	10	2	0	0	79	101	2	34	12	15.8	4.33	76	.312	.384	7	.226	1	-8	-9	0	-0.8
1945	Cle-A	8	11	.421	25	19	11	3	1	159^1	171	3	59	38	13.1	3.73	87	.279	.344	17	.293	3	-6	-8	3	-0.3
1946	*Bos-A	7	6	.538	21	11	6	1	0	106^2	117	4	49	16	14.1	3.71	99	.279	.356	5	.119	-2	-2	-1	-0	-0.3
1947	Pit-N	5	4	.556	37	6	2	0	0	115^2	143	14	37	23	14.4	4.67	90	.304	.361	7	.219	1	-8	-6	1	-0.4
Total	10	97	96	.503	303	198	84	13	9	1666^1	1815	98	608	431	13.2	3.96	97	.278	.342	140	.226	12	-11	-23	10	0.2
● **JIM BAGBY**	Bagby, James Charles Jacob Sr. "Sarge" b: 10/5/1889, Barnett, Ga. d: 7/28/54, Marietta, Ga. BB/TR, 6', 170 lbs. Deb: 4/22/12 F																									
1912	Cin-N	2	1	.667	5	1	0	0	0	17^1	17	2	9	10	13.5	3.12	108	.270	.361	0	.000	-1	1	0	0	0.0
1916	Cle-A	16	16	.500	48	27	14	3	5	272^2	253	2	67	88	10.8	2.61	115	.251	.303	15	.167	-1	7	12	-3	1.0
1917	Cle-A	23	13	.639	49	37	26	8	7	320^2	277	6	73	83	10.0	1.96	144	.235	.283	25	.231	3	25	31	-3	3.6
1918	Cle-A	17	16	.515	**45**	31	23	2	6	271^1	274	0	78	57	11.7	2.69	112	.276	.330	21	.212	-0	3	10	-2	0.8
1919	Cle-A	17	11	.607	35	32	21	0	3	241^1	258	3	44	61	11.4	2.80	120	.275	.310	23	.258	5	12	15	-0	2.1
1920	*Cle-A	**31**	12	**.721**	**48**	38	**30**	3	0	**339**^{2}	338	9	79	73	11.2	2.89	132	.266	.311	33	.252	6	34	34	-7	3.3
1921	Cle-A	14	12	.538	40	26	13	0	4	191^2	238	14	44	37	13.4	4.70	91	.308	.348	15	.197	-1	-9	-9	-2	-1.1
1922	Cle-A	4	5	.444	25	10	4	0	1	98^1	134	5	39	25	16.1	6.32	63	.340	.404	11	.262	3	-25	-25	1	-2.0
1923	Pit-N	3	2	.600	21	6	2	0	3	68^2	95	6	25	16	15.9	5.24	76	.336	.392	1	.050	-2	-9	-9	-1	-1.1
Total	9	127	88	.591	316	208	133	16	29	1821^2	1884	47	458	450	11.7	3.11	110	.273	.321	144	.218	11	38	62	-15	6.6
● **STAN BAHNSEN**	Bahnsen, Stanley Raymond b: 12/15/44, Council Bluffs, Ia. BR/TR, 6'2", 203 lbs. Deb: 9/09/66																									
1966	NY-A	1	1	.500	4	3	1	0	1	23	15	3	7	16	8.6	3.52	94	.181	.244	1	.143	-0	-0	-1	-0	-0.1
1968	NY-A	17	12	.586	37	34	10	1	0	267^1	216	14	68	162	9.6	2.05	141	.221	.273	4	.049	-4	27	25	-2	2.3
1969	NY-A	9	16	.360	40	33	5	2	1	220^2	222	28	90	130	12.7	3.83	91	.260	.331	5	.083	-3	-5	-9	1	-1.1
1970	NY-A	14	11	.560	36	35	6	2	0	232^2	227	23	75	116	11.8	3.33	106	.256	.316	11	.149	-0	10	5	1	0.6
1971	NY-A	14	12	.538	36	34	14	3	0	242	221	20	72	110	11.1	3.35	97	.248	.308	12	.152	0	3	-3	3	0.0
1972	Chi-A	21	16	.568	43	41	5	1	0	252^1	263	22	73	157	12.2	3.60	87	.268	.323	14	.152	-1	-15	-13	2	-1.3
1973	Chi-A	18	21	.462	42	42	14	4	0	282^1	290	20	117	120	13.1	3.57	111	.269	.343	0	—	0	8	12	2	1.5
1974	Chi-A	12	15	.444	38	35	10	1	0	216^1	230	17	110	102	14.3	4.70	79	.277	.364	0	—	0	-26	-23	1	-2.3
1975	Chi-A	4	6	.400	12	12	2	0	0	67^1	78	9	40	31	16.2	6.01	64	.291	.389	0	—	0	-17	-16	-0	-1.5
	Oak-A	6	7	.462	21	16	2	0	0	100	88	2	37	49	11.5	3.24	112	.238	.313	0	.000	0	6	4	0	0.4
	Yr	10	13	.435	33	28	4	0	0	167^1	166	11	77	80	13.2	4.36	85	.259	.342	0	.000	0	-11	-12	0	-1.1
1976	Oak-A	8	7	.533	35	14	1	1	0	143	124	13	43	82	10.6	3.34	101	.232	.292	0	—	0	3	0	1	0.1
1977	Oak-A	1	2	.333	11	2	0	0	1	22	24	5	13	21	15.5	6.14	66	.286	.388	0	—	0	-5	-5	-1	-0.5
	Mon-N	8	9	.471	23	22	3	1	0	127^1	142	14	38	58	12.7	4.81	79	.283	.333	5	.119	-1	-13	-14	-0	-1.5
1978	Mon-N	1	5	.167	44	1	0	0	7	75	74	9	31	44	12.6	3.84	92	.261	.334	1	.091	-1	-2	-3	-0	-0.4
1979	Mon-N	3	1	.750	55	0	0	0	5	94^1	80	10	42	71	11.6	3.15	116	.236	.320	1	.071	-0	6	5	-0	0.5
1980	Mon-N	7	6	.538	57	0	0	0	4	91^1	80	7	33	48	11.1	3.05	117	.235	.302	1	.111	1	6	5	-0	0.6
1981	*Mon-N	2	1	.667	25	3	0	0	1	49	45	7	24	28	12.9	4.96	70	.247	.338	1	.111	-0	-8	-8	-1	-1.0
1982	Cal-A	0	1	.000	7	0	0	0	0	9^2	13	0	8	5	19.6	4.66	87	.310	.420	0	—	0	-1	-1	-0	-0.1
	Phi-N	0	0	—	8	0	0	0	0	13^1	8	0	3	9	7.4	1.35	271	.182	.234	0	—	0	3	3	-0	0.4
Total	16	146	149	.495	574	327	73	16	20	2529	2440	223	924	1359	12.1	3.60	97	.255	.323	56	.117	-8	-20	-35	4	-3.4

YEAR TM/L	W	L	PCT	G	GS	CG	SH	SV	IP	H	HR	BB	SO	RAT	ERA	ERA+	OAV	OOB	BH	AVG	PB	PR	/A	PD	TPI
● ED BAHR Bahr, Edson Garfield b: 10/16/19, Rouleau, Sask., Canada BR/TR, 6'1.5", 172 lbs. Deb: 5/01/46																									
1946 Pit-N	8	6	.571	27	14	7	0	0	136^{2}	128	8	52	44	12.2	2.63	134	.254	.330	8	.178	-1	12	14	-0	1.4
1947 Pit-N	3	5	.375	19	11	1	0	0	82^{1}	82	5	43	25	14.0	4.59	92	.263	.358	2	.087	-2	-5	-3	-1	-0.6
Total 2	11	11	.500	46	25	8	0	0	219	210	13	95	69	12.9	3.37	112	.257	.341	10	.147	-3	7	10	-1	0.8
● GROVER BAICHLEY Baichley, Grover Cleveland b: 1/7/1890, Toledo, Ill. d: 6/30/56, San Jose, Cal. BR/TR, 5'9.5", 165 lbs. Deb: 8/24/14																									
1914 StL-A	0	0	—	4	0	0	0	0	7	9	0	3	3	15.4	5.14	53	.346	.414	0	.000	-0	-2	-2	0	-0.2
● SCOTT BAILES Bailes, Scott Alan b: 12/18/61, Chillicothe, Ohio BL/TL, 6'2", 175 lbs. Deb: 4/09/86																									
1986 Cle-A	10	10	.500	62	10	0	0	7	112^{2}	123	12	43	60	13.3	4.95	84	.276	.342	0	—	0	-10	-10	-1	-1.0
1987 Cle-A	7	8	.467	39	17	0	0	6	120^{1}	145	21	47	65	14.7	4.64	98	.296	.362	0	—	0	-2	-2	0	-0.2
1988 Cle-A	9	14	.391	37	21	5	2	0	145	149	22	46	53	12.2	4.90	84	.266	.324	0	—	0	-15	-13	-0	-1.4
1989 Cle-A	5	9	.357	34	11	0	0	0	113^{2}	116	7	29	47	11.7	4.28	93	.269	.320	0	—	0	-5	-4	0	-0.5
1990 Cal-A	2	0	1.000	27	0	0	0	0	35^{1}	46	8	20	16	17.1	6.37	60	.315	.401	0	—	0	-10	-10	1	-0.8
1991 Cal-A	1	2	.333	42	0	0	0	0	51^{2}	41	5	22	41	11.7	4.18	98	.218	.313	0	—	0	-0	-0	0	0.0
1992 Cal-A	3	1	.750	32	0	0	0	0	38^{2}	59	7	28	25	20.5	7.45	52	.351	.447	0	—	0	-15	-15	-0	-1.4
Total 7	37	44	.457	273	59	5	2	13	617^{1}	679	82	235	307	13.6	4.93	84	.280	.347	0	—	0	-57	-54	-0	-5.3
● SWEETBREADS BAILEY Bailey, Abraham Lincoln b: 2/12/1895, Joliet, Ill. d: 9/27/39, Joliet, Ill. BR/TR, 6', 184 lbs. Deb: 5/23/19																									
1919 Chi-N	3	5	.375	21	5	0	0	0	71^{1}	75	2	20	19	12.4	3.15	91	.288	.346	7	.389	3	-2	-2	2	0.3
1920 Chi-N	1	2	.333	21	1	0	0	0	36^{2}	55	1	11	8	16.7	7.12	45	.359	.410	1	.143	-0	-16	-16	1	-1.6
1921 Chi-N	0	0	—	3	0	0	0	0	5	6	0	2	2	16.2	3.60	106	.300	.391	0	—	0	0	0	0	0.0
Bro-N	0	0	—	7	0	0	0	0	24^{1}	35	1	7	6	15.9	5.18	75	.368	.417	0	.000	-0	-4	-3	-0	-0.4
Yr	0	0	—	10	0	0	0	0	29^{1}	41	1	9	8	15.6	4.91	79	.353	.405	0	.000	-0	-4	-3	-0	-0.4
Total 3	4	7	.364	52	6	0	0	0	137^{1}	171	4	40	35	14.3	4.59	69	.324	.379	8	.267	2	-22	-22	2	-1.7
● HARVEY BAILEY Bailey, Harvey Francis b: 11/24/1876, Adrian, Mich. d: 7/10/22, Toledo, Ohio TL, 6', Deb: 6/30/1899																									
1899 Bos-N	6	4	.600	12	11	8	0	0	86^{2}	83	7	35	26	12.9	3.95	105	.252	.335	8	.235	0	-1	2	-1	0.1
1900 Bos-N	0	0	—	4	1	0	0	0	20	24	0	11	9	16.6	4.95	83	.296	.394	2	.222	0	-3	-2	1	-0.1
Total 2	6	4	.600	16	12	8	0	0	106^{2}	107	7	46	35	13.6	4.13	100	.261	.347	10	.233	0	-4	0	-0	0.0
● HOWARD BAILEY Bailey, Howard L b: 7/31/57, Grand Haven, Mich. BR/TL, 6', 195 lbs. Deb: 4/12/81																									
1981 Det-A	1	4	.200	9	5	0	0	0	36^{2}	45	4	13	17	15.0	7.36	51	.308	.377	0	—	0	-15	-15	1	-1.4
1982 Det-A	0	0	—	8	0	0	0	1	10	6	0	2	3	7.2	0.00	—	.182	.229	0	—	0	5	5	0	0.5
1983 Det-A	5	5	.500	33	3	0	0	0	72	69	11	25	21	12.0	4.88	80	.255	.322	0	—	0	-7	-8	0	-0.7
Total 3	6	9	.400	50	8	0	0	1	118^{2}	120	15	40	41	12.5	5.23	74	.267	.333	0	—	0	-17	-18	1	-1.6
● JIM BAILEY Bailey, James Hopkins b: 12/16/34, Strawberry Plains, Tenn. BB/TL, 6'2.5", 210 lbs. Deb: 9/10/59 F																									
1959 Cin-N	0	1	.000	3	1	0	0	0	11^{2}	17	1	6	7	18.5	6.17	66	.333	.414	0	.000	-0	-3	-3	-0	-0.3
● KING BAILEY Bailey, Leonard C. b: 11/1870, Virginia BL/TL, 6' ", 185 lbs. Deb: 9/21/1895																									
1895 Cin-N	1	0	1.000	1	1	1	0	0	8	13	0	0	0	15.8	5.63	88	.359	.376	2	.500	1	-1	-1	0	0.0
● STEVE BAILEY Bailey, Steven John b: 2/12/42, Bronx, N.Y. BR/TR, 6'1", 194 lbs. Deb: 4/14/67																									
1967 Cle-A	2	5	.286	32	1	0	0	2	64^{2}	62	5	42	46	14.9	3.90	84	.259	.377	0	.000	-1	-5	-5	0	-0.6
1968 Cle-A	0	1	.000	2	1	0	0	0	5	4	1	2	1	10.8	3.60	82	.235	.316	0	—	0	-0	-0	-0	-0.1
Total 2	2	6	.250	34	2	0	0	2	69^{2}	66	6	44	47	14.6	3.88	84	.258	.373	0	.000	-1	-5	-5	-0	-0.7
● BILL BAILEY Bailey, William F. b: 4/12/1889, Ft.Smith, Ark. d: 11/2/26, Houston, Tex. BL/TL, 5'11", 165 lbs. Deb: 9/17/07																									
1907 StL-A	4	1	.800	6	5	3	0	0	48^{1}	39	0	15	17	10.8	2.42	104	.223	.299	3	.150	-1	1	1	-1	-0.2
1908 StL-A	3	5	.375	22	12	7	0	0	106^{2}	85	2	50	42	11.6	3.04	79	.220	.314	3	.088	-2	-8	-8	-2	-1.3
1909 StL-A	9	10	.474	32	20	17	1	0	199	174	2	75	114	11.5	2.44	99	.248	.325	22	.286	5	1	-1	-1	0.4
1910 StL-A	3	18	.143	34	20	13	0	0	192^{1}	186	2	97	90	13.7	3.32	74	.262	.359	13	.206	0	-17	-18	-1	-2.0
1911 StL-A	0	3	.000	7	2	2	0	0	31^{2}	42	1	16	8	17.1	4.55	74	.339	.423	0	.000	-2	-4	-4	0	-0.5
1912 StL-A	0	1	.000	3	2	0	0	0	10^{2}	15	0	10	2	21.1	9.28	36	.341	.463	1	.500	1	-7	-7	-1	-0.6
1914 Bal-F	7	9	.438	19	18	10	1	0	128^{2}	106	2	68	131	12.7	3.08	110	.230	.338	7	.163	-0	2	4	3	0.7
1915 Bal-F	6	19	.240	36	23	11	2	0	190^{1}	179	8	115	98	14.3	4.63	69	.255	.366	15	.231	1	-34	-31	-1	-3.2
Chi-F	3	1	.750	5	5	3	3	0	33^{1}	23	1	10	24	8.9	2.16	129	.202	.266	2	.222	0	3	2	1	0.4
Yr	9	20	.310	41	28	14	5	0	223^{2}	202	9	125	122	13.2	4.27	73	.245	.344	17	.230	1	-31	-28	-1	-2.8
1918 Det-A	1	2	.333	8	4	1	0	0	37^{2}	53	0	26	13	19.1	5.97	45	.368	.468	1	.077	-1	-13	-14	1	-1.4
1921 StL-N	2	5	.286	19	6	3	1	0	74	95	1	22	20	14.5	4.26	86	.330	.381	2	.091	-2	-4	-5	1	-0.5
1922 StL-N	0	2	.000	12	0	0	0	0	31^{2}	38	1	23	11	17.3	5.40	72	.325	.436	2	.286	0	-5	-5	1	-0.4
Total 11	38	76	.333	203	117	70	8	0	1084^{1}	1035	20	527	570	13.3	3.57	80	.261	.354	71	.194	-1	-85	-85	-1	-8.6
● BOB BAILOR Bailor, Robert Michael b: 7/10/51, Connellsville, Pa. BR/TR, 5'11", 170 lbs. Deb: 9/06/75 C♦																									
1980 Tor-A	0	0	—	3	0	0	0	0	2^{1}	4	0	1	0	19.3	7.71	56	.364	.417	82	.236	2	-1	-1	-0	-0.1
● LOREN BAIN Bain, Herbert Loren b: 7/4/22, Staples, Minn. BR/TR, 6', 190 lbs. Deb: 6/23/45																									
1945 NY-N	0	0	—	3	0	0	0	0	8	10	1	4	1	16.9	7.88	50	.323	.417	1	.333	0	-4	-4	-0	-0.3
● DOUG BAIR Bair, Charles Douglas b: 8/22/49, Defiance, Ohio BR/TR, 6', 180 lbs. Deb: 9/13/76																									
1976 Pit-N	0	0	—	4	0	0	0	0	6^{1}	4	0	5	4	12.8	5.68	61	.174	.321	0	—	0	-2	-2	-0	-0.2
1977 Oak-A	4	6	.400	45	0	0	0	8	83^{1}	78	11	57	68	14.6	3.46	116	.253	.370	0	—	0	6	5	1	0.7
1978 Cin-N	7	6	.538	70	0	0	0	28	100^{1}	87	6	38	91	11.2	1.97	180	.236	.307	2	.143	-0	18	18	-1	1.8
1979 *Cin-N	11	7	.611	65	0	0	0	16	94^{1}	93	7	51	86	14.0	4.29	87	.256	.353	0	.000	-1	-6	-6	-1	-0.7
1980 Cin-N	3	6	.333	61	0	0	0	6	85	91	7	39	62	13.9	4.24	84	.277	.355	0	.000	-0	-6	-6	2	-0.5
1981 Cin-N	2	2	.500	24	0	0	0	0	39	42	5	17	16	13.6	5.77	62	.271	.343	1	.333	1	-10	-10	-1	-1.0
StL-N	2	0	1.000	11	0	0	0	1	15^{2}	13	0	2	14	8.6	3.45	103	.224	.250	0	.000	-0	0	0	-0	0.0
Yr	4	2	.667	35	0	0	0	1	54^{2}	55	5	19	30	12.2	5.10	70	.258	.319	1	.167	1	-10	-9	-1	-1.0
1982 *StL-N	5	3	.625	63	0	0	0	8	91^{2}	69	7	36	68	10.4	2.55	142	.211	.291	1	.077	-1	11	11	0	1.1
1983 StL-N	1	1	.500	26	0	0	0	1	29^{2}	24	4	13	21	11.2	3.03	119	.224	.308	0	.000	-0	2	2	-0	0.2
Det-A	7	3	.700	27	1	0	0	4	55^{2}	51	8	19	39	11.5	3.88	101	.242	.307	0	—	0	1	0	-0	0.2
1984 Det-A	5	3	.625	47	1	0	0	4	93^{2}	82	10	36	57	11.3	3.75	105	.238	.310	0	—	0	3	2	1	0.3
1985 Det-A	2	0	1.000	21	3	0	0	0	49	54	3	25	30	14.7	6.24	65	.281	.367	0	—	0	-11	-12	1	-1.0
StL-N	0	0	—	2	0	0	0	0	2	1	0	2	0	13.5	0.00	—	.167	.375	0	—	0	1	1	-0	0.1
1986 Oak-A	2	3	.400	31	0	0	0	4	45	37	5	18	40	11.0	3.00	129	.224	.301	0	—	0	6	4	0	1.0
1987 Phi-N	2	0	1.000	11	0	0	0	0	13^{2}	17	4	5	10	14.5	5.93	72	.309	.367	0	.000	-0	-3	-3	-0	-0.3
1988 Tor-A	0	0	—	10	0	0	0	0	13^{1}	14	2	3	8	11.5	4.05	97	.280	.321	0	—	0	-0	-0	-0	-0.1
1989 Pit-N	2	3	.400	44	0	0	0	1	67^{1}	52	4	28	56	10.7	2.27	148	.211	.292	1	.200	0	9	8	1	1.0
1990 Pit-N	0	0	—	22	0	0	0	0	24^{1}	30	3	11	19	15.2	4.81	75	.306	.376	0	.000	-0	-3	-3	0	-0.3
Total 15	55	43	.561	584	5	0	0	81	909^{1}	839	86	405	689	12.4	3.63	103	.246	.328	5	.096	-2	15	10	2	2.3
● BOB BAIRD Baird, Robert Allen b: 1/16/40, Knoxville, Tenn. d: 4/11/74, Chattanooga, Tenn. BL/TL, 6'4", 195 lbs. Deb: 9/03/62																									
1962 Was-A	0	1	.000	3	3	0	0	0	10^{2}	13	0	8	3	17.7	6.75	60	.310	.420	0	.000	-0	-3	-3	-0	-0.3
1963 Was-A	0	3	.000	5	3	0	0	0	11^{2}	12	1	7	7	15.4	7.71	48	.261	.370	1	.333	0	-5	-5	-0	-0.5

YEAR	TM/L	W	L	PCT	G	GS	CG	SH	SV	IP	H	HR	BB	SO	RAT	ERA	ERA+	OAV	OOB	BH	AVG	PB	PR	/A	PD	TPI
Total	2	0	4	.000	8	6	0	0	0	22^1	25	1	15	10	16.5	7.25	53	.284	.394	1	.167	-0	-9	-8	-1	-0.8
● JERSEY BAKELY Bakely, Edward Enoch (b: Edward Enoch Bakley) b: 4/17/1864, Blackwood, N.J. d: 2/17/15, Philadelphia, Pa. BR/TR, Deb: 5/11/1883																										
1883	Phi-a	5	3	.625	8	8	7	0	0	61^1	65	0	12	14	11.3	3.23	108	.255	.288	5	.192	1	1	2	-0	0.2
1884	Phi-U	14	25	.359	39	38	38	1	0	344^2	390	0	76	204	12.2	4.47	64	.267	.303	22	.132	-7	-55	-61	-3	-5.8
	Wil-U	0	2	.000	2	2	2	0	0	17	24	0	1	9	13.2	4.24	78	.312	.321	0	.000	-1	-2	-2	0	-0.2
	KC-U	2	3	.400	5	5	3	0	0	33	29	0	4	13	9.0	2.45	113	.220	.243	3	.150	-1	2	1	-1	0.0
	Yr	16	30	.348	46	45	43	1	0	394^2	443	0	81	226	11.9	4.29	67	.265	.299	25	.130	-8	-56	-62	-4	-6.0
1888	Cle-a	25	33	.431	61	61	60	4	0	532^2	518	14	128	212	11.2	2.97	104	.246	.294	26	.134	-5	5	7	-1	0.2
1889	Cle-N	12	22	.353	36	34	33	2	0	304^1	296	9	106	105	12.1	2.96	136	.247	.313	15	.135	-1	36	36	2	3.4
1890	Cle-P	12	25	.324	43	38	32	0	0	326^1	412	13	147	67	15.6	4.47	89	.295	.365	28	.203	-2	-9	-18	-3	-1.7
1891	Was-a	2	10	.167	13	12	11	0	0	104^1	127	6	60	32	16.6	5.35	70	.290	.383	10	.222	-0	-19	-19	-2	-1.7
	Bal-a	4	2	.667	8	6	5	0	0	59	48	1	30	13	12.1	2.29	163	.215	.310	2	.095	0	9	10	-1	0.8
	Yr	6	12	.333	21	18	16	0	0	163^1	175	7	90	45	14.7	4.24	88	.262	.351	12	.182	-0	-9	-9	-3	-0.9
Total	6	76	125	.378	215	204	191	7	0	1782^2	1909	43	564	669	12.7	3.66	94	.262	.318	111	.153	-16	-32	-43	-9	-4.8
● DAVE BAKENHASTER Bakenhaster, David Lee b: 3/5/45, Columbus, O. BR/TR, 5'10", 168 lbs. Deb: 6/20/64																										
1964	StL-N	0	0	—	2	0	0	0	0	3	9	1	1	0	30.0	6.00	63	.474	.500	0	—	0	-1	-1	0	-0.1
● AL BAKER Baker, Albert Jones b: 2/28/06, Batesville, Miss. d: 11/6/82, Kenedy, Tex. BR/TR, 5'11", 170 lbs. Deb: 8/20/38																										
1938	Bos-A	0	0	—	3	0	0	0	0	7^2	13	2	2	2	18.8	9.39	53	.371	.421	0	.000	-1	-4	-4	-0	-0.4
● BOCK BAKER Baker, Charles "Smiling Bock" b: 7/17/1878, Troy, N.Y. d: 8/17/40, New York, N.Y. TL , 5'9", 181 lbs. Deb: 4/28/01																										
1901	Cle-A	0	1	.000	1	1	1	0	0	8	23	0	6	0	33.8	5.63	63	.499	.565	0	.000	-1	-2	-2	0	-0.2
	Phi-A	0	1	.000	1	1	0	0	0	6	6	0	6	1	18.0	10.50	36	.257	.409	1	.333	0	-5	-4	-0	-0.4
	Yr	0	2	.000	2	2	1	0	0	14	29	0	12	1	26.4	7.71	47	.412	.498	1	.143	-1	-6	-6	-0	-0.6
● ERNIE BAKER Baker, Earnest Gould b: 8/8/1875, Concord, Mich. d: 10/25/45, Homer, Mich. BR/TR, 5'10", 160 lbs. Deb: 8/18/05																										
1905	Cin-N	0	0	—	1	0	0	0	0	4	7	1	0	1	18.0	4.50	73	.412	.444	0	.000	-0	-1	-1	-0	-0.1
● JESSE BAKER Baker, Jesse Ormond b: 6/3/1888, Anderson Island, Wash. d: 9/26/72, Tacoma, Wash. BL/TL, 5'11", 188 lbs. Deb: 4/23/11																										
1911	Chi-A	2	7	.222	22	8	3	0	1	94	101	3	30	51	12.9	3.93	82	.288	.351	3	.103	-2	-6	-7	1	-0.7
● KIRTLEY BAKER Baker, Kirtley "Whitey" b: 6/24/1869, Aurora, Ind. d: 4/15/27, Covington, Ky. BR/TR, 5'9", 160 lbs. Deb: 5/07/1890 ♦																										
1890	Pit-N	3	19	.136	25	21	19	2	0	178^1	209	11	86	76	15.9	5.60	59	.283	.374	10	.147	-2	-40	-46	-0	-3.8
1893	Bal-N	3	8	.273	15	12	8	0	0	91^2	138	5	58	26	19.7	8.44	56	.337	.426	17	.298	3	-38	-38	3	-2.5
1894	Bal-N	0	1	.000	1	0	0	0	0	0	1	0	2	0	—	∞	—	1.000	1.000	0	.000	-0	-5	-5	-0	-0.3
1898	Was-N	2	3	.400	6	5	4	0	0	47	56	1	18	7	14.2	3.06	120	.293	.354	5	.278	2	3	3	-1	0.4
1899	Was-N	1	7	.125	11	6	3	0	0	54	79	3	22	6	17.8	6.83	57	.340	.411	3	.158	-1	-18	-18	2	-1.4
Total	5	9	38	.191	58	44	34	2	0	371	483	20	186	115	17.0	6.28	60	.307	.392	35	.211	1	-99	-103	4	-7.6
● NEAL BAKER Baker, Neal Vernon b: 4/30/04, Laporte, Tex. d: 1/5/82, Houston, Tex. BR/TR, 6'1", 175 lbs. Deb: 6/26/27																										
1927	Phi-A	0	0	—	5	2	0	0	0	17^1	27	2	7	3	17.7	5.71	75	.365	.420	1	.167	-0	-3	-3	0	-0.3
● NORM BAKER Baker, Norman Leslie b: 10/14/1863, Philadelphia, Pa. d: 2/20/49, Hurffville, N.J. Deb: 5/21/1883																										
1883	Pit-a	0	2	.000	3	3	2	0	0	19	24	0	11	5	16.6	3.32	97	.289	.372	0	.000	-1	-0	-0	-1	-0.2
1885	Lou-a	13	12	.520	25	24	24	1	0	217	210	3	69	79	12.0	3.40	95	.241	.304	18	.207	-1	-4	-4	-2	-0.6
1890	Bal-a	1	1	.500	2	2	2	0	0	17	16	0	6	10	11.6	3.71	109	.241	.304	0	.000	-1	0	1	0	0.0
Total	3	14	15	.483	30	29	28	1	0	253	250	3	86	94	12.3	3.42	96	.245	.309	18	.170	-4	-3	-4	-2	-0.8
● STEVE BAKER Baker, Steven Byrne b: 8/30/56, Eugene, Ore. BR/TR, 6', 185 lbs. Deb: 5/25/78																										
1978	Det-A	2	4	.333	15	10	0	0	0	63^1	66	6	42	39	15.3	4.55	85	.276	.384	0	—	0	-6	-5	-1	-0.8
1979	Det-A	1	7	.125	21	12	0	0	1	84	97	13	51	54	16.5	6.64	65	.296	.400	0	—	0	-23	-22	-1	-2.2
1982	Oak-A	1	1	.500	5	3	0	0	0	25^2	30	3	4	14	11.9	4.56	86	.288	.315	0	—	0	-1	-2	-0	-0.2
1983	Oak-A	3	3	.500	35	1	0	0	5	54	59	4	26	23	14.5	4.33	89	.282	.367	0	—	0	-2	-3	-1	0.1
	StL-N	0	1	.000	8	0	0	0	0	10	10	0	4	1	13.5	1.80	201	.286	.375	0	—	0	2	2	0	0.2
Total	4	7	16	.304	84	26	0	0	6	237	262	26	127	131	15.1	5.13	78	.286	.379	0	—	0	-29	-29	-3	-2.9
● TOM BAKER Baker, Thomas Calvin "Rattlesnake" b: 6/11/13, Nursery, Tex. d: 1/3/91, Fort Worth, Tex. BR/TR, 6'1.5", 180 lbs. Deb: 8/15/35																										
1935	Bro-N	1	0	1.000	11	1	1	0	0	42	48	2	20	10	14.6	4.29	93	.277	.352	9	.474	3	-1	-1	-1	0.1
1936	Bro-N	1	8	.111	35	8	2	0	2	87^2	98	3	48	35	15.2	4.72	88	.288	.379	7	.233	1	-7	-6	0	-0.4
1937	Bro-N	0	1	.000	7	0	0	0	0	8^1	14	1	5	2	21.6	8.64	47	.378	.465	0	—	0	-4	-4	0	-0.4
	NY-N	1	0	1.000	13	0	0	0	0	31	30	0	16	11	13.4	4.06	96	.268	.359	2	.222	-0	-1	-1	-0	-0.1
	Yr	1	1	.500	20	0	0	0	0	39^1	44	1	21	13	14.9	5.03	78	.293	.380	2	.222	-0	-5	-5	-0	-0.5
1938	NY-N	0	0	—	2	0	0	0	0	4	5	0	3	0	18.0	6.75	56	.313	.421	0	—	0	-1	-1	0	-0.1
Total	4	3	9	.250	68	9	3	0	2	173	195	6	92	58	15.1	4.73	85	.288	.375	18	.310	5	-14	-13	-1	-0.9
● TOM BAKER Baker, Thomas Henry b: 5/6/34, Port Townsend, Wash. d: 3/9/80, Port Townsend, Wash BL/TL, 6', 195 lbs. Deb: 8/02/63																										
1963	Chi-N	0	1	.000	10	1	0	0	0	18	20	2	7	14	14.0	3.00	117	.282	.354	0	.000	-0	1	1	0	0.1
● MIKE BALAS Balas, Mitchell Francis (b: Mitchell Francis Balaski) b: 5/17/10, Lowell, Mass. BR/TR, 6', 195 lbs. Deb: 4/27/38																										
1938	Bos-N	0	0	—	1	0	0	0	0	1^1	3	0	0	0	20.3	6.75	51	.375	.375	0	—	0	-0	-0	-0	-0.1
● JACK BALDSCHUN Baldschun, Jack Edward b: 10/16/36, Greenville, O. BR/TR, 6', 190 lbs. Deb: 4/28/61																										
1961	Phi-N	5	3	.625	**65**	0	0	0	3	99^2	90	7	49	59	13.0	3.88	105	.243	.339	0	.000	-1	2	2	0	0.1
1962	Phi-N	12	7	.632	67	0	0	0	13	112^2	95	6	58	95	12.4	2.96	131	.231	.328	1	.063	-1	12	11	1	1.1
1963	Phi-N	11	7	.611	65	0	0	0	16	113^2	99	7	42	89	11.4	2.30	141	.232	.306	0	.000	-2	13	12	1	1.2
1964	Phi-N	6	9	.400	71	0	0	0	21	118^1	111	8	40	96	11.7	3.12	111	.246	.312	4	.250	1	6	5	1	0.8
1965	Phi-N	5	8	.385	65	0	0	0	6	99	102	4	42	81	13.5	3.82	91	.273	.352	0	.000	-1	-3	-4	1	-0.4
1966	Cin-N	1	5	.167	42	0	0	0	0	57^1	71	4	25	44	15.7	5.49	71	.318	.397	1	.333	0	-12	-10	0	-1.0
1967	Cin-N	0	0	—	9	0	0	0	0	13	15	0	9	12	16.6	4.15	90	.283	.387	0	.000	-0	-1	-1	-0	-0.1
1969	SD-N	7	2	.778	61	0	0	0	1	77	80	7	29	67	13.0	4.79	74	.264	.332	1	.250	0	-10	-11	-0	-1.1
1970	SD-N	1	0	1.000	12	0	0	0	0	13^1	24	2	4	12	18.9	10.13	39	.375	.412	0	—	0	-9	-9	-0	-0.9
Total	9	48	41	.539	457	0	0	0	60	704	687	45	298	555	12.9	3.69	98	.257	.336	7	.090	-3	-3	-5	4	-0.3
● LADY BALDWIN Baldwin, Charles Busted b: 4/8/1859, Ormel, N.Y. d: 3/7/37, Hastings, Mich. BL/TL, 5'11", 160 lbs. Deb: 9/30/1884 ♦																										
1884	Mil-U	1	1	.500	2	2	2	0	0	17	7	0	1	21	4.2	2.65	62	.117	.131	6	.222	1	1	-2	-0	-0.1
1885	Det-N	11	9	.550	21	20	19	1	1	179^1	137	2	28	135	**8.3**	1.86	153	**.197**	**.228**	30	.242	3	19	20	2	2.4
1886	Det-N	**42**	13	.764	56	56	55	**7**	0	487	371	11	100	**323**	**8.7**	2.24	148	**.202**	**.243**	41	.201	3	58	58	4	6.0
1887	*Det-N	13	10	.565	24	24	24	1	0	211	225	8	61	60	12.4	3.84	105	.269	.323	23	.271	3	6	5	1	0.7
1888	Det-N	3	3	.500	6	6	5	0	0	53	76	5	15	26	15.6	5.43	51	.322	.365	6	.261	2	-15	-16	-1	-1.3
1890	Bro-N	1	0	1.000	2	1	0	0	0	7^2	15	0	4	4	22.3	7.04	49	.398	.456	0	.000	-0	-3	-3	0	-0.2
	Buf-P	2	5	.286	7	7	7	0	0	62	90	5	24	13	17.0	4.50	91	.325	.385	8	.286	1	-2	-3	-0	-0.1
Total	6	73	41	.640	118	116	112	9	1	1017	921	31	233	582	10.3	2.85	118	.232	.276	114	.231	12	64	59	5	7.4

YEAR TM/L	W	L	PCT	G	GS	CG	SH	SV	IP	H	HR	BB	SO	RAT	ERA	ERA+	OAV	OOB	BH	AVG	PB	PR	/A	PD	TPI

● **KID BALDWIN**   Baldwin, Clarence Geoghan b: 11/1/1864, Newport, Ky. d: 7/12/1897, Cincinnati, Ohio BR/TR, 5'6", 147 lbs. Deb: 7/27/1884 ♦

| 1885 | Cin-a | 0 | 0 | — | 2 | 1 | 0 | 0 | 0 | 4 | 5 | 0 | 6 | 1 | 24.8 | 9.00 | 36 | .294 | .478 | 17 | .135 | -0 | -3 | -3 | 0 | -0.2 |

● **DAVE BALDWIN**   Baldwin, David George b: 3/30/38, Tucson, Ariz. BR/TR, 6'2", 200 lbs. Deb: 9/06/66

1966	Was-A	0	0	—	4	0	0	0	0	7	8	0	4	4	11.6	3.86	90	.267	.290	0	—	0	-0	-0	-0	-0.1
1967	Was-A	2	4	.333	58	0	0	0	12	68²	53	2	20	52	10.1	1.70	186	.215	.285	0	.000	-0	12	11	1	1.3
1968	Was-A	0	2	.000	40	0	0	0	5	42	40	7	12	30	11.1	4.07	72	.260	.313	0	.000	-0	-5	-5	1	-0.5
1969	Was-A	2	4	.333	43	0	0	0	4	66²	57	4	34	51	13.0	4.05	86	.236	.342	0	.000	-1	-3	-4	-0	-0.6
1970	Mil-A	2	1	.667	28	0	0	0	1	35¹	25	4	18	26	11.0	2.55	149	.205	.307	1	.500	0	5	5	2	0.8
1973	Chi-A	0	0	—	3	0	0	0	0	5	7	0	4	1	19.8	3.60	110	.368	.478	0	—	0	0	0	0	0.0
Total	6	6	11	.353	176	0	0	0	22	224²	190	17	89	164	11.5	3.08	108	.234	.316	1	.067	-1	8	6	4	0.9

● **HARRY BALDWIN**   Baldwin, Howard Edward b: 6/3/1900, Baltimore, Md. d: 1/23/58, Baltimore, Md. BR/TR, 5'11", 160 lbs. Deb: 5/04/24

1924	*NY-N	3	1	.750	10	2	1	0	0	33²	42	5	11	5	14.2	4.28	86	.309	.361	4	.364	1	-2	-2	-0	-0.2
1925	NY-N	0	0	—	1	0	0	0	0	1	3	0	1	0	36.0	9.00	45	.500	.571	0	—	0	-1	-1	-0	-0.1
Total	2	3	1	.750	11	2	1	0	0	34²	45	5	12	5	14.8	4.41	83	.317	.370	4	.364	1	-2	-3	-0	-0.3

● **MARK BALDWIN**   Baldwin, Marcus Elmore "Fido" b: 10/29/1863, Pittsburgh, Pa. d: 11/10/29, Pittsburgh, Pa. BR/TR, 6', 190 lbs. Deb: 5/02/1887

1887	Chi-N	18	17	.514	40	39	35	1	1	334	329	23	122	164	12.6	3.40	132	.248	.319	26	.187	-4	25	41	-3	2.8
1888	Chi-N	13	15	.464	30	30	27	2	0	251	241	13	99	157	12.7	2.76	110	.249	.327	16	.151	-1	2	7	2	0.8
1889	Col-a	27	34	.443	63	59	54	6	1	513²	458	9	274	368	13.2	3.61	100	.231	.331	39	.188	1	14	1	1	0.2
1890	Chi-P	34	24	.586	59	57	54	1	0	501	498	10	249	211	13.7	3.31	131	.248	.336	45	.209	-1	52	58	4	5.0
1891	Pit-N	22	28	.440	53	50	48	2	0	437²	385	10	227	197	13.1	2.76	119	.227	.327	29	.153	-3	29	26	1	2.1
1892	Pit-N	26	27	.491	56	53	45	0	0	440¹	447	11	194	157	13.6	3.47	95	.253	.334	18	.101	-12	-9	-9	-2	-2.0
1893	Pit-N	0	0	—	1	1	0	0	0	2¹	6	0	1	0	27.0	11.57	39	.465	.503	0	.000	-0	-2	-2	-0	-0.2
	NY-N	16	20	.444	45	39	33	2	2	331¹	335	6	141	100	13.3	4.10	114	.255	.332	17	.127	-10	21	20	-3	0.6
	Yr	16	20	.444	46	40	33	2	2	333²	341	6	142	100	13.4	4.15	112	.257	.334	17	.126	-10	19	19	-3	0.4
Total	7	156	165	.486	347	328	296	14	4	2811¹	2699	82	1307	1354	13.2	3.36	114	.244	.330	188	.162	-30	132	142	0	9.3

● **O. F. BALDWIN**   Baldwin, Orson F. b: 11/3/1881, Carson City, Mich. d: 2/16/42, Los Angeles, Cal. TR, 185 lbs. Deb: 9/06/08

| 1908 | StL-N | 1 | 3 | .250 | 4 | 4 | 0 | 0 | 0 | 14² | 16 | 0 | 11 | 5 | 18.4 | 6.14 | 38 | .302 | .448 | 0 | .000 | -1 | -6 | -6 | -0 | -0.7 |

● **RICK BALDWIN**   Baldwin, Rickey Alan b: 6/1/53, Fresno, Cal. BL/TR, 6'3", 180 lbs. Deb: 4/10/75

1975	NY-N	3	5	.375	54	0	0	0	6	97¹	97	4	34	54	12.5	3.33	104	.263	.332	3	.200	0	3	1	1	0.2
1976	NY-N	0	0	—	11	0	0	0	0	22²	14	0	10	9	10.3	2.38	138	.189	.302	1	.333	0	3	2	0	0.3
1977	NY-N	1	2	.333	40	0	0	0	1	62²	62	6	31	23	14.1	4.45	84	.265	.363	2	.500	1	-4	-5	1	-0.3
Total	3	4	7	.364	105	0	0	0	7	182²	173	10	75	86	12.8	3.60	98	.256	.339	6	.273	1	2	-1	1	0.2

● **JEFF BALLARD**   Ballard, Jeffrey Scott b: 8/13/63, Billings, Mont. BL/TL, 6'2", 198 lbs. Deb: 5/09/87

1987	Bal-A	2	8	.200	14	14	0	0	0	69²	100	15	35	27	17.4	6.59	67	.344	.414	0	—	0	-17	-17	0	-1.4
1988	Bal-A	8	12	.400	25	25	6	1	0	153¹	167	15	42	41	12.6	4.40	89	.278	.332	0	—	0	-7	-9	-2	-0.9
1989	Bal-A	18	8	.692	35	35	4	1	0	215¹	240	16	57	62	12.6	3.43	111	.287	.336	0	—	0	11	9	4	1.5
1990	Bal-A	2	11	.154	44	17	0	0	0	133¹	152	22	42	50	13.3	4.93	77	.289	.345	0	—	0	-15	-17	-1	-1.5
1991	Bal-A	6	12	.333	26	22	0	0	0	123²	153	16	28	37	13.3	5.60	71	.302	.341	0	—	0	-21	-23	-1	-2.0
Total	5	36	51	.414	144	113	10	2	0	695¹	812	84	204	217	13.3	4.63	84	.294	.346	0	—	0	-49	-56	1	-4.3

● **JAY BALLER**   Baller, Jay Scot b: 10/6/60, Stayton, Ohio BR/TR, 6'7", 225 lbs. Deb: 9/19/82

1982	Phi-N	0	0	—	4	1	0	0	0	8	7	1	2	7	11.3	3.38	109	.226	.294	0	—	0	0	0	-0	0.1
1985	Chi-N	2	3	.400	20	4	0	0	1	52	52	8	17	31	12.1	3.46	115	.260	.321	0	.000	-1	1	3	-0	0.2
1986	Chi-N	2	4	.333	36	0	0	0	5	53²	58	7	28	42	14.8	5.37	75	.275	.365	0	.000	-1	-10	-8	-1	-1.0
1987	Chi-N	0	1	.000	23	0	0	0	0	29¹	38	4	20	27	17.8	6.75	63	.325	.423	1	1.000	0	-9	-8	-0	-0.8
1990	KC-A	0	1	.000	3	0	0	0	0	2¹	4	1	2	1	27.0	15.43	43	.364	.500	0	—	0	-3	-3	-0	-0.2
1992	Phi-N	0	0	—	8	0	0	0	0	11	10	5	10	9	16.4	8.18	43	.250	.400	0	—	0	-6	-6	-0	-0.6
Total	6	4	9	.308	94	5	0	0	6	156¹	169	26	79	117	14.6	5.24	77	.277	.365	1	.071	-1	-26	-21	-2	-2.3

● **MARK BALLINGER**   Ballinger, Mark Alan b: 1/31/49, Glendale, Cal. BR/TR, 6'6", 205 lbs. Deb: 8/06/71

| 1971 | Cle-A | 1 | 2 | .333 | 18 | 0 | 0 | 0 | 0 | 34² | 30 | 3 | 13 | 25 | 11.4 | 4.67 | 82 | .233 | .308 | 1 | .200 | -0 | -5 | -3 | -0 | -0.4 |

● **WIN BALLOU**   Ballou, Noble Winfield b: 11/30/1897, Mount Morgan, Ky. d: 1/30/63, San Francisco, Cal BR/TL, 5'10.5", 170 lbs. Deb: 8/24/25

1925	*Was-A	1	1	.500	10	1	1	0	0	27²	38	1	13	13	16.6	4.55	93	.342	.411	1	.143	-0	-0	-1	0	-0.1
1926	StL-A	11	10	.524	43	14	5	0	2	154	186	12	71	59	15.3	4.79	90	.311	.387	2	.048	-3	-13	-9	3	-0.8
1927	StL-A	5	6	.455	21	11	4	0	0	90¹	105	4	46	17	15.1	4.78	91	.309	.393	1	.036	-4	-6	-4	-0	-0.8
1929	Bro-N	2	3	.400	25	1	0	0	0	57²	69	5	38	20	16.7	6.71	69	.304	.404	1	.063	-2	-13	-13	2	-1.2
Total	4	19	20	.487	99	27	10	0	2	329²	398	22	168	109	15.6	5.11	86	.312	.394	5	.054	-9	-33	-27	5	-2.9

● **TONY BALSAMO**   Balsamo, Anthony Fred b: 11/21/37, Brooklyn, N.Y. BR/TR, 6'2", 185 lbs. Deb: 4/14/62

| 1962 | Chi-N | 0 | 1 | .000 | 18 | 0 | 0 | 0 | 0 | 29¹ | 34 | 1 | 20 | 27 | 16.9 | 6.44 | 64 | .293 | .401 | 1 | .200 | -0 | -8 | -7 | 1 | -0.6 |

● **GEORGE BAMBERGER**   Bamberger, George Irvin b: 8/1/25, Staten Island, N.Y. BR/TR, 6', 175 lbs. Deb: 4/19/51 MC

1951	NY-N	0	0	—	2	0	0	0	0	2	4	2	2	1	27.0	18.00	22	.444	.545	0	—	0	-3	-3	-0	-0.3
1952	NY-N	0	0	—	5	0	0	0	0	4	6	1	6	0	27.0	9.00	41	.353	.522	0	—	0	-2	-2	-0	-0.2
1959	Bal-A	0	0	—	3	1	0	0	1	8¹	15	1	2	2	18.4	7.56	50	.405	.436	0	.000	-0	-3	-3	-0	-0.3
Total	3	0	0	—	10	1	0	0	1	14¹	25	4	10	3	22.0	9.42	40	.397	.479	0	.000	-0	-9	-9	-0	-0.8

● **SAL BANDO**   Bando, Salvatore Leonard b: 2/13/44, Cleveland, O. BR/TR, 6', 205 lbs. Deb: 9/03/66 FC♦

| 1979 | Mil-A | 0 | 0 | — | 1 | 0 | 0 | 0 | 0 | 3 | 3 | 0 | 0 | 0 | 9.0 | 6.00 | 69 | .231 | .231 | 117 | .246 | 1 | -1 | -1 | -0 | -0.1 |

● **EDDIE BANE**   Bane, Edward Norman b: 3/22/52, Chicago, Ill. BR/TL, 5'9", 160 lbs. Deb: 7/04/73

1973	Min-A	0	5	.000	23	6	0	0	2	60¹	62	5	40	42	14.0	4.92	80	.270	.359	0	—	0	-7	-6	1	-0.8
1975	Min-A	3	1	.750	4	4	0	0	0	28¹	28	2	15	14	14.0	2.86	135	.262	.358	0	—	0	3	3	-1	0.1
1976	Min-A	4	7	.364	17	15	1	0	0	79¹	92	6	39	24	14.9	5.11	71	.290	.368	0	—	0	-14	-13	-2	-1.7
Total	3	7	13	.350	44	25	1	0	2	168	182	13	84	80	14.4	4.66	81	.278	.363	0	—	0	-19	-17	-1	-2.4

● **DICK BANEY**   Baney, Richard Lee b: 11/1/46, Fullerton, Cal. BR/TR, 6', 185 lbs. Deb: 7/11/69

1969	Sea-A	1	0	1.000	9	1	0	0	0	18²	21	2	7	9	13.5	3.86	94	.292	.354	0	.000	-0	-0	-0	-0	-0.1
1973	Cin-N	2	1	.667	11	1	0	0	2	30²	26	1	6	17	10.6	2.93	116	.234	.298	2	.222	1	2	2	-1	0.1
1974	Cin-N	1	0	1.000	22	1	0	0	1	41	51	4	17	12	14.9	5.49	64	.305	.370	0	.000	-1	-9	-9	-1	-1.1
Total	3	4	1	.800	42	3	0	0	3	90¹	98	7	30	38	13.2	4.28	81	.280	.344	2	.125	-0	-7	-8	-3	-1.1

● **DAN BANKHEAD**   Bankhead, Daniel Robert b: 5/3/20, Empire, Ala. d: 5/2/76, Houston, Tex. BR/TR, 6'1", 184 lbs. Deb: 8/26/47

1947	*Bro-N	0	0	—	4	0	0	0	1	10	15	1	8	6	21.6	7.20	57	.341	.453	1	.250	1	-3	-3	-0	-0.2
1950	Bro-N	9	4	.692	41	12	2	1	3	129¹	119	16	88	96	14.5	5.50	75	.252	.371	9	.231	1	-19	-20	-1	-1.9
1951	Bro-N	0	1	.000	7	1	0	0	0	14	27	5	14	9	26.4	15.43	25	.422	.526	0	.000	-0	-18	-18	-0	-1.6
Total	3	9	5	.643	52	13	2	1	4	153¹	161	22	110	111	16.1	6.52	63	.277	.395	10	.222	2	-41	-41	-1	-3.7

● SCOTT BANKHEAD Bankhead, Michael Scott b: 7/31/63, Raleigh, N.C. BR/TR, 5'10", 175 lbs. Deb: 5/25/86

YEAR	TM/L	W	L	PCT	G	GS	CG	SH	SV	IP	H	HR	BB	SO	RAT	ERA	ERA+	OAV	OOB	BH	AVG	PB	PR	/A	PD	TPI
1986	KC-A	8	9	.471	24	17	0	0	0	121	121	14	37	94	12.0	4.61	92	.259	.318	0	—	0	-6	-5	-0	-0.6
1987	Sea-A	9	8	.529	27	25	2	0	0	149^1	168	35	37	95	12.5	5.42	87	.283	.329	0	—	0	-16	-12	-2	-1.4
1988	Sea-A	7	9	.438	21	21	2	1	0	135	115	8	38	102	10.3	3.07	136	.224	.278	0	—	0	13	16	-1	1.6
1989	Sea-A	14	6	.700	33	33	3	2	0	210^1	187	19	63	140	10.8	3.34	121	.239	.298	0	—	0	13	16	-2	1.5
1990	Sea-A	0	2	.000	4	4	0	0	0	13	18	2	7	10	17.3	11.08	36	.333	.410	0	—	0	-10	-10	-0	-1.0
1991	Sea-A	3	6	.333	17	9	0	0	0	60^2	73	8	21	28	14.2	4.90	84	.297	.357	0	—	0	-5	-5	-0	-0.5
1992	Cin-N	10	4	.714	54	0	0	0	1	70^2	57	4	29	53	11.3	2.93	125	.218	.304	2	.222	0	5	6	-2	0.5
Total	7	51	44	.537	180	109	7	3	1	760	739	90	232	522	11.7	4.12	102	.253	.311	2	.222	0	-7	6	-8	0.1

● BILL BANKS Banks, William John (b: William John Yerrick) b: 2/26/1874, Danville, Pa. d: 9/8/36, Danville, Pa. BR/TR, 5'11", 150 lbs. Deb: 9/27/1895

YEAR	TM/L	W	L	PCT	G	GS	CG	SH	SV	IP	H	HR	BB	SO	RAT	ERA	ERA+	OAV	OOB	BH	AVG	PB	PR	/A	PD	TPI
1895	Bos-N	1	0	1.000	1	1	1	0	0	7	7	0	4	4	14.1	0.00	—	.256	.352	0	.000	-1	4	4	0	0.3
1896	Bos-N	0	3	.000	4	3	2	0	0	23	42	2	13	6	22.3	10.57	43	.389	.463	3	.273	0	-16	-15	-1	-1.2
Total	2	1	3	.250	5	4	3	0	0	30	49	2	17	10	20.4	8.10	58	.362	.441	3	.214	-1	-12	-11	-1	-0.9

● WILLIE BANKS Banks, Willie Anthony b: 2/27/69, Jersey City, N.J. BR/TR, 6'1", 190 lbs. Deb: 7/31/91

YEAR	TM/L	W	L	PCT	G	GS	CG	SH	SV	IP	H	HR	BB	SO	RAT	ERA	ERA+	OAV	OOB	BH	AVG	PB	PR	/A	PD	TPI
1991	Min-A	1	1	.500	5	3	0	0	0	17^1	21	1	12	16	17.1	5.71	75	.288	.388	0	—	0	-3	-3	-1	-0.6
1992	Min-A	4	4	.500	16	12	0	0	0	71	80	6	37	37	15.1	5.70	71	.288	.375	0	—	0	-14	-13	-0	-1.5
Total	2	5	5	.500	21	15	0	0	0	88^1	101	7	49	53	15.5	5.71	71	.288	.378	0	—	0	-17	-16	-1	-2.1

● FLOYD BANNISTER Bannister, Floyd Franklin b: 6/10/55, Pierre, S.D. BL/TL, 6'1", 195 lbs. Deb: 4/19/77

YEAR	TM/L	W	L	PCT	G	GS	CG	SH	SV	IP	H	HR	BB	SO	RAT	ERA	ERA+	OAV	OOB	BH	AVG	PB	PR	/A	PD	TPI
1977	Hou-N	8	9	.471	24	23	4	1	0	142^2	138	11	68	112	13.2	4.04	88	.254	.341	9	.188	0	-2	-7	-1	-0.8
1978	Hou-N	3	9	.250	28	16	2	2	0	110^1	120	13	63	94	15.0	4.81	69	.280	.374	5	.161	0	-15	-18	-2	-2.0
1979	Sea-A	10	15	.400	30	30	6	2	0	182^1	185	25	68	115	12.7	4.05	108	.260	.328	0	—	0	3	6	-2	0.3
1980	Sea-A	9	13	.409	32	32	8	0	0	217^2	200	24	66	155	11.1	3.47	119	.239	.296	0	—	0	14	16	-1	1.5
1981	Sea-A	9	9	.500	21	20	5	2	0	121^1	128	14	39	85	12.6	4.45	87	.268	.327	0	—	0	-11	-8	-1	-1.0
1982	Sea-A★	12	13	.480	35	35	5	3	0	247	225	32	77	**209**	11.1	3.43	124	.243	.303	0	—	0	18	22	-1	2.1
1983	•Chi-A	16	10	.615	34	34	5	2	0	217^1	191	19	71	193	10.9	3.35	125	.233	.295	0	—	0	17	20	-1	1.8
1984	Chi-A	14	11	.560	34	33	4	0	0	218	211	30	80	152	12.3	4.83	86	.252	.322	0	.000	0	-20	-16	-2	-1.8
1985	Chi-A	10	14	.417	34	34	4	1	0	210^2	211	30	100	198	13.5	4.87	89	.261	.346	0	—	0	-17	-13	-1	-1.4
1986	Chi-A	10	14	.417	28	27	6	1	0	165^1	162	17	48	92	11.5	3.54	122	.259	.314	0	—	0	12	14	-1	1.2
1987	Chi-A	16	11	.593	34	34	11	2	0	228^2	216	38	49	124	10.4	3.58	128	.246	.286	0	—	0	22	25	-3	2.2
1988	KC-A	12	13	.480	31	31	2	0	0	189^1	182	22	68	113	12.1	4.33	92	.248	.316	0	—	0	-8	-7	-0	-0.7
1989	KC-A	4	1	.800	14	14	0	0	0	75^1	87	8	18	35	12.7	4.66	83	.290	.332	0	—	0	-7	-7	1	-0.6
1991	Cal-A	0	0	—	16	0	0	0	0	25	25	5	10	16	12.6	3.96	104	.266	.337	0	—	0	0	0	-1	0.0
1992	Tex-A	1	1	.500	36	0	0	0	0	37	39	3	21	30	15.3	6.32	60	.281	.387	0	—	0	-10	-10	0	-0.8
Total	15	134	143	.484	431	363	62	16	0	2388	2320	291	846	1723	12.1	4.06	102	.253	.319	14	.175	1	-3	16	-15	-0.0

● JIMMY BANNON Bannon, James Henry "Foxy Grandpa" b: 5/5/1871, Amesbury, Mass. d: 3/24/48, Glen Rock, N.J. BR/TR, 5'5", 160 lbs. Deb: 6/15/1893 F♦

YEAR	TM/L	W	L	PCT	G	GS	CG	SH	SV	IP	H	HR	BB	SO	RAT	ERA	ERA+	OAV	OOB	BH	AVG	PB	PR	/A	PD	TPI
1893	StL-N	0	1	.000	1	1	0	0	0	4	10	1	5	1	38.3	22.50	21	.458	.590	36	.336	0	-8	-8	-0	-0.5
1894	Bos-N	0	0	—	1	0	0	0	0	2	4	1	1	0	22.5	0.00	—	.410	.465	166	.336	0	1	1	0	0.1
1895	Bos-N	0	0	—	1	0	0	0	0	3	4	0	2	1	18.0	6.00	85	.315	.408	171	.350	0	-0	-0	0	0.0
Total	3	0	1	.000	3	1	0	0	0	9	18	2	8	2	28.0	12.00	42	.406	.516	459	.320	1	-7	-7	-0	-0.4

● JACK BANTA Banta, John Kay b: 6/24/25, Hutchinson, Kan. BL/TR, 6'2.5", 175 lbs. Deb: 9/18/47

YEAR	TM/L	W	L	PCT	G	GS	CG	SH	SV	IP	H	HR	BB	SO	RAT	ERA	ERA+	OAV	OOB	BH	AVG	PB	PR	/A	PD	TPI
1947	Bro-N	0	1	.000	3	1	0	0	0	7^2	7	1	4	3	14.1	7.04	59	.226	.333	0	.000	-0	-3	-2	1	-0.2
1948	Bro-N	0	1	.000	2	1	0	0	0	3^1	5	0	5	1	27.0	8.10	49	.385	.556	0	.000	-0	-2	-2	-0	-0.2
1949	•Bro-N	10	6	.625	48	12	2	1	3	152^1	125	12	68	97	11.8	3.37	122	.223	.314	5	.109	-2	11	12	1	1.1
1950	Bro-N	4	4	.500	16	5	1	0	2	41^1	39	2	36	15	17.0	4.35	94	.252	.402	2	.167	-0	-1	-1	-1	-0.2
Total	4	14	12	.538	69	19	3	1	5	204^2	176	15	113	116	13.1	3.78	108	.232	.339	7	.115	-2	6	7	0	0.5

● STEVE BARBER Barber, Stephen David b: 2/22/39, Takoma Park, Md. BL/TL, 6', 200 lbs. Deb: 4/21/60

YEAR	TM/L	W	L	PCT	G	GS	CG	SH	SV	IP	H	HR	BB	SO	RAT	ERA	ERA+	OAV	OOB	BH	AVG	PB	PR	/A	PD	TPI
1960	Bal-A	10	7	.588	36	27	6	1	2	181^2	148	10	113	112	13.1	3.22	118	.226	.343	3	.056	-3	13	12	0	0.9
1961	Bal-A	18	12	.600	37	34	14	**8**	1	248^1	194	13	130	150	11.8	3.33	117	.218	.319	13	.162	2	19	16	4	2.2
1962	Bal-A	9	6	.600	28	19	5	2	0	140^1	145	9	61	89	13.3	3.46	109	.262	.337	3	.071	-2	8	5	1	0.4
1963	Bal-A†	20	13	.606	39	36	11	2	0	258^2	253	12	92	180	12.1	2.75	128	.258	.324	12	.138	-0	25	22	2	2.6
1964	Bal-A	9	13	.409	36	26	4	0	1	157	144	15	81	118	13.3	3.84	93	.248	.347	7	.149	1	-4	-5	3	-0.2
1965	Bal-A	15	10	.600	37	32	7	2	0	220^2	177	16	81	130	10.6	2.69	129	.224	.297	5	.077	-2	19	19	1	2.0
1966	Bal-A☆	10	5	.667	25	22	5	3	0	133^1	104	6	49	91	10.5	2.30	145	.218	.294	3	.068	-3	17	15	1	1.5
1967	Bal-A	4	9	.308	15	15	1	1	0	74^2	47	5	61	48	13.6	4.10	77	.185	.353	2	.091	-1	-7	-8	0	-0.9
	NY-A	6	9	.400	17	17	3	1	0	97^2	103	4	54	70	14.7	4.05	77	.278	.375	5	.172	1	-9	-10	-1	-1.0
	Yr	10	18	.357	32	32	4	2	0	172^1	150	9	115	118	14.0	4.07	77	.238	.358	7	.137	1	-16	-18	-1	-1.9
1968	NY-A	6	5	.545	20	19	3	1	0	128^1	127	7	64	87	13.6	3.23	90	.256	.345	2	.051	-1	-4	-5	0	-0.6
1969	Sea-A	4	7	.364	25	16	0	0	0	86^1	99	9	48	69	15.4	4.80	76	.292	.381	5	.200	1	-11	-11	0	-1.0
1970	Chi-N	0	1	.000	5	0	0	0	0	5^2	10	0	6	3	25.4	9.53	47	.417	.533	0	—	0	-3	-3	-0	-0.3
	Atl-N	0	1	.000	5	2	0	0	0	14^2	17	3	5	11	14.1	4.91	87	.288	.354	1	.250	0	-1	-1	-0	-0.1
	Yr	0	2	.000	10	2	0	0	0	20^1	27	3	11	14	17.3	6.20	70	.325	.411	1	.250	0	-5	-4	-0	-0.4
1971	Atl-N	3	1	.750	39	3	0	0	2	75	92	6	25	40	14.3	4.80	77	.301	.357	2	.154	-0	-11	-9	0	-1.0
1972	Atl-N	0	0	—	5	0	0	0	0	15^2	18	1	6	6	14.4	5.74	66	.290	.362	1	.200	-0	-4	-3	1	-0.3
	Cal-A	4	4	.500	34	3	0	0	2	58	37	4	30	34	10.6	2.02	144	.188	.298	1	.143	1	7	6	-1	0.7
1973	Cal-A	3	2	.600	50	1	0	0	4	89^1	90	5	32	58	12.6	3.53	101	.265	.333	0	—	0	3	0	-1	0.6
1974	SF-N	0	1	.000	13	0	0	0	1	13^2	13	0	12	13	16.5	5.27	72	.255	.397	0	—	0	-3	-2	-1	-0.3
Total	15	121	106	.533	466	272	59	21	13	1999	1818	125	950	1309	12.7	3.36	105	.245	.334	65	.115	-6	54	38	10	5.2

● STEVE BARBER Barber, Steven Lee b: 3/13/48, Grand Rapids, Mich. BR/TR, 6'1", 190 lbs. Deb: 4/09/70

YEAR	TM/L	W	L	PCT	G	GS	CG	SH	SV	IP	H	HR	BB	SO	RAT	ERA	ERA+	OAV	OOB	BH	AVG	PB	PR	/A	PD	TPI
1970	Min-A	0	0	—	18	0	0	0	2	27^1	26	1	18	14	15.1	4.61	81	.263	.387	0	.000	-0	-3	-3	-0	-0.3
1971	Min-A	1	0	1.000	4	2	0	0	0	11^2	8	2	13	4	16.2	6.17	58	.190	.382	0	.000	-1	-4	-3	-0	-0.4
Total	2	1	0	1.000	22	2	0	0	2	39	34	3	31	18	15.5	5.08	72	.241	.385	0	.000	-1	-6	-6	-1	-0.7

● FRANK BARBERICH Barberich, Frank Frederick b: 2/3/1882, New Town, N.Y. d: 5/1/65, Ocala, Fla. BB/TR, 5'10.5", 175 lbs. Deb: 9/17/07

YEAR	TM/L	W	L	PCT	G	GS	CG	SH	SV	IP	H	HR	BB	SO	RAT	ERA	ERA+	OAV	OOB	BH	AVG	PB	PR	/A	PD	TPI
1907	Bos-N	1	1	.500	2	2	1	0	0	12^1	19	0	5	1	17.5	5.84	44	.358	.414	0	.000	-1	-5	-5	0	-0.5
1910	Bos-A	0	0	—	2	0	0	0	0	5	7	0	2	0	16.2	7.20	35	.350	.409	0	.000	-0	-3	-3	0	-0.3
Total	2	1	1	.500	4	2	1	0	0	17^1	26	0	7	1	17.1	6.23	41	.356	.412	0	.000	-1	-7	-7	0	-0.8

● CURT BARCLAY Barclay, Curtis Cordell b: 8/22/31, Chicago, Ill. d: 3/25/85, Missoula, Montana BR/TR, 6'3", 210 lbs. Deb: 4/21/57

YEAR	TM/L	W	L	PCT	G	GS	CG	SH	SV	IP	H	HR	BB	SO	RAT	ERA	ERA+	OAV	OOB	BH	AVG	PB	PR	/A	PD	TPI
1957	NY-N	9	9	.500	37	28	5	2	0	183	196	21	48	67	12.1	3.44	114	.274	.321	11	.190	0	9	10	3	1.3
1958	SF-N	1	0	1.000	6	1	0	0	0	16	16	3	5	6	13.5	2.81	136	.258	.343	4	.667	2	2	2	0	0.4
1959	SF-N	0	0	—	1	0	0	0	0	0^1	2	0	2	0	108.0	54.00	7	.500	.667	0	—	0	-2	-2	-0	-0.2
Total	3	10	9	.526	44	29	5	2	0	199^1	214	24	55	73	12.4	3.48	113	.274	.325	15	.234	2	9	10	3	1.5

● RAY BARE Bare, Raymond Douglas b: 4/15/49, Miami, Fla. BR/TR, 6'2", 195 lbs. Deb: 7/30/72

YEAR	TM/L	W	L	PCT	G	GS	CG	SH	SV	IP	H	HR	BB	SO	RAT	ERA	ERA+	OAV	OOB	BH	AVG	PB	PR	/A	PD	TPI
1972	StL-N	0	1	.000	14	0	0	0	1	16^2	18	0	6	5	13.0	0.54	630	.281	.343	0	—	0	5	5	-0	0.5
1974	StL-N	1	2	.333	10	3	0	0	0	24^1	25	2	9	6	12.6	5.92	60	.281	.347	1	.200	-0	-6	-6	1	-0.6
1975	Det-A	8	13	.381	29	21	6	1	0	150^2	174	10	47	71	13.3	4.48	90	.293	.346	0	—	0	-12	-8	2	-1.0
1976	Det-A	7	8	.467	30	21	3	2	0	134	157	13	51	59	14.0	4.63	80	.293	.354	0	—	0	-17	-14	1	-1.4

YEAR	TM/L	W	L	PCT	G	GS	CG	SH	SV	IP	H	HR	BB	SO	RAT	ERA	ERA+	OAV	OOB	BH	AVG	PB	PR	/A	PD	TPI
1977	Det-A	0	2	.000	5	4	0	0	0	14^1	24	3	7	4	19.5	12.56	34	.381	.443	0	—	0	-14	-13	1	-1.4
Total	5	16	26	.381	88	49	9	3	1	340	398	28	120	145	13.7	4.79	80	.296	.354	1	.200	-0	-43	-36	4	-3.9

● **JOHN BARFIELD** Barfield, John David b: 10/15/64, Pine Bluff, Ark. BL/TL, 6'1", 185 lbs. Deb: 9/07/89

YEAR	TM/L	W	L	PCT	G	GS	CG	SH	SV	IP	H	HR	BB	SO	RAT	ERA	ERA+	OAV	OOB	BH	AVG	PB	PR	/A	PD	TPI
1989	Tex-A	0	1	.000	4	2	0	0	0	11^2	15	0	4	9	14.7	6.17	64	.319	.373	0	—	0	-3	-3	-0	-0.4
1990	Tex-A	4	3	.571	33	0	0	0	1	44^1	42	2	13	17	11.4	4.67	84	.268	.327	0	—	0	-4	-4	0	-0.4
1991	Tex-A	4	4	.500	28	9	0	0	1	83^1	96	11	22	27	12.7	4.54	89	.289	.333	0	—	0	-4	-5	-0	-0.4
Total	3	8	8	.500	65	11	0	0	2	139^1	153	13	39	53	12.5	4.72	85	.285	.335	0	—	0	-11	-11	-0	-1.2

● **CLYDE BARFOOT** Barfoot, Clyde Raymond "Foots" b: 7/8/1891, Richmond, Va. d: 3/11/71, Highland Park, Cal BR/TR, 6', 170 lbs. Deb: 4/13/22

YEAR	TM/L	W	L	PCT	G	GS	CG	SH	SV	IP	H	HR	BB	SO	RAT	ERA	ERA+	OAV	OOB	BH	AVG	PB	PR	/A	PD	TPI
1922	StL-N	4	5	.444	42	2	1	0	2	117^2	139	2	30	19	13.7	4.21	92	.307	.363	12	.353	5	-1	-4	1	0.1
1923	StL-N	3	3	.500	33	2	1	1	1	101^1	112	7	27	23	12.4	3.73	105	.289	.337	7	.189	-1	3	2	0	0.1
1926	Det-A	1	2	.333	11	1	0	0	2	31^1	42	4	9	7	14.6	4.88	83	.318	.362	1	.200	0	-3	-3	1	-0.2
Total	3	8	10	.444	86	5	2	1	5	250^1	293	13	66	49	13.3	4.10	95	.301	.353	20	.263	4	-1	-5	1	0.0

● **GREG BARGAR** Bargar, Greg Robert b: 1/27/59, Inglewood, Cal. BR/TR, 6'2", 185 lbs. Deb: 7/17/83

YEAR	TM/L	W	L	PCT	G	GS	CG	SH	SV	IP	H	HR	BB	SO	RAT	ERA	ERA+	OAV	OOB	BH	AVG	PB	PR	/A	PD	TPI
1983	Mon-N	2	0	1.000	8	3	0	0	0	20	23	6	8	9	14.4	6.75	53	.271	.340	1	.167	-0	-7	-7	-1	-0.7
1984	Mon-N	0	1	.000	3	1	0	0	0	8	8	1	7	2	16.9	7.88	43	.286	.429	0	.000	-0	-4	-4	0	-0.4
1986	StL-N	0	2	.000	22	0	0	0	0	27^1	36	3	10	12	16.1	5.60	65	.330	.402	0	.000	-0	-6	-6	1	-0.6
Total	3	2	3	.400	33	4	0	0	0	55^1	67	10	25	23	15.6	6.34	57	.302	.382	1	.111	-0	-16	-17	0	-1.7

● **CY BARGER** Barger, Eros Bolivar b: 5/18/1885, Jamestown, Ky. d: 9/23/64, Columbia, Ky. BL/TR, 6', 160 lbs. Deb: 8/30/06

YEAR	TM/L	W	L	PCT	G	GS	CG	SH	SV	IP	H	HR	BB	SO	RAT	ERA	ERA+	OAV	OOB	BH	AVG	PB	PR	/A	PD	TPI
1906	NY-A	0	0	—	2	1	0	0	1	5^1	7	0	3	3	16.9	10.13	29	.319	.401	1	.333	0	-4	-4	-0	-0.4
1907	NY-A	0	0	—	1	0	0	0	0	6	10	0	1	0	18.0	3.00	93	.372	.415	0	.000	-0	-0	-0	-1	-0.1
1910	Bro-N	15	15	.500	35	30	25	2	1	271^2	267	2	107	87	12.6	2.88	105	.275	.351	24	.231	3	5	5	2	1.0
1911	Bro-N	11	15	.423	30	30	21	1	0	217^1	224	4	71	60	12.5	3.52	95	.279	.342	33	.228	1	-3	-4	1	-0.2
1912	Bro-N	1	9	.100	16	11	6	0	0	94	120	4	42	30	15.9	5.46	61	.326	.401	7	.189	-0	-21	-22	1	-2.0
1914	Pit-F	10	16	.385	33	26	18	1	1	228^1	252	7	63	70	12.7	4.34	73	.290	.342	17	.205	0	-29	-29	-2	-3.1
1915	Pit-F	9	8	.529	34	13	8	1	6	153	130	1	47	47	10.6	2.29	131	.238	.303	15	.278	2	13	12	-1	1.5
Total	7	46	63	.422	151	111	78	5	9	975^2	1010	18	334	297	12.7	3.56	89	.280	.346	97	.227	7	-40	-43	-0	-3.3

● **LEN BARKER** Barker, Leonard Harold b: 7/7/55, Fort Knox, Ky. BR/TR, 6'5", 225 lbs. Deb: 9/14/76

YEAR	TM/L	W	L	PCT	G	GS	CG	SH	SV	IP	H	HR	BB	SO	RAT	ERA	ERA+	OAV	OOB	BH	AVG	PB	PR	/A	PD	TPI
1976	Tex-A	1	0	1.000	2	2	1	1	0	15	7	0	6	7	9.0	2.40	149	.149	.273	0	—	0	2	2	-0	0.2
1977	Tex-A	4	1	.800	15	3	0	0	1	47^1	36	1	24	51	11.6	2.66	153	.217	.319	0	—	0	7	7	1	0.8
1978	Tex-A	1	5	.167	29	0	0	0	4	52^1	63	6	29	33	16.2	4.82	78	.304	.395	0	—	0	-6	-6	0	-0.6
1979	Cle-A	6	6	.500	29	19	2	0	0	137^1	146	6	70	93	14.3	4.92	87	.277	.364	0	—	0	-11	-10	-1	-1.1
1980	Cle-A	19	12	.613	36	36	8	1	0	246^1	237	17	92	**187**	12.1	4.17	98	.252	.320	0	—	0	-4	-3	-2	-0.4
1981	Cle-A★	8	7	.533	22	22	9	3	0	154^1	150	7	46	**127**	11.5	3.91	93	.249	.303	0	—	0	-4	-5	-0	-0.5
1982	Cle-A	15	11	.577	33	33	10	1	0	244^2	211	17	88	187	11.1	3.90	105	.232	.301	0	—	0	5	5	-0	0.5
1983	Cle-A	8	13	.381	24	24	4	1	0	149^2	150	16	52	105	12.3	5.11	83	.266	.330	0	—	0	-17	-15	-1	-1.7
	Atl-N	1	3	.250	6	6	0	0	0	33	31	0	14	21	12.3	3.82	102	.248	.324	1	.125	-0	-1	0	1	0.1
1984	Atl-N	7	8	.467	21	20	1	0	0	126^1	120	10	38	95	11.4	3.85	100	.254	.312	2	.053	-1	-4	0	3	0.2
1985	Atl-N	2	9	.182	20	18	0	0	0	73^2	84	10	37	47	14.9	6.35	61	.288	.370	0	.000	-2	-23	-21	-1	-2.3
1987	Mil-A	2	1	.667	11	11	0	0	0	43^2	54	6	17	22	15.0	5.36	85	.303	.371	0	—	0	-4	-4	-0	-0.6
Total	11	74	76	.493	248	194	35	7	5	1323^2	1289	96	513	975	12.4	4.34	93	.256	.327	3	.048	-3	-59	-48	-1	-5.4

● **JEFF BARKLEY** Barkley, Jeffrey Carver b: 11/21/59, Hickory, N.C. BB/TR, 6'3", 185 lbs. Deb: 9/16/84

YEAR	TM/L	W	L	PCT	G	GS	CG	SH	SV	IP	H	HR	BB	SO	RAT	ERA	ERA+	OAV	OOB	BH	AVG	PB	PR	/A	PD	TPI
1984	Cle-A	0	0	—	3	0	0	0	0	4	6	0	1	4	15.8	6.75	61	.353	.389	0	—	0	-1	-1	0	-0.2
1985	Cle-A	0	3	.000	21	0	0	0	1	41	37	5	15	30	11.4	5.27	78	.243	.311	0	—	0	-5	-5	0	-0.4
Total	2	0	3	.000	24	0	0	0	1	45	43	5	16	34	11.8	5.40	76	.254	.319	0	—	0	-6	-6	0	-0.6

● **MIKE BARLOW** Barlow, Michael Roswell b: 4/30/48, Stamford, N.Y. BL/TR, 6'6", 215 lbs. Deb: 6/18/75

YEAR	TM/L	W	L	PCT	G	GS	CG	SH	SV	IP	H	HR	BB	SO	RAT	ERA	ERA+	OAV	OOB	BH	AVG	PB	PR	/A	PD	TPI
1975	StL-N	0	0	—	9	0	0	0	0	7^2	11	0	3	2	17.6	4.70	80	.355	.429	0	—	0	-1	-1	-0	-0.1
1976	Hou-N	2	2	.500	16	0	0	0	0	22	27	0	17	11	18.0	4.50	71	.318	.431	0	.000	-0	-2	-3	1	-0.3
1977	Cal-A	4	2	.667	20	1	0	0	1	59	53	3	27	25	12.8	4.58	86	.249	.344	0	—	0	-3	-4	0	-0.1
1978	Cal-A	0	0	—	1	0	0	0	0	2	3	0	0	1	13.5	4.50	80	.375	.375	0	—	0	-0	-0	-0	0.0
1979	*Cal-A	1	1	.500	35	0	0	0	0	86	106	8	30	33	14.7	5.13	79	.314	.376	0	—	0	-9	-10	-0	-0.8
1980	Tor-A	3	1	.750	40	1	0	0	5	55	57	4	21	19	13.1	4.09	105	.273	.345	0	—	0	-0	1	-0	-0.1
1981	Tor-A	0	0	—	12	0	0	0	0	15	22	1	6	5	19.2	4.20	94	.338	.427	0	—	0	-1	-0	0	-0.1
Total	7	10	6	.625	133	2	0	0	6	246^2	279	16	104	96	14.5	4.63	86	.294	.373	0	.000	-0	-17	-18	0	-1.5

● **CHARLIE BARNABE** Barnabe, Charles Edward b: 6/12/1900, Russell Gulch, Colo. d: 8/16/77, Waco, Tex. BL/TL, 5'11.5", 164 lbs. Deb: 4/14/27

YEAR	TM/L	W	L	PCT	G	GS	CG	SH	SV	IP	H	HR	BB	SO	RAT	ERA	ERA+	OAV	OOB	BH	AVG	PB	PR	/A	PD	TPI
1927	Chi-A	0	5	.000	17	4	1	0	0	61	86	2	20	5	16.4	5.31	76	.351	.411	3	.158	1	-8	-9	1	-0.7
1928	Chi-A	0	2	.000	7	2	0	0	0	9^2	17	0	0	3	16.8	6.52	62	.395	.409	4	.500	2	-3	-3	1	0.1
Total	2	0	7	.000	24	6	1	0	0	70^2	103	2	20	8	16.4	5.48	74	.358	.411	7	.259	3	-11	-11	1	-0.6

● **BRIAN BARNES** Barnes, Brian Keith b: 3/25/67, Roanoke Rapids, N.C. BL/TL, 5'9", 170 lbs. Deb: 9/14/90

YEAR	TM/L	W	L	PCT	G	GS	CG	SH	SV	IP	H	HR	BB	SO	RAT	ERA	ERA+	OAV	OOB	BH	AVG	PB	PR	/A	PD	TPI
1990	Mon-N	1	1	.500	4	4	1	0	0	28	25	2	7	23	10.3	2.89	126	.236	.283	0	.000	-1	3	2	0	0.2
1991	Mon-N	5	8	.385	28	27	1	0	0	160	135	16	84	117	12.7	4.22	86	.233	.336	4	.082	-1	-10	-11	1	-1.0
1992	Mon-N	6	6	.500	21	17	0	0	0	100	77	9	46	65	11.3	2.97	117	.213	.307	8	.276	2	6	6	0	0.9
Total	3	12	15	.444	53	48	2	0	0	288	237	27	137	205	12.0	3.66	98	.226	.321	12	.138	1	-1	-3	2	0.1

● **FRANK BARNES** Barnes, Frank b: 8/26/28, Longwood, Miss. BR/TR, 6', 170 lbs. Deb: 9/22/57

YEAR	TM/L	W	L	PCT	G	GS	CG	SH	SV	IP	H	HR	BB	SO	RAT	ERA	ERA+	OAV	OOB	BH	AVG	PB	PR	/A	PD	TPI
1957	StL-N	0	1	.000	3	1	0	0	0	10	13	0	9	5	19.8	4.50	88	.317	.440	0	.000	-0	-1	-1	-0	-0.1
1958	StL-N	1	1	.500	8	1	0	0	0	19	19	3	16	17	17.5	7.58	54	.260	.407	1	.167	-0	-8	-7	-0	-0.8
1960	StL-N	0	1	.000	4	1	0	0	1	7^2	8	1	9	8	21.1	3.52	116	.267	.450	0	.000	-0	0	0	-0	0.0
Total	3	1	3	.250	15	3	0	0	1	36^2	40	4	34	30	18.9	5.89	69	.278	.425	1	.100	-1	-8	-7	-1	-0.9

● **FRANK BARNES** Barnes, Frank Samuel "Lefty" b: 1/9/1900, Dallas, Tex. d: 9/27/67, Houston, Tex. BL/TL, 6'2.5", 195 lbs. Deb: 4/18/29

YEAR	TM/L	W	L	PCT	G	GS	CG	SH	SV	IP	H	HR	BB	SO	RAT	ERA	ERA+	OAV	OOB	BH	AVG	PB	PR	/A	PD	TPI
1929	Det-A	0	1	.000	4	1	0	0	0	5	10	0	3	0	25.2	7.20	60	.400	.483	0	.000	-0	-2	-2	0	-0.1
1930	NY-A	0	1	.000	2	2	0	0	0	12^1	13	0	13	2	19.7	8.03	54	.283	.450	2	.333	1	-5	-5	1	-0.2
Total	2	0	2	.000	6	3	0	0	0	17^1	23	0	16	2	21.3	7.79	55	.324	.461	2	.286	1	-6	-7	2	-0.3

● **JESSE BARNES** Barnes, Jesse Lawrence "Nubby" b: 8/26/1892, Perkins, Okla. d: 9/9/61, Santa Rosa, N.Mex. BL/TR, 6', 170 lbs. Deb: 7/30/15 F

YEAR	TM/L	W	L	PCT	G	GS	CG	SH	SV	IP	H	HR	BB	SO	RAT	ERA	ERA+	OAV	OOB	BH	AVG	PB	PR	/A	PD	TPI
1915	Bos-N	3	0	1.000	9	3	2	0	0	45^1	41	1	10	16	10.9	1.39	186	.244	.302	3	.176	0	7	6	-1	0.6
1916	Bos-N	6	15	.286	33	18	9	3	1	163	154	3	37	55	10.8	2.37	105	.254	.302	9	.188	0	4	2	4	0.7
1917	Bos-N	13	21	.382	50	33	27	2	1	295	261	3	50	107	9.6	2.68	95	.241	.277	24	.238	4	1	-4	3	0.3
1918	NY-N	6	1	.857	9	9	4	2	0	54^2	53	0	13	12	10.9	1.81	145	.255	.299	4	.222	-0	6	5	2	0.8
1919	NY-N	**25**	9	.735	38	34	23	4	1	295^2	263	8	35	92	9.1	2.40	117	.236	.260	32	.267	5	17	13	3	2.3
1920	NY-N	20	15	.571	43	35	23	2	0	292^2	271	9	56	63	10.1	2.64	113	.250	.288	22	.204	-2	16	11	3	1.2
1921	*NY-N	15	9	.625	42	31	15	1	6	258^2	298	13	44	56	12.0	3.10	118	.299	.331	19	.207	-1	20	16	1	1.6
1922	*NY-N	13	8	.619	37	30	14	2	0	212^2	236	10	38	52	11.7	3.51	114	.278	.311	14	.182	-1	14	12	3	1.3
1923	NY-N	3	1	.750	12	4	1	0	1	36	48	1	13	12	15.3	6.25	61	.329	.384	3	.273	0	-9	-10	1	-0.8
	Bos-N	10	14	.417	31	23	12	5	2	195^1	204	8	43	41	11.4	2.76	144	.270	.310	10	.147	-4	27	27	3	2.6
	Yr	13	15	.464	43	27	13	5	3	231^1	252	9	56	53	12.0	3.31	120	.280	.322	13	.165	-4	18	17	4	1.8
1924	Bos-N	15	20	.429	37	32	21	**4**	0	267^2	292	7	53	49	11.6	3.23	118	.284	.319	20	.222	-1	19	18	1	1.7

YEAR TM/L	W	L	PCT	G	GS	CG	SH	SV	IP	H	HR	BB	SO	RAT	ERA	ERA+	OAV	OOB	BH	AVG	PB	PR	/A	PD	TPI
1925 Bos-N	11	16	.407	32	28	17	0	0	216^1	255	14	63	55	13.3	4.53	88	.297	.346	16	.198	-0	-6	-13	-2	-1.4
1926 Bro-N	10	11	.476	31	24	10	1	1	158	204	6	35	29	13.7	5.24	73	.321	.358	14	.237	-0	-25	-25	-1	-2.4
1927 Bro-N	2	10	.167	18	10	2	0	0	78^2	106	5	25	14	15.0	5.72	69	.331	.380	5	.217	-0	-16	-15	-0	-1.5
Total 13	152	150	.503	422	314	180	26	13	2569^2	2686	88	515	653	11.3	3.22	104	.273	.310	195	.214	0	74	41	20	7.0

● JUNIE BARNES

Barnes, Junie Shoaf "Lefty" b: 12/1/11, Linwood, N.C. d: 12/31/63, Jacksonville, N.C. BL/TL, 5'11.5", 170 lbs. Deb: 9/12/34

YEAR TM/L	W	L	PCT	G	GS	CG	SH	SV	IP	H	HR	BB	SO	RAT	ERA	ERA+	OAV	OOB	BH	AVG	PB	PR	/A	PD	TPI
1934 Cin-N	0	0	—	2	0	0	0	0	0^1	0	0	1	0	27.0	0.00	—	.000	.500	0	—	0	0	0	0	0.0

● RICH BARNES

Barnes, Richard Monroe b: 7/21/59, Palm Beach, Fla. BR/TL, 6'4", 186 lbs. Deb: 7/18/82

YEAR TM/L	W	L	PCT	G	GS	CG	SH	SV	IP	H	HR	BB	SO	RAT	ERA	ERA+	OAV	OOB	BH	AVG	PB	PR	/A	PD	TPI
1982 Chi-A	0	2	.000	6	2	0	0	1	17	21	1	4	6	14.3	4.76	85	.292	.346	0	—	0	-1	-1	0	-0.1
1983 Cle-A	1	1	.500	4	2	0	0	0	11^2	18	0	10	2	21.6	6.94	61	.375	.483	0	—	0	-4	-4	-0	-0.5
Total 2	1	3	.250	10	4	0	0	1	28^2	39	1	14	8	17.3	5.65	73	.325	.404	0	—	0	-5	-5	0	-0.6

● BOB BARNES

Barnes, Robert Avery "Lefty" b: 1/6/02, Washburn, Ill. BL/TL, 5'11.5", 150 lbs. Deb: 7/08/24

YEAR TM/L	W	L	PCT	G	GS	CG	SH	SV	IP	H	HR	BB	SO	RAT	ERA	ERA+	OAV	OOB	BH	AVG	PB	PR	/A	PD	TPI
1924 Chi-A	0	0	—	2	0	0	0	0	4^2	14	1	0	1	27.0	19.29	21	.519	.519	0	.000	-0	-8	-8	0	-0.6

● ROSS BARNES

Barnes, Roscoe Charles b: 5/8/1850, Lima, N.Y. d: 2/5/15, Chicago, Ill. BR/TR, 5'8.5", 145 lbs. Deb: 5/05/1871 U♦

YEAR TM/L	W	L	PCT	G	GS	CG	SH	SV	IP	H	HR	BB	SO	RAT	ERA	ERA+	OAV	OOB	BH	AVG	PB	PR	/A	PD	TPI
1876 Chi-N	0	0	—	1	0	0	0	0	1^1	7	0	0	0	47.3	20.25	12	.538	.538	138	.429	1	-3	-3	0	-0.2

● VIRGIL BARNES

Barnes, Virgil Jennings "Zeke" b: 3/5/1897, Ontario, Kan. d: 7/24/58, Wichita, Kan. BR/TR, 6', 165 lbs. Deb: 9/25/19 F

YEAR TM/L	W	L	PCT	G	GS	CG	SH	SV	IP	H	HR	BB	SO	RAT	ERA	ERA+	OAV	OOB	BH	AVG	PB	PR	/A	PD	TPI
1919 NY-N	0	0	—	1	0	0	0	0	2	6	0	1	1	31.5	18.00	16	.545	.583	0	—	0	-3	-3	-0	-0.3
1920 NY-N	0	1	.000	1	1	0	0	0	7	9	0	1	2	12.9	3.86	78	.310	.333	0	.000	-0	-1	-1	0	0.0
1922 NY-N	1	0	1.000	22	3	1	0	2	51^2	46	1	11	16	9.9	3.48	115	.243	.285	2	.167	-1	4	3	0	0.3
1923 *NY-N	2	3	.400	22	2	0	0	1	53	59	2	19	6	13.2	3.91	98	.285	.345	0	.000	-2	1	-0	0	-0.2
1924 *NY-N	16	10	.615	35	29	15	1	3	229^1	239	10	57	59	11.6	3.06	120	.270	.314	14	.182	-2	21	15	2	1.5
1925 NY-N	15	11	.577	32	27	17	1	2	221^2	242	9	53	53	12.0	3.53	114	.281	.323	9	.101	-8	18	12	0	0.4
1926 NY-N	8	13	.381	31	25	9	2	1	185	183	4	56	54	11.8	2.87	131	.261	.318	3	.054	-7	20	18	-1	1.0
1927 NY-N	14	11	.560	35	29	12	2	2	228^2	251	14	51	66	12.0	3.98	97	.283	.325	9	.108	-7	-1	-3	-1	-1.1
1928 NY-N	3	3	.500	10	9	3	1	0	55^1	71	3	18	11	14.5	5.04	77	.330	.382	2	.091	-2	-6	-7	-1	-0.9
Bos-N	2	7	.222	16	10	1	0	0	60^1	86	3	26	7	16.7	5.82	67	.344	.406	1	.059	-1	-12	-13	-1	-1.4
Yr	5	10	.333	26	19	4	1	0	115^2	157	6	44	18	15.6	5.45	72	.338	.395	3	.077	-3	-19	-20	-1	-2.3
Total 9	61	59	.508	205	135	58	7	11	1094	1192	46	293	275	12.3	3.66	105	.282	.329	40	.108	-30	38	22	1	-0.7

● REX BARNEY

Barney, Rex Edward b: 12/19/24, Omaha, Neb. BR/TR, 6'3", 185 lbs. Deb: 8/18/43

YEAR TM/L	W	L	PCT	G	GS	CG	SH	SV	IP	H	HR	BB	SO	RAT	ERA	ERA+	OAV	OOB	BH	AVG	PB	PR	/A	PD	TPI
1943 Bro-N	2	2	.500	9	8	1	0	0	45^1	36	4	41	23	15.7	6.35	53	.217	.378	1	.056	-2	-15	-15	-0	-1.6
1946 Bro-N	2	5	.286	16	9	1	0	0	53^2	46	2	51	36	16.3	5.87	58	.240	.399	4	.235	1	-15	-15	-0	-1.4
1947 *Bro-N	5	2	.714	28	9	0	0	0	77^2	66	4	59	36	14.7	4.75	87	.240	.378	3	.111	-1	-6	-5	-1	-0.7
1948 Bro-N	15	13	.536	44	34	12	4	0	246^2	193	17	122	138	11.7	3.10	129	.217	.315	14	.167	-2	23	25	-4	1.9
1949 *Bro-N	9	8	.529	38	20	6	2	1	140^2	108	15	89	80	12.8	4.41	93	.216	.338	10	.213	0	-6	-5	-3	-0.8
1950 Bro-N	2	1	.667	20	1	0	0	0	33^2	25	6	48	23	20.0	6.42	64	.214	.449	1	.125	0	-9	-9	-1	-0.9
Total 6	35	31	.530	155	81	20	6	1	597^2	474	48	410	336	13.5	4.31	91	.221	.350	33	.164	-4	-26	-24	-9	-3.5

● EDGAR BARNHART

Barnhart, Edgar Vernon b: 9/16/04, Providence, Mo. d: 9/14/84, Columbia, Mo. BL/TL, 5'10", 160 lbs. Deb: 9/23/24

YEAR TM/L	W	L	PCT	G	GS	CG	SH	SV	IP	H	HR	BB	SO	RAT	ERA	ERA+	OAV	OOB	BH	AVG	PB	PR	/A	PD	TPI
1924 StL-A	0	0	—	1	0	0	0	0	1	0	0	2	0	18.0	0.00	—	.000	.400	0	—	0	0	1	0	0.1

● LES BARNHART

Barnhart, Leslie Earl "Barney" b: 2/23/05, Hoxie, Kan. d: 10/7/71, Scottsdale, Ariz. BR/TR, 6', 180 lbs. Deb: 9/22/28

YEAR TM/L	W	L	PCT	G	GS	CG	SH	SV	IP	H	HR	BB	SO	RAT	ERA	ERA+	OAV	OOB	BH	AVG	PB	PR	/A	PD	TPI
1928 Cle-A	0	1	.000	2	1	0	0	0	9	13	1	4	1	17.0	7.00	59	.325	.386	1	.500	0	-3	-3	-1	-0.3
1930 Cle-A	1	0	1.000	1	1	0	0	0	8^1	12	0	4	1	17.3	6.48	74	.364	.432	0	.000	-1	-2	-2	0	-0.2
Total 2	1	1	.500	3	2	0	0	0	17^1	25	1	8	2	17.1	6.75	66	.342	.407	1	.200	-0	-5	-4	-0	-0.5

● GEORGE BARNICLE

Barnicle, George Bernard "Barney" b: 8/26/17, Fitchburg, Mass. d: 10/10/90, Largo, Fla. BR/TR, 6'2", 175 lbs. Deb: 9/06/39

YEAR TM/L	W	L	PCT	G	GS	CG	SH	SV	IP	H	HR	BB	SO	RAT	ERA	ERA+	OAV	OOB	BH	AVG	PB	PR	/A	PD	TPI
1939 Bos-N	2	2	.500	6	1	0	0	0	18^1	16	1	8	15	11.8	4.91	75	.235	.316	0	.000	-1	-2	-2	0	-0.3
1940 Bos-N	1	0	1.000	13	2	1	0	0	32^2	28	1	31	11	17.9	7.44	50	.233	.414	0	.000	-1	-13	-14	1	-1.4
1941 Bos-N	0	1	.000	1	1	0	0	0	6^2	5	0	4	2	13.5	6.75	53	.238	.385	0	.000	-0	-2	-2	0	-0.2
Total 3	3	3	.500	20	4	1	0	0	57^2	49	2	43	28	15.5	6.55	56	.234	.382	0	.000	-2	-17	-18	1	-1.9

● ED BARNOWSKI

Barnowski, Edward Anthony b: 8/23/43, Scranton, Pa. BR/TR, 6'2", 195 lbs. Deb: 9/08/65

YEAR TM/L	W	L	PCT	G	GS	CG	SH	SV	IP	H	HR	BB	SO	RAT	ERA	ERA+	OAV	OOB	BH	AVG	PB	PR	/A	PD	TPI
1965 Bal-A	0	0	—	4	0	0	0	0	4^1	3	0	7	6	20.8	2.08	167	.200	.455	0	—	0	1	1	-0	0.1
1966 Bal-A	0	0	—	2	0	0	0	0	3	4	0	1	2	15.0	3.00	111	.364	.417	0	—	0	0	0	0	0.0
Total 2	0	0	—	6	0	0	0	0	7^1	7	0	8	8	18.4	2.45	139	.269	.441	0	—	0	1	1	0	0.1

● SALOME BAROJAS

Barojas, Salome (Romero) b: 6/16/57, Cordoba, Mex. BR/TR, 5'9", 188 lbs. Deb: 4/11/82

YEAR TM/L	W	L	PCT	G	GS	CG	SH	SV	IP	H	HR	BB	SO	RAT	ERA	ERA+	OAV	OOB	BH	AVG	PB	PR	/A	PD	TPI
1982 Chi-A	6	6	.500	61	0	0	0	21	106^2	96	9	46	56	12.1	3.54	114	.244	.324	0	—	0	6	6	3	0.9
1983 *Chi-A	3	3	.500	52	0	0	0	12	87^1	70	2	32	38	11.0	2.47	169	.224	.306	0	—	0	15	17	0	1.5
1984 Chi-A	3	2	.600	24	0	0	0	1	39^1	48	3	19	18	15.3	4.58	91	.310	.385	0	—	0	-3	-2	1	-0.3
Sea-A	6	5	.545	19	14	0	0	1	95^1	88	12	41	37	12.5	3.97	101	.249	.332	0	—	0	0	0	1	0.1
Yr	9	7	.563	43	14	0	0	2	134^2	136	15	60	55	13.3	4.14	97	.268	.349	0	—	0	-2	-2	2	-0.2
1985 Sea-A	0	5	.000	17	4	0	0	0	52^2	65	6	33	27	16.7	5.98	70	.305	.398	0	—	0	-11	-10	0	-1.0
1988 Phi-N	0	0	—	6	0	0	0	0	8^2	7	1	8	1	15.6	8.31	43	.250	.417	0	—	0	-5	-5	-0	-0.5
Total 5	18	21	.462	179	18	0	0	35	390	374	33	179	177	13.0	3.95	103	.257	.342	0	—	0	4	6	5	0.7

● JIM BARR

Barr, James Leland b: 2/10/48, Lynwood, Cal. BR/TR, 6'3", 205 lbs. Deb: 7/31/71

YEAR TM/L	W	L	PCT	G	GS	CG	SH	SV	IP	H	HR	BB	SO	RAT	ERA	ERA+	OAV	OOB	BH	AVG	PB	PR	/A	PD	TPI
1971 *SF-N	1	1	.500	17	0	0	0	0	35^1	33	3	5	16	9.9	3.57	95	.254	.287	0	.000	-0	-0	-1	1	0.0
1972 SF-N	8	10	.444	44	18	8	2	2	179	166	16	41	86	10.6	2.87	122	.246	.292	9	.184	1	12	12	1	1.5
1973 SF-N	11	17	.393	41	33	8	3	2	231^1	240	24	49	88	11.4	3.81	100	.268	.310	10	.152	-1	-4	0	-1	-0.1
1974 SF-N	13	9	.591	44	27	11	5	2	239^2	223	17	47	84	10.2	2.74	139	.251	.290	18	.254	5	23	28	1	3.7
1975 SF-N	13	14	.481	35	33	12	2	0	244	244	17	58	77	11.3	3.06	124	.265	.310	9	.118	-3	15	20	3	2.2
1976 SF-N	15	12	.556	37	37	8	3	0	252^1	260	9	60	75	11.5	2.89	126	.266	.310	12	.162	2	17	21	3	2.9
1977 SF-N	12	16	.429	38	38	6	2	0	234^1	286	18	56	97	13.3	4.76	82	.306	.347	10	.132	-2	-22	-22	3	-2.1
1978 SF-N	8	11	.421	32	25	5	2	1	163	180	7	35	44	11.9	3.53	98	.281	.319	5	.100	-2	1	-2	1	-0.4
1979 Cal-A	10	12	.455	36	25	5	0	0	197	217	22	55	69	12.6	4.20	97	.287	.338	0	—	0	0	-3	2	0.1
1980 Cal-A	1	4	.200	24	7	0	0	1	68	90	12	23	22	15.4	5.56	71	.323	.380	0	—	0	-12	-12	-1	-1.2
1982 SF-N	4	3	.571	53	9	1	1	2	128^2	125	9	20	36	10.4	3.29	109	.262	.297	8	.250	1	4	4	0	0.6
1983 SF-N	5	3	.625	53	0	0	0	2	92^2	106	7	20	47	12.3	3.98	89	.294	.332	2	.133	-0	-4	-5	0	-0.5
Total 12	101	112	.474	454	252	64	20	12	2065^1	2170	161	469	741	11.6	3.56	105	.273	.316	83	.162	0	31	42	12	6.7

● BOB BARR

Barr, Robert Alexander b: 3/12/08, Newton, Mass. BR/TR, 6', 175 lbs. Deb: 9/11/35

YEAR TM/L	W	L	PCT	G	GS	CG	SH	SV	IP	H	HR	BB	SO	RAT	ERA	ERA+	OAV	OOB	BH	AVG	PB	PR	/A	PD	TPI
1935 Bro-N	0	0	—	2	0	0	0	0	2^1	5	0	2	0	27.0	3.86	103	.385	.467	0	—	0	0	0	-0	0.0

● BOB BARR

Barr, Robert McClelland b: 12/1856, Washington, D.C. d: 3/11/30, Washington, D.C. BR/TR, 6'1", 192 lbs. Deb: 6/23/1883

YEAR TM/L	W	L	PCT	G	GS	CG	SH	SV	IP	H	HR	BB	SO	RAT	ERA	ERA+	OAV	OOB	BH	AVG	PB	PR	/A	PD	TPI
1883 Pit-a	6	18	.250	26	23	19	0	1	203^1	263	5	28	81	12.9	4.38	73	.294	.316	35	.246	3	-24	-26	1	-1.9
1884 Was-a	9	23	.281	32	32	32	2	0	281	311	9	31	138	11.4	3.46	88	.258	.284	20	.148	-2	-7	-13	-1	-1.3
Ind-a	3	11	.214	16	16	15	0	0	132	160	2	19	69	12.5	4.98	66	.275	.304	12	.185	0	-25	-25	-1	-2.2
Yr	12	34	.261	48	48	47	2	0	413	471	11	50	207	11.5	3.94	79	.262	.284	32	.160	-2	-32	-38	-2	-3.5
1886 Was-N	3	18	.143	22	22	21	1	0	190^2	216	7	54	80	12.7	4.30	76	.273	.320	13	.165	-2	-21	-21	-1	-2.1
1890 Roc-a	28	24	.538	57	54	52	3	0	493^1	458	7	219	209	12.6	3.25	110	.239	.321	36	.179	-1	34	17	3	1.8

YEAR	TM/L	W	L	PCT	G	GS	CG	SH	SV	IP	H	HR	BB	SO	RAT	ERA	ERA+	OAV	OOB	BH	AVG	PB	PR	/A	PD	TPI
1891	NY-N	0	4	.000	5	4	2	0	0	27	47	1	12	11	20.7	5.33	60	.368	.434	1	.091	-0	-6	-6	0	-0.6
Total	5	49	98	.333	158	151	141	6	1	1327^1	1455	31	363	588	12.6	3.83	87	.264	.313	117	.185	-3	-49	-74	1	-6.3

● STEVE BARR

Barr, Steven Charles b: 9/8/51, St.Louis, Mo. BL/TL, 6'4", 200 lbs. Deb: 10/01/74

YEAR	TM/L	W	L	PCT	G	GS	CG	SH	SV	IP	H	HR	BB	SO	RAT	ERA	ERA+	OAV	OOB	BH	AVG	PB	PR	/A	PD	TPI
1974	Bos-A	1	0	1.000	1	1	1	0	0	9	7	0	6	3	13.0	4.00	96	.212	.333	0	—	0	-0	-0	0	-0.4
1975	Bos-A	0	1	.000	3	2	0	0	0	7	11	1	7	2	23.1	2.57	158	.367	.486	0	—	0	1	1	-0	-0.5
1976	Tex-A	2	6	.250	20	10	3	0	0	67^2	70	10	44	27	15.2	5.59	64	.269	.375	0	—	0	-16	-15	0	-1.5
Total	3	3	7	.300	24	13	4	0	0	83^2	88	11	57	32	15.6	5.16	71	.272	.382	0	—	0	-15	-14	0	-2.4

● RED BARRETT

Barrett, Charles Henry b: 2/14/15, Santa Barbara, Cal d: 7/28/90, Wilson, N.C. BR/TR, 5'11", 183 lbs. Deb: 9/15/37

YEAR	TM/L	W	L	PCT	G	GS	CG	SH	SV	IP	H	HR	BB	SO	RAT	ERA	ERA+	OAV	OOB	BH	AVG	PB	PR	/A	PD	TPI
1937	Cin-N	0	0	—	1	0	0	0	0	3^1	5	0	2	1	9.9	1.42	263	.227	.292	0	.000	-0	2	2	-0	0.1
1938	Cin-N	2	0	1.000	6	2	2	0	0	28^2	28	2	15	5	13.5	3.14	116	.257	.347	1	.143	-0	2	2	-0	0.1
1939	Cin-N	0	0	—	2	0	0	0	0	5^1	5	0	1	1	10.1	1.69	227	.263	.300	0	.000	-0	1	1	0	0.1
1940	Cin-N	1	0	1.000	3	0	0	0	0	2^2	5	0	1	0	20.3	6.75	56	.455	.500	0	—	0	-1	-1	0	-0.1
1943	Bos-N	12	18	.400	38	31	14	3	0	255	240	11	63	64	10.8	3.18	107	.250	.298	11	.136	-4	6	7	1	0.4
1944	Bos-N	9	16	.360	42	30	11	1	2	230^1	257	13	63	54	12.6	4.06	94	.279	.327	13	.173	-1	-12	-6	2	-0.6
1945	Bos-N	2	3	.400	9	5	2	0	2	38	43	6	16	13	14.2	4.74	81	.281	.353	2	.222	-0	-4	-4	1	-0.2
	StL-N	21	9	.700	36	29	22	3	0	246^2	244	12	38	63	10.3	2.74	137	.256	.285	10	.112	-5	29	28	-1	2.2
	Yr	**23**	12	.657	45	34	**24**	3	2	**284^2**	287	18	54	76	10.8	3.00	125	.259	.294	12	.122	-5	25	24	0	2.0
1946	StL-N	3	2	.600	23	9	1	1	2	67	75	5	24	22	13.6	4.03	86	.282	.346	1	.059	-1	-5	-4	1	-0.5
1947	Bos-N	11	12	.478	36	30	12	3	1	210^2	200	16	53	53	10.9	3.55	110	.244	.292	8	.111	-2	12	8	-0	0.6
1948	*Bos-N	7	8	.467	34	13	3	0	0	128^1	132	9	26	40	11.1	3.65	105	.268	.305	7	.179	-1	4	3	1	0.3
1949	Bos-N	1	1	.500	23	0	0	0	0	44^1	58	4	10	17	14.2	5.68	66	.326	.368	1	.200	-0	-8	-9	1	-0.8
Total	11	69	69	.500	253	149	67	11	7	1263^1	1292	78	312	333	11.5	3.53	105	.264	.309	54	.136	-16	28	26	5	1.6

● FRANK BARRETT

Barrett, Francis Joseph "Red" b: 7/1/13, Ft.Lauderdale, Fla BR/TR, 6'2", 173 lbs. Deb: 10/01/39

YEAR	TM/L	W	L	PCT	G	GS	CG	SH	SV	IP	H	HR	BB	SO	RAT	ERA	ERA+	OAV	OOB	BH	AVG	PB	PR	/A	PD	TPI
1939	StL-N	0	1	.000	1	0	0	0	0	1^2	1	0	1	3	10.8	5.40	76	.167	.286	0	—	0	-0	-0	0	0.0
1944	Bos-A	8	7	.533	38	2	0	0	8	90^1	93	5	42	40	13.5	3.69	92	.271	.352	4	.143	-1	-3	-3	-0	-0.4
1945	Bos-A	4	3	.571	37	0	0	0	3	86	77	0	29	35	11.1	2.62	130	.249	.314	5	.250	1	7	8	-1	0.8
1946	Bos-N	2	4	.333	23	0	0	0	1	35^1	35	2	17	12	13.5	5.09	67	.252	.338	0	.000	-1	-7	-7	1	-0.7
1950	Pit-N	1	2	.333	5	0	0	0	0	4^1	5	1	1	0	12.5	4.15	106	.357	.400	0	—	0	-0	0	0	0.1
Total	5	15	17	.469	104	2	0	0	12	217^2	211	8	90	90	12.5	3.51	98	.260	.336	9	.167	-1	-2	-2	1	-0.2

● TIM BARRETT

Barrett, Timothy Wayne b: 1/24/61, Huntingburg, Ind. BL/TR, 6'1", 185 lbs. Deb: 7/18/88

YEAR	TM/L	W	L	PCT	G	GS	CG	SH	SV	IP	H	HR	BB	SO	RAT	ERA	ERA+	OAV	OOB	BH	AVG	PB	PR	/A	PD	TPI
1988	Mon-N	0	0	—	4	0	0	0	1	9^1	10	2	2	5	11.6	5.79	62	.270	.308	0	.000	-0	-2	-2	0	-0.2

● DICK BARRETT

Barrett, Tracy Souter "Kewpie Dick" (a.k.a. Richard Oliver 1933 And Richard Oliver Barrett 1934-43)
b: 9/28/06, Montoursville, Pa d: 10/30/66, Seattle, Wash. BR/TR, 5'9", 175 lbs. Deb: 6/27/33

YEAR	TM/L	W	L	PCT	G	GS	CG	SH	SV	IP	H	HR	BB	SO	RAT	ERA	ERA+	OAV	OOB	BH	AVG	PB	PR	/A	PD	TPI
1933	Phi-A	4	4	.500	15	7	3	0	0	70^1	74	2	49	26	15.9	5.76	74	.272	.385	6	.286	2	-12	-12	0	-0.9
1934	Bos-N	1	3	.250	15	3	0	0	0	32^1	50	2	12	14	17.3	6.68	57	.365	.416	1	.143	-0	-9	-10	1	-0.9
1943	Chi-N	0	4	.000	15	4	0	0	0	45	52	2	28	20	16.2	4.80	70	.291	.389	1	.111	-1	-7	-7	-0	-0.8
	Phi-N	10	9	.526	23	20	10	2	1	169^1	137	5	51	65	10.1	2.39	141	.221	.282	7	.143	-0	19	18	0	2.1
	Yr	10	13	.435	38	24	10	2	1	214^1	189	7	79	85	11.3	2.90	116	.236	.306	8	.138	-1	12	11	0	1.3
1944	Phi-N	12	18	.400	37	27	11	1	0	221^1	223	7	88	74	12.8	3.86	94	.262	.333	16	.216	2	-6	-6	2	-0.2
1945	Phi-N	8	20	.286	36	30	8	0	1	190^2	217	11	92	72	14.9	5.38	71	.281	.363	9	.145	-1	-33	-33	1	-3.2
Total	5	35	58	.376	141	91	32	3	2	729	753	29	320	271	13.4	4.28	86	.266	.343	40	.180	1	-49	-50	4	-3.9

● BILL BARRETT

Barrett, William Joseph "Whispering Bill" b: 5/28/1900, Cambridge, Mass. d: 1/26/51, Cambridge, Mass. BR/TR, 6', 175 lbs. Deb: 5/13/21 ♦

YEAR	TM/L	W	L	PCT	G	GS	CG	SH	SV	IP	H	HR	BB	SO	RAT	ERA	ERA+	OAV	OOB	BH	AVG	PB	PR	/A	PD	TPI
1921	Phi-A	1	0	1.000	4	0	0	0	0	5	2	0	9	2	19.8	7.20	62	.133	.458	7	.233	0	-2	-2	0	-0.1

● FRANCISCO BARRIOS

Barrios, Francisco Javier (Jimenez)
b: 6/10/53, Hermosillo, Mex. d: 4/9/82, Hermosillo, Mexico BR/TR, 6'3", 195 lbs. Deb: 8/18/74

YEAR	TM/L	W	L	PCT	G	GS	CG	SH	SV	IP	H	HR	BB	SO	RAT	ERA	ERA+	OAV	OOB	BH	AVG	PB	PR	/A	PD	TPI
1974	Chi-A	0	0	—	2	0	0	0	0	2	7	0	2	2	40.5	27.00	14	.538	.600	0	—	0	-5	-5	-0	-0.6
1976	Chi-A	5	9	.357	35	14	6	0	3	141^2	136	13	46	81	11.8	4.32	83	.255	.318	0	—	0	-13	-12	-1	-1.3
1977	Chi-A	14	7	.667	33	31	9	0	0	231^1	241	22	58	119	11.8	4.12	99	.267	.315	0	—	0	-2	-1	-1	-0.2
1978	Chi-A	9	15	.375	33	32	9	2	0	195^2	180	13	85	79	12.5	4.05	94	.246	.330	0	—	0	-6	-5	2	-0.3
1979	Chi-A	8	3	.727	15	15	2	0	0	94^2	88	9	33	28	12.0	3.61	118	.242	.314	0	—	0	6	7	-1	0.5
1980	Chi-A	1	1	.500	3	3	0	0	0	16^1	21	4	8	2	16.5	4.96	81	.323	.405	0	—	0	-2	-2	-0	-0.2
1981	Chi-A	1	3	.250	8	7	1	0	0	36^1	45	3	14	12	14.9	3.96	90	.292	.355	0	—	0	-1	-2	-0	-0.2
Total	7	38	38	.500	129	102	27	2	3	718	718	64	246	323	12.4	4.15	94	.260	.326	0	—	0	-22	-20	-1	-2.3

● FRANK BARRON

Barron, Frank John b: 8/6/1890, St.Mary's, W.Va. d: 9/18/64, St.Mary's, W.Va. BL/TL, 6'1", 175 lbs. Deb: 8/19/14

YEAR	TM/L	W	L	PCT	G	GS	CG	SH	SV	IP	H	HR	BB	SO	RAT	ERA	ERA+	OAV	OOB	BH	AVG	PB	PR	/A	PD	TPI
1914	Was-A	0	0	—	1	0	0	0	0	1	1	0	0	1	9.0	0.00	—	.333	.333	0	—	0	0	0	0	0.0

● ED BARRY

Barry, Edward "Jumbo" b: 10/2/1882, Madison, Wis. d: 6/19/20, Montague, Mass. TL, 6'3", 185 lbs. Deb: 8/21/05

YEAR	TM/L	W	L	PCT	G	GS	CG	SH	SV	IP	H	HR	BB	SO	RAT	ERA	ERA+	OAV	OOB	BH	AVG	PB	PR	/A	PD	TPI
1905	Bos-A	1	2	.333	7	5	2	0	0	40^2	38	2	15	18	12.4	2.88	94	.249	.328	1	.091	-0	-1	-1	-2	-0.3
1906	Bos-A	0	3	.000	3	3	3	0	0	21	23	2	5	10	13.3	6.00	46	.281	.345	1	.111	-0	-8	-8	0	-0.7
1907	Bos-A	0	1	.000	2	2	1	0	0	17^1	13	1	5	6	9.9	2.08	124	.210	.280	0	.000	-0	1	1	-0	0.0
Total	3	1	6	.143	12	10	6	0	0	79	74	5	25	34	12.1	3.53	76	.250	.323	2	.087	-1	-8	-7	-2	-1.0

● HARDIN BARRY

Barry, Hardin "Finn" b: 3/26/1891, Susanville, Cal. d: 11/5/69, Carson City, Nev. BR/TR, 6', 185 lbs. Deb: 6/21/12

YEAR	TM/L	W	L	PCT	G	GS	CG	SH	SV	IP	H	HR	BB	SO	RAT	ERA	ERA+	OAV	OOB	BH	AVG	PB	PR	/A	PD	TPI
1912	Phi-A	0	0	—	3	0	0	0	0	13	18	0	4	3	15.9	7.62	40	.360	.418	0	.000	-0	-6	-7	-0	-0.6

● TOM BARRY

Barry, Thomas Arthur b: 4/10/1879, St.Louis, Mo. d: 6/4/46, St.Louis, Mo. TR, 5'9", 155 lbs. Deb: 4/15/04

YEAR	TM/L	W	L	PCT	G	GS	CG	SH	SV	IP	H	HR	BB	SO	RAT	ERA	ERA+	OAV	OOB	BH	AVG	PB	PR	/A	PD	TPI
1904	Phi-N	0	1	.000	1	1	0	0	0	0^2	6	0	1	1	94.5	40.50	7	.667	.700	0	—	0	-3	-3	0	-0.3

● BOB BARTHELSON

Barthelson, Robert Edward b: 7/15/24, New Haven, Conn. BR/TR, 6', 185 lbs. Deb: 7/04/44

YEAR	TM/L	W	L	PCT	G	GS	CG	SH	SV	IP	H	HR	BB	SO	RAT	ERA	ERA+	OAV	OOB	BH	AVG	PB	PR	/A	PD	TPI
1944	NY-N	1	1	.500	7	1	0	0	0	9^2	13	2	5	4	16.8	4.66	79	.310	.383	0	—	0	-1	-1	-0	-0.1

● JOHN BARTHOLD

Barthold, John Francis "Hans" b: 4/14/1882, Philadelphia, Pa. d: 11/4/46, Fairview Village, Pa. BB/TR, 5'11", 180 lbs. Deb: 5/17/04

YEAR	TM/L	W	L	PCT	G	GS	CG	SH	SV	IP	H	HR	BB	SO	RAT	ERA	ERA+	OAV	OOB	BH	AVG	PB	PR	/A	PD	TPI
1904	Phi-A	0	0	—	4	0	0	0	0	10^2	12	0	8	5	17.7	5.06	53	.284	.410	1	.333	1	-3	-3	0	-0.2

● LES BARTHOLOMEW

Bartholomew, Lester Justin b: 4/4/03, Madison, Wis. d: 9/19/72, Barrington, Ill. BR/TL, 5'11.5", 195 lbs. Deb: 4/11/28

YEAR	TM/L	W	L	PCT	G	GS	CG	SH	SV	IP	H	HR	BB	SO	RAT	ERA	ERA+	OAV	OOB	BH	AVG	PB	PR	/A	PD	TPI
1928	Pit-N	0	0	—	6	0	0	0	0	22^2	31	2	9	6	15.9	7.15	57	.356	.417	1	.143	-0	-8	-8	-0	-0.7
1932	Chi-A	0	0	—	3	0	0	0	0	5^1	5	0	6	1	18.6	5.06	85	.250	.423	0	.000	-0	-0	-0	0	-0.1
Total	2	0	0	—	9	0	0	0	0	28	36	2	15	7	16.4	6.75	61	.336	.418	1	.125	-0	-8	-8	-0	-0.8

● BILL BARTLEY

Bartley, William Jackson b: 1/8/1885, Cincinnati, Ohio d: 5/17/65, Cincinnati, Ohio BR/TR, 5'11.5", 190 lbs. Deb: 9/15/03

YEAR	TM/L	W	L	PCT	G	GS	CG	SH	SV	IP	H	HR	BB	SO	RAT	ERA	ERA+	OAV	OOB	BH	AVG	PB	PR	/A	PD	TPI
1903	NY-N	0	0	—	1	0	0	0	0	3	3	0	4	2	21.0	0.00	—	.273	.467	0	.000	-0	1	1	0	0.1
1906	Phi-A	0	0	—	3	0	0	0	1	8^2	10	0	6	6	16.6	9.35	29	.292	.398	1	.333	1	-6	-6	1	-0.5
1907	Phi-A	0	1	.000	15	3	2	0	0	56^1	44	0	19	16	10.1	2.24	117	.217	.284	2	.095	-2	2	2	-0	0.1
Total	3	0	1	.000	19	3	2	0	1	68	57	0	29	24	11.4	3.04	87	.230	.311	3	.120	-1	-3	-3	0	-0.3

● SHAWN BARTON

Barton, Shawn Edward b: 5/14/63, Los Angeles, Cal. BR/TL, 6'3", 195 lbs. Deb: 8/06/92

YEAR	TM/L	W	L	PCT	G	GS	CG	SH	SV	IP	H	HR	BB	SO	RAT	ERA	ERA+	OAV	OOB	BH	AVG	PB	PR	/A	PD	TPI
1992	Sea-A	0	1	.000	14	0	0	0	0	12^1	10	1	7	4	12.4	2.92	137	.238	.347	0	—	0	1	1	0	0.2

YEAR TM/L	W	L	PCT	G	GS	CG	SH	SV	IP	H	HR	BB	SO	RAT	ERA	ERA+	OAV	OOB	BH	AVG	PB	PR	/A	PD	TPI
● **CHARLIE BARTSON** Bartson, Charles Franklin b: 3/13/1865, Peoria, Ill. d: 6/9/36, Peoria, Ill. 6', 170 lbs. Deb: 5/14/1890																								
1890 Chi-P	8	10	.444	25	19	16	0	1	188	222	8	66	47	14.4	4.26	102	.281	.347	13	.173	-2	-1	2	4	0.3
● **JIM BASKETTE** Baskette, James Blaine "Big Jim" b: 12/10/1887, Athens, Tenn. d: 7/30/42, Athens, Tenn. BR/TR, 6'2", 185 lbs. Deb: 9/22/11																								
1911 Cle-A	1	2	.333	4	2	2	0	0	21¹	21	0	9	8	13.1	3.38	101	.273	.356	2	.333	1	-0	0	-0	0.0
1912 Cle-A	8	4	.667	29	11	7	1	1	116	109	2	46	51	12.6	3.18	107	.252	.334	5	.125	-1	2	3	-3	0.0
1913 Cle-A	0	0	—	2	1	0	0	0	4²	8	1	2	0	19.3	5.79	53	.400	.455	1	1.000	1	-1	-1	0	0.0
Total 3	9	6	.600	35	14	9	1	1	142	138	3	57	59	12.9	3.30	103	.261	.342	8	.170	1	0	2	-3	0.0
● **NORM BASS** Bass, Norman Delaney b: 1/21/39, Laurel, Miss. BR/TR, 6'3", 205 lbs. Deb: 4/23/61																								
1961 KC-A	11	11	.500	40	23	6	2	0	170²	164	17	82	74	13.2	4.69	88	.255	.343	7	.119	-2	-13	-11	-3	-1.5
1962 KC-A	2	6	.250	22	10	0	0	0	75¹	96	7	46	33	17.0	6.09	68	.317	.407	1	.045	-2	-18	-16	1	-1.6
1963 KC-A	0	0	—	3	1	0	0	0	7²	11	2	9	4	23.5	11.74	33	.333	.476	0	.000	-0	-7	-7	-0	-0.7
Total 3	13	17	.433	65	34	6	2	0	253²	271	26	137	111	14.6	5.32	77	.277	.368	8	.098	-4	-37	-34	-2	-3.8
● **DICK BASS** Bass, Richard William b: 7/7/06, Rogersville, Tenn. d: 2/3/89, Graceville, Fla. BR/TR, 6'2", 175 lbs. Deb: 9/21/39																								
1939 Was-A	0	1	.000	1	1	0	0	0	8	7	0	6	1	15.8	6.75	64	.241	.389	0	.000	-0	-2	-2	-0	-0.2
● **CHARLIE BASTIAN** Bastian, Charles J. b: 7/4/1860, Philadelphia, Pa. d: 1/18/32, Pennsauken, N.J. BR/TR, 5'6.5", 145 lbs. Deb: 8/18/1884 ♦																								
1884 Wil-U	0	0	—	1	0	0	0	0	6	6	0	0	2	9.0	3.00	110	.243	.243	12	.200	0	0	-0	-0	0.0
● **JOE BATCHELDER** Batchelder, Joseph Edmund "Win" b: 7/11/1898, Wenham, Mass. d: 5/5/89, Beverly, Mass. BR/TL, 5'7", 165 lbs. Deb: 9/29/23																								
1923 Bos-N	1	0	1.000	4	1	1	0	0	9	12	2	1	2	14.0	7.00	57	.353	.389	0	.000	0	-3	-3	-0	-0.3
1924 Bos-N	0	0	—	3	0	0	0	0	4²	4	0	2	2	11.6	3.86	99	.235	.316	0	.000	-0	-0	-0	-0	0.0
1925 Bos-N	0	0	—	4	0	0	0	0	7	10	0	1	2	14.1	5.14	78	.357	.379	0	.000	-0	-1	-1	0	-0.1
Total 3	1	0	1.000	11	1	1	0	0	20²	26	2	4	6	13.5	5.66	70	.329	.369	0	.000	-0	-4	-4	0	-0.4
● **DICK BATES** Bates, Charles Richard b: 10/7/45, McArthur, Ohio BL/TR, 6', 190 lbs. Deb: 4/27/69																								
1969 Sea-A	0	0	—	1	0	0	0	0	1²	3	1	3	3	32.4	27.00	13	.375	.545	0	—	0	-4	-4	0	-0.4
● **FRANK BATES** Bates, Creed Frank b: Chattanooga, Tenn. Deb: 10/07/1898																								
1898 Cle-N	2	1	.667	4	4	4	0	0	29	30	0	11	5	13.0	3.10	117	.265	.335	1	.111	0	2	2	-0	0.2
1899 StL-N	0	0	—	2	0	0	0	0	8²	7	0	5	0	12.5	1.04	383	.221	.327	1	.333	1	3	3	0	0.3
Cle-N	1	18	.053	20	19	17	0	0	153	239	6	105	13	21.6	7.24	51	.355	.458	14	.215	1	-57	-60	0	-4.8
Yr	1	18	.053	22	19	17	0	0	161²	246	6	110	13	21.1	6.90	54	.349	.452	15	.221	1	-55	-58	0	-4.5
Total 2	3	19	.136	26	23	21	0	0	190²	276	6	121	18	19.9	6.33	58	.337	.437	16	.208	1	-53	-56	-0	-4.3
● **JOHN BATES** Bates, John Deb: 8/25/1889																								
1889 KC-a	0	1	.000	1	1	1	0	0	8	15	0	5	3	22.5	13.50	31	.387	.458	0	.000	-1	-9	-8	0	-0.6
● **MIGUEL BATISTA** Batista, Miguel Jerez (Decartes) b: 2/19/71, Santo Domingo, D.R. BR/TR, 6', 160 lbs. Deb: 4/11/92																								
1992 Pit-N	0	0	—	1	0	0	0	0	2	4	1	3	1	31.5	9.00	38	.400	.538	0	—	0	-1	-0	-0	-0.1
● **JOE BATTIN** Battin, Joseph V. b: 11/11/1851, Philadelphia, Pa. d: 12/10/37, Akron, Ohio BR/TR, Deb: 8/11/1871 MU♦																								
1877 StL-N	0	0	—	1	0	0	0	0	3²	3	0	1	1	9.8	4.91	53	.200	.250	45	.199	0	-1	-1	-0	-0.1
1883 Pit-a	0	0	—	2	0	0	0	0	4	9	0	1	0	22.5	2.25	143	.420	.446	83	.214	0	0	0	-0	0.0
Total 2	0	0	—	3	0	0	0	0	7²	12	0	2	1	16.4	3.52	83	.330	.364	313	.218	0	-0	-1	-0	-0.1
● **CHRIS BATTON** Batton, Christopher Sean b: 8/24/54, Los Angeles, Cal. BR/TR, 6'4", 195 lbs. Deb: 9/19/76																								
1976 Oak-A	0	0	—	2	1	0	0	0	4	5	1	3	4	18.0	9.00	37	.313	.421	0	—	0	-2	-3	-0	-0.2
● **LOU BAUER** Bauer, Louis Walter b: 11/30/1898, Egg Harbor City, N.J. d: 2/4/79, Pomona, N.J. BR/TR, 6', 175 lbs. Deb: 8/13/18																								
1918 Phi-A	0	0	—	1	0	0	0	0	0	0	0	2	0	—	∞	—	—	1.000	0	—	0	-1	-1	0	-0.1
● **AL BAUERS** Bauers, Albert J. b: 1850, Columbus, Ohio d: 9/6/13, Wilkes-Barre, Pa. TL, Deb: 9/22/1884 U																								
1884 Col-a	1	2	.333	3	3	3	0	0	25	22	1	14	13	13.0	4.68	65	.224	.321	3	.273	0	-4	-5	-0	-0.4
1886 StL-N	0	4	.000	4	4	3	0	0	28²	31	1	27	13	18.2	5.97	54	.267	.406	2	.167	-1	-8	-9	-1	-0.8
Total 2	1	6	.143	7	7	6	0	0	53²	53	2	41	26	15.8	5.37	58	.248	.369	5	.217	-0	-12	-13	-1	-1.2
● **RUSS BAUERS** Bauers, Russell Lee b: 5/10/14, Townsend, Wis. BL/TR, 6'3", 195 lbs. Deb: 8/20/36																								
1936 Pit-N	0	0	—	1	1	0	0	0	1¹	2	1	4	0	47.3	33.75	12	.500	.778	0	—	0	-4	-4	-0	-0.4
1937 Pit-N	13	6	.684	34	19	11	2	1	187²	174	2	80	118	12.4	2.88	134	.245	.325	15	.217	1	22	21	3	2.5
1938 Pit-N	13	14	.481	40	34	12	2	3	243	207	7	99	112	11.6	3.07	124	.233	.314	21	.239	4	19	20	-3	2.0
1939 Pit-N	2	4	.333	15	8	1	0	0	53²	46	4	25	12	12.1	3.35	114	.240	.330	4	.211	-0	3	3	-1	0.2
1940 Pit-N	0	2	.000	15	2	0	0	0	30²	42	2	18	11	18.2	7.63	50	.323	.413	2	.286	0	-13	-13	0	-1.2
1941 Pit-N	1	3	.250	8	5	1	0	0	37¹	40	1	25	20	15.7	5.54	65	.267	.371	5	.357	1	-8	-8	-1	-0.8
1946 Chi-N	2	1	.667	15	2	2	0	1	43¹	45	1	19	22	13.5	3.53	94	.273	.351	3	.300	1	-1	-1	-0	-0.0
1950 StL-A	0	0	—	1	0	0	0	0	2	6	0	1	0	31.5	4.50	110	.600	.636	0	—	0	0	0	0	0.0
Total 8	31	30	.508	129	71	27	4	6	599	562	17	271	300	12.7	3.53	107	.250	.334	50	.242	7	19	17	-2	2.3
● **FRANK BAUMANN** Baumann, Frank Matt "The Beau" b: 7/1/33, St.Louis, Mo. BL/TL, 6'1", 210 lbs. Deb: 7/31/55																								
1955 Bos-A	2	1	.667	7	5	0	0	0	34	38	2	17	27	14.8	5.82	74	.281	.366	3	.231	-0	-7	-6	0	-0.6
1956 Bos-A	2	1	.667	7	1	0	0	0	24²	22	3	14	18	13.1	3.28	141	.234	.333	3	.333	-0	1	2	-1	0.4
1957 Bos-A	1	0	1.000	4	1	0	0	0	12	13	1	3	7	12.8	3.75	106	.277	.333	1	.500	0	0	-0	-0	0.0
1958 Bos-A	2	2	.500	10	7	2	0	0	52¹	56	4	27	31	15.0	4.47	90	.276	.372	3	.214	1	-4	-3	-1	-0.2
1959 Bos-A	6	4	.600	26	10	2	0	1	95²	96	11	55	49	14.3	4.05	100	.259	.357	6	.207	1	-2	0	1	0.1
1960 Chi-A	13	6	.684	47	20	7	2	3	185¹	169	11	53	71	10.8	**2.67**	142	.247	.302	8	.154	1	25	23	2	2.2
1961 Chi-A	10	13	.435	53	23	5	1	3	187²	249	22	59	75	14.9	5.61	70	.318	.368	16	.262	6	-33	-35	1	-2.7
1962 Chi-A	7	6	.538	40	10	3	1	4	119²	117	10	36	55	11.7	3.38	115	.258	.316	8	.267	4	8	7	0	1.2
1963 Chi-A	2	1	.667	24	1	0	0	0	50¹	52	2	17	31	12.3	3.04	115	.265	.324	1	.091	-0	3	3	0	0.3
1964 Chi-A	0	3	.000	22	0	0	0	0	32	40	4	16	19	15.8	6.19	56	.320	.397	0	.000	-0	-9	-10	-0	-1.1
1965 Chi-N	0	1	.000	4	0	0	0	0	3²	4	0	3	2	17.2	7.36	50	.286	.412	0	—	0	-2	-1	0	-0.2
Total 11	45	38	.542	244	78	19	4	13	797¹	856	70	300	384	13.2	4.11	95	.276	.342	49	.218	14	-19	-19	-2	-0.6
● **GEORGE BAUMGARDNER** Baumgardner, George Washington b: 7/22/1891, Barboursville, W.Va. d: 12/13/70, Barboursville, W.Va. BL/TR, 5'11", 178 lbs. Deb: 4/14/12																								
1912 StL-A	11	13	.458	30	27	18	2	0	218¹	222	1	79	102	12.9	3.38	98	.274	.346	11	.145	-0	-2	-2	-0	-0.1
1913 StL-A	10	19	.345	38	31	23	2	1	253¹	267	6	84	78	12.8	3.13	94	.283	.348	13	.167	2	-5	-5	-2	-0.5
1914 StL-A	14	13	.519	45	18	9	3	3	183²	152	3	84	93	12.0	2.79	97	.229	.323	7	.132	-1	-2	-1	-0	-0.4
1915 StL-A	0	2	.000	7	1	1	0	0	22¹	29	1	6	9	16.1	4.43	65	.358	.435	0	.000	-1	-4	-4	-1	-0.4
1916 StL-A	1	0	1.000	4	2	0	0	0	8	12	0	3	4	19.1	7.88	35	.364	.447	0	.000	0	-4	-5	-1	-0.5
Total 5	36	47	.434	124	79	51	7	4	685²	682	10	263	283	12.8	3.22	93	.269	.345	31	.144	-0	-16	-17	-2	-1.9
● **ROSS BAUMGARTEN** Baumgarten, Ross b: 5/27/55, Highland Park, Ill. BL/TL, 6'1", 180 lbs. Deb: 8/16/78																								
1978 Chi-A	2	2	.500	7	4	1	0	0	39	39	9	15	15.3	5.87	65	.315	.382	0	—	0	-5	-5	-0	0.2
1979 Chi-A	13	8	.619	28	28	4	3	0	190²	175	18	83	72	12.2	3.54	120	.243	.322	0	—	0	14	15	-0	1.5
1980 Chi-A	2	12	.143	24	23	3	1	0	136	127	10	52	66	11.9	3.44	117	.256	.327	0	—	0	9	9	2	1.1

YEAR	TM/L	W	L	PCT	G	GS	CG	SH	SV	IP	H	HR	BB	SO	RAT	ERA	ERA+	OAV	OOB	BH	AVG	PB	PR	/A	PD	TPI
1981	Chi-A	5	9	.357	19	19	2	1	0	101^2	101	9	40	52	12.6	4.07	88	.260	.331	0	—	0	-5	-6	0	-0.6
1982	Pit-N	0	5	.000	12	10	0	0	0	44	60	3	27	17	17.8	6.75	55	.347	.435	1	.083	-1	-15	-15	0	-1.5
Total	5	22	36	.379	90	84	10	6	0	495^1	492	43	211	222	12.8	4.02	99	.263	.339	1	.083	-1	-2	-2	2	-0.1

● HARRY BAUMGARTNER
Baumgartner, Harry E. b: 10/8/1892, S.Pittsburg, Tenn. d: 12/3/30, Augusta, Ga. BR/TR, 5′11″, 175 lbs. Deb: 9/06/20

YEAR	TM/L	W	L	PCT	G	GS	CG	SH	SV	IP	H	HR	BB	SO	RAT	ERA	ERA+	OAV	OOB	BH	AVG	PB	PR	/A	PD	TPI
1920	Det-A	0	1	.000	9	0	0	0	0	18	18	1	6	7	12.0	4.00	93	.273	.333	1	.250	0	-0	-1	0	0.0

● STAN BAUMGARTNER
Baumgartner, Stanwood Fulton b: 12/14/1894, Houston, Tex. d: 10/4/55, Philadelphia, Pa. BL/TL, 6′, 175 lbs. Deb: 6/26/14

YEAR	TM/L	W	L	PCT	G	GS	CG	SH	SV	IP	H	HR	BB	SO	RAT	ERA	ERA+	OAV	OOB	BH	AVG	PB	PR	/A	PD	TPI
1914	Phi-N	2	2	.500	15	3	2	1	0	60^1	60	0	16	24	11.6	3.28	90	.270	.325	1	.053	-1	-3	-2	-1	-0.5
1915	Phi-N	0	2	.000	16	1	0	0	0	48^1	38	2	23	27	11.5	2.42	113	.226	.323	1	.083	-1	2	2	1	0.2
1916	Phi-N	0	0	—	1	0	0	0	0	4	5	0	1	0	13.5	2.25	118	.333	.375	0	.000	-0	0	0	-0	0.0
1921	Phi-N	3	6	.333	22	7	2	0	0	66^2	103	8	22	13	17.1	7.02	60	.355	.404	6	.200	0	-24	-21	-1	-2.0
1922	Phi-N	1	1	.500	6	1	0	0	0	9^2	18	1	5	2	21.4	6.52	72	.409	.469	1	.333	0	-3	-2	0	-0.1
1924	Phi-A	13	6	.684	36	16	12	1	4	181	181	6	73	45	12.8	2.88	**149**	.271	.347	13	.217	-0	27	28	-2	2.5
1925	Phi-A	6	3	.667	37	11	2	1	3	113^1	120	2	35	18	12.9	3.57	130	.275	.338	7	.233	-0	10	14	-1	1.2
1926	Phi-A	1	1	.500	10	1	0	0	0	22^1	28	0	10	0	15.3	4.03	103	.326	.396	1	.333	0	-0	0	1	0.1
Total	8	26	21	.553	143	40	18	3	7	505^2	553	19	185	129	13.4	3.70	109	.287	.354	30	.190	-1	9	19	-3	1.4

● GEORGE BAUSEWINE
Bausewine, George W. b: 3/22/1869, Philadelphia, Pa. d: 7/29/47, Norristown, Pa. 6′2″, Deb: 9/14/1889 U

YEAR	TM/L	W	L	PCT	G	GS	CG	SH	SV	IP	H	HR	BB	SO	RAT	ERA	ERA+	OAV	OOB	BH	AVG	PB	PR	/A	PD	TPI
1889	Phi-a	1	4	.200	7	6	6	0	0	55^1	64	1	33	18	17.2	3.90	97	.281	.393	1	.048	-2	-0	-1	0	-0.2

● ED BAUTA
Bauta, Eduardo (Galvez) b: 1/6/35, Florida Camaguey, Cuba BR/TR, 6′3″, 200 lbs. Deb: 7/06/60

YEAR	TM/L	W	L	PCT	G	GS	CG	SH	SV	IP	H	HR	BB	SO	RAT	ERA	ERA+	OAV	OOB	BH	AVG	PB	PR	/A	PD	TPI
1960	StL-N	0	0	—	9	0	0	0	1	15^2	14	4	11	6	14.9	6.32	65	.237	.366	0	.000	-0	-4	-4	-0	-0.4
1961	StL-N	2	0	1.000	13	0	0	0	5	19^1	12	2	5	12	7.9	1.40	315	.171	.227	2	.500	1	6	6	-0	0.7
1962	StL-N	1	0	1.000	20	0	0	0	1	32^1	28	5	21	25	13.9	5.01	85	.239	.360	1	.250	0	-4	-3	0	-0.2
1963	StL-N	3	4	.429	38	0	0	0	3	52^2	55	2	21	30	13.3	3.93	90	.279	.355	0	.000	-1	-4	-2	-1	-0.4
	NY-N	0	0	—	9	0	0	0	0	19	22	0	9	13	14.7	5.21	67	.289	.365	0	.000	-0	-4	-4	-0	-0.4
	Yr	3	4	.429	47	0	0	0	3	71^2	77	2	30	43	13.4	4.27	83	.278	.349	0	.000	-1	-8	-6	-1	-0.8
1964	NY-N	0	2	.000	8	0	0	0	1	10	17	1	3	3	18.0	5.40	66	.395	.435	0	—	0	-2	-2	0	-0.2
Total	5	6	6	.500	97	0	0	0	11	149	148	14	70	89	13.4	4.35	89	.263	.349	3	.176	-0	-13	-8	-1	-0.9

● JOSE BAUTISTA
Bautista, Jose Joaquin (Arias) b: 7/25/64, Bani, D.R. BR/TR, 6′1″, 205 lbs. Deb: 4/09/88

YEAR	TM/L	W	L	PCT	G	GS	CG	SH	SV	IP	H	HR	BB	SO	RAT	ERA	ERA+	OAV	OOB	BH	AVG	PB	PR	/A	PD	TPI
1988	Bal-A	6	15	.286	33	25	3	0	0	171^2	171	21	45	76	11.7	4.30	91	.258	.311	0	—	0	-6	-8	-1	-0.6
1989	Bal-A	3	4	.429	15	10	0	0	0	78	84	17	15	30	11.5	5.31	71	.274	.310	0	—	0	-12	-13	-1	-1.3
1990	Bal-A	1	0	1.000	22	0	0	0	0	26^2	28	4	7	15	11.8	4.05	94	.272	.318	0	—	0	-0	-1	-0	-0.1
1991	Bal-A	0	1	.000	5	0	0	0	0	5^1	13	1	5	3	32.1	16.88	23	.464	.559	0	—	0	-8	-8	0	-0.6
Total	4	10	20	.333	75	35	3	0	0	281^2	296	43	72	124	12.0	4.79	81	.269	.319	0	—	0	-27	-29	-2	-2.6

● BILL BAYNE
Bayne, William Lear "Beverly" b: 4/18/1899, Pittsburgh, Pa. d: 5/22/81, St.Louis, Mo. BL/TL, 5′9″, 160 lbs. Deb: 9/20/19

YEAR	TM/L	W	L	PCT	G	GS	CG	SH	SV	IP	H	HR	BB	SO	RAT	ERA	ERA+	OAV	OOB	BH	AVG	PB	PR	/A	PD	TPI
1919	StL-A	1	1	.500	2	2	1	0	0	12	16	0	6	0	16.5	5.25	63	.320	.393	2	.400	0	-3	-3	0	-0.2
1920	StL-A	5	6	.455	18	13	6	1	0	99^2	102	3	41	38	13.5	3.70	106	.279	.363	6	.171	-2	1	2	-2	-0.2
1921	StL-A	11	5	.688	47	14	6	1	3	164	167	8	80	82	13.8	4.72	95	.270	.358	18	.300	5	-8	-4	-1	0.0
1922	StL-A	4	5	.444	26	9	3	0	2	92^2	86	5	37	38	12.8	4.56	91	.249	.338	7	.233	-1	-5	-4	-2	-0.7
1923	StL-A	2	2	.500	19	2	0	0	0	46	49	4	31	15	16.2	4.50	93	.287	.405	3	.231	-0	-3	-2	-1	-0.3
1924	StL-A	1	3	.250	22	3	0	0	0	50^2	47	4	29	20	14.9	4.44	102	.250	.373	6	.429	3	-1	0	-1	0.2
1928	Cle-A	2	5	.286	37	6	3	0	3	108^2	128	3	43	39	15.0	5.13	81	.309	.388	11	.367	3	-13	-12	2	-0.8
1929	Bos-A	5	5	.500	27	6	2	0	0	84^1	111	9	29	26	15.8	6.72	64	.326	.392	8	.320	2	-23	-23	1	-1.8
1930	Bos-A	0	0	—	1	0	0	0	0	4	5	1	1	1	13.5	4.50	102	.294	.333	1	.500	0	0	0	0	0.0
Total	9	31	32	.492	199	55	21	2	8	662	711	37	297	259	14.4	4.84	87	.283	.370	62	.290	11	-55	-45	-3	-3.8

● WALTER BEALL
Beall, Walter Esau b: 7/29/1899, Washington, D.C. d: 1/28/59, Suitland, Md. BR/TR, 5′10″, 178 lbs. Deb: 9/03/24

YEAR	TM/L	W	L	PCT	G	GS	CG	SH	SV	IP	H	HR	BB	SO	RAT	ERA	ERA+	OAV	OOB	BH	AVG	PB	PR	/A	PD	TPI
1924	NY-A	2	0	1.000	4	2	0	0	0	23	19	2	17	18	14.1	3.52	118	.237	.371	1	.143	-1	2	2	-1	0.0
1925	NY-A	0	1	.000	8	1	0	0	0	11^1	11	0	19	8	26.2	12.71	34	.282	.541	0	.000	-1	-10	-11	0	-0.9
1926	NY-A	2	4	.333	20	9	1	0	1	81^2	71	2	68	56	16.0	3.53	109	.240	.392	3	.136	0	4	3	1	0.3
1927	NY-A	0	0	—	1	0	0	0	0	1	1	0	0	0	9.0	9.00	43	.333	.333	0	—	0	-1	-1	-0	-0.1
1929	Was-A	1	0	1.000	3	0	0	0	0	7	8	0	7	3	19.3	3.86	110	.348	.500	0	.000	-1	0	0	0	0.0
Total	5	5	5	.500	36	12	1	0	1	124	110	4	111	85	16.7	4.43	90	.249	.410	4	.114	-1	-4	-6	0	-0.7

● ALEX BEAM
Beam, Alexander Rodger b: 11/21/1870, Johnstown, Pa. d: 4/17/38, Nogales, Ariz. Deb: 5/25/1889

YEAR	TM/L	W	L	PCT	G	GS	CG	SH	SV	IP	H	HR	BB	SO	RAT	ERA	ERA+	OAV	OOB	BH	AVG	PB	PR	/A	PD	TPI
1889	Pit-N	1	1	.500	2	2	2	0	0	18	11	0	15	1	13.0	6.50	58	.171	.328	1	.167	0	-5	-6	-0	-0.4

● ERNIE BEAM
Beam, Ernest Joseph b: 3/17/1867, Mansfield, Ohio d: 9/12/18, Mansfield, Ohio 185 lbs. Deb: 5/02/1895

YEAR	TM/L	W	L	PCT	G	GS	CG	SH	SV	IP	H	HR	BB	SO	RAT	ERA	ERA+	OAV	OOB	BH	AVG	PB	PR	/A	PD	TPI
1895	Phi-N	0	2	.000	9	1	1	0	**3**	24^2	33	1	25	3	21.5	11.31	42	.316	.452	2	.182	-1	-18	-18	-0	-1.4

● CHARLIE BEAMON
Beamon, Charles Alfonzo Sr. b: 12/25/34, Oakland, Cal. BR/TR, 5′11″, 195 lbs. Deb: 9/26/56 F

YEAR	TM/L	W	L	PCT	G	GS	CG	SH	SV	IP	H	HR	BB	SO	RAT	ERA	ERA+	OAV	OOB	BH	AVG	PB	PR	/A	PD	TPI
1956	Bal-A	2	0	1.000	2	1	1	1	0	13	9	0	8	14	11.8	1.38	283	.191	.309	0	.000	-1	4	4	0	0.3
1957	Bal-A	0	0	—	4	1	0	0	0	8^2	8	1	7	5	16.6	5.19	69	.229	.372	0	.000	-0	-1	-2	-0	-0.2
1958	Bal-A	1	3	.250	21	3	0	0	0	49^2	47	3	21	26	13.4	4.35	83	.266	.363	0	.000	-1	-3	-4	2	-0.3
Total	3	3	3	.500	27	5	1	1	0	71^1	64	4	36	45	13.5	3.91	93	.247	.354	0	.000	-2	-1	-2	2	-0.2

● BELVE BEAN
Bean, Beveric Benton "Bill" b: 4/23/05, Mullin, Tex. d: 6/1/88, Comanche, Tex. BR/TR, 6′1.5″, 197 lbs. Deb: 5/30/30

YEAR	TM/L	W	L	PCT	G	GS	CG	SH	SV	IP	H	HR	BB	SO	RAT	ERA	ERA+	OAV	OOB	BH	AVG	PB	PR	/A	PD	TPI
1930	Cle-A	3	3	.500	23	3	1	0	2	74^1	99	7	32	19	15.9	5.45	89	.331	.396	9	.346	2	-7	-5	0	-0.3
1931	Cle-A	0	1	.000	4	0	0	0	0	7	11	0	4	3	20.6	6.43	72	.379	.471	0	.000	-0	-2	-1	0	-0.1
1933	Cle-A	1	2	.333	27	2	0	0	0	70^1	80	6	20	41	12.9	5.25	85	.300	.351	4	.182	-1	-8	-6	1	-0.6
1934	Cle-A	5	1	.833	21	1	0	0	0	51^1	53	2	21	20	13.5	3.86	118	.265	.344	3	.200	0	4	4	1	0.4
1935	Cle-A	0	0	—	1	0	0	0	0	1	2	1	0	0	18.0	9.00	50	.400	.400	0	—	0	-1	-0	-0	-0.1
	Was-A	2	0	1.000	10	2	0	0	0	31	43	5	19	6	18.0	7.26	60	.339	.425	3	.375	2	-10	-10	-1	-0.7
	Yr	2	0	1.000	11	2	0	0	0	32	45	6	19	6	18.0	7.31	59	.341	.424	3	.375	2	-10	-11	-1	-0.8
Total	5	11	7	.611	86	8	1	0	2	235	288	21	96	89	14.9	5.32	86	.311	.378	19	.264	4	-22	-19	1	-1.4

● DAVE BEARD
Beard, Charles David b: 10/2/59, Atlanta, Ga. BL/TR, 6′5″, 215 lbs. Deb: 7/16/80

YEAR	TM/L	W	L	PCT	G	GS	CG	SH	SV	IP	H	HR	BB	SO	RAT	ERA	ERA+	OAV	OOB	BH	AVG	PB	PR	/A	PD	TPI
1980	Oak-A	0	1	.000	13	0	0	0	1	16	12	0	7	12	11.3	3.38	112	.218	.317	0	—	0	1	1	-0	0.4
1981	*Oak-A	1	1	.500	8	0	0	0	3	13	9	1	4	15	9.7	2.77	126	.191	.269	0	—	0	1	1	0	0.1
1982	Oak-A	10	9	.526	54	2	0	0	11	91^2	85	9	35	73	11.9	3.44	114	.244	.315	0	—	0	6	5	-0	0.8
1983	Oak-A	5	5	.500	43	0	0	0	10	61	55	8	36	40	13.7	5.61	69	.246	.355	0	—	0	-10	-12	-1	-0.9
1984	Sea-A	3	2	.600	43	0	0	0	5	76	88	15	33	40	14.8	5.80	69	.291	.369	0	—	0	-15	-15	-0	-1.4
1985	Chi-N	0	0	—	9	0	0	0	0	12^2	16	2	7	4	16.3	6.39	62	.314	.397	0	—	0	-4	-3	-0	-0.4
1989	Det-A	0	2	.000	2	1	0	0	0	5^1	9	2	2	1	20.3	5.06	75	.375	.444	0	—	0	-1	-1	0	0.0
Total	7	19	20	.487	172	3	0	0	30	275^2	274	37	124	185	13.3	4.70	83	.261	.344	0	—	0	-21	-25	-2	-1.4

● MIKE BEARD
Beard, Michael Richard b: 6/21/50, Little Rock, Ark. BL/TL, 6′1″, 185 lbs. Deb: 9/07/74

YEAR	TM/L	W	L	PCT	G	GS	CG	SH	SV	IP	H	HR	BB	SO	RAT	ERA	ERA+	OAV	OOB	BH	AVG	PB	PR	/A	PD	TPI
1974	Atl-N	0	0	—	6	0	0	0	0	9^1	5	1	1	7	6.8	2.89	131	.156	.206	0	—	0	1	1	0	0.1
1975	Atl-N	4	0	1.000	34	2	0	0	0	70^1	71	4	28	27	12.9	3.20	118	.265	.339	1	.111	-0	3	4	0	0.5
1976	Atl-N	0	2	.000	30	0	0	0	1	33^2	38	1	14	8	13.9	4.28	89	.299	.369	0	.000	-0	-3	-2	1	-0.1
1977	Atl-N	0	0	—	4	0	0	0	0	4^2	14	3	2	1	30.9	9.64	46	.452	.485	0	—	0	-3	-3	0	-0.3
Total	4	4	2	.667	74	2	0	0	1	118	128	9	45	43	13.4	3.74	102	.279	.348	1	.100	-0	-2	1	1	0.2

YEAR TM/L	W	L	PCT	G	GS	CG	SH	SV	IP	H	HR	BB	SO	RAT	ERA	ERA+	OAV	OOB	BH	AVG	PB	PR	/A	PD	TPI

● **RALPH BEARD** Beard, Ralph William b: 2/11/29, Cincinnati, Ohio BR/TR, 6'5", 200 lbs. Deb: 6/29/54

| 1954 StL-N | 0 | 4 | .000 | 13 | 10 | 0 | 0 | 0 | 58 | 62 | 2 | 28 | 17 | 14.3 | 3.72 | 110 | .278 | .364 | 1 | .059 | -1 | 2 | 2 | -1 | 0.0 |

● **GENE BEARDEN** Bearden, Henry Eugene b: 9/5/20, Lexa, Ark. BL/TL, 6'3", 204 lbs. Deb: 5/10/47

1947 Cle-A	0	0	—	1	0	0	0	0	0¹	2	0	1	0	81.0	81.00	4	.667	.750	0	—	0	-3	-3	0	-0.3
1948 *Cle-A	20	7	.741	37	29	15	6	1	229²	187	9	106	80	11.6	2.43	167	.229	.320	23	.256	5	47	42	3	5.2
1949 Cle-A	8	8	.500	32	19	5	0	0	127	140	6	92	41	16.6	5.10	78	.286	.401	5	.111	-3	-13	-16	4	-1.4
1950 Cle-A	1	3	.250	14	3	0	0	0	45¹	57	5	32	10	17.7	6.15	70	.328	.432	2	.154	1	-8	-9	-1	-0.8
Was-A	3	5	.375	12	9	4	0	0	68¹	81	1	33	20	15.3	4.21	107	.297	.377	5	.227	1	3	2	0	0.3
Yr	4	8	.333	26	12	4	0	0	113²	138	6	65	30	16.2	4.99	89	.309	.399	7	.200	2	-5	-7	-0	-0.5
1951 Was-A	0	0	—	1	1	0	0	0	2²	6	0	2	1	27.0	16.88	24	.429	.500	0	—	0	-4	-4	-0	-0.3
Det-A	3	4	.429	37	4	2	1	0	106	112	6	58	38	14.5	4.33	96	.275	.366	6	.188	1	-2	-2	-0	-0.1
Yr	3	4	.429	38	5	2	1	0	108²	118	6	60	39	14.8	4.64	90	.280	.371	6	.188	1	-6	-6	-0	-0.4
1952 StL-A	7	8	.467	34	16	3	0	0	150²	158	13	78	45	14.2	4.30	91	.270	.357	23	.354	6	-10	-6	1	0.1
1953 Chi-A	3	3	.500	25	3	0	0	0	58¹	48	8	33	24	12.5	2.93	137	.223	.327	4	.190	-1	7	7	0	0.6
Total 7	45	38	.542	193	84	29	7	1	788¹	791	48	435	259	14.1	3.96	103	.266	.361	68	.236	10	17	12	7	3.3

● **GARY BEARE** Beare, Gary Ray b: 8/22/52, San Diego, Cal. BR/TR, 6'4", 205 lbs. Deb: 9/07/76

1976 Mil-A	2	3	.400	6	5	2	0	0	41	43	4	15	32	12.7	3.29	106	.274	.337	0	—	0	1	1	-0	0.2
1977 Mil-A	3	3	.500	17	6	0	0	0	58²	63	6	38	32	15.6	6.44	63	.276	.382	0	—	0	-16	-15	2	-1.3
Total 2	5	6	.455	23	11	2	0	0	99²	106	10	53	64	14.4	5.15	74	.275	.364	0	—	0	-15	-15	1	-1.1

● **LARRY BEARNARTH** Bearnarth, Lawrence Donald b: 9/11/41, New York, N.Y. BR/TR, 6'2", 203 lbs. Deb: 4/16/63 C

1963 NY-N	3	8	.273	58	2	0	0	4	126¹	127	7	47	48	12.8	3.42	102	.268	.340	6	.200	—	-2	1	2	0.5
1964 NY-N	5	5	.500	44	1	0	0	3	78	79	6	38	31	13.7	4.15	86	.271	.360	2	.143	-0	-5	-5	3	-0.3
1965 NY-N	3	5	.375	40	3	0	0	1	60²	75	6	28	16	15.9	4.60	77	.304	.384	1	.111	0	-7	-7	0	-0.7
1966 NY-N	2	3	.400	29	1	0	0	0	54²	59	11	20	27	13.2	4.45	82	.281	.346	1	.111	-0	-5	-5	1	-0.4
1971 Mil-A	0	0	—	2	0	0	0	0	3	10	1	2	2	36.0	18.00	19	.556	.600	0	—	0	-5	-5	0	-0.4
Total 5	13	21	.382	173	7	0	0	8	322²	350	31	135	124	13.9	4.13	86	.282	.358	10	.161	1	-24	-21	7	-1.3

● **KEVIN BEARSE** Bearse, Kevin Gerard b: 11/7/65, Jersey City, N.J. BL/TL, 6'2", 195 lbs. Deb: 4/15/90

| 1990 Cle-A | 0 | 2 | .000 | 3 | 3 | 0 | 0 | 0 | 7² | 16 | 2 | 5 | 2 | 27.0 | 12.91 | 30 | .421 | .511 | 0 | — | 0 | -8 | -8 | -0 | -0.7 |

● **CHRIS BEASLEY** Beasley, Christopher Charles b: 6/23/62, Jackson, Tenn. BR/TR, 6'2", 190 lbs. Deb: 7/20/91

| 1991 Cal-A | 0 | 1 | .000 | 22 | 0 | 0 | 0 | 0 | 26² | 26 | 2 | 10 | 14 | 12.5 | 3.38 | 122 | .257 | .330 | 0 | — | 0 | 2 | 2 | 0 | 0.3 |

● **ED BEATIN** Beatin, Ebenezer Ambrose b: 8/10/1866, Baltimore, Md. d: 5/9/25, Baltimore, Md. BR/TL, 5'9", 162 lbs. Deb: 8/02/1887

1887 Det-N	1	1	.500	2	2	2	0	0	18	13	2	8	6	11.0	4.00	101	.203	.301	0	.000	-1	0	0	-0	-0.1
1888 Det-N	5	7	.417	12	12	12	1	0	107	111	6	16	44	10.9	2.86	97	.251	.280	5	-0	-1	0	4		0.4
1889 Cle-N	20	15	.571	36	36	35	3	0	317²	316	12	141	126	13.1	3.57	113	.251	.330	14	.116	-5	16	16	-1	0.9
1890 Cle-N	22	30	.423	54	54	53	1	0	474¹	518	11	186	155	13.6	3.83	93	.269	.339	27	.141	-9	-14	-13	3	-1.7
1891 Cle-N	0	3	.000	5	4	2	0	0	29	39	1	21	4	20.5	5.28	66	.310	.432	1	.077	-2	-6	-6	-0	-0.6
Total 5	48	56	.462	109	108	104	5	0	946	997	32	372	335	13.3	3.68	99	.262	.332	56	.144	-12	-4	-4	1	-1.1

● **JIM BEATTIE** Beattie, James Louis b: 7/4/54, Hampton, Va. BR/TR, 6'6", 220 lbs. Deb: 4/25/78

1978 *NY-A	6	9	.400	25	22	0	0	0	128	123	8	51	65	12.8	3.73	97	.255	.336	0	—	0	1	-2	1	-0.1
1979 NY-A	3	6	.333	15	13	1	1	0	76	85	5	41	32	14.9	5.21	78	.294	.382	0	—	0	-8	-10	1	-0.8
1980 Sea-A	5	15	.250	33	29	3	0	0	187¹	205	19	98	67	14.7	4.85	85	.286	.375	0	—	0	-17	-15	0	-1.5
1981 Sea-A	3	2	.600	13	9	0	0	1	66²	59	2	18	36	10.7	2.97	130	.232	.288	0	—	0	5	7	0	0.7
1982 Sea-A	8	12	.400	28	26	6	1	0	172¹	149	13	65	140	11.2	3.34	127	.233	.305	0	—	0	14	17	1	1.6
1983 Sea-A	10	15	.400	30	29	8	2	0	196²	197	12	66	132	12.2	3.84	111	.259	.321	0	—	0	5	9	3	1.0
1984 Sea-A	12	16	.429	32	32	12	2	0	211	206	13	75	119	12.2	3.41	117	.260	.328	0	—	0	14	13	1	1.6
1985 Sea-A	5	6	.455	18	15	1	1	0	70¹	93	9	33	45	16.5	7.29	58	.316	.391	0	—	0	-25	-24	1	-2.3
1986 Sea-A	0	6	.000	9	7	0	0	0	40¹	57	7	14	24	16.5	6.02	70	.341	.402	0	—	0	-8	-8	1	-0.7
Total 9	52	87	.374	203	182	31	7	1	1148²	1174	88	461	660	13.0	4.17	98	.267	.341	0	—	0	-20	-12	7	-0.5

● **BLAINE BEATTY** Beatty, Gordon Blaine b: 4/25/64, Victoria, Tex. BL/TL, 6'2", 185 lbs. Deb: 9/16/89

1989 NY-N	0	0	—	2	1	0	0	0	6	5	1	2	3	10.5	1.50	218	.217	.280	1	.500	0	1	1	0	0.2
1991 NY-N	0	0	—	5	0	0	0	0	9²	9	0	4	7	12.1	2.79	130	.250	.325	0	—	0	1	1	0	0.1
Total 2	0	0	—	7	1	0	0	0	15²	14	1	6	10	11.5	2.30	152	.237	.308	1	.500	0	2	2	0	0.3

● **JOHNNY BEAZLEY** Beazley, John Andrew "Nig" b: 5/25/18, Nashville, Tenn. d: 4/21/90, Nashville, Tenn. BR/TR, 6'1.5", 190 lbs. Deb: 9/28/41

1941 StL-N	1	0	1.000	1	1	1	0	0	9	10	3	0	4	13.0	1.00	376	.294	.351	0	.000	-0	3	3	-0	0.3
1942 *StL-N	21	6	.778	43	23	13	3	3	215¹	181	4	73	91	10.7	2.13	161	.226	.293	10	.137	-1	28	31	0	3.4
1946 *StL-N	7	5	.583	19	18	5	0	0	103	109	6	55	36	14.7	4.46	77	.275	.368	8	.242	1	-12	-11	-1	-1.1
1947 Bos-N	2	0	1.000	9	2	2	0	0	28²	30	1	19	12	15.4	4.40	89	.273	.380	0	.000	-1	-1	-2	-0	-0.3
1948 Bos-N	0	1	.000	3	2	0	0	0	16	19	2	7	4	14.6	4.50	85	.284	.351	0	.000	-0	-1	-1	-0	-0.2
1949 Bos-N	0	0	—	1	0	0	0	0	2	0	0	1	0	0.0	0.00	—	.000	.000	0	—	0	1	1	-0	0.1
Total 6	31	12	.721	76	46	21	3	3	374	349	13	157	147	12.3	3.01	116	.247	.325	18	.150	-1	18	20	-1	2.2

● **BUCK BECANNON** Becannon, James Melvin b: 8/22/1859, New York, N.Y. d: 11/5/23, New York, N.Y. 5'10", 165 lbs. Deb: 10/15/1884 ♦

1884 *NY-a	1	0	1.000	1	1	0	0	0	6	2	0	2	2	6.0	1.50	208	.091	.167	0	.000	-0	1	1	0	0.1
1885 NY-a	2	8	.200	10	10	10	0	0	85	108	5	24	13	14.5	6.25	47	.296	.348	10	.303	2	-28	-31	0	-2.3
Total 2	3	8	.273	11	11	10	0	0	91	110	5	26	15	13.9	5.93	50	.284	.337	10	.244	1	-27	-30	0	-2.2

● **GEORGE BECHTEL** Bechtel, George A. b: 1848, Philadelphia, Pa. 5'11", 165 lbs. Deb: 5/20/1871 ♦

1871 Ath-n	1	2	.333	3	3	2	0	0	26	43	0	11	1	18.7	7.96	51	.319	.370	33	.351	1	-11	-11		-0.6
1873 Phi-n	0	2	.000	3	2	1	0	0	16	27	0	2	1	16.3	4.50	73	.318	.333	63	.244	0	-2	-2		-0.1
1874 Phi-n	1	3	.250	6	4	4	0	0	42	64	0	0		13.7	3.86	79	.320	.320	44	.291	1	-4	-4		-0.2
1875 Cen-n	2	12	.143	14	14	14	0	0	126	170	0	3		12.4	3.93	61	.277	.281	17	.274	3	-21	-21		-1.5
Ath-n	3	1	.750	4	4	4	0	0	36	45	0	3		12.0	2.25	117	.298	.312	46	.280	0	1	2		0.2
Yr	5	13	.278	18	18	18	0	0	162	215	0	6		12.3	3.56	69	.281	.287	63	.279	3	-20	-20		-1.3
Total 4 n	7	20	.259	30	27	25	0	0	246	349	0	19	1	13.5	4.13	59	.295	.306	277	.284	6	-46	-46		-2.2

● **GEORGE BECK** Beck, Ernest George B. b: 2/21/1890, South Bend, Ind. d: 10/29/73, South Bend, Ind. BR/TR, 5'11", 165 lbs. Deb: 5/15/14

| 1914 Cle-A | 0 | 0 | — | 1 | 0 | 0 | 0 | 0 | 1 | 1 | 0 | 0 | 0 | 18.0 | 0.00 | — | .250 | .400 | 0 | — | 0 | 0 | 0 | -0 | 0.0 |

● **FRANK BECK** Beck, Frank J. b: 1862, Poughkeepsie, N.Y. TR, Deb: 5/02/1884 ♦

1884 Pit-a	0	3	.000	3	3	3	0	0	25	33	0	6	11	15.8	6.12	55	.306	.370	4	.333	1	-8	-8	0	-0.6
Bal-U	0	2	.000	2	2	1	0	0	9	17	0	4	7	21.0	8.00	41	.378	.429	2	.100	-1	-5	-5	0	-0.4
Total 1	0	5	.000	5	5	4	0	0	34	50	0	10	18	17.2	6.62	51	.327	.387	6	.188	-0	-13	-12	0	-1.0

● **RICH BECK** Beck, Richard Henry b: 1/21/41, Pasco, Wash. BB/TR, 6'3", 190 lbs. Deb: 9/14/65

| 1965 NY-A | 2 | 1 | .667 | 3 | 3 | 1 | 1 | 0 | 21 | 22 | 1 | 7 | 10 | 12.4 | 2.14 | 159 | .275 | .333 | 0 | .000 | -0 | 3 | 3 | 0 | 0.3 |

YEAR	TM/L	W	L	PCT	G	GS	CG	SH	SV	IP	H	HR	BB	SO	RAT	ERA	ERA+	OAV	OOB	BH	AVG	PB	PR	/A	PD	TPI
● ROD BECK		Beck, Rodney Roy b: 8/3/68, Burbank, Cal. BR/TR, 6'1", 215 lbs. Deb: 5/06/91																								
1991	SF-N	1	1	.500	31	0	0	0	1	52^1	53	4	13	38	11.5	3.78	95	.273	.322	1	.500	0	-1	-1	0	0.0
1992	SF-N	3	3	.500	65	0	0	0	17	92	62	4	15	87	7.7	1.76	190	.190	.230	1	.500	0	18	16	-0	1.8
Total	2	4	4	.500	96	0	0	0	18	144^1	115	8	28	125	9.1	2.49	138	.221	.264	2	.500	1	17	15	0	1.8
● BOOM-BOOM BECK		Beck, Walter William b: 10/16/04, Decatur, Ill. d: 5/7/87, Champaign, Ill. BR/TR, 6'2", 200 lbs. Deb: 9/22/24 C																								
1924	StL-A	0	0	—	1	0	0	0	0	1	2	0	1	0	27.0	0.00	—	.667	.750	0	—	0	0	1	0	0.1
1927	StL-A	1	0	1.000	3	1	1	0	0	11^1	15	0	5	6	16.7	5.56	78	.333	.412	1	.250	-0	-2	-2	-0	-0.2
1928	StL-A	2	3	.400	16	4	2	0	0	49	52	4	20	17	14.0	4.41	95	.289	.373	6	.429	1	-2	-1	-0	0.0
1933	Bro-N	12	20	.375	43	35	15	3	1	257	270	9	69	89	12.3	3.54	91	.267	.321	18	.189	0	-6	-9	-0	-0.9
1934	Bro-N	2	6	.250	22	9	2	0	0	57	72	6	32	24	17.2	7.42	53	.301	.395	4	.235	1	-21	-22	1	-1.9
1939	Phi-N	7	14	.333	34	16	12	0	3	182^2	203	11	64	77	13.3	4.73	85	.284	.345	9	.132	-3	-16	-15	-0	-1.7
1940	Phi-N	4	9	.308	29	15	4	0	0	129^1	147	13	41	38	13.7	4.31	90	.286	.349	2	.056	-3	-7	-6	1	-0.8
1941	Phi-N	1	9	.100	34	7	2	0	0	95^1	104	8	35	34	13.3	4.63	80	.276	.341	3	.120	-2	-11	-10	-3	-1.4
1942	Phi-N	0	1	.000	26	1	0	0	0	53	69	4	17	10	14.8	4.75	70	.325	.378	4	.333	1	-8	-9	-1	-0.8
1943	Phi-N	0	0	—	4	0	0	0	0	13^2	24	1	5	3	20.4	9.88	34	.393	.456	2	.500	1	-10	-10	-0	-0.9
1944	Det-A	1	2	.333	28	2	0	0	1	74	67	5	27	25	11.8	3.89	92	.243	.317	7	.318	2	-4	-3	-2	-0.3
1945	Cin-N	2	4	.333	11	5	2	0	1	47^2	42	0	12	9	10.4	3.40	111	.236	.288	3	.214	-0	2	2	0	0.2
	Pit-N	6	1	.857	14	5	4	0	0	63	54	2	14	20	9.7	2.14	184	.234	.278	2	.125	-1	12	13	-0	1.2
	Yr	8	5	.615	25	10	6	0	1	110^2	96	2	26	29	9.9	2.68	144	.234	.280	5	.167	-1	14	15	-0	1.4
Total	12	38	69	.355	265	100	44	3	6	1034	1121	63	342	352	13.1	4.30	86	.277	.340	61	.187	-2	-72	-71	-5	-7.4
● CHARLIE BECKER		Becker, Charles S. "Buck" b: 10/14/1888, Washington, D.C. d: 7/30/28, Washington, D, C. BL/TL, 6'2", 180 lbs. Deb: 8/02/11																								
1911	Was-A	3	5	.375	11	5	5	1	0	71^1	80	2	23	31	13.9	4.04	81	.268	.335	5	.227	-0	-5	-6	-0	-0.6
1912	Was-A	0	0	—	4	0	0	0	0	9	8	0	6	5	14.0	3.00	111	.258	.378	1	.500	0	0	0	-0	0.0
Total	2	3	5	.375	15	5	5	1	0	80^1	88	2	29	36	13.9	3.92	84	.267	.340	6	.250	0	-5	-6	-1	-0.6
● BOB BECKER		Becker, Robert Charles b: 8/15/1875, Syracuse, N.Y. d: 10/11/51, Syracuse, N.Y. TL , Deb: 9/06/1897																								
1897	Phi-N	0	2	.000	5	2	2	0	0	24	32	0	7	10	15.0	5.63	75	.317	.367	1	.111	-0	-3	-4	-0	-0.4
1898	Phi-N	0	0	—	1	0	0	0	0	5	6	0	5	0	19.8	10.80	32	.295	.434	0	.000	0	-4	-4	0	-0.3
Total	2	0	2	.000	6	2	2	0	0	29	38	0	12	10	15.8	6.52	62	.313	.380	1	.100	-0	-7	-8	-0	-0.7
● JAKE BECKLEY		Beckley, Jacob Peter "Eagle Eye" b: 8/4/1867, Hannibal, Mo. d: 6/25/18, Kansas City, Mo. BL/TL, 5'10", 200 lbs. Deb: 6/20/1888 H♦																								
1902	Cin-N	0	1	.000	1	1	0	0	0	4	9	0	1	2	22.5	6.75	44	.442	.468	175	.330	0	-2	-2	1	-0.1
● JIM BECKMAN		Beckman, James Joseph b: 3/1/05, Cincinnati, Ohio BR/TR, 5'10", 172 lbs. Deb: 7/27/27																								
1927	Cin-N	0	1	.000	4	1	0	0	0	12^1	18	2	6	0	18.2	5.84	65	.340	.417	0	.000	0	-3	-3	-1	-0.3
1928	Cin-N	0	1	.000	6	0	0	0	0	15^1	19	1	9	4	16.4	5.87	67	.306	.394	0	.000	-0	-3	-3	-0	-0.4
Total	2	0	2	.000	10	1	0	0	0	27^2	37	3	15	4	17.2	5.86	66	.322	.405	0	.000	-0	-6	-6	-1	-0.7
● BILL BECKMANN		Beckmann, William Aloysius b: 12/8/07, Clayton, Mo. d: 1/2/90, Florissant, Mo. BR/TR, 6', 175 lbs. Deb: 5/02/39																								
1939	Phi-A	7	11	.389	27	19	7	2	0	155^1	198	15	41	20	13.9	5.39	87	.312	.355	13	.250	0	-13	-12	-2	-1.1
1940	Phi-A	8	4	.667	34	9	6	2	1	127^1	132	11	35	47	11.9	4.17	107	.265	.314	8	.205	-1	3	4	-2	0.1
1941	Phi-A	5	9	.357	22	15	4	0	1	130	141	11	33	28	12.2	4.57	92	.270	.315	9	.191	0	-6	-6	-3	-0.8
1942	Phi-A	0	1	.000	5	1	0	0	0	20^1	24	1	9	10	14.6	7.08	53	.289	.359	2	.500	1	-8	-7	-1	-0.6
	StL-N	1	0	1.000	2	0	0	0	0	7	4	0	1	3	6.4	0.00	—	.200	.238	0	.000	-0	3	3	0	0.3
Total	4	21	25	.457	90	44	17	4	2	440	499	38	119	108	12.7	4.79	92	.284	.330	32	.224	1	-22	-18	-7	-2.1
● JOE BECKWITH		Beckwith, Thomas Joseph b: 1/28/55, Opelika, Ala. BL/TR, 6'3", 200 lbs. Deb: 7/21/79																								
1979	LA-N	1	2	.333	17	0	0	0	2	37^1	42	4	15	28	13.7	4.34	84	.284	.350	0	.000	-1	-3	-3	0	-0.3
1980	LA-N	3	3	.500	38	0	0	0	0	59^2	60	1	23	40	12.7	1.96	178	.263	.333	0	.000	0	11	10	-1	1.0
1982	LA-N	2	1	.667	19	1	0	0	1	40	38	2	14	33	11.7	2.70	128	.252	.315	0	.000	-1	4	3	-1	0.2
1983	*LA-N	3	4	.429	42	3	0	0	1	71	73	5	35	50	13.8	3.55	101	.264	.348	1	.200	0	1	0	1	0.1
1984	KC-A	8	4	.667	49	1	0	0	2	100^2	92	13	25	75	10.6	3.40	119	.247	.298	0	—	0	7	7	0	0.7
1985	*KC-A	1	5	.167	49	0	0	0	1	95	99	9	32	80	12.7	4.07	102	.269	.333	0	—	0	1	1	0	0.1
1986	LA-N	0	0	—	15	0	0	0	0	18^1	28	5	6	13	16.7	6.87	50	.350	.395	0	—	0	-6	-7	-1	-0.8
Total	7	18	19	.486	229	5	0	0	7	422	432	39	150	319	12.6	3.54	107	.266	.331	1	.053	-1	14	12	-0	1.0
● JULIO BECQUER		Becquer, Julio (Villegas) b: 12/20/31, Havana, Cuba BL/TL, 5'11.5", 178 lbs. Deb: 9/13/55 ♦																								
1960	Was-A	0	0	—	1	0	0	0	0	1	1	1	0	0	9.0	9.00	43	.250	.250	75	.252	0	-1	-1	-0	-0.1
1961	Min-A	0	0	—	1	0	0	0	0	1^1	4	0	1	0	33.8	20.25	21	.500	.556	20	.238	0	-2	-2	-0	-0.2
Total	2	0	0	—	2	0	0	0	0	2^1	5	1	1	0	23.1	15.43	26	.417	.462	238	.244	0	-3	-3	-0	-0.3
● PHIL BEDGOOD		Bedgood, Phillip Burlette b: 3/8/1898, Harrison, Ga. d: 11/8/27, Fort Pierce, Fla. BR/TR, 6'3", 218 lbs. Deb: 9/20/22																								
1922	Cle-A	1	0	1.000	1	1	1	0	0	9	7	0	4	5	14.0	4.00	100	.233	.378	0	.000	-0	0	0	-0	0.0
1923	Cle-A	0	2	.000	9	2	0	0	0	18^2	16	0	14	7	15.4	5.30	75	.246	.395	1	.250	0	-3	-3	-0	-0.2
Total	2	1	2	.333	10	3	1	0	0	27^2	23	0	18	12	15.0	4.88	82	.242	.390	1	.167	0	-3	-3	-0	-0.2
● HUGH BEDIENT		Bedient, Hugh Carpenter b: 10/23/1889, Gerry, N.Y. d: 7/21/65, Jamestown, N.Y. BR/TR, 6', 185 lbs. Deb: 4/26/12																								
1912	*Bos-A	20	9	.690	41	28	19	0	2	231	206	6	55	122	10.3	2.92	116	.240	.288	14	.192	1	10	12	1	1.4
1913	Bos-A	15	14	.517	43	28	15	1	5	259	255	0	67	122	11.4	2.78	106	.261	.312	10	.125	-3	4	5	-4	-0.3
1914	Bos-A	8	12	.400	42	16	7	1	2	177^1	187	4	45	70	12.0	3.60	75	.281	.331	5	.100	-2	-17	-18	-1	-2.2
1915	Buf-F	16	18	.471	53	30	16	2	**10**	269^1	284	5	69	106	11.9	3.17	98	.274	.321	9	.108	-4	-4	-2	-2	-0.9
Total	4	59	53	.527	179	102	57	4	19	936^2	932	15	236	420	11.4	3.08	99	.263	.312	38	.133	-8	-7	-3	-7	-2.0
● ANDY BEDNAR		Bednar, Andrew Jackson b: 8/16/08, Streator, Ill. d: 11/26/37, Graham, Tex. BR/TR, 5'10.5", 180 lbs. Deb: 9/06/30																								
1930	Pit-N	0	0	—	2	0	0	0	0	1^1	4	0	1	1	33.8	27.00	18	.500	.556	0	—	0	-3	-3	0	-0.3
1931	Pit-N	0	0	—	3	0	0	0	0	4	10	1	0	2	22.5	11.25	34	.476	.476	0	—	0	-3	-3	0	-0.3
Total	2	0	0	—	5	0	0	0	0	5^1	14	1	1	3	25.3	15.19	27	.483	.500	0	—	0	-7	-7	0	-0.6
● STEVE BEDROSIAN		Bedrosian, Stephen Wayne b: 12/6/57, Methuen, Mass. BR/TR, 6'3", 200 lbs. Deb: 8/14/81																								
1981	Atl-N	1	2	.333	15	1	0	0	0	24^1	15	2	15	9	11.5	4.44	81	.169	.295	0	.000	-0	-3	-2	-0	-0.3
1982	*Atl-N	8	6	.571	64	3	0	0	11	137^2	102	7	57	123	10.7	2.42	154	.206	.293	1	.038	-2	18	20	-0	1.9
1983	Atl-N	9	10	.474	70	1	0	0	19	120	100	11	51	114	11.6	3.60	108	.229	.315	2	.105	-1	0	4	0	0.3
1984	Atl-N	9	6	.600	40	4	0	0	11	83^2	65	5	33	81	10.6	2.37	163	.210	.289	2	.118	-1	11	14	-1	1.3
1985	Atl-N	7	15	.318	37	37	0	0	0	206^2	198	17	111	134	13.7	3.83	100	.254	.351	5	.078	-4	-6	0	-2	-0.6
1986	Phi-N	8	6	.571	68	0	0	0	29	90^1	79	12	34	82	11.3	3.39	114	.232	.301	1	.200	0	3	5	-1	0.5
1987	Phi-N★	5	3	.625	65	0	0	0	**40**	89	79	11	28	74	10.9	2.83	150	.237	.298	0	.000	-0	12	14	-1	1.2
1988	Phi-N	6	6	.500	57	0	0	0	28	74^1	75	6	27	61	12.3	3.75	95	.257	.320	0	.000	-0	-3	-2	-0	-0.2
1989	Phi-N	2	3	.400	28	0	0	0	6	33^2	21	7	17	24	10.4	3.21	110	.183	.293	0	—	0	1	1	-0	0.1
	*SF-N	1	4	.200	40	0	0	0	17	51	35	5	22	34	10.1	2.65	127	.192	.279	1	.167	-0	5	4	-1	0.3
	Yr	3	7	.300	68	0	0	0	23	84^2	56	12	39	58	10.1	2.87	120	.187	.280	1	.167	-0	6	5	-2	0.4
1990	SF-N	9	9	.500	68	0	0	0	17	79^1	72	6	44	43	13.4	4.20	87	.241	.342	2	.500	1	-4	-5	0	-0.4
1991	*Min-A	5	3	.625	56	0	0	0	6	77^1	70	11	35	44	12.6	4.42	96	.243	.331	0	—	0	-3	-1	-1	-0.3
Total	11	70	73	.490	608	46	0	0	184	1067^1	911	100	474	823	11.9	3.39	113	.230	.316	14	.094	-8	34	52	-8	3.8

● FRED BEEBE
Beebe, Frederick Leonard b: 12/31/1880, Lincoln, Neb. d: 10/30/57, Elgin, Ill. BR/TR, 6'1", 190 lbs. Deb: 4/17/06

YEAR	TM/L	W	L	PCT	G	GS	CG	SH	SV	IP	H	HR	BB	SO	RAT	ERA	ERA+	OAV	OOB	BH	AVG	PB	PR	/A	PD	TPI
1906	Chi-N	6	1	.857	14	6	4	0	1	70	56	1	32	55	12.0	2.70	98	.210	.306	3	.103	-1	-1	-0	-1	-0.3
	StL-N	9	9	.500	20	19	16	1	0	160^{2}	115	1	68	116	10.8	3.02	87	.208	.305	10	.172	0	-7	-7	-0	-0.8
	Yr	15	10	.600	34	25	20	1	1	230^{2}	171	2	100	**171**	10.9	2.93	90	.207	.300	13	.149	-1	-7	-8	-1	-1.1
1907	StL-N	7	19	.269	31	29	24	4	0	238^{1}	192	1	109	141	11.7	2.72	92	.230	.326	11	.128	-3	-7	-6	1	-0.8
1908	StL-N	5	13	.278	29	19	12	0	0	174^{1}	134	3	66	72	10.5	2.63	90	**.193**	.267	7	.125	-2	-5	-5	2	-0.6
1909	StL-N	15	21	.417	44	34	18	1	1	287^{2}	256	5	104	105	11.5	2.82	90	.229	.299	18	.167	-2	-7	-9	1	-1.1
1910	Cin-N	12	14	.462	35	26	11	2	0	214^{1}	193	3	94	93	12.3	3.07	95	.246	.333	12	.164	-2	-1	-4	3	-0.3
1911	Phi-N	3	3	.500	9	8	3	0	0	48^{1}	52	2	24	20	14.7	4.47	77	.297	.391	5	.263	2	-6	-6	1	-0.3
1916	Cle-A	5	3	.625	20	12	5	1	2	100^{2}	92	1	37	32	11.6	2.41	125	.251	.321	6	.214	1	5	7	-0	0.8
Total	7	62	83	.428	202	153	93	9	4	1294^{1}	1090	17	534	634	11.6	2.86	93	.227	.311	72	.158	-8	-28	-30	6	-3.4

● ED BEECHER
Beecher, Edward H. b: 7/2/1860, Guilford, Conn. d: 9/12/35, Hartford, Conn. BL/TL, 5'10", 185 lbs. Deb: 6/28/1887 ♦

YEAR	TM/L	W	L	PCT	G	GS	CG	SH	SV	IP	H	HR	BB	SO	RAT	ERA	ERA+	OAV	OOB	BH	AVG	PB	PR	/A	PD	TPI
1890	Buf-P	0	0	—	1	0	0	0	0	6	10	0	3	0	19.5	12.00	34	.356	.418	159	.297	0	-5	-5	-0	-0.4

● ROY BEECHER
Beecher, Leroy "Colonel" b: 5/10/1884, Swanton, Ohio d: 10/11/52, Toledo, Ohio BL/TR, 6'2", 180 lbs. Deb: 9/29/07

YEAR	TM/L	W	L	PCT	G	GS	CG	SH	SV	IP	H	HR	BB	SO	RAT	ERA	ERA+	OAV	OOB	BH	AVG	PB	PR	/A	PD	TPI
1907	NY-N	0	2	.000	2	2	2	0	0	14	17	0	6	5	14.8	2.57	96	.293	.359	0	.000	-1	-0	-0	-0	-0.1
1908	NY-N	0	0	—	2	0	0	0	1	5^{2}	11	0	3	0	22.2	7.94	30	.440	.500	1	.333	1	-4	-3	0	-0.3
Total	2	0	2	.000	4	2	2	0	1	19^{2}	28	0	9	5	16.9	4.12	60	.337	.402	1	.125	-0	-4	-4	0	-0.4

● FRED BEENE
Beene, Freddy Ray b: 11/24/42, Angleton, Tex. BB/TR, 5'9", 160 lbs. Deb: 9/18/68

YEAR	TM/L	W	L	PCT	G	GS	CG	SH	SV	IP	H	HR	BB	SO	RAT	ERA	ERA+	OAV	OOB	BH	AVG	PB	PR	/A	PD	TPI
1968	Bal-A	0	0	—	1	0	0	0	0	1	2	0	1	1	27.0	9.00	33	.500	.600	0	—	0	-1	-1	0	-0.1
1969	Bal-A	0	0	—	2	0	0	0	0	2^{2}	2	0	1	0	10.1	0.00	—	.200	.273	0	—	0	1	1	0	0.1
1970	Bal-A	0	0	—	4	0	0	0	0	6	8	1	5	4	19.5	6.00	61	.320	.433	0	—	0	-2	-2	-0	-0.2
1972	NY-A	1	3	.250	29	1	0	0	3	57^{2}	55	3	24	37	12.5	2.34	126	.256	.333	0	.000	-1	5	4	0	0.3
1973	NY-A	6	0	1.000	19	4	0	0	1	91	67	5	27	49	9.4	1.68	218	.209	.273	0	—	0	22	20	1	2.5
1974	NY-A	0	0	—	6	0	0	0	1	10	9	1	2	10	10.8	2.70	129	.231	.286	0	—	0	1	1	0	0.3
	Cle-A	4	4	.500	32	0	0	0	2	73	68	7	26	35	11.7	4.93	73	.246	.314	0	—	0	-11	-11	1	-0.9
	Yr	4	4	.500	38	0	0	0	3	83	77	8	28	45	11.5	4.66	77	.244	.307	0	—	0	-10	-10	1	-0.6
1975	Cle-A	1	0	1.000	19	1	0	0	1	46^{2}	63	4	25	20	17.6	6.94	54	.323	.408	0	—	0	-16	-16	0	-1.6
Total	7	12	7	.632	112	6	0	0	8	288	274	21	111	156	12.3	3.63	97	.253	.326	0	.000	-1	-1	-4	2	0.4

● ANDY BEENE
Beene, Ramon Andrew b: 10/13/56, Freeport, Tex. BR/TR, 6'3", 205 lbs. Deb: 9/22/83

YEAR	TM/L	W	L	PCT	G	GS	CG	SH	SV	IP	H	HR	BB	SO	RAT	ERA	ERA+	OAV	OOB	BH	AVG	PB	PR	/A	PD	TPI
1983	Mil-A	0	0	—	1	0	0	0	0	2	3	0	1	0	18.0	4.50	83	.333	.400	0	—	0	-0	-0	-0	0.8
1984	Mil-A	0	2	.000	5	3	0	0	0	18^{2}	28	1	9	11	18.8	11.09	35	.350	.429	0	—	0	-15	-15	0	-1.1
Total	2	0	2	.000	6	3	0	0	0	20^{2}	31	1	10	11	18.7	10.45	37	.348	.426	0	—	0	-15	-15	0	-0.3

● CLARENCE BEERS
Beers, Clarence Scott b: 12/9/18, ElDorado, Kan. BR/TR, 6', 175 lbs. Deb: 5/02/48

YEAR	TM/L	W	L	PCT	G	GS	CG	SH	SV	IP	H	HR	BB	SO	RAT	ERA	ERA+	OAV	OOB	BH	AVG	PB	PR	/A	PD	TPI
1948	StL-N	0	0	—	1	0	0	0	0	0^{2}	3	0	1	0	54.0	13.50	30	.500	.571	0	—	0	-1	-1	-0	-0.1

● JOE BEGGS
Beggs, Joseph Stanley "Fireman" b: 11/4/10, Rankin, Pa. d: 7/19/83, Indianapolis, Ind BR/TR, 6'1", 182 lbs. Deb: 4/19/38

YEAR	TM/L	W	L	PCT	G	GS	CG	SH	SV	IP	H	HR	BB	SO	RAT	ERA	ERA+	OAV	OOB	BH	AVG	PB	PR	/A	PD	TPI
1938	NY-A	3	2	.600	14	9	4	0	0	58^{1}	69	7	20	8	13.7	5.40	84	.299	.355	5	.250	1	-4	-6	2	-0.3
1940	*Cin-N	12	3	.800	37	1	0	0	**7**	76^{2}	68	1	21	25	10.6	2.00	190	.243	.298	4	.190	-0	**16**	**15**	1	1.7
1941	Cin-N	4	3	.571	37	0	0	0	5	57	57	2	27	19	13.3	3.79	95	.313	.402	3	.300	1	-1	-1	0	0.0
1942	Cin-N	6	5	.545	38	0	0	0	8	88^{2}	65	4	33	24	10.0	2.13	154	.206	.283	0	.000	-3	12	11	3	1.2
1943	Cin-N	7	6	.538	39	4	4	2	6	115^{1}	121	0	25	28	11.4	2.34	142	.276	.315	5	.143	-1	**13**	**12**	1	1.4
1944	Cin-N	1	0	1.000	1	1	1	0	0	9	8	0	0	2	8.0	2.00	174	.222	.222	0	.000	-1	2	1	0	0.1
1946	Cin-N	12	10	.545	28	22	14	2	1	190	175	15	39	38	10.2	2.32	144	.247	.287	14	.222	2	23	22	1	2.8
1947	Cin-N	0	3	.000	11	4	0	0	0	32^{1}	42	4	6	11	13.4	5.29	78	.316	.345	1	.091	-1	-4	-4	1	-0.4
	NY-N	3	3	.500	32	0	0	0	2	66	81	6	18	23	13.6	4.23	96	.300	.346	1	.077	-1	-1	-1	-0	-0.2
	Yr	3	6	.333	43	4	0	0	2	98^{1}	123	10	24	34	13.5	4.58	89	.305	.346	2	.083	-2	-6	-5	0	-0.6
1948	NY-N	0	0	—	1	0	0	0	0	0^{1}	2	0	0	0	54.0	0.00	—	.667	.667	0	—	0	0	0	0	0.0
Total	9	48	35	.578	238	41	23	4	29	693^{2}	688	39	189	178	11.4	2.96	122	.265	.316	33	.167	-3	55	50	8	6.3

● ED BEGLEY
Begley, Edward N. (b: Edward N. Bagley) b: 1863, New York, N.Y. d: 7/24/19, Waterbury, Conn. Deb: 5/03/1884

YEAR	TM/L	W	L	PCT	G	GS	CG	SH	SV	IP	H	HR	BB	SO	RAT	ERA	ERA+	OAV	OOB	BH	AVG	PB	PR	/A	PD	TPI
1884	NY-N	12	18	.400	31	30	30	0	0	266	296	9	99	104	13.4	4.16	72	.263	.323	22	.182	-3	-35	-35	-2	-3.4
1885	NY-a	4	9	.308	15	14	10	0	0	115	131	5	48	44	14.6	4.93	60	.278	.355	9	.173	-0	-21	-25	1	-2.1
Total	2	16	27	.372	46	44	40	0	0	381	427	14	147	148	13.7	4.39	68	.268	.333	31	.179	-3	-56	-60	-1	-5.5

● PETIE BEHAN
Behan, Charles Frederick b: 12/11/1887, Dallas City, Pa. d: 1/22/57, Bradford, Pa. BR/TR, 5'10", 160 lbs. Deb: 9/16/21

YEAR	TM/L	W	L	PCT	G	GS	CG	SH	SV	IP	H	HR	BB	SO	RAT	ERA	ERA+	OAV	OOB	BH	AVG	PB	PR	/A	PD	TPI
1921	Phi-N	0	1	.000	2	2	1	0	0	10^{2}	17	0	1	3	15.2	5.91	72	.354	.367	0	.000	-1	-3	-2	-0	-0.3
1922	Phi-N	4	2	.667	7	5	3	1	0	47^{1}	49	3	14	13	12.2	2.47	189	.259	.314	5	.250	0	9	12	-1	1.1
1923	Phi-N	3	12	.200	31	17	5	0	2	131	182	11	57	27	16.5	5.50	84	.336	.401	8	.186	-2	-22	-13	-1	-1.5
Total	3	7	15	.318	40	24	9	1	2	189	248	14	72	43	15.3	4.76	97	.319	.378	13	.194	-3	-16	-3	-2	-0.7

● RICK BEHENNA
Behenna, Richard Kipp b: 3/6/60, Miami, Fla. BR/TR, 6'2", 170 lbs. Deb: 4/12/83

YEAR	TM/L	W	L	PCT	G	GS	CG	SH	SV	IP	H	HR	BB	SO	RAT	ERA	ERA+	OAV	OOB	BH	AVG	PB	PR	/A	PD	TPI
1983	Atl-N	3	3	.500	14	6	0	0	0	37^{1}	37	7	12	17	12.1	4.58	85	.255	.316	4	.333	2	-4	-3	-0	-0.2
	Cle-A	0	2	.000	5	4	0	0	0	26	22	0	14	9	12.8	4.15	102	.232	.336	0	—	0	-0	0	0	-0.2
1984	Cle-A	0	3	.000	3	3	0	0	0	9^{2}	17	5	8	6	24.2	13.97	29	.386	.491	0	—	0	-11	-11	0	-1.0
1985	Cle-A	0	2	.000	4	4	0	0	0	19^{2}	29	3	8	4	16.9	7.78	53	.354	.411	0	—	0	-8	-8	-1	-0.7
Total	3	3	10	.231	26	17	0	0	0	92^{2}	105	15	42	36	14.6	6.12	66	.287	.365	4	.333	2	-23	-21	-1	-2.1

● MEL BEHNEY
Behney, Melvin Brian b: 9/2/47, Newark, N.J. BL/TL, 6'2", 180 lbs. Deb: 8/14/70

YEAR	TM/L	W	L	PCT	G	GS	CG	SH	SV	IP	H	HR	BB	SO	RAT	ERA	ERA+	OAV	OOB	BH	AVG	PB	PR	/A	PD	TPI
1970	Cin-N	0	2	.000	5	1	0	0	0	10	15	1	8	2	20.7	4.50	90	.341	.442	0	.000	-0	-1	-1	-0	-0.1

● HANK BEHRMAN
Behrman, Henry Bernard b: 6/27/21, Brooklyn, N.Y. d: 1/20/87, New York, N.Y. BR/TR, 5'11", 174 lbs. Deb: 4/17/46

YEAR	TM/L	W	L	PCT	G	GS	CG	SH	SV	IP	H	HR	BB	SO	RAT	ERA	ERA+	OAV	OOB	BH	AVG	PB	PR	/A	PD	TPI
1946	Bro-N	11	5	.688	47	11	2	0	4	150^{2}	138	3	69	78	12.5	2.93	115	.241	.325	4	.095	-3	8	8	-2	0.3
1947	*Bro-N	0	0	—	2	0	0	0	0	3^{2}	3	1	4	2	17.2	9.82	42	.231	.412	0	—	0	-2	-2	0	-0.2
	Pit-N	0	2	.000	10	2	0	0	0	24^{2}	33	6	17	11	19.0	9.12	46	.347	.456	0	.000	-1	-14	-13	-1	-1.4
	*Bro-N	5	3	.625	38	6	0	0	8	88^{1}	94	9	44	31	14.1	5.30	78	.274	.357	6	.231	1	-12	-11	-1	-1.2
	Yr	5	5	.500	50	8	0	0	8	116^{2}	130	16	65	44	15.0	6.25	66	.287	.376	6	.188	-0	-28	-27	-2	-2.8
1948	Bro-N	5	4	.556	34	4	2	1	7	91	95	7	42	42	13.8	4.05	99	.268	.350	3	.107	-2	-1	-1	-0	-0.3
1949	NY-N	3	3	.500	43	4	1	1	0	71^{1}	64	5	52	25	14.6	4.92	81	.239	.363	1	.077	-1	-7	-7	-0	-0.8
Total	4	24	17	.585	174	27	5	2	19	429^{2}	427	31	228	189	13.9	4.40	87	.259	.352	14	.122	-5	-28	-28	-5	-3.6

● TIM BELCHER
Belcher, Timothy Wayne b: 10/19/61, Mount Gilead, Ohio BR/TR, 6'3", 210 lbs. Deb: 9/06/87

YEAR	TM/L	W	L	PCT	G	GS	CG	SH	SV	IP	H	HR	BB	SO	RAT	ERA	ERA+	OAV	OOB	BH	AVG	PB	PR	/A	PD	TPI
1987	LA-N	4	2	.667	6	5	0	0	0	34	30	2	7	23	9.8	2.38	166	.240	.280	2	.200	0	6	6	-0	0.6
1988	*LA-N	12	6	.667	36	27	4	1	4	179^{2}	143	8	51	152	9.8	2.91	115	.217	.275	4	.071	-1	11	8	-1	0.7
1989	LA-N	15	12	.556	39	30	**10**	**8**	1	230	182	20	80	200	10.5	2.82	121	.217	.291	7	.100	-2	17	15	-2	1.3
1990	LA-N	9	9	.500	24	24	5	2	0	153	136	17	48	102	10.9	4.00	91	.240	.302	7	.163	1	-4	-6	-2	-0.7
1991	LA-N	10	9	.526	33	33	2	1	0	209^{1}	189	10	75	156	11.4	2.62	137	.240	.307	8	.119	-2	25	23	-2	2.1
1992	Cin-N	15	14	.517	35	34	2	1	0	227^{2}	201	17	80	149	11.2	3.91	94	.238	.307	8	.105	-2	-10	-6	-0	-0.9
Total	6	65	52	.556	173	153	23	13	5	1033^{2}	881	74	341	782	10.8	3.20	111	.231	.296	36	.112	-6	45	40	-6	3.1

YEAR TM/L	W	L	PCT	G	GS	CG	SH	SV	IP	H	HR	BB	SO	RAT	ERA	ERA+	OAV	OOB	BH	AVG	PB	PR	/A	PD	TPI
● STAN BELINDA Belinda, Stanley Peter b: 8/6/66, Huntingdon, Pa. BR/TR, 6'3", 185 lbs. Deb: 9/08/89																									
1989 Pit-N	0	1	.000	8	0	0	0	0	10^1	13	0	2	10	13.1	6.10	55	.295	.326	0	—	0	-3	-3	-0	-0.4
1990 *Pit-N	3	4	.429	55	0	0	0	8	58^1	48	4	29	55	12.0	3.55	102	.227	.324	0	.000	-0	2	0	-1	-0.1
1991 *Pit-N	7	5	.583	60	0	0	0	16	78^1	50	10	35	71	10.2	3.45	104	.184	.286	0	.000	-0	2	1	-1	0.0
1992 *Pit-N	6	4	.600	59	0	0	0	18	71^1	58	8	29	57	11.0	3.15	108	.223	.301	2	.667	1	3	2	-1	0.2
Total 4	16	14	.533	182	0	0	0	42	218^1	169	22	95	193	11.1	3.50	100	.215	.303	2	.133	1	3	0	-3	-0.3
● BO BELINSKY Belinsky, Robert b: 12/7/36, New York, N.Y. BL/TL, 6'2", 191 lbs. Deb: 4/18/62																									
1962 LA-A	10	11	.476	33	31	5	3	1	187^1	149	12	122	145	13.6	3.56	109	.216	.344	10	.167	1	9	6	-0	0.7
1963 LA-A	2	9	.182	13	13	2	0	0	76^2	78	12	35	60	13.7	5.75	60	.262	.347	2	.074	-2	-18	-20	1	-2.0
1964 LA-A	9	8	.529	23	22	4	1	0	135^1	120	8	49	91	11.6	2.86	115	.240	.315	4	.095	-1	11	6	-1	0.5
1965 Phi-N	4	9	.308	30	14	3	0	1	109^2	103	13	48	71	12.9	4.84	71	.248	.334	6	.188	1	-16	-17	-1	-1.8
1966 Phi-N	0	2	.000	9	1	0	0	0	15^1	14	3	5	8	12.9	2.93	123	.250	.344	1	.333	0	1	1	0	0.1
1967 Hou-N	3	9	.250	27	18	0	0	0	115^1	112	12	54	80	13.6	4.68	71	.255	.347	3	.077	-2	-17	-18	-2	-2.2
1969 Pit-N	0	3	.000	8	3	0	0	0	17^2	17	1	14	15	16.8	4.58	76	.266	.412	0	.000	-0	-2	-2	0	-0.2
1970 Cin-N	0	0	—	3	0	0	0	0	8	10	0	6	6	18.0	4.50	90	.294	.400	1	1.000	1	-0	-0	-0	0.0
Total 8	28	51	.354	146	102	14	4	2	665^1	603	61	333	476	13.2	4.10	86	.241	.340	27	.131	-2	-32	-43	-4	-4.9
● CHARLIE BELL Bell, Charles C. b: 8/12/1868, Cincinnati, Ohio d: 2/7/37, Cincinnati, Ohio TR, Deb: 10/13/1889 F♦																									
1889 KC-a	1	0	1.000	1	1	1	0	0	9	4	0	3	3	8.0	1.00	418	.130	.231	1	.167	0	3	3	1	0.4
1891 Lou-a	2	6	.250	10	9	8	0	0	77	93	4	20	16	14.1	4.68	78	.289	.346	1	.036	-2	-8	-9	-2	-1.0
Cin-a	1	0	1.000	1	1	1	0	0	9	2	0	3	1	6.0	0.00	—	.070	.183	2	.500	1	4	4	0	0.6
Yr	3	6	.333	11	10	9	0	0	86	95	4	23	17	12.5	4.19	88	.265	.311	3	.094	-2	-4	-5	-1	-0.4
Total 2	4	6	.400	12	11	10	0	0	95	99	4	26	20	12.8	3.88	97	.259	.323	4	.105	-2	-2	-1	-1	0.0
● ERIC BELL Bell, Eric Alvin b: 10/27/63, Modesto, Cal. BL/TL, 6'3", 195 lbs. Deb: 9/24/85																									
1985 Bal-A	0	0	—	4	0	0	0	0	5^2	4	1	4	4	12.7	4.76	85	.200	.333	0	—	0	-0	-0	0	0.1
1986 Bal-A	1	2	.333	4	4	0	0	0	23^1	23	4	14	18	14.3	5.01	82	.258	.359	0	—	0	-2	-2	-1	-0.2
1987 Bal-A	10	13	.435	33	29	2	0	0	165	174	32	78	111	13.9	5.45	81	.271	.351	0	—	0	-18	-19	-1	-1.9
1991 Cle-A	4	0	1.000	10	0	0	0	0	18	5	0	5	7	5.5	0.50	830	.091	.180	0	—	0	7	7	-0	0.7
1992 Cle-A	0	2	.000	7	1	0	0	0	15^1	22	1	9	10	18.8	7.63	53	.349	.438	0	—	0	-6	-6	1	-0.6
Total 5	15	17	.469	58	34	2	0	0	227^1	228	38	110	150	13.5	5.15	84	.262	.348	0	—	0	-20	-21	-2	-1.9
● GARY BELL Bell, Gary b: 11/17/36, San Antonio, Tex. BR/TR, 6'1", 198 lbs. Deb: 6/01/58																									
1958 Cle-A	12	10	.545	33	23	10	0	1	182	141	17	73	110	10.8	3.31	110	.213	.296	11	.196	2	9	7	-2	0.6
1959 Cle-A	16	11	.593	44	28	12	1	5	234	208	28	105	136	12.2	4.04	91	.238	.323	18	.240	3	-5	-9	-2	-0.8
1960 Cle-A★	9	10	.474	28	23	6	2	1	154^2	139	15	82	109	13.3	4.13	90	.242	.344	7	.149	-0	-4	-7	1	-0.6
1961 Cle-A	12	16	.429	34	34	11	2	0	228^1	214	32	100	163	12.6	4.10	96	.245	.326	16	.198	1	-2	-4	-1	-0.4
1962 Cle-A	10	9	.526	57	6	1	0	12	107^2	104	14	52	80	13.3	4.26	91	.264	.354	5	.208	1	-4	-5	-1	-0.4
1963 Cle-A	8	5	.615	58	7	0	0	5	119	91	13	52	98	11.1	2.95	123	.208	.298	3	.115	-1	9	9	1	0.9
1964 Cle-A	8	6	.571	56	2	0	0	4	106	106	15	53	89	13.8	4.33	83	.260	.351	6	.375	2	-8	-9	-1	-0.7
1965 Cle-A	6	5	.545	60	0	0	0	17	103^2	86	7	50	86	12.0	3.04	115	.226	.319	1	.063	-0	5	5	-1	0.4
1966 Cle-A☆	14	15	.483	40	37	12	0	0	254^1	211	19	79	194	10.4	3.22	107	.228	.291	10	.132	-1	6	6	2	0.8
1967 Cle-A	1	5	.167	9	9	1	0	0	60^2	50	7	24	39	11.1	3.71	88	.234	.314	0	.000	-2	-3	-3	1	-0.4
*Bos-A	12	8	.600	29	24	8	0	3	165^1	143	16	47	115	10.6	3.16	110	.231	.290	12	.203	1	1	6	-1	0.7
Yr	13	13	.500	38	33	9	0	3	226	193	23	71	154	10.7	3.31	104	.231	.295	12	.162	-0	-2	3	0	0.3
1968 Bos-A☆	11	11	.500	35	27	9	3	1	199^1	177	7	68	103	11.3	3.12	101	.239	.308	13	.220	2	-3	1	0	0.3
1969 Sea-A	2	6	.250	13	11	1	1	2	61^1	76	8	34	30	16.4	4.70	77	.305	.393	3	.214	1	-7	-7	0	-0.6
Chi-A	0	0	—	23	2	0	0	0	38^2	48	8	23	26	17.0	6.28	61	.308	.403	0	.000	-0	-11	-10	0	-1.1
Yr	2	6	.250	36	13	1	1	2	100	124	16	57	56	16.5	5.31	70	.302	.390	3	.158	1	-19	-18	0	-1.7
Total 12	121	117	.508	519	233	71	9	51	2015	1794	206	842	1378	12.0	3.68	98	.239	.320	105	.185	9	-17	-18	-3	-1.3
● GEORGE BELL Bell, George Glenn "Farmer" b: 11/2/1874, Greenwood, N.Y. d: 12/25/41, New York, N.Y. BR/TR, 6', 195 lbs. Deb: 4/17/07																									
1907 Bro-N	8	16	.333	35	27	20	3	1	263^2	222	1	77	88	10.4	2.25	104	.238	.300	8	.095	-3	6	3	2	0.3
1908 Bro-N	4	15	.211	29	21	12	2	1	155^1	162	3	45	63	12.1	3.59	65	.270	.324	8	.170	1	-21	-22	1	-2.1
1909 Bro-N	16	15	.516	33	30	29	6	1	256	236	5	73	95	11.0	2.71	96	.251	.307	15	.167	1	-3	-3	2	0.0
1910 Bro-N	10	27	.270	44	36	25	4	1	310	267	4	82	102	10.2	2.64	115	.241	.296	13	.134	-4	13	13	-3	0.6
1911 Bro-N	5	6	.455	19	12	6	2	0	101	123	2	28	28	13.6	4.28	78	.315	.364	4	.121	-1	-10	-11	2	-1.0
Total 5	43	79	.352	160	126	92	17	4	1086	1010	15	305	376	11.0	2.85	94	.254	.310	48	.137	-6	-14	-20	4	-2.2
● HI BELL Bell, Herman S b: 7/16/1897, Mt.Sherman, Ky. d: 6/7/49, Glendale, Cal. BR/TR, 6', 185 lbs. Deb: 4/16/24																									
1924 StL-N	3	8	.273	28	11	5	0	1	113^1	124	5	29	29	12.5	4.92	77	.292	.344	2	.065	-2	-13	-14	0	-1.6
1926 *StL-N	6	6	.500	27	7	3	0	2	85	82	1	17	27	10.7	3.18	123	.255	.296	3	.120	-1	6	7	-1	0.4
1927 StL-N	1	3	.250	25	1	0	0	0	57^1	71	5	22	31	14.8	3.92	101	.317	.381	1	.091	-1	-0	0	0	-0.1
1929 StL-N	0	2	.000	7	0	0	0	0	13	19	1	4	4	15.9	6.92	67	.339	.383	0	.000	-0	-3	-3	-0	-0.4
1930 *StL-N	4	3	.571	39	9	2	0	**8**	115^1	143	4	23	42	13.1	3.90	129	.299	.334	2	.077	-3	**14**	**14**	1	1.1
1932 NY-N	8	4	.667	35	10	3	0	2	120	132	12	16	25	11.3	3.68	101	.280	.307	3	.088	-2	3	0	-1	-0.2
1933 *NY-N	6	5	.545	38	7	1	1	5	105^1	100	4	20	24	10.4	2.05	157	.246	.285	4	.138	-1	**15**	**14**	-1	1.3
1934 NY-N	4	3	.571	22	2	0	0	6	54	72	2	12	9	14.3	3.67	105	.319	.358	2	.105	-1	2	1	-1	-0.1
Total 8	32	34	.485	221	47	14	1	24	663^1	743	34	143	191	12.2	3.69	107	.285	.326	17	.096	-12	23	19	-4	0.4
● JERRY BELL Bell, Jerry Houston b: 10/6/47, Madison, Tenn. BB/TR, 6'4", 190 lbs. Deb: 9/06/71																									
1971 Mil-A	2	1	.667	8	0	0	0	0	14^2	10	0	6	8	9.8	3.07	113	.200	.286	0	—	0	1	1	-0	0.0
1972 Mil-A	5	1	.833	25	3	0	0	0	70^2	50	1	33	20	11.0	1.66	183	.209	.313	1	.071	-1	11	11	1	1.2
1973 Mil-A	9	9	.500	31	25	8	0	1	183^2	185	14	70	57	12.7	3.97	95	.263	.334	0	—	0	-3	-4	1	-0.2
1974 Mil-A	1	0	1.000	5	0	0	0	0	14	17	2	5	4	14.1	2.57	141	.315	.373	0	—	0	2	2	-0	0.2
Total 4	17	11	.607	69	28	8	0	1	283	262	17	114	89	12.2	3.28	109	.250	.329	1	.071	-1	10	9	1	1.2
● RALPH BELL Bell, Ralph Albert "Lefty" b: 11/6/1890, Kohoka, Mo. d: 10/18/59, Burlington, Iowa BL/TL, 5'11.5", 170 lbs. Deb: 7/16/12																									
1912 Chi-A	0	0	—	3	0	0	0	0	6	8	1	8	5	24.0	9.00	36	.333	.500	0	.000	-0	-4	-4	0	-0.4
● BILL BELL Bell, William Samuel "Ding Dong" b: 10/24/33, Goldsboro, N.C. d: 10/11/62, Durham, N.C. BR/TR, 6'3", 200 lbs. Deb: 9/05/52																									
1952 Pit-N	0	1	.000	4	1	0	0	0	15^2	16	3	13	4	16.7	4.60	87	.254	.382	0	.000	-0	-2	-1	0	-0.1
1955 Pit-N	0	0	—	1	0	0	0	0	1	0	0	1	0	9.0	0.00	—	.000	.250	0	—	0	0	0	-0	0.0
Total 2	0	1	.000	5	1	0	0	0	16^2	16	3	14	4	16.2	4.32	93	.242	.375	0	.000	-0	-1	-1	0	-0.1
● CHIEF BENDER Bender, Charles Albert b: 5/5/1884, Crow Wing Co., Minn d: 5/22/54, Philadelphia, Pa. BR/TR, 6'2", 185 lbs. Deb: 4/20/03 CH																									
1903 Phi-A	17	14	.548	36	33	29	2	0	270	239	6	65	127	10.9	3.07	100	.237	.299	22	.183	-1	-3	-0	-1	-0.2
1904 Phi-A	10	11	.476	29	20	18	4	0	203^2	167	1	59	149	10.2	2.87	93	.225	.286	18	.228	3	-6	-4	-2	-0.4
1905 *Phi-A	18	11	.621	35	23	18	4	0	229	193	5	90	142	11.4	2.83	94	.230	.309	20	.217	2	-4	-4	3	0.0
1906 Phi-A	15	10	.600	36	27	24	0	**3**	238^1	208	5	48	159	10.0	2.53	108	.238	.284	25	.253	6	4	5	-1	1.3
1907 Phi-A	16	8	.667	33	24	20	4	3	219^1	185	1	34	112	9.2	2.05	127	.231	.265	23	.230	3	12	14	-2	1.7
1908 Phi-A	8	9	.471	18	17	14	2	1	138^2	121	1	21	85	9.4	1.75	146	.236	.270	11	.220	3	10	13	-2	1.6
1909 Phi-A	18	8	.692	34	29	24	5	1	250	196	1	45	161	8.9	1.66	145	.214	.254	20	.215	4	23	21	2	3.1
1910 *Phi-A	23	5	**.821**	30	28	25	3	0	250	182	1	47	155	8.6	1.58	150	.207	.255	25	.269	8	26	22	2	3.7

YEAR TM/L	W	L	PCT	G	GS	CG	SH	SV	IP	H	HR	BB	SO	RAT	ERA	ERA+	OAV	OOB	BH	AVG	PB	PR	/A	PD	TPI
1911 *Phi-A	17	5	**.773**	31	24	16	2	3	216^1	198	2	58	114	10.8	2.16	146	.252	.307	13	.165	-3	28	24	1	2.1
1912 Phi-A	13	8	.619	27	19	12	1	2	171	169	1	33	90	10.7	2.74	112	.277	.315	9	.150	-1	11	6	-2	0.4
1913 *Phi-A	21	10	.677	48	21	14	2	**13**	236^2	208	2	59	135	10.3	2.21	125	.228	.277	12	.154	0	19	15	-2	1.4
1914 *Phi-A	17	3	**.850**	28	23	14	7	2	179	159	4	55	107	10.8	2.26	115	.240	.299	9	.145	0	10	7	-0	0.8
1915 Bal-F	4	16	.200	26	23	15	0	1	178^1	198	5	37	89	12.2	3.99	80	.298	.342	16	.267	4	-19	-16	-1	-1.3
1916 Phi-N	7	7	.500	27	13	4	0	3	122^2	137	3	34	43	13.3	3.74	71	.287	.347	12	.279	4	-15	-15	2	-1.1
1917 Phi-N	8	2	.800	20	10	8	4	2	113	84	1	26	43	9.3	1.67	168	.215	.277	8	.205	1	13	14	-2	1.6
1925 Chi-A	0	0	—	1	0	0	0	0	1	1	1	1	0	18.0	18.00	23	.333	.500	0	—	0	-2	-2	-0	-0.1
Total 16	212	127	.625	459	334	255	40	34	3017	2645	40	712	1711	10.3	2.46	112	.239	.290	243	.212	33	107	100	-5	14.6

● ANDY BENES Benes, Andrew Charles b: 8/20/67, Evansville, Ind. BR/TR, 6'6", 235 lbs. Deb: 8/11/89

YEAR TM/L	W	L	PCT	G	GS	CG	SH	SV	IP	H	HR	BB	SO	RAT	ERA	ERA+	OAV	OOB	BH	AVG	PB	PR	/A	PD	TPI
1989 SD-N	6	3	.667	10	10	0	0	0	66^2	51	7	31	66	11.2	3.51	100	.213	.305	6	.250	2	-0	-0	0	0.2
1990 SD-N	10	11	.476	32	31	2	0	0	192^1	177	18	69	140	11.6	3.60	106	.242	.309	6	.100	-2	4	5	-3	0.0
1991 SD-N	15	11	.577	33	33	4	1	0	223	194	23	59	167	10.4	3.03	125	.232	.286	2	.032	-2	16	19	-1	1.8
1992 SD-N	13	14	.481	34	34	2	2	0	231^1	230	14	61	169	11.5	3.35	108	.264	.316	10	.149	2	4	7	0	1.0
Total 4	44	39	.530	109	108	8	3	0	713^1	652	62	220	542	11.1	3.33	112	.244	.304	24	.113	-0	24	31	-3	3.0

● RAY BENGE Benge, Raymond Adelphia b: 4/22/02, Jacksonville, Tex. BR/TR, 5'9.5", 160 lbs. Deb: 9/26/25

YEAR TM/L	W	L	PCT	G	GS	CG	SH	SV	IP	H	HR	BB	SO	RAT	ERA	ERA+	OAV	OOB	BH	AVG	PB	PR	/A	PD	TPI
1925 Cle-A	1	0	1.000	2	2	1	1	0	11^2	9	0	3	3	9.3	1.54	286	.205	.255	2	.400	0	4	4	-1	0.4
1926 Cle-A	1	0	1.000	8	0	0	0	0	11^2	15	0	4	3	14.7	3.86	105	.313	.365	1	.333	0	0	0	0	0.1
1928 Phi-N	8	18	.308	40	28	12	1	1	201^2	219	15	88	68	13.9	4.55	94	.286	.363	12	.207	0	-13	-6	-2	-0.8
1929 Phi-N	11	15	.423	38	27	9	2	4	199	255	24	77	78	15.2	6.29	83	.322	.385	15	.203	-3	-35	-24	-3	-2.6
1930 Phi-N	11	15	.423	38	29	14	0	1	225^2	305	22	81	70	15.4	5.70	96	.328	.382	18	.205	-4	-18	-6	-1	-0.9
1931 Phi-N	14	18	.438	38	31	16	2	2	247	251	12	61	117	11.6	3.17	134	.262	.310	18	.205	-2	19	30	-2	2.7
1932 Phi-N	13	12	.520	41	28	13	2	6	222^1	247	15	58	89	12.5	4.05	109	.281	.329	13	.173	-3	-4	9	-1	0.5
1933 Bro-N	10	17	.370	37	30	16	2	1	228^2	238	11	55	74	11.8	3.42	94	.268	.315	14	.184	0	-2	-5	-3	-0.8
1934 Bro-N	14	12	.538	36	32	14	1	0	227	252	11	61	64	12.5	4.32	90	.272	.319	15	.169	-2	-7	-11	-1	-1.3
1935 Bro-N	9	9	.500	23	17	5	1	1	124^2	142	12	47	39	13.7	4.48	89	.289	.353	9	.191	-1	-6	-7	-2	-0.9
1936 Bos-N	7	9	.438	21	19	2	0	0	115	161	6	38	32	15.7	5.79	66	.333	.382	6	.140	-3	-23	-25	-2	-2.7
Phi-N	1	4	.200	15	6	0	0	1	45^2	70	3	19	13	17.5	4.73	96	.350	.406	0	.000	-2	-4	-1	-2	-0.4
Yr	8	13	.381	36	25	2	0	1	160^2	231	9	57	45	16.1	5.49	73	.337	.388	6	.113	-4	-26	-26	-4	-3.1
1938 Cin-N	1	1	.500	9	0	0	0	2	15^1	13	1	6	5	11.2	4.11	89	.228	.302	1	.333	0	-1	-1	-0	-0.1
Total 12	101	130	.437	346	249	102	12	19	1875^1	2177	132	598	655	13.5	4.52	95	.292	.347	124	.188	-17	-89	-46	-18	-6.8

● HENRY BENN Benn, Henry Omer b: 1/25/1890, Viola, Wis. d: 6/4/67, Madison, Wis. BR/TR, 6', 190 lbs. Deb: 9/24/14

YEAR TM/L	W	L	PCT	G	GS	CG	SH	SV	IP	H	HR	BB	SO	RAT	ERA	ERA+	OAV	OOB	BH	AVG	PB	PR	/A	PD	TPI
1914 Cle-A	0	0	—	1	0	0	0	0	1	0	0	0	1	0.0	0.00	—	.000	.000	0	—	0	0	0	-0	0.0

● DAVE BENNETT Bennett, David Hans b: 11/7/45, Berkeley, Cal. BR/TR, 6'5", 195 lbs. Deb: 6/12/64 F

YEAR TM/L	W	L	PCT	G	GS	CG	SH	SV	IP	H	HR	BB	SO	RAT	ERA	ERA+	OAV	OOB	BH	AVG	PB	PR	/A	PD	TPI
1964 Phi-N	0	0	—	1	0	0	0	0	1	2	0	0	1	18.0	9.00	39	.400	.400	0	—	0	-1	-1	0	-0.1

● DENNIS BENNETT Bennett, Dennis John b: 10/5/39, Oakland, Cal. BL/TL, 6'5", 205 lbs. Deb: 5/12/62 F

YEAR TM/L	W	L	PCT	G	GS	CG	SH	SV	IP	H	HR	BB	SO	RAT	ERA	ERA+	OAV	OOB	BH	AVG	PB	PR	/A	PD	TPI
1962 Phi-N	9	9	.500	31	24	7	2	3	174^2	144	17	68	149	11.2	3.81	102	.224	.304	8	.127	-1	3	1	-1	0.0
1963 Phi-N	9	5	.643	23	16	6	1	1	119^1	102	12	33	82	10.5	2.64	122	.231	.290	9	.225	3	9	8	0	1.2
1964 Phi-N	12	14	.462	41	32	7	2	1	208	222	23	58	125	12.3	3.68	94	.280	.333	13	.197	3	-3	-5	-1	-0.3
1965 Bos-A	5	7	.417	34	18	3	0	0	141^2	152	15	53	85	13.4	4.38	85	.279	.350	7	.179	2	-15	-10	-1	-1.0
1966 Bos-A	3	3	.500	16	13	0	0	0	75	75	9	23	47	11.9	3.24	117	.261	.318	3	.130	1	2	5	-1	0.5
1967 Bos-A	4	3	.571	13	11	4	1	0	69^2	72	12	22	34	12.4	3.88	90	.268	.328	3	.120	-0	-5	-3	-0	-0.4
NY-N	1	1	.500	8	6	0	0	0	26^1	37	4	7	14	15.4	5.13	66	.336	.381	2	.250	0	-5	-5	0	-0.5
1968 Cal-A	0	5	.000	16	7	1	0	1	48^1	46	6	17	36	12.5	3.54	82	.250	.327	1	.077	-1	-3	-3	1	-0.4
Total 7	43	47	.478	182	127	28	6	6	863	850	98	281	572	12.1	3.69	96	.260	.324	46	.166	7	-18	-13	-2	-0.9

● FRANK BENNETT Bennett, Francis Allen "Chip" b: 10/27/04, Mardela Springs, Md. d: 3/18/66, New Castle, Del. BR/TR, 5'10.5", 163 lbs. Deb: 9/17/27

YEAR TM/L	W	L	PCT	G	GS	CG	SH	SV	IP	H	HR	BB	SO	RAT	ERA	ERA+	OAV	OOB	BH	AVG	PB	PR	/A	PD	TPI
1927 Bos-A	0	1	.000	4	1	0	0	0	12^1	15	0	6	1	15.3	2.92	145	.333	.412	0	.000	-1	2	2	0	0.1
1928 Bos-A	0	0	—	1	0	0	0	0	1	1	0	0	0	9.0	0.00	—	.250	.250	0	—	0	0	0	0	0.1
Total 2	0	1	.000	5	1	0	0	0	13^1	16	0	6	1	14.9	2.70	156	.327	.400	0	.000	-1	2	2	0	0.2

● ALLEN BENSON Benson, Allen Wilbert "Bullet Ben" b: 7/12/08, Hurley, S.Dak. BR/TR, 6'1", 185 lbs. Deb: 8/19/34

YEAR TM/L	W	L	PCT	G	GS	CG	SH	SV	IP	H	HR	BB	SO	RAT	ERA	ERA+	OAV	OOB	BH	AVG	PB	PR	/A	PD	TPI
1934 Was-A	0	1	.000	2	2	0	0	0	9^2	19	0	5	4	24.2	12.10	36	.413	.491	0	.000	-0	-8	-8	-0	-0.7

● CY BENTLEY Bentley, Clytus G. b: 11/23/1850, East Haven, Conn. d: 2/26/1873, Middletown, Conn. Deb: 4/26/1872

YEAR TM/L	W	L	PCT	G	GS	CG	SH	SV	IP	H	HR	BB	SO	RAT	ERA	ERA+	OAV	OOB	BH	AVG	PB	PR	/A	PD	TPI
1872 Man-n	2	15	.118	18	17	16	0	0	154	273	4	12	5	16.7	6.14	60	.319	.329	27	.235	-0	-41	-42		-2.8

● JACK BENTLEY Bentley, John Needles b: 3/8/1895, Sandy Spring, Md. d: 10/24/69, Olney, Md. BL/TL, 5'11.5", 200 lbs. Deb: 9/06/13 ♦

YEAR TM/L	W	L	PCT	G	GS	CG	SH	SV	IP	H	HR	BB	SO	RAT	ERA	ERA+	OAV	OOB	BH	AVG	PB	PR	/A	PD	TPI
1913 Was-A	1	0	1.000	3	1	0	0	1	11	5	0	2	5	5.7	0.00	—	.147	.194	0	.000	-0	4	4	0	0.4
1914 Was-A	5	7	.417	30	11	3	2	**4**	125^1	110	3	53	55	11.9	2.37	119	.249	.334	11	.275	2	5	6	-1	0.8
1915 Was-A	0	2	.000	4	2	0	0	0	11^1	8	0	3	0	8.7	0.79	374	.200	.256	0	.000	-0	3	3	-0	0.2
1916 Was-A	0	0	—	2	0	0	0	0	1^1	0	0	1	1	6.8	0.00	—	.000	.250	0	—	0	0	0	0	0.1
1923 *NY-N	13	8	.619	31	26	12	1	3	183	198	10	67	80	13.3	4.48	85	.277	.343	38	.427	15	-10	-13	-1	0.1
1924 *NY-N	16	5	.762	28	24	13	1	1	188	196	11	56	60	12.3	3.78	97	.273	.329	26	.265	4	2	-2	-1	0.0
1925 NY-N	11	9	.550	28	22	11	0	0	157	200	10	59	47	14.9	5.04	80	.323	.383	30	.303	5	-14	-18	-1	-0.7
1926 Phi-N	0	2	.000	7	3	0	0	0	25^1	37	2	10	7	16.7	8.17	51	.327	.382	62	.258	1	-12	-11	-0	-1.0
NY-N	0	0	—	1	0	0	0	0	2	0	0	2	1	9.0	0.00	—	.000	.250	1	.250	-0	1	1	-0	0.1
Yr	0	2	.000	8	3	0	0	0	27^1	37	2	12	8	16.1	7.57	54	.311	.374	63	.258	1	-11	-11	-0	-0.9
1927 NY-N	0	0	—	4	0	0	0	0	9^2	7	1	10	3	16.8	2.79	138	.206	.400	2	.222	1	1	1	-0	0.2
Total 9	46	33	.582	138	89	39	4	9	714	761	37	263	259	13.1	4.01	91	.280	.346	170	.291	27	-20	-28	-3	0.2

● AL BENTON Benton, John Alton b: 3/18/11, Noble, Okla. d: 4/14/68, Lynwood, Cal. BR/TR, 6'4", 215 lbs. Deb: 4/18/34

YEAR TM/L	W	L	PCT	G	GS	CG	SH	SV	IP	H	HR	BB	SO	RAT	ERA	ERA+	OAV	OOB	BH	AVG	PB	PR	/A	PD	TPI
1934 Phi-A	7	9	.438	32	21	7	0	1	155	145	7	88	58	13.6	4.88	90	.249	.349	6	.109	-4	-7	-9	0	-1.1
1935 Phi-A	3	4	.429	27	9	0	0	0	78^1	110	7	47	42	18.2	7.70	59	.328	.413	1	.040	-3	-28	-27	-1	-2.8
1938 Det-A	5	3	.625	19	10	6	0	0	95^1	93	10	39	33	12.6	3.30	151	.259	.333	4	.121	-3	16	18	1	1.5
1939 Det-A	6	8	.429	37	16	3	0	5	150	182	11	58	67	14.5	4.56	107	.294	.355	4	.091	-4	1	5	0	0.1
1940 Det-A	6	10	.375	42	0	0	0	**17**	79^1	93	5	36	50	14.6	4.42	107	.294	.366	0	.000	-3	-0	3	-0	0.0
1941 Det-A☆	15	6	.714	38	14	7	1	7	157^2	130	11	65	63	11.3	2.97	153	**.221**	.302	3	.060	-5	21	28	-0	2.2
1942 Det-A★	7	13	.350	35	30	9	1	2	226^2	210	9	84	110	11.7	2.90	136	.246	.314	5	.075	-6	19	26	-1	2.1
1945 *Det-A†	13	8	.619	31	27	12	5	3	191^2	175	7	63	76	11.3	2.02	174	.241	.303	4	.063	-6	29	32	2	3.1
1946 Det-A	11	7	.611	28	15	6	1	1	140^2	132	9	58	60	12.2	3.65	100	.245	.319	9	.184	-1	-2	0	1	0.0
1947 Det-A	6	7	.462	36	14	4	0	7	133	147	11	61	33	14.1	4.40	86	.288	.365	6	.154	-2	-10	-9	-0	-1.1
1948 Det-A	2	2	.500	30	0	0	0	3	44^1	45	4	36	18	16.6	5.68	77	.273	.406	2	.182	-0	-7	-6	0	-0.6
1949 Cle-A	9	6	.600	40	11	4	2	10	135^2	116	7	51	41	11.1	2.12	188	.238	.312	5	.132	-2	31	28	-2	2.4
1950 Cle-A	4	2	.667	36	0	0	0	4	63	57	7	30	26	12.6	3.57	121	.243	.331	1	.083	-1	7	5	-1	0.4
1952 Bos-A	4	3	.571	24	0	0	0	6	37^2	37	1	17	20	12.9	2.39	165	.268	.348	0	.000	-1	5	6	-0	0.5
Total 14	98	88	.527	455	167	58	10	66	1688^1	1672	106	733	697	12.9	3.66	115	.259	.336	50	.098	-41	74	102	-1	6.7

● RUBE BENTON Benton, John Clebon b: 6/27/1887, Clinton, N.C. d: 12/12/37, Dothan, Ala. BL/TL, 6'1", 190 lbs. Deb: 6/28/10

YEAR TM/L	W	L	PCT	G	GS	CG	SH	SV	IP	H	HR	BB	SO	RAT	ERA	ERA+	OAV	OOB	BH	AVG	PB	PR	/A	PD	TPI
1910 Cin-N	0	1	.000	12	2	0	0	0	38	44	1	23	15	16.1	4.74	62	.282	.378	1	.091	-1	-7	-8	1	-0.8

YEAR TM/L	W	L	PCT	G	GS	CG	SH	SV	IP	H	HR	BB	SO	RAT	ERA	ERA+	OAV	OOB	BH	AVG	PB	PR	/A	PD	TPI
1911 Cin-N	3	3	.500	6	6	5	0	0	44^2	44	0	23	28	14.1	2.01	164	.270	.370	2	.143	-0	7	6	-1	0.5
1912 Cin-N	18	20	.474	**50**	39	22	2	2	302	316	2	118	162	13.5	3.10	108	.278	.356	14	.135	-6	10	9	2	0.4
1913 Cin-N	11	7	.611	23	22	9	1	0	144^1	140	4	60	68	13.0	3.49	93	.265	.350	10	.208	1	-5	-4	-1	-0.4
1914 Cin-N	16	18	.471	41	31	16	5	2	271	223	3	95	121	10.9	2.96	99	.228	.303	13	.143	-3	-5	-1	0	-0.4
1915 Cin-N	6	13	.316	35	21	6	2	4	176^1	165	2	67	83	12.6	3.32	86	.257	.340	11	.208	-0	-11	-9	2	-0.8
NY-N	3	5	.375	10	7	3	0	1	60^2	57	0	9	26	10.5	2.82	91	.253	.297	5	.217	1	-0	-2	-0	-0.1
Yr	9	18	.333	45	28	9	2	5	237	222	2	76	109	11.5	3.19	87	.252	.315	16	.211	1	-12	-11	2	-0.9
1916 NY-N	16	8	.667	38	30	15	3	2	238^2	210	5	58	115	10.5	2.87	85	.241	.296	7	.090	-4	-7	-11	-1	-1.8
1917 *NY-N	15	9	.625	35	25	14	3	3	215	190	5	41	70	10.0	2.72	94	.238	.281	12	.167	-1	-0	-4	-2	-0.7
1918 NY-N	1	2	.333	3	3	2	0	0	24	17	0	3	9	7.5	1.88	140	.202	.230	1	.143	1	2	2	0	0.3
1919 NY-N	17	11	.607	35	28	11	1	2	209	181	5	52	53	10.2	2.63	107	.237	.289	13	.194	-1	7	4	-1	0.3
1920 NY-N	9	16	.360	33	25	12	4	2	193^1	222	8	31	52	11.9	3.03	99	.291	.321	6	.092	-6	2	-1	4	-0.3
1921 NY-N	5	2	.714	18	9	3	1	0	72	72	2	17	11	11.1	2.88	128	.266	.309	3	.143	-1	7	6	-1	0.5
1923 Cin-N	14	10	.583	33	26	15	0	1	219	243	10	57	59	12.5	3.66	106	.284	.333	23	.287	4	8	5	1	0.9
1924 Cin-N	7	9	.438	32	15	6	1	1	162^2	166	2	24	42	10.7	2.77	136	.266	.297	12	.261	2	20	18	1	2.2
1925 Cin-N	9	10	.474	33	16	6	1	1	146^2	182	3	34	36	13.3	4.05	102	.301	.340	9	.200	1	4	1	-1	0.0
Total 15	150	144	.510	437	305	145	24	21	2517^1	2472	52	712	950	11.7	3.09	102	.261	.319	142	.172	-14	33	13	4	-0.2

● LARRY BENTON Benton, Lawrence James b: 11/20/1897, St.Louis, Mo. d: 4/3/53, Amberly Village, O. BR/TR, 5'11", 165 lbs. Deb: 4/25/23

1923 Bos-N	5	9	.357	35	9	1	0	0	128	141	4	57	42	14.2	4.99	80	.293	.373	5	.161	-1	-14	-14	1	-1.3
1924 Bos-N	5	7	.417	30	13	4	0	1	128	129	4	64	41	13.8	4.15	92	.274	.365	3	.091	-3	-4	-5	-0	-0.7
1925 Bos-N	14	7	.667	31	21	16	2	1	183^1	170	6	70	49	11.9	3.09	130	.249	.320	14	.241	2	24	19	-1	1.9
1926 Bos-N	14	14	.500	43	27	12	1	1	231^2	244	10	81	103	12.9	3.85	92	.280	.346	12	.154	-3	-1	-8	-3	-1.3
1927 Bos-N	4	2	.667	11	10	3	0	0	60^1	72	3	27	25	15.1	4.48	83	.310	.387	4	.222	1	-4	-5	-1	-0.5
NY-N	13	5	.722	29	23	8	1	2	173	183	9	54	65	12.4	3.95	98	.275	.331	8	.160	-2	-1	-2	-0	-0.4
Yr	17	7	**.708**	40	33	11	1	2	233^1	255	12	81	90	13.0	4.09	93	.284	.344	12	.176	-1	-4	-7	-1	-0.9
1928 NY-N	**25**	9	**.735**	42	35	**28**	2	4	310^1	299	14	71	90	10.7	2.73	143	.258	.300	16	.143	-3	43	41	-0	3.8
1929 NY-N	11	17	.393	39	30	14	3	3	237	276	16	61	63	12.8	4.14	111	.297	.340	9	.105	-6	15	12	1	0.6
1930 NY-N	1	3	.250	8	4	1	0	1	30	42	8	14	16	16.8	7.80	61	.323	.389	3	.300	2	-9	-10	-0	-0.8
Cin-N	7	12	.368	35	22	9	0	1	177^2	246	7	45	47	14.7	5.12	94	.337	.375	11	.177	-2	-3	-6	-3	-0.9
Yr	8	15	.348	43	26	10	0	2	207^2	288	15	59	63	15.0	5.50	87	.334	.377	14	.194	-0	-12	-16	-3	-1.7
1931 Cin-N	10	15	.400	38	23	12	2	2	204^1	240	6	53	35	12.9	3.35	112	.299	.343	11	.167	-1	12	9	1	0.9
1932 Cin-N	6	13	.316	35	21	7	0	2	179^2	201	10	27	35	11.4	4.31	90	.285	.311	11	.204	0	-9	-9	-1	-0.9
1933 Cin-N	10	11	.476	34	19	7	2	2	152^2	160	5	36	33	11.7	3.71	91	.271	.316	9	.170	-1	-6	-5	-2	-0.8
1934 Cin-N	0	1	.000	16	1	0	0	2	29	53	1	7	5	18.6	6.52	63	.393	.423	2	.286	0	-8	-8	-0	-0.7
1935 Bos-N	2	3	.400	29	0	0	0	0	72	103	6	24	21	16.0	6.88	55	.338	.388	4	.200	0	-23	-25	-1	-2.3
Total 13	127	128	.498	455	258	122	13	22	2297	2559	109	691	670	12.8	4.03	98	.288	.341	122	.165	-17	13	-16	-8	-3.4

● SID BENTON Benton, Sidney Wright b: 8/4/1895, Buckner, Ark. d: 3/8/77, Fayetteville, Ark. BR/TR, 6'1", 170 lbs. Deb: 4/18/22

1922 StL-N	0	0	—	1	0	0	0	0	0	0	0	2	0	—	—	—	—	1.000	0	—	0	0	0	0	0.0

● JOE BENZ Benz, Joseph Louis "Blitzen" or "Butcher Boy" b: 1/21/1886, New Alsace, Ind. d: 4/22/57, Chicago, Ill. BR/TR, 6'1.5", 196 lbs. Deb: 8/16/11

1911 Chi-A	3	2	.600	12	6	1	0	0	55^2	52	0	13	28	10.8	2.26	142	.251	.302	1	.059	-2	7	6	1	0.5
1912 Chi-A	13	17	.433	42	31	12	3	0	238^2	231	5	70	97	11.7	2.90	110	.259	.319	10	.132	-5	11	8	1	0.4
1913 Chi-A	7	10	.412	33	17	6	1	1	151	146	1	59	79	12.3	2.74	107	.254	.325	9	.180	-1	3	3	4	0.7
1914 Chi-A	14	19	.424	48	35	16	4	2	283^1	245	4	66	142	9.9	2.26	119	.236	.282	12	.130	-3	15	14	6	1.9
1915 Chi-A	15	11	.577	39	28	17	2	0	238^1	209	4	43	81	9.6	2.11	141	.238	.276	10	.127	-5	22	23	3	2.2
1916 Chi-A	9	5	.643	28	16	6	4	0	142	108	0	32	57	9.1	2.03	136	.214	.265	3	.065	-3	13	12	1	1.0
1917 Chi-A	7	3	.700	19	13	7	2	0	94^2	76	1	23	25	9.6	2.47	108	.220	.272	5	.167	-1	2	2	0	0.1
1918 Chi-A	8	8	.500	29	17	10	1	0	154	156	1	28	30	10.9	2.63	104	.269	.304	11	.216	-1	3	2	3	0.5
1919 Chi-A	0	0	—	1	0	0	0	0	2	2	0	0	0	9.0	0.00	—	.250	.250	0	—	0	1	1	0	0.1
Total 9	76	75	.503	251	163	75	17	3	1359^2	1225	16	334	539	10.5	2.43	119	.243	.294	61	.138	-20	76	70	19	7.4

● JUAN BERENGUER Berenguer, Juan Bautista b: 11/30/54, Aguadulce, Pan. BR/TR, 5'11", 215 lbs. Deb: 8/17/78

1978 NY-N	0	2	.000	5	3	0	0	0	13	17	1	11	8	20.1	8.31	42	.327	.453	0	.000	-0	-7	-7	-0	-0.7
1979 NY-N	1	1	.500	5	5	0	0	0	30^2	28	2	12	25	12.0	2.93	124	.252	.331	1	.143	0	3	2	-1	0.2
1980 NY-N	0	1	.000	6	0	0	0	0	9^1	9	1	10	7	18.3	5.79	61	.250	.413	0	—	0	-2	-2	0	-0.2
1981 KC-A	0	4	.000	8	3	0	0	0	19^2	22	4	16	20	18.3	8.69	41	.289	.426	0	—	0	-11	-11	-1	-1.1
Tor-A	2	9	.182	12	11	1	0	0	71	62	7	35	29	12.7	4.31	91	.235	.331	0	—	0	-5	-3	-1	-0.5
Yr	2	13	.133	20	14	1	0	0	90^2	84	11	51	49	13.7	5.26	73	.243	.346	0	—	0	-16	-14	-2	-1.6
1982 Det-A	0	0	—	2	1	0	0	0	6^2	5	0	9	8	18.9	6.75	60	.200	.412	0	—	0	-2	-2	-0	-0.2
1983 Det-A	9	5	.643	37	19	2	1	1	157^2	110	19	71	129	10.7	3.14	124	.193	.289	0	—	0	16	13	-2	1.3
1984 Det-A	11	10	.524	31	27	2	1	0	168^1	146	14	79	118	12.3	3.48	113	.232	.323	0	—	0	10	8	-1	0.7
1985 Det-A	5	6	.455	31	13	0	0	0	95	96	12	48	82	13.7	5.59	73	.259	.346	0	—	0	-15	-16	1	-1.5
1986 SF-N	2	3	.400	46	4	0	0	4	73^1	64	4	44	72	13.5	2.70	130	.242	.354	1	.143	-0	8	7	-1	0.6
1987 *Min-A	8	1	.889	47	6	0	0	4	112	100	10	47	110	11.8	3.94	117	.238	.315	0	—	0	6	8	-1	0.6
1988 Min-A	8	4	.667	57	1	0	0	2	100	74	7	61	99	12.2	3.96	103	.207	.325	0	—	0	0	1	0	0.0
1989 Min-A	9	3	.750	56	0	0	0	3	106	96	11	47	93	12.3	3.48	119	.246	.330	0	—	0	5	8	-1	0.5
1990 Min-A	8	5	.615	51	0	0	0	0	100^1	85	9	58	77	13.0	3.41	122	.232	.340	0	—	0	6	8	-2	0.7
1991 Atl-N	0	3	.000	49	0	0	0	17	64^1	43	5	20	53	9.2	2.24	174	.189	.263	0	.000	-1	10	12	-0	1.2
1992 Atl-N	3	1	.750	28	0	0	0	1	33^1	35	7	16	19	14.0	5.13	73	.269	.354	0	.000	-0	-6	-5	-0	-0.6
KC-A	1	4	.200	19	2	0	0	0	44^2	42	3	20	26	12.7	5.64	71	.247	.330	0	—	0	-8	-8	-0	-0.9
Total 15	67	62	.519	490	95	5	2	32	1205^1	1034	116	604	975	12.5	3.90	103	.232	.328	2	.083	-1	7	14	-11	0.1

● BRUCE BERENYI Berenyi, Bruce Michael b: 8/21/54, Bryan, Ohio BR/TR, 6'3", 215 lbs. Deb: 7/05/80

1980 Cin-N	2	2	.500	6	6	0	0	0	27^2	34	1	23	19	18.5	7.81	46	.318	.438	0	.000	-1	-13	-13	-0	-1.3
1981 Cin-N	9	6	.600	21	20	5	3	0	126	97	3	77	106	12.4	3.50	101	.211	.324	8	.190	1	-0	1	-1	0.1
1982 Cin-N	9	18	.333	34	34	4	1	0	222^1	208	8	96	157	12.4	3.36	110	.255	.335	15	.242	3	6	8	2	1.4
1983 Cin-N	9	14	.391	32	31	4	1	0	186^1	173	9	102	151	13.4	3.86	98	.247	.345	12	.218	2	-5	-1	3	0.3
1984 Cin-N	3	7	.300	13	11	0	0	0	51	63	0	42	53	18.5	6.00	63	.306	.423	1	.063	-1	-14	-13	0	-1.3
NY-N	9	6	.600	19	19	0	0	0	115	100	6	53	81	12.1	3.76	94	.238	.325	9	.243	2	-2	-3	-1	-0.2
Yr	12	13	.480	32	30	0	0	0	166	163	6	95	134	14.0	4.45	81	.260	.358	10	.189	0	-16	-15	-1	-1.5
1985 NY-N	1	0	1.000	3	3	0	0	0	13^2	8	0	10	10	12.5	2.63	131	.170	.328	1	.250	0	1	1	0	0.2
1986 NY-N	2	2	.500	14	7	0	0	0	39^2	47	5	22	30	15.9	6.35	56	.299	.389	0	.000	-1	-12	-12	-0	-1.3
Total 7	44	55	.444	142	131	13	5	0	781^2	730	32	425	607	13.4	4.03	91	.251	.347	46	.197	5	-38	-32	3	-2.1

● HEINIE BERGER Berger, Charles b: 1/7/1882, Lasalle, Ill. d: 2/10/54, Lakewood, Ohio TR, 5'9", Deb: 5/06/07

1907 Cle-A	3	3	.500	14	7	5	1	0	87^1	74	0	20	50	9.8	2.99	84	.231	.279	5	.179	0	-4	-5	-1	-0.7
1908 Cle-A	13	8	.619	29	24	16	0	0	199^1	152	1	66	101	10.0	2.12	113	.219	.290	8	.108	-4	6	6	-0	0.1
1909 Cle-A	13	14	.481	34	29	19	4	1	247	221	2	58	162	10.6	2.73	94	.256	.312	11	.133	-1	-7	-5	0	-0.7
1910 Cle-A	3	4	.429	13	8	2	0	0	65^1	57	0	32	24	12.7	3.03	85	.243	.341	3	.143	-1	-4	-3	-1	-0.5
Total 4	32	29	.525	90	68	42	5	1	599	504	3	176	337	10.5	2.60	96	.238	.303	27	.131	-6	-9	-7	-2	-1.8

YEAR TM/L	W	L	PCT	G	GS	CG	SH	SV	IP	H	HR	BB	SO	RAT	ERA	ERA+	OAV	OOB	BH	AVG	PB	PR	/A	PD	TPI

● **JACK BERLY**   Berly, John Chambers   b: 5/24/03, Natchitoches, La.   d: 6/26/77, Houston, Tex.   BR/TR, 5'11.5", 190 lbs.   Deb: 4/22/24

1924 StL-N	0	0	—	4	0	0	0	0	8	8	2	4	2	13.5	5.63	67	.267	.353	0	.000	-0	-2	-2	0	-0.2
1931 NY-N	7	8	.467	27	11	4	1	0	111¹	114	6	51	45	13.7	3.88	95	.270	.354	6	.171	-1	-0	-2	1	-0.2
1932 Phi-N	1	2	.333	21	1	1	0	2	46	61	4	21	15	16.2	7.63	58	.333	.405	0	.000	-2	-19	-16	1	-1.6
1933 Phi-N	2	3	.400	13	6	1	1	0	50	62	5	22	4	15.5	5.04	76	.307	.381	4	.308	0	-9	-7	1	-0.6
Total 4	10	13	.435	65	18	6	2	2	215¹	245	17	98	66	14.6	5.02	78	.292	.371	10	.167	-2	-30	-27	3	-2.6

● **VICTOR BERNAL**   Bernal, Victor Hugo   b: 10/6/53, Los Angeles, Cal.   BR/TR, 6'1", 175 lbs.   Deb: 4/06/77

| 1977 SD-N | 1 | 1 | .500 | 15 | 0 | 0 | 0 | 0 | 20¹ | 23 | 4 | 9 | 6 | 14.2 | 5.31 | 67 | .287 | .360 | 0 | .000 | -0 | -3 | -4 | -0 | -0.4 |

● **DWIGHT BERNARD**   Bernard, Dwight Vern   b: 5/31/52, Mt.Vernon, Ill.   BR/TR, 6'2", 170 lbs.   Deb: 6/29/78

1978 NY-N	1	4	.200	30	1	0	0	0	48	54	4	27	26	15.2	4.31	81	.297	.388	1	.200	0	-4	-4	0	-0.4
1979 NY-N	0	3	.000	32	1	0	0	0	44	59	2	26	20	17.4	4.70	77	.331	.417	0	—	0	-5	-5	-0	-0.5
1981 *Mil-A	0	0	—	6	0	0	0	0	5	5	0	6	1	19.8	3.60	95	.263	.440	0	—	0	-0	-0	-0	0.1
1982 *Mil-A	3	1	.750	47	0	0	0	6	79	78	4	27	45	12.1	3.76	101	.263	.326	0	—	0	3	0	-1	0.1
Total 4	4	8	.333	115	2	0	0	6	176	196	10	86	92	14.5	4.14	88	.290	.371	1	.200	1	-6	-9	-1	-0.7

● **JOE BERNARD**   Bernard, Joseph Carl "J.C."   b: 3/24/1882, Brighton, Ill.   d: 9/22/60, Springfield, Ill   BR/TR, 6'1", 175 lbs.   Deb: 9/23/09

| 1909 StL-N | 0 | 0 | — | 1 | 0 | 0 | 0 | 0 | 1 | 1 | 0 | 2 | 2 | 27.0 | 0.00 | — | .250 | .500 | 0 | — | 0 | 0 | 0 | 0 | 0.0 |

● **BILL BERNHARD**   Bernhard, William Henry "Strawberry Bill"   b: 3/16/1871, Clarence, N.Y.   d: 3/30/49, San Diego, Cal.   BB/TR, 6'1", 205 lbs.   Deb: 4/24/1899

1899 Phi-N	6	6	.500	21	12	10	1	0	132¹	120	3	36	23	11.0	2.65	139	.242	.301	13	.241	0	18	15	-0	1.4
1900 Phi-N	15	10	.600	32	27	20	0	2	218²	284	3	74	49	14.9	4.77	76	.313	.368	14	.154	-5	-26	-28	1	-2.8
1901 Phi-A	17	10	.630	31	27	26	1	0	257	328	6	50	58	13.3	4.52	84	.307	.339	20	.187	-1	-24	-21	4	-1.7
1902 Phi-A	1	0	1.000	1	1	1	0	0	9	7	0	3	1	10.0	1.00	367	.215	.282	0	.000	-1	3	3	-1	0.1
Cle-A	17	5	.773	27	24	22	3	1	217	169	4	34	57	8.6	2.20	157	.216	.253	18	.200	-1	33	30	1	3.1
Yr	18	5	**.783**	28	25	23	3	1	226	176	4	37	58	**8.7**	2.15	161	**.216**	**.254**	18	.191	-2	36	33	1	3.2
1903 Cle-A	14	6	.700	20	19	18	3	0	165²	151	1	21	60	9.3	2.12	135	.242	.267	12	.185	-0	16	14	1	1.5
1904 Cle-A	23	13	.639	38	37	35	4	0	320²	323	4	55	137	10.7	2.13	119	.263	.296	22	.177	-1	17	14	-1	1.4
1905 Cle-A	7	13	.350	22	19	17	0	0	174¹	185	5	34	56	11.4	3.36	79	.273	.309	6	.087	-6	-13	-14	0	-2.1
1906 Cle-A	16	15	.516	31	30	23	2	0	255¹	235	1	47	85	10.1	2.54	103	.248	.287	21	.212	2	4	2	2	0.6
1907 Cle-A	0	4	.000	8	4	3	0	0	42	58	0	11	19	14.8	3.21	78	.329	.369	3	.200	0	-3	-3	0	-0.3
Total 9	116	82	.586	231	200	175	14	3	1792	1860	26	365	545	11.3	3.04	102	.268	.307	129	.180	-13	23	11	7	1.2

● **WALTER BERNHARDT**   Bernhardt, Walter Jacob   b: 5/20/1893, Pleasant Village, Pa.   d: 7/26/58, Watertown, N.Y.   BR/TR, 6'2", 175 lbs.   Deb: 7/16/18

| 1918 NY-A | 0 | 0 | — | 1 | 0 | 0 | 0 | 0 | 0² | 0 | 0 | 0 | 1 | 0.0 | 0.00 | — | .000 | .000 | 0 | — | 0 | 0 | 0 | 0 | 0.0 |

● **JOE BERRY**   Berry, Jonas Arthur "Jittery Joe"   b: 12/16/04, Huntsville, Ark.   d: 9/27/58, Anaheim, Cal.   BL/TR, 5'10.5", 145 lbs.   Deb: 9/06/42

1942 Chi-N	0	0	—	2	0	0	0	0	2	7	0	2	1	40.5	18.00	18	.538	.600	0	—	0	-3	-3	0	-0.3
1944 Phi-A	10	8	.556	53	0	0	0	**12**	111¹	78	4	23	44	8.3	1.94	179	.192	.238	3	.120	-1	18	**19**	2	2.2
1945 Phi-A	8	7	.533	**52**	0	0	0	5	130¹	114	5	38	51	10.5	2.35	146	.232	.287	5	.143	-1	15	16	1	1.7
1946 Phi-A	0	1	.000	5	0	0	0	0	13	15	1	3	5	13.2	2.77	128	.288	.339	1	.333	0	1	1	0	0.2
Cle-A	3	6	.333	21	0	0	0	1	37¹	32	4	21	16	12.8	3.38	98	.235	.338	2	.286	0	1	-0	-1	-0.1
Yr	3	7	.300	26	0	0	0	1	50¹	47	5	24	21	12.7	3.22	105	.249	.333	3	.300	1	2	-1	-0	0.1
Total 4	21	22	.488	133	0	0	0	18	294	246	14	87	117	10.3	2.45	140	.224	.282	11	.157	-2	31	32	3	3.7

● **FRANK BERTAINA**   Bertaina, Frank Louis   b: 4/14/44, San Francisco, Cal.   BL/TL, 5'11", 180 lbs.   Deb: 8/01/64

1964 Bal-A	1	0	1.000	6	4	1	1	0	26	18	3	13	18	10.7	2.77	129	.198	.298	0	.000	-1	2	2	0	0.2
1965 Bal-A	0	0	—	2	1	0	0	0	6	9	0	4	5	19.5	6.00	58	.360	.448	0	.000	-0	-2	-2	0	-0.2
1966 Bal-A	2	5	.286	16	9	0	0	0	63¹	52	3	36	46	13.1	3.13	107	.226	.341	2	.105	-1	2	1	-2	-0.1
1967 Bal-A	1	1	.500	5	2	0	0	0	21²	17	4	14	19	12.9	3.32	95	.224	.344	1	.111	-0	-0	-0	-1	-0.1
Was-A	6	5	.545	18	17	4	4	0	95²	90	8	37	67	11.9	2.92	108	.251	.322	2	.057	-2	3	3	-1	0.0
Yr	7	6	.538	23	19	4	4	0	117¹	107	12	51	86	12.1	2.99	106	.246	.325	3	.068	-3	3	2	-1	-0.1
1968 Was-A	7	13	.350	27	23	1	0	0	127¹	133	15	69	81	14.7	4.66	63	.273	.369	5	.132	-3	-24	-25	-0	-2.7
1969 Was-A	1	3	.250	14	5	0	0	0	35²	43	8	23	25	16.7	6.56	53	.291	.386	4	.364	2	-12	-12	0	-1.0
Bal-A	0	0	—	3	0	0	0	0	6	1	0	3	5	6.0	0.00	—	.063	.211	1	1.000	1	2	2	-0	0.3
Yr	1	3	.250	17	5	0	0	0	41²	44	8	26	30	15.1	5.62	62	.267	.366	5	.417	3	-9	-10	0	-0.7
1970 StL-N	1	2	.333	8	5	0	0	0	31¹	36	1	15	14	14.6	3.16	130	.293	.370	1	.143	0	3	3	0	0.4
Total 7	19	29	.396	99	66	6	5	0	413	399	42	214	280	13.6	3.84	85	.257	.350	16	.127	-1	-24	-27	-2	-3.2

● **LEFTY BERTRAND**   Bertrand, Roman Mathias   b: 2/28/09, Cobden, Minn.   BR/TL, 6', 180 lbs.   Deb: 4/15/36

| 1936 Phi-N | 0 | 0 | — | 1 | 0 | 0 | 0 | 0 | 2 | 3 | 1 | 2 | 1 | 22.5 | 9.00 | 50 | .333 | .455 | 0 | — | 0 | -1 | -1 | -0 | -0.1 |

● **FRED BESANA**   Besana, Frederick Cyril   b: 4/5/31, Lincoln, Cal.   BR/TL, 6'3.5", 200 lbs.   Deb: 4/18/56

| 1956 Bal-A | 1 | 0 | 1.000 | 7 | 2 | 0 | 0 | 0 | 17² | 22 | 0 | 14 | 7 | 19.4 | 5.60 | 70 | .310 | .437 | 0 | .000 | -0 | -3 | -3 | 1 | -0.3 |

● **HERMAN BESSE**   Besse, Herman A.   b: 8/16/11, St.Louis, Mo.   d: 8/13/72, Los Angeles, Cal.   BL/TL, 6'2", 190 lbs.   Deb: 4/19/40

1940 Phi-A	0	3	.000	17	5	0	0	0	53	70	10	34	19	18.2	8.83	50	.315	.413	5	.263	2	-26	-26	-1	-2.2
1941 Phi-A	2	0	1.000	6	2	1	0	0	19²	28	4	12	8	18.3	10.07	42	.329	.412	1	.200	-0	-13	-13	0	-1.1
1942 Phi-A	2	9	.182	30	14	4	0	1	133	163	7	69	78	16.0	6.16	61	.300	.383	12	.226	2	-37	-35	-2	-3.4
1943 Phi-A	1	1	.500	5	1	0	0	0	16¹	18	2	4	3	12.7	3.31	103	.295	.348	0	.000	-1	-0	-0	0	-0.1
1946 Phi-A	0	2	.000	7	3	0	0	1	20²	19	1	9	10	12.2	5.23	68	.247	.326	0	.000	-0	-4	-4	0	-0.4
Total 5	5	15	.250	65	25	5	0	2	242²	298	24	128	118	16.1	6.79	58	.302	.386	18	.200	2	-80	-77	-3	-7.2

● **DON BESSENT**   Bessent, Fred Donald   b: 3/13/31, Jacksonville, Fla.   d: 7/7/90, Jacksonville, Fla.   BR/TR, 6', 175 lbs.   Deb: 7/17/55

1955 *Bro-N	8	1	.889	24	2	1	0	3	63¹	51	7	21	29	10.2	2.70	150	.220	.285	2	.100	-2	9	10	-0	0.8
1956 *Bro-N	4	3	.571	38	0	0	0	9	79¹	63	6	31	52	10.7	2.50	159	.221	.297	2	.111	-1	11	13	-1	1.1
1957 Bro-N	1	3	.250	27	0	0	0	0	44	58	5	19	24	15.8	5.73	73	.328	.393	1	.250	0	-9	-8	-0	-0.8
1958 LA-N	1	0	1.000	19	0	0	0	0	24¹	24	3	17	13	15.5	3.33	123	.270	.393	0	.000	-0	2	2	1	0.3
Total 4	14	7	.667	108	2	1	0	12	211	196	20	88	118	12.2	3.33	122	.250	.327	5	.114	-3	13	17	-1	1.4

● **KARL BEST**   Best, Karl Jon   b: 3/6/59, Aberdeen, Was.   BR/TR, 6'4", 210 lbs.   Deb: 8/19/83

1983 Sea-A	0	1	.000	4	0	0	0	0	5¹	14	2	5	3	35.4	13.50	32	.483	.583	0	—	0	-6	-5	-0	-0.7
1984 Sea-A	1	1	.500	5	0	0	0	0	6	7	0	6	6	10.5	3.00	133	.292	.292	0	—	0	1	1	-0	0.1
1985 Sea-A	2	1	.667	15	0	0	0	4	32¹	25	1	6	32	8.9	1.95	216	.207	.250	0	—	0	8	8	-0	0.8
1986 Sea-A	2	3	.400	26	0	0	0	1	35²	35	3	21	23	14.4	4.04	105	.255	.358	0	—	0	1	1	-0	0.8
1988 Min-A	0	0	—	11	0	0	0	0	12	15	1	7	9	16.5	6.00	68	.306	.393	0	—	0	-3	-3	-0	-0.4
Total 5	5	6	.455	61	0	0	0	5	91¹	96	7	39	73	13.7	4.04	104	.267	.345	0	—	0	2	2	-0	-0.2

● **JIM BETHKE**   Bethke, James Charles   b: 11/5/46, Falls City, Neb.   BR/TR, 6'3", 185 lbs.   Deb: 4/12/65

| 1965 NY-N | 2 | 0 | 1.000 | 25 | 0 | 0 | 0 | 0 | 40 | 41 | 3 | 22 | 19 | 15.5 | 4.27 | 83 | .266 | .379 | 0 | .000 | -0 | -3 | -3 | 1 | -0.3 |

● **JEFF BETTENDORF**   Bettendorf, Jeffrey Allen   b: 12/10/60, Lompoc, Cal.   BR/TR, 6'3", 180 lbs.   Deb: 4/08/84

| 1984 Oak-A | 0 | 0 | — | 3 | 0 | 0 | 0 | 1 | 9² | 9 | 3 | 5 | 5 | 13.0 | 4.66 | 80 | .243 | .333 | 0 | — | 0 | -1 | -1 | -0 | 0.3 |

● **HARRY BETTS** Betts, Harold Matthew "Chubby" or "Ginger" b: 6/19/1881, Alliance, Ohio d: 5/22/46, San Antonio, Tex. BR/TR, 5'10", 200 lbs. Deb: 9/22/03

YEAR	TM/L	W	L	PCT	G	GS	CG	SH	SV	IP	H	HR	BB	SO	RAT	ERA	ERA+	OAV	OOB	BH	AVG	PB	PR	/A	PD	TPI
1903	StL-N	0	1	.000	1	1	1	0	0	9	11	0	5	2	18.0	10.00	33	.297	.409	0	.000	-0	-7	-7	-0	-0.5
1913	Cin-N	0	0	—	1	0	0	0	0	3^1	1	0	3	0	13.5	2.70	120	.143	.455	0	.000	-0	0	0	-0	0.0
Total	2	0	1	.000	2	1	1	0	0	12^1	12	0	8	2	16.8	8.03	41	.273	.418	0	.000	-1	-7	-7	-0	-0.5

● **HUCK BETTS** Betts, Walter Martin b: 2/18/1897, Millsboro, Del. d: 6/13/87, Millsboro, Del. BR/TR, 5'11", 170 lbs. Deb: 4/26/20

YEAR	TM/L	W	L	PCT	G	GS	CG	SH	SV	IP	H	HR	BB	SO	RAT	ERA	ERA+	OAV	OOB	BH	AVG	PB	PR	/A	PD	TPI
1920	Phi-N	1	1	.500	27	4	1	0	0	88^1	86	3	33	18	12.3	3.57	96	.261	.332	2	.080	-2	-4	-1	-1	-0.4
1921	Phi-N	3	7	.300	32	2	1	0	4	100^2	141	8	14	28	14.2	4.47	95	.337	.365	8	.267	0	-8	-3	0	-0.2
1922	Phi-N	1	0	1.000	7	0	0	0	0	15	23	3	8	4	18.6	9.60	49	.348	.419	0	.000	-0	-9	-8	-0	-0.8
1923	Phi-N	2	4	.333	19	4	3	0	1	84^1	100	7	14	18	12.6	3.09	149	.314	.351	3	.097	-4	9	14	0	1.1
1924	Phi-N	7	10	.412	37	9	2	0	2	144^1	160	8	42	46	12.9	4.30	104	.286	.341	7	.156	-3	-7	3	-2	-0.2
1925	Phi-N	4	5	.444	35	7	1	0	1	97^1	146	10	38	28	17.3	5.55	86	.342	.400	10	.294	2	-14	-8	1	-0.5
1932	Bos-N	13	11	.542	31	27	16	3	1	221^2	229	9	35	32	10.7	2.80	134	.267	.295	19	.241	2	27	24	-2	2.4
1933	Bos-N	11	11	.500	35	26	17	2	4	242	225	9	55	40	10.4	2.79	110	.248	.290	17	.224	2	15	7	4	1.5
1934	Bos-N	17	10	.630	40	27	10	2	3	213	258	17	42	69	12.8	4.06	94	.296	.330	13	.188	1	0	-6	-2	-0.6
1935	Bos-N	2	9	.182	44	19	2	1	0	159^2	213	9	40	40	14.4	5.47	69	.321	.362	7	.159	-0	-26	-30	1	-2.8
Total	10	61	68	.473	307	125	53	8	16	1366^1	1581	83	321	323	12.7	3.93	98	.292	.334	86	.197	-3	-18	-9	-0	-0.5

● **BILL BEVENS** Bevens, Floyd Clifford b: 10/21/16, Hubbard, Ore. d: 10/26/91, Salem, Ore. BR/TR, 6'3.5", 210 lbs. Deb: 5/12/44

YEAR	TM/L	W	L	PCT	G	GS	CG	SH	SV	IP	H	HR	BB	SO	RAT	ERA	ERA+	OAV	OOB	BH	AVG	PB	PR	/A	PD	TPI
1944	NY-A	4	1	.800	8	5	3	0	0	43^2	44	4	13	16	12.0	2.68	130	.273	.331	1	.063	-2	4	4	-0	0.2
1945	NY-A	13	9	.591	29	25	14	2	0	184	174	12	68	76	11.9	3.67	94	.254	.322	7	.111	-4	-6	-4	1	-0.9
1946	NY-A	16	13	.552	31	31	18	3	0	249^2	213	11	78	120	10.5	2.23	154	.232	.293	7	.083	-4	35	34	-4	2.8
1947	*NY-A	7	13	.350	28	23	11	1	0	165	167	13	77	77	13.4	3.82	93	.264	.345	7	.121	-3	-2	-5	-0	-0.9
Total	4	40	36	.526	96	84	46	6	0	642^1	598	40	236	289	11.7	3.08	113	.250	.318	22	.100	-13	31	29	-4	1.2

● **LOU BEVIL** Bevil, Louis Eugene (b: Louis Eugene Bevilacqua) b: 11/27/22, Nelson, Ill. d: 2/1/73, Dixon, Ill. BB/TR, 5'11.5", 190 lbs. Deb: 9/02/42

YEAR	TM/L	W	L	PCT	G	GS	CG	SH	SV	IP	H	HR	BB	SO	RAT	ERA	ERA+	OAV	OOB	BH	AVG	PB	PR	/A	PD	TPI
1942	Was-A	0	1	.000	4	1	0	0	0	9^2	9	0	11	2	19.6	6.52	56	.265	.457	0	.000	-0	-3	-3	-0	-0.4

● **BEN BEVILLE** Beville, Clarence Benjamin b: 8/28/1877, Colusa, Cal. d: 1/5/37, Yountville, Cal. BR/TR, 5'9", 190 lbs. Deb: 5/24/01

YEAR	TM/L	W	L	PCT	G	GS	CG	SH	SV	IP	H	HR	BB	SO	RAT	ERA	ERA+	OAV	OOB	BH	AVG	PB	PR	/A	PD	TPI
1901	Bos-A	0	2	.000	2	2	1	0	0	9	8	0	9	1	18.0	4.00	88	.235	.409	2	.286	0	-0	-0	-0	0.0

● **JIM BIBBY** Bibby, James Blair b: 10/29/44, Franklinton, N.C. BR/TR, 6'5", 235 lbs. Deb: 9/04/72

YEAR	TM/L	W	L	PCT	G	GS	CG	SH	SV	IP	H	HR	BB	SO	RAT	ERA	ERA+	OAV	OOB	BH	AVG	PB	PR	/A	PD	TPI
1972	StL-N	1	3	.250	6	6	0	0	0	40^1	29	4	19	28	10.9	3.35	102	.206	.304	1	.125	0	0	0	0	0.1
1973	StL-N	0	2	.000	6	3	0	0	0	16	19	2	17	12	21.4	9.56	38	.306	.469	0	.000	0	-10	-11	0	-1.0
	Tex-A	9	10	.474	26	23	11	2	1	180^1	121	14	106	155	11.6	3.24	115	**.192**	.314	0	—	0	11	10	-2	0.8
1974	Tex-A	19	19	.500	41	41	11	5	0	264	255	25	113	149	12.9	4.74	75	.255	.336	0	—	0	-33	-34	1	-3.4
1975	Tex-A	2	6	.250	12	12	4	1	0	68^1	73	2	28	31	13.6	5.00	75	.274	.348	0	—	0	-9	-9	-1	-1.0
	Cle-A	5	9	.357	24	12	2	0	1	112^2	99	7	50	62	11.9	3.20	118	.235	.316	0	—	0	7	7	1	0.8
	Yr	7	15	.318	36	24	6	1	1	181	172	9	78	93	12.4	3.88	97	.248	.324	0	—	0	-2	-2	0	-0.2
1976	Cle-A	13	7	.650	34	21	4	3	1	163^1	162	6	56	84	12.1	3.20	109	.266	.329	0	—	0	6	5	-1	0.5
1977	Cle-A	12	13	.480	37	30	9	2	2	206^2	197	17	73	141	11.9	3.57	110	.250	.317	0	—	0	11	9	-2	0.7
1978	Pit-N	8	7	.533	34	14	3	2	1	107	100	10	39	72	11.9	3.53	105	.246	.315	4	.129	1	1	2	0	0.3
1979	*Pit-N	12	4	.750	34	17	4	1	0	137^2	110	9	47	103	10.5	2.81	138	.218	.290	8	.178	2	14	16	-2	1.8
1980	Pit-N★	19	6	**.760**	35	34	6	1	0	238^1	210	20	88	144	11.5	3.32	110	.238	.312	12	.156	2	7	8	-2	0.9
1981	Pit-N	6	3	.667	14	14	2	2	0	93^2	79	4	26	48	10.3	2.50	144	.225	.282	4	.143	1	10	11	-1	1.3
1983	Pit-N	5	12	.294	29	12	0	0	2	78	92	10	51	44	16.6	6.69	55	.297	.398	2	.111	-1	-27	-26	-0	-2.7
1984	Tex-A	0	0	—	8	0	0	0	0	16^1	19	1	10	6	16.0	4.41	94	.297	.392	0	—	0	-1	-0	-0	-0.1
Total	12	111	101	.524	340	239	56	19	8	1722^2	1565	131	723	1079	12.2	3.76	98	.243	.323	31	.148	5	-11	-11	-8	-1.0

● **VERN BICKFORD** Bickford, Vernon Edgell b: 8/17/20, Hellier, Ky. d: 5/6/60, Concord, Va. BR/TR, 6', 185 lbs. Deb: 4/24/48

YEAR	TM/L	W	L	PCT	G	GS	CG	SH	SV	IP	H	HR	BB	SO	RAT	ERA	ERA+	OAV	OOB	BH	AVG	PB	PR	/A	PD	TPI
1948	*Bos-N	11	5	.688	33	22	10	1	1	146	125	9	63	60	11.8	3.27	117	.226	.309	10	.204	1	11	9	-1	0.9
1949	Bos-N★	16	11	.593	37	36	15	2	0	230^2	246	20	106	101	14.0	4.25	89	.273	.354	15	.185	-0	-5	-12	2	-1.1
1950	Bos-N	19	14	.576	40	39	**27**	2	0	**311^2**	293	25	122	126	12.2	3.47	111	.248	.321	16	.138	-4	23	13	-1	0.8
1951	Bos-N	11	9	.550	25	20	12	3	0	164^2	146	7	76	76	12.5	3.12	118	.240	.330	6	.115	-2	15	10	3	1.1
1952	Bos-N	7	12	.368	26	22	7	1	0	161^1	165	7	64	62	12.9	3.74	97	.269	.340	9	.176	-0	-0	-2	1	-0.2
1953	Mil-N	2	5	.286	20	9	2	0	1	58	60	8	35	25	15.1	5.28	74	.279	.385	1	.067	-1	-6	-9	1	-0.8
1954	Bal-A	0	1	.000	1	1	0	0	0	4	5	0	1	0	13.5	9.00	40	.333	.375	0	.000	-0	-2	-2	0	-0.2
Total	7	66	57	.537	182	149	73	9	2	1076^1	1040	76	467	450	12.8	3.71	102	.254	.335	57	.156	-6	36	7	3	0.5

● **DAN BICKHAM** Bickham, Daniel Denison b: 10/31/1864, Dayton, Ohio d: 3/3/51, Dayton, Ohio BR/TR, 5'10", 160 lbs. Deb: 8/13/1886

YEAR	TM/L	W	L	PCT	G	GS	CG	SH	SV	IP	H	HR	BB	SO	RAT	ERA	ERA+	OAV	OOB	BH	AVG	PB	PR	/A	PD	TPI
1886	Cin-a	1	0	1.000	1	1	1	0	0	9	13	0	3	6	16.0	3.00	117	.351	.400	1	.333	0	0	1	0	0.1

● **CHARLIE BICKNELL** Bicknell, Charles Stephen "Bud" b: 7/27/28, Plainfield, N.J. BR/TR, 5'11", 170 lbs. Deb: 4/22/48

YEAR	TM/L	W	L	PCT	G	GS	CG	SH	SV	IP	H	HR	BB	SO	RAT	ERA	ERA+	OAV	OOB	BH	AVG	PB	PR	/A	PD	TPI
1948	Phi-N	0	1	.000	17	1	0	0	0	25^2	29	5	17	5	16.1	5.96	66	.287	.390	0	.000	-1	-6	-6	-1	-0.7
1949	Phi-N	0	0	—	13	0	0	0	0	28^1	32	3	17	4	16.2	7.62	52	.291	.395	0	.000	0	-11	-12	-0	-1.1
Total	2	0	1	.000	30	1	0	0	0	54	61	8	34	9	16.2	6.83	58	.289	.393	0	.000	-0	-17	-17	-1	-1.8

● **MIKE BIELECKI** Bielecki, Michael Joseph b: 7/31/59, Baltimore, Md. BR/TR, 6'3", 200 lbs. Deb: 9/14/84

YEAR	TM/L	W	L	PCT	G	GS	CG	SH	SV	IP	H	HR	BB	SO	RAT	ERA	ERA+	OAV	OOB	BH	AVG	PB	PR	/A	PD	TPI
1984	Pit-N	0	0	—	4	0	0	0	0	4^1	4	0	0	1	8.3	0.00	—	.250	.250	0	—	0	2	2	0	0.2
1985	Pit-N	2	3	.400	12	7	0	0	0	45^2	45	5	31	22	15.2	4.53	79	.257	.372	0	.000	-1	-5	-5	1	-0.5
1986	Pit-N	6	11	.353	31	27	0	0	0	148^2	149	10	83	83	14.2	4.66	82	.262	.358	3	.063	-3	-16	-14	-1	-1.7
1987	Pit-N	2	3	.400	8	8	2	0	0	45^2	43	6	12	25	11.0	4.73	87	.250	.303	1	.063	-1	-3	-3	-0	-0.4
1988	Chi-N	2	2	.500	19	5	0	0	0	48^1	55	4	16	33	13.2	3.35	108	.284	.338	1	.100	-0	1	1	-0	0.1
1989	*Chi-N	18	7	**.720**	33	33	4	3	0	212^1	187	16	81	147	11.4	3.14	120	.237	.308	3	.043	-5	8	15	-1	0.9
1990	Chi-N	8	11	.421	36	29	0	0	1	168	188	13	70	103	14.1	4.93	83	.287	.361	7	.163	-0	-21	-16	3	-1.4
1991	Chi-N	13	11	.542	39	25	0	0	0	172	169	18	54	72	11.8	4.50	86	.262	.321	3	.065	-2	-16	-12	1	-1.4
	Atl-N	0	0	—	2	0	0	0	0	1^2	2	0	2	3	21.6	0.00	—	.286	.444	0	—	0	1	1	0	0.1
	Yr	13	11	.542	41	25	0	0	0	173^2	171	18	56	75	11.8	4.46	87	.259	.317	3	.065	-2	-15	-11	1	-1.3
1992	Atl-N	2	4	.333	19	14	1	1	0	80^2	77	2	27	62	11.7	2.57	146	.254	.317	3	.125	-1	8	11	1	1.1
Total	9	53	52	.505	203	148	7	4	1	927^1	919	74	376	551	12.7	4.05	95	.261	.334	21	.079	-14	-41	-20	2	-3.0

● **HARRY BIEMILLER** Biemiller, Harry Lee b: 10/9/1897, Baltimore, Md. d: 5/25/65, Orlando, Fla. BR/TR, 6'1", 171 lbs. Deb: 8/26/20

YEAR	TM/L	W	L	PCT	G	GS	CG	SH	SV	IP	H	HR	BB	SO	RAT	ERA	ERA+	OAV	OOB	BH	AVG	PB	PR	/A	PD	TPI
1920	Was-A	1	0	1.000	5	2	1	0	0	17	21	1	13	10	18.0	4.76	78	.318	.430	0	.000	-1	-2	-2	1	-0.2
1925	Cin-N	0	1	.000	23	1	0	0	2	47	45	2	21	9	14.0	4.02	102	.280	.386	0	.000	-0	1	0	2	0.1
Total	2	1	1	.500	28	3	1	0	2	64	66	3	34	19	15.0	4.22	95	.291	.399	0	.000	-1	-1	-1	2	-0.1

● **LOU BIERBAUER** Bierbauer, Louis W. b: 9/28/1865, Erie, Pa. d: 1/31/26, Erie, Pa. BL/TR, 5'8", 140 lbs. Deb: 4/17/1886 ♦

YEAR	TM/L	W	L	PCT	G	GS	CG	SH	SV	IP	H	HR	BB	SO	RAT	ERA	ERA+	OAV	OOB	BH	AVG	PB	PR	/A	PD	TPI
1886	Phi-a	0	0	—	2	0	0	0	0	10^2	8	0	5	1	11.0	4.22	83	.178	.260	118	.226	-0	-1	-1	-1	-0.1
1887	Phi-a	0	0	—	1	0	0	0	1	1	0	0	0	1	0.0	0.00	—	.000	.000	144	.272	0	0	0	0	0.0
1888	Phi-a	0	0	—	1	0	0	0	0	3	5	0	0	3	15.0	0.00	—	.358	.358	143	.267	0	1	1	-0	0.1
Total	3	0	0	—	4	0	0	0	1	14^2	13	0	5	5	11.0	3.07	112	.210	.269	1521	.267	0	1	1	-1	0.0

● **LYLE BIGBEE** Bigbee, Lyle Randolph "Al" b: 8/22/1893, Sweet Home, Ore. d: 8/5/42, Portland, Ore. BL/TR, 6', 180 lbs. Deb: 4/15/20 F♦

YEAR	TM/L	W	L	PCT	G	GS	CG	SH	SV	IP	H	HR	BB	SO	RAT	ERA	ERA+	OAV	OOB	BH	AVG	PB	PR	/A	PD	TPI
1920	Phi-A	0	3	.000	12	2	0	0	0	45	66	5	25	12	18.2	8.00	50	.369	.446	14	.187	0	-21	-20	0	-1.7
1921	Pit-N	0	0	—	5	0	0	0	0	8	4	0	4	1	9.0	1.13	341	.154	.267	0	.000	-0	2	2	-0	0.2

YEAR TM/L	W	L	PCT	G	GS	CG	SH	SV	IP	H	HR	BB	SO	RAT	ERA	ERA+	OAV	OOB	BH	AVG	PB	PR	/A	PD	TPI
Total 2	0	3	.000	17	2	0	0	0	53	70	5	29	13	16.8	6.96	57	.341	.423	14	.182	-0	-19	-17	0	-1.5
● **CHARLIE BIGGS**	Biggs, Charles Orval b: 9/15/06, French Lick, Ind. d: 5/24/54, French Lick, Ind. BR/TR, 6'1", 185 lbs. Deb: 9/03/32																								
1932 Chi-A	1	1	.500	6	4	0	0	0	24^{2}	32	2	12	1	17.1	6.93	62	.314	.402	1	.111	-0	-7	-7	-0	-0.7
● **LARRY BIITTNER**	Biittner, Lawrence David b: 7/27/45, Pocahontas, Ia. BL/TL, 6'2", 205 lbs. Deb: 7/17/70 ♦																								
1977 Chi-N	0	0	—	1	0	0	0	0	1^{1}	5	3	1	3	40.5	40.50	11	.556	.600	147	.298	0	-5	-5	0	-0.4
● **JIM BILBREY**	Bilbrey, James Melvin b: 4/20/24, Rickman, Tenn. d: 12/26/85, Toledo, Ohio BR/TR, 6'2.5", 205 lbs. Deb: 5/17/49																								
1949 StL-A	0	0	—	1	0	0	0	0	1	1	0	3	0	36.0	18.00	25	.250	.571	0	—	0	-2	-1	0	-0.1
● **EMIL BILDILLI**	Bildilli, Emil "Hill Billy" b: 9/16/12, Diamond, Ind. d: 9/16/46, Hartford City, Ind. BR/TL, 5'10", 170 lbs. Deb: 8/24/37																								
1937 StL-A	0	1	.000	4	1	0	0	0	8	12	1	3	2	16.9	10.13	48	.353	.405	0	.000	-0	-5	-5	1	-0.4
1938 StL-A	1	2	.333	5	3	2	0	0	21^{2}	33	3	11	11	18.3	7.06	70	.359	.427	2	.250	-0	-5	-5	-0	-0.4
1939 StL-A	1	1	.500	2	2	2	0	0	19	21	0	6	8	12.8	3.32	147	.266	.318	0	.000	-1	3	3	0	0.3
1940 StL-A	2	4	.333	28	11	3	0	1	97	113	12	52	32	15.5	5.57	82	.298	.386	6	.200	-1	-13	-11	3	-0.8
1941 StL-A	0	0	—	2	0	0	0	0	2^{1}	5	0	3	2	30.9	11.57	37	.417	.533	0	—	0	-2	-2	0	-0.2
Total 5	4	8	.333	41	17	7	0	1	148	184	16	75	55	15.9	5.84	80	.309	.388	8	.178	-2	-22	-19	4	-1.5
● **HARRY BILLIARD**	Billiard, Harry Pree "Pree" b: 11/11/1883, Monroe, Ind. d: 6/3/23, Wooster, Ohio BR/TR, 6', 190 lbs. Deb: 7/31/08																								
1908 NY-A	0	0	—	6	0	0	0	0	17	15	1	14	10	18.0	2.65	94	.234	.410	1	.200	-0	-0	-0	-1	-0.1
1914 Ind-F	8	7	.533	32	16	5	0	2	125^{2}	117	4	63	45	13.4	3.72	93	.257	.356	7	.184	-1	-7	-4	-2	-0.6
1915 New-F	0	1	.000	14	2	0	0	1	28^{1}	32	0	28	7	20.0	5.72	50	.291	.447	2	.333	0	-8	-9	1	-0.8
Total 3	8	8	.500	52	18	5	0	3	171	164	5	105	62	14.9	3.95	83	.260	.379	10	.204	-0	-16	-13	-2	-1.5
● **JACK BILLINGHAM**	Billingham, John Eugene b: 2/21/43, Orlando, Fla. BR/TR, 6'4", 215 lbs. Deb: 4/11/68																								
1968 LA-N	3	0	1.000	50	1	0	0	8	70^{2}	54	0	30	46	11.0	2.17	128	.215	.304	0	.000	0	6	5	1	0.6
1969 Hou-N	6	7	.462	52	4	1	0	2	82^{2}	92	12	29	71	13.7	4.25	83	.290	.359	1	.071	0	-6	-6	-0	-0.7
1970 Hou-N	13	9	.591	46	24	8	2	0	187^{2}	190	10	63	134	12.6	3.98	97	.259	.326	6	.103	-2	1	-2	1	-0.3
1971 Hou-N	10	16	.385	33	33	8	3	0	228^{1}	205	9	68	139	11.4	3.39	99	.243	.311	9	.123	-3	2	-1	0	-0.3
1972 *Cin-N	12	12	.500	36	31	8	4	1	217^{2}	197	18	64	137	11.1	3.18	101	.241	.301	5	.070	-4	7	1	-1	-0.4
1973 *Cin-N☆	19	10	.655	40	40	16	**7**	0	$\mathbf{293}^{1}$	257	20	95	155	11.1	3.04	112	.236	.303	6	.065	-5	20	12	2	0.9
1974 Cin-N	19	11	.633	36	35	8	3	0	212^{1}	233	16	64	103	12.8	3.94	88	.288	.345	5	.075	-5	-8	-11	1	-1.6
1975 *Cin-N	15	10	.600	33	32	5	0	0	208	222	22	76	79	13.3	4.11	87	.279	.348	7	.108	-1	-11	-12	-2	-1.5
1976 *Cin-N	12	10	.545	34	29	5	2	1	177	190	17	62	76	13.0	4.32	81	.279	.343	14	.237	3	-16	-16	-1	-1.4
1977 Cin-N	10	10	.500	36	23	3	2	0	161^{2}	195	16	56	76	14.5	5.23	75	.306	.371	9	.161	-1	-24	-23	2	-2.2
1978 Det-A	15	8	.652	30	30	10	4	0	201^{2}	218	16	65	59	13.0	3.88	100	.284	.346	0	—	0	-3	-0	-1	-0.2
1979 Det-A	10	7	.588	35	19	2	0	3	158	163	13	60	59	13.1	3.30	131	.275	.348	0	—	0	16	18	-1	1.7
1980 Det-A	0	0	—	8	0	0	0	0	7^{1}	11	1	6	3	20.9	7.36	56	.355	.459	0	—	0	-3	-3	0	-0.3
Bos-A	1	3	.250	7	4	0	0	0	24^{1}	45	6	12	4	22.6	11.10	38	.413	.488	0	—	0	-19	-19	-0	-1.8
Yr	1	3	.250	15	4	0	0	0	31^{2}	56	7	18	7	22.2	10.23	41	.397	.479	0	—	0	-22	-21	-0	-2.1
Total 13	145	113	.562	476	305	74	27	15	2230^{2}	2272	176	750	1141	12.6	3.83	94	.268	.335	62	.111	-16	-37	-59	0	-7.5
● **JOSH BILLINGS**	Billings, Haskell Clark b: 9/27/07, New York, N.Y. d: 12/26/83, Greenbrae, Cal. BR/TR, 5'11", 180 lbs. Deb: 8/17/27																								
1927 Det-A	5	4	.556	10	9	5	0	0	67	64	3	39	18	14.6	4.84	87	.259	.373	7	.259	0	-5	-5	-1	-0.4
1928 Det-A	5	10	.333	21	16	3	1	0	110^{2}	118	4	59	48	14.8	5.12	80	.276	.371	10	.286	3	-13	-12	-0	-1.0
1929 Det-A	0	1	.000	8	0	0	0	0	19^{1}	27	0	9	1	17.2	5.12	84	.365	.440	0	.000	-1	-2	-2	1	-0.1
Total 3	10	15	.400	39	25	8	1	0	197	209	7	107	67	15.0	5.03	83	.279	.378	17	.250	2	-20	-19	0	-1.5
● **DOUG BIRD**	Bird, James Douglas b: 3/5/50, Corona, Cal. BR/TR, 6'4", 180 lbs. Deb: 4/29/73																								
1973 KC-A	4	4	.500	54	0	0	0	20	102^{1}	81	10	30	83	9.9	2.99	137	.217	.279	0	—	0	9	13	-2	0.8
1974 KC-A	7	6	.538	55	1	1	0	10	92^{1}	100	6	27	62	12.5	2.73	140	.286	.339	0	—	0	9	11	1	1.2
1975 KC-A	9	6	.600	51	4	0	0	11	105^{1}	100	7	40	81	12.1	3.25	119	.258	.331	0	—	0	6	7	-1	0.6
1976 *KC-A	12	10	.545	39	27	2	1	2	197^{2}	191	17	31	107	10.2	3.37	104	.251	.283	0	—	0	3	3	-2	0.1
1977 *KC-A	11	4	.733	53	5	0	0	14	118^{1}	120	14	29	83	11.6	3.88	104	.270	.319	0	—	0	2	2	-1	0.1
1978 *KC-A	6	6	.500	40	6	0	0	1	98^{2}	110	8	31	48	13.0	5.29	72	.284	.340	0	—	0	-17	-16	-0	-1.7
1979 Phi-N	2	0	1.000	32	1	1	0	0	61	73	7	16	33	13.4	5.16	74	.305	.354	1	.167	0	-10	-9	-1	-1.0
1980 NY-A	3	0	1.000	22	1	0	0	1	50^{2}	47	3	14	17	11.0	2.66	147	.257	.313	0	—	0	8	7	1	0.8
1981 NY-A	5	1	.833	17	4	0	0	0	53^{1}	58	5	16	28	12.5	2.70	132	.280	.332	0	—	0	6	5	0	0.6
Chi-N	4	5	.444	12	12	2	1	0	75^{1}	72	5	16	34	10.6	3.58	103	.254	.297	2	.100	-1	-1	1	-1	-0.1
1982 Chi-N	9	14	.391	35	33	2	1	0	191	230	26	30	71	12.4	5.14	73	.297	.325	8	.143	-2	-33	-30	-2	-3.3
1983 Bos-A	1	4	.200	22	6	0	0	1	67^{2}	91	14	16	33	14.5	6.65	65	.324	.365	0	—	0	-19	-17	-0	-1.8
Total 11	73	60	.549	432	100	8	3	60	1213^{2}	1273	122	296	680	11.8	3.99	96	.272	.319	11	.134	-2	-36	-23	-8	-3.7
● **RED BIRD**	Bird, James Edward b: 4/25/1890, Stephenville, Tex. d: 3/23/72, Murfreesboro, Ark. BL/TL, 5'11", 170 lbs. Deb: 9/17/21																								
1921 Was-A	0	0	—	1	0	0	0	0	5	5	0	1	2	12.6	5.40	76	.294	.368	0	.000	-0	-1	-1	0	-0.1
● **MIKE BIRKBECK**	Birkbeck, Michael Lawrence b: 3/10/61, Orrville, Ohio BR/TR, 6'1", 190 lbs. Deb: 8/17/86																								
1986 Mil-A	1	1	.500	7	4	0	0	0	22	24	0	12	13	14.7	4.50	96	.282	.371	0	—	0	-1	-0	-0	-0.1
1987 Mil-A	1	4	.200	10	10	1	0	0	45	63	8	19	25	16.4	6.20	74	.335	.396	0	—	0	-9	-8	1	-0.7
1988 Mil-A	10	8	.556	23	23	0	0	0	124	141	10	37	64	13.0	4.72	84	.285	.336	0	—	0	-10	-10	2	-0.8
1989 Mil-A	0	4	.000	9	9	1	0	0	44^{2}	57	4	22	31	16.5	5.44	71	.310	.392	0	—	0	-8	-8	-0	-0.8
1992 NY-N	0	1	.000	1	1	0	0	0	7	12	3	1	2	16.7	9.00	39	.387	.406	0	.000	-0	-4	-4	0	-0.4
Total 5	12	18	.400	50	47	2	0	0	242^{2}	297	25	91	135	14.5	5.23	78	.302	.364	0	.000	-0	-32	-31	2	-2.8
● **RALPH BIRKOFER**	Birkofer, Ralph Joseph "Lefty" b: 11/5/08, Cincinnati, Ohio d: 3/16/71, Cincinnati, Ohio BL/TL, 5'11", 213 lbs. Deb: 4/25/33																								
1933 Pit-N	4	2	.667	9	8	3	1	0	50^{2}	43	1	17	20	10.8	2.31	144	.229	.296	7	.318	1	6	6	-0	0.7
1934 Pit-N	11	12	.478	41	24	11	0	1	204	227	11	66	71	13.1	4.10	100	.277	.335	17	.227	1	-1	0	-2	-0.1
1935 Pit-N	9	7	.563	37	18	8	1	1	150^{1}	173	5	42	80	13.2	4.07	101	.283	.335	14	.241	2	-1	1	-3	0.0
1936 Pit-N	7	5	.583	34	13	2	0	0	109^{1}	130	4	41	44	14.5	4.69	86	.295	.362	9	.220	-0	-8	-8	-3	-1.0
1937 Bro-N	0	2	.000	11	1	0	0	0	29^{2}	45	3	9	9	16.4	6.67	60	.341	.383	3	.273	1	-9	-9	-1	-0.8
Total 5	31	28	.525	132	64	24	2	2	544	618	24	175	224	13.4	4.19	96	.282	.340	50	.242	5	-13	-10	-8	-1.2
● **BABE BIRRER**	Birrer, Werner Joseph b: 7/4/28, Buffalo, N.Y. BR/TR, 6', 195 lbs. Deb: 6/05/55																								
1955 Det-A	4	3	.571	36	3	1	0	3	80^{1}	77	9	29	28	11.9	4.15	93	.248	.313	3	.158	2	-2	-3	-1	-0.1
1956 Bal-A	0	0	—	4	0	0	0	0	5^{1}	9	0	1	1	16.9	6.75	58	.360	.385	0	.000	-0	-2	-2	-0	-0.2
1958 LA-N	0	0	—	16	0	0	0	1	34	43	4	7	16	13.5	4.50	91	.309	.347	4	.571	2	-2	-2	-1	-0.1
Total 3	4	3	.571	56	3	1	0	4	119^{2}	129	13	37	45	12.6	4.36	90	.272	.326	7	.259	4	-5	-6	-2	-0.4
● **TIM BIRTSAS**	Birtsas, Timothy Dean b: 9/5/60, Pontiac, Mich. BL/TL, 6'7", 240 lbs. Deb: 5/03/85																								
1985 Oak-A	10	6	.625	29	25	2	0	0	141^{1}	124	18	91	94	13.9	4.01	96	.238	.354	0	—	0	2	-2	-3	-0.3
1986 Oak-A	0	0	—	2	0	0	0	0	2	2	1	4	1	27.0	22.50	17	.286	.545	0	—	0	-4	-4	-0	-0.2
1988 Cin-N	1	3	.250	36	4	0	0	0	64^{1}	61	6	24	38	12.3	4.20	85	.250	.325	0	.000	-1	-5	-4	-1	-0.7
1989 Cin-N	2	2	.500	42	1	0	0	1	69^{2}	68	5	27	57	12.7	3.75	96	.261	.337	1	.250	1	-2	-1	-1	-0.1
1990 Cin-N	1	3	.250	29	0	0	0	0	51^{1}	69	7	24	41	16.5	3.86	102	.325	.397	0	.000	-0	-0	0	0	0.0
Total 5	14	14	.500	138	30	2	0	1	328^{2}	324	37	170	231	13.8	4.08	93	.260	.354	1	.056	-0	-10	-11	-4	-1.3

YEAR TM/L	W	L	PCT	G	GS	CG	SH	SV	IP	H	HR	BB	SO	RAT	ERA	ERA+	OAV	OOB	BH	AVG	PB	PR	/A	PD	TPI
● FRANK BISCAN Biscan, Frank Stephen "Porky" b: 3/13/20, Mt.Olive, Ill. d: 5/22/59, St.Louis, Mo. BL/TL, 5'11", 190 lbs. Deb: 5/03/42																									
1942 StL-A	0	1	.000	11	0	0	0	1	27	13	1	11	10	8.0	2.33	159	.143	.235	0	.000	-0	4	4	0	0.4
1946 StL-A	1	1	.500	16	0	0	0	1	22^2	28	0	22	9	19.9	5.16	72	.318	.455	0	.000	-0	-4	-4	-0	-0.4
1948 StL-A	6	7	.462	47	4	1	0	2	98^2	129	3	71	45	19.1	6.11	75	.322	.435	5	.192	1	-20	-17	0	-1.5
Total 3	7	9	.438	74	4	1	0	4	148^1	170	4	104	64	17.2	5.28	81	.294	.409	5	.143	-0	-20	-17	0	-1.5
● CHARLIE BISHOP Bishop, Charles Tuller b: 1/1/24, Atlanta, Ga. BR/TR, 6'2", 195 lbs. Deb: 8/22/52																									
1952 Phi-A	2	2	.500	6	5	1	0	0	30^2	29	2	24	17	15.6	6.46	61	.238	.363	1	.111	-0	-9	-9	0	-0.8
1953 Phi-A	3	14	.176	39	20	1	1	2	160^2	174	15	86	66	14.8	5.66	76	.282	.375	5	.089	-4	-30	-24	2	-2.6
1954 Phi-A	4	6	.400	20	12	4	0	1	96	98	10	50	34	14.3	4.41	89	.275	.372	4	.121	-2	-7	-5	-2	-0.9
1955 KC-A	1	0	1.000	4	0	0	0	0	6^2	6	1	8	4	23.0	5.40	77	.261	.500	1	.500	0	-1	-1	-0	-0.1
Total 4	10	22	.313	69	37	6	1	3	294	307	28	168	121	14.9	5.33	77	.275	.376	11	.110	-6	-47	-39	1	-4.4
● JIM BISHOP Bishop, James Morton b: 1/28/1898, Montgomery City, Mo. d: 9/20/73, Montgomery City, Mo. BR/TR, 6', 195 lbs. Deb: 4/26/23																									
1923 Phi-N	0	3	.000	15	0	0	0	1	32^2	48	2	11	5	17.1	6.34	73	.353	.413	0	.000	-2	-8	-6	1	-0.7
1924 Phi-N	0	1	.000	7	1	0	0	0	16^2	24	3	7	3	16.7	6.48	69	.348	.408	1	.200	-0	-5	-4	0	-0.4
Total 2	0	4	.000	22	1	0	0	1	49^1	72	5	18	8	17.0	6.39	71	.351	.412	1	.067	-2	-13	-10	1	-1.1
● LLOYD BISHOP Bishop, Lloyd Clifton b: 4/25/1890, Conway Springs, Kan. d: 6/18/68, Wichita, Kan. BR/TR, 6', 180 lbs. Deb: 9/05/14																									
1914 Cle-A	0	1	.000	3	1	0	0	0	8	14	0	3	1	19.1	5.63	51	.389	.436	0	.000	-0	-3	-2	-0	-0.3
● BILL BISHOP Bishop, William Henry "Lefty" b: 10/22/1900, Houtzdale, Pa. d: 2/14/56, St.Joseph, Mo. BL/TL, 5'8", 170 lbs. Deb: 9/15/21																									
1921 Phi-A	0	0	—	2	0	0	0	0	7	8	0	10	4	23.1	9.00	50	.267	.450	0	.000	-1	-4	-4	0	-0.3
● BILL BISHOP Bishop, William Robinson b: 12/27/1869, Adamsburg, Pa. d: 12/15/32, Pittsburgh, Pa. Deb: 7/13/1886																									
1886 Pit-a	0	1	.000	2	2	2	0	0	17	17	0	11	4	15.4	3.18	107	.221	.326	1	.143	-1	1	0	-1	-0.1
1887 Pit-N	0	3	.000	3	3	3	0	0	27	45	2	22	4	23.0	13.33	29	.354	.457	0	.000	-1	-28	-28	-0	-1.9
1889 Chi-N	0	0	—	2	0	0	0	**2**	3	6	0	6	1	36.0	18.00	23	.403	.575	0	.000	0	-5	-5	-0	-0.4
Total 3	0	4	.000	7	5	5	0	2	47	68	2	39	9	21.1	9.96	37	.311	.422	1	.059	-2	-32	-33	-1	-2.4
● HI BITHORN Bithorn, Hiram Gabriel (Sosa) b: 3/18/16, Santurce, P.R. d: 1/1/52, ElMante, Mex. BR/TR, 6'1", 200 lbs. Deb: 4/15/42																									
1942 Chi-N	9	14	.391	38	16	9	0	2	171^1	191	8	81	65	14.3	3.68	87	.296	.374	7	.123	-1	-7	-9	-1	-1.1
1943 Chi-N	18	12	.600	39	30	19	**7**	2	249^2	227	8	65	86	10.6	2.60	129	.244	.294	16	.174	-0	22	21	1	2.4
1946 Chi-N	6	5	.545	26	7	2	1	1	86^2	97	5	25	34	12.7	3.84	86	.283	.332	5	.179	-0	-4	-5	-0	-0.6
1947 Chi-A	1	0	1.000	2	0	0	0	0	2	2	0	0	0	9.0	0.00	—	.286	.286	0	—	0	1	1	-0	0.1
Total 4	34	31	.523	105	53	30	8	5	509^2	517	21	171	185	12.2	3.16	104	.268	.328	28	.158	-2	12	7	-0	0.8
● JOE BITKER Bitker, Joseph Anthony b: 2/12/64, Glendale, Cal. BR/TR, 6'1", 175 lbs. Deb: 7/31/90																									
1990 Oak-A	0	0	—	1	0	0	0	0	3	1	0	1	2	6.0	0.00	—	.111	.200	0	—	0	1	1	0	0.4
Tex-A	0	0	—	5	0	0	0	0	9	7	0	3	6	11.0	3.00	131	.212	.297	0	—	0	1	1	0	0.1
Yr	0	0	—	6	0	0	0	0	12	8	0	4	8	9.8	2.25	172	.190	.277	0	—	0	2	2	0	0.5
1991 Tex-A	1	0	1.000	9	0	0	0	0	14^2	17	4	8	16	15.3	6.75	60	.274	.357	0	—	0	-4	-4	-0	-0.4
Total 2	1	0	1.000	15	0	0	0	0	26^2	25	4	12	24	12.8	4.73	84	.240	.325	0	—	0	-2	-2	0	0.1
● JEFF BITTIGER Bittiger, Jeffrey Scott b: 4/13/62, Jersey City, N.J. BR/TR, 5'10", 175 lbs. Deb: 9/02/86																									
1986 Phi-N	1	1	.500	3	3	0	0	0	14^2	16	2	7	8	14.7	5.52	70	.271	.358	1	.333	1	-3	-3	0	-0.2
1987 Min-A	1	0	1.000	3	1	0	0	0	8^1	11	2	0	5	13.0	5.40	85	.314	.333	0	—	0	-1	-1	0	-0.1
1988 Chi-A	2	4	.333	25	7	0	0	0	61^2	59	11	29	33	12.8	4.23	94	.255	.338	0	—	0	-2	-2	-1	-0.3
1989 Chi-A	0	1	.000	2	1	0	0	0	9^2	9	2	6	7	14.0	6.52	58	.257	.366	0	—	0	-3	-3	-0	-0.3
Total 4	4	6	.400	33	12	0	0	0	94^1	95	17	42	53	13.3	4.77	84	.264	.344	1	.333	1	-8	-8	-1	-0.9
● JIM BIVIN Bivin, James Nathaniel b: 12/11/09, Jackson, Miss. d: 11/7/82, Pueblo, Colo. BR/TR, 6', 155 lbs. Deb: 4/16/35																									
1935 Phi-N	2	9	.182	47	14	0	0	1	161^2	220	20	65	54	16.0	5.79	78	.316	.377	7	.146	-1	-32	-23	-1	-2.3
● DAVE BLACK Black, David b: 4/19/1892, Chicago, Ill. d: 10/27/36, Pittsburgh, Pa. BL/TL, 6'2", 175 lbs. Deb: 5/02/14																									
1914 Chi-F	1	0	1.000	8	1	1	0	0	25	28	1	4	19	11.5	6.12	48	.311	.340	2	.286	1	-8	-9	0	-0.8
1915 Chi-F	6	7	.462	25	10	2	0	0	121^1	104	3	33	43	10.6	2.45	114	.241	.304	4	.108	-2	8	5	2	0.4
Bal-F	1	3	.250	8	4	1	0	0	34	32	2	15	10	13.0	3.71	86	.260	.350	3	.250	0	-3	-2	1	-0.1
Yr	7	10	.412	33	14	3	0	0	155^1	136	5	48	53	10.8	2.72	106	.243	.305	7	.143	-2	5	3	2	0.3
1923 Bos-A	0	0	—	2	0	0	0	0	1	2	0	0	0	18.0	0.00	—	.500	.500	0	—	0	0	0	-0	0.0
Total 3	8	10	.444	43	15	4	0	0	181^1	166	6	52	72	11.2	3.18	91	.256	.319	9	.161	-1	-2	-6	2	-0.5
● DON BLACK Black, Donald Paul b: 7/20/16, Salix, Iowa d: 4/21/59, Cuyahoga Falls, O. BR/TR, 6', 185 lbs. Deb: 4/24/43																									
1943 Phi-A	6	16	.273	33	26	12	1	1	208	193	8	110	65	13.4	4.20	81	.247	.344	13	.188	-1	-21	-19	0	-2.0
1944 Phi-A	10	12	.455	29	27	8	0	0	177^1	177	6	75	78	13.0	4.06	86	.259	.336	11	.186	-1	-12	-11	-0	-1.2
1945 Phi-A	5	11	.313	26	18	8	0	0	125^1	154	5	69	47	16.0	5.17	66	.307	.391	6	.162	-2	-25	-24	-1	-2.8
1946 Cle-A	1	2	.333	18	4	0	0	0	43^2	45	5	21	15	13.8	4.53	73	.273	.358	2	.200	0	-5	-6	1	-0.5
1947 Cle-A	10	12	.455	30	28	8	3	0	190^2	177	17	85	72	12.4	3.92	89	.249	.330	12	.182	-1	-5	-9	1	-1.0
1948 Cle-A	2	2	.500	18	10	1	0	0	52	57	5	40	16	17.0	5.37	76	.282	.403	3	.200	-0	-6	-8	0	-0.7
Total 6	34	55	.382	154	113	37	4	1	797	803	46	400	293	13.7	4.35	80	.264	.352	47	.184	-4	-74	-76	0	-8.2
● BUD BLACK Black, Harry Ralston b: 6/30/57, San Mateo, Cal. BL/TL, 6'2", 180 lbs. Deb: 9/05/81																									
1981 Sea-A	0	0	—	2	0	0	0	0	1	2	0	3	0	45.0	0.00	—	.500	.714	0	—	0	0	0	0	-0.1
1982 KC-A	4	6	.400	22	14	0	0	0	88^1	92	10	34	40	13.1	4.58	89	.269	.340	0	—	0	-5	-5	-0	-0.5
1983 KC-A	10	7	.588	24	24	3	0	0	161^1	159	19	43	58	11.4	3.79	107	.257	.308	0	—	0	5	5	2	0.7
1984 *KC-A	17	12	.586	35	35	8	1	0	257	226	22	64	140	**10.3**	3.12	129	.233	**.283**	0	—	0	25	26	3	3.0
1985 *KC-A	10	15	.400	33	33	5	2	0	205^2	216	17	59	122	12.4	4.33	96	.268	.324	0	—	0	-4	-4	-1	-0.5
1986 KC-A	5	10	.333	56	4	0	0	9	121	100	14	43	68	11.2	3.20	133	.225	.303	0	—	0	13	14	1	1.4
1987 KC-A	8	6	.571	29	18	0	0	1	122^1	126	16	35	61	12.2	3.60	126	.265	.322	0	—	0	12	13	-0	1.2
1988 KC-A	2	1	.667	17	0	0	0	0	22	23	2	11	19	13.9	4.91	81	.267	.351	0	—	0	-2	-2	-0	-0.3
Cle-A	2	3	.400	16	7	0	0	1	59	59	6	23	44	13.1	5.03	82	.262	.341	0	—	0	-7	-6	1	-0.5
Yr	4	4	.500	33	7	0	0	1	81	82	8	34	63	13.3	5.00	82	.264	.344	0	—	0	-9	-8	0	-0.8
1989 Cle-A	12	11	.522	33	32	6	3	0	222^1	213	14	52	88	10.8	3.36	118	.252	.296	0	—	0	13	15	-1	1.5
1990 Cle-A	11	10	.524	29	29	5	2	0	191	171	17	58	103	11.0	3.53	111	.236	.296	0	—	0	8	8	-0	0.8
Tor-A	2	1	.667	3	2	0	0	0	15^2	10	2	3	3	8.0	4.02	98	.189	.246	0	—	0	-0	-0	1	0.0
Yr	13	11	.542	32	31	5	2	0	206^2	181	19	61	106	10.6	3.57	110	.230	.286	0	—	0	8	8	0	0.8
1991 SF-N	12	16	.429	34	34	3	3	0	214^1	201	25	71	104	11.6	3.99	90	.251	.315	13	.183	1	-7	-10	2	-0.7
1992 SF-N	10	12	.455	28	28	2	1	0	177	178	23	59	82	12.1	3.97	84	.263	.323	3	.056	-3	-9	-12	1	-1.4
Total 12	105	110	.488	361	260	32	12	11	1858	1776	187	558	932	11.5	3.76	105	.251	.310	16	.128	-1	41	41	8	4.6
● JOE BLACK Black, Joseph b: 2/8/24, Plainfield, N.J. BR/TR, 6'2", 220 lbs. Deb: 5/01/52																									
1952 *Bro-N	15	4	.789	56	2	1	0	15	142^1	102	9	41	85	9.1	2.15	169	.201	.262	5	.139	-1	**25**	**24**	-2	2.2
1953 *Bro-N	6	3	.667	34	3	0	0	5	72^2	74	12	27	42	12.6	5.33	80	.259	.325	4	.235	0	-8	-9	-0	-0.9
1954 Bro-N	0	0	—	5	0	0	0	0	7	11	3	5	3	20.6	11.57	35	.355	.444	0	—	0	-6	-6	-0	-0.6
1955 Bro-N	1	0	1.000	6	0	0	0	0	15^1	15	1	5	9	11.7	2.93	138	.273	.333	1	.333	0	2	2	-0	0.2

YEAR	TM/L	W	L	PCT	G	GS	CG	SH	SV	IP	H	HR	BB	SO	RAT	ERA	ERA+	OAV	OOB	BH	AVG	PB	PR	/A	PD	TPI
	Cin-N	5	2	.714	32	11	1	0	3	102¹	106	13	25	54	11.5	4.22	100	.263	.306	3	.100	-3	-2	0	-0	-0.3
	Yr	6	2	.750	38	11	1	0	3	117²	121	14	30	63	11.5	4.05	104	.264	.309	4	.121	-2	-0	2	-1	-0.1
1956	Cin-N	3	2	.600	32	0	0	0	2	61²	61	11	25	27	12.6	4.52	88	.256	.327	0	.000	-1	-5	-4	-1	-0.6
1957	Was-A	0	1	.000	7	0	0	0	0	12²	22	4	1	2	16.3	7.11	55	.393	.404	0	—	0	-5	-5	0	-0.4
Total	6	30	12	.714	172	16	2	0	25	414	391	53	129	222	11.3	3.91	102	.248	.306	13	.135	-5	1	3	-3	-0.4

● **BOB BLACK**   Black, Robert Benjamin b: 12/10/1862, Cincinnati, Ohio d: 3/21/33, Sioux City, Iowa   Deb: 8/17/1884 ♦

| 1884 | KC-U | 4 | 9 | .308 | 16 | 15 | 13 | 0 | 0 | 123 | 127 | 1 | 17 | 93 | 10.5 | 3.22 | 86 | .249 | .273 | 36 | .247 | 4 | -3 | -6 | 2 | -0.1 |

● **BUD BLACK**   Black, William Carroll b: 7/9/32, St.Louis, Mo. BR/TR, 6'3", 197 lbs.   Deb: 9/13/52

1952	Det-A	0	1	.000	2	2	0	0	0	8	14	0	5	0	21.4	10.13	38	.389	.463	0	.000	-0	-6	-6	-0	-0.5
1955	Det-A	1	1	.500	3	2	1	1	0	14	12	0	8	7	14.1	1.29	299	.231	.355	1	.250	0	4	4	0	0.4
1956	Det-A	1	1	.500	5	1	0	0	0	10	10	2	5	7	13.5	3.60	114	.256	.341	0	.000	-0	1	1	0	0.0
Total	3	2	3	.400	10	5	1	1	0	32	36	2	18	14	15.8	4.22	93	.283	.381	1	.111	-1	-1	-1	0	-0.1

● **CHARLIE BLACKBURN**   Blackburn, Foster Edwin b: 1/6/1895, Chicago, Ill. d: 3/9/84, New Port Richey, Fla. BR/TR, 6'1", 165 lbs.   Deb: 4/17/15

1915	KC-F	0	1	.000	7	2	0	0	0	15²	19	2	13	7	18.4	8.62	34	.306	.427	0	.000	-1	-10	-10	0	-1.0
1921	Chi-A	0	0	—	1	0	0	0	0	1	0	0	1	0	9.0	0.00	—	.000	.333	0	—	0	0	0	-0	0.0
Total	2	0	1	.000	8	2	0	0	0	16²	19	2	14	7	17.8	8.10	37	.297	.423	0	.000	-1	-9	-9	0	-1.0

● **GEORGE BLACKBURN**   Blackburn, George W. "Smiling George" b: 9/21/1871, Ozark, Mo. TR, 5'11", 184 lbs.   Deb: 7/06/1897

| 1897 | Bal-N | 2 | 2 | .500 | 5 | 4 | 3 | 0 | 0 | 33 | 34 | 2 | 12 | 1 | 12.8 | 6.82 | 61 | .264 | .332 | 1 | .077 | -2 | -9 | -10 | -1 | -0.9 |

● **JIM BLACKBURN**   Blackburn, James Ray "Bones" b: 6/19/24, Warsaw, Ky. d: 10/26/69, Cincinnati, Ohio BR/TR, 6'4", 175 lbs.   Deb: 7/24/48

1948	Cin-N	0	2	.000	16	0	0	0	0	32¹	38	1	14	10	14.5	4.18	94	.302	.371	0	.000	-0	-1	-1	-0	-0.2
1951	Cin-N	0	0	—	2	0	0	0	0	3²	8	3	2	1	29.5	17.18	24	.444	.545	0	—	-0	-5	-5	-0	-0.4
Total	2	0	2	.000	18	0	0	0	0	36	46	4	16	11	16.0	5.50	71	.319	.395	0	.000	-0	-6	-6	-0	-0.6

● **RON BLACKBURN**   Blackburn, Ronald Hamilton b: 4/23/35, Mt.Airy, N.C. BR/TR, 6'0.5", 160 lbs.   Deb: 4/15/58

1958	Pit-N	2	1	.667	38	2	0	0	3	63²	61	7	27	31	12.9	3.39	114	.261	.345	2	.286	1	4	3	1	0.5
1959	Pit-N	1	1	.500	26	0	0	0	1	44¹	50	5	15	19	13.6	3.65	106	.286	.349	1	.200	1	1	1	-1	0.1
Total	2	3	2	.600	64	2	0	0	4	108	111	12	42	50	13.2	3.50	110	.271	.346	3	.250	2	5	4	0	0.6

● **LENA BLACKBURNE**   Blackburne, Russell Aubrey "Slats" b: 10/23/1886, Clifton Heights, Pa. d: 2/29/68, Riverside, N.J. BR/TR, 5'11", 160 lbs.   Deb: 4/14/10 MC♦

| 1929 | Chi-A | 0 | 0 | — | 1 | 0 | 0 | 0 | 0 | 0¹ | 1 | 0 | 0 | 0 | 27.0 | 0.00 | — | 1.000 | 1.000 | 0 | — | 0 | 0 | 0 | 0 | 0.0 |

● **EWELL BLACKWELL**   Blackwell, Ewell "The Whip" b: 10/23/22, Fresno, Cal. BR/TR, 6'6", 195 lbs.   Deb: 4/21/42

1942	Cin-N	0	0	—	2	0	0	0	0	3	3	0	3	1	18.0	6.00	55	.231	.375	0	.000	-0	-1	-1	0	-0.1
1946	Cin-N★	9	13	.409	33	25	10	5	0	194¹	160	1	79	100	11.3	2.45	136	.226	.307	6	.107	-3	21	19	4	2.3
1947	Cin-N★	22	8	.733	33	33	23	6	0	273	227	10	95	193	10.7	2.47	166	.234	.304	13	.123	-5	48	49	5	5.3
1948	Cin-N★	7	9	.438	22	20	4	1	1	138²	134	12	52	114	12.3	4.54	86	.251	.323	11	.229	1	-9	-10	5	0.1
1949	Cin-N★	5	5	.500	30	4	0	0	1	76²	80	7	34	55	13.7	4.23	99	.271	.352	4	.211	-0	-2	-0	1	0.1
1950	Cin-N★	17	15	.531	40	32	18	1	4	261	203	12	112	188	11.3	2.97	143	.210	.301	13	.146	-2	34	37	2	3.7
1951	Cin-N★	16	15	.516	38	32	11	2	2	232²	204	16	97	120	12.0	3.44	118	.233	.315	24	.293	8	13	16	0	2.5
1952	Cin-N	3	12	.200	23	17	3	0	0	102	107	6	60	48	15.2	5.38	70	.275	.379	5	.156	-0	-19	-18	-0	-1.9
	★NY-A	1	0	1.000	5	2	0	0	1	16	12	0	12	7	13.5	0.56	591	.203	.338	1	.200	-0	6	5	-0	0.5
1953	NY-A	2	0	1.000	8	4	0	0	1	19²	17	2	13	11	14.2	3.66	101	.233	.356	0	.000	-1	1	-0	-0	-0.1
1955	KC-A	0	1	.000	2	0	0	0	0	4	3	1	5	2	20.3	6.75	62	.250	.500	0	—	0	-1	-1	-0	-0.1
Total	10	82	78	.512	236	169	69	15	10	1321	1150	67	562	839	12.0	3.30	120	.235	.319	77	.174	-3	91	96	16	11.8

● **GEORGE BLAEHOLDER**   Blaeholder, George Franklin b: 1/26/04, Orange, Cal. d: 12/29/47, Garden Grove, Cal. BR/TR, 5'11", 175 lbs.   Deb: 4/20/25

1925	StL-A	0	0	—	2	0	0	0	0	2	6	3	1	1	36.0	31.50	15	.600	.667	0	—	0	-6	-6	-0	-0.5
1927	StL-A	0	1	.000	1	1	1	0	0	9	8	1	4	2	13.0	5.00	87	.258	.361	1	.333	0	-1	-1	0	0.0
1928	StL-A	10	15	.400	38	26	9	1	3	214¹	235	23	52	87	12.1	4.37	96	.280	.324	15	.211	2	-8	-4	5	0.2
1929	StL-A	14	15	.483	42	24	13	4	2	222	237	18	61	72	12.1	4.18	106	.275	.323	9	.122	-4	2	6	6	0.8
1930	StL-A	11	13	.458	37	23	10	1	4	191¹	235	20	46	70	13.3	4.61	106	.303	.343	12	.185	-1	1	6	-1	0.3
1931	StL-A	11	15	.423	35	32	13	1	0	226²	280	15	56	79	13.4	4.53	102	.295	.335	11	.143	-3	-4	3	3	0.3
1932	StL-A	14	14	.500	42	36	16	1	0	258¹	304	19	76	80	13.3	4.70	103	.290	.340	12	.136	-4	-6	4	0	0.1
1933	StL-A	15	19	.441	38	36	14	3	0	255²	283	24	69	63	12.4	4.72	99	.280	.326	14	.182	-1	-12	-2	3	0.1
1934	StL-A	14	18	.438	39	33	14	1	3	234¹	276	16	68	66	13.2	4.22	118	.296	.343	7	.093	-6	7	10	1	1.4
1935	StL-A	1	1	.500	6	2	0	0	0	17²	25	3	6	0	15.8	7.13	67	.342	.392	0	.000	-1	-5	-5	1	-0.4
	Phi-A	6	10	.375	23	22	10	1	0	149	173	10	49	22	13.4	3.99	114	.289	.343	2	.043	-6	8	9	2	0.5
	Yr	7	11	.389	29	24	10	1	0	166²	198	13	55	22	13.7	4.32	106	.295	.348	2	.040	-7	3	5	2	0.1
1936	Cle-A	8	4	.667	35	16	6	1	0	134¹	158	21	47	30	13.9	5.09	99	.295	.356	6	.130	-3	-1	-2	-0	-0.2
Total	11	104	125	.454	338	251	106	14	12	1914¹	2220	173	535	572	13.0	4.54	103	.290	.337	89	.142	-26	-26	30	20	2.6

● **DENNIS BLAIR**   Blair, Dennis Herman b: 6/5/54, Middletown, Ohio BR/TR, 6'5", 182 lbs.   Deb: 5/26/74

1974	Mon-N	11	7	.611	22	22	4	1	0	146	113	7	72	76	11.7	3.27	117	.210	.308	6	.118	-2	6	9	3	1.0
1975	Mon-N	8	15	.348	30	27	1	0	0	163¹	150	14	106	82	14.3	3.80	101	.251	.366	7	.143	-1	-3	0	-1	-0.2
1976	Mon-N	0	2	.000	5	4	1	0	0	15²	21	1	11	9	19.5	4.02	92	.300	.410	0	.000	0	-1	-1	0	-0.1
1980	SD-N	0	1	.000	5	1	0	0	0	14	18	3	3	11	13.5	6.43	53	.310	.344	1	.200	0	-4	-5	-1	-0.5
Total	4	19	25	.432	62	54	6	1	0	339	302	25	192	178	13.4	3.69	103	.239	.344	14	.128	-4	-3	4	1	0.2

● **WILLIE BLAIR**   Blair, William Allen b: 12/18/65, Paintsville, Ky. BR/TR, 6'1", 185 lbs.   Deb: 4/11/90

1990	Tor-A	3	5	.375	27	6	0	0	0	68²	66	4	28	43	12.5	4.06	97	.250	.324	0	—	0	-1	-1	-1	-0.2
1991	Cle-A	2	3	.400	11	5	0	0	0	36	58	7	10	19	17.3	6.75	62	.377	.418	0	—	0	-11	-10	-0	-1.0
1992	Hou-N	5	7	.417	29	8	0	0	0	78²	74	5	25	48	11.6	4.00	83	.249	.312	1	.059	-1	-4	-6	-1	-0.8
Total	3	10	15	.400	67	19	0	0	0	183¹	198	16	63	104	13.0	4.57	81	.277	.339	1	.059	-1	-16	-17	-2	-2.0

● **BILL BLAIR**   Blair, William Ellsworth b: 9/17/1863, Pittsburgh, Pa. d: 2/22/1890, Pittsburgh, Pa. BL/TL, 5'8.5", 172 lbs.   Deb: 7/19/1888

| 1888 | Phi-a | 1 | 3 | .250 | 4 | 4 | 3 | 0 | 0 | 31 | 29 | 0 | 8 | 16 | 11.0 | 2.61 | 114 | .239 | .291 | 4 | .308 | 1 | 2 | 1 | 1 | 0.3 |

● **DICK BLAISDELL**   Blaisdell, Howard Carleton b: 6/18/1862, Bradford, Mass. d: 8/20/1886, Malden, Mass.   Deb: 7/09/1884

| 1884 | KC-U | 0 | 3 | .000 | 3 | 3 | 3 | 0 | 0 | 26 | 49 | 0 | 4 | 8 | 18.3 | 8.65 | 32 | .377 | .396 | 5 | .313 | 1 | -16 | -17 | -1 | -1.2 |

● **ED BLAKE**   Blake, Edward James b: 12/23/25, E.St.Louis, Ill. BR/TR, 5'11", 175 lbs.   Deb: 5/01/51

1951	Cin-N	0	0	—	3	0	0	0	0	4	10	3	1	1	24.8	11.25	36	.476	.500	0	—	0	-3	-3	0	-0.3
1952	Cin-N	0	0	—	2	0	0	0	0	3	2	0	3	1	9.0	0.00	—	.250	.250	0	—	0	1	1	0	0.2
1953	Cin-N	0	0	—	1	0	0	0	0	0	1	0	1	0	—	∞	—	1.000	1.000	0	—	0	-2	-2	0	-0.2
1957	KC-A	0	0	—	2	0	0	0	0	1²	1	1	2	0	16.2	5.40	73	.167	.375	0	—	0	-0	-0	-0	-0.1
Total	4	0	0	—	8	0	0	0	0	8²	14	4	4	1	19.7	8.31	48	.375	.432	0	—	0	-4	-4	1	-0.3

● **SHERIFF BLAKE**   Blake, John Frederick b: 9/17/1899, Ansted, W.Va. d: 10/31/82, Beckley, W.Va. BB/TR, 6', 180 lbs.   Deb: 6/29/20

| 1920 | Pit-N | 0 | 0 | — | 6 | 0 | 0 | 0 | 0 | 13¹ | 21 | 0 | 6 | 7 | 18.9 | 8.10 | 40 | .368 | .438 | 1 | .250 | -0 | -7 | -7 | 0 | -0.7 |
| 1924 | Chi-N | 6 | 6 | .500 | 29 | 11 | 4 | 0 | 1 | 106¹ | 123 | 3 | 44 | 42 | 14.3 | 4.57 | 85 | .299 | .370 | 9 | .290 | 1 | -8 | -8 | 1 | -0.6 |

YEAR	TM/L	W	L	PCT	G	GS	CG	SH	SV	IP	H	HR	BB	SO	RAT	ERA	ERA+	OAV	OOB	BH	AVG	PB	PR	/A	PD	TPI
1925	Chi-N	10	18	.357	36	31	14	0	2	231^1	260	17	114	93	14.7	4.86	89	.287	.370	12	.152	-4	-15	-14	0	-1.6
1926	Chi-N	11	12	.478	39	27	11	4	1	197^2	204	7	92	95	13.8	3.60	107	.280	.366	14	.215	-1	5	5	2	0.6
1927	Chi-N	13	14	.481	32	27	13	2	0	224^1	238	3	82	64	13.0	3.29	117	.282	.348	16	.193	-2	16	14	3	1.5
1928	Chi-N	17	11	.607	34	29	16	**4**	1	240^2	209	4	101	78	11.7	2.47	156	.240	.321	19	.216	0	41	37	-2	3.6
1929	*Chi-N	14	13	.519	35	30	13	1	1	218^1	244	8	103	70	14.4	4.29	108	.291	.370	14	.173	-2	10	8	-2	0.4
1930	Chi-N	10	14	.417	34	24	7	0	0	186^2	213	14	99	80	15.2	4.82	101	.291	.378	15	.227	-1	3	1	3	0.2
1931	Chi-N	0	4	.000	16	5	0	0	0	50	64	4	26	29	16.4	5.22	74	.312	.392	8	.500	3	-8	-8	1	-0.4
	Phi-N	4	5	.444	14	9	1	0	1	71	90	2	35	31	16.2	5.58	76	.305	.384	6	.240	0	-13	-11	2	-0.8
	Yr	4	9	.308	30	14	1	0	1	121	154	6	61	60	16.2	5.43	75	.307	.386	14	.341	3	-21	-18	3	-1.2
1937	StL-A	2	2	.500	15	1	0	0	1	36^2	55	5	20	12	18.4	7.61	63	.350	.424	1	.100	-1	-12	-11	0	-1.1
	StL-N	0	3	.000	14	2	2	0	0	43^2	45	1	18	20	13.0	3.71	107	.271	.342	3	.300	0	1	1	0	0.2
Total	10	87	102	.460	304	196	81	11	8	1620	1766	68	740	621	14.1	4.13	101	.284	.363	118	.211	-6	12	9	9	1.3
● **AL BLANCHE**	Blanche, Prosby Albert (b: Prosper Belangio) b: 9/21/09, Somerville, Mass. BR/TR, 6′, 178 lbs. Deb: 8/23/35																									
1935	Bos-N	0	0	—	6	0	0	0	0	17^1	14	0	5	4	9.9	1.56	243	.230	.288	1	.167	-0	5	4	0	0.4
1936	Bos-N	0	1	.000	11	0	0	0	1	16	20	1	8	4	16.3	6.19	62	.303	.387	1	.250	0	-4	-4	1	-0.3
Total	2	0	1	.000	17	0	0	0	1	33^1	34	1	13	8	13.0	3.78	101	.268	.340	2	.200	-0	1	0	1	0.1
● **GIL BLANCO**	Blanco, Gilbert Henry b: 12/15/45, Phoenix, Ariz. BL/TL, 6′5″, 205 lbs. Deb: 4/24/65																									
1965	NY-A	1	1	.500	17	1	0	0	0	20^1	16	1	12	14	12.8	3.98	85	.232	.354	0	—	0	-1	-1	-1	-0.2
1966	KC-A	2	4	.333	11	8	0	0	0	38^1	31	3	36	21	16.7	4.70	72	.237	.415	2	.167	-0	-5	-6	0	-0.6
Total	2	3	5	.375	28	9	0	0	0	58^2	47	4	48	35	15.3	4.45	76	.235	.395	2	.167	-0	-7	-7	-0	-0.8
● **FRED BLANDING**	Blanding, Frederick James "Fritz" b: 2/8/1888, Redlands, Cal. d: 7/16/50, Salem, Va. BR/TR, 6′, 185 lbs. Deb: 9/15/10																									
1910	Cle-A	2	2	.500	6	5	4	1	0	45^1	43	0	12	25	11.7	2.78	93	.254	.319	2	.111	-1	-1	-1	-1	-0.3
1911	Cle-A	7	11	.389	29	16	11	0	2	176	190	5	60	80	13.1	3.68	93	.283	.347	17	.262	2	-7	-5	0	-0.3
1912	Cle-A	18	14	.563	39	31	23	1	1	262	259	4	79	75	11.7	2.92	117	.267	.324	21	.226	1	12	14	0	1.7
1913	Cle-A	15	10	.600	41	22	14	3	0	215	234	6	72	63	12.9	2.55	119	.282	.341	21	.244	4	9	12	-2	1.5
1914	Cle-A	3	9	.250	29	12	5	0	1	116	133	0	54	35	14.6	3.96	73	.301	.378	4	.103	-2	-16	-14	1	-1.6
Total	5	45	46	.495	144	86	57	5	4	814^1	859	15	277	278	12.7	3.13	102	.279	.341	65	.216	4	-3	6	-2	1.0
● **FRED BLANK**	Blank, Frederick August b: 6/18/1874, Desoto, Mo. d: 2/5/36, St.Louis, Mo. BL/TL, 6′0.5″, 175 lbs. Deb: 6/20/1894																									
1894	Cin-N	0	1	.000	1	1	1	0	0	8	5	0	9	1	15.8	4.50	124	.178	.378	0	.000	-1	1	1	1	0.1
● **HOMER BLANKENSHIP**	Blankenship, Homer "Si" b: 8/4/02, Bonham, Tex. d: 6/22/74, Longview, Tex. BR/TR, 6′, 185 lbs. Deb: 9/06/22 F																									
1922	Chi-A	0	0	—	4	0	0	0	0	13	21	1	5	3	18.0	4.85	84	.389	.441	0	.000	-1	-1	-1	-0	-0.2
1923	Chi-A	1	1	.500	4	0	0	0	1	5	9	0	1	1	18.0	3.60	110	.429	.455	0	—	0	0	0	0	0.0
1928	Pit-N	0	2	.000	5	2	1	0	0	21^2	27	1	9	6	15.0	5.82	70	.321	.387	3	.375	1	-4	-4	1	-0.3
Total	3	1	3	.250	13	2	1	0	1	39^2	57	2	15	10	16.3	5.22	78	.358	.414	3	.250	0	-5	-5	1	-0.5
● **KEVIN BLANKENSHIP**	Blankenship, Kevin De Wayne b: 1/26/63, Anaheim, Cal. BR/TR, 6′, 180 lbs. Deb: 9/20/88																									
1988	Atl-N	0	1	.000	2	2	0	0	0	10^2	7	0	7	5	12.7	3.38	109	.194	.341	0	.000	-0	0	0	-0	0.0
	Chi-N	1	0	1.000	1	1	0	0	0	5	7	2	1	4	14.4	7.20	50	.318	.348	0	.000	-0	-2	-2	-0	-0.2
	Yr	1	1	.500	3	3	0	0	0	15^2	14	2	8	9	12.6	4.60	79	.237	.328	0	.000	-1	-2	-2	-1	-0.2
1989	Chi-N	0	0	—	2	0	0	0	0	5^1	4	0	2	2	10.1	1.69	223	.200	.273	0	.000	-0	1	1	-0	0.1
1990	Chi-N	0	2	.000	3	2	0	0	0	12^1	13	1	6	5	13.9	5.84	70	.265	.345	0	.000	-0	-3	-2	0	-0.3
Total	3	1	3	.250	8	5	0	0	0	33^1	31	3	16	16	13.0	4.59	83	.244	.333	0	.000	-1	-4	-3	-1	-0.4
● **TED BLANKENSHIP**	Blankenship, Theodore b: 5/10/01, Bonham, Tex. d: 1/14/45, Atoka, Okla. BR/TR, 6′1″, 170 lbs. Deb: 7/02/22 F																									
1922	Chi-A	8	10	.444	24	15	7	0	1	127^2	124	4	47	42	12.2	3.81	107	.266	.335	7	.171	-1	3	4	0	0.3
1923	Chi-A	9	14	.391	44	23	9	1	0	204^2	219	8	100	57	14.2	4.35	91	.287	.372	16	.211	2	-8	-9	-1	-0.8
1924	Chi-A	7	6	.538	25	11	7	0	1	129^1	167	1	38	36	14.3	5.01	82	.317	.364	15	.326	5	-11	-13	-2	-0.9
1925	Chi-A	17	8	.680	40	23	16	3	1	232	218	11	69	81	11.1	3.03	137	.253	.308	18	.205	2	35	29	-4	2.5
1926	Chi-A	13	10	.565	29	26	15	1	1	209^1	217	13	65	66	12.2	3.61	107	.273	.328	10	.132	-2	10	6	-2	0.2
1927	Chi-A	12	17	.414	37	34	11	3	0	236^2	280	14	74	51	13.5	5.06	80	.299	.352	15	.188	3	-24	-27	-3	-2.4
1928	Chi-A	9	11	.450	27	22	8	0	0	158	186	9	80	36	15.3	4.61	88	.306	.388	10	.169	-2	-10	-10	-2	-1.3
1929	Chi-A	0	2	.000	8	1	0	0	0	18^1	28	3	9	7	18.2	8.84	48	.359	.425	1	.250	-0	-9	-9	-1	-0.9
1930	Chi-A	2	1	.667	7	1	0	0	0	14^2	23	0	7	2	19.0	9.20	50	.371	.443	1	.200	-0	-7	-7	-1	-0.7
Total	9	77	79	.494	241	156	73	8	4	1330^2	1462	63	489	378	13.3	4.29	94	.287	.351	93	.196	7	-22	-36	-15	-4.0
● **CY BLANTON**	Blanton, Darrell Elijah b: 7/6/08, Waurika, Okla. d: 9/13/45, Norman, Okla. BL/TR, 5′11.5″, 180 lbs. Deb: 9/23/34																									
1934	Pit-N	0	1	.000	1	1	0	0	0	8	5	1	4	5	11.3	3.38	122	.161	.278	0	.000	0	1	1	0	0.1
1935	Pit-N	18	13	.581	35	31	23	**4**	1	254^1	220	3	55	142	**9.8**	**2.58**	**159**	**.229**	**.272**	13	.134	-4	**41**	**43**	2	**4.2**
1936	Pit-N	13	15	.464	44	32	15	**4**	3	235^2	235	9	55	127	11.2	3.51	115	.257	.301	13	.155	-3	13	14	1	1.2
1937	Pit-N★	14	12	.538	36	34	14	4	0	242^2	250	13	76	143	12.3	3.30	117	.266	.324	14	.165	-0	17	15	-0	1.4
1938	Pit-N	11	7	.611	29	25	10	1	0	172^2	190	13	46	80	12.4	3.70	103	.281	.329	13	.203	-1	2	2	2	0.3
1939	Pit-N	2	3	.400	10	6	1	0	0	42	45	4	10	11	11.8	4.29	90	.266	.307	4	.286	1	-2	-2	-0	-0.1
1940	Phi-N	4	3	.571	13	10	5	0	0	77	82	7	21	24	12.2	4.32	90	.272	.322	2	.083	-1	-4	-4	0	-0.5
1941	Phi-N☆	6	13	.316	28	25	7	1	0	163^2	186	11	57	64	13.5	4.51	82	.284	.344	6	.118	-2	-16	-15	-3	-1.9
1942	Phi-N	0	4	.000	6	3	0	0	0	22^1	30	3	13	15	17.7	5.64	59	.345	.436	1	.125	-0	-6	-6	0	-0.6
Total	9	68	71	.489	202	167	75	14	4	1218^1	1243	64	337	611	11.8	3.55	110	.262	.314	66	.154	-12	45	49	2	4.1
● **WADE BLASINGAME**	Blasingame, Wade Allen b: 11/22/43, Deming, N.Mex. BL/TL, 6′1″, 185 lbs. Deb: 9/17/63																									
1963	Mil-N	0	0	—	2	0	0	0	0	3	7	0	2	6	27.0	12.00	27	.467	.529	0	—	0	-3	-3	0	-0.3
1964	Mil-N	9	5	.643	28	13	3	1	2	116^2	113	15	51	70	12.7	4.24	83	.257	.334	7	.175	3	-9	-9	0	-0.6
1965	Mil-N	16	10	.615	38	36	10	1	1	224^2	200	17	116	117	12.9	3.77	94	.244	.341	15	.185	3	-6	-6	1	-0.2
1966	Atl-N	3	7	.300	16	12	0	0	0	67^2	71	5	25	34	13.0	5.32	68	.272	.340	5	.217	1	-13	-13	-0	-1.2
1967	Atl-N	1	0	1.000	10	4	0	0	0	25^1	27	1	21	20	17.4	4.62	72	.287	.422	1	.143	0	-4	-4	0	-0.3
	Hou-N	4	7	.364	15	14	0	0	0	77	91	9	27	46	14.0	5.96	56	.298	.359	4	.182	2	-22	-23	-0	-2.1
	Yr	5	7	.417	25	18	0	0	0	102^1	118	10	48	66	14.8	5.63	59	.295	.373	5	.172	2	-26	-26	0	-2.4
1968	Hou-N	1	2	.333	22	2	0	0	1	36	45	3	10	22	13.8	4.75	62	.308	.353	0	.000	0	-7	-7	1	-0.7
1969	Hou-N	0	5	.000	26	5	0	0	1	52	66	4	33	33	17.5	5.37	66	.306	.402	0	.000	-1	-10	-11	0	-1.2
1970	Hou-N	3	3	.500	13	13	1	0	0	77^2	76	4	23	55	11.7	3.48	112	.261	.320	2	.083	-0	5	3	0	0.4
1971	Hou-N	9	11	.450	30	28	2	0	0	158^1	177	11	45	93	13.4	4.60	73	.285	.346	10	.204	4	-20	-22	1	-1.7
1972	Hou-N	0	0	—	10	0	0	0	0	8^1	4	1	8	9	15.1	8.64	39	.148	.378	0	—	0	-5	-5	0	-0.5
	NY-A	0	1	.000	12	1	0	0	0	17	14	5	11	7	13.8	4.24	70	.250	.382	0	.000	0	-2	-2	1	-0.2
Total	10	46	51	.474	222	128	16	2	5	863^2	891	75	372	512	13.5	4.52	77	.271	.350	44	.166	13	-96	-101	4	-8.6
● **STEVE BLASS**	Blass, Stephen Robert b: 4/18/42, Canaan, Conn. BR/TR, 6′, 165 lbs. Deb: 5/10/64																									
1964	Pit-N	5	8	.385	24	13	3	1	0	104^2	107	9	45	67	13.2	4.04	87	.266	.341	2	.067	-1	-6	-6	0	-0.7
1966	Pit-N	11	7	.611	34	25	1	0	0	155^2	173	12	46	76	12.8	3.87	92	.284	.336	12	.231	1	-5	-5	-3	-0.7
1967	Pit-N	6	8	.429	32	16	2	0	0	126^2	126	12	47	72	12.4	3.55	95	.261	.329	5	.128	-1	-3	-3	0	-0.3
1968	Pit-N	18	6	**.750**	33	31	12	7	0	220^1	191	13	57	132	10.3	2.12	138	.234	.288	11	.138	-1	21	20	-1	2.1
1969	Pit-N	16	10	.615	38	32	9	0	2	210	207	21	86	147	12.8	4.46	78	.258	.335	21	.250	6	-20	-23	3	-1.5
1970	Pit-N	10	12	.455	31	31	6	1	0	196^2	187	14	73	120	12.1	3.52	111	.254	.326	8	.114	-2	11	8	0	0.6

YEAR TM/L	W	L	PCT	G	GS	CG	SH	SV	IP	H	HR	BB	SO	RAT	ERA	ERA+	OAV	OOB	BH	AVG	PB	PR	/A	PD	TPI
1971 *Pit-N	15	8	.652	33	33	12	**5**	0	240	226	16	68	136	11.1	2.85	119	.249	.303	10	.120	-3	16	14	1	1.4
1972 *Pit-N★	19	8	.704	33	32	11	2	0	249^{2}	227	18	84	117	11.4	2.49	134	.246	.311	15	.183	1	27	23	2	3.0
1973 Pit-N	3	9	.250	23	18	1	0	0	88^{2}	109	11	84	27	20.8	9.85	36	.313	.462	10	.417	4	-61	-62	1	-5.3
1974 Pit-N	0	0	—	1	0	0	0	0	5	5	2	7	2	21.6	9.00	38	.238	.429	0	.000	-0	-3	-3	0	-0.3
Total 10	103	76	.575	282	231	57	16	2	1597^{1}	1558	128	597	896	12.4	3.63	94	.258	.328	94	.172	4	-21	-37	3	-1.7
● **STEVE BLATERIC** Blateric, Stephen Lawrence b: 3/20/44, Denver, Colo. BR/TR, 6'3", 200 lbs. Deb: 9/17/71																									
1971 Cin-N	0	0	—	2	0	0	0	0	2^{2}	5	2	0	4	20.3	13.50	25	.385	.429	0	—	0	-3	-3	0	-0.3
1972 NY-A	0	0	—	1	0	0	0	0	4	2	0	0	4	4.5	0.00	—	.143	.143	0	.000	-0	1	1	0	0.2
1975 Cal-A	0	0	—	2	0	0	0	0	4^{1}	9	0	1	5	20.8	6.23	57	.429	.455	0	—	0	-1	-1	-0	0.3
Total 3	0	0	—	5	0	0	0	0	11	16	2	1	13	14.7	5.73	57	.333	.360	0	.000	-0	-3	-3	0	0.2
● **HENRY BLAUVELT** Blauvelt, Henry Russell b: 4/8/1873, Nyack, N.Y. d: 12/28/26, Portland, Ore. Deb: 6/22/1890																									
1890 Roc-a	0	0	—	2	0	0	0	0	12^{1}	19	0	8	5	19.7	10.22	35	.342	.425	3	.500	1	-9	-9	0	-0.6
● **GARY BLAYLOCK** Blaylock, Gary Nelson b: 10/11/31, Clarkton, Mo. BR/TR, 6', 196 lbs. Deb: 4/10/59 C																									
1959 StL-N	4	5	.444	26	12	3	0	0	100	117	14	43	61	14.6	5.13	83	.298	.371	4	.118	0	-13	-10	1	-0.9
NY-A	0	1	.000	15	1	0	0	0	25^{2}	30	0	15	20	16.1	3.51	104	.306	.404	1	.500	1	1	0	-0	0.1
Total 1	4	6	.400	41	13	3	0	0	125^{2}	147	14	58	81	14.9	4.80	86	.300	.377	5	.139	1	-12	-10	0	-0.8
● **BOB BLAYLOCK** Blaylock, Robert Edward b: 6/28/35, Chattanooga, Okla BR/TR, 6'1", 185 lbs. Deb: 7/22/56																									
1956 StL-N	1	6	.143	14	6	0	0	0	41	45	7	24	39	15.1	6.37	59	.276	.369	1	.091	-1	-12	-12	0	-1.2
1959 StL-N	0	1	.000	3	1	0	0	0	9	8	1	3	3	11.0	4.00	106	.229	.289	0	.000	-0	-0	0	0	0.0
Total 2	1	7	.125	17	7	0	0	0	50	53	8	27	42	14.4	5.94	65	.268	.356	1	.083	-1	-12	-12	0	-1.2
● **RAY BLEMKER** Blemker, Ray b: 8/9/37, Huntingburg, Ind. BR/TL, 5'11", 190 lbs. Deb: 7/03/60																									
1960 KC-A	0	0	—	1	0	0	0	0	1^{2}	3	1	2	0	32.4	27.00	15	.375	.545	0	—	0	-4	-4	-0	-0.4
● **CLARENCE BLETHEN** Blethen, Clarence Waldo "Climax" b: 7/11/1893, Dover-Foxcroft, Maine d: 4/11/73, Frederick, Md. BL/TR, 5'11", 165 lbs. Deb: 9/17/23																									
1923 Bos-A	0	0	—	5	0	0	0	0	17^{2}	29	0	7	2	18.3	7.13	58	.382	.434	0	.000	-1	-6	-6	-1	-0.7
1929 Bro-N	0	0	—	2	0	0	0	0	2	4	0	3	0	31.5	9.00	51	.444	.583	0	—	0	-1	-1	0	-0.1
Total 2	0	0	—	7	0	0	0	0	19^{2}	33	0	10	2	19.7	7.32	57	.388	.453	0	.000	-1	-7	-7	-1	-0.8
● **BOB BLEWETT** Blewett, Robert Lawrence b: 6/28/1877, Fond Du Lac, Wis. d: 3/17/58, Sedro Woolley, Wash. BL/TL, 5'11", 170 lbs. Deb: 6/17/02																									
1902 NY-N	0	2	.000	5	3	2	0	0	28	39	0	7	8	15.1	4.82	58	.329	.371	0	.000	-1	-6	-6	-1	-0.8
● **ELMER BLISS** Bliss, Elmer Ward b: 3/9/1875, Penfield, Pa. d: 3/18/62, Bradford, Pa. BL/TR, 6', 180 lbs. Deb: 9/28/03 ♦																									
1903 NY-A	1	0	1.000	1	0	0	0	0	7	4	0	0	3	5.1	0.00	—	.167	.167	0	.000	-0	2	2	-0	0.2
● **TERRY BLOCKER** Blocker, Terry Fennell b: 8/18/59, Columbia, S.C. BL/TL, 6'2", 195 lbs. Deb: 4/11/85 ♦																									
1989 Atl-N	0	0	—	1	0	0	0	0	1	0	0	2	0	18.0	0.00	—	.000	.500	7	.226	0	0	0	0	0.0
● **JOE BLONG** Blong, Joseph Myles b: 9/17/1853, St.Louis, Mo. d: 9/16/1892, St.Louis, Mo. BR/TR, Deb: 5/04/1875 ♦																									
1875 RS-n	3	12	.200	15	15	12	1	0	129	169	0	2		11.9	*3.35*	72	.285	.287	10	.147	-3	-13	-13		-1.3
1876 StL-N	0	0	—	1	0	0	0	0	4	2	0	1	0	6.8	0.00	—	.154	.214	62	.235	0	1	1	0	0.1
1877 StL-N	10	9	.526	25	21	17	0	0	187^{1}	203	0	38	51	11.6	2.74	95	.262	.296	47	.216	0	1	-3	-2	-0.4
Total 2	10	9	.526	26	21	17	0	0	191^{1}	205	0	39	51	11.5	2.68	97	.260	.295	109	.226	0	2	-2	-1	-0.3
● **VIDA BLUE** Blue, Vida Rochelle b: 7/28/49, Mansfield, La. BB/TL, 6', 189 lbs. Deb: 7/20/69																									
1969 Oak-A	1	1	.500	12	4	0	0	1	42	49	13	18	24	14.4	6.64	52	.290	.358	0	.000	-0	-14	-15	-1	-1.6
1970 Oak-A	2	0	1.000	6	6	2	2	0	38^{2}	20	0	12	35	7.7	2.09	169	.152	.228	3	.200	2	7	6	0	0.9
1971 *Oak-A★	24	8	.750	39	39	24	**8**	0	312	209	19	88	301	**8.7**	**1.82**	183	**.189**	**.252**	12	.118	-2	57	53	-4	5.4
1972 *Oak-A	6	10	.375	25	23	5	4	0	151	117	11	48	111	9.9	2.80	101	.215	.280	2	.044	-2	4	1	-2	-0.4
1973 *Oak-A	20	9	.690	37	37	13	4	0	263^{2}	214	26	105	158	11.0	3.28	108	.224	.303	0	.000	0	16	8	-2	0.6
1974 *Oak-A	17	15	.531	40	40	12	1	0	282^{1}	246	17	98	174	11.0	3.25	102	.236	.303	0	—	0	11	2	-5	-0.1
1975 *Oak-A★	22	11	.667	39	38	13	2	1	278	243	21	99	189	11.2	3.01	120	.236	.307	0	—	0	24	19	-2	1.8
1976 Oak-A	18	13	.581	37	37	20	6	0	298^{1}	268	9	63	166	10.0	2.35	143	.239	.280	0	—	0	**39**	33	-3	3.3
1977 Oak-A†	14	19	.424	38	38	16	1	0	279^{2}	284	23	86	157	11.9	3.83	105	.264	.319	0	.000	0	7	6	-1	0.5
1978 SF-N★	18	10	.643	35	35	9	4	0	258	233	12	70	171	10.6	2.79	124	.246	.298	6	.076	2	23	19	-2	2.0
1979 SF-N	14	14	.500	34	34	10	0	0	237	246	23	111	138	13.6	5.01	70	.272	.352	10	.120	0	-34	-40	2	-3.7
1980 SF-N†	14	10	.583	31	31	10	3	0	224	202	14	61	129	10.6	2.97	119	.242	.294	5	.074	-4	16	14	2	1.3
1981 SF-N★	8	6	.571	18	18	1	0	0	124^{2}	97	7	54	63	11.0	2.45	140	.217	.303	7	.200	2	14	14	2	2.0
1982 KC-A	13	12	.520	31	31	6	2	0	181	163	20	80	103	12.1	3.78	108	.238	.318	0	—	0	6	6	-0	0.6
1983 KC-A	0	5	.000	19	14	1	0	0	85^{1}	96	12	35	53	14.0	6.01	68	.286	.357	0	—	0	-18	-18	-0	-1.8
1985 SF-N	8	8	.500	33	20	1	0	0	131	115	17	80	103	13.5	4.47	77	.240	.350	4	.133	1	-13	-15	0	-1.4
1986 SF-N	10	10	.500	28	28	0	0	0	156^{2}	137	19	77	100	12.3	3.27	107	.239	.329	4	.093	1	8	4	-1	0.5
Total 17	209	161	.565	502	473	143	37	2	3343^{1}	2939	263	1185	2175	11.2	3.27	108	.237	.305	53	.104	-1	152	95	-17	9.9
● **JIM BLUEJACKET** Bluejacket, James (b: James Smith) b: 7/8/1887, Adair, Okla. d: 3/26/47, Pekin, Ill. BR/TR, 6'2.5", 200 lbs. Deb: 8/06/14 F																									
1914 Bro-F	4	5	.444	17	7	3	1	1	67	77	2	19	29	12.9	3.76	85	.302	.350	3	.136	-0	-4	-4	1	-0.4
1915 Bro-F	10	11	.476	24	21	10	2	0	162^{2}	155	2	75	48	12.7	3.15	96	.258	.340	8	.131	-4	-2	-2	-4	-1.0
1916 Cin-N	0	1	.000	3	2	0	0	0	7	12	0	3	1	19.3	7.71	34	.400	.455	0	.000	-0	-4	-4	-0	-0.5
Total 3	14	17	.452	44	30	13	3	1	236^{2}	244	4	97	78	13.0	3.46	88	.275	.347	11	.129	-4	-10	-11	-3	-1.9
● **CLINT BLUME** Blume, Clinton Willis b: 10/17/1898, Brooklyn, N.Y. d: 6/12/73, Islip, L.I., N.Y. BR/TR, 5'11", 175 lbs. Deb: 9/30/22																									
1922 NY-N	1	0	1.000	1	1	1	0	0	9	7	0	1	2	8.0	1.00	400	.212	.235	1	1.000	1	3	3	-1	0.4
1923 NY-N	2	0	1.000	12	1	0	0	0	24	22	0	20	2	16.5	3.75	102	.265	.419	0	.000	-0	1	0	-1	-0.1
Total 2	3	0	1.000	13	2	1	0	0	33	29	0	21	4	14.2	3.00	129	.250	.374	1	.167	1	4	3	-1	0.3
● **BERT BLYLEVEN** Blyleven, Rik Aalbert b: 4/6/51, Zeist, Holland BR/TR, 6'3", 207 lbs. Deb: 6/05/70																									
1970 *Min-A	10	9	.526	27	25	5	1	0	164	143	17	47	135	10.5	3.18	117	.232	.289	7	.140	-1	10	10	-2	0.7
1971 Min-A	16	15	.516	38	38	17	5	0	278^{1}	267	21	59	224	10.7	2.81	126	.255	.298	12	.132	-3	20	23	-0	2.2
1972 Min-A	17	17	.500	39	38	11	3	0	287^{1}	247	22	69	228	10.2	2.73	118	.233	.286	15	.160	-1	11	15	1	1.8
1973 Min-A★	20	17	.541	40	40	25	**9**	0	325	296	16	67	258	10.3	2.52	**157**	.242	.287	0	—	0	**47**	**52**	-2	**5.6**
1974 Min-A	17	17	.500	37	37	19	3	0	281	244	14	77	249	10.6	2.66	141	.233	.292	0	—	0	30	34	0	3.7
1975 Min-A	15	10	.600	35	35	20	3	0	275^{2}	219	24	84	233	10.0	3.00	128	.219	.283	0	—	0	24	26	3	3.0
1976 Min-A	4	5	.444	12	12	4	0	0	95^{1}	101	3	35	75	13.2	3.12	116	.283	.354	0	—	0	4	5	0	0.6
Tex-A	9	11	.450	24	24	14	6	0	202^{1}	182	11	46	144	10.5	2.76	130	.242	.293	0	—	0	17	19	2	2.3
Yr	13	16	.448	36	36	18	6	0	297^{2}	283	14	81	219	11.2	2.87	125	.254	.309	0	—	0	21	24	2	2.9
1977 Tex-A	14	12	.538	30	30	15	5	0	234^{2}	181	20	69	182	**9.9**	2.72	150	.214	.279	0	—	0	35	35	0	3.8
1978 Pit-N	14	10	.583	34	34	11	4	0	243^{2}	217	17	66	182	10.7	3.03	122	.235	.290	11	.129	-2	15	18	1	1.8
1979 *Pit-N	12	5	.706	37	37	4	0	0	237^{1}	238	21	92	172	12.7	3.60	108	.265	.338	9	.129	-3	3	7	-2	0.2
1980 Pit-N	8	13	.381	34	32	5	2	0	216^{2}	219	20	59	168	11.5	3.82	95	.262	.311	5	.082	-4	-5	-4	-0	-0.9
1981 Cle-A	11	7	.611	20	20	9	1	0	159^{1}	145	9	40	107	10.7	2.88	126	.245	.298	0	—	0	14	13	-2	1.3
1982 Cle-A	2	2	.500	4	4	0	0	0	20^{1}	16	2	11	19	12.0	4.87	84	.211	.310	0	—	0	-2	-2	0	-0.2
1983 Cle-A	7	10	.412	24	24	5	0	0	156^{1}	160	8	44	123	12.3	3.91	108	.267	.328	0	—	0	3	6	1	0.7

YEAR	TM/L	W	L	PCT	G	GS	CG	SH	SV	IP	H	HR	BB	SO	RAT	ERA	ERA+	OAV	OOB	BH	AVG	PB	PR	/A	PD	TPI
1984	Cle-A	19	7	.731	33	32	12	4	0	245	204	19	74	170	10.4	2.87	143	.224	.287	0	—	0	31	33	0	3.6
1985	Cle-A★	9	11	.450	23	23	15	4	0	179^{2}	163	14	49	129	11.0	3.26	127	.240	.298	0	—	0	18	18	-1	1.7
	Min-A	8	5	.615	14	14	9	1	0	114	101	9	26	77	10.2	3.00	147	.237	.284	0	—	0	15	18	-0	1.7
	Yr	17	16	.515	37	37	**24**	**5**	0	**293^{2}**	264	23	75	**206**	10.5	3.16	134	.236	.286	0	—	0	32	35	-1	3.4
1986	Min-A	17	14	.548	36	36	16	3	0	**271^{2}**	262	50	58	215	10.9	4.01	107	.250	.295	0	—	0	5	9	-1	0.8
1987	*Min-A	15	12	.556	37	37	8	1	0	267	249	46	101	196	12.1	4.01	115	.249	.323	0	—	0	13	18	2	1.9
1988	Min-A	10	17	.370	33	33	7	0	0	207^{1}	240	21	51	145	13.3	5.43	75	.294	.348	0	—	0	-34	-31	-1	-3.1
1989	Cal-A	17	5	.773	33	33	8	**5**	0	241	225	14	44	131	10.3	2.73	140	.248	.289	0	—	0	31	29	1	3.2
1990	Cal-A	8	7	.533	23	23	2	0	0	134	163	15	25	69	13.1	5.24	73	.303	.342	0	—	0	-20	-21	0	-2.0
1992	Cal-A	8	12	.400	25	24	1	0	0	133	150	17	29	70	12.5	4.74	82	.285	.329	0	—	0	-12	-12	-1	-1.3
Total	22	287	250	.534	692	685	242	60	0	4970	4632	430	1322	3701	11.1	3.31	117	.247	.303	59	.131	-14	271	318	1	33.1

● **MIKE BLYZKA** Blyzka, Michael John b: 12/25/28, Hamtramck, Mich. BR/TR, 5′11.5″, 190 lbs. Deb: 4/21/53

1953	StL-A	2	6	.250	33	9	2	0	0	94^{1}	110	6	56	23	15.8	6.39	66	.292	.383	0	.000	-3	-25	-23	-1	-2.6
1954	Bal-A	1	5	.167	37	0	0	0	1	86^{1}	83	2	51	35	14.0	4.69	76	.254	.354	2	.133	-1	-9	-11	0	-1.1
Total	2	3	11	.214	70	9	2	0	1	180^{2}	193	8	107	58	14.9	5.58	70	.274	.370	2	.053	-4	-34	-34	-0	-3.7

● **CHARLIE BOARDMAN** Boardman, Charles Louis b: 4/27/1893, Seneca Falls, N.Y. d: 8/10/68, Sacramento, Cal. BL/TL, 6′2.5″, 194 lbs. Deb: 9/26/13

1913	Phi-A	0	2	.000	2	2	1	0	0	9	10	0	6	4	16.0	2.00	138	.294	.400	0	.000	-0	1	1	-0	0.0
1914	Phi-A	0	0	—	2	0	0	0	0	7^{1}	10	0	4	2	17.2	4.91	53	.357	.438	0	.000	-0	-2	-2	-0	-0.2
1915	StL-N	1	0	1.000	3	1	1	0	0	19	12	0	15	7	12.8	2.84	98	.188	.342	2	.286	0	-0	-0	-0	0.0
Total	3	1	2	.333	7	3	2	0	0	35^{1}	32	0	25	13	14.5	3.06	90	.254	.377	2	.167	-0	-1	-1	-1	-0.2

● **RANDY BOCKUS** Bockus, Randy Walter b: 10/5/60, Canton, Ohio BL/TR, 6′2″, 190 lbs. Deb: 9/10/86

1986	SF-N	0	0	—	5	0	0	0	0	7	7	1	6	4	16.7	2.57	137	.241	.371	0	.000	-0	1	1	1	0.1
1987	SF-N	1	0	1.000	12	0	0	0	0	17^{1}	17	2	4	9	10.9	3.63	106	.266	.309	0	.000	-0	1	0	-0	0.0
1988	SF-N	1	1	.500	20	0	0	0	0	32	35	2	13	18	13.8	4.78	68	.297	.371	1	.167	0	-5	-5	0	-0.5
1989	Det-A	0	0	—	2	0	0	0	0	5^{1}	7	0	2	2	15.2	5.06	75	.333	.391	0	—	0	-1	-1	-0	-0.1
Total	4	2	1	.667	39	0	0	0	0	61^{2}	66	5	25	33	13.4	4.23	83	.284	.357	1	.125	-0	-4	-5	1	-0.5

● **MIKE BODDICKER** Boddicker, Michael James b: 8/23/57, Cedar Rapids, Iowa BR/TR, 5′11″, 172 lbs. Deb: 10/04/80

1980	Bal-A	0	1	.000	1	1	0	0	0	7^{1}	6	1	5	4	13.5	6.14	64	.207	.324	0	—	0	-2	-2	-0	-0.1
1981	Bal-A	0	0	—	2	0	0	0	0	5^{2}	6	1	2	2	12.7	4.76	76	.261	.320	0	—	0	-1	-1	-0	-0.1
1982	Bal-A	1	0	1.000	7	0	0	0	0	25^{2}	25	2	12	20	13.0	3.51	115	.258	.339	0	—	0	2	2	0	0.2
1983	*Bal-A	16	8	.667	27	26	10	**5**	0	179	141	13	52	120	9.7	2.77	143	**.216**	.274	0	—	0	26	24	3	2.9
1984	Bal-A☆	**20**	11	.645	34	34	16	4	0	261^{1}	218	23	81	128	10.5	**2.79**	139	.228	.292	0	—	0	**35**	31	6	4.0
1985	Bal-A	12	17	.414	32	32	9	2	0	203^{1}	227	13	89	135	14.2	4.07	99	.286	.361	0	—	0	2	-1	6	0.5
1986	Bal-A	14	12	.538	33	33	7	0	0	218^{1}	214	30	74	175	12.3	4.70	88	.255	.323	0	—	0	-13	-14	3	-0.9
1987	Bal-A	10	12	.455	33	33	7	2	0	226	212	29	78	152	11.8	4.18	105	.248	.316	0	—	0	7	5	4	0.9
1988	Bal-A	6	12	.333	21	21	4	0	0	147	149	14	51	100	12.9	3.86	101	.265	.338	0	—	0	2	1	-1	0.0
	*Bos-A	7	3	.700	15	14	1	1	0	89	85	3	26	56	11.5	2.63	156	.257	.317	0	—	0	13	15	2	1.8
	Yr	13	15	.464	36	35	5	1	0	236	234	17	77	156	12.0	3.39	117	.256	.316	0	—	0	15	15	1	1.8
1989	Bos-A	15	11	.577	34	34	3	2	0	211^{2}	217	19	71	145	12.7	4.00	103	.267	.333	0	—	0	-3	2	1	0.3
1990	*Bos-A	17	8	.680	34	34	4	0	0	228	225	16	69	143	12.0	3.36	121	.258	.319	0	—	0	14	18	1	2.0
1991	KC-A	12	12	.500	30	29	1	0	0	180^{2}	188	13	59	79	13.0	4.08	101	.272	.340	0	—	0	0	1	2	0.2
1992	KC-A	1	4	.200	29	8	0	0	3	86^{2}	92	5	37	47	14.2	4.98	80	.269	.354	0	—	0	-10	-10	1	-0.9
Total	13	131	111	.541	332	299	62	16	3	2069^{2}	2005	182	706	1306	12.1	3.75	108	.255	.323	0	—	0	72	72	28	10.8

● **GEORGE BOEHLER** Boehler, George Henry b: 1/2/1892, Lawrenceburg, Ind. d: 6/23/58, Lawrenceburg, Ind BR/TR, 6′2″, 180 lbs. Deb: 9/13/12

1912	Det-A	0	2	.000	5	4	2	0	0	32	50	0	14	15	18.6	6.47	50	.365	.431	1	.100	-1	-11	-11	1	-1.0
1913	Det-A	0	1	.000	1	1	1	0	0	8	11	0	6	2	21.4	6.75	43	.355	.487	1	.333	1	-3	-3	1	-0.2
1914	Det-A	2	3	.400	18	6	2	0	0	63	54	1	48	37	15.7	3.57	79	.242	.394	3	.176	1	-6	-5	-0	-0.5
1915	Det-A	1	1	.500	8	0	0	0	0	15	19	0	4	7	14.4	1.80	168	.328	.381	3	.750	2	2	2	-0	0.4
1916	Det-A	1	1	.500	5	2	1	0	0	13^{1}	12	0	9	8	15.5	4.73	61	.261	.404	0	.000	0	-3	-3	1	-0.2
1920	StL-A	0	1	.000	3	1	0	0	0	7	10	1	4	2	18.0	7.71	51	.303	.378	0	.000	0	-3	-3	0	-0.3
1921	StL-A	0	0	—	1	0	0	0	0	1	1	0	0	0	9.0	0.00	—	.500	.500	0	—	0	0	0	-0	0.0
1923	Pit-N	1	3	.250	10	3	1	0	0	28^{1}	33	1	26	12	19.1	6.04	66	.314	.455	3	.300	1	-6	-6	-0	-0.6
1926	Bro-N	1	0	1.000	10	1	0	0	0	34^{2}	42	1	23	10	17.7	4.41	87	.302	.412	3	.250	0	-2	-2	-1	-0.2
Total	9	6	12	.333	61	18	7	0	0	202^{1}	232	4	134	93	17.1	4.71	70	.300	.415	14	.233	3	-33	-32	1	-2.6

● **JOE BOEHLING** Boehling, John Joseph b: 3/20/1891, Richmond, Va. d: 9/8/41, Richmond, Va. BL/TL, 5′11″, 168 lbs. Deb: 6/20/12

1912	Was-A	0	0	—	3	0	0	0	0	5	4	0	6	2	21.6	7.20	46	.235	.480	0	—	0	-2	-2	0	-0.2
1913	Was-A	17	7	.708	38	25	18	3	4	235^{1}	197	3	82	110	11.0	2.14	138	.229	.303	19	.221	1	21	21	2	2.7
1914	Was-A	12	8	.600	27	24	14	2	1	196	180	3	76	91	12.2	3.03	93	.258	.339	17	.239	4	-6	-5	2	0.1
1915	Was-A	14	13	.519	40	32	14	2	0	229^{1}	217	5	119	108	13.5	3.22	92	.255	.352	13	.173	0	-7	-6	2	-0.4
1916	Was-A	9	11	.450	27	19	7	2	0	139^{2}	134	1	54	52	12.3	3.09	90	.260	.333	7	.171	1	-4	-5	4	-0.1
	Cle-A	2	4	.333	12	9	3	0	0	60^{2}	63	0	23	18	13.1	2.67	113	.281	.353	5	.263	1	1	2	1	0.4
	Yr	11	15	.423	39	28	10	2	0	200^{1}	197	1	77	70	12.4	2.97	96	.265	.336	12	.200	1	-3	-2	4	0.3
1917	Cle-A	1	6	.143	12	7	1	0	0	46^{1}	50	1	16	11	13.4	4.66	61	.291	.361	3	.188	-0	-10	-9	-0	-1.0
1920	Cle-A	0	1	.000	3	2	0	0	0	13	16	0	10	4	18.0	4.85	78	.333	.448	2	.500	1	-2	-2	0	0.0
Total	7	55	50	.524	162	118	57	9	5	925^{1}	861	13	386	396	12.5	2.97	98	.254	.337	66	.212	7	-10	-5	11	1.5

● **LARRY BOERNER** Boerner, Lawrence Hyer b: 1/21/05, Staunton, Va. d: 10/16/69, Staunton, Va. BR/TR, 6′4.5″, 175 lbs. Deb: 6/30/32

1932	Bos-A	0	4	.000	21	5	0	0	0	61	71	2	37	19	16.4	5.02	90	.302	.404	0	.000	-3	-4	-4	0	-0.5

● **JOE BOEVER** Boever, Joseph Martin b: 10/4/60, Kirkwood, Mo. BR/TR, 6′1″, 200 lbs. Deb: 7/19/85

1985	StL-N	0	0	—	13	0	0	0	0	16^{1}	17	3	4	20	11.6	4.41	80	.270	.313	0	—	0	-1	-2	-0	-0.2
1986	StL-N	0	1	.000	11	0	0	0	0	21^{2}	19	2	11	8	12.5	1.66	219	.232	.323	1	.500	0	5	5	-0	0.5
1987	Atl-N	1	0	1.000	14	0	0	0	0	18^{1}	29	4	12	18	20.1	7.36	59	.367	.451	0	—	0	-7	-6	-0	-0.6
1988	Atl-N	0	2	.000	16	0	0	0	1	20^{1}	12	1	1	7	6.2	1.77	208	.182	.206	0	—	0	4	4	0	0.5
1989	Atl-N	4	11	.267	66	0	0	0	21	82^{1}	78	6	34	68	12.4	3.94	93	.252	.328	0	.000	-0	-4	-3	1	-0.2
1990	Atl-N	1	3	.250	33	0	0	0	8	42^{1}	40	6	35	35	15.9	4.68	86	.252	.387	0	.000	-0	-4	-3	-1	-0.4
	Phi-N	2	3	.400	34	0	0	0	6	46	37	0	16	40	10.4	2.15	178	.215	.282	0	.000	-0	8	9	0	0.9
	Yr	3	6	.333	67	0	0	0	14	88^{1}	77	6	51	75	13.0	3.36	117	.231	.333	0	.000	-0	4	6	-1	0.5
1991	Phi-N	3	5	.375	68	0	0	0	0	98^{1}	90	10	54	89	13.2	3.84	95	.245	.341	1	.333	0	-2	-2	-1	-0.3
1992	Hou-N	3	6	.333	**81**	0	0	0	2	111^{1}	103	3	45	67	12.3	2.51	133	.248	.327	0	.000	-1	12	10	0	1.1
Total	8	14	31	.311	336	0	0	0	38	457	425	35	212	352	12.7	3.41	107	.248	.333	2	.125	-0	11	13	-1	1.3

● **JOHN BOGART** Bogart, John Renzie "Big John" b: 9/21/1900, Bloomsburg, Pa. d: 12/7/86, Clarence, N.Y. BR/TR, 6′2″, 195 lbs. Deb: 9/17/20

1920	Det-A	2	1	.667	4	3	0	0	0	23^{2}	16	0	18	5	12.9	3.04	122	.195	.340	2	.250	-0	2	2	-1	0.1

● **RAY BOGGS** Boggs, Raymond Joseph "Lefty" b: 12/12/04, Reamsville, Kan. d: 11/27/89, Grand Junction, Colo. BL/TL, 6′0.5″, 170 lbs. Deb: 9/01/28

1928	Bos-N	0	0	—	4	0	0	0	0	5	2	0	7	0	21.6	5.40	72	.167	.545	0	—	0	-1	-1	-0	-0.1

● TOMMY BOGGS Boggs, Thomas Winton b: 10/25/55, Poughkeepsie, N.Y. BR/TR, 6'2", 200 lbs. Deb: 7/19/76

YEAR	TM/L	W	L	PCT	G	GS	CG	SH	SV	IP	H	HR	BB	SO	RAT	ERA	ERA+	OAV	OOB	BH	AVG	PB	PR	/A	PD	TPI
1976	Tex-A	1	7	.125	13	13	3	0	0	90^1	87	7	34	36	12.2	3.49	103	.257	.326	0	—	0	0	1	-1	-0.1
1977	Tex-A	0	3	.000	6	6	0	0	0	27^1	40	1	12	15	17.5	5.93	69	.351	.417	0	—	0	-6	-6	-0	-0.6
1978	Atl-N	2	8	.200	16	12	1	1	0	59	80	8	26	21	16.3	6.71	60	.323	.389	3	.167	0	-21	-17	-2	-1.8
1979	Atl-N	0	2	.000	3	3	0	0	0	12^2	21	0	4	1	18.5	6.39	63	.362	.413	1	.250	0	-4	-3	0	-0.3
1980	Atl-N	12	9	.571	32	26	4	3	0	192^1	180	14	46	84	10.8	3.42	109	.249	.298	10	.159	-2	4	7	-2	0.3
1981	Atl-N	3	13	.188	25	24	2	0	0	142^2	140	11	54	81	12.4	4.10	87	.265	.336	7	.152	-1	-10	-8	-1	-1.0
1982	Atl-N	2	2	.500	10	10	0	0	0	46^1	43	2	22	29	13.0	3.30	113	.253	.345	4	.235	0	2	2	-0	0.3
1983	Atl-N	0	0	—	5	0	0	0	0	6^1	8	1	1	5	12.8	5.68	68	.320	.346	0	—	0	-1	-1	-0	-0.1
1985	Tex-A	0	0	—	4	0	0	0	0	7	13	3	2	6	19.3	11.57	37	.382	.417	0	—	0	-6	-6	0	-0.5
Total	9	20	44	.313	114	94	10	4	0	584	612	47	201	278	12.7	4.22	89	.273	.337	25	.169	-2	-41	-31	-5	-3.8

● WARREN BOGLE Bogle, Warren Frederick b: 10/19/46, Passaic, N.J. BL/TL, 6'4", 220 lbs. Deb: 7/31/68

YEAR	TM/L	W	L	PCT	G	GS	CG	SH	SV	IP	H	HR	BB	SO	RAT	ERA	ERA+	OAV	OOB	BH	AVG	PB	PR	/A	PD	TPI
1968	Oak-A	0	0	—	16	1	0	0	0	23	26	3	8	26	13.3	4.30	65	.283	.340	0	.000	-0	-3	-4	1	-0.4

● BRIAN BOHANON Bohanon, Brian Edward b: 8/1/68, Denton, Tex. BL/TL, 6'2", 210 lbs. Deb: 4/10/90

YEAR	TM/L	W	L	PCT	G	GS	CG	SH	SV	IP	H	HR	BB	SO	RAT	ERA	ERA+	OAV	OOB	BH	AVG	PB	PR	/A	PD	TPI
1990	Tex-A	0	3	.000	11	6	0	0	0	34	40	6	18	15	15.9	6.62	59	.296	.387	0	—	0	-10	-10	1	-0.9
1991	Tex-A	4	3	.571	11	11	1	0	0	61^1	66	4	23	34	13.4	4.84	83	.274	.342	0	—	0	-5	-6	-1	-0.5
1992	Tex-A	1	1	.500	18	7	0	0	0	45^2	57	7	25	29	16.4	6.31	61	.297	.381	0	—	0	-12	-13	-0	-1.1
Total	3	5	7	.417	40	24	1	0	0	141	163	17	66	78	14.9	5.74	69	.287	.366	0	—	0	-27	-28	0	-2.5

● PAT BOHEN Bohen, Leo Ignatius b: 9/30/1891, Oakland, Iowa d: 4/8/42, Napa, Cal. BR/TR, 5'10.5", 155 lbs. Deb: 10/01/13

YEAR	TM/L	W	L	PCT	G	GS	CG	SH	SV	IP	H	HR	BB	SO	RAT	ERA	ERA+	OAV	OOB	BH	AVG	PB	PR	/A	PD	TPI
1913	Phi-A	0	1	.000	1	1	1	0	0	8	3	0	2	5	5.6	1.13	245	.115	.179	0	.000	-0	2	1	-0	0.1
1914	Pit-N	0	0	—	1	0	0	0	0	1	2	0	2	0	45.0	18.00	15	.500	.714	0	.000	-0	-2	-2	-0	-0.2
Total	2	0	1	.000	2	1	1	0	0	9	5	0	4	5	10.0	3.00	92	.167	.286	0	.000	-1	-0	-0	-0	-0.1

● CHARLIE BOHN Bohn, Charles b: 1857, Cleveland, Ohio d: 8/1/03, Cleveland, Ohio Deb: 6/20/1882 ♦

YEAR	TM/L	W	L	PCT	G	GS	CG	SH	SV	IP	H	HR	BB	SO	RAT	ERA	ERA+	OAV	OOB	BH	AVG	PB	PR	/A	PD	TPI
1882	Lou-a	1	1	.500	2	2	2	0	0	18	21	0	3	1	12.0	3.00	83	.273	.300	2	.154	-0	-1	-1	0	-0.1

● JOHN BOHNET Bohnet, John Kelly b: 1/18/61, Pasadena, Cal. BB/TL, 6', 175 lbs. Deb: 5/10/82

YEAR	TM/L	W	L	PCT	G	GS	CG	SH	SV	IP	H	HR	BB	SO	RAT	ERA	ERA+	OAV	OOB	BH	AVG	PB	PR	/A	PD	TPI
1982	Cle-A	0	0	—	3	3	0	0	0	11^2	11	4	7	4	14.7	6.94	59	.250	.365	0	—	0	-4	-4	0	-0.3

● DAN BOITANO Boitano, Danny Jon b: 3/22/53, Sacramento, Cal. BR/TR, 6', 185 lbs. Deb: 10/01/78

YEAR	TM/L	W	L	PCT	G	GS	CG	SH	SV	IP	H	HR	BB	SO	RAT	ERA	ERA+	OAV	OOB	BH	AVG	PB	PR	/A	PD	TPI
1978	Phi-N	0	0	—	1	0	0	0	0	1	0	0	1	0	9.0	0.00	—	.000	.250	0	—	0	0	0	0	0.0
1979	Mil-A	0	0	—	5	0	0	0	0	6	6	1	3	5	13.5	1.50	278	.273	.360	0	—	0	2	2	0	0.2
1980	Mil-A	0	1	.000	11	0	0	0	0	17^2	26	7	6	11	16.8	8.15	47	.342	.398	0	—	0	-8	-8	0	-0.6
1981	NY-N	2	1	.667	15	0	0	0	0	16^1	21	2	5	8	15.4	5.51	63	.309	.373	0	—	0	-4	-4	0	-0.4
1982	Tex-A	0	0	—	19	0	0	0	0	30^1	33	5	13	28	14.2	5.34	72	.280	.361	0	—	0	-4	-5	-0	-0.3
Total	5	2	2	.500	51	0	0	0	0	71^1	86	15	28	52	15.0	5.68	67	.300	.372	0	—	0	-14	-15	-0	-1.1

● DICK BOKELMANN Bokelmann, Richard Werner b: 10/26/26, Arlington Heights, Ill. BR/TR, 6'0.5", 180 lbs. Deb: 8/03/51

YEAR	TM/L	W	L	PCT	G	GS	CG	SH	SV	IP	H	HR	BB	SO	RAT	ERA	ERA+	OAV	OOB	BH	AVG	PB	PR	/A	PD	TPI
1951	StL-N	3	3	.500	20	1	0	0	3	52^1	49	2	31	22	13.9	3.78	105	.245	.349	0	.000	-2	1	1	-1	-0.2
1952	StL-N	0	1	.000	11	0	0	0	0	12^2	20	0	7	5	19.2	9.24	40	.357	.429	0	—	0	-8	-8	1	-0.7
1953	StL-N	0	0	—	3	0	0	0	0	3	4	0	0	0	12.0	6.00	71	.308	.308	0	—	0	-1	-1	0	0.0
Total	3	3	4	.429	34	1	0	0	3	68	73	2	38	27	14.8	4.90	80	.271	.364	0	.000	-2	-7	-7	0	-0.9

● JOE BOKINA Bokina, Joseph b: 4/4/10, Northampton, Mass. BR/TR, 6', 184 lbs. Deb: 4/16/36

YEAR	TM/L	W	L	PCT	G	GS	CG	SH	SV	IP	H	HR	BB	SO	RAT	ERA	ERA+	OAV	OOB	BH	AVG	PB	PR	/A	PD	TPI
1936	Was-A	0	2	.000	5	1	0	0	0	8^1	15	0	6	5	22.7	8.64	55	.395	.477	0	.000	-0	-3	-4	-0	-0.3

● BERNIE BOLAND Boland, Bernard Anthony b: 1/21/1892, Rochester, N.Y. d: 9/12/73, Detroit, Mich. BR/TR, 5'8.5", 168 lbs. Deb: 4/14/15

YEAR	TM/L	W	L	PCT	G	GS	CG	SH	SV	IP	H	HR	BB	SO	RAT	ERA	ERA+	OAV	OOB	BH	AVG	PB	PR	/A	PD	TPI
1915	Det-A	13	7	.650	45	18	8	1	2	202^2	167	2	75	72	11.0	3.11	98	.230	.307	11	.175	-1	-4	-2	0	-0.3
1916	Det-A	10	3	.769	46	9	5	1	3	130^1	111	1	73	59	13.0	3.94	73	.240	.349	8	.250	2	-16	-15	-3	-1.8
1917	Det-A	16	11	.593	43	28	13	3	6	238	192	0	95	89	11.1	2.68	99	.226	.308	4	.056	-5	-1	-1	0	-0.7
1918	Det-A	14	10	.583	29	25	14	4	0	204	176	1	67	63	11.0	2.65	101	.236	.304	12	.174	0	3	0	-1	-0.1
1919	Det-A	14	16	.467	35	30	18	1	1	242^2	222	7	80	71	11.3	3.04	105	.253	.318	8	.108	-3	5	4	-2	0.0
1920	Det-A	0	2	.000	4	3	1	0	0	17^1	23	0	14	4	20.3	7.79	48	.348	.476	1	.143	-0	-8	-8	0	-0.7
1921	StL-A	1	4	.200	7	6	0	0	0	27	34	2	28	6	21.0	9.33	48	.309	.453	1	.100	-1	-15	-15	-0	-1.3
Total	7	68	53	.562	209	119	59	10	12	1062	925	13	432	364	11.7	3.25	91	.241	.322	45	.138	-8	-35	-36	-5	-4.9

● BILL BOLDEN Bolden, William Horace "Big Bill" b: 5/9/1893, Dandridge, Tenn. d: 12/8/66, Jefferson City, Tenn. BR/TR, 6'4", 200 lbs. Deb: 6/27/19

YEAR	TM/L	W	L	PCT	G	GS	CG	SH	SV	IP	H	HR	BB	SO	RAT	ERA	ERA+	OAV	OOB	BH	AVG	PB	PR	/A	PD	TPI
1919	StL-N	0	1	.000	3	1	0	0	0	12	17	0	4	4	16.5	5.25	53	.340	.400	1	.333	0	-3	-3	0	-0.3

● STEW BOLEN Bolen, Stewart O'Neal b: 10/12/02, Jackson, Ala. d: 8/30/69, Mobile, Ala. BL/TL, 5'11", 180 lbs. Deb: 4/15/26

YEAR	TM/L	W	L	PCT	G	GS	CG	SH	SV	IP	H	HR	BB	SO	RAT	ERA	ERA+	OAV	OOB	BH	AVG	PB	PR	/A	PD	TPI
1926	StL-A	0	0	—	5	0	0	0	0	14^2	21	2	6	7	16.6	6.14	70	.356	.415	2	.500	1	-3	-3	-0	-0.2
1927	StL-A	0	1	.000	3	1	1	0	0	9^2	14	0	5	7	17.7	8.38	52	.368	.442	1	.333	0	-5	-4	0	-0.4
1931	Phi-N	3	12	.200	28	16	2	0	0	98^2	117	5	63	55	16.8	6.39	66	.297	.399	5	.156	-1	-28	-23	0	-2.3
1932	Phi-N	0	0	—	5	0	0	0	0	16	18	0	10	3	16.9	2.81	157	.281	.395	1	.143	-0	2	3	-0	0.2
Total	4	3	13	.188	41	17	3	0	0	139	170	7	84	72	16.8	6.09	70	.306	.403	9	.196	-0	-34	-28	-0	-2.7

● BOBBY BOLIN Bolin, Bobby Donald b: 1/29/39, Hickory Grove, S.C. BR/TR, 6'4", 200 lbs. Deb: 4/18/61

YEAR	TM/L	W	L	PCT	G	GS	CG	SH	SV	IP	H	HR	BB	SO	RAT	ERA	ERA+	OAV	OOB	BH	AVG	PB	PR	/A	PD	TPI
1961	SF-N	2	2	.500	37	1	0	0	5	48	37	6	37	48	14.4	3.19	120	.210	.356	2	.286	0	5	3	-1	0.3
1962	*SF-N	7	3	.700	41	5	2	0	5	92	84	10	35	74	12.1	3.62	105	.243	.321	6	.261	2	3	2	-1	0.3
1963	SF-N	10	6	.625	47	12	2	0	7	137^1	128	13	57	134	12.6	3.28	98	.242	.324	5	.143	2	0	-1	-2	-0.2
1964	SF-N	6	9	.400	38	23	5	3	1	174^2	143	16	77	146	11.9	3.25	110	.220	.313	5	.100	0	6	6	-1	0.6
1965	SF-N	14	6	.700	45	13	2	0	2	163	125	17	56	135	10.2	2.76	130	.214	.288	9	.167	1	14	15	-2	1.6
1966	SF-N	11	10	.524	36	34	10	4	1	224^1	174	25	70	143	10.2	2.89	127	.211	.281	13	.171	3	18	19	-2	2.3
1967	SF-N	6	8	.429	37	15	0	0	0	120	120	16	50	69	13.0	4.88	67	.258	.333	8	.242	2	-20	-21	-1	-2.1
1968	SF-N	10	5	.667	34	19	6	3	0	176^2	128	9	46	126	9.1	1.99	148	.200	.258	5	.091	-1	20	19	-1	2.0
1969	SF-N	7	7	.500	30	22	2	0	0	146^1	149	17	49	102	12.6	4.43	79	.260	.326	6	.154	3	-14	-15	-1	-1.3
1970	Mil-A	5	11	.313	32	20	3	0	1	132	131	20	67	81	13.8	4.91	77	.256	.346	7	.194	2	-18	-16	-1	-1.6
	Bos-A	2	0	1.000	6	0	0	0	2	8	2	0	5	8	9.0	0.00	—	.080	.258	0	.000	-0	3	4	0	0.4
	Yr	7	11	.389	38	20	3	0	3	140	133	20	72	89	13.2	4.63	82	.243	.332	7	.189	2	-14	-13	-1	-1.2
1971	Bos-A	5	3	.625	52	0	0	0	6	69^2	74	7	24	51	12.7	4.26	87	.273	.332	3	.250	0	-6	-4	-1	-0.5
1972	Bos-A	0	1	.000	21	0	0	0	5	30^2	24	3	11	27	10.6	2.93	109	.209	.283	0	.000	-0	0	1	-0	0.1
1973	Bos-A	3	4	.429	39	0	0	0	15	53^1	45	5	13	31	10.0	2.70	149	.232	.284	0	—	0	7	8	1	0.9
Total	13	88	75	.540	495	164	32	10	50	1576	1364	164	597	1175	11.5	3.40	103	.231	.308	69	.163	15	18	19	-13	2.8

● GREG BOLLO Bollo, Gregory Gene b: 11/16/43, Detroit, Mich. BR/TR, 6'4", 183 lbs. Deb: 5/09/65

YEAR	TM/L	W	L	PCT	G	GS	CG	SH	SV	IP	H	HR	BB	SO	RAT	ERA	ERA+	OAV	OOB	BH	AVG	PB	PR	/A	PD	TPI
1965	Chi-A	0	0	—	15	0	0	0	0	22^2	12	5	9	16	9.1	3.57	89	.152	.256	0	—	0	-0	-1	0	-0.1
1966	Chi-A	0	1	.000	3	1	0	0	0	7	7	0	3	4	14.1	2.57	123	.269	.367	0	.000	-0	1	0	-0	0.0
Total	2	0	1	.000	18	1	0	0	0	29^2	19	5	12	20	10.3	3.34	96	.181	.283	0	.000	-0	0	-0	0	-0.1

● TOM BOLTON Bolton, Thomas Edward b: 5/6/62, Nashville, Tenn. BL/TL, 6'3", 175 lbs. Deb: 5/17/87

YEAR	TM/L	W	L	PCT	G	GS	CG	SH	SV	IP	H	HR	BB	SO	RAT	ERA	ERA+	OAV	OOB	BH	AVG	PB	PR	/A	PD	TPI
1987	Bos-A	1	0	1.000	29	0	0	0	0	61^2	83	5	27	49	16.3	4.38	104	.329	.399	0	—	0	1	1	0	-0.1
1988	Bos-A	1	3	.250	28	0	0	0	1	30^1	35	1	14	21	14.5	4.75	87	.285	.358	0	—	0	-3	-2	1	-0.4
1989	Bos-A	0	4	.000	4	4	0	0	0	17^1	21	1	10	9	16.1	8.31	49	.292	.378	0	—	0	-9	-8	-0	-1.2

YEAR	TM/L	W	L	PCT	G	GS	CG	SH	SV	IP	H	HR	BB	SO	RAT	ERA	ERA+	OAV	OOB	BH	AVG	PB	PR	/A	PD	TPI
1990	*Bos-A	10	5	.667	21	16	3	0	0	119^{2}	111	6	47	65	12.1	3.38	120	.251	.327	0	—	0	7	9	1	0.6
1991	Bos-A	8	9	.471	25	19	0	0	0	110	136	16	51	64	15.4	5.24	82	.308	.381	0	—	0	-14	-11	-1	-1.5
1992	Bos-A	1	2	.333	21	1	0	0	0	29	34	0	14	23	15.5	3.41	122	.286	.370	0	—	0	2	2	0	-0.1
	Cin-N	3	3	.500	16	8	0	0	0	46^{1}	52	9	23	27	15.0	5.24	70	.284	.370	0	.000	-1	-9	-8	0	-1.0
Total	6	24	26	.480	144	48	3	0	1	414^{1}	472	38	186	258	14.5	4.54	92	.289	.365	0	.000	-1	-25	-17	2	-3.7

● MARK BOMBACK Bomback, Mark Vincent b: 4/14/53, Portsmouth, Va. BR/TR, 5'11", 170 lbs. Deb: 9/12/78

YEAR	TM/L	W	L	PCT	G	GS	CG	SH	SV	IP	H	HR	BB	SO	RAT	ERA	ERA+	OAV	OOB	BH	AVG	PB	PR	/A	PD	TPI
1978	Mil-A	0	0	—	2	1	0	0	0	1^{2}	5	1	1	1	32.4	16.20	23	.500	.545	0	—	0	-2	-2	-0	-0.2
1980	NY-N	10	8	.556	36	25	2	1	0	162^{2}	191	17	49	68	13.5	4.09	87	.297	.350	10	.233	3	-9	-10	2	-0.4
1981	Tor-A	5	5	.500	20	11	0	0	0	90^{1}	84	6	35	33	12.0	3.89	101	.251	.323	0	—	0	-2	1	0	0.1
1982	Tor-A	1	5	.167	16	8	0	0	0	59^{2}	87	10	25	22	17.3	6.03	74	.343	.408	0	—	0	-13	-10	0	-1.4
Total	4	16	18	.471	74	45	2	1	0	314^{1}	367	34	110	124	13.9	4.47	86	.295	.356	10	.233	3	-27	-22	3	-1.9

● TOMMY BOND Bond, Thomas Henry b: 4/2/1856, Granard, Ireland d: 1/24/41, Boston, Mass. BR/TR, 5'7.5", 160 lbs. Deb: 5/05/1874 MU♦

YEAR	TM/L	W	L	PCT	G	GS	CG	SH	SV	IP	H	HR	BB	SO	RAT	ERA	ERA+	OAV	OOB	BH	AVG	PB	PR	/A	PD	TPI
1874	Atl-n	22	32	.407	55	55	55	1	0	497	609	16	10		11.2	*3.19*	88	.268	.271	54	.219	-1	-10	-21		-1.5
1875	Har-n	19	16	.543	40	39	37	6	0	352	301	3	10		8.0	*1.56*	**166**	.215	.220	78	.270	4	35	40		3.9
1876	Har-N	31	13	.705	45	45	45	6	0	408	355	2	13	88	8.1	1.68	141	.220	.227	50	.275	1	29	32	5	3.3
1877	Bos-N	**40**	17	**.702**	58	58	58	**6**	0	521	530	5	36	**170**	**9.8**	**2.11**	133	.249	**.261**	59	.228	-4	**41**	41	3	3.6
1878	Bos-N	**40**	19	**.678**	**59**	59	**57**	**9**	0	**532^{2}**	571	5	33	**182**	10.2	2.06	115	.269	.280	50	.212	-4	15	18	2	1.3
1879	Bos-N	43	19	.694	64	64	59	**11**	0	555^{1}	543	8	24	155	**9.2**	**1.96**	**126**	.251	.259	62	.241	2	33	**32**	7	**3.8**
1880	Bos-N	26	29	.473	63	57	49	3	0	493	559	1	45	118	11.0	2.67	85	.274	.290	62	.220	-2	-16	-22	10	-1.3
1881	Bos-N	0	3	.000	3	3	2	0	0	25^{1}	40	3	2	2	14.9	4.26	62	.360	.372	2	.200	-0	-4	-5	1	-0.4
1882	Wor-N	0	1	.000	2	2	0	0	0	12^{1}	12	0	7	2	13.9	4.38	71	.218	.306	4	.133	-1	-2	-2	-0	-0.2
1884	Bos-U	13	9	.591	23	21	19	0	0	189	185	3	14	128	9.5	3.00	98	.239	.253	48	.296	4	0	-1	3	0.4
	Ind-a	0	5	.000	5	5	5	0	0	43	62	5	4	15	14.2	5.65	58	.310	.330	3	.130	-1	-11	-11	-1	-1.1
Total	2 n	41	48	.461	95	94	92	7	0	849	910	19	20		9.9	*2.51*	109	.248	.252	132	.246	2	25	21		2.4
Total	8	193	115	.627	322	314	294	35	0	2779^{2}	2857	32	178	860	9.8	2.25	112	.255	.267	340	.236	2	83	82	30	9.4

● RICKY BONES Bones, Ricardo Ricky b: 4/7/69, Salinas, P.R. BR/TR, 5'10", 175 lbs. Deb: 8/11/91

YEAR	TM/L	W	L	PCT	G	GS	CG	SH	SV	IP	H	HR	BB	SO	RAT	ERA	ERA+	OAV	OOB	BH	AVG	PB	PR	/A	PD	TPI
1991	SD-N	4	6	.400	11	11	0	0	0	54	57	3	18	31	12.5	4.83	79	.269	.326	1	.077	-0	-7	-6	-1	-0.8
1992	Mil-A	9	10	.474	31	28	0	0	0	163^{1}	169	27	48	65	12.5	4.57	83	.264	.324	0	—	0	-12	-14	-1	-1.4
Total	2	13	16	.448	42	39	0	0	0	217^{1}	226	30	66	96	12.5	4.64	82	.265	.324	1	.077	-0	-18	-20	-3	-2.2

● JULIO BONETTI Bonetti, Julio Giacomo b: 7/14/11, Genoa, Italy d: 6/17/52, Belmont, Cal. BR/TR, 6', 180 lbs. Deb: 4/22/37

YEAR	TM/L	W	L	PCT	G	GS	CG	SH	SV	IP	H	HR	BB	SO	RAT	ERA	ERA+	OAV	OOB	BH	AVG	PB	PR	/A	PD	TPI
1937	StL-A	4	11	.267	28	16	7	0	1	143^{1}	190	13	60	43	15.8	5.84	83	.321	.385	7	.149	-2	-19	-16	2	-1.4
1938	StL-A	2	3	.400	17	0	0	0	0	28^{1}	41	1	13	7	17.2	6.35	78	.350	.415	0	.000	-1	-5	-4	0	-0.5
1940	Chi-N	0	0	—	1	0	0	0	0	1^{1}	3	0	4	0	47.3	20.25	19	.429	.636	0	—	0	-2	-2	-0	-0.2
Total	3	6	14	.300	46	16	7	0	1	173	234	14	77	50	16.3	6.03	80	.327	.394	7	.127	-3	-27	-23	2	-2.1

● HANK BONEY Boney, Henry Tate "Haney" b: 10/28/03, Wallace, N.C. BR/TR, 5'11", 176 lbs. Deb: 6/28/27

YEAR	TM/L	W	L	PCT	G	GS	CG	SH	SV	IP	H	HR	BB	SO	RAT	ERA	ERA+	OAV	OOB	BH	AVG	PB	PR	/A	PD	TPI
1927	NY-N	0	0	—	3	0	0	0	0	4	4	0	2	0	13.5	2.25	171	.267	.353	0	—	0	1	1	-0	0.0

● TINY BONHAM Bonham, Ernest Edward b: 8/16/13, Ione, Cal. d: 9/15/49, Pittsburgh, Pa. BR/TR, 6'2", 215 lbs. Deb: 8/08/40

YEAR	TM/L	W	L	PCT	G	GS	CG	SH	SV	IP	H	HR	BB	SO	RAT	ERA	ERA+	OAV	OOB	BH	AVG	PB	PR	/A	PD	TPI
1940	NY-A	9	3	.750	12	12	10	3	0	99^{1}	83	4	13	37	8.7	1.90	212	.224	.250	7	.189	0	27	24	-2	2.2
1941	*NY-A	9	6	.600	23	14	7	1	2	126^{2}	118	12	31	43	10.7	2.98	132	.246	.294	8	.160	-1	16	13	-3	1.0
1942	*NY-A☆	21	5	**.808**	28	27	**22**	**6**	0	226	199	11	24	71	**8.9**	2.27	152	.237	**.259**	9	.122	-2	**35**	29	-4	2.5
1943	*NY-A☆	15	8	.652	28	26	17	4	1	225^{2}	197	13	52	71	10.0	2.27	142	.236	.282	15	.197	0	26	24	-5	2.2
1944	NY-A	12	9	.571	26	25	17	1	0	213^{2}	228	14	41	54	11.3	2.99	116	.273	.307	10	.133	-3	10	12	-3	0.6
1945	NY-A	8	11	.421	23	23	12	0	0	180^{2}	186	11	22	42	10.4	3.29	105	.265	.288	15	.238	3	2	4	-3	0.3
1946	NY-A	5	8	.385	18	14	6	2	3	104^{2}	97	6	23	30	10.3	3.70	93	.243	.284	4	.129	-0	-2	-3	-2	-0.5
1947	Pit-N	11	8	.579	33	18	7	3	3	149^{2}	167	17	35	63	12.3	3.85	110	.277	.319	7	.156	-0	3	6	-3	0.3
1948	Pit-N	6	10	.375	22	20	7	0	0	135^{2}	145	18	23	42	11.3	4.31	94	.276	.310	8	.163	-2	-5	-4	-4	-0.9
1949	Pit-N	7	4	.636	18	14	5	1	0	89	81	11	23	25	10.5	4.25	99	.246	.295	1	.045	-2	-2	-0	-2	-0.3
Total	10	103	72	.589	231	193	110	21	9	1551	1501	117	287	478	10.4	3.06	120	.254	.289	84	.161	-7	110	105	-29	7.4

● BILL BONHAM Bonham, William Gordon b: 10/1/48, Glendale, Cal. BR/TR, 6'3", 195 lbs. Deb: 4/07/71

YEAR	TM/L	W	L	PCT	G	GS	CG	SH	SV	IP	H	HR	BB	SO	RAT	ERA	ERA+	OAV	OOB	BH	AVG	PB	PR	/A	PD	TPI
1971	Chi-N	2	1	.667	33	2	0	0	0	60	63	6	36	41	15.6	4.65	85	.281	.392	2	.167	-0	-8	-5	1	-0.4
1972	Chi-N	1	1	.500	19	4	0	0	4	57^{2}	56	4	25	49	12.8	3.12	122	.260	.340	4	.286	1	2	4	0	0.6
1973	Chi-N	7	5	.583	44	15	3	0	6	152	126	10	64	121	11.5	3.02	131	.230	.315	4	.093	-3	11	16	4	1.8
1974	Chi-N	11	22	.333	44	36	10	2	1	242^{2}	246	13	109	191	13.4	3.86	99	.263	.343	12	.143	-3	-6	-1	5	0.1
1975	Chi-N	13	15	.464	38	36	7	2	0	229^{1}	254	15	109	165	14.4	4.71	82	.281	.361	15	.183	-0	-28	-22	1	-2.1
1976	Chi-N	9	13	.409	32	31	3	0	0	196	215	11	96	110	14.4	4.27	90	.283	.365	13	.200	1	-17	-9	0	-0.8
1977	Chi-N	10	13	.435	34	34	1	0	0	214^{2}	207	15	82	134	12.2	4.36	101	.254	.324	15	.231	1	-11	1	3	0.5
1978	Cin-N	11	5	.688	23	23	1	0	0	140^{1}	151	9	50	83	13.0	3.53	101	.276	.337	8	.186	2	1	0	3	0.6
1979	Cin-N	9	7	.563	29	29	2	0	0	175^{2}	173	14	60	78	12.3	3.79	98	.261	.330	8	.140	-1	-1	-1	0	-0.2
1980	Cin-N	2	1	.667	4	4	0	0	0	19	21	1	5	13	12.3	4.74	75	.276	.321	0	.000	-0	-2	-2	-0	-0.3
Total	10	75	83	.475	300	214	27	4	11	1487^{1}	1512	98	636	985	13.2	4.01	97	.266	.343	81	.172	-2	-59	-20	18	-0.2

● JOE BONIKOWSKI Bonikowski, Joseph Peter b: 1/16/41, Philadelphia, Pa. BR/TR, 6', 175 lbs. Deb: 4/12/62

YEAR	TM/L	W	L	PCT	G	GS	CG	SH	SV	IP	H	HR	BB	SO	RAT	ERA	ERA+	OAV	OOB	BH	AVG	PB	PR	/A	PD	TPI
1962	Min-A	5	7	.417	30	13	3	0	2	99^{2}	95	6	38	45	12.1	3.88	105	.255	.325	4	.148	-1	1	2	1	0.3

● BILL BONNESS Bonness, William John "Lefty" b: 12/15/23, Cleveland, Ohio d: 12/3/77, Detroit, Mich. BR/TL, 6'4", 200 lbs. Deb: 9/26/44

YEAR	TM/L	W	L	PCT	G	GS	CG	SH	SV	IP	H	HR	BB	SO	RAT	ERA	ERA+	OAV	OOB	BH	AVG	PB	PR	/A	PD	TPI
1944	Cle-A	0	1	.000	2	1	0	0	0	7	11	0	5	1	23.1	7.71	43	.367	.486	0	.000	-0	-3	-3	0	-0.4

● GUS BONO Bono, Adlai Wendell b: 8/29/1894, Doe Run, Mo. d: 12/3/48, Dearborn, Mich. BR/TR, 5'11", 175 lbs. Deb: 9/13/20

YEAR	TM/L	W	L	PCT	G	GS	CG	SH	SV	IP	H	HR	BB	SO	RAT	ERA	ERA+	OAV	OOB	BH	AVG	PB	PR	/A	PD	TPI
1920	Was-A	0	2	.000	4	1	0	0	0	12^{1}	17	0	6	4	16.8	8.76	43	.315	.383	0	.000	-0	-7	-7	0	-0.6

● GREG BOOKER Booker, Gregory Scott b: 6/22/60, Lynchburg, Va. BR/TR, 6'6", 233 lbs. Deb: 9/11/83

YEAR	TM/L	W	L	PCT	G	GS	CG	SH	SV	IP	H	HR	BB	SO	RAT	ERA	ERA+	OAV	OOB	BH	AVG	PB	PR	/A	PD	TPI
1983	SD-N	0	1	.000	6	1	0	0	0	11^{2}	18	2	9	5	20.8	7.71	45	.375	.474	0	.000	-0	-5	-5	0	-0.5
1984	*SD-N	1	1	.500	32	1	0	0	0	57^{1}	67	4	27	28	14.8	3.30	108	.295	.370	2	.286	1	2	2	0	0.3
1985	SD-N	0	1	.000	17	0	0	0	0	22^{1}	20	3	17	7	15.3	6.85	52	.247	.384	0	.000	-0	-8	-8	-0	-0.9
1986	SD-N	1	0	1.000	9	0	0	0	0	11	10	0	4	7	11.5	1.64	223	.233	.298	0	—	0	3	2	-0	0.2
1987	SD-N	1	1	.500	44	0	0	0	1	68^{1}	62	5	30	17	12.5	3.16	125	.246	.333	0	.000	-1	7	6	-0	0.5
1988	SD-N	2	2	.500	34	2	0	0	0	63^{2}	68	5	19	43	12.4	3.39	100	.278	.332	2	.250	1	0	0	1	0.1
1989	SD-N	0	1	.000	11	0	0	0	0	19	15	2	10	8	11.8	4.26	82	.224	.325	0	—	0	-2	-2	0	-0.2
	Min-A	0	0	—	6	0	0	0	0	8^{2}	11	1	2	3	13.5	4.15	100	.306	.342	0	—	0	-0	-0	1	-0.5
1990	SF-N	0	0	—	2	0	0	0	0	2	7	0	0	1	31.5	13.50	27	.538	.538	0	—	0	-2	-2	-0	-0.2
Total	8	5	7	.417	161	4	0	0	1	264	278	22	118	119	13.7	3.89	94	.275	.353	4	.174	1	-6	-7	1	-1.2

● RED BOOLES Booles, Seabron Jesse b: 7/14/1880, Bernice, La. d: 3/16/55, Monroe, La. BL/TL, 5'10", 150 lbs. Deb: 7/30/09

YEAR	TM/L	W	L	PCT	G	GS	CG	SH	SV	IP	H	HR	BB	SO	RAT	ERA	ERA+	OAV	OOB	BH	AVG	PB	PR	/A	PD	TPI
1909	Cle-A	0	1	.000	4	1	0	0	0	22^{2}	20	0	8	6	11.5	1.99	129	.235	.309	1	.167	0	1	1	-0	0.2

● DANNY BOONE Boone, Daniel Hugh b: 1/14/54, Long Beach, Cal. BL/TL, 5'8", 150 lbs. Deb: 4/11/81 F

YEAR	TM/L	W	L	PCT	G	GS	CG	SH	SV	IP	H	HR	BB	SO	RAT	ERA	ERA+	OAV	OOB	BH	AVG	PB	PR	/A	PD	TPI
1981	SD-N	1	0	1.000	37	0	0	0	2	63^{1}	63	2	21	43	12.1	2.84	115	.267	.329	2	.500	1	5	3	1	0.5
1982	SD-N	1	0	1.000	10	0	0	0	1	16	21	2	3	8	13.5	5.63	61	.323	.353	1	.200	0	-4	-4	0	-0.4
	Hou-N	0	1	.000	10	0	0	0	1	12^{2}	7	1	4	4	7.8	3.55	93	.171	.244	0	.000	-0	0	-0	0	0.0

YEAR	TM/L	W	L	PCT	G	GS	CG	SH	SV	IP	H	HR	BB	SO	RAT	ERA	ERA+	OAV	OOB	BH	AVG	PB	PR	/A	PD	TPI
	Yr	1	1	.500	20	0	0	0	2	28^{2}	28	3	7	12	11.0	4.71	72	.264	.310	1	.167	0	-4	-4	0	-0.4
1990	Bal-A	0	0	—	4	1	0	0	0	9^{2}	12	1	3	2	14.9	2.79	136	.308	.372	0	—	0	1	1	0	0.4
Total	3	2	1	.667	61	1	0	0	4	101^{2}	103	6	31	57	12.0	3.36	99	.270	.329	3	.300	1	2	-0	1	0.5

● GEORGE BOONE Boone, George Morris b: 3/1/1871, Louisville, Ky. d: 9/24/10, Louisville, Ky. Deb: 4/23/1891

YEAR	TM/L	W	L	PCT	G	GS	CG	SH	SV	IP	H	HR	BB	SO	RAT	ERA	ERA+	OAV	OOB	BH	AVG	PB	PR	/A	PD	TPI
1891	Lou-a	0	0	—	4	1	0	0	1	15	15	0	9	4	14.4	7.80	47	.252	.350	2	.333	0	-7	-7	-0	-0.6

● DAN BOONE Boone, James Albert b: 1/19/1895, Samantha, Ala. d: 5/11/68, Tuscaloosa, Ala. BR/TR, 6'2", 190 lbs. Deb: 9/10/19

YEAR	TM/L	W	L	PCT	G	GS	CG	SH	SV	IP	H	HR	BB	SO	RAT	ERA	ERA+	OAV	OOB	BH	AVG	PB	PR	/A	PD	TPI
1919	Phi-A	0	1	.000	3	2	0	0	0	14^{2}	24	0	10	1	20.9	6.75	51	.375	.459	0	.000	-1	-6	-5	1	-0.5
1921	Det-A	0	0	—	1	0	0	0	0	2	1	0	2	0	13.5	0.00	—	.200	.429	0	.000	-0	1	1	0	0.1
1922	Cle-A	4	6	.400	11	10	4	2	0	75^{1}	87	3	19	9	12.8	4.06	99	.298	.343	5	.192	-1	-0	-0	1	0.0
1923	Cle-A	4	6	.400	27	4	2	0	0	70^{1}	93	3	31	15	16.3	6.01	66	.322	.393	4	.211	0	-16	-16	3	-1.2
Total	4	8	13	.381	42	16	6	2	0	162^{1}	205	6	62	25	15.0	5.10	77	.315	.378	9	.180	-1	-21	-21	4	-1.6

● AMOS BOOTH Booth, Amos Smith "Darling" b: 9/14/1853, Cincinnati, O. d: 7/1/21, Miamisburg, Ohio BR/TR, Deb: 4/25/1876 ♦

YEAR	TM/L	W	L	PCT	G	GS	CG	SH	SV	IP	H	HR	BB	SO	RAT	ERA	ERA+	OAV	OOB	BH	AVG	PB	PR	/A	PD	TPI
1876	Cin-N	0	1	.000	3	1	0	0	0	9^{2}	22	0	0	0	20.5	9.31	24	.431	.431	71	.261	0	-8	-8	-0	-0.6
1877	Cin-N	1	7	.125	12	8	6	0	0	86	114	1	13	18	13.3	3.56	74	.296	.319	27	.172	-1	-7	-9	-1	-0.9
Total	2	1	8	.111	15	9	6	0	0	95^{2}	136	1	13	18	14.0	4.14	63	.312	.332	98	.224	-1	-15	-16	-1	-1.5

● EDDIE BOOTH Booth, Edward H. b: Brooklyn, N.Y. Deb: 4/26/1872 ♦

YEAR	TM/L	W	L	PCT	G	GS	CG	SH	SV	IP	H	HR	BB	SO	RAT	ERA	ERA+	OAV	OOB	BH	AVG	PB	PR	/A	PD	TPI
1876	NY-N	0	0	—	1	0	0	0	0	5	16	0	0	0	28.8	10.80	20	.471	.471	49	.215	-0	-5	-5	-0	-0.4

● JOHN BOOZER Boozer, John Morgan b: 7/6/38, Columbia, S.C. d: 1/24/86, Lexington, S.C. BR/TR, 6'3", 205 lbs. Deb: 7/22/62

YEAR	TM/L	W	L	PCT	G	GS	CG	SH	SV	IP	H	HR	BB	SO	RAT	ERA	ERA+	OAV	OOB	BH	AVG	PB	PR	/A	PD	TPI
1962	Phi-N	0	0	—	9	0	0	0	0	20^{1}	22	3	10	13	14.2	5.75	67	.282	.364	0	.000	-0	-4	-4	-0	-0.4
1963	Phi-N	3	4	.429	26	8	2	0	1	83	67	11	33	69	11.0	2.93	110	.227	.307	3	.143	-0	3	3	-2	0.1
1964	Phi-N	3	4	.429	22	3	0	0	2	60^{1}	64	6	18	51	12.5	5.07	68	.271	.328	1	.077	-1	-10	-11	1	-1.1
1966	Phi-N	0	0	—	2	2	0	0	0	5^{1}	8	1	3	5	18.6	6.75	53	.348	.423	0	.000	-0	-2	-2	0	-0.2
1967	Phi-N	5	4	.556	28	7	1	0	1	74^{2}	86	6	24	48	13.4	4.10	83	.292	.347	4	.211	1	-6	-6	0	-0.5
1968	Phi-N	2	2	.500	38	0	0	0	5	68^{2}	76	3	15	49	12.2	3.67	82	.279	.322	1	.111	-0	-5	-5	0	-0.6
1969	Phi-N	1	2	.333	46	2	0	0	6	82	91	12	36	47	13.9	4.28	83	.283	.356	3	.333	1	-6	-7	-1	-0.7
Total	7	14	16	.467	171	22	3	0	15	394^{1}	414	42	139	282	12.8	4.09	82	.272	.336	12	.162	-0	-30	-31	-2	-3.4

● PEDRO BORBON Borbon, Pedro (Rodriguez) b: 12/2/46, Valverde, Mao, D.R. BR/TR, 6'2", 185 lbs. Deb: 4/09/69 F

YEAR	TM/L	W	L	PCT	G	GS	CG	SH	SV	IP	H	HR	BB	SO	RAT	ERA	ERA+	OAV	OOB	BH	AVG	PB	PR	/A	PD	TPI
1969	Cal-A	2	3	.400	22	0	0	0	0	41	55	5	11	20	15.4	6.15	57	.324	.378	0	.000	-0	-12	-12	-0	-1.3
1970	Cin-N	0	2	.000	12	1	0	0	0	17^{1}	21	2	6	6	15.6	6.75	60	.309	.390	0	.000	-0	-5	-5	2	-0.4
1971	Cin-N	0	0	—	3	0	0	0	0	4^{1}	3	1	1	4	8.3	4.15	81	.200	.250	0	—	0	-0	-0	-0	-0.1
1972	*Cin-N	8	3	.727	62	2	0	0	11	122	115	5	32	48	11.1	3.17	101	.254	.307	1	.048	-1	4	1	-1	-0.1
1973	*Cin-N	11	4	.733	80	0	0	0	14	121	137	4	35	60	12.9	2.16	158	.298	.349	5	.333	1	**20**	17	-0	1.9
1974	Cin-N	10	7	.588	73	0	0	0	14	139	133	11	32	53	10.9	3.24	108	.255	.303	5	.192	-0	6	4	-1	0.3
1975	*Cin-N	9	5	.643	67	0	0	0	5	125	145	6	21	29	12.2	2.95	122	.301	.334	7	.292	2	9	9	-1	1.0
1976	*Cin-N	4	3	.571	69	1	0	0	8	121	135	4	31	53	12.6	3.35	105	.292	.342	4	.222	0	2	2	-0	0.2
1977	Cin-N	10	5	.667	73	0	0	0	18	127	131	7	24	48	11.2	3.19	123	.268	.307	4	.182	-0	10	10	-2	0.9
1978	Cin-N	8	2	.800	62	0	0	0	4	99^{1}	102	6	27	35	12.0	4.98	71	.274	.328	2	.182	-0	-16	-16	-0	-1.7
1979	Cin-N	2	2	.500	30	0	0	0	2	44^{2}	48	2	8	23	11.3	3.43	109	.277	.309	2	.333	0	2	2	0	0.2
	SF-N	4	3	.571	30	0	0	0	3	46	56	7	13	26	13.5	4.89	71	.303	.348	1	.333	0	-6	-7	-1	-0.8
	Yr	6	5	.545	60	0	0	0	5	90^{2}	104	9	21	49	12.4	4.17	87	.287	.326	3	.333	1	-4	-6	-1	-0.6
1980	StL-N	1	0	1.000	10	0	0	0	1	19	17	3	10	4	12.8	3.79	97	.250	.346	1	.250	0	-0	-0	-0	0.0
Total	12	69	39	.639	593	4	0	0	80	1026^{2}	1098	63	251	409	12.1	3.52	101	.280	.328	32	.205	2	14	3	-4	0.1

● PEDRO BORBON Borbon, Pedro Felix b: 11/15/67, Mao, D.R. BR/TL, 6'1", 205 lbs. Deb: 10/02/92 F

YEAR	TM/L	W	L	PCT	G	GS	CG	SH	SV	IP	H	HR	BB	SO	RAT	ERA	ERA+	OAV	OOB	BH	AVG	PB	PR	/A	PD	TPI
1992	Atl-N	0	1	.000	2	0	0	0	0	1^{1}	2	0	1	1	20.3	6.75	55	.333	.429	0	—	0	-0	-0	0	-0.1

● GEORGE BORCHERS Borchers, George Benard "Chief" b: 4/18/1869, Sacramento, Cal. d: 10/24/38, Sacramento, Cal. BB/TR, 5'10", 180 lbs. Deb: 5/18/1888

YEAR	TM/L	W	L	PCT	G	GS	CG	SH	SV	IP	H	HR	BB	SO	RAT	ERA	ERA+	OAV	OOB	BH	AVG	PB	PR	/A	PD	TPI
1888	Chi-N	4	4	.500	10	10	7	1	0	67	67	2	29	26	13.7	3.49	87	.251	.338	2	.061	-3	-5	-3	0	-0.5
1895	Lou-N	0	1	.000	1	1	0	0	0	0^{2}	1	0	3	0	54.0	27.00	17	.341	.674	0	—	0	-2	-2	-0	-0.1
Total	2	4	5	.444	11	11	7	1	0	67^{2}	68	2	32	26	14.1	3.72	82	.252	.344	2	.061	-3	-6	-5	-0	-0.6

● JOE BORDEN Borden, Joseph Emley (a.k.a. Joseph Emley Josephs In 1875)
b: 5/9/1854, Jacobstown, N.J. d: 10/14/29, Yeadon, Pa. BR/TR, 5'9", 140 lbs. Deb: 7/24/1875

YEAR	TM/L	W	L	PCT	G	GS	CG	SH	SV	IP	H	HR	BB	SO	RAT	ERA	ERA+	OAV	OOB	BH	AVG	PB	PR	/A	PD	TPI
1875	Phi-n	2	4	.333	7	7	7	2	0	66	47	0	7		**7.4**	*1.64*	154	**.181**	**.203**	3	.107	-3	6	6		0.3
1876	Bos-N	11	12	.478	29	24	16	2	1	218^{1}	257	4	51	34	12.7	2.89	78	.276	.313	25	.207	-3	-14	-15	-2	-1.8

● RICH BORDI Bordi, Richard Albert b: 4/18/59, San Francisco, Cal. BR/TR, 6'7", 220 lbs. Deb: 7/16/80

YEAR	TM/L	W	L	PCT	G	GS	CG	SH	SV	IP	H	HR	BB	SO	RAT	ERA	ERA+	OAV	OOB	BH	AVG	PB	PR	/A	PD	TPI
1980	Oak-A	0	0	—	1	0	0	0	0	2	4	0	0	0	18.0	4.50	84	.400	.400	0	—	0	-0	-0	-0	0.0
1981	Oak-A	0	0	—	2	0	0	0	0	2	1	0	1	0	9.0	0.00	—	.143	.250	0	—	0	1	1	-0	0.1
1982	Sea-A	0	2	.000	7	2	0	0	0	13	18	4	1	10	13.8	8.31	51	.310	.333	0	—	0	-6	-6	-0	-0.7
1983	Chi-N	0	2	.000	11	1	0	0	1	25^{1}	34	2	12	20	16.3	4.97	76	.321	.390	0	.000	-0	-4	-3	0	-0.4
1984	Chi-N	5	2	.714	31	7	0	0	4	83^{1}	78	11	20	41	10.6	3.46	113	.242	.287	1	.053	-1	1	4	-1	0.2
1985	NY-A	6	8	.429	51	3	0	0	2	98	95	5	29	64	11.5	3.21	124	.253	.308	0	—	0	10	9	-1	0.9
1986	Bal-A	6	4	.600	52	1	0	0	3	107	105	13	41	83	12.6	4.46	93	.254	.327	0	—	0	-3	-4	1	-0.2
1987	NY-A	3	1	.750	16	1	0	0	0	33	42	7	12	23	14.7	7.64	57	.309	.365	0	—	0	-12	-12	-1	-1.1
1988	Oak-A	0	1	.000	2	2	0	0	0	7^{2}	6	0	5	6	12.9	4.70	80	.214	.333	0	—	0	-1	-1	-0	0.0
Total	9	20	20	.500	173	17	0	0	10	371^{1}	383	42	121	247	12.4	4.34	93	.263	.322	1	.043	-2	-13	-12	-2	-1.2

● BILL BORDLEY Bordley, William Clarke b: 1/9/58, Los Angeles, Cal. BR/TL, 6'3", 185 lbs. Deb: 6/30/80

YEAR	TM/L	W	L	PCT	G	GS	CG	SH	SV	IP	H	HR	BB	SO	RAT	ERA	ERA+	OAV	OOB	BH	AVG	PB	PR	/A	PD	TPI
1980	SF-N	2	3	.400	8	6	0	0	0	30^{2}	34	3	21	11	16.1	4.70	75	.288	.396	1	.167	0	-4	-4	1	-0.3

● PAUL BORIS Boris, Paul Stanley b: 12/13/55, Irvington, N.J. BR/TR, 6'2", 200 lbs. Deb: 5/21/82

YEAR	TM/L	W	L	PCT	G	GS	CG	SH	SV	IP	H	HR	BB	SO	RAT	ERA	ERA+	OAV	OOB	BH	AVG	PB	PR	/A	PD	TPI
1982	Min-A	1	2	.333	23	0	0	0	0	49^{2}	46	8	19	30	12.1	3.99	106	.246	.322	0	—	0	0	1	-1	-0.1

● FRANK BORK Bork, Frank Bernard b: 7/13/40, Buffalo, N.Y. BR/TL, 6'2", 175 lbs. Deb: 4/15/64

YEAR	TM/L	W	L	PCT	G	GS	CG	SH	SV	IP	H	HR	BB	SO	RAT	ERA	ERA+	OAV	OOB	BH	AVG	PB	PR	/A	PD	TPI
1964	Pit-N	2	2	.500	33	2	0	0	2	42	51	6	11	31	13.5	4.07	86	.295	.341	1	.200	0	-2	-3	0	-0.2

● TOM BORLAND Borland, Thomas Bruce "Spike" b: 2/14/33, ElDorado, Kan. BL/TL, 6'3", 172 lbs. Deb: 5/15/60

YEAR	TM/L	W	L	PCT	G	GS	CG	SH	SV	IP	H	HR	BB	SO	RAT	ERA	ERA+	OAV	OOB	BH	AVG	PB	PR	/A	PD	TPI
1960	Bos-A	0	4	.000	26	4	0	0	3	51	67	4	23	32	15.9	6.53	62	.322	.390	0	.000	-2	-15	-14	0	-1.5
1961	Bos-A	0	0	—	1	0	0	0	0	1	3	0	0	0	27.0	18.00	23	.500	.500	0	—	0	-2	-2	-0	-0.1
Total	2	0	4	.000	27	4	0	0	3	52	70	4	23	32	16.1	6.75	60	.327	.392	0	.000	-2	-17	-16	0	-1.6

● HANK BOROWY Borowy, Henry Ludwig b: 5/12/16, Bloomfield, N.J. BR/TR, 6', 175 lbs. Deb: 4/18/42

YEAR	TM/L	W	L	PCT	G	GS	CG	SH	SV	IP	H	HR	BB	SO	RAT	ERA	ERA+	OAV	OOB	BH	AVG	PB	PR	/A	PD	TPI
1942	*NY-A	15	4	.789	25	21	13	4	1	178^{1}	157	6	66	85	11.3	2.52	136	.233	.301	11	.157	-1	22	18	1	2.0
1943	*NY-A	14	9	.609	29	27	14	3	0	217^{1}	195	11	72	113	11.1	2.82	114	.241	.305	15	.203	3	12	10	1	1.5
1944	NY-A★	17	12	.586	35	30	19	3	2	252^{2}	224	15	88	107	11.1	2.64	132	.236	.301	12	.133	-3	22	24	1	2.3
1945	NY-A†	10	5	.667	18	18	7	1	0	132^{1}	107	6	58	35	11.3	3.13	111	.221	.305	11	.220	1	3	5	1	0.8
	*Chi-N	11	2	.846	15	14	11	1	1	122^{1}	105	2	47	47	11.2	2.13	171	.231	.303	7	.171	0	23	21	-1	2.2
1946	Chi-N	12	10	.545	32	28	8	1	0	201	220	9	61	95	12.6	3.76	88	.274	.326	13	.181	1	-8	-10	0	-0.9
1947	Chi-N	8	12	.400	40	25	7	1	2	183	190	19	63	75	12.5	4.38	90	.267	.328	7	.125	-1	-6	-9	0	-0.9

YEAR	TM/L	W	L	PCT	G	GS	CG	SH	SV	IP	H	HR	BB	SO	RAT	ERA	ERA+	OAV	OOB	BH	AVG	PB	PR	/A	PD	TPI
1948	Chi-N	5	10	.333	39	17	2	1	1	127	156	9	49	50	14.5	4.89	80	.308	.369	8	.222	2	-13	-14	2	-1.0
1949	Phi-N	12	12	.500	28	28	12	1	0	193^1	188	19	63	43	11.7	4.19	94	.259	.319	13	.213	3	-3	-5	-2	-0.4
1950	Phi-N	0	0	—	3	0	0	0	0	6^1	5	0	4	3	12.8	5.68	71	.250	.375	0	—	0	-1	-1	-0	-0.1
	Pit-N	1	3	.250	11	3	0	0	0	25^1	32	6	9	9	14.9	6.39	69	.311	.372	1	.167	-0	-6	-6	0	-0.5
	Yr	1	3	.250	14	3	0	0	0	31^2	37	6	13	12	14.5	6.25	69	.301	.372	1	.167	-0	-7	-7	0	-0.6
	Det-A	1	1	.500	13	2	1	0	0	32^2	23	3	16	12	10.7	3.31	142	.205	.305	1	.143	-1	5	5	-0	0.4
1951	Det-A	2	2	.500	26	1	0	0	0	45^1	58	3	27	16	17.1	6.95	60	.314	.404	0	.000	-1	-14	-14	1	-1.4
Total	10	108	82	.568	314	214	94	16	7	1717	1660	108	623	690	12.0	3.50	104	.254	.320	99	.173	3	35	24	5	4.0
● **CHRIS BOSIO**	Bosio, Christopher Louis b: 4/3/63, Carmichael, Cal. BR/TR, 6'3", 235 lbs. Deb: 8/03/86																									
1986	Mil-A	0	4	.000	10	4	0	0	0	34^2	41	9	13	29	14.0	7.01	62	.293	.353	0	—	0	-11	-10	0	-1.1
1987	Mil-A	11	8	.579	46	19	2	1	2	170	187	18	50	150	12.6	5.24	87	.276	.327	0	—	0	-15	-13	1	-1.2
1988	Mil-A	7	15	.318	38	22	9	1	6	182	190	13	38	84	11.4	3.36	118	.268	.307	0	—	0	12	12	3	1.6
1989	Mil-A	15	10	.600	33	33	8	2	0	234^2	225	16	48	173	10.7	2.95	130	.249	.291	0	—	0	24	23	1	2.6
1990	Mil-A	4	9	.308	20	20	4	1	0	132^2	131	15	38	76	11.7	4.00	97	.258	.313	0	—	0	-1	-2	2	0.0
1991	Mil-A	14	10	.583	32	32	5	1	0	204^2	187	15	58	117	11.1	3.25	122	.244	.304	0	—	0	19	16	-1	1.7
1992	Mil-A	16	6	.727	33	33	4	2	0	231^1	223	21	44	120	10.5	3.62	105	.254	.293	0	—	0	8	5	0	0.7
Total	7	67	62	.519	212	163	32	8	8	1190	1184	107	289	749	11.3	3.76	106	.258	.306	0	—	0	37	32	6	4.3
● **SHAWN BOSKIE**	Boskie, Shawn Kealoha b: 3/28/67, Hawthorne, Nev. BR/TR, 6'3", 205 lbs. Deb: 5/20/90																									
1990	Chi-N	5	6	.455	15	15	1	0	0	97^2	99	8	31	49	12.1	3.69	111	.265	.323	8	.222	2	1	4	0	0.6
1991	Chi-N	4	9	.308	28	20	0	0	0	129	150	14	52	62	14.4	5.23	74	.294	.364	7	.171	2	-22	-19	1	-1.7
1992	Chi-N	5	11	.313	23	18	0	0	0	91^2	96	14	36	39	13.4	5.01	72	.284	.360	5	.185	1	-15	-14	1	-1.2
Total	3	14	26	.350	66	53	1	0	0	318^1	345	36	119	150	13.4	4.69	82	.282	.351	20	.192	4	-36	-29	2	-2.3
● **DICK BOSMAN**	Bosman, Richard Allen b: 2/17/44, Kenosha, Wis. BR/TR, 6'3", 208 lbs. Deb: 6/01/66 C																									
1966	Was-A	2	6	.250	13	7	0	0	0	39	60	4	12	20	16.6	7.62	45	.361	.404	3	.250	0	-18	-18	-1	-1.8
1967	Was-A	3	1	.750	7	7	2	1	0	51^1	38	3	10	25	8.4	1.75	180	.204	.245	3	.200	0	8	8	-1	1.0
1968	Was-A	2	9	.182	46	10	0	0	1	139	139	9	35	63	11.5	3.69	79	.262	.312	6	.200	1	-11	-12	-0	-1.2
1969	Was-A	14	5	.737	31	26	5	2	1	193	156	11	39	99	9.2	**2.19**	**158**	.220	.262	6	.094	-1	31	27	1	3.0
1970	Was-A	16	12	.571	36	34	7	3	0	230^2	212	16	71	134	11.1	3.00	118	.245	.304	11	.138	-2	18	14	0	1.3
1971	Was-A	12	16	.429	35	35	7	1	0	236^2	245	29	71	113	12.2	3.73	89	.272	.329	7	.093	-1	-7	-11	-2	-1.5
1972	Tex-A	8	10	.444	29	29	1	1	0	173^1	183	11	48	105	12.3	3.63	83	.273	.327	5	.094	-2	-11	-12	1	-1.4
1973	Tex-A	2	5	.286	7	7	1	1	0	40^1	42	6	17	14	13.4	4.24	88	.268	.343	0	—	0	-2	-2	-0	-0.3
	Cle-A	1	8	.111	22	17	2	0	0	97	130	19	29	41	15.3	6.22	63	.320	.374	0	—	0	-26	-25	-1	-2.5
	Yr	3	13	.188	29	24	3	1	0	137^1	172	25	46	55	14.7	5.64	69	.304	.363	0	—	0	-28	-27	-1	-2.8
1974	Cle-A	7	5	.583	25	18	2	1	0	127^1	126	13	29	56	11.0	4.10	88	.255	.298	0	—	0	-7	-7	-2	-0.9
1975	Cle-A	0	2	.000	6	3	0	0	0	28^2	33	3	8	11	13.8	4.08	93	.292	.355	0	—	0	-1	-1	-0	-0.1
	*Oak-A	11	4	.733	22	21	2	0	0	122^2	112	12	24	42	10.2	3.52	103	.240	.281	0	—	0	3	1	-1	0.1
	Yr	11	6	.647	28	24	2	0	0	151^1	145	15	32	53	10.7	3.63	101	.248	.290	0	—	0	3	0	-1	0.0
1976	Oak-A	4	2	.667	27	15	0	0	0	112	118	13	19	34	11.1	4.10	82	.274	.306	0	—	0	-7	-9	0	-0.9
Total	11	82	85	.491	306	229	29	10	2	1591	1594	149	412	757	11.5	3.67	93	.261	.312	41	.125	-4	-29	-46	-5	-5.2
● **MEL BOSSER**	Bosser, Melvin Edward b: 2/8/20, Johnstown, Pa. BR/TR, 6', 173 lbs. Deb: 4/29/45																									
1945	Cin-N	2	0	1.000	7	2	0	0	0	16	9	0	17	3	14.6	3.38	111	.158	.351	0	.000	-1	1	1	-0	0.0
● **ANDY BOSWELL**	Boswell, Andrew Cottrell b: 9/5/1874, New Gretna, N.J. d: 2/3/36, Ocean City, N.J. 6'1", 165 lbs. Deb: 5/10/1895																									
1895	NY-N	2	2	.500	5	4	3	0	0	34	41	1	22	18	17.5	5.82	80	.294	.401	3	.188	-1	-4	-4	-1	-0.5
	Was-N	1	2	.333	6	3	3	0	0	30	44	1	19	12	19.5	6.00	80	.336	.428	4	.286	0	-4	-4	-0	-0.3
	Yr	3	4	.429	11	7	6	0	0	64	85	2	41	30	18.0	5.91	80	.311	.404	7	.233	-1	-8	-8	-1	-0.8
● **DAVE BOSWELL**	Boswell, David Wilson b: 1/20/45, Baltimore, Md. BR/TR, 6'3", 185 lbs. Deb: 9/18/64																									
1964	Min-A	2	0	1.000	4	4	0	0	0	23^1	21	4	12	25	12.7	4.24	84	.236	.327	2	.222	0	-2	-2	1	-0.1
1965	*Min-A	6	5	.545	27	12	1	0	0	106	77	20	46	85	10.9	3.40	105	.204	.298	12	.316	4	1	2	-1	0.5
1966	Min-A	12	5	.706	28	21	8	1	0	169^1	120	19	65	173	10.1	3.14	115	.197	.280	9	.143	-1	6	9	1	0.9
1967	Min-A	14	12	.538	37	32	11	3	0	222^2	162	14	107	204	11.2	3.27	106	.202	.302	16	.219	4	-1	5	-1	0.8
1968	Min-A	10	13	.435	34	28	7	2	0	190	148	19	87	143	11.5	3.32	93	.213	.307	14	.233	5	-7	-5	-2	-0.2
1969	*Min-A	20	12	.625	39	38	10	0	0	256^1	215	18	99	190	11.3	3.23	113	.226	.304	16	.170	3	11	12	-2	1.3
1970	Min-A	3	7	.300	18	15	0	0	0	68^2	80	12	44	45	16.5	6.42	58	.292	.394	4	.160	-0	-21	-21	-1	-2.1
1971	Det-A	0	0	—	3	0	0	0	0	4^1	3	0	6	3	18.7	6.23	58	.200	.429	0	—	0	-1	-1	0	-0.1
	Bal-A	1	2	.333	15	1	0	0	0	24^2	32	4	15	14	17.1	4.38	77	.305	.392	1	.200	0	-3	-3	0	-0.3
	Yr	1	2	.333	18	1	0	0	0	29	35	4	21	17	17.4	4.66	73	.289	.394	1	.200	0	-4	-4	0	-0.4
Total	8	68	56	.548	205	151	37	6	0	1065^1	858	110	481	882	11.6	3.52	99	.219	.310	74	.202	14	-17	-4	-4	0.7
● **DEREK BOTELHO**	Botelho, Derek Wayne b: 8/2/56, Long Beach, Cal. BR/TR, 6'2", 180 lbs. Deb: 7/18/82																									
1982	KC-A	2	1	.667	8	4	0	0	0	24	25	4	8	12	12.4	4.13	99	.275	.333	0	—	0	-0	-0	-0	0.0
1985	Chi-N	1	3	.250	11	7	1	0	0	44	52	8	23	23	15.8	5.32	75	.299	.387	2	.143	-0	-8	-6	-0	-0.7
Total	2	3	4	.429	19	11	1	0	0	68	77	12	31	35	14.6	4.90	82	.291	.369	2	.143	-0	-9	-7	-1	-0.7
● **KENT BOTTENFIELD**	Bottenfield, Kent Dennis b: 11/14/68, Portland, Ore. BB/TR, 6'3", 225 lbs. Deb: 7/06/92																									
1992	Mon-N	1	2	.333	10	4	0	0	1	32^1	26	1	11	14	10.6	2.23	157	.217	.288	3	.375	1	5	5	-1	0.5
● **RALPH BOTTING**	Botting, Ralph Wayne b: 5/12/55, Houlton, Maine BL/TL, 6', 195 lbs. Deb: 6/28/79																									
1979	Cal-A	2	0	1.000	12	1	0	0	0	29^2	46	6	15	22	18.8	8.80	46	.362	.434	0	—	0	-15	-16	-0	-1.4
1980	Cal-A	0	3	.000	6	6	0	0	0	26^1	40	1	13	12	18.1	5.81	68	.348	.414	0	—	0	-5	-6	-0	-0.5
Total	2	2	3	.400	18	7	0	0	0	56	86	7	28	34	18.5	7.39	54	.355	.424	0	—	0	-20	-21	-0	-1.9
● **BOB BOTZ**	Botz, Robert Allen b: 4/28/35, Milwaukee, Wis. BR/TR, 5'11", 170 lbs. Deb: 5/08/62																									
1962	LA-A	2	1	.667	35	0	0	0	2	63	71	7	11	24	12.0	3.43	113	.285	.321	0	.000	-1	4	3	-1	0.1
● **DENIS BOUCHER**	Boucher, Denis b: 3/7/68, Montreal, Que., Can. BR/TL, 6'1", 195 lbs. Deb: 4/12/91																									
1991	Tor-A	0	3	.000	7	7	0	0	0	35^1	39	6	16	16	14.5	4.58	92	.279	.361	0	—	0	-2	-1	1	-0.2
	Cle-A	1	4	.200	5	5	0	0	0	22^2	35	6	8	13	17.1	8.34	50	.350	.398	0	—	0	-11	-11	0	-0.9
	Yr	1	7	.125	12	12	0	0	0	58	74	12	24	29	15.2	6.05	69	.305	.367	0	—	0	-13	-12	1	-1.1
1992	Cle-A	2	2	.500	8	7	0	0	0	41	48	9	20	17	15.1	6.37	63	.302	.383	0	—	0	-11	-11	-1	-1.1
Total	2	3	9	.250	20	19	0	0	0	99	122	21	44	46	15.4	6.18	67	.306	.379	0	—	0	-24	-23	0	-2.2
● **CARL BOULDIN**	Bouldin, Carl Edward b: 9/17/39, Germantown, Ky. BB/TR, 6'2", 180 lbs. Deb: 9/02/61																									
1961	Was-A	0	1	.000	2	1	0	0	0	3^1	9	0	2	2	29.7	16.20	25	.500	.550	0	.000	-0	-5	-5	0	-0.4
1962	Was-A	1	2	.333	6	3	1	0	0	20	26	0	9	12	16.2	5.85	69	.321	.396	0	.000	-1	-4	-4	-0	-0.5
1963	Was-A	2	2	.500	10	3	0	0	0	23^1	31	3	8	10	15.0	5.79	64	.307	.358	0	.000	-1	-6	-5	0	-0.6
1964	Was-A	0	3	.000	9	3	0	0	0	25	30	2	11	12	15.5	5.40	69	.294	.374	0	.000	-0	-5	-5	-0	-0.6
Total	4	3	8	.273	27	10	1	0	0	71^2	96	5	30	36	16.2	6.15	62	.318	.385	0	.000	-2	-19	-19	0	-2.1
● **JAKE BOULTES**	Boultes, Jacob John b: 8/6/1884, St.Louis, Mo. d: 12/24/55, St.Louis, Mo. TR , 6'3", Deb: 4/18/07																									
1907	Bos-N	5	9	.357	24	12	11	0	0	139^2	140	1	50	49	12.8	2.71	94	.266	.338	9	.132	-2	-4	-2	4	0.0

YEAR TM/L	W	L	PCT	G	GS	CG	SH	SV	IP	H	HR	BB	SO	RAT	ERA	ERA+	OAV	OOB	BH	AVG	PB	PR	/A	PD	TPI
1908 Bos-N	3	5	.375	17	5	1	0	0	74^2	80	7	8	28	10.7	3.01	80	.274	.296	3	.143	-1	-5	-5	-0	-0.7
1909 Bos-N	0	0	—	1	0	0	0	0	8	9	2	0	1	11.3	6.75	42	.290	.313	1	.333	0	-4	-3	-0	-0.3
Total 3	8	14	.364	42	17	12	0	0	222^1	229	10	58	78	12.0	2.96	85	.269	.324	13	.141	-2	-13	-11	4	-1.0

● JIM BOUTON

Bouton, James Alan b: 3/8/39, Newark, N.J. BR/TR, 6', 185 lbs. Deb: 4/22/62

YEAR TM/L	W	L	PCT	G	GS	CG	SH	SV	IP	H	HR	BB	SO	RAT	ERA	ERA+	OAV	OOB	BH	AVG	PB	PR	/A	PD	TPI
1962 NY-A	7	7	.500	36	16	3	1	2	133	124	9	59	71	12.4	3.99	94	.254	.334	2	.063	-2	-0	-4	0	-0.5
1963 *NY-A★	21	7	.750	40	30	12	6	1	249^1	191	18	87	148	10.1	2.53	139	.212	.284	6	.072	-6	31	27	-1	2.2
1964 *NY-A	18	13	.581	38	37	11	4	0	271^1	227	32	60	125	9.7	3.02	120	.225	.273	13	.130	-3	18	18	-3	1.3
1965 NY-A	4	15	.211	30	25	2	0	0	151^1	158	23	60	97	13.3	4.82	71	.269	.342	4	.093	-0	-23	-24	-0	-2.5
1966 NY-A	3	8	.273	24	19	3	0	1	120^1	117	13	38	65	11.7	2.69	123	.257	.315	4	.105	-1	10	8	1	0.9
1967 NY-A	1	0	1.000	17	1	0	0	0	44^1	47	5	18	31	13.4	4.67	67	.275	.347	0	.000	-0	-7	-8	0	-0.9
1968 NY-A	1	1	.500	12	3	1	0	0	44	49	5	9	24	12.3	3.68	79	.287	.330	0	.000	-0	-3	-4	1	-0.3
1969 Sea-A	2	1	.667	57	1	0	0	1	92	77	12	38	68	11.4	3.91	93	.219	.299	0	.000	-1	-3	-3	1	-0.3
Hou-N	0	2	.000	16	1	1	0	1	30^2	32	1	12	32	13.5	4.11	86	.267	.343	0	.000	-0	-2	-2	0	-0.2
1970 Hou-N	4	6	.400	29	6	1	0	0	73^1	84	5	33	49	14.5	5.40	72	.285	.359	6	.353	2	-11	-12	-0	-1.0
1978 Atl-N	1	3	.250	5	5	0	0	0	29	25	4	21	10	14.3	4.97	82	.234	.359	0	.000	-1	-4	-3	-0	-0.4
Total 10	62	63	.496	304	144	34	11	6	1238^2	1131	127	435	720	11.5	3.57	99	.243	.311	35	.101	-13	5	-5	-1	-1.7

● RYAN BOWEN

Bowen, Ryan Eugene b: 2/10/68, Hanford, Cal. BR/TR, 6', 185 lbs. Deb: 7/22/91

YEAR TM/L	W	L	PCT	G	GS	CG	SH	SV	IP	H	HR	BB	SO	RAT	ERA	ERA+	OAV	OOB	BH	AVG	PB	PR	/A	PD	TPI
1991 Hou-N	6	4	.600	14	13	0	0	0	71^2	73	4	36	49	14.1	5.15	68	.268	.360	4	.182	1	-12	-13	-2	-1.3
1992 Hou-N	0	7	.000	11	9	0	0	0	33^2	48	8	30	22	21.4	10.96	30	.333	.455	1	.111	-0	-28	-28	-1	-2.8
Total 2	6	11	.353	25	22	0	0	0	105^1	121	12	66	71	16.4	7.01	49	.291	.394	5	.161	1	-40	-42	-2	-4.1

● CY BOWEN

Bowen, Sutherland McCoy b: 2/17/1871, Kingston, Ind. d: 1/25/25, Greensburg, Ind. BR/TR, 6', 175 lbs. Deb: 4/28/1896

YEAR TM/L	W	L	PCT	G	GS	CG	SH	SV	IP	H	HR	BB	SO	RAT	ERA	ERA+	OAV	OOB	BH	AVG	PB	PR	/A	PD	TPI
1896 NY-N	0	1	.000	2	1	1	0	0	12	12	0	9	3	18.0	6.00	70	.258	.411	1	.333	0	-2	-2	0	-0.1

● FRANK BOWERMAN

Bowerman, Frank Eugene "Mike" b: 12/5/1868, Romeo, Mich. d: 11/30/48, Romeo, Mich. BR/TR, 6'2", 190 lbs. Deb: 8/24/1895 M♦

YEAR TM/L	W	L	PCT	G	GS	CG	SH	SV	IP	H	HR	BB	SO	RAT	ERA	ERA+	OAV	OOB	BH	AVG	PB	PR	/A	PD	TPI
1904 NY-N	0	0	—	1	0	0	0	0	1	3	0	1	0	36.0	9.00	30	.429	.500	67	.232	0	-1	-1	-0	-0.1

● STEW BOWERS

Bowers, Stewart Cole "Doc" b: 2/26/15, New Freedom, Pa. BB/TR, 6', 170 lbs. Deb: 8/05/35 ♦

YEAR TM/L	W	L	PCT	G	GS	CG	SH	SV	IP	H	HR	BB	SO	RAT	ERA	ERA+	OAV	OOB	BH	AVG	PB	PR	/A	PD	TPI
1935 Bos-A	2	1	.667	10	2	1	0	0	23^2	26	1	17	5	16.4	3.42	139	.283	.394	1	.200	0	3	3	0	0.4
1936 Bos-A	0	0	—	5	0	0	0	0	5^2	10	1	2	0	19.1	9.53	56	.370	.414	0	—	0	-3	-3	-0	-0.3
Total 2	2	1	.667	15	2	1	0	0	29^1	36	2	19	5	16.9	4.60	106	.303	.399	1	.200	0	-0	1	-0	0.1

● GRANT BOWLER

Bowler, Grant Tierney "Moose" b: 10/24/07, Denver, Col. d: 6/25/68, Denver, Colo. BR/TR, 6', 190 lbs. Deb: 8/21/31

YEAR TM/L	W	L	PCT	G	GS	CG	SH	SV	IP	H	HR	BB	SO	RAT	ERA	ERA+	OAV	OOB	BH	AVG	PB	PR	/A	PD	TPI
1931 Chi-A	0	1	.000	13	3	1	0	0	35^1	40	1	24	15	16.3	5.35	80	.288	.393	1	.100	-0	-4	-4	-1	-0.5
1932 Chi-A	0	0	—	4	0	0	0	0	6^1	15	1	3	2	25.6	15.63	28	.484	.529	0	.000	-0	-8	-8	0	-0.7
Total 2	0	1	.000	17	3	1	0	0	41^2	55	2	27	17	17.7	6.91	62	.324	.416	1	.083	-1	-12	-12	-1	-1.2

● CHARLIE BOWLES

Bowles, Charles James b: 3/15/17, Norwood, Mass. BR/TR, 6'3", 180 lbs. Deb: 9/25/43

YEAR TM/L	W	L	PCT	G	GS	CG	SH	SV	IP	H	HR	BB	SO	RAT	ERA	ERA+	OAV	OOB	BH	AVG	PB	PR	/A	PD	TPI
1943 Phi-A	1	1	.500	2	2	2	0	0	18	17	0	4	6	10.5	3.00	113	.258	.300	1	.125	-1	1	1	0	0.0
1945 Phi-A	0	3	.000	8	4	1	0	0	33^1	35	3	23	11	15.7	5.13	67	.273	.384	5	.238	0	-7	-6	0	-0.6
Total 2	1	4	.200	10	6	3	0	0	51^1	52	3	27	17	13.9	4.38	78	.268	.357	6	.207	-0	-6	-5	0	-0.6

● EMMETT BOWLES

Bowles, Emmett Jerome "Chief" b: 8/2/1898, Wanette, Okla. d: 9/3/59, Flagstaff, Ariz. BR/TR, 6', 180 lbs. Deb: 9/12/22

YEAR TM/L	W	L	PCT	G	GS	CG	SH	SV	IP	H	HR	BB	SO	RAT	ERA	ERA+	OAV	OOB	BH	AVG	PB	PR	/A	PD	TPI
1922 Chi-A	0	0	—	1	0	0	0	0	1	2	0	1	0	27.0	27.00	15	.500	.600	0	—	0	-3	-3	-0	-0.2

● ABE BOWMAN

Bowman, Alvah Edson b: 1/25/1893, Greenup, Ill. d: 10/11/79, Longview, Tex. BR/TR, 6'1", 190 lbs. Deb: 5/19/14

YEAR TM/L	W	L	PCT	G	GS	CG	SH	SV	IP	H	HR	BB	SO	RAT	ERA	ERA+	OAV	OOB	BH	AVG	PB	PR	/A	PD	TPI
1914 Cle-A	2	7	.222	22	10	2	1	0	72^2	74	0	45	27	15.2	4.46	65	.277	.389	1	.048	-2	-14	-13	-0	-1.6
1915 Cle-A	0	1	.000	2	1	0	0	0	1^1	1	0	3	0	27.0	20.25	15	.250	.571	0	—	0	-3	-3	1	-0.2
Total 2	2	8	.200	24	11	2	1	0	74	75	0	48	27	15.4	4.74	61	.277	.393	1	.048	-2	-16	-15	0	-1.8

● JOE BOWMAN

Bowman, Joseph Emil b: 6/17/10, Kansas City, Kan. d: 11/22/90, Kansas City, Mo. BL/TR, 6'2", 190 lbs. Deb: 4/18/32 ♦

YEAR TM/L	W	L	PCT	G	GS	CG	SH	SV	IP	H	HR	BB	SO	RAT	ERA	ERA+	OAV	OOB	BH	AVG	PB	PR	/A	PD	TPI
1932 Phi-A	0	1	.000	7	0	0	0	0	11	14	2	6	4	18.8	8.18	55	.318	.434	1	1.000	0	-5	-4	1	-0.3
1934 NY-N	5	4	.556	30	10	3	0	3	107^1	119	9	36	36	13.2	3.61	107	.279	.338	5	.172	0	5	3	-0	0.3
1935 Phi-N	7	10	.412	33	17	6	1	1	148^1	157	13	56	58	13.2	4.25	107	.269	.337	13	.194	0	-4	5	-0	0.5
1936 Phi-N	9	20	.310	40	28	12	0	1	203^2	243	14	53	80	13.4	5.04	90	.289	.336	15	.195	-1	-23	-11	-2	-1.4
1937 Pit-N	8	8	.500	30	19	7	0	1	128	161	11	35	38	13.9	4.57	85	.306	.351	10	.213	1	-9	-10	0	-0.8
1938 Pit-N	3	4	.429	17	1	0	0	1	60	68	2	20	25	13.2	4.65	82	.285	.340	7	.333	2	-6	-6	-1	-0.4
1939 Pit-N	10	14	.417	37	27	10	1	1	184^2	217	15	43	58	13.0	4.48	86	.292	.336	33	.344	12	-12	-13	0	-0.1
1940 Pit-N	9	10	.474	32	24	10	0	2	187^2	209	10	66	57	13.5	4.46	85	.274	.337	22	.244	9	-13	-14	0	-0.4
1941 Pit-N	3	2	.600	18	7	1	1	1	69^1	77	3	28	22	13.8	2.99	121	.278	.346	8	.258	1	5	5	-0	0.6
1944 Bos-A	12	8	.600	26	24	10	1	0	168^1	175	14	64	53	12.9	4.81	71	.269	.336	20	.200	3	-26	-26	-2	-2.5
1945 Bos-A	0	2	.000	3	3	0	0	0	11^2	18	1	9	0	20.8	9.26	37	.360	.458	2	.222	0	-8	-8	-0	-0.7
Cin-N	11	13	.458	25	24	15	1	0	185^2	198	8	68	71	13.2	3.59	105	.270	.338	5	.070	-5	4	4	-2	-0.3
Total 11	77	96	.445	298	184	74	5	11	1465^2	1656	102	484	502	13.4	4.40	89	.282	.341	141	.221	24	-89	-77	-7	-5.5

● BOB BOWMAN

Bowman, Robert James b: 10/3/10, Keystone, W.Va. d: 9/4/72, Bluefield, W.Va. BR/TR, 5'10.5", 160 lbs. Deb: 4/21/39

YEAR TM/L	W	L	PCT	G	GS	CG	SH	SV	IP	H	HR	BB	SO	RAT	ERA	ERA+	OAV	OOB	BH	AVG	PB	PR	/A	PD	TPI
1939 StL-N	13	5	.722	51	15	4	2	**9**	169^1	141	8	60	78	10.7	2.60	158	.232	.302	4	.085	-3	25	28	-1	2.5
1940 StL-N	7	5	.583	28	17	7	0	0	114^1	118	9	43	43	13.0	4.33	92	.267	.337	2	.061	-2	-6	-4	-0	-0.7
1941 NY-N	6	7	.462	29	6	2	0	1	80^1	100	10	36	25	15.3	5.71	65	.302	.372	1	.048	-1	-19	-18	1	-1.8
1942 Chi-N	0	0	—	1	0	0	0	0	1	1	0	0	0	9.0	0.00	—	.250	.250	0	—	0	0	0	-0	0.0
Total 4	26	17	.605	109	38	13	2	10	365	360	27	139	146	12.5	3.82	104	.260	.330	7	.069	-6	0	6	-1	0.0

● BOB BOWMAN

Bowman, Robert Leroy b: 5/10/31, Laytonville, Cal. BR/TR, 6'1", 195 lbs. Deb: 4/16/55 ♦

YEAR TM/L	W	L	PCT	G	GS	CG	SH	SV	IP	H	HR	BB	SO	RAT	ERA	ERA+	OAV	OOB	BH	AVG	PB	PR	/A	PD	TPI
1959 Phi-N	0	1	.000	5	0	0	0	0	6	5	1	5	0	15.0	6.00	68	.227	.370	10	.127	-0	-1	-1	0	-0.1

● ROGER BOWMAN

Bowman, Roger Clinton b: 8/18/27, Amsterdam, N.Y. BR/TL, 6', 175 lbs. Deb: 9/22/49

YEAR TM/L	W	L	PCT	G	GS	CG	SH	SV	IP	H	HR	BB	SO	RAT	ERA	ERA+	OAV	OOB	BH	AVG	PB	PR	/A	PD	TPI
1949 NY-N	0	0	—	2	2	0	0	0	6^1	6	1	7	4	18.5	4.26	93	.261	.433	0	.000	-0	-0	-0	1	0.0
1951 NY-N	2	4	.333	9	5	0	0	0	26^1	35	2	22	24	19.8	6.15	64	.297	.411	0	.000	-0	-6	-7	-1	-0.7
1952 NY-N	0	0	—	2	1	0	0	0	3	6	0	3	3	30.0	12.00	31	.429	.556	0	.000	-0	-3	-3	-0	-0.3
1953 Pit-N	0	4	.000	30	2	0	0	0	65^1	65	9	29	36	13.1	4.82	93	.261	.341	2	.286	1	-4	-3	0	-0.2
1955 Pit-N	0	3	.000	7	2	0	0	0	16^2	25	2	10	8	19.4	8.64	48	.347	.434	1	.500	0	-9	-8	0	-0.7
Total 5	2	11	.154	50	12	0	0	0	117^2	137	14	71	75	16.2	5.81	73	.288	.385	3	.167	0	-22	-20	1	-1.9

● SUMNER BOWMAN

Bowman, Sumner Sallade b: 2/9/1867, Millersburg, Pa. d: 1/11/54, Millersburg, Pa. BL/TL, 6', 160 lbs. Deb: 6/11/1890

YEAR TM/L	W	L	PCT	G	GS	CG	SH	SV	IP	H	HR	BB	SO	RAT	ERA	ERA+	OAV	OOB	BH	AVG	PB	PR	/A	PD	TPI
1890 Phi-N	0	0	—	1	1	0	0	0	8	11	0	2	2	15.8	7.88	46	.317	.371	2	.500	1	-4	-4	-0	-0.3
Pit-N	2	5	.286	9	7	6	0	0	70^2	100	1	50	22	20.5	6.62	50	.323	.435	10	.278	2	-24	-26	-0	-1.9
Yr	2	5	.286	10	8	6	0	0	78^2	111	1	52	24	19.9	6.75	49	.322	.426	12	.300	2	-28	-30	-0	-2.2
1891 Phi-a	2	5	.286	8	8	8	0	0	68	73	0	37	22	15.2	3.44	111	.265	.362	13	.241	0	2	3	-1	0.2
Total 2	4	10	.286	18	16	14	0	0	146^2	184	1	89	46	17.8	5.22	68	.297	.400	25	.266	3	-26	-27	-1	-2.0

● TED BOWSFIELD

Bowsfield, Edward Oliver b: 1/10/35, Vernon, B.C., Canada BR/TL, 6'1", 190 lbs. Deb: 7/20/58

YEAR TM/L	W	L	PCT	G	GS	CG	SH	SV	IP	H	HR	BB	SO	RAT	ERA	ERA+	OAV	OOB	BH	AVG	PB	PR	/A	PD	TPI
1958 Bos-A	4	2	.667	16	10	2	0	0	65^2	58	3	36	38	13.0	3.84	104	.233	.332	4	.154	-1	-1	1	1	0.1
1959 Bos-A	0	1	.000	5	2	0	0	0	9	16	2	9	4	25.0	15.00	27	.390	.500	0	.000	-0	-11	-11	-0	-1.0
1960 Bos-A	1	2	.333	17	2	0	0	2	21	20	1	13	18	14.6	5.14	79	.260	.374	1	.250	0	-3	-3	1	-0.2

YEAR	TM/L	W	L	PCT	G	GS	CG	SH	SV	IP	H	HR	BB	SO	RAT	ERA	ERA+	OAV	OOB	BH	AVG	PB	PR	/A	PD	TPI
	Cle-A	3	4	.429	11	6	1	1	0	40^2	47	1	20	14	14.8	5.09	73	.296	.374	1	.100	-0	-5	-6	1	-0.6
	Yr	4	6	.400	28	8	1	1	2	61^2	67	2	33	32	14.6	5.11	75	.280	.368	2	.143	-0	-8	-9	1	-0.8
1961	LA-A	11	8	.579	41	21	4	1	0	157	154	18	63	88	12.5	3.73	121	.255	.327	7	.137	-1	5	14	-1	1.1
1962	LA-A	9	8	.529	34	25	1	0	1	139	154	12	40	52	12.7	4.40	88	.277	.328	6	.162	1	-7	-8	-3	-1.0
1963	KC-A	5	7	.417	41	11	2	1	3	111^1	115	14	47	67	13.3	4.45	86	.269	.345	1	.043	-1	-10	-7	2	-0.7
1964	KC-A	4	7	.364	50	9	2	1	0	118^2	135	12	31	45	12.9	4.10	93	.285	.334	2	.095	-1	-6	-4	0	-0.5
Total	7	37	39	.487	215	86	12	4	6	662^1	699	63	259	326	13.2	4.35	92	.270	.339	22	.127	-4	-38	-24	1	-2.8
● **OIL CAN BOYD** Boyd, Dennis Ray b: 10/6/59, Meridian, Miss. BR/TR, 6'1", 155 lbs. Deb: 9/13/82																										
1982	Bos-A	0	1	.000	3	1	0	0	0	8^1	11	2	2	2	14.0	5.40	80	.314	.351	0	—	0	-1	-1	-0	-0.1
1983	Bos-A	4	8	.333	15	13	5	0	0	98^2	103	9	23	43	11.6	3.28	132	.269	.312	0	—	0	9	12	-1	0.7
1984	Bos-A	12	12	.500	29	26	10	3	0	197^2	207	18	53	134	11.9	4.37	95	.269	.317	0	—	0	-8	-5	2	-0.3
1985	Bos-A	15	13	.536	35	35	13	3	0	272^1	273	26	67	154	11.4	3.70	116	.261	.308	0	—	0	13	18	3	2.0
1986	*Bos-A	16	10	.615	30	30	10	0	0	214^1	222	32	45	129	11.3	3.78	110	.265	.304	0	—	0	9	9	1	1.0
1987	Bos-A	1	3	.250	7	7	0	0	0	36^2	47	6	9	12	14.2	5.89	77	.315	.363	0	—	0	-6	-6	1	-0.5
1988	Bos-A	9	7	.563	23	23	1	0	0	129^2	147	25	41	71	13.2	5.34	77	.289	.344	0	—	0	-20	-18	-1	-1.9
1989	Bos-A	3	2	.600	10	10	0	0	0	59	57	8	19	26	11.6	4.42	93	.253	.311	0	—	0	-4	-2	1	-0.3
1990	Mon-N	10	6	.625	31	31	3	3	0	190^2	164	19	52	113	10.3	2.93	125	.233	.289	3	.051	-4	18	15	-1	1.0
1991	Mon-N	6	8	.429	19	19	1	1	0	120^1	115	9	40	82	11.6	3.52	103	.256	.316	3	.083	-1	2	1	-1	-0.1
	Tex-A	2	7	.222	12	12	0	0	0	62	81	12	17	33	14.2	6.68	60	.314	.356	0	—	0	-18	-18	-1	-1.7
Total	10	78	77	.503	214	207	43	10	0	1389^2	1427	166	368	799	11.7	4.04	101	.266	.315	6	.063	-5	-5	5	3	-0.2
● **JAKE BOYD** Boyd, Jacob Henry b: 1/19/1874, Martinsburg, W.Va. d: 8/12/32, Gettysburg, Pa. TL , 160 lbs. Deb: 9/20/1894 ♦																										
1894	Was-N	0	3	.000	3	3	3	0	0	19	37	1	14	3	24.6	8.53	62	.403	.487	3	.143	-1	-7	-7	0	-0.5
1895	Was-N	2	11	.154	14	12	8	0	0	85^1	126	1	35	16	18.0	7.07	68	.337	.409	42	.268	1	-22	-21	1	-1.5
1896	Was-N	1	2	.333	4	2	2	0	0	32	45	0	15	6	18.6	6.75	65	.329	.418	1	.077	-2	-8	-8	0	-0.7
Total	3	3	16	.158	21	17	13	0	0	136^1	208	2	64	25	19.1	7.20	66	.346	.423	46	.241	-2	-37	-37	2	-2.7
● **GARY BOYD** Boyd, Gary Lee b: 8/22/46, Pasadena, Cal. BR/TR, 6'4", 200 lbs. Deb: 8/01/69																										
1969	Cle-A	0	2	.000	8	3	0	0	0	11	8	1	14	9	18.0	9.00	42	.205	.415	0	.000	-0	-7	-6	-0	-0.7
● **RAY BOYD** Boyd, Raymond C. b: 2/11/1887, Hortonville, Ind. d: 2/11/20, Hortonville, Ind. BR/TR, 5'10", 160 lbs. Deb: 9/24/10																										
1910	StL-A	0	2	.000	3	2	1	0	0	14^1	16	0	5	6	13.8	4.40	56	.286	.355	1	.200	-0	-3	-3	-1	-0.4
1911	Cin-N	2	2	.500	7	4	3	0	1	44	34	0	19	20	11.3	2.66	124	.206	.296	1	.083	-0	4	3	-0	0.3
Total	2	2	4	.333	10	6	4	0	1	58^1	50	0	24	26	11.9	3.09	101	.226	.310	2	.118	-0	1	0	-1	-0.1
● **BILL BOYD** Boyd, William J. b: 12/22/1852, New York, N.Y. d: 9/30/12, Jamaica, N.Y. Deb: 4/22/1872 MU♦																										
1875	Atl-n	0	0	—	1	0	0	0	0	1^2	4	0	0		21.6	*5.40*	43	.444	.444	44	.297	0	-1	-1		0.0
● **CLOYD BOYER** Boyer, Cloyd Victor "Junior" b: 9/1/27, Alba, Mo. BR/TR, 6'1", 188 lbs. Deb: 4/23/49 FC																										
1949	StL-N	0	0	—	4	1	0	0	0	3^1	5	0	7	0	32.4	10.80	39	.357	.571	0	—	0	-3	-2	0	-0.2
1950	StL-N	7	7	.500	36	14	6	1	1	120^1	105	15	49	82	11.7	3.52	122	.233	.312	6	.182	0	8	10	0	1.1
1951	StL-N	2	5	.286	19	8	1	0	1	63^1	68	9	46	40	16.6	5.26	75	.286	.408	4	.200	0	-9	-9	-2	-1.0
1952	StL-N	6	6	.500	23	14	4	2	0	110^1	108	11	47	44	13.0	4.24	88	.258	.338	8	.211	2	-6	-6	-2	-0.7
1955	KC-A	5	5	.500	30	11	2	0	0	98^1	107	21	69	32	16.7	6.22	67	.282	.402	2	.069	-2	-25	-22	-1	-2.4
Total	5	20	23	.465	112	48	13	3	2	395^2	393	56	218	198	14.3	4.73	86	.262	.362	20	.167	0	-34	-30	-4	-3.2
● **HENRY BOYLE** Boyle, Henry J. "Handsome Henry" b: 9/20/1860, Philadelphia, Pa. d: 5/25/32, Philadelphia, Pa. TR , Deb: 7/09/1884 ♦																										
1884	StL-U	15	3	.833	19	16	16	2	1	150	118	3	10	88	7.7	1.74	170	.202	.215	68	.260	3	21	20	-1	1.9
1885	StL-N	16	24	.400	42	39	39	1	0	366^2	346	2	100	133	10.9	2.75	100	.239	.288	52	.202	1	3	-0	-1	0.0
1886	StL-N	9	15	.375	25	24	23	2	0	210	183	5	46	101	9.8	**1.76**	**184**	.220	.261	27	.250	4	36	34	1	3.8
1887	Ind-N	13	24	.351	38	38	37	0	0	328	356	11	69	85	12.0	3.65	114	.265	.307	27	.191	-1	15	18	-4	1.2
1888	Ind-N	15	22	.405	37	37	36	3	0	323	315	11	58	98	10.7	3.26	91	.245	.283	18	.144	-3	-15	-11	3	-1.1
1889	Ind-N	21	23	.477	46	45	38	2	0	378^2	422	14	95	97	12.6	3.92	106	.273	.321	38	.245	5	4	11	-5	1.1
Total	6	89	111	.445	207	199	189	10	1	1756^1	1740	46	378	602	11.0	3.06	112	.247	.289	230	.219	8	65	71	-7	6.9
● **HARRY BOYLES** Boyles, Harry "Stretch" b: 11/29/11, Granite City, Ill. BR/TR, 6'5", 185 lbs. Deb: 8/03/38																										
1938	Chi-A	0	4	.000	9	2	1	0	1	29^1	31	2	25	18	17.8	5.22	94	.263	.400	1	.125	-1	-1	-1	1	0.0
1939	Chi-A	0	0	—	2	0	0	0	0	3^1	4	0	6	1	27.0	10.80	44	.308	.526	0	.000	-0	-2	-2	-0	-0.2
Total	2	0	4	.000	11	2	1	0	1	32^2	35	2	31	19	18.7	5.79	84	.267	.415	1	.111	-1	-4	-3	1	-0.2
● **GENE BRABENDER** Brabender, Eugene Mathew b: 8/16/41, Madison, Wis. BR/TR, 6'5.5", 225 lbs. Deb: 5/11/66																										
1966	Bal-A	4	3	.571	31	1	0	0	2	71	57	4	29	62	11.0	3.55	94	.229	.312	1	.077	-1	-1	-2	0	-0.2
1967	Bal-A	6	4	.600	14	14	3	1	0	94	77	6	23	71	9.7	3.35	94	.220	.270	2	.071	-1	-1	-2	-0	-0.4
1968	Bal-A	6	7	.462	37	15	3	2	3	125	116	9	48	92	12.0	3.31	88	.248	.322	3	.086	-0	-5	-5	-1	-0.7
1969	Sea-A	13	14	.481	40	29	7	1	0	202^1	193	26	103	139	13.7	4.36	83	.254	.353	9	.129	-1	-17	-16	-3	-2.0
1970	Mil-A	6	15	.286	29	21	2	0	1	128^2	127	8	79	76	14.5	6.02	63	.255	.359	4	.098	-2	-33	-32	-0	-3.3
Total	5	35	43	.449	151	80	15	4	6	621	570	53	282	440	12.6	4.25	80	.245	.332	19	.102	-5	-56	-58	-3	-6.6
● **JACK BRACKEN** Bracken, John James b: 4/14/1881, Cleveland, Ohio d: 7/16/54, Highland Park, Mich. BR/TR, 5'11", 175 lbs. Deb: 8/07/01																										
1901	Cle-A	4	8	.333	12	12	12	0	0	100	137	4	31	18	15.1	6.21	57	.322	.368	10	.227	0	-28	-30	-1	-2.5
● **JOHN BRACKENRIDGE** Brackenridge, John Givler b: 12/24/1880, Harrisburg, Pa. d: 3/20/53, Harrisburg, Pa. BR/TR, 6', Deb: 4/15/04																										
1904	Phi-N	0	1	.000	7	1	0	0	0	34	37	4	16	11	15.1	5.56	48	.298	.396	2	.154	-0	-11	-11	2	-0.9
● **DON BRADEY** Bradey, Donald Eugene b: 10/4/34, Charlotte, N.C. BR/TR, 5'9", 180 lbs. Deb: 9/25/64																										
1964	Hou-N	0	2	.000	3	1	0	0	0	2^1	6	0	3	2	34.7	19.29	18	.429	.529	0	—	0	-4	-4	-0	-0.4
● **LARRY BRADFORD** Bradford, Larry b: 12/21/49, Chicago, Ill. BR/TL, 6'1", 200 lbs. Deb: 9/24/77																										
1977	Atl-N	0	0	—	2	0	0	0	0	2^2	3	1	0	1	10.1	3.38	132	.273	.273	0	—	0	0	0	0	0.0
1979	Atl-N	1	0	1.000	21	0	0	0	2	19	11	0	10	11	10.4	0.95	427	.172	.293	0	.000	-0	6	7	0	0.7
1980	Atl-N	3	4	.429	56	0	0	0	4	55^1	49	3	22	32	11.7	2.44	153	.243	.320	0	.000	-0	7	8	-0	0.8
1981	Atl-N	2	0	1.000	25	0	0	0	1	26^2	26	1	12	14	12.8	3.71	96	.268	.349	1	1.000	0	-1	-0	0	0.0
Total	4	6	4	.600	104	0	0	0	7	103^2	89	5	44	58	11.7	2.52	150	.238	.321	1	.200	-0	13	14	1	1.5
● **BILL BRADFORD** Bradford, William D b: 8/28/21, Choctaw, Ark. BR/TR, 6'2", 180 lbs. Deb: 4/24/56																										
1956	KC-A	0	0	—	1	0	0	0	0	2	2	2	1	0	13.5	9.00	48	.250	.333	0	—	0	-1	-1	0	-0.1
● **FRED BRADLEY** Bradley, Fred Langdon b: 7/31/20, Parsons, Kan. BR/TR, 6'1", 180 lbs. Deb: 5/01/48																										
1948	Chi-A	0	0	—	8	0	0	0	0	15^2	11	2	4	2	9.2	4.60	93	.190	.254	0	.000	-0	-1	-1	0	-0.1
1949	Chi-A	0	0	—	1	1	0	0	0	2	4	0	3	0	31.5	13.50	31	.444	.583	0	.000	-0	-2	-2	0	-0.2
Total	2	0	0	—	9	1	0	0	0	17^2	15	2	7	2	11.7	5.60	76	.224	.307	0	.000	-0	-3	-3	0	-0.3
● **FOGHORN BRADLEY** Bradley, George H. b: 7/1/1855, Milford, Mass. d: 4/3/1900, Philadelphia, Pa. BR/TR, Deb: 8/23/1876 U																										
1876	Bos-N	9	10	.474	22	21	16	1	1	173^1	201	1	16	16	11.3	2.49	91	.263	.279	19	.232	-1	-4	-5	-1	-0.5

YEAR	TM/L	W	L	PCT	G	GS	CG	SH	SV	IP	H	HR	BB	SO	RAT	ERA	ERA+	OAV	OOB	BH	AVG	PB	PR	/A	PD	TPI
● **GEORGE BRADLEY**	Bradley, George Washington "Grin" b: 7/13/1852, Reading, Pa. d: 10/2/31, Philadelphia, Pa. BR/TR, 5'10.5", 175 lbs. Deb: 5/04/1875 ♦																									
1875	StL-n	33	26	.559	60	60	57	4	0	535^2	538	3	16		9.3	*2.05*	108	.240	.245	62	.244	7	24	10		1.5
1876	StL-N	45	19	.703	64	64	63	**16**	0	573	470	3	38	103	**8.0**	**1.23**	**174**	**.211**	**.224**	66	.249	4	**69**	58	1	5.7
1877	Chi-N	18	23	.439	50	44	35	2	0	394	452	4	39	59	11.2	3.31	90	.269	.286	52	.243	0	-22	-15	1	-1.4
1879	Tro-N	13	40	.245	54	54	53	3	0	487	590	12	26	133	11.4	2.85	88	.275	.284	62	.247	4	-19	-19	4	-0.7
1880	Pro-N	13	8	.619	28	20	16	4	1	196	158	2	6	54	**7.5**	1.38	160	.210	**.217**	70	.227	1	22	18	1	2.0
1881	Cle-N	2	4	.333	6	6	5	0	0	51	70	2	3	6	12.9	3.88	67	.320	.329	60	.249	0	-6	-7	-1	-0.6
1882	Cle-N	6	9	.400	18	16	15	0	0	147	164	5	22	32	11.4	3.73	75	.264	.289	21	.183	-3	-14	-15	3	-1.3
1883	Phi-a	16	7	.696	26	23	22	0	0	214^1	215	7	22	56	10.0	3.15	111	.244	.263	73	.234	0	4	8	-1	0.6
1884	Cin-U	25	15	.625	41	38	36	3	0	342	350	7	23	168	9.8	2.71	117	.248	.260	43	.190	-4	12	17	2	1.2
Total	8	138	125	.525	287	265	245	28	1	2404^1	2469	42	179	611	9.9	2.50	106	.248	.262	456	.228	3	45	41	11	5.5
● **HERB BRADLEY**	Bradley, Herbert Theodore b: 1/3/03, Agenda, Kan. d: 10/16/59, Clay Center, Kan. BR/TR, 6', 170 lbs. Deb: 5/09/27																									
1927	Bos-A	1	1	.500	6	2	2	0	0	23	16	0	7	6	9.8	3.13	135	.198	.278	3	.429	1	3	3	-0	0.3
1928	Bos-A	0	3	.000	15	5	1	1	0	47^1	64	2	16	14	15.6	7.23	57	.339	.396	2	.154	-1	-17	-16	1	-1.5
1929	Bos-A	0	0	—	3	0	0	0	0	4	7	1	2	0	20.3	6.75	63	.438	.500	0	.000	-0	-1	-1	0	-0.1
Total	3	1	4	.200	24	7	3	1	0	74^1	87	3	25	20	14.0	5.93	70	.304	.368	5	.238	-0	-15	-15	1	-1.3
● **BERT BRADLEY**	Bradley, Steven Bert b: 12/23/56, Athens, Ga. BB/TR, 6'1", 190 lbs. Deb: 9/03/83																									
1983	Oak-A	0	0	—	6	0	0	0	0	8^1	14	1	4	3	19.4	6.48	59	.400	.462	0	—	0	-2	-2	1	-0.1
● **TOM BRADLEY**	Bradley, Thomas William b: 3/16/47, Asheville, N.C. BR/TR, 6'3", 185 lbs. Deb: 9/09/69																									
1969	Cal-A	0	1	.000	3	0	0	0	0	2	9	1	0	2	40.5	27.00	13	.600	.600	0	—	0	-5	-5	0	-0.5
1970	Cal-A	2	5	.286	17	11	1	1	0	69^2	71	3	33	53	13.6	4.13	87	.270	.354	3	.167	0	-3	-4	-0	-0.4
1971	Chi-A	15	15	.500	45	39	7	6	2	285^2	273	16	74	206	11.0	2.96	121	.248	.297	15	.156	-1	16	20	-2	1.9
1972	Chi-A	15	14	.517	40	40	11	2	0	260	225	19	65	209	10.1	2.98	105	.231	.280	12	.132	-2	2	4	-0	0.2
1973	SF-N	13	12	.520	35	34	6	1	0	224	212	26	69	136	11.4	3.90	98	.246	.304	15	.195	1	-6	-2	-2	-0.3
1974	SF-N	8	11	.421	30	21	2	0	0	134^1	152	15	52	72	13.7	5.16	74	.282	.346	3	.075	-2	-23	-20	-1	-2.4
1975	SF-N	2	3	.400	13	6	0	0	0	42	57	6	18	13	16.3	6.21	61	.326	.392	0	.000	-1	-12	-11	0	-1.2
Total	7	55	61	.474	183	151	27	10	2	1017^2	999	86	311	691	11.7	3.72	96	.254	.311	48	.145	-5	-31	-19	-5	-2.7
● **BILL BRADLEY**	Bradley, William Joseph b: 2/13/1878, Cleveland, Ohio d: 3/11/54, Cleveland, Ohio BR/TR, 6', 185 lbs. Deb: 8/26/1899 M♦																									
1901	Cle-A	0	0	—	1	0	0	0	0	1	4	0	0	0	36.0	0.00	—	.581	.581	151	.293	0	0	0	-0	0.0
● **JOE BRADSHAW**	Bradshaw, Joe Siah b: 8/17/1897, Roellen, Tenn. d: 1/30/85, Tavares, Fla. BR/TR, 6'2.5", 200 lbs. Deb: 5/09/29																									
1929	Bro-N	0	0	—	2	0	0	0	0	4	3	0	4	1	20.3	4.50	103	.231	.474	0	—	0	0	0	0	0.0
● **NEAL BRADY**	Brady, Cornelius Joseph b: 3/4/1897, Covington, Ky. d: 6/19/47, Fort Mitchell, Ky BR/TR, 6'0.5", 197 lbs. Deb: 9/25/15																									
1915	NY-A	0	0	—	2	1	0	0	0	8^2	9	0	7	6	16.6	3.12	94	.281	.410	0	.000	-1	-0	-0	-0	-0.1
1917	NY-A	1	0	1.000	2	1	0	0	0	9	6	0	5	4	11.0	2.00	134	.188	.297	1	.500	0	1	1	0	0.2
1925	Cin-N	1	3	.250	20	3	2	0	1	63^2	73	4	20	12	13.7	4.66	88	.289	.350	6	.240	1	-3	-4	0	-0.3
Total	3	2	3	.400	24	5	2	0	1	81^1	88	4	32	22	13.7	4.20	91	.278	.351	7	.226	1	-2	-3	1	-0.2
● **JIM BRADY**	Brady, James Joseph "Diamond Jim" b: 3/2/36, Jersey City, N.J. BL/TL, 6'2", 185 lbs. Deb: 5/12/56																									
1956	Det-A	0	0	—	6	0	0	0	0	6^1	15	3	11	3	36.9	28.42	14	.484	.619	0	—	0	-17	-17	0	-1.4
● **KING BRADY**	Brady, James Ward b: 5/28/1881, Elmer, N.J. d: 8/21/47, Albany, N.Y. BR/TR, 6', 190 lbs. Deb: 9/21/05																									
1905	Phi-N	1	1	.500	2	2	2	0	0	13	19	0	2	3	14.5	3.46	84	.333	.356	1	.200	-0	-1	-1	-0	-0.1
1906	Pit-N	1	1	.500	3	2	1	0	0	23	30	0	4	14	13.3	2.35	114	.313	.340	1	.100	-1	1	1	-1	-0.1
1907	Pit-N	0	0	—	1	0	0	0	0	2	2	0	1	0	13.5	0.00	—	.286	.375	0	—	0	1	1	-0	0.0
1908	Bos-A	1	0	1.000	1	1	1	1	0	9	8	0	0	3	8.0	0.00	—	.242	.242	0	.000	-0	2	2	-0	0.2
1912	Bos-N	0	0	—	1	0	0	0	0	2^2	5	0	3	0	27.0	20.25	18	.313	.421	0	.000	-0	-5	-5	0	-0.4
Total	5	3	2	.600	8	5	4	1	0	49^2	64	0	10	20	13.4	3.08	89	.306	.338	2	.111	-1	-2	-2	-1	-0.4
● **BILL BRADY**	Brady, William Aloysius "King" b: 8/18/1889, New York, N.Y. TR, 6'2", Deb: 4/13/12																									
1912	Bos-N	0	0	—	1	0	0	0	0	1	2	0	0	0	18.0	0.00	—	.500	.500	0	—	0	0	0	-0	0.0
● **DICK BRAGGINS**	Braggins, Richard Realf b: 12/25/1879, Mercer, Pa. d: 8/16/63, Lake Wales, Fla. BR/TR, 5'11", 170 lbs. Deb: 5/16/01																									
1901	Cle-A	1	2	.333	4	3	2	0	0	32	44	1	15	1	16.9	4.78	74	.323	.394	2	.154	-1	-4	-4	0	-0.4
● **ASA BRAINARD**	Brainard, Asa "Count" b: 1841, Albany, N.Y. d: 12/29/1888, Denver, Colo. TR, 5'8.5", 150 lbs. Deb: 5/05/1871 ♦																									
1871	Oly-n	12	15	.444	30	30	30	0	0	264	361	4	37	13	13.6	4.50	93	.288	.308	30	.224	-6	-8	-10		-0.9
1872	Oly-n	2	7	.222	9	9	9	0	0	79	147	0	5	1	17.3	6.38	58	.332	.339	16	.390	4	-23	-24		-1.3
	Man-n	0	2	.000	2	2	1	0	0	8	14	1	0	0	15.8	7.88	47	.286	.286	5	.200	-0	-4	-4		-0.3
	Yr	2	9	.182	11	11	10	0	0	87	161	1	5	1	17.2	6.52	56	.327	.334	21	.318	4	-27	-28		-1.6
1873	Bal-n	5	7	.417	14	14	12	0	0	108^2	182	0	9	3	15.8	4.14	79	.323	.334	18	.261	1	-11	-11		-0.7
1874	Bal-n	5	22	.185	29	27	25	0	0	239	403	1	27		16.2	*4.93*	62	.326	.341	50	.253	-0	-51	-50		-3.7
Total	4 n	24	53	.312	84	82	77	0	0	698^2	1107	6	78	17	15.3	*4.84*	63	.312	.327	119	.255	-2	-143	-140		-6.9
● **AL BRAITHWOOD**	Braithwood, Alfred b: 2/15/1892, Braceville, Ill. d: 11/24/60, Rowlesburg, W.Va. BR/TL, 6'1.5", 145 lbs. Deb: 9/01/15																									
1915	Pit-F	0	0	—	2	0	0	0	0	3	0	0	0	2	0.0	0.00	—	.000	.000	0	—	0	1	1	-0	0.1
● **ERV BRAME**	Brame, Ervin Beckham b: 10/12/01, Big Rock, Tenn. d: 11/22/49, Hopkinsville, Ky. BL/TR, 6'2", 190 lbs. Deb: 4/14/28																									
1928	Pit-N	7	4	.636	24	11	6	0	0	95^2	110	5	44	22	14.6	5.08	80	.291	.366	13	.265	4	-12	-11	-1	-0.8
1929	Pit-N	16	11	.593	37	28	19	1	0	229^2	250	17	71	68	12.6	4.55	105	.278	.331	36	.310	12	4	6	-4	1.2
1930	Pit-N	17	8	.680	32	29	**22**	0	1	235^2	291	21	56	55	13.4	4.70	106	.305	.346	41	.353	11	7	7	-3	1.4
1931	Pit-N	9	13	.409	26	21	15	2	0	179^2	211	14	45	33	12.8	4.21	91	.295	.336	26	.274	6	-7	-7	-2	-0.3
1932	Pit-N	3	1	.750	23	3	0	0	0	51	84	6	16	10	17.6	7.41	51	.365	.407	5	.250	1	-20	-20	-1	-1.9
Total	5	52	37	.584	142	92	62	3	1	791^2	946	63	232	188	13.5	4.76	94	.298	.347	121	.306	33	-27	-25	-11	-0.4
● **RALPH BRANCA**	Branca, Ralph Theodore Joseph "Hawk" b: 1/6/26, Mt.Vernon, N.Y. BR/TR, 6'3", 220 lbs. Deb: 6/12/44																									
1944	Bro-N	0	2	.000	21	1	0	0	1	44^2	46	2	32	16	16.7	7.05	50	.274	.405	0	.000	-1	-17	-17	-0	-1.8
1945	Bro-N	5	6	.455	16	15	7	0	1	109^2	73	4	79	69	12.5	3.04	124	.189	.327	4	.100	-3	9	9	0	0.7
1946	Bro-N	3	1	.750	24	10	2	2	3	67^1	62	4	41	42	13.8	3.88	87	.246	.352	2	.111	0	-3	-4	-1	-0.5
1947	*Bro-N☆	21	12	.636	43	36	15	4	1	280	251	22	98	148	11.4	2.67	155	.240	.309	12	.124	-3	43	46	-4	4.0
1948	Bro-N★	14	9	.609	36	28	11	1	1	215^2	189	24	80	122	11.4	3.51	114	.232	.304	15	.203	1	11	12	-4	0.9
1949	*Bro-N☆	13	5	.722	34	27	9	2	1	186^2	181	21	91	109	13.2	4.39	93	.253	.339	5	.081	-2	-7	-6	-4	-1.2
1950	Bro-N	7	9	.438	43	15	5	0	7	142	152	24	55	100	13.1	4.69	87	.271	.336	4	.118	1	-9	-9	-1	-0.9
1951	Bro-N	13	12	.520	42	27	13	3	3	204	180	19	85	118	11.8	3.26	120	.237	.316	11	.175	-1	16	15	-3	1.1
1952	Bro-N	4	2	.667	16	7	2	0	0	61	52	8	21	26	11.4	3.84	95	.232	.309	3	.158	-0	-1	-1	-1	-0.3
1953	Bro-N	0	0	—	7	0	0	0	0	11	15	4	5	5	18.0	9.82	43	.341	.431	0	—	0	-7	-7	0	-0.6
	Det-A	4	7	.364	17	14	7	0	1	102	98	7	31	50	11.6	4.15	98	.253	.311	4	.118	-1	-2	-1	-1	-0.3
1954	Det-A	3	3	.500	17	5	0	0	0	45^1	63	10	30	15	18.9	5.76	64	.330	.426	4	.308	2	-10	-10	-0	-0.9
	NY-A	1	0	1.000	5	3	0	0	0	12^2	9	0	13	7	16.3	2.84	121	.209	.404	2	.500	1	1	1	0	0.2
	Yr	4	3	.571	22	8	0	0	0	58	72	10	43	22	18.0	5.12	71	.304	.413	6	.353	2	-9	-10	-0	-0.7
1956	Bro-N	0	0	—	1	0	0	0	0	2	1	0	2	2	13.5	0.00	—	.143	.333	0	—	0	1	1	0	0.1

YEAR	TM/L	W	L	PCT	G	GS	CG	SH	SV	IP	H	HR	BB	SO	RAT	ERA	ERA+	OAV	OOB	BH	AVG	PB	PR	/A	PD	TPI
Total	12	88	68	.564	322	188	71	12	19	1484	1372	149	663	829	12.5	3.79	104	.245	.328	66	.142	-6	25	27	-18	0.5
● **HARVEY BRANCH**	Branch, Harvey Alfred b: 2/8/39, Memphis, Tenn. BR/TL, 6', 175 lbs. Deb: 9/18/62																									
1962	StL-N	0	1	.000	1	1	0	0	0	5	5	1	5	2	18.0	5.40	79	.263	.417	0	.000	-0	-1	-1	0	0.0
● **NORM BRANCH**	Branch, Norman Downs "Red" b: 3/22/15, Spokane, Wash. d: 11/21/71, Navasota, Tex. BR/TR, 6'3", 200 lbs. Deb: 5/05/41																									
1941	NY-A	5	1	.833	27	0	0	0	2	47	37	2	26	28	12.1	2.87	137	.224	.330	0	.000	-1	7	6	1	0.5
1942	NY-A	0	1	.000	10	0	0	0	2	15^2	18	3	16	13	19.5	6.32	54	.290	.436	1	.333	0	-5	-5	0	-0.4
Total	2	5	2	.714	37	0	0	0	4	62^2	55	5	42	41	13.9	3.73	102	.242	.361	1	.077	-1	2	1	1	0.1
● **ROY BRANCH**	Branch, Roy b: 7/12/53, St.Louis, Mo. BR/TR, 6', 175 lbs. Deb: 9/11/79																									
1979	Sea-A	0	1	.000	2	2	0	0	0	11^1	12	2	7	6	15.1	7.94	55	.273	.373	0	—	0	-5	-5	-0	-0.4
● **CHICK BRANDOM**	Brandom, Chester Milton b: 3/31/1887, Coldwater, Kan. d: 10/7/58, Santa Ana, Cal. BR/TR, 5'8", 161 lbs. Deb: 9/03/08																									
1908	Pit-N	1	0	1.000	3	1	1	0	1	17	13	0	4	8	9.5	0.53	435	.228	.290	1	.143	-0	3	3	0	0.4
1909	Pit-N	1	0	1.000	13	2	0	0	2	40^2	33	0	10	21	9.7	1.11	246	.239	.295	1	.100	-1	7	7	1	0.9
1915	New-F	1	1	.500	16	1	1	0	0	50^1	55	0	15	15	12.7	3.40	84	.293	.348	2	.200	1	-2	-3	1	-0.2
Total	3	3	1	.750	32	4	2	0	3	108	101	0	29	44	11.1	2.08	131	.264	.320	4	.148	-0	8	8	2	1.1
● **BUCKY BRANDON**	Brandon, Darrell G b: 7/8/40, Nacogdoches, Tex. BR/TR, 6'2", 200 lbs. Deb: 4/19/66																									
1966	Bos-A	8	8	.500	40	17	5	2	2	157^2	129	13	70	101	11.6	3.31	115	.222	.310	8	.182	2	2	9	0	1.2
1967	Bos-A	5	11	.313	39	19	2	0	3	157^2	147	21	59	96	12.2	4.17	84	.245	.320	8	.186	1	-16	-12	-0	-1.2
1968	Bos-A	0	0	—	8	0	0	0	0	12^2	19	1	9	10	20.6	6.39	49	.333	.433	0	.000	-0	-5	-5	0	-0.5
1969	Sea-A	0	1	.000	8	1	0	0	0	15	15	4	16	10	19.8	8.40	43	.250	.423	0	—	0	-8	-8	0	-0.8
	Min-A	0	0	—	3	0	0	0	0	3^1	5	1	3	1	21.6	2.70	135	.357	.471	0	.000	0	0	0	-0	0.0
	Yr	0	1	.000	11	1	0	0	0	18^1	20	5	19	11	19.1	7.36	49	.263	.411	0	.000	0	-8	-8	-0	-0.8
1971	Phi-N	6	6	.500	52	0	0	0	4	83	81	5	47	44	13.9	3.90	90	.264	.362	2	.154	-0	-4	-4	-1	-0.5
1972	Phi-N	7	7	.500	42	6	0	0	2	104^1	106	9	46	67	13.6	3.45	104	.268	.353	1	.067	-1	0	2	-2	-0.1
1973	Phi-N	2	4	.333	36	0	0	0	2	56^1	54	5	25	25	13.1	5.43	70	.261	.349	1	.200	0	-11	-10	0	-1.0
Total	7	28	37	.431	228	43	7	2	13	590	556	59	275	354	13.0	4.04	90	.250	.339	20	.164	1	-42	-27	-2	-2.9
● **ED BRANDT**	Brandt, Edward Arthur "Big Ed" b: 2/17/05, Spokane, Wash. d: 11/1/44, Spokane, Wash. BL/TL, 6'1", 190 lbs. Deb: 4/26/28																									
1928	Bos-N	9	21	.300	38	31	12	1	0	225^1	234	22	109	84	14.0	5.07	77	.273	.359	17	.243	5	-27	-29	2	-2.1
1929	Bos-N	8	13	.381	26	21	13	0	0	167^2	196	12	83	50	15.2	5.53	85	.302	.385	15	.234	2	-15	-16	2	-1.0
1930	Bos-N	4	11	.267	41	13	4	1	1	147^1	168	15	59	65	13.9	5.01	99	.291	.356	12	.240	1	-1	-1	2	0.1
1931	Bos-N	18	11	.621	33	29	23	3	2	250	228	11	77	112	11.1	2.92	130	.244	.304	21	.256	5	26	24	3	3.4
1932	Bos-N	16	16	.500	35	31	19	2	1	254	271	11	57	79	11.8	3.97	95	.275	.318	19	.207	-0	-3	-6	1	-0.5
1933	Bos-N	18	14	.563	41	32	23	4	4	287^2	256	10	77	104	10.5	2.60	118	.245	.298	30	.309	9	24	15	-0	2.6
1934	Bos-N	16	14	.533	40	28	20	3	5	255	249	13	83	106	11.9	3.53	108	.254	.315	23	.240	4	15	8	-3	1.0
1935	Bos-N	5	19	.208	29	25	12	0	0	174^2	224	12	66	61	15.0	5.00	76	.319	.378	13	.210	-0	-19	-24	1	-2.1
1936	Bro-N	11	13	.458	38	29	12	1	2	234	246	14	65	104	12.1	3.50	118	.268	.319	16	.190	0	14	16	-2	1.4
1937	Pit-N	11	10	.524	33	25	7	2	2	176^1	177	11	67	74	12.6	3.11	124	.263	.332	10	.169	1	16	15	1	1.7
1938	Pit-N	5	4	.556	24	14	5	1	0	96^1	93	3	35	38	12.0	3.46	110	.250	.314	11	.297	3	4	4	-1	0.6
Total	11	121	146	.453	378	278	150	18	17	2268^1	2342	134	778	877	12.5	3.86	101	.269	.332	187	.236	29	34	5	6	5.1
● **BILL BRANDT**	Brandt, William George b: 3/21/15, Aurora, Ind. d: 5/16/68, Fort Wayne, Ind. BR/TR, 5'8.5", 170 lbs. Deb: 9/20/41																									
1941	Pit-N	0	1	.000	2	1	0	0	0	7	5	0	3	0	10.3	3.86	94	.200	.286	0	.000	-0	-0	-0	-0	0.0
1942	Pit-N	1	1	.500	3	3	1	0	0	16^1	23	1	5	4	15.4	4.96	68	.343	.389	1	.143	-0	-3	-3	-0	-0.4
1943	Pit-N	4	1	.800	29	3	0	0	0	57^1	57	3	19	17	12.1	3.14	111	.248	.308	1	.143	-0	2	2	-0	0.2
Total	3	5	3	.625	34	7	1	0	0	80^2	85	4	27	21	12.6	3.57	97	.264	.323	2	.133	-1	-2	-1	-1	-0.2
● **CLIFF BRANTLEY**	Brantley, Clifford b: 4/12/68, Staten Island, N.Y. BR/TR, 6'1", 190 lbs. Deb: 9/03/91																									
1991	Phi-N	2	2	.500	6	5	0	0	0	31^2	26	0	19	25	13.4	3.41	107	.228	.348	0	.000	-1	1	1	0	0.0
1992	Phi-N	2	6	.250	28	9	0	0	0	76^1	71	6	58	32	15.7	4.60	76	.251	.386	3	.214	1	-9	-9	0	-0.8
Total	2	4	8	.333	34	14	0	0	0	108	97	6	77	57	15.0	4.25	83	.244	.375	3	.136	0	-8	-8	0	-0.8
● **JEFF BRANTLEY**	Brantley, Jeffrey Hoke b: 9/5/63, Florence, Ala. BR/TR, 5'11", 180 lbs. Deb: 8/05/88																									
1988	SF-N	0	1	.000	9	1	0	0	1	20^2	22	2	6	11	12.6	5.66	58	.275	.333	1	.500	0	-5	-6	1	-0.5
1989	*SF-N	7	1	.875	59	1	0	0	0	97^1	101	10	37	69	12.9	4.07	83	.271	.340	1	.083	-1	-6	-8	0	-0.8
1990	SF-N★	5	3	.625	55	0	0	0	19	86^2	77	3	33	61	11.7	1.56	234	.240	.317	2	.286	1	22	20	0	2.2
1991	SF-N	5	2	.714	67	0	0	0	15	95^1	78	8	52	81	12.7	2.45	146	.225	.335	0	.000	-0	13	12	-1	1.2
1992	SF-N	7	7	.500	56	4	0	0	7	91^2	67	8	45	86	11.3	2.95	114	.207	.310	1	.111	0	6	4	-1	0.4
Total	5	24	14	.632	246	6	0	0	42	391^2	345	31	173	308	12.2	2.94	118	.239	.326	5	.152	0	29	23	-1	2.5
● **KITTY BRASHEAR**	Brashear, Norman C. b: 8/27/1877, Mansfield, Ohio d: 12/22/34, Los Angeles, Cal. BR/TR, Deb: 6/25/1899 F																									
1899	Lou-N	1	0	1.000	3	0	0	0	0	8	8	0	2	5	12.4	4.50	86	.260	.326	1	.500	0	-1	-1	0	0.0
● **JOHN BRAUN**	Braun, John Paul b: 12/26/39, Madison, Wis. BR/TR, 6'5", 218 lbs. Deb: 10/02/64																									
1964	Mil-N	0	0	—	1	0	0	0	0	2	2	0	1	1	13.5	0.00	—	.286	.375	0	—	0	1	1	-0	0.1
● **GARLAND BRAXTON**	Braxton, Edgar Garland b: 6/10/1900, Snow Camp, N.C. d: 2/25/66, Norfolk, Va. BB/TL, 5'11", 152 lbs. Deb: 5/27/21																									
1921	Bos-N	1	3	.250	17	2	0	0	0	37^1	44	0	17	16	15.2	4.82	76	.310	.391	0	.000	-1	-4	-5	1	-0.5
1922	Bos-N	1	2	.333	25	4	2	0	0	66^2	75	3	24	15	13.9	3.38	118	.286	.355	1	.063	-2	5	5	-1	0.2
1925	NY-A	1	1	.500	3	2	0	0	0	19^1	26	1	5	11	14.9	6.52	65	.338	.386	2	.333	0	-5	-5	0	-0.4
1926	NY-A	5	1	.833	37	1	0	0	2	67^1	71	1	19	30	12.0	2.67	144	.275	.325	6	.300	1	10	9	0	1.0
1927	Was-A	10	9	.526	**58**	2	0	0	**13**	155^1	144	5	33	96	10.4	2.95	138	.246	.289	9	.231	0	**20**	**19**	-2	1.7
1928	Was-A	13	11	.542	38	24	15	2	6	218^1	177	7	44	94	**9.3**	**2.51**	**160**	**.222**	**.267**	9	.125	-4	37	36	0	3.3
1929	Was-A	12	10	.545	37	20	9	0	4	182	219	6	51	59	13.5	4.85	88	.299	.346	8	.148	-1	-12	-12	-1	-1.3
1930	Was-A	3	2	.600	15	0	0	0	5	27^1	22	3	9	7	10.2	3.29	140	.222	.287	0	.000	-1	4	4	-1	0.2
	Chi-A	4	10	.286	19	10	2	0	1	90^2	127	9	33	44	16.0	6.45	72	.333	.388	2	.087	-2	-18	-18	-1	-1.8
	Yr	7	12	.368	34	10	2	0	6	118	149	12	42	51	14.6	5.72	81	.310	.367	2	.071	-2	-14	-14	-2	-1.6
1931	Chi-A	0	3	.000	17	3	0	0	1	47^1	71	1	23	28	18.3	6.85	62	.338	.409	1	.091	-1	-13	-14	1	-1.2
	StL-A	0	0	—	11	1	0	0	0	18	27	2	10	7	19.0	10.50	44	.370	.452	2	.667	1	-12	-12	-0	-1.0
	Yr	0	3	.000	28	4	0	0	1	65^1	98	3	33	35	18.2	7.85	56	.344	.414	3	.214	0	-25	-25	0	-2.2
1933	StL-A	0	1	.000	5	1	0	0	0	8^1	11	0	8	5	21.6	9.72	48	.289	.426	0	.000	-0	-5	-5	-0	-0.4
Total	10	50	53	.485	282	70	28	2	32	938	1014	38	276	412	12.6	4.13	101	.278	.332	40	.156	-8	8	2	-5	-0.2
● **AL BRAZLE**	Brazle, Alpha Eugene "Cotton" b: 10/19/13, Loyal, Okla. d: 10/24/73, Grand Junction, Colo. BL/TL, 6'2", 185 lbs. Deb: 7/25/43																									
1943	*StL-N	8	2	.800	13	9	8	1	0	88	74	0	29	26	10.5	1.53	219	.231	.295	9	.281	2	18	18	0	2.4
1946	*StL-N	11	10	.524	37	15	6	2	0	153^1	152	1	55	58	12.3	3.29	105	.261	.327	11	.212	-0	2	3	0	0.2
1947	StL-N	14	8	.636	44	19	7	0	4	168	186	7	48	85	12.6	2.84	146	.284	.335	14	.219	1	23	24	3	2.8
1948	StL-N	10	6	.625	42	23	6	2	1	156^1	171	8	50	55	12.7	3.80	108	.281	.335	8	.145	-2	3	5	3	0.6
1949	StL-N	14	8	.636	39	25	9	1	0	206^1	208	18	61	75	12.0	3.18	131	.263	.321	11	.134	-5	20	22	-0	1.8
1950	StL-N	11	9	.550	46	12	3	0	6	164^2	188	12	80	47	14.9	4.10	105	.296	.378	13	.213	-1	1	4	-1	0.2
1951	StL-N	6	5	.545	56	8	5	0	7	154^1	139	13	60	66	11.9	3.09	128	.245	.322	5	.109	-3	**15**	**15**	-2	1.0
1952	StL-N	12	5	.706	46	6	3	1	**16**	109^1	75	7	42	55	9.7	2.72	137	.198	.280	4	.125	-1	12	12	-2	1.0

YEAR	TM/L	W	L	PCT	G	GS	CG	SH	SV	IP	H	HR	BB	SO	RAT	ERA	ERA+	OAV	OOB	BH	AVG	PB	PR	/A	PD	TPI
1953	StL-N	6	7	.462	60	0	0	0	**18**	92	101	8	43	57	14.3	4.21	101	.280	.360	5	.333	1	1	1	2	0.3
1954	StL-N	5	4	.556	58	0	0	0	8	84^1	93	10	24	30	12.8	4.16	99	.288	.343	0	.000	-2	-1	-0	-1	-0.3
Total	10	97	64	.602	441	117	47	7	60	1376^2	1387	84	492	554	12.4	3.31	120	.266	.332	80	.177	-9	93	103	3	10.0

● HARRY BRECHEEN

Brecheen, Harry David "Harry The Cat" b: 10/14/14, Broken Bow, Okla. BL/TL, 5'10", 160 lbs. Deb: 4/22/40 C

YEAR	TM/L	W	L	PCT	G	GS	CG	SH	SV	IP	H	HR	BB	SO	RAT	ERA	ERA+	OAV	OOB	BH	AVG	PB	PR	/A	PD	TPI
1940	StL-N	0	0	—	3	0	0	0	0	3^1	2	0	2	4	10.8	0.00	—	.167	.286	0	—	0	1	1	0	0.2
1943	*StL-N	9	6	.600	29	13	8	1	4	135^1	98	4	39	68	9.3	2.26	149	.206	.270	8	.190	1	17	17	1	2.0
1944	*StL-N	16	5	.762	30	22	13	3	0	189^1	174	8	46	88	10.6	2.85	124	.242	.290	11	.162	1	16	14	-0	1.5
1945	StL-N	15	4	**.789**	24	18	13	3	2	157^1	136	5	44	63	10.6	2.52	149	.238	.298	7	.123	-1	22	21	-1	2.0
1946	*StL-N	15	15	.500	36	30	14	**5**	3	231^1	212	8	67	117	11.0	2.49	139	.244	.301	11	.133	-3	24	25	2	2.5
1947	StL-N★	16	11	.593	29	28	18	1	1	223^1	220	20	66	89	11.6	3.30	125	.260	.316	20	.241	5	19	21	1	2.7
1948	StL-N☆	20	7	**.741**	33	30	21	**7**	1	233^1	193	6	49	**149**	**9.4**	**2.24**	**183**	.222	**.265**	12	.146	-1	45	**48**	1	**5.2**
1949	StL-N	14	11	.560	32	31	14	2	1	214^2	207	18	65	88	11.7	3.35	124	.252	.312	21	.273	5	16	19	-1	2.4
1950	StL-N	8	11	.421	27	23	12	2	1	163^1	151	18	45	80	11.0	3.80	113	.244	.298	14	.241	4	6	9	-0	1.2
1951	StL-N	8	4	.667	24	16	5	0	2	138^2	134	11	54	57	12.3	3.25	122	.256	.327	12	.218	2	11	11	-0	1.3
1952	StL-N	7	5	.583	25	13	4	1	2	100^1	82	12	28	54	10.1	3.32	112	.223	.283	6	.207	1	5	4	2	0.8
1953	StL-A	5	13	.278	26	16	3	0	1	117^1	122	7	31	44	12.0	3.07	137	.269	.320	7	.179	-1	12	15	2	1.6
Total	12	133	92	.591	318	240	125	25	18	1907^2	1731	117	536	901	10.9	2.92	133	.242	.298	129	.192	11	194	205	6	23.4

● BILL BRECKINRIDGE

Breckinridge, William Robertson b: 10/16/07, Tulsa, Okla. d: 8/23/58, Tulsa, Okla. BR/TR, 5'11", 175 lbs. Deb: 6/30/29

YEAR	TM/L	W	L	PCT	G	GS	CG	SH	SV	IP	H	HR	BB	SO	RAT	ERA	ERA+	OAV	OOB	BH	AVG	PB	PR	/A	PD	TPI
1929	Phi-A	0	0	—	3	1	0	0	0	10	10	0	16	2	23.4	8.10	52	.270	.491	0	.000	-1	-4	-4	-1	-0.5

● FRED BREINING

Breining, Fred Lawrence b: 11/15/55, San Francisco, Cal. BR/TR, 6'4", 185 lbs. Deb: 9/04/80

YEAR	TM/L	W	L	PCT	G	GS	CG	SH	SV	IP	H	HR	BB	SO	RAT	ERA	ERA+	OAV	OOB	BH	AVG	PB	PR	/A	PD	TPI
1980	SF-N	0	0	—	5	0	0	0	0	6^2	8	0	4	3	17.6	5.40	65	.333	.448	0	—	0	-1	-1	-0	-0.2
1981	SF-N	5	2	.714	45	1	0	0	1	77^2	66	4	38	37	12.3	2.55	135	.243	.340	0	.000	-1	8	8	-0	0.7
1982	SF-N	11	6	.647	54	9	2	0	0	143^1	146	6	52	98	12.5	3.08	117	.269	.334	6	.207	1	8	8	1	1.1
1983	SF-N	11	12	.478	32	32	6	0	0	202^2	202	15	60	117	11.9	3.82	93	.259	.316	10	.149	1	-4	-6	-1	-0.6
1984	Mon-N	0	0	—	4	0	0	0	0	6^2	4	0	5	5	12.2	1.35	254	.190	.346	0	.000	-0	2	2	-0	0.1
Total	5	27	20	.574	140	42	8	0	1	437	426	25	159	260	12.2	3.34	106	.260	.329	16	.148	1	12	10	-0	1.1

● ALONZO BREITENSTEIN

Breitenstein, Alonzo b: 11/9/1857, Utica, N.Y. d: 6/19/32, Utica, N.Y. Deb: 7/07/1883

YEAR	TM/L	W	L	PCT	G	GS	CG	SH	SV	IP	H	HR	BB	SO	RAT	ERA	ERA+	OAV	OOB	BH	AVG	PB	PR	/A	PD	TPI
1883	Phi-N	0	1	.000	1	1	0	0	0	5	8	0	2	0	18.0	9.00	34	.320	.370	0	.000	-0	-3	-3	-0	-0.3

● TED BREITENSTEIN

Breitenstein, Theodore P. "Theo" b: 6/1/1869, St.Louis, Mo. d: 5/3/35, St.Louis, Mo. BL/TL, 5'9", 167 lbs. Deb: 4/28/1891

YEAR	TM/L	W	L	PCT	G	GS	CG	SH	SV	IP	H	HR	BB	SO	RAT	ERA	ERA+	OAV	OOB	BH	AVG	PB	PR	/A	PD	TPI
1891	StL-a	2	0	1.000	6	1	1	1	1	28^2	15	2	14	13	9.1	2.20	191	.150	.254	0	.000	-2	5	6	-1	0.4
1892	StL-N	9	19	.321	39	32	28	1	0	282^1	280	8	148	126	13.8	4.69	68	.248	.339	16	.122	-4	-44	-47	3	-4.1
1893	StL-N	19	24	.442	48	42	38	1	1	382^2	359	8	156	102	12.3	**3.18**	**149**	.241	.316	29	.181	-5	63	66	2	5.5
1894	StL-N	27	23	.540	**56**	50	**46**	1	0	**447^1**	497	21	191	140	14.1	4.79	113	.278	.352	40	.220	-1	27	31	3	2.6
1895	StL-N	19	30	.388	54	50	**46**	1	1	429^2	458	16	178	127	13.6	4.44	109	.269	.343	42	.193	-7	16	19	3	1.3
1896	StL-N	18	26	.409	44	43	37	1	0	339^2	376	12	138	114	13.8	4.48	97	.278	.347	42	.259	3	-4	-5	4	0.2
1897	Cin-N	23	12	.657	40	39	32	2	0	320^1	345	3	91	98	12.5	3.62	126	.273	.326	33	.266	3	25	33	-0	3.2
1898	Cin-N	20	14	.588	39	37	32	3	0	315^2	313	2	123	68	12.7	3.42	112	.257	.330	26	.215	1	7	15	3	1.7
1899	Cin-N	13	9	.591	26	24	21	0	0	210^2	219	2	71	59	12.8	3.59	109	.268	.333	37	.352	9	6	8	-0	1.5
1900	Cin-N	10	10	.500	24	20	18	1	0	192^1	205	4	79	39	13.9	3.65	101	.272	.352	24	.190	-0	1	0	2	0.2
1901	StL-N	0	3	.000	3	3	1	0	0	15	24	1	14	3	22.8	6.60	48	.358	.469	2	.333	0	-5	-6	1	-0.4
Total	11	160	170	.485	379	341	300	12	3	2964^1	3091	79	1203	889	13.3	4.04	109	.265	.338	291	.216	-3	96	121	20	12.1

● AD BRENNAN

Brennan, Addison Foster b: 7/18/1881, Laharpe, Kan. d: 1/7/62, Kansas City, Mo. BL/TL, 5'11", 170 lbs. Deb: 5/19/10

YEAR	TM/L	W	L	PCT	G	GS	CG	SH	SV	IP	H	HR	BB	SO	RAT	ERA	ERA+	OAV	OOB	BH	AVG	PB	PR	/A	PD	TPI
1910	Phi-N	2	0	1.000	19	5	2	0	0	73^1	72	2	28	28	12.6	2.33	134	.264	.339	7	.280	1	6	6	-2	0.7
1911	Phi-N	2	1	.667	5	3	1	0	0	22^2	22	0	12	12	13.9	3.57	96	.259	.357	2	.222	-0	-0	-0	0	0.0
1912	Phi-N	11	9	.550	27	19	13	1	2	174	185	4	49	78	12.3	3.57	102	.274	.326	15	.254	4	-3	1	2	0.7
1913	Phi-N	14	12	.538	40	25	12	1	1	207	204	5	46	94	11.1	2.39	139	.268	.314	11	.164	-2	19	22	0	2.1
1914	Chi-F	5	5	.500	16	11	5	1	0	85^2	84	6	21	31	11.2	3.57	83	.256	.305	8	.250	1	-3	-6	-1	-0.6
1915	Chi-F	3	9	.250	19	13	7	2	0	106	117	4	30	40	13.1	3.74	75	.287	.346	5	.185	1	-8	-11	-2	-1.3
1918	Was-A	0	0	—	2	1	0	0	0	5^1	7	0	5	0	21.9	5.06	54	.241	.371	0	.000	-0	-1	-1	-0	-0.2
	Cle-A	0	0	—	1	0	0	0	0	3	3	0	3	0	18.0	3.00	100	.333	.500	0	—	0	-0	0	-0	0.0
	Yr	0	0	—	3	1	0	0	0	8^1	10	0	8	0	19.4	4.32	65	.256	.383	0	.000	-0	-1	-1	-0	-0.2
Total	7	37	36	.507	129	77	40	5	3	677	694	21	194	283	12.1	3.11	104	.270	.327	48	.218	5	8	10	-2	1.4

● DON BRENNAN

Brennan, James Donald b: 12/2/03, Augusta, Maine d: 4/26/53, Boston, Mass. BR/TR, 6', 210 lbs. Deb: 4/16/33

YEAR	TM/L	W	L	PCT	G	GS	CG	SH	SV	IP	H	HR	BB	SO	RAT	ERA	ERA+	OAV	OOB	BH	AVG	PB	PR	/A	PD	TPI
1933	NY-A	5	1	.833	18	10	3	0	3	85	92	4	47	46	14.7	4.98	78	.275	.365	7	.259	2	-7	-10	1	-0.7
1934	Cin-N	4	3	.571	28	7	2	0	2	78	89	3	35	31	14.4	3.81	107	.290	.364	5	.227	0	2	2	-1	0.2
1935	Cin-N	5	5	.500	38	5	2	1	5	114^1	101	4	44	48	11.7	3.15	126	.242	.320	3	.100	-1	11	11	-2	0.7
1936	Cin-N	5	2	.714	41	4	0	0	9	94^1	117	2	35	40	14.6	4.39	87	.305	.364	2	.080	-2	-4	-6	-0	-0.8
1937	Cin-N	1	1	.500	10	0	0	0	0	16	25	1	10	6	19.7	6.75	55	.347	.427	0	.000	-1	-5	-5	0	-0.6
	*NY-N	1	0	1.000	6	0	0	0	0	9^1	12	0	9	1	21.2	6.75	58	.316	.458	0	.000	0	-3	-3	-0	-0.3
	Yr	2	1	.667	16	0	0	0	0	25^1	37	1	19	7	20.3	6.75	56	.336	.438	0	.000	-0	-8	-8	-0	-0.9
Total	5	21	12	.636	141	26	7	1	19	397	436	14	180	172	14.1	4.19	94	.281	.358	17	.155	-2	-5	-12	-2	-1.5

● TOM BRENNAN

Brennan, Thomas Martin b: 10/30/52, Chicago, Ill. BR/TR, 6'1", 180 lbs. Deb: 9/05/81

YEAR	TM/L	W	L	PCT	G	GS	CG	SH	SV	IP	H	HR	BB	SO	RAT	ERA	ERA+	OAV	OOB	BH	AVG	PB	PR	/A	PD	TPI
1981	Cle-A	2	2	.500	7	6	1	0	0	48^1	49	5	14	15	11.7	3.17	114	.259	.310	0	—	0	3	2	1	0.4
1982	Cle-A	4	2	.667	30	4	0	0	2	92^2	112	9	10	46	12.0	4.27	95	.300	.322	0	—	0	-2	-2	0	-0.2
1983	Cle-A	2	2	.500	11	5	1	1	0	39^2	45	3	8	21	12.3	3.86	110	.288	.327	0	—	0	1	2	-0	0.1
1984	Chi-A	0	1	.000	4	1	0	0	0	6^2	8	1	3	3	14.9	4.05	103	.308	.379	0	—	0	-0	0	0	0.0
1985	LA-N	1	3	.250	12	4	0	0	0	31^2	41	2	11	17	14.8	7.39	47	.333	.388	1	.125	-0	-13	-14	1	-1.2
Total	5	9	10	.474	64	20	2	1	2	219	255	20	46	102	12.5	4.40	89	.294	.332	1	.125	-0	-12	-12	3	-0.9

● WILLIAM BRENNAN

Brennan, William Raymond b: 1/15/63, Tampa, Fla. BR/TR, 6'3", 200 lbs. Deb: 7/19/88

YEAR	TM/L	W	L	PCT	G	GS	CG	SH	SV	IP	H	HR	BB	SO	RAT	ERA	ERA+	OAV	OOB	BH	AVG	PB	PR	/A	PD	TPI
1988	LA-N	0	1	.000	4	2	0	0	0	9^1	13	0	6	7	18.3	6.75	49	.342	.432	0	.000	-0	-3	-4	0	-0.4

● JIM BRENNEMAN

Brenneman, James Leroy b: 2/13/41, San Diego, Cal. BR/TR, 6'2", 180 lbs. Deb: 7/09/65

YEAR	TM/L	W	L	PCT	G	GS	CG	SH	SV	IP	H	HR	BB	SO	RAT	ERA	ERA+	OAV	OOB	BH	AVG	PB	PR	/A	PD	TPI
1965	NY-A	0	0	—	3	0	0	0	0	2	5	1	3	2	36.0	18.00	19	.455	.571	0	—	0	-3	-3	-0	-0.3

● BERT BRENNER

Brenner, Delbert Henry "Dutch" b: 7/18/1887, Minneapolis, Minn d: 4/11/71, St.Louis Park, Minn. BR/TR, 6', 175 lbs. Deb: 9/21/12

YEAR	TM/L	W	L	PCT	G	GS	CG	SH	SV	IP	H	HR	BB	SO	RAT	ERA	ERA+	OAV	OOB	BH	AVG	PB	PR	/A	PD	TPI
1912	Cle-A	1	0	1.000	2	1	1	0	0	13	14	0	4	3	12.5	2.77	123	.286	.340	0	.000	-1	1	1	0	0.0

● LYNN BRENTON

Brenton, Lynn Davis "Buck" or "Herb" b: 10/7/1890, Peoria, Ill. d: 10/14/68, Los Angeles, Cal. BR/TR, 5'10", 165 lbs. Deb: 8/10/13

YEAR	TM/L	W	L	PCT	G	GS	CG	SH	SV	IP	H	HR	BB	SO	RAT	ERA	ERA+	OAV	OOB	BH	AVG	PB	PR	/A	PD	TPI
1913	Cle-A	0	0	—	1	0	0	0	0	2	4	0	0	2	18.0	9.00	34	.400	.400	0	—	0	-1	-1	-0	-0.1
1915	Cle-A	2	3	.400	11	5	1	1	0	51	60	1	20	18	14.5	3.35	91	.308	.378	2	.118	-1	-2	-2	-1	-0.4
1920	Cin-N	2	1	.667	5	1	1	0	1	18^1	17	0	4	13	10.3	4.91	62	.236	.276	2	.250	0	-4	-4	2	-0.2
1921	Cin-N	1	8	.111	17	9	2	0	1	60	80	0	17	19	14.7	4.05	88	.342	.389	2	.133	-0	-2	-3	2	-0.1
Total	4	5	12	.294	34	15	4	1	2	131^1	161	1	41	52	14.0	3.97	83	.315	.369	6	.150	-1	-9	-10	3	-0.8

● ROGER BRESNAHAN

Bresnahan, Roger Philip "The Duke Of Tralee"
b: 6/11/1879, Toledo, Ohio d: 12/4/44, Toledo, Ohio BR/TR, 5'9", 200 lbs. Deb: 8/27/1897 MCH♦

YEAR	TM/L	W	L	PCT	G	GS	CG	SH	SV	IP	H	HR	BB	SO	RAT	ERA	ERA+	OAV	OOB	BH	AVG	PB	PR	/A	PD	TPI
1897	Was-N	4	0	1.000	6	5	3	1	0	41	52	1	10	12	14.3	3.95	110	.306	.356	6	.375	1	2	2	-0	0.2

YEAR TM/L	W	L	PCT	G	GS	CG	SH	SV	IP	H	HR	BB	SO	RAT	ERA	ERA+	OAV	OOB	BH	AVG	PB	PR	/A	PD	TPI
1901 Bal-A	0	1	.000	2	1	0	0	0	6	10	0	4	3	21.0	6.00	64	.366	.447	79	.268	0	-2	-1	0	-0.1
1910 StL-N	0	0	—	1	0	0	0	0	3^1	6	0	1	0	18.9	0.00	—	.400	.438	65	.278	0	1	1	1	0.2
Total 3	4	1	.800	9	6	3	1	0	50^1	68	1	15	15	15.4	3.93	107	.321	.374	1252	.279	2	1	1	0	0.3

● **RUBE BRESSLER** Bressler, Raymond Bloom b: 10/23/1894, Coder, Pa. d: 11/7/66, Cincinnati, Ohio BR/TL, 6', 187 lbs. Deb: 4/24/14 ♦

YEAR TM/L	W	L	PCT	G	GS	CG	SH	SV	IP	H	HR	BB	SO	RAT	ERA	ERA+	OAV	OOB	BH	AVG	PB	PR	/A	PD	TPI
1914 Phi-A	10	4	.714	29	10	8	1	2	147^2	112	1	56	96	10.5	1.77	148	.220	.302	11	.216	4	16	14	-2	1.7
1915 Phi-A	4	17	.190	32	20	7	1	0	178^1	183	3	118	69	15.5	5.20	56	.283	.399	8	.145	1	-45	-45	0	-4.3
1916 Phi-A	0	2	.000	4	2	0	0	0	15	16	0	14	8	19.2	6.60	43	.296	.457	1	.200	1	-6	-6	-0	-0.6
1917 Cin-N	0	0	—	2	1	0	0	0	9	15	0	5	2	20.0	6.00	44	.429	.500	1	.200	-0	-3	-3	-0	-0.4
1918 Cin-N	8	5	.615	17	13	10	0	0	128	124	3	39	37	11.5	2.46	108	.261	.318	17	.274	4	4	3	3	1.1
1919 Cin-N	2	4	.333	13	4	1	0	0	41^2	37	1	8	13	9.7	3.46	80	.248	.287	34	.206	2	-3	-3	1	-0.2
1920 Cin-N	2	0	1.000	10	2	1	1	0	20^1	24	0	2	4	11.5	1.77	172	.300	.317	8	.267	0	3	3	0	0.4
Total 7	26	32	.448	107	52	27	3	2	540	511	8	242	229	12.8	3.40	81	.262	.348	1170	.301	12	-34	-38	1	-2.3

● **HERB BRETT** Brett, Herbert James "Duke" b: 5/23/1900, Lawrenceville, Va. d: 11/25/74, St.Petersburg, Fla BR/TR, 6', 175 lbs. Deb: 8/08/24

YEAR TM/L	W	L	PCT	G	GS	CG	SH	SV	IP	H	HR	BB	SO	RAT	ERA	ERA+	OAV	OOB	BH	AVG	PB	PR	/A	PD	TPI
1924 Chi-N	0	0	—	1	1	0	0	0	5^1	6	0	7	1	21.9	5.06	77	.300	.481	0	.000	-0	-1	-1	-0	-0.1
1925 Chi-N	1	1	.500	10	1	0	0	0	17^1	12	0	3	6	8.3	3.63	119	.194	.242	0	.000	-0	1	1	1	0.2
Total 2	1	1	.500	11	2	0	0	0	22^2	18	0	10	7	11.5	3.97	106	.220	.312	0	.000	-1	1	1	0	0.1

● **KEN BRETT** Brett, Kenneth Alven b: 9/18/48, Brooklyn, N.Y. BL/TL, 5'11", 195 lbs. Deb: 9/27/67 F

YEAR TM/L	W	L	PCT	G	GS	CG	SH	SV	IP	H	HR	BB	SO	RAT	ERA	ERA+	OAV	OOB	BH	AVG	PB	PR	/A	PD	TPI
1967 *Bos-A	0	0	—	1	0	0	0	0	2	3	0	0	2	13.5	4.50	77	.375	.375	0	—	0	-0	-0	-0	0.0
1969 Bos-A	2	3	.400	8	8	0	0	0	39^1	41	6	22	23	15.1	5.26	72	.275	.379	3	.300	2	-7	-6	0	-0.4
1970 Bos-A	8	9	.471	41	14	1	0	2	139^1	118	17	79	155	12.9	4.07	97	.223	.327	13	.317	6	-6	-2	1	0.6
1971 Bos-A	0	3	.000	29	2	0	0	1	59	57	7	35	57	14.2	5.34	69	.253	.356	2	.200	-0	-12	-11	-0	-1.2
1972 Mil-A	7	12	.368	26	22	2	1	0	133	121	13	49	74	11.6	4.53	67	.242	.311	10	.227	2	-22	-22	-2	-2.3
1973 Phi-N	13	9	.591	31	25	10	1	0	211^2	206	19	74	111	11.9	3.44	110	.259	.322	20	.250	9	5	8	2	2.0
1974 *Pit-N★	13	9	.591	27	27	10	3	0	191	192	9	52	96	11.6	3.30	104	.257	.308	27	.310	10	7	3	-0	1.4
1975 *Pit-N	9	5	.643	23	16	4	1	0	118	110	10	43	47	11.8	3.36	106	.250	.320	12	.231	4	3	2	0	0.7
1976 NY-A	0	0	—	2	0	0	0	1	2^1	2	0	0	1	7.7	0.00	—	.222	.222	0	—	0	1	1	-0	0.1
Chi-A	10	12	.455	27	26	16	1	1	200^2	171	5	76	91	11.2	3.32	107	.234	.308	1	.083	2	4	5	1	0.6
Yr	10	12	.455	29	26	16	1	2	203	173	5	76	92	11.2	3.28	109	.233	.307	1	.083	2	5	6	0	0.7
1977 Chi-A	6	4	.600	13	13	2	0	0	82^2	101	10	15	39	12.7	5.01	82	.305	.337	0	—	0	-9	-8	-0	-0.8
Cal-A	7	10	.412	21	21	5	0	0	142	157	15	38	41	12.5	4.25	92	.287	.337	0	—	0	-3	-5	2	0.0
Yr	13	14	.481	34	34	7	0	0	224^2	258	25	53	80	12.6	4.53	88	.293	.335	0	—	0	-12	-14	2	-0.8
1978 Cal-A	3	5	.375	31	10	1	1	1	100	100	12	42	43	12.9	4.95	73	.262	.336	0	—	0	-13	-15	2	-1.1
1979 Min-A	0	0	—	9	0	0	0	0	12^2	16	1	6	3	15.6	4.97	88	.320	.393	0	—	0	-1	-1	0	-0.4
LA-N	4	3	.571	30	0	0	0	2	47	52	1	12	13	12.4	3.45	105	.277	.323	3	.273	1	1	1	2	0.3
1980 KC-A	0	0	—	8	0	0	0	1	13^1	8	0	5	4	9.5	0.00	—	.174	.269	0	—	0	6	6	0	0.6
1981 KC-A	1	1	.500	22	0	0	0	2	32^1	35	2	14	7	13.9	4.18	86	.282	.360	0	—	0	-2	-2	0	-0.1
Total 14	83	85	.494	349	184	51	8	11	1526^1	1490	127	562	807	12.2	3.93	93	.257	.325	91	.262	36	-47	-46	8	-0.0

● **MARV BREUER** Breuer, Marvin Howard "Baby Face" b: 4/29/14, Rolla, Mo. d: 1/17/91, Rolla, Mo. BR/TR, 6'2", 185 lbs. Deb: 5/04/39

YEAR TM/L	W	L	PCT	G	GS	CG	SH	SV	IP	H	HR	BB	SO	RAT	ERA	ERA+	OAV	OOB	BH	AVG	PB	PR	/A	PD	TPI
1939 NY-A	0	0	—	1	0	0	0	0	1	2	0	1	0	27.0	9.00	48	.667	.750	0	—	0	-0	-1	0	0.0
1940 NY-A	8	9	.471	27	22	10	0	0	164	175	20	61	71	13.0	4.55	89	.267	.329	2	.037	-4	-3	-10	-1	-1.4
1941 *NY-A	9	7	.563	26	18	7	1	2	141	131	10	49	77	11.6	4.09	96	.243	.308	4	.087	-3	1	-2	-1	-0.6
1942 *NY-A	8	9	.471	27	19	6	0	1	164^1	157	11	37	72	10.7	3.07	112	.252	.295	3	.056	-3	11	7	-2	0.2
1943 NY-A	0	1	.000	5	1	0	0	0	14	22	0	6	6	18.0	8.36	39	.349	.406	1	.333	0	-8	-8	0	-0.7
Total 5	25	26	.490	86	60	23	1	3	484^1	487	41	154	226	12.0	4.03	94	.258	.315	10	.064	-10	0	-13	-3	-2.5

● **JIM BREWER** Brewer, James Thomas b: 11/17/37, Merced, Cal. d: 11/16/87, Tyler, Tex. BL/TL, 6'2", 195 lbs. Deb: 7/17/60 C

YEAR TM/L	W	L	PCT	G	GS	CG	SH	SV	IP	H	HR	BB	SO	RAT	ERA	ERA+	OAV	OOB	BH	AVG	PB	PR	/A	PD	TPI
1960 Chi-N	0	3	.000	5	4	0	0	0	21^2	25	2	6	7	13.3	5.82	65	.272	.323	1	.167	0	-5	-5	0	-0.5
1961 Chi-N	1	7	.125	36	11	0	0	0	86^2	116	17	21	57	14.3	5.82	72	.321	.360	4	.182	0	-17	-16	-2	-1.7
1962 Chi-N	0	1	.000	6	1	0	0	0	5^2	10	2	3	1	20.6	9.53	44	.435	.500	0	—	0	-4	-3	0	-0.3
1963 Chi-N	3	2	.600	29	1	0	0	0	49^2	59	10	15	35	13.4	4.89	72	.294	.343	0	.000	0	-9	-8	-1	-0.9
1964 LA-N	4	3	.571	34	5	1	1	1	93	79	5	25	63	10.1	3.00	108	.232	.284	6	.273	2	6	2	-1	0.3
1965 *LA-N	3	2	.600	19	2	0	0	2	49^1	33	1	28	31	11.1	1.82	179	.196	.311	0	.000	-1	9	8	0	0.8
1966 *LA-N	0	2	.000	13	0	0	0	2	22	17	0	11	8	11.5	3.68	90	.221	.318	0	—	0	-0	-1	0	-0.1
1967 LA-N	5	4	.556	30	11	0	0	1	100^2	78	8	31	74	9.8	2.68	116	.218	.283	1	.045	-1	8	5	-1	0.3
1968 LA-N	8	3	.727	54	0	0	0	14	76^1	59	5	33	75	10.8	2.48	112	.219	.304	2	.222	0	4	2	0	0.3
1969 LA-N	7	6	.538	59	0	0	0	20	88^1	71	5	41	92	11.8	2.55	131	.221	.317	1	.091	0	10	8	0	0.9
1970 LA-N	7	6	.538	58	0	0	0	24	89	66	10	33	91	10.0	3.13	122	.207	.281	1	.083	-0	9	7	0	0.7
1971 LA-N	6	5	.545	55	0	0	0	22	81^1	55	4	24	66	8.7	1.88	172	.194	.257	3	.333	1	14	12	1	1.5
1972 LA-N	8	7	.533	51	0	0	0	17	78^1	41	6	25	69	7.8	1.26	264	.157	.236	0	.000	0	19	18	-0	2.0
1973 LA-N★	6	8	.429	56	0	0	0	20	71^2	58	8	25	56	10.4	3.01	114	.229	.299	2	.400	1	5	3	0	0.4
1974 *LA-N	4	4	.500	24	0	0	0	0	39^1	29	5	10	26	8.9	2.52	135	.207	.260	0	.000	-0	5	4	-1	0.3
1975 LA-N	3	1	.750	21	0	0	0	2	33	44	2	12	21	15.5	5.18	66	.333	.393	0	.000	-0	-6	-7	0	-0.7
Cal-A	1	0	1.000	21	0	0	0	5	34^2	38	2	11	22	12.7	1.82	195	.279	.333	0	—	0	8	7	-1	1.2
1976 Cal-A	3	1	.750	13	0	0	0	2	20	20	0	6	16	11.7	2.70	123	.256	.310	0	—	0	2	1	0	0.2
Total 17	69	65	.515	584	35	1	1	132	1040^2	898	92	360	810	11.0	3.07	111	.236	.303	21	.150	1	59	38	-4	4.7

● **JACK BREWER** Brewer, John Herndon "Buddy" b: 7/21/19, Los Angeles, Cal. BR/TR, 6'2", 170 lbs. Deb: 7/15/44

YEAR TM/L	W	L	PCT	G	GS	CG	SH	SV	IP	H	HR	BB	SO	RAT	ERA	ERA+	OAV	OOB	BH	AVG	PB	PR	/A	PD	TPI
1944 NY-N	1	4	.200	14	7	2	0	0	55	66	8	16	21	13.9	5.56	66	.288	.343	4	.211	0	-12	-12	-1	-1.2
1945 NY-N	8	6	.571	28	21	8	0	0	159^2	162	14	58	49	12.6	3.83	102	.260	.326	10	.179	-1	-1	1	-3	-0.2
1946 NY-N	0	0	—	1	0	0	0	0	2	3	0	2	3	22.5	13.50	25	.333	.455	0	—	0	-2	-2	-0	-0.2
Total 3	9	10	.474	43	28	10	0	0	216^2	231	22	76	73	13.0	4.36	88	.268	.332	14	.187	-1	-15	-12	-3	-1.6

● **TOM BREWER** Brewer, Thomas Austin b: 9/3/31, Wadesboro, S.C. BR/TR, 6'1", 175 lbs. Deb: 4/18/54

YEAR TM/L	W	L	PCT	G	GS	CG	SH	SV	IP	H	HR	BB	SO	RAT	ERA	ERA+	OAV	OOB	BH	AVG	PB	PR	/A	PD	TPI
1954 Bos-A	10	9	.526	33	23	7	0	0	162^2	152	15	95	69	14.1	4.65	88	.249	.356	16	.267	3	-17	-10	-2	-0.9
1955 Bos-A	11	10	.524	31	28	9	2	0	192^2	198	21	87	91	13.7	4.20	102	.263	.346	11	.151	-2	-5	2	3	0.3
1956 Bos-A★	19	9	.679	32	32	15	4	0	244^1	200	14	112	127	11.7	3.50	132	.220	.309	28	.298	5	18	30	4	4.1
1957 Bos-A	16	13	.552	32	32	15	2	0	238^1	225	24	93	128	12.3	3.85	103	.250	.325	19	.202	-1	-2	4	6	0.8
1958 Bos-A	12	12	.500	33	32	10	1	0	227^1	227	21	93	124	13.0	3.72	108	.259	.335	16	.195	-0	1	7	4	1.2
1959 Bos-A	10	12	.455	36	32	11	3	2	215^1	219	14	88	121	12.9	3.76	108	.265	.338	8	.111	-4	2	7	4	0.7
1960 Bos-A	10	15	.400	34	29	8	1	1	186^2	220	13	72	60	14.4	4.82	84	.301	.368	12	.194	0	-20	-16	3	-1.3
1961 Bos-A	3	2	.600	10	9	0	1	0	42	37	4	29	13	14.1	3.43	122	.242	.363	4	.286	1	3	3	1	0.6
Total 8	91	82	.526	241	217	75	13	3	1509^1	1478	126	669	733	13.1	4.00	104	.257	.338	114	.207	2	-19	27	22	5.5

● **ALAN BRICE** Brice, Alan Healey b: 10/1/37, New York, N.Y. BR/TR, 6'5", 215 lbs. Deb: 9/22/61

YEAR TM/L	W	L	PCT	G	GS	CG	SH	SV	IP	H	HR	BB	SO	RAT	ERA	ERA+	OAV	OOB	BH	AVG	PB	PR	/A	PD	TPI
1961 Chi-A	0	1	.000	3	0	0	0	0	3^1	4	0	3	3	18.9	0.00	—	.308	.438	0	—	0	1	1	-0	0.1

● **RALPH BRICKNER** Brickner, Ralph Harold "Brick" b: 5/2/25, Cincinnati, Ohio BR/TR, 6'3.5", 215 lbs. Deb: 5/04/52

YEAR TM/L	W	L	PCT	G	GS	CG	SH	SV	IP	H	HR	BB	SO	RAT	ERA	ERA+	OAV	OOB	BH	AVG	PB	PR	/A	PD	TPI
1952 Bos-A	3	1	.750	14	1	0	0	1	33	32	1	11	9	11.7	2.18	181	.264	.326	2	.250	0	5	6	-1	0.7

● **MARSHALL BRIDGES** Bridges, Marshall "Sheriff" b: 6/2/31, Jackson, Miss. d: 9/3/90, Jackson, Miss. BB/TL, 6'1", 180 lbs. Deb: 6/17/59

YEAR TM/L	W	L	PCT	G	GS	CG	SH	SV	IP	H	HR	BB	SO	RAT	ERA	ERA+	OAV	OOB	BH	AVG	PB	PR	/A	PD	TPI
1959 StL-N	6	3	.667	27	4	1	0	1	76	67	10	37	76	12.3	4.26	99	.240	.329	5	.217	2	-3	-0	-2	0.0

YEAR	TM/L	W	L	PCT	G	GS	CG	SH	SV	IP	H	HR	BB	SO	RAT	ERA	ERA+	OAV	OOB	BH	AVG	PB	PR	/A	PD	TPI
1960	StL-N	2	2	.500	20	1	0	0	1	31^1	33	2	16	27	14.4	3.45	119	.266	.355	0	.000	-0	1	2	-0	0.1
	Cin-N	4	0	1.000	14	0	0	0	2	25^1	14	1	7	26	7.5	1.07	359	.161	.223	1	.250	0	8	8	-0	0.8
	Yr	6	2	.750	34	1	0	0	3	56^2	47	3	23	53	11.1	2.38	167	.220	.295	1	.100	-0	9	10	-1	0.9
1961	Cin-N	0	1	.000	13	0	0	0	0	20^2	26	4	11	17	16.5	7.84	52	.317	.404	0	.000	-0	-9	-9	-0	-0.9
1962	*NY-A	8	4	.667	52	0	0	0	18	71^2	49	4	48	66	12.2	3.14	119	.194	.323	0	.000	-2	7	5	2	0.5
1963	NY-A	2	0	1.000	23	0	0	0	1	33	27	2	30	35	15.8	3.82	92	.237	.400	0	—	0	-1	-1	2	0.1
1964	Was-A	0	3	.000	17	0	0	0	2	30	37	3	17	16	16.2	5.70	65	.303	.388	0	.000	-0	-7	-7	-0	-0.7
1965	Was-A	1	2	.333	40	0	0	0	0	57^1	62	3	25	39	13.7	2.67	130	.268	.340	1	.143	0	5	5	-0	0.6
Total	7	23	15	.605	206	5	1	0	25	345^1	315	29	191	302	13.3	3.75	102	.244	.343	7	.119	0	1	3	1	0.5
● TOMMY BRIDGES Bridges, Thomas Jefferson Davis b: 12/28/06, Gordonsville, Tenn d: 4/19/68, Nashville, Tenn. BR/TR, 5'10.5", 155 lbs. Deb: 8/13/30 C																										
1930	Det-A	3	2	.600	8	5	2	0	0	37^2	28	4	23	17	12.2	4.06	118	.215	.333	3	.300	1	2	3	-0	0.3
1931	Det-A	8	16	.333	35	23	8	2	0	173	182	13	108	105	15.1	4.99	92	.263	.363	8	.148	-2	-12	-8	-1	-1.1
1932	Det-A	14	12	.538	34	26	10	**4**	1	201	174	14	119	108	13.2	3.36	140	.233	.339	11	.164	-1	25	30	-1	2.7
1933	Det-A	14	12	.538	33	28	17	2	2	233	192	8	110	120	11.9	3.09	140	**.226**	.319	16	.205	2	31	32	1	3.4
1934	*Det-A☆	22	11	.667	36	35	23	3	1	275	249	16	104	151	11.7	3.67	120	.241	.312	12	.122	-4	25	22	-2	1.5
1935	*Det-A☆	21	10	.677	36	34	23	4	1	274^1	277	22	113	**163**	12.9	3.51	119	.259	.332	26	.239	3	29	20	-1	2.1
1936	Det-A†	**23**	11	.676	39	38	26	5	0	294^2	289	21	115	**175**	12.5	3.60	137	.255	.326	25	.212	0	47	44	2	4.3
1937	Det-A★	15	12	.556	34	31	18	3	0	245^1	267	15	91	138	13.2	4.07	115	.274	.338	23	.240	2	15	16	1	1.8
1938	Det-A	13	9	.591	25	20	13	0	1	151	171	14	58	101	13.8	4.59	109	.287	.353	7	.130	-1	3	7	-1	0.4
1939	Det-A★	17	7	.708	29	26	16	2	2	198	186	11	61	129	11.5	3.50	140	.243	.304	14	.197	0	25	31	-0	2.9
1940	*Det-A☆	12	9	.571	29	28	12	2	0	197^2	171	11	88	133	11.8	3.37	141	.229	.311	12	.176	-2	22	30	-1	2.7
1941	Det-A	9	12	.429	25	22	10	1	0	147^2	128	10	70	90	12.1	3.41	133	.233	.320	4	.085	-3	12	19	2	1.7
1942	Det-A	9	7	.563	23	22	11	2	1	174	164	6	61	97	11.8	2.74	144	.246	.313	6	.095	-3	18	23	1	2.3
1943	Det-A	12	7	.632	25	22	11	3	0	191^2	159	9	61	124	10.3	2.39	147	.226	.287	14	.219	2	19	24	-1	2.9
1945	*Det-A	1	0	1.000	4	1	0	0	0	11	14	2	2	6	13.1	3.27	107	.311	.340	0	.000	-0	0	0	1	0.0
1946	Det-A	1	1	.500	9	1	0	0	1	21^1	24	5	8	17	13.9	5.91	62	.279	.347	0	.000	0	-6	-5	0	-0.5
Total	16	194	138	.584	424	362	200	33	10	2826^1	2675	181	1192	1674	12.4	3.57	126	.248	.325	181	.180	-6	256	291	-3	27.4
● BUTTONS BRIGGS Briggs, Herbert Theodore b: 7/8/1875, Poughkeepsie, N.Y. d: 2/18/11, Cleveland, Ohio BR/TR, 6'1", 180 lbs. Deb: 4/23/1896																										
1896	Chi-N	12	8	.600	26	21	19	0	1	194	202	6	108	84	15.1	4.31	105	.266	.369	10	.128	-6	1	5	-3	-0.4
1897	Chi-N	4	17	.190	22	22	21	0	0	186^2	246	6	85	60	16.4	5.26	85	.315	.388	13	.160	-6	-20	-16	-1	-2.0
1898	Chi-N	1	3	.250	4	4	3	0	0	30	38	0	10	14	14.7	5.70	63	.306	.363	6	.429	2	-7	-7	-0	-0.5
1904	Chi-N	19	11	.633	34	30	28	3	3	277	252	3	77	112	10.9	2.05	130	.246	.304	16	.170	-0	21	19	-4	1.6
1905	Chi-N	8	8	.500	20	20	13	5	0	168	141	1	52	68	10.7	2.14	139	.237	.304	3	.053	-4	16	16	-2	0.9
Total	5	44	47	.484	106	97	84	8	4	855^2	879	16	332	338	13.1	3.41	104	.268	.342	48	.148	-15	12	14	-10	-0.4
● JOHN BRIGGS Briggs, Jonathan Tift b: 1/24/34, Natoma, Cal. BR/TR, 5'10", 175 lbs. Deb: 4/17/56																										
1956	Chi-N	0	0	—	3	0	0	0	0	5^1	5	1	4	1	20.3	1.69	223	.238	.429	0	—	0	1	1	0	0.1
1957	Chi-N	0	1	.000	3	0	0	0	0	4^1	7	2	3	1	20.8	12.46	31	.368	.455	0	—	0	-4	-4	-0	-0.4
1958	Chi-N	5	5	.500	20	17	3	1	0	95^2	99	12	45	46	13.6	4.52	87	.270	.352	9	.257	2	-6	-6	-1	-0.5
1959	Cle-A	0	1	.000	4	1	0	0	0	12^2	12	1	3	5	10.7	2.13	173	.245	.288	0	.000	-0	2	2	-0	0.2
1960	Cle-A	4	2	.667	21	2	0	0	1	36^1	32	4	15	19	11.9	4.46	84	.250	.333	1	.125	-0	-2	-3	-1	-0.4
	KC-A	0	2	.000	8	1	0	0	0	11^1	19	3	12	8	24.6	12.71	31	.380	.500	0	.000	-0	-11	-11	-0	-1.1
	Yr	4	4	.500	29	3	0	0	1	47^2	51	7	27	27	14.7	6.42	59	.282	.375	1	.091	-1	-13	-14	-1	-1.5
Total	5	9	11	.450	59	21	3	1	1	165^2	174	23	82	80	14.2	5.00	77	.275	.363	10	.208	1	-20	-21	-2	-2.1
● NELSON BRILES Briles, Nelson Kelley b: 8/5/43, Dorris, Cal. BR/TR, 5'11", 200 lbs. Deb: 4/19/65																										
1965	StL-N	3	3	.500	37	2	0	0	4	82^1	79	4	26	52	12.1	3.50	110	.258	.328	2	.133	-0	0	3	-1	0.2
1966	StL-N	4	15	.211	49	17	0	0	6	154	162	14	54	100	13.0	3.21	112	.279	.348	3	.079	-2	7	6	1	0.6
1967	*StL-N	14	5	.737	49	14	4	2	6	155^1	139	8	40	94	10.7	2.43	135	.236	.290	6	.150	0	16	15	-2	1.5
1968	*StL-N	19	11	.633	33	33	13	4	0	243^2	251	18	55	141	11.6	2.81	103	.266	.311	11	.138	1	5	2	-2	0.1
1969	StL-N	15	13	.536	36	33	10	3	0	227^2	218	17	63	126	11.2	3.52	102	.251	.303	8	.105	-1	2	1	-1	-0.1
1970	StL-N	6	7	.462	30	19	1	1	0	106^2	129	14	36	59	14.1	6.24	66	.297	.353	7	.179	1	-26	-25	-2	-2.5
1971	*Pit-N	8	4	.667	37	14	4	2	1	136	131	12	35	76	11.2	3.04	111	.250	.301	10	.256	4	6	5	-1	0.9
1972	*Pit-N	14	11	.560	28	27	9	2	0	195^2	185	14	43	120	10.5	3.08	108	.249	.291	11	.157	-0	8	5	-1	0.5
1973	Pit-N	14	13	.519	33	33	7	1	0	218^2	201	19	51	94	10.4	2.84	124	.244	.288	14	.194	3	20	16	0	2.1
1974	KC-A	5	7	.417	18	17	3	0	0	103	118	9	21	41	12.3	4.02	95	.293	.331	0	—	0	-5	-2	-1	-0.7
1975	KC-A	6	6	.500	24	16	3	0	2	112	127	19	25	73	12.6	4.26	90	.285	.330	0	—	0	-6	-5	0	-0.6
1976	Tex-A	11	9	.550	32	31	7	1	1	210	224	17	47	98	11.7	3.26	110	.273	.314	0	—	0	6	8	-3	0.4
1977	Tex-A	6	4	.600	28	15	2	1	1	108^1	114	13	30	57	12.5	4.24	96	.275	.333	0	—	0	-2	-2	-1	-0.3
	Bal-A	0	0	—	2	0	0	0	1	4	5	2	0	2	11.3	6.75	56	.294	.294	0	—	0	-1	-1	-0	-0.1
	Yr	6	4	.600	30	15	2	1	2	112^1	119	15	30	59	11.9	4.33	94	.271	.318	0	—	0	-3	-3	-1	-0.4
1978	Bal-A	4	4	.500	16	8	1	0	0	54^1	58	6	21	30	13.4	4.64	75	.279	.351	0	—	0	-5	-7	-1	-0.8
Total	14	129	112	.535	452	279	64	17	22	2111^2	2141	186	547	1163	11.7	3.44	102	.264	.314	72	.154	5	25	19	-14	1.2
● FRANK BRILL Brill, Francis Hasbrouck (b: Francis Hasbrouck Briell) b: 3/30/1864, Astoria, L.I., N.Y. d: 11/19/44, Flushing, N.Y. BR/TR, 5'8", 155 lbs. Deb: 6/23/1884																										
1884	Det-N	2	10	.167	12	12	12	1	0	103	148	7	26	18	15.2	5.50	53	.312	.348	6	.136	-3	-29	-30	-2	-2.7
● JIM BRILLHEART Brillheart, James Benson b: 9/28/03, Dublin, Va. d: 9/2/72, Radford, Va. BR/TL, 5'11", 170 lbs. Deb: 4/17/22																										
1922	Was-A	4	6	.400	31	10	3	0	1	119^2	120	3	72	47	15.0	3.61	107	.275	.388	3	.083	-3	6	3	-2	-0.2
1923	Was-A	0	1	.000	12	0	0	0	0	18	27	1	12	8	20.0	7.00	54	.360	.455	0	.000	-0	-6	-6	0	-0.6
1927	Chi-N	4	2	.667	32	12	4	0	0	128^2	140	4	38	36	12.7	4.13	94	.286	.343	1	.023	-5	-3	-4	-1	-1.0
1931	Bos-A	0	0	—	11	1	0	0	0	19^2	27	2	15	7	19.2	5.49	78	.325	.429	2	.500	2	-2	-3	1	0.0
Total	4	8	9	.471	86	23	7	0	1	286	314	10	137	98	14.6	4.19	93	.290	.376	6	.070	-8	-6	-9	-2	-1.8
● BRAD BRINK Brink, Bradford Albert b: 1/20/65, Roseville, Cal. BR/TR, 6'2", 195 lbs. Deb: 5/17/92																										
1992	Phi-N	0	4	.000	8	7	0	0	0	41^1	53	2	13	16	14.6	4.14	85	.308	.360	1	.083	-0	-3	-3	-0	-0.3
● JOHN BRISCOE Briscoe, John Eric b: 9/22/67, LaGrange, Ill. BR/TR, 6'3", 185 lbs. Deb: 4/18/91																										
1991	Oak-A	0	0	—	11	0	0	0	0	14	12	3	10	9	14.1	7.07	54	.235	.361	0	—	0	-5	-5	-0	-0.3
1992	Oak-A	0	1	.000	2	2	0	0	0	7	12	0	9	4	27.0	6.43	59	.400	.538	0	—	0	-2	-2	-0	-0.1
Total	2	0	1	.000	13	2	0	0	0	21	24	3	19	13	18.4	6.86	56	.296	.430	0	—	0	-7	-7	-0	-0.4
● LOU BRISSIE Brissie, Leland Victor b: 6/5/24, Anderson, S.C. BL/TL, 6'4", 215 lbs. Deb: 9/28/47																										
1947	Phi-A	0	1	.000	1	1	0	0	0	7	9	1	5	4	18.0	6.43	59	.310	.412	0	.000	-0	-2	-2	0	-0.2
1948	Phi-A	14	10	.583	39	25	11	0	5	194	202	6	95	127	13.9	4.13	104	.269	.352	18	.237	0	3	3	-2	0.2
1949	Phi-A★	16	11	.593	34	29	18	0	3	229^1	220	20	118	118	13.5	4.28	96	.251	.344	24	.267	3	-2	-4	-4	-0.5
1950	Phi-A	7	19	.269	46	31	15	2	8	246	237	22	117	101	13.1	4.02	113	.253	.338	15	.172	-3	15	14	-0	1.0
1951	Phi-A	0	2	.000	2	2	0	0	0	13^1	20	0	8	3	18.9	6.75	63	.357	.438	1	.200	-0	-4	-4	-0	-0.4
	Cle-A	4	3	.571	54	4	1	0	9	112^1	90	5	61	50	12.3	3.20	118	.223	.329	6	.261	0	11	7	-2	0.6
	Yr	4	5	.444	56	6	1	0	9	125^2	110	5	69	53	13.0	3.58	107	.239	.342	7	.250	0	8	4	-2	0.2
1952	Cle-A	3	2	.600	42	1	0	0	2	82^2	68	5	34	28	11.1	3.48	96	.221	.299	3	.250	1	2	-1	1	0.0
1953	Cle-A	0	0	—	16	0	0	0	2	13	21	2	13	5	23.5	7.62	49	.389	.507	0	—	0	-5	-6	-0	-0.6

YEAR	TM/L	W	L	PCT	G	GS	CG	SH	SV	IP	H	HR	BB	SO	RAT	ERA	ERA+	OAV	OOB	BH	AVG	PB	PR	/A	PD	TPI
Total	7	44	48	.478	234	93	45	2	29	897^{2}	867	61	451	436	13.4	4.07	102	.254	.343	67	.227	1	19	8	-7	0.1

● JIM BRITT Britt, James Edward b: 2/25/1856, Brooklyn, N.Y. d: 2/28/23, San Francisco, Cal Deb: 5/02/1872

YEAR	TM/L	W	L	PCT	G	GS	CG	SH	SV	IP	H	HR	BB	SO	RAT	ERA	ERA+	OAV	OOB	BH	AVG	PB	PR	/A	PD	TPI
1872	Atl-n	9	28	.243	37	37	37	0	0	336	561	6	19	13	15.5	5.06	91	.323	.331	39	.248	-8	-50	-17		-1.6
1873	Atl-n	17	36	.321	54	54	**51**	1	0	480^{2}	696	6	40	15	13.8	3.89	78	.300	.312	47	.196	-2	-34	-46		-3.2
Total	2 n	26	64	.289	91	91	88	1	0	816^{2}	1257	12	59	28	14.5	4.38	69	.310	.320	86	.217	-11	-102	-122		-4.8

● JACK BRITTIN Brittin, John Albert b: 3/4/24, Athens, Ill. BR/TR, 5'11", 175 lbs. Deb: 9/15/50

YEAR	TM/L	W	L	PCT	G	GS	CG	SH	SV	IP	H	HR	BB	SO	RAT	ERA	ERA+	OAV	OOB	BH	AVG	PB	PR	/A	PD	TPI
1950	Phi-N	0	0	—	3	0	0	0	0	4	2	0	3	3	11.3	4.50	90	.143	.294	0	—	0	-0	-0	0	0.0
1951	Phi-N	0	0	—	3	0	0	0	0	4	5	0	6	3	24.8	9.00	43	.294	.478	0	—	0	-2	-2	0	-0.2
Total	2	0	0	—	6	0	0	0	0	8	7	0	9	6	18.0	6.75	58	.226	.400	0	—	0	-2	-2	0	-0.2

● JIM BRITTON Britton, James Allan b: 3/25/44, N.Tonawanda, N.Y. BR/TR, 6'5", 225 lbs. Deb: 9/20/67

YEAR	TM/L	W	L	PCT	G	GS	CG	SH	SV	IP	H	HR	BB	SO	RAT	ERA	ERA+	OAV	OOB	BH	AVG	PB	PR	/A	PD	TPI
1967	Atl-N	0	2	.000	2	2	0	0	0	13^{1}	15	2	2	4	11.5	6.08	55	.278	.304	0	.000	-0	-4	-4	-0	-0.5
1968	Atl-N	4	6	.400	34	9	2	2	3	90	81	1	34	61	11.7	3.10	97	.245	.320	3	.143	-0	-1	-1	0	-0.2
1969	*Atl-N	7	5	.583	24	13	2	1	1	88	69	10	49	60	12.1	3.78	95	.218	.323	4	.190	0	-2	-2	-1	-0.2
1971	Mon-N	2	3	.400	16	6	0	0	0	45^{2}	49	10	27	23	15.4	5.72	62	.274	.375	0	.000	-1	-11	-11	-1	-1.3
Total	4	13	16	.448	76	30	4	3	4	237	214	23	112	148	12.5	4.03	83	.243	.332	7	.127	-2	-18	-18	-2	-2.2

● TONY BRIZZOLARA Brizzolara, Anthony John b: 1/14/57, Santa Monica, Cal. BR/TR, 6'5", 215 lbs. Deb: 5/19/79

YEAR	TM/L	W	L	PCT	G	GS	CG	SH	SV	IP	H	HR	BB	SO	RAT	ERA	ERA+	OAV	OOB	BH	AVG	PB	PR	/A	PD	TPI
1979	Atl-N	6	9	.400	20	19	2	0	0	107^{1}	133	6	33	64	14.2	5.28	77	.303	.356	1	.029	-3	-18	-15	0	-1.7
1983	Atl-N	1	0	1.000	14	0	0	0	1	20^{1}	22	2	6	17	12.4	3.54	109	.278	.329	0	—	0	0	1	-0	0.0
1984	Atl-N	1	2	.333	10	4	0	0	0	29	33	4	13	17	14.3	5.28	73	.284	.357	0	.000	-1	-5	-5	0	-0.6
Total	3	8	11	.421	44	23	2	0	1	156^{2}	188	12	52	98	14.0	5.06	79	.297	.353	1	.024	-4	-24	-19	-0	-2.3

● JOHNNY BROACA Broaca, John Joseph b: 10/3/09, Lawrence, Mass. d: 5/16/85, Lawrence, Mass. BR/TR, 5'11", 190 lbs. Deb: 6/02/34

YEAR	TM/L	W	L	PCT	G	GS	CG	SH	SV	IP	H	HR	BB	SO	RAT	ERA	ERA+	OAV	OOB	BH	AVG	PB	PR	/A	PD	TPI
1934	NY-A	12	9	.571	26	24	13	1	0	177^{1}	203	9	65	74	13.7	4.16	98	.284	.344	2	.030	-6	7	-2	-2	-1.0
1935	NY-A	15	7	.682	29	27	14	2	0	201	199	16	79	78	12.4	3.58	113	.254	.323	12	.150	-4	19	10	-3	0.4
1936	NY-A	12	7	.632	37	27	12	1	3	206	235	16	66	84	13.2	4.24	110	.284	.337	9	.110	-6	18	10	-2	0.1
1937	NY-A	1	4	.200	7	6	3	0	0	44	58	5	17	9	15.3	4.70	94	.324	.383	0	.000	-2	-0	-1	-1	-0.4
1939	Cle-A	4	2	.667	22	2	0	0	0	46	53	5	28	13	15.8	4.70	94	.288	.382	0	.000	-1	-0	-1	-0	-0.3
Total	5	44	29	.603	121	86	42	4	3	674^{1}	748	51	255	258	13.4	4.08	105	.278	.341	23	.091	-19	44	15	-8	-1.2

● PETE BROBERG Broberg, Peter Sven b: 3/2/50, W.Palm Beach, Fla. BR/TR, 6'3", 205 lbs. Deb: 6/20/71

YEAR	TM/L	W	L	PCT	G	GS	CG	SH	SV	IP	H	HR	BB	SO	RAT	ERA	ERA+	OAV	OOB	BH	AVG	PB	PR	/A	PD	TPI
1971	Was-A	5	9	.357	18	18	7	1	0	124^{2}	104	10	53	89	12.1	3.47	95	.228	.322	5	.114	0	-0	-2	-1	-0.3
1972	Tex-A	5	12	.294	39	25	3	2	1	176^{1}	153	14	85	133	12.8	4.29	70	.237	.338	4	.078	-2	-24	-25	1	-2.8
1973	Tex-A	5	9	.357	22	20	6	1	0	118^{2}	130	8	66	57	15.2	5.61	66	.283	.379	0	—	0	-24	-25	-0	-2.4
1974	Tex-A	0	4	.000	12	2	0	0	0	29	29	7	13	15	13.3	8.07	44	.264	.347	0	—	0	-14	-15	-0	-1.3
1975	Mil-A	14	16	.467	38	32	7	2	0	220^{1}	219	17	106	100	13.9	4.13	93	.263	.357	0	—	0	-9	-7	-0	-0.7
1976	Mil-A	1	7	.125	20	11	1	0	0	92^{1}	99	5	72	28	17.1	4.97	70	.281	.409	0	—	0	-15	-15	-1	-1.6
1977	Chi-N	1	2	.333	22	0	0	0	0	36	34	8	18	20	13.0	4.75	92	.256	.344	0	.000	-1	-3	-1	0	-0.2
1978	Oak-A	10	12	.455	35	26	2	0	0	165^{2}	174	16	65	94	13.1	4.62	79	.269	.338	0	—	0	-16	-18	1	-1.7
Total	8	41	71	.366	206	134	26	6	1	963	942	85	478	536	13.8	4.56	78	.259	.353	9	.089	-3	-105	-109	-0	-11.0

● DOUG BROCAIL Brocail, Douglas Keith b: 5/16/67, Clearfield, Pa. BL/TR, 6'5", 220 lbs. Deb: 9/08/92

YEAR	TM/L	W	L	PCT	G	GS	CG	SH	SV	IP	H	HR	BB	SO	RAT	ERA	ERA+	OAV	OOB	BH	AVG	PB	PR	/A	PD	TPI
1992	SD-N	0	0	—	3	3	0	0	0	14	17	2	5	15	14.1	6.43	56	.298	.355	1	.200	0	-5	-4	0	-0.4

● LEW BROCKETT Brockett, Lewis Albert "King" b: 7/23/1880, Brownsville, Ill. d: 9/19/60, Norris City, Ill. BR/TR, 5'10.5", 168 lbs. Deb: 4/25/07

YEAR	TM/L	W	L	PCT	G	GS	CG	SH	SV	IP	H	HR	BB	SO	RAT	ERA	ERA+	OAV	OOB	BH	AVG	PB	PR	/A	PD	TPI
1907	NY-A	1	2	.333	8	4	1	0	0	46^{1}	58	1	26	13	16.7	6.22	45	.308	.397	4	.182	-0	-19	-18	-1	-1.9
1909	NY-A	10	8	.556	26	18	10	3	1	170	148	3	59	70	11.3	2.12	119	.245	.318	17	.283	3	7	8	4	1.8
1911	NY-A	2	4	.333	16	8	2	0	0	75^{1}	73	3	39	25	14.0	4.66	77	.256	.356	12	.308	2	-11	-9	1	-0.6
Total	3	13	14	.481	50	30	13	3	1	291^{2}	279	7	124	108	12.8	3.43	83	.259	.343	33	.273	5	-23	-19	3	-0.7

● DICK BRODOWSKI Brodowski, Richard Stanley b: 7/26/32, Bayonne, N.J. BR/TR, 6'2", 190 lbs. Deb: 6/15/52

YEAR	TM/L	W	L	PCT	G	GS	CG	SH	SV	IP	H	HR	BB	SO	RAT	ERA	ERA+	OAV	OOB	BH	AVG	PB	PR	/A	PD	TPI
1952	Bos-A	5	5	.500	20	12	4	0	0	114^{2}	111	12	50	42	12.9	4.40	90	.252	.333	8	.205	1	-9	-6	0	-0.5
1955	Bos-A	1	0	1.000	16	0	0	0	0	32	36	5	25	10	17.4	5.63	76	.295	.419	5	.500	3	-6	-5	1	-0.1
1956	Was-A	0	3	.000	7	3	1	0	0	17^{2}	31	5	12	8	21.9	9.17	47	.397	.478	0	.000	-1	-10	-10	0	-0.9
1957	Was-A	0	1	.000	6	0	0	0	0	11^{1}	12	2	10	4	18.3	11.12	35	.261	.404	0	.000	-0	-9	-9	0	-0.9
1958	Cle-A	1	0	1.000	5	0	0	0	0	10	3	0	6	12	8.1	0.00	—	.100	.250	0	.000	-0	4	4	-0	0.4
1959	Cle-A	2	2	.500	18	0	0	0	5	30	19	3	21	9	12.9	1.80	205	.181	.333	2	.333	0	7	6	-1	0.6
Total	6	9	11	.450	72	15	5	0	5	215^{2}	212	27	124	85	14.4	4.76	84	.258	.361	15	.242	3	-23	-19	0	-1.4

● ERNIE BROGLIO Broglio, Ernest Gilbert b: 8/27/35, Berkeley, Cal. BR/TR, 6'2", 200 lbs. Deb: 4/11/59

YEAR	TM/L	W	L	PCT	G	GS	CG	SH	SV	IP	H	HR	BB	SO	RAT	ERA	ERA+	OAV	OOB	BH	AVG	PB	PR	/A	PD	TPI
1959	StL-N	7	12	.368	35	25	6	3	0	181^{1}	174	20	89	133	13.1	4.72	90	.250	.335	6	.098	-3	-15	-10	1	-1.1
1960	StL-N	**21**	9	**.700**	52	24	9	3	0	226^{1}	172	18	100	188	10.9	2.74	**149**	.213	.301	14	.206	3	26	**34**	1	4.1
1961	StL-N	9	12	.429	29	26	7	2	0	174^{2}	166	19	75	113	12.5	4.12	107	.248	.325	9	.145	-2	-2	5	-1	0.2
1962	StL-N	12	9	.571	34	30	11	4	0	222^{1}	193	22	93	132	11.7	3.00	143	.237	.316	10	.139	-2	23	31	1	3.1
1963	StL-N	18	8	.692	39	35	11	5	0	250	202	24	90	145	10.7	2.99	119	.216	.287	10	.112	-3	8	16	0	1.4
1964	StL-N	3	5	.375	11	11	3	1	0	69^{1}	65	7	26	36	11.9	3.50	109	.247	.317	2	.095	-0	0	2	-0	0.2
	Chi-N	4	7	.364	18	16	3	0	1	100^{1}	111	12	30	46	12.6	4.04	92	.281	.332	10	.286	3	-6	-4	-1	-0.2
	Yr	7	12	.368	29	27	6	1	1	169^{2}	176	19	56	82	12.3	3.82	98	.267	.324	12	.214	2	-5	-1	-2	0.0
1965	Chi-N	1	6	.143	26	6	0	0	0	50^{2}	63	7	46	22	19.4	6.93	53	.313	.441	0	.000	-0	-19	-18	-1	-2.0
1966	Chi-N	2	6	.250	15	11	2	0	1	62^{1}	70	14	38	34	15.6	6.35	58	.290	.387	7	.368	3	-19	-19	2	-1.4
Total	8	77	74	.510	259	184	52	18	2	1337^{1}	1216	143	587	849	12.2	3.74	107	.242	.322	68	.158	-2	-3	39	1	4.3

● KEN BRONDELL Brondell, Kenneth Leroy b: 10/17/21, Bradshaw, Neb. BR/TR, 6'1", 195 lbs. Deb: 5/03/44

YEAR	TM/L	W	L	PCT	G	GS	CG	SH	SV	IP	H	HR	BB	SO	RAT	ERA	ERA+	OAV	OOB	BH	AVG	PB	PR	/A	PD	TPI
1944	NY-N	0	1	.000	7	2	1	0	0	19^{1}	27	3	8	1	16.3	8.38	44	.329	.389	0	.000	-1	-10	-10	-1	-1.1

● JIM BRONSTAD Bronstad, James Warren b: 6/22/36, Ft.Worth, Tex. BR/TR, 6'3", 196 lbs. Deb: 6/07/59

YEAR	TM/L	W	L	PCT	G	GS	CG	SH	SV	IP	H	HR	BB	SO	RAT	ERA	ERA+	OAV	OOB	BH	AVG	PB	PR	/A	PD	TPI
1959	NY-A	0	3	.000	16	3	0	0	2	29^{1}	34	2	13	14	14.7	5.22	70	.288	.364	0	.000	-0	-4	-5	0	-0.5
1963	Was-A	1	3	.250	25	0	0	0	1	57^{1}	66	9	22	22	14.0	5.65	66	.297	.363	0	.000	-1	-13	-12	1	-1.3
1964	Was-A	0	1	.000	4	0	0	0	0	7	10	0	2	9	15.4	5.14	72	.345	.387	0	—	0	-1	-1	-0	-0.1
Total	3	1	7	.125	45	3	0	0	3	93^{2}	110	11	37	45	14.3	5.48	67	.298	.365	0	.000	-2	-18	-19	2	-1.9

● IKE BROOKENS Brookens, Edward Dwain b: 1/3/49, Chambersburg, Pa. BR/TR, 6'5", 170 lbs. Deb: 6/17/75

YEAR	TM/L	W	L	PCT	G	GS	CG	SH	SV	IP	H	HR	BB	SO	RAT	ERA	ERA+	OAV	OOB	BH	AVG	PB	PR	/A	PD	TPI
1975	Det-A	0	0	—	3	0	0	0	0	10^{1}	11	3	5	8	14.8	5.23	77	.282	.378	0	—	0	-2	-1	0	-0.2

● HARRY BROOKS Brooks, Harry Frank b: 11/30/1865, Philadelphia d: 12/5/45, Philadelphia, Pa. Deb: 7/24/1886 ♦

YEAR	TM/L	W	L	PCT	G	GS	CG	SH	SV	IP	H	HR	BB	SO	RAT	ERA	ERA+	OAV	OOB	BH	AVG	PB	PR	/A	PD	TPI
1886	NY-a	0	1	.000	1	1	0	0	0	2	9	0	2	0	49.5	36.00	9	.429	.478	0	.000	-0	-7	-7	-0	-0.5

● JIM BROSNAN Brosnan, James Patrick b: 10/24/29, Cincinnati, O. BR/TR, 6'4", 210 lbs. Deb: 4/15/54

YEAR	TM/L	W	L	PCT	G	GS	CG	SH	SV	IP	H	HR	BB	SO	RAT	ERA	ERA+	OAV	OOB	BH	AVG	PB	PR	/A	PD	TPI
1954	Chi-N	1	0	1.000	18	0	0	0	0	33^{1}	44	9	18	17	17.0	9.45	44	.331	.414	1	.125	-0	-20	-19	1	-1.8
1956	Chi-N	5	9	.357	30	10	1	1	1	95	95	9	45	51	13.3	3.79	100	.270	.353	4	.182	-0	-0	-0	-1	-0.1
1957	Chi-N	5	5	.500	41	5	1	0	0	98^{2}	79	11	46	73	11.5	3.38	115	.219	.310	5	.250	2	6	5	1	0.8
1958	Chi-N	3	4	.429	8	8	2	0	0	51^{2}	41	3	29	24	12.2	3.14	125	.225	.332	2	.105	-1	5	4	1	0.5
	StL-N	8	4	.667	33	12	2	0	7	115	107	10	50	65	12.4	3.44	120	.250	.330	3	.097	-1	6	9	0	0.8

YEAR	TM/L	W	L	PCT	G	GS	CG	SH	SV	IP	H	HR	BB	SO	RAT	ERA	ERA+	OAV	OOB	BH	AVG	PB	PR	/A	PD	TPI
	Yr	11	8	.579	41	20	4	0	7	166^2	148	13	79	89	12.3	3.35	121	.241	.329	5	.100	-2	11	13	1	1.3
1959	StL-N	1	3	.250	20	1	0	0	2	33	34	5	15	18	13.6	4.91	86	.276	.360	2	.286	1	-4	-2	1	-0.1
	Cin-N	8	3	.727	26	9	1	1	2	83^1	79	7	26	56	11.9	3.35	121	.248	.314	1	.043	-2	6	7	1	0.5
	Yr	9	6	.600	46	10	1	1	4	116^1	113	12	41	74	12.3	3.79	108	.255	.324	3	.100	-1	2	4	1	0.4
1960	Cin-N	7	2	.778	57	2	0	0	12	99	79	4	22	62	9.2	2.36	162	.225	.271	3	.200	2	15	16	-0	1.8
1961	*Cin-N	10	4	.714	53	0	0	0	16	80	77	7	18	40	10.7	3.04	134	.249	.291	2	.154	-0	9	9	1	1.0
1962	Cin-N	4	4	.500	48	0	0	0	13	64^2	76	6	18	51	13.1	3.34	120	.292	.338	0	.000	-1	4	5	-1	0.4
1963	Cin-N	0	1	.000	6	0	0	0	0	4^2	8	2	3	4	21.2	7.71	43	.421	.500	0	—	0	-2	-2	0	-0.2
	Chi-A	3	8	.273	45	0	0	0	14	73	71	7	22	46	11.5	2.84	124	.263	.318	4	.308	1	6	5	-0	0.6
Total	9	55	47	.539	385	47	7	2	67	831^1	790	80	312	507	12.0	3.54	111	.254	.324	27	.153	1	31	36	3	4.2

● **TERRY BROSS** Bross, Terrence Paul b: 3/30/66, ElPaso, Tex. BR/TR, 6'9", 234 lbs. Deb: 9/04/91

YEAR	TM/L	W	L	PCT	G	GS	CG	SH	SV	IP	H	HR	BB	SO	RAT	ERA	ERA+	OAV	OOB	BH	AVG	PB	PR	/A	PD	TPI
1991	NY-N	0	0	—	8	0	0	0	0	10	7	1	3	5	9.0	1.80	202	.200	.263	0	—	0	2	2	-0	0.2

● **FRANK BROSSEAU** Brosseau, Franklin Lee b: 7/31/44, Drayton, N.D. BR/TR, 6'1", 180 lbs. Deb: 9/10/69

YEAR	TM/L	W	L	PCT	G	GS	CG	SH	SV	IP	H	HR	BB	SO	RAT	ERA	ERA+	OAV	OOB	BH	AVG	PB	PR	/A	PD	TPI
1969	Pit-N	0	0	—	2	0	0	0	0	1^2	2	0	2	2	21.6	10.80	32	.286	.444	0	—	0	-1	-1	-0	-0.1
1971	Pit-N	0	0	—	1	0	0	0	0	2	1	0	0	0	4.5	0.00	—	.200	.200	0	—	0	1	1	0	0.1
Total	2	0	0	—	3	0	0	0	0	3^2	3	0	2	2	12.3	4.91	70	.250	.357	0	—	0	-1	-1	0	0.0

● **DAN BROUTHERS** Brouthers, Dennis Joseph "Big Dan" b: 5/8/1858, Sylvan Lake, N.Y. d: 8/2/32, E.Orange, N.J. BL/TL, 6'2", 207 lbs. Deb: 6/23/1879 H♦

YEAR	TM/L	W	L	PCT	G	GS	CG	SH	SV	IP	H	HR	BB	SO	RAT	ERA	ERA+	OAV	OOB	BH	AVG	PB	PR	/A	PD	TPI
1879	Tro-N	0	2	.000	3	2	2	0	0	21	35	0	8	6	18.4	5.57	45	.343	.391	46	.274	1	-7	-7	-1	-0.6
1883	Buf-N	0	0	—	1	0	0	0	0	2	9	0	3	2	54.0	31.50	10	.643	.706	159	.374	1	-6	-6	-0	-0.4
Total	2	0	2	.000	4	2	2	0	0	23	44	0	11	8	21.5	7.83	33	.379	.433	2296	.342	1	-13	-13	-1	-1.0

● **FRANK BROWER** Brower, Frank Willard "Turkeyfoot" b: 3/26/1893, Gainesville, Va. d: 11/20/60, Baltimore, Md. BL/TR, 6'2", 180 lbs. Deb: 8/14/20 ♦

YEAR	TM/L	W	L	PCT	G	GS	CG	SH	SV	IP	H	HR	BB	SO	RAT	ERA	ERA+	OAV	OOB	BH	AVG	PB	PR	/A	PD	TPI
1924	Cle-A	0	0	—	4	0	0	0	0	9^2	7	0	4	0	11.2	0.93	459	.212	.316	30	.280	1	4	4	-0	0.4

● **ALTON BROWN** Brown, Alton Leo "Deacon" b: 4/16/25, Norfolk, Va. BR/TR, 6'2", 195 lbs. Deb: 4/21/51

YEAR	TM/L	W	L	PCT	G	GS	CG	SH	SV	IP	H	HR	BB	SO	RAT	ERA	ERA+	OAV	OOB	BH	AVG	PB	PR	/A	PD	TPI
1951	Was-A	0	0	—	7	0	0	0	0	11^2	14	1	12	7	20.8	9.26	44	.298	.450	0	.000	-0	-7	-7	-0	-0.7

● **BOARDWALK BROWN** Brown, Carroll William b: 2/20/1887, Woodbury, N.J. d: 2/8/77, Burlington, N.J. BR/TR, 6'1.5", 178 lbs. Deb: 9/27/11

YEAR	TM/L	W	L	PCT	G	GS	CG	SH	SV	IP	H	HR	BB	SO	RAT	ERA	ERA+	OAV	OOB	BH	AVG	PB	PR	/A	PD	TPI
1911	Phi-A	0	1	.000	2	1	1	0	0	12	12	0	2	6	10.5	4.50	70	.267	.298	0	.000	-1	-2	-2	0	-0.2
1912	Phi-A	13	11	.542	34	24	15	3	0	199	204	2	87	64	13.6	3.66	84	.283	.367	11	.145	-3	-8	-13	3	-1.3
1913	Phi-A	17	11	.607	43	35	11	3	1	235^1	200	6	87	70	11.4	2.94	94	.219	.294	13	.159	-1	-0	-5	-2	-0.9
1914	Phi-A	1	6	.143	15	8	2	0	0	66	64	1	26	20	12.3	4.09	64	.268	.340	0	.000	-2	-10	-11	0	-1.3
	NY-A	5	5	.500	20	14	8	0	1	122^1	123	2	42	57	12.2	3.24	85	.271	.334	8	.182	1	-7	-6	3	-0.2
	Yr	6	11	.353	35	22	10	0	1	188^1	187	3	68	77	12.2	3.54	77	.270	.336	8	.125	-0	-17	-17	3	-1.5
1915	NY-A	2	6	.250	19	11	5	0	1	96^2	95	4	47	34	13.7	4.10	72	.275	.370	6	.188	-1	-12	-13	-0	-1.4
Total	5	38	40	.487	133	93	42	6	3	731^1	698	15	291	251	12.5	3.47	83	.257	.334	38	.147	-6	-39	-49	4	-5.3

● **CHARLIE BROWN** Brown, Charles E. b: 1878, Baltimore, Md. TL , 6', 180 lbs. Deb: 8/04/1897

YEAR	TM/L	W	L	PCT	G	GS	CG	SH	SV	IP	H	HR	BB	SO	RAT	ERA	ERA+	OAV	OOB	BH	AVG	PB	PR	/A	PD	TPI
1897	Cle-N	1	2	.333	4	4	2	0	0	24^1	30	2	17	8	19.2	7.77	58	.300	.427	3	.273	0	-9	-9	-0	-0.7

● **BUSTER BROWN** Brown, Charles Edward "Yank" b: 8/31/1881, Boone, Iowa d: 2/9/14, Sioux City, Iowa BR/TR, 6', 180 lbs. Deb: 6/22/05

YEAR	TM/L	W	L	PCT	G	GS	CG	SH	SV	IP	H	HR	BB	SO	RAT	ERA	ERA+	OAV	OOB	BH	AVG	PB	PR	/A	PD	TPI
1905	StL-N	8	11	.421	23	21	17	3	0	178^2	172	5	62	57	12.3	2.97	100	.260	.332	6	.092	-3	1	0	3	0.0
1906	StL-N	8	16	.333	32	27	21	0	0	238^1	208	2	112	109	12.5	2.64	99	.234	.327	14	.165	0	-0	-0	2	0.2
1907	StL-N	1	6	.143	9	8	6	0	0	63^2	57	2	45	17	15.1	3.39	74	.263	.401	7	.269	2	-7	-6	2	-0.3
	Phi-N	9	6	.600	21	16	13	4	0	130	118	3	56	38	12.5	2.42	100	.246	.333	10	.189	2	1	-0	-1	0.1
	Yr	10	12	.455	30	24	19	4	0	193^2	175	5	101	55	13.1	2.74	89	.250	.349	17	.215	3	-6	-6	1	-0.2
1908	Phi-N	0	0	—	3	0	0	0	0	7	9	0	5	3	19.3	2.57	94	.346	.469	1	.200	-0	-0	-0	1	0.1
1909	Phi-N	0	0	—	7	1	0	0	0	25	22	1	16	10	14.0	3.24	80	.259	.382	0	.000	-1	-2	-2	0	-0.3
	Bos-N	4	8	.333	18	17	8	2	0	123^1	108	1	56	32	12.5	3.14	90	.244	.339	7	.146	-2	-7	-4	1	-0.6
	Yr	4	8	.333	25	18	8	2	0	148^1	130	2	72	42	12.7	3.16	88	.246	.344	7	.123	-3	-9	-6	1	-0.9
1910	Bos-N	9	23	.281	46	29	16	1	2	263	251	4	94	88	11.9	2.67	125	.268	.337	16	.198	0	11	19	1	2.3
1911	Bos-N	8	18	.308	42	25	13	0	2	241	258	11	116	76	14.3	4.29	89	.284	.371	21	.250	4	-24	-13	0	-0.8
1912	Bos-N	4	15	.211	31	21	12	0	0	168^1	146	7	66	68	11.4	4.01	89	.239	.315	13	.213	1	-11	-8	0	-0.7
1913	Bos-N	0	0	—	2	0	0	0	0	13^1	19	0	3	3	16.2	4.73	70	.396	.453	0	.000	-0	-2	-2	-0	-0.2
Total	9	51	103	.331	234	165	106	10	4	1451^2	1368	36	631	501	12.8	3.21	96	.258	.343	95	.182	4	-41	-18	8	-0.2

● **CURLY BROWN** Brown, Charles Roy "Lefty" b: 12/9/1888, Spring Hill, Kan. d: 6/10/68, Spring Hill, Kan. BL/TL, 5'10.5", 165 lbs. Deb: 9/08/11

YEAR	TM/L	W	L	PCT	G	GS	CG	SH	SV	IP	H	HR	BB	SO	RAT	ERA	ERA+	OAV	OOB	BH	AVG	PB	PR	/A	PD	TPI
1911	StL-A	1	2	.333	3	2	2	0	0	23	22	0	5	8	11.0	2.74	123	.247	.295	0	.000	-1	2	2	0	0.0
1912	StL-A	1	3	.250	16	4	2	1	0	64^2	69	0	35	28	14.9	4.87	68	.277	.373	5	.208	-0	-11	-11	-3	-1.3
1913	StL-A	1	1	.500	2	2	2	0	0	14	12	0	4	3	10.3	2.57	114	.245	.302	2	.400	1	1	1	-0	0.1
1915	Cin-N	0	2	.000	7	3	0	0	0	27	26	2	6	13	11.3	4.67	61	.245	.298	4	.364	1	-6	-5	-1	-0.6
Total	4	3	8	.273	28	11	6	1	0	128^2	129	2	50	52	12.9	4.20	76	.262	.337	11	.224	0	-15	-14	-4	-1.8

● **CLINT BROWN** Brown, Clinton Harold b: 7/8/03, Blackash, Pa. d: 12/31/55, Rocky River, Ohio BL/TR, 6'1", 190 lbs. Deb: 9/27/28

YEAR	TM/L	W	L	PCT	G	GS	CG	SH	SV	IP	H	HR	BB	SO	RAT	ERA	ERA+	OAV	OOB	BH	AVG	PB	PR	/A	PD	TPI
1928	Cle-A	0	1	.000	2	1	1	0	0	11	14	0	2	2	13.1	4.91	84	.304	.333	1	.200	-0	-1	-1	0	-0.1
1929	Cle-A	0	2	.000	3	1	1	0	0	16^1	18	0	6	1	13.2	3.31	134	.286	.348	0	.000	-1	2	2	1	0.2
1930	Cle-A	11	13	.458	35	31	16	**3**	1	213^2	271	14	51	54	13.7	4.97	97	.314	.356	18	.247	2	-8	-3	2	0.1
1931	Cle-A	11	15	.423	39	33	12	2	0	233^1	284	10	55	50	13.1	4.71	98	.295	.333	15	.172	-2	-8	-2	4	0.0
1932	Cle-A	15	12	.556	37	32	21	1	1	262^2	298	14	50	59	12.1	4.08	116	.279	.314	25	.250	6	12	19	2	2.6
1933	Cle-A	11	12	.478	33	23	10	2	1	185	202	10	34	47	11.6	3.41	130	.276	.310	9	.145	-3	18	21	3	2.1
1934	Cle-A	4	3	.571	17	2	0	0	1	50^1	83	3	14	15	17.3	5.90	77	.359	.396	5	.294	2	-8	-8	-0	-0.6
1935	Cle-A	4	3	.571	23	5	1	0	2	49	61	3	14	20	14.0	5.14	88	.300	.349	2	.200	0	-4	-3	1	-0.2
1936	Chi-A	6	2	.750	38	2	0	0	5	83	106	5	24	19	14.4	4.99	104	.315	.366	4	.160	-0	0	2	0	0.2
1937	Chi-A	7	7	.500	**53**	0	0	0	**18**	100	92	7	36	51	11.6	3.42	135	.242	.309	4	.222	1	**13**	**13**	1	1.5
1938	Chi-A	1	3	.250	8	0	0	0	2	13^2	16	0	9	2	16.5	4.61	106	.333	.439	1	.500	1	0	0	1	0.2
1939	Chi-A	11	10	.524	**61**	0	0	0	18	118^1	127	8	27	41	11.7	3.88	122	.281	.322	4	.211	1	10	11	2	1.3
1940	Chi-A	4	6	.400	37	0	0	0	10	66	75	5	16	23	12.7	3.68	120	.284	.330	1	.071	-1	5	5	0	0.5
1941	Cle-A	3	3	.500	41	0	0	0	5	74^1	77	3	28	22	12.8	3.27	120	.279	.348	2	.118	0	7	6	3	0.8
1942	Cle-A	1	1	.500	7	0	0	0	0	9	16	2	2	4	19.0	6.00	57	.356	.396	0	.000	-0	-2	-3	-0	-0.3
Total	15	89	93	.489	434	130	62	8	64	1485^2	1740	84	368	410	12.9	4.26	109	.291	.335	91	.199	6	37	60	19	8.3

● **CURT BROWN** Brown, Curtis Steven b: 1/15/60, Ft.Lauderdale, Fla. BR/TR, 6'5", 200 lbs. Deb: 6/10/83

YEAR	TM/L	W	L	PCT	G	GS	CG	SH	SV	IP	H	HR	BB	SO	RAT	ERA	ERA+	OAV	OOB	BH	AVG	PB	PR	/A	PD	TPI
1983	Cal-A	1	1	.500	10	0	0	0	0	16	25	1	4	7	16.3	7.31	55	.368	.403	0	—	0	-6	-6	-0	-0.6
1984	NY-A	1	1	.500	13	0	0	0	0	16^2	18	1	4	10	11.9	2.70	140	.281	.324	0	—	0	2	2	0	0.3
1986	Mon-N	0	1	.000	6	0	0	0	0	12	15	0	2	4	12.8	3.00	123	.319	.347	0	.000	-0	1	1	0	0.1
1987	Mon-N	0	1	.000	5	0	0	0	0	7	10	2	4	6	18.0	7.71	54	.333	.412	0	—	0	-3	-3	0	-0.3
Total	4	2	4	.333	34	0	0	0	0	51^2	68	4	14	27	14.3	4.88	80	.325	.368	0	.000	-0	-5	-6	-0	-0.5

● **ED BROWN** Brown, Edward P. b: Chicago, Ill. TR , Deb: 8/19/1882 ♦

YEAR	TM/L	W	L	PCT	G	GS	CG	SH	SV	IP	H	HR	BB	SO	RAT	ERA	ERA+	OAV	OOB	BH	AVG	PB	PR	/A	PD	TPI
1882	StL-a	0	0	—	1	0	0	0	0	2	2	0	0	1	9.0	0.00	—	.243	.243	11	.183	-0	1	1	-0	0.0
1884	Tol-a	0	1	.000	1	1	1	0	0	9	19	0	4	1	24.0	9.00	38	.396	.453	27	.176	-0	-6	-6	-0	-0.4
Total	2	0	1	.000	2	1	1	0	0	11	21	0	4	2	21.3	7.36	45	.374	.425	38	.178	-0	-5	-5	-0	-0.4

● ELMER BROWN Brown, Elmer Young "Shook" b: 3/25/1883, Southport, Ind. d: 1/23/55, Indianapolis, Ind. BL/TR, 5'11.5", 172 lbs. Deb: 9/16/11

YEAR	TM/L	W	L	PCT	G	GS	CG	SH	SV	IP	H	HR	BB	SO	RAT	ERA	ERA+	OAV	OOB	BH	AVG	PB	PR	/A	PD	TPI
1911	StL-A	1	1	.500	5	3	1	1	0	16^{2}	16	0	14	5	16.2	6.48	52	.242	.375	1	.125	-1	-6	-6	1	-0.5
1912	StL-A	5	8	.385	23	13	2	1	0	120^{1}	122	2	42	45	13.2	2.99	111	.280	.359	6	.167	-1	4	4	-1	0.3
1913	Bro-N	0	0	—	3	1	0	0	0	13	6	0	10	6	11.8	2.08	159	.158	.347	0	.000	-1	2	2	-0	0.1
1914	Bro-N	1	2	.333	11	4	1	0	0	36^{2}	33	2	23	22	15.5	3.93	73	.402	.563	1	.083	-1	-5	-4	1	-0.5
1915	Bro-N	0	0	—	1	0	0	0	0	2	4	0	3	1	31.5	9.00	31	.500	.636	0	—	0	-1	-1	0	-0.1
Total	5	7	11	.389	43	21	4	2	0	188^{2}	181	4	92	79	14.0	3.48	93	.287	.395	8	.133	-3	-6	-5	0	-0.7

● HAL BROWN Brown, Hector Harold "Skinny" b: 12/11/24, Greensboro, N.C. BR/TR, 6'2", 182 lbs. Deb: 4/19/51

YEAR	TM/L	W	L	PCT	G	GS	CG	SH	SV	IP	H	HR	BB	SO	RAT	ERA	ERA+	OAV	OOB	BH	AVG	PB	PR	/A	PD	TPI
1951	Chi-A	0	0	—	3	0	0	0	1	8^{2}	15	3	4	4	19.7	9.35	43	.385	.442	2	1.000	1	-5	-5	0	-0.3
1952	Chi-A	2	3	.400	24	8	1	0	0	72^{1}	82	8	21	31	12.8	4.23	86	.284	.332	3	.158	1	-4	-5	-0	-0.4
1953	Bos-A	11	6	.647	30	25	6	1	0	166^{1}	177	16	57	62	12.7	4.65	90	.269	.327	17	.293	5	-12	-8	-0	-0.4
1954	Bos-A	1	8	.111	40	5	1	0	0	118	126	6	41	66	13.0	4.12	100	.269	.331	3	.125	-0	-5	-0	1	0.0
1955	Bos-A	1	0	1.000	2	0	0	0	0	4	2	0	2	2	9.0	2.25	191	.143	.250	1	1.000	0	1	1	-0	0.1
	Bal-A	0	4	.000	15	5	1	0	0	57	51	5	26	26	12.2	4.11	93	.241	.324	0	.000	-1	-1	-2	-1	-0.4
	Yr	1	4	.200	17	5	1	0	0	61	53	5	28	28	12.0	3.98	97	.235	.319	1	.059	-1	-0	-1	-1	-0.3
1956	Bal-A	9	7	.563	35	14	4	1	2	151^{2}	142	18	37	57	10.7	4.04	97	.247	.294	8	.190	1	2	-2	0	0.0
1957	Bal-A	7	8	.467	25	20	7	2	1	150	132	17	37	62	10.3	3.90	92	.236	.285	10	.208	2	-2	-5	-1	-0.4
1958	Bal-A	7	5	.583	19	17	4	2	1	96^{2}	96	9	20	44	10.8	3.07	117	.259	.297	4	.148	-0	7	6	-0	0.5
1959	Bal-A	11	9	.550	31	21	2	0	3	164	158	16	32	81	10.5	3.79	100	.252	.290	2	.048	-2	1	-0	-1	-0.3
1960	Bal-A	12	5	.706	30	20	6	1	0	159	155	14	22	66	**10.1**	3.06	125	.258	**.286**	8	.182	3	14	13	-1	1.5
1961	Bal-A	10	6	.625	27	23	6	3	1	166^{2}	153	14	33	61	10.1	3.19	123	.247	.286	7	.140	-0	16	13	-0	1.3
1962	Bal-A	6	4	.600	22	11	0	0	1	85^{2}	88	12	21	25	11.8	4.10	92	.268	.318	8	.286	1	-1	-3	-1	-0.3
	NY-A	0	1	.000	2	1	0	0	0	6^{2}	9	3	2	2	14.9	6.75	56	.333	.379	0	.000	-0	-2	-2	-0	-0.2
	Yr	6	5	.545	24	12	0	0	1	92^{1}	97	15	23	27	11.7	4.29	88	.270	.314	8	.276	1	-3	-5	-1	-0.5
1963	Hou-N	5	11	.313	26	20	6	3	0	141^{1}	137	14	8	68	9.2	3.31	95	.255	.266	4	.093	-2	-0	-2	-3	-0.7
1964	Hou-N	3	15	.167	27	21	3	0	1	132	154	18	26	53	12.4	3.95	86	.292	.327	5	.128	-1	-6	-8	-2	-1.0
Total	14	85	92	.480	358	211	47	13	11	1680	1677	173	389	710	11.1	3.81	99	.260	.303	82	.169	8	2	-10	-10	-1.0

● JACKIE BROWN Brown, Jackie Gene b: 5/31/43, Holdenville, Okla. BR/TR, 6'1", 195 lbs. Deb: 7/02/70 FC

YEAR	TM/L	W	L	PCT	G	GS	CG	SH	SV	IP	H	HR	BB	SO	RAT	ERA	ERA+	OAV	OOB	BH	AVG	PB	PR	/A	PD	TPI
1970	Was-A	2	2	.500	24	5	1	0	0	57	49	8	37	47	13.6	3.95	90	.231	.345	2	.154	-0	-1	-2	-1	-0.4
1971	Was-A	3	4	.429	14	9	0	0	0	47	60	9	27	21	16.9	5.94	56	.316	.404	2	.133	-0	-13	-14	1	-1.4
1973	Tex-A	5	5	.500	25	3	2	1	2	66^{2}	82	7	25	45	14.7	3.92	95	.309	.373	0	—	0	-1	-1	-1	-0.2
1974	Tex-A	13	12	.520	35	26	9	2	0	216^{2}	219	13	74	134	12.3	3.57	100	.265	.329	0	—	0	1	-0	-1	-0.1
1975	Tex-A	5	5	.500	17	7	2	1	0	70^{1}	70	7	35	35	13.7	4.22	89	.266	.357	0	—	0	-3	-4	-2	-0.5
	Cle-A	1	2	.333	25	3	1	0	1	69^{1}	72	9	29	41	13.1	4.28	88	.276	.348	0	—	0	-4	-4	-0	-0.4
	Yr	6	7	.462	42	10	3	1	1	139^{2}	142	16	64	76	13.3	4.25	89	.269	.349	0	—	0	-7	-8	-2	-0.9
1976	Cle-A	9	11	.450	32	27	5	2	0	180	193	14	55	104	12.8	4.25	82	.276	.335	0	—	0	-15	-15	-1	-1.6
1977	Mon-N	9	12	.429	42	25	6	2	0	185^{2}	189	15	71	89	12.8	4.51	84	.264	.334	7	.125	-2	-12	-14	-2	-1.8
Total	7	47	53	.470	214	105	26	8	3	892^{2}	934	82	353	516	13.2	4.18	87	.272	.343	11	.131	-3	-48	-55	-7	-6.4

● KEVIN BROWN Brown, James Kevin b: 3/14/65, Milledgeville, Ga. BR/TR, 6'4", 195 lbs. Deb: 9/30/86

YEAR	TM/L	W	L	PCT	G	GS	CG	SH	SV	IP	H	HR	BB	SO	RAT	ERA	ERA+	OAV	OOB	BH	AVG	PB	PR	/A	PD	TPI
1986	Tex-A	1	0	1.000	1	1	0	0	0	5	6	0	0	4	10.8	3.60	119	.316	.316	0	—	0	0	0	0	0.0
1988	Tex-A	1	1	.500	4	4	1	0	0	23^{1}	33	2	8	12	16.2	4.24	96	.330	.385	0	—	0	-1	-0	-0	-0.1
1989	Tex-A	12	9	.571	28	28	7	0	0	191	167	10	70	104	11.4	3.35	118	.234	.305	0	—	0	11	13	3	1.7
1990	Tex-A	12	10	.545	26	26	6	2	0	180	175	13	60	88	11.9	3.60	109	.255	.318	0	.000	0	6	6	-0	0.6
1991	Tex-A	9	12	.429	33	33	0	0	0	210^{2}	233	17	90	96	14.4	4.40	92	.284	.364	0	—	0	-7	-9	1	-0.8
1992	Tex-A★	**21**	11	.656	35	35	11	1	0	**265^{2}**	262	11	76	173	11.8	3.32	115	.260	.318	0	—	0	18	15	2	1.8
Total	6	56	43	.566	127	127	25	3	0	875^{2}	876	53	304	477	12.4	3.67	107	.262	.329	0	.000	0	28	26	6	3.2

● JIM BROWN Brown, James W. H. b: 12/12/1860, Clinton Co., Pa. d: 4/6/08, Williamsport, Pa. Deb: 4/17/1884 ♦

YEAR	TM/L	W	L	PCT	G	GS	CG	SH	SV	IP	H	HR	BB	SO	RAT	ERA	ERA+	OAV	OOB	BH	AVG	PB	PR	/A	PD	TPI
1884	Alt-U	1	9	.100	11	11	7	0	0	74	99	0	36	39	16.4	5.35	61	.301	.370	22	.250	0	-19	-17	0	-1.3
	NY-N	0	1	.000	1	1	1	0	0	9	10	0	8	2	18.0	5.00	60	.263	.391	0	.000	-1	-2	-2	-0	-0.2
	StP-U	1	4	.200	6	6	4	1	0	36	43	1	14	20	14.3	3.75	44	.277	.337	5	.313	3	-3	-8	0	-0.5
1886	Phi-a	0	1	.000	1	1	1	0	0	8^{1}	9	0	3	4	13.0	3.24	108	.265	.324	0	.000	-1	0	0	-0	0.0
Total	2	2	15	.118	19	19	13	1	0	127^{1}	161	1	61	65	15.7	4.74	59	.289	.360	27	.245	2	-24	-27	0	-2.0

● JOHN BROWN Brown, John J. "Ad" b: Trenton, N.J. Deb: 8/11/1897

YEAR	TM/L	W	L	PCT	G	GS	CG	SH	SV	IP	H	HR	BB	SO	RAT	ERA	ERA+	OAV	OOB	BH	AVG	PB	PR	/A	PD	TPI
1897	Bro-N	0	1	.000	1	1	0	0	0	5	7	0	4	0	25.2	7.20	57	.328	.494	1	.500	0	-2	-2	0	-0.1

● JOPHERY BROWN Brown, Jophery Clifford b: 1/22/45, Grambling, La. BL/TR, 6'2", 190 lbs. Deb: 9/21/68

YEAR	TM/L	W	L	PCT	G	GS	CG	SH	SV	IP	H	HR	BB	SO	RAT	ERA	ERA+	OAV	OOB	BH	AVG	PB	PR	/A	PD	TPI
1968	Chi-N	0	0	—	1	0	0	0	0	2	2	0	1	0	13.5	4.50	70	.286	.375	0	—	0	-0	-0	0	0.0

● JOE BROWN Brown, Joseph E. b: 4/4/1859, Warren, Pa. d: 6/28/1888, Warren, Pa. Deb: 8/16/1884 ♦

YEAR	TM/L	W	L	PCT	G	GS	CG	SH	SV	IP	H	HR	BB	SO	RAT	ERA	ERA+	OAV	OOB	BH	AVG	PB	PR	/A	PD	TPI
1884	Chi-N	4	2	.667	7	6	5	0	0	50	56	4	7	27	11.3	4.68	67	.258	.281	13	.213	-1	-9	-9	-0	-0.8
1885	Bal-a	0	4	.000	4	4	4	0	0	38	52	0	4	9	13.3	5.68	57	.306	.322	3	.158	-1	-10	-10	-0	-0.9
Total	2	4	6	.400	11	10	9	0	0	88	108	4	11	36	12.2	5.11	62	.279	.299	16	.200	-2	-20	-19	-1	-1.7

● JOE BROWN Brown, Joseph Henry b: 7/3/1900, Little Rock, Ark. d: 3/7/50, Los Angeles, Cal. BR/TR, 6', 176 lbs. Deb: 5/17/27

YEAR	TM/L	W	L	PCT	G	GS	CG	SH	SV	IP	H	HR	BB	SO	RAT	ERA	ERA+	OAV	OOB	BH	AVG	PB	PR	/A	PD	TPI
1927	Chi-A	0	0	—	1	1	0	0	0	0	2	0	1	0	—	∞	—	1.000	1.000	0	—	0	-3	-3	0	-0.2

● KEITH BROWN Brown, Keith Edward b: 2/14/64, Flagstaff, Ariz. BB/TR, 6'4", 215 lbs. Deb: 8/25/88

YEAR	TM/L	W	L	PCT	G	GS	CG	SH	SV	IP	H	HR	BB	SO	RAT	ERA	ERA+	OAV	OOB	BH	AVG	PB	PR	/A	PD	TPI
1988	Cin-N	2	1	.667	4	3	0	0	0	16^{1}	14	1	4	6	9.9	2.76	130	.237	.286	0	.000	-0	1	1	0	0.1
1990	Cin-N	0	0	—	8	0	0	0	0	11^{1}	12	2	3	8	11.9	4.76	83	.286	.333	0	—	0	-1	-1	0	-0.1
1991	Cin-N	0	0	—	11	0	0	0	0	12	15	0	6	4	15.8	2.25	169	.306	.382	0	—	0	2	2	0	0.2
1992	Cin-N	0	1	.000	2	2	0	0	0	8	10	2	5	5	16.9	4.50	81	.313	.405	0	.000	-0	-1	-1	-0	-0.1
Total	4	2	2	.500	25	5	0	0	0	47^{2}	51	5	18	23	13.0	3.40	110	.280	.345	0	.000	-1	1	2	-0	0.1

● KEVIN BROWN Brown, Kevin Dewayne b: 3/5/66, Oroville, Cal. BL/TL, 6'1", 185 lbs. Deb: 7/27/90

YEAR	TM/L	W	L	PCT	G	GS	CG	SH	SV	IP	H	HR	BB	SO	RAT	ERA	ERA+	OAV	OOB	BH	AVG	PB	PR	/A	PD	TPI
1990	NY-N	0	0	—	2	0	0	0	0	2	2	0	1	0	13.5	0.00	—	.250	.333	0	—	0	1	1	0	0.1
	Mil-A	1	1	.500	5	3	0	0	0	21	14	1	7	12	9.4	2.57	151	.182	.259	0	—	0	3	3	1	0.4
1991	Mil-A	2	4	.333	15	10	0	0	0	63^{2}	66	6	34	30	14.3	5.51	72	.270	.362	0	—	0	-10	-11	0	-1.0
1992	Sea-A	0	0	—	2	0	0	0	0	3	4	1	3	2	21.0	9.00	44	.333	.467	0	—	0	-2	-2	0	-0.2
Total	3	3	5	.375	24	13	0	0	0	89^{2}	86	8	45	44	13.3	4.82	82	.252	.343	0	—	0	-8	-9	1	-0.7

● LEW BROWN Brown, Lewis J. "Blower" b: 2/1/1858, Leominster, Mass. d: 1/16/1889, Boston, Mass. BR/TR, 5'10.5", 185 lbs. Deb: 6/17/1876 ♦

YEAR	TM/L	W	L	PCT	G	GS	CG	SH	SV	IP	H	HR	BB	SO	RAT	ERA	ERA+	OAV	OOB	BH	AVG	PB	PR	/A	PD	TPI
1878	Pro-N	0	0	—	1	0	0	0	0	1	0	0	4	0	36.0	18.00	12	.000	.500	74	.305	0	-2	-2	0	-0.1
1884	Bos-U	0	0	—	1	0	0	0	1	1	6	0	1	0	63.0	36.00	8	.659	.692	75	.231	0	-4	-4	-0	-0.3
Total	2	0	0	—	2	0	0	0	1	2	6	0	5	0	49.5	27.00	10	.458	.607	379	.248	0	-5	-5	0	-0.4

● LLOYD BROWN Brown, Lloyd Andrew "Gimpy" b: 12/25/04, Beeville, Tex. d: 1/14/74, Opalocka, Fla. BL/TL, 5'9", 170 lbs. Deb: 7/17/25

YEAR	TM/L	W	L	PCT	G	GS	CG	SH	SV	IP	H	HR	BB	SO	RAT	ERA	ERA+	OAV	OOB	BH	AVG	PB	PR	/A	PD	TPI
1925	Bro-N	0	3	.000	17	5	1	0	0	63^{1}	79	1	25	23	15.1	4.12	101	.319	.385	2	.087	-2	1	0	0	-0.2
1928	Was-A	4	4	.500	27	10	2	0	1	107	112	7	40	38	13.0	4.04	99	.273	.341	5	.161	0	0	-0	3	0.3
1929	Was-A	8	7	.533	40	15	7	1	0	168	186	7	69	48	13.7	4.18	101	.297	.368	11	.220	3	1	1	2	0.5
1930	Was-A	16	12	.571	38	22	10	1	0	197	220	6	65	59	13.2	4.25	108	.293	.354	14	.215	2	9	8	3	1.2

YEAR	TM/L	W	L	PCT	G	GS	CG	SH	SV	IP	H	HR	BB	SO	RAT	ERA	ERA+	OAV	OOB	BH	AVG	PB	PR	/A	PD	TPI
1931	Was-A	15	14	.517	42	32	15	1	0	258^2	256	13	79	79	11.7	3.20	134	.257	.311	22	.229	3	34	31	1	3.4
1932	Was-A	15	12	.556	46	24	10	2	5	202^2	239	11	55	53	13.1	4.44	97	.296	.342	7	.100	-5	1	-3	1	-0.6
1933	StL-A	1	6	.143	8	6	0	0	0	39	57	1	17	7	17.1	7.15	65	.350	.411	3	.273	1	-12	-11	1	-0.8
	Bos-A	8	11	.421	33	21	9	2	1	163^1	180	4	64	37	13.4	4.02	109	.281	.347	16	.281	6	5	6	4	1.7
	Yr	9	17	.346	41	27	9	2	1	202^1	237	5	81	44	14.1	4.63	96	.295	.360	19	.279	7	-8	-4	5	0.9
1934	Cle-A	5	10	.333	38	15	5	0	6	117	116	7	51	39	13.0	3.85	118	.263	.342	7	.233	1	8	9	0	0.9
1935	Cle-A	8	7	.533	42	8	4	2	4	122	123	6	37	45	12.0	3.61	125	.265	.323	4	.108	-2	**11**	**12**	1	1.0
1936	Cle-A	8	10	.444	24	16	12	1	1	140^1	166	13	45	34	13.7	4.17	121	.294	.349	10	.222	2	14	14	1	1.5
1937	Cle-A	2	6	.250	31	5	2	0	0	77	107	4	27	32	16.0	6.55	70	.329	.386	4	.167	-1	-16	-17	1	-1.5
1940	Phi-N	1	3	.250	18	2	0	0	3	37^2	58	3	16	16	17.7	6.21	63	.354	.411	1	.077	-1	-10	-10	0	-1.0
Total	12	91	105	.464	404	181	77	10	21	1693	1899	83	590	510	13.3	4.20	105	.288	.348	106	.192	7	45	42	19	6.4

● MACE BROWN

Brown, Mace Stanley b: 5/21/09, North English, Ia. BR/TR, 6'1", 190 lbs. Deb: 5/21/35 C

YEAR	TM/L	W	L	PCT	G	GS	CG	SH	SV	IP	H	HR	BB	SO	RAT	ERA	ERA+	OAV	OOB	BH	AVG	PB	PR	/A	PD	TPI
1935	Pit-N	4	1	.800	18	5	2	0	0	72^2	84	5	22	28	13.1	3.59	114	.287	.337	4	.167	-0	3	4	2	0.5
1936	Pit-N	10	11	.476	47	10	3	0	3	165	178	8	55	56	12.8	3.87	105	.275	.332	10	.167	-2	3	3	1	0.2
1937	Pit-N	7	2	.778	50	2	0	0	**7**	107^2	109	2	45	60	13.0	4.18	92	.261	.334	9	.300	2	-3	-4	-1	-0.3
1938	Pit-N★	15	9	.625	**51**	2	0	0	5	132^2	155	5	44	55	13.5	3.80	100	.294	.349	5	.132	-2	-0	-0	-0	-0.2
1939	Pit-N	9	13	.409	47	19	8	1	7	200^1	232	8	52	71	12.8	3.37	114	.293	.338	7	.109	-4	12	10	1	0.7
1940	Pit-N	10	9	.526	48	17	5	1	**7**	173	181	5	49	73	12.1	3.49	109	.267	.318	6	.115	-1	7	6	1	0.6
1941	Pit-N	0	0	—	1	0	0	0	0	1^1	2	0	0	0	13.5	0.00	—	.333	.333	0	—	0	1	1	0	0.1
	Bro-N	3	2	.600	24	0	0	0	3	42^2	31	3	26	22	12.2	3.16	116	.208	.330	0	.000	-1	2	2	1	0.2
	Yr	3	2	.600	25	0	0	0	3	44	33	3	26	22	12.3	3.07	119	.213	.330	0	.000	-1	3	3	1	0.3
1942	Bos-A	9	3	.750	34	0	0	0	6	60^1	56	4	28	20	12.5	3.43	109	.255	.339	1	.067	-1	2	2	1	0.2
1943	Bos-A	6	6	.500	**49**	0	0	0	9	93^1	71	2	51	40	11.8	2.12	156	.222	.329	1	.059	-1	**12**	**12**	0	1.2
1946	*Bos-A	3	1	.750	18	0	0	0	1	26^1	26	2	16	10	14.4	2.05	179	.268	.372	0	.000	-1	4	5	1	0.5
Total	10	76	57	.571	387	55	18	2	48	1075^1	1125	44	388	435	12.7	3.46	110	.271	.335	43	.137	-11	43	43	6	3.7

● MARK BROWN

Brown, Mark Anthony b: 7/13/59, Bellows Falls, Vt. BB/TR, 6'2", 190 lbs. Deb: 8/09/84

YEAR	TM/L	W	L	PCT	G	GS	CG	SH	SV	IP	H	HR	BB	SO	RAT	ERA	ERA+	OAV	OOB	BH	AVG	PB	PR	/A	PD	TPI
1984	Bal-A	1	2	.333	9	0	0	0	0	23	22	2	7	10	11.7	3.91	99	.256	.319	0	—	0	0	-0	-0	0.0
1985	Min-A	0	0	—	6	0	0	0	0	15^2	21	1	7	5	16.1	6.89	64	.333	.400	0	—	0	-5	-4	-0	-0.5
Total	2	1	2	.333	15	0	0	0	0	38^2	43	3	14	15	13.5	5.12	80	.289	.354	0	—	0	-5	-4	-1	-0.5

● MIKE BROWN

Brown, Michael Gary b: 3/4/59, Camden County, N.J. BR/TR, 6'2", 195 lbs. Deb: 9/16/82

YEAR	TM/L	W	L	PCT	G	GS	CG	SH	SV	IP	H	HR	BB	SO	RAT	ERA	ERA+	OAV	OOB	BH	AVG	PB	PR	/A	PD	TPI
1982	Bos-A	1	0	1.000	3	0	0	0	0	6	7	0	1	4	12.0	0.00	—	.304	.333	0	—	0	3	3	-0	0.3
1983	Bos-A	6	6	.500	19	18	3	1	0	104	110	12	43	35	13.4	4.67	93	.276	.350	0	—	0	-7	-4	-1	-0.5
1984	Bos-A	1	8	.111	15	11	0	0	0	67	104	9	19	32	16.9	6.85	61	.347	.391	0	—	0	-21	-20	0	-1.9
1985	Bos-A	0	0	—	2	1	0	0	0	3^1	9	0	3	3	32.4	21.60	20	.500	.571	0	—	0	-6	-6	-0	-0.6
1986	Bos-A	4	4	.500	15	10	0	0	0	57^1	72	10	25	32	15.4	5.34	78	.316	.386	0	—	0	-7	-7	0	-0.7
	Sea-A	0	2	.000	6	2	0	0	0	15^2	19	4	11	9	17.2	7.47	57	.302	.405	0	—	0	-6	-6	0	-0.5
	Yr	4	6	.400	21	12	0	0	0	73	91	14	36	41	15.7	5.79	72	.308	.384	0	—	0	-13	-13	1	-1.2
1987	Sea-A	0	0	—	1	0	0	0	0	0^1	3	0	0	0	81.0	54.00	9	.750	.750	0	—	0	-2	-2	0	-0.3
Total	6	12	20	.375	61	42	3	1	0	253^2	324	35	102	115	15.3	5.75	74	.313	.378	0	—	0	-47	-42	0	-4.2

● MORDECAI BROWN

Brown, Mordecai Peter Centennial "Three Finger" or "Miner"
b: 10/19/1876, Nyesville, Ind. d: 2/14/48, Terre Haute, Ind. BB/TR, 5'10", 175 lbs. Deb: 4/19/03 MH

YEAR	TM/L	W	L	PCT	G	GS	CG	SH	SV	IP	H	HR	BB	SO	RAT	ERA	ERA+	OAV	OOB	BH	AVG	PB	PR	/A	PD	TPI
1903	StL-N	9	13	.409	26	24	19	1	0	201	231	7	59	83	13.3	2.60	126	.293	.347	15	.195	-1	15	15	2	1.6
1904	Chi-N	15	10	.600	26	23	21	4	1	212^1	155	1	50	81	**8.9**	1.86	143	**.199**	**.253**	19	.213	1	21	19	-1	2.1
1905	Chi-N	18	12	.600	30	24	24	4	0	249	219	3	44	89	9.5	2.17	138	.235	.271	13	.140	-1	23	23	-0	2.2
1906	*Chi-N	26	6	.813	36	32	27	**9**	3	277^1	198	1	61	144	**8.5**	**1.04**	**254**	.202	**.252**	20	.204	1	**49**	**49**	2	**6.4**
1907	*Chi-N	20	6	.769	34	27	20	6	3	233	180	2	40	107	8.7	1.39	179	.221	.262	13	.153	-0	28	29	4	**3.8**
1908	*Chi-N	29	9	.763	44	31	27	9	**5**	312^1	214	1	49	123	7.7	1.47	160	.195	.232	25	.207	1	31	31	-1	3.6
1909	Chi-N	**27**	9	.750	**50**	34	**32**	8	7	**342^2**	246	1	53	172	8.0	1.31	194	.202	.239	22	.176	1	**49**	**47**	-1	5.4
1910	*Chi-N	25	14	.641	46	31	**27**	**6**	**7**	295^1	256	3	64	143	**9.9**	1.86	155	.232	**.277**	18	.175	-0	39	34	3	3.9
1911	Chi-N	21	11	.656	**53**	27	21	0	**13**	270	267	5	55	129	10.9	2.80	118	.262	.303	23	.253	5	18	15	-4	1.6
1912	Chi-N	5	6	.455	15	8	5	2	0	88^2	92	2	20	34	11.5	2.64	126	.274	.317	9	.290	2	8	7	-2	0.7
1913	Cin-N	11	12	.478	39	16	11	1	6	173^1	174	7	44	41	11.4	2.91	112	.277	.325	11	.204	-0	6	7	-1	0.5
1914	StL-F	12	6	.667	26	18	13	2	0	175	172	7	43	81	11.2	3.29	103	.254	.302	15	.254	2	-2	2	-2	0.1
	Bro-F	2	5	.286	9	8	5	0	0	57^2	63	1	18	32	12.6	4.21	76	.276	.329	4	.211	-0	-6	-7	-0	-0.7
	Yr	14	11	.560	35	26	18	2	0	232^2	235	8	61	113	11.4	3.52	95	.259	.306	19	.244	2	-8	-5	-3	-0.6
1915	Chi-F	17	8	.680	35	25	17	3	4	236^1	189	2	64	95	9.9	2.09	133	.220	.279	24	.293	6	25	18	3	3.0
1916	Chi-N	2	3	.400	12	4	2	0	0	48^1	52	0	9	21	12.1	3.91	74	.289	.337	4	.250	0	-7	-5	-0	-0.6
Total	14	239	130	.648	481	332	271	55	49	3172^1	2708	43	673	1375	9.8	2.06	139	.233	.278	235	.206	16	295	283	1	33.6

● MYRL BROWN

Brown, Myrl Lincoln b: 10/10/1894, Waynesboro, Pa. d: 2/23/81, Harrisburg, Pa. BR/TR, 5'11", 172 lbs. Deb: 8/19/22

YEAR	TM/L	W	L	PCT	G	GS	CG	SH	SV	IP	H	HR	BB	SO	RAT	ERA	ERA+	OAV	OOB	BH	AVG	PB	PR	/A	PD	TPI
1922	Pit-N	3	1	.750	7	5	2	0	0	34^2	42	2	13	9	14.3	5.97	68	.296	.355	3	.273	1	-7	-7	1	-0.5

● NORM BROWN

Brown, Norman b: 2/1/19, Evergreen, N.C. BB/TR, 6'3", 180 lbs. Deb: 10/03/43

YEAR	TM/L	W	L	PCT	G	GS	CG	SH	SV	IP	H	HR	BB	SO	RAT	ERA	ERA+	OAV	OOB	BH	AVG	PB	PR	/A	PD	TPI
1943	Phi-A	0	0	—	1	1	0	0	0	7	5	0	0	1	6.4	0.00	—	.185	.185	0	.000	-0	3	3	0	0.3
1946	Phi-A	0	1	.000	4	0	0	0	0	7^1	8	2	6	3	17.2	6.14	58	.267	.389	0	—	0	-2	-2	-0	-0.2
Total	2	0	1	.000	5	1	0	0	0	14^1	13	2	6	4	11.9	3.14	111	.228	.302	0	.000	-0	0	1	0	0.1

● PAUL BROWN

Brown, Paul Dwayne b: 6/18/41, Ft.Smith, Ark. BR/TR, 6'1", 190 lbs. Deb: 7/23/61 F

YEAR	TM/L	W	L	PCT	G	GS	CG	SH	SV	IP	H	HR	BB	SO	RAT	ERA	ERA+	OAV	OOB	BH	AVG	PB	PR	/A	PD	TPI
1961	Phi-N	0	1	.000	5	1	0	0	0	10	13	3	8	1	19.8	8.10	50	.325	.449	1	.500	0	-5	-4	-0	-0.4
1962	Phi-N	0	6	.000	23	9	0	0	1	63^2	74	9	33	29	15.5	5.94	65	.298	.387	2	.154	0	-14	-15	-1	-1.4
1963	Phi-N	0	1	.000	6	2	0	0	0	15^1	15	2	5	11	12.9	4.11	79	.238	.314	1	.500	0	-1	-1	0	-0.1
1968	Phi-N	0	0	—	2	0	0	0	0	4	6	0	1	4	15.8	9.00	33	.353	.389	0	—	0	-3	-3	-0	-0.3
Total	4	0	8	.000	36	12	0	0	1	93	108	14	47	45	15.6	6.00	63	.293	.382	4	.235	1	-23	-23	-0	-2.2

● RAY BROWN

Brown, Paul Percival b: 1/31/1889, Chicago, Ill. d: 5/29/55, Los Angeles, Cal. BR/TR, 6'1", 172 lbs. Deb: 9/29/09

YEAR	TM/L	W	L	PCT	G	GS	CG	SH	SV	IP	H	HR	BB	SO	RAT	ERA	ERA+	OAV	OOB	BH	AVG	PB	PR	/A	PD	TPI
1909	Chi-N	1	0	1.000	1	1	1	0	0	9	5	0	4	2	9.0	2.00	127	.172	.273	0	.000	-0	1	1	-0	0.0

● STUB BROWN

Brown, Richard P. b: 8/3/1870, Baltimore, Md. d: 3/11/48, Baltimore, Md. TL, 6'2", 220 lbs. Deb: 8/15/1893

YEAR	TM/L	W	L	PCT	G	GS	CG	SH	SV	IP	H	HR	BB	SO	RAT	ERA	ERA+	OAV	OOB	BH	AVG	PB	PR	/A	PD	TPI
1893	Bal-N	0	0	—	2	0	0	0	0	9	13	0	5	0	19.0	6.00	79	.328	.416	1	.200	-0	-1	-1	-0	-0.2
1894	Bal-N	4	0	1.000	9	6	3	0	0	49^2	59	3	24	8	15.2	4.89	112	.292	.370	2	.087	-4	2	3	-1	-0.1
1897	Cin-N	0	1	.000	2	1	1	0	0	13	17	1	8	2	17.3	4.15	110	.313	.401	0	.000	-1	0	1	0	0.0
Total	3	4	1	.800	13	7	4	0	0	71^2	89	4	37	10	16.1	4.90	106	.301	.382	3	.091	-5	1	2	-1	-0.3

● BOB BROWN

Brown, Robert Murray b: 4/1/11, Dorchester, Mass. d: 8/30/90, Pembroke, Mass. BR/TR, 6'0.5", 190 lbs. Deb: 4/21/30

YEAR	TM/L	W	L	PCT	G	GS	CG	SH	SV	IP	H	HR	BB	SO	RAT	ERA	ERA+	OAV	OOB	BH	AVG	PB	PR	/A	PD	TPI
1930	Bos-N	0	0	—	3	0	0	0	0	6	10	0	8	1	27.0	10.50	47	.417	.563	0	.000	-0	-4	-4	0	-0.3
1931	Bos-N	0	1	.000	3	1	0	0	0	6^1	9	0	3	2	17.1	8.53	44	.375	.444	1	.500	-0	-3	-3	0	-0.3
1932	Bos-N	14	7	.667	35	28	9	0	1	213	187	6	104	110	12.4	3.30	114	.238	.329	13	.194	-0	14	11	-1	1.0
1933	Bos-N	0	0	—	5	0	0	0	0	6^2	6	0	3	3	12.2	2.70	114	.250	.333	0	.000	-0	0	0	-0	0.0
1934	Bos-N	1	3	.250	16	8	2	1	0	58^1	59	2	36	21	15.1	5.71	67	.262	.371	5	.238	0	-11	-12	-1	-1.2
1935	Bos-N	1	8	.111	15	10	2	1	0	65	79	2	36	17	15.9	6.37	59	.302	.386	2	.105	-1	-17	-19	-1	-1.9
1936	Bos-N	0	2	.000	2	2	0	0	0	8^1	10	1	3	5	14.0	5.40	71	.278	.333	0	.000	-0	-1	-1	0	-0.1

YEAR	TM/L	W	L	PCT	G	GS	CG	SH	SV	IP	H	HR	BB	SO	RAT	ERA	ERA+	OAV	OOB	BH	AVG	PB	PR	/A	PD	TPI
Total	7	16	21	.432	79	49	13	2	1	363^2	360	11	193	159	13.8	4.48	84	.261	.354	21	.183	-1	-22	-28	-3	-2.8
● SCOTT BROWN	Brown, Scott Edward b: 8/30/56, DeQuincy, La. BR/TR, 6'2", 220 lbs. Deb: 8/11/81																									
1981	Cin-N	1	0	1.000	10	0	0	0	0	13	16	0	1	7	11.8	2.77	128	.314	.327	0	.000	-0	1	1	-0	0.1
● STEVE BROWN	Brown, Steven Elbert b: 2/12/57, San Francisco, Cal. BR/TR, 6'5", 200 lbs. Deb: 8/01/83																									
1983	Cal-A	2	3	.400	12	4	2	1	0	46	45	4	16	23	11.9	3.52	114	.256	.318	0	—	0	3	3	-0	0.3
1984	Cal-A	0	1	.000	3	3	0	0	0	11	16	0	9	5	20.5	9.00	44	.340	.446	0	—	0	-6	-6	-0	-0.6
Total	2	2	4	.333	15	7	2	1	0	57	61	4	25	28	13.6	4.58	87	.274	.347	0	—	0	-3	-4	-0	-0.3
● TOM BROWN	Brown, Thomas Dale b: 8/10/49, Lafayette, La. BR/TR, 6'1", 170 lbs. Deb: 9/14/78																									
1978	Sea-A	0	0	—	6	0	0	0	0	13	14	2	4	8	12.5	4.15	92	.286	.340	0	—	0	-1	-1	0	0.0
● TOM BROWN	Brown, Thomas Tarlton b: 9/21/1860, Liverpool, England d: 10/25/27, Washington, D.C. BL/TR, 5'10", 168 lbs. Deb: 7/06/1882 MU♦																									
1882	Bal-a	0	0	—	2	0	0	0	0	8^1	13	0	6	2	20.5	1.08	255	.334	.423	55	.304	1	1	2	-1	0.1
1883	Col-a	0	1	.000	3	1	1	0	0	14	14	0	10	6	15.4	5.79	53	.244	.356	115	.274	1	-4	-4	-1	-0.4
1884	Col-a	2	1	.667	4	0	0	0	0	19	27	0	7	5	16.1	7.11	43	.281	.330	123	.273	1	-8	-9	-1	-0.7
1885	Pit-a	0	0	—	2	0	0	0	0	6	0	0	3	2	9.0	3.00	107	.000	.207	134	.307	1	0	0	-0	0.0
1886	Pit-a	0	0	—	1	0	0	0	0	2	2	0	5	1	31.5	9.00	38	.125	.333	131	.285	0	-1	-1	0	-0.1
Total	5	2	2	.500	12	1	1	0	0	49^1	56	0	31	16	16.4	5.29	57	.242	.339	1952	.265	4	-12	-12	-2	-1.1
● JUMBO BROWN	Brown, Walter George b: 4/30/07, Greene, R.I. d: 10/2/66, Freeport, N.Y. BR/TR, 6'4", 295 lbs. Deb: 8/26/25																									
1925	Chi-N	0	0	—	2	0	0	0	0	6	5	0	4	0	13.5	3.00	144	.217	.333	0	.000	-0	1	1	0	0.1
1927	Cle-A	0	2	.000	8	0	0	0	0	18^2	19	3	26	8	22.2	6.27	67	.284	.489	2	.667	1	-4	-4	0	-0.3
1928	Cle-A	0	1	.000	5	0	0	0	0	14^2	19	0	15	12	20.9	6.75	61	.365	.507	2	.667	1	-4	-4	-0	-0.3
1932	NY-A	5	2	.714	19	3	3	1	1	55^2	58	1	30	31	14.6	4.53	90	.270	.364	4	.174	-1	-0	-3	1	-0.2
1933	NY-A	7	5	.583	21	8	1	0	0	74	78	3	52	55	15.8	5.23	74	.269	.380	5	.179	-0	-8	-11	-0	-1.1
1935	NY-A	6	5	.545	20	8	3	1	0	87^1	94	2	37	41	13.5	3.61	112	.279	.350	10	.313	3	8	4	0	0.7
1936	NY-A	1	4	.200	20	3	0	0	1	64	93	4	29	19	17.2	5.91	79	.352	.416	0	.000	-3	-6	-9	1	-0.9
1937	Cin-N	1	0	1.000	4	1	0	0	0	9^2	16	0	3	4	17.7	8.38	45	.390	.432	0	.000	0	-5	-5	-0	-0.5
	NY-N	1	0	1.000	4	0	0	0	0	8^2	5	0	5	4	10.4	1.04	374	.172	.294	0	—	0	3	3	1	0.3
	Yr	2	0	1.000	8	1	0	0	0	18^1	21	0	8	8	14.2	4.91	78	.300	.372	0	.000	0	-2	-2	0	-0.2
1938	NY-N	5	3	.625	43	0	0	0	5	90	65	5	28	42	9.4	1.80	209	.204	.271	3	.188	1	**20**	**20**	-1	1.9
1939	NY-N	4	0	1.000	31	0	0	0	7	56^1	69	1	25	24	15.2	4.15	95	.304	.375	4	.364	1	-1	-1	0	0.0
1940	NY-N	2	4	.333	41	0	0	0	**7**	55^1	49	5	25	31	12.0	3.42	114	.232	.314	1	.100	-1	3	3	-1	0.1
1941	NY-N	1	5	.167	31	0	0	0	**8**	57	49	2	21	30	11.1	3.32	111	.238	.308	1	.111	-1	2	2	-1	0.1
Total	12	33	31	.516	249	23	7	2	29	597^1	619	26	300	301	13.9	4.07	99	.271	.357	32	.204	2	7	-4	-0	-0.1
● WALTER BROWN	Brown, Walter Irving b: 4/23/15, Jamestown, N.Y. d: 2/3/91, Westfield, N.Y. BR/TR, 5'11", 175 lbs. Deb: 5/16/47																									
1947	StL-A	1	0	1.000	19	0	0	0	0	46	50	3	28	10	15.3	4.89	79	.294	.394	0	.000	-1	-6	-5	0	-0.6
● CAL BROWNING	Browning, Calvin Duane b: 3/16/38, Burns Flat, Okla. BL/TL, 5'11", 190 lbs. Deb: 6/12/60																									
1960	StL-N	0	0	—	1	0	0	0	0	0^2	5	1	1	0	81.0	40.50	10	.714	.750	0	—	0	-3	-3	-0	-0.2
● FRANK BROWNING	Browning, Frank "Dutch" b: 10/29/1882, Falmouth, Ky. d: 5/19/48, San Antonio, Tex. BR/TR, 5'5", 145 lbs. Deb: 4/16/10																									
1910	Det-A	2	2	.500	11	6	2	0	3	49	51	0	10	16	11.2	2.57	102	.262	.298	0	.000	-2	-0	0	1	-0.1
● PETE BROWNING	Browning, Louis Rogers "The Gladiator" b: 6/17/1861, Louisville, Ky. d: 9/10/05, Louisville, Ky. BR/TR, 6', 180 lbs. Deb: 5/02/1882 ♦																									
1884	Lou-a	0	1	.000	1	1	0	0	0	0^1	2	0	2	0	135.0	54.00	6	1.000	1.000	150	.336	0	-2	-2	0	-0.1
● TOM BROWNING	Browning, Thomas Leo b: 4/28/60, Casper, Wyoming BL/TL, 6'1", 190 lbs. Deb: 9/09/84																									
1984	Cin-N	1	0	1.000	3	3	0	0	0	23^1	27	0	5	14	12.3	1.54	245	.303	.340	1	.143	-0	5	6	-0	0.6
1985	Cin-N	20	9	.690	38	38	6	4	0	261^1	242	29	73	155	11.0	3.55	107	.245	.299	17	.193	2	1	7	-2	0.8
1986	Cin-N	14	13	.519	39	39	4	2	0	243^1	225	26	70	147	10.9	3.81	102	.245	.299	14	.163	-1	-3	2	-3	-0.2
1987	Cin-N	10	13	.435	32	31	2	0	0	183	201	27	61	117	13.1	5.02	85	.284	.345	8	.154	0	-19	-16	-2	-1.6
1988	Cin-N	18	5	.783	36	36	5	2	0	250^2	205	36	64	124	9.9	3.41	105	.224	.280	12	.145	1	1	5	-3	0.3
1989	Cin-N	15	12	.556	37	37	9	2	0	249^2	241	31	64	118	11.1	3.39	106	.255	.304	7	.090	-3	3	6	-1	0.1
1990	*Cin-N	15	9	.625	35	35	2	1	0	227^2	235	24	52	99	11.5	3.80	104	.266	.311	7	.093	-3	-0	4	-2	-0.2
1991	Cin-N☆	14	14	.500	36	36	1	0	0	230^1	241	32	56	115	11.8	4.18	91	.266	.312	12	.171	2	-13	-10	-3	-1.2
1992	Cin-N	6	5	.545	16	16	0	0	0	87	108	6	28	33	14.3	5.07	72	.311	.366	7	.226	1	-15	-14	0	-1.2
Total	9	113	80	.585	272	271	29	11	0	1756^1	1725	211	473	922	11.4	3.86	99	.257	.309	85	.149	-1	-39	-10	-16	-2.6
● BRUCE BRUBAKER	Brubaker, Bruce Ellsworth b: 12/29/41, Harrisburg, Pa. BR/TR, 6'1", 198 lbs. Deb: 4/15/67																									
1967	LA-N	0	0	—	1	0	0	0	0	1^1	3	1	0	2	20.3	20.25	15	.429	.429	0	—	0	-3	-3	0	-0.2
1970	Mil-A	0	0	—	1	0	0	0	0	2	2	1	1	0	13.5	9.00	42	.250	.333	0	—	0	-1	-1	-0	-0.1
Total	2	0	0	—	2	0	0	0	0	3^1	5	2	1	2	16.2	13.50	26	.333	.375	0	—	0	-4	-4	0	-0.3
● LOU BRUCE	Bruce, Louis R. b: 1/16/1877, St.Regis, N.Y. d: 2/9/68, Ilion, N.Y. BL/TR, 5'5", 145 lbs. Deb: 6/22/04 ♦																									
1904	Phi-A	0	0	—	2	0	0	0	0	11	11	1	2	2	10.6	4.91	55	.261	.295	27	.267	0	-3	-3	0	-0.2
● BOB BRUCE	Bruce, Robert James b: 5/16/33, Detroit, Mich. BR/TR, 6'3", 210 lbs. Deb: 9/14/59																									
1959	Det-A	0	1	.000	2	1	0	0	0	2	2	1	3	1	22.5	9.00	45	.250	.455	0	—	0	-1	-1	-0	-0.1
1960	Det-A	4	7	.364	34	15	1	0	0	130	127	16	56	76	13.0	3.74	106	.250	.331	7	.179	0	2	3	1	0.4
1961	Det-A	1	2	.333	14	6	0	0	0	44^2	57	6	24	25	16.7	4.43	92	.320	.407	1	.111	0	-2	-2	-1	-0.2
1962	Hou-N	10	9	.526	32	27	6	0	0	175	164	16	82	135	13.3	4.06	92	.248	.342	11	.200	5	-2	-6	0	-0.1
1963	Hou-N	5	9	.357	30	25	1	1	0	170^1	162	7	60	123	12.2	3.59	88	.250	.321	7	.127	2	-6	-8	-1	-0.8
1964	Hou-N	15	9	.625	35	29	9	4	0	202^1	191	8	33	135	10.1	2.76	124	.246	.279	12	.190	2	18	15	-0	1.9
1965	Hou-N	9	18	.333	35	34	7	1	0	229^2	241	22	38	145	11.3	3.72	90	.270	.307	9	.122	-1	-5	-9	0	-1.1
1966	Hou-N	3	13	.188	25	23	1	0	0	129^2	160	16	29	71	13.7	5.34	64	.301	.346	3	.077	-2	-25	-28	0	-2.9
1967	Atl-N	2	3	.400	12	7	1	0	1	38^2	42	3	15	22	13.5	4.89	68	.269	.337	2	.167	0	-7	-7	-1	-0.7
Total	9	49	71	.408	219	167	26	6	1	1122^1	1146	95	340	733	12.3	3.85	91	.263	.323	52	.150	6	-28	-43	-2	-3.6
● FRED BRUCKBAUER	Bruckbauer, Frederick John b: 5/27/38, New Ulm, Minn. BR/TR, 6'1", 185 lbs. Deb: 4/25/61																									
1961	Min-A	0	0	—	1	0	0	0	0	0	3	0	1	0	—	∞	—	1.000	1.000	0	—	0	-3	-3	0	-0.3
● ANDY BRUCKMILLER	Bruckmiller, Andrew b: 1/1/1882, McKeesport, Pa. d: 1/12/70, McKeesport, Pa. BR/TR, 5'11", 175 lbs. Deb: 6/26/05																									
1905	Det-A	0	0	—	1	0	0	0	0	1	4	0	1	1	45.0	27.00	10	.586	.639	0	.000	-0	-3	-3	-0	-0.3
● MIKE BRUHERT	Bruhert, Michael Edwin b: 6/24/51, Jamaica, N.Y. BR/TR, 6'6", 220 lbs. Deb: 4/09/78																									
1978	NY-N	4	11	.267	27	22	1	1	0	133^2	171	6	34	56	13.9	4.78	73	.317	.359	3	.075	-3	-18	-19	-0	-2.2
● JACK BRUNER	Bruner, Jack Raymond b: 7/1/24, Waterloo, Iowa BL/TL, 6'1", 185 lbs. Deb: 9/16/49																									
1949	Chi-A	1	2	.333	4	2	0	0	0	7^2	10	0	8	4	21.1	8.22	51	.357	.500	0	.000	-0	-3	-3	-0	-0.4
1950	Chi-A	0	0	—	9	0	0	0	0	12^1	7	0	14	8	16.1	3.65	123	.184	.415	0	—	0	1	1	-0	0.1
	StL-A	1	2	.333	13	1	0	0	1	35	36	4	23	16	15.7	4.63	107	.267	.381	0	.000	-1	-0	1	-1	-0.1
	Yr	1	2	.333	22	1	0	0	1	47^1	43	4	37	24	15.6	4.37	110	.247	.385	0	.000	-1	1	2	-1	0.0
Total	2	2	4	.333	26	3	0	0	1	55	53	4	45	28	16.5	4.91	96	.264	.406	0	.000	-1	-2	-1	-1	-0.4

YEAR TM/L	W	L	PCT	G	GS	CG	SH	SV	IP	H	HR	BB	SO	RAT	ERA	ERA+	OAV	OOB	BH	AVG	PB	PR	/A	PD	TPI
● ROY BRUNER	Bruner, Walter Roy b: 2/10/17, Cecilia, Ky. d: 11/30/86, St.Matthews, Ky. BR/TR, 6', 165 lbs. Deb: 9/14/39																								
1939 Phi-N	0	4	.000	4	4	2	0	0	27	38	3	13	11	17.0	6.67	60	.339	.408	1	.111	-1	-8	-8	-1	-0.8
1940 Phi-N	0	0	—	2	0	0	0	0	6^1	5	2	6	4	15.6	5.68	69	.227	.393	1	.500	0	-1	-1	0	-0.1
1941 Phi-N	0	3	.000	13	1	0	0	0	29^1	37	1	25	13	19.0	4.91	75	.336	.459	0	.000	-0	-4	-4	-1	-0.5
Total 3	0	7	.000	19	5	2	0	0	62^2	80	6	44	28	17.8	5.74	67	.328	.431	2	.118	-1	-14	-13	-1	-1.4
● GEORGE BRUNET	Brunet, George Stuart "Lefty" b: 6/8/35, Houghton, Mich. d: 10/25/91, Poza Rica, Mex. BR/TL, 6'1", 210 lbs. Deb: 9/14/56																								
1956 KC-A	0	0	—	6	1	0	0	0	9	10	1	11	5	21.0	7.00	62	.286	.457	0	.000	-0	-3	-3	0	-0.3
1957 KC-A	0	1	.000	4	2	0	0	0	11^1	13	2	4	3	13.5	5.56	71	.277	.333	0	.000	-0	-2	-2	-0	-0.2
1959 KC-A	0	0	—	2	0	0	0	0	4^2	10	2	7	7	34.7	11.57	35	.435	.581	0	—	0	-4	-4	1	-0.3
1960 KC-A	0	2	.000	3	2	0	0	0	10^1	12	0	10	4	20.0	4.35	91	.308	.460	0	.000	-0	-1	-0	1	0.0
Mil-N	2	0	1.000	17	6	0	0	0	49^2	53	6	22	39	13.8	5.07	68	.275	.352	1	.091	-1	-7	-9	0	-1.0
1961 Mil-N	0	0	—	5	0	0	0	0	5	7	1	2	0	16.2	5.40	69	.412	.474	0	—	0	-1	-1	0	-0.1
1962 Hou-N	2	4	.333	17	11	2	0	0	54	62	2	21	36	13.8	4.50	83	.291	.355	1	.059	-1	-3	-5	1	-0.5
1963 Hou-N	0	3	.000	5	2	0	0	0	12^2	24	2	6	11	21.3	7.11	44	.393	.448	0	.000	-0	-5	-6	0	-0.6
Bal-A	0	1	.000	16	0	0	0	1	20	25	3	9	13	15.7	5.40	65	.301	.376	0	.000	-0	-4	-4	0	-0.4
1964 LA-A	2	2	.500	10	7	0	0	0	42^1	38	2	25	36	13.4	3.61	91	.237	.341	2	.182	0	0	-2	-0	-0.1
1965 Cal-A	9	11	.450	41	26	8	3	2	197	149	9	69	141	10.1	2.56	133	.209	.282	3	.054	-2	20	18	-1	1.6
1966 Cal-A	13	13	.500	41	32	8	2	0	212	183	21	106	148	12.5	3.31	101	.234	.329	7	.103	-2	3	1	-0	0.0
1967 Cal-A	11	19	.367	40	37	7	2	1	250	203	19	90	165	10.7	3.31	95	.223	.295	6	.077	-4	-2	-5	-2	-1.2
1968 Cal-A	13	17	.433	39	36	8	5	0	245^1	191	23	68	132	9.6	2.86	102	.215	.273	6	.081	-3	3	1	-2	-0.5
1969 Cal-A	6	7	.462	23	19	2	2	0	100^2	98	15	39	56	12.3	3.84	91	.255	.325	1	.037	-1	-2	-4	-1	-0.6
Sea-A	2	5	.286	12	11	2	0	0	63^2	70	11	28	37	13.9	5.37	68	.280	.353	3	.150	1	-12	-12	1	-1.1
Yr	8	12	.400	35	30	4	2	0	164^1	168	26	67	93	12.9	4.44	80	.264	.334	4	.085	-0	-15	-16	-0	-1.7
1970 Was-A	8	6	.571	24	20	2	1	0	118	124	10	48	67	13.2	4.42	80	.275	.346	6	.158	1	-9	-11	-1	-1.1
Pit-N	1	1	.500	12	1	0	0	0	16^2	19	1	9	17	15.7	2.70	144	.311	.408	0	.000	-0	2	2	0	0.2
1971 StL-N	0	1	.000	7	0	0	0	0	9^1	12	3	7	4	18.3	5.79	62	.316	.422	1	.333	0	-2	-2	-0	-0.2
Total 15	69	93	.426	324	213	39	15	4	1431^2	1303	133	581	921	12.0	3.62	92	.244	.320	37	.089	-13	-31	-46	-4	-6.4
● TOM BRUNO	Bruno, Thomas Michael b: 1/26/53, Chicago, Ill. BR/TR, 6'5", 210 lbs. Deb: 8/01/76																								
1976 KC-A	1	0	1.000	12	0	0	0	0	17^1	20	3	9	11	15.1	6.75	52	.290	.372	0	—	0	-6	-6	-0	-0.7
1977 Tor-A	0	1	.000	12	0	0	0	0	18^1	30	4	13	9	21.6	7.85	53	.366	.458	0	—	0	-8	-7	0	-0.7
1978 StL-N	4	3	.571	18	3	0	0	1	49^2	38	3	17	33	10.0	1.99	176	.209	.276	1	.083	-1	9	8	-1	0.8
1979 StL-N	2	3	.400	27	1	0	0	0	38^1	37	1	22	27	14.3	4.23	89	.253	.359	1	.200	0	-2	-2	-0	-0.2
Total 4	7	7	.500	69	4	0	0	1	123^2	125	11	61	80	13.8	4.22	87	.261	.348	2	.118	-1	-7	-7	-1	-0.8
● WARREN BRUSSTAR	Brusstar, Warren Scott b: 2/2/52, Oakland, Cal. BR/TR, 6'3", 200 lbs. Deb: 5/06/77																								
1977 *Phi-N	7	2	.778	46	0	0	0	3	71^1	64	7	24	46	11.2	2.65	151	.250	.317	0	.000	-1	10	11	1	1.1
1978 *Phi-N	6	3	.667	58	0	0	0	0	88^2	74	0	30	60	10.9	2.33	153	.239	.312	1	.143	0	12	12	2	1.6
1979 Phi-N	1	0	1.000	13	0	0	0	1	14^1	23	1	4	3	17.0	6.91	55	.383	.422	0	—	0	-5	-5	0	-0.5
1980 *Phi-N	2	2	.500	26	0	0	0	0	38^2	42	3	13	21	12.8	3.72	102	.286	.344	0	.000	-0	-1	0	0	0.0
1981 *Phi-N	0	1	.000	14	0	0	0	0	12^1	12	0	10	8	16.8	4.38	83	.250	.390	0	—	0	-1	-1	0	-0.1
1982 Phi-N	2	3	.400	22	0	0	0	2	22^2	31	2	5	11	14.7	4.76	77	.348	.389	0	.000	-0	-3	-3	0	-0.3
Chi-A	2	0	1.000	10	0	0	0	0	18^1	19	2	3	8	11.3	3.44	117	.257	.295	0	—	0	1	1	1	0.2
1983 Chi-N	3	1	.750	59	0	0	0	1	80^1	67	1	37	46	11.9	2.35	161	.234	.326	0	.000	-0	11	13	0	1.3
1984 *Chi-N	1	1	.500	41	0	0	0	3	63^2	57	4	21	36	11.2	3.11	126	.247	.312	1	.200	1	3	6	-0	0.6
1985 Chi-N	4	3	.571	51	0	0	0	4	74^1	87	8	36	34	15.3	6.05	66	.292	.374	1	.143	0	-20	-17	-2	-1.9
Total 9	28	16	.636	340	0	0	0	14	484^2	476	28	183	273	12.5	3.51	109	.265	.337	3	.094	-1	8	17	2	2.0
● CLAY BRYANT	Bryant, Claiborne Henry b: 11/16/11, Madison Heights, Va. BR/TR, 6'2.5", 195 lbs. Deb: 4/19/35 C																								
1935 Chi-N	1	2	.333	9	1	0	0	2	22^2	34	1	7	13	16.3	5.16	76	.358	.402	2	.333	2	-3	-3	-0	-0.1
1936 Chi-N	1	2	.333	26	0	0	0	0	57^1	57	0	24	35	13.0	3.30	121	.259	.337	5	.417	1	**5**	**4**	1	0.6
1937 Chi-N	9	3	.750	38	10	4	1	3	135^1	117	1	78	75	13.0	4.26	94	.232	.336	14	.311	5	-5	-4	-3	-0.2
1938 *Chi-N	19	11	.633	44	30	17	3	2	270^1	235	6	125	**135**	12.0	3.10	124	.235	.321	24	.226	4	21	22	-3	2.4
1939 Chi-N	2	1	.667	4	4	2	0	0	31^1	42	3	14	9	16.4	5.74	69	.307	.375	3	.214	0	-6	-6	-1	-0.6
1940 Chi-N	0	1	.000	8	0	0	0	0	26^1	26	2	14	5	13.7	4.78	78	.265	.357	3	.333	1	-3	-3	0	-0.2
Total 6	32	20	.615	129	45	23	4	7	543^1	511	13	262	272	12.9	3.73	104	.249	.335	51	.266	13	8	10	-6	1.9
● RON BRYANT	Bryant, Ronald Raymond b: 11/12/47, Redlands, Cal. BB/TL, 6', 190 lbs. Deb: 9/29/67																								
1967 SF-N	0	0	—	1	0	0	0	0	4	3	0	0	2	9.0	4.50	73	.200	.250	0	.000	-0	-1	-1	-0	-0.1
1969 SF-N	4	3	.571	16	8	0	0	1	57^2	60	8	25	30	13.6	4.37	80	.271	.351	3	.188	1	-5	-6	-0	-0.5
1970 SF-N	5	8	.385	34	11	1	0	0	96	103	7	38	66	13.4	4.78	83	.274	.344	3	.111	-1	-8	-9	1	-0.8
1971 *SF-N	7	10	.412	27	22	3	2	0	140	146	9	49	79	12.7	3.79	90	.272	.336	10	.200	1	-5	-6	0	-0.6
1972 SF-N	14	7	.667	35	28	11	4	0	214	176	20	77	107	10.7	2.90	120	.224	.295	12	.171	1	13	14	-4	1.1
1973 SF-N	**24**	12	.667	41	39	8	0	0	270	240	23	115	143	12.1	3.53	108	.234	.316	16	.168	1	4	9	0	1.0
1974 SF-N	3	15	.167	41	23	0	0	0	126^2	142	11	68	75	15.2	5.61	68	.286	.376	4	.129	-1	-28	-26	-0	-2.7
1975 StL-N	0	1	.000	10	1	0	0	0	8^2	20	2	7	7	28.0	16.62	23	.444	.519	0	.000	-0	-13	-12	0	-1.2
Total 8	57	56	.504	205	132	23	6	1	917	890	80	379	509	12.7	4.02	91	.254	.331	48	.165	0	-42	-36	-4	-3.8
● T.R. BRYDEN	Bryden, Thomas Ray b: 1/17/59, Moses Lake, Wash. BR/TR, 6'4", 190 lbs. Deb: 4/10/86																								
1986 Cal-A	2	1	.667	16	0	0	0	0	34^1	38	4	21	25	16.0	6.55	63	.290	.396	0	—	0	-9	-9	0	-0.8
● TOD BRYNAN	Brynan, Charles Ruley b: 7/1863, Philadelphia, Pa. d: 5/10/25, Philadelphia, Pa. BR/TR, Deb: 6/22/1888																								
1888 Chi-N	2	1	.667	3	3	2	0	0	25	29	2	7	11	13.7	6.48	47	.271	.328	2	.182	0	-10	-10	-1	-0.8
1891 Bos-N	0	1	.000	1	1	0	0	0	1	4	0	3	0	63.0	54.00	7	.572	.701	0	—	0	-6	-6	-0	-0.4
Total 2	2	2	.500	4	4	2	0	0	26	33	2	10	11	15.6	8.31	37	.289	.357	2	.182	0	-16	-15	-1	-1.2
● JIM BUCHANAN	Buchanan, James Forrest b: 7/1/1876, Chatham Hill, Va. d: 6/15/49, Norfolk, Neb. BL/TR, 5'10", 165 lbs. Deb: 4/16/05																								
1905 StL-A	5	9	.357	22	15	12	1	**2**	141^1	149	2	27	54	11.3	3.50	73	.272	.308	7	.152	-0	-13	-15	0	-1.6
● BOB BUCHANAN	Buchanan, Robert Gordon b: 5/3/61, Ridley Park, Pa. BL/TL, 6'1", 185 lbs. Deb: 7/13/85																								
1985 Cin-N	1	0	1.000	14	0	0	0	0	16	25	4	9	3	19.1	8.44	45	.368	.442	0	.000	-0	-9	-8	0	-0.8
1989 KC-A	0	0	—	2	0	0	0	0	3^1	5	1	3	3	21.6	16.20	24	.333	.444	0	—	0	-5	-5	-0	-0.4
Total 2	1	0	1.000	16	0	0	0	0	19^1	30	5	12	6	19.6	9.78	39	.361	.442	0	.000	-0	-13	-13	-0	-1.2
● GARLAND BUCKEYE	Buckeye, Garland Maiers "Gob" b: 10/16/1897, Heron Lake, Minn. d: 11/14/75, Stone Lake, Wis. BB/TL, 6', 260 lbs. Deb: 6/19/18																								
1918 Was-A	0	0	—	1	0	0	0	0	2	3	0	6	2	40.5	18.00	15	.333	.600	0	—	0	-3	-3	0	-0.3
1925 Cle-A	13	8	.619	30	18	11	1	0	153	161	3	58	49	13.2	3.65	121	.267	.338	14	.226	2	13	13	-1	1.4
1926 Cle-A	6	9	.400	32	18	5	1	0	165^2	160	3	69	36	12.8	3.10	131	.264	.345	12	.200	2	17	18	-2	1.7
1927 Cle-A	10	17	.370	35	25	13	2	1	204^2	231	6	74	38	13.6	3.96	106	.296	.360	19	.268	3	4	6	-1	0.7
1928 Cle-A	1	5	.167	9	6	0	0	0	35	58	2	5	6	16.7	6.69	62	.389	.417	1	.111	-1	-10	-10	-0	-1.0
NY-N	0	0	—	1	0	0	0	0	3^2	9	1	2	3	27.0	14.73	27	.409	.458	1	.500	1	-4	-4	0	-0.3
Total 5	30	39	.435	108	67	29	4	1	564	622	15	214	134	13.6	3.91	108	.287	.356	47	.230	7	16	19	-3	2.2

YEAR	TM/L	W	L	PCT	G	GS	CG	SH	SV	IP	H	HR	BB	SO	RAT	ERA	ERA+	OAV	OOB	BH	AVG	PB	PR	/A	PD	TPI
● **ED BUCKINGHAM**	Buckingham, Edward Taylor b: 5/12/1874, Metuchen, N.J. d: 7/30/42, Bridgeport, Conn. Deb: 8/30/1895																									
1895	Was-N	0	0	—	1	1	0	0	0	3	6	0	2	1	24.0	6.00	80	.408	.479	0	.000	-0	-0	-0	0	0.0
● **JESS BUCKLES**	Buckles, Jesse Robert "Jim" b: 5/20/1890, LaVerne, Cal. d: 8/2/75, Westminster, Cal. BL/TL, 6'2.5", 205 lbs. Deb: 9/17/16																									
1916	NY-A	0	0	—	2	0	0	0	0	4	3	0	1	2	9.0	2.25	128	.188	.235	0	.000	-0	0	0	-0	0.0
● **JOHN BUCKLEY**	Buckley, John Edward b: 3/20/1869, Marlboro, Mass. d: 5/3/42, Westborough, Mass. BL/TR, 6'1", 200 lbs. Deb: 7/15/1890																									
1890	Buf-P	1	3	.250	4	4	4	0	0	34	49	5	16	4	17.2	7.68	53	.323	.388	0	.000	-2	-13	-14	0	-1.1
● **MIKE BUDNICK**	Budnick, Michael Joe b: 9/15/19, Astoria, Ore. BR/TR, 6'1", 200 lbs. Deb: 4/18/46																									
1946	NY-N	2	3	.400	35	7	1	1	3	88^1	75	13	48	36	12.5	3.16	109	.231	.330	6	.300	3	2	3	1	0.7
1947	NY-N	0	0	—	7	1	0	0	0	12	16	0	10	6	19.5	10.50	39	.314	.426	1	.250	0	-9	-9	0	-0.7
Total	2	2	3	.400	42	8	1	1	3	100^1	91	13	58	42	13.4	4.04	87	.242	.343	7	.292	3	-6	-6	1	0.0
● **CHARLIE BUFFINTON**	Buffinton, Charles G. b: 6/14/1861, Fall River, Mass. d: 9/23/07, Fall River, Mass. BR/TR, 6'1", 180 lbs. Deb: 5/17/1882 M♦																									
1882	Bos-N	2	3	.400	5	5	4	1	0	42	53	2	14	17	14.4	4.07	70	.296	.347	13	.260	0	-5	-6	1	-0.4
1883	Bos-N	25	14	.641	43	41	34	4	1	333	346	4	51	188	10.7	3.03	102	.254	.281	81	.238	0	4	3	-1	0.1
1884	Bos-N	48	16	.750	67	67	63	8	0	587	506	15	76	417	8.9	2.15	135	.219	.244	94	.267	12	54	48	3	5.8
1885	Bos-N	22	27	.449	51	50	49	6	0	434^1	425	10	112	242	11.1	2.88	93	.246	.292	81	.240	5	-3	-9	6	0.0
1886	Bos-N	7	10	.412	18	17	16	0	0	151	203	4	39	47	14.4	4.59	70	.308	.346	51	.290	4	-21	-23	-1	-1.8
1887	Phi-N	21	17	.553	40	38	35	1	0	332^1	352	16	92	160	12.1	3.66	116	.264	.313	72	.268	2	15	21	7	2.6
1888	Phi-N	28	17	.622	46	46	43	6	0	400^1	324	6	59	199	8.7	1.91	155	.213	.244	29	.181	-1	42	47	10	**5.8**
1889	Phi-N	28	16	.636	47	43	37	2	0	380	390	10	121	153	12.2	3.24	134	.257	.315	32	.208	-3	33	47	2	4.1
1890	Phi-P	19	15	.559	36	33	28	0	1	283^1	312	8	126	89	14.1	3.81	112	.268	.343	41	.273	4	13	15	1	1.5
1891	Bos-a	29	9	**.763**	48	43	33	2	1	363^2	303	8	120	158	**10.6**	2.55	137	.219	**.284**	34	.188	0	47	38	6	3.9
1892	Bal-N	4	8	.333	13	13	9	0	0	97	130	4	46	30	16.6	4.92	70	.309	.381	15	.349	4	-18	-16	2	-0.9
Total	11	233	152	.605	414	396	351	30	3	3404	3344	87	856	1700	11.2	2.96	114	.246	.292	543	.245	27	162	161	35	20.7
● **BOB BUHL**	Buhl, Robert Ray b: 8/12/28, Saginaw, Mich. BR/TR, 6'2", 190 lbs. Deb: 4/17/53																									
1953	Mil-N	13	8	.619	30	18	8	3	0	154^1	133	9	73	83	12.2	2.97	132	.235	.326	6	.113	-2	23	16	1	1.4
1954	Mil-N	2	7	.222	31	14	2	1	3	110^1	117	5	65	57	15.0	4.00	93	.277	.376	1	.032	-2	1	-3	-0	-0.6
1955	Mil-N	13	11	.542	38	27	11	1	1	201^2	168	13	109	117	12.4	3.21	117	.227	.327	6	.105	-3	18	12	-1	0.8
1956	Mil-N	18	8	.692	38	33	13	2	0	216^2	190	18	105	86	12.3	3.32	104	.236	.326	7	.096	-3	11	3	0	0.0
1957	*Mil-N	18	7	**.720**	34	31	14	2	0	216^2	191	15	121	117	13.0	2.74	128	.241	.341	6	.082	-3	27	18	-2	1.3
1958	Mil-N	5	2	.714	11	10	3	0	1	73	74	5	30	27	12.9	3.45	102	.260	.332	5	.200	0	4	1	1	0.2
1959	Mil-N	15	9	.625	31	25	12	**4**	0	198	181	19	74	105	11.7	2.86	124	.243	.313	4	.057	-4	24	15	3	1.4
1960	Mil-N★	16	9	.640	36	33	11	2	0	238^2	202	23	103	121	11.6	3.09	111	.229	.312	14	.157	-2	18	9	3	1.0
1961	Mil-N	9	10	.474	32	28	9	1	0	188^1	180	23	98	77	13.5	4.11	91	.256	.351	4	.067	-3	-2	-8	1	-1.0
1962	Mil-N	0	1	.000	1	1	0	0	0	2	6	0	4	1	45.0	22.50	17	.545	.667	0	.000	-0	-4	-4	-0	-0.4
	Chi-N	12	13	.480	34	30	8	1	0	212	204	23	94	109	12.9	3.69	112	.255	.338	0	.000	-6	6	11	-2	0.3
	Yr	12	14	.462	35	31	8	1	0	214	210	23	98	110	13.2	3.87	107	.259	.343	0	.000	-6	2	7	-2	-0.1
1963	Chi-N	11	14	.440	37	34	6	0	0	226	219	24	62	108	11.3	3.38	104	.259	.312	8	.108	-3	-2	3	1	0.1
1964	Chi-N	15	14	.517	36	35	11	3	0	227^2	208	22	68	107	11.1	3.83	97	.244	.303	7	.096	-2	-8	-3	2	-0.3
1965	Chi-N	13	11	.542	32	31	2	0	0	184^1	207	26	57	92	12.9	4.39	84	.284	.335	4	.060	-4	-17	-15	0	-1.9
1966	Chi-N	0	0	—	1	1	0	0	0	2^1	4	1	1	1	19.3	15.43	24	.400	.455	0	.000	-0	-3	-3	0	-0.3
	Phi-N	6	8	.429	32	18	1	0	1	132	156	10	39	59	13.6	4.77	75	.298	.351	4	.098	-1	-17	-17	1	-1.8
	Yr	6	8	.429	33	19	1	0	1	134^1	160	11	40	60	13.7	4.96	73	.299	.352	4	.095	-2	-20	-20	1	-2.1
1967	Phi-N	0	0	—	3	0	0	0	0	3	6	2	2	1	24.0	12.00	28	.462	.533	0	—	0	-3	-3	0	-0.3
Total	15	166	132	.557	457	369	111	20	6	2587	2446	238	1105	1268	12.5	3.55	103	.251	.330	76	.089	-41	75	36	8	-0.1
● **DE WAYNE BUICE**	Buice, De Wayne Allison b: 8/20/57, Lynwood, Cal. BR/TR, 6', 170 lbs. Deb: 4/25/87																									
1987	Cal-A	6	7	.462	57	0	0	0	17	114	87	12	40	109	10.2	3.39	127	.213	.287	0	—	0	13	11	0	1.1
1988	Cal-A	2	4	.333	32	0	0	0	3	41^1	45	5	19	38	13.9	5.88	66	.287	.364	0	—	0	-9	-9	0	-0.8
1989	Tor-A	1	0	1.000	7	0	0	0	0	17	13	2	13	10	13.8	5.82	65	.220	.361	0	—	0	-4	-4	0	-0.3
Total	3	9	11	.450	96	0	0	0	20	172^1	145	19	72	157	11.4	4.23	98	.232	.314	0	—	0	1	-2	0	0.0
● **CY BUKER**	Buker, Cyril Owen b: 2/5/19, Greenwood, Wis. BL/TR, 5'11", 190 lbs. Deb: 5/17/45																									
1945	Bro-N	7	2	.778	42	4	0	0	5	87^1	90	2	45	48	14.0	3.30	114	.268	.356	3	.188	-0	5	4	-1	0.3
● **JIM BULLINGER**	Bullinger, James Eric b: 8/21/65, New Orleans, La. BR/TR, 6'2", 185 lbs. Deb: 5/27/92																									
1992	Chi-N	2	8	.200	39	9	1	0	7	85	72	9	54	36	13.8	4.66	77	.233	.354	5	.250	2	-11	-10	2	-0.6
● **RED BULLOCK**	Bullock, Malton Joseph b: 10/12/11, Biloxi, Miss. d: 6/27/88, Pascagoula, Miss. BL/TL, 6'1", 192 lbs. Deb: 5/19/36																									
1936	Phi-A	0	2	.000	12	2	0	0	0	16^2	19	0	37	7	30.2	14.04	36	.271	.523	0	.000	-1	-17	-17	0	-1.4
● **WALLY BUNKER**	Bunker, Wallace Edward b: 1/25/45, Seattle, Wash. BR/TR, 6'2", 197 lbs. Deb: 9/29/63																									
1963	Bal-A	0	1	.000	1	1	0	0	0	4	10	1	3	1	29.3	13.50	26	.476	.542	1	.500	0	-4	-4	-0	-0.4
1964	Bal-A	19	5	**.792**	29	29	12	1	0	214	161	17	62	96	9.5	2.69	133	.207	.269	5	.069	-2	22	21	1	2.2
1965	Bal-A	10	8	.556	34	27	4	1	2	189	170	16	58	84	11.0	3.38	103	.242	.303	4	.073	-1	2	2	-1	-0.1
1966	*Bal-A	10	6	.625	29	24	3	0	0	142^2	151	16	48	89	12.7	4.29	78	.269	.329	5	.104	-0	-14	-15	-1	-1.7
1967	Bal-A	3	7	.300	29	9	1	0	1	88	83	7	31	51	11.9	4.09	77	.254	.322	2	.077	-2	-8	-9	1	-1.0
1968	Bal-A	2	0	1.000	18	10	2	1	0	71	59	4	14	44	9.4	2.41	121	.225	.267	2	.111	-0	5	4	-0	0.4
1969	KC-A	12	11	.522	35	31	10	1	2	222^2	198	29	62	130	10.7	3.23	114	.238	.294	10	.143	0	10	11	3	1.6
1970	KC-A	2	11	.154	24	15	2	1	0	121^2	109	16	50	59	11.8	4.22	89	.238	.313	2	.065	-0	-7	-6	-1	-0.8
1971	KC-A	2	3	.400	7	6	0	0	0	32^1	35	7	6	15	11.4	5.01	68	.271	.304	0	.000	-1	-6	-6	-0	-0.7
Total	9	60	52	.536	206	152	34	5	5	1085^1	976	113	334	569	11.0	3.51	99	.240	.300	31	.094	-5	-1	-3	1	-0.5
● **JIM BUNNING**	Bunning, James Paul David b: 10/23/31, Southgate, Ky. BR/TR, 6'3", 195 lbs. Deb: 7/20/55																									
1955	Det-A	3	5	.375	15	8	0	0	1	51	59	8	32	37	16.6	6.35	60	.291	.395	3	.200	-0	-14	-14	0	-1.3
1956	Det-A	5	1	.833	15	3	0	0	1	53^1	55	6	28	34	14.0	3.71	111	.257	.343	6	.333	2	3	2	-1	0.3
1957	Det-A★	**20**	8	.714	45	30	14	1	1	**267^1**	214	33	72	182	10.0	2.69	143	.218	.279	20	.213	3	**33**	**35**	-5	3.5
1958	Det-A	14	12	.538	35	34	10	3	0	219^2	188	28	79	177	11.3	3.52	115	.228	.304	14	.187	-1	6	12	-3	0.9
1959	Det-A★	17	13	.567	40	35	14	1	1	249^2	220	37	75	**201**	11.0	3.89	104	.234	.298	17	.191	1	-1	5	-5	0.1
1960	Det-A	11	14	.440	36	34	10	3	0	252	217	20	64	**201**	10.4	2.79	**142**	.236	.293	13	.160	-2	**30**	**33**	-1	**3.0**
1961	Det-A★	17	11	.607	38	37	12	4	1	268	232	25	71	194	10.5	3.19	128	.229	.285	13	.130	-4	25	27	-2	2.2
1962	Det-A★	19	10	.655	41	35	12	2	6	258	262	28	74	184	12.2	3.59	113	.261	.320	23	.242	4	11	14	-5	1.3
1963	Det-A★	12	13	.480	39	35	6	2	1	248^1	245	38	69	196	11.6	3.88	97	.254	.307	13	.155	-1	-7	-4	-2	-0.6
1964	Phi-N★	19	8	.704	41	39	13	5	2	284^1	248	23	46	219	9.7	2.63	132	.233	.274	12	.121	-2	29	27	-4	2.2
1965	Phi-N	19	9	.679	39	39	15	7	0	291	253	23	62	268	10.1	2.60	133	.232	.281	22	.214	4	30	28	0	3.6
1966	Phi-N★	19	14	.576	43	41	16	**5**	1	314	260	26	55	252	9.6	2.41	149	.223	.270	19	.179	1	42	41	-3	4.3
1967	Phi-N	17	15	.531	40	40	16	**6**	0	**302^1**	241	18	73	**253**	9.7	2.29	149	.217	.273	17	.163	2	**36**	**38**	-3	**4.3**
1968	Pit-N	4	14	.222	27	26	3	1	0	160	168	14	48	95	12.6	3.88	75	.272	.333	5	.098	-2	-16	-17	-3	-2.3
1969	Pit-N	10	9	.526	25	25	4	0	0	156	147	10	49	124	11.7	3.81	92	.249	.313	2	.043	-3	-4	-6	-3	-1.2
	LA-N	3	1	.750	9	9	1	0	0	56^1	65	5	10	33	12.1	3.36	99	.288	.321	2	.111	-1	1	-0	-1	-0.2
	Yr	13	10	.565	34	34	5	0	0	212^1	212	15	59	157	11.5	3.69	93	.257	.307	4	.062	-4	-2	-6	-4	-1.4

YEAR	TM/L	W	L	PCT	G	GS	CG	SH	SV	IP	H	HR	BB	SO	RAT	ERA	ERA+	OAV	OOB	BH	AVG	PB	PR	/A	PD	TPI
1970	Phi-N	10	15	.400	34	33	4	0	0	219	233	19	56	147	12.2	4.11	97	.274	.325	9	.127	-2	-2	-3	-1	-0.6
1971	Phi-N	5	12	.294	29	16	1	0	1	110	126	11	37	58	13.8	5.48	64	.297	.362	3	.120	0	-25	-24	-0	-2.5
Total	17	224	184	.549	591	519	151	40	16	3760^1	3433	372	1000	2855	11.0	3.27	114	.242	.299	213	.167	-1	179	192	-41	17.0

● DAVE BURBA Burba, David Allen b: 7/7/66, Dayton, Ohio BR/TR, 6'4", 220 lbs. Deb: 9/08/90

YEAR	TM/L	W	L	PCT	G	GS	CG	SH	SV	IP	H	HR	BB	SO	RAT	ERA	ERA+	OAV	OOB	BH	AVG	PB	PR	/A	PD	TPI
1990	Sea-A	0	0	—	6	0	0	0	0	8	8	0	2	4	12.4	4.50	88	.267	.333	0	—	0	-1	-0	0	-0.1
1991	Sea-A	2	2	.500	22	2	0	0	1	36^2	34	6	14	16	11.8	3.68	112	.245	.314	0	—	0	2	2	-0	0.1
1992	SF-N	2	7	.222	23	11	0	0	0	70^2	80	4	31	47	14.4	4.97	67	.287	.362	1	.067	-1	-11	-13	-1	-1.4
Total	3	4	9	.308	51	13	0	0	1	115^1	122	10	47	67	13.4	4.53	80	.272	.345	1	.067	-1	-10	-11	-1	-1.4

● BILL BURBACH Burbach, William David b: 8/22/47, Dickeyville, Wis. BR/TR, 6'4", 215 lbs. Deb: 4/11/69

YEAR	TM/L	W	L	PCT	G	GS	CG	SH	SV	IP	H	HR	BB	SO	RAT	ERA	ERA+	OAV	OOB	BH	AVG	PB	PR	/A	PD	TPI
1969	NY-A	6	8	.429	31	24	2	1	0	140^2	112	15	102	82	13.8	3.65	95	.219	.351	4	.100	-1	-0	-3	-1	-0.4
1970	NY-A	0	2	.000	4	4	0	0	0	16^2	23	2	9	10	17.8	10.26	34	.324	.407	0	.000	-1	-12	-12	-0	-1.2
1971	NY-A	0	1	.000	2	0	0	0	0	3^1	6	0	5	3	29.7	10.80	30	.400	.550	0	.000	-0	-3	-3	-0	-0.3
Total	3	6	11	.353	37	28	2	1	0	160^2	141	17	116	95	14.6	4.48	78	.236	.363	4	.085	-2	-15	-18	-1	-1.9

● LARRY BURCHART Burchart, Larry Wayne b: 2/8/46, Tulsa, Okla. BR/TR, 6'3", 205 lbs. Deb: 4/10/69

YEAR	TM/L	W	L	PCT	G	GS	CG	SH	SV	IP	H	HR	BB	SO	RAT	ERA	ERA+	OAV	OOB	BH	AVG	PB	PR	/A	PD	TPI
1969	Cle-A	0	2	.000	29	0	0	0	0	42^1	42	2	24	26	14.2	4.25	89	.266	.366	0	—	0	-3	-2	-1	-0.3

● FRED BURCHELL Burchell, Frederick Duff b: 7/14/1879, Perth Amboy, N.J. d: 11/20/51, Jordan, N.Y. BR/TL, 5'11", 190 lbs. Deb: 4/17/03

YEAR	TM/L	W	L	PCT	G	GS	CG	SH	SV	IP	H	HR	BB	SO	RAT	ERA	ERA+	OAV	OOB	BH	AVG	PB	PR	/A	PD	TPI
1903	Phi-N	0	3	.000	6	3	2	0	0	44	48	0	14	12	13.1	2.86	114	.293	.356	3	.188	-1	2	2	-0	0.1
1907	Bos-A	0	1	.000	2	1	0	0	0	10	8	0	2	6	9.9	2.70	96	.221	.281	1	.200	-0	-0	-0	-0	-0.1
1908	Bos-A	10	8	.556	31	19	9	0	0	179^2	161	2	65	94	11.9	2.96	83	.247	.326	17	.246	1	-11	-10	-2	-1.2
1909	Bos-A	3	3	.500	10	5	1	0	0	52	51	1	11	12	11.1	2.94	85	.271	.318	3	.158	-0	-3	-3	1	-0.3
Total	4	13	15	.464	49	28	12	0	0	285^2	268	3	92	124	11.8	2.93	89	.258	.328	24	.220	-0	-12	-10	-2	-1.5

● FREDDIE BURDETTE Burdette, Freddie Thomason b: 9/15/36, Moultrie, Ga. BR/TR, 6'1", 170 lbs. Deb: 9/05/62

YEAR	TM/L	W	L	PCT	G	GS	CG	SH	SV	IP	H	HR	BB	SO	RAT	ERA	ERA+	OAV	OOB	BH	AVG	PB	PR	/A	PD	TPI
1962	Chi-N	0	0	—	8	0	0	0	1	9^2	5	2	8	5	12.1	3.72	111	.161	.333	0	.000	-0	0	0	-0	0.0
1963	Chi-N	0	0	—	4	0	0	0	0	4^2	5	1	2	1	13.5	3.86	91	.313	.389	0	—	0	-0	-0	0	0.0
1964	Chi-N	1	0	1.000	18	0	0	0	0	20	17	2	10	4	12.6	3.15	118	.243	.346	1	1.000	0	1	1	-0	0.2
Total	3	1	0	1.000	30	0	0	0	1	34^1	27	5	20	10	12.6	3.41	112	.231	.348	1	.500	0	1	2	-0	0.2

● LEW BURDETTE Burdette, Selva Lewis b: 11/22/26, Nitro, W.Va. BR/TR, 6'2", 190 lbs. Deb: 9/26/50 C

YEAR	TM/L	W	L	PCT	G	GS	CG	SH	SV	IP	H	HR	BB	SO	RAT	ERA	ERA+	OAV	OOB	BH	AVG	PB	PR	/A	PD	TPI
1950	NY-A	0	0	—	2	0	0	0	0	1^1	3	0	0	0	20.3	6.75	64	.500	.500	0	—	0	-0	-0	0	0.0
1951	Bos-N	0	0	—	3	0	0	0	0	4^1	6	0	5	1	24.9	6.23	59	.375	.545	0	.000	-0	-1	-1	0	-0.1
1952	Bos-N	6	11	.353	45	9	5	0	7	137	138	8	47	47	12.3	3.61	100	.265	.328	4	.114	-0	2	-0	1	0.0
1953	Mil-N	15	5	.750	46	13	6	1	8	175	177	7	56	58	12.2	3.24	121	.264	.326	9	.170	-1	20	13	2	1.3
1954	Mil-N	15	14	.517	38	32	13	4	0	238	224	17	62	79	11.0	2.76	135	.251	.302	7	.089	-4	35	26	1	2.3
1955	Mil-N	13	8	.619	42	33	11	2	0	230	253	25	73	70	13.0	4.03	93	.280	.337	20	.233	3	0	-7	2	-0.3
1956	Mil-N	19	10	.655	39	35	16	**6**	1	256^1	234	22	52	110	10.1	**2.70**	128	.241	.282	16	.186	1	30	22	1	2.5
1957	*Mil-N★	17	9	.654	37	33	14	1	0	256^2	260	25	59	78	11.3	3.72	94	.264	.307	13	.148	1	5	-6	2	-0.4
1958	*Mil-N	20	10	**.667**	40	36	19	3	0	275^1	279	18	50	113	10.9	2.91	121	.264	.301	24	.242	8	**32**	19	3	3.0
1959	Mil-N★	**21**	15	.583	41	39	20	**4**	1	289^2	312	38	38	105	10.9	4.07	87	.273	.297	21	.202	6	-4	-17	0	-1.1
1960	Mil-N	19	13	.594	45	32	**18**	4	4	275^2	277	19	35	83	10.3	3.36	102	.260	.287	16	.176	5	12	2	5	1.2
1961	Mil-N	18	11	.621	40	36	14	3	0	**272**^{1}	295	31	33	92	10.9	4.00	94	.273	.296	21	.204	5	1	-8	2	-0.1
1962	Mil-N	10	9	.526	37	19	6	1	2	143^2	172	26	23	59	12.3	4.89	78	.298	.327	9	.176	0	-15	-17	1	-1.6
1963	Mil-N	6	5	.545	15	13	4	1	0	84	71	15	24	28	10.3	3.64	88	.228	.285	1	.038	-0	-3	-4	-0	-0.5
	StL-N	3	8	.273	21	14	3	0	2	98	106	6	16	45	11.8	3.77	94	.278	.319	3	.097	-1	-5	-2	-2	-0.5
	Yr	9	13	.409	36	27	7	1	2	182	177	21	40	73	11.1	3.71	92	.255	.302	4	.070	-2	-9	-6	-2	-1.0
1964	StL-N	1	0	1.000	8	0	0	0	0	10	10	1	3	3	11.7	1.80	211	.256	.310	0	.000	-0	2	2	-0	0.2
	Chi-N	9	9	.500	28	17	8	2	0	131	152	15	19	40	11.8	4.88	76	.292	.319	12	.279	6	-20	-17	2	-0.9
	Yr	10	9	.526	36	17	8	2	0	141	162	16	22	43	11.8	4.66	80	.289	.317	12	.273	6	-18	-15	2	-0.7
1965	Chi-N	0	2	.000	7	3	0	0	0	20^1	26	3	4	5	13.7	5.31	69	.299	.337	2	.333	1	-4	-4	-0	-0.3
	Phi-N	3	3	.500	19	9	1	1	0	70^2	95	5	17	23	14.9	5.48	63	.329	.376	6	.300	1	-15	-16	0	-1.4
	Yr	3	5	.375	26	12	1	1	0	91	121	8	21	28	14.5	5.44	65	.321	.365	8	.308	2	-19	-20	0	-1.7
1966	Cal-A	7	2	.778	54	0	0	0	5	79^2	80	4	12	27	10.5	3.39	99	.268	.298	1	.125	-0	0	-0	-1	-0.1
1967	Cal-A	1	0	1.000	19	0	0	0	1	18^1	16	4	0	8	8.3	4.91	64	.232	.243	0	—	0	-3	-4	0	-0.4
Total	18	203	144	.585	626	373	158	33	31	3067^1	3186	289	628	1074	11.4	3.66	99	.268	.308	185	.183	29	68	-18	19	2.8

● BILL BURDICK Burdick, William Byron b: 10/11/1859, Austin, Minn. d: 10/23/49, Spokane, Wash. BR/TR, Deb: 7/23/1888

YEAR	TM/L	W	L	PCT	G	GS	CG	SH	SV	IP	H	HR	BB	SO	RAT	ERA	ERA+	OAV	OOB	BH	AVG	PB	PR	/A	PD	TPI
1888	Ind-N	10	10	.500	20	20	20	0	0	176	168	12	43	55	11.1	2.81	105	.242	.292	10	.147	-3	1	3	-0	0.0
1889	Ind-N	2	4	.333	10	4	2	0	1	45^2	58	7	13	16	14.0	4.53	92	.300	.344	2	.118	-0	-3	-2	-0	-0.2
Total	2	12	14	.462	30	24	22	0	1	221^2	226	19	56	71	11.7	3.17	101	.255	.304	12	.141	-3	-2	1	-0	-0.2

● TOM BURGMEIER Burgmeier, Thomas Henry b: 8/2/43, St.Paul, Minn. BL/TL, 5'11", 185 lbs. Deb: 4/10/68 C

YEAR	TM/L	W	L	PCT	G	GS	CG	SH	SV	IP	H	HR	BB	SO	RAT	ERA	ERA+	OAV	OOB	BH	AVG	PB	PR	/A	PD	TPI
1968	Cal-A	1	4	.200	56	2	0	0	5	72^2	65	5	24	33	11.0	4.33	67	.250	.313	0	.000	0	-11	-12	4	-0.9
1969	KC-A	3	1	.750	31	0	0	0	0	54	67	5	21	23	14.8	4.17	88	.316	.380	3	.167	-0	-3	-3	2	-0.1
1970	KC-A	6	6	.500	41	0	0	0	1	68^1	59	6	23	43	10.8	3.16	118	.236	.300	2	.143	-0	4	4	2	0.6
1971	KC-A	9	7	.563	67	0	0	0	17	88^1	71	3	30	44	11.0	1.73	198	.223	.303	5	.250	2	17	17	3	2.3
1972	KC-A	6	2	.750	51	0	0	0	9	55^1	67	0	33	18	16.4	4.23	72	.313	.407	4	.333	1	-7	-7	1	-0.6
1973	KC-A	0	0	—	6	0	0	0	1	10	13	2	4	4	16.2	5.40	76	.310	.383	0	—	0	-2	-1	-0	-0.5
1974	Min-A	5	3	.625	50	0	0	0	4	91^2	92	7	26	34	11.8	4.52	83	.270	.325	0	—	0	-9	-8	3	-0.7
1975	Min-A	5	8	.385	46	0	0	0	11	75^2	76	7	23	41	11.9	3.09	125	.264	.321	0	—	0	6	6	0	0.6
1976	Min-A	8	1	.889	57	0	0	0	1	115^1	95	11	29	45	9.8	2.50	144	.226	.279	0	—	0	13	14	2	1.6
1977	Min-A	6	4	.600	61	0	0	0	7	97^1	113	15	33	35	13.7	5.09	78	.299	.358	0	—	0	-11	-12	1	-1.0
1978	Bos-A	2	1	.667	35	1	0	0	4	61^1	74	7	23	24	14.7	4.40	93	.302	.369	0	—	0	-4	-2	1	-0.3
1979	Bos-A	3	2	.600	44	0	0	0	4	88^2	89	8	16	60	11.1	2.74	161	.263	.304	0	—	0	15	16	1	1.3
1980	Bos-A☆	5	4	.556	62	0	0	0	24	99	87	3	20	54	9.9	2.00	211	.241	.285	0	—	0	22	24	3	2.8
1981	Bos-A	4	5	.444	32	0	0	0	6	59^2	61	5	17	35	12.4	2.87	135	.268	.329	0	—	0	5	7	1	0.5
1982	Bos-A	7	0	1.000	40	0	0	0	2	102^1	98	6	22	44	10.7	2.29	188	.259	.303	0	—	0	20	23	2	2.2
1983	Oak-A	6	7	.462	49	0	0	0	4	96	89	2	32	39	11.3	2.81	137	.244	.305	0	—	0	13	11	2	1.3
1984	Oak-A	3	0	1.000	17	0	0	0	2	23	15	2	8	8	9.0	2.35	159	.190	.264	0	—	0	4	4	0	0.7
Total	17	79	55	.590	745	3	0	0	102	1258^2	1231	94	384	584	11.8	3.23	118	.261	.321	14	.212	2	72	81	27	9.8

● SANDY BURK Burk, Charles Sanford b: 4/22/1887, Columbus, Ohio d: 10/11/34, Brooklyn, N.Y. BR/TR, 5'8", 155 lbs. Deb: 9/12/10

YEAR	TM/L	W	L	PCT	G	GS	CG	SH	SV	IP	H	HR	BB	SO	RAT	ERA	ERA+	OAV	OOB	BH	AVG	PB	PR	/A	PD	TPI
1910	Bro-N	0	3	.000	4	3	1	0	0	19^1	17	0	27	14	21.4	6.05	50	.258	.484	0	.000	-1	-6	-6	0	-0.7
1911	Bro-N	1	3	.250	13	7	1	0	0	58	54	1	47	15	16.1	5.12	65	.261	.405	2	.105	-1	-11	-12	0	-1.2
1912	Bro-N	0	0	—	2	0	0	0	0	8^1	9	0	3	2	13.0	3.24	103	.273	.333	1	.250	0	0	0	0	0.0
	StL-N	1	3	.250	12	4	2	0	1	44^2	37	0	12	17	10.1	2.42	142	.236	.294	0	.000	-2	5	5	-1	0.2
	Yr	1	3	.250	14	4	2	0	1	53	46	0	15	19	10.5	2.55	134	.242	.301	1	.067	-1	5	5	-1	0.2
1913	StL-N	0	2	.000	19	5	0	0	1	70	81	1	33	29	15.4	5.14	63	.290	.377	2	.091	-2	-15	-15	-0	-1.7
1915	Pit-F	2	0	1.000	2	2	1	0	0	18	8	0	11	9	9.5	1.00	301	.140	.279	1	.167	-0	4	4	-1	0.4
Total	5	4	11	.267	52	21	5	0	2	218^1	206	2	133	86	14.5	4.25	77	.258	.372	6	.090	-5	-23	-24	-2	-3.0

YEAR	TM/L	W	L	PCT	G	GS	CG	SH	SV	IP	H	HR	BB	SO	RAT	ERA	ERA+	OAV	OOB	BH	AVG	PB	PR	/A	PD	TPI

● ELMER BURKART   Burkart, Elmer Robert "Swede" b: 2/1/17, Torresdale, Pa. BR/TR, 6'2", 190 lbs. Deb: 9/14/36

1936	Phi-N	0	0	—	2	2	0	0	0	7²	4	0	12	2	18.8	3.52	129	.160	.432	0	.000	-0	0	1	0	0.1
1937	Phi-N	0	0	—	7	0	0	0	0	16	20	0	9	4	16.3	6.19	70	.323	.408	0	.000	-1	-4	-3	-0	-0.4
1938	Phi-N	0	1	.000	2	1	1	0	0	10	12	0	3	1	14.4	4.50	86	.286	.348	0	.000	-0	-1	-1	-0	-0.1
1939	Phi-N	1	0	1.000	5	0	0	0	0	8¹	11	0	2	2	14.0	4.32	93	.344	.382	1	1.000	1	-0	-0	-0	0.0
Total	4	1	1	.500	16	3	1	0	0	42	47	0	26	9	15.9	4.93	85	.292	.394	1	.083	-1	-5	-3	-0	-0.4

● JOHN BURKE   Burke, John Patrick b: 1/27/1877, Hazelton, Pa. d: 8/4/50, Jersey City, N.J. BR/TR, Deb: 6/27/02 ♦

| 1902 | NY-N | 0 | 1 | .000 | 2 | 1 | 1 | 0 | 0 | 14 | 21 | 0 | 3 | 3 | 15.4 | 5.79 | 48 | .345 | .376 | 2 | .154 | -0 | -5 | -5 | 0 | -0.5 |

● BOBBY BURKE   Burke, Robert James "Lefty" b: 1/23/07, Joliet, Ill. d: 2/8/71, Joliet, Ill. BL/TL, 6'0.5", 150 lbs. Deb: 4/16/27

1927	Was-A	3	2	.600	36	6	1	0	0	100	91	6	32	20	11.7	3.96	103	.245	.316	3	.125	-2	2	1	0	-0.1
1928	Was-A	2	4	.333	26	7	2	1	0	85¹	87	1	18	27	11.3	3.90	103	.277	.320	5	.250	1	1	1	0	0.2
1929	Was-A	6	8	.429	37	17	4	0	0	141	154	6	55	51	13.6	4.79	89	.279	.349	6	.140	-3	-8	-9	-2	-1.2
1930	Was-A	3	4	.429	24	4	2	0	3	74¹	62	2	29	35	11.4	3.63	127	.229	.310	4	.174	-1	8	8	-1	0.5
1931	Was-A	8	3	.727	30	13	3	1	2	128²	124	6	50	38	12.3	4.27	101	.255	.327	10	.213	-0	2	0	0	0.0
1932	Was-A	3	6	.333	22	10	2	0	0	91	98	4	44	32	14.1	5.14	84	.272	.353	4	.200	0	-7	-8	-1	-0.8
1933	Was-A	4	3	.571	25	6	4	1	0	64	64	1	31	28	13.6	3.23	129	.256	.343	4	.235	0	7	7	0	0.7
1934	Was-A	8	8	.500	37	15	7	1	0	168	155	8	72	52	12.2	3.21	134	.245	.323	13	.228	2	24	21	0	2.2
1935	Was-A	1	8	.111	15	10	2	0	0	66¹	90	7	27	16	16.1	7.46	58	.327	.391	4	.182	-0	-22	-23	1	-2.0
1937	Phi-N	0	0	—	2	0	0	0	0	1	0	1	0	2	—	∞	—	.500	.750	0	—	0	-1	-1	-0	-0.1
Total	10	38	46	.452	254	88	27	4	5	918²	926	35	360	299	12.8	4.29	99	.263	.336	54	.194	-3	6	-3	-3	-0.6

● STEVE BURKE   Burke, Steven Michael b: 3/5/55, Stockton, Cal. BB/TR, 6'2", 200 lbs. Deb: 9/10/77

1977	Sea-A	0	1	.000	6	0	0	0	0	15²	12	0	7	6	10.9	2.87	143	.226	.317	0	—	0	2	2	0	0.3
1978	Sea-A	0	1	.000	18	0	0	0	0	49	46	2	24	16	13.0	3.49	109	.258	.350	0	—	0	1	2	0	0.2
Total	2	0	2	.000	24	0	0	0	0	64²	58	2	31	22	12.5	3.34	116	.251	.342	0	—	0	4	4	0	0.5

● TIM BURKE   Burke, Timothy Philip b: 2/19/59, Omaha, Neb. BR/TR, 6'3", 205 lbs. Deb: 4/08/85

1985	Mon-N	9	4	.692	**78**	0	0	0	8	120¹	86	9	44	87	10.2	2.39	142	.204	.290	1	.100	-0	**16**	13	1	1.5
1986	Mon-N	9	7	.563	68	2	0	0	4	101¹	103	7	46	82	13.6	2.93	126	.262	.345	0	.000	-0	9	9	1	1.0
1987	Mon-N	7	0	1.000	55	0	0	0	18	91	64	3	17	58	8.0	1.19	354	.196	.235	0	.000	-1	**29**	**30**	1	3.1
1988	Mon-N	3	5	.375	61	0	0	0	18	82	84	7	25	42	12.3	3.40	106	.272	.332	0	.000	-0	2	0	0	0.2
1989	Mon-N★	9	3	.750	68	0	0	0	28	84²	68	6	22	54	9.6	2.55	138	.225	.278	0	.000	-0	9	9	1	1.1
1990	Mon-N	3	3	.500	58	0	0	0	20	75	71	6	21	47	11.3	2.52	145	.247	.303	1	.167	-0	11	9	2	1.2
1991	Mon-N	3	4	.429	37	0	0	0	5	46	41	3	14	25	11.5	4.11	88	.243	.316	0	.000	-0	-2	-3	-0	-0.3
	NY-N	3	3	.500	35	0	0	0	1	55²	55	5	12	34	10.8	2.75	132	.255	.294	0	.000	-1	6	6	1	0.6
	Yr	6	7	.462	72	0	0	0	6	101²	96	8	26	59	10.8	3.36	108	.246	.293	0	.000	-1	4	3	1	0.3
1992	NY-N	1	2	.333	15	0	0	0	0	15²	26	1	3	7	16.7	5.74	61	.366	.392	0	—	0	-4	-4	-0	-0.4
	NY-A	2	2	.500	23	0	0	0	0	27²	26	2	15	14	13.7	3.25	124	.250	.350	0	—	0	2	2	1	0.2
Total	8	49	33	.598	498	2	0	0	102	699¹	624	49	219	444	11.1	2.72	135	.240	.304	2	.045	-2	76	74	7	8.2

● WALTER BURKE   Burke, Walter R. b: California d: 3/3/11, Memphis, Tenn. 6', 200 lbs. Deb: 6/10/1882 ♦

1882	Buf-N	0	1	.000	1	1	0	0	0	4	10	0	0	0	22.5	11.25	26	.435	.435	0	.000	-1	-4	-4	-1	-0.3
1883	Buf-N	0	0	—	1	1	0	0	0	8	9	0	3	1	13.5	5.63	56	.243	.300	1	.200	-0	-2	-2	-0	-0.2
1884	Bos-U	19	15	.559	38	36	34	0	0	322	326	10	31	255	10.0	2.85	103	.246	.263	41	.223	1	6	3	-4	-0.1
1887	Det-N	0	1	.000	2	2	1	0	0	15	21	0	5	3	16.8	6.00	67	.318	.384	2	.250	-0	-3	-3	-0	-0.3
Total	4	19	17	.528	42	40	35	0	0	349	366	10	39	259	10.5	3.15	95	.252	.272	44	.219	-1	-3	-6	-4	-0.9

● BILLY BURKE   Burke, William Ignatius b: 7/11/1889, Clinton, Mass. d: 2/9/67, Worcester, Mass. BL/TL, 5'10", 165 lbs. Deb: 4/30/10

1910	Bos-N	1	0	1.000	19	1	1	0	0	64	68	1	29	22	13.9	4.08	82	.302	.387	4	.190	-1	-7	-5	-1	-0.7
1911	Bos-N	0	1	.000	2	1	0	0	0	3¹	6	0	5	1	29.7	18.90	20	.429	.579	1	1.000	0	-6	-6	-0	-0.5
Total	2	1	1	.500	21	2	1	0	0	67¹	74	1	34	23	14.7	4.81	70	.310	.400	5	.227	-0	-13	-11	-2	-1.2

● JESSE BURKETT   Burkett, Jesse Cail "Crab" b: 12/4/1868, Wheeling, W.Va. d: 5/27/53, Worcester, Mass. BL/TL, 5'8", 155 lbs. Deb: 4/22/1890 CH♦

1890	NY-N	3	10	.231	21	12	6	0	0	118	134	3	92	82	18.3	5.57	63	.277	.407	124	.309	8	-26	-27	2	-1.7
1894	Cle-N	0	0	—	1	0	0	0	0	4	6	0	1	0	15.8	4.50	121	.342	.378	187	.358	0	0	0	-0	0.0
1902	StL-A	0	1	.000	1	0	0	0	0	1	4	0	1	2	45.0	9.00	39	.585	.638	169	.306	0	-1	-1	0	-0.1
Total	3	3	11	.214	23	12	6	0	0	123	144	3	94	84	18.4	5.56	64	.284	.409	2850	.338	9	-26	-27	2	-1.8

● JOHN BURKETT   Burkett, John David b: 11/28/64, New Brighton, Pa. BR/TR, 6'2", 205 lbs. Deb: 9/15/87

1987	SF-N	0	0	—	3	0	0	0	0	6	7	2	3	5	16.5	4.50	85	.304	.407	0	.000	-0	-0	-0	0	0.0
1990	SF-N	14	7	.667	33	32	2	0	1	204	201	18	61	118	11.7	3.79	96	.257	.314	3	.048	-3	-0	-3	-1	-0.7
1991	SF-N	12	11	.522	36	34	3	1	0	206²	223	19	60	131	12.8	4.18	86	.277	.335	5	.091	-1	-11	-14	-1	-1.6
1992	SF-N	13	9	.591	32	32	3	1	0	189²	194	13	45	107	11.5	3.84	87	.264	.310	1	.018	-3	-7	-10	-3	-1.7
Total	4	39	27	.591	104	98	8	2	1	606¹	625	52	169	361	12.1	3.95	89	.267	.321	9	.052	-8	-19	-28	-4	-4.0

● KEN BURKHART   Burkhart, Kenneth William (b: Kenneth William Burkhardt) b: 11/18/16, Knoxville, Tenn. BR/TR, 6'1", 190 lbs. Deb: 4/21/45 U

1945	StL-N	18	8	.692	42	22	12	4	2	217¹	206	9	66	67	11.4	2.90	129	.251	.309	13	.181	1	22	20	-1	2.0
1946	StL-N	6	3	.667	25	13	5	2	2	100	111	4	36	32	13.4	2.88	120	.282	.346	5	.147	-0	6	6	-2	0.5
1947	StL-N	3	6	.333	34	6	1	0	1	95	108	13	23	44	12.8	5.21	79	.292	.340	3	.125	-1	-12	-11	1	-1.2
1948	StL-N	0	0	—	20	0	0	0	0	37¹	50	4	14	16	15.9	5.54	74	.331	.395	1	.250	0	-7	-6	1	-0.5
	Cin-N	0	3	.000	16	0	0	0	0	41²	42	3	16	14	12.7	6.91	57	.255	.324	3	.333	2	-14	-14	-0	-1.2
	Yr	0	3	.000	36	0	0	0	0	79	92	7	30	30	14.0	6.27	64	.289	.352	4	.308	2	-20	-20	1	-1.7
1949	Cin-N	0	0	—	11	0	0	0	1	28¹	29	2	10	8	12.4	3.18	132	.282	.345	2	.286	0	3	3	0	0.4
Total	5	27	20	.574	148	41	18	6	7	519²	546	35	165	181	12.5	3.84	99	.273	.332	27	.180	2	-2	-1	-2	-0.0

● WALLY BURNETTE   Burnette, Wallace Harper b: 6/20/29, Blairs, Va. BR/TR, 6'0.5", 178 lbs. Deb: 7/15/56

1956	KC-A	6	8	.429	18	14	4	1	0	121¹	115	13	39	54	11.6	2.89	150	.252	.314	2	.051	-5	17	19	-1	1.5
1957	KC-A	7	12	.368	38	9	1	0	1	113	115	8	44	57	12.7	4.30	92	.268	.338	8	.250	1	-6	-4	2	-0.1
1958	KC-A	1	1	.500	12	4	0	0	0	28¹	29	2	14	11	13.7	3.49	112	.264	.347	1	.167	-0	1	1	0	0.1
Total	3	14	21	.400	68	27	5	1	1	262²	259	23	97	122	12.3	3.56	116	.260	.328	11	.143	-4	11	16	1	1.5

● DENNIS BURNS   Burns, Dennis b: 5/24/1898, Tiff City, Mo. d: 5/21/69, Tulsa, Okla. BR/TR, 5'10", 180 lbs. Deb: 9/22/23

1923	Phi-A	2	1	.667	4	3	2	0	0	27	21	1	7	8	9.3	2.00	205	.210	.262	1	.111	-1	6	6	-0	0.6
1924	Phi-A	6	8	.429	37	17	7	0	1	154	191	3	68	26	15.2	5.08	84	.314	.384	6	.143	-2	-15	-14	-0	-1.5
Total	2	8	9	.471	41	20	9	0	1	181	212	4	75	34	14.3	4.62	92	.299	.367	7	.137	-3	-9	-7	-0	-0.9

● FARMER BURNS   Burns, James "Slab" b: Ashtabula, Ohio TR, 5'7", 168 lbs. Deb: 7/06/01

| 1901 | StL-N | 0 | 0 | — | 1 | 0 | 0 | 0 | 0 | 1 | 2 | 0 | 1 | 0 | 36.0 | 9.00 | 35 | .411 | .583 | 0 | — | 0 | -1 | -1 | -0 | 0.0 |

● DICK BURNS   Burns, Richard Simon b: 12/26/1863, Holyoke, Mass. d: 11/11/37, Holyoke, Mass. BL/TL, 140 lbs. Deb: 5/03/1883 ♦

1883	Det-N	2	12	.143	17	13	13	0	0	127²	178	8	33	30	14.5	4.51	69	.301	.339	26	.186	-2	-19	-20	-0	-1.8
1884	Cin-U	23	15	.605	40	40	34	1	0	329²	298	7	47	167	9.4	2.46	129	.225	.252	107	.306	11	21	26	0	3.3
1885	StL-N	0	0	—	1	1	0	0	0	3	3	0	0	2	9.0	9.00	31	.250	.250	12	.222	0	-2	-2	1	-0.1

YEAR	TM/L	W	L	PCT	G	GS	CG	SH	SV	IP	H	HR	BB	SO	RAT	ERA	ERA+	OAV	OOB	BH	AVG	PB	PR	/A	PD	TPI
Total	3	25	27	.481	58	53	47	1	0	460^1	473	15	80	199	10.8	3.07	103	.248	.278	145	.267	10	-1	4	1	1.4

● BRITT BURNS Burns, Robert Britt b: 6/8/59, Houston, Tex. BL/TL, 6'5", 218 lbs. Deb: 8/05/78

YEAR	TM/L	W	L	PCT	G	GS	CG	SH	SV	IP	H	HR	BB	SO	RAT	ERA	ERA+	OAV	OOB	BH	AVG	PB	PR	/A	PD	TPI
1978	Chi-A	0	2	.000	2	2	0	0	0	7^2	14	2	3	3	20.0	12.91	29	.378	.425	0	—	0	-8	-8	0	-0.7
1979	Chi-A	0	0	—	6	0	0	0	0	5	10	1	1	2	19.8	5.40	79	.435	.458	0	—	0	-1	-1	-0	-0.1
1980	Chi-A	15	13	.536	34	32	11	1	0	238	213	17	63	133	10.6	2.84	142	.241	.295	0	—	0	32	31	-1	3.3
1981	Chi-A☆	10	6	.625	24	23	5	1	0	156^2	139	14	49	108	11.1	2.64	135	.238	.303	0	—	0	18	16	-4	1.5
1982	Chi-A	13	5	.722	28	28	5	1	0	169^1	168	12	67	116	12.6	4.04	100	.257	.329	0	—	0	1	-0	-3	-0.3
1983	*Chi-A	10	11	.476	29	26	8	4	0	173^2	165	14	55	115	11.7	3.58	117	.249	.311	0	—	0	9	12	-2	0.9
1984	Chi-A	4	12	.250	34	16	2	0	3	117	130	7	45	85	13.8	5.00	83	.280	.349	0	—	0	-13	-11	-0	-1.1
1985	Chi-A	18	11	.621	36	34	8	4	0	227	206	26	79	172	11.4	3.96	109	.242	.308	0	—	0	5	9	-1	0.6
Total	8	70	60	.538	193	161	39	11	3	1094^1	1045	93	362	734	11.8	3.66	111	.251	.315	0	—	0	42	49	-11	4.1

● TOM BURNS Burns, Thomas Everett b: 3/30/1857, Honesdale, Pa. d: 3/19/02, Jersey City, N.J. BR/TR, 5'7", 152 lbs. Deb: 5/01/1880 MU♦

YEAR	TM/L	W	L	PCT	G	GS	CG	SH	SV	IP	H	HR	BB	SO	RAT	ERA	ERA+	OAV	OOB	BH	AVG	PB	PR	/A	PD	TPI
1880	Chi-N	0	0	—	1	0	0	0	0	1^1	2	0	2	1	27.0	0.00	—	.250	.400	103	.309	0	0	0	0	0.0

● OYSTER BURNS Burns, Thomas P. b: 9/6/1864, Philadelphia, Pa. d: 11/11/28, Brooklyn, N.Y. BR/TR, 5'8", 183 lbs. Deb: 8/18/1884 ♦

YEAR	TM/L	W	L	PCT	G	GS	CG	SH	SV	IP	H	HR	BB	SO	RAT	ERA	ERA+	OAV	OOB	BH	AVG	PB	PR	/A	PD	TPI
1884	Bal-a	0	0	—	2	0	0	0	**1**	9	12	0	2	6	14.0	3.00	116	.343	.378	39	.298	1	0	0	-0	0.1
1885	Bal-a	7	4	.636	15	11	10	1	**3**	105^2	112	2	21	30	12.4	3.58	91	.266	.321	74	.231	2	-4	-4	-1	-0.2
1887	Bal-a	1	0	1.000	3	0	0	0	0	11^1	16	0	4	2	18.3	9.53	43	.291	.371	188	.341	2	-7	-7	-1	-0.5
1888	Bal-a	0	1	.000	5	0	0	0	0	12^2	12	0	3	2	10.7	4.26	70	.241	.284	97	.298	2	-2	-2	-0	-0.1
Total	4	8	5	.615	25	11	10	1	4	138^2	152	2	30	40	12.9	4.09	81	.271	.326	1389	.300	7	-12	-12	-2	-0.7

● TODD BURNS Burns, Todd Edward b: 7/6/63, Maywood, Cal. BR/TR, 6'2", 186 lbs. Deb: 5/31/88

YEAR	TM/L	W	L	PCT	G	GS	CG	SH	SV	IP	H	HR	BB	SO	RAT	ERA	ERA+	OAV	OOB	BH	AVG	PB	PR	/A	PD	TPI
1988	*Oak-A	8	2	.800	17	14	2	0	1	102^2	93	8	34	57	11.2	3.16	120	.241	.304	0	—	0	9	7	-1	0.9
1989	*Oak-A	6	5	.545	50	2	0	0	8	96^1	66	3	28	49	8.9	2.24	164	.196	.260	0	—	0	18	15	-1	1.7
1990	*Oak-A	3	3	.500	43	2	0	0	3	78^2	78	8	32	43	12.6	2.97	125	.263	.334	0	—	0	8	6	-1	0.9
1991	Oak-A	1	0	1.000	9	0	0	0	0	13^1	10	2	8	3	12.2	3.38	114	.217	.333	0	—	0	1	1	0	0.4
1992	Tex-A	3	5	.375	35	10	0	0	1	103	97	8	32	55	11.6	3.84	99	.248	.311	0	—	0	1	-0	-1	-0.1
Total	5	21	15	.583	154	28	2	0	13	394	344	29	134	207	11.1	3.08	122	.236	.303	0	—	0	37	29	-4	3.8

● BILL BURNS Burns, William Thomas "Sleepy Bill" b: 1/29/1880, San Saba, Tex. d: 6/6/53, Ramona, Cal. BB/TL, 6'2", 195 lbs. Deb: 4/18/08

YEAR	TM/L	W	L	PCT	G	GS	CG	SH	SV	IP	H	HR	BB	SO	RAT	ERA	ERA+	OAV	OOB	BH	AVG	PB	PR	/A	PD	TPI
1908	Was-A	6	11	.353	23	19	11	2	0	165	135	3	18	55	8.6	1.69	135	.229	.257	8	.148	-1	13	11	3	1.5
1909	Was-A	1	1	.500	6	4	1	0	0	29^1	25	0	7	13	10.7	1.23	198	.229	.294	2	.182	-0	4	4	0	0.5
	Chi-A	7	13	.350	23	19	10	3	0	168	161	2	34	50	10.9	2.04	115	.264	.312	10	.172	2	8	6	1	0.9
	Yr	8	14	.364	29	23	11	3	0	197^1	186	2	41	63	10.7	1.92	123	.258	.305	12	.174	1	12	10	1	1.4
1910	Chi-A	0	0	—	1	0	0	0	0	0^1	0	0	1	0	27.0	0.00	—	.000	.500	0	—	0	0	0	0	0.0
	Cin-N	8	13	.381	31	21	13	2	0	178^2	183	3	49	57	12.3	3.48	84	.273	.333	16	.262	2	-9	-11	1	-0.9
1911	Cin-N	1	0	1.000	6	3	0	0	1	17^2	17	1	3	5	11.7	3.06	108	.254	.315	3	.429	2	1	0	1	0.3
	Phi-N	6	10	.375	21	14	8	3	1	121	132	5	26	47	12.2	3.42	101	.287	.333	6	.150	-1	-0	0	2	0.0
	Yr	7	10	.412	27	17	8	3	2	138^2	149	6	29	52	11.9	3.38	102	.281	.326	9	.191	0	0	1	3	0.3
1912	Det-A	1	4	.200	6	5	2	0	0	38^2	52	0	9	6	14.7	5.35	61	.338	.382	3	.231	1	-9	-9	-0	-0.7
Total	5	30	52	.366	117	85	45	10	2	718^2	705	14	147	233	11.1	2.72	100	.265	.313	48	.197	4	8	1	7	1.6

● PETE BURNSIDE Burnside, Peter Willits b: 7/2/30, Evanston, Ill. BR/TL, 6'2", 190 lbs. Deb: 9/20/55

YEAR	TM/L	W	L	PCT	G	GS	CG	SH	SV	IP	H	HR	BB	SO	RAT	ERA	ERA+	OAV	OOB	BH	AVG	PB	PR	/A	PD	TPI
1955	NY-N	1	0	1.000	2	2	1	0	0	12^2	10	1	9	2	13.5	2.84	142	.204	.328	1	.200	0	2	2	-0	0.2
1957	NY-N	1	4	.200	10	9	1	1	0	30^2	47	5	13	18	17.9	8.80	45	.356	.418	0	.000	-1	-17	-17	-0	-1.7
1958	SF-N	0	0	—	6	1	0	0	0	10^2	20	3	5	4	21.1	6.75	56	.400	.455	0	—	0	-3	-3	-0	-0.3
1959	Det-A	1	3	.250	30	0	0	0	1	62	55	7	25	49	11.9	3.77	108	.237	.317	0	.000	-1	1	2	0	0.1
1960	Det-A	7	7	.500	31	15	2	0	2	113^2	122	14	50	71	13.9	4.28	93	.277	.356	4	.148	-1	-5	-4	-1	-0.6
1961	Was-A	4	9	.308	33	16	4	2	2	113^1	106	11	51	56	12.7	4.53	89	.251	.335	2	.059	-3	-6	-6	-1	-1.0
1962	Was-A	5	11	.313	40	20	6	0	2	149^2	152	20	51	74	12.3	4.45	91	.263	.325	2	.057	-3	-8	-7	-2	-1.1
1963	Bal-A	0	1	.000	6	0	0	0	0	7^1	11	0	2	6	17.2	4.91	72	.344	.400	0	.000	-0	-1	-1	-0	-0.2
	Was-A	0	1	.000	38	1	0	0	0	67^1	84	12	24	23	14.4	6.15	60	.308	.364	1	.091	-0	-19	-18	-1	-2.0
	Yr	0	2	.000	44	1	0	0	0	74^2	95	12	26	29	14.6	6.03	61	.310	.364	1	.083	-1	-20	-19	-2	-2.2
Total	8	19	36	.345	196	64	14	3	7	567^1	607	73	230	303	13.5	4.81	82	.275	.347	10	.076	-8	-57	-53	-6	-6.6

● SHELDON BURNSIDE Burnside, Sheldon John b: 12/22/54, South Bend, Ind. BR/TL, 6'5", 200 lbs. Deb: 9/04/78

YEAR	TM/L	W	L	PCT	G	GS	CG	SH	SV	IP	H	HR	BB	SO	RAT	ERA	ERA+	OAV	OOB	BH	AVG	PB	PR	/A	PD	TPI
1978	Det-A	0	0	—	2	0	0	0	0	4	4	0	2	3	13.5	9.00	43	.250	.333	0	—	0	-2	-2	-0	-0.4
1979	Det-A	1	1	.500	10	0	0	0	0	21^1	28	2	8	13	15.6	6.33	68	.333	.398	0	—	0	-5	-5	0	-0.7
1980	Cin-N	1	0	1.000	7	0	0	0	0	4^2	6	1	1	2	13.5	1.93	185	.333	.368	0	.000	-0	1	1	1	0.1
Total	3	2	1	.667	19	0	0	0	0	30	38	3	11	18	15.0	6.00	69	.322	.385	0	.000	-0	-6	-6	1	-1.0

● GEORGE BURPO Burpo, George Harvie b: 6/19/22, Jenkins, Ky. BR/TL, 6', 195 lbs. Deb: 6/09/46

YEAR	TM/L	W	L	PCT	G	GS	CG	SH	SV	IP	H	HR	BB	SO	RAT	ERA	ERA+	OAV	OOB	BH	AVG	PB	PR	/A	PD	TPI
1946	Cin-N	0	0	—	2	0	0	0	0	2^1	4	0	5	1	34.7	15.43	22	.400	.600	0	—	0	-3	-3	-0	-0.3

● HARRY BURRELL Burrell, Harry J. b: 5/26/1869, Bethel, Vt. d: 12/11/14, Omaha, Neb. BR/TR, Deb: 9/13/1891

YEAR	TM/L	W	L	PCT	G	GS	CG	SH	SV	IP	H	HR	BB	SO	RAT	ERA	ERA+	OAV	OOB	BH	AVG	PB	PR	/A	PD	TPI
1891	StL-a	4	2	.667	7	4	3	0	0	43	51	4	21	19	15.5	4.81	87	.285	.366	5	.227	-0	-5	-3	-0	-0.3

● AL BURRIS Burris, Alva Burton b: 1/28/1874, Warwick, Md. d: 3/24/38, Salisbury, Md. BR/TR, Deb: 6/22/1894

YEAR	TM/L	W	L	PCT	G	GS	CG	SH	SV	IP	H	HR	BB	SO	RAT	ERA	ERA+	OAV	OOB	BH	AVG	PB	PR	/A	PD	TPI
1894	Phi-N	0	0	—	1	0	0	0	0	5	14	0	2	0	28.8	18.00	28	.493	.526	2	.500	1	-7	-7	0	-0.4

● RAY BURRIS Burris, Bertram Ray b: 8/22/50, Idabel, Okla. BR/TR, 6'5", 200 lbs. Deb: 4/08/73 C

YEAR	TM/L	W	L	PCT	G	GS	CG	SH	SV	IP	H	HR	BB	SO	RAT	ERA	ERA+	OAV	OOB	BH	AVG	PB	PR	/A	PD	TPI
1973	Chi-N	1	1	.500	31	1	0	0	0	64^2	65	2	27	57	12.8	2.92	135	.261	.333	1	.143	0	5	7	1	0.9
1974	Chi-N	3	5	.375	40	5	0	0	1	75	91	8	26	40	14.5	6.60	58	.300	.363	1	.077	-1	-25	-23	-1	-2.5
1975	Chi-N	15	10	.600	36	35	8	2	0	238^1	259	25	73	108	12.7	4.12	93	.281	.337	15	.183	1	-13	-7	-4	-1.1
1976	Chi-N	15	13	.536	37	36	10	4	0	249	251	22	70	112	11.8	3.11	124	.263	.317	9	.111	-5	11	21	0	1.8
1977	Chi-N	14	16	.467	39	39	5	1	0	221	270	29	67	105	13.8	4.72	93	.305	.356	12	.174	1	-20	-8	3	-0.5
1978	Chi-N	7	13	.350	40	32	4	1	1	198^2	210	15	79	94	13.5	4.76	85	.274	.349	7	.115	-1	-26	-16	2	-1.6
1979	Chi-N	0	0	—	14	0	0	0	0	21^2	23	0	15	14	16.2	6.23	66	.284	.402	0	.000	0	-6	-5	0	-0.5
	NY-A	1	3	.250	15	0	0	0	0	27^2	40	5	10	19	16.3	6.18	66	.342	.394	0	—	0	-6	-6	-0	-0.5
	NY-N	0	2	.000	4	4	0	0	0	21^2	21	2	6	10	11.6	3.32	109	.247	.304	1	.167	-0	1	1	0	0.1
1980	NY-N	7	13	.350	29	29	1	0	0	170^1	181	20	54	83	12.6	4.02	88	.277	.336	5	.098	-2	-8	-9	-1	-1.3
1981	*Mon-N	9	7	.563	22	21	4	0	0	135^2	117	9	41	52	10.7	3.05	114	.235	.297	7	.189	1	7	7	-1	0.7
1982	Mon-N	4	14	.222	37	15	2	0	2	123^2	143	14	53	55	14.4	4.73	77	.297	.369	5	.179	1	-16	-15	-1	-1.5
1983	Mon-N	4	7	.364	40	17	2	1	0	154	139	13	56	100	11.5	3.68	97	.244	.314	9	.231	3	-1	-2	0	0.2
1984	Oak-A	13	10	.565	34	28	5	1	0	211^2	193	15	90	93	12.4	3.15	119	.244	.327	0	—	0	20	14	-3	1.1
1985	Mil-A	9	13	.409	29	28	6	0	0	170^1	182	25	53	81	12.6	4.81	87	.272	.328	0	—	0	-13	-12	-1	-1.2
1986	StL-N	4	5	.444	23	10	0	0	0	82	92	13	32	34	14.0	5.60	65	.287	.359	4	.148	0	-17	-18	-1	-1.8
1987	Mil-A	2	2	.500	10	2	0	0	0	23	33	4	12	8	17.6	5.87	78	.351	.425	0	—	0	-4	-3	0	-0.4
Total	15	108	134	.446	480	302	47	10	4	2188^1	2310	221	764	1065	12.9	4.17	93	.274	.338	76	.151	-1	-110	-75	-6	-8.1

● JOHN BURROWS Burrows, John b: 10/30/13, Winnfield, La. d: 4/27/87, Coal Run, Ohio BR/TL, 5'10", 200 lbs. Deb: 4/25/43

YEAR	TM/L	W	L	PCT	G	GS	CG	SH	SV	IP	H	HR	BB	SO	RAT	ERA	ERA+	OAV	OOB	BH	AVG	PB	PR	/A	PD	TPI
1943	Phi-A	0	1	.000	4	1	0	0	0	7^2	8	0	9	3	21.1	8.22	41	.276	.462	0	.000	-0	-4	-4	-0	-0.4
	Chi-N	0	2	.000	23	1	0	0	2	32^2	25	0	16	18	11.8	3.86	87	.205	.307	2	.667	1	-2	-2	0	0.0
1944	Chi-N	0	0	—	3	0	0	0	0	3	7	0	3	1	30.0	18.00	20	.467	.556	0	—	0	-5	-5	0	-0.5

YEAR TM/L	W	L	PCT	G	GS	CG	SH	SV	IP	H	HR	BB	SO	RAT	ERA	ERA+	OAV	OOB	BH	AVG	PB	PR	/A	PD	TPI
Total 2	0	3	.000	30	2	0	0	2	43^1	40	0	28	22	14.7	5.61	60	.241	.360	2	.500	1	-11	-11	0	-0.9

● JIM BURTON Burton, Jim Scott b: 10/27/49, Royal Oak, Mich. BR/TL, 6'3", 195 lbs. Deb: 6/10/75

YEAR TM/L	W	L	PCT	G	GS	CG	SH	SV	IP	H	HR	BB	SO	RAT	ERA	ERA+	OAV	OOB	BH	AVG	PB	PR	/A	PD	TPI
1975 *Bos-A	1	2	.333	29	4	0	0	1	53	58	6	19	39	13.1	2.89	141	.276	.336	0	—	0	5	7	0	0.1
1977 Bos-A	0	0	—	1	0	0	0	0	2^2	2	0	1	3	10.1	0.00	—	.200	.273	0	—	0	1	1	-0	-0.6
Total 2	1	2	.333	30	4	0	0	1	55^2	60	6	20	42	12.9	2.75	149	.273	.333	0	—	0	6	8	-0	-0.5

● MOE BURTSCHY Burtschy, Edward Frank b: 4/18/22, Cincinnati, Ohio BR/TR, 6'3", 208 lbs. Deb: 6/17/50

YEAR TM/L	W	L	PCT	G	GS	CG	SH	SV	IP	H	HR	BB	SO	RAT	ERA	ERA+	OAV	OOB	BH	AVG	PB	PR	/A	PD	TPI
1950 Phi-A	0	1	.000	9	1	0	0	0	19	22	2	21	12	20.8	7.11	64	.289	.449	0	.000	-0	-5	-5	0	-0.5
1951 Phi-A	0	0	—	7	0	0	0	0	17	18	0	12	4	16.4	5.29	81	.277	.397	1	.333	0	-2	-2	0	-0.2
1954 Phi-A	5	4	.556	46	0	0	0	4	94^2	80	7	53	54	13.4	3.80	103	.234	.350	2	.118	-1	-1	1	0	0.0
1955 KC-A	2	0	1.000	7	0	0	0	0	11^1	17	0	10	9	22.2	10.32	40	.354	.475	1	.333	0	-8	-8	-0	-0.7
1956 KC-A	3	1	.750	21	0	0	0	0	43^1	41	6	30	18	15.4	3.95	110	.263	.392	1	.125	-1	1	2	2	0.3
Total 5	10	6	.625	90	1	0	0	4	185^1	178	15	126	97	15.4	4.71	88	.259	.385	5	.139	-1	-15	-12	1	-1.1

● DENNIS BURTT Burtt, Dennis Allen b: 11/29/57, San Diego, Cal. BB/TR, 6', 180 lbs. Deb: 9/04/85

YEAR TM/L	W	L	PCT	G	GS	CG	SH	SV	IP	H	HR	BB	SO	RAT	ERA	ERA+	OAV	OOB	BH	AVG	PB	PR	/A	PD	TPI
1985 Min-A	2	2	.500	5	2	0	0	0	28^1	20	2	7	9	8.6	3.81	116	.200	.252	0	—	0	1	2	0	0.0
1986 Min-A	0	0	—	3	0	0	0	0	2	7	1	3	1	45.0	31.50	14	.538	.625	0	—	0	-6	-6	-0	-0.6
Total 2	2	2	.500	8	2	0	0	0	30^1	27	3	10	10	11.0	5.64	78	.239	.301	0	—	0	-5	-4	0	-0.6

● DICK BURWELL Burwell, Richard Matthew b: 1/23/40, Alton, Ill. BR/TR, 6'1", 190 lbs. Deb: 9/13/60

YEAR TM/L	W	L	PCT	G	GS	CG	SH	SV	IP	H	HR	BB	SO	RAT	ERA	ERA+	OAV	OOB	BH	AVG	PB	PR	/A	PD	TPI
1960 Chi-N	0	0	—	3	1	0	0	0	9^2	11	2	7	1	17.7	5.59	68	.306	.432	1	.333	0	-2	-2	-0	-0.2
1961 Chi-N	0	0	—	2	0	0	0	0	4	6	0	4	0	22.5	9.00	46	.375	.500	0	.000	-0	-2	-2	0	-0.2
Total 2	0	0	—	5	1	0	0	0	13^2	17	2	11	1	19.1	6.59	59	.327	.453	1	.250	0	-4	-4	0	-0.4

● BILL BURWELL Burwell, William Edwin b: 3/27/1895, Jarbalo, Kan. d: 6/11/73, Ormond Beach, Fla BL/TR, 5'11", 175 lbs. Deb: 5/01/20 MC

YEAR TM/L	W	L	PCT	G	GS	CG	SH	SV	IP	H	HR	BB	SO	RAT	ERA	ERA+	OAV	OOB	BH	AVG	PB	PR	/A	PD	TPI
1920 StL-A	6	4	.600	33	2	0	0	4	113^1	133	5	42	30	14.2	3.65	107	.303	.369	7	.167	-2	2	3	-0	0.1
1921 StL-A	2	4	.333	33	3	1	0	2	84^1	102	2	29	17	14.2	5.12	87	.309	.368	6	.240	-0	-8	-6	-1	-0.7
1928 Pit-N	1	0	1.000	4	1	0	0	0	20^2	18	2	8	2	11.3	5.23	78	.234	.306	2	.222	-0	-3	-3	1	-0.2
Total 3	9	8	.529	70	6	1	0	6	218^1	253	9	79	49	13.9	4.37	95	.299	.363	15	.197	-2	-9	-5	-1	-0.8

● STEVE BUSBY Busby, Steven Lee b: 9/29/49, Burbank, Cal. BR/TR, 6'2", 205 lbs. Deb: 9/08/72

YEAR TM/L	W	L	PCT	G	GS	CG	SH	SV	IP	H	HR	BB	SO	RAT	ERA	ERA+	OAV	OOB	BH	AVG	PB	PR	/A	PD	TPI
1972 KC-A	3	1	.750	5	5	3	0	0	40	28	1	8	31	8.1	1.57	192	.200	.243	3	.200	0	7	6	-1	0.8
1973 KC-A	16	15	.516	37	37	7	1	0	238^1	246	18	105	174	13.5	4.23	97	.271	.350	0	—	0	-11	-3	2	-0.6
1974 KC-A☆	22	14	.611	38	38	20	3	0	292^1	284	14	92	198	11.9	3.39	113	.258	.320	0	—	0	8	14	3	1.4
1975 KC-A★	18	12	.600	34	34	18	3	0	260^1	233	18	81	160	11.0	3.08	125	.242	.303	0	—	0	20	22	4	2.5
1976 KC-A	3	3	.500	13	13	1	0	0	71^2	58	7	49	29	13.8	4.40	80	.218	.346	0	—	0	-7	-7	-0	-0.8
1978 KC-A	1	0	1.000	7	5	0	0	0	21^1	24	2	15	10	17.3	7.59	50	.282	.402	0	—	0	-9	-9	0	-1.0
1979 KC-A	6	6	.500	22	12	4	0	0	94^1	71	10	64	45	12.9	3.63	118	.220	.349	0	—	0	6	7	2	0.7
1980 KC-A	1	3	.250	11	6	0	0	0	42^1	59	3	19	12	17.0	6.17	66	.335	.406	0	—	0	-10	-10	-0	-1.0
Total 8	70	54	.565	167	150	53	7	0	1060^2	1003	73	433	659	12.4	3.72	105	.253	.330	3	.200	0	4	20	10	2.0

● DON BUSCHHORN Buschhorn, Donald Lee b: 4/29/46, Independence, Mo. BR/TR, 6', 170 lbs. Deb: 5/15/65

YEAR TM/L	W	L	PCT	G	GS	CG	SH	SV	IP	H	HR	BB	SO	RAT	ERA	ERA+	OAV	OOB	BH	AVG	PB	PR	/A	PD	TPI
1965 KC-A	0	1	.000	12	3	0	0	0	31	36	7	8	9	13.1	4.35	80	.295	.344	2	.500	1	-3	-3	-0	-0.3

● GUY BUSH Bush, Guy Terrell "The Mississippi Mudcat" b: 8/23/01, Aberdeen, Miss. d: 7/2/85, Shannon, Miss. BR/TR, 6', 175 lbs. Deb: 9/17/23

YEAR TM/L	W	L	PCT	G	GS	CG	SH	SV	IP	H	HR	BB	SO	RAT	ERA	ERA+	OAV	OOB	BH	AVG	PB	PR	/A	PD	TPI
1923 Chi-N	0	0	—	1	0	0	0	0	1	1	0	0	2	9.0	0.00	—	.250	.250	0	—	0	0	0	0	0.0
1924 Chi-N	2	5	.286	16	8	4	0	0	80^2	91	7	24	36	13.1	4.02	97	.285	.339	4	.154	-1	-1	-1	-2	-0.4
1925 Chi-N	6	13	.316	42	15	5	0	**4**	182	213	15	52	76	13.3	4.30	101	.300	.350	11	.193	-2	-1	0	4	0.2
1926 Chi-N	13	9	.591	35	16	7	2	2	157^1	149	3	42	32	11.1	2.86	134	.258	.311	8	.167	-3	17	17	-1	1.4
1927 Chi-N	10	10	.500	36	22	9	1	2	193^1	177	3	79	62	12.2	3.03	128	.250	.330	8	.123	-4	19	18	0	1.4
1928 Chi-N	15	6	.714	42	24	9	2	2	204^1	229	10	86	61	14.1	3.83	100	.293	.367	6	.082	-6	4	0	-1	-0.6
1929 *Chi-N	18	7	.720	**50**	29	18	2	**8**	270^2	277	16	107	82	12.9	3.66	126	.265	.335	15	.165	-4	32	29	0	2.3
1930 Chi-N	15	10	.600	46	25	11	0	3	225	291	22	86	75	15.2	6.20	79	.316	.376	22	.282	3	-31	-33	1	-2.5
1931 Chi-N	16	8	.667	39	24	14	1	2	180^1	190	9	66	54	12.9	4.49	86	.268	.332	7	.123	-2	-13	-13	4	-1.1
1932 *Chi-N	19	11	.633	40	30	15	1	0	238^2	262	13	70	73	12.8	3.21	118	.278	.332	15	.179	0	18	15	1	1.5
1933 Chi-N	20	12	.625	41	32	20	4	2	259	261	9	68	84	11.5	2.75	119	.257	.304	11	.125	-1	17	15	4	1.9
1934 Chi-N	18	10	.643	40	27	15	1	2	209^1	213	15	54	75	11.5	3.83	101	.262	.309	16	.229	1	5	1	1	0.3
1935 Pit-N	11	11	.500	41	25	8	1	2	204^1	237	16	40	42	12.4	4.32	95	.285	.321	8	.127	-1	-7	-5	-1	-0.7
1936 Pit-N	1	3	.250	16	0	0	0	2	34^2	49	3	11	10	15.6	5.97	68	.336	.382	3	.333	0	-8	-7	1	-0.6
Bos-N	4	5	.444	15	11	5	0	0	90^1	98	2	20	28	11.8	3.39	113	.281	.320	3	.120	-1	6	4	1	0.4
Yr	5	8	.385	31	11	5	0	2	125	147	5	31	38	12.8	4.10	95	.297	.338	6	.176	0	-1	-3	1	-0.2
1937 Bos-N	8	15	.348	32	20	11	1	1	180^2	201	8	48	56	12.4	3.54	101	.282	.328	6	.111	-2	8	1	1	0.0
1938 StL-N	0	1	.000	6	0	0	0	1	6	6	1	3	1	13.5	4.50	88	.286	.375	0	—	0	-0	-0	-0	-0.1
1945 Cin-N	0	0	—	4	0	0	0	1	4^1	5	0	3	1	16.6	8.31	45	.278	.381	0	—	0	-2	-2	-0	-0.2
Total 17	176	136	.564	542	308	151	16	34	2722	2950	152	859	850	12.7	3.86	103	.277	.334	143	.161	-21	64	40	12	3.2

● JOE BUSH Bush, Leslie Ambrose "Bullet Joe" b: 11/27/1892, Brainerd, Minn. d: 11/1/74, Ft.Lauderdale, Fla. BR/TR, 5'9", 173 lbs. Deb: 9/30/12

YEAR TM/L	W	L	PCT	G	GS	CG	SH	SV	IP	H	HR	BB	SO	RAT	ERA	ERA+	OAV	OOB	BH	AVG	PB	PR	/A	PD	TPI
1912 Phi-A	0	0	—	1	1	0	0	0	8	14	0	4	3	20.3	7.88	39	.368	.429	2	.500	1	-4	-4	-0	-0.3
1913 *Phi-A	15	6	.714	39	16	6	1	3	200^1	199	3	66	81	12.1	3.82	72	.248	.310	11	.157	-0	-20	-24	4	-2.1
1914 *Phi-A	16	12	.571	38	22	14	2	3	206	184	2	81	109	11.9	3.06	85	.242	.322	14	.189	2	-7	-10	-0	-0.9
1915 Phi-A	5	15	.250	25	18	8	0	0	145^2	137	3	89	89	14.2	4.14	71	.263	.375	7	.143	-3	-19	-20	0	-2.2
1916 Phi-A	15	24	.385	40	33	25	8	0	286^2	222	3	130	157	11.1	2.57	111	.219	.310	14	.140	-4	8	9	5	1.2
1917 Phi-A	11	17	.393	37	31	17	4	2	233^1	207	3	111	121	12.3	2.47	111	.241	.328	16	.200	1	5	7	0	1.0
1918 *Bos-A	15	15	.500	36	31	26	7	2	272^2	241	3	91	125	11.1	2.11	127	.242	.307	27	.276	6	20	17	3	3.1
1919 Bos-A	0	0	—	3	2	0	0	0	9	11	0	4	3	15.0	5.00	60	.324	.395	2	.400	1	-2	-2	0	-0.2
1920 Bos-A	15	15	.500	35	32	18	0	1	243^2	287	3	94	88	14.4	4.25	86	.300	.369	25	.245	2	-12	-16	3	-1.2
1921 Bos-A	16	9	.640	37	32	21	3	1	254^1	244	10	93	96	12.1	3.50	121	.260	.330	39	.325	6	22	20	1	2.9
1922 *NY-A	26	7	**.788**	39	30	20	0	3	255^1	240	16	85	92	11.5	3.31	121	.252	.314	31	.326	8	21	20	1	2.8
1923 *NY-A	19	15	.559	37	30	22	3	0	275^2	263	7	117	125	12.6	3.43	115	.260	.340	31	.274	7	17	16	1	2.4
1924 NY-A	17	16	.515	39	31	19	3	1	252	262	9	109	80	13.5	3.57	116	.273	.352	42	.339	13	18	16	2	3.1
1925 StL-A	14	14	.500	33	28	15	2	0	208^2	230	18	91	63	13.9	5.09	92	.284	.357	26	.255	3	-16	-10	2	-0.2
1926 Was-A	1	8	.111	12	11	3	0	0	71^1	83	6	35	27	15.5	6.69	58	.292	.380	7	.233	1	-21	-22	0	-2.0
Pit-N	6	6	.500	19	11	9	2	3	110^2	97	7	35	38	10.9	3.01	131	.236	.299	13	.265	3	10	11	-1	1.3
1927 Pit-N	1	2	.333	5	3	0	0	0	6^2	14	1	5	1	25.7	13.50	30	.412	.487	3	.600	1	-7	-7	0	-0.5
NY-N	1	1	.500	3	2	1	0	0	12	18	1	5	6	17.3	7.50	51	.340	.397	2	.500	1	-5	-5	-0	-0.4
Yr	2	3	.400	8	5	1	0	0	18^2	32	2	10	7	20.3	9.64	41	.368	.433	5	.556	2	-12	-12	0	-0.9
1928 Phi-A	2	1	.667	11	2	1	0	1	35^1	39	1	18	15	14.8	5.09	79	.300	.389	1	.067	-1	-4	-4	1	-0.4
Total 17	195	183	.516	489	366	225	35	20	3087^1	2992	96	1263	1319	12.6	3.51	99	.259	.335	313	.253	49	4	-8	21	7.4

● JACK BUSHELMAN Bushelman, John Francis b: 8/29/1885, Cincinnati, Ohio d: 10/26/55, Roanoke, Va. BR/TR, 6'2", 175 lbs. Deb: 10/05/09

YEAR TM/L	W	L	PCT	G	GS	CG	SH	SV	IP	H	HR	BB	SO	RAT	ERA	ERA+	OAV	OOB	BH	AVG	PB	PR	/A	PD	TPI
1909 Cin-N	0	1	.000	1	1	1	0	0	7	7	1	4	3	14.1	2.57	101	.241	.333	0	.000	-0	0	0	-0	-0.1
1911 Bos-A	0	1	.000	3	1	1	0	0	12	8	0	10	5	14.3	3.00	109	.186	.352	0	.000	-0	0	0	-0	0.0
1912 Bos-A	1	0	1.000	3	0	0	0	0	7^2	9	0	5	5	16.4	4.70	72	.310	.412	0	.000	-0	-1	-1	-0	-0.1
Total 3	1	2	.333	7	2	2	0	0	26^2	24	1	19	13	14.9	3.38	93	.238	.364	0	.000	-1	-1	-1	-0	-0.2

YEAR TM/L	W	L	PCT	G	GS	CG	SH	SV	IP	H	HR	BB	SO	RAT	ERA	ERA+	OAV	OOB	BH	AVG	PB	PR	/A	PD	TPI

● FRANK BUSHEY Bushey, Francis Clyde b: 8/1/06, Wheaton, Kan. d: 3/18/72, Topeka, Kan. BR/TR, 6′, 180 lbs. Deb: 9/17/27

1927 Bos-A	0	0	—	1	0	0	0	0	1¹	2	0	2	0	27.0	6.75	63	.500	.667			0	-0	-0	0	0.0
1930 Bos-A	0	1	.000	11	0	0	0	0	30	34	1	15	4	15.3	6.30	73	.306	.398	1	.111	-1	-6	-6	0	-0.6
Total 2	0	1	.000	12	0	0	0	0	31¹	36	1	17	4	15.8	6.32	73	.313	.410	1	.111	-1	-6	-6	0	-0.6

● TOM BUSKEY Buskey, Thomas William b: 2/20/47, Harrisburg, Pa. BR/TR, 6′3″, 220 lbs. Deb: 8/05/73

1973 NY-A	0	1	.000	8	0	0	0	1	16²	18	2	4	8	12.4	5.40	68	.286	.338	0	—	0	-3	-3	-0	-0.1
1974 NY-A	0	1	.000	4	0	0	0	1	5²	10	1	3	3	22.2	6.35	55	.400	.483	0	—	0	-2	-2	-0	0.0
Cle-A	2	6	.250	51	0	0	0	17	93	93	10	33	40	12.3	3.19	113	.263	.327	0	—	0	4	4	1	0.6
Yr	2	7	.222	55	0	0	0	18	98²	103	11	36	43	12.8	3.38	107	.271	.336	0	—	0	3	3	1	0.6
1975 Cle-A	5	3	.625	50	0	0	0	7	77	69	7	29	29	11.6	2.57	147	.252	.326	0	—	0	10	10	2	1.3
1976 Cle-A	5	4	.556	39	0	0	0	1	94¹	88	9	34	32	11.9	3.63	96	.256	.328	0	—	0	-1	-1	0	0.0
1977 Cle-A	0	0	—	21	0	0	0	0	34	45	6	8	15	14.3	5.29	74	.313	.353	0	—	0	-5	-5	-0	-0.3
1978 Tor-A	0	1	.000	8	0	0	0	0	13¹	14	1	5	7	12.8	3.38	116	.275	.339	0	—	0	1	1	0	0.0
1979 Tor-A	6	10	.375	44	0	0	0	7	78²	74	10	25	44	11.4	3.43	126	.249	.310	0	—	0	7	8	2	0.8
1980 Tor-A	3	1	.750	33	0	0	0	0	66²	68	11	26	34	12.7	4.45	97	.278	.347	0	—	0	-3	-1	0	-0.5
Total 8	21	27	.438	258	0	0	0	34	479¹	479	57	167	212	12.3	3.66	105	.267	.332	0	—	0	9	11	5	1.8

● MAX BUTCHER Butcher, Albert Maxwell b: 9/21/10, Holden, W.Va. d: 9/15/57, Man, W.Va. BR/TR, 6′2″, 220 lbs. Deb: 4/20/36

1936 Bro-N	6	6	.500	38	15	5	0	2	147²	154	11	59	55	13.0	3.96	104	.268	.337	6	.125	-3	1	3	-2	-0.1
1937 Bro-N	11	15	.423	39	24	8	1	0	191²	203	12	75	57	13.4	4.27	94	.280	.354	10	.161	-1	-8	-5	-3	-0.3
1938 Bro-N	5	4	.556	24	8	3	0	2	72²	104	9	39	21	17.8	6.56	59	.334	.410	4	.160	0	-22	-21	1	-1.9
Phi-N	4	8	.333	12	12	11	0	0	98¹	94	6	31	29	11.6	2.93	133	.253	.314	9	.257	1	9	10	0	1.2
Yr	9	12	.429	36	20	14	0	2	171	198	15	70	50	14.2	4.47	87	.290	.358	13	.217	1	-13	-11	2	-0.7
1939 Phi-N	2	13	.133	19	16	3	0	0	104¹	131	10	51	27	15.8	5.61	71	.308	.383	7	.184	-1	-20	-19	-2	-2.0
Pit-N	4	4	.500	14	12	5	2	0	86²	104	2	23	21	13.2	3.43	112	.297	.340	3	.097	-2	5	4	2	0.4
Yr	6	17	.261	33	28	8	2	0	191	235	12	74	48	14.6	4.62	85	.302	.363	10	.145	-3	-15	-15	-0	-1.6
1940 Pit-N	8	9	.471	35	24	6	2	2	136¹	161	13	46	40	13.7	6.01	63	.290	.346	15	.300	4	-33	-33	1	-2.7
1941 Pit-N	17	12	.586	33	32	19	0	0	236	249	11	66	61	12.1	3.05	118	.265	.314	15	.183	-1	15	15	0	1.5
1942 Pit-N	5	8	.385	24	18	9	0	1	150²	144	7	44	49	11.3	2.93	116	.247	.303	7	.143	-2	6	8	0	0.6
1943 Pit-N	10	8	.556	33	21	10	2	1	193²	191	4	57	45	11.6	2.60	134	.262	.317	10	.164	-1	17	19	0	1.9
1944 Pit-N	13	11	.542	35	27	13	5	1	199	216	8	46	43	11.9	3.12	119	.273	.314	12	.190	0	11	13	3	1.6
1945 Pit-N	10	8	.556	28	20	12	2	0	169¹	184	7	46	42	12.4	3.03	130	.277	.328	12	.222	0	15	17	1	1.9
Total 10	95	106	.473	334	229	104	14	9	1786¹	1935	100	583	485	12.8	3.73	101	.276	.333	110	.184	-6	-3	11	8	2.1

● JOHN BUTCHER Butcher, John Daniel b: 3/8/57, Glendale, Cal. BR/TR, 6′4″, 190 lbs. Deb: 9/08/80

1980 Tex-A	3	3	.500	6	6	1	0	0	35¹	34	2	13	27	12.0	4.08	96	.248	.313	0	—	0	-0	-1	0	0.2
1981 Tex-A	1	2	.333	5	3	1	1	0	27²	18	0	8	19	8.5	1.63	213	.186	.248	0	—	0	6	6	0	0.6
1982 Tex-A	1	5	.167	18	13	2	0	1	94¹	102	10	34	39	13.2	4.87	80	.280	.345	0	—	0	-8	-10	2	-0.8
1983 Tex-A	6	6	.500	38	6	1	1	5	123	128	8	41	58	12.4	3.51	114	.270	.329	0	—	0	8	7	0	0.8
1984 Min-A	13	11	.542	34	34	8	1	0	225	242	18	53	83	12.0	3.44	122	.276	.320	0	—	0	14	19	-1	1.6
1985 Min-A	11	14	.440	34	33	8	2	0	207²	239	24	43	92	12.5	4.98	88	.289	.328	0	—	0	-19	-13	0	-1.4
1986 Min-A	0	3	.000	16	10	1	0	0	70	82	11	24	29	13.8	6.30	68	.294	.352	0	—	0	-17	-16	0	-1.6
Cle-A	1	5	.167	13	8	1	1	0	50²	86	6	13	16	18.1	6.93	60	.381	.421	0	—	0	-15	-16	-1	-1.4
Yr	1	8	.111	29	18	2	1	0	120²	168	17	37	45	15.5	6.56	65	.330	.379	0	—	0	-32	-31	0	-3.0
Total 7	36	49	.424	164	113	23	6	6	833²	931	79	229	363	12.7	4.42	94	.284	.334	0	—	0	-32	-24	1	-1.7

● MIKE BUTCHER Butcher, Michael Dana b: 5/10/65, Davenport, Iowa BR/TR, 6′1″, 200 lbs. Deb: 7/08/92

| 1992 Cal-A | 2 | 2 | .500 | 19 | 0 | 0 | 0 | 0 | 27² | 29 | 3 | 13 | 24 | 14.3 | 3.25 | 120 | .264 | .352 | 0 | — | 0 | 2 | 2 | -0 | 0.2 |

● SAL BUTERA Butera, Salvatore Philip b: 9/25/52, Richmond Hill, N.Y BR/TR, 6′, 190 lbs. Deb: 4/10/80 ♦

1985 Mon-N	0	0	—	1	0	0	0	0	1	0	0	0	0	0.0	0.00	—	.000	.000	24	.200	0	0	0	-0	0.0
1986 Cin-N	0	0	—	1	0	0	0	0	1	0	0	1	1	9.0	0.00	—	.000	.250	27	.239	0	0	0	0	0.0
Total 2	0	0	—	2	0	0	0	0	2	0	0	1	1	4.5	0.00	—	.000	.143	182	.227	0	1	1	-0	0.0

● BILL BUTLAND Butland, Wilburn Rue b: 3/22/18, Terre Haute, Ind. BR/TL, 6′5″, 185 lbs. Deb: 5/29/40

1940 Bos-A	1	2	.333	3	3	1	0	0	21	27	0	10	5	15.9	5.57	81	.307	.378	0	.000	-1	-3	-3	1	-0.3
1942 Bos-A	7	1	.875	23	10	6	2	1	111¹	85	8	33	46	9.8	2.51	149	.206	.270	1	.036	-1	14	15	0	1.6
1946 Bos-A	1	0	1.000	5	2	0	0	0	16¹	23	3	13	10	19.8	11.02	33	.343	.450	1	.250	0	-14	-13	-1	-1.2
1947 Bos-A	0	0	—	1	0	0	0	0	2	3	0	0	1	13.5	4.50	86	.333	.333	0	—	0	-0	-0	-0	0.0
Total 4	9	3	.750	32	15	7	2	1	150²	138	11	56	62	11.8	3.88	99	.240	.310	2	.051	-2	-2	-1	1	0.1

● CECIL BUTLER Butler, Cecil Dean "Slewfoot" b: 10/23/37, Dallas, Ga. BR/TR, 6′4″, 195 lbs. Deb: 4/23/62

1962 Mil-N	2	0	1.000	9	2	1	0	0	31	26	4	9	22	10.2	2.61	145	.217	.271	0	.000	-1	5	4	0	0.4
1964 Mil-N	0	0	—	2	0	0	0	0	4¹	7	2	0	2	14.5	8.31	42	.368	.368	0	—	0	-2	-2	0	-0.2
Total 2	2	0	1.000	11	2	1	0	0	35¹	33	6	9	24	10.7	3.31	114	.237	.284	0	.000	-1	2	2	0	0.2

● CHARLIE BUTLER Butler, Charles Thomas b: 5/12/06, Green Cove Springs, Fla. d: 5/10/64, Brunswick, Ga. BR/TL, 6′1.5″, 210 lbs. Deb: 5/01/33

| 1933 Phi-N | 0 | 0 | — | 1 | 0 | 0 | 0 | 0 | 1 | 1 | 1 | 0 | 0 | 27.0 | 9.00 | 42 | .500 | .500 | 0 | — | 0 | -1 | -1 | -0 | -0.1 |

● IKE BUTLER Butler, Isaac Burr b: 8/22/1873, Langston, Mich. d: 3/17/48, Oakland, Cal. TR, 6′, 175 lbs. Deb: 8/05/02

| 1902 Bal-A | 1 | 10 | .091 | 16 | 14 | 12 | 0 | 0 | 116¹ | 168 | 1 | 45 | 13 | 16.6 | 5.34 | 71 | .338 | .395 | 6 | .113 | -3 | -23 | -20 | -1 | -2.1 |

● BILL BUTLER Butler, William Franklin b: 3/12/47, Hyattsville, Md. BL/TL, 6′2″, 210 lbs. Deb: 4/09/69

1969 KC-A	9	10	.474	34	29	5	4	0	193²	174	15	91	156	12.5	3.90	94	.240	.328	3	.050	-4	-6	-5	-3	-1.1
1970 KC-A	4	12	.250	25	25	2	1	0	140²	117	17	87	75	13.1	3.77	99	.229	.342	2	.045	-3	-1	-1	-2	-0.6
1971 KC-A	1	2	.333	14	6	0	0	0	44¹	45	6	18	32	12.8	3.45	99	.268	.339	1	.083	-1	0	-0	-0	-0.1
1972 Cle-A	0	0	—	6	2	0	0	0	11²	9	1	10	6	14.7	1.54	208	.220	.373	0	.000	-0	2	2	-0	0.2
1974 Min-A	4	6	.400	26	12	2	0	1	98²	91	9	56	79	13.5	4.10	91	.251	.353	0	—	0	-5	-4	-2	-0.9
1975 Min-A	5	4	.556	23	8	1	0	0	81²	100	12	35	55	14.9	5.95	65	.301	.368	0	—	0	-20	-19	-0	-2.0
1977 Min-A	0	1	.000	6	4	0	0	0	21	19	5	15	5	15.0	6.86	58	.244	.372	0	—	0	-7	-7	-1	-0.6
Total 7	23	35	.397	134	86	10	5	1	591²	555	65	312	408	13.3	4.21	88	.250	.345	6	.051	-7	-37	-33	-9	-5.1

● TOM BUTTERS Butters, Thomas Arden b: 4/8/38, Delaware, O. BR/TR, 6′2″, 195 lbs. Deb: 9/08/62

1962 Pit-N	0	0	—	4	0	0	0	0	6	5	0	6	10	18.0	1.50	262	.238	.429	0	—	0	2	2	0	0.2
1963 Pit-N	0	0	—	6	1	0	0	0	16¹	15	1	8	11	13.8	4.41	75	.259	.368	0	—	0	-2	-2	-0	-0.2
1964 Pit-N	2	2	.500	28	4	0	0	0	64¹	52	3	37	58	12.5	2.38	148	.221	.327	1	.333	0	8	8	-1	0.8
1965 Pit-N	0	1	.000	5	0	0	0	0	9	9	2	5	6	14.0	7.00	50	.250	.341	2	.182	0	-3	-3	0	-0.4
Total 4	2	3	.400	43	5	0	0	0	95²	81	6	56	85	13.2	3.10	113	.231	.342	3	.200	0	4	4	-1	0.4

● FRANK BUTTERY Buttery, Frank b: 5/13/1851, Silver Mine, Conn. d: 12/16/02, Silver Mine, Conn. Deb: 4/26/1872 ♦

| 1872 Man-n | 3 | 2 | .600 | 6 | 5 | 5 | 0 | 0 | 49 | 81 | 0 | 1 | 0 | 15.1 | 5.14 | 71 | .331 | .333 | 25 | .269 | -0 | -8 | -8 | | -0.5 |

● RALPH BUXTON Buxton, Ralph Stanley "Buck" b: 6/7/11, Weyburn, Sask., Can BR/TR, 5′11.5″, 163 lbs. Deb: 9/11/38

| 1938 Phi-A | 0 | 1 | .000 | 5 | 0 | 0 | 0 | 0 | 9¹ | 12 | 1 | 5 | 9 | 16.4 | 4.82 | 100 | .324 | .405 | 0 | .000 | -0 | -0 | 0 | -0 | 0.0 |

YEAR	TM/L	W	L	PCT	G	GS	CG	SH	SV	IP	H	HR	BB	SO	RAT	ERA	ERA+	OAV	OOB	BH	AVG	PB	PR	/A	PD	TPI
1949	NY-A	0	1	.000	14	0	0	0	2	26^2	22	3	16	14	12.8	4.05	100	.229	.339	0	.000	-0	0	-0	-0	-0.1
Total	2	0	2	.000	19	0	0	0	2	36	34	4	21	23	13.8	4.25	100	.256	.357	0	.000	-1	0	-0	-0	-0.1

● JOHN BUZHARDT

Buzhardt, John William b: 8/17/36, Prosperity, S.C. BR/TR, 6'2", 198 lbs. Deb: 9/10/58

YEAR	TM/L	W	L	PCT	G	GS	CG	SH	SV	IP	H	HR	BB	SO	RAT	ERA	ERA+	OAV	OOB	BH	AVG	PB	PR	/A	PD	TPI
1958	Chi-N	3	0	1.000	6	2	1	0	0	24^1	16	2	7	9	8.5	1.85	212	.184	.245	1	.125	-0	6	6	1	0.6
1959	Chi-N	4	5	.444	31	10	1	1	0	101^1	107	12	29	33	12.2	4.97	79	.271	.322	2	.069	-1	-12	-12	1	-1.2
1960	Phi-N	5	16	.238	30	29	5	0	0	200^1	198	14	68	73	12.0	3.86	100	.259	.321	10	.161	-1	-2	0	-1	-0.1
1961	Phi-N	6	18	.250	41	27	6	1	0	202^1	200	28	65	92	12.1	4.49	91	.263	.326	6	.105	-2	-10	-9	0	-1.1
1962	Chi-A	8	12	.400	28	25	8	2	0	152^1	156	16	59	64	12.9	4.19	93	.264	.335	6	.118	-2	-4	-5	2	-0.5
1963	Chi-A	9	4	.692	19	18	6	3	0	126^1	100	8	31	59	9.7	2.42	145	.216	.273	4	.083	-3	17	15	1	1.5
1964	Chi-A	10	8	.556	31	25	8	3	0	160	150	13	35	97	10.6	2.98	116	.250	.295	11	.204	2	11	8	0	1.1
1965	Chi-A	13	8	.619	32	30	4	1	1	188^2	167	12	56	108	11.0	3.01	106	.242	.305	7	.125	0	10	4	-1	0.3
1966	Chi-A	6	11	.353	33	22	5	4	1	150^1	144	13	30	66	10.7	3.83	83	.248	.289	5	.116	-1	-7	-11	3	-1.0
1967	Chi-A	3	9	.250	28	7	0	0	0	88^2	100	11	37	33	14.5	3.96	78	.294	.373	4	.200	0	-7	-8	0	-0.9
	Bal-A	0	1	.000	7	1	0	0	0	11^2	14	1	5	7	14.7	4.63	68	.298	.365	0	.000	-0	-2	-2	0	-0.2
	Yr	3	10	.231	35	8	0	0	0	100^1	114	12	42	40	14.0	4.04	77	.288	.356	4	.190	0	-9	-10	1	-1.1
	Hou-N	0	0	—	1	0	0	0	0	0^2	0	0	0	0	0.0	0.00	—	.000	.000	0	—	0	0	0	0	0.0
1968	Hou-N	4	4	.500	39	4	0	0	5	83^2	73	0	35	37	12.0	3.12	95	.239	.325	4	.250	1	-1	-2	1	0.0
Total	11	71	96	.425	326	200	44	15	7	1490^2	1425	130	457	678	11.6	3.66	97	.253	.314	60	.135	-7	-1	-16	7	-1.5

● BUD BYERLY

Byerly, Eldred William b: 10/26/20, Webster Groves, Mo BR/TR, 6'2.5", 185 lbs. Deb: 9/26/43

YEAR	TM/L	W	L	PCT	G	GS	CG	SH	SV	IP	H	HR	BB	SO	RAT	ERA	ERA+	OAV	OOB	BH	AVG	PB	PR	/A	PD	TPI
1943	StL-N	1	0	1.000	2	2	0	0	0	13	14	0	5	6	13.2	3.46	97	.280	.345	0	.000	-0	-0	-0	-0	-0.1
1944	*StL-N	2	2	.500	9	4	2	0	0	42^1	37	2	20	13	12.1	3.40	104	.228	.313	2	.167	-0	1	1	1	0.1
1945	StL-N	4	5	.444	33	8	2	0	0	95	111	3	41	39	14.5	4.74	79	.288	.358	5	.217	1	-10	-10	2	-0.7
1950	Cin-N	0	1	.000	4	1	0	0	0	14^2	12	1	4	5	9.8	2.45	173	.218	.271	0	.000	-0	3	3	-0	0.2
1951	Cin-N	2	1	.667	40	0	0	0	0	66	69	6	25	28	13.1	3.27	125	.267	.337	0	.000	-0	5	6	1	0.6
1952	Cin-N	0	1	.000	12	2	0	0	1	24^2	29	0	7	14	13.1	5.11	74	.309	.356	1	.200	0	-4	-4	0	-0.4
1956	Was-A	2	4	.333	25	0	0	0	4	51^2	45	6	14	19	10.6	2.96	146	.243	.303	1	.091	-1	7	8	0	0.7
1957	Was-A	6	6	.500	47	0	0	0	6	95	94	6	22	39	11.1	3.13	125	.264	.309	1	.067	-1	7	8	1	0.9
1958	Was-A	2	0	1.000	17	0	0	0	1	24	34	4	11	13	17.3	6.75	56	.347	.418	0	.000	-0	-8	-8	-0	-0.8
	Bos-A	1	2	.333	18	0	0	0	0	30^1	31	1	7	16	11.6	1.78	225	.272	.320	0	.000	-1	7	7	-0	0.7
	Yr	3	2	.600	35	0	0	0	1	54^1	65	5	18	29	13.9	3.98	99	.302	.359	0	.000	-1	-1	-0	-0	-0.1
1959	SF-N	1	0	1.000	11	0	0	0	0	13	11	2	5	4	11.1	1.38	275	.234	.308	0	—	0	4	4	1	0.4
1960	SF-N	1	0	1.000	19	0	0	0	2	22	32	3	6	13	16.0	5.32	65	.340	.386	0	.000	-0	-4	-4	-0	-0.5
Total	11	22	22	.500	237	17	4	0	14	491^2	519	34	167	209	12.7	3.70	105	.273	.335	10	.118	-4	8	10	4	1.1

● HARRY BYRD

Byrd, Harry Gladwin b: 2/3/25, Darlington, S.C. d: 5/14/85, Darlington, S.C. BR/TR, 6'1", 188 lbs. Deb: 4/21/50

YEAR	TM/L	W	L	PCT	G	GS	CG	SH	SV	IP	H	HR	BB	SO	RAT	ERA	ERA+	OAV	OOB	BH	AVG	PB	PR	/A	PD	TPI
1950	Phi-A	0	0	—	6	0	0	0	0	10^2	25	3	9	2	30.4	16.88	27	.481	.571	0	.000	-0	-15	-15	-0	-1.3
1952	Phi-A	15	15	.500	37	28	15	3	2	228^1	244	12	98	116	13.8	3.31	120	.274	.351	10	.133	-3	9	16	0	1.4
1953	Phi-A	11	20	.355	40	37	11	2	0	236^2	279	23	115	122	15.5	5.51	78	.294	.379	18	.222	-1	-40	-32	-1	-3.3
1954	NY-A	9	7	.563	25	21	5	1	0	132^1	131	10	43	52	12.3	2.99	115	.258	.324	9	.196	1	11	7	-1	0.6
1955	Bal-A	3	2	.600	14	8	1	1	1	65^1	64	7	28	25	13.6	4.55	84	.261	.354	3	.158	-0	-4	-5	-1	-0.6
	Chi-A	4	6	.400	25	12	1	1	1	91	85	10	30	44	11.6	4.65	85	.251	.315	2	.067	-3	-7	-7	0	-1.0
	Yr	7	8	.467	39	20	2	2	2	156^1	149	17	58	69	12.0	4.61	85	.251	.320	5	.102	-3	-11	-12	-1	-1.6
1956	Chi-A	0	1	.000	3	1	0	0	0	4^1	9	0	4	0	27.0	10.38	39	.474	.565	0	.000	-0	-3	-3	0	-0.3
1957	Det-A	4	3	.571	37	1	0	0	5	59	53	6	28	20	12.7	3.36	115	.249	.342	0	.000	-1	3	3	-1	0.2
Total	7	46	54	.460	187	108	33	8	9	827^2	890	71	355	381	14.0	4.35	91	.277	.356	42	.160	-8	-46	-36	-3	-4.3

● JEFF BYRD

Byrd, Jeffrey Alan b: 11/11/56, LaMesa, Cal. BR/TR, 6'3", 195 lbs. Deb: 6/20/77

YEAR	TM/L	W	L	PCT	G	GS	CG	SH	SV	IP	H	HR	BB	SO	RAT	ERA	ERA+	OAV	OOB	BH	AVG	PB	PR	/A	PD	TPI
1977	Tor-A	2	13	.133	17	17	1	0	0	87^1	98	5	68	40	17.1	6.18	68	.286	.404	0	—	0	-21	-19	1	-1.9

● JERRY BYRNE

Byrne, Gerald Wilford b: 2/2/07, Parnell, Mich. d: 8/11/55, Lansing, Mich. BR/TR, 6', 170 lbs. Deb: 8/31/29

YEAR	TM/L	W	L	PCT	G	GS	CG	SH	SV	IP	H	HR	BB	SO	RAT	ERA	ERA+	OAV	OOB	BH	AVG	PB	PR	/A	PD	TPI
1929	Chi-A	0	1	.000	3	1	0	0	0	7^1	11	0	6	1	20.9	7.36	58	.379	.486	0	.000	-0	-3	-3	-0	-0.3

● TOMMY BYRNE

Byrne, Thomas Joseph b: 12/31/19, Baltimore, Md. BL/TL, 6'1", 182 lbs. Deb: 4/27/43

YEAR	TM/L	W	L	PCT	G	GS	CG	SH	SV	IP	H	HR	BB	SO	RAT	ERA	ERA+	OAV	OOB	BH	AVG	PB	PR	/A	PD	TPI
1943	NY-A	2	1	.667	11	2	0	0	0	31^2	28	1	35	22	18.8	6.54	49	.248	.437	1	.091	-0	-11	-12	0	-1.2
1946	NY-A	0	1	.000	4	1	0	0	0	9^1	7	1	8	5	15.4	5.79	60	.194	.356	2	.222	0	-2	-2	0	-0.2
1947	NY-A	0	0	—	4	1	0	0	0	4^1	5	0	6	2	22.8	4.15	85	.294	.478	0	—	0	-0	-0	0	0.0
1948	NY-A	8	5	.615	31	11	5	1	2	133^2	79	8	101	93	12.7	3.30	124	.172	.332	15	.326	5	15	12	-1	1.6
1949	*NY-A	15	7	.682	32	30	12	3	0	196	125	11	179	129	14.6	3.72	109	**.183**	.362	16	.193	1	10	7	-3	0.5
1950	NY-A☆	15	9	.625	31	31	10	2	0	203^1	188	23	160	118	16.2	4.74	91	.245	.387	22	.272	7	-4	-10	-2	-0.5
1951	NY-A	2	1	.667	9	3	0	0	0	21	16	0	36	14	23.6	6.86	56	.213	.482	2	.222	1	-6	-7	-0	-0.6
	StL-A	4	10	.286	19	17	7	2	0	122^2	104	5	114	57	16.9	3.82	115	.235	.404	16	.281	3	4	8	-1	1.1
	Yr	6	11	.353	28	20	7	2	0	143^2	120	5	150	71	17.7	4.26	101	.230	.413	18	.273	4	-2	1	-1	0.5
1952	StL-A	7	14	.333	29	24	14	0	0	196	182	16	112	91	14.0	4.68	84	.247	.354	21	.250	5	-22	-17	-4	-1.5
1953	Chi-A	2	0	1.000	6	6	0	0	0	16	18	0	26	4	24.8	10.13	40	.295	.506	3	.167	1	-11	-11	0	-0.9
	Was-A	0	5	.000	6	5	2	0	0	33^2	35	3	22	22	15.5	4.28	91	.276	.387	1	.059	-1	-1	-1	0	-0.2
	Yr	2	5	.286	12	11	2	0	0	49^2	53	3	48	26	18.5	6.16	64	.282	.430	4	.114	-0	-12	-12	1	-1.1
1954	NY-A	3	2	.600	5	5	4	1	0	40	36	1	19	24	12.4	2.70	127	.240	.325	7	.368	4	5	3	0	0.8
1955	*NY-A	16	5	**.762**	27	22	9	3	2	160	137	12	87	76	13.0	3.15	119	.237	.344	16	.205	4	14	11	-1	1.3
1956	*NY-A	7	3	.700	37	8	1	0	6	109^2	108	9	72	52	14.9	3.36	115	.262	.374	14	.269	6	10	6	1	1.2
1957	*NY-A	4	6	.400	30	4	1	0	2	84^2	70	8	60	57	14.6	4.36	82	.227	.364	7	.189	4	-5	-7	-1	-0.5
Total	13	85	69	.552	281	170	65	12	12	1362	1138	98	1037	766	14.9	4.11	97	.229	.371	143	.238	40	-5	-20	-11	0.9

● MARTY BYSTROM

Bystrom, Martin Eugene b: 7/26/58, Coral Gables, Fla. BR/TR, 6'5", 200 lbs. Deb: 9/07/80

YEAR	TM/L	W	L	PCT	G	GS	CG	SH	SV	IP	H	HR	BB	SO	RAT	ERA	ERA+	OAV	OOB	BH	AVG	PB	PR	/A	PD	TPI
1980	*Phi-N	5	0	1.000	6	5	1	1	0	36	26	1	9	21	8.8	1.50	252	.195	.246	1	.071	-1	8	9	1	1.1
1981	Phi-N	4	3	.571	9	9	1	0	0	53^2	55	3	16	24	12.1	3.35	108	.264	.320	2	.118	-1	1	2	1	0.1
1982	Phi-N	5	6	.455	19	16	1	0	0	89	93	2	35	50	13.4	4.85	76	.277	.354	3	.125	-0	-12	-12	-1	-1.3
1983	Phi-N	6	9	.400	24	23	1	1	0	119^1	136	6	44	87	14.1	4.60	77	.285	.353	9	.237	2	-13	-14	-1	-1.3
1984	Phi-N	4	4	.500	11	11	0	0	0	56^2	66	5	22	36	14.0	5.08	71	.283	.345	3	.158	-0	-9	-9	-0	-1.0
	NY-A	2	2	.500	7	7	0	0	0	39^1	34	3	13	24	11.0	2.97	127	.230	.296	0	—	0	4	4	-1	0.7
1985	NY-A	3	2	.600	8	8	0	0	0	41	44	8	19	16	14.0	5.71	70	.280	.362	0	—	0	-7	-8	0	-0.5
Total	6	29	26	.527	84	79	4	2	0	435	454	28	158	258	13.0	4.26	86	.268	.336	18	.161	-0	-28	-28	-1	-2.2

● GREG CADARET

Cadaret, Gregory James b: 2/27/62, Detroit, Mich. BL/TL, 6'3", 205 lbs. Deb: 7/05/87

YEAR	TM/L	W	L	PCT	G	GS	CG	SH	SV	IP	H	HR	BB	SO	RAT	ERA	ERA+	OAV	OOB	BH	AVG	PB	PR	/A	PD	TPI
1987	Oak-A	6	2	.750	29	0	0	0	0	39^2	37	6	24	30	14.1	4.54	91	.252	.360	0	—	0	-0	-2	1	0.4
1988	*Oak-A	5	2	.714	58	0	0	0	3	71^2	60	2	36	64	12.2	2.89	131	.226	.320	0	—	0	9	7	0	0.8
1989	Oak-A	0	0	—	26	0	0	0	0	27^2	21	0	19	14	13.0	2.28	162	.214	.342	0	—	0	5	4	1	0.5
	NY-A	5	5	.500	20	13	3	1	0	92^1	109	7	38	66	14.5	4.58	84	.298	.367	0	—	0	-7	-7	0	-0.7
	Yr	5	5	.500	46	13	3	1	0	120	130	7	57	80	14.2	4.05	94	.279	.360	0	—	0	-2	-3	1	-0.2
1990	NY-A	5	4	.556	54	6	0	0	3	121^1	120	8	64	80	13.7	4.15	96	.268	.361	0	—	0	-3	-2	2	0.0
1991	NY-A	8	6	.571	68	5	0	0	3	121^2	110	8	59	105	12.6	3.62	114	.246	.337	0	—	0	6	7	1	0.8
1992	NY-A	4	8	.333	46	11	1	1	1	103^2	104	12	74	73	15.6	4.25	95	.267	.387	0	—	0	-4	-2	1	-0.2
Total	6	33	27	.550	301	35	4	2	10	578	561	43	314	432	13.8	3.91	102	.260	.356	0	—	0	5	4	6	1.6

YEAR	TM/L	W	L	PCT	G	GS	CG	SH	SV	IP	H	HR	BB	SO	RAT	ERA	ERA+	OAV	OOB	BH	AVG	PB	PR	/A	PD	TPI
● **LEON CADORE**	Cadore, Leon Joseph "Caddy" b: 11/20/1890, Chicago, Ill. d: 3/16/58, Spokane, Wash. BR/TR, 6'1", 190 lbs. Deb: 4/28/15																									
1915	Bro-N	0	2	.000	7	2	1	0	0	21	28	0	8	12	16.3	5.57	50	.337	.409	0	.000	-1	-7	-7	0	-0.8
1916	Bro-N	0	0	—	1	0	0	0	0	6	10	0	0	2	15.0	4.50	60	.370	.370	0	.000	-0	-1	-1	0	-0.1
1917	Bro-N	13	13	.500	37	30	21	1	3	264	231	3	63	115	10.3	2.45	114	.241	.292	24	.261	5	8	10	-2	1.5
1918	Bro-N	1	0	1.000	2	2	1	1	0	17	6	0	2	5	4.8	0.53	526	.115	.164	0	.000	-0	4	4	0	0.5
1919	Bro-N	14	12	.538	35	27	16	3	0	250^2	228	5	39	94	9.8	2.37	125	.245	.280	14	.161	-3	15	17	-3	1.1
1920	*Bro-N	15	14	.517	35	30	16	4	0	254^1	256	4	56	79	11.1	2.62	122	.270	.313	20	.220	2	15	17	1	2.3
1921	Bro-N	13	14	.481	35	30	12	1	0	211^2	243	17	46	79	12.5	4.17	93	.292	.334	14	.187	-1	-9	-7	-1	-0.9
1922	Bro-N	8	15	.348	29	21	13	0	0	190^1	224	13	57	49	13.3	4.35	94	.299	.349	19	.268	4	-5	-6	-3	-0.4
1923	Bro-N	4	1	.800	8	4	3	0	0	36	39	2	13	5	13.0	3.25	119	.291	.354	1	.077	-1	3	3	-1	0.0
	Chi-A	0	1	.000	1	1	0	0	0	2^1	6	0	2	3	30.9	23.14	17	.500	.571	0	—	0	-5	-5	-0	-0.4
1924	NY-N	0	0	—	2	0	0	0	0	4	2	0	3	2	11.3	0.00	—	.154	.313	0	—	0	2	2	0	0.2
Total	10	68	72	.486	192	147	83	10	3	1257^1	1273	44	289	445	11.4	3.14	106	.269	.314	92	.208	5	19	27	-8	3.0
● **CHARLIE CADY**	Cady, Charles B. b: 12/1865, Chicago, Ill. d: 6/7/09, Kankakee, Ill. 5'11", 180 lbs. Deb: 9/05/1883 ♦																									
1883	Cle-N	0	1	.000	1	1	1	0	0	8	13	0	4	5	19.1	7.88	40	.361	.425	0	.000	-1	-4	-4	-0	-0.4
1884	CP-U	3	1	.750	4	4	4	0	0	35	37	0	13	15	12.9	2.83	107	.254	.315	2	.100	-1	1	1	-0	0.0
Total	2	3	2	.600	5	5	5	0	0	43	50	0	17	20	14.0	3.77	81	.275	.337	2	.059	-1	-3	-3	-0	-0.4
● **JOHN CAHILL**	Cahill, John Patrick Francis "Patsy" b: 4/30/1865, San Francisco, Cal d: 10/31/01, Pleasanton, Cal. BR/TR, 5'7.5", 168 lbs. Deb: 5/31/1884 ♦																									
1884	Col-a	1	0	1.000	2	1	1	0	0	16	15	0	4	1	12.4	5.06	60	.211	.282	46	.219	0	-3	-4	-0	-0.3
1886	StL-N	1	0	1.000	2	0	0	0	0	12	11	0	3	2	10.5	3.00	108	.268	.318	92	.199	-0	0	0	0	0.0
1887	Ind-N	0	2	.000	6	1	1	0	0	22	40	2	19	5	25.0	14.32	29	.430	.535	54	.205	-1	-25	-25	-1	-1.9
Total	3	2	2	.500	10	2	2	0	0	50	66	2	26	8	17.5	8.64	41	.322	.411	192	.205	-1	-28	-28	-1	-2.2
● **LES CAIN**	Cain, Leslie b: 1/13/48, San Luis Obispo, Cal. BL/TL, 6'1", 200 lbs. Deb: 4/28/68																									
1968	Det-A	1	0	1.000	8	4	0	0	0	24	25	1	20	13	16.9	3.00	100	.269	.398	1	.143	0	-0	0	0	0.1
1970	Det-A	12	7	.632	29	29	5	0	0	180^2	167	15	98	156	13.5	3.84	97	.247	.349	11	.162	0	-2	-2	-0	-0.3
1971	Det-A	10	9	.526	26	26	3	1	0	144^2	121	14	91	118	13.6	4.35	82	.228	.348	8	.145	-0	-14	-12	-1	-1.4
1972	Det-A	0	3	.000	5	5	0	0	0	23^2	18	2	16	16	12.9	3.80	83	.209	.333	1	.143	-0	-2	-2	-0	-0.3
Total	4	23	19	.548	68	64	8	1	0	373	331	32	225	303	13.7	3.98	90	.239	.351	21	.153	-0	-19	-16	-1	-1.9
● **SUGAR CAIN**	Cain, Merritt Patrick b: 4/5/07, Macon, Ga. d: 4/3/75, Atlanta, Ga. BL/TR, 5'11", 190 lbs. Deb: 4/15/32																									
1932	Phi-A	3	4	.429	10	6	3	0	0	45	42	1	28	24	14.0	5.00	90	.256	.365	3	.250	1	-3	-2	-0	-0.2
1933	Phi-A	13	12	.520	38	32	16	1	1	218	244	18	137	43	15.9	4.25	101	.280	.379	16	.200	-1	1	1	-1	-0.1
1934	Phi-A	9	17	.346	36	32	15	0	0	230^2	235	15	128	66	14.3	4.41	99	.266	.360	13	.159	-3	2	-1	-1	-0.4
1935	Phi-A	0	5	.000	6	5	0	0	0	26	39	1	19	5	20.1	6.58	69	.382	.479	0	.000	-1	-6	-6	0	-0.6
	StL-A	9	8	.529	31	24	8	0	0	167^2	197	7	104	68	16.4	5.26	91	.290	.388	11	.193	-3	-15	-9	-3	-1.3
	Yr	9	13	.409	37	29	8	0	0	193^2	236	8	123	73	16.9	5.44	88	.302	.400	11	.169	-4	-21	-15	-3	-1.9
1936	StL-A	1	1	.500	4	3	1	0	0	16^1	20	0	9	8	16.0	6.61	81	.286	.367	2	.286	0	-3	-2	-0	-0.2
	Chi-A	14	10	.583	30	26	14	1	0	195^1	228	18	75	42	14.2	4.75	110	.293	.359	7	.103	-4	6	10	-3	0.2
	Yr	15	11	.577	34	29	15	1	0	211^2	248	18	84	50	14.3	4.89	107	.292	.360	9	.120	-4	3	8	-3	0.0
1937	Chi-A	4	2	.667	18	6	1	0	0	68^2	88	7	51	17	18.2	6.16	75	.325	.432	4	.182	-1	-12	-12	-0	-1.1
1938	Chi-A	0	1	.000	5	3	0	0	0	19^2	26	0	18	6	20.1	4.58	107	.321	.444	0	.000	-1	0	1	-1	-0.1
Total	7	53	60	.469	178	137	58	2	1	987^1	1119	67	569	279	15.5	4.83	96	.287	.380	56	.163	-13	-29	-21	-9	-3.8
● **BOB CAIN**	Cain, Robert Max "Sugar" b: 10/16/24, Longford, Kan. BL/TL, 6', 165 lbs. Deb: 9/18/49 ♦																									
1949	Chi-A	0	0	—	6	0	0	0	1	11	7	0	5	5	9.8	2.45	170	.179	.273	0	.000	-0	2	2	-0	0.1
1950	Chi-A	9	12	.429	34	23	11	1	2	171^2	153	12	109	77	14.0	3.93	114	.244	.361	12	.197	-0	12	11	0	1.0
1951	Chi-A	1	2	.333	4	4	1	0	0	26^1	25	3	13	3	14.0	3.76	107	.248	.350	3	.333	1	1	1	-0	0.1
	Det-A	11	10	.524	35	22	6	1	2	149^1	135	12	82	58	13.7	4.70	89	.239	.347	13	.245	2	-10	-9	0	-0.7
	Yr	12	12	.500	39	26	7	1	2	175^2	160	15	95	61	13.6	4.56	91	.240	.344	16	.258	3	-9	-8	-0	-0.6
1952	StL-A	12	10	.545	29	27	8	1	2	170	169	15	62	70	12.3	4.13	95	.264	.331	8	.138	-1	-9	-4	-2	-0.8
1953	StL-A	4	10	.286	32	13	1	0	1	99^2	129	8	45	36	15.8	6.23	67	.310	.379	6	.200	0	-25	-22	-2	-2.3
Total	5	37	44	.457	140	89	27	3	8	628	618	50	316	249	13.7	4.50	93	.259	.351	42	.196	0	-27	-21	-4	-2.6
● **CHARLIE CALDWELL**	Caldwell, Charles William "Chuck" b: 8/2/01, Bristol, Va. d: 11/1/57, Princeton, N.J. BR/TR, 5'10", 180 lbs. Deb: 7/07/25																									
1925	NY-A	0	0	—	3	0	0	0	0	2^2	7	0	3	1	33.8	16.88	25	.467	.556	0	.000	-0	-4	-4	-0	-0.4
● **EARL CALDWELL**	Caldwell, Earl Welton "Teach" b: 4/9/05, Sparks, Tex. d: 9/15/81, Mission, Tex. BR/TR, 6'1", 178 lbs. Deb: 9/08/28																									
1928	Phi-N	1	4	.200	5	5	1	1	0	34^2	46	5	17	6	16.4	5.71	75	.348	.423	1	.111	-0	-7	-6	0	-0.5
1935	StL-A	3	2	.600	6	5	2	1	0	36^2	34	2	17	5	12.5	3.68	130	.245	.327	2	.182	-0	3	5	1	0.5
1936	StL-A	7	16	.304	41	25	10	2	2	189	252	15	83	59	16.7	6.00	90	.319	.394	11	.190	-1	-20	-13	-1	-1.3
1937	StL-A	0	0	—	9	2	0	0	0	29	39	3	13	8	16.8	6.83	71	.317	.391	2	.222	0	-7	-6	0	-0.6
1945	Chi-A	6	7	.462	27	11	5	1	4	105^1	108	8	37	45	12.6	3.59	92	.265	.331	8	.216	-0	-3	-3	3	0.0
1946	Chi-A	13	4	.765	39	0	0	0	8	90^2	60	2	29	42	8.9	2.08	164	.186	.255	3	.167	1	**14**	**13**	1	1.6
1947	Chi-A	1	4	.200	40	0	0	0	8	54^1	53	4	30	22	13.9	3.64	100	.261	.359	0	.000	-1	0	0	-1	-0.2
1948	Chi-A	1	5	.167	25	1	0	0	3	39	53	3	22	10	17.8	5.31	80	.335	.423	0	.000	-0	-4	-5	-0	-0.5
	Bos-A	1	1	.500	8	0	0	0	0	9	11	2	11	5	23.0	13.00	34	.333	.511	1	.333	0	-9	-9	-0	-0.8
	Yr	2	6	.250	33	1	0	0	3	48	64	5	33	15	18.4	6.75	63	.332	.432	1	.125	-0	-13	-13	-1	-1.3
Total	8	33	43	.434	200	49	18	5	25	587^2	656	44	259	202	14.4	4.69	92	.284	.363	28	.178	-2	-32	-25	3	-1.8
● **RALPH CALDWELL**	Caldwell, Ralph Grant "Lefty" b: 1/18/1884, Philadelphia, Pa. d: 8/5/69, W.Trenton, N.J. BL/TL, 5'9", 155 lbs. Deb: 9/10/04																									
1904	Phi-N	2	2	.500	6	5	5	0	0	41	40	1	15	30	12.5	4.17	64	.242	.313	8	.444	3	-7	-7	0	-0.4
1905	Phi-N	1	3	.250	7	2	1	0	1	34	44	1	7	29	14.3	4.24	69	.321	.367	0	.000	-2	-5	-5	-1	-0.8
Total	2	3	5	.375	13	7	6	0	1	75	84	2	22	59	13.3	4.20	66	.278	.337	8	.242	1	-11	-12	-1	-1.2
● **MIKE CALDWELL**	Caldwell, Ralph Michael b: 1/22/49, Tarboro, N.C. BR/TL, 6', 185 lbs. Deb: 9/04/71																									
1971	SD-N	1	0	1.000	6	0	0	0	0	6^2	4	0	3	5	9.5	0.00	—	.174	.269	1	1.000	1	3	2	0	0.4
1972	SD-N	7	11	.389	42	20	4	2	2	163^2	183	10	49	102	13.0	4.01	82	.282	.337	7	.140	-1	-10	-13	5	-1.0
1973	SD-N	5	14	.263	55	13	3	1	10	149	146	8	53	86	12.1	3.74	93	.260	.326	5	.143	-1	-1	-5	2	-0.4
1974	SF-N	14	5	.737	31	27	6	2	0	189^1	176	17	63	83	11.6	2.95	129	.249	.314	9	.143	-2	14	18	4	2.2
1975	SF-N	7	13	.350	38	21	4	0	1	163^1	194	16	48	57	13.6	4.79	79	.296	.348	7	.159	-0	-21	-18	2	-1.7
1976	SF-N	1	7	.125	50	9	0	0	2	107^1	145	5	20	55	14.0	4.86	75	.324	.356	3	.158	-0	-16	-15	1	-1.4
1977	Cin-N	0	0	—	14	0	0	0	1	24^2	25	1	8	11	12.0	4.01	98	.260	.317	2	.500	2	-0	-0	-0	0.1
	Mil-A	5	8	.385	21	12	2	0	0	94^1	101	6	36	38	13.3	4.58	89	.271	.338	0	—	0	-5	-5	3	-0.2
1978	Mil-A	22	9	.710	37	34	**23**	6	1	293^1	258	14	54	131	9.8	2.36	159	.234	.274	0	—	0	46	45	1	5.2
1979	Mil-A	16	6	**.727**	30	30	16	4	0	235	252	18	39	89	11.3	3.29	126	.278	.311	0	—	0	24	23	5	2.8
1980	Mil-A	13	11	.542	34	33	11	2	1	225^1	248	29	56	74	12.2	4.03	96	.285	.330	0	—	0	0	-4	0	-0.4
1981	*Mil-A	11	9	.550	24	23	3	0	0	144^1	151	18	38	41	11.8	3.93	87	.272	.319	0	—	0	-4	-8	-0	-0.8
1982	*Mil-A	17	13	.567	35	34	12	3	0	258	269	30	58	75	11.4	3.91	97	.271	.311	0	—	0	5	-4	2	0.2
1983	Mil-A	12	11	.522	32	32	10	2	0	228^1	269	35	51	58	12.7	4.53	82	.296	.334	0	—	0	-12	-20	-0	-1.6
1984	Mil-A	6	13	.316	26	19	4	1	0	126	160	11	21	34	13.0	4.64	83	.314	.343	0	—	0	-9	-11	1	-1.0
Total	14	137	130	.513	475	307	98	23	18	2408^2	2581	218	597	939	12.0	3.81	99	.276	.322	34	.157	-2	11	-14	24	2.4

YEAR	TM/L	W	L	PCT	G	GS	CG	SH	SV	IP	H	HR	BB	SO	RAT	ERA	ERA+	OAV	OOB	BH	AVG	PB	PR	/A	PD	TPI
● RAY CALDWELL	Caldwell, Raymond Benjamin "Rube" or "Sum" b: 4/26/1888, Corydon, Pa. d: 8/17/67, Salamanca, N.Y. BL/TR, 6'2", 190 lbs. Deb: 9/09/10 ♦																									
1910	NY-A	1	0	1.000	6	2	1	0	1	19^1	19	1	9	17	13.0	3.72	71	.260	.341	0	.000	-1	-3	-2	-0	-0.4
1911	NY-A	14	14	.500	41	27	19	1	1	255	240	7	79	145	11.7	3.35	107	.260	.327	40	.272	4	-0	7	-3	0.8
1912	NY-A	8	16	.333	30	26	13	3	0	183^1	196	1	67	95	13.2	4.47	80	.277	.344	18	.237	1	-23	-18	1	-1.4
1913	NY-A	9	8	.529	27	16	15	2	1	164^1	131	5	60	87	11.0	2.41	124	.219	.299	28	.289	3	10	11	-1	1.8
1914	NY-A	17	9	.654	31	23	22	5	1	213	153	5	51	92	8.8	1.94	142	.205	.260	22	.195	1	19	19	-2	2.2
1915	NY-A	19	16	.543	36	35	31	3	0	305	266	6	107	130	11.2	2.89	101	.244	.315	35	.243	8	2	1	-3	0.6
1916	NY-A	5	12	.294	21	18	14	1	0	165^2	142	6	65	76	11.7	2.99	97	.243	.327	19	.204	-0	-3	-2	-1	-0.3
1917	NY-A	13	16	.448	32	29	21	1	0	236	199	8	76	102	10.7	2.86	94	.234	.302	32	.258	6	-5	-5	-1	0.3
1918	NY-A	9	8	.529	24	21	14	1	1	176^2	173	2	62	59	12.0	3.06	93	.261	.325	44	.291	5	-5	-4	-3	-0.1
1919	Bos-A	7	4	.636	18	12	6	1	0	86^1	92	1	31	23	13.1	3.96	76	.279	.346	13	.271	1	-7	-9	-2	-0.9
	Cle-A	5	1	.833	6	6	4	1	0	52^2	33	1	19	24	9.2	1.71	196	.181	.266	8	.348	3	9	10	-1	1.3
	Yr	12	5	.706	24	18	10	2	0	139	125	2	50	47	11.5	3.11	101	.243	.312	21	.296	4	2	1	-3	0.4
1920	*Cle-A	20	10	.667	34	33	20	1	0	237^2	286	9	63	80	13.4	3.86	98	.303	.350	19	.213	1	-2	-2	-3	-0.5
1921	Cle-A	6	6	.500	37	12	4	1	4	147	159	7	49	76	12.9	4.90	87	.275	.333	11	.208	0	-10	-10	-0	-1.0
Total	12	133	120	.526	343	260	184	21	9	2242	2089	59	738	1006	11.6	3.22	99	.253	.319	289	.248	32	-20	-4	-19	2.4
● JEFF CALHOUN	Calhoun, Jeffrey Wilton b: 4/11/58, LaGrange, Ga. BL/TL, 6'2", 190 lbs. Deb: 9/02/84																									
1984	Hou-N	0	1	.000	9	0	0	0	0	15^1	5	0	2	11	4.1	1.17	283	.100	.135	0	—	0	4	4	-0	0.4
1985	Hou-N	2	5	.286	44	0	0	0	4	63^2	56	2	24	47	11.3	2.54	136	.243	.315	0	.000	-0	7	6	0	0.7
1986	*Hou-N	1	0	1.000	20	0	0	0	0	26^2	28	3	12	14	13.5	3.71	97	.264	.339	0	—	0	0	-0	-1	-0.1
1987	Phi-N	3	1	.750	42	0	0	0	1	42^2	25	1	26	31	11.0	1.48	287	.168	.295	0	.000	-0	12	13	1	1.4
1988	Phi-N	0	0	—	3	0	0	0	0	2^1	6	2	1	1	27.0	15.43	23	.462	.500	0	—	0	-3	-3	-0	-0.3
Total	5	6	7	.462	118	0	0	0	5	150^2	120	8	65	104	11.1	2.51	147	.219	.303	0	.000	-0	21	20	-0	2.1
● FRED CALIGIURI	Caligiuri, Frederick John b: 10/22/18, W.Hickory, Pa. BR/TR, 6', 190 lbs. Deb: 9/03/41																									
1941	Phi-A	2	2	.500	5	5	4	0	0	43	45	2	14	7	12.3	2.93	143	.257	.312	4	.200	1	6	6	-1	0.6
1942	Phi-A	0	3	.000	13	2	0	0	1	36^2	45	2	18	20	16.0	6.38	59	.300	.382	1	.083	-0	-11	-11	-0	-1.1
Total	2	2	5	.286	18	7	4	0	1	79^2	90	4	32	27	14.0	4.52	89	.277	.345	5	.156	1	-5	-5	-1	-0.5
● WILL CALIHAN	Calihan, William T. b: 1867, Oswego, N.Y. d: 12/20/17, Rochester, N.Y. 5'8", 150 lbs. Deb: 4/17/1890																									
1890	Roc-a	18	15	.545	37	36	31	0	0	296^1	276	4	125	127	12.7	3.28	109	.239	.322	23	.145	-3	19	9	3	0.8
1891	Phi-a	6	6	.500	13	11	11	0	0	112	151	7	47	28	16.9	6.43	59	.312	.387	11	.196	-1	-34	-32	2	-2.5
Total	2	24	21	.533	50	47	42	0	0	408^1	427	11	172	155	13.8	4.14	88	.261	.341	34	.158	-4	-14	-23	4	-1.7
● BEN CALLAHAN	Callahan, Benjamin Franklin b: 5/19/57, Mt.Airy, N.C. BR/TR, 6'7", 230 lbs. Deb: 6/22/83																									
1983	Oak-A	1	2	.333	4	2	0	0	0	9^1	18	0	5	2	22.2	12.54	31	.400	.460	0	—	0	-9	-9	0	-0.5
● NIXEY CALLAHAN	Callahan, James Joseph b: 3/18/1874, Fitchburg, Mass. d: 10/4/34, Boston, Mass. BR/TR, 5'10.5", 180 lbs. Deb: 5/12/1894 M♦																									
1894	Phi-N	1	2	.333	9	2	1	0	2	33^2	64	3	17	9	23.0	9.89	52	.398	.470	5	.238	-1	-17	-18	1	-1.3
1897	Chi-N	12	9	.571	23	22	21	1	0	189^2	221	6	55	52	13.5	4.03	111	.289	.343	105	.292	3	6	9	1	1.2
1898	Chi-N	20	10	.667	31	31	30	2	0	274^1	267	2	71	73	11.4	2.46	146	.253	.307	43	.262	4	35	34	1	4.0
1899	Chi-N	21	12	.636	35	34	33	3	0	294^1	327	5	76	77	13.1	3.06	123	.281	.338	39	.260	4	26	23	5	3.0
1900	Chi-N	13	16	.448	32	32	32	2	0	285^1	347	5	74	77	13.9	3.82	94	.299	.352	27	.235	2	-4	-7	6	0.2
1901	Chi-A	15	8	.652	27	22	20	1	0	215^1	195	4	50	70	10.6	2.42	144	.239	.289	39	.331	8	30	25	6	4.0
1902	Chi-A	16	14	.533	35	31	29	2	0	282^1	287	8	89	75	12.3	3.60	94	.264	.326	51	.234	2	-1	-7	6	0.2
1903	Chi-A	1	2	.333	3	3	3	0	0	28	40	0	5	12	14.8	4.50	62	.334	.366	128	.292	1	-5	-5	1	-0.3
Total	8	99	73	.576	195	177	169	11	2	1603	1748	33	437	445	12.8	3.39	109	.276	.332	901	.273	23	70	54	26	11.0
● JIM CALLAHAN	Callahan, James W. b: Moberly, Mo. Deb: 9/03/1898																									
1898	StL-N	0	2	.000	2	2	1	0	0	8^1	18	2	7	2	29.2	16.20	23	.430	.530	0	.000	-1	-12	-11	0	-0.9
● JOE CALLAHAN	Callahan, Joseph Thomas b: 10/8/16, E.Boston, Mass. d: 5/24/49, S.Boston, Mass. BR/TR, 6'2", 170 lbs. Deb: 9/13/39																									
1939	Bos-N	1	0	1.000	4	1	1	0	0	17^1	17	0	3	8	10.9	3.12	119	.250	.292	0	.000	-0	2	1	0	0.1
1940	Bos-N	0	2	.000	6	2	0	0	0	15	20	1	13	3	19.8	10.20	36	.351	.471	0	.000	-1	-11	-11	1	-1.0
Total	2	1	2	.333	10	3	1	0	0	32^1	37	1	16	11	15.0	6.40	58	.296	.380	0	.000	-1	-9	-10	1	-0.9
● RAY CALLAHAN	Callahan, Raymond James "Pat" b: 8/29/1891, Ashland, Wis. d: 1/23/73, Olympia, Wash. BL/TL, 5'10.5", 170 lbs. Deb: 9/12/15																									
1915	Cin-N	0	0	—	3	0	0	0	0	6^1	12	1	1	4	18.5	8.53	34	.364	.382	1	.333	0	-4	-4	-0	-0.4
● DICK CALMUS	Calmus, Richard Lee b: 1/7/44, Los Angeles, Cal. BR/TR, 6'4", 187 lbs. Deb: 4/22/63																									
1963	LA-N	3	1	.750	21	1	0	0	0	44	32	3	16	25	9.8	2.66	114	.204	.277	0	.000	-1	3	2	-1	0.1
1967	Chi-N	0	0	—	1	1	0	0	0	4^1	5	2	0	1	10.4	8.31	43	.278	.278	1	.500	0	-2	-2	0	-0.2
Total	2	3	1	.750	22	2	0	0	0	48^1	37	5	16	26	9.9	3.17	97	.211	.277	1	.125	-0	1	-1	-1	-0.1
● MARK CALVERT	Calvert, Mark b: 9/29/56, Tulsa, Okla. BR/TR, 6'1", 195 lbs. Deb: 4/17/83																									
1983	SF-N	1	4	.200	18	4	0	0	0	37^1	46	2	34	14	20.0	6.27	56	.307	.444	0	.000	-1	-11	-11	1	-1.1
1984	SF-N	2	4	.333	10	5	1	0	0	32	40	4	9	5	14.1	5.06	69	.303	.352	0	.000	-1	-5	-6	0	-0.6
Total	2	3	8	.273	28	9	1	0	0	69^1	86	6	43	19	17.3	5.71	62	.305	.404	0	.000	-1	-16	-17	1	-1.7
● PAUL CALVERT	Calvert, Paul Leo Emile b: 10/6/17, Montreal, Que., Can. BR/TR, 6', 185 lbs. Deb: 9/24/42																									
1942	Cle-A	0	0	—	1	0	0	0	0	2	0	0	2	2	9.0	0.00	—	.000	.286	0	—	0	1	1	-0	0.1
1943	Cle-A	0	0	—	5	0	0	0	0	8^1	6	0	6	2	14.0	4.32	72	.200	.351	0	.000	-0	-1	-1	0	-0.1
1944	Cle-A	1	3	.250	35	4	0	0	0	77	89	4	38	31	14.8	4.56	72	.289	.367	4	.267	1	-10	-11	2	-0.8
1945	Cle-A	0	0	—	1	0	0	0	0	1^1	3	0	1	1	27.0	13.50	24	.429	.500	0	—	0	-2	-2	0	-0.2
1949	Was-A	6	17	.261	34	23	5	0	1	160^2	175	11	86	52	14.7	5.43	78	.279	.368	7	.137	-2	-22	-21	3	-1.9
1950	Det-A	2	2	.500	32	0	0	0	4	51^1	71	7	25	14	17.2	6.31	74	.324	.398	0	.000	-1	-10	-9	1	-0.8
1951	Det-A	0	0	—	1	0	0	0	0	1	1	0	0	0	9.0	0.00	—	.250	.250	0	—	0	0	0	0	0.1
Total	7	9	22	.290	109	27	5	0	5	301^2	345	22	158	102	15.2	5.31	76	.287	.373	11	.149	-2	-43	-43	5	-3.6
● ERNIE CAMACHO	Camacho, Ernest Carlos b: 2/1/55, Salinas, Cal. BR/TR, 6'1", 180 lbs. Deb: 5/22/80																									
1980	Oak-A	0	0	—	5	0	0	0	0	11^2	20	2	5	9	20.1	6.94	54	.364	.426	0	—	0	-4	-4	-0	-0.4
1981	Pit-N	0	1	.000	7	3	0	0	0	21^2	23	0	15	11	15.8	4.98	72	.295	.409	0	.000	-0	-4	-3	-0	-0.4
1983	Cle-A	0	1	.000	4	0	0	0	0	5^1	5	1	2	2	13.5	5.06	84	.250	.348	0	—	0	-1	-0	-0	-0.2
1984	Cle-A	5	9	.357	69	0	0	0	23	100	83	6	37	48	10.9	2.43	168	.229	.303	0	—	0	17	18	-0	1.8
1985	Cle-A	0	1	.000	2	0	0	0	0	3^1	4	0	1	2	13.5	8.10	51	.333	.385	0	—	0	-1	-1	0	-0.1
1986	Cle-A	2	4	.333	51	0	0	0	20	57^1	60	1	31	36	14.6	4.08	101	.269	.363	0	—	0	1	0	1	0.1
1987	Cle-A	0	1	.000	15	0	0	0	1	13^2	21	1	5	9	19.1	9.22	49	.350	.426	0	—	0	-7	-7	1	-0.6
1988	Hou-N	0	3	.000	13	0	0	0	1	17^2	25	1	12	13	18.8	7.64	43	.352	.446	0	.000	-0	-8	-8	0	-0.9
1989	SF-N	3	0	1.000	13	0	0	0	0	16^1	10	1	11	14	11.6	2.76	122	.175	.309	0	.000	-0	1	1	1	0.2
1990	SF-N	0	0	—	8	0	0	0	0	10	10	1	3	8	11.7	3.60	101	.256	.310	0	—	0	0	0	-0	0.0
	StL-N	0	0	—	6	0	0	0	0	5^2	7	2	6	7	20.6	7.94	48	.318	.464	0	—	0	-3	-3	0	-0.3
	Yr	0	0	—	14	0	0	0	0	15^2	17	3	9	15	14.9	5.17	72	.279	.371	0	—	0	-2	-3	-0	-0.3
Total	10	10	20	.333	193	3	0	0	45	262^2	268	16	128	159	13.8	4.21	94	.268	.356	0	.000	-1	-8	-8	1	-0.8

YEAR	TM/L	W	L	PCT	G	GS	CG	SH	SV	IP	H	HR	BB	SO	RAT	ERA	ERA+	OAV	OOB	BH	AVG	PB	PR	/A	PD	TPI
● FRED CAMBRIA	Cambria, Frederick Dennis b: 1/22/48, Cambria Heights, N.Y. BR/TR, 6'2", 195 lbs. Deb: 8/26/70																									
1970	Pit-N	1	2	.333	6	5	0	0	0	33^1	37	2	12	14	13.5	3.51	111	.272	.336	2	.200	1	2	1	0	0.2
● JACK CAMERON	Cameron, John William "Happy Jack" b: 9/1884, Nova Scotia, Can. d: 8/17/51, Boston, Mass. Deb: 9/13/06 ♦																									
1906	Bos-N	0	0	—	2	1	0	0	0	6	4	0	6	2	15.0	0.00	—	.211	.400	11	.180	-0	2	2	0	0.2
● HARRY CAMNITZ	Camnitz, Henry Richardson b: 10/26/1884, McKinney, Ky. d: 1/6/51, Louisville, Ky. BR/TR, 6'1", 168 lbs. Deb: 4/14/09 F																									
1909	Pit-N	0	0	—	1	0	0	0	0	4	6	0	1	1	15.8	4.50	61	.353	.389	0	.000	-0	-1	-1	0	-0.1
1911	StL-N	1	0	1.000	2	0	0	0	0	2	0	0	1	2	4.5	0.00	—	.000	.143	0	—	0	1	1	-0	0.1
Total	2	1	0	1.000	3	0	0	0	0	6	6	0	2	3	12.0	3.00	98	.261	.320	0	.000	-0	-0	-0	0	0.0
● HOWIE CAMNITZ	Camnitz, Samuel Howard "Red" b: 8/22/1881, Covington, Ky. d: 3/2/60, Louisville, Ky. BR/TR, 5'9", 169 lbs. Deb: 4/22/04 F																									
1904	Pit-N	1	4	.200	10	2	2	0	0	49	48	0	20	21	13.0	4.22	65	.259	.341	1	.063	-1	-8	-8	-1	-1.0
1906	Pit-N	1	0	1.000	2	1	1	1	0	9	6	0	5	5	11.0	2.00	134	.188	.297	0	.000	-0	1	1	-0	0.0
1907	Pit-N	13	8	.619	31	19	15	4	1	180	135	0	59	85	9.9	2.15	113	.211	.281	3	.050	-5	6	6	-0	0.0
1908	Pit-N	16	9	.640	38	26	17	3	2	236^2	182	6	69	118	9.7	1.56	148	.210	.272	6	.083	-3	21	20	-1	1.8
1909	*Pit-N	25	6	**.806**	41	30	20	6	3	283	207	1	68	133	9.0	1.62	168	.211	.267	12	.138	-0	31	35	-3	3.6
1910	Pit-N	12	13	.480	38	31	16	1	2	260	246	1	61	120	11.0	3.22	96	.256	.308	11	.125	-3	-5	-3	-2	-1.0
1911	Pit-N	20	15	.571	40	33	18	1	1	267^2	245	8	84	139	11.2	3.13	110	.248	.309	12	.143	-3	8	9	-3	0.2
1912	Pit-N	22	12	.647	41	32	22	2	2	276^2	256	8	82	121	11.4	2.83	115	.251	.315	23	.235	1	18	13	-3	1.1
1913	Pit-N	6	17	.261	36	21	5	1	2	192^1	203	7	84	64	13.8	3.74	81	.282	.363	9	.153	-1	-12	-16	1	-1.7
	Phi-N	3	3	.500	9	5	1	0	1	49	49	1	23	21	13.6	3.67	91	.268	.356	1	.063	-1	-3	-2	-1	-0.4
	Yr	9	20	.310	45	26	6	1	3	241^1	252	8	107	85	13.5	3.73	83	.277	.354	10	.133	-3	-14	-17	-0	-2.1
1914	Pit-F	14	19	.424	36	34	20	1	1	262	256	8	90	82	12.2	3.23	99	.258	.324	14	.161	-3	-1	-1	-5	-0.9
1915	Pit-F	0	0	—	4	2	0	0	0	20	19	1	11	6	13.5	4.50	67	.257	.353	0	.000	-1	-3	-3	-1	-0.5
Total	11	133	106	.556	326	236	137	20	15	2085^1	1852	41	656	915	11.1	2.75	108	.242	.307	92	.136	-23	54	50	-18	1.2
● RICK CAMP	Camp, Rick Lamar b: 6/10/53, Trion, Ga. BR/TR, 6', 198 lbs. Deb: 9/15/76																									
1976	Atl-N	0	1	.000	5	1	0	0	0	11^1	13	0	2	6	11.9	6.35	60	.302	.333	0	.000	-0	-4	-3	1	-0.3
1977	Atl-N	6	3	.667	54	0	0	0	10	78^2	89	6	47	51	15.7	4.00	111	.283	.377	0	.000	-1	-1	4	-0	0.3
1978	Atl-N	2	4	.333	42	4	0	0	0	74^1	99	5	32	23	16.2	3.75	108	.329	.399	0	.000	-1	-1	2	-0	0.2
1980	Atl-N	6	4	.600	77	0	0	0	22	108^1	92	3	29	33	10.4	1.91	196	.235	.294	1	.111	-0	20	22	4	2.7
1981	Atl-N	9	3	.750	48	0	0	0	17	76	68	5	12	47	9.6	1.78	202	.239	.272	0	.000	-1	14	**15**	0	1.5
1982	*Atl-N	11	13	.458	51	21	3	0	5	177^1	199	18	52	68	12.8	3.65	102	.291	.342	1	.024	-3	-1	1	1	-0.1
1983	Atl-N	10	9	.526	40	16	1	0	0	140	146	16	38	61	12.1	3.79	102	.270	.323	3	.077	-2	-3	1	0	0.0
1984	Atl-N	8	6	.571	31	21	1	0	0	148^2	134	11	63	69	12.0	3.27	118	.245	.325	5	.111	-2	5	10	0	0.9
1985	Atl-N	4	6	.400	66	2	0	0	3	127^2	130	8	61	49	13.8	3.95	97	.263	.349	3	.231	1	-5	-1	-2	-0.2
Total	9	56	49	.533	414	65	5	0	57	942^1	970	72	336	407	12.7	3.37	114	.269	.335	13	.074	-9	25	51	3	5.0
● KID CAMP	Camp, Winfield Scott b: 1870, Columbus, Ohio d: 3/2/1895, Omaha, Neb. 6', 160 lbs. Deb: 5/03/1892 F																									
1892	Pit-N	0	1	.000	4	1	1	0	0	23	31	4	9	6	16.0	6.26	53	.310	.373	1	.091	-1	-8	-8	-1	-0.8
1894	Chi-N	0	1	.000	3	2	2	0	0	22	34	0	12	6	19.2	6.55	86	.349	.426	0	.000	-3	-3	-2	0	-0.3
Total	2	0	2	.000	7	3	3	0	0	45	65	4	21	12	17.6	6.40	69	.329	.399	1	.045	-4	-11	-10	-1	-1.1
● BERT CAMPANERIS	Campaneris, Dagoberto (Blanco) "Campy" (b: Dagoberto Campaneria (Blanco)) b: 3/9/42, Pueblo Nuevo, Cuba BR/TR, 5'10", 160 lbs. Deb: 7/23/64 ♦																									
1965	KC-A	0	0	—	1	0	0	0	0	1	1	0	2	1	27.0	9.00	39	.333	.600	156	.270	0	-1	-1	0	-0.1
● ARCHIE CAMPBELL	Campbell, Archibald Stewart "Iron Man" b: 10/20/03, Maplewood, N.J. d: 12/22/89, Sparks, Nevada BR/TR, 6', 180 lbs. Deb: 4/21/28																									
1928	NY-A	0	1	.000	13	1	0	0	2	24	30	0	11	9	15.4	5.25	72	.288	.357	1	.250	0	-3	-4	-1	-0.4
1929	Was-A	0	1	.000	4	0	0	0	0	4	10	1	5	1	33.8	15.75	27	.500	.600	0	—	0	-5	-5	0	-0.4
1930	Cin-N	2	4	.333	23	3	1	0	4	58	71	2	31	19	16.0	5.43	89	.311	.396	4	.267	0	-3	-4	2	-0.1
Total	3	2	6	.250	40	4	1	0	6	86	111	3	47	29	16.6	5.86	77	.315	.398	5	.263	0	-11	-13	2	-0.9
● DAVE CAMPBELL	Campbell, David Alan b: 9/3/51, Princeton, Ind. BR/TR, 6'3", 210 lbs. Deb: 5/06/77																									
1977	Atl-N	0	6	.000	65	0	0	0	13	88^2	78	7	33	42	11.6	3.05	146	.239	.315	1	.083	-1	9	14	-2	1.1
1978	Atl-N	4	4	.500	53	0	0	0	1	69^1	67	10	49	45	15.7	4.80	84	.258	.385	0	—	0	-9	-6	0	-0.6
Total	2	4	10	.286	118	0	0	0	14	158	145	17	82	87	13.4	3.82	112	.247	.348	1	.083	-1	-1	8	-2	0.5
● HUGH CAMPBELL	Campbell, Hugh F. b: 1846, Scotland d: 3/1/1881, Elizabeth, N.J. Deb: 4/28/1873 F																									
1873	Res-n	2	16	.111	19	18	18	0	0	165	250	7	7	5	14.0	2.84	118	.296	.302	13	.151	-5	8	9		0.5
● JIM CAMPBELL	Campbell, James Marcus b: 5/19/66, Santa Maria, Cal. BL/TL, 5'11", 175 lbs. Deb: 8/21/90																									
1990	KC-A	1	0	1.000	2	2	0	0	0	9^2	15	1	1	2	14.9	8.38	46	.349	.364	0	—	0	-5	-5	-0	-0.4
● JOHN CAMPBELL	Campbell, John Millard b: 9/13/07, Washington, D.C. BR/TR, 6'1.5", 184 lbs. Deb: 7/23/33																									
1933	Was-A	0	0	—	1	0	0	0	0	1	1	0	1	0	18.0	0.00	—	.200	.333	0	—	0	0	0	-0	0.0
● KEVIN CAMPBELL	Campbell, Kevin Wade b: 12/12/64, Marianna, Ark. BR/TR, 6'2", 255 lbs. Deb: 7/19/91																									
1991	Oak-A	1	0	1.000	14	0	0	0	0	23	13	4	14	16	11.0	2.74	140	.167	.301	0	—	0	3	3	0	0.4
1992	Oak-A	2	3	.400	32	5	0	0	1	65	66	4	45	38	15.4	5.12	74	.267	.380	0	—	0	-9	-10	-1	-1.0
Total	2	3	3	.500	46	5	0	0	1	88	79	8	59	54	14.2	4.50	84	.243	.361	0	—	0	-5	-7	-1	-0.6
● MIKE CAMPBELL	Campbell, Michael Thomas b: 2/17/64, Seattle, Wash. BR/TR, 6'3", 210 lbs. Deb: 7/04/87																									
1987	Sea-A	1	4	.200	9	9	1	0	0	49^1	41	9	25	35	12.4	4.74	99	.224	.324	0	—	0	-2	-0	0	-0.4
1988	Sea-A	6	10	.375	20	20	2	0	0	114^2	128	18	43	63	13.4	5.89	71	.280	.342	0	—	0	-24	-22	-1	-2.3
1989	Sea-A	1	2	.333	5	5	0	0	0	21	28	4	10	6	16.3	7.29	55	.301	.369	0	—	0	-8	-8	-0	-1.0
1992	Tex-A	0	1	.000	1	0	0	0	0	3^2	3	1	2	2	12.3	9.82	39	.231	.333	0	—	0	-2	-2	-0	-0.2
Total	4	8	17	.320	35	34	3	0	0	188^2	200	32	80	106	13.5	5.82	74	.268	.341	0	—	0	-36	-32	-1	-3.9
● BILLY CAMPBELL	Campbell, William James b: 11/5/1873, Pittsburgh, Pa. d: 10/6/57, Cincinnati, Ohio BL/TL, 5'10", 165 lbs. Deb: 4/17/05																									
1905	StL-N	1	1	.500	2	2	2	0	0	17	27	0	7	2	18.0	7.41	40	.365	.420	1	.143	-0	-8	-8	1	-0.7
1907	Cin-N	3	0	1.000	3	3	3	0	0	21	19	0	3	4	9.4	2.14	121	.244	.272	2	.250	0	1	1	1	0.2
1908	Cin-N	12	13	.480	35	24	19	2	2	221^1	203	3	44	73	10.5	2.60	89	.252	.299	6	.083	-3	-6	-7	4	-0.7
1909	Cin-N	7	11	.389	30	15	7	0	2	148^1	162	0	39	37	12.7	2.67	97	.288	.344	6	.140	-1	-1	-1	2	0.1
Total	4	23	25	.479	70	44	31	2	4	407^2	411	3	93	116	11.5	2.80	88	.270	.320	15	.115	-4	-15	-16	8	-1.1
● BILL CAMPBELL	Campbell, William Richard b: 8/9/48, Highland Park, Mich. BL/TR, 6'3", 190 lbs. Deb: 7/14/73																									
1973	Min-A	3	3	.500	28	2	0	0	7	51^2	44	5	20	42	11.3	3.14	126	.226	.301	0	—	0	4	5	0	0.2
1974	Min-A	8	7	.533	63	0	0	0	19	120^1	109	4	55	89	12.4	2.62	143	.242	.327	0	—	0	13	15	1	1.4
1975	Min-A	4	6	.400	47	7	2	1	5	121	119	13	46	76	12.4	3.79	102	.262	.333	0	.000	0	-0	1	1	0.1
1976	Min-A	17	5	**.773**	**78**	0	0	0	20	167^2	145	9	62	115	11.4	3.01	120	.234	.309	0	—	0	10	11	-0	0.9
1977	Bos-A★	13	9	.591	69	0	0	0	**31**	140	112	13	60	114	11.4	2.96	152	.224	.313	0	—	0	17	24	2	1.6
1978	Bos-A	7	5	.583	29	0	0	0	4	50^2	62	3	17	47	14.0	3.91	105	.308	.362	0	—	0	-1	1	1	-0.2
1979	Bos-A	3	4	.429	41	0	0	0	9	54^2	55	5	23	25	13.0	4.28	103	.262	.338	0	—	0	-0	1	1	0.0
1980	Bos-A	4	0	1.000	23	0	0	0	0	41^1	44	1	22	17	14.4	4.79	88	.284	.373	0	—	0	-3	-3	-1	-0.5

YEAR	TM/L	W	L	PCT	G	GS	CG	SH	SV	IP	H	HR	BB	SO	RAT	ERA	ERA+	OAV	OOB	BH	AVG	PB	PR	/A	PD	TPI
1981	Bos-A	1	1	.500	30	0	0	0	7	48^1	45	5	20	37	12.1	3.17	122	.245	.319	0	—	0	3	4	0	0.3
1982	Chi-N	3	6	.333	62	0	0	0	8	100	89	6	40	71	11.6	3.69	101	.245	.319	1	.143	-0	-1	0	2	0.3
1983	Chi-N	6	8	.429	**82**	0	0	0	8	122^1	128	4	49	97	13.1	4.49	84	.275	.346	1	.100	-1	-12	-9	2	-0.8
1984	Phi-N	6	5	.545	57	0	0	0	1	81^1	68	2	35	52	11.4	3.43	106	.222	.302	0	.000	-0	1	2	-1	0.0
1985	*StL-N	5	3	.625	50	0	0	0	4	64^1	55	5	21	41	10.9	3.50	101	.230	.298	2	.333	1	1	0	-1	0.0
1986	Det-A	3	6	.333	34	0	0	0	3	55^2	46	5	21	37	11.0	3.88	106	.230	.306	0	—	0	2	1	-1	0.1
1987	Mon-N	0	0	—	7	0	0	0	0	10	18	2	4	4	19.8	8.10	52	.360	.407	0	.000	0	-4	-4	0	-0.4
Total	15	83	68	.550	700	9	2	1	126	1229^1	1139	82	495	864	12.1	3.54	110	.248	.324	4	.154	1	28	49	5	3.0

● CARDELL CAMPER Camper, Cardell b: 7/6/52, Boley, Okla. BR/TR, 6'3", 208 lbs. Deb: 9/11/77

YEAR	TM/L	W	L	PCT	G	GS	CG	SH	SV	IP	H	HR	BB	SO	RAT	ERA	ERA+	OAV	OOB	BH	AVG	PB	PR	/A	PD	TPI
1977	Cle-A	1	0	1.000	3	1	0	0	0	9^1	7	0	4	9	10.6	3.86	102	.200	.282	0	—	0	0	0	-0	0.2

● SAL CAMPFIELD Campfield, William Holton b: 2/19/1868, Meadville, Pa. d: 5/16/52, Meadville, Pa. BR/TR, 6'0.5", Deb: 5/15/1896

YEAR	TM/L	W	L	PCT	G	GS	CG	SH	SV	IP	H	HR	BB	SO	RAT	ERA	ERA+	OAV	OOB	BH	AVG	PB	PR	/A	PD	TPI
1896	NY-N	1	1	.500	6	2	2	0	0	27	31	1	6	6	13.0	4.00	105	.286	.335	2	.167	-0	1	1	-1	0.0

● SAL CAMPISI Campisi, Salvatore John b: 8/11/42, Brooklyn, N.Y. BR/TR, 6'2", 210 lbs. Deb: 8/15/69

YEAR	TM/L	W	L	PCT	G	GS	CG	SH	SV	IP	H	HR	BB	SO	RAT	ERA	ERA+	OAV	OOB	BH	AVG	PB	PR	/A	PD	TPI
1969	StL-N	1	0	1.000	7	0	0	0	0	9^2	4	0	6	7	9.3	0.93	384	.121	.256	0	—	0	3	3	0	0.3
1970	StL-N	2	2	.500	37	0	0	0	4	49^1	53	2	37	26	17.0	2.92	141	.282	.408	0	.000	-0	6	7	-0	0.6
1971	Min-A	0	0	—	6	0	0	0	0	4^1	5	1	4	2	18.7	4.15	86	.294	.429	0	—	0	-0	-0	0	0.0
Total	3	3	2	.600	50	0	0	0	4	63^1	62	3	47	35	15.9	2.70	148	.261	.389	0	.000	-0	9	9	0	0.9

● HUGH CANAVAN Canavan, Hugh Edward "Hugo" b: 5/13/1897, Worcester, Mass. d: 9/4/67, Boston, Mass. BL/TL, 5'8", 160 lbs. Deb: 4/23/18

YEAR	TM/L	W	L	PCT	G	GS	CG	SH	SV	IP	H	HR	BB	SO	RAT	ERA	ERA+	OAV	OOB	BH	AVG	PB	PR	/A	PD	TPI
1918	Bos-N	0	4	.000	11	3	3	0	0	46^2	70	0	15	18	17.4	6.36	42	.366	.427	2	.095	-0	-19	-19	1	-1.8

● JOHN CANDELARIA Candelaria, John Robert "Candy Man" b: 11/6/53, New York, N.Y. BL/TL, 6'7", 232 lbs. Deb: 6/08/75

YEAR	TM/L	W	L	PCT	G	GS	CG	SH	SV	IP	H	HR	BB	SO	RAT	ERA	ERA+	OAV	OOB	BH	AVG	PB	PR	/A	PD	TPI
1975	*Pit-N	8	6	.571	18	18	4	1	0	120^2	95	8	36	95	9.9	2.76	128	.212	.273	6	.140	-0	12	10	-1	0.9
1976	Pit-N	16	7	.696	32	31	11	4	1	220	173	22	60	138	9.6	3.15	111	.216	.273	14	.184	3	9	8	-1	1.1
1977	Pit-N☆	20	5	**.800**	33	33	6	1	0	230^2	197	29	50	133	9.7	**2.34**	**170**	.232	.276	18	.225	4	**40**	42	-2	4.8
1978	Pit-N	12	11	.522	30	29	3	1	1	189	191	15	49	94	11.7	3.24	114	.261	.312	9	.173	4	7	10	-2	1.2
1979	*Pit-N	14	9	.609	33	30	8	0	0	207	201	25	41	101	10.7	3.22	121	.253	.292	9	.132	-1	12	15	0	1.5
1980	Pit-N	11	14	.440	35	34	7	0	1	233^1	246	14	50	97	11.5	4.01	91	.276	.317	15	.195	2	-11	-10	-1	-0.9
1981	Pit-N	2	2	.500	6	6	0	0	0	40^2	42	3	11	14	11.7	3.54	101	.271	.319	3	.231	0	-0	0	-0	0.0
1982	Pit-N	12	7	.632	31	30	1	1	1	174^2	166	13	37	133	10.7	2.94	126	.255	.299	12	.222	3	13	15	-1	1.8
1983	Pit-N	15	8	.652	33	32	2	0	0	197^2	191	15	45	157	10.8	3.23	115	.257	.302	9	.138	-0	9	10	-2	0.9
1984	Pit-N	12	11	.522	33	28	3	1	2	185^1	179	19	34	133	10.4	2.72	132	.256	.291	8	.129	1	18	18	-2	1.8
1985	Pit-N	2	4	.333	37	0	0	0	9	54^1	57	7	14	47	11.9	3.64	98	.275	.324	0	.000	-0	-0	-0	-0	-0.1
	Cal-A	7	3	.700	13	13	1	1	0	71	70	7	24	53	12.3	3.80	108	.262	.330	0	—	0	3	2	-1	0.2
1986	*Cal-A	10	2	.833	16	16	1	1	0	91^2	68	4	26	81	9.5	2.55	161	.206	.270	0	—	0	17	16	-1	1.6
1987	Cal-A	8	6	.571	20	20	0	0	0	116^2	127	17	20	74	11.4	4.71	91	.279	.311	0	—	0	-3	-5	1	-0.1
	NY-N	2	0	1.000	3	3	0	0	0	12^1	17	1	3	10	14.6	5.84	65	.333	.370	1	.200	0	-2	-3	0	-0.3
1988	NY-A	13	7	.650	25	24	6	2	1	157	150	18	23	121	10.0	3.38	116	.248	.278	0	—	0	10	10	0	1.0
1989	NY-A	3	3	.500	10	6	1	0	0	49	49	8	12	37	11.2	5.14	75	.258	.302	0	—	0	-7	-7	-0	-0.7
	Mon-N	0	2	.000	12	0	0	0	0	16^1	17	3	4	14	11.6	3.31	107	.283	.328	0	—	0	0	0	-0	0.0
1990	Min-A	7	3	.700	34	1	0	0	4	58^1	55	9	9	44	9.9	3.39	122	.244	.274	0	—	0	3	5	-1	0.4
	Tor-A	0	3	.000	13	2	0	0	1	21^1	32	2	11	19	19.0	5.48	72	.356	.437	0	—	0	-4	-4	1	-0.3
	Yr	7	6	.538	47	3	0	0	5	79^2	87	11	20	63	12.3	3.95	104	.274	.321	0	—	0	-0	1	-0	0.1
1991	LA-N	1	1	.500	59	0	0	0	2	33^2	31	3	11	38	11.2	3.74	96	.252	.313	0	—	0	-0	-1	-1	-0.1
1992	LA-N	2	5	.286	50	0	0	0	5	25^1	20	1	13	23	11.7	2.84	122	.220	.317	0	—	0	2	2	0	0.2
Total	18	177	119	.598	576	356	54	13	28	2506	2374	243	583	1656	10.7	3.29	115	.251	.297	104	.174	15	126	136	-13	14.9

● MILO CANDINI Candini, Mario Cain b: 8/3/17, Manteca, Cal. BR/TR, 6', 187 lbs. Deb: 5/01/43

YEAR	TM/L	W	L	PCT	G	GS	CG	SH	SV	IP	H	HR	BB	SO	RAT	ERA	ERA+	OAV	OOB	BH	AVG	PB	PR	/A	PD	TPI
1943	Was-A	11	7	.611	28	21	8	3	1	166	144	3	65	67	11.4	2.49	128	.238	.313	9	.161	-1	15	13	1	1.4
1944	Was-A	6	7	.462	28	10	4	2	1	103	110	3	49	31	14.0	4.11	79	.276	.357	10	.313	3	-8	-10	-0	-0.7
1946	Was-A	2	0	1.000	9	0	0	0	1	21^2	15	1	4	6	7.9	2.08	161	.192	.232	2	.333	1	3	3	-0	0.4
1947	Was-A	3	4	.429	38	2	0	0	1	87	96	5	35	31	13.6	5.17	72	.273	.339	3	.167	-0	-14	-14	0	-1.4
1948	Was-A	2	3	.400	35	4	1	0	3	94^1	96	1	63	23	15.3	5.15	84	.267	.378	8	.364	3	-9	-8	0	-0.5
1949	Was-A	0	0	—	3	0	0	0	1	5^2	4	0	1	1	7.9	4.76	89	.200	.238	1	1.000	0	-0	-0	-0	0.0
1950	Phi-N	1	0	1.000	18	0	0	0	0	30	32	2	15	10	14.1	2.70	150	.281	.364	1	.167	-0	5	4	1	0.5
1951	Phi-N	1	0	1.000	15	0	0	0	0	30	33	3	18	14	15.3	6.00	64	.275	.370	1	.333	1	-7	-7	0	-0.6
Total	8	26	21	.553	174	37	13	5	8	537^2	530	18	250	183	13.1	3.92	92	.259	.341	35	.243	6	-15	-19	1	-0.9

● TOM CANDIOTTI Candiotti, Thomas Caesar b: 8/31/57, Walnut Creek, Cal. BR/TR, 6'3", 205 lbs. Deb: 8/08/83

YEAR	TM/L	W	L	PCT	G	GS	CG	SH	SV	IP	H	HR	BB	SO	RAT	ERA	ERA+	OAV	OOB	BH	AVG	PB	PR	/A	PD	TPI
1983	Mil-A	4	4	.500	10	8	2	1	0	55^2	62	4	16	21	12.9	3.23	116	.291	.346	0	—	0	5	3	-1	0.4
1984	Mil-A	2	2	.500	8	6	0	0	0	32^1	38	5	10	23	13.4	5.29	73	.277	.327	0	—	0	-5	-5	-1	-0.5
1986	Cle-A	16	12	.571	36	34	**17**	3	0	252^1	234	18	106	167	12.4	3.57	116	.246	.326	0	—	0	17	16	3	2.0
1987	Cle-A	7	18	.280	32	32	7	2	0	201^2	193	28	93	111	12.9	4.78	95	.250	.333	0	—	0	-7	-6	0	-0.5
1988	Cle-A	14	8	.636	31	31	11	1	0	216^2	225	15	53	137	11.8	3.28	125	.272	.321	0	—	0	16	20	2	2.3
1989	Cle-A	13	10	.565	31	31	4	0	0	206	188	10	55	124	10.8	3.10	128	.242	.295	0	—	0	18	20	4	2.5
1990	Cle-A	15	11	.577	31	29	3	1	0	202	207	23	55	128	11.9	3.65	107	.263	.316	0	—	0	6	6	3	0.9
1991	Cle-A	7	6	.538	15	15	3	0	0	108^1	88	6	28	86	9.8	2.24	185	.218	.272	0	—	0	22	23	-0	2.5
	*Tor-A	6	7	.462	19	19	3	0	0	129^2	114	6	45	81	11.3	2.98	141	.236	.306	0	—	0	16	18	0	1.9
	Yr	13	13	.500	34	34	6	0	0	238	202	12	73	167	10.6	2.65	158	.225	.287	0	—	0	38	41	-0	4.4
1992	LA-N	11	15	.423	32	30	6	2	0	203^2	177	13	63	152	10.7	3.00	115	.237	.299	6	.107	-1	11	10	1	1.1
Total	9	95	93	.505	245	235	56	10	0	1608^1	1526	128	524	1030	11.7	3.45	117	.250	.313	6	.107	-1	100	105	12	12.6

● JOHN CANEIRA Caneira, John Cascaes b: 10/7/52, Waterbury, Conn. BR/TR, 6'3", 180 lbs. Deb: 9/10/77

YEAR	TM/L	W	L	PCT	G	GS	CG	SH	SV	IP	H	HR	BB	SO	RAT	ERA	ERA+	OAV	OOB	BH	AVG	PB	PR	/A	PD	TPI
1977	Cal-A	2	2	.500	6	4	0	0	0	28^2	27	5	16	17	13.5	4.08	96	.252	.350	0	—	0	-0	-1	-1	0.2
1978	Cal-A	0	0	—	2	2	0	0	0	7^2	8	2	3	0	12.9	7.04	51	.286	.355	0	—	0	-3	-3	-0	-0.2
Total	2	2	2	.500	8	6	0	0	0	36^1	35	7	19	17	13.4	4.71	82	.259	.351	0	—	0	-3	-3	-1	0.0

● JOHN CANGELOSI Cangelosi, John Anthony b: 3/10/63, Brooklyn, N.Y. BB/TL, 5'8", 150 lbs. Deb: 6/03/85 ♦

YEAR	TM/L	W	L	PCT	G	GS	CG	SH	SV	IP	H	HR	BB	SO	RAT	ERA	ERA+	OAV	OOB	BH	AVG	PB	PR	/A	PD	TPI
1988	Pit-N	0	0	—	1	0	0	0	0	2	1	0	0	0	4.5	0.00	—	.143	.143	30	.254	0	1	1	-0	0.1

● JOSE CANO Cano, Joselito (Soriano) b: 3/7/62, Boca De Soco, D.R. BR/TR, 6'3", 175 lbs. Deb: 8/28/89

YEAR	TM/L	W	L	PCT	G	GS	CG	SH	SV	IP	H	HR	BB	SO	RAT	ERA	ERA+	OAV	OOB	BH	AVG	PB	PR	/A	PD	TPI
1989	Hou-N	1	1	.500	6	3	1	0	0	23	24	2	7	8	12.1	5.09	67	.267	.320	0	.000	-1	-4	-4	-0	-0.5

● GUY CANTRELL Cantrell, Guy Dewey "Gunner" b: 4/9/04, Clarita, Okla. d: 1/31/61, McAlester, Okla. BR/TR, 6', 190 lbs. Deb: 8/18/25

YEAR	TM/L	W	L	PCT	G	GS	CG	SH	SV	IP	H	HR	BB	SO	RAT	ERA	ERA+	OAV	OOB	BH	AVG	PB	PR	/A	PD	TPI
1925	Bro-N	1	0	1.000	14	3	1	0	0	36	42	0	14	13	14.3	3.00	139	.294	.361	0	.000	-1	5	5	1	0.5
1927	Bro-N	0	0	—	6	0	0	0	0	10	10	0	6	5	14.4	2.70	147	.250	.348	1	.333	0	1	1	0	0.2
	Phi-A	0	2	.000	2	2	2	0	0	18	25	0	7	7	16.0	5.00	85	.338	.395	1	.167	-0	-2	-1	0	-0.2
1930	Det-A	1	5	.167	16	2	1	0	0	35	38	5	20	20	15.2	5.66	85	.271	.366	0	.000	-2	-4	-3	1	-0.4
Total	3	2	7	.222	38	7	4	0	0	99	115	5	47	45	14.9	4.27	103	.290	.368	2	.074	-3	1	1	2	0.1

● BEN CANTWELL Cantwell, Benjamin Caldwell b: 4/13/02, Milan, Tenn. d: 12/4/62, Salem, Mo. BR/TR, 6'1", 168 lbs. Deb: 8/19/27

YEAR	TM/L	W	L	PCT	G	GS	CG	SH	SV	IP	H	HR	BB	SO	RAT	ERA	ERA+	OAV	OOB	BH	AVG	PB	PR	/A	PD	TPI
1927	NY-N	1	1	.500	5	2	1	0	0	19^2	26	1	2	6	13.3	4.12	94	.313	.337	2	.250	0	-0	-1	-0	-0.1
1928	NY-N	1	0	1.000	7	1	0	0	1	18^1	20	1	4	0	12.3	4.42	88	.282	.329	2	.500	1	-1	-1	1	0.0

YEAR	TM/L	W	L	PCT	G	GS	CG	SH	SV	IP	H	HR	BB	SO	RAT	ERA	ERA+	OAV	OOB	BH	AVG	PB	PR	/A	PD	TPI
	Bos-N	3	3	.500	22	9	3	0	0	90	112	7	36	18	15.0	5.10	77	.304	.369	5	.172	-1	-11	-12	1	-1.1
	Yr	4	3	.571	29	10	3	0	1	108^1	132	8	40	18	14.5	4.98	78	.300	.361	7	.212	-0	-12	-13	2	-1.1
1929	Bos-N	4	13	.235	27	20	8	0	2	157	171	11	52	25	12.9	4.47	105	.280	.338	9	.180	0	4	4	4	0.7
1930	Bos-N	9	15	.375	31	21	10	0	2	173^1	213	15	45	43	13.4	4.88	101	.312	.355	19	.302	2	2	1	4	0.7
1931	Bos-N	7	9	.438	33	16	9	2	2	156^1	160	4	34	32	11.2	3.63	104	.262	.301	13	.228	0	4	3	3	0.6
1932	Bos-N	13	11	.542	37	9	3	1	5	146	133	6	33	33	10.5	2.96	127	.247	.296	14	.280	2	15	13	3	1.8
1933	Bos-N	20	10	**.667**	40	29	18	2	2	254^2	242	12	54	57	10.6	2.62	117	.249	.291	12	.141	-1	20	13	4	1.7
1934	Bos-N	5	11	.313	27	19	6	1	5	143^1	163	8	34	45	12.5	4.33	88	.285	.327	12	.279	1	-4	-8	2	-0.5
1935	Bos-N	4	25	.138	39	24	13	0	0	210^2	235	15	44	34	12.0	4.61	82	.282	.320	19	.284	4	-14	-19	2	-1.3
1936	Bos-N	9	9	.500	34	12	4	0	2	133^1	127	8	35	42	11.2	3.04	126	.252	.306	8	.195	-1	15	12	3	1.4
1937	NY-N	0	1	.000	1	1	0	0	0	4	6	1	1	1	15.8	9.00	43	.375	.412	0	—	0	-2	-2	0	-0.2
	Bro-N	0	0	—	13	0	0	0	0	27^1	32	1	8	12	13.2	4.61	88	.288	.336	1	.167	-0	-2	-2	2	0.0
	Yr	0	1	.000	14	1	0	0	0	31^1	38	2	9	13	13.5	5.17	78	.299	.346	1	.167	0	-4	-4	2	-0.2
Total	11	76	108	.413	316	163	75	6	21	1534	1640	90	382	348	12.0	3.91	100	.275	.321	116	.231	8	25	-2	28	3.7

● MIKE CANTWELL Cantwell, Michael Joseph b: 1/15/1896, Washington, D.C. d: 1/5/53, Oteen, N.C. BL/TL, 5'10", 155 lbs. Deb: 8/17/16 F

YEAR	TM/L	W	L	PCT	G	GS	CG	SH	SV	IP	H	HR	BB	SO	RAT	ERA	ERA+	OAV	OOB	BH	AVG	PB	PR	/A	PD	TPI
1916	NY-A	0	0	—	1	0	0	0	0	2	0	0	2	0	9.0	0.00	—	.000	.333	0	—	0	1	1	-0	0.1
1919	Phi-N	1	3	.250	5	3	2	0	0	27^1	36	1	9	6	15.5	5.60	58	.343	.405	2	.222	-0	-8	-7	-1	-0.8
1920	Phi-N	0	3	.000	5	1	0	0	0	23^1	25	1	15	8	16.6	3.86	89	.284	.406	1	.143	-1	-2	-1	0	-0.1
Total	3	1	6	.143	11	4	2	0	0	52^2	61	2	26	14	15.7	4.61	71	.310	.404	3	.188	-1	-9	-8	-1	-0.8

● TOM CANTWELL Cantwell, Thomas Aloysius b: 12/23/1888, Washington, D.C. d: 4/1/68, Washington, D.C. BL/TR, 6', 170 lbs. Deb: 5/19/09 F

YEAR	TM/L	W	L	PCT	G	GS	CG	SH	SV	IP	H	HR	BB	SO	RAT	ERA	ERA+	OAV	OOB	BH	AVG	PB	PR	/A	PD	TPI
1909	Cin-N	1	0	1.000	6	1	1	0	0	21^2	16	0	7	7	10.0	1.66	157	.205	.279	3	.600	1	2	2	-0	0.4
1910	Cin-N	0	0	—	2	0	0	0	0	1^1	2	0	3	0	33.8	13.50	22	.400	.625	0	—	0	-2	-2	-0	-0.2
Total	2	1	0	1.000	8	1	1	0	0	23	18	0	10	7	11.3	2.35	112	.217	.309	3	.600	1	1	1	-0	0.2

● MIKE CAPEL Capel, Michael Lee b: 10/13/61, Marshall, Tex. BR/TR, 6'1", 175 lbs. Deb: 5/07/88

YEAR	TM/L	W	L	PCT	G	GS	CG	SH	SV	IP	H	HR	BB	SO	RAT	ERA	ERA+	OAV	OOB	BH	AVG	PB	PR	/A	PD	TPI
1988	Chi-N	2	1	.667	22	0	0	0	0	29^1	34	5	13	19	15.3	4.91	73	.293	.379	0	.000	-0	-5	-4	-0	-0.5
1990	Mil-A	0	0	—	2	0	0	0	0	0^1	6	0	1	1	216.0	135.00	3	.857	.889	0	—	0	-5	-5	0	-0.4
1991	Hou-N	1	3	.250	25	0	0	0	3	32^2	33	3	15	23	13.2	3.03	116	.266	.345	0	—	0	2	2	0	0.2
Total	3	3	4	.429	49	0	0	0	3	62^1	73	8	29	43	15.3	4.62	77	.296	.379	0	.000	-0	-7	-7	-0	-0.7

● DOUG CAPILLA Capilla, Douglas Edmund b: 1/7/52, Honolulu, Hawaii BL/TL, 5'8", 175 lbs. Deb: 9/12/76

YEAR	TM/L	W	L	PCT	G	GS	CG	SH	SV	IP	H	HR	BB	SO	RAT	ERA	ERA+	OAV	OOB	BH	AVG	PB	PR	/A	PD	TPI
1976	StL-N	1	0	1.000	7	0	0	0	0	8^1	8	0	4	5	13.0	5.40	65	.242	.324	0	—	0	-2	-2	0	-0.2
1977	StL-N	0	0	—	2	0	0	0	0	2^1	2	0	2	1	15.4	15.43	25	.222	.364	0	—	0	-3	-3	0	-0.3
	Cin-N	7	8	.467	22	16	1	0	0	106^1	94	10	59	74	13.1	4.23	93	.237	.338	2	.059	-3	-4	-4	-1	-0.7
	Yr	7	8	.467	24	16	1	0	0	108^2	96	10	61	75	13.2	4.47	88	.236	.339	2	.059	-3	-7	-7	-1	-1.0
1978	Cin-N	0	1	.000	6	3	0	0	0	11	14	1	11	9	20.5	9.82	36	.318	.455	0	.000	-0	-8	-8	-0	-0.8
1979	Cin-N	1	0	1.000	5	0	0	0	0	6^1	7	1	5	0	18.5	8.53	44	.269	.406	1	1.000	0	-3	-3	0	-0.3
	Chi-N	0	1	.000	13	1	0	0	0	17^1	14	1	7	10	10.9	2.60	159	.206	.280	0	—	0	2	3	0	0.3
	Yr	1	1	.500	18	1	0	0	0	23^2	21	2	12	10	12.5	4.18	96	.221	.308	1	1.000	0	-1	-0	1	0.0
1980	Chi-N	2	8	.200	39	11	0	0	0	89^2	82	7	51	51	13.7	4.12	95	.253	.360	4	.190	0	-5	-2	1	-0.1
1981	Chi-N	1	0	1.000	42	0	0	0	0	51	52	1	34	28	15.5	3.18	116	.284	.402	0	.000	-0	2	3	0	0.3
Total	6	12	18	.400	136	31	1	0	0	292^1	273	21	173	178	14.0	4.34	89	.252	.359	7	.115	-3	-21	-15	0	-1.8

● GEORGE CAPPUZZELLO Cappuzzello, George Angelo b: 1/15/54, Youngstown, Ohio BR/TL, 6', 175 lbs. Deb: 5/31/81

YEAR	TM/L	W	L	PCT	G	GS	CG	SH	SV	IP	H	HR	BB	SO	RAT	ERA	ERA+	OAV	OOB	BH	AVG	PB	PR	/A	PD	TPI
1981	Det-A	1	1	.500	18	3	0	0	1	33^2	28	2	18	19	12.8	3.48	108	.222	.329	0	—	0	1	1	-0	0.1
1982	Hou-N	0	1	.000	17	0	0	0	0	19^1	16	2	7	13	12.1	2.79	119	.232	.329	0	.000	-0	2	1	0	0.1
Total	2	1	2	.333	35	3	0	0	1	53	44	4	25	32	12.6	3.23	112	.226	.329	0	.000	-0	2	2	0	0.2

● BUZZ CAPRA Capra, Lee William b: 10/1/47, Chicago, Ill. BR/TR, 5'10", 168 lbs. Deb: 9/15/71

YEAR	TM/L	W	L	PCT	G	GS	CG	SH	SV	IP	H	HR	BB	SO	RAT	ERA	ERA+	OAV	OOB	BH	AVG	PB	PR	/A	PD	TPI
1971	NY-N	0	1	.000	3	0	0	0	0	5^1	3	0	5	6	13.5	8.44	40	.167	.348	0	.000	-0	-3	-3	0	-0.3
1972	NY-N	3	2	.600	14	6	0	0	0	53	50	7	27	45	13.1	4.58	73	.253	.342	3	.250	1	-7	-7	1	-0.5
1973	NY-N	2	7	.222	24	0	0	0	4	42	35	4	28	35	13.9	3.86	94	.233	.361	0	.000	0	-1	-1	0	-0.1
1974	Atl-N☆	16	8	.667	39	27	11	5	1	217	163	13	84	137	10.4	**2.28**	**166**	**.208**	.287	11	.164	0	32	36	-3	3.7
1975	Atl-N	4	7	.364	12	12	5	0	0	78^1	77	8	28	35	12.2	4.25	89	.257	.322	1	.043	-2	-5	-4	1	-0.6
1976	Atl-N	0	1	.000	5	0	0	0	0	9^1	9	0	6	4	14.5	8.68	44	.265	.375	0	—	0	-5	-5	0	-0.5
1977	Atl-N	6	11	.353	45	16	0	0	0	139^1	142	28	80	100	14.6	5.36	83	.263	.362	4	.111	-2	-22	-14	-1	-1.6
Total	7	31	37	.456	142	61	16	5	5	544^1	479	60	258	362	12.4	3.87	100	.237	.326	19	.135	-2	-12	1	-1	0.1

● PAT CARAWAY Caraway, Cecil Bradford Patrick b: 9/26/05, Erath Co., Tex. d: 6/9/74, ElPaso, Tex. BL/TL, 6'4", 175 lbs. Deb: 4/19/30

YEAR	TM/L	W	L	PCT	G	GS	CG	SH	SV	IP	H	HR	BB	SO	RAT	ERA	ERA+	OAV	OOB	BH	AVG	PB	PR	/A	PD	TPI
1930	Chi-A	10	10	.500	38	21	9	1	1	193^1	194	11	57	83	11.8	3.86	120	.267	.323	11	.172	-1	17	16	3	1.7
1931	Chi-A	10	24	.294	51	32	11	1	2	220	268	17	101	55	15.4	6.22	68	.295	.370	14	.194	-1	-45	-48	-1	-4.4
1932	Chi-A	2	6	.250	19	9	1	0	0	64^2	80	6	37	13	16.7	6.82	63	.304	.396	3	.143	-1	-17	-18	0	-1.6
Total	3	22	40	.355	108	62	21	2	3	478	542	34	195	151	14.1	5.35	83	.286	.356	28	.178	-3	-45	-50	2	-4.3

● JOHN CARDEN Carden, John Bruton b: 5/19/21, Killeen, Tex. d: 2/8/49, Mexia, Tex. BR/TR, 6'5", 210 lbs. Deb: 5/18/46

YEAR	TM/L	W	L	PCT	G	GS	CG	SH	SV	IP	H	HR	BB	SO	RAT	ERA	ERA+	OAV	OOB	BH	AVG	PB	PR	/A	PD	TPI
1946	NY-N	0	0	—	1	0	0	0	0	2	4	0	4	1	40.5	22.50	15	.400	.600	0	—	0	-4	-4	-0	-0.4

● CONRAD CARDINAL Cardinal, Conrad Seth b: 3/30/42, Brooklyn, N.Y. BR/TR, 6'1", 190 lbs. Deb: 4/11/63

YEAR	TM/L	W	L	PCT	G	GS	CG	SH	SV	IP	H	HR	BB	SO	RAT	ERA	ERA+	OAV	OOB	BH	AVG	PB	PR	/A	PD	TPI
1963	Hou-N	0	1	.000	6	1	0	0	0	13^1	15	0	7	7	14.9	6.08	52	.283	.367	0	.000	-0	-4	-4	0	-0.4

● BEN CARDONI Cardoni, Armand Joseph "Big Ben" b: 8/21/20, Jessup, Pa. d: 4/2/69, Jessup, Pa. BR/TR, 6'3", 195 lbs. Deb: 8/22/43

YEAR	TM/L	W	L	PCT	G	GS	CG	SH	SV	IP	H	HR	BB	SO	RAT	ERA	ERA+	OAV	OOB	BH	AVG	PB	PR	/A	PD	TPI
1943	Bos-N	0	0	—	11	0	0	0	1	28	38	1	14	5	17.0	6.43	53	.336	.414	0	.000	-1	-9	-9	0	-1.0
1944	Bos-N	0	6	.000	22	5	1	0	0	75^2	83	5	37	24	14.4	3.93	97	.284	.367	4	.235	-0	-3	-1	-1	-0.2
1945	Bos-N	0	0	—	3	0	0	0	0	4	6	0	3	5	22.5	9.00	43	.300	.417	0	—	0	-2	-2	-0	-0.2
Total	3	0	6	.000	36	5	1	0	1	107^2	127	6	54	34	15.4	4.76	78	.299	.382	4	.167	-1	-14	-13	-1	-1.4

● DON CARDWELL Cardwell, Donald Eugene b: 12/7/35, Winston-Salem, N.C. BR/TR, 6'4", 210 lbs. Deb: 4/21/57

YEAR	TM/L	W	L	PCT	G	GS	CG	SH	SV	IP	H	HR	BB	SO	RAT	ERA	ERA+	OAV	OOB	BH	AVG	PB	PR	/A	PD	TPI
1957	Phi-N	4	8	.333	30	19	5	1	1	128^1	122	17	42	92	11.8	4.91	78	.251	.316	7	.200	1	-15	-16	-0	-1.4
1958	Phi-N	3	6	.333	16	14	3	0	0	107^2	99	16	37	77	11.5	4.51	88	.241	.307	8	.211	1	-7	-7	0	-0.6
1959	Phi-N	9	10	.474	25	22	5	1	0	153	135	22	65	106	12.0	4.06	101	.238	.320	3	.055	-3	-2	1	-3	-0.5
1960	Phi-N	1	2	.333	5	4	0	0	0	28^1	28	4	11	21	12.7	4.45	87	.262	.336	2	.250	2	-2	-2	-0	0.0
	Chi-N	8	14	.364	31	26	6	1	0	177	166	19	68	129	12.2	4.37	86	.249	.323	14	.203	3	-12	-12	-2	-1.0
	Yr	9	16	.360	36	30	6	1	0	205^1	194	23	79	150	12.2	4.38	87	.250	.324	16	.208	5	-14	-13	-2	-1.0
1961	Chi-N	15	14	.517	39	38	13	3	0	259^1	243	22	88	156	11.8	3.82	110	.246	.314	10	.105	-1	6	10	2	1.2
1962	Chi-N	7	16	.304	41	29	6	1	4	195^2	205	27	60	104	12.6	4.92	84	.267	.327	9	.148	-0	-21	-17	1	-1.6
1963	Pit-N	13	15	.464	33	32	7	2	0	213^2	195	21	52	112	11.1	3.07	107	.245	.305	6	.085	-2	5	5	-1	0.3
1964	Pit-N	1	2	.333	4	4	1	1	0	19^1	15	1	7	10	11.6	2.79	126	.217	.316	1	.143	-0	2	2	0	0.2
1965	Pit-N	13	10	.565	37	34	12	2	0	240^1	214	21	59	107	10.7	3.18	110	.239	.295	12	.162	3	10	9	2	1.5
1966	Pit-N	6	6	.500	32	14	1	0	1	101^2	112	15	27	60	12.8	4.60	78	.282	.337	3	.103	-1	-11	-12	2	-1.0
1967	NY-N	5	9	.357	26	16	3	3	0	118^1	112	8	39	71	12.0	3.57	95	.249	.319	6	.158	2	-3	-2	2	0.2
1968	NY-N	7	13	.350	29	25	5	1	1	179^2	156	9	50	82	10.8	2.96	102	.233	.296	3	.049	-4	1	1	2	0.0
1969	*NY-N	8	10	.444	30	21	4	0	0	152^1	145	15	47	60	11.6	3.01	121	.252	.314	8	.170	1	10	11	2	1.5
1970	NY-N	0	2	.000	16	1	0	0	0	25	31	3	6	8	14.4	6.48	62	.316	.374	0	.000	-1	-7	-7	0	-0.7

YEAR	TM/L	W	L	PCT	G	GS	CG	SH	SV	IP	H	HR	BB	SO	RAT	ERA	ERA+	OAV	OOB	BH	AVG	PB	PR	/A	PD	TPI
	Atl-N	2	1	.667	16	2	1	1	0	23	31	5	13	16	17.6	9.00	48	.326	.413	2	.400	1	-13	-12	1	-1.1
	Yr	2	3	.400	32	3	1	1	0	48	62	8	19	24	15.4	7.69	54	.312	.374	2	.200	-0	-19	-19	1	-1.8
Total	14	102	138	.425	410	301	72	17	7	2122^{2}	2009	225	671	1211	11.8	3.92	95	.250	.315	94	.135	2	-59	-47	10	-3.0

● TEX CARLETON Carleton, James Otto b: 8/19/06, Comanche, Tex. d: 1/11/77, Fort Worth, Tex. BB/TR, 6'1.5", 180 lbs. Deb: 4/17/32

YEAR	TM/L	W	L	PCT	G	GS	CG	SH	SV	IP	H	HR	BB	SO	RAT	ERA	ERA+	OAV	OOB	BH	AVG	PB	PR	/A	PD	TPI
1932	StL-N	10	13	.435	44	22	9	3	0	196^{1}	198	12	70	113	12.4	4.08	96	.261	.326	9	.150	-2	-4	-3	2	-0.3
1933	StL-N	17	11	.607	44	33	15	4	3	277	263	15	97	147	11.8	3.38	103	.249	.315	17	.187	1	-1	3	-1	0.3
1934	*StL-N	16	11	.593	40	31	16	0	2	240^{2}	260	14	52	103	11.9	4.26	99	.271	.314	17	.193	1	-5	-1	0	0.0
1935	*Chi-N	11	8	.579	31	22	8	0	1	171	169	17	60	84	12.2	3.89	101	.257	.322	8	.129	-3	2	1	2	0.0
1936	Chi-N	14	10	.583	35	26	12	**4**	1	197^{1}	204	14	67	88	12.6	3.65	109	.268	.332	14	.233	6	8	7	2	1.5
1937	Chi-N	16	8	.667	32	27	18	4	0	208^{1}	183	10	94	105	12.1	3.15	126	.236	.321	12	.169	1	18	19	1	2.1
1938	*Chi-N	10	9	.526	33	24	9	0	0	167^{2}	213	11	74	80	15.8	5.42	71	.307	.381	15	.231	3	-30	-30	-0	-2.6
1940	Bro-N	6	6	.500	34	17	4	1	2	149	140	12	47	88	11.5	3.81	105	.245	.305	8	.186	-0	1	3	-1	0.2
Total	8	100	76	.568	293	202	91	16	9	1607^{1}	1630	105	561	808	12.5	3.91	100	.261	.326	100	.185	6	-13	-0	6	1.2

● CISCO CARLOS Carlos, Francisco Manuel b: 9/17/40, Monrovia, Cal. BR/TR, 6'3", 205 lbs. Deb: 8/25/67

YEAR	TM/L	W	L	PCT	G	GS	CG	SH	SV	IP	H	HR	BB	SO	RAT	ERA	ERA+	OAV	OOB	BH	AVG	PB	PR	/A	PD	TPI
1967	Chi-A	2	0	1.000	8	7	1	1	0	41^{2}	23	0	9	27	7.1	0.86	359	.161	.216	1	.063	-1	11	10	0	1.2
1968	Chi-A	4	14	.222	29	21	0	0	0	122^{1}	121	13	37	57	12.4	3.90	78	.258	.326	2	.065	-1	-13	-12	2	-1.3
1969	Chi-A	4	3	.571	25	4	0	0	0	49^{1}	52	4	23	28	14.6	5.66	68	.274	.367	0	.000	-1	-11	-10	1	-1.0
	Was-A	1	1	.500	6	4	0	0	0	17^{2}	23	2	6	5	14.8	4.58	76	.348	.403	1	.200	-1	-2	-2	0	-0.1
	Yr	5	4	.556	31	8	0	0	0	67	75	6	29	33	14.0	5.37	70	.287	.359	1	.067	-0	-13	-12	1	-1.1
1970	Was-A	0	0	—	5	0	0	0	0	6	3	0	4	2	10.5	1.50	237	.150	.292	0	—	0	1	1	0	0.2
Total	4	11	18	.379	73	36	1	1	0	237	222	19	79	119	12.0	3.72	88	.250	.322	4	.065	-3	-13	-12	3	-1.0

● DON CARLSEN Carlsen, Donald Herbert b: 10/15/26, Chicago, Ill. BR/TR, 6'1", 175 lbs. Deb: 4/28/48

YEAR	TM/L	W	L	PCT	G	GS	CG	SH	SV	IP	H	HR	BB	SO	RAT	ERA	ERA+	OAV	OOB	BH	AVG	PB	PR	/A	PD	TPI
1948	Chi-N	0	0	—	1	0	0	0	0	1	5	0	2	1	63.0	36.00	11	.625	.700	0	—	0	-4	-4	0	-0.3
1951	Pit-N	2	3	.400	7	6	2	0	0	43	50	4	14	20	13.6	4.19	101	.292	.349	4	.250	0	-1	0	-1	0.0
1952	Pit-N	0	1	.000	5	1	0	0	0	10	20	1	5	2	22.5	10.80	37	.417	.472	1	.333	0	-8	-8	1	-0.6
Total	3	2	4	.333	13	7	2	0	0	54	75	5	21	23	16.2	6.00	70	.330	.390	5	.263	0	-12	-11	0	-0.9

● HAL CARLSON Carlson, Harold Gust b: 5/17/1892, Rockford, Ill. d: 5/28/30, Chicago, Ill. BR/TR, 6', 180 lbs. Deb: 4/13/17

YEAR	TM/L	W	L	PCT	G	GS	CG	SH	SV	IP	H	HR	BB	SO	RAT	ERA	ERA+	OAV	OOB	BH	AVG	PB	PR	/A	PD	TPI
1917	Pit-N	7	11	.389	34	17	9	1	1	161^{1}	140	0	49	68	10.8	2.90	98	.241	.304	6	.122	-2	-3	-1	2	-0.2
1918	Pit-N	0	1	.000	3	2	0	0	0	12	12	1	5	5	12.8	3.75	77	.286	.362	1	.200	-0	-1	-1	-0	-0.2
1919	Pit-N	8	10	.444	22	14	7	1	0	141	114	0	39	49	9.9	2.23	135	.243	.303	7	.163	-1	11	12	1	1.4
1920	Pit-N	14	13	.519	39	31	16	3	3	246^{2}	262	4	63	62	12.1	3.36	96	.281	.331	23	.271	3	-6	-4	-5	-0.6
1921	Pit-N	4	8	.333	31	10	3	0	4	109^{2}	121	6	23	37	12.0	4.27	90	.290	.330	10	.294	2	-6	-5	1	-0.3
1922	Pit-N	9	12	.429	39	18	6	0	2	145^{1}	193	10	58	64	15.8	5.70	72	.323	.386	15	.268	3	-26	-26	3	-1.9
1923	Pit-N	0	0	—	4	0	0	0	0	13^{1}	19	2	2	4	14.9	4.73	85	.358	.393	0	.000	-0	-1	-1	0	-0.1
1924	Phi-N	8	17	.320	38	24	12	1	2	203^{2}	267	9	55	66	14.4	4.86	92	.329	.374	21	.276	2	-22	-9	1	-0.6
1925	Phi-N	13	14	.481	35	32	18	**4**	0	234	281	19	52	80	13.0	4.23	113	.298	.338	17	.183	-2	1	14	-1	1.0
1926	Phi-N	17	12	.586	35	34	20	3	0	267^{1}	293	9	47	55	11.5	3.23	128	.281	.313	23	.240	2	18	27	-4	2.7
1927	Phi-N	4	5	.444	11	9	4	0	1	63^{2}	80	7	18	13	13.9	5.23	79	.316	.362	6	.240	0	-9	-8	-1	-0.8
	Chi-N	12	8	.600	27	22	15	2	0	184^{1}	201	9	27	27	11.2	3.17	122	.280	.307	11	.164	-3	15	14	-0	1.1
	Yr	16	13	.552	38	31	19	2	1	248	281	16	45	40	11.9	3.70	106	.289	.322	17	.185	-3	6	6	-1	0.3
1928	Chi-N	3	2	.600	20	5	2	0	4	56^{1}	74	4	15	11	14.2	5.91	65	.329	.371	5	.263	0	-12	-13	0	-1.2
1929	*Chi-N	11	5	.688	31	14	6	2	2	111^{2}	131	8	31	35	13.1	5.16	90	.292	.340	9	.231	1	-5	-7	2	-0.4
1930	Chi-N	4	2	.667	8	6	3	0	0	51^{2}	68	5	14	14	14.5	5.05	97	.313	.358	5	.250	0	-0	-1	1	0.0
Total	14	114	120	.487	377	238	121	17	19	2002	2256	93	498	590	12.5	3.97	99	.291	.337	159	.223	5	-49	-8	-0	-0.1

● LEON CARLSON Carlson, Leon Alton "Swede" b: 2/17/1895, Jamestown, N.Y. d: 9/15/61, Jamestown, N.Y. BR/TR, 6'3", 195 lbs. Deb: 5/31/20

YEAR	TM/L	W	L	PCT	G	GS	CG	SH	SV	IP	H	HR	BB	SO	RAT	ERA	ERA+	OAV	OOB	BH	AVG	PB	PR	/A	PD	TPI
1920	Was-A	0	0	—	3	0	0	0	0	12^{1}	14	1	2	3	11.7	3.65	102	.292	.320	1	.167	-0	0	0	-0	-0.1

● STEVE CARLTON Carlton, Steven Norman "Lefty" b: 12/22/44, Miami, Fla. BL/TL, 6'4", 210 lbs. Deb: 4/12/65

YEAR	TM/L	W	L	PCT	G	GS	CG	SH	SV	IP	H	HR	BB	SO	RAT	ERA	ERA+	OAV	OOB	BH	AVG	PB	PR	/A	PD	TPI
1965	StL-N	0	0	—	15	2	0	0	0	25	27	3	8	21	13.0	2.52	153	.287	.350	0	.000	-0	3	4	1	0.4
1966	StL-N	3	3	.500	9	9	2	1	0	52	56	2	18	25	12.8	3.12	115	.280	.339	4	.267	1	3	3	0	0.4
1967	*StL-N	14	9	.609	30	28	11	2	1	193	173	10	62	168	11.1	2.98	110	.238	.300	11	.153	1	8	6	0	0.8
1968	*StL-N★	13	11	.542	34	33	10	5	0	231^{2}	214	11	61	162	10.8	2.99	97	.246	.298	12	.164	2	-0	-2	-1	-0.1
1969	StL-N★	17	11	.607	31	31	12	2	0	236^{1}	185	15	93	210	10.7	2.17	165	.216	.295	17	.213	5	37	37	-1	4.6
1970	StL-N	10	19	.345	34	33	13	2	0	253^{2}	239	25	109	193	12.4	3.73	110	.251	.329	16	.200	2	9	11	-1	1.2
1971	StL-N☆	20	9	.690	37	36	18	4	0	273^{1}	275	23	98	172	12.4	3.56	101	.262	.328	17	.177	1	-3	1	-0	0.2
1972	Phi-N★	**27**	10	.730	41	41	**30**	8	0	**346^{1}**	257	17	87	**310**	9.0	**1.97**	**182**	.206	.259	23	.197	4	**57**	**62**	-2	**7.8**
1973	Phi-N	13	20	.394	40	40	**18**	3	0	**293^{1}**	293	29	113	223	12.5	3.90	97	.260	.329	16	.160	0	-8	-3	-1	-0.4
1974	Phi-N☆	16	13	.552	39	39	17	1	0	291	249	21	136	**240**	12.1	3.22	117	.234	.323	25	.245	2	13	18	-1	2.1
1975	Phi-N	15	14	.517	37	37	14	3	0	255^{1}	217	24	104	192	11.4	3.56	105	.233	.312	14	.156	-0	2	5	-1	0.4
1976	*Phi-N	20	7	**.741**	35	35	13	2	0	252^{2}	224	19	72	195	10.6	3.13	113	.237	.291	20	.217	2	10	12	-4	1.1
1977	*Phi-N☆	**23**	10	.697	36	36	17	2	0	283	229	25	89	198	10.2	2.64	151	.223	.287	26	.268	8	40	43	1	**5.7**
1978	*Phi-N	16	13	.552	34	34	12	3	0	247^{1}	228	30	63	161	10.7	2.84	126	.246	.297	25	.291	7	20	20	1	3.2
1979	Phi-N★	18	11	.621	35	35	13	4	0	251	202	25	89	213	10.6	3.62	106	.219	.292	21	.223	4	3	6	-1	0.8
1980	*Phi-N☆	**24**	9	.727	38	38	13	3	0	**304**	243	15	90	**286**	9.9	2.34	**162**	.218	.278	19	.188	-1	**43**	**49**	-1	**5.4**
1981	*Phi-N☆	13	4	.765	24	24	10	1	0	190	152	9	62	179	10.2	2.42	150	.222	.288	9	.134	-0	23	26	-1	2.8
1982	Phi-N★	**23**	11	.676	38	38	**19**	**6**	0	**295^{2}**	253	17	86	**286**	10.3	3.10	118	.232	.289	22	.218	4	16	18	-1	2.3
1983	*Phi-N	15	16	.484	37	37	8	3	0	**283^{2}**	277	20	84	**275**	11.5	3.11	115	.258	.314	19	.196	3	16	14	-1	1.7
1984	Phi-N	13	7	.650	33	33	1	0	0	229	214	14	79	163	11.5	3.58	102	.246	.309	16	.190	2	0	1	-3	0.1
1985	Phi-N	1	8	.111	16	16	0	0	0	92	84	6	53	48	13.4	3.33	111	.249	.350	5	.179	0	3	4	1	0.5
1986	Phi-N	4	8	.333	16	16	0	0	0	83	102	15	45	62	15.9	6.18	62	.297	.379	7	.206	1	-23	-21	-1	-2.1
	SF-N	1	3	.250	6	6	0	0	0	30	36	4	16	18	15.9	5.10	69	.303	.390	2	.182	1	-5	-5	1	-0.4
	Yr	5	11	.313	22	22	0	0	0	113	138	19	61	80	15.9	5.89	64	.297	.380	9	.200	2	-27	-27	-0	-2.5
	Chi-A	4	3	.571	10	10	0	0	0	63^{1}	58	6	25	40	11.8	3.69	117	.252	.325	0	—	0	3	4	-1	0.1
1987	Cle-A	5	9	.357	23	14	3	0	1	109	111	17	63	71	14.5	5.37	84	.266	.364	0	—	0	-11	-10	-0	-1.0
	Min-A	1	5	.167	9	7	0	0	0	43	54	7	23	20	16.5	6.70	69	.310	.397	0	—	0	-11	-10	0	-1.1
	Yr	6	14	.300	32	21	3	0	1	152	165	24	86	91	15.0	5.74	79	.276	.369	0	—	0	-22	-20	-0	-2.1
1988	Min-A	0	1	.000	4	1	0	0	0	9^{2}	20	5	5	5	23.3	16.76	24	.408	.463	0	—	0	-14	-14	-0	-1.2
Total	24	329	244	.574	741	709	254	55	2	5217^{1}	4672	414	1833	4136	11.3	3.22	115	.240	.308	346	.201	50	236	277	-18	35.3

● DON CARMAN Carman, Donald Wayne b: 8/14/59, Oklahoma City, Okla BL/TL, 6'3", 195 lbs. Deb: 10/01/83

YEAR	TM/L	W	L	PCT	G	GS	CG	SH	SV	IP	H	HR	BB	SO	RAT	ERA	ERA+	OAV	OOB	BH	AVG	PB	PR	/A	PD	TPI
1983	Phi-N	0	0	—	1	0	0	0	1	1	0	0	0	0	0.0	0.00	—	.000	.000	0	—	0	0	0	0	0.0
1984	Phi-N	0	1	.000	11	0	0	0	0	13^{1}	14	2	6	16	13.5	5.40	67	.255	.328	0	.000	-0	-3	-3	-0	-0.3
1985	Phi-N	9	4	.692	71	0	0	0	7	86^{1}	52	6	38	87	9.6	2.08	177	.178	.277	0	.000	-0	14	15	0	1.6
1986	Phi-N	10	5	.667	50	14	2	1	1	134^{1}	113	11	52	98	11.3	3.22	120	.234	.313	0	.000	-3	7	9	2	0.8
1987	Phi-N	13	11	.542	35	35	3	2	0	211	194	34	69	125	11.4	4.22	100	.244	.308	5	.082	-3	-3	0	-3	-0.6
1988	Phi-N	10	14	.417	36	32	2	0	0	201^{1}	211	20	70	116	12.7	4.29	83	.270	.333	3	.048	-5	-19	-16	-3	-2.5
1989	Phi-N	5	15	.250	49	20	0	0	0	149^{1}	152	21	86	81	14.5	5.24	68	.260	.358	1	.029	-3	-29	-28	-1	-3.3
1990	Phi-N	6	2	.750	59	1	0	0	1	86^{2}	69	13	38	58	11.5	4.15	92	.218	.310	3	.273	1	-3	-3	0	-0.3
1991	Cin-N	0	2	.000	28	0	0	0	1	36	40	8	19	15	15.0	5.25	72	.286	.375	0	.000	-1	-6	-6	0	-0.6

YEAR	TM/L	W	L	PCT	G	GS	CG	SH	SV	IP	H	HR	BB	SO	RAT	ERA	ERA+	OAV	OOB	BH	AVG	PB	PR	/A	PD	TPI
1992	Tex-A	0	0	—	2	0	0	0	0	2^1	4	0	0	2	15.4	7.71	50	.364	.364	0	—	0	-1	-1	-0	-0.1
Total	10	53	54	.495	342	102	7	3	11	921^2	849	115	378	598	12.2	4.11	92	.245	.323	12	.057	-15	-42	-32	-5	-5.3

● **CHET CARMICHAEL** Carmichael, Chester Keller b: 1/9/1888, Muncie, Ind. d: 8/22/60, Rochester, N.Y. BR/TR, 5'11.5", 200 lbs. Deb: 9/05/09

YEAR	TM/L	W	L	PCT	G	GS	CG	SH	SV	IP	H	HR	BB	SO	RAT	ERA	ERA+	OAV	OOB	BH	AVG	PB	PR	/A	PD	TPI
1909	Cin-N	0	0	—	2	0	0	0	0	7	9	0	3	2	18.0	0.00	—	.321	.424	0	.000	-0	2	2	-0	0.2

● **EDDIE CARNETT** Carnett, Edwin Elliott "Lefty" b: 10/21/16, Springfield, Mo. BL/TL, 6', 185 lbs. Deb: 4/19/41 ♦

YEAR	TM/L	W	L	PCT	G	GS	CG	SH	SV	IP	H	HR	BB	SO	RAT	ERA	ERA+	OAV	OOB	BH	AVG	PB	PR	/A	PD	TPI
1941	Bos-N	0	0	—	2	0	0	0	0	1^1	4	0	3	2	47.3	20.25	18	.500	.636	0	—	0	-2	-2	0	-0.2
1944	Chi-A	0	0	—	2	0	0	0	0	2	3	1	0	1	13.5	9.00	38	.333	.333	126	.276	1	-1	-1	0	-0.1
1945	Cle-A	0	0	—	2	0	0	0	0	2	0	0	0	1	0.0	0.00	—	.000	.000	16	.219	0	1	1	-0	0.1
Total	3	0	0	—	6	0	0	0	0	5^1	7	1	3	4	16.9	8.44	40	.304	.385	142	.268	1	-3	-3	0	-0.2

● **PAT CARNEY** Carney, Patrick Joseph "Doc" b: 8/7/1876, Holyoke, Mass. d: 1/9/53, Worcester, Mass. BL/TL, 6', 200 lbs. Deb: 9/20/01 ♦

YEAR	TM/L	W	L	PCT	G	GS	CG	SH	SV	IP	H	HR	BB	SO	RAT	ERA	ERA+	OAV	OOB	BH	AVG	PB	PR	/A	PD	TPI
1902	Bos-N	0	1	.000	2	1	0	0	0	5	6	1	3	3	18.0	9.00	31	.297	.413	141	.270	0	-3	-3	-0	-0.3
1903	Bos-N	4	5	.444	10	9	9	0	0	78	93	2	31	29	14.5	4.04	79	.284	.349	94	.240	1	-7	-7	-0	-0.5
1904	Bos-N	0	4	.000	4	2	1	0	0	26^1	40	1	12	5	18.1	5.81	47	.364	.431	57	.204	0	-9	-9	-0	-0.9
Total	3	4	10	.286	16	12	10	0	0	109^1	139	4	46	37	15.6	4.69	66	.303	.372	308	.247	2	-19	-20	-1	-1.7

● **CRIS CARPENTER** Carpenter, Cris Howell b: 4/5/65, St.Augustine, Fla. BR/TR, 6'1", 195 lbs. Deb: 5/14/88

YEAR	TM/L	W	L	PCT	G	GS	CG	SH	SV	IP	H	HR	BB	SO	RAT	ERA	ERA+	OAV	OOB	BH	AVG	PB	PR	/A	PD	TPI
1988	StL-N	2	3	.400	8	8	1	0	0	47^2	56	3	9	24	12.5	4.72	74	.298	.333	2	.143	-0	-7	-7	-0	-0.7
1989	StL-N	4	4	.500	36	5	0	0	0	68	70	4	26	35	13.0	3.18	114	.262	.332	4	.444	1	2	3	-0	0.5
1990	StL-N	0	0	—	4	0	0	0	0	8	5	2	2	6	7.9	4.50	85	.167	.219	0	.000	-0	-1	-1	-0	-0.1
1991	StL-N	10	4	.714	59	0	0	0	0	66	53	6	20	47	10.0	4.23	88	.220	.280	1	.333	0	-4	-4	-0	-0.4
1992	StL-N	5	4	.556	73	0	0	0	1	88	69	10	27	46	10.2	2.97	116	.220	.291	1	.333	0	5	5	-1	0.5
Total	5	21	15	.583	180	13	1	0	1	277^2	253	25	84	158	11.2	3.66	97	.244	.304	8	.267	1	-4	-3	-2	-0.2

● **LEW CARPENTER** Carpenter, Lewis Emmett b: 8/16/13, Woodstock, Ga. d: 4/25/79, Marietta, Ga. BR/TR, 6'2", 195 lbs. Deb: 5/01/43

YEAR	TM/L	W	L	PCT	G	GS	CG	SH	SV	IP	H	HR	BB	SO	RAT	ERA	ERA+	OAV	OOB	BH	AVG	PB	PR	/A	PD	TPI
1943	Was-A	0	0	—	4	0	0	0	0	3^1	1	0	4	1	16.2	0.00	—	.125	.462	0	—	0	1	1	-0	0.1

● **PAUL CARPENTER** Carpenter, Paul Calvin b: 8/12/1894, Granville, Ohio d: 3/14/68, Newark, Ohio BR/TR, 5'11", 165 lbs. Deb: 7/26/16

YEAR	TM/L	W	L	PCT	G	GS	CG	SH	SV	IP	H	HR	BB	SO	RAT	ERA	ERA+	OAV	OOB	BH	AVG	PB	PR	/A	PD	TPI
1916	Pit-N	0	0	—	5	0	0	0	0	7^2	8	0	4	5	14.1	1.17	229	.258	.343	0	.000	-0	1	1	0	0.1

● **BOB CARPENTER** Carpenter, Robert Louis b: 12/12/17, Chicago, Ill. BR/TR, 6'3", 195 lbs. Deb: 9/12/40

YEAR	TM/L	W	L	PCT	G	GS	CG	SH	SV	IP	H	HR	BB	SO	RAT	ERA	ERA+	OAV	OOB	BH	AVG	PB	PR	/A	PD	TPI
1940	NY-N	2	0	1.000	5	3	2	0	0	33	29	2	14	25	11.7	2.73	142	.238	.316	1	.100	-0	4	4	-0	0.4
1941	NY-N	11	6	.647	29	19	8	1	2	131^2	138	15	42	42	12.4	3.83	97	.265	.323	7	.156	-0	-3	-2	-3	-0.5
1942	NY-N	11	10	.524	28	25	12	2	0	185^2	192	13	51	53	11.8	3.15	107	.263	.312	12	.185	-1	3	4	-3	0.1
1946	NY-N	1	3	.250	12	6	1	1	0	39	37	7	18	13	12.7	4.85	71	.245	.325	1	.100	-0	-6	-6	-1	-0.7
1947	NY-N	0	0	—	2	0	0	0	0	3	5	0	3	0	24.0	12.00	34	.385	.500	0	—	0	-3	-3	0	-0.2
	Chi-N	0	1	.000	4	1	0	0	0	7^1	10	1	4	1	17.2	4.91	80	.323	.400	1	1.000	0	-1	-1	0	0.0
	Yr	0	1	.000	6	1	0	0	0	10^1	15	1	7	1	19.2	6.97	57	.341	.431	1	1.000	0	-3	-3	0	-0.2
Total	5	25	20	.556	80	54	23	4	2	399^2	411	38	132	134	12.3	3.60	98	.262	.321	22	.168	-1	-5	-3	-6	-0.9

● **FRANK CARPIN** Carpin, Frank Dominic b: 9/14/38, Brooklyn, N.Y. BL/TL, 5'10", 172 lbs. Deb: 5/25/65

YEAR	TM/L	W	L	PCT	G	GS	CG	SH	SV	IP	H	HR	BB	SO	RAT	ERA	ERA+	OAV	OOB	BH	AVG	PB	PR	/A	PD	TPI
1965	Pit-N	3	1	.750	39	0	0	0	4	39^2	35	0	24	27	14.1	3.18	111	.243	.363	0	.000	-0	2	1	1	0.3
1966	Hou-N	1	0	1.000	10	0	0	0	0	6	9	0	6	2	22.5	7.50	46	.346	.469	0	—	0	-3	-3	-0	-0.3
Total	2	4	1	.800	49	0	0	0	4	45^2	44	0	30	29	15.2	3.74	93	.259	.379	0	.000	-0	-1	-1	1	0.0

● **ALEX CARRASQUEL** Carrasquel, Alejandro Eloy (Aparicio) b: 7/24/12, Caracas, Venez. d: 8/19/69, Caracas, Venez. BR/TR, 6'1", 182 lbs. Deb: 4/23/39

YEAR	TM/L	W	L	PCT	G	GS	CG	SH	SV	IP	H	HR	BB	SO	RAT	ERA	ERA+	OAV	OOB	BH	AVG	PB	PR	/A	PD	TPI
1939	Was-A	5	9	.357	40	17	7	0	2	159^1	165	7	68	41	13.2	4.69	93	.266	.340	7	.167	1	-1	-6	0	-0.4
1940	Was-A	6	2	.750	28	0	0	0	0	48	42	4	29	19	13.3	4.88	86	.240	.348	0	.000	-1	-3	-4	0	-0.4
1941	Was-A	6	2	.750	35	5	4	0	2	96^2	103	7	49	30	14.2	3.44	117	.278	.364	2	.095	0	8	6	4	1.0
1942	Was-A	7	7	.500	35	15	7	1	4	152^1	161	7	53	40	12.7	3.43	107	.267	.327	6	.136	-0	4	4	1	0.5
1943	Was-A	11	7	.611	39	13	4	1	5	144^1	160	3	54	48	13.4	3.68	87	.279	.342	8	.186	1	-6	-8	1	-0.7
1944	Was-A	8	7	.533	43	7	3	0	2	134	143	8	50	35	13.1	3.43	95	.273	.339	7	.194	1	0	-3	1	0.0
1945	Was-A	7	5	.583	35	7	5	2	1	122^2	105	5	40	38	10.6	2.71	114	.228	.289	3	.083	-1	9	5	-0	0.4
1949	Chi-A	0	0	—	3	0	0	0	0	3^2	8	1	4	1	29.5	14.73	28	.421	.522	0	—	0	-4	-4	0	-0.4
Total	8	50	39	.562	258	64	30	4	16	861	887	42	347	252	13.0	3.73	98	.265	.335	33	.144	0	6	-9	8	0.0

● **AMALIO CARRENO** Carreno, Amalio Rafael (Adrian) b: 4/11/64, Chacachacare, Ven. BR/TR, 6', 170 lbs. Deb: 7/07/91

YEAR	TM/L	W	L	PCT	G	GS	CG	SH	SV	IP	H	HR	BB	SO	RAT	ERA	ERA+	OAV	OOB	BH	AVG	PB	PR	/A	PD	TPI
1991	Phi-N	0	0	—	3	0	0	0	0	3^1	5	1	3	2	27.0	16.20	23	.333	.500	0	.000	-0	-5	-5	-0	-0.5

● **BILL CARRICK** Carrick, William Martin "Doughnut Bill" b: 9/5/1873, Erie, Pa. d: 3/7/32, Philadelphia, Pa. TR , Deb: 7/30/1898

YEAR	TM/L	W	L	PCT	G	GS	CG	SH	SV	IP	H	HR	BB	SO	RAT	ERA	ERA+	OAV	OOB	BH	AVG	PB	PR	/A	PD	TPI
1898	NY-N	3	1	.750	5	4	4	0	0	39^2	39	0	21	10	14.7	3.40	102	.255	.364	3	.167	-0	1	0	1	0.0
1899	NY-N	16	27	.372	44	43	**40**	3	0	361^2	485	4	122	60	15.6	4.65	81	.320	.378	18	.138	-6	-32	-36	2	-3.5
1900	NY-N	19	22	.463	**45**	41	32	1	0	341^2	415	7	92	63	13.6	3.53	102	.299	.347	20	.174	-3	6	3	-0	0.0
1901	Was-A	14	22	.389	42	37	34	0	0	324	367	12	93	70	13.3	3.75	98	.282	.338	20	.159	-5	-3	-3	0	-0.7
1902	Was-A	11	17	.393	31	30	28	0	0	257^2	344	10	72	36	14.9	4.86	76	.320	.368	20	.185	-2	-37	-33	-3	-3.3
Total	5	63	89	.414	167	155	138	4	0	1324^2	1650	33	400	239	14.3	4.14	89	.304	.358	81	.163	-16	-64	-68	-0	-7.5

● **DON CARRITHERS** Carrithers, Donald George b: 9/15/49, Lynwood, Cal. BR/TR, 6'2", 180 lbs. Deb: 8/01/70

YEAR	TM/L	W	L	PCT	G	GS	CG	SH	SV	IP	H	HR	BB	SO	RAT	ERA	ERA+	OAV	OOB	BH	AVG	PB	PR	/A	PD	TPI
1970	SF-N	2	1	.667	11	2	0	0	0	22	31	5	14	14	18.4	7.36	54	.333	.421	0	.000	-0	-8	-8	-0	-0.8
1971	*SF-N	5	3	.625	22	12	2	1	1	80^1	77	6	37	41	13.0	4.03	84	.254	.339	3	.176	0	-5	-6	-1	-0.6
1972	SF-N	4	8	.333	25	14	2	0	0	90	108	10	42	42	15.5	5.80	60	.296	.376	6	.207	1	-23	-23	0	-2.3
1973	SF-N	1	2	.333	25	3	0	0	0	58	64	2	35	36	16.0	4.81	79	.278	.383	4	.250	0	-7	-6	1	-0.5
1974	Mon-N	5	2	.714	22	3	0	0	1	60	56	6	17	31	11.4	3.00	128	.249	.310	4	.286	1	4	6	1	0.7
1975	Mon-N	5	3	.625	19	14	5	2	0	101	90	7	38	37	11.8	3.30	116	.240	.317	6	.176	0	4	6	2	0.9
1976	Mon-N	6	12	.333	34	19	2	0	0	140^1	153	9	78	71	15.3	4.43	84	.286	.384	4	.108	-1	-14	-11	1	-1.2
1977	Min-A	0	1	.000	7	0	0	0	0	14^1	16	2	6	3	14.4	6.91	58	.271	.348	0	—	0	-5	-5	0	-0.3
Total	8	28	32	.467	165	67	11	3	3	566	595	47	267	275	14.1	4.45	83	.272	.358	27	.176	0	-55	-48	5	-4.1

● **CLAY CARROLL** Carroll, Clay Palmer "Hawk" b: 5/2/41, Clanton, Ala. BR/TR, 6'1", 200 lbs. Deb: 9/02/64

YEAR	TM/L	W	L	PCT	G	GS	CG	SH	SV	IP	H	HR	BB	SO	RAT	ERA	ERA+	OAV	OOB	BH	AVG	PB	PR	/A	PD	TPI
1964	Mil-N	2	0	1.000	11	1	0	0	1	20^1	15	1	3	17	8.0	1.77	199	.200	.231	0	.000	-0	4	4	1	0.5
1965	Mil-N	0	1	.000	19	1	0	0	1	34^2	35	3	16	16	12.7	4.41	80	.269	.340	0	.000	-1	-3	-3	-0	-0.4
1966	Atl-N	8	7	.533	**73**	3	0	0	11	144^1	127	8	29	67	10.0	2.37	154	.236	.280	3	.100	-2	20	20	1	2.1
1967	Atl-N	6	12	.333	42	7	1	0	0	93	111	6	29	35	13.8	5.52	60	.304	.360	1	.063	-1	-22	-23	1	-2.3
1968	Atl-N	0	1	.000	10	0	0	0	0	22^1	26	1	6	10	12.9	4.84	62	.310	.356	0	.000	-1	-5	-5	0	-0.5
	Cin-N	7	7	.500	58	1	0	0	17	121^2	102	3	32	61	10.4	2.29	138	.230	.290	6	.250	1	9	12	1	1.7
	Yr	7	8	.467	68	1	0	0	17	144	128	4	38	71	10.8	2.69	117	.242	.300	6	.207	1	5	7	2	1.2
1969	Cin-N	12	6	.667	71	4	0	0	7	150^2	149	9	78	90	14.0	3.52	107	.262	.358	6	.207	2	1	4	3	0.9
1970	*Cin-N	9	4	.692	65	0	0	0	16	104^1	104	4	27	63	11.5	2.59	156	.259	.309	1	.071	-1	17	17	1	1.8
1971	Cin-N☆	10	4	.714	61	0	0	0	15	93^2	78	5	42	64	11.7	2.50	134	.234	.324	1	.100	-1	10	9	4	1.3
1972	*Cin-N☆	6	4	.600	**65**	0	0	0	**37**	96	89	5	32	51	11.4	2.25	143	.256	.321	2	.182	0	13	10	1	1.2
1973	*Cin-N	8	8	.500	53	5	0	0	14	92^2	111	5	34	41	14.6	3.69	92	.307	.374	3	.214	0	-0	-3	1	-0.2
1974	Cin-N	12	5	.706	57	3	0	0	6	100^2	96	3	30	46	11.3	2.15	163	.256	.311	3	.167	-0	16	15	2	1.7
1975	*Cin-N	7	5	.583	56	2	0	0	7	96^1	93	2	32	44	12.0	2.62	137	.255	.320	0	.000	-2	11	10	-1	0.8
1976	Chi-A	4	4	.500	29	0	0	0	6	77^1	67	1	24	38	10.8	2.56	139	.242	.307	0	—	0	8	9	0	0.9

YEAR	TM/L	W	L	PCT	G	GS	CG	SH	SV	IP	H	HR	BB	SO	RAT	ERA	ERA+	OAV	OOB	BH	AVG	PB	PR	/A	PD	TPI
1977	StL-N	4	2	.667	51	1	0	0	4	90	77	8	24	34	10.2	2.50	154	.238	.293	1	.091	-1	14	13	1	1.4
	Chi-A	1	3	.250	8	0	0	0	1	11^1	14	3	4	4	14.3	4.76	86	.311	.367	0	—	0	-1	-1	0	-0.1
1978	Pit-N	0	0	—	2	0	0	0	0	4	2	0	3	0	11.3	2.25	164	.143	.294	0	—	0	1	1	0	0.1
Total	15	96	73	.568	731	28	1	0	143	1353^1	1296	67	442	681	11.8	2.94	120	.257	.321	27	.130	-5	93	90	17	10.9

● ED CARROLL Carroll, Edgar Fleischer b: 7/27/07, Baltimore, Md. d: 10/13/84, Rossville, Md. BR/TR, 6'3", 185 lbs. Deb: 5/01/29

YEAR	TM/L	W	L	PCT	G	GS	CG	SH	SV	IP	H	HR	BB	SO	RAT	ERA	ERA+	OAV	OOB	BH	AVG	PB	PR	/A	PD	TPI
1929	Bos-A	1	0	1.000	24	3	0	0	0	67^1	77	6	20	13	13.5	5.61	76	.291	.349	1	.063	-2	-10	-10	0	-1.1

● OWNIE CARROLL Carroll, Owen Thomas b: 11/11/02, Kearny, N.J. d: 6/8/75, Orange, N.J. BR/TR, 5'10.5", 165 lbs. Deb: 6/20/25

YEAR	TM/L	W	L	PCT	G	GS	CG	SH	SV	IP	H	HR	BB	SO	RAT	ERA	ERA+	OAV	OOB	BH	AVG	PB	PR	/A	PD	TPI
1925	Det-A	2	2	.500	10	4	1	0	0	40^2	46	1	28	12	16.8	3.76	114	.293	.406	6	.375	1	3	2	-2	0.2
1927	Det-A	10	6	.625	31	15	8	0	0	172	186	5	73	41	13.9	3.98	106	.281	.358	12	.174	-2	3	4	2	0.4
1928	Det-A	16	12	.571	34	28	19	2	2	231	219	6	87	51	12.2	3.27	126	.262	.337	19	.194	-0	20	21	1	2.2
1929	Det-A	9	17	.346	34	26	12	0	1	202	249	10	86	54	15.3	4.63	93	.310	.383	17	.230	2	-9	-8	2	-0.4
1930	Det-A	0	5	.000	6	3	0	0	0	20^1	30	3	9	4	17.3	10.62	45	.333	.394	1	.143	-1	-13	-13	0	-1.1
	NY-A	0	1	.000	10	1	0	0	0	32^2	49	2	18	8	19.6	6.61	65	.374	.464	2	.200	0	-7	-8	1	-0.7
	Yr	0	6	.000	16	4	0	0	0	53	79	5	27	12	18.7	8.15	55	.357	.437	3	.176	-0	-21	-22	1	-1.8
	Cin-N	0	1	.000	3	2	1	0	0	14	17	3	3	0	12.9	4.50	107	.309	.345	1	.200	-0	1	1	0	0.0
1931	Cin-N	3	9	.250	29	12	4	0	0	107^1	135	6	51	24	15.9	5.53	67	.314	.392	7	.206	0	-20	-21	1	-1.9
1932	Cin-N	10	19	.345	32	26	15	0	1	210	245	7	44	55	12.8	4.50	86	.286	.328	16	.208	2	-14	-15	-1	-1.3
1933	Bro-N	13	15	.464	33	31	11	0	0	226^1	248	9	54	45	12.3	3.78	85	.281	.327	11	.149	-1	-11	-14	3	-1.2
1934	Bro-N	1	3	.250	26	5	0	0	1	74^1	108	9	33	17	17.2	6.42	61	.342	.406	6	.240	1	-19	-21	3	-1.6
Total	9	64	90	.416	248	153	71	2	5	1330^2	1532	61	486	311	14.0	4.43	89	.294	.359	98	.200	2	-68	-72	11	-5.4

● DICK CARROLL Carroll, Richard Thomas "Shadow" b: 7/21/1884, Cleveland, Ohio d: 11/22/45, Cleveland, Ohio BR/TR, 6'2", Deb: 9/25/09

YEAR	TM/L	W	L	PCT	G	GS	CG	SH	SV	IP	H	HR	BB	SO	RAT	ERA	ERA+	OAV	OOB	BH	AVG	PB	PR	/A	PD	TPI
1909	NY-A	0	0	—	2	1	0	0	0	5	7	1	1	1	14.4	3.60	70	.292	.320	1	.500	0	-1	-1	-0	-0.1

● TOM CARROLL Carroll, Thomas Michael b: 11/5/52, Utica, N.Y. BL/TR, 6'3", 190 lbs. Deb: 7/07/74

YEAR	TM/L	W	L	PCT	G	GS	CG	SH	SV	IP	H	HR	BB	SO	RAT	ERA	ERA+	OAV	OOB	BH	AVG	PB	PR	/A	PD	TPI
1974	Cin-N	4	3	.571	16	13	0	0	0	78^1	68	11	44	37	12.9	3.68	95	.231	.331	4	.154	-1	-1	-2	-1	-0.3
1975	Cin-N	4	1	.800	12	7	0	0	0	47	52	1	26	14	15.3	4.98	72	.284	.379	0	.000	-2	-7	-7	-1	-1.0
Total	2	8	4	.667	28	20	0	0	0	125^1	120	12	70	51	13.8	4.16	85	.252	.350	4	.100	-2	-8	-9	-2	-1.3

● KID CARSEY Carsey, Wilfred b: 10/22/1870, New York, N.Y. d: 3/29/60, Miami, Fla. BL/TR, 5'7", 168 lbs. Deb: 4/08/1891 ♦

YEAR	TM/L	W	L	PCT	G	GS	CG	SH	SV	IP	H	HR	BB	SO	RAT	ERA	ERA+	OAV	OOB	BH	AVG	PB	PR	/A	PD	TPI
1891	Was-a	14	37	.275	54	53	46	1	0	415	513	17	161	174	15.2	4.99	75	.294	.362	28	.150	-6	-58	-57	6	-4.6
1892	Phi-N	19	16	.543	43	36	30	1	1	317^2	320	6	104	76	12.4	3.12	104	.251	.314	20	.153	-3	6	5	2	0.3
1893	Phi-N	20	15	.571	39	35	30	1	0	318^1	375	7	124	50	14.6	4.81	95	.285	.355	27	.186	-8	-5	-8	2	-1.1
1894	Phi-N	18	12	.600	35	31	26	0	0	277	349	22	102	41	15.2	5.56	92	.304	.370	34	.272	3	-7	-14	2	-0.7
1895	Phi-N	24	16	.600	44	40	35	0	1	342^1	460	14	118	64	15.7	4.92	97	.317	.376	41	.291	3	-5	-5	-1	-0.3
1896	Phi-N	11	11	.500	27	21	18	1	1	187^1	273	4	72	36	17.0	5.62	77	.337	.397	18	.222	2	-26	-27	1	-2.0
1897	Phi-N	2	1	.667	4	4	2	0	0	28	35	0	16	1	16.7	5.14	82	.303	.393	3	.231	-1	-3	-3	-0	-0.3
	StL-N	3	8	.273	12	11	11	0	0	99	133	5	31	14	15.3	6.00	73	.319	.372	13	.302	2	-19	-18	1	-1.2
	Yr	5	9	.357	16	15	13	0	0	127	168	5	47	15	15.5	5.81	75	.315	.375	16	.286	2	-21	-20	1	-1.5
1898	StL-N	2	12	.143	20	13	10	0	0	123^2	177	2	37	10	16.3	6.33	60	.333	.387	21	.200	-0	-37	-35	2	-2.9
1899	Cle-N	1	8	.111	10	9	8	0	0	77^2	109	2	24	11	15.6	5.68	65	.330	.379	10	.278	1	-16	-17	1	-1.3
	Was-N	1	2	.333	4	3	2	0	0	29	27	0	4	3	9.9	3.72	105	.247	.280	0	.000	-2	0	1	1	-0.1
	Yr	2	10	.167	14	12	10	0	0	106^2	136	2	28	14	13.9	5.15	73	.308	.351	10	.213	-1	-15	-17	2	-1.4
1901	Bro-N	1	0	1.000	2	0	0	0	0	7	9	1	3	4	16.7	10.29	33	.310	.393	0	.000	-0	-5	-5	-0	-0.5
Total	10	116	138	.457	294	256	218	4	3	2222	2780	80	796	484	15.0	4.95	85	.300	.363	221	.213	-9	-175	-183	14	-14.7

● AL CARSON Carson, Albert James "Soldier" b: 8/22/1882, Chicago, Ill. d: 11/26/62, San Diego, Cal. TR , Deb: 5/06/10

YEAR	TM/L	W	L	PCT	G	GS	CG	SH	SV	IP	H	HR	BB	SO	RAT	ERA	ERA+	OAV	OOB	BH	AVG	PB	PR	/A	PD	TPI
1910	Chi-N	0	0	—	2	0	0	0	0	6^2	6	0	1	2	9.5	4.05	71	.240	.269	0	.000	0	-1	-1	0	-0.1

● ARNOLD CARTER Carter, Arnold Lee "Hook" or "Lefty" b: 3/14/18, Rainelle, W.Va. d: 4/12/89, Louisville, Ky. BL/TL, 5'10", 170 lbs. Deb: 4/29/44

YEAR	TM/L	W	L	PCT	G	GS	CG	SH	SV	IP	H	HR	BB	SO	RAT	ERA	ERA+	OAV	OOB	BH	AVG	PB	PR	/A	PD	TPI
1944	Cin-N	11	7	.611	33	18	9	3	3	148^2	143	1	40	33	11.3	2.60	134	.256	.309	12	.250	5	17	15	1	2.2
1945	Cin-N	2	4	.333	13	6	2	1	0	46^2	54	2	13	4	13.3	3.09	122	.286	.338	3	.176	0	4	3	0	0.4
Total	2	13	11	.542	46	24	11	4	3	195^1	197	3	53	37	11.7	2.72	131	.264	.317	15	.231	5	20	18	1	2.6

● NICK CARTER Carter, Conrad Powell b: 5/19/1879, Oatlands, Va. d: 11/23/61, Grasonville, Md. BL/TR, 5'8", 126 lbs. Deb: 4/14/08

YEAR	TM/L	W	L	PCT	G	GS	CG	SH	SV	IP	H	HR	BB	SO	RAT	ERA	ERA+	OAV	OOB	BH	AVG	PB	PR	/A	PD	TPI
1908	Phi-A	2	5	.286	14	5	2	0	0	60^2	58	1	17	17	11.4	2.97	86	.270	.329	2	.100	-2	-4	-3	1	-0.4

● JEFF CARTER Carter, Jeffrey Allen b: 12/3/64, Tampa, Fla. BR/TR, 6'3", 195 lbs. Deb: 7/31/91

YEAR	TM/L	W	L	PCT	G	GS	CG	SH	SV	IP	H	HR	BB	SO	RAT	ERA	ERA+	OAV	OOB	BH	AVG	PB	PR	/A	PD	TPI
1991	Chi-A	0	1	.000	5	2	0	0	0	12	8	1	5	2	9.8	5.25	76	.182	.265	0	—	0	-2	-2	-0	-0.2

● LARRY CARTER Carter, Larry Gene b: 5/22/65, Charleston, W.Va. BR/TR, 6'5", 195 lbs. Deb: 9/06/92

YEAR	TM/L	W	L	PCT	G	GS	CG	SH	SV	IP	H	HR	BB	SO	RAT	ERA	ERA+	OAV	OOB	BH	AVG	PB	PR	/A	PD	TPI
1992	SF-N	1	5	.167	6	6	0	0	0	33	34	6	18	21	14.2	4.64	72	.270	.361	2	.200	0	-4	-5	-1	-0.5

● PAUL CARTER Carter, Paul Warren "Nick" b: 5/1/1894, Lake Park, Ga. d: 9/11/84, Lake Park, Ga. BL/TR, 6'3", 175 lbs. Deb: 9/15/14

YEAR	TM/L	W	L	PCT	G	GS	CG	SH	SV	IP	H	HR	BB	SO	RAT	ERA	ERA+	OAV	OOB	BH	AVG	PB	PR	/A	PD	TPI
1914	Cle-A	1	3	.250	5	4	1	0	0	24^2	35	0	5	9	14.6	2.92	99	.340	.370	0	.000	-1	-0	-0	-0	-0.1
1915	Cle-A	1	1	.500	11	2	2	0	0	42	44	1	18	14	13.3	3.21	95	.272	.344	3	.214	1	-1	-1	1	0.0
1916	Chi-N	2	2	.500	8	5	2	0	0	36	26	1	17	14	10.8	2.75	106	.203	.297	2	.167	-0	-1	1	1	0.2
1917	Chi-N	5	8	.385	23	13	6	0	2	113^1	115	2	19	34	10.9	3.26	89	.276	.313	6	.171	-0	-7	-5	-1	-0.7
1918	Chi-N	3	2	.600	21	4	1	0	2	73	78	2	19	13	12.1	2.71	103	.290	.339	6	.240	0	0	1	2	0.3
1919	Chi-N	5	4	.556	28	7	2	0	1	85	81	1	28	17	11.8	2.65	109	.252	.316	7	.269	1	3	2	-0	0.3
1920	Chi-N	3	6	.333	31	8	2	0	2	106	131	3	36	14	14.6	4.67	69	.324	.387	6	.171	-1	-18	-17	-2	-2.0
Total	7	20	26	.435	127	43	16	0	7	480	510	10	142	115	12.4	3.32	89	.283	.339	30	.195	-1	-24	-19	1	-2.0

● SOL CARTER Carter, Solomon Mobley "Buck" b: 12/23/08, Picayune, Miss. BR/TR, 6', 178 lbs. Deb: 4/15/31

YEAR	TM/L	W	L	PCT	G	GS	CG	SH	SV	IP	H	HR	BB	SO	RAT	ERA	ERA+	OAV	OOB	BH	AVG	PB	PR	/A	PD	TPI
1931	Phi-A	0	0	—	2	0	0	0	0	2^1	1	0	4	1	19.3	19.29	23	.143	.455	0	—	0	-4	-4	1	-0.3

● BOB CARUTHERS Caruthers, Robert Lee "Parisian Bob" b: 1/5/1864, Memphis, Tenn. d: 8/5/11, Peoria, Ill. BL/TR, 5'7", 138 lbs. Deb: 9/07/1884 MU♦

YEAR	TM/L	W	L	PCT	G	GS	CG	SH	SV	IP	H	HR	BB	SO	RAT	ERA	ERA+	OAV	OOB	BH	AVG	PB	PR	/A	PD	TPI
1884	StL-a	7	2	.778	13	7	7	0	0	82^2	61	1	15	58	8.6	2.61	125	.189	.232	21	.256	2	6	6	-1	0.6
1885	*StL-a	**40**	13	**.755**	53	53	53	6	0	482^1	430	3	57	190	9.4	**2.07**	**158**	.230	.260	50	.225	7	**63**	**64**	0	6.7
1886	*StL-a	30	14	.682	44	43	42	2	0	387^1	323	3	86	166	9.7	2.32	148	.217	.263	106	.334	26	48	48	-2	6.8
1887	*StL-a	29	9	**.763**	39	39	39	2	0	341	337	6	61	74	10.9	3.30	138	.247	.287	130	.357	21	38	47	7	6.4
1888	Bro-a	29	15	.659	44	43	42	4	0	391^2	337	4	53	140	9.2	2.39	125	.224	.255	77	.230	10	29	26	1	3.5
1889	*Bro-a	**40**	11	**.784**	56	50	46	**7**	1	445	444	16	104	118	11.3	3.13	119	.252	.298	43	.250	17	35	29	2	4.2
1890	*Bro-N	23	11	.676	37	33	30	1	0	300	292	9	87	64	11.7	3.09	111	.247	.306	63	.265	11	16	12	3	2.3
1891	Bro-N	18	14	.563	38	32	29	2	1	297	323	7	107	69	13.4	3.12	106	.267	.333	48	.281	11	7	6	1	1.7
1892	StL-N	2	10	.167	16	10	10	0	1	101^2	131	10	27	21	14.5	5.84	55	.301	.350	142	.277	5	-29	-30	0	-2.2
Total	9	218	99	.688	340	310	298	24	3	2828^2	2678	59	597	900	10.7	2.83	123	.240	.285	694	.282	110	214	206	11	30.0

● CHUCK CARY Cary, Charles Douglas b: 3/3/60, Whittier, Cal. BL/TL, 6'4", 210 lbs. Deb: 8/22/85

YEAR	TM/L	W	L	PCT	G	GS	CG	SH	SV	IP	H	HR	BB	SO	RAT	ERA	ERA+	OAV	OOB	BH	AVG	PB	PR	/A	PD	TPI
1985	Det-A	0	1	.000	16	0	0	0	2	23^2	16	2	8	22	9.9	3.42	119	.190	.277	0	—	0	2	2	-0	0.2
1986	Det-A	1	2	.333	22	0	0	0	0	31^2	33	3	15	21	13.6	3.41	121	.273	.353	0	—	0	3	3	-0	0.2
1987	Atl-N	1	1	.500	13	0	0	0	1	16^2	17	3	4	15	11.9	3.78	115	.266	.319	0	.000	-0	1	1	0	0.1
1988	Atl-N	0	0	—	7	0	0	0	0	8^1	8	1	4	7	14.0	6.48	57	.250	.351	0	—	0	-3	-3	-0	-0.3
1989	NY-A	4	4	.500	22	11	2	0	0	99^1	78	13	29	79	9.7	3.26	119	.209	.266	0	—	0	7	7	-2	0.6

YEAR	TM/L	W	L	PCT	G	GS	CG	SH	SV	IP	H	HR	BB	SO	RAT	ERA	ERA+	OAV	OOB	BH	AVG	PB	PR	/A	PD	TPI
1990	NY-A	6	12	.333	28	27	2	0	0	156^{2}	155	21	55	134	12.1	4.19	95	.260	.323	0	—	0	-5	-4	-1	-0.5
1991	NY-A	1	6	.143	10	9	0	0	0	53^{1}	61	6	32	34	15.7	5.91	70	.285	.378	0	—	0	-11	-10	-0	-1.0
Total	7	13	26	.333	118	47	4	0	3	389^{2}	368	49	147	312	12.0	4.11	97	.248	.318	0	.000	-0	-7	-5	-4	-0.7
● **SCOTT CARY** Cary, Scott Russell "Red" b: 4/11/23, Kendallville, Ind. BL/TL, 5'11.5", 168 lbs. Deb: 5/01/47																										
1947	Was-A	3	1	.750	23	3	1	0	0	54^{2}	73	5	20	25	15.5	5.93	63	.312	.369	1	.077	-1	-13	-13	-1	-1.5
● **JERRY CASALE** Casale, Jerry Joseph b: 9/27/33, Brooklyn, N.Y. BR/TR, 6'2", 200 lbs. Deb: 9/14/9158																										
1958	Bos-A	0	0	—	2	0	0	0	0	3	1	0	2	3	9.0	0.00	—	.111	.273	0	—	0	1	1	0	0.1
1959	Bos-A	13	8	.619	31	26	9	3	0	179^{2}	162	20	89	93	12.8	4.31	94	.238	.331	10	.169	3	-9	-5	-4	-0.6
1960	Bos-A	2	9	.182	29	14	1	0	0	96^{1}	113	14	67	54	16.9	6.17	66	.294	.400	9	.273	3	-25	-23	-0	-2.0
1961	LA-A	1	5	.167	13	7	0	0	1	42^{2}	52	9	25	35	16.5	6.54	69	.297	.388	6	.462	4	-12	-10	-0	-0.6
	Det-A	0	0	—	3	1	0	0	0	12	15	3	3	6	13.5	5.25	78	.313	.353	0	.000	-0	-2	-2	0	-0.2
	Yr	1	5	.167	16	8	0	0	1	54^{2}	67	12	28	41	15.6	6.26	71	.298	.375	6	.375	3	-14	-11	-0	-0.8
1962	Det-A	1	2	.333	18	1	0	0	0	36^{2}	33	5	18	16	12.5	4.66	87	.236	.323	0	.000	-1	-3	-2	0	-0.3
Total	5	17	24	.415	96	49	10	3	1	370^{1}	376	51	204	207	14.3	5.08	81	.262	.356	25	.216	8	-49	-40	-5	-3.6
● **JOE CASCARELLA** Cascarella, Joseph Thomas "Crooning Joe" b: 6/28/07, Philadelphia, Pa. BR/TR, 5'10.5", 175 lbs. Deb: 4/17/34																										
1934	Phi-A	12	15	.444	42	22	9	2	1	194^{1}	214	8	104	71	14.9	4.68	94	.288	.377	6	.094	-4	-4	-6	2	-0.8
1935	Phi-A	1	6	.143	9	3	1	0	0	32^{1}	29	1	22	15	14.2	5.29	86	.252	.372	1	.125	-1	-3	-3	2	-0.2
	Bos-A	0	3	.000	6	4	0	0	0	17	25	3	11	9	19.1	6.88	69	.329	.414	0	.000	-0	-5	-4	0	-0.4
	Yr	1	9	.100	15	7	1	0	0	49^{1}	54	4	33	24	15.9	5.84	79	.283	.388	1	.100	-1	-8	-7	2	-0.6
1936	Bos-A	0	2	.000	10	1	0	0	0	20^{2}	27	0	9	7	15.7	6.97	76	.329	.396	0	.000	-1	-4	-4	0	-0.4
	Was-A	9	8	.529	22	16	7	1	1	139^{1}	147	7	54	34	13.4	4.07	117	.276	.349	7	.143	-2	15	11	-2	0.6
	Yr	9	10	.474	32	17	7	1	1	160	174	7	63	41	13.7	4.44	109	.283	.355	7	.132	-3	11	7	-2	0.2
1937	Was-A	0	5	.000	10	4	1	0	1	32^{1}	50	3	23	10	20.6	8.07	55	.347	.440	2	.222	-0	-12	-13	0	-1.1
	Cin-N	1	2	.333	11	3	2	0	1	43^{2}	44	1	22	16	13.6	3.92	95	.263	.349	1	.091	-1	-0	-1	-0	-0.2
1938	Cin-N	4	7	.364	33	1	0	0	4	61	66	2	22	30	13.0	4.57	80	.275	.336	3	.167	-1	-5	-6	-0	-0.7
Total	5	27	48	.360	143	54	20	3	8	540^{2}	602	25	267	192	14.6	4.84	91	.287	.370	20	.121	-9	-19	-26	1	-3.2
● **CHARLIE CASE** Case, Charles Emmett b: 9/7/1879, Smith Landing, O. d: 4/16/64, Clairmont, Ohio BR/TR, 6', 170 lbs. Deb: 7/05/01																										
1901	Cin-N	1	2	.333	3	3	3	0	0	27	34	0	6	5	13.3	4.67	69	.305	.341	1	.100	-1	-4	-4	-0	-0.5
1904	Pit-N	10	5	.667	18	17	14	3	0	141	129	0	31	49	10.5	2.94	93	.243	.290	9	.170	0	-3	-3	1	-0.2
1905	Pit-N	11	11	.500	31	24	18	3	1	217	202	2	66	57	11.7	2.57	117	.251	.319	7	.103	-2	10	10	-3	0.5
1906	Pit-N	1	1	.500	2	2	1	0	0	11	8	0	5	3	11.5	5.73	47	.190	.292	1	.500	1	-4	-4	0	-0.3
Total	4	23	19	.548	54	46	36	6	1	396	373	2	108	114	11.4	2.93	99	.250	.310	18	.135	-2	-0	-1	-3	-0.5
● **DAN CASEY** Casey, Daniel Maurice b: 11/20/1862, Binghamton, N.Y. d: 2/8/43, Washington, D.C. BR/TL, 6', 180 lbs. Deb: 8/18/1884 F																										
1884	Wil-U	1	1	.500	2	2	2	0	0	18	23	0	4	10	13.5	1.00	329	.291	.325	1	.167	-1	4	5	-0	0.4
1885	Det-N	4	8	.333	12	12	12	1	0	104	105	1	35	79	12.1	3.29	86	.256	.315	5	.116	-3	-5	-5	1	-0.7
1886	Phi-N	24	18	.571	44	44	39	4	0	369	326	8	104	193	10.5	2.41	137	.223	.275	23	.152	-5	37	36	-1	2.8
1887	Phi-N	28	13	.683	45	45	43	**4**	0	390^{1}	377	15	115	119	11.7	**2.86**	**148**	.246	.305	27	.165	-11	53	60	-2	4.0
1888	Phi-N	14	18	.438	33	33	31	2	0	285^{2}	298	6	48	108	11.1	3.15	94	.259	.291	18	.153	-3	-10	-6	1	-0.9
1889	Phi-N	6	10	.375	20	20	15	1	0	152^{2}	170	4	72	65	14.7	3.77	115	.273	.356	15	.221	-2	4	10	0	0.8
1890	Syr-a	19	22	.463	45	42	40	2	0	360^{2}	365	8	165	169	13.6	4.14	85	.255	.337	26	.162	-3	-11	-24	2	-2.1
Total	7	96	90	.516	201	198	182	14	0	1680^{1}	1664	42	543	743	12.0	3.18	113	.249	.309	115	.162	-26	72	76	1	4.3
● **HUGH CASEY** Casey, Hugh Thomas b: 10/14/13, Atlanta, Ga. d: 7/3/51, Atlanta, Ga. BR/TR, 6'1", 207 lbs. Deb: 4/29/35																										
1935	Chi-N	0	0	—	13	0	0	0	0	25^{2}	29	2	14	10	15.1	3.86	102	.279	.364	1	.167	-0	0	0	0	0.0
1939	Bro-N	15	10	.600	40	25	15	0	1	227^{1}	228	13	54	79	11.6	2.93	137	.260	.311	15	.203	0	25	28	2	3.1
1940	Bro-N	11	8	.579	44	10	5	2	2	154	136	13	51	53	11.3	3.62	110	.237	.306	9	.250	2	4	6	1	1.0
1941	*Bro-N	14	11	.560	45	18	4	1	7	162	155	8	57	61	11.8	3.89	94	.251	.316	6	.120	-1	-5	-4	2	-0.4
1942	Bro-N	6	3	.667	50	2	0	0	**13**	112	91	3	44	54	11.0	2.25	145	.221	.300	4	.148	-0	13	13	-1	1.3
1946	Bro-N	11	5	.688	46	1	0	0	5	99^{2}	101	2	33	31	12.3	1.99	170	.267	.329	3	.136	-1	**16**	**15**	3	1.9
1947	*Bro-N	10	4	.714	46	0	0	0	**18**	76^{2}	75	7	29	40	12.4	3.99	104	.260	.331	1	.056	-1	1	1	0	0.0
1948	Bro-N	3	0	1.000	22	0	0	0	4	36	59	6	17	7	19.5	8.00	50	.391	.459	0	.000	-1	-16	-16	-0	-1.6
1949	Pit-N	4	1	.800	33	0	0	0	5	38^{2}	50	4	14	9	15.1	4.66	90	.314	.374	1	.333	0	-3	-2	-2	-0.3
	NY-A	1	0	1.000	4	0	0	0	0	7^{2}	11	0	8	5	22.3	8.22	49	.324	.452	0	.000	-0	-3	-4	-0	-0.4
Total	9	75	42	.641	343	56	24	3	55	939^{2}	935	58	321	349	12.3	3.45	110	.260	.325	40	.164	-2	32	38	6	4.6
● **BILL CASEY** Casey, William B. b: St.Louis, Mo. Deb: 8/17/1887																										
1887	Phi-a	0	0	—	1	0	0	0	0	1	4	0	1	0	45.0	18.00	24	.667	.714	0	—	0	-2	-2	-0	-0.1
● **CARL CASHION** Cashion, Jay Carl b: 6/6/1891, Mecklenburg, N.C. d: 11/17/35, Lake Millicent, Wis. BL/TR, 6'2", 200 lbs. Deb: 8/04/11																										
1911	Was-A	1	5	.167	11	9	5	0	0	71^{1}	67	4	47	26	15.3	4.16	79	.220	.338	12	.324	2	-6	-7	1	-0.4
1912	Was-A	10	6	.625	26	17	13	1	1	170^{1}	150	4	103	84	13.6	3.17	105	.250	.365	22	.214	2	3	3	-1	0.5
1913	Was-A	1	1	.500	4	3	0	0	0	9	7	0	14	3	24.0	6.00	49	.269	.558	3	.250	0	-3	-3	0	-0.3
1914	Was-A	0	1	.000	2	1	0	0	0	5	4	0	6	1	19.8	10.80	26	.250	.478	0	.000	-0	-4	-4	0	-0.4
Total	4	12	13	.480	43	30	18	1	1	255^{2}	228	8	170	114	14.6	3.70	89	.241	.366	37	.242	5	-11	-11	1	-0.6
● **LARRY CASIAN** Casian, Lawrence Paul b: 10/28/65, Lynwood, Cal. BR/TL, 6', 170 lbs. Deb: 9/09/90																										
1990	Min-A	2	1	.667	5	3	0	0	0	22^{1}	26	2	4	11	12.1	3.22	129	.306	.337	0	—	0	2	2	-0	0.2
1991	Min-A	0	0	—	15	0	0	0	0	18^{1}	28	4	7	6	17.7	7.36	58	.354	.414	0	—	0	-7	-6	0	-0.9
1992	Min-A	1	0	1.000	6	0	0	0	0	6^{2}	7	0	1	2	10.8	2.70	149	.259	.286	0	—	0	1	1	0	-0.1
Total	3	3	1	.750	26	3	0	0	0	47^{1}	61	6	12	19	14.1	4.75	88	.319	.363	0	—	0	-4	-3	1	-0.8
● **CRAIG CASKEY** Caskey, Craig Douglas b: 12/11/49, Visalia, Cal. BB/TL, 5'11", 185 lbs. Deb: 7/19/73																										
1973	Mon-N	0	0	—	9	1	0	0	0	14^{1}	15	3	4	6	12.6	5.65	67	.278	.339	0	.000	-0	-3	-3	0	-0.3
● **ED CASSIAN** Cassian, Edwin b: Connecticut 5'8", 160 lbs. Deb: 6/26/1891																										
1891	Phi-N	1	3	.250	6	4	3	0	0	38	40	0	16	10	14.0	2.84	120	.260	.342	2	.118	-1	2	2	1	0.1
	Was-a	2	4	.333	7	5	5	0	0	53	73	4	35	14	19.2	5.60	67	.316	.417	9	.346	2	-11	-11	0	-0.7
Total	1	3	7	.300	13	9	8	0	0	91	113	4	51	24	17.0	4.45	81	.294	.388	11	.256	1	-9	-9	1	-0.6
● **JOHN CASSIDY** Cassidy, John P. b: 1857, Brooklyn, N.Y. d: 7/2/1891, Brooklyn, N.Y. BR/TL, 5'8", 168 lbs. Deb: 4/24/1875 ♦																										
1875	Atl-n	1	20	.048	30	22	18	0	0	214^{2}	278	6	12		12.2	*3.98*	58	.276	.284	29	.176	-2	-36	-40		-3.3
1877	Har-N	1	1	.500	2	2	2	0	0	18	24	0	1	2	12.5	5.00	49	.320	.329	95	.378	1	-4	-5	-0	-0.4
● **GEORGE CASTER** Caster, George Jasper "Ug" b: 8/4/07, Colton, Cal. d: 12/18/55, Lakewood, Cal. BR/TR, 6'1.5", 180 lbs. Deb: 9/10/34																										
1934	Phi-A	3	2	.600	5	3	2	0	0	37	32	3	14	15	11.9	3.41	129	.235	.320	4	.267	0	4	4	1	0.5
1935	Phi-A	1	4	.200	25	1	0	0	1	63^{1}	86	8	37	24	17.8	6.25	73	.322	.408	5	.227	0	-13	-12	2	-1.0
1937	Phi-A	12	19	.387	34	33	19	3	0	231^{2}	227	23	107	100	13.1	4.43	106	.258	.339	19	.211	-1	5	7	0	0.7
1938	Phi-A	16	20	.444	42	40	20	2	1	281^{1}	310	25	117	112	13.8	4.35	111	.277	.347	20	.198	1	14	15	-2	1.4
1939	Phi-A	9	9	.500	28	17	7	1	0	136	144	16	45	59	12.7	4.90	96	.276	.337	9	.209	-1	-4	-3	0	-0.3
1940	Phi-A	4	19	.174	36	24	11	0	2	178^{1}	234	18	69	75	15.4	6.56	68	.312	.372	8	.129	-3	-43	-42	-1	-4.1
1941	StL-A	3	7	.300	32	9	3	0	3	104^{1}	105	12	37	36	12.4	5.00	86	.259	.324	3	.103	-2	-10	-8	1	-0.9

YEAR	TM/L	W	L	PCT	G	GS	CG	SH	SV	IP	H	HR	BB	SO	RAT	ERA	ERA+	OAV	OOB	BH	AVG	PB	PR	/A	PD	TPI
1942	StL-A	8	2	.800	39	0	0	0	5	80	62	3	39	34	11.7	2.81	132	.217	.317	1	.067	-1	8	8	1	0.8
1943	StL-A	6	8	.429	35	0	0	0	8	76^1	69	4	41	43	13.1	2.12	157	.246	.345	3	.136	-1	10	10	0	1.1
1944	StL-A	6	6	.500	42	0	0	0	**12**	81	91	5	33	46	13.8	2.44	147	.284	.351	5	.250	0	9	10	-0	1.1
1945	StL-A	1	2	.333	10	0	0	0	1	15^2	20	0	7	9	15.5	6.89	51	.308	.375	1	.333	0	-6	-6	-0	-0.6
	*Det-A	5	1	.833	22	0	0	0	2	51^1	47	3	27	23	13.3	3.86	91	.250	.350	2	.182	0	-3	-2	-0	-0.2
	Yr	6	3	.667	32	0	0	0	3	67	67	3	34	32	13.8	4.57	77	.265	.356	3	.214	0	-9	-8	-0	-0.8
1946	Det-A	2	1	.667	26	0	0	0	4	41^1	42	1	24	19	14.6	5.66	65	.264	.364	1	.143	-0	-10	-9	1	-0.9
Total	12	76	100	.432	376	127	62	6	39	1377^2	1469	121	597	595	13.7	4.54	96	.273	.349	81	.184	-7	-39	-27	2	-2.4
● TONY CASTILLO Castillo, Antonio Jose (Jimenez) b: 3/1/63, Quibor, Venez. BL/TL, 5'10", 177 lbs. Deb: 8/14/88																										
1988	Tor-A	1	0	1.000	14	0	0	0	0	15	10	2	2	14	7.2	3.00	131	.200	.231	0	—	0	2	2	0	0.1
1989	Tor-A	1	1	.500	17	0	0	0	1	17^2	23	0	10	10	17.3	6.11	62	.333	.425	0	—	0	-4	-5	-0	-0.3
	Atl-N	0	1	.000	12	0	0	0	0	9^1	8	0	4	5	11.6	4.82	76	.222	.300	0	.000	-0	-1	-1	0	-0.1
1990	Atl-N	5	1	.833	52	3	0	0	1	76^2	93	5	20	64	13.4	4.23	95	.302	.347	1	.143	0	-4	-2	1	-0.1
1991	Atl-N	1	1	.500	7	0	0	0	0	8^2	13	3	5	8	18.7	7.27	53	.342	.419	0	—	0	-3	-3	-0	-0.3
	NY-N	1	0	1.000	10	3	0	0	0	23^2	27	1	6	10	12.5	1.90	191	.281	.324	0	.000	-0	5	5	1	0.5
	Yr	2	1	.667	17	3	0	0	0	32^1	40	4	11	18	14.2	3.34	111	.299	.352	0	.000	-0	1	1	0	0.2
Total	4	9	4	.692	112	6	0	0	2	151	174	11	47	111	13.3	4.17	93	.291	.345	1	.083	-0	-7	-5	1	-0.2
● MANNY CASTILLO Castillo, Esteban Manuel Antonio (Cabrera) b: 4/1/57, Santo Domingo, D.R. BB/TR, 5'9", 160 lbs. Deb: 9/01/80 ♦																										
1983	Sea-A	0	0	—	1	0	0	0	0	2^2	8	3	3	2	40.5	23.63	18	.533	.632	42	.207	1	-6	-6	-0	-0.5
● FRANK CASTILLO Castillo, Frank Anthony b: 4/1/69, ElPaso, Tex. BR/TR, 6'1", 180 lbs. Deb: 6/27/91																										
1991	Chi-N	6	7	.462	18	18	4	0	0	111^2	107	5	33	73	11.3	4.35	89	.252	.306	5	.143	-0	-8	-6	-0	-0.7
1992	Chi-N	10	11	.476	33	33	0	0	0	205^1	179	19	63	135	10.9	3.46	104	.232	.295	6	.092	-2	1	3	-1	0.0
Total	2	16	18	.471	51	51	4	0	0	317	286	24	96	208	11.0	3.78	98	.239	.299	11	.110	-3	-7	-3	-1	-0.7
● BOBBY CASTILLO Castillo, Robert Ernie b: 4/18/55, Los Angeles, Cal. BR/TR, 5'10", 170 lbs. Deb: 9/10/77																										
1977	LA-N	1	0	1.000	6	1	0	0	0	11^1	12	2	2	7	11.1	3.97	96	.279	.311	0	.000	-0	-0	-0	0	0.0
1978	LA-N	0	4	.000	18	0	0	0	1	34	28	2	33	30	16.1	3.97	88	.239	.407	0	.000	-1	-1	-2	0	-0.3
1979	LA-N	2	0	1.000	19	0	0	0	7	24^1	26	0	13	25	14.8	1.11	328	.277	.370	0	.000	-0	7	7	0	0.7
1980	LA-N	8	6	.571	61	0	0	0	5	98^1	70	4	45	60	10.6	2.75	127	.206	.301	1	.111	-0	9	8	1	0.9
1981	*LA-N	2	4	.333	34	1	0	0	5	50^2	50	5	24	35	13.1	5.33	62	.262	.344	4	.444	2	-10	-11	-1	-1.1
1982	Min-A	13	11	.542	40	25	6	1	0	218^2	194	26	85	123	11.5	3.66	116	.241	.313	0	—	0	10	14	-2	1.2
1983	Min-A	8	12	.400	27	25	3	0	0	158^1	170	17	65	90	13.4	4.77	89	.278	.348	0	—	0	-13	-9	1	-0.9
1984	Min-A	2	1	.667	10	2	0	0	0	25^1	14	2	19	7	11.7	1.78	237	.177	.337	0	—	0	6	7	-0	0.6
1985	*LA-N	2	2	.500	35	5	0	0	0	68	59	9	41	57	13.4	5.43	64	.230	.339	1	.100	-0	-14	-15	0	-1.5
Total	9	38	40	.487	250	59	9	1	18	689	623	67	327	434	12.5	3.94	99	.246	.333	6	.154	0	-6	-2	-1	-0.4
● SLICK CASTLEMAN Castleman, Clydell b: 9/8/13, Donelson, Tenn. BR/TR, 6', 185 lbs. Deb: 5/09/34																										
1934	NY-N	1	0	1.000	7	1	0	0	0	16^2	18	1	10	5	15.1	5.40	72	.277	.373	1	.250	1	-2	-3	1	-0.2
1935	NY-N	15	6	.714	29	25	9	1	0	173^2	186	14	64	64	13.0	4.09	94	.268	.330	12	.179	-0	-1	-5	1	-0.4
1936	*NY-N	4	7	.364	29	12	2	1	1	111^2	148	6	56	54	16.8	5.64	69	.323	.403	5	.128	-1	-20	-22	1	-2.1
1937	NY-N	11	6	.647	23	23	10	2	0	160^1	148	19	33	78	10.2	3.31	117	.247	.287	4	.070	-5	11	10	-3	0.3
1938	NY-N	4	5	.444	21	14	4	0	0	90^2	108	4	37	18	14.7	4.17	90	.296	.365	3	.097	-2	-4	-4	-1	-0.7
1939	NY-N	1	2	.333	12	4	0	0	0	33^2	36	1	23	6	15.8	4.54	86	.286	.396	3	.333	1	-2	-2	-1	-0.2
Total	6	36	26	.581	121	79	25	4	1	586^2	644	45	223	225	13.4	4.25	91	.279	.345	28	.135	-6	-19	-25	-2	-3.3
● ROY CASTLETON Castleton, Royal Eugene b: 7/26/1885, Salt Lake City, Utah d: 6/24/67, Los Angeles, Cal. BR/TL, 5'11", 167 lbs. Deb: 4/16/07																										
1907	NY-A	1	1	.500	3	2	1	0	0	16	11	1	3	3	7.9	2.81	100	.196	.237	0	.000	-1	-0	-0	-0	-0.1
1909	Cin-N	1	1	.500	4	1	1	0	0	14	14	0	6	5	14.1	1.93	135	.275	.373	2	.667	1	1	1	0	0.3
1910	Cin-N	1	2	.333	4	2	1	0	0	13^2	15	0	6	5	14.5	3.29	89	.288	.373	0	.000	-1	-0	-1	0	-0.1
Total	3	3	4	.429	11	5	3	0	0	43^2	40	1	15	13	12.0	2.68	104	.252	.328	2	.154	-0	0	0	0	0.1
● PAUL CASTNER Castner, Paul Henry "Lefty" b: 2/16/1897, St.Paul, Minn. d: 3/3/86, St.Paul, Minn. BL/TL, 5'11", 187 lbs. Deb: 8/06/23																										
1923	Chi-A	0	0	—	6	0	0	0	0	10	14	0	5	0	17.1	6.30	63	.326	.396	0	.000	-0	-3	-3	0	-0.3
● BILL CASTRO Castro, William Radhames (Checo) b: 12/13/53, Santiago, D.R. BR/TR, 5'11", 170 lbs. Deb: 8/20/74 C																										
1974	Mil-A	0	0	—	8	0	0	0	0	18	19	2	5	10	12.0	4.50	80	.264	.312	0	—	0	-2	-2	0	-0.2
1975	Mil-A	3	2	.600	18	5	0	0	1	75	78	3	17	25	11.6	2.52	152	.271	.316	0	—	0	10	11	0	1.2
1976	Mil-A	4	6	.400	39	0	0	0	8	70^1	70	4	19	23	11.8	3.45	101	.265	.322	0	—	0	1	0	-0	0.1
1977	Mil-A	8	6	.571	51	0	0	0	13	69^1	76	7	23	28	13.1	4.15	98	.293	.356	0	—	0	-1	-1	1	0.0
1978	Mil-A	5	4	.556	42	0	0	0	8	49^2	43	2	14	17	11.4	1.81	207	.234	.309	0	—	0	11	11	0	1.2
1979	Mil-A	3	1	.750	39	0	0	0	6	44^1	40	2	13	10	10.8	2.03	205	.244	.299	0	—	0	11	11	-0	1.0
1980	Mil-A	2	4	.333	56	0	0	0	8	84^1	89	2	17	32	11.5	2.77	139	.274	.314	0	—	0	12	10	1	1.3
1981	NY-A	1	1	.500	11	0	0	0	0	19	26	2	5	4	14.7	3.79	94	.329	.369	0	—	0	-0	-0	-0	0.0
1982	KC-A	3	2	.600	21	4	0	0	1	75^2	72	8	20	37	11.2	3.45	118	.243	.296	0	—	0	5	5	-1	0.4
1983	KC-A	2	0	1.000	18	0	0	0	0	40^2	51	4	12	17	15.0	6.64	61	.300	.364	0	—	0	-12	-12	0	-1.1
Total	10	31	26	.544	303	9	0	0	45	546^1	564	36	145	203	12.0	3.33	117	.268	.322	0	—	0	35	34	0	3.9
● ELI CATES Cates, Eli Eldo b: 1/26/1877, Greensfork, Ind. d: 5/29/64, Richmond, Ind. BR/TR, 5'9.5", 175 lbs. Deb: 4/20/08 ♦																										
1908	Was-A	4	8	.333	19	10	7	0	0	114^2	112	3	32	33	11.4	2.51	91	.261	.314	11	.186	1	-1	-3	1	0.0
● TED CATHER Cather, Theodore P b: 5/20/1889, Chester, Pa. d: 4/9/45, Elkton, Md. BR/TR, 5'10.5", 178 lbs. Deb: 9/23/12 ♦																										
1913	StL-N	0	0	—	1	0	0	0	0	0^1	1	0	2	0	108.0	54.00	6	.500	.800	39	.213	0	-2	-2	0	-0.2
● HARDIN CATHEY Cathey, Hardin "Lil Abner" b: 7/6/19, Burns, Tenn. BR/TR, 6'4", 190 lbs. Deb: 4/16/42																										
1942	Was-A	1	1	.500	12	2	0	0	0	30^1	44	1	16	8	17.8	7.42	49	.341	.414	3	.375	1	-13	-13	-0	-1.2
● KEEFE CATO Cato, John Keefe b: 5/6/58, Yonkers, N.Y. BR/TR, 6'1", 185 lbs. Deb: 6/13/83																										
1983	Cin-N	1	0	1.000	4	0	0	0	0	3^2	2	0	1	3	7.4	2.45	155	.154	.214	0	—	0	0	1	-0	0.0
1984	Cin-N	0	1	.000	8	0	0	0	1	15^2	22	5	4	12	14.9	8.04	47	.344	.382	2	.500	1	-8	-7	0	-0.6
Total	2	1	1	.500	12	0	0	0	1	19^1	24	5	5	15	13.5	6.98	54	.312	.354	2	.500	1	-7	-7	0	-0.6
● JOHN CATTANACH Cattanach, John Leckie b: 5/10/1863, Providence, R.I. d: 11/10/26, Providence, R.I. 5'10", 190 lbs. Deb: 6/05/1884																										
1884	Pro-N	0	0	—	1	1	0	0	0	5	2	0	4	2	10.8	9.00	31	.100	.250	0	.000	-1	-3	-3	-0	-0.3
	StL-U	1	1	.500	2	2	2	0	0	17	12	0	4	13	8.5	2.12	140	.185	.232	0	.000	-1	2	2	0	0.0
Total	1	1	1	.500	3	3	2	0	0	22	14	0	8	15	9.0	3.68	80	.165	.237	0	.000	-2	-2	-2	-0	-0.3
● BILL CAUDILL Caudill, William Holland b: 7/13/56, Santa Monica, Cal. BR/TR, 6'1", 210 lbs. Deb: 5/12/79																										
1979	Chi-N	1	7	.125	29	12	0	0	0	90	89	16	41	104	13.4	4.80	86	.255	.340	1	.059	-2	-11	-7	1	-0.8
1980	Chi-N	4	6	.400	72	2	0	0	1	127^2	100	10	59	112	11.3	2.19	179	.223	.314	2	.222	0	20	**25**	-1	2.6
1981	Chi-N	1	5	.167	30	10	0	0	0	71	87	9	31	45	15.2	5.83	63	.301	.373	2	.143	0	-18	-17	-1	-1.8
1982	Sea-A	12	9	.571	70	0	0	0	26	95^2	65	9	35	111	9.5	2.35	180	.192	.270	0	—	0	18	20	-1	1.8
1983	Sea-A	2	8	.200	63	0	0	0	26	72^2	70	10	38	73	13.6	4.71	90	.257	.353	0	—	0	-5	-4	-1	-0.7
1984	Oak-A★	9	7	.563	68	0	0	0	36	96^1	77	9	31	89	10.1	2.71	138	.218	.281	0	.000	0	14	11	-2	1.0

YEAR	TM/L	W	L	PCT	G	GS	CG	SH	SV	IP	H	HR	BB	SO	RAT	ERA	ERA+	OAV	OOB	BH	AVG	PB	PR	/A	PD	TPI
1985	Tor-A	4	6	.400	67	0	0	0	14	69^1	53	9	35	46	11.7	2.99	141	.209	.310	0	—	0	9	9	-1	0.8
1986	Tor-A	2	4	.333	40	0	0	0	2	36^1	36	6	17	32	13.6	6.19	68	.254	.342	0	—	0	-8	-8	-1	-0.9
1987	Oak-A	0	0	—	6	0	0	0	1	8	10	3	1	8	12.4	9.00	46	.294	.314	0	—	0	-4	-4	-0	-0.2
Total	9	35	52	.402	445	24	0	0	106	667	587	81	288	620	12.0	3.68	110	.237	.320	5	.122	-1	14	26	-7	1.8

● RED CAUSEY Causey, Cecil Algernon b: 8/11/1893, Georgetown, Fla. d: 11/11/60, Avon Park, Fla. BR/TR, 6'1", 160 lbs. Deb: 4/26/18

YEAR	TM/L	W	L	PCT	G	GS	CG	SH	SV	IP	H	HR	BB	SO	RAT	ERA	ERA+	OAV	OOB	BH	AVG	PB	PR	/A	PD	TPI
1918	NY-N	11	6	.647	29	18	10	2	2	158^1	143	2	42	48	10.9	2.79	94	.245	.304	6	.125	-3	-0	-3	-1	-0.7
1919	NY-N	9	3	.750	19	16	6	0	0	105	99	5	38	25	11.9	3.69	76	.251	.320	5	.132	-1	-9	-10	-1	-1.3
	Bos-N	4	5	.444	10	10	3	0	0	69	81	1	20	14	13.3	4.57	63	.308	.359	2	.095	-2	-13	-13	0	-1.5
	Yr	13	8	.619	29	26	9	0	0	174	180	6	58	39	12.4	4.03	70	.273	.333	7	.119	-3	-22	-23	-1	-2.8
1920	Phi-N	7	14	.333	35	26	11	1	3	181^1	203	4	79	30	14.2	4.32	79	.299	.376	11	.186	-2	-24	-18	-2	-2.3
1921	Phi-N	3	3	.500	7	7	4	0	0	50^2	58	4	11	8	12.4	2.84	149	.294	.335	3	.150	-1	5	8	-0	0.7
	NY-N	1	1	.500	7	1	0	0	0	14^2	13	0	6	1	11.7	2.45	149	.228	.302	1	.333	0	2	2	-0	0.2
	Yr	4	4	.500	14	8	4	0	0	65^1	71	4	17	9	12.1	2.76	149	.278	.324	4	.174	-1	7	10	-0	0.9
1922	NY-N	4	3	.571	24	2	1	0	1	70^2	69	2	34	13	13.1	3.18	126	.262	.347	5	.238	-0	7	6	1	0.7
Total	5	39	35	.527	131	80	35	3	6	649^2	666	18	230	139	12.6	3.59	89	.273	.340	33	.157	-9	-31	-29	-3	-4.2

● PUG CAVET Cavet, Tiller H. b: 12/26/1889, McGregor, Tex. d: 8/4/66, San Luis Obispo, Cal. BL/TL, 6'3", 176 lbs. Deb: 4/25/11

YEAR	TM/L	W	L	PCT	G	GS	CG	SH	SV	IP	H	HR	BB	SO	RAT	ERA	ERA+	OAV	OOB	BH	AVG	PB	PR	/A	PD	TPI
1911	Det-A	0	0	—	1	1	0	0	0	4	6	0	1	1	15.8	4.50	77	.316	.350	0	.000	-0	-1	-0	-0	-0.1
1914	Det-A	7	7	.500	31	14	6	1	2	151^1	129	2	44	51	10.8	2.44	115	.238	.306	5	.106	-2	5	6	1	0.6
1915	Det-A	4	2	.667	17	7	2	0	1	71	83	1	22	26	13.6	4.06	75	.300	.355	6	.250	2	-9	-8	-0	-0.7
Total	3	11	9	.550	49	22	8	1	3	226^1	218	3	67	78	11.8	2.98	97	.260	.323	11	.153	-0	-4	-2	1	-0.2

● JOSE CECENA Cecena, Jose Isabel (Lugo) b: 8/20/63, Ciudad Obregon, Mexico BR/TR, 5'11", 180 lbs. Deb: 4/06/88

YEAR	TM/L	W	L	PCT	G	GS	CG	SH	SV	IP	H	HR	BB	SO	RAT	ERA	ERA+	OAV	OOB	BH	AVG	PB	PR	/A	PD	TPI
1988	Tex-A	0	0	—	22	0	0	0	1	26^1	20	2	23	27	15.4	4.78	85	.213	.378	0	—	0	-2	-2	-0	-0.3

● ART CECCARELLI Ceccarelli, Arthur Edward "Chic" b: 4/2/30, New Haven, Conn. BR/TL, 6', 190 lbs. Deb: 5/03/55

YEAR	TM/L	W	L	PCT	G	GS	CG	SH	SV	IP	H	HR	BB	SO	RAT	ERA	ERA+	OAV	OOB	BH	AVG	PB	PR	/A	PD	TPI
1955	KC-A	4	7	.364	31	16	3	1	0	123^2	123	20	71	68	14.1	5.31	79	.258	.354	3	.079	-3	-19	-16	-2	-2.0
1956	KC-A	0	1	.000	3	2	0	0	0	10	13	3	4	2	16.2	7.20	60	.317	.391	0	.000	-0	-3	-3	1	-0.3
1957	Bal-A	0	5	.000	20	8	1	0	0	58	62	3	31	30	14.7	4.50	80	.278	.371	0	.000	-1	-5	-6	-1	-0.8
1959	Chi-N	5	5	.500	18	15	4	2	0	102	95	19	37	56	11.7	4.76	83	.245	.312	3	.091	-1	-9	-9	-1	-1.1
1960	Chi-N	0	0	—	7	1	0	0	0	13	16	1	4	10	13.8	5.54	68	.296	.345	0	—	0	-3	-3	-0	-0.3
Total	5	9	18	.333	79	42	8	3	0	306^2	309	46	147	166	13.5	5.05	79	.261	.345	6	.068	-6	-38	-37	-3	-4.5

● REX CECIL Cecil, Rex Rolston b: 10/8/16, Lindsay, Okla. d: 10/30/66, Long Beach, Cal. BL/TR, 6'3", 195 lbs. Deb: 8/13/44

YEAR	TM/L	W	L	PCT	G	GS	CG	SH	SV	IP	H	HR	BB	SO	RAT	ERA	ERA+	OAV	OOB	BH	AVG	PB	PR	/A	PD	TPI
1944	Bos-A	4	5	.444	11	9	4	0	0	61	72	5	33	33	15.6	5.16	66	.286	.371	5	.278	1	-12	-12	-0	-1.1
1945	Bos-A	2	5	.286	7	7	1	0	0	45	46	4	27	30	14.6	5.20	66	.261	.360	6	.300	1	-9	-9	1	-0.7
Total	2	6	10	.375	18	16	5	0	0	106	118	9	60	63	15.2	5.18	66	.276	.366	11	.289	2	-21	-21	1	-1.8

● PETE CENTER Center, Marvin Earl b: 4/22/12, Hazel Green, Ky. BR/TR, 6'4", 190 lbs. Deb: 9/11/42

YEAR	TM/L	W	L	PCT	G	GS	CG	SH	SV	IP	H	HR	BB	SO	RAT	ERA	ERA+	OAV	OOB	BH	AVG	PB	PR	/A	PD	TPI
1942	Cle-A	0	0	—	1	0	0	0	0	3^1	7	0	4	0	32.4	16.20	21	.438	.571	0	.000	-0	-5	-5	-0	-0.4
1943	Cle-A	1	2	.333	24	1	0	0	1	42^1	29	3	18	10	10.0	2.76	112	.201	.290	0	.000	-1	3	2	-1	0.1
1945	Cle-A	6	3	.667	31	8	2	0	1	85^2	89	2	28	34	12.4	3.99	81	.270	.329	2	.091	-2	-6	-7	-2	-1.1
1946	Cle-A	0	2	.000	21	0	0	0	1	29	29	2	20	6	15.5	4.97	67	.269	.388	0	.000	-0	-5	-5	-0	-0.6
Total	4	7	7	.500	77	9	2	0	3	160^1	154	7	70	50	12.7	4.10	79	.258	.338	2	.065	-3	-13	-16	-3	-2.0

● RICK CERONE Cerone, Richard Aldo b: 5/19/54, Newark, N.J. BR/TR, 5'11", 192 lbs. Deb: 8/17/75 ♦

YEAR	TM/L	W	L	PCT	G	GS	CG	SH	SV	IP	H	HR	BB	SO	RAT	ERA	ERA+	OAV	OOB	BH	AVG	PB	PR	/A	PD	TPI
1987	NY-A	0	0	—	2	0	0	0	0	2	0	0	1	1	4.5	0.00	—	.000	.143	69	.243	1	1	1	-0	0.1

● JOHN CERUTTI Cerutti, John Joseph b: 4/28/60, Albany, N.Y. BL/TL, 6'2", 200 lbs. Deb: 9/01/85

YEAR	TM/L	W	L	PCT	G	GS	CG	SH	SV	IP	H	HR	BB	SO	RAT	ERA	ERA+	OAV	OOB	BH	AVG	PB	PR	/A	PD	TPI
1985	Tor-A	0	2	.000	4	1	0	0	0	6^2	10	1	4	5	20.3	5.40	78	.323	.417	0	—	0	-1	-1	0	-0.1
1986	Tor-A	9	4	.692	34	20	2	1	1	145^1	150	25	47	89	12.3	4.15	102	.268	.326	0	—	0	0	1	0	0.1
1987	Tor-A	11	4	.733	44	21	2	0	0	151^1	144	30	59	92	12.1	4.40	102	.251	.322	0	—	0	1	2	-2	-0.1
1988	Tor-A	6	7	.462	46	12	0	0	1	123^2	120	12	42	65	12.0	3.13	126	.256	.322	0	—	0	11	11	3	1.4
1989	*Tor-A	11	11	.500	33	31	3	1	0	205^1	214	19	53	69	12.0	3.07	123	.273	.323	0	—	0	19	16	3	2.1
1990	Tor-A	9	9	.500	30	23	0	0	0	140	162	23	49	49	13.8	4.76	83	.297	.359	0	—	0	-13	-13	-0	-1.3
1991	Det-A	3	6	.333	38	8	1	0	2	88^2	94	9	37	29	13.5	4.57	91	.276	.351	0	—	0	-5	-4	1	-0.4
Total	7	49	43	.533	229	116	8	2	4	861	894	119	291	398	12.6	3.94	103	.271	.333	0	—	0	13	12	4	1.7

● RAY CHADWICK Chadwick, Ray Charles b: 11/17/62, Durham, N.C. BB/TR, 6'2", 180 lbs. Deb: 7/29/86

YEAR	TM/L	W	L	PCT	G	GS	CG	SH	SV	IP	H	HR	BB	SO	RAT	ERA	ERA+	OAV	OOB	BH	AVG	PB	PR	/A	PD	TPI
1986	Cal-A	0	5	.000	7	7	0	0	0	27^1	39	5	15	9	18.1	7.24	57	.336	.417	0	—	0	-9	-10	0	-0.8

● LEON CHAGNON Chagnon, Leon Wilbur "Shag" b: 9/28/02, Pittsfield, N.H. d: 7/30/53, Amesbury, Mass. BR/TR, 6', 182 lbs. Deb: 10/05/29

YEAR	TM/L	W	L	PCT	G	GS	CG	SH	SV	IP	H	HR	BB	SO	RAT	ERA	ERA+	OAV	OOB	BH	AVG	PB	PR	/A	PD	TPI
1929	Pit-N	0	0	—	1	1	0	0	0	7	11	1	1	4	15.4	9.00	53	.333	.353	0	.000	-0	-3	-3	0	-0.3
1930	Pit-N	0	3	.000	18	4	3	0	0	62	92	9	23	27	17.4	6.82	73	.355	.418	4	.200	-1	-13	-13	0	-1.1
1932	Pit-N	9	6	.600	30	10	4	1	0	128	140	10	34	52	12.4	3.94	97	.276	.324	9	.225	2	-1	-2	-2	-0.1
1933	Pit-N	6	4	.600	39	5	1	0	1	100	100	2	17	35	10.8	3.69	90	.259	.296	1	.048	-2	-4	-4	-1	-0.7
1934	Pit-N	4	1	.800	33	1	0	0	1	58	68	5	24	19	14.4	4.81	86	.288	.356	3	.231	0	-5	-4	1	-0.3
1935	NY-N	0	2	.000	14	1	0	0	1	38^1	32	7	5	16	8.7	3.52	109	.232	.259	0	.000	-1	2	1	0	0.0
Total	6	19	16	.543	135	22	8	1	3	393^1	443	34	104	153	12.8	4.51	87	.284	.333	17	.162	-2	-24	-25	-1	-2.5

● BOB CHAKALES Chakales, Robert Edward "Chick" b: 8/10/27, Asheville, N.C. BR/TR, 6'1", 185 lbs. Deb: 4/21/51

YEAR	TM/L	W	L	PCT	G	GS	CG	SH	SV	IP	H	HR	BB	SO	RAT	ERA	ERA+	OAV	OOB	BH	AVG	PB	PR	/A	PD	TPI
1951	Cle-A	3	4	.429	17	10	2	1	0	68^1	80	3	43	32	16.2	4.74	80	.292	.388	7	.350	2	-5	-7	-0	-0.5
1952	Cle-A	1	2	.333	5	1	0	0	0	12	19	2	8	7	20.3	9.75	34	.388	.474	2	.500	1	-8	-9	-1	-0.8
1953	Cle-A	0	2	.000	7	3	1	0	0	27	28	2	10	6	13.0	2.67	141	.283	.355	2	.286	0	4	3	0	0.4
1954	Cle-A	2	0	1.000	3	0	0	0	0	10^1	4	0	12	3	13.9	0.87	422	.114	.340	1	.333	1	3	3	-0	0.4
	Bal-A	3	7	.300	38	6	0	0	3	89^1	81	8	43	44	12.6	3.73	96	.245	.333	8	.364	2	-0	-1	0	0.1
	Yr	5	7	.417	41	6	0	0	3	99^2	85	8	55	47	12.7	3.43	105	.232	.334	9	.360	3	3	2	-0	0.5
1955	Chi-A	0	0	—	7	0	0	0	0	12^1	11	2	6	6	12.4	1.46	271	.256	.347	0	.000	-0	3	3	0	0.3
	Was-A	2	3	.400	29	0	0	0	0	54^2	55	4	25	28	13.3	5.27	73	.263	.345	0	.000	-1	-8	-9	1	-0.9
	Yr	2	3	.400	36	0	0	0	0	67	66	6	31	34	13.2	4.57	84	.262	.345	0	.000	-1	-5	-5	1	-0.6
1956	Was-A	4	4	.500	43	1	0	0	4	96	94	3	57	33	14.4	4.03	107	.268	.375	3	.150	-1	1	3	1	0.3
1957	Was-A	0	1	.000	4	2	0	0	0	18^1	20	2	10	12	14.7	5.40	72	.274	.361	1	.143	0	-3	-3	0	-0.2
	Bos-A	0	2	.000	18	0	0	0	3	32	53	5	11	16	18.3	8.16	49	.379	.428	2	.667	1	-16	-15	-1	-1.4
	Yr	0	3	.000	22	2	0	0	3	50^1	73	7	21	28	17.0	7.15	55	.341	.403	3	.300	1	-19	-18	-0	-1.6
Total	7	15	25	.375	171	23	3	1	10	420^1	445	31	225	187	14.5	4.54	85	.277	.369	26	.271	4	-28	-31	1	-2.3

● GEORGE CHALMERS Chalmers, George W. "Dut" b: 6/7/1888, Edinburgh, Scot. d: 8/5/60, Bronx, N.Y. BR/TR, 6'1", 189 lbs. Deb: 9/21/10

YEAR	TM/L	W	L	PCT	G	GS	CG	SH	SV	IP	H	HR	BB	SO	RAT	ERA	ERA+	OAV	OOB	BH	AVG	PB	PR	/A	PD	TPI
1910	Phi-N	1	1	.500	4	3	2	0	0	22	21	0	11	12	13.5	5.32	59	.280	.379	1	.143	-0	-6	-5	1	-0.4
1911	Phi-N	13	10	.565	38	22	11	3	4	208^2	196	5	101	101	13.0	3.11	111	.256	.346	13	.178	-1	7	8	-1	0.6
1912	Phi-N	3	4	.429	12	8	3	0	0	57^2	64	4	37	22	16.1	3.28	111	.296	.404	3	.188	-0	1	2	-2	0.0
1913	Phi-N	3	10	.231	26	13	4	0	1	116	133	3	51	46	14.7	4.81	69	.296	.374	7	.212	-1	-21	-19	1	-1.9
1914	Phi-N	0	3	.000	3	2	1	0	0	18	23	0	15	6	19.5	5.50	53	.324	.448	0	.000	-1	-5	-5	0	-0.6
1915	*Phi-N	8	9	.471	26	20	13	1	1	170^1	159	3	45	82	10.8	2.48	110	.255	.305	10	.169	-0	5	5	1	0.5
1916	Phi-N	1	4	.200	12	8	2	0	0	53^2	49	2	19	21	11.7	3.19	83	.244	.315	0	.000	-2	-3	-3	0	-0.6
Total	7	29	41	.414	121	76	36	4	6	646^1	645	17	279	290	13.1	3.41	93	.269	.348	34	.163	-5	-22	-18	1	-2.4

YEAR TM/L	W	L	PCT	G	GS	CG	SH	SV	IP	H	HR	BB	SO	RAT	ERA	ERA+	OAV	OOB	BH	AVG	PB	PR	/A	PD	TPI
● **CRAIG CHAMBERLAIN** Chamberlain, Craig Philip b: 2/2/57, Hollywood, Cal. BR/TR, 6'1", 190 lbs. Deb: 8/12/79																									
1979 KC-A	4	4	.500	10	10	4	0	0	69^{2}	68	7	18	30	11.2	3.75	114	.261	.311	0	—	0	4	4	-2	0.2
1980 KC-A	0	1	.000	5	0	0	0	0	9^{1}	10	3	5	3	14.5	6.75	60	.270	.357	0	—	0	-3	-3	0	-0.3
Total 2	4	5	.444	15	10	4	0	0	79	78	10	23	33	11.6	4.10	103	.262	.317	0	—	0	1	1	-2	-0.1
● **ELTON CHAMBERLAIN** Chamberlain, Elton P. "Icebox" b: 11/5/1867, Buffalo, N.Y. d: 9/22/29, Baltimore, Md. BR/TB, 5'9", 168 lbs. Deb: 9/13/1886																									
1886 Lou-a	0	3	.000	4	4	4	0	0	31^{1}	39	0	17	18	16.1	6.61	55	.287	.366	3	.158	-0	-11	-10	-0	-0.8
1887 Lou-a	18	16	.529	36	36	35	1	0	309	340	8	117	118	13.7	3.79	116	.274	.343	26	.198	-3	17	21	1	1.5
1888 Lou-a	14	9	.609	24	24	21	1	0	196	177	2	59	119	11.3	2.53	122	.232	.297	18	.191	1	12	12	1	1.3
*StL-a	11	2	.846	14	14	13	1	0	112	61	1	27	57	7.6	1.61	203	.154	.220	5	.100	-3	18	21	-1	1.6
Yr	25	11	.694	38	38	34	2	0	308	238	3	86	176	9.6	2.19	143	.204	.262	23	.160	-3	30	33	0	2.9
1889 StL-a	32	15	.681	53	51	44	3	1	421^{2}	376	18	165	202	11.9	2.97	142	.231	.309	34	.199	-2	41	59	-3	4.8
1890 StL-a	3	1	.750	5	5	3	0	0	35	47	1	26	14	18.8	5.91	73	.312	.413	2	.133	-1	-8	-6	0	-0.6
Col-a	12	6	.667	25	21	19	6	0	175	128	2	70	114	10.6	2.21	162	.198	.284	15	.231	3	32	27	-2	2.6
Yr	15	7	.682	30	26	22	**6**	0	210	175	3	96	128	12.0	2.83	131	.220	.310	17	.213	1	24	21	-2	2.0
1891 Phi-a	22	23	.489	49	46	44	0	0	405^{2}	397	10	206	204	13.6	4.22	91	.248	.338	33	.188	2	-22	-18	0	-1.3
1892 Cin-N	19	23	.452	52	49	43	2	0	406^{1}	391	8	170	169	12.8	3.39	96	.243	.322	36	.225	3	-5	-5	-4	-0.6
1893 Cin-N	16	12	.571	34	27	19	1	0	241	248	3	112	59	14.0	3.73	128	.258	.345	19	.196	-4	25	28	-2	1.9
1894 Cin-N	10	9	.526	23	22	18	1	0	177^{2}	220	10	91	57	16.4	5.77	96	.301	.387	22	.314	5	-9	-4	-1	-0.1
1896 Cle-N	0	1	.000	2	2	1	0	0	11	21	0	5	2	22.1	7.36	62	.399	.461	0	.000	-0	-4	-3	-0	-0.3
Total 10	157	120	.567	321	301	264	16	1	2521^{2}	2445	63	1065	1133	12.9	3.57	112	.247	.327	213	.203	-2	88	119	-11	10.0
● **BILL CHAMBERLAIN** Chamberlain, William Vincent b: 4/21/09, Stoughton, Mass. BR/TL, 5'10.5", 173 lbs. Deb: 8/02/32																									
1932 Chi-A	0	5	.000	12	5	0	0	0	41^{1}	39	3	25	11	13.9	4.57	95	.250	.354	1	.100	-1	-0	-1	-1	-0.2
● **CLIFF CHAMBERS** Chambers, Clifford Day "Lefty" b: 1/10/22, Portland, Ore. BL/TL, 6'3", 208 lbs. Deb: 4/24/48																									
1948 Chi-N	2	9	.182	29	12	3	1	0	103^{2}	100	4	48	51	13.1	4.43	88	.254	.339	4	.133	-1	-5	-6	0	-0.7
1949 Pit-N	13	7	.650	34	21	10	1	0	177^{1}	186	15	58	93	12.6	3.96	106	.268	.329	13	.236	3	2	5	1	0.9
1950 Pit-N	12	15	.444	37	33	11	2	0	249^{1}	262	18	92	93	13.0	4.30	102	.265	.332	26	.289	7	-4	2	-2	0.7
1951 Pit-N	3	6	.333	10	10	2	1	0	59^{2}	64	5	31	19	14.9	5.58	76	.276	.371	7	.333	2	-11	-9	-2	-0.8
StL-N	11	6	.647	21	16	9	1	0	129^{1}	120	13	56	45	12.2	3.83	104	.251	.329	8	.163	0	2	2	-2	0.0
Yr	14	12	.538	31	26	11	2	0	189	184	18	87	64	12.9	4.38	92	.257	.338	15	.214	2	-9	-7	-3	-0.8
1952 StL-N	4	4	.500	26	13	2	1	1	98^{1}	110	8	33	47	13.3	4.12	90	.285	.344	9	.281	3	-4	-4	0	-0.1
1953 StL-N	3	6	.333	32	8	0	0	0	79^{2}	82	7	43	26	14.2	4.86	88	.266	.358	2	.118	-1	-5	-5	0	-0.6
Total 6	48	53	.475	189	113	37	7	1	897^{1}	924	70	361	374	13.1	4.29	96	.266	.338	69	.235	14	-26	-16	-4	-0.6
● **JOHNNIE CHAMBERS** Chambers, Johnnie Monroe b: 9/10/11, Copper Hill, Tenn d: 5/11/77, Palatka, Fla. BL/TR, 6', 185 lbs. Deb: 5/04/37																									
1937 StL-N	0	0	—	2	0	0	0	0	2	5	0	2	1	31.5	18.00	22	.455	.538	0	—	0	-3	-3	-0	-0.3
● **ROME CHAMBERS** Chambers, Richard Jerome b: 8/31/1875, Weaverville, N.C. d: 8/30/02, Weaverville, N.C. BL/TL, 6'2", 173 lbs. Deb: 5/07/00																									
1900 Bos-N	0	0	—	1	0	0	0	1	4	5	0	5	2	22.5	11.25	37	.305	.467	0	.000	-0	-3	-3	-0	-0.3
● **BILL CHAMBERS** Chambers, William Christopher b: 9/13/1889, Cameron, W.Va. d: 3/27/62, Fort Wayne, Ind. BR/TR, 5'9", 185 lbs. Deb: 7/11/10																									
1910 StL-N	0	0	—	1	0	0	0	0	1	1	0	0	0	9.0	0.00	—	.250	.250	0	—	0	0	0	-0	0.0
● **BILL CHAMPION** Champion, Buford Billy b: 9/18/47, Shelby, N.C. BR/TR, 6'4", 188 lbs. Deb: 6/04/69																									
1969 Phi-N	5	10	.333	23	20	4	2	1	116^{2}	130	7	63	70	15.1	5.01	71	.286	.376	6	.171	0	-18	-19	1	-1.8
1970 Phi-N	0	2	.000	7	1	0	0	0	14	21	3	10	12	20.6	9.00	44	.375	.478	0	.000	-0	-8	-8	0	-0.8
1971 Phi-N	3	5	.375	37	9	0	0	0	108^{2}	100	10	48	49	12.5	4.39	80	.249	.334	3	.111	-1	-11	-10	1	-1.1
1972 Phi-N	4	14	.222	30	22	2	0	0	132^{2}	155	11	54	54	14.2	5.09	71	.301	.368	5	.147	0	-24	-22	1	-2.2
1973 Mil-A	5	8	.385	37	11	2	0	1	136^{1}	139	10	62	67	13.5	3.70	102	.267	.350	0	—	0	2	1	2	0.5
1974 Mil-A	11	4	.733	31	23	2	0	0	161^{2}	168	12	49	60	12.1	3.62	100	.270	.323	0	—	0	-0	-0	-1	-0.1
1975 Mil-A	6	6	.500	27	13	3	1	0	110	125	11	55	40	14.7	5.89	65	.290	.370	0	—	0	-26	-25	1	-2.4
1976 Mil-A	0	1	.000	10	3	0	0	0	24^{1}	35	0	13	8	18.1	7.03	50	.361	.441	0	—	0	-9	-10	1	-0.8
Total 8	34	50	.405	202	102	13	3	2	804^{1}	873	64	354	360	13.9	4.69	78	.282	.358	14	.141	-1	-95	-93	4	-8.7
● **DEAN CHANCE** Chance, Wilmer Dean b: 6/1/41, Wayne, O. BR/TR, 6'3", 200 lbs. Deb: 9/11/61																									
1961 LA-A	0	2	.000	5	4	0	0	0	18^{1}	33	0	5	11	19.1	6.87	66	.412	.453	0	.000	-1	-6	-5	1	-0.5
1962 LA-A	14	10	.583	50	24	6	2	8	206^{2}	195	14	66	127	11.6	2.96	130	.250	.313	4	.062	-4	23	21	1	1.7
1963 LA-A	13	18	.419	45	35	6	2	3	248	229	10	90	168	11.9	3.19	107	.243	.316	12	.150	-1	12	6	1	0.7
1964 LA-A★	**20**	9	.690	46	35	**15**	**11**	4	**278^{1}**	194	7	86	207	9.1	**1.65**	**199**	.195	.261	7	.079	-5	**61**	**51**	-2	**4.9**
1965 Cal-A	15	10	.600	36	33	10	4	0	225^{2}	197	12	101	164	12.2	3.15	108	.238	.328	7	.093	-2	8	6	3	0.8
1966 Cal-A	12	17	.414	41	37	11	2	1	259^{2}	206	18	114	180	11.3	3.08	109	.222	.312	2	.026	-6	10	8	2	0.4
1967 Min-A★	20	14	.588	41	39	**18**	5	1	**283^{2}**	244	17	68	220	10.1	2.73	127	.229	.279	3	.033	-6	16	23	2	2.1
1968 Min-A	16	16	.500	43	39	15	6	1	292	224	15	63	234	9.2	2.53	122	.211	.261	5	.054	-6	15	18	3	1.8
1969 *Min-A	5	4	.556	20	15	1	0	0	88^{1}	76	6	35	50	11.7	2.95	124	.233	.315	1	.042	-1	7	7	-1	0.5
1970 Cle-A	9	8	.529	45	19	1	1	4	155	172	18	59	109	13.8	4.24	93	.287	.357	3	.071	-3	-9	-5	-1	-0.9
NY-N	0	1	.000	3	0	0	0	1	2	3	0	2	0	22.5	13.50	30	.500	.625	0	—	0	-2	-2	0	-0.2
1971 Det-A	4	6	.400	31	14	0	0	0	89^{2}	91	5	50	64	14.6	3.51	102	.265	.364	0	.000	-2	-1	1	-0	-0.2
Total 11	128	115	.527	406	294	83	33	23	2147^{1}	1864	122	739	1534	11.2	2.92	119	.234	.305	44	.066	-37	134	131	8	11.1
● **ED CHANDLER** Chandler, Edward Oliver b: 2/17/22, Pinson, Ala. BR/TR, 6'2", 190 lbs. Deb: 4/18/47																									
1947 Bro-N	0	1	.000	15	1	0	0	1	29^{2}	31	7	12	8	13.0	6.37	65	.263	.331	0	.000	0	-8	-7	0	-0.7
● **SPUD CHANDLER** Chandler, Spurgeon Ferdinand b: 9/12/07, Commerce, Ga. d: 1/9/90, S.Pasadena, Fla. BR/TR, 6', 181 lbs. Deb: 5/06/37 C																									
1937 NY-A	7	4	.636	12	10	6	2	0	82^{1}	79	8	20	31	10.9	2.84	156	.253	.300	4	.133	-2	16	15	2	1.4
1938 NY-A	14	5	.737	23	23	14	2	0	172	183	7	47	36	12.1	4.03	113	.271	.320	14	.203	2	15	10	4	1.5
1939 NY-A	3	0	1.000	11	0	0	0	0	19	26	0	9	4	16.6	2.84	153	.329	.398	2	.400	1	4	3	1	0.5
1940 NY-A	8	7	.533	27	24	6	1	0	172	184	12	60	56	13.1	4.60	88	.275	.341	9	.150	1	-4	-11	3	-0.7
1941 *NY-A	10	4	.714	28	20	11	4	4	163^{2}	146	5	60	60	11.3	3.19	123	.239	.307	11	.183	-1	17	13	3	1.5
1942 *NY-A★	16	5	.762	24	24	17	3	0	200^{2}	176	13	74	74	11.4	2.38	145	.237	.309	15	.211	4	29	24	3	3.3
1943 *NY-A☆	**20**	4	**.833**	30	30	**20**	**5**	0	253	197	5	54	134	**9.1**	**1.64**	**197**	.215	**.261**	25	.258	7	**47**	**44**	3	**6.6**
1944 NY-A	0	0	—	1	1	0	0	0	6	6	1	1	1	12.0	4.50	77	.300	.364	0	.000	-0	-1	-1	0	-0.1
1945 NY-A	2	1	.667	4	4	2	1	0	31	30	2	7	12	10.7	4.65	75	.250	.291	4	.333	1	-4	-4	0	-0.3
1946 NY-A☆	20	8	.714	34	32	20	6	2	257^{1}	200	7	90	138	10.2	2.10	164	.218	.288	14	.149	-0	40	39	4	4.8
1947 *NY-A☆	9	5	.643	17	16	13	2	0	128	100	4	41	68	9.9	2.46	144	.214	.277	12	.245	4	18	15	3	2.5
Total 11	109	43	.717	211	184	109	26	6	1485	1327	64	463	614	11.0	2.84	132	.240	.301	110	.201	16	176	149	27	21.0
● **ESTY CHANEY** Chaney, Esty Clyon b: 1/29/1891, Hadley, Pa. d: 2/5/52, Cleveland, Ohio BR/TR, 5'11", 170 lbs. Deb: 8/02/13																									
1913 Bos-A	0	0	—	1	0	0	0	0	1	1	0	2	0	27.0	9.00	33	.200	.429	0	—	0	-1	-1	-0	-0.1
1914 Bro-F	0	0	—	1	0	0	0	0	4	7	0	2	1	20.3	6.75	47	.389	.450	0	.000	-0	-2	-2	-0	-0.2
Total 2	0	0	—	2	0	0	0	0	5	8	0	4	1	21.6	7.20	44	.348	.444	0	.000	-0	-2	-2	-0	-0.3
● **DARRIN CHAPIN** Chapin, Darrin John b: 2/1/66, Warren, Ohio BR/TR, 6', 170 lbs. Deb: 9/21/91																									
1991 NY-A	0	1	.000	3	0	0	0	0	5^{1}	3	0	6	5	15.2	5.06	82	.158	.360	0	—	0	-1	-1	0	0.0

YEAR	TM/L	W	L	PCT	G	GS	CG	SH	SV	IP	H	HR	BB	SO	RAT	ERA	ERA+	OAV	OOB	BH	AVG	PB	PR	/A	PD	TPI
1992	Phi-N	0	0	—	1	0	0	0	0	2	2	1	0	1	9.0	9.00	39	.250	.250	0	—	0	-1	-1	-0	-0.1
Total	2	0	1	.000	4	0	0	0	0	7^1	5	1	6	6	13.5	6.14	65	.185	.333	0	—	0	-2	-2	0	-0.1
● **TINY CHAPLIN**	Chaplin, James Bailey b: 7/13/05, Los Angeles, Cal. d: 3/25/39, National City, Cal BR/TR, 6'1", 195 lbs. Deb: 4/13/28																									
1928	NY-N	0	2	.000	12	1	0	0	0	24	27	0	8	5	13.1	4.50	87	.284	.340	0	.000	-1	-1	-2	-1	-0.3
1930	NY-N	2	6	.250	19	8	3	0	1	73	89	8	16	20	13.4	5.18	91	.305	.349	2	.105	-0	-2	-4	0	-0.3
1931	NY-N	3	0	1.000	16	3	1	0	1	42^1	39	2	16	7	12.1	3.19	116	.242	.318	2	.182	0	3	2	-1	0.2
1936	Bos-N	10	15	.400	40	31	14	0	2	231^2	273	21	62	86	13.1	4.12	93	.294	.340	17	.202	-0	-3	-7	2	-0.6
Total	4	15	23	.395	87	43	18	0	4	371	428	31	102	118	13.1	4.25	94	.290	.340	21	.176	-1	-2	-10	1	-1.0
● **ED CHAPMAN**	Chapman, Edwin Volney b: 11/28/05, Courtland, Miss. BB/TR, 6'1", 185 lbs. Deb: 8/06/33																									
1933	Was-A	0	0	—	6	1	0	0	0	9	10	2	2	4	12.0	8.00	52	.270	.308	0	.000	-0	-4	-4	-0	-0.4
● **FRED CHAPMAN**	Chapman, Frederick Joseph b: 11/24/1872, Little Cooley, Pa. d: 12/14/57, Union City, Pa. BR/TR, 5'8", 165 lbs. Deb: 7/22/1887																									
1887	Phi-a	0	0	—	1	1	1	0	0	5	8	0	2	4	18.0	7.20	60	.364	.417	0	.000	-0	-2	-2	-0	-0.2
● **BEN CHAPMAN**	Chapman, William Benjamin b: 12/25/08, Nashville, Tenn. BR/TR, 6', 190 lbs. Deb: 4/15/30 MC♦																									
1944	Bro-N	5	3	.625	11	9	6	0	0	79^1	75	4	33	37	12.6	3.40	104	.242	.321	14	.368	6	2	1	-2	0.6
1945	Bro-N	3	3	.500	10	7	2	0	0	53^2	64	3	32	23	16.6	5.53	68	.296	.394	3	.136	-1	-10	-11	1	-1.0
	Phi-N	0	0	—	3	0	0	0	0	7	7	0	6	4	16.7	7.71	50	.259	.394	16	.314	0	-3	-3	-0	-0.3
	Yr	3	3	.500	13	7	2	0	0	60^2	71	3	38	27	16.2	5.79	65	.289	.384	19	.260	-0	-13	-14	0	-1.3
1946	Phi-N	0	0	—	1	0	0	0	0	1	1	0	0	1	9.0	0.00	—	.200	.200	0	.000	-0	0	0	0	0.0
Total	3	8	6	.571	25	16	8	0	0	141	147	7	71	65	14.3	4.40	83	.263	.353	1958	.302	6	-11	-12	-1	-0.7
● **BILL CHAPPELLE**	Chappelle, William Hogan "Big Bill" b: 3/22/1884, Waterloo, N.Y. d: 12/31/44, Mineola, N.Y. BR/TR, 6'2", 206 lbs. Deb: 8/20/08																									
1908	Bos-N	2	4	.333	13	7	3	1	0	70^1	60	0	17	23	10.4	1.79	135	.233	.290	1	.048	-1	4	5	1	0.5
1909	Bos-N	1	1	.500	5	3	2	0	0	29	31	0	11	8	13.3	1.86	152	.279	.350	4	.364	2	2	3	1	0.8
	Cin-N	0	0	—	1	0	0	0	1	4	5	0	2	0	18.0	2.25	116	.278	.381	0	.000	-0	0	0	-0	0.0
	Yr	1	1	.500	6	3	2	0	1	33	36	0	13	8	13.6	1.91	146	.277	.347	4	.333	2	3	3	1	0.8
1914	Bro-F	4	2	.667	16	6	4	0	0	74^1	71	1	29	31	12.5	3.15	101	.255	.332	0	.000	-3	0	0	-1	-0.4
Total	3	7	7	.500	35	16	9	1	1	177^2	167	1	59	62	11.9	2.38	118	.251	.321	5	.089	-3	7	9	1	0.9
● **NORM CHARLTON**	Charlton, Norman Wood b: 1/6/63, Fort Polk, La. BB/TL, 6'3", 195 lbs. Deb: 8/19/88																									
1988	Cin-N	4	5	.444	10	10	0	0	0	61^1	60	6	20	39	12.0	3.96	90	.256	.320	0	.000	-1	-4	-3	-0	-0.4
1989	Cin-N	8	3	.727	69	0	0	0	0	95^1	67	5	40	98	10.3	2.93	123	.197	.285	0	.000	-1	6	7	-0	0.7
1990	*Cin-N	12	9	.571	56	16	1	1	2	154^1	131	10	70	117	12.0	2.74	144	.231	.320	5	.135	0	18	21	1	2.3
1991	Cin-N	3	5	.375	39	11	0	0	1	108^1	92	6	34	77	11.0	2.91	131	.236	.307	1	.043	-2	9	11	1	1.1
1992	Cin-N★	4	2	.667	64	0	0	0	26	81^1	79	7	26	90	12.0	2.99	123	.262	.326	1	.200	0	5	6	-1	0.6
Total	5	31	24	.564	238	37	1	1	29	500^2	429	34	190	421	11.4	3.00	125	.234	.312	7	.082	-3	35	42	0	4.3
● **PETE CHARTON**	Charton, Frank Lane b: 12/21/42, Jackson, Tenn. BL/TR, 6'2", 190 lbs. Deb: 4/19/64																									
1964	Bos-A	0	2	.000	25	5	0	0	0	65	67	12	24	37	12.7	5.26	73	.275	.342	1	.100	-0	-12	-10	2	-0.9
● **HAL CHASE**	Chase, Harold Homer "Prince Hal" b: 2/13/1883, Los Gatos, Cal. d: 5/18/47, Colusa, Cal. BR/TL, 6', 175 lbs. Deb: 4/14/05 M♦																									
1908	NY-A	0	0	—	1	0	0	0	0	0^1	0	0	0	0	0.0	0.00	—	.000	.000	104	.257	0	0	0	-0	0.0
● **KEN CHASE**	Chase, Kendall Fay "Lefty" b: 10/6/13, Oneonta, N.Y. d: 1/16/85, Oneonta, N.Y. BL/TL, 6'2", 210 lbs. Deb: 4/23/36																									
1936	Was-A	0	0	—	1	0	0	0	0	2^1	2	0	4	1	23.1	11.57	41	.250	.500	1	1.000	0	-2	-2	-0	-0.1
1937	Was-A	4	3	.571	14	9	4	0	0	76^1	74	4	60	43	15.8	4.13	107	.257	.385	1	.034	-4	4	3	-0	-0.1
1938	Was-A	9	10	.474	32	21	7	0	1	150	151	4	113	64	16.1	5.58	81	.268	.394	10	.208	1	-13	-18	1	-1.4
1939	Was-A	10	19	.345	32	31	15	1	0	232	215	10	114	118	12.8	3.80	114	.243	.330	15	.169	-3	21	14	0	1.1
1940	Was-A	15	17	.469	35	34	20	1	0	261^2	260	14	143	129	14.0	3.23	129	.261	.357	15	.163	-0	33	27	-1	2.6
1941	Was-A	6	18	.250	33	30	8	1	0	205^2	228	11	115	98	15.1	5.08	80	.280	.371	11	.149	-2	-21	-24	1	-2.2
1942	Bos-A	5	1	.833	13	10	4	0	0	80^1	82	5	41	34	13.8	3.81	98	.263	.348	6	.182	1	-1	-1	-1	-0.1
1943	Bos-A	0	4	.000	7	5	0	0	0	27^1	36	0	30	9	21.7	6.91	48	.316	.458	1	.091	-1	-11	-11	0	-1.1
	NY-N	4	12	.250	21	20	4	1	0	129^1	140	7	74	86	15.0	4.11	84	.275	.369	9	.214	0	-10	-9	-1	-1.0
Total	8	53	84	.387	188	160	62	4	1	1165	1188	55	694	582	14.7	4.27	97	.265	.365	69	.165	-8	-0	-19	-0	-2.3
● **JIM CHATTERTON**	Chatterton, James M. b: 10/14/1864, Brooklyn, N.Y. d: 12/15/44, Tewksbury, Mass. Deb: 6/07/1884 ♦																									
1884	KC-U	0	1	.000	1	1	0	0	0	5	11	0	2	2	23.4	3.60	77	.414	.455	2	.133	-0	-0	-0	0	0.0
● **NESTOR CHAVEZ**	Chavez, Nestor Isais (Silva) b: 7/6/47, Chacao, Venez. d: 3/16/69, Maracaibo, Venez. BR/TR, 6', 170 lbs. Deb: 9/09/67																									
1967	SF-N	1	0	1.000	2	0	0	0	0	5	4	0	3	3	12.6	0.00	—	.211	.318	0	.000	-0	2	2	0	0.2
● **DAVE CHEADLE**	Cheadle, David Baird b: 2/19/52, Greensboro, N.C. BL/TL, 6'2", 203 lbs. Deb: 9/16/73																									
1973	Atl-N	0	1	.000	2	0	0	0	0	2	2	1	3	2	22.5	18.00	22	.250	.455	0	—	0	-3	-3	-0	-0.3
● **CHARLIE CHECH**	Chech, Charles William b: 4/27/1878, Madison, Wis. d: 1/31/38, Los Angeles, Cal. BR/TR, 5'11.5", 190 lbs. Deb: 4/14/05																									
1905	Cin-N	14	14	.500	39	25	20	1	0	267^2	300	4	77	79	13.0	2.89	114	.288	.344	17	.191	1	3	12	-0	1.3
1906	Cin-N	1	4	.200	11	5	5	0	3	66	59	1	24	17	12.1	2.32	119	.243	.326	5	.200	1	2	3	0	0.5
1908	Cle-A	11	7	.611	27	20	14	4	0	165^2	136	2	34	51	9.6	1.74	138	.229	.279	5	.104	-1	12	12	1	1.5
1909	Bos-A	7	5	.583	17	13	6	1	0	106^2	107	3	27	40	11.7	2.95	85	.260	.314	3	.083	-2	-6	-5	-0	-0.9
Total	4	33	30	.524	94	63	45	6	3	606	602	10	162	187	11.8	2.52	113	.263	.320	30	.152	-1	12	21	1	2.4
● **VIRGIL CHEEVES**	Cheeves, Virgil Earl "Chief" b: 2/12/01, Oklahoma City, Okla. d: 5/5/79, Dallas, Tex. BR/TR, 6', 195 lbs. Deb: 9/07/20																									
1920	Chi-N	0	0	—	5	2	0	0	0	18	16	0	7	3	11.5	3.50	92	.250	.324	0	.000	-0	-1	-1	-1	-0.2
1921	Chi-N	11	12	.478	37	22	9	1	0	163	192	8	47	39	13.7	4.64	82	.309	.366	8	.167	-2	-15	-15	-3	-1.9
1922	Chi-N	12	11	.522	39	23	9	1	2	182^2	195	9	76	40	13.8	4.09	103	.281	.360	13	.210	2	0	2	-1	0.2
1923	Chi-N	3	4	.429	19	8	0	0	0	71^1	89	8	37	13	16.3	6.18	65	.314	.399	4	.174	-1	-17	-17	-1	-1.7
1924	Cle-A	0	0	—	8	1	0	0	0	17^1	26	2	17	2	22.8	7.79	55	.388	.518	1	.250	0	-7	-7	0	-0.6
1927	NY-N	0	0	—	3	0	0	0	0	6^1	8	1	4	1	17.1	4.26	90	.333	.429	0	—	0	-0	-0	0	0.0
Total	6	26	27	.491	111	56	18	2	2	458^2	526	28	188	98	14.5	4.73	84	.300	.375	26	.184	-1	-40	-38	-5	-4.2
● **ITALO CHELINI**	Chelini, Italo Vincent "Chilly" or "Lefty" b: 10/10/14, San Francisco, Cal d: 8/25/72, San Francisco, Cal BL/TL, 5'10.5", 175 lbs. Deb: 9/12/35																									
1935	Chi-A	0	0	—	2	0	0	0	0	5	7	1	4	1	21.6	12.60	37	.350	.480	1	.500	0	-5	-4	0	-0.4
1936	Chi-A	4	3	.571	18	6	5	0	0	83^2	100	8	30	16	14.0	4.95	105	.291	.348	5	.156	-1	1	2	-1	0.0
1937	Chi-A	0	1	.000	4	0	0	0	0	8^2	15	2	0	3	16.6	10.38	44	.405	.421	0	.000	0	-6	-6	-0	-0.5
Total	3	4	4	.500	24	6	5	0	0	97^1	122	11	34	20	14.6	5.83	88	.304	.362	6	.171	-1	-9	-8	-1	-0.9
● **LARRY CHENEY**	Cheney, Laurance Russell b: 5/2/1886, Belleville, Kan. d: 1/6/69, Daytona Beach, Fla. BR/TR, 6'1.5", 185 lbs. Deb: 9/09/11																									
1911	Chi-N	1	0	1.000	3	1	0	0	0	10	8	0	3	11	9.9	0.00	—	.229	.289	1	.250	0	4	4	1	0.5
1912	Chi-N	**26**	10	.722	42	37	**28**	4	0	303^1	262	5	111	140	11.3	2.85	117	.234	.307	24	.226	5	19	16	-2	1.8
1913	Chi-N	21	14	.600	**54**	36	25	2	**11**	305	271	7	98	136	11.1	2.57	124	.241	.306	20	.192	2	22	21	-0	2.4
1914	Chi-N	20	18	.526	**50**	40	21	6	5	311^1	239	9	140	157	11.2	2.54	109	.215	.308	18	.180	3	9	8	1	1.3
1915	Chi-N	8	9	.471	25	18	6	2	0	131^1	120	1	55	68	12.3	3.56	78	.246	.327	6	.150	-1	-12	-11	2	-1.2
	Bro-N	0	2	.000	5	4	1	0	0	27	16	0	17	11	11.7	1.67	167	.174	.315	1	.143	0	3	3	0	0.4

YEAR TM/L	W	L	PCT	G	GS	CG	SH	SV	IP	H	HR	BB	SO	RAT	ERA	ERA+	OAV	OOB	BH	AVG	PB	PR	/A	PD	TPI
Yr	8	11	.421	30	22	7	2	0	158^{1}	136	1	72	79	11.9	3.24	86	.233	.319	7	.149	-1	-9	-8	2	-0.8
1916 *Bro-N	18	12	.600	41	32	15	5	0	253	178	5	105	166	10.4	1.92	140	**.198**	.289	9	.114	-3	20	21	-1	2.1
1917 Bro-N	8	12	.400	35	24	14	1	2	210^{1}	185	4	73	102	11.3	2.35	119	.239	.309	14	.206	2	8	10	-1	1.3
1918 Bro-N	11	13	.458	32	21	15	0	1	200^{2}	177	2	74	83	11.7	3.00	93	.241	.319	16	.242	2	-5	-5	1	-0.2
1919 Bro-N	1	3	.250	9	4	2	0	0	39	45	1	14	14	14.1	4.15	72	.300	.367	2	.182	-0	-5	-5	-0	-0.6
Bos-N	0	2	.000	8	2	0	0	0	33	35	0	15	13	13.6	3.55	81	.294	.373	2	.182	0	-2	-3	0	-0.2
Phi-N	2	5	.286	9	6	5	0	0	57^{1}	69	2	28	25	15.4	4.55	71	.315	.395	2	.095	-2	-10	-8	-1	-1.2
Yr	3	10	.231	26	12	7	0	0	129^{1}	149	3	57	52	14.4	4.18	73	.304	.378	6	.140	-2	-18	-16	-1	-2.0
Total 9	116	100	.537	313	225	132	20	19	1881^{1}	1605	36	733	926	11.5	2.70	109	.234	.313	115	.186	9	49	52	0	6.4
● **TOM CHENEY** Cheney, Thomas Edgar b: 10/14/34, Morgan, Ga. BR/TR, 6', 180 lbs. Deb: 4/21/57																									
1957 StL-N	0	1	.000	4	3	0	0	0	9	6	0	15	10	21.0	5.00	79	.207	.477	0	.000	-0	-1	-1	0	-0.1
1959 StL-N	0	1	.000	11	2	0	0	0	11^{2}	17	2	11	8	23.1	6.94	61	.354	.492	0	—	0	-4	-4	0	-0.4
1960 *Pit-N	2	2	.500	11	8	1	1	0	52	44	5	33	35	13.3	3.98	94	.238	.353	3	.176	0	-1	-1	-2	-0.2
1961 Pit-N	0	0	—	1	0	0	0	0	0	1	1	4	0	—	∞	—	.500	.833	0	—	0	-4	-4	0	-0.3
Was-A	1	3	.250	10	7	0	0	0	29^{2}	32	8	26	20	17.6	8.80	46	.283	.417	4	.500	2	-16	-16	-1	-1.3
1962 Was-A	7	9	.438	37	23	4	3	1	173^{1}	134	12	97	147	12.1	3.17	127	.213	.320	3	.063	-3	15	17	0	1.4
1963 Was-A	8	9	.471	23	21	7	4	0	136^{1}	99	14	40	97	9.2	2.71	137	.202	.264	5	.109	-3	14	15	-2	1.1
1964 Was-A	1	3	.250	15	6	1	0	1	48^{2}	45	10	13	25	10.7	3.70	100	.245	.294	3	.250	0	-0	0	-0	0.0
1966 Was-A	0	1	.000	3	1	0	0	0	5^{1}	4	1	6	3	18.6	5.06	68	.222	.440	0	—	0	-1	-1	0	0.0
Total 8	19	29	.396	115	71	13	8	2	466	382	53	245	345	12.2	3.77	103	.225	.325	18	.135	-4	2	5	-4	0.2
● **JACK CHESBRO** Chesbro, John Dwight "Happy Jack" b: 6/5/1874, N.Adams, Mass. d: 11/6/31, Conway, Mass. BR/TR, 5'9", 180 lbs. Deb: 7/12/1899 CH																									
1899 Pit-N	6	9	.400	19	17	15	0	0	149	165	3	59	28	14.2	4.11	93	.280	.357	9	.155	-3	-4	-5	-3	-1.0
1900 Pit-N	15	13	.536	32	26	20	3	1	215^{2}	220	4	79	56	12.9	3.67	99	.264	.335	15	.176	-1	1	-1	-2	-0.4
1901 Pit-N	21	10	**.677**	36	28	26	**6**	1	287^{2}	261	4	52	129	10.2	2.38	137	.240	.283	25	.216	2	30	28	-3	2.7
1902 Pit-N	**28**	6	**.824**	35	33	31	**8**	1	286^{1}	242	1	62	136	10.2	2.17	126	.229	.285	20	.179	-2	19	18	-2	1.4
1903 NY-A	21	15	.583	40	36	33	1	0	324^{2}	300	7	74	147	10.6	2.77	113	.245	.292	23	.185	-1	7	13	2	1.4
1904 NY-A	**41**	12	**.774**	**55**	51	**48**	6	0	**454^{2}**	338	4	88	239	8.6	1.82	149	**.208**	.252	41	.236	6	39	**45**	5	**6.7**
1905 NY-A	19	15	.559	41	38	24	3	0	303^{1}	262	5	71	156	10.1	2.20	134	.234	.284	21	.188	0	16	25	1	3.0
1906 NY-A	23	17	.575	**49**	42	24	4	1	325	314	2	75	152	11.0	2.96	100	.257	.304	26	.208	-1	-10	0	-0	-0.1
1907 NY-A	10	10	.500	30	25	17	1	0	206	192	0	46	78	10.7	2.53	110	.249	.296	15	.197	-1	0	6	-0	0.6
1908 NY-A	14	20	.412	45	31	20	3	1	288^{2}	271	6	67	124	11.0	2.93	85	.250	.303	18	.176	-2	-17	-14	1	-1.7
1909 NY-A	0	4	.000	9	4	2	0	0	49^{2}	70	2	13	17	15.6	6.34	40	.347	.394	3	.176	-0	-21	-21	1	-2.0
Bos-A	0	1	.000	1	1	0	0	0	6	7	1	4	3	16.5	4.50	56	.318	.423	1	.500	0	-1	-1	-0	-0.1
Yr	0	5	.000	10	5	2	0	0	55^{2}	77	3	17	20	15.2	6.14	41	.339	.385	4	.211	0	-23	-22	1	-2.1
Total 11	198	132	.600	392	332	260	35	5	2896^{2}	2642	39	690	1265	10.7	2.68	111	.244	.296	217	.197	-2	59	97	-2	10.5
● **BOB CHESNES** Chesnes, Robert Vincent b: 5/6/21, Oakland, Cal. d: 5/23/79, Everett, Wash. BB/TR, 6', 180 lbs. Deb: 5/06/48																									
1948 Pit-N	14	6	.700	25	23	15	0	0	194^{1}	180	13	90	69	12.7	3.57	114	.247	.333	25	.275	7	8	11	3	2.2
1949 Pit-N	7	13	.350	27	25	8	1	1	145^{1}	153	15	82	49	14.9	5.88	71	.276	.374	17	.250	6	-30	-27	3	-1.8
1950 Pit-N	3	3	.500	9	7	2	0	0	39	44	7	17	12	14.8	5.54	79	.293	.376	2	.154	-0	-6	-5	2	-0.3
Total 3	24	22	.522	61	55	25	1	1	378^{2}	377	35	189	130	13.7	4.66	89	.263	.354	44	.256	13	-27	-21	8	0.1
● **MITCH CHETKOVICH** Chetkovich, Mitchell b: 7/21/17, Fairpoint, Ohio d: 8/24/71, Grass Valley, Cal. BR/TR, 6'3.5", 208 lbs. Deb: 4/19/45																									
1945 Phi-N	0	0	—	4	0	0	0	0	3	2	0	3	0	15.0	0.00	—	.182	.357	0	—	0	1	1	-0	0.1
● **TONY CHEVEZ** Chevez, Silvio Antonio (b: Silvio Antonio Aguilera (Chevez)) b: 6/20/54, Telica, Nicaragua BR/TR, 5'11", 177 lbs. Deb: 5/31/77																									
1977 Bal-A	0	0	—	4	0	0	0	0	8	10	3	8	7	22.5	12.38	31	.294	.455	0	—	0	-7	-8	-0	-0.3
● **SCOTT CHIAMPARINO** Chiamparino, Scott Michael b: 8/22/66, San Mateo, Cal. BR/TR, 6'2", 190 lbs. Deb: 9/05/90																									
1990 Tex-A	1	2	.333	6	6	0	0	0	37^{2}	36	1	12	19	11.9	2.63	149	.250	.316	0	—	0	5	5	-1	0.5
1991 Tex-A	1	0	1.000	5	5	0	0	0	22^{1}	26	1	12	8	15.3	4.03	100	.295	.380	0	—	0	0	-0	-1	-0.1
1992 Tex-A	0	4	.000	4	4	0	0	0	25^{1}	25	2	5	13	10.7	3.55	108	.260	.297	0	—	0	1	1	-1	0.3
Total 3	2	6	.250	15	15	0	0	0	85^{1}	87	4	29	40	12.4	3.27	120	.265	.329	0	—	0	7	6	-2	0.7
● **FLOYD CHIFFER** Chiffer, Floyd John b: 4/20/56, Glen Cove, N.Y. BR/TR, 6'2", 185 lbs. Deb: 4/07/82																									
1982 SD-N	4	3	.571	51	0	0	0	4	79^{1}	73	9	34	48	12.6	2.95	116	.247	.333	0	.000	-1	6	4	-0	0.3
1983 SD-N	0	2	.000	15	0	0	0	1	22^{2}	17	0	10	15	10.7	3.18	110	.210	.297	0	.000	-0	1	1	0	0.1
1984 SD-N	1	0	1.000	15	1	0	0	0	28	42	1	16	20	18.6	7.71	46	.347	.423	0	.000	-0	-13	-13	-1	-1.4
Total 3	5	5	.500	81	1	0	0	5	130	132	10	60	83	13.6	4.02	86	.266	.349	0	.000	-1	-6	-8	-1	-1.0
● **HARRY CHILD** Child, Harry Stephen Patrick (b: Harry Stephen Patrick Chesley) b: 5/23/05, Baltimore, Md. d: 11/8/72, Alexandria, Va. BB/TR, 5'11", 187 lbs. Deb: 7/16/30																									
1930 Was-A	0	0	—	5	0	0	0	0	10	10	1	5	5	13.5	6.30	73	.263	.349	1	.250	-0	-2	-2	0	-0.2
● **CHILDERS** Childers b: St.Louis, Mo. Deb: 7/27/1895																									
1895 Lou-N	0	0	—	1	0	0	0	0	0	2	0	6	0	—	∞	—	1.000	1.000	0	—	0	-6	-6	0	-0.4
● **ROCKY CHILDRESS** Childress, Rodney Osborne b: 2/18/62, Santa Rosa, Cal. BR/TR, 6'2", 195 lbs. Deb: 5/17/85																									
1985 Phi-N	0	1	.000	16	1	0	0	0	33^{1}	45	3	9	14	14.6	6.21	59	.326	.367	1	.167	-0	-10	-9	-0	-1.0
1986 Phi-N	0	0	—	2	0	0	0	0	2^{2}	4	0	1	1	16.9	6.75	57	.364	.417	0	—	0	-1	-1	-0	-0.1
1987 Hou-N	1	2	.333	32	0	0	0	0	48^{1}	46	4	18	26	11.9	2.98	131	.260	.328	0	.000	-0	6	5	-0	0.4
1988 Hou-N	1	0	1.000	11	0	0	0	0	23^{1}	26	3	9	24	13.9	6.17	54	.280	.350	1	.250	0	-7	-7	-1	-0.8
Total 4	2	3	.400	61	1	0	0	0	107^{2}	121	10	37	65	13.3	4.76	78	.289	.348	2	.167	-0	-12	-13	-1	-1.5
● **BOB CHIPMAN** Chipman, Robert Howard "Mr. Chips" b: 10/11/18, Brooklyn, N.Y. d: 11/8/73, Huntington, N.Y. BL/TL, 6'2", 190 lbs. Deb: 9/28/41																									
1941 Bro-N	1	0	1.000	1	1	0	0	0	5	3	0	1	3	7.2	0.00	—	.150	.190	0	.000	-0	2	2	-0	0.2
1942 Bro-N	0	0	—	2	0	0	0	0	1^{1}	1	0	2	1	20.3	0.00	—	.250	.500	0	—	0	0	0	0	0.0
1943 Bro-N	0	0	—	1	0	0	0	0	1^{2}	2	0	2	0	21.6	0.00	—	.400	.571	0	—	0	1	1	-0	0.1
1944 Bro-N	3	1	.750	11	3	1	0	0	36^{1}	38	1	24	20	15.4	4.21	84	.270	.376	2	.182	-0	-2	-3	0	-0.3
Chi-N	9	9	.500	26	21	8	1	2	129	147	9	40	41	13.0	3.49	101	.288	.340	5	.104	-2	2	1	-0	-0.2
Yr	12	10	.545	37	24	9	1	2	165^{1}	185	10	64	61	13.6	3.65	97	.284	.348	7	.119	-3	-1	-2	-0	-0.5
1945 *Chi-N	4	5	.444	25	10	3	1	0	72	63	4	34	29	12.3	3.50	104	.230	.317	3	.176	1	2	1	1	0.2
1946 Chi-N	6	5	.545	34	10	5	3	2	109^{1}	103	8	54	42	13.0	3.13	106	.255	.344	2	.061	-3	3	2	-1	-0.1
1947 Chi-N	7	6	.538	32	17	5	1	0	134^{2}	135	6	66	51	13.4	3.68	107	.264	.348	4	.091	-3	6	4	1	0.3
1948 Chi-N	2	1	.667	34	3	0	0	4	60^{1}	73	5	24	16	14.5	3.58	109	.293	.355	4	.250	1	3	2	1	0.4
1949 Chi-N	7	8	.467	38	11	3	1	1	113^{1}	110	7	63	46	13.9	3.97	102	.248	.344	3	.125	-0	1	1	-1	-0.1
1950 Bos-N	7	7	.500	27	12	4	0	1	124	127	10	37	40	12.2	4.43	87	.262	.319	6	.154	-1	-4	-8	-3	-1.1
1951 Bos-N	4	3	.571	33	0	0	0	4	52	59	5	19	17	13.8	4.85	76	.284	.349	1	.100	-1	-5	-7	-0	-0.8
1952 Bos-N	1	1	.500	29	0	0	0	0	41^{2}	28	5	20	16	10.4	2.81	129	.188	.284	2	.400	1	4	4	0	0.5
Total 12	51	46	.526	293	87	29	7	14	880^{2}	889	60	386	322	13.1	3.72	100	.261	.338	32	.128	-8	13	1	-2	-0.9
● **STEVE CHITREN** Chitren, Stephen Vincent b: 6/8/67, Tokyo, Japan BR/TR, 6', 180 lbs. Deb: 9/15/90																									
1990 Oak-A	1	0	1.000	8	0	0	0	0	17^{2}	7	0	4	19	5.6	1.02	365	.117	.172	0	—	0	6	5	0	0.6
1991 Oak-A	1	4	.200	56	0	0	0	4	60^{1}	59	8	32	47	14.2	4.33	89	.258	.358	0	—	0	-2	-3	-0	-0.3

YEAR TM/L	W	L	PCT	G	GS	CG	SH	SV	IP	H	HR	BB	SO	RAT	ERA	ERA+	OAV	OOB	BH	AVG	PB	PR	/A	PD	TPI
Total 2	2	4	.333	64	0	0	0	4	78	66	8	36	66	12.2	3.58	106	.228	.322	0	—	0	4	2	-0	0.3
● NELSON CHITTUM Chittum, Nelson Boyd b: 3/25/33, Harrisonburg, Va. BR/TR, 6'1", 180 lbs. Deb: 8/17/58																									
1958 StL-N	0	1	.000	13	2	0	0	0	29^1	31	5	7	13	12.0	6.44	64	.265	.312	1	.250	0	-8	-8	0	-0.7
1959 Bos-A	3	0	1.000	21	0	0	0	0	30^1	29	0	11	12	11.9	1.19	342	.266	.333	1	.200	0	9	10	1	1.1
1960 Bos-A	0	0	—	6	0	0	0	0	8^1	8	0	6	5	15.1	4.32	94	.242	.359	0	.000	-0	-0	-0	0	0.0
Total 3	3	1	.750	40	2	0	0	0	68	68	5	24	30	12.3	3.84	106	.263	.327	2	.200	0	0	2	1	0.4
● BOB CHLUPSA Chlupsa, Robert Joseph b: 9/16/45, New York, N.Y. BR/TR, 6'7", 215 lbs. Deb: 7/16/70																									
1970 StL-N	0	2	.000	14	0	0	0	0	16^1	26	2	9	10	19.3	8.82	47	.366	.438	0	—	0	-9	-9	1	-0.8
1971 StL-N	0	0	—	1	0	0	0	0	2	3	0	0	1	13.5	9.00	40	.333	.333	0	—	0	-1	-1	0	-0.1
Total 2	0	2	.000	15	0	0	0	0	18^1	29	2	9	11	18.7	8.84	46	.363	.427	0	—	0	-10	-10	1	-0.9
● DON CHOATE Choate, Donald Leon b: 7/2/38, Potosi, Mo. BR/TR, 6', 185 lbs. Deb: 9/12/60																									
1960 SF-N	0	0	—	4	0	0	0	0	8	7	0	4	7	12.4	2.25	155	.233	.324	0	—	0	1	1	0	0.2
● CHIEF CHOUNEAU Chouneau, William (b: William Cadreau) b: 9/2/1889, Cloquet, Minn. d: 9/17/48, Cloquet, Minn. BR/TR, 5'9", 150 lbs. Deb: 10/09/10																									
1910 Chi-A	0	1	.000	1	1	0	0	0	5^1	7	0	0	1	11.8	3.38	71	.292	.292	0	.000	0	-1	-1	-0	0.0
● MIKE CHRIS Chris, Michael b: 10/8/57, Santa Monica, Cal. BL/TL, 6'3", 180 lbs. Deb: 7/31/79																									
1979 Det-A	3	3	.500	13	8	0	0	0	39	46	3	21	31	15.5	6.92	62	.297	.381	0	—	0	-12	-11	1	-1.0
1982 SF-N	0	2	.000	9	6	0	0	0	26	23	2	26	10	17.3	4.85	74	.245	.413	1	.143	-0	-4	-4	1	-0.3
1983 SF-N	0	0	—	7	0	0	0	0	13^1	16	1	16	5	23.0	8.10	44	.308	.486	0	.000	-0	-7	-7	-0	-0.7
Total 3	3	5	.375	29	14	0	0	0	78^1	85	6	63	46	17.3	6.43	61	.282	.411	1	.111	-0	-22	-22	1	-2.0
● GARY CHRISTENSON Christenson, Gary Richard b: 5/5/53, Mineola, N.Y. BL/TL, 6'5", 200 lbs. Deb: 9/01/79																									
1979 KC-A	0	0	—	6	0	0	0	0	10^2	10	1	2	4	10.1	3.38	126	.250	.286	0	—	0	1	1	0	0.1
1980 KC-A	3	0	1.000	24	0	0	0	1	31^1	35	4	18	16	15.8	5.17	78	.278	.377	0	—	0	-4	-4	1	-0.4
Total 2	3	0	1.000	30	0	0	0	1	42	45	5	20	20	14.4	4.71	87	.271	.356	0	—	0	-3	-3	1	-0.3
● LARRY CHRISTENSON Christenson, Larry Richard b: 11/10/53, Everett, Wash. BR/TR, 6'4", 215 lbs. Deb: 4/13/73																									
1973 Phi-N	1	4	.200	10	9	1	0	0	34^1	53	3	20	11	19.4	6.55	58	.366	.446	0	.000	-1	-11	-11	-0	-1.1
1974 Phi-N	1	1	.500	10	1	0	0	2	23	20	2	15	18	13.7	4.30	88	.241	.357	0	.000	-1	-2	-1	-0	-0.2
1975 Phi-N	11	6	.647	29	26	5	2	1	171^2	149	12	45	88	10.2	3.67	102	.236	.288	14	.246	5	-1	1	-3	0.4
1976 Phi-N	13	8	.619	32	29	2	0	0	168^2	199	8	42	54	12.9	3.68	96	.297	.339	10	.196	4	-3	-3	-3	-0.2
1977 *Phi-N	19	6	.760	34	34	5	1	0	219^1	229	21	69	118	12.5	4.06	98	.268	.327	10	.135	1	-4	-2	-2	-0.3
1978 *Phi-N	13	14	.481	33	33	9	3	0	228	209	16	47	131	10.1	3.24	110	.244	.284	5	.075	-2	9	8	-0	0.6
1979 Phi-N	5	10	.333	19	17	2	0	0	106	118	9	30	53	12.7	4.50	85	.291	.342	9	.290	5	-9	-8	-0	-0.3
1980 *Phi-N	5	1	.833	14	14	0	0	0	73^2	62	4	27	49	11.2	4.03	94	.227	.304	7	.368	4	-4	-2	1	0.3
1981 *Phi-N	4	7	.364	20	15	0	0	1	106^2	108	8	30	70	11.7	3.54	102	.267	.319	3	.100	-2	-1	1	-1	-0.1
1982 Phi-N	9	10	.474	33	33	3	0	0	223	212	15	53	145	10.8	3.47	106	.253	.300	5	.075	-3	3	5	-1	0.1
1983 Phi-N	2	4	.333	9	9	0	0	0	48^1	42	2	17	44	11.2	3.91	91	.233	.303	1	.059	-1	-2	-2	1	-0.2
Total 11	83	71	.539	243	220	27	6	4	1402^2	1401	100	395	781	11.7	3.79	98	.262	.315	64	.150	10	-24	-12	-8	-1.0
● CLAY CHRISTIANSEN Christiansen, Clay C. b: 6/28/58, Wichita, Kan. BR/TR, 6'5", 205 lbs. Deb: 5/10/84																									
1984 NY-A	2	4	.333	24	1	0	0	2	38^2	50	4	12	27	14.7	6.05	63	.309	.360	0	—	0	-9	-10	-0	-1.0
● MIKE CHRISTOPHER Christopher, Michael Wayne b: 11/3/63, Petersburg, Va. BR/TR, 6'5", 205 lbs. Deb: 9/10/91																									
1991 LA-N	0	0	—	3	0	0	0	0	4	2	0	3	2	11.3	0.00	—	.167	.333	0	—	0	2	2	0	0.2
1992 Cle-A	0	0	—	10	0	0	0	0	18	17	2	10	13	13.5	3.00	134	.254	.351	0	—	0	2	2	0	0.1
Total 2	0	0	—	13	0	0	0	0	22	19	2	13	15	13.1	2.45	161	.241	.348	0	—	0	4	4	0	0.3
● RUSS CHRISTOPHER Christopher, Russell Ormand b: 9/12/17, Richmond, Cal. d: 12/5/54, Richmond, Cal. BR/TR, 6'3", 180 lbs. Deb: 4/14/42 F																									
1942 Phi-A	4	13	.235	30	18	10	0	1	165	154	8	99	58	14.0	3.82	99	.254	.362	5	.089	-3	-3	-1	6	0.2
1943 Phi-A	5	8	.385	24	15	5	0	2	133	120	3	58	56	12.2	3.45	98	.242	.325	7	.156	-1	-2	-1	8	0.6
1944 Phi-A	14	14	.500	35	24	13	1	1	215^1	200	6	63	84	11.4	2.97	117	.245	.306	18	.222	3	11	12	5	2.3
1945 Phi-A†	13	13	.500	33	27	17	2	2	227^1	213	9	75	100	11.8	3.17	108	.251	.319	13	.171	-1	5	7	7	1.5
1946 Phi-A	5	7	.417	30	13	1	0	2	119^1	119	5	44	79	12.5	4.30	82	.254	.322	5	.139	-0	-11	-10	4	-0.6
1947 Phi-A	10	7	.588	44	0	0	0	12	80^2	70	4	33	33	11.5	2.90	131	.236	.313	2	.125	-0	7	8	1	0.9
1948 *Cle-A	3	2	.600	45	0	0	0	**17**	59	55	3	27	14	12.5	2.90	140	.247	.328	0	.000	-0	9	8	0	0.7
Total 7	54	64	.458	241	97	46	3	35	999^2	931	38	399	424	12.2	3.37	106	.248	.325	50	.158	-3	17	24	31	5.6
● BUBBA CHURCH Church, Emory Nicholas b: 9/12/24, Birmingham, Ala. BR/TR, 6', 180 lbs. Deb: 4/30/50																									
1950 Phi-N	8	6	.571	31	18	8	2	1	142	113	12	56	50	10.7	2.73	149	.225	.303	8	.182	0	22	21	-0	2.1
1951 Phi-N	15	11	.577	38	33	15	4	1	247	246	17	90	104	12.3	3.53	109	.261	.326	22	.256	5	12	9	-2	1.1
1952 Phi-N	0	0	—	2	1	0	0	0	5	11	0	1	3	23.4	10.80	34	.440	.481	0	.000	-0	-4	-4	0	-0.4
Cin-N	5	9	.357	29	22	5	1	0	153^1	173	21	48	47	13.1	4.34	87	.301	.358	12	.240	3	-10	-10	-1	-0.8
Yr	5	9	.357	31	23	5	1	0	158^1	184	21	49	50	13.4	4.55	83	.306	.361	12	.235	3	-14	-14	-1	-1.2
1953 Cin-N	3	3	.500	11	7	2	0	0	43^2	55	9	19	12	15.7	5.98	73	.318	.392	4	.267	1	-8	-8	-0	-0.7
Chi-N	4	5	.444	27	11	1	0	1	104^1	115	16	49	47	14.3	5.00	89	.276	.355	7	.212	1	-8	-6	-1	-0.6
Yr	7	8	.467	38	18	3	0	1	148	170	25	68	59	14.6	5.29	84	.288	.363	11	.229	2	-17	-14	-1	-1.3
1954 Chi-N	1	3	.250	7	3	1	0	0	14^2	21	8	13	8	20.9	9.82	43	.350	.466	0	.000	-1	-9	-9	0	-0.9
1955 Chi-N	0	0	—	2	0	0	0	1	3^1	4	1	1	3	13.5	5.40	76	.286	.333	0	.000	-0	-1	-0	-0	-0.1
Total 6	36	37	.493	147	95	32	7	4	713^1	738	84	277	274	12.9	4.10	97	.272	.342	53	.226	9	-7	-8	-4	-0.3
● LEN CHURCH Church, Leonard b: 3/21/42, Chicago, Ill. d: 4/22/88, Richardson, Tex. BB/TR, 6', 190 lbs. Deb: 8/27/66																									
1966 Chi-N	0	1	.000	4	0	0	0	0	6	10	1	7	3	25.5	7.50	49	.400	.531	0	.000	-0	-3	-3	0	-0.3
● CHUCK CHURN Churn, Clarence Nottingham b: 2/1/30, Bridgetown, Va. BR/TR, 6'3", 205 lbs. Deb: 4/18/57																									
1957 Pit-N	0	0	—	5	0	0	0	0	8^1	9	1	4	4	14.0	4.32	88	.333	.419	0	.000	-0	-0	-0	1	0.0
1958 Cle-A	0	0	—	6	0	0	0	0	8^2	12	1	5	4	17.7	6.23	59	.343	.425	0	—	0	-2	-2	-0	-0.3
1959 *LA-N	3	2	.600	14	0	0	0	1	30^2	28	2	10	24	11.4	4.99	85	.255	.322	1	.167	0	-4	-3	0	-0.2
Total 3	3	2	.600	25	0	0	0	1	47^2	49	4	19	32	13.0	5.10	79	.285	.359	1	.143	0	-6	-6	1	-0.5
● MARK CIARDI Ciardi, Mark Thomas b: 8/19/61, New Brunswick, N.J. BR/TR, 6' ", 180 lbs. Deb: 4/09/87																									
1987 Mil-A	1	1	.500	4	3	0	0	0	16^1	26	5	9	8	19.3	9.37	49	.361	.432	0	—	0	-9	-9	0	-0.8
● AL CICOTTE Cicotte, Alva Warren "Bozo" b: 12/23/29, Melvindale, Mich. d: 11/29/82, Westland, Mich. BR/TR, 6'3", 185 lbs. Deb: 4/22/57																									
1957 NY-A	2	2	.500	20	2	0	0	2	65^1	57	5	30	36	12.1	3.03	118	.237	.325	3	.150	-0	6	4	0	0.4
1958 Was-A	0	3	.000	8	4	0	0	0	28	36	3	14	14	16.1	4.82	79	.316	.391	2	.200	-0	-3	-3	-1	-0.4
Det-A	3	1	.750	14	2	0	0	0	43	50	1	15	21	13.6	3.56	113	.307	.365	3	.176	-1	1	2	1	0.3
Yr	3	4	.429	22	6	0	0	0	71	86	4	29	35	14.6	4.06	97	.309	.375	5	.185	-1	-2	-1	1	-0.1
1959 Cle-A	3	1	.750	26	1	0	0	1	44	46	4	25	23	14.9	5.32	69	.299	.403	1	.333	1	-7	-8	0	-0.7
1961 StL-N	2	6	.250	29	7	0	0	1	75	83	16	34	51	14.3	5.28	83	.283	.362	6	.286	1	-10	-7	0	-0.6
1962 Hou-N	0	0	—	5	0	0	0	0	4^2	8	1	1	4	17.4	3.86	97	.381	.409	0	—	0	0	-0	-0	0.0
Total 5	10	13	.435	102	16	0	0	4	260	280	30	119	149	14.0	4.36	90	.284	.364	15	.211	0	-14	-12	1	-1.0

● EDDIE CICOTTE
Cicotte, Edward Victor "Knuckles" b: 6/19/1884, Detroit, Mich. d: 5/5/69, Detroit, Mich. BB/TR, 5'9", 175 lbs. Deb: 9/03/05

YEAR	TM/L	W	L	PCT	G	GS	CG	SH	SV	IP	H	HR	BB	SO	RAT	ERA	ERA+	OAV	OOB	BH	AVG	PB	PR	/A	PD	TPI
1905	Det-A	1	1	.500	3	1	1	0	0	18	25	0	5	6	15.0	3.50	78	.330	.371	3	.429	1	-2	-2	-1	-0.2
1908	Bos-A	11	12	.478	39	24	17	2	2	207^1	198	0	59	95	11.6	2.43	101	.261	.323	17	.236	3	-1	1	0	0.4
1909	Bos-A	13	5	.722	27	17	10	1	2	159^2	117	3	56	82	9.8	1.97	127	.210	.283	11	.224	3	9	9	-0	1.3
1910	Bos-A	15	11	.577	36	30	20	3	0	250	213	4	86	104	11.2	2.74	93	.233	.308	12	.141	-1	-6	-5	3	-0.4
1911	Bos-A	11	15	.423	35	25	16	1	0	220	236	2	73	106	12.8	2.82	116	.282	.342	10	.141	-2	13	11	1	0.9
1912	Bos-A	1	3	.250	9	6	2	0	0	46	58	0	15	20	14.5	5.67	60	.319	.374	2	.154	0	-12	-12	1	-1.0
	Chi-A	9	7	.563	20	18	13	1	0	152	159	3	37	70	11.6	2.84	113	.277	.320	13	.245	1	8	6	2	1.0
	Yr	10	10	.500	29	24	15	1	0	198	217	3	52	90	12.2	3.50	93	.286	.332	15	.227	1	-4	-6	3	0.0
1913	Chi-A	18	12	.600	41	30	18	3	1	268	224	2	73	121	10.1	1.58	185	.226	.281	13	.143	-3	40	40	7	5.1
1914	Chi-A	11	16	.407	45	30	15	4	3	269^1	220	0	72	122	9.9	2.04	132	.232	.288	14	.163	-1	21	19	7	2.9
1915	Chi-A	13	12	.520	39	26	15	1	3	223^1	216	2	48	106	10.9	3.02	99	.261	.306	14	.209	1	-2	-1	0	0.0
1916	Chi-A	15	7	**.682**	44	19	11	2	5	187	138	1	70	91	10.1	1.78	155	.218	.296	12	.211	2	22	20	1	2.6
1917	*Chi-A	**28**	12	.700	49	35	29	7	4	**346^2**	246	2	70	150	**8.3**	**1.53**	**174**	.203	**.248**	20	.179	1	**44**	**43**	-1	**5.0**
1918	Chi-A	12	19	.387	38	30	24	1	2	266	275	2	40	104	10.7	2.77	99	.271	.300	14	.163	2	0	-1	-0	0.0
1919	*Chi-A	**29**	7	**.806**	40	35	**30**	5	1	**306^2**	256	5	49	110	**9.0**	1.82	175	.228	.261	20	.202	1	48	46	-4	4.8
1920	Chi-A	21	10	.677	37	35	28	4	2	303^1	316	6	74	87	11.6	3.26	115	.275	.320	22	.196	-3	18	17	0	1.5
Total	14	208	149	.583	502	361	249	35	25	3223^1	2897	32	827	1374	10.5	2.38	123	.245	.298	197	.186	4	200	195	15	23.9

● PETE CIMINO
Cimino, Peter William b: 10/17/42, Philadelphia, Pa. BR/TR, 6'2", 195 lbs. Deb: 9/22/65

YEAR	TM/L	W	L	PCT	G	GS	CG	SH	SV	IP	H	HR	BB	SO	RAT	ERA	ERA+	OAV	OOB	BH	AVG	PB	PR	/A	PD	TPI
1965	Min-A	0	0	—	1	0	0	0	0	1	0	0	0	0	0.0	0.00	—	.000	.000	0	—	0	0	0	-0	0.0
1966	Min-A	2	5	.286	35	0	0	0	4	64^2	53	4	30	57	11.7	2.92	123	.222	.311	0	.000	-0	4	5	-1	0.4
1967	Cal-A	3	3	.500	46	1	0	0	1	88^1	73	12	31	80	10.8	3.26	96	.229	.301	5	.417	2	-0	-1	-1	-0.1
1968	Cal-A	0	0	—	4	0	0	0	0	7	7	0	4	2	14.1	2.57	113	.259	.355	0	—	0	0	0	-0	0.0
Total	4	5	8	.385	86	1	0	0	5	161	133	16	65	139	11.2	3.07	108	.226	.306	5	.278	1	4	4	-2	0.3

● LOU CIOLA
Ciola, Louis Alexander b: 9/6/22, Norfolk, Va. BR/TR, 5'9", 165 lbs. Deb: 7/25/43

YEAR	TM/L	W	L	PCT	G	GS	CG	SH	SV	IP	H	HR	BB	SO	RAT	ERA	ERA+	OAV	OOB	BH	AVG	PB	PR	/A	PD	TPI
1943	Phi-A	1	3	.250	12	3	2	0	0	43^2	48	2	22	7	14.6	5.56	61	.273	.357	3	.167	-1	-11	-11	-0	-1.2

● GALEN CISCO
Cisco, Galen Bernard b: 3/7/36, St. Mary's, Ohio BR/TR, 5'11", 215 lbs. Deb: 6/11/61 C

YEAR	TM/L	W	L	PCT	G	GS	CG	SH	SV	IP	H	HR	BB	SO	RAT	ERA	ERA+	OAV	OOB	BH	AVG	PB	PR	/A	PD	TPI
1961	Bos-A	2	4	.333	17	8	0	0	0	52^1	67	5	28	26	16.3	6.71	62	.325	.406	1	.100	-0	-16	-15	-0	-1.4
1962	Bos-A	4	7	.364	23	9	1	0	0	83	95	11	50	43	16.0	6.72	61	.292	.392	2	.080	-1	-25	-24	1	-2.2
	NY-N	1	1	.500	4	2	1	0	0	19^1	15	0	11	13	13.5	3.26	128	.208	.337	0	.000	-1	1	2	-0	0.1
1963	NY-N	7	15	.318	51	17	1	0	4	155^2	165	15	64	81	13.6	4.34	80	.273	.349	5	.132	0	-18	-15	-0	-1.6
1964	NY-N	6	19	.240	36	25	5	2	0	191^2	182	17	54	78	11.4	3.62	99	.256	.313	6	.111	-0	-2	-1	2	0.1
1965	NY-N	4	8	.333	35	17	1	1	0	112^1	119	12	51	58	13.7	4.49	79	.272	.349	7	.259	2	-12	-12	-2	-1.2
1967	Bos-A	0	1	.000	11	0	0	0	1	22^1	21	4	8	8	11.7	3.63	96	.266	.333	0	.000	-0	-1	-0	0	-0.1
1969	KC-A	1	1	.500	15	0	0	0	1	22^1	17	4	15	18	12.9	3.63	102	.215	.340	0	—	0	-0	0	0	0.1
Total	7	25	56	.309	192	78	9	3	2	659	681	68	281	325	13.4	4.56	81	.271	.349	21	.128	-0	-72	-64	1	-6.2

● RALPH CITARELLA
Citarella, Ralph Alexander b: 2/7/58, East Orange, N.J. BR/TR, 6', 180 lbs. Deb: 9/13/83

YEAR	TM/L	W	L	PCT	G	GS	CG	SH	SV	IP	H	HR	BB	SO	RAT	ERA	ERA+	OAV	OOB	BH	AVG	PB	PR	/A	PD	TPI
1983	StL-N	0	0	—	6	0	0	0	0	11	8	0	3	4	9.0	1.64	221	.205	.262	0	.000	-0	2	2	-0	0.2
1984	StL-N	0	1	.000	10	2	0	0	0	22^1	20	0	7	15	12.1	3.63	96	.238	.319	1	.250	0	-0	-0	0	0.0
1987	Chi-A	0	0	—	5	0	0	0	0	11	13	4	4	9	15.5	7.36	62	.302	.388	0	—	0	-4	-3	-0	-0.4
Total	3	0	1	.000	21	2	0	0	0	44^1	41	4	14	28	12.2	4.06	93	.247	.324	1	.200	0	-1	-1	0	-0.2

● BOBBY CLACK
Clack, Robert S. "Gentlemanly Bob" (b: Robert S. Clark) b: 6/1850, England d: 10/22/33, Danvers, Mass. BR/TR, 5'9", 153 lbs. Deb: 5/15/1874 ♦

YEAR	TM/L	W	L	PCT	G	GS	CG	SH	SV	IP	H	HR	BB	SO	RAT	ERA	ERA+	OAV	OOB	BH	AVG	PB	PR	/A	PD	TPI
1876	Cin-N	0	0	—	1	0	0	0	0	2	2	0	0	0	9.0	4.50	49	.250	.250	19	.161	-0	-0	-1	0	0.0

● JIM CLANCY
Clancy, James b: 12/18/55, Chicago, Ill. BR/TR, 6'4", 220 lbs. Deb: 7/26/77

YEAR	TM/L	W	L	PCT	G	GS	CG	SH	SV	IP	H	HR	BB	SO	RAT	ERA	ERA+	OAV	OOB	BH	AVG	PB	PR	/A	PD	TPI
1977	Tor-A	4	9	.308	13	13	4	1	0	76^2	80	7	47	44	14.9	5.05	83	.280	.381	0	—	0	-8	-7	1	-0.7
1978	Tor-A	10	12	.455	31	30	7	0	0	193^2	199	10	91	106	13.5	4.09	96	.270	.351	0	—	0	-7	-4	1	-0.3
1979	Tor-A	2	7	.222	12	11	2	0	0	63^2	65	8	31	33	13.6	5.51	79	.272	.356	0	—	0	-9	-8	0	-0.8
1980	Tor-A	13	16	.448	34	34	15	2	0	250^2	217	19	128	152	12.5	3.30	130	.233	.327	0	—	0	20	28	-0	2.6
1981	Tor-A	6	12	.333	22	22	2	0	0	125	126	12	64	56	14.0	4.90	80	.262	.355	0	—	0	-17	-13	-3	-1.7
1982	Tor-A★	16	14	.533	40	40	11	3	0	266^2	251	26	77	139	11.1	3.71	121	.248	.302	0	—	0	11	23	-2	2.0
1983	Tor-A	15	11	.577	34	34	11	1	0	223	238	23	61	99	12.1	3.91	110	.271	.319	0	—	0	4	10	-2	0.7
1984	Tor-A	13	15	.464	36	36	5	0	0	219^2	249	25	88	118	13.9	5.12	80	.287	.355	0	—	0	-28	-25	0	-2.4
1985	*Tor-A	9	6	.600	23	23	1	0	0	128^2	117	15	37	66	10.8	3.78	111	.241	.295	0	—	0	5	6	-1	0.5
1986	Tor-A	14	14	.500	34	34	6	3	0	219^1	202	24	63	126	11.0	3.94	107	.243	.299	0	—	0	6	7	1	0.7
1987	Tor-A	15	11	.577	37	37	5	1	0	241^1	234	24	80	180	11.7	3.54	127	.255	.315	0	—	0	24	25	2	2.7
1988	Tor-A	11	13	.458	36	31	4	0	1	196^1	207	26	47	118	12.1	4.49	87	.272	.322	0	—	0	-11	-12	-1	-1.3
1989	Hou-N	7	14	.333	33	26	1	0	0	147	155	13	66	91	13.5	5.08	67	.269	.344	6	.146	-0	-26	-28	-3	-3.1
1990	Hou-N	2	8	.200	33	10	0	0	1	76	100	4	33	44	16.1	6.51	57	.322	.392	3	.214	0	-23	-24	1	-2.3
1991	Hou-N	0	3	.000	30	0	0	0	5	55	37	5	20	33	9.3	2.78	126	.193	.269	0	.000	-0	6	4	-1	0.3
	*Atl-N	3	2	.600	24	0	0	0	3	34^2	36	3	14	17	13.2	5.71	68	.267	.340	0	.000	-0	-8	-7	0	-0.8
	Yr	3	5	.375	54	0	0	0	8	89^2	73	8	34	50	10.8	3.91	93	.222	.297	0	.000	-1	-2	-3	-1	-0.5
Total	15	140	167	.456	472	381	74	11	10	2517^1	2513	244	947	1422	12.5	4.23	98	.261	.329	9	.148	-0	-62	-26	-8	-3.9

● BRYAN CLARK
Clark, Bryan Donald b: 7/12/56, Madera, Cal. BL/TL, 6'2", 185 lbs. Deb: 4/11/81

YEAR	TM/L	W	L	PCT	G	GS	CG	SH	SV	IP	H	HR	BB	SO	RAT	ERA	ERA+	OAV	OOB	BH	AVG	PB	PR	/A	PD	TPI
1981	Sea-A	2	5	.286	29	9	1	0	2	93^1	92	3	55	52	14.3	4.34	89	.261	.363	0	—	0	-7	-5	1	-0.4
1982	Sea-A	5	2	.714	37	5	1	1	0	114^2	104	6	58	70	12.7	2.75	154	.241	.331	0	—	0	17	19	1	2.1
1983	Sea-A	7	10	.412	41	17	2	0	0	162^1	160	14	72	76	13.0	3.94	108	.261	.342	0	—	0	2	6	3	0.9
1984	Tor-A	1	2	.333	20	3	0	0	0	45^2	66	6	22	21	17.5	5.91	69	.342	.412	0	—	0	-10	-9	1	-0.8
1985	Cle-A	3	4	.429	31	3	0	0	2	62^2	78	8	34	24	16.1	6.32	65	.311	.393	0	—	0	-15	-15	1	-1.4
1986	Chi-A	0	0	—	5	0	0	0	0	8	8	0	2	5	11.3	4.50	96	.276	.323	0	—	0	-0	-0	-0	-0.1
1987	Chi-A	0	0	—	11	0	0	0	0	18^2	19	1	8	8	13.0	2.41	190	.297	.375	0	—	0	4	4	-1	0.3
1990	Sea-A	2	0	1.000	12	0	0	0	0	11	9	0	10	3	15.5	3.27	121	.237	.396	0	—	0	1	1	0	0.1
Total	8	20	23	.465	186	37	4	1	4	516^1	536	38	261	259	14.0	4.15	100	.272	.359	0	—	0	-8	1	7	0.7

● ED CLARK
Clark, Edward C. b: Cincinnati, Ohio Deb: 7/04/1886

YEAR	TM/L	W	L	PCT	G	GS	CG	SH	SV	IP	H	HR	BB	SO	RAT	ERA	ERA+	OAV	OOB	BH	AVG	PB	PR	/A	PD	TPI
1886	Phi-a	0	1	.000	1	1	1	0	0	8	10	2	2	2	15.8	6.75	52	.294	.368	0	.000	-0	-3	-3	-0	-0.3
1891	Col-a	0	0	—	1	0	0	0	0	2	2	0	0	1	9.0	0.00	—	.252	.252	0	.000	-0	1	1	0	0.1
Total	2	0	1	.000	2	1	1	0	0	10	12	2	2	3	14.4	5.40	65	.286	.348	0	.000	-0	-2	-2	-0	-0.2

● GEORGE CLARK
Clark, George Myron b: 5/19/1891, Smithland, Iowa d: 11/14/40, Sioux City, Iowa BR/TL, 6', 190 lbs. Deb: 5/16/13

YEAR	TM/L	W	L	PCT	G	GS	CG	SH	SV	IP	H	HR	BB	SO	RAT	ERA	ERA+	OAV	OOB	BH	AVG	PB	PR	/A	PD	TPI
1913	NY-A	0	1	.000	11	1	0	0	0	19	22	1	19	5	20.8	9.00	33	.272	.427	2	.500	1	-13	-13	-0	-1.2

● GINGER CLARK
Clark, Harvey Daniel b: 3/7/1879, Wooster, Ohio d: 5/10/43, Lake Charles, La. BR/TR, 5'11", 165 lbs. Deb: 8/11/02

YEAR	TM/L	W	L	PCT	G	GS	CG	SH	SV	IP	H	HR	BB	SO	RAT	ERA	ERA+	OAV	OOB	BH	AVG	PB	PR	/A	PD	TPI
1902	Cle-A	1	0	1.000	1	0	0	0	0	6	10	0	3	1	21.0	6.00	57	.370	.451	2	.500	1	-2	-2	0	-0.1

● MARK CLARK
Clark, Mark Willard b: 5/12/68, Bath, Ill. BR/TR, 6'5", 225 lbs. Deb: 9/06/91

YEAR	TM/L	W	L	PCT	G	GS	CG	SH	SV	IP	H	HR	BB	SO	RAT	ERA	ERA+	OAV	OOB	BH	AVG	PB	PR	/A	PD	TPI
1991	StL-N	1	1	.500	7	2	0	0	0	22^1	17	3	11	13	11.3	4.03	92	.215	.311	0	.000	-1	-1	-1	-0	-0.2
1992	StL-N	3	10	.231	20	20	1	1	0	113^1	117	12	36	44	12.2	4.45	77	.265	.321	5	.139	-1	-12	-13	-2	-1.6
Total	2	4	11	.267	27	22	1	1	0	135^2	134	15	47	57	12.0	4.38	80	.258	.319	5	.116	-1	-13	-13	-2	-1.8

YEAR TM/L	W	L	PCT	G	GS	CG	SH	SV	IP	H	HR	BB	SO	RAT	ERA	ERA+	OAV	OOB	BH	AVG	PB	PR	/A	PD	TPI

● **MIKE CLARK** Clark, Michael John b: 2/12/22, Camden, N.J. BR/TR, 6'4", 190 lbs. Deb: 7/27/52

1952 StL-N	2	0	1.000	12	4	0	0	0	25¹	32	2	14	10	16.3	6.04	61	.311	.393	0	.000	-1	-6	-7	0	-0.7
1953 StL-N	1	0	1.000	23	2	0	0	1	35²	46	2	21	17	17.4	4.79	89	.315	.408	0	.000	-1	-2	-2	1	-0.2
Total 2	3	0	1.000	35	6	0	0	1	61	78	4	35	27	17.0	5.31	76	.313	.402	0	.000	-1	-9	-9	1	-0.9

● **SPIDER CLARK** Clark, Owen F. b: 9/16/1867, Brooklyn, N.Y. d: 2/8/1892, Brooklyn, N.Y. TR, 5'10", 150 lbs. Deb: 5/02/1889 ♦

| 1890 Buf-P | 0 | 0 | — | 1 | 0 | 0 | 0 | 0 | 4 | 8 | 0 | 2 | 2 | 22.5 | 6.75 | 61 | .399 | .453 | 69 | .265 | 0 | -1 | -1 | -0 | -0.1 |

● **PHIL CLARK** Clark, Philip James b: 10/3/32, Albany, Ga. BR/TR, 6'3", 210 lbs. Deb: 4/15/58

1958 StL-N	0	1	.000	7	0	0	0	1	7²	11	2	3	1	16.4	3.52	117	.355	.412	0	.000	-0	0	1	-0	0.0
1959 StL-N	0	1	.000	7	0	0	0	0	7	8	0	8	5	20.6	12.86	33	.286	.444	0	—	0	-7	-7	0	-0.6
Total 2	0	2	.000	14	0	0	0	1	14²	19	2	11	6	18.4	7.98	52	.322	.429	0	.000	-0	-7	-6	-0	-0.6

● **RICKEY CLARK** Clark, Rickey Charles b: 3/21/46, Mt.Clemens, Mich. BR/TR, 6'2", 170 lbs. Deb: 4/22/67

1967 Cal-A	12	11	.522	32	30	1	1	0	174	144	15	69	81	11.3	2.59	121	.224	.305	2	.040	-4	12	11	1	0.9
1968 Cal-A	1	11	.083	21	17	0	0	0	94¹	74	4	54	60	12.3	3.53	82	.217	.326	1	-6	-6	-1	-0.8
1969 Cal-A	0	0	—	6	0	0	0	0	9²	12	2	7	6	17.7	5.59	62	.300	.404	1	.500	N	-2	-2	-1	-0.2
1971 Cal-A	2	1	.667	11	7	1	1	1	44	36	6	28	28	13.5	2.86	113	.220	.340	4	.267	1	3	2	-1	0.2
1972 Cal-A	4	9	.308	26	15	2	0	1	109²	105	10	55	61	13.3	4.51	64	.261	.352	3	.097	-1	-18	-20	1	-2.2
Total 5	19	32	.373	96	70	4	2	2	431²	371	37	213	236	12.4	3.38	90	.233	.328	13	.103	-5	-10	-16	1	-2.1

● **BOB CLARK** Clark, Robert William b: 8/22/1897, Newport, Pa. d: 5/18/44, Carlsbad, N.Mex. BR/TR, 6'3", 188 lbs. Deb: 5/26/20

1920 Cle-A	1	2	.333	11	2	2	1	0	42	59	0	13	8	15.6	3.43	111	.383	.435	2	.200	-0	2	2	-0	0.1
1921 Cle-A	0	0	—	5	0	0	0	0	9¹	23	2	6	2	28.9	14.46	29	.511	.577	0	.000	-1	-11	-11	-0	-1.0
Total 2	1	2	.333	16	2	2	1	0	51¹	82	2	19	10	18.1	5.44	71	.412	.468	2	.154	-1	-9	-9	-1	-0.9

● **TERRY CLARK** Clark, Terry Lee b: 10/18/60, Los Angeles, Cal. BR/TR, 6'2", 190 lbs. Deb: 7/07/88

1988 Cal-A	6	6	.500	15	15	2	1	0	94	120	8	31	39	14.5	5.07	76	.323	.375	0	—	0	-12	-13	0	-1.0
1989 Cal-A	0	2	.000	4	2	0	0	0	11	13	0	3	7	13.1	4.91	78	.310	.356	0	—	0	-1	-1	0	-0.1
1990 Hou-N	0	0	—	1	1	0	0	0	4	9	0	3	2	27.0	13.50	27	.429	.500	1	.500	0	-4	-4	0	-0.3
Total 3	6	8	.429	20	18	2	1	0	109	142	8	37	48	14.8	5.37	72	.326	.379	1	.500	0	-17	-18	0	-1.4

● **OTIE CLARK** Clark, William Otis b: 5/22/18, Boscobel, Wis. BR/TR, 6'1.5", 190 lbs. Deb: 4/17/45

| 1945 Bos-A | 4 | 4 | .500 | 12 | 9 | 4 | 1 | 0 | 82 | 86 | 6 | 19 | 20 | 11.6 | 3.07 | 111 | .268 | .311 | 5 | .208 | 0 | 3 | 3 | -2 | 0.1 |

● **WATTY CLARK** Clark, William Watson "Lefty" b: 5/16/02, St.Joseph, La. d: 3/4/72, Clearwater, Fla. BL/TL, 6'0.5", 175 lbs. Deb: 5/28/24

1924 Cle-A	1	3	.250	12	1	0	0	0	25²	38	0	14	6	18.9	7.01	61	.345	.429	2	.222	1	-8	-8	-0	-0.7
1927 Bro-N	7	2	.778	27	3	1	0	2	73²	74	2	19	32	11.4	2.32	171	.265	.312	3	.143	-1	13	13	0	1.3
1928 Bro-N	12	9	.571	40	19	10	2	3	194²	193	4	50	85	11.4	2.68	148	.259	.306	10	.152	-2	28	28	1	2.7
1929 Bro-N	16	19	.457	41	36	19	3	1	**279**	295	14	71	140	11.9	3.74	123	.270	.316	16	.165	-3	30	27	-0	2.2
1930 Bro-N	13	13	.500	44	24	9	1	6	200	209	20	38	81	11.1	4.18	118	.271	.306	14	.206	0	17	16	0	1.5
1931 Bro-N	14	10	.583	34	28	16	3	1	233¹	243	4	52	96	11.4	3.20	119	.267	.308	21	.250	4	17	16	-3	1.8
1932 Bro-N	20	12	.625	40	36	19	2	0	273	282	15	49	99	11.0	3.49	109	.264	.299	21	.216	1	12	10	1	1.2
1933 Bro-N	2	4	.333	11	8	4	1	1	50²	61	2	6	14	12.4	4.80	67	.303	.333	2	.154	-0	-8	-9	-0	-0.9
NY-N	3	4	.429	16	5	0	0	0	44	58	3	11	11	14.3	4.70	68	.317	.359	3	.273	1	-7	-7	1	-0.6
Yr	5	8	.385	27	13	4	1	1	94²	119	5	17	25	13.0	4.75	68	.307	.338	5	.208	1	-15	-16	1	-1.5
1934 NY-N	1	2	.333	5	4	1	0	0	18²	23	5	5	6	13.5	6.75	57	.295	.337	1	.167	0	-6	-6	0	-0.5
Bro-N	2	0	1.000	17	1	0	0	0	25¹	40	0	9	10	17.8	5.33	73	.345	.397	1	.125	-1	-4	-4	-0	-0.5
Yr	3	2	.600	22	5	1	0	0	44	63	5	14	16	16.0	5.93	66	.325	.373	2	.143	-0	-9	-10	-0	-1.0
1935 Bro-N	13	8	.619	33	25	11	1	0	207	215	11	28	35	10.6	3.30	120	.264	.289	14	.177	-0	16	15	2	1.7
1936 Bro-N	7	11	.389	33	16	1	1	2	120	162	11	28	28	14.3	4.43	93	.316	.351	9	.231	0	-5	-4	0	-0.4
1937 Bro-N	0	0	—	2	0	0	0	0	2¹	4	0	3	0	27.0	7.71	52	.308	.438	0	—	0	-1	-1	-0	-0.1
Total 12	111	97	.534	355	206	91	14	16	1747¹	1897	86	383	643	11.8	3.66	112	.275	.315	117	.196	1	96	87	1	8.7

● **LEFTY CLARKE** Clarke, Alan Thomas b: 3/8/1896, Clarksville, Md. d: 3/11/75, Cheverly, Md. BB/TL, 5'11", 180 lbs. Deb: 10/02/21

| 1921 Cin-N | 0 | 1 | .000 | 1 | 1 | 1 | 0 | 0 | 5 | 7 | 2 | 1 | 2 | 16.2 | 5.40 | 66 | .304 | .360 | 0 | .000 | -0 | -1 | -1 | -0 | -0.1 |

● **HENRY CLARKE** Clarke, Henry Tefft b: 8/28/1875, Bellevue, Neb. d: 3/28/50, Colorado Springs, Colo. BR/TR, Deb: 6/26/1897 ♦

1897 Cle-N	0	4	.000	5	4	3	0	0	30²	32	4	12	3	13.8	6.16	73	.267	.348	7	.280	0	-6	-6	-1	-0.5
1898 Chi-N	1	0	1.000	1	1	1	0	0	9	8	0	5	1	14.0	2.00	179	.237	.352	1	.250	0	2	2	-0	0.2
Total 2	1	4	.200	6	5	4	0	0	39²	40	4	17	4	13.8	5.22	82	.260	.349	8	.276	0	-5	-4	-1	-0.3

● **RUFE CLARKE** Clarke, Rufus Rivers b: 4/13/1900, Estill, S.C. d: 2/8/83, Columbia, S.C. BR/TR, 6'1", 203 lbs. Deb: 9/03/23 F

1923 Det-A	1	1	.500	5	0	0	0	0	6	6	0	6	2	19.5	4.50	86	.300	.481	0	-0	-0	0	0.0
1924 Det-A	0	0	—	2	0	0	0	0	5¹	3	0	5	1	15.2	3.38	122	.158	.360	0	.000	-0	1	0	-0	0.0
Total 2	1	1	.500	7	0	0	0	0	11¹	9	0	11	3	17.5	3.97	100	.231	.423	0	.000	0	0	0	-0	0.0

● **STAN CLARKE** Clarke, Stanley Martin b: 8/9/60, Toledo, Ohio BL/TL, 6'1", 180 lbs. Deb: 6/07/83

1983 Tor-A	1	1	.500	10	0	0	0	0	11	10	2	5	7	12.3	3.27	131	.256	.341	0	—	0	1	1	0	0.0
1985 Tor-A	0	0	—	4	0	0	0	0	4	3	1	2	2	11.3	4.50	94	.214	.313	0	—	0	-0	-0	0	0.0
1986 Tor-A	0	1	.000	10	0	0	0	0	12²	18	4	10	9	19.9	9.24	46	.375	.483	0	—	0	-7	-7	-0	-0.7
1987 Sea-A	2	2	.500	22	0	0	0	0	23	31	5	10	13	16.0	5.48	86	.333	.398	0	—	0	-3	-2	-0	-0.3
1989 KC-A	0	2	.000	2	2	0	0	0	7	14	2	4	2	23.1	15.43	25	.438	.500	0	—	0	-9	-9	-0	-0.7
1990 StL-N	0	0	—	2	0	0	0	0	3¹	2	0	0	3	5.4	2.70	141	.167	.167	0	—	0	0	0	0	0.0
Total 6	3	6	.333	50	2	0	0	0	61	78	16	31	36	16.1	6.79	64	.328	.405	0	—	0	-18	-17	-0	-1.7

● **WEBBO CLARKE** Clarke, Vibert Ernesto b: 6/8/28, Colon, Panama d: 6/14/70, Cristobal, C.Z. BL/TL, 6', 165 lbs. Deb: 9/04/55

| 1955 Was-A | 0 | 0 | — | 7 | 2 | 0 | 0 | 0 | 21¹ | 17 | 2 | 14 | 9 | 13.1 | 4.64 | 83 | .221 | .341 | 1 | .167 | -0 | -2 | -2 | 0 | -0.2 |

● **DAD CLARKE** Clarke, William H. b: 1/7/1865, Oswego, N.Y. d: 6/3/11, Lorain, Ohio BB/TR, Deb: 4/23/1888

1888 Chi-N	1	0	1.000	2	2	1	0	0	16	23	2	6	6	17.4	5.06	60	.315	.383	2	.286	2	-4	-4	0	-0.2
1891 Col-a	1	2	.333	4	3	2	0	0	21	30	0	16	2	20.1	6.86	50	.324	.429	1	.111	0	-7	-8	-0	-0.6
1894 NY-N	3	4	.429	15	6	5	0	1	84	114	3	26	15	15.3	4.93	106	.320	.372	8	.216	-0	4	3	-0	0.1
1895 NY-N	18	15	.545	37	30	27	1	1	281²	336	5	60	67	13.0	3.39	137	.292	.333	29	.240	-2	44	39	-3	2.9
1896 NY-N	17	24	.415	48	40	33	1	1	351	431	9	60	66	12.9	4.26	99	.300	.333	30	.204	-3	4	-2	-3	-0.7
1897 NY-N	2	1	.667	6	4	2	0	0	31	43	1	11	10	16.3	6.10	68	.326	.386	3	.167	-1	-6	-7	-0	-0.6
Lou-N	2	4	.333	7	6	6	0	0	54²	74	3	10	7	14.2	3.95	108	.320	.354	5	.227	-1	2	1	-0	0.1
Yr	4	5	.444	13	10	8	0	0	85²	117	4	21	17	14.7	4.73	89	.321	.361	8	.200	-2	-4	-5	-0	-0.5
1898 Lou-N	0	1	.000	1	1	1	0	0	9	10	1	2	1	14.0	5.00	72	.279	.352	0	.000	-1	-1	-1	-0	-0.2
Total 7	44	51	.463	120	92	77	2	3	848¹	1061	24	191	174	13.6	4.17	106	.302	.344	78	.214	-6	35	23	-6	0.9

● **DAD CLARKSON** Clarkson, Arthur Hamilton b: 8/31/1866, Cambridge, Mass. d: 2/5/11, Somerville, Mass. BR/TR, 5'10", 165 lbs. Deb: 8/20/1891 F

1891 NY-N	1	2	.333	5	2	1	0	0	28	24	0	18	11	14.5	2.89	111	.223	.350	4	.444	2	1	1	0	0.2
1892 Bos-N	1	0	1.000	1	1	1	0	0	7	5	0	3	0	10.3	1.29	273	.192	.276	0	.000	-1	2	2	-0	0.1
1893 StL-N	12	9	.571	24	21	17	1	0	186¹	194	6	79	37	13.9	3.48	136	.260	.342	10	.133	-5	25	26	1	1.8
1894 StL-N	8	17	.320	32	32	24	1	0	233¹	318	9	117	46	17.2	6.36	85	.321	.399	16	.182	-4	-27	-25	1	-2.0

YEAR	TM/L	W	L	PCT	G	GS	CG	SH	SV	IP	H	HR	BB	SO	RAT	ERA	ERA+	OAV	OOB	BH	AVG	PB	PR	/A	PD	TPI
1895	StL-N	1	6	.143	7	7	7	0	0	61	91	7	26	9	17.6	7.38	66	.340	.402	1	.043	-3	-18	-17	-1	-1.6
	Bal-N	12	3	.800	20	14	10	0	0	142	169	5	64	23	15.0	3.87	123	.291	.365	8	.140	-4	14	14	2	0.9
	Yr	13	9	.591	27	21	17	0	0	203	260	12	90	32	15.7	4.92	97	.306	.375	9	.112	-7	-3	-3	1	-0.7
1896	Bal-N	4	2	.667	7	4	3	0	0	47	72	1	18	7	17.6	4.98	86	.348	.405	5	.278	0	-3	-4	-0	-0.3
Total	6	39	39	.500	96	81	63	2	0	704^2	873	26	325	133	15.8	4.90	99	.299	.376	44	.161	-14	-6	-3	2	-0.9

● JOHN CLARKSON

Clarkson, John Gibson b: 7/1/1861, Cambridge, Mass. d: 2/4/09, Belmont, Mass. BR/TR, 5'10", 155 lbs. Deb: 5/02/1882 FH

YEAR	TM/L	W	L	PCT	G	GS	CG	SH	SV	IP	H	HR	BB	SO	RAT	ERA	ERA+	OAV	OOB	BH	AVG	PB	PR	/A	PD	TPI
1882	Wor-N	1	2	.333	3	3	2	0	0	24	49	0	2	3	19.1	4.50	69	.392	.402	4	.364	1	-4	-4	0	-0.2
1884	Chi-N	10	3	.769	14	13	12	0	0	118	94	10	25	102	9.1	2.14	147	.208	.249	22	.262	4	11	13	3	1.9
1885	*Chi-N	**53**	16	.768	**70**	70	**68**	**10**	0	**623**	497	21	97	**308**	8.6	1.85	164	.208	.239	61	.216	2	**67**	**82**	8	**8.9**
1886	*Chi-N	36	17	.679	55	55	50	3	0	466^2	419	20	86	313	9.7	2.41	151	.229	.264	49	.233	1	47	**64**	4	6.4
1887	Chi-N	**38**	21	.644	**60**	59	**56**	2	0	**523**	513	20	92	**237**	10.5	3.08	146	.246	.281	52	.242	3	**58**	**82**	9	**8.3**
1888	Bos-N	33	20	.623	54	54	53	3	0	**483^1**	448	17	119	223	10.7	2.76	103	.236	.284	40	.195	3	5	5	3	0.9
1889	Bos-N	**49**	19	**.721**	**73**	72	**68**	**8**	1	**620**	589	16	203	**284**	**11.7**	**2.73**	**153**	.243	**.306**	54	.206	1	**89**	**99**	11	**10.2**
1890	Bos-N	26	18	.591	44	44	43	2	0	383	370	14	140	138	12.4	3.27	115	.246	.317	43	.249	4	13	21	-1	2.1
1891	Bos-N	33	19	.635	55	51	47	3	**3**	460^2	435	18	154	141	11.8	2.79	131	.240	.305	42	.225	4	28	44	4	4.8
1892	Bos-N	8	6	.571	16	16	15	4	0	145^2	115	4	60	48	11.1	2.35	150	.208	.292	13	.228	1	15	19	0	2.0
	*Cle-N	17	10	.630	29	28	27	1	1	243^1	235	4	72	91	11.5	2.55	133	.244	.299	14	.139	-5	20	23	-1	1.5
	Yr	25	16	.610	45	44	42	5	1	389	350	8	132	139	11.2	2.48	139	.230	.293	27	.171	-4	35	41	-1	3.5
1893	Cle-N	16	17	.485	36	35	31	0	0	295	358	11	95	62	14.0	4.45	110	.291	.344	27	.206	-4	7	14	3	1.1
1894	Cle-N	8	10	.444	22	18	13	1	0	150^2	173	6	46	28	13.1	4.42	124	.285	.335	11	.200	-2	15	17	2	1.3
Total	12	328	178	.648	531	518	485	37	5	4536^1	4295	161	1191	1978	11.0	2.81	134	.240	.291	432	.219	13	371	480	45	49.2

● WALTER CLARKSON

Clarkson, Walter Hamilton b: 11/3/1878, Cambridge, Mass. d: 10/10/46, Cambridge, Mass. BR/TR, 5'10", 150 lbs. Deb: 7/02/04 F

YEAR	TM/L	W	L	PCT	G	GS	CG	SH	SV	IP	H	HR	BB	SO	RAT	ERA	ERA+	OAV	OOB	BH	AVG	PB	PR	/A	PD	TPI
1904	NY-A	1	2	.333	13	4	2	0	1	66^1	63	3	25	43	13.3	5.02	54	.251	.343	7	.269	2	-18	-17	-1	-1.7
1905	NY-A	3	3	.500	9	4	3	0	0	46	40	1	13	35	10.8	3.91	75	.235	.297	1	.053	-2	-6	-5	-1	-0.8
1906	NY-A	9	4	.692	32	16	9	3	0	151	135	6	55	64	11.6	2.32	128	.242	.315	8	.157	-1	6	11	-1	0.9
1907	NY-A	1	1	.500	5	2	0	0	0	17^1	19	1	8	3	14.5	6.23	45	.280	.365	2	.286	0	-7	-7	0	-0.6
	Cle-A	4	6	.400	17	10	9	1	0	90^2	77	1	29	32	10.7	1.99	127	.232	.297	1	.036	-3	6	5	-0	0.1
	Yr	5	7	.417	22	12	9	1	0	108	96	2	37	35	11.3	2.67	96	.239	.307	3	.086	-3	-1	-1	-0	-0.5
1908	Cle-A	0	0	—	2	1	0	0	0	3^1	6	0	2	1	27.0	10.80	22	.400	.526	1	1.000	0	-3	-3	-0	-0.3
Total	5	18	16	.529	78	37	23	4	1	374^2	340	12	132	178	11.8	3.17	88	.244	.319	20	.152	-4	-23	-16	-4	-2.4

● BILL CLARKSON

Clarkson, William Henry "Blackie" b: 9/27/1898, Portsmouth, Va. d: 8/27/71, Raleigh, N.C. BR/TR, 5'11", 160 lbs. Deb: 5/02/27

YEAR	TM/L	W	L	PCT	G	GS	CG	SH	SV	IP	H	HR	BB	SO	RAT	ERA	ERA+	OAV	OOB	BH	AVG	PB	PR	/A	PD	TPI
1927	NY-N	3	9	.250	26	7	2	0	2	86^2	92	3	52	28	15.1	4.36	88	.280	.380	1	.050	-1	-4	-5	0	-0.6
1928	NY-N	0	0	—	4	0	0	0	0	5^2	10	0	1	3	17.5	7.94	49	.455	.478	0	—	0	-2	-3	-0	-0.2
	Bos-N	0	2	.000	19	1	0	0	0	34^2	53	2	22	8	19.7	6.75	58	.349	.434	0	.000	-0	-11	-11	1	-1.0
	Yr	0	2	.000	23	1	0	0	0	40^1	63	2	23	11	19.4	6.92	56	.362	.439	0	.000	-0	-13	-13	1	-1.2
1929	Bos-N	0	1	.000	2	1	0	0	0	7	16	0	4	0	25.7	10.29	45	.485	.541	1	.500	0	-4	-4	0	-0.3
Total	3	3	12	.200	51	9	2	0	2	134	171	5	79	39	16.9	5.44	72	.319	.408	2	.080	-1	-22	-23	1	-2.1

● MARTY CLARY

Clary, Martin Keith b: 4/3/62, Detroit, Mich. BR/TR, 6'4", 190 lbs. Deb: 9/05/87

YEAR	TM/L	W	L	PCT	G	GS	CG	SH	SV	IP	H	HR	BB	SO	RAT	ERA	ERA+	OAV	OOB	BH	AVG	PB	PR	/A	PD	TPI
1987	Atl-N	0	1	.000	7	1	0	0	0	14^2	20	2	4	7	15.3	6.14	71	.328	.379	0	.000	-0	-3	-3	-0	-0.3
1989	Atl-N	4	3	.571	18	17	2	1	0	108^2	103	6	31	30	11.2	3.15	116	.249	.303	5	.161	0	4	6	0	0.7
1990	Atl-N	1	10	.091	33	14	0	0	0	101^2	128	9	39	44	14.9	5.67	71	.308	.368	0	.000	-3	-21	-18	1	-2.0
Total	3	5	14	.263	58	32	2	1	0	225	251	17	74	81	13.1	4.48	86	.282	.339	5	.083	-3	-20	-15	1	-1.6

● GOWELL CLASET

Claset, Gowell Sylvester "Lefty" b: 11/26/07, Battle Creek, Mich d: 3/8/81, St.Petersburg, Fla. BB/TL, 6'3.5", 210 lbs. Deb: 4/12/33

YEAR	TM/L	W	L	PCT	G	GS	CG	SH	SV	IP	H	HR	BB	SO	RAT	ERA	ERA+	OAV	OOB	BH	AVG	PB	PR	/A	PD	TPI
1933	Phi-A	2	0	1.000	8	1	0	0	0	11^1	23	1	11	1	27.0	9.53	45	.426	.523	1	.500	1	-7	-7	0	-0.5

● FRITZ CLAUSEN

Clausen, Frederick William b: 4/26/1869, New York, N.Y. d: 2/11/60, Memphis, Tenn. BR/TL, 5'11", 190 lbs. Deb: 7/23/1892

YEAR	TM/L	W	L	PCT	G	GS	CG	SH	SV	IP	H	HR	BB	SO	RAT	ERA	ERA+	OAV	OOB	BH	AVG	PB	PR	/A	PD	TPI
1892	Lou-N	9	13	.409	24	24	24	2	0	200	181	3	87	94	12.2	3.06	100	.232	.311	13	.155	-3	5	0	-1	-0.3
1893	Lou-N	1	4	.200	5	5	3	0	0	33	41	2	22	4	17.5	6.00	73	.296	.396	3	.214	-1	-5	-6	0	-0.5
	Chi-N	6	2	.750	10	9	8	0	1	76	71	1	39	31	13.6	3.08	150	.240	.338	4	.121	-3	13	13	0	0.9
	Yr	7	6	.538	15	14	11	0	1	109	112	3	61	35	14.7	3.96	115	.257	.355	7	.149	-4	8	7	0	0.4
1894	Chi-N	0	1	.000	1	1	0	0	0	4^1	5	0	3	1	16.6	10.38	54	.286	.391	0	.000	-0	-2	-2	0	-0.2
1896	Lou-N	0	2	.000	2	2	1	0	0	11	17	1	6	4	21.3	6.55	66	.350	.452	0	.000	-1	-3	-3	0	-0.3
Total	4	16	22	.421	42	41	36	2	1	324^1	315	7	157	134	13.4	3.58	101	.246	.334	20	.147	-7	8	2	-0	-0.4

● AL CLAUSS

Clauss, Albert Stanley "Lefty" b: 6/24/1891, New Haven, Conn. d: 9/13/52, New Haven, Conn. BR/TL, 5'10.5", 178 lbs. Deb: 4/22/13

YEAR	TM/L	W	L	PCT	G	GS	CG	SH	SV	IP	H	HR	BB	SO	RAT	ERA	ERA+	OAV	OOB	BH	AVG	PB	PR	/A	PD	TPI
1913	Det-A	0	1	.000	5	1	0	0	0	13^1	11	0	12	1	16.9	4.73	62	.220	.391	0	.000	-1	-3	-3	-0	-0.4

● DANNY CLAY

Clay, Danny Bruce b: 10/24/61, Sun Walley, Cal. BR/TR, 6'1", 190 lbs. Deb: 5/01/88

YEAR	TM/L	W	L	PCT	G	GS	CG	SH	SV	IP	H	HR	BB	SO	RAT	ERA	ERA+	OAV	OOB	BH	AVG	PB	PR	/A	PD	TPI
1988	Phi-N	0	1	.000	17	0	0	0	0	24	27	5	21	12	18.0	6.00	59	.303	.436	0	.000	-0	-7	-7	-1	-0.8

● KEN CLAY

Clay, Kenneth Earl b: 4/6/54, Lynchburg, Va. BR/TR, 6'3", 195 lbs. Deb: 6/07/77

YEAR	TM/L	W	L	PCT	G	GS	CG	SH	SV	IP	H	HR	BB	SO	RAT	ERA	ERA+	OAV	OOB	BH	AVG	PB	PR	/A	PD	TPI
1977	*NY-A	2	3	.400	21	3	0	0	1	55^2	53	6	24	20	12.6	4.37	90	.251	.331	0	—	0	-2	-3	0	-0.2
1978	*NY-A	3	4	.429	28	6	0	0	0	75^2	89	3	21	32	13.3	4.28	85	.291	.340	0	—	0	-4	-6	-1	-0.6
1979	NY-A	1	7	.125	32	5	0	0	2	78^1	88	12	25	28	13.2	5.40	75	.291	.350	0	—	0	-10	-12	0	-1.1
1980	Tex-A	2	3	.400	8	8	0	0	0	43	43	4	29	17	15.7	4.60	85	.256	.375	0	—	0	-3	-3	-1	-0.3
1981	Sea-A	2	7	.222	22	14	0	0	0	101	116	10	42	32	14.3	4.63	83	.294	.366	0	—	0	-11	-9	-2	-1.1
Total	5	10	24	.294	111	36	0	0	3	353^2	389	35	141	129	13.8	4.68	83	.281	.353	0	—	0	-30	-32	-3	-3.3

● MARK CLEAR

Clear, Mark Alan b: 5/27/56, Los Angeles, Cal. BR/TR, 6'4", 215 lbs. Deb: 4/04/79

YEAR	TM/L	W	L	PCT	G	GS	CG	SH	SV	IP	H	HR	BB	SO	RAT	ERA	ERA+	OAV	OOB	BH	AVG	PB	PR	/A	PD	TPI
1979	*Cal-A★	11	5	.688	52	0	0	0	14	109	87	6	68	98	13.0	3.63	112	.219	.337	0	—	0	7	5	-1	0.4
1980	Cal-A	11	11	.500	58	0	0	0	9	106^1	82	2	65	105	12.9	3.30	119	.216	.338	0	—	0	9	7	-1	0.8
1981	Bos-A	8	3	.727	34	0	0	0	9	76^2	69	11	51	82	14.3	4.11	94	.239	.357	0	—	0	-4	-2	-1	-0.4
1982	Bos-A☆	14	9	.609	55	0	0	0	14	105	92	11	61	109	13.7	3.00	144	.238	.352	0	—	0	13	15	-0	1.5
1983	Bos-A	4	5	.444	48	0	0	0	4	96	101	10	68	81	16.1	6.28	69	.273	.390	0	—	0	-24	-21	-1	-2.3
1984	Bos-A	8	3	.727	47	0	0	0	8	67	47	2	70	76	16.0	4.03	103	.198	.385	0	—	0	-0	1	0	0.0
1985	Bos-A	1	3	.250	41	0	0	0	3	55^2	45	1	50	55	16.2	3.72	115	.225	.392	0	—	0	3	3	1	0.4
1986	Mil-A	5	5	.500	59	0	0	0	16	73^2	53	4	36	85	11.0	2.20	197	.201	.299	0	—	0	16	17	-0	1.7
1987	Mil-A	8	5	.615	58	1	0	0	6	78^1	70	9	55	81	14.9	4.48	102	.239	.368	0	—	0	-0	1	1	0.1
1988	Mil-A	1	0	1.000	25	0	0	0	0	29	23	4	21	26	13.7	2.79	142	.215	.344	0	—	0	4	4	-0	0.3
1990	Cal-A	0	0	—	4	0	0	0	0	7^2	5	0	9	6	18.8	5.87	65	.200	.444	0	—	0	-2	-2	-0	-0.2
Total	11	71	49	.592	481	1	0	0	83	804^1	674	60	554	804	14.1	3.85	109	.228	.357	0	—	0	21	30	-3	2.3

● JOE CLEARY

Cleary, Joseph Christopher "Fire" b: 12/3/18, Cork City, Ireland BR/TR, 5'9", 150 lbs. Deb: 8/04/45

YEAR	TM/L	W	L	PCT	G	GS	CG	SH	SV	IP	H	HR	BB	SO	RAT	ERA	ERA+	OAV	OOB	BH	AVG	PB	PR	/A	PD	TPI
1945	Was-A	0	0	—	1	0	0	0	0	0^1	5	0	3	1	216.0	189.00	2	.833	.889	0	—	0	-7	-7	0	-0.5

● ROGER CLEMENS

Clemens, William Roger b: 8/4/62, Dayton, Ohio BR/TR, 6'4", 215 lbs. Deb: 5/15/84

YEAR	TM/L	W	L	PCT	G	GS	CG	SH	SV	IP	H	HR	BB	SO	RAT	ERA	ERA+	OAV	OOB	BH	AVG	PB	PR	/A	PD	TPI
1984	Bos-A	9	4	.692	21	20	5	1	0	133^1	146	13	29	126	11.9	4.32	96	.271	.311	0	—	0	-5	-2	0	-0.3
1985	Bos-A	7	5	.583	15	15	3	1	0	98^1	83	5	37	74	11.3	3.29	130	.228	.304	0	—	0	9	11	0	1.1
1986	*Bos-A★	**24**	4	**.857**	33	33	10	1	0	254	179	21	67	238	**8.9**	**2.48**	**168**	**.195**	**.253**	0	—	0	**48**	**48**	-1	**5.0**
1987	Bos-A	**20**	9	**.690**	36	36	**18**	**7**	0	281^2	248	19	83	256	10.9	2.97	153	.235	.296	0	—	0	46	49	-2	4.8
1988	*Bos-A★	18	12	.600	35	35	**14**	**8**	0	264	217	17	62	**291**	9.7	2.93	140	.220	.270	0	—	0	30	35	-2	3.2

YEAR	TM/L	W	L	PCT	G	GS	CG	SH	SV	IP	H	HR	BB	SO	RAT	ERA	ERA+	OAV	OOB	BH	AVG	PB	PR	/A	PD	TPI
1989	Bos-A	17	11	.607	35	35	8	3	0	253^1	215	20	93	230	11.2	3.13	131	.231	.307	0	—	0	21	27	-1	2.6
1990	*Bos-A☆	21	6	.778	31	31	7	**4**	0	228^1	193	7	54	209	10.0	**1.93**	**211**	.228	.280	0	—	0	**50**	**54**	1	**6.2**
1991	Bos-A★	18	10	.643	35	35	13	**4**	0	**271^1**	219	15	65	**241**	9.6	**2.62**	**164**	.221	.272	0	—	0	**44**	**51**	1	**5.3**
1992	Bos-A★	18	11	.621	32	32	11	**5**	0	246^2	203	11	62	208	10.0	**2.41**	**172**	.224	.280	0	—	0	**42**	**48**	-0	**5.3**
Total	9	152	72	.679	273	272	89	34	0	2031	1703	128	552	1873	10.2	2.80	151	.226	.283	0	—	0	287	320	-3	33.2

● BILL CLEMENSEN Clemensen, William Melville b: 6/20/19, New Brunswick, N.J. BR/TR, 6'1", 193 lbs. Deb: 5/22/39

YEAR	TM/L	W	L	PCT	G	GS	CG	SH	SV	IP	H	HR	BB	SO	RAT	ERA	ERA+	OAV	OOB	BH	AVG	PB	PR	/A	PD	TPI
1939	Pit-N	0	1	.000	12	1	0	0	0	27	32	0	20	13	18.3	7.33	52	.311	.437	2	.333	1	-10	-10	1	-0.8
1941	Pit-N	1	0	1.000	2	1	1	0	0	13	7	0	7	4	9.7	2.77	130	.159	.275	0	.000	-1	1	1	-0	0.0
1946	Pit-N	0	0	—	1	0	0	0	0	2	0	0	0	2	0.0	0.00	—	.000	.000	0	—	0	1	1	-0	0.1
Total	3	1	1	.500	15	2	1	0	0	42	39	0	27	19	14.8	5.57	67	.255	.377	2	.200	0	-8	-8	1	-0.7

● PAT CLEMENTS Clements, Patrick Brian b: 2/2/62, McCloud, Cal. BR/TL, 6', 180 lbs. Deb: 4/09/85

YEAR	TM/L	W	L	PCT	G	GS	CG	SH	SV	IP	H	HR	BB	SO	RAT	ERA	ERA+	OAV	OOB	BH	AVG	PB	PR	/A	PD	TPI
1985	Cal-A	5	0	1.000	41	0	0	0	1	62	47	4	25	19	10.7	3.34	123	.218	.305	0	—	0	6	5	1	0.6
	Pit-N	0	2	.000	27	0	0	0	2	34^1	39	2	15	17	14.2	3.67	97	.289	.360	1	.333	0	-0	-0	-1	-0.1
1986	Pit-N	0	4	.000	65	0	0	0	2	61	53	1	32	31	12.8	2.80	137	.251	.355	0	.000	-1	6	7	1	0.7
1987	NY-A	3	3	.500	55	0	0	0	7	80	91	4	30	36	13.9	4.95	89	.299	.368	0	—	0	-4	-5	1	-0.4
1988	NY-A	0	0	—	6	1	0	0	0	8^1	12	1	4	3	17.3	6.48	61	.343	.410	0	—	0	-2	-2	0	-0.2
1989	SD-N	4	1	.800	23	1	0	0	0	39	39	4	15	18	12.5	3.92	89	.267	.335	0	.000	-1	-2	-2	0	-0.2
1990	SD-N	0	0	—	9	0	0	0	0	13	20	1	7	6	18.7	4.15	92	.357	.429	0	—	0	-1	-0	0	0.0
1991	SD-N	1	0	1.000	12	0	0	0	0	14^1	13	0	9	8	13.8	3.77	101	.255	.367	0	.000	-0	-0	0	0	0.0
1992	SD-N	2	1	.667	27	0	0	0	0	23^2	25	0	12	11	14.8	2.66	136	.281	.379	0	.000	-0	2	3	1	0.3
	Bal-A	2	0	1.000	23	0	0	0	0	24^2	23	0	11	9	13.1	3.28	119	.258	.353	0	—	0	2	2	1	0.3
Total	8	17	11	.607	288	2	0	0	12	360^1	362	17	160	158	13.3	3.77	104	.272	.355	1	.059	-1	6	7	4	1.0

● LANCE CLEMONS Clemons, Lance Levis b: 7/6/47, Philadelphia, Pa. BL/TL, 6'2", 205 lbs. Deb: 8/12/71

YEAR	TM/L	W	L	PCT	G	GS	CG	SH	SV	IP	H	HR	BB	SO	RAT	ERA	ERA+	OAV	OOB	BH	AVG	PB	PR	/A	PD	TPI
1971	KC-A	1	0	1.000	10	3	0	0	0	24	26	2	12	20	14.6	4.13	83	.263	.348	2	.286	2	-2	-2	0	0.0
1972	StL-N	0	1	.000	3	1	0	0	0	5^1	8	1	5	2	23.6	10.13	34	.364	.500	0	.000	-0	-4	-4	0	-0.4
1974	Bos-A	1	0	1.000	6	0	0	0	0	6^1	8	1	4	1	18.5	9.95	39	.296	.406	0	—	0	-4	-4	0	-0.5
Total	3	2	1	.667	19	4	0	0	0	35^2	42	4	21	23	16.7	6.06	58	.284	.384	2	.250	2	-10	-10	0	-0.9

● REGGIE CLEVELAND Cleveland, Reginald Leslie b: 5/23/48, Swift Current, Sask., Canada BR/TR, 6'1", 195 lbs. Deb: 10/01/69

YEAR	TM/L	W	L	PCT	G	GS	CG	SH	SV	IP	H	HR	BB	SO	RAT	ERA	ERA+	OAV	OOB	BH	AVG	PB	PR	/A	PD	TPI
1969	StL-N	0	0	—	1	1	0	0	0	4	7	0	1	3	18.0	9.00	40	.368	.400	0	.000	-0	-2	-2	-0	-0.2
1970	StL-N	0	4	.000	16	1	0	0	0	26	31	3	18	22	17.0	7.62	54	.298	.402	1	.250	0	-10	-10	-1	-1.0
1971	StL-N	12	12	.500	34	34	10	2	0	222	238	20	53	148	12.0	4.01	90	.271	.317	14	.171	-1	-14	-10	-0	-1.2
1972	StL-N	14	15	.483	33	33	11	3	0	230^2	229	21	60	153	11.5	3.94	86	.258	.308	17	.239	3	-13	-14	-1	-1.3
1973	StL-N	14	10	.583	32	32	6	3	0	224	211	13	61	122	11.1	3.01	121	.246	.300	17	.230	4	16	16	-2	1.8
1974	Bos-A	12	14	.462	41	27	10	0	0	221^1	234	25	69	103	12.7	4.31	89	.271	.332	0	—	0	-17	-12	1	-1.2
1975	*Bos-A	13	9	.591	31	20	3	1	0	170^2	173	19	52	78	12.0	4.43	92	.263	.320	0	—	0	-12	-7	-0	-0.7
1976	Bos-A	10	9	.526	41	14	3	0	2	170	159	3	61	76	11.9	3.07	127	.246	.315	0	—	0	8	16	-0	0.7
1977	Bos-A	11	8	.579	36	27	9	1	2	190^1	211	20	43	85	12.2	4.26	105	.281	.323	0	—	0	-4	5	-1	-0.1
1978	Bos-A	0	1	.000	1	0	0	0	0	0^1	1	0	0	0	27.0	0.00	—	.333	.333	0	—	0	0	0	0	-0.2
	Tex-A	5	7	.417	53	0	0	0	12	75^2	65	5	23	46	10.8	3.09	121	.236	.301	0	—	0	6	5	0	0.6
	Yr	5	8	.385	54	0	0	0	12	76	66	5	23	46	10.9	3.08	122	.237	.302	0	—	0	6	6	0	0.4
1979	Mil-A	1	5	.167	29	1	0	0	4	55	77	9	23	22	16.4	6.71	62	.344	.405	0	—	0	-15	-16	-1	-1.6
1980	Mil-A	11	9	.550	45	13	5	2	4	154^1	150	9	49	54	11.9	3.73	104	.254	.317	0	—	0	5	2	-1	0.3
1981	Mil-A	2	3	.400	35	0	0	0	1	64^2	57	5	30	18	12.2	5.15	66	.239	.327	0	—	0	-11	-12	-1	-1.4
Total	13	105	106	.498	428	203	57	12	25	1809	1843	152	543	930	12.1	4.01	95	.264	.321	49	.211	6	-63	-38	-9	-5.5

● TEX CLEVENGER Clevenger, Truman Eugene b: 7/9/32, Visalia, Cal. BR/TR, 6'1", 180 lbs. Deb: 4/18/54

YEAR	TM/L	W	L	PCT	G	GS	CG	SH	SV	IP	H	HR	BB	SO	RAT	ERA	ERA+	OAV	OOB	BH	AVG	PB	PR	/A	PD	TPI
1954	Bos-A	2	4	.333	23	8	1	0	0	67^2	67	9	29	43	13.0	4.79	86	.262	.341	3	.214	0	-8	-5	0	-0.5
1956	Was-A	0	0	—	20	1	0	0	0	31^2	33	4	21	17	15.3	5.40	80	.264	.370	0	.000	-0	-4	-4	-0	-0.4
1957	Was-A	7	6	.538	52	9	2	0	8	139^2	139	11	47	75	12.2	4.19	93	.261	.326	7	.212	1	-6	-5	1	-0.2
1958	Was-A	9	9	.500	**55**	4	0	0	6	124	119	12	50	70	12.3	4.35	88	.251	.324	3	.136	0	-8	-7	3	-0.5
1959	Was-A	8	5	.615	50	7	2	2	8	117^1	114	9	51	71	12.8	3.91	100	.256	.335	4	.174	1	-1	0	4	0.5
1960	Was-A	5	11	.313	53	11	1	0	7	128^2	150	10	49	49	14.1	4.20	93	.298	.363	2	.091	-1	-5	-4	-1	-0.6
1961	LA-A	2	1	.667	12	0	0	0	1	16	13	1	13	11	14.6	1.69	267	.220	.361	0	.000	-0	4	5	1	0.5
	NY-A	1	1	.500	21	0	0	0	0	31^2	35	3	21	14	16.2	4.83	77	.287	.396	1	.250	0	-3	-4	1	-0.3
	Yr	3	2	.600	33	0	0	0	1	47^2	48	4	34	25	15.7	3.78	105	.265	.384	1	.143	0	1	1	1	0.2
1962	NY-A	2	0	1.000	21	0	0	0	0	38	36	3	17	11	12.8	2.84	132	.248	.331	0	.000	-0	5	4	0	0.3
Total	8	36	37	.493	307	40	6	2	30	694^2	706	62	298	361	13.2	4.18	94	.265	.342	20	.157	1	-26	-20	8	-1.2

● STEW CLIBURN Cliburn, Stewart Walker b: 12/19/56, Jackson, Miss. BR/TR, 6', 195 lbs. Deb: 9/17/84 F

YEAR	TM/L	W	L	PCT	G	GS	CG	SH	SV	IP	H	HR	BB	SO	RAT	ERA	ERA+	OAV	OOB	BH	AVG	PB	PR	/A	PD	TPI
1984	Cal-A	0	0	—	1	0	0	0	0	2	3	0	1	1	18.0	13.50	29	.333	.400	0	—	0	-2	-2	0	-0.2
1985	Cal-A	9	3	.750	44	0	0	0	6	99	87	5	26	48	10.4	2.09	197	.241	.294	0	—	0	23	22	1	2.4
1988	Cal-A	4	2	.667	40	1	0	0	0	84	83	11	32	42	13.0	4.07	95	.266	.346	0	—	0	-1	-2	0	0.0
Total	3	13	5	.722	85	1	0	0	6	185	173	16	59	91	11.6	3.11	128	.254	.320	0	—	0	20	18	2	2.2

● JIM CLINTON Clinton, James Lawrence "Big Jim" b: 8/10/1850, New York, N.Y. d: 9/3/21, Brooklyn, N.Y. BR/TR, 5'8.5", 174 lbs. Deb: 5/18/1872 MU♦

YEAR	TM/L	W	L	PCT	G	GS	CG	SH	SV	IP	H	HR	BB	SO	RAT	ERA	ERA+	OAV	OOB	BH	AVG	PB	PR	/A	PD	TPI
1875	Atl-n	1	14	.067	17	14	9	0	0	123	146	0	8		11.3	3.22	71	.268	.279	10	.123	-4	-10	-13		-1.3
1876	Lou-N	0	1	.000	1	1	1	0	0	9	12	0	0	1	12.0	6.00	45	.279	.279	22	.338	0	-4	-3	0	-0.2

● TONY CLONINGER Cloninger, Tony Lee b: 8/13/40, Lincoln, N.C. BR/TR, 6', 210 lbs. Deb: 6/15/61 C

YEAR	TM/L	W	L	PCT	G	GS	CG	SH	SV	IP	H	HR	BB	SO	RAT	ERA	ERA+	OAV	OOB	BH	AVG	PB	PR	/A	PD	TPI
1961	Mil-N	7	2	.778	19	10	3	0	0	84	84	16	33	51	12.6	5.25	71	.258	.328	5	.167	-0	-11	-14	1	-1.3
1962	Mil-N	8	3	.727	24	15	4	1	0	111	113	10	46	69	13.0	4.30	88	.264	.337	4	.103	-2	-4	-6	0	-0.7
1963	Mil-N	9	11	.450	41	18	4	2	1	145^1	131	17	63	100	12.1	3.78	85	.239	.320	5	.135	-0	-8	-9	-2	-1.2
1964	Mil-N	19	14	.576	38	34	15	3	2	242^2	206	20	82	163	10.8	3.56	99	.231	.298	21	.241	3	-1	-1	-0	0.2
1965	Mil-N	24	11	.686	40	38	16	1	1	279	247	20	119	211	11.9	3.29	107	.236	.316	17	.162	2	8	7	-1	0.8
1966	Atl-N	14	11	.560	39	38	11	1	1	257^2	253	29	116	178	13.1	4.12	88	.258	.340	26	.234	10	-15	-14	-0	-0.5
1967	Atl-N	4	7	.364	16	16	1	0	0	76^2	85	13	31	55	13.6	5.17	64	.285	.353	5	.200	1	-15	-16	-0	-1.5
1968	Atl-N	1	3	.250	8	1	0	0	0	19	15	0	11	7	12.3	4.26	70	.227	.338	0	.000	-0	-3	-3	0	-0.3
	Cin-N	4	3	.571	17	17	2	2	0	91^1	81	7	48	65	13.0	4.04	78	.233	.331	7	.206	3	-11	-9	-0	-0.7
	Yr	5	6	.455	25	18	2	2	0	110^1	96	7	59	72	12.9	4.08	77	.231	.331	7	.184	3	-13	-12	-0	-1.0
1969	Cin-N	11	17	.393	35	34	6	2	0	189^2	184	24	103	103	13.9	5.03	75	.250	.346	12	.167	1	-30	-27	-2	-2.8
1970	*Cin-N	9	7	.563	30	18	0	0	1	148	136	10	78	56	13.3	3.83	105	.249	.347	10	.213	3	4	3	2	0.8
1971	Cin-N	3	6	.333	28	8	1	1	0	97^1	79	12	49	51	12.2	3.88	86	.230	.332	7	.259	1	-5	-6	0	-0.5
1972	StL-N	0	2	.000	17	0	0	0	0	26	29	2	19	11	17.0	5.19	66	.293	.412	0	.000	-0	-5	-5	1	-0.5
Total	12	113	97	.538	352	247	63	13	6	1767^2	1643	180	798	1120	12.6	4.07	88	.247	.330	119	.192	21	-96	-98	-2	-8.2

● AL CLOSTER Closter, Alan Edward b: 6/15/43, Creighton, Neb. BL/TL, 6'2", 190 lbs. Deb: 4/19/66

YEAR	TM/L	W	L	PCT	G	GS	CG	SH	SV	IP	H	HR	BB	SO	RAT	ERA	ERA+	OAV	OOB	BH	AVG	PB	PR	/A	PD	TPI
1966	Was-A	0	0	—	1	0	0	0	0	0^1	1	0	2	0	81.0	0.00	—	.500	.750	0	—	0	0	0	0	0.0
1971	NY-A	2	2	.500	14	1	0	0	0	28^1	33	4	13	22	15.2	5.08	64	.289	.372	0	.000	-1	-5	-6	1	-0.6
1972	NY-A	0	0	—	2	0	0	0	0	2^1	2	1	4	2	23.1	11.57	25	.250	.500	0	.000	-0	-2	-2	0	-0.2
1973	Atl-N	0	0	—	4	0	0	0	0	4^1	7	1	4	2	22.8	14.54	27	.389	.500	0	—	0	-5	-5	0	-0.5
Total	4	2	2	.500	21	1	0	0	0	35^1	43	6	23	26	17.3	6.62	50	.303	.407	0	.000	-1	-12	-13	1	-1.3

YEAR TM/L	W	L	PCT	G	GS	CG	SH	SV	IP	H	HR	BB	SO	RAT	ERA	ERA+	OAV	OOB	BH	AVG	PB	PR	/A	PD	TPI

● ED CLOUGH Clough, Edgar George "Big Ed" or "Spec" b: 10/28/06, Wiconisco, Pa. d: 1/30/44, Harrisburg, Pa. BL/TL, 6', 188 lbs. Deb: 8/28/24 ♦

1925 StL-N	0	1	.000	3	1	0	0	0	10	11	1	5	3	15.3	8.10	53	.289	.386	1	.250	-0	-4	-4	-0	-0.4
1926 StL-N	0	0	—	1	0	0	0	0	2	5	0	3	0	40.5	22.50	17	.556	.692	0	.000	-0	-4	-4	-0	-0.4
Total 2	0	1	.000	4	1	0	0	0	12	16	1	8	3	19.5	10.50	40	.340	.456	2	.105	-0	-8	-8	-0	-0.8

● BILL CLOWERS Clowers, William Perry b: 8/14/1898, San Marcos, Tex. d: 1/13/78, Sweeny, Tex. BL/TL, 5'11", 175 lbs. Deb: 7/20/26

| 1926 Bos-A | 0 | 0 | — | 2 | 0 | 0 | 0 | 0 | 1² | 2 | 0 | 0 | 0 | 10.8 | 0.00 | — | .333 | .333 | 0 | — | 0 | 1 | 1 | 0 | 0.1 |

● BRYAN CLUTTERBUCK Clutterbuck, Bryan Richard b: 12/17/59, Detroit, Mich. BR/TR, 6'4", 223 lbs. Deb: 7/18/86

1986 Mil-A	0	1	.000	20	0	0	0	0	56²	68	8	16	38	13.7	4.29	101	.296	.347	0	—	0	-1	0	-0	0.0
1989 Mil-A	2	5	.286	14	11	1	0	0	67¹	73	11	16	29	11.9	4.14	93	.269	.310	0	—	0	-2	-2	-2	-0.4
Total 2	2	6	.250	34	11	1	0	0	124	141	19	32	67	12.7	4.21	96	.281	.327	0	—	0	-3	-2	-2	-0.4

● DAVID CLYDE Clyde, David Eugene b: 4/22/55, Kansas City, Kan. BL/TL, 6'1", 185 lbs. Deb: 6/27/73

1973 Tex-A	4	8	.333	18	18	0	0	0	93¹	106	8	54	74	15.8	5.01	74	.293	.390	0	—	0	-12	-13	-0	-1.1
1974 Tex-A	3	9	.250	28	21	4	0	0	117	129	14	47	52	13.8	4.38	81	.286	.359	0	—	0	-10	-11	-2	-1.2
1975 Tex-A	0	1	.000	1	1	0	0	0	7	6	0	6	2	15.4	2.57	146	.273	.429	0	—	0	1	1	-0	0.1
1978 Cle-A	8	11	.421	28	25	5	0	0	153¹	166	4	60	83	13.4	4.28	87	.280	.350	0	—	0	-9	-9	-1	-1.0
1979 Cle-A	3	4	.429	9	8	1	0	0	45²	50	7	13	17	12.6	5.91	72	.279	.332	0	—	0	-9	-8	-0	-0.8
Total 5	18	33	.353	84	73	10	0	0	416¹	457	33	180	228	14.0	4.63	81	.285	.361	0	—	0	-39	-41	-4	-4.0

● TOM CLYDE Clyde, Thomas Knox b: 8/17/23, Wachapreague, Va. BR/TR, 6'3", 195 lbs. Deb: 5/31/43

| 1943 Phi-A | 0 | 0 | — | 4 | 0 | 0 | 0 | 0 | 6 | 7 | 1 | 4 | 0 | 18.0 | 9.00 | 38 | .304 | .429 | 0 | .000 | -0 | -4 | -4 | -0 | -0.4 |

● ANDY COAKLEY Coakley, Andrew James (a.k.a. Jack McAllister In 1902) b: 11/20/1882, Providence, R.I. d: 9/27/63, New York, N.Y. BL/TR, 6', 165 lbs. Deb: 9/17/02

1902 Phi-A	2	1	.667	3	3	3	0	0	27	25	0	9	9	12.0	2.67	138	.246	.320	3	.375	2	3	3	0	0.5
1903 Phi-A	0	3	.000	6	3	2	0	0	37²	48	2	11	20	14.8	5.50	56	.309	.366	3	.200	-0	-11	-10	-0	-1.0
1904 Phi-A	4	3	.571	8	8	7	2	0	62	48	1	23	33	10.6	1.89	142	.215	.294	2	.087	-2	5	5	0	0.3
1905 *Phi-A	18	8	.692	35	31	21	3	0	255	227	2	73	145	10.8	1.84	145	.240	.298	13	.138	-3	23	23	-1	2.1
1906 Phi-A	7	8	.467	22	16	10	0	0	149	144	0	44	59	11.5	3.14	87	.257	.313	7	.143	-7	-7	-3	-1.2
1907 Cin-N	17	16	.515	37	30	21	1	1	265¹	269	1	79	89	12.0	2.34	111	.274	.332	6	.071	-6	4	8	-3	-0.1
1908 Cin-N	8	18	.308	32	28	20	4	2	242¹	219	3	64	61	10.7	1.86	124	.249	.303	7	.092	-4	14	12	-4	0.3
Chi-N	2	0	1.000	4	3	2	1	0	20¹	14	0	6	7	8.9	0.89	266	.192	.253	0	.000	-1	3	3	0	0.3
Yr	10	18	.357	36	31	22	5	2	262²	233	3	70	68	10.4	1.78	130	.244	.295	7	.085	-5	17	15	-5	0.7
1909 Chi-N	0	1	.000	1	1	0	0	0	2	7	0	3	1	45.0	18.00	14	.583	.667	0	—	0	-3	-3	-0	-0.3
1911 NY-A	0	1	.000	2	1	1	0	0	11²	20	0	2	4	17.0	5.40	67	.377	.400	1	.250	0	-3	-2	0	-0.2
Total 9	58	59	.496	150	124	87	11	3	1072¹	1021	9	314	428	11.4	2.35	111	.256	.314	42	.117	-16	28	32	-12	0.8

● JIM COATES Coates, James Alton b: 8/4/32, Farnham, Va. BR/TR, 6'4", 192 lbs. Deb: 9/21/56

1956 NY-A	0	0	—	2	0	0	0	0	1	4	0	4	0	27.0	13.50	29	.167	.545	0	—	0	-2	-2	-0	-0.2
1959 NY-A	6	1	.857	37	4	2	0	0	100¹	89	10	36	64	11.5	2.87	127	.234	.305	2	.095	-1	11	9	0	0.8
1960 *NY-A★	13	3	.813	35	18	6	2	1	149¹	139	16	66	73	12.5	4.28	84	.248	.330	12	.250	4	-7	-12	-2	-1.0
1961 *NY-A	11	5	.688	43	11	4	1	5	141¹	128	15	53	80	12.0	3.44	108	.243	.321	1	.029	-3	9	4	-0	0.1
1962 *NY-A	7	6	.538	50	6	0	0	6	117²	119	9	50	67	13.3	4.44	84	.263	.343	4	.125	-1	-6	-9	-2	-1.2
1963 Was-A	2	4	.333	20	2	0	0	0	44¹	51	4	21	31	15.2	5.28	70	.297	.383	0	.000	-1	-8	-8	-0	-0.9
Cin-N	0	0	—	9	0	0	0	0	16¹	21	2	7	11	15.4	5.51	61	.313	.378	0	.000	-0	-4	-4	-0	-0.4
1965 Cal-A	2	0	1.000	17	0	0	0	3	28	23	1	16	15	12.5	3.54	96	.228	.333	0	—	0	-0	-0	-0	-0.1
1966 Cal-A	1	1	.500	9	4	1	1	0	31²	32	3	10	16	11.9	3.98	84	.258	.313	1	.091	-1	-2	-2	-0	-0.3
1967 Cal-A	1	2	.333	25	1	0	0	0	52¹	47	5	23	39	12.7	4.30	73	.244	.336	1	.333	1	-6	-7	-0	-0.6
Total 9	43	22	.662	247	46	13	4	15	683¹	650	65	286	396	12.7	4.00	90	.252	.332	21	.131	-3	-15	-30	-4	-3.8

● GEORGE COBB Cobb, George Washington b: San Francisco, Cal. Deb: 4/15/1892

| 1892 Bal-N | 10 | 37 | .213 | 53 | 47 | 42 | 0 | 0 | 394¹ | 495 | 21 | 140 | 159 | 14.9 | 4.86 | 71 | .295 | .356 | 36 | .209 | 6 | -69 | -63 | 2 | -4.8 |

● HERB COBB Cobb, Herbert Edward b: 8/6/04, Pinetops, N.C. d: 1/8/80, Tarboro, N.C. BR/TR, 5'11", 150 lbs. Deb: 4/21/29

| 1929 StL-A | 0 | 0 | — | 1 | 0 | 0 | 0 | 0 | 1 | 3 | 1 | 1 | 0 | 36.0 | 36.00 | 12 | .600 | .667 | 0 | — | 0 | -4 | -4 | -0 | -0.3 |

● TY COBB Cobb, Tyrus Raymond "The Georgia Peach" b: 12/18/1886, Narrows, Ga. d: 7/17/61, Atlanta, Ga. BL/TR, 6'1", 175 lbs. Deb: 8/30/05 MH♦

1918 Det-A	0	0	—	2	0	0	0	0	4	6	0	2	0	18.0	4.50	59	.400	.471	161	.382	1	-1	-1	-0	-0.1
1925 Det-A	0	0	—	1	0	0	0	1	1	0	0	0	0	0.00	—	.000	.000	157	.378	1	0	0	0	0.1
Total 2	0	0	—	3	0	0	0	1	5	6	0	2	0	14.4	3.60	83	.333	.400	4189	.366	2	-0	-0	0	0.0

● JAIME COCANOWER Cocanower, James Stanley b: 2/14/57, San Juan, P.R. BR/TR, 6'4", 200 lbs. Deb: 9/07/83

1983 Mil-A	2	0	1.000	5	3	1	0	0	30	21	1	12	8	10.2	1.80	208	.200	.288	0	—	0	8	6	0	1.0
1984 Mil-A	8	16	.333	33	27	1	0	0	174²	188	13	78	65	14.2	4.02	96	.279	.362	0	—	0	-1	-3	1	-0.1
1985 Mil-A	6	8	.429	24	15	3	1	0	116¹	122	6	73	44	15.7	4.33	96	.274	.386	0	—	0	-2	-2	1	-0.2
1986 Mil-A	0	1	.000	17	2	0	0	0	44²	40	1	38	22	16.1	4.43	98	.248	.398	0	—	0	-1	-1	1	0.1
Total 4	16	25	.390	79	47	5	1	0	365²	371	21	201	139	14.6	3.99	100	.268	.369	0	—	0	3	0	3	0.8

● GOAT COCHRAN Cochran, Alvah Jackson "Al" or "Goat" b: 1/31/1891, Concord, Ga. d: 5/23/47, Atlanta, Ga. BR/TR, 5'10", 175 lbs. Deb: 8/25/15

| 1915 Cin-N | 0 | 0 | — | 1 | 0 | 0 | 0 | 0 | 2 | 5 | 0 | 1 | 1 | 22.5 | 9.00 | 32 | .455 | .455 | 0 | — | 0 | -1 | -1 | -0 | -0.1 |

● GENE COCREHAM Cocreham, Eugene b: 11/14/1884, Luling, Tex. d: 12/27/45, Luling, Tex. BR/TR, 6'3.5", 192 lbs. Deb: 9/25/13

1913 Bos-N	0	1	.000	1	1	0	0	0	8¹	13	0	4	3	19.4	7.56	43	.371	.450	0	.000	-1	-4	-4	0	-0.4
1914 Bos-N	3	4	.429	15	3	1	0	0	44²	48	2	27	15	15.1	4.84	57	.296	.397	1	.100	-0	-10	-10	-1	-1.2
1915 Bos-N	0	0	—	1	0	0	0	0	1²	3	0	0	0	16.2	5.40	48	.429	.429	0	—	0	-1	-1	-0	-0.1
Total 3	3	5	.375	17	4	1	0	0	54²	64	2	31	18	15.8	5.27	54	.314	.407	1	.071	-1	-15	-15	-2	-1.7

● CHRIS CODIROLI Codiroli, Christopher Allen b: 3/26/58, Oxnard, Cal. BR/TR, 6'1", 160 lbs. Deb: 9/11/82

1982 Oak-A	1	2	.333	3	3	0	0	0	16²	16	1	4	5	10.8	4.32	90	.246	.290	0	—	0	-0	-1	0	0.0
1983 Oak-A	12	12	.500	37	31	7	2	1	205²	208	17	72	85	12.6	4.46	86	.264	.331	0	—	0	-9	-14	-2	-1.4
1984 Oak-A	6	4	.600	28	14	1	0	1	89¹	111	16	34	44	14.9	5.84	64	.304	.368	0	—	0	-18	-21	-1	-1.9
1985 Oak-A	14	14	.500	37	37	4	0	0	226	228	23	78	111	12.3	4.46	86	.259	.321	0	—	0	-8	-15	-1	-1.5
1986 Oak-A	5	8	.385	16	16	1	0	0	91²	91	15	38	43	12.9	4.03	96	.250	.324	0	—	0	2	-2	1	0.0
1987 Oak-A	0	2	.000	3	3	0	0	0	11¹	12	1	6	4	16.7	8.74	47	.273	.396	0	—	0	-5	-6	-0	-0.6
1988 Cle-A	0	4	.000	14	2	0	0	0	19¹	32	2	10	12	20.9	9.31	44	.372	.455	0	—	0	-11	-11	-0	-1.2
1990 KC-A	0	1	.000	6	2	0	0	0	10¹	13	1	17	8	29.6	9.58	40	.325	.557	0	—	0	-7	-7	-0	-0.6
Total 8	38	47	.447	144	108	13	2	3	670¹	711	76	261	312	13.4	4.87	79	.270	.341	0	—	0	-58	-76	-2	-7.1

● SLICK COFFMAN Coffman, George David b: 12/11/10, Veto, Ala. BR/TR, 6', 155 lbs. Deb: 5/21/37 F

1937 Det-A	7	5	.583	28	5	1	0	0	101	121	8	39	22	14.5	4.37	107	.295	.361	5	.172	0	3	3	-1	0.3
1938 Det-A	4	4	.500	39	5	1	0	1	95²	120	6	48	31	15.8	6.02	83	.310	.386	4	.167	-0	-13	-11	-1	-1.0
1939 Det-A	2	1	.667	23	1	0	0	1	42¹	51	4	22	10	15.7	6.38	77	.295	.378	0	.000	-1	-8	-7	0	-0.7
1940 StL-A	2	2	.500	31	4	1	0	1	74²	108	5	23	26	15.8	6.27	73	.334	.379	3	.200	-0	-16	-14	-1	-1.2
Total 4	15	12	.556	121	16	3	0	3	313²	400	23	132	89	15.4	5.60	85	.309	.375	12	.164	-0	-34	-28	-1	-2.6

● KEVIN COFFMAN

Coffman, Kevin Reese b: 1/19/65, Austin, Tex. BR/TR, 6'2", 175 lbs. Deb: 9/05/87

YEAR	TM/L	W	L	PCT	G	GS	CG	SH	SV	IP	H	HR	BB	SO	RAT	ERA	ERA+	OAV	OOB	BH	AVG	PB	PR	/A	PD	TPI
1987	Atl-N	2	3	.400	5	5	0	0	0	25^1	31	2	22	14	19.9	4.62	94	.313	.452	1	.100	-0	-2	-1	1	0.0
1988	Atl-N	2	6	.250	18	11	0	0	0	67	62	3	54	24	16.1	5.78	64	.251	.393	5	.227	2	-17	-16	0	-1.4
1990	Chi-N	0	2	.000	8	2	0	0	0	18^1	26	0	19	9	22.1	11.29	36	.333	.464	1	.200	0	-15	-15	1	-1.3
Total	3	4	11	.267	31	18	0	0	0	110^2	119	5	95	47	18.0	6.42	61	.281	.420	7	.189	2	-34	-31	2	-2.7

● DICK COFFMAN

Coffman, Samuel Richard b: 12/18/06, Veto, Ala. d: 3/24/72, Athens, Ala. BR/TR, 6'2", 195 lbs. Deb: 4/28/27 F

YEAR	TM/L	W	L	PCT	G	GS	CG	SH	SV	IP	H	HR	BB	SO	RAT	ERA	ERA+	OAV	OOB	BH	AVG	PB	PR	/A	PD	TPI
1927	Was-A	0	1	.000	5	2	0	0	0	16	20	0	2	5	13.5	3.38	120	.313	.353	1	.333	0	1	1	0	0.2
1928	StL-A	4	5	.444	29	7	3	0	1	85^2	122	7	37	25	16.8	6.09	69	.359	.423	1	.043	-3	-20	-18	0	-1.9
1929	StL-A	1	1	.500	27	3	1	1	1	52^2	61	3	14	11	13.3	5.98	74	.295	.348	0	.000	-1	-10	-9	0	-0.9
1930	StL-A	8	18	.308	38	30	12	1	1	196	250	14	69	54	14.9	5.14	95	.311	.369	9	.136	-5	-11	-6	0	-1.0
1931	StL-A	9	13	.409	32	17	11	2	1	169^1	159	10	51	39	11.3	3.88	119	.241	.298	4	.078	-5	9	14	-2	0.7
1932	StL-A	5	3	.625	9	6	3	0	0	61	66	3	21	14	13.1	3.10	157	.277	.341	1	.045	-2	9	12	-1	0.9
	Was-A	1	6	.143	22	9	2	1	0	76^1	92	2	31	17	14.6	4.83	89	.307	.373	2	.091	-1	-3	-4	-1	-0.6
	Yr	6	9	.400	31	15	5	1	0	137^1	158	5	52	31	13.8	4.06	112	.293	.356	3	.068	-3	6	7	-2	0.3
1933	StL-A	3	7	.300	21	13	3	1	1	81	114	9	39	19	17.2	5.89	79	.329	.399	1	.037	-3	-14	-11	0	-1.2
1934	StL-A	9	10	.474	40	21	6	1	3	173	212	11	59	55	14.2	4.53	110	.303	.358	11	.216	-1	-1	9	0	0.8
1935	StL-A	5	11	.313	41	18	5	0	2	143^2	206	14	46	34	15.9	6.14	78	.335	.383	6	.146	-1	-27	-21	-1	-2.1
1936	*NY-N	7	5	.583	42	2	0	0	7	101^2	119	7	23	26	12.7	3.90	100	.296	.337	4	.200	-0	1	0	1	0.1
1937	*NY-N	8	3	.727	42	1	0	0	3	80	93	4	31	30	14.4	3.04	128	.289	.359	7	.368	2	**8**	**8**	0	1.0
1938	NY-N	8	4	.667	**51**	3	1	1	**12**	111^1	116	3	21	21	11.3	3.48	108	.268	.306	2	.071	-3	4	4	-2	-0.1
1939	NY-N	1	2	.333	28	0	0	0	3	38	50	1	6	9	14.0	3.08	128	.316	.353	0	.000	-1	4	4	-0	0.3
1940	Bos-N	1	5	.167	31	0	0	0	3	48^1	63	4	11	11	14.2	5.40	69	.323	.365	1	.083	-1	-8	-9	-1	-1.0
1945	Phi-N	2	1	.667	14	0	0	0	0	26^1	39	0	2	2	14.0	5.13	75	.351	.363	1	.250	0	-4	-4	1	-0.2
Total	15	72	95	.431	472	132	47	8	38	1460^1	1782	92	463	372	14.1	4.65	96	.302	.357	51	.127	-23	-61	-33	-2	-5.0

● DICK COGAN

Cogan, Richard Henry b: 12/5/1871, Paterson, N.J. d: 5/2/48, Paterson, N.J. BR/TR, 5'7", 150 lbs. Deb: 5/10/1897

YEAR	TM/L	W	L	PCT	G	GS	CG	SH	SV	IP	H	HR	BB	SO	RAT	ERA	ERA+	OAV	OOB	BH	AVG	PB	PR	/A	PD	TPI
1897	Bal-N	0	0	—	1	0	0	0	0	2	4	0	2	0	31.5	13.50	31	.411	.549	0	.000	-0	-2	-2	-0	-0.2
1899	Chi-N	2	3	.400	5	5	5	0	0	44	54	1	24	9	16.8	4.30	87	.301	.396	5	.200	1	-2	-3	-1	-0.2
1900	NY-N	0	0	—	2	0	0	0	0	8	10	0	6	1	18.0	6.75	54	.305	.413	1	.125	-0	-3	-3	-0	-0.3
Total	3	2	3	.400	8	5	5	0	0	54	68	1	32	10	17.5	5.00	75	.307	.406	6	.176	0	-7	-8	-1	-0.7

● HY COHEN

Cohen, Hyman b: 1/29/31, Brooklyn, N.Y. BR/TR, 6'5", 220 lbs. Deb: 4/17/55

YEAR	TM/L	W	L	PCT	G	GS	CG	SH	SV	IP	H	HR	BB	SO	RAT	ERA	ERA+	OAV	OOB	BH	AVG	PB	PR	/A	PD	TPI
1955	Chi-N	0	0	—	7	1	0	0	0	17	28	2	10	4	20.6	7.94	51	.378	.459	0	.000	-0	-7	-7	-0	-0.7

● SYD COHEN

Cohen, Sydney Harry b: 5/7/08, Baltimore, Md. d: 4/9/88, ElPaso, Tex. BB/TL, 5'11", 180 lbs. Deb: 9/18/34 F

YEAR	TM/L	W	L	PCT	G	GS	CG	SH	SV	IP	H	HR	BB	SO	RAT	ERA	ERA+	OAV	OOB	BH	AVG	PB	PR	/A	PD	TPI
1934	Was-A	1	1	.500	3	2	2	0	0	18	25	2	6	6	15.5	7.50	58	.333	.383	3	.273	0	-6	-6	1	-0.4
1936	Was-A	0	2	.000	19	1	0	0	1	36	44	4	14	21	15.3	5.25	91	.303	.377	0	.000	-1	-1	-2	2	-0.1
1937	Was-A	2	4	.333	33	0	0	0	4	55	64	1	17	22	13.3	3.11	142	.299	.351	2	.143	-1	9	8	2	0.8
Total	3	3	7	.300	55	3	2	0	5	109	133	7	37	49	14.3	4.54	100	.306	.365	5	.152	-2	2	-0	5	0.3

● ROCKY COLAVITO

Colavito, Rocco Domenico b: 8/10/33, New York, N.Y. BR/TR, 6'3", 190 lbs. Deb: 9/10/55 C♦

YEAR	TM/L	W	L	PCT	G	GS	CG	SH	SV	IP	H	HR	BB	SO	RAT	ERA	ERA+	OAV	OOB	BH	AVG	PB	PR	/A	PD	TPI
1958	Cle-A	0	0	—	1	0	0	0	0	3	0	0	3	1	9.0	0.00	—	.000	.273	148	.303	1	1	1	0	0.2
1968	NY-A	1	0	1.000	1	0	0	0	0	2^2	1	0	2	1	10.1	0.00	—	.111	.273	20	.220	0	1	1	-0	0.1
Total	2	1	0	1.000	2	0	0	0	0	5^2	1	0	5	2	9.5	0.00	—	.059	.273	1730	.266	1	2	2	0	0.3

● VINCE COLBERT

Colbert, Vincent Norman b: 12/20/45, Washington, D.C. BR/TR, 6'4", 200 lbs. Deb: 5/19/70

YEAR	TM/L	W	L	PCT	G	GS	CG	SH	SV	IP	H	HR	BB	SO	RAT	ERA	ERA+	OAV	OOB	BH	AVG	PB	PR	/A	PD	TPI
1970	Cle-A	1	1	.500	23	0	0	0	2	31	37	4	16	17	15.7	7.26	55	.298	.383	0	.000	-0	-12	-11	0	-1.2
1971	Cle-A	7	6	.538	50	10	2	0	2	142^2	140	11	71	74	13.7	3.97	96	.265	.358	4	.138	-0	-8	-2	0	-0.3
1972	Cle-A	1	7	.125	22	11	1	1	0	74^2	74	8	38	36	14.3	4.58	70	.267	.370	4	.200	1	-13	-11	0	-1.1
Total	3	9	14	.391	95	21	3	1	4	248^1	251	23	125	127	14.1	4.57	80	.270	.365	8	.157	0	-33	-25	1	-2.6

● JIM COLBORN

Colborn, James William b: 5/22/46, Santa Paula, Cal. BR/TR, 6', 191 lbs. Deb: 7/13/69

YEAR	TM/L	W	L	PCT	G	GS	CG	SH	SV	IP	H	HR	BB	SO	RAT	ERA	ERA+	OAV	OOB	BH	AVG	PB	PR	/A	PD	TPI
1969	Chi-N	1	0	1.000	6	2	0	0	0	14^2	15	2	9	4	15.3	3.07	131	.283	.397	0	.000	-0	1	2	0	0.2
1970	Chi-N	3	1	.750	34	5	0	0	4	72^2	88	3	23	50	13.9	3.59	125	.298	.351	1	.067	-1	4	7	1	0.7
1971	Chi-N	0	1	.000	14	0	0	0	0	10^1	18	1	3	2	18.3	6.97	56	.383	.420	0	—	0	-4	-3	0	-0.3
1972	Mil-A	7	7	.500	39	12	4	1	0	147^2	135	14	43	97	11.0	3.11	97	.245	.302	3	.081	-1	-1	-1	-1	-0.4
1973	Mil-A☆	20	12	.625	43	36	22	4	1	314^1	297	21	87	135	11.1	3.18	118	.251	.304	0	—	0	22	20	2	2.4
1974	Mil-A	10	13	.435	33	31	10	1	0	224	230	27	60	83	11.9	4.06	89	.268	.320	0	—	0	-11	-11	0	-1.1
1975	Mil-A	11	13	.458	36	29	8	1	2	206^1	215	18	65	79	12.4	4.27	90	.270	.329	0	—	0	-11	-10	1	-0.9
1976	Mil-A	9	15	.375	32	32	7	0	0	225^2	232	20	54	101	11.5	3.71	94	.268	.312	0	—	0	-5	-5	-0	-0.6
1977	KC-A	18	14	.563	36	35	6	1	0	239	233	22	81	103	12.3	3.62	112	.255	.324	0	—	0	12	11	1	1.2
1978	KC-A	1	2	.333	8	3	0	0	0	28^1	31	4	12	8	14.3	4.76	80	.282	.363	0	—	0	-3	-3	1	-0.3
	Sea-A	3	10	.231	20	19	3	0	0	114^1	125	21	38	26	13.3	5.35	71	.279	.343	0	—	0	-20	-20	3	-1.7
	Yr	4	12	.250	28	22	3	0	0	142^2	156	25	50	34	13.4	5.24	73	.279	.344	0	—	0	-23	-23	3	-2.0
Total	10	83	88	.485	301	204	60	8	7	1597^1	1619	153	475	688	12.0	3.80	98	.265	.322	4	.073	-3	-17	-14	7	-0.8

● TOM COLCOLOUGH

Colcolough, Thomas Bernard b: 10/8/1870, Charleston, S.C. d: 12/10/19, Charleston, S.C. BR/TR, 5'10.5", 180 lbs. Deb: 8/01/1893

YEAR	TM/L	W	L	PCT	G	GS	CG	SH	SV	IP	H	HR	BB	SO	RAT	ERA	ERA+	OAV	OOB	BH	AVG	PB	PR	/A	PD	TPI
1893	Pit-N	1	0	1.000	8	3	1	0	**2**	43^2	45	1	32	7	15.9	4.12	110	.258	.373	2	.143	0	3	2	-1	0.1
1894	Pit-N	8	5	.615	22	14	11	0	0	148^2	207	5	70	29	17.1	7.08	74	.326	.397	14	.200	-3	-29	-30	0	-2.4
1895	Pit-N	1	1	.500	6	5	2	0	0	35^1	38	1	21	15	16.3	5.60	81	.271	.385	5	.333	3	-3	-4	-1	-0.2
1899	NY-N	4	5	.444	11	8	7	0	0	81^2	85	1	41	14	14.2	3.97	95	.268	.357	10	.270	1	-1	-2	1	0.0
Total	4	14	11	.560	47	30	21	0	2	309^1	375	8	164	65	16.1	5.67	82	.296	.382	31	.228	1	-31	-35	0	-2.5

● BERT COLE

Cole, Albert George b: 7/1/1896, San Francisco, Cal. d: 5/30/75, San Mateo, Cal. BL/TL, 6'1", 180 lbs. Deb: 4/19/21

YEAR	TM/L	W	L	PCT	G	GS	CG	SH	SV	IP	H	HR	BB	SO	RAT	ERA	ERA+	OAV	OOB	BH	AVG	PB	PR	/A	PD	TPI
1921	Det-A	7	4	.636	20	11	7	1	1	109^2	134	3	36	22	14.3	4.27	100	.305	.363	13	.283	3	0	0	-1	0.2
1922	Det-A	1	6	.143	23	5	2	1	0	79^1	105	4	39	21	16.4	4.88	80	.313	.387	4	.160	-1	-7	-9	0	-0.9
1923	Det-A	13	5	.722	52	13	6	1	5	163	183	9	61	32	13.7	4.14	93	.284	.351	14	.255	2	-3	-5	-1	-0.4
1924	Det-A	3	9	.250	28	11	2	1	2	109^1	135	4	35	16	14.3	4.69	88	.314	.371	10	.270	1	-6	-7	1	-0.5
1925	Det-A	2	3	.400	14	2	1	0	1	33^2	44	2	15	7	16.0	5.88	73	.336	.408	3	.273	0	-6	-6	1	-0.4
	Cle-A	1	1	.500	13	2	0	0	1	44	55	1	25	9	16.6	6.14	72	.322	.411	2	.154	-0	-9	-8	-0	-0.8
	Yr	3	4	.429	27	4	1	0	2	77^2	99	3	40	16	16.2	6.03	73	.327	.407	5	.208	0	-14	-14	0	-1.2
1927	Chi-A	1	4	.200	27	2	0	0	0	66^2	79	3	19	12	13.6	4.72	86	.309	.363	3	.167	-1	-4	-5	2	-0.4
Total	6	28	32	.467	177	46	18	4	10	605^2	735	26	230	119	14.6	4.67	87	.305	.370	49	.239	5	-34	-40	2	-3.2

● DAVE COLE

Cole, David Bruce b: 8/29/30, Williamsport, Md. BR/TR, 6'2", 175 lbs. Deb: 9/09/50

YEAR	TM/L	W	L	PCT	G	GS	CG	SH	SV	IP	H	HR	BB	SO	RAT	ERA	ERA+	OAV	OOB	BH	AVG	PB	PR	/A	PD	TPI
1950	Bos-N	0	1	.000	4	0	0	0	0	8	7	0	3	8	12.4	1.13	342	.259	.355	0	.000	-0	3	2	-0	0.2
1951	Bos-N	2	4	.333	23	7	1	0	0	67^2	64	3	64	33	17.3	4.26	86	.254	.409	6	.353	3	-2	-4	0	-0.1
1952	Bos-N	1	1	.500	22	3	0	0	0	44^2	38	2	42	22	16.7	4.03	90	.241	.409	0	.000	-1	-1	-2	0	-0.3
1953	Mil-N	0	1	.000	10	0	0	0	0	14^2	17	1	14	13	19.0	8.59	46	.279	.413	1	.500	1	-7	-8	0	-0.6
1954	Chi-N	3	8	.273	18	14	2	1	0	84	74	7	62	37	14.7	5.36	78	.241	.370	6	.214	1	-12	-11	-0	-0.9
1955	Phi-N	0	3	.000	7	3	0	0	0	18^1	21	3	14	6	17.2	6.38	62	.304	.422	1	.200	-0	-5	-5	0	-0.4
Total	6	6	18	.250	84	27	3	1	0	237^1	221	16	199	119	16.2	4.93	79	.253	.395	14	.230	5	-25	-27	1	-2.1

YEAR TM/L	W	L	PCT	G	GS	CG	SH	SV	IP	H	HR	BB	SO	RAT	ERA	ERA+	OAV	OOB	BH	AVG	PB	PR	/A	PD	TPI
● **ED COLE**	Cole, Edward William (b: Edward William Kisleauskas) b: 3/22/09, Wilkes-Barre, Pa. BR/TR, 5'11", 170 lbs. Deb: 4/22/38																								
1938 StL-A	1	5	.167	36	6	1	0	3	88^2	116	8	48	26	17.2	5.18	96	.313	.399	3	.143	-1	-4	-2	-1	-0.4
1939 StL-A	0	2	.000	6	0	0	0	0	6^1	8	1	6	5	19.9	7.11	68	.308	.438	0	.000	-0	-2	-2	0	-0.2
Total 2	1	7	.125	42	6	1	0	3	95	124	9	54	31	17.3	5.31	94	.312	.401	3	.136	-2	-6	-4	-1	-0.6
● **KING COLE**	Cole, Leonard Leslie b: 4/15/1886, Toledo, Iowa d: 1/6/16, Bay City, Mich. BR/TR, 6'1", 170 lbs. Deb: 10/06/09																								
1909 Chi-N	1	0	1.000	1	1	1	1	0	9	6	0	3	1	9.0	0.00	—	.194	.265	3	.750	2	3	3	-0	0.7
1910 *Chi-N	20	4	**.833**	33	29	21	4	1	239^2	174	2	130	114	11.8	**1.80**	**160**	**.211**	.325	21	.231	2	33	29	-1	3.3
1911 Chi-N	18	7	.720	32	27	13	2	0	221^1	188	3	99	101	12.0	3.13	106	.236	.328	12	.152	-2	7	4	-2	0.0
1912 Chi-N	1	2	.333	8	3	0	0	0	19	36	2	8	9	21.8	10.89	31	.409	.469	2	.400	1	-16	-16	0	-1.3
Pit-N	2	2	.500	12	4	2	0	0	49	61	1	18	11	14.9	6.43	51	.330	.395	2	.133	-1	-16	-17	-0	-1.7
Yr	3	4	.429	20	7	2	0	0	68	97	3	26	20	16.5	7.68	43	.353	.413	4	.200	0	-32	-33	0	-3.0
1914 NY-A	11	9	.550	33	15	8	2	0	141^2	151	3	51	43	12.9	3.30	84	.288	.352	2	.048	-3	-9	-9	-3	-1.6
1915 NY-A	3	3	.500	10	6	2	0	1	51	41	2	22	19	11.6	3.18	92	.224	.317	1	.077	-1	-1	-1	-0	-0.3
Total 6	56	27	.675	129	85	47	9	2	730^2	657	13	331	298	12.5	3.12	97	.250	.340	43	.173	-2	-0	-7	-6	-0.9
● **VICTOR COLE**	Cole, Victor Alexander b: 1/23/68, Leningrad, Russia BB/TR, 5'10", 160 lbs. Deb: 6/06/92																								
1992 Pit-N	0	2	.000	8	4	0	0	0	23	23	1	14	12	14.5	5.48	62	.261	.363	0	.000	-0	-5	-5	0	-0.6
● **JOHN COLEMAN**	Coleman, John b: Bristol, Pa. TR, Deb: 6/23/1890																								
1890 Phi-N	0	1	.000	1	1	0	0	0	1^2	4	0	3	2	37.8	21.60	17	.448	.586	0	—	0	-3	-3	-0	-0.3
● **JOHN COLEMAN**	Coleman, John b: Jefferson City, Mo. TL, Deb: 9/25/1895																								
1895 StL-N	0	1	.000	1	1	1	0	0	8	12	1	8	5	23.6	13.50	36	.341	.475	1	.200	-0	-8	-8	0	-0.5
● **JOHN COLEMAN**	Coleman, John Francis b: 3/6/1863, Saratoga Spgs., N.Y d: 5/31/22, Detroit, Mich. BL/TR, 5'9.5", 170 lbs. Deb: 5/01/1883 ♦																								
1883 Phi-N	12	48	.200	65	61	59	3	0	538^1	772	17	48	159	13.7	4.87	63	.309	.322	83	.234	4	-103	-106	1	-8.1
1884 Phi-N	5	15	.250	21	19	14	1	0	154^1	216	9	22	37	13.9	4.90	61	.308	.329	42	.246	2	-33	-33	1	-2.5
Phi-a	0	2	.000	3	2	2	0	0	21	28	0	2	5	14.6	3.43	99	.304	.347	22	.206	0	-0	-0	0	0.0
1885 Phi-a	2	2	.500	8	3	3	0	0	60^1	82	0	5	12	13.0	3.43	100	.366	.380	119	.299	3	-1	0	-0	0.2
1886 Phi-a	1	1	.500	3	1	1	0	0	20^2	18	1	5	2	10.5	2.61	134	.225	.279	121	.246	0	2	2	-0	0.2
1889 Phi-a	3	2	.600	5	5	4	0	0	34	38	2	14	6	14.0	2.91	130	.274	.345	1	.053	-2	4	3	1	0.2
1890 Pit-N	0	2	.000	2	2	1	0	0	14	28	1	6	3	21.9	9.64	34	.403	.451	2	.182	0	-9	-10	-0	-0.7
Total 6	23	72	.242	107	93	84	4	0	842^2	1182	30	102	224	13.8	4.68	67	.311	.330	645	.257	7	-142	-144	3	-10.7
● **JOE COLEMAN**	Coleman, Joseph Howard b: 2/3/47, Boston, Mass. BR/TR, 6'3", 195 lbs. Deb: 9/28/65 FC																								
1965 Was-A	2	0	1.000	2	2	2	0	0	18	9	0	8	7	8.5	1.50	232	.153	.254	0	.000	-1	4	4	1	0.5
1966 Was-A	1	0	1.000	1	1	1	0	0	9	6	0	2	4	8.0	2.00	173	.188	.235	0	.000	-0	1	1	0	0.2
1967 Was-A	8	9	.471	28	22	3	0	0	134	154	6	47	77	14.1	4.63	68	.291	.359	2	.056	-1	-21	-22	-2	-2.6
1968 Was-A	12	16	.429	33	33	12	2	0	223	212	19	51	139	11.1	3.27	89	.250	.302	9	.129	-1	-7	-9	-1	-1.2
1969 Was-A	12	13	.480	40	36	12	4	1	247^2	222	26	100	182	11.9	3.27	106	.243	.322	9	.107	-2	10	5	-1	0.4
1970 Was-A	8	12	.400	39	29	6	1	0	218^2	190	25	89	152	11.6	3.58	99	.233	.311	8	.119	2	3	-1	0	0.2
1971 Det-A	20	9	.690	39	38	16	3	0	286	241	17	96	236	10.8	3.15	114	.229	.298	9	.094	-3	10	14	-2	0.9
1972 *Det-A†	19	14	.576	40	39	9	3	0	280	216	23	110	222	10.8	2.80	112	.214	.297	9	.110	-3	8	11	-1	0.8
1973 Det-A	23	15	.605	40	40	13	2	0	288^1	283	32	93	202	12.0	3.53	116	.258	.322	0	—	0	9	18	-0	1.5
1974 Det-A	14	12	.538	41	41	11	2	0	285^2	272	30	158	177	13.9	4.32	88	.254	.356	0	—	0	-22	-16	2	-1.6
1975 Det-A	10	18	.357	31	31	6	1	0	201	234	27	85	125	14.7	5.55	72	.291	.366	0	—	0	-40	-34	0	-3.4
1976 Det-A	2	5	.286	12	12	1	0	0	66^2	80	1	34	38	16.1	4.86	76	.308	.398	0	—	0	-10	-9	2	-0.7
Chi-N	2	8	.200	39	4	0	0	4	79	72	9	35	66	12.4	4.10	94	.246	.330	2	.154	-0	-5	-2	0	-0.2
1977 Oak-A	4	4	.500	43	12	2	0	2	127^2	114	11	49	55	11.6	2.96	136	.241	.314	0	—	0	16	15	-0	1.5
1978 Oak-A	3	0	1.000	10	0	0	0	0	19^2	12	1	5	4	7.8	1.37	265	.185	.243	0	—	0	5	5	0	0.6
Tor-A	2	0	1.000	31	0	0	0	0	60^2	67	6	30	28	14.5	4.60	85	.286	.370	0	—	0	-6	-5	-1	-0.6
Yr	5	0	1.000	41	0	0	0	0	80^1	79	7	35	32	12.9	3.81	101	.263	.342	0	—	0	-0	0	-1	0.0
1979 SF-N	0	0	—	5	0	0	0	0	3^2	3	0	2	0	14.7	0.00	—	.231	.375	0	—	0	2	1	-0	0.1
Pit-N	0	0	—	10	0	0	0	0	20^2	29	1	9	14	17.0	6.10	64	.326	.394	1	.200	0	-5	-5	-1	-0.6
Yr	0	0	—	15	0	0	0	0	24^1	32	1	11	14	16.3	5.18	74	.308	.379	1	.200	0	-4	-4	-1	-0.5
Total 15	142	135	.513	484	340	94	18	7	2569^1	2416	234	1003	1728	12.3	3.70	97	.250	.327	49	.106	-10	-48	-28	-2	-4.2
● **JOE COLEMAN**	Coleman, Joseph Patrick b: 7/30/22, Medford, Mass. BR/TR, 6'2.5", 200 lbs. Deb: 9/19/42 F																								
1942 Phi-A	0	1	.000	1	0	0	0	0	6	8	0	1	0	13.5	3.00	126	.308	.333	0	.000	-1	0	1	-0	0.0
1946 Phi-A	0	2	.000	4	2	0	0	0	13	19	1	8	8	18.7	5.54	64	.345	.429	2	.400	1	-3	-3	-0	-0.3
1947 Phi-A	6	12	.333	32	21	9	2	1	160^1	171	17	62	65	13.1	4.32	88	.275	.341	7	.146	-1	-11	-9	-2	-1.2
1948 Phi-A★	14	13	.519	33	29	13	3	0	215^2	224	11	90	86	13.1	4.09	105	.269	.341	9	.122	-4	5	5	-1	-0.1
1949 Phi-A	13	14	.481	33	30	18	1	1	240^1	249	12	127	109	14.2	3.86	107	.271	.361	14	.177	0	9	7	-5	0.3
1950 Phi-A	0	5	.000	15	6	2	0	0	54	74	9	50	12	20.7	8.50	54	.332	.454	1	.059	-1	-24	-24	-2	-2.2
1951 Phi-A	1	6	.143	28	9	1	0	1	96^1	117	12	59	34	16.7	5.98	72	.305	.402	7	.259	1	-20	-18	-1	-1.7
1953 Phi-A	3	4	.429	21	9	2	1	0	90	85	8	49	18	13.5	4.00	107	.254	.352	8	.286	2	-0	3	-2	0.3
1954 Bal-A	13	17	.433	33	32	15	4	0	221^1	184	16	96	103	11.5	3.50	102	.232	.317	13	.176	2	6	2	1	0.6
1955 Bal-A	0	1	.000	6	2	0	0	0	11^2	19	5	10	4	23.1	10.80	35	.373	.484	2	.667	1	-9	-9	0	-0.7
Det-A	2	1	.667	17	0	0	0	3	25^1	22	1	14	5	13.1	3.20	120	.239	.346	3	.750	1	2	2	0	0.4
Yr	2	2	.500	23	2	0	0	3	37	41	6	24	9	16.1	5.59	69	.281	.386	5	.714	2	-7	-7	0	-0.3
Total 10	52	76	.406	223	140	60	11	6	1134	1172	92	566	444	13.9	4.38	92	.271	.357	66	.182	2	-44	-44	-12	-4.6
● **PERCY COLEMAN**	Coleman, Pierce D. b: 10/15/1876, Mason, Ohio d: 2/16/48, Van Nuys, Cal. Deb: 7/02/1897																								
1897 StL-N	1	2	.333	12	4	2	0	0	57^1	99	0	32	10	21.5	8.16	54	.376	.454	6	.214	-1	-25	-24	1	-1.9
1898 Cin-N	0	1	.000	1	1	1	0	0	9	13	0	3	2	17.0	3.00	128	.335	.397	0	.000	-1	1	1	-0	0.0
Total 2	1	3	.250	13	5	3	0	0	66^1	112	0	35	12	20.9	7.46	58	.370	.447	6	.194	-2	-24	-23	0	-1.9
● **RIP COLEMAN**	Coleman, Walter Gary b: 7/31/31, Troy, N.Y. BL/TL, 6'2", 185 lbs. Deb: 8/15/55																								
1955 *NY-A	2	1	.667	10	6	0	0	1	29	40	2	16	15	17.7	5.28	71	.331	.413	2	.200	1	-4	-5	0	-0.4
1956 NY-A	3	5	.375	29	9	0	0	2	88^1	97	6	42	42	14.3	3.67	105	.285	.366	1	.042	-3	5	2	0	0.0
1957 KC-A	0	7	.000	19	6	1	1	0	41	53	5	25	15	17.1	5.93	67	.325	.415	0	.000	-1	-10	-9	0	-1.0
1959 KC-A	2	10	.167	29	11	2	0	2	81	85	8	34	54	13.3	4.56	88	.273	.347	2	.080	-2	-6	-5	-0	-0.7
Bal-A	0	0	—	3	0	0	0	0	4	4	0	2	4	13.5	0.00	—	.267	.353	0	—	0	2	2	1	0.3
Yr	2	10	.167	32	11	2	0	2	85	89	8	36	58	13.2	4.34	92	.271	.342	2	.080	-2	-5	-3	1	-0.4
1960 Bal-A	0	2	.000	5	1	0	0	0	4	8	0	5	0	31.5	11.25	34	.444	.583	0	.000	-0	-3	-3	0	-0.3
Total 5	7	25	.219	95	33	3	1	5	247^1	287	21	124	130	15.1	4.58	85	.296	.379	5	.072	-5	-17	-18	2	-2.1
● **ALLAN COLLAMORE**	Collamore, Allan Edward b: 6/5/1887, Worcester, Mass. d: 8/8/80, Battle Creek, Mich. BR/TR, 6', 170 lbs. Deb: 4/15/11																								
1911 Phi-A	0	1	.000	2	0	0	0	0	2	6	0	3	1	49.5	36.00	9	.600	.733	0	—	0	-7	-7	-0	-0.6
1914 Cle-A	3	7	.300	27	8	3	0	0	105^1	100	3	49	32	13.2	3.25	89	.264	.357	3	.094	-2	-6	-4	-1	-0.7
1915 Cle-A	2	5	.286	11	6	5	2	0	64^1	52	1	22	15	10.4	2.38	128	.235	.305	4	.174	0	4	5	1	0.6
Total 3	5	13	.278	40	14	8	2	0	171^2	158	4	74	48	12.6	3.30	89	.259	.347	7	.127	-2	-9	-7	-0	-0.7

YEAR	TM/L	W	L	PCT	G	GS	CG	SH	SV	IP	H	HR	BB	SO	RAT	ERA	ERA+	OAV	OOB	BH	AVG	PB	PR	/A	PD	TPI
● HAP COLLARD	Collard, Earl Clinton b: 8/29/1898, Williams, Ariz. d: 7/9/68, Jamestown, Cal. BR/TR, 6', 170 lbs. Deb: 4/23/27																									
1927	Cle-A	0	0	—	4	0	0	0	0	5^1	8	0	3	2	18.6	5.06	83	.333	.407	0	—	0	-1	-1	0	0.0
1928	Cle-A	0	0	—	1	0	0	0	0	4	4	0	4	1	18.0	2.25	184	.250	.400	1	1.000	0	1	1	-0	0.1
1930	Phi-N	6	12	.333	30	15	4	0	0	127	188	15	39	25	16.3	6.80	80	.350	.397	9	.205	-2	-26	-19	1	-1.7
Total	3	6	12	.333	35	15	4	0	0	136^1	200	15	46	28	16.4	6.60	81	.347	.398	10	.222	-1	-26	-19	1	-1.6
● ORLIN COLLIER	Collier, Orlin Edward b: 2/17/07, E.Prairie, Mo. d: 9/9/44, Memphis, Tenn. BR/TR, 5'11.5", 180 lbs. Deb: 9/11/31																									
1931	Det-A	0	1	.000	2	2	0	0	0	10^1	17	0	7	3	20.9	7.84	59	.362	.444	0	.000	-0	-4	-4	-0	-0.4
● HARRY COLLIFLOWER	Colliflower, James Harry "Collie" b: 3/11/1869, Petersville, Md. d: 8/12/61, Washington, D.C. BL/TL, 5'11.5", 175 lbs. Deb: 7/21/1899 U																									
1899	Cle-N	1	11	.083	14	12	11	0	0	98	152	6	41	8	18.7	8.17	45	.353	.423	23	.303	2	-47	-49	0	-3.7
● DAN COLLINS	Collins, Daniel Thomas b: 7/12/1854, St.Louis, Mo. d: 9/21/1883, New Orleans, La. Deb: 6/08/1874 ♦																									
1874	Chi-n	1	1	.500	2	2	1	0	0	11	21	0	2		18.8	*5.73*	53	.368	.390	1	.083	-1	-3	-3		-0.3
● DON COLLINS	Collins, Donald Edward b: 9/15/52, Lyons, Ga. BR/TL, 6'2", 195 lbs. Deb: 5/04/77																									
1977	Atl-N	3	9	.250	40	6	0	0	2	70^2	82	8	41	27	15.8	5.09	87	.299	.392	0	.000	-2	-9	-5	-1	-0.8
1980	Cle-A	0	0	—	4	0	0	0	0	6	9	0	7	0	24.0	7.50	54	.346	.485	0	—	0	-2	-2	-0	-0.2
Total	2	3	9	.250	44	6	0	0	2	76^2	91	8	48	27	16.4	5.28	84	.303	.401	0	.000	-2	-12	-7	-1	-1.0
● RIP COLLINS	Collins, Harry Warren b: 2/26/1896, Weatherford, Tex. d: 5/27/68, Bryan, Tex. BR/TR, 6'1", 205 lbs. Deb: 4/19/20																									
1920	NY-A	14	8	.636	36	18	10	2	1	187^1	171	6	79	66	12.7	3.22	119	.247	.337	8	.129	-4	12	13	-1	0.8
1921	*NY-A	11	5	.688	28	16	7	2	0	137^1	158	6	78	64	16.1	5.44	78	.293	.392	11	.196	-1	-18	-18	-1	-1.9
1922	Bos-A	14	11	.560	32	29	15	3	0	210^2	219	4	103	69	14.2	3.76	109	.274	.364	12	.158	-3	7	8	-1	0.4
1923	Det-A	3	7	.300	17	14	3	1	0	92^1	104	3	22	25	13.3	4.87	79	.284	.342	3	.111	-2	-9	-10	0	-1.1
1924	Det-A	14	7	.667	34	30	11	1	0	216	199	6	63	75	11.1	3.21	128	.249	.307	11	.145	-4	25	22	0	1.6
1925	Det-A	6	11	.353	26	20	5	0	0	140	149	7	52	33	13.3	4.56	94	.281	.352	5	.119	-4	-3	-4	4	-0.4
1926	Det-A	8	8	.500	30	13	5	3	1	122	128	4	44	44	13.2	2.73	149	.278	.350	6	.154	-1	17	18	1	1.8
1927	Det-A	13	7	.650	30	25	10	1	0	172^2	207	5	59	37	14.3	4.69	90	.312	.375	11	.204	0	-11	-9	5	-0.4
1929	StL-A	11	6	.647	26	20	10	1	1	155^1	162	16	73	47	14.0	4.00	111	.270	.355	17	.274	4	4	7	0	1.1
1930	StL-A	9	7	.563	35	20	6	1	2	171^2	168	11	63	75	12.4	4.35	112	.259	.330	7	.130	-2	6	10	-0	0.7
1931	StL-A	5	5	.500	17	14	2	0	0	107	130	5	38	34	14.2	3.79	122	.307	.366	5	.147	-1	7	10	1	1.0
Total	11	108	82	.568	311	219	84	15	5	1712^1	1795	73	674	569	13.4	3.99	106	.275	.351	96	.165	-18	38	45	9	3.6
● ORTH COLLINS	Collins, Orth Stein "Buck" b: 4/27/1880, Lafayette, Ind. d: 12/13/49, Ft.Lauderdale, Fla BL/TR, 6', 150 lbs. Deb: 6/01/04 ♦																									
1909	Was-A	0	0	—	1	0	0	0	0	1	0	0	0	1	0.0	0.00	—	.000	.000	0	.000	-0	0	0	-0	0.0
● PHIL COLLINS	Collins, Philip Eugene "Fidgety Phil" b: 8/27/01, Chicago, Ill. d: 8/14/48, Chicago, Ill. BR/TR, 5'11", 175 lbs. Deb: 10/07/23																									
1923	Chi-N	1	0	1.000	1	1	0	0	0	5	8	0	1	2	16.2	3.60	111	.400	.429	0	.000	-0	0	0	1	0.0
1929	Phi-N	9	7	.563	43	11	3	0	5	153^1	172	18	83	61	15.2	5.75	90	.284	.374	11	.190	-0	-18	-10	-1	-1.0
1930	Phi-N	16	11	.593	47	25	17	1	3	239	287	22	86	87	14.4	4.78	114	.299	.363	22	.253	3	5	18	-2	1.8
1931	Phi-N	12	16	.429	42	27	16	2	4	240^1	268	14	83	73	13.3	3.86	110	.283	.344	16	.168	-4	0	10	1	0.7
1932	Phi-N	14	12	.538	43	21	6	0	3	184^1	231	21	65	66	14.7	5.27	84	.314	.375	18	.265	3	-29	-18	-0	-1.5
1933	Phi-N	8	13	.381	42	13	5	1	**6**	151	178	9	57	40	14.4	4.11	93	.293	.360	7	.132	-3	-13	-5	-1	-0.9
1934	Phi-N	13	18	.419	45	32	15	0	1	254	277	30	87	72	13.0	4.18	113	.273	.333	15	.170	-5	-3	15	-3	0.7
1935	Phi-N	0	2	.000	3	3	0	0	0	14^2	24	5	9	4	20.3	11.66	39	.348	.423	0	.000	-1	-12	-12	0	-1.0
	StL-N	7	6	.538	26	8	2	0	2	82^2	96	6	26	18	13.6	4.57	90	.290	.347	4	.160	-1	-5	-4	-1	-0.6
	Yr	7	8	.467	29	11	2	0	2	97^1	120	11	35	22	14.6	5.64	74	.300	.361	4	.129	-2	-18	-16	-1	-1.6
Total	8	80	85	.485	292	141	64	4	24	1324^1	1541	125	497	423	14.1	4.66	100	.291	.356	93	.193	-8	-75	-3	-7	-1.8
● RAY COLLINS	Collins, Raymond Williston b: 2/11/1887, Colchester, Vt. d: 1/9/70, Burlington, Vt. BL/TL, 6'1", 185 lbs. Deb: 7/19/09																									
1909	Bos-A	4	3	.571	12	8	4	2	0	73^2	70	2	18	31	10.8	2.81	89	.269	.317	3	.130	-0	-3	-3	1	-0.2
1910	Bos-A	13	11	.542	35	26	18	4	1	244^2	205	1	41	109	9.1	1.62	158	.229	.264	15	.179	-1	25	25	-4	2.4
1911	Bos-A	11	12	.478	31	24	14	0	1	194^2	184	1	44	86	10.7	2.40	136	.256	.302	9	.150	0	20	19	-3	1.6
1912	*Bos-A	13	8	.619	27	24	17	4	0	199^1	192	4	42	82	10.7	2.53	135	.256	.297	11	.169	0	17	19	-3	1.8
1913	Bos-A	19	8	.704	30	30	19	3	0	246^2	242	3	37	88	10.3	2.63	112	.263	.293	12	.150	2	8	9	-4	0.7
1914	Bos-A	20	13	.606	39	30	16	6	0	272^1	252	3	56	72	10.2	2.51	107	.258	.298	11	.139	-0	7	5	-6	-0.1
1915	Bos-A	4	7	.364	25	9	2	0	2	104^2	101	1	31	43	11.4	4.30	65	.261	.317	8	.286	4	-16	-18	-3	-1.7
Total	7	84	62	.575	199	151	90	19	4	1336	1246	15	269	511	10.3	2.51	115	.254	.294	69	.165	6	59	58	-22	4.5
● JACKIE COLLUM	Collum, Jack Dean b: 6/21/27, Victor, Ia. BL/TL, 5'7", 163 lbs. Deb: 9/21/51																									
1951	StL-N	2	1	.667	3	2	1	1	0	17	11	0	10	5	11.1	1.59	250	.204	.328	3	.429	1	4	4	0	0.6
1952	StL-N	0	0	—	2	0	0	0	0	3	2	0	1	0	9.0	0.00	—	.200	.273	0	—	0	1	1	0	0.2
1953	StL-N	0	0	—	7	0	0	0	0	11^1	15	1	4	5	15.1	6.35	67	.326	.380	0	.000	-0	-3	-3	1	-0.2
	Cin-N	7	11	.389	30	12	4	1	3	124^2	123	8	39	51	12.1	3.75	116	.263	.328	10	.278	3	7	8	1	1.1
	Yr	7	11	.389	37	12	4	1	3	136	138	9	43	56	12.4	3.97	109	.269	.333	10	.256	3	5	6	2	0.9
1954	Cin-N	7	3	.700	36	2	1	0	0	79	86	8	32	28	14.0	3.76	112	.283	.361	3	.231	2	3	4	3	0.8
1955	Cin-N	9	8	.529	32	17	5	0	1	134	128	17	37	49	11.2	3.63	117	.254	.308	10	.250	2	6	9	-0	1.1
1956	StL-N	6	2	.750	38	1	0	0	7	60	63	6	27	17	13.8	4.20	90	.281	.364	3	.214	1	-3	-3	1	-0.1
1957	Chi-N	1	1	.500	9	0	0	0	1	10^2	8	0	9	7	15.2	6.75	57	.211	.375	0	—	0	-3	-3	0	-0.3
	Bro-N	0	0	—	3	0	0	0	0	4^1	7	1	1	3	16.6	8.31	50	.368	.400	0	—	0	-2	-2	-0	-0.2
	Yr	1	1	.500	12	0	0	0	1	15	15	1	10	10	15.0	7.20	55	.254	.362	0	—	0	-6	-5	-0	-0.5
1958	LA-N	0	0	—	2	0	0	0	0	3^1	4	2	2	0	16.2	8.10	51	.308	.400	0	.000	-0	-2	-1	0	-0.1
1962	Min-A	0	2	.000	8	3	0	0	0	15^1	29	1	11	5	23.5	11.15	37	.414	.494	0	.000	-1	-12	-12	0	-1.2
	Cle-A	0	0	—	1	0	0	0	0	1^1	4	0	0	1	27.0	13.50	29	.571	.571	0	—	0	-1	-1	0	-0.1
	Yr	0	2	.000	9	3	0	0	0	16^2	33	1	11	6	23.8	11.34	36	.418	.489	0	.000	-1	-14	-13	0	-1.3
Total	9	32	28	.533	171	37	11	2	12	464	480	44	173	171	13.0	4.15	101	.273	.344	29	.246	8	-4	1	6	1.6
● DICK COLPAERT	Colpaert, Richard Charles b: 1/3/44, Fraser, Mich. BR/TR, 5'10", 182 lbs. Deb: 7/21/70																									
1970	Pit-N	1	0	1.000	8	0	0	0	0	10^2	9	3	8	6	14.3	5.91	66	.237	.370	0	—	0	-2	-2	-0	-0.3
● LOYD COLSON	Colson, Loyd Albert b: 11/4/47, Wellington, Tex. BR/TR, 6'1", 190 lbs. Deb: 9/25/70																									
1970	NY-A	0	0	—	1	0	0	0	0	2	3	0	0	3	13.5	4.50	78	.333	.333	0	—	0	-0	-0	0	0.0
● LARRY COLTON	Colton, Lawrence Robert b: 6/8/42, Los Angeles, Cal. BL/TR, 6'3", 200 lbs. Deb: 5/06/68																									
1968	Phi-N	0	0	—	1	0	0	0	0	2	3	0	0	2	13.5	4.50	67	.333	.333	0	—	0	-0	-0	-0	0.0
● GEOFF COMBE	Combe, Geoffrey Wade b: 2/1/56, Melrose, Mass. BR/TR, 6'2", 185 lbs. Deb: 9/02/80																									
1980	Cin-N	0	0	—	4	0	0	0	0	6^2	9	0	4	10	17.6	10.80	33	.346	.433	0	—	0	-5	-5	0	-0.5
1981	Cin-N	1	0	1.000	14	0	0	0	0	17^2	27	3	10	9	18.8	7.64	46	.370	.446	0	—	0	-8	-8	-0	-0.9
Total	2	1	0	1.000	18	0	0	0	0	24^1	36	3	14	19	18.5	8.51	42	.364	.442	0	—	0	-13	-13	-0	-1.4
● PAT COMBS	Combs, Patrick Dennis b: 10/29/66, Newport, R.I. BL/TL, 6'3", 200 lbs. Deb: 9/05/89																									
1989	Phi-N	4	0	1.000	6	6	1	1	0	38^2	36	2	6	30	9.8	2.09	169	.248	.278	2	.167	0	6	6	-1	0.7
1990	Phi-N	10	10	.500	32	31	3	2	0	183^1	179	12	86	108	13.2	4.07	94	.257	.342	9	.150	0	-6	-5	-0	-0.5

YEAR	TM/L	W	L	PCT	G	GS	CG	SH	SV	IP	H	HR	BB	SO	RAT	ERA	ERA+	OAV	OOB	BH	AVG	PB	PR	/A	PD	TPI
1991	Phi-N	2	6	.250	14	13	1	0	0	64^1	64	7	43	41	15.2	4.90	75	.254	.367	2	.133	1	-9	-9	-0	-0.9
1992	Phi-N	1	1	.500	4	4	0	0	0	18^2	20	0	12	11	15.4	7.71	45	.278	.381	1	.125	0	-9	-9	1	-0.8
Total	4	17	17	.500	56	54	5	3	0	305	299	21	147	190	13.3	4.22	88	.257	.343	14	.147	2	-17	-16	-1	-1.5

● JORGE COMELLAS Comellas, Jorge (Pous) "Pancho" b: 12/7/16, Havana, Cuba BR/TR, 6', 190 lbs. Deb: 4/19/45

YEAR	TM/L	W	L	PCT	G	GS	CG	SH	SV	IP	H	HR	BB	SO	RAT	ERA	ERA+	OAV	OOB	BH	AVG	PB	PR	/A	PD	TPI
1945	Chi-N	0	2	.000	7	1	0	0	0	12	11	1	6	6	12.8	4.50	81	.244	.333	0	.000	-0	-1	-1	1	0.0

● STEVE COMER Comer, Steven Michael b: 1/13/54, Minneapolis, Minn. BB/TR, 6'3", 205 lbs. Deb: 4/15/78 C

YEAR	TM/L	W	L	PCT	G	GS	CG	SH	SV	IP	H	HR	BB	SO	RAT	ERA	ERA+	OAV	OOB	BH	AVG	PB	PR	/A	PD	TPI
1978	Tex-A	11	5	.688	30	11	3	2	1	117^1	107	5	37	65	11.1	2.30	163	.249	.310	0	—	0	19	19	1	2.1
1979	Tex-A	17	12	.586	36	36	6	1	0	242^1	230	24	84	86	12.0	3.68	113	.252	.320	0	—	0	14	13	-0	1.3
1980	Tex-A	2	4	.333	12	11	0	0	0	41^2	65	5	22	9	19.2	7.99	49	.367	.443	0	—	0	-18	-19	-0	-1.7
1981	Tex-A	8	2	.800	36	1	0	0	6	77^1	70	1	31	22	11.9	2.56	135	.241	.317	0	—	0	9	8	1	1.0
1982	Tex-A	1	6	.143	37	3	1	0	6	97	133	11	36	23	15.9	5.10	76	.342	.400	0	—	0	-11	-13	-0	-1.1
1983	Phi-N	1	0	1.000	3	1	0	0	0	8^2	11	0	3	1	14.5	5.19	69	.314	.368	0	.000	-0	-2	-2	-0	-0.2
1984	Cle-A	4	8	.333	22	20	1	0	0	117^1	146	11	39	39	14.5	5.68	72	.309	.366	0	—	0	-22	-21	0	-2.0
Total	7	44	37	.543	176	83	11	3	13	701^2	762	57	252	245	13.2	4.13	95	.281	.347	0	.000	-0	-10	-15	1	-0.6

● CHARLIE COMISKEY Comiskey, Charles Albert "Commy" or "The Old Roman"
b: 8/15/1859, Chicago, Ill. d: 10/26/31, Eagle River, Wis. BR/TR, 6', 180 lbs. Deb: 5/02/1882 MH♦

YEAR	TM/L	W	L	PCT	G	GS	CG	SH	SV	IP	H	HR	BB	SO	RAT	ERA	ERA+	OAV	OOB	BH	AVG	PB	PR	/A	PD	TPI
1882	StL-a	0	1	.000	2	1	1	0	0	8	12	0	3	2	16.9	0.00	—	.325	.376	80	.243	0	2	2	0	0.2
1884	StL-a	0	0	—	1	0	0	0	0	4	1	0	0	4	2.3	2.25	145	.059	.059	110	.239	0	0	0	-0	0.0
1889	StL-a	0	0	—	1	0	0	0	0	0^1	0	0	0	0	0.0	0.00	—	.000	.000	168	.286	0	0	0	0	0.0
Total	3	0	1	.000	4	1	1	0	0	12^1	13	0	3	6	11.7	0.73	410	.237	.277	1531	.264	0	3	3	-0	0.2

● JACK COMPTON Compton, Harry Leroy b: 3/9/1882, Lancaster, Ohio d: 7/4/74, Lancaster, Ohio BR/TR, 5'9", 157 lbs. Deb: 9/07/11

YEAR	TM/L	W	L	PCT	G	GS	CG	SH	SV	IP	H	HR	BB	SO	RAT	ERA	ERA+	OAV	OOB	BH	AVG	PB	PR	/A	PD	TPI
1911	Cin-N	0	1	.000	8	3	0	0	1	25^1	19	0	15	6	12.4	3.91	85	.204	.321	2	.333	0	-1	-2	-0	-0.2

● CLINT COMPTON Compton, Robert Clinton b: 11/1/50, Montgomery, Ala. BL/TL, 5'11", 185 lbs. Deb: 10/03/72

YEAR	TM/L	W	L	PCT	G	GS	CG	SH	SV	IP	H	HR	BB	SO	RAT	ERA	ERA+	OAV	OOB	BH	AVG	PB	PR	/A	PD	TPI
1972	Chi-N	0	0	—	1	0	0	0	0	2	2	0	2	0	18.0	9.00	42	.286	.444	0	—	0	-1	-1	-0	-0.1

● KEITH COMSTOCK Comstock, Keith Martin b: 12/23/55, San Francisco, Cal. BL/TL, 6', 175 lbs. Deb: 4/03/84

YEAR	TM/L	W	L	PCT	G	GS	CG	SH	SV	IP	H	HR	BB	SO	RAT	ERA	ERA+	OAV	OOB	BH	AVG	PB	PR	/A	PD	TPI
1984	Min-A	0	0	—	4	0	0	0	0	6^1	6	2	4	2	14.2	8.53	49	.261	.370	0	—	0	-3	-3	0	-0.5
1987	SF-N	2	0	1.000	15	0	0	0	1	20^2	19	1	10	21	12.6	3.05	126	.253	.341	0	.000	-0	2	2	0	0.2
	SD-N	0	1	.000	26	0	0	0	0	36	33	4	21	38	13.5	5.50	72	.252	.355	0	.000	-0	-6	-6	-1	-0.7
	Yr	2	1	.667	41	0	0	0	1	56^2	52	5	31	59	13.2	4.61	85	.251	.349	0	.000	-0	-3	-4	-1	-0.5
1988	SD-N	0	0	—	7	0	0	0	0	8	8	1	3	9	12.4	6.75	50	.250	.314	0	—	0	-3	-3	0	-0.3
1989	Sea-A	1	2	.333	31	0	0	0	0	25^2	26	2	10	22	12.6	2.81	144	.268	.336	0	—	0	3	3	-0	0.1
1990	Sea-A	7	4	.636	60	0	0	0	2	56	40	4	26	50	10.6	2.89	137	.206	.300	0	—	0	6	7	1	0.7
1991	Sea-A	0	0	—	1	0	0	0	0	0^1	2	0	1	0	81.0	54.00	8	.667	.750	0	—	0	-2	-2	0	-0.2
Total	6	10	7	.588	144	0	0	0	3	153	134	14	75	142	12.3	4.06	97	.241	.332	0	.000	-0	-2	-2	0	-0.7

● RALPH COMSTOCK Comstock, Ralph Remick "Commy" b: 11/24/1890, Sylvania, Ohio d: 9/13/66, Toledo, Ohio BR/TR, 5'10", 168 lbs. Deb: 8/26/13

YEAR	TM/L	W	L	PCT	G	GS	CG	SH	SV	IP	H	HR	BB	SO	RAT	ERA	ERA+	OAV	OOB	BH	AVG	PB	PR	/A	PD	TPI
1913	Det-A	2	5	.286	10	7	1	0	1	60^1	90	0	16	37	16.0	5.37	54	.344	.384	5	.227	1	-16	-16	0	-1.5
1915	Bos-A	1	0	1.000	3	0	0	0	0	9	10	2	2	1	12.0	2.00	139	.294	.333	0	.000	0	1	1	0	0.1
	Pit-F	3	3	.500	12	7	3	0	2	52^2	44	3	7	18	8.9	3.25	93	.237	.268	0	.000	-2	-1	-1	-0	-0.4
1918	Pit-N	5	6	.455	15	8	6	0	1	81	78	0	14	44	10.4	3.00	96	.259	.297	5	.192	-0	-2	-1	0	-0.1
Total	3	11	14	.440	40	22	10	0	4	203	222	5	39	100	11.7	3.72	78	.284	.321	10	.152	-1	-19	-18	-0	-1.9

● DAVE CONCEPCION Concepcion, David Ismael (Benitez) b: 6/17/48, Aragua, Venez. BR/TR, 6'1", 180 lbs. Deb: 4/06/70 ♦

YEAR	TM/L	W	L	PCT	G	GS	CG	SH	SV	IP	H	HR	BB	SO	RAT	ERA	ERA+	OAV	OOB	BH	AVG	PB	PR	/A	PD	TPI
1988	Cin-N	0	0	—	1	0	0	0	0	1^1	2	0	0	1	13.5	0.00	—	.333	.333	39	.198	0	1	1	0	0.1

● DAVID CONE Cone, David Bryan b: 1/2/63, Kansas City, Mo. BL/TR, 6'1", 185 lbs. Deb: 6/08/86

YEAR	TM/L	W	L	PCT	G	GS	CG	SH	SV	IP	H	HR	BB	SO	RAT	ERA	ERA+	OAV	OOB	BH	AVG	PB	PR	/A	PD	TPI
1986	KC-A	0	0	—	11	0	0	0	0	22^2	29	2	13	21	17.1	5.56	76	.309	.398	0	—	0	-3	-3	-0	-0.4
1987	NY-N	5	6	.455	21	13	1	0	1	99^1	87	11	44	68	12.3	3.71	102	.239	.329	2	.065	-1	4	1	-0	-0.1
1988	*NY-N★	20	3	**.870**	35	28	8	4	0	231^1	178	10	80	213	10.2	2.22	145	.213	.285	12	.150	1	32	26	-1	2.8
1989	NY-N	14	8	.636	34	33	7	2	0	219^2	183	20	74	190	10.7	3.52	93	.223	.290	18	.234	4	-1	-6	-2	-0.5
1990	NY-N	14	10	.583	31	30	6	2	0	211^2	177	21	65	**233**	10.3	3.23	116	.226	.286	14	.200	3	13	12	-0	1.5
1991	NY-N	14	14	.500	34	34	5	2	0	232^2	204	13	73	**241**	10.9	3.29	111	.235	.298	9	.125	-1	10	9	0	0.9
1992	NY-N★	13	7	.650	27	27	7	**5**	0	196^2	162	12	82	214	11.6	2.88	121	.223	.309	6	.092	-2	14	13	-0	1.2
	*Tor-A	4	3	.571	8	7	0	0	0	53	39	3	29	47	12.1	2.55	160	.206	.321	0	—	0	8	9	-1	0.9
Total	7	84	51	.622	201	172	34	15	1	1267	1059	92	460	1227	11.0	3.10	114	.226	.300	61	.154	4	77	60	-5	6.3

● BOB CONE Cone, Robert Earl b: 2/27/1894, Galveston, Tex. d: 5/24/55, Galveston, Tex. BR/TR, 6'2", 172 lbs. Deb: 7/25/15

YEAR	TM/L	W	L	PCT	G	GS	CG	SH	SV	IP	H	HR	BB	SO	RAT	ERA	ERA+	OAV	OOB	BH	AVG	PB	PR	/A	PD	TPI
1915	Phi-A	0	0	—	1	1	0	0	0	0^2	5	0	0	0	67.5	40.50	7	.714	.714	0	—	0	-3	-3	-0	-0.3

● DICK CONGER Conger, Richard b: 4/3/21, Los Angeles, Cal. d: 2/16/70, Los Angeles, Cal. BR/TR, 6', 185 lbs. Deb: 4/22/40

YEAR	TM/L	W	L	PCT	G	GS	CG	SH	SV	IP	H	HR	BB	SO	RAT	ERA	ERA+	OAV	OOB	BH	AVG	PB	PR	/A	PD	TPI
1940	Det-A	1	0	1.000	2	0	0	0	0	3	2	0	3	1	15.0	3.00	159	.200	.385	0	—	0	0	1	-0	0.0
1941	Pit-N	0	0	—	2	1	0	0	0	4	3	0	3	2	13.5	0.00	—	.214	.353	0	—	0	2	2	-0	0.2
1942	Pit-N	0	0	—	2	1	0	0	0	8^1	9	0	5	3	15.1	2.16	157	.290	.389	0	.000	-0	1	1	1	0.1
1943	Phi-N	2	7	.222	13	10	2	0	0	54^2	72	3	24	18	16.6	6.09	55	.327	.406	1	.063	-1	-16	-17	-0	-1.7
Total	4	3	7	.300	19	12	2	0	0	70	86	3	35	24	16.2	5.14	67	.313	.400	1	.053	-1	-13	-13	0	-1.4

● ALLEN CONKWRIGHT Conkwright, Allen Howard "Red" b: 12/4/1896, Sedalia, Mo. d: 7/30/91, LaMesa, Cal. BR/TR, 5'10", 170 lbs. Deb: 9/16/20

YEAR	TM/L	W	L	PCT	G	GS	CG	SH	SV	IP	H	HR	BB	SO	RAT	ERA	ERA+	OAV	OOB	BH	AVG	PB	PR	/A	PD	TPI
1920	Det-A	2	1	.667	5	2	0	0	1	19^1	29	0	16	4	20.9	6.98	53	.397	.506	1	.200	1	-7	-7	0	-0.6

● GENE CONLEY Conley, Donald Eugene b: 11/10/30, Muskogee, Okla. BR/TR, 6'8", 225 lbs. Deb: 4/17/52

YEAR	TM/L	W	L	PCT	G	GS	CG	SH	SV	IP	H	HR	BB	SO	RAT	ERA	ERA+	OAV	OOB	BH	AVG	PB	PR	/A	PD	TPI
1952	Bos-N	0	3	.000	4	3	0	0	0	12^2	23	4	9	6	24.2	7.82	46	.397	.493	2	.400	1	-6	-6	-0	-0.5
1954	Mil-N★	14	9	.609	28	27	12	2	0	194^1	171	17	79	113	11.9	2.96	126	.240	.322	12	.156	-2	24	16	-1	1.4
1955	Mil-N★	11	7	.611	22	21	10	0	0	158	152	23	52	107	11.7	4.16	90	.254	.315	11	.204	-1	-2	-7	-0	-0.8
1956	Mil-N	8	9	.471	31	19	5	1	3	158^1	169	13	52	68	12.7	3.13	111	.276	.335	7	.156	-0	11	6	-1	0.5
1957	*Mil-N	9	9	.500	35	18	6	1	1	148	133	9	64	61	12.1	3.16	111	.244	.325	9	.196	1	12	6	-0	0.7
1958	Mil-N	0	6	.000	26	7	0	0	2	72	89	8	17	53	13.8	4.88	72	.309	.356	3	.188	1	-7	-11	0	-1.0
1959	Phi-N★	12	7	.632	25	22	12	3	1	180	159	13	42	102	10.1	3.00	**137**	.235	.281	16	.239	2	19	22	-0	2.6
1960	Phi-N	8	14	.364	29	25	9	2	0	183^1	192	10	42	117	11.6	3.68	105	.272	.314	8	.127	-1	2	4	-2	0.1
1961	Bos-A	11	14	.440	33	30	6	2	1	199^2	229	33	65	113	13.4	4.91	85	.287	.343	16	.219	4	-20	-17	-1	-1.3
1962	Bos-A	15	14	.517	34	33	9	2	1	241^2	238	28	68	134	11.6	3.95	105	.256	.310	18	.207	4	1	5	-1	0.7
1963	Bos-A	3	4	.429	9	9	0	0	0	40^2	51	4	21	14	16.2	6.64	57	.305	.386	3	.200	0	-14	-13	-1	-1.3
Total	11	91	96	.487	276	214	69	13	9	1588^2	1606	162	511	888	12.2	3.82	101	.264	.324	105	.192	8	20	6	-6	1.1

● ED CONLEY Conley, Edward J. b: 7/10/1864, Sandwich, Mass. d: 10/16/1894, Cumberland, R.I. 5'11.5", Deb: 7/20/1884

YEAR	TM/L	W	L	PCT	G	GS	CG	SH	SV	IP	H	HR	BB	SO	RAT	ERA	ERA+	OAV	OOB	BH	AVG	PB	PR	/A	PD	TPI
1884	Pro-N	4	4	.500	8	8	8	1	0	71	63	4	22	33	10.8	2.15	131	.223	.280	4	.143	-2	7	5	-1	0.2

● SNIPE CONLEY Conley, James Patrick b: 4/25/1894, Cressona, Pa. d: 1/7/78, DeSoto, Tex. BR/TR, 5'11.5", 179 lbs. Deb: 5/20/14

YEAR	TM/L	W	L	PCT	G	GS	CG	SH	SV	IP	H	HR	BB	SO	RAT	ERA	ERA+	OAV	OOB	BH	AVG	PB	PR	/A	PD	TPI
1914	Bal-F	4	6	.400	35	11	4	2	1	125	112	2	47	86	11.9	2.52	134	.259	.340	4	.114	-3	10	12	-1	0.9
1915	Bal-F	1	4	.200	25	6	4	0	0	86	97	5	32	40	13.9	4.29	74	.314	.386	6	.250	2	-12	-11	-1	-1.0
1918	Cin-N	2	0	1.000	5	0	0	0	1	13^2	17	2	5	2	14.5	5.27	51	.321	.379	1	.250	0	-4	-4	0	-0.4

YEAR TM/L	W	L	PCT	G	GS	CG	SH	SV	IP	H	HR	BB	SO	RAT	ERA	ERA+	OAV	OOB	BH	AVG	PB	PR	/A	PD	TPI
Total 3	7	10	.412	65	17	8	2	2	224²	226	9	84	128	12.8	3.36	97	.284	.360	11	.175	-1	-6	-3	-1	-0.5

● **BOB CONLEY**   Conley, Robert Burns   b: 2/1/34, Mousie, Ky.   BR/TR, 6'1", 188 lbs.   Deb: 9/11/58

| 1958 Phi-N | 0 | 0 | — | 2 | 2 | 0 | 0 | 0 | 8¹ | 9 | 0 | 1 | 0 | 10.8 | 7.56 | 52 | .273 | .294 | 0 | .000 | -0 | -3 | -3 | -0 | -0.3 |

● **BERT CONN**   Conn, Albert Thomas   b: 9/22/1879, Philadelphia, Pa.   d: 11/2/44, Philadelphia, Pa.   TR ,   Deb: 9/16/1898   ◆

1898 Phi-N	0	1	.000	1	1	0	0	0	7	13	1	2	3	19.3	6.43	53	.393	.428	1	.333	1	-2	-2	-0	-0.1
1900 Phi-N	0	2	.000	4	1	1	0	0	17¹	29	0	16	2	26.5	8.31	44	.370	.508	3	.333	1	-9	-9	-1	-0.7
Total 2	0	3	.000	5	2	1	0	0	24¹	42	1	18	5	24.4	7.77	46	.377	.487	8	.267	1	-11	-11	-1	-0.8

● **SARGE CONNALLY**   Connally, George Walter   b: 8/31/1898, McGregor, Tex.   d: 1/27/78, Temple, Tex.   BR/TR, 5'11", 170 lbs.   Deb: 9/10/21

1921 Chi-A	0	1	.000	5	2	0	0	0	22¹	29	0	10	6	16.1	6.45	66	.330	.404	4	.500	2	-5	-5	0	-0.3
1923 Chi-A	0	0	—	3	0	0	0	0	8²	7	0	12	3	20.8	6.23	64	.241	.476	1	.333	0	-2	-2	-0	-0.2
1924 Chi-A	7	13	.350	44	13	6	0	6	160	177	4	68	55	14.3	4.05	102	.290	.369	11	.220	-1	3	1	3	0.3
1925 Chi-A	6	7	.462	40	2	0	0	8	104²	122	2	58	45	15.6	4.64	89	.310	.402	7	.250	1	-3	-6	3	-0.2
1926 Chi-A	6	5	.545	31	8	5	0	3	108¹	128	6	35	47	13.7	3.16	122	.300	.356	5	.156	-1	10	9	2	0.9
1927 Chi-A	10	15	.400	43	18	11	1	5	198¹	217	8	83	58	14.0	4.08	99	.292	.370	22	.328	4	1	-1	1	0.4
1928 Chi-A	2	5	.286	28	5	1	0	2	74¹	89	1	29	28	14.8	4.84	84	.313	.385	2	.105	-2	-7	-7	-0	-0.8
1929 Chi-A	0	0	—	11	0	0	0	0	11¹	13	0	8	3	16.7	4.76	90	.317	.429	0	—	0	-1	-1	-0	-0.1
1931 Cle-A	5	5	.500	17	9	5	0	1	85²	87	7	50	37	15.0	4.20	110	.256	.361	5	.185	1	2	4	-0	0.4
1932 Cle-A	8	6	.571	35	7	4	1	3	112¹	119	6	42	32	13.1	4.33	110	.266	.333	7	.175	-0	2	5	0	0.5
1933 Cle-A	5	3	.625	41	3	1	0	1	103	112	4	49	30	14.3	4.89	91	.271	.353	6	.231	1	-7	-5	-2	-0.6
1934 Cle-A	0	0	—	5	0	0	0	0	5¹	4	0	5	1	15.2	5.06	90	.222	.391	0	.000	-0	-0	-0	-0	-0.0
Total 12	49	60	.450	303	67	33	2	31	994¹	1104	32	449	345	14.4	4.30	98	.288	.368	70	.233	5	-7	-8	5	0.3

● **BILL CONNELLY**   Connelly, William Wirt "Wild Bill"   b: 6/29/25, Alberta, Va.   d: 11/27/80, Richmond, Va.   BL/TR, 6', 175 lbs.   Deb: 8/22/45

1945 Phi-A	1	1	.500	2	1	0	0	0	8	7	0	8	0	16.9	4.50	76	.259	.429	0	.000	0	-1	-1	-0	-0.1
1950 Chi-A	0	0	—	2	0	0	0	0	2¹	5	1	1	0	23.1	11.57	39	.455	.500	0	—	0	-2	-2	-0	-0.2
Det-A	0	0	—	2	0	0	0	0	4	4	1	2	1	13.5	6.75	69	.250	.333	0	.000	0	-1	-1	-0	-0.1
Yr	0	0	—	4	0	0	0	0	6¹	9	2	3	1	17.1	8.53	54	.333	.400	0	.000	0	-3	-3	-0	-0.3
1952 NY-N	5	0	1.000	11	4	0	0	0	31²	22	4	25	22	13.4	4.55	81	.208	.359	4	.364	3	-3	-3	1	0.0
1953 NY-N	0	1	.000	8	2	0	0	0	20¹	33	4	17	11	22.1	11.07	39	.371	.472	0	.000	-1	-15	-15	-0	-1.4
Total 4	6	2	.750	25	7	0	0	0	66¹	71	10	53	34	16.8	6.92	57	.285	.411	4	.211	3	-22	-22	-0	-1.8

● **ED CONNOLLY**   Connolly, Edward Joseph Jr.   b: 12/3/39, Brooklyn, N.Y.   BL/TL, 6'1", 190 lbs.   Deb: 4/19/64   F

1964 Bos-A	4	11	.267	27	15	1	1	0	80²	80	3	64	73	16.7	4.91	76	.261	.398	3	.167	0	-12	-9	-1	-1.1
1967 Cle-A	2	1	.667	15	4	0	0	0	49¹	63	6	34	45	17.9	7.48	44	.315	.417	2	.182	0	-23	-23	-0	-2.3
Total 2	6	12	.333	42	19	1	1	0	130	143	9	98	118	17.2	5.88	62	.282	.405	5	.172	0	-35	-33	-2	-3.4

● **JOHN CONNOR**   Connor, John   b: 8/1854, Scotland   d: 10/13/32, Boston, Mass.   Deb: 7/26/1884

1884 Bos-N	1	4	.200	7	7	7	0	0	60	70	1	18	29	13.2	3.15	92	.275	.322	2	.080	-3	-1	-2	0	-0.4
1885 Buf-N	0	1	.000	1	1	1	0	0	9	14	0	2	0	16.0	4.00	75	.378	.410	0	.000	-0	-1	-1	-1	-0.2
Lou-a	1	3	.250	4	4	4	0	0	35	43	0	12	19	14.7	4.89	66	.295	.356	2	.143	-1	-6	-6	-1	-0.7
Total 2	2	8	.200	12	12	12	0	0	104	127	1	32	48	13.9	3.81	79	.290	.341	4	.095	-4	-9	-9	-1	-1.3

● **JOE CONNORS**   Connors, Joseph P.   b: Paterson, N.J.   Deb: 5/03/1884   ◆

1884 Alt-U	0	1	.000	1	1	1	0	0	9	18	0	5	0	23.0	7.00	47	.391	.451	1	.091	-0	-4	-4	0	-0.3
KC-U	0	1	.000	2	1	1	0	0	12	24	1	0	1	18.0	4.50	61	.391	.391	1	.091	-1	-2	-2	-1	-0.3
Yr	0	2	.000	3	2	2	0	0	21	42	1	5	1	20.1	5.57	54	.391	.418	2	.091	-1	-6	-6	-0	-0.6

● **BILL CONNORS**   Connors, William Joseph   b: 11/2/41, Schenectady, N.Y.   BR/TR, 6'1", 180 lbs.   Deb: 5/03/66   C

1966 Chi-N	0	1	.000	11	0	0	0	0	16	20	4	7	3	15.2	7.31	50	.308	.375	0	—	0	-7	-6	-0	-0.6
1967 NY-N	0	0	—	6	1	0	0	0	13	8	3	5	13	9.7	6.23	54	.170	.264	0	.000	-0	-4	-4	-0	-0.5
1968 NY-N	0	1	.000	9	0	0	0	0	14	21	0	7	8	18.6	9.00	34	.339	.414	1	1.000	1	-9	-9	0	-0.9
Total 3	0	2	.000	26	1	0	0	0	43	49	7	19	24	14.7	7.53	45	.282	.359	1	.500	1	-20	-20	-0	-2.0

● **TED CONOVAR**   Conovar, Theodore "Huck"   b: 3/10/1868, Lexington, Ky.   d: 7/27/10, Paris, Ky.   BR/TR, 5'10.5", 165 lbs.   Deb: 5/26/1889

| 1889 Cin-a | 0 | 0 | — | 1 | 0 | 0 | 0 | 1 | 2 | 4 | 0 | 2 | 1 | 27.0 | 13.50 | 29 | .403 | .503 | 0 | — | 0 | -2 | -2 | -0 | -0.2 |

● **TIM CONROY**   Conroy, Timothy James   b: 4/3/60, McKeesport, Pa.   BL/TL, 5'11", 185 lbs.   Deb: 6/23/78

1978 Oak-A	0	0	—	2	2	0	0	0	4²	3	0	9	0	25.1	7.71	47	.188	.500	0	—	0	-2	-2	-0	-0.2
1982 Oak-A	2	2	.500	5	5	1	0	0	25¹	20	1	18	17	13.5	3.55	110	.222	.352	0	—	0	1	1	-0	0.2
1983 Oak-A	7	10	.412	39	18	3	1	0	162¹	141	17	98	112	13.4	3.94	98	.232	.340	0	—	0	2	-1	-2	-0.2
1984 Oak-A	1	6	.143	38	14	0	0	0	93	82	11	63	69	14.2	5.32	70	.236	.356	0	—	0	-14	-16	-1	-1.5
1985 Oak-A	0	1	.000	16	0	0	0	0	25¹	22	3	15	8	13.5	4.26	90	.237	.349	0	—	0	-0	-1	-0	-0.1
1986 StL-N	5	11	.313	25	21	1	0	0	115¹	122	15	56	79	14.1	5.23	70	.275	.360	4	.138	1	-19	-20	-1	-2.1
1987 StL-N	3	2	.600	10	9	0	0	0	40²	48	0	25	22	16.4	5.53	73	.306	.404	0	.000	-2	-7	-6	-1	-0.8
Total 7	18	32	.360	135	71	5	1	0	466²	438	47	284	307	14.1	4.71	81	.249	.357	4	.091	-1	-38	-47	-6	-4.6

● **JIM CONSTABLE**   Constable, Jimmy Lee "Sheriff"   b: 6/14/33, Jonesboro, Tenn.   BB/TL, 6'1", 185 lbs.   Deb: 6/24/56

1956 NY-N	0	0	—	3	0	0	0	0	4¹	9	0	7	1	35.3	14.54	26	.429	.586	0	—	0	-5	-5	-0	-0.5
1957 NY-N	1	1	.500	16	0	0	0	0	28¹	27	2	7	13	12.1	2.86	138	.262	.333	0	.000	-0	3	3	-0	0.3
1958 SF-N	1	0	1.000	9	0	0	0	1	8	10	1	3	4	14.6	5.63	68	.323	.382	1	1.000	1	-1	-2	1	-0.0
Cle-A	0	1	.000	6	2	0	0	0	9¹	17	1	4	3	21.2	11.57	32	.415	.478	2	1.000	1	-8	-8	-0	-0.7
Was-A	0	1	.000	15	2	0	0	0	27²	29	3	15	25	14.6	4.88	78	.271	.366	1	.250	0	-3	-3	-0	-0.3
Yr	1	2	.000	21	4	0	0	0	37	46	4	19	28	16.1	6.57	57	.309	.391	3	.500	1	-12	-11	-1	-1.0
1962 Mil-N	1	1	.500	3	2	1	1	0	18	14	1	4	12	9.0	2.00	190	.222	.269	0	.000	-0	4	4	-1	0.3
1963 SF-N	0	0	—	4	0	0	0	0	2¹	3	0	1	1	15.4	3.86	83	.333	.400	0	—	0	-0	-0	-0	-0.0
Total 5	3	4	.429	56	6	1	1	2	98	109	8	41	59	14.4	4.87	78	.291	.371	4	.235	2	-11	-11	-1	-0.9

● **SANDY CONSUEGRA**   Consuegra, Sandalio Simeon (Castello)   b: 9/3/20, Potrerillos, Cuba   BR/TR, 5'10", 165 lbs.   Deb: 6/10/50

1950 Was-A	7	8	.467	21	18	8	2	2	124²	132	6	57	38	13.7	4.40	102	.270	.347	7	.175	-1	2	1	0	0.1
1951 Was-A	7	8	.467	40	12	5	0	3	146	140	10	63	31	12.5	4.01	102	.251	.327	10	.233	-0	2	1	1	0.2
1952 Was-A	6	0	1.000	30	2	0	0	5	73²	80	7	27	19	13.1	3.05	116	.276	.338	3	.176	-0	5	4	1	0.3
1953 Was-A	0	0	—	4	0	0	0	0	5	9	0	4	0	23.4	10.80	36	.391	.481	0	—	0	-4	-4	-0	-0.3
Chi-A	7	5	.583	29	13	5	1	3	124	122	9	28	30	11.0	2.54	158	.258	.302	2	.057	-4	20	20	3	2.0
Yr	7	5	.583	33	13	5	1	3	129	131	9	32	30	11.5	2.86	141	.264	.311	2	.057	-4	16	17	3	1.7
1954 Chi-A★	16	3	**.842**	39	17	3	2	3	154	142	9	35	31	10.3	2.69	139	.248	.292	11	.229	1	18	18	1	2.1
1955 Chi-A	6	5	.545	44	7	3	0	7	126¹	120	4	18	35	10.0	2.64	150	.256	.286	3	.103	-2	19	18	-0	1.7
1956 Chi-A	1	2	.333	28	1	0	0	0	38¹	45	4	11	7	13.4	5.17	79	.296	.348	0	.000	-1	-4	-5	-0	-0.5
Bal-A	1	1	.500	4	1	0	0	0	8²	10	2	2	1	12.5	4.15	94	.294	.333	1	.500	0	-0	-0	-0	-0.0
Yr	2	3	.400	32	2	0	0	0	47	55	6	13	8	13.0	4.98	82	.293	.338	1	.167	-0	-4	-5	-0	-0.5
1957 Bal-A	0	0	—	5	0	0	0	0	5	4	0	2	0	7.2	1.80	200	.211	.211	0	—	0	1	1	0	0.1
NY-N	0	0	—	4	0	0	0	0	3²	7	1	1	1	19.6	2.45	160	.389	.421	0	—	0	1	0	0	0.1
Total 8	51	32	.614	248	71	24	5	26	809¹	811	43	246	193	11.8	3.37	119	.262	.318	37	.170	-5	59	57	4	5.8

YEAR TM/L	W	L	PCT	G	GS	CG	SH	SV	IP	H	HR	BB	SO	RAT	ERA	ERA+	OAV	OOB	BH	AVG	PB	PR	/A	PD	TPI

● NARDI CONTRERAS   Contreras, Arnaldo Juan b: 9/19/51, Tampa, Fla. BB/TR, 6'2", 193 lbs. Deb: 5/23/80

| 1980 Chi-A | 0 | 0 | — | 8 | 0 | 0 | 0 | 0 | 13² | 18 | 1 | 7 | 8 | 17.8 | 5.93 | 68 | .333 | .429 | 0 | — | 0 | -3 | -3 | 0 | -0.3 |

● JIM CONWAY   Conway, James P. b: Clifton, Pa. TR , Deb: 5/05/1884 F

1884 Bro-a	3	9	.250	13	13	10	0	0	105¹	132	4	15	25	12.8	4.44	75	.289	.316	6	.128	-4	-14	-13	-2	-1.6
1885 Phi-a	0	1	.000	2	2	1	0	0	12¹	19	0	2	0	15.3	7.30	47	.358	.382	0	.000	-1	-6	-5	-0	-0.5
1889 KC-a	19	19	.500	41	37	33	0	0	335	334	12	90	115	11.8	3.25	129	.252	.306	31	.208	-6	22	35	1	2.6
Total 3	22	29	.431	56	52	44	0	0	452²	485	16	107	140	12.1	3.64	109	.264	.311	37	.183	-11	3	16	-1	0.5

● JERRY CONWAY   Conway, Jerome Patrick b: 6/7/01, Holyoke, Mass. d: 4/16/80, Holyoke, Mass. BL/TL, 6'2", 190 lbs. Deb: 8/31/20

| 1920 Was-A | 0 | 0 | — | 1 | 0 | 0 | 0 | 0 | 2 | 1 | 0 | 1 | 0 | 9.0 | 0.00 | — | .167 | .286 | 0 | — | 0 | 1 | 1 | -0 | 0.1 |

● PETE CONWAY   Conway, Peter J. b: 10/30/1866, Burmont, Pa. d: 1/13/03, Clifton Heights, Pa. BR/TR, 5'10.5", Deb: 8/10/1885 F♦

1885 Buf-N	10	17	.370	27	27	26	0	0	210	256	6	44	94	12.9	4.67	64	.287	.320	10	.111	-4	-43	-39	1	-3.7
1886 KC-N	5	15	.250	23	20	19	0	0	180	236	6	61	81	14.9	5.75	66	.294	.343	47	.242	-1	-49	-39	-2	-3.4
Det-N	6	5	.545	11	11	11	0	0	91	93	1	25	35	11.7	3.36	99	.255	.303	8	.186	1	-1	-0	-0	-0.1
Yr	11	20	.355	34	31	30	0	0	271	329	7	86	116	13.8	4.95	73	.282	.331	55	.232	1	-49	-40	-2	-3.5
1887 *Det-N	8	9	.471	17	17	16	0	0	146	132	3	47	40	11.3	2.90	140	.235	.300	22	.232	0	19	19	3	1.8
1888 Det-N	30	14	.682	45	45	43	4	0	391	315	11	57	176	8.9	2.26	123	.208	**.243**	46	.275	14	26	22	3	3.9
1889 Pit-N	2	1	.667	3	3	2	0	0	22	26	1	16	2	17.2	4.91	76	.285	.392	1	.100	0	-2	-3	0	-0.2
Total 5	61	61	.500	126	123	117	5	0	1040	1058	32	250	428	11.5	3.59	90	.250	.295	134	.224	11	-50	-42	4	-1.7

● DICK CONWAY   Conway, Richard Butler b: 4/25/1865, Lowell, Mass. d: 9/9/26, Lowell, Mass. BL/TR, 5'7.5", 140 lbs. Deb: 7/22/1886 F

1886 Bal-a	2	7	.222	9	9	8	0	0	76²	106	6	43	64	17.8	6.81	50	.312	.394	7	.206	0	-29	-29	2	-2.1
1887 Bos-N	9	15	.375	26	26	25	0	0	222¹	249	10	86	45	13.8	4.66	87	.276	.343	36	.248	2	-14	-15	1	-1.0
1888 Bos-N	4	2	.667	6	6	6	0	0	53	49	2	8	12	10.4	2.38	120	.240	.282	4	.160	-1	3	3	-0	0.2
Total 3	15	24	.385	41	41	39	0	0	352	404	18	137	121	14.2	4.78	78	.279	.347	47	.230	2	-40	-41	2	-2.9

● JOE CONZELMAN   Conzelman, Joseph Harrison b: 7/14/1885, Bristol, Conn. d: 4/17/79, Mountain Brook, Ala. BR/TR, 6', 170 lbs. Deb: 5/01/13

1913 Pit-N	0	1	.000	3	2	1	0	0	15	13	0	5	9	11.4	1.20	251	.245	.322	0	.000	-1	3	3	0	0.3
1914 Pit-N	5	6	.455	33	9	4	1	2	101	88	2	40	39	11.7	2.94	90	.254	.337	3	.111	-2	-2	-3	2	-0.4
1915 Pit-N	1	1	.500	18	1	0	0	0	47¹	41	0	20	22	12.2	3.42	80	.248	.340	1	.091	-1	-4	-4	1	-0.4
Total 3	6	8	.429	54	12	5	1	2	163¹	142	2	65	70	11.8	2.92	93	.252	.336	4	.095	-3	-2	-4	2	-0.5

● DENNIS COOK   Cook, Dennis Bryan b: 10/4/62, LaMarque, Tex. BL/TL, 6'3", 185 lbs. Deb: 9/12/88

1988 SF-N	2	1	.667	4	4	1	0	0	22	9	1	11	13	8.2	2.86	114	.125	.241	0	.000	1	1	1	-1	0.1
1989 SF-N	1	0	1.000	2	2	1	0	0	15	13	1	5	9	10.8	1.80	187	.245	.310	1	.167	1	3	3	0	0.4
Phi-N	6	8	.429	21	16	1	1	0	106	97	17	33	58	11.2	3.99	89	.243	.304	8	.222	1	-6	-5	-1	-0.6
Yr	7	8	.467	23	18	2	1	0	121	110	18	38	67	11.2	3.72	95	.243	.305	9	.214	2	-3	-3	-1	-0.2
1990 Phi-N	8	3	.727	42	13	2	1	1	141²	132	13	54	58	11.9	3.56	107	.250	.322	13	.310	4	4	4	-0	0.8
LA-N	1	1	.500	5	3	0	0	0	14¹	23	7	2	6	15.7	7.53	49	.365	.385	2	.286	1	-6	-6	-0	-0.5
Yr	9	4	.692	47	16	2	1	1	156	155	20	56	64	12.2	3.92	97	.259	.323	15	.306	5	-2	-2	-0	0.3
1991 LA-N	1	0	1.000	20	1	0	0	0	17²	12	0	7	8	9.7	0.51	705	.203	.288	0	.000	-0	6	6	0	0.6
1992 Cle-A	5	7	.417	32	25	1	0	0	158	156	29	50	96	11.8	3.82	106	.255	.314	0	—	0	2	4	-2	0.2
Total 5	24	20	.545	126	64	6	3	1	474²	442	68	162	248	11.6	3.66	103	.248	.312	24	.250	7	5	6	-3	1.0

● EARL COOK   Cook, Earl Davis b: 12/10/08, Stouffville, Ont., BR/TR, 6', 195 lbs. Deb: 9/12/41

| 1941 Det-A | 0 | 0 | — | 1 | 0 | 0 | 0 | 0 | 2 | 4 | 0 | 0 | 1 | 18.0 | 4.50 | 101 | .400 | .400 | 0 | — | 0 | -0 | -0 | -0 | -0.0 |

● GLEN COOK   Cook, Glen Patrick b: 9/8/59, Buffalo, N.Y. BR/TR, 5'11", 180 lbs. Deb: 6/23/85

| 1985 Tex-A | 2 | 3 | .400 | 9 | 7 | 0 | 0 | 0 | 40 | 53 | 12 | 18 | 19 | 16.6 | 9.45 | 45 | .327 | .404 | 0 | — | 0 | -24 | -23 | -1 | -2.1 |

● MIKE COOK   Cook, Michael Horace b: 8/14/63, Charleston, S.C. BR/TR, 6'3", 200 lbs. Deb: 7/01/86

1986 Cal-A	0	2	.000	5	1	0	0	0	9	13	3	7	6	20.0	9.00	46	.333	.435	0	—	0	-5	-5	0	-0.4
1987 Cal-A	1	2	.333	16	1	0	0	0	34¹	34	7	18	27	13.6	5.50	78	.264	.354	0	—	0	-4	-5	1	-0.3
1988 Cal-A	0	1	.000	3	0	0	0	0	3²	4	0	1	2	14.7	4.91	79	.308	.400	0	—	0	-0	-0	-0	0.0
1989 Min-A	0	1	.000	15	0	0	0	0	21¹	22	1	17	15	16.9	5.06	82	.268	.400	0	—	0	-3	-2	-1	-0.7
Total 4	1	6	.143	39	2	0	0	0	68¹	73	11	43	50	15.5	5.80	73	.278	.383	0	—	0	-12	-12	1	-1.4

● ROLLIN COOK   Cook, Rollin Edward b: 10/5/1890, Toledo, Ohio d: 8/11/75, Toledo, Ohio BR/TR, 5'9", 152 lbs. Deb: 7/06/15

| 1915 StL-A | 0 | 0 | — | 5 | 0 | 0 | 0 | 0 | 13² | 16 | 0 | 9 | 7 | 17.1 | 7.24 | 40 | .276 | .382 | 1 | .250 | 0 | -7 | -7 | 0 | -0.6 |

● RON COOK   Cook, Ronald Wayne b: 7/11/47, Jefferson, Tex. BL/TL, 6'1", 175 lbs. Deb: 4/10/70

1970 Hou-N	4	4	.500	41	7	0	0	2	82¹	80	4	42	50	13.7	3.72	104	.274	.371	4	.235	2	3	1	-0	0.3
1971 Hou-N	0	4	.000	5	4	0	0	0	25²	23	2	8	10	11.2	4.91	69	.237	.302	2	.250	0	-4	-4	0	-0.4
Total 2	4	8	.333	46	11	0	0	2	108	103	6	50	60	13.1	4.00	94	.265	.354	6	.240	2	-1	-3	-0	-0.1

● STEVE COOKE   Cooke, Stephen Montague b: 1/14/70, Kanai, Hawaii BR/TL, 6'6", 220 lbs. Deb: 7/28/92

| 1992 Pit-N | 2 | 0 | 1.000 | 11 | 0 | 0 | 0 | 1 | 23 | 22 | 2 | 4 | 10 | 10.2 | 3.52 | 97 | .253 | .286 | 1 | .333 | 0 | -0 | -0 | -0 | 0.0 |

● DANNY COOMBS   Coombs, Daniel Bernard b: 3/23/42, Lincoln, Me. BR/TL, 6'5", 210 lbs. Deb: 9/27/63

1963 Hou-N	0	0	—	1	0	0	0	0	0¹	3	0	0	0	81.0	27.00	12	.750	.750	0	—	0	-1	-1	0	-0.1
1964 Hou-N	1	1	.500	7	1	0	0	0	18	21	1	10	14	16.0	5.00	68	.300	.395	0	.000	-0	-3	-3	-0	-0.4
1965 Hou-N	0	2	.000	26	3	0	0	0	47	54	3	23	35	15.3	4.79	70	.292	.379	1	.111	0	-7	-7	1	-0.7
1966 Hou-N	0	0	—	2	0	0	0	0	2²	4	0	0	3	13.5	3.38	101	.333	.333	0	.000	0	0	-0	0	0.0
1967 Hou-N	3	0	1.000	6	2	0	0	0	24¹	21	0	9	23	11.1	3.33	99	.233	.303	1	.125	0	0	-0	0	0.0
1968 Hou-N	4	3	.571	40	2	0	0	2	46²	52	6	17	29	13.5	3.28	90	.286	.350	4	.400	1	-2	-2	1	0.0
1969 Hou-N	0	1	.000	8	0	0	0	0	8	12	0	2	3	16.9	6.75	52	.364	.417	0	.000	-0	-3	-3	-0	-0.3
1970 SD-N	10	14	.417	35	27	5	1	0	188¹	185	12	76	105	13.4	3.30	121	.256	.329	5	.096	-2	16	14	-2	1.1
1971 SD-N	1	6	.143	19	7	0	0	0	57²	81	10	25	37	16.5	6.24	53	.327	.388	3	.214	1	-18	-19	1	-1.7
Total 9	19	27	.413	144	42	5	1	2	393	433	26	162	249	13.8	4.08	88	.280	.351	14	.140	-0	-17	-21	0	-2.1

● JACK COOMBS   Coombs, John Wesley "Colby Jack" b: 11/18/1882, LeGrand, Iowa d: 4/15/57, Palestine, Tex. BB/TR, 6', 185 lbs. Deb: 7/05/06 MC♦

1906 Phi-A	10	10	.500	23	18	13	1	0	173	144	0	68	90	11.4	2.50	109	.229	.312	16	.239	1	4	4	0	0.6
1907 Phi-A	6	9	.400	23	17	10	2	2	132²	109	2	64	73	12.3	3.12	84	.226	.328	8	.167	0	-8	-8	0	-1.0
1908 Phi-A	7	5	.583	26	18	10	4	0	153	130	1	64	80	11.6	2.00	128	.233	.316	56	.255	4	7	10	1	1.5
1909 Phi-A	12	11	.522	30	24	18	6	1	205²	156	1	73	97	10.3	2.32	104	.213	.289	14	.169	1	4	2	-0	0.3
1910 *Phi-A	**31**	9	.775	**45**	38	35	**13**	1	353	248	0	115	224	9.4	1.30	183	.201	.273	26	.220	3	48	42	-5	4.7
1911 *Phi-A	28	12	.700	47	40	26	1	2	336²	360	8	119	185	13.2	3.53	89	.280	.348	45	.319	14	-7	-14	-3	-0.4
1912 Phi-A	21	10	.677	40	32	23	1	2	262²	227	1	94	120	11.4	3.29	93	.241	.316	28	.255	6	1	-6	-1	-0.1
1913 Phi-A	0	0	—	2	2	0	0	0	5¹	5	0	6	0	20.3	10.13	27	.250	.444	1	.333	1	-4	-4	-0	-0.2
1914 Phi-A	0	1	.000	2	2	0	0	0	2	3	0	1	3	15.4	4.50	58	.267	.353	3	.273	-0	-2	-2	-0	-0.2
1915 Bro-N	15	10	.600	29	24	17	2	0	195²	166	1	91	56	12.6	2.58	108	.236	.337	21	.280	4	4	4	-4	0.5
1916 *Bro-N	13	8	.619	27	21	10	3	0	159	136	3	44	47	10.3	2.66	101	.239	.296	11	.180	-0	-1	0	-6	-0.6
1917 Bro-N	7	11	.389	31	14	9	0	0	141	147	4	49	34	13.0	3.96	71	.284	.355	10	.227	2	-20	-18	-3	-2.1
1918 Bro-N	8	14	.364	27	22	16	2	0	189	191	0	49	44	11.5	3.81	73	.266	.315	19	.168	-0	-22	-22	-3	-2.6

YEAR	TM/L	W	L	PCT	G	GS	CG	SH	SV	IP	H	HR	BB	SO	RAT	ERA	ERA+	OAV	OOB	BH	AVG	PB	PR	/A	PD	TPI
1920	Det-A	0	0	—	2	0	0	0	0	5^{2}	7	0	2	1	14.3	3.18	117	.318	.375	0	.000	-0	0	0	-0	0.0
Total	14	158	110	.590	354	272	187	35	8	2320	2034	38	841	1052	11.5	2.78	99	.241	.316	261	.235	35	4	-8	-25	0.2

● BOBBY COOMBS

Coombs, Raymond Franklin b: 2/2/08, Goodwins Mills, Me. d: 10/21/91, Ogunquit, Me. BR/TR, 5'9.5", 160 lbs. Deb: 6/08/33

YEAR	TM/L	W	L	PCT	G	GS	CG	SH	SV	IP	H	HR	BB	SO	RAT	ERA	ERA+	OAV	OOB	BH	AVG	PB	PR	/A	PD	TPI
1933	Phi-A	0	1	.000	21	0	0	0	2	31^{1}	47	4	20	8	19.2	7.47	57	.348	.432	2	.400	1	-11	-11	-0	-0.9
1943	NY-N	0	1	.000	9	0	0	0	0	16	33	1	8	5	23.1	12.94	27	.423	.477	0	.000	0	-17	-17	0	-1.6
Total	2	0	2	.000	30	0	0	0	2	47^{1}	80	5	28	13	20.5	9.32	43	.376	.448	2	.286	1	-28	-28	-0	-2.5

● WILLIAM COON

Coon, William K. b: 3/21/1855, Pennsylvania d: 8/30/15, Burlington, N.J. Deb: 9/04/1875 ♦

YEAR	TM/L	W	L	PCT	G	GS	CG	SH	SV	IP	H	HR	BB	SO	RAT	ERA	ERA+	OAV	OOB	BH	AVG	PB	PR	/A	PD	TPI
1876	Phi-N	0	0	—	2	0	0	0	0	7	9	0	0	0	11.6	5.14	47	.257	.257	50	.227	-0	-2	-2	-0	-0.2

● JOHNNY COONEY

Cooney, John Walter b: 3/18/01, Cranston, R.I. d: 7/8/86, Sarasota, Fla. BR/TL, 5'10", 165 lbs. Deb: 4/19/21 FMC♦

YEAR	TM/L	W	L	PCT	G	GS	CG	SH	SV	IP	H	HR	BB	SO	RAT	ERA	ERA+	OAV	OOB	BH	AVG	PB	PR	/A	PD	TPI
1921	Bos-N	0	1	.000	8	1	0	0	0	20^{2}	19	3	10	9	12.6	3.92	93	.241	.326	1	.200	-0	-0	-1	0	-0.1
1922	Bos-N	1	2	.333	4	3	1	0	0	25	19	0	6	7	9.4	2.16	185	.224	.283	0	.000	-1	5	5	0	0.4
1923	Bos-N	3	5	.375	23	8	5	2	0	98	92	3	22	23	10.7	3.31	121	.246	.293	25	.379	4	8	7	-2	0.9
1924	Bos-N	8	9	.471	34	19	12	2	2	181	176	4	50	67	11.4	3.18	120	.260	.314	33	.254	2	14	13	-1	1.3
1925	Bos-N	14	14	.500	31	29	20	2	0	245^{2}	267	18	50	65	11.7	3.48	115	.274	.312	33	.320	5	22	14	1	2.3
1926	Bos-N	3	3	.500	19	8	3	1	0	83^{1}	106	0	29	23	15.3	4.00	89	.320	.387	38	.302	3	-2	-4	0	-0.1
1928	Bos-N	3	7	.300	24	6	2	0	1	89^{2}	106	7	31	18	13.8	4.32	91	.303	.360	7	.171	-0	-3	-4	3	-0.1
1929	Bos-N	2	3	.400	14	2	1	0	3	45	57	4	22	11	15.8	5.00	94	.315	.389	23	.319	2	-1	-2	1	0.1
1930	Bos-N	0	0	—	2	0	0	0	0	7	16	2	3	1	25.7	18.00	27	.471	.526	0	.000	-1	-10	-10	1	-0.8
Total	9	34	44	.436	159	76	44	7	6	795^{1}	858	41	223	224	12.4	3.72	106	.278	.331	965	.286	14	32	19	4	3.9

● BOB COONEY

Cooney, Robert Daniel b: 7/12/07, Glens Falls, N.Y. d: 5/4/76, Glens Falls, N.Y. BR/TR, 5'11", 160 lbs. Deb: 9/06/31

YEAR	TM/L	W	L	PCT	G	GS	CG	SH	SV	IP	H	HR	BB	SO	RAT	ERA	ERA+	OAV	OOB	BH	AVG	PB	PR	/A	PD	TPI
1931	StL-A	0	3	.000	5	4	1	0	0	39^{1}	46	1	20	13	15.3	4.12	113	.291	.374	5	.385	1	1	2	-0	0.3
1932	StL-A	1	2	.333	23	3	1	0	1	71	94	8	36	23	16.7	6.97	70	.324	.402	0	.000	-3	-20	-17	-2	-1.9
Total	2	1	5	.167	28	7	2	0	1	110^{1}	140	9	56	36	16.2	5.95	80	.313	.393	5	.143	-2	-19	-14	-2	-1.6

● BILL COONEY

Cooney, William A. "Cush" b: 4/7/1883, Boston, Mass. d: 11/6/28, Roxbury, Mass. TR , Deb: 9/22/09 ♦

YEAR	TM/L	W	L	PCT	G	GS	CG	SH	SV	IP	H	HR	BB	SO	RAT	ERA	ERA+	OAV	OOB	BH	AVG	PB	PR	/A	PD	TPI
1909	Bos-N	0	0	—	3	0	0	0	0	6^{1}	4	0	2	3	8.5	1.42	199	.182	.250	3	.300	0	1	1	-0	0.1

● WILBUR COOPER

Cooper, Arley Wilbur b: 2/24/1892, Bearsville, W.Va. d: 8/7/73, Encino, Cal. BR/TL, 5'11", 175 lbs. Deb: 8/29/12

YEAR	TM/L	W	L	PCT	G	GS	CG	SH	SV	IP	H	HR	BB	SO	RAT	ERA	ERA+	OAV	OOB	BH	AVG	PB	PR	/A	PD	TPI
1912	Pit-N	3	0	1.000	6	4	3	2	0	38	32	1	15	30	11.1	1.66	197	.227	.301	2	.154	-0	7	7	-0	0.6
1913	Pit-N	5	3	.625	30	9	3	1	0	93	98	0	45	39	14.0	3.29	92	.276	.361	2	.077	-1	-1	-3	-2	-0.6
1914	Pit-N	16	15	.516	40	34	19	0	0	266^{2}	246	4	79	102	11.1	2.13	125	.254	.313	19	.207	1	20	16	0	1.9
1915	Pit-N	5	16	.238	38	21	11	1	4	185^{2}	180	4	52	71	11.7	3.30	83	.262	.323	7	.117	-3	-11	-12	1	-1.5
1916	Pit-N	12	11	.522	42	23	16	2	2	246	189	4	74	111	9.8	1.87	144	.215	.279	17	.215	0	21	22	-1	2.6
1917	Pit-N	17	11	.607	40	34	23	7	1	297^{2}	276	4	54	99	10.1	2.36	120	.258	.297	21	.204	2	12	16	-3	1.8
1918	Pit-N	19	14	.576	38	29	26	2	**3**	273^{1}	219	2	65	117	9.7	2.11	136	.223	.279	23	.242	3	20	23	-2	2.8
1919	Pit-N	19	13	.594	35	32	**27**	4	1	286^{2}	229	10	74	106	10.0	2.67	113	.225	.287	29	.287	6	8	11	-5	1.4
1920	Pit-N	24	15	.615	44	37	28	3	2	327	307	4	52	114	10.2	2.39	134	.253	.290	25	.221	1	27	30	-3	2.9
1921	Pit-N	**22**	14	.611	38	38	29	2	0	**327**	341	9	80	134	11.9	3.25	118	.272	.320	31	.254	4	19	21	-3	2.2
1922	Pit-N	23	14	.622	41	37	**27**	4	0	294^{2}	330	13	61	129	12.2	3.18	128	.286	.326	29	.269	9	**30**	**29**	-2	**3.7**
1923	Pit-N	17	19	.472	39	38	26	1	0	294^{2}	331	11	71	77	12.6	3.57	112	.288	.335	28	.262	4	14	14	-1	1.5
1924	Pit-N	20	14	.588	38	35	25	**4**	1	268^{2}	296	13	40	62	11.4	3.28	117	.283	.313	36	.346	10	17	17	-4	2.2
1925	Chi-N	12	14	.462	32	26	13	0	0	212^{1}	249	18	61	41	13.3	4.28	101	.291	.341	17	.207	1	-0	1	-2	-0.1
1926	Chi-N	2	1	.667	8	8	3	2	0	55	65	6	21	18	14.1	4.42	87	.311	.374	7	.389	3	-4	-4	-1	-0.1
	Det-A	0	4	.000	8	3	0	0	0	13^{2}	27	0	9	2	25.7	11.20	36	.443	.534	0	.000	-1	-11	-11	0	-1.0
Total	15	216	178	.548	517	408	279	35	14	3480	3415	103	853	1252	11.3	2.89	116	.262	.312	293	.239	40	168	180	-26	20.3

● CAL COOPER

Cooper, Calvin Asa b: 8/11/22, Great Falls, S.C. BR/TR, 6'2.5", 180 lbs. Deb: 9/14/48

YEAR	TM/L	W	L	PCT	G	GS	CG	SH	SV	IP	H	HR	BB	SO	RAT	ERA	ERA+	OAV	OOB	BH	AVG	PB	PR	/A	PD	TPI
1948	Was-A	0	0	—	1	0	0	0	0	1	5	1	1	0	54.0	45.00	10	.625	.667	0	—	0	-5	-5	-0	-0.4

● DON COOPER

Cooper, Donald James b: 1/15/56, New York, N.Y. BR/TR, 6'1", 185 lbs. Deb: 4/09/81

YEAR	TM/L	W	L	PCT	G	GS	CG	SH	SV	IP	H	HR	BB	SO	RAT	ERA	ERA+	OAV	OOB	BH	AVG	PB	PR	/A	PD	TPI
1981	Min-A	1	5	.167	27	2	0	0	0	58^{2}	61	9	32	33	14.4	4.30	92	.274	.367	0	—	0	-4	-2	-1	-0.7
1982	Min-A	0	1	.000	6	1	0	0	0	11^{1}	14	0	11	5	19.9	9.53	45	.311	.446	0	—	0	-7	-7	-0	-0.8
1983	Tor-A	0	0	—	4	0	0	0	0	5^{1}	8	3	0	5	13.5	6.75	64	.348	.348	0	—	0	-2	-1	-0	-0.6
1985	NY-A	0	0	—	7	0	0	0	0	10	12	2	3	4	13.5	5.40	74	.300	.349	0	—	0	-1	-2	-0	0.0
Total	4	1	6	.143	44	3	0	0	0	85^{1}	95	14	46	47	15.0	5.27	76	.287	.376	0	—	0	-14	-12	-2	-2.1

● GUY COOPER

Cooper, Guy Evans "Rebel" b: 1/28/1893, Rome, Ga. d: 8/2/51, Santa Monica, Cal. BB/TR, 6'1", 185 lbs. Deb: 5/02/14

YEAR	TM/L	W	L	PCT	G	GS	CG	SH	SV	IP	H	HR	BB	SO	RAT	ERA	ERA+	OAV	OOB	BH	AVG	PB	PR	/A	PD	TPI
1914	NY-A	0	0	—	1	0	0	0	0	3	3	0	2	3	15.0	9.00	31	.273	.385	0	.000	-0	-2	-2	0	-0.2
	Bos-A	1	0	1.000	9	1	0	0	0	22	23	1	9	5	14.3	5.32	51	.299	.393	0	.000	-1	-6	-6	-1	-0.9
	Yr	1	0	1.000	10	1	0	0	0	25	26	1	11	8	14.4	5.76	47	.295	.392	0	.000	-1	-8	-8	-1	-1.1
1915	Bos-A	0	0	—	1	0	0	0	0	2	0	0	2	0	9.0	0.00	—	.000	.286	0	—	0	1	1	-0	0.1
Total	2	1	0	1.000	11	1	0	0	0	27	26	1	13	8	14.0	5.33	51	.280	.385	0	.000	-1	-8	-8	-1	-1.0

● MORT COOPER

Cooper, Morton Cecil b: 3/2/13, Atherton, Mo. d: 11/17/58, Little Rock, Ark. BR/TR, 6'2", 210 lbs. Deb: 9/14/38 F

YEAR	TM/L	W	L	PCT	G	GS	CG	SH	SV	IP	H	HR	BB	SO	RAT	ERA	ERA+	OAV	OOB	BH	AVG	PB	PR	/A	PD	TPI
1938	StL-N	2	1	.667	4	3	1	0	1	23^{2}	17	1	12	11	11.4	3.04	130	.195	.300	2	.222	0	2	2	1	0.3
1939	StL-N	12	6	.667	45	26	7	2	4	210^{2}	208	6	97	130	13.1	3.25	127	.260	.342	16	.232	3	16	20	-3	2.1
1940	StL-N	11	12	.478	38	29	16	3	3	230^{2}	225	12	86	95	12.3	3.63	110	.253	.321	13	.157	-2	6	9	-2	0.4
1941	StL-N	13	9	.591	29	25	12	0	0	186^{2}	175	15	69	118	11.9	3.91	96	.244	.313	13	.186	-0	-6	-3	-1	-0.4
1942	*StL-N★	**22**	7	.759	37	35	22	**10**	0	278^{2}	207	9	68	152	**9.0**	**1.78**	**193**	**.204**	**.258**	19	.184	-1	**48**	**51**	-3	**5.4**
1943	*StL-N★	**21**	8	**.724**	37	32	24	6	3	274	228	5	79	141	10.2	2.30	146	.226	.286	17	.170	-1	33	32	-2	3.2
1944	*StL-N	22	7	.759	34	33	22	**7**	1	252^{1}	227	6	60	97	10.4	2.46	143	.239	.288	19	.202	2	32	30	-5	2.9
1945	StL-N	2	0	1.000	4	3	1	0	0	23^{2}	20	1	7	14	10.6	1.52	246	.227	.292	2	.333	1	6	6	-1	0.7
	Bos-N	7	4	.636	20	11	4	1	1	78	77	4	27	45	12.1	3.35	115	.257	.320	6	.231	1	4	4	0	0.5
	Yr	9	4	.692	24	14	5	1	1	101^{2}	97	5	34	59	11.7	2.92	130	.249	.311	8	.250	2	10	10	-0	1.2
1946	Bos-N☆	13	11	.542	28	27	15	4	1	199	181	16	39	83	**9.9**	3.12	110	.239	**.276**	14	.209	1	6	7	-3	0.5
1947	Bos-N	2	5	.286	10	7	2	0	0	46^{2}	48	2	13	15	12.2	4.05	96	.271	.328	0	.000	-1	0	-1	-1	-0.3
	NY-N	1	5	.167	8	8	2	0	0	36^{2}	51	7	13	12	15.7	7.12	57	.323	.374	6	.429	4	-12	-12	-1	-0.9
	Yr	3	10	.231	18	15	4	0	0	83^{1}	99	9	26	27	13.5	5.40	74	.294	.344	6	.222	2	-12	-13	-2	-1.2
1949	Chi-N	0	0	—	1	0	0	0	0	0	2	1	1	0	—	∞	—	1.000	1.000	0	—	0	-3	-3	0	-0.3
Total	11	128	75	.631	295	239	128	33	14	1840^{2}	1666	85	571	913	11.1	2.97	123	.240	.300	127	.194	6	132	143	-20	14.1

● PAT COOPER

Cooper, Orge Patterson b: 11/26/17, Albemarle, N.C. BR/TR, 6'3", 180 lbs. Deb: 5/11/46 ♦

YEAR	TM/L	W	L	PCT	G	GS	CG	SH	SV	IP	H	HR	BB	SO	RAT	ERA	ERA+	OAV	OOB	BH	AVG	PB	PR	/A	PD	TPI
1946	Phi-A	0	0	—	1	0	0	0	0	1	1	0	1	0	18.0	0.00	—	.250	.400	0	—	0	0	0	-0	0.0

● MAYS COPELAND

Copeland, Mays b: 8/31/13, Mountain View, Ark d: 11/29/82, Indio, Cal. BR/TR, 6', 180 lbs. Deb: 4/27/35

YEAR	TM/L	W	L	PCT	G	GS	CG	SH	SV	IP	H	HR	BB	SO	RAT	ERA	ERA+	OAV	OOB	BH	AVG	PB	PR	/A	PD	TPI
1935	StL-N	0	0	—	1	0	0	0	0	0^{2}	2	0	0	0	27.0	13.50	30	.667	.667	0	—	0	-1	-1	0	-0.1

● HENRY COPPOLA

Coppola, Henry Peter b: 8/6/12, E.Douglas, Mass. d: 7/10/90, Norfolk, Mass. BR/TR, 5'11", 175 lbs. Deb: 4/19/35

YEAR	TM/L	W	L	PCT	G	GS	CG	SH	SV	IP	H	HR	BB	SO	RAT	ERA	ERA+	OAV	OOB	BH	AVG	PB	PR	/A	PD	TPI
1935	Was-A	3	4	.429	19	5	2	1	0	59^{1}	72	6	29	19	15.5	5.92	73	.300	.378	1	.071	-0	-10	-11	-0	-1.0
1936	Was-A	0	0	—	6	0	0	0	1	14	17	1	12	2	18.6	4.50	106	.315	.439	1	.333	0	1	0	0	0.1
Total	2	3	4	.429	25	5	2	1	1	73^{1}	89	7	41	21	16.1	5.65	78	.303	.390	2	.118	0	-9	-10	0	-0.9

YEAR	TM/L	W	L	PCT	G	GS	CG	SH	SV	IP	H	HR	BB	SO	RAT	ERA	ERA+	OAV	OOB	BH	AVG	PB	PR	/A	PD	TPI
● **DOUG CORBETT**	Corbett, Douglas Mitchell b: 11/4/52, Sarasota, Fla. BR/TR, 6'1", 185 lbs. Deb: 4/10/80																									
1980	Min-A	8	6	.571	73	0	0	0	23	136^{1}	102	7	42	89	9.6	1.98	220	.213	.278	0	—	0	**31**	**36**	3	3.4
1981	Min-A☆	2	6	.250	**54**	0	0	0	17	87^{2}	80	5	34	60	11.7	2.57	154	.239	.309	0	—	0	11	13	2	1.3
1982	Min-A	0	2	.000	10	0	0	0	3	22	27	3	10	15	15.1	5.32	80	.300	.370	0	—	0	-3	-3	1	-0.4
	Cal-A	1	7	.125	33	0	0	0	8	57	46	8	25	37	11.2	5.05	80	.223	.307	0	—	0	-6	-6	0	-0.6
	Yr	1	9	.100	43	0	0	0	11	79	73	11	35	52	12.3	5.13	80	.247	.326	0	—	0	-9	-9	1	-1.0
1983	Cal-A	1	1	.500	11	0	0	0	0	17^{1}	26	1	4	18	16.1	3.63	110	.351	.392	0	—	0	1	1	-0	0.1
1984	Cal-A	5	1	.833	45	1	0	0	4	85	76	2	30	48	11.4	2.12	187	.244	.314	0	—	0	18	17	0	1.9
1985	Cal-A	3	3	.500	30	0	0	0	0	46	49	7	20	24	13.7	4.89	84	.274	.350	0	—	0	-4	-4	0	-0.3
1986	*Cal-A	4	2	.667	46	0	0	0	10	78^{2}	66	11	22	36	10.2	3.66	112	.231	.288	0	—	0	5	4	1	0.6
1987	Bal-A	0	2	.000	11	0	0	0	1	23	25	5	13	16	14.9	7.83	56	.281	.373	0	—	0	-9	-9	1	-0.7
Total	8	24	30	.444	313	1	0	0	66	553	497	49	200	343	11.4	3.32	125	.242	.312	0	—	0	43	50	8	5.3
● **JOE CORBETT**	Corbett, Joseph A. b: 12/4/1875, San Francisco, Cal. d: 5/2/45, San Francisco, Cal. BR/TR, 5'10", Deb: 8/23/1895																									
1895	Was-N	0	2	.000	3	3	3	0	0	19	26	3	9	3	17.5	5.68	84	.321	.402	2	.133	-1	-2	-2	0	-0.2
1896	*Bal-N	3	0	1.000	8	3	3	0	1	41	31	0	17	28	11.6	2.20	195	.208	.311	6	.273	1	10	9	-1	0.8
1897	*Bal-N	24	8	.750	37	37	34	1	0	313	330	2	115	149	13.4	3.11	134	.269	.342	37	.247	-0	42	37	2	3.4
1904	StL-N	5	8	.385	14	14	12	0	0	108^{2}	110	2	51	68	14.0	4.39	61	.240	.327	9	.209	1	-20	-20	0	-1.8
Total	4	32	18	.640	62	57	52	1	1	481^{2}	497	7	192	248	13.5	3.42	113	.259	.338	54	.235	1	30	24	2	2.2
● **SHERMAN CORBETT**	Corbett, Sherman Stanley b: 11/3/62, New Braunfels, Tex. BL/TL, 6'4", 205 lbs. Deb: 5/29/88																									
1988	Cal-A	2	1	.667	34	0	0	0	1	45^{2}	47	2	23	28	13.8	4.14	93	.273	.359	0	—	0	-1	-1	-0	-0.1
1989	Cal-A	0	0	—	4	0	0	0	0	5^{1}	3	1	1	3	6.8	3.38	113	.158	.200	0	—	0	0	0	-0	0.0
1990	Cal-A	0	0	—	4	0	0	0	0	5	8	0	3	2	19.8	9.00	42	.364	.440	0	—	0	-3	-3	-0	-0.3
Total	3	2	1	.667	42	0	0	0	1	56	58	3	27	33	13.7	4.50	86	.272	.354	0	—	0	-3	-4	-1	-0.4
● **RAY CORBIN**	Corbin, Alton Ray b: 2/12/49, Live Oak, Fla. BR/TR, 6'2", 200 lbs. Deb: 4/06/71																									
1971	Min-A	8	11	.421	52	11	2	0	3	140^{1}	141	19	70	83	13.7	4.10	87	.265	.353	7	.206	1	-10	-9	1	-0.7
1972	Min-A	8	9	.471	31	19	5	3	0	161^{2}	135	12	53	83	10.8	2.62	123	.230	.300	4	.082	-2	8	11	-2	0.7
1973	Min-A	8	5	.615	51	7	1	0	14	148^{1}	124	7	60	83	11.5	3.03	130	.229	.311	0	—	0	13	15	-1	1.4
1974	Min-A	7	6	.538	29	15	1	0	0	112^{1}	133	8	40	50	14.1	5.29	71	.294	.356	0	—	0	-21	-19	1	-2.0
1975	Min-A	5	7	.417	18	11	3	0	0	89^{2}	105	13	38	49	14.6	5.12	75	.295	.366	0	—	0	-13	-13	1	-1.3
Total	5	36	38	.486	181	63	12	3	17	652^{1}	638	59	261	348	12.7	3.84	95	.258	.334	11	.133	-2	-23	-14	-0	-1.9
● **ARCHIE CORBIN**	Corbin, Archie Ray b: 12/30/67, Beaumont, Tex. BR/TR, 6'4", 190 lbs. Deb: 9/10/91																									
1991	KC-A	0	0	—	2	0	0	0	0	2^{1}	3	0	2	1	19.3	3.86	107	.300	.417	0	—	0	0	0	-0	0.0
● **JACK CORCORAN**	Corcoran, John H. b: 1860, Lowell, Mass. Deb: 5/01/1884 ♦																									
1884	Bro-a	0	0	—	1	0	0	0	0	1	0	0	1	0	9.0	0.00	—	.000	.091	39	.211	0	0	0	-0	0.0
● **LARRY CORCORAN**	Corcoran, Lawrence J. b: 8/10/1859, Brooklyn, N.Y. d: 10/14/1891, Newark, N.J. BL/TB, 120 lbs. Deb: 5/01/1880 F♦																									
1880	Chi-N	43	14	.754	63	60	57	4	2	536^{1}	404	6	99	**268**	8.4	1.95	124	.199	.236	66	.231	-0	25	28	6	3.2
1881	Chi-N	**31**	14	.689	45	44	43	4	0	396^{2}	380	10	78	150	10.4	2.31	118	.242	.278	42	.222	-1	20	19	-2	1.4
1882	Chi-N	27	12	**.692**	39	39	38	3	0	355^{2}	281	5	63	170	**8.7**	**1.95**	**147**	**.200**	**.234**	35	.207	-2	38	36	1	3.2
1883	Chi-N	34	20	.630	56	53	51	3	0	473^{2}	483	7	82	216	10.7	2.49	128	.247	.277	55	.209	-1	34	37	1	3.2
1884	Chi-N	35	23	.603	60	59	57	7	0	516^{2}	473	35	116	272	10.3	2.40	130	.229	.270	61	.243	2	33	42	7	4.6
1885	Chi-N	5	2	.714	7	7	6	1	0	59^{1}	63	2	24	10	13.2	3.64	83	.259	.326	6	.273	2	-5	-4	0	-0.2
	NY-N	2	1	.667	3	3	2	0	0	25	24	1	11	10	12.6	2.88	93	.245	.321	5	.357	1	-0	-1	1	0.1
	Yr	7	3	.700	10	10	8	1	0	84^{1}	87	3	35	20	13.0	3.42	86	.255	.324	11	.306	3	-6	-5	1	-0.1
1886	Was-N	0	1	.000	2	1	1	0	0	14	16	0	4	3	12.9	5.79	57	.271	.317	15	.185	0	-4	-4	-0	-0.3
1887	Ind-N	0	2	.000	2	2	1	0	0	15	23	3	19	4	26.4	12.60	33	.338	.494	2	.200	0	-14	-14	0	-0.9
Total	8	177	89	.665	277	268	256	22	2	2392^{1}	2147	69	496	1103	10.0	2.36	122	.226	.264	287	.223	1	127	139	14	14.3
● **MIKE CORCORAN**	Corcoran, Michael b: Brooklyn, N.Y. Deb: 7/15/1884 F																									
1884	Chi-N	0	1	.000	1	1	1	0	0	9	16	1	7	2	23.0	4.00	78	.372	.460	0	.000	-0	-1	-1	-0	-0.1
● **ED COREY**	Corey, Edward Norman "Ike" (b: Abraham Simon Cohen) b: 7/13/1899, Chicago, Ill. d: 9/17/70, Kenosha, Wis. BR/TR, 6', 170 lbs. Deb: 7/02/18																									
1918	Chi-A	0	0	—	1	0	0	0	0	2	2	0	1	0	13.5	4.50	61	.333	.429	0	.000	-0	-0	-0	0	-0.1
● **FRED COREY**	Corey, Frederick Harrison b: 1857, S.Kingston, R.I. d: 11/27/12, Providence, R.I. BR/TR, Deb: 5/01/1878 ♦																									
1878	Pro-N	1	2	.333	5	5	2	0	0	23	22	0	7	7	11.3	2.35	94	.250	.305	3	.143	-1	-0	-0	-1	-0.1
1880	Wor-N	8	9	.471	25	17	9	2	2	148^{1}	131	6	16	47	8.9	2.43	107	.219	.239	24	.174	-3	-1	3	-3	-0.3
1881	Wor-N	6	15	.286	23	21	20	1	0	188^{2}	231	3	31	33	12.5	3.72	81	.299	.326	45	.222	-1	-20	-15	-1	-1.5
1882	Wor-N	1	13	.071	21	14	12	0	0	139	180	5	19	36	12.9	3.56	87	.286	.307	63	.247	1	-10	-7	1	-0.5
1883	Phi-a	10	7	.588	18	16	15	0	0	148^{1}	182	3	24	42	12.5	3.40	103	.283	.309	77	.258	2	-2	2	1	0.4
1885	Phi-a	1	0	1.000	1	1	1	0	0	9	18	2	1	3	19.0	7.00	49	.419	.432	94	.245	0	-4	-4	0	-0.3
Total	6	27	46	.370	93	74	59	3	2	656^{1}	764	19	98	168	11.8	3.32	91	.276	.300	427	.246	-3	-36	-21	-2	-2.3
● **POP CORKHILL**	Corkhill, John Stewart b: 4/11/1858, Parkesburg, Pa. d: 4/4/21, Pennsauken, N.J. BL/TR, 5'10", 180 lbs. Deb: 5/01/1883 ♦																									
1884	Cin-a	1	0	1.000	1	0	0	0	0	5	1	0	2	4	5.4	1.80	185	.063	.167	124	.274	0	1	1	-0	0.1
1885	Cin-a	1	4	.200	8	1	0	0	1	37	36	2	10	12	11.4	3.65	89	.243	.296	111	.252	1	-2	-2	0	-0.1
1886	Cin-a	0	0	—	1	0	0	0	0	0^{2}	1	0	0	1	13.5	13.50	26	.125	.125	143	.265	0	-1	-1	0	-0.1
1887	Cin-a	1	0	1.000	5	0	0	0	0	14^{2}	22	0	5	3	16.6	5.52	79	.324	.370	168	.311	1	-2	-2	-0	-0.1
1888	Cin-a	0	0	—	2	0	0	0	1	5	8	1	0	1	14.4	10.80	29	.349	.349	133	.271	0	-4	-4	-0	-0.4
Total	5	3	4	.429	17	1	0	0	2	62^{1}	68	3	17	21	12.4	4.62	76	.259	.306	1120	.254	2	-8	-8	-1	-0.6
● **MIKE CORKINS**	Corkins, Michael Patrick b: 5/25/46, Riverside, Cal. BR/TR, 6'1", 200 lbs. Deb: 9/08/69																									
1969	SD-N	1	3	.250	6	4	0	0	0	17	27	3	8	13	18.5	8.47	42	.370	.432	0	.000	0	-9	-9	0	-0.9
1970	SD-N	5	6	.455	24	18	1	0	0	111	109	11	79	75	15.6	4.62	86	.258	.379	8	.216	2	-7	-8	-1	-0.7
1971	SD-N	0	0	—	8	0	0	0	0	13	14	1	6	16	13.8	3.46	95	.280	.357	0	—	0	0	-0	-0	0.0
1972	SD-N	6	9	.400	47	9	2	1	6	140	125	14	62	108	12.3	3.54	93	.240	.325	9	.237	2	-1	-4	0	-0.1
1973	SD-N	5	8	.385	47	11	2	0	3	122	130	12	61	82	14.9	4.50	77	.274	.370	7	.212	4	-11	-14	-2	-1.2
1974	SD-N	2	2	.500	25	2	0	0	0	56^{1}	53	5	32	41	13.7	4.79	74	.255	.357	0	.000	-0	-7	-8	-1	-0.9
Total	6	19	28	.404	157	44	5	1	9	459^{1}	458	46	248	335	14.2	4.39	81	.262	.360	24	.202	9	-36	-43	-4	-3.8
● **RHEAL CORMIER**	Cormier, Rheal Paul b: 4/23/67, Moncton, N.B., Can. BL/TL, 5'10", 185 lbs. Deb: 8/15/91																									
1991	StL-N	4	5	.444	11	10	2	0	0	67^{2}	74	5	8	38	11.2	4.12	90	.277	.303	5	.238	1	-3	-3	-1	-0.3
1992	StL-N	10	10	.500	31	30	3	0	0	186	194	15	33	117	11.2	3.68	94	.269	.306	6	.102	-2	-4	-5	1	-0.6
Total	2	14	15	.483	42	40	5	0	0	253^{2}	268	20	41	155	11.2	3.80	93	.272	.305	11	.138	-1	-7	-8	1	-0.9
● **MARDIE CORNEJO**	Cornejo, Nieves Mardie b: 8/5/51, Wellington, Kan. BR/TR, 6'3", 200 lbs. Deb: 4/08/78																									
1978	NY-N	4	2	.667	25	0	0	0	3	36^{2}	37	1	14	17	13.3	2.45	142	.285	.367	0	—	0	5	4	-0	0.4
● **JEFF CORNELL**	Cornell, Jeffery Ray b: 2/10/57, Kansas City, Mo. BB/TR, 5'11", 170 lbs. Deb: 6/02/84																									
1984	SF-N	1	3	.250	23	0	0	0	0	38^{1}	51	4	22	19	17.4	6.10	57	.340	.428	0	.000	-0	-11	-11	-1	-1.2

YEAR	TM/L	W	L	PCT	G	GS	CG	SH	SV	IP	H	HR	BB	SO	RAT	ERA	ERA+	OAV	OOB	BH	AVG	PB	PR	/A	PD	TPI
● TERRY CORNUTT	Cornutt, Terry Stanton b: 10/2/52, Roseburg, Ore. BR/TR, 6'2", 195 lbs. Deb: 4/09/77																								
1977	SF-N	1	2	.333	28	1	0	0	0	44¹	38	4	22	23	12.2	3.86	101	.229	.319	0	.000	-0	0	0	-1	-0.1
1978	SF-N	0	0	—	1	0	0	0	0	3	1	0	0	0	3.0	0.00	—	.100	.100	0	—	0	1	1	-0	0.1
Total	2	1	2	.333	29	1	0	0	0	47¹	39	4	22	23	11.6	3.61	107	.222	.308	0	.000	-0	1	1	-1	0.0
● ED CORREA	Correa, Edwin Josue (Andino) b: 4/29/66, Hato Rey, P.R. BR/TR, 6'2", 192 lbs. Deb: 9/18/85																								
1985	Chi-A	1	0	1.000	5	1	0	0	0	10¹	11	2	11	10	19.2	6.97	62	.275	.431	0	—	0	-3	-3	-0	-0.6
1986	Tex-A	12	14	.462	32	32	4	2	0	202¹	167	15	126	189	13.2	4.23	102	.223	.337	0	—	0	-1	2	3	0.3
1987	Tex-A	3	5	.375	15	15	0	0	0	70	83	17	52	61	17.9	7.59	59	.296	.414	0	—	0	-24	-24	-0	-2.1
Total	3	16	19	.457	52	48	4	2	0	282²	261	34	189	260	14.6	5.16	84	.244	.361	0	—	0	-29	-26	2	-2.4
● FRANK CORRIDON	Corridon, Frank J. "Fiddler" b: 11/25/1880, Newport, R.I. d: 2/21/41, Syracuse, N.Y. BR/TR, 6', 170 lbs. Deb: 4/15/04																								
1904	Chi-N	5	5	.500	12	10	9	0	0	100¹	88	2	37	34	11.8	3.05	87	.240	.321	13	.224	0	-3	-4	3	-0.1
	Phi-N	6	5	.545	12	11	11	1	0	94¹	88	2	28	44	11.8	2.19	122	.250	.320	6	.171	-1	6	5	3	0.8
	Yr	11	10	.524	24	21	20	1	0	194²	176	4	65	78	11.5	2.64	101	.242	.312	19	.204	-1	2	1	6	0.7
1905	Phi-N	10	12	.455	35	26	18	1	1	212	203	2	57	79	11.7	3.48	84	.257	.319	15	.208	4	-11	-13	2	-0.7
1907	Phi-N	18	14	.563	37	32	23	3	2	274	228	0	89	131	10.7	2.46	98	.230	.299	16	.165	-0	-0	-1	5	0.4
1908	Phi-N	14	10	.583	27	24	18	2	1	208¹	178	0	48	50	10.0	2.51	97	.239	.290	9	.123	-2	-3	-2	3	-0.1
1909	Phi-N	7	11	.611	27	19	11	3	0	171	147	0	61	69	11.3	2.11	124	.242	.318	11	.186	-0	9	9	5	1.6
1910	StL-N	6	14	.300	30	18	9	0	3	156	168	1	55	51	13.4	3.81	78	.283	.353	10	.196	-0	-13	-14	3	-1.2
Total	6	70	67	.511	180	140	99	10	7	1216	1100	7	375	458	11.4	2.80	95	.247	.315	80	.180	2	-16	-20	24	0.7
● JIM CORSI	Corsi, James Bernard b: 9/9/61, Newton, Mass. BR/TR, 6'1", 210 lbs. Deb: 6/28/88																								
1988	Oak-A	0	1	.000	11	1	0	0	0	21¹	20	1	6	10	11.0	3.80	100	.260	.313	0	—	0	0	-0	-0	0.1
1989	Oak-A	1	2	.333	22	0	0	0	0	38¹	26	2	10	21	8.7	1.88	196	.194	.255	0	—	0	9	8	-0	0.8
1991	Hou-N	0	5	.000	47	0	0	0	0	77²	76	6	23	53	11.5	3.71	95	.259	.312	0	.000	-0	-0	-2	1	-0.1
1992	*Oak-A	4	2	.667	32	0	0	0	0	44	44	2	18	19	12.7	1.43	264	.273	.346	0	—	0	12	11	1	1.4
Total	4	5	10	.333	112	1	0	0	0	181¹	166	11	57	103	11.1	2.78	131	.249	.309	0	.000	-0	21	17	2	2.2
● BARRY CORT	Cort, Barry Lee b: 4/15/56, Toronto, Ont., Can. BR/TR, 6'5", 210 lbs. Deb: 4/22/77																								
1977	Mil-A	1	1	.500	7	3	1	0	0	24¹	25	1	9	17	12.9	3.33	122	.281	.354	0	—	0	2	2	0	0.2
● AL CORWIN	Corwin, Elmer Nathan b: 12/3/26, Newburgh, N.Y. BR/TR, 6'1", 170 lbs. Deb: 7/25/51																								
1951	*NY-N	5	1	.833	15	8	3	1	1	59	49	7	21	30	10.7	3.66	107	.222	.289	1	.050	-2	2	2	-2	-0.2
1952	NY-N	6	1	.857	21	7	1	0	2	67²	58	5	36	36	12.5	2.66	139	.237	.335	2	.095	-1	8	8	-1	0.6
1953	NY-N	6	4	.600	48	7	2	1	2	106²	122	17	68	49	16.3	4.98	86	.290	.393	9	.281	4	-8	-8	-1	-0.5
1954	NY-N	1	3	.250	20	0	0	0	0	31¹	35	4	14	14	14.1	4.02	100	.297	.371	0	.000	-1	-0	-1	-0	-0.1
1955	NY-N	0	1	.000	13	0	0	0	0	24²	25	3	17	13	15.3	4.01	100	.263	.375	0	.000	-0	0	0	-0	-0.1
Total	5	18	10	.643	117	22	6	2	5	289¹	289	36	156	142	13.9	3.98	101	.263	.356	12	.152	0	2	1	-6	-0.3
● MIKE COSGROVE	Cosgrove, Michael John b: 2/17/51, Phoenix, Ariz. BL/TL, 6'1", 180 lbs. Deb: 9/10/72																								
1972	Hou-N	0	1	.000	7	1	0	0	1	13²	16	2	3	7	12.5	4.61	73	.286	.322	0	.000	-0	-2	-2	-1	-0.3
1973	Hou-N	1	1	.500	13	0	0	0	0	10	11	1	8	2	17.1	1.80	202	.282	.404	0	—	0	2	2	-0	0.2
1974	Hou-N	7	3	.700	45	0	0	0	2	90	76	4	39	47	11.6	3.50	99	.232	.316	1	.056	-1	1	-0	-1	-0.2
1975	Hou-N	1	2	.333	32	3	1	0	5	71¹	62	2	37	32	12.5	3.03	111	.245	.341	2	.154	0	5	3	0	0.3
1976	Hou-N	3	4	.429	22	16	1	1	0	89²	106	6	58	34	16.7	5.52	58	.303	.405	2	.087	-1	-20	-23	-0	-2.4
Total	5	12	11	.522	119	20	2	1	8	274²	271	13	145	122	13.7	4.03	83	.264	.357	5	.089	-2	-14	-21	-2	-2.4
● JIM COSMAN	Cosman, James Henry b: 2/19/43, Brockport, N.Y. BR/TR, 6'4.5", 211 lbs. Deb: 10/02/66																								
1966	StL-N	1	0	1.000	1	1	1	1	0	9	2	0	2	5	5.0	0.00	—	.074	.167	0	.000	-0	4	4	-0	0.4
1967	StL-N	1	0	1.000	10	5	0	0	0	31¹	21	2	24	11	14.4	3.16	104	.198	.370	1	.125	-0	1	0	-1	0.0
1970	Chi-N	0	0	—	1	0	0	0	0	1	3	1	1	0	36.0	27.00	17	.600	.667	0	—	0	-3	-2	0	-0.2
Total	3	2	0	1.000	12	6	1	1	0	41¹	26	3	27	16	12.8	3.05	111	.188	.345	1	.091	-1	2	2	-1	0.2
● JOHN COSTELLO	Costello, John Reilly b: 12/24/60, Bronx, N.Y. BR/TR, 6'1", 190 lbs. Deb: 6/02/88																								
1988	StL-N	5	2	.714	36	0	0	0	1	49²	44	3	25	38	12.5	1.81	192	.235	.325	0	.000	-0	9	9	-1	0.9
1989	StL-N	5	4	.556	48	0	0	0	3	62¹	48	5	20	40	10.1	3.32	109	.213	.283	0	.000	-1	1	2	-1	0.0
1990	StL-N	0	0	—	4	0	0	0	0	4¹	7	1	1	1	18.7	6.23	61	.368	.429	0	—	0	-1	-1	-0	-0.1
	Mon-N	0	0	—	4	0	0	0	0	6¹	5	2	1	1	8.5	5.68	64	.208	.240	0	—	0	-1	-1	-0	-0.2
	Yr	0	0	—	8	0	0	0	0	10²	12	3	2	2	11.8	5.91	63	.273	.304	0	—	0	-3	-3	-0	-0.3
1991	SD-N	1	0	1.000	27	0	0	0	0	35	37	2	17	24	13.9	3.09	123	.276	.358	0	.000	-0	2	3	-0	0.3
Total	4	11	6	.647	119	0	0	0	4	157²	141	13	64	104	11.9	2.97	122	.239	.317	0	.000	-1	10	11	-3	0.9
● DAN COTTER	Cotter, Daniel Joseph b: 4/14/1867, Boston, Mass. d: 9/4/35, Boston, Mass. BR/TR, Deb: 7/16/1890																								
1890	Buf-P	0	1	.000	1	1	1	0	0	9	18	1	7	0	25.0	14.00	29	.399	.480	0	.000	-1	-10	-10	-0	-0.7
● ENSIGN COTTRELL	Cottrell, Ensign Stover b: 8/29/1888, Hoosick Falls, N.Y. d: 2/27/47, Syracuse, N.Y. BL/TL, 5'9.5", 173 lbs. Deb: 6/21/11																								
1911	Pit-N	0	0	—	1	0	0	0	0	1	4	0	1	0	45.0	9.00	38	.667	.714	0	—	0	-1	-1	-0	-0.1
1912	Chi-N	0	0	—	1	0	0	0	0	4	8	0	1	1	20.3	9.00	37	.444	.474	0	.000	-0	-2	-3	-0	-0.2
1913	Phi-A	1	0	1.000	2	1	1	0	0	10	15	0	2	3	15.3	5.40	51	.326	.354	1	.250	1	-3	-3	-0	-0.2
1914	Bos-N	0	1	.000	1	1	0	0	0	1	2	0	3	1	45.0	9.00	31	.333	.556	0	—	0	-1	-1	-0	-0.1
1915	NY-A	0	1	.000	7	0	0	0	0	21¹	29	2	7	7	15.6	3.38	87	.330	.385	0	.000	-1	-1	-1	0	-0.1
Total	5	1	2	.333	12	2	1	0	0	37¹	58	2	14	12	17.6	4.82	61	.354	.408	1	.083	-0	-8	-8	-0	-0.8
● JOHNNY COUCH	Couch, John Daniel b: 3/31/1891, Vaughn, Mont. d: 12/8/75, San Mateo, Cal. BL/TR, 6', 180 lbs. Deb: 4/11/17																								
1917	Det-A	0	0	—	3	0	0	0	0	13¹	13	0	1	1	9.5	2.70	98	.255	.269	0	.000	-0	-0	-0	0	0.0
1922	Cin-N	16	9	.640	43	34	18	2	1	264	301	13	56	45	12.3	3.89	103	.289	.328	12	.132	-3	6	3	1	0.1
1923	Cin-N	2	7	.222	19	8	1	0	0	69¹	98	2	15	14	14.7	5.97	65	.344	.377	4	.174	-1	-15	-12	-1	-1.6
	Phi-N	2	4	.333	11	7	2	0	0	65	91	4	21	18	15.9	5.26	87	.335	.389	6	.250	-1	-9	-5	-0	-0.5
	Yr	4	11	.267	30	15	3	0	0	134¹	189	6	36	32	15.3	5.63	75	.339	.383	10	.213	-1	-24	-21	-1	-2.1
1924	Phi-N	4	8	.333	37	6	3	0	3	137	170	13	39	23	13.8	4.73	94	.306	.352	10	.204	-1	-13	-4	1	-0.4
1925	Phi-N	5	6	.455	34	7	2	1	2	94¹	112	9	39	11	14.5	5.44	88	.298	.365	5	.161	-1	-12	-7	1	-0.7
Total	5	29	34	.460	147	62	26	3	6	643	785	41	171	112	13.5	4.63	91	.304	.350	37	.167	-6	-43	-29	2	-3.1
● MIKE COUCHEE	Couchee, Michael Eugene b: 12/4/57, San Jose, Cal. BR/TR, 6', 190 lbs. Deb: 4/05/83																								
1983	SD-N	0	1	.000	8	0	0	0	0	14	12	1	6	5	11.6	5.14	68	.214	.290	1	.500	0	-2	-3	-0	-0.3
● ED COUGHLIN	Coughlin, Edward E. b: 8/5/1861, Hartford, Conn. d: 12/25/52, Hartford, Conn. Deb: 5/15/1884 ♦																								
1884	Buf-N	0	0	—	1	0	0	0	0	0	3	0	0	0	—	∞	—	.600	.600	1	.250	-0	-3	-3	0	-0.2
● ROSCOE COUGHLIN	Coughlin, William Edward b: 3/15/1868, Walpole, Mass. d: 3/20/51, Chelsea, Mass. TR, 5'10", 160 lbs. Deb: 4/22/1890																								
1890	Chi-N	4	6	.400	11	10	10	0	0	95	102	3	40	29	13.8	4.26	86	.266	.342	10	.256	1	-7	-6	1	-0.4
1891	NY-N	3	4	.429	8	7	6	0	0	61	74	5	23	22	14.8	3.84	83	.289	.354	3	.130	1	-3	-4	1	-0.2
Total	2	7	10	.412	19	17	16	0	0	156	176	8	63	51	14.2	4.10	85	.275	.347	13	.210	2	-11	-11	2	-0.6

● FRITZ COUMBE
Coumbe, Frederick Nicholas b: 12/13/1889, Antrim, Pa. d: 3/21/78, Paradise, Cal. BL/TL, 6', 152 lbs. Deb: 4/22/14

YEAR	TM/L	W	L	PCT	G	GS	CG	SH	SV	IP	H	HR	BB	SO	RAT	ERA	ERA+	OAV	OOB	BH	AVG	PB	PR	/A	PD	TPI
1914	Bos-A	1	2	.333	17	5	1	0	1	62^{1}	49	0	16	17	9.4	1.44	186	.222	.274	2	.111	-1	9	9	0	0.9
	Cle-A	1	5	.167	14	5	2	0	0	55^{1}	59	0	16	22	12.8	3.25	89	.288	.351	6	.261	1	-3	-2	1	-0.1
	Yr	2	7	.222	31	10	3	0	1	117^{2}	108	0	32	39	11.0	2.29	121	.254	.312	8	.195	1	6	6	1	0.8
1915	Cle-A	4	7	.364	30	12	4	1	2	114	123	1	37	37	12.9	3.47	88	.294	.355	10	.270	1	-7	-5	3	-0.2
1916	Cle-A	7	5	.583	29	13	7	2	0	120^{1}	121	1	27	39	11.1	2.02	149	.279	.323	2	.057	-3	11	13	5	1.7
1917	Cle-A	8	6	.571	34	10	4	1	5	134^{1}	119	0	35	30	10.5	2.14	132	.251	.307	6	.154	-1	8	10	3	1.3
1918	Cle-A	13	7	.650	30	17	9	0	3	150	164	4	52	41	13.0	3.06	98	.286	.347	12	.214	-1	-5	-1	5	0.3
1919	Cle-A	1	1	.500	8	2	0	0	1	23^{2}	32	2	9	7	15.6	5.32	63	.348	.406	3	.500	1	-6	-5	0	-0.4
1920	Cin-N	0	1	.000	3	0	0	0	0	14^{2}	17	0	4	7	12.9	4.91	62	.304	.350	3	.231	1	-3	-3	0	-0.2
1921	Cin-N	3	4	.429	28	6	3	0	1	86^{2}	89	2	21	12	11.5	3.22	111	.280	.326	8	.320	1	5	3	2	0.7
Total	8	38	38	.500	193	70	30	4	13	761^{1}	773	10	217	212	11.9	2.80	108	.277	.332	52	.206	-1	10	20	20	4.0

● HARRY COURTNEY
Courtney, Henry Seymour b: 11/19/1898, Asheville, N.C. d: 12/11/54, Lyme, Conn. BL/TL, 6'4", 185 lbs. Deb: 9/13/19

YEAR	TM/L	W	L	PCT	G	GS	CG	SH	SV	IP	H	HR	BB	SO	RAT	ERA	ERA+	OAV	OOB	BH	AVG	PB	PR	/A	PD	TPI
1919	Was-A	3	0	1.000	4	3	2	1	0	26^{1}	25	0	19	6	15.0	2.73	117	.269	.393	2	.200	-0	1	1	-1	0.0
1920	Was-A	8	11	.421	37	24	10	1	0	188	223	6	77	48	14.8	4.74	79	.298	.371	16	.232	4	-20	-21	-3	-2.0
1921	Was-A	6	9	.400	30	15	3	0	1	132^{2}	159	7	71	26	16.1	5.63	73	.305	.397	14	.298	2	-20	-22	-0	-1.9
1922	Was-A	0	1	.000	5	0	0	0	0	10	11	0	9	4	18.0	3.60	107	.306	.444	0	.000	-1	0	0	-0	0.0
	Chi-A	5	6	.455	18	11	5	0	0	86^{2}	100	5	37	28	14.3	4.98	82	.299	.371	9	.273	3	-9	-9	-1	-0.6
	Yr	5	7	.417	23	11	5	0	0	96^{2}	111	5	46	32	14.7	4.84	84	.300	.379	9	.243	2	-9	-8	-1	-0.6
Total	4	22	27	.449	94	53	20	2	1	443^{2}	518	18	213	112	15.2	4.91	79	.299	.382	41	.252	7	-47	-50	-5	-4.5

● HARRY COVELESKI
Coveleski, Harry Frank "The Giant Killer" (b: Harry Frank Kowalewski)
b: 4/23/1886, Shamokin, Pa. d: 8/4/50, Shamokin, Pa. BB/TL, 6', 180 lbs. Deb: 9/10/07 F

YEAR	TM/L	W	L	PCT	G	GS	CG	SH	SV	IP	H	HR	BB	SO	RAT	ERA	ERA+	OAV	OOB	BH	AVG	PB	PR	/A	PD	TPI
1907	Phi-N	1	0	1.000	4	0	0	0	0	20	10	0	3	6	6.3	0.00	—	.147	.194	0	.000	-0	5	5	-0	0.6
1908	Phi-N	4	1	.800	6	5	5	2	0	43^{2}	29	0	12	22	8.9	1.24	196	.196	.265	2	.133	-0	5	6	1	0.8
1909	Phi-N	6	10	.375	24	17	8	2	1	121^{2}	109	0	49	56	12.1	2.74	95	.247	.329	4	.108	-2	-2	-2	1	-0.3
1910	Cin-N	1	1	.500	7	4	2	0	0	39^{1}	35	1	42	27	18.5	5.26	55	.246	.431	1	.063	-1	-10	-10	1	-1.0
1914	Det-A	22	12	.647	44	36	23	5	2	303^{1}	251	4	100	124	10.8	2.49	113	.227	.298	23	.242	5	8	11	7	2.3
1915	Det-A	22	13	.629	**50**	38	20	1	4	312^{2}	271	2	87	150	10.9	2.45	124	.233	.298	18	.175	-2	17	20	4	2.3
1916	Det-A	21	11	.656	44	39	22	3	2	324^{1}	278	6	63	108	9.8	1.97	145	.237	.282	25	.212	1	31	32	4	4.3
1917	Det-A	4	6	.400	16	11	2	0	0	69	70	0	14	15	11.2	2.61	101	.265	.307	5	.227	-0	0	0	2	0.2
1918	Det-A	0	1	.000	3	1	1	0	0	14	17	0	6	3	14.8	3.86	69	.315	.383	1	.250	0	-2	-2	1	-0.1
Total	9	81	55	.596	198	151	83	13	9	1248	1070	13	376	511	10.8	2.39	118	.235	.301	79	.189	-0	55	61	20	9.1

● STAN COVELESKI
Coveleski, Stanley Anthony (b: Stanislaus Kowalewski)
b: 7/13/1889, Shamokin, Pa. d: 3/20/84, South Bend, Ind. BR/TR, 5'11", 166 lbs. Deb: 9/10/12 FH

YEAR	TM/L	W	L	PCT	G	GS	CG	SH	SV	IP	H	HR	BB	SO	RAT	ERA	ERA+	OAV	OOB	BH	AVG	PB	PR	/A	PD	TPI
1912	Phi-A	2	1	.667	5	2	2	1	0	21	18	0	4	9	9.9	3.43	90	.231	.277	1	.143	-0	-0	-1	-1	-0.1
1916	Cle-A	15	13	.536	45	27	11	1	3	232	247	6	58	76	11.9	3.41	88	.278	.323	13	.173	-0	-15	-10	2	-1.0
1917	Cle-A	19	14	.576	45	36	24	**9**	4	298^{1}	202	3	94	133	9.0	1.81	157	**.194**	.261	13	.134	-4	28	34	-4	3.0
1918	Cle-A	22	13	.629	38	33	25	2	1	311	261	2	76	87	9.9	1.82	165	.229	.279	21	.191	-3	33	41	-0	4.5
1919	Cle-A	24	12	.667	43	34	24	4	4	286	286	2	60	118	11.0	2.61	128	.267	.308	20	.213	4	20	23	3	3.2
1920	*Cle-A	24	14	.632	41	38	26	3	2	315	284	6	65	**133**	**10.1**	2.49	153	**.243**	**.285**	25	.225	3	**46**	**46**	3	**5.4**
1921	Cle-A	23	13	.639	43	40	28	2	2	315	341	6	84	99	12.3	3.37	126	.280	.329	18	.155	-6	32	31	7	3.1
1922	Cle-A	17	14	.548	35	33	21	3	2	276^{2}	292	14	64	98	11.6	3.32	121	.274	.316	10	.101	-7	22	21	1	1.5
1923	Cle-A	13	14	.481	33	31	17	**5**	2	228	251	8	42	54	11.6	**2.76**	**143**	.282	.316	7	.089	-8	**31**	30	3	2.6
1924	Cle-A	15	16	.484	37	33	18	2	0	240^{1}	286	6	73	58	13.6	4.04	106	.294	.346	11	.134	-5	5	6	-0	0.1
1925	*Was-A	20	5	**.800**	32	32	15	3	0	241	230	7	73	58	11.4	**2.84**	**149**	.255	.312	9	.111	-7	42	37	0	2.8
1926	Was-A	14	11	.560	36	34	11	3	1	245^{1}	272	1	81	50	12.9	3.12	124	.286	.342	17	.207	1	25	20	1	2.3
1927	Was-A	2	1	.667	5	4	0	0	0	14^{1}	13	0	8	3	13.2	3.14	129	.250	.350	2	.333	0	2	1	-0	0.1
1928	NY-A	5	1	.833	12	8	2	0	0	58	72	5	20	5	14.3	5.74	66	.323	.379	1	.053	-2	-11	-13	1	-1.3
Total	14	215	142	.602	450	385	224	38	21	3082	3055	66	802	981	11.4	2.89	128	.262	.311	168	.159	-34	259	276	16	26.2

● CHET COVINGTON
Covington, Chester Rogers "Chesty" b: 11/6/10, Cairo, Ill. d: 6/11/76, Pembroke Park, Fla. BB/TL, 6'2", 195 lbs. Deb: 4/23/44

YEAR	TM/L	W	L	PCT	G	GS	CG	SH	SV	IP	H	HR	BB	SO	RAT	ERA	ERA+	OAV	OOB	BH	AVG	PB	PR	/A	PD	TPI
1944	Phi-N	1	1	.500	19	0	0	0	0	38^{2}	46	2	8	13	12.6	4.66	78	.297	.331	0	.000	-1	-4	-4	-0	-0.6

● TEX COVINGTON
Covington, William Wilkes b: 3/19/1887, Henryville, Tenn. d: 12/10/31, Denison, Tex. BL/TR, 6'1", 175 lbs. Deb: 4/25/11 F

YEAR	TM/L	W	L	PCT	G	GS	CG	SH	SV	IP	H	HR	BB	SO	RAT	ERA	ERA+	OAV	OOB	BH	AVG	PB	PR	/A	PD	TPI
1911	Det-A	7	1	.875	17	6	5	0	0	83^{2}	94	2	33	29	14.7	4.09	85	.297	.381	6	.188	-1	-7	-6	-1	-0.8
1912	Det-A	3	4	.429	14	9	2	1	0	63^{1}	58	0	30	19	12.9	4.12	79	.253	.347	2	.133	0	-6	-6	-1	-0.6
Total	2	10	5	.667	31	15	7	1	0	147	152	2	63	48	14.0	4.10	82	.278	.367	8	.170	-1	-13	-12	-2	-1.4

● JOE COWLEY
Cowley, Joseph Alan b: 8/15/58, Lexington, Ky. BR/TR, 6'5", 210 lbs. Deb: 4/13/82

YEAR	TM/L	W	L	PCT	G	GS	CG	SH	SV	IP	H	HR	BB	SO	RAT	ERA	ERA+	OAV	OOB	BH	AVG	PB	PR	/A	PD	TPI
1982	Atl-N	1	2	.333	17	8	0	0	0	52^{1}	53	6	16	27	12.0	4.47	83	.265	.323	3	.200	-0	-5	-4	-0	-0.5
1984	NY-A	9	2	.818	16	11	3	1	0	83^{1}	75	12	31	71	11.7	3.56	106	.234	.305	0	—	0	4	2	0	0.5
1985	NY-A	12	6	.667	30	26	1	0	0	159^{2}	132	29	85	97	12.6	3.95	101	.224	.328	0	—	0	4	1	-1	0.2
1986	Chi-A	11	11	.500	27	27	4	0	0	162^{1}	133	20	83	132	12.1	3.88	111	.223	.321	0	—	0	5	8	-1	0.7
1987	Phi-N	0	4	.000	5	4	0	0	0	11^{2}	21	2	17	5	30.9	15.43	27	.389	.548	1	.333	1	-15	-15	-1	-1.3
Total	5	33	25	.569	95	76	8	1	0	469^{1}	414	69	232	332	12.7	4.20	96	.235	.329	4	.222	1	-7	-8	-1	-0.4

● DANNY COX
Cox, Danny Bradford b: 9/21/59, Northampton, England BR/TR, 6'4", 235 lbs. Deb: 8/06/83

YEAR	TM/L	W	L	PCT	G	GS	CG	SH	SV	IP	H	HR	BB	SO	RAT	ERA	ERA+	OAV	OOB	BH	AVG	PB	PR	/A	PD	TPI
1983	StL-N	3	6	.333	12	12	0	0	0	83	92	6	23	36	12.5	3.25	111	.286	.333	2	.074	-2	3	3	1	0.3
1984	StL-N	9	11	.450	29	27	1	1	0	156^{1}	171	9	54	70	13.4	4.03	86	.289	.355	7	.132	0	-8	-10	1	-0.9
1985	*StL-N	18	9	.667	35	35	10	4	0	241	226	19	64	131	10.9	2.88	123	.251	.303	12	.152	1	19	18	-1	1.9
1986	StL-N	12	13	.480	32	32	8	0	0	220	189	14	60	108	10.3	2.90	125	.234	.289	5	.077	-3	20	18	-5	1.1
1987	*StL-N	11	9	.550	31	31	2	0	0	199^{1}	224	17	71	101	13.5	3.88	107	.290	.352	8	.116	-2	4	6	-1	0.4
1988	StL-N	3	8	.273	13	13	0	0	0	86	89	6	25	47	12.0	3.98	87	.272	.326	1	.043	-2	-5	-5	0	-0.7
1991	Phi-N	4	6	.400	23	17	0	0	0	102^{1}	98	14	39	46	12.1	4.57	80	.258	.329	3	.103	-1	-10	-10	-1	-1.2
1992	Phi-N	2	2	.500	9	7	0	0	0	38^{1}	46	3	19	30	15.3	5.40	65	.299	.376	1	.091	-1	-8	-8	1	-0.8
	*Pit-N	3	1	.750	16	0	0	0	3	24^{1}	20	2	8	18	10.4	3.33	102	.225	.289	0	.000	-0	0	0	-0	0.0
	Yr	5	3	.625	25	7	0	0	3	62^{2}	66	5	27	48	13.4	4.60	75	.269	.342	1	.071	-1	-8	-8	0	-0.8
Total	8	65	65	.500	200	174	21	5	3	1150^{2}	1155	90	363	587	12.0	3.57	103	.266	.325	39	.109	-9	16	12	-5	0.1

● ERNIE COX
Cox, Ernest Thompson b: 2/19/1894, Birmingham, Ala. d: 4/29/74, Birmingham, Ala. BL/TR, 6'1", 180 lbs. Deb: 5/05/22

YEAR	TM/L	W	L	PCT	G	GS	CG	SH	SV	IP	H	HR	BB	SO	RAT	ERA	ERA+	OAV	OOB	BH	AVG	PB	PR	/A	PD	TPI
1922	Chi-A	0	0	—	1	0	0	0	0	1	1	0	2	0	27.0	18.00	23	.250	.500	0	—	0	-2	-2	-0	-0.1

● GEORGE COX
Cox, George Melvin b: 11/15/04, Sherman, Tex. BR/TR, 6'1", 170 lbs. Deb: 4/12/28

YEAR	TM/L	W	L	PCT	G	GS	CG	SH	SV	IP	H	HR	BB	SO	RAT	ERA	ERA+	OAV	OOB	BH	AVG	PB	PR	/A	PD	TPI
1928	Chi-A	1	2	.333	26	2	0	0	0	89	110	6	39	22	15.3	5.26	77	.313	.385	2	.077	-2	-12	-12	2	-1.2

● GLENN COX
Cox, Glenn Melvin b: 2/3/31, Montebello, Cal. BR/TR, 6'2", 210 lbs. Deb: 9/20/55

YEAR	TM/L	W	L	PCT	G	GS	CG	SH	SV	IP	H	HR	BB	SO	RAT	ERA	ERA+	OAV	OOB	BH	AVG	PB	PR	/A	PD	TPI
1955	KC-A	0	2	.000	2	2	0	0	0	2^{1}	11	0	1	2	46.3	30.86	14	.611	.632	0	.000	-0	-7	-7	0	-0.6
1956	KC-A	0	2	.000	3	3	1	0	0	23^{1}	15	2	22	6	14.3	4.24	102	.203	.385	0	.000	-1	-0	0	-1	-0.2
1957	KC-A	1	0	1.000	10	0	0	0	0	14^{1}	18	1	9	8	17.0	5.02	79	.321	.415	0	.000	0	-2	-2	0	-0.1
1958	KC-A	0	0	—	2	0	0	0	0	3^{2}	6	1	3	1	22.1	9.82	40	.400	.500	0	—	0	-2	-2	-0	-0.2
Total	4	1	4	.200	17	5	1	0	0	43^{2}	50	4	35	17	17.5	6.39	65	.307	.429	0	.000	-1	-12	-11	-1	-1.1

YEAR TM/L	W	L	PCT	G	GS	CG	SH	SV	IP	H	HR	BB	SO	RAT	ERA	ERA+	OAV	OOB	BH	AVG	PB	PR	/A	PD	TPI

● CASEY COX   Cox, Joseph Casey   b: 7/3/41, Long Beach, Cal.   BR/TR, 6'5", 200 lbs.   Deb: 4/15/66

1966 Was-A	4	5	.444	66	0	0	0	7	113	104	6	35	46	11.4	3.50	99	.250	.314	0	.000	-1	-1	-1	0	-0.1
1967 Was-A	7	4	.636	54	0	0	0	1	73	67	2	21	32	11.3	2.96	107	.250	.314	0	.000	-0	2	2	0	0.2
1968 Was-A	0	1	.000	4	0	0	0	0	7²	7	0	0	4	8.2	2.35	124	.250	.250	0	—	0	1	0	-0	0.0
1969 Was-A	12	7	.632	52	13	4	0	0	171²	161	15	64	73	11.8	2.78	125	.251	.320	5	.106	-2	16	13	-1	1.1
1970 Was-A	8	12	.400	37	30	1	0	1	192¹	211	27	44	68	12.1	4.45	80	.285	.329	7	.121	-2	-16	-19	-2	-2.3
1971 Was-A	5	7	.417	54	11	0	0	7	124¹	131	9	40	43	12.9	3.98	83	.273	.338	2	.077	-1	-7	-9	-1	-1.2
1972 Tex-A	3	5	.375	35	4	0	0	4	65¹	73	7	26	27	13.8	4.41	68	.277	.344	1	.111	1	-10	-10	-1	-1.1
NY-A	0	1	.000	5	1	0	0	0	11²	13	0	3	4	13.9	4.63	64	.289	.360	0	—	0	-2	-2	-0	-0.3
Yr	3	6	.333	40	5	0	0	4	77	86	7	29	31	13.7	4.44	68	.276	.341	1	.111	1	-12	-12	-0	-1.4
1973 NY-A	0	0	—	1	0	0	0	0	3	5	0	1	0	24.0	6.00	61	.357	.471	0	—	0	-1	-1	0	0.0
Total 8	39	42	.481	308	59	5	0	20	762	772	66	234	297	12.2	3.70	91	.266	.327	15	.099	-6	-17	-27	-3	-3.7

● LES COX   Cox, Leslie Warren   b: 8/14/05, Junction, Tex.   d: 10/14/34, San Angelo, Tex.   BR/TR, 6', 164 lbs.   Deb: 9/11/26

| 1926 Chi-A | 0 | 1 | .000 | 2 | 0 | 0 | 0 | 0 | 5 | 6 | 2 | 5 | 3 | 19.8 | 5.40 | 72 | .261 | .393 | 1 | .500 | 0 | -1 | -1 | 0 | -0.1 |

● RED COX   Cox, Plateau Rex   b: 2/16/1895, Laurel Springs, N.C.   d: 10/15/84, Roanoke, Va.   BL/TR, 6'2", 190 lbs.   Deb: 4/17/20

| 1920 Det-A | 0 | 0 | — | 3 | 0 | 0 | 0 | 0 | 5 | 9 | 0 | 3 | 1 | 21.6 | 5.40 | 69 | .375 | .444 | 0 | .000 | -0 | -1 | -1 | -0 | -0.1 |

● TERRY COX   Cox, Terry Lee   b: 3/30/49, Odessa, Tex.   BR/TR, 6'5", 215 lbs.   Deb: 9/07/70

| 1970 Cal-A | 0 | 0 | — | 3 | 0 | 0 | 0 | 0 | 2¹ | 4 | 0 | 0 | 3 | 15.4 | 3.86 | 94 | .400 | .400 | 0 | — | 0 | -0 | -0 | 0 | 0.0 |

● BILL COX   Cox, William Donald   b: 6/23/13, Ashmore, Ill.   d: 2/16/88, Charleston, Ill.   BR/TR, 6'1", 185 lbs.   Deb: 6/06/36

1936 StL-N	0	0	—	2	0	0	0	0	2²	4	0	1	1	16.9	6.75	58	.333	.385	0	—	0	-1	-1	-0	-0.1
1937 Chi-A	1	0	1.000	3	2	1	1	0	12²	9	0	5	8	9.9	0.71	648	.200	.280	1	.250	0	6	5	-0	0.6
1938 Chi-A	0	2	.000	7	1	0	0	0	11²	11	0	13	5	18.5	6.94	70	.244	.414	0	.000	-0	-3	-3	-0	-0.3
StL-A	1	4	.200	22	7	1	0	0	63	81	8	35	16	16.6	7.00	71	.315	.397	1	.059	-1	-15	-14	0	-1.3
Yr	1	6	.143	29	8	1	0	0	74²	92	8	48	21	16.9	6.99	71	.305	.400	1	.053	-2	-18	-17	0	-1.6
1939 StL-A	0	2	.000	4	2	1	0	0	9¹	10	0	8	8	17.4	9.64	50	.256	.383	0	.000	-0	-5	-5	1	-0.4
1940 StL-A	0	1	.000	12	0	0	0	0	17¹	23	3	12	7	18.2	7.27	63	.333	.432	0	.000	-0	-6	-5	-0	-0.5
Total 5	2	9	.182	50	12	3	1	0	116²	138	11	74	45	16.4	6.56	74	.296	.392	2	.080	-2	-24	-22	1	-2.0

● BILL COYLE   Coyle, William Claude   b: Pittsburgh, Pa.   TR ,   Deb: 7/07/1893

| 1893 Bos-N | 0 | 1 | .000 | 2 | 1 | 0 | 0 | 0 | 8 | 14 | 1 | 3 | 2 | 19.1 | 9.00 | 55 | .372 | .418 | 0 | .000 | -1 | -4 | -4 | 0 | -0.3 |

● CHARLIE COZART   Cozart, Charles Rhubin   b: 10/17/19, Lenoir, N.C.   BR/TL, 6', 190 lbs.   Deb: 4/17/45

| 1945 Bos-N | 1 | 0 | 1.000 | 5 | 0 | 0 | 0 | 0 | 8 | 10 | 2 | 15 | 4 | 28.1 | 10.13 | 38 | .303 | .521 | 0 | .000 | -0 | -6 | -6 | 1 | -0.5 |

● ROY CRABB   Crabb, James Roy   b: 8/23/1890, Monticello, Iowa   d: 3/30/40, Lewistown, Mont.   BR/TR, 5'11", 160 lbs.   Deb: 8/10/12

1912 Chi-A	0	1	.000	2	1	0	0	0	8²	6	0	4	3	10.4	1.04	308	.214	.313	0	.000	-0	2	2	0	0.2
Phi-A	2	4	.333	7	7	3	0	0	43¹	48	0	17	12	14.3	3.74	82	.287	.367	0	.000	-2	-2	-3	0	-0.5
Yr	2	5	.286	9	8	3	0	0	52	54	0	21	15	13.7	3.29	94	.277	.359	0	.000	-3	0	-1	0	-0.3

● GEORGE CRABLE   Crable, George E.   b: 12/1885, Nebraska   BL/TL, 6'1", 190 lbs.   Deb: 8/03/10

| 1910 Bro-N | 0 | 0 | — | 2 | 1 | 1 | 0 | 0 | 7¹ | 5 | 0 | 5 | 3 | 14.7 | 4.91 | 62 | .217 | .400 | 0 | .000 | 0 | -2 | -2 | 0 | -0.2 |

● WALT CRADDOCK   Craddock, Walter Anderson   b: 3/25/32, Pax, W.Va.   d: 7/6/80, Parma Heights, O.   BR/TL, 5'11.5", 176 lbs.   Deb: 9/03/55

1955 KC-A	0	2	.000	4	2	0	0	0	15	18	3	10	9	16.8	7.80	54	.300	.400	0	.000	-1	-6	-6	-0	-0.6
1956 KC-A	0	2	.000	2	2	0	0	0	9¹	9	1	10	8	18.3	6.75	64	.265	.432	0	.000	-0	-3	-3	-0	-0.3
1958 KC-A	0	3	.000	23	1	0	0	0	36²	41	4	20	22	15.6	5.89	66	.289	.380	0	.000	-0	-9	-8	0	-0.8
Total 3	0	7	.000	29	5	0	0	0	61	68	8	40	39	16.1	6.49	62	.288	.394	0	.000	-1	-18	-17	0	-1.7

● MOLLY CRAFT   Craft, Maurice Montague   b: 11/28/1895, Portsmouth, Va.   d: 10/25/78, Los Angeles, Cal.   BR/TR, 6'2", 165 lbs.   Deb: 8/08/16

1916 Was-A	0	1	.000	2	1	1	0	0	11	12	0	6	9	14.7	3.27	85	.316	.409	0	.000	-0	-1	-1	0	-0.1
1917 Was-A	0	0	—	8	0	0	0	1	14	17	0	8	2	16.1	3.86	68	.315	.403	1	.500	0	-2	-2	0	-0.1
1918 Was-A	0	0	—	3	0	0	0	0	7	5	0	1	5	7.7	1.29	212	.208	.240	0	.000	-0	1	1	0	0.1
1919 Was-A	0	3	.000	16	2	0	0	1	48²	59	2	18	17	14.6	3.88	83	.309	.374	2	.111	-2	-4	-4	-0	-0.5
Total 4	0	4	.000	29	3	1	0	2	80²	93	2	33	33	14.3	3.57	84	.303	.374	3	.115	-2	-5	-5	1	-0.6

● HOWARD CRAGHEAD   Craghead, Howard Oliver "Judge"   b: 5/25/08, Selma, Cal.   d: 7/15/62, San Zieloe, Cal.   BR/TR, 6'2", 200 lbs.   Deb: 4/30/31

1931 Cle-A	0	0	—	4	0	0	0	0	5²	8	0	2	2	15.9	6.35	73	.320	.370	0	—	0	-1	-1	0	-0.1
1933 Cle-A	0	0	—	11	0	0	0	0	17¹	19	1	10	2	15.6	6.23	71	.292	.395	0	.000	-0	-4	-3	0	-0.4
Total 2	0	0	—	15	0	0	0	0	23	27	1	12	4	15.7	6.26	72	.300	.388	0	.000	-0	-5	-5	0	-0.5

● GEORGE CRAIG   Craig, George McCarthy "Lefty"   b: 11/15/1887, Philadelphia, Pa.   d: 4/23/11, Indianapolis, Ind.   TL,   Deb: 7/12/07

| 1907 Phi-A | 0 | 0 | — | 2 | 0 | 0 | 0 | 0 | 1² | 2 | 0 | 3 | 0 | 37.8 | 10.80 | 24 | .299 | .599 | 0 | .000 | -0 | -2 | -2 | -0 | -0.2 |

● PETE CRAIG   Craig, Peter Joel   b: 7/10/40, Lasalle, Ont., Can.   BL/TR, 6'5", 220 lbs.   Deb: 9/06/64

1964 Was-A	0	0	—	1²	8	1	4	0	1²	8	1	4	0	64.8	48.60	8	.667	.750	0	—	0	-8	-8	-0	-0.7
1965 Was-A	0	3	.000	3	3	0	0	0	14¹	18	1	8	2	16.3	8.16	43	.321	.406	2	.667	1	-7	-7	1	-0.6
1966 Was-A	0	0	—	1	0	0	0	0	2	2	0	1	1	13.5	4.50	77	.250	.333	0	—	0	-0	-0	0	0.0
Total 3	0	3	.000	6	4	0	0	0	18	28	2	13	3	20.5	11.50	30	.368	.461	2	.667	1	-16	-16	0	-1.3

● ROGER CRAIG   Craig, Roger Lee   b: 2/17/30, Durham, N.C.   BR/TR, 6'4", 191 lbs.   Deb: 7/17/55   MC

1955 *Bro-N	5	3	.625	21	10	3	0	2	90²	81	8	43	48	12.4	2.78	146	.238	.325	2	.077	-2	13	13	-1	1.0
1956 *Bro-N	12	11	.522	35	32	8	2	1	199	169	25	87	109	11.8	3.71	107	.231	.316	1	.016	-6	1	6	-2	-0.2
1957 Bro-N	6	9	.400	32	13	1	0	0	111¹	102	18	47	69	12.2	4.61	90	.249	.329	4	.138	-1	-9	-5	1	-0.6
1958 LA-N	2	1	.667	9	2	1	0	0	32	30	3	12	16	11.8	4.50	91	.242	.309	0	.000	-1	-2	-1	-1	-0.3
1959 *LA-N	11	5	.688	29	17	7	4	0	152²	122	13	45	76	9.9	2.06	205	.217	.276	3	.058	-4	32	37	-1	3.4
1960 LA-N	8	3	.727	21	15	6	1	0	115²	99	8	43	69	11.3	3.27	121	.230	.305	2	.056	-2	6	9	-0	0.7
1961 LA-N	5	6	.455	40	14	2	0	2	112²	130	22	52	63	14.9	6.15	71	.288	.367	4	.148	-0	-27	-23	-1	-2.3
1962 NY-N	10	24	.294	42	33	13	0	3	233¹	261	35	70	118	13.0	4.51	93	.288	.343	4	.053	-5	-15	-9	4	-1.0
1963 NY-N	5	22	.185	46	31	14	0	0	236	249	28	58	108	11.9	3.78	92	.267	.314	6	.087	-2	-13	-8	3	-0.8
1964 *StL-N	7	9	.438	39	19	3	0	5	166	180	16	35	84	11.9	3.25	117	.276	.317	10	.208	2	5	10	2	1.5
1965 Cin-N	1	4	.200	40	0	0	0	2	64¹	74	6	23	30	14.3	3.64	103	.289	.359	2	.182	-0	-1	1	-0	0.1
1966 Phi-N	2	1	.667	14	0	0	0	1	22²	31	4	5	13	14.3	5.56	65	.326	.360	0	.000	-0	-5	-5	1	-0.5
Total 12	74	98	.430	368	186	58	7	19	1536¹	1528	186	522	803	12.2	3.83	104	.259	.323	38	.085	-23	-13	25	4	1.0

● GERALD CRAM   Cram, Gerald Allen   b: 12/9/47, Los Angeles, Cal.   BR/TR, 6', 180 lbs.   Deb: 9/03/69

1969 KC-A	0	1	.000	5	2	0	0	0	16²	15	0	6	10	11.3	3.24	114	.231	.296	0	.000	-0	1	1	-0	0.0
1974 NY-N	0	0	—	10	0	0	0	0	22¹	22	1	4	8	10.5	1.61	221	.275	.310	1	.333	0	5	5	0	0.6
1975 NY-N	0	1	.000	4	0	0	0	0	5	7	2	2	2	16.2	5.40	64	.333	.391	0	—	0	-1	-1	0	-0.1
1976 KC-A	0	0	—	4	0	0	0	0	4¹	8	0	1	2	18.7	6.23	56	.421	.450	0	—	0	-1	-1	0	-0.2
Total 4	0	3	.000	23	2	0	0	0	48¹	52	3	13	22	12.1	2.98	120	.281	.328	1	.167	-0	3	3	0	0.3

YEAR TM/L	W	L	PCT	G	GS	CG	SH	SV	IP	H	HR	BB	SO	RAT	ERA	ERA+	OAV	OOB	BH	AVG	PB	PR	/A	PD	TPI

● **DOC CRAMER**   Cramer, Roger Maxwell "Flit"   b: 7/22/05, Beach Haven, N.J.   d: 9/9/90, Manahawkin, N.J.   BL/TR, 6'2", 185 lbs.   Deb: 9/18/29   C◆

| 1938 Bos-A★ | 0 | 0 | — | 1 | 0 | 0 | 0 | 0 | 4 | 3 | 0 | 3 | 1 | 13.5 | 4.50 | 110 | .214 | .353 | 198 | .301 | 0 | 0 | 0 | 0 | 0.0 |

● **BILL CRAMER**   Cramer, William Wendell   b: 5/21/1891, Bedford, Ind.   d: 9/11/66, Fort Wayne, Ind.   BR/TR, 6', 175 lbs.   Deb: 6/25/12

| 1912 Cin-N | 0 | 0 | — | 1 | 0 | 0 | 0 | 0 | 2¹ | 6 | 0 | 0 | 2 | 23.1 | 0.00 | — | .500 | .500 | 0 | .000 | -0 | 1 | 1 | -0 | 0.0 |

● **DOC CRANDALL**   Crandall, James Otis   b: 10/8/1887, Wadena, Ind.   d: 8/17/51, Bell, Cal.   BR/TR, 5'10.5", 180 lbs.   Deb: 4/24/08   ◆

1908 NY-N	12	12	.500	32	24	13	0	0	214²	198	3	59	77	11.2	2.93	82	.248	.307	16	.222	5	-14	-12	-1	-1.1
1909 NY-N	6	4	.600	30	7	4	0	6	122	117	5	33	55	11.3	2.88	89	.252	.305	10	.244	3	-4	-4	2	0.0
1910 NY-N	17	4	.810	42	18	13	2	5	207²	194	10	43	73	10.4	2.56	116	.246	.289	25	.342	10	11	9	-1	2.0
1911 *NY-N	15	5	.750	41	15	9	2	5	198²	199	10	51	94	11.6	2.63	128	.256	.307	27	.239	1	17	16	2	2.4
1912 *NY-N	13	7	.650	37	10	7	0	2	162	181	7	35	60	12.1	3.61	94	.286	.326	25	.313	6	-4	-4	-0	0.3
1913 *NY-N	2	4	.333	24	1	1	0	5	55¹	61	2	13	28	12.2	3.09	101	.293	.338	7	.280	2	1	0	1	0.3
*NY-N	2	0	1.000	11	1	1	0	1	42¹	41	1	11	14	11.1	2.55	122	.248	.295	8	.364	3	3	3	1	0.7
Yr	4	4	.500	35	2	2	0	6	97²	102	3	24	42	11.6	2.86	109	.273	.317	15	.319	5	4	3	1	1.0
1914 StL-F	13	9	.591	27	21	18	1	0	196	194	8	52	84	11.4	3.54	96	.256	.305	86	.309	9	-7	-3	-1	0.6
1915 StL-F	21	15	.583	51	33	22	4	1	312²	307	5	77	117	11.3	2.59	123	.263	.314	40	.284	14	15	21	1	**4.1**
1916 StL-A	0	0	—	2	0	0	0	0	1¹	7	0	1	0	60.8	27.00	10	.636	.692	1	.083	-0	-4	-4	-0	-0.4
1918 Bos-N	1	2	.333	5	3	3	0	0	34	39	1	4	11	11.6	2.38	113	.307	.333	8	.286	1	1	1	0	0.3
Total 10	102	62	.622	302	133	91	9	25	1546²	1538	52	379	606	11.4	2.92	105	.261	.310	253	.285	57	17	23	1	9.2

● **ED CRANE**   Crane, Edward Nicholas "Cannon-Ball"   b: 5/1862, Boston, Mass.   d: 9/19/1896, Rochester, N.Y.   BR/TR, 5'10.5", 204 lbs.   Deb: 4/17/1884   ◆

1884 Bos-U	0	2	.000	4	2	1	0	0	18	17	1	6	13	11.5	4.00	74	.233	.291	1	.285	1	-2	-2	1	-0.1
1886 Was-N	1	7	.125	10	8	7	1	0	70	91	6	53	39	18.5	7.20	46	.313	.419	50	.171	-1	-30	-30	0	-2.5
1888 *NY-N	5	6	.455	12	11	11	2	1	92²	70	3	40	58	10.9	2.43	113	.193	.277	6	.162	1	4	3	1	0.5
1889 *NY-N	14	10	.583	29	25	23	0	0	230	221	10	136	130	14.4	3.68	107	.245	.350	21	.204	3	9	7	-4	0.5
1890 NY-P	16	19	.457	43	35	28	0	0	330¹	323	12	210	174	14.8	4.63	98	.245	.353	46	.315	8	-15	-3	-3	0.1
1891 Cin-a	14	14	.500	32	31	25	1	0	250	216	3	139	122	13.3	**2.45**	**168**	.225	.332	17	.155	-6	35	46	-2	3.5
Cin-N	4	8	.333	15	13	11	1	0	116²	134	3	64	51	15.5	4.09	83	.277	.366	5	.109	-3	-10	-9	0	-1.1
1892 NY-N	16	24	.400	47	43	35	2	1	364¹	350	10	189	174	13.6	3.80	85	.243	.335	40	.245	4	-21	-24	-0	-1.8
1893 NY-N	2	4	.333	10	7	4	0	0	68¹	84	2	41	11	17.3	5.93	79	.293	.393	12	.462	4	-10	-10	-1	-0.4
Bro-N	0	2	.000	2	2	1	0	0	10	19	2	9	5	26.1	13.50	33	.391	.495	2	.400	0	-10	-10	-0	-0.7
Yr	2	6	.250	12	9	5	0	0	78¹	103	4	50	16	17.7	6.89	67	.302	.393	14	.452	5	-19	-20	-1	-1.1
Total 8	72	96	.429	204	177	146	7	2	1550¹	1525	51	887	720	14.3	3.99	95	.247	.347	335	.238	12	-48	-34	-9	-2.0

● **LARRY CRAWFORD**   Crawford, Charles Lowrie   b: 4/27/14, Swissvale, Pa.   BL/TL, 6'1", 165 lbs.   Deb: 7/21/37

| 1937 Phi-N | 0 | 0 | — | 6 | 0 | 0 | 0 | 0 | 6 | 12 | 2 | 1 | 2 | 19.5 | 15.00 | 29 | .387 | .406 | 0 | — | 0 | -7 | -7 | -0 | -0.7 |

● **JIM CRAWFORD**   Crawford, James Frederick "Catfish"   b: 9/29/50, Chicago, Ill.   BL/TL, 6'3", 200 lbs.   Deb: 4/06/73

1973 Hou-N	2	4	.333	48	0	0	0	6	70	69	7	33	56	13.4	4.50	81	.256	.341	3	.231	1	-7	-7	1	-0.5
1975 Hou-N	3	5	.375	44	2	0	0	4	86²	92	6	37	37	13.6	3.63	93	.280	.356	5	.294	2	-0	-3	0	0.0
1976 Det-A	1	8	.111	32	5	1	0	2	109¹	115	4	43	68	13.0	4.53	82	.275	.343	0	—	0	-12	-10	5	-0.8
1977 Det-A	7	8	.467	37	7	0	0	1	126	156	13	50	91	14.8	4.79	90	.310	.373	0	—	0	-10	-7	1	-0.7
1978 Det-A	2	3	.400	20	0	0	0	0	39¹	45	3	19	24	15.1	4.35	89	.292	.377	0	—	0	-3	-2	-0	-0.3
Total 5	15	28	.349	181	14	1	0	13	431¹	477	27	182	276	13.9	4.40	86	.285	.357	8	.267	3	-32	-29	6	-2.3

● **STEVE CRAWFORD**   Crawford, Steven Ray   b: 4/29/58, Pryor, Okla.   BR/TR, 6'5", 225 lbs.   Deb: 9/02/80

1980 Bos-A	2	0	1.000	6	4	0	0	0	32¹	41	3	8	10	13.6	3.62	117	.306	.345	0	—	0	1	2	-0	0.0
1981 Bos-A	0	5	.000	14	11	0	0	0	57²	69	10	18	29	14.0	4.99	77	.301	.360	0	—	0	-9	-7	0	-0.7
1982 Bos-A	1	0	1.000	5	0	0	0	0	9	14	0	0	4	14.0	2.00	215	.341	.341	0	—	0	2	2	0	0.2
1984 Bos-A	5	0	1.000	35	0	0	0	1	62	69	6	21	21	13.2	3.34	125	.286	.346	0	—	0	4	6	-0	0.3
1985 Bos-A	6	5	.545	44	0	0	0	12	91	103	5	28	58	13.0	3.76	114	.289	.340	0	—	0	4	5	1	0.3
1986 *Bos-A	0	2	.000	40	0	0	0	4	57¹	69	5	19	32	13.8	3.92	106	.308	.362	0	—	0	2	2	0	0.1
1987 Bos-A	5	4	.556	29	0	0	0	0	72²	91	13	32	43	15.5	5.33	85	.314	.386	0	—	0	-7	-6	1	-0.6
1989 KC-A	3	1	.750	25	0	0	0	0	54	48	2	19	33	11.7	2.83	136	.242	.318	0	—	0	6	6	2	0.8
1990 KC-A	5	4	.556	46	0	0	0	1	80	79	7	23	54	11.8	4.16	92	.254	.312	0	—	0	-2	-3	1	-0.1
1991 KC-A	3	2	.600	33	0	0	0	1	46²	60	3	18	38	15.2	5.98	69	.311	.373	0	—	0	-10	-10	-0	-1.0
Total 10	30	23	.566	277	16	2	0	19	562²	643	54	186	320	13.5	4.17	99	.290	.348	0	—	0	-8	-3	3	-0.7

● **JACK CREEL**   Creel, Jack Dalton "Tex"   b: 4/23/16, Kyle, Tex.   BR/TR, 6', 165 lbs.   Deb: 4/22/45

| 1945 StL-N | 5 | 4 | .556 | 26 | 8 | 2 | 0 | 2 | 87 | 78 | 5 | 45 | 34 | 13.3 | 4.14 | 90 | .245 | .349 | 2 | .077 | -2 | -3 | -4 | 0 | -0.5 |

● **KEITH CREEL**   Creel, Steven Keith   b: 2/4/59, Dallas, Tex.   BR/TR, 6'2", 180 lbs.   Deb: 5/25/82

1982 KC-A	1	4	.200	9	6	0	0	0	41²	43	8	25	13	14.7	5.40	76	.267	.366	0	—	0	-6	-6	-0	-0.6
1983 KC-A	2	5	.286	25	10	1	0	0	89¹	116	17	35	31	15.4	6.35	64	.320	.382	0	—	0	-23	-23	-1	-2.2
1985 Cle-A	2	5	.286	15	8	0	0	0	62	73	7	23	31	14.2	4.79	86	.296	.360	0	—	0	-4	-5	-1	-0.5
1987 Tex-A	0	0	—	6	0	0	0	0	9²	12	2	5	5	15.8	4.66	96	.293	.370	0	—	0	-0	-0	0	0.0
Total 4	5	14	.263	55	24	1	0	0	202²	244	34	88	80	14.9	5.60	74	.300	.372	0	—	0	-33	-33	-2	-3.3

● **BOB CREMINS**   Cremins, Robert Anthony "Lefty" or "Crooked Arm"   b: 2/15/06, Pelham Manor, N.Y.   BL/TL, 5'11", 178 lbs.   Deb: 8/17/27

| 1927 Bos-A | 0 | 0 | — | 4 | 0 | 0 | 0 | 0 | 5¹ | 5 | 0 | 3 | 0 | 13.5 | 5.06 | 83 | .250 | .348 | 0 | — | 0 | -1 | -0 | 0 | 0.0 |

● **WALKER CRESS**   Cress, Walker James "Foots"   b: 3/6/17, Ben Hur, Va.   BR/TR, 6'5", 205 lbs.   Deb: 4/27/48

1948 Cin-N	0	1	.000	30	2	1	0	0	60	60	2	42	33	15.5	4.50	87	.271	.390	4	.500	2	-4	-4	-1	-0.3
1949 Cin-N	0	0	—	3	0	0	0	0	2	2	0	3	0	22.5	0.00	—	.286	.500	0	—	0	1	1	-0	0.1
Total 2	0	1	.000	33	2	1	0	0	62	62	2	45	33	15.7	4.35	90	.272	.394	4	.500	2	-3	-3	-1	-0.2

● **TIM CREWS**   Crews, Stanley Timothy   b: 4/3/61, Tampa, Fla.   BR/TR, 6', 190 lbs.   Deb: 7/27/87

1987 LA-N	1	1	.500	20	0	0	0	3	29	30	2	8	20	12.4	2.48	160	.268	.328	0	.000	-0	5	5	0	0.5
1988 LA-N	4	0	1.000	42	0	0	0	0	71²	77	3	16	45	11.7	3.14	106	.278	.317	1	.200	0	2	2	-1	0.0
1989 LA-N	0	1	.000	44	0	0	0	0	61²	69	7	23	56	13.7	3.21	106	.284	.351	0	—	0	2	1	0	0.1
1990 LA-N	4	5	.444	66	2	0	0	5	107¹	98	9	24	76	10.3	2.77	132	.238	.282	0	.000	-1	12	11	-1	0.9
1991 LA-N	2	3	.400	60	0	0	0	6	76	75	7	19	53	11.1	3.43	105	.256	.301	0	.000	0	2	1	0	0.2
1992 LA-N	0	3	.000	49	2	0	0	1	78	95	6	20	43	13.5	5.19	62	.310	.357	2	.286	-1	-15	-15	-1	-1.6
Total 6	11	13	.458	281	4	0	0	15	423²	444	34	110	293	11.9	3.44	103	.270	.319	3	.136	-0	9	5	-3	0.1

● **JERRY CRIDER**   Crider, Jerry Stephen   b: 9/2/41, Sioux Falls, S.D.   BR/TR, 6'2", 200 lbs.   Deb: 5/21/69

1969 Min-A	1	0	1.000	21	1	0	0	1	28²	31	3	15	16	15.1	4.71	78	.284	.381	4	.444	2	-3	-3	0	-0.2
1970 Chi-A	4	7	.364	32	8	0	0	4	91	101	13	34	40	13.5	4.45	88	.288	.354	2	.083	-1	-7	-6	-2	-0.9
Total 2	5	7	.417	53	9	0	0	5	119²	132	16	49	56	13.9	4.51	85	.287	.361	6	.182	1	-11	-9	-2	-1.1

● **CHUCK CRIM**   Crim, Charles Robert   b: 7/23/61, Van Nuys, Cal.   BR/TR, 6', 190 lbs.   Deb: 4/08/87

1987 Mil-A	6	8	.429	53	5	0	0	12	130	133	15	39	56	12.1	3.67	125	.266	.323	0	—	0	11	13	-0	1.2
1988 Mil-A	7	6	.538	70	0	0	0	9	105	95	11	28	58	10.7	2.91	136	.247	.302	0	—	0	12	12	0	1.2
1989 Mil-A	9	7	.563	76	0	0	0	7	117²	114	7	36	59	11.6	2.83	136	.259	.318	0	—	0	14	13	-1	1.2

YEAR TM/L	W	L	PCT	G	GS	CG	SH	SV	IP	H	HR	BB	SO	RAT	ERA	ERA+	OAV	OOB	BH	AVG	PB	PR	/A	PD	TPI
1990 Mil-A	3	5	.375	67	0	0	0	11	85^{2}	88	7	23	39	11.9	3.47	112	.261	.312	0	—	0	4	4	0	0.5
1991 Mil-A	8	5	.615	66	0	0	0	3	91^{1}	115	9	25	39	14.0	4.63	86	.305	.351	0	—	0	-5	-7	0	-0.6
1992 Cal-A	7	6	.538	57	0	0	0	1	87	100	11	29	30	14.0	5.17	76	.293	.359	0	—	0	-12	-12	0	-1.2
Total 6	40	37	.519	389	5	0	0	43	616^{2}	645	60	180	281	12.3	3.71	109	.271	.327	0	—	0	24	23	-1	2.3

● JACK CRIMIAN Crimian, John Melvin b: 2/17/26, Philadelphia, Pa. BR/TR, 5'10", 180 lbs. Deb: 7/03/51

YEAR TM/L	W	L	PCT	G	GS	CG	SH	SV	IP	H	HR	BB	SO	RAT	ERA	ERA+	OAV	OOB	BH	AVG	PB	PR	/A	PD	TPI
1951 StL-N	1	0	1.000	11	0	0	0	1	17	24	3	8	5	16.9	9.00	44	.338	.405	1	.333	0	-10	-10	-0	-0.9
1952 StL-N	0	0	—	5	0	0	0	0	8^{1}	15	4	4	4	20.5	9.72	38	.417	.475	0	.000	0	-6	-6	-0	-0.5
1956 KC-A	4	8	.333	54	7	0	0	3	129	129	19	49	59	12.8	5.51	79	.265	.339	5	.227	1	-19	-17	-0	-1.6
1957 Det-A	0	1	.000	4	0	0	0	0	5^{2}	9	1	4	1	20.6	12.71	30	.375	.464	0	—	0	-6	-6	-0	-0.5
Total 4	5	9	.357	74	7	0	0	4	160	177	27	65	69	13.9	6.36	67	.287	.360	6	.231	1	-40	-38	-1	-3.5

● DODE CRISS Criss, Dode b: 3/12/1885, Sherman, Miss. d: 9/8/55, Sherman, Miss. BL/TR, 6'2", 200 lbs. Deb: 4/20/08 ♦

YEAR TM/L	W	L	PCT	G	GS	CG	SH	SV	IP	H	HR	BB	SO	RAT	ERA	ERA+	OAV	OOB	BH	AVG	PB	PR	/A	PD	TPI
1908 StL-A	0	1	.000	9	1	0	0	0	18	15	1	13	9	15.5	6.50	37	.250	.408	28	.341	1	-8	-8	-1	-0.8
1909 StL-A	1	5	.167	11	6	3	0	0	55^{1}	53	0	32	43	14.2	3.42	71	.262	.369	14	.292	5	-6	-6	-1	-0.2
1910 StL-A	2	1	.667	6	0	0	0	0	19^{1}	12	0	9	9	11.6	1.40	177	.176	.309	21	.231	1	2	2	-0	0.4
1911 StL-A	0	2	.000	4	2	0	0	0	18^{1}	24	0	10	9	17.7	8.35	40	.333	.429	21	.253	0	-10	-10	0	-0.8
Total 4	3	9	.250	30	9	3	0	0	111	104	1	64	70	14.5	4.38	59	.259	.375	84	.276	8	-22	-22	-1	-1.4

● BILL CRISTALL Cristall, William Arthur "Lefty" b: 9/12/1878, Odessa, Russia d: 1/28/39, Buffalo, N.Y. BL/TL, 5'7", 145 lbs. Deb: 9/03/01

YEAR TM/L	W	L	PCT	G	GS	CG	SH	SV	IP	H	HR	BB	SO	RAT	ERA	ERA+	OAV	OOB	BH	AVG	PB	PR	/A	PD	TPI
1901 Cle-A	1	5	.167	6	6	5	1	0	48^{1}	54	1	30	12	16.4	4.84	73	.279	.387	7	.350	2	-6	-7	2	-0.3

● LEO CRISTANTE Cristante, Dante Leo b: 12/10/26, Detroit, Mich. d: 8/24/77, Dearborn, Mich. BR/TR, 6'1", 195 lbs. Deb: 4/21/51

YEAR TM/L	W	L	PCT	G	GS	CG	SH	SV	IP	H	HR	BB	SO	RAT	ERA	ERA+	OAV	OOB	BH	AVG	PB	PR	/A	PD	TPI
1951 Phi-N	1	1	.500	10	1	0	0	0	22	28	3	9	6	15.5	4.91	78	.318	.388	1	.167	-0	-2	-3	0	-0.3
1955 Det-A	0	1	.000	20	1	0	0	0	36^{2}	37	1	14	9	12.5	3.19	120	.261	.327	0	.000	-1	3	3	-1	0.0
Total 2	1	2	.333	30	2	0	0	0	58^{2}	65	4	23	15	13.7	3.84	100	.283	.350	1	.077	-1	1	0	-1	-0.3

● MORRIE CRITCHLEY Critchley, Morris Arthur b: 3/26/1850, New London, Conn. d: 3/6/10, Pittsburgh, Pa. 6'1", 190 lbs. Deb: 5/08/1882

YEAR TM/L	W	L	PCT	G	GS	CG	SH	SV	IP	H	HR	BB	SO	RAT	ERA	ERA+	OAV	OOB	BH	AVG	PB	PR	/A	PD	TPI
1882 Pit-a	1	0	1.000	1	1	1	1	0	9	7	0	1	3	8.0	0.00	—	.200	.222	0	.000	-1	3	3	0	0.2
StL-a	0	4	.000	4	4	4	0	0	34	43	3	7	2	13.2	4.24	66	.289	.321	3	.214	-0	-6	-5	-1	-0.6
Yr	1	4	.200	5	5	5	1	0	43	50	3	8	5	12.1	3.35	83	.272	.303	3	.158	-1	-3	-3	-1	-0.4

● CLAUDE CROCKER Crocker, Claude Arthur b: 7/20/24, Caroleen, N.C. BR/TR, 6'2", 185 lbs. Deb: 8/01/44

YEAR TM/L	W	L	PCT	G	GS	CG	SH	SV	IP	H	HR	BB	SO	RAT	ERA	ERA+	OAV	OOB	BH	AVG	PB	PR	/A	PD	TPI
1944 Bro-N	0	0	—	2	0	0	0	0	3^{1}	6	0	5	1	29.7	10.80	33	.400	.550	1	1.000	0	-3	-3	0	-0.2
1945 Bro-N	0	0	—	1	0	0	0	1	2	2	0	1	1	13.5	0.00	—	.286	.375	0	—	0	1	1	-0	0.1
Total 2	0	0	—	3	0	0	0	1	5^{1}	8	0	6	2	23.6	6.75	54	.364	.500	1	1.000	0	-2	-2	0	-0.1

● RAY CRONE Crone, Raymond Hayes b: 8/7/31, Memphis, Tenn. BR/TR, 6'2", 185 lbs. Deb: 4/13/54

YEAR TM/L	W	L	PCT	G	GS	CG	SH	SV	IP	H	HR	BB	SO	RAT	ERA	ERA+	OAV	OOB	BH	AVG	PB	PR	/A	PD	TPI
1954 Mil-N	1	0	1.000	19	2	1	0	1	49	44	6	19	33	11.8	2.02	184	.247	.323	2	.200	-0	11	9	-0	0.9
1955 Mil-N	10	9	.526	33	15	6	1	0	140^{1}	117	11	42	76	10.2	3.46	108	.227	.285	7	.159	-1	9	5	0	0.4
1956 Mil-N	11	10	.524	35	21	6	0	2	169^{2}	173	19	44	73	11.6	3.87	89	.263	.311	6	.122	1	-2	-8	-1	-0.8
1957 Mil-N	3	1	.750	11	5	2	0	0	42^{1}	54	8	15	15	14.7	4.46	78	.312	.367	2	.182	1	-3	-5	1	-0.3
NY-N	4	8	.333	25	17	2	0	1	120^{2}	131	11	40	56	13.0	4.33	91	.272	.331	1	.025	-4	-6	-5	2	-0.6
Yr	7	9	.438	36	22	4	0	1	163	185	19	55	71	13.4	4.36	88	.282	.340	3	.059	-3	-9	-10	3	-0.9
1958 SF-N	1	2	.333	14	1	0	0	0	24	35	5	13	7	18.0	6.75	56	.354	.429	0	.000	-0	-7	-8	-0	-0.8
Total 5	30	30	.500	137	61	17	1	4	546	554	60	173	260	12.1	3.87	95	.263	.321	18	.115	-3	2	-12	2	-1.2

● JACK CRONIN Cronin, John J. b: 5/26/1874, W.New Brighton, S.I., N.Y. d: 7/12/29, Middletown, N.Y. BR/TR, 6' ", 200 lbs. Deb: 8/24/1895

YEAR TM/L	W	L	PCT	G	GS	CG	SH	SV	IP	H	HR	BB	SO	RAT	ERA	ERA+	OAV	OOB	BH	AVG	PB	PR	/A	PD	TPI
1895 Bro-N	0	0	—	2	0	0	0	2	5	10	0	3	1	23.4	10.80	41	.408	.473	1	.500	1	-3	-4	-0	-0.2
1898 Pit-N	2	2	.500	4	4	2	1	0	28	35	0	8	9	13.8	3.54	101	.304	.349	1	.100	-0	0	0	0	0.0
1899 Cin-N	2	2	.500	5	5	5	0	0	41	56	2	16	9	16.9	5.49	71	.324	.398	2	.118	-1	-7	-7	-1	-0.8
1901 Det-A	13	15	.464	30	28	21	1	0	219^{2}	261	6	42	62	12.8	3.89	99	.292	.330	21	.247	1	-6	-1	-3	-0.2
1902 Det-A	0	0	—	4	0	0	0	0	17^{1}	26	1	8	5	19.2	9.35	39	.346	.430	0	.000	-1	-11	-11	0	-1.0
Bal-A	3	5	.375	10	8	8	0	0	75^{2}	66	1	24	20	10.7	2.62	144	.235	.296	4	.148	-2	8	10	2	1.1
Yr	3	5	.375	14	8	8	0	0	93	92	2	32	25	12.0	3.87	97	.257	.317	4	.118	-3	-3	-1	3	0.1
NY-N	5	6	.455	13	12	11	0	0	114	105	3	18	52	9.7	2.45	115	.245	.275	11	.169	-1	4	5	0	0.4
1903 NY-N	6	4	.600	20	11	8	0	1	115^{2}	130	5	37	50	13.5	3.81	88	.284	.345	9	.196	-0	-7	-6	0	-0.6
1904 Bro-N	12	23	.343	40	34	33	4	0	307	284	10	79	110	11.0	2.70	102	.245	.300	17	.157	-3	1	2	0	-0.1
Total 7	43	57	.430	128	102	88	6	3	923^{1}	973	28	235	318	12.1	3.40	96	.270	.320	66	.180	-6	-20	-13	-1	-1.4

● GEORGE CROSBY Crosby, George W. b: 1860, Iowa d: 1/9/13, San Francisco, Cal. Deb: 5/22/1884

YEAR TM/L	W	L	PCT	G	GS	CG	SH	SV	IP	H	HR	BB	SO	RAT	ERA	ERA+	OAV	OOB	BH	AVG	PB	PR	/A	PD	TPI
1884 Chi-N	1	2	.333	3	3	3	0	0	28	27	3	12	11	12.5	3.54	89	.227	.298	4	.308	1	-2	-1	1	0.0

● KEN CROSBY Crosby, Kenneth Stewart b: 12/15/47, New Denver, B.C., Canada BR/TR, 6'2", 179 lbs. Deb: 8/05/75

YEAR TM/L	W	L	PCT	G	GS	CG	SH	SV	IP	H	HR	BB	SO	RAT	ERA	ERA+	OAV	OOB	BH	AVG	PB	PR	/A	PD	TPI
1975 Chi-N	1	0	1.000	9	0	0	0	0	8^{1}	10	0	7	6	18.4	3.24	119	.294	.415	0	—	0	0	1	0	0.1
1976 Chi-N	0	0	—	7	1	0	0	0	12	20	3	8	5	21.0	12.00	32	.377	.459	1	.500	0	-11	-11	0	-1.0
Total 2	1	0	1.000	16	1	0	0	0	20^{1}	30	3	15	11	19.9	8.41	46	.345	.441	1	.500	1	-11	-10	0	-0.9

● LEM CROSS Cross, George Lewis b: 1/9/1872, Sanbornton, N.H. d: 10/9/30, Manchester, N.H. 5'9", 155 lbs. Deb: 8/06/1893

YEAR TM/L	W	L	PCT	G	GS	CG	SH	SV	IP	H	HR	BB	SO	RAT	ERA	ERA+	OAV	OOB	BH	AVG	PB	PR	/A	PD	TPI
1893 Cin-N	0	2	.000	3	3	2	0	0	21	24	3	9	7	14.1	5.57	86	.279	.347	2	.333	1	-2	-2	0	-0.1
1894 Cin-N	3	4	.429	8	7	3	0	0	53	94	8	21	11	20.4	8.49	65	.381	.440	6	.231	-1	-19	-17	-1	-1.3
Total 2	3	6	.333	11	10	5	0	0	74	118	11	30	18	18.6	7.66	70	.355	.416	8	.250	-0	-21	-19	-0	-1.4

● DOUG CROTHERS Crothers, Douglas b: 11/16/1859, Natchez, Miss. d: 3/29/07, St.Louis, Mo. BR/TR, Deb: 8/03/1884

YEAR TM/L	W	L	PCT	G	GS	CG	SH	SV	IP	H	HR	BB	SO	RAT	ERA	ERA+	OAV	OOB	BH	AVG	PB	PR	/A	PD	TPI
1884 KC-U	1	2	.333	3	3	3	0	0	25	26	0	6	11	11.5	1.80	153	.251	.291	2	.133	-1	3	3	-1	0.1
1885 NY-a	7	11	.389	18	18	18	1	0	154	192	4	49	40	14.2	5.08	58	.293	.344	8	.157	0	-31	-36	0	-3.0
Total 2	8	13	.381	21	21	21	1	0	179	218	4	55	51	13.8	4.63	63	.287	.337	10	.152	-1	-28	-34	-0	-2.9

● BILL CROUCH Crouch, Wilmer Elmer b: 8/20/10, Wilmington, Del. d: 12/26/80, Howell, Mich. BB/TR, 6'1", 180 lbs. Deb: 5/09/39 F

YEAR TM/L	W	L	PCT	G	GS	CG	SH	SV	IP	H	HR	BB	SO	RAT	ERA	ERA+	OAV	OOB	BH	AVG	PB	PR	/A	PD	TPI
1939 Bro-N	4	0	1.000	6	3	3	0	0	38^{1}	37	3	14	10	12.0	2.58	156	.255	.321	2	.133	-1	6	6	-1	0.5
1941 Phi-N	2	3	.400	20	5	1	0	1	59	65	4	17	26	12.5	4.42	84	.286	.336	1	.091	-0	-5	-5	2	-0.3
StL-N	1	2	.333	18	4	0	0	6	45	45	2	14	15	11.8	3.00	125	.271	.328	0	.000	-1	3	4	-1	0.2
Yr	3	5	.375	38	9	1	0	7	104	110	6	31	41	12.2	3.81	98	.280	.333	1	.042	-2	-2	-1	1	-0.1
1945 StL-N	1	0	1.000	6	0	0	0	0	13^{1}	12	1	7	4	13.5	3.38	111	.255	.364	0	.000	-0	1	1	0	0.0
Total 3	8	5	.615	50	12	4	0	7	155^{2}	159	10	52	55	12.3	3.47	110	.272	.332	3	.073	-3	4	6	0	0.4

● BILL CROUCH Crouch, William Henry "Skip" b: 12/3/1886, Marshallton, Del. d: 12/22/45, Highland Park, Mich. BL/TL, 6'1", 210 lbs. Deb: 7/12/10 F

YEAR TM/L	W	L	PCT	G	GS	CG	SH	SV	IP	H	HR	BB	SO	RAT	ERA	ERA+	OAV	OOB	BH	AVG	PB	PR	/A	PD	TPI
1910 StL-A	0	0	—	1	1	1	0	0	8	6	0	7	2	14.6	3.38	73	.231	.394	0	.000	-0	-1	-1	-0	-0.1

● ZACH CROUCH Crouch, Zachary Quinn b: 10/26/65, Folsom, Cal. BL/TL, 6'3", 180 lbs. Deb: 6/04/88

YEAR TM/L	W	L	PCT	G	GS	CG	SH	SV	IP	H	HR	BB	SO	RAT	ERA	ERA+	OAV	OOB	BH	AVG	PB	PR	/A	PD	TPI
1988 Bos-A	0	0	—	3	0	0	0	0	1^{1}	4	0	2	0	40.5	6.75	61	.571	.667	0	—	0	-0	-0	0	-0.2

● GENERAL CROWDER Crowder, Alvin Floyd b: 1/11/1899, Winston-Salem, N.C d: 4/3/72, Winston-Salem, N.C. BL/TR, 5'10", 170 lbs. Deb: 7/24/26

YEAR TM/L	W	L	PCT	G	GS	CG	SH	SV	IP	H	HR	BB	SO	RAT	ERA	ERA+	OAV	OOB	BH	AVG	PB	PR	/A	PD	TPI
1926 Was-A	7	4	.636	19	12	6	0	1	100	97	3	60	26	14.3	3.96	98	.261	.367	9	.237	1	1	-1	1	0.1
1927 Was-A	4	7	.364	15	11	4	2	0	67^{1}	58	3	42	22	13.6	4.54	89	.232	.347	3	.136	-1	-3	-4	-1	-0.5
StL-A	3	5	.375	21	8	2	1	3	73^{2}	71	3	42	30	13.9	5.01	87	.260	.361	6	.261	0	-7	-5	-1	-0.6

YEAR	TM/L	W	L	PCT	G	GS	CG	SH	SV	IP	H	HR	BB	SO	RAT	ERA	ERA+	OAV	OOB	BH	AVG	PB	PR	/A	PD	TPI
	Yr	7	12	.368	36	19	6	3	3	141	129	6	84	52	13.7	4.79	88	.246	.351	9	.200	-1	-10	-9	-2	-1.1
1928	StL-A	21	5	**.808**	41	31	19	1	2	244	238	11	91	99	12.2	3.69	114	.258	.325	15	.188	-2	10	14	-5	0.7
1929	StL-A	17	15	.531	40	34	19	**4**	4	266^2	272	22	93	79	12.3	3.92	113	.271	.332	18	.188	-3	10	15	-2	0.9
1930	StL-A	3	7	.300	13	10	5	1	1	77^1	85	11	27	42	13.2	4.66	105	.283	.345	4	.160	-2	-0	2	1	0.1
	Was-A	15	9	.625	27	25	20	0	1	202^1	191	6	69	65	11.6	3.60	128	.249	.312	13	.171	-2	24	22	-4	1.5
	Yr	18	16	.529	40	35	25	1	2	279^2	276	17	96	107	12.0	3.89	120	.259	.320	17	.168	-4	23	24	-3	1.6
1931	Was-A	18	11	.621	44	26	13	1	2	234^1	255	13	72	85	12.6	3.88	111	.275	.328	19	.216	-1	13	11	-3	0.6
1932	Was-A	**26**	13	.667	50	39	21	3	1	**327**	319	17	77	103	10.9	3.33	130	.252	.295	27	.221	2	42	36	-2	3.2
1933	*Was-A★	**24**	15	.615	**52**	35	17	0	4	299^1	311	14	81	110	11.9	3.97	105	.267	.316	19	.186	1	10	7	-3	0.4
1934	Was-A	4	10	.286	29	13	4	0	3	100^2	142	9	38	39	16.1	6.79	64	.326	.380	7	.219	1	-26	-28	-1	-2.5
	*Det-A	5	1	.833	9	9	3	1	0	66^2	81	3	20	30	13.6	4.18	105	.295	.342	4	.133	-2	2	2	-1	-0.2
	Yr	9	11	.450	38	22	7	1	3	167^1	223	12	58	69	15.1	5.75	76	.314	.365	11	.177	-1	-23	-26	-2	-2.7
1935	*Det-A	16	10	.615	33	32	16	2	0	241	269	16	67	59	12.7	4.26	98	.285	.335	17	.183	-2	5	-2	-3	-0.7
1936	Det-A	4	3	.571	9	7	1	0	0	44	64	5	21	10	17.4	8.39	59	.342	.409	3	.150	-1	-16	-17	-0	-1.4
Total	11	167	115	.592	402	292	150	16	22	2344^1	2453	136	800	799	12.5	4.12	105	.270	.330	164	.194	-12	64	52	-24	1.6
● **CAP CROWELL**	Crowell, Minot Joy b: 9/5/1892, Roxbury, Mass. d: 9/30/62, Central Falls, R.I. BR/TR, 6'1", 178 lbs. Deb: 6/23/15																									
1915	Phi-A	2	6	.250	10	8	4	0	0	54^1	56	1	47	15	17.9	5.47	54	.292	.443	5	.227	-0	-15	-15	-0	-1.5
1916	Phi-A	0	5	.000	9	6	1	0	0	39^2	43	0	34	15	17.9	4.99	57	.289	.427	0	.000	-2	-10	-9	-1	-1.2
Total	2	2	11	.154	19	14	5	0	0	94	99	1	81	30	17.9	5.27	55	.290	.436	5	.147	-2	-25	-25	-1	-2.7
● **BILLY CROWELL**	Crowell, William Theodore b: 11/6/1865, Cincinnati, Ohio d: 7/24/35, Ft.Worth, Tex. BR/TR, 5'8.5", 160 lbs. Deb: 4/20/1887																									
1887	Cle-a	14	31	.311	45	45	45	1	0	389^1	541	9	138	72	16.2	4.88	89	.327	.386	22	.141	-13	-25	-23	-3	-3.0
1888	Cle-a	5	13	.278	18	18	16	0	0	150^2	212	8	61	61	16.8	5.79	53	.320	.385	5	.086	-5	-46	-45	-1	-4.1
	Lou-a	0	1	.000	1	1	1	0	0	9	12	1	6	5	19.0	6.00	51	.309	.414	0	.000	-0	-3	-3	0	-0.2
	Yr	5	14	.263	19	19	17	0	0	159^2	224	9	67	66	16.5	5.81	53	.316	.376	5	.082	-5	-49	-48	-0	-4.3
Total	2	19	45	.297	64	64	62	1	0	549	765	18	205	138	16.4	5.15	77	.325	.386	27	.124	-18	-74	-71	-4	-7.3
● **WOODY CROWSON**	Crowson, Thomas Woodrow b: 9/9/18, Fuquay Sprgs., N.C d: 8/14/47, Mayodan, N.C. BR/TR, 6'2", 185 lbs. Deb: 4/17/45																									
1945	Phi-A	0	0	—	1	0	0	0	0	3	2	0	3	2	15.0	6.00	57	.200	.385	0	.000	-0	-1	-1	0	-0.1
● **CAL CRUM**	Crum, Calvin N. b: 7/27/1890, Cooks Mills, Ill. d: 12/7/45, Tulsa, Okla. BR/TR, 6'1", 175 lbs. Deb: 4/17/17																									
1917	Bos-N	0	0	—	1	0	0	0	0	1	1	0	1	0	18.0	0.00	—	.250	.400	0	—	0	0	0	0	0.1
1918	Bos-N	0	1	.000	1	1	0	0	0	2^1	6	0	3	0	38.6	15.43	17	.600	.714	0	.000	-0	-3	-3	0	-0.3
Total	2	0	1	.000	2	1	0	0	0	3^1	7	0	4	0	32.4	10.80	24	.500	.632	0	.000	-0	-3	-3	1	-0.2
● **ROY CRUMPLER**	Crumpler, Roy Maxton b: 7/8/1896, Clinton, N.C. d: 10/6/69, Fayetteville, N.C. BL/TL, 6'1", 195 lbs. Deb: 9/16/20																									
1920	Det-A	1	0	1.000	2	2	1	0	0	13	17	2	11	2	20.1	5.54	67	.315	.439	3	.333	1	-3	-3	-0	-0.2
1925	Phi-N	0	0	—	3	1	0	0	0	4^2	8	0	2	1	19.3	7.71	62	.381	.435	0	.000	-0	-2	-2	0	-0.1
Total	2	1	0	1.000	5	3	1	0	0	17^2	25	2	13	3	19.9	6.11	65	.333	.438	3	.273	1	-4	-4	-0	-0.3
● **DICK CRUTCHER**	Crutcher, Richard Louis b: 11/25/1889, Frankfort, Ky. d: 6/19/52, Frankfort, Ky. BR/TR, 5'9", 148 lbs. Deb: 4/14/14																									
1914	Bos-N	5	7	.417	33	15	5	1	0	158^2	169	4	66	48	13.7	3.46	80	.293	.371	8	.148	-1	-12	-12	1	-1.3
1915	Bos-N	2	2	.500	14	4	1	0	2	43^2	50	1	16	17	14.0	4.33	60	.309	.378	3	.231	1	-8	-8	0	-0.8
Total	2	7	9	.438	47	19	6	1	2	202^1	219	5	82	65	13.7	3.65	75	.296	.373	11	.164	-0	-19	-21	1	-2.1
● **TODD CRUZ**	Cruz, Todd Ruben b: 11/23/55, Highland Park, Mich BR/TR, 6', 175 lbs. Deb: 9/04/78 ♦																									
1984	Bal-A	0	0	—	1	0	0	0	0	1	0	0	0	0	0.0	0.00	—	.000	.000	31	.218	0	0	0	0	0.0
● **VICTOR CRUZ**	Cruz, Victor Manuel (b: b: 12/24/57, Rancho Viejo La Vega, D.R. BR/TR, 5'9", 200 lbs. Deb: 6/24/78																									
1978	Tor-A	7	3	.700	32	0	0	0	9	47^1	28	0	35	51	12.2	1.71	229	.179	.333	0	—	0	11	12	-0	1.1
1979	Cle-A	3	9	.250	61	0	0	0	10	78^2	70	10	44	63	13.2	4.23	100	.244	.346	0	—	0	-0	0	-2	-0.2
1980	Cle-A	6	7	.462	55	0	0	0	12	86	71	10	27	88	10.6	3.45	118	.229	.297	0	—	0	6	6	-1	0.4
1981	Pit-N	1	1	.500	22	0	0	0	1	34	33	6	15	28	13.0	2.65	136	.264	.348	0	.000	-0	3	4	0	0.3
1983	Tex-A	1	3	.250	17	0	0	0	5	25	16	2	10	18	9.7	1.44	278	.184	.276	0	—	0	7	7	-0	0.7
Total	5	18	23	.439	187	0	0	0	37	271	218	28	131	248	11.8	3.09	131	.226	.323	0	.000	-0	27	28	-4	2.3
● **COOKIE CUCCURULLO**	Cuccurullo, Arthur Joseph b: 2/8/18, Asbury Park, N.J. d: 1/23/83, W.Orange, N.J. BL/TL, 5'10", 168 lbs. Deb: 10/03/43																									
1943	Pit-N	0	1	.000	1	1	0	0	0	7	10	0	3	3	16.7	6.43	54	.357	.419	0	—	1	-2	-2	0	-0.1
1944	Pit-N	2	1	.667	32	4	0	0	4	106^1	110	5	44	31	13.3	4.06	91	.270	.346	14	.368	5	-5	-4	1	0.2
1945	Pit-N	1	3	.250	29	4	0	0	1	56^2	68	2	34	17	16.4	5.24	75	.305	.399	3	.214	-0	-9	-8	0	-0.8
Total	3	3	5	.375	62	9	0	0	5	170	188	7	81	51	14.5	4.55	83	.286	.367	17	.327	5	-17	-15	1	-0.7
● **JIM CUDWORTH**	Cudworth, James Alaric "Cuddy" b: 8/22/1858, Fairhaven, Mass. d: 12/21/43, Middleboro, Mass. BR/TR, 6', 165 lbs. Deb: 7/27/1884 ♦																									
1884	KC-U	0	0	—	2	1	1	0	0	17	19	1	3	6	11.6	4.24	65	.264	.294	17	.147	-0	-2	-3	-1	-0.3
● **CHARLIE CUELLAR**	Cuellar, Jesus Patracis b: 9/24/17, Ybor City, Fla. BR/TR, 5'11", 183 lbs. Deb: 7/02/50																									
1950	Chi-A	0	0	—	2	0	0	0	0	1^1	6	0	3	1	60.8	33.75	13	.600	.692	0	—	0	-4	-4	0	-0.4
● **MIKE CUELLAR**	Cuellar, Miguel Angel (Santana) b: 5/8/37, Las Villas, Cuba BL/TL, 5'11", 175 lbs. Deb: 4/18/59																									
1959	Cin-N	0	0	—	2	0	0	0	0	4	7	1	4	5	24.8	15.75	26	.368	.478	0	.000	-0	-5	-5	-0	-0.5
1964	StL-N	5	5	.500	32	7	1	0	4	72	80	8	33	56	14.3	4.50	85	.288	.365	0	.000	-2	-8	-6	1	-0.7
1965	Hou-N	1	4	.200	25	4	0	0	2	56	55	3	21	46	12.4	3.54	95	.262	.332	0	.000	-1	0	-1	0	-0.2
1966	Hou-N	12	10	.545	38	28	11	1	2	227^1	193	10	52	175	9.7	2.22	154	.229	.274	8	.113	-1	35	30	0	3.3
1967	Hou-N★	16	11	.593	36	32	16	3	1	246^1	233	16	63	203	10.9	3.03	109	.248	.296	13	.140	1	9	8	-0	0.9
1968	Hou-N	8	11	.421	28	24	11	2	1	170^2	152	8	45	133	10.4	2.74	108	.237	.289	11	.193	2	5	4	-0	0.7
1969	*Bal-A	23	11	.676	39	39	18	5	0	290^2	213	18	79	182	9.1	2.38	149	.204	**.261**	12	.117	-3	**40**	**38**	-0	**3.8**
1970	*Bal-A☆	**24**	8	**.750**	40	40	**21**	4	0	297^2	273	34	69	190	10.4	3.48	105	.242	.286	10	.089	-4	8	6	-3	-0.2
1971	*Bal-A★	20	9	.690	38	38	21	4	0	292^1	250	30	78	124	10.1	3.08	109	.234	.287	11	.103	-3	12	9	1	0.6
1972	Bal-A	18	12	.600	35	35	17	4	0	248^1	197	21	71	132	9.7	2.57	119	.220	.277	11	.126	-1	13	14	0	1.5
1973	*Bal-A	18	13	.581	38	38	17	2	0	267	265	29	84	140	11.8	3.27	114	.258	.314	0	—	0	16	14	0	1.5
1974	*Bal-A☆	22	10	**.688**	38	38	20	5	0	269^1	253	17	86	106	11.4	3.11	111	.252	.312	0	—	0	15	10	-3	0.8
1975	Bal-A	14	12	.538	36	36	17	5	0	256	229	17	84	105	11.0	3.66	96	.249	.313	0	—	0	3	-4	2	-0.1
1976	Bal-A	4	13	.235	26	19	2	1	1	107	129	8	50	32	15.2	4.96	66	.307	.383	0	—	0	-17	-20	-0	-1.8
1977	Cal-A	0	1	.000	2	1	0	0	0	3^1	9	2	3	3	32.4	18.90	21	.500	.571	0	—	0	-5	-6	-0	-0.3
Total	15	185	130	.587	453	379	172	36	11	2808	2538	222	822	1632	10.8	3.14	109	.243	.299	76	.115	-13	122	92	-2	9.3
● **BOBBY CUELLAR**	Cuellar, Robert b: 8/20/52, Alice, Tex. BR/TR, 5'11", 188 lbs. Deb: 9/09/77																									
1977	Tex-A	0	0	—	4	0	0	0	0	6^2	4	1	2	3	8.1	1.35	302	.182	.250	0	—	0	2	2	-0	0.1
● **BERT CUETO**	Cueto, Dagoberto (Concepcion) b: 8/14/37, San Luis, Pinar, Cuba BR/TR, 6'4", 170 lbs. Deb: 6/18/61																									
1961	Min-A	1	3	.250	7	5	0	0	0	21^1	27	7	10	5	16.0	7.17	59	.300	.376	0	.000	-0	-7	-7	0	-0.7
● **JACK CULLEN**	Cullen, John Patrick b: 10/6/39, Newark, N.J. BR/TR, 5'11", 170 lbs. Deb: 9/09/62																									
1962	NY-A	0	0	—	2	0	0	0	1	3	2	0	2	2	12.0	0.00	—	.182	.308	0	—	0	1	1	-0	0.1
1965	NY-A	3	4	.429	12	9	2	1	0	59	59	2	21	25	12.2	3.05	112	.262	.325	3	.150	-0	3	2	1	0.3

YEAR	TM/L	W	L	PCT	G	GS	CG	SH	SV	IP	H	HR	BB	SO	RAT	ERA	ERA+	OAV	OOB	BH	AVG	PB	PR	/A	PD	TPI
1966	NY-A	1	0	1.000	5	0	0	0	0	11^{1}	11	0	5	7	12.7	3.97	84	.256	.333	0	.000	-0	-1	-1	-0	-0.2
Total	3	4	4	.500	19	9	2	1	1	73^{1}	72	2	28	34	12.3	3.07	111	.258	.326	3	.130	-1	3	3	0	0.2
● NICK CULLOP Cullop, Henry Nicholas "Tomato Face" b: 10/16/1900, St.Louis, Mo. d: 12/8/78, Westerville, Ohio BR/TR, 6', 200 lbs. Deb: 4/14/26 ♦																										
1927	Cle-A	0	0	—	1	0	0	0	0	1	3	0	0	0	27.0	9.00	47	.600	.600	16	.235	0	-1	-1	-0	-0.1
● NICK CULLOP Cullop, Norman Andrew b: 9/17/1887, Chilhowie, Va. d: 4/15/61, Tazewell, Va. BL/TL, 5'11.5", 172 lbs. Deb: 5/20/13																										
1913	Cle-A	3	7	.300	23	8	4	0	0	97^{2}	105	3	35	30	13.2	4.42	69	.291	.358	4	.129	-1	-16	-15	1	-1.6
1914	Cle-A	0	1	.000	1	0	0	0	0	3^{1}	4	0	1	3	13.5	2.70	107	.364	.417	0	.000	-0	0	0	-0	0.0
	KC-F	14	19	.424	44	36	22	4	1	295^{2}	256	6	87	149	10.8	2.34	132	.235	.299	14	.141	-3	28	24	1	2.3
1915	KC-F	22	11	.667	44	36	22	3	2	302^{1}	278	8	67	111	10.5	2.44	120	.249	.297	18	.188	1	20	16	6	2.5
1916	NY-A	13	6	.684	28	22	9	0	1	167	151	4	32	77	10.0	2.05	141	.243	.284	6	.109	-3	14	16	-5	0.9
1917	NY-A	5	9	.357	30	18	5	2	1	146^{1}	161	2	31	27	11.9	3.32	81	.307	.348	7	.159	-1	-11	-10	-0	-1.3
1921	StL-A	0	2	.000	4	1	0	0	0	11^{2}	18	1	6	3	18.5	8.49	53	.340	.407	0	.000	-1	-5	-5	0	-0.5
Total	6	57	55	.509	174	121	62	9	5	1024	973	24	259	400	11.1	2.73	108	.258	.310	49	.149	-9	30	26	3	2.3
● BUD CULLOTON Culloton, Bernard Aloysius b: 5/19/1897, Kingston, N.Y. d: 11/9/76, Kingston, N.Y. BR/TR, 5'11", 180 lbs. Deb: 4/16/25																										
1925	Pit-N	0	1	.000	9	1	0	0	0	21	19	1	1	3	8.6	2.57	173	.241	.250	0	.000	-1	4	4	-0	0.3
1926	Pit-N	0	0	—	4	0	0	0	0	3^{2}	3	0	6	1	22.1	7.36	53	.214	.450	0	—	0	-1	-1	0	-0.1
Total	2	0	1	.000	13	1	0	0	0	24^{2}	22	1	7	4	10.6	3.28	133	.237	.290	0	.000	-1	3	3	-0	0.2
● RAY CULP Culp, Raymond Leonard b: 8/6/41, Elgin, Tex. BR/TR, 6', 200 lbs. Deb: 4/10/63																										
1963	Phi-N★	14	11	.560	34	30	10	5	0	203^{1}	148	15	102	176	11.3	2.97	109	.206	.309	9	.136	-0	7	6	-0	0.6
1964	Phi-N	8	7	.533	30	19	3	1	0	135	139	15	56	96	13.3	4.13	84	.263	.340	5	.114	-1	-9	-10	-1	-1.2
1965	Phi-N	14	10	.583	33	30	11	2	0	204^{1}	188	14	78	134	12.2	3.22	108	.243	.322	6	.088	-2	7	6	-1	0.2
1966	Phi-N	7	4	.636	34	12	1	0	1	110^{2}	106	19	53	100	13.5	5.04	71	.246	.338	2	.077	-2	-18	-18	-1	-2.1
1967	Chi-N	8	11	.421	30	22	4	1	0	152^{2}	138	22	59	111	11.7	3.89	91	.239	.311	5	.098	-1	-9	-6	-1	-0.9
1968	Bos-A	16	6	.727	35	30	11	6	0	216^{1}	166	18	82	190	10.7	2.91	108	.210	.292	8	.114	-1	2	6	-1	0.4
1969	Bos-A★	17	8	.680	32	32	9	2	0	227	195	25	79	172	11.1	3.81	100	.231	.302	12	.152	1	-5	-0	-0	0.0
1970	Bos-A	17	14	.548	33	33	15	1	0	251^{1}	211	22	91	197	11.2	3.04	130	.224	.300	12	.124	-4	19	26	-1	2.2
1971	Bos-A	14	16	.467	35	35	12	3	0	242^{1}	236	21	67	151	11.4	3.60	103	.253	.307	8	.118	-2	-4	2	-2	-0.1
1972	Bos-A	5	8	.385	16	16	4	1	0	105	104	8	53	52	13.7	4.46	72	.260	.351	7	.212	1	-16	-15	0	-1.5
1973	Bos-A	2	6	.250	10	9	0	0	0	50^{1}	46	9	32	32	14.7	4.47	90	.247	.369	0	—	0	-4	-3	0	-0.3
Total	11	122	101	.547	322	268	80	22	1	1898^{1}	1677	188	752	1411	11.8	3.58	99	.235	.314	74	.123	-11	-29	-5	-8	-2.7
● BILL CULP Culp, William Edward b: 6/11/1887, Bellaire, Ohio d: 9/3/69, Arnold, Pa. BB/TR, 6'1.5", 165 lbs. Deb: 9/08/10																										
1910	Phi-N	0	0	—	4	0	0	0	1	6^{2}	8	0	4	4	16.2	8.10	39	.333	.429	0	.000	-0	-4	-4	1	-0.3
● GEORGE CULVER Culver, George Raymond b: 7/8/43, Salinas, Cal. BR/TR, 6'2", 185 lbs. Deb: 9/07/66																										
1966	Cle-A	0	2	.000	5	1	0	0	0	9^{2}	15	1	7	6	21.4	8.38	41	.357	.460	0	.000	-0	-5	-5	0	-0.5
1967	Cle-A	7	3	.700	53	1	0	0	3	75	71	2	31	41	13.0	3.96	82	.258	.346	1	.250	0	-6	-6	1	-0.5
1968	Cin-N	11	16	.407	42	35	5	2	2	226^{1}	229	8	84	114	13.0	3.22	98	.264	.339	8	.121	-1	-6	-2	2	-0.1
1969	Cin-N	5	7	.417	32	13	0	0	4	101^{1}	117	8	52	58	15.8	4.26	88	.291	.384	3	.097	-2	-8	-6	2	-0.6
1970	StL-N	3	3	.500	11	7	2	0	0	56^{2}	64	6	24	23	14.1	4.61	89	.284	.356	3	.176	0	-4	-3	2	-0.1
	Hou-N	3	3	.500	32	0	0	0	3	45	44	1	21	31	13.6	3.20	121	.254	.345	1	.250	0	4	3	-1	0.3
	Yr	6	6	.500	43	7	2	0	3	101^{2}	108	7	45	54	13.8	3.98	101	.270	.348	4	.190	0	1	0	1	0.2
1971	Hou-N	5	8	.385	59	0	0	0	7	95^{1}	89	4	38	57	12.2	2.64	127	.257	.334	1	.091	-1	9	8	1	0.8
1972	Hou-N	6	2	.750	45	0	0	0	2	97^{1}	73	7	43	82	11.2	3.05	110	.212	.309	3	.158	0	4	3	-0	0.4
1973	LA-N	4	4	.500	28	0	0	0	2	42	45	4	21	23	14.4	3.00	115	.292	.381	0	.000	-0	3	2	1	0.3
	Phi-N	3	1	.750	14	0	0	0	0	18^{2}	26	0	15	7	19.8	4.82	79	.342	.451	0	—	0	-2	-2	1	-0.2
	Yr	7	5	.583	42	0	0	0	2	60^{2}	71	4	36	30	15.9	3.56	100	.305	.398	0	.000	-0	1	-0	2	0.1
1974	Phi-N	1	0	1.000	14	0	0	0	0	21^{2}	20	1	16	9	15.4	6.65	57	.267	.402	0	.000	-0	-7	-7	-0	-0.8
Total	9	48	49	.495	335	57	7	2	23	789	793	42	352	451	13.6	3.62	96	.266	.352	20	.124	-4	-18	-13	8	-1.0
● JOHN CUMBERLAND Cumberland, John Sheldon b: 5/10/47, Westbrook, Me. BR/TL, 6', 190 lbs. Deb: 9/27/68																										
1968	NY-A	0	0	—	1	0	0	0	0	2	3	1	1	1	18.0	9.00	32	.333	.400	0	—	0	-1	-1	0	-0.1
1969	NY-A	0	0	—	2	0	0	0	0	4	3	0	4	0	15.8	4.50	77	.231	.412	0	—	0	-0	-0	0	0.0
1970	NY-A	3	4	.429	15	8	1	0	0	64	62	9	15	38	10.8	3.94	89	.252	.295	1	.059	-1	-2	-3	-1	-0.5
	SF-N	2	0	1.000	7	0	0	0	0	11	6	0	4	6	8.2	0.82	486	.158	.238	0	.000	-0	4	4	0	0.4
1971	*SF-N	9	6	.600	45	21	5	2	2	185	153	22	55	65	10.1	2.92	116	.223	.281	7	.119	-2	11	10	-3	0.5
1972	SF-N	0	4	.000	9	6	0	0	0	25	38	6	7	8	16.2	8.64	40	.336	.375	1	.111	-0	-14	-14	-1	-1.5
	StL-N	1	1	.500	14	1	0	0	0	21^{2}	23	6	7	7	12.5	6.65	51	.291	.349	0	.000	-1	-8	-8	-1	-1.0
	Yr	1	5	.167	23	7	0	0	0	46^{2}	61	12	14	15	14.5	7.71	45	.316	.362	1	.071	-1	-22	-22	-2	-2.5
1974	Cal-A	0	1	.000	17	0	0	0	0	21^{2}	24	2	10	12	14.1	3.74	92	.289	.366	0	—	0	-0	-1	-0	-0.1
Total	6	15	16	.484	110	36	6	2	2	334^{1}	312	46	103	137	11.2	3.82	90	.246	.303	9	.099	-5	-11	-14	-6	-2.3
● STEVE CUMMINGS Cummings, Steven Brent b: 7/15/64, Houston, Tex. BB/TR, 6'2", 200 lbs. Deb: 6/24/89																										
1989	Tor-A	2	0	1.000	5	2	0	0	0	21	18	1	11	8	12.9	3.00	126	.231	.333	0	—	0	2	2	-0	0.2
1990	Tor-A	0	0	—	6	2	0	0	0	12^{1}	22	4	5	4	20.4	5.11	77	.431	.491	0	—	0	-2	-2	-0	-0.3
Total	2	2	0	1.000	11	4	0	0	0	33^{1}	40	5	16	12	15.7	3.78	101	.310	.395	0	—	0	0	0	-0	-0.1
● CANDY CUMMINGS Cummings, William Arthur b: 10/18/1848, Ware, Mass. d: 5/16/24, Toledo, Ohio BR/TR, 5'9", 120 lbs. Deb: 4/22/1872 H																										
1872	Mut-n	33	20	.623	**55**	55	**53**	**3**	0	**497**	600	2	30	43	11.4	2.52	137	.270	.280	52	.206	-3	66	51		3.3
1873	Bal-n	28	14	.667	42	42	42	1	0	382	475	4	33	31	12.0	2.66	122	.274	.287	48	.250	2	25	25		2.0
1874	Phi-n	28	26	.519	54	54	52	3	0	482	602	4	21		11.6	*2.88*	106	.271	.278	54	.236	-1	7	9		0.5
1875	Har-n	35	12	.745	48	47	46	**7**	0	417	396	0	6		8.7	*1.60*	162	.235	.237	44	.199	-5	40	46		3.6
1876	Har-N	16	8	.667	24	24	24	5	0	216	215	0	14	26	9.5	1.67	142	.239	.251	17	.162	-8	15	17	-2	0.6
1877	Cin-N	5	14	.263	19	19	16	0	0	155^{2}	219	2	13	11	13.4	4.34	61	.315	.327	14	.200	0	-26	-29	0	-2.4
Total	4 n	124	72	.633	199	198	193	14	0	1778	2073	10	90	74	10.9	*2.43*	128	.264	.272	198	.221	-8	138	135		9.4
Total	2	21	22	.488	43	43	40	5	0	371^{2}	434	2	27	37	11.2	2.78	90	.272	.284	31	.177	-8	-11	-12	-2	-1.8
● BRUCE CUNNINGHAM Cunningham, Bruce Lee b: 9/29/05, San Francisco, Cal. d: 3/8/84, Hayward, Cal. BR/TR, 5'10.5", 165 lbs. Deb: 5/07/29																										
1929	Bos-N	4	6	.400	17	8	4	0	1	91^{2}	100	7	32	22	13.2	4.52	104	.282	.344	4	.148	-0	2	2	1	0.2
1930	Bos-N	5	6	.455	36	6	2	0	0	106^{2}	121	7	41	28	13.7	5.48	90	.289	.352	6	.194	0	-6	-6	3	-0.3
1931	Bos-N	3	12	.200	33	16	6	1	1	136^{2}	157	7	54	32	14.0	4.48	85	.296	.363	3	.071	-4	-9	-10	4	-0.9
1932	Bos-N	1	0	1.000	18	3	0	0	0	47	50	1	19	21	14.0	3.45	109	.281	.363	2	.222	2	2	2	1	0.4
Total	4	13	24	.351	104	33	12	1	2	382	428	22	146	103	13.7	4.64	93	.289	.356	15	.138	-2	-11	-14	9	-0.6
● BERT CUNNINGHAM Cunningham, Ellsworth Elmer b: 11/25/1865, Wilmington, Del. d: 5/14/52, Cragmere, Del. BR/TR, 187 lbs. Deb: 9/15/1887 U																										
1887	Bro-a	0	2	.000	3	3	3	0	0	23	26	0	13	8	16.8	5.09	85	.263	.371	0	.000	-1	-2	-2	-0	-0.2
1888	Bal-a	22	29	.431	51	51	50	0	0	453^{1}	412	8	157	186	11.9	3.39	88	.233	.307	33	.186	-2	-17	-21	0	-2.0
1889	Bal-a	16	19	.457	39	33	29	0	1	279^{1}	306	11	141	140	14.9	4.87	81	.270	.358	27	.206	-3	-32	-29	-0	-2.5
1890	Phi-P	3	9	.250	14	11	11	0	0	108^{2}	133	0	67	33	17.1	5.22	82	.289	.387	6	.115	-4	-12	-11	1	-1.1
	Buf-P	9	15	.375	25	25	24	2	0	211	251	8	134	78	16.7	5.84	70	.283	.381	23	.228	1	-38	-41	-1	-3.0
	Yr	12	24	.333	39	36	35	2	0	319^{2}	384	8	201	111	16.6	5.63	74	.283	.378	29	.190	-3	-50	-52	0	-4.1

YEAR	TM/L	W	L	PCT	G	GS	CG	SH	SV	IP	H	HR	BB	SO	RAT	ERA	ERA+	OAV	OOB	BH	AVG	PB	PR	/A	PD	TPI
1891	Bal-a	11	14	.440	30	25	21	0	0	237^{2}	241	8	138	59	14.8	4.01	93	.254	.355	15	.150	-1	-8	-7	2	-0.6
1895	Lou-N	11	16	.407	31	28	24	1	0	231	299	6	104	49	15.9	4.75	97	.309	.379	30	.300	6	1	-3	2	0.4
1896	Lou-N	7	14	.333	27	20	17	0	1	189^{1}	242	6	74	37	15.8	5.09	85	.308	.380	22	.250	3	-15	-16	2	-0.9
1897	Lou-N	14	13	.519	29	27	25	0	0	234^{2}	286	2	72	49	14.2	4.14	103	.298	.355	22	.237	-1	4	3	2	0.5
1898	Lou-N	28	15	.651	44	42	41	0	0	362	387	8	65	34	11.7	3.16	113	.271	.312	32	.229	2	18	17	-1	1.7
1899	Lou-N	17	17	.500	39	37	33	1	0	323^{2}	385	4	75	36	13.2	3.84	101	.295	.340	40	.260	3	1	1	6	0.8
1900	Chi-N	4	3	.571	8	7	7	0	0	64	84	0	21	7	15.3	4.36	83	.315	.374	4	.148	-1	-5	-5	-1	-0.6
1901	Chi-N	0	1	.000	1	1	1	0	0	9	11	0	3	2	14.0	5.00	65	.299	.352	0	.000	0	-2	-2	1	-0.1
Total	12	142	167	.460	341	310	286	4	2	2726^{2}	3063	61	1064	718	14.1	4.22	91	.277	.349	254	.217	1	-105	-117	12	-7.6

● GEORGE CUNNINGHAM Cunningham, George Harold b: 7/13/1894, Sturgeon Lake, Minn. d: 3/10/72, Chattanooga, Tenn. BR/TR, 5'11", 185 lbs. Deb: 4/14/16 ♦

YEAR	TM/L	W	L	PCT	G	GS	CG	SH	SV	IP	H	HR	BB	SO	RAT	ERA	ERA+	OAV	OOB	BH	AVG	PB	PR	/A	PD	TPI
1916	Det-A	7	10	.412	35	14	5	0	2	150^{1}	146	0	74	68	13.4	2.75	104	.269	.360	11	.268	5	1	2	1	0.9
1917	Det-A	2	7	.222	44	8	4	0	4	139	113	2	51	49	10.9	2.91	91	.227	.304	6	.176	1	-4	-4	0	-0.4
1918	Det-A	6	7	.462	27	14	10	0	1	140	131	0	38	39	11.2	3.15	84	.255	.312	25	.223	3	-6	-8	0	-0.4
1919	Det-A	1	1	.500	17	0	0	0	1	47^{2}	54	0	15	11	14.0	4.91	65	.292	.361	5	.217	2	-9	-9	0	-0.7
Total	4	16	25	.390	123	36	19	0	8	477	444	2	178	167	12.1	3.13	89	.255	.330	47	.224	11	-17	-19	2	-0.6

● MIKE CUNNINGHAM Cunningham, Mody b: 6/14/1882, Lancaster, S.C. d: 12/10/69, Lancaster, S.C. BR/TR, 5'10.5", 175 lbs. Deb: 8/31/06

YEAR	TM/L	W	L	PCT	G	GS	CG	SH	SV	IP	H	HR	BB	SO	RAT	ERA	ERA+	OAV	OOB	BH	AVG	PB	PR	/A	PD	TPI
1906	Phi-A	1	0	1.000	5	1	1	0	0	28	29	1	9	15	12.5	3.21	85	.270	.332	4	.333	1	-2	-2	-0	-0.1

● NIG CUPPY Cuppy, George Joseph (b: George Koppe) b: 7/3/1869, Logansport, Ind. d: 7/27/22, Elkhart, Ind. BR/TR, 5'7", 160 lbs. Deb: 4/16/1892

YEAR	TM/L	W	L	PCT	G	GS	CG	SH	SV	IP	H	HR	BB	SO	RAT	ERA	ERA+	OAV	OOB	BH	AVG	PB	PR	/A	PD	TPI
1892	*Cle-N	28	13	.683	47	42	38	1	1	376	333	9	121	103	11.1	2.51	135	.228	.291	36	.214	1	32	37	3	3.9
1893	Cle-N	17	10	.630	31	30	24	0	0	243^{2}	316	6	75	39	14.8	4.47	109	.305	.357	27	.248	1	5	11	-1	0.9
1894	Cle-N	24	15	.615	43	33	29	**3**	0	316	381	11	128	65	14.8	4.56	120	.295	.363	35	.259	1	27	32	1	2.7
1895	*Cle-N	26	14	.650	47	40	36	1	2	353	384	9	95	91	12.4	3.54	141	.273	.322	40	.286	7	49	57	4	5.8
1896	*Cle-N	25	14	.641	46	40	35	1	1	358	388	8	75	86	11.8	3.12	146	.274	.314	38	.270	7	50	56	4	6.0
1897	Cle-N	10	6	.625	19	17	13	1	0	139^{1}	150	3	26	23	11.7	3.17	142	.273	.312	8	.145	-4	18	21	-1	1.4
1898	Cle-N	9	8	.529	18	15	13	1	0	128	147	4	25	27	12.5	3.30	110	.286	.326	5	.104	-4	4	4	-2	-0.1
1899	StL-N	11	8	.579	21	21	18	1	0	171^{2}	203	3	26	25	12.3	3.15	127	.294	.324	13	.186	-3	14	16	0	1.3
1900	Bos-N	8	4	.667	17	13	9	0	1	105^{1}	107	8	24	23	11.7	3.08	134	.263	.314	11	.262	1	7	12	-1	1.2
1901	Bos-A	4	6	.400	13	11	9	0	0	93^{1}	111	1	14	22	12.2	4.15	85	.292	.320	10	.204	0	-5	-6	-2	-0.7
Total	10	162	98	.623	302	262	224	9	5	2284^{1}	2520	62	609	504	12.6	3.48	127	.275	.325	223	.233	7	201	239	6	22.4

● SAMMY CURRAN Curran, Simon Francis b: 10/30/1874, Dorchester, Mass. d: 5/19/36, Dorchester, Mass. Deb: 8/01/02

YEAR	TM/L	W	L	PCT	G	GS	CG	SH	SV	IP	H	HR	BB	SO	RAT	ERA	ERA+	OAV	OOB	BH	AVG	PB	PR	/A	PD	TPI
1902	Bos-N	0	0	—	1	0	0	0	0	6^{2}	6	0	0	3	8.1	1.35	209	.240	.240	0	.000	-0	1	1	-0	0.0

● LAFAYETTE CURRENCE Currence, Delancy Lafayette b: 12/3/51, Rock Hill, S.C. BB/TL, 5'11", 175 lbs. Deb: 7/24/75

YEAR	TM/L	W	L	PCT	G	GS	CG	SH	SV	IP	H	HR	BB	SO	RAT	ERA	ERA+	OAV	OOB	BH	AVG	PB	PR	/A	PD	TPI
1975	Mil-A	0	2	.000	8	1	0	0	0	18^{2}	25	5	14	7	18.8	7.71	50	.316	.419	0	—	0	-8	-8	-1	-0.8

● CLARENCE CURRIE Currie, Clarence Ffranklin b: 12/30/1878, Glencoe, Ont., Can. d: 7/15/41, Little Chute, Wis BR/TR, Deb: 4/25/02

YEAR	TM/L	W	L	PCT	G	GS	CG	SH	SV	IP	H	HR	BB	SO	RAT	ERA	ERA+	OAV	OOB	BH	AVG	PB	PR	/A	PD	TPI
1902	Cin-N	3	4	.429	10	7	6	1	0	65^{1}	70	1	17	20	12.3	3.72	81	.274	.324	2	.083	-2	-7	-5	1	-0.7
	StL-N	7	5	.583	15	12	10	2	0	124^{2}	125	0	35	30	11.9	2.60	105	.261	.318	9	.196	-0	3	2	2	0.5
	Yr	10	9	.526	25	19	16	3	0	190	195	1	52	50	11.9	2.98	95	.265	.317	11	.157	-3	-4	-3	3	-0.2
1903	StL-N	4	12	.250	22	16	13	1	1	148	155	7	60	52	13.7	4.01	81	.281	.362	4	.085	-3	-12	-12	4	-1.1
	Chi-N	1	2	.333	6	3	2	0	1	33^{1}	35	1	9	9	12.7	2.97	106	.254	.313	5	.417	2	1	1	1	0.3
	Yr	5	14	.263	28	19	15	1	2	181^{1}	190	8	69	61	13.0	3.82	85	.271	.339	9	.153	-1	-11	-12	5	-0.8
Total	2	15	23	.395	53	38	31	4	2	371^{1}	385	9	121	111	12.7	3.39	89	.270	.336	20	.155	-4	-15	-15	8	-1.0

● MURPHY CURRIE Currie, Murphy Archibald b: 8/31/1893, Fayetteville, N.C. d: 6/22/39, Asheboro, N.C. BR/TR, 5'11.5", 185 lbs. Deb: 8/31/16

YEAR	TM/L	W	L	PCT	G	GS	CG	SH	SV	IP	H	HR	BB	SO	RAT	ERA	ERA+	OAV	OOB	BH	AVG	PB	PR	/A	PD	TPI
1916	StL-N	0	0	—	6	0	0	0	0	14^{1}	7	1	9	8	10.0	1.88	140	.149	.286	0	.000	-0	1	1	-1	0.1

● BILL CURRIE Currie, William Cleveland b: 11/29/28, Leary, Ga. BR/TR, 6', 175 lbs. Deb: 4/13/55

YEAR	TM/L	W	L	PCT	G	GS	CG	SH	SV	IP	H	HR	BB	SO	RAT	ERA	ERA+	OAV	OOB	BH	AVG	PB	PR	/A	PD	TPI
1955	Was-A	0	0	—	3	0	0	0	0	4^{1}	7	3	2	2	20.8	12.46	31	.350	.435	0	—	0	-4	-4	0	-0.4

● GEORGE CURRY Curry, George James "Soldier Boy" b: 12/21/1888, Bridgeport, Conn. d: 10/5/63, Stratford, Conn. BR/TR, 6', 185 lbs. Deb: 7/16/11

YEAR	TM/L	W	L	PCT	G	GS	CG	SH	SV	IP	H	HR	BB	SO	RAT	ERA	ERA+	OAV	OOB	BH	AVG	PB	PR	/A	PD	TPI
1911	StL-A	0	3	.000	3	3	0	0	0	15^{2}	19	0	24	2	24.7	7.47	45	.339	.538	0	.000	-1	-7	-7	-0	-0.7

● STEVE CURRY Curry, Stephen Thomas b: 9/13/65, Winter Park, Fla. BR/TR, 6'6", 217 lbs. Deb: 7/10/88

YEAR	TM/L	W	L	PCT	G	GS	CG	SH	SV	IP	H	HR	BB	SO	RAT	ERA	ERA+	OAV	OOB	BH	AVG	PB	PR	/A	PD	TPI
1988	Bos-A	0	1	.000	3	3	0	0	0	11	15	0	14	4	23.7	8.18	50	.357	.518	0	—	0	-5	-5	0	-0.5

● WES CURRY Curry, Wesley b: 4/1/1860, Wilmington, Del. d: 5/19/33, Philadelphia, Pa. Deb: 8/06/1884 U

YEAR	TM/L	W	L	PCT	G	GS	CG	SH	SV	IP	H	HR	BB	SO	RAT	ERA	ERA+	OAV	OOB	BH	AVG	PB	PR	/A	PD	TPI
1884	Ric-a	0	2	.000	2	2	2	0	0	16	15	2	3	1	10.7	5.06	66	.221	.264	2	.250	-0	-3	-3	-0	-0.3

● CLIFF CURTIS Curtis, Clifton Garfield b: 7/3/1883, Delaware, Ohio d: 4/23/43, Newark, Ohio BR/TR, 6'2", 180 lbs. Deb: 8/23/09

YEAR	TM/L	W	L	PCT	G	GS	CG	SH	SV	IP	H	HR	BB	SO	RAT	ERA	ERA+	OAV	OOB	BH	AVG	PB	PR	/A	PD	TPI
1909	Bos-N	4	5	.444	10	9	8	2	0	83	53	1	30	22	9.2	1.41	200	.191	.275	1	.034	-3	11	13	1	1.3
1910	Bos-N	6	24	.200	43	37	12	2	2	251	251	9	124	75	13.9	3.55	94	.277	.371	12	.146	-5	-14	-6	6	-0.5
1911	Bos-N	1	8	.111	12	9	5	0	1	77	79	4	34	23	13.4	4.44	86	.265	.344	7	.250	-0	-9	-5	1	-0.5
	Chi-N	1	2	.333	4	1	0	0	0	7	7	0	5	4	19.3	3.86	86	.241	.405	1	.500	0	-0	-0	0	0.0
	Phi-N	2	1	.667	8	5	3	1	0	45	45	0	15	13	12.2	2.60	132	.260	.323	4	.267	0	4	4	-0	0.4
	Yr	4	11	.267	24	15	8	1	1	129	131	4	54	40	13.0	3.77	97	.259	.332	12	.267	0	-5	-1	0	-0.1
1912	Phi-N	2	5	.286	10	8	2	0	0	50	55	3	17	20	13.7	3.24	112	.286	.357	0	.000	-2	1	2	1	0.1
	Bro-N	4	7	.364	19	9	3	0	1	80	72	4	37	22	12.9	3.94	85	.250	.347	8	.308	1	-5	-5	-0	-0.4
	Yr	6	12	.333	29	17	5	0	1	130	127	7	54	42	12.9	3.67	94	.262	.344	8	.195	-1	-4	-3	1	-0.3
1913	Bro-N	8	9	.471	30	16	6	0	2	151^{2}	145	1	55	57	12.3	3.26	101	.255	.328	6	.122	-3	-1	1	2	-0.1
Total	5	28	61	.315	136	94	39	5	6	744^{2}	707	22	317	236	12.8	3.31	101	.259	.344	39	.159	-11	-13	3	9	0.3

● JACK CURTIS Curtis, Jack Patrick b: 1/11/37, Rhodhiss, N.C. BL/TL, 5'10", 175 lbs. Deb: 4/22/61

YEAR	TM/L	W	L	PCT	G	GS	CG	SH	SV	IP	H	HR	BB	SO	RAT	ERA	ERA+	OAV	OOB	BH	AVG	PB	PR	/A	PD	TPI
1961	Chi-N	10	13	.435	31	27	6	0	0	180^{1}	220	23	51	57	13.6	4.89	85	.303	.350	10	.167	3	-17	-14	0	-1.0
1962	Chi-N	0	2	.000	4	3	0	0	0	18	18	2	6	8	12.0	3.50	118	.277	.338	1	.250	0	1	1	-0	0.1
	Mil-N	4	4	.500	30	5	0	0	1	75^{2}	82	8	27	40	13.2	4.16	91	.282	.347	4	.222	2	-2	-3	-1	-0.2
	Yr	4	6	.400	34	8	0	0	1	93^{2}	100	10	33	48	13.0	4.04	96	.280	.344	5	.227	2	-1	-2	-1	-0.1
1963	Cle-A	0	0	—	4	0	0	0	0	5	8	0	5	3	25.2	18.00	20	.348	.483	0	—	0	-8	-8	0	-0.7
Total	3	14	19	.424	69	35	6	0	1	279	328	33	89	108	13.6	4.84	84	.297	.352	15	.183	5	-26	-24	-1	-1.8

● JACK CURTIS Curtis, John Duffield b: 3/9/48, Newton, Mass. BL/TL, 6'2", 185 lbs. Deb: 8/13/70

YEAR	TM/L	W	L	PCT	G	GS	CG	SH	SV	IP	H	HR	BB	SO	RAT	ERA	ERA+	OAV	OOB	BH	AVG	PB	PR	/A	PD	TPI
1970	Bos-A	0	0	—	1	0	0	0	0	2^{1}	4	1	1	1	19.3	11.57	34	.333	.385	0	—	0	-2	-2	0	-0.2
1971	Bos-A	2	2	.500	5	3	1	0	0	26	30	3	6	19	12.5	3.12	119	.291	.330	1	.111	-0	1	2	-1	0.0
1972	Bos-A	11	8	.579	26	21	8	3	0	154^{1}	161	8	50	106	12.3	3.73	86	.271	.328	5	.094	-3	-12	-9	-0	-1.3
1973	Bos-A	13	13	.500	35	30	10	4	0	221^{1}	225	24	83	101	12.6	3.58	112	.264	.331	0	—	0	6	11	-1	0.9
1974	StL-N	10	14	.417	33	29	5	2	1	195	199	15	83	89	13.1	3.78	94	.267	.342	10	.159	-0	-4	-5	0	-0.5
1975	StL-N	8	9	.471	39	18	4	0	1	146^{2}	151	13	65	67	13.4	3.44	109	.268	.346	8	.211	2	3	5	2	0.9
1976	StL-N	6	11	.353	37	15	3	1	1	134	139	11	65	52	13.7	4.50	79	.276	.359	7	.200	3	-15	-14	0	-1.3
1977	SF-N	3	3	.500	43	9	1	1	1	77	95	5	48	47	16.8	5.49	71	.314	.409	3	.231	1	-14	-14	1	-1.1
1978	SF-N	4	3	.571	46	0	0	0	1	63	60	1	29	38	12.7	3.71	93	.262	.345	0	.000	-0	-1	-2	0	-0.2
1979	SF-N	10	9	.526	27	18	3	2	0	120^{2}	121	15	42	85	12.2	4.18	84	.257	.318	5	.147	1	-6	-9	-1	-0.9
1980	SD-N	10	8	.556	30	27	6	0	0	187	184	9	67	71	12.2	3.51	98	.262	.329	12	.194	1	2	-2	1	0.0

YEAR	TM/L	W	L	PCT	G	GS	CG	SH	SV	IP	H	HR	BB	SO	RAT	ERA	ERA+	OAV	OOB	BH	AVG	PB	PR	/A	PD	TPI
1981	SD-N	2	6	.250	28	8	0	0	0	66^{2}	70	11	30	31	13.6	5.13	63	.275	.353	1	.077	-1	-12	-14	-0	-1.5
1982	SD-N	8	6	.571	26	18	1	1	0	116^{1}	121	15	46	54	13.0	4.10	83	.271	.341	11	.297	3	-6	-9	-1	-0.7
	Cal-A	0	1	.000	8	0	0	0	1	12	16	0	3	10	14.3	6.00	68	.320	.358	0	—	0	-3	-3	-0	-0.3
1983	Cal-A	1	2	.333	37	3	0	0	5	90	89	5	40	36	13.1	3.80	106	.258	.339	0	—	0	3	2	-1	0.1
1984	Cal-A	1	2	.333	17	0	0	0	0	28^{2}	30	4	11	18	12.9	4.40	90	.263	.328	0	—	0	-1	-1	0	-0.1
Total	15	89	97	.478	438	199	42	14	11	1641	1695	140	669	825	13.0	3.96	91	.270	.341	63	.175	4	-61	-63	-1	-6.2
● VERN CURTIS	Curtis, Vernon Eugene "Turk" b: 5/24/20, Cairo, Ill. BR/TR, 6', 170 lbs. Deb: 9/06/43																									
1943	Was-A	0	0	—	2	0	0	0	0	4	3	0	6	1	20.3	6.75	47	.200	.429	0	—	0	-2	-2	-0	-0.2
1944	Was-A	0	1	.000	3	1	0	0	0	9^{2}	8	0	3	2	10.2	2.79	117	.235	.297	0	.000	-0	1	0	-0	0.0
1946	Was-A	0	0	—	11	0	0	0	0	16^{1}	19	1	10	7	16.0	7.16	47	.297	.392	0	.000	-0	-7	-7	0	-0.7
Total	3	0	1	.000	16	1	0	0	0	30	30	1	19	10	14.7	5.70	58	.265	.371	0	.000	-1	-7	-8	-0	-0.9
● ED CUSHMAN	Cushman, Edgar Leander b: 3/27/1852, Eaglesville, Ohio d: 9/26/15, Erie, Pa. BR/TL, Deb: 7/06/1883																									
1883	Buf-N	3	3	.500	7	7	5	0	0	50^{1}	61	0	17	34	13.9	3.93	81	.285	.338	5	.217	-0	-4	-4	-0	-0.4
1884	Mil-U	4	0	1.000	4	4	4	2	0	36	10	0	3	47	3.3	1.00	164	.082	.104	1	.091	0	8	3	-1	0.2
1885	Phi-a	3	7	.300	10	10	10	0	0	87	101	1	17	37	12.5	3.52	98	.269	.306	7	.189	-1	-3	-1	-1	-0.3
	NY-a	8	14	.364	22	22	22	0	0	191	158	2	33	133	9.1	2.78	106	.210	.246	10	.145	-0	10	4	-2	0.1
	Yr	11	21	.344	32	32	32	0	0	278	259	3	50	170	10.1	3.01	103	.229	.263	17	.160	-2	7	3	-3	-0.2
1886	NY-a	17	20	.459	38	37	37	2	0	325^{2}	278	6	99	167	10.4	3.12	109	.220	.277	19	.151	-7	12	10	0	0.4
1887	NY-a	10	15	.400	26	26	25	0	0	220	310	9	83	64	16.4	5.97	71	.325	.384	23	.247	3	-41	-42	-1	-3.0
1890	Tol-a	17	21	.447	40	38	34	0	1	315^{2}	346	5	107	125	13.2	4.19	94	.270	.331	13	.100	-9	-11	-8	-5	-1.9
Total	6	62	80	.437	147	144	137	4	1	1225^{2}	1264	23	359	607	12.1	3.86	92	.254	.308	78	.160	-15	-29	-40	-10	-4.9
● HARVEY CUSHMAN	Cushman, Harvey Barnes b: 7/10/1877, Rockland, Me. d: 12/27/20, Emsworth, Pa. Deb: 8/24/02																									
1902	Pit-N	0	4	.000	4	4	3	0	0	25^{2}	30	0	31	12	22.1	7.36	37	.291	.463	2	.200	-0	-13	-13	-1	-1.2
● MIKE CVENGROS	Cvengros, Michael John b: 12/1/01, Pana, Ill. d: 8/2/70, Hot Springs, Ark. BL/TL, 5'8", 159 lbs. Deb: 9/30/22																									
1922	NY-N	0	1	.000	1	1	1	0	0	9	6	1	3	3	10.0	4.00	100	.194	.286	0	.000	-0	0	0	0	0.0
1923	Chi-A	12	13	.480	40	26	14	0	3	214^{1}	216	6	107	86	14.1	4.41	90	.269	.364	15	.203	-1	-10	-11	0	-1.2
1924	Chi-A	3	12	.200	26	15	2	0	0	105^{2}	119	5	67	36	16.1	5.88	70	.300	.405	6	.200	2	-19	-21	0	-1.7
1925	Chi-A	3	9	.250	22	11	4	0	0	104^{2}	109	7	55	32	14.4	4.30	97	.278	.371	5	.152	-1	1	-2	-0	-0.3
1927	*Pit-N	2	1	.667	23	4	0	0	1	53^{2}	55	3	24	21	13.4	3.35	123	.271	.351	3	.158	-0	3	5	1	0.5
1929	Chi-N	5	4	.556	32	2	0	0	2	64	82	2	29	23	15.8	4.64	99	.319	.390	6	.400	2	1	-0	0	0.2
Total	6	25	40	.385	144	59	21	0	6	551^{1}	587	24	285	201	14.6	4.59	90	.282	.374	35	.201	1	-24	-28	1	-2.5
● JOHN D'ACQUISTO	D'Acquisto, John Francis b: 12/24/51, San Diego, Cal. BR/TR, 6'2", 205 lbs. Deb: 9/02/73																									
1973	SF-N	1	1	.500	7	3	1	0	0	27^{2}	23	4	19	29	13.7	3.58	107	.219	.339	0	.000	-1	0	1	-0	-0.1
1974	SF-N	12	14	.462	38	36	5	1	0	215	182	13	124	167	13.1	3.77	101	.227	.334	8	.113	-1	-4	1	-4	-0.4
1975	SF-N	2	4	.333	10	6	0	0	0	28	29	5	34	22	20.9	10.29	37	.264	.445	0	.000	-0	-21	-20	-1	-1.9
1976	SF-N	3	8	.273	28	19	0	0	0	106	93	5	102	53	16.8	5.35	68	.243	.406	7	.269	2	-22	-20	-0	-1.9
1977	StL-N	0	0	—	3	2	0	0	0	8^{1}	5	0	10	9	17.3	4.32	89	.185	.421	0	.000	-0	-0	-0	-0	-0.1
	SD-N	1	2	.333	17	12	0	0	0	44	49	3	47	45	19.8	6.95	51	.297	.455	0	.000	-0	-15	-17	0	-1.6
	Yr	1	2	.333	20	14	0	0	0	52^{1}	54	3	57	54	19.3	6.54	55	.278	.444	0	.000	-1	-15	-17	0	-1.7
1978	SD-N	4	3	.571	45	3	0	0	10	93	60	2	56	104	11.3	2.13	156	.185	.307	4	.190	1	15	12	-1	1.3
1979	SD-N	9	13	.409	51	11	1	1	2	133^{2}	140	15	86	97	15.4	4.92	72	.275	.383	4	.129	1	-18	-21	-2	-2.2
1980	SD-N	2	3	.400	39	0	0	0	1	67	67	2	36	44	14.0	3.76	91	.270	.365	0	.000	-1	-1	-2	-0	-0.4
	Mon-N	0	2	.000	11	0	0	0	2	20^{2}	14	0	9	15	10.0	2.18	164	.206	.299	0	—	0	3	3	0	0.3
	Yr	2	5	.286	50	0	0	0	3	87^{2}	81	2	45	59	12.9	3.39	102	.252	.343	0	.000	-1	2	1	-0	-0.1
1981	Cal-A	0	0	—	6	0	0	0	0	19^{1}	26	2	12	8	18.2	10.71	34	.338	.433	0	—	0	-15	-15	-0	-1.4
1982	Oak-A	0	1	.000	11	0	0	0	0	17	20	1	9	7	15.4	5.29	74	.290	.372	0	—	0	-2	-3	0	0.0
Total	10	34	51	.400	266	92	7	2	15	779^{2}	708	52	544	600	14.7	4.56	79	.245	.368	23	.127	0	-79	-81	-9	-8.4
● JOHN DAGENHARD	Dagenhard, John Douglas b: 4/25/17, Magnolia, Ohio BR/TR, 6'2", 195 lbs. Deb: 9/28/43																									
1943	Bos-N	1	0	1.000	2	1	1	0	0	11	9	0	4	2	12.3	0.00	—	.225	.326	0	.000	-0	4	4	1	0.6
● PETE DAGLIA	Daglia, Peter George b: 2/28/06, Napa, Cal. d: 3/11/52, Willits, Cal. BR/TR, 6'1", 200 lbs. Deb: 6/08/32																									
1932	Chi-A	2	4	.333	12	5	2	0	0	50	67	4	20	16	16.4	5.76	75	.324	.394	1	.077	-1	-7	-8	-1	-0.9
● JAY DAHL	Dahl, Jay Steven b: 12/6/45, San Bernardino, Cal. d: 6/20/65, Salisbury, N.C. BB/TL, 5'10", 183 lbs. Deb: 9/27/63																									
1963	Hou-N	0	1	.000	1	1	0	0	0	2^{2}	7	0	0	0	23.6	16.88	19	.438	.438	0	—	0	-4	-4	-0	-0.4
● JERRY DAHLKE	Dahlke, Jerome Alexander "Joe" b: 6/8/30, Marathon, Wis. BR/TR, 6', 180 lbs. Deb: 5/06/56																									
1956	Chi-A	0	0	—	5	0	0	0	0	2^{1}	5	0	6	1	42.4	19.29	21	.455	.647	0	—	0	-4	-4	0	-0.4
● SAM DAILEY	Dailey, Samuel Laurence b: 3/31/04, Oakford, Ill. d: 12/2/79, Columbia, Mo. BL/TR, 5'11", 168 lbs. Deb: 7/04/29																									
1929	Phi-N	2	2	.500	20	5	0	0	0	51^{1}	74	5	23	18	17.2	7.54	69	.349	.415	1	.059	-2	-16	-13	-1	-1.5
● VINCE DAILEY	Dailey, Vincent Perry b: 12/25/1864, Osceola, Pa. d: 11/14/19, Hornell, N.Y. 6', 200 lbs. Deb: 4/21/1890 ♦																									
1890	Cle-N	0	1	.000	2	1	0	0	0	7	12	0	7	0	24.4	7.71	46	.367	.478	71	.289	1	-3	-3	0	-0.2
● BILL DAILEY	Dailey, William Garland b: 5/13/35, Arlington, Va. BR/TR, 6'3", 185 lbs. Deb: 8/17/61																									
1961	Cle-A	1	0	1.000	12	0	0	0	0	19	16	0	6	7	10.4	0.95	415	.232	.293	0	.000	-0	6	6	0	0.7
1962	Cle-A	2	2	.500	27	0	0	0	1	42^{2}	43	0	17	24	13.1	3.59	108	.270	.348	0	.000	-0	2	1	-0	0.1
1963	Min-A	6	3	.667	66	0	0	0	21	108^{2}	80	9	19	72	8.2	1.99	183	.208	.246	5	.238	2	20	20	2	2.6
1964	Min-A	1	2	.333	14	0	0	0	0	15^{1}	23	3	17	6	25.8	8.22	44	.377	.537	0	—	0	-8	-8	0	-0.8
Total	4	10	7	.588	119	0	0	0	22	185^{2}	162	12	59	109	11.0	2.76	135	.241	.308	5	.192	1	20	20	3	2.6
● ED DAILY	Daily, Edward M. b: 9/7/1862, Providence, R.I. d: 10/21/1891, Washington, D.C. BR/TR, 5'10.5", 174 lbs. Deb: 5/04/1885 F♦																									
1885	Phi-N	26	23	.531	50	50	49	4	0	440	370	12	90	140	9.4	2.21	126	.217	.256	38	.207	-0	30	28	-4	2.4
1886	Phi-N	16	9	.640	27	23	22	1	0	218	211	7	59	95	11.1	3.06	108	.242	.290	70	.227	3	6	6	2	0.8
1887	Phi-N	0	4	.000	6	5	4	0	0	41^{1}	52	2	25	7	16.8	7.19	59	.289	.376	30	.283	1	-14	-14	1	-0.9
	Was-N	0	1	.000	1	1	1	0	0	7	5	0	6	3	14.1	7.71	53	.208	.367	78	.251	0	-3	-3	0	-0.2
	Yr	0	5	.000	7	6	5	0	0	48^{1}	57	2	31	10	16.4	7.26	58	.279	.374	108	.259	1	-17	-16	1	-1.1
1888	Was-N	2	7	.222	9	8	8	0	0	73^{2}	88	7	19	20	13.4	4.89	57	.278	.325	102	.225	1	-17	-17	0	-1.4
1889	Col-a	0	0	—	2	0	0	0	1	1^{2}	1	0	4	2	27.0	21.60	17	.168	.503	148	.256	0	-3	-3	-0	-0.3
1890	Bro-a	10	15	.400	27	27	27	0	0	235^{2}	252	3	93	82	13.9	4.05	96	.265	.342	94	.239	4	-5	-4	2	0.2
	NY-N	2	0	1.000	2	1	1	0	0	16	6	0	6	0	9.0	2.25	156	.112	.252	2	.133	-1	2	2	1	0.2
	*Lou-a	6	3	.667	12	10	9	1	0	93	83	2	30	31	11.3	1.94	199	.232	.298	20	.250	3	20	20	2	2.4
1891	Lou-a	4	8	.333	15	14	11	0	0	111^{1}	149	6	48	27	16.6	5.74	64	.310	.382	16	.250	2	-25	-26	0	-1.9
Total	7	66	70	.485	151	139	132	6	1	1237^{2}	1217	39	380	407	11.9	3.39	98	.246	.305	616	.239	12	-8	-11	5	1.3
● HUGH DAILY	Daily, Hugh Ignatius "One Arm" (b: Harry Criss) b: 1857, Baltimore, Md. BR/TR, 6'2", 180 lbs. Deb: 5/01/1882																									
1882	Buf-N	15	14	.517	29	29	29	0	0	255^{2}	246	6	70	116	11.1	2.99	98	.234	.282	18	.164	-6	-3	-2	-5	-1.1
1883	Cle-N	23	19	.548	45	43	40	4	1	378^{2}	360	5	99	171	10.9	2.42	130	.243	.291	18	.127	-10	30	31	-1	1.8
1884	CP-U	27	27	.500	56	56	54	5	0	484^{2}	430	11	71	469	9.3	2.43	124	.222	.249	43	.219	-2	32	32	1	2.8

YEAR TM/L	W	L	PCT	G	GS	CG	SH	SV	IP	H	HR	BB	SO	RAT	ERA	ERA+	OAV	OOB	BH	AVG	PB	PR	/A	PD	TPI
Was-U	1	1	.500	2	2	2	0	0	16	16	0	1	14	9.6	2.25	132	.243	.255	0	.000	-1	1	1	-0	0.0
Yr	28	28	.500	58	58	56	5	0	500^{2}	446	11	72	**483**	9.3	2.43	124	.223	.250	43	.214	-3	33	33	1	2.8
1885 StL-N	3	8	.273	11	11	10	1	0	91^{1}	92	5	44	31	13.4	3.94	70	.252	.333	3	.086	-3	-11	-12	-0	-1.3
1886 Was-N	0	6	.000	6	6	6	0	0	49	69	2	40	15	20.0	7.35	45	.332	.440	2	.125	-1	-22	-22	-0	-1.8
1887 Cle-a	4	12	.250	16	16	16	0	0	139^{2}	181	1	44	30	14.7	3.67	118	.311	.362	4	.069	-8	10	10	-1	0.1
Total 6	73	87	.456	165	163	157	10	1	1415	1394	30	369	846	11.2	2.92	108	.245	.291	88	.157	-30	37	38	-6	0.5

● BRUCE DalCANTON

DalCanton, John Bruce b: 6/15/42, California, Pa. BR/TR, 6'2", 205 lbs. Deb: 9/03/67 C

YEAR TM/L	W	L	PCT	G	GS	CG	SH	SV	IP	H	HR	BB	SO	RAT	ERA	ERA+	OAV	OOB	BH	AVG	PB	PR	/A	PD	TPI
1967 Pit-N	2	1	.667	8	2	1	0	0	24	19	1	10	13	11.3	1.88	179	.211	.297	2	.333	1	4	4	-1	0.5
1968 Pit-N	1	1	.500	7	0	0	0	2	17	7	0	6	8	7.9	2.12	138	.127	.238	0	.000	-0	2	2	-1	0.1
1969 Pit-N	8	2	.800	57	0	0	0	5	86^{1}	79	3	49	56	13.3	3.34	105	.252	.353	3	.300	2	2	1	-0	0.3
1970 Pit-N	9	4	.692	41	6	1	0	1	84^{2}	94	7	39	53	14.2	4.57	85	.282	.359	0	.000	-1	-5	-6	-1	-0.8
1971 KC-A	8	6	.571	25	22	2	0	0	141^{1}	144	8	44	58	12.0	3.44	100	.262	.317	4	.087	-3	0	-0	-2	-0.4
1972 KC-A	6	6	.500	35	16	1	0	2	132^{1}	135	7	29	75	11.2	3.40	89	.265	.306	4	.098	-2	-5	-5	-2	-1.0
1973 KC-A	4	3	.571	32	3	1	0	3	97^{1}	108	8	46	38	14.6	4.81	85	.284	.367	0	—	0	-11	-8	0	-0.9
1974 KC-A	8	10	.444	31	22	9	2	0	175^{1}	135	5	82	96	11.4	3.13	122	.211	.306	0	—	0	9	13	0	1.5
1975 KC-A	0	2	.000	4	2	0	0	0	8^{2}	23	0	7	5	32.2	15.58	25	.479	.554	0	—	0	-11	-11	0	-1.0
Atl-N	2	7	.222	26	9	0	0	3	67	63	2	24	38	12.5	3.36	112	.248	.327	2	.105	-1	2	3	1	0.3
1976 Atl-N	3	5	.375	42	1	0	0	1	73^{1}	67	6	42	36	13.6	3.56	106	.244	.348	2	.222	0	-0	2	1	0.3
1977 Chi-A	0	2	.000	8	0	0	0	2	24	20	1	13	9	12.4	3.75	109	.230	.330	0	—	0	1	1	-1	0.0
Total 11	51	49	.510	316	83	15	2	19	931^{1}	894	48	391	485	12.6	3.67	99	.253	.331	17	.113	-3	-12	-5	-3	-1.1

● GENE DALE

Dale, Emmett Eugene b: 6/16/1889, St.Louis, Mo. d: 3/20/58, St.Louis, Mo. BR/TR, 6'3", 179 lbs. Deb: 9/19/11

YEAR TM/L	W	L	PCT	G	GS	CG	SH	SV	IP	H	HR	BB	SO	RAT	ERA	ERA+	OAV	OOB	BH	AVG	PB	PR	/A	PD	TPI
1911 StL-N	0	2	.000	5	2	0	0	0	14^{2}	13	0	16	13	19.0	6.75	50	.250	.443	2	.400	1	-5	-5	0	-0.5
1912 StL-N	0	5	.000	19	3	1	0	0	61^{2}	76	4	51	37	19.0	6.57	52	.311	.436	6	.273	1	-22	-22	-1	-2.0
1915 Cin-N	18	17	.514	49	35	20	4	3	296^{2}	256	6	107	104	11.2	2.46	116	.243	.316	20	.220	2	10	13	-1	1.6
1916 Cin-N	3	4	.429	17	5	2	0	0	69^{2}	80	3	33	23	14.9	5.17	50	.304	.386	3	.143	-0	-20	-20	1	-2.0
Total 4	21	28	.429	90	45	23	4	3	442^{2}	425	13	207	177	13.1	3.60	81	.263	.352	31	.223	3	-37	-34	-1	-2.9

● BUD DALEY

Daley, Leavitt Leo b: 10/7/32, Orange, Cal. BL/TL, 6'1", 185 lbs. Deb: 9/10/55

YEAR TM/L	W	L	PCT	G	GS	CG	SH	SV	IP	H	HR	BB	SO	RAT	ERA	ERA+	OAV	OOB	BH	AVG	PB	PR	/A	PD	TPI
1955 Cle-A	0	1	.000	2	1	0	0	0	7	10	1	1	2	14.1	6.43	62	.333	.355	0	.000	-0	-2	-2	0	-0.2
1956 Cle-A	1	0	1.000	14	0	0	0	0	20^{1}	21	2	14	13	17.7	6.20	68	.273	.417	0	.000	-0	-5	-5	1	-0.4
1957 Cle-A	2	8	.200	34	10	1	0	2	87^{1}	99	7	40	54	15.4	4.43	84	.279	.368	4	.200	0	-6	-7	1	-0.6
1958 KC-A	3	2	.600	26	5	1	0	0	70^{2}	67	5	19	39	11.7	3.31	118	.249	.313	2	.125	-1	4	5	1	0.5
1959 KC-A★	16	13	.552	39	29	12	2	1	216^{1}	212	24	62	125	11.9	3.16	127	.257	.317	23	.295	5	17	20	-0	2.6
1960 KC-A★	16	16	.500	37	35	13	1	0	231	234	27	96	126	13.2	4.56	87	.263	.341	12	.160	1	-18	-15	1	-1.3
1961 KC-A	4	8	.333	16	10	2	0	1	63^{2}	84	6	22	36	15.7	4.95	83	.319	.383	2	.111	-1	-7	-6	1	-0.6
*NY-A	8	9	.471	23	17	7	0	0	129^{2}	127	17	51	83	12.6	3.96	94	.257	.331	6	.133	-1	1	-3	-1	-0.5
Yr	12	17	.414	39	27	9	0	1	193^{1}	211	23	73	119	13.4	4.28	90	.275	.341	8	.127	-2	-6	-9	-0	-1.1
1962 *NY-A	7	5	.583	43	6	0	0	4	105^{1}	105	8	21	55	11.2	3.59	104	.258	.303	5	.185	-0	4	2	-0	0.1
1963 NY-A	0	0	—	1	0	0	0	1	1	2	0	0	0	18.0	0.00	—	.667	.667	0	—	0	0	0	-0	0.0
1964 NY-A	3	2	.600	13	3	0	0	1	35	37	3	25	16	17.0	4.63	78	.274	.402	2	.250	1	-4	-4	1	-0.3
Total 10	60	64	.484	248	116	36	3	10	967^{1}	998	100	351	549	13.1	4.03	97	.266	.339	56	.192	3	-15	-14	4	-0.7

● BILL DALEY

Daley, William b: 6/27/1868, Poughkeepsie, N.Y d: 5/4/22, Poughkeepsie, N.Y. TL , Deb: 7/17/1889

YEAR TM/L	W	L	PCT	G	GS	CG	SH	SV	IP	H	HR	BB	SO	RAT	ERA	ERA+	OAV	OOB	BH	AVG	PB	PR	/A	PD	TPI
1889 Bos-N	3	3	.500	9	7	4	0	0	48	34	1	43	40	14.8	4.31	97	.193	.357	3	.150	-1	-2	-1	3	0.1
1890 Bos-P	18	7	**.720**	34	25	19	2	2	235	246	7	167	110	16.2	3.60	122	.258	.373	17	.155	-5	17	21	-1	1.2
1891 Bos-a	8	6	.571	19	11	10	0	**2**	126^{2}	119	6	81	68	14.7	2.98	117	.240	.355	10	.169	-2	10	7	1	0.4
Total 3	29	16	.644	62	43	33	2	4	409^{2}	399	14	291	218	15.6	3.49	117	.245	.366	30	.159	-8	25	27	3	1.7

● MIKE DALTON

Dalton, Michael Edward b: 3/27/63, Palo Alto, Cal. BR/TL, 6', 215 lbs. Deb: 5/31/91

YEAR TM/L	W	L	PCT	G	GS	CG	SH	SV	IP	H	HR	BB	SO	RAT	ERA	ERA+	OAV	OOB	BH	AVG	PB	PR	/A	PD	TPI
1991 Det-A	0	0	—	4	0	0	0	0	8	12	2	2	4	15.8	3.38	123	.333	.368	0	—	0	1	1	0	0.0

● GEORGE DALY

Daly, George Josephs "Pecks" b: 7/28/1887, Buffalo, N.Y. d: 12/12/57, Buffalo, N.Y. BR/TR, 5'10.5", 175 lbs. Deb: 9/26/09

YEAR TM/L	W	L	PCT	G	GS	CG	SH	SV	IP	H	HR	BB	SO	RAT	ERA	ERA+	OAV	OOB	BH	AVG	PB	PR	/A	PD	TPI
1909 NY-N	0	3	.000	3	3	3	0	0	21	31	0	8	8	17.1	6.00	43	.341	.400	1	.111	-1	-8	-8	-1	-0.9

● BILL DAMMANN

Dammann, William Henry "Wee Willie" b: 8/9/1872, Chicago, Ill. d: 12/6/48, Lynnhaven, Va. BL/TL, 5'7", 155 lbs. Deb: 4/24/1897

YEAR TM/L	W	L	PCT	G	GS	CG	SH	SV	IP	H	HR	BB	SO	RAT	ERA	ERA+	OAV	OOB	BH	AVG	PB	PR	/A	PD	TPI
1897 Cin-N	6	4	.600	16	11	7	1	0	95	122	2	37	21	15.5	4.74	96	.309	.376	5	.161	-1	-4	-2	1	-0.2
1898 Cin-N	16	10	.615	35	22	16	2	2	224^{2}	277	3	67	51	14.1	3.61	106	.301	.353	16	.195	1	0	6	-3	0.4
1899 Cin-N	2	1	.667	9	5	3	1	1	48	74	0	11	2	16.1	4.88	80	.351	.386	1	.056	-2	-5	-5	0	-0.6
Total 3	24	15	.615	60	38	26	4	3	367^{2}	473	5	115	74	14.7	4.06	99	.310	.363	22	.168	-2	-10	-1	-2	-0.4

● ART DANEY

Daney, Arthur Lee b: 7/9/04, Talihina, Okla. d: 3/11/88, Phoenix, Ariz. BR/TR, 5'11", 165 lbs. Deb: 5/25/28

YEAR TM/L	W	L	PCT	G	GS	CG	SH	SV	IP	H	HR	BB	SO	RAT	ERA	ERA+	OAV	OOB	BH	AVG	PB	PR	/A	PD	TPI
1928 Phi-A	0	0	—	1	0	0	0	0	1	1	0	0	0	9.0	0.00	—	.250	.250	0	—	0	0	0	0	0.1

● DAVE DANFORTH

Danforth, David Charles "Dauntless Dave" b: 3/7/1890, Granger, Tex. d: 9/19/70, Baltimore, Md. BL/TL, 6', 167 lbs. Deb: 8/01/11

YEAR TM/L	W	L	PCT	G	GS	CG	SH	SV	IP	H	HR	BB	SO	RAT	ERA	ERA+	OAV	OOB	BH	AVG	PB	PR	/A	PD	TPI
1911 Phi-A	4	1	.800	14	2	1	0	1	33^{2}	29	1	17	21	13.1	3.74	84	.240	.348	1	.167	0	-1	-2	-0	-0.2
1912 Phi-A	0	0	—	3	0	0	0	0	20^{1}	26	0	12	8	16.8	3.98	77	.338	.427	2	.250	0	-2	-2	0	-0.2
1916 Chi-A	6	5	.545	28	8	1	0	2	93^{2}	87	1	37	49	12.2	3.27	85	.259	.338	2	.087	-1	-5	-5	1	-0.6
1917 *Chi-A	11	6	.647	**50**	9	1	1	**9**	173	155	1	74	79	12.1	2.65	100	.244	.325	6	.130	0	0	0	-3	-0.3
1918 Chi-A	6	15	.286	39	11	5	0	2	139	148	1	40	48	12.5	3.43	80	.288	.345	6	.143	-2	-10	-11	0	-1.3
1919 Chi-A	1	2	.333	15	1	0	0	1	41^{2}	58	1	20	17	17.1	7.78	41	.333	.405	1	.111	0	-21	-21	-0	-2.1
1922 StL-A	5	2	.714	20	10	3	0	1	79^{2}	93	1	38	48	14.9	3.28	127	.304	.383	2	.087	-2	7	8	1	0.4
1923 StL-A	16	14	.533	38	26	16	0	1	226^{1}	221	4	87	96	12.7	3.94	106	.262	.340	15	.211	3	1	6	-1	0.7
1924 StL-A	15	12	.556	41	27	11	1	4	219^{2}	246	16	69	65	13.0	4.51	100	.292	.348	13	.171	-2	-7	0	-3	-0.4
1925 StL-A	7	9	.438	38	15	5	0	2	159	172	19	61	53	13.4	4.36	107	.284	.353	8	.174	-2	1	6	-4	0.0
Total 10	71	66	.518	286	109	43	2	23	1186	1235	45	455	484	13.1	3.89	95	.277	.349	56	.160	-6	-37	-25	-10	-4.0

● CHUCK DANIEL

Daniel, Charles Edward b: 9/17/33, Bluffton, Ark. BR/TR, 6'2", 195 lbs. Deb: 9/21/57

YEAR TM/L	W	L	PCT	G	GS	CG	SH	SV	IP	H	HR	BB	SO	RAT	ERA	ERA+	OAV	OOB	BH	AVG	PB	PR	/A	PD	TPI
1957 Det-A	0	0	—	1	0	0	0	0	2^{1}	3	1	0	2	11.6	7.71	50	.333	.333	0	—	0	-1	-1	-0	-0.1

● BENNIE DANIELS

Daniels, Bennie b: 6/17/32, Tuscaloosa, Ala. BL/TR, 6'1.5", 193 lbs. Deb: 9/24/57

YEAR TM/L	W	L	PCT	G	GS	CG	SH	SV	IP	H	HR	BB	SO	RAT	ERA	ERA+	OAV	OOB	BH	AVG	PB	PR	/A	PD	TPI
1957 Pit-N	0	1	.000	1	1	0	0	0	7	5	0	3	2	10.3	1.29	295	.208	.296	0	.000	-0	2	2	1	0.3
1958 Pit-N	0	3	.000	8	5	1	0	0	27^{2}	31	3	15	7	15.3	5.53	70	.290	.382	1	.125	-0	-5	-5	1	-0.4
1959 Pit-N	7	9	.438	34	12	0	0	1	100^{2}	115	9	39	67	13.9	5.45	71	.287	.353	9	.310	6	-17	-18	-1	-1.2
1960 Pit-N	1	3	.250	10	6	0	0	0	40^{1}	52	4	17	16	15.4	7.81	48	.311	.375	3	.188	-0	-18	-18	1	-1.6
1961 Was-A	12	11	.522	32	28	12	1	0	212	184	14	80	110	11.3	3.44	117	.237	.311	15	.197	3	14	14	1	1.8
1962 Was-A	7	16	.304	44	21	3	1	2	161^{1}	172	14	68	66	13.5	4.85	83	.280	.354	6	.130	-1	-16	-15	5	-1.0
1963 Was-A	5	10	.333	35	24	6	1	1	168^{2}	163	19	58	88	11.8	4.38	85	.250	.312	7	.152	1	-14	-12	3	-0.9
1964 Was-A	8	10	.444	33	24	3	2	0	163	147	20	64	73	11.7	3.70	100	.245	.317	6	.128	0	-1	0	3	0.3
1965 Was-A	5	13	.278	33	18	1	0	1	116^{1}	135	16	39	42	13.5	4.72	74	.290	.345	4	.133	0	-16	-16	-0	-1.7
Total 9	45	76	.372	230	139	26	5	5	997	1004	99	383	471	12.6	4.44	86	.264	.332	51	.170	9	-72	-69	12	-4.4

● CHARLIE DANIELS

Daniels, Charles L. b: 7/1/1861, Roxbury, Mass. d: 2/9/38, Boston, Mass. Deb: 4/18/1884

YEAR TM/L	W	L	PCT	G	GS	CG	SH	SV	IP	H	HR	BB	SO	RAT	ERA	ERA+	OAV	OOB	BH	AVG	PB	PR	/A	PD	TPI
1884 Bos-U	0	2	.000	2	2	2	0	0	16^{2}	20	0	2	12	11.9	4.32	68	.278	.298	3	.273	0	-2	-3	-0	-0.2

YEAR TM/L	W	L	PCT	G	GS	CG	SH	SV	IP	H	HR	BB	SO	RAT	ERA	ERA+	OAV	OOB	BH	AVG	PB	PR	/A	PD	TPI

● PETE DANIELS Daniels, Peter J. "Smiling Pete" b: 4/8/1864, County Cavan, Ireland d: 2/13/28, Indianapolis, Ind. BL/TL, Deb: 4/19/1890

1890 Pit-N	1	2	.333	4	4	3	0	0	28	40	1	12	8	17.7	7.07	47	.325	.399	4	.333	1	-11	-12	-0	-0.9
1898 StL-N	1	6	.143	10	6	3	0	0	54²	62	0	14	13	13.0	3.62	105	.283	.335	3	.176	0	-0	1	-0	0.1
Total 2	2	8	.200	14	10	6	0	0	82²	102	1	26	21	14.6	4.79	76	.298	.359	7	.241	1	-11	-11	-0	-0.8

● GEORGE DARBY Darby, George William "Deacon" b: 2/6/1869, Kansas City, Mo. d: 2/25/37, Sacramento, Cal. BR/TR, 5'10.5", 160 lbs. Deb: 4/28/1893

| 1893 Cin-N | 1 | 1 | .500 | 4 | 3 | 2 | 0 | 0 | 29 | 41 | 2 | 18 | 6 | 19.2 | 7.76 | 62 | .323 | .419 | 3 | .300 | 0 | -10 | -10 | 1 | -0.6 |

● PAT DARCY Darcy, Patrick Leonard b: 5/12/50, Troy, Ohio BL/TR, 6'3", 175 lbs. Deb: 9/12/74

1974 Cin-N	1	0	1.000	6	2	0	0	0	17	17	2	8	14	13.2	3.71	94	.262	.342	1	.333	0	-0	-0	-0	0.0
1975 *Cin-N	11	5	.688	27	22	1	0	1	130²	134	4	59	46	13.3	3.58	100	.269	.346	4	.085	-3	1	0	-0	-0.3
1976 Cin-N	2	3	.400	11	4	0	0	2	39	41	2	22	15	14.5	6.23	56	.279	.373	2	.182	1	-12	-12	-1	-1.2
Total 3	14	8	.636	44	28	1	0	3	186²	192	8	89	75	13.5	4.15	86	.270	.352	7	.115	-2	-11	-12	-1	-1.5

● ALVIN DARK Dark, Alvin Ralph "Blackie" b: 1/7/22, Comanche, Okla. BR/TR, 5'11", 185 lbs. Deb: 7/14/46 MC♦

| 1953 NY-N | 0 | 0 | — | 1 | 1 | 0 | 0 | 0 | 1 | 1 | 1 | 1 | 0 | 18.0 | 18.00 | 24 | .250 | .400 | 194 | .300 | 1 | -2 | -2 | -0 | -0.1 |

● RON DARLING Darling, Ronald Maurice b: 8/19/60, Honolulu, Hawaii BR/TR, 6'3", 195 lbs. Deb: 9/06/83

1983 NY-N	1	3	.250	5	5	1	0	0	35¹	31	0	17	23	13.0	2.80	129	.248	.352	1	.100	-1	3	3	0	0.3
1984 NY-N	12	9	.571	33	33	2	2	0	205²	179	17	104	136	12.6	3.81	93	.235	.331	10	.149	-1	-5	-6	2	-0.5
1985 NY-N☆	16	6	.727	36	35	4	2	0	248	214	21	114	167	12.0	2.90	119	.235	.323	13	.171	2	19	15	3	2.3
1986 *NY-N	15	6	.714	34	34	4	2	0	237	203	21	81	184	10.9	2.81	126	.234	.302	8	.099	-2	24	19	3	2.2
1987 NY-N	12	8	.600	32	32	2	0	0	207²	183	24	96	167	12.2	4.29	88	.233	.319	1	.123	1	-5	-12	4	-0.8
1988 *NY-N	17	9	.654	34	34	7	4	0	240²	218	24	60	161	10.6	3.25	99	.245	.297	18	.220	6	5	-1	0	0.5
1989 NY-N	14	14	.500	33	33	4	0	0	217¹	214	19	70	153	11.9	3.52	93	.258	.318	9	.123	1	-1	-6	2	-0.4
1990 NY-N	7	9	.438	33	18	1	0	0	126	135	20	44	99	13.1	4.50	83	.273	.338	4	.129	0	-10	-11	1	-1.0
1991 NY-N	5	6	.455	17	17	0	0	0	102¹	96	9	28	58	11.4	3.87	94	.251	.313	4	.118	-0	-2	-3	-0	-0.3
Mon-N	0	2	.000	3	3	0	0	0	17	25	6	5	11	16.4	7.41	49	.333	.383	1	.167	-0	-7	-7	-0	-0.6
Yr	5	8	.385	20	20	0	0	0	119¹	121	15	33	69	11.7	4.37	83	.259	.309	5	.125	-0	-9	-10	-0	-0.9
Oak-A	3	7	.300	12	12	0	0	0	75	76	7	38	60	12.5	4.08	94	.237	.335	0	—	0	0	-2	0	0.2
1992 *Oak-A	15	10	.600	33	33	4	3	0	206¹	198	15	72	99	12.0	3.66	103	.253	.319	0	—	0	6	3	-1	0.3
Total 10	117	89	.568	305	289	29	13	0	1918¹	1760	183	729	1318	11.9	3.57	99	.246	.319	76	.145	6	28	-7	15	2.2

● BOB DARNELL Darnell, Robert Jack b: 11/6/30, Wewoka, Okla. BR/TR, 5'10", 175 lbs. Deb: 8/10/54

1954 Bro-N	0	0	—	6	1	0	0	0	14¹	15	2	7	5	13.8	3.14	130	.278	.361	0	.000	-0	1	2	0	0.2
1956 Bro-N	0	0	—	1	0	0	0	0	1¹	1	0	0	0	6.8	0.00	—	.200	.200	0	—	0	1	1	-0	0.1
Total 2	0	0	—	7	1	0	0	0	15²	16	2	7	5	13.2	2.87	142	.271	.348	0	.000	-0	2	2	0	0.3

● MIKE DARR Darr, Michael Edward b: 3/23/56, Pomona, Cal. BR/TR, 6'4", 190 lbs. Deb: 9/06/77

| 1977 Tor-A | 0 | 1 | .000 | 1 | 1 | 0 | 0 | 0 | 1¹ | 3 | 1 | 4 | 1 | 54.0 | 33.75 | 12 | .429 | .667 | 0 | — | 0 | -4 | -4 | 0 | -0.4 |

● GEORGE DARROW Darrow, George Oliver b: 7/12/03, Beloit, Kan. d: 3/24/83, Sun City, Ariz. BL/TL, 6', 180 lbs. Deb: 4/22/34

| 1934 Phi-N | 2 | 6 | .250 | 17 | 8 | 2 | 0 | 1 | 49 | 57 | 4 | 28 | 14 | 16.3 | 5.51 | 86 | .302 | .403 | 2 | .133 | 1 | -8 | -4 | 0 | -0.3 |

● BOBBY DARWIN Darwin, Arthur Bobby Lee b: 2/16/43, Los Angeles, Cal. BR/TR, 6'2", 200 lbs. Deb: 9/30/62 ♦

1962 LA-A	0	1	.000	1	1	0	0	0	3¹	8	0	4	6	32.4	10.80	36	.421	.522	0	.000	-0	-3	-3	-0	-0.2
1969 LA-N	0	0	—	3	0	0	0	0	3²	4	0	5	0	27.0	9.82	34	.333	.579	0	—	0	-3	-3	-0	-0.3
Total 2	0	1	.000	4	1	0	0	0	7	12	0	9	6	29.6	10.29	35	.387	.548	559	.251	-0	-5	-5	-0	-0.5

● DANNY DARWIN Darwin, Daniel Wayne b: 10/25/55, Bonham, Tex. BR/TR, 6'3", 190 lbs. Deb: 9/08/78

1978 Tex-A	1	0	1.000	3	1	0	0	0	8²	11	0	1	8	12.5	4.15	90	.324	.343	0	—	0	-0	-0	-0	-0.1
1979 Tex-A	4	4	.500	20	6	1	0	0	78	50	5	30	58	9.8	4.04	103	.186	.280	0	—	0	2	1	-1	0.0
1980 Tex-A	13	4	.765	53	2	0	0	8	109²	98	4	50	104	12.3	2.63	148	.243	.329	0	—	0	17	15	-0	1.7
1981 Tex-A	9	9	.500	22	22	6	2	0	146	115	12	57	98	11.0	3.64	95	.218	.302	0	—	0	-3	-1	-0.2
1982 Tex-A	10	8	.556	56	1	0	0	7	89	95	6	37	61	13.6	3.44	113	.279	.354	0	—	0	6	4	2	0.9
1983 Tex-A	8	13	.381	28	26	9	2	0	183	175	9	62	92	11.8	3.49	115	.250	.313	0	—	0	12	10	1	1.0
1984 Tex-A	8	12	.400	35	32	5	1	0	223²	249	19	54	123	12.4	3.94	105	.279	.323	0	—	0	1	5	-2	0.2
1985 Mil-A	8	18	.308	39	29	11	1	2	217²	212	24	65	125	11.6	3.80	109	.254	.311	0	—	0	8	9	-3	0.6
1986 Mil-A	6	8	.429	27	14	5	1	0	130¹	120	13	35	80	10.9	3.52	123	.246	.300	0	—	0	9	12	1	1.1
Hou-N	5	2	.714	12	8	1	0	0	54¹	50	3	9	40	9.8	2.32	155	.239	.271	1	.063	-1	8	8	-1	0.7
1987 Hou-N	9	10	.474	33	30	3	1	0	195²	184	17	69	134	11.9	3.59	109	.246	.314	12	.182	2	11	7	-2	0.8
1988 Hou-N	8	13	.381	44	20	3	0	3	192	189	20	48	129	11.4	3.84	86	.259	.311	4	.071	-1	-8	-11	-2	-1.1
1989 Hou-N	11	4	.733	68	0	0	0	7	122	92	8	33	104	9.4	2.36	143	.212	.271	2	.118	-1	15	14	1	1.3
1990 Hou-N	11	4	.733	48	17	3	0	2	162²	136	11	31	109	**9.5**	**2.21**	**168**	.225	**.267**	5	.132	1	29	27	-1	2.8
1991 Bos-A	3	6	.333	12	12	0	0	0	68	71	15	15	42	11.9	5.16	83	.263	.311	0	—	0	-8	-7	-0	-0.9
1992 Bos-A	9	9	.500	51	15	2	0	3	161¹	159	11	53	124	12.1	3.96	105	.257	.321	0	—	0	-0	3	-1	0.1
Total 15	123	124	.498	551	235	49	8	32	2142	2006	187	649	1431	11.4	3.50	111	.248	.308	24	.124	-0	102	94	-10	8.9

● DOUG DASCENZO Dascenzo, Douglas Craig b: 6/30/64, Cleveland, Ohio BB/TL, 5'7", 150 lbs. Deb: 9/02/88 ♦

1990 Chi-N	0	0	—	1	0	0	0	0	1	1	0	0	0	9.0	0.00	—	.333	.333	61	.253	0	0	0	0	0.0
1991 Chi-N	0	0	—	3	0	0	0	0	4	2	0	2	2	9.0	0.00	—	.154	.267	61	.255	1	2	2	-0	0.2
Total 2	0	0	—	4	0	0	0	0	5	3	0	2	2	9.0	0.00	—	.188	.278	257	.240	1	2	2	-0	0.2

● LEE DASHNER Dashner, Lee Claire "Lefty" b: 4/25/1887, Renault, Ill. d: 12/16/59, ElDorado, Kan. BB/TL, 5'11.5", 192 lbs. Deb: 8/04/13

| 1913 Cle-A | 0 | 0 | — | 1 | 0 | 0 | 0 | 0 | 1² | 0 | 0 | 0 | 2 | 10.0 | 5.40 | 56 | .000 | .000 | 0 | — | 0 | -0 | -0 | -0 | -0.1 |

● FRANK DASSO Dasso, Francis Joseph Nicholas b: 8/31/17, Chicago, Ill. BR/TR, 5'11.5", 185 lbs. Deb: 4/22/45

1945 Cin-N	4	5	.444	16	12	6	0	0	95²	89	9	53	39	13.4	3.67	102	.253	.351	5	.161	-1	1	1	0	0.1
1946 Cin-N	0	0	—	2	0	0	0	0	1	2	0	2	1	36.0	27.00	12	.400	.571	0	—	0	-3	-3	0	-0.3
Total 2	4	5	.444	18	12	6	0	0	96²	91	9	55	40	13.6	3.91	96	.255	.354	5	.161	-1	-1	-2	0	-0.2

● DAN DAUB Daub, Daniel William "Mickey" b: 1/12/1868, Middletown, Ohio d: 3/25/51, Bradenton, Fla. BR/TR, 5'10", 160 lbs. Deb: 8/31/1892

1892 Cin-N	1	2	.333	4	3	2	0	0	25	23	0	13	7	13.7	2.88	113	.235	.336	0	.000	-1	1	1	0	0.0
1893 Bro-N	6	6	.500	12	12	12	0	0	103	104	3	61	25	14.9	3.84	115	.254	.358	8	.190	-1	9	7	3	0.7
1894 Bro-N	10	12	.455	34	27	15	0	0	224	291	7	91	45	16.1	6.11	81	.311	.383	18	.189	-5	-19	-29	-1	-2.6
1895 Bro-N	10	10	.500	25	21	16	0	0	184²	212	4	51	36	13.4	4.29	102	.284	.339	14	.197	-2	10	2	2	0.2
1896 Bro-N	12	11	.522	32	24	18	0	0	225	255	4	63	53	13.0	3.60	115	.283	.335	19	.226	2	19	13	4	1.6
1897 Bro-N	6	11	.353	19	16	11	0	0	137²	180	8	48	19	15.6	6.08	67	.313	.376	11	.224	2	-27	-30	-2	-2.3
Total 6	45	52	.464	126	103	74	0	0	899¹	1065	26	327	185	14.5	4.75	93	.290	.357	70	.201	-6	-7	-36	8	-2.4

● HOOKS DAUSS Dauss, George August (b: George August Daus) b: 9/22/1889, Indianapolis, Ind d: 7/27/63, St.Louis, Mo. BR/TR, 5'10.5", 168 lbs. Deb: 9/28/12

1912 Det-A	1	1	.500	2	2	2	0	0	17	11	0	9	7	12.2	3.18	103	.186	.324	1	.250	1	0	0	1	0.2
1913 Det-A	13	12	.520	33	29	22	2	0	225	188	4	90	107	11.3	2.48	118	.228	.308	14	.177	3	11	11	-1	1.5
1914 Det-A	18	15	.545	45	35	22	3	**4**	302	286	1	87	150	11.7	2.86	98	.257	.321	21	.216	4	-4	-2	1	0.5
1915 Det-A	24	13	.649	46	35	27	1	2	309²	261	1	115	132	11.2	2.50	121	.235	.313	15	.146	0	15	18	9	3.1
1916 Det-A	19	12	.613	39	29	18	1	4	238²	220	2	90	95	12.3	3.21	89	.257	.339	16	.222	8	-10	-9	2	0.1

YEAR	TM/L	W	L	PCT	G	GS	CG	SH	SV	IP	H	HR	BB	SO	RAT	ERA	ERA+	OAV	OOB	BH	AVG	PB	PR	/A	PD	TPI
1917	Det-A	17	14	.548	37	31	22	6	2	270^2	243	3	87	102	11.2	2.43	109	.245	.311	11	.126	-1	7	7	4	1.1
1918	Det-A	12	16	.429	33	26	21	1	3	249^2	243	3	58	73	11.2	2.99	89	.263	.313	14	.182	3	-6	-9	2	-0.5
1919	Det-A	21	9	.700	34	32	22	2	0	256^1	262	9	63	73	11.6	3.55	90	.267	.315	14	.144	-3	-9	-10	6	-0.7
1920	Det-A	13	21	.382	38	32	18	0	0	270^1	308	11	84	82	13.3	3.56	105	.289	.345	14	.169	1	7	5	8	1.4
1921	Det-A	10	15	.400	32	28	16	0	1	233	275	11	81	68	14.3	4.33	99	.297	.362	23	.261	2	-1	-1	5	0.5
1922	Det-A	13	13	.500	39	25	12	1	4	218^2	251	7	59	78	13.0	4.20	92	.289	.339	15	.208	3	-4	-8	1	-0.4
1923	Det-A	21	13	.618	50	39	22	4	3	316	331	10	78	105	11.8	3.62	107	.272	.319	24	.231	5	13	9	2	1.4
1924	Det-A	12	11	.522	40	10	5	0	6	131^1	155	6	40	44	13.4	4.59	90	.302	.354	5	.132	-2	-5	-7	0	-0.8
1925	Det-A	16	11	.593	35	30	16	1	1	228	238	11	85	58	12.9	3.16	136	.272	.339	15	.185	1	31	29	-1	2.8
1926	Det-A	12	6	.667	35	5	0	0	9	124^1	135	6	49	27	13.3	4.20	97	.287	.354	10	.238	4	-2	-2	-0	0.1
Total	15	222	182	.550	538	388	245	22	40	3390^2	3407	87	1067	1201	12.2	3.30	103	.266	.329	212	.189	32	44	33	38	10.3

● VIC DAVALILLO Davalillo, Victor Jose (Romero) b: 7/31/36, Cabimas, Venez. BL/TL, 5'7", 155 lbs. Deb: 4/09/63 F♦

YEAR	TM/L	W	L	PCT	G	GS	CG	SH	SV	IP	H	HR	BB	SO	RAT	ERA	ERA+	OAV	OOB	BH	AVG	PB	PR	/A	PD	TPI
1969	StL-N	0	0	—	2	0	0	0	0	0	2	0	2	0	—	∞	—	1.000	1.000	26	.265	0	-1	-1	0	-0.1

● CLAUDE DAVENPORT Davenport, Claude Edwin "Big Dave" b: 5/28/1898, Runge, Tex. d: 6/13/76, Corpus Christi, Tex. BR/TR, 6'6", 193 lbs. Deb: 10/02/20 F

YEAR	TM/L	W	L	PCT	G	GS	CG	SH	SV	IP	H	HR	BB	SO	RAT	ERA	ERA+	OAV	OOB	BH	AVG	PB	PR	/A	PD	TPI
1920	NY-N	0	0	—	1	0	0	0	0	2	2	1	1	0	13.5	4.50	67	.250	.333	0	.000	-0	-0	-0	-0	-0.1

● DAVE DAVENPORT Davenport, David W. b: 2/20/1890, DeRidder, La. d: 10/16/54, ElDorado, Ark. BR/TR, 6'6", 220 lbs. Deb: 4/17/14 F

YEAR	TM/L	W	L	PCT	G	GS	CG	SH	SV	IP	H	HR	BB	SO	RAT	ERA	ERA+	OAV	OOB	BH	AVG	PB	PR	/A	PD	TPI
1914	Cin-N	2	2	.500	10	6	3	1	2	54	38	1	30	22	11.8	2.50	117	.202	.321	2	.111	-1	2	3	-0	0.1
	StL-F	8	13	.381	33	26	13	2	4	215^2	204	3	80	142	12.1	3.46	98	.251	.324	6	.088	-6	-6	-2	1	-0.6
1915	StL-F	22	18	.550	**55**	46	**30**	**10**	1	**392^2**	300	5	96	**229**	9.2	2.20	145	**.215**	.268	12	.092	-10	**36**	**43**	-8	2.9
1916	StL-A	12	11	.522	**59**	31	13	1	2	290^2	267	4	100	129	11.6	2.85	96	.256	.326	10	.137	3	-1	-3	-3	-0.4
1917	StL-A	17	17	.500	47	39	20	2	2	280^2	273	5	105	100	12.4	3.08	84	.260	.331	9	.098	-6	-13	-15	-1	-2.3
1918	StL-A	10	11	.476	31	22	12	2	1	180	182	0	69	60	12.9	3.25	84	.273	.347	7	.135	1	-9	-10	2	-0.9
1919	StL-A	2	11	.154	24	16	5	0	0	123^1	135	4	41	37	13.0	3.94	84	.280	.339	3	.077	-4	-10	-9	1	-1.2
Total	6	73	83	.468	259	186	96	18	12	1537	1399	22	521	719	11.5	2.93	101	.248	.316	49	.104	-22	-1	6	-9	-2.4

● LUM DAVENPORT Davenport, Joubert Lum b: 6/27/1900, Tucson, Ariz. d: 4/21/61, Dallas, Tex. BL/TL, 6'1", 165 lbs. Deb: 5/02/21

YEAR	TM/L	W	L	PCT	G	GS	CG	SH	SV	IP	H	HR	BB	SO	RAT	ERA	ERA+	OAV	OOB	BH	AVG	PB	PR	/A	PD	TPI
1921	Chi-A	0	3	.000	13	2	0	0	0	35^1	41	1	32	9	18.8	6.88	62	.318	.457	7	.412	2	-10	-10	-0	-0.8
1922	Chi-A	1	1	.500	9	1	0	0	0	16^2	14	2	13	9	14.6	10.80	38	.233	.370	0	.000	-0	-13	-12	0	-1.1
1923	Chi-A	0	0	—	2	0	0	0	0	4^1	7	0	4	1	22.8	6.23	64	.438	.550	1	1.000	0	-1	-1	0	-0.1
1924	Chi-A	0	0	—	1	0	0	0	0	2	1	0	2	1	13.5	0.00	—	.125	.300	0	—	0	1	1	-0	0.1
Total	4	1	4	.200	25	3	0	0	0	58^1	63	3	51	20	17.7	7.71	54	.296	.434	8	.381	2	-23	-23	-0	-1.9

● MIKE DAVEY Davey, Michael Gerard b: 6/2/52, Spokane, Wash. BR/TL, 6'2", 190 lbs. Deb: 8/13/77

YEAR	TM/L	W	L	PCT	G	GS	CG	SH	SV	IP	H	HR	BB	SO	RAT	ERA	ERA+	OAV	OOB	BH	AVG	PB	PR	/A	PD	TPI
1977	Atl-N	0	0	—	16	0	0	0	2	16	19	1	9	7	15.8	5.06	88	.302	.389	0	.000	-0	-2	-1	-0	-0.1
1978	Atl-N	0	0	—	3	0	0	0	0	2^2	1	0	1	0	6.8	0.00	—	.125	.222	0	—	0	1	1	-0	0.1
Total	2	0	0	—	19	0	0	0	2	18^2	20	1	10	7	14.5	4.34	101	.282	.370	0	.000	-0	-1	0	-0	0.0

● RAY DAVIAULT Daviault, Raymond Joseph Robert b: 5/27/34, Montreal, Que., Can BR/TR, 6'1", 170 lbs. Deb: 4/13/62

YEAR	TM/L	W	L	PCT	G	GS	CG	SH	SV	IP	H	HR	BB	SO	RAT	ERA	ERA+	OAV	OOB	BH	AVG	PB	PR	/A	PD	TPI
1962	NY-N	1	5	.167	36	3	0	0	0	81	92	14	48	51	16.0	6.22	67	.288	.388	1	.067	-1	-21	-18	-1	-2.0

● BOB DAVIDSON Davidson, Robert Banks b: 1/6/63, Bad Kurznach, W.Ger. BR/TR, 6', 185 lbs. Deb: 7/15/89

YEAR	TM/L	W	L	PCT	G	GS	CG	SH	SV	IP	H	HR	BB	SO	RAT	ERA	ERA+	OAV	OOB	BH	AVG	PB	PR	/A	PD	TPI
1989	NY-A	0	0	—	1	0	0	0	0	1	1	1	1	0	18.0	18.00	21	.250	.400	0	—	0	-2	-2	0	-0.1

● TED DAVIDSON Davidson, Thomas Eugene b: 10/4/39, Las Vegas, Nev. BR/TL, 6', 192 lbs. Deb: 7/24/65

YEAR	TM/L	W	L	PCT	G	GS	CG	SH	SV	IP	H	HR	BB	SO	RAT	ERA	ERA+	OAV	OOB	BH	AVG	PB	PR	/A	PD	TPI
1965	Cin-N	4	3	.571	24	1	0	0	1	68^2	57	5	17	54	10.0	2.23	168	.233	.288	0	.000	-2	10	12	0	1.1
1966	Cin-N	5	4	.556	54	0	0	0	4	85^1	82	11	23	54	11.2	3.90	100	.253	.305	0	.000	-2	-3	-0	-0	-0.2
1967	Cin-N	1	0	1.000	9	0	0	0	0	13	13	0	3	6	11.1	4.15	90	.250	.291	0	—	0	-1	-1	0	0.0
1968	Cin-N	1	0	1.000	23	0	0	0	0	21^2	27	3	7	7	14.1	6.23	51	.307	.358	0	.000	-0	-8	-7	0	-0.8
	Atl-N	0	0	—	4	0	0	0	0	6^2	10	2	4	3	18.9	6.75	44	.345	.424	0	—	0	-3	-3	0	-0.3
	Yr	1	0	1.000	27	0	0	0	0	28^1	37	5	11	10	15.2	6.35	49	.316	.375	0	.000	0	-11	-10	0	-1.1
Total	4	11	7	.611	114	1	0	0	5	195^1	189	21	54	124	11.3	3.69	101	.256	.309	0	.000	-3	-5	1	1	-0.2

● JERRY DAVIE Davie, Gerald Lee b: 2/10/33, Detroit, Mich. BR/TR, 6', 180 lbs. Deb: 4/14/59

YEAR	TM/L	W	L	PCT	G	GS	CG	SH	SV	IP	H	HR	BB	SO	RAT	ERA	ERA+	OAV	OOB	BH	AVG	PB	PR	/A	PD	TPI
1959	Det-A	2	2	.500	11	5	1	0	0	36^2	40	8	17	20	15.0	4.17	97	.265	.355	4	.400	2	-1	-0	1	0.2

● GEORGE DAVIES Davies, George Washington b: 2/22/1868, Portage, Wis. d: 9/22/06, Waterloo, Wis. 180 lbs. Deb: 8/18/1891

YEAR	TM/L	W	L	PCT	G	GS	CG	SH	SV	IP	H	HR	BB	SO	RAT	ERA	ERA+	OAV	OOB	BH	AVG	PB	PR	/A	PD	TPI
1891	Mil-a	7	5	.583	12	12	12	1	0	102	94	2	35	61	11.6	2.65	166	.237	.303	9	.243	1	12	20	-1	1.8
1892	Cle-N	10	16	.385	26	26	23	0	0	215^2	201	4	69	95	11.5	2.59	131	.237	.299	12	.138	-5	17	19	3	1.5
1893	Cle-N	0	2	.000	3	3	1	0	0	15	28	1	10	3	22.8	11.40	43	.387	.461	2	.333	0	-11	-11	0	-0.8
	NY-N	1	1	.500	5	1	1	0	0	36^1	41	1	13	7	13.4	6.19	75	.276	.334	4	.333	2	-6	-6	0	-0.3
	Yr	1	3	.250	8	4	2	0	0	51^1	69	2	23	10	16.1	7.71	61	.312	.377	6	.333	2	-17	-17	1	-1.1
Total	3	18	24	.429	46	42	37	1	0	369	364	8	127	166	12.2	3.32	116	.248	.312	27	.190	-2	12	22	2	2.2

● CHICK DAVIES Davies, Lloyd Garrison b: 3/6/1892, Peabody, Mass. d: 9/5/73, Middletown, Conn. BL/TL, 5'8", 145 lbs. Deb: 7/11/14 ♦

YEAR	TM/L	W	L	PCT	G	GS	CG	SH	SV	IP	H	HR	BB	SO	RAT	ERA	ERA+	OAV	OOB	BH	AVG	PB	PR	/A	PD	TPI
1914	Phi-A	1	0	1.000	1	1	1	0	0	9	8	0	3	4	11.0	1.00	261	.258	.324	11	.239	0	2	2	0	0.3
1915	Phi-A	1	2	.333	4	2	0	0	0	15^1	20	0	12	2	19.4	8.80	33	.339	.458	24	.182	0	-10	-10	1	-0.9
1925	NY-N	0	0	—	2	1	0	0	0	7^1	13	0	4	5	20.9	6.14	66	.361	.425	0	.000	-0	-2	-2	0	-0.2
1926	NY-N	2	4	.333	38	1	0	0	**6**	89	96	3	35	27	13.2	3.94	95	.277	.344	4	.222	1	-1	-2	1	0.0
Total	4	4	6	.400	45	5	1	0	6	120^2	137	3	54	38	14.3	4.48	80	.290	.364	39	.193	1	-11	-12	2	-0.8

● CURT DAVIS Davis, Curtis Benton "Coonskin" b: 9/7/03, Greenfield, Mo. d: 10/13/65, Covina, Cal. BR/TR, 6'2", 185 lbs. Deb: 4/21/34

YEAR	TM/L	W	L	PCT	G	GS	CG	SH	SV	IP	H	HR	BB	SO	RAT	ERA	ERA+	OAV	OOB	BH	AVG	PB	PR	/A	PD	TPI
1934	Phi-N	19	17	.528	**51**	31	18	3	5	274^1	283	14	60	99	11.5	2.95	160	.269	.313	20	.211	-2	34	54	9	**6.4**
1935	Phi-N	16	14	.533	44	27	19	3	2	231	264	14	47	74	12.4	3.66	124	.285	.324	13	.173	-1	9	22	2	2.3
1936	Phi-N	2	4	.333	10	8	3	0	0	60^1	71	6	19	18	13.6	4.62	98	.291	.345	4	.154	-2	-4	-1	0	-0.2
	Chi-N	11	9	.550	24	20	10	0	1	153	146	11	31	52	10.5	3.00	133	.251	.290	8	.151	-2	17	17	3	1.7
	Yr	13	13	.500	34	28	13	0	1	213^1	217	17	50	70	11.3	3.46	120	.263	.306	12	.152	-4	13	16	3	1.5
1937	Chi-N	10	5	.667	28	14	8	0	1	123^2	138	7	30	32	12.6	4.08	98	.286	.334	12	.300	4	-2	-1	2	0.4
1938	StL-N	12	8	.600	40	21	8	2	3	173^1	187	9	27	36	11.2	3.63	109	.272	.301	13	.228	3	3	6	1	0.9
1939	StL-N☆	22	16	.579	49	31	13	3	7	248	279	18	48	70	12.0	3.63	113	.280	.315	40	.381	12	8	13	1	2.8
1940	StL-N	0	4	.000	14	7	0	0	1	54	73	4	19	12	15.5	5.17	77	.327	.383	0	.000	-3	-8	-7	1	-0.8
	Bro-N	8	7	.533	22	18	9	0	2	137	135	13	19	46	10.2	3.81	105	.256	.283	6	.128	-1	1	3	1	0.3
	Yr	8	11	.421	36	25	9	0	3	191	208	17	38	58	11.6	4.19	95	.277	.312	6	.091	-3	-7	-4	2	-0.5
1941	*Bro-N	13	7	.650	28	16	10	5	2	154^1	141	6	27	50	9.9	2.97	123	.244	.280	11	.186	2	11	12	4	1.8
1942	Bro-N	15	6	.714	32	26	13	5	2	206	179	10	51	60	10.4	2.36	138	.233	.287	12	.176	-0	22	21	3	2.6
1943	Bro-N	10	13	.435	31	21	8	2	3	164^1	182	8	39	47	12.2	3.78	89	.281	.324	9	.164	-1	-7	-8	2	-0.6
1944	Bro-N	10	11	.476	31	23	12	1	4	194	207	12	39	49	11.6	3.34	106	.270	.310	10	.159	-2	6	5	2	0.5
1945	Bro-N	10	10	.500	24	18	10	0	0	149^2	171	9	21	39	11.7	3.25	116	.280	.308	7	.137	-1	9	8	0	0.8
1946	Bro-N	0	0	—	1	0	0	0	0	2	3	1	2	0	27.0	13.50	25	.375	.545	0	—	0	-2	-2	0	-0.2
Total	13	158	131	.547	429	281	141	24	33	2325	2459	142	479	684	11.6	3.42	116	.270	.310	165	.203	7	96	139	31	18.7

● DIXIE DAVIS Davis, Frank Talmadge b: 10/12/1890, Wilson Mills, N.C. d: 2/4/44, Raleigh, N.C. BR/TR, 5'11", 155 lbs. Deb: 7/12/12

YEAR	TM/L	W	L	PCT	G	GS	CG	SH	SV	IP	H	HR	BB	SO	RAT	ERA	ERA+	OAV	OOB	BH	AVG	PB	PR	/A	PD	TPI
1912	Cin-N	0	1	.000	7	0	0	0	0	26^2	25	0	16	12	14.2	2.70	124	.258	.368	2	.200	-0	2	2	-1	0.1
1915	Chi-A	0	0	—	2	0	0	0	0	3	2	0	2	2	15.0	0.00	—	.250	.455	0	—	0	1	1	0	0.1

YEAR	TM/L	W	L	PCT	G	GS	CG	SH	SV	IP	H	HR	BB	SO	RAT	ERA	ERA+	OAV	OOB	BH	AVG	PB	PR	/A	PD	TPI
1918	Phi-N	0	2	.000	17	2	1	0	0	47	43	1	30	18	14.0	3.06	98	.247	.358	0	.000	-0	-2	-0	-1	-0.2
1920	StL-A	18	12	.600	38	31	22	0	0	269^1	250	10	149	85	13.6	3.17	123	.256	.359	25	.266	3	19	22	-4	2.0
1921	StL-A	16	16	.500	40	36	20	2	0	265^1	279	12	123	100	14.0	4.44	101	.281	.366	20	.211	-3	-5	1	-1	-0.3
1922	StL-A	11	6	.647	25	25	7	2	0	174^1	162	10	87	65	13.3	4.08	102	**.250**	.345	8	.136	-3	-1	1	-0	-0.3
1923	StL-A	4	6	.400	19	17	5	1	0	109^1	106	4	63	36	14.3	3.62	115	.259	.365	10	.250	0	4	7	-2	0.5
1924	StL-A	11	13	.458	29	24	11	5	0	160^1	159	9	72	45	13.3	4.10	110	.263	.347	7	.152	-2	2	7	-1	0.4
1925	StL-A	12	7	.632	35	23	9	0	1	180^1	192	10	106	58	15.2	4.59	102	.279	.380	11	.172	-4	-4	2	1	-0.1
1926	StL-A	3	8	.273	27	7	2	0	1	83	93	7	40	39	14.5	4.66	92	.292	.372	4	.167	-0	-6	-3	-0	-0.4
Total	10	75	71	.514	239	165	77	10	2	1318^2	1311	63	688	460	14.0	3.97	107	.267	.362	87	.197	-10	12	39	-10	1.8
● **IRON DAVIS**	Davis, George Allen b: 3/9/1890, Lancaster, N.Y. d: 6/4/61, Buffalo, N.Y. BB/TR, 5'10.5", 175 lbs. Deb: 7/16/12																									
1912	NY-A	1	4	.200	10	7	5	0	0	54	61	3	28	22	15.3	6.50	55	.293	.385	2	.111	-1	-19	-17	-2	-1.8
1913	Bos-N	0	0	—	2	0	0	0	0	8	7	1	5	3	13.5	4.50	73	.241	.353	0	.000	-0	-1	-1	-0	-0.2
1914	Bos-N	3	3	.500	9	6	4	1	0	55^2	42	1	26	26	11.5	3.40	81	.215	.317	3	.167	0	-4	-4	-2	-0.6
1915	Bos-N	3	3	.500	15	9	4	0	0	73^1	85	2	19	26	13.3	3.80	68	.304	.356	6	.261	1	-9	-10	0	-0.9
Total	4	7	10	.412	36	22	13	1	0	191	195	7	78	77	13.3	4.48	66	.274	.354	11	.180	-0	-33	-33	-3	-3.5
● **STORM DAVIS**	Davis, George Earl b: 12/26/61, Dallas, Tex. BR/TR, 6'4", 207 lbs. Deb: 4/29/82																									
1982	Bal-A	8	4	.667	29	8	1	0	0	100^2	96	8	28	67	11.1	3.49	116	.257	.308	0	—	0	7	6	-0	0.6
1983	*Bal-A	13	7	.650	34	29	6	1	0	200^1	180	14	64	125	11.1	3.59	110	.238	.299	0	—	0	10	8	-2	0.8
1984	Bal-A	14	9	.609	35	31	10	2	1	225	205	7	71	105	11.2	3.12	124	.247	.310	0	—	0	22	19	-3	1.8
1985	Bal-A	10	8	.556	31	28	8	1	0	175	172	11	70	93	12.5	4.53	89	.256	.327	0	—	0	-7	-10	-1	-0.8
1986	Bal-A	9	12	.429	25	25	2	0	0	154	166	16	49	96	12.6	3.62	114	.275	.330	0	—	0	9	9	2	1.1
1987	SD-N	2	7	.222	21	10	0	0	0	62^2	70	5	36	37	15.5	6.18	64	.280	.375	1	.063	-1	-15	-15	0	-1.6
	Oak-A	1	1	.500	5	5	0	0	0	30^1	28	3	11	28	11.6	3.26	126	.241	.307	0	—	0	4	3	-1	0.8
1988	*Oak-A	16	7	.696	33	33	1	0	0	201^2	211	16	91	127	13.5	3.70	102	.274	.352	0	—	0	6	2	-2	0.0
1989	*Oak-A	19	7	.731	31	31	1	0	0	169^1	187	19	68	91	13.7	4.36	84	.288	.358	0	—	0	-9	-13	-2	-1.2
1990	KC-A	7	10	.412	21	20	0	0	0	112	129	9	35	62	13.2	4.74	81	.281	.332	0	—	0	-10	-11	-1	-1.1
1991	KC-A	3	9	.250	51	9	1	1	2	114^1	140	11	46	53	14.7	4.96	83	.306	.370	0	—	0	-11	-11	-1	-1.2
1992	Bal-A	7	3	.700	48	2	0	0	4	89^1	79	5	36	53	11.8	3.43	114	.244	.323	0	—	0	5	5	1	0.5
Total	11	109	84	.565	364	231	30	5	7	1634^2	1663	124	605	937	12.6	3.98	99	.266	.332	1	.063	-1	11	-9	-10	-0.3
● **GEORGE DAVIS**	Davis, George Stacey b: 8/23/1870, Cohoes, N.Y. d: 10/17/40, Philadelphia, Pa. BB/TR, 5'9", 180 lbs. Deb: 4/19/1890 M♦																									
1891	Cle-N	0	1	.000	3	0	0	0	1	4	8	0	3	4	24.8	15.75	22	.401	.479	165	.289	1	-6	-5	-0	-0.5
● **JIM DAVIS**	Davis, James Bennett b: 9/15/24, Red Bluff, Cal. BB/TL, 6', 180 lbs. Deb: 4/18/54																									
1954	Chi-N	11	7	.611	46	12	2	0	4	127^2	114	12	51	58	11.8	3.52	119	.247	.326	2	.063	-1	8	10	1	1.0
1955	Chi-N	7	11	.389	42	16	0	0	3	133^2	122	16	58	62	12.3	4.44	92	.246	.327	1	.027	-4	-6	-5	-1	-1.0
1956	Chi-N	5	7	.417	46	11	2	1	2	120^1	116	11	59	66	13.5	3.66	103	.256	.349	5	.179	-0	1	1	1	0.2
1957	StL-N	0	1	.000	10	0	0	0	1	13^2	18	1	6	5	15.8	5.27	75	.340	.407	0	.000	-0	-2	-2	0	-0.2
	NY-N	1	0	1.000	10	0	0	0	0	11	13	2	5	6	14.7	6.55	60	.283	.353	1	1.000	0	-3	-3	0	-0.3
	Yr	1	1	.500	20	0	0	0	1	24^2	31	3	11	11	15.3	5.84	68	.310	.378	1	.500	0	-5	-5	0	-0.5
Total	4	24	26	.480	154	39	4	1	10	406^1	383	42	179	197	12.7	4.01	100	.253	.337	9	.091	-5	-2	0	1	-0.3
● **JOEL DAVIS**	Davis, Joel Clark b: 1/30/65, Jacksonville, Fla. BL/TR, 6'5", 205 lbs. Deb: 8/11/85																									
1985	Chi-A	3	3	.500	12	11	1	0	0	71^1	71	6	26	37	12.4	4.16	104	.256	.322	0	—	0	-0	1	-2	-0.3
1986	Chi-A	4	5	.444	19	19	1	0	0	105^1	115	9	51	54	14.3	4.70	92	.280	.361	0	—	0	-6	-5	1	-0.6
1987	Chi-A	1	5	.167	13	9	1	0	0	55	56	7	29	25	13.9	5.73	80	.264	.353	0	—	0	-8	-7	-1	-0.9
1988	Chi-A	0	1	.000	5	2	0	0	0	16	21	4	5	10	14.6	6.75	59	.328	.377	0	—	0	-5	-5	-0	-0.5
Total	4	8	14	.364	49	41	3	0	0	247^2	263	26	111	126	13.7	4.91	89	.273	.349	0	—	0	-19	-15	-3	-2.3
● **DAISY DAVIS**	Davis, John Henry Albert b: 11/28/1858, Boston, Mass. d: 11/5/02, Lynn, Mass. TR, Deb: 5/06/1884																									
1884	StL-a	10	12	.455	25	24	20	1	0	198^1	196	1	35	143	11.1	2.90	112	.249	.293	15	.172	-2	8	8	-1	0.4
	Bos-N	1	3	.250	4	4	3	0	0	31	50	2	8	13	16.8	7.84	37	.355	.389	0	.000	-3	-17	-17	0	-1.5
1885	Bos-N	5	6	.455	11	11	10	1	0	94^1	110	2	28	30	13.2	4.29	63	.280	.328	7	.189	-0	-15	-17	-1	-1.6
Total	2	16	21	.432	40	39	33	2	0	323^2	356	5	71	186	12.3	3.78	81	.269	.313	22	.157	-5	-25	-26	-2	-2.7
● **JOHN DAVIS**	Davis, John Kirk b: 1/5/63, Chicago, Ill. BR/TR, 6'7", 215 lbs. Deb: 7/24/87																									
1987	KC-A	5	2	.714	27	0	0	0	2	43^2	29	0	26	24	11.7	2.27	201	.195	.322	0	—	0	11	11	0	0.9
1988	Chi-A	2	5	.286	34	1	0	0	1	63^2	77	5	50	37	18.5	6.64	60	.297	.419	0	—	0	-19	-19	-0	-1.9
1989	Chi-A	0	1	.000	4	0	0	0	1	6	5	2	2	5	10.5	4.50	85	.217	.280	0	—	0	-0	-0	0	0.1
1990	SD-N	0	1	.000	6	0	0	0	0	9^1	9	1	4	7	12.5	5.79	66	.257	.333	0	.000	-0	-2	-2	-0	-0.2
Total	4	7	9	.438	71	1	0	0	4	122^2	120	8	82	73	15.3	4.92	85	.258	.375	0	.000	-0	-11	-10	0	-1.1
● **BUD DAVIS**	Davis, John Wilbur "Country" b: 12/7/1896, Merry Point, Va. d: 5/26/67, Williamsburg, Va. BL/TR, 6', 207 lbs. Deb: 4/19/15																									
1915	Phi-A	0	2	.000	18	2	2	0	0	66^2	65	1	59	18	17.6	4.05	72	.273	.429	8	.308	2	-8	-8	-1	-0.7
● **MARK DAVIS**	Davis, Mark William b: 10/19/60, Livermore, Cal. BL/TL, 6'4", 205 lbs. Deb: 9/12/80																									
1980	Phi-N	0	0	—	2	1	0	0	0	7	4	0	5	5	11.6	2.57	147	.160	.300	1	.500	0	1	1	-0	0.1
1981	Phi-N	1	4	.200	9	9	0	0	0	43	49	7	24	29	15.3	7.74	47	.299	.388	1	.091	-0	-20	-20	-0	-1.9
1983	SF-N	6	4	.600	20	20	2	2	0	111	93	14	50	83	11.8	3.49	101	.227	.315	4	.133	0	2	1	-1	0.0
1984	SF-N	5	17	.227	46	27	1	0	0	174^2	201	25	54	124	13.4	5.36	65	.293	.349	6	.130	0	-34	-36	-2	-3.7
1985	SF-N	5	12	.294	77	1	0	0	7	114^1	89	13	41	131	10.5	3.54	97	.219	.295	3	.250	1	1	-1	-1	-0.1
1986	SF-N	5	7	.417	67	2	0	0	4	84^1	63	6	34	90	10.5	2.99	118	.212	.295	1	.125	0	7	5	-0	0.5
1987	SF-N	4	5	.444	20	11	1	0	0	70^2	72	9	28	51	13.2	4.71	82	.273	.351	5	.217	2	-5	-7	-1	-0.6
	SD-N	5	3	.625	43	0	0	0	2	62^1	51	5	31	47	12.1	3.18	124	.224	.322	2	.286	0	6	5	0	0.6
	Yr	9	8	.529	63	11	1	0	2	133	123	14	59	98	12.5	3.99	98	.247	.329	7	.233	2	1	-1	-0	0.0
1988	SD-N★	5	10	.333	62	0	0	0	28	98^1	70	2	42	102	10.3	2.01	169	.199	.284	2	.200	1	16	15	2	2.0
1989	SD-N★	4	3	.571	70	0	0	0	**44**	92^2	66	6	31	92	9.6	1.85	189	.200	.273	0	.000	-1	17	17	-1	1.6
1990	KC-A	2	7	.222	53	3	0	0	6	68^2	71	9	52	73	16.6	5.11	75	.259	.385	0	—	0	-9	-10	-1	-1.0
1991	KC-A	6	3	.667	29	5	0	0	1	62^2	55	6	39	47	13.6	4.45	93	.240	.353	0	—	0	-2	-2	-0	-0.3
1992	KC-A	1	3	.250	13	6	0	0	0	36^1	42	6	28	19	17.3	7.18	55	.294	.409	0	—	0	-13	-13	0	-1.3
	Atl-N	1	0	1.000	14	0	0	0	0	16^2	22	3	13	15	19.4	7.02	53	.314	.429	0	.000	-0	-7	-6	-1	-0.7
Total	12	50	78	.391	525	85	4	2	92	1042^2	948	111	472	908	12.5	4.07	89	.244	.330	25	.153	4	-42	-51	-4	-4.8
● **PEACHES DAVIS**	Davis, Ray Thomas b: 5/31/05, Glen Rose, Tex. BL/TR, 6'3.5", 190 lbs. Deb: 7/11/36																									
1936	Cin-N	8	8	.500	26	15	5	0	5	125^2	139	7	36	32	12.7	3.58	107	.280	.331	7	.163	-1	6	3	0	0.2
1937	Cin-N	11	13	.458	42	24	11	1	3	218	252	5	51	59	12.6	3.59	104	.295	.337	10	.128	-4	8	3	-3	-0.3
1938	Cin-N	7	12	.368	29	19	11	1	1	167^2	193	9	40	28	12.6	3.97	92	.290	.331	15	.246	1	-3	-6	-3	-0.8
1939	Cin-N	1	0	1.000	20	0	0	0	2	30^2	43	5	11	4	16.1	6.46	59	.341	.399	1	.333	0	-9	-9	0	-0.8
Total	4	27	33	.450	117	58	27	2	11	542	627	26	138	123	12.8	3.87	96	.293	.337	33	.178	-3	2	-8	-6	-1.7
● **BOB DAVIS**	Davis, Robert Edward b: 9/11/33, New York, N, Y. BR/TR, 6', 170 lbs. Deb: 7/26/58																									
1958	KC-A	0	4	.000	8	4	0	0	0	31	45	5	12	22	17.1	7.84	50	.346	.410	1	.167	-0	-14	-14	0	-1.3
1960	KC-A	0	0	—	21	0	0	0	1	32	31	1	22	28	15.2	3.66	109	.263	.383	1	.250	0	1	1	1	0.2

YEAR TM/L	W	L	PCT	G	GS	CG	SH	SV	IP	H	HR	BB	SO	RAT	ERA	ERA+	OAV	OOB	BH	AVG	PB	PR	/A	PD	TPI
Total 2	0	4	.000	29	4	0	0	1	63	76	6	34	50	16.1	5.71	69	.306	.396	2	.200	-0	-13	-12	2	-1.1
● **RON DAVIS** Davis, Ronald Gene b: 8/6/55, Houston, Tex. BR/TR, 6'4", 207 lbs. Deb: 7/29/78																									
1978 NY-A	0	0	—	4	0	0	0	0	2^1	3	0	3	0	23.1	11.57	31	.333	.500	0	—	0	-2	-2	0	-0.1
1979 NY-A	14	2	.875	44	0	0	0	9	85^1	84	5	28	43	11.9	2.85	143	.262	.323	0	.000	0	13	12	1	1.2
1980 *NY-A	9	3	.750	53	0	0	0	7	131	121	9	32	65	10.9	2.95	133	.246	.299	0	.000	0	16	14	0	1.4
1981 *NY-A★	4	5	.444	43	0	0	0	6	73	47	6	25	83	8.9	2.71	132	.186	.259	0	—	0	8	7	-1	0.7
1982 Min-A	3	9	.250	63	0	0	0	22	106	106	16	47	89	13.1	4.42	96	.261	.339	0	—	0	-4	-2	-0	-0.3
1983 Min-A	5	8	.385	66	0	0	0	30	89	89	6	33	84	12.6	3.34	127	.266	.338	0	—	0	7	9	-2	0.5
1984 Min-A	7	11	.389	64	0	0	0	29	83	79	11	41	74	13.2	4.55	92	.253	.344	0	—	0	-5	-3	-0	-0.6
1985 Min-A	2	6	.250	57	0	0	0	25	64^2	55	7	35	72	13.1	3.48	127	.230	.338	0	—	0	5	7	-0	0.2
1986 Min-A	2	6	.250	36	0	0	0	2	38^2	55	7	29	30	20.5	9.08	47	.340	.451	0	—	0	-21	-21	0	-2.1
Chi-N	0	2	.000	17	0	0	0	0	20	31	3	3	10	15.3	7.65	53	.356	.378	0	.000	-0	-9	-8	-1	-0.9
1987 Chi-N	0	0	—	21	0	0	0	0	32^1	43	8	12	31	15.3	5.85	73	.328	.385	0	—	0	-6	-6	-1	-0.6
LA-N	0	0	—	4	0	0	0	0	4	7	0	6	1	31.5	6.75	59	.412	.583	0	—	0	-1	-1	0	-0.1
Yr	0	0	—	25	0	0	0	0	36^1	50	8	18	32	17.1	5.94	71	.336	.411	0	—	0	-8	-7	-0	-0.7
1988 SF-N	1	1	.500	9	0	0	0	0	17^1	15	4	6	15	11.4	4.67	70	.234	.310	0	.000	-0	-2	-3	0	-0.3
Total 11	47	53	.470	481	0	0	0	130	746^2	735	82	300	597	12.7	4.05	101	.260	.336	0	.000	-0	-3	3	-3	-1.0
● **STEVE DAVIS** Davis, Steven Kennon b: 8/4/60, San Antonio, Tex. BL/TL, 6'1", 195 lbs. Deb: 8/25/85																									
1985 Tor-A	2	1	.667	10	5	0	0	0	28	23	5	13	22	11.6	3.54	119	.223	.310	0	—	0	2	2	-0	0.0
1986 Tor-A	0	0	—	3	0	0	0	0	3^2	8	2	5	5	31.9	17.18	25	.471	.591	0	—	0	-5	-5	-0	-0.6
1989 Cle-A	1	1	.500	12	2	0	0	0	25^2	34	2	14	12	16.8	8.06	49	.318	.397	0	—	0	-12	-12	-0	-1.3
Total 3	3	2	.600	25	7	0	0	0	57^1	65	9	32	39	15.2	6.44	64	.286	.375	0	—	0	-15	-15	-1	-1.9
● **WILEY DAVIS** Davis, Wiley Anderson b: 8/1/1875, Seymour, Tenn. d: 9/22/42, Detroit, Mich. BR/TR, 5'10", 165 lbs. Deb: 4/18/1896																									
1896 Cin-N	1	1	.500	2	0	0	0	0	4^1	8	0	2	1	20.8	8.31	55	.391	.446	0	.000	-0	-2	-2	1	-0.1
● **WOODY DAVIS** Davis, Woodrow Wilson "Babe" b: 4/25/13, Nicholls, Ga. BL/TR, 6'1", 200 lbs. Deb: 5/02/38																									
1938 Det-A	0	0	—	2	0	0	0	0	6	3	0	4	1	10.5	1.50	333	.158	.304	0	.000	-0	2	2	-0	0.2
● **MIKE DAVISON** Davison, Michael Lynn b: 8/4/45, Galesburg, Ill. BL/TL, 6'1", 170 lbs. Deb: 10/01/69																									
1969 SF-N	0	0	—	1	0	0	0	0	2	2	0	0	2	9.0	4.50	78	.250	.250	0	—	0	-0	-0	-0	0.0
1970 SF-N	3	5	.375	31	0	0	0	1	36	46	4	22	21	17.0	6.50	61	.324	.415	0	.000	0	-10	-10	1	-0.9
Total 2	3	5	.375	32	0	0	0	1	38	48	4	22	23	16.6	6.39	62	.320	.407	0	.000	0	-10	-10	1	-0.9
● **BILL DAWLEY** Dawley, William Chester b: 2/6/58, Norwich, Conn. BR/TR, 6'4", 240 lbs. Deb: 4/15/83																									
1983 Hou-N★	6	6	.500	48	0	0	0	14	79^2	51	9	22	60	8.4	2.82	120	.185	.247	2	.222	0	7	5	-1	0.4
1984 Hou-N	11	4	.733	60	0	0	0	5	98	82	5	35	47	10.7	1.93	172	.234	.303	3	.333	1	18	15	-1	1.7
1985 Hou-N	5	3	.625	49	0	0	0	2	81	76	7	37	48	12.6	3.56	97	.259	.341	2	.200	0	0	-1	0	0.0
1986 Chi-A	0	7	.000	46	0	0	0	2	97^2	91	10	28	66	11.1	3.32	130	.247	.302	0	.000	0	9	11	-1	1.0
1987 StL-N	5	8	.385	60	0	0	0	2	96^2	93	15	38	65	12.3	4.47	93	.259	.332	2	.167	0	-4	-3	1	-0.2
1988 Phi-N	0	2	.000	8	0	0	0	0	8^2	16	3	4	3	20.8	13.50	26	.381	.435	0	—	0	-10	-10	-0	-1.0
1989 Oak-A	0	0	—	4	0	0	0	0	9	11	0	2	3	14.0	4.00	92	.297	.350	0	—	0	-0	-0	-0	0.0
Total 7	27	30	.474	275	0	0	0	25	470^2	420	49	166	292	11.3	3.42	109	.243	.311	9	.214	3	21	16	-2	1.9
● **JOE DAWSON** Dawson, Ralph Fenton b: 3/9/1897, Bow, Wash. d: 1/4/78, Longview, Tex. BR/TR, 5'11", 182 lbs. Deb: 7/04/24																									
1924 Cle-A	1	2	.333	4	4	0	0	0	20^1	24	0	21	7	20.4	6.64	64	.300	.451	2	.286	0	-5	-5	1	-0.4
1927 *Pit-N	3	7	.300	20	7	4	0	0	80^2	80	2	32	17	12.5	4.46	92	.268	.338	5	.200	-1	-5	-3	-1	-0.4
1928 Pit-N	7	7	.500	31	7	1	0	3	128^2	116	6	56	36	12.1	3.29	123	.242	.322	12	.279	4	10	11	-3	1.1
1929 Pit-N	0	1	.000	4	0	0	0	0	8^2	13	2	3	2	16.6	8.31	57	.342	.390	1	.500	1	-3	-3	-0	-0.3
Total 4	11	17	.393	59	18	5	0	3	238^1	233	10	112	62	13.1	4.15	99	.260	.343	20	.260	3	-4	-1	-3	0.0
● **REX DAWSON** Dawson, Rexford Paul b: 2/10/1889, Skagit Co., Wash. d: 10/20/58, Indianapolis, Ind. BL/TR, 6', 185 lbs. Deb: 10/03/13																									
1913 Was-A	0	0	—	1	0	0	0	0	1	1	0	0	1	9.0	0.00	—	.250	.250	0	—	0	0	0	-0	0.0
● **PEA RIDGE DAY** Day, Clyde Henry b: 8/26/1899, Pea Ridge, Ark. d: 3/21/34, Kansas City, Mo. BR/TR, 6', 190 lbs. Deb: 9/19/24																									
1924 StL-N	1	1	.500	3	3	1	0	0	17^2	22	0	6	3	14.3	4.58	82	.306	.359	1	.125	-1	-1	-2	-0	-0.3
1925 StL-N	2	4	.333	17	4	1	0	1	40	53	5	7	13	14.2	6.30	69	.325	.364	2	.154	-1	-9	-9	-1	-0.9
1926 Cin-N	0	0	—	4	0	0	0	0	7^1	13	1	2	2	18.4	7.36	50	.406	.441	0	.000	-0	-3	-3	-0	-0.3
1931 Bro-N	2	2	.500	22	2	1	0	1	57^1	75	5	13	30	13.8	4.55	84	.315	.351	4	.222	0	-4	-5	-1	-0.5
Total 4	5	7	.417	46	9	3	0	2	122^1	163	11	28	48	14.3	5.30	75	.323	.362	7	.171	-2	-18	-18	-2	-2.0
● **BILL DAY** Day, William M. b: 7/28/1867, Wilmington, Del. d: 8/16/23, Wilmington, Del. TR, 5'8", 150 lbs. Deb: 8/20/1889																									
1889 Phi-N	0	3	.000	4	3	2	0	0	19	16	0	23	20	18.5	5.21	83	.221	.409	0	.000	-2	-3	-2	-0	-0.3
1890 Phi-N	1	1	.500	4	2	2	0	0	23^2	26	0	12	9	14.5	3.04	120	.271	.352	1	.100	-1	1	2	-1	0.0
Pit-N	0	6	.000	6	6	6	0	0	50	66	1	24	10	16.4	5.22	63	.308	.381	1	.043	-3	-9	-11	1	-1.0
Yr	1	7	.125	10	8	8	0	0	73^2	92	1	36	19	15.8	4.52	75	.297	.372	2	.061	-4	-8	-9	1	-1.0
Total 2	1	10	.091	14	11	10	0	0	92^2	108	1	59	39	16.3	4.66	77	.282	.380	2	.047	-6	-10	-11	0	-1.3
● **KEN DAYLEY** Dayley, Kenneth Grant b: 2/25/59, Jerome, Idaho BL/TL, 6', 175 lbs. Deb: 5/13/82																									
1982 Atl-N	5	6	.455	20	11	0	0	0	71^1	79	9	25	34	13.1	4.54	82	.286	.346	5	.250	1	-7	-6	-2	-0.8
1983 Atl-N	5	8	.385	24	16	0	0	0	104^2	100	12	39	70	12.1	4.30	90	.257	.328	7	.219	2	-8	-5	-2	-0.6
1984 Atl-N	0	3	.000	4	4	0	0	0	18^2	28	5	6	10	16.9	5.30	73	.341	.393	2	.500	1	-4	-3	0	-0.2
StL-N	0	2	.000	3	2	0	0	0	5	16	1	5	0	37.8	18.00	19	.615	.677	0	—	0	-8	-8	0	-0.8
Yr	0	5	.000	7	6	0	0	0	23^2	44	6	11	10	20.9	7.99	47	.404	.458	2	.500	1	-12	-11	0	-1.0
1985 *StL-N	4	4	.500	57	0	0	0	11	65^1	65	2	18	62	11.4	2.76	128	.263	.313	2	.400	1	6	6	2	0.8
1986 StL-N	0	3	.000	31	0	0	0	5	38^2	42	1	11	33	12.6	3.26	112	.275	.327	1	.200	0	2	2	0	0.2
1987 *StL-N	9	5	.643	53	0	0	0	4	61	52	2	33	63	12.8	2.66	156	.234	.339	0	—	0	10	10	-1	1.0
1988 StL-N	2	7	.222	54	0	0	0	5	55^1	48	2	19	38	11.1	2.77	126	.239	.308	0	.000	-0	4	4	-0	0.4
1989 StL-N	4	3	.571	71	0	0	0	12	75^1	63	3	30	40	11.1	2.87	127	.228	.304	0	.000	-1	5	6	-2	0.5
1990 StL-N	4	4	.500	58	0	0	0	2	73^1	63	5	30	51	11.4	3.56	107	.233	.310	0	.000	-1	2	2	-0	0.1
1991 Tor-A	0	0	—	8	0	0	0	0	4^1	7	0	5	3	27.0	6.23	67	.368	.520	0	—	0	-1	-1	0	-0.1
Total 10	33	45	.423	383	33	0	0	39	573	563	42	221	404	12.4	3.64	103	.261	.331	17	.210	3	1	7	-5	0.5
● **REN DEAGLE** Deagle, Lorenzo Burroughs b: 6/26/1858, New York, N.Y. d: 12/24/36, Kansas City, Mo. BR/TR, 5'9", 190 lbs. Deb: 5/17/1883																									
1883 Cin-a	10	8	.556	18	18	17	1	0	148	136	0	34	48	10.3	2.31	141	.228	.270	9	.129	-5	16	15	-1	0.8
1884 Cin-a	3	1	.750	4	4	4	1	0	34	39	0	9	12	13.0	5.03	66	.322	.374	0	.000	-2	-7	-6	-0	-0.7
Lou-a	4	6	.400	12	12	8	0	0	87^1	80	0	13	23	10.3	2.58	120	.238	.281	6	.133	-3	7	5	1	0.3
Yr	7	7	.500	16	16	12	1	0	121^1	119	0	22	35	11.0	3.26	97	.260	.304	6	.103	-5	-0	-1	1	-0.4
Total 2	17	15	.531	34	34	29	2	0	269^1	255	0	56	83	10.7	2.74	117	.242	.286	15	.117	-9	16	14	-1	0.4
● **COT DEAL** Deal, Ellis Fergason b: 1/23/23, Arapaho, Okla. BB/TR, 5'10.5", 185 lbs. Deb: 9/11/47 C																									
1947 Bos-A	0	1	.000	5	2	0	0	0	12^2	20	0	7	6	19.2	9.24	42	.364	.435	2	.500	1	-8	-8	0	-0.7
1948 Bos-A	1	0	1.000	4	0	0	0	0	4	3	0	3	2	13.5	0.00	—	.200	.333	0	—	0	2	2	0	0.2
1950 StL-N	0	0	—	3	0	0	0	0	1	3	0	2	1	45.0	18.00	24	.500	.625	0	—	0	-2	-2	-0	-0.2

YEAR	TM/L	W	L	PCT	G	GS	CG	SH	SV	IP	H	HR	BB	SO	RAT	ERA	ERA+	OAV	OOB	BH	AVG	PB	PR	/A	PD	TPI
1954	StL-N	2	3	.400	33	0	0	0	1	71^{2}	85	14	36	25	15.7	6.28	65	.297	.383	2	.100	0	-18	-17	-0	-1.6
Total	4	3	4	.429	45	2	0	0	1	89^{1}	111	14	48	34	16.4	6.55	63	.307	.394	4	.167	1	-25	-24	-0	-2.3
● CHUBBY DEAN	Dean, Alfred Lovill b: 8/24/16, Mt.Airy, N.C. d: 12/21/70, Riverside, Cal. BL/TL, 5'11", 181 lbs. Deb: 4/14/36 ♦																									
1937	Phi-A	1	0	1.000	2	1	0	0	0	9	7	0	6	4	13.0	4.00	118	.219	.342	81	.262	0	1	1	0	0.1
1938	Phi-A	2	1	.667	6	1	0	0	0	23	22	3	15	3	14.5	3.52	137	.250	.359	6	.300	2	3	3	1	0.5
1939	Phi-A	5	8	.385	54	1	0	0	7	116^{2}	132	8	80	39	16.4	5.25	90	.289	.395	27	.351	8	-8	-7	1	0.3
1940	Phi-A	6	13	.316	30	19	8	1	1	159^{1}	220	21	63	38	16.0	6.61	67	.324	.381	26	.289	4	-39	-38	1	-2.7
1941	Phi-A	2	4	.333	18	7	2	0	0	75^{2}	90	9	35	22	14.9	6.19	68	.294	.367	9	.243	2	-17	-17	0	-1.3
	Cle-A	1	4	.200	8	8	2	0	0	53^{1}	57	3	24	14	13.7	4.39	90	.282	.358	4	.160	0	-1	-3	1	-0.1
	Yr	3	8	.273	26	15	4	0	0	129	147	12	59	36	14.4	5.44	75	.289	.363	13	.210	2	-19	-19	1	-1.4
1942	Cle-A	8	11	.421	27	22	8	0	1	172^{2}	170	7	66	46	12.3	3.81	91	.261	.329	27	.267	8	-3	-7	-3	-0.2
1943	Cle-A	5	5	.500	17	9	3	0	0	76	83	1	34	29	14.0	4.50	69	.281	.358	9	.196	1	-10	-12	-1	-1.2
Total	7	30	46	.395	162	68	23	1	9	685^{2}	781	52	323	195	14.5	5.08	79	.288	.364	287	.274	25	-75	-80	-1	-4.6
● DORY DEAN	Dean, Charles Wilson b: 11/6/1852, Cincinnati, Ohio d: 5/4/35, Nashville, Tenn. BR/TR, Deb: 6/22/1876																									
1876	Cin-N	4	26	.133	30	30	26	0	0	262^{2}	397	1	24	22	14.4	3.73	59	.322	.335	36	.261	1	-42	-45	-1	-3.6
● HARRY DEAN	Dean, James Harry b: 5/12/15, Rockmart, Ga. d: 6/1/60, Rockmart, Ga. BR/TR, 6'4", 185 lbs. Deb: 4/16/41																									
1941	Was-A	0	0	—	2	0	0	0	0	2	2	0	3	0	27.0	4.50	90	.250	.500	0	—	0	-0	-0	-0	0.0
● DIZZY DEAN	Dean, Jay Hanna b: 1/16/11, Lucas, Ark. d: 7/17/74, Reno, Nevada BR/TR, 6'2", 182 lbs. Deb: 9/28/30 FCH																									
1930	StL-N	1	0	1.000	1	1	1	0	0	9	3	0	3	5	6.0	1.00	502	.103	.188	1	.333	0	4	4	1	0.5
1932	StL-N	18	15	.545	46	33	16	**4**	2	**286**	280	14	102	**191**	12.2	3.30	119	.260	.327	25	.258	5	18	20	-1	2.4
1933	StL-N	20	18	.526	**48**	34	**26**	3	4	293	279	11	64	**199**	10.7	3.04	114	.250	.293	19	.181	1	10	14	-5	1.1
1934	*StL-N★	**30**	7	**.811**	50	33	24	**7**	7	311^{2}	288	14	75	**195**	10.7	2.66	159	.241	.289	29	.246	4	49	54	-2	5.7
1935	StL-N★	**28**	12	.700	50	36	**29**	3	5	**325^{1}**	324	16	77	**190**	11.2	3.04	135	.256	.300	30	.234	4	35	38	-5	3.7
1936	StL-N★	24	13	.649	**51**	34	**28**	2	**11**	**315**	310	21	53	195	10.5	3.17	124	.253	.285	27	.223	1	30	27	-4	2.5
1937	StL-N★	13	10	.565	27	25	17	4	1	197^{1}	200	9	33	120	10.7	2.69	148	.259	.291	15	.227	2	27	28	-3	2.8
1938	*Chi-N	7	1	.875	13	10	3	1	0	74^{2}	63	2	8	22	8.7	1.81	212	.226	.250	5	.192	-0	16	17	-1	1.7
1939	Chi-N	6	4	.600	19	13	7	2	0	96^{1}	98	4	17	27	10.8	3.36	117	.261	.294	5	.147	-1	6	6	-1	0.4
1940	Chi-N	3	3	.500	10	9	3	0	0	54	68	4	20	18	14.7	5.17	73	.306	.364	4	.222	0	-8	-9	1	-0.7
1941	Chi-N	0	0	—	1	1	0	0	0	1	3	0	0	1	27.0	18.00	19	.429	.429	0	—	0	-2	-2	0	-0.2
1947	StL-A	0	0	—	1	1	0	0	0	4	3	0	1	0	9.0	0.00	—	.231	.286	1	1.000	0	2	2	-0	0.2
Total	12	150	83	.644	317	230	154	26	30	1967^{1}	1919	95	453	1163	11.0	3.02	130	.253	.298	161	.225	16	187	201	-20	20.1
● PAUL DEAN	Dean, Paul Dee "Daffy" b: 8/14/13, Lucas, Ark. d: 3/17/81, Springdale, Ark. BR/TR, 6', 175 lbs. Deb: 4/18/34 F																									
1934	*StL-N	19	11	.633	39	26	16	5	2	233^{1}	225	19	52	150	10.9	3.43	123	.248	.292	20	.241	1	16	21	-6	1.6
1935	StL-N	19	12	.613	46	33	19	2	5	269^{2}	261	16	55	143	10.8	3.37	122	.249	.292	12	.133	-5	19	22	-6	1.1
1936	StL-N	5	5	.500	17	14	5	0	1	92	113	3	20	28	13.1	4.60	86	.300	.337	2	.059	-4	-6	-7	-3	-1.3
1937	StL-N	0	0	—	1	0	0	0	0	0	1	0	2	0	—	∞	—	1.000	1.000	0	—	0	-3	-3	0	-0.3
1938	StL-N	3	1	.750	5	4	2	1	0	31	37	3	5	14	12.2	2.61	151	.298	.326	2	.182	-0	4	5	-1	0.4
1939	StL-N	0	1	.000	16	2	0	0	0	43	54	4	10	16	13.6	6.07	68	.310	.351	1	.111	-1	-10	-9	-0	-1.0
1940	NY-N	4	4	.500	27	7	2	0	0	99^{1}	110	8	29	32	12.6	3.90	100	.281	.330	3	.115	-2	-1	-0	-1	-0.3
1941	NY-N	0	0	—	5	0	0	0	0	5^{2}	8	0	3	3	17.5	3.18	116	.320	.393	0	—	0	0	0	-0	0.0
1943	StL-A	0	0	—	3	1	0	0	0	13^{1}	16	0	3	1	13.5	3.38	99	.296	.345	0	.000	-0	-0	-0	-0	-0.1
Total	9	50	34	.595	159	87	44	8	8	787^{1}	825	53	179	387	11.7	3.75	109	.266	.309	40	.156	-11	20	28	-18	0.1
● WAYLAND DEAN	Dean, Wayland Ogden b: 6/20/02, Richmond, W.Va. d: 4/10/30, Huntington, W.Va. BB/TR, 6'1", 178 lbs. Deb: 4/17/24																									
1924	*NY-N	6	12	.333	26	20	6	0	0	125^{2}	139	9	45	39	13.5	5.01	73	.280	.346	8	.200	1	-16	-19	3	-1.5
1925	NY-N	10	7	.588	33	14	6	1	1	151^{1}	169	13	50	53	13.3	4.64	87	.282	.342	12	.235	3	-6	-10	0	-0.7
1926	Phi-N	8	16	.333	33	26	15	1	0	203^{2}	245	9	89	52	14.9	4.91	84	.307	.379	27	.265	5	-24	-17	-1	-1.3
1927	Phi-N	0	1	.000	2	0	0	0	0	3	6	0	2	1	24.0	12.00	34	.500	.571	2	.667	1	-3	-3	0	-0.1
	Chi-N	0	0	—	2	0	0	0	0	2	0	0	2	2	13.5	0.00	—	.000	.429	0	—	0	1	1	0	0.1
	Yr	0	1	.000	4	0	0	0	0	5	6	0	4	3	19.8	7.20	56	.375	.524	2	.667	1	-2	-2	0	0.0
Total	4	24	36	.400	96	60	27	2	1	485^{2}	559	31	188	147	14.1	4.87	82	.293	.360	49	.250	10	-48	-47	2	-3.5
● DENNIS DeBARR	DeBarr, Dennis Lee b: 1/16/53, Cheyenne, Wyo. BL/TL, 6'2", 190 lbs. Deb: 5/14/77																									
1977	Tor-A	0	1	.000	14	0	0	0	0	21^{1}	29	1	8	10	15.6	5.91	71	.337	.394	0	—	0	-4	-4	-0	-0.4
● JOE DeBERRY	DeBerry, Joseph Gaddy b: 11/29/1896, Mt.Gilead, N.C. d: 10/9/44, Southern Pines, N.C BL/TR, 6'1", 175 lbs. Deb: 8/24/20																									
1920	StL-A	2	4	.333	10	7	3	1	0	54^{2}	65	2	20	12	14.3	4.94	79	.307	.372	3	.167	-1	-7	-6	0	-0.6
1921	StL-A	0	1	.000	10	1	0	0	0	12^{1}	15	0	10	1	18.2	6.57	68	.300	.417	0	.000	-0	-3	-3	0	-0.3
Total	2	2	5	.286	20	8	3	1	0	67	80	2	30	13	15.0	5.24	77	.305	.381	3	.150	-1	-10	-9	0	-0.9
● DAVE DeBUSSCHERE	DeBusschere, David Albert b: 10/16/40, Detroit, Mich. BR/TR, 6'6", 225 lbs. Deb: 4/22/62																									
1962	Chi-A	0	0	—	12	0	0	0	0	18	5	1	23	8	14.5	2.00	195	.089	.363	0	—	0	4	4	0	0.4
1963	Chi-A	3	4	.429	24	10	1	1	0	84^{1}	80	9	34	53	12.6	3.09	113	.249	.329	1	.045	-2	5	4	0	0.3
Total	2	3	4	.429	36	10	1	1	0	102^{1}	85	10	57	61	12.9	2.90	123	.225	.335	1	.045	-2	9	8	0	0.7
● ART DECATUR	Decatur, Arthur Rue b: 1/14/1894, Cleveland, Ohio d: 4/25/66, Talladega, Ala. BR/TR, 6'1", 190 lbs. Deb: 4/15/22																									
1922	Bro-N	3	4	.429	29	2	1	0	1	87^{2}	87	3	29	31	12.0	2.77	147	.265	.327	2	.080	-2	13	13	-2	0.9
1923	Bro-N	3	3	.500	36	5	2	0	3	97^{2}	101	3	32	25	12.4	2.58	150	.264	.325	0	.000	-3	**15**	**14**	-2	0.9
1924	Bro-N	10	9	.526	31	10	3	0	1	126^{1}	156	12	27	38	13.3	4.13	91	.308	.348	5	.114	-3	-4	-5	-2	-1.1
1925	Bro-N	0	0	—	1	0	0	0	0	1	3	0	0	0	27.0	18.00	23	.600	.600	0	—	0	-2	-2	-0	-0.1
	Phi-N	4	13	.235	25	15	4	0	2	128	170	13	35	31	14.6	5.27	91	.316	.360	2	.049	-5	-14	-7	-2	-1.3
	Yr	4	13	.235	26	15	4	0	2	129	173	13	35	31	14.7	5.37	89	.319	.362	2	.049	-5	-16	-9	-2	-1.4
1926	Phi-N	0	0	—	2	1	0	0	0	3	6	0	2	0	24.0	6.00	69	.375	.444	0	.000	-0	-1	-1	-0	-0.1
1927	Phi-N	3	5	.375	29	3	0	0	0	94^{2}	130	11	20	27	14.6	7.42	56	.334	.373	6	.222	0	-37	-35	-2	-3.4
Total	6	23	34	.404	153	36	10	0	7	538^{1}	653	42	145	152	13.6	4.51	92	.302	.349	15	.094	-14	-29	-23	-10	-4.2
● MARTY DECKER	Decker, Dee Martin b: 6/7/57, Upland, Cal. BR/TR, 5'10", 168 lbs. Deb: 9/20/83																									
1983	SD-N	0	0	—	4	0	0	0	0	8^{2}	5	1	3	9	9.3	2.08	168	.167	.265	0	—	0	1	1	0	0.1
● JOE DECKER	Decker, George Henry b: 6/16/47, Storm Lake, Ia. BR/TR, 6', 180 lbs. Deb: 9/18/69																									
1969	Chi-N	1	0	1.000	4	1	0	0	0	12^{1}	10	0	6	13	11.7	2.92	138	.222	.314	0	.000	-0	1	2	-0	0.1
1970	Chi-N	2	7	.222	24	17	1	0	0	108^{2}	108	12	56	79	13.9	4.64	97	.263	.357	6	.176	1	-7	-2	-1	-0.2
1971	Chi-N	3	2	.600	21	4	0	0	0	45^{2}	62	2	25	37	17.1	4.73	83	.343	.422	2	.250	1	-6	-4	1	-0.3
1972	Chi-N	1	0	1.000	5	1	0	0	0	12^{2}	9	1	4	7	9.2	2.13	179	.188	.250	0	.000	-0	2	2	-0	0.2
1973	Min-A	10	10	.500	29	24	6	3	0	170^{1}	167	12	88	109	13.7	4.17	95	.260	.352	0	—	0	-7	-4	0	-0.4
1974	Min-A	16	14	.533	37	37	11	1	0	248^{2}	234	24	97	158	12.1	3.29	114	.252	.324	0	—	0	9	13	-2	1.1
1975	Min-A	1	3	.250	10	7	1	0	0	26^{1}	25	2	36	8	20.8	8.54	45	.260	.462	0	—	0	-14	-14	-0	-1.4
1976	Min-A	2	7	.222	13	12	0	0	0	58	60	3	51	35	17.4	5.28	68	.273	.412	0	—	0	-11	-11	1	-1.1
1979	Sea-A	0	1	.000	9	2	0	0	0	27^{1}	27	2	14	12	13.5	4.28	102	.255	.342	0	—	0	-0	0	1	0.0
Total	9	36	44	.450	152	105	19	4	0	710	702	58	377	458	13.8	4.17	95	.262	.355	8	.174	1	-34	-18	-1	-2.0

YEAR	TM/L	W	L	PCT	G	GS	CG	SH	SV	IP	H	HR	BB	SO	RAT	ERA	ERA+	OAV	OOB	BH	AVG	PB	PR	/A	PD	TPI

● JEFF DEDMON Dedmon, Jeffrey Linden b: 3/4/60, Torrance, Cal. BL/TR, 6'2", 200 lbs. Deb: 9/02/83

1983	Atl-N	0	0	—	5	0	0	0	0	4	10	1	0	3	22.5	13.50	29	.455	.455	0	—	0	-4	-4	0	-0.4
1984	Atl-N	4	3	.571	54	0	0	0	4	81	86	5	35	51	13.7	3.78	102	.277	.354	0	.000	-1	-2	1	2	0.2
1985	Atl-N	6	3	.667	60	0	0	0	0	86	84	5	49	41	14.0	4.08	94	.264	.364	1	.111	-0	-5	-2	3	0.1
1986	Atl-N	6	6	.500	57	0	0	0	3	99²	90	8	39	58	12.0	2.98	133	.242	.320	2	.125	-1	8	11	2	1.2
1987	Atl-N	3	4	.429	53	3	0	0	4	89²	82	8	42	40	12.5	3.91	111	.246	.332	4	.250	1	2	4	1	0.6
1988	Cle-A	1	0	1.000	21	0	0	0	1	33²	35	3	21	17	15.8	4.54	90	.276	.391	0	—	0	-2	-2	1	0.0
Total	6	20	16	.556	250	3	0	0	12	394	387	30	186	210	13.3	3.84	105	.261	.348	7	.149	-0	-3	8	9	1.7

● DUMMY DEEGAN Deegan, William John b: 11/16/1874, Bronx, N.Y. d: 5/17/57, Bronx, N.Y. Deb: 8/03/01

| 1901 | NY-N | 0 | 1 | .000 | 2 | 1 | 1 | 0 | 0 | 17 | 27 | 0 | 6 | 8 | 17.5 | 6.35 | 52 | .357 | .404 | 0 | .000 | -1 | -6 | -6 | 0 | -0.5 |

● JOHN DEERING Deering, John Thomas b: 6/25/1879, Lynn, Mass. d: 2/15/43, Beverly, Mass. TR, Deb: 5/12/03

1903	Det-A	3	4	.429	10	8	5	0	0	60²	77	3	24	14	15.1	3.86	75	.308	.371	8	.333	2	-6	-6	-1	-0.5
	NY-A	4	3	.571	9	7	6	1	0	60	59	0	18	14	11.7	3.75	83	.256	.313	1	.043	-3	-5	-4	-1	-0.8
	Yr	7	7	.500	19	15	11	1	0	120²	136	3	42	28	13.4	3.80	79	.283	.342	9	.191	-0	-11	-11	-2	-1.3

● MIKE DEGERICK Degerick, Michael Arthur b: 4/1/43, New York, N.Y. BR/TR, 6'2", 178 lbs. Deb: 9/04/61

1961	Chi-A	0	0	—	1	0	0	0	0	1²	2	0	1	0	16.2	5.40	72	.400	.500	0	—	0	-0	-0	0	0.0
1962	Chi-A	0	0	—	1	0	0	0	0	1	1	0	1	0	18.0	0.00	—	.250	.400	0	—	0	0	0	0	0.1
Total	2	0	0	—	2	0	0	0	0	2²	3	0	2	0	16.9	3.38	116	.333	.455	0	—	0	0	0	0	0.1

● PEP DEININGER Deininger, Otto Charles b: 10/10/1877, Wasseralfingen, Germany d: 9/25/50, Boston, Mass. BL/TL, 5'8.5", 180 lbs. Deb: 4/26/02 ♦

| 1902 | Bos-A | 0 | 0 | — | 2 | 1 | 0 | 0 | 0 | 12 | 19 | 3 | 9 | 2 | 22.5 | 9.75 | 37 | .358 | .469 | 2 | .333 | 1 | -8 | -8 | -1 | -0.6 |

● JOSE DeJESUS DeJesus, Jose Luis b: 1/6/65, Brooklyn, N.Y. BR/TR, 6'5", 175 lbs. Deb: 9/09/88

1988	KC-A	0	1	.000	2	1	0	0	0	2²	6	0	5	2	37.1	27.00	15	.429	.579	0	—	0	-7	-7	-0	-0.6
1989	KC-A	0	0	—	3	1	0	0	0	8	7	1	8	2	16.9	4.50	85	.241	.405	0	—	0	-1	-1	-0	0.0
1990	Phi-N	7	8	.467	22	22	3	1	0	130	97	10	73	87	11.9	3.74	102	.210	.321	3	.079	-1	1	1	-1	0.0
1991	Phi-N	10	9	.526	31	29	3	0	1	181²	147	7	128	118	13.8	3.42	107	.224	.355	8	.129	-1	5	5	-3	0.1
Total	4	17	18	.486	58	53	6	1	1	322¹	257	18	214	209	13.3	3.77	99	.222	.346	11	.110	-2	-1	-1	-3	-0.5

● TOMMY de la CRUZ de la Cruz, Tomas (Rivero) b: 9/18/11, Marianao, Cuba d: 9/6/58, Havana, Cuba BR/TR, 6'2", 168 lbs. Deb: 4/20/44

| 1944 | Cin-N | 9 | 9 | .500 | 34 | 20 | 9 | 3 | 1 | 191¹ | 170 | 9 | 45 | 65 | 10.2 | 3.25 | 108 | .238 | .284 | 9 | .155 | -0 | 8 | 5 | -0 | 0.5 |

● JIM DELAHANTY Delahanty, James Christopher b: 6/20/1879, Cleveland, Ohio d: 10/17/53, Cleveland, Ohio BR/TR, 5'10.5", 170 lbs. Deb: 4/19/01 F♦

1904	Bos-N	0	0	—	1	0	0	0	0	3¹	5	0	1	0	16.2	0.00	—	.357	.400	142	.285	0	1	1	0	0.1
1905	Bos-N	0	0	—	1	1	0	0	0	2	5	1	0	0	22.5	4.50	69	.500	.500	119	.258	0	-0	-0	0	0.0
Total	2	0	0	—	2	1	0	0	0	5¹	10	1	1	0	18.6	1.69	171	.417	.440	1159	.283	1	1	1	0	0.1

● ART DELANEY Delaney, Arthur Dewey "Swede" (b: Arthur Dewey Helenius)
b: 1/5/1895, Chicago, Ill. d: 5/2/70, Hayward, Cal. BR/TR, 5'10.5", 178 lbs. Deb: 4/16/24

1924	StL-N	1	0	1.000	8	1	1	0	0	20	19	0	6	2	11.2	1.80	210	.250	.305	2	.286	0	5	4	0	0.5
1928	Bos-N	9	17	.346	39	22	8	0	2	192¹	197	11	56	45	11.9	3.79	103	.267	.319	9	.143	-3	4	2	1	0.1
1929	Bos-N	3	5	.375	20	8	3	1	0	75	103	6	35	17	16.7	6.12	76	.336	.405	3	.143	-0	-12	-12	-1	-1.1
Total	3	13	22	.371	67	31	12	1	2	287¹	319	17	97	64	13.1	4.26	96	.285	.343	14	.154	-2	-3	-5	0	-0.5

● FRANCISCO DeLA ROSA DeLa Rosa, Francisco (Jimenez) b: 3/3/66, LaRomana, D.R. BB/TR, 5'11", 185 lbs. Deb: 9/07/91

| 1991 | Bal-A | 0 | 0 | — | 2 | 0 | 0 | 0 | 0 | 4 | 6 | 0 | 2 | 1 | 18.0 | 4.50 | 88 | .353 | .421 | 0 | — | 0 | -0 | -0 | -0 | 0.2 |

● JOSE DeLEON DeLeon, Jose (Chestaro) b: 12/20/60, LaVega, D.R. BR/TR, 6'3", 215 lbs. Deb: 7/23/83

1983	Pit-N	7	3	.700	15	15	3	2	0	108	75	5	47	118	10.3	2.83	131	.196	.285	2	.059	-1	10	10	-1	1.0
1984	Pit-N	7	13	.350	30	28	5	1	0	192¹	147	10	92	153	11.3	3.74	96	.214	.310	5	.085	-4	-3	-3	-3	-1.0
1985	Pit-N	2	19	.095	31	25	1	0	3	162²	138	15	89	149	12.7	4.70	76	.231	.334	2	.056	-2	-20	-20	-1	-2.3
1986	Pit-N	1	3	.250	9	1	0	0	1	16¹	17	2	17	11	19.3	8.27	46	.266	.427	0	.000	0	-8	-8	0	-0.8
	Chi-A	4	5	.444	13	13	1	0	0	79	49	7	42	68	10.8	2.96	145	.179	.297	0	—	0	11	12	0	1.3
1987	Chi-A	11	12	.478	33	31	2	0	0	206	177	24	97	153	12.4	4.02	114	.230	.324	0	—	0	10	13	-3	0.8
1988	StL-N	13	10	.565	34	34	3	1	0	225²	198	13	86	208	11.4	3.67	95	.237	.310	10	.139	-0	-6	-5	-2	-0.8
1989	StL-N	16	12	.571	36	36	5	3	0	244²	173	16	80	**201**	9.5	3.05	119	**.197**	.269	8	.096	-4	12	16	-4	0.8
1990	StL-N	7	19	.269	32	32	0	0	0	182²	168	15	86	164	12.8	4.43	86	.246	.335	6	.107	-1	-13	-13	-2	-1.6
1991	StL-N	5	9	.357	28	28	1	0	0	162²	144	15	61	118	11.7	2.71	137	.239	.315	2	.043	-4	18	18	-2	1.4
1992	StL-N	2	7	.222	29	15	0	0	0	102¹	95	7	43	72	12.3	4.57	75	.245	.324	1	.048	-1	-12	-13	-1	-1.6
	Phi-N	0	1	.000	3	3	0	0	0	15	16	0	5	7	12.6	3.00	117	.281	.339	2	.400	-1	1	1	-0	0.1
	Yr	2	8	.200	32	18	0	0	0	117¹	111	7	48	79	12.2	4.37	79	.246	.324	3	.115	-0	-11	-12	-1	-1.5
Total	10	75	113	.399	293	261	21	7	4	1697	1397	129	745	1422	11.6	3.73	101	.225	.312	38	.092	-16	-2	7	-19	-2.7

● LUIS DeLEON DeLeon, Luis Antonio (Tricoche) b: 8/19/58, Ponce, P.R. BR/TR, 6'1", 153 lbs. Deb: 9/06/81

1981	StL-N	0	1	.000	10	0	0	0	0	15¹	11	1	3	8	8.2	2.35	151	.200	.241	0	.000	-0	2	2	-0	0.2
1982	SD-N	9	5	.643	61	0	0	0	15	102	77	10	16	60	8.3	2.03	169	.212	.247	1	.091	0	18	16	1	1.8
1983	SD-N	6	6	.500	63	0	0	0	13	111	89	8	27	94	9.5	2.68	130	.224	.288	2	.143	0	12	10	-2	0.9
1984	SD-N	2	2	.500	32	0	0	0	0	42²	44	12	12	44	12.7	5.48	65	.256	.319	0	.000	-0	-9	-9	-1	-1.0
1985	SD-N	0	3	.000	29	0	0	0	3	38²	39	6	10	31	12.1	4.19	84	.267	.327	1	.200	-0	-3	-3	-0	-0.3
1987	Bal-A	0	2	.000	11	0	0	0	1	20²	19	1	8	13	12.6	4.79	92	.253	.341	0	—	0	-1	-1	-1	0.0
1989	Sea-A	0	0	—	1	1	0	0	0	4	5	1	1	2	15.8	2.25	179	.313	.389	0	—	0	1	1	-0	0.1
Total	7	17	19	.472	207	1	0	0	32	334¹	284	39	77	248	10.0	3.12	114	.232	.284	4	.114	-0	20	16	-2	1.5

● FLAME DELHI Delhi, Lee William b: 11/5/1892, Harqua Hala, Ariz. d: 5/9/66, Greenbrae, Cal. BR/TR, 6'2.5", 198 lbs. Deb: 4/16/12

| 1912 | Chi-A | 0 | 0 | — | 1 | 0 | 0 | 0 | 0 | 3 | 7 | 0 | 3 | 2 | 30.0 | 9.00 | 36 | .412 | .500 | 0 | — | 0 | -2 | -2 | 0 | -0.1 |

● WHEEZER DELL Dell, William George b: 6/11/1887, Tuscarora, Nev. d: 8/24/66, Independence, Cal. BR/TR, 6'4", 210 lbs. Deb: 4/22/12

1912	StL-N	0	0	—	3	0	0	0	0	2¹	3	0	3	0	23.1	11.57	30	.188	.316	0	—	0	-2	-2	-0	-0.2
1915	Bro-N	11	10	.524	40	24	12	4	1	215	166	5	100	94	11.5	2.34	119	.218	.315	10	.152	-1	10	10	0	1.1
1916	*Bro-N	8	9	.471	32	16	9	2	1	155	143	2	43	76	11.0	2.26	118	.256	.314	4	.091	-2	6	7	-1	0.4
1917	Bro-N	0	4	.000	17	4	0	0	1	58	55	3	25	28	12.7	3.72	75	.263	.347	1	.063	-2	-7	-6	-1	-0.9
Total	4	19	23	.452	92	44	21	6	3	430¹	367	10	171	198	11.5	2.55	108	.237	.319	15	.119	-5	7	9	-2	0.4

● IKE DELOCK Delock, Ivan Martin b: 11/11/29, Highland Park, Mich. BR/TR, 5'11", 175 lbs. Deb: 4/17/52

1952	Bos-A	4	9	.308	39	7	1	1	5	95	88	9	50	46	13.3	4.26	92	.245	.341	1	.045	-1	-6	-3	-0	-0.5
1953	Bos-A	3	1	.750	23	1	0	0	1	48²	60	2	20	22	15.2	4.44	95	.308	.378	1	.100	-1	-2	-1	-1	-0.3
1955	Bos-A	9	7	.563	29	18	6	0	3	143²	136	16	61	88	12.6	3.76	114	.247	.326	7	.143	-1	3	8	-1	0.7
1956	Bos-A	13	7	.650	48	8	1	0	9	128¹	122	12	80	105	14.5	4.21	110	.252	.363	3	.103	-2	-1	6	0	0.4
1957	Bos-A	9	8	.529	49	2	0	0	11	94	80	11	45	62	12.3	3.83	104	.230	.323	1	.048	-1	-0	2	-1	0.0
1958	Bos-A	14	8	.636	31	19	9	1	2	160	155	13	56	82	11.5	3.37	119	.252	.315	3	.063	-4	7	11	-1	0.7
1959	Bos-A	11	6	.647	28	17	4	0	0	134¹	120	12	62	55	12.3	2.95	138	.236	.322	3	.064	-3	14	17	-2	1.2
1960	Bos-A	9	10	.474	24	23	3	1	0	129¹	145	21	52	49	14.0	4.73	85	.283	.354	3	.116	-3	-12	-10	-1	-1.3
1961	Bos-A	6	9	.400	28	28	3	1	0	156	185	24	52	80	13.8	4.90	85	.293	.349	5	.104	-2	-15	-13	-2	-1.6

YEAR	TM/L	W	L	PCT	G	GS	CG	SH	SV	IP	H	HR	BB	SO	RAT	ERA	ERA+	OAV	OOB	BH	AVG	PB	PR	/A	PD	TPI
1962	Bos-A	4	5	.444	17	13	4	2	0	86¹	89	10	24	49	11.8	3.75	110	.268	.317	2	.087	-1	2	4	-1	0.1
1963	Bos-A	1	2	.333	6	6	1	0	0	32	31	4	12	23	12.1	4.50	84	.246	.312	0	.000	-2	-3	-3	-0	-0.4
	Bal-A	1	3	.250	7	5	0	0	0	30¹	25	7	16	11	12.2	5.04	70	.236	.336	0	.000	-1	-5	-5	-0	-0.6
	Yr	2	5	.286	13	11	1	0	0	62¹	56	11	28	34	12.1	4.76	77	.240	.322	0	.000	-3	-8	-8	-0	-1.0
Total	11	84	75	.528	329	147	32	6	31	1238	1236	141	530	672	13.0	4.03	102	.259	.336	31	.086	-21	-19	12	-9	-1.6

● **RAMON de los SANTOS**   de los Santos, Ramon (Genero) b: 1/19/49, Santo Domingo, D.R.   BL/TL, 6'1", 175 lbs.   Deb: 8/21/74

| 1974 | Hou-N | 1 | 1 | .500 | 12 | 0 | 0 | 0 | 0 | 12¹ | 11 | 0 | 9 | 7 | 14.6 | 2.19 | 158 | .234 | .357 | 0 | — | 0 | 2 | 2 | 0 | 0.2 |

● **RICH DeLUCIA**   DeLucia, Richard Anthony b: 10/7/64, Reading, Pa.   BR/TR, 6', 180 lbs.   Deb: 9/08/90

1990	Sea-A	1	2	.333	5	5	0	0	0	36	30	2	9	20	9.8	2.00	198	.226	.275	0	—	0	8	8	-1	0.7
1991	Sea-A	12	13	.480	32	31	0	0	0	182	176	31	78	98	12.8	5.09	81	.260	.339	0	—	0	-20	-20	-2	-2.1
1992	Sea-A	3	6	.333	30	11	0	0	1	83²	100	13	35	66	14.7	5.49	73	.293	.362	0	—	0	-14	-14	-1	-1.5
Total	3	16	21	.432	67	47	0	0	1	301²	306	46	122	184	12.9	4.83	84	.266	.339	0	—	0	-27	-26	-3	-2.9

● **FRED DEMARAIS**   Demarais, Frederick b: 11/1/1866, Canada d: 3/6/19, Stamford, Conn.   TR,   Deb: 7/26/1890

| 1890 | Chi-N | 0 | 0 | — | 1 | 0 | 0 | 0 | 0 | 2 | 1 | 0 | 1 | 2 | 9.0 | 0.00 | — | .144 | .252 | 0 | .000 | -0 | 1 | 1 | 0 | 0.1 |

● **AL DEMAREE**   Demaree, Albert Wentworth b: 9/8/1884, Quincy, Ill. d: 4/30/62, Los Angeles, Cal.   BL/TR, 6', 170 lbs.   Deb: 9/26/12

1912	NY-N	1	0	1.000	2	2	1	1	0	16	17	0	2	11	10.7	1.69	200	.288	.311	0	.000	-1	3	3	0	0.2
1913	*NY-N	13	4	.765	31	24	11	2	2	199²	176	4	38	76	9.9	2.21	141	.243	.286	7	.106	-3	22	20	-3	1.4
1914	NY-N	10	17	.370	38	30	13	2	0	224	219	3	77	89	12.2	3.09	86	.263	.331	9	.132	-2	-8	-11	-1	-1.5
1915	Phi-N	14	11	.560	32	26	13	3	1	209²	201	4	58	69	11.2	3.05	90	.260	.314	12	.176	0	-7	-7	-5	-1.3
1916	Phi-N	19	14	.576	39	35	25	4	1	285	252	4	48	130	9.7	2.62	101	.242	.281	11	.109	-4	-0	1	-6	-1.1
1917	Chi-N	5	9	.357	24	18	6	1	1	141¹	125	5	37	43	10.4	2.55	114	.244	.297	5	.122	-2	3	5	1	0.5
	NY-N	4	5	.444	15	11	1	0	0	78¹	70	1	17	23	10.1	2.64	97	.239	.283	2	.111	-1	1	-1	0	-0.2
	Yr	9	14	.391	39	29	7	1	1	219²	195	6	54	66	10.2	2.58	107	.241	.290	7	.119	-2	3	5	1	0.3
1918	NY-N	8	6	.571	26	14	8	2	1	142	143	5	25	39	10.8	2.47	106	.262	.297	6	.128	-3	5	2	-0	-0.1
1919	Bos-N	6	6	.500	25	13	6	0	3	128	147	8	35	34	12.9	3.80	75	.300	.348	2	.048	-5	-13	-13	-2	-2.1
Total	8	80	72	.526	232	173	84	15	9	1424	1350	34	337	514	10.9	2.77	100	.256	.304	54	.118	-20	6	0	-16	-4.2

● **LARRY DEMERY**   Demery, Lawrence Calvin b: 6/4/53, Bakersfield, Cal.   BR/TR, 6', 170 lbs.   Deb: 6/02/74

1974	*Pit-N	6	6	.500	19	15	2	0	0	95¹	95	12	51	51	13.8	4.25	81	.262	.354	5	.152	0	-7	-9	-1	-0.9
1975	*Pit-N	7	5	.583	45	8	1	0	4	114²	95	7	43	59	11.1	2.90	122	.230	.307	3	.125	1	9	8	-1	-0.9
1976	Pit-N	10	7	.588	36	15	4	1	2	145	123	8	58	72	11.4	3.17	110	.234	.313	5	.125	-1	5	5	-0	0.4
1977	Pit-N	6	5	.545	39	8	0	0	1	90¹	100	13	47	35	14.6	5.08	78	.279	.363	3	.150	-0	-12	-11	-0	-1.2
Total	4	29	23	.558	139	46	7	1	7	445¹	413	40	199	217	12.5	3.72	97	.249	.331	16	.137	-0	-4	-6	-2	-0.8

● **HARRY DeMILLER**   DeMiller, Harry b: 11/12/1867, Wooster, Ohio d: 10/19/28, Santa Ana, Cal.   BR/TL,   Deb: 8/20/1892

| 1892 | Chi-N | 1 | 1 | .500 | 4 | 2 | 2 | 0 | 0 | 24 | 29 | 1 | 16 | 15 | 17.3 | 6.38 | 52 | .287 | .390 | 3 | .300 | 1 | -8 | -8 | -0 | -0.6 |

● **DON DeMOLA**   DeMola, Donald John b: 7/5/52, Glen Cove, N.Y.   BR/TR, 6'2", 185 lbs.   Deb: 4/13/74

1974	Mon-N	1	0	1.000	25	1	0	0	0	57²	46	7	21	47	10.5	3.12	123	.223	.295	0	.000	-1	3	5	-1	0.4
1975	Mon-N	4	7	.364	60	0	0	0	1	97²	92	8	42	63	12.7	4.15	92	.251	.335	0	.000	-1	-6	-4	-3	-0.8
Total	2	5	7	.417	85	1	0	0	1	155¹	138	15	63	110	11.9	3.77	102	.241	.321	0	.000	-2	-3	1	-3	-0.4

● **BEN DeMOTT**   DeMott, Benjamin Harrison b: 4/2/1889, Green Village, N.J. d: 7/5/63, Somerville, N.J.   BR/TR, 6', 192 lbs.   Deb: 8/12/10

1910	Cle-A	0	3	.000	6	4	1	0	0	28¹	45	0	8	13	17.2	5.40	48	.388	.432	3	.167	-0	-9	-9	-0	-0.9
1911	Cle-A	0	1	.000	1	1	0	0	0	3²	10	0	2	2	29.5	12.27	28	.588	.632	0	—	-0	-4	-4	0	-0.3
Total	2	0	4	.000	7	5	1	0	0	32	55	0	10	15	18.6	6.19	43	.414	.458	3	.136	-0	-13	-12	1	-1.2

● **CON DEMPSEY**   Dempsey, Cornelius Francis b: 9/16/23, San Francisco, Cal.   BR/TR, 6'4", 190 lbs.   Deb: 4/28/51

| 1951 | Pit-N | 0 | 2 | .000 | 3 | 2 | 0 | 0 | 0 | 7 | 11 | 2 | 4 | 3 | 19.3 | 9.00 | 47 | .393 | .469 | 0 | .000 | -0 | -4 | -4 | 0 | -0.4 |

● **RICK DEMPSEY**   Dempsey, John Rikard b: 9/13/49, Fayetteville, Tenn.   BR/TR, 6', 190 lbs.   Deb: 9/23/69 ♦

| 1991 | Mil-A | 0 | 0 | — | 2 | 0 | 0 | 0 | 0 | 2 | 3 | 0 | 1 | 0 | 18.0 | 4.50 | 88 | .333 | .400 | 34 | .231 | 2 | -0 | -0 | -0 | 0.0 |

● **MARK DEMPSEY**   Dempsey, Mark Steven b: 12/17/57, Dayton, Ohio   BR/TR, 6'6", 220 lbs.   Deb: 9/04/82

| 1982 | SF-N | 0 | 0 | — | 3 | 1 | 0 | 0 | 0 | 5² | 11 | 1 | 2 | 4 | 20.6 | 7.94 | 45 | .440 | .481 | 0 | .000 | -0 | -3 | -3 | 0 | -0.3 |

● **BILL DENEHY**   Denehy, William Francis b: 3/31/46, Middletown, Conn.   BB/TR, 6'3", 200 lbs.   Deb: 4/16/67

1967	NY-N	1	7	.125	15	8	0	0	0	53²	51	8	29	35	13.4	4.70	72	.248	.340	0	.000	-1	-8	-8	-1	-0.9
1968	Was-A	0	0	—	3	0	0	0	0	2	4	0	4	1	36.0	9.00	32	.444	.615	0	—	0	-1	-1	0	-0.1
1971	Det-A	0	3	.000	31	1	0	0	1	49	47	4	28	27	14.5	4.22	85	.250	.359	0	.000	-1	-4	-3	-0	-0.3
Total	3	1	10	.091	49	9	0	0	1	104²	102	12	61	63	14.4	4.56	76	.253	.357	0	.000	0	-13	-13	-1	-1.3

● **BRIAN DENMAN**   Denman, Brian John b: 2/12/56, Minneapolis, Minn.   BR/TR, 6'4", 205 lbs.   Deb: 8/22/82

| 1982 | Bos-A | 3 | 4 | .429 | 9 | 9 | 2 | 1 | 0 | 49 | 55 | 6 | 9 | 9 | 11.8 | 4.78 | 90 | .282 | .314 | 0 | — | 0 | -4 | -3 | -0 | -0.5 |

● **DON DENNIS**   Dennis, Donald Ray b: 3/3/42, Uniontown, Kan.   BR/TR, 6'2", 190 lbs.   Deb: 6/18/65

1965	StL-N	2	3	.400	41	0	0	0	6	55	47	3	16	29	10.5	2.29	168	.236	.296	2	.400	1	8	9	2	1.3
1966	StL-N	4	2	.667	38	1	0	0	2	59²	73	8	17	25	13.7	4.98	72	.302	.350	1	.083	-1	-9	-9	3	-0.8
Total	2	6	5	.545	79	1	0	0	8	114²	120	11	33	54	12.2	3.69	101	.272	.326	3	.176	-1	0	4	0	0.5

● **JERRY DENNY**   Denny, Jeremiah Dennis (b: Jeremiah Dennis Eldridge)
b: 3/16/1859, New York, N.Y. d: 8/16/27, Houston, Tex.   BR/TR, 5'11.5", 180 lbs.   Deb: 5/02/1881 ♦

| 1888 | Ind-N | 0 | 0 | — | 1 | 0 | 0 | 0 | 0 | 4 | 5 | 1 | 4 | 1 | 20.3 | 9.00 | 33 | .278 | .409 | 137 | .261 | 0 | -3 | -3 | 0 | -0.2 |

● **JOHN DENNY**   Denny, John Allen b: 11/8/52, Prescott, Ariz.   BR/TR, 6'3", 190 lbs.   Deb: 9/12/74

1974	StL-N	0	0	—	2	0	0	0	0	2	3	0	1	0	13.5	0.00	—	.273	.273	0	—	0	1	1	-0	0.1
1975	StL-N	10	7	.588	25	24	3	2	0	136	149	5	51	72	13.4	3.97	95	.280	.346	10	.227	1	-5	-3	2	-0.1
1976	StL-N	11	9	.550	30	30	8	3	0	207	189	11	74	74	11.8	**2.52**	**140**	.246	.318	15	.224	2	23	**23**	1	**3.0**
1977	StL-N	8	8	.500	26	26	3	1	0	149²	165	9	62	60	14.0	4.51	85	.281	.355	5	.098	-3	-10	-11	3	-1.1
1978	StL-N	14	11	.560	33	33	11	2	0	234	200	13	74	103	10.8	2.96	119	.238	.304	13	.178	2	16	14	8	2.7
1979	StL-N	8	11	.421	31	31	5	2	0	206	206	24	100	99	13.5	4.85	78	.264	.350	9	.129	-1	-26	-25	2	-2.5
1980	Cle-A	8	6	.571	16	16	4	1	0	108²	116	4	47	59	13.9	4.39	93	.284	.365	0	—	0	-4	-4	1	-0.3
1981	Cle-A	10	6	.625	19	19	6	3	0	145²	139	4	66	94	12.9	3.15	115	.254	.338	0	—	0	8	8	5	1.4
1982	Cle-A	6	11	.353	21	21	5	0	0	138¹	126	11	73	94	13.3	5.01	81	.240	.340	0	—	0	-14	-14	1	-1.3
	Phi-N	0	2	.000	4	4	0	0	0	22¹	18	1	10	19	11.3	4.03	91	.217	.301	1	.167	1	-1	-1	0	0.1
1983	*Phi-N	19	6	**.760**	36	36	7	1	0	242²	229	9	53	139	10.6	2.37	150	.250	.294	13	.169	0	**34**	32	1	**3.8**
1984	Phi-N	7	7	.500	22	22	2	0	0	154¹	122	11	29	94	9.0	2.45	148	.214	.257	9	.191	0	20	20	4	2.8
1985	Phi-N	11	14	.440	33	33	6	2	0	230²	252	15	83	123	13.2	3.82	96	.282	.345	10	.123	-2	-6	-4	1	-0.4
1986	Cin-N	11	10	.524	27	27	2	1	0	171¹	179	15	56	115	12.6	4.20	92	.272	.333	12	.222	2	-9	-6	3	-0.9
Total	13	123	108	.532	325	322	62	18	0	2148²	2093	137	778	1146	12.3	3.59	104	.258	.327	97	.170	3	25	30	31	8.0

● **EDDIE DENT**   Dent, Elliott Estill b: 12/8/1887, Baltimore, Md. d: 11/25/74, Birmingham, Ala.   BR/TR, 6'1", 190 lbs.   Deb: 8/31/09

| 1909 | Bro-N | 2 | 4 | .333 | 6 | 5 | 4 | 0 | 0 | 42 | 47 | 2 | 15 | 17 | 13.3 | 4.29 | 61 | .307 | .369 | 1 | .067 | -1 | -8 | -8 | -1 | -1.0 |

YEAR	TM/L	W	L	PCT	G	GS	CG	SH	SV	IP	H	HR	BB	SO	RAT	ERA	ERA+	OAV	OOB	BH	AVG	PB	PR	/A	PD	TPI
1911	Bro-N	2	1	.667	5	3	1	0	0	31^2	30	0	10	3	11.9	3.69	90	.256	.326	1	.100	-0	-1	-1	0	-0.1
1912	Bro-N	0	0	—	1	0	0	0	0	1	4	0	1	1	45.0	36.00	9	.571	.625	0	.000	-0	-4	-4	0	-0.3
Total	3	4	5	.444	12	8	5	0	0	74^2	81	2	26	21	13.1	4.46	65	.292	.357	2	.077	-2	-13	-13	-0	-1.4

● ROGER DENZER

Denzer, Roger "Peaceful Valley" b: 10/5/1871, Leseur, Minn. d: 9/18/49, Leseur, Minn. BL/TR, 6', 180 lbs. Deb: 4/24/1897

YEAR	TM/L	W	L	PCT	G	GS	CG	SH	SV	IP	H	HR	BB	SO	RAT	ERA	ERA+	OAV	OOB	BH	AVG	PB	PR	/A	PD	TPI
1897	Chi-N	2	8	.200	12	10	8	0	0	94^2	125	4	34	17	15.3	5.13	87	.315	.372	6	.154	-3	-9	-7	-1	-0.9
1901	NY-N	2	6	.250	11	9	3	1	0	61^2	69	2	5	22	10.8	3.36	99	.281	.295	2	.091	-1	-0	-0	-2	-0.3
Total	2	4	14	.222	23	19	11	1	0	156^1	194	6	39	39	13.5	4.43	90	.302	.344	8	.131	-4	-9	-8	-2	-1.2

● GEORGE DERBY

Derby, George H. "Jonah" b: 7/6/1857, Webster, Mass. d: 7/4/25, Philadelphia, Pa. BL/TR, 6', 175 lbs. Deb: 5/02/1881

YEAR	TM/L	W	L	PCT	G	GS	CG	SH	SV	IP	H	HR	BB	SO	RAT	ERA	ERA+	OAV	OOB	BH	AVG	PB	PR	/A	PD	TPI
1881	Det-N	29	26	.527	56	55	55	**9**	0	494^2	505	3	86	**212**	10.8	2.20	132	.251	.281	44	.186	-11	**32**	**39**	2	**3.0**
1882	Det-N	17	20	.459	40	39	38	3	0	362	386	8	81	182	11.6	3.26	90	.256	.294	29	.195	-6	-14	-13	1	-1.6
1883	Buf-N	2	10	.167	14	13	12	0	1	107^2	173	3	15	34	15.7	5.85	54	.334	.353	14	.237	-1	-32	-32	1	-2.6
Total	3	48	56	.462	110	107	105	12	1	964^1	1064	14	182	428	11.6	3.01	98	.263	.295	87	.196	-18	-15	-5	4	-1.2

● PAUL DERRINGER

Derringer, Samuel Paul "Duke" b: 10/17/06, Springfield, Ky. d: 11/17/87, Sarasota, Fla. BR/TR, 6'3.5", 205 lbs. Deb: 4/16/31

YEAR	TM/L	W	L	PCT	G	GS	CG	SH	SV	IP	H	HR	BB	SO	RAT	ERA	ERA+	OAV	OOB	BH	AVG	PB	PR	/A	PD	TPI
1931	*StL-N	18	8	**.692**	35	23	15	4	2	211^2	225	9	65	134	12.5	3.36	117	.274	.330	7	.097	-6	12	14	-0	0.8
1932	StL-N	11	14	.440	39	30	14	1	0	233^1	296	6	67	78	14.1	4.05	97	.310	.356	13	.178	-0	-4	-3	-2	-0.5
1933	StL-N	0	2	.000	3	2	1	0	0	17	24	0	9	3	18.0	4.24	82	.353	.436	0	.000	-1	-2	-1	0	-0.2
	Cin-N	7	25	.219	33	31	16	2	1	231	240	4	51	86	11.5	3.23	105	.271	.315	14	.184	-1	3	4	1	0.4
	Yr	7	27	.206	36	33	17	2	1	248	264	4	60	89	11.9	3.30	103	.277	.323	14	.173	-2	1	3	1	0.2
1934	Cin-N	15	21	.417	47	31	18	1	4	261	297	8	59	122	12.4	3.59	114	.283	.323	18	.196	0	14	14	-2	1.3
1935	Cin-N★	22	13	.629	45	33	20	3	2	276^2	295	13	49	120	11.3	3.51	113	.271	.305	13	.140	-5	16	14	3	1.2
1936	Cin-N	19	19	.500	**51**	37	13	2	5	282^1	331	11	42	121	12.0	4.02	95	.289	.316	18	.200	-1	0	-6	0	-0.6
1937	Cin-N	10	14	.417	43	26	12	1	1	222^2	240	7	55	94	11.9	4.04	92	.271	.313	16	.200	1	-3	-8	1	-0.6
1938	Cin-N☆	21	14	.600	41	37	**26**	4	3	**307**	315	20	49	132	10.7	2.93	124	.262	.291	21	.176	-0	29	24	-2	2.3
1939	*Cin-N★	25	7	**.781**	38	35	28	5	0	301	321	15	35	128	10.7	2.93	131	.272	.295	23	.209	0	33	30	-3	2.8
1940	*Cin-N★	20	12	.625	37	37	26	3	0	296^2	280	17	48	115	**10.0**	3.06	124	.246	**.276**	18	.167	-2	26	24	-4	1.9
1941	Cin-N★	12	14	.462	29	28	17	2	1	228^1	233	16	54	76	11.3	3.31	109	.266	.309	13	.155	-3	8	7	-1	0.4
1942	Cin-N†	10	11	.476	29	27	13	1	0	208^2	203	4	49	68	11.0	3.06	107	.250	.296	9	.132	-2	6	5	-4	-0.1
1943	Chi-N	10	14	.417	32	22	10	2	3	174	184	7	39	75	11.5	3.57	93	.264	.303	13	.224	1	-4	-4	-4	-0.8
1944	Chi-N	7	13	.350	42	16	7	0	3	180	205	13	39	69	12.2	4.15	85	.284	.321	9	.158	-2	-11	-12	-1	-1.5
1945	*Chi-N†	16	11	.593	35	30	15	1	4	213^2	223	8	51	86	11.6	3.45	106	.265	.308	15	.200	0	8	5	-2	0.3
Total	15	223	212	.513	579	445	251	32	29	3645	3912	158	761	1507	11.6	3.46	108	.272	.310	220	.175	-19	131	108	-17	7.1

● JIM DERRINGTON

Derrington, Charles James "Blackie" b: 11/29/39, Compton, Cal. BL/TL, 6'3", 190 lbs. Deb: 9/30/56

YEAR	TM/L	W	L	PCT	G	GS	CG	SH	SV	IP	H	HR	BB	SO	RAT	ERA	ERA+	OAV	OOB	BH	AVG	PB	PR	/A	PD	TPI
1956	Chi-A	0	1	.000	1	1	0	0	0	6	9	2	6	3	22.5	7.50	55	.375	.500	1	.500	0	-2	-2	-0	-0.2
1957	Chi-A	0	1	.000	20	5	0	0	0	37	29	4	29	14	14.4	4.86	77	.216	.360	0	.000	-0	-4	-5	-1	-0.6
Total	2	0	2	.000	21	6	0	0	0	43	38	6	35	17	15.5	5.23	72	.241	.381	1	.167	0	-7	-7	-1	-0.8

● JIM DESHAIES

Deshaies, James Joseph b: 6/23/60, Massena, N.Y. BL/TL, 6'4", 225 lbs. Deb: 8/07/84

YEAR	TM/L	W	L	PCT	G	GS	CG	SH	SV	IP	H	HR	BB	SO	RAT	ERA	ERA+	OAV	OOB	BH	AVG	PB	PR	/A	PD	TPI
1984	NY-A	0	1	.000	2	2	0	0	0	7	14	1	7	5	27.0	11.57	33	.438	.538	0	—	0	-6	-6	0	-0.5
1985	Hou-N	0	0	—	2	0	0	0	0	3	1	0	0	2	3.0	0.00	—	.100	.100	0	—	0	1	1	-0	0.1
1986	Hou-N	12	5	.706	26	26	1	1	0	144	124	16	59	128	11.6	3.25	111	.234	.313	2	.047	-1	7	6	-2	0.3
1987	Hou-N	11	6	.647	26	25	1	0	0	152	149	22	57	104	12.2	4.62	85	.257	.324	5	.094	-0	-9	-12	-1	-1.2
1988	Hou-N	11	14	.440	31	31	3	2	0	207	164	20	72	127	10.3	3.00	111	.218	.288	3	.048	-4	10	7	-2	0.1
1989	Hou-N	15	10	.600	34	34	6	3	0	225^2	180	15	79	153	10.5	2.91	116	.217	.288	9	.120	-2	15	12	-1	0.9
1990	Hou-N	7	12	.368	34	34	2	0	0	209^1	186	21	84	119	12.0	3.78	98	.245	.326	4	.063	-3	0	-2	-1	-0.6
1991	Hou-N	5	12	.294	28	28	1	0	0	161	156	19	72	98	12.8	4.98	70	.259	.339	4	.098	-1	-23	-26	-2	-2.8
1992	SD-N	4	7	.364	15	15	0	0	0	96	92	6	33	46	11.8	3.28	111	.258	.323	6	.207	1	2	4	1	0.6
Total	9	65	67	.492	198	195	14	6	0	1205	1066	120	463	782	11.6	3.68	97	.239	.314	33	.090	-11	-2	-16	-7	-3.1

● JIMMIE DeSHONG

DeShong, James Brooklyn b: 11/30/09, Harrisburg, Pa. BR/TR, 5'11", 165 lbs. Deb: 4/12/32

YEAR	TM/L	W	L	PCT	G	GS	CG	SH	SV	IP	H	HR	BB	SO	RAT	ERA	ERA+	OAV	OOB	BH	AVG	PB	PR	/A	PD	TPI
1932	Phi-A	0	0	—	6	0	0	0	0	10	17	3	9	5	24.3	11.70	39	.378	.491	0	.000	-0	-8	-8	0	-0.7
1934	NY-A	6	7	.462	31	12	6	0	3	133^2	126	6	56	40	12.4	4.11	99	.243	.319	8	.190	2	6	-1	-0	0.1
1935	NY-A	4	1	.800	29	3	0	0	3	69	64	6	33	30	12.9	3.26	124	.242	.331	1	.071	-1	9	6	2	0.7
1936	Was-A	18	10	.643	34	31	16	2	2	223^2	255	11	96	59	14.2	4.63	103	.285	.356	15	.190	2	10	4	-2	0.4
1937	Was-A	14	15	.483	37	34	20	0	1	264^1	290	15	124	86	14.2	4.90	90	.280	.359	19	.202	2	-8	-14	1	-1.0
1938	Was-A	5	8	.385	31	14	1	0	0	131^1	160	11	83	41	16.7	6.58	69	.310	.407	12	.261	2	-26	-30	0	-2.4
1939	Was-A	0	3	.000	7	6	1	0	0	40^2	56	7	31	12	19.3	8.63	50	.337	.442	3	.200	0	-18	-19	1	-1.5
Total	7	47	44	.516	175	100	44	2	9	872^2	968	59	432	273	14.6	5.08	87	.281	.363	58	.198	7	-35	-63	3	-4.4

● SHORTY DesJARDIEN

DesJardien, Paul Raymond b: 8/24/1893, Coffeyville, Kan. d: 3/7/56, Monrovia, Cal. BR/TR, 6'4.5", 205 lbs. Deb: 5/20/16

YEAR	TM/L	W	L	PCT	G	GS	CG	SH	SV	IP	H	HR	BB	SO	RAT	ERA	ERA+	OAV	OOB	BH	AVG	PB	PR	/A	PD	TPI
1916	Cle-A	0	0	—	1	0	0	0	0	1	1	0	1	0	18.0	18.00	17	.200	.333	0	—	0	-2	-2	-0	-0.2

● RUBE DESSAU

Dessau, Frank Rolland b: 3/29/1883, New Galilee, Pa. d: 5/6/52, York, Pa. BB/TR, 5'11", 175 lbs. Deb: 9/22/07

YEAR	TM/L	W	L	PCT	G	GS	CG	SH	SV	IP	H	HR	BB	SO	RAT	ERA	ERA+	OAV	OOB	BH	AVG	PB	PR	/A	PD	TPI
1907	Bos-N	0	1	.000	2	2	1	0	0	9^1	13	0	10	1	23.1	10.61	24	.394	.545	0	.000	-0	-8	-8	-0	-0.8
1910	Bro-N	2	3	.400	19	0	0	0	1	51^1	67	0	29	24	17.7	5.79	52	.328	.424	1	.067	-1	-16	-16	-1	-1.8
Total	2	2	4	.333	21	2	1	0	1	60^2	80	0	39	25	18.5	6.53	45	.338	.443	1	.053	-1	-24	-24	-2	-2.6

● TOM DETTORE

Dettore, Thomas Anthony b: 11/17/47, Canonsburg, Pa. BL/TR, 6'4", 200 lbs. Deb: 6/11/73

YEAR	TM/L	W	L	PCT	G	GS	CG	SH	SV	IP	H	HR	BB	SO	RAT	ERA	ERA+	OAV	OOB	BH	AVG	PB	PR	/A	PD	TPI
1973	Pit-N	0	1	.000	12	1	0	0	0	22^2	33	1	14	13	19.9	5.96	59	.340	.439	0	.000	-0	-6	-6	-0	-0.7
1974	Chi-N	3	5	.375	16	9	0	0	0	64^2	64	4	31	43	14.1	4.18	91	.255	.351	5	.250	2	-4	-3	0	-0.1
1975	Chi-N	5	4	.556	36	5	0	0	0	85^1	88	8	31	46	13.5	5.38	71	.270	.350	6	.250	1	-17	-15	0	-1.4
1976	Chi-N	0	1	.000	4	0	0	0	0	7	11	3	2	4	16.7	10.29	38	.355	.394	0	—	0	-5	-5	-0	-0.5
Total	4	8	11	.421	68	15	0	0	0	179^2	196	16	78	106	14.6	5.21	73	.278	.365	11	.229	2	-32	-28	0	-2.7

● MEL DEUTSCH

Deutsch, Melvin Elliott b: 7/26/15, Caldwell, Tex. BR/TR, 6'4", 215 lbs. Deb: 4/21/46

YEAR	TM/L	W	L	PCT	G	GS	CG	SH	SV	IP	H	HR	BB	SO	RAT	ERA	ERA+	OAV	OOB	BH	AVG	PB	PR	/A	PD	TPI
1946	Bos-A	0	0	—	3	0	0	0	0	6^1	7	1	3	2	14.2	5.68	64	.280	.357	0	.000	-0	-2	-1	-0	-0.2

● CHARLIE DEVENS

Devens, Charles b: 1/1/10, Milton, Mass. BR/TR, 6'1", 180 lbs. Deb: 9/24/32

YEAR	TM/L	W	L	PCT	G	GS	CG	SH	SV	IP	H	HR	BB	SO	RAT	ERA	ERA+	OAV	OOB	BH	AVG	PB	PR	/A	PD	TPI
1932	NY-A	1	0	1.000	1	1	1	0	0	9	6	0	7	4	13.0	2.00	204	.200	.351	0	.000	0	2	2	-0	0.2
1933	NY-A	3	3	.500	14	8	2	0	0	62	59	1	50	23	15.8	4.35	89	.250	.381	2	.095	-1	-1	-3	-1	-0.4
1934	NY-A	1	0	1.000	1	1	1	0	0	11	9	0	5	4	11.5	1.64	248	.225	.311	1	.500	1	3	3	0	0.6
Total	3	5	3	.625	16	10	4	0	0	82	74	1	62	31	14.9	3.73	105	.242	.370	3	.120	0	5	2	-1	0.4

● ADRIAN DEVINE

Devine, Paul Adrian b: 12/2/51, Galveston, Tex. BR/TR, 6'4", 205 lbs. Deb: 6/27/73

YEAR	TM/L	W	L	PCT	G	GS	CG	SH	SV	IP	H	HR	BB	SO	RAT	ERA	ERA+	OAV	OOB	BH	AVG	PB	PR	/A	PD	TPI
1973	Atl-N	2	3	.400	24	1	0	0	4	32^1	45	6	12	15	16.4	6.40	61	.338	.401	1	.250	0	-10	-9	-1	-0.9
1975	Atl-N	1	0	1.000	5	2	0	0	0	16^1	19	2	7	8	14.9	4.41	86	.284	.360	0	.000	-1	-1	-1	-0	-0.2
1976	Atl-N	5	6	.455	48	1	0	0	9	73	72	3	26	48	12.2	3.21	118	.255	.320	0	.000	-2	2	5	-1	0.3
1977	Tex-A	11	6	.647	56	2	0	0	15	105^2	102	8	31	67	11.7	3.58	114	.259	.319	0	—	0	6	6	2	0.8
1978	Atl-N	5	4	.556	31	6	0	0	3	65^1	84	3	25	26	15.0	5.92	68	.323	.382	1	.091	-1	-17	-14	0	-1.5
1979	Atl-N	1	2	.333	40	0	0	0	0	66^2	84	8	25	22	15.0	3.24	125	.311	.374	0	.000	-1	4	6	-0	0.5
1980	Tex-A	1	1	.500	13	0	0	0	0	28	49	4	9	8	19.0	4.82	81	.377	.421	0	—	0	-2	-3	-0	-0.3
Total	7	26	22	.542	217	12	0	0	31	387^1	455	34	135	194	14.0	4.21	95	.296	.357	2	.049	-4	-19	-9	0	-1.3

YEAR TM/L	W	L	PCT	G	GS	CG	SH	SV	IP	H	HR	BB	SO	RAT	ERA	ERA+	OAV	OOB	BH	AVG	PB	PR	/A	PD	TPI
● **JIM DEVINE**	Devine, Walter James b: 10/5/1858, Brooklyn, N.Y. d: 1/11/05, Syracuse, N.Y. TL, Deb: 5/08/1883 ♦																								
1883 Bal-a	1	1	.500	2	2	1	0	0	11	15	0	1	3	13.1	7.36	47	.305	.319	2	.222	-0	-5	-5	-1	-0.4
● **HAL DEVINEY**	Deviney, Harold John b: 4/11/1893, Newton, Mass. d: 1/4/33, Westwood, Mass. BR/TR, Deb: 7/30/20																								
1920 Bos-A	0	0	—	1	0	0	0	0	3	7	0	2	0	27.0	15.00	24	.500	.563	2	1.000	2	-4	-4	-0	-0.2
● **JIM DEVLIN**	Devlin, James Alexander b: 1849, Philadelphia, Pa. d: 10/10/1883, Philadelphia, Pa. BR/TR, 5'11", 175 lbs. Deb: 4/21/1873 ♦																								
1875 Chi-n	7	16	.304	28	24	24	0	0	224	254	0	11		10.6	*2.89*	87	.255	.263	92	.292	7	-11	-10		-0.3
1876 Lou-N	30	35	.462	**68**	68	**66**	5	0	**622**	566	3	37	**122**	8.7	1.56	174	.224	.235	94	.315	4	51	**80**	1	**7.9**
1877 Lou-N	35	25	.583	**61**	61	**61**	4	0	**559**	617	4	41	141	10.6	2.25	**147**	.270	.283	72	.269	-1	34	**65**	2	**6.3**
Total 2	65	60	.520	129	129	127	9	0	1181	1183	7	78	263	9.6	1.89	159	.246	.258	166	.293	3	86	145	3	14.2
● **JIM DEVLIN**	Devlin, James H. b: 4/16/1866, Troy, N.Y. d: 12/14/1900, Troy, N.Y. TL, Deb: 6/28/1886																								
1886 NY-N	0	0	—	1	0	0	0	1	2	3	0	4	2	31.5	18.00	18	.250	.438	0	.000	-0	-3	-3	0	-0.3
1887 Phi-N	0	2	.000	2	2	2	0	0	18	20	0	10	6	16.5	6.00	71	.267	.375	2	.333	0	-4	-4	0	-0.2
1888 *StL-a	6	5	.545	11	11	10	0	0	90^1	82	3	20	45	11.0	3.19	102	.233	.290	11	.297	2	-1	1	0	0.3
1889 StL-a	5	3	.625	9	8	5	0	0	60	56	0	24	37	13.1	2.40	176	.239	.329	5	.192	-2	10	12	1	1.0
Total 4	11	10	.524	23	21	17	0	1	170^1	161	3	58	90	12.5	3.38	109	.239	.317	18	.257	1	1	6	2	0.8
● **CHARLIE DEWALD**	Dewald, Charles H. b: 9/1867, Newark, N.J. d: 8/22/04, Cleveland, Ohio TL, Deb: 9/02/1890																								
1890 Cle-P	2	0	1.000	2	2	2	0	0	14	13	0	5	6	11.6	0.64	618	.236	.299	3	.375	1	6	5	-0	0.5
● **MARK DEWEY**	Dewey, Mark Alan b: 1/3/65, Grand Rapids, Mich. BR/TR, 6', 185 lbs. Deb: 8/24/90																								
1990 SF-N	1	1	.500	14	0	0	0	0	22^2	22	1	5	11	10.7	2.78	131	.259	.300	0	.000	0	3	2	-0	0.2
1992 NY-N	1	0	1.000	20	0	0	0	0	33^1	37	2	10	24	12.7	4.32	81	.280	.331	0	.000	-0	-3	-3	0	-0.3
Total 2	2	1	.667	34	0	0	0	0	56	59	3	15	35	11.9	3.70	96	.272	.319	0	.000	0	-0	-1	0	-0.1
● **CARLOS DIAZ**	Diaz, Carlos Antonio b: 1/7/58, Kapotte, Hawaii BR/TL, 6', 170 lbs. Deb: 6/30/82																								
1982 Atl-N	3	2	.600	19	0	0	0	1	25^1	31	3	9	16	14.2	4.62	81	.307	.364	0	.000	-0	-3	-3	0	-0.3
NY-N	0	0	—	4	0	0	0	0	3^2	6	0	4	0	24.5	0.00	—	.353	.476	0	—	0	1	1	0	0.2
Yr	3	2	.600	23	0	0	0	1	29	37	3	13	16	15.5	4.03	92	.311	.379	0	.000	-0	-1	-1	0	-0.1
1983 NY-N	3	1	.750	54	0	0	0	2	83^1	62	1	35	64	10.6	2.05	177	.211	.297	0	.000	-0	15	15	1	1.6
1984 LA-N	1	0	1.000	37	0	0	0	1	41	47	4	24	36	15.6	5.49	64	.285	.376	0	.000	-0	-9	-9	-1	-1.0
1985 *LA-N	6	3	.667	46	0	0	0	0	79^1	70	7	18	73	10.0	2.61	133	.230	.273	0	.000	-0	9	8	-1	0.7
1986 LA-N	0	0	—	19	0	0	0	0	25^1	33	2	7	18	14.2	4.26	81	.317	.360	0	.000	-0	-2	-2	0	-0.2
Total 5	13	6	.684	179	0	0	0	4	258	249	17	97	207	12.1	3.21	111	.253	.320	0	.000	-1	12	10	-0	1.0
● **ROB DIBBLE**	Dibble, Robert Keith b: 1/24/64, Bridgeport, Conn. BL/TR, 6'4", 230 lbs. Deb: 6/29/88																								
1988 Cin-N	1	1	.500	37	0	0	0	0	59^1	43	2	21	59	9.9	1.82	197	.207	.283	0	.000	-0	11	12	-1	1.1
1989 Cin-N	10	5	.667	74	0	0	0	2	99	62	4	39	141	9.5	2.09	172	.176	.264	0	.000	-1	15	17	-1	1.6
1990 *Cin-N★	8	3	.727	68	0	0	0	11	98	62	3	34	136	8.9	1.74	226	.183	.259	0	.000	-1	**22**	**24**	-0	2.4
1991 Cin-N★	3	5	.375	67	0	0	0	31	82^1	67	5	25	124	10.1	3.17	120	.223	.282	0	.000	-0	5	6	-0	0.6
1992 Cin-N	3	5	.375	63	0	0	0	25	70^1	48	3	31	110	10.4	3.07	119	.193	.287	2	.400	1	3	5	-1	0.5
Total 5	25	19	.568	309	0	0	0	69	409	282	17	150	570	9.7	2.35	158	.195	.273	2	.083	-1	57	63	-3	6.2
● **PEDRO DIBUT**	Dibut, Pedro (Villafana) b: 11/18/1892, Cienfuegos, Cuba d: 12/4/79, Hialeah, Fla. BR/TR, 5'8", 190 lbs. Deb: 5/01/24																								
1924 Cin-N	3	0	1.000	7	2	2	0	0	36^2	24	1	12	15	8.8	2.21	170	.188	.257	3	.273	1	7	6	1	0.9
1925 Cin-N	0	0	—	1	0	0	0	0	0	3	0	0	0	—	∞	—	1.000	1.000	0	—	0	-2	-2	0	-0.2
Total 2	3	0	1.000	8	2	2	0	0	36^2	27	1	12	15	9.6	2.70	139	.206	.273	3	.273	1	5	4	1	0.7
● **LEO DICKERMAN**	Dickerman, Leo Louis b: 10/31/1896, DeSoto, Mo. d: 4/30/82, Atkins, Ark. BR/TR, 6'4", 192 lbs. Deb: 4/21/23																								
1923 Bro-N	8	12	.400	35	20	7	1	0	159^2	180	4	72	58	14.3	3.72	104	.283	.357	13	.250	3	5	3	2	0.8
1924 Bro-N	0	0	—	7	2	0	0	0	19^2	20	0	16	9	17.4	5.49	68	.263	.404	1	.167	-0	-4	-4	0	-0.3
StL-N	7	4	.636	18	13	8	1	0	119^2	108	6	51	28	12.0	2.41	157	.249	.328	9	.231	1	19	18	0	2.0
Yr	7	4	.636	25	15	8	1	0	139^1	128	6	67	37	12.6	2.84	133	.250	.337	10	.222	1	16	14	1	1.7
1925 StL-N	4	11	.267	29	20	7	2	1	130^2	135	10	79	40	14.9	5.58	77	.273	.376	5	.114	-3	-19	-18	4	-1.6
Total 3	19	27	.413	89	55	22	4	1	429^2	443	20	218	135	14.0	4.00	99	.270	.358	28	.199	1	2	-1	6	0.9
● **GEORGE DICKERSON**	Dickerson, George Clark b: 12/1/1892, Renner, Tex. d: 7/9/38, Los Angeles, Cal. BR/TR, 6'1", 170 lbs. Deb: 8/02/17																								
1917 Cle-A	0	0	—	1	0	0	0	0	1	0	0	0	0	0.0	0.00	—	.000	.000	0	—	0	0	0	-0	0.0
● **EMERSON DICKMAN**	Dickman, George Emerson b: 11/12/14, Buffalo, N.Y. d: 4/27/81, New York, N.Y. BR/TR, 6'2", 175 lbs. Deb: 6/27/36																								
1936 Bos-A	0	0	—	1	0	0	0	0	1	2	0	1	2	27.0	9.00	59	.400	.500	0	—	0	-0	-0	0	0.0
1938 Bos-A	5	5	.500	32	11	3	1	0	104	117	9	54	22	15.1	5.28	93	.288	.377	10	.286	4	-6	-4	-0	-0.1
1939 Bos-A	8	3	.727	48	1	0	0	5	113^2	126	10	43	46	13.6	4.43	107	.282	.349	2	.056	-4	2	4	3	0.2
1940 Bos-A	8	6	.571	35	9	2	0	3	100	121	15	38	40	14.7	6.03	75	.291	.356	3	.107	-2	-18	-17	2	-1.6
1941 Bos-A	1	1	.500	9	3	1	0	0	31	37	4	17	16	15.7	6.39	65	.301	.386	1	.091	-1	-8	-8	-1	-0.9
Total 5	22	15	.595	125	24	6	1	8	349^2	403	38	153	126	14.6	5.33	88	.288	.363	16	.145	-2	-30	-25	4	-2.4
● **JIM DICKSON**	Dickson, James Edward b: 4/20/38, Portland, Ore. BL/TR, 6'1", 185 lbs. Deb: 7/02/63																								
1963 Hou-N	0	1	.000	13	0	0	0	2	14^2	22	0	2	6	14.7	6.14	51	.344	.364	0	.000	-0	-5	-5	-0	-0.6
1964 Cin-N	1	0	1.000	4	0	0	0	0	5	8	0	5	6	23.4	7.20	50	.444	.565	0	—	0	-2	-2	0	-0.2
1965 KC-A	3	2	.600	68	0	0	0	0	85^2	68	6	47	54	12.3	3.47	101	.220	.327	0	.000	-0	-0	0	-1	-0.1
1966 KC-A	1	0	1.000	24	1	0	0	1	37	37	4	23	20	14.6	5.35	63	.264	.368	1	.250	0	-8	-8	-0	-0.8
Total 4	5	3	.625	109	1	0	0	3	142^1	135	10	77	86	13.5	4.36	79	.254	.351	1	.143	-0	-15	-15	-1	-1.7
● **LANCE DICKSON**	Dickson, Lance Michael b: 10/19/69, Fullerton, Cal. BR/TL, 6', 185 lbs. Deb: 8/09/90																								
1990 Chi-N	0	3	.000	3	3	0	0	0	13^2	20	2	4	4	15.8	7.24	56	.370	.414	0	.000	-0	-5	-5	1	-0.4
● **MURRY DICKSON**	Dickson, Murry Monroe b: 8/21/16, Tracy, Mo. d: 9/21/89, Kansas City, Kan. BR/TR, 5'10.5", 157 lbs. Deb: 9/30/39																								
1939 StL-N	0	0	—	1	0	0	0	0	3^2	1	0	1	2	4.9	0.00	—	.091	.167	0	.000	-0	2	2	0	0.2
1940 StL-N	0	0	—	1	1	0	0	0	1^2	5	0	1	0	32.4	16.20	25	.500	.545	0	—	0	-2	-2	-0	-0.2
1942 StL-N	6	3	.667	36	7	2	0	2	120^2	91	1	61	66	11.4	2.91	118	.216	.316	8	.190	-0	5	7	1	0.8
1943 *StL-N	8	2	.800	31	7	2	0	0	115^2	119	4	49	44	13.1	3.58	94	.269	.343	9	.265	1	-3	-3	-0	-0.2
1946 *StL-N	15	6	**.714**	47	19	12	2	1	184^1	160	8	56	82	10.7	2.88	120	.234	.295	18	.277	5	11	12	4	2.2
1947 StL-N	13	16	.448	47	25	11	4	3	231^2	211	16	88	111	11.7	3.07	135	.243	.315	17	.213	1	25	27	1	2.9
1948 StL-N	12	16	.429	42	29	11	1	1	252^1	257	39	85	113	12.2	4.14	99	.265	.325	27	.281	4	-5	-1	1	0.4
1949 Pit-N	12	14	.462	44	20	11	2	0	224^1	216	17	80	89	12.1	3.29	128	.255	.324	17	.202	1	19	23	5	2.9
1950 Pit-N	10	15	.400	51	22	8	0	3	225	227	20	83	76	12.5	3.80	115	.260	.326	21	.256	3	9	15	2	1.9
1951 Pit-N	20	16	.556	45	35	19	3	2	288^2	294	32	101	112	12.5	4.02	105	.262	.327	30	.273	5	-2	7	4	1.6
1952 Pit-N	14	21	.400	43	34	21	2	2	277^2	278	26	76	112	11.5	3.57	112	.261	.311	24	.224	2	5	13	4	2.1
1953 Pit-N★	10	19	.345	45	26	10	1	4	200^2	240	27	58	88	13.5	4.53	99	.298	.348	7	.115	-4	-5	-1	-0	-0.5
1954 Phi-N	10	20	.333	40	31	12	4	3	226^1	256	31	73	64	13.2	3.78	107	.286	.342	15	.190	0	7	7	3	0.9
1955 Phi-N	12	11	.522	36	28	12	4	0	216	190	27	82	92	11.5	3.50	113	.238	.312	18	.220	1	13	11	1	1.3
1956 Phi-N	0	3	.000	3	3	0	0	0	23	20	1	12	1	12.5	5.09	73	.241	.337	3	.333	1	-3	-3	0	-0.3
StL-N	13	8	.619	28	27	12	3	0	196^1	175	20	57	109	10.7	3.07	123	.240	.296	19	.247	4	15	16	4	2.5

YEAR	TM/L	W	L	PCT	G	GS	CG	SH	SV	IP	H	HR	BB	SO	RAT	ERA	ERA+	OAV	OOB	BH	AVG	PB	PR	/A	PD	TPI
	Yr	13	11	.542	31	30	12	3	0	219^1	195	21	69	110	10.9	3.28	115	.240	.301	22	.256	4	12	12	4	2.2
1957	StL-N	5	3	.625	14	13	3	1	0	74	87	8	25	29	13.7	4.14	96	.296	.353	6	.222	1	-2	-1	2	0.1
1958	KC-A	9	5	.643	27	9	3	0	1	99	99	12	31	46	12.0	3.27	119	.258	.317	9	.257	2	5	7	2	1.2
	*NY-A	1	2	.333	6	2	0	0	1	20^1	18	4	12	9	13.7	5.75	61	.237	.348	2	.286	0	-4	-5	-0	-0.5
	Yr	10	7	.588	33	11	3	0	2	119^1	117	16	43	55	12.1	3.70	104	.253	.318	11	.262	2	1	2	2	0.7
1959	KC-A	2	1	.667	38	0	0	0	0	71	85	9	27	36	14.2	4.94	81	.290	.350	3	.176	-1	-9	-7	-0	-0.8
Total	18	172	181	.487	625	338	149	27	23	3052^1	3029	302	1058	1281	12.2	3.66	110	.260	.323	253	.231	26	81	120	32	18.5

● WALT DICKSON Dickson, Walter R. "Hickory" b: 12/3/1878, New Summerfield, Tex. d: 12/9/18, Ardmore, Okla. BR/TR, 5'11.5", 175 lbs. Deb: 4/26/10

YEAR	TM/L	W	L	PCT	G	GS	CG	SH	SV	IP	H	HR	BB	SO	RAT	ERA	ERA+	OAV	OOB	BH	AVG	PB	PR	/A	PD	TPI
1910	NY-N	1	0	1.000	12	1	0	0	0	29^2	31	1	9	9	12.1	5.46	54	.272	.325	1	.250	0	-8	-8	-1	-0.9
1912	Bos-N	3	19	.136	36	20	9	1	1	189	233	2	61	47	14.1	3.86	93	.320	.375	10	.167	-2	-9	-6	2	-0.5
1913	Bos-N	6	7	.462	19	15	8	0	0	128	118	4	45	47	11.5	3.23	102	.249	.316	8	.178	-1	-0	1	-1	-0.2
1914	Pit-F	9	19	.321	40	32	19	3	1	256^2	262	5	74	63	11.9	3.16	101	.273	.327	7	.084	-7	1	1	-0	-0.7
1915	Pit-F	7	5	.583	27	11	4	0	0	96^2	115	5	33	36	14.0	4.19	72	.316	.376	4	.129	-0	-12	-13	0	-1.3
Total	5	26	50	.342	134	79	40	4	2	700	759	17	222	202	12.7	3.60	91	.288	.345	30	.135	-10	-29	-26	0	-3.6

● GEORGE DIEHL Diehl, George Krause b: 2/25/18, Emmaus, Pa. d: 8/24/86, Kingsport, Tenn. BR/TR, 6'2", 196 lbs. Deb: 4/19/42

YEAR	TM/L	W	L	PCT	G	GS	CG	SH	SV	IP	H	HR	BB	SO	RAT	ERA	ERA+	OAV	OOB	BH	AVG	PB	PR	/A	PD	TPI
1942	Bos-N	0	0	—	1	0	0	0	0	3^2	2	0	2	0	12.3	2.45	136	.167	.333	0	.000	-0	0	0	0	0.0
1943	Bos-N	0	0	—	1	0	0	0	0	4	4	0	3	1	15.8	4.50	76	.267	.389	0	.000	-0	-0	-0	1	0.0
Total	2	0	0	—	2	0	0	0	0	7^2	6	0	5	1	14.1	3.52	96	.222	.364	0	.000	-0	-0	-0	1	0.0

● LARRY DIERKER Dierker, Lawrence Edward b: 9/22/46, Hollywood, Cal BR/TR, 6'4", 215 lbs. Deb: 9/22/64

YEAR	TM/L	W	L	PCT	G	GS	CG	SH	SV	IP	H	HR	BB	SO	RAT	ERA	ERA+	OAV	OOB	BH	AVG	PB	PR	/A	PD	TPI
1964	Hou-N	0	1	.000	3	1	0	0	0	9	7	1	3	5	10.0	2.00	171	.219	.286	0	.000	-0	2	1	-1	0.1
1965	Hou-N	7	8	.467	26	19	1	0	0	146^2	135	16	37	109	10.7	3.50	96	.240	.290	5	.100	-1	1	-2	-2	-0.5
1966	Hou-N	10	8	.556	29	28	8	2	0	187	173	17	45	108	10.5	3.18	108	.240	.285	10	.149	1	9	5	-1	0.5
1967	Hou-N	6	5	.545	15	15	4	0	0	99	95	4	25	68	11.0	3.36	98	.252	.300	7	.226	2	0	-1	-1	0.0
1968	Hou-N	12	15	.444	32	32	10	1	0	233^2	206	14	89	161	11.7	3.31	89	.240	.317	5	.068	-3	-9	-9	-2	-1.6
1969	Hou-N★	20	13	.606	39	37	20	4	0	305^1	240	18	72	232	9.2	2.33	152	.214	**.262**	17	.144	-1	43	41	-1	4.4
1970	Hou-N	16	12	.571	37	36	17	2	1	269^2	263	31	82	191	11.7	3.87	100	.254	.313	16	.174	-0	5	0	-1	-0.1
1971	Hou-N†	12	6	.667	24	23	6	2	0	159	150	8	33	91	10.5	2.72	124	.248	.289	4	.074	-3	13	11	0	0.9
1972	Hou-N	15	8	.652	31	31	12	5	0	214^2	209	14	51	115	11.1	3.40	99	.256	.304	13	.167	-0	1	-1	-2	-0.3
1973	Hou-N	1	1	.500	14	3	0	0	0	27	27	3	13	18	14.0	4.33	84	.265	.359	0	.000	-0	-2	-2	-0	-0.3
1974	Hou-N	11	10	.524	33	33	7	3	0	223^2	189	18	82	150	11.1	2.90	120	.232	.307	14	.197	1	18	14	0	1.6
1975	Hou-N	14	16	.467	34	34	14	2	0	232	225	24	91	127	12.5	4.00	84	.260	.335	7	.092	-4	-10	-16	-1	-2.1
1976	Hou-N	13	14	.481	28	28	7	4	0	187^2	171	9	72	112	11.9	3.69	86	.243	.319	9	.141	-0	-4	-10	-1	-1.2
1977	StL-N	2	6	.250	11	9	0	0	0	39^1	40	7	16	6	13.3	4.58	84	.267	.345	0	.000	-1	-3	-3	-0	-0.5
Total	14	139	123	.531	356	329	106	25	1	2333^2	2130	184	711	1493	11.1	3.31	103	.243	.303	107	.136	-11	65	29	-12	0.9

● BILL DIETRICH Dietrich, William John "Bullfrog" b: 3/29/10, Philadelphia, Pa. d: 6/20/78, Philadelphia, Pa. BR/TR, 6', 185 lbs. Deb: 4/13/33

YEAR	TM/L	W	L	PCT	G	GS	CG	SH	SV	IP	H	HR	BB	SO	RAT	ERA	ERA+	OAV	OOB	BH	AVG	PB	PR	/A	PD	TPI
1933	Phi-A	0	1	.000	8	1	0	0	0	17	13	1	19	4	16.9	5.82	74	.236	.432	1	.333	1	-3	-3	0	-0.2
1934	Phi-A	11	12	.478	39	23	14	4	3	207^2	201	12	114	88	13.8	4.68	94	.255	.351	15	.208	3	-4	-7	-2	-0.5
1935	Phi-A	7	13	.350	43	15	8	1	3	185^1	203	7	101	59	14.8	5.39	84	.276	.364	5	.083	-6	-19	-17	-1	-2.2
1936	Phi-A	4	6	.400	21	4	0	0	3	71^2	91	4	40	34	16.5	6.53	78	.305	.388	3	.111	-2	-12	-11	1	-1.0
	Was-A	0	1	.000	5	0	0	0	0	8^1	13	0	6	4	20.5	9.72	49	.351	.442	0	—	0	-4	-5	0	-0.4
	Chi-A	4	4	.500	14	11	6	1	0	82^2	93	8	36	39	14.2	4.68	111	.284	.356	8	.267	1	3	5	-0	0.4
	Yr	8	11	.421	40	15	6	1	3	162^2	197	12	82	77	15.5	5.75	89	.297	.375	11	.193	-1	-13	-11	1	-1.0
1937	Chi-A	8	10	.444	29	20	7	1	1	143^1	162	15	72	62	14.7	4.90	94	.285	.366	8	.182	1	-4	-5	1	-0.3
1938	Chi-A	2	4	.333	8	7	1	0	0	48	49	7	31	11	15.0	5.44	90	.259	.364	1	.063	-1	-3	-3	-0	-0.4
1939	Chi-A	7	8	.467	25	19	2	0	0	127^2	134	14	56	43	13.5	5.22	91	.272	.349	8	.216	2	-8	-7	-1	-0.5
1940	Chi-A	10	6	.625	23	17	6	1	0	149^2	154	10	65	43	13.2	4.03	110	.266	.340	12	.240	3	6	7	-2	0.8
1941	Chi-A	5	8	.385	19	15	4	1	0	109^1	114	7	50	26	13.8	5.35	77	.263	.345	3	.088	0	-15	-15	-2	-1.5
1942	Chi-A	6	11	.353	26	23	6	0	0	160	173	16	70	39	13.9	4.89	74	.277	.355	5	.104	-1	-22	-23	-0	-2.4
1943	Chi-A	12	10	.545	26	26	12	2	0	186^2	180	4	53	52	11.3	2.80	119	.253	.307	8	.143	0	10	11	1	1.4
1944	Chi-A	16	17	.485	36	36	15	2	0	246	269	15	68	70	12.4	3.62	95	.279	.328	9	.117	-3	-5	-5	-1	-0.9
1945	Chi-A	7	10	.412	18	16	6	3	0	122^1	136	4	36	43	12.7	4.19	79	.279	.329	6	.167	0	-11	-12	0	-1.2
1946	Chi-A	3	3	.500	11	9	3	0	1	62	63	4	24	20	12.6	2.61	131	.267	.335	1	.053	-2	6	6	1	0.5
1947	Phi-A	5	2	.714	11	9	2	1	0	60^2	48	0	40	18	13.4	3.12	122	.223	.350	1	.063	-2	4	5	-1	0.2
1948	Phi-A	1	2	.333	4	2	0	0	0	15^1	21	0	9	5	17.6	5.87	73	.356	.441	0	.000	-0	-3	-3	0	-0.3
Total	16	108	128	.458	366	253	92	17	11	2003^2	2117	128	890	660	13.6	4.48	92	.271	.348	94	.150	-5	-85	-84	-3	-8.5

● DUTCH DIETZ Dietz, Lloyd Arthur b: 2/9/12, Cincinnati, Ohio d: 10/29/72, Beaumont, Tex. BR/TR, 5'11.5", 180 lbs. Deb: 4/26/40

YEAR	TM/L	W	L	PCT	G	GS	CG	SH	SV	IP	H	HR	BB	SO	RAT	ERA	ERA+	OAV	OOB	BH	AVG	PB	PR	/A	PD	TPI
1940	Pit-N	0	1	.000	4	2	0	0	0	15^1	22	2	4	8	15.3	5.87	65	.355	.394	1	.143	-0	-3	-4	-0	-0.4
1941	Pit-N	7	2	.778	33	6	4	1	0	100^1	88	6	33	22	11.0	2.33	155	.233	.298	4	.160	-1	15	14	0	1.5
1942	Pit-N	6	9	.400	40	13	3	0	3	134^1	139	8	57	35	13.2	3.95	86	.268	.342	7	.200	1	-10	-8	-2	-1.0
1943	Pit-N	0	3	.000	8	0	0	0	0	9	12	0	4	4	17.0	6.00	58	.324	.405	0	—	0	-3	-3	1	-0.2
	Phi-N	1	1	.500	21	0	0	0	2	36	42	2	15	10	14.3	6.50	52	.292	.358	1	.167	0	-12	-13	-0	-1.3
	Yr	1	4	.200	29	0	0	0	2	45	54	2	19	14	14.6	6.40	53	.297	.363	1	.167	0	-15	-15	0	-1.5
Total	4	14	16	.467	106	21	7	1	6	295	303	18	113	79	12.8	3.87	90	.266	.334	13	.178	-0	-14	-13	-1	-1.4

● REESE DIGGS Diggs, Reese Wilson "Diggsy" b: 9/22/15, Mathews, Va. d: 10/30/78, Baltimore, Md. BB/TR, 6'2", 180 lbs. Deb: 9/15/34

YEAR	TM/L	W	L	PCT	G	GS	CG	SH	SV	IP	H	HR	BB	SO	RAT	ERA	ERA+	OAV	OOB	BH	AVG	PB	PR	/A	PD	TPI
1934	Was-A	1	2	.333	4	3	2	0	0	21^1	26	3	15	2	17.3	6.75	64	.313	.418	2	.250	0	-5	-6	-0	-0.5

● JACK DiLAURO DiLauro, Jack Edward b: 5/3/43, Akron, Ohio BB/TL, 6'2", 185 lbs. Deb: 5/15/69

YEAR	TM/L	W	L	PCT	G	GS	CG	SH	SV	IP	H	HR	BB	SO	RAT	ERA	ERA+	OAV	OOB	BH	AVG	PB	PR	/A	PD	TPI
1969	NY-N	1	4	.200	23	4	0	0	1	63^2	50	4	18	27	9.6	2.40	152	.216	.272	0	.000	-1	8	9	-0	0.8
1970	Hou-N	1	3	.250	42	0	0	0	3	33^2	34	4	17	23	13.6	4.28	91	.262	.347	0	.000	-0	-1	-1	-0	-0.2
Total	2	2	7	.222	65	4	0	0	4	97^1	84	8	35	50	11.0	3.05	122	.232	.300	0	.000	-2	8	7	-1	0.6

● GORDON DILLARD Dillard, Gordon Lee b: 5/20/64, Salinas, Cal. BL/TL, 6'1", 190 lbs. Deb: 8/12/88

YEAR	TM/L	W	L	PCT	G	GS	CG	SH	SV	IP	H	HR	BB	SO	RAT	ERA	ERA+	OAV	OOB	BH	AVG	PB	PR	/A	PD	TPI
1988	Bal-A	0	0	—	2	1	0	0	0	3	3	1	4	2	21.0	6.00	65	.273	.467	0	—	0	-1	-1	0	0.0
1989	Phi-N	0	0	—	5	0	0	0	0	4	7	0	0	2	15.8	6.75	53	.368	.368	0	—	0	-1	-1	0	-0.1
Total	2	0	0	—	7	1	0	0	0	7	10	1	4	4	18.0	6.43	58	.333	.412	0	—	0	-2	-2	0	-0.1

● HARLEY DILLINGER Dillinger, Harley Hugh "Hoke" or "Lefty" b: 10/30/1894, Pomeroy, Ohio d: 1/8/59, Cleveland, Ohio BR/TL, 5'11", 175 lbs. Deb: 8/16/14

YEAR	TM/L	W	L	PCT	G	GS	CG	SH	SV	IP	H	HR	BB	SO	RAT	ERA	ERA+	OAV	OOB	BH	AVG	PB	PR	/A	PD	TPI
1914	Cle-A	0	1	.000	11	2	1	0	0	33^2	41	0	25	11	17.9	4.54	64	.325	.441	0	.000	-1	-7	-6	-1	-0.9

● BILL DILLMAN Dillman, William Howard b: 5/25/45, Trenton, N.J. BR/TR, 6'2", 180 lbs. Deb: 4/14/67

YEAR	TM/L	W	L	PCT	G	GS	CG	SH	SV	IP	H	HR	BB	SO	RAT	ERA	ERA+	OAV	OOB	BH	AVG	PB	PR	/A	PD	TPI
1967	Bal-A	5	9	.357	32	15	2	1	3	124	115	13	33	69	11.0	4.35	72	.249	.303	5	.161	-0	-15	-17	-1	-1.9
1970	Mon-N	2	3	.400	18	0	0	0	0	30^2	28	4	18	17	13.8	5.28	78	.255	.364	0	.000	-0	-4	-4	0	-0.4
Total	2	7	12	.368	50	15	2	1	3	154^2	143	17	51	86	11.5	4.54	74	.250	.316	5	.152	-1	-20	-21	-1	-2.3

● STEVE DILLON Dillon, Stephen Edward b: 3/20/43, Yonkers, N.Y. BL/TL, 5'10", 160 lbs. Deb: 9/05/63

YEAR	TM/L	W	L	PCT	G	GS	CG	SH	SV	IP	H	HR	BB	SO	RAT	ERA	ERA+	OAV	OOB	BH	AVG	PB	PR	/A	PD	TPI
1963	NY-N	0	0	—	1	0	0	0	0	1^2	3	0	0	1	16.2	10.80	32	.429	.429	0	—	0	-1	-1	0	-0.1
1964	NY-N	0	0	—	2	0	0	0	0	3	4	1	2	2	18.0	9.00	40	.333	.429	0	—	0	-2	-2	-0	-0.2
Total	2	0	0	—	3	0	0	0	0	4^2	7	1	2	3	17.4	9.64	37	.368	.429	0	—	0	-3	-3	-0	-0.3

YEAR TM/L	W	L	PCT	G	GS	CG	SH	SV	IP	H	HR	BB	SO	RAT	ERA	ERA+	OAV	OOB	BH	AVG	PB	PR	/A	PD	TPI
● FRANK DIMICHELE Dimichele, Frank Lawrence b: 2/16/65, Philadelphia, Pa. BR/TL, 6'3", 205 lbs. Deb: 4/08/88																									
1988 Cal-A	0	0	—	4	0	0	0	0	4^2	5	2	2	1	13.5	9.64	40	.263	.333	0	—	0	-3	-3	-0	-0.3
● BILL DINNEEN Dinneen, William Henry "Big Bill" b: 4/5/1876, Syracuse, N.Y. d: 1/13/55, Syracuse, N.Y. BR/TR, 6'1", 190 lbs. Deb: 4/22/1898 U																									
1898 Was-N	9	16	.360	29	27	22	0	0	218^1	238	6	88	83	14.1	4.00	92	.275	.353	8	.100	-5	-9	-8	0	-1.1
1899 Was-N	14	20	.412	37	35	30	0	0	291	350	6	106	91	14.4	3.93	100	.297	.361	36	.303	5	-2	-0	4	0.8
1900 Bos-N	20	14	.588	40	37	33	1	0	320^2	304	11	105	107	11.7	3.12	133	.250	.314	35	.280	2	21	**36**	2	**3.8**
1901 Bos-N	15	18	.455	37	34	31	0	0	309^1	295	8	77	141	11.0	2.94	123	.250	.299	31	.211	0	13	23	-1	2.2
1902 Bos-A	21	21	.500	42	42	39	2	0	371^1	348	9	99	136	11.0	2.93	122	.248	.302	18	.128	-7	27	27	-6	1.3
1903 *Bos-A	21	13	.618	37	34	32	6	**2**	299	255	6	66	148	9.8	2.26	134	.230	.276	17	.160	-1	23	26	-1	2.5
1904 Bos-A	23	14	.622	37	37	37	5	0	335^2	283	8	63	153	9.3	2.20	122	.230	.268	25	.208	-1	15	18	-2	1.7
1905 Bos-A	12	14	.462	31	29	23	2	1	243^2	235	7	50	97	10.8	3.73	72	.255	.299	13	.148	-3	-29	-28	0	-3.2
1906 Bos-A	8	19	.296	28	27	22	1	0	218^2	209	4	52	60	10.8	2.92	94	.255	.300	7	.111	-2	-6	-4	-3	-0.9
1907 Bos-A	0	4	.000	5	5	3	0	0	32^2	42	5	8	8	14.1	5.23	49	.314	.357	0	.000	-1	-10	-10	-1	-1.1
StL-A	7	10	.412	24	16	15	2	4	155^1	153	3	33	38	11.1	2.43	104	.259	.304	10	.204	2	2	1	-3	0.0
Yr	7	14	.333	29	21	18	2	**4**	188	195	8	41	46	11.5	2.92	87	.269	.313	10	.169	0	-8	-8	-4	-1.1
1908 StL-A	14	7	.667	27	16	11	1	0	167	133	2	53	39	10.2	2.10	114	.231	.300	12	.203	0	5	5	-3	0.3
1909 StL-A	6	7	.462	17	13	8	3	0	112	112	3	29	26	11.4	3.46	70	.267	.316	7	.194	2	-12	-13	-0	-1.2
Total 12	170	177	.490	391	352	306	23	7	3074^2	2957	78	829	1127	11.3	3.01	107	.254	.308	219	.192	-9	38	71	-15	5.1
● RON DIORIO Diorio, Ronald Michael b: 7/15/46, Waterbury, Conn. BR/TR, 6'6", 212 lbs. Deb: 8/09/73																									
1973 Phi-N	0	0	—	23	0	0	0	1	19^1	18	1	6	11	11.2	2.33	163	.257	.316	0	—	0	3	3	-0	0.3
1974 Phi-N	0	0	—	2	0	0	0	0	1	2	1	1	0	27.0	18.00	21	.400	.500	0	—	0	-2	-2	0	-0.1
Total 2	0	0	—	25	0	0	0	1	20^1	20	2	7	11	12.0	3.10	122	.267	.329	0	—	0	1	2	0	0.2
● FRANK DiPINO DiPino, Frank Michael b: 10/22/56, Syracuse, N.Y. BL/TL, 6', 180 lbs. Deb: 9/14/81																									
1981 Mil-A	0	0	—	2	0	0	0	0	2^1	0	0	3	3	11.6	0.00	—	.000	.300	0	—	0	1	1	-0	0.3
1982 Hou-N	2	2	.500	6	6	0	0	0	28^1	32	1	11	25	13.7	6.04	55	.302	.368	0	.000	-1	-8	-9	-1	-0.9
1983 Hou-N	3	4	.429	53	0	0	0	20	71^1	52	2	20	67	9.2	2.65	128	.205	.265	1	.167	1	8	6	1	0.8
1984 Hou-N	4	9	.308	57	0	0	0	14	75^1	74	3	36	65	13.3	3.35	99	.260	.345	0	.000	-1	2	-0	0	-0.1
1985 Hou-N	3	7	.300	54	0	0	0	6	76	69	7	43	49	13.5	4.03	86	.248	.353	2	.167	-0	-4	-5	-2	-0.7
1986 Hou-N	1	3	.250	31	0	0	0	3	40^1	27	5	16	27	10.0	3.57	101	.189	.280	1	.200	0	1	0	0	0.1
Chi-N	2	4	.333	30	0	0	0	0	40	47	6	14	43	13.7	5.17	78	.297	.355	0	.000	-0	-6	-5	1	-0.4
Yr	3	7	.300	61	0	0	0	3	80^1	74	11	30	70	11.7	4.37	87	.243	.311	1	.167	-0	-6	-5	2	-0.3
1987 Chi-N	3	3	.500	69	0	0	0	4	80	75	7	34	61	12.4	3.15	136	.252	.330	1	.500	0	8	10	1	1.1
1988 Chi-N	2	3	.400	63	0	0	0	6	90^1	102	6	32	69	13.4	4.98	72	.285	.344	1	.100	-0	-15	-14	-0	-1.6
1989 StL-N	9	0	1.000	67	0	0	0	0	88^1	73	6	20	44	9.5	2.45	148	.227	.273	1	.077	-1	10	12	0	1.2
1990 StL-N	5	2	.714	62	0	0	0	3	81	92	8	31	49	13.8	4.56	84	.294	.359	1	.250	0	-7	-7	1	-0.6
1992 StL-N	0	0	—	9	0	0	0	0	11	9	0	3	8	9.8	1.64	210	.220	.273	1	1.000	0	2	2	0	0.3
Total 11	34	37	.479	503	6	0	0	56	684^1	652	51	263	510	12.1	3.76	97	.254	.326	9	.125	-1	-8	-8	2	-0.5
● GEORGE DISCH Disch, George Charles b: 3/15/1879, Lincoln, Mo. d: 8/25/50, Rapid City, S.D. 5'11", Deb: 8/08/05																									
1905 Det-A	0	2	.000	8	3	1	0	0	47^2	43	1	8	14	10.0	2.64	104	.242	.282	2	.105	-2	0	1	-0	-0.1
● ALEC DISTASO Distaso, Alec John b: 12/23/48, Los Angeles, Cal. BR/TR, 6'2", 200 lbs. Deb: 4/20/69																									
1969 Chi-N	0	0	—	2	0	0	0	0	4^2	6	0	1	1	13.5	3.86	104	.316	.350	0	—	0	-0	0	0	0.0
● ART DITMAR Ditmar, Arthur John b: 4/3/29, Winthrop, Mass. BR/TR, 6'2", 196 lbs. Deb: 4/19/54																									
1954 Phi-A	1	4	.200	14	5	0	0	0	39^1	50	4	36	14	19.9	6.41	61	.314	.444	1	.125	0	-12	-11	-0	-1.1
1955 KC-A	12	12	.500	35	22	7	1	1	175^1	180	23	86	79	14.0	5.03	83	.270	.360	13	.210	-0	-21	-17	1	-1.6
1956 KC-A	12	22	.353	44	34	14	2	1	254^1	254	30	108	126	13.1	4.42	98	.262	.340	13	.143	-4	-7	-3	-1	-0.8
1957 *NY-A	8	3	.727	46	11	0	0	6	127^1	128	9	35	64	11.7	3.25	110	.261	.313	7	.200	-0	8	5	-1	0.4
1958 *NY-A	9	8	.529	38	13	4	0	4	139^2	124	14	38	52	10.8	3.42	103	.237	.295	11	.250	-0	5	2	-2	0.1
1959 NY-A	13	9	.591	38	25	7	1	1	202	156	17	52	96	**9.6**	2.90	126	.211	**.270**	15	.197	1	22	17	-1	1.8
1960 *NY-A	15	9	.625	34	28	8	1	0	200	195	25	56	65	11.3	3.06	117	.256	.308	11	.159	0	18	12	-2	1.0
1961 NY-A	2	3	.400	12	8	1	0	0	54^1	59	9	14	24	12.4	4.64	80	.285	.336	1	.053	-2	-4	-6	1	-0.6
KC-A	0	5	.000	20	5	0	0	1	54	60	6	23	19	14.2	5.67	73	.286	.362	2	.167	-0	-10	-9	-0	-0.9
Yr	2	8	.200	32	13	1	0	1	108^1	119	15	37	43	13.1	5.15	76	.281	.341	3	.097	-2	-14	-15	0	-1.5
1962 KC-A	0	2	.000	6	5	0	0	0	21^2	31	1	13	13	19.1	6.65	63	.323	.414	1	.167	-0	-6	-6	-0	-0.6
Total 9	72	77	.483	287	156	41	5	14	1268	1237	138	461	552	12.3	3.98	97	.256	.326	75	.178	-4	-7	-17	-6	-2.3
● SONNY DIXON Dixon, John Craig b: 11/5/24, Charlotte, N.C. BB/TR, 6'2.5", 205 lbs. Deb: 4/20/53																									
1953 Was-A	5	8	.385	43	6	3	0	3	120	123	13	31	40	11.7	3.75	104	.267	.316	4	.154	0	3	2	2	0.4
1954 Was-A	1	2	.333	16	0	0	0	1	29^2	26	3	12	7	11.5	3.03	117	.236	.311	0	.000	-1	2	2	1	0.2
Phi-A	5	7	.417	38	6	1	0	4	107^1	136	8	27	42	13.9	4.86	80	.308	.352	7	.250	2	-14	-11	3	-0.7
Yr	6	9	.400	**54**	6	1	0	5	137	162	11	39	49	13.4	4.47	86	.293	.343	7	.206	1	-11	-10	3	-0.5
1955 KC-A	0	0	—	2	0	0	0	0	1^2	6	1	0	0	32.4	16.20	26	.545	.545	0	—	0	-2	-2	0	-0.2
1956 NY-A	0	1	.000	3	0	0	0	1	4^1	5	0	5	1	20.8	2.08	186	.294	.455	0	.000	-0	1	1	0	0.1
Total 4	11	18	.379	102	12	4	0	9	263	296	25	75	90	12.9	4.17	93	.284	.335	11	.180	1	-9	-9	6	-0.2
● KEN DIXON Dixon, Kenneth John b: 10/17/60, Monroe, Va. BB/TR, 5'11", 166 lbs. Deb: 9/22/84																									
1984 Bal-A	0	1	.000	2	2	0	0	0	13	14	1	4	8	12.5	4.15	93	.269	.321	0	—	0	-0	-0	0	0.0
1985 Bal-A	8	4	.667	34	18	3	1	1	162	144	20	64	108	11.7	3.67	110	.237	.312	0	—	0	9	7	-1	0.6
1986 Bal-A	11	13	.458	35	33	2	0	0	202^1	194	33	83	170	12.4	4.58	90	.249	.322	0	—	0	-9	-10	-1	-1.0
1987 Bal-A	7	10	.412	34	15	0	0	5	105	128	31	27	91	13.4	6.43	68	.292	.334	0	—	0	-23	-24	-0	-2.2
Total 4	26	28	.481	105	68	5	1	6	482^1	480	85	178	377	12.4	4.66	89	.256	.322	0	—	0	-24	-28	-2	-2.6
● TOM DIXON Dixon, Thomas Earl b: 4/23/55, Orlando, Fla. BR/TR, 5'11", 175 lbs. Deb: 7/30/77																									
1977 Hou-N	1	0	1.000	9	4	1	0	0	30^1	40	0	7	15	14.2	3.26	109	.320	.361	0	.000	-1	2	1	0	0.0
1978 Hou-N	7	11	.389	30	19	3	2	1	140	140	8	40	66	11.6	3.99	83	.265	.318	4	.100	-2	-6	-11	-1	-1.3
1979 Hou-N	1	2	.333	19	1	0	0	0	25^2	39	2	15	9	18.9	6.66	53	.348	.425	1	1.000	0	-8	-9	1	-0.8
1983 Mon-N	0	1	.000	4	0	0	0	0	3^2	6	1	1	4	19.6	9.82	37	.375	.444	0	—	0	-3	-3	-0	-0.3
Total 4	9	14	.391	62	24	4	2	1	199^2	225	11	63	94	13.1	4.33	78	.288	.343	5	.104	-2	-15	-21	-0	-2.4
● BILL DOAK Doak, William Leopold "Spittin' Bill" b: 1/28/1891, Pittsburgh, Pa. d: 11/26/54, Bradenton, Fla. BR/TR, 6'0.5", 165 lbs. Deb: 9/01/12																									
1912 Cin-N	0	0	—	1	1	0	0	0	2	4	0	1	0	22.5	4.50	75	.444	.500	0	—	0	-0	-0	-0	0.0
1913 StL-N	2	8	.200	15	12	5	1	1	93	79	4	39	51	11.9	3.10	104	.236	.325	1	.032	-4	1	1	1	-0.1
1914 StL-N	19	6	.760	36	33	16	7	1	256	193	2	87	118	10.1	**1.72**	**162**	.216	.290	10	.118	-3	30	31	5	3.7
1915 StL-N	16	18	.471	38	36	19	3	1	276	263	4	85	124	11.6	2.64	106	.261	.323	15	.174	1	3	5	7	1.4
1916 StL-N	12	8	.600	29	26	11	2	0	192	177	5	55	82	11.0	2.63	101	.251	.308	8	.129	-2	-0	0	3	0.1
1917 StL-N	16	20	.444	44	37	16	3	2	281^1	257	6	85	111	11.2	3.10	87	.250	.312	12	.126	-4	-12	-13	5	-1.4
1918 StL-N	9	15	.375	31	23	16	1	1	211	191	3	60	74	10.9	2.43	111	.249	.306	12	.182	1	8	7	5	1.5
1919 StL-N	13	14	.481	31	29	13	3	0	202^2	182	5	55	69	10.6	3.11	90	.246	.299	7	.109	-4	-4	-7	5	-0.7
1920 StL-N	20	12	.625	39	37	20	5	1	270	256	7	80	90	11.4	2.53	118	.253	.312	10	.114	-6	18	14	0	0.9
1921 StL-N	15	6	**.714**	32	28	13	1	1	208^2	224	3	37	83	11.4	**2.59**	142	.278	.313	10	.143	-3	28	25	2	2.4

YEAR TM/L	W	L	PCT	G	GS	CG	SH	SV	IP	H	HR	BB	SO	RAT	ERA	ERA+	OAV	OOB	BH	AVG	PB	PR	/A	PD	TPI
1922 StL-N	11	13	.458	37	29	8	2	2	180^1	222	12	69	73	14.7	5.54	70	.311	.374	7	.130	-3	-29	-34	0	-3.3
1923 StL-N	8	13	.381	30	26	7	2	0	185	199	4	69	53	13.2	3.26	120	.279	.346	3	.045	-8	15	13	3	0.8
1924 StL-N	2	1	.667	11	1	0	0	3	22	25	0	14	7	16.0	3.27	116	.313	.415	1	.200	-0	1	1	1	0.2
Bro-N	11	5	.688	21	16	8	2	0	149^1	130	8	35	32	10.1	3.07	122	.239	.289	10	.179	-0	13	11	3	1.4
Yr	13	6	.684	32	17	8	2	3	171^1	155	8	49	39	10.9	3.10	121	.249	.307	11	.180	-1	15	12	3	1.6
1927 Bro-N	11	8	.579	27	20	6	1	0	145	153	6	40	32	12.2	3.48	114	.271	.322	6	.128	-3	7	8	1	0.6
1928 Bro-N	3	8	.273	28	12	4	1	3	99^1	104	1	35	12	13.0	3.26	122	.271	.340	3	.111	-2	8	8	3	0.8
1929 StL-N	1	2	.333	3	2	0	0	0	9	17	1	5	3	22.0	12.00	39	.415	.478	0	.000	0	-7	-7	-0	-0.6
Total 16	169	157	.518	453	368	162	34	16	2782^2	2676	71	851	1014	11.6	2.98	107	.259	.319	115	.127	-41	80	64	43	7.7

● WALT DOANE Doane, Walter Rudolph b: 3/12/1887, Bellevue, Idaho d: 10/19/35, W.Brandywine, Pa. BL/TR, 6', 165 lbs. Deb: 9/20/09 ♦

YEAR TM/L	W	L	PCT	G	GS	CG	SH	SV	IP	H	HR	BB	SO	RAT	ERA	ERA+	OAV	OOB	BH	AVG	PB	PR	/A	PD	TPI
1909 Cle-A	0	1	.000	1	1	0	0	0	5	10	0	1	2	19.8	5.40	47	.400	.423	1	.111	-0	-2	-2	-0	-0.2
1910 Cle-A	0	0	—	6	0	0	0	0	17^2	31	1	8	7	20.4	5.60	46	.413	.476	2	.286	1	-6	-6	-1	-0.6
Total 2	0	1	.000	7	1	0	0	0	22^2	41	1	9	9	20.3	5.56	46	.410	.464	3	.188	1	-8	-8	-1	-0.8

● JOHN DOBB Dobb, John Kenneth "Lefty" b: 11/15/01, Muskegon, Mich. d: 7/31/91, Muskegon, Mich. BR/TL, 6'2", 180 lbs. Deb: 8/13/24

YEAR TM/L	W	L	PCT	G	GS	CG	SH	SV	IP	H	HR	BB	SO	RAT	ERA	ERA+	OAV	OOB	BH	AVG	PB	PR	/A	PD	TPI
1924 Chi-A	0	0	—	2	0	0	0	0	2	4	0	1	2	22.5	9.00	46	.400	.455	0	—	0	-1	-1	-0	-0.1

● RAY DOBENS Dobens, Raymond Joseph "Lefty" b: 7/28/06, Nashua, N.H. d: 4/21/80, Stuart, Fla. BL/TL, 5'8", 175 lbs. Deb: 7/07/29

YEAR TM/L	W	L	PCT	G	GS	CG	SH	SV	IP	H	HR	BB	SO	RAT	ERA	ERA+	OAV	OOB	BH	AVG	PB	PR	/A	PD	TPI
1929 Bos-A	0	0	—	11	2	0	0	0	28^1	32	0	9	4	13.3	3.81	112	.302	.362	3	.375	1	1	1	-1	0.1

● JESS DOBERNIC Dobernic, Andrew Joseph b: 11/20/17, Mt.Olive, Ill. BR/TR, 5'10", 170 lbs. Deb: 7/02/39

YEAR TM/L	W	L	PCT	G	GS	CG	SH	SV	IP	H	HR	BB	SO	RAT	ERA	ERA+	OAV	OOB	BH	AVG	PB	PR	/A	PD	TPI
1939 Chi-A	0	1	.000	4	0	0	0	0	3^1	3	0	6	1	27.0	13.50	35	.231	.500	0	.000	-0	-3	-3	0	-0.3
1948 Chi-N	7	2	.778	54	0	0	0	1	85^2	67	8	40	48	11.3	3.15	124	.213	.303	2	.200	-0	8	7	-2	0.5
1949 Chi-N	0	0	—	4	0	0	0	0	4	9	2	4	0	29.3	20.25	20	.450	.542	0	—	0	-7	-7	-0	-0.7
Cin-N	0	0	—	14	0	0	0	0	19^1	28	7	16	6	20.5	9.78	43	.329	.436	0	.000	0	-12	-12	0	-1.1
Yr	0	0	—	18	0	0	0	0	23^1	37	9	20	6	22.0	11.57	36	.352	.456	0	.000	0	-20	-19	-0	-1.8
Total 3	7	3	.700	76	0	0	0	1	112^1	107	17	66	55	14.0	5.21	76	.247	.349	2	.154	-0	-15	-15	-2	-1.6

● CHUCK DOBSON Dobson, Charles Thomas b: 1/10/44, Kansas City, Mo. BR/TR, 6'4", 200 lbs. Deb: 4/19/66

YEAR TM/L	W	L	PCT	G	GS	CG	SH	SV	IP	H	HR	BB	SO	RAT	ERA	ERA+	OAV	OOB	BH	AVG	PB	PR	/A	PD	TPI
1966 KC-A	4	6	.400	14	14	1	0	0	83^2	71	7	50	61	13.2	4.09	83	.234	.346	3	.115	-1	-6	-6	1	-0.6
1967 KC-A	10	10	.500	32	29	4	1	0	197^2	172	17	75	110	11.4	3.69	86	.233	.306	13	.181	0	-10	-11	-0	-1.2
1968 Oak-A	12	14	.462	35	34	11	3	0	225^1	197	20	80	168	11.2	3.00	94	.234	.303	15	.200	2	-0	-4	2	-0.1
1969 Oak-A	15	13	.536	35	35	11	1	0	235^1	244	16	80	137	12.4	3.86	89	.270	.330	8	.101	-3	-6	-11	-2	-1.6
1970 Oak-A	16	15	.516	41	40	13	**5**	0	267	230	32	92	149	11.0	3.74	95	.229	.297	11	.118	-3	-1	-6	-2	-1.1
1971 Oak-A	15	5	.750	30	30	7	1	0	189	185	24	71	100	12.2	3.81	88	.259	.327	13	.197	3	-7	-10	0	-0.7
1973 Oak-A	0	1	.000	1	1	0	0	0	2^1	6	1	2	3	30.9	7.71	46	.429	.500	0	—	0	-1	-1	0	-0.1
1974 Cal-A	2	3	.400	5	5	2	0	0	30	39	3	13	16	15.6	5.70	60	.315	.380	0	—	0	-7	-8	-0	-0.7
1975 Cal-A	0	2	.000	9	2	0	0	0	28	30	5	13	14	14.5	6.75	53	.275	.363	0	—	0	-9	-10	-1	-1.0
Total 9	74	69	.517	202	190	49	11	0	1258^1	1174	125	476	758	11.9	3.78	87	.247	.318	63	.153	-2	-48	-68	-1	-7.1

● JOE DOBSON Dobson, Joseph Gordon "Burrhead" b: 1/20/17, Durant, Okla. BR/TR, 6'2", 197 lbs. Deb: 4/26/39

YEAR TM/L	W	L	PCT	G	GS	CG	SH	SV	IP	H	HR	BB	SO	RAT	ERA	ERA+	OAV	OOB	BH	AVG	PB	PR	/A	PD	TPI
1939 Cle-A	2	3	.400	35	3	0	0	1	78	87	3	51	27	16.0	5.88	75	.290	.395	1	.056	-2	-11	-13	1	-1.3
1940 Cle-A	3	7	.300	40	7	2	1	3	100	101	8	48	57	13.4	4.95	85	.268	.351	3	.125	-1	-6	-8	-0	-0.8
1941 Bos-A	12	5	.706	27	18	7	1	0	134^1	136	8	67	69	13.7	4.49	93	.262	.349	7	.149	0	-5	-5	-2	-0.6
1942 Bos-A	11	9	.550	30	23	10	3	0	182^2	155	9	68	72	11.1	3.30	113	.231	.303	10	.145	-1	7	9	2	1.0
1943 Bos-A	7	11	.389	25	20	9	3	0	164^1	144	4	57	63	11.0	3.12	106	.239	.305	5	.096	-3	3	4	-2	-0.2
1946 *Bos-A	13	7	.650	32	24	9	1	0	166^2	148	11	68	91	11.7	3.24	113	.234	.309	5	.100	-2	5	8	2	0.8
1947 Bos-A	18	8	.692	33	31	15	1	1	228^2	203	15	73	110	10.9	2.95	132	.238	**.299**	16	.208	1	19	24	-2	2.5
1948 Bos-A☆	16	10	.615	38	32	16	5	2	245^1	237	14	92	116	12.1	3.56	123	.253	.320	17	.202	1	20	23	-1	2.2
1949 Bos-A	14	12	.538	33	27	12	2	2	212^2	219	12	97	87	13.5	3.85	113	.269	.348	10	.147	-1	8	12	-1	0.9
1950 Bos-A	15	10	.600	39	27	12	1	4	206^2	217	15	81	81	13.0	4.18	117	.275	.343	15	.214	1	9	16	1	1.8
1951 Chi-A	7	6	.538	28	21	6	0	3	146^2	136	17	51	67	11.5	3.62	111	.248	.312	3	.065	-6	8	7	0	0.1
1952 Chi-A	14	10	.583	29	25	11	3	1	200^2	164	11	60	101	10.0	2.51	145	.222	.280	12	.190	0	26	25	-2	2.5
1953 Chi-A	5	5	.500	23	15	3	1	1	100^2	96	10	37	50	11.9	3.67	110	.249	.314	2	.069	-2	4	4	-1	0.1
1954 Bos-A	0	0	—	2	0	0	0	0	2^2	5	0	1	1	20.3	6.75	61	.385	.429	0	—	0	-1	-1	0	-0.1
Total 14	137	103	.571	414	273	112	22	18	2170	2048	137	851	992	12.1	3.62	112	.250	.322	106	.152	-15	86	105	-5	8.9

● PAT DOBSON Dobson, Patrick Edward b: 2/12/42, Depew, N.Y. BR/TR, 6'3", 190 lbs. Deb: 5/31/67 C

YEAR TM/L	W	L	PCT	G	GS	CG	SH	SV	IP	H	HR	BB	SO	RAT	ERA	ERA+	OAV	OOB	BH	AVG	PB	PR	/A	PD	TPI
1967 Det-A	1	2	.333	28	1	0	0	0	49^1	38	6	27	34	12.2	2.92	112	.216	.327	0	.000	-1	2	2	-1	0.1
1968 *Det-A	5	8	.385	47	10	2	1	7	125	89	13	48	93	10.0	2.66	113	.200	.281	4	.143	0	4	5	1	0.7
1969 Det-A	5	10	.333	49	9	1	0	9	105	100	10	39	64	12.0	3.60	104	.253	.322	2	.091	-1	0	2	0	0.1
1970 SD-N	14	15	.483	40	34	8	1	1	251	257	28	78	185	12.2	3.76	106	.265	.322	10	.141	-0	8	6	-0	0.5
1971 *Bal-A	20	8	.714	38	37	18	4	1	282^1	248	24	63	187	10.0	2.90	116	.235	.279	10	.110	-3	18	14	-1	1.1
1972 Bal-A☆	16	18	.471	38	36	13	3	0	268^1	220	13	69	161	9.8	2.65	116	.224	.278	12	.141	-2	12	13	-2	1.1
1973 Atl-N	3	7	.300	12	10	1	1	0	57^2	73	1	19	23	14.5	4.99	79	.315	.369	1	.067	-1	-9	-7	0	-0.8
NY-A	9	8	.529	22	21	6	1	0	142^1	150	22	34	70	11.8	4.17	88	.266	.311	0	—	0	-6	-8	0	-0.8
1974 NY-A	19	15	.559	39	39	12	2	0	281	282	23	75	157	11.6	3.07	113	.262	.312	0	—	0	17	13	-1	1.3
1975 NY-A	11	14	.440	33	30	7	1	0	207^2	205	21	83	129	12.5	4.07	89	.261	.333	0	—	0	-7	-10	-0	-1.0
1976 Cle-A	16	12	.571	35	35	6	0	0	217^1	226	13	65	117	12.1	3.48	100	.272	.327	0	—	0	1	0	-1	0.0
1977 Cle-A	3	12	.200	33	17	0	0	1	133^1	155	23	65	81	14.9	6.14	64	.299	.378	0	—	0	-31	-33	0	-3.0
Total 11	122	129	.486	414	279	74	14	19	2120^1	2043	197	665	1301	11.6	3.54	100	.255	.314	39	.123	-8	10	-3	-3	-0.7

● GEORGE DOCKINS Dockins, George Woodrow "Lefty" b: 5/5/17, Clyde, Kan. BL/TL, 6', 175 lbs. Deb: 5/05/45

YEAR TM/L	W	L	PCT	G	GS	CG	SH	SV	IP	H	HR	BB	SO	RAT	ERA	ERA+	OAV	OOB	BH	AVG	PB	PR	/A	PD	TPI
1945 StL-N	8	6	.571	31	12	5	2	0	126^1	132	4	38	33	12.1	3.21	117	.269	.321	6	.176	1	8	8	-1	0.8
1947 Bro-N	0	0	—	4	0	0	0	0	5^1	10	2	2	1	20.3	11.81	35	.400	.444	0	.000	-0	-5	-5	0	-0.4
Total 2	8	6	.571	35	12	5	2	0	131^2	142	6	40	34	12.4	3.55	106	.275	.327	6	.171	1	4	3	-0	0.4

● SAM DODGE Dodge, Samuel Edward b: 12/9/1889, Neath, Pa. d: 4/5/66, Utica, N.Y. BR/TR, 6'1", 170 lbs. Deb: 9/24/21

YEAR TM/L	W	L	PCT	G	GS	CG	SH	SV	IP	H	HR	BB	SO	RAT	ERA	ERA+	OAV	OOB	BH	AVG	PB	PR	/A	PD	TPI
1921 Bos-A	0	0	—	1	0	0	0	0	1	1	0	1	0	18.0	9.00	47	.500	.667	0	—	0	-1	-1	-0	-0.1
1922 Bos-A	0	0	—	3	0	0	0	0	6	11	0	3	3	21.0	4.50	91	.379	.438	0	.000	-0	-0	-0	0	0.0
Total 2	0	0	—	4	0	0	0	0	7	12	0	4	3	20.6	5.14	80	.387	.457	0	.000	-0	-1	-1	0	-0.1

● FRED DOE Doe, Alfred George "Count" b: 4/18/1864, Rockport, Mass. d: 10/4/38, Quincy, Mass. BR/TR, 5'10", 165 lbs. Deb: 8/23/1890

YEAR TM/L	W	L	PCT	G	GS	CG	SH	SV	IP	H	HR	BB	SO	RAT	ERA	ERA+	OAV	OOB	BH	AVG	PB	PR	/A	PD	TPI
1890 Buf-P	0	1	.000	1	1	1	0	0	6	10	0	7	2	25.5	12.00	34	.356	.485	0	.000	-0	-5	-5	0	-0.4
Pit-P	0	0	—	1	0	0	0	0	4	4	0	2	2	13.5	4.50	87	.249	.332	1	.500	0	-0	-0	-0	0.0
Yr	0	1	.000	2	1	1	0	0	10	14	0	9	4	20.7	9.00	45	.317	.433	1	.250	-0	-5	-6	-0	-0.4

● ED DOHENY Doheny, Edward R. b: 11/24/1874, Northfield, Vt. d: 12/29/16, Medfield, Mass. BL/TL, 5'10.5", 165 lbs. Deb: 9/16/1895

YEAR TM/L	W	L	PCT	G	GS	CG	SH	SV	IP	H	HR	BB	SO	RAT	ERA	ERA+	OAV	OOB	BH	AVG	PB	PR	/A	PD	TPI
1895 NY-N	0	3	.000	3	3	3	0	0	25^2	37	2	19	9	20.7	6.66	70	.332	.442	1	.100	-0	-5	-6	-0	-0.5
1896 NY-N	6	7	.462	17	15	9	0	0	108^1	112	3	59	39	14.7	4.49	94	.265	.363	6	.150	-2	-1	-3	-0	-0.5
1897 NY-N	4	4	.500	10	10	10	0	0	85	69	0	45	37	12.9	2.12	196	.220	.333	7	.200	-1	21	19	3	1.9
1898 NY-N	7	19	.269	28	27	23	0	0	213	238	1	101	96	15.2	3.68	95	.280	.370	14	.163	-1	-2	-5	3	-0.3
1899 NY-N	14	17	.452	35	33	30	1	0	265^1	282	2	156	115	16.1	4.51	83	.272	.386	27	.241	0	-19	-22	5	-1.5
1900 NY-N	4	14	.222	20	18	12	0	0	133^2	148	2	96	44	17.9	5.45	66	.280	.411	12	.222	-0	-26	-27	2	-2.2

YEAR TM/L	W	L	PCT	G	GS	CG	SH	SV	IP	H	HR	BB	SO	RAT	ERA	ERA+	OAV	OOB	BH	AVG	PB	PR	/A	PD	TPI
1901 NY-N	2	5	.286	10	6	6	0	0	74	88	1	17	36	13.5	4.50	73	.293	.344	10	.345	3	-10	-10	0	-0.6
Pit-N	6	2	.750	11	10	6	1	0	76^{2}	68	1	22	28	11.2	2.00	164	.236	.302	3	.115	0	11	11	-2	1.0
Yr	8	7	.533	21	16	12	1	0	150^{2}	156	2	39	64	11.9	3.23	102	.263	.314	13	.236	4	2	1	-1	0.4
1902 Pit-N	16	4	.800	22	21	19	2	0	188^{1}	161	0	61	88	11.2	2.53	108	.231	.305	12	.156	-2	5	4	-1	0.1
1903 Pit-N	16	8	.667	27	25	22	2	2	222^{2}	209	1	89	75	12.8	3.19	101	.252	.338	19	.209	-1	2	1	5	0.5
Total 9	75	83	.475	183	168	140	6	2	1392^{2}	1412	13	665	567	14.3	3.75	94	.263	.359	111	.198	-4	-24	-37	15	-2.1

● JOHN DOHERTY Doherty, John Harold b: 6/11/67, New York, N.Y. BR/TR, 6'4", 200 lbs. Deb: 4/08/92

YEAR TM/L	W	L	PCT	G	GS	CG	SH	SV	IP	H	HR	BB	SO	RAT	ERA	ERA+	OAV	OOB	BH	AVG	PB	PR	/A	PD	TPI
1992 Det-A	7	4	.636	47	11	0	0	3	116	131	4	25	37	12.4	3.88	103	.287	.329	0	—	0	1	1	1	0.2

● JOHN DOLAN Dolan, John b: 9/12/1867, Newport, Ky. d: 5/8/48, Springfield, Ohio TR, 5'10", 170 lbs. Deb: 9/05/1890

YEAR TM/L	W	L	PCT	G	GS	CG	SH	SV	IP	H	HR	BB	SO	RAT	ERA	ERA+	OAV	OOB	BH	AVG	PB	PR	/A	PD	TPI
1890 Cin-N	1	1	.500	2	2	2	0	0	18	17	3	10	9	14.0	4.50	79	.242	.344	1	.125	-1	-2	-2	-0	-0.2
1891 Col-a	12	11	.522	27	24	19	0	0	203^{1}	216	8	84	68	13.3	4.16	83	.263	.332	7	.090	-4	-10	-16	-2	-1.8
1893 StL-N	0	1	.000	3	1	1	0	1	17^{1}	26	1	7	1	17.7	4.15	114	.336	.399	1	.143	0	1	1	-0	0.1
1895 Chi-N	0	1	.000	2	2	1	0	0	11	16	0	6	1	18.8	6.55	78	.334	.419	0	.000	-0	-2	-2	0	-0.1
Total 4	13	14	.481	34	29	23	0	1	249^{2}	275	12	107	79	13.9	4.29	84	.271	.342	9	.094	-5	-13	-19	-2	-2.0

● COZY DOLAN Dolan, Patrick Henry b: 12/3/1872, Cambridge, Mass. d: 3/29/07, Louisville, Ky. BL/TL, 5'10", 160 lbs. Deb: 8/09/1892 ♦

YEAR TM/L	W	L	PCT	G	GS	CG	SH	SV	IP	H	HR	BB	SO	RAT	ERA	ERA+	OAV	OOB	BH	AVG	PB	PR	/A	PD	TPI
1892 Was-N	2	2	.500	5	4	3	0	0	37	39	0	15	8	13.4	4.38	74	.260	.331	3	.231	0	-4	-5	-1	-0.4
1895 Bos-N	11	7	.611	25	21	18	3	1	198^{1}	215	11	67	47	13.4	4.27	120	.272	.340	20	.241	-1	11	18	4	1.7
1896 Bos-N	1	4	.200	6	5	3	0	0	41	55	1	27	14	18.7	4.83	94	.318	.419	2	.143	-1	-2	-1	-0	-0.3
1905 Bos-N	0	1	.000	2	0	0	0	0	4	7	2	1	1	18.0	9.00	34	.368	.400	119	.275	1	-3	-3	-0	-0.3
1906 Bos-N	0	1	.000	2	0	0	0	0	12	12	1	6	7	13.5	4.50	60	.300	.391	136	.248	0	-2	-2	-1	-0.3
Total 5	14	15	.483	40	30	24	3	1	292^{1}	328	15	116	77	14.2	4.43	105	.280	.354	858	.269	-1	-0	7	2	0.4

● TOM DOLAN Dolan, Thomas J. b: 1/10/1859, New York, N.Y. d: 1/16/13, St.Louis, Mo. BR/TR, Deb: 9/30/1879 ♦

YEAR TM/L	W	L	PCT	G	GS	CG	SH	SV	IP	H	HR	BB	SO	RAT	ERA	ERA+	OAV	OOB	BH	AVG	PB	PR	/A	PD	TPI
1883 StL-a	0	0	—	1	0	0	0	0	4	4	0	0	0	9.0	4.50	77	.244	.244	63	.214	-0	-1	-0	0	0.0

● ART DOLL Doll, Arthur James "Moose" b: 5/7/13, Chicago, Ill. d: 4/28/78, Calumet City, Ill. BR/TR, 6'1", 190 lbs. Deb: 9/21/35 ♦

YEAR TM/L	W	L	PCT	G	GS	CG	SH	SV	IP	H	HR	BB	SO	RAT	ERA	ERA+	OAV	OOB	BH	AVG	PB	PR	/A	PD	TPI
1936 Bos-N	0	1	.000	1	1	0	0	0	8	11	1	2	2	15.8	3.38	114	.355	.412	0	.000	-0	1	0	-0	0.0
1938 Bos-N	0	0	—	3	0	0	0	0	4	4	0	3	1	15.8	2.25	153	.286	.412	1	1.000	0	1	1	0	0.1
Total 2	0	1	.000	4	1	0	0	0	12	15	1	5	3	15.8	3.00	123	.333	.412	2	.154	0	1	1	0	0.1

● RED DONAHUE Donahue, Francis Rostell b: 1/23/1873, Waterbury, Conn. d: 8/25/13, Philadelphia, Pa. BR/TR, Deb: 5/06/1893

YEAR TM/L	W	L	PCT	G	GS	CG	SH	SV	IP	H	HR	BB	SO	RAT	ERA	ERA+	OAV	OOB	BH	AVG	PB	PR	/A	PD	TPI
1893 NY-N	0	0	—	2	0	0	0	1	5	8	1	3	1	23.4	9.00	52	.351	.468	0	.000	-0	-2	-2	0	-0.2
1895 StL-N	0	1	.000	1	1	1	0	0	8	9	2	3	2	14.6	6.75	72	.280	.359	0	.000	-1	-2	-2	0	-0.2
1896 StL-N	7	24	.226	32	32	28	0	0	267	376	6	98	70	16.4	5.80	75	.329	.389	17	.159	-8	-43	-43	-1	-4.1
1897 StL-N	10	35	.222	**46**	42	**38**	1	1	348	484	16	106	64	15.8	6.13	72	.326	.380	33	.213	-3	-70	-67	5	-5.2
1898 Phi-N	16	17	.485	35	35	33	1	0	284^{1}	327	7	80	57	13.3	3.55	97	.286	.340	16	.143	-7	2	-3	4	-0.6
1899 Phi-N	21	8	.724	35	31	27	4	0	279	292	6	63	51	11.8	3.39	109	.269	.316	20	.180	-5	15	9	3	0.6
1900 Phi-N	15	10	.600	32	24	21	2	0	240	299	6	50	41	13.4	3.60	100	.304	.344	20	.222	-1	3	0	-1	-0.1
1901 Phi-N	21	13	.618	35	34	34	1	1	304^{1}	307	2	60	89	11.1	2.60	131	.260	.301	11	.094	-9	24	27	-2	1.6
1902 StL-A	22	11	.667	35	34	33	2	0	316^{1}	322	7	65	63	11.2	2.76	128	.264	.306	11	.093	-10	29	27	7	2.4
1903 StL-A	8	7	.533	16	15	14	0	0	131	145	0	22	51	11.5	2.75	106	.280	.309	8	.157	-2	3	2	0	0.1
Cle-A	7	9	.438	16	15	14	4	0	136^{2}	142	3	12	45	10.5	2.44	117	.267	.291	8	.151	-1	8	6	1	0.6
Yr	15	16	.484	32	30	28	4	0	267^{2}	287	3	34	96	11.0	2.59	111	.273	.300	16	.154	-3	11	9	2	0.7
1904 Cle-A	19	14	.576	35	32	30	6	0	277	281	2	49	127	10.9	2.40	106	.264	.299	17	.168	-1	6	4	2	0.5
1905 Cle-A	6	12	.333	20	18	14	1	0	137^{2}	132	2	25	45	10.7	3.40	78	.253	.295	4	.075	-5	-11	-12	1	-1.6
1906 Det-A	13	14	.481	28	28	26	3	0	241	260	1	54	82	12.0	2.73	101	.278	.323	10	.123	-4	-1	1	-0	-0.4
Total 13	165	175	.485	368	341	313	25	3	2975^{1}	3384	61	690	788	12.7	3.61	96	.285	.331	175	.152	-57	-40	-51	19	-6.6

● DEACON DONAHUE Donahue, John Stephen Michael b: 6/23/20, Chicago, Ill. BR/TR, 6', 180 lbs. Deb: 9/16/43

YEAR TM/L	W	L	PCT	G	GS	CG	SH	SV	IP	H	HR	BB	SO	RAT	ERA	ERA+	OAV	OOB	BH	AVG	PB	PR	/A	PD	TPI
1943 Phi-N	0	0	—	2	0	0	0	0	4	4	0	1	1	13.5	4.50	75	.235	.316	0	—	0	-0	-1	0	-0.1
1944 Phi-N	0	2	.000	6	0	0	0	0	9^{1}	18	0	2	2	19.3	7.71	47	.429	.455	0	.000	-0	-4	-4	0	-0.4
Total 2	0	2	.000	8	0	0	0	0	13^{1}	22	0	3	3	17.6	6.75	52	.373	.413	0	.000	-0	-5	-5	0	-0.5

● ATLEY DONALD Donald, Richard Atley "Swampy" b: 8/19/10, Morton, Miss. BL/TR, 6'1", 186 lbs. Deb: 4/21/38

YEAR TM/L	W	L	PCT	G	GS	CG	SH	SV	IP	H	HR	BB	SO	RAT	ERA	ERA+	OAV	OOB	BH	AVG	PB	PR	/A	PD	TPI
1938 NY-A	0	1	.000	2	2	0	0	0	12	7	0	14	6	16.5	5.25	86	.175	.400	1	.167	-0	-1	-1	0	-0.1
1939 NY-A	13	3	.813	24	20	11	2	1	153	144	12	60	55	12.0	3.71	118	.247	.317	15	.250	3	16	11	-1	1.1
1940 NY-A	8	3	.727	24	11	6	1	0	118^{2}	113	11	59	60	13.2	3.03	133	.249	.339	6	.146	-2	18	13	-3	0.8
1941 *NY-A	9	5	.643	22	20	10	0	0	159	141	11	69	71	12.1	3.57	110	.237	.320	5	.081	-4	10	6	-0	0.2
1942 *NY-A	11	3	.786	20	19	10	1	0	147^{2}	133	6	45	53	10.8	3.11	111	.239	.296	9	.148	-1	9	5	-2	0.2
1943 NY-A	6	4	.600	22	15	2	0	0	119^{1}	134	10	38	57	13.0	4.60	70	.276	.329	6	.128	-2	-17	-18	-2	-2.3
1944 NY-A	13	10	.565	30	19	9	0	0	159	173	13	59	48	13.2	3.34	104	.280	.345	10	.182	-0	2	3	-1	0.1
1945 NY-A	5	4	.556	9	9	6	2	0	63^{2}	62	3	25	19	12.3	2.97	117	.248	.316	5	.208	0	3	4	-2	0.2
Total 8	65	33	.663	153	115	54	6	1	932^{1}	907	66	369	369	12.4	3.52	107	.253	.325	57	.160	-7	39	24	-11	0.2

● ED DONALDS Donalds, Edward Alexander "Erston" b: 6/22/1885, Bidwell, Ohio d: 7/3/50, Columbus, Ohio BR/TR, 5'11", 180 lbs. Deb: 9/01/12

YEAR TM/L	W	L	PCT	G	GS	CG	SH	SV	IP	H	HR	BB	SO	RAT	ERA	ERA+	OAV	OOB	BH	AVG	PB	PR	/A	PD	TPI
1912 Cin-N	1	0	1.000	1	0	0	0	0	4	7	0	0	1	15.8	4.50	75	.438	.438	0	.000	-0	-0	-1	0	-0.1

● MIKE DONLIN Donlin, Michael Joseph "Turkey Mike" b: 5/30/1878, Peoria, Ill. d: 9/24/33, Hollywood, Cal. BL/TL, 5'9", 170 lbs. Deb: 7/19/1899 ♦

YEAR TM/L	W	L	PCT	G	GS	CG	SH	SV	IP	H	HR	BB	SO	RAT	ERA	ERA+	OAV	OOB	BH	AVG	PB	PR	/A	PD	TPI
1899 StL-N	0	1	.000	3	1	0	0	0	15^{1}	15	1	14	6	17.6	7.63	52	.256	.408	86	.323	1	-6	-6	1	-0.4
1902 Cin-N	0	0	—	1	0	0	0	0	1	1	0	0	0	9.0	0.00	—	.260	.260	41	.287	0	0	0	-0	0.0
Total 2	0	1	.000	4	1	0	0	0	16^{1}	16	1	14	6	17.1	7.16	55	.256	.400	1282	.333	1	-6	-6	1	-0.4

● ED DONNELLY Donnelly, Edward "Big Ed" or "Ned" (b: Edward O'Donnell)
b: 7/29/1880, Hampton, N.Y. d: 11/28/57, Rutland, Vt. BR/TR, 6'1", 205 lbs. Deb: 9/19/11

YEAR TM/L	W	L	PCT	G	GS	CG	SH	SV	IP	H	HR	BB	SO	RAT	ERA	ERA+	OAV	OOB	BH	AVG	PB	PR	/A	PD	TPI
1911 Bos-N	3	2	.600	5	4	4	1	0	36^{2}	33	0	9	16	10.8	2.45	156	.236	.291	1	.071	-2	4	6	-0	0.4
1912 Bos-N	5	10	.333	37	18	10	0	0	184^{1}	225	10	72	67	14.7	4.35	82	.304	.370	19	.275	3	-19	-16	1	-1.2
Total 2	8	12	.400	42	22	14	1	0	221	258	10	81	83	14.1	4.03	90	.293	.357	20	.241	1	-15	-10	1	-0.8

● ED DONNELLY Donnelly, Edward Vincent b: 12/10/34, Allen, Mich. BR/TR, 6', 175 lbs. Deb: 8/01/59

YEAR TM/L	W	L	PCT	G	GS	CG	SH	SV	IP	H	HR	BB	SO	RAT	ERA	ERA+	OAV	OOB	BH	AVG	PB	PR	/A	PD	TPI
1959 Chi-N	1	1	.500	9	0	0	0	0	14^{1}	18	1	9	6	17.0	3.14	126	.305	.397	0	—	0	1	1	0	0.1

● FRANK DONNELLY Donnelly, Franklin Marion b: 10/7/1869, Tamaroa, Ill. d: 2/3/53, Canton, Ill. 5'6", 180 lbs. Deb: 8/15/1893

YEAR TM/L	W	L	PCT	G	GS	CG	SH	SV	IP	H	HR	BB	SO	RAT	ERA	ERA+	OAV	OOB	BH	AVG	PB	PR	/A	PD	TPI
1893 Chi-N	3	1	.750	7	5	3	0	**2**	42	51	1	17	6	15.4	5.36	86	.291	.367	8	.444	4	-3	-3	-0	0.0

● BLIX DONNELLY Donnelly, Sylvester Urban b: 1/21/14, Olivia, Minn. d: 6/20/76, Olivia, Minn. BR/TR, 5'10", 178 lbs. Deb: 5/06/44

YEAR TM/L	W	L	PCT	G	GS	CG	SH	SV	IP	H	HR	BB	SO	RAT	ERA	ERA+	OAV	OOB	BH	AVG	PB	PR	/A	PD	TPI
1944 *StL-N	2	1	.667	27	4	2	1	2	76^{1}	61	2	34	45	11.4	2.12	166	.218	.307	1	.063	-1	13	12	1	1.2
1945 StL-N†	8	10	.444	31	23	9	4	2	166^{1}	157	10	87	76	13.5	3.52	106	.250	.346	7	.130	-2	5	4	-4	-0.2
1946 StL-N	1	2	.333	13	0	0	0	0	13^{2}	17	1	10	11	18.4	3.95	87	.347	.467	0	—	0	-1	-1	-0	-0.1
Phi-N	3	4	.429	12	8	2	0	1	76^{1}	64	7	24	38	10.6	2.95	116	.220	.284	7	.280	2	4	4	-1	0.6
Yr	4	6	.400	25	8	2	0	1	90	81	8	34	49	11.7	3.10	111	.238	.310	7	.280	2	3	3	-1	0.5
1947 Phi-N	4	6	.400	38	10	5	1	5	120^{2}	113	6	46	31	12.1	2.98	134	.265	.340	2	.063	-2	14	14	-0	1.2
1948 Phi-N	5	7	.417	26	19	8	1	2	131^{2}	125	13	49	46	11.9	3.69	107	.261	.330	10	.222	2	4	4	-3	0.3
1949 Phi-N	2	1	.667	23	10	1	0	0	78^{1}	84	7	40	36	14.4	5.06	78	.294	.382	4	.174	-1	-9	-10	-2	-1.2

YEAR	TM/L	W	L	PCT	G	GS	CG	SH	SV	IP	H	HR	BB	SO	RAT	ERA	ERA+	OAV	OOB	BH	AVG	PB	PR	/A	PD	TPI
1950	Phi-N	2	4	.333	14	1	0	0	0	21	30	5	10	10	17.1	4.29	94	.330	.396	1	.200	-0	-0	-1	0	0.0
1951	Bos-N	0	1	.000	6	0	0	0	0	7^1	8	1	6	3	18.4	7.36	50	.286	.429	0	.000	-0	-3	-3	0	-0.3
Total	8	27	36	.429	190	75	27	7	12	691^2	659	52	306	296	12.8	3.49	109	.257	.340	32	.159	-1	27	24	-8	1.5

● JIM DONOHUE

Donohue, James Thomas b: 10/31/38, St.Louis, Mo. BR/TR, 6'4", 190 lbs. Deb: 4/11/61

YEAR	TM/L	W	L	PCT	G	GS	CG	SH	SV	IP	H	HR	BB	SO	RAT	ERA	ERA+	OAV	OOB	BH	AVG	PB	PR	/A	PD	TPI
1961	Det-A	1	1	.500	14	0	0	0	1	20^1	23	2	15	20	16.8	3.54	116	.287	.400	0	.000	-0	1	1	-0	0.1
	LA-A	4	6	.400	38	7	0	0	5	100^1	93	16	50	79	12.8	4.31	105	.246	.334	4	.148	-1	-3	2	-0	0.1
	Yr	5	7	.417	52	7	0	0	6	120^2	116	18	65	99	13.5	4.18	106	.253	.346	4	.143	-1	-2	4	-1	0.2
1962	LA-A	1	0	1.000	12	1	0	0	0	24^1	24	4	11	14	13.7	3.70	104	.258	.349	1	.250	0	1	0	-1	0.0
	Min-A	0	1	.000	6	1	0	0	1	10^1	12	2	6	3	15.7	6.97	59	.324	.419	0	.000	-0	-3	-3	1	-0.3
	Yr	1	1	.500	18	2	0	0	1	34^2	36	6	17	17	13.8	4.67	84	.273	.356	1	.167	0	-3	-3	-0	-0.3
Total	2	6	8	.429	70	9	0	0	7	155^1	152	24	82	116	13.7	4.29	101	.259	.351	5	.147	-1	-5	1	-1	-0.1

● PETE DONOHUE

Donohue, Peter Joseph b: 11/5/1900, Athens, Tex. d: 2/23/88, Ft.Worth, Tex. BR/TR, 6'2", 185 lbs. Deb: 7/01/21

YEAR	TM/L	W	L	PCT	G	GS	CG	SH	SV	IP	H	HR	BB	SO	RAT	ERA	ERA+	OAV	OOB	BH	AVG	PB	PR	/A	PD	TPI
1921	Cin-N	7	6	.538	21	11	7	0	1	118^1	117	5	26	44	10.9	3.35	107	.263	.304	8	.211	1	6	3	2	0.6
1922	Cin-N	18	9	**.667**	33	30	18	2	1	242	257	7	43	66	11.3	3.12	128	.276	.312	16	.182	-3	26	23	1	2.1
1923	Cin-N	21	15	.583	42	36	19	2	3	274^1	304	3	68	84	12.5	3.38	114	.278	.326	24	.250	3	19	15	1	1.7
1924	Cin-N	16	9	.640	35	32	16	3	0	222^1	248	9	36	72	11.9	3.60	105	.285	.321	14	.192	-0	7	4	-1	0.2
1925	Cin-N	21	14	.600	42	38	**27**	3	2	**301**	310	3	49	78	10.8	3.08	133	.268	.299	32	.294	7	40	34	-3	3.8
1926	Cin-N	**20**	14	.588	47	38	17	**5**	2	**285^2**	298	6	39	73	10.9	3.37	109	.268	.298	33	.311	9	14	10	-3	1.6
1927	Cin-N	6	16	.273	33	24	12	1	1	190^2	253	3	32	48	13.5	4.11	92	.328	.356	16	.250	1	-4	-7	0	-0.5
1928	Cin-N	7	11	.389	23	18	8	0	0	150	180	10	32	37	12.9	4.74	83	.309	.348	7	.146	-0	-13	-13	1	-1.2
1929	Cin-N	10	13	.435	32	24	7	0	0	177^2	243	12	51	30	15.1	5.42	84	.331	.377	20	.333	4	-14	-17	0	-1.1
1930	Cin-N	1	3	.250	8	5	2	0	1	34^1	53	0	13	4	17.6	6.29	77	.363	.419	1	.100	-1	-5	-6	1	-0.5
	NY-N	7	6	.538	18	11	4	0	1	86^2	135	6	18	26	16.1	6.13	77	.360	.392	9	.273	1	-11	-13	-2	-1.2
	Yr	8	9	.471	26	16	6	0	2	121	188	6	31	30	16.4	6.17	77	.360	.398	10	.233	0	-16	-19	-0	-1.7
1931	NY-N	0	1	.000	4	1	0	0	0	11^1	14	1	4	4	14.3	5.56	66	.311	.367	0	.000	-0	-2	-2	-0	-0.3
	Cle-A	0	0	—	2	0	0	0	0	5^1	9	1	5	4	23.6	8.44	55	.429	.538	0	.000	-0	-2	-2	-0	-0.2
1932	Bos-A	0	1	.000	4	2	0	0	0	12^2	18	2	6	1	17.1	7.82	57	.340	.407	0	.000	-0	-5	-5	1	-0.4
Total	12	134	118	.532	344	270	137	16	12	2112^1	2439	68	422	571	12.4	3.87	103	.293	.330	180	.246	21	56	25	-1	4.6

● LINO DONOSO

Donoso, Lino (Galeta) b: 9/23/22, Havana, Cuba d: 10/13/90, Veracruz, Mexico BL/TL, 5'11", 160 lbs. Deb: 6/18/55

YEAR	TM/L	W	L	PCT	G	GS	CG	SH	SV	IP	H	HR	BB	SO	RAT	ERA	ERA+	OAV	OOB	BH	AVG	PB	PR	/A	PD	TPI
1955	Pit-N	4	6	.400	25	9	3	0	1	95	106	16	35	38	13.5	5.31	78	.287	.351	5	.185	-1	-13	-13	0	-1.3
1956	Pit-N	0	0	—	3	0	0	0	0	1^2	2	0	1	1	16.2	0.00	—	.250	.333	0	—	0	1	1	0	0.1
Total	2	4	6	.400	28	9	3	0	1	96^2	108	16	36	39	13.5	5.21	79	.286	.350	5	.185	-1	-13	-12	0	-1.2

● DICK DONOVAN

Donovan, Richard Edward b: 12/7/27, Boston, Mass. BL/TR, 6'3", 205 lbs. Deb: 4/24/50

YEAR	TM/L	W	L	PCT	G	GS	CG	SH	SV	IP	H	HR	BB	SO	RAT	ERA	ERA+	OAV	OOB	BH	AVG	PB	PR	/A	PD	TPI
1950	Bos-N	0	2	.000	10	3	0	0	0	29^2	28	4	34	9	19.4	8.19	47	.255	.438	1	.167	1	-13	-14	-0	-1.2
1951	Bos-N	0	0	—	8	2	0	0	0	13^2	17	0	11	4	18.4	5.27	70	.298	.412	1	.333	1	-2	-2	0	-0.1
1952	Bos-N	0	2	.000	7	2	0	0	1	13	18	1	12	6	22.2	5.54	65	.346	.485	0	.000	-0	-3	-3	1	-0.3
1954	Det-A	0	0	—	2	0	0	0	0	6	9	1	5	2	21.0	10.50	35	.360	.467	0	.000	-0	-5	-5	-0	-0.4
1955	Chi-A☆	15	9	.625	29	24	11	5	0	187	186	17	48	88	11.4	3.32	119	.261	.311	17	.224	5	13	13	1	1.9
1956	Chi-A	12	10	.545	34	31	14	3	0	234^2	212	22	59	120	10.6	3.64	113	.240	.292	20	.222	8	13	12	2	2.1
1957	Chi-A	16	6	**.727**	28	28	**16**	2	0	220^2	203	17	45	88	10.4	2.77	135	.247	.293	12	.145	2	25	24	0	2.8
1958	Chi-A	15	14	.517	34	34	16	4	0	248	240	23	53	127	10.9	3.01	121	.251	.295	9	.112	-1	21	17	-1	1.6
1959	*Chi-A	9	10	.474	31	29	5	1	0	179^2	171	15	58	71	11.7	3.66	103	.247	.310	8	.131	1	4	2	-2	0.1
1960	Chi-A	6	1	.857	33	8	0	0	3	78^2	87	13	25	30	12.8	5.38	70	.283	.337	3	.130	-0	-13	-14	1	-1.3
1961	Was-A★	10	10	.500	23	22	11	2	0	168^2	138	10	35	62	**9.4**	**2.40**	**167**	.224	**.269**	10	.179	2	30	30	-1	3.4
1962	Cle-A★	20	10	.667	34	34	16	**5**	0	250^2	255	23	47	94	10.9	3.59	108	.263	.299	16	.180	6	11	8	-1	1.3
1963	Cle-A	11	13	.458	30	30	7	3	0	206	211	27	28	84	10.7	4.24	85	.265	.295	9	.130	-1	-14	-14	-1	-1.6
1964	Cle-A	7	9	.438	30	23	5	0	1	158^1	181	19	29	83	12.1	4.55	79	.290	.324	7	.146	3	-16	-17	1	-1.3
1965	Cle-A	1	3	.250	12	3	0	0	0	22^2	32	6	6	12	15.1	5.96	58	.333	.373	0	.000	-1	-6	-6	-0	-0.7
Total	15	122	99	.552	345	273	101	25	5	2017^1	1988	198	495	880	11.3	3.67	104	.258	.306	113	.163	24	45	31	-0	6.3

● TOM DONOVAN

Donovan, Thomas Joseph b: 1/1/1873, West Troy, N.Y. d: 3/25/33, Watervliet, N.Y. BR/TR, 6'2", 168 lbs. Deb: 9/10/01 F♦

YEAR	TM/L	W	L	PCT	G	GS	CG	SH	SV	IP	H	HR	BB	SO	RAT	ERA	ERA+	OAV	OOB	BH	AVG	PB	PR	/A	PD	TPI
1901	Cle-A	0	0	—	1	0	0	0	0	7	16	0	3	0	27.0	5.14	69	.442	.510	18	.254	0	-1	-1	0	-0.1

● BILL DONOVAN

Donovan, Willard Earl b: 7/6/16, Maywood, Ill. BR/TL, 6'2", 198 lbs. Deb: 4/19/42

YEAR	TM/L	W	L	PCT	G	GS	CG	SH	SV	IP	H	HR	BB	SO	RAT	ERA	ERA+	OAV	OOB	BH	AVG	PB	PR	/A	PD	TPI
1942	Bos-N	3	6	.333	31	10	2	0	0	89^1	97	2	32	23	13.0	3.43	97	.283	.344	6	.240	1	-1	-1	2	0.3
1943	Bos-N	1	0	1.000	7	0	0	0	0	14^2	17	0	9	1	16.0	1.84	185	.304	.400	1	.333	0	3	3	1	0.4
Total	2	4	6	.400	38	10	2	0	0	104	114	2	41	24	13.4	3.20	105	.286	.352	7	.250	1	1	2	3	0.7

● BILL DONOVAN

Donovan, William Edward "Wild Bill" b: 10/13/1876, Lawrence, Mass. d: 12/9/23, Forsyth, N.Y. BR/TR, 5'11", 190 lbs. Deb: 4/22/1898 M♦

YEAR	TM/L	W	L	PCT	G	GS	CG	SH	SV	IP	H	HR	BB	SO	RAT	ERA	ERA+	OAV	OOB	BH	AVG	PB	PR	/A	PD	TPI
1898	Was-N	1	6	.143	17	7	6	0	0	88	88	0	69	36	16.8	4.30	85	.258	.394	17	.165	-1	-7	-6	-0	-0.6
1899	Bro-N	1	2	.333	5	2	2	0	1	25	35	0	13	11	17.3	4.32	91	.330	.403	3	.231	-0	-1	-1	-0	-0.1
1900	Bro-N	1	2	.333	5	4	2	0	0	31	36	0	18	13	16.5	6.68	58	.290	.392	0	.000	-2	-10	-10	1	-0.9
1901	Bro-N	**25**	15	.625	**45**	38	36	2	**3**	351	324	1	152	226	12.4	2.77	121	.244	.324	23	.170	-1	22	23	-1	2.0
1902	Bro-N	17	15	.531	35	33	30	4	1	297^2	250	1	111	170	11.1	2.78	99	.228	.303	28	.174	-1	-0	-1	1	0.0
1903	Det-A	17	16	.515	35	34	**34**	4	0	307	247	3	95	187	10.1	2.29	127	.220	.283	30	.242	4	23	21	-3	2.4
1904	Det-A	17	16	.515	34	34	30	3	0	293	251	5	94	137	10.9	2.46	104	.232	.300	38	.271	5	5	3	0	1.0
1905	Det-A	18	15	.545	34	32	27	5	0	280^2	236	2	101	135	11.1	2.60	105	.229	.304	25	.192	1	2	4	-3	0.3
1906	Det-A	9	15	.375	25	25	22	0	0	211^2	221	4	72	85	12.8	3.15	88	.272	.337	11	.121	-5	-11	-9	-0	-1.5
1907	*Det-A	25	4	**.862**	32	28	27	3	1	271	222	3	82	123	10.4	2.19	119	.225	.290	29	.266	7	11	13	-6	1.6
1908	*Det-A	18	7	.720	29	28	25	6	0	242^2	210	2	53	141	10.0	2.08	117	.231	.278	13	.159	0	9	9	-6	0.3
1909	*Det-A	8	7	.533	21	17	13	4	2	140^1	121	0	60	76	12.0	2.31	109	.235	.322	9	.200	1	3	3	-2	0.2
1910	Det-A	17	7	.708	26	23	20	3	0	206^2	184	4	61	107	11.0	2.44	108	.243	.305	10	.145	-2	2	4	-6	-0.5
1911	Det-A	10	9	.526	20	19	15	1	0	168^1	160	4	64	81	12.1	3.31	104	.250	.321	12	.200	4	1	3	-5	0.2
1912	Det-A	1	0	1.000	3	1	0	0	0	10	5	0	2	6	7.2	0.90	362	.147	.216	1	.077	-1	3	3	-0	0.2
1915	NY-A	0	3	.000	9	1	0	0	0	33^2	35	1	10	17	12.3	4.81	61	.278	.336	1	.083	-1	-7	-7	-1	-0.9
1916	NY-A	0	0	—	1	0	0	0	0	1	1	0	1	0	18.0	0.00	—	.250	.400	0	—	0	0	0	-0	0.0
1918	Det-A	1	0	1.000	2	1	0	0	0	6	5	0	1	1	9.0	1.50	177	.227	.261	1	.500	0	1	1	-0	0.1
Total	18	186	139	.572	378	327	289	35	8	2964^2	2631	30	1059	1552	11.5	2.69	106	.239	.310	251	.193	7	44	54	-31	3.8

● JOHN DOPSON

Dopson, John Robert b: 7/14/63, Baltimore, Md. BL/TR, 6'4", 205 lbs. Deb: 9/04/85

YEAR	TM/L	W	L	PCT	G	GS	CG	SH	SV	IP	H	HR	BB	SO	RAT	ERA	ERA+	OAV	OOB	BH	AVG	PB	PR	/A	PD	TPI
1985	Mon-N	0	2	.000	4	3	0	0	0	13	25	4	4	4	20.1	11.08	31	.379	.414	0	.000	0	-11	-11	-0	-1.0
1988	Mon-N	3	11	.214	26	26	1	0	0	168^2	150	15	58	101	11.2	3.04	118	.235	.300	3	.059	-3	8	10	-3	0.5
1989	Bos-A	12	8	.600	29	28	2	0	0	169^1	166	14	69	95	12.6	3.99	103	.257	.330	0	—	0	-2	2	3	0.5
1990	Bos-A	0	0	—	4	4	0	0	0	17^2	13	2	9	9	11.2	2.04	200	.200	.297	0	—	0	4	4	1	0.5
1991	Bos-A	0	0	—	1	0	0	0	0	1	2	0	1	0	27.0	18.00	24	.500	.600	0	—	0	-2	-2	0	-0.2
1992	Bos-A	7	11	.389	25	25	0	0	0	141^1	159	17	38	55	12.7	4.08	102	.287	.335	0	—	0	-2	1	1	-0.1
Total	6	22	32	.407	89	86	3	0	0	511	515	52	179	264	12.3	3.84	102	.261	.324	3	.055	-3	-5	5	2	0.2

● JOHN DORAN

Doran, John F. b: 1869, New Jersey TL , 5'11", 175 lbs. Deb: 4/11/1891

YEAR	TM/L	W	L	PCT	G	GS	CG	SH	SV	IP	H	HR	BB	SO	RAT	ERA	ERA+	OAV	OOB	BH	AVG	PB	PR	/A	PD	TPI
1891	Lou-a	5	10	.333	15	14	12	1	0	126	160	3	75	55	17.7	5.43	67	.299	.398	10	.189	-2	-24	-25	-0	-2.2

YEAR TM/L	W	L	PCT	G	GS	CG	SH	SV	IP	H	HR	BB	SO	RAT	ERA	ERA+	OAV	OOB	BH	AVG	PB	PR	/A	PD	TPI

● MIKE DORGAN　Dorgan, Michael Cornelius　b: 10/2/1853, Middletown, Conn.　d: 4/26/09, Syracuse, N.Y.　BR/TR, 5'9", 180 lbs.　Deb: 5/08/1877　FM♦

1879 Syr-N	0	0	—	2	0	0	0	0	12	13	0	8	8	11.3	2.25	105	.260	.288	72	.267	0	0	0	0	0.1
1880 Pro-N	0	0	—	1	0	0	0	0	8	4	0	0	2	4.5	1.13	196	.138	.138	79	.246	0	1	1	0	0.2
1883 NY-N	0	1	.000	1	1	0	0	0	7	8	0	6	3	18.0	3.86	80	.286	.412	61	.234	0	-1	-1	-0	-0.1
1884 NY-N	8	6	.571	14	14	12	0	0	113	98	5	51	90	11.9	3.50	85	.215	.294	94	.276	2	-7	-7	1	-0.4
Total 4	8	7	.533	18	15	13	0	0	140	123	5	59	103	11.7	3.28	88	.218	.293	802	.274	3	-6	-6	1	-0.3

● HARRY DORISH　Dorish, Harry　b: 7/13/21, Swoyersville, Pa.　BR/TR, 5'11", 206 lbs.　Deb: 4/15/47　C

1947 Bos-A	7	8	.467	41	9	2	0	2	136	149	6	54	50	13.5	4.70	83	.283	.351	5	.143	-1	-15	-12	1	-1.3
1948 Bos-A	0	1	.000	9	0	0	0	0	14¹	18	1	6	5	15.1	5.65	78	.281	.343	1	.250	-0	-2	-2	-0	-0.2
1949 Bos-A	0	0	—	5	0	0	0	0	7²	7	1	1	5	9.4	2.35	186	.241	.267	0	—	0	2	2	0	0.2
1950 StL-A	4	9	.308	29	13	4	0	0	109	162	13	36	36	17.1	6.44	77	.337	.394	5	.161	-4	-23	-18	-1	-1.7
1951 Chi-A	5	6	.455	32	4	2	1	0	96²	101	6	31	29	12.3	3.54	114	.272	.328	8	.258	0	6	5	0	0.6
1952 Chi-A	8	4	.667	39	1	1	0	11	91	66	4	42	47	10.8	2.47	148	.208	.303	2	.091	-1	12	12	2	1.3
1953 Chi-A	10	6	.625	55	6	2	0	18	145²	140	9	52	69	12.2	3.40	118	.254	.325	7	.171	-1	10	10	2	1.1
1954 Chi-A	6	4	.600	37	6	2	1	6	109	88	9	29	48	9.7	2.72	137	.228	.284	3	.111	-2	12	12	-1	1.0
1955 Chi-A	2	0	1.000	13	0	0	0	1	17	16	0	9	6	13.2	1.59	249	.258	.352	1	.333	0	4	4	1	0.5
Bal-A	3	3	.500	35	1	0	0	6	65²	58	4	28	22	11.9	3.15	121	.238	.319	0	.000	-1	6	5	1	0.4
Yr	5	3	.625	48	1	0	0	7	82²	74	4	37	28	12.2	2.83	136	.242	.326	1	.077	-1	10	9	1	0.9
1956 Bal-A	0	0	—	13	0	0	0	0	19²	22	3	3	4	11.4	4.12	95	.297	.325	0	—	0	0	-0	1	0.0
Bos-A	0	2	.000	15	0	0	0	0	22²	23	1	10	11	13.1	3.57	129	.277	.355	0	—	0	1	3	1	0.4
Yr	0	2	.000	28	0	0	0	0	42¹	45	4	13	15	12.3	3.83	112	.283	.337	0	—	0	2	2	2	0.4
Total 10	45	43	.511	323	40	13	2	44	834¹	850	57	301	332	12.6	3.83	106	.267	.333	32	.157	-6	14	20	6	2.3

● GUS DORNER　Dorner, Augustus　b: 8/18/1876, Chambersburg, Pa.　d: 5/4/56, Chambersburg, Pa.　BR/TR, 5'10", 176 lbs.　Deb: 9/17/02

1902 Cle-A	3	1	.750	4	4	4	1	0	36	33	1	13	5	11.8	1.25	275	.244	.315	5	.385	2	9	9	-0	1.2
1903 Cle-A	4	5	.444	12	8	4	2	0	73²	83	4	24	28	13.3	4.52	63	.283	.342	2	.080	-2	-13	-14	0	-1.5
1906 Cin-N	0	1	.000	2	1	1	0	0	15	16	0	4	5	12.6	1.20	230	.276	.333	0	.000	-1	2	3	-0	0.2
Bos-N	8	25	.242	34	32	29	0	0	273¹	264	5	103	104	12.6	3.65	74	.260	.338	14	.140	-4	-31	-29	3	-3.2
Yr	8	26	.235	36	33	30	0	0	288¹	280	5	107	109	12.6	3.53	76	.261	.337	14	.133	-5	-29	-27	2	-3.0
1907 Bos-N	12	16	.429	36	31	24	2	0	271¹	253	4	92	85	11.9	3.12	82	.255	.327	12	.130	-4	-19	-17	-3	-2.5
1908 Bos-N	8	19	.296	38	28	14	3	0	216¹	176	3	77	41	11.1	3.54	68	.224	.305	12	.179	-1	-28	-27	2	-2.9
1909 Bos-N	1	2	.333	5	2	0	0	1	24²	17	1	17	7	13.1	2.55	110	.198	.343	1	.167	-0	0	1	-0	0.0
Total 6	36	69	.343	131	106	76	8	1	910¹	842	18	330	275	12.1	3.37	78	.250	.327	46	.149	-10	-80	-74	1	-8.7

● BERT DORR　Dorr, Charles Albert　b: 2/2/1862, New York　d: 6/16/14, Dickinson Town, N.Y.　Deb: 8/24/1882

| 1882 StL-a | 2 | 6 | .250 | 8 | 8 | 8 | 0 | 0 | 66 | 53 | 0 | 1 | 34 | 7.4 | 2.59 | 108 | .205 | .208 | 4 | .154 | -2 | 1 | 2 | 1 | 0.1 |

● CAL DORSETT　Dorsett, Calvin Leavelle "Preacher"　b: 6/10/13, Lone Oak, Tex.　d: 10/22/70, Elk City, Okla.　BR/TR, 6', 180 lbs.　Deb: 8/19/40

1940 Cle-A	0	0	—	1	0	0	0	0	1	1	1	0	0	9.0	9.00	47	.250	.250	0	—	0	-1	-1	-0	-0.1
1941 Cle-A	0	1	.000	5	2	0	0	0	11¹	21	1	10	5	24.6	10.32	38	.382	.477	0	.000	0	-8	-8	-0	-0.7
1947 Cle-A	0	0	—	2	0	0	0	0	1¹	3	1	3	1	40.5	27.00	13	.500	.667	0	—	0	-3	-3	0	-0.3
Total 3	0	1	.000	8	2	0	0	0	13²	25	2	13	6	25.0	11.85	33	.385	.487	0	.000	-0	-12	-12	-0	-1.1

● JIM DORSEY　Dorsey, James Edward　b: 8/2/55, Oak Park, Ill.　BR/TR, 6'7", 190 lbs.　Deb: 9/02/80

1980 Cal-A	1	2	.333	4	4	0	0	0	15²	25	2	8	8	19.5	9.19	43	.368	.442	0	—	0	-9	-9	-0	-0.8
1984 Bos-A	0	0	—	2	0	0	0	0	2²	6	0	2	4	27.0	10.13	41	.462	.533	0	—	0	-2	-2	-0	-0.2
1985 Bos-A	0	1	.000	2	1	0	0	0	5¹	12	2	10	2	37.1	20.25	21	.444	.595	0	—	0	-10	-9	-0	-0.8
Total 3	1	3	.250	8	5	0	0	0	23²	43	4	20	14	24.3	11.79	34	.398	.496	0	—	0	-20	-20	-0	-1.8

● JERRY DORSEY　Dorsey, Michael Jeremiah　b: 1854, Canada　d: 11/3/38, Auburn, N.Y.　Deb: 7/09/1884　♦

| 1884 Bal-U | 0 | 1 | .000 | 1 | 1 | 0 | 0 | 0 | 4 | 7 | 1 | 0 | 3 | 15.8 | 9.00 | 37 | .360 | .360 | 0 | .000 | -1 | -3 | -3 | -0 | -0.2 |

● JACK DOSCHER　Doscher, John Henry Jr.　b: 7/27/1880, Troy, N.Y.　d: 5/27/71, Park Ridge, N.J.　BL/TL, 6'1", 205 lbs.　Deb: 7/02/03　F

1903 Chi-N	0	1	.000	1	1	0	0	0	3	6	0	2	5	27.0	12.00	26	.429	.529	0	.000	-0	-3	-3	-0	-0.2
Bro-N	0	0	—	3	0	0	0	0	7	8	1	9	4	23.1	7.71	41	.296	.486	0	.000	-0	-3	-4	-0	-0.4
Yr	0	1	.000	4	1	0	0	0	10	14	1	11	9	23.4	9.00	35	.333	.481	0	.000	-1	-6	-6	-0	-0.6
1904 Bro-N	0	0	—	2	0	0	0	0	6¹	1	0	1	2	2.8	0.00	—	.053	.100	1	.500	0	2	2	0	0.2
1905 Bro-N	1	5	.167	12	7	6	0	0	71	60	1	30	33	11.8	3.17	91	.232	.318	2	.083	-2	-1	-2	-2	-0.6
1906 Bro-N	0	1	.000	2	1	1	0	0	14	12	0	4	10	10.3	1.29	196	.250	.308	0	.000	-1	2	2	-0	0.1
1908 Cin-N	1	3	.250	7	4	3	0	0	44¹	31	1	22	7	11.4	1.83	126	.196	.306	2	.133	0	3	3	-0	0.2
Total 5	2	10	.167	27	13	10	0	0	145²	118	3	68	61	12.0	2.84	95	.225	.323	5	.100	-3	-1	-2	-3	-0.7

● RICHARD DOTSON　Dotson, Richard Elliott　b: 1/10/59, Cincinnati, Ohio　BR/TR, 6', 204 lbs.　Deb: 9/04/79

1979 Chi-A	2	0	1.000	5	5	1	0	0	24¹	28	0	6	13	12.6	3.70	115	.286	.327	0	—	0	1	1	0	0.2
1980 Chi-A	12	10	.545	33	32	8	1	0	198	185	20	87	109	12.6	4.27	94	.247	.331	0	—	0	-5	-5	1	-0.4
1981 Chi-A	9	8	.529	24	24	5	4	0	141	145	13	49	73	12.6	3.77	95	.270	.336	0	—	0	-2	-3	-0	-0.3
1982 Chi-A	11	15	.423	34	31	3	1	0	196²	219	19	73	109	13.6	3.84	105	.282	.348	0	—	0	5	4	-1	0.4
1983 *Chi-A	22	7	.759	35	35	8	1	0	240	209	19	106	137	12.1	3.23	130	.240	.328	0	—	0	22	26	4	3.1
1984 Chi-A★	14	15	.483	32	32	14	1	0	245²	216	24	103	120	11.9	3.59	116	.238	.321	0	—	0	11	15	-0	1.6
1985 Chi-A	3	4	.429	9	9	0	0	0	52¹	53	5	17	33	12.6	4.47	97	.261	.327	0	—	0	-2	-1	-0	-0.1
1986 Chi-A	10	17	.370	34	34	3	1	0	197	226	24	69	110	13.6	5.48	79	.289	.348	0	—	0	-29	-26	-1	-2.5
1987 Chi-A	11	12	.478	31	31	7	2	0	211¹	201	24	86	114	12.2	4.17	110	.249	.321	0	—	0	7	10	2	1.1
1988 NY-A	12	9	.571	32	29	4	0	0	171	178	27	72	77	13.4	5.00	79	.266	.341	0	—	0	-20	-20	-1	-2.1
1989 NY-A	2	5	.286	11	9	1	0	0	51²	69	8	17	14	15.2	5.57	69	.317	.369	0	—	0	-10	-10	-1	-1.0
Chi-A	3	7	.300	17	17	1	0	0	99²	112	8	41	55	13.8	3.88	98	.282	.349	0	—	0	-0	-1	-0	-0.1
Yr	5	12	.294	28	26	2	0	0	151¹	181	16	58	69	14.2	4.46	86	.293	.354	0	—	0	-10	-11	-1	-1.1
1990 KC-A	0	4	.000	8	7	0	0	0	28²	43	3	14	9	17.9	8.48	45	.355	.422	0	—	0	-15	-15	-0	-1.4
Total 12	111	113	.496	305	295	55	11	0	1857¹	1884	194	740	973	12.9	4.23	97	.264	.337	0	—	0	-35	-25	2	-1.5

● GARY DOTTER　Dotter, Gary Richard　b: 8/7/42, St.Louis, Mo.　BL/TL, 6'1", 180 lbs.　Deb: 9/10/61

1961 Min-A	0	0	—	2	0	0	0	0	6	6	0	4	2	15.0	9.00	47	.273	.385	0	.000	-0	-3	-3	-0	-0.3
1963 Min-A	0	0	—	2	0	0	0	0	2	0	0	0	2	0.0	0.00	—	.000	.000	0	—	0	1	1	0	0.1
1964 Min-A	0	0	—	3	0	0	0	0	4¹	3	1	3	6	12.5	2.08	172	.188	.316	0	—	0	1	1	-0	0.1
Total 3	0	0	—	7	0	0	0	0	12¹	9	1	7	10	11.7	5.11	76	.205	.314	0	.000	-0	-2	-2	0	-0.1

● BABE DOTY　Doty, Elmer L.　b: 12/17/1867, Genoa, Ohio　d: 11/20/29, Toledo, Ohio　BL/TR, 6', 160 lbs.　Deb: 8/18/1890

| 1890 Tol-a | 1 | 0 | 1.000 | 1 | 1 | 1 | 0 | 0 | 9 | 9 | 0 | 4 | 4 | 10.0 | 1.00 | 395 | .252 | .273 | 0 | .000 | -0 | 3 | 3 | -0 | 0.2 |

● TOM DOUGHERTY　Dougherty, Thomas James "Sugar Boy"　b: 5/30/1881, Chicago, Ill.　d: 11/6/53, Milwaukee, Wis.　BL/TR,　Deb: 4/24/04

| 1904 Chi-A | 1 | 0 | 1.000 | 1 | 0 | 0 | 0 | 0 | 2 | 0 | 0 | 0 | 0 | 0.0 | 0.00 | — | .000 | .000 | 0 | .000 | -0 | 1 | 1 | 0 | 0.1 |

● WHAMMY DOUGLAS　Douglas, Charles William　b: 2/17/35, Carrboro, N.C.　BR/TR, 6'2", 185 lbs.　Deb: 7/29/57

| 1957 Pit-N | 3 | 3 | .500 | 11 | 8 | 0 | 0 | 0 | 47 | 48 | 5 | 30 | 28 | 15.5 | 3.26 | 116 | .270 | .384 | 1 | .063 | -1 | 3 | 3 | -0 | 0.1 |

YEAR	TM/L	W	L	PCT	G	GS	CG	SH	SV	IP	H	HR	BB	SO	RAT	ERA	ERA+	OAV	OOB	BH	AVG	PB	PR	/A	PD	TPI
● **LARRY DOUGLAS** Douglas, Lawrence Howard b: 6/5/1890, Jellico, Tenn. d: 11/4/49, Jellico, Tenn. 6'3", 175 lbs. Deb: 6/17/15																										
1915	Bal-F	1	0	1.000	2	0	0	0	0	3	3	0	2	1	15.0	3.00	106	.273	.385	0	—	0	0	0	0	0.0
● **PHIL DOUGLAS** Douglas, Phillip Brooks "Shufflin' Phil" b: 6/17/1890, Cedartown, Ga. d: 8/1/52, Sequatchie Valley, Tenn. BR/TR, 6'3", 190 lbs. Deb: 8/30/12																										
1912	Chi-A	0	1	.000	3	1	0	0	0	12^1	21	0	6	7	19.7	7.30	44	.382	.443	0	.000	-0	-5	-6	0	-0.5
1914	Cin-N	11	18	.379	45	25	13	0	1	239^1	186	7	92	121	10.9	2.56	115	.223	.308	10	.137	-2	6	10	-2	0.6
1915	Cin-N	1	5	.167	8	7	0	0	0	46^2	53	0	23	29	14.7	5.40	53	.299	.380	2	.118	-1	-14	-13	0	-1.4
	Bro-N	5	5	.500	20	13	5	1	0	116^2	104	1	17	63	9.7	2.62	106	.241	.278	6	.154	-1	2	2	0	0.1
	Chi-N	1	1	.500	4	4	2	1	0	25	17	0	7	18	9.0	2.16	129	.187	.253	0	.000	-1	2	2	0	0.1
	Yr	7	11	.389	32	24	7	2	0	188^1	174	1	47	110	10.6	3.25	86	.247	.295	8	.125	-3	-10	-9	1	-1.2
1917	Chi-N	14	20	.412	**51**	37	20	5	1	293^1	269	13	50	151	10.0	2.55	114	.250	.287	11	.126	-4	5	11	4	1.3
1918	*Chi-N	10	9	.526	25	19	11	2	2	156^2	145	2	31	51	10.2	2.13	131	.246	.285	14	.255	1	11	11	3	1.8
1919	Chi-N	10	6	.625	25	19	8	4	0	161^2	133	0	34	63	9.4	2.00	144	.230	.275	8	.157	-2	16	16	5	2.2
	NY-N	2	4	.333	8	6	4	0	0	51^1	53	0	6	21	10.5	2.10	133	.264	.288	0	.000	-2	5	4	0	0.2
	Yr	12	10	.545	33	25	12	4	0	213	186	0	40	84	9.6	2.03	141	.238	.276	8	.121	-4	21	20	5	2.4
1920	NY-N	14	10	.583	46	21	10	3	2	226	225	6	55	71	11.2	2.71	111	.263	.309	11	.151	-4	11	7	1	0.4
1921	*NY-N	15	10	.600	40	27	13	**3**	2	221^2	266	17	55	55	13.1	4.22	87	.308	.351	16	.198	0	-11	-14	1	-1.2
1922	NY-N	11	4	.733	24	21	9	1	0	157^2	154	6	35	33	**11.0**	**2.63**	**152**	**.257**	**.302**	12	.207	1	26	24	0	2.5
Total	9	94	93	.503	299	200	95	20	8	1708^1	1626	52	411	683	10.9	2.80	111	.256	.305	90	.161	-16	53	58	13	6.1
● **KIP DOWD** Dowd, James Joseph b: 2/16/1889, Holyoke, Mass. d: 12/20/60, Holyoke, Mass. BR/TR, 5'10.5", 160 lbs. Deb: 7/05/10																										
1910	Pit-N	0	0	—	1	0	0	0	0	2	4	0	2	1	31.5	0.00	—	.400	.538	0	—	0	1	1	-0	0.1
● **DAVE DOWLING** Dowling, David Barclay b: 8/23/42, Baton Rouge, La. BR/TL, 6'2", 181 lbs. Deb: 10/03/64																										
1964	StL-N	0	0	—	1	0	0	0	0	1	2	0	0	0	18.0	0.00	—	.400	.400	0	—	0	0	0	-0	0.0
1966	Chi-N	1	0	1.000	1	1	1	0	0	9	10	0	0	3	10.0	2.00	184	.270	.270	0	.000	-0	2	2	-0	0.1
Total	2	1	0	1.000	2	1	1	0	0	10	12	0	0	3	10.8	1.80	205	.286	.286	0	.000	-0	2	2	-0	0.1
● **PETE DOWLING** Dowling, Henry Peter b: St.Louis, Mo. d: 6/30/05, Hot Lake, Ore. TL , 5'11", Deb: 7/17/1897																										
1897	Lou-N	1	2	.333	4	4	2	0	0	26	39	0	8	3	18.3	5.88	72	.343	.415	2	.200	-0	-5	-5	-0	-0.4
1898	Lou-N	13	20	.394	36	32	30	0	0	285^2	284	7	120	84	13.4	4.16	86	.257	.342	21	.196	1	-17	-18	-1	-1.6
1899	Lou-N	13	17	.433	34	32	29	0	0	289^2	321	4	93	88	13.4	3.11	124	.280	.343	27	.233	-1	24	24	-0	2.2
1901	Mil-A	1	4	.200	10	4	3	0	1	49^2	71	1	14	25	16.1	5.62	64	.331	.383	4	.211	1	-11	-11	0	-0.9
	Cle-A	11	22	.333	33	30	28	2	0	256^1	269	1	104	99	13.7	3.86	92	.267	.345	16	.162	-5	-6	-9	0	-1.1
	Yr	12	26	.316	43	34	31	2	1	306	340	2	118	124	14.0	4.15	86	.277	.349	20	.169	-4	-16	-20	1	-2.0
Total	4	39	65	.375	117	102	92	2	1	907^1	984	13	339	299	13.8	3.87	95	.274	.348	70	.199	-5	-14	-19	-1	-1.8
● **AL DOWNING** Downing, Alphonso Erwin b: 6/28/41, Trenton, N.J. BR/TL, 5'11", 177 lbs. Deb: 7/19/61																										
1961	NY-A	0	1	.000	5	1	0	0	0	9	7	0	12	12	20.0	8.00	46	.212	.435	0	.000	-0	-4	-4	0	-0.4
1962	NY-A	0	0	—	1	0	0	0	0	1	0	0	0	1	0.0	0.00	—	.000	.000	0	—	0	0	0	0	0.0
1963	*NY-A	13	5	.722	24	22	10	4	0	175^2	114	7	80	171	9.9	2.56	137	**.184**	.277	6	.103	-2	21	19	-1	1.7
1964	*NY-A	13	8	.619	37	35	11	1	2	244	201	18	120	**217**	11.8	3.47	104	.223	.314	15	.176	1	4	4	0	0.5
1965	NY-A	12	14	.462	35	32	8	2	0	212	185	16	105	179	12.4	3.40	100	.237	.329	8	.108	-1	1	0	0	0.0
1966	NY-A	10	11	.476	30	30	1	0	0	200	178	23	79	152	11.6	3.56	94	.235	.309	7	.100	-2	-3	-5	-4	-1.1
1967	NY-A★	14	10	.583	31	28	10	4	0	201^2	158	13	61	171	10.0	2.63	119	.217	.283	8	.121	1	13	11	-1	1.3
1968	NY-A	3	3	.500	15	12	1	0	0	61^1	54	7	20	40	11.0	3.52	82	.237	.301	3	.176	0	-4	-4	-0	-0.5
1969	NY-A	7	5	.583	30	15	5	1	0	130^2	117	12	49	85	11.4	3.38	103	.240	.309	6	.136	-0	4	1	-2	0.0
1970	Oak-A	3	3	.500	10	6	1	0	0	41	39	5	22	26	13.6	3.95	90	.252	.348	2	.182	-0	-1	-2	2	0.0
	Mil-A	2	10	.167	17	16	1	0	0	94^1	79	8	59	53	13.5	3.34	113	.232	.350	2	.083	-2	4	5	0	0.3
	Yr	5	13	.278	27	22	2	0	0	135^1	118	13	81	79	13.4	3.52	105	.237	.347	4	.114	-2	3	3	2	0.3
1971	LA-N	20	9	.690	37	36	12	**5**	0	262^1	245	16	84	136	11.4	2.68	121	.247	.308	16	.174	2	23	16	-1	1.9
1972	LA-N	9	9	.500	31	30	7	4	0	202^2	196	13	67	117	12.0	2.98	112	.254	.319	8	.121	-1	11	8	5	1.3
1973	LA-N	9	9	.500	30	28	5	2	0	193	155	19	68	124	10.4	3.31	104	.219	.289	5	.088	-1	7	3	1	0.2
1974	*LA-N	5	6	.455	21	16	1	1	0	98^1	94	7	45	63	13.0	3.66	93	.255	.341	5	.172	-0	-0	-3	1	-0.2
1975	LA-N	2	1	.667	22	6	0	0	1	74^2	59	6	28	39	10.7	2.89	118	.215	.293	0	.000	-1	6	4	1	0.4
1976	LA-N	1	2	.333	17	3	0	0	0	46^2	43	3	18	30	11.8	3.86	88	.250	.321	0	.000	-1	-2	-2	0	-0.3
1977	LA-N	0	1	.000	12	1	0	0	0	20	22	4	16	23	17.1	6.75	57	.278	.400	0	.000	-0	-6	-7	-0	-0.7
Total	17	123	107	.535	405	317	73	24	3	2268^1	1946	177	933	1639	11.5	3.22	105	.232	.311	91	.127	-7	75	44	2	4.4
● **DAVE DOWNS** Downs, David Ralph b: 6/21/52, Logan, Utah BR/TR, 6'5", 220 lbs. Deb: 9/02/72 F																										
1972	Phi-N	1	1	.500	4	4	1	1	0	23	25	1	3	5	11.3	2.74	131	.294	.326	2	.250	0	2	2	0	0.3
● **KELLY DOWNS** Downs, Kelly Robert b: 10/25/60, Ogden, Utah BR/TR, 6'4", 200 lbs. Deb: 7/29/86 F																										
1986	SF-N	4	4	.500	14	14	1	0	0	88^1	78	5	30	64	11.3	2.75	128	.236	.305	5	.172	0	9	8	0	0.8
1987	*SF-N	12	9	.571	41	28	4	3	1	186	185	14	67	137	12.4	3.63	106	.258	.324	8	.143	-0	9	4	-4	0.0
1988	SF-N	13	9	.591	27	26	6	3	0	168	140	11	47	118	10.2	3.32	98	.225	.283	9	.167	2	2	-1	0	0.1
1989	*SF-N	4	8	.333	18	15	0	0	0	82^2	82	7	26	49	11.9	4.79	70	.261	.320	2	.091	-1	-12	-13	-1	-1.5
1990	SF-N	3	2	.600	13	9	0	0	0	63	56	2	20	31	11.1	3.43	106	.233	.298	0	.000	-1	3	2	1	0.1
1991	SF-N	10	4	.714	45	11	0	0	0	111^2	99	12	53	62	12.5	4.19	85	.239	.329	2	.087	-1	-6	-8	1	-0.8
1992	SF-N	1	2	.333	19	7	0	0	0	62^1	65	4	24	33	13.3	3.47	97	.275	.350	0	.000	-1	0	-1	-1	-0.4
	*Oak-A	5	5	.500	18	13	0	0	0	82	72	4	46	38	13.4	3.29	115	.237	.345	0	—	0	6	4	-1	0.6
Total	7	52	43	.547	195	123	11	6	1	844	777	59	313	532	11.9	3.60	99	.244	.317	26	.123	-2	12	-5	-5	-1.1
● **TOM DOWSE** Dowse, Thomas Joseph b: 8/12/1866, Ireland d: 12/14/46, Riverside, Cal. BR/TR, 5'11", 175 lbs. Deb: 4/21/1890 ♦																										
1890	Cle-N	0	0	—	1	0	0	0	0	5	6	0	1	0	12.6	5.40	66	.288	.321	33	.208	-0	-1	-1	0	-0.1
● **JESS DOYLE** Doyle, Jesse Herbert b: 4/14/1898, Knoxville, Tenn. d: 4/15/61, Belleville, Ill. BR/TR, 5'11", 175 lbs. Deb: 4/14/25																										
1925	Det-A	4	7	.364	45	3	0	0	8	118^1	158	6	50	31	16.2	5.93	73	.340	.410	8	.242	3	-20	-21	-1	-1.7
1926	Det-A	0	0	—	2	0	0	0	1	4^1	6	0	1	2	14.5	4.15	98	.316	.350	1	1.000	0	-0	-0	-0	0.0
1927	Det-A	0	0	—	7	0	0	0	0	12^1	16	0	5	5	15.3	8.03	52	.314	.375	1	.333	0	-5	-5	0	-0.5
1931	StL-A	0	0	—	1	0	0	0	0	1	3	0	1	0	36.0	27.00	17	.500	.571	0	—	0	-3	-2	-0	-0.2
Total	4	4	7	.364	55	3	0	0	9	136	183	6	57	38	16.2	6.22	69	.338	.406	10	.270	3	-28	-29	-1	-2.4
● **JOHN DOYLE** Doyle, John Aloysius b: 1858, Nova Scotia, Canada d: 12/24/15, Providence, R.I. Deb: 7/26/1882																										
1882	StL-a	0	3	.000	3	3	3	0	0	24	41	0	3	5	16.5	2.63	107	.355	.371	2	.182	-0	0	0	-1	0.0
● **SLOW JOE DOYLE** Doyle, Judd Bruce b: 9/15/1881, Clay Center, Kan. d: 11/21/47, Tannersville, N.Y. BR/TR, 5'8", 150 lbs. Deb: 8/25/06																										
1906	NY-A	2	1	.667	9	6	3	2	0	45^1	34	1	13	28	9.5	2.38	124	.211	.275	3	.214	-0	2	3	0	0.3
1907	NY-A	11	11	.500	29	23	15	1	1	193^2	169	2	67	94	11.3	2.65	106	.237	.308	8	.138	-2	-2	3	-3	-0.1
1908	NY-A	1	1	.500	12	4	2	1	0	48	42	1	14	20	10.9	2.63	95	.235	.297	3	.214	0	-1	-1	-2	-0.2
1909	NY-A	8	6	.571	17	15	8	3	0	125^2	103	3	37	57	10.2	2.58	98	.232	.294	7	.167	0	-1	-1	-4	-0.4
1910	NY-A	0	2	.000	3	2	1	0	0	12^1	19	0	5	6	18.2	8.03	33	.365	.431	1	.250	0	-8	-7	1	-0.7
	Cin-N	0	0	—	5	0	0	0	0	11^1	16	0	11	4	21.4	6.35	46	.327	.450	0	.000	-0	-4	-4	-1	-0.5
Total	5	22	21	.512	75	50	29	7	1	436^1	383	7	147	209	11.2	2.85	95	.240	.309	22	.163	-1	-15	-7	-7	-1.6

● PAUL DOYLE Doyle, Paul Sinnott b: 10/2/39, Philadelphia, Pa. BL/TL, 5'11", 172 lbs. Deb: 5/28/69

YEAR	TM/L	W	L	PCT	G	GS	CG	SH	SV	IP	H	HR	BB	SO	RAT	ERA	ERA+	OAV	OOB	BH	AVG	PB	PR	/A	PD	TPI
1969	*Atl-N	2	0	1.000	36	0	0	0	4	39	31	4	16	25	10.8	2.08	174	.231	.313	0	.000	-0	7	7	1	0.7
1970	Cal-A	3	1	.750	40	0	0	0	5	42	43	7	21	34	13.9	5.14	70	.267	.355	0	.000	-0	-7	-7	1	-0.7
	SD-N	0	2	.000	9	0	0	0	2	7	9	0	6	2	19.3	6.43	62	.360	.484	0	.000	-0	-2	-2	1	-0.1
1972	Cal-A	0	0	—	2	0	0	0	0	2^1	2	0	3	4	19.3	0.00	—	.250	.455	0	—	0	1	1	0	0.1
Total	3	5	3	.625	87	0	0	0	11	90^1	85	11	46	65	13.2	3.79	96	.259	.352	0	.000	-1	-1	-2	3	0.0

● CARL DOYLE Doyle, William Carl b: 7/30/12, Knoxville, Tenn. d: 9/4/51, Knoxville, Tenn. BR/TR, 6'1", 185 lbs. Deb: 8/05/35

YEAR	TM/L	W	L	PCT	G	GS	CG	SH	SV	IP	H	HR	BB	SO	RAT	ERA	ERA+	OAV	OOB	BH	AVG	PB	PR	/A	PD	TPI
1935	Phi-A	2	7	.222	14	9	3	0	0	79^2	86	3	72	34	18.1	5.99	76	.282	.422	4	.133	-2	-14	-13	1	-1.3
1936	Phi-A	0	3	.000	8	6	1	0	0	38^2	66	4	29	12	23.3	10.94	47	.369	.469	4	.267	1	-25	-25	-1	-2.0
1939	Bro-N	1	2	.333	5	1	1	1	1	17^2	8	1	7	7	7.6	1.02	395	.136	.227	1	.167	0	6	6	0	0.7
1940	Bro-N	0	0	—	3	0	0	0	1	5^2	18	3	6	4	44.5	27.00	15	.545	.651	1	1.000	1	-15	-14	0	-1.1
	StL-N	3	3	.500	21	5	1	0	0	81	99	7	41	44	16.2	5.89	68	.294	.380	6	.200	2	-18	-17	-0	-1.5
	Yr	3	3	.500	24	5	1	0	1	86^2	117	10	47	48	17.7	7.27	55	.313	.398	7	.226	3	-33	-32	0	-2.6
Total	4	6	15	.286	51	21	6	1	2	222^2	277	18	155	101	18.1	6.95	63	.303	.414	16	.195	1	-66	-63	-0	-5.2

● TOM DOZIER Dozier, Thomas Dean b: 9/5/61, San Pablo, Cal. BR/TR, 6'2", 190 lbs. Deb: 5/17/86

YEAR	TM/L	W	L	PCT	G	GS	CG	SH	SV	IP	H	HR	BB	SO	RAT	ERA	ERA+	OAV	OOB	BH	AVG	PB	PR	/A	PD	TPI
1986	Oak-A	0	0	—	4	0	0	0	0	6^1	6	1	5	4	15.6	5.68	68	.261	.393	0	—	0	-1	-1	-0	0.5

● BUZZ DOZIER Dozier, William Joseph b: 8/31/27, Waco, Tex. BR/TR, 6'3", 185 lbs. Deb: 9/12/47

YEAR	TM/L	W	L	PCT	G	GS	CG	SH	SV	IP	H	HR	BB	SO	RAT	ERA	ERA+	OAV	OOB	BH	AVG	PB	PR	/A	PD	TPI
1947	Was-A	0	0	—	2	0	0	0	0	4^2	2	0	1	2	5.8	0.00	—	.133	.188	0	.000	-0	2	2	0	0.2
1949	Was-A	0	0	—	2	0	0	0	0	6^1	12	0	6	1	25.6	11.37	37	.429	.529	0	.000	-0	-5	-5	-0	-0.5
Total	2	0	0	—	4	0	0	0	0	11	14	0	7	3	17.2	6.55	62	.326	.420	0	.000	-0	-3	-3	-0	-0.3

● DOUG DRABEK Drabek, Douglas Dean b: 7/25/62, Victoria, Tex. BR/TR, 6'1", 185 lbs. Deb: 5/30/86

YEAR	TM/L	W	L	PCT	G	GS	CG	SH	SV	IP	H	HR	BB	SO	RAT	ERA	ERA+	OAV	OOB	BH	AVG	PB	PR	/A	PD	TPI
1986	NY-A	7	8	.467	27	21	0	0	0	131^2	126	13	50	76	12.2	4.10	100	.251	.323	0	—	0	1	-0	-1	-0.1
1987	Pit-N	11	12	.478	29	28	1	1	0	176^1	165	22	46	120	10.8	3.88	106	.247	.296	7	.119	-1	4	4	1	0.4
1988	Pit-N	15	7	.682	33	32	3	1	0	219^1	194	21	50	127	10.3	3.08	111	.239	.288	13	.171	3	9	8	-1	1.1
1989	Pit-N	14	12	.538	35	34	8	5	0	244^1	215	21	69	123	10.6	2.80	120	.238	.295	8	.104	-2	19	15	-0	1.4
1990	*Pit-N	**22**	6	**.786**	33	33	9	3	0	231^1	190	15	56	131	9.7	2.76	131	.225	.275	18	.214	5	26	22	2	3.1
1991	*Pit-N	15	14	.517	35	35	5	2	0	234^2	245	16	62	142	11.9	3.07	116	.274	.323	15	.179	1	16	13	2	1.7
1992	*Pit-N	15	11	.577	34	34	10	4	0	256^2	218	17	54	177	9.7	2.77	123	.231	.277	14	.157	1	21	18	1	2.2
Total	7	99	70	.586	226	217	36	16	0	1494^1	1353	125	387	896	10.6	3.11	116	.243	.295	75	.160	7	96	80	3	9.8

● MOE DRABOWSKY Drabowsky, Myron Walter b: 7/21/35, Ozanna, Poland BR/TR, 6'2", 200 lbs. Deb: 8/07/56 C

YEAR	TM/L	W	L	PCT	G	GS	CG	SH	SV	IP	H	HR	BB	SO	RAT	ERA	ERA+	OAV	OOB	BH	AVG	PB	PR	/A	PD	TPI
1956	Chi-N	2	4	.333	9	7	3	0	0	51	37	1	39	36	13.8	2.47	153	.207	.355	4	.250	0	7	7	-0	0.8
1957	Chi-N	13	15	.464	36	33	12	2	0	239^2	214	22	94	170	11.9	3.53	110	.242	.321	15	.183	2	9	9	0	1.2
1958	Chi-N	9	11	.450	22	20	4	1	0	125^2	118	19	73	77	14.0	4.51	87	.245	.350	7	.156	-1	-8	-8	-0	-0.9
1959	Chi-N	5	10	.333	31	23	3	1	0	141^2	138	21	75	70	13.7	4.13	96	.251	.344	5	.111	-1	-3	-3	-0	-0.4
1960	Chi-N	3	1	.750	32	7	0	0	1	50^1	71	3	23	26	17.0	6.44	59	.338	.406	0	.000	-1	-15	-15	-1	-1.6
1961	Mil-N	0	2	.000	16	0	0	0	2	25^1	26	4	18	5	16.0	4.62	81	.277	.398	1	.250	0	-2	-2	0	-0.2
1962	Cin-N	2	6	.250	23	10	1	0	1	83	84	13	31	56	13.1	4.99	81	.267	.344	0	.000	-2	-10	-9	-1	-1.1
	KC-A	1	1	.500	10	3	0	0	0	28	29	8	10	19	12.9	5.14	81	.266	.333	1	.167	-0	-4	-3	0	-0.3
1963	KC-A	7	13	.350	26	22	9	2	0	174^1	135	16	64	109	10.7	3.05	126	.214	.295	10	.161	1	11	15	-2	1.6
1964	KC-A	5	13	.278	53	21	1	0	1	168^1	176	24	72	119	13.7	5.29	72	.273	.353	1	.023	-4	-31	-28	1	-3.2
1965	KC-A	1	5	.167	14	5	0	0	0	38^2	44	5	18	25	15.1	4.42	79	.291	.378	1	.091	-1	-4	-4	-0	-0.5
1966	*Bal-A	6	0	1.000	44	3	0	0	7	96	62	10	29	98	8.6	2.81	118	.181	.247	8	.364	4	7	6	-1	0.9
1967	Bal-A	7	5	.583	43	0	0	0	12	95^1	66	7	25	96	8.8	1.60	196	.194	.253	7	.350	2	17	16	0	2.2
1968	Bal-A	4	4	.500	45	0	0	0	7	61^1	35	3	25	46	9.4	1.91	153	.166	.267	2	.286	0	7	7	-0	0.8
1969	KC-A	11	9	.550	52	0	0	0	11	98	68	10	30	76	9.2	2.94	125	.190	.256	4	.235	1	7	8	1	1.1
1970	KC-A	1	2	.333	24	0	0	0	2	35^2	28	3	12	38	10.6	3.28	114	.217	.294	1	.250	0	2	2	0	0.2
	*Bal-A	4	2	.667	21	0	0	0	1	33^1	30	7	15	21	12.4	3.78	96	.233	.317	0	.000	-1	-0	-0	-0	-0.1
	Yr	5	4	.556	45	0	0	0	3	69	58	10	27	59	11.2	3.52	105	.221	.296	1	.111	-0	1	1	-0	0.1
1971	StL-N	6	1	.857	51	0	0	0	8	60^1	45	2	33	49	11.9	3.43	105	.207	.317	1	.167	-0	0	1	-1	0.0
1972	StL-N	1	1	.500	30	0	0	0	2	27^2	29	4	14	22	14.3	2.60	131	.259	.346	0	.000	-0	3	2	-1	0.2
	Chi-A	0	0	—	7	0	0	0	0	7^1	6	0	2	4	9.8	2.45	127	.240	.296	0	.000	-0	0	1	-0	0.0
Total	17	88	105	.456	589	154	33	6	55	1641	1441	182	702	1162	12.1	3.71	100	.236	.321	68	.162	-0	-5	2	-5	0.7

● DICK DRAGO Drago, Richard Anthony b: 6/25/45, Toledo, Ohio BR/TR, 6'1", 190 lbs. Deb: 4/11/69

YEAR	TM/L	W	L	PCT	G	GS	CG	SH	SV	IP	H	HR	BB	SO	RAT	ERA	ERA+	OAV	OOB	BH	AVG	PB	PR	/A	PD	TPI
1969	KC-A	11	13	.458	41	26	10	2	1	200^2	190	19	65	108	11.5	3.77	98	.248	.308	3	.058	-3	-3	-2	2	-0.3
1970	KC-A	9	15	.375	35	34	7	1	0	240	239	20	72	127	11.9	3.75	100	.266	.325	4	.053	-6	-1	-0	-1	-0.7
1971	KC-A	17	11	.607	35	34	15	4	0	241^1	251	14	46	109	11.4	2.98	115	.276	.318	10	.130	1	13	12	0	1.4
1972	KC-A	12	17	.414	34	33	11	2	0	239^1	230	22	51	135	10.8	3.01	101	.254	.298	4	.059	-2	1	1	-3	-0.5
1973	KC-A	12	14	.462	37	33	10	1	0	212^2	252	16	76	98	14.2	4.23	97	.300	.363	0	—	0	-10	-3	1	-0.2
1974	Bos-A	7	10	.412	33	18	8	0	3	175^2	165	17	56	90	11.6	3.48	110	.251	.315	0	—	0	3	7	-2	0.1
1975	*Bos-A	2	2	.500	40	2	0	0	15	72^2	69	5	31	43	12.4	3.84	106	.247	.323	0	—	0	-1	2	0	-0.1
1976	Cal-A	7	8	.467	43	0	0	0	6	79^1	80	7	31	43	13.2	4.42	75	.264	.342	0	—	0	-8	-10	-2	-0.9
1977	Cal-A	0	1	.000	13	0	0	0	2	21	22	3	3	15	10.7	3.00	130	.272	.298	0	—	0	2	2	-0	0.4
	Bal-A	6	3	.667	36	0	0	0	3	39^2	49	2	15	20	14.7	3.63	104	.308	.371	0	—	0	2	1	-0	0.4
	Yr	6	4	.600	49	0	0	0	5	60^2	71	5	18	35	13.4	3.41	112	.293	.345	0	—	0	4	3	-1	0.8
1978	Bos-A	4	4	.500	37	1	0	0	7	77^1	71	5	32	42	12.5	3.03	136	.246	.329	0	—	0	6	9	-1	0.8
1979	Bos-A	10	6	.625	53	1	0	0	13	89	85	6	21	67	11.0	3.03	145	.254	.304	0	—	0	12	14	-0	1.3
1980	Bos-A	7	7	.500	43	7	1	0	3	132^2	127	17	44	63	11.9	4.14	102	.251	.317	0	.000	0	-2	1	-1	0.0
1981	Sea-A	4	6	.400	39	0	0	0	5	53^2	71	4	15	27	14.4	5.53	70	.324	.368	0	—	0	-11	-10	0	-1.0
Total	13	108	117	.480	519	189	62	10	58	1875	1901	157	558	987	12.1	3.62	103	.266	.324	21	.077	-10	4	23	-5	0.7

● BRIAN DRAHMAN Drahman, Brian Stacy b: 11/7/66, Kenton, Ky. BR/TR, 6'3", 205 lbs. Deb: 4/16/91

YEAR	TM/L	W	L	PCT	G	GS	CG	SH	SV	IP	H	HR	BB	SO	RAT	ERA	ERA+	OAV	OOB	BH	AVG	PB	PR	/A	PD	TPI
1991	Chi-A	3	2	.600	28	0	0	0	0	30^2	21	4	13	18	10.0	3.23	123	.193	.279	0	—	0	3	3	-0	0.4
1992	Chi-A	0	0	—	5	0	0	0	0	7	6	0	2	1	10.3	2.57	149	.222	.276	0	—	0	1	1	-0	0.2
Total	2	3	2	.600	33	0	0	0	0	37^2	27	4	15	19	10.0	3.11	127	.199	.278	0	—	0	4	4	-0	0.6

● LOGAN DRAKE Drake, Logan Gaffney "L.G." b: 12/26/1900, Spartanburg, S.C. d: 6/1/40, Columbia, S.C. BR/TR, 5'10.5", 165 lbs. Deb: 9/21/22

YEAR	TM/L	W	L	PCT	G	GS	CG	SH	SV	IP	H	HR	BB	SO	RAT	ERA	ERA+	OAV	OOB	BH	AVG	PB	PR	/A	PD	TPI
1922	Cle-A	0	0	—	1	0	0	0	0	3	4	0	2	1	18.0	3.00	134	.364	.462	0	.000	-0	0	0	-0	0.0
1923	Cle-A	0	0	—	4	0	0	0	0	4^1	2	0	4	2	14.5	4.15	95	.133	.350	0	—	0	-0	-0	-0	0.0
1924	Cle-A	0	1	.000	5	1	0	0	0	11^1	18	0	10	8	23.0	10.32	41	.400	.518	0	.000	-0	-8	-8	-0	-0.7
Total	3	0	1	.000	10	1	0	0	0	18^2	24	0	16	11	20.3	7.71	54	.338	.472	0	.000	-0	-7	-7	-1	-0.7

● TOM DRAKE Drake, Thomas Kendall b: 8/7/14, Birmingham, Ala. d: 7/2/88, Birmingham, Ala. BR/TR, 6'1", 185 lbs. Deb: 4/24/39

YEAR	TM/L	W	L	PCT	G	GS	CG	SH	SV	IP	H	HR	BB	SO	RAT	ERA	ERA+	OAV	OOB	BH	AVG	PB	PR	/A	PD	TPI
1939	Cle-A	0	1	.000	8	1	0	0	0	15	23	2	19	1	26.4	9.00	49	.377	.537	0	.000	-0	-7	-8	0	-0.7
1941	Bro-N	1	1	.500	10	2	0	0	0	24^2	26	2	9	12	12.8	4.38	84	.280	.343	2	.400	0	-2	-2	-0	-0.2
Total	2	1	2	.333	18	3	0	0	0	39^2	49	4	28	13	17.9	6.13	65	.318	.429	2	.286	0	-9	-10	0	-0.9

● DAVE DRAVECKY Dravecky, David Francis b: 2/14/56, Youngstown, Ohio BR/TL, 6'1", 195 lbs. Deb: 6/15/82

YEAR	TM/L	W	L	PCT	G	GS	CG	SH	SV	IP	H	HR	BB	SO	RAT	ERA	ERA+	OAV	OOB	BH	AVG	PB	PR	/A	PD	TPI
1982	SD-N	5	3	.625	31	10	0	0	2	105	86	8	33	59	10.3	2.57	133	.225	.288	3	.130	-0	12	10	2	1.2
1983	SD-N★	14	10	.583	28	28	9	1	0	183^2	181	18	44	74	11.2	3.58	97	.262	.309	6	.098	-1	1	-2	1	-0.3

YEAR TM/L	W	L	PCT	G	GS	CG	SH	SV	IP	H	HR	BB	SO	RAT	ERA	ERA+	OAV	OOB	BH	AVG	PB	PR	/A	PD	TPI
1984 *SD-N	9	8	.529	50	14	3	2	8	156^2	125	12	51	71	10.3	2.93	122	.222	.291	4	.098	-1	11	11	-2	0.9
1985 SD-N	13	11	.542	34	31	7	2	0	214^2	200	18	57	105	10.8	2.93	120	.249	.300	8	.116	-0	16	14	-1	1.4
1986 SD-N	9	11	.450	26	26	3	1	0	161^1	149	17	54	87	11.4	3.07	119	.246	.309	7	.140	0	12	10	0	1.2
1987 SD-N	3	7	.300	30	10	1	0	0	79	71	10	31	60	12.0	3.76	105	.240	.318	3	.167	0	3	2	0	0.1
*SF-N	7	5	.583	18	18	4	3	0	112^1	115	8	33	78	12.0	3.20	120	.272	.328	5	.132	0	11	8	1	1.0
Yr	10	12	.455	48	28	5	3	0	191^1	186	18	64	138	11.9	3.43	113	.257	.319	8	.143	1	14	10	1	1.1
1988 SF-N	2	2	.500	7	7	1	0	0	37	33	4	8	19	10.0	3.16	103	.243	.285	1	.100	-0	1	0	0	0.0
1989 SF-N	2	0	1.000	2	2	0	0	0	13	8	2	4	5	9.0	3.46	97	.182	.265	1	.333	1	0	-0	0	0.1
Total 8	64	57	.529	226	146	28	9	10	1062^2	968	97	315	558	11.0	3.13	115	.245	.304	38	.121	-1	67	54	1	5.6

● TOM DREES Drees, Thomas Kent b: 6/17/63, Des Moines, Iowa BB/TL, 6'6", 210 lbs. Deb: 9/03/91

YEAR TM/L	W	L	PCT	G	GS	CG	SH	SV	IP	H	HR	BB	SO	RAT	ERA	ERA+	OAV	OOB	BH	AVG	PB	PR	/A	PD	TPI
1991 Chi-A	0	0	—	4	0	0	0	0	7^1	10	4	6	2	19.6	12.27	32	.345	.457	0	—	0	-7	-7	-0	-0.5

● CLEM DREISEWERD Dreisewerd, Clemens Johann "Steamboat" b: 1/24/16, Old Monroe, Mo. BL/TL, 6'1.5", 195 lbs. Deb: 8/29/44

YEAR TM/L	W	L	PCT	G	GS	CG	SH	SV	IP	H	HR	BB	SO	RAT	ERA	ERA+	OAV	OOB	BH	AVG	PB	PR	/A	PD	TPI
1944 Bos-A	2	4	.333	7	7	3	0	0	48^2	52	2	9	9	11.3	4.07	84	.268	.300	3	.188	0	-3	-4	-1	-0.4
1945 Bos-A	0	1	.000	2	2	0	0	0	9^2	13	0	2	3	14.9	4.66	73	.325	.372	0	.000	-0	-1	-1	-0	-0.2
1946 *Bos-A	4	1	.800	20	1	0	0	0	47^1	50	3	15	19	12.4	4.18	88	.276	.332	0	.000	-1	-4	-3	1	-0.3
1948 StL-A	0	2	.000	13	0	0	0	1	22^1	28	6	8	6	14.5	5.64	81	.318	.375	0	.000	-1	-3	-3	-0	-0.3
NY-N	0	0	—	4	0	0	0	1	12^2	17	3	5	2	15.6	5.68	69	.321	.379	1	.250	1	-2	-2	-0	-0.2
Total 4	6	8	.429	46	10	3	0	2	140^2	160	14	39	39	12.8	4.54	82	.288	.336	4	.105	-1	-14	-13	-1	-1.4

● KIRK DRESSENDORFER Dressendorfer, Kirk Richard b: 4/8/69, Houston, Tex. BR/TR, 5'11", 190 lbs. Deb: 4/13/91

YEAR TM/L	W	L	PCT	G	GS	CG	SH	SV	IP	H	HR	BB	SO	RAT	ERA	ERA+	OAV	OOB	BH	AVG	PB	PR	/A	PD	TPI
1991 Oak-A	3	3	.500	7	7	0	0	0	34^2	33	5	21	17	14.0	5.45	70	.244	.346	0	—	0	-5	-6	-0	-0.3

● BOB DRESSER Dresser, Robert Nicholson b: 10/4/1878, Newton, Mass. d: 7/27/24, Duxbury, Mass. BL/TL, Deb: 8/13/02

YEAR TM/L	W	L	PCT	G	GS	CG	SH	SV	IP	H	HR	BB	SO	RAT	ERA	ERA+	OAV	OOB	BH	AVG	PB	PR	/A	PD	TPI
1902 Bos-N	0	1	.000	1	1	1	0	0	9	12	0	0	8	12.0	3.00	94	.319	.319	1	.250	0	-0	-0	-0	0.0

● ROB DRESSLER Dressler, Robert Anthony b: 2/2/54, Portland, Ore. BR/TR, 6'3", 180 lbs. Deb: 9/07/75

YEAR TM/L	W	L	PCT	G	GS	CG	SH	SV	IP	H	HR	BB	SO	RAT	ERA	ERA+	OAV	OOB	BH	AVG	PB	PR	/A	PD	TPI
1975 SF-N	1	0	1.000	3	2	1	0	0	16^1	17	0	4	6	11.6	1.10	345	.274	.318	0	.000	-0	5	5	0	0.6
1976 SF-N	3	10	.231	25	19	0	0	0	107^2	125	8	35	33	13.5	4.43	82	.291	.347	4	.129	-1	-11	-10	1	-1.0
1978 StL-N	0	1	.000	3	2	0	0	0	13	12	0	4	4	11.1	2.08	169	.267	.327	0	.000	-0	2	2	-0	0.2
1979 Sea-A	3	2	.600	21	11	2	0	0	104	134	11	22	36	13.5	4.93	88	.312	.345	0	—	0	-8	-7	-0	-0.7
1980 Sea-A	4	10	.286	30	14	3	0	0	149^1	161	14	33	50	11.9	3.98	104	.280	.322	0	—	0	1	3	1	0.4
Total 5	11	23	.324	82	48	6	0	0	390^1	449	33	98	129	12.7	4.17	96	.291	.335	4	.105	-2	-12	-7	2	-0.5

● DAVE DREW Drew, David Deb: 5/14/1884 ♦

YEAR TM/L	W	L	PCT	G	GS	CG	SH	SV	IP	H	HR	BB	SO	RAT	ERA	ERA+	OAV	OOB	BH	AVG	PB	PR	/A	PD	TPI
1884 Phi-U	0	1	.000	1	0	0	0	0	7	7	0	0	2	9.0	3.86	74	.243	.243	4	.444	1	-1	-1	-0	-0.1

● KARL DREWS Drews, Karl August b: 2/22/20, Staten Island, N.Y d: 8/15/63, Dania, Fla. BR/TR, 6'4", 198 lbs. Deb: 9/08/46

YEAR TM/L	W	L	PCT	G	GS	CG	SH	SV	IP	H	HR	BB	SO	RAT	ERA	ERA+	OAV	OOB	BH	AVG	PB	PR	/A	PD	TPI
1946 NY-A	0	1	.000	3	1	0	0	0	6^1	6	0	6	4	18.5	8.53	40	.250	.419	0	.000	-0	-4	-4	-0	-0.4
1947 *NY-A	6	6	.500	30	10	0	0	1	91^2	92	6	55	45	14.9	4.91	72	.264	.373	1	.037	-2	-12	-14	1	-1.6
1948 NY-A	2	3	.400	19	2	0	0	1	38	35	3	31	11	15.6	3.79	108	.248	.384	0	.000	-1	2	1	1	0.1
StL-A	3	2	.600	20	2	0	0	2	38	43	3	38	11	19.2	8.05	57	.289	.433	0	.000	-0	-16	-15	0	-1.4
Yr	5	5	.500	39	4	0	0	3	76	78	6	69	22	17.4	5.92	73	.269	.409	0	.000	-1	-14	-14	1	-1.3
1949 StL-A	4	12	.250	31	23	3	1	0	139^2	180	11	66	35	16.4	6.64	68	.317	.397	0	.000	-5	-38	-33	-1	-3.5
1951 Phi-N	1	0	1.000	5	3	1	0	0	23	29	2	7	13	15.7	6.26	61	.296	.367	2	.250	1	-6	-6	0	-0.5
1952 Phi-N	14	15	.483	33	30	15	5	0	228^2	213	13	52	96	10.6	2.72	135	.252	.298	9	.110	-2	26	24	0	2.4
1953 Phi-N	9	10	.474	47	27	6	0	3	185^1	218	26	50	72	13.5	4.52	93	.293	.346	7	.119	-2	-5	-6	2	-0.7
1954 Phi-N	1	0	1.000	8	0	0	0	0	16	18	2	8	6	14.6	5.63	72	.300	.382	0	.000	-1	-3	-3	0	-0.3
Cin-N	4	4	.500	22	9	1	1	0	60	79	6	19	29	15.0	6.00	70	.326	.380	2	.167	1	-13	-12	0	-1.0
Yr	5	4	.556	30	9	1	1	0	76	97	8	27	35	14.9	5.92	70	.320	.380	2	.125	1	-16	-15	0	-1.3
Total 8	44	53	.454	218	107	26	7	7	826^2	913	72	332	322	13.9	4.76	84	.284	.357	21	.083	-12	-68	-68	3	-6.9

● DENNY DRISCOLL Driscoll, John F. b: 11/19/1855, Lowell, Mass. d: 7/11/1886, Lowell, Mass. BL/TL, 5'10.5", 160 lbs. Deb: 7/01/1880 ♦

YEAR TM/L	W	L	PCT	G	GS	CG	SH	SV	IP	H	HR	BB	SO	RAT	ERA	ERA+	OAV	OOB	BH	AVG	PB	PR	/A	PD	TPI
1880 Buf-N	1	3	.250	6	4	4	0	0	41^2	48	1	9	17	12.3	3.89	63	.270	.305	10	.154	-1	-7	-7	0	-0.7
1882 Pit-a	13	9	.591	23	23	23	0	0	201	162	0	12	59	7.8	**1.21**	**216**	.206	.218	11	.138	-2	33	31	-4	2.5
1883 Pit-a	18	21	.462	41	40	35	1	0	336^1	427	3	39	79	12.5	3.99	81	.290	.309	27	.182	-4	-26	-29	6	-2.4
1884 Lou-a	6	6	.500	13	13	10	0	0	102	110	3	7	16	10.5	3.44	90	.252	.267	9	.188	-1	-2	-4	2	-0.2
Total 4	38	39	.494	83	80	72	1	0	681	747	7	67	171	10.8	3.08	97	.260	.277	60	.167	-9	-2	-8	4	-0.8

● MICHAEL DRISCOLL Driscoll, Michael Columbus b: 10/19/1892, Rockland, Mass. d: 3/22/53, Foxboro, Mass. BR/TR, 6'1", 160 lbs. Deb: 7/06/16

YEAR TM/L	W	L	PCT	G	GS	CG	SH	SV	IP	H	HR	BB	SO	RAT	ERA	ERA+	OAV	OOB	BH	AVG	PB	PR	/A	PD	TPI
1916 Phi-A	0	1	.000	1	0	0	0	0	5	6	0	2	0	14.4	5.40	53	.273	.333	0	.000	-0	-1	-1	1	-0.1

● TOM DROHAN Drohan, Thomas F b: 8/26/1887, Fall River, Mass. d: 9/17/26, Kewanee, Ill. BR/TR, 5'10", 175 lbs. Deb: 5/01/13

YEAR TM/L	W	L	PCT	G	GS	CG	SH	SV	IP	H	HR	BB	SO	RAT	ERA	ERA+	OAV	OOB	BH	AVG	PB	PR	/A	PD	TPI
1913 Was-A	0	0	—	2	0	0	0	0	2	5	1	0	2	22.5	9.00	33	.500	.500	0	—	0	-1	-1	0	-0.1

● DICK DROTT Drott, Richard Fred "Hummer" b: 7/1/36, Cincinnati, Ohio d: 8/16/85, Glendale Heights, Ill. BR/TR, 6', 185 lbs. Deb: 4/16/57

YEAR TM/L	W	L	PCT	G	GS	CG	SH	SV	IP	H	HR	BB	SO	RAT	ERA	ERA+	OAV	OOB	BH	AVG	PB	PR	/A	PD	TPI
1957 Chi-N	15	11	.577	38	32	7	3	0	229	200	22	129	170	13.2	3.58	108	.234	.340	8	.100	-5	8	8	-1	0.2
1958 Chi-N	7	11	.389	39	31	4	0	0	167^1	156	23	99	127	14.0	5.43	72	.245	.352	15	.273	3	-28	-28	1	-2.4
1959 Chi-N	1	2	.333	8	6	1	1	0	27^1	25	5	26	15	16.8	5.93	67	.245	.398	1	.125	-0	-6	-6	-0	-0.6
1960 Chi-N	0	6	.000	23	9	0	0	0	55^1	63	7	42	32	17.6	7.16	53	.296	.419	1	.100	-1	-21	-21	-0	-2.1
1961 Chi-N	1	4	.200	35	8	0	0	0	98	75	13	51	48	11.7	4.22	99	.215	.317	6	.273	2	-2	-0	-2	-0.1
1962 Hou-N	1	0	1.000	6	1	0	0	0	13	12	1	9	10	14.5	7.62	49	.240	.356	0	.000	-0	-5	-6	-0	-0.6
1963 Hou-N	2	12	.143	27	14	2	1	0	97^2	95	13	49	58	13.8	4.98	63	.257	.353	3	.130	-1	-18	-20	-1	-2.2
Total 7	27	46	.370	176	101	14	5	0	687^2	626	84	405	460	13.8	4.78	80	.243	.351	34	.168	-2	-72	-74	-5	-7.8

● LOUIS DRUCKE Drucke, Louis Frank b: 12/3/1888, Waco, Tex. d: 9/22/55, Waco, Tex. BR/TR, 6'1", 188 lbs. Deb: 9/25/09

YEAR TM/L	W	L	PCT	G	GS	CG	SH	SV	IP	H	HR	BB	SO	RAT	ERA	ERA+	OAV	OOB	BH	AVG	PB	PR	/A	PD	TPI
1909 NY-N	2	1	.667	3	3	2	0	0	24	20	0	13	8	12.4	2.25	114	.227	.327	1	.125	-0	1	1	-0	0.0
1910 NY-N	12	10	.545	34	27	15	0	0	215^1	174	3	82	151	11.2	2.47	120	.228	.312	15	.214	4	14	12	2	1.8
1911 NY-N	4	4	.500	15	10	4	0	0	75^2	83	1	41	42	15.7	4.04	83	.281	.384	2	.087	-1	-5	-6	1	-0.6
1912 NY-N	0	0	—	1	0	0	0	1	2	5	0	1	0	27.0	13.50	25	.417	.462	0	—	0	-2	-2	-0	-0.2
Total 4	18	15	.545	53	40	21	0	1	317	282	4	137	201	12.4	2.90	105	.243	.333	18	.178	2	7	5	2	1.0

● CARL DRUHOT Druhot, Carl A. "Collie" b: 9/1/1882, Ohio d: 2/11/18, Portland, Ore. BL/TL, 5'7", 150 lbs. Deb: 4/18/06

YEAR TM/L	W	L	PCT	G	GS	CG	SH	SV	IP	H	HR	BB	SO	RAT	ERA	ERA+	OAV	OOB	BH	AVG	PB	PR	/A	PD	TPI
1906 Cin-N	2	2	.500	4	3	1	0	0	25	27	0	7	14	13.0	4.32	64	.270	.330	2	.222	0	-5	-4	-1	-0.5
StL-N	6	7	.462	15	13	12	1	0	130^1	117	1	46	45	11.6	2.62	100	.238	.310	13	.232	1	0	0	1	0.2
Yr	8	9	.471	19	16	13	1	0	155^1	144	1	53	59	11.7	2.90	91	.243	.310	15	.231	1	-5	-4	-1	-0.3
1907 StL-N	0	1	.000	1	1	0	0	0	2^1	3	0	4	1	30.9	15.43	16	.600	.800	0	—	0	-3	-3	0	-0.3
Total 2	8	10	.444	20	17	13	1	0	157^2	147	1	57	60	12.1	3.08	86	.247	.321	15	.231	1	-8	-8	-0	-0.6

● TIM DRUMMOND Drummond, Timothy Darnell b: 12/24/64, LaPlata, Md. BR/TR, 6'3", 170 lbs. Deb: 9/12/87

YEAR TM/L	W	L	PCT	G	GS	CG	SH	SV	IP	H	HR	BB	SO	RAT	ERA	ERA+	OAV	OOB	BH	AVG	PB	PR	/A	PD	TPI
1987 Pit-N	0	0	—	6	0	0	0	0	6	5	0	3	5	12.0	4.50	91	.227	.320	0	.000	-0	-0	-0	0	0.0
1989 Min-A	0	0	—	8	0	0	0	1	16^1	16	0	8	9	14.3	3.86	107	.246	.347	0	—	0	0	1	-0	-0.4
1990 Min-A	3	5	.375	35	4	0	0	1	91	104	8	36	49	13.9	4.35	95	.295	.362	0	—	0	-5	-2	-1	-0.6
Total 3	3	5	.375	49	4	0	0	2	113^1	125	8	47	63	13.9	4.29	97	.284	.357	0	.000	-0	-5	-2	-1	-1.0

YEAR TM/L	W	L	PCT	G	GS	CG	SH	SV	IP	H	HR	BB	SO	RAT	ERA	ERA+	OAV	OOB	BH	AVG	PB	PR	/A	PD	TPI

● DON DRYSDALE   Drysdale, Donald Scott   b: 7/23/36, Van Nuys, Cal.   BR/TR, 6'6", 216 lbs.   Deb: 4/17/56   H

1956 *Bro-N	5	5	.500	25	12	2	0	0	99	95	9	31	55	11.7	2.64	150	.255	.317	5	.192	1	12	15	1	1.8
1957 Bro-N	17	9	.654	34	29	9	4	0	221	197	17	61	148	10.8	2.69	155	.236	.294	9	.123	-0	29	36	5	4.5
1958 LA-N	12	13	.480	44	29	6	1	0	211²	214	21	72	131	12.8	4.17	98	.263	.333	15	.227	9	-5	-2	3	1.0
1959 *LA-N★	17	13	.567	44	36	15	4	2	270²	237	26	93	242	11.6	3.46	122	.233	.308	15	.165	4	15	23	2	3.0
1960 LA-N	15	14	.517	41	36	15	5	2	269	214	27	72	246	9.9	2.84	140	.215	.275	13	.157	2	27	34	4	4.4
1961 LA-N☆	13	10	.565	40	37	10	3	0	244	236	29	83	182	12.5	3.69	118	.254	.329	16	.193	5	9	18	-1	2.2
1962 LA-N★	25	9	.735	43	41	19	2	1	314¹	272	21	78	232	10.3	2.83	128	.230	.283	22	.198	5	39	28	1	3.4
1963 *LA-N★	19	17	.528	42	42	17	3	0	315¹	287	25	57	251	10.1	2.63	115	.242	.283	16	.167	4	23	14	3	2.3
1964 LA-N★	18	16	.529	40	40	21	5	0	321¹	242	15	68	237	9.0	2.18	148	.207	.256	19	.173	4	48	38	2	4.9
1965 *LA-N★	23	12	.657	44	42	20	7	1	308¹	270	36	66	210	10.2	2.77	118	.232	.280	39	.300	20	26	17	0	4.2
1966 *LA-N	13	16	.448	40	40	11	3	0	273²	279	21	45	177	11.2	3.42	96	.265	.306	20	.189	4	6	-4	-1	-0.1
1967 LA-N★	13	16	.448	38	38	9	3	0	282	269	19	60	196	10.8	2.74	113	.251	.296	12	.129	-0	20	11	3	1.5
1968 LA-N★	14	12	.538	31	31	12	8	0	239	201	11	56	155	10.1	2.15	129	.231	.286	14	.177	1	22	16	2	2.4
1969 LA-N	5	4	.556	12	12	1	1	0	62²	71	9	13	24	12.4	4.45	75	.291	.332	3	.136	0	-6	-8	-0	-0.7
Total 14	209	166	.557	518	465	167	49	6	3432	3084	280	855	2486	10.7	2.95	121	.239	.294	218	.186	59	266	230	25	34.8

● MONK DUBIEL   Dubiel, Walter John   b: 2/12/19, Hartford, Conn.   d: 10/23/69, Hartford, Conn.   BR/TR, 6', 190 lbs.   Deb: 4/19/44

1944 NY-A	13	13	.500	30	28	19	3	0	232	217	12	86	79	11.8	3.38	103	.248	.316	15	.181	-2	1	3	0	0.1
1945 NY-A	10	9	.526	26	20	9	1	0	151¹	157	9	62	45	13.0	4.64	75	.266	.335	16	.276	4	-21	-20	-2	-1.8
1948 Phi-N	8	10	.444	37	17	6	2	4	150¹	139	13	58	42	11.9	3.89	101	.248	.320	7	.167	0	1	1	-2	0.0
1949 Chi-N	6	9	.400	32	20	3	1	4	147²	142	16	54	52	12.0	4.14	97	.250	.317	10	.286	3	-2	-2	1	0.3
1950 Chi-N	6	10	.375	39	12	4	2	2	142²	152	12	67	51	13.9	4.16	101	.270	.348	9	.200	1	-0	1	2	0.3
1951 Chi-N	2	2	.500	22	0	0	0	1	54²	46	3	22	19	11.2	2.30	178	.232	.309	0	.000	-1	10	11	0	1.0
1952 Chi-N	0	0	—	1	0	0	0	0	0²	1	0	0	1	13.5	0.00	—	.333	.333	0	—	0	0	0	0	0.0
Total 7	45	53	.459	187	97	41	9	11	879¹	854	65	349	289	12.4	3.87	98	.254	.325	57	.207	5	-11	-6	-0	-0.1

● BRIAN DuBOIS   DuBois, Brian Andrew   b: 4/18/67, Joliet, Ill.   BL/TL, 5'10", 195 lbs.   Deb: 8/17/89

1989 Det-A	0	4	.000	6	5	0	0	0	36	29	2	17	13	12.0	1.75	218	.218	.316	0	—	0	9	8	-0	1.1
1990 Det-A	3	5	.375	12	11	0	0	0	58¹	70	9	22	34	14.3	5.09	78	.310	.373	0	—	0	-8	-7	-1	-0.9
Total 2	3	9	.250	18	16	0	0	0	94¹	99	11	39	47	13.5	3.82	102	.276	.352	0	—	0	1	1	-1	0.2

● JEAN DUBUC   Dubuc, Jean Joseph Octave Arthur "Chauncey"   b: 9/15/1888, St.Johnsbury, Vt.   d: 8/28/58, Fort Myers, Fla.   BR/TR, 5'10.5", 185 lbs.   Deb: 6/25/08   C♦

1908 Cin-N	5	6	.455	15	9	7	1	0	85¹	62	2	41	32	11.4	2.74	84	.205	.309	4	.138	-1	-4	-4	1	-0.5
1909 Cin-N	2	5	.286	19	5	2	0	0	71¹	72	0	46	19	15.4	3.66	71	.269	.384	3	.167	0	-8	-8	-0	-0.9
1912 Det-A	17	10	.630	37	26	23	2	3	250	217	2	109	97	12.0	2.77	118	.235	.321	29	.269	6	15	14	4	2.5
1913 Det-A	15	14	.517	36	28	22	1	2	242²	228	1	91	73	12.1	2.89	101	.252	.325	36	.267	5	1	1	8	1.9
1914 Det-A	13	14	.481	36	27	15	2	1	224	216	4	76	70	12.0	3.46	81	.257	.324	28	.226	7	-18	-16	3	-0.6
1915 Det-A	17	12	.586	39	33	22	5	2	258	231	6	88	74	11.5	3.21	94	.245	.316	23	.205	4	-8	-5	1	-0.4
1916 Det-A	10	10	.500	36	16	8	1	1	170¹	134	1	84	40	11.8	2.96	97	.233	.336	20	.256	5	-2	-2	4	0.8
1918 *Bos-A	0	1	.000	2	1	1	0	0	10²	11	1	5	1	13.5	4.22	64	.268	.348	1	.167	0	-2	-2	-0	-0.2
1919 NY-N	6	4	.600	36	5	1	0	3	132	119	4	37	32	10.8	2.66	105	.246	.303	6	.143	-1	4	2	2	0.2
Total 9	85	76	.528	256	150	101	12	13	1444¹	1290	20	577	438	11.9	3.04	96	.244	.324	150	.230	21	-22	-21	23	2.8

● JIM DUCKWORTH   Duckworth, James Raymond   b: 5/24/39, National City, Cal.   BR/TR, 6'4", 194 lbs.   Deb: 4/13/63

1963 Was-A	4	12	.250	37	15	2	0	0	120²	131	13	67	66	15.5	6.04	61	.278	.379	0	.000	-3	-32	-31	-1	-3.5
1964 Was-A	1	6	.143	30	4	0	0	3	56	52	9	25	56	12.9	4.34	85	.244	.332	2	.222	0	-4	-4	0	-0.3
1965 Was-A	2	2	.500	17	8	0	0	0	64	45	11	36	74	11.7	3.94	88	.202	.318	0	.000	-2	-3	-2	-1	-0.6
1966 Was-A	0	3	.000	5	4	0	0	0	14¹	14	2	10	14	15.7	5.02	69	.259	.385	0	.000	-0	-3	-2	-0	-0.3
KC-A	0	2	.000	8	0	0	0	1	12	14	2	10	10	18.8	9.00	38	.292	.424	0	.000	-0	-7	-7	-0	-0.8
Yr	0	5	.000	13	4	0	0	1	26¹	28	4	20	24	16.7	6.84	50	.269	.392	0	.000	-1	-10	-10	-1	-1.1
Total 4	7	25	.219	97	29	2	0	4	267	256	37	148	220	14.2	5.26	69	.253	.358	2	.034	-5	-50	-49	-2	-5.5

● CLISE DUDLEY   Dudley, Elzie Clise   b: 8/8/03, Graham, N.C.   d: 1/12/89, Moncks Corner, S.C   BL/TR, 6'1", 195 lbs.   Deb: 4/18/29

1929 Bro-N	6	14	.300	35	21	8	1	0	156²	202	9	64	33	15.9	5.69	81	.315	.385	5	.098	-1	-17	-19	2	-1.6
1930 Bro-N	2	4	.333	21	7	2	0	1	66²	103	3	27	18	17.8	6.35	77	.371	.430	5	.208	0	-10	-11	1	-0.9
1931 Phi-N	8	14	.364	30	24	8	0	0	179	206	10	56	50	13.5	3.52	121	.287	.343	18	.214	0	7	14	1	1.6
1932 Phi-N	1	1	.500	13	0	0	0	1	17²	23	1	8	5	15.8	7.13	62	.329	.397	4	.286	3	-6	-5	0	-0.2
1933 Pit-N	0	0	—	1	0	0	0	0	0¹	6	0	1	0	189.0	135.00	2	.857	.875	0	—	0	-5	-5	0	-0.4
Total 5	17	33	.340	100	52	18	1	2	420¹	540	25	156	106	15.3	5.03	90	.315	.378	32	.185	2	-31	-24	4	-1.5

● HAL DUES   Dues, Hal Joseph   b: 9/22/54, LaMarque, Tex.   BR/TR, 6'3", 180 lbs.   Deb: 9/09/77

1977 Mon-N	1	1	.500	6	4	0	0	0	23	26	2	9	9	13.7	4.30	88	.265	.327	0	.000	-1	-1	-1	0	-0.2
1978 Mon-N	5	6	.455	25	12	1	0	1	99	85	9	42	36	11.9	2.36	149	.240	.327	6	.194	0	13	13	-0	1.4
1980 Mon-N	0	1	.000	6	1	0	0	0	12¹	17	1	4	2	15.3	6.57	54	.333	.382	0	.000	-0	-4	-4	0	-0.4
Total 3	6	8	.429	37	17	1	0	1	134¹	128	8	55	47	12.5	3.08	116	.254	.333	6	.154	-1	8	7	0	0.8

● LARRY DUFF   Duff, Cecil Elba   b: 11/30/1897, Radersburg, Mont.   d: 11/10/69, Bend, Ore.   BL/TR, 6'1", 175 lbs.   Deb: 9/05/22

| 1922 Chi-A | 1 | 1 | .500 | 3 | 1 | 0 | 0 | 0 | 12² | 16 | 1 | 3 | 7 | 13.5 | 4.97 | 82 | .340 | .380 | 2 | .400 | 0 | -1 | -1 | -0 | -0.1 |

● JIM DUFFALO   Duffalo, James Francis   b: 11/25/35, Helvetia, Pa.   BR/TR, 6'1", 175 lbs.   Deb: 4/12/61

1961 SF-N	5	1	.833	24	4	1	0	1	61²	59	9	32	37	13.6	4.23	90	.257	.352	5	.294	3	-1	-3	-1	-0.1
1962 SF-N	1	2	.333	24	2	0	0	0	42	42	3	23	29	13.9	3.64	104	.256	.348	0	.000	-0	1	1	-0	0.0
1963 SF-N	4	2	.667	34	5	0	0	2	75¹	56	3	37	55	11.3	2.87	112	.209	.309	2	.111	-1	4	3	1	0.3
1964 SF-N	5	1	.833	35	3	1	0	3	74	57	9	31	55	10.9	2.92	122	.209	.294	1	.071	-1	5	5	-1	0.4
1965 SF-N	0	1	.000	2	0	0	0	0	0¹	1	0	2	0	81.0	27.00	13	.500	.750	0	—	-0	-1	-1	0	-0.1
Cin-N	0	1	.000	22	0	0	0	0	44¹	33	3	30	34	13.8	3.45	109	.212	.356	0	.000	-1	0	1	1	0.1
Yr	0	2	.000	24	0	0	0	0	44²	34	3	32	34	14.3	3.63	103	.215	.364	0	.000	-1	-0	1	1	0.0
Total 5	15	8	.652	141	14	2	0	6	297²	248	27	155	210	12.5	3.39	106	.227	.329	8	.127	0	8	7	-1	0.6

● JOHN DUFFIE   Duffie, John Brown   b: 10/4/45, Greenwood, S.C.   BR/TR, 6'7", 210 lbs.   Deb: 9/18/67

| 1967 LA-N | 0 | 2 | .000 | 2 | 2 | 0 | 0 | 0 | 9² | 11 | 1 | 4 | 6 | 14.0 | 2.79 | 111 | .282 | .349 | 0 | .000 | -0 | 1 | 0 | -0 | 0.0 |

● BERNIE DUFFY   Duffy, Bernard Allen   b: 8/18/1893, Vinson, Okla.   d: 2/9/62, Abilene, Tex.   BR/TR, 5'11", 180 lbs.   Deb: 9/20/13

| 1913 Pit-N | 0 | 0 | — | 3 | 2 | 0 | 0 | 0 | 11¹ | 18 | 0 | 3 | 8 | 16.7 | 5.56 | 54 | .360 | .396 | 1 | .250 | 0 | -3 | -3 | 0 | -0.3 |

● DAN DUGAN   Dugan, Daniel Phillip   b: 2/22/07, Plainfield, N.J.   d: 6/25/68, Green Brook, N.J.   BL/TL, 6'1.5", 187 lbs.   Deb: 9/05/28

1928 Chi-A	0	0	—	1	0	0	0	0	0¹	0	0	0	0	0.00	0.00	—	.000	.000	0	—	0	0	0	0	0.0
1929 Chi-A	1	4	.200	19	2	0	0	1	65	77	8	19	15	13.6	6.65	64	.300	.353	3	.150	-1	-17	-17	-2	-1.8
Total 2	1	4	.200	20	2	0	0	1	65¹	77	8	19	15	13.5	6.61	65	.298	.351	3	.150	-1	-17	-17	-2	-1.8

● ED DUGAN   Dugan, Edward John   b: 1864, Brooklyn, N.Y.   Deb: 8/05/1884   F

| 1884 Ric-a | 5 | 14 | .263 | 20 | 20 | 20 | 0 | 0 | 166¹ | 196 | 5 | 15 | 60 | 11.5 | 4.49 | 74 | .267 | .284 | 8 | .114 | -4 | -23 | -22 | -2 | -2.4 |

● BILL DUGGLEBY Duggleby, William James "Frosty Bill" b: 3/16/1874, Utica, N.Y. d: 8/30/44, Redfield, N.Y. TR , Deb: 4/21/1898

YEAR	TM/L	W	L	PCT	G	GS	CG	SH	SV	IP	H	HR	BB	SO	RAT	ERA	ERA+	OAV	OOB	BH	AVG	PB	PR	/A	PD	TPI
1898	Phi-N	3	3	.500	9	5	4	0	0	54	70	4	18	12	15.7	5.50	62	.311	.378	5	.238	2	-11	-12	1	-0.8
1901	Phi-N	19	12	.613	34	28	25	5	0	275^{2}	294	9	40	94	11.1	2.87	118	.271	.301	19	.171	-3	14	16	5	1.8
1902	Phi-A	1	1	.500	2	2	2	0	0	17	19	0	4	4	12.2	3.18	116	.283	.323	0	.000	-1	1	1	1	0.1
	Phi-N	11	17	.393	33	28	25	0	1	258^{2}	282	2	57	60	12.2	3.38	83	.277	.322	17	.173	-1	-17	-16	2	-1.6
1903	Phi-N	13	16	.448	36	30	28	3	2	264^{1}	318	4	79	57	13.9	3.75	87	.303	.358	24	.231	2	-14	-14	1	-1.0
1904	Phi-N	12	13	.480	32	27	22	2	1	223^{2}	265	3	53	55	13.2	3.78	71	.292	.338	14	.171	0	-26	-27	0	-2.7
1905	Phi-N	18	17	.514	38	36	27	1	0	289^{1}	270	10	83	75	11.4	2.46	119	.253	.315	11	.109	-2	18	15	-2	1.2
1906	Phi-N	13	19	.406	42	30	22	5	2	280^{1}	241	5	66	83	10.2	2.25	116	.227	.280	14	.141	-2	12	11	1	1.2
1907	Phi-N	0	2	.000	5	2	2	0	0	29	43	2	11	8	18.3	7.45	33	.371	.447	1	.111	0	-16	-16	1	-1.4
	Pit-N	2	2	.500	9	3	1	1	0	40^{1}	34	0	12	4	10.7	2.68	91	.239	.308	2	.154	-0	-1	-1	1	0.0
	Yr	2	4	.333	14	5	3	1	0	69^{1}	77	2	23	12	13.2	4.67	52	.293	.354	3	.136	0	-17	-17	2	-1.4
Total	8	92	102	.474	240	191	158	17	6	1732^{1}	1836	39	423	452	12.1	3.18	93	.272	.323	107	.166	-4	-41	-44	11	-3.2

● MARTIN DUKE Duke, Martin F. "Duck" (b: Martin F. Duck) b: 1867, Zanesville, Ohio d: 12/31/1898, Minneapolis, Minn. TL , Deb: 8/24/1891

YEAR	TM/L	W	L	PCT	G	GS	CG	SH	SV	IP	H	HR	BB	SO	RAT	ERA	ERA+	OAV	OOB	BH	AVG	PB	PR	/A	PD	TPI
1891	Was-a	0	3	.000	4	3	2	0	0	23	36	0	19	5	21.5	7.43	50	.345	.446	1	.111	-1	-9	-9	-0	-0.8

● JAN DUKES Dukes, Noble Jan b: 8/16/45, Cheyenne, Wyo. BL/TL, 5'11", 175 lbs. Deb: 9/06/69

YEAR	TM/L	W	L	PCT	G	GS	CG	SH	SV	IP	H	HR	BB	SO	RAT	ERA	ERA+	OAV	OOB	BH	AVG	PB	PR	/A	PD	TPI
1969	Was-A	0	2	.000	8	0	0	0	0	11	8	0	4	3	9.8	2.45	141	.216	.293	0	.000	0	1	1	-0	0.1
1970	Was-A	0	0	—	5	0	0	0	0	6^{2}	6	0	1	4	10.8	2.70	132	.240	.296	0	.000	-0	1	1	0	0.1
1972	Tex-A	0	0	—	3	0	0	0	0	2^{1}	1	0	5	0	23.1	3.86	78	.167	.545	0	—	0	-0	-0	0	0.0
Total	3	0	2	.000	16	0	0	0	0	20	15	0	10	7	11.7	2.70	128	.221	.329	0	.000	0	2	2	-0	0.2

● TOM DUKES Dukes, Thomas Earl b: 8/31/42, Knoxville, Tenn. BR/TR, 6'2", 185 lbs. Deb: 8/15/67

YEAR	TM/L	W	L	PCT	G	GS	CG	SH	SV	IP	H	HR	BB	SO	RAT	ERA	ERA+	OAV	OOB	BH	AVG	PB	PR	/A	PD	TPI
1967	Hou-N	0	2	.000	17	0	0	0	1	23^{2}	25	2	11	23	14.5	5.32	62	.275	.365	1	.500	0	-5	-5	-0	-0.6
1968	Hou-N	2	2	.500	43	0	0	0	4	52^{2}	62	3	28	37	15.7	4.27	69	.291	.379	0	.000	-0	-8	-8	0	-0.9
1969	SD-N	1	0	1.000	13	0	0	0	1	22^{1}	26	2	10	15	14.5	7.25	49	.295	.367	0	.000	-0	-9	-9	0	-0.9
1970	SD-N	1	6	.143	53	0	0	0	10	69	62	7	25	56	11.6	4.04	98	.246	.319	0	.000	-1	0	-1	-0	-0.2
1971	*Bal-A	1	5	.167	28	0	0	0	4	38^{1}	40	4	8	30	11.5	3.52	95	.263	.304	1	.143	0	-0	-1	-1	-0.1
1972	Cal-A	0	1	.000	7	0	0	0	1	11	11	1	0	8	9.8	1.64	178	.262	.279	0	—	0	2	2	-1	0.1
Total	6	5	16	.238	161	0	0	0	21	217	226	19	82	169	13.1	4.35	79	.270	.341	2	.095	-1	-20	-22	-2	-2.6

● BOB DULIBA Duliba, Robert John b: 1/9/35, Glen Lyon, Pa. BR/TR, 5'10", 185 lbs. Deb: 8/11/59

YEAR	TM/L	W	L	PCT	G	GS	CG	SH	SV	IP	H	HR	BB	SO	RAT	ERA	ERA+	OAV	OOB	BH	AVG	PB	PR	/A	PD	TPI
1959	StL-N	0	1	.000	11	0	0	0	1	22^{2}	19	2	12	14	12.3	2.78	153	.237	.337	0	.000	-0	3	4	1	0.4
1960	StL-N	4	4	.500	27	0	0	0	0	40^{2}	49	6	16	23	14.4	4.20	97	.310	.374	1	.200	-0	-2	-0	-0	-0.1
1962	StL-N	2	0	1.000	28	0	0	0	2	39^{1}	33	3	17	22	11.4	2.06	207	.239	.323	0	.000	-1	8	10	0	0.9
1963	LA-A	1	1	.500	6	0	0	0	1	7^{2}	3	0	6	4	10.6	1.17	292	.125	.300	0	.000	-0	2	2	-0	0.2
1964	LA-A	6	4	.600	58	0	0	0	9	72^{2}	80	5	22	33	12.8	3.59	91	.287	.341	0	.000	-1	0	-2	1	-0.3
1965	Bos-A	4	2	.667	39	0	0	0	1	64^{1}	60	6	22	27	11.5	3.78	99	.248	.311	0	.000	-1	-2	-0	-0	-0.1
1967	KC-A	0	0	—	7	0	0	0	0	9^{2}	13	3	1	6	13.0	6.52	49	.342	.359	0	—	0	-4	-4	-0	-0.4
Total	7	17	12	.586	176	0	0	0	14	257	257	25	96	129	12.4	3.47	108	.268	.335	1	.038	-2	6	8	1	0.6

● GEORGE DUMONT Dumont, George Henry "Pea Soup" b: 11/13/1895, Minneapolis, Minn. d: 10/13/56, Minneapolis, Minn. BR/TR, 5'11", 163 lbs. Deb: 9/14/15

YEAR	TM/L	W	L	PCT	G	GS	CG	SH	SV	IP	H	HR	BB	SO	RAT	ERA	ERA+	OAV	OOB	BH	AVG	PB	PR	/A	PD	TPI
1915	Was-A	2	1	.667	6	4	3	2	0	40	23	0	12	18	8.3	2.02	147	.169	.247	2	.167	-0	4	4	-1	0.3
1916	Was-A	2	3	.400	17	5	2	0	1	53	37	0	17	21	9.3	3.06	91	.194	.263	1	.071	-0	-1	-2	-1	-0.3
1917	Was-A	5	14	.263	37	23	8	2	2	204^{2}	171	3	76	65	11.1	2.55	103	.227	.303	2	.034	-5	3	2	-3	-0.7
1918	Was-A	1	1	.500	4	1	1	0	0	14	18	0	6	12	15.4	5.14	53	.295	.358	1	.333	1	-4	-4	0	-0.3
1919	Bos-A	0	4	.000	13	2	0	0	0	35^{1}	45	1	19	12	16.6	4.33	70	.326	.411	0	.000	-0	-4	-5	0	-0.5
Total	5	10	23	.303	77	35	14	4	3	347	294	4	130	128	11.3	2.85	96	.230	.306	6	.064	-5	-3	-4	-5	-1.5

● DAN DUMOULIN Dumoulin, Daniel Lynn b: 8/20/53, Kokomo, Ind. BR/TR, 6', 175 lbs. Deb: 9/05/77

YEAR	TM/L	W	L	PCT	G	GS	CG	SH	SV	IP	H	HR	BB	SO	RAT	ERA	ERA+	OAV	OOB	BH	AVG	PB	PR	/A	PD	TPI
1977	Cin-N	0	0	—	5	0	0	0	0	5^{1}	12	0	3	5	25.3	13.50	29	.462	.517	0	—	0	-6	-6	0	-0.5
1978	Cin-N	1	0	1.000	3	0	0	0	0	5	7	0	3	2	19.8	1.80	197	.368	.478	0	—	0	1	1	0	0.1
Total	2	1	0	1.000	8	0	0	0	0	10^{1}	19	0	6	7	22.6	7.84	48	.422	.500	0	—	0	-5	-5	0	-0.4

● NICK DUMOVICH Dumovich, Nicholas b: 1/2/02, Sacramento, Cal. d: 12/12/78, Laguna Hills, Cal. BL/TL, 6', 170 lbs. Deb: 4/20/23

YEAR	TM/L	W	L	PCT	G	GS	CG	SH	SV	IP	H	HR	BB	SO	RAT	ERA	ERA+	OAV	OOB	BH	AVG	PB	PR	/A	PD	TPI
1923	Chi-N	3	5	.375	28	8	1	0	1	94	118	4	45	23	15.9	4.60	87	.319	.397	7	.241	1	-6	-6	1	-0.4

● ED DUNDON Dundon, Edward Joseph "Dummy" b: 7/10/1859, Columbus, Ohio d: 8/18/1893, Columbus, Ohio TR , Deb: 6/02/1883 ♦

YEAR	TM/L	W	L	PCT	G	GS	CG	SH	SV	IP	H	HR	BB	SO	RAT	ERA	ERA+	OAV	OOB	BH	AVG	PB	PR	/A	PD	TPI
1883	Col-a	3	16	.158	20	19	16	0	0	166^{2}	213	7	38	31	13.6	4.48	69	.292	.327	15	.161	-3	-22	-26	0	-2.4
1884	Col-a	6	4	.600	11	9	7	0	0	81	85	9	15	37	11.1	3.78	80	.249	.281	12	.140	-1	-5	-7	1	-0.5
Total	2	9	20	.310	31	28	23	0	0	247^{2}	298	16	53	68	12.8	4.25	72	.278	.312	27	.151	-4	-27	-33	1	-2.9

● JIM DUNEGAN Dunegan, James William b: 8/6/47, Burlington, Iowa BR/TR, 6'1", 205 lbs. Deb: 5/28/70

YEAR	TM/L	W	L	PCT	G	GS	CG	SH	SV	IP	H	HR	BB	SO	RAT	ERA	ERA+	OAV	OOB	BH	AVG	PB	PR	/A	PD	TPI
1970	Chi-N	0	2	.000	7	0	0	0	0	13^{1}	13	2	12	3	16.9	4.73	95	.277	.424	1	.250	0	-1	-0	0	0.0

● WILEY DUNHAM Dunham, Henry Huston b: 1/30/1877, Piketown, Ohio d: 1/16/34, Cleveland, Ohio 6'1", 180 lbs. Deb: 5/24/02

YEAR	TM/L	W	L	PCT	G	GS	CG	SH	SV	IP	H	HR	BB	SO	RAT	ERA	ERA+	OAV	OOB	BH	AVG	PB	PR	/A	PD	TPI
1902	StL-N	2	3	.400	7	5	3	0	1	38	47	1	13	15	14.9	5.68	48	.303	.368	1	.083	-1	-12	-12	-0	-1.3

● DAVEY DUNKLE Dunkle, Edward Perks b: 8/30/1872, Phillipsburg, Pa. d: 11/19/41, Lock Haven, Pa. BB/TR, 6'2", 220 lbs. Deb: 8/28/1897

YEAR	TM/L	W	L	PCT	G	GS	CG	SH	SV	IP	H	HR	BB	SO	RAT	ERA	ERA+	OAV	OOB	BH	AVG	PB	PR	/A	PD	TPI
1897	Phi-N	5	2	.714	7	7	7	0	0	62	72	0	23	9	13.9	3.48	121	.288	.350	4	.174	-1	6	5	-1	0.3
1898	Phi-N	1	4	.200	12	7	4	0	0	68^{1}	83	1	38	21	17.1	6.98	49	.297	.399	6	.214	-0	-26	-27	-1	-2.4
1899	Was-N	0	2	.000	4	2	2	0	0	26	46	3	14	9	21.1	10.04	39	.383	.452	3	.273	-0	-18	-18	-0	-1.4
1903	Chi-A	4	4	.500	12	7	6	0	1	82	96	1	31	26	14.2	4.06	69	.291	.356	10	.303	2	-10	-11	-2	-1.1
	Was-A	5	9	.357	14	13	10	0	0	108^{1}	111	4	33	51	12.4	4.24	74	.264	.325	4	.098	-4	-15	-13	-2	-1.8
	Yr	9	13	.409	26	20	16	0	1	190^{1}	207	5	64	77	13.1	4.16	72	.275	.336	14	.189	-2	-25	-25	-4	-2.9
1904	Was-A	2	9	.182	12	11	7	0	0	74^{1}	95	1	23	23	14.5	4.96	54	.311	.363	4	.143	-2	-20	-19	-1	-2.1
Total	5	17	30	.362	61	47	36	0	1	421	503	10	162	139	14.6	5.02	65	.295	.363	31	.189	-5	-83	-83	-7	-8.5

● FRED DUNLAP Dunlap, Frederick C. "Sure Shot" b: 5/21/1859, Philadelphia, Pa. d: 12/1/02, Philadelphia, Pa. BR/TR, 5'8", 165 lbs. Deb: 5/01/1880 M♦

YEAR	TM/L	W	L	PCT	G	GS	CG	SH	SV	IP	H	HR	BB	SO	RAT	ERA	ERA+	OAV	OOB	BH	AVG	PB	PR	/A	PD	TPI
1884	StL-U	0	0	—	1	0	0	0	1	0^{2}	2	0	0	1	27.0	13.50	22	.491	.491	185	.412	1	-1	-1	0	-0.1
1887	*Det-N	0	0	—	1	0	0	0	0	2	4	0	0	1	18.0	4.50	90	.500	.500	72	.265	0	-0	-0	-0	0.0
Total	2	0	0	—	2	0	0	0	1	2^{2}	6	0	0	2	20.3	6.75	56	.497	.497	1159	.292	1	-1	-1	-0	-0.1

● JACK DUNLEAVY Dunleavy, John Francis b: 9/14/1879, Harrison, N.J. d: 4/12/44, S.Norwalk, Conn. TL , 5'6", 167 lbs. Deb: 5/30/03 ♦

YEAR	TM/L	W	L	PCT	G	GS	CG	SH	SV	IP	H	HR	BB	SO	RAT	ERA	ERA+	OAV	OOB	BH	AVG	PB	PR	/A	PD	TPI
1903	StL-N	6	8	.429	14	13	9	0	0	102	101	2	57	51	14.6	4.06	80	.264	.371	48	.249	2	-9	-9	1	-0.6
1904	StL-N	1	4	.200	7	5	5	0	0	55	63	4	23	28	14.2	4.42	61	.275	.344	40	.233	1	-10	-11	1	-0.8
Total	2	7	12	.368	21	18	14	0	0	157	164	6	80	79	14.5	4.18	73	.268	.361	193	.241	3	-19	-20	1	-1.4

● JIM DUNN Dunn, James William "Bill" b: 2/25/31, Valdosta, Ga. BR/TR, 6'0.5", 185 lbs. Deb: 8/26/52

YEAR	TM/L	W	L	PCT	G	GS	CG	SH	SV	IP	H	HR	BB	SO	RAT	ERA	ERA+	OAV	OOB	BH	AVG	PB	PR	/A	PD	TPI
1952	Pit-N	0	0	—	3	0	0	0	0	5^{1}	4	0	3	2	11.8	3.38	118	.190	.292	0	.000	-0	0	0	0	0.0

● JACK DUNN Dunn, John Joseph b: 10/6/1872, Meadville, Pa. d: 10/22/28, Towson, Md. BR/TR, 5'9", Deb: 5/06/1897 ♦

YEAR	TM/L	W	L	PCT	G	GS	CG	SH	SV	IP	H	HR	BB	SO	RAT	ERA	ERA+	OAV	OOB	BH	AVG	PB	PR	/A	PD	TPI
1897	Bro-N	14	9	.609	25	21	21	0	0	216^{2}	251	6	66	26	13.5	4.57	90	.288	.344	29	.221	-2	-6	-11	1	-1.0
1898	Bro-N	16	21	.432	41	37	31	0	0	322^{2}	352	10	82	66	12.5	3.60	100	.276	.327	41	.246	0	0	-0	-1	-0.1
1899	Bro-N	23	13	.639	41	34	29	2	2	299^{1}	323	8	86	48	12.8	3.70	106	.275	.334	30	.246	-0	5	7	3	0.9

YEAR	TM/L	W	L	PCT	G	GS	CG	SH	SV	IP	H	HR	BB	SO	RAT	ERA	ERA+	OAV	OOB	BH	AVG	PB	PR	/A	PD	TPI
1900	Bro-N	3	4	.429	10	7	5	0	0	63	88	1	28	6	17.0	5.57	69	.329	.399	6	.231	-0	-13	-12	1	-1.0
	Phi-N	5	5	.500	10	9	9	1	0	80	87	2	29	12	13.6	4.84	75	.276	.347	10	.303	1	-10	-11	-1	-0.9
	Yr	8	9	.471	20	16	14	1	0	143	175	3	57	18	14.9	5.16	72	.299	.366	16	.271	1	-23	-23	1	-1.9
1901	Phi-N	0	1	.000	2	2	0	0	0	4^2	11	0	7	1	38.6	21.21	16	.451	.599	1	1.000	1	-9	-9	-0	-0.7
	Bal-A	3	3	.500	9	6	6	0	0	59^2	74	2	21	5	14.5	3.62	107	.301	.358	90	.249	0	0	2	1	0.2
1902	NY-N	0	3	.000	3	2	2	0	0	26^2	28	0	12	6	13.5	3.71	76	.270	.345	72	.211	0	-3	-3	1	-0.2
1904	NY-N	0	0	—	1	0	0	0	1	4	3	1	3	1	13.5	4.50	61	.167	.286	56	.309	0	-1	-1	-0	-0.1
Total	7	64	59	.520	142	118	103	3	3	1076^2	1217	30	334	171	13.4	4.11	92	.283	.342	397	.245	0	-36	-38	5	-2.9

● MIKE DUNNE Dunne, Michael Dennis b: 10/27/62, South Bend, Ind. BR/TR, 6'4", 190 lbs. Deb: 6/05/87

YEAR	TM/L	W	L	PCT	G	GS	CG	SH	SV	IP	H	HR	BB	SO	RAT	ERA	ERA+	OAV	OOB	BH	AVG	PB	PR	/A	PD	TPI
1987	Pit-N	13	6	.684	23	23	5	1	0	163^1	143	10	68	72	11.7	3.03	136	.240	.319	5	.094	-1	19	20	2	2.2
1988	Pit-N	7	11	.389	30	28	1	0	0	170	163	15	88	70	13.6	3.92	87	.255	.349	5	.109	-1	-9	-10	0	-1.1
1989	Pit-N	1	1	.500	3	3	0	0	0	14^1	21	1	9	4	19.5	7.53	45	.328	.419	1	.250	0	-6	-7	0	-0.6
	Sea-A	2	9	.182	15	15	1	0	0	85^1	104	7	37	38	15.1	5.27	76	.307	.378	0	—	0	-13	-12	0	-1.1
1990	SD-N	0	3	.000	10	6	0	0	0	28^2	28	4	17	15	14.1	5.65	68	.241	.338	0	.000	-1	-6	-6	1	-0.6
1992	Chi-A	2	0	1.000	4	1	0	0	0	12^2	12	0	6	6	13.5	4.26	90	.255	.352	0	—	0	-0	-1	0	0.0
Total	5	25	30	.455	85	76	7	1	0	474^1	471	37	225	205	13.4	4.08	93	.261	.347	11	.101	-1	-16	-15	3	-1.2

● ANDY DUNNING Dunning, Andrew Jackson b: 8/12/1871, New York, N.Y. d: 6/21/52, New York, N.Y. BR/TR, 6', 175 lbs. Deb: 5/23/1889

YEAR	TM/L	W	L	PCT	G	GS	CG	SH	SV	IP	H	HR	BB	SO	RAT	ERA	ERA+	OAV	OOB	BH	AVG	PB	PR	/A	PD	TPI
1889	Pit-N	0	2	.000	2	2	2	0	0	18	20	1	16	4	18.0	7.00	54	.273	.403	0	.000	-1	-6	-7	0	-0.6
1891	NY-N	0	1	.000	1	1	0	0	0	2	3	1	3	2	27.0	4.50	71	.334	.501	0	—	0	-0	-0	-0	0.0
Total	2	0	3	.000	3	3	2	0	0	20	23	2	19	6	18.9	6.75	55	.280	.415	0	.000	-1	-6	-7	0	-0.6

● STEVE DUNNING Dunning, Steven John b: 5/15/49, Denver, Colo. BR/TR, 6'2", 205 lbs. Deb: 6/14/70

YEAR	TM/L	W	L	PCT	G	GS	CG	SH	SV	IP	H	HR	BB	SO	RAT	ERA	ERA+	OAV	OOB	BH	AVG	PB	PR	/A	PD	TPI
1970	Cle-A	4	9	.308	19	17	0	0	0	94^1	93	16	54	77	14.4	4.96	80	.261	.364	5	.161	-1	-13	-11	1	-1.0
1971	Cle-A	8	14	.364	31	29	3	1	1	184	173	25	109	132	14.0	4.50	85	.254	.361	10	.182	1	-21	-14	2	-1.1
1972	Cle-A	6	4	.600	16	16	1	0	0	105	98	16	43	52	12.1	3.26	99	.248	.322	9	.273	5	-2	-0	-1	0.5
1973	Cle-A	0	2	.000	4	3	0	0	0	18	17	2	13	10	15.0	6.50	60	.250	.370	0	—	0	-5	-5	-0	-0.5
	Tex-A	2	6	.250	23	12	2	0	0	94^1	101	11	52	38	14.7	5.34	70	.275	.367	0	—	0	-16	-17	-0	-1.7
	Yr	2	8	.200	27	15	2	0	0	112^1	118	13	65	48	14.7	5.53	68	.271	.367	0	—	0	-21	-22	-0	-2.2
1974	Tex-A	0	0	—	1	0	0	0	0	2^1	3	2	3	1	23.1	19.29	18	.333	.500	0	—	0	-4	-4	0	-0.3
1976	Cal-A	0	0	—	4	0	0	0	0	6	9	2	6	4	22.5	7.50	44	.310	.429	0	—	0	-3	-3	-0	-0.1
	Mon-N	2	6	.250	32	7	1	0	0	91^1	93	6	33	72	12.6	4.14	90	.274	.342	2	.133	-0	-6	-4	0	-0.4
1977	Oak-A	1	0	1.000	6	0	0	0	0	18^1	17	2	10	4	13.3	3.93	102	.254	.351	0	—	0	0	0	0	0.1
Total	7	23	41	.359	136	84	7	1	1	613^2	604	82	323	390	13.8	4.56	82	.261	.355	26	.194	6	-71	-58	3	-4.5

● FRANK DUPEE Dupee, Frank Oliver b: 4/29/1877, Monkton, Vt. d: 8/14/56, Portland, Me. TL , 6'1", 200 lbs. Deb: 8/24/01

YEAR	TM/L	W	L	PCT	G	GS	CG	SH	SV	IP	H	HR	BB	SO	RAT	ERA	ERA+	OAV	OOB	BH	AVG	PB	PR	/A	PD	TPI
1901	Chi-A	0	1	.000	1	1	0	0	0	0	0	0	3	0	—	∞	—	—	1.000	0	—	0	-3	-3	0	-0.2

● MIKE DUPREE Dupree, Michael Dennis b: 5/29/53, Kansas City, Kan. BR/TR, 6'1", 185 lbs. Deb: 4/13/76

YEAR	TM/L	W	L	PCT	G	GS	CG	SH	SV	IP	H	HR	BB	SO	RAT	ERA	ERA+	OAV	OOB	BH	AVG	PB	PR	/A	PD	TPI
1976	SD-N	0	0	—	12	0	0	0	0	15^2	18	4	7	5	14.4	9.19	36	.286	.357	1	1.000	0	-10	-10	0	-1.0

● KID DURBIN Durbin, Blaine Alphonsus b: 9/10/1886, Kansas d: 9/11/43, Kirkwood, Mo. BL/TL, 5'8", 155 lbs. Deb: 4/24/07 ♦

YEAR	TM/L	W	L	PCT	G	GS	CG	SH	SV	IP	H	HR	BB	SO	RAT	ERA	ERA+	OAV	OOB	BH	AVG	PB	PR	/A	PD	TPI
1907	Chi-N	0	1	.000	5	1	1	0	1	16^2	14	0	10	5	13.5	5.40	46	.233	.352	6	.333	1	-5	-5	0	-0.5

● RYNE DUREN Duren, Rinold George b: 2/22/29, Cazenovia, Wis. BR/TR, 6'1", 195 lbs. Deb: 9/25/54

YEAR	TM/L	W	L	PCT	G	GS	CG	SH	SV	IP	H	HR	BB	SO	RAT	ERA	ERA+	OAV	OOB	BH	AVG	PB	PR	/A	PD	TPI
1954	Bal-A	0	0	—	1	0	0	0	0	2	3	0	1	2	18.0	9.00	40	.333	.400	0	—	0	-1	-1	-0	-0.1
1957	KC-A	0	3	.000	14	6	0	0	1	42^2	37	4	30	37	14.6	5.27	75	.236	.365	1	.071	-1	-7	-6	0	-0.7
1958	*NY-A☆	6	4	.600	44	1	0	0	**20**	75^2	40	4	43	87	10.7	2.02	175	.157	.296	1	.077	0	15	13	0	1.4
1959	NY-A★	3	6	.333	41	0	0	0	14	76^2	49	6	43	96	11.2	1.88	194	.181	.301	0	.000	-1	17	15	-0	1.5
1960	*NY-A	3	4	.429	42	1	0	0	9	49	27	3	49	67	15.2	4.96	72	.160	.369	0	.000	-1	-6	-7	1	-0.7
1961	NY-A	0	1	.000	4	0	0	0	0	5	2	2	4	7	10.8	5.40	69	.125	.300	0	—	0	-1	-1	-0	-0.1
	LA-A☆	6	12	.333	40	14	1	1	2	99	87	13	75	108	15.0	5.18	87	.233	.366	1	.040	-2	-13	-7	-1	-1.1
	Yr	6	13	.316	44	14	1	1	2	104	89	15	79	115	14.8	5.19	86	.229	.363	1	.040	-2	-14	-8	-2	-1.2
1962	LA-A	2	9	.182	42	3	0	0	8	71^1	53	1	57	74	14.6	4.42	87	.206	.363	1	.067	-1	-4	-4	-1	-0.6
1963	Phi-N	6	2	.750	33	7	1	0	2	87^1	65	6	52	84	12.6	3.30	98	.210	.332	3	.143	1	-0	-1	-1	-0.1
1964	Phi-N	0	0	—	2	0	0	0	0	3	5	0	1	5	21.0	6.00	58	.357	.438	0	—	0	-1	-1	-0	-0.1
	Cin-N	0	2	.000	26	0	0	0	1	43^2	41	1	15	39	12.2	2.89	125	.248	.322	0	.000	-0	3	4	-1	0.3
	Yr	0	2	.000	28	0	0	0	1	46^2	46	1	16	44	12.5	3.09	117	.256	.327	0	.000	-0	2	3	-1	0.2
1965	Phi-N	0	0	—	6	0	0	0	0	11	10	0	4	6	12.3	3.27	106	.270	.357	0	.000	-0	0	0	0	0.0
	Was-A	1	1	.500	16	0	0	0	0	23	24	0	18	18	17.6	6.65	52	.286	.429	0	—	0	-8	-8	-0	-0.9
Total	10	27	44	.380	311	32	2	1	57	589^1	443	40	392	630	13.4	3.83	98	.209	.344	7	.061	-5	-5	-6	-4	-1.2

● DON DURHAM Durham, Donald Gary b: 3/21/49, Yosemite, Ky. BR/TR, 6', 170 lbs. Deb: 7/16/72

YEAR	TM/L	W	L	PCT	G	GS	CG	SH	SV	IP	H	HR	BB	SO	RAT	ERA	ERA+	OAV	OOB	BH	AVG	PB	PR	/A	PD	TPI
1972	StL-N	2	7	.222	10	8	1	0	0	47^2	42	1	22	35	12.1	4.34	78	.240	.325	7	.500	4	-5	-5	-1	-0.1
1973	Tex-A	0	4	.000	15	4	0	0	1	40^1	49	7	23	23	16.3	7.59	49	.304	.395	0	—	0	-17	-17	-1	-1.7
Total	2	2	11	.154	25	12	1	0	1	88	91	8	45	58	14.0	5.83	61	.271	.359	7	.500	4	-22	-22	-1	-1.8

● ED DURHAM Durham, Edward Fant "Bull" b: 8/17/08, Chester, S.C. d: 4/27/76, Chester, S.C. BL/TR, 5'11", 170 lbs. Deb: 4/19/29

YEAR	TM/L	W	L	PCT	G	GS	CG	SH	SV	IP	H	HR	BB	SO	RAT	ERA	ERA+	OAV	OOB	BH	AVG	PB	PR	/A	PD	TPI
1929	Bos-A	1	0	1.000	14	1	0	0	0	22^1	34	2	14	6	19.3	9.27	46	.374	.457	0	.000	-0	-12	-12	-0	-1.2
1930	Bos-A	4	15	.211	33	12	6	1	1	140	144	9	43	28	12.2	4.69	98	.270	.326	4	.098	-4	-1	-1	-0	-0.5
1931	Bos-A	8	10	.444	38	15	7	2	0	165^1	175	9	50	53	12.5	4.25	101	.266	.322	3	.056	-6	2	1	-2	-0.6
1932	Bos-A	6	13	.316	34	22	4	0	0	175^1	187	13	49	52	12.3	3.80	118	.274	.327	7	.123	-3	13	14	1	1.1
1933	Chi-A	10	6	.625	24	21	6	0	0	138^2	137	12	46	65	12.2	4.48	95	.256	.320	10	.217	0	-3	-4	-1	-0.4
Total	5	29	44	.397	143	71	23	3	1	641^2	677	45	202	204	12.5	4.45	99	.271	.329	24	.119	-14	-0	-3	-3	-1.6

● JOHN DURHAM Durham, John Garfield b: 10/7/1881, Douglass, Kan. d: 5/7/49, Coffeyville, Kan. BR/TR, 6', 175 lbs. Deb: 9/15/02

YEAR	TM/L	W	L	PCT	G	GS	CG	SH	SV	IP	H	HR	BB	SO	RAT	ERA	ERA+	OAV	OOB	BH	AVG	PB	PR	/A	PD	TPI
1902	Chi-A	1	1	.500	3	3	3	0	0	20	21	0	16	3	16.6	5.85	58	.270	.395	1	.067	-1	-5	-5	0	-0.5

● BULL DURHAM Durham, Louis Raphael (b: Louis Raphael Staub) b: 6/27/1877, New Oxford, Pa. d: 6/28/60, Bentley, Kan. BR/TR, 5'10", Deb: 9/15/04

YEAR	TM/L	W	L	PCT	G	GS	CG	SH	SV	IP	H	HR	BB	SO	RAT	ERA	ERA+	OAV	OOB	BH	AVG	PB	PR	/A	PD	TPI
1904	Bro-N	2	0	1.000	2	2	1	0	0	11	10	0	5	1	12.3	3.27	84	.250	.333	1	.250	0	-1	-1	-0	-0.1
1907	Was-A	0	0	—	2	0	0	0	0	5	10	0	4	1	27.0	12.60	19	.415	.516	0	.000	-0	-6	-6	-0	-0.6
1908	NY-N	0	0	—	1	0	0	0	0	2	2	0	1	2	13.5	9.00	27	.250	.333	0	—	0	-1	-1	-0	-0.2
1909	NY-N	0	0	—	4	0	0	0	1	11	15	0	2	2	13.9	3.27	78	.326	.354	0	.000	-0	-1	-1	-0	-0.1
Total	4	2	0	1.000	9	2	1	0	1	29	37	0	12	6	15.5	5.28	49	.313	.381	1	.143	-0	-9	-9	-1	-1.0

● RICH DURNING Durning, Richard Knott b: 10/10/1892, Louisville, Ky. d: 9/23/48, Castle Point, N.Y BL/TL, 6'2", 178 lbs. Deb: 4/16/17

YEAR	TM/L	W	L	PCT	G	GS	CG	SH	SV	IP	H	HR	BB	SO	RAT	ERA	ERA+	OAV	OOB	BH	AVG	PB	PR	/A	PD	TPI
1917	Bro-N	0	0	—	1	0	0	0	0	1	0	0	0	0	0.0	0.00	—	.000	.000	0	—	0	0	0	-0	0.0
1918	Bro-N	0	0	—	1	0	0	0	0	2	3	0	4	0	31.5	13.50	21	.375	.583	0	—	0	-2	-2	0	-0.2
Total	2	0	0	—	2	0	0	0	0	3	3	0	4	0	21.0	9.00	31	.273	.467	0	—	0	-2	-2	0	-0.2

● JESSE DURYEA Duryea, James Newton "Cyclone Jim" b: 9/7/1859, Osage, Iowa d: 8/19/42, Algona, Iowa BR/TR, 5'10", 175 lbs. Deb: 4/20/1889

YEAR	TM/L	W	L	PCT	G	GS	CG	SH	SV	IP	H	HR	BB	SO	RAT	ERA	ERA+	OAV	OOB	BH	AVG	PB	PR	/A	PD	TPI
1889	Cin-a	32	19	.627	53	48	38	2	1	401	372	9	127	183	11.6	2.56	153	.238	.302	44	.272	6	**57**	**60**	0	5.9
1890	Cin-N	16	12	.571	33	32	29	2	0	274	270	11	60	108	11.1	2.92	122	.250	.294	15	.152	-0	20	19	0	1.9
1891	Cin-N	1	9	.100	10	10	8	0	0	77	101	4	25	23	15.5	5.38	63	.305	.366	1	.031	-4	-17	-17	-0	-1.8
	StL-a	1	1	.500	3	3	2	0	0	24	19	0	10	13	10.9	3.38	125	.210	.289	4	.364	1	1	2	0	0.3

YEAR	TM/L	W	L	PCT	G	GS	CG	SH	SV	IP	H	HR	BB	SO	RAT	ERA	ERA+	OAV	OOB	BH	AVG	PB	PR	/A	PD	TPI
1892	Cin-N	2	5	.286	9	7	5	0	0	68	55	3	26	21	11.1	3.57	91	.212	.292	3	.111	-1	-2	-2	1	-0.2
	Was-N	3	11	.214	18	15	13	1	2	127	102	6	45	48	11.1	2.41	135	.211	.291	6	.120	-3	12	12	4	1.3
	Yr	5	16	.238	27	22	18	1	2	195	157	9	71	69	10.9	2.82	116	.211	.287	9	.117	-4	10	10	4	1.1
1893	Was-N	4	10	.286	17	15	9	0	0	117	182	8	56	20	19.3	7.54	61	.345	.420	13	.277	2	-37	-38	0	-2.7
Total	5	59	67	.468	143	130	104	5	3	1088	1101	41	349	416	12.5	3.45	109	.254	.318	86	.201	0	34	36	5	4.7
● ERV DUSAK	Dusak, Ervin Frank "Four Sack" b: 7/29/20, Chicago, Ill. BR/TR, 6'2", 185 lbs. Deb: 9/18/41 ♦																									
1948	StL-N	0	0	—	1	0	0	0	0	1	0	0	1	0	9.0	0.00	—	.000	.250	65	.209	0	0	0	-0	0.0
1950	StL-N	0	2	.000	14	2	0	0	1	36^1	27	2	27	16	13.6	3.72	116	.211	.353	1	.083	-0	2	2	0	0.2
1951	StL-N	0	0	—	5	0	0	0	0	10	14	0	7	8	18.9	7.20	55	.333	.429	1	.500	1	-4	-4	0	-0.2
	Pit-N	0	1	.000	3	1	0	0	0	6^2	10	2	9	2	27.0	12.15	35	.357	.526	12	.308	1	-6	-6	-0	-0.5
	Yr	0	1	.000	8	1	0	0	0	16^2	24	2	16	10	22.1	9.18	44	.343	.471	13	.317	2	-10	-9	-0	-0.7
Total	3	0	3	.000	23	3	0	0	1	54	51	4	44	26	16.2	5.33	79	.254	.393	251	.243	2	-8	-7	-0	-0.5
● CARL DUSER	Duser, Carl Robert b: 7/22/32, Hazleton, Pa. BL/TL, 6'1", 175 lbs. Deb: 9/15/56																									
1956	KC-A	1	1	.500	2	2	0	0	0	6	14	0	2	5	24.0	9.00	48	.452	.485	0	.000	-0	-3	-3	0	-0.3
1958	KC-A	0	0	—	1	0	0	0	0	2	5	0	1	0	27.0	4.50	87	.500	.545	0	—	0	-0	-0	-0	0.0
Total	2	1	1	.500	3	2	0	0	0	8	19	0	3	5	24.8	7.88	54	.463	.500	0	.000	-0	-3	-3	0	-0.3
● BOB DUSTAL	Dustal, Robert Andrew b: 9/28/35, Sayreville, N.J. BR/TR, 6', 172 lbs. Deb: 4/09/63																									
1963	Det-A	0	1	.000	7	0	0	0	0	6	10	0	5	4	22.5	9.00	42	.357	.455	0	—	0	-4	-4	1	-0.3
● BILL DUZEN	Duzen, William George b: 2/21/1870, Buffalo, N.Y. d: 3/11/44, Buffalo, N.Y. BR/TR, 5'11", 165 lbs. Deb: 9/21/1890																									
1890	Buf-P	0	2	.000	2	2	2	0	0	13	20	2	14	5	23.5	13.85	30	.338	.465	1	.250	1	-14	-14	-0	-0.9
● FRANK DWYER	Dwyer, John Francis b: 3/25/1868, Lee, Mass. d: 2/4/43, Pittsfield, Mass. BR/TR, 5'8", 145 lbs. Deb: 9/20/1888 MC																									
1888	Chi-N	4	1	.800	5	5	5	1	0	42	32	1	9	17	8.8	1.07	283	.198	.240	4	.190	-0	8	9	0	1.0
1889	Chi-N	16	13	.552	32	30	27	0	0	276	307	14	72	63	12.6	3.59	116	.273	.321	27	.200	-2	13	17	-2	1.2
1890	Chi-P	3	6	.333	12	6	6	0	1	69^1	98	4	25	17	16.0	6.23	70	.319	.371	14	.264	-0	-15	-15	1	-1.1
1891	Cin-a	13	19	.406	35	31	29	1	0	289	332	10	124	101	14.5	4.52	91	.279	.351	40	.284	3	-25	-13	1	-0.7
	Mil-a	6	4	.600	10	10	10	0	0	86	92	2	21	27	12.2	2.20	200	.264	.314	9	.225	-2	15	21	-0	1.8
	Yr	19	23	.452	45	41	39	1	0	375	424	12	145	128	13.8	3.98	105	.274	.337	49	.271	2	-11	8	1	1.1
1892	StL-N	2	8	.200	10	10	6	0	0	64	90	1	24	16	16.3	5.63	57	.319	.377	2	.080	-1	-17	-17	1	-1.5
	Cin-N	19	10	.655	33	27	24	3	1	259^1	251	6	49	45	10.6	2.33	141	.244	.282	21	.163	-4	28	27	-1	2.1
	Yr	21	18	.538	43	37	30	3	1	323^1	341	7	73	61	11.7	2.98	109	.260	.301	23	.149	-5	11	10	-1	0.6
1893	Cin-N	18	15	.545	37	30	28	1	**2**	287^1	332	17	93	53	13.5	4.13	116	.281	.336	24	.200	-3	17	21	3	1.7
1894	Cin-N	19	22	.463	45	40	34	1	1	348	471	27	106	49	15.3	5.07	110	.320	.371	46	.267	1	10	19	1	1.6
1895	Cin-N	18	15	.545	37	31	23	2	0	280^1	355	10	74	46	14.2	4.24	117	.304	.353	30	.265	2	17	23	-0	2.0
1896	Cin-N	24	11	.686	36	34	30	3	1	288^2	321	8	60	57	12.2	3.15	146	.279	.321	29	.264	4	39	47	-2	4.3
1897	Cin-N	18	13	.581	37	31	22	0	0	247^1	315	5	56	41	13.9	3.78	120	.307	.350	25	.266	-0	15	21	-3	1.6
1898	Cin-N	16	10	.615	31	28	24	0	0	240	257	3	42	29	11.8	3.04	126	.272	.314	12	.141	-5	15	21	-2	1.5
1899	Cin-N	0	5	.000	5	5	2	0	0	32^2	48	1	9	2	16.0	5.51	71	.341	.384	4	.364	1	-6	-6	0	-0.4
Total	12	176	152	.537	365	318	270	12	6	2810	3301	109	764	563	13.3	3.85	115	.286	.336	287	.230	-6	113	177	-4	15.1
● BEN DYER	Dyer, Benjamin Franklin b: 2/13/1893, Chicago, Ill. d: 8/7/59, Kenosha, Wis. BR/TR, 5'10", 170 lbs. Deb: 5/23/14 ♦																									
1918	Det-A	0	0	—	2	0	0	0	0	1^2	0	0	0	0	0.0	0.00	—	.000	.000	5	.278	0	1	0	0	0.1
● EDDIE DYER	Dyer, Edwin Hawley b: 10/11/1900, Morgan City, La. d: 4/20/64, Houston, Tex. BL/TL, 5'11.5", 168 lbs. Deb: 7/08/22 M♦																									
1922	StL-N	0	0	—	2	0	0	0	0	3^2	7	0	0	3	17.2	2.45	157	.412	.412	1	.333	0	1	1	0	0.1
1923	StL-N	2	1	.667	4	3	2	1	0	22	30	0	5	7	14.7	4.09	95	.333	.375	12	.267	0	-0	-0	-0	0.0
1924	StL-N	8	11	.421	29	15	7	1	0	136^2	174	6	51	23	15.1	4.61	82	.331	.395	18	.237	1	-11	-13	1	-0.9
1925	StL-N	4	3	.571	27	5	1	0	3	82^1	93	4	24	25	13.6	4.15	104	.278	.340	3	.097	-2	1	2	0	0.0
1926	StL-N	1	0	1.000	6	0	0	0	0	9^1	7	0	14	4	21.2	11.57	34	.219	.468	1	.500	0	-8	-8	0	-0.7
1927	StL-N	0	0	—	1	0	0	0	0	2	5	1	2	1	31.5	18.00	22	.500	.583	0	—	0	-3	-3	-0	-0.3
Total	6	15	15	.500	69	23	10	2	3	256	316	11	96	63	14.9	4.75	84	.313	.380	35	.223	1	-21	-22	1	-1.8
● MIKE DYER	Dyer, Michael Lawrence b: 9/8/66, Upland, Cal. BR/TR, 6'3", 195 lbs. Deb: 6/29/89																									
1989	Min-A	4	7	.364	16	12	1	0	0	71	74	2	37	37	14.3	4.82	86	.273	.365	0	—	0	-7	-5	-1	-0.8
● JIMMY DYGERT	Dygert, James Henry "Sunny Jim" b: 7/5/1884, Utica, N.Y. d: 2/8/36, New Orleans, La. BR/TR, 5'10", 185 lbs. Deb: 9/08/05																									
1905	Phi-A	1	4	.200	6	3	2	0	0	35^1	41	2	11	24	13.8	4.33	61	.291	.351	4	.267	0	-7	-7	2	-0.5
1906	Phi-A	11	13	.458	35	25	15	4	0	213^2	175	1	91	106	11.6	2.70	101	.227	.316	13	.176	-0	-0	1	1	0.1
1907	Phi-A	21	8	.724	42	28	18	5	1	261^2	200	2	85	151	10.3	2.34	112	**.214**	.289	12	.128	-4	6	8	-1	0.3
1908	Phi-A	11	15	.423	41	27	15	5	1	238^2	184	3	97	164	11.0	2.87	89	.220	.309	6	.080	-7	-12	-8	3	-1.4
1909	Phi-A	9	5	.643	32	13	6	1	0	137^1	117	1	50	79	11.7	2.42	99	.242	.327	9	.214	1	1	-0	-2	-0.2
1910	Phi-A	4	4	.500	19	8	6	1	0	99^1	81	0	49	59	12.1	2.54	94	.231	.331	3	.083	-2	-0	-2	-2	-0.7
Total	6	57	49	.538	175	104	62	16	2	986	798	9	383	583	11.3	2.65	97	.227	.312	47	.140	-11	-12	-8	-0	-2.4
● JIMMY DYKES	Dykes, James Joseph b: 11/10/1896, Philadelphia, Pa. d: 6/15/76, Philadelphia, Pa. BR/TR, 5'9", 185 lbs. Deb: 5/06/18 MC♦																									
1927	Phi-A	0	0	—	2	0	0	0	1	2	2	0	1	0	13.5	4.50	95	.333	.429	135	.324	1	-0	-0	-0	0.0
● ARNOLD EARLEY	Earley, Arnold Carl b: 6/4/33, Lincoln Park, Mich. BL/TL, 6'1", 200 lbs. Deb: 9/27/60																									
1960	Bos-A	0	1	.000	2	0	0	0	0	4	9	1	4	5	29.3	15.75	26	.429	.520	0	.000	0	-5	-5	-0	-0.5
1961	Bos-A	2	4	.333	33	0	0	0	7	49^2	42	3	34	44	13.8	3.99	105	.226	.345	0	.000	-1	0	1	0	0.0
1962	Bos-A	4	5	.444	38	3	0	0	5	68^1	76	8	46	59	16.2	5.80	71	.281	.388	2	.200	0	-14	-13	1	-1.2
1963	Bos-A	3	7	.300	53	4	0	0	1	115^2	124	13	43	97	13.6	4.75	80	.270	.343	5	.278	1	-14	-12	0	-1.2
1964	Bos-A	1	1	.500	25	3	1	0	1	50^1	51	3	18	45	12.5	2.68	144	.266	.332	1	.111	0	5	7	1	0.8
1965	Bos-A	0	1	.000	57	0	0	0	0	74^1	79	5	29	47	13.4	3.63	103	.271	.344	0	.000	-0	-1	1	-0	0.0
1966	Chi-N	2	1	.667	13	0	0	0	0	17^2	14	1	9	12	11.7	3.57	103	.226	.324	0	.000	-0	0	0	-1	-0.1
1967	Hou-N	0	0	—	2	0	0	0	0	1^1	5	1	1	1	40.5	27.00	12	.625	.667	0	—	0	-4	-4	0	-0.3
Total	8	12	20	.375	223	10	1	0	14	381^1	400	35	184	310	14.1	4.48	87	.269	.354	8	.157	0	-33	-25	1	-2.5
● TOM EARLEY	Earley, Thomas Francis Aloysius b: 2/19/17, Roxbury, Mass. d: 4/5/88, Nantucket, Mass. BR/TR, 6', 180 lbs. Deb: 9/27/38																									
1938	Bos-N	1	0	1.000	2	1	1	0	0	11	8	2	1	4	8.2	3.27	105	.186	.222	0	.000	-1	1	0	-0	0.0
1939	Bos-N	1	4	.200	14	2	0	0	1	40	49	1	19	9	15.7	4.72	78	.304	.385	3	.300	0	-4	-5	1	-0.4
1940	Bos-N	2	0	1.000	4	1	1	1	0	16^1	16	1	3	5	11.6	3.86	96	.267	.323	2	.400	1	-0	-0	-0	0.1
1941	Bos-N	6	8	.429	33	13	6	1	3	138^2	120	9	46	54	11.0	2.53	141	.233	.300	11	.234	1	17	16	-1	1.7
1942	Bos-N	6	11	.353	27	18	6	0	1	112^2	120	10	55	28	14.1	4.71	71	.276	.359	4	.118	-1	-18	-17	0	-1.8
1945	Bos-N	2	1	.667	11	2	1	0	0	41	36	4	19	4	12.1	4.61	83	.235	.320	3	.214	1	-4	-4	0	-0.3
Total	6	18	24	.429	91	37	15	2	5	359^2	349	27	143	104	12.5	3.78	94	.256	.330	23	.202	2	-7	-9	-0	-0.7
● BILL EARLEY	Earley, William Albert b: 1/30/56, Cincinnati, Ohio BR/TL, 6'4", 200 lbs. Deb: 9/22/86																									
1986	StL-N	0	0	—	3	0	0	0	0	3	0	0	2	2	6.0	0.00	—	.000	.182	0	—	0	1	1	-0	0.1
● GEORGE EARNSHAW	Earnshaw, George Livingston "Moose" b: 2/15/1900, New York, N.Y. d: 12/1/76, Little Rock, Ark. BR/TR, 6'4", 210 lbs. Deb: 6/03/28 C																									
1928	Phi-A	7	7	.500	26	22	7	3	1	158^1	143	7	100	117	13.9	3.81	105	.240	.351	14	.246	1	4	4	-1	0.3

YEAR	TM/L	W	L	PCT	G	GS	CG	SH	SV	IP	H	HR	BB	SO	RAT	ERA	ERA+	OAV	OOB	BH	AVG	PB	PR	/A	PD	TPI
1929	*Phi-A	**24**	8	.750	44	33	13	3	1	254^{2}	233	8	125	149	12.8	3.29	129	**.241**	.331	15	.172	-2	27	27	-3	2.0
1930	*Phi-A	22	13	.629	49	39	20	**3**	2	296	299	20	139	193	13.3	4.44	105	.266	.347	26	.228	1	7	8	-1	0.6
1931	*Phi-A	21	7	.750	43	30	23	3	6	281^{2}	255	16	75	152	10.6	3.67	122	.236	.288	30	.263	6	22	26	0	3.1
1932	Phi-A	19	13	.594	36	33	21	1	0	245^{1}	262	28	94	109	13.2	4.77	95	.270	.336	26	.286	4	-8	-7	1	-0.2
1933	Phi-A	5	10	.333	21	18	4	0	0	117^{2}	153	8	58	37	16.2	5.97	72	.311	.385	8	.182	-0	-22	-22	1	-1.9
1934	Chi-A	14	11	.560	33	30	16	2	0	227	242	28	104	97	13.9	4.52	105	.270	.349	16	.203	-0	-1	5	-1	0.5
1935	Chi-A	1	2	.333	3	3	0	0	0	18	26	2	11	8	18.5	9.00	51	.342	.425	2	.286	0	-9	-9	-0	-0.7
	Bro-N	8	12	.400	25	22	6	2	0	166	175	14	53	72	12.4	4.12	96	.270	.325	13	.217	1	-2	-3	0	-0.2
1936	Bro-N	4	9	.308	19	13	4	1	1	93	113	7	30	40	14.1	5.32	78	.297	.354	8	.242	1	-13	-12	-0	-1.1
	StL-N	2	1	.667	20	6	1	0	1	57^{2}	80	4	20	28	16.1	6.40	62	.333	.392	4	.222	-0	-15	-16	1	-1.4
	Yr	6	10	.375	39	19	5	1	2	150^{2}	193	11	50	68	14.7	5.73	71	.310	.364	12	.235	0	-29	-28	1	-2.5
Total	9	127	93	.577	319	249	115	18	12	1915^{1}	1981	142	809	1002	13.2	4.38	100	.265	.339	162	.230	9	-10	0	-2	1.0

● LOGAN EASLEY

Easley, Kenneth Logan b: 11/4/61, Salt Lake City, Utah BR/TR, 6'1", 185 lbs. Deb: 4/09/87

YEAR	TM/L	W	L	PCT	G	GS	CG	SH	SV	IP	H	HR	BB	SO	RAT	ERA	ERA+	OAV	OOB	BH	AVG	PB	PR	/A	PD	TPI
1987	Pit-N	1	1	.500	17	0	0	0	1	26^{1}	23	5	17	21	14.0	5.47	75	.242	.363	0	.000	-0	-4	-4	1	-0.3
1989	Pit-N	1	0	1.000	10	0	0	0	1	12^{1}	8	1	7	6	11.7	4.38	77	.190	.320	0	.000	-0	-1	-1	-0	-0.2
Total	2	2	1	.667	27	0	0	0	2	38^{2}	31	6	24	27	13.3	5.12	75	.226	.350	0	.000	-0	-5	-5	1	-0.5

● MAL EASON

Eason, Malcolm Wayne "Kid" b: 3/13/1879, Brookville, Pa. d: 4/16/70, Douglas, Ariz. TR , Deb: 10/01/00 U

YEAR	TM/L	W	L	PCT	G	GS	CG	SH	SV	IP	H	HR	BB	SO	RAT	ERA	ERA+	OAV	OOB	BH	AVG	PB	PR	/A	PD	TPI
1900	Chi-N	1	0	1.000	1	1	1	0	0	9	9	0	3	2	12.0	1.00	361	.260	.319	0	.000	-1	3	3	-0	0.2
1901	Chi-N	8	17	.320	27	25	23	1	0	220^{2}	246	9	60	68	13.0	3.59	90	.280	.335	12	.138	-5	-7	-9	-2	-1.4
1902	Chi-N	1	1	.500	2	2	2	0	0	18	21	0	2	4	11.5	1.00	270	.291	.310	1	.200	0	4	3	0	0.5
	Bos-N	9	11	.450	27	26	20	2	0	206^{1}	237	4	59	50	13.4	2.75	103	.288	.344	6	.083	-7	1	2	-1	-0.5
	Yr	10	12	.455	29	28	22	2	0	224^{1}	258	4	61	54	13.2	2.61	108	.288	.341	7	.091	-7	4	5	-0	0.0
1903	Det-A	2	5	.286	7	6	6	1	0	56^{1}	60	1	19	21	13.3	3.36	87	.272	.341	2	.100	-2	-2	-3	1	-0.3
1905	Bro-N	5	21	.192	27	27	20	3	0	207	230	5	72	64	13.3	4.30	67	.292	.355	14	.173	-1	-30	-32	1	-3.1
1906	Bro-N	10	17	.370	34	26	18	3	1	227	212	1	74	64	11.7	3.25	78	.256	.323	8	.091	-4	-16	-18	1	-2.3
Total	6	36	72	.333	125	113	90	10	1	944^{1}	1015	20	289	273	12.8	3.39	85	.278	.338	43	.121	-19	-47	-54	2	-6.9

● CARL EAST

East, Carlton William b: 8/27/1894, Marietta, Ga. d: 1/15/53, Whitesburg, Ga. BL/TR, 6'2", 178 lbs. Deb: 8/24/15 ♦

YEAR	TM/L	W	L	PCT	G	GS	CG	SH	SV	IP	H	HR	BB	SO	RAT	ERA	ERA+	OAV	OOB	BH	AVG	PB	PR	/A	PD	TPI
1915	StL-A	0	0	—	1	1	0	0	0	3^{1}	6	0	2	1	21.6	16.20	18	.400	.471	0	.000	-0	-5	-5	-0	-0.4

● HUGH EAST

East, Gordon Hugh b: 7/7/19, Birmingham, Ala. d: 11/2/81, Charleston, S.C. BR/TR, 6'2", 185 lbs. Deb: 9/13/41

YEAR	TM/L	W	L	PCT	G	GS	CG	SH	SV	IP	H	HR	BB	SO	RAT	ERA	ERA+	OAV	OOB	BH	AVG	PB	PR	/A	PD	TPI
1941	NY-N	1	1	.500	2	2	0	0	0	15^{2}	19	0	9	4	16.1	3.45	107	.297	.384	2	.222	0	0	0	-0	0.1
1942	NY-N	0	2	.000	4	1	0	0	0	7^{1}	15	1	7	2	27.0	9.82	34	.429	.524	1	.500	2	-5	-5	0	-0.3
1943	NY-N	1	3	.250	13	5	1	0	0	40^{1}	51	4	25	21	17.0	5.36	64	.298	.388	1	.077	-1	-9	-9	-1	-1.0
Total	3	2	6	.250	19	8	1	0	0	63^{1}	85	5	41	27	17.9	5.40	65	.315	.405	4	.167	1	-14	-13	-1	-1.2

● JAMIE EASTERLY

Easterly, James Morris b: 2/17/53, Houston, Tex. BL/TL, 5'9", 180 lbs. Deb: 4/06/74

YEAR	TM/L	W	L	PCT	G	GS	CG	SH	SV	IP	H	HR	BB	SO	RAT	ERA	ERA+	OAV	OOB	BH	AVG	PB	PR	/A	PD	TPI
1974	Atl-N	0	0	—	3	0	0	0	0	2^{2}	6	0	4	0	33.8	16.88	22	.400	.526	0	—	0	-4	-4	0	-0.4
1975	Atl-N	2	9	.182	21	13	0	0	0	68^{2}	73	5	42	34	15.3	4.98	76	.275	.379	1	.056	-2	-10	-9	-1	-1.1
1976	Atl-N	1	1	.500	4	4	0	0	0	22	23	0	13	11	14.7	4.91	77	.280	.379	1	.111	-1	-3	-3	0	-0.3
1977	Atl-N	2	4	.333	22	5	0	0	1	58^{2}	72	5	30	37	16.1	6.14	72	.303	.387	4	.267	1	-15	-11	-1	-1.1
1978	Atl-N	3	6	.333	37	6	0	0	1	78	91	9	45	42	15.9	5.65	72	.299	.393	4	.211	1	-18	-14	0	-1.4
1979	Atl-N	0	0	—	4	0	0	0	0	2^{2}	7	0	3	3	33.8	13.50	30	.467	.556	0	—	0	-3	-3	0	-0.3
1981	*Mil-A	3	3	.500	44	0	0	0	4	62	46	0	34	31	11.6	3.19	107	.219	.328	0	—	0	3	2	0	0.2
1982	Mil-A	0	2	.000	28	0	0	0	2	30^{2}	39	6	15	16	15.8	4.70	81	.312	.386	0	—	0	-2	-3	1	-0.1
1983	Mil-A	0	1	.000	12	0	0	0	1	11^{2}	14	0	10	6	20.1	3.86	97	.350	.500	0	.000	0	0	-0	-0	0.0
	Cle-A	4	2	.667	41	0	0	0	3	57	69	4	22	39	14.7	3.63	117	.309	.377	0	—	0	3	4	0	0.4
	Yr	4	3	.571	53	0	0	0	4	68^{2}	83	4	32	45	15.3	3.67	113	.312	.390	0	.000	0	3	4	0	0.4
1984	Cle-A	3	1	.750	26	1	0	0	2	69^{1}	74	3	23	42	12.7	3.38	121	.273	.332	0	—	0	5	5	0	0.5
1985	Cle-A	4	1	.800	50	7	0	0	0	98^{2}	96	9	53	58	14.0	3.92	105	.264	.363	0	—	0	2	2	-0	0.3
1986	Cle-A	0	2	.000	13	0	0	0	0	17^{2}	27	3	12	9	19.9	7.64	54	.365	.453	0	—	0	-7	-7	-0	-0.6
1987	Cle-A	1	1	.500	16	0	0	0	0	31^{2}	26	4	13	22	11.4	4.55	99	.218	.301	0	—	0	-0	-0	0	0.0
Total	13	23	33	.411	321	36	0	0	14	611^{1}	663	48	319	350	14.7	4.62	87	.283	.373	10	.161	-0	-49	-40	-0	-3.9

● JACK EASTON

Easton, John S. b: 2/28/1867, Bridgeport, Ohio d: 11/28/03, Steubenville, Ohio Deb: 9/23/1889

YEAR	TM/L	W	L	PCT	G	GS	CG	SH	SV	IP	H	HR	BB	SO	RAT	ERA	ERA+	OAV	OOB	BH	AVG	PB	PR	/A	PD	TPI
1889	Col-a	1	0	1.000	4	1	1	0	1	18	13	0	21	7	18.5	3.50	104	.196	.410	0	.000	-1	1	0	-0	-0.1
1890	Col-a	15	14	.517	37	29	23	0	1	255^{2}	213	4	125	147	12.6	3.52	102	.220	.321	19	.178	0	10	2	1	0.3
1891	Col-a	5	10	.333	18	16	13	0	0	135^{1}	145	3	59	52	14.6	4.52	77	.265	.352	15	.238	2	-12	-16	1	-1.1
	StL-a	3	2	.600	7	6	4	0	0	47^{2}	48	3	23	22	14.2	5.10	83	.253	.346	5	.179	-1	-7	-5	-2	-0.6
	Col-a	0	2	.000	2	2	2	0	0	15	15	2	4	13	12.6	3.60	96	.252	.320	0	.000	-1	0	-0	-1	-0.1
	Yr	8	14	.364	27	24	19	0	0	198	208	8	86	87	13.5	4.59	79	.255	.327	20	.196	-0	-19	-21	-1	-1.8
1892	StL-N	2	0	1.000	5	2	2	0	0	31	38	2	26	4	19.5	6.39	50	.290	.419	3	.176	-0	-11	-11	0	-0.9
1894	Pit-N	0	1	.000	3	1	1	0	0	19^{2}	26	0	4	1	15.1	4.12	127	.315	.368	0	.000	-1	3	2	-1	0.0
Total	5	26	29	.473	76	57	46	0	2	522^{1}	498	14	262	246	14.0	4.12	89	.243	.343	42	.176	-3	-16	-27	-1	-2.5

● RAWLY EASTWICK

Eastwick, Rawlins Jackson b: 10/24/50, Camden, N.J. BR/TR, 6'3", 180 lbs. Deb: 9/12/74

YEAR	TM/L	W	L	PCT	G	GS	CG	SH	SV	IP	H	HR	BB	SO	RAT	ERA	ERA+	OAV	OOB	BH	AVG	PB	PR	/A	PD	TPI
1974	Cin-N	0	0	—	8	0	0	0	2	17^{2}	12	1	5	14	8.7	2.04	171	.188	.246	0	.000	-0	3	3	-0	0.3
1975	*Cin-N	5	3	.625	58	0	0	0	**22**	90	77	6	25	61	10.4	2.60	138	.229	.287	1	.067	-1	10	10	-1	0.8
1976	*Cin-N	11	5	.688	71	0	0	0	**26**	107^{2}	93	3	27	70	10.2	2.09	168	.232	.284	0	.000	-2	17	17	-2	1.4
1977	Cin-N	2	2	.500	23	0	0	0	7	43^{1}	40	3	8	17	10.0	2.91	135	.244	.279	1	.167	-0	5	5	-1	0.4
	StL-N	3	7	.300	41	1	0	0	4	53^{2}	74	6	21	30	15.9	4.70	82	.332	.389	2	.400	1	-5	-5	-1	-0.5
	Yr	5	9	.357	64	1	0	0	11	97	114	9	29	47	13.3	3.90	100	.295	.344	3	.273	1	0	-0	-2	-0.1
1978	NY-A	2	1	.667	8	0	0	0	0	24^{2}	22	2	4	13	9.9	3.28	110	.232	.270	0	—	0	1	1	-0	0.2
	*Phi-N	2	1	.667	22	0	0	0	0	40^{1}	31	5	18	14	10.9	4.02	89	.209	.295	0	.000	-0	-2	-2	-1	-0.3
1979	Phi-N	3	6	.333	51	0	0	0	6	82^{2}	90	8	25	47	12.6	4.90	78	.284	.338	0	.000	-1	-11	-10	-2	-1.3
1980	KC-A	0	1	.000	14	0	0	0	0	22	37	2	8	5	19.2	5.32	76	.363	.420	0	—	0	-3	-3	1	-0.3
1981	Chi-N	0	1	.000	30	0	0	0	1	43^{1}	43	2	15	24	12.0	2.28	162	.264	.326	0	.000	-0	6	7	0	0.7
Total	8	28	27	.509	326	1	0	0	68	525^{1}	519	38	156	295	11.7	3.31	112	.258	.314	4	.071	-4	22	22	-7	1.4

● CRAIG EATON

Eaton, Craig b: 9/7/54, Glendale, Ohio BR/TR, 5'11", 175 lbs. Deb: 9/05/79

YEAR	TM/L	W	L	PCT	G	GS	CG	SH	SV	IP	H	HR	BB	SO	RAT	ERA	ERA+	OAV	OOB	BH	AVG	PB	PR	/A	PD	TPI
1979	KC-A	0	0	—	5	0	0	0	0	10	8	0	3	4	9.9	2.70	158	.222	.282	0	—	0	2	2	0	0.1

● ZEB EATON

Eaton, Zebulon Vance "Red" b: 2/2/20, Cooleemee, N.C. d: 12/17/89, W.Palm Beach, Fla. BR/TR, 5'10", 185 lbs. Deb: 4/18/44

YEAR	TM/L	W	L	PCT	G	GS	CG	SH	SV	IP	H	HR	BB	SO	RAT	ERA	ERA+	OAV	OOB	BH	AVG	PB	PR	/A	PD	TPI
1944	Det-A	0	0	—	6	0	0	0	0	15^{2}	19	2	8	4	15.5	5.74	62	.322	.403	1	.100	-1	-4	-4	-0	-0.5
1945	*Det-A	4	2	.667	17	3	0	0	0	53^{1}	48	0	40	15	15.4	4.05	87	.247	.384	8	.250	2	-4	-3	0	-0.1
Total	2	4	2	.667	23	3	0	0	0	69	67	2	48	19	15.4	4.43	80	.265	.388	9	.214	2	-8	-7	-0	-0.6

● GARY EAVE

Eave, Gary Louis b: 7/22/63, Monroe, La. BR/TR, 6'4", 200 lbs. Deb: 4/12/88

YEAR	TM/L	W	L	PCT	G	GS	CG	SH	SV	IP	H	HR	BB	SO	RAT	ERA	ERA+	OAV	OOB	BH	AVG	PB	PR	/A	PD	TPI
1988	Atl-N	0	0	—	5	0	0	0	0	5	7	0	3	0	18.0	9.00	41	.333	.417	0	—	0	-3	-3	-0	-0.3
1989	Atl-N	2	0	1.000	3	3	0	0	0	20^{2}	15	0	12	9	12.2	1.31	279	.200	.318	0	.000	-1	5	5	-1	0.5
1990	Sea-A	0	3	.000	8	5	0	0	0	30	27	5	20	16	14.7	4.20	94	.241	.366	0	—	0	-1	-1	0	-0.1
Total	3	2	3	.400	16	8	0	0	0	55^{2}	49	5	35	25	14.1	3.56	107	.236	.354	0	.000	-1	1	2	-1	0.1

● **VALLIE EAVES** Eaves, Vallie Ennis "Chief" b: 9/6/11, Allen, Okla. d: 4/19/60, Norman, Okla. BR/TR, 6'2.5", 180 lbs. Deb: 9/12/35

YEAR TM/L	W	L	PCT	G	GS	CG	SH	SV	IP	H	HR	BB	SO	RAT	ERA	ERA+	OAV	OOB	BH	AVG	PB	PR	/A	PD	TPI
1935 Phi-A	1	2	.333	3	3	1	0	0	14	12	0	15	6	17.4	5.14	88	.240	.415	0	.000	-1	-1	-1	-0	-0.2
1939 Chi-A	0	1	.000	2	1	1	0	0	11^2	11	1	8	5	15.4	4.63	102	.250	.377	2	.333	0	-0	0	-0	0.0
1940 Chi-A	0	2	.000	5	3	0	0	0	18^2	22	2	24	11	22.7	6.75	66	.301	.480	0	.000	-1	-5	-5	-1	-0.6
1941 Chi-N	3	3	.500	12	7	4	0	0	58^2	56	4	21	24	12.3	3.53	99	.253	.327	2	.100	-1	1	-0	-1	-0.3
1942 Chi-N	0	0	—	2	0	0	0	0	3	4	0	2	0	21.0	9.00	36	.308	.438	0	—	0	-2	-2	-0	-0.2
Total 5	4	8	.333	24	14	6	0	0	106	105	7	70	46	15.4	4.58	86	.262	.379	4	.114	-3	-7	-8	-3	-1.3

● **EDDIE EAYRS** Eayrs, Edwin b: 11/10/1890, Blackstone, Mass. d: 11/30/69, Warwick, R.I. BL/TL, 5'7", 160 lbs. Deb: 6/30/13 ◆

YEAR TM/L	W	L	PCT	G	GS	CG	SH	SV	IP	H	HR	BB	SO	RAT	ERA	ERA+	OAV	OOB	BH	AVG	PB	PR	/A	PD	TPI
1913 Pit-N	0	0	—	2	0	0	0	0	8	8	0	6	5	15.8	2.25	134	.267	.389	1	.167	-0	1	1	-0	0.0
1920 Bos-N	1	2	.333	7	3	0	0	0	26^1	36	1	12	7	17.1	5.47	56	.346	.424	80	.328	2	-7	-7	1	-0.5
1921 Bos-N	0	0	—	2	0	0	0	0	4^2	9	0	9	1	34.7	17.36	21	.391	.563	1	.067	-2	-7	-7	-0	-0.7
Total 3	1	2	.333	11	3	0	0	0	39	53	1	27	13	18.9	6.23	50	.338	.441	83	.306	0	-13	-14	0	-1.2

● **HARRY ECCLES** Eccles, Harry Josiah "Bugs" b: 7/9/1893, Kennedy, N.Y. d: 6/2/55, Jamestown, N.Y. BL/TL, 6'2", 170 lbs. Deb: 9/13/15

YEAR TM/L	W	L	PCT	G	GS	CG	SH	SV	IP	H	HR	BB	SO	RAT	ERA	ERA+	OAV	OOB	BH	AVG	PB	PR	/A	PD	TPI
1915 Phi-A	0	1	.000	5	1	0	0	1	21	18	2	6	13	10.3	4.71	62	.240	.296	1	.167	-0	-4	-4	-1	-0.5

● **DENNIS ECKERSLEY** Eckersley, Dennis Lee b: 10/3/54, Oakland, Cal. BR/TR, 6'2", 190 lbs. Deb: 4/12/75

YEAR TM/L	W	L	PCT	G	GS	CG	SH	SV	IP	H	HR	BB	SO	RAT	ERA	ERA+	OAV	OOB	BH	AVG	PB	PR	/A	PD	TPI
1975 Cle-A	13	7	.650	34	24	6	2	2	186^2	147	16	90	152	11.8	2.60	145	.215	.312	0	—	0	24	24	-3	2.3
1976 Cle-A	13	12	.520	36	30	9	3	1	199^1	155	13	78	200	10.7	3.43	102	.214	.295	0	—	0	2	1	-1	0.1
1977 Cle-A★	14	13	.519	33	33	12	3	0	247^1	214	31	54	191	10.0	3.53	112	.231	**.278**	0	—	0	15	11	-3	0.9
1978 Bos-A	20	8	.714	35	35	16	3	0	268^1	258	30	71	162	11.3	2.99	138	.251	.304	0	—	0	23	34	-2	3.0
1979 Bos-A	17	10	.630	33	33	17	2	0	246^2	234	29	59	150	10.9	2.99	**148**	.250	.298	0	—	0	34	**39**	1	4.1
1980 Bos-A	12	14	.462	30	30	8	0	0	197^2	188	25	44	121	10.7	4.28	99	.248	.291	0	—	0	-5	-1	-1	-0.3
1981 Bos-A	9	8	.529	23	23	8	2	0	154	160	9	35	79	11.6	4.27	91	.267	.310	0	—	0	-10	-7	-1	-0.8
1982 Bos-A★	13	13	.500	33	33	11	3	0	224^1	228	31	43	127	11.0	3.73	115	.261	.297	0	—	0	9	14	-1	1.2
1983 Bos-A	9	13	.409	28	28	2	0	0	176^1	223	27	39	77	13.7	5.61	77	.303	.343	0	—	0	-30	-25	-1	-2.4
1984 Bos-A	4	4	.500	9	9	2	0	0	64^2	71	10	13	33	11.8	5.01	83	.284	.322	0	—	0	-7	-6	1	-0.8
*Chi-N	10	8	.556	24	24	2	0	0	160^1	152	11	36	81	10.8	3.03	129	.250	.296	6	.109	-3	10	16	1	1.5
1985 Chi-N	11	7	.611	25	25	6	2	0	169^1	145	15	19	117	8.9	3.08	129	.229	.255	7	.125	0	10	17	0	1.9
1986 Chi-N	6	11	.353	33	32	1	0	0	201	226	21	43	137	12.2	4.57	88	.285	.324	11	.159	1	-19	-12	-0	-1.1
1987 Oak-A	6	8	.429	54	2	0	0	16	115^2	99	11	17	113	9.3	3.03	136	.228	.262	0	—	0	18	14	-1	1.5
1988 *Oak-A★	4	2	.667	60	0	0	0	**45**	72^2	52	5	11	70	7.9	2.35	161	.198	.233	0	—	0	13	12	-1	1.1
1989 *Oak-A	4	0	1.000	51	0	0	0	33	57^2	32	5	3	55	5.6	1.56	236	.162	.178	0	—	0	15	14	-0	1.5
1990 *Oak-A★	4	2	.667	63	0	0	0	48	73^1	41	2	4	73	5.5	0.61	605	.160	.172	0	—	0	27	25	-2	2.5
1991 Oak-A★	5	4	.556	67	0	0	0	43	76	60	11	9	87	8.3	2.96	129	.208	.235	0	—	0	10	7	0	0.8
1992 *Oak-A★	7	1	.875	69	0	0	0	**51**	80	62	5	11	93	8.3	1.91	198	.211	.242	0	—	0	18	17	1	1.8
Total 18	181	145	.555	740	361	100	20	239	2971^1	2747	307	679	2118	10.6	3.43	117	.243	.290	24	.133	-1	154	196	-12	18.8

● **AL ECKERT** Eckert, Albert George "Obbie" b: 5/17/06, Milwaukee, Wis. d: 4/20/74, Milwaukee, Wis. BL/TL, 5'10", 174 lbs. Deb: 4/21/30

YEAR TM/L	W	L	PCT	G	GS	CG	SH	SV	IP	H	HR	BB	SO	RAT	ERA	ERA+	OAV	OOB	BH	AVG	PB	PR	/A	PD	TPI
1930 Cin-N	0	1	.000	2	1	0	0	0	5	7	0	4	1	19.8	7.20	67	.304	.407	0	.000	-0	-1	-1	0	-0.1
1931 Cin-N	0	1	.000	14	1	0	0	0	18^2	26	3	9	5	16.9	9.16	41	.325	.393	1	.333	0	-11	-11	-0	-1.1
1935 StL-N	0	0	—	2	0	0	0	0	3	7	0	1	1	24.0	12.00	34	.467	.500	0	—	0	-3	-3	-0	-0.3
Total 3	0	2	.000	18	2	0	0	0	26^2	40	3	14	7	18.2	9.11	44	.339	.409	1	.250	0	-15	-15	0	-1.5

● **CHARLIE ECKERT** Eckert, Charles William "Buzz" b: 8/8/1897, Philadelphia, Pa. d: 8/22/86, Trevose, Pa. BR/TR, 5'10.5", 165 lbs. Deb: 9/18/19

YEAR TM/L	W	L	PCT	G	GS	CG	SH	SV	IP	H	HR	BB	SO	RAT	ERA	ERA+	OAV	OOB	BH	AVG	PB	PR	/A	PD	TPI
1919 Phi-A	0	1	.000	2	1	1	0	0	16	17	1	3	6	11.3	3.94	87	.270	.303	1	.167	-0	-1	-1	0	-0.1
1920 Phi-A	0	0	—	2	0	0	0	0	5^2	8	0	1	1	15.9	4.76	84	.421	.476	0	.000	-0	-1	-0	-0	-0.1
1922 Phi-A	0	2	.000	21	0	0	0	0	50	61	7	23	15	15.3	4.68	91	.319	.395	1	.091	-1	-4	-2	2	-0.2
Total 3	0	3	.000	25	1	1	0	0	71^2	86	8	27	22	14.4	4.52	90	.315	.381	2	.111	-2	-5	-4	1	-0.4

● **DON EDDY** Eddy, Donald Eugene b: 10/25/46, Mason City, Iowa BR/TL, 5'11", 170 lbs. Deb: 9/07/70

YEAR TM/L	W	L	PCT	G	GS	CG	SH	SV	IP	H	HR	BB	SO	RAT	ERA	ERA+	OAV	OOB	BH	AVG	PB	PR	/A	PD	TPI
1970 Chi-A	0	0	—	7	0	0	0	0	11^2	10	0	6	9	12.3	2.31	168	.244	.340	0	—	0	2	2	0	0.2
1971 Chi-A	0	2	.000	22	0	0	0	0	22^2	19	3	19	14	15.1	2.38	151	.232	.376	1	1.000	1	3	3	-1	0.4
Total 2	0	2	.000	29	0	0	0	0	34^1	29	3	25	23	14.2	2.36	157	.236	.365	1	1.000	1	5	5	-1	0.6

● **STEVE EDDY** Eddy, Steven Allen b: 8/21/57, Sterling, Ill. BR/TR, 6'2", 185 lbs. Deb: 6/13/79

YEAR TM/L	W	L	PCT	G	GS	CG	SH	SV	IP	H	HR	BB	SO	RAT	ERA	ERA+	OAV	OOB	BH	AVG	PB	PR	/A	PD	TPI
1979 Cal-A	1	1	.500	7	4	0	0	0	32^1	36	1	20	7	16.1	4.73	86	.290	.397	0	—	0	-2	-2	0	-0.1

● **JOE EDELEN** Edelen, Benny Joe b: 9/16/55, Durant, Okla. BR/TR, 6', 165 lbs. Deb: 4/18/81

YEAR TM/L	W	L	PCT	G	GS	CG	SH	SV	IP	H	HR	BB	SO	RAT	ERA	ERA+	OAV	OOB	BH	AVG	PB	PR	/A	PD	TPI
1981 StL-N	1	0	1.000	13	0	0	0	0	17^1	29	2	3	10	17.1	9.35	38	.367	.398	1	.333	0	-11	-11	-0	-1.1
Cin-N	1	0	1.000	5	0	0	0	0	12^2	5	1	0	5	3.6	0.71	500	.128	.128	0	.000	-0	4	4	-1	0.4
Yr	2	0	1.000	18	0	0	0	0	30	34	3	3	15	11.1	5.70	62	.283	.301	1	.200	0	-7	-7	-1	-0.7
1982 Cin-N	0	0	—	9	0	0	0	0	15^1	22	2	8	11	17.6	8.80	42	.344	.417	1	.500	0	-9	-9	-0	-0.8
Total 2	2	0	1.000	27	0	0	0	0	45^1	56	5	11	26	13.5	6.75	53	.308	.351	2	.286	0	-16	-16	-1	-1.5

● **ED EDELEN** Edelen, Edward Joseph "Doc" b: 3/16/12, Bryantown, Md. d: 2/1/82, LaPlata, Md. BR/TR, 6', 191 lbs. Deb: 8/20/32

YEAR TM/L	W	L	PCT	G	GS	CG	SH	SV	IP	H	HR	BB	SO	RAT	ERA	ERA+	OAV	OOB	BH	AVG	PB	PR	/A	PD	TPI
1932 Was-A	0	0	—	2	0	0	0	0	1	0	0	6	0	54.0	27.00	16	.000	.600	0	—	0	-3	-3	-0	-0.2

● **JOHN EDELMAN** Edelman, John Rogers b: 7/27/35, Philadelphia, Pa. BR/TR, 6'3", 185 lbs. Deb: 6/02/55

YEAR TM/L	W	L	PCT	G	GS	CG	SH	SV	IP	H	HR	BB	SO	RAT	ERA	ERA+	OAV	OOB	BH	AVG	PB	PR	/A	PD	TPI
1955 Mil-N	0	0	—	5	0	0	0	0	5^2	7	0	8	3	23.8	11.12	34	.304	.484	0	—	0	-4	-5	0	-0.4

● **CHARLIE EDEN** Eden, Charles M. b: 1/18/1855, Lexington, Ky. d: 9/17/20, Cincinnati, Ohio BR/TR, Deb: 8/17/1877 ◆

YEAR TM/L	W	L	PCT	G	GS	CG	SH	SV	IP	H	HR	BB	SO	RAT	ERA	ERA+	OAV	OOB	BH	AVG	PB	PR	/A	PD	TPI
1884 Pit-a	0	1	.000	2	1	1	0	0	12	12	1	3	3	12.0	6.00	56	.255	.314	33	.270	1	-4	-4	-1	-0.3
1885 Pit-a	1	2	.333	4	1	0	0	0	15^2	22	0	3	5	14.4	5.17	62	.314	.342	103	.254	1	-3	-3	-1	-0.3
Total 2	1	3	.250	6	2	1	0	0	27^2	34	1	6	8	13.3	5.53	59	.291	.331	244	.261	1	-7	-7	-1	-0.6

● **TOM EDENS** Edens, Thomas Patrick b: 6/9/61, Ontario, Ore. BR/TR, 6'3", 185 lbs. Deb: 6/02/87

YEAR TM/L	W	L	PCT	G	GS	CG	SH	SV	IP	H	HR	BB	SO	RAT	ERA	ERA+	OAV	OOB	BH	AVG	PB	PR	/A	PD	TPI
1987 NY-N	0	0	—	2	2	0	0	0	8	15	2	4	4	21.4	6.75	56	.417	.475	0	.000	-0	-2	-3	0	-0.2
1990 Mil-A	4	5	.444	35	6	0	0	2	89	89	8	33	40	12.7	4.45	87	.262	.334	0	—	0	-5	-6	-1	-0.6
1991 Min-A	2	2	.500	8	6	0	0	0	33	34	2	10	19	12.0	4.09	104	.256	.308	0	—	0	0	1	0	0.1
1992 Min-A	6	3	.667	52	0	0	0	3	76^1	65	1	36	57	12.1	2.83	142	.236	.334	0	—	0	9	10	-1	0.9
Total 4	12	10	.545	97	14	0	0	5	206^1	203	13	83	120	12.7	3.88	103	.259	.334	0	.000	-0	2	2	-1	0.2

● **BUTCH EDGE** Edge, Claude Lee b: 7/18/56, Houston, Tex. BR/TR, 6'3", 203 lbs. Deb: 8/13/79

YEAR TM/L	W	L	PCT	G	GS	CG	SH	SV	IP	H	HR	BB	SO	RAT	ERA	ERA+	OAV	OOB	BH	AVG	PB	PR	/A	PD	TPI
1979 Tor-A	3	4	.429	9	9	1	0	0	51^2	60	6	24	19	14.8	5.23	83	.283	.359	0	—	0	-6	-5	-0	-0.5

● **BILL EDGERTON** Edgerton, William Albert b: 8/16/41, South Bend, Ind. BL/TL, 6'2", 185 lbs. Deb: 9/03/66

YEAR TM/L	W	L	PCT	G	GS	CG	SH	SV	IP	H	HR	BB	SO	RAT	ERA	ERA+	OAV	OOB	BH	AVG	PB	PR	/A	PD	TPI
1966 KC-A	0	1	.000	6	1	0	0	0	8^1	10	0	7	3	18.4	3.24	105	.303	.425	0	—	0	0	0	0	0.0
1967 KC-A	1	0	1.000	7	0	0	0	0	8^1	11	1	3	6	16.2	2.16	147	.324	.395	0	—	0	1	1	0	0.1
1969 Sea-A	0	1	.000	4	0	0	0	0	4	10	1	0	2	24.8	13.50	27	.455	.478	0	—	0	-4	-4	0	-0.4
Total 3	1	2	.333	17	1	0	0	0	20^2	31	2	10	11	18.7	4.79	70	.348	.426	0	—	0	-3	-3	1	-0.3

● **GEORGE EDMONDSON** Edmondson, George Henderson "Big Ed" b: 5/18/1896, Waxahachie, Tex. d: 7/11/73, Waco, Tex. BR/TR, 6'1", 179 lbs. Deb: 8/15/22

YEAR TM/L	W	L	PCT	G	GS	CG	SH	SV	IP	H	HR	BB	SO	RAT	ERA	ERA+	OAV	OOB	BH	AVG	PB	PR	/A	PD	TPI
1922 Cle-A	0	0	—	2	0	0	0	0	2	4	0	0	0	18.0	9.00	45	.444	.444	0	—	0	-1	-1	0	-0.1
1923 Cle-A	0	0	—	1	0	0	0	0	4	8	0	3	0	27.0	11.25	35	.444	.545	0	.000	-0	-3	-3	0	-0.3

YEAR	TM/L	W	L	PCT	G	GS	CG	SH	SV	IP	H	HR	BB	SO	RAT	ERA	ERA+	OAV	OOB	BH	AVG	PB	PR	/A	PD	TPI
1924	Cle-A	0	0	—	5	1	0	0	0	8	10	1	5	3	16.9	9.00	47	.294	.385	1	.333	0	-4	-4	-0	-0.4
Total	3	0	0	—	8	1	0	0	0	14	22	1	8	3	19.9	9.64	43	.361	.443	1	.250	-0	-9	-9	0	-0.8
● **PAUL EDMONDSON**	Edmondson, Paul Michael b: 2/12/43, Kansas City, Kan. d: 2/13/70, Santa Barbara, Cal. BR/TR, 6'5", 195 lbs. Deb: 6/20/69																									
1969	Chi-A	1	6	.143	14	13	1	0	0	87^2	72	5	39	46	11.8	3.70	104	.227	.319	5	.172	-1	-1	2	3	0.4
● **BOB EDMONDSON**	Edmondson, Robert E. b: 4/30/1879, Paris, Ky. d: 8/14/31, Lawrence, Kan. BR/TR, 5'11", 185 lbs. Deb: 9/15/06 ♦																									
1906	Was-A	0	1	.000	2	1	1	0	0	10	10	0	2	0	10.8	4.50	59	.263	.300	1	.333	0	-2	-2	0	-0.2
● **SAM EDMONSTON**	Edmonston, Samuel Sherwood "Big Sam" b: 8/30/1883, Washington, D.C. d: 4/12/79, Corpus Christi, Tex. BL/TL, 5'11.5", 185 lbs. Deb: 6/24/07																									
1907	Was-A	0	0	—	1	0	0	0	0	3	8	0	1	0	27.0	9.00	27	.487	.516	0	.000	-0	-2	-2	0	-0.2
● **EDWARDS**	Edwards Deb: 9/11/1875																									
1875	Atl-n	0	1	.000	1	1	0	0	0	2	6	0	0		27.0	*9.00*	26	.429	.429	1	.200	-0	-1	-1		-0.1
● **FOSTER EDWARDS**	Edwards, Foster Hamilton "Eddie" b: 9/1/03, Holstein, Iowa d: 1/4/80, Orleans, Mass. BR/TR, 6'3", 175 lbs. Deb: 7/02/25																									
1925	Bos-N	0	0	—	1	0	0	0	0	2	6	0	1	1	31.5	9.00	45	.545	.583	0	—	0	-1	-1	-0	-0.1
1926	Bos-N	2	0	1.000	3	3	1	0	0	25	20	0	13	4	11.9	0.72	492	.230	.330	0	.000	-1	9	8	-0	0.7
1927	Bos-N	2	8	.200	29	11	1	0	0	92	95	2	45	37	14.0	4.99	74	.274	.362	1	.045	-2	-11	-13	-1	-1.5
1928	Bos-N	2	1	.667	21	3	2	0	0	49^1	67	2	23	17	16.8	5.66	69	.327	.400	1	.091	-1	-9	-10	0	-1.0
1930	NY-A	0	0	—	2	0	0	0	0	1^2	5	0	2	1	37.8	21.60	20	.500	.583	0	—	0	-3	-3	-0	-0.3
Total	5	6	9	.400	56	17	4	0	0	170	193	4	84	60	14.9	4.76	79	.292	.377	2	.048	-4	-16	-19	-1	-2.2
● **JIM JOE EDWARDS**	Edwards, James Corbette "Little Joe" b: 12/14/1894, Banner, Miss. d: 1/19/65, Sarepta, Miss. BR/TL, 6'2", 185 lbs. Deb: 5/14/22																									
1922	Cle-A	3	8	.273	25	7	0	0	0	92^2	113	1	40	44	15.3	4.47	90	.313	.389	2	.087	-2	-4	-5	-1	-0.7
1923	Cle-A	10	10	.500	38	21	8	1	1	179^1	200	5	75	68	14.1	3.71	107	.286	.359	7	.119	-5	5	5	-1	-0.1
1924	Cle-A	4	3	.571	10	7	5	1	0	57	64	3	34	15	15.5	2.84	150	.305	.402	3	.150	-1	9	9	0	0.8
1925	Cle-A	0	3	.000	13	3	1	0	0	36	60	0	23	12	21.0	8.25	54	.382	.464	1	.111	-1	-15	-15	1	-1.4
	Chi-A	1	2	.333	9	4	1	1	0	45^1	46	4	23	20	13.9	3.97	105	.263	.352	3	.176	-1	2	1	1	0.1
	Yr	1	5	.167	22	7	2	1	0	81^1	106	4	46	32	16.9	5.86	73	.318	.403	4	.154	-2	-13	-14	2	-1.3
1926	Chi-A	6	9	.400	32	16	8	3	1	142	140	4	63	41	12.9	4.18	92	.264	.343	5	.109	-3	-3	-5	-1	-0.9
1928	Cin-N	2	2	.500	18	1	0	0	2	32	43	1	20	11	17.7	7.59	52	.347	.438	3	.300	0	-13	-13	-1	-1.3
Total	6	26	37	.413	145	59	23	6	4	584^1	666	18	278	211	14.7	4.37	92	.295	.376	24	.130	-13	-19	-23	-1	-3.5
● **SHERMAN EDWARDS**	Edwards, Sherman Stanley b: 7/25/09, Mt.Ida, Ark. d: 3/8/92, ElDorado, Ark. BR/TR, 6', 165 lbs. Deb: 9/21/34																									
1934	Cin-N	0	0	—	1	0	0	0	0	3	4	0	1	1	15.0	3.00	136	.333	.385	0	.000	-0	0	0	0	0.0
● **WAYNE EDWARDS**	Edwards, Wayne Maurice b: 3/7/64, Burbank, Cal. BL/TL, 6'5", 185 lbs. Deb: 9/11/89																									
1989	Chi-A	0	0	—	7	0	0	0	0	7^1	7	1	3	9	12.3	3.68	103	.269	.345	0	—	0	0	0	0	0.1
1990	Chi-A	5	3	.625	42	5	0	0	2	95	81	6	41	63	11.8	3.22	119	.234	.321	0	—	0	7	6	0	0.7
1991	Chi-A	0	2	.000	13	0	0	0	0	23^1	22	2	17	12	15.0	3.86	103	.259	.382	0	—	0	1	0	-0	0.0
Total	3	5	5	.500	62	5	0	0	2	125^2	110	9	61	84	12.5	3.37	114	.241	.334	0	—	0	8	7	0	0.8
● **HARRY EELLS**	Eells, Harry Archibald "Slippery" b: 2/14/1881, Ida Grove, Iowa d: 10/15/40, Los Angeles, Cal. BR/TR, 6'1", 195 lbs. Deb: 4/22/06																									
1906	Cle-A	4	5	.444	14	8	6	1	0	86^1	77	1	48	35	13.4	2.61	101	.242	.348	6	.188	0	1	0	1	0.1
● **WISH EGAN**	Egan, Aloysius Jerome b: 6/16/1881, Evart, Mich. d: 4/13/51, Detroit, Mich. BR/TR, 6'3", 185 lbs. Deb: 9/03/02																									
1902	Det-A	0	2	.000	3	3	2	0	0	22	23	0	6	0	11.9	2.86	127	.269	.317	2	.250	-0	2	2	1	0.3
1905	StL-N	6	15	.286	23	19	18	0	0	171^1	189	2	39	29	12.4	3.57	83	.285	.333	6	.102	-3	-11	-11	5	-1.0
1906	StL-N	2	9	.182	16	12	7	0	0	86^1	97	3	27	23	13.1	4.59	57	.278	.333	2	.069	-2	-19	-19	1	-2.0
Total	3	8	26	.235	42	34	27	0	0	279^2	309	5	72	52	12.6	3.83	76	.282	.332	10	.104	-5	-28	-28	6	-2.7
● **JIM EGAN**	Egan, James K. "Troy Terrier" b: 1858, Derby, Conn. d: 9/26/1884, New Haven, Conn. TL , Deb: 5/15/1882 ♦																									
1882	Tro-N	4	6	.400	12	10	10	0	0	100	133	2	24	20	14.1	4.14	68	.315	.352	23	.200	-2	-14	-15	-2	-1.6
● **RIP EGAN**	Egan, John Joseph b: 7/9/1871, Philadelphia, Pa. d: 12/22/50, Cranston, R.I. 5'11", 168 lbs. Deb: 4/30/1894 U																									
1894	Was-N	0	0	—	1	0	0	0	0	5	8	1	2	2	18.0	10.80	49	.357	.410	0	.000	-0	-3	-3	0	-0.2
● **DICK EGAN**	Egan, Richard Wallis b: 3/24/37, Berkeley, Cal. BL/TL, 6'4", 193 lbs. Deb: 4/09/63 C																									
1963	Det-A	0	1	.000	20	0	0	0	0	21	25	4	3	16	12.0	5.14	73	.287	.311	0	—	0	-4	-3	0	-0.3
1964	Det-A	0	0	—	23	0	0	0	2	34^1	33	4	17	21	13.4	4.46	82	.246	.336	0	.000	-0	-3	-3	1	-0.3
1966	Cal-A	0	0	—	11	0	0	0	0	14^1	17	2	6	11	14.4	4.40	76	.309	.377	0	.000	-0	-2	-2	-0	-0.2
1967	LA-N	1	1	.500	20	0	0	0	0	31^2	34	3	15	20	15.1	6.25	50	.272	.368	0	.000	-0	-10	-11	-1	-1.2
Total	4	1	2	.333	74	0	0	0	2	101^1	109	13	41	68	13.8	5.15	67	.272	.347	0	.000	-1	-18	-19	0	-2.0
● **BRUCE EGLOFF**	Egloff, Bruce Edward b: 4/10/65, Denver, Colo. BR/TR, 6'2", 215 lbs. Deb: 4/13/91																									
1991	Cle-A	0	0	—	6	0	0	0	0	5^2	8	0	4	8	19.1	4.76	87	.333	.429	0	—	0	-0	-0	0	0.0
● **HOWARD EHMKE**	Ehmke, Howard Jonathan "Bob" b: 4/24/1894, Silver Creek, N.Y. d: 3/17/59, Philadelphia, Pa. BR/TR, 6'3", 190 lbs. Deb: 4/12/15																									
1915	Buf-F	0	2	.000	18	2	0	0	0	53^2	69	2	25	18	16.6	5.53	56	.325	.409	0	.000	-2	-15	-14	2	-1.5
1916	Det-A	3	1	.750	5	4	4	0	0	37^1	34	0	15	15	11.8	3.13	91	.252	.327	2	.143	-1	-1	-1	1	-0.1
1917	Det-A	10	15	.400	35	25	13	4	2	206	174	3	88	90	11.7	2.97	89	.243	.330	17	.246	2	-7	-7	2	-0.3
1919	Det-A	17	10	.630	33	31	20	2	0	248^2	255	5	107	79	13.3	3.18	100	.274	.353	23	.253	3	1	0	4	0.7
1920	Det-A	15	18	.455	38	33	23	2	3	268^1	250	8	124	98	13.0	3.25	115	.253	.344	25	.238	2	16	14	6	2.2
1921	Det-A	13	14	.481	30	22	13	1	0	196^1	220	15	81	68	14.4	4.54	94	.286	.364	21	.284	2	-6	-6	1	-0.2
1922	Det-A	17	17	.500	45	30	16	1	1	279^2	299	12	101	108	13.6	4.22	92	.281	.356	16	.157	-3	-5	-10	2	-1.2
1923	Bos-A	20	17	.541	43	39	28	2	3	316^2	318	12	119	121	13.0	3.78	109	.272	.349	25	.223	-2	7	12	5	1.5
1924	Bos-A	19	17	.528	45	36	26	4	4	**315**	324	9	81	119	11.9	3.46	126	.265	.316	28	.222	-3	27	32	2	3.1
1925	Bos-A	9	20	.310	34	31	**22**	0	1	260^2	285	8	85	95	13.2	3.73	122	.285	.348	13	.148	-6	19	24	5	2.2
1926	Bos-A	3	10	.231	14	14	7	1	0	97^1	115	3	45	38	15.2	5.46	75	.303	.382	5	.147	-1	-16	-15	1	-1.4
	Phi-A	12	4	.750	20	18	10	1	0	147^1	125	1	50	55	10.9	2.81	148	.232	.302	7	.152	-2	20	22	0	2.1
	Yr	15	14	.517	34	32	17	2	0	244^2	240	4	95	93	12.5	3.86	107	.260	.332	12	.150	-3	4	7	1	0.7
1927	Phi-A	12	10	.545	30	27	10	1	0	189^2	200	13	60	68	13.0	4.22	101	.281	.349	14	.206	-1	-2	1	3	0.2
1928	Phi-A	9	8	.529	23	18	5	1	0	139^1	135	6	44	34	11.8	3.62	111	.254	.316	11	.239	1	7	6	0	0.8
1929	*Phi-A	7	2	.778	11	8	2	0	0	54^2	48	2	15	20	10.5	3.29	129	.233	.288	2	.105	-2	6	6	0	0.4
1930	Phi-A	0	1	.000	3	1	0	0	0	10	22	4	2	4	24.3	11.70	40	.458	.509	1	.333	0	-8	-8	0	-0.6
Total	15	166	166	.500	427	339	199	20	14	2820^2	2873	103	1042	1030	12.9	3.75	105	.271	.343	210	.208	-11	44	53	32	7.9
● **RED EHRET**	Ehret, Philip Sydney b: 8/31/1868, Louisville, Ky. d: 7/28/40, Cincinnati, Ohio BR/TR, 6', 175 lbs. Deb: 7/07/1888 ♦																									
1888	KC-a	3	2	.600	7	6	5	0	0	52	58	1	22	12	14.4	3.98	86	.272	.348	12	.190	-1	-5	-3	1	-0.3
1889	Lou-a	10	29	.256	45	38	35	1	0	364	441	11	115	135	14.2	4.80	80	.290	.347	65	.252	2	-38	-38	3	-2.7
1890	*Lou-a	25	14	.641	43	38	35	4	2	359	351	5	79	174	11.2	2.53	152	.248	.296	31	.212	-3	53	53	-3	4.4
1891	Lou-a	13	13	.500	26	24	23	2	0	220^2	225	2	70	76	12.5	3.47	105	.255	.318	22	.242	1	6	5	0	0.5
1892	Pit-N	16	20	.444	39	36	32	0	0	316	290	7	83	101	11.3	2.65	124	.234	.294	34	.258	3	22	23	-4	2.1
1893	Pit-N	18	18	.500	39	35	32	**4**	0	314^1	322	3	115	70	13.2	3.44	133	.257	.331	24	.176	-5	43	39	1	2.9
1894	Pit-N	19	21	.475	46	38	31	1	0	346^2	441	12	128	102	15.0	5.14	102	.306	.367	23	.170	-10	7	4	-1	-0.6

YEAR	TM/L	W	L	PCT	G	GS	CG	SH	SV	IP	H	HR	BB	SO	RAT	ERA	ERA+	OAV	OOB	BH	AVG	PB	PR	/A	PD	TPI
1895	StL-N	6	19	.240	37	32	18	0	0	231^{2}	360	11	88	55	17.8	6.02	80	.349	.405	21	.219	-2	-32	-30	0	-2.5
1896	Cin-N	18	14	.563	34	33	29	2	0	276^{2}	298	5	74	60	12.4	3.42	135	.273	.324	20	.196	-3	29	37	1	3.0
1897	Cin-N	8	10	.444	34	19	11	0	2	184^{1}	256	3	47	43	15.4	4.78	95	.326	.374	13	.197	-3	-10	-5	-1	-0.7
1898	Lou-N	3	7	.300	12	10	9	0	0	89	130	3	20	20	15.5	5.76	62	.337	.375	9	.225	1	-21	-22	-1	-1.9
Total	11	139	167	.454	362	309	260	14	4	2754^{1}	3172	63	841	848	13.6	4.02	105	.282	.339	274	.217	-20	55	62	-4	4.2

● RUBE EHRHARDT Ehrhardt, Welton Claude b: 11/20/1894, Beecher, Ill. d: 4/27/80, Chicago Heights, Ill. BR/TR, 6'2", 190 lbs. Deb: 7/18/24

YEAR	TM/L	W	L	PCT	G	GS	CG	SH	SV	IP	H	HR	BB	SO	RAT	ERA	ERA+	OAV	OOB	BH	AVG	PB	PR	/A	PD	TPI
1924	Bro-N	5	3	.625	15	9	6	2	0	83^{2}	71	5	17	13	9.6	2.26	166	.232	.275	4	.138	-2	15	14	-2	1.1
1925	Bro-N	10	14	.417	36	24	12	0	1	207^{2}	239	10	62	47	13.2	5.03	83	.293	.345	15	.211	2	-17	-20	4	-1.3
1926	Bro-N	2	5	.286	44	1	0	0	4	97	101	5	35	25	12.6	3.90	98	.275	.338	6	.250	0	-1	-1	-2	-0.2
1927	Bro-N	3	7	.300	46	3	2	0	2	95^{2}	90	3	37	22	12.2	3.57	111	.264	.341	6	.250	1	4	4	3	0.8
1928	Bro-N	1	3	.250	28	2	1	0	2	54	74	1	27	12	17.0	4.67	85	.352	.429	4	.286	0	-4	-4	1	-0.3
1929	Cin-N	1	2	.333	24	1	1	1	1	49^{1}	58	2	22	9	14.8	4.74	96	.305	.380	2	.182	-0	-0	-1	1	-0.1
Total	6	22	34	.393	193	40	22	3	10	587^{1}	633	26	200	128	12.9	4.15	97	.284	.345	37	.214	1	-4	-7	5	0.0

● HACK EIBEL Eibel, Henry Hack b: 12/6/1893, Brooklyn, N.Y. d: 10/16/45, Macon, Ga. BL/TL, 5'11", 220 lbs. Deb: 6/13/12 ♦

YEAR	TM/L	W	L	PCT	G	GS	CG	SH	SV	IP	H	HR	BB	SO	RAT	ERA	ERA+	OAV	OOB	BH	AVG	PB	PR	/A	PD	TPI
1920	Bos-A	0	0	—	3	0	0	0	0	10^{1}	10	0	3	5	11.3	3.48	105	.270	.325	8	.186	-0	0	0	-0	0.0

● JUAN EICHELBERGER Eichelberger, Juan Tyrone b: 10/21/53, St.Louis, Mo. BR/TR, 6'3", 205 lbs. Deb: 9/07/78

YEAR	TM/L	W	L	PCT	G	GS	CG	SH	SV	IP	H	HR	BB	SO	RAT	ERA	ERA+	OAV	OOB	BH	AVG	PB	PR	/A	PD	TPI
1978	SD-N	0	0	—	3	0	0	0	0	3^{1}	4	0	2	2	16.2	10.80	31	.267	.353	0	—	0	-3	-3	0	-0.3
1979	SD-N	1	1	.500	3	3	1	0	0	21	15	1	11	12	11.1	3.43	103	.211	.317	2	.400	1	1	0	-0	0.1
1980	SD-N	4	2	.667	15	13	0	0	0	88^{2}	73	8	55	43	13.1	3.65	94	.233	.350	3	.111	-1	-1	-2	-1	-0.4
1981	SD-N	8	8	.500	25	24	3	1	0	141^{1}	136	5	74	81	13.6	3.50	93	.259	.353	4	.087	-3	-0	-4	1	-0.6
1982	SD-N	7	14	.333	31	24	8	0	0	177^{2}	171	23	72	74	12.4	4.20	81	.251	.325	5	.091	-2	-12	-15	-1	-1.8
1983	Cle-A	4	11	.267	28	15	2	0	0	134	132	10	59	56	13.0	4.90	86	.259	.338	0	—	0	-13	-10	-1	-1.1
1988	Atl-N	2	0	1.000	20	0	0	0	0	37^{1}	44	3	10	13	13.0	3.86	95	.297	.342	0	.000	-0	-2	-1	1	0.0
Total	7	26	36	.419	125	79	14	1	0	603^{1}	575	50	283	281	12.9	4.10	87	.254	.339	14	.103	-4	-29	-35	-2	-4.1

● MARK EICHHORN Eichhorn, Mark Anthony b: 11/21/60, San Jose, Cal. BR/TR, 6'4", 200 lbs. Deb: 8/30/82

YEAR	TM/L	W	L	PCT	G	GS	CG	SH	SV	IP	H	HR	BB	SO	RAT	ERA	ERA+	OAV	OOB	BH	AVG	PB	PR	/A	PD	TPI
1982	Tor-A	0	3	.000	7	7	0	0	0	38	40	4	14	16	12.8	5.45	82	.260	.321	0	—	0	-6	-4	-1	-0.6
1986	Tor-A	14	6	.700	69	0	0	0	10	157	105	8	45	166	9.0	1.72	245	.191	.261	0	—	0	**43**	**44**	2	4.4
1987	Tor-A	10	6	.625	**89**	0	0	0	4	127^{2}	110	14	52	96	11.8	3.17	142	.234	.318	0	—	0	18	19	2	2.0
1988	Tor-A	0	3	.000	37	0	0	0	1	66^{2}	79	3	27	28	15.1	4.18	94	.304	.382	0	—	0	-2	-2	1	-0.1
1989	Atl-N	5	5	.500	45	0	0	0	0	68^{1}	70	6	19	49	11.9	4.35	84	.275	.327	0	.000	-0	-6	-5	2	-0.4
1990	Cal-A	2	5	.286	60	0	0	0	13	84^{2}	98	2	23	69	13.5	3.08	124	.289	.345	0	—	0	8	7	1	0.9
1991	Cal-A	3	3	.500	70	0	0	0	1	81^{2}	63	2	13	49	8.6	1.98	207	.219	.257	0	—	0	19	19	2	2.1
1992	Cal-A	2	4	.333	42	0	0	0	2	56^{2}	51	2	18	42	11.0	2.38	164	.238	.297	0	—	0	10	10	1	1.1
	*Tor-A	2	0	1.000	23	0	0	0	0	31	35	1	7	19	12.8	4.35	94	.285	.333	0	—	0	-1	-1	1	-0.1
	Yr	4	4	.500	65	0	0	0	2	87^{2}	86	3	25	61	11.6	3.08	129	.253	.308	0	—	0	8	9	2	1.0
Total	8	38	35	.521	442	7	0	0	31	711^{2}	651	42	218	534	11.4	3.02	136	.245	.310	0	.000	-0	82	86	10	9.3

● DAVE EILAND Eiland, David William b: 7/5/66, Dade City, Fla. BR/TR, 6'3", 210 lbs. Deb: 8/03/88

YEAR	TM/L	W	L	PCT	G	GS	CG	SH	SV	IP	H	HR	BB	SO	RAT	ERA	ERA+	OAV	OOB	BH	AVG	PB	PR	/A	PD	TPI
1988	NY-A	0	0	—	3	3	0	0	0	12^{2}	15	6	4	7	14.9	6.39	62	.294	.368	0	—	0	-3	-3	0	-0.3
1989	NY-A	1	3	.250	6	6	0	0	0	34^{1}	44	5	13	11	15.5	5.77	67	.328	.396	0	—	0	-7	-7	-1	-0.7
1990	NY-A	2	1	.667	5	5	0	0	0	30^{1}	31	2	5	16	10.7	3.56	111	.254	.283	0	—	0	1	1	-0	0.1
1991	NY-A	2	5	.286	18	13	0	0	0	72^{2}	87	10	23	18	14.0	5.33	78	.302	.360	0	—	0	-10	-10	-2	-1.1
1992	SD-N	0	2	.000	7	7	0	0	0	27	33	1	5	10	12.7	5.67	64	.287	.317	1	.111	1	-6	-6	0	-0.6
Total	5	5	11	.313	39	34	0	0	0	177	210	24	50	62	13.6	5.24	76	.296	.348	1	.111	1	-26	-25	-3	-2.6

● DAVE EILERS Eilers, David Louis b: 12/3/36, Oldenburg, Tex. BR/TR, 5'11", 188 lbs. Deb: 7/27/64

YEAR	TM/L	W	L	PCT	G	GS	CG	SH	SV	IP	H	HR	BB	SO	RAT	ERA	ERA+	OAV	OOB	BH	AVG	PB	PR	/A	PD	TPI
1964	Mil-N	0	0	—	6	0	0	0	0	7^{2}	11	1	1	1	15.3	4.70	75	.333	.371	0	—	0	-1	-1	-0	-0.1
1965	Mil-N	0	0	—	6	0	0	0	0	3^{2}	8	1	0	1	19.6	12.27	29	.421	.421	0	—	0	-4	-4	0	-0.4
	NY-N	1	1	.500	11	0	0	0	2	18	20	2	4	9	13.0	4.00	88	.274	.329	1	1.000	0	-1	-1	-0	-0.1
	Yr	1	1	.500	17	0	0	0	2	21^{2}	28	3	4	10	14.1	5.40	65	.304	.347	1	1.000	0	-4	-5	-0	-0.5
1966	NY-N	1	1	.500	23	0	0	0	0	34^{2}	39	7	7	14	12.2	4.67	78	.287	.326	0	.000	-0	-4	-4	1	-0.4
1967	Hou-N	6	4	.600	35	0	0	0	1	59^{1}	68	3	17	27	13.3	3.94	84	.296	.352	0	.000	-1	-4	-4	-0	-0.5
Total	4	8	6	.571	81	0	0	0	3	123^{1}	146	14	29	52	13.3	4.45	78	.297	.345	1	.111	-0	-13	-14	-0	-1.5

● JAKE EISENHART Eisenhart, Jacob Henry b: 10/3/22, Perkasie, Pa. d: 12/20/87, Huntingdon, Pa. BL/TL, 6'3.5", 195 lbs. Deb: 6/10/44

YEAR	TM/L	W	L	PCT	G	GS	CG	SH	SV	IP	H	HR	BB	SO	RAT	ERA	ERA+	OAV	OOB	BH	AVG	PB	PR	/A	PD	TPI
1944	Cin-N	0	0	—	1	0	0	0	0	0^{1}	0	0	1	0	27.0	0.00	—	.000	.500	0	—	0	0	0	0	0.0

● HARRY EISENSTAT Eisenstat, Harry b: 10/10/15, Brooklyn, N.Y. BL/TL, 5'11", 185 lbs. Deb: 5/19/35

YEAR	TM/L	W	L	PCT	G	GS	CG	SH	SV	IP	H	HR	BB	SO	RAT	ERA	ERA+	OAV	OOB	BH	AVG	PB	PR	/A	PD	TPI
1935	Bro-N	0	1	.000	2	0	0	0	0	4^{2}	9	0	2	2	21.2	13.50	29	.429	.478	0	.000	-0	-5	-5	1	-0.4
1936	Bro-N	1	2	.333	5	2	1	0	0	14^{1}	22	1	6	5	17.6	5.65	73	.344	.400	1	.333	0	-3	-2	0	-0.2
1937	Bro-N	3	3	.500	13	4	0	0	0	47^{2}	61	2	11	12	13.8	3.97	102	.308	.348	0	.000	-1	-0	0	1	0.0
1938	Det-A	9	6	.600	32	9	5	0	4	125^{1}	131	7	29	37	11.6	3.73	134	.266	.308	5	.139	-1	15	18	1	1.6
1939	Det-A	2	2	.500	10	2	1	0	0	29^{2}	39	3	9	6	14.6	6.98	70	.315	.361	3	.375	1	-8	-7	1	-0.5
	Cle-A	6	7	.462	26	11	4	1	2	103^{2}	109	8	23	38	11.5	3.30	133	.265	.304	8	.250	1	15	13	-1	1.1
	Yr	8	9	.471	36	13	5	1	2	133^{1}	148	11	32	44	12.2	4.12	110	.277	.317	11	.275	1	7	6	-0	0.6
1940	Cle-A	1	4	.200	27	3	0	0	4	71^{2}	78	6	12	27	11.3	3.14	134	.282	.311	6	.273	1	**10**	9	-0	0.9
1941	Cle-A	1	1	.500	21	0	0	0	2	34	43	2	16	11	16.1	4.24	93	.312	.391	2	.333	1	-0	-1	-1	-0.1
1942	Cle-A	2	1	.667	29	1	0	0	2	47^{2}	58	1	6	19	12.1	2.45	140	.304	.325	1	.250	0	6	5	-0	0.5
Total	8	25	27	.481	165	32	11	1	14	478^{2}	550	30	114	157	12.6	3.84	114	.287	.328	26	.211	1	30	29	0	2.9

● ED EITELJORG Eiteljorg, Edward Henry b: 10/14/1871, Berlin, Germany d: 12/7/42, Greencastle, Ind. BR/TR, 6'2", 190 lbs. Deb: 5/02/1890

YEAR	TM/L	W	L	PCT	G	GS	CG	SH	SV	IP	H	HR	BB	SO	RAT	ERA	ERA+	OAV	OOB	BH	AVG	PB	PR	/A	PD	TPI
1890	Chi-N	0	1	.000	1	1	0	0	0	2	5	0	1	1	27.0	22.50	16	.458	.503	0	.000	-0	-4	-4	-0	-0.3
1891	Was-a	1	5	.167	8	7	6	0	0	61^{1}	79	3	41	23	18.9	6.16	61	.302	.414	5	.192	-1	-17	-17	2	-1.2
Total	2	1	6	.143	9	8	6	0	0	63^{1}	84	3	42	24	19.2	6.68	56	.308	.417	5	.185	-1	-21	-21	1	-1.5

● HEINIE ELDER Elder, Henry Knox b: 8/23/1890, Seattle, Wash. d: 11/13/58, Long Beach, Cal. BL/TL, 6'2", 200 lbs. Deb: 7/07/13

YEAR	TM/L	W	L	PCT	G	GS	CG	SH	SV	IP	H	HR	BB	SO	RAT	ERA	ERA+	OAV	OOB	BH	AVG	PB	PR	/A	PD	TPI
1913	Det-A	0	0	—	1	0	0	0	0	3^{1}	4	0	5	0	24.3	8.10	36	.286	.474	0	.000	-0	-2	-2	-0	-0.2

● CAL ELDRED Eldred, Calvin John b: 11/24/67, Cedar Rapids, Iowa BR/TR, 6'4", 215 lbs. Deb: 9/24/91

YEAR	TM/L	W	L	PCT	G	GS	CG	SH	SV	IP	H	HR	BB	SO	RAT	ERA	ERA+	OAV	OOB	BH	AVG	PB	PR	/A	PD	TPI
1991	Mil-A	2	0	1.000	3	3	0	0	0	16	20	2	6	10	14.6	4.50	88	.299	.356	0	—	0	-1	-1	-0	0.0
1992	Mil-A	11	2	.846	14	14	2	1	0	100^{1}	76	4	23	62	9.1	1.79	213	.207	.257	0	—	0	24	23	-0	2.6
Total	2	13	2	.867	17	17	2	1	0	116^{1}	96	6	29	72	9.8	2.17	177	.221	.273	0	—	0	23	22	-1	2.6

● HOD ELLER Eller, Horace Owen b: 7/5/1894, Muncie, Ind. d: 7/18/61, Indianapolis, Ind BR/TR, 5'11.5", 185 lbs. Deb: 4/16/17

YEAR	TM/L	W	L	PCT	G	GS	CG	SH	SV	IP	H	HR	BB	SO	RAT	ERA	ERA+	OAV	OOB	BH	AVG	PB	PR	/A	PD	TPI
1917	Cin-N	10	5	.667	37	11	7	1	1	152^{1}	131	2	37	77	10.1	2.36	111	.239	.290	6	.133	-2	6	4	-2	0.1
1918	Cin-N	16	12	.571	37	22	14	0	1	217^{2}	205	1	59	84	11.2	2.36	113	.253	.309	11	.157	-2	10	8	-4	0.1
1919	*Cin-N	19	9	.679	38	30	16	7	2	248^{1}	216	7	50	137	9.8	2.39	116	.238	.281	26	.280	7	14	11	-3	1.6
1920	Cin-N	13	12	.520	35	22	15	1	0	210^{1}	208	6	52	76	11.3	2.95	103	.266	.315	22	.253	1	4	2	-1	0.2
1921	Cin-N	2	2	.500	13	3	0	0	1	34^{1}	46	3	15	7	16.0	4.98	72	.322	.386	3	.231	0	-5	-5	-1	-0.6
Total	5	60	40	.600	160	88	52	9	5	863	806	19	213	381	10.8	2.62	108	.253	.303	68	.221	4	30	19	-11	1.4

YEAR	TM/L	W	L	PCT	G	GS	CG	SH	SV	IP	H	HR	BB	SO	RAT	ERA	ERA+	OAV	OOB	BH	AVG	PB	PR	/A	PD	TPI
● **JOE ELLICK**	Ellick, Joseph J. b: 4/3/1854, Cincinnati, Ohio d: 4/21/23, Kansas City, Kan. 5'10", 162 lbs. Deb: 5/13/1875 MU♦																									
1878	Mil-N	0	1	.000	1	0	0	0	0	3	1	0	1	0	6.0	3.00	88	.100	.182	2	.154	-0	-0	-0	-0	0.0
● **BRUCE ELLINGSEN**	Ellingsen, Harold Bruce b: 4/26/49, Pocatello, Idaho BL/TL, 6', 180 lbs. Deb: 7/04/74																									
1974	Cle-A	1	1	.500	16	2	0	0	0	42	45	5	17	16	13.3	3.21	112	.278	.346	0	—	0	2	2	-0	0.2
● **CLAUDE ELLIOTT**	Elliott, Claude Judson "Chaucer" or "Old Pardee" b: 11/17/1879, Pardeeville, Wis. d: 6/21/23, Pardeeville, Wis. BR/TR, 6', 190 lbs. Deb: 4/16/04																									
1904	Cin-N	3	1	.750	9	6	4	1	0	57^{2}	53	1	23	19	12.5	2.97	99	.247	.331	5	.208	1	-1	-0	0	0.1
	NY-N	0	1	.000	3	1	1	0	0	15	21	2	3	8	14.4	3.00	91	.328	.358	1	.200	0	-0	-0	-1	-0.1
	Yr	3	2	.600	12	7	5	1	0	72^{2}	74	3	26	27	12.4	2.97	97	.261	.324	6	.207	1	-2	-1	-1	0.0
1905	NY-N	0	1	.000	10	2	2	0	**6**	38	41	3	12	20	12.8	4.03	73	.270	.327	3	.188	-0	-4	-5	1	-0.5
Total	2	3	3	.500	22	9	7	1	6	110^{2}	115	6	38	47	12.8	3.33	87	.267	.333	9	.200	1	-6	-5	0	-0.5
● **HAL ELLIOTT**	Elliott, Harold William b: 5/29/1899, Mt.Clemens, Mich. d: 4/25/63, Honolulu, Hawaii BR/TR, 6'1.5", 170 lbs. Deb: 4/19/29																									
1929	Phi-N	3	7	.300	40	8	2	0	2	114^{1}	146	5	59	32	16.1	6.06	86	.313	.390	5	.167	-1	-17	-11	1	-0.9
1930	Phi-N	6	11	.353	**48**	11	2	0	0	117^{1}	191	7	58	37	19.2	7.67	71	.382	.447	3	.094	-3	-35	-29	2	-2.6
1931	Phi-N	0	2	.000	16	4	0	0	2	33	46	5	19	8	18.0	9.55	44	.338	.423	1	.111	-0	-21	-19	0	-1.8
1932	Phi-N	2	4	.333	16	7	0	0	0	57^{2}	70	5	38	13	16.9	5.77	76	.297	.394	3	.167	-0	-12	-9	-1	-1.0
Total	4	11	24	.314	120	30	4	0	4	322^{1}	453	22	174	90	17.6	6.95	73	.338	.415	12	.135	-5	-85	-68	2	-6.3
● **GLENN ELLIOTT**	Elliott, Herbert Glenn "Lefty" b: 11/11/19, Sapulpa, Okla d: 7/27/69, Portland, Ore. BB/TL, 5'10", 170 lbs. Deb: 4/17/47																									
1947	Bos-N	0	1	.000	11	0	0	0	1	19	18	4	11	8	13.7	4.74	82	.269	.372	1	.500	0	-1	-2	0	-0.1
1948	Bos-N	1	0	1.000	1	1	0	0	0	3	5	0	1	2	18.0	3.00	128	.357	.400	0	.000	-0	0	0	-0	0.0
1949	Bos-N	3	4	.429	22	6	1	0	0	68^{1}	70	7	27	15	12.8	3.95	96	.269	.338	1	.059	-1	1	-1	1	-0.2
Total	3	4	5	.444	34	7	1	0	1	90^{1}	93	11	39	25	13.2	4.08	93	.273	.347	2	.095	-1	-0	-3	1	-0.3
● **JUMBO ELLIOTT**	Elliott, James Thomas b: 10/22/1900, St.Louis, Mo. d: 1/7/70, Terre Haute, Ind. BR/TL, 6'3", 235 lbs. Deb: 4/21/23																									
1923	StL-A	0	0	—	1	0	0	0	0	1	1	0	3	0	36.0	27.00	15	.333	.667	0	—	0	-3	-3	-0	-0.2
1925	Bro-N	0	2	.000	3	1	0	0	0	10^{2}	17	0	9	3	22.8	8.44	50	.362	.474	0	.000	-1	-5	-5	-0	-0.5
1927	Bro-N	6	13	.316	30	21	12	2	3	188^{1}	188	5	60	99	11.9	3.30	120	.269	.327	9	.141	-1	13	14	-4	0.9
1928	Bro-N	9	14	.391	41	21	7	2	1	192	194	8	64	74	12.4	3.89	102	.268	.332	12	.176	2	2	2	-3	0.1
1929	Bro-N	1	2	.333	6	3	0	0	0	19	21	2	16	7	18.0	6.63	70	.280	.413	1	.250	0	-4	-4	-0	-0.4
1930	Bro-N	10	7	.588	35	21	6	2	1	198^{1}	204	16	70	59	12.7	3.95	124	.271	.337	10	.147	-2	23	21	-3	1.5
1931	Phi-N	**19**	14	.576	**52**	30	12	2	5	249	288	15	83	99	13.6	4.27	100	.287	.344	11	.122	-7	-11	-1	-5	-1.2
1932	Phi-N	11	10	.524	39	22	8	0	0	166	210	14	47	62	14.0	5.42	81	.300	.346	12	.197	-1	-28	-19	-2	-2.1
1933	Phi-N	6	10	.375	35	21	6	0	2	161^{2}	188	8	49	43	13.4	3.84	99	.295	.348	12	.231	0	-9	-0	-4	-0.4
1934	Phi-N	0	1	.000	3	1	0	0	0	5^{1}	8	0	4	1	21.9	10.13	47	.333	.448	0	.000	-0	-4	-3	-0	-0.3
	Bos-N	1	1	.500	7	3	0	0	0	15^{1}	19	2	9	6	17.0	5.87	65	.284	.377	1	.250	0	-3	-3	-0	-0.3
	Yr	1	2	.333	10	4	0	0	0	20^{2}	27	2	13	7	17.9	6.97	58	.293	.387	1	.200	0	-7	-7	-0	-0.6
Total	10	63	74	.460	252	144	51	8	12	1206^{2}	1338	70	414	453	13.3	4.24	100	.283	.344	68	.163	-8	-29	2	-21	-2.9
● **DOCK ELLIS**	Ellis, Dock Phillip b: 3/11/45, Los Angeles, Cal. BB/TR, 6'3", 210 lbs. Deb: 6/18/68																									
1968	Pit-N	6	5	.545	26	10	2	0	0	104	82	4	38	52	10.5	2.51	117	.213	.285	2	.069	-1	5	5	0	0.4
1969	Pit-N	11	17	.393	35	33	8	2	0	218^{2}	206	14	76	173	11.8	3.58	97	.250	.316	6	.088	-3	0	-2	1	-0.5
1970	*Pit-N	13	10	.565	30	30	9	4	0	201^{2}	194	9	87	128	13.0	3.21	121	.257	.342	7	.100	-3	19	15	2	1.5
1971	*Pit-N★	19	9	.679	31	31	11	2	0	226^{2}	207	15	63	137	10.8	3.06	111	.239	.292	16	.203	2	10	8	0	1.2
1972	*Pit-N	15	7	.682	25	25	4	1	0	163^{1}	156	6	33	96	10.6	2.70	123	.253	.294	9	.153	-1	14	11	-1	1.0
1973	Pit-N	12	14	.462	28	28	3	1	0	192	176	7	55	122	11.1	3.05	115	.240	.299	7	.108	-3	13	10	1	0.9
1974	Pit-N	12	9	.571	26	26	9	0	0	176^{2}	163	13	41	91	10.7	3.16	109	.242	.292	12	.214	3	9	6	-1	0.8
1975	*Pit-N	8	9	.471	27	24	5	2	0	140	163	9	43	69	13.4	3.79	93	.292	.345	4	.111	0	-3	-4	-1	-0.5
1976	*NY-A	17	8	.680	32	32	8	1	0	211^{2}	195	14	76	65	11.7	3.19	107	.247	.316	0	—	0	8	5	-3	0.3
1977	NY-A	1	1	.500	3	3	1	0	0	19^{2}	18	1	8	5	11.9	1.83	215	.237	.310	0	—	0	5	5	-0	0.5
	Oak-A	1	5	.167	7	7	0	0	0	26	35	5	14	11	17.3	9.69	42	.315	.397	0	—	0	-16	-16	-0	-1.4
	Tex-A	10	6	.625	23	22	7	1	1	167^{1}	158	13	42	90	10.8	2.90	140	.254	.301	0	—	0	21	22	-2	2.1
	Yr	12	12	.500	33	32	8	1	1	213	211	19	64	106	11.6	3.63	112	.260	.314	0	—	0	10	10	-2	1.2
1978	Tex-A	9	7	.563	22	22	3	0	0	141^{1}	131	15	46	45	11.4	4.20	89	.245	.307	0	—	0	-7	-7	0	-0.7
1979	Tex-A	1	5	.167	10	9	0	0	0	46^{2}	64	5	16	10	15.4	5.98	69	.323	.374	0	—	0	-9	-9	-0	-0.8
	NY-N	3	7	.300	17	14	1	0	0	85	110	9	34	41	15.4	6.04	60	.320	.383	2	.077	-1	-22	-23	0	-2.3
	Pit-N	0	0	—	3	1	0	0	0	7	9	1	2	1	14.1	2.57	151	.346	.393	0	.000	-0	1	1	-0	0.1
	Yr	3	7	.300	20	15	1	0	0	92	119	10	36	42	15.2	5.77	63	.316	.375	2	.074	-2	-21	-22	0	-2.2
Total	12	138	119	.537	345	317	71	14	1	2127^{2}	2067	140	674	1136	11.8	3.46	103	.255	.315	65	.133	-7	49	26	-3	2.6
● **JIM ELLIS**	Ellis, James Russell b: 3/25/45, Tulare, Cal. BR/TL, 6'2", 185 lbs. Deb: 8/11/67																									
1967	Chi-N	1	1	.500	8	1	0	0	0	16^{2}	20	1	9	8	15.7	3.24	109	.313	.397	1	.200	0	0	1	-0	0.1
1969	StL-N	0	0	—	2	1	0	0	0	5^{1}	7	0	3	0	16.9	1.69	212	.318	.400	0	—	0	1	1	-0	0.1
Total	2	1	1	.500	10	2	0	0	0	22	27	1	12	8	16.0	2.86	124	.314	.398	1	.200	0	1	2	-1	0.2
● **SAMMY ELLIS**	Ellis, Samuel Joseph b: 2/11/41, Youngstown, Ohio BL/TR, 6'1", 180 lbs. Deb: 4/14/62 C																									
1962	Cin-N	2	2	.500	8	4	0	0	0	28	29	6	29	27	19.0	6.75	60	.269	.428	2	.200	-0	-9	-8	-0	-0.8
1964	Cin-N	10	3	.769	52	5	2	0	14	122^{1}	101	9	28	125	9.6	2.57	140	.223	.270	2	.083	-0	13	14	0	1.5
1965	Cin-N☆	22	10	.688	44	39	15	2	2	263^{2}	222	22	104	183	11.3	3.79	99	.226	.304	12	.125	-1	-7	-1	-3	-0.6
1966	Cin-N	12	19	.387	41	36	7	0	0	221	226	35	78	154	12.5	5.29	74	.264	.328	8	.114	-3	-41	-34	-3	-3.9
1967	Cin-N	8	11	.421	32	27	8	1	0	175^{2}	197	18	67	80	13.7	3.84	98	.286	.353	4	.082	-2	-9	-2	-1	-0.6
1968	Cal-A	9	10	.474	42	24	3	0	2	164	150	22	56	93	11.6	3.95	74	.244	.313	2	.045	-3	-18	-19	-2	-2.6
1969	Chi-A	0	3	.000	10	5	0	0	0	29^{1}	42	6	16	15	18.1	5.83	66	.336	.415	1	.167	0	-7	-6	0	-0.6
Total	7	63	58	.521	229	140	35	3	18	1004	967	118	378	677	12.3	4.15	88	.253	.323	31	.104	-9	-78	-58	-9	-7.6
● **GEORGE ELLISON**	Ellison, George Russell b: 1/24/1895, California d: 1/20/78, San Francisco, Cal BR/TR, 6'3", 185 lbs. Deb: 8/21/20																									
1920	Cle-A	0	0	—	1	0	0	0	0	1	0	0	2	1	18.0	0.00	—	.000	.400	0	—	0	0	0	0	0.1
● **DICK ELLSWORTH**	Ellsworth, Richard Clark b: 3/22/40, Lusk, Wyo. BL/TL, 6'4", 195 lbs. Deb: 6/22/58 F																									
1958	Chi-N	0	1	.000	1	1	0	0	0	2^{1}	4	0	3	0	30.9	15.43	25	.364	.533	0	.000	-0	-3	-3	-0	-0.3
1960	Chi-N	7	13	.350	31	27	6	0	0	176^{2}	170	12	72	94	12.4	3.72	102	.257	.332	2	.042	-3	1	1	-0	-0.2
1961	Chi-N	10	11	.476	37	31	7	1	0	186^{2}	213	23	48	91	12.7	3.86	108	.292	.338	2	.036	-5	4	7	3	0.5
1962	Chi-N	9	20	.310	37	33	6	0	1	208^{2}	241	23	77	113	13.9	5.09	81	.291	.355	7	.113	1	-27	-22	0	-2.0
1963	Chi-N	22	10	.688	37	37	19	4	0	290^{2}	223	14	75	185	9.3	2.11	**167**	.210	.263	9	.096	-3	38	**45**	2	**5.3**
1964	Chi-N☆	14	18	.438	37	36	16	1	0	256^{2}	267	34	71	148	12.0	3.75	99	.266	.317	4	.046	-6	-6	-1	2	-0.5
1965	Chi-N	14	15	.483	36	34	8	0	1	222^{1}	227	22	57	130	11.7	3.81	97	.265	.313	7	.096	-2	-7	-3	2	-0.3
1966	Chi-N	8	22	.267	38	37	9	0	0	269^{1}	321	28	51	144	12.6	3.98	92	.294	.328	14	.156	-0	-11	-9	2	-0.8
1967	Phi-N	6	7	.462	32	21	3	1	0	125^{1}	152	6	36	45	13.9	4.38	78	.306	.359	4	.108	-1	-14	-14	2	-1.4
1968	Bos-A	16	7	.696	31	28	10	1	0	196	196	16	37	106	11.0	3.03	104	.260	.301	4	.056	-5	-1	3	-0	-0.3
1969	Bos-A	0	0	—	2	2	0	0	0	12	16	1	4	4	15.0	3.75	101	.320	.370	0	.000	-0	-0	0	-0	0.0
	Cle-A	6	9	.400	34	22	3	1	0	135	162	10	40	48	13.8	4.13	91	.301	.354	6	.133	-1	-8	-6	0	-0.7
	Yr	6	9	.400	36	24	3	1	0	147	178	11	44	52	13.9	4.10	92	.302	.356	6	.125	-2	-8	-5	0	-0.7

YEAR	TM/L	W	L	PCT	G	GS	CG	SH	SV	IP	H	HR	BB	SO	RAT	ERA	ERA+	OAV	OOB	BH	AVG	PB	PR	/A	PD	TPI
1970	Cle-A	3	3	.500	29	1	0	0	2	43^{2}	49	4	14	13	13.2	4.53	87	.299	.358	0	.000	-0	-4	-3	1	-0.2
	Mil-A	0	0	—	14	0	0	0	1	15^{2}	11	0	3	9	8.6	1.72	220	.196	.250	0	—	0	3	4	-0	0.4
	Yr	3	3	.500	43	1	0	0	3	59^{1}	60	4	17	22	11.8	3.79	103	.269	.324	0	.000	-0	-1	1	1	0.2
1971	Mil-A	0	1	.000	11	0	0	0	0	14^{2}	22	1	7	10	18.4	4.91	71	.361	.435	0	.000	-0	-2	-2	-0	-0.3
Total	13	115	137	.456	407	310	87	9	5	2155^{2}	2274	194	595	1140	12.2	3.72	100	.272	.324	59	.088	-25	-37	-2	12	-0.8
● STEVE ELLSWORTH Ellsworth, Steven Clark b: 7/30/60, Chicago, Ill. BR/TR, 6'8", 220 lbs. Deb: 4/07/88 F																										
1988	Bos-A	1	6	.143	8	7	0	0	0	36	47	7	16	16	16.0	6.75	61	.315	.386	0	—	0	-11	-11	-0	-1.1
● DON ELSTON Elston, Donald Ray b: 4/6/29, Campbellstown, Ohio BR/TR, 6', 170 lbs. Deb: 9/17/53																										
1953	Chi-N	0	1	.000	2	1	0	0	0	5	11	1	0	2	19.8	14.40	31	.458	.458	0	.000	-0	-6	-6	-0	-0.5
1957	Bro-N	0	0	—	1	0	0	0	0	1	1	0	0	1	9.0	0.00	—	.250	.250	0	—	0	0	0	0	0.1
	Chi-N	6	7	.462	39	14	2	0	8	144	139	15	55	102	12.4	3.56	109	.259	.334	4	.108	-2	5	5	0	0.3
	Yr	6	7	.462	40	14	2	0	8	145	140	15	55	103	12.4	3.54	109	.259	.333	4	.108	-2	5	5	0	0.4
1958	Chi-N	9	8	.529	**69**	0	0	0	10	97	75	9	39	84	10.7	2.88	136	.214	.294	5	.357	1	**12**	**11**	1	1.4
1959	Chi-N★	10	8	.556	**65**	0	0	0	13	97^{2}	77	11	46	82	11.6	3.32	119	.218	.313	4	.211	0	7	7	-0	0.7
1960	Chi-N	8	9	.471	60	0	0	0	11	127	109	17	55	85	11.9	3.40	111	.231	.316	3	.125	-1	5	5	-2	0.3
1961	Chi-N	6	7	.462	58	0	0	0	8	93^{1}	108	11	45	59	15.3	5.59	75	.297	.383	2	.182	-0	-16	-15	0	-1.4
1962	Chi-N	4	8	.333	57	0	0	0	8	66^{1}	57	6	32	37	12.2	2.44	170	.247	.341	0	.000	-1	11	13	1	1.3
1963	Chi-N	4	1	.800	51	0	0	0	4	70	57	6	21	41	10.3	2.83	124	.226	.291	0	.000	-0	4	5	-1	0.5
1964	Chi-N	2	5	.286	48	0	0	0	1	54^{1}	68	4	34	26	17.4	5.30	70	.330	.432	1	.167	-0	-11	-10	1	-0.9
Total	9	49	54	.476	450	15	2	0	63	755^{2}	702	80	327	519	12.6	3.69	106	.251	.335	19	.153	-4	11	17	1	1.8
● NARCISO ELVIRA Elvira, Narciso Chicho (Delgado) b: 10/29/67, Vera Cruz, Mex. BL/TL, 5'10", 160 lbs. Deb: 9/09/90																										
1990	Mil-A	0	0	—	4	0	0	0	0	5	6	0	5	6	19.8	5.40	72	.300	.440	0	—	0	-1	-1	0	0.0
● BONES ELY Ely, William Frederick b: 6/7/1863, N.Girard, Pa. d: 1/10/52, Berkeley, Cal. BR/TR, 6'1", 155 lbs. Deb: 6/19/1884 ♦																										
1884	Buf-N	0	1	.000	1	1	0	0	0	5	17	1	5	4	39.6	14.40	22	.500	.564	0	.000	-1	-6	-6	-0	-0.5
1886	Lou-a	0	4	.000	6	4	4	0	**1**	44	53	0	26	28	16.2	5.32	68	.280	.367	5	.156	-1	-9	-8	0	-0.8
1890	Syr-a	0	0	—	1	0	0	0	0	2	7	0	0	0	31.5	22.50	16	.542	.542	130	.262	0	-4	-4	0	-0.3
1894	StL-N	0	0	—	1	0	0	0	0	1	0	0	3	0	27.0	0.00	—	.000	.510	156	.306	0	1	1	0	0.0
Total	4	0	5	.000	9	5	4	0	1	52	77	1	34	32	19.2	6.75	54	.322	.407	1331	.258	-2	-19	-18	0	-1.6
● HARRY ELY Ely, Harry Deb: 9/24/1892																										
1892	Bal-N	0	1	.000	1	1	1	0	0	7	14	0	7	0	29.6	7.71	44	.400	.523	0	.000	-0	-3	-3	-0	-0.3
● ALAN EMBREE Embree, Alan Duane b: 1/23/70, Vancouver, Wash. BL/TL, 6'2", 185 lbs. Deb: 9/15/92																										
1992	Cle-A	0	2	.000	4	4	0	0	0	18	19	3	8	12	14.0	7.00	58	.271	.354	0	—	0	-6	-6	-1	-0.6
● RED EMBREE Embree, Charles Willard b: 8/30/17, ElMonte, Cal. BR/TR, 6', 165 lbs. Deb: 9/10/41																										
1941	Cle-A	0	1	.000	1	1	0	0	0	4	7	0	3	4	24.8	6.75	58	.438	.550	0	.000	-0	-1	-1	-0	-0.1
1942	Cle-A	3	4	.429	19	6	2	0	0	63	58	0	31	44	13.0	3.86	89	.242	.333	2	.133	-0	-1	-3	-0	-0.3
1944	Cle-A	0	1	.000	3	1	0	0	0	3^{1}	2	0	5	4	18.9	13.50	24	.167	.412	0	—	0	-4	-4	0	-0.4
1945	Cle-A	4	4	.500	8	8	5	1	0	70	56	3	26	42	10.5	1.93	168	.215	.287	3	.143	-1	11	10	1	1.2
1946	Cle-A	8	12	.400	28	26	8	0	0	200	170	15	79	87	11.3	3.47	95	.227	.302	13	.186	1	1	-3	-1	-0.4
1947	Cle-A	8	10	.444	27	21	6	0	0	162^{2}	137	13	67	56	11.3	3.15	110	.233	.313	9	.173	-1	10	6	1	0.5
1948	NY-A	5	3	.625	20	8	4	0	0	76^{2}	77	6	30	25	12.7	3.76	109	.261	.331	4	.148	-1	5	3	-1	0.0
1949	StL-A	3	13	.188	35	19	4	0	1	127^{1}	146	13	89	24	16.8	5.37	84	.294	.405	6	.162	-1	-17	-12	-0	-1.3
Total	8	31	48	.392	141	90	29	1	1	707	653	50	330	286	12.6	3.72	98	.246	.331	37	.166	-4	4	-5	-2	-0.8
● SLIM EMBREY Embrey, Charles Akin b: 8/17/01, Columbia, Tenn. d: 10/10/47, Nashville, Tenn. BR/TR, 6'2", 184 lbs. Deb: 10/01/23																										
1923	Chi-A	0	0	—	1	0	0	0	0	2^{2}	7	0	2	1	30.4	10.13	39	.500	.563	0	—	0	-2	-2	0	-0.1
● CHARLIE EMIG Emig, Charles H. b: Bellevue, Ky. TL, Deb: 9/04/1896																										
1896	Lou-N	0	1	.000	1	1	1	0	0	8	12	1	7	1	24.8	7.88	55	.343	.489	0	.000	-1	-3	-3	1	-0.2
● SLIM EMMERICH Emmerich, William Peter b: 9/29/19, Allentown, Pa. BR/TR, 6'1", 170 lbs. Deb: 5/14/45																										
1945	NY-N	4	4	.500	31	7	1	0	0	100	111	8	33	27	13.1	4.86	80	.278	.334	3	.120	-2	-12	-11	-0	-1.2
1946	NY-N	0	0	—	2	0	0	0	0	4	6	1	0	1	13.5	4.50	76	.400	.400	0	—	0	-0	-0	0	0.0
Total	2	4	4	.500	33	7	1	0	0	104	117	9	33	28	13.1	4.85	80	.282	.336	3	.120	-2	-12	-11	-0	-1.2
● BOB EMSLIE Emslie, Robert Daniel b: 1/27/1859, Guelph, Ont., Can. d: 4/26/43, St.Thomas, Ont., Canada BR/TR, 5'11", Deb: 7/25/1883 U																										
1883	Bal-a	9	13	.409	24	23	21	1	0	201^{1}	188	3	41	62	10.2	3.17	110	.231	.268	16	.165	-3	3	7	2	0.5
1884	Bal-a	32	17	.653	50	50	50	4	0	455^{1}	419	5	88	264	10.3	2.75	126	.224	.264	37	.190	-5	25	36	-1	2.9
1885	Bal-a	3	10	.231	13	13	11	0	0	107	131	0	30	27	14.0	4.29	76	.298	.350	12	.235	0	-12	-12	-1	-1.1
	Phi-a	0	4	.000	4	4	3	0	0	28^{2}	37	1	6	9	13.5	6.28	55	.291	.323	1	.083	-1	-10	-9	1	-0.8
	Yr	3	14	.176	17	17	14	0	0	135^{2}	168	1	36	36	13.5	4.71	70	.294	.336	13	.206	-1	-22	-21	-1	-1.9
Total	3	44	44	.500	91	90	85	5	0	792^{1}	775	9	165	362	10.9	3.19	108	.239	.279	66	.186	-9	6	22	1	1.5
● LUIS ENCARNACION Encarnacion, Luis Martin Lora (b: Luis Martin Lora (Encarcnacion)) b: 10/20/63, Santo Domingo, D.R. BR/TR, 5'10", 178 lbs. Deb: 7/27/90																										
1990	KC-A	0	0	—	4	0	0	0	0	10^{1}	14	1	4	8	15.7	7.84	49	.311	.367	0	—	0	-5	-5	-0	-0.4
● JOE ENGEL Engel, Joseph William b: 3/12/1893, Washington, D.C. d: 6/12/69, Chattanooga, Tenn BR/TL, 6'1.5", 183 lbs. Deb: 5/30/12																										
1912	Was-A	2	5	.286	17	10	2	0	1	75	70	2	50	29	14.9	3.96	84	.253	.375	1	.059	-1	-5	-5	1	-0.5
1913	Was-A	8	9	.471	36	24	6	2	0	164^{2}	124	2	85	70	12.0	3.06	97	.207	.317	3	.061	-5	-2	-2	-1	-0.8
1914	Was-A	7	5	.583	35	15	1	0	3	124^{1}	108	2	75	41	13.6	2.97	95	.254	.372	3	.107	1	-3	-2	-0	-0.2
1915	Was-A	0	3	.000	11	3	0	0	0	33^{2}	30	0	19	9	13.9	3.21	93	.261	.380	0	.000	-1	-1	-1	0	-0.1
1917	Cin-N	0	1	.000	1	1	1	0	0	8	12	0	6	2	20.3	5.63	47	.353	.450	0	.000	-0	-3	-3	0	-0.3
1919	Cle-A	0	0	—	1	0	0	0	0	0	0	0	3	0	—	∞	—	—	1.000	0	—	0	-2	-2	0	-0.2
1920	Was-A	0	0	—	1	0	0	0	0	1^{2}	0	0	4	0	27.0	21.60	17	.000	.556	0	.000	-0	-3	-3	-0	-0.3
Total	7	17	23	.425	102	53	10	2	4	407^{1}	344	6	242	151	13.5	3.38	88	.237	.355	7	.067	-6	-20	-18	-0	-2.4
● STEVE ENGEL Engel, Steven Michael b: 12/31/61, Cincinnati, Ohio BR/TL, 6'3", 216 lbs. Deb: 7/30/85																										
1985	Chi-N	1	5	.167	11	8	1	0	1	51^{2}	61	10	26	29	15.2	5.57	72	.298	.377	3	.188	2	-11	-9	-0	-0.8
● RICK ENGLE Engle, Richard Douglas b: 4/7/57, Corbin, Ky. BR/TL, 5'11.5", 181 lbs. Deb: 9/02/81																										
1981	Mon-N	0	0	—	1	0	0	0	0	2	6	0	1	2	31.5	18.00	19	.500	.538	0	—	0	-3	-3	-0	-0.3
● JACK ENRIGHT Enright, Jackson Percy b: 11/29/1895, Fort Worth, Tex. d: 8/18/75, Pompano Beach, Fla BR/TR, 5'11", 177 lbs. Deb: 9/26/17																										
1917	NY-A	0	1	.000	1	1	0	0	0	5	5	0	3	1	14.4	5.40	50	.294	.400	0	.000	-0	-2	-2	1	-0.1
● TERRY ENYART Enyart, Terry Gene b: 10/10/50, Ironton, Ohio BR/TL, 6'2", 190 lbs. Deb: 6/17/74																										
1974	Mon-N	0	0	—	2	0	0	0	0	1^{2}	4	0	4	2	43.2	16.20	24	.444	.615	0	—	0	-2	-2	-0	-0.2
● JOHNNY ENZMANN Enzmann, John "Gentleman John" b: 3/4/1890, Brooklyn, N.Y. d: 3/14/84, Riverhead, N.Y. BR/TR, 5'10", 165 lbs. Deb: 7/10/14																										
1914	Bro-N	1	0	1.000	7	1	0	0	0	19	21	1	8	5	15.2	4.74	60	.300	.395	0	.000	-1	-4	-4	1	-0.4

YEAR TM/L	W	L	PCT	G	GS	CG	SH	SV	IP	H	HR	BB	SO	RAT	ERA	ERA+	OAV	OOB	BH	AVG	PB	PR	/A	PD	TPI
1918 Cle-A	5	7	.417	30	14	8	0	2	136^{2}	130	2	29	38	10.8	2.37	127	.263	.310	7	.149	-3	6	10	0	0.8
1919 Cle-A	3	2	.600	14	4	2	0	0	55^{1}	67	0	8	13	12.5	2.28	147	.312	.342	2	.133	-0	6	7	-1	0.5
1920 Phi-N	2	3	.400	16	1	1	0	0	58^{2}	79	1	16	35	15.3	3.84	89	.320	.373	4	.167	1	-5	-3	-0	-0.2
Total 4	11	12	.478	67	20	11	0	2	269^{2}	297	4	61	91	12.4	2.84	111	.289	.338	13	.141	-3	3	10	-0	0.7

● AL EPPERLY Epperly, Albert Paul "Tub" or "Pard" b: 5/7/18, Glidden, Iowa BL/TR, 6'2", 194 lbs. Deb: 4/25/38

YEAR TM/L	W	L	PCT	G	GS	CG	SH	SV	IP	H	HR	BB	SO	RAT	ERA	ERA+	OAV	OOB	BH	AVG	PB	PR	/A	PD	TPI
1938 Chi-N	2	0	1.000	9	4	1	0	0	27	28	1	15	10	14.3	3.67	104	.264	.355	2	.250	1	0	0	0	0.2
1950 Bro-N	0	0	—	5	0	0	0	0	9	14	1	5	3	19.0	5.00	82	.378	.452	0	—	0	-1	-1	-0	-0.1
Total 2	2	0	1.000	14	4	1	0	0	36	42	2	20	13	15.5	4.00	97	.294	.380	2	.250	1	-0	-0	-0	0.1

● GREG ERARDI Erardi, Joseph Gregory b: 5/31/54, Syracuse, N.Y. BR/TR, 6'1", 190 lbs. Deb: 9/06/77

YEAR TM/L	W	L	PCT	G	GS	CG	SH	SV	IP	H	HR	BB	SO	RAT	ERA	ERA+	OAV	OOB	BH	AVG	PB	PR	/A	PD	TPI
1977 Sea-A	0	1	.000	5	0	0	0	0	9	12	3	6	5	18.0	6.00	69	.300	.391	0	—	0	-2	-2	-0	-0.2

● EDDIE ERAUTT Erautt, Edward Lorenz Sebastian b: 9/26/24, Portland, Ore. BR/TR, 6', 186 lbs. Deb: 4/16/47 F

YEAR TM/L	W	L	PCT	G	GS	CG	SH	SV	IP	H	HR	BB	SO	RAT	ERA	ERA+	OAV	OOB	BH	AVG	PB	PR	/A	PD	TPI
1947 Cin-N	4	9	.308	36	10	2	0	0	119	146	5	53	43	15.2	5.07	81	.307	.379	2	.069	-1	-13	-13	1	-1.3
1948 Cin-N	0	0	—	2	0	0	0	0	3	3	0	1	0	12.0	6.00	65	.250	.308	0	—	0	-1	-1	-0	-0.1
1949 Cin-N	4	11	.267	39	9	1	0	1	112^{2}	99	9	61	43	13.0	3.36	125	.247	.351	4	.174	0	**9**	**10**	-1	1.0
1950 Cin-N	4	2	.667	33	2	1	0	1	65^{1}	82	9	22	35	15.2	5.65	75	.307	.373	2	.154	0	-11	-10	-0	-1.0
1951 Cin-N	0	0	—	30	0	0	0	0	39^{1}	50	4	23	20	17.4	5.72	71	.314	.411	0	.000	-0	-8	-7	1	-0.7
1953 Cin-N	0	0	—	4	0	0	0	0	4^{2}	11	1	3	1	27.0	5.79	75	.500	.560	0	.000	-0	-1	-1	0	-0.1
StL-N	3	1	.750	20	1	0	0	0	35^{2}	43	6	16	15	15.4	6.31	67	.299	.377	1	.167	-0	-8	-8	0	-0.7
Yr	3	1	.750	24	1	0	0	0	40^{1}	54	7	19	16	16.7	6.25	68	.325	.401	1	.143	-0	-9	-9	0	-0.8
Total 6	15	23	.395	164	22	4	0	2	379^{2}	434	34	179	157	14.9	4.86	86	.293	.376	9	.120	-2	-33	-29	0	-2.9

● DON ERICKSON Erickson, Don Lee b: 12/13/31, Springfield, Ill. BR/TR, 6', 175 lbs. Deb: 9/01/58

YEAR TM/L	W	L	PCT	G	GS	CG	SH	SV	IP	H	HR	BB	SO	RAT	ERA	ERA+	OAV	OOB	BH	AVG	PB	PR	/A	PD	TPI
1958 Phi-N	0	1	.000	9	0	0	0	1	11^{2}	11	3	9	9	15.4	4.63	86	.244	.370	0	.000	-0	-1	-1	-0	-0.1

● ERIC ERICKSON Erickson, Eric George Adolph b: 3/13/1895, Goteborg, Sweden d: 5/19/65, Jamestown, N.Y. BR/TR, 6'2", 190 lbs. Deb: 10/06/14

YEAR TM/L	W	L	PCT	G	GS	CG	SH	SV	IP	H	HR	BB	SO	RAT	ERA	ERA+	OAV	OOB	BH	AVG	PB	PR	/A	PD	TPI
1914 NY-N	0	1	.000	1	1	0	0	0	5	8	0	3	3	19.8	0.00	—	.364	.440	0	.000	-0	2	1	-0	0.1
1916 Det-A	0	0	—	8	0	0	0	0	16	13	0	8	7	12.4	2.81	102	.220	.324	0	.000	-1	0	0	-1	-0.1
1918 Det-A	4	5	.444	12	9	8	0	1	94^{1}	81	2	29	48	10.8	2.48	107	.240	.306	4	.121	-2	3	2	-3	-0.3
1919 Det-A	0	2	.000	3	2	0	0	0	14^{2}	17	0	10	4	17.2	6.75	47	.293	.406	1	.200	-0	-6	-6	0	-0.5
Was-A	6	11	.353	20	15	7	1	0	132	130	7	63	86	13.6	3.95	81	.254	.344	7	.146	-1	-11	-11	-3	-1.5
Yr	6	13	.316	23	17	7	1	0	146^{2}	147	7	73	90	13.9	4.23	76	.258	.349	8	.151	-2	-16	-17	-3	-2.0
1920 Was-A	12	16	.429	39	27	12	0	1	239^{1}	231	13	128	87	13.9	3.84	97	.264	.365	23	.277	4	-1	-3	-4	-0.3
1921 Was-A	8	10	.444	32	22	9	3	0	179	181	7	65	71	12.8	3.62	114	.269	.341	9	.150	-3	13	10	-3	0.3
1922 Was-A	4	12	.250	30	17	6	2	2	141^{2}	144	8	73	61	14.0	4.96	78	.279	.372	6	.133	-2	-14	-17	-2	-2.0
Total 7	34	57	.374	145	93	42	6	4	822	805	37	379	367	13.3	3.85	93	.264	.352	50	.179	-6	-14	-23	-15	-4.3

● HAL ERICKSON Erickson, Harold James b: 7/17/19, Portland, Ore. BR/TR, 6'5", 230 lbs. Deb: 4/14/53

YEAR TM/L	W	L	PCT	G	GS	CG	SH	SV	IP	H	HR	BB	SO	RAT	ERA	ERA+	OAV	OOB	BH	AVG	PB	PR	/A	PD	TPI
1953 Det-A	0	1	.000	18	0	0	0	1	32^{1}	43	4	10	19	15.3	4.73	86	.323	.379	0	.000	-1	-3	-2	-0	-0.3

● PAUL ERICKSON Erickson, Paul Walford "Li'L Abner" b: 12/14/15, Zion, Ohio BR/TR, 6'2", 200 lbs. Deb: 6/29/41

YEAR TM/L	W	L	PCT	G	GS	CG	SH	SV	IP	H	HR	BB	SO	RAT	ERA	ERA+	OAV	OOB	BH	AVG	PB	PR	/A	PD	TPI
1941 Chi-N	5	7	.417	32	15	7	1	1	141	126	2	64	85	12.3	3.70	95	.234	.318	7	.152	0	-1	-3	-1	-0.4
1942 Chi-N	1	6	.143	18	7	1	0	0	63	70	4	41	26	15.9	5.43	59	.288	.391	3	.143	-1	-15	-16	0	-1.7
1943 Chi-N	1	3	.250	15	4	0	0	0	42^{2}	47	4	22	24	15.0	6.12	55	.280	.370	3	.200	0	-13	-13	-1	-1.4
1944 Chi-N	5	9	.357	33	15	5	3	1	124^{1}	113	5	67	82	13.0	3.55	100	.243	.338	2	.056	-1	1	-0	2	0.0
1945 *Chi-N	7	4	.636	28	9	3	0	3	108^{1}	94	5	48	53	12.4	3.32	110	.233	.325	5	.156	0	6	4	-0	0.4
1946 Chi-N	9	7	.563	32	14	5	1	0	137	119	2	65	70	12.3	2.43	137	.232	.321	2	.050	-4	15	14	-1	0.9
1947 Chi-N	7	12	.368	40	20	6	0	1	174	179	17	93	82	14.3	4.34	91	.268	.362	15	.250	3	-6	-8	1	-0.4
1948 Chi-N	0	0	—	3	0	0	0	0	5^{2}	7	0	6	4	20.6	6.35	61	.292	.433	0	.000	-0	-2	-2	0	-0.2
Phi-N	2	0	1.000	4	2	0	0	0	17^{1}	19	2	17	5	18.7	5.19	76	.292	.439	1	.143	-0	-2	-2	0	-0.2
NY-N	0	0	—	2	0	0	0	0	1	0	0	2	1	18.0	0.00	—	.000	.400	0	—	0	0	0	0	0.0
Yr	2	0	1.000	9	2	0	0	0	24	26	2	25	10	19.1	5.25	75	.283	.436	1	.125	-0	-3	-4	0	-0.4
Total 8	37	48	.435	207	86	27	5	6	814^{1}	774	41	425	432	13.5	3.86	93	.250	.345	38	.147	-2	-16	-26	-0	-3.0

● RALPH ERICKSON Erickson, Ralph Lief b: 6/25/04, Dubois, Idaho BL/TL, 6'1", 175 lbs. Deb: 9/11/29

YEAR TM/L	W	L	PCT	G	GS	CG	SH	SV	IP	H	HR	BB	SO	RAT	ERA	ERA+	OAV	OOB	BH	AVG	PB	PR	/A	PD	TPI
1929 Pit-N	0	0	—	1	0	0	0	0	1	2	0	2	0	36.0	27.00	18	.500	.667	0	—	0	-2	-2	-0	-0.2
1930 Pit-N	1	0	1.000	7	0	0	0	0	14	21	1	10	2	19.9	7.07	70	.375	.470	1	.250	-0	-3	-3	0	-0.3
Total 2	1	0	1.000	8	0	0	0	0	15	23	1	12	2	21.0	8.40	59	.383	.486	1	.250	-0	-6	-6	0	-0.5

● ROGER ERICKSON Erickson, Roger Farrell b: 8/30/56, Springfield, Ill. BR/TR, 6'3", 190 lbs. Deb: 4/06/78

YEAR TM/L	W	L	PCT	G	GS	CG	SH	SV	IP	H	HR	BB	SO	RAT	ERA	ERA+	OAV	OOB	BH	AVG	PB	PR	/A	PD	TPI
1978 Min-A	14	13	.519	37	37	14	0	0	265^{2}	268	19	79	121	12.0	3.96	96	.263	.321	0	—	0	-6	-4	0	-0.4
1979 Min-A	3	10	.231	24	21	0	0	0	123	154	17	48	47	14.9	5.63	78	.310	.372	0	—	0	-19	-17	-0	-1.8
1980 Min-A	7	13	.350	32	27	7	0	0	191^{1}	198	13	56	97	12.1	3.25	134	.268	.322	0	—	0	17	24	-0	2.5
1981 Min-A	3	8	.273	14	14	1	0	0	91^{1}	93	7	31	44	12.2	3.84	103	.262	.321	0	—	0	-2	1	-0	-0.1
1982 Min-A	4	3	.571	7	7	2	0	0	40^{2}	56	6	12	12	15.3	4.87	87	.326	.373	0	—	0	-4	-3	1	-0.3
NY-A	4	5	.444	16	11	0	0	1	70^{2}	86	5	17	37	13.1	4.46	89	.301	.340	0	—	0	-3	-4	-1	-0.4
Yr	8	8	.500	23	18	2	0	1	111^{1}	142	11	29	49	13.8	4.61	89	.308	.349	0	—	0	-7	-7	-1	-0.7
1983 NY-A	0	1	.000	5	0	0	0	0	16^{2}	13	1	8	7	11.3	4.32	90	.213	.304	0	—	0	-0	-1	0	0.1
Total 6	35	53	.398	135	117	24	0	1	799^{1}	868	68	251	365	12.8	4.13	99	.277	.334	0	—	0	-18	-4	-1	-0.4

● SCOTT ERICKSON Erickson, Scott Gavin b: 2/2/68, Long Beach, Cal. BR/TR, 6'4", 220 lbs. Deb: 6/25/90

YEAR TM/L	W	L	PCT	G	GS	CG	SH	SV	IP	H	HR	BB	SO	RAT	ERA	ERA+	OAV	OOB	BH	AVG	PB	PR	/A	PD	TPI
1990 Min-A	8	4	.667	19	17	1	0	0	113	108	9	51	53	13.1	2.87	145	.256	.343	0	—	0	13	16	-0	1.7
1991 *Min-A	**20**	8	**.714**	32	32	5	3	0	204	189	13	71	108	11.7	3.18	134	.248	.317	0	—	0	21	25	1	2.5
1992 Min-A	13	12	.520	32	32	5	3	0	212	197	18	83	101	12.2	3.40	119	.252	.330	0	—	0	13	15	2	1.6
Total 3	41	24	.631	83	81	11	6	0	529	494	40	205	262	12.2	3.20	130	.251	.328	0	—	0	47	56	3	5.8

● DICK ERRICKSON Errickson, Richard Merriwell "Lief" b: 3/5/14, Vineland, N.J. BL/TR, 6'1", 175 lbs. Deb: 4/27/38

YEAR TM/L	W	L	PCT	G	GS	CG	SH	SV	IP	H	HR	BB	SO	RAT	ERA	ERA+	OAV	OOB	BH	AVG	PB	PR	/A	PD	TPI
1938 Bos-N	9	7	.563	34	10	6	1	6	122^{2}	113	1	56	40	12.5	3.15	109	.246	.330	4	.114	-1	9	4	2	0.4
1939 Bos-N	6	9	.400	28	11	3	0	1	128^{1}	143	6	54	33	13.9	4.00	92	.293	.365	10	.227	1	-1	-4	2	-0.2
1940 Bos-N	12	13	.480	34	29	17	3	4	236^{1}	241	8	90	34	12.6	3.16	118	.270	.338	13	.157	-2	18	15	1	1.5
1941 Bos-N	6	12	.333	38	23	5	2	1	165^{2}	192	12	62	45	14.0	4.78	75	.287	.351	8	.178	-0	-21	-22	1	-2.2
1942 Bos-N	2	5	.286	21	4	0	0	1	59^{1}	76	8	20	15	14.6	5.01	67	.309	.361	2	.125	-1	-11	-11	-1	-1.3
Chi-N	1	1	.500	13	0	0	0	0	24	39	1	8	9	18.0	4.13	78	.411	.462	0	.000	-1	-2	-2	1	-0.2
Yr	3	6	.333	34	4	0	0	1	83^{1}	115	9	28	24	15.6	4.75	69	.337	.389	2	.095	-1	-13	-13	-0	-1.5
Total 5	36	47	.434	168	77	31	6	13	736^{1}	804	36	290	176	13.5	3.85	93	.282	.350	37	.162	-5	-9	-21	5	-2.0

● CARL ERSKINE Erskine, Carl Daniel "Oisk" b: 12/13/26, Anderson, Ind. BR/TR, 5'10", 165 lbs. Deb: 7/25/48

YEAR TM/L	W	L	PCT	G	GS	CG	SH	SV	IP	H	HR	BB	SO	RAT	ERA	ERA+	OAV	OOB	BH	AVG	PB	PR	/A	PD	TPI
1948 Bro-N	6	3	.667	17	9	3	0	0	64	51	5	35	29	12.2	3.23	124	.231	.339	2	.095	-2	5	5	-1	0.3
1949 *Bro-N	8	1	.889	22	3	2	0	0	79^{2}	68	6	51	49	13.7	4.63	89	.235	.354	3	.115	-2	-5	-5	0	-0.6
1950 Bro-N	7	6	.538	22	13	3	0	1	103	109	15	35	50	12.7	4.72	87	.273	.333	9	.243	2	-7	-7	-1	-0.6
1951 Bro-N	16	12	.571	46	19	7	0	4	189^{2}	206	23	78	95	13.6	4.46	88	.280	.351	8	.131	-2	-11	-11	-0	-1.4
1952 *Bro-N	14	6	.700	33	26	10	4	2	206^{2}	167	17	71	131	10.5	2.70	135	.220	.289	10	.152	-0	24	22	2	2.5
1953 *Bro-N	20	6	**.769**	39	33	16	4	3	246^{2}	213	21	95	187	11.3	3.54	120	.230	.304	20	.215	0	20	20	-2	1.8
1954 Bro-N★	18	15	.545	38	37	12	2	1	260^{1}	239	31	92	166	11.6	4.15	98	.243	.311	14	.159	-1	-2	-2	-0	-0.4

YEAR TM/L	W	L	PCT	G	GS	CG	SH	SV	IP	H	HR	BB	SO	RAT	ERA	ERA+	OAV	OOB	BH	AVG	PB	PR	/A	PD	TPI
1955 *Bro-N	11	8	.579	31	29	7	2	1	194^2	185	29	64	84	11.5	3.79	107	.253	.313	15	.203	-0	5	6	-2	0.3
1956 *Bro-N	13	11	.542	31	28	8	1	0	186^1	189	25	57	95	11.9	4.25	93	.264	.320	8	.121	-4	-10	-6	1	-0.9
1957 Bro-N	5	3	.625	15	7	1	0	0	66	62	8	20	26	11.2	3.55	118	.248	.304	2	.091	-2	2	5	-1	0.2
1958 LA-N	4	4	.500	31	9	2	1	0	98^1	115	14	35	54	13.7	5.13	80	.297	.355	1	.037	-3	-13	-11	1	-1.3
1959 LA-N	0	3	.000	10	3	0	0	1	23^1	33	5	13	15	17.7	7.71	55	.320	.397	0	.000	-1	-10	-9	-0	-1.0
Total 12	122	78	.610	335	216	71	14	13	1718^2	1637	199	646	981	12.0	4.00	101	.252	.321	92	.156	-14	-0	6	-4	-1.1

● CHICO ESCARREGA Escarrega, Ernesto (Acosta) b: 12/27/49, Los Mochis, Mex. BR/TR, 5'11", 185 lbs. Deb: 4/26/82

YEAR TM/L	W	L	PCT	G	GS	CG	SH	SV	IP	H	HR	BB	SO	RAT	ERA	ERA+	OAV	OOB	BH	AVG	PB	PR	/A	PD	TPI
1982 Chi-A	1	3	.250	38	2	0	0	1	73^2	73	3	16	33	10.9	3.67	110	.263	.303	0	—	0	3	3	-1	0.3

● DUKE ESPER Esper, Charles H. b: 7/28/1868, Salem, N.J. d: 8/31/10, Philadelphia, Pa. TL, 5'11.5", 185 lbs. Deb: 4/18/1890

YEAR TM/L	W	L	PCT	G	GS	CG	SH	SV	IP	H	HR	BB	SO	RAT	ERA	ERA+	OAV	OOB	BH	AVG	PB	PR	/A	PD	TPI
1890 Phi-a	8	9	.471	18	16	14	1	0	143^2	176	1	67	61	15.5	4.89	78	.293	.368	18	.295	4	-16	-17	1	-1.0
Pit-N	0	2	.000	2	2	2	0	0	17	18	0	10	9	15.4	5.29	62	.263	.365	1	.143	-1	-3	-4	0	-0.3
Phi-N	5	0	1.000	5	5	4	0	0	41	40	1	16	18	12.3	3.07	119	.248	.316	3	.158	-1	2	3	0	0.2
Yr	5	2	.714	7	7	6	0	0	58	58	1	26	27	13.0	3.72	95	.251	.327	4	.154	-2	-1	-1	1	-0.1
1891 Phi-N	20	15	.571	39	36	25	1	1	296	302	8	121	108	13.1	3.56	96	.254	.327	27	.220	1	-7	-5	1	-0.3
1892 Phi-N	11	6	.647	21	18	14	0	1	160^1	171	2	58	45	12.9	3.42	95	.262	.324	17	.243	2	-2	-3	-1	-0.2
Pit-N	2	0	1.000	3	3	1	0	0	18^1	18	0	12	5	14.7	5.40	61	.247	.353	0	.000	-1	-4	-4	-0	-0.5
Yr	13	6	.684	24	21	15	0	1	178^2	189	2	70	50	13.0	3.63	90	.260	.325	17	.215	0	-7	-7	-1	-0.7
1893 Was-N	12	28	.300	42	36	34	0	0	334^1	442	14	156	78	16.4	4.71	98	.309	.381	41	.287	7	-2	-3	1	0.4
1894 Was-N	5	10	.333	18	14	7	0	0	116	177	8	39	24	16.9	7.45	71	.346	.395	14	.259	1	-27	-28	0	-1.9
*Bal-N	10	2	.833	16	9	8	0	2	101	107	1	36	25	12.8	3.92	139	.269	.331	10	.222	-1	16	17	1	1.4
Yr	15	12	.556	34	23	15	0	2	217	284	9	75	49	14.9	5.81	92	.312	.365	24	.242	0	-12	-11	1	-0.5
1895 *Bal-N	10	12	.455	34	25	16	1	1	218^1	248	2	79	39	13.5	3.92	122	.282	.341	16	.178	-6	21	20	-2	1.0
1896 Bal-N	14	5	.737	20	18	14	1	0	155^2	168	3	39	19	12.1	3.58	119	.273	.319	13	.197	-2	13	12	-2	0.7
1897 StL-N	1	6	.143	8	8	7	0	0	61^1	95	5	12	8	15.8	5.28	83	.350	.380	8	.320	1	-7	-6	1	-0.3
1898 StL-N	3	5	.375	10	8	6	0	0	64^2	86	1	22	14	15.0	5.98	63	.317	.368	10	.370	2	-17	-16	0	-1.2
Total 9	101	100	.502	236	198	152	4	5	1727^2	2048	46	667	453	14.3	4.39	96	.288	.351	178	.241	5	-33	-33	1	-2.0

● NINO ESPINOSA Espinosa, Arnulfo Acevedo (b: Arnulfo Acevedo (Espinosa)) b: 8/15/53, Villa Altagracia, d: 12/25/87, Villa Altagracia, BR/TR, 6'1", 192 lbs. Deb: 9/13/74

YEAR TM/L	W	L	PCT	G	GS	CG	SH	SV	IP	H	HR	BB	SO	RAT	ERA	ERA+	OAV	OOB	BH	AVG	PB	PR	/A	PD	TPI
1974 NY-N	0	0	—	2	1	0	0	0	9	12	1	0	2	12.0	5.00	71	.324	.324	1	.500	0	-1	-1	0	-0.1
1975 NY-N	0	1	.000	2	0	0	0	0	3	8	0	1	2	27.0	18.00	19	.471	.500	0	—	0	-5	-5	-0	-0.5
1976 NY-N	4	4	.500	12	5	0	0	0	41^2	41	3	13	30	11.7	3.67	90	.265	.321	0	.000	-1	-1	-2	-1	-0.3
1977 NY-N	10	13	.435	32	29	7	1	0	200	188	17	55	105	11.2	3.42	109	.249	.304	8	.129	-1	11	7	-0	0.6
1978 NY-N	11	15	.423	32	32	6	1	0	203^2	230	24	75	76	13.6	4.73	74	.292	.355	14	.209	2	-26	-28	2	-2.4
1979 Phi-N	14	12	.538	33	33	8	3	0	212	211	20	65	88	11.8	3.65	105	.262	.319	14	.194	2	2	4	0	0.6
1980 Phi-N	3	5	.375	12	12	1	0	0	76^1	73	9	19	13	11.1	3.77	100	.250	.300	3	.115	-1	-1	0	-1	-0.2
1981 Phi-N	2	5	.286	14	14	2	0	0	73^2	98	11	24	22	15.0	6.11	59	.333	.386	4	.200	-0	-21	-20	-1	-2.1
Tor-A	0	0	—	1	0	0	0	0	1	4	0	0	0	36.0	9.00	44	.667	.667	0	—	0	-1	-1	-0	-0.2
Total 8	44	55	.444	140	126	24	5	0	820^1	865	85	252	338	12.4	4.17	88	.275	.331	44	.171	1	-44	-46	0	-4.6

● ALVARO ESPINOZA Espinoza, Alvaro Alberto b: 2/19/62, Valencia, Venez. BR/TR, 6', 170 lbs. Deb: 9/14/84 ♦

YEAR TM/L	W	L	PCT	G	GS	CG	SH	SV	IP	H	HR	BB	SO	RAT	ERA	ERA+	OAV	OOB	BH	AVG	PB	PR	/A	PD	TPI
1991 NY-A	0	0	—	1	0	0	0	0	0^2	0	0	0	0	0.0	0.00	—	.000	.000	123	.256	1	0	0	0	0.0

● MARK ESSER Esser, Mark Gerald b: 4/1/56, Erie, Pa. BR/TL, 6'1", 190 lbs. Deb: 4/22/79

YEAR TM/L	W	L	PCT	G	GS	CG	SH	SV	IP	H	HR	BB	SO	RAT	ERA	ERA+	OAV	OOB	BH	AVG	PB	PR	/A	PD	TPI
1979 Chi-A	0	0	—	2	0	0	0	0	1^2	2	0	4	1	32.4	16.20	26	.286	.545	0	—	0	-2	-2	-0	-0.2

● BILL ESSICK Essick, William Earl "Vinegar Bill" b: 12/18/1881, Grand Ridge, Ill. d: 10/12/51, Los Angeles, Cal. TR, 5'10", 175 lbs. Deb: 9/12/06

YEAR TM/L	W	L	PCT	G	GS	CG	SH	SV	IP	H	HR	BB	SO	RAT	ERA	ERA+	OAV	OOB	BH	AVG	PB	PR	/A	PD	TPI
1906 Cin-N	2	2	.500	6	4	3	0	0	39^1	39	1	16	16	13.0	2.97	93	.273	.354	1	.077	-1	-1	-1	-1	-0.3
1907 Cin-N	0	2	.000	3	2	2	0	0	21^2	23	0	8	7	13.3	2.91	89	.274	.344	0	.000	-1	-1	-1	1	-0.1
Total 2	2	4	.333	9	6	5	0	0	61	62	1	24	23	13.1	2.95	91	.273	.350	1	.048	-2	-3	-2	-0	-0.4

● DICK ESTELLE Estelle, Richard Henry b: 1/18/42, Lakewood, N.J. BB/TL, 6'2", 170 lbs. Deb: 9/04/64

YEAR TM/L	W	L	PCT	G	GS	CG	SH	SV	IP	H	HR	BB	SO	RAT	ERA	ERA+	OAV	OOB	BH	AVG	PB	PR	/A	PD	TPI
1964 SF-N	1	2	.333	6	6	0	0	0	41^2	39	3	23	23	13.4	3.02	118	.247	.343	1	.067	-1	2	3	-1	0.1
1965 SF-N	0	0	—	6	1	0	0	0	11^1	12	0	8	6	16.7	3.97	91	.261	.382	0	.000	0	-1	-0	0	0.0
Total 2	1	2	.333	12	7	0	0	0	53	51	3	31	29	14.1	3.23	111	.250	.352	1	.063	-0	2	2	-1	0.1

● GEORGE ESTOCK Estock, George John b: 11/2/24, Stirling, N.J. BR/TR, 6', 185 lbs. Deb: 4/21/51

YEAR TM/L	W	L	PCT	G	GS	CG	SH	SV	IP	H	HR	BB	SO	RAT	ERA	ERA+	OAV	OOB	BH	AVG	PB	PR	/A	PD	TPI
1951 Bos-N	0	1	.000	37	1	0	0	3	60^1	56	2	37	11	13.9	4.33	85	.258	.366	2	.286	1	-2	-4	0	-0.3

● CHUCK ESTRADA Estrada, Charles Leonard b: 2/15/38, San Luis Obispo, Cal. BR/TR, 6'1", 185 lbs. Deb: 4/21/60 C

YEAR TM/L	W	L	PCT	G	GS	CG	SH	SV	IP	H	HR	BB	SO	RAT	ERA	ERA+	OAV	OOB	BH	AVG	PB	PR	/A	PD	TPI
1960 Bal-A★	**18**	11	.621	36	25	12	1	2	208^2	162	18	101	144	12.0	3.58	106	**.218**	.323	9	.141	-0	7	5	-0	0.5
1961 Bal-A	15	9	.625	33	31	6	1	0	212	159	19	132	160	12.8	3.69	106	**.207**	.331	8	.114	-3	8	5	-2	0.0
1962 Bal-A	9	17	.346	34	33	6	0	0	223^1	199	24	121	165	13.3	3.83	98	.240	.343	10	.152	-0	3	-2	-3	-0.5
1963 Bal-A	3	2	.600	8	7	0	0	0	31^1	26	2	19	16	13.2	4.60	77	.226	.341	1	.100	-1	-3	-4	-1	-0.5
1964 Bal-A	3	2	.600	17	6	0	0	0	54^2	62	8	21	32	14.0	5.27	68	.282	.350	2	.143	-0	-10	-10	-1	-1.2
1966 Chi-N	1	1	.500	9	1	0	0	0	12^1	16	2	5	3	16.1	7.30	50	.314	.386	0	.000	-0	-5	-5	-0	-0.6
1967 NY-N	1	2	.333	9	2	0	0	0	22	28	5	17	15	18.8	9.41	36	.326	.442	0	.000	-1	-15	-15	-0	-1.5
Total 7	50	44	.532	146	105	24	2	2	764^1	652	78	416	535	13.0	4.07	93	.232	.339	30	.129	-5	-15	-25	-8	-3.8

● OSCAR ESTRADA Estrada, Oscar b: 2/15/04, Havana, Cuba d: 1/2/78, Havana, Cuba BL/TL, 5'8", 160 lbs. Deb: 4/21/29

YEAR TM/L	W	L	PCT	G	GS	CG	SH	SV	IP	H	HR	BB	SO	RAT	ERA	ERA+	OAV	OOB	BH	AVG	PB	PR	/A	PD	TPI
1929 StL-A	0	0	—	1	0	0	0	0	1	1	0	1	0	18.0	0.00	—	.250	.400	0	—	0	0	0	0	0.1

● JOHN EUBANK Eubank, John Franklin "Honest John" b: 9/9/1872, Servia, Ind. d: 11/3/58, Bellevue, Mich. BR/TR, 6'2", 215 lbs. Deb: 9/19/05

YEAR TM/L	W	L	PCT	G	GS	CG	SH	SV	IP	H	HR	BB	SO	RAT	ERA	ERA+	OAV	OOB	BH	AVG	PB	PR	/A	PD	TPI
1905 Det-A	1	0	1.000	3	2	0	0	0	17^1	13	0	3	1	8.8	2.08	132	.210	.258	5	.357	1	1	1	-0	0.3
1906 Det-A	4	10	.286	24	12	7	1	2	135	147	0	35	38	12.7	3.53	78	.280	.335	13	.206	-0	-13	-12	1	-1.1
1907 Det-A	3	3	.500	15	8	4	1	0	81	88	0	20	17	12.2	2.67	98	.279	.326	4	.129	-1	-1	-0	1	-0.2
Total 3	8	13	.381	42	22	11	2	2	233^1	248	0	58	56	12.2	3.12	87	.275	.326	22	.204	-1	-13	-11	1	-1.0

● UEL EUBANKS Eubanks, Uel Melvin "Poss" b: 2/14/03, Quinlan, Tex. d: 11/21/54, Dallas, Tex. BR/TR, 6'3", 175 lbs. Deb: 7/20/22

YEAR TM/L	W	L	PCT	G	GS	CG	SH	SV	IP	H	HR	BB	SO	RAT	ERA	ERA+	OAV	OOB	BH	AVG	PB	PR	/A	PD	TPI
1922 Chi-N	0	0	—	2	0	0	0	0	1^2	5	0	4	1	48.6	27.00	16	.556	.692	1	1.000	1	-4	-4	0	-0.3

● FRANK EUFEMIA Eufemia, Frank Anthony b: 12/23/59, Bronx, N.Y. BR/TR, 5'11", 185 lbs. Deb: 5/21/85

YEAR TM/L	W	L	PCT	G	GS	CG	SH	SV	IP	H	HR	BB	SO	RAT	ERA	ERA+	OAV	OOB	BH	AVG	PB	PR	/A	PD	TPI
1985 Min-A	4	2	.667	39	0	0	0	2	61^2	56	7	21	30	11.2	3.79	116	.250	.314	0	—	0	2	4	1	0.5

● CHICK EVANS Evans, Charles Franklin b: 10/15/1889, Arlington, Vt. d: 9/2/16, Schenectady, N.Y. BR/TR, Deb: 9/19/09

YEAR TM/L	W	L	PCT	G	GS	CG	SH	SV	IP	H	HR	BB	SO	RAT	ERA	ERA+	OAV	OOB	BH	AVG	PB	PR	/A	PD	TPI
1909 Bos-N	0	3	.000	4	3	1	0	0	21^2	25	0	14	11	16.2	4.57	62	.305	.406	0	.000	-1	-5	-4	-0	-0.6
1910 Bos-N	1	1	.500	13	1	0	0	2	31	28	1	27	12	16.8	5.23	64	.275	.439	1	.100	-1	-8	-7	0	-0.7
Total 2	1	4	.200	17	4	1	0	2	52^2	53	1	41	23	16.6	4.96	63	.288	.425	1	.053	-2	-12	-11	0	-1.3

● ROY EVANS Evans, Roy b: 3/19/1874, Knoxville, Tenn. d: 8/15/15, Galveston, Tex. BR/TR, 6', 180 lbs. Deb: 5/15/1897

YEAR TM/L	W	L	PCT	G	GS	CG	SH	SV	IP	H	HR	BB	SO	RAT	ERA	ERA+	OAV	OOB	BH	AVG	PB	PR	/A	PD	TPI
1897 StL-N	0	0	—	3	0	0	0	0	13	33	1	13	4	31.8	9.69	45	.469	.552	0	.000	0	-8	-8	-0	-0.6
Lou-N	5	4	.556	9	8	6	0	0	59^1	66	4	24	20	14.9	4.10	104	.279	.365	3	.130	-2	1	1	-1	-0.1
Yr	5	4	.556	12	8	6	0	0	72^1	99	5	37	24	17.9	5.10	84	.323	.410	3	.115	-2	-6	-7	-1	-0.7
1898 Was-N	3	3	.500	7	6	4	0	0	50^2	50	0	25	11	14.6	3.38	109	.256	.361	1	.053	-2	1	2	-1	-0.1

YEAR TM/L	W	L	PCT	G	GS	CG	SH	SV	IP	H	HR	BB	SO	RAT	ERA	ERA+	OAV	OOB	BH	AVG	PB	PR	/A	PD	TPI
1899 Was-N	3	4	.429	7	7	6	0	0	54	60	1	25	27	14.2	5.67	69	.281	.356	4	.200	-1	-11	-11	0	-0.9
1902 NY-N	8	13	.381	23	17	17	0	0	176	186	2	58	48	13.0	3.17	89	.271	.337	8	.148	-1	-8	-7	2	-0.7
Bro-N	5	6	.455	13	11	11	2	0	97^1	91	0	33	35	11.7	2.68	103	.247	.313	9	.265	2	1	1	-3	0.0
Yr	13	19	.406	36	28	28	2	0	273^1	277	2	91	83	12.2	3.00	93	.260	.320	17	.193	1	-7	-6	-2	-0.7
1903 Bro-N	5	9	.357	15	12	9	0	0	110	121	1	41	42	13.8	3.27	98	.297	.371	5	.172	-0	-0	-1	-1	-0.2
StL-A	0	4	.000	7	7	4	0	0	54	66	1	14	24	13.8	4.17	70	.300	.350	2	.105	-1	-7	-8	0	-0.8
Total 5	29	43	.403	84	68	57	2	0	614^1	673	10	233	211	13.8	3.66	88	.281	.354	32	.159	-4	-30	-30	-5	-3.4

● RED EVANS Evans, Russell Edison b: 11/12/06, Chicago, Ill. d: 6/14/82, Lakeview, Ark. BR/TR, 5'11", 168 lbs. Deb: 4/24/36

YEAR TM/L	W	L	PCT	G	GS	CG	SH	SV	IP	H	HR	BB	SO	RAT	ERA	ERA+	OAV	OOB	BH	AVG	PB	PR	/A	PD	TPI
1936 Chi-A	0	3	.000	17	0	0	0	1	47^1	70	4	22	19	17.5	7.61	68	.338	.402	2	.133	-1	-14	-13	1	-1.1
1939 Bro-N	1	8	.111	24	6	0	0	1	64^1	74	4	26	28	14.0	5.18	78	.284	.348	4	.308	1	-9	-8	1	-0.6
Total 2	1	11	.083	41	6	0	0	2	111^2	144	8	48	47	15.5	6.21	73	.308	.372	6	.214	-0	-23	-21	3	-1.7

● JAKE EVANS Evans, Uriah L. P. "Bloody Jake" b: 9/1856, Baltimore, Md. d: 1/16/07, Baltimore, Md. TR, 5'8", 154 lbs. Deb: 5/01/1879 ♦

YEAR TM/L	W	L	PCT	G	GS	CG	SH	SV	IP	H	HR	BB	SO	RAT	ERA	ERA+	OAV	OOB	BH	AVG	PB	PR	/A	PD	TPI
1880 Tro-N	0	0	—	1	0	0	0	0	4	11	0	0	0	24.8	13.50	19	.524	.524	46	.256	0	-5	-5	0	-0.4
1882 Wor-N	0	1	.000	1	1	1	0	0	8	13	1	0	2	14.6	5.63	55	.317	.317	71	.213	-0	-2	-2	-0	-0.2
1883 Cle-N	0	0	—	1	0	0	0	0	3	0	0	0	1	0.0	0.00	—	.000	.000	79	.238	0	1	1	1	0.2
Total 3	0	1	.000	3	1	1	0	0	15	24	1	0	3	14.4	6.60	45	.338	.338	435	.238	-0	-6	-6	1	-0.4

● ART EVANS Evans, William Arthur b: 8/3/11, Elvins, Mo. d: 1/8/52, Wichita, Kan. BB/TL, 6'1.5", 181 lbs. Deb: 6/20/32

YEAR TM/L	W	L	PCT	G	GS	CG	SH	SV	IP	H	HR	BB	SO	RAT	ERA	ERA+	OAV	OOB	BH	AVG	PB	PR	/A	PD	TPI
1932 Chi-A	0	0	—	7	0	0	0	0	18	19	1	10	6	14.5	3.00	144	.257	.345	0	.000	-0	3	3	1	0.3

● BILL EVANS Evans, William James b: 2/10/1894, Reidsville, N.C. d: 12/21/46, Burlington, N.C. BR/TR, 6', 175 lbs. Deb: 8/13/16

YEAR TM/L	W	L	PCT	G	GS	CG	SH	SV	IP	H	HR	BB	SO	RAT	ERA	ERA+	OAV	OOB	BH	AVG	PB	PR	/A	PD	TPI
1916 Pit-N	2	5	.286	13	6	3	0	0	63	57	2	16	21	10.9	3.00	89	.249	.306	3	.150	-1	-3	-2	2	-0.1
1917 Pit-N	0	4	.000	8	2	1	0	0	26^2	24	0	14	5	13.2	3.38	84	.231	.328	1	.111	-0	-2	-2	-0	-0.2
1919 Pit-N	0	4	.000	7	3	2	0	0	36^2	41	1	18	15	14.5	5.65	54	.297	.378	0	.000	-1	-11	-11	1	-1.2
Total 3	2	13	.133	28	11	6	0	0	126^1	122	3	48	41	12.4	3.85	73	.259	.333	4	.100	-2	-16	-14	2	-1.5

● BILL EVANS Evans, William Lawrence b: 3/25/19, Quanah, Texas d: 11/30/83, Grand Junction, Colo. BR/TR, 6'2", 180 lbs. Deb: 4/21/49

YEAR TM/L	W	L	PCT	G	GS	CG	SH	SV	IP	H	HR	BB	SO	RAT	ERA	ERA+	OAV	OOB	BH	AVG	PB	PR	/A	PD	TPI
1949 Chi-A	0	1	.000	4	0	0	0	0	6^1	6	0	8	1	19.9	7.11	59	.261	.452	0	.000	-0	-2	-2	-0	-0.2
1951 Bos-A	0	0	—	9	0	0	0	0	15^1	15	0	8	3	13.5	4.11	109	.268	.359	0	.000	-1	0	1	-0	0.0
Total 2	0	1	.000	13	0	0	0	0	21^2	21	0	16	4	15.4	4.98	88	.266	.389	0	.000	-1	-2	-1	-1	-0.2

● LEON EVERITT Everitt, Edward Leon b: 1/12/47, Marshall, Tex. BL/TR, 6'1.5", 195 lbs. Deb: 4/21/69

YEAR TM/L	W	L	PCT	G	GS	CG	SH	SV	IP	H	HR	BB	SO	RAT	ERA	ERA+	OAV	OOB	BH	AVG	PB	PR	/A	PD	TPI
1969 SD-N	0	1	.000	5	0	0	0	0	15^2	18	4	12	11	17.8	8.04	44	.300	.425	0	.000	-0	-8	-8	0	-0.7

● BOB EWING Ewing, George Lemuel "Long Bob" b: 4/24/1873, New Hampshire, O. d: 6/20/47, Wapakoneta, Ohio BR/TR, 6'1.5", 170 lbs. Deb: 4/19/02

YEAR TM/L	W	L	PCT	G	GS	CG	SH	SV	IP	H	HR	BB	SO	RAT	ERA	ERA+	OAV	OOB	BH	AVG	PB	PR	/A	PD	TPI
1902 Cin-N	5	6	.455	15	12	10	0	0	117^2	126	1	47	44	13.5	2.98	100	.274	.345	12	.169	-1	-3	0	-1	-0.2
1903 Cin-N	14	13	.519	29	28	27	1	1	246^2	254	3	64	104	12.0	2.77	128	.265	.317	24	.253	4	14	22	4	3.0
1904 Cin-N	11	13	.458	26	24	22	0	0	212	198	3	58	99	11.0	2.46	119	.253	.308	25	.258	5	7	11	-1	1.7
1905 Cin-N	20	11	.645	40	34	30	4	0	311^2	284	5	79	164	10.8	2.51	132	.246	.301	32	.262	4	17	27	-3	3.1
1906 Cin-N	13	14	.481	33	32	26	2	0	287^2	248	4	60	145	9.7	2.38	116	.238	.281	14	.139	-3	8	12	1	1.0
1907 Cin-N	17	19	.472	41	37	32	2	0	332^2	279	2	85	147	10.0	1.73	150	.231	.286	19	.154	-1	27	**32**	-6	3.0
1908 Cin-N	17	15	.531	37	32	23	4	3	293^2	247	5	57	95	9.5	2.21	105	.241	.284	14	.149	-1	5	3	-3	-0.1
1909 Cin-N	11	12	.478	31	29	14	2	0	218^1	195	1	63	86	10.9	2.43	107	.238	.298	8	.110	-4	4	4	-4	-0.4
1910 Phi-N	16	14	.533	34	32	20	4	0	255^1	235	5	86	102	11.6	3.00	104	.251	.318	20	.222	2	1	4	-2	0.4
1911 Phi-N	0	1	.000	4	3	1	0	0	24	29	2	14	12	16.1	7.88	44	.309	.398	2	.333	0	-12	-12	-0	-1.0
1912 StL-N	0	0	—	1	1	0	0	0	1^1	2	0	1	0	20.3	0.00	—	.333	.429	0	—	0	1	1	0	0.1
Total 11	124	118	.512	291	264	205	19	4	2301	2097	31	614	998	10.8	2.49	116	.247	.302	170	.195	5	69	102	-16	10.6

● JOHN EWING Ewing, John "Long Jong" b: 6/1/1863, Cincinnati, Ohio d: 4/23/1895, Denver, Colo. TR, Deb: 6/18/1883 F♦

YEAR TM/L	W	L	PCT	G	GS	CG	SH	SV	IP	H	HR	BB	SO	RAT	ERA	ERA+	OAV	OOB	BH	AVG	PB	PR	/A	PD	TPI
1888 Lou-a	8	13	.381	21	21	21	2	0	191	175	3	34	87	10.2	2.83	109	.235	.276	16	.203	-1	5	5	0	0.4
1889 Lou-a	6	30	.167	40	39	37	1	0	331	407	6	147	155	15.4	4.87	79	.293	.367	23	.172	-6	-37	-37	2	-3.3
1890 NY-P	18	12	.600	35	31	27	1	2	267^1	293	6	104	145	13.9	4.24	107	.267	.339	24	.211	-2	-0	9	0	0.5
1891 NY-N	21	8	**.724**	33	30	28	5	0	269^1	237	2	105	138	11.8	**2.27**	141	.227	.305	23	.204	-2	32	28	0	2.4
Total 4	53	63	.457	129	121	113	9	2	1058^2	1112	17	390	525	13.2	3.68	101	.260	.329	87	.192	-11	-1	3	3	0.0

● BUCK EWING Ewing, William b: 10/17/1859, Hoaglands, Ohio d: 10/20/06, Cincinnati, Ohio BR/TR, 5'10", 188 lbs. Deb: 9/09/1880 FMH♦

YEAR TM/L	W	L	PCT	G	GS	CG	SH	SV	IP	H	HR	BB	SO	RAT	ERA	ERA+	OAV	OOB	BH	AVG	PB	PR	/A	PD	TPI
1882 Tro-N	0	0	—	1	0	0	0	0	1	2	0	1	0	27.0	9.00	31	.400	.500	89	.271	0	-1	-1	0	0.0
1884 NY-N	0	1	.000	1	1	1	0	0	8	7	0	4	3	12.4	1.13	265	.241	.333	106	.277	0	2	2	-0	0.2
1885 NY-N	0	1	.000	1	0	0	0	0	2	4	0	3	0	31.5	4.50	59	.444	.583	104	.304	0	-0	-0	-0	0.0
1888 *NY-N	0	0	—	2	0	0	0	0	7	8	1	4	6	16.7	2.57	107	.174	.255	127	.306	1	0	0	-0	0.0
1889 *NY-N	2	0	1.000	3	2	2	0	0	20	23	0	8	12	13.9	4.05	97	.280	.344	133	.327	2	-0	-0	-0	0.0
1890 NY-P	0	1	.000	1	1	1	0	0	9	11	1	3	2	14.0	4.00	114	.289	.340	119	.338	1	0	1	-0	0.1
Total 6	2	3	.400	9	4	4	0	0	47	55	2	23	23	15.1	3.45	105	.263	.339	1625	.303	4	1	1	-1	0.3

● GEORGE EYRICH Eyrich, George Lincoln b: 3/3/25, Reading, Pa. BR/TR, 5'11", 175 lbs. Deb: 6/13/43

YEAR TM/L	W	L	PCT	G	GS	CG	SH	SV	IP	H	HR	BB	SO	RAT	ERA	ERA+	OAV	OOB	BH	AVG	PB	PR	/A	PD	TPI
1943 Phi-N	0	0	—	9	0	0	0	0	18^2	27	1	9	5	17.4	3.38	100	.342	.409	0	.000	-0	0	-0	-0	0.0

● RED FABER Faber, Urban Charles b: 9/6/1888, Cascade, Iowa d: 9/25/76, Chicago, Ill. BB/TR, 6'2", 180 lbs. Deb: 4/17/14 CH

YEAR TM/L	W	L	PCT	G	GS	CG	SH	SV	IP	H	HR	BB	SO	RAT	ERA	ERA+	OAV	OOB	BH	AVG	PB	PR	/A	PD	TPI
1914 Chi-A	10	9	.526	40	19	11	2	**4**	181^1	154	3	64	88	11.4	2.68	100	.239	.319	8	.145	1	1	0	2	0.3
1915 Chi-A	24	14	.632	**50**	32	21	2	2	299^2	264	3	99	182	11.2	2.55	117	.240	.309	11	.131	2	13	14	-0	1.8
1916 Chi-A	17	9	.654	35	25	15	3	1	205^1	167	1	61	87	10.2	2.02	137	.228	.292	6	.095	-3	19	17	2	1.7
1917 *Chi-A	16	13	.552	41	29	16	3	3	248	224	1	85	84	11.6	1.92	138	.247	.319	4	.058	-4	20	20	2	2.0
1918 Chi-A	4	1	.800	11	9	5	1	1	80^2	70	3	23	26	10.4	1.23	223	.245	.301	1	.042	-2	14	14	1	1.5
1919 Chi-A	11	9	.550	25	20	9	0	0	162^1	185	7	45	45	13.2	3.83	83	.287	.341	10	.185	-0	-11	-12	0	-1.2
1920 Chi-A	23	13	.639	40	39	28	2	1	319	332	8	88	108	12.0	2.99	126	.277	.328	11	.106	-4	29	28	-1	2.2
1921 Chi-A	25	15	.625	43	39	**32**	4	1	330^2	293	10	87	124	**10.5**	**2.48**	**171**	**.242**	**.297**	16	.148	-4	**66**	**65**	1	**6.3**
1922 Chi-A	21	17	.553	43	38	**31**	4	2	**352**	334	10	83	148	**10.8**	**2.81**	**145**	.252	**.299**	25	.200	-2	**48**	**49**	1	**4.8**
1923 Chi-A	14	11	.560	32	31	15	2	0	232^1	233	6	62	91	11.7	3.41	116	.259	.311	15	.217	3	15	14	2	2.0
1924 Chi-A	9	11	.450	21	20	9	0	0	161^1	173	5	58	47	13.0	3.85	107	.282	.346	8	.148	-2	7	5	-2	0.1
1925 Chi-A	12	11	.522	34	32	16	1	0	238	266	8	59	71	12.4	3.78	110	.289	.333	8	.104	-4	16	10	1	0.7
1926 Chi-A	15	9	.625	27	25	13	1	0	184^2	203	3	57	65	12.8	3.56	109	.281	.335	9	.150	-0	9	6	-3	0.3
1927 Chi-A	4	7	.364	18	15	6	0	0	110^2	131	2	41	39	14.4	4.55	89	.312	.380	10	.270	2	-5	-6	2	-0.2
1928 Chi-A	13	9	.591	27	27	16	2	0	201^1	223	11	68	43	13.2	3.75	108	.286	.347	8	.114	-3	6	7	1	0.4
1929 Chi-A	13	13	.500	31	31	15	1	0	234	241	10	61	68	12.0	3.88	110	.273	.327	10	.128	-3	9	10	2	0.9
1930 Chi-A	8	13	.381	29	26	10	0	1	169	188	7	49	62	12.9	4.21	110	.283	.337	2	.041	-5	8	8	2	0.5
1931 Chi-A	10	14	.417	44	19	5	1	1	184	210	11	57	49	13.2	3.82	112	.285	.339	4	.075	-3	12	9	-2	0.4
1932 Chi-A	2	11	.154	42	5	0	0	6	106	123	0	38	26	13.8	3.74	116	.290	.350	4	.222	3	**9**	7	-0	0.9
1933 Chi-A	3	4	.429	36	2	0	0	5	86^1	92	2	28	18	12.6	3.44	123	.275	.332	0	.000	-3	8	8	-1	0.4
Total 20	254	213	.544	669	483	273	29	28	4086^2	4106	111	1213	1471	11.9	3.15	119	.266	.323	170	.134	-30	294	274	11	25.8

● ROY FACE Face, Elroy Leon b: 2/20/28, Stephentown, N.Y. BR/TR, 5'8", 155 lbs. Deb: 4/16/53

YEAR TM/L	W	L	PCT	G	GS	CG	SH	SV	IP	H	HR	BB	SO	RAT	ERA	ERA+	OAV	OOB	BH	AVG	PB	PR	/A	PD	TPI
1953 Pit-N	6	8	.429	41	13	2	0	0	119	145	19	30	56	13.4	6.58	68	.297	.340	4	.133	-2	-30	-28	-1	-2.8
1955 Pit-N	5	7	.417	42	10	4	0	5	125^2	128	10	40	84	12.0	3.58	115	.268	.325	3	.115	-1	6	7	-1	0.6
1956 Pit-N	12	13	.480	**68**	3	0	0	6	135^1	131	16	42	96	11.6	3.52	107	.256	.314	5	.192	-0	4	4	1	0.5

YEAR	TM/L	W	L	PCT	G	GS	CG	SH	SV	IP	H	HR	BB	SO	RAT	ERA	ERA+	OAV	OOB	BH	AVG	PB	PR	/A	PD	TPI
1957	Pit-N	4	6	.400	59	1	0	0	10	93^2	97	9	24	53	11.7	3.07	123	.270	.318	2	.125	-1	8	7	-2	0.5
1958	Pit-N	5	2	.714	57	0	0	0	**20**	84	77	6	22	47	10.6	2.89	134	.244	.293	0	.000	-1	10	9	1	0.9
1959	Pit-N★	18	1	**.947**	57	0	0	0	10	93^1	91	5	25	69	11.3	2.70	143	.266	.318	3	.231	0	13	12	-0	1.2
1960	*Pit-N★	10	8	.556	**68**	0	0	0	24	114^2	93	11	29	72	9.6	2.90	129	.226	.277	7	.412	2	11	11	1	1.5
1961	Pit-N★	6	12	.333	62	0	0	0	**17**	92	94	12	10	55	10.3	3.82	105	.267	.289	3	.273	0	2	2	2	0.4
1962	Pit-N	8	7	.533	63	0	0	0	**28**	91	74	7	18	45	9.2	1.88	209	.231	.274	1	.083	-1	**21**	**21**	-1	1.9
1963	Pit-N	3	9	.250	56	0	0	0	16	69^2	75	6	19	41	12.5	3.23	102	.285	.340	2	.250	0	0	1	1	0.2
1964	Pit-N	3	3	.500	55	0	0	0	4	79^2	82	11	27	63	12.4	5.20	68	.269	.330	0	.000	-0	-15	-15	0	-1.6
1965	Pit-N	5	2	.714	16	0	0	0	0	20^1	20	1	7	19	12.0	2.66	132	.263	.325	0	.000	-0	2	2	-1	0.1
1966	Pit-N	6	6	.500	54	0	0	0	18	70	68	9	24	67	12.0	2.70	132	.262	.326	0	.000	-1	7	7	1	0.7
1967	Pit-N	7	5	.583	61	0	0	0	17	74^1	62	5	22	41	10.2	2.42	139	.230	.288	0	.000	-1	8	8	-1	0.7
1968	Pit-N	2	4	.333	43	0	0	0	13	52	46	3	7	34	9.5	2.60	113	.238	.272	0	.000	-0	2	2	-0	0.1
	Det-A	0	0	—	2	0	0	0	0	1	2	0	1	1	27.0	0.00	—	.500	.600	0	—	0	0	0	0	0.0
1969	Mon-N	4	2	.667	44	0	0	0	5	59^1	62	11	15	34	11.7	3.94	93	.263	.307	1	.500	0	-2	-2	-1	-0.2
Total	16	104	95	.523	848	27	6	0	193	1375	1347	141	362	877	11.3	3.48	109	.260	.310	31	.160	-4	48	48	0	4.7

● TONY FAETH Faeth, Anthony Joseph b: 7/9/1893, Aberdeen, S.D. d: 12/22/82, St.Paul, Minn. BR/TR, 6', 180 lbs. Deb: 8/10/19

YEAR	TM/L	W	L	PCT	G	GS	CG	SH	SV	IP	H	HR	BB	SO	RAT	ERA	ERA+	OAV	OOB	BH	AVG	PB	PR	/A	PD	TPI
1919	Cle-A	0	0	—	6	0	0	0	0	18^1	13	0	10	7	11.3	0.49	682	.224	.338	0	.000	-1	6	6	-0	0.5
1920	Cle-A	0	0	—	13	0	0	0	0	25	31	0	20	14	18.7	4.32	88	.333	.456	0	.000	-1	-1	-1	-0	-0.2
Total	2	0	0	—	19	0	0	0	0	43^1	44	0	30	21	15.6	2.70	134	.291	.412	0	.000	-1	4	4	-0	0.3

● EVERETT FAGAN Fagan, Everett Joseph b: 1/13/18, Pottersville, N.J. d: 2/16/83, Morristown, N.J. BR/TR, 6', 195 lbs. Deb: 4/24/43

YEAR	TM/L	W	L	PCT	G	GS	CG	SH	SV	IP	H	HR	BB	SO	RAT	ERA	ERA+	OAV	OOB	BH	AVG	PB	PR	/A	PD	TPI
1943	Phi-A	2	6	.250	18	2	0	0	3	37^1	41	4	14	9	13.7	6.27	54	.283	.354	0	.000	-0	-12	-12	0	-1.2
1946	Phi-A	0	1	.000	20	0	0	0	0	45	47	2	24	12	14.8	4.80	74	.264	.361	4	.286	1	-6	-6	-0	-0.6
Total	2	2	7	.222	38	2	0	0	3	82^1	88	6	38	21	14.3	5.47	64	.272	.358	4	.190	1	-19	-18	0	-1.8

● BILL FAGAN Fagan, William A. "Clinkers" b: 2/15/1869, Troy, N.Y. d: 3/21/30, Troy, N.Y. TL , 5'11", 165 lbs. Deb: 9/15/1887

YEAR	TM/L	W	L	PCT	G	GS	CG	SH	SV	IP	H	HR	BB	SO	RAT	ERA	ERA+	OAV	OOB	BH	AVG	PB	PR	/A	PD	TPI
1887	NY-a	1	4	.200	6	6	6	0	0	45	55	1	24	12	16.2	4.00	106	.306	.393	3	.143	-2	1	1	0	0.0
1888	KC-a	5	11	.313	17	17	15	0	0	142^1	179	4	75	49	16.1	5.69	60	.296	.375	14	.215	-1	-42	-36	1	-2.9
Total	2	6	15	.286	23	23	21	0	0	187^1	234	5	99	61	16.1	5.28	69	.299	.379	17	.198	-3	-40	-34	1	-2.9

● FRANK FAHEY Fahey, Francis Raymond b: 1/22/1896, Milford, Mass. d: 3/19/54, Boston, Mass. BB/TR, 6'1", 190 lbs. Deb: 4/25/18 ♦

YEAR	TM/L	W	L	PCT	G	GS	CG	SH	SV	IP	H	HR	BB	SO	RAT	ERA	ERA+	OAV	OOB	BH	AVG	PB	PR	/A	PD	TPI
1918	Phi-A	0	0	—	3	0	0	0	0	9	5	0	14	1	20.0	6.00	49	.200	.500	3	.176	-0	-3	-3	-1	-0.4

● JERRY FAHR Fahr, Gerald Warren b: 12/9/24, Marmaduke, Ark. BR/TR, 6'5", 185 lbs. Deb: 4/29/51

YEAR	TM/L	W	L	PCT	G	GS	CG	SH	SV	IP	H	HR	BB	SO	RAT	ERA	ERA+	OAV	OOB	BH	AVG	PB	PR	/A	PD	TPI
1951	Cle-A	0	0	—	5	0	0	0	0	5^2	11	0	2	0	20.6	4.76	80	.500	.542	0	—	0	-0	-1	-0	-0.1

● PETE FAHRER Fahrer, Clarence Willie b: 3/10/1890, Holgate, Ohio d: 6/10/67, Fremont, Mich. BL/TR, 6', 190 lbs. Deb: 8/17/14

YEAR	TM/L	W	L	PCT	G	GS	CG	SH	SV	IP	H	HR	BB	SO	RAT	ERA	ERA+	OAV	OOB	BH	AVG	PB	PR	/A	PD	TPI
1914	Cin-N	0	0	—	5	0	0	0	0	8	8	0	4	2	13.5	1.13	260	.308	.400	0	.000	-0	1	2	0	0.2

● JIM FAIRBANK Fairbank, James Lee "Lee" or "Smoky" b: 3/17/1881, Deansboro, N.Y. d: 12/27/55, Utica, N.Y. BR/TR, 5'10", 185 lbs. Deb: 9/18/03

YEAR	TM/L	W	L	PCT	G	GS	CG	SH	SV	IP	H	HR	BB	SO	RAT	ERA	ERA+	OAV	OOB	BH	AVG	PB	PR	/A	PD	TPI
1903	Phi-A	1	1	.500	4	1	1	0	0	24	33	1	12	10	16.9	4.88	63	.325	.397	1	.100	-1	-5	-5	1	-0.4
1904	Phi-A	0	1	.000	3	1	1	0	0	17	19	0	13	6	18.0	6.35	42	.283	.414	0	.000	-1	-7	-7	1	-0.7
Total	2	1	2	.333	7	2	2	0	0	41	52	1	25	16	17.3	5.49	53	.309	.404	1	.063	-1	-12	-12	2	-1.1

● RAGS FAIRCLOTH Faircloth, James Lamar b: 8/19/1892, Kenton, Tenn. d: 10/5/53, Tucson, Ariz. BR/TR, 5'11", 160 lbs. Deb: 5/06/19

YEAR	TM/L	W	L	PCT	G	GS	CG	SH	SV	IP	H	HR	BB	SO	RAT	ERA	ERA+	OAV	OOB	BH	AVG	PB	PR	/A	PD	TPI
1919	Phi-N	0	0	—	2	0	0	0	0	2	5	0	0	0	22.5	9.00	36	.625	.625	0	—	0	-1	-1	0	-0.1

● HECTOR FAJARDO Fajardo, Hector (Nabaratte) b: 11/16/70, Sahuayo, Mexico BR/TR, 6'4", 185 lbs. Deb: 8/10/91

YEAR	TM/L	W	L	PCT	G	GS	CG	SH	SV	IP	H	HR	BB	SO	RAT	ERA	ERA+	OAV	OOB	BH	AVG	PB	PR	/A	PD	TPI
1991	Pit-N	0	0	—	2	2	0	0	0	6^1	10	0	7	8	24.2	9.95	36	.357	.486	0	.000	-0	-4	-4	-0	-0.5
	Tex-A	0	2	.000	4	3	0	0	0	19	25	2	4	15	14.2	5.68	71	.329	.370	0	—	0	-3	-3	-0	-0.3
Total	1	0	2	.000	6	5	0	0	0	25^1	35	2	11	23	16.7	6.75	58	.337	.405	0	.000	-0	-8	-8	-1	-0.8

● PETE FALCONE Falcone, Peter Frank b: 10/1/53, Brooklyn, N.Y. BL/TL, 6'2", 185 lbs. Deb: 4/13/75

YEAR	TM/L	W	L	PCT	G	GS	CG	SH	SV	IP	H	HR	BB	SO	RAT	ERA	ERA+	OAV	OOB	BH	AVG	PB	PR	/A	PD	TPI
1975	SF-N	12	11	.522	34	32	3	1	0	190	171	16	111	131	13.5	4.17	91	.244	.350	4	.062	-5	-12	-8	-1	-1.3
1976	StL-N	12	16	.429	32	32	9	2	0	212	173	12	93	138	11.4	3.23	110	.222	.306	8	.129	-2	6	7	-4	0.2
1977	StL-N	4	8	.333	27	22	1	1	1	124	130	19	61	75	14.1	5.44	71	.273	.359	10	.244	2	-21	-22	-1	-2.0
1978	StL-N	2	7	.222	19	14	0	0	0	75	94	9	48	28	17.3	5.76	61	.319	.417	5	.238	1	-18	-19	-2	-1.9
1979	NY-N	6	14	.300	33	31	1	1	0	184	194	24	76	113	13.3	4.16	88	.276	.347	9	.173	0	-9	-11	-3	-1.4
1980	NY-N	7	10	.412	37	23	1	0	1	157^1	163	16	58	109	12.8	4.52	79	.269	.335	6	.146	-1	-16	-17	-3	-2.1
1981	NY-N	5	3	.625	35	9	3	1	1	95^1	84	3	36	56	11.3	2.55	137	.241	.312	4	.182	1	10	10	-2	1.0
1982	NY-N	8	10	.444	40	23	3	0	2	171	159	24	71	101	12.2	3.84	94	.252	.329	6	.113	-2	-5	-4	-3	-0.9
1983	Atl-N	9	4	.692	33	15	2	0	0	106^2	102	14	60	59	13.8	3.63	107	.256	.355	3	.115	-1	-0	3	-2	0.0
1984	Atl-N	5	7	.417	35	16	2	1	2	120	115	15	57	55	12.9	4.13	93	.252	.335	7	.212	1	-7	-4	-1	-0.4
Total	10	70	90	.438	325	217	25	7	7	1435^1	1385	152	671	865	13.0	4.07	90	.257	.341	62	.149	-6	-71	-63	-20	-8.8

● CHET FALK Falk, Chester Emanuel "Spot" b: 5/15/05, Austin, Tex. d: 1/7/82, Austin, Tex. BL/TL, 6'2", 170 lbs. Deb: 4/20/25 F

YEAR	TM/L	W	L	PCT	G	GS	CG	SH	SV	IP	H	HR	BB	SO	RAT	ERA	ERA+	OAV	OOB	BH	AVG	PB	PR	/A	PD	TPI
1925	StL-A	0	0	—	13	0	0	0	0	25	38	2	17	7	19.8	8.28	56	.362	.451	5	.625	2	-11	-10	0	-0.6
1926	StL-A	4	4	.500	18	8	3	0	0	74	95	1	27	7	15.6	5.35	80	.338	.408	6	.194	-1	-11	-9	-1	-1.0
1927	StL-A	1	0	1.000	9	0	0	0	0	15^2	25	1	10	2	20.1	5.74	76	.352	.432	1	.200	-0	-3	-2	0	-0.2
Total	3	5	4	.556	40	8	3	0	0	114^2	158	4	54	16	17.1	6.04	73	.346	.422	12	.273	1	-25	-21	0	-1.8

● CY FALKENBERG Falkenberg, Frederick Peter b: 12/17/1880, Chicago, Ill. d: 4/14/61, San Francisco, Cal BR/TR, 6'5", 180 lbs. Deb: 4/21/03

YEAR	TM/L	W	L	PCT	G	GS	CG	SH	SV	IP	H	HR	BB	SO	RAT	ERA	ERA+	OAV	OOB	BH	AVG	PB	PR	/A	PD	TPI
1903	Pit-N	1	5	.167	10	6	3	0	0	56	65	0	32	24	15.9	3.86	84	.295	.390	4	.190	-0	-4	-4	2	-0.2
1905	Was-A	7	2	.778	12	10	6	2	0	75^1	71	1	31	35	12.4	3.82	69	.250	.328	4	.125	-2	-10	-10	-1	-1.3
1906	Was-A	14	20	.412	40	36	30	2	1	298^2	277	1	108	178	12.0	2.86	92	.249	.323	18	.170	1	-6	-8	1	-0.5
1907	Was-A	6	17	.261	32	24	17	1	1	233^2	195	0	77	108	10.8	2.35	103	.229	.299	12	.140	-3	5	2	2	0.1
1908	Was-A	6	2	.750	17	8	5	1	0	82^2	70	2	21	34	10.1	1.96	117	.236	.291	6	.222	0	4	3	1	0.4
	Cle-A	2	4	.333	8	7	2	0	0	46^1	52	1	10	17	12.4	3.88	62	.284	.328	2	.118	-1	-8	-8	-1	-1.0
	Yr	8	6	.571	25	15	7	1	0	129	122	3	31	51	10.8	2.65	88	.253	.301	8	.182	-1	-4	-5	0	-0.6
1909	Cle-A	10	9	.526	24	18	13	2	0	165	135	0	50	82	10.4	2.40	107	.231	.297	9	.173	-1	1	3	3	0.5
1910	Cle-A	14	13	.519	37	29	18	3	1	256^2	246	3	75	107	11.5	2.95	88	.261	.320	15	.183	-0	-12	-10	3	-0.8
1911	Cle-A	8	5	.615	15	13	7	0	1	106^2	117	0	24	46	12.2	3.29	104	.282	.326	7	.175	-1	1	1	1	0.0
1913	Cle-A	23	10	.697	39	36	23	6	0	276	238	2	88	166	10.8	2.22	137	.235	.299	10	.119	-2	22	25	-2	2.3
1914	Ind-F	25	16	.610	**49**	43	33	**9**	3	**377**^{1}	332	5	89	**236**	10.2	2.22	156	.236	.284	21	.168	-3	41	**52**	3	5.8
1915	New-F	9	11	.450	25	21	14	0	1	172	175	6	47	76	12.1	3.24	88	.268	.326	3	.053	-6	-4	-8	1	-1.3
	Bro-F	3	3	.500	7	7	5	1	0	48	31	1	12	20	8.3	1.50	201	.189	.249	1	.067	-1	8	8	-0	0.8
	Yr	12	14	.462	32	28	19	1	1	220	206	7	59	96	10.9	2.86	101	.250	.301	4	.056	-7	4	0	1	-0.5
1917	Phi-A	2	6	.250	15	8	4	0	0	80^2	86	1	26	35	12.5	3.35	82	.293	.350	5	.185	0	-6	-5	1	-0.4
Total	12	130	123	.514	330	266	180	27	8	2275	2090	23	690	1164	11.3	2.68	106	.248	.310	117	.152	-20	34	41	13	4.4

● ED FALLENSTEIN Fallenstein, Edward Joseph "Jack" (b: Edward Joseph Valestin)
b: 12/22/08, Newark, N.J. d: 11/24/71, Orange, N.J. BR/TR, 6'3", 180 lbs. Deb: 4/16/31

YEAR	TM/L	W	L	PCT	G	GS	CG	SH	SV	IP	H	HR	BB	SO	RAT	ERA	ERA+	OAV	OOB	BH	AVG	PB	PR	/A	PD	TPI
1931	Phi-N	0	0	—	24	0	0	0	0	41^2	56	2	26	15	17.7	7.13	60	.333	.423	1	.200	0	-15	-13	0	-1.3
1933	Bos-N	2	1	.667	9	4	1	1	0	35	43	1	13	5	14.7	3.60	85	.305	.368	3	.375	1	-1	-2	-0	-0.1
Total	2	2	1	.667	33	4	1	1	0	76^2	99	3	39	20	16.3	5.52	67	.320	.398	4	.308	1	-16	-16	-0	-1.4

YEAR	TM/L	W	L	PCT	G	GS	CG	SH	SV	IP	H	HR	BB	SO	RAT	ERA	ERA+	OAV	OOB	BH	AVG	PB	PR	/A	PD	TPI
● **BOB FALLON**	Fallon, Robert Joseph b: 2/18/60, Bronx, N.Y. BL/TL, 6'3", 200 lbs. Deb: 4/26/84																									
1984	Chi-A	0	0	—	3	3	0	0	0	14^{2}	12	0	11	10	14.1	3.68	113	.235	.371	0	—	0	1	1	0	0.1
1985	Chi-A	0	0	—	10	0	0	0	0	16	25	5	9	17	19.1	6.19	70	.362	.436	0	—	0	-4	-3	1	-0.6
Total	2	0	0	—	13	3	0	0	0	30^{2}	37	5	20	27	16.7	4.99	85	.308	.407	0	—	0	-3	-3	1	-0.5
● **CLIFF FANNIN**	Fannin, Clifford Bryson "Mule" b: 5/13/24, Louisa, Ky. d: 12/11/66, Sandusky, Ohio BL/TR, 6', 170 lbs. Deb: 9/02/45																									
1945	StL-A	0	0	—	5	0	0	0	0	10^{1}	8	0	5	5	11.3	2.61	135	.222	.317	0	.000	-0	1	1	-0	0.1
1946	StL-A	5	2	.714	27	7	4	1	2	86^{2}	76	4	42	52	12.4	3.01	124	.236	.326	5	.161	-1	5	7	-0	0.6
1947	StL-A	6	8	.429	26	18	6	2	1	145^{2}	134	10	77	77	13.1	3.58	108	.245	.340	9	.196	-0	2	5	0	0.5
1948	StL-A	10	14	.417	34	29	10	3	1	213^{2}	198	14	104	102	12.8	4.17	109	.245	.332	11	.169	-0	3	9	-2	0.7
1949	StL-A	8	14	.364	30	25	5	0	1	143	177	15	93	57	17.0	6.17	73	.308	.404	9	.164	-2	-31	-26	-3	-2.8
1950	StL-A	5	9	.357	25	16	3	0	1	102	116	18	58	42	15.4	6.53	76	.280	.369	6	.176	-2	-22	-18	-0	-1.8
1951	StL-A	0	2	.000	7	1	0	0	0	15^{1}	20	6	5	11	14.7	6.46	68	.317	.368	1	.250	-0	-4	-4	0	-0.3
1952	StL-A	0	2	.000	10	2	0	0	0	16^{1}	34	5	9	6	23.7	12.67	31	.453	.512	0	.000	0	-16	-16	-1	-1.5
Total	8	34	51	.400	164	98	28	6	6	733	763	72	393	352	14.2	4.85	89	.269	.358	41	.173	-6	-63	-42	-6	-4.5
● **JACK FANNING**	Fanning, John Jacob b: 1863, S.Orange, N.J. d: 6/10/17, Aberdeen, Wash. 5'9", 163 lbs. Deb: 9/20/1889																									
1889	Ind-N	0	1	.000	1	1	0	0	0	1	3	0	2	0	45.0	18.00	23	.503	.628	0	.000	-0	-2	-2	0	-0.1
1894	Phi-N	1	3	.250	5	4	2	0	0	32^{1}	45	4	20	7	18.6	8.07	63	.326	.418	2	.154	-1	-10	-11	-0	-0.8
Total	2	1	4	.200	6	5	2	0	0	33^{1}	48	4	22	7	19.4	8.37	61	.333	.428	2	.143	-1	-11	-12	0	-0.9
● **HARRY FANOK**	Fanok, Harry Michael "The Flame Thrower" b: 5/11/40, Whippany, N.J. BB/TR, 6', 180 lbs. Deb: 4/16/63																									
1963	StL-N	2	1	.667	12	0	0	0	1	25^{2}	24	3	21	25	16.1	5.26	67	.255	.397	2	.400	1	-6	-5	-0	-0.4
1964	StL-N	0	0	—	4	0	0	0	0	7^{2}	5	0	3	10	9.4	5.87	65	.179	.258	0	.000	-0	-2	-2	-0	-0.2
Total	2	2	1	.667	16	0	0	0	1	33^{1}	29	3	24	35	14.6	5.40	67	.238	.367	2	.333	1	-8	-7	-0	-0.6
● **FRANK FANOVICH**	Fanovich, Frank Joseph "Lefty" b: 1/11/22, New York, N.Y. BL/TL, 5'11", 180 lbs. Deb: 4/25/49																									
1949	Cin-N	0	2	.000	29	1	0	0	0	43^{1}	44	2	28	27	15.4	5.40	77	.257	.368	0	.000	-0	-7	-6	0	-0.6
1953	Phi-A	0	3	.000	26	3	0	0	0	61^{2}	62	5	37	37	15.3	5.55	77	.273	.389	2	.182	-0	-11	-9	-1	-0.9
Total	2	0	5	.000	55	4	0	0	0	105	106	7	65	64	15.3	5.49	77	.266	.380	2	.133	-1	-17	-14	-0	-1.5
● **STAN FANSLER**	Fansler, Stanley Robert b: 2/12/65, Elkins, W.V.A BR/TR, 5'11", 180 lbs. Deb: 9/06/86																									
1986	Pit-N	0	3	.000	5	5	0	0	0	24	20	2	15	13	13.1	3.75	102	.247	.365	1	.167	-0	-0	0	-0	0.0
● **HARRY FANWELL**	Fanwell, Harry Clayton b: 10/16/1886, Patapsco, Md. d: 7/15/65, Baltimore, Md. BB/TR, 6', 175 lbs. Deb: 7/23/10																									
1910	Cle-A	2	9	.182	17	11	5	1	0	92	87	0	38	30	12.8	3.62	71	.260	.347	1	.033	-3	-11	-11	1	-1.4
● **ED FARMER**	Farmer, Edward Joseph b: 10/18/49, Evergreen Park, Ill BR/TR, 6'5", 210 lbs. Deb: 6/09/71																									
1971	Cle-A	5	4	.556	43	4	0	0	4	78^{2}	77	9	41	48	13.8	4.35	88	.263	.359	1	.071	-1	-8	-5	-0	-0.6
1972	Cle-A	2	5	.286	46	1	0	0	7	61^{1}	51	10	27	33	11.6	4.40	73	.231	.317	1	.143	-0	-9	-8	0	-0.9
1973	Cle-A	0	2	.000	16	0	0	0	1	17^{1}	25	4	5	10	15.6	4.67	84	.325	.366	0	—	0	-2	-1	-0	-0.2
	Det-A	3	0	1.000	24	0	0	0	2	45	52	3	27	28	16.2	5.00	82	.292	.391	0	—	0	-6	-5	-1	-0.5
	Yr	3	2	.600	40	0	0	0	3	62^{1}	77	7	32	38	16.0	4.91	82	.301	.383	0	—	0	-8	-6	-1	-0.7
1974	Phi-N	2	1	.667	14	3	0	0	0	31	41	5	27	20	19.7	8.42	45	.323	.442	1	.111	-1	-17	-16	-0	-1.6
1977	Bal-A	0	0	—	1	0	0	0	0	0	1	0	1	0	—	∞	—	1.000	1.000	0	—	0	-1	-1	0	0.3
1978	Mil-A	1	0	1.000	3	0	0	0	1	11	7	1	4	6	9.0	0.82	459	.175	.250	0	—	0	4	4	-0	0.4
1979	Tex-A	2	0	1.000	11	2	0	0	0	33	30	2	19	25	13.9	4.36	95	.252	.364	0	—	0	-1	-1	-0	0.0
	Chi-A	3	7	.300	42	3	0	0	14	81^{1}	66	2	34	48	11.2	2.43	175	.219	.301	0	—	0	16	16	0	1.7
	Yr	5	7	.417	53	5	0	0	14	114^{1}	96	4	53	73	11.8	2.99	141	.226	.314	0	—	0	16	16	0	1.7
1980	Chi-A★	7	9	.438	64	0	0	0	30	99^{2}	92	6	56	54	13.5	3.34	121	.244	.343	0	—	0	8	8	1	0.8
1981	Chi-A	3	3	.500	42	0	0	0	10	52^{2}	53	5	34	42	15.0	4.61	78	.262	.371	0	—	0	-6	-6	1	-0.6
1982	Phi-N	2	6	.250	47	4	0	0	6	76	66	2	50	58	13.7	4.86	75	.234	.349	0	.000	-1	-11	-10	0	-1.2
1983	Phi-N	0	6	.000	12	3	0	0	0	26^{2}	35	2	20	16	18.9	6.08	59	.307	.415	1	.167	-0	-7	-7	0	-0.7
	Oak-A	0	0	—	5	1	0	0	0	10^{1}	15	1	0	7	13.1	3.48	111	.366	.366	0	—	0	1	0	-0	0.0
Total	11	30	43	.411	370	21	0	0	75	624	611	52	345	395	14.0	4.30	89	.257	.355	4	.085	-3	-38	-31	0	-3.1
● **HOWARD FARMER**	Farmer, Howard Earl b: 11/18/66, Gary, Ind. BR/TR, 6'3", 185 lbs. Deb: 7/02/90																									
1990	Mon-N	0	3	.000	6	4	0	0	0	23	26	9	10	14	14.1	7.04	52	.302	.375	2	.400	1	-8	-9	1	-0.7
● **JIM FARR**	Farr, James Alfred b: 5/18/56, Waverly, N.Y. BR/TR, 6'1", 195 lbs. Deb: 9/07/82																									
1982	Tex-A	0	0	—	5	0	0	0	0	18	20	0	7	6	13.5	2.50	155	.278	.342	0	—	0	3	3	-0	0.3
● **STEVE FARR**	Farr, Steven Michael b: 12/12/56, LaPlata, Md. BR/TR, 5'11", 198 lbs. Deb: 5/16/84																									
1984	Cle-A	3	11	.214	31	16	0	0	1	116	106	14	46	83	12.2	4.58	89	.245	.325	0	—	0	-8	-6	1	-0.6
1985	*KC-A	2	1	.667	16	3	0	0	1	37^{2}	34	2	20	36	13.4	3.11	134	.245	.348	0	—	0	4	4	0	0.5
1986	KC-A	8	4	.667	56	0	0	0	8	109^{1}	90	10	39	83	10.9	3.13	136	.228	.304	0	—	0	13	14	1	1.3
1987	KC-A	4	3	.571	47	0	0	0	1	91	97	9	44	88	14.1	4.15	110	.270	.353	0	—	0	3	4	-1	0.1
1988	KC-A	5	4	.556	62	1	0	0	20	82^{2}	74	5	30	72	11.5	2.50	159	.240	.312	0	—	0	13	14	-1	1.3
1989	KC-A	2	5	.286	51	2	0	0	18	63^{1}	75	5	22	56	13.9	4.12	93	.296	.355	0	—	0	-2	-2	-0	-0.2
1990	KC-A	13	7	.650	57	6	1	1	1	127	99	6	48	94	10.8	1.98	193	.220	.302	0	—	0	**27**	**26**	0	2.9
1991	NY-A	5	5	.500	60	0	0	0	23	70	57	4	20	60	10.5	2.19	189	.219	.288	0	—	0	15	15	1	1.6
1992	NY-A	2	2	.500	50	0	0	0	30	52	34	2	19	37	9.5	1.56	260	.186	.270	0	—	0	14	14	-1	1.4
Total	9	44	42	.512	430	28	1	1	103	749	666	57	288	609	11.8	3.10	132	.240	.317	0	—	0	80	83	-0	8.3
● **JOHN FARRELL**	Farrell, John Edward b: 8/4/62, Monmouth Beach, N.J. BR/TR, 6'4", 210 lbs. Deb: 8/18/87																									
1987	Cle-A	5	1	.833	10	9	1	0	0	69	68	7	22	28	12.4	3.39	133	.256	.324	0	—	0	8	9	-0	0.8
1988	Cle-A	14	10	.583	31	30	4	0	0	210^{1}	216	15	67	92	12.5	4.24	97	.269	.332	0	—	0	-6	-3	-0	-0.5
1989	Cle-A	9	14	.391	31	31	7	2	0	208	196	14	71	132	11.9	3.63	109	.244	.311	0	—	0	6	8	-2	0.5
1990	Cle-A	4	5	.444	17	17	1	0	0	96^{2}	108	10	33	44	13.2	4.28	91	.286	.345	0	—	0	-4	-4	-0	-0.4
Total	4	32	30	.516	89	87	13	2	0	584	588	46	193	296	12.4	3.93	104	.261	.326	0	—	0	4	9	-3	0.4
● **KERBY FARRELL**	Farrell, Major Kerby b: 9/3/13, Leapwood, Tenn. d: 12/17/75, Nashville, Tenn. BL/TL, 5'11", 172 lbs. Deb: 4/24/43 MC♦																									
1943	Bos-N	0	1	.000	5	0	0	0	0	23	24	1	9	4	12.9	4.30	79	.276	.344	75	.268	1	-2	-2	-0	-0.2
● **TURK FARRELL**	Farrell, Richard Joseph b: 4/8/34, Boston, Mass. d: 6/10/77, Great Yarmouth, England BR/TR, 6'4", 220 lbs. Deb: 9/21/56																									
1956	Phi-N	0	1	.000	1	1	0	0	0	4^{1}	6	0	3	0	20.8	12.46	30	.353	.476	0	.000	-0	-4	-4	0	-0.3
1957	Phi-N	10	2	.833	52	0	0	0	10	83^{1}	74	2	36	54	12.1	2.38	160	.242	.326	1	.111	0	**14**	13	0	1.4
1958	Phi-N★	8	9	.471	54	0	0	0	11	94	84	7	40	73	11.9	3.35	118	.244	.323	5	.208	0	6	6	-2	0.5
1959	Phi-N	1	6	.143	38	0	0	0	6	57	61	9	25	31	13.6	4.74	87	.288	.363	1	.167	-0	-5	-4	-0	-0.4
1960	Phi-N	10	6	.625	59	0	0	0	11	103^{1}	88	3	29	70	10.5	2.70	144	.239	.302	3	.200	1	12	14	-1	1.4
1961	Phi-N	2	1	.667	5	0	0	0	0	9^{2}	10	3	6	10	15.8	6.52	63	.270	.386	1	.500	0	-3	-3	-0	-0.3
	LA-N	6	6	.500	50	0	0	0	10	89	107	12	43	80	15.3	5.06	86	.296	.373	0	.000	-3	-10	-7	-2	-1.1
	Yr	8	7	.533	55	0	0	0	10	98^{2}	117	15	49	90	15.2	5.20	83	.293	.372	1	.050	-2	-13	-10	-2	-1.4
1962	Hou-N★	10	20	.333	43	29	11	2	4	241^{2}	210	21	55	203	10.1	3.02	124	.233	.280	14	.179	2	25	19	-2	2.0
1963	Hou-N	14	13	.519	34	26	12	0	1	202^{1}	161	12	35	141	8.8	3.02	104	.219	.256	9	.143	1	6	3	-2	0.3

YEAR TM/L	W	L	PCT	G	GS	CG	SH	SV	IP	H	HR	BB	SO	RAT	ERA	ERA+	OAV	OOB	BH	AVG	PB	PR	/A	PD	TPI
1964 Hou-N★	11	10	.524	32	27	7	0	0	198^1	196	21	52	117	11.4	3.27	105	.261	.311	5	.072	-3	6	3	-1	-0.1
1965 Hou-N★	11	11	.500	33	29	8	3	1	208^1	202	18	35	122	10.4	3.50	96	.252	.286	10	.135	-1	1	-3	-2	-0.6
1966 Hou-N	6	10	.375	32	21	3	0	2	152^2	167	23	28	101	11.5	4.60	74	.278	.310	7	.146	-0	-17	-20	-2	-2.2
1967 Hou-N	1	0	1.000	7	0	0	0	0	11^2	11	0	7	10	14.7	4.63	72	.244	.358	0	.000	-0	-2	-2	0	-0.2
Phi-N	9	6	.600	50	1	0	0	12	92	76	6	15	68	9.0	2.05	166	.228	.263	2	.105	-0	14	14	-1	1.4
Yr	10	6	.625	57	1	0	0	12	103^2	87	6	22	78	9.5	2.34	145	.229	.273	2	.100	-0	12	12	-1	1.2
1968 Phi-N	4	6	.400	54	0	0	0	12	83	83	7	32	57	12.7	3.47	87	.271	.344	1	.167	-0	-4	-4	-0	-0.5
1969 Phi-N	3	4	.429	46	0	0	0	3	74^1	92	8	27	40	14.5	4.00	89	.307	.366	0	.000	-0	-3	-4	-2	-0.6
Total 14	106	111	.488	590	134	41	5	83	1705	1628	152	468	1177	11.2	3.45	103	.254	.307	59	.135	-3	35	21	-17	0.7

● **JEFF FASSERO** Fassero, Jeffrey Joseph b: 1/5/63, Springfield, Ill. BL/TL, 6'1", 180 lbs. Deb: 5/04/91

YEAR TM/L	W	L	PCT	G	GS	CG	SH	SV	IP	H	HR	BB	SO	RAT	ERA	ERA+	OAV	OOB	BH	AVG	PB	PR	/A	PD	TPI
1991 Mon-N	2	5	.286	51	0	0	0	8	55^1	39	1	17	42	9.3	2.44	148	.196	.263	0	.000	0	8	7	1	0.8
1992 Mon-N	8	7	.533	70	0	0	0	1	85^2	81	1	34	63	12.3	2.84	123	.249	.324	1	.143	0	6	6	0	0.7
Total 2	10	12	.455	121	0	0	0	9	141	120	2	51	105	11.1	2.68	132	.229	.301	1	.100	0	14	13	1	1.5

● **FAST** Fast b: Milwaukee, Wis. Deb: 7/11/1887

YEAR TM/L	W	L	PCT	G	GS	CG	SH	SV	IP	H	HR	BB	SO	RAT	ERA	ERA+	OAV	OOB	BH	AVG	PB	PR	/A	PD	TPI
1887 Ind-N	0	1	.000	4	2	1	0	**1**	15^2	25	1	8	0	20.1	10.34	40	.347	.427	2	.182	-1	-11	-11	0	-0.9

● **DARCY FAST** Fast, Darcy Rae b: 3/10/47, Dallas, Ore. BL/TL, 6'3", 195 lbs. Deb: 6/15/68

YEAR TM/L	W	L	PCT	G	GS	CG	SH	SV	IP	H	HR	BB	SO	RAT	ERA	ERA+	OAV	OOB	BH	AVG	PB	PR	/A	PD	TPI
1968 Chi-N	0	1	.000	8	1	0	0	0	10	8	1	8	10	14.4	5.40	59	.216	.356	0	.000	-0	-3	-2	0	-0.3

● **JACK FASZHOLZ** Faszholz, John Edward "Preacher" b: 4/11/27, St.Louis, Mo. BR/TR, 6'3", 205 lbs. Deb: 4/25/53

YEAR TM/L	W	L	PCT	G	GS	CG	SH	SV	IP	H	HR	BB	SO	RAT	ERA	ERA+	OAV	OOB	BH	AVG	PB	PR	/A	PD	TPI
1953 StL-N	0	0	—	4	1	0	0	0	11^2	16	3	1	7	13.9	6.94	61	.327	.353	0	.000	-0	-3	-3	-1	-0.4

● **BILL FAUL** Faul, William Alvan b: 4/21/40, Cincinnati, Ohio BR/TR, 5'10", 190 lbs. Deb: 9/19/62

YEAR TM/L	W	L	PCT	G	GS	CG	SH	SV	IP	H	HR	BB	SO	RAT	ERA	ERA+	OAV	OOB	BH	AVG	PB	PR	/A	PD	TPI
1962 Det-A	0	0	—	1	0	0	0	0	1^2	4	1	3	2	43.2	32.40	13	.444	.615	0	—	0	-5	-5	-0	-0.4
1963 Det-A	5	6	.455	28	10	2	0	1	97	93	14	48	64	13.5	4.64	81	.251	.343	4	.148	0	-11	-10	-2	-1.2
1964 Det-A	0	0	—	1	1	0	0	0	5	5	2	2	1	12.6	10.80	34	.250	.318	0	.000	-0	-4	-4	-0	-0.4
1965 Chi-N	6	6	.500	17	16	5	3	0	96^2	83	12	18	59	9.7	3.54	104	.232	.275	3	.100	-1	0	2	-2	-0.1
1966 Chi-N	1	4	.200	17	6	1	0	0	51^1	47	12	18	32	12.1	5.08	72	.242	.319	0	.000	-2	-8	-8	-1	-1.0
1970 SF-N	0	0	—	7	0	0	0	1	9^2	15	1	6	6	19.6	7.45	53	.357	.438	0	—	0	-4	-4	-0	-0.4
Total 6	12	16	.429	71	33	8	3	2	261^1	247	42	95	164	12.2	4.72	79	.249	.322	7	.097	-2	-32	-29	-5	-3.5

● **JIM FAULKNER** Faulkner, James Leroy "Lefty" b: 7/27/1899, Beatrice, Neb. d: 6/1/62, W.Palm Beach, Fla. BB/TL, 6'3", 190 lbs. Deb: 9/15/27

YEAR TM/L	W	L	PCT	G	GS	CG	SH	SV	IP	H	HR	BB	SO	RAT	ERA	ERA+	OAV	OOB	BH	AVG	PB	PR	/A	PD	TPI
1927 NY-N	1	0	1.000	3	1	0	0	0	9^2	13	0	5	2	17.7	3.72	104	.317	.404	1	.500	1	0	0	-0	0.1
1928 NY-N	9	8	.529	38	8	3	0	2	117^1	131	5	41	32	13.4	3.53	111	.289	.351	9	.231	1	6	5	1	0.6
1930 Bro-N	0	0	—	2	1	0	0	1	0^1	2	1	1	0	81.0	81.00	6	.667	.750	0	—	0	-3	-3	0	-0.2
Total 3	10	8	.556	43	10	3	0	3	127^1	146	6	47	34	13.9	3.75	104	.293	.359	10	.244	2	3	2	1	0.5

● **BUCK FAUSETT** Fausett, Robert Shaw "Leaky" b: 4/8/08, Sheridan, Ark. BL/TR, 5'10", 170 lbs. Deb: 4/18/44 ♦

YEAR TM/L	W	L	PCT	G	GS	CG	SH	SV	IP	H	HR	BB	SO	RAT	ERA	ERA+	OAV	OOB	BH	AVG	PB	PR	/A	PD	TPI
1944 Cin-N	0	0	—	2	0	0	0	0	10^2	13	0	7	3	18.6	5.91	59	.295	.415	3	.097	-0	-3	-3	0	-0.3

● **CHARLIE FAUST** Faust, Charles Victor "Victory" b: 10/9/1880, Marion, Kan. d: 6/18/15, Fort Steilacoom, Wash. BR/TR, 6'2", Deb: 10/07/11

YEAR TM/L	W	L	PCT	G	GS	CG	SH	SV	IP	H	HR	BB	SO	RAT	ERA	ERA+	OAV	OOB	BH	AVG	PB	PR	/A	PD	TPI
1911 NY-N	0	0	—	2	0	0	0	0	2	2	0	0	0	9.0	4.50	75	.250	.250	0	—	0	-0	-0	0	0.0

● **CLAY FAUVER** Fauver, Clayton King "Cayt" b: 8/1/1872, N.Eaton, Ohio d: 3/3/42, Chatsworth, Ga. BB/TR, 5'10", Deb: 9/07/1899

YEAR TM/L	W	L	PCT	G	GS	CG	SH	SV	IP	H	HR	BB	SO	RAT	ERA	ERA+	OAV	OOB	BH	AVG	PB	PR	/A	PD	TPI
1899 Lou-N	1	0	1.000	1	1	1	0	0	9	11	0	2	1	13.0	0.00	—	.301	.337	0	.000	-1	4	4	-0	0.3

● **VERN FEAR** Fear, Luvern Carl b: 8/21/24, Everly, Iowa d: 9/6/76, Spencer, Iowa BB/TR, 6', 170 lbs. Deb: 8/03/52

YEAR TM/L	W	L	PCT	G	GS	CG	SH	SV	IP	H	HR	BB	SO	RAT	ERA	ERA+	OAV	OOB	BH	AVG	PB	PR	/A	PD	TPI
1952 Chi-N	0	0	—	4	0	0	0	0	8	9	1	3	4	14.6	7.88	49	.290	.371	0	.000	-0	-4	-4	-0	-0.4

● **JACK FEE** Fee, John b: 12/23/1867, Carbondale, Pa. d: 3/3/13, Carbondale, Pa. Deb: 9/14/1889

YEAR TM/L	W	L	PCT	G	GS	CG	SH	SV	IP	H	HR	BB	SO	RAT	ERA	ERA+	OAV	OOB	BH	AVG	PB	PR	/A	PD	TPI
1889 Ind-N	2	2	.500	7	3	2	0	0	40	39	2	31	10	17.1	4.27	98	.248	.391	3	.143	-2	-1	-0	1	-0.1

● **HARRY FELDMAN** Feldman, Harry b: 11/10/19, New York, N.Y. d: 3/16/62, Fort Smith, Ark. BR/TR, 6', 175 lbs. Deb: 9/10/41

YEAR TM/L	W	L	PCT	G	GS	CG	SH	SV	IP	H	HR	BB	SO	RAT	ERA	ERA+	OAV	OOB	BH	AVG	PB	PR	/A	PD	TPI
1941 NY-N	1	1	.500	3	3	1	1	0	20^1	21	0	6	9	12.0	3.98	93	.280	.333	1	.167	0	-1	-1	-0	-0.1
1942 NY-N	7	1	.875	31	6	2	1	0	114	100	5	73	49	13.7	3.16	106	.236	.350	11	.282	3	2	3	-0	0.6
1943 NY-N	4	5	.444	31	10	1	0	0	104^2	114	7	58	49	15.1	4.30	80	.279	.374	4	.133	-1	-11	-10	0	-1.1
1944 NY-N	11	13	.458	40	27	8	1	2	205^1	214	18	91	70	13.5	4.16	88	.266	.342	15	.205	0	-13	-11	-2	-1.4
1945 NY-N	12	13	.480	35	30	10	3	1	217^2	213	14	69	74	11.7	3.27	120	.251	.308	7	.097	-3	13	16	-2	1.1
1946 NY-N	0	2	.000	3	2	0	0	0	4	9	1	3	3	27.0	18.00	19	.474	.545	0	.000	-0	-6	-6	-0	-0.6
Total 6	35	35	.500	143	78	22	6	3	666	671	45	300	254	13.2	3.80	96	.260	.339	38	.172	-1	-16	-10	-5	-1.5

● **HARRY FELIX** Felix, Harry b: 1870, Brooklyn, N.Y. d: 10/17/61, Miami, Fla. BR/TR, 5'7.5", 160 lbs. Deb: 10/05/01

YEAR TM/L	W	L	PCT	G	GS	CG	SH	SV	IP	H	HR	BB	SO	RAT	ERA	ERA+	OAV	OOB	BH	AVG	PB	PR	/A	PD	TPI
1901 NY-N	0	0	—	1	0	0	0	0	2	3	0	0	0	13.5	0.00	—	.344	.344	0	.000	-0	1	1	-0	0.0
1902 Phi-N	1	3	.250	9	5	3	0	0	45	61	1	11	10	14.4	5.60	50	.323	.360	5	.135	-1	-14	-14	-1	-1.4
Total 2	1	3	.250	10	5	3	0	0	47	64	1	11	10	14.4	5.36	53	.324	.359	5	.132	-1	-13	-13	-1	-1.4

● **BOB FELLER** Feller, Robert William "Rapid Robert" b: 11/3/18, Van Meter, Iowa BR/TR, 6', 185 lbs. Deb: 7/19/36 H

YEAR TM/L	W	L	PCT	G	GS	CG	SH	SV	IP	H	HR	BB	SO	RAT	ERA	ERA+	OAV	OOB	BH	AVG	PB	PR	/A	PD	TPI
1936 Cle-A	5	3	.625	14	8	5	0	1	62	52	1	47	76	15.0	3.34	151	.229	.371	3	.136	-2	12	12	-1	0.9
1937 Cle-A	9	7	.563	26	19	9	0	1	148^2	116	4	106	150	13.6	3.39	136	.218	.351	9	.170	-1	20	20	1	1.9
1938 Cle-A☆	17	11	.607	39	36	20	2	1	277^2	225	13	208	**240**	14.3	4.08	114	**.220**	.356	17	.181	2	22	17	-2	1.5
1939 Cle-A★	**24**	9	.727	39	35	**24**	4	1	**296^2**	227	13	142	**246**	11.3	2.85	154	**.210**	.303	21	.212	5	**58**	**51**	0	**5.6**
1940 Cle-A★	**27**	11	.711	**43**	37	**31**	**4**	4	**320^1**	245	13	118	**261**	**10.3**	**2.61**	161	**.210**	**.285**	18	.157	1	**63**	**57**	-4	**5.5**
1941 Cle-A★	**25**	13	.658	**44**	40	28	**6**	2	**343**	284	15	194	**260**	12.7	3.15	125	.226	.332	18	.150	2	38	30	-1	3.1
1945 Cle-A	5	3	.625	9	9	7	1	0	72	50	1	35	59	10.9	2.50	130	.192	.293	4	.160	-0	7	6	-1	0.5
1946 Cle-A★	**26**	15	.634	**48**	42	**36**	**10**	4	**371^1**	277	11	153	**348**	10.5	2.18	152	.208	.291	16	.129	-2	**55**	46	-1	4.9
1947 Cle-A☆	**20**	11	.645	42	37	20	**5**	3	**299**	230	17	127	**196**	**10.9**	2.68	130	.215	.300	18	.184	2	**34**	27	2	3.2
1948 ★Cle-A†	19	15	.559	44	38	18	2	3	280^1	255	20	116	**164**	12.0	3.56	114	.241	.317	9	.095	-8	23	15	-1	0.6
1949 Cle-A	15	14	.517	36	28	15	0	0	211	198	18	84	108	12.1	3.75	106	.248	.320	17	.236	4	10	6	-4	0.6
1950 Cle-A★	16	11	.593	35	34	16	3	0	247	230	20	103	119	12.3	3.43	126	.247	.325	10	.120	-2	32	25	-4	1.8
1951 Cle-A	**22**	8	**.733**	33	32	16	4	0	249^2	239	22	95	111	12.3	3.50	108	.253	.325	10	.123	-4	17	8	-3	0.1
1952 Cle-A	9	13	.409	30	30	11	0	0	191^2	219	13	83	81	14.3	4.74	71	.288	.360	7	.117	1	-23	-30	-0	-2.9
1953 Cle-A	10	7	.588	25	25	10	1	0	175^2	163	16	60	60	11.6	3.59	105	.251	.317	6	.107	-2	8	3	1	0.2
1954 Cle-A	13	3	.813	19	19	9	1	0	140	127	13	39	59	10.9	3.09	119	.239	.294	9	.188	1	10	9	-2	0.8
1955 Cle-A	4	4	.500	25	11	2	1	0	83	71	7	31	25	11.2	3.47	115	.235	.308	1	.048	-2	5	5	-1	0.2
1956 Cle-A	0	4	.000	19	4	2	0	1	58	63	7	23	18	13.3	4.97	85	.280	.347	0	.000	-2	-5	-5	-1	-0.7
Total 18	266	162	.621	570	484	279	44	21	3827	3271	224	1764	2581	12.0	3.25	122	.231	.319	193	.151	-6	385	301	-22	27.8

● **TERRY FELTON** Felton, Terry Lane b: 10/29/57, Texarkana, Ark. BR/TR, 6'1", 180 lbs. Deb: 9/28/79

YEAR TM/L	W	L	PCT	G	GS	CG	SH	SV	IP	H	HR	BB	SO	RAT	ERA	ERA+	OAV	OOB	BH	AVG	PB	PR	/A	PD	TPI
1979 Min-A	0	0	—	1	0	0	0	0	2	0	0	0	1	0.0	0.00	—	.000	.000	0	—	0	1	1	-0	-0.2
1980 Min-A	0	3	.000	5	4	0	0	0	17^2	20	2	9	14	15.3	7.13	61	.286	.375	0	—	0	-6	-5	-0	-0.5
1981 Min-A	0	0	—	1	0	0	0	0	1^1	4	1	2	1	40.5	40.50	10	.500	.600	0	—	0	-5	-5	0	-0.5
1982 Min-A	0	13	.000	48	6	0	0	3	117^1	99	18	76	92	13.7	4.99	85	.230	.351	0	—	0	-12	-10	-2	-1.2
Total 4	0	16	.000	55	10	0	0	3	138^1	123	21	87	108	14.0	5.53	77	.240	.355	0	—	0	-22	-20	-3	-2.4

YEAR	TM/L	W	L	PCT	G	GS	CG	SH	SV	IP	H	HR	BB	SO	RAT	ERA	ERA+	OAV	OOB	BH	AVG	PB	PR	/A	PD	TPI
● HOD FENNER	Fenner, Horace Alfred b: 7/12/1897, Martin, Mich. d: 11/20/54, Detroit, Mich. BR/TR, 5'10.5", 165 lbs. Deb: 9/09/21																									
1921	Chi-A	0	0	—	2	1	0	0	0	7	14	0	3	1	21.9	7.71	55	.452	.500	0	.000	-0	-3	-3	-0	-0.3
● STAN FERENS	Ferens, Stanley "Lefty" b: 3/5/15, Wendell, Pa. BB/TL, 5'11", 170 lbs. Deb: 6/10/42																									
1942	StL-A	3	4	.429	19	3	1	0	0	69	76	2	21	23	12.7	3.78	98	.279	.331	3	.143	-1	-1	-1	-0	-0.1
1946	StL-A	2	9	.182	34	6	1	0	0	88	100	3	38	28	14.4	4.50	83	.293	.369	4	.167	-1	-10	-8	-1	-0.9
Total	2	5	13	.278	53	9	2	0	0	157	176	5	59	51	13.6	4.18	89	.287	.353	7	.156	-1	-11	-8	-1	-1.0
● CHARLIE FERGUSON	Ferguson, Charles Augustus b: 5/10/1875, Okemos, Mich. d: 5/17/31, Sault Ste.Marie, Mich. TR , 5'11", Deb: 9/20/01																									
1901	Chi-N	0	0	—	1	0	0	0	0	2	1	0	2	0	13.5	0.00	—	.149	.344	0	.000	-0	1	1	-0	0.0
● CHARLIE FERGUSON	Ferguson, Charles J. b: 4/17/1863, Charlottesville, Va. d: 4/29/1888, Philadelphia, Pa. BB/TR, 6', 165 lbs. Deb: 5/01/1884																									
1884	Phi-N	21	25	.457	50	47	46	2	1	416^{2}	443	13	93	194	11.6	3.54	84	.253	.291	50	.246	7	-26	-26	-2	-1.8
1885	Phi-N	26	20	.565	48	45	45	5	0	405	345	5	81	197	9.5	2.22	126	.219	.257	72	.306	17	27	26	1	4.2
1886	Phi-N	30	9	.769	48	45	43	4	**2**	395^{2}	317	11	69	212	8.8	1.98	167	.210	.244	66	.253	12	**59**	58	5	**7.1**
1887	Phi-N	22	10	.688	37	33	31	2	**1**	297^{1}	297	13	47	125	10.7	3.00	141	.254	.289	89	.337	14	36	41	1	4.9
Total	4	99	64	.607	183	170	165	13	4	1514^{2}	1402	42	290	728	10.1	2.67	122	.233	.270	277	.288	49	95	97	6	14.4
● GEORGE FERGUSON	Ferguson, George Cecil "Cecil" b: 8/19/1886, Ellsworth, Ind. d: 9/5/43, Orlando, Fla. BR/TR, 5'10", 165 lbs. Deb: 4/19/06																									
1906	NY-N	2	0	1.000	22	1	1	1	**7**	52^{1}	43	1	24	32	11.9	2.58	101	.229	.322	5	.333	2	**0**	**0**	1	0.3
1907	NY-N	3	2	.600	15	5	4	0	1	64	63	2	20	37	12.4	2.11	118	.266	.336	1	.056	-1	3	3	-0	0.1
1908	Bos-N	11	11	.500	37	20	13	3	0	208	168	1	84	98	11.3	2.47	98	.230	.316	11	.169	1	-2	-1	-3	-0.4
1909	Bos-N	5	23	.179	36	30	19	3	0	226^{2}	235	2	83	87	13.1	3.73	76	.282	.355	15	.205	1	-28	-23	0	-2.3
1910	Bos-N	7	7	.500	26	14	10	1	0	123	110	3	58	40	12.8	3.80	87	.254	.351	7	.175	-1	-11	-7	-0	-0.7
1911	Bos-N	1	3	.250	6	3	0	0	0	24	40	3	12	4	19.5	9.75	39	.388	.452	2	.286	1	-17	-16	-0	-1.3
Total	6	29	46	.387	142	73	47	8	8	698	659	12	281	298	12.6	3.34	83	.261	.343	41	.188	3	-55	-44	-2	-4.3
● ALEX FERGUSON	Ferguson, James Alexander b: 2/16/1897, Montclair, N.J. d: 4/26/76, Sepulveda, Cal. BR/TR, 6', 180 lbs. Deb: 8/16/18																									
1918	NY-A	0	0	—	1	0	0	0	0	1^{2}	2	0	2	1	21.6	0.00	—	.333	.500	0	.000	-0	1	1	-0	0.0
1921	NY-A	3	1	.750	17	4	1	0	1	56^{1}	64	4	27	9	15.2	5.91	72	.296	.385	4	.211	-1	-10	-10	-0	-1.0
1922	Bos-A	9	16	.360	39	27	10	1	2	198^{1}	201	5	62	44	12.2	4.31	95	.265	.326	6	.092	-6	-6	-4	-1	-1.1
1923	Bos-A	9	13	.409	34	27	11	0	0	198^{1}	229	5	67	72	13.8	4.04	102	.297	.360	6	.097	-5	-1	2	-1	-0.5
1924	Bos-A	14	17	.452	41	32	15	0	2	237^{2}	259	6	108	78	14.1	3.79	115	.286	.366	12	.140	-7	12	15	1	1.0
1925	Bos-A	0	2	.000	5	4	0	0	1	15^{2}	22	6	5	5	16.1	10.91	42	.314	.368	0	.000	-0	-11	-11	-0	-1.0
	NY-A	4	2	.667	21	5	0	0	1	54^{1}	83	3	42	20	21.0	7.79	55	.358	.460	2	.133	-1	-20	-21	1	-1.9
	*Was-A	5	1	.833	7	6	3	0	0	55^{1}	52	2	23	24	12.5	3.25	130	.256	.338	1	.050	-2	7	6	-1	0.2
	Yr	9	5	.643	33	15	3	0	2	125^{1}	157	11	70	49	16.4	6.18	69	.309	.395	3	.077	-4	-25	-26	-1	-2.7
1926	Was-A	3	4	.429	19	4	0	0	1	47^{2}	69	4	18	16	17.0	7.74	50	.343	.405	2	.182	-0	-20	-21	0	-1.9
1927	Phi-N	8	16	.333	31	31	16	0	0	227	280	15	65	73	13.9	4.84	85	.313	.363	7	.100	-5	-23	-18	0	-2.1
1928	Phi-N	5	10	.333	34	19	5	1	2	131^{2}	162	14	48	50	14.8	5.67	75	.312	.376	1	.026	-5	-25	-21	2	-2.2
1929	Phi-N	1	2	.333	5	4	1	0	0	12^{2}	19	2	10	3	20.6	12.08	43	.345	.446	0	.000	-1	-10	-10	0	-0.8
	Bro-N	0	1	.000	3	3	0	0	0	2	7	2	1	1	36.0	22.50	21	.583	.615	1	1.000	0	-4	-4	0	-0.3
	Yr	1	3	.250	8	7	1	0	0	14^{2}	26	4	11	4	22.7	13.50	38	.388	.474	1	.200	-0	-14	-14	1	-1.1
Total	10	61	85	.418	257	166	62	2	10	1238^{2}	1449	68	478	396	14.3	4.90	86	.299	.367	42	.106	-34	-112	-96	1	-11.6
● BOB FERGUSON	Ferguson, Robert Lester b: 4/18/19, Birmingham, Ala. BR/TR, 6'1.5", 180 lbs. Deb: 4/29/44																									
1944	Cin-N	0	3	.000	9	2	0	0	1	16	24	3	10	9	20.3	9.00	39	.358	.456	1	.333	0	-10	-10	0	-0.9
● BOB FERGUSON	Ferguson, Robert V. b: 1/31/1845, Brooklyn, N.Y. d: 5/3/1894, Brooklyn, N.Y. BB/TR, 5'9.5", 149 lbs. Deb: 5/18/1871 MU♦																									
1871	Mut-n	0	0	—	1	0	0	0	0	1	8	0	0	0	72.0	27.00	14	.571	.571	38	.241	-0	-3	-3		-0.2
1873	Atl-n	0	1	.000	4	1	1	0	0	19^{1}	41	2	2	0	20.0	6.05	50	.380	.391	59	.259	1	-6	-6		-0.4
1874	Atl-n	0	1	.000	1	1	1	0	0	9	12	0	3		15.0	*4.00*	70	.273	.319	63	.256	0	-1	-1		-0.1
1875	Har-n	0	0	—	1	0	0	0	0	2	9	1	0		40.5	*13.50*	19	.643	.643	88	.240	0	-2	-2		-0.2
1877	Har-N	1	1	.500	3	2	2	0	0	25	38	0	2	1	14.4	3.96	61	.352	.364	65	.256	0	-3	-4	0	-0.3
1883	Phi-N	0	0	—	1	0	0	0	0	1	2	0	0	0	18.0	9.00	34	.286	.286	85	.258	0	-1	-1	0	0.0
Total	4 n	0	2	.000	7	2	2	0	0	31^{1}	70	3	5	0	21.5	*6.61*	45	.389	.405	293	.252	1	-12	-13		-0.9
Total	2	1	1	.500	4	2	2	0	0	26	40	0	2	1	14.5	4.15	59	.348	.359	625	.271	1	-4	-5	0	-0.3
● ALEX FERNANDEZ	Fernandez, Alexander b: 8/13/69, Miami Beach, Fla. BR/TR, 6'2", 200 lbs. Deb: 8/02/90																									
1990	Chi-A	5	5	.500	13	13	3	0	0	87^{2}	89	6	34	61	12.9	3.80	101	.265	.338	0	—	0	1	0	-0	0.1
1991	Chi-A	9	13	.409	34	32	2	0	0	191^{2}	186	16	88	145	13.0	4.51	88	.259	.341	0	—	0	-9	-11	1	-0.9
1992	Chi-A	8	11	.421	29	29	4	2	0	187^{2}	199	21	50	95	12.3	4.27	90	.270	.324	0	—	0	-7	-9	2	-0.7
Total	3	22	29	.431	76	74	9	2	0	467	474	43	172	301	12.7	4.28	91	.265	.334	0	—	0	-15	-21	2	-1.5
● SID FERNANDEZ	Fernandez, Charles Sidney b: 10/12/62, Honolulu, Hawaii BL/TL, 6'1", 220 lbs. Deb: 9/20/83																									
1983	LA-N	0	1	.000	2	1	0	0	0	6	7	0	7	9	22.5	6.00	60	.280	.455	1	1.000	0	-2	-2	0	-0.1
1984	NY-N	6	6	.500	15	15	0	0	0	90	74	8	34	62	10.8	3.50	101	.226	.299	5	.179	-0	1	0	-2	-0.2
1985	NY-N	9	9	.500	26	26	3	0	0	170^{1}	108	14	80	180	10.0	2.80	123	**.181**	.280	11	.212	2	15	12	-0	1.5
1986	*NY-N★	16	6	.727	32	31	2	1	1	204^{1}	161	13	91	200	11.2	3.52	100	.216	.303	11	.162	1	4	0	-3	-0.1
1987	NY-N★	12	8	.600	28	27	3	1	0	156	130	16	67	134	11.8	3.81	99	.224	.313	7	.163	1	5	-1	-3	-0.2
1988	*NY-N	12	10	.545	31	31	1	1	0	187	127	15	70	189	9.8	3.03	106	**.191**	.274	14	.250	5	9	4	-3	0.7
1989	NY-N	14	5	.737	35	32	6	2	0	219^{1}	157	21	75	198	9.8	2.83	115	.198	.272	15	.211	4	16	11	-4	1.2
1990	NY-N	9	14	.391	30	30	2	1	0	179^{1}	130	18	67	181	10.1	3.46	108	**.200**	.280	11	.190	1	7	6	-2	0.4
1991	NY-N	1	3	.250	8	8	0	0	0	44	36	4	9	31	9.2	2.86	127	.222	.263	2	.154	0	4	4	1	0.5
1992	NY-N	14	11	.560	32	32	5	2	0	214^{2}	162	12	67	193	9.8	2.73	128	.210	.277	15	.203	2	19	18	-2	2.0
Total	10	93	73	.560	239	233	22	8	1	1471	1092	121	567	1377	10.4	3.17	110	.205	.286	92	.198	17	77	53	-17	5.7
● DON FERRARESE	Ferrarese, Donald Hugh b: 6/19/29, Oakland, Cal. BR/TL, 5'9", 170 lbs. Deb: 4/11/55																									
1955	Bal-A	0	0	—	6	0	0	0	0	9	8	0	11	5	19.0	3.00	127	.276	.475	0	.000	-0	1	1	-0	0.1
1956	Bal-A	4	10	.286	36	14	3	1	2	102	86	8	64	81	13.5	5.03	78	.229	.345	1	.036	-3	-10	-13	1	-1.4
1957	Bal-A	1	1	.500	8	2	0	0	0	19	14	1	12	13	12.3	4.74	76	.200	.317	0	.000	-0	-2	-2	0	-0.3
1958	Cle-A	3	4	.429	28	10	2	0	1	94^{2}	91	5	46	62	13.1	3.71	98	.254	.341	3	.115	-1	1	-1	-1	-0.4
1959	Cle-A	5	3	.625	15	10	4	0	0	76	58	6	51	45	13.0	3.20	115	.219	.347	7	.259	2	6	4	0	0.7
1960	Chi-A	0	1	.000	5	0	0	0	0	4	8	2	9	4	38.3	18.00	21	.400	.586	1	.500	0	-6	-6	-0	-0.6
1961	Phi-N	5	12	.294	42	14	3	1	1	138^{2}	120	14	68	89	12.3	3.76	108	.234	.325	6	.171	-1	4	5	-3	0.2
1962	Phi-N	0	1	.000	5	0	0	0	0	6^{2}	9	1	3	6	16.2	8.10	48	.310	.375	1	1.000	0	-3	-3	0	-0.2
	StL-N	1	4	.200	38	0	0	0	1	56^{2}	55	2	31	45	13.8	2.70	158	.270	.369	1	.200	1	8	10	1	1.2
	Yr	1	5	.167	43	0	0	0	1	63^{1}	64	3	34	51	14.1	3.27	129	.274	.368	2	.333	1	5	7	1	1.0
Total	8	19	36	.345	183	50	12	2	5	506^{2}	449	39	295	350	13.3	4.00	98	.241	.347	20	.156	-2	-2	-5	-1	-0.7
● BILL FERRAZZI	Ferrazzi, William Joseph b: 4/19/07, W.Quincy, Mass. BR/TR, 6'2.5", 200 lbs. Deb: 9/07/35																									
1935	Phi-A	1	2	.333	3	2	0	0	0	7	7	0	5	0	15.4	5.14	88	.269	.387	0	.000	0	-1	-0	0	0.0
● TONY FERREIRA	Ferreira, Anthony Ross b: 10/4/62, Riverside, Cal. BL/TL, 6'1", 160 lbs. Deb: 9/17/85																									
1985	KC-A	0	0	—	2	0	0	0	0	5^{2}	6	0	2	5	12.7	7.94	52	.273	.333	0	—	0	-2	-2	0	-0.2

● **WES FERRELL** Ferrell, Wesley Cheek b: 2/2/08, Greensboro, N.C. d: 12/9/76, Sarasota, Fla. BR/TR, 6'2", 195 lbs. Deb: 9/09/27 F♦

YEAR	TM/L	W	L	PCT	G	GS	CG	SH	SV	IP	H	HR	BB	SO	RAT	ERA	ERA+	OAV	OOB	BH	AVG	PB	PR	/A	PD	TPI
1927	Cle-A	0	0	—	1	0	0	0	0	1	3	0	2	0	45.0	27.00	16	.600	.714	0	—	0	-3	-3	-0	-0.2
1928	Cle-A	0	2	.000	2	2	1	0	0	16	15	0	5	4	11.3	2.25	184	.242	.299	1	.250	1	3	3	0	0.4
1929	Cle-A	21	10	.677	43	25	18	1	5	242^2	256	7	109	100	13.6	3.60	124	.279	.358	22	.237	4	17	23	3	2.9
1930	Cle-A	25	13	.658	43	35	25	1	3	296^2	299	14	106	143	12.3	3.31	146	.262	.325	35	.297	9	44	50	-3	5.4
1931	Cle-A	22	12	.647	40	35	**27**	2	3	276^1	276	9	130	123	13.3	3.75	123	.255	.336	37	.319	18	19	27	5	4.9
1932	Cle-A	23	13	.639	38	34	26	3	1	287^2	299	17	104	105	12.6	3.66	130	.264	.326	31	.242	5	26	35	1	3.9
1933	Cle-A☆	11	12	.478	28	26	16	1	0	201	225	8	70	41	13.3	4.21	106	.282	.341	38	.271	8	2	5	1	1.7
1934	Bos-A	14	5	.737	26	23	17	3	1	181	205	4	49	67	12.6	3.63	132	.282	.327	22	.282	9	17	24	-2	3.0
1935	Bos-A	**25**	14	.641	41	38	**31**	3	0	**322^1**	336	16	108	110	12.5	3.52	135	.267	.326	52	.347	22	34	44	2	**6.9**
1936	Bos-A	20	15	.571	39	38	**28**	3	0	**301**	330	11	119	106	13.6	4.19	127	.274	.343	36	.267	12	28	38	-3	4.4
1937	Bos-A	3	6	.333	12	11	5	0	0	73^1	111	14	34	31	17.9	7.61	62	.348	.412	12	.364	6	-24	-23	2	-1.3
	Was-A	11	13	.458	25	24	21	0	0	207^2	214	11	88	92	13.2	3.94	112	.265	.339	27	.255	5	16	11	-1	1.4
	Yr	14	19	.424	37	35	**26**	0	0	**281**	325	25	122	123	14.4	4.90	92	.288	.359	39	.281	11	-9	-12	1	0.1
1938	Was-A	13	8	.619	23	22	9	0	0	149	193	12	68	36	15.8	5.92	76	.311	.380	11	.224	6	-19	-23	1	-1.4
	NY-A	2	2	.500	5	4	1	0	0	30	52	6	18	7	21.0	8.10	56	.388	.461	2	.167	0	-11	-12	1	-0.9
	Yr	15	10	.600	28	26	10	0	0	179	245	18	86	43	16.6	6.28	72	.324	.393	13	.213	6	-30	-35	2	-2.3
1939	NY-A	1	2	.333	3	3	1	0	0	19^1	14	2	17	6	14.4	4.66	94	.219	.383	1	.125	-0	-0	-1	0	-0.1
1940	Bro-N	0	0	—	1	0	0	0	0	4	4	0	4	4	20.3	6.75	59	.250	.429	0	.000	-0	-1	-1	1	-0.1
1941	Bos-N	2	1	.667	4	3	1	0	0	14	13	1	9	10	14.8	5.14	69	.241	.359	2	.500	2	-2	-2	-0	-0.1
Total	15	193	128	.601	374	323	227	17	13	2623	2845	132	1040	985	13.4	4.04	117	.275	.343	329	.280	105	147	195	6	30.8

● **TOM FERRICK** Ferrick, Thomas Jerome b: 1/6/15, New York, N.Y. BR/TR, 6'2.5", 220 lbs. Deb: 4/19/41 C

YEAR	TM/L	W	L	PCT	G	GS	CG	SH	SV	IP	H	HR	BB	SO	RAT	ERA	ERA+	OAV	OOB	BH	AVG	PB	PR	/A	PD	TPI
1941	Phi-A	8	10	.444	36	4	2	1	7	119^1	130	8	33	30	12.3	3.77	111	.275	.322	9	.205	1	5	6	3	0.9
1942	Cle-A	3	2	.600	31	2	2	0	3	81^1	56	3	32	28	9.7	1.99	173	.200	.282	4	.211	0	**15**	**13**	2	1.6
1946	Cle-A	0	0	—	9	0	0	0	1	18	25	3	4	9	14.5	5.00	66	.321	.354	2	.667	1	-3	-3	0	-0.2
	StL-A	4	1	.800	25	1	0	0	5	32^1	26	1	5	13	8.6	2.78	134	.224	.256	0	.000	-1	3	3	0	0.3
	Yr	4	1	.800	34	1	0	0	6	50^1	51	4	9	22	10.7	3.58	100	.263	.296	2	.286	1	-0	0	0	0.1
1947	Was-A	1	7	.125	31	0	0	0	9	60	57	1	20	23	11.6	3.15	118	.256	.317	1	.100	-1	4	4	2	0.5
1948	Was-A	2	5	.286	37	0	0	0	10	73^2	75	3	38	34	13.8	4.15	105	.261	.348	1	.067	-1	1	2	1	0.2
1949	StL-A	6	4	.600	50	0	0	0	6	104^1	102	9	41	34	12.4	3.88	117	.258	.329	3	.143	-1	4	7	2	0.8
1950	StL-A	1	3	.250	16	0	0	0	2	24	24	2	7	6	11.6	4.13	120	.267	.320	1	.250	-0	1	2	1	0.3
	*NY-A	8	4	.667	30	0	0	0	9	56^2	49	5	22	20	11.3	3.65	118	.233	.306	2	.143	0	6	4	1	0.5
	Yr	9	7	.563	46	0	0	0	11	80^2	73	7	29	26	11.4	3.79	118	.243	.310	3	.167	0	7	6	1	0.8
1951	NY-A	1	1	.500	9	0	0	0	1	12	21	4	7	3	21.0	7.50	51	.389	.459	1	1.000	0	-5	-5	-0	-0.4
	Was-A	2	0	1.000	22	0	0	0	2	41^2	36	3	7	17	9.3	2.38	172	.234	.267	2	.286	0	8	8	0	0.9
	Yr	3	1	.750	31	0	0	0	3	53^2	57	7	14	20	11.9	3.52	115	.274	.320	3	.375	1	4	3	0	0.5
1952	Was-A	4	3	.571	27	0	0	0	1	50^2	53	2	11	28	11.4	3.02	118	.273	.312	1	.200	1	4	3	1	0.5
Total	9	40	40	.500	323	7	4	1	56	674	654	44	227	245	11.8	3.47	117	.256	.317	27	.184	1	42	44	11	5.9

● **BOB FERRIS** Ferris, Robert Eugene b: 5/7/55, Arlington, Va. BR/TR, 6'6", 225 lbs. Deb: 9/12/79

YEAR	TM/L	W	L	PCT	G	GS	CG	SH	SV	IP	H	HR	BB	SO	RAT	ERA	ERA+	OAV	OOB	BH	AVG	PB	PR	/A	PD	TPI
1979	Cal-A	0	0	—	2	0	0	0	0	6	5	1	3	2	12.0	1.50	271	.217	.308	0	—	0	2	2	0	0.5
1980	Cal-A	0	2	.000	5	3	0	0	0	15^1	23	2	9	4	18.8	5.87	67	.354	.432	0	—	0	-3	-3	0	-0.3
Total	2	0	2	.000	7	3	0	0	0	21^1	28	3	12	6	16.9	4.64	86	.318	.400	0	—	0	-1	-2	0	0.2

● **DAVE FERRISS** Ferriss, David Meadow "Boo" b: 12/5/21, Shaw, Miss. BL/TR, 6'2", 208 lbs. Deb: 4/29/45 C

YEAR	TM/L	W	L	PCT	G	GS	CG	SH	SV	IP	H	HR	BB	SO	RAT	ERA	ERA+	OAV	OOB	BH	AVG	PB	PR	/A	PD	TPI
1945	Bos-A†	21	10	.677	35	31	26	5	2	264^2	263	6	85	94	12.1	2.96	115	.264	.327	32	.267	11	12	13	5	3.2
1946	*Bos-A☆	25	6	**.806**	40	35	26	6	3	274	274	14	71	106	11.4	3.25	113	.259	.308	24	.209	2	8	13	0	1.6
1947	Bos-A	12	11	.522	33	28	14	1	0	218^1	241	14	92	64	14.0	4.04	96	.287	.362	27	.273	7	-8	-4	-1	0.3
1948	Bos-A	7	3	.700	31	9	1	0	3	115^1	127	7	61	30	15.2	5.23	84	.286	.381	9	.243	2	-12	-11	1	-0.8
1949	Bos-A	0	0	—	4	0	0	0	0	6^2	7	1	4	1	16.2	4.05	108	.292	.414	1	1.000	1	0	0	-0	0.1
1950	Bos-A	0	0	—	1	0	0	0	0	1	2	0	1	1	27.0	18.00	27	.500	.600	0	—	0	-1	-1	0	-0.1
Total	6	65	30	.684	144	103	67	12	8	880	914	42	314	296	12.8	3.64	103	.272	.338	93	.250	23	-2	10	5	4.3

● **CY FERRY** Ferry, Alfred Joseph b: 9/27/1878, Hudson, N.Y. d: 9/27/38, Pittsfield, Mass. BR/TR, 6'1", 170 lbs. Deb: 5/12/04 F

YEAR	TM/L	W	L	PCT	G	GS	CG	SH	SV	IP	H	HR	BB	SO	RAT	ERA	ERA+	OAV	OOB	BH	AVG	PB	PR	/A	PD	TPI
1904	Det-A	0	1	.000	3	1	1	0	0	13	12	0	11	4	16.6	6.23	41	.246	.395	2	.333	1	-5	-5	0	-0.5
1905	Cle-A	0	0	—	1	1	0	0	0	2	3	1	0	2	22.5	13.50	20	.347	.470	0	.000	-0	-2	-2	0	-0.2
Total	2	0	1	.000	4	2	1	0	0	15	15	1	11	6	17.4	7.20	36	.261	.406	2	.286	1	-8	-8	0	-0.7

● **JACK FERRY** Ferry, John Francis b: 4/7/1887, Pittsfield, Mass. d: 8/29/54, Pittsfield, Mass. BR/TR, 5'11", 175 lbs. Deb: 9/04/10 F

YEAR	TM/L	W	L	PCT	G	GS	CG	SH	SV	IP	H	HR	BB	SO	RAT	ERA	ERA+	OAV	OOB	BH	AVG	PB	PR	/A	PD	TPI
1910	Pit-N	1	2	.333	6	3	2	0	0	31	26	0	8	12	10.2	2.32	133	.230	.287	3	.333	1	2	3	0	0.4
1911	Pit-N	6	4	.600	26	8	4	1	3	85^2	83	3	27	32	11.8	3.15	109	.260	.322	9	.310	3	2	3	-2	0.4
1912	Pit-N	2	0	1.000	11	3	1	1	1	39	33	1	23	10	13.2	3.00	109	.234	.345	1	.077	-1	2	1	1	0.1
1913	Pit-N	1	0	1.000	4	0	0	0	0	5	4	0	2	2	10.8	5.40	56	.286	.375	0	—	0	-1	-1	0	-0.1
Total	4	10	6	.625	47	14	7	2	4	160^2	146	4	60	56	11.8	3.02	110	.249	.323	13	.255	3	5	5	-1	0.8

● **ALEX FERSON** Ferson, Alexander "Colonel" b: 7/14/1866, Philadelphia, Pa. d: 12/5/57, Boston, Mass. BR/TR, 5'9", 165 lbs. Deb: 5/04/1889

YEAR	TM/L	W	L	PCT	G	GS	CG	SH	SV	IP	H	HR	BB	SO	RAT	ERA	ERA+	OAV	OOB	BH	AVG	PB	PR	/A	PD	TPI
1889	Was-N	17	17	.500	36	34	28	1	0	288^1	319	9	105	85	13.6	3.90	101	.272	.338	13	.114	-5	4	1	-2	-0.4
1890	Buf-P	1	7	.125	10	10	7	0	0	71	88	5	40	13	16.4	5.45	75	.291	.376	7	.219	1	-10	-11	0	-0.7
1892	Bal-N	0	1	.000	2	1	1	0	0	9	17	1	6	8	23.0	11.00	31	.386	.460	0	.000	-1	-8	-8	-0	-0.7
Total	3	18	25	.419	48	45	36	1	0	368^1	424	15	151	106	14.4	4.37	91	.279	.349	20	.133	-5	-14	-17	-3	-1.8

● **LOU FETTE** Fette, Louis Henry William b: 3/15/07, Alma, Mo. d: 1/3/81, Warrensburg, Mo. BR/TR, 6'1.5", 200 lbs. Deb: 4/26/37

YEAR	TM/L	W	L	PCT	G	GS	CG	SH	SV	IP	H	HR	BB	SO	RAT	ERA	ERA+	OAV	OOB	BH	AVG	PB	PR	/A	PD	TPI
1937	Bos-N	20	10	.667	35	33	23	**5**	0	259	243	5	81	70	11.4	2.88	124	.251	.311	22	.239	3	30	20	0	2.4
1938	Bos-N	11	13	.458	33	32	17	3	1	239^2	235	11	79	83	11.9	3.15	109	.258	.320	16	.188	0	17	7	2	0.9
1939	Bos-N★	10	10	.500	27	26	11	**6**	0	146	123	7	61	35	11.4	2.96	125	.229	.309	3	.061	-4	16	12	3	1.1
1940	Bos-N	0	5	.000	7	5	0	0	0	32^1	38	0	18	2	15.9	5.57	67	.302	.393	3	.375	1	-6	-7	-1	-0.6
	Bro-N	0	0	—	2	0	0	0	0	3	3	0	2	0	15.0	0.00	—	.300	.417	0	—	0	1	1	-0	0.1
	Yr	0	5	.000	9	5	0	0	0	35^1	41	0	20	2	15.5	5.09	73	.299	.389	3	.375	1	-5	-5	-1	-0.5
1945	Bos-N	0	2	.000	5	1	0	0	0	11	16	1	7	4	19.6	5.73	67	.356	.453	0	.000	-0	-2	-2	0	-0.2
Total	5	41	40	.506	109	97	51	14	1	691	658	24	248	194	11.9	3.15	113	.253	.321	44	.186	-0	55	32	4	3.7

● **MIKE FETTERS** Fetters, Michael Lee b: 12/19/64, Van Nuys, Cal. BR/TR, 6'4", 200 lbs. Deb: 9/01/89

YEAR	TM/L	W	L	PCT	G	GS	CG	SH	SV	IP	H	HR	BB	SO	RAT	ERA	ERA+	OAV	OOB	BH	AVG	PB	PR	/A	PD	TPI
1989	Cal-A	0	0	—	1	0	0	0	0	3^1	5	1	1	4	16.2	8.10	47	.333	.375	0	—	0	-2	-2	0	0.0
1990	Cal-A	1	1	.500	26	2	0	0	1	67^2	77	9	20	35	13.2	4.12	93	.287	.341	0	—	0	-2	-2	1	0.0
1991	Cal-A	2	5	.286	19	4	0	0	0	44^2	53	4	28	24	16.9	4.84	85	.305	.410	0	—	0	-4	-4	-1	-0.4
1992	Mil-A	5	1	.833	50	0	0	0	2	62^2	38	3	24	43	9.9	1.87	204	.185	.292	0	—	0	14	14	1	1.5
Total	4	8	7	.533	96	6	0	0	3	178^1	173	17	73	106	13.0	3.58	108	.261	.345	0	—	0	8	6	1	1.1

● **JOHN FICK** Fick, John Ralph b: 5/18/21, Baltimore, Md. d: 6/9/58, Somers Point, N.J. BL/TL, 5'10", 150 lbs. Deb: 7/29/44

YEAR	TM/L	W	L	PCT	G	GS	CG	SH	SV	IP	H	HR	BB	SO	RAT	ERA	ERA+	OAV	OOB	BH	AVG	PB	PR	/A	PD	TPI
1944	Phi-N	0	0	—	4	0	0	0	0	5^1	3	0	3	2	11.8	3.38	107	.150	.292	0	—	0	0	0	-0	0.0

● **MARK FIDRYCH** Fidrych, Mark Steven "The Bird" b: 8/14/54, Worcester, Mass. BR/TR, 6'3", 175 lbs. Deb: 4/20/76

YEAR	TM/L	W	L	PCT	G	GS	CG	SH	SV	IP	H	HR	BB	SO	RAT	ERA	ERA+	OAV	OOB	BH	AVG	PB	PR	/A	PD	TPI
1976	Det-A★	19	9	.679	31	29	**24**	4	0	250^1	217	12	53	97	9.8	**2.34**	**159**	.235	.279	0	—	0	33	**38**	5	**5.0**
1977	Det-A†	6	4	.600	11	11	7	1	0	81	82	2	12	42	10.6	2.89	148	.269	.299	0	—	0	11	13	-1	0.8

YEAR	TM/L	W	L	PCT	G	GS	CG	SH	SV	IP	H	HR	BB	SO	RAT	ERA	ERA+	OAV	OOB	BH	AVG	PB	PR	/A	PD	TPI
1978	Det-A	2	0	1.000	3	3	2	0	0	22	17	1	5	10	9.0	2.45	157	.213	.259	0	—	0	3	3	1	0.4
1979	Det-A	0	3	.000	4	4	0	0	0	14²	23	3	9	5	20.3	10.43	41	.371	.458	0	—	0	-10	-10	-0	-1.0
1980	Det-A	2	3	.400	9	9	1	0	0	44¹	58	5	20	16	16.0	5.68	72	.309	.378	0	—	0	-8	-8	1	-0.7
Total	5	29	19	.604	58	56	34	5	0	412¹	397	23	99	170	11.0	3.10	126	.255	.302	0	—	0	28	37	5	4.5

● **CLARENCE FIEBER**   Fieber, Clarence Thomas "Lefty" b: 9/4/13, San Francisco, Cal d: 8/20/85, Redwood City, Cal BL/TL, 6'4", 187 lbs. Deb: 5/18/32

| 1932 | Chi-A | 1 | 0 | 1.000 | 3 | 0 | 0 | 0 | 0 | 5¹ | 6 | 0 | 3 | 1 | 15.2 | 1.69 | 256 | .273 | .360 | 0 | — | 0 | 2 | 2 | 0 | 0.2 |

● **JIM FIELD**   Field, James C. b: 4/24/1863, Philadelphia, Pa. d: 5/13/53, Atlantic City, N.J 6'1", 170 lbs. Deb: 6/02/1883 ♦

| 1890 | Roc-a | 1 | 0 | 1.000 | 2 | 1 | 1 | 0 | 1 | 9² | 7 | 0 | 4 | 2 | 11.2 | 2.79 | 128 | .196 | .295 | 38 | .202 | 0 | 1 | 1 | -0 | 0.1 |

● **JOCKO FIELDS**   Fields, John Joseph b: 10/20/1864, Cork, Ireland d: 10/14/50, Jersey City, N.J. BR/TR, 5'10", 160 lbs. Deb: 5/31/1887 ♦

| 1887 | Pit-N | 0 | 0 | — | 1 | 0 | 0 | 0 | 0 | 1 | 0 | 0 | 2 | 0 | 18.0 | 0.00 | — | .000 | .286 | 44 | .268 | 0 | 0 | 0 | -0 | 0.0 |

● **LOU FIENE**   Fiene, Louis Henry "Big Finn" b: 12/29/1884, Ft.Dodge, Iowa d: 12/22/64, Chicago, Ill. BR/TR, 6', 175 lbs. Deb: 5/07/06

1906	Chi-A	1	1	.500	6	2	1	0	0	31	35	0	9	12	13.6	2.90	87	.288	.352	2	.200	0	-1	-1	0	-0.1
1907	Chi-A	0	1	.000	6	1	1	0	0	26	30	0	7	15	13.5	4.15	58	.291	.348	2	.182	-0	-5	-5	-0	-0.5
1908	Chi-A	0	1	.000	1	1	1	0	0	9	9	0	1	3	10.0	4.00	58	.257	.278	0	.000	-0	-2	-2	0	-0.2
1909	Chi-A	2	5	.286	13	6	4	0	0	72	75	1	18	24	12.3	4.13	57	.284	.341	2	.069	-2	-13	-14	1	-1.6
Total	4	3	8	.273	26	10	7	0	0	138	149	1	35	54	12.7	3.85	62	.284	.341	6	.113	-2	-20	-22	2	-2.4

● **DANNY FIFE**   Fife, Danny Wayne b: 10/5/49, Harrisburg, Ill. BR/TR, 6'3", 175 lbs. Deb: 8/18/73

1973	Min-A	3	2	.600	10	7	1	0	0	51²	54	4	29	18	15.0	4.35	91	.270	.371	0	—	0	-3	-2	-0	-0.3
1974	Min-A	0	0	—	4	0	0	0	0	4²	10	0	4	3	28.9	17.36	22	.417	.517	0	—	0	-7	-7	-0	-0.7
Total	2	3	2	.600	14	7	1	0	0	56¹	64	4	33	21	16.1	5.43	73	.286	.387	0	—	0	-10	-9	-0	-1.0

● **JACK FIFIELD**   Fifield, John Proctor b: 10/5/1871, Enfield, N.H. d: 11/27/39, Syracuse, N.Y. BR/TR, 5'11", 160 lbs. Deb: 4/28/1897

1897	Phi-N	5	18	.217	27	26	21	0	0	210²	263	8	80	38	15.0	5.51	76	.303	.368	18	.234	3	-28	-31	1	-2.3
1898	Phi-N	11	9	.550	21	21	18	2	0	171¹	170	2	60	31	13.0	3.31	104	.257	.335	7	.109	-4	6	2	-3	-0.4
1899	Phi-N	3	8	.273	14	11	9	1	1	92²	110	0	36	8	14.6	4.08	90	.294	.363	9	.257	1	-2	-4	-1	-0.2
	Was-N	2	4	.333	6	6	6	0	0	47	73	1	17	12	17.6	6.13	64	.353	.408	4	.200	-0	-12	-12	-1	-1.0
	Yr	5	12	.294	20	17	15	1	1	139²	183	1	53	20	15.3	4.77	79	.313	.372	13	.236	1	-14	-16	-0	-1.2
Total	3	21	39	.350	68	64	54	3	1	521²	616	11	193	89	14.5	4.59	83	.292	.361	38	.194	-0	-36	-44	-2	-3.9

● **FRANK FIGGEMEIER**   Figgemeier, Frank Y. b: 4/22/1874, St.Louis, Mo. d: 4/15/15, St.Louis, Mo. Deb: 9/25/1894

| 1894 | Phi-N | 0 | 1 | .000 | 1 | 1 | 1 | 0 | 0 | 8 | 12 | 1 | 4 | 2 | 21.4 | 11.25 | 45 | .342 | .452 | 1 | .333 | 0 | -5 | -5 | 0 | -0.3 |

● **ED FIGUEROA**   Figueroa, Eduardo (Padilla) b: 10/14/48, Ciales, P.R. BR/TR, 6'1", 190 lbs. Deb: 4/09/74

1974	Cal-A	2	8	.200	25	12	5	1	0	105¹	119	3	36	49	13.6	3.67	94	.294	.357	0	—	0	-1	-3	0	-0.2
1975	Cal-A	16	13	.552	33	32	16	2	0	244²	213	14	84	139	11.1	2.91	122	.233	.301	0	—	0	24	17	1	2.0
1976	*NY-A	19	10	.655	34	34	14	4	0	256²	237	13	94	119	11.7	3.02	113	.246	.315	0	—	0	14	11	-3	0.9
1977	*NY-A	16	11	.593	32	32	12	2	0	239¹	228	19	75	104	11.5	3.57	110	.252	.312	0	—	0	13	10	-2	0.9
1978	*NY-A	20	9	.690	35	35	12	2	0	253	233	22	77	92	11.1	2.99	121	.248	.307	0	—	0	22	18	-0	1.9
1979	NY-A	4	6	.400	16	16	4	1	0	104²	109	6	35	42	12.4	4.13	99	.275	.333	0	—	0	1	-1	0	0.1
1980	NY-A	3	3	.500	15	9	0	0	1	58	90	3	24	16	17.8	6.98	56	.363	.421	0	—	0	-19	-20	1	-1.8
	Tex-A	0	7	.000	8	8	0	0	0	39²	62	9	12	9	16.8	5.90	66	.365	.407	0	—	0	-8	-9	1	-0.8
	Yr	3	10	.231	23	17	0	0	1	97²	152	12	36	25	17.3	6.54	60	.360	.410	0	—	0	-27	-29	1	-2.6
1981	Oak-A	0	0	—	2	1	0	0	0	8¹	8	1	6	1	16.2	5.40	64	.258	.378	0	—	0	-2	-2	-0	-0.2
Total	8	80	67	.544	200	179	63	12	1	1309²	1299	90	443	571	12.1	3.51	104	.261	.324	0	—	0	44	23	-4	2.8

● **TOM FILER**   Filer, Thomas Carson b: 12/1/56, Philadelphia, Pa. BR/TR, 6'1", 198 lbs. Deb: 6/08/82

1982	Chi-N	1	2	.333	8	8	0	0	0	40²	50	5	18	15	15.0	5.53	67	.301	.370	1	.083	-1	-9	-8	2	-0.7
1985	Tor-A	7	0	1.000	11	9	0	0	0	48²	38	6	18	24	10.4	3.88	108	.222	.296	0	—	0	1	2	-1	0.1
1988	Mil-A	5	8	.385	19	16	2	1	0	101²	108	8	33	39	12.6	4.43	90	.281	.339	0	—	0	-5	-5	3	-0.3
1989	Mil-A	7	3	.700	13	13	0	0	0	72¹	74	6	23	20	12.6	3.61	106	.271	.337	0	—	0	2	2	1	0.3
1990	Mil-A	2	3	.400	7	4	0	0	0	22	26	4	9	8	14.3	6.14	63	.289	.354	0	—	0	-5	-6	-1	-0.5
1992	NY-N	0	1	.000	9	1	0	0	0	22	18	2	6	9	9.8	2.05	171	.222	.276	0	.000	-0	4	4	0	0.4
Total	6	22	17	.564	67	51	2	1	0	307¹	314	29	107	115	12.5	4.25	92	.269	.333	1	.067	-1	-12	-12	-0	-0.7

● **EDDIE FILES**   Files, Charles Edward b: 5/19/1883, Portland, Me. d: 5/10/54, Cornish, Maine BR/TR, Deb: 10/03/08

| 1908 | Phi-A | 0 | 0 | — | 2 | 0 | 0 | 0 | 0 | 9 | 8 | 0 | 3 | 4 | 13.0 | 6.00 | 43 | .286 | .394 | 0 | .000 | -0 | -4 | -3 | -0 | -0.4 |

● **MARC FILLEY**   Filley, Marcus Lucius b: 2/28/12, Troy, N.Y. BR/TR, 5'11", 172 lbs. Deb: 4/19/34

| 1934 | Was-A | 0 | 0 | — | 1 | 0 | 0 | 0 | 0 | 0¹ | 2 | 0 | 0 | 0 | 54.0 | 27.00 | 16 | .667 | .667 | 0 | — | 0 | -1 | -1 | 0 | -0.1 |

● **DANA FILLINGIM**   Fillingim, Dana b: 11/6/1893, Columbus, Ga. d: 2/3/61, Tuskegee, Ala. BL/TR, 5'10", 175 lbs. Deb: 8/02/15

1915	Phi-A	0	5	.000	8	4	1	0	0	39¹	42	0	32	17	17.2	3.43	85	.313	.449	2	.167	-0	-2	-2	-0	-0.3
1918	Bos-N	7	6	.538	14	13	10	4	0	113	99	0	28	29	10.5	2.23	120	.243	.300	9	.214	0	7	6	-0	0.7
1919	Bos-N	6	13	.316	32	19	9	0	2	186¹	185	2	39	50	10.9	3.38	85	.270	.312	16	.246	1	-10	-11	2	-0.8
1920	Bos-N	12	21	.364	37	30	22	2	0	272	292	8	79	66	12.4	3.11	98	.287	.340	16	.174	-2	1	-2	5	0.2
1921	Bos-N	15	10	.600	44	22	11	3	1	239²	249	10	56	54	11.5	3.45	106	.272	.316	21	.247	5	9	5	-1	0.8
1922	Bos-N	5	9	.357	25	12	5	1	2	117	143	6	37	25	13.9	4.54	88	.311	.363	6	.158	-2	-6	-7	-1	-0.9
1923	Bos-N	1	9	.100	35	12	1	0	0	100¹	141	6	36	27	16.0	5.20	77	.345	.399	7	.226	1	-13	-14	-0	-1.2
1925	Phi-N	1	0	1.000	5	1	0	0	0	8²	19	0	6	2	26.0	10.38	46	.432	.500	0	.000	-0	-6	-5	-0	-0.5
Total	8	47	73	.392	200	113	59	10	5	1076¹	1170	32	313	270	12.5	3.56	93	.287	.340	77	.209	4	-21	-30	5	-2.0

● **PETE FILSON**   Filson, William Peter b: 9/28/58, Darby, Pa. BB/TL, 6'2", 195 lbs. Deb: 5/15/82

1982	Min-A	0	2	.000	5	3	0	0	0	12¹	17	2	8	10	18.2	8.76	48	.321	.410	0	—	0	-6	-6	-0	-0.6
1983	Min-A	4	1	.800	26	8	0	0	1	90	87	9	29	49	11.7	3.40	125	.252	.312	0	—	0	7	8	-2	0.7
1984	Min-A	6	5	.545	55	7	0	0	1	118²	106	14	54	59	12.4	4.10	103	.238	.325	0	—	0	-1	1	-1	-0.1
1985	Min-A	4	5	.444	40	6	1	0	2	95²	93	13	30	42	11.6	3.67	120	.251	.307	0	—	0	5	8	-1	0.7
1986	Min-A	0	0	—	4	0	0	0	0	6¹	13	1	2	4	22.7	5.68	76	.406	.457	0	—	0	-1	-1	-0	-0.1
	Chi-A	0	1	.000	3	1	0	0	0	11²	14	4	5	4	14.7	6.17	70	.286	.352	0	—	0	-3	-2	-0	-0.3
	Yr	0	1	.000	7	1	0	0	0	18	27	5	7	8	17.0	6.00	72	.329	.382	0	—	0	-4	-3	-1	-0.4
1987	NY-A	1	0	1.000	7	2	0	0	0	22	26	2	9	10	14.7	3.27	134	.299	.371	0	—	0	3	3	1	0.4
1990	KC-A	0	4	.000	8	7	0	0	0	35	42	6	13	9	14.7	5.91	65	.282	.348	0	—	0	-8	-8	-0	-0.7
Total	7	15	18	.455	148	34	1	0	4	391²	398	51	150	187	12.8	4.18	102	.260	.329	0	—	0	-5	3	-4	0.0

● **JOEL FINCH**   Finch, Joel D b: 8/20/56, South Bend, Ind. BR/TR, 6'2", 175 lbs. Deb: 6/12/79

| 1979 | Bos-A | 0 | 3 | .000 | 15 | 7 | 0 | 0 | 0 | 57¹ | 65 | 5 | 25 | 25 | 14.3 | 4.87 | 91 | .289 | .363 | 0 | .000 | 0 | -4 | -3 | 1 | -0.2 |

● **BILL FINCHER**   Fincher, William Allen b: 5/26/1894, Atlanta, Ga. d: 5/7/46, Shreveport, La. BR/TR, 6'1", 180 lbs. Deb: 4/23/16

| 1916 | StL-A | 0 | 1 | .000 | 12 | 1 | 0 | 0 | 0 | 21 | 22 | 0 | 7 | 5 | 12.4 | 2.14 | 128 | .282 | .341 | 1 | .250 | 0 | 2 | 1 | 1 | 0.3 |

● **TOMMY FINE**   Fine, Thomas Morgan b: 10/10/14, Cleburne, Tex. BB/TR, 6', 180 lbs. Deb: 4/26/47

| 1947 | Bos-A | 1 | 2 | .333 | 9 | 7 | 1 | 0 | 0 | 36 | 41 | 0 | 19 | 10 | 15.3 | 5.50 | 71 | .285 | .372 | 3 | .333 | 1 | -7 | -6 | 2 | -0.4 |

YEAR TM/L	W	L	PCT	G	GS	CG	SH	SV	IP	H	HR	BB	SO	RAT	ERA	ERA+	OAV	OOB	BH	AVG	PB	PR	/A	PD	TPI
1950 StL-A	0	1	.000	14	0	0	0	0	36^2	53	6	25	6	19.1	8.10	61	.342	.433	4	.333	1	-14	-13	-0	-1.0
Total 2	1	3	.250	23	7	1	0	0	72^2	94	6	44	16	17.2	6.81	65	.314	.404	7	.333	2	-22	-19	1	-1.4
● ROLLIE FINGERS	Fingers, Roland Glen b: 8/25/46, Steubenville, Ohio BR/TR, 6'4", 195 lbs. Deb: 9/15/68 H																								
1968 Oak-A	0	0	—	1	0	0	0	0	1^1	4	1	1	0	40.5	27.00	10	.571	.667	0	—	0	-4	-4	-0	-0.3
1969 Oak-A	6	7	.462	60	8	1	1	12	119	116	13	41	61	12.2	3.71	93	.257	.325	5	.200	0	-1	-4	2	-0.1
1970 Oak-A	7	9	.438	45	19	1	0	2	148	137	13	48	79	11.4	3.65	97	.250	.312	4	.103	-0	1	-2	1	-0.2
1971 *Oak-A	4	6	.400	48	8	2	1	17	129^1	94	14	30	98	9.2	2.99	111	.207	.268	7	.212	1	7	5	2	0.8
1972 *Oak-A	11	9	.550	65	0	0	0	21	111^1	85	8	32	113	9.5	2.51	113	.212	.272	6	.316	2	7	4	-0	0.7
1973 *Oak-A★	7	8	.467	62	2	0	0	22	126^2	107	5	39	110	10.7	1.92	185	.226	.290	0	.000	0	27	23	-1	2.3
1974 *Oak-A★	9	5	.643	**76**	0	0	0	18	119	104	5	29	95	10.1	2.65	125	.240	.289	0	—	0	13	9	2	1.2
1975 *Oak-A☆	10	6	.625	**75**	0	0	0	24	126^2	95	13	33	115	9.5	2.98	122	.213	.276	0	.000	0	11	9	0	0.9
1976 Oak-A☆	13	11	.542	70	0	0	0	20	134^2	118	3	40	113	11.0	2.47	136	.243	.310	0	—	0	16	13	2	1.6
1977 SD-N	8	9	.471	**78**	0	0	0	**35**	132^1	123	12	36	113	10.9	2.99	118	.248	.300	1	.050	-2	13	8	-0	0.6
1978 SD-N★	6	13	.316	67	0	0	0	**37**	107^1	84	4	29	72	9.6	2.52	132	.212	.267	2	.167	-0	13	10	0	1.0
1979 SD-N	9	9	.500	54	0	0	0	13	83^2	91	7	37	65	13.9	4.52	78	.281	.356	1	.083	-1	-7	-9	-1	-1.1
1980 SD-N	11	9	.550	66	0	0	0	23	103	101	3	32	69	11.6	2.80	123	.263	.320	5	.278	2	9	7	-1	0.9
1981 *Mil-A★	6	3	.667	47	0	0	0	**28**	78	55	3	13	61	8.0	1.04	330	.198	.236	0	—	0	**23**	**21**	0	2.3
1982 Mil-A★	5	6	.455	50	0	0	0	29	79^2	63	5	20	71	9.5	2.60	146	.220	.273	0	—	0	13	11	0	1.1
1984 Mil-A	1	2	.333	33	0	0	0	23	46	38	5	13	40	10.0	1.96	197	.213	.267	0	—	0	10	10	-0	1.1
1985 Mil-A	1	6	.143	47	0	0	0	17	55^1	59	9	19	24	12.7	5.04	83	.272	.331	0	—	0	-6	-5	1	-0.4
Total 17	114	118	.491	944	37	4	2	341	1701^1	1474	123	492	1299	10.6	2.90	119	.235	.295	31	.172	3	145	105	6	12.4
● HERMAN FINK	Fink, Herman Adam b: 8/22/11, Concord, N.C. d: 8/24/80, Salisbury, N.C. BR/TR, 6'2", 198 lbs. Deb: 9/16/35																								
1935 Phi-A	0	3	.000	5	3	0	0	0	15^2	18	0	10	2	16.7	9.19	49	.290	.397	1	.200	-0	-8	-8	0	-0.7
1936 Phi-A	8	16	.333	34	24	9	0	3	188^2	222	18	78	53	14.3	5.39	95	.294	.360	8	.125	-4	-7	-6	-2	-1.0
1937 Phi-A	2	1	.667	28	3	1	0	1	80	82	6	35	18	13.3	4.05	116	.263	.339	5	.208	-1	5	6	-0	0.5
Total 3	10	20	.333	67	30	10	0	4	284^1	322	24	123	73	14.1	5.22	95	.285	.356	14	.151	-5	-11	-8	-2	-1.2
● PEMBROKE FINLAYSON	Finlayson, Pembroke b: 7/31/1888, Cheraw, S.C. d: 3/6/12, Brooklyn, N.Y. BR/TR, Deb: 6/06/08																								
1908 Bro-N	0	0	—	1	0	0	0	0	0^1	0	0	4	0	108.0	135.00	2	.000	.800	0	—	0	-5	-5	0	-0.4
1909 Bro-N	0	0	—	1	0	0	0	0	7	7	0	4	2	14.1	5.14	50	.212	.297	0	.000	-0	-2	-2	-0	-0.2
Total 2	0	0	—	2	0	0	0	0	7^1	7	0	8	2	18.4	11.05	23	.206	.357	0	.000	-0	-7	-7	-0	-0.6
● CHUCK FINLEY	Finley, Charles Edward b: 11/26/62, Monroe, La. BL/TL, 6'6", 220 lbs. Deb: 5/29/86																								
1986 *Cal-A	3	1	.750	25	0	0	0	0	46^1	40	2	23	37	12.4	3.30	124	.235	.330	0	—	0	4	4	1	0.5
1987 Cal-A	2	7	.222	35	3	0	0	0	90^2	102	7	43	63	14.7	4.67	92	.287	.369	0	—	0	-2	-4	-0	-0.4
1988 Cal-A	9	15	.375	31	31	2	0	0	194^1	191	15	82	111	12.9	4.17	93	.263	.343	0	—	0	-4	-7	-1	-0.8
1989 Cal-A☆	16	9	.640	29	29	9	1	0	199^2	171	13	82	156	11.5	2.57	148	.233	.312	0	—	0	29	28	-3	2.6
1990 Cal-A★	18	9	.667	32	32	7	2	0	236	210	17	81	177	11.2	2.40	159	.243	.309	0	—	0	39	37	-2	4.0
1991 Cal-A	18	9	.667	34	34	4	2	0	227^1	205	23	101	171	12.4	3.80	108	.244	.331	0	—	0	7	8	-3	0.5
1992 Cal-A	7	12	.368	31	31	4	1	0	204^1	212	24	98	124	13.8	3.96	99	.277	.362	0	—	0	-1	-1	-3	-0.3
Total 7	73	62	.541	217	160	26	6	0	1198^2	1131	101	510	839	12.5	3.45	114	.254	.334	0	—	0	73	65	-11	6.1
● HAPPY FINNERAN	Finneran, Joseph Ignatius "Smokey Joe" b: 10/29/1891, E.Orange, N.J. d: 2/3/42, Orange, N.J. BR/TR, 5'10.5", 169 lbs. Deb: 8/20/12																								
1912 Phi-N	0	2	.000	14	4	0	0	1	46^1	50	2	10	10	11.8	2.53	144	.282	.324	2	.200	0	5	6	-0	0.6
1913 Phi-N	0	0	—	3	0	0	0	0	5	12	0	2	0	25.2	7.20	46	.462	.500	2	.667	1	-2	-2	-0	-0.1
1914 Bro-F	12	11	.522	27	23	13	2	1	175^1	153	6	60	54	11.2	3.18	100	.237	.308	7	.127	-4	0	0	-1	-0.5
1915 Bro-F	10	12	.455	37	24	12	1	2	215^1	197	2	87	68	12.2	2.80	108	.249	.331	11	.149	-3	6	5	-1	0.2
1918 Det-A	0	2	.000	5	2	0	0	1	13^2	22	0	8	2	19.8	9.88	27	.393	.469	0	.000	-0	-11	-11	1	-1.1
NY-A	3	6	.333	23	13	4	0	0	114^1	134	7	35	34	13.5	3.78	75	.305	.359	9	.231	1	-13	-12	-1	-1.3
Yr	3	8	.273	28	15	4	0	1	128	156	7	43	36	14.1	4.43	63	.315	.372	9	.214	0	-23	-23	-0	-2.4
Total 5	25	33	.431	109	66	29	3	5	570	568	17	202	168	12.4	3.30	93	.266	.335	31	.168	-5	-15	-14	-2	-2.2
● STEVE FIREOVID	Fireovid, Stephen John b: 6/6/57, Bryan, Ohio BB/TR, 6'2", 195 lbs. Deb: 9/06/81																								
1981 SD-N	0	1	.000	5	4	0	0	0	26^1	30	2	7	11	12.6	2.73	119	.294	.339	1	.143	-0	2	2	0	0.1
1983 SD-N	0	0	—	3	0	0	0	0	5	4	0	2	1	10.8	1.80	194	.235	.316	0	—	0	1	1	0	0.1
1984 Phi-N	0	0	—	6	0	0	0	0	5^2	4	0	0	3	6.4	1.59	229	.200	.200	0	—	0	1	1	0	0.2
1985 Chi-A	0	0	—	4	0	0	0	0	7	17	0	2	2	24.4	5.14	84	.472	.500	0	—	0	-1	-1	-0	-0.1
1986 Sea-A	2	0	1.000	10	1	0	0	0	21	28	1	4	10	14.1	4.29	99	.333	.371	0	—	0	-0	-0	-0	0.0
1992 Tex-A	1	0	1.000	3	0	0	0	0	6^2	10	0	4	0	18.9	4.05	94	.370	.452	0	—	0	-0	-0	0	0.3
Total 6	3	1	.750	31	5	0	0	0	71^2	93	3	19	27	14.2	3.39	110	.325	.369	1	.143	-0	3	3	0	0.6
● TED FIRTH	Firth, John E. b: 1856, Massachusetts d: 6/23/02, Tewksbury, Mass. Deb: 8/15/1884																								
1884 Ric-a	0	1	.000	1	1	1	0	0	9	14	0	5	0	19.0	8.00	41	.326	.396	1	.333	0	-5	-5	-0	-0.4
● CARL FISCHER	Fischer, Charles William b: 11/5/05, Medina, N.Y. d: 12/10/63, Medina, N.Y. BR/TL, 6', 180 lbs. Deb: 7/19/30																								
1930 Was-A	1	1	.500	8	4	1	0	1	33^1	37	0	18	21	15.4	4.86	95	.285	.380	0	.000	-1	-1	-1	1	-0.1
1931 Was-A	13	9	.591	46	23	7	0	3	191	207	12	80	96	13.6	4.38	98	.273	.344	8	.121	-5	-0	-2	-4	-1.0
1932 Was-A	3	2	.600	12	7	1	1	1	50^2	57	4	31	23	15.6	4.97	87	.282	.378	3	.200	1	-3	-4	-2	-0.5
StL-A	3	7	.300	24	11	4	0	0	97	122	12	45	35	15.5	5.57	87	.310	.380	9	.265	1	-12	-8	-1	-0.8
Yr	6	9	.400	36	18	5	1	1	147^2	179	16	76	58	15.5	5.36	87	.300	.379	12	.245	1	-15	-11	-3	-1.3
1933 Det-A	11	15	.423	35	22	9	0	3	182^2	176	5	84	93	13.0	3.55	122	.251	.334	9	.145	-3	15	15	-2	1.0
1934 Det-A	6	4	.600	20	15	4	1	1	95	107	5	38	39	13.8	4.36	101	.288	.356	2	.065	-3	1	0	-2	-0.4
1935 Det-A	0	1	.000	3	1	0	0	0	12	16	2	5	7	16.5	6.00	69	.320	.393	0	.000	-0	-2	-2	-0	-0.3
Chi-A	5	5	.500	24	11	3	1	0	88^2	102	7	39	31	14.5	6.19	75	.283	.356	4	.190	-0	-17	-15	-1	-1.5
Yr	5	6	.455	27	12	3	1	0	100^2	118	9	44	38	14.7	6.17	74	.286	.358	4	.174	-1	-19	-18	-1	-1.8
1937 Cle-A	0	1	.000	2	0	0	0	0	0^2	2	0	1	1	40.5	27.00	17	.667	.750	0	—	0	-2	-2	0	-0.1
Was-A	4	5	.444	17	11	2	0	2	72	74	6	31	30	13.1	4.38	101	.270	.344	3	.136	-1	2	0	-2	-0.2
Yr	4	6	.400	19	11	2	0	2	72^2	76	6	32	31	13.4	4.58	97	.274	.350	3	.136	-1	0	-1	-2	-0.3
Total 7	46	50	.479	191	105	31	3	11	823	900	53	372	376	14.0	4.63	96	.277	.354	38	.145	-12	-18	-18	-14	-3.9
● HANK FISCHER	Fischer, Henry William "Bulldog" b: 1/11/40, Yonkers, N.Y. BR/TR, 6', 190 lbs. Deb: 4/16/62																								
1962 Mil-N	2	3	.400	29	0	0	0	4	37^1	43	4	20	29	15.2	5.30	72	.291	.375	0	.000	-0	-6	-6	-0	-0.6
1963 Mil-N	4	3	.571	31	6	1	0	0	74^1	74	8	28	72	13.0	4.96	65	.262	.340	2	.105	-0	-14	-14	-1	-1.6
1964 Mil-N	11	10	.524	37	28	9	5	2	168^1	177	17	39	99	11.7	4.01	88	.265	.309	8	.154	1	-9	-9	-1	-1.0
1965 Mil-N	8	9	.471	31	19	2	0	0	122^2	126	18	39	79	12.3	3.89	91	.270	.331	4	.108	-1	-5	-5	-2	-0.9
1966 Atl-N	2	3	.400	14	8	0	0	0	48^1	55	3	14	22	13.0	3.91	93	.296	.348	0	.000	-2	-2	-1	-1	-0.4
Cin-N	0	6	.000	11	9	0	0	0	38	53	3	15	24	16.8	6.63	59	.331	.399	1	.091	-1	-13	-12	-0	-1.3
Yr	2	9	.182	25	17	0	0	0	86^1	108	6	29	46	14.6	5.11	73	.309	.366	1	.042	-2	-14	-13	-2	-1.7
Bos-A	2	3	.400	6	5	1	0	0	31	35	4	11	26	13.6	2.90	131	.287	.351	2	.222	0	2	3	0	0.4
1967 Bos-A	1	2	.333	9	2	1	0	1	26^2	24	3	8	18	11.1	2.36	148	.229	.289	1	.143	-0	3	3	-0	0.3
Total 6	30	39	.435	168	77	14	5	7	546^2	587	60	174	369	12.8	4.23	84	.275	.334	18	.118	-3	-43	-41	-5	-5.1

YEAR	TM/L	W	L	PCT	G	GS	CG	SH	SV	IP	H	HR	BB	SO	RAT	ERA	ERA+	OAV	OOB	BH	AVG	PB	PR	/A	PD	TPI
● JEFF FISCHER																										
Fischer, Jeffrey Thomas b: 8/17/63, W.Palm Beach, Fla. BR/TR, 6'3", 185 lbs. Deb: 6/19/87																										
1987	Mon-N	0	1	.000	4	2	0	0	0	13^2	21	3	5	6	17.1	8.56	49	.362	.413	1	.200	0	-7	-7	-0	-0.6
1989	LA-N	0	0	—	2	0	0	0	0	3^1	7	1	0	2	18.9	13.50	25	.438	.438	0	—	0	-4	-4	-0	-0.4
Total	2	0	1	.000	6	2	0	0	0	17	28	4	5	8	17.5	9.53	42	.378	.418	1	.200	0	-11	-10	-0	-1.0
● RUBE FISCHER																										
Fischer, Reuben Walter b: 9/19/16, Carlock, S.D. BR/TR, 6'4", 190 lbs. Deb: 9/12/41																										
1941	NY-N	1	0	1.000	2	1	1	0	0	11	10	0	6	9	13.1	2.45	151	.238	.333	1	.333	0	1	2	-0	0.2
1943	NY-N	5	10	.333	22	17	4	0	1	130^2	140	4	59	47	13.8	4.61	75	.281	.360	11	.256	3	-18	-17	-2	-1.6
1944	NY-N	6	14	.300	38	18	2	1	2	128^2	128	7	87	39	15.5	5.18	71	.266	.384	5	.125	-2	-22	-22	-2	-2.5
1945	NY-N	3	8	.273	31	4	0	0	1	76^2	90	6	49	27	16.4	5.63	69	.288	.387	4	.211	2	-16	-15	-1	-1.4
1946	NY-N	1	2	.333	15	1	0	0	0	35^2	48	3	21	14	17.4	6.31	55	.316	.399	1	.111	-1	-11	-11	0	-1.2
Total	5	16	34	.320	108	41	7	1	4	382^2	416	20	222	136	15.2	5.10	71	.280	.377	22	.193	2	-66	-63	-5	-6.5
● TODD FISCHER																										
Fischer, Todd Richard b: 9/15/60, Columbus, Ohio BR/TR, 5'10", 170 lbs. Deb: 5/29/86																										
1986	Cal-A	0	0	—	9	0	0	0	0	17	18	4	8	7	13.8	4.24	97	.286	.366	0	—	0	-0	-0	-0	0.0
● BILL FISCHER																										
Fischer, William Charles b: 10/11/30, Wausau, Wis. BR/TR, 6', 190 lbs. Deb: 4/21/56 C																										
1956	Chi-A	0	0	—	3	0	0	0	0	1^2	6	0	1	2	37.8	21.60	19	.545	.583	0	—	0	-3	-3	0	-0.3
1957	Chi-A	7	8	.467	33	11	3	1	1	124	139	1	35	48	12.8	3.48	107	.291	.344	6	.150	-2	4	3	-1	0.1
1958	Chi-A	2	3	.400	17	3	0	0	0	36^1	43	6	13	16	13.9	6.69	54	.301	.359	1	.143	-0	-12	-12	1	-1.1
	Det-A	2	4	.333	22	0	0	0	2	30^2	46	6	13	16	17.3	7.63	53	.362	.421	0	.000	0	-13	-12	0	-1.2
	Was-A	0	3	.000	3	3	0	0	0	21	24	1	5	10	12.9	3.86	99	.320	.370	1	.200	0	-0	-0	0	0.1
	Yr	4	10	.286	42	6	0	0	2	88	113	13	31	42	14.8	6.34	60	.325	.382	2	.154	0	-25	-25	2	-2.2
1959	Was-A	9	11	.450	34	29	6	1	0	187^1	211	16	43	62	12.4	4.28	92	.281	.324	7	.130	-2	-9	-8	4	-0.6
1960	Was-A	3	5	.375	20	7	1	0	0	77	85	7	17	31	11.9	4.91	79	.281	.320	3	.158	1	-9	-9	1	-0.6
	Det-A	5	3	.625	20	6	1	0	0	55	50	6	18	24	11.1	3.44	115	.244	.305	4	.364	2	3	3	0	0.6
	Yr	8	8	.500	40	13	2	0	0	132	135	13	35	55	11.6	4.30	91	.265	.313	7	.233	3	-6	-6	2	0.0
1961	Det-A	3	2	.600	26	1	0	0	3	46^2	54	10	17	18	13.7	5.01	82	.292	.351	0	.000	-1	-5	-5	-0	-0.6
	KC-A	1	0	1.000	15	0	0	0	2	21	26	2	6	12	13.7	3.86	107	.321	.368	0	.000	-0	0	1	0	0.0
	Yr	4	2	.667	41	1	0	0	5	67^2	80	12	23	30	13.7	4.66	88	.301	.356	0	.000	-1	-5	-4	-0	-0.6
1962	KC-A	4	12	.250	34	16	5	0	2	127^2	150	16	8	38	11.2	3.95	105	.293	.305	4	.105	-2	0	3	-1	0.0
1963	KC-A	9	6	.600	45	2	0	0	3	95^2	86	13	29	34	11.1	3.57	108	.242	.305	1	.067	-0	1	3	-1	0.2
1964	Min-A	0	1	.000	9	0	0	0	0	7^1	16	2	5	2	25.8	7.36	49	.471	.538	0	—	0	-3	-3	0	-0.3
Total	9	45	58	.437	281	78	16	2	13	831^1	936	86	210	313	12.5	4.34	90	.287	.333	27	.136	-4	-46	-39	5	-3.7
● LEO FISHEL																										
Fishel, Leo b: 12/13/1877, Babylon, N.Y. d: 5/19/60, Hempstead, N.Y. BR/TR, 6', 175 lbs. Deb: 5/03/1899																										
1899	NY-N	0	1	.000	1	1	1	0	0	9	9	0	6	6	17.0	6.00	63	.260	.399	1	.250	-0	-2	-2	0	-0.2
● BRIAN FISHER																										
Fisher, Brian Kevin b: 3/18/62, Honolulu, Hawaii BR/TR, 6'4", 210 lbs. Deb: 5/07/85																										
1985	NY-A	4	4	.500	55	0	0	0	14	98^1	77	4	29	85	9.7	2.38	168	.216	.275	0	—	0	19	18	0	1.8
1986	NY-A	9	5	.643	62	0	0	0	6	96^2	105	14	37	67	13.3	4.93	83	.277	.343	0	—	0	-8	-9	-1	-1.0
1987	Pit-N	11	9	.550	37	26	6	3	0	185^1	185	27	72	117	12.7	4.52	91	.262	.334	11	.190	5	-9	-8	-1	-0.6
1988	Pit-N	8	10	.444	33	22	1	1	1	146^1	157	13	57	66	13.5	4.61	74	.277	.348	2	.048	-2	-19	-20	-2	-2.5
1989	Pit-N	0	3	.000	9	3	0	0	1	17	25	2	10	8	18.5	7.94	42	.329	.407	0	.000	-1	-8	-9	-0	-0.9
1990	Hou-N	0	0	—	4	0	0	0	0	5	9	1	0	1	16.2	7.20	52	.409	.409	0	—	0	-2	-2	-0	-0.2
1992	Sea-A	4	3	.571	22	14	0	0	1	91^1	80	9	47	26	12.6	4.53	88	.234	.328	0	—	0	-6	-6	-0	-0.6
Total	7	36	34	.514	222	65	7	4	23	640	638	70	252	370	12.7	4.39	89	.261	.332	13	.124	2	-33	-36	-5	-4.0
● CHAUNCEY FISHER																										
Fisher, Chauncey Burr "Peach" or "Whoa Bill" b: 1/8/1872, Anderson, Ind. d: 4/27/39, Los Angeles, Cal. BR/TR, 5'11", 175 lbs. Deb: 9/20/1893 F																										
1893	Cle-N	0	2	.000	2	2	2	0	0	18	26	0	9	9	17.5	5.50	89	.328	.397	2	.250	-0	-2	-1	0	-0.1
1894	Cle-N	0	2	.000	3	2	0	0	0	11	22	0	5	0	22.9	11.45	48	.410	.469	0	.000	-1	-7	-7	1	-0.5
	Cin-N	2	8	.200	11	11	10	0	0	91	134	4	44	14	17.6	7.32	76	.338	.404	10	.233	-1	-20	-18	-1	-1.5
	Yr	2	10	.167	14	13	10	0	0	102	156	4	49	14	18.1	7.76	71	.346	.410	10	.213	-2	-28	-25	-1	-2.0
1896	Cin-N	10	7	.588	27	15	13	2	2	159^2	199	9	36	25	13.5	4.45	104	.303	.344	14	.246	0	-2	3	-0	0.2
1897	Bro-N	9	7	.563	20	13	11	1	1	149	184	5	43	31	13.8	4.23	97	.301	.349	12	.203	-1	1	-2	-2	-0.4
1901	NY-N	0	0	—	1	1	0	0	0	4	11	0	2	1	29.3	15.75	21	.490	.531	0	.000	-0	-6	-6	-0	-0.5
	StL-N	0	0	—	1	0	0	0	0	3	7	0	1	0	24.0	15.00	21	.449	.482	0	.000	-0	-4	-4	0	-0.3
	Yr	0	0	—	2	1	0	0	0	7	18	0	3	1	27.0	15.43	21	.473	.511	0	.000	-0	-9	-9	0	-0.8
Total	5	21	26	.447	65	44	36	3	3	435^2	583	18	140	80	15.1	5.37	86	.318	.368	38	.218	-3	-39	-35	-2	-3.1
● CLARENCE FISHER																										
Fisher, Clarence Henry b: 8/27/1898, Letart, W.Va. d: 11/2/65, Point Pleasant, W.Va. BR/TR, 6', 174 lbs. Deb: 9/14/19																										
1919	Was-A	0	0	—	2	0	0	0	0	4	8	0	3	1	24.8	13.50	24	.421	.500	0	—	0	-5	-5	0	-0.4
1920	Was-A	0	1	.000	2	0	0	0	0	3^2	5	0	5	0	24.5	9.82	38	.714	.833	0	.000	-0	-2	-2	1	-0.2
Total	2	0	1	.000	4	0	0	0	0	7^2	13	0	8	1	24.7	11.74	29	.500	.618	0	.000	-0	-7	-7	1	-0.6
● DON FISHER																										
Fisher, Donald Raymond b: 2/6/16, Cleveland, Ohio d: 7/29/73, Mayfield Heights Ohio BR/TR, 6', 210 lbs. Deb: 8/25/45																										
1945	NY-N	1	0	1.000	2	1	1	1	0	18	12	0	7	4	10.5	2.00	196	.190	.292	1	.143	-0	4	4	-0	0.4
● EDDIE FISHER																										
Fisher, Eddie Gene b: 7/16/36, Shreveport, La. BR/TR, 6'2.5", 200 lbs. Deb: 6/22/59																										
1959	SF-N	2	6	.250	17	5	0	0	1	40	57	8	8	15	14.8	7.87	48	.339	.373	0	.000	-1	-17	-18	-1	-1.8
1960	SF-N	1	0	1.000	3	1	1	0	0	12^2	11	2	2	7	9.2	3.55	98	.244	.277	3	.600	1	0	-0	0	0.1
1961	SF-N	0	2	.000	15	1	0	0	1	33^2	36	7	9	16	12.0	5.35	71	.267	.313	1	.143	0	-5	-6	-0	-0.6
1962	Chi-A	9	5	.643	57	12	2	1	5	182^2	169	17	45	88	10.6	3.10	126	.245	.293	6	.130	-0	18	16	0	1.7
1963	Chi-A	9	8	.529	33	15	2	1	0	120^2	114	14	28	67	10.7	3.95	89	.244	.290	5	.139	-1	-4	-6	1	-0.6
1964	Chi-A	6	3	.667	59	2	0	0	9	125	86	13	32	74	8.7	3.02	114	.192	.250	3	.167	-0	8	6	0	0.6
1965	Chi-A★	15	7	.682	**82**	0	0	0	24	165^1	118	13	43	90	**8.9**	2.40	133	.205	.262	4	.138	0	20	15	1	1.7
1966	Chi-A	1	3	.250	23	0	0	0	6	35^1	27	1	17	18	11.5	2.29	138	.214	.313	0	.000	-0	4	3	0	0.4
	Bal-A	5	3	.625	44	0	0	0	13	71^2	60	4	19	39	10.2	2.64	126	.226	.282	2	.154	0	6	6	-0	0.6
	Yr	6	6	.500	**67**	0	0	0	19	107	87	5	36	57	10.5	2.52	130	.221	.289	2	.133	-0	11	9	-0	1.0
1967	Bal-A	4	3	.571	46	0	0	0	1	89^2	82	7	26	53	11.2	3.61	87	.245	.307	1	.200	0	-4	-5	-1	-0.5
1968	Cle-A	4	2	.667	54	0	0	0	4	94^2	87	8	17	42	10.1	2.85	104	.248	.286	0	.000	-1	1	1	1	0.1
1969	Cal-A	3	2	.600	52	1	0	0	2	96^2	100	9	28	47	12.0	3.63	96	.272	.326	0	.000	-1	-0	-2	0	-0.3
1970	Cal-A	4	4	.500	67	2	0	0	8	130^1	117	15	35	74	10.6	3.04	119	.239	.292	1	.091	-1	10	8	1	1.0
1971	Cal-A	10	8	.556	57	3	0	0	3	119	92	11	50	82	10.9	2.72	119	.211	.295	1	.063	-0	10	7	-0	0.6
1972	Cal-A	4	5	.444	43	1	0	0	4	81^1	73	6	31	32	11.5	3.76	77	.247	.319	2	.118	-1	-6	-8	-0	-1.0
	Chi-A	0	1	.000	6	4	0	0	0	22^1	31	1	9	10	16.1	4.43	70	.348	.408	0	.000	-1	-3	-3	0	-0.4
	Yr	4	6	.400	49	5	0	0	4	103^2	104	7	40	42	12.5	3.91	76	.267	.336	2	.083	-1	-10	-11	-0	-1.4
1973	Chi-A	6	7	.462	26	16	2	0	0	110^2	135	12	38	57	14.3	4.88	81	.301	.360	0	—	0	-13	-11	0	-1.1
	StL-N	2	1	.667	6	0	0	0	0	7	3	1	1	1	6.4	1.29	283	.125	.192	1	1.000	0	2	2	-0	0.2
Total	15	85	70	.548	690	63	7	2	81	1538^2	1398	149	438	812	10.9	3.41	101	.243	.299	30	.122	-4	26	5	3	0.7
● ED FISHER																										
Fisher, Edward Fredrick b: 10/31/1876, Wayne, Mich. d: 7/24/51, Spokane, Wash. BR/TR, 6'2", 200 lbs. Deb: 9/05/02																										
1902	Det-A	0	0	—	1	0	0	0	0	4	4	0	1	0	11.3	0.00	—	.261	.306	0	.000	-0	2	2	-0	0.1

YEAR TM/L	W	L	PCT	G	GS	CG	SH	SV	IP	H	HR	BB	SO	RAT	ERA	ERA+	OAV	OOB	BH	AVG	PB	PR	/A	PD	TPI
● FRITZ FISHER Fisher, Frederick Brown b: 11/28/41, Adrian, Mich. BL/TL, 6'1", 180 lbs. Deb: 4/19/64																									
1964 Det-A	0	0	—	1	0	0	0	0	0^1	2	0	2	1	108.0	108.00	3	.667	.800	0	—	0	-4	-4	0	-0.3
● GEORGE FISHER Fisher, George C. b: Wilmington, Del. Deb: 7/17/1884 ♦																									
1884 Phi-U	1	7	.125	8	8	8	0	0	70^2	76	0	13	42	11.3	3.57	80	.257	.288	8	.222	0	-4	-5	-1	-0.5
1885 Buf-N	0	1	.000	1	1	1	0	0	9	10	0	2	4	12.0	5.00	60	.256	.293	0	.000	-1	-2	-2	0	-0.2
Total 2	1	8	.111	9	9	9	0	0	79^2	86	0	15	46	11.4	3.73	77	.257	.289	13	.140	-0	-6	-7	-1	-0.7
● HARRY FISHER Fisher, Harry Devereux b: 1/3/26, Newbury, Ont., Can. d: 9/20/81, Waterloo, Ont., Ca BL/TR, 6', 180 lbs. Deb: 9/16/51 ♦																									
1952 Pit-N	1	2	.333	8	3	0	0	0	18^1	17	4	13	5	15.7	6.87	58	.266	.405	5	.333	1	-6	-6	-1	-0.5
● JACK FISHER Fisher, John Howard "Fat Jack" b: 3/4/39, Frostburg, Md. BR/TR, 6'2", 215 lbs. Deb: 4/14/59																									
1959 Bal-A	1	6	.143	27	7	1	1	2	88^2	76	7	38	52	11.7	3.05	124	.230	.311	3	.130	-1	8	7	-1	0.6
1960 Bal-A	12	11	.522	40	20	8	3	2	197^2	174	13	78	99	11.6	3.41	111	.241	.317	11	.183	2	10	9	0	1.1
1961 Bal-A	10	13	.435	36	25	10	1	1	196	205	17	75	118	13.0	3.90	100	.270	.339	5	.089	-2	3	0	-3	-0.5
1962 Bal-A	7	9	.438	32	25	4	0	1	152	173	23	56	81	13.7	5.09	74	.284	.346	5	.102	-1	-19	-23	-1	-2.3
1963 SF-N	6	10	.375	36	12	2	0	1	116	132	12	38	57	13.6	4.58	70	.284	.344	3	.103	1	-17	-18	-0	-1.8
1964 NY-N	10	17	.370	40	34	8	1	0	227^2	256	23	56	115	12.7	4.23	85	.283	.331	12	.158	1	-18	-16	-1	-1.7
1965 NY-N	8	24	.250	43	36	10	0	1	253^2	252	22	68	116	11.5	3.94	90	.259	.310	12	.154	0	-11	-12	2	-1.0
1966 NY-N	11	14	.440	38	33	10	2	0	230	229	26	54	127	11.4	3.68	99	.260	.309	6	.090	-2	-2	-1	3	0.0
1967 NY-N	9	18	.333	39	30	7	1	0	220^1	251	21	64	117	13.0	4.70	72	.287	.339	7	.100	-2	-32	-32	1	-3.4
1968 Chi-A	8	13	.381	35	28	2	0	0	180^2	176	14	48	80	11.5	2.99	101	.257	.312	6	.113	-1	-0	1	-0	-0.1
1969 Cin-N	4	4	.500	34	15	0	0	1	113	137	15	30	55	13.7	5.50	68	.295	.345	4	.121	-1	-24	-22	-2	-2.5
Total 11	86	139	.382	400	265	62	9	9	1975^2	2061	193	605	1017	12.4	4.06	88	.269	.326	74	.125	-6	-102	-106	-1	-11.6
● MAURICE FISHER Fisher, Maurice Wayne b: 2/16/31, Uniondale, Ind. BR/TR, 6'5", 210 lbs. Deb: 4/16/55																									
1955 Cin-N	0	0	—	1	0	0	0	0	2^2	5	1	2	1	23.6	6.75	63	.385	.467	0	.000	-0	-1	-1	-0	-0.1
● RAY FISHER Fisher, Raymond Lyle "Chic" b: 10/4/1887, Middlebury, Vt. d: 11/3/82, Ann Arbor, Mich. BR/TR, 5'11.5", 180 lbs. Deb: 7/02/10																									
1910 NY-A	5	3	.625	17	7	3	0	1	92^1	95	0	18	42	11.3	2.92	91	.274	.315	3	.103	-2	-4	-3	1	-0.4
1911 NY-A	10	11	.476	29	22	8	2	0	171^2	178	3	55	99	12.5	3.25	111	.269	.330	7	.119	-3	2	7	4	0.7
1912 NY-A	2	8	.200	17	13	5	0	0	90^1	107	2	32	47	14.0	5.88	61	.312	.374	2	.065	-4	-26	-23	3	-2.2
1913 NY-A	12	16	.429	43	31	14	1	1	246^1	244	3	71	92	11.8	3.18	94	.261	.319	22	.278	3	-7	-5	2	0.0
1914 NY-A	10	12	.455	29	26	17	2	1	209	177	2	61	86	10.4	2.28	121	.241	.303	9	.138	-2	11	11	4	1.4
1915 NY-A	18	11	.621	30	28	20	4	0	247^2	219	7	62	97	10.4	2.11	139	.243	.295	9	.108	-5	23	23	-0	2.0
1916 NY-A	11	8	.579	31	21	9	1	2	179	191	4	51	56	12.4	3.17	91	.285	.339	11	.177	1	-7	-5	-1	-0.6
1917 NY-A	8	9	.471	23	18	12	3	0	144	126	3	43	64	10.7	2.19	123	.243	.304	9	.180	-0	8	8	1	1.0
1919 *Cin-N	14	5	.737	26	20	12	5	1	174^1	141	5	38	41	9.3	2.17	128	.226	.271	16	.271	3	14	12	3	2.1
1920 Cin-N	10	11	.476	33	22	10	1	1	201	189	5	50	56	11.1	2.73	111	.249	.302	17	.243	1	9	7	2	1.1
Total 10	100	94	.515	278	208	110	19	7	1755^2	1667	34	481	680	11.2	2.82	105	.257	.312	105	.179	-8	23	30	19	5.1
● TOM FISHER Fisher, Thomas Chalmers "Red" b: 11/1/1880, Anderson, Ind. d: 9/3/72, Anderson, Ind. BR/TR, 5'10.5", 185 lbs. Deb: 4/17/04 F																									
1904 Bos-N	6	16	.273	31	21	19	2	0	214	257	5	82	84	14.7	4.25	65	.302	.370	21	.212	3	-36	-35	-5	-3.7
● TOM FISHER Fisher, Thomas Gene b: 4/4/42, Cleveland, Ohio BR/TR, 6', 180 lbs. Deb: 9/20/67																									
1967 Bal-A	0	0	—	2	0	0	0	0	3^1	2	0	2	1	10.8	0.00	—	.182	.308	0	—	0	1	1	-0	0.1
● CHEROKEE FISHER Fisher, William Charles b: 12/1845, Philadelphia, Pa. d: 9/26/12, New York, N.Y. BR/TR, 5'9", 164 lbs. Deb: 5/06/1871 ♦																									
1871 Rok-n	4	16	.200	24	24	22	**1**	0	213	295	3	31	15	13.8	4.35	94	.281	.302	28	.228	-3	-3	-6		-0.6
1872 Bal-n	10	1	.909	19	11	9	1	**1**	110^1	89	0	11	20	**8.2**	2.53	148	**.189**	**.207**	52	.230	-1	15	15		1.0
1873 Ath-n	3	4	.429	13	5	5	0	1	84^1	90	1	10	14	**10.7**	**1.81**	**188**	**.227**	**.246**	66	.261	1	13	15		1.1
1874 Har-n	14	23	.378	39	35	31	0	0	317	405	1	10		11.8	*3.04*	104	.275	.279	54	.223	-5	-1	4		0.0
1875 Phi-n	22	19	.537	41	41	36	2	0	356^2	345	6	9		8.9	*1.92*	131	.232	.237	41	.232	-1	21	24		1.9
1876 Cin-N	4	20	.167	28	24	22	0	0	229^1	294	6	6	29	11.8	3.02	73	.285	.289	32	.248	-1	-18	-21	-2	-2.0
1878 Pro-N	0	1	.000	1	1	1	0	0	9	14	0	0	2	14.0	4.00	55	.304	.304	0	.000	-0	-2	-2	0	-0.2
Total 5 n	53	63	.457	136	116	103	4	2	1081^1	1224	11	71	49	10.8	*2.78*	116	.251	.262	241	.236	-10	45	53		3.4
Total 2	4	21	.160	29	25	23	0	0	238^1	308	6	6	31	11.9	3.06	72	.285	.289	32	.235	-10	-20	-23	-2	-2.2
● MAX FISKE Fiske, Maximilian Patrick "Ski" b: 10/12/1888, Chicago, Ill. d: 5/15/28, Chicago, Ill. BR/TR, 5'11", 185 lbs. Deb: 4/19/14																									
1914 Chi-F	12	12	.500	38	22	7	0	0	198	161	7	59	87	10.3	3.14	94	.231	.298	16	.235	1	2	-4	-0	-0.3
● PAUL FITTERY Fittery, Paul Clarence b: 10/10/1887, Lebanon, Pa. d: 1/28/74, Cartersville, Ga. BB/TL, 5'8.5", 156 lbs. Deb: 9/05/14																									
1914 Cin-N	0	2	.000	8	4	2	0	0	43^2	41	0	12	21	11.1	3.09	95	.246	.300	1	.059	-1	-1	-1	0	-0.2
1917 Phi-N	1	1	.500	17	2	1	0	0	55^2	69	1	27	13	16.3	4.53	62	.317	.404	2	.091	-1	-11	-11	1	-1.1
Total 2	1	3	.250	25	6	3	0	0	99^1	110	1	39	34	14.0	3.90	73	.286	.360	3	.077	-2	-13	-11	2	-1.3
● JOHN FITZGERALD Fitzgerald, John Francis b: 9/15/33, Brooklyn, N.Y. BL/TL, 6'3", 190 lbs. Deb: 9/28/58																									
1958 SF-N	0	0	—	1	1	0	0	0	3	1	1	1	3	6.0	3.00	127	.111	.200	0	.000	-0	0	0	0	0.0
● JOHN FITZGERALD Fitzgerald, John H. b: 5/30/1870, Natick, Mass. d: 3/31/21, Boston, Mass. Deb: 7/18/1891																									
1891 Bos-a	1	1	.500	6	3	2	0	1	32	49	2	11	16	17.4	5.63	62	.340	.394	1	.071	-1	-7	-8	0	-0.7
● JOHN FITZGERALD Fitzgerald, John J. Deb: 4/18/1890																									
1890 Roc-a	3	8	.273	11	11	8	1	0	78	77	0	45	35	14.8	4.04	88	.250	.357	6	.194	-0	-1	-4	1	-0.3
● JOHN FITZGERALD Fitzgerald, John T. b: Leadville, Col. Deb: 6/04/1891																									
1891 Lou-a	14	18	.438	33	32	29	3	0	276	280	6	95	111	12.7	3.59	102	.254	.321	19	.170	0	4	2	-4	-0.1
1892 Lou-N	1	3	.250	4	4	4	0	0	34	45	2	11	3	15.1	4.24	72	.306	.359	2	.133	-0	-4	-4	-1	-0.5
Total 2	15	21	.417	37	36	33	3	0	310	325	8	106	114	12.9	3.66	98	.260	.325	21	.165	-0	1	-2	-4	-0.6
● PAUL FITZKE Fitzke, Paul Frederick Herman "Bob" b: 7/30/1900, Lacrosse, Wis. d: 6/30/50, Sacramento, Cal. BR/TR, 5'11.5", 185 lbs. Deb: 9/01/24																									
1924 Cle-A	0	0	—	1	0	0	0	0	4	5	0	3	1	18.0	4.50	95	.313	.421	0	.000	-0	-0	-0	-0	0.0
● AL FITZMORRIS Fitzmorris, Alan James b: 3/21/46, Buffalo, N.Y. BB/TR, 6'2", 190 lbs. Deb: 9/08/69																									
1969 KC-A	1	1	.500	7	0	0	0	2	10^2	9	1	4	3	11.0	4.22	87	.237	.310	0	.000	-0	-1	-1	-0	-0.1
1970 KC-A	8	5	.615	43	11	2	0	1	117^2	112	14	52	47	12.5	4.44	84	.254	.333	9	.290	4	-9	-9	1	-0.5
1971 KC-A	7	5	.583	36	15	2	0	1	127^1	112	6	55	53	11.9	4.17	82	.245	.327	11	.250	2	-10	-10	2	-0.7
1972 KC-A	2	5	.286	38	2	0	0	3	101	99	10	28	51	11.4	3.74	81	.252	.303	4	.174	1	-8	-8	2	-0.6
1973 KC-A	8	3	.727	15	13	3	1	0	89	88	5	25	26	11.4	2.83	145	.259	.310	0	—	0	10	13	2	1.0
1974 KC-A	13	6	.684	34	27	9	4	1	190	189	8	63	53	11.9	2.79	137	.260	.319	0	—	0	17	22	3	2.5
1975 KC-A	16	12	.571	35	35	11	3	0	242	239	16	76	78	11.9	3.57	108	.262	.322	0	—	0	6	7	1	0.8
1976 KC-A	15	11	.577	35	33	8	2	0	220^1	227	6	56	80	11.6	3.06	114	.273	.320	0	—	0	11	11	3	1.5
1977 Cle-A	6	10	.375	29	21	1	0	0	133	164	12	53	54	14.8	5.41	73	.306	.369	0	—	0	-20	-22	-0	-1.9
1978 Cle-A	0	1	.000	7	0	0	0	0	14^1	19	3	7	5	17.0	6.28	59	.333	.415	0	—	0	-4	-4	-0	-0.3
Cal-A	1	0	1.000	9	2	0	0	0	31^2	26	2	14	8	11.4	1.71	212	.236	.323	0	—	0	7	7	-0	1.0
Yr	1	1	.500	16	2	0	0	0	46	45	5	21	13	12.9	3.13	117	.268	.349	0	—	0	3	3	-0	0.7

YEAR	TM/L	W	L	PCT	G	GS	CG	SH	SV	IP	H	HR	BB	SO	RAT	ERA	ERA+	OAV	OOB	BH	AVG	PB	PR	/A	PD	TPI
Total	10	77	59	.566	288	159	36	11	7	1277	1284	83	433	458	12.2	3.65	101	.265	.327	24	.242	7	-1	5	12	2.7
● FREDDIE FITZSIMMONS	Fitzsimmons, Frederick Landis "Fat Freddie" b: 7/28/01, Mishawaka, Ind. d: 11/18/79, Yucca Valley, Cal. BR/TR, 5'11", 185 lbs. Deb: 8/12/25 MC																									
1925	NY-N	6	3	.667	10	8	6	1	0	74^2	70	4	18	17	10.6	2.65	152	.248	.293	9	.310	2	13	12	2	1.5
1926	NY-N	14	10	.583	37	26	12	0	0	219	224	7	58	48	11.8	2.88	130	.272	.322	11	.128	-6	23	21	3	1.8
1927	NY-N	17	10	.630	42	31	14	1	3	244^2	260	15	67	78	12.2	3.72	104	.275	.325	18	.207	-0	6	4	2	0.5
1928	NY-N	20	9	.690	40	32	16	1	1	261^1	264	13	65	67	11.5	3.68	106	.268	.316	18	.191	1	9	6	2	0.9
1929	NY-N	15	11	.577	37	31	14	4	1	221^2	242	14	66	55	12.6	4.10	112	.285	.338	15	.183	-2	15	12	4	1.3
1930	NY-N	19	7	**.731**	41	29	17	1	1	224^1	230	26	59	76	11.6	4.25	111	.266	.314	22	.265	5	18	12	7	2.1
1931	NY-N	18	11	.621	35	33	19	4	0	253^2	242	16	62	78	10.8	3.05	121	.251	.296	21	.228	8	23	18	8	**3.6**
1932	NY-N	11	11	.500	35	31	11	0	0	237^2	287	18	83	65	14.1	4.43	84	.299	.356	19	.221	4	-15	-19	7	-0.9
1933	*NY-N	16	11	.593	36	35	13	1	0	251^2	243	14	72	65	11.3	2.90	111	.251	.305	19	.200	3	12	9	6	1.8
1934	NY-N	18	14	.563	38	37	14	3	1	263^1	266	12	51	73	10.9	3.04	127	.261	.297	22	.232	5	30	24	5	3.4
1935	NY-N	4	8	.333	18	15	6	**4**	0	94	104	7	22	23	12.2	4.02	96	.281	.323	8	.258	1	-0	-2	1	0.1
1936	*NY-N	10	7	.588	28	17	7	0	2	141	147	6	39	35	11.9	3.32	117	.274	.323	7	.149	-2	11	9	1	0.7
1937	NY-N	2	2	.500	6	4	1	1	0	27^1	28	3	8	13	11.9	4.61	84	.272	.324	3	.300	2	-2	-2	-0	-0.1
	Bro-N	4	8	.333	13	13	4	0	0	90^2	91	2	32	29	12.3	4.27	95	.263	.327	5	.167	-1	-4	-2	1	-0.2
	Yr	6	10	.375	19	17	5	1	0	118	119	5	40	42	12.2	4.35	92	.265	.327	8	.200	1	-6	-5	1	-0.3
1938	Bro-N	11	8	.579	27	26	12	3	0	202^2	205	8	43	38	11.1	3.02	129	.261	.302	12	.171	-1	17	20	6	2.6
1939	Bro-N	7	9	.438	27	20	5	0	3	151^1	178	6	28	44	12.4	3.87	104	.293	.327	11	.234	3	1	3	5	1.1
1940	Bro-N	16	2	**.889**	20	18	11	4	1	134^1	120	5	25	35	9.8	2.81	142	.233	.269	5	.106	-2	15	18	1	1.7
1941	*Bro-N	6	1	.857	13	12	3	1	0	82^2	78	3	26	19	11.5	2.07	177	.245	.305	4	.143	-0	14	15	2	1.9
1942	Bro-N	0	0	—	1	1	0	0	0	3	6	1	1	0	21.0	15.00	22	.400	.438	1	.500	0	-4	-4	0	-0.3
1943	Bro-N	3	4	.429	9	7	1	0	0	44^2	50	6	21	12	14.5	5.44	62	.281	.360	1	.071	-1	-10	-10	0	-1.1
Total	19	217	146	.598	513	426	186	29	13	3223^2	3335	186	846	870	11.8	3.51	111	.268	.316	231	.200	20	174	144	60	22.4
● PATSY FLAHERTY	Flaherty, Patrick Joseph b: 6/29/1876, Mansfield, Pa. d: 1/23/68, Alexandria, La. BL/TL, 5'8", 165 lbs. Deb: 9/08/1899 ♦																									
1899	Lou-N	2	3	.400	5	4	4	0	0	39	41	0	5	5	10.8	2.31	167	.270	.298	5	.208	1	7	7	-1	0.6
1900	Pit-N	0	0	—	4	1	0	0	0	22	30	0	9	5	17.2	6.14	59	.324	.401	1	.111	-1	-6	-6	1	-0.5
1903	Chi-A	11	25	.306	40	34	29	2	1	293^2	338	9	50	65	12.3	3.74	75	.288	.324	14	.137	-3	-25	-30	3	-3.1
1904	Chi-A	1	2	.333	5	5	4	0	0	43	36	1	10	14	9.8	2.09	117	.228	.279	4	.333	2	2	2	1	0.6
	Pit-N	19	9	.679	29	28	28	5	0	242	210	3	59	54	10.4	2.05	134	.232	.287	22	.212	5	19	19	5	3.3
1905	Pit-N	10	10	.500	27	20	15	0	1	187^2	197	2	49	44	12.1	3.50	86	.272	.324	15	.197	2	-10	-10	2	-0.7
1907	Bos-N	12	15	.444	27	25	23	0	0	217	197	4	59	34	10.9	2.70	95	.248	.306	22	.191	2	-5	-3	2	0.2
1908	Bos-N	12	18	.400	31	31	21	0	0	244	221	6	81	50	11.4	3.25	74	.236	.303	12	.140	-0	-24	-23	2	-2.4
1910	Phi-N	0	0	—	1	0	0	0	0	0^1	1	0	1	0	54.0	0.00	—	.333	.500	1	.500	0	0	0	0	0.0
1911	Bos-N	0	2	.000	4	2	1	0	0	14	21	0	8	0	20.6	7.07	54	.350	.451	27	.287	1	-6	-5	-0	-0.4
Total	9	67	84	.444	173	150	125	7	2	1302^2	1292	25	331	271	11.6	3.10	89	.259	.312	123	.197	10	-49	-50	14	-2.4
● MIKE FLANAGAN	Flanagan, Michael Kendall b: 12/16/51, Manchester, N.H. BL/TL, 6', 195 lbs. Deb: 9/05/75																									
1975	Bal-A	0	1	.000	2	1	0	0	0	9^2	9	0	6	7	14.0	2.79	126	.250	.357	0	—	0	1	1	0	0.3
1976	Bal-A	3	5	.375	20	10	4	0	0	85	83	7	33	56	12.3	4.13	79	.260	.330	0	—	0	-6	-8	0	-0.5
1977	Bal-A	15	10	.600	36	33	15	2	1	235	235	17	70	149	11.8	3.64	104	.266	.321	0	—	0	11	4	-0	0.8
1978	Bal-A☆	19	15	.559	40	40	17	2	0	281^1	271	22	87	167	11.5	4.03	87	.257	.315	0	—	0	-8	-17	-2	-1.4
1979	*Bal-A	**23**	9	.719	39	38	16	**5**	0	265^2	245	23	70	190	10.8	3.08	130	.245	.297	0	—	0	33	27	-0	2.9
1980	Bal-A	16	13	.552	37	37	12	2	0	251^1	278	27	71	128	12.6	4.12	96	.287	.337	0	—	0	-2	-5	0	-0.4
1981	Bal-A	9	6	.600	20	20	3	2	0	116	108	11	37	72	11.4	4.19	87	.244	.305	0	—	0	-7	-7	1	-0.6
1982	Bal-A	15	11	.577	36	35	11	1	0	236	233	24	76	103	11.9	3.97	102	.259	.319	0	—	0	3	2	0	0.2
1983	*Bal-A	12	4	.750	20	20	3	1	0	125^1	135	10	31	50	12.1	3.30	120	.278	.324	0	—	0	11	9	-1	1.0
1984	Bal-A	13	13	.500	34	34	10	2	0	226^2	213	24	81	115	11.7	3.53	110	.250	.316	0	—	0	11	8	-1	0.9
1985	Bal-A	4	5	.444	15	15	1	0	0	86	101	14	28	42	13.7	5.13	79	.297	.354	0	—	0	-9	-10	-0	-0.9
1986	Bal-A	7	11	.389	29	28	2	0	0	172	179	15	66	96	12.9	4.24	98	.270	.337	0	—	0	-1	-2	-2	-0.3
1987	Bal-A	3	6	.333	16	16	4	0	0	94^2	102	9	36	50	13.1	4.94	89	.278	.342	0	—	0	-5	-6	-0	-0.4
	Tor-A	3	2	.600	7	7	0	0	0	49^1	46	3	15	43	11.1	2.37	189	.237	.292	0	—	0	11	12	-0	1.0
	Yr	6	8	.429	23	23	4	0	0	144	148	12	51	93	12.4	4.06	109	.263	.325	0	—	0	6	6	-1	0.6
1988	Tor-A	13	13	.500	34	34	2	1	0	211	220	23	80	99	13.1	4.18	94	.271	.341	0	—	0	-5	-6	1	-0.6
1989	*Tor-A	8	10	.444	30	30	1	1	0	171^2	186	10	47	47	12.5	3.93	96	.283	.335	0	—	0	-1	-3	1	-0.1
1990	Tor-A	2	2	.500	5	5	0	0	0	20^1	28	3	8	5	15.9	5.31	74	.329	.387	0	—	0	-3	-3	0	-0.4
1991	Bal-A	2	7	.222	64	1	0	0	3	98^1	84	6	25	55	10.3	2.38	166	.236	.292	0	—	0	19	17	2	2.2
1992	Bal-A	0	0	—	42	0	0	0	0	34^2	50	3	23	17	20.3	8.05	49	.338	.443	0	—	0	-16	-16	1	-1.5
Total	18	167	143	.539	526	404	101	19	4	2770	2806	251	890	1491	12.1	3.90	100	.266	.325	0	—	0	36	-3	-1	2.2
● RAY FLANIGAN	Flanigan, Raymond Arthur b: 1/8/23, Morgantown, W.Va. BR/TR, 6', 190 lbs. Deb: 9/20/46																									
1946	Cle-A	0	1	.000	3	1	0	0	0	9	11	1	8	2	19.0	11.00	30	.289	.413	1	.500	1	-7	-8	0	-0.6
● TOM FLANIGAN	Flanigan, Thomas Anthony b: 9/6/34, Cincinnati, Ohio BR/TL, 6'3", 175 lbs. Deb: 4/14/54																									
1954	Chi-A	0	0	—	2	0	0	0	0	1^2	1	0	1	0	10.8	0.00	—	.200	.333	0	—	0	1	1	0	0.1
1958	StL-N	0	0	—	1	0	0	0	0	1	2	1	1	0	27.0	9.00	46	.500	.600	0	—	0	-1	-1	-0	-0.1
Total	2	0	0	—	3	0	0	0	0	2^2	3	1	2	0	16.9	3.38	115	.333	.455	0	—	0	0	0	0	0.0
● JACK FLATER	Flater, John William b: 9/22/1880, Sandymount, Md. d: 3/20/70, Westminster, Md. BR/TR, 5'10", 175 lbs. Deb: 9/18/08																									
1908	Phi-A	1	3	.250	5	3	3	0	0	39^1	35	0	12	8	11.2	2.06	125	.252	.320	2	.133	-0	1	2	2	0.4
● JOHN FLAVIN	Flavin, John Thomas b: 5/7/42, Albany, Cal. BL/TL, 6'2", 208 lbs. Deb: 8/25/64																									
1964	Chi-N	0	1	.000	5	1	0	0	0	4^2	11	0	3	5	27.0	13.50	28	.500	.560	0	.000	-0	-5	-5	-0	-0.5
● FRANK FLEET	Fleet, Frank H. b: 1848, New York, N.Y. d: 6/13/1900, New York, N.Y. Deb: 10/18/1871 ♦																									
1871	Mut-n	0	1	.000	1	1	1	0	0	9	20	0	3	0	23.0	10.00	38	.370	.404	2	.333	0	-6	-6		-0.3
1873	Res-n	0	3	.000	3	3	2	0	0	24	57	0	0	1	21.4	5.63	60	.399	.399	23	.256	0	-6	-6		-0.4
1875	StL-n	2	1	.667	3	3	3	0	0	27	33	0	3		12.0	*2.33*	95	.277	.295	1	.063	-2	0	-0		-0.2
	Atl-n	0	1	.000	2	1	1	0	0	15^1	24	1	0		14.1	*4.70*	49	.312	.312	25	.223	-0	-4	-4		-0.3
	Yr	2	2	.500	5	4	4	0	0	42^1	57	1	3		12.8	*3.19*	71	.291	.302	26	.203	-2	-3	-4		-0.5
Total	3 n	2	6	.250	9	8	7	0	0	75^1	134	1	6	1	16.7	*4.78*	47	.341	.351	86	.231	-2	-19	-21		-1.2
● DAVE FLEMING	Fleming, David Anthony b: 11/7/69, Jackson Heights, N.Y. BL/TL, 6'3", 200 lbs. Deb: 8/06/91																									
1991	Sea-A	1	0	1.000	9	3	0	0	0	17^2	19	3	3	11	12.7	6.62	62	.284	.342	0	—	0	-5	-5	1	-0.4
1992	Sea-A	17	10	.630	33	33	7	4	0	228^1	225	13	60	112	11.4	3.39	118	.257	.307	0	—	0	14	15	-0	1.6
Total	2	18	10	.643	42	36	7	4	0	246	244	16	63	123	11.5	3.62	110	.258	.310	0	—	0	9	10	1	1.2
● BILL FLEMING	Fleming, Leslie Fletchard b: 7/31/13, Rowland, Cal. BR/TR, 6', 190 lbs. Deb: 8/21/40																									
1940	Bos-A	1	2	.333	10	6	1	0	0	46^1	53	4	20	24	14.6	4.86	93	.290	.366	0	.000	-2	-2	-2	-1	-0.4
1941	Bos-A	1	1	.500	16	1	0	0	1	41^1	32	4	24	20	12.2	3.92	106	.212	.320	2	.222	1	1	1	1	0.2
1942	Chi-N	5	6	.455	33	14	4	2	2	134^1	117	9	63	59	12.3	3.01	106	.230	.318	2	.051	-4	4	3	-1	-0.2
1943	Chi-N	0	1	.000	11	0	0	0	0	32^1	41	2	12	12	15.6	6.40	52	.311	.381	0	.000	-1	-11	-11	1	-1.1

YEAR TM/L	W	L	PCT	G	GS	CG	SH	SV	IP	H	HR	BB	SO	RAT	ERA	ERA+	OAV	OOB	BH	AVG	PB	PR	/A	PD	TPI
1944 Chi-N	9	10	.474	39	18	9	1	0	158^{1}	163	6	62	42	12.8	3.13	113	.269	.337	9	.170	-1	9	7	1	0.8
1946 Chi-N	0	1	.000	14	1	0	0	0	29^{1}	37	2	12	10	15.3	6.14	54	.301	.368	0	.000	-0	-9	-9	0	-1.0
Total 6	16	21	.432	123	40	14	3	3	442	443	27	193	167	13.2	3.79	94	.260	.339	13	.104	-7	-8	-11	1	-1.7
● **VAN FLETCHER** Fletcher, Alfred Vanoide b: 8/6/24, East Bend, N.C. BR/TR, 6'2", 185 lbs. Deb: 4/12/55																									
1955 Det-A	0	0	—	9	0	0	0	0	12	13	1	2	4	11.3	3.00	128	.260	.288	0	—	0	1	1	-0	0.1
● **SAM FLETCHER** Fletcher, Samuel S. b: Altoona, Pa. TR, 6'2", 210 lbs. Deb: 10/06/09																									
1909 Bro-N	0	1	.000	1	1	1	0	0	9	13	0	2	5	15.0	8.00	32	.351	.385	0	.000	-0	-5	-5	-0	-0.5
1912 Cin-N	0	0	—	2	0	0	0	0	9^{2}	15	1	11	3	24.2	12.10	28	.366	.500	2	.500	1	-9	-9	0	-0.7
Total 2	0	1	.000	3	1	1	0	0	18^{2}	28	1	13	8	19.8	10.13	30	.359	.451	2	.286	0	-15	-15	0	-1.2
● **TOM FLETCHER** Fletcher, Thomas Wayne b: 6/28/42, Elmira, N.Y. BB/TL, 6', 170 lbs. Deb: 9/12/62 F																									
1962 Det-A	0	0	—	1	0	0	0	0	2	2	0	2	1	18.0	0.00	—	.250	.400	0	—	0	1	1	0	0.1
● **JOHN FLINN** Flinn, John Richard b: 9/2/54, Merced, Cal. BR/TR, 6', 175 lbs. Deb: 5/06/78																									
1978 Bal-A	1	1	.500	13	0	0	0	0	15^{2}	24	3	13	8	21.3	8.04	43	.348	.451	0	—	0	-7	-8	0	-0.3
1979 Bal-A	0	0	—	4	0	0	0	0	2^{2}	2	0	1	0	10.1	0.00	—	.222	.300	0	—	0	1	1	0	0.3
1980 Mil-A	2	1	.667	20	1	0	0	2	37	31	3	20	15	12.4	3.89	99	.220	.317	0	—	0	1	-0	-0	0.0
1982 Bal-A	2	0	1.000	5	0	0	0	0	13^{2}	13	1	3	13	10.5	1.32	306	.260	.302	0	—	0	4	4	-0	0.4
Total 4	5	2	.714	42	1	0	0	2	69	70	7	37	36	14.0	4.17	92	.260	.350	0	—	0	-1	-3	-0	0.4
● **HILLY FLITCRAFT** Flitcraft, Hildreth Milton b: 8/21/23, Woodstown, N.J. BL/TL, 6'2", 180 lbs. Deb: 8/31/42																									
1942 Phi-N	0	0	—	3	0	0	0	0	3^{1}	6	0	2	1	21.6	8.10	41	.429	.500	0	—	0	-2	-2	0	-0.2
● **MORT FLOHR** Flohr, Moritz Herman "Dutch" b: 8/15/11, Canisteo, N.Y. BL/TL, 6', 173 lbs. Deb: 6/08/34																									
1934 Phi-A	0	2	.000	14	3	0	0	0	30^{2}	34	3	33	6	20.0	5.87	75	.296	.456	4	.333	1	-5	-5	1	-0.3
● **JESSE FLORES** Flores, Jesse (Sandoval) b: 11/2/14, Guadalajara, Mexico d: 12/17/91, Orange, Cal. BR/TR, 5'10", 175 lbs. Deb: 4/16/42																									
1942 Chi-N	0	1	.000	4	0	0	0	0	5^{1}	5	1	2	6	11.8	3.38	95	.227	.292	0	—	0	-0	-0	0	0.0
1943 Phi-A	12	14	.462	31	27	13	0	0	231^{1}	208	13	70	113	11.0	3.11	109	.240	.301	14	.175	-0	5	7	1	0.9
1944 Phi-A	9	11	.450	27	25	11	2	0	185^{2}	172	8	49	65	10.9	3.39	103	.245	.298	11	.172	-0	1	2	-1	0.1
1945 Phi-A	7	10	.412	29	24	9	4	1	191^{1}	180	6	63	52	11.6	3.43	100	.250	.314	9	.148	-2	-1	-0	-3	-0.5
1946 Phi-A	9	7	.563	29	15	8	4	1	155	147	8	38	48	10.8	2.32	153	.249	.295	11	.250	3	20	21	-2	2.5
1947 Phi-A	4	13	.235	28	20	4	0	0	151^{1}	139	10	59	41	11.8	3.39	112	.244	.315	10	.227	1	5	7	-1	0.8
1950 Cle-A	3	3	.500	28	2	1	1	4	53	53	3	25	27	13.4	3.74	116	.261	.345	0	.000	-2	5	4	-2	0.0
Total 7	44	59	.427	176	113	46	11	6	973	904	49	306	352	11.3	3.18	112	.246	.307	55	.181	-0	35	41	-7	3.8
● **BEN FLOWERS** Flowers, Bennett b: 6/15/27, Wilson, N.C. BR/TR, 6'4", 195 lbs. Deb: 9/29/51																									
1951 Bos-A	0	0	—	1	0	0	0	0	3	2	0	1	2	9.0	0.00	—	.200	.273	0	.000	-0	1	1	-0	0.1
1953 Bos-A	1	4	.200	32	6	1	1	3	79^{1}	87	6	24	36	12.7	3.86	109	.280	.333	3	.158	-0	1	3	1	0.3
1955 Det-A	0	0	—	4	0	0	0	0	6	5	1	2	2	10.5	6.00	64	.238	.304	0	.000	-0	-1	-1	0	-0.1
StL-N	1	0	1.000	4	4	0	0	0	27^{1}	27	1	12	19	12.8	3.62	112	.255	.331	1	.100	-1	1	1	-0	0.0
1956 StL-N	1	1	.500	3	3	0	0	0	11^{2}	15	1	5	5	15.4	6.94	54	.341	.408	0	.000	-0	-4	-4	0	-0.4
Phi-N	0	2	.000	32	0	0	0	0	41	54	9	10	22	14.3	5.71	65	.331	.374	0	.000	0	-9	-9	1	-0.8
Yr	1	3	.250	35	3	0	0	0	52^{2}	69	10	15	27	14.5	5.98	62	.330	.378	0	.000	-0	-13	-13	1	-1.2
Total 4	3	7	.300	76	13	1	1	3	168^{1}	190	18	54	86	13.2	4.49	90	.290	.346	4	.111	-2	-10	-9	1	-0.9
● **DICKIE FLOWERS** Flowers, Charles Richard b: 1850, Philadelphia, Pa. d: 10/5/1892, Philadelphia, Pa. Deb: 6/03/1871 ♦																									
1871 Tro-n	0	0	—	1	0	0	0	0	1	1	0	0	0	9.0	0.00	—	.333	.333	33	.314	0	0	0		0.0
● **WES FLOWERS** Flowers, Charles Wesley b: 8/13/13, Vanndale, Ark. d: 12/31/88, Wynne, Ark. BL/TL, 6'1.5", 190 lbs. Deb: 8/08/40																									
1940 Bro-N	1	1	.500	5	2	0	0	0	21	23	2	10	8	15.4	3.43	117	.299	.400	1	.200	-0	1	1	0	0.1
1944 Bro-N	1	1	.500	9	1	0	0	0	17^{1}	26	3	13	3	20.8	7.79	46	.333	.435	3	.600	1	-8	-8	-0	-0.7
Total 2	2	2	.500	14	3	0	0	0	38^{1}	49	5	23	11	17.8	5.40	70	.316	.418	4	.400	1	-7	-7	-0	-0.6
● **CARNEY FLYNN** Flynn, Cornelius Francis Xavier b: 1/23/1875, Cincinnati, Ohio d: 2/10/47, Cincinnati, Ohio BL/TL, 5'11", 165 lbs. Deb: 7/17/1894																									
1894 Cin-N	0	2	.000	2	1	0	0	0	7^{2}	16	4	10	4	31.7	17.61	32	.420	.550	0	.000	-1	-10	-10	-0	-0.7
1896 NY-N	0	2	.000	3	2	1	0	0	10^{2}	18	0	8	4	26.2	11.81	36	.370	.503	2	.500	2	-9	-9	0	-0.6
Was-N	0	1	.000	4	1	1	0	0	20	43	0	10	3	24.7	8.55	52	.428	.489	2	.250	-0	-9	-9	-1	-0.8
Yr	0	3	.000	7	3	2	0	0	30^{2}	61	0	18	7	23.8	9.68	45	.396	.465	4	.333	1	-18	-18	-1	-1.4
Total 2	0	5	.000	9	4	2	0	0	38^{1}	77	4	28	11	26.5	11.27	41	.412	.506	4	.267	1	-29	-29	-1	-2.1
● **JOCKO FLYNN** Flynn, John A. b: 6/30/1864, Lawrence, Mass. d: 12/30/07, Lawrence, Mass. 5'6.5", 143 lbs. Deb: 5/01/1886 ♦																									
1886 Chi-N	23	6	**.793**	32	29	28	2	1	257	207	9	63	146	9.5	2.24	163	.210	.257	41	.200	2	31	40	2	4.1
● **STU FLYTHE** Flythe, Stuart Mcguire b: 12/5/11, Conway, N.C. d: 10/18/63, Durham, N.C. BR/TR, 6'2", 175 lbs. Deb: 5/31/36																									
1936 Phi-A	0	0	—	17	3	0	0	0	39^{1}	49	4	61	14	25.9	13.04	39	.302	.500	4	.267	0	-35	-35	-0	-2.8
● **GENE FODGE** Fodge, Eugene Arlan "Suds" b: 7/9/31, South Bend, Ind. BR/TR, 6', 175 lbs. Deb: 4/20/58																									
1958 Chi-N	1	1	.500	16	4	1	0	0	39^{2}	47	5	11	15	13.2	4.76	82	.296	.341	0	.000	-1	-4	-4	0	-0.4
● **JIM FOGARTY** Fogarty, James G. b: 2/12/1864, San Francisco, Cal d: 5/20/1891, Philadelphia, Pa. BR/TR, 5'10.5", 180 lbs. Deb: 5/01/1884 FM♦																									
1884 Phi-N	0	0	—	1	0	0	0	0	1	2	0	0	1	18.0	0.00	—	.333	.333	80	.212	0	0	0	0	0.0
1886 Phi-N	0	1	.000	1	0	0	0	0	6	7	1	0	4	10.5	0.00	—	.250	.250	82	.293	0	2	2	0	0.3
1887 Phi-N	0	0	—	1	0	0	0	0	3	3	0	1	0	12.0	9.00	47	.200	.250	129	.261	0	-2	-2	-0	-0.1
1889 Phi-N	0	0	—	4	0	0	0	0	4	4	0	2	0	13.5	9.00	48	.252	.336	129	.259	1	-2	-2	-0	-0.2
Total 4	0	1	.000	7	0	0	0	0	14	16	1	3	5	12.2	4.50	84	.247	.280	709	.246	2	-1	-1	0	0.0
● **CURRY FOLEY** Foley, Charles Joseph b: 1/14/1856, Milltown, Ireland d: 10/20/1898, Boston, Mass. TL, 180 lbs. Deb: 5/13/1879 ♦																									
1879 Bos-N	9	9	.500	21	16	16	1	0	161^{2}	175	1	15	57	10.6	2.51	99	.252	.268	46	.315	5	-0	-0	-2	0.2
1880 Bos-N	14	14	.500	36	28	21	1	0	238	264	1	40	68	11.5	3.89	58	.274	.303	97	.292	8	-40	-43	1	-3.4
1881 Buf-N	3	4	.429	10	6	2	0	0	41	70	1	5	2	16.5	5.27	53	.337	.352	96	.256	1	-11	-11	-0	-1.0
1882 Buf-N	0	0	—	1	0	0	0	0	1	2	0	0	0	18.0	18.00	16	.333	.333	104	.305	0	-2	-2	-0	-0.1
1883 Buf-N	1	0	1.000	1	0	0	0	0	1	0	0	4	0	36.0	0.00	—	.000	.667	30	.270	0	0	0	-0	0.0
Total 5	27	27	.500	69	50	39	2	0	442^{2}	511	3	64	127	11.7	3.54	68	.273	.297	373	.286	14	-53	-56	-2	-4.3
● **JOHN FOLEY** Foley, John J b: Hannibal, Mo. TL, Deb: 9/18/1885																									
1885 Pro-N	0	1	.000	1	1	1	0	0	8	6	0	5	2	12.4	4.50	59	.188	.297	0	.000	0	-1	-2	0	-0.1
● **TOM FOLEY** Foley, Thomas Michael b: 9/9/59, Columbus, Ga. BL/TR, 6'1", 175 lbs. Deb: 4/09/83 ♦																									
1989 Mon-N	0	0	—	1	0	0	0	0	0^{1}	1	1	0	0	27.0	27.00	13	.500	.500	86	.229	0	-1	-1	0	-0.1
● **RICH FOLKERS** Folkers, Richard Nevin b: 10/17/46, Waterloo, Iowa BL/TL, 6'2", 180 lbs. Deb: 6/10/70																									
1970 NY-N	0	2	.000	16	1	0	0	2	29^{1}	36	6	25	15	18.7	6.44	62	.313	.436	2	.333	0	-8	-8	1	-0.6
1972 StL-N	1	0	1.000	9	0	0	0	0	13^{1}	12	0	5	7	11.5	3.38	101	.240	.309	0	.000	-0	0	0	-0	0.0
1973 StL-N	4	4	.500	34	9	1	0	3	82^{1}	74	10	34	44	12.1	3.61	101	.239	.321	2	.100	-1	0	0	-0	-0.1

YEAR	TM/L	W	L	PCT	G	GS	CG	SH	SV	IP	H	HR	BB	SO	RAT	ERA	ERA+	OAV	OOB	BH	AVG	PB	PR	/A	PD	TPI
1974	StL-N	6	2	.750	55	0	0	0	2	90	65	4	38	57	10.5	3.00	119	.207	.297	1	.100	-1	6	6	-1	0.4
1975	SD-N	6	11	.353	45	15	4	0	0	142	155	8	39	87	12.4	4.18	83	.278	.327	6	.167	1	-9	-11	-0	-1.1
1976	SD-N	2	3	.400	33	3	0	0	0	59^2	67	10	25	26	14.2	5.28	62	.279	.352	0	.000	-0	-12	-13	-0	-1.4
1977	Mil-A	0	1	.000	3	0	0	0	0	6^1	7	2	4	6	15.6	4.26	95	.269	.367	0	—	0	-0	-0	0	0.0
Total	7	19	23	.452	195	28	5	0	7	423	416	40	170	242	12.6	4.11	86	.258	.332	11	.143	-1	-22	-27	-1	-2.8

● LEW FONSECA Fonseca, Lewis Albert b: 1/21/1899, Oakland, Cal. d: 11/26/89, Ely, Iowa BR/TR, 5'10.5", 180 lbs. Deb: 4/13/21 M♦

YEAR	TM/L	W	L	PCT	G	GS	CG	SH	SV	IP	H	HR	BB	SO	RAT	ERA	ERA+	OAV	OOB	BH	AVG	PB	PR	/A	PD	TPI
1932	Chi-A	0	0	—	1	0	0	0	0	1	0	0	0	0	0.0	0.00	—	.000	.000	5	.135	-0	0	0	-0	0.0

● RAY FONTENOT Fontenot, Silton Ray b: 8/8/57, Lake Charles, La. BL/TL, 6', 175 lbs. Deb: 6/30/83

YEAR	TM/L	W	L	PCT	G	GS	CG	SH	SV	IP	H	HR	BB	SO	RAT	ERA	ERA+	OAV	OOB	BH	AVG	PB	PR	/A	PD	TPI
1983	NY-A	8	2	.800	15	15	3	1	0	97^1	101	3	25	27	11.7	3.33	117	.266	.314	0	—	0	8	6	1	0.8
1984	NY-A	8	9	.471	35	24	0	0	0	169^1	189	8	58	85	13.3	3.61	105	.290	.351	0	—	0	7	3	0	0.4
1985	Chi-N	6	10	.375	38	23	0	0	0	154^2	177	23	45	70	12.9	4.36	91	.294	.343	2	.049	-4	-13	-6	2	-0.9
1986	Chi-N	3	5	.375	42	0	0	0	2	56	57	5	21	24	12.5	3.86	105	.266	.332	1	.167	-0	-1	1	-1	0.0
	Min-A	0	0	—	15	0	0	0	0	16^1	27	3	4	10	18.2	9.92	43	.360	.407	0	.000	0	-10	-10	0	-1.0
Total	4	25	26	.490	145	62	3	1	2	493^2	551	42	153	216	12.9	4.03	98	.287	.341	3	.063	-4	-10	-5	2	-0.7

● JIM FOOR Foor, James Emerson b: 1/13/49, St.Louis, Mo. BL/TL, 6'2", 170 lbs. Deb: 4/09/71

YEAR	TM/L	W	L	PCT	G	GS	CG	SH	SV	IP	H	HR	BB	SO	RAT	ERA	ERA+	OAV	OOB	BH	AVG	PB	PR	/A	PD	TPI
1971	Det-A	0	0	—	3	0	0	0	0	1	2	0	4	2	54.0	18.00	20	.400	.667	0	—	0	-2	-2	0	-0.2
1972	Det-A	1	0	1.000	7	0	0	0	0	3^2	6	1	6	2	29.5	14.73	21	.353	.522	0	—	0	-5	-5	0	-0.5
1973	Pit-N	0	0	—	3	0	0	0	0	1^1	2	0	1	1	20.3	0.00	—	.286	.375	0	—	0	1	1	0	0.1
Total	3	1	0	1.000	13	0	0	0	0	6	10	1	11	5	31.5	12.00	28	.345	.525	0	—	0	-6	-6	0	-0.6

● DAVY FORCE Force, David W. "Wee Davy" or "Tom Thumb" b: 7/27/1849, New York, N.Y. d: 6/21/18, Englewood, N.J. BR/TR, 5'4", 130 lbs. Deb: 5/05/1871 ♦

YEAR	TM/L	W	L	PCT	G	GS	CG	SH	SV	IP	H	HR	BB	SO	RAT	ERA	ERA+	OAV	OOB	BH	AVG	PB	PR	/A	PD	TPI
1873	Bal-n	1	1	.500	3	1	1	0	0	18	23	0	0	0	11.5	3.50	93	.264	.264	86	.368	1	-0	-0		0.0
1874	Chi-n	0	0	—	1	0	0	0	0	7	22	4	0		28.3	*12.86*	24	.440	.440	93	.314	0	-8	-8		-0.5
Total	2 n	1	1	.500	4	1	1	0	0	25	45	4	0	0	16.2	*6.12*	50	.328	.328	437	.335	2	-9	-9		-0.5

● DAVE FORD Ford, David Alan b: 12/29/56, Cleveland, Ohio BR/TR, 6'4", 190 lbs. Deb: 9/02/78

YEAR	TM/L	W	L	PCT	G	GS	CG	SH	SV	IP	H	HR	BB	SO	RAT	ERA	ERA+	OAV	OOB	BH	AVG	PB	PR	/A	PD	TPI
1978	Bal-A	1	0	1.000	2	1	0	0	0	15	10	0	2	5	7.2	0.00	—	.196	.226	0	—	0	6	6	-0	1.6
1979	Bal-A	2	1	.667	9	2	0	0	2	30	23	2	7	7	9.0	2.10	191	.219	.268	0	—	0	7	6	0	1.0
1980	Bal-A	1	3	.250	25	3	1	0	1	69^2	66	11	13	22	10.5	4.26	93	.251	.291	0	—	0	-2	-2	-1	-0.3
1981	Bal-A	1	2	.333	15	2	0	0	0	40	61	2	10	12	16.0	6.52	56	.359	.394	0	—	0	-13	-13	-0	-1.3
Total	4	5	6	.455	51	8	1	0	3	154^2	160	15	32	46	11.3	4.02	96	.272	.311	0	—	0	-1	-3	-1	1.0

● WHITEY FORD Ford, Edward Charles "Chairman Of The Board" b: 10/21/28, New York, N.Y. BL/TL, 5'10", 181 lbs. Deb: 7/01/50 CH

YEAR	TM/L	W	L	PCT	G	GS	CG	SH	SV	IP	H	HR	BB	SO	RAT	ERA	ERA+	OAV	OOB	BH	AVG	PB	PR	/A	PD	TPI
1950	*NY-A	9	1	.900	20	12	7	2	1	112	87	7	52	59	11.3	2.81	153	.216	.309	7	.194	0	22	18	-0	1.8
1953	*NY-A	18	6	.750	32	30	11	3	0	207	187	13	110	110	13.1	3.00	123	.245	.344	20	.267	6	23	16	0	2.2
1954	NY-A★	16	8	.667	34	28	11	3	1	210^2	170	10	101	125	11.6	2.82	122	.227	.319	10	.161	2	21	14	1	1.8
1955	*NY-A★	**18**	7	.720	39	33	**18**	5	2	253^2	188	20	113	137	10.7	2.63	143	.208	.297	14	.163	2	38	31	-0	3.4
1956	*NY-A★	19	6	**.760**	31	30	18	2	1	225^2	187	13	84	141	11.0	**2.47**	156	.228	.303	17	.218	3	42	35	5	4.5
1957	*NY-A	11	5	.688	24	17	5	0	0	129^1	114	10	53	84	11.7	2.57	139	.237	.313	6	.143	-1	17	15	2	1.6
1958	*NY-A☆	14	7	.667	30	29	15	**7**	1	219^1	174	14	62	145	**9.8**	**2.01**	**176**	.217	**.276**	15	.205	2	**43**	**37**	1	**4.5**
1959	NY-A★	16	10	.615	35	29	9	2	1	204	194	13	89	114	12.5	3.04	120	.250	.328	15	.231	7	19	14	4	2.5
1960	*NY-A★	12	9	.571	33	29	8	**4**	0	192^2	168	15	65	85	10.9	3.08	116	.235	.299	8	.151	2	17	11	1	1.4
1961	*NY-A★	**25**	4	**.862**	39	39	11	3	0	**283**	242	23	92	209	10.7	3.21	116	.229	.292	17	.177	3	26	16	0	1.9
1962	*NY-A	17	8	.680	38	37	7	0	0	257^2	243	22	69	160	11.0	2.90	129	.246	.298	10	.118	-1	31	24	4	2.9
1963	*NY-A	**24**	7	**.774**	38	37	13	3	1	**269^1**	240	26	56	189	10.0	2.74	128	.241	.283	13	.141	0	27	23	-0	2.4
1964	*NY-A☆	17	6	.739	39	36	12	8	1	244^2	212	10	57	172	10.0	2.13	170	.230	.276	8	.119	1	41	40	2	4.9
1965	NY-A	16	13	.552	37	36	9	2	1	244^1	241	22	50	162	10.8	3.24	105	.258	.297	15	.183	2	6	4	2	0.9
1966	NY-A	2	5	.286	22	9	0	0	0	73	79	8	24	43	12.7	2.47	135	.277	.333	0	.000	-2	8	7	3	0.9
1967	NY-A	2	4	.333	7	7	2	1	0	44	40	2	9	21	10.0	1.64	191	.247	.287	2	.154	-0	8	7	2	1.1
Total	16	236	106	.690	498	438	156	45	10	3170^1	2766	228	1086	1956	11.0	2.75	133	.235	.301	177	.173	25	386	315	26	38.7

● GENE FORD Ford, Eugene Matthew b: 6/23/12, Ft.Dodge, Iowa d: 9/7/70, Emmetsburg, Iowa BR/TR, 6'2", 195 lbs. Deb: 6/17/36

YEAR	TM/L	W	L	PCT	G	GS	CG	SH	SV	IP	H	HR	BB	SO	RAT	ERA	ERA+	OAV	OOB	BH	AVG	PB	PR	/A	PD	TPI
1936	Bos-N	0	0	—	2	1	0	0	0	2	2	0	3	0	22.5	13.50	28	.250	.455	0	—	0	-2	-2	0	-0.2
1938	Chi-A	0	0	—	4	0	0	0	0	14	21	1	12	2	21.2	10.29	48	.350	.458	1	.167	-0	-9	-8	0	-0.7
Total	2	0	0	—	6	1	0	0	0	16	23	1	15	2	21.4	10.69	44	.338	.458	1	.167	-0	-11	-11	0	-0.9

● GENE FORD Ford, Eugene Wyman b: 4/16/1881, Milton, N.S., Can. d: 8/23/73, Dunedin, Fla. BR/TR, 6', 170 lbs. Deb: 5/05/05 F

YEAR	TM/L	W	L	PCT	G	GS	CG	SH	SV	IP	H	HR	BB	SO	RAT	ERA	ERA+	OAV	OOB	BH	AVG	PB	PR	/A	PD	TPI
1905	Det-A	0	1	.000	7	1	1	0	0	35	51	0	14	20	17.2	5.66	48	.340	.404	0	.000	-1	-12	-11	0	-1.2

● WENTY FORD Ford, Percival Edmund Wentworth b: 11/25/46, Nassau, Bahamas d: 7/8/80, Nassau, Bahamas BR/TR, 5'11", 165 lbs. Deb: 9/10/73

YEAR	TM/L	W	L	PCT	G	GS	CG	SH	SV	IP	H	HR	BB	SO	RAT	ERA	ERA+	OAV	OOB	BH	AVG	PB	PR	/A	PD	TPI
1973	Atl-N	1	2	.333	4	2	1	0	0	16^1	17	3	8	4	14.3	5.51	71	.279	.371	2	.400	1	-3	-3	0	-0.2

● RUSS FORD Ford, Russell William b: 4/25/1883, Brandon, Man., Can. d: 1/24/60, Rockingham, N.C. BR/TR, 5'11", 175 lbs. Deb: 4/28/09 F

YEAR	TM/L	W	L	PCT	G	GS	CG	SH	SV	IP	H	HR	BB	SO	RAT	ERA	ERA+	OAV	OOB	BH	AVG	PB	PR	/A	PD	TPI
1909	NY-A	0	0	—	1	0	0	0	0	3	4	0	4	2	33.0	9.00	28	.333	.579	0	.000	-0	-2	-2	0	-0.2
1910	NY-A	26	6	.813	36	33	29	8	1	299^2	194	4	70	209	8.2	1.65	161	.188	.245	20	.208	4	29	34	-3	4.2
1911	NY-A	22	11	.667	37	33	26	1	0	281^1	251	3	76	158	10.6	2.27	158	.237	.291	20	.196	-3	34	41	-1	4.0
1912	NY-A	13	21	.382	36	35	30	0	0	291^2	317	10	79	112	12.4	3.55	101	.280	.329	32	.286	5	-7	1	1	0.9
1913	NY-A	12	18	.400	33	28	15	1	2	237	244	9	58	72	11.6	2.66	112	.275	.322	12	.162	0	7	9	-4	0.6
1914	Buf-F	21	6	**.778**	35	26	19	5	**6**	247^1	190	11	41	123	8.7	1.82	**181**	.214	.254	10	.128	-3	38	40	0	4.2
1915	Buf-F	5	9	.357	21	15	7	0	0	127^1	140	7	48	34	13.5	4.52	69	.285	.352	12	.279	3	-21	-20	-0	-1.7
Total	7	99	71	.582	199	170	126	15	9	1487^1	1340	44	376	710	10.6	2.59	124	.243	.296	106	.209	8	77	103	-5	12.0

● TOM FORD Ford, Thomas Walter b: 1866, Chattanooga, Tenn. d: 5/27/17, Chattanooga, Tenn. 5'10.5", 155 lbs. Deb: 5/06/1890

YEAR	TM/L	W	L	PCT	G	GS	CG	SH	SV	IP	H	HR	BB	SO	RAT	ERA	ERA+	OAV	OOB	BH	AVG	PB	PR	/A	PD	TPI
1890	Col-a	0	0	—	1	0	0	0	0	2	0	0	3	0	13.5	0.00	—	.000	.336	0	.000	-0	1	1	0	0.1
	Bro-a	0	6	.000	7	6	6	0	0	49	70	2	32	12	18.7	5.14	76	.325	.413	1	.033	-3	-7	-7	0	-0.8
	Yr	0	6	.000	8	6	6	0	0	51	70	2	35	12	18.5	4.94	79	.317	.410	1	.032	-3	-6	-6	1	-0.7

● HAPPY FOREMAN Foreman, August b: 7/20/1897, Memphis, Tenn. d: 2/13/53, New York, N.Y. BL/TL, 5'7", 160 lbs. Deb: 9/03/24

YEAR	TM/L	W	L	PCT	G	GS	CG	SH	SV	IP	H	HR	BB	SO	RAT	ERA	ERA+	OAV	OOB	BH	AVG	PB	PR	/A	PD	TPI
1924	Chi-A	0	0	—	3	0	0	0	0	4	7	0	4	1	24.8	2.25	183	.467	.579	0	.000	-0	1	1	-0	0.0
1926	Bos-A	0	0	—	3	0	0	0	0	7^1	3	0	5	3	9.8	3.68	111	.130	.286	0	.000	-0	0	0	1	0.1
Total	2	0	0	—	6	0	0	0	0	11^1	10	0	9	4	15.1	3.18	129	.263	.404	0	.000	-1	1	1	0	0.1

● FRANK FOREMAN Foreman, Francis Isaiah "Monkey" b: 5/1/1863, Baltimore, Md. d: 11/19/57, Baltimore, Md. BL/TL, 6', 160 lbs. Deb: 5/15/1884 F♦

YEAR	TM/L	W	L	PCT	G	GS	CG	SH	SV	IP	H	HR	BB	SO	RAT	ERA	ERA+	OAV	OOB	BH	AVG	PB	PR	/A	PD	TPI
1884	CP-U	1	2	.333	3	3	1	0	0	18	23	0	2	10	12.5	4.00	75	.291	.309	1	.091	-1	-2	-2	-0	-0.3
	KC-U	0	1	.000	1	1	1	0	0	8	17	0	2	5	21.4	5.63	49	.406	.433	0	.000	-0	-2	-3	1	-0.2
	Yr	1	3	.250	4	4	2	0	0	26	40	0	4	15	15.2	4.50	65	.331	.352	1	.071	-2	-4	-5	1	-0.5
1885	Bal-a	2	1	.667	3	3	2	0	0	27	33	0	9	11	14.3	6.00	54	.284	.341	4	.286	1	-8	-8	-0	-0.6
1889	Bal-a	23	21	.523	51	48	43	5	0	414	364	8	137	180	11.8	3.52	112	.229	.306	26	.144	-10	15	19	-2	0.6
1890	Cin-N	13	10	.565	25	24	20	0	0	198^1	201	6	89	57	14.1	3.95	90	.255	.345	10	.133	-1	-8	-9	-3	-1.0
1891	Was-a	18	20	.474	43	41	39	1	1	345^1	381	9	142	170	14.8	3.73	100	.271	.355	34	.222	9	-0	1	-1	0.9
1892	Was-N	2	4	.333	11	7	4	0	0	60	53	3	37	16	14.3	3.30	99	.228	.345	13	.464	7	-0	-0	-1	0.6
	Bal-N	0	3	.000	4	3	2	0	0	25	40	4	11	5	18.7	6.84	50	.348	.409	4	.174	0	-10	-9	0	-0.8
	Yr	2	7	.222	15	10	6	0	0	85	93	7	48	21	15.0	4.34	76	.263	.353	17	.333	8	-10	-10	-1	-0.2

YEAR	TM/L	W	L	PCT	G	GS	CG	SH	SV	IP	H	HR	BB	SO	RAT	ERA	ERA+	OAV	OOB	BH	AVG	PB	PR	/A	PD	TPI
1893	NY-N	0	1	.000	2	1	0	0	0	5^2	19	1	10	0	47.6	27.00	17	.531	.641	0	.000	-1	-14	-14	-0	-1.0
1895	Cin-N	11	14	.440	32	27	19	0	1	219	253	11	92	55	14.8	4.11	121	.285	.362	29	.309	4	16	21	-3	1.9
1896	Cin-N	14	7	.667	27	22	17	0	1	185^2	212	2	62	33	13.7	3.97	116	.285	.346	18	.243	-1	8	13	-0	1.0
1901	Bos-A	0	1	.000	1	1	1	0	0	8	8	1	2	1	13.5	9.00	39	.257	.342	0	.000	-1	-5	-5	-0	-0.4
	Bal-A	12	6	.667	24	22	18	1	1	191^1	225	2	58	41	13.6	3.67	105	.290	.344	26	.325	5	-0	4	-3	0.6
	Yr	12	7	.632	25	23	19	1	1	199^1	233	3	60	42	13.5	3.88	99	.288	.341	26	.310	4	-5	-1	-3	0.2
1902	Bal-A	0	2	.000	2	2	2	0	0	16^1	28	0	6	2	18.7	6.06	62	.377	.423	3	.429	1	-5	-4	1	-0.2
Total	11	96	93	.508	229	205	169	7	4	1721^2	1857	47	659	586	13.9	3.97	100	.268	.344	169	.224	12	-15	3	-13	1.1

● BROWNIE FOREMAN

Foreman, John Davis b: 8/6/1875, Baltimore, Md. d: 10/10/26, Baltimore, Md. BL/TL, 5′8″, 150 lbs. Deb: 7/18/1895 F

YEAR	TM/L	W	L	PCT	G	GS	CG	SH	SV	IP	H	HR	BB	SO	RAT	ERA	ERA+	OAV	OOB	BH	AVG	PB	PR	/A	PD	TPI
1895	Pit-N	8	6	.571	19	16	12	0	2	139^2	131	0	64	54	13.8	3.22	140	**.244**	.346	3	.065	-5	24	20	2	1.4
1896	Pit-N	3	3	.500	9	9	5	0	0	61^2	73	4	35	18	16.9	6.57	64	.292	.396	3	.150	0	-15	-16	1	-1.2
	Cin-N	1	3	.250	4	4	3	1	0	23	41	2	16	9	23.1	11.35	41	.383	.472	2	.200	-0	-18	-17	-0	-1.3
	Yr	4	6	.400	13	13	8	1	0	84^2	114	6	51	27	17.8	7.87	55	.312	.399	5	.167	0	-33	-33	1	-2.5
Total	2	12	12	.500	32	29	20	1	2	224^1	245	6	115	81	15.6	4.97	89	.274	.375	8	.105	-5	-9	-13	3	-1.1

● BILL FORMAN

Forman, William Orange b: 10/10/1886, Venango, Pa. d: 10/3/58, Uniontown, Pa. BB/TR, 5′11″, 180 lbs. Deb: 9/20/09

YEAR	TM/L	W	L	PCT	G	GS	CG	SH	SV	IP	H	HR	BB	SO	RAT	ERA	ERA+	OAV	OOB	BH	AVG	PB	PR	/A	PD	TPI
1909	Was-A	0	2	.000	2	2	1	0	0	11	8	0	7	2	13.9	4.91	50	.211	.362	1	.333	0	-3	-3	1	-0.2
1910	Was-A	0	0	—	1	0	0	0	0	0^2	1	0	0	0	13.5	13.50	18	.333	.333	0	—	0	-1	-1	-0	-0.1
Total	2	0	2	.000	3	2	1	0	0	11^2	9	0	7	2	13.9	5.40	45	.220	.360	1	.333	1	-4	-4	1	-0.3

● MIKE FORNIELES

Fornieles, Jose Miguel (Torres) b: 1/18/32, Havana, Cuba BR/TR, 5′11″, 172 lbs. Deb: 9/02/52

YEAR	TM/L	W	L	PCT	G	GS	CG	SH	SV	IP	H	HR	BB	SO	RAT	ERA	ERA+	OAV	OOB	BH	AVG	PB	PR	/A	PD	TPI
1952	Was-A	2	2	.500	4	2	2	1	0	26^1	13	1	11	12	8.2	1.37	260	.143	.235	0	.000	-1	7	6	-0	0.6
1953	Chi-A	8	7	.533	39	16	5	0	3	153	160	8	61	72	13.1	3.59	112	.270	.340	4	.098	-3	7	7	2	0.6
1954	Chi-A	1	2	.333	15	6	0	0	1	42	41	4	14	18	11.8	4.29	87	.252	.311	3	.273	0	-3	-3	1	-0.1
1955	Chi-A	6	3	.667	26	9	2	0	2	86^1	84	12	29	23	12.0	3.86	102	.255	.319	3	.103	-2	1	1	0	-0.1
1956	Chi-A	0	1	.000	6	0	0	0	0	15^2	22	1	6	6	16.1	4.60	89	.306	.359	1	.200	0	-1	-1	-0	-0.1
	Bal-A	4	7	.364	30	11	1	1	1	111	109	7	25	53	10.9	3.97	99	.266	.308	5	.167	-1	2	-1	2	0.1
	Yr	4	8	.333	36	11	1	1	1	126^2	131	8	31	59	11.5	4.05	97	.271	.315	6	.171	-1	2	-2	2	0.0
1957	Bal-A	2	6	.250	15	4	1	1	0	57	57	4	17	43	11.7	4.26	84	.257	.310	5	.278	1	-3	-4	1	-0.3
	Bos-A	8	7	.533	25	18	7	1	2	125^1	136	7	38	64	12.7	3.52	113	.271	.327	6	.136	-2	4	7	-1	0.3
	Yr	10	13	.435	40	22	8	2	2	182^1	193	11	55	107	12.4	3.75	103	.267	.321	11	.177	-1	1	2	-1	0.0
1958	Bos-A	4	6	.400	37	7	1	0	1	110^2	123	10	33	49	13.2	4.96	81	.284	.343	6	.207	-0	-15	-12	-0	-1.3
1959	Bos-A	5	3	.625	46	0	0	0	11	82	77	6	29	54	11.7	3.07	132	.254	.321	3	.158	-1	7	9	-0	0.9
1960	Bos-A	10	5	.667	**70**	0	0	0	**14**	109	86	6	49	64	11.6	2.64	153	.219	.315	6	.400	2	15	17	1	2.0
1961	Bos-A★	9	8	.529	57	2	1	0	15	119^1	121	18	54	70	13.3	4.68	89	.265	.345	5	.156	0	-9	-7	2	-0.5
1962	Bos-A	3	6	.333	42	1	0	0	5	82^1	96	14	37	36	15.4	5.36	77	.303	.390	3	.188	-0	-13	-11	-0	-1.1
1963	Bos-A	0	0	—	9	0	0	0	0	14	16	0	5	5	13.5	6.43	59	.286	.344	1	.333	1	-4	-4	-0	-0.4
	Min-A	1	1	.500	11	0	0	0	0	22^2	24	0	13	7	15.5	4.76	76	.273	.379	1	.167	0	-3	-3	-1	-0.3
	Yr	1	1	.500	20	0	0	0	0	36^2	40	0	18	12	14.7	5.40	68	.276	.364	2	.222	1	-7	-7	-1	-0.7
Total	12	63	64	.496	432	76	20	4	55	1156^2	1165	98	421	576	12.6	3.96	100	.263	.332	52	.169	-6	-7	2	4	0.3

● KEN FORSCH

Forsch, Kenneth Roth b: 9/8/46, Sacramento, Cal. BR/TR, 6′4″, 210 lbs. Deb: 9/07/70 F

YEAR	TM/L	W	L	PCT	G	GS	CG	SH	SV	IP	H	HR	BB	SO	RAT	ERA	ERA+	OAV	OOB	BH	AVG	PB	PR	/A	PD	TPI
1970	Hou-N	1	2	.333	4	4	1	0	0	24	28	1	5	13	12.4	5.63	69	.298	.333	0	.000	-1	-4	-5	-0	-0.5
1971	Hou-N	8	8	.500	33	23	7	2	0	188^1	162	8	53	131	10.5	2.53	133	.230	.288	8	.136	-1	20	17	-2	1.5
1972	Hou-N	6	8	.429	30	24	1	0	0	156^1	163	19	62	113	13.0	3.91	86	.273	.341	6	.146	-1	-8	-10	-3	-1.3
1973	Hou-N	9	12	.429	46	26	5	0	4	201^1	197	18	74	149	12.3	4.20	86	.257	.325	4	.065	-4	-12	-13	-2	-1.9
1974	Hou-N	8	7	.533	70	0	0	0	10	103^1	98	3	37	48	12.1	2.79	124	.255	.326	0	.000	-1	10	8	-0	0.7
1975	Hou-N	4	8	.333	34	9	2	0	2	109	114	9	30	54	12.1	3.22	105	.277	.330	1	.045	-1	5	2	-0	0.1
1976	Hou-N★	4	3	.571	52	0	0	0	19	92	76	5	26	49	10.2	2.15	148	.226	.286	1	.091	-0	14	11	1	1.2
1977	Hou-N	5	8	.385	42	5	0	0	8	86	80	2	28	45	11.5	2.72	131	.246	.310	1	.077	-1	11	8	1	0.9
1978	Hou-N	10	6	.625	52	6	4	2	7	133^1	136	2	37	71	11.7	2.70	123	.268	.319	5	.185	0	13	9	1	1.0
1979	Hou-N	11	6	.647	26	24	10	2	0	177^2	155	14	35	58	**9.6**	3.04	116	.236	**.275**	8	.138	0	14	9	2	1.2
1980	*Hou-N	12	13	.480	32	32	6	3	0	222^1	230	15	41	84	11.3	3.20	103	.266	.304	18	.234	3	10	2	1	0.8
1981	Cal-A★	11	7	.611	20	20	10	**4**	0	153	143	7	27	55	10.2	2.88	126	.250	.289	0	—	0	13	13	1	1.5
1982	Cal-A	13	11	.542	37	35	12	4	0	228	225	25	57	73	11.6	3.87	105	.258	.311	0	—	0	5	5	-2	0.3
1983	Cal-A	11	12	.478	31	31	11	1	0	219^1	226	21	61	81	11.9	4.06	99	.266	.318	0	—	0	-0	-1	-1	-0.2
1984	Cal-A	1	1	.500	2	2	1	0	0	16^1	14	2	3	10	9.4	2.20	180	.237	.274	0	—	0	3	3	1	0.5
1986	Cal-A	0	1	.000	10	0	0	0	1	17	24	4	10	13	19.1	9.53	43	.343	.439	0	—	0	-10	-10	0	-1.0
Total	16	114	113	.502	521	241	70	18	51	2127^1	2071	155	586	1047	11.4	3.37	106	.257	.311	52	.136	-5	83	48	-3	4.8

● BOB FORSCH

Forsch, Robert Herbert b: 1/13/50, Sacramento, Cal. BR/TR, 6′4″, 200 lbs. Deb: 7/07/74 F

YEAR	TM/L	W	L	PCT	G	GS	CG	SH	SV	IP	H	HR	BB	SO	RAT	ERA	ERA+	OAV	OOB	BH	AVG	PB	PR	/A	PD	TPI
1974	StL-N	7	4	.636	19	14	5	2	0	100	84	5	34	39	10.7	2.97	120	.230	.298	7	.241	1	7	7	-0	0.9
1975	StL-N	15	10	.600	34	34	7	4	0	230	213	14	70	108	11.2	2.86	131	.244	.303	24	.308	10	20	23	2	3.8
1976	StL-N	8	10	.444	33	32	2	0	0	194	209	17	71	76	13.1	3.94	90	.277	.341	11	.177	1	-10	-9	1	-0.7
1977	StL-N	20	7	.741	35	35	8	2	0	217^1	210	20	69	95	11.7	3.48	111	.251	.311	12	.167	0	10	9	-1	0.8
1978	StL-N	11	17	.393	34	34	7	3	0	233^2	205	15	97	114	11.8	3.70	95	.238	.318	15	.181	3	-3	-5	1	-0.1
1979	StL-N	11	11	.500	33	32	7	1	0	218^2	215	16	52	92	11.1	3.83	98	.262	.309	8	.110	-0	-2	-2	1	-0.1
1980	StL-N	11	10	.524	31	31	8	0	0	214^2	225	12	33	87	11.0	3.77	98	.273	.304	23	.295	9	-4	-2	2	1.0
1981	StL-N	10	5	.667	20	20	1	0	0	124^1	106	7	29	41	10.1	3.18	112	.232	.284	5	.122	-1	4	5	0	0.5
1982	*StL-N	15	9	.625	36	34	6	2	1	233	238	16	54	69	11.4	3.48	104	.268	.313	15	.205	3	3	4	-2	0.5
1983	StL-N	10	12	.455	34	30	6	2	0	187	190	23	54	56	11.9	4.28	85	.266	.320	13	.241	4	-14	-14	-0	-1.1
1984	StL-N	2	5	.286	16	11	1	0	0	52^1	64	6	19	21	14.3	6.02	58	.303	.361	4	.250	1	-14	-15	0	-1.4
1985	*StL-N	9	6	.600	34	19	3	1	2	136	132	11	47	48	12.0	3.90	91	.258	.323	11	.244	4	-5	-6	-0	-0.2
1986	StL-N	14	10	.583	33	33	3	0	0	230	211	19	68	104	11.0	3.25	112	.247	.304	13	.171	3	12	10	-1	1.3
1987	*StL-N	11	7	.611	33	30	2	1	0	179	189	15	45	89	12.0	4.32	96	.273	.321	17	.298	8	-5	-3	-1	0.4
1988	StL-N	9	4	.692	30	12	1	1	0	108^2	111	8	38	40	12.4	3.73	93	.270	.333	7	.280	2	-3	-3	-2	-0.3
	Hou-N	1	4	.200	6	6	0	0	0	27^2	42	2	6	14	16.3	6.51	51	.359	.400	1	.143	0	-9	-10	-0	-1.0
	Yr	10	8	.556	36	18	1	1	0	136^1	153	10	44	54	13.1	4.29	80	.287	.344	8	.250	2	-13	-13	-2	-1.3
1989	Hou-N	4	5	.444	37	15	0	0	0	108^1	133	10	46	40	15.0	5.32	64	.303	.370	4	.167	-0	-22	-23	-1	-2.5
Total	16	168	136	.553	498	422	67	19	3	2794^2	2777	216	832	1133	11.8	3.76	97	.261	.318	190	.213	49	-35	-33	-3	1.8

● TERRY FORSTER

Forster, Terry Jay b: 1/14/52, Sioux Falls, S.D. BL/TL, 6′3″, 210 lbs. Deb: 4/11/71

YEAR	TM/L	W	L	PCT	G	GS	CG	SH	SV	IP	H	HR	BB	SO	RAT	ERA	ERA+	OAV	OOB	BH	AVG	PB	PR	/A	PD	TPI
1971	Chi-A	2	3	.400	45	3	0	0	1	49^2	46	5	23	48	12.7	3.99	90	.241	.326	2	.400	1	-3	-2	0	-0.1
1972	Chi-A	6	5	.545	62	0	0	0	29	100	75	0	44	104	11.0	2.25	139	.208	.300	10	.526	4	9	10	1	1.8
1973	Chi-A	6	11	.353	51	12	4	0	16	172^2	174	7	78	120	13.1	3.23	122	.266	.344	0	.000	0	11	14	5	1.9
1974	Chi-A	7	8	.467	59	1	0	0	**24**	134^1	120	6	48	105	11.8	3.62	103	.245	.322	0	—	0	0	2	3	0.5
1975	Chi-A	3	3	.500	17	1	0	0	4	37	30	0	24	32	13.1	2.19	177	.236	.358	0	—	0	7	7	2	0.8
1976	Chi-A	2	12	.143	29	16	1	0	1	111^1	126	7	41	70	13.6	4.37	82	.288	.351	0	—	0	-10	-10	2	-0.9
1977	Pit-N	6	4	.600	33	6	0	0	1	87^1	90	7	32	58	12.8	4.43	90	.269	.337	9	.346	3	-5	-4	-0	-0.2
1978	*LA-N	5	4	.556	47	0	0	0	22	65^1	56	2	23	46	10.9	1.93	182	.233	.300	4	.500	2	12	11	-0	1.4
1979	LA-N	1	2	.333	17	0	0	0	2	16^1	18	0	11	8	16.0	5.51	66	.295	.403	0	—	0	-3	-3	1	-0.3
1980	LA-N	0	0	—	9	0	0	0	0	11^2	10	0	4	2	10.8	3.09	113	.222	.286	0	—	0	1	1	0	0.1
1981	*LA-N	0	1	.000	21	0	0	0	0	30^2	37	1	15	17	15.3	4.11	81	.308	.385	0	.000	-0	-2	-3	1	-0.2

YEAR TM/L	W	L	PCT	G	GS	CG	SH	SV	IP	H	HR	BB	SO	RAT	ERA	ERA+	OAV	OOB	BH	AVG	PB	PR	/A	PD	TPI
1982 LA-N	5	6	.455	56	0	0	0	3	83	66	3	31	52	11.0	3.04	114	.221	.302	0	.000	-0	5	4	1	0.5
1983 Atl-N	3	2	.600	56	0	0	0	13	79^{1}	60	3	31	54	10.6	2.16	180	.217	.301	4	.500	2	13	15	1	1.9
1984 Atl-N	2	0	1.000	25	0	0	0	5	26^{2}	30	1	7	10	12.5	2.70	143	.297	.343	2	.667	1	3	3	0	0.5
1985 Atl-N	2	3	.400	46	0	0	0	1	59^{1}	49	7	28	37	11.7	2.28	169	.222	.309	0	.000	-0	9	10	-1	1.0
1986 Cal-A	4	1	.800	41	0	0	0	5	41	47	2	17	28	14.7	3.51	117	.297	.376	0	—	0	3	3	1	0.4
Total 16	54	65	.454	614	39	5	0	127	1105^{2}	1034	51	457	791	12.3	3.23	114	.251	.330	31	.397	11	48	57	16	9.1

● TIM FORTUGNO Fortugno, Timothy Shawn b: 4/11/62, Clinton, Mass. BL/TL, 6'1", 195 lbs. Deb: 7/20/92

YEAR TM/L	W	L	PCT	G	GS	CG	SH	SV	IP	H	HR	BB	SO	RAT	ERA	ERA+	OAV	OOB	BH	AVG	PB	PR	/A	PD	TPI
1992 Cal-A	1	1	.500	14	5	1	1	1	41^{2}	37	5	19	31	12.1	5.18	75	.236	.318	0	—	0	-6	-6	-0	-0.6

● GARY FORTUNE Fortune, Garrett Reese b: 10/11/1894, High Point, N.C. d: 9/23/55, Washington, D.C. BB/TR, 5'11.5", 176 lbs. Deb: 10/05/16

YEAR TM/L	W	L	PCT	G	GS	CG	SH	SV	IP	H	HR	BB	SO	RAT	ERA	ERA+	OAV	OOB	BH	AVG	PB	PR	/A	PD	TPI
1916 Phi-N	0	1	.000	1	1	0	0	0	5	2	0	4	3	10.8	3.60	74	.118	.286	0	.000	-0	-1	-1	-0	-0.1
1918 Phi-N	0	2	.000	5	2	1	0	0	31	41	2	19	10	17.7	8.13	37	.333	.427	2	.200	0	-18	-18	-0	-1.6
1920 Bos-A	0	2	.000	14	3	1	0	0	41^{2}	46	0	23	10	14.9	5.83	63	.282	.371	2	.167	-0	-9	-10	-1	-1.0
Total 3	0	5	.000	20	6	2	0	0	77^{2}	89	2	46	23	15.8	6.61	51	.294	.389	4	.167	-0	-28	-28	-1	-2.7

● JERRY FOSNOW Fosnow, Gerald Eugene b: 9/21/40, Deshler, Ohio BR/TL, 6'4", 195 lbs. Deb: 6/29/64

YEAR TM/L	W	L	PCT	G	GS	CG	SH	SV	IP	H	HR	BB	SO	RAT	ERA	ERA+	OAV	OOB	BH	AVG	PB	PR	/A	PD	TPI
1964 Min-A	0	1	.000	7	0	0	0	0	10^{2}	13	3	8	9	17.7	10.97	33	.302	.412	0	—	0	-9	-9	-0	-0.9
1965 Min-A	3	3	.500	29	0	0	0	2	46^{2}	33	7	25	35	11.4	4.44	80	.193	.299	0	.000	-1	-5	-5	0	-0.5
Total 2	3	4	.429	36	0	0	0	2	57^{1}	46	10	33	44	12.6	5.65	63	.215	.323	0	.000	-1	-14	-13	0	-1.4

● LARRY FOSS Foss, Larry Curtis b: 4/18/36, Castleton, Kan. BR/TR, 6'2", 187 lbs. Deb: 9/18/61

YEAR TM/L	W	L	PCT	G	GS	CG	SH	SV	IP	H	HR	BB	SO	RAT	ERA	ERA+	OAV	OOB	BH	AVG	PB	PR	/A	PD	TPI
1961 Pit-N	1	1	.500	3	3	0	0	0	15^{1}	15	3	11	9	16.4	5.87	68	.273	.412	1	.167	-0	-3	-3	-0	-0.3
1962 NY-N	0	1	.000	5	1	0	0	0	11^{2}	17	2	7	3	19.3	4.63	90	.362	.455	0	.000	-0	-1	-1	-0	-0.1
Total 2	1	2	.333	8	4	0	0	0	27	32	5	18	12	17.7	5.33	76	.314	.431	1	.143	-0	-4	-4	-0	-0.4

● TONY FOSSAS Fossas, Emilio Antonio (Morejon) b: 9/23/57, Havana, Cuba BL/TL, 6', 195 lbs. Deb: 5/15/88

YEAR TM/L	W	L	PCT	G	GS	CG	SH	SV	IP	H	HR	BB	SO	RAT	ERA	ERA+	OAV	OOB	BH	AVG	PB	PR	/A	PD	TPI
1988 Tex-A	0	0	—	5	0	0	0	0	5^{2}	11	0	2	0	20.6	4.76	86	.423	.464	0	—	0	-1	-0	0	-0.2
1989 Mil-A	2	2	.500	51	0	0	0	1	61	57	3	22	42	11.8	3.54	108	.256	.325	0	—	0	2	2	0	0.3
1990 Mil-A	2	3	.400	32	0	0	0	0	29^{1}	44	5	10	24	16.6	6.44	60	.331	.378	0	—	0	-8	-8	-0	-0.8
1991 Bos-A	3	2	.600	64	0	0	0	1	57	49	3	28	29	12.6	3.47	124	.236	.335	0	—	0	4	5	1	0.6
1992 Bos-A	1	2	.333	60	0	0	0	2	29^{2}	31	1	14	19	14.0	2.43	171	.279	.365	0	—	0	5	6	1	0.4
Total 5	8	9	.471	212	0	0	0	4	182^{2}	192	12	76	114	13.5	3.84	105	.274	.349	0	—	0	2	4	2	0.3

● ALAN FOSTER Foster, Alan Benton b: 12/8/46, Pasadena, Cal. BR/TR, 6', 180 lbs. Deb: 4/25/67

YEAR TM/L	W	L	PCT	G	GS	CG	SH	SV	IP	H	HR	BB	SO	RAT	ERA	ERA+	OAV	OOB	BH	AVG	PB	PR	/A	PD	TPI
1967 LA-N	0	1	.000	4	2	0	0	0	16^{2}	10	0	3	15	7.0	2.16	143	.169	.210	0	.000	-0	2	2	0	0.2
1968 LA-N	1	1	.500	3	3	0	0	0	15^{2}	11	1	2	10	7.5	1.72	160	.200	.228	1	.250	0	2	2	-0	0.2
1969 LA-N	3	9	.250	24	15	2	2	0	102^{2}	119	11	29	59	13.3	4.38	76	.290	.342	2	.074	-1	-9	-12	-0	-1.3
1970 LA-N	10	13	.435	33	33	7	1	0	198^{2}	200	22	81	83	12.8	4.26	90	.264	.337	7	.109	-1	-5	-9	-1	-1.2
1971 Cle-A	8	12	.400	36	26	3	0	0	181^{2}	158	19	82	97	12.1	4.16	92	.232	.318	2	.039	-5	-14	-7	-4	-1.6
1972 Cal-A	0	1	.000	8	0	0	0	0	12^{2}	12	3	6	11	14.2	4.97	59	.245	.351	0	—	0	-3	-3	0	-0.3
1973 StL-N	13	9	.591	35	29	6	2	0	203^{2}	195	17	63	106	11.6	3.14	116	.254	.315	13	.191	1	12	11	-2	1.1
1974 StL-N	7	10	.412	31	25	5	1	0	162^{1}	167	16	61	78	12.8	3.88	92	.268	.336	8	.167	-1	-5	-6	-1	-0.7
1975 SD-N	3	1	.750	17	4	1	0	0	44^{2}	41	1	21	20	12.5	2.42	144	.244	.328	1	.091	-1	6	5	0	0.5
1976 SD-N	3	6	.333	26	11	2	0	0	86^{1}	75	9	35	22	11.5	3.22	102	.235	.313	1	.056	-0	3	0	-1	0.0
Total 10	48	63	.432	217	148	26	6	0	1025^{1}	988	99	383	501	12.2	3.74	96	.254	.324	35	.119	-8	-10	-15	-9	-3.1

● ED FOSTER Foster, Eddy Lee "Slim" b: Birmingham, Ala. d: 3/1/29, Montgomery, Ala. BR/TR, 6'1", Deb: 7/31/08

YEAR TM/L	W	L	PCT	G	GS	CG	SH	SV	IP	H	HR	BB	SO	RAT	ERA	ERA+	OAV	OOB	BH	AVG	PB	PR	/A	PD	TPI
1908 Cle-A	1	0	1.000	6	1	1	0	2	21	16	1	12	11	12.9	2.14	112	.229	.357	0	.000	-1	1	1	-1	-0.1

● RUBE FOSTER Foster, George b: 1/5/1888, Lehigh, Okla d: 3/1/76, Bokoshe, Okla. BR/TR, 5'7.5", 170 lbs. Deb: 4/10/13

YEAR TM/L	W	L	PCT	G	GS	CG	SH	SV	IP	H	HR	BB	SO	RAT	ERA	ERA+	OAV	OOB	BH	AVG	PB	PR	/A	PD	TPI
1913 Bos-A	3	4	.429	19	8	4	1	0	68^{1}	64	1	28	36	12.6	3.16	93	.249	.332	2	.095	-1	-2	-2	-0	-0.4
1914 Bos-A	14	8	.636	32	27	17	5	0	211^{2}	164	2	52	89	9.5	1.70	158	.218	.274	11	.175	0	24	23	-0	2.7
1915 *Bos-A	19	8	.704	37	33	21	5	1	255^{1}	217	3	86	82	11.0	2.11	132	.237	.310	23	.277	7	23	19	1	2.9
1916 *Bos-A	14	7	.667	33	19	9	3	2	182^{1}	173	0	86	53	13.0	3.06	90	.263	.352	11	.177	0	-5	-6	2	-0.5
1917 Bos-A	8	7	.533	17	16	9	1	0	124^{2}	108	0	53	34	11.9	2.53	102	.243	.329	11	.268	2	2	1	1	0.4
Total 5	58	34	.630	138	103	60	15	3	842^{1}	726	6	305	294	11.3	2.36	116	.240	.315	58	.215	8	43	36	2	5.1

● LARRY FOSTER Foster, Larry Lynn b: 12/24/37, Lansing, Mich. BL/TR, 6', 185 lbs. Deb: 9/18/63

YEAR TM/L	W	L	PCT	G	GS	CG	SH	SV	IP	H	HR	BB	SO	RAT	ERA	ERA+	OAV	OOB	BH	AVG	PB	PR	/A	PD	TPI
1963 Det-A	0	0	—	1	0	0	0	0	2	4	0	1	1	22.5	13.50	28	.364	.417	0	—	0	-2	-2	0	-0.2

● STEVE FOSTER Foster, Stephen Eugene b: 8/16/66, Dallas, Tex. BR/TR, 6', 180 lbs. Deb: 8/22/91

YEAR TM/L	W	L	PCT	G	GS	CG	SH	SV	IP	H	HR	BB	SO	RAT	ERA	ERA+	OAV	OOB	BH	AVG	PB	PR	/A	PD	TPI
1991 Cin-N	0	0	—	11	0	0	0	0	14	7	1	4	11	7.1	1.93	197	.143	.208	0	—	0	3	3	-0	0.3
1992 Cin-N	1	1	.500	31	1	0	0	2	50	52	4	13	34	11.7	2.88	127	.275	.322	1	.200	0	3	4	1	0.6
Total 2	1	1	.500	42	1	0	0	2	64	59	5	17	45	10.7	2.67	138	.248	.298	1	.200	0	6	7	1	0.9

● STEVE FOUCAULT Foucault, Steven Raymond b: 10/3/49, Duluth, Minn. BL/TR, 6', 205 lbs. Deb: 4/07/73

YEAR TM/L	W	L	PCT	G	GS	CG	SH	SV	IP	H	HR	BB	SO	RAT	ERA	ERA+	OAV	OOB	BH	AVG	PB	PR	/A	PD	TPI
1973 Tex-A	2	4	.333	32	0	0	0	8	55^{2}	54	6	31	28	14.2	3.88	96	.262	.367	0	—	0	-0	-1	1	0.2
1974 Tex-A	8	9	.471	69	0	0	0	12	144^{1}	123	8	40	106	10.5	2.24	159	.234	.295	0	—	0	22	21	1	2.4
1975 Tex-A	8	4	.667	59	0	0	0	10	107	96	10	55	56	13.0	4.12	91	.249	.349	0	—	0	-4	-4	-1	-0.5
1976 Tex-A	8	8	.500	46	0	0	0	5	75^{2}	68	9	25	41	11.5	3.33	108	.249	.321	0	—	0	2	2	2	0.4
1977 Det-A	7	7	.500	44	0	0	0	13	74^{1}	64	7	17	58	9.8	3.15	136	.226	.270	0	—	0	8	9	-1	0.9
1978 Det-A	2	4	.333	24	0	0	0	4	37^{1}	48	1	21	18	16.9	3.13	123	.324	.412	0	—	0	3	3	-1	0.0
KC-A	0	0	—	3	0	0	0	0	2^{1}	5	0	1	0	23.1	3.86	99	.417	.462	0	—	0	-0	-0	0	-0.2
Yr	2	4	.333	27	0	0	0	4	39^{2}	53	1	22	18	17.0	3.18	122	.323	.403	0	—	0	3	3	-0	-0.2
Total 6	35	36	.493	277	0	0	0	52	496^{2}	458	41	190	307	12.1	3.21	117	.250	.326	0	—	0	29	30	1	3.2

● JACK FOURNIER Fournier, John Frank b: 9/29/1892, AuSable, Mich. d: 9/5/73, Tacoma, Wash. BL/TR, 6', 195 lbs. Deb: 4/13/12 ♦

YEAR TM/L	W	L	PCT	G	GS	CG	SH	SV	IP	H	HR	BB	SO	RAT	ERA	ERA+	OAV	OOB	BH	AVG	PB	PR	/A	PD	TPI
1922 StL-N	0	0	—	1	0	0	0	0	1	0	0	0	0	0.0	0.00	—	.000	.000	119	.295	0	0	0	0	0.1

● HENRY FOURNIER Fournier, Julius Henry "Frenchy" b: 8/8/1865, Syracuse, N.Y. d: 12/8/45, Detroit, Mich. TL , Deb: 8/22/1894

YEAR TM/L	W	L	PCT	G	GS	CG	SH	SV	IP	H	HR	BB	SO	RAT	ERA	ERA+	OAV	OOB	BH	AVG	PB	PR	/A	PD	TPI
1894 Cin-N	1	3	.250	6	4	4	0	0	45	71	4	20	5	18.6	5.40	103	.354	.418	2	.105	-3	-0	1	0	-0.1

● DAVE FOUTZ Foutz, David Luther "Scissors" b: 9/7/1856, Carroll Co., Md. d: 3/5/1897, Waverly, Ind. BR/TR, 6'2", 161 lbs. Deb: 7/29/1884 FM♦

YEAR TM/L	W	L	PCT	G	GS	CG	SH	SV	IP	H	HR	BB	SO	RAT	ERA	ERA+	OAV	OOB	BH	AVG	PB	PR	/A	PD	TPI
1884 StL-a	15	6	.714	25	25	19	2	0	206^{2}	167	7	36	95	9.2	2.18	150	.212	.255	27	.227	1	25	25	3	2.7
1885 *StL-a	33	14	.702	47	46	46	2	0	407^{2}	351	8	92	147	10.2	2.63	125	.227	.278	59	.248	5	28	29	7	3.7
1886 *StL-a	**41**	16	**.719**	59	57	55	11	**1**	504	418	5	144	283	10.2	**2.11**	**163**	.216	.274	116	.280	11	**75**	75	2	**8.0**
1887 *StL-a	25	12	.676	40	38	36	1	0	339^{1}	369	7	90	94	12.4	3.87	117	.258	.306	151	.357	16	16	25	0	3.3
1888 Bro-a	12	7	.632	23	19	19	0	0	176	146	3	35	73	9.5	2.51	119	.218	.262	156	.277	6	11	9	3	1.6
1889 *Bro-a	3	0	1.000	12	4	3	0	0	59^{2}	70	2	19	21	13.4	4.37	85	.284	.335	152	.275	3	-3	-4	1	-0.1
1890 *Bro-N	2	1	.667	5	2	2	0	**2**	29	29	0	6	4	11.2	1.86	185	.252	.295	154	.303	2	6	5	-1	0.5
1891 Bro-N	3	2	.600	6	5	5	0	0	52	51	1	16	14	11.8	3.29	100	.247	.304	134	.257	1	0	0	-0	0.1
1892 Bro-N	13	8	.619	27	20	17	0	1	203	210	3	63	56	12.3	3.41	93	.256	.313	41	.186	0	-3	-6	3	-0.3
1893 Bro-N	0	0	—	6	0	0	0	0	18	28	2	8	3	18.0	7.50	59	.345	.403	137	.246	1	-6	-6	1	-0.4
1894 Bro-N	0	0	—	1	0	0	0	0	2	4	0	1	0	22.5	13.50	37	.410	.465	90	.307	0	-2	-2	-0	-0.1
Total 11	147	66	.690	251	216	202	16	4	1997^{1}	1843	38	510	790	10.9	2.84	124	.235	.286	1253	.276	46	147	148	18	19.0

YEAR	TM/L	W	L	PCT	G	GS	CG	SH	SV	IP	H	HR	BB	SO	RAT	ERA	ERA+	OAV	OOB	BH	AVG	PB	PR	/A	PD	TPI
● JESSE FOWLER Fowler, Jesse Peter "Pete" b: 10/30/1898, Spartanburg, S.C. d: 9/23/73, Columbia, S.C. BR/TL, 5'10.5", 158 lbs. Deb: 7/29/24 F																										
1924	StL-N	1	1	.500	13	3	0	0	0	32^2	28	0	18	5	13.2	4.41	86	.226	.333	2	.222	0	-2	-2	-1	-0.3
● ART FOWLER Fowler, John Arthur b: 7/3/22, Converse, S.C. BR/TR, 5'11", 180 lbs. Deb: 4/17/54 FC																										
1954	Cin-N	12	10	.545	40	29	8	1	0	227^2	256	20	85	93	13.6	3.83	109	.286	.351	6	.100	-1	6	9	-1	0.7
1955	Cin-N	11	10	.524	46	28	8	3	2	207^2	198	20	63	94	11.4	3.90	109	.250	.306	12	.200	-0	3	8	-1	0.6
1956	Cin-N	11	11	.500	45	23	8	0	1	177^2	191	15	35	86	11.4	4.05	98	.278	.313	7	.146	-0	-6	-1	1	-0.1
1957	Cin-N	3	0	1.000	33	7	1	0	0	87^2	111	11	24	45	14.1	6.47	64	.310	.357	3	.176	0	-25	-23	0	-2.2
1959	LA-N	3	4	.429	36	0	0	0	2	61	70	8	23	47	13.7	5.31	80	.294	.356	1	.083	-1	-9	-7	0	-0.8
1961	LA-A	5	8	.385	53	3	0	0	11	89	68	12	29	78	9.8	3.64	124	.209	.274	1	.077	-1	4	9	-1	0.6
1962	LA-A	4	3	.571	48	0	0	0	5	77	67	6	25	38	10.9	2.81	138	.234	.298	3	.273	1	10	9	-0	1.0
1963	LA-A	5	3	.625	57	0	0	0	10	89^1	70	5	19	53	9.0	2.42	142	.219	.263	2	.222	0	12	10	-1	1.0
1964	LA-A	0	2	.000	4	0	0	0	1	7	8	2	5	5	18.0	10.29	32	.296	.424	0	.000	-0	-5	-5	0	-0.5
Total	9	54	51	.514	362	90	25	4	32	1024	1039	99	308	539	11.9	4.03	102	.265	.320	35	.152	-3	-10	7	-3	0.3
● DICK FOWLER Fowler, Richard John b: 3/30/21, Toronto, Ont., Can. d: 5/22/72, Oneonta, N.Y. BR/TR, 6'4.5", 215 lbs. Deb: 9/13/41																										
1941	Phi-A	1	2	.333	4	3	1	0	0	24	26	4	8	8	12.8	3.38	124	.289	.347	0	.000	-1	2	2	-0	0.1
1942	Phi-A	6	11	.353	31	17	4	0	1	140	159	13	45	38	13.1	4.95	76	.287	.341	8	.160	-1	-20	-18	-2	-2.2
1945	Phi-A	1	2	.333	7	3	2	1	0	37^1	41	1	18	21	14.2	4.82	71	.283	.362	8	.444	3	-6	-6	-1	-0.3
1946	Phi-A	9	16	.360	32	28	14	1	0	205^2	213	16	75	89	12.7	3.28	108	.263	.327	13	.183	-1	5	6	-1	0.4
1947	Phi-A	12	11	.522	36	31	16	3	0	227^1	210	12	85	75	11.8	2.81	136	.249	.319	14	.171	-3	23	25	-2	2.2
1948	Phi-A	15	8	.652	29	26	16	2	2	204^2	221	15	76	50	13.2	3.78	113	.281	.348	14	.171	-2	12	12	-1	0.8
1949	Phi-A	15	11	.577	31	28	15	4	1	213^2	210	13	115	43	13.8	3.75	110	.262	.357	18	.234	3	11	9	1	1.2
1950	Phi-A	1	5	.167	11	9	2	0	0	66^2	75	7	56	15	18.1	6.48	70	.300	.434	5	.192	-1	-14	-14	0	-1.3
1951	Phi-A	5	11	.313	22	22	4	0	0	125	141	11	72	29	15.4	5.62	76	.291	.384	8	.190	-0	-21	-19	-1	-1.8
1952	Phi-A	1	2	.333	18	3	1	0	0	58^2	71	4	28	14	15.8	6.44	61	.302	.386	0	.000	-2	-18	-16	1	-1.8
Total	10	66	79	.455	221	170	75	11	4	1303	1367	96	578	382	13.6	4.11	97	.273	.351	88	.186	-6	-27	-19	-6	-2.7
● ALAN FOWLKES Fowlkes, Alan Kim b: 8/8/58, Brawley, Cal. BR/TR, 6'2", 190 lbs. Deb: 4/07/82																										
1982	SF-N	4	2	.667	21	15	1	0	0	85	111	12	24	50	14.8	5.19	69	.321	.373	3	.115	-1	-15	-15	-0	-1.6
1985	Cal-A	0	0	—	2	0	0	0	0	7	8	4	4	5	15.4	9.00	46	.276	.364	0	—	0	-4	-4	0	-0.3
Total	2	4	2	.667	23	15	1	0	0	92	119	16	28	55	14.9	5.48	66	.317	.373	3	.115	-1	-19	-19	-0	-1.9
● HENRY FOX Fox, Henry (b: Henry Fuchs) b: 11/18/1874, Scranton, Pa. d: 6/6/27, Scranton, Pa. Deb: 9/04/02																										
1902	Phi-N	0	0	—	1	0	0	0	1	1	2	0	1	1	27.0	18.00	16	.413	.513	0	—	0	-2	-2	0	-0.2
● HOWIE FOX Fox, Howard Francis b: 3/1/21, Coburg, Ore. d: 10/9/55, San Antonio, Tex. BR/TR, 6'3", 210 lbs. Deb: 9/28/44																										
1944	Cin-N	0	0	—	2	0	0	0	0	2^1	2	0	0	0	7.7	0.00	—	.222	.222	0	.000	-0	1	1	-0	0.1
1945	Cin-N	8	13	.381	45	15	7	0	0	164^1	169	6	77	54	13.8	4.93	76	.268	.353	13	.283	3	-21	-21	4	-1.4
1946	Cin-N	0	0	—	4	0	0	0	0	5	12	2	5	1	30.6	18.00	19	.462	.548	0	—	0	-8	-8	0	-0.8
1948	Cin-N	6	9	.400	34	24	5	0	1	171	185	11	62	63	13.1	4.53	86	.280	.343	12	.200	1	-11	-12	1	-0.9
1949	Cin-N	6	19	.240	38	30	9	0	0	215	221	13	77	60	12.6	3.98	105	.265	.330	17	.236	2	2	5	6	1.2
1950	Cin-N	11	8	.579	34	22	10	1	1	187	196	14	85	64	13.6	4.33	98	.269	.347	11	.175	-0	-4	-2	3	0.1
1951	Cin-N	9	14	.391	40	30	9	4	2	228	239	15	69	57	12.2	3.83	107	.272	.326	8	.114	-2	3	6	1	0.5
1952	Phi-N	2	7	.222	13	11	2	0	0	62	70	8	26	16	13.9	5.08	72	.287	.356	1	.048	-1	-9	-10	1	-1.0
1954	Bal-A	1	2	.333	38	0	0	0	2	73^2	80	2	34	27	14.2	3.67	98	.289	.371	4	.250	1	0	-1	1	0.1
Total	9	43	72	.374	248	132	42	5	6	1108^1	1174	71	435	342	13.2	4.33	92	.274	.343	66	.189	2	-46	-42	17	-2.1
● JOHN FOX Fox, John Joseph b: 2/7/1859, Roxbury, Mass. d: 4/18/1893, Boston, Mass. Deb: 6/02/1881																										
1881	Bos-N	6	8	.429	17	16	12	0	0	124^1	144	0	39	30	13.2	3.33	80	.279	.329	21	.178	-4	-8	-9	1	-1.1
1883	Bal-a	6	13	.316	20	19	18	0	0	165^1	209	2	32	49	13.1	4.03	86	.289	.320	14	.152	-4	-13	-10	-1	-1.3
1884	Pit-a	1	6	.143	7	7	7	0	0	59	76	2	16	22	14.5	5.64	60	.291	.339	6	.240	0	-16	-15	1	-1.2
1886	Was-N	0	1	.000	1	1	1	0	0	8	11	0	11	3	24.8	9.00	37	.314	.478	1	.333	0	-5	-5	0	-0.4
Total	4	13	28	.317	45	43	38	0	0	356^2	440	4	98	104	13.7	4.16	76	.287	.331	42	.176	-7	-42	-40	0	-4.0
● TERRY FOX Fox, Terrence Edward b: 7/31/35, Chicago, Ill. BR/TR, 6', 175 lbs. Deb: 9/04/60																										
1960	Mil-N	0	0	—	5	0	0	0	0	8^1	6	0	6	5	13.0	4.32	79	.200	.333	0	.000	-0	-1	-1	-0	-0.1
1961	Det-A	5	2	.714	39	0	0	0	12	57^1	42	6	16	32	9.6	1.41	290	.200	.266	2	.167	-0	17	17	1	1.8
1962	Det-A	3	1	.750	44	0	0	0	16	58	48	2	16	23	10.1	1.71	238	.227	.285	2	.250	2	15	15	0	1.8
1963	Det-A	8	6	.571	46	0	0	0	11	80^1	81	9	20	35	11.5	3.59	104	.263	.312	1	.091	-0	0	1	0	0.2
1964	Det-A	4	3	.571	32	0	0	0	5	61^1	77	4	16	28	13.9	3.39	108	.316	.360	3	.250	1	2	2	1	0.3
1965	Det-A	6	4	.600	42	0	0	0	10	77^2	59	7	31	34	10.8	2.78	125	.214	.300	0	.000	-1	6	6	2	0.7
1966	Det-A	0	1	.000	4	0	0	0	1	10	9	3	2	6	9.9	6.30	55	.243	.282	0	.000	-0	-3	-3	0	-0.3
	Phi-N	3	2	.600	36	0	0	0	4	44^1	57	3	17	22	15.4	4.47	80	.322	.388	0	.000	-0	-4	-4	-0	-0.5
Total	7	29	19	.604	248	0	0	0	59	397	379	34	124	185	11.7	2.99	125	.254	.316	8	.123	1	31	33	4	3.9
● BILL FOXEN Foxen, William Aloysius b: 5/31/1884, Tenafly, N.J. d: 4/17/37, Brooklyn, N.Y. BL/TL, 5'11.5", 165 lbs. Deb: 5/05/08																										
1908	Phi-N	7	7	.500	22	16	10	2	0	147^1	126	2	53	52	11.4	1.95	124	.240	.319	5	.094	-3	7	8	2	0.8
1909	Phi-N	3	7	.300	18	7	5	1	0	83^1	65	0	32	37	10.9	3.35	78	.219	.303	5	.208	3	-7	-7	4	0.1
1910	Phi-N	5	5	.500	16	9	5	0	0	77^2	73	2	40	33	13.4	2.55	123	.268	.368	4	.174	-1	4	5	2	0.6
	Chi-N	0	0	—	2	0	0	0	0	5	7	0	3	2	18.0	9.00	32	.350	.435	0	.000	-0	-3	-3	-0	-0.4
	Yr	5	5	.500	18	9	5	0	0	82^2	80	2	43	35	13.4	2.94	106	.271	.364	4	.160	-1	1	2	1	0.2
1911	Chi-N	1	1	.500	3	1	0	0	0	13	12	0	12	6	16.6	2.08	160	.255	.407	1	.250	1	2	2	1	0.3
Total	4	16	20	.444	61	33	20	3	0	326^1	283	4	140	130	12.1	2.56	105	.244	.333	15	.142	0	3	4	8	1.4
● JIMMIE FOXX Foxx, James Emory "Beast" or "Double X" b: 10/22/07, Sudlersville, Md. d: 7/21/67, Miami, Fla. BR/TR, 6', 195 lbs. Deb: 5/01/25 H♦																										
1939	Bos-A☆	0	0	—	1	0	0	0	0	1	0	0	0	1	0.0	0.00	—	.000	.000	168	.360	1	1	1	0	0.1
1945	Phi-N	1	0	1.000	9	2	0	0	0	22^2	13	0	14	10	11.1	1.59	241	.171	.308	60	.268	2	6	6	-1	0.7
Total	2	1	0	1.000	10	2	0	0	0	23^2	13	0	14	11	10.6	1.52	254	.165	.298	2646	.325	3	6	6	-1	0.8
● PAUL FOYTACK Foytack, Paul Eugene b: 11/16/30, Scranton, Pa. BR/TR, 5'11", 180 lbs. Deb: 4/21/53																										
1953	Det-A	0	0	—	6	0	0	0	0	9^2	15	1	9	7	23.3	11.17	36	.375	.500	0	.000	-0	-8	-8	-0	-0.7
1955	Det-A	0	1	.000	22	1	0	0	0	49^2	48	4	36	38	15.2	5.26	73	.259	.380	1	.091	-1	-7	-8	-0	-0.9
1956	Det-A	15	13	.536	43	33	16	1	1	256	211	24	142	184	12.5	3.59	115	.226	.330	11	.122	-6	16	15	-1	0.8
1957	Det-A	14	11	.560	38	27	8	1	1	212	175	19	104	118	12.0	3.14	123	.226	.321	14	.222	1	15	17	-2	1.6
1958	Det-A	15	13	.536	39	33	16	2	1	230	198	23	77	135	10.9	3.44	117	.233	.299	18	.240	3	8	15	-2	1.7
1959	Det-A	14	14	.500	39	37	11	2	1	240^1	239	34	64	110	11.4	4.64	87	.259	.308	9	.111	-4	-21	-16	-2	-2.1
1960	Det-A	2	11	.154	28	13	1	0	2	96^2	108	11	49	38	14.6	6.14	64	.286	.369	7	.280	2	-24	-23	-2	-2.2
1961	Det-A	11	10	.524	32	20	6	0	0	169^2	152	27	56	89	11.1	3.93	104	.238	.301	12	.222	2	2	3	-3	0.2
1962	Det-A	10	7	.588	29	21	5	1	0	143^2	145	18	86	63	14.5	4.39	93	.259	.359	6	.143	-1	-7	-5	0	-0.6
1963	Det-A	0	1	.000	9	0	0	0	1	17^2	18	4	8	7	13.2	8.66	43	.265	.342	0	.000	-0	-10	-10	-0	-1.0
	LA-A	5	5	.500	25	8	0	0	0	70^1	68	9	29	37	12.4	3.71	92	.255	.328	4	.267	1	-1	-2	-1	-0.2
	Yr	5	6	.455	34	8	0	0	1	88	86	13	37	44	12.6	4.70	74	.256	.330	4	.211	1	-11	-12	-1	-1.2
1964	LA-A	0	1	.000	2	0	0	0	0	2^1	4	2	2	1	23.1	15.43	21	.364	.462	0	—	0	-3	-3	-0	-0.3
Total	11	86	87	.497	312	193	63	7	7	1498	1381	176	662	827	12.4	4.14	97	.246	.327	82	.178	-3	-39	-24	-13	-3.7

YEAR	TM/L	W	L	PCT	G	GS	CG	SH	SV	IP	H	HR	BB	SO	RAT	ERA	ERA+	OAV	OOB	BH	AVG	PB	PR	/A	PD	TPI
● KEN FRAILING	Frailing, Kenneth Douglas b: 1/19/48, Marion, Wis. BL/TL, 6', 190 lbs. Deb: 9/01/72																									
1972	Chi-A	1	0	1.000	4	0	0	0	0	3	3	1	1	1	12.0	3.00	104	.250	.308	0	—	0	0	0	0	0.0
1973	Chi-A	0	0	—	10	0	0	0	0	18^1	18	1	7	15	12.8	1.96	202	.254	.329	0	—	0	4	4	-0	0.2
1974	Chi-N	6	9	.400	55	16	1	0	1	125^1	150	11	43	71	13.9	3.88	98	.296	.353	8	.258	1	-4	-1	0	0.0
1975	Chi-N	2	5	.286	41	0	0	0	1	53	61	6	26	39	15.1	5.43	71	.293	.377	1	.143	0	-11	-9	2	-0.8
1976	Chi-N	1	2	.333	6	3	0	0	0	18^2	20	0	5	10	12.1	2.41	160	.274	.321	0	.000	-0	2	3	0	0.3
Total	5	10	16	.385	116	19	1	0	2	218^1	252	19	82	136	13.9	3.96	97	.290	.354	9	.220	1	-8	-3	2	-0.3
● OSSIE FRANCE	France, Osman Beverly "O. B." b: 10/4/1858, Greensburg, Ohio d: 5/2/47, Akron, Ohio BL/TL, 5'8", 155 lbs. Deb: 7/14/1890																									
1890	Chi-N	0	0	—	1	0	0	0	0	2	3	0	2	0	22.5	13.50	27	.336	.458	0	.000	-0	-2	-2	-0	-0.2
● EARL FRANCIS	Francis, Earl Coleman b: 7/14/35, Slab Fork, W.Va. BR/TR, 6'2", 215 lbs. Deb: 6/30/60																									
1960	Pit-N	1	0	1.000	7	0	0	0	0	18	14	0	4	8	9.5	2.00	188	.222	.279	0	.000	-1	4	4	-0	0.3
1961	Pit-N	2	8	.200	23	15	0	0	0	102^2	110	4	47	53	13.9	4.21	95	.274	.351	3	.107	-1	-2	-3	0	-0.3
1962	Pit-N	9	8	.529	36	23	5	1	0	176	153	8	83	121	12.2	3.07	128	.235	.323	10	.164	1	17	17	1	2.0
1963	Pit-N	4	6	.400	33	13	0	0	0	97^1	107	6	43	72	14.2	4.53	73	.284	.363	8	.308	3	-13	-13	0	-1.1
1964	Pit-N	0	1	.000	2	1	0	0	0	6^1	7	2	1	6	12.8	8.53	41	.269	.321	0	.000	-0	-4	-4	-0	-0.4
1965	StL-N	0	0	—	2	0	0	0	0	5^1	7	1	3	3	16.9	5.06	76	.318	.400	0	.000	-0	-1	-1	-0	-0.1
Total	6	16	23	.410	103	52	5	1	0	405^2	398	21	181	263	13.0	3.77	100	.258	.340	21	.172	2	1	0	1	0.4
● RAY FRANCIS	Francis, Ray James b: 3/8/1893, Sherman, Tex. d: 7/6/34, Atlanta, Ga. BL/TL, 6'1.5", 182 lbs. Deb: 4/18/22																									
1922	Was-A	7	18	.280	39	26	15	2	2	225	265	7	66	64	13.5	4.28	90	.303	.356	13	.167	-2	-6	-10	-1	-1.2
1923	Det-A	5	8	.385	33	6	0	0	1	79^1	95	2	28	27	14.4	4.42	87	.308	.374	3	.143	-1	-4	-5	-0	-0.6
1925	NY-A	0	0	—	4	0	0	0	0	4^2	5	0	3	1	17.4	7.71	55	.278	.409	0	—	0	-2	-2	-0	-0.2
	Bos-A	0	2	.000	6	4	0	0	0	28	44	3	13	4	18.6	7.71	59	.373	.439	1	.125	-0	-10	-10	0	-0.8
	Yr	0	2	.000	10	4	0	0	0	32^2	49	3	16	5	18.2	7.71	58	.358	.429	1	.125	-0	-12	-12	-0	-1.0
Total	3	12	28	.300	82	36	15	2	3	337	409	12	110	96	14.2	4.65	84	.310	.368	17	.159	-4	-22	-27	-1	-2.8
● JOHN FRANCO	Franco, John Anthony b: 9/17/60, Brooklyn, N.Y. BL/TL, 5'10", 180 lbs. Deb: 4/24/84																									
1984	Cin-N	6	2	.750	54	0	0	0	4	79^1	74	3	36	55	12.7	2.61	145	.256	.343	0	.000	-0	9	10	1	1.1
1985	Cin-N	12	3	.800	67	0	0	0	12	99	83	5	40	61	11.3	2.18	173	.234	.314	2	.333	0	16	**18**	2	2.1
1986	Cin-N☆	6	6	.500	74	0	0	0	29	101	90	7	44	84	12.1	2.94	132	.242	.325	0	.000	-0	9	10	1	1.2
1987	Cin-N★	8	5	.615	68	0	0	0	32	82	76	6	27	61	11.3	2.52	168	.245	.306	0	.000	-0	14	16	-1	1.4
1988	Cin-N	6	6	.500	70	0	0	0	**39**	86	60	3	27	46	9.1	1.57	228	.198	.264	0	.000	-0	**18**	**19**	1	2.2
1989	Cin-N☆	4	8	.333	60	0	0	0	32	80^2	77	3	36	60	12.6	3.12	115	.258	.337	1	.333	0	3	4	1	0.6
1990	NY-N★	5	3	.625	55	0	0	0	**33**	67^2	66	4	21	56	11.6	2.53	148	.252	.307	0	.000	-1	10	9	1	1.0
1991	NY-N	5	9	.357	52	0	0	0	30	55^1	61	2	18	45	13.0	2.93	124	.271	.328	0	.000	-0	5	4	1	0.5
1992	NY-N	6	2	.750	31	0	0	0	15	33	24	1	11	20	9.5	1.64	213	.209	.278	0	.000	-0	7	7	2	0.9
Total	9	58	44	.569	531	0	0	0	226	684	611	34	260	488	11.5	2.49	152	.242	.314	3	.115	-1	89	98	7	11.0
● TERRY FRANCONA	Francona, Terry Jon b: 4/22/59, Aberdeen, S.D. BL/TL, 6'1", 190 lbs. Deb: 8/19/81 F♦																									
1989	Mil-A	0	0	—	1	0	0	0	0	1	0	0	0	1	0.0	0.00	—	.000	.000	54	.232	1	0	0	0	0.0
● CHARLIE FRANK	Frank, Charles b: 5/30/1870, Mobile, Ala. d: 5/24/22, Memphis, Tenn. 5'10", 170 lbs. Deb: 8/18/1893 ♦																									
1894	StL-N	0	0	—	2	0	0	0	0	3	6	1	7	1	39.0	15.00	36	.410	.601	89	.279	0	-3	-3	-0	-0.2
● FRED FRANKHOUSE	Frankhouse, Frederick Meloy b: 4/9/04, Port Royal, Pa. d: 8/17/89, Port Royal, Pa. BR/TR, 5'11", 175 lbs. Deb: 9/11/27																									
1927	StL-N	5	1	.833	6	6	5	1	0	50	41	2	16	20	10.4	2.70	146	.218	.283	5	.250	0	7	7	-1	0.7
1928	StL-N	3	2	.600	21	10	1	0	1	84	91	6	36	29	14.1	3.96	101	.277	.358	5	.185	1	0	0	1	0.2
1929	StL-N	7	2	.778	30	12	6	0	1	133^1	149	9	43	37	13.2	4.12	113	.289	.349	15	.288	4	9	8	3	1.3
1930	StL-N	2	3	.400	8	1	0	0	0	19^2	31	1	11	4	19.2	7.32	69	.373	.447	0	.000	-1	-5	-5	0	-0.5
	Bos-N	7	6	.538	27	11	3	1	0	110^2	138	13	43	30	14.9	5.61	88	.313	.377	14	.359	4	-8	-8	-0	-0.4
	Yr	9	9	.500	35	12	3	1	0	130^1	169	14	54	34	15.5	5.87	84	.323	.388	14	.318	3	-13	-13	0	-0.9
1931	Bos-N	8	8	.500	26	15	6	0	1	127^1	125	4	43	50	12.1	4.03	94	.252	.315	6	.150	-0	-2	-3	1	-0.3
1932	Bos-N	4	6	.400	37	6	3	0	0	108^2	113	7	45	35	13.3	3.56	106	.278	.355	3	.100	-1	4	2	3	0.4
1933	Bos-N	16	15	.516	43	30	14	2	2	244^2	249	12	77	83	12.1	3.16	97	.267	.324	19	.237	4	5	-3	4	0.6
1934	Bos-N★	17	9	.654	37	31	13	2	1	233^2	239	10	77	78	12.3	3.20	120	.262	.322	17	.200	1	22	16	-0	1.8
1935	Bos-N	11	15	.423	40	29	10	1	0	230^2	278	12	81	64	14.2	4.76	80	.293	.352	20	.263	6	-19	-25	3	-1.5
1936	Bro-N	13	10	.565	41	31	9	1	2	234^1	236	18	89	84	12.6	3.65	113	.257	.325	13	.143	-4	10	13	1	0.9
1937	Bro-N	10	13	.435	33	26	9	1	0	179^1	214	8	78	64	14.9	4.27	95	.297	.369	11	.190	-0	-7	-5	3	-0.2
1938	Bro-N	3	5	.375	30	8	2	1	0	93^2	92	6	44	32	13.5	4.04	97	.256	.344	4	.154	-1	-3	-1	1	-0.1
1939	Bos-N	0	2	.000	23	0	0	0	4	38	37	3	18	12	13.3	2.61	142	.253	.339	0	.000	-1	6	5	-1	0.3
Total	13	106	97	.522	402	216	81	10	12	1888	2033	111	701	622	13.2	3.92	100	.275	.341	132	.208	11	18	-0	18	3.2
● JACK FRANKLIN	Franklin, Jack Wilford b: 10/20/19, Paris, Ill. d: 11/15/91, Panama City, Fla. BR/TR, 5'11.5", 170 lbs. Deb: 6/12/44																									
1944	Bro-N	0	0	—	1	0	0	0	0	2	2	1	4	0	36.0	13.50	26	.250	.571	0	—	0	-2	-2	-0	-0.2
● JAY FRANKLIN	Franklin, John William b: 3/16/53, Arlington, Va. BR/TR, 6'2", 180 lbs. Deb: 9/04/71																									
1971	SD-N	0	1	.000	3	1	0	0	0	5^2	5	3	4	4	14.3	6.35	52	.250	.375	0	.000	-0	-2	-2	0	-0.2
● CHICK FRASER	Fraser, Charles Carrolton b: 3/17/1871, Chicago, Ill. d: 5/8/40, Wendell, Idaho BR/TR, 5'10.5", 188 lbs. Deb: 4/19/1896 C																									
1896	Lou-N	12	27	.308	43	38	36	0	1	349^1	396	9	166	91	15.2	4.87	89	.283	.371	22	.151	-9	-20	-21	3	-2.1
1897	Lou-N	15	19	.441	35	34	32	0	0	286^1	332	11	133	70	15.3	4.09	104	.288	.372	18	.161	-4	7	6	6	0.6
1898	Lou-N	7	17	.292	26	26	20	1	0	203	230	4	100	58	15.7	5.32	67	.283	.377	13	.167	-2	-39	-39	4	-3.3
	Cle-N	2	3	.400	6	6	6	0	0	42	49	2	12	19	14.4	5.57	65	.289	.357	4	.250	0	-9	-9	0	-0.8
	Yr	9	20	.310	32	32	26	1	0	245	279	6	112	77	14.6	5.36	67	.278	.354	17	.181	-2	-48	-48	4	-4.1
1899	Phi-N	21	12	.636	35	33	29	4	0	270^2	278	1	85	68	12.8	3.36	110	.265	.333	21	.179	-2	15	10	2	0.9
1900	Phi-N	15	9	.625	29	26	22	1	0	223^1	250	7	93	58	14.2	3.14	115	.282	.357	22	.259	3	14	12	3	1.7
1901	Phi-A	22	16	.579	40	37	35	2	0	331	344	6	132	110	13.8	3.81	99	.265	.347	26	.187	-4	-5	-1	2	-0.3
1902	Phi-N	12	13	.480	27	26	24	3	0	224	238	2	74	97	13.1	3.42	82	.272	.339	15	.174	0	-16	-15	-0	-1.5
1903	Phi-N	12	17	.414	31	29	26	1	1	250	260	8	97	104	13.4	4.50	73	.267	.344	19	.204	4	-34	-34	2	-2.5
1904	Phi-N	14	24	.368	42	36	32	2	1	302	287	5	100	127	11.9	3.25	82	.246	.311	17	.155	-1	-17	-19	2	-1.8
1905	Bos-N	14	21	.400	39	38	35	2	0	334^1	320	8	149	130	13.0	3.28	94	.254	.340	35	.224	3	-10	-7	-1	-0.4
1906	Cin-N	10	20	.333	31	28	25	2	0	236	221	1	80	58	11.8	2.67	103	.259	.329	14	.171	-1	-1	2	1	0.2
1907	Chi-N	8	5	.615	22	15	9	2	1	138^1	112	1	46	41	10.5	2.28	110	.229	.299	3	.067	-3	3	3	0	0.0
1908	Chi-N	11	9	.550	26	17	11	2	2	162^2	141	4	61	66	11.5	2.27	104	.244	.323	6	.120	-2	2	2	4	0.4
1909	Chi-N	0	0	—	1	0	0	0	0	3	2	0	4	1	18.0	0.00	—	.222	.462	0	.000	-0	1	1	-0	0.1
Total	14	175	212	.452	433	389	342	22	6	3356	3460	69	1332	1098	13.4	3.68	92	.267	.345	235	.179	-16	-109	-108	29	-8.8
● WILLIE FRASER	Fraser, William Patrick b: 5/26/64, New York, N.Y. BR/TR, 6'1", 208 lbs. Deb: 9/10/86																									
1986	Cal-A	0	0	—	1	1	0	0	0	4^1	6	0	1	2	14.5	8.31	49	.353	.389	0	—	0	-2	-2	-0	-0.1
1987	Cal-A	10	10	.500	36	23	5	1	1	176^2	160	26	63	106	11.7	3.92	110	.240	.312	0	—	0	10	7	-3	0.7
1988	Cal-A	12	13	.480	34	32	2	0	0	194^2	203	33	80	86	13.5	5.41	71	.267	.344	0	—	0	-31	-34	-1	-3.2
1989	Cal-A	4	7	.364	44	0	0	0	2	91^2	80	6	23	46	10.6	3.24	118	.235	.293	0	—	0	7	6	0	0.7
1990	Cal-A	5	4	.556	45	0	0	0	2	76	69	4	24	32	11.0	3.08	124	.241	.300	0	—	0	7	6	-1	0.5

YEAR	TM/L	W	L	PCT	G	GS	CG	SH	SV	IP	H	HR	BB	SO	RAT	ERA	ERA+	OAV	OOB	BH	AVG	PB	PR	/A	PD	TPI
1991	Tor-A	0	2	.000	13	1	0	0	0	26^1	33	4	11	12	16.1	6.15	68	.303	.382	0	—	0	-6	-6	-0	-0.8
	StL-N	3	3	.500	35	0	0	0	0	49^1	44	9	21	25	12.4	4.93	75	.242	.330	0	.000	-0	-7	-7	-1	-0.8
Total	6	34	39	.466	208	57	7	1	5	619	595	82	223	309	12.3	4.39	91	.252	.323	0	.000	-0	-22	-28	-6	-3.0
● VIC FRASIER Frasier, Victor Patrick b: 8/5/04, Ruston, La. d: 1/10/77, Jacksonville, Tex. BR/TR, 6', 182 lbs. Deb: 4/18/31																										
1931	Chi-A	13	15	.464	46	29	13	2	4	254	258	11	127	87	13.8	4.46	95	.259	.345	18	.209	1	-2	-6	-1	-0.5
1932	Chi-A	3	13	.188	29	21	4	0	0	146	180	14	70	33	15.7	6.23	69	.297	.374	4	.091	-3	-28	-31	2	-2.8
1933	Chi-A	1	1	.500	10	1	0	0	0	20^1	32	2	11	4	19.0	8.85	48	.368	.439	0	.000	-1	-10	-10	1	-0.9
	Det-A	5	5	.500	20	14	4	0	0	104^1	129	9	59	26	16.3	6.64	65	.312	.399	7	.189	-0	-27	-27	0	-2.4
	Yr	6	6	.500	30	15	4	0	0	124^2	161	11	70	30	16.7	7.00	61	.321	.406	7	.171	-1	-38	-37	2	-3.3
1934	Det-A	1	3	.250	8	2	0	0	0	22^2	30	0	12	11	17.1	5.96	74	.313	.394	2	.286	0	-4	-4	2	-0.2
1937	Bos-N	0	0	—	3	0	0	0	0	8	12	1	1	2	14.6	5.63	64	.364	.382	0	.000	-0	-2	-2	0	-0.2
1939	Chi-A	0	1	.000	10	1	0	0	0	23^2	45	0	11	7	21.3	10.27	46	.405	.459	2	.286	0	-15	-15	0	-1.2
Total	6	23	38	.377	126	68	21	2	4	579	686	37	291	170	15.4	5.77	75	.293	.373	33	.177	-3	-88	-94	4	-8.2
● GEORGE FRAZIER Frazier, George Allen b: 10/13/54, Oklahoma City, Okla BR/TR, 6'5", 205 lbs. Deb: 5/25/78																										
1978	StL-N	0	3	.000	14	0	0	0	0	22	22	2	6	8	11.5	4.09	86	.250	.298	1	.333	0	-1	-1	0	-0.1
1979	StL-N	2	4	.333	25	0	0	0	0	32^1	35	3	12	14	13.4	4.45	84	.278	.345	0	.000	-0	-3	-2	-0	-0.3
1980	StL-N	1	4	.200	22	0	0	0	3	23	24	2	7	11	12.1	2.74	135	.273	.326	0	—	0	2	2	0	0.3
1981	*NY-A	0	1	.000	16	0	0	0	3	27^2	26	1	11	17	12.0	1.63	220	.245	.316	0	—	0	6	6	-0	0.7
1982	NY-A	4	4	.500	63	0	0	0	1	111^2	103	7	39	69	11.8	3.47	115	.252	.325	0	—	0	8	6	0	0.8
1983	NY-A	4	4	.500	61	0	0	0	8	115^1	94	5	45	78	11.1	3.43	113	.227	.307	0	—	0	8	6	0	0.9
1984	Cle-A	3	2	.600	22	0	0	0	1	44^1	45	3	14	24	12.0	3.65	112	.259	.314	0	—	0	2	2	-1	0.0
	*Chi-N	6	3	.667	37	0	0	0	3	63^2	53	4	26	58	11.3	4.10	95	.221	.300	2	.286	0	-4	-1	-1	-0.2
1985	Chi-N	7	8	.467	51	0	0	0	2	76	88	11	52	46	16.9	6.39	62	.299	.410	0	.000	-1	-24	-20	-0	-2.2
1986	Chi-N	2	4	.333	35	0	0	0	0	51^2	63	5	34	41	17.1	5.40	75	.310	.412	0	.000	-0	-10	-8	-1	-1.0
	Min-A	1	1	.500	15	0	0	0	6	26^2	23	2	16	25	13.2	4.39	98	.232	.339	0	—	0	-1	-0	0	-0.2
1987	*Min-A	5	5	.500	54	0	0	0	2	81^1	77	9	51	58	14.4	4.98	93	.258	.369	0	—	0	-5	-3	-1	-0.6
Total	10	35	43	.449	415	0	0	0	29	675^2	653	54	313	449	13.1	4.20	96	.257	.342	3	.143	-1	-20	-14	-4	-1.9
● BUCK FREEMAN Freeman, Alexander Vernon b: 7/5/1893, Mart, Tex. d: 2/21/53, Fort Sam Houston, Tex. BB/TR, 5'10", 167 lbs. Deb: 4/13/21																										
1921	Chi-N	9	10	.474	38	20	6	0	3	177^1	189	12	70	42	13.6	4.11	93	.281	.356	11	.208	0	-6	-6	-1	-0.7
1922	Chi-N	0	1	.000	11	1	0	0	1	25^2	47	0	10	10	20.7	8.77	48	.412	.468	1	.125	-0	-13	-13	1	-1.1
Total	2	9	11	.450	49	21	6	0	4	203	236	12	80	52	14.5	4.70	82	.300	.372	12	.197	-0	-20	-19	-0	-1.8
● HARVEY FREEMAN Freeman, Harvey Bayard "Buck" b: 12/22/1897, Nottville, Mich. d: 1/10/70, Kalamazoo, Mich. BR/TR, 5'10", 160 lbs. Deb: 7/10/21																										
1921	Phi-A	1	4	.200	18	4	2	0	0	48	65	2	35	5	19.7	7.69	58	.346	.461	1	.083	-2	-18	-17	1	-1.6
● HERSH FREEMAN Freeman, Hershell Baskin "Buster" b: 7/1/28, Gadsden, Ala. BR/TR, 6'3", 220 lbs. Deb: 9/10/52																										
1952	Bos-A	1	0	1.000	4	1	1	0	0	13^2	13	1	5	5	12.5	3.29	120	.260	.339	2	.500	1	1	1	0	0.2
1953	Bos-A	1	4	.200	18	2	0	0	0	39	50	2	17	15	15.5	5.54	76	.316	.383	1	.091	-1	-7	-6	-0	-0.7
1955	Bos-A	0	0	—	2	0	0	0	0	1^2	1	0	1	1	10.8	0.00	—	.200	.333	0	—	0	1	1	-0	0.1
	Cin-N	7	4	.636	52	0	0	0	11	91^2	94	3	30	37	12.4	2.16	196	.276	.338	3	.167	1	**19**	**21**	1	2.3
1956	Cin-N	14	5	.737	64	0	0	0	18	108^2	112	2	34	50	12.2	3.40	117	.274	.331	1	.056	-1	5	7	-0	0.6
1957	Cin-N	7	2	.778	52	0	0	0	8	83^2	90	14	14	36	11.5	4.52	91	.277	.313	2	.200	0	-6	-4	-1	-0.4
1958	Cin-N	0	0	—	3	0	0	0	0	7^2	4	0	5	7	10.6	3.52	118	.154	.290	0	.000	-0	0	1	0	0.1
	Chi-N	0	1	.000	9	0	0	0	0	13	23	3	3	7	18.0	8.31	47	.354	.382	0	.000	-0	-6	-6	0	-0.6
	Yr	0	1	.000	12	0	0	0	0	20^2	27	3	8	14	15.2	6.53	61	.293	.350	0	.000	-0	-6	-6	0	-0.5
Total	6	30	16	.652	204	3	1	0	37	359	387	25	109	158	12.6	3.74	110	.281	.336	9	.143	-0	6	15	1	1.6
● JIMMY FREEMAN Freeman, Jimmy Lee b: 6/29/51, Carlsbad, N.Mex. BL/TL, 6'4", 180 lbs. Deb: 9/01/72																										
1972	Atl-N	2	2	.500	6	6	1	0	0	36	40	5	22	18	15.5	6.00	63	.278	.373	1	.077	-0	-10	-9	-1	-1.0
1973	Atl-N	0	2	.000	13	5	0	0	1	37^1	50	7	25	20	18.1	7.71	51	.327	.421	2	.154	-0	-17	-16	-1	-1.6
Total	2	2	4	.333	19	11	1	0	1	73^1	90	12	47	38	16.8	6.87	56	.303	.398	3	.115	-1	-27	-25	-2	-2.6
● BUCK FREEMAN Freeman, John Frank b: 10/30/1871, Catasauqua, Pa. d: 6/25/49, Wilkes-Barre, Pa. BL/TL, 5'9", 169 lbs. Deb: 6/27/1891 ♦																										
1891	Was-a	3	2	.600	5	4	4	0	0	44	35	0	33	28	14.7	3.89	96	.211	.355	4	.222	0	-1	-1	-0	0.0
1899	Was-N	0	0	—	2	0	0	0	0	7	15	3	3	0	27.0	7.71	51	.430	.513	187	.318	1	-3	-3	0	-0.2
Total	2	3	2	.600	7	4	4	0	0	51	50	3	36	28	16.4	4.41	85	.249	.381	1235	.293	1	-4	-4	-0	-0.2
● JULIE FREEMAN Freeman, Julius Benjamin b: 11/7/1868, Missouri d: 6/10/21, St.Louis, Mo. BR, Deb: 10/10/1888																										
1888	StL-a	0	1	.000	1	1	0	0	0	6^1	7	0	4	1	17.1	4.26	77	.270	.388	1	.333	0	-1	-1	-0	-0.1
● MARK FREEMAN Freeman, Mark Price b: 12/7/30, Memphis, Tenn. BR/TR, 6'4", 220 lbs. Deb: 4/18/59																										
1959	KC-A	0	0	—	3	0	0	0	0	3^2	6	0	3	1	22.1	9.82	41	.375	.474	0	—	0	-2	-2	-0	-0.2
	NY-A	0	0	—	1	1	0	0	0	7	6	0	2	4	11.6	2.57	142	.240	.321	0	.000	-0	1	1	-0	0.1
	Yr	0	0	—	4	1	0	0	0	10^2	12	0	5	5	15.2	5.06	74	.286	.375	0	.000	-0	-1	-2	-0	-0.1
1960	Chi-N	3	3	.500	30	8	1	0	1	76^2	70	10	33	50	12.7	5.63	67	.240	.327	3	.150	-0	-16	-16	-2	-1.8
Total	2	3	3	.500	34	9	1	0	1	87^1	82	10	38	55	13.0	5.56	68	.246	.334	3	.136	-1	-17	-17	-2	-1.9
● MARVIN FREEMAN Freeman, Marvin b: 4/10/63, Chicago, Ill. BR/TR, 6'7", 200 lbs. Deb: 9/16/86																										
1986	Phi-N	2	0	1.000	3	3	0	0	0	16	6	0	10	8	9.0	2.25	171	.120	.267	0	.000	-1	3	3	-0	0.2
1988	Phi-N	2	3	.400	11	11	0	0	0	51^2	55	2	43	37	17.2	6.10	58	.276	.407	3	.214	0	-15	-15	0	-1.4
1989	Phi-N	0	0	—	1	1	0	0	0	3	2	0	5	0	21.0	6.00	59	.182	.438	0	.000	-0	-1	-1	-0	-0.1
1990	Phi-N	0	2	.000	16	3	0	0	1	32^1	34	5	14	26	14.2	5.57	69	.264	.349	0	.000	-1	-6	-6	0	-0.7
	Atl-N	1	0	1.000	9	0	0	0	0	15^2	7	0	3	12	6.9	1.72	234	.130	.203	0	—	0	4	4	-0	0.4
	Yr	1	2	.333	25	3	0	0	1	48	41	5	17	38	11.3	4.31	90	.220	.293	0	.000	-1	-3	-2	-0	-0.3
1991	Atl-N	1	0	1.000	34	0	0	0	1	48	37	2	13	34	9.8	3.00	130	.214	.277	0	.000	-1	4	5	-1	0.4
1992	*Atl-N	7	5	.583	58	0	0	0	3	64^1	61	7	29	41	12.7	3.22	116	.251	.333	2	.500	1	2	4	-1	0.4
Total	6	13	10	.565	132	18	0	0	5	231	202	16	117	158	12.8	4.01	94	.235	.333	5	.125	-1	-11	-6	-2	-0.8
● JAKE FREEZE Freeze, Carl Alexander b: 4/25/1900, Huntington, Ark. d: 4/9/83, San Angelo, Tex. BR/TR, 5'8", 150 lbs. Deb: 7/01/25																										
1925	Chi-A	0	0	—	2	0	0	0	0	3^2	5	1	3	1	19.6	2.45	169	.333	.444	0	.000	-0	1	1	-0	0.0
● DAVE FREISLEBEN Freisleben, David James b: 10/31/51, Coraopolis, Pa. BR/TR, 5'11", 200 lbs. Deb: 4/26/74																										
1974	SD-N	9	14	.391	33	31	6	2	0	211^2	194	13	112	130	13.3	3.66	97	.241	.339	11	.172	2	-1	-2	-0	-0.1
1975	SD-N	5	14	.263	36	27	4	1	0	181	206	11	82	77	14.7	4.28	81	.289	.368	4	.083	-1	-13	-16	0	-1.7
1976	SD-N	10	13	.435	34	24	6	3	1	172	163	10	66	81	12.2	3.51	93	.248	.321	7	.189	1	-0	-5	2	-0.1
1977	SD-N	7	9	.438	33	23	1	0	0	138^2	140	21	71	72	13.8	4.61	77	.266	.356	5	.135	0	-11	-16	-2	-1.8
1978	SD-N	0	3	.000	12	4	0	0	0	26^2	41	3	15	16	18.9	6.08	55	.363	.438	0	.000	-1	-7	-8	-0	-0.9
	Cle-A	1	4	.200	12	10	0	0	0	44^1	52	4	31	19	17.3	7.11	53	.299	.411	0	—	0	-16	-17	-0	-1.5
1979	Tor-A	2	3	.400	42	2	0	0	3	91	101	5	53	35	15.4	4.95	88	.294	.391	0	—	0	-7	-6	-1	-0.6
Total	6	34	60	.362	202	121	17	6	4	865^1	897	67	430	430	14.1	4.30	83	.269	.357	27	.141	2	-56	-71	-2	-6.7
● TONY FREITAS Freitas, Antonio b: 5/5/08, Mill Valley, Cal. BR/TL, 5'8", 161 lbs. Deb: 5/31/32																										
1932	Phi-A	12	5	.706	23	18	10	1	0	150^1	150	11	48	31	12.1	3.83	118	.263	.325	8	.148	-1	11	12	1	1.1

YEAR TM/L	W	L	PCT	G	GS	CG	SH	SV	IP	H	HR	BB	SO	RAT	ERA	ERA+	OAV	OOB	BH	AVG	PB	PR	/A	PD	TPI
1933 Phi-A	2	4	.333	19	9	2	0	1	64^1	90	8	24	15	16.2	7.27	59	.337	.396	1	.063	-1	-21	-21	0	-2.0
1934 Cin-N	6	12	.333	30	18	5	0	1	152^2	194	6	25	37	13.1	4.01	102	.311	.341	9	.191	0	1	1	2	0.4
1935 Cin-N	5	10	.333	31	18	5	0	2	143^2	174	6	38	51	13.4	4.57	87	.295	.340	6	.130	-0	-9	-9	1	-0.9
1936 Cin-N	0	2	.000	4	0	0	0	0	7	6	0	2	1	10.3	1.29	297	.240	.296	0	.000	-0	2	2	-0	0.2
Total 5	25	33	.431	107	63	22	1	4	518	614	31	137	135	13.2	4.48	94	.296	.343	24	.145	-2	-16	-16	4	-1.2

● LARRY FRENCH French, Lawrence Herbert b: 11/1/07, Visalia, Cal. d: 2/9/87, San Diego, Cal. BR/TL, 6'1", 195 lbs. Deb: 4/18/29

YEAR TM/L	W	L	PCT	G	GS	CG	SH	SV	IP	H	HR	BB	SO	RAT	ERA	ERA+	OAV	OOB	BH	AVG	PB	PR	/A	PD	TPI
1929 Pit-N	7	5	.583	30	13	6	0	1	123	130	10	62	49	14.3	4.90	97	.276	.364	8	.190	-1	-3	-2	1	-0.1
1930 Pit-N	17	18	.486	42	35	21	3	1	274^2	325	20	89	90	13.8	4.36	114	.295	.351	22	.242	1	19	19	-1	1.7
1931 Pit-N	15	13	.536	39	33	20	1	1	275^2	301	9	70	73	12.1	3.26	118	.278	.322	17	.179	-1	18	18	-1	1.6
1932 Pit-N	18	16	.529	**47**	33	19	3	4	274^1	301	17	62	72	11.9	3.02	126	.276	.316	19	.207	1	26	24	-4	2.2
1933 Pit-N	18	13	.581	47	35	21	5	1	291^1	290	9	55	88	10.8	2.72	122	.257	.294	15	.149	-2	20	19	-4	1.5
1934 Pit-N	12	18	.400	49	35	16	3	1	263^2	299	8	59	103	12.3	3.58	115	.281	.321	16	.190	-0	14	16	-3	1.2
1935 *Chi-N	17	10	.630	42	30	16	**4**	2	246^1	279	10	44	90	11.9	2.96	133	.286	.318	12	.141	-3	29	27	1	2.4
1936 Chi-N	18	9	.667	43	28	16	**4**	3	252^1	262	16	54	104	11.5	3.39	118	.266	.308	18	.212	0	18	17	-3	1.4
1937 Chi-N	16	10	.615	42	28	11	4	0	208	229	17	65	100	12.8	3.98	100	.274	.327	9	.127	-4	-2	0	2	-0.2
1938 *Chi-N	10	19	.345	43	27	10	3	0	201^1	210	17	62	83	12.2	3.80	101	.271	.326	13	.210	2	-0	1	1	0.4
1939 Chi-N	15	8	.652	36	21	10	2	1	194	205	7	50	98	11.9	3.29	120	.269	.314	14	.192	1	13	14	2	1.7
1940 Chi-N★	14	14	.500	40	33	18	3	2	246	240	12	64	107	11.3	3.29	114	.256	.306	14	.165	1	15	12	2	1.6
1941 Chi-N	5	14	.263	26	18	6	1	0	138	161	10	43	60	13.4	4.63	76	.285	.338	9	.191	1	-15	-17	-1	-1.7
*Bro-N	0	0	—	6	1	0	0	0	15^2	16	1	4	8	12.1	3.45	106	.267	.323	1	.250	0	0	0	-0	0.1
Yr	5	14	.263	32	19	6	1	0	153^2	177	11	47	68	13.2	4.51	78	.282	.333	10	.196	1	-15	-17	-1	-1.6
1942 Bro-N	15	4	**.789**	38	14	8	4	0	147^2	127	1	36	62	10.2	1.83	178	.233	.287	12	.300	4	24	24	-1	3.0
Total 14	197	171	.535	570	384	198	40	17	3152	3375	164	819	1187	12.1	3.44	114	.272	.320	199	.188	0	178	171	-7	16.8

● BILL FRENCH French, William b: Baltimore, Md. Deb: 4/14/1873 ♦

YEAR TM/L	W	L	PCT	G	GS	CG	SH	SV	IP	H	HR	BB	SO	RAT	ERA	ERA+	OAV	OOB	BH	AVG	PB	PR	/A	PD	TPI
1873 Mar-n	0	1	.000	1	1	1	0	0	9	30	1	0	0	30.0	12.00	27	.462	.462	4	.222	-0	-9	-9		-0.5

● BENNY FREY Frey, Benjamin Rudolph b: 4/6/06, Dexter, Mich. d: 11/1/37, Jackson, Mich. BR/TR, 5'10", 165 lbs. Deb: 9/18/29

YEAR TM/L	W	L	PCT	G	GS	CG	SH	SV	IP	H	HR	BB	SO	RAT	ERA	ERA+	OAV	OOB	BH	AVG	PB	PR	/A	PD	TPI
1929 Cin-N	1	2	.333	3	3	2	0	0	24	29	2	8	1	13.9	4.13	111	.302	.356	3	.375	1	2	1	1	0.3
1930 Cin-N	11	18	.379	44	28	14	2	1	245	295	15	62	43	13.2	4.70	103	.305	.349	25	.284	4	7	3	6	1.2
1931 Cin-N	8	12	.400	34	17	7	1	2	133^2	166	2	36	19	13.7	4.92	76	.319	.365	14	.318	4	-16	-18	4	-1.0
1932 StL-N	0	2	.000	2	0	0	0	0	3	6	0	2	0	24.0	12.00	33	.600	.667	0	.000	-0	-3	-3	-0	-0.3
Cin-N	4	10	.286	28	15	5	0	0	131^1	159	10	30	27	13.0	4.32	89	.299	.338	9	.205	-0	-6	-7	3	-0.4
Yr	4	12	.250	30	15	5	0	0	134^1	165	10	32	27	13.3	4.49	86	.305	.345	9	.200	-0	-9	-9	2	-0.7
1933 Cin-N	6	4	.600	37	9	1	1	0	132	144	4	21	12	11.3	3.82	89	.281	.309	11	.262	3	-7	-6	2	-0.1
1934 Cin-N	11	16	.407	39	30	12	2	2	245^1	288	10	42	33	12.2	3.52	116	.289	.319	14	.171	-0	15	15	4	1.9
1935 Cin-N	6	10	.375	38	13	3	1	3	114^1	164	6	32	24	15.7	6.85	58	.335	.381	11	.344	4	-36	-36	2	-2.9
1936 Cin-N	10	8	.556	31	12	5	0	0	131^1	164	5	30	20	13.3	4.25	90	.296	.332	11	.250	2	-3	-6	0	-0.4
Total 8	57	82	.410	256	127	49	7	8	1160	1415	54	263	179	13.1	4.50	90	.303	.341	98	.255	17	-47	-55	21	-1.7

● STEVE FREY Frey, Steven Francis b: 7/29/63, Meadowbrook, Pa. BR/TL, 5'9", 170 lbs. Deb: 5/10/89

YEAR TM/L	W	L	PCT	G	GS	CG	SH	SV	IP	H	HR	BB	SO	RAT	ERA	ERA+	OAV	OOB	BH	AVG	PB	PR	/A	PD	TPI
1989 Mon-N	3	2	.600	20	0	0	0	0	21^1	29	4	11	15	17.3	5.48	64	.326	.406	0	—	0	-5	-5	-0	-0.5
1990 Mon-N	8	2	.800	51	0	0	0	9	55^2	44	4	29	29	12.0	2.10	174	.219	.320	0	.000	-0	10	10	-0	1.0
1991 Mon-N	0	1	.000	31	0	0	0	1	39^2	43	3	23	21	15.2	4.99	72	.281	.379	0	.000	-0	-6	-6	-1	-0.7
1992 Cal-A	4	2	.667	51	0	0	0	4	45^1	39	6	22	24	12.5	3.57	109	.238	.335	0	—	0	2	2	0	0.2
Total 4	15	7	.682	153	0	0	0	14	162	155	17	85	89	13.6	3.67	101	.255	.352	0	.000	0	2	1	-1	0.0

● BERNIE FRIBERG Friberg, Bernard Albert (b: Gustaf Bernhard Friberg) b: 8/18/1899, Manchester, N.H. d: 12/8/58, Lynn, Mass. BR/TR, 5'11", 178 lbs. Deb: 8/20/19 ♦

YEAR TM/L	W	L	PCT	G	GS	CG	SH	SV	IP	H	HR	BB	SO	RAT	ERA	ERA+	OAV	OOB	BH	AVG	PB	PR	/A	PD	TPI
1925 Phi-N	0	0	—	1	0	0	0	0	4	4	0	3	1	15.8	4.50	106	.286	.412	82	.270	0	-0	0	-0	0.0

● MARION FRICANO Fricano, Marion John b: 7/15/23, Brant, N.Y. d: 5/18/76, Tijuana, Mex. BR/TR, 6', 170 lbs. Deb: 9/06/52

YEAR TM/L	W	L	PCT	G	GS	CG	SH	SV	IP	H	HR	BB	SO	RAT	ERA	ERA+	OAV	OOB	BH	AVG	PB	PR	/A	PD	TPI
1952 Phi-A	1	0	1.000	2	0	0	0	0	5	5	0	1	0	10.8	1.80	220	.238	.273	0	—	0	1	1	0	0.1
1953 Phi-A	9	12	.429	39	23	10	0	0	211	206	21	90	67	12.9	3.88	110	.257	.337	10	.145	-3	3	10	-2	0.5
1954 Phi-A	5	11	.313	37	20	4	0	1	151^2	163	17	64	43	13.7	5.16	76	.275	.349	4	.098	-3	-24	-21	-2	-2.6
1955 KC-A	0	0	—	10	0	0	0	0	20	19	2	9	5	12.6	3.15	133	.253	.333	2	.667	1	2	2	0	0.4
Total 4	15	23	.395	88	43	14	0	1	387^2	393	40	164	115	13.2	4.32	96	.264	.341	16	.142	-5	-19	-8	-3	-1.6

● SKIPPER FRIDAY Friday, Grier William b: 10/26/1897, Gastonia, N.C. d: 8/25/62, Gastonia, N.C. BR/TR, 5'11", 170 lbs. Deb: 6/17/23

YEAR TM/L	W	L	PCT	G	GS	CG	SH	SV	IP	H	HR	BB	SO	RAT	ERA	ERA+	OAV	OOB	BH	AVG	PB	PR	/A	PD	TPI
1923 Was-A	0	1	.000	7	2	1	0	0	30	35	2	22	9	17.7	6.90	55	.313	.434	2	.222	0	-10	-10	1	-0.9

● CY FRIED Fried, Arthur Edwin b: 7/23/1897, San Antonio, Tex. d: 10/10/70, San Antonio, Tex. BL/TL, 5'11.5", 150 lbs. Deb: 9/17/20

YEAR TM/L	W	L	PCT	G	GS	CG	SH	SV	IP	H	HR	BB	SO	RAT	ERA	ERA+	OAV	OOB	BH	AVG	PB	PR	/A	PD	TPI
1920 Det-A	0	0	—	2	0	0	0	0	1^2	3	0	4	0	37.8	16.20	23	.500	.700	0	—	0	-2	-2	0	-0.2

● BOB FRIEDRICH Friedrich, Robert George b: 8/30/06, Cincinnati, Ohio BR/TR, 5'11.5", 165 lbs. Deb: 5/17/32

YEAR TM/L	W	L	PCT	G	GS	CG	SH	SV	IP	H	HR	BB	SO	RAT	ERA	ERA+	OAV	OOB	BH	AVG	PB	PR	/A	PD	TPI
1932 Was-A	0	0	—	2	0	0	0	0	4	4	0	7	2	27.0	11.25	38	.250	.500	0	.000	-0	-3	-3	-0	-0.3

● BILL FRIEL Friel, William Edward b: 4/1/1876, Renovo, Pa. d: 12/24/59, St.Louis, Mo. BL/TR, 5'10", 165 lbs. Deb: 5/03/01 FU♦

YEAR TM/L	W	L	PCT	G	GS	CG	SH	SV	IP	H	HR	BB	SO	RAT	ERA	ERA+	OAV	OOB	BH	AVG	PB	PR	/A	PD	TPI
1902 StL-A	0	0	—	1	0	0	0	0	4	4	0	0	0	9.0	4.50	78	.261	.261	64	.240	0	-0	-0	-0	-0.1

● DANNY FRIEND Friend, Daniel Sebastian b: 4/18/1873, Cincinnati, Ohio d: 6/1/42, Chillicothe, Ohio TL, 5'9", 175 lbs. Deb: 9/10/1895

YEAR TM/L	W	L	PCT	G	GS	CG	SH	SV	IP	H	HR	BB	SO	RAT	ERA	ERA+	OAV	OOB	BH	AVG	PB	PR	/A	PD	TPI
1895 Chi-N	2	2	.500	5	5	5	0	0	41	50	5	14	10	14.7	5.27	97	.296	.360	4	.235	-1	-2	-1	0	-0.1
1896 Chi-N	18	14	.563	36	33	28	1	0	290^2	298	11	139	86	14.7	4.74	96	.263	.363	30	.238	-1	-12	-6	-2	-0.8
1897 Chi-N	12	11	.522	24	24	23	0	0	203	244	5	86	58	15.4	4.52	99	.295	.373	25	.284	2	-5	-1	-2	-0.1
1898 Chi-N	0	2	.000	2	2	2	0	0	17	20	1	10	4	16.4	5.29	68	.291	.389	2	.286	0	-3	-3	2	-0.1
Total 4	32	29	.525	67	64	58	1	0	551^2	612	22	249	158	15.0	4.71	96	.279	.368	61	.256	1	-22	-12	-2	-1.1

● BOB FRIEND Friend, Robert Bartmess "Warrior" b: 11/24/30, Lafayette, Ind. BR/TR, 6', 190 lbs. Deb: 4/28/51

YEAR TM/L	W	L	PCT	G	GS	CG	SH	SV	IP	H	HR	BB	SO	RAT	ERA	ERA+	OAV	OOB	BH	AVG	PB	PR	/A	PD	TPI
1951 Pit-N	6	10	.375	34	22	3	1	0	149^2	173	12	68	41	14.5	4.27	99	.293	.366	4	.091	-2	-5	-1	0	-0.3
1952 Pit-N	7	17	.292	35	23	6	1	0	185	186	15	84	75	13.3	4.18	95	.258	.338	3	.058	-4	-9	-4	1	-0.7
1953 Pit-N	8	11	.421	32	24	8	0	0	170^2	193	18	57	66	13.3	4.90	91	.286	.344	7	.135	-3	-12	-8	1	-0.9
1954 Pit-N	7	12	.368	35	20	4	2	2	170^1	204	16	58	73	13.9	5.07	83	.302	.358	14	.275	5	-19	-17	-1	-1.2
1955 Pit-N	14	9	.609	44	20	9	2	2	200^1	178	18	52	98	10.4	**2.83**	**145**	.242	.294	10	.164	-2	**27**	**29**	3	3.1
1956 Pit-N★	17	17	.500	49	42	19	4	3	**314^1**	310	25	85	166	11.4	3.46	109	.258	.308	16	.165	-1	11	11	-1	1.0
1957 Pit-N	14	18	.438	40	38	17	3	0	**277**	273	28	68	143	11.1	3.38	112	.257	.303	16	.184	1	15	13	-1	1.3
1958 Pit-N★	**22**	14	.611	38	38	16	1	0	274	299	25	61	135	12.0	3.68	105	.281	.322	10	.106	-4	8	6	-0	0.2
1959 Pit-N	8	19	.296	35	35	7	2	0	234^2	267	19	52	104	12.5	4.03	96	.283	.325	12	.164	0	-2	-4	0	-0.4
1960 *Pit-N★	18	12	.600	38	37	16	4	1	275^2	266	18	45	183	10.2	3.00	125	.251	.281	6	.068	-5	23	23	0	1.9
1961 Pit-N	14	19	.424	41	35	10	1	1	236	271	16	45	108	12.2	3.85	104	.289	.324	11	.139	-3	5	4	-1	0.0
1962 Pit-N	18	14	.563	39	36	13	**5**	1	261^2	280	23	53	144	11.5	3.06	129	.273	.310	11	.121	-3	26	25	0	2.2
1963 Pit-N	17	16	.515	39	38	12	4	0	268^2	236	13	44	144	9.5	2.34	141	.233	.269	9	.105	-3	28	28	-1	2.8
1964 Pit-N	13	18	.419	35	35	13	3	0	240^1	253	10	50	128	11.5	3.33	105	.271	.310	5	.070	-3	5	5	2	0.4
1965 Pit-N	8	12	.400	34	34	8	2	0	222	221	17	47	74	11.2	3.24	108	.260	.305	3	.042	-5	7	7	0	0.1
1966 NY-A	1	4	.200	12	8	0	0	0	44^2	61	2	9	22	14.1	4.84	69	.330	.361	0	.000	-1	-7	-7	1	-0.8
NY-N	5	8	.385	22	12	2	1	1	86	101	11	16	30	12.3	4.40	83	.289	.322	1	.034	-3	-8	-7	-2	-1.2

YEAR	TM/L	W	L	PCT	G	GS	CG	SH	SV	IP	H	HR	BB	SO	RAT	ERA	ERA+	OAV	OOB	BH	AVG	PB	PR	/A	PD	TPI
Total	16	197	230	.461	602	497	163	36	11	3611	3772	286	894	1734	11.7	3.58	107	.269	.315	138	.121	-36	94	100	2	7.5
● PETE FRIES	Fries, Peter Martin b: 10/30/1857, Scranton, Pa. d: 7/30/37, Chicago, Ill. BL/TL, 5′8″, 160 lbs. Deb: 8/10/1883 ♦																									
1883	Col-a	0	3	.000	3	3	3	0	0	25	34	1	14	7	17.3	6.48	48	.305	.382	3	.300	1	-9	-9	0	-0.7
● JOHN FRILL	Frill, John Edmond b: 4/3/1879, Reading, Pa. d: 9/28/18, Westerly, R.I. BR/TL, 5′10.5″, 170 lbs. Deb: 4/16/10																									
1910	NY-A	2	2	.500	10	5	3	1	1	48^1	55	1	5	27	11.4	4.47	59	.289	.311	2	.111	-1	-10	-10	0	-1.1
1912	StL-A	0	1	.000	3	3	0	0	0	4^1	16	1	1	2	37.4	20.77	16	.571	.600	1	.500	0	-8	-8	0	-0.7
	Cin-N	1	0	1.000	3	2	0	0	0	15	19	0	1	4	13.2	6.00	56	.345	.379	1	.250	0	-4	-4	0	-0.4
Total	2	3	3	.500	16	10	3	1	1	67^2	90	2	7	33	13.4	5.85	49	.330	.356	4	.167	-1	-23	-22	0	-2.2
● DANNY FRISELLA	Frisella, Daniel Vincent "Bear" b: 3/4/46, San Francisco, Cal. d: 1/1/77, Phoenix, Ariz. BL/TR, 6′, 195 lbs. Deb: 7/27/67																									
1967	NY-N	1	6	.143	14	11	0	0	0	74	68	6	33	51	12.3	3.41	100	.249	.330	2	.087	-1	-0	-0	-0	-0.1
1968	NY-N	2	4	.333	19	4	0	0	2	50^2	53	5	17	47	12.4	3.91	77	.270	.329	1	.083	-1	-5	-5	0	-0.6
1969	NY-N	0	0	—	3	0	0	0	0	4^2	8	1	3	5	21.2	7.71	47	.381	.458	0	.000	-0	-2	-2	-0	-0.2
1970	NY-N	8	3	.727	30	1	0	0	1	65^2	49	4	34	54	11.4	3.02	133	.204	.303	4	.308	1	8	7	-0	0.8
1971	NY-N	8	5	.615	53	0	0	0	12	90^2	76	6	30	93	10.8	1.99	172	.227	.296	3	.231	1	15	14	1	1.7
1972	NY-N	5	8	.385	39	0	0	0	9	67^1	63	8	20	46	11.1	3.34	101	.243	.297	2	.286	0	1	0	1	0.2
1973	Atl-N	1	2	.333	42	0	0	0	8	45	40	5	23	27	12.8	4.20	94	.241	.337	1	.500	0	-3	-1	-0	-0.1
1974	Atl-N	3	4	.429	36	1	0	0	6	41^2	37	4	28	27	14.0	5.18	73	.240	.357	0	.000	0	-7	-7	-0	-0.7
1975	SD-N	1	6	.143	65	0	0	0	9	97^2	86	7	51	67	12.8	3.13	111	.242	.340	1	.200	0	5	4	-0	0.4
1976	StL-N	0	0	—	18	0	0	0	1	22^2	19	3	13	11	12.7	3.97	89	.232	.337	0	.000	-0	-1	-1	0	-0.1
	Mil-A	5	2	.714	32	0	0	0	9	49^1	30	4	34	43	11.9	2.74	128	.175	.316	0	—	0	4	4	0	0.5
Total	10	34	40	.459	351	17	0	0	57	609^1	529	53	286	471	12.1	3.32	106	.235	.323	14	.179	1	14	13	0	1.8
● EMIL FRISK	Frisk, John Emil b: 10/15/1874, Kalkaska, Mich. d: 1/27/22, Seattle, Wash. BL/TR, 6′1″, 190 lbs. Deb: 9/02/1899 ♦																									
1899	Cin-N	3	6	.333	9	9	9	0	0	68^1	81	1	17	17	13.7	3.95	99	.294	.349	7	.280	1	-1	-0	-0	0.1
1901	Det-A	5	4	.556	11	7	6	0	0	74^2	94	1	26	22	14.7	4.34	89	.304	.361	15	.313	2	-6	-4	3	0.1
Total	2	8	10	.444	20	16	15	0	0	143	175	2	43	39	14.2	4.15	94	.299	.355	135	.267	3	-6	-4	2	0.2
● CHARLIE FRITZ	Fritz, Charles Cornelius b: 6/18/1882, Mobile, Ala. d: 7/30/43, Mobile, Ala. TL , Deb: 10/05/07																									
1907	Phi-A	0	0	—	1	1	0	0	0	3	0	0	3	1	12.0	3.00	87	.000	.321	0	.000	-0	-0	-0	-0	-0.1
● BILL FROATS	Froats, William John b: 10/20/30, New York, N.Y. BL/TL, 6′, 180 lbs. Deb: 4/22/55																									
1955	Det-A	0	0	—	1	0	0	0	0	2	0	0	2	0	9.0	0.00	—	.000	.333	0	—	0	1	1	0	0.1
● SAM FROCK	Frock, Samuel William b: 12/23/1882, Baltimore, Md. d: 11/3/25, Baltimore, Md. BR/TR, 6′, 168 lbs. Deb: 9/21/07																									
1907	Bos-N	1	2	.333	5	3	3	1	0	33^1	28	1	11	12	11.1	2.97	86	.243	.320	1	.071	-1	-2	-2	-2	-0.5
1909	Pit-N	2	1	.667	8	4	3	0	1	36^1	44	0	4	11	12.6	2.48	110	.299	.331	2	.143	-1	1	1	0	0.1
1910	Pit-N	0	0	—	1	0	0	0	0	2	2	0	2	1	22.5	4.50	69	.400	.625	0	—	0	-0	-0	0	0.0
	Bos-N	12	19	.387	45	29	13	2	2	255^1	245	8	91	170	12.0	3.21	104	.262	.330	16	.190	-3	-5	3	1	0.2
	Yr	12	19	.387	46	29	13	2	2	257^1	247	8	93	171	12.0	3.22	103	.263	.332	16	.190	-3	-5	3	2	0.2
1911	Bos-N	0	1	.000	4	1	1	0	0	16	29	0	5	8	19.7	5.63	68	.426	.473	1	.200	-0	-4	-3	0	-0.3
Total	4	15	23	.395	63	37	20	3	3	343	348	9	113	202	12.4	3.23	99	.274	.339	20	.171	-5	-11	-1	0	-0.5
● TODD FROHWIRTH	Frohwirth, Todd Gerard b: 9/28/62, Milwaukee, Wis. BR/TR, 6′4″, 190 lbs. Deb: 8/10/87																									
1987	Phi-N	1	0	1.000	10	0	0	0	0	11	12	0	2	9	11.5	0.00	—	.293	.326	0	.000	-0	5	5	0	0.5
1988	Phi-N	1	2	.333	12	0	0	0	0	12	16	2	11	11	20.3	8.25	43	.327	.450	0	—	0	-6	-6	1	-0.6
1989	Phi-N	1	0	1.000	45	0	0	0	0	62^2	56	4	18	39	11.1	3.59	99	.240	.303	0	.000	-0	-1	-0	-0	-0.1
1990	Phi-N	0	1	.000	5	0	0	0	0	1	3	0	6	1	81.0	18.00	21	.500	.750	0	—	0	-2	-2	0	-0.2
1991	Bal-A	7	3	.700	51	0	0	0	3	96^1	64	2	29	77	8.8	1.87	211	.190	.256	0	—	0	**24**	**22**	3	3.0
1992	Bal-A	4	3	.571	65	0	0	0	4	106	97	4	41	58	12.0	2.46	159	.247	.323	0	—	0	17	17	3	2.0
Total	6	14	9	.609	188	0	0	0	7	289	248	12	107	195	11.3	2.71	142	.234	.309	0	.000	-0	38	36	6	4.6
● ART FROMME	Fromme, Arthur Henry b: 9/3/1883, Quincy, Ill. d: 8/24/56, Los Angeles, Cal. BR/TR, 6′, 178 lbs. Deb: 9/14/06																									
1906	StL-N	1	2	.333	3	3	3	1	0	25	19	0	10	11	10.8	1.44	183	.221	.309	2	.222	0	3	3	1	0.5
1907	StL-N	5	13	.278	23	16	13	2	0	145^2	138	3	67	67	12.9	2.90	86	.256	.343	10	.182	0	-7	-6	0	-0.6
1908	StL-N	5	13	.278	20	14	9	2	0	116	102	1	50	62	11.9	2.72	87	.218	.296	5	.139	-1	-5	-5	-0	-0.7
1909	Cin-N	19	13	.594	37	34	22	4	2	279^1	195	2	101	126	9.6	1.90	137	.201	.278	18	.191	2	22	22	2	3.0
1910	Cin-N	3	4	.429	11	5	1	0	0	49^1	44	2	39	10	15.3	2.92	100	.260	.402	2	.133	-1	1	-0	0	-0.1
1911	Cin-N	10	11	.476	38	26	11	1	0	208	190	8	79	107	12.3	3.46	96	.248	.331	14	.189	-1	-1	-3	1	-0.4
1912	Cin-N	16	18	.471	43	37	23	3	0	296	285	7	88	120	11.7	2.74	123	.260	.321	9	.087	-9	22	21	-0	1.1
1913	Cin-N	1	4	.200	9	7	2	0	0	56	55	1	21	24	12.7	4.18	78	.274	.351	3	.143	-0	-6	-6	-1	-0.7
	NY-N	11	6	.647	26	13	3	0	0	112^1	112	5	29	50	11.5	4.01	78	.260	.310	6	.171	-0	-10	-11	1	-1.0
	Yr	12	10	.545	35	20	5	0	0	168^1	167	6	50	74	11.7	4.06	78	.263	.319	9	.161	-1	-16	-17	1	-1.7
1914	NY-N	9	5	.643	38	12	3	1	2	138	142	7	44	57	12.6	3.20	83	.283	.349	7	.226	1	-6	-8	3	-0.4
1915	NY-N	0	1	.000	4	1	0	0	0	12^1	15	1	2	4	12.4	5.84	44	.306	.333	1	.333	1	-4	-4	0	-0.4
Total	10	80	90	.471	252	168	90	14	4	1438	1297	37	530	638	11.7	2.90	100	.246	.320	77	.162	-8	8	2	7	0.3
● DAVE FROST	Frost, Carl David b: 11/17/52, Long Beach, Cal. BR/TR, 6′6″, 235 lbs. Deb: 9/11/77																									
1977	Chi-A	1	1	.500	4	3	0	0	0	23^2	30	0	3	15	12.9	3.04	134	.323	.351	0	—	0	3	3	-0	0.3
1978	Cal-A	5	4	.556	11	10	2	1	0	80^1	71	6	24	30	10.9	2.58	140	.240	.301	0	—	0	11	9	1	1.5
1979	*Cal-A	16	10	.615	36	33	12	2	1	239^1	226	17	77	107	11.6	3.57	114	.251	.314	0	—	0	17	13	-1	1.2
1980	Cal-A	4	8	.333	15	15	2	0	0	78^1	97	8	21	28	13.8	5.29	74	.308	.355	0	—	0	-11	-12	-1	-1.2
1981	Cal-A	1	8	.111	12	9	0	0	0	47^1	44	3	19	16	12.2	5.51	66	.250	.327	0	—	0	-10	-10	0	-1.0
1982	KC-A	6	6	.500	21	14	0	0	0	81^2	103	7	30	26	15.0	5.51	74	.313	.376	0	—	0	-13	-13	-1	-1.4
Total	6	33	37	.471	99	84	16	3	1	550^2	571	41	174	222	12.4	4.10	96	.271	.330	0	—	0	-3	-9	-3	-0.6
● JOHNSON FRY	Fry, Johnson "Jay" b: 11/21/01, Huntington, W.Va. d: 4/7/59, Carmi, Ill. BR/TR, 6′1″, 150 lbs. Deb: 8/24/23																									
1923	Cle-A	0	0	—	1	0	0	0	0	3^2	6	0	4	0	24.5	12.27	32	.353	.476	1	1.000	1	-3	-3	-0	-0.2
● CHARLIE FRYE	Frye, Charles Andrew b: 7/17/14, Hickory, N.C. d: 5/25/45, Hickory, N.C. BR/TR, 6′1″, 175 lbs. Deb: 7/28/40																									
1940	Phi-N	0	6	.000	15	5	1	0	0	50^1	58	3	26	18	15.0	4.65	84	.291	.373	5	.263	1	-4	-4	-1	-0.3
● WOODIE FRYMAN	Fryman, Woodrow Thompson b: 4/15/40, Ewing, Ky. BR/TL, 6′2″, 205 lbs. Deb: 4/15/66																									
1966	Pit-N	12	9	.571	36	28	9	3	1	181^2	182	13	47	105	11.4	3.81	94	.261	.309	10	.159	-1	-4	-5	-2	-0.8
1967	Pit-N	3	8	.273	28	18	3	1	1	113^1	121	12	44	74	13.4	4.05	83	.276	.348	4	.118	-1	-9	-9	2	-0.8
1968	Phi-N☆	12	14	.462	34	32	10	5	0	213^2	198	12	64	151	11.3	2.78	108	.246	.306	6	.085	-2	5	5	-1	0.2
1969	Phi-N	12	15	.444	36	35	10	1	0	228^1	243	15	89	150	13.5	4.41	80	.270	.343	9	.118	-2	-21	-22	-1	-2.4
1970	Phi-N	8	6	.571	27	20	4	3	0	127^2	122	11	43	97	11.7	4.09	98	.253	.315	5	.128	-2	-1	-1	-0	-0.3
1971	Phi-N	10	7	.588	37	17	3	2	2	149^1	133	7	46	104	11.0	3.38	104	.242	.304	7	.189	0	1	2	2	0.5
1972	Phi-N	4	10	.286	23	17	3	2	1	119^2	131	15	39	69	12.9	4.36	82	.279	.337	5	.152	1	-12	-10	1	-0.9
	*Det-A	10	3	.769	16	14	6	1	0	113^2	93	6	31	72	10.4	2.06	153	.220	.285	5	.125	-2	13	14	-1	1.3
1973	Det-A	6	13	.316	34	29	1	0	0	169^2	200	23	64	119	14.2	5.36	76	.294	.357	0	—	0	-29	-24	1	-2.4
1974	Det-A	6	9	.400	27	22	4	1	0	141^2	120	16	67	92	12.1	4.32	88	.233	.326	0	—	0	-11	-8	-1	-1.0
1975	Mon-N	9	12	.429	38	20	7	3	3	157	141	10	68	118	12.3	3.32	115	.239	.323	10	.204	1	5	9	1	1.2

YEAR	TM/L	W	L	PCT	G	GS	CG	SH	SV	IP	H	HR	BB	SO	RAT	ERA	ERA+	OAV	OOB	BH	AVG	PB	PR	/A	PD	TPI
1976	Mon-N☆	13	13	.500	34	32	4	2	2	216^{1}	218	14	76	123	12.6	3.37	110	.263	.332	7	.109	-3	3	8	-0	0.5
1977	Cin-N	5	5	.500	17	12	0	0	1	75^{1}	83	13	45	57	15.5	5.38	73	.292	.393	7	.318	2	-12	-12	1	-1.0
1978	Chi-N	2	4	.333	13	9	0	0	0	55^{2}	64	6	37	28	16.3	5.17	78	.309	.414	1	.063	-1	-10	-7	1	-0.7
	Mon-N	5	7	.417	19	17	4	3	1	94^{2}	93	4	37	53	12.6	3.61	98	.260	.334	2	.059	-2	-0	-1	-0	-0.4
	Yr	7	11	.389	32	26	4	3	1	150^{1}	157	10	74	81	14.0	4.19	89	.276	.362	3	.060	-3	-10	-8	1	-1.1
1979	Mon-N	3	6	.333	44	0	0	0	10	58	52	4	22	44	11.9	2.79	131	.248	.328	0	.000	-1	6	6	1	0.6
1980	Mon-N	7	4	.636	61	0	0	0	17	80	61	1	30	59	10.5	2.25	158	.209	.287	2	.167	-0	12	12	-1	1.2
1981	*Mon-N	5	3	.625	35	0	0	0	7	43	38	1	14	25	11.1	1.88	185	.247	.314	2	.667	1	8	8	0	1.0
1982	Mon-N	9	4	.692	60	0	0	0	12	69^{2}	66	3	26	46	12.0	3.75	97	.259	.330	2	.222	0	-1	-1	1	0.1
1983	Mon-N	0	3	.000	6	0	0	0	0	3	8	1	1	1	27.0	21.00	17	.571	.600	0	—	0	-6	-6	0	-0.5
Total	18	141	155	.476	625	322	68	27	58	2411^{1}	2367	187	890	1587	12.4	3.77	96	.259	.329	84	.138	-12	-63	-43	4	-4.6
● CHARLIE FUCHS	Fuchs, Charles Thomas b: 11/18/13, Union City, N.J. d: 6/10/69, Weehawken, N.J. BB/TR, 5'8", 168 lbs. Deb: 4/17/42																									
1942	Det-A	3	3	.500	9	4	1	1	0	36^{2}	43	5	19	15	15.5	6.63	60	.285	.368	1	.077	-1	-12	-11	1	-1.1
1943	Phi-N	2	7	.222	17	9	4	1	1	77^{2}	76	4	34	12	13.1	4.29	79	.266	.350	2	.091	-2	-8	-8	-1	-1.1
	StL-A	0	0	—	13	0	0	0	0	35^{2}	42	4	11	9	13.6	4.04	82	.294	.348	0	.000	-1	-3	-3	-0	-0.4
1944	Bro-N	1	0	1.000	8	0	0	0	0	15^{2}	25	2	9	5	20.1	5.74	62	.347	.427	0	.000	0	-4	-4	1	-0.3
Total	3	6	10	.375	47	13	5	2	1	165^{2}	186	15	73	41	14.4	4.89	72	.285	.363	3	.070	-4	-27	-25	0	-2.9
● MIGUEL FUENTES	Fuentes, Miguel (Pinet) b: 5/10/46, Loiza, P.R. d: 1/29/70, Loiza, P.R. BR/TR, 6', 160 lbs. Deb: 9/01/69																									
1969	Sea-A	1	3	.250	8	4	1	0	0	26	29	1	16	14	15.6	5.19	70	.284	.381	2	.333	0	-5	-5	-1	-0.5
● OSCAR FUHR	Fuhr, Oscar Lawrence b: 8/22/1893, Defiance, Mo. d: 3/27/75, Dallas, Tex. BL/TL, 6'0.5", 176 lbs. Deb: 4/19/21																									
1921	Chi-N	0	0	—	1	0	0	0	0	4	11	1	0	2	24.8	9.00	42	.500	.500	0	.000	-0	-2	-2	0	-0.2
1924	Bos-A	3	6	.333	23	10	4	1	0	80^{1}	100	1	39	30	16.1	5.94	74	.310	.392	4	.182	-1	-15	-14	1	-1.3
1925	Bos-A	0	6	.000	39	6	0	0	0	91^{1}	138	7	30	27	16.9	6.60	69	.364	.415	5	.250	0	-22	-21	1	-1.8
Total	3	3	12	.200	63	16	4	1	0	175^{2}	249	9	69	59	16.7	6.35	70	.344	.407	9	.209	-1	-40	-37	2	-3.3
● JOHN FULGHAM	Fulgham, John Thomas b: 6/9/56, St.Louis, Mo. BR/TR, 6'2", 205 lbs. Deb: 6/19/79																									
1979	StL-N	10	6	.625	20	19	10	2	0	146	123	10	26	75	9.4	2.53	149	.227	.267	6	.143	1	20	20	-2	2.1
1980	StL-N	4	6	.400	15	14	4	1	0	85^{1}	66	7	32	48	10.4	3.38	109	.219	.296	0	.000	-3	2	3	-0	0.0
Total	2	14	12	.538	35	33	14	3	0	231^{1}	189	17	58	123	9.8	2.84	132	.224	.277	6	.087	-2	22	23	-2	2.1
● ED FULLER	Fuller, Edward Ashton b: 3/22/1868, Washington, D.C. d: 3/16/35, Hyattsville, Md. BR/TR, 6', 158 lbs. Deb: 7/11/1886																									
1886	Was-N	0	1	.000	2	1	1	0	0	13	15	0	5	3	13.8	6.92	47	.375	.444	1	.143	-0	-5	-5	-0	-0.5
● CURT FULLERTON	Fullerton, Curtis Hooper b: 9/13/1898, Ellsworth, Me. d: 1/2/75, Winthrop, Mass. BL/TR, 6', 162 lbs. Deb: 4/14/21																									
1921	Bos-A	0	1	.000	4	1	1	0	0	15^{1}	22	3	10	4	19.4	8.80	48	.355	.452	0	.000	-0	-8	-8	-1	-0.7
1922	Bos-A	1	4	.200	31	3	0	0	0	64^{1}	70	4	35	17	15.4	5.46	75	.290	.391	2	.250	1	-10	-10	1	-0.7
1923	Bos-A	2	15	.118	37	15	6	0	1	143^{1}	167	9	71	37	15.3	5.09	81	.300	.385	11	.297	2	-18	-16	-2	-1.5
1924	Bos-A	7	12	.368	33	20	9	0	2	152	166	1	73	33	14.5	4.32	101	.283	.368	3	.071	-4	-2	1	-0	-0.3
1925	Bos-A	0	3	.000	4	2	0	0	0	22^{2}	22	1	9	3	13.1	3.18	143	.259	.344	2	.200	-0	3	3	1	0.4
1933	Bos-A	0	2	.000	6	2	2	0	0	25^{1}	36	1	13	10	17.8	8.53	51	.364	.442	2	.222	0	-12	-12	-1	-1.0
Total	6	10	37	.213	115	43	18	0	3	423	483	19	211	104	15.2	5.11	83	.296	.384	20	.182	-1	-46	-40	-1	-3.8
● CHICK FULMER	Fulmer, Charles John b: 2/12/1851, Philadelphia, Pa. d: 2/15/40, Philadelphia, Pa. BR/TR, 6', 158 lbs. Deb: 8/23/1871 FU♦																									
1873	Phi-n	0	0	—	2	0	0	0	0	5	7	0	1	0	14.4	3.60	92	.304	.333	66	.280	0	-0	-0		0.0
● CHRIS FULMER	Fulmer, Christopher b: 7/4/1858, Tamaqua, Pa. d: 11/9/31, Tamaqua, Pa. BR/TR, 5'8", 165 lbs. Deb: 8/04/1884 ♦																									
1886	Bal-a	0	0	—	1	0	0	0	0	2	2	0	1	0	13.5	4.50	76	.250	.333	66	.244	0	-0	-0	-0	0.0
● BILL FULTON	Fulton, William David b: 10/22/63, Pittsburgh, Pa. BR/TR, 6'3", 195 lbs. Deb: 9/12/87																									
1987	NY-A	1	0	1.000	3	0	0	0	0	4^{2}	9	4	1	2	21.2	11.57	38	.409	.458	0	—	0	-4	-4	0	-0.3
● FRANK FUNK	Funk, Franklin Ray b: 8/30/35, Washington, D.C. BR/TR, 6', 175 lbs. Deb: 9/03/60 C																									
1960	Cle-A	4	2	.667	9	0	0	0	1	31^{2}	27	3	9	18	10.2	1.99	188	.248	.305	1	.111	-0	7	6	0	0.6
1961	Cle-A	11	11	.500	56	0	0	0	11	92^{1}	79	9	31	64	11.1	3.31	119	.234	.306	1	.059	-1	7	6	0	0.5
1962	Cle-A	2	1	.667	47	0	0	0	6	80^{2}	62	11	32	49	10.9	3.24	120	.212	.298	1	.067	-1	7	6	-0	0.4
1963	Mil-N	3	3	.500	25	0	0	0	0	43^{2}	42	3	13	19	11.5	2.68	120	.258	.316	0	.000	-0	3	3	-1	0.2
Total	4	20	17	.541	137	0	0	0	18	248^{1}	210	26	85	150	11.0	3.01	125	.233	.305	3	.067	-3	23	21	-1	1.7
● TOM FUNK	Funk, Thomas James b: 3/13/62, Kansas City, Mo. BL/TL, 6'2", 210 lbs. Deb: 7/24/86																									
1986	Hou-N	0	0	—	8	0	0	0	0	8^{1}	10	1	6	2	17.3	6.48	56	.286	.390	0	.000	-0	-3	-3	0	-0.3
● EDDIE FUSSELBACK	Fusselback, Edward L. b: 7/17/1856, Philadelphia, Pa. d: 4/14/26, Philadelphia, Pa. 5'6", 156 lbs. Deb: 5/03/1882 ♦																									
1882	StL-a	1	2	.333	4	2	2	0	**1**	23	34	0	2	3	14.1	4.70	60	.322	.335	31	.228	0	-5	-5	-1	-0.5
● FRED FUSSELL	Fussell, Frederick Morris "Moonlight Ace" b: 10/7/1895, Sheridan, Mo. d: 10/23/66, Syracuse, N.Y. BL/TL, 5'10", 155 lbs. Deb: 9/23/22																									
1922	Chi-N	1	1	.500	3	2	1	0	0	19	24	0	8	4	15.2	4.74	89	.333	.400	0	.000	-1	-1	-1	0	-0.1
1923	Chi-N	3	5	.375	28	2	1	0	3	76^{1}	90	2	31	38	14.6	5.54	72	.298	.369	4	.200	-0	-13	-13	0	-1.2
1928	Pit-N	8	9	.471	28	20	9	2	1	159^{2}	183	6	41	43	12.7	3.61	112	.295	.340	7	.121	-3	7	8	-3	0.2
1929	Pit-N	2	2	.500	21	3	0	0	1	39^{2}	68	8	8	18	17.5	8.62	55	.389	.418	4	.250	2	-17	-17	-0	-1.3
Total	4	14	17	.452	80	27	11	2	5	294^{2}	365	16	88	103	14.0	4.86	85	.312	.363	15	.150	-2	-25	-23	-2	-2.4
● FRANK GABLER	Gabler, Frank Harold "The Great Gabbo" b: 11/6/11, E.Highlands, Cal. d: 11/1/67, Long Beach, Cal. BR/TR, 6'1", 175 lbs. Deb: 4/19/35																									
1935	NY-N	2	1	.667	26	1	0	0	0	60	79	6	20	24	14.9	5.70	68	.315	.365	2	.125	-1	-11	-12	0	-1.2
1936	*NY-N	9	8	.529	43	14	5	0	6	161^{2}	170	11	34	46	11.5	3.12	125	.274	.315	10	.208	2	16	14	-1	1.4
1937	NY-N	0	0	—	6	0	0	0	0	9	20	1	2	3	22.0	10.00	39	.455	.478	0	—	0	-6	-6	-0	-0.6
	Bos-N	4	7	.364	19	9	2	1	2	76	84	7	16	19	11.8	5.09	70	.283	.319	4	.182	0	-10	-13	-0	-1.2
	Yr	4	7	.364	25	9	2	1	2	85	104	8	18	22	12.9	5.61	64	.305	.340	4	.182	0	-16	-19	-0	-1.8
1938	Bos-N	0	0	—	1	0	0	0	0	0^{1}	3	0	1	0	108.0	81.00	4	1.000	1.000	0	—	0	-3	-3	0	-0.3
	Chi-A	1	7	.125	18	7	3	0	0	69^{1}	101	12	34	17	17.7	9.09	54	.348	.418	5	.238	0	-33	-32	-1	-2.8
Total	4	16	23	.410	113	31	10	1	8	376^{1}	457	37	107	109	13.6	5.26	76	.303	.351	21	.196	1	-47	-53	-2	-4.7
● GABE GABLER	Gabler, John Richard b: 10/2/30, Kansas City, Mo. BB/TR, 6'2", 165 lbs. Deb: 9/18/59																									
1959	NY-A	1	1	.500	3	1	0	0	0	19^{1}	21	1	10	11	14.9	2.79	130	.284	.376	0	.000	-1	2	2	0	0.1
1960	NY-A	3	3	.500	21	4	0	0	1	52	46	2	32	19	13.5	4.15	86	.242	.351	1	.091	-0	-2	-3	0	-0.4
1961	Was-A	3	8	.273	29	9	0	0	4	92^{2}	104	5	37	33	13.8	4.86	83	.283	.351	5	.200	1	-9	-9	1	-0.6
Total	3	7	12	.368	53	14	0	0	5	164	171	8	79	63	13.8	4.39	87	.271	.354	6	.143	-0	-8	-10	1	-0.9
● KEN GABLES	Gables, Kenneth Harlin "Coral" b: 1/31/19, Walnut Grove, Mo. d: 1/2/60, Walnut Grove, Mo. BR/TR, 5'11", 210 lbs. Deb: 4/18/45																									
1945	Pit-N	11	7	.611	29	16	6	0	1	138^{2}	139	5	46	49	12.3	4.15	95	.256	.319	4	.103	-3	-5	-3	-2	-0.8
1946	Pit-N	2	4	.333	32	7	0	0	1	100^{2}	113	3	52	39	14.8	5.27	67	.281	.365	6	.250	2	-21	-20	-2	-2.0
1947	Pit-N	0	0	—	1	0	0	0	0	0^{1}	3	1	0	0	81.0	54.00	8	.750	.750	0	—	0	-2	-2	-0	-0.2
Total	3	13	11	.542	62	23	6	0	2	239^{2}	255	9	98	88	13.4	4.69	80	.269	.340	10	.159	-1	-28	-25	-4	-3.0

YEAR TM/L	W	L	PCT	G	GS	CG	SH	SV	IP	H	HR	BB	SO	RAT	ERA	ERA+	OAV	OOB	BH	AVG	PB	PR	/A	PD	TPI

● **JOHN GADDY** Gaddy, John Wilson "Sheriff" b: 2/5/14, Wadesboro, N.C. d: 5/3/66, Albemarle, N.C. BR/TR, 6'0.5", 182 lbs. Deb: 9/27/38

| 1938 Bro-N | 2 | 0 | 1.000 | 2 | 2 | 1 | 0 | 0 | 13 | 13 | 0 | 4 | 3 | 12.5 | 0.69 | 564 | .255 | .321 | 0 | .000 | -1 | 4 | 5 | -0 | 0.4 |

● **BRENT GAFF** Gaff, Brent Allen b: 10/5/58, Fort Wayne, Ind. BR/TR, 6'2", 200 lbs. Deb: 7/07/82

1982 NY-N	0	3	.000	7	5	0	0	0	31²	41	3	10	14	14.8	4.55	80	.323	.377	0	.000	-0	-3	-3	-0	-0.4
1983 NY-N	1	0	1.000	4	0	0	0	0	10¹	18	0	1	4	16.5	6.10	59	.360	.373	0	.000	-0	-3	-3	-0	-0.3
1984 NY-N	3	2	.600	47	0	0	0	1	84¹	77	4	36	42	12.2	3.63	97	.247	.327	-1	.000	-1	-0	-1	-0	-0.1
Total 3	4	5	.444	58	5	0	0	1	126¹	136	7	47	60	13.2	4.06	88	.278	.344	-1	.000	-1	-7	-7	0	-0.8

● **CHARLIE GAGUS** Gagus, Charles Frederick b: 3/25/1862, San Francisco, Cal d: 1/16/17, San Francisco, Cal Deb: 8/07/1884

| 1884 Was-U | 10 | 9 | .526 | 23 | 21 | 19 | 0 | 0 | 177¹ | 143 | 2 | 38 | 156 | 9.2 | 2.54 | 117 | .206 | .247 | 38 | .247 | 1 | 9 | 8 | 1 | 0.9 |

● **NEMO GAINES** Gaines, Willard Roland b: 12/23/1897, Alexandria, Va. d: 1/26/79, Warrenton, Va. BL/TL, 6', 180 lbs. Deb: 6/26/21

| 1921 Was-A | 0 | 0 | — | 4 | 0 | 0 | 0 | 0 | 4² | 5 | 0 | 2 | 1 | 13.5 | 0.00 | — | .294 | .368 | 0 | .000 | -0 | 2 | 2 | -0 | 0.2 |

● **FRED GAISER** Gaiser, Frederick Jacob b: 8/31/1885, Stuttgart, Germany d: 10/9/18, Trenton, N.J. Deb: 9/03/08

| 1908 StL-N | 0 | 0 | — | 1 | 0 | 0 | 0 | 0 | 2¹ | 4 | 0 | 3 | 2 | 27.0 | 7.71 | 31 | .444 | .583 | 0 | .000 | -0 | -1 | -1 | 0 | -0.1 |

● **DAN GAKELER** Gakeler, Daniel Michael b: 5/1/64, Mt.Holly, N.J. BR/TR, 6'6", 215 lbs. Deb: 6/09/91

| 1991 Det-A | 1 | 4 | .200 | 31 | 7 | 0 | 0 | 2 | 73² | 73 | 5 | 39 | 43 | 13.8 | 5.74 | 72 | .256 | .348 | 0 | — | 0 | -13 | -13 | 0 | -1.3 |

● **BOB GALASSO** Galasso, Robert Joseph b: 1/13/52, Connellsville, Pa. BL/TR, 6'1", 205 lbs. Deb: 7/24/77

1977 Sea-A	0	6	.000	11	7	0	0	0	35	57	8	8	21	17.5	9.00	46	.365	.407	0	—	0	-19	-19	-0	-1.7
1979 Mil-A	3	1	.750	31	0	0	0	3	51¹	64	5	26	28	15.8	4.38	95	.299	.375	0	—	0	-1	-1	-0	-0.2
1981 Sea-A	1	1	.500	13	1	0	0	1	31²	32	2	13	14	12.8	4.83	80	.264	.336	0	—	0	-4	-3	-0	-0.4
Total 3	4	8	.333	55	8	0	0	4	118	153	15	47	63	15.5	5.87	69	.312	.375	0	—	0	-24	-24	-1	-2.3

● **MILT GALATZER** Galatzer, Milton b: 5/4/07, Chicago, Il.. d: 1/29/76, San Francisco, Cal BL/TL, 5'10", 168 lbs. Deb: 6/25/33 ◆

| 1936 Cle-A | 0 | 0 | — | 1 | 0 | 0 | 0 | 0 | 6 | 7 | 0 | 5 | 3 | 18.0 | 4.50 | 112 | .292 | .414 | 23 | .237 | 0 | 0 | 0 | 0 | 0.0 |

● **RICH GALE** Gale, Richard Blackwell b: 1/19/54, Littleton, N.H. BR/TR, 6'7", 225 lbs. Deb: 4/30/78 C

1978 KC-A	14	8	.636	31	30	9	3	0	192¹	171	10	100	88	12.8	3.09	124	.244	.340	0	—	0	14	16	-2	1.5
1979 KC-A	9	10	.474	34	31	2	1	0	181²	197	19	99	103	14.9	5.65	75	.278	.369	0	—	0	-29	-28	-1	-2.7
1980 *KC-A	13	9	.591	32	28	6	1	1	190²	169	16	78	97	11.8	3.92	103	.239	.316	0	—	0	2	3	-1	0.2
1981 KC-A	6	6	.500	19	15	2	0	0	101²	107	14	38	47	13.0	5.40	67	.270	.336	0	—	0	-20	-20	-2	-2.2
1982 SF-N	7	14	.333	33	29	2	0	0	170¹	193	9	81	102	14.7	4.23	85	.294	.376	6	.125	-1	-12	-12	-1	-1.1
1983 Cin-N	4	6	.400	33	7	0	0	1	89²	103	8	43	53	14.8	5.82	65	.286	.364	3	.150	-1	-22	-20	-1	-2.0
1984 Bos-A	2	3	.400	13	4	0	0	0	43²	57	6	18	28	15.7	5.56	75	.315	.380	0	—	0	-8	-7	-0	-0.7
Total 7	55	56	.495	195	144	21	5	2	970	997	82	457	518	13.7	4.54	86	.269	.351	9	.132	2	-73	-69	-5	-7.0

● **DENNY GALEHOUSE** Galehouse, Dennis Ward b: 12/7/11, Marshallville, Ohio BR/TR, 6'1", 195 lbs. Deb: 4/30/34

1934 Cle-A	0	0	—	1	0	0	0	0	1	2	0	1	0	27.0	18.00	25	.500	.600	0	—	0	-2	-1	-0	-0.1
1935 Cle-A	1	0	1.000	5	1	1	0	0	13	16	1	9	8	18.0	9.00	50	.314	.426	1	.250	-0	-7	-6	-0	-0.6
1936 Cle-A	8	7	.533	36	15	5	0	1	148¹	161	5	68	71	14.0	4.85	104	.280	.358	8	.170	-0	3	3	-2	0.1
1937 Cle-A	9	14	.391	36	29	7	0	3	200²	238	11	83	78	14.4	4.57	101	.302	.369	15	.208	-1	1	1	1	0.0
1938 Cle-A	7	8	.467	36	12	5	1	0	114	119	12	65	66	14.6	4.34	107	.275	.371	6	.154	-1	6	4	0	0.3
1939 Bos-A	9	10	.474	30	18	6	1	0	146²	160	6	52	68	13.1	4.54	104	.276	.337	2	.064	-3	3	3	0	0.0
1940 Bos-A	6	6	.500	25	20	5	0	0	120	155	10	41	53	14.7	5.18	87	.313	.366	3	.077	-4	-11	-9	1	-1.1
1941 StL-A	9	10	.474	30	24	11	2	0	190¹	183	10	68	61	12.1	3.64	118	.253	.320	13	.191	-0	11	14	1	1.4
1942 StL-A	12	12	.500	32	28	12	3	1	192¹	193	5	79	75	12.9	3.60	103	.262	.337	14	.194	1	1	2	1	0.4
1943 StL-A	11	11	.500	31	28	14	2	1	224	217	8	74	114	11.7	2.77	120	.255	.315	-3	.125	-3	13	14	-3	0.8
1944 *StL-A	9	10	.474	24	19	6	2	0	153	162	6	44	80	12.2	3.12	115	.266	.316	3	.063	-4	5	8	-2	0.2
1946 StL-A	8	12	.400	30	24	11	2	0	180	194	9	52	90	12.3	3.65	102	.273	.322	5	.091	-4	-3	-2	-0	-0.4
1947 StL-A	1	3	.250	9	4	0	0	1	32¹	42	3	16	11	16.1	6.12	63	.311	.384	-1	.000	-1	-9	-8	-0	-0.9
Bos-A	11	7	.611	21	21	11	3	0	149	150	7	34	38	11.1	3.32	117	.260	.301	5	.096	-4	6	9	-1	0.4
Yr	12	10	.545	30	25	11	3	1	181¹	192	10	50	49	12.0	3.82	102	.269	.317	5	.083	-5	-2	1	-1	-0.5
1948 Bos-A	8	8	.500	27	15	6	1	3	137¹	152	10	46	38	13.1	4.00	110	.282	.341	7	.167	-0	4	6	-2	0.4
1949 Bos-A	0	0	—	2	0	0	0	0	2	4	1	3	0	31.5	13.50	32	.400	.538	0	—	0	-2	-2	-0	-0.2
Total 15	109	118	.480	375	258	100	17	13	2004	2148	104	735	851	13.0	3.97	105	.275	.338	92	.138	-26	20	40	-8	0.7

● **DOUG GALLAGHER** Gallagher, Douglas Eugene b: 2/21/40, Fremont, Ohio BR/TL, 6'3.5", 195 lbs. Deb: 4/09/62

| 1962 Det-A | 0 | 4 | .000 | 9 | 2 | 0 | 0 | 1 | 25 | 31 | 2 | 15 | 14 | 16.6 | 4.68 | 87 | .290 | .377 | 2 | .333 | 1 | -2 | -2 | 0 | -0.1 |

● **ED GALLAGHER** Gallagher, Edward Michael "Lefty" b: 11/28/10, Dorchester, Mass. d: 12/22/81, Hyannis, Mass. BB/TL, 6'2", 197 lbs. Deb: 7/08/32

| 1932 Bos-A | 0 | 3 | .000 | 9 | 3 | 0 | 0 | 0 | 23² | 30 | 3 | 28 | 6 | 22.1 | 12.55 | 36 | .323 | .479 | 0 | .000 | -1 | -21 | -21 | 0 | -1.8 |

● **BILL GALLAGHER** Gallagher, William John b: Philadelphia, Pa. TL , Deb: 5/02/1883 ◆

1883 Bal-a	0	5	.000	7	5	4	0	0	51²	79	0	6	19	14.8	5.40	64	.330	.346	10	.164	-1	-12	-11	-1	-1.0
1884 Phi-U	1	2	.333	3	3	3	0	0	25	32	3	4	12	13.0	3.24	89	.291	.316	1	.091	-1	-1	0	-0	-0.2
Total 2	1	7	.125	10	8	7	0	0	76²	111	3	10	31	14.2	4.70	70	.318	.337	11	.138	-2	-13	-12	-1	-1.2

● **BERT GALLIA** Gallia, Melvin Allys b: 10/14/1891, Beeville, Tex. d: 3/19/76, Devine, Tex. BR/TR, 6', 165 lbs. Deb: 9/04/12

1912 Was-A	0	0	—	2	0	0	0	0	2	0	0	3	0	13.5	0.00	—	.000	.333	0	—	0	1	1	-0	0.1
1913 Was-A	1	5	.167	31	4	0	0	3	96	85	2	46	46	12.9	4.13	72	.222	.317	2	.087	-2	-13	-12	2	-1.3
1914 Was-A	0	0	—	2	0	0	0	0	6	3	0	4	4	10.5	4.50	63	.120	.241	0	.000	-1	-1	-0	-0	-0.2
1915 Was-A	17	11	.607	43	29	14	3	1	259²	220	2	64	130	10.0	2.29	130	.234	.286	14	.165	-2	19	20	-2	1.8
1916 Was-A	17	12	.586	49	31	13	1	2	283²	278	3	99	120	12.2	2.76	101	.266	.334	18	.194	1	2	1	-3	-0.2
1917 Was-A	9	13	.409	42	23	9	1	1	207²	191	1	93	84	12.5	2.99	88	.258	.344	14	.209	2	-8	-8	-1	-0.9
1918 StL-A	8	6	.571	19	17	10	1	0	124	126	1	61	48	14.0	3.48	79	.268	.359	6	.130	-3	-10	-10	-1	-1.4
1919 StL-A	12	14	.462	34	25	14	1	1	222¹	220	10	92	83	13.0	3.60	92	.264	.343	11	.153	-2	-9	-7	-2	-0.7
1920 StL-A	0	1	.000	2	1	0	0	0	3²	8	0	3	0	27.0	7.36	53	.400	.478	0	.000	-0	-1	-1	-0	-0.2
Phi-N	2	6	.250	18	5	1	0	2	72	79	2	29	35	13.9	4.50	76	.287	.362	4	.174	-1	-11	-9	-1	-1.0
Total 9	66	68	.493	242	135	61	7	10	1277	1210	21	494	550	12.3	3.14	94	.256	.331	69	.167	-7	-31	-28	-3	-4.0

● **PHIL GALLIVAN** Gallivan, Philip Joseph b: 5/29/07, Seattle, Wash. d: 11/24/69, St.Paul, Minn. BR/TR, 6', 170 lbs. Deb: 4/21/31

1931 Bro-N	0	1	.000	6	1	0	0	0	15¹	23	2	7	1	17.6	5.28	72	.354	.417	0	.000	-0	-2	-3	1	-0.2
1932 Chi-A	1	3	.250	13	3	1	0	0	33¹	49	4	24	12	20.0	7.56	57	.338	.435	3	.375	-1	-11	-12	-0	-1.0
1934 Chi-A	4	7	.364	35	7	3	0	1	126²	155	14	64	55	15.6	5.61	84	.295	.373	9	.225	1	-16	-12	-1	-1.2
Total 3	5	11	.313	54	11	4	0	1	175¹	227	20	95	68	16.6	5.95	77	.309	.389	12	.235	-1	-30	-27	-1	-2.4

● **BALVINO GALVEZ** Galvez, Balvino (Jerez) b: 3/31/64, San Pedro De Macoris, D.R. BR/TR, 6', 170 lbs. Deb: 5/07/86

| 1986 LA-N | 0 | 1 | .000 | 10 | 0 | 0 | 0 | 0 | 14 | 11 | 2 | 9 | 14 | 13.5 | 3.92 | 88 | .241 | .341 | 0 | .000 | -0 | -0 | -1 | 0 | -0.1 |

● **JIM GALVIN** Galvin, James Francis "Pud", "Gentle Jeems" or "The Little Steam Engine" b: 12/25/1856, St.Louis, Mo. d: 3/7/02, Pittsburgh, Pa. BR/TR, 5'8", 190 lbs. Deb: 5/22/1875 MUH

| 1875 StL-n | 4 | 2 | .667 | 8 | 7 | 7 | 1 | 0 | 62 | 53 | 0 | 1 | | 7.8 | 2.18 | 102 | .209 | .213 | 6 | .128 | -1 | 2 | 0 | | -0.1 |

YEAR	TM/L	W	L	PCT	G	GS	CG	SH	SV	IP	H	HR	BB	SO	RAT	ERA	ERA+	OAV	OOB	BH	AVG	PB	PR	/A	PD	TPI
1879	Buf-N	37	27	.578	66	66	65	6	0	593	585	3	31	136	9.3	2.28	115	.243	.253	66	.249	5	14	22	3	2.9
1880	Buf-N	20	35	.364	58	54	46	5	0	458^{2}	528	5	32	128	11.0	2.71	91	.273	.284	51	.212	-4	-17	-13	1	-1.4
1881	Buf-N	28	24	.538	56	53	48	5	0	474	546	4	46	136	11.2	2.37	117	.274	.291	50	.212	-1	21	21	7	2.6
1882	Buf-N	28	23	.549	52	51	48	3	0	445^{1}	476	8	40	162	10.4	3.17	93	.256	.272	44	.214	-5	-13	-12	1	-1.5
1883	Buf-N	46	29	.613	**76**	75	**72**	**5**	0	**656**^{1}	676	9	50	279	10.0	2.72	117	.251	.265	71	.220	-4	31	34	-0	2.5
1884	Buf-N	46	22	.676	72	72	71	**12**	0	636^{1}	566	23	63	369	8.9	1.99	158	.227	.246	49	.179	-14	70	82	7	7.1
1885	Buf-N	13	19	.406	33	32	31	3	1	284	356	8	37	93	12.5	4.09	73	.292	.313	23	.189	-2	-40	-35	4	-2.9
	Pit-a	3	7	.300	11	11	9	0	0	88^{1}	97	2	7	27	10.6	3.67	88	.266	.280	4	.105	-3	-4	-4	-1	-0.7
1886	Pit-a	29	21	.580	50	50	49	2	0	434^{2}	457	3	75	72	11.2	2.67	127	.263	.296	49	.253	2	38	35	3	3.5
1887	Pit-N	28	21	.571	49	48	47	2	0	440^{2}	490	12	67	76	11.6	3.29	118	.269	.299	41	.212	-2	38	29	8	3.0
1888	Pit-N	23	25	.479	50	50	49	6	0	437^{1}	446	9	53	107	10.4	2.63	101	.255	.280	25	.143	-5	10	2	4	0.0
1889	Pit-N	23	16	.590	41	40	38	4	0	341	392	19	78	77	12.7	4.17	90	.280	.322	28	.187	-0	-6	-16	1	-1.2
1890	Pit-P	12	13	.480	26	25	23	1	0	217	275	3	49	35	13.8	4.35	90	.296	.337	20	.206	-1	-3	-11	4	-0.6
1891	Pit-N	14	14	.500	33	31	23	2	0	246^{2}	256	10	62	46	12.1	2.88	114	.258	.310	18	.165	-5	13	11	0	0.6
1892	Pit-N	5	6	.455	12	12	10	0	0	96	104	0	28	29	12.4	2.63	126	.265	.314	5	.122	-2	7	7	-0	0.4
	StL-N	5	6	.455	12	12	10	0	0	92	102	4	26	27	12.8	3.23	99	.270	.322	2	.051	-5	1	-0	-2	-0.6
	Yr	10	12	.455	24	24	20	0	0	188	206	4	54	56	12.6	2.92	111	.268	.318	7	.087	-7	8	7	-2	-0.2
Total	14	360	308	.539	697	682	639	56	1	5941^{1}	6352	122	744	1799	10.8	2.87	109	.261	.284	546	.202	-46	160	162	39	13.7

● LOU GALVIN Galvin, Louis J. b: 4/1862, St.Paul, Minn. d: 6/17/1895, Deb: 10/01/1884

YEAR	TM/L	W	L	PCT	G	GS	CG	SH	SV	IP	H	HR	BB	SO	RAT	ERA	ERA+	OAV	OOB	BH	AVG	PB	PR	/A	PD	TPI
1884	StP-U	0	2	.000	3	3	3	0	0	25	21	0	10	17	11.2	2.88	57	.213	.285	2	.222	0	0	-3	-1	-0.3

● BOB GAMBLE Gamble, Robert J. b: 2/1867, Hazelton, Pa. TR, 5'10", 155 lbs. Deb: 5/02/1888

YEAR	TM/L	W	L	PCT	G	GS	CG	SH	SV	IP	H	HR	BB	SO	RAT	ERA	ERA+	OAV	OOB	BH	AVG	PB	PR	/A	PD	TPI
1888	Phi-a	0	1	.000	1	1	1	0	0	9	10	0	3	2	13.0	8.00	37	.271	.326	1	.333	0	-5	-5	-0	-0.4

● GUSSIE GANNON Gannon, James Edward b: 11/26/1873, Erie, Pa. d: 4/12/66, Erie, Pa. BL/TL, 5'11", 154 lbs. Deb: 6/15/1895

YEAR	TM/L	W	L	PCT	G	GS	CG	SH	SV	IP	H	HR	BB	SO	RAT	ERA	ERA+	OAV	OOB	BH	AVG	PB	PR	/A	PD	TPI
1895	Pit-N	0	0	—	1	0	0	0	0	5	7	0	2	0	16.2	1.80	251	.326	.383	0	.000	-0	2	2	-0	0.1

● JOE GANNON Gannon, Joseph b: St.Louis, Mo. Deb: 8/28/1898

YEAR	TM/L	W	L	PCT	G	GS	CG	SH	SV	IP	H	HR	BB	SO	RAT	ERA	ERA+	OAV	OOB	BH	AVG	PB	PR	/A	PD	TPI
1898	StL-N	0	1	.000	1	1	1	0	0	9	13	0	5	2	19.0	11.00	34	.335	.424	0	.000	-1	-7	-7	-0	-0.6

● JIM GANTNER Gantner, James Elmer b: 1/5/53, Fond Du Lac, Wis. BL/TR, 6', 180 lbs. Deb: 9/03/76 ♦

YEAR	TM/L	W	L	PCT	G	GS	CG	SH	SV	IP	H	HR	BB	SO	RAT	ERA	ERA+	OAV	OOB	BH	AVG	PB	PR	/A	PD	TPI
1979	Mil-A	0	0	—	1	0	0	0	0	1	2	0	0	0	18.0	0.00	—	.400	.400	59	.284	1	0	0	0	0.1

● GENE GARBER Garber, Henry Eugene b: 11/13/47, Lancaster, Pa. BR/TR, 5'10", 175 lbs. Deb: 6/17/69

YEAR	TM/L	W	L	PCT	G	GS	CG	SH	SV	IP	H	HR	BB	SO	RAT	ERA	ERA+	OAV	OOB	BH	AVG	PB	PR	/A	PD	TPI
1969	Pit-N	0	0	—	2	1	0	0	0	5	6	3	1	3	12.6	5.40	65	.333	.368	0	.000	-0	-1	-1	-0	-0.1
1970	Pit-N	0	3	.000	14	0	0	0	0	22^{1}	22	4	10	7	13.7	5.24	74	.275	.370	2	.667	1	-3	-3	1	-0.2
1972	Pit-N	0	0	—	4	0	0	0	0	6^{1}	7	3	3	3	14.2	7.11	47	.269	.345	0	.000	-0	-3	-3	0	-0.3
1973	KC-A	9	9	.500	48	8	4	0	11	152^{2}	164	14	49	60	12.7	4.24	97	.283	.341	0	—	0	-7	-2	1	-0.1
1974	KC-A	1	2	.333	17	0	0	0	1	28	35	3	13	14	15.8	4.82	79	.313	.389	0	—	0	-4	-3	-0	-0.7
	Phi-N	4	0	1.000	34	0	0	0	4	48	39	1	31	27	13.3	2.06	183	.236	.360	0	.000	-0	8	9	0	1.0
1975	Phi-N	10	12	.455	**71**	0	0	0	14	110	104	13	27	69	10.9	3.60	104	.254	.304	2	.167	-0	0	2	-0	0.1
1976	*Phi-N	9	3	.750	59	0	0	0	11	92^{2}	78	4	30	92	10.9	2.82	126	.228	.298	2	.286	1	7	8	1	1.0
1977	*Phi-N	8	6	.571	64	0	0	0	19	103^{1}	82	6	23	78	9.3	2.35	170	.220	.270	0	.000	-1	18	19	2	2.0
1978	Phi-N	2	1	.667	22	0	0	0	3	38^{2}	26	1	11	24	9.3	1.40	256	.191	.267	0	.000	-0	9	9	-0	1.0
	Atl-N	4	4	.500	43	0	0	0	22	78^{1}	58	11	13	61	8.4	2.53	160	.204	.244	1	.091	-1	9	13	1	1.5
	Yr	6	5	.545	65	0	0	0	25	117	84	12	24	85	8.5	2.15	181	.199	.245	1	.071	-1	18	**23**	1	2.5
1979	Atl-N	6	16	.273	68	0	0	0	25	106	121	10	24	56	12.7	4.33	94	.283	.328	3	.300	1	-7	-3	1	-0.1
1980	Atl-N	5	5	.500	68	0	0	0	7	82^{1}	95	6	24	51	13.0	3.83	98	.288	.336	1	.500	0	-2	-1	2	0.1
1981	Atl-N	4	6	.400	35	0	0	0	2	58^{2}	49	2	20	34	10.6	2.61	137	.214	.277	0	.000	-1	6	6	2	0.8
1982	*Atl-N	8	10	.444	69	0	0	0	30	119^{1}	100	4	32	68	10.1	2.34	160	.231	.288	2	.133	0	17	18	2	2.2
1983	Atl-N	4	5	.444	43	0	0	0	9	60^{2}	72	8	23	45	14.4	4.60	84	.300	.366	0	.000	0	-7	-5	2	-0.3
1984	Atl-N	3	6	.333	62	0	0	0	11	106	103	7	24	55	11.0	3.06	126	.254	.299	2	.143	-0	6	9	1	1.0
1985	Atl-N	6	6	.500	59	0	0	0	1	97^{1}	98	8	25	66	11.6	3.61	107	.263	.313	1	.200	0	-0	3	1	0.4
1986	Atl-N	5	5	.500	61	0	0	0	24	78	76	3	20	56	11.2	2.54	157	.260	.310	1	.167	0	10	12	1	1.4
1987	Atl-N	8	10	.444	49	0	0	0	10	69^{1}	87	7	28	48	15.1	4.41	98	.311	.375	0	.000	-0	-3	-1	2	0.1
	KC-A	0	0	—	13	0	0	0	8	14^{1}	13	1	1	3	9.4	2.51	181	.245	.273	0	—	0	3	3	0	0.2
1988	KC-A	0	4	.000	26	0	0	0	6	32^{2}	29	4	13	20	12.1	3.58	111	.238	.321	0	—	0	1	1	0	0.1
Total	19	96	113	.459	931	9	4	0	218	1510	1464	123	445	940	11.6	3.34	116	.257	.314	17	.148	-0	59	92	20	11.1

● BOB GARBER Garber, Robert Mitchell b: 9/10/28, Hunker, Pa. BR/TR, 6'1", 190 lbs. Deb: 5/13/56

YEAR	TM/L	W	L	PCT	G	GS	CG	SH	SV	IP	H	HR	BB	SO	RAT	ERA	ERA+	OAV	OOB	BH	AVG	PB	PR	/A	PD	TPI
1956	Pit-N	0	0	—	2	0	0	0	0	4	3	1	3	3	13.5	2.25	168	.200	.333	0	—	0	1	1	-0	0.0

● RICH GARCES Garces, Richard Aron (Mendoza) b: 5/18/71, Maracay, Venez. BR/TR, 6', 187 lbs. Deb: 9/18/90

YEAR	TM/L	W	L	PCT	G	GS	CG	SH	SV	IP	H	HR	BB	SO	RAT	ERA	ERA+	OAV	OOB	BH	AVG	PB	PR	/A	PD	TPI
1990	Min-A	0	0	—	5	0	0	0	2	5^{2}	4	0	4	1	12.7	1.59	261	.200	.333	0	—	0	1	2	0	-0.1

● MIKE GARCIA Garcia, Edward Miguel "The Big Bear" b: 11/17/23, San Gabriel, Cal. d: 1/13/86, Fairview Park, O. BR/TR, 6'1", 200 lbs. Deb: 10/03/48

YEAR	TM/L	W	L	PCT	G	GS	CG	SH	SV	IP	H	HR	BB	SO	RAT	ERA	ERA+	OAV	OOB	BH	AVG	PB	PR	/A	PD	TPI
1948	Cle-A	0	0	—	1	0	0	0	0	2	3	0	0	1	13.5	0.00	—	.333	.333	0	—	0	1	1	0	0.1
1949	Cle-A	14	5	.737	41	20	8	5	2	175^{2}	154	6	60	94	11.1	**2.36**	**169**	.241	.308	12	.235	3	36	32	1	3.6
1950	Cle-A	11	11	.500	33	29	11	0	0	184	191	15	74	76	13.0	3.86	112	.266	.334	13	.200	-0	15	10	2	1.1
1951	Cle-A	20	13	.606	47	30	15	1	6	254	239	10	82	118	11.5	3.15	120	.246	.307	18	.212	1	27	18	1	2.0
1952	Cle-A☆	22	11	.667	46	36	19	**6**	4	292^{1}	284	9	87	143	11.6	2.37	141	.253	.310	13	.137	-1	42	32	2	3.4
1953	Cle-A★	18	9	.667	38	35	21	3	0	271^{2}	260	18	81	134	11.4	3.25	116	.250	.307	24	.250	4	23	15	-0	1.9
1954	*Cle-A†	19	8	.704	45	34	13	**5**	5	258^{2}	220	6	71	129	**10.2**	**2.64**	**139**	.229	**.284**	11	.136	-2	**31**	**30**	0	2.9
1955	Cle-A	11	13	.458	38	31	6	2	3	210^{2}	230	17	56	120	12.3	4.02	99	.278	.327	15	.217	2	-1	-1	-1	0.0
1956	Cle-A	11	12	.478	35	30	8	4	0	197^{2}	213	18	74	119	13.3	3.78	111	.272	.339	7	.115	-3	8	9	-0	0.5
1957	Cle-A	12	8	.600	38	27	9	1	0	211^{1}	221	14	73	110	12.8	3.75	99	.269	.333	12	.160	-1	1	-1	-2	-0.4
1958	Cle-A	1	0	1.000	6	1	0	0	0	8	15	2	7	2	25.9	9.00	41	.395	.500	0	.000	-0	-5	-5	0	-0.5
1959	Cle-A	3	6	.333	29	8	1	0	1	72	72	4	31	49	12.9	4.00	92	.265	.340	1	.071	-1	-1	-3	0	-0.4
1960	Chi-A	0	0	—	15	0	0	0	2	17^{2}	23	2	10	8	16.8	4.58	82	.338	.423	1	.333	0	-1	-2	0	-0.1
1961	Was-A	0	1	.000	16	0	0	0	0	19	23	1	13	14	17.5	4.74	85	.287	.394	0	—	0	-2	-2	-1	-0.2
Total	14	142	97	.594	428	281	111	27	23	2174^{2}	2148	122	719	1117	12.0	3.27	117	.257	.319	127	.182	1	174	134	2	13.9

● MIGUEL GARCIA Garcia, Miguel Angel (Silfontes) b: 4/19/66, Caracas, Venez. BL/TL, 5'11", 173 lbs. Deb: 4/30/87

YEAR	TM/L	W	L	PCT	G	GS	CG	SH	SV	IP	H	HR	BB	SO	RAT	ERA	ERA+	OAV	OOB	BH	AVG	PB	PR	/A	PD	TPI
1987	Cal-A	0	0	—	1	0	0	0	0	1^{2}	3	0	3	0	32.4	16.20	27	.375	.545	0	—	0	-2	-2	0	-0.1
	Pit-N	0	0	—	1	0	0	0	0	0^{2}	0	0	0	0	0.0	0.00	—	.000	.000	0	—	0	0	0	-0	0.0
1988	Pit-N	0	0	—	1	0	0	0	0	2	3	1	2	2	27.0	4.50	76	.375	.545	0	—	0	-0	-0	-0	0.0
1989	Pit-N	0	2	.000	11	0	0	0	0	16	25	2	7	9	18.0	8.44	40	.357	.416	1	1.000	0	-9	-9	0	-0.9
Total	3	0	2	.000	14	0	0	0	0	20^{1}	31	3	12	11	19.5	8.41	41	.352	.436	1	1.000	0	-11	-11	0	-1.0

● RALPH GARCIA Garcia, Ralph b: 12/14/48, Los Angeles, Cal. BR/TR, 6', 195 lbs. Deb: 9/26/72

YEAR	TM/L	W	L	PCT	G	GS	CG	SH	SV	IP	H	HR	BB	SO	RAT	ERA	ERA+	OAV	OOB	BH	AVG	PB	PR	/A	PD	TPI
1972	SD-N	0	0	—	3	0	0	0	0	5	4	0	3	3	12.6	1.80	183	.211	.318	0	—	0	1	1	0	0.1
1974	SD-N	0	0	—	8	0	0	0	0	10^{1}	15	1	7	9	19.2	6.10	58	.357	.449	0	—	0	-3	-3	0	-0.3
Total	2	0	0	—	11	0	0	0	0	15^{1}	19	1	10	12	17.0	4.70	74	.311	.408	0	—	0	-2	-2	0	-0.2

YEAR TM/L	W	L	PCT	G	GS	CG	SH	SV	IP	H	HR	BB	SO	RAT	ERA	ERA+	OAV	OOB	BH	AVG	PB	PR	/A	PD	TPI

● **RAMON GARCIA** Garcia, Ramon (Garcia) b: 3/5/24, LaEsperanza, Cuba BR/TR, 5'10", 170 lbs. Deb: 4/19/48

| 1948 Was-A | 0 | 0 | — | 4 | 0 | 0 | 0 | 0 | 3² | 11 | 0 | 4 | 2 | 39.3 | 17.18 | 25 | .524 | .615 | 1 | 1.000 | 0 | -5 | -5 | 0 | -0.4 |

● **RAMON GARCIA** Garcia, Ramon Antonio (Fortunato) b: 12/9/69, Guanare, Venez. BR/TR, 6'2", 200 lbs. Deb: 5/31/91

| 1991 Chi-A | 4 | 4 | .500 | 16 | 15 | 0 | 0 | 0 | 78¹ | 79 | 13 | 31 | 40 | 12.9 | 5.40 | 74 | .269 | .343 | 0 | — | 0 | -11 | -12 | 1 | -1.0 |

● **ART GARDINER** Gardiner, Arthur Cecil b: 12/26/1899, Brooklyn, N.Y. d: 10/21/54, Copiague, N.Y. BR/TR, Deb: 9/25/23

| 1923 Phi-N | 0 | 0 | — | 1 | 0 | 0 | 0 | 0 | 0 | 1 | 0 | 1 | 0 | — | — | 1.000 | 1.000 | 0 | — | 0 | 0 | 0 | 0 | 0.0 |

● **MIKE GARDINER** Gardiner, Michael James b: 10/19/65, Sarnia, Ont., Can. BB/TR, 6', 185 lbs. Deb: 9/08/90

1990 Sea-A	0	2	.000	5	3	0	0	0	12²	22	1	5	6	20.6	10.66	37	.379	.446	0	—	0	-10	-9	0	-0.9
1991 Bos-A	9	10	.474	22	22	0	0	0	130	140	18	47	91	12.9	4.85	89	.274	.335	0	—	0	-11	-8	-0	-1.1
1992 Bos-A	4	10	.286	28	18	0	0	0	130²	126	12	58	79	12.8	4.75	83	.253	.333	0	—	0	-12	-9	-0	-1.0
Total 3	13	22	.371	55	43	0	0	0	273¹	288	31	110	176	13.2	5.07	83	.270	.340	0	—	0	-32	-26	0	-3.0

● **CHRIS GARDNER** Gardner, Christopher John b: 3/30/69, Long Beach, Cal. BR/TR, 6', 175 lbs. Deb: 9/10/91

| 1991 Hou-N | 1 | 2 | .333 | 5 | 4 | 0 | 0 | 0 | 24² | 19 | 5 | 14 | 12 | 12.0 | 4.01 | 87 | .218 | .327 | 0 | .000 | -0 | -1 | -1 | 1 | -0.1 |

● **GID GARDNER** Gardner, Frank Washington b: 6/9/1859, Attleboro, Mass. d: 8/1/14, Cambridge, Mass. 165 lbs. Deb: 8/23/1879 ♦

1879 Tro-N	0	2	.000	2	2	2	0	0	14	27	0	0	3	17.4	5.79	43	.365	.365	1	.167	-0	-5	-5	-1	-0.5
1880 Cle-N	1	8	.111	9	9	9	0	0	77	80	2	20	21	11.7	2.57	91	.254	.299	6	.188	0	-2	-2	-0	-0.2
1883 Bal-a	1	0	1.000	2	0	0	0	0	7	9	1	1	2	12.9	5.14	68	.293	.315	44	.273	1	-1	-1	-0	-0.1
1884 CP-U	0	1	.000	1	1	0	0	0	6	10	0	1	4	16.5	6.00	50	.349	.371	38	.255	0	-2	-2	0	-0.1
1885 Bal-a	0	1	.000	1	1	1	0	0	9	16	2	6	3	23.0	10.00	33	.372	.460	37	.218	0	-7	-7	0	-0.5
Total 5	2	12	.143	15	13	12	0	0	113	142	5	28	33	13.6	3.90	65	.289	.329	178	.233		-17	-17	-1	-1.4

● **HARRY GARDNER** Gardner, Harry Ray b: 6/1/1887, Quincy, Mich. d: 8/2/61, Canby, Ore. BR/TR, 6'2", 180 lbs. Deb: 4/17/11

1911 Pit-N	1	1	.500	13	3	2	0	2	42	39	2	20	24	13.1	4.50	76	.244	.335	3	.214	0	-5	-5	-1	-0.6
1912 Pit-N	0	0	—	1	0	0	0	0	0¹	3	0	1	0	108.0	0.00	—	.500	.571	0	—	0	0	0	0	0.0
Total 2	1	1	.500	14	3	2	0	2	42¹	42	2	21	24	13.8	4.46	77	.253	.344	3	.214	0	-5	-5	-1	-0.6

● **JIM GARDNER** Gardner, James Anderson b: 10/4/1874, Pittsburgh, Pa. d: 4/24/05, Pittsburgh, Pa. TR , Deb: 6/20/1895

1895 Pit-N	8	2	.800	11	10	8	0	0	85¹	99	1	27	31	13.9	2.64	171	.286	.348	9	.265	1	20	18	-1	1.6
1897 Pit-N	5	5	.500	14	11	8	0	0	95¹	115	4	32	35	14.7	5.19	80	.296	.363	12	.158	-1	-9	-11	-0	-1.0
1898 Pit-N	10	13	.435	25	22	19	1	0	185¹	179	3	48	41	11.4	3.21	111	.252	.307	14	.154	-2	8	7	-2	0.4
1899 Pit-N	1	0	1.000	6	3	0	0	0	32¹	52	1	13	2	18.1	7.52	51	.361	.414	3	.231	0	-13	-13	-2	-1.2
1902 Chi-N	1	2	.333	3	3	2	0	0	25	23	0	10	6	11.9	2.88	94	.244	.317	2	.200	0	-0	-0	-0	-0.0
Total 5	25	22	.532	59	49	37	1	0	423¹	468	9	130	115	13.2	3.85	100	.278	.338	40	.179	-1	6	1	-4	-0.2

● **MARK GARDNER** Gardner, Mark Allan b: 3/1/62, Los Angeles, Cal. BR/TR, 6'1", 190 lbs. Deb: 5/16/89

1989 Mon-N	0	3	.000	7	4	0	0	0	26¹	26	2	11	21	13.3	5.13	69	.250	.333	1	.167	-0	-5	-5	-0	-0.5
1990 Mon-N	7	9	.438	27	26	3	3	0	152²	129	13	61	135	11.7	3.42	107	.230	.315	5	.114	-1	6	4	2	0.5
1991 Mon-N	9	11	.450	27	27	0	0	0	168¹	139	17	75	107	11.7	3.85	94	.230	.319	5	.091	-2	-3	-4	-2	-0.9
1992 Mon-N	12	10	.545	33	30	0	0	0	179²	179	15	60	132	12.4	4.36	80	.259	.327	7	.140	1	-17	-17	-1	-1.8
Total 4	28	33	.459	94	87	3	3	0	527	473	47	207	395	12.0	3.96	90	.241	.321	18	.116	-3	-19	-22	-1	-2.7

● **GLENN GARDNER** Gardner, Miles Glenn b: 1/25/16, Burnsville, N.C. d: 7/7/64, Rochester, N.Y. BR/TR, 5'11", 180 lbs. Deb: 7/21/45

| 1945 StL-N | 3 | 1 | .750 | 17 | 4 | 2 | 1 | 1 | 54² | 50 | 2 | 27 | 20 | 12.7 | 3.29 | 114 | .242 | .329 | 7 | .333 | 2 | 3 | 3 | -1 | 0.4 |

● **ROB GARDNER** Gardner, Richard Frank b: 12/19/44, Binghamton, N.Y. BR/TL, 6'1", 176 lbs. Deb: 9/01/65

1965 NY-N	0	2	.000	5	4	0	0	0	28	23	4	7	19	9.6	3.21	110	.217	.265	0	.000	-1	1	1	0	0.1
1966 NY-N	4	8	.333	41	17	3	0	1	133²	147	15	64	74	14.4	5.12	71	.285	.367	7	.171	-0	-22	-22	0	-2.3
1967 Chi-N	0	2	.000	18	5	0	0	0	31²	33	2	6	16	11.1	3.98	89	.260	.293	0	.000	-0	-2	-2	-0	-0.1
1968 Cle-A	0	0	—	5	0	0	0	0	2²	5	0	2	6	23.6	6.75	44	.417	.500	0	—	0	-1	-1	-0	-0.1
1970 NY-A	1	0	1.000	1	1	0	0	0	7¹	8	2	4	6	14.7	4.91	72	.276	.364	1	.333	1	-1	-1	0	-0.1
1971 Oak-A	0	0	—	4	1	0	0	0	7²	8	1	3	2	12.9	2.35	142	.267	.333	1	.500	1	1	1	0	0.2
NY-A	0	0	—	2	0	0	0	0	3	3	0	2	5	15.0	3.00	108	.273	.348	0	—	0	0	0	-0	0.0
Yr	0	0	—	6	1	0	0	0	10²	11	1	5	7	13.5	2.53	131	.268	.348	1	.500	1	1	1	0	0.2
1972 NY-A	8	5	.615	20	14	1	0	0	97	91	9	28	58	11.0	3.06	96	.243	.296	3	.107	-1	-0	-1	-1	-0.3
1973 Oak-A	0	0	—	3	0	0	0	0	7¹	10	2	4	2	17.2	4.91	72	.370	.452	0	—	0	-1	-1	0	-0.1
Mil-A	1	1	.500	10	0	0	0	1	12²	17	0	13	5	22.0	9.95	38	.327	.470	0	—	0	-9	-9	-0	-0.7
Yr	1	1	.500	13	0	0	0	1	20	27	2	17	7	20.2	8.10	45	.342	.464	0	—	0	-10	-10	0	-0.5
Total 8	14	18	.438	109	42	4	0	2	331	345	35	133	193	13.1	4.35	78	.269	.339	12	.138	-2	-34	-35	-0	-3.2

● **WES GARDNER** Gardner, Wesley Brian b: 4/29/61, Benton, Ark. BR/TR, 6'4", 197 lbs. Deb: 7/29/84

1984 NY-N	1	1	.500	21	0	0	0	1	25¹	34	0	8	19	14.9	6.39	55	.321	.368	0	.000	-0	-8	-8	-0	-0.9
1985 NY-N	0	2	.000	9	0	0	0	0	12	18	1	8	11	19.5	5.25	66	.375	.464	0	—	0	-2	-2	0	-0.2
1986 Bos-A	0	0	—	1	0	0	0	0	1	1	0	0	1	9.0	9.00	46	.333	.333	0	—	0	-1	-1	0	-0.1
1987 Bos-A	3	6	.333	49	1	0	0	10	89²	98	17	42	70	14.3	5.42	84	.279	.359	0	—	0	-10	-9	-1	-1.0
1988 *Bos-A	8	6	.571	36	18	1	0	2	149	119	17	64	106	11.2	3.50	117	.220	.305	0	—	0	8	10	1	1.0
1989 Bos-A	3	7	.300	22	16	0	0	0	86	97	10	47	81	15.2	5.97	69	.287	.376	0	—	0	-20	-18	-1	-2.1
1990 Bos-A	3	7	.300	34	9	0	0	0	77¹	77	6	35	58	13.3	4.89	83	.259	.341	0	—	0	-8	-7	-0	-0.9
1991 SD-N	0	1	.000	14	0	0	0	1	20¹	27	1	12	9	17.3	7.08	54	.310	.394	0	.000	-0	-8	-8	0	-0.8
KC-A	0	0	—	3	0	0	0	0	5²	5	0	2	3	11.1	1.59	259	.208	.269	0	—	0	2	2	0	0.1
Total 8	18	30	.375	189	44	1	0	14	466¹	476	52	218	358	13.5	4.90	84	.265	.347	0	.000	-0	-47	-40	-2	-4.9

● **BILL GARDNER** Gardner, William A. b: 9/1868, Baltimore, Md. Deb: 8/09/1887

| 1887 Bal-a | 0 | 1 | .000 | 3 | 2 | 1 | 0 | 0 | 13 | 23 | 0 | 10 | 3 | 23.5 | 11.08 | 37 | .426 | .523 | 3 | .273 | 0 | -10 | -10 | -0 | -0.8 |

● **BILL GARFIELD** Garfield, William Milton b: 10/26/1867, Sheffield, Ohio d: 12/16/41, Danville, Ill. BR/TR, 5'11.5", 160 lbs. Deb: 7/10/1889

1889 Pit-N	0	2	.000	4	2	2	0	0	29	45	2	17	4	19.6	7.76	48	.344	.423	0	.000	-2	-12	-13	0	-1.1
1890 Cle-N	1	7	.125	9	8	7	0	0	70	91	3	35	16	17.2	4.89	73	.305	.393	4	.154	-1	-10	-10	-0	-1.0
Total 2	1	9	.100	13	10	9	0	0	99	136	5	52	20	17.9	5.73	63	.317	.402	4	.103	-3	-22	-23	0	-2.1

● **BOB GARIBALDI** Garibaldi, Robert Roy b: 3/3/42, Stockton, Cal. BL/TR, 6'4", 210 lbs. Deb: 7/15/62

1962 SF-N	0	0	—	9	0	0	0	1	12¹	13	1	5	9	13.1	5.11	74	.265	.333	0	.000	-0	-2	-2	0	-0.2
1963 SF-N	0	1	.000	8	0	0	0	0	8	8	0	4	4	14.6	1.13	284	.276	.382	0	.000	-0	2	2	0	0.2
1966 SF-N	0	0	—	1	0	0	0	0	1	1	0	0	0	9.0	0.00	—	.250	.250	0	—	0	0	0	-0	0.0
1969 SF-N	0	1	.000	5	1	0	0	0	5	6	0	2	1	14.4	1.80	194	.316	.381	0	.000	-0	1	1	0	0.1
Total 4	0	2	.000	15	1	0	0	2	26¹	28	1	11	14	13.7	3.08	116	.277	.354	0	.000	-0	2	1	0	0.1

● **LOU GARLAND** Garland, Louis Lyman b: 7/16/05, Archie, Mo. d: 8/30/90, Idaho Falls, Idaho BR/TR, 6'2.5", 200 lbs. Deb: 8/31/31

| 1931 Chi-A | 0 | 2 | .000 | 7 | 2 | 0 | 0 | 0 | 16² | 30 | 2 | 14 | 4 | 24.3 | 10.26 | 41 | .400 | .500 | 0 | .000 | -0 | -11 | -11 | 1 | -1.0 |

● **WAYNE GARLAND** Garland, Marcus Wayne b: 10/26/50, Nashville, Tenn. BR/TR, 6', 195 lbs. Deb: 9/13/73

| 1973 Bal-A | 0 | 1 | .000 | 4 | 1 | 0 | 0 | 0 | 16 | 14 | 1 | 7 | 10 | 11.8 | 3.94 | 95 | .233 | .313 | 0 | — | 0 | -0 | -0 | -0 | 0.0 |

YEAR TM/L	W	L	PCT	G	GS	CG	SH	SV	IP	H	HR	BB	SO	RAT	ERA	ERA+	OAV	OOB	BH	AVG	PB	PR	/A	PD	TPI
1974 *Bal-A	5	5	.500	20	6	0	0	1	91	68	5	26	40	9.6	2.97	116	.211	.276	0	—	0	7	5	-1	0.6
1975 Bal-A	2	5	.286	29	1	0	0	4	87^1	80	7	31	46	11.5	3.71	95	.252	.321	0	—	0	1	-2	-0	0.0
1976 Bal-A	20	7	.741	38	25	14	4	1	232^1	224	10	64	113	11.4	2.67	122	.255	.309	0	—	0	22	15	2	2.0
1977 Cle-A	13	19	.406	38	38	21	1	0	282^2	281	23	88	118	11.8	3.60	110	.261	.318	0	—	0	14	11	-0	1.1
1978 Cle-A	2	3	.400	6	6	0	0	0	29^2	43	6	16	13	18.2	7.89	47	.347	.426	0	—	0	-14	-14	0	-1.2
1979 Cle-A	4	10	.286	18	14	2	0	0	94^2	120	11	34	40	14.9	5.23	81	.318	.379	0	—	0	-11	-10	-1	-1.1
1980 Cle-A	6	9	.400	25	20	4	1	0	150^1	163	18	48	55	13.0	4.61	88	.276	.337	0	—	0	-10	-9	-1	-1.0
1981 Cle-A	3	7	.300	12	10	2	1	0	56	89	8	14	15	16.6	5.79	63	.374	.409	0	—	0	-13	-13	0	-1.3
Total 9	55	66	.455	190	121	43	7	6	1040	1082	89	328	450	12.4	3.89	96	.272	.330	0	—	0	-4	-18	-2	-0.9

● MIKE GARMAN Garman, Michael Douglas b: 9/16/49, Caldwell, Idaho BR/TR, 6'3", 215 lbs. Deb: 9/22/69

YEAR TM/L	W	L	PCT	G	GS	CG	SH	SV	IP	H	HR	BB	SO	RAT	ERA	ERA+	OAV	OOB	BH	AVG	PB	PR	/A	PD	TPI
1969 Bos-A	1	0	1.000	2	2	0	0	0	12^1	13	0	10	10	16.8	4.38	87	.277	.404	2	.400	1	-1	-1	0	0.0
1971 Bos-A	1	1	.500	3	3	0	0	0	18^2	15	3	9	6	12.1	3.86	96	.217	.316	2	.333	0	-1	-0	-1	-0.1
1972 Bos-A	0	1	.000	3	1	0	0	0	3^1	4	1	2	1	16.2	10.80	30	.286	.375	0	—	0	-3	-3	-0	-0.3
1973 Bos-A	0	0	—	12	0	0	0	0	22	32	1	15	9	19.2	5.32	76	.352	.443	0	—	0	-4	-3	-0	-0.7
1974 StL-N	7	2	.778	64	0	0	0	6	81^2	66	4	27	45	10.5	2.64	135	.227	.297	1	.100	-1	9	8	-0	0.8
1975 StL-N	3	8	.273	66	0	0	0	10	79	73	3	48	48	13.9	2.39	157	.245	.352	0	.000	-0	11	12	-1	1.1
1976 Chi-N	2	4	.333	47	2	0	0	1	76^1	79	7	35	37	13.8	4.95	78	.273	.358	0	.000	-1	-12	-9	0	-1.0
1977 *LA-N	4	4	.500	49	0	0	0	12	62^2	60	7	22	29	12.1	2.73	140	.254	.323	0	.000	-1	8	8	-1	0.6
1978 LA-N	0	1	.000	10	0	0	0	0	16^1	15	3	3	5	9.9	4.41	80	.259	.295	0	—	0	-2	-2	-0	-0.2
Mon-N	4	6	.400	47	0	0	0	13	61^1	54	5	31	23	12.5	4.40	80	.238	.329	0	.000	-1	-6	-6	-0	-0.7
Yr	4	7	.364	57	0	0	0	13	77^2	69	8	34	28	11.9	4.40	80	.242	.323	0	.000	-1	-7	-8	-1	-0.9
Total 9	22	27	.449	303	8	0	0	42	433^2	411	34	202	213	12.9	3.63	102	.254	.340	5	.119	-2	-0	4	-3	-0.5

● WILLIE GARONI Garoni, William b: 7/28/1877, Ft.Lee, N.J. d: 9/9/14, Ft.Lee, N.J. BR/TR, 6'1", 165 lbs. Deb: 9/07/1899

YEAR TM/L	W	L	PCT	G	GS	CG	SH	SV	IP	H	HR	BB	SO	RAT	ERA	ERA+	OAV	OOB	BH	AVG	PB	PR	/A	PD	TPI
1899 NY-N	0	1	.000	3	1	1	0	0	10	12	0	2	2	12.6	4.50	83	.297	.330	0	.000	-1	-1	-1	0	-0.1

● SCOTT GARRELTS Garrelts, Scott William b: 10/30/61, Urbana, Ill. BR/TR, 6'4", 195 lbs. Deb: 10/02/82

YEAR TM/L	W	L	PCT	G	GS	CG	SH	SV	IP	H	HR	BB	SO	RAT	ERA	ERA+	OAV	OOB	BH	AVG	PB	PR	/A	PD	TPI
1982 SF-N	0	0	—	1	0	0	0	0	2	3	0	2	4	22.5	13.50	27	.333	.455	0	—	0	-2	-2	0	-0.2
1983 SF-N	2	2	.500	5	5	1	1	0	35^2	33	4	19	16	13.6	2.52	140	.254	.358	2	.222	0	4	4	0	0.5
1984 SF-N	2	3	.400	21	3	0	0	0	43	45	6	34	32	16.7	5.65	62	.274	.402	1	.100	-0	-10	-10	-1	-1.1
1985 SF-N☆	9	6	.600	74	0	0	0	13	105^2	76	2	58	106	11.7	2.30	149	.198	.308	2	.222	1	15	13	2	1.7
1986 SF-N	13	9	.591	53	18	2	0	10	173^2	144	17	74	125	11.4	3.11	113	.231	.314	8	.178	2	12	8	2	1.3
1987 *SF-N	11	7	.611	64	0	0	0	12	106^1	70	10	55	127	10.6	3.22	119	.192	.298	2	.200	0	10	7	-1	0.7
1988 SF-N	5	9	.357	65	0	0	0	13	98	80	3	46	86	11.8	3.58	91	.226	.318	1	.077	-1	-1	-3	-1	-0.5
1989 *SF-N	14	5	.737	30	29	2	1	0	193^1	149	11	46	119	**9.1**	**2.28**	**148**	.212	**.260**	9	.136	1	26	23	-0	2.6
1990 SF-N	12	11	.522	31	31	4	2	0	182	190	16	70	80	13.0	4.15	88	.272	.341	4	.061	-3	-7	-10	-1	-1.5
1991 SF-N	1	1	.500	8	3	0	0	0	19^2	25	5	9	8	15.6	6.41	56	.313	.382	0	.000	-0	-6	-6	-0	-0.7
Total 10	69	53	.566	352	89	9	4	48	959^1	815	74	413	703	11.6	3.29	107	.232	.315	29	.125	-1	41	24	1	2.8

● CLARENCE GARRETT Garrett, Clarence Raymond "Laz" b: 3/6/1891, Reader, W.Va. d: 2/11/77, Moundsville, W.Va. BR/TR, 6'5.5", 185 lbs. Deb: 9/13/15

YEAR TM/L	W	L	PCT	G	GS	CG	SH	SV	IP	H	HR	BB	SO	RAT	ERA	ERA+	OAV	OOB	BH	AVG	PB	PR	/A	PD	TPI
1915 Cle-A	2	2	.500	4	4	2	0	0	23^1	19	1	6	5	10.0	2.31	132	.224	.283	0	.000	-0	2	2	1	0.3

● GREG GARRETT Garrett, Gregory b: 3/12/48, Atascadero, Cal. BB/TL, 6', 200 lbs. Deb: 4/24/70

YEAR TM/L	W	L	PCT	G	GS	CG	SH	SV	IP	H	HR	BB	SO	RAT	ERA	ERA+	OAV	OOB	BH	AVG	PB	PR	/A	PD	TPI
1970 Cal-A	5	6	.455	32	7	0	0	0	74^2	48	6	44	53	11.2	2.65	136	.190	.312	1	.067	-1	9	8	-0	0.7
1971 Cin-N	0	1	.000	2	1	0	0	0	8^2	7	0	10	2	17.7	1.04	323	.250	.447	1	.333	0	2	2	-0	0.3
Total 2	5	7	.417	34	8	0	0	0	83^1	55	6	54	55	11.9	2.48	144	.196	.327	2	.111	-1	11	10	-0	1.0

● CLIFF GARRISON Garrison, Clifford William b: 8/13/05, Belmont, Okla. BR/TR, 6', 180 lbs. Deb: 4/16/28

YEAR TM/L	W	L	PCT	G	GS	CG	SH	SV	IP	H	HR	BB	SO	RAT	ERA	ERA+	OAV	OOB	BH	AVG	PB	PR	/A	PD	TPI
1928 Bos-A	0	0	—	6	0	0	0	0	16	22	2	6	0	15.8	7.88	52	.361	.418	0	.000	-0	-7	-7	1	-0.6

● JIM GARRY Garry, James Thomas b: 9/21/1869, Great Barrington, Mass. d: 1/15/17, Pittsfield, Mass. Deb: 5/02/1893

YEAR TM/L	W	L	PCT	G	GS	CG	SH	SV	IP	H	HR	BB	SO	RAT	ERA	ERA+	OAV	OOB	BH	AVG	PB	PR	/A	PD	TPI
1893 Bos-N	0	1	.000	1	0	0	0	0	1	5	0	4	2	81.0	63.00	8	.628	.753	0	.000	-0	-6	-6	0	-0.4

● NED GARVER Garver, Ned Franklin b: 12/25/25, Ney, Ohio BR/TR, 5'10.5", 180 lbs. Deb: 4/28/48

YEAR TM/L	W	L	PCT	G	GS	CG	SH	SV	IP	H	HR	BB	SO	RAT	ERA	ERA+	OAV	OOB	BH	AVG	PB	PR	/A	PD	TPI
1948 StL-A	7	11	.389	38	24	7	0	5	198	200	14	95	75	13.5	3.41	134	.268	.352	19	.288	4	19	25	1	3.1
1949 StL-A	12	17	.414	41	32	16	1	3	223^2	245	14	102	70	14.1	3.98	114	.277	.354	14	.187	2	5	14	0	1.6
1950 StL-A	13	18	.419	37	31	**22**	1	2	260	264	18	108	85	13.0	3.39	**146**	.264	.338	26	.286	4	24	30	2	3.8
1951 StL-A★	20	12	.625	33	30	**24**	1	0	246	237	17	96	84	12.4	3.73	118	.255	.328	29	.305	8	**34**	**45**	2	**5.4**
1952 StL-A	7	10	.412	21	21	7	2	0	148^2	130	14	55	60	11.4	3.69	106	.235	.309	9	.184	0	-0	4	-0	0.4
Det-A	1	0	1.000	1	1	1	0	0	9	9	1	3	3	12.0	2.00	190	.265	.324	0	.000	0	2	2	0	0.3
Yr	8	10	.444	22	22	8	2	0	157^2	139	15	58	63	11.2	3.60	109	.235	.304	9	.176	0	1	5	0	0.7
1953 Det-A	11	11	.500	30	26	13	0	1	198^1	228	16	66	69	13.4	4.45	91	.290	.347	11	.153	-1	-10	-8	1	-0.8
1954 Det-A	14	11	.560	35	32	16	3	1	246^1	216	20	62	93	10.3	2.81	131	.236	.287	13	.165	-0	25	24	2	2.7
1955 Det-A	12	16	.429	33	32	16	1	0	230^2	251	21	67	83	12.6	3.98	97	.279	.333	17	.224	4	-1	-4	0	0.2
1956 Det-A	0	2	.000	6	3	1	0	0	17^2	15	2	13	6	14.8	4.08	101	.234	.372	0	.000	-0	0	0	1	0.0
1957 KC-A	6	13	.316	24	23	6	1	0	145^1	120	13	55	61	11.1	3.84	103	.223	.301	8	.182	0	-1	2	-0	0.2
1958 KC-A	12	11	.522	31	28	10	3	1	201	192	24	66	72	11.6	4.03	97	.244	.304	12	.174	0	-6	-3	5	0.3
1959 KC-A	10	13	.435	32	30	9	2	1	201^1	214	22	42	61	11.6	3.71	108	.270	.309	20	.282	7	3	7	-0	1.3
1960 KC-A	4	9	.308	28	15	5	2	0	122^1	110	15	35	50	10.8	3.83	104	.240	.296	2	.074	-1	1	2	-0	0.1
1961 LA-A	0	3	.000	12	2	0	0	0	29	40	2	16	9	17.4	5.59	81	.348	.427	0	.000	-1	-5	-3	1	-0.3
Total 14	129	157	.451	402	330	153	18	12	2477^1	2471	213	881	881	12.3	3.73	112	.260	.325	180	.218	26	78	122	14	17.3

● JERRY GARVIN Garvin, Theodore Jared b: 10/21/55, Oakland, Cal. BL/TL, 6'3", 195 lbs. Deb: 4/10/77

YEAR TM/L	W	L	PCT	G	GS	CG	SH	SV	IP	H	HR	BB	SO	RAT	ERA	ERA+	OAV	OOB	BH	AVG	PB	PR	/A	PD	TPI
1977 Tor-A	10	18	.357	34	34	12	1	0	244^2	247	33	85	127	12.4	4.19	100	.264	.328	0	—	0	-4	0	5	0.4
1978 Tor-A	4	12	.250	26	22	3	0	0	144^2	189	20	48	67	15.0	5.54	71	.319	.374	0	—	0	-29	-26	1	-2.5
1979 Tor-A	0	1	.000	8	1	0	0	0	22^2	15	2	10	14	10.7	2.78	156	.197	.307	0	—	0	4	4	-0	0.4
1980 Tor-A	4	7	.364	61	0	0	0	8	82^2	70	6	27	52	10.6	2.29	188	.233	.296	0	—	0	16	19	1	1.9
1981 Tor-A	1	2	.333	35	4	0	0	0	53	46	3	23	25	11.7	3.40	116	.240	.321	0	—	0	2	3	0	0.3
1982 Tor-A	1	1	.500	32	4	0	0	0	58^1	81	10	26	35	16.7	7.25	62	.335	.401	0	—	0	-21	-18	2	-2.2
Total 6	20	41	.328	196	65	15	1	8	606	648	74	219	320	13.0	4.43	94	.277	.342	0	—	0	-32	-18	9	-1.7

● NED GARVIN Garvin, Virgil Lee b: 1/1/1874, Navasota, Tex. d: 6/16/08, Fresno, Cal. TR, 6'3.5", 160 lbs. Deb: 7/13/1896

YEAR TM/L	W	L	PCT	G	GS	CG	SH	SV	IP	H	HR	BB	SO	RAT	ERA	ERA+	OAV	OOB	BH	AVG	PB	PR	/A	PD	TPI
1896 Phi-N	0	1	.000	2	1	1	0	0	13	19	0	7	4	18.0	7.62	57	.337	.411	0	.000	-1	-5	-5	-0	-0.5
1899 Chi-N	9	13	.409	24	23	22	4	0	199	202	1	42	69	11.6	2.85	132	.263	.311	11	.155	-5	22	20	1	1.5
1900 Chi-N	10	18	.357	30	28	25	1	0	246^1	225	4	63	107	11.1	2.41	150	.243	.303	14	.154	-5	**35**	33	4	3.1
1901 Mil-A	7	20	.259	37	27	22	1	2	257^1	258	4	90	122	12.7	3.46	104	.258	.328	10	.108	-9	6	4	4	-0.1
1902 Chi-A	10	10	.500	23	19	16	2	0	175^1	169	3	43	55	11.2	2.21	153	.254	.306	9	.153	-3	27	23	3	2.3
Bro-N	1	1	.500	2	2	2	1	0	18	15	0	4	7	9.5	1.00	276	.227	.271	1	.143	-0	4	4	0	0.4
1903 Bro-N	15	18	.455	38	34	30	2	2	298	277	2	84	154	11.3	3.08	104	.248	.308	8	.075	-8	6	4	8	0.3
1904 Bro-N	5	15	.250	23	22	16	2	0	181^2	141	6	78	86	11.1	1.68	163	.218	.308	8	.127	-4	21	21	4	2.4
NY-A	0	1	.000	2	2	0	0	0	12	14	0	2	8	12.0	2.25	121	.292	.320	0	.000	-1	0	1	1	0.1
Total 7	57	97	.370	181	158	134	13	4	1400^2	1320	20	413	612	11.6	2.72	125	.249	.312	61	.122	-35	117	104	24	9.5

YEAR TM/L	W	L	PCT	G	GS	CG	SH	SV	IP	H	HR	BB	SO	RAT	ERA	ERA+	OAV	OOB	BH	AVG	PB	PR	/A	PD	TPI

● HARRY GASPAR
Gaspar, Harry Lambert b: 4/28/1883, Kingsley, Iowa d: 5/14/40, Orange, Cal. BR/TR, 6', 180 lbs. Deb: 4/21/09

1909 Cin-N	19	11	.633	44	29	19	4	b	260	228	0	57	65	10.2	2.01	130	.242	.291	10	.122	-3	17	17	-5	1.0
1910 Cin-N	15	17	.469	48	31	16	4	7	275	257	6	75	74	11.4	2.59	113	.255	.317	14	.115	-3	14	10	-2	0.5
1911 Cin-N	11	17	.393	44	32	11	2	4	253²	272	9	69	76	12.6	3.30	100	.283	.340	13	.153	-2	3	0	-1	-0.4
1912 Cin-N	1	3	.250	7	6	2	0	0	36²	38	0	16	13	13.5	4.17	81	.277	.357	3	.250	0	-3	-3	-0	-0.3
Total 4	46	48	.489	143	98	48	10	13	825¹	795	15	217	228	11.5	2.69	110	.261	.318	36	.135	-8	31	25	-8	0.8

● CHARLIE GASSAWAY
Gassaway, Charles Cason "Sheriff" b: 8/12/18, Gassaway, Ga. d: 1/15/92, Miami, Fla. BL/TL, 6'2.5", 210 lbs. Deb: 9/25/44

1944 Chi-N	0	1	.000	2	2	0	0	0	11²	20	3	10	7	23.1	7.71	46	.385	.484	1	.250	0	-5	-5	-0	-0.5
1945 Phi-A	4	7	.364	24	11	4	0	0	118	114	4	55	50	13.0	3.74	92	.252	.336	6	.154	-2	-5	-4	-1	-0.8
1946 Cle-A	1	1	.500	13	6	0	0	0	50²	54	2	26	23	14.9	3.91	85	.273	.368	1	.067	-1	-2	-3	-0	-0.4
Total 3	5	9	.357	39	19	4	0	0	180¹	188	9	91	80	14.2	4.04	84	.268	.357	8	.138	-3	-12	-13	-2	-1.7

● MILT GASTON
Gaston, Nathaniel Milton b: 1/27/1896, Ridgefield Park, N.J. BR/TR, 6'1", 185 lbs. Deb: 4/20/24 F

1924 NY-A	5	3	.625	29	2	0	0	1	86	92	3	44	24	14.9	4.50	92	.286	.382	6	.222	-1	-3	-3	-1	-0.5
1925 StL-A	15	14	.517	42	30	16	0	1	238²	284	8	101	84	14.7	4.41	106	.305	.376	21	.262	-2	-0	7	-2	0.7
1926 StL-A	10	18	.357	32	28	14	1	0	214¹	227	13	101	39	13.9	4.33	99	.283	.366	13	.167	-2	-7	-1	-1	-0.3
1927 StL-A	13	17	.433	37	30	21	0	1	254	275	18	100	77	13.4	5.00	87	.281	.350	25	.260	6	-24	-18	1	-1.1
1928 Was-A	6	12	.333	28	22	8	3	0	148²	179	3	53	45	14.0	5.51	73	.302	.360	7	.143	-3	-24	-25	1	-2.5
1929 Bos-A	12	19	.387	39	29	20	1	2	243²	265	15	81	83	12.9	3.73	115	.289	.348	15	.192	0	14	15	-1	1.3
1930 Bos-A	13	20	.394	38	34	20	2	2	273	272	15	98	99	12.2	3.92	117	.259	.323	20	.204	-4	22	21	1	1.7
1931 Bos-A	2	13	.133	23	18	4	0	0	119	137	4	41	33	13.5	4.46	96	.291	.348	6	.158	-2	-1	-2	-0	-0.4
1932 Chi-A	7	17	.292	28	25	7	1	1	166²	183	10	73	44	13.9	4.00	108	.279	.352	14	.233	2	9	6	2	0.9
1933 Chi-A	8	12	.400	30	25	7	1	0	167	177	9	60	39	12.8	4.85	87	.272	.334	8	.154	-0	-11	-11	-1	-1.1
1934 Chi-A	6	19	.240	29	28	10	1	0	194	247	16	84	48	15.4	5.85	81	.313	.379	10	.147	-3	-29	-24	3	-2.2
Total 11	97	164	.372	355	271	127	10	8	2105	2338	114	836	615	13.7	4.55	97	.287	.355	145	.200	-4	-54	-35	0	-3.5

● WELCOME GASTON
Gaston, Welcome Thornburg b: 12/19/1872, Guernsey Co., Ohio d: 12/13/44, Columbus, Ohio TL, Deb: 10/06/1898

1898 Bro-N	1	1	.500	2	2	0	0	0	16	17	0	9	0	14.6	2.81	128	.270	.362	1	.125	-0	1	1	-0	0.1
1899 Bro-N	0	0	—	1	0	0	0	0	3	3	0	4	0	24.0	3.00	130	.260	.484	1	1.000	1	0	0	-0	0.1
Total 2	1	1	.500	3	2	0	0	0	19	20	0	13	0	16.1	2.84	128	.269	.384	2	.222	1	2	2	-0	0.2

● HANK GASTRIGHT
Gastright, Henry Carl (b: Henry Carl Gastreich)
b: 3/29/1865, Covington, Ky. d: 10/9/37, Cold Springs, Ky. BR/TR, 6'2", 190 lbs. Deb: 4/19/1889

1889 Col-a	10	16	.385	32	26	21	0	0	222²	255	8	104	115	14.7	4.57	79	.279	.355	17	.181	-4	-18	-23	-0	-2.2
1890 Col-a	30	14	.682	48	45	41	4	0	401¹	312	8	135	199	10.4	2.94	122	.208	.281	36	.213	3	42	29	-4	2.5
1891 Col-a	12	19	.387	35	33	28	1	0	283²	280	7	136	109	13.5	3.78	92	.249	.336	23	.197	2	-2	-10	1	-0.6
1892 Was-N	3	3	.500	11	7	6	0	0	79²	94	3	38	32	15.3	5.08	64	.282	.361	4	.138	0	-16	-16	-1	-1.5
1893 Pit-N	3	1	.750	9	5	4	0	0	59	74	3	39	12	17.7	6.25	73	.298	.399	4	.042	-3	-10	-11	-1	-1.1
Bos-N	12	4	.750	19	18	16	0	0	156	179	9	76	27	15.2	5.13	96	.279	.364	13	.191	-3	-8	-3	-2	-0.6
Yr	15	5	.750	28	23	19	0	0	215	253	12	115	39	15.8	5.44	89	.284	.371	14	.152	-6	-19	-15	-1	-1.7
1894 Bro-N	2	6	.250	16	8	6	1	2	93	135	1	55	20	19.0	6.39	77	.335	.423	7	.171	-2	-11	-15	-1	-1.3
1896 Cin-N	0	0	—	1	0	0	0	0	6	8	0	1	0	13.5	4.50	102	.317	.343	0	.000	-0	-0	-0	-0	0.0
Total 7	72	63	.533	171	142	121	6	2	1301¹	1337	39	584	514	13.7	4.20	92	.258	.339	101	.186	-7	-23	-51	-7	-4.8

● AUBREY GATEWOOD
Gatewood, Aubrey Lee b: 11/17/38, Little Rock, Ark. BR/TR, 6'1", 170 lbs. Deb: 9/11/63

1963 LA-A	1	1	.500	4	3	1	0	0	24	12	0	16	13	10.5	1.50	228	.148	.289	0	.000	-1	6	5	-0	0.5
1964 LA-A	3	3	.500	15	7	0	0	0	60¹	59	4	12	25	10.7	2.24	147	.258	.298	2	.100	-1	9	7	-0	0.6
1965 Cal-N	4	5	.444	46	3	0	0	0	92	91	5	37	37	12.6	3.42	99	.266	.339	3	.214	1	0	-0	-1	0.0
1970 Atl-N	0	0	—	3	0	0	0	0	2	4	0	2	0	31.5	4.50	95	.364	.500	—	—	0	-0	-0	-0	0.0
Total 4	8	9	.471	68	13	1	0	0	178¹	166	9	67	75	11.9	2.78	122	.250	.322	5	.119	-1	15	12	-1	1.1

● CHIPPY GAW
Gaw, George Joseph b: 3/13/1892, W.Newton, Mass. d: 5/26/68, Boston, Mass. BR/TR, 5'11", 180 lbs. Deb: 4/20/20

| 1920 Chi-N | 1 | 1 | .500 | 6 | 1 | 0 | 0 | 0 | 13 | 16 | 1 | 3 | 4 | 13.8 | 4.85 | 66 | .320 | .370 | 1 | .250 | -0 | -2 | -2 | -0 | -0.3 |

● DALE GEAR
Gear, Dale Dudley b: 2/2/1872, Lone Elm, Kan. d: 9/23/51, Topeka, Kan. BR/TR, 5'11", 165 lbs. Deb: 8/15/1896 ♦

1896 Cle-N	0	2	.000	3	2	2	0	0	23	35	1	6	6	16.8	5.48	83	.346	.394	6	.400	2	-3	-2	-0	-0.1
1901 Was-A	4	11	.267	24	16	14	1	1	163	199	9	22	35	12.4	4.03	91	.297	.324	47	.236	0	-7	-7	2	-0.4
Total 2	4	13	.235	27	18	16	1	1	186	234	10	28	41	13.0	4.21	90	.304	.333	57	.239	2	-9	-9	2	-0.5

● DINTY GEARIN
Gearin, Dennis John b: 10/15/1897, Providence, R.I. d: 3/11/59, Providence, R.I. BL/TL, 5'4", 148 lbs. Deb: 8/06/23

1923 *NY-N	1	1	.500	6	2	1	0	0	24	23	1	10	9	12.4	3.38	113	.264	.340	2	.286	0	2	1	-0	0.1
1924 NY-N	1	2	.333	6	3	2	0	0	29	30	3	16	4	14.3	2.48	148	.275	.368	3	.333	0	4	4	-0	0.4
Bos-N	0	1	.000	1	1	0	0	0	0	3	0	2	0	—	∞	—	1.000	1.000	0	—	0	-5	-5	-0	-0.4
Yr	1	3	.250	7	4	2	0	0	29	33	3	18	4	15.8	4.03	91	.295	.392	3	.333	0	-1	-1	-0	0.0
Total 2	2	4	.333	13	6	3	0	0	53	56	4	28	13	14.3	3.74	100	.281	.370	5	.313	1	1	0	-1	0.1

● BOB GEARY
Geary, Robert Norton "Speed" b: 5/10/1891, Cincinnati, Ohio d: 1/3/80, Cincinnati, Ohio BR/TR, 5'11", 168 lbs. Deb: 4/25/18

1918 Phi-A	2	5	.286	16	7	6	2	4	87	94	0	31	22	13.2	2.69	109	.289	.357	4	.148	-1	1	2	-1	0.1
1919 Phi-A	0	3	.000	9	2	1	0	0	32¹	32	1	18	9	13.9	4.73	72	.264	.360	5	.500	0	-5	-5	0	-0.3
1921 Cin-N	1	1	.500	10	1	0	0	0	29	38	1	2	10	12.4	4.34	82	.333	.345	2	.250	0	-2	-3	-0	-0.3
Total 3	3	9	.250	35	10	7	2	4	148¹	164	2	51	41	13.2	3.46	92	.293	.355	11	.244	1	-6	-5	-1	-0.5

● BOB GEBHARD
Gebhard, Robert Henry b: 1/3/43, Lamberton, Minn. BR/TR, 6'2", 210 lbs. Deb: 8/02/71 C

1971 Min-A	1	2	.333	17	0	0	0	0	18	17	0	11	13	14.5	3.00	118	.243	.354	0	—	0	1	1	1	0.2
1972 Min-A	0	1	.000	13	0	0	0	1	21	36	3	13	13	21.9	8.57	37	.371	.455	0	—	0	-13	-13	1	-1.2
1974 Mon-N	0	0	—	1	0	0	0	0	2	5	1	0	0	22.5	4.50	85	.500	.500	0	—	0	-0	-0	0	0.0
Total 3	1	3	.250	31	0	0	0	1	41	58	4	24	26	18.7	5.93	57	.328	.417	0	—	0	-12	-12	1	-1.0

● PETE GEBRIAN
Gebrian, Peter "Gabe" b: 8/10/23, Bayonne, N.J. BR/TR, 6', 170 lbs. Deb: 5/06/47

| 1947 Chi-A | 2 | 3 | .400 | 27 | 4 | 0 | 0 | 5 | 66¹ | 61 | 7 | 33 | 17 | 13.0 | 4.48 | 82 | .247 | .340 | 0 | .000 | -2 | -6 | -6 | -1 | -0.9 |

● JIM GEDDES
Geddes, James Lee b: 3/23/49, Columbus, Ohio BR/TR, 6'2", 200 lbs. Deb: 4/28/72

1972 Chi-A	0	0	—	5	1	0	0	0	10¹	12	1	10	3	20.0	6.97	45	.293	.442	0	.000	-0	-4	-4	-0	-0.5
1973 Chi-A	0	0	—	6	1	0	0	0	15²	14	0	14	7	17.8	2.87	138	.255	.431	—	—	0	2	2	0	0.2
Total 2	0	0	—	11	2	0	0	0	26	26	1	24	10	18.7	4.50	81	.271	.435	0	.000	-0	-3	-3	-0	-0.3

● JOE GEDEON
Gedeon, Elmer Joseph b: 12/5/1893, Sacramento, Cal. d: 5/19/41, San Francisco, Cal BR/TR, 6', 167 lbs. Deb: 5/13/13 ♦

| 1913 Was-A | 0 | 0 | — | 1 | 0 | 0 | 0 | 0 | 1 | 1 | 0 | 0 | 0 | 9.0 | 0.00 | — | .250 | .250 | 13 | .183 | 0 | 0 | -0 | -0 | 0.1 |

● COUNT GEDNEY
Gedney, Alfred W. b: 5/10/1849, Brooklyn, N.Y. d: 3/26/22, Hackensack, N.J. 5'9", 140 lbs. Deb: 4/27/1872 ♦

| 1875 Mut-n | 1 | 0 | 1.000 | 2 | 1 | 1 | 0 | 0 | 11 | 7 | 0 | 1 | | 6.5 | 1.64 | 158 | .179 | .200 | 54 | .203 | | 1 | 1 | | 0.1 |

● JOHNNY GEE
Gee, John Alexander "Whiz" b: 12/7/15, Syracuse, N.Y. d: 1/23/88, Cortland, N.Y. BL/TL, 6'9", 225 lbs. Deb: 9/17/39

| 1939 Pit-N | 1 | 2 | .333 | 3 | 3 | 1 | 0 | 0 | 19² | 20 | 0 | 10 | 16 | 13.7 | 4.12 | 93 | .253 | .337 | 0 | .000 | -1 | -0 | -1 | 1 | -0.1 |
| 1941 Pit-N | 0 | 2 | .000 | 3 | 2 | 0 | 0 | 0 | 7¹ | 10 | 0 | 5 | 2 | 18.4 | 6.14 | 59 | .294 | .385 | 1 | .333 | 0 | -2 | -2 | -0 | -0.2 |

YEAR	TM/L	W	L	PCT	G	GS	CG	SH	SV	IP	H	HR	BB	SO	RAT	ERA	ERA+	OAV	OOB	BH	AVG	PB	PR	/A	PD	TPI
1943	Pit-N	4	4	.500	15	10	2	0	0	82	89	5	27	18	12.7	4.28	81	.280	.336	3	.115	-1	-8	-7	-3	-1.1
1944	Pit-N	0	0	—	4	0	0	0	0	11^1	20	0	5	3	19.9	7.15	52	.377	.431	1	.500	0	-4	-4	-0	-0.4
	NY-N	0	0	—	4	0	0	0	0	4^2	5	0	0	3	9.6	0.00	—	.263	.263	0	—	0	2	2	0	0.2
	Yr	0	0	—	8	0	0	0	0	16	25	0	5	6	16.9	5.06	73	.347	.390	1	.500	0	-3	-2	0	-0.2
1945	NY-N	0	0	—	2	0	0	0	1	3	5	0	2	1	21.0	9.00	43	.385	.467	0	.000	-0	-2	-2	0	-0.2
1946	NY-N	2	4	.333	13	6	1	0	0	47^1	60	3	15	22	14.6	3.99	86	.308	.363	3	.231	0	-3	-3	-1	-0.4
Total	6	7	12	.368	44	21	4	0	1	175^1	209	8	64	65	14.1	4.41	80	.294	.354	8	.157	-1	-18	-17	-3	-2.2

● BILLY GEER

Geer, William Henry Harrison (b: George Harrison Geer) b: 8/13/1849, Syracuse, N.Y. TR , 5'8", 160 lbs. Deb: 10/15/1874 ♦

1884	Bro-a	0	0	—	2	0	0	0	0	5	14	0	3	1	30.6	12.60	26	.609	.654	82	.210	0	-5	-5	-0	-0.4

● HENRY GEHRING

Gehring, Henry b: 1/24/1881, St.Paul, Minn. d: 4/18/12, Kansas City, Mo. BR/TR, Deb: 7/16/07

1907	Was-A	3	7	.300	15	9	8	2	0	87	92	1	14	31	11.1	3.31	73	.273	.304	9	.205	3	-7	-9	-2	-0.8
1908	Was-A	0	1	.000	3	1	0	0	0	5	9	0	2	0	23.4	14.40	16	.450	.542	3	.600	2	-7	-7	0	-0.5
Total	2	3	8	.273	18	10	8	2	0	92	101	1	16	31	11.7	3.91	62	.283	.319	12	.245	5	-14	-15	-2	-1.3

● PAUL GEHRMAN

Gehrman, Paul Arthur "Dutch" b: 5/3/12, Marquam, Ore. d: 10/23/86, Bend, Ore. BR/TR, 6', 195 lbs. Deb: 9/15/37

1937	Cin-N	0	1	.000	2	1	0	0	0	9^1	11	0	5	1	15.4	2.89	129	.282	.364	0	.000	-0	1	1	0	0.1

● GARY GEIGER

Geiger, Gary Merle b: 4/4/37, Sand Ridge, Ill. BL/TR, 6', 168 lbs. Deb: 4/15/58 ♦

1958	Cle-A	0	0	—	1	0	0	0	0	2	2	0	1	2	13.5	9.00	41	.286	.375	45	.231	0	-1	-1	0	-0.1

● EMIL GEIS

Geis, Emil Michael b: 3/1861, Villmar, Germany BR/TR, 5'11", 170 lbs. Deb: 7/19/1882

1882	Bal-a	4	9	.308	13	13	10	1	0	95^2	84	2	22	10	10.0	4.80	57	.220	.263	6	.146	-2	-22	-22	-3	-2.1

● BILL GEIS

Geis, William J. (b: William J. Geiss) b: 7/15/1858, Chicago, Ill. d: 9/18/24, Chicago, Ill. 5'10", 164 lbs. Deb: 5/01/1884 F♦

1884	Det-N	0	0	—	1	0	0	0	0	5	14	0	2	1	28.8	14.40	20	.424	.457	50	.177	-0	-6	-6	0	-0.5

● DAVE GEISEL

Geisel, John David b: 1/18/55, Windber, Pa. BL/TL, 6'3", 210 lbs. Deb: 6/13/78

1978	Chi-N	1	0	1.000	18	1	0	0	0	23^1	27	0	11	15	14.7	4.24	95	.278	.352	0	.000	-0	-2	-1	-0	-0.1
1979	Chi-N	0	0	—	7	0	0	0	0	15	10	0	4	5	9.0	0.60	686	.189	.259	0	.000	-0	5	6	-0	0.6
1981	Chi-N	2	0	1.000	11	2	0	0	0	16	11	0	10	7	11.8	0.56	657	.204	.328	0	.000	-0	5	6	-0	0.6
1982	Tor-A	1	1	.500	16	2	0	0	0	31^2	32	6	17	22	14.5	3.98	113	.260	.359	0	—	0	0	2	-0	-0.2
1983	Tor-A	0	3	.000	47	0	0	0	5	52^1	47	4	31	50	13.8	4.64	93	.240	.349	0	—	0	-3	-2	-1	-0.4
1984	Sea-A	1	1	.500	20	3	0	0	3	43^1	47	2	9	28	12.0	4.15	96	.273	.317	0	—	0	-1	-1	-1	-0.1
1985	Sea-A	0	0	—	12	0	0	0	0	27	35	3	15	17	16.7	6.33	67	.310	.391	0	—	0	-7	-6	-0	-0.7
Total	7	5	5	.500	131	8	0	0	8	208^2	209	15	97	144	13.5	4.01	104	.259	.343	0	.000	-1	-2	4	-3	-0.3

● VERN GEISHERT

Geishert, Vernon William b: 1/10/46, Madison, Wis. BR/TR, 6'1", 215 lbs. Deb: 8/26/69

1969	Cal-A	1	1	.500	11	3	0	0	1	31	32	4	7	18	11.6	4.65	75	.267	.313	0	.000	-1	-4	-4	0	-0.5

● EMIL GEISS

Geiss, Emil August b: 3/20/1867, Chicago, Ill. d: 10/4/11, Chicago, Ill. BR/TR, Deb: 5/18/1887 F♦

1887	Chi-N	0	1	.000	1	1	1	0	0	9	17	0	3	4	20.0	8.00	56	.395	.435	1	.083	-1	-4	-4	0	-0.3

● CHARLIE GELBERT

Gelbert, Charles Magnus b: 1/26/06, Scranton, Pa. d: 1/13/67, Easton, Pa. BR/TR, 5'11", 170 lbs. Deb: 4/16/29 ♦

1940	Was-A	0	0	—	2	0	0	0	0	4	5	2	3	1	18.0	9.00	46	.278	.381	20	.370	1	-2	-2	0	-0.2

● JOHN GELNAR

Gelnar, John Richard b: 6/25/43, Granite, Okla BR/TR, 6'1.5", 190 lbs. Deb: 8/04/64

1964	Pit-N	0	0	—	7	0	0	0	0	9	11	2	1	4	12.0	5.00	70	.314	.333	0	—	0	-1	-1	-0	-0.2
1967	Pit-N	0	1	.000	10	1	0	0	0	19	30	4	11	5	20.4	8.05	42	.375	.462	1	.167	0	-10	-10	0	-1.0
1969	Sea-A	3	10	.231	39	10	0	0	3	108^2	103	7	26	69	11.1	3.31	110	.250	.302	1	.053	-2	4	4	-0	0.2
1970	Mil-A	4	3	.571	53	0	0	0	4	92^1	98	7	23	48	12.3	4.19	90	.277	.330	1	.083	-1	-5	-4	1	-0.3
1971	Mil-A	0	0	—	2	0	0	0	0	1^1	3	0	1	0	27.0	13.50	26	.429	.500	0	—	0	-1	-1	0	-0.1
Total	5	7	14	.333	111	11	0	0	7	230^1	245	20	62	126	12.5	4.18	88	.276	.332	3	.081	-2	-14	-13	1	-1.4

● JOE GENEWICH

Genewich, Joseph Edward b: 1/15/1897, Elmira, N.Y. d: 12/21/85, Lockport, N.Y. BR/TR, 6', 174 lbs. Deb: 9/13/22

1922	Bos-N	0	2	.000	6	2	1	0	0	23	29	2	11	4	15.7	7.04	57	.319	.392	1	.167	-0	-8	-8	-0	-0.7
1923	Bos-N	13	14	.481	43	24	12	1	1	227^1	272	15	46	54	12.9	3.72	107	.303	.341	19	.247	2	7	7	2	1.0
1924	Bos-N	10	19	.345	34	27	11	2	1	200^1	258	4	65	43	14.9	5.21	73	.329	.386	10	.167	-2	-30	-31	-0	-3.1
1925	Bos-N	12	10	.545	34	21	10	0	0	169	185	4	41	34	12.4	3.99	100	.279	.327	15	.273	1	5	0	-1	0.1
1926	Bos-N	8	16	.333	37	26	12	2	2	216	239	6	63	59	12.8	3.88	92	.288	.342	11	.164	-1	-1	-8	1	-0.8
1927	Bos-N	11	8	.579	40	19	7	0	1	181	199	7	54	38	12.7	3.83	97	.279	.332	11	.193	-1	2	-2	0	-0.3
1928	Bos-N	3	7	.300	13	11	4	0	0	80^2	88	14	18	15	12.2	4.13	95	.280	.325	1	.038	-3	-1	-2	1	-0.4
	NY-N	11	4	.733	26	18	10	2	3	158^1	136	10	54	37	10.9	3.18	123	.232	.298	13	.203	-1	14	13	1	1.2
	Yr	14	11	.560	39	29	14	2	3	239	224	24	72	52	11.2	3.50	112	.248	.304	14	.156	-4	13	11	2	0.8
1929	NY-N	3	7	.300	21	9	1	0	1	85	133	9	30	19	17.4	6.78	68	.359	.409	12	.375	3	-19	-21	0	-1.6
1930	NY-N	2	5	.286	18	9	3	0	3	61	71	6	20	13	13.6	5.61	84	.297	.354	3	.150	-1	-4	-6	2	-0.4
Total	9	73	92	.442	272	166	71	7	12	1401^2	1610	77	402	316	13.1	4.29	91	.293	.345	96	.207	-3	-35	-58	5	-5.0

● GARY GENTRY

Gentry, Gary Edward b: 10/6/46, Phoenix, Ariz. BR/TR, 6', 183 lbs. Deb: 4/10/69

1969	*NY-N	13	12	.520	35	35	6	3	0	233^2	192	24	81	154	10.7	3.43	107	.222	.293	6	.081	-4	4	6	1	0.3
1970	NY-N	9	9	.500	32	29	5	2	1	188^1	155	19	86	134	11.9	3.68	109	.224	.318	4	.068	-2	8	7	-2	0.3
1971	NY-N	12	11	.522	32	31	8	3	0	203^1	167	16	82	155	11.3	3.23	105	.224	.305	5	.074	-5	5	4	-1	-0.2
1972	NY-N	7	10	.412	32	26	3	0	0	164	153	20	75	120	12.8	4.01	84	.250	.338	5	.104	-1	-10	-12	2	-1.1
1973	Atl-N	4	6	.400	16	14	3	0	1	86^2	74	7	35	42	11.4	3.43	115	.231	.308	7	.233	1	2	5	-1	0.5
1974	Atl-N	0	0	—	3	1	0	0	0	6^2	4	1	2	0	9.5	1.35	280	.167	.259	0	.000	-0	2	2	-0	0.2
1975	Atl-N	1	1	.500	7	2	0	0	0	20	25	3	8	10	14.8	4.95	76	.313	.375	0	.000	-1	-3	-3	0	-0.3
Total	7	46	49	.484	157	138	25	8	2	902^2	770	90	369	615	11.6	3.56	103	.231	.312	27	.095	-12	8	9	-1	-0.3

● RUFE GENTRY

Gentry, James Ruffus b: 5/18/18, Winston-Salem, N.C BR/TR, 6'1", 180 lbs. Deb: 9/10/43 F

1943	Det-A	1	3	.250	4	4	2	0	0	29^1	30	2	12	8	13.5	3.68	96	.268	.349	0	.000	-1	-1	-1	-0	-0.2
1944	Det-A	12	14	.462	37	30	10	3	0	203^2	211	9	108	68	14.3	4.24	84	.273	.365	15	.197	-1	-18	-15	1	-1.6
1946	Det-A	0	0	—	2	0	0	0	0	3	4	0	7	1	33.0	15.00	24	.333	.579	0	—	0	-4	-4	-0	-0.4
1947	Det-A	0	0	—	1	0	0	0	0	0^1	1	0	2	0	81.0	81.00	5	.500	.750	0	—	0	-3	-3	0	-0.3
1948	Det-A	0	0	—	4	0	0	0	0	6^2	5	0	5	1	14.9	2.70	162	.208	.367	1	1.000	0	1	1	-0	0.2
Total	5	13	17	.433	48	34	12	3	0	243	251	11	134	78	14.5	4.37	82	.272	.368	16	.184	-2	-25	-21	0	-2.3

● CHRIS GEORGE

George, Christopher Sean b: 9/24/66, Pittsburgh, Pa. BR/TR, 6'2", 200 lbs. Deb: 10/01/91

1991	Mil-A	0	0	—	2	1	0	0	0	6	8	0	0	2	12.0	3.00	132	.333	.333	0	—	0	1	1	-0	0.2

● LEFTY GEORGE

George, Thomas Edward b: 8/13/1886, Pittsburgh, Pa. d: 5/13/55, York, Pa. BL/TL, 6', 155 lbs. Deb: 4/14/11

1911	StL-A	4	9	.308	27	13	6	1	0	116^1	136	3	51	23	15.2	4.18	81	.256	.332	5	.114	-3	-11	-10	-1	-1.4
1912	Cle-A	0	5	.000	11	5	2	0	0	44^1	69	1	18	18	18.1	4.87	70	.373	.434	3	.214	1	-8	-7	0	-0.6
1915	Cin-N	2	2	.500	5	3	2	1	0	28	24	1	8	11	11.9	3.86	74	.242	.330	4	.333	2	-3	-3	1	0.0
1918	Bos-N	1	5	.167	9	5	4	0	0	54^1	56	0	21	22	13.3	2.32	116	.281	.359	2	.091	-2	3	2	2	0.3
Total	4	7	21	.250	52	26	14	2	0	243	285	5	98	74	14.9	3.85	82	.281	.355	14	.152	-2	-19	-19	1	-1.7

YEAR TM/L	W	L	PCT	G	GS	CG	SH	SV	IP	H	HR	BB	SO	RAT	ERA	ERA+	OAV	OOB	BH	AVG	PB	PR	/A	PD	TPI
● **BILL GEORGE** George, William M. b: 1/27/1865, Bellaire, Ohio d: 8/23/16, Wheeling, W.Va. BR/TL, 5'8", 165 lbs. Deb: 5/11/1887 ♦																									
1887 NY-N	3	9	.250	13	13	11	0	0	108	126	1	89	49	19.1	5.25	72	.292	.428	9	.170	-3	-14	-18	2	-1.6
1888 *NY-N	2	1	.667	4	3	3	1	0	33^2	18	0	11	26	8.0	1.34	205	.149	.226	9	.231	1	6	5	-0	0.6
1889 Col-a	0	0	—	2	0	0	0	0	8	11	1	3	3	15.8	7.88	46	.317	.371	4	.235	-0	-4	-4	0	-0.3
Total 3	5	10	.333	19	16	14	1	0	149^2	155	2	103	78	16.4	4.51	78	.264	.387	26	.210	-2	-12	-16	2	-1.3
● **OSCAR GEORGY** Georgy, Oscar John b: 11/25/16, New Orleans, La. BR/TR, 6'3.5", 180 lbs. Deb: 6/04/38																									
1938 NY-N	0	0	—	1	0	0	0	0	1	2	0	1	0	27.0	18.00	21	.400	.500	0	—	0	-2	-2	-0	-0.2
● **DAVE GERARD** Gerard, David Frederick b: 8/6/36, New York, N.Y. BR/TR, 6'2", 205 lbs. Deb: 4/10/62																									
1962 Chi-N	2	3	.400	39	0	0	0	3	58^2	67	10	28	30	14.7	4.91	84	.289	.368	3	.375	1	-6	-5	-0	-0.4
● **GEORGE GERBERMAN** Gerberman, George Alois b: 3/8/42, ElCampo, Tex. BR/TR, 6', 180 lbs. Deb: 9/23/62																									
1962 Chi-N	0	0	—	1	1	0	0	0	5^1	3	1	5	1	13.5	1.69	246	.158	.333	0	.000	0	1	1	-0	0.2
● **RUSTY GERHARDT** Gerhardt, Allen Russell b: 8/13/50, Baltimore, Md. BB/TL, 5'9", 175 lbs. Deb: 7/27/74																									
1974 SD-N	2	1	.667	23	1	0	0	1	35^2	44	1	17	22	15.9	7.07	50	.308	.389	1	.167	-0	-14	-14	-0	-1.5
● **AL GERHEAUSER** Gerheauser, Albert "Lefty" b: 6/24/17, St.Louis, Mo. d: 5/28/72, Springfield, Mo. BL/TL, 6'3", 190 lbs. Deb: 4/24/43																									
1943 Phi-N	10	19	.345	38	31	11	2	0	215	222	10	70	92	12.3	3.60	94	.263	.321	8	.113	-3	-5	-5	-1	-1.0
1944 Phi-N	8	16	.333	30	29	10	2	0	182^2	210	8	65	66	13.6	4.58	79	.285	.344	15	.231	3	-20	-20	-2	-1.8
1945 Pit-N	5	10	.333	32	14	5	0	1	140^1	170	5	54	55	14.4	3.91	101	.304	.366	12	.250	3	-2	1	2	0.5
1946 Pit-N	2	2	.500	35	3	1	0	0	81^2	92	2	25	32	13.0	3.97	89	.286	.339	7	.333	2	-5	-4	1	-0.1
1948 StL-A	0	3	.000	14	2	0	0	0	23^1	32	0	10	10	16.6	7.33	62	.317	.384	2	.333	0	-8	-7	-0	-0.7
Total 5	25	50	.333	149	79	27	4	1	643	726	25	224	255	13.4	4.13	88	.283	.342	44	.209	6	-40	-36	-0	-3.1
● **STEVE GERKIN** Gerkin, Stephen Paul "Splinter" b: 11/19/15, Grafton, W.Va. d: 11/9/78, Bay Pines, Fla. BR/TR, 6'1", 162 lbs. Deb: 5/13/45																									
1945 Phi-A	0	12	.000	21	12	3	0	0	102	112	4	27	25	12.5	3.62	95	.285	.336	2	.059	-4	-3	-2	0	-0.6
● **LES GERMAN** German, Lester Stanley b: 6/1/1869, Baltimore, Md. d: 6/10/34, Germantown, Md. BR/TR, 5'8", 165 lbs. Deb: 8/27/1890																									
1890 Bal-a	5	11	.313	17	16	15	0	0	132^1	147	2	54	37	14.6	4.83	84	.273	.353	6	.118	-2	-14	-11	-2	-1.3
1893 NY-N	8	8	.500	20	18	14	0	0	152	162	6	70	35	14.3	4.14	112	.265	.349	23	.311	3	9	9	-1	0.8
1894 NY-N	9	8	.529	23	15	10	0	1	134	178	7	66	17	17.1	5.78	91	.316	.397	17	.298	0	-7	-8	2	-0.4
1895 NY-N	7	11	.389	25	18	16	0	0	178^1	243	7	78	36	16.7	5.96	78	.320	.390	29	.261	2	-23	-26	-0	-1.9
1896 NY-N	0	0	—	1	0	0	0	0	2^2	9	0	1	0	33.8	13.50	31	.540	.566	0	.000	-0	-3	-3	-0	-0.2
Was-N	2	20	.091	28	20	14	0	1	166^2	240	6	74	20	17.2	6.32	70	.334	.400	16	.229	-0	-36	-35	1	-2.8
Yr	2	20	.091	29	20	14	0	1	169^1	249	6	75	20	17.5	6.43	68	.339	.404	16	.225	-1	-39	-38	1	-3.0
1897 Was-N	3	5	.375	15	5	4	0	0	83^2	117	2	33	2	16.9	5.59	78	.328	.395	15	.341	2	-12	-12	-1	-0.8
Total 6	34	63	.351	129	92	73	0	2	849^2	1096	30	376	147	16.2	5.49	83	.307	.382	106	.260	5	-86	-86	-0	-6.6
● **ED GERNER** Gerner, Edwin Frederick "Lefty" b: 7/22/1897, Philadelphia, Pa. d: 5/15/70, Philadelphia, Pa. BL/TL, 5'8.5", 175 lbs. Deb: 5/14/19																									
1919 Cin-N	1	0	1.000	5	1	0	0	0	17	22	0	3	2	14.3	3.18	87	.333	.380	1	.167	0	-0	-1	1	0.0
● **LEFTY GERVAIS** Gervais, Lucien Edward b: 7/6/1890, Grover, Wis. d: 10/19/50, Los Angeles, Cal. BL/TL, 5'10", 165 lbs. Deb: 4/17/13																									
1913 Bos-N	0	1	.000	5	2	1	0	0	15^2	18	0	4	1	12.6	5.74	57	.383	.431	0	.000	-0	-4	-4	-0	-0.5
● **CHARLIE GESSNER** Gessner, Charles J. b: Philadelphia, Pa. Deb: 7/19/1886																									
1886 Phi-a	0	1	.000	1	1	1	0	0	8	13	0	5	0	22.5	9.00	39	.351	.455	1	.250	-0	-5	-5	-0	-0.4
● **AL GETTEL** Gettel, Allen Jones b: 9/17/17, Norfolk, Va. BR/TR, 6'3.5", 200 lbs. Deb: 4/20/45																									
1945 NY-A	9	8	.529	27	17	9	0	3	154^2	141	11	53	67	11.7	3.90	89	.243	.314	16	.281	2	-9	-7	-1	-0.7
1946 NY-A	6	7	.462	26	11	5	2	0	103	89	6	40	54	11.4	2.97	116	.229	.305	4	.125	-2	6	5	0	0.4
1947 Cle-A	11	10	.524	31	21	9	2	0	149	122	12	62	64	11.3	3.20	109	.229	.313	15	.294	4	8	5	1	1.0
1948 Cle-A	0	1	.000	5	2	0	0	0	7^2	15	2	10	4	30.5	17.61	23	.385	.520	0	.000	-0	-11	-12	-0	-1.1
Chi-A	8	10	.444	22	19	7	0	1	148	154	7	60	49	13.3	4.01	106	.268	.342	13	.241	0	5	4	-1	0.4
Yr	8	11	.421	27	21	7	0	1	155^2	169	9	70	53	14.0	4.68	91	.275	.353	13	.228	-0	-7	-7	-1	-0.7
1949 Chi-A	2	5	.286	19	7	1	1	1	63	69	12	26	22	13.9	6.43	65	.283	.357	3	.167	-0	-16	-16	-1	-1.5
Was-A	0	2	.000	16	1	0	0	1	34^2	43	4	24	7	17.4	5.45	78	.314	.416	0	.000	-1	-5	-5	1	-0.5
Yr	2	7	.222	35	8	1	1	2	97^2	112	16	50	29	14.9	6.08	69	.292	.374	3	.115	-1	-20	-20	-0	-2.0
1951 NY-N	1	2	.333	30	1	0	0	0	57^1	52	12	25	36	12.1	4.87	80	.240	.318	1	.083	-1	-6	-6	1	-0.6
1955 StL-N	1	0	1.000	8	0	0	0	0	17	26	6	10	7	19.1	9.00	45	.361	.439	3	.500	1	-9	-9	-1	-0.8
Total 7	38	45	.458	184	79	31	5	6	734^1	711	72	310	310	12.7	4.28	88	.255	.334	55	.228	3	-37	-40	-1	-3.4
● **CHARLIE GETTIG** Gettig, Charles Henry b: 12/1870, Baltimore, Md. d: 4/11/35, Baltimore, Md. 5'10", 172 lbs. Deb: 8/05/1896 ♦																									
1896 NY-N	1	0	1.000	4	1	1	0	1	14	20	0	8	5	19.3	9.64	44	.332	.427	3	.333	1	-8	-8	0	-0.6
1897 NY-N	1	1	.500	3	2	2	0	0	19	23	0	9	7	16.1	5.21	80	.297	.384	15	.200	-0	-2	-2	0	-0.2
1898 NY-N	6	3	.667	17	8	7	0	0	115	141	1	39	14	14.7	3.83	91	.299	.363	49	.250	2	-3	-5	1	-0.1
1899 NY-N	7	8	.467	18	15	12	0	0	128	161	3	54	25	15.4	4.43	85	.307	.376	24	.247	1	-8	-10	-1	-0.8
Total 4	15	12	.556	42	26	22	0	1	276	345	4	110	51	15.4	4.50	82	.304	.374	91	.241	3	-21	-25	1	-1.7
● **TOM GETTINGER** Gettinger, Thomas L. b: 1870, Mobile, Ala. BL/TL, 5'10", 180 lbs. Deb: 9/21/1889 ♦																									
1895 Lou-N	0	0	—	2	0	0	0	0	6^1	13	1	1	0	19.9	7.11	65	.415	.433	70	.269	0	-2	-2	0	-0.1
● **CHARLIE GETZIEN** Getzien, Charles H. "Pretzels" b: 2/14/1864, Germany d: 6/19/32, Chicago, Ill. BR/TR, 5'10", 172 lbs. Deb: 8/13/1884																									
1884 Det-N	5	12	.294	17	17	17	1	0	147^1	118	2	25	107	8.7	1.95	148	.204	.237	6	.109	-4	17	15	-2	1.0
1885 Det-N	12	25	.324	37	37	37	1	0	330	360	8	92	110	12.3	3.03	94	.264	.311	29	.212	-1	-8	-7	-2	-0.9
1886 Det-N	30	11	.732	43	43	42	1	0	386^2	388	6	85	172	11.0	3.03	110	.250	.288	29	.176	-3	12	12	-2	0.5
1887 *Det-N	29	13	**.690**	43	42	41	2	0	366^2	373	24	106	135	11.8	3.73	109	.254	.305	29	.186	-2	14	13	0	0.8
1888 Det-N	19	25	.432	46	46	45	2	0	404	411	13	54	202	10.5	3.05	91	.251	.279	41	.246	9	-9	-13	-2	-0.6
1889 Ind-N	18	22	.450	45	44	36	0	1	349	395	27	100	139	13.0	4.54	92	.277	.328	25	.180	2	-20	-14	-3	-1.2
1890 Bos-N	23	17	.575	40	40	39	4	0	350	342	5	82	140	11.0	3.19	118	.248	.292	34	.231	5	15	22	-2	2.2
1891 Bos-N	4	5	.444	11	9	7	0	0	89	112	4	23	29	13.7	3.84	95	.296	.337	7	.171	1	-5	-2	1	0.0
Cle-N	0	1	.000	1	1	1	0	0	9	12	1	4	4	16.0	8.00	43	.308	.373	0	.000	-1	-5	-5	-1	-0.4
Yr	4	6	.400	12	10	8	0	0	98	124	5	27	33	13.9	4.22	86	.297	.340	7	.156	1	-10	-6	0	-0.4
1892 StL-N	5	8	.385	13	13	12	0	0	108	159	5	31	32	16.3	5.67	56	.329	.377	9	.200	1	-29	-30	-1	-2.5
Total 9	145	139	.511	296	292	277	11	1	2539^2	2670	95	602	1070	11.7	3.46	99	.259	.302	209	.198	8	-17	-9	-13	-1.1
● **RUBE GEYER** Geyer, Jacob Bowman b: 3/26/1884, Allegheny, Pa. d: 10/12/62, Ford Township, Minn. BR/TR, 5'10", 170 lbs. Deb: 4/24/10																									
1910 StL-N	0	1	.000	4	0	0	0	0	4	5	0	3	5	18.0	4.50	66	.294	.400	0	.000	-0	-1	-1	-0	-0.1
1911 StL-N	9	6	.600	29	11	7	1	0	148^2	141	7	56	46	12.3	3.27	103	.259	.335	13	.228	1	2	2	-1	0.1
1912 StL-N	7	14	.333	41	18	5	0	0	181	191	4	84	61	13.9	3.28	104	.288	.371	11	.208	-0	3	3	0	0.3
1913 StL-N	1	5	.167	30	4	2	0	1	78^2	83	6	38	21	14.1	5.26	61	.282	.368	2	.091	-2	-18	-18	-1	-2.0
Total 4	17	26	.395	104	33	14	1	1	412^1	420	17	181	133	13.4	3.67	92	.276	.358	26	.195	-1	-14	-14	-2	-1.7
● **TONY GHELFI** Ghelfi, Anthony Paul b: 8/23/61, LaCrosse, Wis. BR/TR, 6'3", 185 lbs. Deb: 9/01/83																									
1983 Phi-N	1	1	.500	3	3	0	0	0	14^1	15	2	6	14	13.2	3.14	114	.268	.339	1	.250	0	1	1	1	0.2

● BOB GIALLOMBARDO Giallombardo, Robert Paul b: 5/20/37, Brooklyn, N.Y. BL/TL, 6', 175 lbs. Deb: 6/21/58

YEAR	TM/L	W	L	PCT	G	GS	CG	SH	SV	IP	H	HR	BB	SO	RAT	ERA	ERA+	OAV	OOB	BH	AVG	PB	PR	/A	PD	TPI
1958	LA-N	1	1	.500	6	5	0	0	0	26^1	29	3	15	14	15.0	3.76	109	.284	.376	1	.167	-0	1	1	0	0.1

● JOE GIARD Giard, Joseph Oscar "Peco" b: 10/7/1898, Ware, Mass. d: 7/10/56, Worcester, Mass. BL/TL, 5'10.5", 170 lbs. Deb: 4/18/25

YEAR	TM/L	W	L	PCT	G	GS	CG	SH	SV	IP	H	HR	BB	SO	RAT	ERA	ERA+	OAV	OOB	BH	AVG	PB	PR	/A	PD	TPI
1925	StL-A	10	5	.667	30	21	9	4	0	160^2	179	13	87	43	15.2	5.04	93	.295	.388	3	.057	-6	-12	-7	2	-1.0
1926	StL-A	3	10	.231	22	15	2	0	0	90	113	7	67	18	18.1	7.00	61	.318	.428	8	.276	0	-30	-27	-1	-2.5
1927	NY-A	0	0	—	16	0	0	0	0	27	38	1	19	10	19.0	8.00	48	.352	.449	2	.286	0	-12	-12	-0	-1.2
Total	3	13	15	.464	68	36	11	4	0	277^2	330	21	173	71	16.5	5.96	75	.309	.408	13	.146	-6	-53	-46	1	-4.7

● JOE GIBBON Gibbon, Joseph Charles b: 4/10/35, Hickory, Miss. BR/TL, 6'4", 210 lbs. Deb: 4/17/60

YEAR	TM/L	W	L	PCT	G	GS	CG	SH	SV	IP	H	HR	BB	SO	RAT	ERA	ERA+	OAV	OOB	BH	AVG	PB	PR	/A	PD	TPI
1960	*Pit-N	4	2	.667	27	9	0	0	0	80^1	87	5	31	60	13.2	4.03	93	.277	.342	4	.211	1	-2	-3	0	-0.2
1961	Pit-N	13	10	.565	30	29	7	3	0	195^1	185	16	57	145	11.3	3.32	120	.251	.309	8	.136	-2	16	15	-0	1.3
1962	Pit-N	3	4	.429	19	8	0	0	0	57	53	4	24	26	12.2	3.63	108	.250	.326	3	.176	-0	2	2	1	0.3
1963	Pit-N	5	12	.294	37	22	5	0	1	147^1	147	7	54	110	12.6	3.30	100	.258	.328	4	.093	-2	-0	-0	1	-0.1
1964	Pit-N	10	7	.588	28	24	3	0	0	146^2	145	10	54	97	12.6	3.68	95	.262	.334	12	.255	3	-2	-3	1	0.1
1965	Pit-N	4	9	.308	31	15	1	0	1	105^2	85	7	34	63	10.5	4.51	78	.221	.291	3	.115	-0	-11	-12	0	-1.2
1966	SF-N	4	6	.400	37	10	1	0	1	81	86	4	16	48	11.6	3.67	100	.275	.314	3	.200	0	-1	0	1	0.2
1967	SF-N	6	2	.750	28	10	3	1	1	82	65	4	33	63	11.1	3.07	107	.220	.305	1	.042	-1	3	2	2	0.3
1968	SF-N	1	2	.333	29	0	0	0	1	40	33	3	19	22	12.1	1.57	187	.234	.333	0	.000	-0	6	6	0	0.7
1969	SF-N	1	3	.250	16	0	0	0	2	20	15	1	13	9	13.0	3.60	97	.211	.341	0	.000	-0	-0	-0	1	0.1
	Pit-N	5	1	.833	35	0	0	0	9	51^1	38	5	17	35	10.0	1.93	181	.208	.282	0	.000	-1	9	9	1	0.9
	Yr	6	4	.600	51	0	0	0	11	71^1	53	6	30	44	10.7	2.40	146	.208	.296	0	.000	-1	9	9	2	1.0
1970	*Pit-N	0	1	.000	41	0	0	0	5	41	44	2	24	26	15.4	4.83	81	.280	.383	0	.000	-0	-4	-4	0	-0.4
1971	Cin-N	5	6	.455	50	0	0	0	11	64^1	54	3	32	34	12.2	2.94	114	.239	.336	0	.000	-0	4	3	1	0.4
1972	Cin-N	0	0	—	2	0	0	0	0	0^1	3	1	1	1	108.0	54.00	6	.750	.800	0	—	0	-2	-2	0	-0.2
	Hou-N	0	0	—	9	0	0	0	0	7^1	13	2	5	4	23.3	9.82	34	.394	.487	0	—	0	-5	-5	1	-0.5
	Yr	0	0	—	11	0	0	0	0	7^2	16	3	6	5	27.0	11.74	29	.432	.523	0	—	0	-7	-7	1	-0.7
Total	13	61	65	.484	419	127	20	4	32	1119^2	1053	74	414	743	12.1	3.52	102	.251	.323	38	.144	-2	12	8	11	1.7

● NORWOOD GIBSON Gibson, Norwood Ringold "Gibby" b: 3/11/1877, Peoria, Ill. d: 7/7/59, Peoria, Ill. BR/TR, 5'10", 165 lbs. Deb: 4/29/03

YEAR	TM/L	W	L	PCT	G	GS	CG	SH	SV	IP	H	HR	BB	SO	RAT	ERA	ERA+	OAV	OOB	BH	AVG	PB	PR	/A	PD	TPI
1903	Bos-A	13	9	.591	24	21	17	2	0	183^1	166	2	65	76	11.6	3.19	95	.241	.312	17	.266	4	-5	-3	0	0.1
1904	Bos-A	17	14	.548	33	32	29	1	0	273	216	8	81	112	9.9	2.21	121	.219	.280	6	.065	-7	12	14	-3	0.5
1905	Bos-A	4	7	.364	23	17	9	0	0	134	118	9	55	67	12.0	3.69	73	.238	.320	4	.095	-2	-15	-15	-2	-2.0
1906	Bos-A	0	2	.000	5	2	1	0	0	18^2	25	2	7	3	15.4	5.30	52	.324	.380	1	.200	0	-5	-5	-0	-0.6
Total	4	34	32	.515	85	72	56	3	0	609	525	21	208	258	11.0	2.93	95	.233	.302	28	.138	-4	-14	-9	-5	-2.0

● PAUL GIBSON Gibson, Paul Marshall b: 1/4/60, Southampton, N.Y. BL/TR, 6', 165 lbs. Deb: 4/08/88

YEAR	TM/L	W	L	PCT	G	GS	CG	SH	SV	IP	H	HR	BB	SO	RAT	ERA	ERA+	OAV	OOB	BH	AVG	PB	PR	/A	PD	TPI
1988	Det-A	4	2	.667	40	1	0	0	0	92	83	6	34	50	11.6	2.93	130	.240	.312	0	—	0	11	9	0	1.1
1989	Det-A	4	8	.333	45	13	0	0	0	132	129	11	57	77	13.1	4.64	82	.259	.342	0	—	0	-11	-12	-0	-1.2
1990	Det-A	5	4	.556	61	0	0	0	3	97^1	99	10	44	56	13.3	3.05	130	.269	.349	0	—	0	9	10	0	1.0
1991	Det-A	5	7	.417	68	0	0	0	8	96	112	10	48	52	15.3	4.59	90	.297	.381	0	—	0	-5	-5	-0	-0.6
1992	NY-N	0	1	.000	43	1	0	0	0	62	70	7	25	49	13.8	5.23	67	.287	.353	0	.000	-0	-12	-12	-1	-1.4
Total	5	18	22	.450	257	15	0	0	11	479^1	493	44	208	284	13.4	4.06	95	.269	.347	0	.000	-0	-8	-10	-1	-1.1

● BOB GIBSON Gibson, Robert b: 11/9/35, Omaha, Neb. BR/TR, 6'1.5", 195 lbs. Deb: 4/15/59 CH

YEAR	TM/L	W	L	PCT	G	GS	CG	SH	SV	IP	H	HR	BB	SO	RAT	ERA	ERA+	OAV	OOB	BH	AVG	PB	PR	/A	PD	TPI
1959	StL-N	3	5	.375	13	9	2	1	0	75^2	77	4	39	48	13.9	3.33	127	.273	.363	3	.115	-1	5	8	-0	0.7
1960	StL-N	3	6	.333	27	12	2	0	0	86^2	97	7	48	69	15.2	5.61	73	.284	.374	5	.179	-0	-18	-15	1	-1.4
1961	StL-N	13	12	.520	35	27	10	2	1	211^1	186	13	119	166	13.2	3.24	136	.239	.344	13	.197	2	19	27	1	3.1
1962	StL-N★	15	13	.536	32	30	15	**5**	1	233^2	174	15	95	208	10.7	2.85	**150**	.204	.291	20	.263	6	28	37	1	**4.7**
1963	StL-N	18	9	.667	36	33	14	2	0	254^2	224	19	96	204	11.8	3.39	105	.233	.311	18	.207	8	-3	4	-2	1.1
1964	*StL-N	19	12	.613	40	36	17	2	1	287^1	250	25	86	245	10.8	3.01	127	.232	.294	15	.156	1	17	26	-1	2.7
1965	StL-N★	20	12	.625	38	36	20	6	1	299	243	34	103	270	10.7	3.07	125	.222	.295	25	.240	9	16	26	-2	3.8
1966	StL-N†	21	12	.636	35	35	20	**5**	0	280^1	210	20	78	225	9.4	2.44	147	.207	.267	20	.200	3	36	36	-1	4.2
1967	*StL-N★	13	7	.650	24	24	10	2	0	175^1	151	10	40	147	10.0	2.98	110	.231	.278	8	.133	1	8	6	0	0.8
1968	*StL-N☆	22	9	.710	34	34	28	**13**	0	304^2	198	11	62	**268**	**7.9**	**1.12**	**258**	**.184**	**.233**	16	.170	4	**63**	**60**	-3	**8.1**
1969	StL-N★	20	13	.606	35	35	**28**	4	0	314	251	12	95	269	10.2	2.18	164	.219	.285	29	.246	8	49	49	-2	**6.3**
1970	StL-N★	**23**	7	**.767**	34	34	23	3	0	294	262	13	88	274	10.8	3.12	132	.237	.296	33	.303	12	30	32	-1	4.6
1971	StL-N	16	13	.552	31	31	20	**5**	0	245^2	215	14	76	185	10.9	3.04	118	.232	.296	15	.172	2	12	15	0	2.0
1972	StL-N★	19	11	.633	34	34	23	4	0	278	226	14	88	208	10.3	2.46	138	.224	.288	20	.194	7	31	29	2	4.3
1973	StL-N	12	10	.545	25	25	13	1	0	195	159	12	57	142	10.1	2.77	132	.224	.284	12	.185	2	19	19	-1	2.2
1974	StL-N	11	13	.458	33	33	9	1	0	240	236	24	104	129	12.9	3.83	93	.259	.338	17	.210	3	-6	-7	-1	-0.6
1975	StL-N	3	10	.231	22	14	1	0	2	109	120	10	62	60	15.4	5.04	75	.287	.384	5	.179	0	-17	-16	-0	-1.5
Total	17	251	174	.591	528	482	255	56	6	3884^1	3279	257	1336	3117	10.9	2.91	127	.228	.299	274	.206	68	290	335	-10	45.1

● BOB GIBSON Gibson, Robert Louis b: 6/19/57, Philadelphia, Pa. BR/TR, 6', 195 lbs. Deb: 4/13/83

YEAR	TM/L	W	L	PCT	G	GS	CG	SH	SV	IP	H	HR	BB	SO	RAT	ERA	ERA+	OAV	OOB	BH	AVG	PB	PR	/A	PD	TPI
1983	Mil-A	3	4	.429	27	7	0	0	2	80^2	71	6	46	46	13.2	3.90	96	.237	.340	0	—	0	1	-2	-1	0.2
1984	Mil-A	2	5	.286	18	9	1	1	0	69	61	10	47	54	14.1	4.96	78	.236	.354	0	—	0	-7	-9	0	-0.5
1985	Mil-A	6	7	.462	41	1	0	0	11	92^1	86	10	49	53	13.3	3.90	107	.260	.357	0	—	0	3	3	-0	0.3
1986	Mil-A	1	2	.333	11	1	0	0	0	26^2	23	3	23	11	15.5	4.73	92	.232	.377	0	—	0	-2	-1	-0	-0.3
1987	NY-N	0	0	—	1	0	0	0	0	1	0	0	1	2	9.0	0.00	—	.000	.250	0	—	0	0	0	0	0.1
Total	5	12	18	.400	98	18	1	1	13	269^2	241	29	166	166	13.7	4.24	94	.243	.353	0	—	0	-5	-8	-1	-0.2

● ROBERT GIBSON Gibson, Robert Murray b: 8/20/1869, Duncansville, Pa. d: 12/19/49, Pittsburgh, Pa. BR/TR, 6'3", 185 lbs. Deb: 6/04/1890

YEAR	TM/L	W	L	PCT	G	GS	CG	SH	SV	IP	H	HR	BB	SO	RAT	ERA	ERA+	OAV	OOB	BH	AVG	PB	PR	/A	PD	TPI
1890	Chi-N	1	0	1.000	1	1	1	0	0	9	6	0	2	1	8.0	0.00	—	.184	.231	0	.000	-0	4	4	0	0.4
	Pit-N	0	3	.000	3	3	2	0	0	12	24	0	23	3	37.5	17.25	19	.403	.584	3	.231	-0	-18	-19	-1	-1.4
	Yr	1	3	.250	4	4	3	0	0	21	30	0	25	4	24.9	9.86	35	.325	.483	3	.176	-1	-15	-15	-0	-1.0

● SAM GIBSON Gibson, Samuel Braxton b: 8/5/1899, King, N.C. d: 1/31/83, High Point, N.C. BL/TR, 6'2", 198 lbs. Deb: 4/19/26

YEAR	TM/L	W	L	PCT	G	GS	CG	SH	SV	IP	H	HR	BB	SO	RAT	ERA	ERA+	OAV	OOB	BH	AVG	PB	PR	/A	PD	TPI
1926	Det-A	12	9	.571	35	24	16	2	2	196^1	199	6	75	61	12.8	3.48	117	.269	.341	18	.250	2	12	13	0	1.4
1927	Det-A	11	12	.478	33	26	11	0	0	184^2	201	9	86	76	14.4	3.80	111	.285	.369	14	.212	-1	7	8	-1	0.5
1928	Det-A	5	8	.385	20	18	5	1	0	119^2	155	4	53	29	16.2	5.42	76	.322	.397	12	.286	2	-18	-17	-1	-1.5
1930	NY-A	0	1	.000	2	2	0	0	0	6	14	1	6	3	30.0	15.00	29	.424	.513	1	.333	0	-7	-7	0	-0.5
1932	NY-N	4	8	.333	41	5	1	1	3	81^2	107	7	30	39	15.3	4.85	77	.322	.382	5	.263	0	-9	-10	-1	-1.0
Total	5	32	38	.457	131	75	33	4	5	588^1	676	27	250	208	14.5	4.28	95	.295	.370	50	.248	3	-15	-14	-3	-1.1

● GEORGE GICK Gick, George Edward b: 10/18/15, Dunnington, Ind. BB/TR, 6', 190 lbs. Deb: 10/03/37

YEAR	TM/L	W	L	PCT	G	GS	CG	SH	SV	IP	H	HR	BB	SO	RAT	ERA	ERA+	OAV	OOB	BH	AVG	PB	PR	/A	PD	TPI
1937	Chi-A	0	0	—	1	0	0	0	1	2	0	0	0	1	0.0	0.00	—	.000	.000	0	—	0	1	1	-0	0.1
1938	Chi-A	0	0	—	1	0	0	0	0	1	0	0	0	1	9.0	0.00	—	.000	.250	0	—	0	1	1	0	0.0
Total	2	0	0	—	2	0	0	0	1	3	0	0	0	2	3.0	0.00	—	.000	.100	0	—	0	2	2	-0	0.1

● BRETT GIDEON Gideon, Byron Brett b: 8/8/63, Ozona, Tex. BR/TR, 6'2", 200 lbs. Deb: 7/05/87

YEAR	TM/L	W	L	PCT	G	GS	CG	SH	SV	IP	H	HR	BB	SO	RAT	ERA	ERA+	OAV	OOB	BH	AVG	PB	PR	/A	PD	TPI
1987	Pit-N	1	5	.167	29	0	0	0	3	36^2	34	6	10	31	11.0	4.66	88	.243	.298	1	1.000	1	-2	-2	-0	-0.2
1989	Mon-N	0	0	—	4	0	0	0	0	4^2	5	1	5	2	19.3	1.93	183	.294	.455	0	—	0	1	1	-0	0.1
1990	Mon-N	0	0	—	1	0	0	0	0	1	2	0	4	0	54.0	9.00	41	.500	.750	0	—	0	-1	-1	0	0.0
Total	3	1	5	.167	34	0	0	0	3	42^1	41	7	19	33	13.0	4.46	90	.255	.337	1	1.000	1	-2	-2	-0	-0.1

YEAR TM/L	W	L	PCT	G	GS	CG	SH	SV	IP	H	HR	BB	SO	RAT	ERA	ERA+	OAV	OOB	BH	AVG	PB	PR	/A	PD	TPI
● **JIM GIDEON** Gideon, James Leslie b: 9/26/53, Taylor, Tex. BR/TR, 6'3", 190 lbs. Deb: 9/14/75																									
1975 Tex-A	0	0	—	1	1	0	0	0	5²	7	1	5	2	19.1	7.94	47	.292	.414	0	—	0	-3	-3	-0	-0.2
● **FLOYD GIEBELL** Giebell, Floyd George b: 12/10/09, Pennsboro, W.Va. BL/TR, 6'2.5", 172 lbs. Deb: 4/21/39																									
1939 Det-A	1	1	.500	9	0	0	0	0	15¹	19	1	12	9	18.2	2.93	167	.317	.431	0	.000	-0	3	3	-0	0.2
1940 Det-A	2	0	1.000	2	2	2	1	0	18	14	2	4	11	9.0	1.00	476	.206	.250	0	.000	-1	7	8	-0	0.7
1941 Det-A	0	0	—	17	2	0	0	0	34¹	45	3	26	10	18.6	6.03	75	.313	.418	2	.333	-0	-7	-6	-0	-0.5
Total 3	3	1	.750	28	4	2	1	0	67²	78	6	42	30	16.0	3.99	117	.287	.382	2	.143	-1	2	5	-1	0.4
● **PAUL GIEL** Giel, Paul Robert b: 2/29/32, Winona, Minn. BR/TR, 5'11", 185 lbs. Deb: 7/10/54																									
1954 NY-N	0	0	—	6	0	0	0	0	4¹	8	0	2	4	20.8	8.31	49	.421	.476	0	—	0	-2	-2	-0	-0.2
1955 NY-N	4	4	.500	34	2	0	0	0	82¹	70	8	50	47	13.3	3.39	119	.233	.346	1	.053	-2	6	6	-1	0.3
1958 SF-N	4	5	.444	29	9	0	0	0	92	89	12	55	55	14.3	4.70	81	.259	.365	2	.074	-2	-8	-9	1	-0.9
1959 Pit-N	0	0	—	4	0	0	0	0	7²	17	0	6	3	27.0	14.09	27	.472	.548	0	—	0	-9	-9	-0	-0.8
1960 Pit-N	2	0	1.000	16	0	0	0	0	33	35	3	15	21	13.6	5.73	65	.276	.352	0	.000	-1	-7	-7	-1	-0.9
1961 Min-A	1	0	1.000	12	0	0	0	0	19¹	24	4	17	14	19.1	9.78	43	.289	.410	1	.500	0	-12	-12	0	-1.1
KC-A	0	0	—	1	0	0	0	0	1²	6	1	3	1	48.6	37.80	11	.600	.692	0	—	0	-6	-6	-0	-0.5
Yr	1	0	1.000	13	0	0	0	0	21	30	7	20	15	21.4	12.00	35	.319	.439	1	.500	0	-19	-18	-0	-1.6
Total 6	11	9	.550	102	11	0	0	0	240¹	249	30	148	145	15.0	5.39	73	.271	.374	4	.073	-4	-38	-39	-0	-4.1
● **BOB GIGGIE** Giggie, Robert Thomas b: 8/13/33, Dorchester, Mass. BR/TR, 6'1", 200 lbs. Deb: 4/18/59																									
1959 Mil-N	1	0	1.000	13	0	0	0	0	20	24	2	10	15	15.3	4.05	87	.316	.395	0	.000	-0	-0	-1	1	0.0
1960 Mil-N	0	0	—	3	0	0	0	0	4¹	5	0	4	5	18.7	4.15	83	.278	.409	0	—	-0	-0	-0	-0	0.0
KC-A	1	0	1.000	10	0	0	0	0	18²	24	1	15	8	18.8	5.79	69	.333	.448	0	.000	-0	-4	-4	-0	-0.4
1962 KC-A	1	1	.500	4	2	0	0	0	14¹	17	1	3	4	13.2	6.28	66	.293	.339	0	.000	-1	-4	-3	-1	-0.4
Total 3	3	1	.750	30	2	0	0	1	57¹	70	4	32	32	16.2	5.18	74	.313	.401	0	.000	-1	-8	-9	-0	-0.8
● **JOE GILBERT** Gilbert, Joe Dennis b: 4/20/52, Jasper, Tex. BR/TL, 6'1", 167 lbs. Deb: 4/30/72																									
1972 Mon-N	0	1	.000	22	0	0	0	1	33	41	3	18	25	16.1	8.45	42	.306	.388	0	.000	-0	-18	-18	-1	-1.9
1973 Mon-N	1	2	.333	21	0	0	0	1	29	30	1	19	17	15.2	4.97	77	.270	.377	0	.000	0	-4	-4	-0	-0.4
Total 2	1	3	.250	43	0	0	0	1	62	71	4	37	42	15.7	6.82	54	.290	.383	0	.000	-0	-23	-22	-0	-2.3
● **BILL GILBERT** Gilbert, Wilmer M. b: 5/12/1870, Havre De Grace, Md 6', 180 lbs. Deb: 9/15/1892																									
1892 Bal-N	0	1	.000	2	1	1	0	0	14	14	1	17	5	19.9	5.79	59	.250	.425	2	.333	1	-4	-4	-1	-0.3
● **BILL GILBRETH** Gilbreth, William Freeman b: 9/3/47, Abilene, Tex. BL/TL, 6', 180 lbs. Deb: 6/25/71																									
1971 Det-A	2	1	.667	9	5	2	0	0	30	28	4	21	14	15.3	4.80	75	.264	.395	2	.182	-0	-4	-4	0	-0.4
1972 Det-A	0	0	—	2	0	0	0	0	5	10	1	4	2	25.2	16.20	19	.476	.560	0	.000	-0	-7	-7	-0	-0.7
1974 Cal-A	0	0	—	3	0	0	0	0	1¹	2	0	1	0	20.3	13.50	25	.400	.500	0	—	0	-1	-1	-0	-0.1
Total 3	2	1	.667	14	5	2	0	0	36¹	40	5	26	16	16.8	6.69	53	.303	.425	2	.167	-0	-13	-13	-0	-1.2
● **BOB GILKS** Gilks, Robert James b: 7/2/1864, Cincinnati, Ohio d: 8/21/44, Brunswick, Ga. BR/TR, 5'8", 178 lbs. Deb: 8/25/1887 ♦																									
1887 Cle-a	7	5	.583	13	13	12	1	0	108	104	1	42	28	12.9	3.08	141	.245	.326	26	.313	1	15	15	2	1.6
1888 Cle-a	0	2	.000	4	2	2	0	1	21	26	1	8	3	15.0	8.14	38	.293	.358	111	.229	0	-12	-12	-0	-1.0
1890 Cle-N	2	2	.500	4	3	3	0	0	31²	34	0	9	5	13.4	4.26	84	.266	.334	116	.213	-0	-2	-2	-1	-0.3
Total 3	9	9	.500	21	18	17	1	1	160²	164	2	59	36	13.3	3.98	101	.256	.332	320	.231	1	0	1	1	0.3
● **ED GILL** Gill, Edward James b: 8/7/1895, Somerville, Mass. BL/TR, 5'10", 165 lbs. Deb: 7/05/19																									
1919 Was-A	1	1	.500	16	2	0	0	0	37¹	38	0	21	7	14.7	4.82	67	.260	.361	0	.000	-1	-7	-7	-1	-0.8
● **GEORGE GILL** Gill, George Lloyd b: 2/13/09, Catchings, Miss. BR/TR, 6'1", 185 lbs. Deb: 5/04/37																									
1937 Det-A	11	4	.733	31	10	4	1	1	127²	146	11	42	40	13.3	4.51	104	.285	.340	7	.140	-3	2	2	1	0.1
1938 Det-A	12	9	.571	24	23	13	1	0	164	195	15	50	30	13.6	4.12	121	.296	.348	6	.105	-4	12	16	-1	1.0
1939 Det-A	0	1	.000	3	1	0	0	0	8²	14	1	3	1	17.7	8.31	59	.368	.415	0	.000	-0	-4	-3	-0	-0.3
StL-A	1	12	.077	27	11	5	0	0	95	139	10	34	24	16.7	7.11	68	.343	.398	4	.154	-2	-26	-24	1	-2.1
Yr	1	13	.071	30	12	5	0	0	103²	153	11	37	25	16.8	7.21	68	.345	.400	4	.143	-2	-30	-27	1	-2.4
Total 3	24	26	.480	85	45	22	2	1	395¹	494	37	129	95	14.3	5.05	96	.306	.360	17	.126	-9	-16	-9	2	-1.3
● **HADDIE GILL** Gill, Harold Edward b: 1/23/1899, Brockton, Mass. d: 8/1/32, Brockton, Mass. BL/TL, 5'11", 165 lbs. Deb: 8/16/23																									
1923 Cin-N	0	0	—	1	0	0	0	0	1	1	0	1	1	18.0	0.00	—	.333	.500	0	—	0	0	0	0	0.0
● **CLARAL GILLENWATER** Gillenwater, Claral Lewis b: 5/20/1900, Sims, Ind. d: 2/26/78, Bradenton, Fla. BR/TR, 6', 187 lbs. Deb: 8/20/23																									
1923 Chi-A	1	3	.250	5	3	1	1	0	21¹	28	2	6	2	14.8	5.48	72	.337	.389	0	.000	-1	-4	-4	0	-0.4
● **TOM GILLES** Gilles, Thomas Bradford b: 7/2/62, Peoria, Ill. BR/TR, 6'1", 185 lbs. Deb: 6/07/90																									
1990 Tor-A	1	0	1.000	2	0	0	0	0	1¹	2	0	1	0	13.5	6.75	58	.333	.333	0	—	0	-0	-0	0	0.0
● **JOHN GILLESPIE** Gillespie, John Patrick "Silent John" b: 2/25/1900, Oakland, Cal. d: 2/15/54, Vallejo, Cal. BR/TR, 5'11.5", 172 lbs. Deb: 4/12/22																									
1922 Cin-N	3	3	.500	31	4	1	0	0	77²	84	2	29	21	13.6	4.52	88	.294	.367	2	.133	-1	-4	-5	1	-0.4
● **BOB GILLESPIE** Gillespie, Robert William "Bunch" b: 10/8/18, Columbus, Ohio BR/TR, 6'4", 187 lbs. Deb: 5/11/44																									
1944 Det-A	0	1	.000	7	0	0	0	0	11	7	0	12	4	15.5	6.55	54	.194	.396	0	.000	-0	-4	-4	-0	-0.4
1947 Chi-A	5	8	.385	25	17	1	0	0	118	133	4	53	36	14.3	4.73	77	.291	.366	2	.061	-2	-13	-14	3	-1.4
1948 Chi-A	0	4	.000	25	6	1	0	0	72	81	3	33	19	14.4	5.13	83	.287	.364	0	.000	-2	-7	-7	-0	-0.9
1950 Bos-A	0	0	—	1	0	0	0	0	1¹	2	1	4	0	40.5	20.25	24	.333	.600	0	—	0	-2	-2	-0	-0.2
Total 4	5	13	.278	58	23	2	0	0	202¹	223	8	102	59	14.5	5.07	76	.286	.369	2	.039	-5	-26	-27	3	-2.9
● **PAUL GILLIFORD** Gilliford, Paul Gant "Gorilla" b: 1/12/45, Bryn Mawr, Pa. BR/TL, 5'11", 210 lbs. Deb: 9/20/67																									
1967 Bal-A	0	0	—	2	0	0	0	0	3	6	1	1	2	21.0	12.00	26	.429	.467	0	—	0	-3	-3	-0	-0.3
● **JACK GILLIGAN** Gilligan, John Patrick b: 10/18/1884, Chicago, Ill. d: 11/19/80, Modesto, Cal. BB/TR, 6', 190 lbs. Deb: 9/16/09																									
1909 StL-A	1	2	.333	3	3	3	0	0	23	28	1	9	4	15.3	5.48	44	.315	.390	1	.111	-1	-8	-8	-1	-0.8
1910 StL-A	0	3	.000	9	5	2	0	0	39¹	37	0	28	10	15.1	3.66	68	.253	.377	3	.200	-0	-5	-5	0	-0.5
Total 2	1	5	.167	12	8	5	0	0	62¹	65	1	37	14	15.2	4.33	57	.277	.382	4	.167	-1	-13	-13	-0	-1.3
● **GEORGE GILLPATRICK** Gillpatrick, George F. b: 2/28/1875, Holden, Mo. d: 12/15/41, Kansas City, Mo. Deb: 5/22/1898																									
1898 StL-N	0	2	.000	7	3	1	0	0	35	42	0	19	12	16.2	6.94	55	.295	.386	2	.125	-2	-13	-12	-1	-1.2
● **FRANK GILMORE** Gilmore, Frank T. "Shadow" b: 4/27/1864, Webster, Mass. d: 7/21/29, Hartford, Conn. BR Deb: 9/11/1886																									
1886 Was-N	4	4	.500	9	9	9	1	0	75	57	3	22	75	9.5	2.52	130	.200	.257	0	.000	-4	7	6	-1	0.2
1887 Was-N	7	20	.259	28	27	27	1	0	234²	247	7	92	114	13.5	3.87	105	.262	.336	6	.065	-11	5	5	-3	-0.7
1888 Was-N	1	9	.100	12	11	10	0	0	95²	131	4	29	23	15.7	6.59	43	.323	.378	1	.024	-4	-40	-40	-2	-3.9
Total 3	12	33	.267	49	47	46	2	0	405¹	435	14	143	212	13.3	4.26	85	.266	.333	7	.043	-20	-28	-29	-6	-4.4
● **LEN GILMORE** Gilmore, Leonard Preston "Meow" b: 11/3/17, Clinton, Ind. BR/TR, 6'3", 175 lbs. Deb: 10/01/44																									
1944 Pit-N	0	1	.000	1	1	1	0	0	8	13	2	0	0	14.6	7.88	47	.361	.361	0	.000	-0	-4	-4	1	-0.3

YEAR TM/L	W	L	PCT	G	GS	CG	SH	SV	IP	H	HR	BB	SO	RAT	ERA	ERA+	OAV	OOB	BH	AVG	PB	PR	/A	PD	TPI
● **JOHN GILROY**	Gilroy, John M. b: 10/26/1869, Washington, D.C. d: 8/4/1897, Norfolk, Va. Deb: 8/30/1895																								
1895 Was-N	1	4	.200	8	4	2	0	0	41^{1}	63	3	24	2	19.8	6.53	73	.345	.432	7	.241	-1	-8	-8	1	-0.6
1896 Was-N	0	0	—	1	0	0	0	0	2	0	0	1	0	4.5	0.00	—	.000	.148	0	.000	-0	1	1	0	0.1
Total 2	1	4	.200	9	4	2	0	0	43^{1}	63	3	25	2	19.1	6.23	77	.334	.423	7	.233	-1	-7	-7	1	-0.5
● **HAL GILSON**	Gilson, Harold "Lefty" b: 2/9/42, Los Angeles, Cal. BR/TL, 6'5", 195 lbs. Deb: 4/14/68																								
1968 StL-N	0	2	.000	13	0	0	0	2	21^{2}	27	1	11	19	15.8	4.57	63	.310	.388	0	.000	-0	-4	-4	-1	-0.6
Hou-N	0	0	—	2	0	0	0	0	3^{2}	7	0	1	1	22.1	7.36	40	.412	.474	0	—	0	-2	-2	0	-0.2
Yr	0	2	.000	15	0	0	0	2	25^{1}	34	1	12	20	16.7	4.97	58	.327	.402	0	.000	-0	-6	-6	-1	-0.8
● **BILLY GING**	Ging, William Joseph b: 11/7/1872, Elmira, N.Y. d: 9/14/50, Elmira, N.Y. BR/TR, 5'10", 170 lbs. Deb: 9/25/1899																								
1899 Bos-N	1	0	1.000	1	1	1	0	0	8	5	0	5	2	11.3	1.13	370	.180	.305	0	.000	-0	2	3	-0	0.2
● **JOE GINGRAS**	Gingras, Joseph Elzead John b: 1/10/1894, New York, N.Y. d: 9/6/47, Jersey City, N.J. BR/TR, 6'2", 188 lbs. Deb: 6/18/15																								
1915 KC-F	0	0	—	2	0	0	0	0	4	6	0	1	2	15.8	6.75	43	.353	.389	0	.000	-0	-2	-2	-0	-0.2
● **CHARLIE GIRARD**	Girard, Charles August b: 12/16/1884, Brooklyn, N.Y. d: 8/6/36, Brooklyn, N.Y. BR/TR, 5'10", 175 lbs. Deb: 9/14/10																								
1910 Phi-N	1	2	.333	7	1	0	0	1	26^{2}	33	2	12	11	15.9	6.41	49	.308	.388	1	.125	-0	-10	-10	-1	-1.1
● **DAVE GIUSTI**	Giusti, David John b: 11/27/39, Seneca Falls, N.Y. BR/TR, 5'11", 195 lbs. Deb: 4/13/62																								
1962 Hou-N	2	3	.400	22	5	0	0	0	73^{2}	82	7	30	43	13.7	5.62	66	.280	.347	7	.292	2	-14	-15	1	-1.2
1964 Hou-N	0	0	—	8	0	0	0	0	25^{2}	24	1	8	16	11.2	3.16	108	.253	.311	2	.286	1	1	1	1	0.3
1965 Hou-N	8	7	.533	38	13	4	1	3	131^{1}	132	13	46	92	12.3	4.32	78	.259	.321	6	.171	2	-11	-14	1	-1.1
1966 Hou-N	15	14	.517	34	33	9	4	0	210	215	23	54	131	11.7	4.20	81	.260	.310	17	.230	5	-14	-18	-1	-1.5
1967 Hou-N	11	15	.423	37	33	8	1	1	221^{2}	231	20	58	157	11.9	4.18	79	.265	.313	13	.155	3	-20	-21	-2	-2.1
1968 Hou-N	11	14	.440	37	34	12	2	1	251	226	15	67	186	10.6	3.19	93	.239	.293	15	.183	2	-6	-7	3	-0.2
1969 StL-N	3	7	.300	22	12	2	1	0	99^{2}	96	7	37	62	12.1	3.61	99	.255	.323	5	.200	1	-0	-0	1	0.2
1970 *Pit-N	9	3	.750	66	1	0	0	26	103	98	7	39	85	12.0	3.06	128	.259	.328	3	.188	2	11	10	0	1.1
1971 *Pit-N	5	6	.455	58	0	0	0	**30**	86	79	5	31	55	11.6	2.93	115	.241	.308	1	.059	-1	5	4	-1	0.2
1972 *Pit-N	7	4	.636	54	0	0	0	22	74^{2}	59	3	20	54	9.5	1.93	172	.219	.273	0	.000	-1	13	12	1	1.2
1973 Pit-N★	9	2	.818	67	0	0	0	20	98^{2}	89	9	37	64	11.5	2.37	148	.241	.310	4	.308	1	14	13	-2	1.3
1974 *Pit-N	7	5	.583	64	2	0	0	12	105^{2}	101	2	40	53	12.0	3.32	104	.258	.327	1	.111	-0	3	1	1	0.3
1975 *Pit-N	5	4	.556	61	0	0	0	17	91^{2}	79	3	42	38	11.9	2.95	120	.237	.322	3	.300	1	7	6	0	0.7
1976 Pit-N	5	4	.556	40	0	0	0	6	58^{1}	59	5	27	24	13.3	4.32	81	.267	.347	0	.000	-0	-5	-5	0	-0.6
1977 Oak-A	3	3	.500	40	0	0	0	6	60^{1}	54	4	20	28	11.0	2.98	135	.245	.308	0	—	0	7	7	0	0.8
Chi-N	0	2	.000	20	0	0	0	1	25^{1}	30	2	14	15	15.6	6.04	73	.297	.383	0	.000	-0	-6	-5	-0	-0.5
Total 15	100	93	.518	668	133	35	9	145	1716^{2}	1654	126	570	1103	11.7	3.60	95	.253	.315	77	.187	17	-14	-33	2	-1.1
● **DAN GLADDEN**	Gladden, Clinton Daniel b: 7/7/57, San Jose, Cal. BR/TR, 5'11", 180 lbs. Deb: 9/05/83 ♦																								
1988 Min-A	0	0	—	1	0	0	0	0	1	0	0	0	0	0.0	0.00	—	.000	.000	155	.269	1	0	0	0	0.0
1989 Min-A	0	0	—	1	0	0	0	0	1	2	0	1	0	27.0	9.00	46	.400	.500	136	.295	1	-1	-1	0	-0.1
Total 2	0	0	—	2	0	0	0	0	2	2	0	1	0	13.5	4.50	91	.250	.333	1120	.270	2	-0	-0	0	-0.1
● **FRED GLADDING**	Gladding, Fred Earl b: 6/28/36, Flat Rock, Mich. BL/TR, 6', 225 lbs. Deb: 7/01/61 C																								
1961 Det-A	1	0	1.000	8	0	0	0	0	16^{1}	18	1	11	11	17.1	3.31	124	.286	.408	0	.000	-0	1	1	-0	0.1
1962 Det-A	0	0	—	6	0	0	0	0	5	3	0	2	4	9.0	0.00	—	.176	.263	0	—	0	2	2	0	0.3
1963 Det-A	1	1	.500	22	0	0	0	7	27^{1}	19	1	14	24	10.9	1.98	189	.198	.300	0	.000	-0	5	5	0	0.6
1964 Det-A	7	4	.636	42	0	0	0	7	67^{1}	57	7	27	59	11.5	3.07	119	.233	.314	0	.000	-1	4	4	1	0.4
1965 Det-A	6	2	.750	46	0	0	0	5	70	63	6	29	43	12.3	2.83	123	.239	.323	0	.000	-1	5	5	-1	0.4
1966 Det-A	5	0	1.000	51	0	0	0	2	74	62	6	29	57	11.2	3.28	106	.230	.307	0	.000	-0	1	2	-1	0.1
1967 Det-A	6	4	.600	42	1	0	0	12	77	62	6	19	64	9.9	1.99	164	.227	.287	0	.000	-2	11	11	-0	1.0
1968 Hou-N	0	0	—	7	0	0	0	2	4^{1}	8	0	3	2	24.9	14.54	20	.421	.522	0	—	0	-6	-6	-0	-0.6
1969 Hou-N	4	8	.333	57	0	0	0	**29**	72^{2}	83	2	27	40	13.7	4.21	84	.289	.352	1	.100	-0	-5	-5	0	-0.6
1970 Hou-N	7	4	.636	63	0	0	0	18	71	84	4	24	46	14.1	4.06	96	.293	.354	0	.000	-1	-0	-1	1	-0.1
1971 Hou-N	4	5	.444	48	0	0	0	12	51^{1}	51	0	22	17	14.0	2.10	160	.268	.365	0	.000	-0	8	7	-1	0.6
1972 Hou-N	5	6	.455	42	0	0	0	14	48^{2}	38	1	12	18	9.6	2.77	121	.222	.281	0	.000	-1	4	3	-1	0.2
1973 Hou-N	2	0	1.000	16	0	0	0	1	16	18	4	4	9	12.4	4.50	81	.290	.333	0	—	0	-1	-2	0	-0.1
Total 13	48	34	.585	450	1	0	0	109	601	566	38	223	394	12.2	3.13	113	.252	.327	1	.016	-6	29	28	-2	2.3
● **FRED GLADE**	Glade, Frederick Monroe "Lucky" b: 1/25/1876, Dubuque, Iowa d: 11/21/34, Grand Island, Neb. BR/TR, 5'10", 175 lbs. Deb: 5/27/02																								
1902 Chi-N	0	1	.000	1	1	1	0	0	8	13	0	3	3	19.1	9.00	30	.364	.428	1	.333	1	-6	-6	0	-0.4
1904 StL-A	18	15	.545	35	34	30	6	1	289	248	2	58	156	9.9	2.27	109	.233	.281	19	.186	1	10	7	1	1.1
1905 StL-A	6	25	.194	32	32	28	2	0	275	257	3	58	127	10.6	2.81	91	.249	.295	9	.092	-6	-5	-8	4	-1.1
1906 StL-A	15	14	.517	35	32	28	4	1	266^{2}	215	4	59	96	9.6	2.36	109	.224	.275	13	.137	-4	10	7	-3	0.0
1907 StL-A	13	9	.591	24	22	18	2	0	202	187	2	45	71	10.7	2.67	94	.248	.298	15	.205	2	-3	-3	-4	-0.6
1908 NY-A	0	4	.000	5	5	2	0	0	32	30	0	14	11	13.5	4.22	59	.275	.378	0	.000	-1	-6	-6	-1	-0.8
Total 6	52	68	.433	132	126	107	14	2	1072^{2}	950	11	237	464	10.3	2.62	97	.240	.291	57	.150	-7	1	-10	-3	-1.8
● **JOHN GLAISER**	Glaiser, John Burke "Bert" b: 7/28/1894, Yoakum, Tex. d: 3/7/59, Houston, Tex. BL/TR, 5'8", 165 lbs. Deb: 4/20/20																								
1920 Det-A	0	0	—	9	1	0	0	1	17	23	1	8	3	16.9	6.35	59	.354	.432	0	.000	-0	-5	-5	1	-0.4
● **TOM GLASS**	Glass, Thomas Joseph b: 4/29/1898, Greensboro, N.C. d: 12/15/81, Greensboro, N.C. BR/TR, 6'3", 170 lbs. Deb: 6/12/25																								
1925 Phi-A	1	0	1.000	2	0	0	0	0	5	9	0	0	2	16.2	5.40	86	.409	.409	0	.000	-0	-1	-0	-0	-0.1
● **JACK GLASSCOCK**	Glasscock, John Wesley "Pebbly Jack" b: 7/22/1859, Wheeling, W.Va. d: 2/24/47, Wheeling, W.Va. BR/TR, 5'8", 160 lbs. Deb: 5/01/1879 M♦																								
1884 Cle-N	0	0	—	2	0	0	0	0	5	8	0	2	1	18.0	5.40	58	.333	.385	70	.249	0	-1	-1	1	-0.1
1887 Ind-N	0	0	—	1	0	0	0	0	1	0	0	0	1	0.0	0.00	—	.000	.000	142	.294	0	0	0	0	0.0
1888 Ind-N	0	0	—	1	0	0	0	0	0^{1}	1	0	2	1	108.0	54.00	5	1.000	1.000	119	.269	0	-2	-2	0	-0.2
1889 Ind-N	0	0	—	1	0	0	0	0	0^{2}	3	0	3	0	81.0	0.00	—	.603	.752	205	.352	0	0	0	-0	0.0
Total 4	0	0	—	5	0	0	0	0	7	12	0	7	3	25.7	6.43	53	.364	.488	2040	.290	1	-2	-2	1	-0.3
● **LUKE GLAVENICH**	Glavenich, Luke Frank b: 1/17/1893, Jackson, Cal. d: 5/22/35, Stockton, Cal. BR/TR, 5'9.5", 189 lbs. Deb: 4/12/13																								
1913 Cle-A	0	0	—	1	0	0	0	0	1	3	0	3	1	54.0	9.00	34	.500	.667	0	—	0	-1	-1	-0	-0.1
● **TOM GLAVINE**	Glavine, Thomas Michael b: 3/25/66, Concord, Mass. BL/TL, 6'1", 190 lbs. Deb: 8/17/87																								
1987 Atl-N	2	4	.333	9	9	0	0	0	50^{1}	55	5	33	20	16.3	5.54	78	.279	.391	2	.125	-0	-8	-7	1	-0.6
1988 Atl-N	7	17	.292	34	34	1	0	0	195^{1}	201	12	63	84	12.5	4.56	81	.270	.333	11	.183	1	-24	-19	2	-1.7
1989 Atl-N	14	8	.636	29	29	6	4	0	186	172	20	40	90	10.4	3.68	99	.243	.285	10	.149	0	-4	-1	1	0.1
1990 Atl-N	10	12	.455	33	33	1	0	0	214^{1}	232	18	78	129	13.1	4.28	94	.281	.343	7	.113	0	-12	-6	1	-0.4
1991 *Atl-N★	**20**	11	.645	34	34	**9**	1	0	246^{2}	201	17	69	192	9.9	2.55	**152**	.222	.279	17	.230	4	31	**37**	3	**4.9**
1992 *Atl-N★	**20**	8	.714	33	33	7	**5**	0	225	197	6	70	129	10.8	2.76	136	.235	.295	19	.247	4	19	25	-0	3.3
Total 6	73	60	.549	172	172	24	10	0	1117^{2}	1058	78	353	644	11.5	3.60	106	.251	.311	66	.185	10	2	29	7	5.6
● **RALPH GLAZE**	Glaze, Daniel Ralph b: 3/13/1882, Denver, Col. d: 10/31/68, Atascadero, Cal. BR/TR, 5'9", 165 lbs. Deb: 6/01/06																								
1906 Bos-A	4	6	.400	19	10	7	0	0	123	110	4	32	56	10.8	3.59	77	.242	.301	10	.182	0	-12	-11	0	-1.1
1907 Bos-A	9	13	.409	32	21	11	1	0	182^{1}	150	4	48	68	10.0	2.32	111	.226	.283	11	.180	0	5	5	-4	0.2

YEAR	TM/L	W	L	PCT	G	GS	CG	SH	SV	IP	H	HR	BB	SO	RAT	ERA	ERA+	OAV	OOB	BH	AVG	PB	PR	/A	PD	TPI
1908	Bos-A	2	2	.500	10	3	2	0	0	34^2	43	1	5	13	12.5	3.38	73	.253	.274	1	.077	-1	-4	-4	-1	-0.6
Total	3	15	21	.417	61	34	20	1	0	340	303	9	85	137	10.6	2.89	91	.235	.288	22	.171	-1	-11	-10	-4	-1.5
● **WHITEY GLAZNER**	Glazner, Charles Franklin b: 9/17/1893, Sycamore, Ala. d: 6/6/89, Orlando, Fla. BR/TR, 5'9", 165 lbs. Deb: 9/26/20																									
1920	Pit-N	0	0	—	2	0	0	0	0	8^2	9	0	2	1	11.4	3.12	103	.300	.344	0	.000	-0	0	0	-0	-0.1
1921	Pit-N	14	5	.737	36	25	15	0	1	234	214	5	58	88	10.9	2.77	139	**.250**	.306	10	.132	-3	26	28	-4	2.1
1922	Pit-N	11	12	.478	34	26	10	1	1	193	238	9	52	77	13.6	4.38	93	.309	.354	16	.246	3	-6	-7	0	-0.3
1923	Pit-N	2	1	.667	7	4	1	1	1	30	29	5	11	8	12.0	3.30	122	.250	.315	4	.333	2	2	2	0	0.4
	Phi-N	7	14	.333	28	23	12	2	1	161^1	195	11	63	51	14.7	4.69	98	.304	.371	9	.170	-0	-12	-1	-0	-0.3
	Yr	9	15	.375	35	27	13	3	2	191^1	224	16	74	59	14.3	4.47	101	.296	.363	13	.200	1	-10	1	0	0.1
1924	Phi-N	7	16	.304	35	24	8	2	0	156^2	210	14	63	41	15.9	5.92	75	.339	.403	8	.157	-4	-36	-25	1	-2.7
Total	5	41	48	.461	142	102	46	6	4	783^2	895	44	249	266	13.4	4.21	99	.295	.353	47	.181	-3	-25	-3	-3	-0.9
● **JOE GLEASON**	Gleason, Joseph Paul b: 7/9/1895, Phelps, N.Y. d: 9/8/90, Phelps, N.Y. BR/TR, 5'10.5", 175 lbs. Deb: 9/11/20																									
1920	Was-A	0	0	—	3	0	0	0	0	8	14	2	6	2	23.6	13.50	28	.326	.420	0	.000	1	-9	-9	0	-0.7
1922	Was-A	2	2	.500	8	5	3	0	0	40^2	53	3	18	12	15.9	4.65	83	.319	.389	2	.143	-0	-3	-4	-0	-0.4
Total	2	2	2	.500	11	5	3	0	0	48^2	67	5	24	14	17.2	6.10	63	.321	.396	2	.125	0	-11	-12	0	-1.1
● **BILL GLEASON**	Gleason, William b: 1868, Cleveland, Ohio d: 12/2/1893, Cleveland, Ohio Deb: 4/24/1890																									
1890	Cle-P	0	1	.000	1	1	0	0	0	4	14	1	6	0	45.0	27.00	15	.537	.624	0	.000	-0	-10	-10	-0	-0.6
● **KID GLEASON**	Gleason, William J. b: 10/26/1866, Camden, N.J. d: 1/2/33, Philadelphia, Pa. BB/TR, 5'7", 158 lbs. Deb: 4/20/1888 FMC♦																									
1888	Phi-N	7	16	.304	24	23	23	0	0	199^2	199	11	53	89	11.9	2.84	105	.252	.309	17	.205	0	0	3	-3	0.0
1889	Phi-N	9	15	.375	29	21	15	0	1	205	242	8	97	64	15.3	5.58	78	.285	.364	25	.253	3	-36	-28	1	-2.1
1890	Phi-N	38	17	.691	60	55	54	6	**2**	506	479	8	167	222	11.8	2.63	139	.242	.306	47	.210	-5	53	58	-0	4.7
1891	Phi-N	24	22	.522	53	44	40	1	1	418	431	10	165	100	13.1	3.51	97	.256	.328	53	.248	6	-8	-5	-3	-0.2
1892	StL-N	20	24	.455	47	45	43	2	0	400	389	11	151	133	12.4	3.33	96	.245	.314	50	.215	8	-2	-6	5	0.7
1893	StL-N	21	22	.488	48	45	37	1	1	380^1	436	18	187	86	15.0	4.61	103	.279	.360	51	.256	3	2	5	1	0.8
1894	StL-N	2	6	.250	8	8	6	0	0	58	75	2	21	9	15.4	6.05	89	.310	.372	7	.250	-0	-5	-4	1	-0.2
	*Bal-N	15	5	.750	21	20	19	0	0	172	224	3	44	35	14.2	4.45	123	.311	.354	30	.349	4	17	19	-2	1.8
	Yr	17	11	.607	29	28	25	0	0	230	299	5	65	44	14.4	4.85	112	.310	.356	37	.325	4	12	15	-0	1.6
1895	*Bal-N	2	4	.333	9	5	3	0	1	50^1	77	4	21	6	18.1	6.97	68	.345	.409	130	.309	2	-12	-12	-0	-0.9
Total	8	138	131	.513	299	266	240	10	6	2389^1	2552	75	906	744	13.3	3.79	103	.265	.333	1944	.261	21	10	29	-0	4.6
● **JERRY GLEATON**	Gleaton, Jerry Don b: 9/14/57, Brownwood, Tex. BL/TL, 6'3", 210 lbs. Deb: 7/11/79																									
1979	Tex-A	0	1	.000	5	2	0	0	0	9^2	15	0	2	2	16.8	6.52	64	.375	.419	0	—	0	-2	-3	0	-0.2
1980	Tex-A	0	0	—	5	0	0	0	0	7	5	0	4	2	11.6	2.57	151	.208	.321	0	—	0	1	1	0	0.2
1981	Sea-A	4	7	.364	20	13	1	0	0	85^1	88	10	38	31	13.5	4.75	81	.273	.354	0	—	0	-10	-8	-1	-1.1
1982	Sea-A	0	0	—	3	0	0	0	0	4^2	7	3	2	1	19.3	13.50	31	.333	.417	0	—	0	-5	-5	-0	-0.5
1984	Chi-A	1	2	.333	11	1	0	0	2	18^1	20	2	6	4	13.3	3.44	121	.286	.351	0	—	0	1	1	-1	-0.2
1985	Chi-A	1	0	1.000	31	0	0	0	1	29^2	37	3	13	22	15.2	5.76	75	.316	.385	0	—	0	-5	-5	-0	-0.5
1987	KC-A	4	4	.500	48	0	0	0	5	50^2	38	4	28	44	11.7	4.26	107	.216	.324	0	—	0	1	2	1	0.1
1988	KC-A	0	4	.000	42	0	0	0	3	38	33	2	17	29	12.6	3.55	112	.232	.327	0	—	0	2	2	-0	0.1
1989	KC-A	0	0	—	15	0	0	0	0	14^1	20	0	6	9	16.3	5.65	68	.345	.406	0	—	0	-3	-3	-0	-0.3
1990	Det-A	1	3	.250	57	0	0	0	13	82^2	62	5	25	56	9.8	2.94	135	.213	.282	0	—	0	9	9	-0	0.9
1991	Det-A	3	2	.600	47	0	0	0	2	75^1	74	7	39	47	13.5	4.06	102	.269	.360	0	—	0	0	1	0	0.0
1992	Pit-N	1	0	1.000	23	0	0	0	0	31^2	34	4	19	18	15.1	4.26	80	.283	.381	0	.000	0	-3	-3	0	-0.3
Total	12	15	23	.395	307	16	1	0	26	447^1	433	40	199	265	12.9	4.25	95	.261	.345	0	.000	0	-14	-10	-0	-1.8
● **MARTIN GLENDON**	Glendon, Martin J. b: 2/8/1877, Milwaukee, Wis. d: 11/6/50, Norwood Park, Ill. 5'8", 165 lbs. Deb: 4/18/02																									
1902	Cin-N	0	1	.000	1	1	0	0	0	3	5	0	4	0	27.0	12.00	25	.370	.513	0	.000	-0	-3	-3	0	-0.3
1903	Cle-A	1	2	.333	3	3	3	0	0	27^2	20	0	7	9	8.8	0.98	292	.202	.255	0	.000	-1	6	6	1	0.7
Total	2	1	3	.250	4	4	3	0	0	30^2	25	0	11	9	10.6	2.05	140	.222	.292	0	.000	-1	3	3	1	0.4
● **BOB GLENN**	Glenn, Burdette b: 6/16/1894, W.Sunbury, Pa. d: 6/3/77, Richmond, Cal. Deb: 7/27/20																									
1920	StL-N	0	0	—	2	0	0	0	0	2	2	0	0	0	9.0	0.00	—	.222	.222	0	—	0	1	1	0	0.1
● **SAL GLIATTO**	Gliatto, Salvador Michael b: 5/7/02, Chicago, Ill. BB/TR, 5'8.5", 150 lbs. Deb: 4/19/30																									
1930	Cle-A	0	0	—	8	0	0	0	2	15	21	1	9	7	19.2	6.60	73	.328	.427	0	.000	-0	-3	-3	-0	-0.3
● **ED GLYNN**	Glynn, Edward Paul b: 6/3/53, Flushing, N.Y. BR/TL, 6'2", 180 lbs. Deb: 9/19/75																									
1975	Det-A	0	2	.000	3	1	0	0	0	14^2	11	1	8	8	11.7	4.30	93	.220	.328	0	—	0	-1	-0	0	-0.1
1976	Det-A	1	3	.250	5	4	1	0	0	23^2	22	3	20	17	16.0	6.08	61	.265	.408	0	—	0	-7	-6	-1	-0.7
1977	Det-A	2	1	.667	8	3	0	0	0	27^1	36	3	12	13	15.8	5.27	81	.316	.381	0	—	0	-4	-3	-0	-0.7
1978	Det-A	0	0	—	10	0	0	0	0	14^2	11	3	4	9	9.2	3.07	126	.208	.263	0	—	0	1	1	1	0.2
1979	NY-N	1	4	.200	46	0	0	0	7	60	57	3	40	32	14.9	3.00	121	.259	.378	0	.000	-0	5	4	-1	0.3
1980	NY-N	3	3	.500	38	0	0	0	1	52^1	49	5	23	32	12.4	4.13	86	.246	.324	0	.000	-1	-3	-3	1	-0.4
1981	Cle-A	0	0	—	4	0	0	0	0	7^2	5	0	4	4	10.6	1.17	309	.192	.300	0	—	0	2	2	-0	0.2
1982	Cle-A	5	2	.714	47	0	0	0	4	49^2	43	6	30	54	13.2	4.17	98	.232	.340	0	—	0	-1	-0	-0	-0.1
1983	Cle-A	0	2	.000	11	0	0	0	0	12^1	22	2	6	13	20.4	5.84	73	.373	.431	0	—	0	-2	-2	-0	-0.4
1985	Mon-N	0	0	—	3	0	0	0	0	2^1	5	0	4	2	34.7	19.29	18	.455	.600	0	—	0	-4	-4	-0	-0.4
Total	10	12	17	.414	175	8	1	0	12	264^2	261	26	151	184	14.1	4.25	90	.261	.359	0	.000	-1	-13	-12	-2	-2.1
● **JOT GOAR**	Goar, Joshua Mercer b: 1/31/1870, New Lisbon, Ind. d: 4/4/47, New Castle, Ind. BR/TR, 5'9", 160 lbs. Deb: 4/18/1896																									
1896	Pit-N	0	1	.000	3	0	0	0	0	13^1	36	1	8	3	30.4	16.88	25	.485	.540	1	.167	-0	-19	-19	-1	-1.4
1898	Cin-N	0	0	—	1	0	0	0	0	2	4	0	1	0	22.5	9.00	43	.411	.466	0	—	0	-1	-1	0	-0.1
Total	2	0	1	.000	4	0	0	0	0	15^1	40	1	9	3	29.3	15.85	26	.476	.532	1	.167	-0	-20	-20	-0	-1.5
● **GEORGE GOETZ**	Goetz, George Burt b: Greencastle, Ind. 6'2", 180 lbs. Deb: 6/17/1889																									
1889	Bal-a	1	0	1.000	1	1	0	0	0	9	12	0	0	2	12.0	4.00	99	.310	.310	0	.000	-1	-0	-0	0	0.0
● **JOHN GOETZ**	Goetz, John Hardy b: 10/24/37, Goetzville, Mich. BR/TR, 6', 185 lbs. Deb: 4/16/60																									
1960	Chi-N	0	0	—	4	0	0	0	0	6^1	10	2	4	6	19.9	12.79	30	.370	.452	0	.000	-0	-6	-6	0	-0.6
● **BILL GOGOLEWSKI**	Gogolewski, William Joseph b: 10/26/47, Oshkosh, Wis. BL/TR, 6'4", 190 lbs. Deb: 9/03/70																									
1970	Was-A	2	2	.500	8	5	0	0	0	33^2	33	2	25	19	15.8	4.81	74	.260	.386	0	.000	-0	-4	-5	1	-0.4
1971	Was-A	6	5	.545	27	17	4	1	0	124^1	112	5	39	70	11.1	2.75	120	.241	.302	5	.156	0	10	8	-0	0.9
1972	Tex-A	4	11	.267	36	21	2	1	2	150^2	136	9	58	95	11.9	4.24	71	.239	.316	5	.125	-1	-20	-21	-0	-2.4
1973	Tex-A	3	6	.333	49	1	0	0	6	123^2	139	10	48	77	13.7	4.22	88	.286	.351	0	—	0	-6	-7	2	-0.5
1974	Cle-A	0	0	—	5	0	0	0	0	13^2	15	1	2	3	11.9	4.61	78	.283	.321	0	—	0	-2	-2	1	0.0
1975	Chi-A	0	0	—	19	0	0	0	2	55	61	5	28	37	14.7	5.24	74	.292	.378	0	—	0	-9	-8	1	-0.8
Total	6	15	24	.385	144	44	6	2	10	501	496	32	200	301	12.7	4.02	85	.260	.334	10	.127	-1	-30	-34	5	-3.2
● **JIM GOLDEN**	Golden, James Edward b: 3/20/36, Eldon, Mo. BL/TR, 6', 175 lbs. Deb: 9/30/60																									
1960	LA-N	1	0	1.000	1	1	0	0	0	7	6	1	4	4	12.9	6.43	62	.240	.345	1	.333	1	-2	-2	-0	-0.1
1961	LA-N	1	1	.500	28	0	0	0	0	42	52	7	20	18	15.4	5.79	75	.306	.379	0	.000	-0	-8	-7	-0	-0.7

YEAR	TM/L	W	L	PCT	G	GS	CG	SH	SV	IP	H	HR	BB	SO	RAT	ERA	ERA+	OAV	OOB	BH	AVG	PB	PR	/A	PD	TPI
1962	Hou-N	7	11	.389	37	18	5	2	1	152^2	163	13	50	88	12.6	4.07	92	.270	.326	12	.222	4	-2	-6	1	-0.1
1963	Hou-N	0	1	.000	3	1	0	0	0	6^1	12	0	2	5	19.9	5.68	55	.429	.467	0	—	0	-2	-2	0	-0.2
Total	4	9	13	.409	69	20	5	2	1	208	233	21	76	115	13.4	4.54	85	.282	.343	13	.217	4	-14	-16	0	-1.1

● MIKE GOLDEN Golden, Michael Henry b: 9/11/1851, Shirley, Mass. d: 1/11/29, Rockford, Ill. BR/TR, 5′8″, 168 lbs. Deb: 5/05/1875 ♦

YEAR	TM/L	W	L	PCT	G	GS	CG	SH	SV	IP	H	HR	BB	SO	RAT	ERA	ERA+	OAV	OOB	BH	AVG	PB	PR	/A	PD	TPI
1875	Wes-n	1	12	.077	13	13	13	0	0	112	110	0	14		10.0	*2.81*	96	.225	.247	6	.130	-4	-4	-1		-0.4
	Chi-n	6	7	.462	14	14	12	1	0	119	129	0	11		10.6	*2.87*	87	.252	.268	40	.258	1	-5	-5		-0.4
	Yr	7	19	.269	27	27	25	1	0	231	239	0	25		10.3	*2.84*	91	.239	.258	46	.229	-4	-10	-6		-0.8
1878	Mil-N	3	13	.188	22	18	15	0	0	161	217	1	33	52	14.0	4.14	63	.295	.325	44	.206	-2	-33	-27	0	-2.5

● ROY GOLDEN Golden, Roy Kramer b: 7/12/1888, Madisonville, Ill d: 10/4/61, Norwood, Ohio BR/TR, 6′1″, 195 lbs. Deb: 9/07/10

YEAR	TM/L	W	L	PCT	G	GS	CG	SH	SV	IP	H	HR	BB	SO	RAT	ERA	ERA+	OAV	OOB	BH	AVG	PB	PR	/A	PD	TPI
1910	StL-N	2	3	.400	7	6	3	0	0	42^2	44	3	33	31	16.7	4.43	67	.286	.418	4	.267	1	-7	-7	1	-0.5
1911	StL-N	4	9	.308	30	25	6	0	0	148^2	127	6	129	81	15.8	5.02	67	.240	.394	5	.114	-1	-27	-27	-0	-2.7
Total	2	6	12	.333	37	31	9	0	0	191^1	171	9	162	112	16.0	4.89	67	.250	.399	9	.153	-1	-33	-34	1	-3.2

● FRED GOLDSMITH Goldsmith, Fred Ernest b: 5/15/1856, New Haven, Conn. d: 3/28/39, Berkley, Mich. BR/TR, 6′1″, 195 lbs. Deb: 10/23/1875 U♦

YEAR	TM/L	W	L	PCT	G	GS	CG	SH	SV	IP	H	HR	BB	SO	RAT	ERA	ERA+	OAV	OOB	BH	AVG	PB	PR	/A	PD	TPI
1879	Tro-N	2	4	.333	8	7	7	0	0	63	61	0	1	31	8.9	1.57	159	.237	.240	9	.237	0	6	6	-0	0.7
1880	Chi-N	21	3	**.875**	26	24	22	4	1	210^1	189	2	18	90	8.9	1.75	138	.231	.247	37	.261	2	14	16	2	1.9
1881	Chi-N	24	13	.649	39	39	37	5	0	330	328	4	44	76	10.1	2.59	106	.247	.271	38	.241	3	7	5	5	1.1
1882	Chi-N	28	17	.622	45	45	45	4	0	405	377	7	38	109	9.2	2.42	119	.236	.254	42	.230	-1	22	20	-2	1.4
1883	Chi-N	25	19	.568	46	45	40	2	0	383^1	456	14	39	82	11.6	3.15	101	.277	.294	52	.221	-0	-0	2	1	0.2
1884	Chi-N	9	11	.450	21	21	20	1	0	188	245	11	29	34	13.1	4.26	74	.298	.322	11	.136	-3	-27	-24	-3	-2.5
	Bal-a	3	1	.750	4	4	3	0	0	30	29	0	2	11	9.6	2.70	128	.238	.256	2	.143	-0	2	3	1	0.3
Total	6	112	68	.622	189	185	174	16	1	1609^2	1685	38	171	433	10.4	2.73	106	.256	.275	191	.224	-1	24	28	4	3.1

● HAL GOLDSMITH Goldsmith, Harold Eugene b: 8/18/1898, Peconic, N.Y. d: 10/20/85, Riverhead, N.Y. BR/TR, 6′, 174 lbs. Deb: 6/23/26

YEAR	TM/L	W	L	PCT	G	GS	CG	SH	SV	IP	H	HR	BB	SO	RAT	ERA	ERA+	OAV	OOB	BH	AVG	PB	PR	/A	PD	TPI
1926	Bos-N	5	7	.417	19	15	5	0	0	101	135	2	28	16	14.6	4.37	81	.333	.377	8	.211	0	-6	-9	1	-0.8
1927	Bos-N	1	3	.250	22	5	1	0	1	71^2	83	4	26	13	13.7	3.52	106	.289	.348	5	.238	0	3	2	0	0.2
1928	Bos-N	0	0	—	4	0	0	0	0	8^1	14	2	1	1	16.2	3.24	121	.359	.375	0	.000	-0	1	1	0	0.1
1929	StL-N	0	0	—	2	0	0	0	0	4	3	1	1	0	9.0	6.75	69	.214	.267	0	.000	-0	-1	-1	-0	-0.1
Total	4	6	10	.375	47	20	6	0	1	185	235	9	56	30	14.2	4.04	90	.315	.364	13	.210	0	-3	-8	1	-0.6

● IZZY GOLDSTEIN Goldstein, Isidore b: 6/6/08, New York, N.Y. BB/TR, 6′, 160 lbs. Deb: 4/24/32

YEAR	TM/L	W	L	PCT	G	GS	CG	SH	SV	IP	H	HR	BB	SO	RAT	ERA	ERA+	OAV	OOB	BH	AVG	PB	PR	/A	PD	TPI
1932	Det-A	3	2	.600	16	6	2	0	0	56^1	63	2	41	14	17.1	4.47	105	.276	.393	5	.294	1	0	1	0	0.2

● DAVE GOLTZ Goltz, David Allan b: 6/23/49, Pelican Rapids, Minn. BR/TR, 6′4″, 215 lbs. Deb: 7/18/72

YEAR	TM/L	W	L	PCT	G	GS	CG	SH	SV	IP	H	HR	BB	SO	RAT	ERA	ERA+	OAV	OOB	BH	AVG	PB	PR	/A	PD	TPI
1972	Min-A	3	3	.500	15	11	2	0	1	91	75	5	26	38	10.0	2.67	120	.224	.280	3	.103	-1	4	5	-0	0.5
1973	Min-A	6	4	.600	32	10	1	0	1	106^1	138	11	32	65	14.6	5.25	75	.318	.368	0	—	0	-17	-15	1	-1.5
1974	Min-A	10	10	.500	28	24	5	1	1	174^1	192	14	45	89	12.6	3.25	115	.282	.333	0	—	0	7	10	1	1.1
1975	Min-A	14	14	.500	32	32	15	1	0	243	235	18	72	128	11.6	3.67	105	.255	.313	0	—	0	3	5	1	0.6
1976	Min-A	14	14	.500	36	35	13	4	0	249^1	239	14	91	133	12.1	3.36	107	.254	.323	0	—	0	4	7	0	0.7
1977	Min-A	**20**	11	.645	39	39	19	2	0	303	284	23	91	186	11.2	3.36	119	.247	.304	0	—	0	24	21	-1	2.2
1978	Min-A	15	10	.600	29	29	13	2	0	220^1	209	12	67	116	11.3	2.49	153	.253	.309	0	—	0	31	32	0	3.6
1979	Min-A	14	13	.519	36	35	12	1	0	250^2	282	22	69	132	12.6	4.16	105	.288	.336	0	—	0	1	6	-1	0.5
1980	LA-N	7	11	.389	35	27	2	2	1	171^1	198	12	59	91	13.5	4.31	81	.299	.356	6	.128	0	-13	-15	-0	-1.6
1981	*LA-N	2	7	.222	26	8	0	0	1	77	83	4	25	48	12.6	4.09	81	.288	.345	1	.059	-1	-5	-7	1	-0.7
1982	LA-N	0	1	.000	2	1	0	0	0	3^2	6	0	0	3	14.7	4.91	71	.353	.353	0	.000	-0	-1	-1	0	0.0
	*Cal-A	8	5	.615	28	7	1	0	3	86	82	4	32	49	12.0	4.08	99	.252	.320	0	—	0	-0	-0	-2	-0.2
1983	Cal-A	0	6	.000	15	6	0	0	0	63^2	81	10	37	27	16.8	6.22	65	.315	.403	0	—	0	-15	-16	-0	-1.5
Total	12	113	109	.509	353	264	83	13	8	2039^2	2104	149	646	1105	12.2	3.69	104	.269	.327	10	.106	-1	23	33	0	3.7

● LUIS GOMEZ Gomez, Luis (Sanchez) b: 8/19/51, Guadalajara, Mex. BR/TR, 5′9″, 150 lbs. Deb: 4/28/74 ♦

YEAR	TM/L	W	L	PCT	G	GS	CG	SH	SV	IP	H	HR	BB	SO	RAT	ERA	ERA+	OAV	OOB	BH	AVG	PB	PR	/A	PD	TPI
1981	Atl-N	0	0	—	1	0	0	0	0	1	3	0	2	0	45.0	27.00	13	.500	.625	7	.200	0	-3	-3	-0	-0.2

● RUBEN GOMEZ Gomez, Ruben (Colon) b: 7/13/27, Arroyo, P.R. BR/TR, 6′, 175 lbs. Deb: 4/17/53

YEAR	TM/L	W	L	PCT	G	GS	CG	SH	SV	IP	H	HR	BB	SO	RAT	ERA	ERA+	OAV	OOB	BH	AVG	PB	PR	/A	PD	TPI
1953	NY-N	13	11	.542	29	26	13	3	0	204	166	17	101	113	12.0	3.40	126	.218	.313	15	.208	-0	20	20	2	2.2
1954	*NY-N	17	9	.654	37	32	10	4	0	221^2	202	20	109	106	12.9	2.88	140	.244	.337	14	.173	0	29	28	2	3.0
1955	NY-N	9	10	.474	33	31	9	3	1	185^1	207	20	63	79	13.5	4.56	88	.285	.348	18	.300	4	-11	-11	3	-0.5
1956	NY-N	7	17	.292	40	31	4	2	0	196^1	191	19	77	76	12.7	4.58	83	.259	.337	11	.183	-0	-18	-17	2	-1.5
1957	NY-N	15	13	.536	38	36	16	1	0	238^1	233	28	71	92	11.7	3.78	104	.254	.311	16	.184	1	3	4	2	0.8
1958	SF-N	10	12	.455	42	30	8	1	1	207^2	204	21	77	112	12.5	4.38	87	.261	.334	14	.200	1	-10	-13	2	-1.0
1959	Phi-N	3	8	.273	20	12	2	1	1	72^1	90	12	24	37	14.2	6.10	67	.300	.352	3	.176	0	-17	-16	2	-1.4
1960	Phi-N	0	3	.000	22	1	0	0	1	52^1	68	7	9	24	13.4	5.33	73	.321	.351	1	.083	-1	-9	-8	-1	-1.0
1962	Cle-A	1	2	.333	15	4	0	0	1	45^1	50	5	25	21	15.3	4.37	89	.292	.389	3	.231	0	-2	-2	1	-0.2
	Min-A	1	1	.500	6	2	1	0	0	19^1	17	3	11	8	13.0	4.66	88	.254	.359	0	.000	-0	-1	-1	0	-0.2
	Yr	2	3	.400	21	6	1	0	1	64^2	67	8	36	29	14.3	4.45	88	.276	.369	3	.167	-0	-3	-4	1	-0.4
1967	Phi-N	0	0	—	7	0	0	0	0	11^1	8	2	7	9	11.9	3.97	86	.211	.333	0	—	0	-1	-1	1	0.0
Total	10	76	86	.469	289	205	63	15	5	1454	1436	154	574	677	12.7	4.09	97	.259	.334	95	.199	6	-17	-18	14	0.2

● LEFTY GOMEZ Gomez, Vernon Louis "Goofy" b: 11/26/08, Rodeo, Cal. d: 2/17/89, Greenbrae, Cal. BL/TL, 6′2″, 173 lbs. Deb: 4/29/30 H

YEAR	TM/L	W	L	PCT	G	GS	CG	SH	SV	IP	H	HR	BB	SO	RAT	ERA	ERA+	OAV	OOB	BH	AVG	PB	PR	/A	PD	TPI
1930	NY-A	2	5	.286	15	6	2	0	1	60	66	12	28	22	14.3	5.55	78	.280	.358	3	.150	-2	-6	-8	1	-0.8
1931	NY-A	21	9	.700	40	26	17	1	3	243	206	7	85	150	10.9	2.67	149	.226	.295	11	.133	-3	46	35	-1	3.0
1932	*NY-A	24	7	.774	37	31	21	1	1	265^1	266	23	105	176	12.7	4.21	97	.259	.329	18	.173	-1	8	-4	-3	-0.8
1933	NY-A★	16	10	.615	35	30	14	4	2	234^2	218	16	106	**163**	12.4	3.18	122	.240	.319	9	.112	-3	29	18	-4	1.1
1934	NY-A★	**26**	5	**.839**	38	33	**25**	**6**	1	**281^2**	223	12	96	**158**	**10.2**	**2.33**	174	**.215**	**.282**	13	.131	-3	**68**	54	-2	4.9
1935	NY-A★	12	15	.444	34	30	15	2	1	246	223	18	86	138	11.4	3.18	127	.242	.309	10	.120	-6	35	24	1	1.7
1936	*NY-A☆	13	7	.650	31	30	10	0	0	188^2	184	6	122	105	14.6	4.39	106	.254	.362	10	.145	-2	14	6	-1	0.2
1937	*NY-A★	**21**	11	.656	34	34	25	**6**	0	278^1	233	10	93	**194**	10.6	**2.33**	191	**.223**	.287	21	.200	-1	**71**	**65**	-3	**6.2**
1938	*NY-A★	18	12	.600	32	32	20	**4**	0	239	239	7	99	129	12.8	3.35	135	.260	.332	13	.151	-2	38	31	2	2.9
1939	*NY-A☆	12	8	.600	26	26	14	2	0	198	173	11	84	102	11.8	3.41	128	.235	.316	11	.151	-2	27	21	-1	1.7
1940	NY-A	3	3	.500	9	5	0	0	0	27^1	37	2	18	14	18.4	6.59	61	.325	.421	0	.000	-1	-7	-8	-1	-0.9
1941	NY-A	15	5	**.750**	23	23	8	2	0	156^1	151	10	103	76	14.7	3.74	105	.250	.360	9	.153	-1	7	3	-4	-0.1
1942	NY-A	6	4	.600	13	13	2	0	0	80	67	4	65	41	15.1	4.27	80	.237	.383	5	.152	-1	-5	-7	-2	-1.0
1943	Was-A	0	1	.000	1	1	0	0	0	4^2	4	0	5	0	17.4	5.79	55	.250	.429	0	.000	-0	-1	-1	1	-0.1
Total	14	189	102	.649	368	320	173	28	9	2503	2290	138	1095	1468	12.2	3.34	125	.242	.321	133	.147	-27	322	229	-15	18.0

● JOE GONZALES Gonzales, Joe Madrid "Smokey" b: 3/19/15, San Francisco, Cal BR/TR, 5′9″, 175 lbs. Deb: 8/28/37

YEAR	TM/L	W	L	PCT	G	GS	CG	SH	SV	IP	H	HR	BB	SO	RAT	ERA	ERA+	OAV	OOB	BH	AVG	PB	PR	/A	PD	TPI
1937	Bos-A	1	2	.333	8	2	2	0	0	31	37	1	11	11	13.9	4.35	109	.291	.348	0	.000	-2	1	1	0	0.0

● VINCE GONZALES Gonzales, Wenceslao (O'Reilly)
b: 9/28/25, Quivican, Cuba d: 3/11/81, Ciudad Del Carmen Campeche, Mexico BL/TL, 6′1″, 165 lbs. Deb: 4/13/55

YEAR	TM/L	W	L	PCT	G	GS	CG	SH	SV	IP	H	HR	BB	SO	RAT	ERA	ERA+	OAV	OOB	BH	AVG	PB	PR	/A	PD	TPI
1955	Was-A	0	0	—	1	0	0	0	0	2	6	0	3	1	40.5	27.00	14	.500	.600	0	—	0	-5	-5	-0	-0.4

● GERMAN GONZALEZ Gonzalez, German Jose (Caraballo) b: 3/7/62, Rio Caribe, Venez. BR/TR, 6′, 170 lbs. Deb: 8/05/88

YEAR	TM/L	W	L	PCT	G	GS	CG	SH	SV	IP	H	HR	BB	SO	RAT	ERA	ERA+	OAV	OOB	BH	AVG	PB	PR	/A	PD	TPI
1988	Min-A	0	0	—	16	0	0	0	1	21^1	20	4	8	19	12.2	3.38	121	.244	.319	0	—	0	1	2	0	0.1
1989	Min-A	3	2	.600	22	0	0	0	0	29	32	2	11	25	14.6	4.66	89	.274	.356	0	—	0	-2	-2	-0	-0.2

YEAR	TM/L	W	L	PCT	G	GS	CG	SH	SV	IP	H	HR	BB	SO	RAT	ERA	ERA+	OAV	OOB	BH	AVG	PB	PR	/A	PD	TPI
Total	2	3	2	.600	38	0	0	0	1	50^1	52	6	19	44	13.6	4.11	100	.261	.341	0	—	0	-1	-0	0	-0.1
● JULIO GONZALEZ Gonzalez, Julio Enrique (Herrera) b: 12/20/20, Banes, Cuba d: 2/15/91, Banes, Cuba BR/TR, 5'11", 150 lbs. Deb: 8/09/49																										
1949	Was-A	0	0	—	13	0	0	0	0	34^1	33	3	27	5	16.0	4.72	90	.256	.389	1	.200	0	-2	-2	-0	-0.1
● RALPH GOOD Good, Ralph Nelson "Holy" b: 4/25/1886, Monticello, Me. d: 11/24/65, Waterville, Maine BR/TR, 6', 165 lbs. Deb: 7/01/10																										
1910	Bos-N	0	0	—	2	0	0	0	0	9	6	0	2	4	10.0	2.00	166	.188	.278	0	.000	-0	1	1	0	0.1
● WILBUR GOOD Good, Wilbur David "Lefty" b: 9/28/1885, Punxsutawney, Pa. d: 12/30/63, Brooksville, Fla. BL/TL, 5'6", 165 lbs. Deb: 8/18/05 ♦																										
1905	NY-A	0	2	.000	5	2	0	0	0	19	18	1	14	13	15.2	4.74	62	.251	.374	3	.375	1	-4	-4	0	-0.3
● HERB GOODALL Goodall, Herbert Frank b: 3/10/1870, Mansfield, Pa. d: 1/20/38, Mansfield, Pa. BR/TR, 5'9", 180 lbs. Deb: 4/29/1890																										
1890	Lou-a	8	5	.615	18	13	8	1	**4**	109	94	2	51	46	12.8	3.39	114	.226	.324	19	.422	5	6	6	1	1.1
● JOHN GOODELL Goodell, John Henry William "Lefty" b: 4/5/07, Muskogee, Okla. BR/TL, 5'10", 165 lbs. Deb: 4/19/28																										
1928	Chi-A	0	0	—	2	0	0	0	0	3	6	0	2	0	27.0	18.00	23	.500	.600	0	—	0	-5	-5	0	-0.4
● DWIGHT GOODEN Gooden, Dwight Eugene "Doc" b: 11/16/64, Tampa, Fla. BR/TR, 6'3", 198 lbs. Deb: 4/07/84																										
1984	NY-N★	17	9	.654	31	31	7	3	0	218	161	7	73	**276**	**9.7**	2.60	136	**.202**	**.270**	14	.200	1	24	23	1	2.7
1985	NY-N☆	**24**	4	.857	35	35	**16**	8	0	**276^2**	198	13	69	**268**	8.8	**1.53**	**226**	.201	.254	21	.226	6	**63**	**59**	2	**8.0**
1986	*NY-N★	17	6	.739	33	33	12	2	0	250	197	17	80	200	10.1	2.84	124	.215	.280	7	.086	-3	24	19	2	2.0
1987	NY-N	15	7	**.682**	25	25	7	3	0	179^2	162	11	53	148	10.9	3.21	118	.244	.301	14	.219	2	17	11	-0	1.4
1988	*NY-N★	18	9	.667	34	34	10	3	0	248^1	242	8	57	175	11.1	3.19	101	.256	.303	16	.178	2	7	1	5	0.9
1989	NY-N	9	4	.692	19	17	0	0	1	118^1	93	9	47	101	10.8	2.89	113	.211	.290	8	.200	2	8	5	0	0.7
1990	NY-N	19	7	.731	34	34	2	1	0	232^2	229	10	70	223	11.8	3.83	98	.258	.317	14	.187	4	-1	-2	2	0.3
1991	NY-N	13	7	.650	27	27	3	1	0	190	185	12	56	150	11.6	3.60	101	.257	.313	15	.238	4	2	1	1	0.6
1992	NY-N	10	13	.435	31	31	3	0	0	206	197	11	70	145	11.8	3.67	95	.255	.319	19	.264	6	-4	-4	1	0.4
Total	9	142	66	.683	269	267	60	21	1	1919^2	1664	98	575	1686	10.6	2.99	118	.233	.293	128	.198	24	141	113	13	17.0
● ART GOODWIN Goodwin, Arthur Ingram b: 2/27/1877, Whitley Twnshp, Pa d: 6/19/43, Franklin Township, Greene County, Pa. TR , 5'8", 195 lbs. Deb: 10/07/05																										
1905	NY-A	0	0	—	1	0	0	0	0	0^1	2	0	2	0	108.0	81.00	4	.680	.809	0	—	0	-3	-3	0	-0.3
● CLYDE GOODWIN Goodwin, Clyde Samuel b: 11/12/1886, Shade, Ohio d: 10/12/63, Dayton, Ohio BR/TR, 5'11", 145 lbs. Deb: 9/18/06																										
1906	Was-A	0	2	.000	4	3	1	0	0	22^1	20	0	13	9	13.7	4.43	59	.243	.352	1	.200	-0	-4	-4	-1	-0.5
● JIM GOODWIN Goodwin, James Patrick b: 8/15/26, St.Louis, Mo. BL/TL, 6'1", 170 lbs. Deb: 4/24/48																										
1948	Chi-A	0	0	—	8	1	0	0	1	10^1	9	0	12	3	19.2	8.71	49	.237	.431	1	.500	0	-5	-5	0	-0.4
● MARV GOODWIN Goodwin, Marvin Mardo b: 1/16/1891, Gordonsville, Va. d: 10/21/25, Houston, Tex. BR/TR, 5'11", 168 lbs. Deb: 9/07/16																										
1916	Was-A	0	0	—	3	0	0	0	0	5^2	5	0	3	1	12.7	3.18	88	.217	.308	0	.000	-0	-0	-0	-0	-0.1
1917	StL-N	6	4	.600	14	12	6	3	0	85^1	70	1	19	38	9.4	2.21	122	.222	.266	4	.174	-0	5	5	2	0.7
1919	StL-N	11	9	.550	33	17	7	0	0	179	163	3	33	48	10.3	2.51	111	.245	.289	12	.200	1	8	6	-1	0.7
1920	StL-N	3	8	.273	32	12	3	0	1	116^1	153	1	28	23	14.4	4.95	60	.314	.357	7	.200	-0	-23	-25	-3	-2.8
1921	StL-N	1	2	.333	14	4	1	0	1	36^1	47	1	9	7	14.1	3.72	99	.315	.358	0	.000	-1	0	-0	0	0.0
1922	StL-N	0	0	—	2	0	0	0	0	4	3	0	3	0	13.5	2.25	172	.250	.400	0	—	0	1	1	0	0.1
1925	Cin-N	0	2	.000	4	3	2	0	0	20^2	26	2	5	4	13.9	4.79	86	.317	.364	1	.250	0	-1	-2	1	-0.1
Total	7	21	25	.457	102	48	19	3	2	447^1	467	8	100	121	11.7	3.30	90	.269	.315	24	.186	0	-11	-17	0	-1.5
● RAY GORDINIER Gordinier, Raymond Cornelius "Gordy" b: 4/11/1892, Rochester, N.Y. d: 11/15/60, Rochester, N.Y. BB/TR, 5'8.5", 170 lbs. Deb: 9/17/21																										
1921	Bro-N	1	0	1.000	3	3	0	0	0	12	10	0	8	4	13.5	5.25	74	.227	.346	1	.250	0	-2	-2	0	-0.1
1922	Bro-N	0	0	—	5	0	0	0	0	11^1	13	3	8	5	16.7	8.74	47	.289	.396	0	.000	-0	-6	-6	-0	-0.6
Total	2	1	0	1.000	8	3	0	0	0	23^1	23	3	16	9	15.0	6.94	57	.258	.371	1	.167	-0	-8	-8	0	-0.7
● DON GORDON Gordon, Donald Thomas b: 10/10/59, New York, N.Y. BR/TR, 6'1", 175 lbs. Deb: 4/10/86																										
1986	Tor-A	0	1	.000	14	0	0	0	1	21^2	28	1	8	13	15.4	7.06	60	.311	.374	0	—	0	-7	-7	-1	-0.7
1987	Tor-A	0	0	—	5	0	0	0	0	11	8	2	3	3	9.0	4.09	110	.200	.256	0	—	0	0	0	-0	0.0
	Cle-A	0	3	.000	21	0	0	0	1	39^2	49	3	12	20	14.7	4.08	111	.295	.357	0	—	0	2	2	1	0.3
	Yr	0	3	.000	26	0	0	0	1	50^2	57	5	15	23	13.5	4.09	111	.277	.338	0	—	0	2	2	1	0.3
1988	Cle-A	3	4	.429	38	0	0	0	1	59^1	65	5	19	20	13.2	4.40	93	.284	.347	0	—	0	-3	-2	1	-0.2
Total	3	3	8	.273	78	0	0	0	3	131^2	150	11	42	56	13.7	4.72	91	.286	.348	0	—	0	-8	-6	1	-0.6
● TOM GORDON Gordon, Thomas b: 11/18/67, Sebring, Fla. BR/TR, 5'9", 160 lbs. Deb: 9/08/88																										
1988	KC-A	0	2	.000	5	2	0	0	0	15^2	16	1	7	18	13.2	5.17	77	.267	.343	0	—	0	-2	-2	0	-0.2
1989	KC-A	17	9	.654	49	16	1	1	1	163	122	10	86	153	11.5	3.64	106	.210	.312	0	—	0	4	4	3	0.6
1990	KC-A	12	11	.522	32	32	6	1	0	195^1	192	17	99	175	13.5	3.73	103	.257	.347	0	—	0	4	2	1	0.3
1991	KC-A	9	14	.391	45	14	1	0	1	158	129	16	87	167	12.5	3.87	106	.221	.325	0	—	0	4	4	0	0.4
1992	KC-A	6	10	.375	40	11	0	0	0	117^2	116	9	55	98	13.4	4.59	87	.258	.344	0	—	0	-9	-8	1	-0.8
Total	5	44	46	.489	171	75	8	2	2	649^2	575	53	334	611	12.8	3.93	100	.237	.333	0	—	0	1	0	4	0.3
● CHARLIE GORIN Gorin, Charles Perry b: 2/6/28, Waco, Tex. BL/TL, 5'10", 165 lbs. Deb: 5/29/54																										
1954	Mil-N	0	1	.000	5	0	0	0	0	9^2	5	0	6	12	10.2	1.86	200	.152	.282	0	.000	-0	2	2	-0	0.1
1955	Mil-N	0	0	—	2	0	0	0	0	0^1	1	0	3	0	108.0	54.00	7	.500	.800	0	—	0	-2	-2	0	-0.2
Total	2	0	1	.000	7	0	0	0	0	10	6	0	9	12	13.5	3.60	103	.171	.341	0	.000	-0	1	0	-0	-0.1
● JACK GORMAN Gorman, John F. "Stooping Jack" b: 1859, St.Louis, Mo. d: 9/9/1889, St.Louis, Mo. Deb: 7/01/1883 ♦																										
1884	Pit-a	1	2	.333	3	3	3	0	0	25	22	0	5	10	10.1	4.68	72	.212	.255	4	.148	-0	-4	-4	0	-0.4
● TOM GORMAN Gorman, Thomas Aloysius b: 1/4/25, New York, N.Y. BR/TR, 6'1", 190 lbs. Deb: 7/16/52																										
1952	*NY-A	6	2	.750	12	6	1	1	1	60^2	63	8	22	31	12.9	4.60	72	.272	.340	2	.087	-1	-6	-9	-0	-1.0
1953	*NY-A	4	5	.444	40	1	0	0	6	77	65	5	32	38	12.0	3.39	109	.226	.317	2	.133	-1	5	3	-0	0.2
1954	NY-A	0	0	—	23	0	0	0	2	36^2	30	1	14	31	11.0	2.21	156	.222	.300	0	.000	-0	6	5	0	0.5
1955	KC-A	7	6	.538	57	0	0	0	18	109	98	11	36	46	11.4	3.55	118	.246	.314	2	.083	-2	5	8	-1	0.5
1956	KC-A	9	10	.474	52	13	1	0	3	171^1	168	23	68	56	12.5	3.83	113	.258	.330	2	.051	-4	6	9	-0	0.6
1957	KC-A	5	9	.357	38	12	3	1	3	124^2	125	18	33	66	11.5	3.83	103	.261	.310	4	.121	-2	-1	2	-0	0.0
1958	KC-A	4	4	.500	50	1	0	0	8	89^2	86	8	20	44	10.9	3.51	111	.258	.306	2	.118	-1	3	4	-1	0.2
1959	KC-A	1	0	1.000	17	0	0	0	1	20^1	24	3	14	9	17.3	7.08	57	.293	.402	0	—	0	-7	-7	-1	-0.8
Total	8	36	36	.500	289	33	5	2	42	689^1	659	77	239	321	12.0	3.77	105	.254	.321	14	.090	-10	11	14	-4	0.2
● TOM GORMAN Gorman, Thomas David "Big Tom" b: 3/16/16, New York, N.Y. d: 8/11/86, Closter, N.J. BR/TL, 6'2", 200 lbs. Deb: 9/14/39 U																										
1939	NY-N	0	0	—	4	0	0	0	0	5	7	0	1	2	14.4	7.20	55	.350	.381	0	.000	-0	-2	-2	0	-0.2
● TOM GORMAN Gorman, Thomas Patrick b: 12/16/57, Portland, Ore. BL/TL, 6'4", 200 lbs. Deb: 9/02/81																										
1981	Mon-N	0	0	—	9	0	0	0	0	15	12	0	6	13	11.4	4.20	83	.222	.311	0	—	0	-1	-1	1	-0.1
1982	Mon-N	1	0	1.000	5	0	0	0	0	7	8	0	4	6	15.4	5.14	71	.286	.375	0	—	0	-1	-1	0	-0.1
	NY-N	0	1	.000	3	1	0	0	0	9^1	8	0	0	7	7.7	0.96	376	.235	.235	0	.000	-0	3	3	0	0.3
	Yr	1	1	.500	8	1	0	0	0	16^1	16	0	4	13	11.0	2.76	132	.254	.299	0	.000	-0	2	2	0	0.2
1983	NY-N	1	4	.200	25	4	0	0	0	49^1	45	3	15	30	10.9	4.93	74	.245	.302	1	.250	0	-7	-7	0	-0.8

YEAR	TM/L	W	L	PCT	G	GS	CG	SH	SV	IP	H	HR	BB	SO	RAT	ERA	ERA+	OAV	OOB	BH	AVG	PB	PR	/A	PD	TPI
1984	NY-N	6	0	1.000	36	0	0	0	0	57^{2}	51	6	13	40	10.1	2.97	119	.238	.285	0	.000	-0	4	4	0	0.4
1985	NY-N	4	4	.500	34	2	0	0	0	52^{2}	56	8	18	32	12.6	5.13	67	.277	.336	0	.000	-1	-9	-10	1	-0.9
1986	Phi-N	0	1	.000	8	0	0	0	0	11^{2}	21	0	5	8	20.1	7.71	50	.382	.433	0	.000	-0	-5	-5	0	-0.5
1987	SD-N	0	0	—	6	0	0	0	0	11	11	1	5	8	13.1	4.09	97	.262	.340	0	—	0	-0	-0	-0	-0.1
Total	7	12	10	.545	126	7	0	0	0	213^{2}	212	18	66	144	11.8	4.34	83	.261	.318	1	.071	-1	-17	-18	2	-1.8

● JOE GORMLEY Gormley, Joseph b: 12/20/1866, Summit Hill, Pa. d: 7/2/50, Summit Hill, Pa. BL/TL, Deb: 6/16/1891

YEAR	TM/L	W	L	PCT	G	GS	CG	SH	SV	IP	H	HR	BB	SO	RAT	ERA	ERA+	OAV	OOB	BH	AVG	PB	PR	/A	PD	TPI
1891	Phi-N	0	1	.000	1	1	1	0	0	8	10	0	5	2	16.9	5.63	61	.295	.385	0	.000	-1	-2	-2	0	-0.2

● HANK GORNICKI Gornicki, Henry Frank b: 1/14/11, Niagara Falls, N.Y BR/TR, 6'1", 145 lbs. Deb: 4/17/41

YEAR	TM/L	W	L	PCT	G	GS	CG	SH	SV	IP	H	HR	BB	SO	RAT	ERA	ERA+	OAV	OOB	BH	AVG	PB	PR	/A	PD	TPI
1941	StL-N	1	0	1.000	4	1	1	1	0	11^{1}	6	0	9	6	12.7	3.18	118	.158	.333	1	.250	0	1	1	-0	0.1
	Chi-N	0	0	—	1	0	0	0	0	2	3	0	0	2	13.5	4.50	78	.375	.375	0	—	0	-0	-0	0	0.0
	Yr	1	0	1.000	5	1	1	1	0	13^{1}	9	0	9	8	12.2	3.38	110	.191	.321	1	.250	0	0	1	0	0.1
1942	Pit-N	5	6	.455	25	14	7	2	2	112	89	2	40	48	10.4	2.57	132	.215	.286	4	.114	-1	9	10	-1	0.9
1943	Pit-N	9	13	.409	42	19	4	1	4	147	165	10	47	63	13.1	3.98	87	.286	.342	7	.175	-1	-10	-8	-1	-1.0
1946	Pit-N	0	0	—	7	0	0	0	0	12^{2}	12	0	11	4	16.3	3.55	99	.255	.397	0	.000	-0	-0	-0	-0	-0.1
Total	4	15	19	.441	79	34	12	4	6	285	275	12	107	123	12.2	3.38	102	.254	.323	12	.146	-2	-0	2	-2	-0.1

● JOHNNY GORSICA Gorsica, John Joseph Perry (b: John Joseph Perry Gorczyca) b: 3/29/15, Bayonne, N.J. BR/TR, 6'2", 180 lbs. Deb: 4/22/40

YEAR	TM/L	W	L	PCT	G	GS	CG	SH	SV	IP	H	HR	BB	SO	RAT	ERA	ERA+	OAV	OOB	BH	AVG	PB	PR	/A	PD	TPI
1940	*Det-A	7	7	.500	29	20	5	2	0	160	170	10	57	68	13.0	4.33	110	.272	.337	12	.194	1	1	8	5	1.3
1941	Det-A	9	11	.450	33	21	8	1	2	171	193	14	55	59	13.2	4.47	102	.281	.336	17	.298	4	-6	1	4	0.9
1942	Det-A	3	2	.600	28	0	0	0	4	53	63	2	26	19	15.6	4.75	83	.310	.397	1	.100	-0	-6	-5	4	-0.1
1943	Det-A	4	5	.444	35	4	1	0	5	96^{1}	88	3	40	45	12.1	3.36	105	.247	.327	4	.174	0	-1	2	3	0.5
1944	Det-A	6	14	.300	34	19	8	1	4	162	192	5	32	47	12.7	4.11	87	.296	.333	7	.135	-1	-12	-10	3	-0.8
1946	Det-A	0	0	—	14	0	0	0	1	23^{2}	28	5	11	14	14.8	4.56	80	.301	.375	2	.667	1	-3	-2	-0	-0.2
1947	Det-A	2	0	1.000	31	0	0	0	1	57^{2}	44	5	26	20	11.2	3.75	101	.208	.300	2	.200	0	-0	0	1	0.2
Total	7	31	39	.443	204	64	22	4	17	723^{2}	778	44	247	272	13.0	4.18	98	.276	.338	45	.207	5	-28	-7	20	1.8

● RICH GOSSAGE Gossage, Richard Michael "Goose" b: 7/5/51, Colorado Springs, Colo. BR/TR, 6'3", 217 lbs. Deb: 4/16/72

YEAR	TM/L	W	L	PCT	G	GS	CG	SH	SV	IP	H	HR	BB	SO	RAT	ERA	ERA+	OAV	OOB	BH	AVG	PB	PR	/A	PD	TPI
1972	Chi-A	7	1	.875	36	1	0	0	2	80	72	2	44	57	13.5	4.27	73	.247	.353	0	.000	-2	-11	-10	-1	-1.4
1973	Chi-A	0	4	.000	20	4	1	0	0	49^{2}	57	9	37	33	17.6	7.43	53	.311	.435	0	—	0	-20	-19	-0	-1.9
1974	Chi-A	4	6	.400	39	3	0	0	1	89^{1}	92	4	47	64	14.2	4.13	90	.272	.364	0	—	0	-5	-4	0	-0.4
1975	Chi-A★	9	8	.529	62	0	0	0	**26**	141^{2}	99	3	70	130	11.1	1.84	210	.201	.306	0	—	0	**30**	**32**	1	3.5
1976	Chi-A☆	9	17	.346	31	29	15	0	1	224	214	16	90	135	12.6	3.94	91	.254	.333	0	—	0	-10	-9	-1	-1.0
1977	Pit-N★	11	9	.550	72	0	0	0	26	133	78	9	49	151	8.7	1.62	245	.170	.253	5	.217	1	**34**	35	-1	3.5
1978	*NY-A★	10	11	.476	63	0	0	0	**27**	134^{1}	87	9	59	122	9.9	2.01	180	.187	.281	0	—	0	**26**	**24**	-1	2.4
1979	NY-A	5	3	.625	36	0	0	0	18	58^{1}	48	5	19	41	10.3	2.62	155	.227	.291	0	—	0	10	9	-1	0.9
1980	*NY-A★	6	2	.750	64	0	0	0	**33**	99	74	5	37	103	10.2	2.27	173	.211	.288	0	—	0	19	18	-1	1.8
1981	*NY-A†	3	2	.600	32	0	0	0	20	46^{2}	22	2	14	48	7.1	0.77	463	.141	.216	0	—	0	15	15	0	1.6
1982	NY-A☆	4	5	.444	56	0	0	0	30	93	63	5	28	102	8.8	2.23	179	.196	.261	0	—	0	19	18	-1	1.8
1983	NY-A	13	5	.722	57	0	0	0	22	87^{1}	82	5	25	90	11.1	2.27	172	.248	.303	0	—	0	17	16	-2	1.4
1984	*SD-N★	10	6	.625	62	0	0	0	25	102^{1}	75	6	36	84	9.9	2.90	123	.204	.277	4	.182	0	8	8	-1	0.7
1985	SD-N★	5	3	.625	50	0	0	0	26	79	64	1	17	52	9.3	1.82	194	.226	.272	0	.000	-1	16	15	-1	1.4
1986	SD-N	5	7	.417	45	0	0	0	21	64^{2}	69	8	20	63	12.7	4.45	82	.273	.331	0	.000	-1	-5	-6	-1	-0.8
1987	SD-N	5	4	.556	40	0	0	0	11	52	47	4	19	44	11.4	3.12	127	.244	.311	0	.000	-0	6	5	-1	0.4
1988	Chi-N	4	4	.500	46	0	0	0	13	43^{2}	50	3	15	30	14.0	4.33	83	.291	.358	0	.000	-0	-4	-4	-0	-0.4
1989	SF-N	2	1	.667	31	0	0	0	4	43^{2}	32	2	27	24	12.2	2.68	126	.212	.331	0	.000	-0	4	3	-1	0.3
	NY-A	1	0	1.000	11	0	0	0	1	14^{1}	14	0	3	6	11.3	3.77	103	.275	.327	0	—	0	0	0	0	0.0
1991	Tex-A	4	2	.667	44	0	0	0	1	40^{1}	33	4	16	28	11.6	3.57	113	.228	.317	0	—	0	2	2	-1	0.1
1992	Oak-A	0	2	.000	30	0	0	0	0	38	32	5	19	26	12.6	2.84	133	.230	.331	0	—	0	5	4	-0	0.7
Total	20	117	102	.534	927	37	16	0	308	1714^{1}	1404	107	691	1433	11.2	2.93	127	.227	.309	9	.106	-3	156	152	-13	14.6

● JIM GOTT Gott, James William b: 8/3/59, Hollywood, Cal. BR/TR, 6'4", 220 lbs. Deb: 4/09/82

YEAR	TM/L	W	L	PCT	G	GS	CG	SH	SV	IP	H	HR	BB	SO	RAT	ERA	ERA+	OAV	OOB	BH	AVG	PB	PR	/A	PD	TPI
1982	Tor-A	5	10	.333	30	23	1	1	0	136	134	15	66	82	13.4	4.43	101	.255	.341	0	—	0	-5	1	-0	0.0
1983	Tor-A	9	14	.391	34	30	6	1	0	176^{2}	195	15	68	121	13.7	4.74	91	.280	.349	0	—	0	-13	-9	-1	-0.9
1984	Tor-A	7	6	.538	35	12	1	1	2	109^{2}	93	7	49	73	11.9	4.02	102	.233	.322	0	—	0	-0	1	-1	-0.3
1985	SF-N	7	10	.412	26	26	2	0	0	148^{1}	144	10	51	78	11.9	3.88	89	.254	.317	10	.196	4	-5	-7	1	-0.3
1986	SF-N	0	0	—	9	2	0	0	1	13	16	0	13	9	20.1	7.62	46	.314	.453	0	.000	0	-6	-6	-0	-0.6
1987	SF-N	1	0	1.000	30	3	0	0	0	56	53	4	32	63	14.0	4.50	85	.244	.347	1	.100	1	-3	-4	0	-0.3
	Pit-N	0	2	.000	25	0	0	0	13	31	28	0	8	27	10.5	1.45	283	.233	.281	0	.000	-0	9	9	-0	0.9
	Yr	1	2	.333	55	3	0	0	13	87	81	4	40	90	12.5	3.41	115	.238	.318	1	.091	0	6	5	-0	0.6
1988	Pit-N	6	6	.500	67	0	0	0	34	77^{1}	68	9	22	76	10.7	3.49	97	.243	.303	0	.000	-0	-0	-1	-0	-0.1
1989	Pit-N	0	0	—	1	0	0	0	0	0^{2}	1	0	1	1	27.0	0.00	—	.333	.500	0	—	0	0	0	0	0.0
1990	LA-N	3	5	.375	50	0	0	0	3	62	59	5	34	44	13.5	2.90	126	.257	.352	0	.000	-0	6	5	-0	0.5
1991	LA-N	4	3	.571	55	0	0	0	2	76	63	5	32	73	11.4	2.96	121	.223	.305	1	.500	0	6	5	1	0.7
1992	LA-N	3	3	.500	68	0	0	0	6	88	72	4	41	75	11.7	2.45	141	.225	.315	1	.500	0	10	10	1	1.2
Total	11	45	59	.433	430	96	10	3	61	974^{2}	926	74	417	722	12.6	3.84	101	.251	.330	13	.183	5	-1	4	-0	0.8

● TED GOULAIT Goulait, Theodore Lee b: 8/11/1889, St.Clair, Mich. d: 7/15/36, St.Clair, Mich. BR/TR, 5'9.5", 172 lbs. Deb: 9/28/12

YEAR	TM/L	W	L	PCT	G	GS	CG	SH	SV	IP	H	HR	BB	SO	RAT	ERA	ERA+	OAV	OOB	BH	AVG	PB	PR	/A	PD	TPI
1912	NY-N	0	0	—	1	1	1	0	0	7	11	0	4	6	19.3	6.43	53	.367	.441	1	.500	0	-2	-2	0	-0.2

● AL GOULD Gould, Albert Frank "Pudgy" b: 1/20/1893, Muscatine, Iowa d: 8/8/82, San Jose, Cal. BR/TR, 5'6.5", 160 lbs. Deb: 7/11/16

YEAR	TM/L	W	L	PCT	G	GS	CG	SH	SV	IP	H	HR	BB	SO	RAT	ERA	ERA+	OAV	OOB	BH	AVG	PB	PR	/A	PD	TPI
1916	Cle-A	5	7	.417	30	9	6	1	1	106^{2}	101	0	40	41	12.2	2.53	119	.256	.329	3	.103	-2	4	6	-1	0.3
1917	Cle-A	4	4	.500	27	7	1	0	0	94	95	1	52	24	14.4	3.64	78	.281	.382	5	.208	1	-10	-8	2	-0.7
Total	2	9	11	.450	57	16	7	1	1	200^{2}	196	1	92	65	13.2	3.05	96	.267	.354	8	.151	-1	-7	-3	1	-0.4

● CHARLIE GOULD Gould, Charles Harvey b: 8/21/1847, Cincinnati, Ohio d: 4/10/17, Flushing, N.Y. BR/TR, 6', 172 lbs. Deb: 5/05/1871 M♦

YEAR	TM/L	W	L	PCT	G	GS	CG	SH	SV	IP	H	HR	BB	SO	RAT	ERA	ERA+	OAV	OOB	BH	AVG	PB	PR	/A	PD	TPI
1876	Cin-N	0	0	—	2	0	0	0	0	4^{1}	10	0	0	0	20.8	0.00	—	.400	.400	65	.252	0	1	1	-0	0.1

● LARRY GOWELL Gowell, Lawrence Clyde b: 5/2/48, Lewiston, Me. BR/TR, 6'2", 182 lbs. Deb: 9/21/72

YEAR	TM/L	W	L	PCT	G	GS	CG	SH	SV	IP	H	HR	BB	SO	RAT	ERA	ERA+	OAV	OOB	BH	AVG	PB	PR	/A	PD	TPI
1972	NY-A	0	1	.000	2	1	0	0	0	7	3	0	2	7	6.4	1.29	229	.143	.217	1	1.000	1	1	1	0	0.3

● MAURO GOZZO Gozzo, Mauro Paul b: 3/7/66, New Britain, Conn. BR/TR, 6'2", 210 lbs. Deb: 8/08/89

YEAR	TM/L	W	L	PCT	G	GS	CG	SH	SV	IP	H	HR	BB	SO	RAT	ERA	ERA+	OAV	OOB	BH	AVG	PB	PR	/A	PD	TPI
1989	Tor-A	4	1	.800	9	3	0	0	0	31^{2}	35	1	9	10	12.8	4.83	78	.289	.344	0	—	0	-3	-4	-0	-0.4
1990	Cle-A	0	0	—	2	0	0	0	0	3	2	0	2	2	12.0	0.00	—	.182	.308	0	—	0	1	1	-0	0.1
1991	Cle-A	0	0	—	2	2	0	0	0	4^{2}	9	0	7	3	30.9	19.29	22	.450	.593	0	—	0	-8	-8	-0	-0.7
1992	Min-A	0	0	—	2	0	0	0	0	1^{2}	7	2	0	1	37.8	27.00	15	.583	.583	0	—	0	-4	-4	-0	-0.6
Total	4	4	1	.800	15	5	0	0	0	41	53	3	18	16	15.8	7.02	55	.323	.393	0	—	0	-14	-15	-1	-1.6

● AL GRABOWSKI Grabowski, Alfons Francis b: 9/6/01, Syracuse, N.Y. d: 10/29/66, Memphis, N.Y. BL/TL, 5'11.5", 175 lbs. Deb: 9/11/29 F

YEAR	TM/L	W	L	PCT	G	GS	CG	SH	SV	IP	H	HR	BB	SO	RAT	ERA	ERA+	OAV	OOB	BH	AVG	PB	PR	/A	PD	TPI
1929	StL-N	3	2	.600	6	6	4	2	0	50	44	0	8	22	9.4	2.52	185	.227	.257	4	.250	2	12	12	-0	1.4
1930	StL-N	6	4	.600	33	8	1	0	1	107	122	7	49	43	14.6	4.79	105	.295	.373	12	.364	3	2	3	-0	0.4
Total	2	9	6	.600	39	14	5	2	1	157	166	7	57	65	13.0	4.07	120	.273	.338	16	.327	4	14	15	-0	1.8

● REGGIE GRABOWSKI Grabowski, Reginald John b: 7/16/07, Syracuse, N.Y. d: 4/2/55, Syracuse, N.Y. BR/TR, 6'0.5", 185 lbs. Deb: 4/15/32 F

YEAR	TM/L	W	L	PCT	G	GS	CG	SH	SV	IP	H	HR	BB	SO	RAT	ERA	ERA+	OAV	OOB	BH	AVG	PB	PR	/A	PD	TPI
1932	Phi-N	2	2	.500	14	2	0	0	0	34^{1}	38	2	22	15	16.3	3.67	120	.273	.380	0	.000	-1	1	3	-1	0.2

YEAR	TM/L	W	L	PCT	G	GS	CG	SH	SV	IP	H	HR	BB	SO	RAT	ERA	ERA+	OAV	OOB	BH	AVG	PB	PR	/A	PD	TPI
1933	Phi-N	1	3	.250	10	5	4	1	0	48	38	4	10	9	9.2	2.44	157	.220	.266	2	.125	-1	5	7	-1	0.6
1934	Phi-N	1	3	.250	27	5	0	0	0	65^1	114	13	23	13	19.3	9.23	51	.384	.433	1	.056	-2	-38	-33	-1	-3.3
Total	3	4	8	.333	51	12	4	1	0	147^2	190	19	55	37	15.3	5.73	76	.312	.375	3	.075	-4	-32	-23	-3	-2.5

● **JOHN GRAFF** Graff, John F. b: Philadelphia, Pa. Deb: 7/19/1893

YEAR	TM/L	W	L	PCT	G	GS	CG	SH	SV	IP	H	HR	BB	SO	RAT	ERA	ERA+	OAV	OOB	BH	AVG	PB	PR	/A	PD	TPI
1893	Was-N	0	1	.000	2	1	1	0	0	12	21	2	13	4	26.3	11.25	41	.372	.496	1	.200	-0	-9	-9	-0	-0.7

● **PEACHES GRAHAM** Graham, George Frederick b: 3/23/1877, Aledo, Ill. d: 7/25/39, Long Beach, Cal. BR/TR, 5'9", 180 lbs. Deb: 9/14/02 F♦

YEAR	TM/L	W	L	PCT	G	GS	CG	SH	SV	IP	H	HR	BB	SO	RAT	ERA	ERA+	OAV	OOB	BH	AVG	PB	PR	/A	PD	TPI
1903	Chi-N	0	1	.000	1	1	0	0	0	5	9	0	3	4	23.4	5.40	58	.429	.520	0	.000	-0	-1	-1	0	-0.1

● **SKINNY GRAHAM** Graham, Kyle b: 8/14/1899, Oak Grove, Ala. d: 12/1/73, Oak Grove, Ala. BR/TR, 6'2", 172 lbs. Deb: 9/03/24

YEAR	TM/L	W	L	PCT	G	GS	CG	SH	SV	IP	H	HR	BB	SO	RAT	ERA	ERA+	OAV	OOB	BH	AVG	PB	PR	/A	PD	TPI
1924	Bos-N	0	4	.000	5	4	1	0	0	33	33	0	11	15	12.0	3.82	100	.287	.349	0	.000	-1	0	0	-0	-0.1
1925	Bos-N	7	12	.368	34	23	5	0	1	157	177	6	62	32	13.9	4.41	91	.296	.365	6	.136	-2	-3	-7	-2	-1.0
1926	Bos-N	3	3	.500	15	4	1	0	0	36^1	54	3	19	7	18.6	7.93	45	.370	.449	2	.167	-1	-17	-18	0	-1.7
1929	Det-A	1	3	.250	13	6	2	0	1	51^2	70	2	33	7	18.5	5.57	77	.340	.438	2	.105	-1	-8	-7	-1	-0.8
Total	4	11	22	.333	67	37	9	0	2	278	334	11	125	61	15.1	5.02	79	.314	.390	10	.122	-5	-27	-32	-3	-3.6

● **OSCAR GRAHAM** Graham, Oscar M. b: 7/20/1878, Plattsmouth, Neb. d: 10/15/31, Moline, Ill. TL, 6'0.5", Deb: 4/16/07

YEAR	TM/L	W	L	PCT	G	GS	CG	SH	SV	IP	H	HR	BB	SO	RAT	ERA	ERA+	OAV	OOB	BH	AVG	PB	PR	/A	PD	TPI
1907	Was-A	4	9	.308	20	14	6	0	0	104	116	3	29	44	13.3	3.98	61	.284	.345	11	.229	2	-17	-18	0	-1.5

● **BILL GRAHAM** Graham, William James b: 7/22/1884, Owosso, Mich. d: 2/15/36, Holt, Mich. TL, 6', Deb: 4/18/08

YEAR	TM/L	W	L	PCT	G	GS	CG	SH	SV	IP	H	HR	BB	SO	RAT	ERA	ERA+	OAV	OOB	BH	AVG	PB	PR	/A	PD	TPI
1908	StL-A	6	7	.462	21	13	7	0	0	117^1	104	0	32	47	11.4	2.30	104	.240	.310	5	.119	-3	1	1	-0	-0.2
1909	StL-A	8	14	.364	34	21	13	3	1	187^1	171	3	60	82	11.3	3.12	77	.256	.322	10	.159	-0	-13	-15	1	-1.5
1910	StL-A	0	8	.000	9	6	1	0	0	43	46	2	13	12	13.2	3.56	70	.297	.366	2	.154	-0	-5	-5	-2	-0.8
Total	3	14	29	.326	64	40	21	3	1	347^2	321	5	105	141	11.6	2.90	83	.256	.323	17	.144	-3	-17	-19	-1	-2.5

● **BILL GRAHAM** Graham, William Albert b: 1/21/37, Flemingsburg, Ky. BR/TR, 6'3", 217 lbs. Deb: 10/02/66

YEAR	TM/L	W	L	PCT	G	GS	CG	SH	SV	IP	H	HR	BB	SO	RAT	ERA	ERA+	OAV	OOB	BH	AVG	PB	PR	/A	PD	TPI
1966	Det-A	0	0	—	1	0	0	0	0	2	2	0	0	2	9.0	0.00	—	.250	.250	0	—	0	1	1	-0	0.1
1967	NY-N	1	2	.333	5	3	1	0	0	27^1	20	3	11	14	10.2	2.63	129	.200	.279	1	.125	-0	2	2	-1	0.1
Total	2	1	2	.333	6	3	1	0	0	29^1	22	3	11	16	10.1	2.45	138	.204	.277	1	.125	-0	3	3	-1	0.2

● **JOE GRAHE** Grahe, Joseph Milton b: 8/14/67, W.Palm Beach, Fla. BR/TR, 6'1", 196 lbs. Deb: 8/04/90

YEAR	TM/L	W	L	PCT	G	GS	CG	SH	SV	IP	H	HR	BB	SO	RAT	ERA	ERA+	OAV	OOB	BH	AVG	PB	PR	/A	PD	TPI
1990	Cal-A	3	4	.429	8	8	0	0	0	43^1	51	3	23	25	16.0	4.98	77	.293	.385	0	—	0	-5	-6	1	-0.4
1991	Cal-A	3	7	.300	18	10	1	0	0	73	84	2	33	40	14.8	4.81	85	.288	.366	0	—	0	-6	-6	0	-0.6
1992	Cal-A	5	6	.455	46	7	0	0	21	94^2	85	5	39	39	12.4	3.52	111	.246	.332	0	—	0	4	4	0	0.6
Total	3	11	17	.393	72	25	1	0	21	211	220	10	95	104	13.9	4.27	93	.271	.356	0	—	0	-7	-7	2	-0.4

● **TOMMY GRAMLY** Gramly, Bert Thomas b: 4/19/45, Dallas, Tex. BR/TR, 6'3", 175 lbs. Deb: 4/18/68

YEAR	TM/L	W	L	PCT	G	GS	CG	SH	SV	IP	H	HR	BB	SO	RAT	ERA	ERA+	OAV	OOB	BH	AVG	PB	PR	/A	PD	TPI
1968	Cle-A	0	1	.000	3	0	0	0	0	3^1	3	0	2	1	13.5	2.70	110	.250	.357	0	—	0	0	0	-0	0.0

● **HANK GRAMPP** Grampp, Henry Erchardt b: 9/28/03, New York, N.Y. d: 3/24/86, New York, N.Y. BR/TR, 6'1", 185 lbs. Deb: 6/02/27

YEAR	TM/L	W	L	PCT	G	GS	CG	SH	SV	IP	H	HR	BB	SO	RAT	ERA	ERA+	OAV	OOB	BH	AVG	PB	PR	/A	PD	TPI
1927	Chi-N	0	0	—	2	0	0	0	0	3	4	0	1	3	15.0	9.00	43	.333	.385	0	—	0	-2	-2	0	-0.2
1929	Chi-N	0	1	.000	1	1	0	0	0	2	4	0	3	0	36.0	27.00	17	.500	.667	0	—	0	-5	-5	-0	-0.4
Total	2	0	1	.000	3	1	0	0	0	5	8	0	4	3	23.4	16.20	26	.400	.520	0	—	0	-7	-7	0	-0.6

● **JACK GRANEY** Graney, John Gladstone b: 6/10/1886, St.Thomas, Ont., Can. d: 4/20/78, Louisiana, Mo. BL/TL, 5'9", 180 lbs. Deb: 4/30/08 ♦

YEAR	TM/L	W	L	PCT	G	GS	CG	SH	SV	IP	H	HR	BB	SO	RAT	ERA	ERA+	OAV	OOB	BH	AVG	PB	PR	/A	PD	TPI
1908	Cle-A	0	0	—	2	0	0	0	0	3^1	6	0	1	0	18.9	5.40	44	.400	.438	0	—	0	-1	-1	-0	-0.1

● **WAYNE GRANGER** Granger, Wayne Allan b: 3/15/44, Springfield, Mass. BR/TR, 6'2", 165 lbs. Deb: 6/05/68

YEAR	TM/L	W	L	PCT	G	GS	CG	SH	SV	IP	H	HR	BB	SO	RAT	ERA	ERA+	OAV	OOB	BH	AVG	PB	PR	/A	PD	TPI
1968	*StL-N	4	2	.667	34	0	0	0	4	44	40	2	12	27	11.0	2.25	129	.238	.297	1	.200	0	4	3	2	0.6
1969	Cin-N	9	6	.600	**90**	0	0	0	27	144^2	143	10	40	68	11.8	2.80	134	.262	.320	2	.095	-0	13	15	1	1.7
1970	*Cin-N	6	5	.545	67	0	0	0	**35**	84^2	79	5	27	38	11.4	2.66	152	.252	.313	1	.100	-1	13	13	2	1.4
1971	Cin-N	7	6	.538	**70**	0	0	0	11	100	94	8	28	51	11.1	3.33	101	.251	.304	1	.143	1	2	0	3	0.5
1972	Min-A	4	6	.400	63	0	0	0	19	89^2	83	7	28	45	11.3	3.01	107	.243	.304	2	.200	0	0	2	-0	0.2
1973	StL-N	2	4	.333	33	0	0	0	5	46^2	50	3	21	14	14.1	4.24	86	.284	.367	0	.000	-0	-3	-3	-0	-0.3
	NY-A	0	1	.000	7	0	0	0	0	15^1	19	1	3	10	13.5	1.76	208	.279	.319	0	—	0	4	3	-1	0.4
1974	Chi-A	0	0	—	5	0	0	0	0	7^2	16	1	3	4	22.3	8.22	45	.432	.475	0	—	0	-4	-4	0	-0.4
1975	Hou-N	2	5	.286	55	0	0	0	5	74	76	7	23	30	12.5	3.65	92	.264	.327	0	.000	-1	-0	-2	1	-0.2
1976	Mon-N	1	0	1.000	27	0	0	0	2	32	32	3	16	16	14.1	3.66	102	.264	.360	0	.000	-0	-1	0	-0	0.0
Total	9	35	35	.500	451	0	0	0	108	638^2	632	47	201	303	12.0	3.14	113	.260	.322	7	.103	-1	27	28	8	3.9

● **GEORGE GRANT** Grant, George Addison b: 1/6/03, E.Tallassee, Ala. d: 3/25/86, Montgomery, Ala. BR/TR, 5'11.5", 175 lbs. Deb: 9/17/23

YEAR	TM/L	W	L	PCT	G	GS	CG	SH	SV	IP	H	HR	BB	SO	RAT	ERA	ERA+	OAV	OOB	BH	AVG	PB	PR	/A	PD	TPI
1923	StL-A	0	0	—	4	0	0	0	0	8^2	15	0	3	2	18.7	5.19	80	.395	.439	0	.000	-0	-1	-1	0	-0.1
1924	StL-A	1	2	.333	22	2	0	0	0	51^1	69	4	25	11	16.7	6.31	72	.325	.399	0	.000	-2	-12	-10	-1	-1.2
1925	StL-A	0	2	.000	12	0	0	0	0	16^1	26	2	8	7	18.7	6.06	77	.400	.466	1	.250	-0	-3	-3	0	-0.2
1927	Cle-A	4	6	.400	25	3	2	0	1	74^2	85	1	40	19	15.1	4.46	94	.300	.387	2	.095	-2	-3	-2	0	-0.4
1928	Cle-A	10	8	.556	28	18	6	1	0	155^1	196	7	76	39	15.9	5.04	82	.319	.395	11	.183	-2	-17	-15	2	-1.4
1929	Cle-A	0	2	.000	12	0	0	0	0	24	41	2	23	5	24.0	10.50	42	.414	.525	0	.000	-0	-17	-16	0	-1.4
1931	Pit-N	0	0	—	11	0	0	0	0	17	28	0	7	6	19.1	7.41	52	.364	.424	0	.000	-0	-7	-7	0	-0.7
Total	7	15	20	.429	114	23	8	1	1	347^1	460	16	182	89	16.7	5.65	75	.331	.410	14	.135	-8	-59	-54	3	-5.4

● **JIM GRANT** Grant, James Ronald b: 8/4/1894, Coalville, Iowa d: 11/30/85, Des Moines, Iowa BR/TL, 5'11", 180 lbs. Deb: 4/21/23

YEAR	TM/L	W	L	PCT	G	GS	CG	SH	SV	IP	H	HR	BB	SO	RAT	ERA	ERA+	OAV	OOB	BH	AVG	PB	PR	/A	PD	TPI
1923	Phi-N	0	0	—	2	0	0	0	0	4	10	0	4	0	33.8	13.50	34	.588	.682	0	.000	-0	-4	-4	0	-0.4

● **MUDCAT GRANT** Grant, James Timothy "Jim" b: 8/13/35, Lacoochee, Fla. BR/TR, 6'1", 186 lbs. Deb: 4/17/58

YEAR	TM/L	W	L	PCT	G	GS	CG	SH	SV	IP	H	HR	BB	SO	RAT	ERA	ERA+	OAV	OOB	BH	AVG	PB	PR	/A	PD	TPI
1958	Cle-A	10	11	.476	44	28	11	1	4	204	173	20	104	111	12.3	3.84	95	.228	.321	5	.076	-4	-2	-4	-2	-1.0
1959	Cle-A	10	7	.588	38	19	6	1	3	165^1	140	23	81	85	12.1	4.14	89	.232	.325	11	.200	1	-5	-8	-0	-0.7
1960	Cle-A	9	8	.529	33	19	5	0	0	159^2	147	26	78	75	12.8	4.40	85	.243	.332	16	.281	3	-9	-12	-1	-1.0
1961	Cle-A	15	9	.625	35	35	11	3	0	244^2	207	32	109	146	11.7	3.86	102	.227	.312	15	.170	1	4	2	1	0.3
1962	Cle-A	7	10	.412	26	23	6	1	0	149^2	128	24	81	90	12.6	4.27	91	.233	.331	8	.151	-0	-5	-7	-0	-0.7
1963	Cle-A☆	13	14	.481	38	32	10	2	1	229^1	213	30	87	157	11.9	3.69	98	.243	.314	13	.188	3	-2	-2	-3	-0.2
1964	Cle-A	3	4	.429	13	9	1	0	0	62	82	11	25	43	15.7	5.95	60	.324	.387	6	.273	4	-16	-16	0	-1.2
	Min-A	11	9	.550	26	23	10	1	1	166	162	21	36	75	10.7	2.82	127	.248	.288	10	.167	0	15	14	0	1.5
	Yr	14	13	.519	39	32	11	1	1	228	244	32	61	118	12.0	3.67	98	.269	.315	16	.195	4	-1	-2	1	0.3
1965	*Min-A★	**21**	7	**.750**	41	39	14	**6**	0	270^1	252	34	61	142	10.4	3.30	108	.247	.289	15	.155	2	5	8	1	1.2
1966	Min-A	13	13	.500	35	35	10	3	0	249	248	23	49	110	11.0	3.25	111	.260	.300	15	.192	2	5	10	2	1.5
1967	Min-A	5	6	.455	27	14	2	0	0	95^1	121	10	17	50	13.1	4.72	73	.315	.346	5	.179	0	-16	-13	-2	-1.6
1968	LA-N	6	4	.600	37	4	1	0	3	94^2	77	1	19	35	9.7	2.09	132	.226	.279	4	.129	0	9	7	1	0.9
1969	Mon-N	1	6	.143	11	10	1	0	0	50^2	64	7	14	20	14.0	4.80	77	.299	.345	2	.125	-1	-7	-6	0	-0.7
	StL-N	7	5	.583	30	3	1	0	7	63^1	62	9	22	35	12.2	4.12	87	.252	.319	5	.294	2	-4	-4	-1	-0.3
	Yr	8	11	.421	41	13	2	0	7	114	126	16	36	55	12.9	4.42	82	.273	.328	7	.212	1	-10	-10	-1	-1.0
1970	Oak-A	6	2	.750	72	0	0	0	24	123^1	104	8	30	54	10.0	1.82	194	.235	.288	2	.222	2	**26**	**24**	1	2.7
	Pit-N	2	1	.667	8	0	0	0	0	12	8	2	2	4	7.5	2.25	173	.190	.227	0	.000	-0	2	2	0	0.2
1971	Pit-N	5	3	.625	42	0	0	0	7	75	79	8	28	22	13.0	3.60	94	.274	.341	2	.250	1	-1	-2	1	0.0
	*Oak-A	1	0	1.000	15	0	0	0	3	27^1	25	3	6	13	10.2	1.98	169	.243	.284	1	.333	0	5	4	-0	0.5
Total	14	145	119	.549	571	293	89	18	53	2441^2	2292	292	849	1267	11.7	3.63	100	.248	.313	135	.178	16	5	-3	-3	1.4

YEAR	TM/L	W	L	PCT	G	GS	CG	SH	SV	IP	H	HR	BB	SO	RAT	ERA	ERA+	OAV	OOB	BH	AVG	PB	PR	/A	PD	TPI
● MARK GRANT Grant, Mark Andrew b: 10/24/63, Aurora, Ill. BR/TR, 6'2", 205 lbs. Deb: 4/27/84																										
1984	SF-N	1	4	.200	11	10	0	0	1	53^2	56	6	19	32	12.7	6.37	55	.272	.336	0	.000	-1	-17	-17	-0	-1.8
1986	SF-N	0	1	.000	4	1	0	0	0	10	6	0	5	5	9.9	3.60	98	.176	.282	0	.000	-0	0	-0	-0	0.0
1987	SF-N	1	2	.333	16	8	0	0	1	61	66	6	21	32	13.0	3.54	109	.282	.344	1	.083	-0	4	2	-1	0.1
	SD-N	6	7	.462	17	17	2	1	0	102^1	104	16	52	58	13.7	4.66	85	.263	.348	3	.094	-1	-7	-8	-1	-0.9
	Yr	7	9	.438	33	25	2	1	1	163^1	170	22	73	90	13.4	4.24	92	.269	.345	4	.091	-1	-3	-6	-1	-0.8
1988	SD-N	2	8	.200	33	11	0	0	0	97^2	97	14	36	61	12.4	3.69	92	.268	.338	0	.000	-1	-3	-3	0	-0.4
1989	SD-N	8	2	.800	50	0	0	0	2	116^1	105	11	32	69	10.8	3.33	105	.248	.305	1	.050	-0	2	2	-0	0.2
1990	SD-N	1	1	.500	26	0	0	0	0	39	47	5	19	29	15.2	4.85	79	.305	.382	1	.500	0	-5	-4	1	-0.3
	Atl-N	1	2	.333	33	1	0	0	3	52^1	61	4	18	40	13.8	4.64	87	.293	.352	1	.250	1	-5	-4	-0	-0.3
	Yr	2	3	.400	59	1	0	0	3	91^1	108	9	37	69	14.4	4.73	83	.296	.362	2	.333	1	-10	-8	0	-0.6
1992	Sea-A	2	4	.333	23	10	0	0	0	81	100	6	22	42	13.8	3.89	103	.311	.358	0	—	0	0	1	-1	-0.1
Total	7	22	31	.415	213	58	2	1	7	613^1	642	68	224	368	12.9	4.18	89	.274	.340	7	.067	-3	-29	-31	-3	-3.5
● RICK GRAPENTHIN Grapenthin, Richard Ray b: 4/16/58, Linn Grove, Iowa BR/TR, 6'2", 205 lbs. Deb: 5/03/83																										
1983	Mon-N	0	1	.000	1	0	0	0	0	4	4	2	1	3	11.3	9.00	40	.267	.313	0	.000	-0	-2	-2	0	-0.2
1984	Mon-N	1	2	.333	13	1	0	0	2	23	19	3	7	9	10.2	3.52	97	.235	.295	1	.200	0	0	-0	0	0.0
1985	Mon-N	0	0	—	5	0	0	0	0	7	13	0	8	4	28.3	14.14	24	.394	.524	1	1.000	0	-8	-8	-0	-0.8
Total	3	1	3	.250	19	1	0	0	2	34	36	5	16	16	14.0	6.35	54	.279	.363	2	.286	0	-10	-11	0	-1.0
● LOU GRASMICK Grasmick, Louis Junior b: 9/11/24, Baltimore, Md. BR/TR, 6', 195 lbs. Deb: 4/22/48																										
1948	Phi-N	0	0	—	2	0	0	0	0	5	3	1	8	2	19.8	7.20	55	.176	.440	1	1.000	0	-2	-2	0	-0.1
● DON GRATE Grate, Donald "Buckeye" b: 8/27/23, Greenfield, Ohio BR/TR, 6'2.5", 180 lbs. Deb: 7/06/45																										
1945	Phi-N	0	1	.000	4	2	0	0	0	8^1	18	0	12	6	32.4	17.28	22	.439	.566	0	.000	-0	-12	-12	-0	-1.1
1946	Phi-N	1	0	1.000	3	0	0	0	0	8	4	0	2	2	6.8	1.13	305	.160	.222	0	.000	0	2	2	-0	0.2
Total	2	1	1	.500	7	2	0	0	0	16^1	22	0	14	8	19.8	9.37	39	.333	.450	0	.000	-0	-10	-10	-1	-0.9
● MARK GRATER Grater, Mark Anthony b: 1/19/64, Rochester, Pa. BR/TR, 5'10", 205 lbs. Deb: 6/12/91																										
1991	StL-N	0	0	—	3	0	0	0	0	3	5	0	2	0	21.0	0.00	—	.385	.467	0	—	0	1	1	-0	0.1
● FRANK GRAVES Graves, Frank M. b: 11/2/1860, Cincinnati, Ohio 6', 163 lbs. Deb: 5/10/1886 ♦																										
1886	StL-N	0	0	—	1	0	0	0	0	7	10	0	1	2	14.1	9.00	36	.323	.344	21	.152	-0	-4	-4	-0	-0.4
● CHARLIE GRAY Gray, Charles b: 1867, Indianapolis, Ind. Deb: 4/23/1890																										
1890	Pit-N	1	4	.200	5	4	3	0	0	31	48	0	24	10	21.2	7.55	44	.343	.443	3	.200	-0	-14	-15	-1	-1.2
● DAVE GRAY Gray, David Alexander b: 1/7/43, Ogden, Utah BR/TR, 6'1", 190 lbs. Deb: 6/14/64																										
1964	Bos-A	0	0	—	9	1	0	0	0	13	18	3	20	17	26.3	9.00	43	.321	.500	1	1.000	0	-8	-7	0	-0.7
● CHUMMY GRAY Gray, George Edward b: 7/17/1873, Rockland, Me. d: 8/14/13, Rockland, Maine TR, 5'11.5", 163 lbs. Deb: 9/14/1899																										
1899	Pit-N	3	3	.500	9	7	6	0	0	70^2	85	1	24	9	14.4	3.44	111	.297	.360	1	.038	-3	3	3	2	0.1
● JEFF GRAY Gray, Jeffrey Edward b: 4/10/63, Richmond, Va. BR/TR, 6'1", 175 lbs. Deb: 6/21/88																										
1988	Cin-N	0	0	—	5	0	0	0	0	9^1	12	0	4	5	15.4	3.86	93	.333	.400	0	.000	-0	-0	-0	0	0.0
1990	*Bos-A	2	4	.333	41	0	0	0	9	50^2	53	3	15	50	12.3	4.44	92	.268	.322	0	—	0	-3	-2	-0	-0.3
1991	Bos-A	2	3	.400	50	0	0	0	1	61^2	39	7	10	41	7.3	2.34	184	.181	.220	0	—	0	12	13	1	1.4
Total	3	4	7	.364	96	0	0	0	10	121^2	104	10	29	96	10.0	3.33	125	.231	.281	0	.000	-0	9	11	1	1.1
● JOHNNY GRAY Gray, John Leonard b: 12/11/27, W.Palm Beach, Fla. BR/TR, 6'4", 226 lbs. Deb: 7/18/54																										
1954	Phi-A	3	12	.200	18	16	5	0	0	105	111	10	91	51	17.3	6.51	60	.273	.406	1	.029	-4	-33	-30	0	-3.2
1955	KC-A	0	3	.000	8	5	0	0	0	26^2	28	2	24	11	17.9	6.41	65	.277	.421	1	.125	-1	-7	-7	-1	-0.7
1957	Cle-A	1	3	.250	7	3	1	1	0	20	21	1	13	3	15.3	5.85	64	.288	.395	0	.000	-1	-5	-5	-0	-0.5
1958	Phi-N	0	0	—	15	0	0	0	0	17^1	12	3	14	10	13.5	4.15	95	.222	.382	0	.000	-0	-0	-0	-0	-0.1
Total	4	4	18	.182	48	24	6	1	0	169	172	16	142	75	16.8	6.18	64	.271	.405	2	.043	-5	-45	-42	-1	-4.5
● SAM GRAY Gray, Samuel David "Sad Sam" b: 10/15/1897, Van Alstyne, Tex. d: 4/16/53, McKinney, Tex. BR/TR, 5'10", 175 lbs. Deb: 4/19/24																										
1924	Phi-A	8	7	.533	34	19	8	2	2	151^2	169	5	89	54	15.7	3.98	108	.284	.383	10	.175	-2	4	5	-1	0.2
1925	Phi-A	16	8	.667	32	28	14	4	3	203^2	199	11	63	80	11.7	3.27	142	.260	.319	12	.179	-2	25	31	-3	2.5
1926	Phi-A	11	12	.478	38	18	5	0	0	150^2	164	9	50	82	13.0	3.64	114	.279	.340	11	.216	1	6	9	-2	0.8
1927	Phi-A	9	6	.600	37	13	3	1	3	133^1	153	4	51	49	14.0	4.59	93	.295	.362	8	.190	-1	-7	-5	0	-0.6
1928	StL-A	20	12	.625	35	31	21	2	3	262^2	256	11	86	102	11.8	3.19	132	.260	.320	19	.188	-2	25	30	3	3.1
1929	StL-A	18	15	.545	43	37	23	**4**	1	**305**	336	18	96	109	12.8	3.72	119	.285	.340	19	.184	-2	18	24	-1	2.0
1930	StL-A	4	15	.211	27	24	7	0	0	167^2	215	17	52	51	14.5	6.28	78	.316	.368	11	.204	-2	-30	-26	-1	-2.5
1931	StL-A	11	24	.314	43	37	13	0	2	258	323	20	54	88	13.3	5.09	91	.297	.332	14	.177	-1	-20	-13	-1	-1.4
1932	StL-A	7	12	.368	52	18	7	3	4	206^2	250	9	53	79	13.2	4.53	107	.294	.336	13	.210	-0	-1	7	-1	0.6
1933	StL-A	7	4	.636	38	6	0	0	4	112	131	7	45	36	14.2	4.10	114	.301	.368	7	.219	1	2	7	-1	0.8
Total	10	111	115	.491	379	231	101	16	22	1951^1	2196	111	639	730	13.2	4.18	108	.286	.343	124	.191	-10	23	68	-7	5.5
● TED GRAY Gray, Ted Glenn b: 12/31/24, Detroit, Mich. BB/TL, 5'11", 175 lbs. Deb: 5/15/46																										
1946	Det-A	0	2	.000	3	2	0	0	1	11^2	17	4	5	5	17.0	8.49	43	.340	.400	0	.000	-0	-6	-6	-0	-0.6
1948	Det-A	6	2	.750	26	11	3	1	0	85^1	73	2	72	60	15.6	4.22	104	.236	.385	7	.241	1	1	1	-0	0.2
1949	Det-A	10	10	.500	34	27	8	3	1	195	163	11	103	96	12.5	3.51	119	.227	.328	8	.127	-3	15	14	1	1.2
1950	Det-A★	10	7	.588	27	21	7	0	1	149^1	139	22	72	102	12.8	4.40	107	.248	.335	7	.140	-2	3	5	-2	0.1
1951	Det-A	7	14	.333	34	28	9	1	1	197^1	194	17	95	131	13.5	4.06	103	.256	.343	9	.143	-3	1	3	-1	-0.2
1952	Det-A	12	17	.414	35	32	13	2	0	224	212	21	101	138	12.7	4.14	92	.249	.331	13	.171	-2	-12	-8	1	-0.9
1953	Det-A	10	15	.400	30	28	8	0	0	176	166	25	76	115	12.7	4.60	88	.252	.336	14	.230	2	-12	-10	-1	-0.9
1954	Det-A	3	5	.375	19	10	2	0	0	72	70	8	56	29	16.0	5.38	69	.268	.401	1	.045	-2	-13	-13	-1	-1.7
1955	Chi-A	0	0	—	2	1	0	0	0	3	9	0	2	1	33.0	18.00	22	.500	.550	0	—	0	-5	-5	0	-0.4
	Cle-A	0	0	—	2	0	0	0	0	2	5	1	2	1	31.5	18.00	22	.455	.538	0	—	0	-3	-3	0	-0.3
	NY-A	0	0	—	1	1	0	0	0	3	3	0	0	1	9.0	3.00	125	.300	.300	0	.000	-0	0	0	-0	0.0
	Bal-A	1	2	.333	9	1	0	0	0	15^1	21	3	11	8	18.8	8.22	46	.344	.444	0	.000	-0	-7	-8	1	-0.7
	Yr	1	2	.333	14	3	0	0	0	23^1	38	4	15	11	20.4	9.64	40	.376	.457	0	.000	-0	-15	-15	1	-1.4
Total	9	59	74	.444	222	162	50	7	4	1134	1072	114	595	687	13.5	4.37	94	.251	.346	59	.159	-10	-38	-30	-4	-4.2
● DOLLY GRAY Gray, William Denton b: 12/4/1878, Ishpeming, Mich. d: 4/4/56, Yuba City, Cal. BL/TL, 6'2", 160 lbs. Deb: 4/13/09																										
1909	Was-A	5	19	.208	36	26	19	0	0	218	210	1	77	87	12.2	3.59	68	.258	.329	13	.146	-1	-27	-28	-1	-3.3
1910	Was-A	8	19	.296	34	29	21	3	0	229	216	3	65	84	11.4	2.63	95	.249	.309	21	.247	4	-3	-4	2	0.2
1911	Was-A	2	13	.133	28	15	6	0	0	121	160	4	40	42	15.1	5.06	65	.331	.385	10	.227	1	-23	-24	1	-2.1
Total	3	15	51	.227	98	70	46	3	0	568	586	8	182	213	12.5	3.52	75	.271	.333	44	.202	3	-53	-56	2	-5.2
● ELI GRBA Grba, Eli b: 8/9/34, Chicago, Ill. BR/TR, 6'2", 207 lbs. Deb: 7/10/59																										
1959	NY-A	2	5	.286	19	6	0	0	0	50^1	52	6	39	23	16.3	6.44	57	.269	.392	3	.214	1	-14	-16	-0	-1.5
1960	*NY-A	6	4	.600	24	9	1	0	1	80^2	65	9	46	32	12.6	3.68	97	.226	.337	5	.238	2	2	-1	-1	0.1
1961	LA-A	11	13	.458	40	30	8	0	2	211^2	197	26	114	105	13.5	4.25	106	.242	.340	15	.234	5	-5	6	-1	1.0
1962	LA-A	8	9	.471	40	29	1	0	1	176^1	185	19	75	90	13.4	4.54	85	.267	.340	12	.207	3	-11	-13	1	-1.0

YEAR	TM/L	W	L	PCT	G	GS	CG	SH	SV	IP	H	HR	BB	SO	RAT	ERA	ERA+	OAV	OOB	BH	AVG	PB	PR	/A	PD	TPI
1963	LA-A	1	2	.333	12	1	0	0	0	17^1	14	2	10	5	13.0	4.67	73	.222	.338	0	.000	-0	-2	-2	0	-0.2
Total	5	28	33	.459	135	75	10	0	4	536^1	513	62	284	255	13.6	4.48	90	.250	.345	35	.219	10	-31	-27	-1	-1.6
● **BILL GREASON** Greason, William Henry "Booster" b: 9/3/24, Atlanta, Ga. BR/TR, 5'10", 170 lbs. Deb: 5/31/54																										
1954	StL-N	0	1	.000	3	2	0	0	0	4	8	4	4	2	27.0	13.50	30	.421	.522	0	.000	-0	-4	-4	0	-0.4
● **CHRIS GREEN** Green, Christopher De Wayne b: 9/5/60, Los Angeles, Cal. BL/TL, 6'2", 214 lbs. Deb: 4/17/84																										
1984	Pit-N	0	0	—	4	0	0	0	0	3	5	0	1	3	18.0	6.00	60	.417	.462	0	—	0	-1	-1	0	-0.1
● **ED GREEN** Green, Edward M. b: 1850, Philadelphia, Pa. d: 3/22/17, Ogden, Utah Deb: 4/22/1890																										
1890	Phi-a	7	15	.318	25	22	20	1	1	191	267	4	94	56	17.3	5.80	66	.321	.393	15	.119	-4	-41	-42	3	-3.4
● **FRED GREEN** Green, Fred Allen b: 9/14/33, Titusville, N.J. BR/TL, 6'4", 190 lbs. Deb: 4/15/59 F																										
1959	Pit-N	1	2	.333	17	1	0	0	1	37^1	37	2	15	20	12.5	3.13	123	.259	.329	0	.000	-1	3	3	0	0.3
1960	*Pit-N	8	4	.667	45	0	0	0	3	70	61	4	33	49	12.2	3.21	117	.243	.333	3	.375	3	4	4	-1	0.7
1961	Pit-N	0	0	—	13	0	0	0	0	20^2	27	2	9	4	15.7	4.79	83	.321	.387	0	.000	-0	-2	-2	1	-0.2
1962	Was-A	0	1	.000	5	0	0	0	0	7	7	3	6	2	16.7	6.43	63	.250	.382	0	—	0	-2	-2	0	-0.2
1964	Pit-N	0	0	—	8	0	0	0	0	7^1	10	1	0	2	12.3	1.23	286	.323	.323	0	—	0	2	2	-0	0.2
Total	5	9	7	.563	88	1	0	0	4	142^1	142	12	63	77	13.0	3.48	110	.264	.343	3	.176	2	6	5	0	0.8
● **DALLAS GREEN** Green, George Dallas b: 8/4/34, Newport, Del. BL/TR, 6'5", 210 lbs. Deb: 6/18/60 M																										
1960	Phi-N	3	6	.333	23	10	5	1	0	108^2	100	10	44	51	12.1	4.06	96	.248	.325	7	.206	1	-4	-2	-1	-0.2
1961	Phi-N	2	4	.333	42	10	1	1	1	128	160	8	47	51	14.7	4.85	84	.315	.375	5	.152	0	-12	-11	0	-1.0
1962	Phi-N	6	6	.500	37	10	2	0	1	129^1	145	10	43	58	13.4	3.83	101	.289	.352	2	.063	-1	2	1	2	0.2
1963	Phi-N	7	5	.583	40	14	4	0	2	120	134	10	38	68	13.1	3.23	100	.286	.342	3	.086	-1	1	0	1	0.0
1964	Phi-N	2	1	.667	25	0	0	0	0	42	63	4	14	21	16.9	5.79	60	.362	.416	0	.000	-0	-10	-11	-1	-1.2
1965	Was-A	0	0	—	6	2	0	0	0	14^1	14	0	3	6	10.7	3.14	111	.241	.279	0	.000	-0	1	1	0	0.0
1966	NY-N	0	0	—	4	0	0	0	0	5	6	2	2	1	14.4	5.40	67	.333	.400	0	—	0	-1	-1	0	-0.1
1967	Phi-N	0	0	—	8	0	0	0	0	15	25	2	6	12	19.2	9.00	38	.362	.421	0	.000	-0	-9	-9	1	-0.9
Total	8	20	22	.476	185	46	12	2	4	562^1	647	46	197	268	13.7	4.26	88	.294	.356	17	.120	-3	-33	-33	3	-3.2
● **HARVEY GREEN** Green, Harvey George "Buck" b: 2/9/15, Kenosha, Wis. d: 7/24/70, Franklin, La. BB/TR, 6'2.5", 185 lbs. Deb: 9/12/35																										
1935	Bro-N	0	0	—	2	0	0	0	0	1	2	0	3	0	54.0	9.00	44	.400	.667	0	—	0	-1	-1	-0	-0.1
● **TOMMY GREENE** Greene, Ira Thomas b: 4/6/67, Lumberton, N.C. BR/TR, 6'5", 225 lbs. Deb: 9/10/89																										
1989	Atl-N	1	2	.333	4	4	1	1	0	26^1	22	5	6	17	9.6	4.10	89	.234	.280	1	.100	-1	-2	-1	-0	-0.2
1990	Atl-N	1	0	1.000	5	2	0	0	0	12^1	14	3	9	4	17.5	8.03	50	.286	.407	0	.000	-0	-6	-5	-0	-0.6
	Phi-N	2	3	.400	10	7	0	0	0	39	36	5	17	17	12.2	4.15	92	.247	.325	2	.182	0	-2	-1	-0	-0.1
	Yr	3	3	.500	15	9	0	0	0	51^1	50	8	26	21	13.3	5.08	76	.255	.342	2	.167	0	-7	-7	-1	-0.7
1991	Phi-N	13	7	.650	36	27	3	2	0	207^2	177	19	66	154	10.7	3.38	108	.230	.294	19	.268	7	7	7	-3	1.2
1992	Phi-N	3	3	.500	13	12	0	0	0	64^1	75	5	34	39	15.2	5.32	66	.291	.373	3	.125	-1	-13	-13	-1	-1.5
Total	4	20	15	.571	68	52	4	3	0	349^2	324	37	132	231	11.8	4.04	91	.246	.317	25	.214	6	-15	-15	-4	-1.2
● **JUNE GREENE** Greene, Julius Foust b: 6/25/1899, Ramseur, N.C. d: 3/19/74, Glendora, Cal. BL/TR, 6'2.5", 185 lbs. Deb: 4/20/28 ♦																										
1928	Phi-N	0	0	—	1	0	0	0	0	2	5	0	0	0	22.5	9.00	47	.556	.556	3	.500	2	-1	-1	0	0.1
1929	Phi-N	0	0	—	5	0	0	0	0	13^2	33	2	9	4	29.6	19.76	26	.465	.542	4	.211	0	-23	-22	0	-1.7
Total	2	0	0	—	6	0	0	0	0	15^2	38	2	9	4	28.7	18.38	28	.475	.543	7	.280	2	-24	-23	1	-1.6
● **NELSON GREENE** Greene, Nelson George "Lefty" b: 9/20/1900, Philadelphia, Pa. d: 4/6/83, Lebanon, Pa. BL/TL, 6', 185 lbs. Deb: 4/28/24																										
1924	Bro-N	0	1	.000	4	1	0	0	0	9	14	1	2	3	16.0	4.00	94	.350	.381	0	.000	-0	-0	-0	0	0.0
1925	Bro-N	2	0	1.000	11	0	0	0	1	22	45	4	7	4	21.3	10.64	39	.417	.452	2	.286	0	-16	-16	0	-1.4
Total	2	2	1	.667	15	1	0	0	1	31	59	5	9	7	19.7	8.71	47	.399	.433	2	.250	-0	-16	-16	1	-1.4
● **KENT GREENFIELD** Greenfield, Kent b: 7/1/02, Guthrie, Ky. d: 3/14/78, Guthrie, Ky. BR/TR, 6'1", 180 lbs. Deb: 9/28/24																										
1924	NY-N	0	1	.000	1	1	0	0	0	3	9	1	1	1	30.0	15.00	24	.500	.526	0	—	0	-4	-4	-0	-0.3
1925	NY-N	12	8	.600	29	21	12	0	0	171^2	195	4	64	66	13.7	3.88	104	.288	.352	5	.081	-6	7	3	1	-0.2
1926	NY-N	13	12	.520	39	28	8	1	1	222^2	206	17	82	74	11.8	3.96	95	.251	.322	6	.092	-5	-3	-5	-2	-1.2
1927	NY-N	2	2	.500	12	1	0	0	0	20	39	3	13	4	24.3	9.45	41	.411	.491	0	.000	-0	-12	-12	0	-1.2
	Bos-N	11	14	.440	27	26	11	1	0	190	203	3	59	59	12.6	3.84	97	.282	.341	11	.172	-1	2	-3	-0	-0.4
	Yr	13	16	.448	39	27	11	1	0	210	242	6	72	63	13.7	4.37	85	.297	.357	11	.167	-2	-11	-15	-0	-1.6
1928	Bos-N	3	11	.214	32	23	5	0	0	143^2	173	6	60	30	14.9	5.32	73	.307	.378	2	.053	-4	-21	-23	1	-2.4
1929	Bos-N	0	0	—	6	2	0	0	0	15^2	33	1	15	7	28.7	10.91	43	.465	.568	0	.000	-1	-11	-11	1	-0.9
	Bro-N	0	0	—	6	0	0	0	0	8^2	13	1	3	1	16.6	8.31	56	.382	.432	0	.000	-0	-3	-4	0	-0.3
	Yr	0	0	—	12	2	0	0	0	24^1	46	2	18	8	23.7	9.99	47	.430	.512	0	.000	-1	-14	-14	1	-1.2
Total	6	41	48	.461	152	102	36	2	1	775^1	871	36	297	242	13.8	4.54	85	.290	.358	24	.101	-17	-46	-58	-0	-6.9
● **JOHN GREENING** Greening, John A. (b: John A. Greenig) b: Philadelphia, Pa. Deb: 5/09/1888																										
1888	Was-N	0	1	.000	1	1	1	0	0	9	17	2	4	2	21.0	11.00	25	.405	.457	0	.000	-0	-8	-8	-0	-0.6
● **BOB GREENWOOD** Greenwood, Robert Chandler "Greenie" b: 3/13/28, Cananea, Mexico BR/TR, 6'5", 200 lbs. Deb: 4/21/54																										
1954	Phi-N	1	2	.333	11	4	0	0	0	36^2	28	2	18	9	11.3	3.19	127	.209	.303	0	.000	-1	4	3	0	0.3
1955	Phi-N	0	0	—	1	0	0	0	0	2^1	7	1	0	0	27.0	15.43	26	.500	.500	0	.000	-0	-3	-3	-0	-0.3
Total	2	1	2	.333	12	4	0	0	0	39	35	3	18	9	12.2	3.92	103	.236	.319	0	.000	-1	1	0	0	0.0
● **DAVE GREGG** Gregg, David Charles "Highpockets" b: 3/14/1891, Chehalis, Wash. d: 11/12/65, Clarkston, Wash. BR/TR, 6'1", 185 lbs. Deb: 6/15/13 F																										
1913	Cle-A	0	0	—	1	0	0	0	0	1	2	0	0	0	27.0	18.00	17	.400	.500	0	—	0	-2	-2	0	-0.1
● **HAL GREGG** Gregg, Harold Dana "Skeets" b: 7/11/21, Anaheim, Cal. BR/TR, 6'3.5", 195 lbs. Deb: 8/18/43																										
1943	Bro-N	0	3	.000	5	4	0	0	0	18^2	21	2	21	7	20.3	9.64	35	.304	.467	0	.000	0	-13	-13	-0	-1.2
1944	Bro-N	9	16	.360	39	31	6	0	2	197^2	201	12	137	92	15.8	5.46	65	.258	.376	14	.206	-0	-41	-42	0	-4.1
1945	Bro-N†	18	13	.581	42	34	13	2	2	254^1	221	5	120	139	12.3	3.47	108	.232	.323	20	.220	3	9	8	-0	1.1
1946	Bro-N	6	4	.600	26	16	4	1	2	117^1	103	3	44	54	11.4	2.99	113	.236	.308	4	.125	-1	5	5	-2	0.2
1947	*Bro-N	4	5	.444	37	16	2	1	1	104^1	115	6	55	59	15.0	5.87	70	.272	.361	9	.265	2	-21	-20	0	-1.7
1948	Pit-N	2	4	.333	22	8	1	0	1	74^1	72	3	34	25	13.2	4.60	88	.255	.342	6	.273	2	-5	-4	-0	-0.3
1949	Pit-N	1	1	.500	8	1	0	0	0	18^2	20	1	8	9	14.0	3.38	125	.303	.387	0	.000	-0	1	2	-0	0.1
1950	Pit-N	0	1	.000	5	1	0	0	0	5^1	10	2	7	3	30.4	13.50	32	.400	.545	0	.000	-0	-6	-5	0	-0.5
1952	NY-N	0	1	.000	16	4	1	0	1	36^1	42	7	17	13	15.1	4.71	79	.286	.367	1	.125	-0	-4	-4	-1	-0.5
Total	9	40	48	.455	200	115	27	4	9	827	805	41	443	401	13.9	4.54	82	.253	.350	54	.205	4	-73	-74	-3	-6.9
● **VEAN GREGG** Gregg, Sylveanus Augustus b: 4/13/1885, Chehalis, Wash. d: 7/29/64, Aberdeen, Was. BR/TL, 6'1", 185 lbs. Deb: 4/12/11 F																										
1911	Cle-A	23	7	.767	34	26	22	5	0	244^2	172	2	86	125	**9.9**	**1.80**	**189**	**.205**	.286	14	.165	-4	42	44	0	4.2
1912	Cle-A	20	13	.606	37	34	26	1	2	271^1	242	4	90	184	11.3	2.59	132	.246	.316	17	.175	-3	22	25	-2	2.1
1913	Cle-A	20	13	.606	44	34	23	3	3	285^2	258	2	124	166	12.4	2.24	136	.246	.334	13	.131	-5	22	25	-3	2.0
1914	Cle-A	9	3	.750	17	12	6	1	0	96^2	88	0	48	56	12.9	3.07	94	.251	.347	6	.176	1	-4	-2	-0	-0.2
	Bos-A	3	4	.429	12	9	4	0	0	68^1	71	0	37	24	14.2	3.95	68	.283	.375	4	.211	0	-9	-10	-1	-1.1
	Yr	12	7	.632	29	21	10	1	0	165	159	0	85	80	13.3	3.44	82	.263	.354	10	.189	1	-13	-12	-2	-1.3

YEAR	TM/L	W	L	PCT	G	GS	CG	SH	SV	IP	H	HR	BB	SO	RAT	ERA	ERA+	OAV	OOB	BH	AVG	PB	PR	/A	PD	TPI
1915	Bos-A	4	2	.667	18	9	3	1	3	75	71	2	32	43	13.0	3.36	83	.260	.348	7	.350	2	-4	-5	0	-0.3
1916	Bos-A	2	5	.286	21	7	3	0	0	77^2	71	0	30	41	12.1	3.01	92	.259	.339	2	.111	-1	-2	-2	-0	-0.4
1918	Phi-A	9	14	.391	30	25	17	3	2	199^1	180	4	67	63	11.4	3.12	94	.251	.320	12	.169	-3	-7	-4	-1	-0.9
1925	Was-A	2	2	.500	26	5	1	0	2	74^1	87	3	38	18	15.4	4.12	103	.318	.404	3	.214	0	2	1	-1	0.0
Total	8	92	63	.594	239	161	105	14	12	1393	1240	17	552	720	11.9	2.70	118	.248	.328	78	.171	-12	63	73	-8	5.4

● FRANK GREGORY Gregory, Frank Ernst b: 7/25/1888, Spring Valley Township, Wis. d: 11/5/55, Beloit, Wis. BR/TR, 5'11", 185 lbs. Deb: 9/05/12

YEAR	TM/L	W	L	PCT	G	GS	CG	SH	SV	IP	H	HR	BB	SO	RAT	ERA	ERA+	OAV	OOB	BH	AVG	PB	PR	/A	PD	TPI
1912	Cin-N	2	0	1.000	4	2	1	0	0	15^2	19	0	7	4	15.5	4.60	73	.297	.375	1	.200	0	-2	-2	-1	-0.3

● LEE GREGORY Gregory, Grover Leroy b: 6/2/38, Bakersfield, Cal. BL/TL, 6'1", 180 lbs. Deb: 4/17/64

YEAR	TM/L	W	L	PCT	G	GS	CG	SH	SV	IP	H	HR	BB	SO	RAT	ERA	ERA+	OAV	OOB	BH	AVG	PB	PR	/A	PD	TPI
1964	Chi-N	0	0	—	11	0	0	0	0	18	23	3	5	8	14.0	3.50	106	.333	.378	1	.077	0	0	0	0	0.0

● HOWIE GREGORY Gregory, Howard Watterson b: 11/18/1886, Hannibal, Mo. d: 5/30/70, Tulsa, Okla. BL/TR, 6', 175 lbs. Deb: 4/16/11

YEAR	TM/L	W	L	PCT	G	GS	CG	SH	SV	IP	H	HR	BB	SO	RAT	ERA	ERA+	OAV	OOB	BH	AVG	PB	PR	/A	PD	TPI
1911	StL-A	0	1	.000	3	1	0	0	0	7	11	0	4	1	19.3	5.14	66	.393	.469	0	.000	-0	-1	-1	-0	-0.2

● PAUL GREGORY Gregory, Paul Edwin "Pop" b: 6/9/08, Tomnolen, Miss. BR/TR, 6'2", 180 lbs. Deb: 4/20/32

YEAR	TM/L	W	L	PCT	G	GS	CG	SH	SV	IP	H	HR	BB	SO	RAT	ERA	ERA+	OAV	OOB	BH	AVG	PB	PR	/A	PD	TPI
1932	Chi-A	5	3	.625	33	9	3	0	0	117^2	125	8	51	39	13.6	4.51	96	.273	.348	3	.079	-3	-0	-2	3	-0.2
1933	Chi-A	4	11	.267	23	17	5	0	0	103^2	124	10	47	18	14.9	4.95	86	.296	.368	5	.143	-1	-8	-8	1	-0.8
Total	2	9	14	.391	56	26	8	0	0	221^1	249	18	98	57	14.2	4.72	91	.284	.358	8	.110	-4	-8	-11	4	-1.0

● BILL GREIF Greif, William Briley b: 4/25/50, Ft.Stockton, Tex. BR/TR, 6'5", 205 lbs. Deb: 7/19/71

YEAR	TM/L	W	L	PCT	G	GS	CG	SH	SV	IP	H	HR	BB	SO	RAT	ERA	ERA+	OAV	OOB	BH	AVG	PB	PR	/A	PD	TPI
1971	Hou-N	1	1	.500	7	3	0	0	0	16	18	1	8	14	15.8	5.06	66	.290	.389	1	.333	0	-3	-3	0	-0.3
1972	SD-N	5	16	.238	34	22	2	1	2	125^1	143	18	47	91	14.2	5.60	59	.287	.357	1	.030	-3	-30	-32	-2	-3.7
1973	SD-N	10	17	.370	36	31	9	3	1	199^1	181	20	62	120	11.2	3.21	108	.246	.309	6	.098	-2	10	6	-1	0.3
1974	SD-N	9	19	.321	43	35	7	1	1	226	244	17	95	137	14.1	4.66	76	.279	.359	4	.071	-2	-26	-28	0	-2.9
1975	SD-N	4	6	.400	59	1	0	0	9	72	74	7	38	43	14.6	3.88	90	.269	.368	0	.000	-0	-2	-3	-2	-0.5
1976	SD-N	1	3	.250	5	5	0	0	0	22^1	27	2	11	5	15.3	8.06	41	.297	.373	0	.000	-1	-11	-12	0	-1.2
	StL-N	1	5	.167	47	0	0	0	6	54^2	60	5	26	32	14.5	4.12	86	.290	.374	0	.000	0	-4	-4	-1	-0.4
	Yr	2	8	.200	52	5	0	0	6	77	87	7	37	37	14.7	5.26	66	.291	.373	0	.000	-1	-15	-15	-0	-1.6
Total	6	31	67	.316	231	97	18	5	19	715^2	747	70	287	442	13.5	4.41	78	.272	.349	12	.072	-6	-66	-76	-5	-8.7

● BILL GREVELL Grevell, William J. b: 3/5/1898, Williamstown, N.J. d: 6/21/23, Philadelphia, Pa. BR/TR, 5'11", 170 lbs. Deb: 5/14/19

YEAR	TM/L	W	L	PCT	G	GS	CG	SH	SV	IP	H	HR	BB	SO	RAT	ERA	ERA+	OAV	OOB	BH	AVG	PB	PR	/A	PD	TPI
1919	Phi-A	0	0	—	5	2	0	0	0	12	15	0	18	3	25.5	14.25	24	.306	.500	0	.000	-1	-15	-14	1	-1.3

● GREYSON Greyson TL, Deb: 8/27/1873

YEAR	TM/L	W	L	PCT	G	GS	CG	SH	SV	IP	H	HR	BB	SO	RAT	ERA	ERA+	OAV	OOB	BH	AVG	PB	PR	/A	PD	TPI
1873	Was-n	1	6	.143	7	7	7	0	0	63	112	3	7	3	17.0	5.43	62	.357	.371	4	.143	-2	-15	-15		-1.1

● LEE GRIFFETH Griffeth, Leon Clifford b: 5/20/25, Carmel, N.Y. BB/TL, 5'11.5", 180 lbs. Deb: 6/25/46

YEAR	TM/L	W	L	PCT	G	GS	CG	SH	SV	IP	H	HR	BB	SO	RAT	ERA	ERA+	OAV	OOB	BH	AVG	PB	PR	/A	PD	TPI
1946	Phi-A	0	0	—	10	0	0	0	0	15^1	13	1	6	4	12.3	2.93	121	.232	.328	0	.000	0	1	1	-0	0.1

● HANK GRIFFIN Griffin, James Linton "Pepper" b: 7/11/1886, Whitehouse, Tex. d: 2/11/50, Terrell, Tex. BR/TR, 6', 165 lbs. Deb: 5/05/11

YEAR	TM/L	W	L	PCT	G	GS	CG	SH	SV	IP	H	HR	BB	SO	RAT	ERA	ERA+	OAV	OOB	BH	AVG	PB	PR	/A	PD	TPI
1911	Chi-N	0	0	—	1	1	0	0	0	1	1	1	3	1	36.0	18.00	18	.250	.571	0	—	0	-2	-2	0	-0.2
	Bos-N	0	6	.000	15	6	1	0	0	82^2	96	3	34	30	14.8	5.23	73	.305	.383	7	.233	-0	-17	-13	0	-1.2
	Yr	0	6	.000	16	7	1	0	0	83^2	97	4	37	31	15.1	5.38	71	.304	.387	7	.233	-0	-18	-14	0	-1.4
1912	Bos-N	0	0	—	3	0	0	0	0	1^2	3	0	3	0	37.8	27.00	13	.750	.875	0	—	0	-4	-4	-0	-0.4
Total	2	0	6	.000	19	7	1	0	0	85^1	100	4	40	31	15.5	5.80	66	.310	.397	7	.233	-0	-23	-19	0	-1.8

● MARTY GRIFFIN Griffin, Martin John b: 9/2/01, San Francisco, Cal d: 11/19/51, Los Angeles, Cal. BR/TR, 6'2", 200 lbs. Deb: 7/25/28

YEAR	TM/L	W	L	PCT	G	GS	CG	SH	SV	IP	H	HR	BB	SO	RAT	ERA	ERA+	OAV	OOB	BH	AVG	PB	PR	/A	PD	TPI
1928	Bos-A	0	3	.000	11	3	0	0	0	37^2	42	0	17	9	14.1	5.02	82	.300	.376	4	.308	1	-4	-4	-0	-0.3

● MIKE GRIFFIN Griffin, Michael Leroy b: 6/26/57, Colusa, Cal. BR/TR, 6'5", 197 lbs. Deb: 9/17/79

YEAR	TM/L	W	L	PCT	G	GS	CG	SH	SV	IP	H	HR	BB	SO	RAT	ERA	ERA+	OAV	OOB	BH	AVG	PB	PR	/A	PD	TPI
1979	NY-A	0	0	—	3	0	0	0	1	4^1	5	0	2	5	14.5	4.15	98	.313	.389	0	—	0	0	-0	-0	0.2
1980	NY-A	2	4	.333	13	9	0	0	0	54	64	6	23	25	14.7	4.83	81	.287	.356	0	—	0	-5	-5	-0	-0.4
1981	NY-A	0	0	—	2	0	0	0	0	4^1	5	0	0	4	10.4	2.08	172	.278	.278	0	—	0	1	1	0	0.2
	Chi-N	2	5	.286	16	9	0	0	1	52	64	4	9	20	12.6	4.50	82	.302	.330	2	.154	-0	-6	-5	0	-0.5
1982	SD-N	0	1	.000	7	0	0	0	0	10^1	9	0	3	4	10.5	3.48	98	.237	.293	0	.000	-0	0	-0	-0	0.0
1987	Bal-A	3	5	.375	23	6	1	0	1	74^1	78	9	33	42	13.8	4.36	101	.269	.350	0	—	0	1	0	-1	0.2
1989	Cin-N	0	0	—	3	0	0	0	0	4^1	10	0	3	1	27.0	12.46	29	.500	.565	1	1.000	0	-4	-4	0	-0.4
Total	6	7	15	.318	67	24	1	0	3	203^2	235	19	73	101	13.8	4.60	87	.288	.349	3	.200	-0	-13	-13	-1	-0.7

● PAT GRIFFIN Griffin, Patrick Richard b: 5/6/1893, Niles, Ohio d: 6/7/27, Youngstown, Ohio BR/TR, 6'2", 180 lbs. Deb: 7/23/14

YEAR	TM/L	W	L	PCT	G	GS	CG	SH	SV	IP	H	HR	BB	SO	RAT	ERA	ERA+	OAV	OOB	BH	AVG	PB	PR	/A	PD	TPI
1914	Cin-N	0	0	—	1	0	0	0	0	1	3	0	2	0	45.0	9.00	33	.750	.833	0	—	0	-1	-1	0	0.0

● TOM GRIFFIN Griffin, Thomas James b: 2/22/48, Los Angeles, Cal. BR/TR, 6'3", 210 lbs. Deb: 4/10/69

YEAR	TM/L	W	L	PCT	G	GS	CG	SH	SV	IP	H	HR	BB	SO	RAT	ERA	ERA+	OAV	OOB	BH	AVG	PB	PR	/A	PD	TPI
1969	Hou-N	11	10	.524	31	31	6	3	0	188^1	156	19	93	200	12.2	3.54	100	.220	.317	9	.145	2	1	0	-2	0.0
1970	Hou-N	3	13	.188	23	20	2	1	0	111^1	118	9	72	72	15.6	5.74	68	.275	.383	2	.061	-2	-21	-23	-1	-2.5
1971	Hou-N	0	6	.000	10	6	0	0	0	37^2	44	4	20	29	15.8	4.78	70	.288	.377	1	.111	-0	-5	-6	1	-0.6
1972	Hou-N	5	4	.556	39	5	1	1	3	94^1	92	7	38	83	12.7	3.24	104	.258	.334	7	.280	3	2	1	-1	0.4
1973	Hou-N	4	6	.400	25	12	4	0	0	99^2	83	10	46	69	11.8	4.15	87	.229	.320	3	.107	0	-5	-6	0	-0.5
1974	Hou-N	14	10	.583	34	34	8	3	0	211	202	14	89	110	12.6	3.54	98	.250	.328	20	.294	8	2	-2	1	0.7
1975	Hou-N	3	8	.273	17	13	3	1	0	79^1	89	11	46	56	15.5	5.33	63	.288	.384	3	.136	-0	-15	-17	1	-1.7
1976	Hou-N	5	3	.625	20	2	0	0	0	41^2	44	4	37	33	17.7	6.05	53	.278	.418	0	.000	-0	-12	-13	0	-1.4
	SD-N	4	3	.571	11	11	2	0	0	70^1	56	0	42	36	12.7	2.94	111	.222	.336	2	.077	-2	4	3	-0	0.1
	Yr	9	6	.600	31	13	2	0	0	112	100	4	79	69	14.5	4.10	79	.242	.364	2	.065	-2	-7	-11	-0	-1.3
1977	SD-N	6	9	.400	38	20	0	0	0	151^1	144	17	88	79	14.1	4.46	79	.254	.359	6	.133	1	-9	-16	-2	-1.6
1978	Cal-A	3	4	.429	24	4	0	0	0	56	63	8	31	35	15.3	4.02	90	.279	.368	0	—	0	-2	-3	1	-0.2
1979	SF-N	5	6	.455	59	3	0	0	2	94^1	83	9	46	82	12.7	3.91	89	.237	.333	1	.071	-1	-2	-4	2	-0.4
1980	SF-N	5	1	.833	42	4	0	0	0	107^2	80	8	49	79	11.5	2.76	128	.212	.315	2	.111	0	10	9	0	1.0
1981	SF-N	8	8	.500	22	22	3	1	0	129^1	121	8	57	83	12.9	3.76	91	.249	.336	8	.195	2	-4	-5	2	-0.1
1982	Pit-N	1	3	.250	6	4	0	0	0	22^1	32	5	15	8	19.3	8.87	42	.330	.425	2	.222	0	-13	-13	0	-1.2
Total	14	77	94	.450	401	191	29	10	5	1494^2	1407	133	769	1054	13.4	4.07	86	.249	.345	66	.163	12	-69	-94	1	-8.0

● CLARK GRIFFITH Griffith, Clark Calvin "The Old Fox"
b: 11/20/1869, Clear Creek, Mo. d: 10/27/55, Washington, D.C. BR/TR, 5'6.5", 156 lbs. Deb: 4/11/1891 MH♦

YEAR	TM/L	W	L	PCT	G	GS	CG	SH	SV	IP	H	HR	BB	SO	RAT	ERA	ERA+	OAV	OOB	BH	AVG	PB	PR	/A	PD	TPI
1891	StL-a	11	8	.579	27	17	12	0	0	186^1	195	8	58	68	12.9	3.33	126	.260	.326	12	.156	-4	8	18	0	1.3
	Bos-a	3	1	.750	7	4	3	0	0	40	47	3	15	20	15.1	5.62	62	.283	.360	4	.174	2	-8	-9	-1	-0.7
	Yr	14	9	.609	34	21	15	0	0	226^1	242	11	73	88	12.7	3.74	109	.260	.317	16	.160	-2	-0	9	-1	0.6
1893	Chi-N	1	2	.333	4	2	2	0	0	19^2	24	1	5	9	13.7	5.03	92	.292	.340	2	.182	-1	-1	-1	1	-0.1
1894	Chi-N	21	14	.600	36	30	28	0	0	261^1	328	12	85	71	14.7	4.92	114	.304	.362	33	.232	-0	12	20	1	1.6
1895	Chi-N	26	14	.650	42	41	39	0	0	353	434	11	91	79	13.9	3.93	130	.298	.348	46	.319	6	34	46	1	4.5
1896	Chi-N	23	11	.676	36	35	35	0	0	317^2	370	3	70	81	12.8	3.54	128	.289	.331	36	.267	3	29	35	1	3.4
1897	Chi-N	21	18	.538	41	38	**38**	1	1	343^2	410	3	86	102	13.4	3.72	120	.294	.342	38	.235	3	23	28	3	3.0
1898	Chi-N	24	10	.706	38	38	36	4	0	325^2	305	1	64	97	10.8	**1.88**	**191**	.246	.294	20	.164	-2	63	62	1	6.2
1899	Chi-N	22	14	.611	38	38	35	0	0	319^2	329	5	65	73	11.5	2.79	134	.266	.310	31	.258	5	38	34	6	4.4
1900	Chi-N	14	13	.519	30	30	27	**4**	0	248	245	6	51	61	11.3	3.05	118	.258	.306	24	.253	5	18	15	-1	1.8
1901	Chi-A	24	7	**.774**	35	30	26	**5**	1	266^2	275	4	50	67	11.1	2.67	131	.263	.299	27	.303	13	30	24	0	3.5

YEAR	TM/L	W	L	PCT	G	GS	CG	SH	SV	IP	H	HR	BB	SO	RAT	ERA	ERA+	OAV	OOB	BH	AVG	PB	PR	/A	PD	TPI
1902	Chi-A	15	9	.625	28	24	20	3	0	213	247	11	47	51	13.1	4.18	81	.290	.339	20	.217	1	-14	-19	-1	-1.7
1903	NY-A	14	11	.560	25	24	22	2	0	213	201	3	33	69	10.1	2.70	116	.249	.283	11	.159	2	6	10	-3	0.9
1904	NY-A	7	5	.583	16	11	8	1	0	100^1	91	3	16	36	10.0	2.87	94	.243	.281	6	.143	-1	-3	-2	-1	-0.4
1905	NY-A	9	6	.600	25	7	4	2	1	101^2	82	1	15	46	8.7	1.68	175	.222	.254	7	.219	1	11	14	-2	1.5
1906	NY-A	2	2	.500	17	2	1	0	2	59^2	58	0	15	16	11.6	3.02	98	.258	.316	2	.111	-1	-2	-0	1	0.0
1907	NY-A	0	0	—	4	0	0	0	0	8^1	15	0	6	5	22.7	8.64	32	.390	.472	0	.000	-0	-6	-5	0	-0.6
1909	Cin-N	0	1	.000	1	1	1	0	0	6	11	0	2	3	19.5	6.00	43	.379	.419	0	.000	-0	-2	-2	1	-0.2
1912	Was-A	0	0	—	1	0	0	0	0	0	1	1	0	0	—	∞	—	1.000	1.000	0	.000	-0	-1	-1	0	-0.1
1913	Was-A	0	0	—	1	0	0	0	0	1	1	0	0	0	9.0	0.00	—	.250	.250	1	1.000	1	0	0	-0	0.1
1914	Was-A	0	0	—	1	0	0	0	1	1	1	0	0	1	9.0	0.00	—	.250	.250	1	1.000	1	0	0	-0	0.0
Total	20	237	146	.619	453	372	337	22	6	3385^2	3670	76	774	955	12.3	3.31	121	.274	.322	321	.233	34	233	266	7	28.4

● FRANK GRIFFITH Griffith, Frank Wesley b: 11/18/1872, Gilman, Ill. d: 12/13/08, BL/TL, Deb: 8/13/1892

YEAR	TM/L	W	L	PCT	G	GS	CG	SH	SV	IP	H	HR	BB	SO	RAT	ERA	ERA+	OAV	OOB	BH	AVG	PB	PR	/A	PD	TPI
1892	Chi-N	0	1	.000	1	1	0	0	0	4	3	1	6	3	20.3	11.25	30	.200	.429	0	.000	-0	-4	-4	-0	-0.3
1894	Cle-N	1	2	.333	7	6	3	0	0	42^1	64	5	37	15	23.4	9.99	55	.344	.474	8	.333	2	-22	-21	-0	-1.4
Total	2	1	3	.250	8	7	3	0	0	46^1	67	6	43	18	23.1	10.10	52	.333	.471	8	.320	2	-25	-25	-0	-1.7

● HAL GRIGGS Griggs, Harold Lloyd b: 8/24/28, Shannon, Ga. BR/TR, 6', 170 lbs. Deb: 4/18/56

YEAR	TM/L	W	L	PCT	G	GS	CG	SH	SV	IP	H	HR	BB	SO	RAT	ERA	ERA+	OAV	OOB	BH	AVG	PB	PR	/A	PD	TPI
1956	Was-A	1	6	.143	34	12	1	0	1	98^2	120	14	76	48	18.0	6.02	72	.307	.421	0	.000	-1	-20	-19	1	-1.7
1957	Was-A	0	1	.000	2	2	0	0	0	13^2	11	1	7	12	11.9	3.29	118	.229	.327	1	.250	0	1	1	0	0.1
1958	Was-A	3	11	.214	32	21	3	0	0	137	138	20	74	69	14.1	5.52	69	.262	.355	5	.122	-2	-27	-26	-0	-2.8
1959	Was-A	2	8	.200	37	10	2	1	2	97^2	103	8	52	43	14.4	5.25	75	.270	.359	1	.056	-2	-15	-15	-0	-1.6
Total	4	6	26	.188	105	45	6	1	3	347	372	43	209	172	15.2	5.50	73	.276	.375	7	.089	-5	-61	-58	1	-6.0

● GUIDO GRILLI Grilli, Guido John b: 1/9/39, Memphis, Tenn. BL/TL, 6', 188 lbs. Deb: 4/12/66

YEAR	TM/L	W	L	PCT	G	GS	CG	SH	SV	IP	H	HR	BB	SO	RAT	ERA	ERA+	OAV	OOB	BH	AVG	PB	PR	/A	PD	TPI
1966	Bos-A	0	1	.000	6	0	0	0	0	4^2	5	1	9	4	27.0	7.71	49	.278	.519	1	.500	0	-2	-2	0	-0.2
	KC-A	0	1	.000	16	0	0	0	1	15^2	19	0	11	8	19.0	6.89	49	.302	.429	0	—	0	-6	-6	-1	-0.7
	Yr	0	2	.000	22	0	0	0	1	20^1	24	1	20	12	20.8	7.08	49	.296	.452	1	.500	0	-8	-8	-1	-0.9

● STEVE GRILLI Grilli, Stephen Joseph b: 5/2/49, Brooklyn, N.Y. BR/TR, 6'2", 170 lbs. Deb: 9/19/75

YEAR	TM/L	W	L	PCT	G	GS	CG	SH	SV	IP	H	HR	BB	SO	RAT	ERA	ERA+	OAV	OOB	BH	AVG	PB	PR	/A	PD	TPI
1975	Det-A	0	0	—	3	0	0	0	0	6^2	3	0	6	5	12.2	1.35	297	.136	.321	0	—	0	2	2	0	0.0
1976	Det-A	3	1	.750	36	0	0	0	3	66	63	5	41	36	14.9	4.64	80	.258	.376	0	—	0	-8	-7	2	-0.6
1977	Det-A	1	2	.333	30	2	0	0	0	72^2	71	8	49	49	15.2	4.83	89	.265	.384	0	—	0	-6	-4	-1	-0.5
1979	Tor-A	0	0	—	1	0	0	0	0	2^1	1	0	0	1	3.9	0.00	—	.143	.143	0	—	0	1	1	-0	0.0
Total	4	4	3	.571	70	2	0	0	3	147^2	138	13	96	91	14.7	4.51	89	.255	.375	0	—	0	-12	-8	1	-1.1

● JOHN GRIM Grim, John Helm b: 8/9/1867, Lebanon, Ky. d: 7/28/61, Indianapolis, Ind BR/TR, 6'2", 175 lbs. Deb: 9/29/1888 ♦

YEAR	TM/L	W	L	PCT	G	GS	CG	SH	SV	IP	H	HR	BB	SO	RAT	ERA	ERA+	OAV	OOB	BH	AVG	PB	PR	/A	PD	TPI
1890	Roc-a	0	0	—	1	0	0	0	0	3^1	3	0	4	3	18.9	0.00	—	.233	.415	51	.266	0	1	1	-0	0.1

● BOB GRIM Grim, Robert Anton b: 3/8/30, New York, Ny. BR/TR, 6'1", 185 lbs. Deb: 4/18/54

YEAR	TM/L	W	L	PCT	G	GS	CG	SH	SV	IP	H	HR	BB	SO	RAT	ERA	ERA+	OAV	OOB	BH	AVG	PB	PR	/A	PD	TPI
1954	NY-A	20	6	.769	37	20	8	1	0	199	175	9	85	108	11.9	3.26	106	.244	.327	10	.143	-1	10	4	-1	0.2
1955	*NY-A	7	5	.583	26	11	1	1	4	92^1	81	9	42	63	12.3	4.19	89	.238	.326	3	.120	-1	-2	-5	0	-0.5
1956	NY-A	6	1	.857	26	6	1	0	5	74^2	64	3	31	48	11.7	2.77	139	.235	.318	1	.063	-0	11	9	-1	0.8
1957	*NY-A★	12	8	.600	46	0	0	0	**19**	72	60	5	36	52	12.0	2.63	137	.239	.334	1	.111	1	9	8	0	0.9
1958	NY-A	0	1	.000	11	0	0	0	0	16^1	12	3	10	11	12.7	5.51	64	.211	.338	0	.000	-0	-3	-4	-0	-0.4
	KC-A	7	6	.538	26	14	5	1	0	113^2	118	7	41	54	12.8	3.56	110	.269	.336	6	.188	-1	3	4	-1	0.3
	Yr	7	7	.500	37	14	5	1	0	130	130	10	51	65	12.7	3.81	101	.262	.335	6	.182	-1	-1	1	-1	-0.1
1959	KC-A	6	10	.375	40	9	3	1	4	125^1	124	10	57	65	13.2	4.09	98	.260	.343	3	.094	-1	-3	-1	-2	-0.4
1960	Cle-A	0	1	.000	3	0	0	0	0	2^1	6	0	1	2	27.0	11.57	32	.500	.538	0	—	0	-2	-2	0	-0.2
	Cin-N	2	2	.500	26	0	0	0	2	30^1	32	3	10	22	12.5	4.45	86	.274	.331	0	.000	-0	-2	-2	-0	-0.3
	StL-N	1	0	1.000	15	0	0	0	0	20^2	22	1	9	15	13.5	3.05	134	.272	.344	0	.000	-0	2	2	0	0.3
	Yr	3	2	.600	41	0	0	0	2	51	54	4	19	37	12.9	3.88	101	.267	.330	0	.000	-0	-1	0	-0	0.0
1962	KC-A	0	1	.000	12	0	0	0	3	13	14	0	8	3	15.2	6.23	67	.292	.393	0	.000	-0	-3	-3	1	-0.3
Total	8	61	41	.598	268	60	18	4	37	759^2	708	50	330	443	12.5	3.61	104	.252	.334	24	.127	-4	19	11	-4	0.4

● BURLEIGH GRIMES Grimes, Burleigh Arland "Ol' Stubblebeard"
b: 8/9/1893, Emerald, Wis. d: 12/6/85, Clear Lake, Wis. BR/TR, 5'10", 175 lbs. Deb: 9/10/16 MCH

YEAR	TM/L	W	L	PCT	G	GS	CG	SH	SV	IP	H	HR	BB	SO	RAT	ERA	ERA+	OAV	OOB	BH	AVG	PB	PR	/A	PD	TPI
1916	Pit-N	2	3	.400	6	5	4	0	0	45^2	40	1	10	20	9.9	2.36	114	.241	.284	3	.176	-0	1	2	1	0.2
1917	Pit-N	3	16	.158	37	17	8	1	0	194	186	5	70	72	12.2	3.53	81	.260	.331	16	.232	2	-18	-15	1	-1.3
1918	Bro-N	19	9	.679	**40**	28	19	7	1	269^2	210	3	76	113	9.7	2.14	130	.216	.276	18	.200	0	19	19	4	2.7
1919	Bro-N	10	11	.476	25	21	13	1	0	181^1	179	2	60	82	12.2	3.47	86	.256	.321	17	.246	1	-11	-10	1	-0.9
1920	*Bro-N	23	11	**.676**	40	33	25	5	2	303^2	271	5	67	131	10.1	2.22	144	.238	.282	34	.306	11	31	33	3	5.3
1921	Bro-N	**22**	13	.629	37	35	**30**	2	0	302^1	313	6	76	**136**	11.7	2.83	138	.274	.322	27	.237	2	32	**36**	4	**4.4**
1922	Bro-N	17	14	.548	36	34	18	1	1	259	324	17	84	99	14.4	4.76	85	.308	.363	22	.237	4	-19	-20	4	-1.0
1923	Bro-N	21	18	.538	39	38	**33**	2	0	**327**	356	9	100	119	12.9	3.58	108	.280	.338	30	.238	3	15	11	5	1.9
1924	Bro-N	22	13	.629	38	36	**30**	1	1	**310^2**	351	15	91	135	13.0	3.82	98	.287	.339	37	.298	6	1	-3	5	0.8
1925	Bro-N	12	19	.387	33	31	19	0	0	246^2	305	15	102	73	15.1	5.04	83	.309	.377	24	.250	5	-21	-23	8	-0.9
1926	Bro-N	12	13	.480	30	29	18	1	0	225^1	238	4	88	64	13.2	3.71	103	.276	.346	18	.222	1	3	3	3	0.6
1927	NY-N	19	8	.704	39	34	15	2	2	259^2	274	12	87	102	12.7	3.54	109	.276	.337	18	.188	-0	11	9	5	1.3
1928	Pit-N	**25**	14	.641	**48**	37	**28**	**4**	3	**330^2**	311	11	77	97	10.8	2.99	135	.248	.297	42	.321	11	36	39	6	5.7
1929	Pit-N	17	7	.708	33	29	18	2	2	232^2	245	11	70	62	12.3	3.13	**152**	.269	.324	26	.286	6	**41**	**42**	3	**5.0**
1930	Bos-N	3	5	.375	11	9	1	0	0	49	72	4	22	15	17.8	7.35	67	.353	.424	3	.188	-0	-13	-13	0	-1.1
	*StL-N	13	6	.684	22	19	10	1	0	152^1	174	5	43	58	13.1	3.01	166	.293	.345	15	.263	2	33	34	1	3.6
	Yr	16	11	.593	33	28	11	1	0	201^1	246	9	65	73	14.1	4.07	123	.307	.362	18	.247	2	20	21	2	2.5
1931	*StL-N	17	9	.654	29	28	17	3	0	212^1	240	11	59	67	13.1	3.65	108	.286	.340	14	.184	-2	5	7	3	0.8
1932	*Chi-N	6	11	.353	30	18	5	1	1	141^1	174	8	50	36	14.3	4.78	79	.297	.354	11	.250	1	-14	-16	1	-1.3
1933	Chi-N	3	6	.333	17	7	3	1	3	69^2	71	2	29	12	13.0	3.49	94	.277	.353	3	.150	-0	-1	-2	1	-0.2
	StL-N	0	1	.000	4	3	0	0	1	13^2	15	1	8	4	15.8	5.27	66	.263	.364	1	.200	0	-3	-3	-1	-0.3
	Yr	3	7	.300	21	10	3	1	4	83^1	86	3	37	16	13.4	3.78	87	.274	.352	4	.160	-0	-4	-4	-0	-0.5
1934	StL-N	2	1	.667	4	0	0	0	0	7^2	5	1	2	1	8.2	3.52	120	.179	.233	0	—	0	0	1	0	0.1
	Pit-N	1	2	.333	8	4	0	0	0	27^1	36	0	10	9	15.5	7.24	57	.310	.370	1	.143	-0	-10	-10	1	-0.9
	Yr	3	3	.500	12	4	0	0	0	35	41	1	12	10	13.9	6.43	64	.285	.344	1	.143	-0	-9	-9	1	-0.8
	NY-A	1	2	.333	10	0	0	0	1	18	22	0	14	5	18.5	5.50	74	.319	.440	0	.000	-0	-2	-3	1	-0.2
Total	19	270	212	.560	616	495	314	35	18	4179^2	4412	148	1295	1512	12.5	3.53	107	.273	.331	380	.248	52	118	121	58	24.3

● JOHN GRIMES Grimes, John Thomas b: 4/17/1869, Wooodstock, Md. d: 1/17/64, San Francisco, Cal BR/TR, 5'11", 160 lbs. Deb: 7/28/1897

YEAR	TM/L	W	L	PCT	G	GS	CG	SH	SV	IP	H	HR	BB	SO	RAT	ERA	ERA+	OAV	OOB	BH	AVG	PB	PR	/A	PD	TPI
1897	StL-N	0	2	.000	3	1	1	0	0	19^2	24	0	8	4	17.4	5.95	74	.298	.402	2	.286	1	-4	-3	1	-0.1

● JASON GRIMSLEY Grimsley, Jason Alan b: 8/7/67, Cleveland, Tex. BR/TR, 6'3", 180 lbs. Deb: 9/08/89

YEAR	TM/L	W	L	PCT	G	GS	CG	SH	SV	IP	H	HR	BB	SO	RAT	ERA	ERA+	OAV	OOB	BH	AVG	PB	PR	/A	PD	TPI
1989	Phi-N	1	3	.250	4	4	0	0	0	18^1	19	2	19	7	18.7	5.89	60	.268	.422	0	.000	-1	-5	-5	0	-0.5
1990	Phi-N	3	2	.600	11	11	0	0	0	57^1	47	1	43	41	14.4	3.30	116	.227	.365	3	.188	0	3	3	1	0.5
1991	Phi-N	1	7	.125	12	12	0	0	0	61	54	4	41	42	14.5	4.87	75	.242	.367	1	.059	-1	-8	-8	1	-0.8
Total	3	5	12	.294	27	27	0	0	0	136^2	120	7	103	90	15.0	4.35	85	.240	.374	4	.105	-1	-10	-10	3	-0.8

YEAR TM/L	W	L	PCT	G	GS	CG	SH	SV	IP	H	HR	BB	SO	RAT	ERA	ERA+	OAV	OOB	BH	AVG	PB	PR	/A	PD	TPI
● **ROSS GRIMSLEY** Grimsley, Ross Albert I b: 6/4/22, Americus, Kan. BL/TL, 6', 175 lbs. Deb: 9/03/51 F																									
1951 Chi-A	0	0	—	7	0	0	0	0	14	12	1	10	8	14.1	3.86	105	.235	.361	0	.000	-0	0	0	-1	-0.1
● **ROSS GRIMSLEY** Grimsley, Ross Albert Ii b: 1/7/50, Topeka, Kan. BL/TL, 6'3", 200 lbs. Deb: 5/16/71 F																									
1971 Cin-N	10	7	.588	26	26	6	3	0	161^1	151	15	43	67	10.9	3.57	94	.250	.302	6	.118	-1	-2	-4	-1	-0.6
1972 Cin-N	14	8	.636	30	28	4	1	1	197^2	194	18	50	79	11.1	3.05	105	.260	.307	8	.121	-2	9	4	-0	0.1
1973 Cin-N	13	10	.565	38	36	8	1	1	242^1	245	24	68	90	11.6	3.23	105	.266	.317	5	.061	-6	12	5	-2	-0.3
1974 Bal-A	18	13	.581	40	39	17	4	1	295^2	267	26	76	158	10.5	3.07	112	.244	.295	0	—	0	18	12	0	1.4
1975 Bal-A	10	13	.435	35	32	8	1	0	197	210	29	47	89	11.8	4.07	86	.276	.319	0	—	0	-6	-12	0	-1.0
1976 Bal-A	8	7	.533	28	19	2	0	0	136^2	143	8	35	41	11.8	3.95	83	.270	.317	0	—	0	-7	-10	-1	-1.1
1977 Bal-A	14	10	.583	34	34	11	2	0	218^1	230	24	74	53	12.6	3.96	96	.277	.337	0	—	0	2	-4	2	-0.2
1978 Mon-N☆	20	11	.645	36	36	19	3	0	263	237	17	67	84	10.5	3.05	116	.243	.293	13	.144	-1	15	14	1	1.5
1979 Mon-N	10	9	.526	32	27	2	0	0	151^1	199	18	41	42	14.5	5.35	68	.322	.367	11	.200	1	-27	-28	-0	-2.7
1980 Mon-N	2	4	.333	11	7	0	0	0	41^1	61	5	12	11	16.1	6.31	56	.351	.396	2	.222	0	-12	-13	0	-1.2
Cle-A	4	5	.444	14	11	2	0	0	74^2	103	11	24	18	15.4	6.75	60	.331	.381	0	—	0	-23	-22	-1	-2.1
1982 Bal-A	1	2	.333	21	0	0	0	0	60	65	7	22	18	13.1	5.25	77	.283	.345	0	—	0	-8	-8	0	-0.8
Total 11	124	99	.556	345	295	79	15	3	2039^1	2105	202	559	750	11.8	3.81	92	.270	.320	45	.127	-9	-29	-67	-1	-7.0
● **DAN GRINER** Griner, Donald Dexter "Rusty" b: 3/7/1888, Centerville, Tenn. d: 6/3/50, Bishopville, S.C. BL/TR, 6'1.5", 200 lbs. Deb: 8/17/12																									
1912 StL-N	3	4	.429	12	7	2	0	0	54	59	3	15	20	12.8	3.17	108	.278	.335	1	.077	-0	1	2	-1	0.0
1913 StL-N	10	22	.313	34	34	18	1	0	225	279	12	66	79	14.2	5.08	64	.312	.366	21	.259	5	-47	-46	2	-3.8
1914 StL-N	9	13	.409	37	16	11	2	2	179	163	3	57	74	11.2	2.51	111	.254	.318	14	.255	4	5	6	-1	0.9
1915 StL-N	5	11	.313	37	18	9	3	3	150^1	137	4	46	46	11.4	2.81	99	.259	.328	14	.269	4	-1	-0	-2	0.2
1916 StL-N	0	0	—	4	0	0	0	1	11	15	0	3	3	15.5	4.09	65	.341	.396	1	.250	0	-2	-2	0	-0.2
1918 Bro-N	1	5	.167	11	6	3	1	0	54^1	47	0	15	22	11.4	2.15	129	.267	.348	1	.071	-1	4	4	0	0.4
Total 6	28	55	.337	135	81	43	7	6	673^2	700	22	202	244	12.5	3.49	86	.280	.342	52	.237	12	-39	-37	-2	-2.5
● **LEE GRISSOM** Grissom, Lee Theo b: 10/23/07, Sherman, Tex. BB/TL, 6'3", 200 lbs. Deb: 9/02/34 F																									
1934 Cin-N	0	1	.000	4	1	0	0	0	7	13	0	7	4	25.7	15.43	26	.382	.488	0	.000	-0	-9	-9	-0	-0.8
1935 Cin-N	1	1	.500	3	3	1	0	0	21	31	0	4	13	15.0	3.86	103	.333	.361	0	.000	-1	0	0	0	0.0
1936 Cin-N	1	1	.500	6	4	0	0	0	24^1	33	1	9	13	15.5	6.29	61	.320	.375	0	.000	-1	-6	-7	-0	-0.7
1937 Cin-N★	12	17	.414	50	30	14	**5**	6	223^2	193	7	93	149	11.7	3.26	114	.232	.313	7	.109	-3	16	12	-2	0.6
1938 Cin-N	2	3	.400	14	7	0	0	0	51	60	4	22	16	14.8	5.29	69	.300	.375	3	.188	-0	-9	-9	-0	-1.0
1939 *Cin-N	9	7	.563	33	21	3	0	0	153^2	145	14	56	53	11.8	4.10	93	.249	.316	4	.085	-2	-3	-5	-2	-0.9
1940 NY-A	0	0	—	5	0	0	0	0	4^2	4	0	2	1	11.6	0.00	—	.250	.333	0	—	0	2	2	0	0.2
Bro-N	2	5	.286	14	10	3	1	0	73^2	59	3	34	56	11.4	2.81	142	.215	.302	5	.217	0	9	10	-1	1.0
1941 Bro-N	0	0	—	4	1	0	0	1	11^1	10	2	8	5	14.3	2.38	154	.238	.360	1	.500	0	2	2	-0	0.2
Phi-N	2	13	.133	29	18	2	0	0	131^1	120	4	70	74	13.2	3.97	93	.242	.338	6	.167	-1	-5	-4	-1	-0.5
Yr	2	13	.133	33	19	2	0	1	142^2	130	6	78	79	13.2	3.85	96	.242	.340	7	.184	-0	-3	-2	-1	-0.3
Total 8	29	48	.377	162	95	23	6	7	701^2	668	35	305	384	12.6	3.89	97	.250	.329	26	.127	-8	-3	-8	-6	-1.9
● **MARV GRISSOM** Grissom, Marvin Edward b: 3/31/18, Los Molinos, Cal. BR/TR, 6'3", 195 lbs. Deb: 9/10/46 FC																									
1946 NY-N	0	2	.000	4	3	0	0	0	18^2	17	1	13	9	14.9	4.34	79	.254	.383	1	.200	-0	-2	-2	1	-0.1
1949 Det-A	2	4	.333	27	2	0	0	0	39^1	56	6	34	17	20.8	6.41	65	.335	.450	2	.222	1	-10	-10	0	-0.9
1952 Chi-A	12	10	.545	28	24	7	1	0	166	156	6	79	97	12.9	3.74	98	.250	.337	8	.151	-1	-1	-2	-2	-0.4
1953 Bos-A	2	6	.250	13	11	1	1	0	59^1	61	5	30	31	14.0	4.70	89	.266	.354	0	.000	-3	-5	-3	-1	-0.7
NY-N	4	2	.667	21	7	3	0	0	84^1	83	6	31	46	12.3	3.95	109	.255	.321	2	.074	-2	3	3	1	0.3
1954 *NY-N★	10	7	.588	56	3	1	1	19	122^1	100	13	50	64	11.6	2.35	171	.226	.314	5	.156	-1	23	23	-0	2.2
1955 NY-N	5	4	.556	55	0	0	0	8	89^1	76	6	41	49	12.4	2.92	138	.237	.334	2	.154	-1	11	11	0	1.0
1956 NY-N	1	1	.500	43	2	0	0	7	80^2	71	3	16	49	9.8	1.56	242	.241	.282	1	.091	-0	**20**	**20**	-1	2.0
1957 NY-N	4	4	.500	55	0	0	0	14	82^2	74	6	23	51	10.8	2.61	151	.243	.301	2	.167	0	12	12	1	1.4
1958 SF-N	7	5	.583	51	0	0	0	10	65^1	71	11	26	46	14.1	3.99	95	.287	.367	0	.000	-1	-0	-1	0	-0.2
1959 StL-N	0	0	—	3	0	0	0	0	2	6	2	0	0	27.0	22.50	19	.500	.500	0	—	0	-4	-4	0	-0.4
Total 10	47	45	.511	356	52	12	3	58	810	771	65	343	459	12.7	3.41	115	.254	.335	23	.122	-7	47	47	-0	4.2
● **CONNIE GROB** Grob, Conrad George b: 11/9/32, Cross Plains, Wis. BL/TR, 6'0.5", 180 lbs. Deb: 4/22/56																									
1956 Was-A	4	5	.444	37	1	0	0	1	79^1	121	14	26	27	16.8	7.83	55	.353	.400	6	.333	2	-32	-31	1	-2.7
● **JOHNNY GRODZICKI** Grodzicki, John "Grod" b: 2/26/17, Nanticoke, Pa. BR/TR, 6'1.5", 200 lbs. Deb: 4/18/41 C																									
1941 StL-N	2	1	.667	5	1	0	0	0	13^1	6	0	11	10	11.5	1.35	279	.130	.298	0	.000	0	3	4	-0	0.4
1946 StL-N	0	0	—	3	0	0	0	0	4	4	1	4	2	18.0	9.00	38	.250	.400	0	—	0	-2	-2	0	-0.2
1947 StL-N	0	1	.000	16	0	0	0	0	23^1	21	5	19	8	15.4	5.40	77	.253	.392	0	.000	-0	-3	-3	0	-0.3
Total 3	2	2	.500	24	1	0	0	0	40^2	31	6	34	20	14.4	4.43	89	.214	.363	0	.000	0	-3	-2	0	-0.1
● **STEVE GROMEK** Gromek, Stephen Joseph b: 1/15/20, Hamtramck, Mich. BB/TR, 6'2", 180 lbs. Deb: 8/18/41																									
1941 Cle-A	1	1	.500	9	2	1	0	2	23^1	25	0	11	19	13.9	4.24	93	.266	.343	1	.167	-0	-0	-1	-1	-0.2
1942 Cle-A	2	0	1.000	14	0	0	0	0	44^1	46	2	23	14	14.0	3.65	94	.267	.354	5	.333	3	0	-1	-1	0.1
1943 Cle-A	0	0	—	3	0	0	0	0	4	6	0	0	4	13.5	9.00	35	.353	.353	2	1.000	1	-3	-3	-0	-0.2
1944 Cle-A	10	9	.526	35	21	12	2	1	203^2	160	5	70	115	10.3	2.56	129	**.219**	.290	19	.260	5	20	17	-3	2.0
1945 Cle-A†	19	9	.679	33	30	21	3	1	251	229	6	66	101	10.7	2.55	128	.243	.295	21	.231	3	23	20	-3	2.2
1946 Cle-A	5	15	.250	29	21	5	2	4	153^2	159	20	47	75	12.2	4.33	76	.264	.321	11	.196	0	-14	-18	-1	-1.8
1947 Cle-A	3	5	.375	29	7	0	0	4	84^1	77	8	36	39	12.2	3.74	93	.240	.318	7	.318	2	-0	-2	-0	-0.1
1948 *Cle-A	9	3	.750	38	9	4	1	2	130	109	10	51	50	11.5	2.84	143	.226	.307	6	.146	-1	21	18	-1	1.5
1949 Cle-A	4	6	.400	27	12	3	0	0	92	86	8	40	22	12.5	3.33	120	.250	.332	4	.167	-0	9	7	0	0.7
1950 Cle-A	10	7	.588	31	13	4	1	0	113^1	94	10	36	43	10.6	3.65	119	.226	.292	6	.158	-2	12	9	-0	0.6
1951 Cle-A	7	4	.636	27	8	4	0	1	107^1	98	6	29	40	11.0	2.77	137	.238	.295	8	.296	3	16	12	1	1.6
1952 Cle-A	7	7	.500	29	13	3	1	1	122^2	109	14	28	65	10.2	3.67	91	.232	.278	3	.100	-0	0	-4	-3	-0.7
1953 Cle-A	1	1	.500	5	1	0	0	0	11	11	0	3	8	12.3	3.27	115	.268	.333	0	.000	-0	1	1	-0	0.0
Det-A	6	8	.429	19	17	6	1	1	125^2	138	17	36	59	13.0	4.51	90	.276	.335	3	.073	-4	-7	-6	-1	-1.1
Yr	7	9	.438	24	18	6	1	1	136^2	149	17	39	67	12.9	4.41	92	.275	.333	3	.070	-5	-6	-6	-1	-1.1
1954 Det-A	18	16	.529	36	32	17	4	1	252^2	236	26	57	102	10.9	2.74	135	.246	.297	15	.190	1	28	27	-3	2.7
1955 Det-A	13	10	.565	28	25	8	2	0	181	183	26	37	73	11.4	3.98	97	.261	.307	9	.167	4	-0	-3	-2	-0.1
1956 Det-A	8	6	.571	40	13	4	0	4	141	142	25	47	64	12.6	4.28	96	.263	.332	4	.148	2	-2	-3	-2	-0.3
1957 Det-A	0	1	.000	15	1	0	0	1	23^2	32	3	13	11	17.5	6.08	63	.333	.418	0	.000	-0	-6	-6	-1	-0.7
Total 17	123	108	.532	447	225	92	17	23	2064^2	1940	186	630	904	11.5	3.41	108	.247	.309	124	.197	15	96	63	-21	6.2
● **BOB GROOM** Groom, Robert b: 9/12/1884, Belleville, Ill. d: 2/19/48, Belleville, Ill. BR/TR, 6'2", 175 lbs. Deb: 4/13/09																									
1909 Was-A	7	26	.212	44	31	17	1	0	260^2	218	2	105	131	11.6	2.87	85	.229	.314	8	.091	-5	-11	-13	4	-1.6
1910 Was-A	12	17	.414	34	30	22	3	0	257^2	244	8	77	98	11.5	2.76	90	.260	.322	11	.120	-6	-7	-8	-2	-1.6
1911 Was-A	13	17	.433	37	32	20	2	2	254^2	280	9	67	135	12.5	3.82	86	.282	.332	11	.134	-4	-13	-15	1	-1.7
1912 Was-A	24	13	.649	43	40	28	2	1	316	287	3	94	179	11.0	2.62	127	.246	.305	12	.117	-7	24	25	-2	1.7
1913 Was-A	16	16	.500	37	36	17	4	0	264^1	258	8	81	156	11.7	3.23	91	.254	.312	15	.163	1	-9	-8	2	-0.7
1914 StL-F	13	20	.394	42	34	23	1	1	280^2	281	9	75	167	11.5	3.24	104	.262	.312	15	.160	-2	-1	4	-0	0.2
1915 StL-F	11	11	.500	37	26	11	4	2	209	200	6	73	111	11.8	3.27	98	.261	.327	10	.152	-2	-6	-2	0	-0.4

YEAR	TM/L	W	L	PCT	G	GS	CG	SH	SV	IP	H	HR	BB	SO	RAT	ERA	ERA+	OAV	OOB	BH	AVG	PB	PR	/A	PD	TPI
1916	StL-A	13	9	.591	41	26	8	1	4	217^1	174	1	98	92	11.4	2.57	107	.226	.315	7	.111	-2	6	4	2	0.4
1917	StL-A	8	19	.296	38	28	11	4	3	232^2	193	3	95	82	11.3	2.94	88	.233	.315	8	.111	-4	-7	-9	-1	-1.5
1918	Cle-A	2	2	.500	14	5	0	0	0	43^1	70	0	18	8	18.5	7.06	43	.380	.438	1	.083	-1	-21	-20	0	-2.1
Total	10	119	150	.442	367	288	157	22	13	2336^1	2205	49	783	1159	11.7	3.10	95	.254	.319	98	.128	-32	-44	-41	2	-7.3

● **BUDDY GROOM** Groom, Wedsel Gary b: 7/10/65, Dallas, Tex. BL/TL, 6'2", 200 lbs. Deb: 6/18/92

YEAR	TM/L	W	L	PCT	G	GS	CG	SH	SV	IP	H	HR	BB	SO	RAT	ERA	ERA+	OAV	OOB	BH	AVG	PB	PR	/A	PD	TPI
1992	Det-A	0	5	.000	12	7	0	0	1	38^2	48	4	22	15	16.3	5.82	69	.320	.407	0	—	0	-8	-8	-0	-0.8

● **DON GROSS** Gross, Donald John b: 6/30/31, Weidman, Mich. BL/TL, 5'11", 186 lbs. Deb: 7/21/55

YEAR	TM/L	W	L	PCT	G	GS	CG	SH	SV	IP	H	HR	BB	SO	RAT	ERA	ERA+	OAV	OOB	BH	AVG	PB	PR	/A	PD	TPI
1955	Cin-N	4	5	.444	17	11	2	1	0	67^1	79	11	16	33	12.8	4.14	102	.298	.340	3	.158	-1	-1	1	0	0.0
1956	Cin-N	3	0	1.000	19	7	2	0	0	69^1	69	4	20	47	11.7	1.95	204	.257	.310	2	.105	-1	14	16	1	1.7
1957	Cin-N	7	9	.438	43	16	5	0	1	148^1	152	21	33	73	11.4	4.31	95	.264	.307	5	.109	-2	-7	-3	-0	-0.6
1958	Pit-N	5	7	.417	40	3	0	0	7	74^2	67	5	38	59	12.8	3.98	97	.241	.334	1	.056	-1	-0	-1	1	-0.1
1959	Pit-N	1	1	.500	21	0	0	0	2	33	28	3	10	15	10.6	3.55	109	.228	.291	0	.000	-0	1	1	1	0.2
1960	Pit-N	0	0	—	5	0	0	0	0	5^1	5	1	0	3	8.4	3.38	111	.238	.238	0	—	0	0	0	-0	0.0
Total	6	20	22	.476	145	37	9	1	10	398	400	45	117	230	11.8	3.73	108	.261	.316	11	.106	-5	8	14	2	1.2

● **GREG GROSS** Gross, Gregory Eugene b: 8/1/52, York, Pa. BL/TL, 5'11", 175 lbs. Deb: 9/05/73 ♦

YEAR	TM/L	W	L	PCT	G	GS	CG	SH	SV	IP	H	HR	BB	SO	RAT	ERA	ERA+	OAV	OOB	BH	AVG	PB	PR	/A	PD	TPI
1986	Phi-N	0	0	—	1	0	0	0	0	0^2	1	0	1	2	27.0	0.00	—	.333	.500	25	.248	0	0	0	0	0.0
1989	Hou-N	0	0	—	1	0	0	0	0	1	3	0	1	1	36.0	18.00	19	.500	.571	15	.200	0	-2	-2	0	-0.2
Total	2	0	0	—	2	0	0	0	0	1^2	4	0	2	3	32.4	10.80	33	.444	.545	1073	.287	0	-1	-1	0	-0.2

● **KEVIN GROSS** Gross, Kevin Frank b: 6/8/61, Downey, Cal. BR/TR, 6'5", 215 lbs. Deb: 6/25/83

YEAR	TM/L	W	L	PCT	G	GS	CG	SH	SV	IP	H	HR	BB	SO	RAT	ERA	ERA+	OAV	OOB	BH	AVG	PB	PR	/A	PD	TPI
1983	Phi-N	4	6	.400	17	17	1	1	0	96	100	13	35	66	12.9	3.56	100	.265	.333	3	.091	-1	1	0	0	0.0
1984	Phi-N	8	5	.615	44	14	1	0	1	129	140	8	44	84	13.2	4.12	88	.277	.341	2	.067	-2	-8	-7	1	-0.8
1985	Phi-N	15	13	.536	38	31	6	2	0	205^2	194	11	81	151	12.3	3.41	108	.251	.328	9	.138	0	4	6	1	0.8
1986	Phi-N	12	12	.500	37	36	7	2	0	241^2	240	28	94	154	12.7	4.02	96	.259	.333	15	.188	3	-8	-5	-1	-0.2
1987	Phi-N	9	16	.360	34	33	3	1	0	200^2	205	26	87	110	13.5	4.35	97	.267	.350	12	.190	2	-6	-2	-2	-0.2
1988	Phi-N★	12	14	.462	33	33	5	1	0	231^2	209	18	89	162	12.0	3.69	96	.239	.317	13	.173	1	-6	-3	-0	-0.3
1989	Mon-N	11	12	.478	31	31	4	3	0	201^1	188	20	88	158	12.6	4.38	81	.247	.330	9	.141	1	-20	-19	-0	-1.9
1990	Mon-N	9	12	.429	31	26	2	1	0	163^1	171	9	65	111	13.2	4.57	80	.272	.344	10	.200	4	-14	-17	-2	-1.6
1991	LA-N	10	11	.476	46	10	0	0	3	115^2	123	10	50	95	13.6	3.58	100	.275	.351	7	.280	2	1	0	-0	0.3
1992	LA-N	8	13	.381	34	30	4	3	0	204^2	182	11	77	158	11.5	3.17	109	.241	.313	6	.095	-1	8	7	-1	0.5
Total	10	98	114	.462	345	261	33	14	4	1789^2	1752	154	710	1249	12.7	3.89	95	.257	.332	86	.157	9	-48	-40	-4	-3.4

● **KIP GROSS** Gross, Kip Lee b: 8/24/64, Scottsbluff, Neb. BR/TR, 6'2", 195 lbs. Deb: 4/21/90

YEAR	TM/L	W	L	PCT	G	GS	CG	SH	SV	IP	H	HR	BB	SO	RAT	ERA	ERA+	OAV	OOB	BH	AVG	PB	PR	/A	PD	TPI
1990	Cin-N	0	0	—	5	0	0	0	0	6^1	6	0	2	3	11.4	4.26	93	.273	.333	0	—	0	-0	-0	0	0.0
1991	Cin-N	6	4	.600	29	9	1	0	0	85^2	93	8	40	40	14.0	3.47	110	.279	.357	2	.091	-1	2	3	0	0.2
1992	LA-N	1	1	.500	16	1	0	0	0	23^2	32	1	10	14	16.0	4.18	83	.323	.385	2	1.000	1	-2	-2	1	0.0
Total	3	7	5	.583	50	10	1	0	0	115^2	131	9	52	57	14.2	3.66	102	.289	.362	4	.167	-0	-0	1	1	0.2

● **WAYNE GROSS** Gross, Wayne Dale b: 1/14/52, Riverside, Cal. BL/TR, 6'2", 210 lbs. Deb: 8/21/76 ♦

YEAR	TM/L	W	L	PCT	G	GS	CG	SH	SV	IP	H	HR	BB	SO	RAT	ERA	ERA+	OAV	OOB	BH	AVG	PB	PR	/A	PD	TPI
1983	Oak-A	0	0	—	1	0	0	0	0	2^1	2	0	1	0	15.4	0.00	—	.222	.364	79	.233	1	1	1	-0	0.1

● **HARLEY GROSSMAN** Grossman, Harley Joseph b: 5/5/30, Evansville, Ind. BR/TR, 6', 170 lbs. Deb: 4/22/52

YEAR	TM/L	W	L	PCT	G	GS	CG	SH	SV	IP	H	HR	BB	SO	RAT	ERA	ERA+	OAV	OOB	BH	AVG	PB	PR	/A	PD	TPI
1952	Was-A	0	0	—	1	0	0	0	0	0^1	2	1	0	0	54.0	54.00	7	.667	.667	0	—	0	-2	-2	0	-0.2

● **ERNIE GROTH** Groth, Ernest John "Dango" b: 12/24/1884, Cedarsburg, Wis. d: 5/23/50, Milwaukee, Wis. BR/TR, 5'11", 175 lbs. Deb: 9/06/04

YEAR	TM/L	W	L	PCT	G	GS	CG	SH	SV	IP	H	HR	BB	SO	RAT	ERA	ERA+	OAV	OOB	BH	AVG	PB	PR	/A	PD	TPI
1904	Chi-N	0	2	.000	3	2	2	0	1	16	22	1	6	9	16.3	5.63	47	.310	.372	0	.000	-1	-5	-5	-0	-0.6

● **ERNEST GROTH** Groth, Ernest William b: 5/3/22, Beaver Falls, Pa. BR/TR, 5'9", 185 lbs. Deb: 9/11/47

YEAR	TM/L	W	L	PCT	G	GS	CG	SH	SV	IP	H	HR	BB	SO	RAT	ERA	ERA+	OAV	OOB	BH	AVG	PB	PR	/A	PD	TPI
1947	Cle-A	0	0	—	2	0	0	0	0	1^1	0	0	1	1	6.8	0.00	—	.000	.250	0	—	0	1	1	0	0.1
1948	Cle-A	0	0	—	1	0	0	0	0	1	1	0	2	0	27.0	9.00	45	.250	.500	0	—	0	-1	-1	-0	-0.1
1949	Chi-A	0	1	.000	3	0	0	0	0	5	2	2	3	1	10.8	5.40	77	.125	.300	0	—	0	-1	-1	-0	-0.1
Total	3	0	1	.000	6	0	0	0	0	7^1	3	2	6	2	12.3	4.91	82	.130	.333	0	—	0	-1	-1	-0	-0.1

● **ORVAL GROVE** Grove, Orval Leroy b: 8/29/19, Mineral, Kan. d: 4/20/92, Carmichael, Cal. BR/TR, 6'3", 196 lbs. Deb: 5/28/40

YEAR	TM/L	W	L	PCT	G	GS	CG	SH	SV	IP	H	HR	BB	SO	RAT	ERA	ERA+	OAV	OOB	BH	AVG	PB	PR	/A	PD	TPI
1940	Chi-A	0	0	—	3	0	0	0	0	6	4	0	4	1	12.0	3.00	147	.182	.308	0	.000	-0	1	1	-0	0.1
1941	Chi-A	0	0	—	2	0	0	0	0	7	9	2	5	5	18.0	10.29	40	.321	.424	0	.000	-0	-5	-5	0	-0.4
1942	Chi-A	4	6	.400	12	8	4	0	0	66^1	77	1	33	21	15.1	5.16	70	.283	.363	5	.227	1	-11	-11	1	-0.9
1943	Chi-A	15	9	.625	32	25	18	3	2	216^1	192	9	72	76	11.1	2.75	122	.239	.304	12	.182	2	13	14	1	1.9
1944	Chi-A☆	14	15	.483	34	33	11	2	0	234^2	237	11	71	105	12.1	3.72	92	.263	.322	8	.104	-3	-8	-8	4	-0.8
1945	Chi-A	14	12	.538	33	30	16	4	1	217	233	12	68	54	12.7	3.44	96	.273	.330	7	.099	-4	-2	-3	2	-0.5
1946	Chi-A	8	13	.381	33	26	10	1	0	205^1	213	10	78	60	12.9	3.02	113	.272	.340	7	.108	-2	11	9	2	0.8
1947	Chi-A	6	8	.429	25	19	6	1	0	135^2	158	10	70	33	15.4	4.44	82	.296	.382	7	.146	-0	-11	-12	-1	-1.3
1948	Chi-A	2	10	.167	32	11	1	0	1	87^2	110	6	42	18	15.9	6.16	69	.315	.393	2	.095	-2	-18	-19	2	-1.7
1949	Chi-A	0	0	—	1	0	0	0	0	0^2	4	1	1	1	81.0	54.00	8	.667	.750	0	—	0	-4	-4	0	-0.3
Total	10	63	73	.463	207	152	66	11	4	1176^2	1237	62	444	374	13.1	3.78	93	.272	.340	48	.129	-9	-33	-37	10	-3.1

● **LEFTY GROVE** Grove, Robert Moses b: 3/6/1900, Lonaconing, Md. d: 5/22/75, Norwalk, Ohio BL/TL, 6'3", 190 lbs. Deb: 4/14/25 H

YEAR	TM/L	W	L	PCT	G	GS	CG	SH	SV	IP	H	HR	BB	SO	RAT	ERA	ERA+	OAV	OOB	BH	AVG	PB	PR	/A	PD	TPI
1925	Phi-A	10	12	.455	45	18	5	0	1	197	207	11	131	**116**	15.7	4.75	98	.278	.390	8	.123	-6	-8	-2	2	-0.6
1926	Phi-A	13	13	.500	45	33	20	1	6	258	227	6	101	**194**	11.7	**2.51**	**166**	.244	.322	8	.099	-5	**43**	**48**	-1	4.2
1927	Phi-A	20	13	.606	51	28	14	1	9	262^1	251	6	79	**174**	11.4	3.19	134	.252	.309	10	.125	-3	28	31	-1	2.7
1928	Phi-A	**24**	8	.750	39	31	24	4	4	261^2	228	10	64	**183**	10.1	2.58	156	.229	.277	15	.170	1	**43**	**42**	-3	**4.0**
1929	*Phi-A	20	6	**.769**	42	37	19	2	4	275^1	278	8	81	**170**	11.8	**2.81**	**151**	.262	.316	22	.216	1	**44**	**43**	-3	**4.0**
1930	*Phi-A	**28**	5	**.848**	**50**	32	22	2	**9**	291	273	8	60	**209**	**10.5**	**2.54**	**184**	**.247**	**.288**	22	.200	0	**68**	**69**	0	**6.6**
1931	*Phi-A	**31**	4	**.886**	41	30	**27**	**4**	5	288^2	249	10	62	**175**	**9.7**	**2.06**	**218**	.229	**.271**	23	.200	-2	**74**	**78**	-2	**7.5**
1932	Phi-A	25	10	.714	44	30	**27**	**4**	7	291^2	269	13	79	188	**10.8**	**2.84**	**159**	.241	**.292**	18	.168	0	**53**	**55**	-2	**5.1**
1933	Phi-A★	**24**	8	**.750**	45	28	**21**	2	6	275^1	280	12	83	114	12.0	3.20	134	.261	.316	9	.086	-7	33	33	0	2.6
1934	Bos-A	8	8	.500	22	12	5	0	0	109^1	149	5	32	43	15.0	6.50	74	.320	.365	6	.162	-0	-24	-21	-1	-1.9
1935	Bos-A☆	20	12	.625	35	30	23	2	1	273	269	6	65	121	**11.1**	**2.70**	**176**	.257	.302	7	.079	-6	**53**	**62**	2	5.9
1936	Bos-A★	17	12	.586	35	30	22	**6**	2	253^1	237	14	65	130	**10.9**	**2.81**	**189**	.246	**.297**	11	.138	-3	**63**	**71**	0	**6.6**
1937	Bos-A☆	17	9	.654	32	32	21	3	0	262	269	9	83	153	12.1	3.02	157	.261	.317	13	.143	-3	46	50	-1	4.6
1938	Bos-A★	14	4	.778	24	21	12	1	1	163^2	169	8	52	99	12.2	**3.08**	**160**	.263	.319	8	.148	-1	31	34	-0	3.1
1939	Bos-A☆	15	4	**.789**	23	23	17	2	0	191	180	8	58	81	11.3	**2.54**	**186**	.249	.305	9	.134	-1	44	46	-3	4.2
1940	Bos-A	7	6	.538	22	21	9	1	0	153^1	159	20	50	62	12.3	3.99	113	.269	.328	8	.151	-1	7	9	0	0.7
1941	Bos-A	7	7	.500	21	21	10	0	0	134	155	8	42	54	13.4	4.37	95	.287	.340	5	.111	-1	-3	-3	-2	-0.6
Total	17	300	141	.680	616	457	298	35	55	3940^2	3849	162	1187	2266	11.6	3.06	148	.255	.311	202	.148	-38	595	643	-15	58.7

● **CHARLIE GROVER** Grover, Charles Burt "Bugs" (Born Charles Byrd Grover)
b: 6/20/1890, Huntington Township, Ohio d: 5/24/71, Emmett, Mich. BL/TR, 6'1.5", 185 lbs. Deb: 9/09/13

YEAR	TM/L	W	L	PCT	G	GS	CG	SH	SV	IP	H	HR	BB	SO	RAT	ERA	ERA+	OAV	OOB	BH	AVG	PB	PR	/A	PD	TPI
1913	Det-A	0	0	—	2	1	0	0	0	10^2	9	0	7	2	13.5	3.38	86	.265	.390	0	.000	-0	-1	-1	0	-0.1

● **TOM GRUBBS** Grubbs, Thomas Dillard "Judge" b: 2/22/1894, Mt.Sterling, Ky. d: 1/28/86, Mt.Sterling, Ky. BR/TR, 6'2", 165 lbs. Deb: 10/03/20

YEAR	TM/L	W	L	PCT	G	GS	CG	SH	SV	IP	H	HR	BB	SO	RAT	ERA	ERA+	OAV	OOB	BH	AVG	PB	PR	/A	PD	TPI
1920	NY-N	0	1	.000	1	1	0	0	0	5	9	0	0	0	16.2	7.20	42	.409	.409	0	.000	-0	-2	-2	-0	-0.3

YEAR	TM/L	W	L	PCT	G	GS	CG	SH	SV	IP	H	HR	BB	SO	RAT	ERA	ERA+	OAV	OOB	BH	AVG	PB	PR	/A	PD	TPI
● **HENRY GRUBER** Gruber, Henry John b: 12/14/1863, Hamden, Conn. d: 9/26/32, New Haven, Conn. BR/TR, Deb: 7/28/1887																										
1887	Det-N	4	3	.571	7	7	7	0	0	62^{1}	63	3	21	12	12.1	2.74	148	.262	.322	4	.167	1	9	9	-1	0.7
1888	Det-N	11	14	.440	27	25	25	3	0	240	196	8	41	71	9.0	2.29	121	.213	.249	13	.141	-1	15	13	1	1.2
1889	Cle-N	7	16	.304	25	23	23	0	1	205	198	6	94	74	13.2	3.64	111	.246	.331	7	.101	-2	8	9	-0	0.7
1890	Cle-P	22	23	.489	48	44	39	1	0	383^{1}	464	15	204	110	16.0	4.27	93	.287	.372	36	.221	6	-2	-13	1	-0.4
1891	Cle-N	17	22	.436	44	40	35	1	0	348^{2}	407	10	119	79	13.8	4.13	84	.281	.338	23	.163	1	-30	-26	2	-2.0
Total	5	61	78	.439	151	139	129	5	1	1239^{1}	1328	42	479	346	13.4	3.67	99	.264	.332	83	.170	4	1	-7	3	0.2
● **AL GRUNWALD** Grunwald, Alfred Henry "Stretch" b: 2/13/30, Los Angeles, Cal. BL/TL, 6'4", 210 lbs. Deb: 4/18/55																										
1955	Pit-N	0	0	—	3	0	0	0	0	7^{2}	7	1	7	2	16.4	4.70	88	.241	.389	2	.500	1	-1	-0	-0	0.0
1959	KC-A	0	1	.000	6	1	0	0	1	11^{1}	18	1	11	9	23.0	7.94	50	.360	.475	0	.000	-1	-5	-5	0	-0.5
Total	2	0	1	.000	9	1	0	0	1	19	25	2	18	11	20.4	6.63	61	.316	.443	2	.250	0	-6	-5	-0	-0.5
● **JOE GRZENDA** Grzenda, Joseph Charles b: 6/8/37, Scranton, Pa. BR/TL, 6'2", 180 lbs. Deb: 4/26/61																										
1961	Det-A	1	0	1.000	4	0	0	0	0	5^{2}	9	2	2	0	17.5	7.94	52	.375	.423	1	1.000	0	-2	-2	0	-0.2
1964	KC-A	0	2	.000	20	0	0	0	0	25	34	2	13	17	17.3	5.40	71	.324	.403	0	.000	-0	-5	-4	1	-0.4
1966	KC-A	0	2	.000	21	0	0	0	0	22	28	1	12	14	16.4	3.27	104	.337	.421	0	.000	-0	0	0	1	0.1
1967	NY-N	0	0	—	11	0	0	0	0	16^{2}	14	0	8	9	12.4	2.16	157	.237	.338	0	.000	-0	2	2	-1	0.2
1969	*Min-A	4	1	.800	38	0	0	0	3	48^{2}	52	4	17	24	12.9	3.88	94	.281	.345	0	.000	0	-1	-1	1	0.0
1970	Was-A	3	6	.333	49	3	0	0	6	84^{2}	86	8	34	38	13.1	5.00	71	.267	.343	0	.000	-1	-12	-14	0	-1.5
1971	Was-A	5	2	.714	46	0	0	0	5	70^{1}	54	2	17	56	9.2	1.92	172	.217	.270	1	.143	-0	12	11	-0	1.1
1972	StL-N	1	0	1.000	30	0	0	0	0	35	46	1	17	15	17.0	5.66	60	.326	.410	0	.000	-0	-9	-9	0	-0.9
Total	8	14	13	.519	219	3	0	0	14	308	323	20	120	173	13.2	4.00	88	.277	.349	2	.067	-2	-15	-17	3	-1.6
● **CECILIO GUANTE** Guante, Cecilio (Magallane) b: 2/1/60, Villa Mella, D.R. BR/TR, 6'3", 205 lbs. Deb: 5/01/82																										
1982	Pit-N	0	0	—	10	0	0	0	0	27	28	1	5	26	11.7	3.33	111	.264	.310	0	.000	-1	1	1	-0	0.0
1983	Pit-N	2	6	.250	49	0	0	0	9	100^{1}	90	5	46	82	12.4	3.32	112	.241	.327	2	.091	-1	3	4	-1	0.3
1984	Pit-N	2	3	.400	27	0	0	0	2	41^{1}	32	3	16	30	10.9	2.61	138	.224	.311	0	.000	-0	4	5	-1	0.4
1985	Pit-N	4	6	.400	63	0	0	0	5	109	84	5	40	92	10.7	2.72	131	.214	.295	1	.059	-1	10	10	-1	0.9
1986	Pit-N	5	2	.714	52	0	0	0	4	78	65	11	29	63	11.2	3.35	115	.225	.302	0	.000	-0	3	4	-2	0.3
1987	NY-A	3	2	.600	23	0	0	0	1	44	42	8	20	46	12.9	5.73	77	.247	.330	0	—	0	-6	-7	-1	-0.6
1988	NY-A	5	6	.455	56	0	0	0	11	75	59	10	22	61	10.3	2.88	137	.213	.283	0	—	0	9	9	-2	0.8
	Tex-A	0	0	—	7	0	0	0	1	4^{2}	8	1	4	4	23.1	1.93	212	.400	.500	0	—	0	1	1	-0	-0.1
	Yr	5	6	.455	63	0	0	0	12	79^{2}	67	11	26	65	10.5	2.82	140	.221	.283	0	—	0	10	10	-2	0.7
1989	Tex-A	6	6	.500	50	0	0	0	2	69	66	7	36	69	13.8	3.91	101	.249	.348	0	—	0	-0	0	-1	-0.1
1990	Cle-A	2	3	.400	26	1	0	0	0	46^{2}	38	10	18	30	11.4	5.01	78	.220	.304	0	—	0	-6	-6	0	-0.5
Total	9	29	34	.460	363	1	0	0	35	595	512	61	236	503	11.7	3.48	110	.232	.313	3	.061	-3	20	23	-8	1.4
● **MARK GUBICZA** Gubicza, Mark Steven b: 8/14/62, Philadelphia, Pa. BR/TR, 6'6", 215 lbs. Deb: 4/06/84																										
1984	KC-A	10	14	.417	29	29	4	2	0	189	172	13	75	111	12.0	4.05	99	.243	.320	0	—	0	-1	-0	2	0.1
1985	*KC-A	14	10	.583	29	28	0	0	0	177^{1}	160	14	77	99	12.3	4.06	102	.238	.321	0	—	0	2	2	2	0.4
1986	KC-A	12	6	.667	35	24	3	2	0	180^{2}	155	8	84	118	12.2	3.64	117	.233	.324	0	—	0	11	12	3	1.5
1987	KC-A	13	18	.419	35	35	10	2	0	241^{2}	231	18	120	166	13.3	3.98	114	.259	.350	0	—	0	13	15	4	1.7
1988	KC-A★	20	8	.714	35	35	8	4	0	269^{2}	237	11	83	183	10.9	2.70	147	.234	.296	0	—	0	38	38	3	**4.5**
1989	KC-A★	15	11	.577	36	36	8	2	0	255	252	10	63	173	11.3	3.04	127	.259	.307	0	—	0	24	23	2	2.7
1990	KC-A	4	7	.364	16	16	2	0	0	94	101	5	38	71	13.7	4.50	85	.283	.358	0	—	0	-6	-7	0	-0.6
1991	KC-A	9	12	.429	26	26	0	0	0	133	168	10	42	89	14.6	5.68	72	.308	.364	0	—	0	-23	-23	2	-2.0
1992	KC-A	7	6	.538	18	18	2	1	0	111^{1}	110	8	36	81	11.9	3.72	107	.259	.318	0	—	0	3	3	0	0.3
Total	9	104	92	.531	259	247	37	13	0	1651^{2}	1586	97	618	1091	12.2	3.75	109	.254	.325	0	—	0	59	63	19	8.6
● **MARV GUDAT** Gudat, Marvin John b: 8/27/05, Goliad, Tex. d: 3/1/54, Los Angeles, Cal. BL/TL, 5'11", 162 lbs. Deb: 5/21/29 ♦																										
1929	Cin-N	1	1	.500	7	2	2	0	0	26^{2}	29	0	4	0	11.1	3.38	135	.282	.308	2	.200	-0	4	4	-1	0.2
1932	*Chi-N	0	0	—	1	0	0	0	0	1	1	0	0	2	9.0	0.00	—	.250	.250	24	.255	0	0	0	0	0.0
Total	2	1	1	.500	8	2	2	0	0	27^{2}	30	0	4	2	11.1	3.25	139	.280	.306	26	.250	-0	4	4	-1	0.2
● **LEE GUETTERMAN** Guetterman, Arthur Lee b: 11/22/58, Chattanooga, Tenn. BL/TL, 6'8", 225 lbs. Deb: 9/12/84																										
1984	Sea-A	0	0	—	3	0	0	0	0	4^{1}	9	0	2	2	22.8	4.15	96	.450	.500	0	—	0	-0	-0	0	0.0
1986	Sea-A	0	4	.000	41	4	1	0	0	76	108	7	30	38	16.8	7.34	58	.347	.412	0	—	0	-27	-26	0	-2.5
1987	Sea-A	11	4	.733	25	17	2	1	0	113^{1}	117	13	35	42	12.2	3.81	124	.267	.324	0	—	0	8	11	1	1.0
1988	NY-A	1	2	.333	20	2	0	0	0	40^{2}	49	2	14	15	14.2	4.65	85	.306	.366	0	—	0	-3	-3	-0	-0.3
1989	NY-A	5	5	.500	70	0	0	0	13	103	98	6	26	51	10.8	2.45	158	.258	.305	0	—	0	16	16	2	1.9
1990	NY-A	11	7	.611	64	0	0	0	2	93	80	6	26	48	10.3	3.39	117	.236	.290	0	—	0	5	6	1	0.7
1991	NY-A	3	4	.429	64	0	0	0	6	88	91	6	25	35	12.2	3.68	112	.268	.323	0	—	0	4	4	0	0.4
1992	NY-A	1	1	.500	15	0	0	0	0	22^{2}	35	5	13	5	19.1	9.53	42	.354	.429	0	—	0	-14	-14	0	-1.4
	NY-N	3	4	.429	43	0	0	0	2	43^{1}	57	5	14	15	15.0	5.82	60	.324	.377	0	.000	-0	-11	-11	-1	-1.3
Total	8	35	31	.530	345	23	3	1	23	584^{1}	644	50	185	251	12.9	4.37	94	.284	.341	0	.000	-0	-21	-17	4	-1.5
● **WHITEY GUESE** Guese, Theodore b: 1/24/1872, New Bremen, Ohio d: 4/8/51, Wapakoneta, Ohio BR/TR, 6'0.5", 200 lbs. Deb: 7/13/01																										
1901	Cin-N	1	4	.200	6	5	4	0	0	44^{1}	62	5	14	11	16.0	6.09	53	.328	.383	3	.200	1	-14	-14	-2	-1.3
● **RON GUIDRY** Guidry, Ronald Ames b: 8/28/50, Lafayette, La. BL/TL, 5'11", 162 lbs. Deb: 7/27/75																										
1975	NY-A	0	1	.000	10	1	0	0	0	15^{2}	15	0	9	15	14.4	3.45	106	.259	.368	0	—	0	1	0	-1	0.1
1976	*NY-A	0	0	—	7	0	0	0	0	16	20	1	4	12	13.5	5.63	61	.294	.333	0	—	0	-4	-4	0	-0.3
1977	*NY-A	16	7	.696	31	25	9	5	1	210^{2}	174	12	65	176	10.2	2.82	140	.224	.284	0	—	0	29	26	-1	2.7
1978	*NY-A★	**25**	3	**.893**	35	35	16	**9**	0	273^{2}	187	13	72	248	**8.6**	**1.74**	**208**	**.193**	**.250**	0	—	0	**61**	**57**	2	**6.8**
1979	NY-A★	18	8	.692	33	30	15	2	2	236^{1}	203	20	71	201	10.4	**2.78**	146	.236	.294	0	—	0	38	34	-0	3.5
1980	*NY-A	17	10	.630	37	29	5	3	1	219^{2}	215	19	80	166	12.1	3.56	110	.260	.326	0	—	0	11	9	2	1.2
1981	*NY-A	11	5	.688	23	21	0	0	0	127	100	12	26	104	**9.0**	2.76	129	.214	**.257**	0	—	0	13	11	1	1.3
1982	NY-A☆	14	8	.636	34	33	6	1	0	222	216	22	69	162	11.6	3.81	105	.254	.311	0	—	0	6	4	-2	0.3
1983	NY-A†	21	9	.700	31	31	**21**	3	0	250^{1}	232	26	60	156	10.6	3.42	114	.244	.291	0	—	0	18	13	-0	1.3
1984	NY-A	10	11	.476	29	28	5	1	0	195^{2}	223	24	44	127	12.4	4.51	84	.287	.327	0	—	0	-11	-16	-0	-1.6
1985	NY-A	**22**	6	**.786**	34	33	11	2	0	259	243	28	42	143	9.9	3.27	122	.248	.279	0	—	0	25	21	-1	2.0
1986	NY-A	9	12	.429	30	30	5	0	0	192^{1}	202	28	38	140	11.3	3.98	103	.265	.301	0	—	0	4	2	-1	0.1
1987	NY-A	5	8	.385	22	17	2	0	0	117^{2}	111	14	38	96	11.5	3.67	119	.248	.308	0	—	0	10	9	-0	0.9
1988	NY-A	2	3	.400	12	10	0	0	0	56	57	7	15	32	11.9	4.18	94	.259	.312	0	—	0	-1	-1	-1	-0.2
Total	14	170	91	.651	368	323	95	26	4	2392	2198	226	633	1778	10.7	3.29	119	.244	.294	0	—	0	201	167	-3	18.1
● **SKIP GUINN** Guinn, Drannon Eugene b: 10/25/44, St.Charles, Mo. BR/TL, 5'10", 180 lbs. Deb: 5/07/68																										
1968	Atl-N	0	0	—	3	0	0	0	0	5	3	0	3	4	10.8	3.60	83	.167	.286	0	—	0	-0	-0	-0	-0.1
1969	Hou-N	1	2	.333	28	0	0	0	0	27	34	3	21	33	18.7	6.67	53	.304	.418	0	.000	-0	-9	-9	-0	-1.0
1971	Hou-N	0	0	—	4	0	0	0	1	4^{2}	1	0	3	3	7.7	0.00	—	.067	.222	0	—	0	2	2	-0	0.2
Total	3	1	2	.333	35	0	0	0	1	36^{2}	38	3	27	40	16.2	5.40	64	.262	.382	0	.000	-0	-8	-8	-0	-0.9
● **LEFTY GUISE** Guise, Witt Orison b: 9/18/09, Driggs, Ark. d: 8/13/68, Little Rock, Ark. BL/TL, 6'2", 172 lbs. Deb: 9/13/40																										
1940	Cin-N	0	0	—	2	0	0	0	0	7^{2}	8	0	5	1	16.4	1.17	323	.296	.424	1	.333	0	2	2	0	0.3

YEAR	TM/L	W	L	PCT	G	GS	CG	SH	SV	IP	H	HR	BB	SO	RAT	ERA	ERA+	OAV	OOB	BH	AVG	PB	PR	/A	PD	TPI
● DON GULLETT Gullett, Donald Edward b: 1/6/51, Lynn, Ky. BR/TL, 6', 190 lbs. Deb: 4/10/70																										
1970	*Cin-N	5	2	.714	44	2	0	0	6	77^2	54	4	44	76	11.4	2.43	166	.196	.306	4	.211	1	14	14	-1	1.4
1971	Cin-N	16	6	**.727**	35	31	4	3	0	217^2	196	14	64	107	10.8	2.65	127	.242	.299	9	.120	-2	20	17	-2	1.4
1972	*Cin-N	9	10	.474	31	16	2	0	2	134^2	127	15	43	96	11.4	3.94	81	.250	.309	8	.211	2	-7	-11	-2	-1.2
1973	*Cin-N	18	8	.692	45	30	7	4	2	228^1	198	24	69	153	10.6	3.51	97	.232	.292	12	.188	3	4	-3	-0	0.0
1974	Cin-N	17	11	.607	36	35	10	3	0	243	201	22	88	183	10.8	3.04	115	.222	.292	19	.237	4	16	12	-0	1.6
1975	*Cin-N	15	4	**.789**	22	22	8	3	0	159^2	127	11	56	98	10.4	2.42	148	.218	.289	14	.226	3	21	21	-1	2.5
1976	*Cin-N	11	3	.786	23	20	4	0	1	126	119	8	48	64	11.9	3.00	117	.253	.322	8	.182	-0	7	7	-0	0.7
1977	*NY-A	14	4	.778	22	22	7	1	0	158^1	137	14	69	116	11.8	3.58	110	.232	.314	0	—	0	8	6	-2	0.5
1978	NY-A	4	2	.667	8	8	2	0	0	44^2	46	3	20	28	13.5	3.63	100	.269	.349	0	—	0	1	-0	0	0.0
Total	9	109	50	.686	266	186	44	14	11	1390	1205	115	501	921	11.1	3.11	113	.233	.302	74	.194	10	83	63	-8	6.9
● BILL GULLICKSON Gullickson, William Lee b: 2/20/59, Marshall, Minn. BR/TR, 6'3", 215 lbs. Deb: 9/26/79																										
1979	Mon-N	0	0	—	1	0	0	0	0	1	2	0	0	0	18.0	0.00	—	.500	.500	0	—	0	0	0	0	0.0
1980	Mon-N	10	5	.667	24	19	5	2	0	141	127	6	50	120	11.4	3.00	119	.238	.305	7	.175	0	9	9	0	1.0
1981	*Mon-N	7	9	.438	22	22	3	2	0	157^1	142	3	34	115	10.3	2.80	125	.239	.284	7	.152	0	12	12	-1	1.2
1982	Mon-N	12	14	.462	34	34	6	0	0	236^2	231	25	61	155	11.3	3.57	102	.254	.304	10	.122	-2	1	2	-4	-0.4
1983	Mon-N	17	12	.586	34	34	10	1	0	242^1	230	19	59	120	10.9	3.75	96	.251	.299	11	.134	1	-3	-4	-1	-0.5
1984	Mon-N	12	9	.571	32	32	3	0	0	226^2	230	27	37	100	10.6	3.61	95	.265	.295	8	.110	-2	-1	-5	-4	-1.1
1985	Mon-N	14	12	.538	29	29	4	1	0	181^1	187	8	47	68	11.7	3.52	96	.271	.318	12	.188	2	1	-3	-1	-0.2
1986	Cin-N	15	12	.556	37	37	6	2	0	244^2	245	24	60	121	11.3	3.38	114	.264	.310	6	.076	-4	9	13	-2	0.7
1987	Cin-N	10	11	.476	27	27	3	1	0	165	172	33	39	89	11.6	4.85	87	.267	.310	11	.208	2	-14	-11	-2	-1.1
	NY-A	4	2	.667	8	8	1	0	0	48	46	7	11	28	10.9	4.88	90	.253	.299	0	—	0	-2	-3	-1	-0.2
1990	Hou-N	10	14	.417	32	32	2	1	0	193^1	221	21	61	73	13.2	3.82	97	.287	.341	9	.158	2	-1	-2	-3	-0.4
1991	Det-A	**20**	9	.690	35	35	4	0	0	226^1	256	22	44	91	12.1	3.90	107	.288	.324	0	—	0	5	6	-3	0.4
1992	Det-A	14	13	.519	34	34	4	1	0	221^2	228	35	50	64	11.3	4.34	92	.267	.308	0	—	0	-10	-9	-0	-0.9
Total	12	145	122	.543	349	343	51	11	0	2285^1	2317	230	553	1144	11.4	3.73	101	.264	.309	81	.141	-1	7	5	-21	-1.5
● AD GUMBERT Gumbert, Addison Courtney b: 10/10/1868, Pittsburgh, Pa. d: 4/23/25, Pittsburgh, Pa. BR/TR, 5'10", 200 lbs. Deb: 9/15/1888 F																										
1888	Chi-N	3	3	.500	6	6	5	0	0	48^2	44	0	10	16	10.9	3.14	96	.234	.291	8	.333	2	-2	-1	-1	0.1
1889	Chi-N	16	13	.552	31	28	25	2	0	246^1	258	16	76	91	12.7	3.62	115	.261	.323	44	.288	11	11	15	-1	2.2
1890	Bos-P	23	12	.657	39	33	27	1	0	277^1	338	18	86	81	14.1	3.96	111	.288	.342	35	.241	5	8	14	2	1.6
1891	Chi-N	17	11	.607	32	31	24	1	0	256^1	282	5	90	73	13.4	3.58	93	.269	.333	32	.305	11	-7	-7	1	0.6
1892	Chi-N	22	19	.537	46	45	39	0	0	382^2	399	11	107	118	12.2	3.41	97	.258	.312	42	.236	4	-5	-4	1	0.1
1893	Pit-N	11	7	.611	22	20	16	2	0	162^2	207	5	78	40	16.0	5.15	88	.301	.376	21	.221	1	-9	-11	-2	-0.9
1894	Pit-N	15	14	.517	37	31	26	0	0	269	372	13	84	65	15.5	6.02	87	.324	.374	33	.292	5	-21	-23	1	-1.4
1895	Bro-N	11	16	.407	33	26	20	0	1	234	288	11	69	45	14.2	5.08	87	.298	.352	35	.361	10	-8	-18	-1	-0.6
1896	Bro-N	0	4	.000	5	4	2	0	0	31	34	2	11	3	13.1	3.77	109	.276	.336	2	.182	-0	2	1	1	0.2
	Phi-N	5	3	.625	11	10	7	1	0	77^1	99	0	23	14	14.7	4.54	95	.308	.362	9	.265	1	-2	-2	-1	-0.1
	Yr	5	7	.417	16	14	9	1	0	108^1	133	2	34	17	14.2	4.32	99	.300	.355	11	.244	1	1	-1	0	0.1
Total	9	123	102	.547	262	234	191	7	1	1985^1	2321	81	634	546	13.8	4.27	97	.283	.341	261	.273	50	-31	-33	1	1.8
● HARRY GUMBERT Gumbert, Harry Edward "Gunboat" b: 11/5/09, Elizabeth, Pa. BR/TR, 6'2", 185 lbs. Deb: 9/12/35																										
1935	NY-N	1	2	.333	6	3	1	0	0	23^2	35	1	10	11	17.1	6.08	63	.330	.388	0	.000	-1	-5	-6	-0	-0.7
1936	*NY-N	11	3	.786	39	15	3	0	0	140^2	157	7	54	52	13.6	3.90	100	.281	.346	11	.250	2	2	-0	3	0.5
1937	*NY-N	10	11	.476	34	24	10	1	1	200^1	194	11	62	65	11.7	3.68	106	.257	.317	13	.181	-1	5	5	8	1.1
1938	NY-N	15	13	.536	38	33	14	1	0	235^2	238	13	84	84	12.6	4.01	94	.261	.328	13	.155	-3	-6	-6	8	-0.2
1939	NY-N	18	11	.621	36	34	14	2	0	243^2	257	21	81	81	12.5	4.32	91	.271	.329	18	.200	-0	-11	-11	6	-0.5
1940	NY-N	12	14	.462	35	30	14	2	2	237	230	17	81	77	11.9	3.76	103	.252	.316	17	.195	2	2	3	4	0.9
1941	NY-N	1	1	.500	5	5	1	0	0	32^1	34	3	18	9	14.5	4.45	83	.266	.356	2	.167	-0	-3	-3	1	-0.2
	StL-N	11	5	.688	33	17	8	3	1	144^1	139	7	30	53	10.6	2.74	137	.251	.291	17	.321	6	14	16	4	2.7
	Yr	12	6	.667	38	22	9	3	1	176^2	173	10	48	62	11.3	3.06	123	.254	.304	19	.292	5	11	14	4	2.5
1942	*StL-N	9	5	.643	38	19	5	0	5	163	156	3	59	52	11.9	3.26	105	.250	.315	6	.111	-3	1	3	5	0.5
1943	StL-N	10	5	.667	21	19	7	3	0	133	115	4	32	40	9.9	2.84	118	.237	.284	7	.156	-2	8	8	2	0.8
1944	StL-N	4	2	.667	10	7	3	0	1	61^1	60	1	19	16	11.6	2.49	141	.258	.313	4	.190	-0	8	7	1	0.8
	Cin-N	10	8	.556	24	19	11	2	2	155^1	157	7	40	40	11.5	3.30	106	.262	.310	5	.096	-2	5	3	2	0.4
	Yr	14	10	.583	34	26	14	2	3	216^2	217	8	59	56	11.5	3.07	114	.261	.311	9	.123	-2	13	10	3	1.2
1946	Cin-N	6	8	.429	36	10	5	0	4	119	112	8	42	44	11.7	3.25	103	.248	.314	8	.250	1	2	1	1	0.3
1947	Cin-N	10	10	.500	46	0	0	0	10	90^1	88	3	47	43	13.5	3.89	106	.260	.351	6	.273	1	2	2	0	0.3
1948	Cin-N	10	8	.556	**61**	0	0	0	**17**	106^1	123	5	34	25	13.3	3.47	113	.291	.344	1	.040	-1	6	5	4	0.8
1949	Cin-N	4	3	.571	29	0	0	0	2	40^2	58	5	8	12	14.8	5.53	76	.341	.374	0	.000	-0	-7	-6	1	-0.5
	Pit-N	1	4	.200	16	0	0	0	3	27^2	30	5	18	5	15.6	5.86	72	.270	.372	1	.250	0	-6	-5	1	-0.4
	Yr	5	7	.417	45	0	0	0	5	68^1	88	10	26	17	15.0	5.66	74	.312	.370	1	.167	-0	-12	-11	2	-0.9
1950	Pit-N	0	0	—	1	0	0	0	0	1^2	3	0	2	0	27.0	5.40	81	.333	.455	1	1.000	0	-0	-0	0	0.1
Total	15	143	113	.559	508	235	96	14	48	2156	2186	121	721	709	12.2	3.68	102	.263	.323	130	.184	-1	18	17	50	6.7
● BILLY GUMBERT Gumbert, William Skeen b: 8/8/1865, Pittsburgh, Pa. d: 4/13/46, Pittsburgh, Pa. BR/TR, 6'1.5", 200 lbs. Deb: 6/19/1890 F																										
1890	Pit-N	4	6	.400	10	10	8	0	0	79^1	96	0	31	18	15.3	5.22	63	.290	.365	9	.243	2	-15	-17	1	-1.2
1892	Pit-N	3	2	.600	6	3	2	0	0	39^2	30	0	23	3	12.3	1.36	242	.201	.312	2	.111	-1	8	9	-1	0.7
1893	Lou-N	0	0	—	1	1	0	0	0	0^2	2	0	5	0	94.5	27.00	16	.503	.780	1	1.000	1	-2	-2	-0	-0.1
Total	3	7	8	.467	17	14	10	0	0	119^2	128	0	59	21	14.7	4.06	81	.264	.355	12	.214	2	-8	-10	-1	-0.6
● DAVE GUMPERT Gumpert, David Lawrence b: 5/5/58, South Haven, Mich. BR/TR, 6'1", 190 lbs. Deb: 7/25/82																										
1982	Det-A	0	0	—	5	1	0	0	1	2	7	1	2	0	40.5	27.00	15	.700	.750	0	—	0	-5	-5	-0	-0.5
1983	Det-A	0	2	.000	26	0	0	0	2	44^1	43	1	7	14	10.2	2.64	148	.257	.287	0	—	0	7	6	-1	0.6
1985	Chi-N	1	0	1.000	9	0	0	0	0	10^1	12	0	7	4	16.5	3.48	115	.279	.380	0	.000	-0	0	1	-0	0.0
1986	Chi-N	2	0	1.000	38	0	0	0	2	59^2	60	4	28	45	13.4	4.37	92	.267	.350	0	.000	-1	-4	-2	-1	-0.4
1987	KC-A	0	0	—	8	0	0	0	0	19^1	27	3	6	13	15.4	6.05	75	.333	.379	0	—	0	-3	-3	0	-0.4
Total	5	3	2	.600	86	1	0	0	5	135^2	149	9	50	76	13.3	4.31	95	.283	.347	0	.000	-1	-6	-4	-2	-0.7
● RANDY GUMPERT Gumpert, Randall Pennington b: 1/23/18, Monocacy, Pa. BR/TR, 6'3", 205 lbs. Deb: 6/13/36																										
1936	Phi-A	1	2	.333	22	3	2	0	2	62^1	74	2	32	9	15.3	4.76	107	.295	.375	6	.273	0	2	**2**	-1	0.2
1937	Phi-A	0	0	—	10	1	0	0	0	12	16	1	15	5	24.0	12.00	39	.333	.500	1	.333	0	-10	-10	0	-0.8
1938	Phi-A	0	2	.000	4	2	0	0	0	12^1	24	1	10	1	24.8	10.95	44	.393	.479	1	.250	0	-8	-8	1	-0.6
1946	NY-A	11	3	.786	33	12	4	0	1	132^2	113	8	32	63	9.8	2.31	150	.229	.276	6	.128	-2	18	17	-1	1.5
1947	NY-A	4	1	.800	24	6	2	0	0	56^1	71	4	28	25	15.8	5.43	65	.311	.387	1	.071	-1	-11	-12	0	-1.3
1948	NY-A	1	0	1.000	15	0	0	0	0	25	27	0	6	12	12.2	2.88	142	.267	.315	0	—	0	4	3	0	0.3
	Chi-A	2	6	.250	16	11	6	1	0	97^1	103	6	13	31	10.9	3.79	112	.275	.303	4	.138	-2	5	5	-1	0.2
	Yr	3	6	.333	31	11	6	1	0	122^1	130	6	19	43	11.1	3.60	117	.273	.303	4	.138	-2	9	8	-1	0.5
1949	Chi-A	13	16	.448	34	32	18	3	1	234	223	22	83	78	11.8	3.81	110	.253	.318	16	.190	-1	10	9	1	0.9
1950	Chi-A	5	12	.294	40	17	6	1	0	155^1	165	15	58	48	13.2	4.75	94	.275	.343	3	.071	-4	-3	-5	-0	-0.8
1951	Chi-A☆	9	8	.529	33	16	7	1	2	141^2	156	20	34	45	12.1	4.32	93	.272	.314	15	.333	3	-3	-4	-3	-0.4
1952	Bos-A	1	0	1.000	10	1	0	0	1	19^2	15	1	5	6	9.6	4.12	96	.205	.266	0	.000	-1	-1	-0	-0	-0.1
	Was-A	4	9	.308	20	12	2	0	0	104	112	12	30	29	12.7	4.24	84	.273	.330	7	.206	0	-7	-8	-1	-0.8

YEAR TM/L	W	L	PCT	G	GS	CG	SH	SV	IP	H	HR	BB	SO	RAT	ERA	ERA+	OAV	OOB	BH	AVG	PB	PR	/A	PD	TPI
Yr	5	9	.357	30	13	2	0	1	123^2	127	13	35	35	12.2	4.22	86	.262	.318	7	.179	-0	-8	-8	-1	-0.9
Total 10	51	59	.464	261	113	47	6	7	1052^2	1099	92	346	352	12.5	4.17	98	.268	.328	60	.182	-8	-4	-10	-5	-1.7
● **ERIC GUNDERSON**	Gunderson, Eric Andrew b: 3/29/66, Portland, Ore. BR/TL, 6′, 175 lbs. Deb: 4/11/90																								
1990 SF-N	1	2	.333	7	4	0	0	0	19^2	24	2	11	14	16.0	5.49	66	.293	.376	0	.000	-1	-4	-4	0	-0.4
1991 SF-N	0	0	—	2	0	0	0	1	3^1	6	0	1	2	18.9	5.40	66	.353	.389	0	—	0	-1	-1	0	-0.1
1992 Sea-A	2	1	.667	9	0	0	0	0	9^1	12	1	5	2	17.4	8.68	46	.324	.419	0	—	0	-5	-5	0	-0.5
Total 3	3	3	.500	18	4	0	0	1	32^1	42	3	17	18	16.7	6.40	58	.309	.390	0	.000	-1	-9	-10	1	-1.0
● **RED GUNKEL**	Gunkel, Woodward William b: 4/15/1894, Sheffield, Ill. d: 4/19/54, Chicago, Ill. BB/TR, 5′8″, 158 lbs. Deb: 6/18/16																								
1916 Cle-A	0	0	—	1	0	0	0	0	1	0	0	1	1	18.0	0.00	—	.000	.500	0	—	0	0	0	-0	0.0
● **LARRY GURA**	Gura, Lawrence Cyril b: 11/26/47, Joliet, Ill. BB/TL, 6′1″, 185 lbs. Deb: 4/30/70																								
1970 Chi-N	1	3	.250	20	3	1	0	1	38	35	6	23	21	14.0	3.79	119	.254	.364	0	.000	-1	1	3	0	0.2
1971 Chi-N	0	0	—	6	0	0	0	1	3	6	0	1	2	21.0	6.00	66	.400	.438	0	.000	-0	-1	-1	-0	-0.1
1972 Chi-N	0	0	—	7	0	0	0	0	12^1	11	3	3	13	10.2	3.65	104	.250	.298	0	.000	-0	-0	0	0	0.0
1973 Chi-N	2	4	.333	21	7	0	0	0	64^2	79	10	11	43	12.7	4.87	81	.296	.326	3	.200	0	-9	-7	1	-0.6
1974 NY-A	5	1	.833	8	8	4	2	0	56	54	2	12	17	10.6	2.41	145	.248	.287	0	—	0	8	7	-0	0.8
1975 NY-A	7	8	.467	26	20	5	0	0	151^1	173	13	41	65	12.9	3.51	104	.295	.344	0	—	0	5	2	-0	0.3
1976 *KC-A	4	0	1.000	20	2	1	1	1	62^2	47	4	20	22	9.8	2.30	152	.213	.281	0	—	0	9	8	1	1.0
1977 *KC-A	8	5	.615	52	6	1	1	10	106^1	108	8	28	46	11.6	3.13	129	.265	.314	0	—	0	11	11	0	1.1
1978 *KC-A	16	4	.800	35	26	8	2	0	221^2	183	13	60	81	10.0	2.72	141	.229	.286	0	—	0	26	27	2	3.1
1979 KC-A	13	12	.520	39	33	7	1	0	233^2	226	29	73	85	11.8	4.47	95	.253	.315	0	—	0	-7	-5	1	-0.5
1980 *KC-A☆	18	10	.643	36	36	16	4	0	283^1	272	20	76	113	11.2	2.95	137	.255	.307	0	—	0	34	35	1	3.7
1981 *KC-A	11	8	.579	23	23	12	2	0	172^1	139	11	35	61	9.3	2.72	133	.223	.269	0	—	0	18	17	0	1.9
1982 KC-A	18	12	.600	37	37	8	3	0	248	251	31	64	98	11.6	4.03	101	.261	.311	0	—	0	1	1	2	0.4
1983 KC-A	11	18	.379	34	31	5	0	0	200^1	220	23	76	57	13.7	4.90	83	.284	.354	0	—	0	-19	-18	3	-1.5
1984 KC-A	12	9	.571	31	25	3	0	0	168^2	175	26	67	68	13.1	5.18	78	.269	.341	0	—	0	-22	-22	1	-2.0
1985 KC-A	0	0	—	3	0	0	0	1	4^1	7	1	4	2	22.8	12.46	33	.368	.478	0	—	0	-4	-4	0	-0.4
Chi-N	0	3	.000	5	4	0	0	0	20^1	34	4	6	7	18.1	8.41	47	.370	.414	0	.000	-0	-11	-10	0	-0.9
Total 16	126	97	.565	403	261	71	16	14	2047	2020	204	600	801	11.7	3.76	105	.260	.317	3	.091	-2	39	45	11	6.5
● **CHARLIE GUTH**	Guth, Charles J. b: 1856, Chicago, Ill. d: 7/5/1883, Cambridge, Mass. Deb: 9/30/1880																								
1880 Chi-N	1	0	1.000	1	1	1	0	0	9	12	0	1	7	13.0	5.00	48	.293	.310	1	.250	0	-3	-3	-0	-0.2
● **MARK GUTHRIE**	Guthrie, Mark Andrew b: 9/22/65, Buffalo, N.Y. BB/TR, 6′4″, 195 lbs. Deb: 7/25/89																								
1989 Min-A	2	4	.333	13	8	0	0	0	57^1	66	7	21	38	13.8	4.55	91	.292	.355	0	—	0	-4	-3	-0	-0.7
1990 Min-A	7	9	.438	24	21	3	1	0	144^2	154	8	39	101	12.1	3.79	109	.276	.325	0	—	0	2	6	1	0.2
1991 *Min-A	7	5	.583	41	12	0	0	2	98	116	11	41	72	14.5	4.32	99	.303	.372	0	—	0	-2	-1	-1	-0.1
1992 Min-A	2	3	.400	54	0	0	0	5	75	59	7	23	76	9.8	2.88	140	.215	.276	0	—	0	9	10	-0	0.9
Total 4	18	21	.462	132	41	3	1	7	375	395	33	124	287	12.5	3.86	108	.274	.333	0	—	0	4	12	-1	0.3
● **JOSE GUZMAN**	Guzman, Jose Alberto (Mirabal) b: 4/9/63, Santa Isabel, P.R. BR/TR, 6′2″, 195 lbs. Deb: 9/10/85																								
1985 Tex-A	3	2	.600	5	5	0	0	0	32^2	27	3	14	24	11.3	2.76	153	.214	.293	0	—	0	5	5	0	0.5
1986 Tex-A	9	15	.375	29	29	2	0	0	172^1	199	23	60	87	13.8	4.54	95	.293	.355	0	—	0	-7	-5	0	-0.5
1987 Tex-A	14	14	.500	37	30	6	0	0	208^1	196	30	82	143	12.1	4.67	96	.251	.324	0	—	0	-5	-4	1	-0.3
1988 Tex-A	11	13	.458	30	30	6	2	0	206^2	180	20	82	157	11.6	3.70	110	.231	.308	0	—	0	6	9	-0	0.7
1991 Tex-A	13	7	.650	25	25	5	1	0	169^2	152	10	84	125	12.7	3.08	131	.239	.331	0	—	0	19	18	2	2.1
1992 Tex-A	16	11	.593	33	33	5	0	0	224	229	17	73	179	12.3	3.66	105	.268	.329	0	—	0	7	4	-0	0.4
Total 6	66	62	.516	159	152	24	3	0	1013^2	983	103	395	715	12.4	3.90	106	.255	.328	0	—	0	25	27	3	2.9
● **JUAN GUZMAN**	Guzman, Juan Andres (Correa) b: 10/28/66, Santo Domingo, P.R. BR/TR, 5′11″, 190 lbs. Deb: 6/07/91																								
1991 *Tor-A	10	3	.769	23	23	1	0	0	138^2	98	6	66	123	10.9	2.99	141	.197	.296	0	—	0	17	19	-2	1.7
1992 *Tor-A★	16	5	.762	28	28	1	0	0	180^2	135	6	72	165	10.4	2.64	155	.207	.287	0	—	0	26	29	-2	2.9
Total 2	26	8	.765	51	51	2	0	0	319^1	233	12	138	288	10.6	2.79	148	.203	.291	0	—	0	43	48	-4	4.6
● **JOHNNY GUZMAN**	Guzman, Ramon Dionny (Estrella) b: 1/21/71, Hatillo Palma, D.R. BR/TL, 5′10″, 155 lbs. Deb: 6/08/91																								
1991 Oak-A	1	0	1.000	5	0	0	0	0	5	11	0	2	3	23.4	9.00	43	.500	.542	0	—	0	-3	-3	0	-0.3
1992 Oak-A	0	0	—	2	0	0	0	0	3	8	0	0	0	27.0	12.00	31	.471	.500	0	—	0	-3	-3	-0	-0.3
Total 2	1	0	1.000	7	0	0	0	0	8	19	0	2	3	24.8	10.13	38	.487	.524	0	—	0	-5	-6	0	-0.6
● **SANTIAGO GUZMAN**	Guzman, Santiago Donovan (b: Santiago Donovan (Guzman)) b: 7/25/49, San Pedro De Macoris, D.R. BR/TR, 6′2″, 180 lbs. Deb: 9/30/69																								
1969 StL-N	0	1	.000	1	1	0	0	0	7^1	9	2	3	7	14.7	4.91	73	.321	.387	1	.333	0	-1	-1	-0	-0.1
1970 StL-N	1	1	.500	8	3	1	0	0	13^2	14	1	13	9	17.8	7.24	57	.275	.422	1	.200	-0	-5	-5	-0	-0.5
1971 StL-N	0	0	—	2	1	0	0	0	10	6	0	2	13	7.2	0.00	—	.162	.205	0	.000	-0	4	4	-0	0.4
1972 StL-N	0	0	—	1	0	0	0	0	1	1	1	0	0	9.0	9.00	38	.250	.250	0	—	0	-1	-1	0	-0.1
Total 4	1	2	.333	12	5	1	0	0	32	30	4	18	29	13.5	4.50	85	.250	.348	2	.222	0	-3	-2	-1	-0.3
● **BRUNO HAAS**	Haas, Bruno Philip "Boon" b: 5/5/1891, Worcester, Mass. d: 6/5/52, Sarasota, Fla. BB/TL, 5′10″, 180 lbs. Deb: 6/23/15 ♦																								
1915 Phi-A	0	1	.000	6	2	1	0	0	14^1	23	0	28	7	32.0	11.93	25	.404	.600	1	.056	-1	-14	-14	0	-1.4
● **MOOSE HAAS**	Haas, Bryan Edmund b: 4/22/56, Baltimore, Md. BR/TR, 6′, 180 lbs. Deb: 9/08/76																								
1976 Mil-A	0	1	.000	5	2	0	0	0	16	12	0	12	9	13.5	3.94	89	.207	.343	0	—	0	-1	-1	1	0.0
1977 Mil-A	10	12	.455	32	32	6	0	0	197^2	195	21	84	113	12.8	4.33	94	.261	.338	0	—	0	-6	-6	-2	-0.8
1978 Mil-A	2	3	.400	7	6	2	0	1	30^2	33	6	8	32	12.0	6.16	61	.273	.318	0	—	0	-8	-8	-0	-0.8
1979 Mil-A	11	11	.500	29	28	8	1	0	184^2	198	26	59	95	12.5	4.78	87	.275	.330	0	—	0	-12	-13	-1	-1.3
1980 Mil-A	16	15	.516	33	33	14	3	0	252^1	246	25	56	146	10.8	3.10	125	.258	.300	0	—	0	26	21	-0	2.2
1981 *Mil-A	11	7	.611	24	22	5	0	0	137^1	146	10	40	64	12.3	4.46	77	.275	.327	0	—	0	-12	-16	-1	-1.7
1982 *Mil-A	11	8	.579	32	27	3	0	1	193^1	232	15	39	104	12.8	4.47	85	.302	.339	0	—	0	-8	-15	-2	-1.5
1983 Mil-A	13	3	.813	25	25	7	3	0	179	170	12	42	75	10.7	3.27	114	.251	.296	0	—	0	16	9	-1	0.9
1984 Mil-A	9	11	.450	31	30	4	0	0	189^1	205	15	43	84	11.8	3.99	96	.279	.318	0	—	0	-0	-3	3	0.2
1985 Mil-A	8	8	.500	27	26	6	1	0	161^2	165	21	25	78	10.6	3.84	108	.260	.289	0	—	0	5	6	-1	0.5
1986 Oak-A	7	2	.778	12	12	1	0	0	72^1	58	4	19	40	9.7	2.74	141	.218	.273	0	—	0	12	9	-0	1.1
1987 Oak-A	2	2	.500	9	9	0	0	0	40^2	57	7	9	13	14.6	5.75	72	.335	.369	0	—	0	-6	-7	-0	-0.7
Total 12	100	83	.546	266	252	56	8	2	1655	1717	162	436	853	11.8	4.01	97	.269	.317	0	—	0	6	-23	-5	-1.9
● **DAVE HAAS**	Haas, Robert David b: 10/19/65, Independence, Mo. BR/TR, 6′1″, 200 lbs. Deb: 9/08/91																								
1991 Det-A	1	0	1.000	11	0	0	0	0	10^2	8	1	12	6	17.7	6.75	62	.242	.457	0	—	0	-3	-3	-0	-0.3
1992 Det-A	5	3	.625	12	11	1	1	0	61^2	68	8	16	29	12.4	3.94	101	.276	.323	0	—	0	-0	0	-0	0.0
Total 2	6	3	.667	23	11	1	1	0	72^1	76	9	28	35	13.2	4.35	92	.272	.343	0	—	0	-3	-3	-1	-0.3
● **BOB HABENICHT**	Habenicht, Robert Julius "Hobby" b: 2/13/26, St.Louis, Mo. d: 12/24/80, Richmond, Va. BR/TR, 6′2″, 185 lbs. Deb: 4/17/51																								
1951 StL-N	0	0	—	3	0	0	0	0	5	5	0	9	1	25.2	7.20	55	.278	.519	0	.000	0	-2	-2	0	-0.1
1953 StL-A	0	0	—	1	0	0	0	0	1^2	1	0	1	1	16.2	5.40	78	.167	.375	0	—	0	-0	-0	-0	0.0
Total 2	0	0	—	4	0	0	0	0	6^2	6	0	10	2	23.0	6.75	60	.250	.486	0	.000	0	-2	-2	0	-0.1

YEAR TM/L	W	L	PCT	G	GS	CG	SH	SV	IP	H	HR	BB	SO	RAT	ERA	ERA+	OAV	OOB	BH	AVG	PB	PR	/A	PD	TPI
● **JOHN HABYAN** Habyan, John Gabriel b: 1/29/63, Bay Shore, N.Y. BR/TR, 6'1", 195 lbs. Deb: 9/09/85																									
1985 Bal-A	1	0	1.000	2	0	0	0	0	2^2	3	0	0	2	10.1	0.00	—	.250	.250	0	—	0	1	1	0	0.2
1986 Bal-A	1	3	.250	6	5	0	0	0	26^1	24	3	18	14	14.4	4.44	93	.250	.368	0	—	0	-1	-1	-0	-0.1
1987 Bal-A	6	7	.462	27	13	0	0	1	116^1	110	20	40	64	11.8	4.80	92	.248	.313	0	—	0	-4	-5	1	-0.4
1988 Bal-A	1	0	1.000	7	0	0	0	0	14^2	22	2	4	4	16.0	4.30	91	.355	.394	0	—	0	-1	-1	0	0.1
1990 NY-A	0	0	—	6	0	0	0	0	8^2	10	0	2	4	13.5	2.08	191	.294	.351	0	—	0	2	2	-0	0.2
1991 NY-A	4	2	.667	66	0	0	0	2	90	73	2	20	70	9.5	2.30	180	.225	.275	0	—	0	18	18	0	1.9
1992 NY-A	5	6	.455	56	0	0	0	7	72^2	84	6	21	44	13.3	3.84	105	.295	.347	0	—	0	1	2	1	0.3
Total 7	18	18	.500	170	18	0	0	10	331^1	326	33	105	202	11.9	3.75	112	.260	.320	0	—	0	16	16	2	2.2
● **WARREN HACKER** Hacker, Warren Louis b: 11/21/24, Marissa, Ill. BR/TR, 6'1", 185 lbs. Deb: 9/24/48																									
1948 Chi-N	0	1	.000	3	1	0	0	0	3	7	0	3	0	30.0	21.00	19	.438	.526	0	—	0	-6	-6	0	-0.5
1949 Chi-N	5	8	.385	30	12	3	0	0	125^2	141	7	53	40	14.2	4.23	95	.283	.356	7	.184	-1	-3	-3	1	-0.3
1950 Chi-N	0	1	.000	5	3	1	0	1	15^1	20	3	8	5	16.4	5.28	80	.313	.389	0	.000	-1	-2	-2	1	-0.2
1951 Chi-N	0	0	—	2	0	0	0	0	1^1	3	0	0	2	27.0	13.50	30	.500	.571	0	—	0	-1	-1	0	-0.1
1952 Chi-N	15	9	.625	33	20	12	5	1	185	144	17	31	84	**8.6**	2.58	149	**.212**	**.247**	7	.121	-2	24	26	-4	2.2
1953 Chi-N	12	19	.387	39	32	9	0	2	221^2	225	35	54	106	11.4	4.38	101	.254	.299	17	.218	1	-2	2	-3	0.0
1954 Chi-N	6	13	.316	39	18	4	1	2	158^2	157	28	37	80	11.2	4.25	99	.257	.304	13	.236	1	-3	-1	-1	-0.1
1955 Chi-N	11	15	.423	35	30	13	0	3	213	202	38	43	80	10.4	4.27	96	.245	.285	18	.250	2	-5	-4	-4	-0.6
1956 Chi-N	3	13	.188	34	24	4	0	0	168	190	28	44	65	12.6	4.66	81	.285	.330	8	.148	-2	-17	-17	-3	-2.1
1957 Cin-N	3	2	.600	15	6	0	0	0	43^1	50	5	13	18	13.7	5.19	79	.294	.355	1	.125	-0	-6	-5	-0	-0.6
Phi-N	4	4	.500	20	10	1	0	0	74	72	10	18	33	11.1	4.50	85	.257	.304	6	.261	1	-5	-6	-1	-0.6
Yr	7	6	.538	35	16	1	0	0	117^1	122	15	31	51	11.8	4.76	82	.267	.315	7	.226	1	-11	-11	-1	-1.2
1958 Phi-N	0	1	.000	9	1	0	0	0	17	24	2	8	4	16.9	7.41	53	.329	.395	0	.000	-0	-7	-7	-0	-0.7
1961 Chi-A	3	3	.500	42	0	0	0	8	57^1	62	8	8	40	11.1	3.77	104	.272	.300	1	.111	-1	2	1	-1	-0.1
Total 12	62	89	.411	306	157	47	6	17	1283^1	1297	181	320	557	11.5	4.21	96	.259	.307	78	.195	-2	-32	-22	-15	-3.7
● **JIM HACKETT** Hackett, James Joseph "Sunny Jim" b: 10/1/1877, Jacksonville, Ill. d: 3/28/61, Douglas, Mich. BR/TR, 6'2", 185 lbs. Deb: 9/14/02 ♦																									
1902 StL-N	0	3	.000	4	3	3	0	0	30^1	46	0	16	7	18.7	6.23	44	.348	.422	6	.286	1	-12	-12	-0	-1.0
1903 StL-N	1	3	.250	7	6	5	0	1	48^1	47	0	18	21	12.7	3.72	88	.249	.324	80	.228	1	-2	-2	0	-0.2
Total 2	1	6	.143	11	9	8	0	1	78^2	93	0	34	28	15.0	4.69	65	.290	.365	86	.231	2	-14	-14	-0	-1.2
● **HARVEY HADDIX** Haddix, Harvey "The Kitten" b: 9/18/25, Medway, Ohio BL/TL, 5'9.5", 170 lbs. Deb: 8/20/52 C																									
1952 StL-N	2	2	.500	7	6	3	0	0	42	31	4	10	31	9.2	2.79	133	.201	.259	3	.214	0	4	4	-1	0.5
1953 StL-N☆	20	9	.690	36	33	19	**6**	1	253	220	24	69	163	10.4	3.06	139	.232	.287	28	.289	10	35	34	1	4.6
1954 StL-N†	18	13	.581	43	35	13	3	4	259^2	247	26	77	184	11.3	3.57	115	.249	.305	18	.194	3	14	16	-0	1.9
1955 StL-N★	12	16	.429	37	30	9	2	1	208	216	27	62	150	12.2	4.46	91	.268	.325	12	.164	0	-10	-9	1	-0.7
1956 StL-N	1	0	1.000	4	4	1	1	0	23^2	28	3	10	16	14.5	5.32	71	.298	.365	2	.222	1	-4	-4	-0	-0.3
Phi-N	12	8	.600	31	26	11	2	2	206^2	196	23	55	154	11.2	3.48	107	.247	.301	22	.237	4	7	5	-1	1.0
Yr	13	8	.619	35	30	12	3	2	230^1	224	26	65	170	11.5	3.67	102	.253	.308	24	.235	5	3	1	-1	0.7
1957 Phi-N	10	13	.435	27	25	8	1	0	170^2	176	18	39	136	11.4	4.06	94	.264	.306	21	.309	7	-3	-5	-2	0.0
1958 Cin-N	8	7	.533	29	26	8	1	0	184	191	28	43	110	11.8	3.52	118	.268	.315	11	.180	3	9	13	-1	1.6
1959 Pit-N	12	12	.500	31	29	14	2	0	224^1	189	26	49	149	**9.6**	3.13	124	.228	**.273**	12	.145	-0	20	18	-0	1.9
1960 *Pit-N	11	10	.524	29	28	4	0	1	172^1	189	13	38	101	11.9	3.97	94	.277	.316	17	.254	4	-4	-4	3	0.3
1961 Pit-N	10	6	.625	29	22	5	2	0	156	159	15	41	99	11.7	4.10	97	.266	.316	8	.143	0	-1	-2	0	-0.2
1962 Pit-N	9	6	.600	28	20	4	0	0	141^1	146	17	42	101	12.1	4.20	94	.264	.319	13	.250	4	-4	-4	-1	0.0
1963 Pit-N	3	4	.429	49	1	0	0	1	70	67	7	20	70	11.7	3.34	99	.256	.318	2	.182	1	-0	-0	0	0.0
1964 Bal-A	5	5	.500	49	0	0	0	10	89^2	68	4	23	90	9.3	2.31	155	.211	.268	0	.000	-2	13	13	1	1.2
1965 Bal-A	3	2	.600	24	0	0	0	1	33^2	31	5	23	21	15.0	3.48	100	.248	.373	0	.000	-0	-0	-0	-0	0.0
Total 14	136	113	.546	453	285	99	20	21	2235	2154	240	601	1575	11.3	3.63	108	.252	.305	169	.212	35	75	74	1	11.8
● **GEORGE HADDOCK** Haddock, George Silas "Gentleman George" b: 12/25/1866, Portsmouth, N.H. d: 4/18/26, Boston, Mass. BR/TR, 5'11", 155 lbs. Deb: 9/27/1888																									
1888 Was-N	0	2	.000	2	2	2	0	0	16	9	0	2	3	6.8	2.25	125	.148	.188	1	.200	0	1	1	0	0.2
1889 Was-N	11	19	.367	33	31	30	0	0	276^1	299	10	123	106	14.0	4.20	94	.268	.345	25	.223	7	-6	-8	0	0.0
1890 Buf-P	9	26	.257	35	34	31	0	0	290^2	366	15	149	123	16.4	5.76	71	.295	.376	36	.247	7	-49	-54	4	-3.1
1891 Bos-a	34	11	.756	51	47	37	**5**	1	379^2	330	8	137	169	11.4	2.49	140	.226	.299	45	.243	8	**52**	42	6	5.0
1892 Bro-N	29	13	.690	46	44	39	3	1	381^1	340	11	163	153	12.2	3.14	101	.229	.311	28	.177	-1	6	1	2	0.2
1893 Bro-N	8	9	.471	23	20	12	0	0	151	193	10	89	37	17.2	5.60	79	.302	.393	24	.282	4	-16	-20	-3	-1.5
1894 Phi-N	4	3	.571	10	7	5	0	0	56	63	0	34	7	15.8	5.79	88	.281	.378	5	.172	-1	-3	-4	1	-0.3
Was-N	0	4	.000	4	4	4	0	0	29	50	2	17	1	21.1	8.69	61	.375	.449	3	.188	-0	-11	-11	-0	-0.8
Yr	4	7	.364	14	11	9	0	0	85	113	2	51	8	17.5	6.78	76	.315	.402	8	.178	-1	-14	-15	1	-1.1
Total 7	95	87	.522	204	189	160	8	2	1580	1650	56	714	599	13.8	4.07	93	.259	.340	167	.227	24	-25	-53	11	-0.3
● **BUMP HADLEY** Hadley, Irving Darius b: 7/5/04, Lynn, Mass. d: 2/15/63, Lynn, Mass. BR/TR, 5'11", 190 lbs. Deb: 4/20/26																									
1926 Was-A	0	0	—	1	0	0	0	0	3	6	0	2	0	24.0	12.00	32	.429	.500	0	—	0	-3	-3	-0	-0.2
1927 Was-A	14	6	.700	30	27	13	0	0	198^2	177	2	86	60	12.3	2.85	142	.244	.332	19	.271	2	28	27	0	2.9
1928 Was-A	12	13	.480	33	31	16	3	0	231^2	236	4	100	80	13.4	3.54	113	.268	.348	17	.210	1	13	12	-0	1.3
1929 Was-A	6	16	.273	37	27	7	1	0	195^1	196	10	85	98	13.2	5.62	75	.263	.342	6	.097	-4	-30	-30	1	-3.1
1930 Was-A	15	11	.577	42	34	15	1	2	260^1	242	6	105	162	12.2	3.73	123	.247	.323	21	.226	1	27	25	-1	2.4
1931 Was-A	11	10	.524	**55**	11	2	1	8	179^2	145	4	92	124	11.9	3.06	140	**.218**	.314	9	.167	-1	26	25	2	2.4
1932 Chi-A	1	1	.500	3	2	1	0	1	18^2	17	2	8	13	12.1	3.86	112	.262	.342	1	.167	-0	1	1	0	0.1
StL-A	13	20	.394	40	33	12	1	1	229^2	244	21	163	132	16.3	5.53	88	.274	.391	22	.282	5	-27	-17	-3	-1.4
Yr	14	21	.400	43	35	13	1	2	248^1	261	23	171	145	15.9	5.40	89	.273	.388	23	.274	4	-25	-16	-3	-1.3
1933 StL-A	15	20	.429	45	36	19	2	3	**316^2**	309	17	141	149	12.9	3.92	119	.256	.335	17	.156	-4	13	26	-3	1.9
1934 StL-A	10	16	.385	39	32	7	2	1	213	212	14	127	79	14.6	4.35	115	.257	.361	13	.203	-1	3	15	-0	1.3
1935 Was-A	10	15	.400	35	32	13	0	0	230^1	268	18	102	77	14.6	4.92	88	.292	.366	15	.195	1	-12	-15	1	-1.2
1936 *NY-A	14	4	.778	31	17	8	1	1	173^2	194	12	89	74	14.7	4.35	107	.283	.366	16	.235	2	13	6	1	0.8
1937 *NY-A	11	8	.579	29	25	6	0	0	178^1	199	16	83	70	14.4	5.30	84	.281	.358	11	.169	1	-13	-17	1	-1.5
1938 NY-A	9	8	.529	29	17	8	1	1	167^1	165	13	66	61	12.6	3.60	126	.254	.325	5	.093	-1	22	17	3	1.7
1939 *NY-A	12	6	.667	26	18	7	1	2	154	132	10	85	65	12.9	2.98	146	.237	.342	11	.177	-0	28	24	2	2.4
1940 NY-A	3	5	.375	25	2	0	0	2	80	88	4	52	39	15.9	5.74	70	.276	.379	3	.111	-1	-12	-15	0	-1.5
1941 NY-N	1	0	1.000	3	2	0	0	0	13	19	1	9	4	19.4	6.23	59	.345	.438	0	.000	-0	-4	-4	-0	-0.4
Phi-A	4	6	.400	25	9	1	0	3	102^1	131	13	47	31	15.8	5.01	84	.310	.381	4	.129	-1	-10	-9	-1	-1.0
Total 16	161	165	.494	528	355	135	14	25	2945^2	2980	167	1442	1318	13.7	4.24	105	.263	.350	190	.189	-1	65	69	2	6.9
● **MICKEY HAEFNER** Haefner, Milton Arnold b: 10/9/12, Lenzburg, Ill. BL/TL, 5'8", 160 lbs. Deb: 4/22/43																									
1943 Was-A	11	5	.688	36	13	8	1	6	165^1	126	4	60	65	10.3	2.29	140	.208	.283	6	.133	0	19	17	-0	1.8
1944 Was-A	12	15	.444	31	28	18	3	1	228	221	7	71	86	11.7	3.04	107	.251	.310	11	.157	-0	10	5	1	0.6
1945 Was-A	16	14	.533	37	28	19	1	3	238^1	226	10	69	83	11.4	3.47	89	.247	.305	20	.244	4	-3	-10	1	-0.6
1946 Was-A	14	11	.560	33	27	17	2	1	227^2	220	10	80	85	12.1	2.85	118	.251	.317	15	.203	4	17	13	-1	1.7
1947 Was-A	10	14	.417	31	28	14	4	1	193	195	8	85	77	13.2	3.64	102	.264	.343	8	.136	-1	1	2	-1	0.0
1948 Was-A	5	13	.278	28	20	4	0	0	147^2	151	7	61	45	13.3	4.02	108	.265	.342	7	.163	-1	4	5	2	0.6
1949 Was-A	5	5	.500	19	12	4	1	0	91^2	85	7	53	23	13.7	4.42	96	.249	.353	5	.200	1	-2	-2	1	0.0
Chi-A	4	6	.400	14	12	4	1	1	80^1	84	9	41	17	14.6	4.37	95	.275	.370	6	.261	2	-2	-2	0	0.0

YEAR TM/L	W	L	PCT	G	GS	CG	SH	SV	IP	H	HR	BB	SO	RAT	ERA	ERA+	OAV	OOB	BH	AVG	PB	PR	/A	PD	TPI
Yr	9	11	.450	33	24	8	2	1	172	169	16	94	40	14.0	4.40	96	.260	.358	11	.229	2	-4	-3	1	0.0
1950 Chi-A	1	6	.143	24	9	2	0	0	70^2	83	11	45	17	16.6	5.73	78	.299	.400	4	.200	0	-9	-10	-1	-0.9
Bos-N	0	2	.000	8	2	1	0	0	24	23	3	12	10	13.1	5.63	68	.247	.333	2	.286	1	-4	-5	-0	-0.4
Total 8	78	91	.462	261	179	91	13	13	1466^2	1414	76	577	508	12.5	3.50	102	.252	.326	84	.188	8	31	13	1	2.8
● **BUD HAFEY** Hafey, Daniel Albert b: 8/6/12, Berkeley, Cal. d: 7/27/86, Sacramento, Cal. BR/TR, 6', 185 lbs. Deb: 4/21/35 F♦																									
1939 Phi-N	0	0	—	2	0	0	0	0	1^1	7	0	1	1	54.0	33.75	12	.700	.727	9	.176	-0	-4	-4	0	-0.4
● **LEO HAFFORD** Hafford, Leo Edgar b: 9/17/1883, Somerville, Mass. d: 10/2/11, Willimantic, Conn. TR, 6', 170 lbs. Deb: 4/15/06																									
1906 Cin-N	1	1	.500	3	1	1	0	0	19	13	0	11	5	11.8	0.95	291	.191	.313	2	.222	-0	4	4	-1	0.4
● **FRANK HAFNER** Hafner, Francis R. b: 8/14/1867, Hannibal, Mo. d: 3/2/57, Hannibal, Mo. TR, Deb: 5/05/1888																									
1888 KC-a	0	2	.000	2	2	2	0	0	18	24	2	16	5	20.5	7.00	49	.309	.433	0	.000	-1	-8	-7	-0	-0.6
● **ART HAGAN** Hagan, Arthur Charles b: 3/17/1863, Providence, R.I. d: 3/25/36, Providence, R.I. TR, Deb: 6/30/1883																									
1883 Phi-N	1	14	.067	17	16	15	0	0	137	207	2	33	39	15.8	5.45	57	.342	.376	6	.102	-5	-35	-36	-1	-3.3
Buf-N	0	2	.000	2	2	1	0	0	15	17	0	6	7	13.8	3.60	88	.270	.333	0	.000	-1	-1	-1	0	-0.1
Yr	1	16	.059	19	18	16	0	0	152	224	2	39	46	15.6	5.27	59	.335	.371	6	.091	-7	-36	-37	-1	-3.4
1884 Buf-N	1	2	.333	3	3	3	0	0	26	53	1	4	4	19.7	5.88	54	.384	.401	4	.308	0	-8	-8	-1	-0.7
Total 2	2	18	.100	22	21	19	0	0	178	277	3	43	50	16.2	5.36	58	.343	.376	10	.127	-6	-44	-45	-2	-4.1
● **CASEY HAGEMAN** Hageman, Kurt Moritz b: 5/12/1887, Mt.Oliver, Pa. d: 4/1/64, New Bedford, Pa. BR/TR, 5'10.5", 186 lbs. Deb: 9/18/11																									
1911 Bos-A	0	2	.000	2	2	2	0	0	17	16	2	5	8	11.6	2.12	155	.262	.328	0	.000	-0	2	2	-1	0.1
1912 Bos-A	0	0	—	2	1	0	0	0	1^1	5	0	3	1	54.0	27.00	13	.500	.615	0	—	0	-4	-3	-0	-0.3
1914 StL-N	2	4	.333	12	7	2	0	0	55^1	43	0	20	21	11.1	2.44	115	.215	.302	2	.125	-1	2	2	1	0.3
Chi-N	1	1	.500	16	1	0	0	1	46^2	44	0	12	17	11.4	3.47	80	.254	.314	7	.467	3	-4	-4	-1	-0.2
Yr	3	5	.375	28	8	2	0	1	102	87	0	32	38	10.8	2.91	96	.230	.295	9	.290	2	-1	-1	-0	0.1
Total 3	3	7	.300	32	11	4	0	1	120^1	108	2	40	47	11.7	3.07	93	.243	.318	9	.257	2	-3	-3	-1	-0.1
● **KEVIN HAGEN** Hagen, Kevin Eugene b: 3/8/60, Renton, Wash. BR/TR, 6'2", 185 lbs. Deb: 6/04/83																									
1983 StL-N	2	2	.500	9	4	0	0	0	22^1	34	0	7	7	16.5	4.84	75	.362	.406	0	.000	-1	-3	-3	0	-0.4
1984 StL-N	1	0	1.000	4	0	0	0	0	7^1	9	0	1	2	12.3	2.45	141	.300	.323	0	—	0	1	1	-0	0.1
Total 2	3	2	.600	13	4	0	0	0	29^2	43	0	8	9	15.5	4.25	84	.347	.386	0	.000	-1	-2	-2	-0	-0.3
● **RIP HAGERMAN** Hagerman, Zeriah Zequiel b: 6/20/1888, Linden, Kan. d: 1/30/30, Albuquerque, N.Mex BR/TR, 6'2", 200 lbs. Deb: 4/16/09																									
1909 Chi-N	4	4	.500	13	7	4	1	0	79	64	0	28	32	10.7	1.82	140	.225	.298	3	.130	-0	7	6	-0	0.6
1914 Cle-A	9	15	.375	37	26	12	3	0	198	189	3	118	112	14.2	3.09	93	.265	.374	1	.016	-6	-8	-4	-3	-1.4
1915 Cle-A	6	14	.300	29	22	7	0	0	151	156	4	77	69	14.2	3.52	87	.277	.370	4	.105	-3	-10	-8	-3	-1.4
1916 Cle-A	0	0	—	2	0	0	0	0	3^2	5	1	2	1	22.1	12.27	25	.333	.474	0	.000	-0	-4	-4	-0	-0.4
Total 4	19	33	.365	81	55	23	4	0	431^2	414	8	225	214	13.6	3.09	93	.263	.360	8	.065	-9	-14	-10	-6	-2.6
● **NOODLES HAHN** Hahn, Frank George b: 4/29/1879, Nashville, Tenn. d: 2/6/60, Candler, N.C. BL/TL, 5'9", 160 lbs. Deb: 4/18/1899																									
1899 Cin-N	23	8	.742	38	34	32	4	0	309	280	3	68	**145**	10.4	2.68	146	.242	.289	16	.147	-4	40	43	-4	3.2
1900 Cin-N	16	20	.444	39	37	29	**4**	0	311^1	306	4	89	**132**	11.6	3.27	112	.257	.311	24	.209	-0	15	14	-0	1.3
1901 Cin-N	22	19	.537	42	42	**41**	2	0	**375^1**	370	12	69	**239**	10.7	2.71	118	.256	.293	24	.170	-1	26	20	-0	2.0
1902 Cin-N	23	12	.657	36	36	35	6	0	321	282	2	58	142	9.7	1.77	170	.236	.275	22	.185	0	36	44	-2	4.7
1903 Cin-N	22	12	.647	34	34	34	5	0	296	297	3	47	127	10.7	2.52	141	.262	.297	18	.161	-2	25	34	-1	3.1
1904 Cin-N	16	18	.471	35	34	33	2	0	297^2	258	3	35	98	9.1	2.06	143	.234	.262	17	.172	1	23	29	-0	3.2
1905 Cin-N	5	3	.625	13	8	5	1	0	77	85	0	9	17	11.2	2.81	118	.272	.297	4	.167	-1	2	4	-2	0.1
1906 NY-A	3	2	.600	6	6	3	1	0	42	38	0	6	17	10.1	3.86	77	.244	.286	4	.333	2	-5	-4	-1	-0.4
Total 8	130	94	.580	243	231	212	25	0	2029^1	1916	27	381	917	10.4	2.55	133	.249	.289	129	.176	-6	161	187	-11	17.2
● **FRED HAHN** Hahn, Frederick Aloys b: 2/16/29, Nyack, N.Y. d: 8/16/84, Valhalla, N.Y. BR/TL, 6'3", 174 lbs. Deb: 4/19/52																									
1952 StL-N	0	0	—	1	0	0	0	0	2	2	0	1	0	13.5	0.00	—	.250	.333	0	—	0	1	1	0	0.1
● **HAL HAID** Haid, Harold Augustine b: 12/21/1897, Barberton, Ohio d: 8/13/52, Los Angeles, Cal. BR/TR, 5'10.5", 150 lbs. Deb: 9/05/19																									
1919 StL-A	0	0	—	1	0	0	0	0	2	5	0	3	1	36.0	18.00	18	.556	.667	0	—	0	-3	-3	0	-0.3
1928 StL-N	2	2	.500	27	0	0	0	**5**	47	39	1	11	21	9.8	2.30	174	.218	.267	3	.375	1	9	9	0	1.0
1929 StL-N	9	9	.500	38	12	8	0	4	154^2	171	8	66	41	14.1	4.07	115	.284	.360	4	.082	-3	11	10	-1	0.5
1930 StL-N	3	2	.600	20	0	0	0	2	33	38	1	14	13	15.0	4.09	123	.297	.379	0	.000	-0	3	3	1	0.3
1931 Bos-N	0	2	.000	27	0	0	0	1	56	59	3	16	20	12.5	4.50	84	.263	.321	1	.125	-0	-4	-4	2	-0.3
1933 Chi-A	0	0	—	6	0	0	0	0	14^2	18	2	13	7	20.3	7.98	53	.310	.452	1	.250	0	-6	-6	0	-0.5
Total 6	14	15	.483	119	12	8	0	12	307^1	330	15	123	103	13.7	4.16	106	.275	.349	9	.125	-3	10	9	2	0.7
● **JESSE HAINES** Haines, Jesse Joseph "Pop" b: 7/22/1893, Clayton, Ohio d: 8/5/78, Dayton, Ohio BR/TR, 6', 190 lbs. Deb: 7/20/18 CH																									
1918 Cin-N	0	0	—	1	0	0	0	0	5	5	0	1	2	10.8	1.80	148	.294	.333	1	1.000	0	1	0	0	0.1
1920 StL-N	13	20	.394	**47**	37	19	4	2	301^2	303	9	80	120	11.7	2.98	100	.270	.324	19	.176	-1	5	0	-5	-0.7
1921 StL-N	18	12	.600	37	29	13	**3**	0	244^1	261	15	56	84	12.0	3.50	105	.286	.333	17	.181	-3	8	5	2	0.3
1922 StL-N	11	9	.550	29	26	11	2	0	183	207	10	45	62	12.6	3.84	101	.284	.329	12	.167	-2	5	1	1	0.0
1923 StL-N	20	13	.606	37	36	23	1	0	266	283	7	75	73	12.3	3.11	125	.275	.328	20	.202	-2	26	23	0	2.1
1924 StL-N	8	19	.296	35	31	16	1	0	222^2	275	14	66	69	14.0	4.41	86	.309	.360	14	.189	-2	-13	-15	-1	-1.8
1925 StL-N	13	14	.481	29	25	15	0	0	207	234	11	52	63	12.5	4.57	95	.290	.334	13	.176	-2	-7	-6	-1	-0.8
1926 *StL-N	13	4	.765	33	21	14	3	1	183	186	10	48	46	11.6	3.25	120	.265	.314	13	.213	-1	12	13	-3	0.9
1927 StL-N	24	10	.706	38	36	**25**	**6**	1	300^2	273	11	77	89	10.6	2.72	145	.245	.297	23	.202	-1	40	41	1	4.2
1928 *StL-N	20	8	.714	33	28	20	1	0	240^1	238	14	72	77	11.8	3.18	126	.266	.324	16	.184	-1	21	22	-3	1.7
1929 StL-N	13	10	.565	28	25	12	0	0	179^2	230	21	73	59	15.3	5.71	82	.313	.376	11	.159	-3	-20	-21	-4	-2.4
1930 *StL-N	13	8	.619	29	24	14	0	1	182	215	15	54	68	13.4	4.30	117	.298	.348	16	.246	1	14	14	-3	1.1
1931 StL-N	12	3	.800	19	17	8	2	0	122^1	134	2	28	27	11.9	3.02	131	.278	.318	6	.133	-2	12	13	-1	0.9
1932 StL-N	3	5	.375	20	10	4	1	0	85^1	116	4	16	27	14.0	4.75	83	.326	.357	5	.185	0	-8	-8	-1	-0.8
1933 StL-N	9	6	.600	32	10	5	0	1	115^1	113	3	37	37	11.8	2.50	139	.252	.311	2	.067	-2	11	13	-2	0.9
1934 *StL-N	4	4	.500	37	6	0	0	1	90	86	6	19	17	10.9	3.50	121	.262	.311	3	.158	-1	**6**	**7**	2	0.8
1935 StL-N	6	5	.545	30	12	3	0	2	115^1	110	4	28	24	10.8	3.59	114	.252	.299	9	.273	1	6	7	-2	0.6
1936 StL-N	7	5	.583	25	9	4	0	1	99^1	110	4	24	19	12.0	3.90	101	.284	.323	5	.167	-1	1	1	-0	0.0
1937 StL-N	3	3	.500	16	6	2	0	0	65^2	81	5	23	18	14.4	4.52	88	.303	.361	4	.182	-0	-4	-4	-1	-0.5
Total 19	210	158	.571	555	388	208	24	10	3208^2	3460	165	871	981	12.3	3.64	108	.280	.330	209	.186	-21	114	104	-21	6.6
● **JIM HAISLIP** Haislip, James Clifton "Slim" b: 8/4/1891, Farmersville, Tex. d: 1/22/70, Dallas, Tex. BR/TR, 6'1", 186 lbs. Deb: 8/27/13																									
1913 Phi-N	0	0	—	1	0	0	0	0	3	4	0	3	0	21.0	6.00	56	.400	.538	0	.000	-0	-1	-1	-0	-0.1
● **ED HALBRITER** Halbriter, Edward L. b: 2/2/1860, Auburn, N.Y. d: 8/9/36, Los Angeles, Cal. Deb: 5/23/1882																									
1882 Phi-a	0	1	.000	1	1	1	0	0	8	17	1	4	4	23.6	7.88	38	.406	.458	0	.000	-1	-5	-4	-0	-0.4
● **DAD HALE** Hale, Ray Luther b: 2/18/1879, Allegan, Mich. d: 2/1/46, Allegan, Mich. BR/TR, 5'10", 180 lbs. Deb: 4/21/02																									
1902 Bos-N	1	4	.200	8	6	3	0	0	47	69	1	18	12	16.9	6.32	45	.341	.397	0	.000	-1	-18	-18	-0	-1.8
Bal-A	0	1	.000	3	2	1	0	0	14	21	0	6	6	18.0	4.50	84	.346	.414	0	.000	-1	-1	-1	-1	-0.2
Total 1	1	5	.167	11	8	4	0	0	61	90	1	24	18	17.1	5.90	51	.342	.401	0	.000	-2	-20	-19	-1	-2.0

YEAR	TM/L	W	L	PCT	G	GS	CG	SH	SV	IP	H	HR	BB	SO	RAT	ERA	ERA+	OAV	OOB	BH	AVG	PB	PR	/A	PD	TPI
● **ED HALICKI** Halicki, Edward Louis b: 10/4/50, Newark, N.J. BR/TR, 6'7", 220 lbs. Deb: 7/08/74																										
1974	SF-N	1	8	.111	16	11	2	0	0	74^1	84	6	31	40	14.2	4.24	90	.275	.345	6	.240	1	-5	-4	-1	-0.3
1975	SF-N	9	13	.409	24	23	7	2	0	159^2	143	6	59	153	11.6	3.49	109	.240	.312	6	.113	-2	2	5	-1	0.3
1976	SF-N	12	14	.462	32	31	8	4	0	186^1	171	10	61	130	11.3	3.62	100	.246	.309	9	.170	1	-3	0	-0	0.1
1977	SF-N	16	12	.571	37	37	7	2	0	257^2	241	27	70	168	11.1	3.32	118	.244	.298	15	.176	3	17	17	-3	1.7
1978	SF-N	9	10	.474	29	28	9	4	1	199	166	11	45	105	9.9	2.85	121	.221	**.271**	9	.136	-2	16	13	-2	1.0
1979	SF-N	5	8	.385	33	19	3	1	0	125^2	134	12	47	81	13.2	4.58	76	.266	.333	7	.206	1	-12	-15	0	-1.4
1980	SF-N	0	0	—	11	2	0	0	0	25	29	5	10	14	14.0	5.40	65	.293	.358	1	.167	-0	-5	-5	0	-0.5
	Cal-A	3	1	.750	10	6	0	0	0	35^1	39	5	11	16	12.7	4.84	81	.279	.331	0	—	0	-3	-4	-1	-0.4
Total	7	55	66	.455	192	157	36	13	1	1063	1007	82	334	707	11.6	3.62	102	.247	.308	53	.165	3	8	8	-7	0.5
● **DREW HALL** Hall, Andrew Clark b: 3/27/63, Louisville, Ky. BL/TL, 6'4", 205 lbs. Deb: 9/14/86																										
1986	Chi-N	1	2	.333	5	4	1	0	1	23^2	24	3	10	21	12.9	4.56	89	.267	.340	1	.143	0	-2	-1	-0	-0.2
1987	Chi-N	1	1	.500	21	0	0	0	0	32^2	40	4	14	20	14.9	6.89	62	.308	.375	0	.000	-0	-10	-9	-0	-1.0
1988	Chi-N	1	1	.500	19	0	0	0	1	22^1	26	4	9	22	14.5	7.66	47	.295	.367	0	.000	0	-10	-10	0	-1.0
1989	Tex-A	2	1	.667	38	0	0	0	0	58^1	42	3	33	45	12.0	3.70	107	.207	.326	0	—	0	1	2	0	0.2
1990	Mon-N	4	7	.364	42	0	0	0	3	58^1	52	6	29	40	12.5	5.09	72	.242	.332	0	.000	-0	-8	-9	1	-0.9
Total	5	9	12	.429	125	4	1	0	5	195^1	184	20	95	148	13.0	5.21	75	.253	.343	1	.063	-1	-30	-29	-0	-2.9
● **CHARLEY HALL** Hall, Charles Louis "Sea Lion" (b: Carlos Clolo) b: 7/27/1885, Ventura, Cal. d: 12/6/43, Ventura, Cal. BL/TR, 6'1", 187 lbs. Deb: 7/12/06																										
1906	Cin-N	4	8	.333	14	9	9	1	1	95	86	1	50	49	13.6	3.32	83	.258	.368	6	.128	-1	-7	-6	0	-0.8
1907	Cin-N	4	2	.667	11	8	5	0	0	68	51	0	43	25	13.0	2.51	103	.226	.359	7	.269	1	-0	1	-1	0.1
1909	Bos-A	6	4	.600	11	7	3	0	0	59^2	59	0	17	27	11.9	2.56	98	.271	.332	3	.158	-1	-1	-0	-0	-0.1
1910	Bos-A	12	9	.571	35	16	13	0	2	188^2	142	6	73	95	10.7	1.91	134	.207	.292	17	.207	3	13	14	0	2.0
1911	Bos-A	8	7	.533	32	10	6	0	**4**	146^1	149	3	72	83	13.9	3.75	87	.279	.370	9	.141	-1	-7	-8	-2	-1.0
1912	*Bos-A	15	8	.652	34	20	9	2	2	191	178	3	70	83	11.9	3.02	113	.257	.329	20	.267	5	6	8	1	1.5
1913	Bos-A	5	4	.556	35	4	2	0	2	105	97	1	46	48	12.7	3.43	86	.235	.319	9	.214	1	-6	-6	-1	-0.6
1916	StL-N	0	4	.000	10	5	2	0	1	42^2	45	1	14	15	12.4	5.48	48	.280	.337	2	.143	-1	-14	-13	0	-1.4
1918	Det-A	0	1	.000	6	1	0	0	0	13^1	14	1	6	2	13.5	6.75	39	.269	.345	0	.000	-0	-6	-6	-1	-0.7
Total	9	54	47	.535	188	80	49	3	12	909^2	821	16	391	427	12.4	3.09	95	.248	.334	73	.197	7	-21	-17	-2	-1.0
● **BERT HALL** Hall, Herbert Ernest b: 10/15/1888, Portland, Ore. d: 7/18/48, Seattle, Wash. BR/TR, 5'10", 178 lbs. Deb: 8/21/11																										
1911	Phi-N	0	1	.000	7	1	0	0	0	18	19	0	13	8	16.5	4.00	86	.297	.423	1	.333	0	-1	-1	-1	-0.2
● **HERB HALL** Hall, Herbert Silas "Iron Duke" b: 6/5/1893, Steelville, Ill. d: 7/1/70, Fresno, Cal. BB/TR, 6'4", 220 lbs. Deb: 4/28/18																										
1918	Det-A	0	0	—	3	0	0	0	0	6	12	0	7	1	31.5	15.00	18	.500	.636	0	.000	-0	-8	-8	0	-0.8
● **JOHN HALL** Hall, John Sylvester b: 1/9/24, Muskogee, Okla. BR/TR, 6'2.5", 170 lbs. Deb: 4/21/48																										
1948	Bro-N	0	0	—	3	0	0	0	0	4^1	4	1	2	2	12.5	6.23	64	.267	.353	0	—	0	-1	-1	0	-0.1
● **MARC HALL** Hall, Marcus b: 8/12/1887, Joplin, Mo. d: 2/24/15, Joplin, Mo. BR/TR, 6'1.5", 190 lbs. Deb: 8/20/10																										
1910	StL-A	1	7	.125	8	7	5	0	0	46^1	50	0	31	25	16.3	4.27	58	.289	.406	1	.067	-2	-9	-9	1	-1.0
1913	Det-A	10	12	.455	30	21	8	1	0	165	154	1	79	69	12.8	3.27	89	.255	.344	4	.089	-3	-6	-6	0	-0.9
1914	Det-A	4	6	.400	25	8	1	0	0	90^1	88	1	27	18	11.5	2.69	104	.267	.322	1	.043	-2	1	1	0	-0.1
Total	3	15	25	.375	63	36	14	1	0	301^2	292	2	137	112	12.9	3.25	87	.264	.348	6	.072	-7	-15	-15	1	-2.0
● **DICK HALL** Hall, Richard Wallace b: 9/27/30, St.Louis, Mo. BR/TR, 6'6", 200 lbs. Deb: 4/15/52 ♦																										
1955	Pit-N	6	6	.500	15	13	4	0	1	94^1	92	8	28	46	11.6	3.91	105	.253	.310	7	.175	1	1	2	-2	0.2
1956	Pit-N	0	7	.000	19	9	1	0	1	62^1	64	8	21	27	12.3	4.76	79	.270	.329	10	.345	2	-7	-7	-1	-0.4
1957	Pit-N	0	0	—	8	0	0	0	0	10	17	4	5	7	20.7	10.80	35	.362	.434	0	.000	-0	-8	-8	-0	-0.8
1959	Pit-N	0	0	—	2	1	0	0	0	8^2	12	1	1	3	13.5	3.12	124	.333	.351	0	.000	-0	1	1	-0	0.0
1960	KC-A	8	13	.381	29	28	9	1	0	182^1	183	28	38	79	11.1	4.05	98	.261	.301	6	.107	-3	-4	-1	-1	-0.4
1961	Bal-A	7	5	.583	29	13	4	2	4	122^1	102	10	30	92	9.7	3.09	126	.227	.275	5	.139	-0	13	11	1	1.2
1962	Bal-A	6	6	.500	43	6	1	0	6	118^1	102	9	19	71	9.2	2.28	165	.230	.262	4	.167	1	22	19	-0	2.1
1963	Bal-A	5	5	.500	47	3	0	0	12	111^2	91	12	16	74	8.9	2.98	118	.224	.260	13	.464	6	8	7	1	1.4
1964	Bal-A	9	1	.900	45	0	0	0	7	87^2	58	8	16	52	7.6	1.85	193	.188	.228	2	.125	-0	17	17	-0	1.8
1965	Bal-A	11	8	.579	48	0	0	0	12	93^2	84	8	11	79	9.1	3.07	113	.243	.266	5	.333	3	4	4	-1	0.6
1966	Bal-A	6	2	.750	32	0	0	0	7	66	59	8	8	44	9.5	3.95	84	.233	.265	2	.167	0	-4	-5	-0	-0.5
1967	Phi-N	10	8	.556	48	1	1	0	8	86	83	5	12	49	10.2	2.20	155	.255	.286	1	.071	-1	11	12	1	1.3
1968	Phi-N	4	1	.800	32	0	0	0	0	46	53	6	5	31	11.5	4.89	61	.296	.319	1	.333	0	-10	-10	-0	-1.1
1969	*Bal-A	5	2	.714	39	0	0	0	6	65^2	49	3	9	31	8.1	1.92	186	.213	.246	2	.286	1	12	12	-1	1.3
1970	*Bal-A	10	5	.667	32	0	0	0	3	61^1	51	8	6	30	8.4	3.08	118	.229	.249	1	.083	-1	4	4	-1	0.2
1971	Bal-A	6	6	.500	27	0	0	0	1	43^1	52	4	11	26	13.3	4.98	67	.302	.348	2	.400	1	-7	-8	-1	-0.8
Total	16	93	75	.554	495	74	20	3	68	1259^2	1152	130	236	741	10.0	3.32	111	.244	.283	150	.210	9	55	50	-7	6.1
● **BOB HALL** Hall, Robert Lewis b: 12/22/23, Swissvale, Pa. d: 3/12/83, St.Petersburg, Fla BR/TR, 6'2", 195 lbs. Deb: 4/23/49																										
1949	Bos-N	6	4	.600	31	6	2	0	0	74^1	77	7	41	43	14.4	4.36	87	.272	.366	8	.364	2	-3	-5	-2	-0.4
1950	Bos-N	0	2	.000	21	4	0	0	0	50^1	58	8	33	22	16.6	6.97	55	.293	.399	1	.083	-1	-16	-17	-0	-1.7
1953	Pit-N	3	12	.200	37	17	6	1	1	152	172	17	72	68	14.5	5.39	83	.286	.364	6	.158	0	-19	-15	-1	-1.5
Total	3	9	18	.333	89	27	8	1	1	276^2	307	32	146	133	14.9	5.40	77	.284	.371	15	.208	2	-37	-38	-3	-3.6
● **TOM HALL** Hall, Tom Edward b: 11/23/47, Thomasville, N.C. BL/TL, 6', 155 lbs. Deb: 6/09/68																										
1968	Min-A	2	1	.667	8	4	0	0	0	29^2	27	1	12	18	12.1	2.43	127	.239	.317	0	.000	-1	2	2	-0	0.1
1969	*Min-A	8	7	.533	31	18	5	2	0	140^2	129	12	50	92	11.5	3.33	110	.243	.308	8	.186	1	5	5	-2	0.4
1970	*Min-A	11	6	.647	52	11	1	0	4	155^1	94	11	66	184	9.4	2.55	146	.173	.265	8	.182	-0	20	20	-2	1.9
1971	Min-A	4	7	.364	48	11	0	0	9	129^2	104	13	58	137	11.2	3.33	107	.216	.300	9	.265	2	2	3	1	0.6
1972	*Cin-N	10	1	.909	47	7	1	1	8	124^1	77	13	56	134	9.8	2.61	123	.173	.269	3	.100	-1	12	8	-2	0.6
1973	*Cin-N	8	5	.615	54	7	0	0	8	103^2	74	13	48	96	10.6	3.47	98	.202	.295	1	.045	-2	2	-1	-2	-0.5
1974	Cin-N	3	1	.750	40	1	0	0	1	64	54	9	30	48	11.8	4.08	86	.232	.319	0	.000	-1	-3	-4	-0	-0.5
1975	Cin-N	0	0	—	2	0	0	0	0	2	2	0	2	3	18.0	0.00	—	.250	.400	0	—	0	1	1	0	0.1
	NY-N	4	3	.571	34	4	0	0	1	60^2	58	10	31	48	13.6	4.75	73	.254	.351	2	.400	1	-8	-9	-0	-0.9
	Yr	4	3	.571	36	4	0	0	1	62^2	60	10	33	51	13.8	4.60	75	.254	.353	2	.400	1	-7	-8	-0	-0.8
1976	NY-N	1	1	.500	5	0	0	0	0	4^2	5	0	5	2	19.3	5.79	57	.250	.400	0	—	0	-1	-1	0	-0.1
	*KC-A	1	1	.500	31	0	0	0	1	30^1	28	4	18	25	13.6	4.45	79	.246	.348	0	—	0	-3	-3	1	-0.3
1977	KC-A	0	0	—	6	0	0	0	0	7^2	4	2	6	10	11.7	3.52	115	.154	.313	0	—	0	0	0	0	0.1
Total	10	52	33	.612	358	63	7	3	32	852^2	656	88	382	797	11.0	3.27	107	.211	.299	31	.161	-1	28	22	-8	1.5
● **BILL HALL** Hall, William Bernard "Beanie" b: 2/22/1894, Charleston, W.Va. d: 8/15/47, Newport, Ky. BR/TR, 6'2", 250 lbs. Deb: 7/04/13																										
1913	Bro-N	0	0	—	3	0	0	0	0	4^2	4	0	5	3	19.3	5.79	57	.267	.476	0	.000	-0	-1	-1	-0	-0.2
● **JOHN HALLA** Halla, John Arthur b: 5/13/1884, St.Louis, Mo. d: 9/30/47, ElSegundo, Cal. BL/TL, 5'11", 175 lbs. Deb: 8/18/05																										
1905	Cle-A	0	0	—	3	0	0	0	0	12^2	12	0	0	4	9.2	2.84	93	.251	.267	1	.200	-0	-0	-0	-0	-0.1
● **BILL HALLAHAN** Hallahan, William Anthony "Wild Bill" b: 8/4/02, Binghamton, N.Y. d: 7/8/81, Binghamton, N.Y. BR/TL, 5'10.5", 170 lbs. Deb: 4/16/25																										
1925	StL-N	1	0	1.000	6	0	0	0	0	15^1	14	0	11	8	14.7	3.52	123	.259	.385	1	.333	0	1	1	0	0.2

YEAR	TM/L	W	L	PCT	G	GS	CG	SH	SV	IP	H	HR	BB	SO	RAT	ERA	ERA+	OAV	OOB	BH	AVG	PB	PR	/A	PD	TPI
1926	*StL-N	1	4	.200	19	3	0	0	0	56^2	45	1	32	28	12.4	3.65	107	.260	.379	4	.250	0	**1**	**2**	-1	0.1
1929	StL-N	4	4	.500	20	12	5	0	0	93^2	94	6	60	52	14.8	4.42	106	.269	.376	4	.154	-1	3	3	1	0.2
1930	*StL-N	15	9	.625	35	32	13	2	2	237^1	233	15	126	**177**	13.6	4.66	108	.260	.351	10	.123	-6	8	9	-0	0.2
1931	*StL-N	**19**	9	.679	37	30	16	3	4	248^2	242	10	112	**159**	12.8	3.29	120	.259	.339	8	.099	-4	16	18	-2	1.1
1932	StL-N	12	7	.632	25	22	13	1	1	176^1	169	10	69	108	12.1	3.11	126	.253	.323	12	.214	2	15	16	-1	1.7
1933	StL-N★	16	13	.552	36	32	16	2	0	244^1	245	6	98	93	12.6	3.50	99	.260	.330	12	.150	-0	-4	-1	-3	-0.4
1934	*StL-N	8	12	.400	32	26	10	2	0	162^2	195	2	66	70	14.4	4.26	99	.294	.358	10	.182	-1	-4	-1	-0	-0.2
1935	StL-N	15	8	.652	40	23	8	2	1	181^1	196	7	57	73	12.6	3.42	120	.275	.329	8	.143	-2	12	14	-1	1.1
1936	StL-N	2	2	.500	9	6	1	0	0	37	58	4	17	16	18.2	6.32	62	.360	.421	5	.556	3	-9	-10	0	-0.7
	Cin-N	5	9	.357	23	19	5	2	0	135	150	3	57	32	13.9	4.33	88	.287	.359	9	.191	1	-5	-8	1	-0.6
	Yr	7	11	.389	32	25	6	2	0	172	208	7	74	48	14.8	4.76	81	.305	.373	14	.250	3	-14	-17	1	-1.3
1937	Cin-N	3	9	.250	21	9	2	0	0	63	90	3	29	18	17.3	6.14	61	.345	.414	2	.095	-1	-16	-17	0	-1.7
1938	Phi-N	1	8	.111	21	10	1	0	0	89	107	4	45	22	15.6	5.46	71	.295	.376	5	.192	-0	-17	-16	-0	-1.5
Total	12	102	94	.520	324	224	90	14	8	1740^1	1838	71	779	856	13.6	4.03	102	.274	.351	90	.162	-9	2	12	-6	-0.5

● JACK HALLETT Hallett, Jack Price b: 11/13/14, Toledo, Ohio d: 6/11/82, Toledo, Ohio BR/TR, 6'4", 215 lbs. Deb: 9/13/40

YEAR	TM/L	W	L	PCT	G	GS	CG	SH	SV	IP	H	HR	BB	SO	RAT	ERA	ERA+	OAV	OOB	BH	AVG	PB	PR	/A	PD	TPI
1940	Chi-A	1	1	.500	2	2	1	0	0	14	15	1	6	9	14.1	6.43	69	.273	.355	2	.400	0	-3	-3	0	-0.2
1941	Chi-A	5	5	.500	22	6	3	0	0	74^2	96	7	38	25	16.5	6.03	68	.306	.386	4	.154	0	-16	-16	-0	-1.5
1942	Pit-N	0	1	.000	3	3	2	0	0	22^1	23	0	8	16	12.5	4.84	70	.274	.337	3	.375	2	-4	-4	0	-0.2
1943	Pit-N	1	2	.333	9	4	2	1	0	47^2	36	0	11	11	9.1	1.70	205	.212	.264	4	.286	2	9	9	-1	1.2
1946	Pit-N	5	7	.417	35	9	3	1	0	115	107	0	39	64	11.4	3.29	107	.267	.332	6	.231	0	2	3	0	0.4
1948	NY-N	0	0	—	2	0	0	0	0	4	3	0	4	3	15.8	4.50	87	.214	.389	0	.000	-0	-0	-0	-0	-0.1
Total	6	12	16	.429	73	24	11	2	0	277^2	280	8	106	128	12.7	4.05	92	.270	.340	19	.237	4	-12	-10	-1	-0.4

● BILL HALLMAN Hallman, William Wilson b: 3/31/1867, Pittsburgh, Pa. d: 9/11/20, Philadelphia, Pa. BR/TR, 5'8", 160 lbs. Deb: 4/23/1888 M♦

YEAR	TM/L	W	L	PCT	G	GS	CG	SH	SV	IP	H	HR	BB	SO	RAT	ERA	ERA+	OAV	OOB	BH	AVG	PB	PR	/A	PD	TPI
1896	Phi-N	0	0	—	1	0	0	0	0	2	4	0	2	0	27.0	18.00	24	.411	.511	150	.320	0	-3	-3	-0	-0.2

● CHARLIE HALLSTROM Hallstrom, Charles E. "Swedish Wonder" b: 1/22/1864, Jonkoping, Sweden d: 5/6/49, Chicago, Ill. Deb: 9/23/1885

YEAR	TM/L	W	L	PCT	G	GS	CG	SH	SV	IP	H	HR	BB	SO	RAT	ERA	ERA+	OAV	OOB	BH	AVG	PB	PR	/A	PD	TPI
1885	Pro-N	0	1	.000	1	1	1	0	0	9	18	3	6	0	24.0	11.00	24	.409	.480	0	.000	-1	-8	-8	-0	-0.6

● DOC HAMANN Hamann, Elmer Joseph b: 12/21/1900, New Ulm, Minn. d: 1/11/73, Milwaukee, Wis. BR/TR, 6'1", 180 lbs. Deb: 9/21/22

YEAR	TM/L	W	L	PCT	G	GS	CG	SH	SV	IP	H	HR	BB	SO	RAT	ERA	ERA+	OAV	OOB	BH	AVG	PB	PR	/A	PD	TPI
1922	Cle-A	0	0	—	1	0	0	0	0	0	3	0	3	0	—	∞	—	1.000	1.000	0	—	0	-6	-6	0	-0.5

● ROGER HAMBRIGHT Hambright, Roger Dee b: 3/26/49, Sunnyside, Wash. BR/TR, 5'10", 180 lbs. Deb: 7/19/71

YEAR	TM/L	W	L	PCT	G	GS	CG	SH	SV	IP	H	HR	BB	SO	RAT	ERA	ERA+	OAV	OOB	BH	AVG	PB	PR	/A	PD	TPI
1971	NY-A	3	1	.750	18	0	0	0	2	26^2	22	5	10	14	10.8	4.39	74	.224	.296	1	.500	0	-3	-3	0	-0.3

● JOHN HAMILL Hamill, John Alexander Charles b: 12/18/1860, New York, N.Y. d: 12/6/11, Bristol, R.I. BR/TR, 5'8", 158 lbs. Deb: 5/01/1884

YEAR	TM/L	W	L	PCT	G	GS	CG	SH	SV	IP	H	HR	BB	SO	RAT	ERA	ERA+	OAV	OOB	BH	AVG	PB	PR	/A	PD	TPI
1884	Was-a	2	17	.105	19	19	18	1	0	156^2	197	8	43	50	14.1	4.48	68	.287	.333	7	.099	-3	-21	-25	-1	-2.4

● DAVE HAMILTON Hamilton, David Edward b: 12/13/47, Seattle, Wash. BL/TL, 6', 190 lbs. Deb: 5/29/72

YEAR	TM/L	W	L	PCT	G	GS	CG	SH	SV	IP	H	HR	BB	SO	RAT	ERA	ERA+	OAV	OOB	BH	AVG	PB	PR	/A	PD	TPI
1972	*Oak-A	6	6	.500	25	14	1	0	0	101^1	94	7	31	55	11.2	2.93	97	.249	.307	4	.154	2	1	-1	-0	0.1
1973	Oak-A	6	4	.600	16	11	1	0	0	69^2	74	8	24	34	12.8	4.39	81	.274	.336	0	—	0	-4	-7	-1	-0.6
1974	Oak-A	7	4	.636	29	18	1	1	0	117	104	10	48	69	12.1	3.15	105	.241	.324	0	—	0	6	2	-0	0.3
1975	Oak-A	1	2	.333	11	4	0	0	0	35^2	42	4	18	20	15.1	4.04	90	.290	.368	0	—	0	-1	-2	-0	-0.1
	Chi-A	6	5	.545	30	1	0	0	6	69^2	63	4	29	51	11.9	2.84	136	.246	.323	0	—	0	7	8	0	0.8
	Yr	7	7	.500	41	5	0	0	6	105^1	105	8	47	71	13.0	3.25	117	.261	.339	0	—	0	6	6	0	0.7
1976	Chi-A	6	6	.500	45	1	0	0	10	90^1	81	4	45	62	13.0	3.59	99	.243	.340	0	—	0	-1	-0	-1	-0.1
1977	Chi-A	4	5	.444	55	0	0	0	9	67^1	71	6	33	45	13.9	3.61	113	.270	.351	0	—	0	3	4	0	0.4
1978	StL-N	0	0	—	13	0	0	0	0	14	16	5	6	8	14.1	6.43	55	.296	.367	0	.000	-0	-4	-5	0	-0.5
	Pit-N	0	2	.000	16	0	0	0	1	26^1	23	2	12	15	12.0	3.42	108	.221	.302	0	.000	-1	0	1	-0	0.0
	Yr	0	2	.000	29	0	0	0	1	40^1	39	7	18	23	12.7	4.46	81	.247	.324	0	.000	-1	-4	-4	-0	-0.5
1979	Oak-A	3	4	.429	40	7	1	0	5	82^2	80	5	43	52	13.5	3.70	109	.261	.353	0	—	0	5	3	1	0.4
1980	Oak-A	0	3	.000	21	1	0	0	0	30	44	6	28	23	22.5	11.40	33	.344	.472	0	—	0	-25	-25	-0	-2.4
Total	9	39	41	.488	301	57	4	1	31	704	692	61	317	434	13.1	3.85	93	.259	.341	4	.121	1	-12	-22	-2	-1.7

● EARL HAMILTON Hamilton, Earl Andrew b: 7/19/1891, Gibson, Ill. d: 11/17/68, Anaheim, Cal. BL/TL, 5'8", 160 lbs. Deb: 4/14/11

YEAR	TM/L	W	L	PCT	G	GS	CG	SH	SV	IP	H	HR	BB	SO	RAT	ERA	ERA+	OAV	OOB	BH	AVG	PB	PR	/A	PD	TPI
1911	StL-A	5	12	.294	32	17	10	1	0	177	191	4	69	55	13.4	3.97	85	.284	.354	6	.107	-1	-12	-12	1	-1.1
1912	StL-A	11	14	.440	41	26	17	1	2	249^2	228	2	86	139	11.6	3.24	102	.248	.319	13	.178	-0	2	2	-2	0.1
1913	StL-A	13	12	.520	31	24	19	3	1	217^1	197	3	83	101	12.0	2.57	114	.241	.318	10	.135	-2	9	9	-1	0.7
1914	StL-A	17	18	.486	44	35	20	5	2	302^1	265	5	100	111	11.2	2.50	108	.239	.307	15	.176	4	8	7	-4	0.7
1915	StL-A	9	17	.346	35	27	13	1	0	204	203	4	69	63	12.5	2.87	100	.274	.346	7	.113	-2	2	-0	-2	-0.4
1916	StL-A	0	0	—	1	0	0	0	0	4	4	0	4	0	18.0	9.00	31	.250	.400	0	—	0	-3	-3	-0	-0.3
	Det-A	1	2	.333	5	5	3	0	0	37^1	34	0	22	7	14.5	2.65	108	.254	.375	1	.077	-1	1	1	1	0.1
	StL-A	5	7	.417	22	12	3	0	0	91^1	97	2	26	25	12.3	3.05	90	.284	.339	0	.000	-1	-2	-3	-1	-0.6
	Yr	6	9	.400	28	17	6	0	0	132^2	135	2	52	32	12.8	3.12	89	.273	.344	1	.027	-2	-4	-5	-1	-0.8
1917	StL-A	0	9	.000	27	8	2	0	1	83	86	1	41	19	14.0	3.14	83	.274	.361	7	.368	3	-4	-5	-1	-0.3
1918	Pit-N	6	0	1.000	6	6	6	1	0	54	47	0	13	20	10.0	0.83	345	.242	.290	6	.286	1	12	12	-0	1.7
1919	Pit-N	8	11	.421	28	19	9	1	1	160^1	167	3	49	39	12.4	3.31	91	.280	.340	7	.135	-2	-7	-5	2	-0.7
1920	Pit-N	10	13	.435	39	23	12	0	3	230^1	223	2	69	74	11.5	3.24	99	.258	.314	10	.149	-3	-3	-1	-0	-0.4
1921	Pit-N	13	15	.464	35	30	12	2	0	225	237	5	58	59	12.1	3.36	114	.272	.323	12	.160	-0	11	12	4	1.5
1922	Pit-N	11	7	.611	33	14	9	1	2	160	183	6	40	34	12.6	3.99	102	.296	.339	9	.155	-2	2	1	-1	-0.1
1923	Pit-N	7	9	.438	28	15	5	0	1	141	148	6	42	42	12.2	3.77	106	.271	.324	9	.173	-2	4	4	2	0.4
1924	Phi-N	0	1	.000	3	0	0	0	0	6	9	0	2	2	18.0	10.50	42	.391	.462	0	.000	-0	-4	-4	0	-0.4
Total	14	116	147	.441	410	261	140	16	13	2342^2	2319	43	773	790	12.1	3.16	102	.264	.329	112	.153	-9	13	15	-4	0.9

● JACK HAMILTON Hamilton, Jack Edwin b: 12/25/38, Burlington, Iowa BR/TR, 6', 200 lbs. Deb: 4/13/62

YEAR	TM/L	W	L	PCT	G	GS	CG	SH	SV	IP	H	HR	BB	SO	RAT	ERA	ERA+	OAV	OOB	BH	AVG	PB	PR	/A	PD	TPI
1962	Phi-N	9	12	.429	41	26	4	1	2	182	185	18	107	101	14.7	5.09	76	.268	.370	3	.056	-4	-23	-25	2	-2.5
1963	Phi-N	2	1	.667	19	1	0	0	1	30	22	3	17	23	11.7	5.40	60	.200	.307	0	.000	-0	-7	-7	1	-0.7
1964	Det-A	0	1	.000	5	1	0	0	0	15	24	2	8	5	19.8	8.40	44	.364	.440	0	.000	-0	-8	-8	1	-0.7
1965	Det-A	1	1	.500	4	1	0	0	0	4^1	6	1	4	3	20.8	14.54	24	.316	.435	0	—	0	-5	-5	0	-0.5
1966	NY-N	6	13	.316	57	13	3	1	13	148^2	138	13	88	93	14.0	3.93	92	.248	.356	5	.132	-1	-5	-5	1	-0.5
1967	NY-N	2	0	1.000	17	1	0	0	1	31^1	24	2	16	22	11.8	3.73	91	.205	.306	1	.200	1	-1	-1	-0	-0.1
	Cal-A	9	6	.600	26	20	0	0	0	119^1	104	6	63	74	12.7	3.24	97	.239	.337	6	.158	-0	-0	-1	-0	-0.2
1968	Cal-A	3	1	.750	21	2	1	0	2	38	34	0	15	18	11.6	3.32	88	.246	.320	1	.143	-0	-1	-2	-0	-0.2
1969	Cle-A	0	2	.000	20	0	0	0	1	30^2	37	2	23	13	17.6	4.40	86	.316	.429	0	.000	-0	-3	-2	-0	-0.3
	Chi-A	0	3	.000	8	0	0	0	0	12^1	23	1	7	5	21.9	11.68	33	.411	.476	0	—	0	-11	-11	-0	-1.0
	Yr	0	5	.000	28	0	0	0	1	43	60	3	30	18	18.8	6.49	58	.345	.441	0	.000	-0	-14	-13	-0	-1.3
Total	8	32	40	.444	218	65	8	2	20	611^2	597	48	348	357	14.1	4.53	78	.259	.359	16	.107	-5	-66	-67	4	-6.7

● JEFF HAMILTON Hamilton, Jeffrey Robert b: 3/19/64, Flint, Mich. BR/TR, 6'3", 207 lbs. Deb: 6/28/86 ♦

YEAR	TM/L	W	L	PCT	G	GS	CG	SH	SV	IP	H	HR	BB	SO	RAT	ERA	ERA+	OAV	OOB	BH	AVG	PB	PR	/A	PD	TPI
1989	LA-N	0	1	.000	1	0	0	0	0	1^2	2	0	1	2	16.2	5.40	63	.286	.375	134	.245	0	-0	-0	0	0.0

● STEVE HAMILTON Hamilton, Steve Absher b: 11/30/35, Columbia, Ky. BL/TL, 6'7", 195 lbs. Deb: 4/23/61 C

YEAR	TM/L	W	L	PCT	G	GS	CG	SH	SV	IP	H	HR	BB	SO	RAT	ERA	ERA+	OAV	OOB	BH	AVG	PB	PR	/A	PD	TPI
1961	Cle-A	0	0	—	2	0	0	0	0	3	2	0	3	4	15.0	3.00	131	.200	.385	1	1.000	0	0	0	0	0.1
1962	Was-A	3	8	.273	41	10	1	0	2	107^1	103	10	39	83	12.2	3.77	107	.248	.317	2	.077	-1	2	3	1	0.3

YEAR	TM/L	W	L	PCT	G	GS	CG	SH	SV	IP	H	HR	BB	SO	RAT	ERA	ERA+	OAV	OOB	BH	AVG	PB	PR	/A	PD	TPI
1963	Was-A	0	1	.000	3	0	0	0	0	2	5	0	2	1	31.5	13.50	27	.556	.636	0	—	0	-2	-2	0	-0.2
	*NY-A	5	1	.833	34	0	0	0	5	62^1	49	3	24	63	10.7	2.60	135	.220	.298	4	.286	1	7	6	1	0.9
	Yr	5	2	.714	37	0	0	0	5	64^1	54	3	26	64	11.3	2.94	120	.232	.312	4	.286	1	5	4	1	0.7
1964	*NY-A	7	2	.778	30	3	1	0	3	60^1	55	6	15	49	10.4	3.28	110	.246	.293	4	.200	1	2	2	0	0.3
1965	NY-A	3	1	.750	46	1	0	0	5	58^1	47	2	16	51	9.7	1.39	245	.214	.267	1	.167	0	13	13	-2	1.3
1966	NY-A	8	3	.727	44	3	1	1	3	90	69	8	22	57	9.4	3.00	111	.218	.276	1	.053	-1	4	3	-1	0.1
1967	NY-A	2	4	.333	44	0	0	0	4	62	57	7	23	55	11.8	3.48	90	.250	.321	1	.111	-0	-2	-2	0	-0.3
1968	NY-A	2	2	.500	40	0	0	0	11	50^2	37	0	13	42	9.1	2.13	136	.211	.270	0	.000	0	5	4	0	0.6
1969	NY-A	3	4	.429	38	0	0	0	2	57	39	7	21	39	9.5	3.32	105	.194	.270	0	.000	-1	2	1	-1	-0.1
1970	NY-A	4	3	.571	35	0	0	0	3	45^1	36	3	16	33	10.5	2.78	126	.222	.296	0	.000	-1	5	4	0	0.3
	Chi-A	0	0	—	3	0	0	0	0	3	4	0	1	3	15.0	6.00	65	.333	.385	0	—	0	-1	-1	0	-0.1
	Yr	4	3	.571	38	0	0	0	3	48^1	40	3	17	36	10.6	2.98	119	.227	.295	0	.000	-1	4	3	1	0.2
1971	*SF-N	2	2	.500	39	0	0	0	4	44^2	29	4	11	38	8.3	3.02	112	.186	.244	0	.000	-0	2	2	-0	0.1
1972	Chi-N	1	0	1.000	22	0	0	0	0	17	24	1	8	13	17.5	4.76	80	.333	.407	0	.000	-0	-2	-2	-0	-0.2
Total	12	40	31	.563	421	17	3	1	42	663	556	51	214	531	10.6	3.05	114	.229	.295	14	.125	-2	36	32	-1	3.1
● **LUKE HAMLIN**	Hamlin, Luke Daniel "Hot Potato" b: 7/3/04, Ferris Center, Mich. d: 2/18/78, Clare, Mich. BL/TR, 6'2", 168 lbs. Deb: 9/18/33																									
1933	Det-A	1	0	1.000	3	3	0	0	0	16^2	20	3	10	10	16.2	4.86	89	.294	.385	2	.400	1	-1	-1	-1	0.0
1934	Det-A	2	3	.400	20	5	1	0	1	75^1	87	11	44	30	15.7	5.38	82	.289	.380	6	.231	-0	-7	-8	-0	-0.8
1937	Bro-N	11	13	.458	39	25	11	1	1	185^2	183	4	48	93	11.2	3.59	113	.252	.298	11	.186	-1	7	9	-3	0.6
1938	Bro-N	12	15	.444	44	30	10	3	6	237^1	243	14	65	97	11.8	3.68	106	.263	.313	11	.141	-3	3	6	-4	-0.1
1939	Bro-N	20	13	.606	40	36	19	2	0	269^2	255	27	54	88	10.3	3.64	111	.248	.285	13	.126	-5	8	12	-5	0.2
1940	Bro-N	9	8	.529	33	25	9	2	0	182^1	183	17	34	91	10.8	3.06	131	.256	.292	5	.086	-5	16	19	-4	1.1
1941	Bro-N	8	8	.500	30	20	5	1	1	136	139	14	41	58	12.0	4.24	87	.261	.316	6	.146	-1	-9	-9	-2	-1.1
1942	Pit-N	4	4	.500	23	14	6	1	0	112	128	3	19	38	11.9	3.94	86	.281	.312	9	.243	1	-8	-7	-2	-0.9
1944	Phi-A	6	12	.333	29	23	9	2	0	190	204	13	38	58	11.6	3.74	93	.271	.309	13	.232	3	-7	-6	-5	-0.8
Total	9	73	76	.490	261	181	70	12	9	1405	1442	106	353	563	11.6	3.77	103	.262	.308	76	.164	-9	2	16	-25	-1.8
● **PETE HAMM**	Hamm, Peter Whitfield b: 9/20/47, Buffalo, N.Y. BR/TR, 6'5", 210 lbs. Deb: 7/29/70																									
1970	Min-A	0	2	.000	10	0	0	0	0	16^1	17	3	7	3	13.2	5.51	68	.262	.333	0	.000	-0	-3	-3	-1	-0.4
1971	Min-A	2	4	.333	13	8	1	0	0	44	55	7	18	16	15.1	6.75	53	.309	.376	3	.273	1	-16	-16	0	-1.5
Total	2	2	6	.250	23	8	1	0	0	60^1	72	10	25	19	14.6	6.41	56	.296	.364	3	.250	1	-19	-19	-0	-1.9
● **ATLEE HAMMAKER**	Hammaker, Charlton Atlee b: 1/24/58, Carmel, Cal. BB/TL, 6'3", 200 lbs. Deb: 8/13/81																									
1981	KC-A	1	3	.250	10	6	0	0	0	39	44	2	12	11	12.9	5.54	65	.286	.337	0	—	0	-8	-8	-1	-0.9
1982	SF-N	12	8	.600	29	27	4	1	0	175	189	16	28	102	11.3	4.11	87	.278	.309	4	.068	-4	-10	-10	1	-1.3
1983	SF-N★	10	9	.526	23	23	8	3	0	172^1	147	9	32	127	**9.5**	**2.25**	**157**	.228	**.267**	6	.102	-1	26	25	1	2.7
1984	SF-N	2	0	1.000	6	6	0	0	0	33	32	2	9	24	11.2	2.18	161	.256	.306	2	.182	1	5	5	0	0.6
1985	SF-N	5	12	.294	29	29	1	1	0	170^2	161	17	47	100	11.0	3.74	92	.247	.298	4	.085	-2	-3	-6	1	-0.8
1987	*SF-N	10	10	.500	31	27	2	0	0	168^1	159	22	57	107	11.7	3.58	107	.248	.313	7	.123	-1	9	5	-1	0.3
1988	SF-N	9	9	.500	43	17	3	1	5	144^2	136	11	41	65	11.2	3.73	87	.248	.304	4	.121	-0	-5	-8	2	-0.6
1989	*SF-N	6	6	.500	28	9	0	0	0	76^2	78	5	23	30	12.0	3.76	90	.271	.327	7	.368	2	-2	-3	-1	-0.2
1990	SF-N	4	5	.444	25	6	0	0	0	67^1	69	7	21	28	12.0	4.28	85	.273	.328	1	.059	-1	-4	-5	-1	-0.6
	SD-N	0	4	.000	9	1	0	0	0	19^1	16	1	6	16	10.2	4.66	82	.213	.272	1	.500	0	-2	-2	-0	-0.2
	Yr	4	9	.308	34	7	0	0	0	86^2	85	8	27	44	11.6	4.36	84	.256	.312	2	.105	-0	-5	-7	-1	-0.8
1991	SD-N	0	1	.000	1	1	0	0	0	4^2	8	0	3	1	21.2	5.79	66	.364	.440	0	.000	-0	-1	-1	0	-0.1
Total	10	59	67	.468	234	152	18	6	5	1071	1039	92	279	611	11.2	3.61	98	.254	.304	36	.118	-7	6	-8	1	-1.1
● **CHRIS HAMMOND**	Hammond, Christopher Andrew b: 1/21/66, Atlanta, Ga. BL/TL, 6'1", 190 lbs. Deb: 7/16/90 F																									
1990	Cin-N	0	2	.000	3	3	0	0	0	11^1	13	2	12	4	19.9	6.35	62	.302	.455	0	.000	-0	-3	-3	0	-0.3
1991	Cin-N	7	7	.500	20	18	0	0	0	99^2	92	4	48	50	12.8	4.06	94	.250	.340	12	.353	5	-4	-3	0	0.2
1992	Cin-N	7	10	.412	28	26	0	0	0	147^1	149	13	55	79	12.6	4.21	87	.266	.334	6	.136	2	-12	-9	-0	-0.8
Total	3	14	19	.424	51	47	0	0	0	258^1	254	19	115	133	13.0	4.25	88	.261	.342	18	.222	6	-19	-15	0	-0.9
● **GRANNY HAMNER**	Hamner, Granville Wilbur b: 4/26/27, Richmond, Va. BR/TR, 5'10", 163 lbs. Deb: 9/14/44 F♦																									
1956	Phi-N	0	1	.000	3	1	0	0	0	8^1	10	0	2	4	13.0	4.32	86	.294	.333	90	.224	1	-1	-1	-0	0.0
1957	Phi-N	0	0	—	1	0	0	0	0	1	1	0	0	1	9.0	0.00	—	.250	.250	114	.227	0	0	0	0	0.0
1962	KC-A	0	1	.000	3	0	0	0	0	4	10	0	6	0	36.0	9.00	46	.476	.593	0	—	0	-2	-2	0	-0.2
Total	3	0	2	.000	7	1	0	0	0	13^1	21	0	8	5	19.6	5.40	71	.356	.433	1529	.262	1	-2	-2	-0	-0.2
● **RALPH HAMNER**	Hamner, Ralph Conant "Bruz" b: 9/12/16, Gibsland, La. BR/TR, 6'3", 165 lbs. Deb: 4/28/46																									
1946	Chi-A	2	7	.222	25	7	1	0	1	71^1	80	2	39	29	15.6	4.42	77	.276	.371	3	.167	0	-7	-8	-1	-0.9
1947	Chi-N	1	2	.333	3	3	2	0	0	25	24	0	16	14	14.4	2.52	157	.267	.377	1	.125	-0	4	4	-1	0.3
1948	Chi-N	5	9	.357	27	17	5	0	0	111^1	110	12	69	53	14.9	4.69	83	.259	.369	6	.182	1	-9	-10	2	-0.7
1949	Chi-N	0	2	.000	6	1	0	0	0	12^1	22	1	8	3	22.6	8.76	46	.407	.492	0	.000	-0	-6	-6	1	-0.5
Total	4	8	20	.286	61	28	8	0	1	220	236	15	132	99	15.5	4.58	82	.275	.378	10	.164	0	-18	-20	1	-1.8
● **GARRY HANCOCK**	Hancock, Ronald Garry b: 1/23/54, Tampa, Fla. BL/TL, 6', 175 lbs. Deb: 7/16/78 ♦																									
1984	Oak-A	0	0	—	1	0	0	0	0	1^1	0	0	0	0	0.0	0.00	—	.000	.000	13	.217	0	1	1	0	0.1
● **RICH HAND**	Hand, Richard Allen b: 7/10/48, Bellevue, Wash. BR/TR, 6'1", 195 lbs. Deb: 4/09/70																									
1970	Cle-A	6	13	.316	35	25	3	1	3	159^2	132	27	69	110	11.6	3.83	103	.228	.314	6	.146	-1	-2	2	0	0.1
1971	Cle-A	2	6	.250	15	12	0	0	0	60^2	74	6	38	26	17.2	5.79	66	.311	.414	2	.125	-1	-16	-13	-1	-1.5
1972	Tex-A	10	14	.417	30	28	2	1	0	170^2	139	12	103	109	12.9	3.32	91	.226	.340	8	.154	1	-5	-6	-0	-0.5
1973	Tex-A	2	3	.400	8	7	1	0	0	41^2	49	2	19	14	15.1	5.40	69	.290	.368	0	—	0	-7	-8	-1	-0.7
	Cal-A	4	3	.571	16	6	0	0	0	54^2	58	5	21	19	13.2	3.62	98	.274	.342	0	—	0	1	-0	1	0.2
	Yr	6	6	.500	24	13	1	0	0	96^1	107	7	40	33	13.8	4.39	82	.277	.347	0	—	0	-6	-8	0	-0.5
Total	4	24	39	.381	104	78	6	2	3	487^1	452	52	250	278	13.2	4.01	88	.249	.345	16	.147	-1	-29	-25	-1	-2.4
● **JIM HANDIBOE**	Handiboe, James Edward "Nick" b: 7/17/1866, Columbus, Ohio d: 11/8/42, Columbus, Ohio BR/TR, 5'11", 160 lbs. Deb: 5/28/1886																									
1886	Pit-a	7	7	.500	14	14	12	1	0	114	82	1	33	83	10.0	3.32	102	.195	.273	5	.114	-2	2	1	-0	-0.2
● **VERN HANDRAHAN**	Handrahan, James Vernon b: 11/27/38, Charlottetown, P.E.I., Canada BL/TR, 6'2", 185 lbs. Deb: 4/14/64																									
1964	KC-A	0	1	.000	18	1	0	0	0	35^2	33	9	25	18	15.1	6.06	63	.252	.380	2	.222	0	-10	-9	0	-0.9
1966	KC-A	0	1	.000	16	1	0	0	1	25^1	20	5	15	18	12.8	4.26	80	.227	.346	0	.000	-0	-2	-2	0	-0.3
Total	2	0	2	.000	34	2	0	0	1	61	53	14	40	36	14.2	5.31	69	.242	.366	2	.167	-0	-12	-11	0	-1.2
● **BILL HANDS**	Hands, William Alfred b: 5/6/40, Hackensack, N.J. BR/TR, 6'2", 185 lbs. Deb: 6/03/65																									
1965	SF-N	0	2	.000	4	2	0	0	0	6	13	0	6	5	28.5	16.50	22	.433	.528	0	.000	-0	-9	-9	0	-0.8
1966	Chi-N	8	13	.381	41	26	0	0	2	159	168	17	59	93	13.1	4.58	80	.272	.340	2	.041	-3	-17	-16	1	-1.8
1967	Chi-N	7	8	.467	49	11	3	1	6	150	134	9	48	84	11.0	2.46	144	.239	.301	4	.105	-1	15	18	-0	1.9
1968	Chi-N	16	10	.615	38	34	11	4	0	258^2	221	26	36	148	9.2	2.89	109	.231	.264	5	.061	-5	3	8	-0	0.3
1969	Chi-N	20	14	.588	41	41	18	3	0	300	268	21	73	181	10.4	2.49	162	.237	.287	9	.092	-5	37	**51**	1	5.3
1970	Chi-N	18	15	.545	39	38	12	2	1	265	278	20	76	170	12.2	3.70	122	.269	.322	10	.133	1	10	24	1	2.7
1971	Chi-N	12	18	.400	36	35	14	1	0	242^1	248	27	50	128	11.1	3.42	115	.260	.298	6	.083	-3	1	14	-0	1.1

YEAR	TM/L	W	L	PCT	G	GS	CG	SH	SV	IP	H	HR	BB	SO	RAT	ERA	ERA+	OAV	OOB	BH	AVG	PB	PR	/A	PD	TPI
1972	Chi-N	11	8	.579	32	28	6	3	0	189	168	12	47	96	10.3	3.00	127	.237	.286	1	.018	-5	10	17	-2	1.1
1973	Min-A	7	10	.412	39	15	3	1	2	142	138	14	41	78	11.5	3.49	114	.252	.307	0	—	0	5	7	-1	0.6
1974	Min-A	4	5	.444	35	10	0	0	3	115^1	130	9	25	74	12.4	4.45	84	.284	.327	0	—	0	-11	-9	-1	-1.1
	Tex-A	2	0	1.000	2	2	1	1	0	14	11	0	3	4	9.0	1.93	185	.208	.250	0	—	0	3	3	0	0.3
	Yr	6	5	.545	37	12	1	1	3	129^1	141	9	28	78	11.8	4.18	89	.274	.311	0	—	0	-8	-6	-1	-0.8
1975	Tex-A	6	7	.462	18	18	4	1	0	109^2	118	12	28	67	12.2	4.02	93	.271	.319	0	—	0	-3	-3	0	-0.3
Total	11	111	110	.502	374	260	72	17	14	1951	1895	167	492	1128	11.2	3.35	114	.253	.302	37	.078	-21	44	104	-0	9.3

● CHRIS HANEY Haney, Christopher Deane b: 11/16/68, Baltimore, Md. BL/TL, 6'3", 185 lbs. Deb: 6/21/91 F

YEAR	TM/L	W	L	PCT	G	GS	CG	SH	SV	IP	H	HR	BB	SO	RAT	ERA	ERA+	OAV	OOB	BH	AVG	PB	PR	/A	PD	TPI
1991	Mon-N	3	7	.300	16	16	0	0	0	84^2	94	6	43	51	14.7	4.04	90	.280	.363	2	.074	-2	-3	-4	1	-0.5
1992	Mon-N	2	3	.400	9	6	1	1	0	38	40	6	10	27	12.8	5.45	64	.270	.333	2	.222	0	-8	-8	-0	-0.8
	KC-A	2	3	.400	7	7	1	1	0	42	35	5	16	27	10.9	3.86	103	.226	.298	0	—	0	0	1	-1	-0.1
Total	2	7	13	.350	32	29	2	2	0	164^2	169	17	69	105	13.3	4.32	85	.264	.341	4	.111	-1	-11	-12	-0	-1.4

● DON HANKINS Hankins, Donald Wayne b: 2/9/02, Pendleton, Ind. d: 5/16/63, Winston-Salem, N.C BR/TR, 6'3", 183 lbs. Deb: 4/23/27

YEAR	TM/L	W	L	PCT	G	GS	CG	SH	SV	IP	H	HR	BB	SO	RAT	ERA	ERA+	OAV	OOB	BH	AVG	PB	PR	/A	PD	TPI
1927	Det-A	2	1	.667	20	1	0	0	2	42^2	67	1	13	10	16.9	6.33	67	.383	.426	1	.143	-1	-10	-10	0	-1.0

● FRANK HANKINSON Hankinson, Frank Edward b: 4/29/1856, New York, N.Y. d: 4/5/11, Palisades Park, N.J BR/TR, 5'11", 168 lbs. Deb: 5/01/1878 ♦

YEAR	TM/L	W	L	PCT	G	GS	CG	SH	SV	IP	H	HR	BB	SO	RAT	ERA	ERA+	OAV	OOB	BH	AVG	PB	PR	/A	PD	TPI
1878	Chi-N	0	1	.000	1	1	1	0	0	9	11	0	0	4	11.0	6.00	40	.282	.282	64	.267	0	-4	-4	-0	-0.3
1879	Chi-N	15	10	.600	26	25	25	2	0	230^2	248	0	27	69	10.7	2.50	103	.255	.275	31	.181	-4	-0	2	4	0.1
1880	Cle-N	1	1	.500	4	2	2	0	1	25	20	0	3	8	8.3	1.08	218	.215	.240	55	.209	-0	4	4	1	0.4
1885	NY-a	0	0	—	1	0	0	0	0	2	2	1	1	0	13.5	4.50	66	.500	.600	81	.224	0	-0	-0	-0	0.0
Total	4	16	12	.571	32	28	28	2	1	266^2	281	1	31	81	10.5	2.50	102	.253	.274	747	.228	-4	-0	1	5	0.2

● JIM HANLEY Hanley, James Patrick b: 10/13/1885, Providence, R.I. d: 5/1/61, Elmhurst, N.J. BR/TL, 5'11", 165 lbs. Deb: 7/03/13

YEAR	TM/L	W	L	PCT	G	GS	CG	SH	SV	IP	H	HR	BB	SO	RAT	ERA	ERA+	OAV	OOB	BH	AVG	PB	PR	/A	PD	TPI
1913	NY-A	0	0	—	1	0	0	0	0	4	5	0	4	2	20.3	6.75	44	.313	.450	0	.000	-0	-2	-2	0	-0.2

● PRESTON HANNA Hanna, Preston Lee b: 9/10/54, Pensacola, Fla. BR/TR, 6'1", 195 lbs. Deb: 9/13/75

YEAR	TM/L	W	L	PCT	G	GS	CG	SH	SV	IP	H	HR	BB	SO	RAT	ERA	ERA+	OAV	OOB	BH	AVG	PB	PR	/A	PD	TPI
1975	Atl-N	0	0	—	4	0	0	0	0	5^2	7	0	5	2	22.2	1.59	238	.304	.467	0	—	0	1	1	-0	0.1
1976	Atl-N	0	0	—	5	0	0	0	0	8	11	0	4	3	16.9	4.50	84	.333	.405	0	.000	-0	-1	-1	-0	-0.1
1977	Atl-N	2	6	.250	17	9	1	0	1	60	69	6	34	37	15.8	4.95	90	.285	.378	1	.071	-0	-7	-3	1	-0.2
1978	Atl-N	7	13	.350	29	28	0	0	0	140^1	132	10	93	90	14.6	5.13	79	.251	.367	9	.184	1	-24	-17	-0	-1.7
1979	Atl-N	1	1	.500	6	4	0	0	0	24^1	27	1	15	15	15.5	2.96	137	.284	.382	0	.000	-0	2	3	1	0.4
1980	Atl-N	2	0	1.000	32	2	0	0	0	79^1	63	3	44	35	12.5	3.18	118	.224	.335	2	.143	0	4	5	-1	0.5
1981	Atl-N	2	1	.667	20	1	0	0	0	35^1	45	2	23	22	17.3	6.37	56	.341	.439	1	.250	0	-11	-11	2	-0.9
1982	Atl-N	3	0	1.000	20	1	0	0	0	36	36	3	28	17	16.0	3.75	99	.277	.405	2	.400	1	-1	-0	-1	0.0
	Oak-A	0	4	.000	23	2	1	0	0	48^1	54	3	33	32	16.4	5.59	70	.287	.396	0	—	0	-8	-9	-0	-0.9
Total	8	17	25	.405	156	47	2	0	1	437^1	444	28	279	253	15.1	4.61	86	.269	.378	15	.161	1	-45	-31	1	-2.8

● GERRY HANNAHS Hannahs, Gerald Ellis b: 3/6/53, Binghamton, N.Y. BL/TL, 6'3", 210 lbs. Deb: 9/08/76

YEAR	TM/L	W	L	PCT	G	GS	CG	SH	SV	IP	H	HR	BB	SO	RAT	ERA	ERA+	OAV	OOB	BH	AVG	PB	PR	/A	PD	TPI
1976	Mon-N	2	0	1.000	3	3	0	0	0	16	20	2	12	10	18.0	6.75	55	.323	.432	3	.375	1	-6	-5	-0	-0.5
1977	Mon-N	1	5	.167	8	7	0	0	0	37	43	7	17	21	14.6	4.86	78	.291	.364	0	.000	-0	-4	-4	-0	-0.5
1978	LA-N	0	0	—	1	0	0	0	0	2	3	0	0	5	13.5	9.00	39	.333	.333	0	—	0	-1	-1	0	-0.1
1979	LA-N	0	2	.000	4	2	0	0	1	16	10	2	13	6	12.9	3.38	108	.175	.329	1	.250	0	1	0	0	0.1
Total	4	3	7	.300	16	12	0	0	1	71	76	11	42	42	15.0	5.07	74	.275	.371	4	.211	1	-10	-10	-1	-1.0

● JIM HANNAN Hannan, James John b: 1/7/40, Jersey City, N.J. BR/TR, 6'3", 205 lbs. Deb: 4/17/62

YEAR	TM/L	W	L	PCT	G	GS	CG	SH	SV	IP	H	HR	BB	SO	RAT	ERA	ERA+	OAV	OOB	BH	AVG	PB	PR	/A	PD	TPI
1962	Was-A	2	4	.333	42	3	0	0	4	68	56	6	49	39	13.9	3.31	122	.230	.360	1	.091	-1	5	5	0	0.5
1963	Was-A	2	2	.500	13	2	0	0	0	27^2	23	2	17	14	13.0	4.88	76	.228	.339	0	.000	-0	-4	-4	0	-0.4
1964	Was-A	4	7	.364	49	7	0	0	3	106	108	13	45	67	13.0	4.16	89	.266	.339	3	.150	-1	-6	-5	-1	-0.7
1965	Was-A	1	1	.500	4	1	1	1	0	14^2	18	0	6	5	15.3	4.91	71	.340	.417	0	.000	-0	-2	-2	-1	-0.3
1966	Was-A	3	9	.250	30	18	2	0	0	114	125	9	59	68	14.8	4.26	81	.288	.377	2	.067	-2	-10	-10	-0	-1.2
1967	Was-A	1	1	.500	8	2	0	0	0	21^2	28	3	7	14	15.0	5.40	59	.315	.371	0	.000	-0	-5	-5	0	-0.6
1968	Was-A	10	6	.625	25	22	4	1	0	140^1	147	4	50	75	12.9	3.01	97	.272	.338	3	.064	-2	-1	-2	-0	-0.4
1969	Was-A	7	6	.538	35	28	1	1	0	158^1	138	17	91	72	13.1	3.64	95	.238	.343	6	.115	-2	-0	-3	-1	-0.6
1970	Was-A	9	11	.450	42	17	1	1	0	128	119	17	54	61	12.2	4.01	89	.250	.328	4	.129	-0	-4	-6	1	-0.6
1971	Det-A	1	0	1.000	7	0	0	0	0	11	7	1	7	6	12.3	3.27	110	.189	.333	0	.000	-0	0	0	1	0.1
	Mil-A	1	1	.500	21	1	0	0	0	32^1	38	7	21	17	16.7	5.01	69	.295	.397	0	.000	-0	-6	-6	-0	-0.7
	Yr	2	1	.667	28	1	0	0	0	43^1	45	8	28	23	15.4	4.57	77	.269	.378	0	.000	-1	-5	-5	0	-0.6
Total	10	41	48	.461	276	101	9	4	7	822	807	79	406	438	13.4	3.88	89	.261	.350	19	.091	-9	-34	-38	-1	-4.9

● LOY HANNING Hanning, Loy Vernon b: 10/18/17, Bunker, Mo. d: 6/24/86, Anaconda, Mo. BR/TR, 6'2", 175 lbs. Deb: 9/20/39

YEAR	TM/L	W	L	PCT	G	GS	CG	SH	SV	IP	H	HR	BB	SO	RAT	ERA	ERA+	OAV	OOB	BH	AVG	PB	PR	/A	PD	TPI
1939	StL-A	0	1	.000	4	1	0	0	0	10	6	1	4	8	9.0	3.60	135	.158	.238	0	.000	-0	1	1	0	0.1
1942	StL-A	1	1	.500	11	0	0	0	0	17^1	26	2	12	9	20.3	7.79	48	.356	.453	1	.250	0	-8	-8	1	-0.7
Total	2	1	2	.333	15	1	0	0	0	27^1	32	3	16	17	16.1	6.26	66	.288	.383	1	.200	-0	-7	-6	1	-0.6

● ANDY HANSEN Hansen, Andrew Viggo "Swede" b: 11/12/24, Lake Worth, Fla. BR/TR, 6'3", 190 lbs. Deb: 6/30/44

YEAR	TM/L	W	L	PCT	G	GS	CG	SH	SV	IP	H	HR	BB	SO	RAT	ERA	ERA+	OAV	OOB	BH	AVG	PB	PR	/A	PD	TPI
1944	NY-N	3	3	.500	23	4	0	0	1	52^2	63	3	32	15	16.7	6.49	56	.301	.402	2	.167	0	-17	-17	1	-1.5
1945	NY-N	4	3	.571	23	13	4	0	3	92^2	98	7	28	37	12.4	4.66	84	.273	.329	0	.000	-3	-9	-8	2	-0.9
1947	NY-N	1	5	.167	27	9	1	0	0	82^1	78	8	38	18	12.7	4.37	93	.248	.330	4	.190	-0	-3	-3	1	-0.2
1948	NY-N	5	3	.625	36	9	3	0	1	100	96	4	36	27	11.9	2.97	133	.255	.320	1	.050	-0	11	11	-1	1.0
1949	NY-N	2	6	.250	33	2	0	0	1	66^1	58	7	28	26	11.7	4.61	86	.234	.312	0	.000	-1	-4	-5	0	-0.5
1950	NY-N	0	1	.000	31	1	0	0	3	57	64	8	26	19	14.4	5.53	74	.279	.355	0	.000	-1	-9	-9	-0	-1.0
1951	Phi-N	3	1	.750	24	0	0	0	0	39	34	4	7	11	9.7	2.54	152	.228	.268	1	.333	1	6	6	1	0.8
1952	Phi-N	5	6	.455	43	0	0	0	4	77^1	76	6	27	18	12.3	3.26	112	.259	.328	2	.182	1	4	3	1	0.5
1953	Phi-N	0	2	.000	30	1	0	0	3	51^1	60	6	24	17	14.9	4.03	104	.296	.373	2	.286	0	1	1	1	0.2
Total	9	23	30	.434	270	39	8	0	16	618^2	627	53	246	188	12.9	4.22	93	.263	.335	12	.102	-3	-19	-20	5	-1.6

● SNIPE HANSEN Hansen, Roy Emil Frederick b: 2/21/07, Chicago, Ill. d: 9/11/78, Chicago, Ill. BB/TL, 6'3", 195 lbs. Deb: 7/05/30

YEAR	TM/L	W	L	PCT	G	GS	CG	SH	SV	IP	H	HR	BB	SO	RAT	ERA	ERA+	OAV	OOB	BH	AVG	PB	PR	/A	PD	TPI
1930	Phi-N	0	7	.000	22	9	1	0	0	84^1	123	8	38	25	17.4	6.72	81	.364	.431	3	.111	-3	-16	-12	-1	-1.3
1932	Phi-N	10	10	.500	39	23	5	0	2	191	215	13	51	56	12.8	3.72	118	.278	.328	8	.127	-4	3	15	-2	0.9
1933	Phi-N	6	14	.300	32	22	8	0	1	168^1	199	12	30	47	12.5	4.44	86	.294	.328	9	.155	-3	-21	-12	-1	-1.6
1934	Phi-N	6	12	.333	50	16	5	2	3	151	194	15	61	40	15.4	5.42	87	.307	.371	10	.233	-0	-23	-12	1	-1.0
1935	Phi-N	0	1	.000	2	1	0	0	0	4^1	8	0	5	0	27.0	12.46	36	.421	.542	0	.000	-0	-4	-4	0	-0.4
	StL-A	0	1	.000	10	0	0	0	0	26^2	44	2	9	8	18.2	8.78	55	.364	.412	1	.143	-1	-13	-12	-1	-1.1
Total	5	22	45	.328	155	71	19	2	6	625^2	783	50	194	176	14.3	5.01	90	.306	.358	31	.155	-10	-73	-36	-3	-4.5

● ROY HANSEN Hansen, Roy Inglof "Ing" b: 3/6/1898, Beloit, Wis. d: 2/9/77, Beloit, Wis. BR/TR, 6', 165 lbs. Deb: 5/28/18

YEAR	TM/L	W	L	PCT	G	GS	CG	SH	SV	IP	H	HR	BB	SO	RAT	ERA	ERA+	OAV	OOB	BH	AVG	PB	PR	/A	PD	TPI
1918	Was-A	1	0	1.000	5	0	0	0	0	9	10	0	3	2	14.0	3.00	91	.278	.350	0	—	0	-0	-0	0	0.0

● F. C. HANSFORD Hansford, F. C. TL, 6', 180 lbs. Deb: 6/09/1898

YEAR	TM/L	W	L	PCT	G	GS	CG	SH	SV	IP	H	HR	BB	SO	RAT	ERA	ERA+	OAV	OOB	BH	AVG	PB	PR	/A	PD	TPI
1898	Bro-N	0	0	—	1	0	0	0	0	7	10	0	5	0	19.3	3.86	93	.332	.428	0	.000	-1	-0	-0	-0	-0.1

● DON HANSKI Hanski, Donald Thomas (b: Donald Thomas Hanyzewski) b: 2/27/16, Laporte, Ind. d: 9/2/57, Worth, Ill. BL/TL, 5'11", 180 lbs. Deb: 5/06/43 ♦

YEAR	TM/L	W	L	PCT	G	GS	CG	SH	SV	IP	H	HR	BB	SO	RAT	ERA	ERA+	OAV	OOB	BH	AVG	PB	PR	/A	PD	TPI
1943	Chi-A	0	0	—	1	0	0	0	0	1	1	0	1	0	18.0	0.00	—	.333	.500	5	.238	0	0	0	-0	0.0
1944	Chi-A	0	0	—	2	0	0	0	0	3	5	0	2	0	21.0	12.00	29	.357	.438	0	.000	-0	-3	-3	-0	-0.3

YEAR TM/L	W	L	PCT	G	GS	CG	SH	SV	IP	H	HR	BB	SO	RAT	ERA	ERA+	OAV	OOB	BH	AVG	PB	PR	/A	PD	TPI
Total 2	0	0	—	3	0	0	0	0	4	6	0	3	0	20.3	9.00	38	.353	.450	5	.227	-0	-2	-2	-0	-0.3
● OLLIE HANSON	Hanson, Earl Sylvester b: 1/19/1896, Holbrook, Mass. d: 8/19/51, Clifton, N.J. BR/TR, 5'11", 178 lbs. Deb: 4/27/21																								
1921 Chi-N	0	2	.000	2	2	1	0	0	9	9	0	6	2	16.0	7.00	55	.265	.390	0	.000	-0	-3	-3	0	-0.3
● ERIK HANSON	Hanson, Erik Brian b: 5/18/65, Kinnelon, N.J. BR/TR, 6'6", 210 lbs. Deb: 9/05/88																								
1988 Sea-A	2	3	.400	6	6	0	0	0	41^{2}	35	4	12	36	10.4	3.24	128	.230	.291	0	—	0	3	4	-0	0.4
1989 Sea-A	9	5	.643	17	17	1	0	0	113^{1}	103	7	32	75	11.1	3.18	127	.243	.304	0	—	0	9	11	0	1.0
1990 Sea-A	18	9	.667	33	33	5	1	0	236	205	15	68	211	10.5	3.24	122	.232	.289	0	—	0	17	19	-0	1.9
1991 Sea-A	8	8	.500	27	27	2	1	0	174^{2}	182	16	56	143	12.4	3.81	108	.269	.327	0	—	0	5	6	-1	0.5
1992 Sea-A	8	17	.320	31	30	6	1	0	186^{2}	209	14	57	112	13.2	4.82	83	.287	.345	0	—	0	-18	-17	0	-1.7
Total 5	45	42	.517	114	113	14	3	0	752^{1}	734	56	225	577	11.7	3.76	107	.256	.314	0	—	0	17	22	-1	2.1
● ED HANYZEWSKI	Hanyzewski, Edward Michael b: 9/18/20, Union Mills, Ind. d: 10/8/91, Fargo, N.D. BR/TR, 6'1", 200 lbs. Deb: 5/12/42																								
1942 Chi-N	1	1	.500	6	1	0	0	0	19	17	2	8	6	11.8	3.79	84	.254	.333	1	.200	-0	-1	-1	0	-0.1
1943 Chi-N	8	7	.533	33	16	3	0	0	130	120	2	45	55	11.6	2.56	130	.243	.309	2	.049	-4	12	11	2	0.9
1944 Chi-N	2	5	.286	14	7	3	0	0	58^{1}	61	6	20	19	12.7	4.47	79	.261	.322	1	.059	-1	-6	-6	3	-0.4
1945 Chi-N	0	0	—	2	1	0	0	0	4^{2}	7	1	1	0	15.4	5.79	63	.350	.381	0	.000	0	-1	-1	0	-0.1
1946 Chi-N	1	0	1.000	3	0	0	0	0	6	8	0	5	1	21.0	4.50	74	.348	.483	0	.000	-0	-1	-1	0	-0.1
Total 5	12	13	.480	58	25	6	0	0	218	213	11	79	81	12.2	3.30	102	.254	.321	4	.062	-5	4	2	5	0.2
● MEL HARDER	Harder, Melvin Leroy "Chief" b: 10/15/09, Beemer, Neb. BR/TR, 6'1", 195 lbs. Deb: 4/24/28 MC																								
1928 Cle-A	0	2	.000	23	1	0	0	1	49	64	4	32	15	17.6	6.61	63	.335	.430	0	.000	-1	-14	-13	-1	-1.5
1929 Cle-A	1	0	1.000	11	0	0	0	0	17^{2}	24	2	5	4	16.3	5.60	79	.333	.400	0	.000	-0	-3	-2	-0	-0.3
1930 Cle-A	11	10	.524	36	19	7	0	2	175^{1}	205	9	68	44	14.2	4.21	115	.295	.361	9	.143	-4	9	12	-1	0.6
1931 Cle-A	13	14	.481	40	24	9	0	1	194	229	8	72	63	14.2	4.36	106	.289	.352	19	.253	1	0	6	0	0.7
1932 Cle-A	15	13	.536	39	32	17	1	0	254^{2}	277	9	68	90	12.3	3.75	127	.272	.319	17	.181	-0	21	28	3	2.9
1933 Cle-A	15	17	.469	43	31	14	2	4	253	254	10	67	81	11.5	**2.95**	**151**	.259	.309	16	.190	-1	**37**	**42**	8	**4.9**
1934 Cle-A★	20	12	.625	44	29	17	**6**	4	255^{1}	246	6	81	91	11.8	2.61	**174**	.254	.316	14	.161	-1	54	**55**	2	**5.5**
1935 Cle-A★	22	11	.667	42	35	17	4	2	287^{1}	313	6	53	95	11.5	3.29	137	.275	.307	21	.206	-1	37	39	5	4.2
1936 Cle-A★	15	15	.500	36	30	13	0	1	224^{2}	294	13	71	84	14.9	5.17	97	.313	.365	11	.138	-4	-3	-3	0	-0.6
1937 Cle-A★	15	12	.556	38	30	13	0	2	233^{2}	269	9	86	95	13.8	4.28	108	.288	.350	15	.174	-1	9	9	2	0.8
1938 Cle-A	17	10	.630	38	29	15	2	4	240	257	16	62	102	12.2	3.83	121	.271	.319	10	.114	-5	26	22	2	1.8
1939 Cle-A	15	9	.625	29	26	12	1	1	208	213	15	64	67	12.1	3.50	126	.269	.326	10	.139	-1	26	21	-2	1.7
1940 Cle-A	12	11	.522	31	25	5	0	0	186^{1}	200	16	59	76	12.8	4.06	104	.278	.337	11	.177	-1	7	3	1	0.4
1941 Cle-A	5	4	.556	15	10	1	0	1	68^{2}	76	8	37	21	15.1	5.24	75	.279	.370	2	.080	-2	-8	-10	1	-1.0
1942 Cle-A	13	14	.481	29	29	13	4	0	198^{2}	179	8	82	74	12.0	3.44	100	.240	.317	8	.119	-3	5	0	1	-0.1
1943 Cle-A	8	7	.533	19	18	6	1	0	135^{1}	126	7	61	40	12.5	3.06	102	.254	.337	10	.213	1	4	1	-0	0.2
1944 Cle-A	12	10	.545	30	27	12	2	0	196^{1}	211	5	69	64	13.0	3.71	89	.278	.341	16	.216	1	-6	-9	-1	-0.9
1945 Cle-A	3	7	.300	11	11	2	0	0	76	93	3	23	16	13.7	3.67	88	.303	.352	2	.080	-2	-3	-4	1	-0.5
1946 Cle-A	5	4	.556	13	12	4	1	0	92^{1}	85	4	31	21	11.3	3.41	97	.249	.311	3	.086	-2	1	-1	-2	-0.5
1947 Cle-A	6	4	.600	15	15	4	1	0	80	91	3	27	17	13.4	4.50	77	.289	.347	5	.179	0	-7	-9	-1	-1.0
Total 20	223	186	.545	582	433	181	25	23	3426^{1}	3706	161	1118	1160	12.8	3.80	113	.276	.334	199	.165	-27	190	182	18	17.3
● JIM HARDIN	Hardin, James Warren b: 8/6/43, Morris Chapel, Tenn. d: 3/9/91, Key West, Fla. BR/TR, 6', 175 lbs. Deb: 6/23/67																								
1967 Bal-A	8	3	.727	19	14	5	2	0	111	85	5	27	64	9.3	2.27	139	.211	.266	5	.135	-0	12	11	-1	1.1
1968 Bal-A	18	13	.581	35	35	16	2	0	244	188	20	70	160	9.9	2.51	117	.212	.277	7	.085	-3	13	11	-0	0.9
1969 Bal-A	6	7	.462	30	20	3	1	1	137^{2}	128	18	43	64	11.6	3.60	99	.248	.313	7	.156	2	0	-0	-1	0.0
1970 Bal-A	6	5	.545	36	19	3	2	1	145^{1}	150	13	26	78	11.0	3.53	103	.267	.301	3	.067	-1	3	2	-2	-0.1
1971 Bal-A	0	0	—	6	0	0	0	0	5^{2}	12	0	3	3	23.8	4.76	70	.480	.536	0	—	0	-1	-1	0	-0.1
NY-A	0	2	.000	12	3	0	0	0	28^{1}	35	3	9	14	14.3	5.08	64	.313	.369	0	.000	-0	-5	-6	-0	-0.7
Yr	0	2	.000	18	3	0	0	0	34	47	3	12	17	15.9	5.03	65	.343	.400	0	.000	-0	-6	-7	-0	-0.8
1972 Atl-N	5	2	.714	26	9	1	0	2	79^{2}	93	11	24	25	13.4	4.41	86	.287	.340	2	.095	1	-8	-5	-1	-0.5
Total 6	43	32	.573	164	100	28	7	4	751^{2}	691	70	202	408	11.0	3.18	104	.244	.300	24	.103	-3	14	11	-5	0.6
● CHARLIE HARDING	Harding, Charles Harold "Slim" b: 1/3/1891, Nashville, Tenn. d: 10/30/71, Bold Srpings, Tenn BR/TR, 6'2.5", 172 lbs. Deb: 9/18/13																								
1913 Det-A	0	0	—	1	0	0	0	0	2	3	0	1	0	18.0	4.50	65	.375	.444	0	—	0	-0	-0	0	0.0
● ALEX HARDY	Hardy, David Alexander "Dooney" b: 1877, Toronto, Ont., Canada d: 4/22/40, Toronto, Ont., Can. TL, Deb: 9/04/02																								
1902 Chi-N	2	2	.500	4	4	4	1	0	35	29	0	12	12	10.5	3.60	75	.226	.292	3	.214	0	-3	-3	-1	-0.4
1903 Chi-N	1	1	.500	3	3	1	0	0	12^{2}	21	0	7	4	20.6	6.39	49	.375	.453	1	.167	0	-4	-5	0	-0.3
Total 2	3	3	.500	7	7	5	1	0	47^{2}	50	0	19	16	13.2	4.34	65	.271	.342	4	.200	0	-8	-8	-0	-0.7
● RED HARDY	Hardy, Francis Joseph b: 1/6/23, Marmarth, N.Dak. BR/TR, 5'11", 175 lbs. Deb: 6/20/51																								
1951 NY-N	0	0	—	2	0	0	0	0	1^{1}	4	0	1	0	40.5	6.75	58	.571	.667	0	—	0	-0	-0	0	0.0
● HARRY HARDY	Hardy, Harry b: 11/5/1875, Steubenville, Ohio d: 9/4/43, Steubenville, Ohio BL/TL, 5'6", 155 lbs. Deb: 9/26/05																								
1905 Was-A	1	1	.500	3	2	2	0	0	24	20	0	6	10	9.8	1.88	141	.228	.277	1	.111	-1	2	2	-1	0.0
1906 Was-A	0	3	.000	5	3	2	0	0	20	35	0	12	4	21.1	9.00	29	.385	.457	0	.000	-1	-14	-14	1	-1.3
Total 2	1	4	.200	8	5	4	0	0	44	55	0	18	14	14.9	5.11	52	.308	.371	1	.067	-1	-12	-12	-0	-1.3
● LARRY HARDY	Hardy, Howard Lawrence b: 1/10/48, Goose Creek, Tex. BR/TR, 5'10", 180 lbs. Deb: 4/28/74																								
1974 SD-N	9	4	.692	76	1	0	0	2	101^{2}	129	9	44	57	15.3	4.69	76	.317	.384	0	.000	-1	-12	-13	1	-1.3
1975 SD-N	0	0	—	3	0	0	0	0	2^{2}	8	3	2	3	33.8	13.50	26	.500	.556	0	—	0	-3	-3	-0	-0.3
1976 Hou-N	0	0	—	15	0	0	0	3	21^{2}	34	2	10	10	18.3	7.06	45	.362	.423	0	.000	-0	-9	-9	0	-1.0
Total 3	9	4	.692	94	1	0	0	5	126	171	14	56	70	16.2	5.29	66	.331	.396	0	.000	-1	-24	-25	1	-2.6
● JACK HARDY	Hardy, John Graydon b: 10/8/59, St.Petersburg, Fla. BR/TR, 6'2", 175 lbs. Deb: 5/23/89																								
1989 Chi-A	0	0	—	5	0	0	0	0	12^{1}	14	1	5	4	14.6	6.57	58	.286	.364	0	—	0	-4	-4	1	-0.2
● STEVE HARGAN	Hargan, Steven Lowell b: 9/8/42, Ft.Wayne, Ind. BR/TR, 6'3", 180 lbs. Deb: 8/03/65																								
1965 Cle-A	4	3	.571	17	8	1	0	2	60^{1}	55	2	28	37	12.5	3.43	101	.246	.332	1	.053	-1	0	0	0	-0.1
1966 Cle-A	13	10	.565	38	21	7	3	0	192	173	9	45	132	10.3	2.48	138	.241	.286	7	.121	-2	20	20	0	2.1
1967 Cle-A☆	14	13	.519	30	29	15	**6**	0	223	180	9	72	141	10.3	2.62	125	.224	.290	11	.164	1	15	16	1	2.1
1968 Cle-A	8	15	.348	32	27	4	2	0	158^{1}	139	11	81	78	12.8	4.15	71	.241	.340	9	.176	1	-21	-21	-2	-2.4
1969 Cle-A	5	14	.263	32	23	1	1	0	143^{2}	145	14	81	76	14.3	5.70	66	.265	.363	7	.159	-1	-33	-31	2	-3.1
1970 Cle-A	11	3	.786	23	19	8	1	1	142^{2}	101	14	53	72	9.9	2.90	136	.201	.281	5	.111	-2	13	17	1	1.7
1971 Cle-A	1	13	.071	37	16	1	0	1	113^{1}	138	18	56	52	15.9	6.19	62	.304	.388	2	.063	-3	-34	-30	-2	-3.5
1972 Cle-A	0	3	.000	12	1	0	0	0	20	23	1	15	10	17.1	5.85	55	.291	.404	0	.000	-0	-6	-6	1	-0.6
1974 Tex-A	12	9	.571	37	27	8	2	0	186^{2}	202	15	48	98	12.3	3.95	90	.275	.324	0	—	0	-7	-8	2	-0.7
1975 Tex-A	9	10	.474	33	26	8	1	0	189^{1}	203	17	62	93	12.9	3.80	99	.275	.336	0	—	0	-1	-1	2	0.1
1976 Tex-A	8	8	.500	35	8	2	1	1	124^{1}	127	8	38	63	12.2	3.62	99	.261	.318	0	—	0	-1	-0	-0	-0.1
1977 Tor-A	1	3	.250	6	5	1	0	0	29^{1}	36	2	14	11	15.3	5.22	80	.308	.382	0	—	0	-4	-3	0	-0.3
Tex-A	1	0	1.000	6	0	0	0	0	12^{1}	22	2	5	10	19.7	8.76	47	.393	.443	0	—	0	-6	-6	-0	-0.7
Yr	2	3	.400	12	5	1	0	0	41^{2}	58	4	19	21	16.6	6.26	66	.335	.401	0	—	0	-10	-10	0	-1.0
Atl-N	0	3	.000	16	5	0	0	0	36^{2}	49	3	16	18	16.0	6.87	65	.325	.389	0	.000	-1	-12	-10	1	-0.9

YEAR	TM/L	W	L	PCT	G	GS	CG	SH	SV	IP	H	HR	BB	SO	RAT	ERA	ERA+	OAV	OOB	BH	AVG	PB	PR	/A	PD	TPI
Total	12	87	107	.448	354	215	56	17	4	1632	1593	125	614	891	12.4	3.92	91	.257	.328	42	.129	-8	-77	-64	6	-6.4
● **ALAN HARGESHEIMER** Hargesheimer, Alan Robert b: 11/21/56, Chicago, Ill. BR/TR, 6'3", 195 lbs. Deb: 7/14/80																										
1980	SF-N	4	6	.400	15	13	0	0	0	75	82	3	32	40	13.7	4.32	82	.285	.356	4	.182	1	-6	-7	-1	-0.7
1981	SF-N	1	2	.333	6	3	0	0	0	18^2	20	1	9	6	14.5	4.34	79	.299	.390	1	.200	0	-2	-2	0	-0.2
1983	Chi-N	0	0	—	5	0	0	0	0	4	6	0	2	5	18.0	9.00	42	.375	.444	0	—	0	-2	-2	-0	-0.2
1986	KC-A	0	1	.000	5	1	0	0	0	13	18	1	7	4	18.0	6.23	68	.340	.426	0	—	0	-3	-3	-0	-0.4
Total	4	5	9	.357	31	17	0	0	0	110^2	126	5	50	55	14.5	4.72	77	.297	.374	5	.185	1	-13	-14	-1	-1.5
● **MIKE HARKEY** Harkey, Michael Anthony b: 10/25/66, San Diego, Cal. BR/TR, 6'5", 220 lbs. Deb: 9/05/88																										
1988	Chi-N	0	3	.000	5	5	0	0	0	34^2	33	0	15	18	13.0	2.60	139	.248	.333	1	.091	-1	3	4	-1	0.3
1990	Chi-N	12	6	.667	27	27	2	1	0	173^2	153	14	59	94	11.3	3.26	125	.234	.305	14	.250	4	10	16	-1	2.0
1991	Chi-N	0	2	.000	4	4	0	0	0	18^2	21	3	6	15	13.0	5.30	73	.273	.325	2	.400	1	-3	-3	0	-0.2
1992	Chi-N	4	0	1.000	7	7	0	0	0	38	34	4	15	21	11.8	1.89	190	.243	.321	4	.267	1	7	7	-0	0.9
Total	4	16	11	.593	43	43	2	1	0	265	241	21	95	148	11.8	3.12	126	.240	.312	21	.241	5	17	24	-2	3.0
● **JOHN HARKINS** Harkins, John Joseph "Pa" b: 4/12/1859, New Brunswick, N.J d: 11/20/40, New Brunswick, N.J BR/TR, 6'1", 205 lbs. Deb: 5/02/1884																										
1884	Cle-N	12	32	.273	46	45	42	3	0	391	399	7	108	192	11.7	3.68	86	.249	.297	47	.205	-5	-30	-23	-1	-2.4
1885	Bro-a	14	20	.412	34	34	33	1	0	293	303	7	56	141	11.2	3.75	88	.250	.287	42	.264	6	-16	-15	4	-0.4
1886	Bro-a	15	16	.484	34	33	33	0	0	292^1	286	6	114	118	12.5	3.60	97	.244	.313	32	.225	3	-5	-4	2	0.2
1887	Bro-a	10	14	.417	24	24	22	0	0	199	262	6	77	36	15.6	6.02	72	.309	.369	23	.235	-0	-38	-38	-1	-3.0
1888	Bal-a	0	1	.000	1	1	1	0	0	8	12	0	3	2	16.9	6.75	44	.335	.386	0	.000	-0	-3	-3	0	-0.3
Total	5	51	83	.381	139	137	131	4	0	1183^1	1262	26	358	489	12.5	4.09	85	.259	.312	144	.228	4	-93	-81	5	-5.9
● **SPEC HARKNESS** Harkness, Frederick Harvey b: 12/13/1887, Los Angeles, Cal. d: 5/16/52, Compton, Cal. BR/TR, 5'11", 180 lbs. Deb: 6/13/10																										
1910	Cle-A	10	7	.588	26	16	6	1	1	136^1	132	2	55	60	12.5	3.04	85	.268	.345	7	.140	-1	-8	-7	-1	-1.0
1911	Cle-A	2	2	.500	12	6	3	0	0	53^1	62	1	21	25	14.0	4.22	81	.310	.376	6	.316	1	-5	-5	-2	-0.5
Total	2	12	9	.571	38	22	9	1	1	189^2	194	3	76	85	13.0	3.37	84	.280	.354	13	.188	-0	-13	-12	-3	-1.5
● **DICK HARLEY** Harley, Henry Risk b: 8/18/1874, Springfield, Ohio d: 5/16/61, Springfield, Ohio BR/TR, Deb: 4/15/05																										
1905	Bos-N	2	5	.286	9	4	4	1	0	65^2	72	5	19	19	12.6	4.66	67	.286	.338	1	.045	-2	-12	-11	2	-1.2
● **LARRY HARLOW** Harlow, Larry Duane b: 11/13/51, Colorado Springs, Colo. BL/TL, 6'2", 185 lbs. Deb: 9/20/75 ♦																										
1978	Bal-A	0	0	—	1	0	0	0	0	0^2	2	1	4	1	81.0	67.50	5	.500	.750	112	.243	1	-5	-5	0	-0.4
● **BILL HARMAN** Harman, William Bell b: 1/2/19, Bridgewater, Va. BR/TR, 6'4", 200 lbs. Deb: 6/17/41 ♦																										
1941	Phi-N	0	0	—	5	0	0	0	0	13	15	0	8	3	15.9	4.85	76	.319	.418	1	.071	-0	-2	-2	-0	-0.2
● **BOB HARMON** Harmon, Robert Green "Hickory Bob" b: 10/15/1887, Liberal, Mo. d: 11/27/61, Monroe, La. BB/TR, 6', 187 lbs. Deb: 6/23/09																										
1909	StL-N	6	11	.353	21	17	10	0	0	159	155	6	65	48	12.7	3.68	69	.265	.342	13	.255	4	-19	-20	-0	-1.8
1910	StL-N	13	15	.464	43	33	15	0	2	236	227	1	133	87	14.0	4.46	67	.258	.360	14	.184	2	-37	-39	2	-3.5
1911	StL-N	23	16	.590	51	41	28	2	4	348	290	10	181	144	12.4	3.13	108	.235	.336	17	.153	0	11	10	1	1.1
1912	StL-N	18	18	.500	43	34	15	3	0	268	284	4	116	73	13.5	3.93	87	.281	.357	23	.232	1	-15	-15	4	-1.0
1913	StL-N	8	21	.276	42	27	16	1	2	273^1	291	6	99	66	13.0	3.92	83	.286	.353	24	.261	5	-22	-21	2	-1.4
1914	Pit-N	13	17	.433	37	30	19	2	3	245	226	3	55	61	10.6	2.53	105	.252	.300	12	.140	-1	7	3	-1	0.0
1915	Pit-N	16	17	.485	37	32	25	5	1	269^2	242	6	62	86	10.2	2.50	109	.247	.294	14	.147	1	7	7	4	1.3
1916	Pit-N	8	11	.421	31	17	10	2	0	172^2	175	4	39	62	11.2	2.81	95	.267	.309	6	.109	-3	-4	-2	3	-0.2
1918	Pit-N	2	7	.222	16	9	5	0	0	82^1	76	3	12	7	9.6	2.62	110	.254	.283	4	.148	-1	1	2	0	0.2
Total	9	107	133	.446	321	240	143	15	12	2054	1966	43	762	634	12.1	3.33	90	.260	.331	127	.184	7	-71	-76	14	-5.3
● **PETE HARNISCH** Harnisch, Peter Thomas b: 9/23/66, Commack, N.Y. BB/TR, 6'1", 195 lbs. Deb: 9/13/88																										
1988	Bal-A	0	2	.000	2	2	0	0	0	13	13	1	9	10	15.2	5.54	70	.260	.373	0	—	0	-2	-2	0	-0.2
1989	Bal-A	5	9	.357	18	17	2	0	0	103^1	97	10	64	70	14.5	4.62	82	.249	.362	0	—	0	-8	-9	-1	-0.9
1990	Bal-A	11	11	.500	31	31	3	0	0	188^2	189	17	86	122	13.2	4.34	87	.261	.341	0	—	0	-9	-11	-2	-1.3
1991	Hou-N★	12	9	.571	33	33	4	2	0	216^2	169	14	83	172	10.7	2.70	130	**.212**	.291	6	.097	-1	24	19	-3	1.6
1992	Hou-N	9	10	.474	34	34	0	0	0	206^2	182	18	64	164	10.9	3.70	90	.233	.296	11	.164	2	-5	-8	-3	-1.0
Total	5	37	41	.474	118	117	9	2	0	728^1	650	60	306	538	12.0	3.73	96	.237	.318	17	.132	1	-1	-12	-8	-1.8
● **JACK HARPER** Harper, Charles William b: 4/2/1878, Galloway, Pa. d: 9/30/50, Jamestown, N.Y. BR/TR, 6', 178 lbs. Deb: 9/18/1899																										
1899	Cle-N	1	4	.200	5	5	5	0	0	37	44	3	12	14	14.4	3.89	95	.295	.359	2	.182	1	-0	-1	-0	0.0
1900	StL-N	0	1	.000	1	1	0	0	0	3	4	0	2	0	18.0	12.00	30	.319	.413	0	.000	-0	-3	-3	0	-0.2
1901	StL-N	23	13	.639	39	37	28	1	0	308^2	294	7	99	128	11.8	3.62	88	.249	.315	20	.172	0	-10	-15	1	-1.3
1902	StL-A	15	11	.577	29	26	20	2	0	222^1	224	8	81	74	12.7	4.13	85	.262	.332	17	.205	-0	-14	-15	1	-1.3
1903	Cin-N	8	9	.471	17	15	13	0	0	135	143	2	70	45	14.9	4.33	82	.271	.367	14	.250	2	-16	-12	1	-0.8
1904	Cin-N	23	9	.719	35	35	31	6	0	293^2	262	2	85	125	10.9	2.30	128	.234	.293	18	.159	-2	14	21	-5	1.4
1905	Cin-N	9	13	.409	26	23	15	1	1	179^1	189	2	69	70	13.3	3.86	86	.271	.344	10	.167	1	-17	-11	-0	-1.1
1906	Cin-N	1	4	.200	5	5	3	0	0	36^2	38	1	20	10	14.7	4.17	66	.286	.387	3	.273	1	-6	-6	-1	-0.6
	Chi-N	0	0	—	1	1	0	0	0	1	0	0	0	0	0.0	0.00	—	.000	.000	0	—	0	0	0	0	0.0
	Yr	1	4	.200	6	6	3	0	0	37^2	38	1	20	10	13.9	4.06	68	.275	.367	3	.273	1	-6	-5	-1	-0.6
Total	8	80	64	.556	158	148	115	10	1	1216^2	1198	25	438	466	12.5	3.55	92	.256	.327	84	.186	3	-51	-39	-3	-3.9
● **GEORGE HARPER** Harper, George B. b: 8/17/1866, Milwaukee, Wis. d: 12/11/31, Stockton, Cal. Deb: 7/11/1894																										
1894	Phi-N	6	6	.500	12	9	7	0	0	86^1	128	3	49	24	18.7	5.32	96	.340	.419	6	.150	-3	0	-2	-1	-0.5
1896	Bro-N	4	8	.333	16	11	7	0	0	86	106	4	39	22	15.5	5.55	74	.300	.375	6	.162	0	-11	-14	1	-1.0
Total	2	10	14	.417	28	20	14	0	0	172^1	234	7	88	46	17.1	5.43	85	.321	.398	12	.156	-3	-11	-16	0	-1.5
● **HARRY HARPER** Harper, Harry Clayton b: 4/24/1895, Hackensack, N.J. d: 4/23/63, New York, N.Y. BL/TL, 6'2", 165 lbs. Deb: 6/27/13																										
1913	Was-A	0	0	—	4	0	0	0	0	12^2	10	1	5	9	11.4	3.55	83	.204	.291	1	.250	0	-1	-1	0	-0.1
1914	Was-A	2	1	.667	23	3	1	0	2	57	45	1	35	50	13.4	3.47	81	.211	.336	3	.250	0	-5	-4	-1	-0.6
1915	Was-A	4	4	.500	19	10	5	2	2	86^1	66	1	40	54	11.2	1.77	168	.222	.317	0	.000	-4	11	11	-2	0.6
1916	Was-A	14	10	.583	36	34	13	2	0	249^2	209	4	101	149	11.5	2.45	114	.235	.319	18	.207	1	10	9	-4	0.7
1917	Was-A	11	12	.478	31	31	10	4	0	179^1	145	1	106	99	12.8	3.01	87	.230	.345	7	.117	-3	-7	-8	-3	-1.5
1918	Was-A	11	10	.524	35	32	14	3	1	244	182	1	104	78	10.8	2.18	125	.212	.303	11	.134	-4	16	15	-5	0.7
1919	Was-A	6	21	.222	35	31	8	0	0	208	220	3	97	87	14.1	3.72	86	.284	.370	11	.169	-2	-11	-12	-1	-1.6
1920	Bos-A	5	14	.263	27	22	11	1	0	162^2	163	9	66	71	12.8	3.04	120	.275	.349	6	.120	-2	14	11	-3	0.5
1921	*NY-A	4	3	.571	8	7	4	0	0	52^2	52	3	25	22	13.5	3.76	113	.263	.351	2	.125	-1	3	3	-2	0.0
1923	Bro-N	0	1	.000	1	1	0	0	0	3^2	8	2	3	4	27.0	14.73	26	.421	.500	0	.000	-0	-4	-4	-0	-0.4
Total	10	57	76	.429	219	171	66	12	5	1256	1100	26	582	623	12.3	2.87	105	.243	.335	59	.147	-15	26	21	-21	-1.7
● **JACK HARPER** Harper, John Wesley b: 8/5/1893, Hendricks, W.Va. d: 6/18/27, Halstead, Kan. BR/TR, 5'11", 180 lbs. Deb: 4/17/15																										
1915	Phi-A	0	0	—	3	0	0	0	0	8^2	5	0	1	3	6.2	3.12	94	.161	.188	0	.000	-0	-0	-0	0	0.0
● **BILL HARPER** Harper, William Homer "Blue Sleeve" b: 6/14/1889, Bertand, Mo. d: 6/17/51, Somerville, Tenn. BB/TR, 6'1", 180 lbs. Deb: 6/10/11																										
1911	StL-A	0	0	—	2	0	0	0	0	8	9	0	4	6	15.8	6.75	50	.300	.400	0	.000	-0	-3	-3	0	-0.3

YEAR	TM/L	W	L	PCT	G	GS	CG	SH	SV	IP	H	HR	BB	SO	RAT	ERA	ERA+	OAV	OOB	BH	AVG	PB	PR	/A	PD	TPI
● **SLIM HARRELL** Harrell, Oscar Martin b: 7/31/1890, Grandview, Tex. d: 4/30/71, Hillsboro, Tex. BR/TR, 6'3", 180 lbs. Deb: 6/21/12																										
1912	Phi-A	0	0	—	1	0	0	0	0	3	4	0	0	1	12.0	0.00	—	.364	.364	0	.000	-0	1	1	-0	0.1
● **RAY HARRELL** Harrell, Raymond James "Cowboy" b: 2/16/12, Petrolia, Tex. d: 1/28/84, Alexandria, La. BR/TR, 6'1", 185 lbs. Deb: 4/16/35																										
1935	StL-N	1	1	.500	11	1	0	0	0	29^2	39	4	11	13	15.2	6.67	61	.320	.376	0	.000	-1	-9	-8	-0	-0.9
1937	StL-N	3	7	.300	35	15	1	1	1	96^2	99	7	59	41	14.9	5.87	68	.263	.366	1	.045	-2	-21	-20	-1	-2.2
1938	StL-N	2	3	.400	32	3	1	0	2	63	78	6	29	32	15.7	4.86	81	.308	.386	0	.000	-1	-7	-6	0	-0.7
1939	Chi-N	0	2	.000	4	2	0	0	0	17^1	29	2	6	5	18.2	8.31	47	.387	.432	0	.000	-1	-8	-8	0	-0.8
	Phi-N	3	7	.300	22	10	4	0	0	94^2	101	6	56	35	15.3	5.42	74	.270	.371	3	.115	-1	-16	-15	-3	-1.8
	Yr	3	9	.250	26	12	4	0	0	112	130	8	62	40	15.8	5.87	68	.290	.381	3	.097	-2	-24	-23	-3	-2.6
1940	Pit-N	0	0	—	3	0	0	0	0	3^1	5	0	2	3	18.9	8.10	47	.333	.412	0	—	0	-2	-2	-0	-0.2
1945	NY-N	0	0	—	12	0	0	0	0	25^1	34	1	14	7	17.4	4.97	79	.343	.430	1	.200	1	-3	-3	0	-0.2
Total	6	9	20	.310	119	31	6	1	3	330	385	26	177	136	15.6	5.70	70	.293	.381	5	.069	-5	-66	-63	-3	-6.8
● **BILL HARRELSON** Harrelson, William Charles b: 11/17/45, Tahlequah, Okla. BB/TR, 6'5", 215 lbs. Deb: 7/31/68																										
1968	Cal-A	1	6	.143	10	5	1	0	0	33^2	28	4	26	22	14.7	5.08	57	.226	.364	1	.100	-0	-8	-8	-0	-1.0
● **ANDY HARRINGTON** Harrington, Andrew Francis b: 11/13/1888, Wakefield, Mass. d: 11/12/38, Malden, Mass. BR/TR, 6', 193 lbs. Deb: 9/08/13																										
1913	Cin-N	0	0	—	1	0	0	0	0	4	6	0	1	1	15.8	9.00	36	.353	.389	1	.500	0	-3	-3	-0	-0.2
● **BILL HARRINGTON** Harrington, William Womble b: 10/3/27, Sanford, N.C. BR/TR, 5'11", 160 lbs. Deb: 4/16/53																										
1953	Phi-A	0	0	—	1	0	0	0	0	2	5	0	0	0	22.5	13.50	32	.500	.500	0	—	0	-2	-2	-0	-0.2
1955	KC-A	3	3	.500	34	1	0	0	2	76^2	69	6	41	26	13.1	4.11	102	.246	.347	2	.118	-1	-1	1	-1	0.0
1956	KC-A	2	2	.500	23	1	0	0	1	37^2	40	3	26	14	15.8	6.45	67	.274	.384	0	.000	-1	-10	-9	-0	-0.9
Total	3	5	5	.500	58	2	0	0	3	116^1	114	9	67	40	14.2	5.03	84	.261	.362	2	.083	-1	-13	-10	-1	-1.1
● **BEN HARRIS** Harris, Ben Franklin b: 12/17/1889, Donelson, Tenn. d: 4/29/27, St.Louis, Mo. BR/TR, 6', 220 lbs. Deb: 4/19/14																										
1914	KC-F	7	7	.500	31	14	5	0	1	154	179	7	41	40	13.2	4.09	75	.303	.354	9	.200	1	-15	-17	1	-1.5
1915	KC-F	0	0	—	1	0	0	0	0	2	1	0	0	0	4.5	0.00	—	.143	.143	0	—	0	1	1	0	0.1
Total	2	7	7	.500	32	14	5	0	1	156	180	7	41	40	13.1	4.04	76	.301	.352	9	.200	1	-14	-17	1	-1.4
● **LUM HARRIS** Harris, Chalmer Luman b: 1/17/15, New Castle, Ala. BR/TR, 6'1", 180 lbs. Deb: 4/19/41 MC																										
1941	Phi-A	4	4	.500	33	10	5	0	2	131^2	134	16	51	49	12.8	4.78	88	.260	.329	11	.275	2	-9	-9	-1	-0.8
1942	Phi-A	11	15	.423	26	20	10	1	0	166	146	14	70	60	11.8	3.74	101	.234	.313	10	.161	-2	-2	1	-1	-0.1
1943	Phi-A	7	21	.250	32	27	15	1	1	216^1	241	17	63	55	12.8	4.20	81	.279	.330	12	.171	-1	-22	-19	-0	-2.1
1944	Phi-A	10	9	.526	23	22	12	2	0	174^1	193	8	26	33	11.3	3.30	105	.281	.308	10	.169	-1	2	3	-1	0.3
1946	Phi-A	3	14	.176	34	12	4	0	0	125^1	153	11	48	33	14.4	5.24	68	.308	.369	8	.222	1	-24	-24	3	-1.9
1947	Was-A	0	0	—	3	0	0	0	0	6^1	7	0	7	2	19.9	2.84	131	.318	.483	0	.000	-0	1	1	1	0.1
Total	6	35	63	.357	151	91	46	4	3	820	874	66	265	232	12.6	4.16	88	.273	.329	51	.190	-0	-54	-47	1	-4.5
● **BUBBA HARRIS** Harris, Charles b: 2/15/26, Sulligent, Ala. BR/TR, 6'4", 204 lbs. Deb: 4/29/48																										
1948	Phi-A	5	2	.714	45	0	0	0	5	93^2	89	2	35	32	12.0	4.13	104	.249	.317	3	.125	-1	2	2	-0	0.0
1949	Phi-A	1	1	.500	37	0	0	0	3	84^1	92	12	42	18	14.4	5.44	75	.286	.370	3	.125	-2	-12	-12	2	-1.1
1951	Phi-A	0	0	—	3	0	0	0	0	4	4	0	5	2	22.5	9.00	48	.250	.455	0	—	0	-2	-2	0	-0.2
	Cle-A	0	0	—	2	0	0	0	0	4	5	0	4	1	20.3	4.50	84	.333	.474	0	—	0	-0	-0	0	0.0
	Yr	0	0	—	5	0	0	0	0	8	9	0	9	3	20.3	6.75	60	.281	.439	0	—	0	-2	-2	0	-0.2
Total	3	6	3	.667	87	0	0	0	8	186	190	14	86	53	13.5	4.84	87	.267	.349	6	.125	-3	-12	-13	2	-1.3
● **GREG HARRIS** Harris, Greg Allen b: 11/2/55, Lynwood, Cal. BB/TR, 6', 175 lbs. Deb: 5/20/81																										
1981	NY-N	3	5	.375	16	14	0	0	1	68^2	65	8	28	54	12.5	4.46	78	.245	.322	4	.182	0	-7	-7	-1	-0.8
1982	Cin-N	2	6	.250	34	10	1	0	1	91^1	96	12	37	67	13.3	4.83	77	.274	.346	3	.167	-0	-12	-11	0	-1.2
1983	Cin-N	0	0	—	1	0	0	0	0	1	2	0	3	1	54.0	27.00	14	.500	.750	0	.000	-0	-3	-3	0	-0.2
1984	Mon-N	0	1	.000	15	0	0	0	2	17^2	10	0	7	15	9.7	2.04	168	.172	.284	0	.000	-0	3	3	0	0.3
	*SD-N	2	1	.667	19	1	0	0	1	36^2	28	3	18	30	11.8	2.70	132	.209	.312	3	.375	1	4	4	-0	0.5
	Yr	2	2	.500	34	1	0	0	3	54^1	38	3	25	45	10.8	2.48	142	.196	.294	3	.333	1	7	6	-0	0.8
1985	Tex-A	5	4	.556	58	0	0	0	11	113	74	7	43	111	9.7	2.47	171	.186	.274	0	—	0	21	22	1	2.3
1986	Tex-A	10	8	.556	73	0	0	0	20	111^1	103	12	42	95	11.8	2.83	152	.251	.322	0	—	0	17	18	1	1.8
1987	Tex-A	5	10	.333	42	19	0	0	0	140^2	157	18	56	106	13.9	4.86	92	.281	.351	0	—	0	-6	-6	0	-0.5
1988	Phi-N	4	6	.400	66	1	0	0	1	107	80	7	52	71	11.4	2.36	151	.209	.311	3	.333	1	13	14	-0	1.7
1989	Phi-N	2	2	.500	44	0	0	0	1	75^1	64	7	43	51	13.0	3.58	99	.234	.342	1	.167	1	-1	-0	1	0.1
	Bos-A	2	2	.500	15	0	0	0	0	28	21	1	15	25	11.6	2.57	159	.208	.310	0	—	0	4	5	0	0.2
1990	*Bos-A	13	9	.591	34	30	1	0	0	184^1	186	13	77	117	13.1	4.00	102	.265	.342	0	—	0	-2	1	3	0.2
1991	Bos-A	11	12	.478	53	21	1	0	2	173	157	13	69	127	12.0	3.85	112	.243	.321	0	—	0	5	9	2	1.1
1992	Bos-A	4	9	.308	70	2	1	0	4	107^2	82	6	60	73	12.2	2.51	165	.215	.327	0	—	0	17	20	0	2.0
Total	12	63	75	.457	540	98	4	0	44	1255^2	1125	107	550	943	12.3	3.55	114	.241	.326	14	.215	3	52	67	8	7.5
● **GREG HARRIS** Harris, Gregory Wade b: 12/1/63, Greensboro, N.C. BR/TR, 6'3", 190 lbs. Deb: 9/14/88																										
1988	SD-N	2	0	1.000	3	1	1	0	0	18	13	0	3	15	8.0	1.50	226	.200	.235	0	.000	-1	4	4	-0	0.3
1989	SD-N	8	9	.471	56	8	0	0	6	135	106	8	52	106	10.7	2.60	134	.215	.293	1	.053	-1	13	13	1	1.5
1990	SD-N	8	8	.500	73	0	0	0	9	117^1	92	6	49	97	11.1	2.30	166	.220	.307	1	.083	-0	19	20	0	2.1
1991	SD-N	9	5	.643	20	20	3	2	0	133	116	16	27	95	9.7	2.23	170	.233	.274	3	.083	-2	21	23	-1	2.3
1992	SD-N	4	8	.333	20	20	1	0	0	118	113	13	35	66	11.4	4.12	88	.252	.309	4	.129	1	-8	-6	0	-0.6
Total	5	31	30	.508	172	49	5	2	15	521^1	440	43	166	379	10.6	2.74	134	.229	.293	9	.086	-2	50	54	1	5.6
● **HERB HARRIS** Harris, Herbert Benjamin "Hub" or "Lefty" b: 4/24/13, Chicago, Ill. BL/TL, 6'1", 175 lbs. Deb: 7/21/36																										
1936	Phi-N	0	0	—	4	0	0	0	0	7	14	0	5	0	25.7	10.29	44	.438	.526	0	.000	-0	-5	-4	0	-0.4
● **JOE HARRIS** Harris, Joseph White b: 2/1/1882, Melrose, Mass. d: 4/12/66, Melrose, Mass. BR/TR, 6'1", 198 lbs. Deb: 9/22/05																										
1905	Bos-A	1	2	.333	3	3	3	0	0	23	16	0	8	14	9.4	2.35	115	.198	.270	1	.111	-1	1	1	-0	0.0
1906	Bos-A	2	21	.087	30	24	20	1	2	235	211	5	67	99	10.9	3.52	78	.243	.302	13	.160	-2	-22	-20	6	-1.7
1907	Bos-A	0	7	.000	12	5	3	0	0	59	57	0	13	24	10.8	3.05	85	.256	.300	4	.190	-0	-3	-3	0	-0.3
Total	3	3	30	.091	45	32	26	1	2	317	284	5	88	137	10.8	3.35	81	.242	.299	18	.162	-3	-24	-22	6	-2.0
● **MICKEY HARRIS** Harris, Maurice Charles b: 1/30/17, New York, N.Y. d: 4/15/71, Farmington, Mich. BL/TL, 6', 195 lbs. Deb: 4/23/40																										
1940	Bos-A	4	2	.667	13	9	3	0	0	68^1	83	8	26	36	14.6	5.00	90	.292	.356	6	.273	2	-5	-4	0	-0.1
1941	Bos-A	8	14	.364	35	22	11	1	1	194	189	6	86	111	12.9	3.25	128	.250	.328	6	.109	2	19	20	-1	2.1
1946	*Bos-A☆	17	9	.654	34	30	15	0	0	222^2	236	18	76	131	12.7	3.64	101	.268	.329	18	.231	4	-3	1	-1	0.3
1947	Bos-A	5	4	.556	15	6	1	0	0	51^2	42	3	23	35	11.3	2.44	159	.225	.310	5	.417	3	7	8	0	1.2
1948	Bos-A	7	10	.412	20	17	6	1	0	113^2	120	10	59	42	14.3	5.30	83	.273	.360	2	.063	-1	-13	-12	-2	-1.3
1949	Bos-A	2	3	.400	7	6	2	0	0	37^2	53	3	20	14	17.7	5.02	87	.323	.400	1	.083	-1	-3	-3	0	-0.3
	Was-A	2	12	.143	23	19	4	0	0	129	151	8	55	54	14.4	5.16	82	.292	.360	8	.205	1	-14	-13	-2	-1.2
	Yr	4	15	.211	30	25	6	0	0	166^2	204	11	75	68	15.1	5.13	83	.299	.368	9	.176	1	-17	-16	-2	-1.5
1950	Was-A	5	9	.357	**53**	0	0	0	**15**	98	93	10	46	41	12.9	4.78	94	.247	.330	4	.235	1	-2	-3	-1	-0.3
1951	Was-A	6	8	.429	41	0	0	0	4	87^1	87	6	43	47	13.5	3.81	107	.260	.347	3	.188	0	3	3	-1	0.2
1952	Was-A	0	0	—	1	0	0	0	0	1	1	1	0	0	9.0	9.00	40	.250	.250	0	—	0	-1	-1	-0	-0.1

YEAR	TM/L	W	L	PCT	G	GS	CG	SH	SV	IP	H	HR	BB	SO	RAT	ERA	ERA+	OAV	OOB	BH	AVG	PB	PR	/A	PD	TPI
	Cle-A	3	0	1.000	29	0	0	0	1	46^2	42	6	21	23	12.3	4.63	72	.249	.335	1	.200	-0	-5	-7	0	-0.7
	Yr	3	0	1.000	30	0	0	0	1	47^2	43	7	21	23	12.3	4.72	71	.249	.333	1	.200	-0	-6	-7	-0	-0.8
Total	9	59	71	.454	271	109	42	2	21	1050	1097	79	455	534	13.4	4.18	98	.267	.342	54	.188	11	-16	-9	-7	-0.2

● REGGIE HARRIS Harris, Reginald Allen b: 8/12/68, Waynesboro, Va. BR/TR, 6'1", 180 lbs. Deb: 7/04/90

YEAR	TM/L	W	L	PCT	G	GS	CG	SH	SV	IP	H	HR	BB	SO	RAT	ERA	ERA+	OAV	OOB	BH	AVG	PB	PR	/A	PD	TPI
1990	Oak-A	1	0	1.000	16	1	0	0	0	41^1	25	5	21	31	10.5	3.48	107	.176	.291	0	—	0	2	1	-0	0.3
1991	Oak-A	0	0	—	2	0	0	0	0	3	5	0	3	2	24.0	12.00	32	.455	.571	0	—	0	-3	-3	-0	-0.3
Total	2	1	0	1.000	18	1	0	0	0	44^1	30	5	24	33	11.4	4.06	92	.196	.313	0	—	0	-1	-2	-1	0.0

● BOB HARRIS Harris, Robert Arthur b: 5/1/17, Gillette, Wyo. d: 8/8/89, North Platte, Neb. BR/TR, 6', 185 lbs. Deb: 9/19/38

YEAR	TM/L	W	L	PCT	G	GS	CG	SH	SV	IP	H	HR	BB	SO	RAT	ERA	ERA+	OAV	OOB	BH	AVG	PB	PR	/A	PD	TPI
1938	Det-A	1	0	1.000	3	1	1	0	0	10	14	0	4	7	16.2	7.20	69	.318	.375	1	.333	0	-3	-2	0	-0.1
1939	Det-A	1	1	.500	5	1	0	0	0	18	18	4	8	9	13.0	4.00	122	.269	.347	2	.400	0	1	2	0	0.2
	StL-A	3	12	.200	28	16	6	0	0	126	162	5	71	48	16.6	5.71	85	.321	.405	7	.189	-0	-15	-12	3	-0.9
	Yr	4	13	.235	33	17	6	0	0	144	180	9	79	57	16.2	5.50	89	.315	.398	9	.214	-0	-14	-10	3	-0.7
1940	StL-A	11	15	.423	35	28	8	1	1	193^2	225	24	85	49	14.5	4.93	93	.290	.362	15	.250	3	-12	-7	-0	-0.4
1941	StL-A	12	14	.462	34	29	9	2	1	186^2	237	18	85	57	15.6	5.21	83	.312	.383	7	.115	-3	-22	-19	-2	-2.2
1942	StL-A	1	5	.167	6	6	0	0	0	33^2	37	2	17	9	14.4	5.61	66	.268	.348	0	.000	-1	-7	-7	-1	-0.8
	Phi-A	1	5	.167	16	8	2	1	0	78	77	5	24	26	11.7	2.88	131	.253	.308	7	.269	1	7	8	2	1.2
	Yr	2	10	.167	22	14	2	1	0	111^2	114	7	41	35	12.5	3.71	101	.258	.321	7	.194	0	-1	1	2	0.4
Total	5	30	52	.366	127	89	26	4	2	646	770	58	294	205	14.9	4.96	89	.297	.370	39	.193	1	-51	-38	3	-3.0

● GENE HARRIS Harris, Tyrone Eugene b: 12/5/64, Sebring, Fla. BR/TR, 5'11", 190 lbs. Deb: 4/05/89

YEAR	TM/L	W	L	PCT	G	GS	CG	SH	SV	IP	H	HR	BB	SO	RAT	ERA	ERA+	OAV	OOB	BH	AVG	PB	PR	/A	PD	TPI
1989	Mon-N	1	1	.500	11	0	0	0	0	20	16	1	10	11	11.7	4.95	71	.242	.342	0	.000	-0	-3	-3	2	-0.2
	Sea-A	1	4	.200	10	6	0	0	1	33^1	47	3	15	14	17.0	6.48	62	.353	.423	0	—	0	-10	-9	-1	-1.1
1990	Sea-A	1	2	.333	25	0	0	0	0	38	31	5	30	43	14.7	4.74	84	.217	.356	0	—	0	-4	-3	-0	-0.4
1991	Sea-A	0	0	—	8	0	0	0	1	13^1	15	1	10	6	16.9	4.05	102	.273	.385	0	—	0	0	0	-0	0.0
1992	Sea-A	0	0	—	8	0	0	0	0	9	8	3	6	6	14.0	7.00	57	.235	.350	0	—	0	-3	-3	-0	-0.3
	SD-N	0	2	.000	14	1	0	0	0	21^1	15	0	9	19	10.5	2.95	123	.195	.287	1	.333	0	1	2	0	0.2
Total	4	3	9	.250	76	7	0	0	2	135	132	13	80	99	14.3	5.00	78	.260	.364	1	.250	0	-18	-17	0	-1.8

● BUDDY HARRIS Harris, Walter Francis b: 12/5/48, Philadelphia, Pa. BR/TR, 6'7", 245 lbs. Deb: 9/10/70

YEAR	TM/L	W	L	PCT	G	GS	CG	SH	SV	IP	H	HR	BB	SO	RAT	ERA	ERA+	OAV	OOB	BH	AVG	PB	PR	/A	PD	TPI
1970	Hou-N	0	0	—	2	0	0	0	0	6^1	6	3	0	2	8.5	5.68	68	.240	.240	0	.000	-0	-1	-1	-0	-0.1
1971	Hou-N	1	1	.500	20	0	0	0	0	30^2	33	3	16	21	14.4	6.46	52	.275	.360	0	.000	-0	-10	-11	-1	-1.2
Total	2	1	1	.500	22	0	0	0	0	37	39	6	16	23	13.4	6.32	55	.269	.342	0	.000	-0	-11	-12	-1	-1.3

● BILL HARRIS Harris, William Milton b: 6/23/1900, Wylie, Tex. d: 8/21/65, Indian Trail, N.C. BR/TR, 6'1", 180 lbs. Deb: 4/22/23

YEAR	TM/L	W	L	PCT	G	GS	CG	SH	SV	IP	H	HR	BB	SO	RAT	ERA	ERA+	OAV	OOB	BH	AVG	PB	PR	/A	PD	TPI
1923	Cin-N	3	2	.600	22	3	1	0	0	69^2	79	3	18	18	12.9	5.17	75	.292	.342	6	.353	1	-9	-10	0	-0.8
1924	Cin-N	0	0	—	3	0	0	0	0	7	10	0	2	5	15.4	9.00	42	.323	.364	1	1.000	0	-4	-4	0	-0.3
1931	Pit-N	2	2	.500	4	4	3	1	0	31	21	0	9	10	8.7	0.87	442	.194	.256	1	.091	-1	10	10	0	1.1
1932	Pit-N	10	9	.526	37	17	4	0	2	168	178	6	38	63	11.9	3.64	105	.271	.317	10	.182	-1	4	3	-2	0.1
1933	Pit-N	4	4	.500	31	0	0	0	5	58^2	68	1	14	19	12.7	3.22	103	.289	.332	0	.000	-1	1	1	-1	-0.1
1934	Pit-N	0	0	—	11	2	0	0	0	19	28	2	7	8	17.1	6.63	62	.350	.409	1	.500	0	-5	-5	0	-0.5
1938	Bos-A	5	5	.500	13	11	5	1	1	80^1	83	5	21	26	11.8	4.03	122	.268	.316	6	.214	-0	7	8	-0	0.7
Total	7	24	22	.522	121	37	13	2	8	433^2	467	17	109	149	12.2	3.92	101	.276	.324	25	.203	-1	4	2	-2	0.2

● BILL HARRIS Harris, William Thomas b: 12/3/31, Duguayville, N.B., Canada BL/TR, 5'8", 187 lbs. Deb: 9/27/57

YEAR	TM/L	W	L	PCT	G	GS	CG	SH	SV	IP	H	HR	BB	SO	RAT	ERA	ERA+	OAV	OOB	BH	AVG	PB	PR	/A	PD	TPI
1957	Bro-N	0	1	.000	1	1	0	0	0	7	9	1	1	3	12.9	3.86	108	.321	.345	1	.500	0	0	0	0	0.1
1959	LA-N	0	0	—	1	0	0	0	0	1^2	0	0	3	0	16.2	0.00	—	.000	.375	0	—	0	1	1	0	0.1
Total	2	0	1	.000	2	1	0	0	0	8^2	9	1	4	3	13.5	3.12	134	.273	.351	1	.500	0	1	1	0	0.2

● BOB HARRISON Harrison, Robert Lee b: 9/22/30, St.Louis, Mo. BL/TR, 5'11", 178 lbs. Deb: 9/23/55

YEAR	TM/L	W	L	PCT	G	GS	CG	SH	SV	IP	H	HR	BB	SO	RAT	ERA	ERA+	OAV	OOB	BH	AVG	PB	PR	/A	PD	TPI
1955	Bal-A	0	0	—	1	0	0	0	0	2	3	0	4	0	31.5	9.00	42	.500	.700	0	—	0	-1	-1	-0	-0.1
1956	Bal-A	0	0	—	1	1	0	0	0	1^2	3	0	5	0	43.2	16.20	24	.375	.615	0	—	0	-2	-2	-0	-0.2
Total	2	0	0	—	2	1	0	0	0	3^2	6	0	9	0	36.8	12.27	31	.429	.652	0	—	0	-3	-3	-0	-0.3

● RORIC HARRISON Harrison, Roric Edward b: 9/20/46, Los Angeles, Cal. BR/TR, 6'3", 195 lbs. Deb: 4/18/72

YEAR	TM/L	W	L	PCT	G	GS	CG	SH	SV	IP	H	HR	BB	SO	RAT	ERA	ERA+	OAV	OOB	BH	AVG	PB	PR	/A	PD	TPI
1972	Bal-A	3	4	.429	39	2	0	0	4	94	68	2	34	62	10.1	2.30	134	.209	.292	2	.118	1	8	8	-1	1.0
1973	Atl-N	11	8	.579	38	22	3	0	5	177^1	161	15	98	130	13.3	4.16	94	.242	.342	3	.056	-2	-10	-5	-1	-0.8
1974	Atl-N	6	11	.353	20	20	3	0	0	126	148	12	49	46	14.3	4.71	80	.294	.360	7	.184	3	-15	-13	-2	-1.3
1975	Atl-N	3	4	.429	15	7	2	0	1	54^2	58	7	19	22	12.7	4.77	79	.266	.325	3	.200	1	-7	-6	0	-0.6
	Cle-A	7	7	.500	19	19	4	0	0	126	137	9	46	52	13.4	4.79	79	.275	.341	0	—	0	-14	-14	-1	-1.5
1978	Min-A	0	1	.000	9	0	0	0	0	12	18	0	11	7	21.8	7.50	51	.346	.460	0	—	0	-5	-5	-0	-0.6
Total	5	30	35	.462	140	70	12	0	10	590	590	45	257	319	13.1	4.24	87	.261	.340	15	.121	2	-43	-35	-5	-3.8

● TOM HARRISON Harrison, Thomas James b: 1/18/45, Trail, B.C., Canada BR/TR, 6'3", 200 lbs. Deb: 5/07/65 ♦

YEAR	TM/L	W	L	PCT	G	GS	CG	SH	SV	IP	H	HR	BB	SO	RAT	ERA	ERA+	OAV	OOB	BH	AVG	PB	PR	/A	PD	TPI
1965	KC-A	0	0	—	1	0	0	0	0	1	2	0	1	0	27.0	9.00	39	.667	.750	0	—	0	-1	-1	-0	-0.1

● SLIM HARRISS Harriss, William Jennings Bryan b: 12/11/1896, Brownwood, Tex. d: 9/19/63, Temple, Tex. BR/TR, 6'6", 180 lbs. Deb: 4/19/20

YEAR	TM/L	W	L	PCT	G	GS	CG	SH	SV	IP	H	HR	BB	SO	RAT	ERA	ERA+	OAV	OOB	BH	AVG	PB	PR	/A	PD	TPI
1920	Phi-A	9	14	.391	31	25	11	1	0	192	226	5	57	60	13.5	4.08	99	.305	.359	7	.106	-7	-6	-1	3	-0.5
1921	Phi-A	11	16	.407	39	28	14	0	2	227^2	258	16	73	92	13.4	4.27	104	.290	.350	12	.148	-7	0	5	-1	-0.3
1922	Phi-A	9	20	.310	47	32	13	0	3	229^2	262	19	94	102	14.1	5.02	85	.290	.359	13	.176	-4	-25	-19	1	-2.2
1923	Phi-A	10	16	.385	46	28	9	0	6	209^1	221	9	95	89	13.7	4.00	103	.280	.359	4	.066	-8	-0	3	5	0.0
1924	Phi-A	6	10	.375	36	12	4	1	2	123	138	5	62	45	14.9	4.68	92	.291	.377	7	.167	-3	-6	-5	4	-0.4
1925	Phi-A	19	12	.613	46	33	15	2	1	252^2	263	8	95	95	13.0	3.49	133	.268	.336	18	.205	-3	25	33	4	3.2
1926	Phi-A	3	5	.375	12	10	2	0	0	57	66	0	22	13	13.9	4.11	102	.289	.352	1	.059	-2	-1	0	0	-0.1
	Bos-A	6	10	.375	21	18	6	1	0	113	135	0	33	34	13.5	4.46	91	.311	.362	7	.206	-0	-6	-5	1	-0.4
	Yr	9	15	.375	33	28	8	1	0	170	201	0	55	47	13.7	4.34	95	.304	.359	8	.157	-2	-6	-4	1	-0.5
1927	Bos-A	14	21	.400	44	27	11	1	1	217^2	253	8	66	77	13.6	4.18	101	.298	.355	8	.121	-5	-1	1	1	-0.3
1928	Bos-A	8	11	.421	27	15	4	1	1	128^1	141	5	33	37	12.3	4.63	89	.287	.335	5	.139	-3	-8	-7	-2	-1.1
Total	9	95	135	.413	349	228	89	7	16	1750^1	1963	75	630	644	13.5	4.25	100	.290	.354	82	.145	-41	-27	3	15	-2.1

● EARL HARRIST Harrist, Earl "Irish" b: 8/20/19, Dubach, La. BR/TR, 6', 178 lbs. Deb: 8/18/45

YEAR	TM/L	W	L	PCT	G	GS	CG	SH	SV	IP	H	HR	BB	SO	RAT	ERA	ERA+	OAV	OOB	BH	AVG	PB	PR	/A	PD	TPI
1945	Cin-N	2	4	.333	14	5	1	0	0	62^1	60	2	27	15	12.7	3.61	104	.249	.327	0	.000	-2	1	1	-1	-0.2
1947	Chi-A	3	8	.273	33	4	0	0	5	93^2	85	3	49	55	13.2	3.56	103	.248	.347	5	.208	-0	2	1	1	0.1
1948	Chi-A	1	3	.250	11	1	0	0	0	23	23	4	13	14	15.3	5.87	73	.267	.382	0	.000	-1	-4	-4	0	-0.5
	Was-A	3	3	.500	23	4	0	0	0	60^2	70	1	37	21	16.3	4.60	94	.293	.394	3	.167	-1	-2	-2	-1	-0.3
	Yr	4	6	.400	34	5	0	0	0	83^2	93	5	50	35	15.7	4.95	87	.284	.383	3	.136	-2	-6	-6	-1	-0.8
1952	StL-A	2	8	.200	36	9	1	0	5	116^2	119	7	47	49	13.6	4.01	98	.269	.352	3	.097	-3	-4	-1	1	-0.3
1953	Chi-A	1	0	1.000	7	0	0	0	0	8^1	9	1	5	1	15.1	7.56	53	.290	.389	0	.000	-0	-3	-3	-0	-0.3
	Det-A	0	2	.000	8	1	0	0	0	18^2	25	2	15	7	19.3	8.68	47	.333	.444	0	.000	-0	-10	-10	1	-0.9
	Yr	1	2	.333	15	1	0	0	0	27	34	3	20	8	18.0	8.33	49	.321	.429	0	.000	-0	-13	-13	1	-1.2
Total	5	12	28	.300	132	24	2	0	10	383^1	391	20	193	162	14.2	4.34	90	.268	.361	11	.115	-7	-21	-18	0	-2.4

● JACK HARSHMAN Harshman, John Elvin b: 7/12/27, San Diego, Cal. BL/TL, 6'2", 185 lbs. Deb: 9/16/48 ♦

YEAR	TM/L	W	L	PCT	G	GS	CG	SH	SV	IP	H	HR	BB	SO	RAT	ERA	ERA+	OAV	OOB	BH	AVG	PB	PR	/A	PD	TPI
1952	NY-N	0	2	.000	2	2	0	0	0	6^1	12	2	6	6	25.6	14.21	26	.429	.529	0	.000	-0	-7	-7	0	-0.6
1954	Chi-A	14	8	.636	35	21	9	4	1	177	157	7	96	134	13.1	2.95	127	.238	.339	8	.143	3	15	15	-1	1.9

YEAR	TM/L	W	L	PCT	G	GS	CG	SH	SV	IP	H	HR	BB	SO	RAT	ERA	ERA+	OAV	OOB	BH	AVG	PB	PR	/A	PD	TPI
1955	Chi-A	11	7	.611	32	23	9	0	0	179^1	144	16	97	116	12.3	3.36	117	.224	.330	11	.183	4	12	12	-0	1.5
1956	Chi-A	15	11	.577	34	30	15	4	0	226^2	183	14	102	143	11.4	3.10	132	.221	.308	12	.169	6	27	25	-2	2.9
1957	Chi-A	8	8	.500	30	26	6	0	1	151^1	142	16	82	83	13.6	4.10	91	.250	.349	10	.222	5	-5	-6	-3	-0.4
1958	Bal-A	12	15	.444	34	29	17	3	4	236^1	204	20	75	161	10.7	2.89	124	.231	.294	16	.195	7	23	18	1	3.2
1959	Bal-A	0	6	.000	14	8	0	0	0	47^1	58	6	28	24	16.7	6.85	55	.319	.415	2	.200	1	-16	-16	1	-1.3
	Bos-A	2	3	.400	8	2	0	0	0	24^2	29	2	10	14	14.2	6.57	62	.284	.348	1	.143	0	-7	-7	-1	-0.7
	Cle-A	5	1	.833	13	6	5	1	1	66	46	6	13	35	8.0	2.59	142	.179	.219	7	.206	2	9	8	-0	1.0
	Yr	7	10	.412	35	16	5	1	1	138	133	14	51	73	12.0	4.76	79	.244	.308	10	.196	3	-14	-15	1	-1.0
1960	Cle-A	2	4	.333	15	8	0	0	0	54^1	50	7	30	25	13.3	3.98	94	.243	.339	3	.176	-0	-1	-1	-1	-0.2
Total	8	69	65	.515	217	155	61	12	7	1169^1	1025	96	539	741	12.2	3.50	109	.235	.323	76	.179	29	50	41	-5	7.3

● OSCAR HARSTAD Harstad, Oscar Theander b: 5/24/1892, Parkland, Wash. d: 11/14/85, Corvallis, Ore. BR/TR, 6', 174 lbs. Deb: 4/23/15

YEAR	TM/L	W	L	PCT	G	GS	CG	SH	SV	IP	H	HR	BB	SO	RAT	ERA	ERA+	OAV	OOB	BH	AVG	PB	PR	/A	PD	TPI
1915	Cle-A	3	5	.375	32	7	4	0	1	82	81	1	35	35	12.8	3.40	90	.270	.348	2	.125	-1	-4	-3	2	-0.3

● BILLY HART Hart, Robert Lee b: 5/16/1866, Palmyra, Mo. d: 5/14/44, Hannibal, Mo. 5'8", Deb: 7/13/1890

YEAR	TM/L	W	L	PCT	G	GS	CG	SH	SV	IP	H	HR	BB	SO	RAT	ERA	ERA+	OAV	OOB	BH	AVG	PB	PR	/A	PD	TPI
1890	StL-a	12	8	.600	26	24	20	0	0	201^1	188	6	66	95	12.1	3.67	118	.240	.312	15	.192	-1	5	15	-3	1.0

● BILL HART Hart, William Franklin b: 7/19/1865, Louisville, Ky. d: 9/19/36, Cincinnati, Ohio TR, 5'10", 163 lbs. Deb: 7/26/1886 U

YEAR	TM/L	W	L	PCT	G	GS	CG	SH	SV	IP	H	HR	BB	SO	RAT	ERA	ERA+	OAV	OOB	BH	AVG	PB	PR	/A	PD	TPI
1886	Phi-a	9	13	.409	22	22	22	2	0	186	183	7	66	78	12.4	3.19	110	.234	.299	10	.137	-5	5	6	1	0.3
1887	Phi-a	1	2	.333	3	3	3	0	0	26	28	1	17	4	15.9	4.50	95	.272	.380	1	.077	-2	-1	-1	0	-0.2
1892	Bro-N	9	12	.429	28	23	16	2	1	195	188	3	96	65	13.4	3.28	97	.243	.332	24	.192	2	0	-2	3	0.3
1895	Pit-N	14	17	.452	36	29	24	0	1	261^2	293	4	135	85	15.2	4.75	95	.279	.369	25	.236	-2	1	-7	6	-0.2
1896	StL-N	12	29	.293	42	41	37	0	0	336	411	11	141	65	15.2	5.12	85	.299	.370	30	.186	-5	-28	-29	6	-2.2
1897	StL-N	9	27	.250	39	38	31	0	0	294^2	395	10	148	67	17.1	6.26	70	.318	.398	39	.250	-1	-64	-61	3	-4.7
1898	Pit-N	5	9	.357	16	15	13	1	1	125	141	4	44	19	13.8	4.82	74	.282	.349	12	.240	0	-17	-18	0	-1.5
1901	Cle-A	7	11	.389	20	19	16	0	0	157^2	180	3	57	48	14.1	3.77	94	.283	.352	14	.219	-2	-2	-4	2	-0.3
Total	8	66	120	.355	206	190	162	5	3	1582	1819	43	704	431	14.8	4.65	86	.282	.359	155	.207	-14	-105	-114	22	-8.5

● CHUCK HARTENSTEIN Hartenstein, Charles Oscar "Twiggy" b: 5/26/42, Seguin, Tex. BR/TR, 5'11", 165 lbs. Deb: 9/11/65 C♦

YEAR	TM/L	W	L	PCT	G	GS	CG	SH	SV	IP	H	HR	BB	SO	RAT	ERA	ERA+	OAV	OOB	BH	AVG	PB	PR	/A	PD	TPI
1966	Chi-N	0	0	—	5	0	0	0	0	9^1	8	0	3	4	11.6	1.93	191	.222	.300	0	—	0	2	2	0	0.2
1967	Chi-N	9	5	.643	45	0	0	0	10	73	74	4	17	20	11.3	3.08	115	.278	.324	1	.063	-1	2	4	-0	0.3
1968	Chi-N	2	4	.333	28	0	0	0	1	35^2	41	3	11	17	13.4	4.54	70	.291	.346	0	.000	-0	-6	-5	-0	-0.7
1969	Pit-N	5	4	.556	56	0	0	0	10	95^2	84	9	27	44	10.8	3.95	88	.241	.303	1	.071	-1	-4	-5	1	-0.4
1970	Pit-N	1	1	.500	17	0	0	0	1	23^2	25	3	8	14	12.5	4.56	85	.278	.337	0	.000	-0	-1	-2	1	-0.1
	StL-N	0	0	—	6	0	0	0	0	13^1	24	1	5	9	19.6	8.78	47	.375	.420	0	.000	0	-7	-7	0	-0.6
	Yr	1	1	.500	23	0	0	0	1	37	49	4	13	23	15.1	6.08	65	.316	.369	0	.000	-0	-8	-9	1	-0.7
	Bos-A	0	3	.000	17	0	0	0	1	19	21	6	12	12	16.1	8.05	49	.288	.395	0	.000	0	-9	-9	-1	-0.9
1977	Tor-A	0	2	.000	13	0	0	0	0	27^1	40	8	6	15	15.5	6.59	64	.348	.385	0	—	0	-8	-7	-0	-0.7
Total	6	17	19	.472	187	0	0	0	23	297	317	34	89	135	12.6	4.52	80	.280	.337	2	.054	-2	-31	-29	2	-2.9

● FRANK HARTER Harter, Franklin Pierce "Chief" b: 9/19/1886, Keyesport, Ill. d: 4/14/59, Breese, Ill. BR/TR, 5'11", 165 lbs. Deb: 8/31/12

YEAR	TM/L	W	L	PCT	G	GS	CG	SH	SV	IP	H	HR	BB	SO	RAT	ERA	ERA+	OAV	OOB	BH	AVG	PB	PR	/A	PD	TPI
1912	Cin-N	1	2	.333	6	3	1	0	0	29^1	25	1	11	12	11.0	3.07	110	.234	.305	1	.091	-1	1	1	-1	-0.1
1913	Cin-N	1	1	.500	17	2	0	0	0	46^2	47	3	19	10	12.7	3.86	84	.272	.344	2	.143	-1	-3	-3	-1	-0.5
1914	Ind-F	1	2	.333	6	1	1	0	0	24^2	33	0	7	8	14.6	4.01	86	.330	.374	0	.000	-1	-2	-1	-0	-0.3
Total	3	3	5	.375	29	6	2	0	0	100^2	105	4	37	30	12.7	3.67	91	.276	.341	3	.091	-3	-4	-4	-2	-0.9

● MIKE HARTLEY Hartley, Michael Edward b: 8/31/61, Hawthorne, Cal. BR/TR, 6'1", 192 lbs. Deb: 9/10/89

YEAR	TM/L	W	L	PCT	G	GS	CG	SH	SV	IP	H	HR	BB	SO	RAT	ERA	ERA+	OAV	OOB	BH	AVG	PB	PR	/A	PD	TPI
1989	LA-N	0	1	.000	5	0	0	0	0	6	2	0	0	4	3.0	1.50	228	.100	.100	0	.000	-0	1	1	0	0.1
1990	LA-N	6	3	.667	32	6	1	1	1	79^1	58	7	30	76	10.2	2.95	124	.200	.280	1	.077	-1	7	6	-0	0.5
1991	LA-N	2	0	1.000	40	0	0	0	1	57	53	7	37	44	14.7	4.42	81	.245	.363	0	.000	-0	-5	-5	0	-0.6
	Phi-N	2	1	.667	18	0	0	0	1	26^1	21	4	10	19	11.6	3.76	98	.219	.312	0	.000	-0	-0	-0	-1	-0.1
	Yr	4	1	.800	58	0	0	0	2	83^1	74	11	47	63	13.4	4.21	86	.234	.339	0	.000	-1	-5	-6	-1	-0.7
1992	Phi-N	7	6	.538	46	0	0	0	0	55	54	5	23	53	12.9	3.44	102	.255	.333	0	.000	-0	0	0	-0	0.0
Total	4	17	11	.607	141	6	1	1	3	223^2	188	23	100	196	12.0	3.50	103	.225	.316	1	.043	-2	4	2	-1	-0.1

● CHARLIE HARTMAN Hartman, Charles Otto b: 8/10/1888, Los Angeles, Cal. d: 10/22/60, Los Angeles, Cal. Deb: 6/24/08

YEAR	TM/L	W	L	PCT	G	GS	CG	SH	SV	IP	H	HR	BB	SO	RAT	ERA	ERA+	OAV	OOB	BH	AVG	PB	PR	/A	PD	TPI
1908	Bos-A	0	0	—	1	0	0	0	0	2	1	0	2	1	13.5	4.50	55	.143	.333	0	—	0	-0	-0	0	0.0

● BOB HARTMAN Hartman, Robert Louis b: 8/28/37, Kenosha, Wis. BR/TL, 5'11", 185 lbs. Deb: 4/26/59

YEAR	TM/L	W	L	PCT	G	GS	CG	SH	SV	IP	H	HR	BB	SO	RAT	ERA	ERA+	OAV	OOB	BH	AVG	PB	PR	/A	PD	TPI
1959	Mil-N	0	0	—	3	0	0	0	0	1^2	6	0	2	1	43.2	27.00	13	.545	.615	0	—	0	-4	-4	-0	-0.4
1962	Cle-A	0	1	.000	8	2	0	0	0	17^1	14	1	8	11	11.4	3.12	124	.209	.293	0	.000	-1	2	1	-0	0.1
Total	2	0	1	.000	11	2	0	0	0	19	20	1	10	12	14.2	5.21	74	.256	.341	0	.000	-1	-3	-3	-0	-0.3

● RAY HARTRANFT Hartranft, Raymond Joseph b: 9/19/1890, Quakertown, Pa. d: 2/10/55, Spring City, Pa. BL/TL, 6'1", 195 lbs. Deb: 6/16/13

YEAR	TM/L	W	L	PCT	G	GS	CG	SH	SV	IP	H	HR	BB	SO	RAT	ERA	ERA+	OAV	OOB	BH	AVG	PB	PR	/A	PD	TPI
1913	Phi-N	0	0	—	1	0	0	0	0	1	3	0	1	1	36.0	9.00	37	.500	.571	0	—	0	-1	-1	0	-0.1

● JEFF HARTSOCK Hartsock, Jeffrey Roger b: 11/19/66, Hamilton, Ohio BR/TR, 6', 190 lbs. Deb: 9/12/92

YEAR	TM/L	W	L	PCT	G	GS	CG	SH	SV	IP	H	HR	BB	SO	RAT	ERA	ERA+	OAV	OOB	BH	AVG	PB	PR	/A	PD	TPI
1992	Chi-N	0	0	—	4	0	0	0	0	9^1	15	2	4	6	18.3	6.75	53	.375	.432	0	.000	-0	-3	-3	0	-0.3

● CLINT HARTUNG Hartung, Clinton Clarence "Floppy" or "The Hondo Hurricane" b: 8/10/22, Hondo, Tex. BR/TR, 6'4", 215 lbs. Deb: 4/15/47 ♦

YEAR	TM/L	W	L	PCT	G	GS	CG	SH	SV	IP	H	HR	BB	SO	RAT	ERA	ERA+	OAV	OOB	BH	AVG	PB	PR	/A	PD	TPI
1947	NY-N	9	7	.563	23	20	8	1	0	138	140	15	69	54	13.8	4.57	89	.263	.350	29	.309	9	-8	-8	-1	0.1
1948	NY-N	8	8	.500	36	19	6	2	1	153^1	146	15	72	42	13.1	4.75	83	.258	.347	10	.179	2	-14	-14	-0	-1.2
1949	NY-N	9	11	.450	33	25	8	0	0	154^2	156	16	86	48	14.3	5.00	80	.260	.357	12	.190	4	-17	-18	2	-1.2
1950	NY-N	3	3	.500	20	8	1	0	0	65^1	87	10	44	23	18.3	6.61	62	.326	.425	13	.302	4	-18	-18	2	-1.0
Total	4	29	29	.500	112	72	23	3	1	511^1	529	56	271	167	14.3	5.02	80	.269	.361	90	.238	19	-56	-57	3	-3.3

● PAUL HARTZELL Hartzell, Paul Franklin b: 11/2/53, Bloomsburg, Pa. BR/TR, 6'5", 200 lbs. Deb: 4/10/76

YEAR	TM/L	W	L	PCT	G	GS	CG	SH	SV	IP	H	HR	BB	SO	RAT	ERA	ERA+	OAV	OOB	BH	AVG	PB	PR	/A	PD	TPI
1976	Cal-A	7	4	.636	37	15	7	2	2	166	166	6	43	51	11.9	2.77	120	.266	.323	0	—	0	14	10	1	1.7
1977	Cal-A	8	12	.400	41	23	6	0	4	189^1	200	14	38	79	11.5	3.57	110	.274	.313	0	—	0	10	7	1	0.8
1978	Cal-A	6	10	.375	54	12	5	0	6	157	168	8	41	55	12.3	3.44	105	.278	.329	0	—	0	6	3	1	0.7
1979	Min-A	6	10	.375	28	26	4	0	0	163	193	18	44	44	13.3	5.36	82	.301	.350	0	—	0	-21	-18	1	-1.6
1980	Bal-A	0	2	.000	6	0	0	0	0	17^2	22	3	9	5	15.8	6.62	60	.310	.387	0	—	0	-5	-5	-1	-0.5
1984	Mil-A	0	1	.000	4	1	0	0	0	10^1	17	0	6	3	20.0	7.84	49	.370	.442	0	—	0	-4	-5	0	-0.4
Total	6	27	39	.409	170	77	22	2	12	703^1	766	49	181	237	12.4	3.90	98	.282	.332	0	—	0	-0	-7	3	0.7

● BRYAN HARVEY Harvey, Bryan Stanley b: 6/2/63, Chattanooga, Tenn. BR/TR, 6'2", 215 lbs. Deb: 5/16/87

YEAR	TM/L	W	L	PCT	G	GS	CG	SH	SV	IP	H	HR	BB	SO	RAT	ERA	ERA+	OAV	OOB	BH	AVG	PB	PR	/A	PD	TPI
1987	Cal-A	0	0	—	3	0	0	0	0	5	6	0	2	3	14.4	0.00	—	.300	.364	0	—	0	2	2	-0	0.3
1988	Cal-A	7	5	.583	50	0	0	0	17	76	59	4	20	67	9.5	2.13	181	.214	.269	0	—	0	15	15	-2	1.4
1989	Cal-A	3	3	.500	51	0	0	0	25	55	36	6	41	78	12.6	3.44	111	.183	.324	0	—	0	3	2	0	0.3
1990	Cal-A	4	4	.500	54	0	0	0	25	64^1	45	4	35	82	11.2	3.22	119	.201	.309	0	—	0	5	4	-0	0.5
1991	Cal-A☆	2	4	.333	67	0	0	0	**46**	78^2	51	6	17	101	7.9	1.60	256	.178	.227	0	—	0	22	22	-0	2.2
1992	Cal-A	0	4	.000	25	0	0	0	13	28^2	22	4	11	34	10.4	2.83	138	.208	.282	0	—	0	4	3	-1	0.3
Total	6	16	20	.444	250	0	0	0	126	307^2	219	24	126	365	10.2	2.49	157	.197	.281	0	—	0	51	49	-3	5.0

● ERWIN HARVEY Harvey, Ervin King "Zaza" b: 1/5/1879, Saratoga, Cal. d: 6/3/54, Santa Monica, Cal. BL/TL, 6', 190 lbs. Deb: 5/03/00 ♦

YEAR	TM/L	W	L	PCT	G	GS	CG	SH	SV	IP	H	HR	BB	SO	RAT	ERA	ERA+	OAV	OOB	BH	AVG	PB	PR	/A	PD	TPI
1900	Chi-N	0	0	—	1	0	0	0	0	4	3	0	1	0	9.0	0.00	—	.208	.260	0	.000	-1	2	2	-0	0.1

YEAR TM/L	W	L	PCT	G	GS	CG	SH	SV	IP	H	HR	BB	SO	RAT	ERA	ERA+	OAV	OOB	BH	AVG	PB	PR	/A	PD	TPI
1901 Chi-A	3	6	.333	16	9	5	0	1	92	91	2	34	27	12.8	3.62	96	.255	.330	10	.250	2	0	-1	2	0.2
Total 2	3	6	.333	17	9	5	0	1	96	94	2	35	27	12.7	3.47	101	.253	.328	86	.332	1	2	0	2	0.3
● HERB HASH	Hash, Herbert Howard b: 2/13/11, Woolwine, Va. BR/TR, 6'1", 180 lbs. Deb: 4/19/40																								
1940 Bos-A	7	7	.500	34	12	3	1	3	120	123	11	84	36	15.9	4.95	91	.266	.385	7	.175	-0	-8	-6	1	-0.5
1941 Bos-A	1	0	1.000	4	0	0	0	1	8^{1}	7	1	7	3	15.1	5.40	77	.226	.368	0	.000	-0	-1	-1	0	-0.1
Total 2	8	7	.533	38	12	3	1	4	128^{1}	130	12	91	39	15.8	4.98	90	.264	.384	7	.167	-1	-9	-7	1	-0.6
● ANDY HASSLER	Hassler, Andrew Earl b: 10/18/51, Texas City, Tex. BL/TL, 6'5", 220 lbs. Deb: 5/30/71																								
1971 Cal-A	0	3	.000	6	4	0	0	0	18^{2}	25	0	15	13	19.8	3.86	84	.333	.451	0	.000	-1	-1	-1	0	-0.2
1973 Cal-A	0	4	.000	7	4	1	0	0	31^{2}	33	0	19	19	15.6	3.69	96	.262	.372	0	—	0	0	-1	-0	0.3
1974 Cal-A	7	11	.389	23	22	10	2	1	162	132	10	79	76	12.2	2.61	132	.225	.326	0	—	0	18	15	0	1.7
1975 Cal-A	3	12	.200	30	18	6	1	0	133^{1}	158	12	53	82	14.6	5.94	60	.303	.373	0	—	0	-32	-35	1	-2.9
1976 Cal-A	0	6	.000	14	4	0	0	0	47^{1}	50	3	17	16	12.7	5.13	65	.284	.347	0	—	0	-8	-10	-0	-0.5
*KC-A	5	6	.455	19	14	4	1	0	99^{2}	89	2	39	45	11.6	2.89	121	.242	.314	0	—	0	7	7	1	0.7
Yr	5	12	.294	33	18	4	1	0	147	139	5	56	61	11.9	3.61	95	.254	.323	0	—	0	-2	-3	1	0.2
1977 *KC-A	9	6	.600	29	27	3	1	0	156^{1}	166	7	75	83	14.2	4.20	96	.270	.354	0	—	0	-2	-3	0	-0.3
1978 KC-A	1	4	.200	11	9	1	0	0	58^{1}	76	1	24	26	15.7	4.32	88	.317	.383	0	—	0	-4	-3	-1	-0.4
Bos-A	2	1	.667	13	2	0	0	1	30	38	0	13	23	15.3	3.00	137	.302	.367	0	—	0	3	4	-0	0.3
Yr	3	5	.375	24	11	1	0	1	88^{1}	114	1	37	49	15.4	3.87	101	.308	.371	0	—	0	-1	0	-1	-0.1
1979 Bos-A	1	2	.333	8	0	0	0	0	15^{1}	23	0	7	7	18.2	8.80	50	.365	.437	0	—	0	-8	-7	-0	-0.9
NY-N	4	5	.444	29	8	1	0	4	80^{1}	74	5	42	53	13.0	3.70	98	.252	.345	0	.000	-2	0	-1	1	-0.2
1980 Pit-N	0	0	—	6	0	0	0	0	11^{2}	9	2	4	4	10.0	3.86	94	.243	.317	0	.000	-0	-0	-0	1	0.0
Cal-A	5	1	.833	41	0	0	0	10	83	67	8	37	75	11.4	2.49	158	.214	.299	0	—	0	14	13	-1	1.4
1981 Cal-A	4	3	.571	42	0	0	0	5	75^{2}	72	8	33	44	12.5	3.21	114	.262	.341	0	—	0	4	4	1	0.4
1982 *Cal-A	2	1	.667	54	0	0	0	4	71^{1}	58	5	40	38	12.9	2.78	146	.232	.347	0	—	0	10	10	2	1.2
1983 Cal-A	0	5	.000	42	0	0	0	4	36^{1}	42	2	17	20	14.6	5.45	74	.302	.378	0	—	0	-6	-6	1	-0.5
1984 StL-N	1	0	1.000	3	0	0	0	0	2^{1}	4	2	2	1	23.1	11.57	30	.364	.462	0	—	0	-2	-2	0	-0.2
1985 StL-N	0	1	.000	10	0	0	0	0	10	9	0	4	5	11.7	1.80	196	.225	.295	0	—	0	2	2	-0	0.2
Total 14	44	71	.383	387	112	26	5	29	1123^{1}	1125	67	520	630	13.4	3.83	97	.264	.349	0	.000	-3	-5	-15	4	0.1
● CHARLIE HASTINGS	Hastings, Charles Morton b: 11/11/1870, Ironton, Ohio d: 8/3/34, Parkersburg, W.Va. 5'11", 179 lbs. Deb: 5/03/1893																								
1893 Cle-N	4	5	.444	15	9	6	0	1	92	128	5	33	14	16.2	4.70	104	.320	.379	7	.179	0	-0	2	-2	0.0
1896 Pit-N	5	10	.333	17	13	9	0	1	104	126	1	44	19	15.3	5.88	71	.297	.372	8	.216	-0	-18	-19	1	-1.5
1897 Pit-N	5	4	.556	16	10	9	0	0	118	138	3	47	42	14.6	4.58	91	.289	.362	10	.233	3	-3	-5	-1	-0.3
1898 Pit-N	4	10	.286	19	13	12	0	0	137^{1}	142	2	52	40	13.4	3.41	104	.265	.341	10	.233	2	3	2	1	0.5
Total 4	18	29	.383	67	45	36	0	2	451^{1}	534	11	176	115	14.7	4.55	91	.291	.362	35	.216	5	-18	-21	-1	-1.3
● BOB HASTY	Hasty, Robert Keller b: 5/3/1896, Canton, Ga. d: 5/28/72, Dallas, Ga. BR/TR, 6'3", 210 lbs. Deb: 9/11/19																								
1919 Phi-A	0	2	.000	2	2	1	0	0	12	15	1	4	5	14.3	5.25	65	.306	.358	1	.333	0	-3	-2	-1	-0.3
1920 Phi-A	1	3	.250	19	4	1	0	0	71^{2}	91	5	28	12	14.9	5.02	80	.323	.384	6	.250	0	-10	-8	2	-0.6
1921 Phi-A	5	16	.238	35	22	9	0	0	179^{1}	238	8	40	46	14.1	4.87	92	.331	.368	20	.294	2	-12	-8	0	-0.5
1922 Phi-A	9	14	.391	28	26	14	1	0	192^{1}	225	20	41	33	12.6	4.26	100	.298	.336	15	.200	-2	-5	-0	-2	-0.4
1923 Phi-A	13	15	.464	44	36	10	1	1	243^{1}	274	11	72	56	13.1	4.44	93	.291	.347	17	.193	-3	-12	-9	-1	-1.2
1924 Phi-A	1	3	.250	18	4	0	0	0	52^{2}	57	4	30	15	15.0	5.64	76	.282	.378	1	.077	-1	-8	-8	2	-0.7
Total 6	29	53	.354	146	94	35	2	1	751^{1}	900	49	215	167	13.5	4.65	91	.305	.355	60	.221	-3	-49	-35	-0	-3.7
● MICKEY HATCHER	Hatcher, Michael Vaughn b: 3/15/55, Cleveland, Ohio BR/TR, 6'2", 200 lbs. Deb: 8/03/79 ♦																								
1989 LA-N	0	0	—	1	0	0	0	0	1	0	0	3	0	36.0	9.00	38	.000	.667	66	.295	0	-1	-1	0	-0.1
● GIL HATFIELD	Hatfield, Gilbert "Colonel" b: 1/27/1855, Hoboken, N.J. d: 5/27/21, Hoboken, N.J. TR, 5'9.5", 168 lbs. Deb: 9/24/1885 F♦																								
1889 NY-N	2	4	.333	6	5	5	0	0	52	53	2	25	28	13.7	3.98	99	.256	.339	23	.184	-0	0	-0	0	0.0
1890 NY-P	1	1	.500	3	0	0	0	1	7^{2}	8	1	4	3	15.3	3.52	129	.257	.360	80	.279	0	1	1	-0	0.0
1891 Was-a	0	0	—	4	0	0	0	0	18	29	1	14	3	21.5	11.00	34	.351	.445	128	.256	1	-15	-15	-0	-1.1
Total 3	3	5	.375	13	5	5	0	1	77^{2}	90	4	43	34	15.6	5.56	71	.281	.369	295	.248	1	-14	-14	-0	-1.1
● JOHN HATFIELD	Hatfield, John Van Buskirk b: 7/20/1847, New Jersey d: 2/20/09, Long Island City, N.Y. 5'10", 165 lbs. Deb: 5/18/1871 FM♦																								
1874 Mut-n	0	1	.000	3	0	0	0	0	8	11	0	1		13.5	2.25	137	.324	.343	68	.235	-0	1	1		0.1
● HILLY HATHAWAY	Hathaway, Hillary Houston b: 9/12/69, Jacksonville, Fla. BL/TL, 6'4", 195 lbs. Deb: 9/08/92																								
1992 Cal-A	0	0	—	2	1	0	0	0	5^{2}	8	1	3	1	17.5	7.94	49	.333	.407	0	—	0	-3	-3	-0	-0.2
● RAY HATHAWAY	Hathaway, Ray Wilson b: 10/13/16, Greenville, Ohio BR/TR, 6', 165 lbs. Deb: 4/20/45																								
1945 Bro-N	0	1	.000	4	1	0	0	0	9	11	1	6	3	17.0	4.00	94	.297	.395	0	.000	-0	-0	-0	0	0.0
● JOE HATTEN	Hatten, Joseph Hilarian b: 11/17/16, Bancroft, Iowa d: 12/16/88, Redding, Cal. BR/TL, 6', 176 lbs. Deb: 4/21/46																								
1946 Bro-N	14	11	.560	42	30	13	1	2	222	207	10	110	85	13.1	2.84	119	.253	.347	6	.076	-6	14	13	-2	0.6
1947 *Bro-N	17	8	.680	42	32	11	3	0	225^{1}	211	9	105	76	12.8	3.63	114	.252	.339	17	.205	0	11	12	3	1.5
1948 Bro-N	13	10	.565	42	30	11	1	0	208^{2}	228	9	94	73	14.0	3.58	112	.283	.360	13	.206	1	9	10	4	1.5
1949 *Bro-N	12	8	.600	37	29	11	2	2	187^{1}	194	15	69	58	12.7	4.18	98	.271	.337	12	.179	-1	-3	-2	0	-0.3
1950 Bro-N	2	2	.500	23	8	2	1	0	68^{2}	82	10	31	29	14.8	4.59	89	.294	.365	2	.111	-1	-3	-4	-1	-0.5
1951 Bro-N	1	0	1.000	11	6	0	0	0	49^{1}	55	3	21	22	13.9	4.56	86	.281	.350	2	.133	-1	-3	-3	1	-0.4
Chi-N	2	6	.250	23	6	1	0	0	75^{1}	82	8	37	23	14.3	5.14	80	.281	.364	4	.235	0	-10	-9	-0	-0.9
Yr	3	6	.333	34	12	1	0	0	124^{2}	137	11	58	45	14.1	4.91	82	.281	.358	6	.188	-1	-13	-12	1	-1.3
1952 Chi-N	4	4	.500	13	8	2	0	0	50^{1}	65	6	25	15	16.3	6.08	63	.314	.391	1	.067	-1	-13	-12	1	-1.2
Total 7	65	49	.570	233	149	51	8	4	1087	1124	70	492	381	13.5	3.87	101	.271	.351	57	.160	-8	1	5	6	0.3
● CLYDE HATTER	Hatter, Clyde Melno b: 8/7/08, Poplar Hill, Ky. d: 10/16/37, Yosemite, Ky. BR/TL, 5'11", 170 lbs. Deb: 4/23/35																								
1935 Det-A	0	0	—	8	2	0	0	0	33^{1}	44	2	30	15	20.3	7.56	55	.319	.444	3	.300	0	-12	-13	-1	-1.2
1937 Det-A	1	0	1.000	3	0	0	0	0	9^{1}	17	0	11	4	28.0	11.57	40	.415	.547	0	.000	-0	-7	-7	-0	-0.6
Total 2	1	0	1.000	11	2	0	0	0	42^{2}	61	2	41	19	21.9	8.44	51	.341	.468	3	.231	0	-19	-20	-1	-1.8
● CHRIS HAUGHEY	Haughey, Christopher Francis "Bud" b: 10/3/25, Astoria, N.Y. BR/TR, 6'1", 180 lbs. Deb: 10/03/43																								
1943 Bro-N	0	1	.000	1	0	0	0	0	7	5	0	10	0	19.3	3.86	87	.238	.484	0	.000	-0	-0	-0	-0	-0.1
● PHIL HAUGSTAD	Haugstad, Philip Donald b: 2/23/24, Black River Falls Wis. BR/TR, 6'2", 165 lbs. Deb: 9/01/47																								
1947 Bro-N	1	0	1.000	6	1	0	0	0	12^{2}	14	1	4	4	12.8	2.84	145	.298	.353	0	.000	-0	2	2	-0	0.1
1948 Bro-N	0	0	—	1	0	0	0	0	1	1	0	0	0	9.0	0.00	—	.333	.333	0	—	0	0	0	0	0.1
1951 Bro-N	0	1	.000	21	1	0	0	0	30^{2}	28	4	24	22	16.1	6.46	61	.233	.374	0	.000	0	-9	-9	0	-0.8
1952 Cin-N	0	0	—	9	0	0	0	0	12	8	1	13	2	16.5	6.75	56	.190	.393	0	.000	-0	-4	-4	0	-0.4
Total 4	1	1	.500	37	2	0	0	0	56^{1}	51	6	41	28	15.3	5.59	70	.241	.374	0	.000	-0	-10	-10	1	-1.0
● TOM HAUSMAN	Hausman, Thomas Matthew b: 3/31/53, Mobridge, S.D. BR/TR, 6'5", 200 lbs. Deb: 4/26/75																								
1975 Mil-A	3	6	.333	29	9	1	0	0	112	110	7	47	46	13.1	4.10	93	.258	.340	0	—	0	-4	-3	1	-0.3
1976 Mil-A	0	0	—	3	0	0	0	0	3^{1}	3	0	3	1	16.2	5.40	65	.250	.400	0	—	0	-1	-1	0	0.1
1978 NY-N	3	3	.500	10	10	0	0	0	51^{2}	58	6	9	16	11.8	4.70	74	.287	.321	3	.176	1	-6	-7	0	-0.7

YEAR	TM/L	W	L	PCT	G	GS	CG	SH	SV	IP	H	HR	BB	SO	RAT	ERA	ERA+	OAV	OOB	BH	AVG	PB	PR	/A	PD	TPI
1979	NY-N	2	6	.250	19	10	1	0	2	78^{2}	65	6	19	33	10.1	2.75	133	.226	.284	3	.115	-1	9	8	0	0.7
1980	NY-N	6	5	.545	55	4	0	0	1	122	125	12	26	53	11.4	3.98	89	.266	.309	1	.063	-1	-5	-6	1	-0.6
1981	NY-N	0	1	.000	20	0	0	0	0	33	28	2	7	13	9.5	2.18	160	.235	.278	0	.000	0	5	5	0	0.5
1982	NY-N	1	2	.333	21	0	0	0	0	36^{2}	44	4	6	16	12.8	4.42	82	.295	.331	0	.000	-0	-3	-3	-1	-0.4
	Atl-N	0	0	—	3	0	0	0	0	3^{2}	6	0	4	2	24.5	4.91	76	.500	.625	0	—	0	-1	-0	0	0.0
	Yr	1	2	.333	24	0	0	0	0	40^{1}	50	4	10	18	13.4	4.46	82	.299	.339	0	.000	-0	-4	-4	-0	-0.4
Total	7	15	23	.395	160	33	2	0	3	441	439	37	121	180	11.8	3.80	96	.262	.317	7	.111	-2	-7	-8	2	-0.7
● CLEM HAUSMANN	Hausmann, Clemens Raymond b: 8/17/19, Houston, Tex. d: 8/29/72, Baytown, Tex. BR/TR, 5'9", 165 lbs. Deb: 4/28/44																									
1944	Bos-A	4	7	.364	32	12	3	0	2	137	139	6	69	43	13.9	3.42	99	.266	.355	3	.079	-2	0	-0	-0	-0.3
1945	Bos-A	5	7	.417	31	13	4	2	2	125	131	5	60	30	13.9	5.04	68	.270	.352	4	.103	-3	-23	-23	2	-2.4
1949	Phi-A	0	0	—	1	0	0	0	0	1	0	0	2	0	18.0	9.00	46	.000	.500	0	—	0	-1	-1	0	0.0
Total	3	9	14	.391	64	25	7	2	4	263	270	11	131	73	13.9	4.21	81	.267	.354	7	.091	-5	-24	-23	2	-2.7
● BRAD HAVENS	Havens, Bradley David b: 11/17/59, Highland Park, Mich BL/TL, 6'1", 196 lbs. Deb: 6/05/81																									
1981	Min-A	3	6	.333	14	12	1	1	0	78	76	6	24	43	11.7	3.58	110	.257	.315	0	—	0	1	3	-1	0.0
1982	Min-A	10	14	.417	33	32	4	1	0	208^{2}	201	32	80	129	12.1	4.31	98	.250	.318	0	—	0	-6	-2	-3	-0.5
1983	Min-A	5	8	.385	16	14	1	0	0	80^{1}	110	11	38	40	16.6	8.18	52	.333	.402	0	—	0	-37	-35	-2	-3.5
1985	Bal-A	0	1	.000	8	1	0	0	0	14^{1}	20	4	10	19	18.8	8.79	46	.333	.429	0	—	0	-7	-8	-0	-0.6
1986	Bal-A	3	3	.500	46	0	0	0	1	71	64	7	29	57	11.8	4.56	91	.248	.324	0	—	0	-3	-3	1	-0.2
1987	LA-N	0	0	—	31	1	0	0	1	35^{1}	30	2	23	23	13.8	4.33	92	.227	.346	0	.000	-0	-1	-1	-1	-0.2
1988	LA-N	0	0	—	9	0	0	0	0	9^{2}	15	1	4	8	17.7	4.66	72	.357	.413	0	.000	-0	-1	-1	1	-0.1
	Cle-A	2	3	.400	28	0	0	0	1	57^{1}	62	7	17	30	12.4	3.14	131	.273	.324	0	—	0	5	6	-0	0.5
1989	Cle-A	0	0	—	7	0	0	0	0	13^{1}	18	3	7	6	16.9	4.05	98	.353	.431	0	—	0	-0	-0	1	0.0
	Det-A	1	2	.333	13	1	0	0	0	22^{2}	28	3	14	15	17.9	5.56	69	.308	.417	0	—	0	-4	-4	0	-0.4
	Yr	1	2	.333	20	1	0	0	0	36	46	6	21	21	17.5	5.00	77	.319	.417	0	—	0	-4	-5	1	-0.4
Total	8	24	37	.393	205	61	6	2	3	590^{2}	624	76	246	370	13.3	4.81	86	.272	.344	0	.000	-0	-54	-46	-4	-5.0
● ED HAWK	Hawk, Edward b: 5/11/1890, Neosho, Mo. d: 3/26/36, Neosho, Mo. BL/TR, 5'11", 175 lbs. Deb: 9/07/11																									
1911	StL-A	0	4	.000	5	4	4	0	0	37^{2}	38	1	8	14	11.9	3.35	101	.253	.309	2	.154	-1	-0	0	0	0.0
● BILL HAWKE	Hawke, William Victor "Dick" b: 4/28/1870, Elsmere, Del. d: 12/11/02, Wilmington, Del. BR/TR, 5'8.5", 169 lbs. Deb: 7/28/1892																									
1892	StL-N	5	5	.500	14	11	10	1	0	97^{1}	108	2	45	55	14.9	3.70	86	.270	.355	4	.089	-4	-4	-5	0	-0.9
1893	StL-N	0	1	.000	1	1	0	0	0	5^{1}	9	0	3	1	20.3	5.06	93	.363	.432	1	.333	0	-0	-0	-0	0.0
	Bal-N	11	16	.407	29	29	22	1	0	225	248	8	108	69	14.6	4.76	100	.271	.354	16	.172	-4	-2	-0	0	-0.4
	Yr	11	17	.393	30	30	22	1	0	230^{1}	257	8	111	70	14.7	4.77	100	.274	.356	17	.177	-4	-3	-1	0	-0.4
1894	*Bal-N	16	9	.640	32	25	17	0	3	206	264	9	78	68	15.5	5.81	94	.308	.374	28	.304	2	-11	-8	1	-0.4
Total	3	32	31	.508	76	66	49	2	3	533^{2}	629	19	234	193	15.0	4.98	95	.286	.363	49	.210	-6	-18	-15	1	-1.7
● ANDY HAWKINS	Hawkins, Melton Andrew b: 1/21/60, Waco, Tex. BR/TR, 6'3", 223 lbs. Deb: 7/17/82																									
1982	SD-N	2	5	.286	15	10	1	0	0	63^{2}	66	4	27	25	13.4	4.10	84	.274	.352	0	.000	-2	-4	-5	-1	-0.7
1983	SD-N	5	7	.417	21	19	4	1	0	119^{2}	106	8	48	59	12.0	2.93	119	.244	.326	2	.065	-1	9	7	1	0.7
1984	*SD-N	8	9	.471	36	22	2	1	0	146	143	13	72	77	13.4	4.68	76	.254	.341	8	.195	1	-18	-18	-1	-1.9
1985	SD-N	18	8	.692	33	33	5	2	0	228^{2}	229	18	65	69	11.7	3.15	112	.267	.321	6	.078	-4	11	10	-1	0.5
1986	SD-N	10	8	.556	37	35	3	1	0	209^{1}	218	24	75	117	12.8	4.30	85	.268	.334	10	.149	-1	-14	-15	-2	-1.7
1987	SD-N	3	10	.231	24	20	0	0	0	117^{2}	131	16	49	51	13.9	5.05	78	.287	.358	5	.156	-0	-13	-14	0	-1.4
1988	SD-N	14	11	.560	33	33	4	2	0	217^{2}	196	16	76	91	11.5	3.35	101	.244	.314	7	.113	-2	2	1	-3	-0.3
1989	NY-A	15	15	.500	34	34	5	2	0	208^{1}	238	23	76	98	13.8	4.80	81	.290	.355	0	—	0	-21	-21	-3	-2.3
1990	NY-A	5	12	.294	28	26	2	1	0	157^{2}	156	20	82	74	13.7	5.37	74	.260	.351	0	—	0	-26	-24	-2	-2.6
1991	NY-A	0	2	.000	4	3	0	0	0	12^{2}	23	5	6	5	20.6	9.95	42	.383	.439	0	—	0	-8	-8	1	-0.6
	Oak-A	4	4	.500	15	14	1	0	0	77	68	5	36	40	12.7	4.79	80	.237	.332	0	—	0	-6	-8	0	-0.8
	Yr	4	6	.400	19	17	1	0	0	89^{2}	91	10	42	45	13.9	5.52	70	.262	.350	0	—	0	-14	-16	1	-1.4
Total	10	84	91	.480	280	249	27	10	0	1558^{1}	1574	152	612	706	12.9	4.22	87	.265	.338	38	.117	-8	-86	-96	-11	-11.1
● WYNN HAWKINS	Hawkins, Wynn Firth "Hawk" b: 2/20/36, E.Palestine, Ohio BR/TR, 6'3", 195 lbs. Deb: 4/22/60																									
1960	Cle-A	4	4	.500	15	9	1	0	0	66	68	10	39	39	14.7	4.23	88	.269	.369	2	.100	-1	-3	-4	1	-0.4
1961	Cle-A	7	9	.438	30	21	3	1	1	133	139	16	59	51	13.5	4.06	97	.270	.347	4	.108	-2	-1	-2	-1	-0.4
1962	Cle-A	1	0	1.000	3	0	0	0	0	3^{2}	9	1	1	0	24.5	7.36	53	.429	.455	0	—	0	-1	-1	-0	-0.1
Total	3	12	13	.480	48	30	4	1	1	202^{2}	216	27	99	90	14.1	4.17	93	.274	.357	6	.105	-2	-5	-7	-1	-0.9
● PINK HAWLEY	Hawley, Emerson P. b: 12/5/1872, Beaver Dam, Wis. d: 9/19/38, Beaver Dam, Wis. BL/TR, 5'10", 185 lbs. Deb: 8/13/1892																									
1892	StL-N	6	14	.300	20	20	18	0	0	166^{1}	160	4	63	63	12.7	3.19	100	.243	.319	12	.169	-2	2	0	-2	-0.3
1893	StL-N	5	17	.227	31	24	21	0	1	227	249	6	103	73	14.7	4.60	103	.270	.356	26	.286	7	2	3	-3	0.6
1894	StL-N	19	27	.413	53	41	36	0	0	392^{2}	481	14	149	120	14.9	4.90	110	.298	.365	43	.264	1	18	22	2	2.0
1895	Pit-N	31	22	.585	**56**	50	44	**4**	1	**444^{1}**	449	7	122	142	12.2	3.18	142	.258	.319	57	.308	13	**79**	66	2	**6.9**
1896	Pit-N	22	21	.512	49	43	37	2	0	378	382	2	157	137	13.5	3.57	118	.260	.343	39	.239	2	33	26	3	2.8
1897	Pit-N	18	18	.500	40	39	33	0	0	311^{1}	362	7	94	88	13.9	4.80	87	.288	.350	30	.231	-2	-17	-22	0	-1.9
1898	Cin-N	27	11	.711	43	37	32	3	0	331	357	5	91	69	12.8	3.37	114	.273	.331	24	.185	-5	9	17	-5	0.7
1899	Cin-N	14	17	.452	34	29	25	0	1	250^{1}	289	7	65	46	13.4	4.24	92	.289	.344	22	.218	-1	-11	-9	-2	-1.1
1900	NY-N	18	18	.500	41	38	**34**	2	0	329^{1}	377	7	89	80	13.3	3.53	103	.287	.341	25	.203	-2	6	3	4	0.5
1901	Mil-A	7	14	.333	26	23	17	0	0	182^{1}	228	3	41	50	13.7	4.59	78	.302	.346	19	.260	2	-19	-20	1	-1.5
Total	10	167	179	.483	393	344	297	11	3	3012^{2}	3334	62	974	868	13.5	3.96	107	.277	.342	297	.241	13	103	89	-0	8.7
● SCOTT HAWLEY	Hawley, Scott Deb: 9/22/1894																									
1894	Bos-N	0	1	.000	1	1	1	0	0	7	10	0	7	1	24.4	7.71	74	.332	.485	0	.000	-1	-2	-2	0	-0.1
● HAL HAYDEL	Haydel, John Harold b: 7/9/44, Houma, La. BR/TR, 6', 190 lbs. Deb: 9/07/70																									
1970	Min-A	2	0	1.000	4	0	0	0	0	9	7	2	4	4	11.0	3.00	124	.226	.314	2	.667	2	1	1	-0	0.3
1971	Min-A	4	2	.667	31	0	0	0	1	40	33	3	20	29	12.4	4.27	83	.243	.348	1	.333	0	-4	-3	0	-0.3
Total	2	6	2	.750	35	0	0	0	1	49	40	5	24	33	12.1	4.04	89	.240	.342	3	.500	2	-3	-2	-0	0.0
● LEFTY HAYDEN	Hayden, Eugene Franklin b: 4/14/35, San Francisco, Cal BL/TL, 6'2", 175 lbs. Deb: 6/26/58																									
1958	Cin-N	0	0	—	3	0	0	0	0	3^{2}	5	0	1	3	14.7	4.91	84	.313	.353	0	—	0	-0	-0	-0	0.0
● BEN HAYES	Hayes, Ben Joseph b: 8/4/57, Niagara Falls, N.Y. BR/TR, 6'1", 180 lbs. Deb: 6/25/82																									
1982	Cin-N	2	0	1.000	26	0	0	0	2	45^{2}	37	3	22	38	11.6	1.97	188	.219	.309	0	.000	-0	8	9	-1	0.8
1983	Cin-N	4	6	.400	60	0	0	0	7	69^{1}	82	8	37	44	15.6	6.49	59	.301	.387	0	.000	-1	-22	-21	0	-2.2
Total	2	6	6	.500	86	0	0	0	9	115	119	11	59	82	14.0	4.70	80	.270	.357	0	.000	-1	-14	-12	-1	-1.4
● JIM HAYES	Hayes, James Millard "Whitey" b: 2/25/12, Montevallo, Ala. BL/TR, 6'1", 168 lbs. Deb: 7/13/35																									
1935	Was-A	2	4	.333	7	4	1	0	0	28	38	0	23	9	19.6	8.36	52	.322	.433	2	.250	-0	-12	-13	-1	-1.2
● JOE HAYNES	Haynes, Joseph Walton b: 9/21/17, Lincolnton, Ga. d: 1/6/67, Hopkins, Minn. BR/TR, 6'2.5", 190 lbs. Deb: 4/24/39 C																									
1939	Was-A	8	12	.400	27	20	10	1	0	173	186	10	78	64	13.8	5.36	81	.276	.352	14	.209	0	-14	-19	-1	-1.8
1940	Was-A	3	6	.333	22	7	1	0	0	63^{1}	85	4	34	23	17.1	6.54	64	.327	.407	2	.105	-1	-15	-17	-1	-1.7
1941	Chi-A	0	0	—	8	0	0	0	0	28	30	0	11	18	13.2	3.86	106	.280	.347	3	.273	0	1	1	-0	0.1

YEAR	TM/L	W	L	PCT	G	GS	CG	SH	SV	IP	H	HR	BB	SO	RAT	ERA	ERA+	OAV	OOB	BH	AVG	PB	PR	/A	PD	TPI
1942	Chi-A	8	5	.615	**40**	1	1	0	6	103	88	6	47	35	12.1	2.62	137	.234	.324	5	.179	0	12	11	0	1.2
1943	Chi-A	7	2	.778	35	2	1	0	3	109^{1}	114	2	32	37	12.2	2.96	113	.263	.316	9	.265	2	4	5	-1	0.6
1944	Chi-A	5	6	.455	33	12	8	0	2	154^{1}	148	5	43	44	11.1	2.57	134	.254	.306	10	.200	1	15	15	0	1.8
1945	Chi-A	5	5	.500	14	13	8	1	1	104	92	5	29	34	10.6	3.55	94	.237	.291	7	.175	-2	-2	-3	1	-0.4
1946	Chi-A	7	9	.438	32	23	9	0	2	177^{1}	203	14	60	60	13.6	3.76	91	.289	.349	14	.246	3	-5	-7	1	-0.3
1947	Chi-A	14	6	.700	29	22	7	2	0	182	174	5	61	50	11.7	**2.42**	**151**	.250	.312	17	.262	2	26	25	0	3.0
1948	Chi-A☆	9	10	.474	27	22	6	0	0	149^{2}	167	13	52	40	13.3	3.97	107	.284	.344	8	.160	-1	5	5	-2	0.2
1949	Was-A	2	9	.182	37	10	0	0	2	96^{1}	106	6	55	19	15.3	6.26	68	.283	.380	6	.240	1	-22	-21	1	-1.9
1950	Was-A	7	5	.583	27	10	1	1	0	101^{2}	124	14	46	15	15.5	5.84	77	.305	.382	7	.200	1	-14	-15	1	-1.2
1951	Was-A	1	4	.200	26	3	1	0	2	73	85	9	37	18	15.2	4.56	90	.290	.372	7	.333	2	-4	-4	-1	-0.2
1952	Was-A	0	3	.000	22	2	0	0	3	66	70	2	35	18	14.5	4.50	79	.275	.364	2	.105	-1	-6	-7	-1	-0.8
Total	14	76	82	.481	379	147	53	5	21	1581	1672	95	620	475	13.2	4.01	96	.272	.342	111	.213	7	-20	-31	-2	-1.4

● RAY HAYWARD

Hayward, Raymond Alton b: 4/27/61, Enid, Okla. BL/TL, 6′1″, 190 lbs. Deb: 9/20/86

YEAR	TM/L	W	L	PCT	G	GS	CG	SH	SV	IP	H	HR	BB	SO	RAT	ERA	ERA+	OAV	OOB	BH	AVG	PB	PR	/A	PD	TPI
1986	SD-N	0	2	.000	3	3	0	0	0	10	16	1	4	6	18.0	9.00	41	.340	.392	0	.000	-0	-6	-6	-0	-0.6
1987	SD-N	0	0	—	4	0	0	0	0	6	12	3	3	2	22.5	16.50	24	.444	.500	0	.000	-0	-8	-8	1	-0.7
1988	Tex-A	4	6	.400	12	12	1	1	0	62^{2}	63	6	35	37	14.1	5.46	75	.276	.373	0	—	0	-10	-10	1	-0.9
Total	3	4	8	.333	19	15	1	1	0	78^{2}	91	10	42	45	15.2	6.75	60	.301	.387	0	.000	-1	-25	-24	1	-2.2

● BILL HAYWOOD

Haywood, William Kiernan b: 4/21/37, Colon, Panama BR/TR, 6′3″, 205 lbs. Deb: 7/28/68

YEAR	TM/L	W	L	PCT	G	GS	CG	SH	SV	IP	H	HR	BB	SO	RAT	ERA	ERA+	OAV	OOB	BH	AVG	PB	PR	/A	PD	TPI
1968	Was-A	0	0	—	14	0	0	0	0	23	27	1	12	10	16.0	4.70	62	.314	.410	0	—	0	-4	-5	-0	-0.5

● ED HEAD

Head, Edward Marvin b: 1/25/18, Selma, La. d: 1/31/80, Bastrop, La. BR/TR, 6′1″, 175 lbs. Deb: 7/27/40

YEAR	TM/L	W	L	PCT	G	GS	CG	SH	SV	IP	H	HR	BB	SO	RAT	ERA	ERA+	OAV	OOB	BH	AVG	PB	PR	/A	PD	TPI
1940	Bro-N	1	2	.333	13	5	2	0	0	39^{1}	40	0	18	13	13.3	4.12	97	.260	.337	2	.182	-0	-1	-1	-1	-0.2
1942	Bro-N	10	6	.625	36	15	5	1	4	136^{2}	118	11	47	78	11.1	3.56	92	.231	.300	13	.333	4	-4	-4	0	0.0
1943	Bro-N	9	10	.474	47	18	7	3	6	169^{2}	166	8	66	83	12.3	3.66	92	.250	.318	7	.152	-2	-5	-6	1	-0.7
1944	Bro-N	4	3	.571	9	8	5	1	0	63^{1}	54	2	19	17	10.4	2.70	132	.232	.290	5	.263	1	6	6	-1	0.6
1946	Bro-N	3	2	.600	13	7	3	1	1	56	56	3	24	17	12.9	3.21	105	.267	.342	5	.313	2	1	1	-1	0.2
Total	5	27	23	.540	118	53	22	6	11	465	434	24	174	208	11.8	3.48	98	.245	.314	32	.244	5	-2	-4	-1	-0.1

● RALPH HEAD

Head, Ralph b: 8/30/1893, Tallapoosa, Ga. d: 10/8/62, Muscadine, Ala. BR/TR, 5′10″, 175 lbs. Deb: 4/18/23

YEAR	TM/L	W	L	PCT	G	GS	CG	SH	SV	IP	H	HR	BB	SO	RAT	ERA	ERA+	OAV	OOB	BH	AVG	PB	PR	/A	PD	TPI
1923	Phi-N	2	9	.182	35	13	5	0	0	132^{1}	185	13	57	24	16.5	6.66	69	.341	.404	3	.071	-5	-39	-30	-1	-3.3

● TOM HEALEY

Healey, Thomas F. b: 1853, Cranston, R.I. d: 2/6/1891, Lewiston, Maine TR , Deb: 6/13/1878

YEAR	TM/L	W	L	PCT	G	GS	CG	SH	SV	IP	H	HR	BB	SO	RAT	ERA	ERA+	OAV	OOB	BH	AVG	PB	PR	/A	PD	TPI
1878	Pro-N	0	3	.000	3	3	3	0	0	24	27	1	7	2	12.8	3.00	74	.278	.327	2	.222	0	-2	-2	-0	-0.2
	Ind-N	6	4	.600	11	10	9	0	1	89	98	1	13	18	11.2	2.22	91	.270	.295	8	.178	-1	1	-2	-0	-0.2
	Yr	6	7	.462	14	13	12	0	**1**	113	125	2	20	20	11.5	2.39	87	.272	.302	10	.185	-1	-1	-4	-0	-0.4

● JOHN HEALY

Healy, John J. "Egyptian" or "Long John" b: 10/27/1866, Cairo, Ill. d: 3/16/1899, St.Louis, Mo. BR/TR, 6′2″, 158 lbs. Deb: 9/11/1885

YEAR	TM/L	W	L	PCT	G	GS	CG	SH	SV	IP	H	HR	BB	SO	RAT	ERA	ERA+	OAV	OOB	BH	AVG	PB	PR	/A	PD	TPI
1885	StL-N	1	7	.125	8	8	8	0	0	66	54	0	20	32	10.1	3.00	92	.210	.267	1	.042	-3	-1	-2	1	-0.4
1886	StL-N	17	23	.425	43	41	39	3	0	353^{2}	315	5	118	213	11.0	2.88	112	.230	.291	14	.097	-11	17	14	-2	0.1
1887	Ind-N	12	29	.293	41	41	40	3	0	341	415	24	108	75	14.2	5.17	80	.294	.350	24	.174	-4	-42	-39	-4	-3.7
1888	Ind-N	12	24	.333	37	37	36	1	0	321^{1}	347	13	87	124	12.6	3.89	76	.267	.320	30	.229	4	-37	-33	1	-2.7
1889	Was-N	1	11	.083	13	12	10	0	0	101	139	2	38	49	16.2	6.24	63	.317	.378	10	.222	1	-25	-26	2	-1.8
	Chi-N	1	4	.200	5	5	5	0	0	46	48	4	18	22	13.7	4.50	92	.261	.339	2	.100	-2	-2	-2	-0	-0.3
	Yr	2	15	.118	18	17	15	0	0	147	187	6	56	71	15.1	5.69	70	.298	.359	12	.185	-1	-27	-27	1	-2.1
1890	Tol-a	22	21	.512	46	46	44	2	0	389	326	5	127	225	11.0	2.89	137	.221	.293	34	.218	5	42	46	-2	4.8
1891	Bal-a	8	10	.444	23	22	19	0	0	170^{1}	179	6	57	54	12.7	3.75	100	.261	.322	9	.141	-2	-1	-0	-5	-0.6
1892	Bal-N	3	6	.333	9	8	5	0	0	68^{1}	82	4	21	24	13.8	4.74	72	.286	.339	6	.222	1	-11	-10	-0	-0.8
	Lou-N	1	1	.500	2	2	2	0	0	18^{1}	15	0	5	4	9.8	1.96	156	.214	.267	2	.286	1	3	2	-1	0.3
	Yr	4	7	.364	11	10	7	0	0	86^{2}	97	4	26	28	12.8	4.15	81	.270	.320	8	.235	1	-8	-8	-1	-0.5
Total	8	78	136	.364	227	222	208	9	0	1875	1920	63	599	822	12.4	3.84	94	.257	.318	132	.174	-11	-57	-50	-10	-5.1

● CHARLIE HEARD

Heard, Charles b: 1/30/1872, Philadelphia, Pa. d: 2/20/45, Philadelphia, Pa. BR/TR, 6′2″, 190 lbs. Deb: 7/14/1890 ♦

YEAR	TM/L	W	L	PCT	G	GS	CG	SH	SV	IP	H	HR	BB	SO	RAT	ERA	ERA+	OAV	OOB	BH	AVG	PB	PR	/A	PD	TPI
1890	Pit-N	0	6	.000	6	6	5	0	0	44	75	5	32	13	22.3	8.39	39	.365	.455	8	.186	-1	-24	-25	-1	-2.0

● JAY HEARD

Heard, Jehosie b: 1/17/20, Atlanta, Ga. BL/TL, 5′7″, 155 lbs. Deb: 4/24/54

YEAR	TM/L	W	L	PCT	G	GS	CG	SH	SV	IP	H	HR	BB	SO	RAT	ERA	ERA+	OAV	OOB	BH	AVG	PB	PR	/A	PD	TPI
1954	Bal-A	0	0	—	2	0	0	0	0	3^{1}	6	1	3	2	24.3	13.50	27	.375	.474	0	—	0	-4	-4	0	-0.3

● BUNNY HEARN

Hearn, Bunn b: 5/21/1891, Chapel Hill, N.C. d: 10/10/59, Wilson, N.C. BL/TL, 5′11″, 190 lbs. Deb: 9/17/10

YEAR	TM/L	W	L	PCT	G	GS	CG	SH	SV	IP	H	HR	BB	SO	RAT	ERA	ERA+	OAV	OOB	BH	AVG	PB	PR	/A	PD	TPI
1910	StL-N	1	3	.250	5	5	4	0	0	39	49	2	16	14	15.2	5.08	59	.322	.391	2	.133	-0	-9	-9	-1	-0.9
1911	StL-N	0	0	—	2	0	0	0	0	2^{2}	7	1	0	1	23.6	13.50	25	.538	.538	0	.000	-0	-3	-3	-0	-0.3
1913	NY-N	1	1	.500	2	2	1	0	0	13	13	0	7	8	13.8	2.77	113	.277	.370	2	.400	1	1	1	-0	0.1
1915	Pit-F	6	11	.353	29	17	8	1	0	175^{2}	187	6	37	49	11.6	3.38	89	.285	.326	10	.189	0	-7	-7	-1	-0.8
1918	Bos-N	5	6	.455	17	12	9	1	0	126^{1}	119	2	29	30	10.5	2.49	108	.256	.300	8	.178	-1	4	3	1	0.3
1920	Bos-N	0	3	.000	11	4	2	0	0	43	54	3	11	9	13.8	5.65	54	.329	.375	2	.143	-1	-12	-12	0	-1.3
Total	6	13	24	.351	66	40	24	2	0	399^{2}	429	14	100	111	12.0	3.56	82	.287	.333	24	.180	-1	-26	-29	-1	-2.9

● BUNNY HEARN

Hearn, Elmer Lafayette b: 1/13/04, Brooklyn, N.Y. d: 3/31/74, Venice, Fla. BL/TL, 5′8″, 160 lbs. Deb: 4/13/26

YEAR	TM/L	W	L	PCT	G	GS	CG	SH	SV	IP	H	HR	BB	SO	RAT	ERA	ERA+	OAV	OOB	BH	AVG	PB	PR	/A	PD	TPI
1926	Bos-N	4	9	.308	34	12	3	0	2	117^{1}	121	2	56	40	13.6	4.22	84	.276	.358	3	.100	-2	-5	-9	2	-0.9
1927	Bos-N	0	2	.000	8	0	0	0	0	12^{2}	16	0	9	5	17.8	4.26	87	.327	.431	2	.400	1	-0	-1	0	0.0
1928	Bos-N	1	0	1.000	7	0	0	0	0	10	6	0	8	8	13.5	6.30	62	.167	.333	0	.000	-0	-3	-3	-0	-0.3
1929	Bos-N	2	0	1.000	10	1	0	0	0	18^{1}	18	2	9	12	13.3	4.42	106	.277	.365	0	.000	0	1	1	1	0.1
Total	4	7	11	.389	59	13	3	0	2	158^{1}	161	4	82	65	13.9	4.38	85	.273	.363	5	.132	-2	-8	-12	2	-1.1

● JIM HEARN

Hearn, James Tolbert b: 4/11/21, Atlanta, Ga. BR/TR, 6′3″, 205 lbs. Deb: 4/17/47

YEAR	TM/L	W	L	PCT	G	GS	CG	SH	SV	IP	H	HR	BB	SO	RAT	ERA	ERA+	OAV	OOB	BH	AVG	PB	PR	/A	PD	TPI
1947	StL-N	12	7	.632	37	21	4	1	1	162	151	9	63	57	11.9	3.22	128	.248	.319	8	.145	-1	15	16	-1	1.4
1948	StL-N	8	6	.571	34	13	3	0	1	89^{2}	92	9	35	27	12.9	4.22	97	.271	.342	5	.200	-0	-3	-1	-2	-0.4
1949	StL-N	1	3	.250	17	4	0	0	0	42	48	3	23	18	15.6	5.14	81	.294	.388	1	.100	-0	-5	-5	0	-0.5
1950	StL-N	0	1	.000	6	0	0	0	0	9	12	1	6	4	18.0	10.00	43	.333	.429	1	1.000	0	-6	-6	-0	-0.5
	NY-N	11	3	.786	16	16	11	5	0	125	72	8	38	54	7.9	1.94	211	.169	.237	6	.136	-0	31	30	0	3.2
	Yr	11	4	.733	22	16	11	**5**	0	134	84	9	44	58	8.6	2.49	165	.182	.253	7	.156	0	25	24	0	2.7
1951	*NY-N	17	9	.654	34	34	11	0	0	211^{1}	204	21	82	66	12.3	3.62	108	.251	.321	12	.162	-0	8	7	5	1.2
1952	NY-N☆	14	7	.667	37	34	11	1	1	223^{2}	208	16	97	89	12.5	3.78	98	.245	.326	14	.182	4	-1	-2	4	0.6
1953	NY-N	9	12	.429	36	32	6	0	0	196^{2}	206	22	84	77	13.4	4.53	95	.266	.341	9	.136	0	-5	-5	2	-0.3
1954	NY-N	8	8	.500	29	18	3	2	1	130	137	10	66	45	14.2	4.15	97	.272	.359	5	.111	-1	-1	-2	1	-0.1
1955	NY-N	14	16	.467	39	33	11	1	0	226^{2}	225	27	66	86	11.7	3.73	108	.260	.314	12	.156	1	8	7	2	1.1
1956	NY-N	5	11	.313	30	19	2	0	1	129^{1}	124	17	44	66	11.9	3.97	95	.254	.319	4	.098	-3	-3	-3	-0	-0.6
1957	Phi-N	5	1	.833	36	4	1	0	3	74	79	6	18	46	12.0	3.65	104	.274	.321	0	.000	-2	2	1	1	0.0
1958	Phi-N	5	3	.625	39	1	0	0	0	73^{1}	88	6	27	33	14.1	4.17	95	.292	.351	0	.000	-1	-2	-2	-1	-0.4
1959	Phi-N	0	2	.000	6	0	0	0	0	11	15	2	6	1	17.2	5.73	72	.333	.412	0	.000	0	-2	-2	0	-0.1
Total	13	109	89	.551	396	229	63	10	8	1703^{2}	1661	157	655	669	12.4	3.81	105	.255	.326	77	.141	-3	35	35	11	4.6

● SPENCER HEATH

Heath, Spencer Paul b: 11/5/1894, Chicago, Ill. d: 1/25/30, Chicago, Ill. BB/TR, 6′, 170 lbs. Deb: 5/04/20

YEAR	TM/L	W	L	PCT	G	GS	CG	SH	SV	IP	H	HR	BB	SO	RAT	ERA	ERA+	OAV	OOB	BH	AVG	PB	PR	/A	PD	TPI
1920	Chi-A	0	0	—	4	0	0	0	0	7	19	1	2	0	27.0	15.43	24	.475	.500	0	.000	-1	-9	-9	-0	-0.8

YEAR TM/L	W	L	PCT	G	GS	CG	SH	SV	IP	H	HR	BB	SO	RAT	ERA	ERA+	OAV	OOB	BH	AVG	PB	PR	/A	PD	TPI
● **JEFF HEATHCOCK**	Heathcock, Ronald Jeffrey b: 11/18/59, Covina, Cal. BR/TR, 6'4", 205 lbs. Deb: 9/03/83																								
1983 Hou-N	2	1	.667	6	3	0	0	1	28	19	1	4	12	7.7	3.21	106	.181	.218	0	.000	-1	1	1	0	0.0
1985 Hou-N	3	1	.750	14	7	1	0	1	56^1	50	9	13	25	10.2	3.36	103	.239	.287	1	.063	0	1	1	0	0.1
1987 Hou-N	4	2	.667	19	2	0	0	1	42^2	44	4	9	15	11.4	3.16	124	.277	.320	0	.000	-1	4	4	-0	0.2
1988 Hou-N	0	5	.000	17	1	0	0	0	31	33	2	16	12	14.5	5.81	57	.275	.365	0	.000	-0	-8	-9	0	-0.9
Total 4	9	9	.500	56	13	1	0	3	158	146	16	42	64	10.9	3.76	94	.246	.300	1	.029	-2	-1	-4	0	-0.6
● **NEAL HEATON**	Heaton, Neal b: 3/3/60, Holtsville, N.Y. BL/TL, 6'1", 205 lbs. Deb: 9/03/82																								
1982 Cle-A	0	2	.000	8	4	0	0	0	31	32	1	16	14	13.9	5.23	78	.260	.345	0	—	0	-4	-4	-0	-0.4
1983 Cle-A	11	7	.611	39	16	4	3	7	149^1	157	11	44	75	12.2	4.16	102	.269	.321	0	—	0	-2	1	-2	-0.2
1984 Cle-A	12	15	.444	38	34	4	1	0	198^2	231	21	75	75	13.9	5.21	78	.293	.354	0	—	0	-27	-25	-3	-2.7
1985 Cle-A	9	17	.346	36	33	5	1	0	207^2	244	19	80	82	14.3	4.90	84	.298	.365	0	—	0	-17	-18	-3	-1.9
1986 Cle-A	3	6	.333	12	12	2	0	0	74^1	73	8	34	24	13.1	4.24	98	.254	.335	0	—	0	-1	-1	-0	-0.1
Min-A	4	9	.308	21	17	3	0	1	124^1	128	18	47	66	12.7	3.98	108	.273	.340	0	—	0	3	4	-1	0.4
Yr	7	15	.318	33	29	5	0	1	198^2	201	26	81	90	12.8	4.08	104	.266	.337	0	—	0	2	4	-1	0.3
1987 Mon-N	13	10	.565	32	32	3	1	0	193^1	207	25	37	105	11.5	4.52	93	.273	.310	14	.209	2	-9	-7	-1	-0.6
1988 Mon-N	3	10	.231	32	11	0	0	2	97^1	98	14	43	43	13.3	4.99	72	.271	.354	3	.143	-0	-17	-15	-0	-1.7
1989 Pit-N	6	7	.462	42	18	1	0	0	147^1	127	12	55	67	11.5	3.05	110	.233	.311	9	.214	1	7	5	1	0.6
1990 Pit-N☆	12	9	.571	30	24	0	0	0	146	143	17	38	68	11.3	3.45	105	.263	.314	2	.047	-2	6	3	-0	0.1
1991 Pit-N	3	3	.500	42	1	0	0	0	68^2	72	6	21	34	12.7	4.33	83	.275	.338	4	.286	2	-5	-6	-1	-0.5
1992 KC-A	3	1	.750	31	0	0	0	0	41	43	5	22	29	14.5	4.17	95	.274	.367	0	—	0	-1	-1	-0	-0.2
Mil-A	0	0	—	1	0	0	0	0	1	0	0	1	2	9.0	0.00	—	.000	.250	0	—	0	0	0	0	0.1
Yr	3	1	.750	32	0	0	0	0	42	43	5	23	31	14.1	4.07	98	.262	.353	0	—	0	-1	-0	-0	-0.1
Total 11	79	96	.451	364	202	22	6	10	1480	1555	157	513	684	12.8	4.34	91	.273	.336	32	.171	2	-67	-62	-11	-7.1
● **DAVE HEAVERLO**	Heaverlo, David Wallace b: 8/25/50, Ellensburg, Wash. BR/TR, 6'1", 210 lbs. Deb: 4/14/75																								
1975 SF-N	3	1	.750	42	0	0	0	1	64	62	2	31	35	13.2	2.39	159	.262	.349	2	.500	1	9	10	1	1.2
1976 SF-N	4	4	.500	61	0	0	0	1	75	85	2	15	40	12.2	4.44	82	.289	.328	1	.333	0	-8	-7	1	-0.6
1977 SF-N	5	1	.833	56	0	0	0	1	98^2	92	10	21	58	10.6	2.55	153	.251	.297	0	.000	-0	15	15	2	1.7
1978 Oak-A	3	6	.333	69	0	0	0	10	130	141	11	41	71	12.8	3.25	112	.281	.339	0	—	0	7	6	3	0.9
1979 Oak-A	4	11	.267	62	0	0	0	9	85^2	97	7	42	40	15.0	4.20	96	.294	.380	0	.000	0	0	-2	0	-0.1
1980 Sea-A	6	3	.667	60	0	0	0	4	78^2	75	9	35	42	13.2	3.89	106	.253	.342	0	—	0	1	2	-2	0.0
1981 Oak-A	1	0	1.000	6	0	0	0	0	5^2	7	0	3	2	15.9	1.59	219	.292	.370	0	—	0	1	1	-0	0.3
Total 7	26	26	.500	356	0	0	0	26	537^2	559	41	188	288	12.8	3.41	113	.273	.339	3	.231	1	26	26	4	3.4
● **WALLY HEBERT**	Hebert, Wallace Andrew "Preacher" b: 8/21/07, Lake Charles, La. BL/TL, 6'1", 195 lbs. Deb: 5/01/31																								
1931 StL-A	6	7	.462	23	13	5	0	0	103	128	11	43	26	15.2	5.07	91	.306	.375	9	.209	-2	-8	-5	-2	-0.8
1932 StL-A	1	12	.077	35	15	2	0	1	108^1	145	6	45	29	16.0	6.48	75	.322	.386	12	.353	2	-24	-20	0	-1.5
1933 StL-A	4	6	.400	33	10	3	0	0	88^1	114	4	35	19	15.3	5.30	88	.308	.369	9	.391	3	-10	-6	-1	-0.4
1943 Pit-N	10	11	.476	34	23	12	1	0	184	197	3	45	41	11.9	2.98	117	.272	.316	13	.220	1	8	10	1	1.4
Total 4	21	36	.368	125	61	22	1	1	483^2	584	24	168	115	14.1	4.63	91	.298	.355	43	.270	5	-34	-21	-1	-1.3
● **GUY HECKER**	Hecker, Guy Jackson b: 4/3/1856, Youngsville, Pa. d: 12/3/38, Wooster, Ohio BR/TR, 6', 190 lbs. Deb: 5/02/1882 MU♦																								
1882 Lou-a	6	6	.500	13	11	10	0	0	104	75	0	5	33	**6.9**	1.30	191	**.188**	**.198**	94	.276	4	16	14	3	2.0
1883 Lou-a	26	23	.531	51	50	49	3	0	451	509	4	72	153	11.6	3.33	90	.267	.293	88	.273	11	-1	-17	3	-0.3
1884 Lou-a	**52**	20	.722	**75**	73	**72**	6	0	**670^2**	526	4	56	**385**	**8.0**	**1.80**	**172**	.204	**.226**	94	.297	26	108	**96**	7	**12.9**
1885 Lou-a	30	23	.566	53	53	51	2	0	480	454	6	54	209	9.9	2.18	148	.237	.265	81	.273	9	57	56	5	**6.7**
1886 Lou-a	26	23	.531	49	48	45	2	0	420^2	390	6	118	133	11.1	2.87	127	.231	.285	117	.341	19	27	36	1	5.2
1887 Lou-a	18	12	.600	34	32	32	2	1	285^1	325	9	50	58	12.1	4.16	105	.272	.307	118	.319	10	4	7	5	1.9
1888 Lou-a	8	17	.320	26	25	25	0	0	223^1	251	5	43	63	12.3	3.39	91	.274	.313	48	.227	2	-8	-8	1	-0.4
1889 Lou-a	5	13	.278	19	16	15	0	0	151^1	215	7	47	33	15.9	5.59	69	.324	.373	93	.284	4	-29	-29	1	-2.0
1890 Pit-N	2	9	.182	14	12	11	0	0	119^2	160	9	44	32	15.6	5.11	64	.311	.369	77	.226	1	-21	-24	-1	-1.9
Total 9	173	146	.542	334	320	310	15	1	2906	2905	50	489	1099	10.7	2.92	114	.247	.281	810	.283	86	154	128	24	24.1
● **HARRY HEDGPETH**	Hedgpeth, Harry Malcolm b: 9/4/1888, Fayetteville, N.C. d: 7/30/66, Richmond, Va. BL/TL, 6'1.5", 194 lbs. Deb: 10/03/13																								
1913 Was-A	0	0	—	1	0	0	0	1	1	1	0	0	0	9.0	0.00	—	.250	.250	0	—	0	0	0	0	0.1
● **MIKE HEDLUND**	Hedlund, Michael David "Red" b: 8/11/46, Dallas, Tex. BR/TR, 6'1", 190 lbs. Deb: 5/08/65																								
1965 Cle-A	0	0	—	6	0	0	0	0	5^1	6	0	5	4	18.6	5.06	69	.286	.423	0	.000	-0	-1	-1	-0	-0.1
1968 Cle-A	0	0	—	3	0	0	0	0	1^2	6	0	2	0	48.6	10.80	27	.545	.643	0	—	0	-1	-1	0	-0.1
1969 KC-A	3	6	.333	34	16	1	0	2	125	123	8	40	74	11.8	3.24	114	.259	.318	5	.152	-1	5	6	1	0.8
1970 KC-A	2	3	.400	9	0	0	0	0	15	18	6	7	5	15.0	7.20	52	.300	.373	0	.000	-0	-6	-6	-0	-0.7
1971 KC-A	15	8	.652	32	30	7	1	0	205^2	168	15	72	76	10.5	2.71	126	.227	.296	6	.088	-3	17	16	3	1.8
1972 KC-A	5	7	.417	29	16	1	0	0	113	119	10	41	52	13.1	4.78	63	.275	.343	6	.188	-0	-22	-22	1	-2.3
Total 6	25	24	.510	113	62	9	1	2	465^2	440	39	167	211	11.9	3.56	96	.253	.321	17	.123	-5	-7	-8	5	-0.6
● **DANNY HEEP**	Heep, Daniel William b: 7/3/57, San Antonio, Tex. BL/TL, 5'11", 185 lbs. Deb: 8/31/79 ♦																								
1988 *LA-N	0	0	—	1	0	0	0	0	2	2	1	0	0	9.0	9.00	37	.222	.222	36	.242	0	-1	-1	-0	-0.1
1990 *Bos-A	0	0	—	1	0	0	0	0	1	4	0	0	0	36.0	9.00	45	.667	.667	12	.174	0	-1	-1	0	-0.1
Total 2	0	0	—	2	0	0	0	0	3	6	1	0	0	18.0	9.00	40	.400	.400	503	.257	1	-2	-2	-0	-0.2
● **BOB HEFFNER**	Heffner, Robert Frederic b: 9/13/38, Allentown, Pa. BR/TR, 6'4", 205 lbs. Deb: 6/19/63																								
1963 Bos-A	4	9	.308	20	19	3	1	0	124^2	131	15	36	77	12.2	4.26	89	.267	.319	5	.116	-1	-9	-7	-0	-0.8
1964 Bos-A	7	9	.438	55	10	1	1	6	158^2	152	20	44	112	11.3	4.08	94	.251	.305	7	.159	0	-8	-4	-1	-0.5
1965 Bos-A	0	2	.000	27	1	0	0	0	49	59	9	18	42	14.3	7.16	52	.304	.366	0	.000	-1	-20	-19	-1	-2.0
1966 Cle-A	0	1	.000	5	1	0	0	0	13	12	1	3	7	10.4	3.46	99	.240	.283	0	.000	0	-0	-0	-1	0.0
1968 Cal-A	0	0	—	7	0	0	0	0	8	6	0	6	3	13.5	2.25	129	.240	.387	0	—	0	1	1	-0	0.1
Total 5	11	21	.344	114	31	4	2	6	353^1	360	45	107	241	12.0	4.51	84	.264	.320	12	.128	-1	-36	-29	-2	-3.2
● **RANDY HEFLIN**	Heflin, Randolph Rutherford b: 9/11/18, Fredericksburg, Va. BL/TR, 6', 185 lbs. Deb: 6/09/45																								
1945 Bos-A	4	10	.286	20	14	6	2	0	102	102	3	61	39	14.7	4.06	84	.272	.380	3	.086	-3	-8	-7	1	-1.0
1946 Bos-A	0	1	.000	5	1	0	0	0	14^2	16	0	12	6	17.8	2.45	149	.296	.433	2	.667	1	2	2	1	0.4
Total 2	4	11	.267	25	15	6	2	0	116^2	118	3	73	45	15.1	3.86	89	.275	.387	5	.132	-2	-6	-5	2	-0.6
● **JAKE HEHL**	Hehl, Herman Jacob b: 12/8/1899, Brooklyn, N.Y. d: 7/4/61, Brooklyn, N.Y. BR/TR, 5'11", 180 lbs. Deb: 6/20/18																								
1918 Bro-N	0	0	—	1	0	0	0	0	1	0	0	0	0	9.0	0.00	—	.000	.250	0	—	0	0	0	0	0.1
● **EMMETT HEIDRICK**	Heidrick, John Emmett "Snags" b: 7/9/1876, Queenstown, Pa. d: 1/20/16, Clarion, Pa. BL/TR, 6', 185 lbs. Deb: 9/14/1898 ♦																								
1902 StL-A	0	0	—	1	0	0	0	0	1	0	0	0	0	0.0	0.00	—	.000	.000	129	.289	0	0	0	-0	0.0
● **FRANK HEIFER**	Heifer, Franklin "Heck" b: 1/18/1854, Reading, Pa. d: 8/29/1893, Reading, Pa. 5'10.5", 175 lbs. Deb: 6/04/1875 ♦																								
1875 Bos-n	0	0	—	2	0	0	0	1	2^1	7	0	0		27.0	7.71	31	.500	.500	14	.275	1	-1	-1		-0.1
● **FRED HEIMACH**	Heimach, Frederick Amos "Lefty" b: 1/27/01, Camden, N.J. d: 6/1/73, Ft.Myers, Fla. BL/TL, 6', 175 lbs. Deb: 10/01/20																								
1920 Phi-A	0	1	.000	1	1	0	0	0	5	13	0	1	0	25.2	14.40	28	.542	.560	0	.000	-0	-6	-6	1	-0.4

YEAR	TM/L	W	L	PCT	G	GS	CG	SH	SV	IP	H	HR	BB	SO	RAT	ERA	ERA+	OAV	OOB	BH	AVG	PB	PR	/A	PD	TPI
1921	Phi-A	1	0	1.000	1	1	1	1	0	9	7	0	1	1	8.0	0.00	—	.226	.250	1	.250	-0	4	4	1	0.6
1922	Phi-A	7	11	.389	37	19	7	0	1	171^2	220	18	63	47	15.0	5.03	85	.316	.375	15	.250	2	-19	-15	1	-1.1
1923	Phi-A	6	12	.333	40	19	10	0	0	208^1	238	14	69	63	13.5	4.32	95	.292	.352	30	.254	2	-8	-5	0	-0.2
1924	Phi-A	14	12	.538	40	26	10	0	0	198	243	2	60	60	14.0	4.73	91	.306	.357	29	.322	6	-11	-10	2	-0.1
1925	Phi-A	0	1	.000	10	0	0	0	0	20^1	24	2	9	6	15.0	3.98	117	.312	.391	1	.167	-0	1	2	0	0.1
1926	Phi-A	1	0	1.000	13	1	0	0	0	31^2	28	1	5	8	9.4	2.84	147	.239	.270	1	.100	-1	4	5	2	0.5
	Bos-A	2	9	.182	20	13	6	0	0	102	119	5	42	17	14.2	5.65	72	.303	.370	13	.295	2	-18	-18	3	-1.1
	Yr	3	9	.250	33	14	6	0	0	133^2	147	6	47	25	13.1	4.98	82	.288	.348	14	.259	2	-14	-13	5	-0.6
1928	NY-A	2	3	.400	13	9	5	0	0	68	66	3	16	25	11.0	3.31	114	.250	.295	5	.167	-1	6	3	0	0.2
1929	NY-A	11	6	.647	35	10	3	3	4	134^2	141	4	29	26	11.6	4.01	96	.272	.314	9	.184	1	4	-2	2	0.0
1930	Bro-N	0	2	.000	9	0	0	0	1	7^1	14	0	3	1	20.9	4.91	100	.424	.472	1	.250	-0	0	0	0	0.0
1931	Bro-N	9	7	.563	31	10	7	1	1	135^1	145	6	23	43	11.2	3.46	110	.274	.306	12	.197	1	6	5	4	1.0
1932	Bro-N	9	4	.692	36	15	7	0	0	167^2	203	7	28	30	12.7	3.97	96	.299	.333	9	.164	1	-2	-3	1	-0.1
1933	Bro-N	0	1	.000	10	3	0	0	0	29^2	49	2	11	7	18.8	10.01	32	.374	.431	2	.200	-0	-22	-22	-0	-2.1
Total	13	62	69	.473	296	127	56	5	7	1288^2	1510	64	360	334	13.2	4.46	90	.296	.346	128	.236	12	-61	-61	16	-2.7

● GORMAN HEIMUELLER Heimueller, Gorman John b: 9/24/55, Los Angeles, Cal. BL/TL, 6′4″, 195 lbs. Deb: 7/12/83

YEAR	TM/L	W	L	PCT	G	GS	CG	SH	SV	IP	H	HR	BB	SO	RAT	ERA	ERA+	OAV	OOB	BH	AVG	PB	PR	/A	PD	TPI
1983	Oak-A	3	5	.375	16	14	2	1	0	83^2	93	8	29	31	13.2	4.41	87	.286	.346	0	—	0	-3	-5	2	0.0
1984	Oak-A	0	1	.000	6	0	0	0	0	14^2	21	2	7	3	17.2	6.14	61	.344	.412	0	—	0	-3	-4	0	0.0
Total	2	3	6	.333	22	14	2	1	0	98^1	114	10	36	34	13.8	4.67	82	.295	.357	0	—	0	-7	-9	3	0.0

● DON HEINKEL Heinkel, Donald Elliott b: 10/20/59, Racine, Wis. BL/TR, 6′, 185 lbs. Deb: 4/07/88

YEAR	TM/L	W	L	PCT	G	GS	CG	SH	SV	IP	H	HR	BB	SO	RAT	ERA	ERA+	OAV	OOB	BH	AVG	PB	PR	/A	PD	TPI
1988	Det-A	0	0	—	21	0	0	0	1	36^1	30	4	12	30	10.7	3.96	96	.219	.287	0	—	0	0	-1	-0	0.0
1989	StL-N	1	1	.500	7	5	0	0	0	26^1	40	2	7	16	16.1	5.81	62	.348	.385	0	.000	-0	-7	-6	0	-0.6
Total	2	1	1	.500	28	5	0	0	1	62^2	70	6	19	46	12.9	4.74	79	.278	.331	0	.000	-0	-7	-7	0	-0.6

● KEN HEINTZELMAN Heintzelman, Kenneth Alphonse b: 10/14/15, Peruque, Mo. BR/TL, 5′11.5″, 185 lbs. Deb: 10/03/37 F

YEAR	TM/L	W	L	PCT	G	GS	CG	SH	SV	IP	H	HR	BB	SO	RAT	ERA	ERA+	OAV	OOB	BH	AVG	PB	PR	/A	PD	TPI
1937	Pit-N	1	0	1.000	1	1	1	0	0	9	6	0	3	4	10.0	2.00	193	.207	.303	0	.000	-1	2	2	-1	0.1
1938	Pit-N	0	0	—	1	0	0	0	0	2	1	0	3	1	18.0	9.00	42	.167	.444	0	—	0	-1	-1	0	-0.1
1939	Pit-N	1	1	.500	17	2	1	1	0	35^2	35	2	18	18	13.4	5.05	76	.250	.335	2	.222	0	-4	-5	-0	-0.5
1940	Pit-N	8	8	.500	39	16	5	2	3	165	193	7	65	71	14.3	4.47	85	.292	.359	9	.167	-1	-11	-12	3	-1.1
1941	Pit-N	11	11	.500	35	24	13	2	0	196	206	8	83	81	13.3	3.44	105	.272	.345	8	.127	-2	4	4	1	0.3
1942	Pit-N	8	11	.421	27	18	5	3	0	130	143	9	63	39	14.3	4.57	74	.281	.361	3	.086	-2	-18	-17	-2	-2.1
1946	Pit-N	8	12	.400	32	24	6	2	1	157^2	165	7	86	57	14.3	3.77	94	.271	.362	6	.136	-1	-6	-4	2	-0.4
1947	Pit-N	0	0	—	2	1	0	0	0	4	9	2	6	2	33.8	20.25	21	.409	.536	0	—	0	-7	-7	-0	-0.6
	Phi-N	7	10	.412	24	19	8	0	1	136	144	12	46	55	12.7	4.04	99	.277	.338	5	.116	-2	0	-0	-3	-0.5
	Yr	7	10	.412	26	20	8	0	1	140	153	14	52	57	13.3	4.50	89	.282	.347	5	.116	-2	-7	-8	-3	-1.1
1948	Phi-N	6	11	.353	27	16	5	2	2	130	117	10	45	57	11.3	4.29	92	.241	.307	5	.135	-1	-5	-5	-1	-0.7
1949	Phi-N	17	10	.630	33	32	15	**5**	0	250	239	19	93	65	12.0	3.02	130	.255	.323	13	.157	-1	28	26	-3	2.3
1950	*Phi-N	3	9	.250	23	17	4	1	0	125^1	122	10	54	39	12.6	4.09	99	.250	.325	2	.053	-3	1	-1	-2	-0.6
1951	Phi-N	6	12	.333	35	12	3	0	2	118^1	119	13	53	55	13.4	4.18	92	.267	.350	3	.107	-1	-3	-4	-1	-0.7
1952	Phi-N	1	3	.250	23	1	0	0	1	42^2	41	1	12	20	11.2	3.16	115	.266	.319	0	.000	-0	3	2	-1	0.1
Total	13	77	98	.440	319	183	66	18	10	1501^2	1540	100	630	564	13.1	3.93	96	.267	.341	56	.127	-15	-18	-23	-7	-4.5

● CLARENCE HEISE Heise, Clarence Edward "Lefty" b: 8/7/07, Topeka, Kan. BL/TL, 5′10″, 172 lbs. Deb: 4/22/34

YEAR	TM/L	W	L	PCT	G	GS	CG	SH	SV	IP	H	HR	BB	SO	RAT	ERA	ERA+	OAV	OOB	BH	AVG	PB	PR	/A	PD	TPI
1934	StL-N	0	0	—	1	0	0	0	0	2	3	1	0	1	13.5	4.50	94	.300	.300	0	—	0	-0	-0	-0	0.0

● JIM HEISE Heise, James Edward b: 10/2/32, Scottdale, Pa. BR/TR, 6′1″, 185 lbs. Deb: 6/29/57

YEAR	TM/L	W	L	PCT	G	GS	CG	SH	SV	IP	H	HR	BB	SO	RAT	ERA	ERA+	OAV	OOB	BH	AVG	PB	PR	/A	PD	TPI
1957	Was-A	0	3	.000	8	2	0	0	0	19	25	2	16	8	19.4	8.05	48	.329	.446	0	.000	-0	-9	-9	-0	-0.9

● ROY HEISER Heiser, Le Roy Barton b: 6/22/42, Baltimore, Md. BR/TR, 6′4″, 190 lbs. Deb: 9/02/61

YEAR	TM/L	W	L	PCT	G	GS	CG	SH	SV	IP	H	HR	BB	SO	RAT	ERA	ERA+	OAV	OOB	BH	AVG	PB	PR	/A	PD	TPI
1961	Was-A	0	0	—	3	0	0	0	0	5^2	6	1	9	1	25.4	6.35	63	.261	.485	0	.000	-0	-1	-1	-0	-0.2

● CRESE HEISMANN Heismann, Christian Ernest b: 4/16/1880, Cincinnati, Ohio d: 11/19/51, Cincinnati, Ohio BR/TL, 6′2″, 175 lbs. Deb: 9/25/01

YEAR	TM/L	W	L	PCT	G	GS	CG	SH	SV	IP	H	HR	BB	SO	RAT	ERA	ERA+	OAV	OOB	BH	AVG	PB	PR	/A	PD	TPI
1901	Cin-N	0	1	.000	3	2	1	0	0	13^2	18	1	6	6	17.8	5.93	54	.315	.408	2	.400	1	-4	-4	-1	-0.3
1902	Cin-N	2	1	.667	5	3	2	0	0	33	33	1	10	15	13.1	2.45	122	.260	.338	3	.214	0	1	2	0	0.2
	Bal-A	0	3	.000	3	3	2	0	0	16	20	1	12	2	19.1	8.44	45	.306	.428	1	.143	-1	-9	-8	-0	-0.8
Total	2	2	5	.286	11	8	5	0	0	62^2	71	3	28	23	15.7	4.74	69	.285	.379	6	.231	0	-11	-10	-1	-0.9

● HARRY HEITMANN Heitmann, Henry Anton b: 10/6/1896, Albany, N.Y. d: 12/15/58, Brooklyn, N.Y. BR/TR, 6′, 175 lbs. Deb: 7/27/18

YEAR	TM/L	W	L	PCT	G	GS	CG	SH	SV	IP	H	HR	BB	SO	RAT	ERA	ERA+	OAV	OOB	BH	AVG	PB	PR	/A	PD	TPI
1918	Bro-N	0	1	.000	1	1	0	0	0	0^1	4	0	0	0	108.0	108.00	3	1.000	1.000	0	—	0	-4	-4	0	-0.4

● MEL HELD Held, Melvin Nicholas "Country" b: 4/12/29, Edon, Ohio BR/TR, 6′1″, 178 lbs. Deb: 4/27/56

YEAR	TM/L	W	L	PCT	G	GS	CG	SH	SV	IP	H	HR	BB	SO	RAT	ERA	ERA+	OAV	OOB	BH	AVG	PB	PR	/A	PD	TPI
1956	Bal-A	0	0	—	4	0	0	0	0	7	7	1	3	4	12.9	5.14	76	.318	.400	0	—	0	-1	-1	0	0.0

● HORACE HELMBOLD Helmbold, Horace b: Philadelphia, Pa. Deb: 10/11/1890

YEAR	TM/L	W	L	PCT	G	GS	CG	SH	SV	IP	H	HR	BB	SO	RAT	ERA	ERA+	OAV	OOB	BH	AVG	PB	PR	/A	PD	TPI
1890	Phi-a	0	1	.000	1	1	1	0	0	7	17	0	6	3	29.6	14.14	27	.451	.526	0	.000	-0	-8	-8	0	-0.6

● RUSS HEMAN Heman, Russell Fredrick b: 2/10/33, Olive, Cal. BR/TR, 6′4″, 200 lbs. Deb: 4/20/61

YEAR	TM/L	W	L	PCT	G	GS	CG	SH	SV	IP	H	HR	BB	SO	RAT	ERA	ERA+	OAV	OOB	BH	AVG	PB	PR	/A	PD	TPI
1961	Cle-A	0	0	—	6	0	0	0	1	10	8	0	8	4	15.3	3.60	109	.216	.370	0	.000	-0	0	0	0	0.0
	LA-A	0	0	—	6	0	0	0	0	10	4	1	2	2	6.3	1.80	251	.125	.200	0	.000	-0	2	3	0	0.3
	Yr	0	0	—	12	0	0	0	1	20	12	1	10	6	10.3	2.70	156	.171	.284	0	.000	-0	3	3	0	0.3

● GEORGE HEMMING Hemming, George Earl "Old Wax Figger"
b: 12/15/1868, Carrollton, Ohio d: 6/3/30, Springfield, Mass. BR/TR, 5′11″, 170 lbs. Deb: 4/21/1890

YEAR	TM/L	W	L	PCT	G	GS	CG	SH	SV	IP	H	HR	BB	SO	RAT	ERA	ERA+	OAV	OOB	BH	AVG	PB	PR	/A	PD	TPI
1890	Cle-P	0	1	.000	3	1	1	0	0	21	25	1	19	3	19.7	6.86	58	.283	.421	2	.182	-1	-6	-7	1	-0.5
	Bro-P	8	4	.667	19	11	11	0	3	123	117	3	59	32	13.1	3.80	117	.240	.326	9	.158	-4	6	9	0	0.4
	Yr	8	5	.615	22	12	12	0	**3**	144	142	4	78	35	13.9	4.25	103	.246	.338	11	.162	-5	-0	2	1	-0.1
1891	Bro-N	8	15	.348	27	22	19	1	1	199^2	231	11	84	83	14.7	4.96	67	.279	.353	13	.159	-1	-36	-37	1	-3.1
1892	Cin-N	0	1	.000	1	0	0	0	0	6	10	1	2	0	18.0	7.50	44	.357	.400	1	.333	0	-3	-3	0	-0.2
	Lou-N	2	2	.500	4	4	4	0	0	35	36	1	17	12	13.6	4.63	66	.255	.335	1	.077	-1	-5	-6	0	-0.6
	Yr	2	3	.400	5	4	4	0	0	41	46	2	19	12	14.3	5.05	61	.272	.346	2	.125	-1	-8	-9	0	-0.8
1893	Lou-N	18	17	.514	41	32	32	1	1	332	369	7	176	79	15.2	5.10	86	.273	.363	32	.203	-2	-16	-26	2	-2.0
1894	Lou-N	13	19	.406	35	32	32	1	1	294^1	358	7	133	66	15.3	4.37	117	.297	.371	33	.252	2	31	24	-1	1.9
	*Bal-N	4	0	1.000	6	6	4	0	0	45^1	48	0	26	4	15.1	3.57	153	.269	.368	6	.286	1	9	9	-0	0.8
	Yr	17	19	.472	41	38	36	1	1	339^2	406	7	159	70	15.0	4.27	121	.291	.365	39	.257	3	40	33	-1	2.7
1895	Bal-N	20	13	.606	34	31	26	1	0	262^1	288	10	96	43	13.4	4.05	118	.275	.339	33	.282	3	21	21	-3	1.7
1896	Bal-N	15	6	.714	25	21	20	3	0	202	233	9	54	33	12.9	4.19	102	.287	.333	25	.258	4	4	2	-3	0.3
1897	Lou-N	3	4	.429	9	8	7	0	0	67	80	5	25	7	14.2	5.10	83	.294	.355	5	.179	-1	-6	-6	1	-0.6
Total	8	91	82	.526	204	168	156	7	6	1587^2	1795	55	691	362	14.4	4.53	98	.279	.353	160	.223	1	-1	-19	-2	-1.9

● BERNIE HENDERSON Henderson, Bernard "Barnyard" b: 4/12/1899, Douglassville, Tex d: 6/6/66, Linden, Tex. BR/TR, 5′9″, 175 lbs. Deb: 9/05/21

YEAR	TM/L	W	L	PCT	G	GS	CG	SH	SV	IP	H	HR	BB	SO	RAT	ERA	ERA+	OAV	OOB	BH	AVG	PB	PR	/A	PD	TPI
1921	Cle-A	0	1	.000	2	1	0	0	0	3	5	0	0	1	15.0	9.00	47	.333	.333	0	.000	0	-2	-2	-0	-0.1

● ED HENDERSON Henderson, Edward J. (b: Eugene J. Ball) b: 12/25/1884, Newark, N.J. d: 1/15/64, New York, N.Y. BL/TL, 5′9″, 168 lbs. Deb: 5/15/14

YEAR	TM/L	W	L	PCT	G	GS	CG	SH	SV	IP	H	HR	BB	SO	RAT	ERA	ERA+	OAV	OOB	BH	AVG	PB	PR	/A	PD	TPI
1914	Pit-F	0	1	.000	6	1	1	0	0	16	14	2	8	4	12.4	3.94	81	.241	.333	0	.000	-0	-1	-1	-1	-0.2

YEAR	TM/L	W	L	PCT	G	GS	CG	SH	SV	IP	H	HR	BB	SO	RAT	ERA	ERA+	OAV	OOB	BH	AVG	PB	PR	/A	PD	TPI
	Ind-F	1	0	1.000	2	1	1	0	0	10	8	0	4	1	13.5	4.50	77	.229	.357	0	.000	-1	-1	-1	-0	-0.2
	Yr	1	1	.500	8	2	2	0	0	26	22	2	12	5	12.8	4.15	79	.237	.343	0	.000	-1	-3	-2	-1	-0.4

● HARDIE HENDERSON Henderson, James Harding b: 10/31/1862, Philadelphia, Pa. d: 2/6/03, Philadelphia, Pa. BR/TR, Deb: 5/02/1883 U

YEAR	TM/L	W	L	PCT	G	GS	CG	SH	SV	IP	H	HR	BB	SO	RAT	ERA	ERA+	OAV	OOB	BH	AVG	PB	PR	/A	PD	TPI
1883	Phi-N	0	1	.000	1	1	1	0	0	9	26	0	2	2	28.0	19.00	16	.481	.500	2	.250	0	-16	-16	-0	-0.9
	Bal-a	10	32	.238	45	42	38	0	0	358^{1}	383	4	87	145	11.8	4.02	87	.256	.297	31	.162	-7	-28	-21	-2	-2.5
1884	Bal-a	27	23	.540	52	52	50	4	0	439^{1}	382	9	116	346	10.5	2.62	132	.216	.271	46	.227	3	31	41	1	4.3
1885	Bal-a	25	35	.417	61	61	59	0	0	539^{1}	539	7	117	263	11.3	3.19	102	.253	.298	51	.223	3	4	4	-0	0.7
1886	Bal-a	3	15	.167	19	19	19	0	0	171^{1}	188	0	66	88	13.8	4.62	74	.252	.320	16	.235	2	-22	-23	2	-1.6
	Bro-a	10	4	.714	14	14	14	0	0	124	112	2	51	49	11.8	2.90	120	.232	.306	9	.180	-1	8	8	0	0.6
	Yr	13	19	.406	33	33	33	0	0	295^{1}	300	2	117	137	12.7	3.90	88	.242	.308	25	.212	1	-15	-15	2	-1.0
1887	Bro-a	5	8	.385	13	12	12	0	0	111^{2}	127	3	63	28	15.7	3.95	109	.281	.375	5	.122	-3	4	4	1	0.2
1888	Pit-N	1	3	.250	5	5	4	0	0	35^{1}	43	0	20	9	16.6	5.35	50	.289	.380	5	.278	1	-10	-11	0	-0.9
Total	6	81	121	.401	210	206	197	4	0	1788^{1}	1800	25	522	930	11.9	3.50	98	.247	.302	165	.204	-2	-30	-13	2	-0.1

● JOE HENDERSON Henderson, Joseph Lee b: 7/4/46, Lake Cormorant, Miss. BL/TR, 6'2", 195 lbs. Deb: 6/07/74

YEAR	TM/L	W	L	PCT	G	GS	CG	SH	SV	IP	H	HR	BB	SO	RAT	ERA	ERA+	OAV	OOB	BH	AVG	PB	PR	/A	PD	TPI
1974	Chi-A	1	0	1.000	5	3	0	0	0	15	21	2	11	12	19.2	8.40	44	.328	.427	0	.000	0	-8	-8	0	-0.8
1976	Cin-N	2	0	1.000	4	0	0	0	0	11	9	0	8	7	13.9	0.00	—	.225	.354	0	—	0	4	4	0	0.5
1977	Cin-N	0	2	.000	7	0	0	0	0	9	17	2	6	8	23.0	12.00	33	.386	.460	0	.000	-0	-8	-8	-0	-0.8
Total	3	3	2	.600	16	3	0	0	0	35	47	4	25	27	18.5	6.69	55	.318	.416	0	.000	0	-12	-12	-0	-1.1

● BILL HENDERSON Henderson, William Maxwell b: 11/4/01, Pensacola, Fla. d: 10/6/66, Pensacola, Fla. BR/TR, 6', 190 lbs. Deb: 6/20/30

YEAR	TM/L	W	L	PCT	G	GS	CG	SH	SV	IP	H	HR	BB	SO	RAT	ERA	ERA+	OAV	OOB	BH	AVG	PB	PR	/A	PD	TPI
1930	NY-A	0	0	—	3	0	0	0	0	8	7	1	4	2	12.4	4.50	96	.250	.344	1	.500	0	0	-0	0	0.0

● BOB HENDLEY Hendley, Charles Robert b: 4/30/39, Macon, Ga. BR/TL, 6'2", 190 lbs. Deb: 6/23/61

YEAR	TM/L	W	L	PCT	G	GS	CG	SH	SV	IP	H	HR	BB	SO	RAT	ERA	ERA+	OAV	OOB	BH	AVG	PB	PR	/A	PD	TPI
1961	Mil-N	5	7	.417	19	13	3	0	0	97	96	8	39	44	12.5	3.90	96	.262	.333	1	.032	-3	1	-2	1	-0.3
1962	Mil-N	11	13	.458	35	29	7	2	1	200	188	17	59	112	11.1	3.60	105	.247	.301	7	.119	1	8	4	1	0.6
1963	Mil-N	9	9	.500	41	24	7	3	3	169^{1}	153	16	64	105	11.6	3.93	82	.244	.315	5	.106	-1	-12	-13	1	-1.4
1964	SF-N	10	11	.476	30	29	4	1	0	163^{1}	161	18	59	104	12.2	3.64	98	.258	.325	5	.106	-1	-2	-1	-2	-0.5
1965	SF-N	0	0	—	8	2	0	0	0	15	27	6	13	8	24.6	12.60	29	.397	.500	0	.000	-0	-15	-15	0	-1.4
	Chi-N	4	4	.500	18	10	2	0	0	62	59	9	25	38	12.3	4.35	85	.244	.317	0	.000	-2	-6	-5	1	-0.6
	Yr	4	4	.500	26	12	2	0	0	77	86	15	38	46	14.6	5.96	62	.277	.357	0	.000	-2	-21	-20	1	-2.0
1966	Chi-N	4	5	.444	43	6	0	0	7	89^{2}	98	10	39	65	13.8	3.91	94	.285	.358	3	.167	1	-3	-2	1	-0.1
1967	Chi-N	2	0	1.000	7	0	0	0	1	12^{1}	17	4	3	10	14.6	6.57	54	.315	.351	0	.000	-1	-4	-4	-0	-0.5
	NY-N	3	3	.500	15	13	2	0	0	70^{2}	65	11	28	36	12.0	3.44	99	.241	.314	2	.111	-0	-1	-0	-2	-0.2
	Yr	5	3	.625	22	13	2	0	1	83	82	15	31	46	12.4	3.90	87	.253	.320	2	.083	-1	-5	-5	-2	-0.7
Total	7	48	52	.480	216	126	25	6	12	879^{1}	864	99	329	522	12.3	3.97	90	.257	.325	23	.095	-6	-34	-38	0	-4.4

● ED HENDRICKS Hendricks, Edward "Big Ed" b: 6/20/1886, Zeeland, Mich. d: 11/28/30, Jackson, Mich. BL/TL, 6'3", 200 lbs. Deb: 9/15/10

YEAR	TM/L	W	L	PCT	G	GS	CG	SH	SV	IP	H	HR	BB	SO	RAT	ERA	ERA+	OAV	OOB	BH	AVG	PB	PR	/A	PD	TPI
1910	NY-N	0	1	.000	4	1	1	0	1	12	12	0	4	2	12.0	3.75	79	.261	.320	0	.000	-1	-1	-1	-1	-0.2

● ELLIE HENDRICKS Hendricks, Elrod Jerome b: 12/22/40, Charlotte Amalie, V.I. BL/TR, 6'1", 175 lbs. Deb: 4/13/68 C♦

YEAR	TM/L	W	L	PCT	G	GS	CG	SH	SV	IP	H	HR	BB	SO	RAT	ERA	ERA+	OAV	OOB	BH	AVG	PB	PR	/A	PD	TPI
1978	Bal-A	0	0	—	1	0	0	0	0	2^{1}	1	0	1	0	7.7	0.00	—	.125	.222	6	.333	1	1	1	-0	0.1

● DON HENDRICKSON Hendrickson, Donald William b: 7/14/15, Kewanna, Ind. d: 1/19/77, Norfolk, Va. BR/TR, 6'2", 204 lbs. Deb: 7/04/45

YEAR	TM/L	W	L	PCT	G	GS	CG	SH	SV	IP	H	HR	BB	SO	RAT	ERA	ERA+	OAV	OOB	BH	AVG	PB	PR	/A	PD	TPI
1945	Bos-N	4	8	.333	37	2	1	0	5	73^{1}	74	8	39	14	14.0	4.91	78	.261	.353	3	.167	-0	-9	-9	-1	-1.0
1946	Bos-N	0	1	.000	2	0	0	0	0	2	4	0	2	2	27.0	4.50	76	.364	.462	0	.000	-0	-0	-0	-0	0.0
Total	2	4	9	.308	39	2	1	0	5	75^{1}	78	8	41	16	14.3	4.90	78	.265	.357	3	.158	-0	-9	-9	-1	-1.0

● CLAUDE HENDRIX Hendrix, Claude Raymond b: 4/13/1889, Olathe, Kan. d: 3/22/44, Allentown, Pa. BR/TR, 6', 195 lbs. Deb: 6/07/11

YEAR	TM/L	W	L	PCT	G	GS	CG	SH	SV	IP	H	HR	BB	SO	RAT	ERA	ERA+	OAV	OOB	BH	AVG	PB	PR	/A	PD	TPI
1911	Pit-N	4	6	.400	22	12	6	1	1	118^{2}	85	1	53	57	10.5	2.73	126	.204	.295	4	.098	-1	9	9	4	1.2
1912	Pit-N	24	9	**.727**	39	32	25	4	1	288^{2}	256	6	105	176	11.5	2.59	126	.246	.320	39	.322	15	26	22	5	4.2
1913	Pit-N	14	15	.483	42	25	17	2	3	241	216	3	89	138	11.6	2.84	106	.248	.321	27	.273	9	10	5	2	1.6
1914	Chi-F	**29**	10	.744	**49**	37	**34**	6	5	362	262	6	77	189	**8.6**	**1.69**	175	**.203**	**.251**	30	.231	5	**61**	51	6	**7.0**
1915	Chi-F	16	15	.516	40	31	26	5	4	285	256	7	84	107	10.8	3.00	93	.241	.298	30	.265	12	1	-7	-4	0.1
1916	Chi-N	8	16	.333	36	24	15	3	2	218	193	4	67	117	11.0	2.68	108	.242	.306	16	.200	2	-2	5	2	1.1
1917	Chi-N	10	12	.455	40	21	13	1	1	215	202	3	72	81	11.6	2.60	112	.257	.322	22	.256	4	3	7	-2	1.1
1918	*Chi-N	20	7	**.741**	32	27	21	3	0	233	229	2	54	86	11.1	2.78	100	.259	.305	24	.264	9	-0	0	1	1.1
1919	Chi-N	10	14	.417	33	25	15	2	0	206^{1}	208	3	42	69	11.3	2.62	110	.266	.311	15	.192	-0	7	6	1	0.8
1920	Chi-N	9	12	.429	27	23	12	0	0	203^{2}	216	6	54	72	12.1	3.58	90	.273	.322	15	.181	-2	-10	-8	-1	-1.1
Total	10	144	116	.554	360	257	184	27	17	2371^{1}	2123	41	697	1092	10.9	2.65	113	.243	.303	222	.241	52	105	93	14	17.1

● LAFAYETTE HENION Henion, Lafayette Marion b: 6/7/1899, Eureka, Cal. d: 7/22/55, San Luis Obispo, Cal. BR/TR, 5'11", 154 lbs. Deb: 9/10/19

YEAR	TM/L	W	L	PCT	G	GS	CG	SH	SV	IP	H	HR	BB	SO	RAT	ERA	ERA+	OAV	OOB	BH	AVG	PB	PR	/A	PD	TPI
1919	Bro-N	0	0	—	1	0	0	0	0	3	2	0	2	2	12.0	6.00	50	.200	.333	0	.000	-0	-1	-1	-0	-0.1

● TOM HENKE Henke, Thomas Anthony b: 12/21/57, Kansas City, Mo. BR/TR, 6'5", 215 lbs. Deb: 9/10/82

YEAR	TM/L	W	L	PCT	G	GS	CG	SH	SV	IP	H	HR	BB	SO	RAT	ERA	ERA+	OAV	OOB	BH	AVG	PB	PR	/A	PD	TPI
1982	Tex-A	1	0	1.000	8	0	0	0	0	15^{2}	14	0	8	9	13.2	1.15	337	.246	.348	0	—	0	5	5	0	0.9
1983	Tex-A	1	0	1.000	8	0	0	0	1	16	16	1	4	17	11.3	3.38	119	.262	.308	0	—	0	1	1	0	0.2
1984	Tex-A	1	1	.500	25	0	0	0	2	28^{1}	36	0	20	25	18.1	6.35	65	.313	.419	0	—	0	-7	-7	-0	-0.8
1985	*Tor-A	3	3	.500	28	0	0	0	13	40	29	4	8	42	8.3	2.02	208	.206	.248	0	—	0	9	10	-0	0.9
1986	Tor-A	9	5	.643	63	0	0	0	27	91^{1}	63	6	32	118	9.5	3.35	126	.191	.265	0	—	0	8	9	-2	0.7
1987	Tor-A★	0	6	.000	72	0	0	0	**34**	94	62	10	25	128	8.3	2.49	180	.188	.245	0	—	0	**21**	**21**	1	2.1
1988	Tor-A	4	4	.500	52	0	0	0	25	68	60	6	24	66	11.4	2.91	135	.237	.308	0	—	0	8	8	0	0.8
1989	*Tor-A	8	3	.727	64	0	0	0	20	89	66	5	25	116	9.4	1.92	196	.205	.266	0	—	0	19	18	0	1.9
1990	Tor-A	2	4	.333	61	0	0	0	32	74^{2}	58	8	19	75	9.4	2.17	182	.213	.267	0	—	0	14	15	-1	1.3
1991	*Tor-A	0	2	.000	49	0	0	0	32	50^{1}	33	4	11	53	7.9	2.32	181	.184	.232	0	—	0	10	11	-1	0.7
1992	*Tor-A	3	2	.600	57	0	0	0	34	55^{2}	40	5	22	46	10.0	2.26	180	.197	.276	0	—	0	10	11	-1	0.8
Total	11	32	30	.516	487	0	0	0	220	623	477	49	198	695	9.9	2.64	155	.211	.277	0	—	0	99	101	-3	9.5

● WELDON HENLEY Henley, Weldon b: 10/25/1880, Jasper, Ga. d: 11/16/60, Palatka, Fla. BR/TR, 6', 175 lbs. Deb: 4/23/03

YEAR	TM/L	W	L	PCT	G	GS	CG	SH	SV	IP	H	HR	BB	SO	RAT	ERA	ERA+	OAV	OOB	BH	AVG	PB	PR	/A	PD	TPI
1903	Phi-A	12	10	.545	29	21	13	1	0	186^{1}	186	3	67	86	12.8	3.91	78	.259	.333	9	.132	-4	-20	-18	-1	-2.2
1904	Phi-A	15	17	.469	36	34	31	5	0	295^{2}	245	3	76	130	10.3	2.53	106	.227	.288	24	.222	2	2	5	4	1.2
1905	Phi-A	4	11	.267	25	19	13	1	0	183^{2}	155	4	67	82	11.2	2.60	102	.230	.306	11	.169	-1	1	1	4	0.4
1907	Bro-N	1	5	.167	7	7	5	0	0	56	54	2	21	11	12.2	3.05	77	.273	.345	4	.200	1	-4	-4	2	-0.3
Total	4	32	43	.427	97	81	62	7	0	721^{2}	640	12	231	309	11.3	2.94	93	.240	.309	48	.184	-2	-20	-16	9	-0.9

● MIKE HENNEMAN Henneman, Michael Alan b: 12/11/61, St.Charles, Mo. BR/TR, 6'4", 205 lbs. Deb: 5/11/87

YEAR	TM/L	W	L	PCT	G	GS	CG	SH	SV	IP	H	HR	BB	SO	RAT	ERA	ERA+	OAV	OOB	BH	AVG	PB	PR	/A	PD	TPI
1987	*Det-A	11	3	.786	55	0	0	0	7	96^{2}	86	8	30	75	11.1	2.98	142	.238	.301	0	.000	0	16	13	0	1.3
1988	Det-A	9	6	.600	65	0	0	0	22	91^{1}	72	7	24	58	9.7	1.87	204	.218	.275	0	—	0	**21**	**20**	-1	2.0
1989	Det-A☆	11	4	.733	60	0	0	0	8	90	84	4	51	69	14.0	3.70	103	.251	.358	0	—	0	2	1	0	0.1
1990	Det-A	8	6	.571	69	0	0	0	22	94^{1}	90	4	33	50	12.0	3.05	130	.253	.321	0	—	0	9	9	1	1.0
1991	Det-A	10	2	.833	60	0	0	0	21	84^{1}	81	2	34	61	12.3	2.88	144	.258	.330	0	—	0	11	12	-0	1.1
1992	Det-A	2	6	.250	60	0	0	0	24	77^{1}	75	6	20	58	11.1	3.96	101	.256	.304	0	—	0	-0	0	1	0.0
Total	6	51	27	.654	369	0	0	0	104	534	488	31	192	371	11.7	3.05	131	.245	.316	0	.000	0	59	56	0	5.5

YEAR TM/L	W	L	PCT	G	GS	CG	SH	SV	IP	H	HR	BB	SO	RAT	ERA	ERA+	OAV	OOB	BH	AVG	PB	PR	/A	PD	TPI

● GEORGE HENNESSEY Hennessey, George "Three Star" b: 10/28/07, Slatington, Pa. d: 1/15/88, Princeton, N.J. BR/TR, 5'10", 168 lbs. Deb: 9/02/37

1937 StL-A	0	1	.000	5	0	0	0	0	7	15	2	6	4	27.0	10.29	47	.500	.583	0	—	0	-4	-4	0	-0.4
1942 Phi-N	1	1	.500	5	1	0	0	0	17	11	1	10	2	11.1	2.65	125	.180	.296	0	.000	-1	1	1	-0	0.0
1945 Chi-N	0	0	—	2	0	0	0	0	3²	7	0	1	2	19.6	7.36	50	.438	.471	0	—	0	-1	-2	0	-0.1
Total 3	1	2	.333	12	1	0	0	0	27²	33	3	17	8	16.3	5.20	72	.308	.403	0	.000	-1	-5	-5	-0	-0.5

● PHIL HENNIGAN Hennigan, Phillip Winston b: 4/10/46, Jasper, Tex. BR/TR, 5'11.5", 185 lbs. Deb: 9/02/69

1969 Cle-A	2	1	.667	9	0	0	0	0	16¹	14	0	4	10	10.5	3.31	114	.241	.302	0	.000	-0	1	1	-1	0.0
1970 Cle-A	6	3	.667	42	1	0	0	3	71²	69	7	44	43	14.7	4.02	99	.263	.377	1	.143	1	-2	-0	1	0.1
1971 Cle-A	4	3	.571	57	0	0	0	14	82	80	13	51	69	14.7	4.94	77	.261	.371	0	.000	-0	-13	-10	-1	-1.2
1972 Cle-A	5	3	.625	38	1	0	0	5	67¹	54	8	18	44	9.9	2.67	120	.226	.286	1	.083	-0	3	4	-1	0.3
1973 NY-N	0	4	.000	30	0	0	0	3	43¹	50	6	16	22	13.9	6.23	58	.289	.353	1	.333	1	-12	-13	-1	-1.3
Total 5	17	14	.548	176	2	0	0	25	280²	267	34	133	188	13.2	4.26	86	.257	.347	3	.100	1	-25	-18	-2	-2.1

● PETE HENNING Henning, Ernest Herman b: 12/28/1887, Crown Point, Ind. d: 11/4/39, Dyer, Ind. BR/TR, 5'11", 185 lbs. Deb: 4/17/14

1914 KC-F	5	10	.333	28	14	7	0	2	138	153	5	58	45	14.2	4.83	64	.291	.369	8	.182	1	-25	-27	0	-2.5
1915 KC-F	9	15	.375	40	20	15	1	2	207	181	5	76	73	11.3	3.17	92	.235	.307	14	.206	-0	-3	-6	4	-0.3
Total 2	14	25	.359	68	34	22	1	4	345	334	10	134	118	12.5	3.83	78	.258	.332	22	.196	0	-28	-32	4	-2.8

● RICK HENNINGER Henninger, Richard Lee b: 1/11/48, Hastings, Neb. BR/TR, 6'6", 225 lbs. Deb: 9/03/73

| 1973 Tex-A | 1 | 0 | 1.000 | 6 | 2 | 0 | 0 | 0 | 23 | 23 | 1 | 11 | 6 | 13.3 | 2.74 | 136 | .261 | .343 | 0 | — | 0 | 3 | 3 | -1 | 0.3 |

● RANDY HENNIS Hennis, Randall Philip b: 12/16/65, Clearlake, Cal. BR/TR, 6'6", 220 lbs. Deb: 9/17/90

| 1990 Hou-N | 0 | 0 | — | 3 | 1 | 0 | 0 | 0 | 9² | 1 | 0 | 3 | 4 | 4.7 | 0.00 | — | .033 | .147 | 0 | .000 | -0 | 4 | 4 | -0 | 0.4 |

● DWAYNE HENRY Henry, Dwayne Allen b: 2/16/62, Elkton, Md. BR/TR, 6'3", 205 lbs. Deb: 9/07/84

1984 Tex-A	0	1	.000	3	0	0	0	0	4¹	5	0	7	2	24.9	8.31	50	.294	.500	0	—	0	-2	-2	-0	-0.3
1985 Tex-A	2	2	.500	16	0	0	0	3	21	16	0	7	20	9.9	2.57	164	.211	.277	0	—	0	4	4	-0	0.4
1986 Tex-A	1	0	1.000	19	0	0	0	0	19¹	14	1	22	17	17.2	4.66	92	.209	.411	0	—	0	-1	-1	0	-0.1
1987 Tex-A	0	0	—	5	0	0	0	0	10	12	2	9	7	18.9	9.00	50	.293	.420	0	—	0	-5	-5	-0	-0.5
1988 Tex-A	0	1	.000	11	0	0	0	1	10¹	15	1	9	10	23.5	8.71	47	.326	.466	0	—	0	-5	-5	-0	-0.6
1989 Atl-N	0	2	.000	12	0	0	0	1	12²	12	2	5	16	12.1	4.26	86	.250	.321	0	—	0	-1	-1	-0	-0.1
1990 Atl-N	2	2	.500	34	0	0	0	0	38¹	41	3	25	34	15.5	5.63	72	.273	.377	0	—	0	-8	-7	-1	-0.7
1991 Hou-N	3	2	.600	52	0	0	0	2	67²	51	7	39	51	12.2	3.19	110	.219	.336	0	.000	-0	4	2	-1	0.2
1992 Cin-N	3	3	.500	60	0	0	0	0	83²	59	4	44	72	11.2	3.33	110	.199	.304	1	.250	0	2	3	0	0.4
Total 9	11	13	.458	212	0	0	0	7	267¹	225	20	167	229	13.4	4.21	91	.231	.347	1	.200	0	-14	-11	-2	-1.3

● EARL HENRY Henry, Earl Clifford "Hook" b: 6/10/17, Roseville, Ohio BL/TL, 5'11", 172 lbs. Deb: 9/23/44

1944 Cle-A	1	1	.500	2	2	1	0	0	17²	18	0	3	5	10.7	4.58	72	.269	.300	0	—	-0	-2	-3	-0	-0.3
1945 Cle-A	0	3	.000	15	1	0	0	0	21²	20	0	20	10	17.0	5.40	60	.253	.410	2	.500	1	-5	-5	1	-0.4
Total 2	1	4	.200	17	3	1	0	0	39¹	38	0	23	15	14.2	5.03	65	.260	.365	2	.222	0	-7	-8	1	-0.7

● BUTCH HENRY Henry, Floyd Bluford b: 10/7/68, ElPaso, Tex. BL/TL, 6'1", 195 lbs. Deb: 4/09/92

| 1992 Hou-N | 6 | 9 | .400 | 28 | 28 | 2 | 1 | 0 | 165² | 185 | 16 | 41 | 96 | 12.3 | 4.02 | 83 | .285 | .329 | 8 | .148 | 1 | -10 | -12 | 1 | -1.1 |

● DUTCH HENRY Henry, Frank John b: 5/12/02, Cleveland, Ohio d: 8/23/68, Cleveland, Ohio BL/TL, 6'1", 175 lbs. Deb: 9/16/21

1921 StL-A	0	0	—	1	0	0	0	0	2	2	0	0	1	9.0	4.50	100	.250	.250	1	1.000	0	-0	-0	0	0.0
1922 StL-A	0	0	—	4	0	0	0	0	5	7	0	5	3	21.6	5.40	77	.280	.400	0	—	0	-1	-1	0	-0.1
1923 Bro-N	4	6	.400	17	9	5	2	0	94¹	105	9	28	28	12.9	3.91	99	.281	.334	8	.229	1	1	-0	-0	0.0
1924 Bro-N	1	2	.333	16	4	0	0	0	46	69	0	15	11	16.4	5.67	66	.352	.398	5	.250	1	-9	-10	-1	-0.9
1927 NY-N	11	6	.647	45	15	7	1	4	163²	184	6	31	40	11.8	4.23	91	.278	.311	13	.236	1	-6	-7	-2	-0.7
1928 NY-N	3	6	.333	17	8	4	0	1	64	82	4	25	23	15.2	3.80	103	.325	.388	3	.158	-1	1	1	1	0.1
1929 NY-N	5	6	.455	27	9	4	0	1	101¹	129	10	31	27	14.3	3.82	120	.316	.366	7	.250	2	10	9	1	0.8
Chi-A	1	0	1.000	2	1	1	0	0	15	20	1	7	2	16.2	6.00	71	.308	.375	1	.143	0	-3	-3	-1	-0.3
1930 Chi-A	2	17	.105	35	16	4	0	0	155	211	12	48	35	15.3	4.88	95	.331	.381	12	.235	1	-4	-4	3	-0.1
Total 8	27	43	.386	164	62	25	3	6	646¹	809	42	190	170	14.0	4.39	95	.308	.356	50	.231	5	-10	-16	0	-1.2

● JIM HENRY Henry, James Francis b: 6/26/10, Danville, Pa. d: 8/15/76, Memphis, Tenn. BR/TR, 6'2", 175 lbs. Deb: 4/23/36

1936 Bos-A	5	1	.833	21	8	2	0	0	76¹	75	10	40	36	13.8	4.60	116	.255	.348	3	.115	-1	4	6	0	0.4
1937 Bos-A	1	0	1.000	3	2	1	0	0	15¹	15	2	11	8	15.3	5.28	90	.263	.382	0	.000	-1	-1	-1	-0	-0.1
1939 Phi-N	0	1	.000	9	1	0	0	1	23	24	3	8	7	12.9	5.09	79	.276	.344	0	.000	-1	-3	-3	-1	-0.4
Total 3	6	2	.750	33	11	3	0	1	114²	114	15	59	51	13.8	4.79	104	.260	.352	3	.083	-2	-0	2	-1	-0.1

● JOHN HENRY Henry, John Michael b: 9/2/1863, Springfield, Mass. d: 6/11/39, Hartford, Conn. TL, Deb: 8/13/1884 ◆

1884 Cle-N	1	4	.200	5	5	5	1	0	42	46	2	26	23	15.4	3.64	87	.257	.351	4	.154	-1	-3	-2	1	-0.3
1885 Bal-a	2	7	.222	9	9	9	0	0	71	71	0	13	31	10.9	4.31	76	.247	.284	9	.265	1	-8	-8	2	-0.4
1886 Was-N	1	3	.250	4	4	4	0	0	27²	35	1	15	19	16.3	4.23	78	.285	.362	5	.357	1	-3	-3	-0	-0.2
Total 3	4	14	.222	18	18	18	1	0	140²	152	3	54	73	13.3	4.09	79	.258	.322	53	.243	1	-14	-13	2	-0.9

● DOUG HENRY Henry, Richard Douglas b: 12/10/63, Sacramento, Cal. BR/TR, 6'4", 185 lbs. Deb: 7/15/91

1991 Mil-A	2	1	.667	32	0	0	0	15	36	16	1	14	28	7.5	1.00	397	.133	.224	0	—	0	12	12	-1	1.3
1992 Mil-A	1	4	.200	68	0	0	0	29	65	64	6	24	52	12.2	4.02	95	.256	.321	0	—	0	-1	-1	0	0.0
Total 2	3	5	.375	100	0	0	0	44	101	80	7	38	80	10.5	2.94	132	.216	.289	0	—	0	12	10	-0	1.3

● BILL HENRY Henry, William Francis b: 2/15/42, Long Beach, Cal. BL/TL, 6'3", 195 lbs. Deb: 9/13/66

| 1966 NY-A | 0 | 0 | — | 2 | 0 | 0 | 0 | 0 | 3 | 0 | 0 | 2 | 3 | 6.0 | 0.00 | — | .000 | .200 | 0 | — | 0 | 1 | 1 | 0 | 0.2 |

● BILL HENRY Henry, William Rodman b: 10/15/27, Alice, Tex. BL/TL, 6'2", 180 lbs. Deb: 4/17/52

1952 Bos-A	5	4	.556	13	10	5	0	0	76²	75	7	36	23	13.3	3.87	102	.254	.339	8	.258	2	-2	1	-1	0.2
1953 Bos-A	5	5	.500	21	12	4	1	1	85²	86	4	33	56	12.9	3.26	129	.260	.334	6	.188	-0	7	9	-1	0.8
1954 Bos-A	3	7	.300	24	13	3	1	0	95²	104	9	49	38	14.5	4.52	91	.270	.354	4	.118	-2	-8	-4	-1	-0.7
1955 Bos-A	2	4	.333	17	7	0	0	0	59²	56	7	21	23	11.6	3.32	129	.247	.310	2	.105	-1	4	6	0	0.6
1958 Chi-N	5	4	.556	44	0	0	0	0	81¹	63	8	17	58	9.0	2.88	136	.214	.259	4	.235	1	10	9	-1	1.0
1959 Chi-N	9	8	.529	65	0	0	0	12	134¹	111	19	26	115	9.2	2.68	147	.227	.267	6	.194	0	19	**19**	-1	1.9
1960 Cin-N★	1	5	.167	51	0	0	0	17	67²	62	8	20	58	11.4	3.19	120	.247	.313	0	.000	-1	4	3	0	0.5
1961 *Cin-N	2	1	.667	47	0	0	0	16	53¹	50	8	15	53	11.0	2.19	185	.244	.295	0	.000	-1	11	11	0	1.0
1962 Cin-N	4	2	.667	40	0	0	0	11	37¹	40	5	20	35	14.7	4.58	88	.280	.372	1	.333	-0	-3	-2	-1	-0.3
1963 Cin-N	1	3	.250	47	0	0	0	14	52	55	4	11	45	11.6	4.15	81	.279	.321	1	.167	-0	-5	-5	0	-0.5
1964 Cin-N	2	2	.500	37	0	0	0	6	52	31	2	12	28	8.0	0.87	418	.170	.234	3	.500	1	15	16	0	1.8
1965 Cin-N	1	0	1.000	3	0	0	0	0	5	3	0	1	5	7.2	0.00	—	.176	.222	0	—	0	2	2	-0	0.2
SF-N	2	2	.500	35	0	0	0	4	42	40	2	8	35	10.5	3.64	99	.248	.288	1	.200	0	-0	-0	-1	-0.1
Yr	4	2	.667	38	0	0	0	4	47	43	2	9	40	10.1	3.26	111	.242	.282	1	.200	0	1	2	-1	0.1
1966 SF-N	1	1	.500	35	0	0	0	1	22	15	2	6	15	10.6	2.45	149	.190	.289	0	.000	-0	3	3	0	0.3
1967 SF-N	2	0	1.000	28	1	0	0	2	21²	16	1	9	23	11.2	2.08	158	.198	.293	0	—	0	3	3	-0	0.3
1968 SF-N	0	2	.000	7	1	0	0	0	5	4	0	4	9	14.4	5.40	54	.250	.400	0	—	0	-1	-1	0	-0.1

YEAR	TM/L	W	L	PCT	G	GS	CG	SH	SV	IP	H	HR	BB	SO	RAT	ERA	ERA+	OAV	OOB	BH	AVG	PB	PR	/A	PD	TPI
	Pit-N	0	0	—	10	0	0	0	0	16^{2}	29	2	3	9	18.4	8.10	36	.382	.420	0	.000	-0	-9	-10	-1	-1.1
	Yr	0	2	.000	17	1	0	0	0	21^{2}	33	2	6	9	17.0	7.48	39	.355	.406	0	.000	-0	-11	-11	-1	-1.2
1969	Hou-N	0	0	—	3	0	0	0	0	5	2	0	2	2	7.2	0.00	—	.111	.200	0	—	0	2	2	-0	0.2
Total	16	46	50	.479	527	44	12	2	90	913	842	89	296	621	11.5	3.26	119	.244	.308	36	.177	-0	51	63	-6	6.0

● ROY HENSHAW Henshaw, Roy Knikelbine b: 7/29/11, Chicago, Ill. BR/TL, 5'8", 155 lbs. Deb: 4/15/33

YEAR	TM/L	W	L	PCT	G	GS	CG	SH	SV	IP	H	HR	BB	SO	RAT	ERA	ERA+	OAV	OOB	BH	AVG	PB	PR	/A	PD	TPI
1933	Chi-N	2	1	.667	21	0	0	0	0	38^{2}	32	0	20	16	12.6	4.19	78	.230	.335	2	.200	-0	-4	-4	-1	-0.5
1935	*Chi-N	13	5	.722	31	18	7	3	1	142^{2}	135	6	68	53	13.1	3.28	120	.249	.337	13	.255	2	12	10	-3	0.8
1936	Chi-N	6	5	.545	39	14	6	2	1	129^{1}	152	8	56	69	14.8	3.97	100	.296	.370	6	.136	-2	1	0	-2	-0.4
1937	Bro-N	5	12	.294	42	16	5	0	2	156^{1}	176	14	69	98	14.3	5.07	80	.278	.352	8	.167	-2	-20	-18	0	-1.9
1938	StL-N	5	11	.313	27	15	4	0	0	130	132	7	48	34	12.5	4.02	99	.266	.332	9	.220	-0	-3	-1	-1	-0.2
1942	Det-A	2	4	.333	23	2	0	0	1	61^{2}	63	3	27	24	13.3	4.09	97	.269	.347	1	.083	-1	-3	-1	-1	-0.2
1943	Det-A	0	2	.000	26	3	0	0	2	71^{1}	75	2	33	33	14.0	3.79	93	.276	.360	2	.111	-1	-4	-2	0	-0.4
1944	Det-A	0	0	—	7	1	0	0	0	12^{1}	17	0	6	10	16.8	8.76	41	.315	.383	0	.000	-1	-7	-7	0	-0.7
Total	8	33	40	.452	216	69	22	5	7	742^{1}	782	40	327	337	13.7	4.16	94	.271	.349	41	.179	-5	-29	-22	-8	-3.5

● PHIL HENSIEK Hensiek, Philip Frank "Sid" b: 10/13/01, St.Louis, Mo. d: 2/21/72, St.Louis, Mo. BR/TR, 6', 160 lbs. Deb: 8/15/35

YEAR	TM/L	W	L	PCT	G	GS	CG	SH	SV	IP	H	HR	BB	SO	RAT	ERA	ERA+	OAV	OOB	BH	AVG	PB	PR	/A	PD	TPI
1935	Was-A	0	3	.000	6	1	0	0	1	13	21	2	9	6	20.8	9.69	45	.356	.441	2	.667	1	-8	-8	-0	-0.6

● CHUCK HENSLEY Hensley, Charles Floyd b: 3/11/59, Tulare, Cal. BL/TL, 6'3", 190 lbs. Deb: 5/10/86

YEAR	TM/L	W	L	PCT	G	GS	CG	SH	SV	IP	H	HR	BB	SO	RAT	ERA	ERA+	OAV	OOB	BH	AVG	PB	PR	/A	PD	TPI
1986	SF-N	0	0	—	11	0	0	0	1	7^{1}	5	2	2	6	8.6	2.45	143	.179	.233	0	—	0	1	1	0	0.1

● PAT HENTGEN Hentgen, Patrick George b: 11/13/68, Detroit, Mich. BR/TR, 6'2", 200 lbs. Deb: 9/03/91

YEAR	TM/L	W	L	PCT	G	GS	CG	SH	SV	IP	H	HR	BB	SO	RAT	ERA	ERA+	OAV	OOB	BH	AVG	PB	PR	/A	PD	TPI
1991	Tor-A	0	0	—	3	1	0	0	0	7^{1}	5	1	3	3	12.3	2.45	171	.208	.345	0	—	0	1	1	0	-0.1
1992	Tor-A	5	2	.714	28	2	0	0	0	50^{1}	49	7	32	39	14.5	5.36	76	.254	.360	0	—	0	-8	-7	-1	-1.0
Total	2	5	2	.714	31	3	0	0	0	57^{2}	54	8	35	42	14.2	4.99	82	.249	.358	0	—	0	-7	-6	-0	-1.1

● BILL HEPLER Hepler, William Lewis b: 9/25/45, Covington, Va. BL/TL, 6', 160 lbs. Deb: 4/23/66

YEAR	TM/L	W	L	PCT	G	GS	CG	SH	SV	IP	H	HR	BB	SO	RAT	ERA	ERA+	OAV	OOB	BH	AVG	PB	PR	/A	PD	TPI
1966	NY-N	3	3	.500	37	3	0	0	0	69	71	3	51	25	16.3	3.52	103	.274	.399	3	.214	0	1	1	-1	0.1

● RON HERBEL Herbel, Ronald Samuel b: 1/16/38, Denver, Colo. BR/TR, 6'1", 195 lbs. Deb: 9/10/63

YEAR	TM/L	W	L	PCT	G	GS	CG	SH	SV	IP	H	HR	BB	SO	RAT	ERA	ERA+	OAV	OOB	BH	AVG	PB	PR	/A	PD	TPI
1963	SF-N	0	0	—	2	0	0	0	0	1^{1}	1	0	1	1	13.5	6.75	47	.200	.333	0	—	0	-1	-1	0	-0.1
1964	SF-N	9	9	.500	40	22	7	2	1	161	162	7	61	98	12.6	3.07	116	.259	.328	0	.000	-4	8	9	2	0.7
1965	SF-N	12	9	.571	47	21	1	0	1	170^{2}	172	16	47	106	11.7	3.85	94	.261	.313	1	.020	-4	-6	-5	2	-0.7
1966	SF-N	4	5	.444	32	18	0	0	1	129^{2}	149	15	39	55	13.2	4.16	88	.291	.344	1	.026	-4	-8	-7	-1	-1.2
1967	SF-N	4	5	.444	42	11	1	1	1	125^{2}	125	10	35	52	11.6	3.08	107	.268	.322	3	.107	0	4	3	4	0.7
1968	SF-N	0	0	—	28	2	0	0	0	42^{2}	55	5	15	18	15.0	3.38	87	.309	.366	0	.000	-0	-2	-2	1	-0.2
1969	SF-N	4	1	.800	39	4	2	0	1	87^{1}	92	7	23	34	12.0	4.02	87	.275	.323	0	.000	-1	-4	-5	0	-0.7
1970	SD-N	7	5	.583	64	1	0	0	9	111	114	14	39	53	12.7	4.95	80	.266	.333	0	.000	-1	-11	-12	-0	-1.3
	NY-N	2	2	.500	12	0	0	0	1	13	14	1	2	8	11.1	1.38	291	.275	.302	0	—	0	4	4	-0	0.4
	Yr	9	7	.563	**76**	1	0	0	10	124	128	15	41	61	12.3	4.57	87	.262	.319	0	.000	-1	-7	-8	-1	-0.9
1971	Atl-N	0	1	.000	25	0	0	0	1	51^{2}	61	6	23	22	15.3	5.23	71	.300	.383	1	.091	-1	-10	-9	0	-1.0
Total	9	42	37	.532	331	79	11	3	16	894	945	81	285	447	12.6	3.83	94	.273	.332	6	.029	-16	-25	-25	7	-3.4

● ERNIE HERBERT Herbert, Ernie Albert "Tex" b: 1/30/1887, Hale, Mo. d: 1/13/68, Dallas, Tex. BR/TR, 5'10", 165 lbs. Deb: 7/27/13

YEAR	TM/L	W	L	PCT	G	GS	CG	SH	SV	IP	H	HR	BB	SO	RAT	ERA	ERA+	OAV	OOB	BH	AVG	PB	PR	/A	PD	TPI
1913	Cin-N	0	0	—	6	0	0	0	0	17^{1}	12	0	5	5	9.3	2.08	156	.179	.247	1	.250	0	2	2	-1	0.2
1914	StL-F	1	1	.500	18	2	0	0	1	50^{1}	56	2	27	24	15.6	3.75	90	.293	.392	7	.538	3	-3	-2	-2	-0.2
1915	StL-F	1	0	1.000	11	1	1	0	0	48	48	1	18	23	12.9	3.38	95	.253	.327	5	.278	1	-2	-1	-1	0.0
Total	3	2	1	.667	35	3	1	0	1	115^{2}	116	3	50	52	13.5	3.35	98	.259	.344	13	.371	4	-3	-1	-4	0.0

● FRED HERBERT Herbert, Frederick (b: Herbert Frederick Kemman) b: 3/4/1887, Lagrange, Ill. d: 5/29/63, Tice, Fla. BR/TR, 6', 185 lbs. Deb: 9/25/15

YEAR	TM/L	W	L	PCT	G	GS	CG	SH	SV	IP	H	HR	BB	SO	RAT	ERA	ERA+	OAV	OOB	BH	AVG	PB	PR	/A	PD	TPI
1915	NY-N	1	1	.500	2	2	1	0	0	17	12	0	4	6	8.5	1.06	242	.197	.246	1	.167	-0	3	3	0	0.3

● RAY HERBERT Herbert, Raymond Ernest b: 12/15/29, Detroit, Mich. BR/TR, 5'11", 185 lbs. Deb: 8/27/50

YEAR	TM/L	W	L	PCT	G	GS	CG	SH	SV	IP	H	HR	BB	SO	RAT	ERA	ERA+	OAV	OOB	BH	AVG	PB	PR	/A	PD	TPI
1950	Det-A	1	2	.333	8	3	1	0	1	22^{1}	20	1	12	5	12.9	3.63	129	.244	.340	2	.286	0	2	3	1	0.3
1951	Det-A	4	0	1.000	5	0	0	0	0	12^{2}	8	0	9	9	12.1	1.42	294	.190	.333	0	.000	-0	4	4	-0	0.3
1953	Det-A	4	6	.400	43	3	0	0	6	87^{2}	109	5	46	37	15.9	5.24	78	.308	.387	3	.158	-0	-12	-11	3	-0.8
1954	Det-A	3	6	.333	42	4	0	0	0	84^{1}	114	6	50	44	17.7	5.87	63	.334	.422	3	.176	2	-20	-20	2	-1.6
1955	KC-A	1	8	.111	23	11	2	0	0	87^{2}	99	10	40	30	14.4	6.26	67	.292	.368	4	.190	0	-22	-20	2	-1.7
1958	KC-A	8	8	.500	42	16	5	0	3	175	161	20	55	108	11.3	3.50	112	.248	.311	10	.192	1	5	8	2	1.2
1959	KC-A	11	11	.500	37	26	10	2	1	183^{2}	196	24	62	99	12.7	4.85	83	.275	.334	12	.211	2	-20	-17	-1	-1.6
1960	KC-A	14	15	.483	37	33	14	0	1	252^{2}	256	17	72	122	11.9	3.28	121	.267	.323	13	.171	1	17	20	3	2.4
1961	KC-A	3	6	.333	13	12	1	0	0	83^{2}	103	10	30	34	14.5	5.38	77	.303	.363	3	.107	-1	-13	-12	0	-1.2
	Chi-A	9	6	.600	21	20	4	0	0	137^{2}	142	15	36	50	11.6	4.05	97	.265	.311	12	.226	4	-0	-2	1	0.3
	Yr	12	12	.500	34	32	5	0	0	221^{1}	245	25	66	84	12.6	4.55	88	.278	.328	15	.185	3	-13	-14	1	-0.9
1962	Chi-A★	20	9	**.690**	35	35	12	2	0	236^{2}	228	13	74	115	11.5	3.27	119	.255	.312	16	.195	5	18	17	3	2.6
1963	Chi-A	13	10	.565	33	33	14	**7**	0	224^{2}	230	12	35	105	10.7	3.24	108	.265	.295	14	.222	6	10	7	2	1.6
1964	Chi-A	6	7	.462	20	19	1	1	0	111^{2}	117	14	17	40	11.0	3.47	100	.275	.306	5	.139	-1	2	-0	-1	-0.2
1965	Phi-N	5	8	.385	25	19	4	1	1	130^{2}	162	13	19	51	12.5	3.86	90	.309	.334	11	.268	3	-5	-6	0	-0.3
1966	Phi-N	2	5	.286	23	2	0	0	2	50^{1}	55	7	14	15	12.5	4.29	84	.293	.345	1	.077	-1	-4	-4	-0	-0.5
Total	14	104	107	.493	407	236	68	13	15	1881^{1}	2000	167	571	864	12.4	4.01	96	.276	.331	109	.192	20	-38	-36	18	0.8

● GIL HEREDIA Heredia, Gilbert b: 10/26/65, Nogales, Ariz. BR/TR, 6'1", 190 lbs. Deb: 9/01/91

YEAR	TM/L	W	L	PCT	G	GS	CG	SH	SV	IP	H	HR	BB	SO	RAT	ERA	ERA+	OAV	OOB	BH	AVG	PB	PR	/A	PD	TPI
1991	SF-N	0	2	.000	7	4	0	0	0	33	27	4	7	13	9.3	3.82	94	.233	.276	3	.429	1	-0	-1	-1	0.0
1992	SF-N	2	3	.400	13	4	0	0	0	30	32	3	16	15	14.7	5.40	62	.278	.371	1	.167	-0	-6	-7	-1	-0.8
	Mon-N	0	0	—	7	1	0	0	0	14^{2}	12	1	4	7	9.8	1.84	189	.250	.308	0	.000	-0	3	3	0	0.3
	Yr	2	3	.400	20	5	0	0	0	44^{2}	44	4	20	22	12.9	4.23	80	.268	.348	1	.111	-0	-4	-4	-1	-0.5
Total	2	2	5	.286	27	9	0	0	0	77^{2}	71	8	27	35	11.5	4.06	86	.254	.322	4	.250	1	-4	-5	-2	-0.5

● UBALDO HEREDIA Heredia, Ubaldo Jose (Martinez) b: 5/4/56, Ciudad Bolivar, Ven. BR/TR, 6'2", 180 lbs. Deb: 5/12/87

YEAR	TM/L	W	L	PCT	G	GS	CG	SH	SV	IP	H	HR	BB	SO	RAT	ERA	ERA+	OAV	OOB	BH	AVG	PB	PR	/A	PD	TPI
1987	Mon-N	0	1	.000	2	2	0	0	0	10	10	2	3	6	12.6	5.40	78	.263	.333	0	.000	-0	-1	-1	0	-0.1

● ART HERMAN Herman, Arthur b: 5/11/1871, Louisville, Ky. d: 9/20/55, Los Angeles, Cal. Deb: 6/29/1896

YEAR	TM/L	W	L	PCT	G	GS	CG	SH	SV	IP	H	HR	BB	SO	RAT	ERA	ERA+	OAV	OOB	BH	AVG	PB	PR	/A	PD	TPI
1896	Lou-N	4	6	.400	14	12	9	0	0	94^{1}	122	4	36	13	15.3	5.63	77	.311	.371	5	.139	-4	-13	-14	-1	-1.5
1897	Lou-N	0	1	.000	3	2	1	0	0	18	23	1	5	4	14.0	4.00	107	.308	.351	2	.333	1	1	1	0	0.2
Total	2	4	7	.364	17	14	10	0	0	112^{1}	145	5	41	17	15.1	5.37	80	.310	.368	7	.167	-2	-13	-13	-1	-1.3

● JESUS HERNAIZ Hernaiz, Jesus Rafael (Rodriguez) b: 1/8/45, Santurce, P.R. BR/TR, 6'2", 175 lbs. Deb: 6/14/74

YEAR	TM/L	W	L	PCT	G	GS	CG	SH	SV	IP	H	HR	BB	SO	RAT	ERA	ERA+	OAV	OOB	BH	AVG	PB	PR	/A	PD	TPI
1974	Phi-N	2	3	.400	27	0	0	0	1	41^{1}	53	6	25	16	17.0	5.88	64	.323	.413	0	.000	-0	-10	-10	-0	-1.0

● XAVIER HERNANDEZ Hernandez, Francis Xavier b: 8/16/65, Port Arthur, Tex. BL/TR, 6'2", 185 lbs. Deb: 6/04/89

YEAR	TM/L	W	L	PCT	G	GS	CG	SH	SV	IP	H	HR	BB	SO	RAT	ERA	ERA+	OAV	OOB	BH	AVG	PB	PR	/A	PD	TPI
1989	Tor-A	1	0	1.000	7	0	0	0	0	22^{2}	25	2	8	7	13.5	4.76	79	.278	.343	0	—	0	-2	-3	-1	-0.3
1990	Hou-N	2	1	.667	34	1	0	0	0	62^{1}	60	8	24	24	12.7	4.62	80	.256	.336	1	.333	0	-6	-6	-1	-0.7
1991	Hou-N	2	7	.222	32	6	0	0	3	63	66	6	32	55	14.0	4.71	74	.263	.346	0	.000	-0	-7	-8	0	-0.9
1992	Hou-N	9	1	.900	77	0	0	0	7	111	81	5	42	96	10.2	2.11	159	.200	.281	0	.000	-1	17	15	-2	1.4
Total	4	14	9	.609	150	7	0	0	10	259	232	21	106	182	12.0	3.58	98	.237	.317	1	.045	-1	2	-2	-3	-0.5

● EVELIO HERNANDEZ
Hernandez, Gregorio Evelio (Lopez) b: 12/24/30, Guanabacoa, Havana, Cuba BR/TR, 6'1", 195 lbs. Deb: 9/12/56

YEAR	TM/L	W	L	PCT	G	GS	CG	SH	SV	IP	H	HR	BB	SO	RAT	ERA	ERA+	OAV	OOB	BH	AVG	PB	PR	/A	PD	TPI
1956	Was-A	1	1	.500	4	4	1	0	0	22^2	24	2	8	9	12.7	4.76	91	.276	.337	2	.182	-0	-2	-1	-0	-0.2
1957	Was-A	0	0	—	14	2	0	0	0	36	38	2	20	15	14.5	4.25	92	.268	.358	0	.000	-1	-2	-1	-1	-0.3
Total	2	1	1	.500	18	6	1	0	0	58^2	62	4	28	24	13.8	4.45	91	.271	.350	2	.118	-1	-3	-3	-1	-0.5

● WILLIE HERNANDEZ
Hernandez, Guillermo (Villanueva) b: 11/14/54, Aguada, P.R. BL/TL, 6'3", 180 lbs. Deb: 4/09/77

YEAR	TM/L	W	L	PCT	G	GS	CG	SH	SV	IP	H	HR	BB	SO	RAT	ERA	ERA+	OAV	OOB	BH	AVG	PB	PR	/A	PD	TPI
1977	Chi-N	8	7	.533	67	1	0	0	4	110	94	11	28	78	10.1	3.03	145	.234	.285	1	.063	-2	11	17	3	1.8
1978	Chi-N	8	2	.800	54	0	0	0	3	59^2	57	6	35	38	14.0	3.77	107	.263	.368	0	.000	-0	-1	2	1	0.2
1979	Chi-N	4	4	.500	51	2	0	0	0	79	85	8	39	53	14.6	5.01	82	.281	.370	2	.250	0	-11	-8	-0	-0.8
1980	Chi-N	1	9	.100	53	7	0	0	0	108^1	115	8	45	75	13.5	4.40	89	.276	.349	4	.211	0	-10	-6	2	-0.4
1981	Chi-N	0	0	—	12	0	0	0	2	13^2	14	0	8	13	14.5	3.95	94	.280	.379	0	—	0	-1	-0	0	0.0
1982	Chi-N	4	6	.400	75	0	0	0	10	75	74	3	24	54	11.9	3.00	124	.268	.329	0	.000	-0	5	6	2	0.9
1983	Chi-N	1	0	1.000	11	1	0	0	1	19^2	16	0	6	18	10.1	3.20	118	.222	.282	1	.500	0	1	1	0	0.2
	*Phi-N	8	4	.667	63	0	0	0	7	95^2	93	9	26	75	11.3	3.29	108	.254	.305	5	.385	2	4	3	-0	0.5
	Yr	9	4	.692	74	1	0	0	8	115^1	109	9	32	93	11.1	3.28	110	.249	.301	6	.400	2	4	4	0	0.7
1984	*Det-A★	9	3	.750	**80**	0	0	0	32	140^1	96	6	36	112	8.7	1.92	204	.194	.254	0	—	0	**32**	**31**	-1	3.1
1985	Det-A★	8	10	.444	74	0	0	0	31	106^2	82	13	14	76	8.2	2.70	151	.210	.239	0	.000	0	17	16	-2	1.5
1986	Det-A☆	8	7	.533	64	0	0	0	24	88^2	87	13	21	77	11.5	3.55	116	.251	.304	0	—	0	6	6	1	0.6
1987	*Det-A	3	4	.429	45	0	0	0	8	49	53	8	20	30	13.4	3.67	115	.276	.344	0	—	0	4	3	-1	0.2
1988	Det-A	6	5	.545	63	0	0	0	10	67^2	50	8	31	59	11.3	3.06	125	.208	.309	0	—	0	7	6	1	0.8
1989	Det-A	2	2	.500	32	0	0	0	15	31^1	36	4	16	30	15.2	5.74	66	.293	.379	0	—	0	-6	-7	0	-0.6
Total	13	70	63	.526	744	11	0	0	147	1044^2	952	97	349	788	11.4	3.38	118	.245	.311	13	.206	1	57	70	6	8.0

● JEREMY HERNANDEZ
Hernandez, Jeremy Stuart b: 7/6/66, Burbank, Cal. BR/TR, 6'5", 195 lbs. Deb: 9/02/91

YEAR	TM/L	W	L	PCT	G	GS	CG	SH	SV	IP	H	HR	BB	SO	RAT	ERA	ERA+	OAV	OOB	BH	AVG	PB	PR	/A	PD	TPI
1991	SD-N	0	0	—	9	0	0	0	2	14^1	8	0	5	9	8.2	0.00	—	.157	.232	0	.000	-0	6	6	0	0.7
1992	SD-N	1	4	.200	26	0	0	0	1	36^2	39	4	11	25	12.5	4.17	87	.291	.349	0	.000	-0	-3	-2	0	-0.2
Total	2	1	4	.200	35	0	0	0	3	51	47	4	16	34	11.3	3.00	123	.254	.317	0	.000	-0	3	4	1	0.5

● MANNY HERNANDEZ
Hernandez, Manuel Antonio (Montas) b: 5/7/61, LaRomana, D.R. BR/TR, 6', 150 lbs. Deb: 6/05/86

YEAR	TM/L	W	L	PCT	G	GS	CG	SH	SV	IP	H	HR	BB	SO	RAT	ERA	ERA+	OAV	OOB	BH	AVG	PB	PR	/A	PD	TPI
1986	Hou-N	2	3	.400	9	4	0	0	0	27^2	33	2	12	9	14.6	3.90	92	.306	.375	0	.000	-1	-1	-1	-0	-0.2
1987	Hou-N	0	4	.000	6	3	0	0	0	21^2	25	1	5	12	12.9	5.40	73	.301	.348	0	.000	-0	-3	-4	0	-0.4
1989	NY-N	0	0	—	1	0	0	0	0	1	0	0	0	1	0.0	0.00	—	.000	.000	0	—	0	0	0	0	0.0
Total	3	2	7	.222	16	7	0	0	0	50^1	58	3	17	22	13.6	4.47	83	.299	.358	0	.000	-1	-3	-4	0	-0.6

● RAMON HERNANDEZ
Hernandez, Ramon (Gonzalez) b: 8/31/40, Carolina, P.R. BB/TL, 5'9", 170 lbs. Deb: 4/11/67

YEAR	TM/L	W	L	PCT	G	GS	CG	SH	SV	IP	H	HR	BB	SO	RAT	ERA	ERA+	OAV	OOB	BH	AVG	PB	PR	/A	PD	TPI
1967	Atl-N	0	2	.000	46	0	0	0	5	51^2	60	5	14	28	13.2	4.18	79	.296	.347	0	.000	-0	-5	-5	1	-0.5
1968	Chi-N	0	0	—	8	0	0	0	0	9	14	1	0	3	15.0	9.00	35	.350	.366	0	—	0	-6	-6	0	-0.6
1971	Pit-N	0	1	.000	10	0	0	0	4	12^1	5	0	2	7	5.1	0.73	463	.122	.163	1	.500	0	4	4	0	0.5
1972	*Pit-N	5	0	1.000	53	0	0	0	14	70	50	3	22	47	9.6	1.67	199	.194	.265	2	.167	0	14	13	0	1.4
1973	Pit-N	4	5	.444	59	0	0	0	11	89^2	71	5	25	64	10.0	2.41	146	.218	.282	1	.125	0	12	11	1	1.3
1974	*Pit-N	5	2	.714	58	0	0	0	2	68^2	68	3	18	33	11.5	2.75	125	.258	.310	1	.250	1	7	5	-1	0.6
1975	*Pit-N	7	2	.778	46	0	0	0	5	64	62	0	28	43	12.7	2.95	120	.252	.328	0	.000	-0	5	4	1	0.5
1976	Pit-N	2	2	.500	37	0	0	0	3	43	42	3	16	17	12.3	3.56	98	.262	.333	0	.000	-0	-0	-0	-1	-0.1
	Chi-N	0	0	—	2	0	0	0	0	1^2	2	0	0	1	10.8	0.00	—	.333	.333	0	—	0	1	1	0	0.1
	Yr	2	2	.500	39	0	0	0	3	44^2	44	3	16	18	12.1	3.43	102	.257	.321	0	.000	-0	0	0	-0	0.0
1977	Chi-N	0	0	—	6	0	0	0	1	7^2	11	1	3	4	16.4	8.22	53	.306	.359	0	.000	-0	-4	-3	0	-0.3
	Bos-A	0	1	.000	12	0	0	0	1	12^2	14	2	7	8	15.6	5.68	79	.280	.379	0	—	0	-2	-2	-0	-0.2
Total	9	23	15	.605	337	0	0	0	46	430^1	399	23	135	255	11.5	3.03	115	.245	.308	5	.125	1	25	22	1	2.7

● ROBERTO HERNANDEZ
Hernandez, Roberto Manuel (Rodriguez) b: 11/11/64, Santurce, P.R. BR/TR, 6'4", 220 lbs. Deb: 9/02/91

YEAR	TM/L	W	L	PCT	G	GS	CG	SH	SV	IP	H	HR	BB	SO	RAT	ERA	ERA+	OAV	OOB	BH	AVG	PB	PR	/A	PD	TPI
1991	Chi-A	1	0	1.000	9	3	0	0	0	15	18	1	7	6	15.0	7.80	51	.290	.362	0	—	0	-6	-6	-0	-0.6
1992	Chi-A	7	3	.700	43	0	0	0	12	71	45	4	20	68	8.7	1.65	232	.180	.252	0	—	0	18	17	-0	1.7
Total	2	8	3	.727	52	3	0	0	12	86	63	5	27	74	9.8	2.72	141	.202	.274	0	—	0	12	11	-1	1.1

● RUDY HERNANDEZ
Hernandez, Rudolph Albert (Fuentes) b: 12/10/31, Santiago, D.R. BR/TR, 6'3", 185 lbs. Deb: 7/03/60

YEAR	TM/L	W	L	PCT	G	GS	CG	SH	SV	IP	H	HR	BB	SO	RAT	ERA	ERA+	OAV	OOB	BH	AVG	PB	PR	/A	PD	TPI
1960	Was-A	4	1	.800	21	0	0	0	0	34^2	34	2	21	22	14.5	4.41	88	.262	.368	1	.167	-0	-2	-2	-0	-0.3
1961	Was-A	0	1	.000	7	0	0	0	0	9	8	0	3	4	11.0	3.00	134	.250	.314	0	—	0	1	1	0	0.1
Total	2	4	2	.667	28	0	0	0	0	43^2	42	2	24	26	13.8	4.12	95	.259	.358	1	.167	-0	-1	-1	-0	-0.2

● WALT HERRELL
Herrell, Walter William "Reds" b: 2/19/1889, Rockville, Md. d: 1/23/49, Front Royal, Va. Deb: 6/10/11

YEAR	TM/L	W	L	PCT	G	GS	CG	SH	SV	IP	H	HR	BB	SO	RAT	ERA	ERA+	OAV	OOB	BH	AVG	PB	PR	/A	PD	TPI
1911	Was-A	0	0	—	1	0	0	0	0	2	5	0	2	0	31.5	18.00	18	.556	.636	0	.000	-0	-3	-3	0	-0.3

● BOBBY HERRERA
Herrera, Procopio Rodriguez "Tito" (b: Procopio Rodriguez (Herrera)) b: 7/26/26, Nuevo Laredo, Mex BR/TR, 6', 184 lbs. Deb: 4/19/51

YEAR	TM/L	W	L	PCT	G	GS	CG	SH	SV	IP	H	HR	BB	SO	RAT	ERA	ERA+	OAV	OOB	BH	AVG	PB	PR	/A	PD	TPI
1951	StL-A	0	0	—	3	0	0	0	0	2^1	6	2	4	1	42.4	27.00	16	.462	.611	0	—	0	-6	-6	-0	-0.5

● TROY HERRIAGE
Herriage, William Troy "Dutch" b: 12/20/30, Tipton, Okla. BR/TR, 6'1", 170 lbs. Deb: 4/25/56

YEAR	TM/L	W	L	PCT	G	GS	CG	SH	SV	IP	H	HR	BB	SO	RAT	ERA	ERA+	OAV	OOB	BH	AVG	PB	PR	/A	PD	TPI
1956	KC-A	1	13	.071	31	16	1	0	0	103	135	16	64	59	17.9	6.64	65	.321	.418	3	.120	-1	-28	-26	-2	-2.8

● TOM HERRIN
Herrin, Thomas Edward b: 9/12/29, Shreveport, La. BR/TR, 6'3", 190 lbs. Deb: 4/13/54

YEAR	TM/L	W	L	PCT	G	GS	CG	SH	SV	IP	H	HR	BB	SO	RAT	ERA	ERA+	OAV	OOB	BH	AVG	PB	PR	/A	PD	TPI
1954	Bos-A	1	2	.333	14	1	0	0	0	28^1	34	3	22	8	17.8	7.31	56	.315	.431	1	.125	-1	-11	-10	1	-0.9

● ART HERRING
Herring, Arthur L "Red" or "Sandy" b: 3/10/07, Altus, Okla. BR/TR, 5'7", 168 lbs. Deb: 9/12/29

YEAR	TM/L	W	L	PCT	G	GS	CG	SH	SV	IP	H	HR	BB	SO	RAT	ERA	ERA+	OAV	OOB	BH	AVG	PB	PR	/A	PD	TPI
1929	Det-A	2	1	.667	4	4	2	0	0	32	38	0	19	15	16.3	4.78	90	.302	.397	3	.214	1	-2	-2	0	-0.1
1930	Det-A	3	3	.500	23	6	1	0	0	77^2	97	2	36	16	15.8	5.33	90	.315	.392	3	.130	-2	-6	-5	-0	-0.6
1931	Det-A	7	13	.350	35	16	9	0	1	165	186	8	67	64	14.2	4.31	106	.281	.355	11	.200	-1	1	5	2	0.6
1932	Det-A	1	2	.333	12	0	0	0	2	22^1	25	2	15	12	16.5	5.24	90	.284	.394	0	.000	-0	-2	-1	0	-0.1
1933	Det-A	1	2	.333	24	3	1	0	0	61	61	6	20	20	12.1	3.84	112	.264	.325	1	.077	-1	3	3	-1	0.2
1934	Bro-N	2	4	.333	14	4	2	0	0	49^1	63	2	29	15	16.8	6.20	63	.307	.393	2	.143	1	-12	-13	-0	-1.2
1939	Chi-A	0	0	—	7	0	0	0	0	14^1	13	2	5	8	11.9	5.65	84	.250	.328	0	.000	-0	-2	-1	0	-0.2
1944	Bro-N	3	4	.429	12	6	3	1	1	55^1	59	3	17	19	12.5	3.42	104	.277	.333	3	.200	0	1	1	0	0.2
1945	Bro-N	7	4	.636	22	15	7	2	2	124	103	11	43	34	10.8	3.48	108	.222	.292	4	.095	-2	4	4	1	0.2
1946	Bro-N	7	2	.778	35	2	0	0	5	86	91	2	29	34	12.7	3.35	101	.277	.338	4	.182	0	1	0	2	0.2
1947	Pit-N	1	3	.250	11	0	0	0	2	10^2	18	3	4	6	18.6	8.44	50	.360	.407	0	.000	-0	-5	-5	-0	-0.5
Total	11	34	38	.472	199	56	25	3	13	697^2	754	41	284	243	13.6	4.32	96	.276	.349	31	.149	-5	-18	-14	4	-1.3

● HERB HERRING
Herring, Herbert Lee b: 7/22/1891, Danville, Ark. d: 4/22/64, Tucson, Ariz. BR/TR, 5'11", 178 lbs. Deb: 9/04/12

YEAR	TM/L	W	L	PCT	G	GS	CG	SH	SV	IP	H	HR	BB	SO	RAT	ERA	ERA+	OAV	OOB	BH	AVG	PB	PR	/A	PD	TPI
1912	Was-A	0	0	—	1	0	0	0	0	1	1	0	1	0	18.0	0.00	—	.250	.400	0	—	0	0	0	-0	0.0

● LEFTY HERRING
Herring, Silas Clarke b: 3/4/1880, Philadelphia, Pa. d: 2/11/65, Massapequa, N.Y. BL/TL, 5'11", 160 lbs. Deb: 5/16/1899 ♦

YEAR	TM/L	W	L	PCT	G	GS	CG	SH	SV	IP	H	HR	BB	SO	RAT	ERA	ERA+	OAV	OOB	BH	AVG	PB	PR	/A	PD	TPI
1899	Was-N	0	0	—	2	0	0	0	0	2	0	0	2	0	9.0	0.00	—	.000	.260	1	1.000	1	1	1	0	0.2

● BILL HERRING
Herring, William Francis "Smoke" b: 10/31/1893, New York, N.Y. d: 9/10/62, Honesdale, Pa. BR/TR, 6'3", 185 lbs. Deb: 6/26/15

YEAR	TM/L	W	L	PCT	G	GS	CG	SH	SV	IP	H	HR	BB	SO	RAT	ERA	ERA+	OAV	OOB	BH	AVG	PB	PR	/A	PD	TPI
1915	Bro-F	0	0	—	3	0	0	0	0	3	5	1	2	3	24.0	15.00	20	.385	.500	0	—	0	-4	-4	-0	-0.4

● LEROY HERRMANN
Herrmann, Leroy George b: 2/27/06, Steward, Ill. d: 7/3/72, Livermore, Cal. BR/TR, 5'10", 185 lbs. Deb: 7/30/32

YEAR	TM/L	W	L	PCT	G	GS	CG	SH	SV	IP	H	HR	BB	SO	RAT	ERA	ERA+	OAV	OOB	BH	AVG	PB	PR	/A	PD	TPI
1932	Chi-N	2	1	.667	7	0	0	0	0	12^2	18	0	9	5	19.2	6.39	59	.346	.443	1	.500	0	-4	-4	-0	-0.3

YEAR TM/L	W	L	PCT	G	GS	CG	SH	SV	IP	H	HR	BB	SO	RAT	ERA	ERA+	OAV	OOB	BH	AVG	PB	PR	/A	PD	TPI
1933 Chi-N	0	1	.000	9	1	0	0	1	21	26	3	8	4	16.3	5.57	59	.299	.384	1	.167	-0	-5	-5	-1	-0.7
1935 Cin-N	3	5	.375	29	8	2	0	0	108	124	9	31	30	13.6	3.58	111	.297	.357	8	.267	1	5	5	-0	0.6
Total 3	5	7	.417	45	9	2	0	1	141^{2}	168	12	48	39	14.5	4.13	93	.302	.370	10	.263	1	-4	-4	-1	-0.4

● MARTY HERRMANN Herrmann, Martin John "Lefty" b: 1/10/1893, Oldenburg, Ind. d: 9/11/56, Cincinnati, Ohio BL/TL, 5'10", 150 lbs. Deb: 7/10/18 F

YEAR TM/L	W	L	PCT	G	GS	CG	SH	SV	IP	H	HR	BB	SO	RAT	ERA	ERA+	OAV	OOB	BH	AVG	PB	PR	/A	PD	TPI
1918 Bro-N	0	0	—	1	0	0	0	0	1	0	0	1	0	9.0	0.00	—	.000	.250	0	—	0	0	0	-0	0.0

● FRANK HERSHEY Hershey, Frank b: 12/13/1877, Gorham, N.Y. d: 12/15/49, Canadaigua, N.Y. TR, 175 lbs. Deb: 4/20/05

YEAR TM/L	W	L	PCT	G	GS	CG	SH	SV	IP	H	HR	BB	SO	RAT	ERA	ERA+	OAV	OOB	BH	AVG	PB	PR	/A	PD	TPI
1905 Bos-N	0	1	.000	1	1	0	0	0	4	5	0	2	1	15.8	6.75	46	.313	.389	0	.000	-0	-2	-2	-0	-0.2

● OREL HERSHISER Hershiser, Orel Leonard b: 9/16/58, Buffalo, N.Y. BR/TR, 6'3", 192 lbs. Deb: 9/01/83

YEAR TM/L	W	L	PCT	G	GS	CG	SH	SV	IP	H	HR	BB	SO	RAT	ERA	ERA+	OAV	OOB	BH	AVG	PB	PR	/A	PD	TPI
1983 LA-N	0	0	—	8	0	0	0	1	8	7	1	6	5	14.6	3.38	106	.233	.361	0	—	0	0	0	0	0.0
1984 LA-N	11	8	.579	45	20	8	**4**	2	189^{2}	160	9	50	150	10.2	2.66	133	.225	.279	10	.200	2	20	18	1	2.2
1985 *LA-N	19	3	**.864**	36	34	9	5	0	239^{2}	179	8	68	157	9.5	2.03	171	.206	.268	15	.197	3	42	39	2	5.0
1986 LA-N	14	14	.500	35	35	8	1	0	231^{1}	213	13	86	153	11.8	3.85	90	.243	.314	17	.239	4	-3	-10	1	-0.6
1987 LA-N★	16	16	.500	37	35	10	1	1	**264^{2}**	247	17	74	190	11.2	3.06	130	.247	.305	19	.211	4	30	27	1	**3.3**
1988 *LA-N★	**23**	8	.742	35	34	**15**	**8**	1	**267**	208	18	73	178	9.6	2.26	147	.213	.271	11	.129	-0	**35**	**32**	6	**4.3**
1989 LA-N☆	15	15	.500	35	33	8	4	0	**256^{2}**	226	9	77	178	10.7	2.31	148	.240	.299	14	.182	3	**34**	**31**	4	**4.4**
1990 LA-N	1	1	.500	4	4	0	0	0	25^{1}	26	1	4	16	11.0	4.26	86	.260	.295	0	.000	-1	-1	-2	-0	-0.3
1991 LA-N	7	2	.778	21	21	0	0	0	112	112	3	32	73	12.0	3.46	104	.259	.317	8	.258	3	3	2	1	0.6
1992 LA-N	10	15	.400	33	33	1	0	0	210^{2}	209	15	69	130	12.2	3.67	94	.257	.322	15	.221	4	-4	-5	3	0.2
Total 10	116	82	.586	289	249	59	23	5	1805	1587	94	539	1230	10.8	2.87	123	.235	.296	109	.196	21	154	132	19	19.1

● JOE HESKETH Hesketh, Joseph Thomas b: 2/15/59, Lackawanna, N.Y. BR/TL, 6'2", 170 lbs. Deb: 8/07/84

YEAR TM/L	W	L	PCT	G	GS	CG	SH	SV	IP	H	HR	BB	SO	RAT	ERA	ERA+	OAV	OOB	BH	AVG	PB	PR	/A	PD	TPI
1984 Mon-N	2	2	.500	11	5	1	1	1	45	38	2	15	32	10.6	1.80	190	.233	.298	1	.100	0	9	8	-0	0.9
1985 Mon-N	10	5	.667	25	25	2	1	0	155^{1}	125	10	45	113	9.8	2.49	136	.222	.280	4	.091	-1	19	16	-1	1.5
1986 Mon-N	6	5	.545	15	15	0	0	0	82^{2}	92	11	31	67	13.6	5.01	74	.283	.349	0	.000	-2	-12	-12	-1	-1.5
1987 Mon-N	0	0	—	18	0	0	0	1	28^{2}	23	2	15	31	12.6	3.14	134	.211	.317	0	.000	-0	3	3	-1	0.2
1988 Mon-N	4	3	.571	60	0	0	0	9	72^{2}	63	1	35	64	12.1	2.85	126	.242	.332	0	.000	0	5	6	1	0.8
1989 Mon-N	6	4	.600	43	0	0	0	3	48^{1}	54	5	26	44	14.9	5.77	61	.292	.379	1	.500	0	-12	-12	1	-1.1
1990 Mon-N	1	0	1.000	2	0	0	0	0	3	2	0	2	3	12.0	0.00	—	.200	.333	0	—	0	1	1	0	0.1
Atl-N	0	2	.000	31	0	0	0	5	31	30	5	12	21	12.5	5.81	69	.248	.321	0	.000	-0	-7	-6	-0	-0.7
Yr	1	2	.333	33	0	0	0	5	34	32	5	14	24	12.4	5.29	76	.244	.322	0	.000	-0	-6	-5	-0	-0.6
Bos-A	0	4	.000	12	2	0	0	0	25^{2}	37	2	11	26	16.8	3.51	116	.333	.393	0	—	0	1	2	-0	0.1
1991 Bos-A	12	4	.750	39	17	0	0	0	153^{1}	142	19	53	104	11.4	3.29	131	.250	.314	0	—	0	14	17	0	1.7
1992 Bos-A	8	9	.471	30	25	1	0	1	148^{2}	162	15	58	104	13.4	4.36	95	.276	.343	0	—	0	-7	-3	0	-0.3
Total 9	49	38	.563	286	89	4	2	20	794^{1}	768	72	303	609	12.2	3.63	106	.256	.325	6	.070	-2	14	19	-1	1.7

● OTTO HESS Hess, Otto C. b: 10/10/1878, Berne, Switzerland d: 2/25/26, Tucson, Ariz. BL/TL, 6'1", 170 lbs. Deb: 8/03/02 ♦

YEAR TM/L	W	L	PCT	G	GS	CG	SH	SV	IP	H	HR	BB	SO	RAT	ERA	ERA+	OAV	OOB	BH	AVG	PB	PR	/A	PD	TPI
1902 Cle-A	2	4	.333	7	4	4	0	0	43^{2}	67	0	23	13	18.8	5.98	58	.351	.424	1	.071	-1	-12	-12	1	-1.1
1904 Cle-A	8	7	.533	21	16	15	4	0	151^{1}	134	2	31	64	10.1	1.67	152	.238	.284	12	.120	-3	16	15	-0	1.3
1905 Cle-A	10	15	.400	26	25	22	4	0	213^{2}	179	1	72	109	10.9	3.16	83	.229	.300	44	.254	5	-12	-12	1	-0.8
1906 Cle-A	20	17	.541	43	36	33	7	**3**	333^{2}	274	4	85	167	10.2	1.83	143	.227	.289	31	.201	1	32	**29**	-2	3.2
1907 Cle-A	6	6	.500	17	14	7	0	1	93^{1}	84	1	37	36	13.1	2.89	87	.242	.341	4	.133	-1	-4	-4	-1	-0.5
1908 Cle-A	0	0	—	4	0	0	0	0	7	11	0	1	2	15.4	5.14	47	.407	.429	0	.000	-1	-2	-2	0	-0.3
1912 Bos-N	12	17	.414	33	31	21	0	0	254	270	3	90	80	13.3	3.76	95	.283	.354	23	.245	3	-10	-5	-4	-0.5
1913 Bos-N	7	17	.292	29	27	19	2	0	218^{1}	231	12	70	80	12.7	3.83	86	.279	.340	26	.313	9	-15	-13	1	-0.4
1914 Bos-N	5	6	.455	14	11	7	1	1	89	89	2	33	24	12.8	3.03	91	.271	.347	11	.234	1	-2	-3	2	0.1
1915 Bos-N	0	1	.000	4	1	1	0	0	14	16	0	6	5	15.4	3.86	67	.286	.375	2	.400	1	-2	-2	-0	-0.1
Total 10	70	90	.438	198	165	129	18	5	1418	1355	25	448	580	11.9	2.98	98	.257	.324	154	.216	14	-11	-11	-2	0.9

● GEORGE HESSELBACHER Hesselbacher, George Edward b: 1/18/1895, Philadelphia, Pa. d: 2/18/80, Rydal, Pa. BR/TR, 6'2", 175 lbs. Deb: 6/29/16

YEAR TM/L	W	L	PCT	G	GS	CG	SH	SV	IP	H	HR	BB	SO	RAT	ERA	ERA+	OAV	OOB	BH	AVG	PB	PR	/A	PD	TPI
1916 Phi-A	0	4	.000	6	4	2	0	0	26	37	3	22	6	20.4	7.27	39	.349	.461	1	.125	-0	-13	-13	1	-1.2

● LARRY HESTERFER Hesterfer, Lawrence b: 6/9/1878, Newark, N.J. d: 9/22/43, Cedar Grove, N.J. BR/TL, 5'8", 145 lbs. Deb: 9/05/01

YEAR TM/L	W	L	PCT	G	GS	CG	SH	SV	IP	H	HR	BB	SO	RAT	ERA	ERA+	OAV	OOB	BH	AVG	PB	PR	/A	PD	TPI
1901 NY-N	0	1	.000	1	1	1	0	0	6	15	0	3	2	27.0	7.50	44	.466	.511	0	.000	0	-3	-3	-0	-0.2

● JOHNNY HETKI Hetki, John Edward b: 5/12/22, Leavenworth, Kan. BR/TR, 6'1", 205 lbs. Deb: 9/14/45

YEAR TM/L	W	L	PCT	G	GS	CG	SH	SV	IP	H	HR	BB	SO	RAT	ERA	ERA+	OAV	OOB	BH	AVG	PB	PR	/A	PD	TPI
1945 Cin-N	1	2	.333	5	2	2	0	0	32^{2}	28	1	11	9	10.7	3.58	105	.235	.300	1	.091	-1	1	1	1	0.0
1946 Cin-N	6	6	.500	32	11	4	0	1	126^{1}	121	3	31	41	10.9	2.99	112	.253	.300	11	.333	3	6	5	-1	0.8
1947 Cin-N	3	4	.429	37	5	2	0	0	96	110	7	48	33	14.9	5.81	71	.287	.368	6	.222	1	-19	-18	0	-1.7
1948 Cin-N	0	1	.000	3	0	0	0	0	6^{2}	8	0	3	3	14.9	9.45	41	.286	.355	0	.000	0	-4	-4	-0	-0.4
1950 Cin-N	1	2	.333	22	1	0	0	0	53	53	9	27	21	14.1	5.09	83	.265	.361	2	.222	0	-6	-5	-0	-0.5
1952 StL-A	0	1	.000	3	1	0	0	0	9^{1}	15	2	2	4	16.4	3.86	101	.357	.386	0	.000	0	-0	0	0	0.0
1953 Pit-N	3	6	.333	54	2	0	0	3	118^{1}	120	9	33	37	11.7	3.95	113	.266	.318	5	.208	1	4	7	0	0.8
1954 Pit-N	4	4	.500	58	1	0	0	9	83	102	11	30	27	14.3	4.99	84	.297	.353	2	.222	-0	-8	-7	-1	-0.8
Total 8	18	26	.409	214	23	8	0	13	525^{1}	557	42	185	175	12.8	4.39	91	.272	.335	27	.235	5	-26	-23	-2	-1.8

● ERIC HETZEL Hetzel, Eric Paul b: 9/25/63, Crowley, La. BR/TR, 6'3", 175 lbs. Deb: 7/01/89

YEAR TM/L	W	L	PCT	G	GS	CG	SH	SV	IP	H	HR	BB	SO	RAT	ERA	ERA+	OAV	OOB	BH	AVG	PB	PR	/A	PD	TPI
1989 Bos-A	2	3	.400	12	11	0	0	0	50^{1}	61	7	28	33	16.3	6.26	66	.296	.386	0	—	0	-13	-12	-1	-1.3
1990 Bos-A	1	4	.200	9	8	0	0	0	35	39	3	21	20	15.7	5.91	69	.281	.379	0	—	0	-8	-7	-0	-0.8
Total 2	3	7	.300	21	19	0	0	0	85^{1}	100	10	49	53	16.0	6.12	67	.290	.383	0	—	0	-21	-19	-2	-2.1

● ED HEUSSER Heusser, Edward Burlton "The Wild Elk Of The Wasatch" b: 5/7/09, Mill Creek, Utah d: 3/1/56, Aurora, Cal. BB/TR, 6'0.5", 187 lbs. Deb: 4/25/35

YEAR TM/L	W	L	PCT	G	GS	CG	SH	SV	IP	H	HR	BB	SO	RAT	ERA	ERA+	OAV	OOB	BH	AVG	PB	PR	/A	PD	TPI
1935 StL-N	5	5	.500	33	11	2	0	2	123^{1}	125	5	27	39	11.2	2.92	140	.263	.305	4	.118	-1	15	16	-1	1.4
1936 StL-N	7	3	.700	42	3	0	0	3	104^{1}	130	6	38	26	14.8	5.43	73	.310	.373	7	.269	3	-16	-17	-0	-1.4
1938 Phi-N	0	0	—	1	0	0	0	0	1	2	1	1	0	27.0	27.00	14	.400	.500	0	—	0	-3	-3	-0	-0.2
1940 Phi-A	6	13	.316	41	6	2	0	5	110	144	11	42	39	15.4	4.99	89	.308	.368	5	.167	1	-7	-7	1	-0.5
1943 Cin-N	4	3	.571	26	10	2	1	0	91	97	4	23	28	11.9	3.46	96	.275	.319	5	.185	-1	-1	-1	-1	-0.3
1944 Cin-N	13	11	.542	30	23	17	4	2	192^{2}	165	9	42	42	9.7	**2.38**	**146**	.231	.275	15	.217	1	26	24	-1	2.5
1945 Cin-N	11	16	.407	31	30	18	4	1	223	248	10	60	56	12.6	3.71	101	.280	.328	19	.247	4	2	1	0	0.5
1946 Cin-N	7	14	.333	29	21	9	1	2	167^{2}	167	11	39	47	11.1	3.22	104	.260	.304	11	.208	1	4	2	-2	0.2
1948 Phi-N	3	2	.600	33	0	0	0	3	74	89	9	28	22	14.2	4.99	79	.299	.359	3	.158	-1	-8	-9	0	-0.9
Total 9	56	67	.455	266	104	50	10	18	1087	1167	66	300	299	12.3	3.69	101	.274	.324	69	.206	8	11	6	-5	1.3

● JOE HEVING Heving, Joseph William b: 9/2/1900, Covington, Ky. d: 4/11/70, Covington, Ky. BR/TR, 6'1", 185 lbs. Deb: 4/29/30 F

YEAR TM/L	W	L	PCT	G	GS	CG	SH	SV	IP	H	HR	BB	SO	RAT	ERA	ERA+	OAV	OOB	BH	AVG	PB	PR	/A	PD	TPI
1930 NY-N	7	5	.583	41	2	0	0	6	89^{2}	109	7	27	37	13.8	5.22	91	.309	.360	5	.227	-0	-2	-5	4	-0.1
1931 NY-N	1	6	.143	22	0	0	0	3	42^{1}	48	4	11	26	13.0	4.89	76	.277	.328	1	.125	-0	-5	-6	1	-0.5
1933 Chi-A	7	5	.583	40	6	3	1	6	118	113	6	27	47	10.8	2.67	159	.249	.295	8	.211	0	21	21	0	2.1
1934 Chi-A	1	7	.125	33	2	0	0	4	88	133	12	48	40	18.8	7.26	65	.343	.419	5	.185	1	-27	-25	1	-2.1
1937 Cle-A	8	4	.667	40	0	0	0	5	72^{2}	92	6	30	35	15.4	4.83	95	.311	.378	5	.263	0	-2	-2	1	0.0
1938 Cle-A	1	1	.500	3	0	0	0	0	6	10	0	5	0	22.5	9.00	52	.370	.469	0	.000	-0	-3	-3	-0	-0.3
Bos-A	8	1	.889	16	11	7	1	2	82	94	5	22	34	12.8	3.73	132	.283	.330	4	.133	-2	10	11	2	1.1
Yr	9	2	.818	19	11	7	1	2	88	104	5	27	34	13.5	4.09	120	.290	.341	4	.129	-2	7	8	2	0.8
1939 Bos-A	11	3	.786	46	5	1	0	7	107	124	8	34	43	13.5	3.70	128	.295	.350	6	.188	-1	**11**	**12**	0	1.0

YEAR TM/L	W	L	PCT	G	GS	CG	SH	SV	IP	H	HR	BB	SO	RAT	ERA	ERA+	OAV	OOB	BH	AVG	PB	PR	/A	PD	TPI
1940 Bos-A	12	7	.632	39	7	4	0	3	119	129	7	42	55	13.2	4.01	112	.272	.335	8	.200	0	5	6	0	0.6
1941 Cle-A	5	2	.714	27	3	2	1	5	70^{2}	63	2	31	18	12.1	2.29	172	.240	.323	0	.000	-1	15	13	2	1.4
1942 Cle-A	5	3	.625	27	2	0	0	3	46^{1}	52	4	25	13	15.3	4.86	71	.278	.369	0	.000	-1	-6	-7	0	-0.8
1943 Cle-A	1	1	.500	30	1	0	0	9	72	58	1	34	34	11.8	2.75	113	.230	.326	1	.071	-0	4	3	2	0.4
1944 Cle-A	8	3	.727	**63**	1	0	0	10	119^{2}	106	2	41	46	11.2	1.96	169	.239	.307	4	.182	-1	**20**	18	1	1.9
1945 Bos-N	1	0	1.000	3	0	0	0	0	5^{1}	5	0	3	1	15.2	3.38	114	.294	.429	0	.000	-0	0	0	1	0.1
Total 13	76	48	.613	430	40	17	3	63	1038^{2}	1136	64	380	429	13.3	3.90	108	.279	.344	47	.170	-4	40	36	14	4.8
● **JAKE HEWITT** Hewitt, Charles Jacob b: 6/6/1870, Maidsville, W.Va. d: 5/18/59, Morgantown, W.Va. BL/TL, 5'7", 150 lbs. Deb: 8/06/1895																									
1895 Pit-N	1	0	1.000	4	2	1	0	2	13	13	0	2	4	11.1	4.15	109	.256	.298	1	.167	-1	1	1	-0	0.0
● **GREG HEYDEMAN** Heydeman, Gregory George b: 1/2/52, Carmel, Cal. BR/TR, 6', 180 lbs. Deb: 9/02/73																									
1973 LA-N	0	0	—	1	0	0	0	0	2	2	0	1	1	18.0	4.50	76	.222	.364	0	—	0	-0	-0	-0	0.0
● **JOHN HEYNER** Heyner, John b: Hyde Park, Ill. Deb: 8/19/1890																									
1890 Pit-N	0	0	—	1	0	0	0	0	4	7	2	5	1	27.0	13.50	24	.371	.503	0	.000	-0	-4	-5	0	-0.4
● **GREG HIBBARD** Hibbard, James Gregory b: 9/13/64, New Orleans, La. BL/TL, 6', 180 lbs. Deb: 5/31/89																									
1989 Chi-A	6	7	.462	23	23	2	0	0	137^{1}	142	5	41	55	12.1	3.21	118	.268	.323	0	—	0	10	9	1	1.1
1990 Chi-A	14	9	.609	33	33	3	1	0	211	202	11	55	92	11.2	3.16	121	.255	.308	0	—	0	18	16	-1	1.6
1991 Chi-A	11	11	.500	32	29	5	0	0	194	196	23	57	71	11.8	4.31	92	.266	.320	0	—	0	-5	-7	-1	-0.8
1992 Chi-A	10	7	.588	31	28	0	0	1	176	187	17	57	69	12.8	4.40	87	.277	.340	0	—	0	-9	-11	2	-0.9
Total 4	41	34	.547	119	113	10	1	1	718^{1}	727	56	210	287	12.0	3.78	102	.266	.322	0	—	0	14	6	2	1.0
● **JOHN HIBBARD** Hibbard, John Denison b: 12/2/1864, Chicago, Ill. d: 11/17/37, Hollywood, Cal. TL, Deb: 7/31/1884																									
1884 Chi-N	1	1	.500	2	2	2	1	0	17	18	1	9	4	14.3	2.65	118	.300	.391	0	.000	-1	1	1	-0	0.0
● **BRYAN HICKERSON** Hickerson, Bryan David b: 10/13/63, Bemidji, Minn. BL/TL, 6'2", 195 lbs. Deb: 7/25/91																									
1991 SF-N	2	2	.500	17	6	0	0	0	50	53	3	17	43	12.6	3.60	99	.275	.333	0	.000	-1	0	-0	-1	-0.3
1992 SF-N	5	3	.625	61	1	0	0	0	87^{1}	74	7	21	68	9.9	3.09	108	.236	.286	0	.000	-0	4	3	-2	0.0
Total 2	7	5	.583	78	7	0	0	0	137^{1}	127	10	38	111	10.9	3.28	105	.250	.304	0	.000	-2	4	2	-3	-0.3
● **JIM HICKEY** Hickey, James Robert "Sid" b: 10/22/20, N.Abington, Mass. BR/TR, 6'1", 204 lbs. Deb: 4/25/42																									
1942 Bos-N	0	1	.000	1	1	0	0	0	1^{1}	4	1	2	0	40.5	20.25	16	.500	.600	0	.000	-0	-3	-3	-0	-0.2
1944 Bos-N	0	0	—	8	0	0	0	0	9^{1}	15	0	5	3	20.3	4.82	79	.366	.447	0	.000	-0	-1	-1	0	-0.1
Total 2	0	1	.000	9	1	0	0	0	10^{2}	19	1	7	3	22.8	6.75	56	.388	.474	0	.000	-0	-4	-4	0	-0.3
● **JOHN HICKEY** Hickey, John William b: 11/3/1881, Minneapolis, Minn. d: 12/28/41, Seattle, Wash. BR/TL, 5'10", 170 lbs. Deb: 4/16/04																									
1904 Cle-A	0	1	.000	2	2	1	0	0	12^{1}	14	0	11	5	18.2	7.30	35	.286	.417	0	.000	-1	-6	-7	0	-0.6
● **KEVIN HICKEY** Hickey, Kevin John b: 2/25/57, Chicago, Ill. BL/TL, 6'1", 200 lbs. Deb: 4/14/81																									
1981 Chi-A	0	2	.000	41	0	0	0	3	44^{1}	38	3	18	17	11.6	3.65	98	.232	.311	0	—	0	0	-0	1	0.2
1982 Chi-A	4	4	.500	60	0	0	0	6	78	73	4	30	38	12.1	3.00	134	.256	.331	0	—	0	9	9	2	1.1
1983 Chi-A	1	2	.333	23	0	0	0	5	20^{2}	23	5	11	8	14.8	5.23	80	.264	.347	0	—	0	-3	-2	-0	-0.5
1989 Bal-A	2	3	.400	51	0	0	0	2	49^{1}	38	3	23	28	11.3	2.92	130	.220	.315	0	—	0	5	5	-0	0.5
1990 Bal-A	1	3	.250	37	0	0	0	1	26^{1}	26	3	13	17	13.3	5.13	74	.265	.351	0	—	0	-4	-4	0	-0.3
1991 Bal-A	1	0	1.000	19	0	0	0	0	14	15	3	6	10	13.5	9.00	44	.278	.350	0	—	0	-8	-8	-0	-0.7
Total 6	9	14	.391	231	0	0	0	17	232^{2}	213	21	101	118	12.3	3.91	99	.247	.329	0	—	0	1	-1	2	0.3
● **CHARLIE HICKMAN** Hickman, Charles Taylor "Cheerful Charlie" or "Piano Legs" b: 3/4/1876, Taylortown, Dunkard Township, Pa. d: 4/19/34, Morgantown, W.Va. BR/TR, 5'11.5", 215 lbs. Deb: 9/08/1897 ♦																									
1897 *Bos-N	0	0	—	2	0	0	0	1	7^{2}	10	0	5	0	17.6	5.87	76	.312	.405	2	.667	2	-1	-1	0	0.0
1898 Bos-N	1	2	.333	6	3	3	1	2	33	22	0	13	9	9.5	2.18	169	.189	.270	15	.259	0	5	6	-1	0.5
1899 Bos-N	6	0	1.000	11	9	5	2	1	66^{1}	52	3	40	14	13.6	4.48	93	.216	.346	25	.397	6	-5	-2	-1	0.2
1901 NY-N	3	5	.375	9	9	6	0	0	65	76	1	26	11	14.5	4.57	72	.290	.360	113	.278	2	-9	-9	1	-0.6
1902 Cle-A	0	1	.000	1	1	1	0	0	8	11	0	5	1	19.1	7.88	44	.327	.428	161	.378	1	-4	-4	-0	-0.3
1907 Was-A	0	0	—	1	0	0	0	0	5	4	0	5	2	16.2	3.60	67	.221	.390	55	.278	0	-1	-1	1	0.0
Total 6	10	8	.556	30	22	15	3	4	185	175	4	94	37	13.7	4.28	86	.249	.347	1176	.295	11	-14	-12	-1	-0.2
● **ERNIE HICKMAN** Hickman, Ernest P. b: 1856, E.St.Louis, Ill. d: 11/19/1891, E.St.Louis, Ill Deb: 6/07/1884																									
1884 KC-U	4	13	.235	17	17	15	0	0	137^{1}	172	5	36	68	13.6	4.52	61	.287	.327	12	.167	-3	-23	-27	-1	-2.5
● **JIM HICKMAN** Hickman, James Lucius b: 5/10/37, Henning, Tenn. BR/TR, 6'4", 205 lbs. Deb: 4/14/62 ♦																									
1967 LA-N	0	0	—	1	0	0	0	0	2	2	1	0	0	9.0	4.50	69	.286	.286	16	.163	0	-0	-0	-0	0.0
● **JESSE HICKMAN** Hickman, Jesse Owens b: 2/18/39, Lecompte, La. BR/TR, 6'2", 186 lbs. Deb: 6/05/65																									
1965 KC-A	0	1	.000	12	0	0	0	0	15^{1}	9	3	8	16	10.0	5.87	59	.184	.298	0	—	0	-4	-4	-0	-0.4
1966 KC-A	0	0	—	1	0	0	0	0	1	0	0	1	0	9.0	0.00	—	.000	.333	0	—	0	0	0	-0	0.0
Total 2	0	1	.000	13	0	0	0	0	16^{1}	9	3	9	16	9.9	5.51	63	.176	.300	0	—	0	-4	-4	-0	-0.4
● **KIRBY HIGBE** Higbe, Walter Kirby b: 4/8/15, Columbia, S.C. d: 5/6/85, Columbia, S.C. BR/TR, 5'11", 190 lbs. Deb: 10/03/37																									
1937 Chi-N	1	0	1.000	1	0	0	0	0	5	4	1	1	2	9.0	5.40	74	.182	.217	0	.000	-0	-1	-1	-0	-0.1
1938 Chi-N	0	0	—	2	2	0	0	0	10	10	1	6	4	14.4	5.40	71	.263	.364	0	.000	-0	-2	-2	1	-0.2
1939 Chi-N	2	1	.667	9	2	0	0	0	22^{2}	12	0	22	16	13.5	3.18	124	.158	.347	2	.286	1	2	2	-0	0.2
Phi-N	10	14	.417	34	26	14	1	2	187^{1}	208	10	101	79	15.3	4.85	83	.283	.378	11	.167	-2	-19	-18	-4	-2.3
Yr	12	15	.444	43	28	14	1	2	210	220	10	123	95	15.1	4.67	86	.272	.374	13	.178	-2	-18	-16	-4	-2.1
1940 Phi-N☆	14	19	.424	41	36	20	1	1	283	242	12	121	**137**	11.6	3.72	105	.232	.313	17	.165	-2	4	6	-1	0.4
1941 *Bro-N	**22**	9	.710	**48**	39	19	2	3	298	244	17	132	121	11.5	3.14	117	.220	.306	21	.188	1	16	17	-5	1.4
1942 Bro-N	16	11	.593	38	32	13	2	0	221^{2}	180	17	106	115	11.7	3.25	100	.223	.315	8	.104	-4	2	0	-1	-0.6
1943 Bro-N	13	10	.565	35	27	8	1	0	185	189	4	95	108	14.1	3.70	91	.264	.354	9	.138	-2	-6	-7	-1	-1.0
1946 Bro-N★	17	8	.680	42	29	11	3	1	210^{2}	178	6	107	134	12.2	3.03	111	.229	.323	10	.130	-4	9	8	1	0.5
1947 Bro-N	2	0	1.000	4	3	0	0	0	15^{2}	18	0	12	10	17.8	5.17	80	.295	.419	1	.200	0	-2	-2	0	-0.1
Pit-N	11	17	.393	46	30	10	1	5	225	204	22	110	99	12.7	3.72	113	.240	.329	10	.139	-2	8	13	-4	0.7
Yr	13	17	.433	50	33	10	1	5	240^{2}	222	22	122	109	13.0	3.81	111	.243	.334	11	.143	-1	7	11	-4	0.6
1948 Pit-N	8	7	.533	56	8	3	0	10	158	140	11	83	86	12.9	3.36	121	.240	.337	10	.208	1	10	12	-1	1.2
1949 Pit-N	0	2	.000	7	1	0	0	0	15^{1}	25	2	12	5	21.7	13.50	31	.379	.474	0	.000	-0	-16	-16	0	-1.4
NY-N	2	0	1.000	37	2	0	0	2	80^{1}	72	12	41	38	12.8	3.47	115	.242	.335	1	.067	-0	5	5	-1	0.3
Yr	2	2	.500	44	3	0	0	2	95^{2}	97	14	53	43	14.2	5.08	79	.266	.361	1	.056	-1	-11	-11	-1	-1.1
1950 NY-N	0	3	.000	18	1	0	0	0	34^{2}	37	2	30	17	17.4	4.93	83	.285	.419	1	.250	0	-3	-3	1	-0.2
Total 12	118	101	.539	418	238	98	11	24	1952^{1}	1763	117	979	971	12.8	3.69	102	.241	.333	101	.153	-14	7	14	-16	-1.2
● **IRV HIGGINBOTHAM** Higginbotham, Irving Clinton b: 4/26/1882, Homer, Neb. d: 6/12/59, Seattle, Wash. BR/TR, 6'1", 196 lbs. Deb: 8/11/06																									
1906 StL-N	1	4	.200	7	6	4	0	0	47^{1}	50	1	11	14	11.8	3.23	81	.266	.310	4	.222	0	-3	-3	1	-0.2
1908 StL-N	3	8	.273	19	11	7	1	0	107	113	0	33	38	12.5	3.20	74	.270	.328	5	.132	-2	-10	-10	-1	-1.4
1909 StL-N	1	0	1.000	3	1	1	0	0	11^{1}	5	0	2	2	5.6	1.59	159	.143	.189	0	.000	-0	1	1	-1	0.0
Chi-N	5	2	.714	19	6	4	0	1	78	64	0	20	32	10.0	2.19	116	.213	.269	6	.231	1	4	3	-1	0.2

YEAR TM/L	W	L	PCT	G	GS	CG	SH	SV	IP	H	HR	BB	SO	RAT	ERA	ERA+	OAV	OOB	BH	AVG	PB	PR	/A	PD	TPI
Yr	6	2	.750	22	7	5	0	1	89^1	69	0	22	34	9.5	2.12	120	.205	.260	6	.207	0	5	4	-2	0.2
Total 3	10	14	.417	48	24	16	1	1	243^2	232	1	66	86	11.3	2.81	88	.246	.300	15	.176	-1	-8	-9	-2	-1.4

● **DENNIS HIGGINS** Higgins, Dennis Dean b: 8/4/39, Jefferson City, Mo. BR/TR, 6'4", 190 lbs. Deb: 4/12/66

YEAR TM/L	W	L	PCT	G	GS	CG	SH	SV	IP	H	HR	BB	SO	RAT	ERA	ERA+	OAV	OOB	BH	AVG	PB	PR	/A	PD	TPI
1966 Chi-A	1	0	1.000	42	1	0	0	5	93	66	9	33	86	10.1	2.52	126	.202	.286	3	.176	0	9	7	1	0.8
1967 Chi-A	1	2	.333	9	0	0	0	0	12^1	13	0	10	8	19.0	5.84	53	.271	.426	0	.000	-0	-4	-4	0	-0.4
1968 Was-A	4	4	.500	59	0	0	0	13	99^2	81	8	46	66	11.7	3.25	90	.226	.319	2	.133	-0	-3	-4	-1	-0.6
1969 Was-A	10	9	.526	55	0	0	0	16	85^1	79	7	56	71	14.6	3.48	100	.252	.371	1	.091	-1	1	-0	-1	-0.2
1970 Cle-A	4	6	.400	58	0	0	0	11	90^1	82	8	54	82	13.7	3.99	99	.248	.358	3	.250	1	-3	-0	1	0.1
1971 StL-N	1	0	1.000	3	0	0	0	0	7	6	0	2	6	10.3	3.86	93	.240	.296	0	.000	-0	-0	-0	0	0.0
1972 StL-N	1	2	.333	15	1	0	0	1	22^2	19	0	22	20	16.3	3.97	86	.226	.387	0	.000	-0	-1	-1	-0	-0.2
Total 7	22	23	.489	241	2	0	0	46	410^1	346	32	223	339	12.8	3.42	98	.233	.340	9	.155	0	-0	-3	-1	-0.5

● **EDDIE HIGGINS** Higgins, Thomas Edward "Doc" or "Irish" b: 3/18/1888, Nevada, Ill. d: 2/14/59, Elgin, Ill. BR/TR, 6'0.5", 174 lbs. Deb: 5/14/09

YEAR TM/L	W	L	PCT	G	GS	CG	SH	SV	IP	H	HR	BB	SO	RAT	ERA	ERA+	OAV	OOB	BH	AVG	PB	PR	/A	PD	TPI
1909 StL-N	3	3	.500	16	5	5	0	0	66	68	4	17	15	11.7	4.50	56	.273	.322	4	.190	-0	-14	-14	0	-1.5
1910 StL-N	0	1	.000	2	0	0	0	0	10^1	15	0	7	1	19.2	4.35	68	.349	.440	2	.400	1	-2	-2	1	0.0
Total 2	3	4	.429	18	5	5	0	0	76^1	83	4	24	16	12.7	4.48	58	.284	.341	6	.231	1	-15	-16	1	-1.5

● **ED HIGH** High, Edward T. "Lefty" b: 12/26/1876, Baltimore, Md. d: 2/10/26, Baltimore, Md. TL, Deb: 7/04/01

YEAR TM/L	W	L	PCT	G	GS	CG	SH	SV	IP	H	HR	BB	SO	RAT	ERA	ERA+	OAV	OOB	BH	AVG	PB	PR	/A	PD	TPI
1901 Det-A	1	0	1.000	4	1	1	0	0	18	21	0	6	4	14.0	3.50	110	.288	.350	0	.000	-1	0	1	-0	0.0

● **TEDDY HIGUERA** Higuera, Teodoro Valenzuela (Valenzuela) b: 11/9/58, Los Mochis, Mexico BB/TL, 5'10", 178 lbs. Deb: 4/23/85

YEAR TM/L	W	L	PCT	G	GS	CG	SH	SV	IP	H	HR	BB	SO	RAT	ERA	ERA+	OAV	OOB	BH	AVG	PB	PR	/A	PD	TPI
1985 Mil-A	15	8	.652	32	30	7	2	0	212^1	186	22	63	127	10.7	3.90	107	.235	.293	0	—	0	6	6	-3	0.4
1986 Mil-A★	20	11	.645	34	34	15	4	0	248^1	226	26	74	207	11.0	2.79	155	.241	.299	0	—	0	38	42	-1	4.2
1987 Mil-A	18	10	.643	35	35	14	3	0	261^2	236	24	87	240	11.2	3.85	119	.241	.304	0	—	0	18	21	-2	1.7
1988 Mil-A	16	9	.640	31	31	8	1	0	227^1	168	15	59	192	**9.2**	2.45	162	.207	**.265**	0	—	0	**38**	38	1	4.3
1989 Mil-A	9	6	.600	22	22	2	1	0	135^1	125	9	48	91	11.8	3.46	111	.248	.318	0	—	0	6	6	-2	0.4
1990 Mil-A	11	10	.524	27	27	4	1	0	170	167	16	50	129	11.6	3.76	103	.256	.312	0	—	0	3	2	-1	0.1
1991 Mil-A	3	2	.600	7	6	0	0	0	36^1	37	2	10	33	11.9	4.46	89	.262	.316	0	—	0	-1	-2	-0	-0.2
Total 7	92	56	.622	188	185	50	12	0	1291^1	1145	114	391	1019	10.9	3.37	123	.238	.298	0	—	0	107	113	-8	10.9

● **WHITEY HILCHER** Hilcher, Walter Frank b: 2/28/09, Chicago, Ill. d: 11/21/62, Minneapolis, Minn. BR/TR, 6', 174 lbs. Deb: 9/17/31

YEAR TM/L	W	L	PCT	G	GS	CG	SH	SV	IP	H	HR	BB	SO	RAT	ERA	ERA+	OAV	OOB	BH	AVG	PB	PR	/A	PD	TPI
1931 Cin-N	0	1	.000	2	1	0	0	0	12	16	0	4	5	15.8	3.00	125	.320	.382	0	.000	-1	1	1	-0	0.0
1932 Cin-N	0	3	.000	11	2	0	0	0	18^2	24	3	10	4	16.4	7.71	50	.316	.395	1	.333	0	-8	-8	0	-0.7
1935 Cin-N	2	0	1.000	4	2	1	1	0	19^1	19	0	5	9	11.2	2.79	142	.264	.312	1	.167	-0	3	3	1	0.3
1936 Cin-N	1	2	.333	14	1	0	0	0	35	44	3	14	10	15.2	6.17	62	.299	.364	0	.000	-1	-8	-9	-1	-1.0
Total 4	3	6	.333	31	6	1	1	0	85	103	6	33	28	14.6	5.29	73	.299	.363	2	.095	-1	-13	-14	-0	-1.4

● **ORAL HILDEBRAND** Hildebrand, Oral Clyde b: 4/7/07, Indianapolis, Ind. d: 9/8/77, Southport, Ind. BR/TR, 6'3", 175 lbs. Deb: 9/08/31

YEAR TM/L	W	L	PCT	G	GS	CG	SH	SV	IP	H	HR	BB	SO	RAT	ERA	ERA+	OAV	OOB	BH	AVG	PB	PR	/A	PD	TPI
1931 Cle-A	2	1	.667	5	2	2	0	0	26^2	25	0	13	6	13.8	4.39	105	.243	.345	2	.182	-1	-0	1	-0	0.0
1932 Cle-A	8	6	.571	27	15	7	0	0	129^1	124	7	62	49	12.9	3.69	129	.249	.333	7	.146	-3	11	15	-2	0.9
1933 Cle-A☆	16	11	.593	36	31	15	**6**	0	220^1	205	8	88	90	12.0	3.76	118	.245	.318	16	.190	-1	13	17	-0	1.5
1934 Cle-A	11	9	.550	33	28	10	1	1	198	225	14	99	72	14.9	4.50	101	.282	.364	13	.171	-1	-0	1	1	0.0
1935 Cle-A	9	8	.529	34	20	8	0	5	171^1	171	12	63	49	12.4	3.94	114	.263	.331	9	.164	-2	10	11	-0	0.8
1936 Cle-A	10	11	.476	36	21	9	0	4	174^2	197	10	83	65	14.6	4.90	103	.283	.362	12	.190	0	3	3	-1	0.1
1937 StL-A	8	17	.320	30	27	12	1	1	201^1	228	18	87	75	14.2	5.14	94	.284	.356	14	.200	-1	-12	-7	-1	-0.8
1938 StL-A	8	10	.444	23	23	10	0	0	163	194	18	73	66	14.9	5.69	87	.297	.370	15	.254	1	-16	-13	-3	-1.3
1939 *NY-A	10	4	.714	21	15	7	1	2	126^2	102	11	41	50	10.2	3.06	143	.219	.284	8	.182	-1	22	18	-1	1.6
1940 NY-A	1	1	.500	13	0	0	0	0	19^1	19	1	14	5	15.8	1.86	217	.268	.395	0	.000	-0	5	5	-0	0.4
Total 10	83	78	.516	258	182	80	9	13	1430^2	1490	99	623	527	13.4	4.35	107	.267	.343	96	.187	-9	36	50	-8	3.2

● **TOM HILGENDORF** Hilgendorf, Thomas Eugene b: 3/10/42, Clinton, Iowa BB/TL, 6'1", 190 lbs. Deb: 8/15/69

YEAR TM/L	W	L	PCT	G	GS	CG	SH	SV	IP	H	HR	BB	SO	RAT	ERA	ERA+	OAV	OOB	BH	AVG	PB	PR	/A	PD	TPI
1969 StL-N	0	0	—	6	0	0	0	2	6^1	3	0	2	2	7.1	1.42	251	.150	.227	1	1.000	1	2	2	-0	0.2
1970 StL-N	0	4	.000	23	0	0	0	3	20^2	22	0	13	13	15.2	3.92	105	.272	.372	0	.000	-0	0	0	0	0.1
1972 Cle-A	3	1	.750	19	5	1	0	0	47	51	4	21	25	14.2	2.68	120	.283	.365	1	.077	-1	2	3	0	0.3
1973 Cle-A	5	3	.625	48	1	1	0	6	94^2	87	9	36	58	12.0	3.14	125	.242	.316	0	—	0	7	8	1	0.9
1974 Cle-A	4	3	.571	35	0	0	0	3	48^1	58	6	17	23	14.2	4.84	75	.302	.362	0	—	0	-7	-7	0	-0.6
1975 Phi-N	7	3	.700	53	0	0	0	0	96^2	81	6	38	52	11.2	2.14	174	.230	.307	3	.250	1	16	17	1	2.0
Total 6	19	14	.576	184	6	2	0	14	313^2	302	25	127	173	12.5	3.04	122	.255	.331	5	.185	1	20	24	2	2.9

● **CARMEN HILL** Hill, Carmen Proctor "Specs" or "Bunker" b: 10/1/1895, Royalton, Minn. d: 1/1/90, Indianapolis, Ind. BR/TR, 6'1", 180 lbs. Deb: 8/24/15

YEAR TM/L	W	L	PCT	G	GS	CG	SH	SV	IP	H	HR	BB	SO	RAT	ERA	ERA+	OAV	OOB	BH	AVG	PB	PR	/A	PD	TPI
1915 Pit-N	2	1	.667	8	3	2	1	0	47	42	0	13	24	10.9	1.15	238	.255	.317	2	.154	0	8	8	1	1.1
1916 Pit-N	0	0	—	2	0	0	0	0	6^1	11	0	5	5	24.2	8.53	31	.611	.708	0	—	0	-4	-4	-0	-0.4
1918 Pit-N	2	3	.400	6	4	3	0	0	43^2	24	0	17	15	8.5	1.24	232	.160	.246	2	.167	0	7	8	0	1.0
1919 Pit-N	0	0	—	4	0	0	0	0	5	12	0	1	1	23.4	9.00	34	.480	.500	0	—	0	-3	-3	0	-0.3
1922 NY-N	2	1	.667	8	4	0	0	0	28^1	33	0	5	6	12.1	4.76	84	.295	.325	2	.182	-0	-2	-2	1	-0.2
1926 Pit-N	3	3	.500	6	6	4	1	0	39^2	42	2	9	8	12.0	3.40	116	.288	.338	3	.176	-1	2	2	1	0.3
1927 *Pit-N	22	11	.667	43	31	22	2	3	277^2	260	12	80	95	11.2	3.24	127	.249	.305	22	.212	2	21	27	1	2.9
1928 Pit-N	16	10	.615	36	31	16	1	2	237	229	16	81	73	11.9	3.53	115	.259	.324	20	.233	2	12	14	-3	1.3
1929 Pit-N	2	3	.400	27	3	0	0	3	79	94	4	35	28	14.7	3.99	120	.297	.366	1	.036	-3	6	7	0	0.3
StL-N	0	0	—	3	1	0	0	0	8^2	10	2	8	1	19.7	8.31	56	.303	.452	0	.000	-0	-3	-4	0	-0.3
Yr	2	3	.400	30	4	0	0	3	87^2	104	6	43	29	15.2	4.41	108	.297	.376	1	.032	-4	**3**	**3**	0	0.0
1930 StL-N	0	1	.000	4	2	0	0	0	14^2	12	2	13	8	15.3	7.36	68	.240	.397	1	.333	0	-4	-4	-0	-0.3
Total 10	49	33	.598	147	85	47	5	8	787	769	38	267	264	12.0	3.44	116	.261	.326	53	.191	-0	40	49	1	5.4

● **RED HILL** Hill, Clifford Joseph b: 1/20/1893, Marshall, Tex. d: 8/11/38, ElPaso, Tex. BB/TL, Deb: 4/21/17

YEAR TM/L	W	L	PCT	G	GS	CG	SH	SV	IP	H	HR	BB	SO	RAT	ERA	ERA+	OAV	OOB	BH	AVG	PB	PR	/A	PD	TPI
1917 Phi-A	0	0	—	1	0	0	0	0	2^2	5	0	1	0	20.3	6.75	41	.385	.429	0	—	0	-1	-1	0	-0.1

● **DAVE HILL** Hill, David Burnham b: 11/11/37, New Orleans, La. BR/TL, 6'2", 170 lbs. Deb: 8/22/57

YEAR TM/L	W	L	PCT	G	GS	CG	SH	SV	IP	H	HR	BB	SO	RAT	ERA	ERA+	OAV	OOB	BH	AVG	PB	PR	/A	PD	TPI
1957 KC-A	0	0	—	2	0	0	0	0	2^1	6	3	3	1	34.7	27.00	15	.462	.563	0	—	0	-6	-6	-0	-0.5

● **DONNIE HILL** Hill, Donald Earl b: 11/12/60, Pomona, Cal. BB/TR, 5'10", 160 lbs. Deb: 7/25/83 ♦

YEAR TM/L	W	L	PCT	G	GS	CG	SH	SV	IP	H	HR	BB	SO	RAT	ERA	ERA+	OAV	OOB	BH	AVG	PB	PR	/A	PD	TPI
1990 Cal-A	0	0	—	1	0	0	0	0	1	0	0	1	1	9.0	0.00	—	.000	.250	93	.264	1	0	0	0	0.0

● **GARRY HILL** Hill, Garry Alton b: 11/3/46, Rutherfordton, N.C. BR/TR, 6'2", 195 lbs. Deb: 6/12/69

YEAR TM/L	W	L	PCT	G	GS	CG	SH	SV	IP	H	HR	BB	SO	RAT	ERA	ERA+	OAV	OOB	BH	AVG	PB	PR	/A	PD	TPI
1969 Atl-N	0	1	.000	1	1	0	0	0	2^1	6	1	1	2	27.0	15.43	23	.462	.500	0	—	0	-3	-3	0	-0.3

● **HERBERT HILL** Hill, Herbert Lee b: 8/19/1891, Hutchins, Tex. d: 9/2/70, Farmers Branch, Tex. BR/TR, 5'11.5", 175 lbs. Deb: 7/17/15

YEAR TM/L	W	L	PCT	G	GS	CG	SH	SV	IP	H	HR	BB	SO	RAT	ERA	ERA+	OAV	OOB	BH	AVG	PB	PR	/A	PD	TPI
1915 Cle-A	0	0	—	1	0	0	0	0	2	1	0	2	0	13.5	0.00	—	.250	.500	0	—	0	1	1	-0	0.1

● **KEN HILL** Hill, Kenneth Wade b: 12/14/65, Lynn, Mass. BR/TR, 6'2", 175 lbs. Deb: 9/03/88

YEAR TM/L	W	L	PCT	G	GS	CG	SH	SV	IP	H	HR	BB	SO	RAT	ERA	ERA+	OAV	OOB	BH	AVG	PB	PR	/A	PD	TPI
1988 StL-N	0	1	.000	4	1	0	0	0	14	16	0	6	6	14.1	5.14	68	.286	.355	0	.000	-0	-3	-3	0	-0.3
1989 StL-N	7	15	.318	33	33	2	1	0	196^2	186	9	99	112	13.3	3.80	96	.252	.344	9	.153	-0	-7	-4	0	-0.4
1990 StL-N	5	6	.455	17	14	1	0	0	78^2	79	7	33	58	12.9	5.49	69	.264	.339	4	.211	1	-15	-15	0	-1.3
1991 StL-N	11	10	.524	30	30	0	0	0	181^1	147	15	67	121	10.9	3.57	104	.224	.302	5	.100	-1	2	3	0	0.2
1992 Mon-N	16	9	.640	33	33	3	3	0	218	187	13	75	150	10.9	2.68	130	.230	.298	11	.177	5	20	19	1	2.9

YEAR	TM/L	W	L	PCT	G	GS	CG	SH	SV	IP	H	HR	BB	SO	RAT	ERA	ERA+	OAV	OOB	BH	AVG	PB	PR	/A	PD	TPI
Total	5	39	41	.488	117	111	6	4	0	688^2	615	44	280	447	11.9	3.61	101	.240	.319	29	.150	4	-2	1	2	1.1

● MILT HILL Hill, Milton Giles b: 8/22/65, Atlanta, Ga. BR/TR, 6', 180 lbs. Deb: 8/01/91

YEAR	TM/L	W	L	PCT	G	GS	CG	SH	SV	IP	H	HR	BB	SO	RAT	ERA	ERA+	OAV	OOB	BH	AVG	PB	PR	/A	PD	TPI
1991	Cin-N	1	1	.500	22	0	0	0	0	33^1	36	1	8	20	11.9	3.78	101	.295	.338	0	.000	-0	-0	0	-1	-0.1
1992	Cin-N	0	0	—	14	0	0	0	1	20	15	1	5	10	9.4	3.15	116	.211	.273	0	—	0	1	1	-0	0.1
Total	2	1	1	.500	36	0	0	0	1	53^1	51	2	13	30	11.0	3.54	106	.264	.314	0	.000	-0	0	1	-1	0.0

● BILL HILL Hill, William Cicero "Still Bill" b: 8/2/1874, Chattanooga, Tenn. d: 1/28/38, Cincinnati, Ohio BL/TL, 6'1", 201 lbs. Deb: 4/18/1896 F

YEAR	TM/L	W	L	PCT	G	GS	CG	SH	SV	IP	H	HR	BB	SO	RAT	ERA	ERA+	OAV	OOB	BH	AVG	PB	PR	/A	PD	TPI
1896	Lou-N	9	28	.243	43	39	32	0	2	319^2	353	14	155	104	14.8	4.31	100	.278	.364	24	.207	-5	2	1	4	0.0
1897	Lou-N	7	17	.292	27	26	20	1	0	199	209	6	69	55	13.3	3.62	118	.268	.341	7	.095	-8	15	14	2	0.7
1898	Cin-N	13	14	.481	33	32	26	2	0	262	261	3	119	75	13.6	3.98	96	.258	.346	13	.133	-8	-11	-4	1	-1.0
1899	Cle-N	3	6	.333	11	10	7	0	0	72^1	96	0	39	26	17.3	6.97	53	.318	.403	4	.129	-2	-25	-26	0	-2.3
	Bal-N	3	4	.429	8	7	6	0	0	61	64	1	18	17	12.5	3.25	122	.269	.329	7	.292	1	4	5	1	0.6
	Bro-N	1	0	1.000	2	1	1	0	1	11	11	0	6	3	13.9	0.82	478	.260	.352	3	.600	2	4	4	-0	0.6
	Yr	7	10	.412	21	18	14	0	1	144^1	171	1	63	46	14.6	4.93	78	.291	.359	14	.233	0	-17	-18	1	-1.1
Total	4	36	69	.343	124	115	92	3	3	925	994	24	406	280	14.2	4.16	99	.273	.355	58	.167	-20	-11	-6	7	-1.4

● HOMER HILLEBRAND Hillebrand, Homer Hiller Henry "Doc" b: 10/10/1879, Freeport, Ill. d: 1/20/74, Elsinore, Cal. BR/TL, 5'8", 165 lbs. Deb: 4/24/05 ♦

YEAR	TM/L	W	L	PCT	G	GS	CG	SH	SV	IP	H	HR	BB	SO	RAT	ERA	ERA+	OAV	OOB	BH	AVG	PB	PR	/A	PD	TPI
1905	Pit-N	5	2	.714	10	6	4	0	1	60^2	43	0	19	37	9.5	2.82	107	.198	.269	26	.236	1	1	1	-1	0.2
1906	Pit-N	3	2	.600	7	5	4	1	0	53	42	1	21	32	10.9	2.21	121	.220	.300	5	.238	1	3	3	1	0.6
1908	Pit-N	0	0	—	1	0	0	0	0	1	1	0	0	1	9.0	0.00	—	.333	.333	0	—	0	0	0	-0	0.0
Total	3	8	4	.667	18	11	8	1	1	114^2	86	1	40	70	10.1	2.51	113	.209	.284	31	.237	2	4	4	1	0.8

● SHAWN HILLEGAS Hillegas, Shawn Patrick b: 8/21/64, Dos Palos, Cal. BR/TR, 6'2", 208 lbs. Deb: 8/09/87

YEAR	TM/L	W	L	PCT	G	GS	CG	SH	SV	IP	H	HR	BB	SO	RAT	ERA	ERA+	OAV	OOB	BH	AVG	PB	PR	/A	PD	TPI
1987	LA-N	4	3	.571	12	10	0	0	0	58	52	5	31	51	12.9	3.57	111	.241	.336	0	.000	-1	3	3	-1	0.1
1988	LA-N	3	4	.429	11	10	0	0	0	56^2	54	5	17	30	11.8	4.13	81	.250	.314	2	.133	0	-4	-5	-1	-0.6
	Chi-A	3	2	.600	6	6	0	0	0	40	30	4	18	26	11.0	3.15	126	.207	.299	0	—	0	4	4	-0	0.4
1989	Chi-A	7	11	.389	50	13	0	0	3	119^2	132	12	51	76	14.0	4.74	80	.279	.353	0	—	0	-11	-12	-1	-1.3
1990	Chi-A	0	0	—	7	0	0	0	0	11^1	4	0	5	5	7.1	0.79	481	.111	.220	0	—	0	4	4	0	0.5
1991	Cle-A	3	4	.429	51	3	0	0	7	83	67	7	46	66	12.5	4.34	96	.223	.330	0	—	0	-2	-2	-0	-0.2
1992	NY-A	1	8	.111	21	9	1	1	0	78^1	96	12	33	46	14.8	5.51	73	.306	.372	0	—	0	-14	-13	-1	-1.5
	Oak-A	0	0	—	5	0	0	0	0	7^2	8	1	4	3	14.1	2.35	161	.276	.364	0	—	0	1	1	-0	0.3
	Yr	1	8	.111	26	9	1	1	0	86	104	13	37	49	14.8	5.23	77	.301	.368	0	—	0	-12	-12	-1	-1.2
Total	6	21	32	.396	163	51	1	1	10	454^2	443	46	205	303	13.0	4.30	90	.256	.338	2	.069	-1	-19	-21	-5	-2.3

● FRANK HILLER Hiller, Frank Walter "Dutch" b: 7/13/20, Newark, N.J. d: 1/8/87, West Chester, Pa. BR/TR, 6', 200 lbs. Deb: 5/25/46

YEAR	TM/L	W	L	PCT	G	GS	CG	SH	SV	IP	H	HR	BB	SO	RAT	ERA	ERA+	OAV	OOB	BH	AVG	PB	PR	/A	PD	TPI
1946	NY-A	0	2	.000	3	1	0	0	0	11^1	13	2	6	4	15.1	4.76	72	.295	.380	1	.250	0	-2	-2	-0	-0.2
1948	NY-A	5	2	.714	22	5	1	0	0	62^1	59	8	30	25	13.0	4.04	101	.244	.330	6	.375	2	2	0	0	0.2
1949	NY-A	0	2	.000	4	0	0	0	1	7^2	9	0	7	3	18.8	5.87	69	.290	.421	1	.500	0	-1	-2	-0	-0.1
1950	Chi-N	12	5	.706	38	17	9	2	1	153	153	16	32	55	11.1	3.53	119	.258	.300	5	.114	-3	10	11	1	0.9
1951	Chi-N	6	12	.333	24	21	6	2	1	141^1	147	17	31	50	11.9	4.84	85	.268	.317	6	.125	-2	-14	-12	1	-1.2
1952	Cin-N	5	8	.385	28	15	6	1	1	124^1	129	7	37	50	12.5	4.63	81	.271	.331	5	.167	1	-12	-12	0	-1.1
1953	NY-N	2	1	.667	19	1	0	0	0	33^2	43	6	15	10	16.6	6.15	70	.303	.385	2	.500	1	-7	-7	1	-0.5
Total	7	30	32	.484	138	60	22	5	4	533^2	553	56	158	197	12.4	4.42	92	.266	.325	26	.176	-1	-24	-22	3	-2.0

● JOHN HILLER Hiller, John Frederick b: 4/8/43, Toronto, Ont., Canada BR/TL, 6', 195 lbs. Deb: 9/06/65

YEAR	TM/L	W	L	PCT	G	GS	CG	SH	SV	IP	H	HR	BB	SO	RAT	ERA	ERA+	OAV	OOB	BH	AVG	PB	PR	/A	PD	TPI
1965	Det-A	0	0	—	5	0	0	0	1	6	5	0	1	4	9.0	0.00	—	.227	.261	0	—	0	2	2	-0	0.2
1966	Det-A	0	0	—	1	0	0	0	0	2	2	0	2	1	18.0	9.00	39	.286	.444	0	—	0	-1	-1	-0	-0.1
1967	Det-A	4	3	.571	23	6	2	2	3	65	57	4	9	49	9.1	2.63	124	.233	.260	2	.133	-0	4	5	-0	0.5
1968	*Det-A	9	6	.600	39	12	4	1	2	128	92	9	51	78	10.1	2.39	126	.200	.280	3	.081	-2	8	9	-0	0.7
1969	Det-A	4	4	.500	40	8	1	1	4	99^1	97	13	44	74	12.9	3.99	94	.257	.336	6	.286	2	-4	-3	-1	-0.2
1970	Det-A	6	6	.500	47	5	1	1	3	104	82	12	46	89	11.3	3.03	123	.219	.307	0	.000	-2	8	8	-1	0.5
1972	*Det-A	1	2	.333	24	3	1	0	3	44^1	39	4	13	26	11.2	2.03	155	.232	.299	0	.000	-0	5	5	1	0.6
1973	Det-A	10	5	.667	**65**	0	0	0	**38**	125^1	89	7	39	124	9.2	1.44	285	.198	.262	0	—	0	**33**	**37**	0	3.6
1974	Det-A☆	17	14	.548	59	0	0	0	13	150	127	10	62	134	11.5	2.64	144	.231	.312	0	—	0	16	19	-2	1.7
1975	Det-A	2	3	.400	36	0	0	0	14	70^2	52	6	36	87	11.2	2.17	185	.205	.303	0	—	0	13	15	-0	1.4
1976	Det-A	12	8	.600	56	1	1	1	13	121	93	7	67	117	12.0	2.38	156	.219	.329	0	.000	0	15	**18**	-1	1.8
1977	Det-A	8	14	.364	45	8	3	0	7	124	120	15	61	115	13.2	3.56	121	.258	.345	0	—	0	7	10	-1	0.9
1978	Det-A	9	4	.692	51	0	0	0	15	92^1	64	6	35	74	9.6	2.34	165	.202	.281	0	—	0	15	16	-1	1.5
1979	Det-A	4	7	.364	43	0	0	0	9	79^1	83	14	55	46	15.7	5.22	83	.274	.385	0	—	0	-9	-8	-0	-0.8
1980	Det-A	1	0	1.000	11	0	0	0	0	30^2	38	3	14	18	15.3	4.40	93	.309	.380	0	—	0	-1	-1	-0	-0.1
Total	15	87	76	.534	545	43	13	6	125	1242	1040	110	535	1036	11.5	2.83	133	.229	.312	11	.109	-3	112	130	-8	12.2

● DAVE HILLMAN Hillman, Darius Dutton b: 9/14/27, Dungannon, Va. BR/TR, 5'11", 168 lbs. Deb: 4/30/55

YEAR	TM/L	W	L	PCT	G	GS	CG	SH	SV	IP	H	HR	BB	SO	RAT	ERA	ERA+	OAV	OOB	BH	AVG	PB	PR	/A	PD	TPI
1955	Chi-N	0	0	—	25	3	0	0	0	57^2	63	10	25	23	13.9	5.31	77	.283	.357	1	.100	0	-8	-8	0	-0.8
1956	Chi-N	0	2	.000	2	2	0	0	0	12^1	11	0	5	6	11.7	2.19	172	.216	.286	0	.000	-1	2	2	0	0.2
1957	Chi-N	6	11	.353	32	14	1	0	1	103^1	115	13	37	53	13.2	4.35	89	.280	.340	0	.000	-2	-5	-6	-0	-0.8
1958	Chi-N	4	8	.333	31	16	3	0	1	125^2	132	12	31	65	11.7	3.15	124	.265	.308	6	.146	-1	11	11	-0	1.0
1959	Chi-N	8	11	.421	39	24	4	1	0	191	178	17	43	88	10.5	3.53	112	.248	.292	9	.150	1	9	9	1	1.1
1960	Bos-A	0	3	.000	16	3	0	0	0	36^2	41	6	12	14	13.0	5.65	72	.281	.335	0	.000	-0	-7	-7	0	-0.7
1961	Bos-A	3	2	.600	28	1	0	0	0	78	70	8	23	39	10.7	2.77	151	.242	.298	0	.000	-2	11	12	0	1.1
1962	Cin-N	0	0	—	2	0	0	0	0	3^2	8	0	1	0	22.1	9.82	41	.421	.450	0	—	0	-2	-2	-0	-0.2
	NY-N	0	0	—	13	1	0	0	1	15^2	21	5	8	8	17.2	6.32	66	.333	.417	0	.000	-0	-4	-4	0	-0.4
	Yr	0	0	—	15	1	0	0	1	19^1	29	5	9	8	18.2	6.98	59	.354	.424	0	.000	-0	-7	-6	-0	-0.6
Total	8	21	37	.362	188	64	8	1	3	624	639	71	185	296	11.9	3.87	103	.264	.317	16	.098	-5	6	8	1	0.5

● ERIC HILLMAN Hillman, John Eric b: 4/27/66, Gary, Ind. BL/TL, 6'10", 225 lbs. Deb: 5/18/92

YEAR	TM/L	W	L	PCT	G	GS	CG	SH	SV	IP	H	HR	BB	SO	RAT	ERA	ERA+	OAV	OOB	BH	AVG	PB	PR	/A	PD	TPI
1992	NY-N	2	2	.500	11	8	0	0	0	52^1	67	9	10	16	13.6	5.33	66	.318	.354	1	.077	-1	-11	-11	-1	-1.2

● CHARLIE HILSEY Hilsey, Charles T. b: 3/23/1864, Philadelphia, Pa. d: 10/31/18, Philadelphia, Pa. 5'7", 180 lbs. Deb: 9/27/1883 ♦

YEAR	TM/L	W	L	PCT	G	GS	CG	SH	SV	IP	H	HR	BB	SO	RAT	ERA	ERA+	OAV	OOB	BH	AVG	PB	PR	/A	PD	TPI
1883	Phi-N	0	3	.000	3	3	3	0	0	26	36	1	4	8	13.8	5.54	56	.305	.328	1	.100	-1	-7	-7	-0	-0.7
1884	Phi-a	2	1	.667	3	3	3	0	0	27	29	0	5	10	11.3	4.67	73	.257	.288	5	.208	0	-4	-4	1	-0.3
Total	2	2	4	.333	6	6	6	0	0	53	65	1	9	18	12.6	5.09	64	.281	.308	6	.176	-1	-11	-11	0	-1.0

● HOWARD HILTON Hilton, Howard James b: 1/3/64, Oxnard, Cal. BR/TR, 6'3", 230 lbs. Deb: 4/09/90

YEAR	TM/L	W	L	PCT	G	GS	CG	SH	SV	IP	H	HR	BB	SO	RAT	ERA	ERA+	OAV	OOB	BH	AVG	PB	PR	/A	PD	TPI
1990	StL-N	0	0	—	2	0	0	0	0	3	2	0	3	2	15.0	0.00	—	.182	.357	0	—	0	1	1	-0	0.1

● SAM HINDS Hinds, Samuel Russell b: 7/11/53, Frederick, Md. BR/TR, 6'6", 215 lbs. Deb: 5/21/77

YEAR	TM/L	W	L	PCT	G	GS	CG	SH	SV	IP	H	HR	BB	SO	RAT	ERA	ERA+	OAV	OOB	BH	AVG	PB	PR	/A	PD	TPI
1977	Mil-A	0	3	.000	29	1	0	0	2	72^1	72	5	40	46	14.2	4.73	86	.266	.364	0	—	0	-5	-5	-0	-0.6

● PAUL HINES Hines, Paul A. b: 3/1/1852, Washington, D.C. d: 7/10/35, Hyattsville, Md. BR/TR, 5'9.5", 173 lbs. Deb: 4/20/1872 ♦

YEAR	TM/L	W	L	PCT	G	GS	CG	SH	SV	IP	H	HR	BB	SO	RAT	ERA	ERA+	OAV	OOB	BH	AVG	PB	PR	/A	PD	TPI
1884	*Pro-N	0	0	—	1	0	0	0	0	1	3	0	0	0	27.0	0.00	—	.500	.500	148	.302	0	0	0	-0	0.0

● PAUL HINRICHS Hinrichs, Paul Edwin "Herky" b: 8/31/25, Marengo, Iowa BR/TR, 6', 180 lbs. Deb: 5/16/51

YEAR	TM/L	W	L	PCT	G	GS	CG	SH	SV	IP	H	HR	BB	SO	RAT	ERA	ERA+	OAV	OOB	BH	AVG	PB	PR	/A	PD	TPI
1951	Bos-A	0	0	—	4	0	0	0	0	3^1	7	1	4	1	29.7	21.60	21	.412	.524	0	—	0	-6	-6	0	-0.6

YEAR TM/L	W	L	PCT	G	GS	CG	SH	SV	IP	H	HR	BB	SO	RAT	ERA	ERA+	OAV	OOB	BH	AVG	PB	PR	/A	PD	TPI
● **DUTCH HINRICHS** Hinrichs, William Louis b: 4/27/1889, Orange, Cal. d: 8/18/72, Kingsburg, Cal. BR/TR, 6'3", 195 lbs. Deb: 6/25/10																									
1910 Was-A	0	1	.000	3	0	0	0	1	7	10	0	3	5	16.7	2.57	97	.357	.419	0	.000	-1	-0	-0	-0	-0.1
● **JERRY HINSLEY** Hinsley, Jerry Dean b: 4/9/44, Hugo, Okla. BR/TR, 5'11", 165 lbs. Deb: 4/18/64																									
1964 NY-N	0	2	.000	9	2	0	0	0	15¹	21	0	7	11	16.4	8.22	44	.313	.378	0	.000	-0	-8	-8	-1	-0.8
1967 NY-N	0	0	—	2	0	0	0	0	5	6	0	4	3	18.0	3.60	94	.316	.435	0	—	0	-0	-0	0	0.0
Total 2	0	2	.000	11	2	0	0	0	20¹	27	0	11	14	16.8	7.08	50	.314	.392	0	.000	-0	-8	-8	-1	-0.8
● **RICH HINTON** Hinton, Richard Michael b: 5/22/47, Tucson, Ariz. BL/TL, 6'2", 185 lbs. Deb: 7/17/71																									
1971 Chi-A	3	4	.429	18	2	0	0	0	24¹	27	1	6	15	12.6	4.44	81	.310	.362	0	.000	-0	-3	-2	1	-0.2
1972 NY-A	1	0	1.000	7	3	0	0	0	16²	20	2	8	13	15.1	4.86	61	.299	.373	0	.000	-0	-3	-4	-0	-0.5
Tex-A	0	1	.000	5	0	0	0	0	11¹	7	1	10	4	13.5	2.38	126	.171	.333	1	.500	1	1	1	0	0.2
Yr	1	1	.500	12	3	0	0	0	28	27	3	18	17	14.5	3.86	77	.245	.352	1	.200	1	-2	-3	-0	-0.3
1975 Chi-A	1	0	1.000	15	0	0	0	0	37¹	41	3	15	30	13.5	4.82	80	.270	.335	0	—	0	-4	-4	1	-0.3
1976 Cin-N	1	2	.333	12	1	0	0	0	17²	30	4	11	8	20.9	7.64	46	.380	.456	0	.000	-0	-8	-8	-0	-0.9
1978 Chi-A	2	6	.250	29	4	2	0	1	80²	78	5	28	48	12.0	4.02	95	.261	.328	0	—	0	-2	-2	-1	-0.3
1979 Chi-A	1	2	.333	16	2	0	0	2	41²	57	4	8	27	14.5	6.05	70	.331	.368	0	—	0	-8	-8	1	-0.7
Sea-A	0	2	.000	14	1	0	0	0	20	23	4	5	7	13.5	5.40	81	.284	.341	0	—	0	-3	-2	-0	-0.2
Yr	1	4	.200	30	3	0	0	2	61²	80	8	13	34	13.9	5.84	73	.310	.348	0	—	0	-11	-11	-0	-0.9
Total 6	9	17	.346	116	13	2	0	3	249²	283	24	91	152	13.7	4.87	78	.289	.354	1	.143	0	-31	-30	0	-2.9
● **HERB HIPPAUF** Hippauf, Herbert August b: 5/9/40, New York, N.Y. BR/TL, 6', 180 lbs. Deb: 4/27/66																									
1966 Atl-N	0	1	.000	3	0	0	0	0	2²	6	0	1	1	23.6	13.50	27	.462	.500	0	—	0	-3	-3	-0	-0.3
● **HARLEY HISNER** Hisner, Harley Parnell b: 11/6/26, Naples, Ind. BR/TR, 6'1", 185 lbs. Deb: 9/30/51																									
1951 Bos-A	0	1	.000	1	1	0	0	0	6	7	0	4	3	16.5	4.50	99	.292	.393	1	.500	0	-0	-0	0	0.0
● **STERLING HITCHCOCK** Hitchcock, Sterling Alex b: 4/29/71, Fayetteville, N.C. BL/TL, 6'1", 200 lbs. Deb: 9/11/92																									
1992 NY-A	0	2	.000	3	3	0	0	0	13	23	2	6	6	20.8	8.31	49	.377	.441	0	—	0	-6	-6	0	-0.6
● **BRUCE HITT** Hitt, Bruce Smith b: 3/14/1897, Comanche, Tex. d: 11/10/73, Portland, Ore. BR/TR, 6'1", 190 lbs. Deb: 9/23/17																									
1917 StL-N	0	0	—	2	0	0	0	0	4	7	1	1	1	18.0	9.00	30	.368	.400	0	.000	-0	-3	-3	0	-0.3
● **ROY HITT** Hitt, Roy Wesley "Rhino" b: 6/22/1887, Carleton, Neb. d: 2/8/56, Pomona, Cal. BL/TL, 5'10", 200 lbs. Deb: 4/27/07																									
1907 Cin-N	6	10	.375	21	18	14	2	0	153¹	143	2	56	63	12.4	3.40	76	.258	.339	10	.179	-0	-16	-14	-1	-1.6
● **LLOYD HITTLE** Hittle, Lloyd Eldon "Red" b: 2/21/24, Lodi, Cal. BR/TL, 5'10.5", 164 lbs. Deb: 6/12/49																									
1949 Was-A	5	7	.417	36	9	3	2	0	109	123	3	57	32	14.9	4.21	101	.285	.369	4	.143	-2	-0	1	-1	-0.2
1950 Was-A	2	4	.333	11	4	1	0	0	43¹	60	1	17	9	16.0	4.98	90	.326	.383	1	.077	-1	-2	-2	1	-0.2
Total 2	7	11	.389	47	13	4	2	0	152¹	183	3	74	41	15.2	4.43	98	.298	.373	5	.122	-3	-2	-2	0	-0.4
● **MYRIL HOAG** Hoag, Myril Oliver b: 3/9/08, Davis, Cal. d: 7/28/71, High Springs, Fla BR/TR, 5'11", 180 lbs. Deb: 4/15/31 ◆																									
1939 StL-A★	0	0	—	1	0	0	0	0	1	0	0	0	0	0.0	0.00	—	.000	.000	142	.295	0	1	1	0	0.1
1945 Cle-A	0	0	—	2	0	0	0	0	3	3	0	1	0	12.0	0.00	—	.300	.364	27	.211	0	1	1	0	0.1
Total 2	0	0	—	3	0	0	0	0	4	3	0	1	0	9.0	0.00	—	.214	.267	854	.271	1	2	2	0	0.2
● **ED HOBAUGH** Hobaugh, Edward Russell b: 6/27/34, Kittanning, Pa. BR/TR, 6', 176 lbs. Deb: 4/19/61																									
1961 Was-A	7	9	.438	26	18	3	0	0	126¹	142	12	64	67	14.7	4.42	91	.281	.363	4	.098	-2	-6	-6	0	-0.7
1962 Was-A	2	1	.667	26	2	0	0	1	69¹	66	9	25	37	11.8	3.76	107	.258	.324	2	.167	0	2	2	-1	0.2
1963 Was-A	0	0	—	9	1	0	0	0	16	20	3	6	11	15.8	6.19	60	.308	.384	1	.500	2	-5	-4	0	-0.3
Total 3	9	10	.474	61	21	3	0	1	211²	228	24	95	115	13.9	4.34	92	.276	.352	7	.127	-1	-8	-8	-0	-0.8
● **GLEN HOBBIE** Hobbie, Glen Frederick b: 4/24/36, Witt, Ill. BR/TR, 6'2", 195 lbs. Deb: 9/20/57																									
1957 Chi-N	0	0	—	2	0	0	0	0	4¹	6	0	5	3	22.8	10.38	37	.333	.478	0	.000	-0	-3	-3	0	-0.3
1958 Chi-N	10	6	.625	55	16	2	1	2	168¹	163	13	93	91	14.1	3.74	105	.252	.353	7	.146	-2	4	3	4	0.5
1959 Chi-N	16	13	.552	46	33	10	3	0	234	204	15	106	138	12.2	3.69	107	.236	.324	9	.151	-3	7	7	1	0.5
1960 Chi-N	16	20	.444	46	36	16	4	1	258²	253	27	101	134	12.6	3.97	95	.256	.330	13	.151	1	-6	-5	4	0.0
1961 Chi-N	7	13	.350	36	29	7	2	2	198²	207	26	54	103	12.1	4.26	98	.268	.321	11	.167	2	-5	-2	3	0.4
1962 Chi-N	5	14	.263	42	23	5	0	0	162	198	19	62	87	14.6	5.22	79	.304	.367	6	.122	-2	-23	-19	1	-2.0
1963 Chi-N	7	10	.412	36	24	4	1	0	165¹	172	17	49	94	12.4	3.92	90	.270	.328	4	.080	-2	-12	-8	-1	-1.2
1964 Chi-N	0	3	.000	8	4	0	0	0	27¹	39	4	10	14	16.5	7.90	47	.325	.382	0	.000	-0	-13	-13	0	-1.2
StL-N	1	2	.333	13	5	1	0	1	44¹	41	4	15	18	11.6	4.26	89	.241	.306	2	.154	1	-4	-2	1	0.0
Yr	1	5	.167	21	9	1	0	1	71²	80	8	25	32	13.3	5.65	67	.275	.334	2	.111	1	-17	-15	1	-1.2
Total 8	62	81	.434	284	170	45	11	6	1263	1283	125	495	682	12.9	4.20	93	.264	.337	52	.131	-5	-55	-42	13	-3.3
● **JOHN HOBBS** Hobbs, John Douglas b: 11/11/56, Philadelphia, Pa. BR/TL, 6'3", 190 lbs. Deb: 8/31/81																									
1981 Min-A	0	0	—	4	0	0	0	0	5²	5	0	6	1	20.6	3.18	124	.238	.448	0	—	0	0	0	-0	0.0
● **HARRY HOCH** Hoch, Harry Keller b: 1/9/1887, Woodside, Del. d: 10/26/81, Lewes, Del. BR/TL, 5'10.5", 165 lbs. Deb: 4/16/08																									
1908 Phi-N	2	1	.667	3	3	2	0	0	26	20	0	13	4	12.1	2.77	88	.211	.318	1	.200	1	-1	-1	0	0.0
1914 StL-A	0	2	.000	15	2	1	0	0	54	55	1	27	13	14.0	3.00	90	.284	.377	1	.056	-2	-2	-2	2	-0.2
1915 StL-A	0	4	.000	12	3	1	0	0	40	52	2	26	9	18.2	7.20	40	.311	.413	2	.200	-0	-19	-19	-0	-1.9
Total 3	2	7	.222	30	8	4	0	0	120	127	3	66	26	15.0	4.35	62	.279	.378	4	.121	-1	-22	-22	2	-2.1
● **CHUCK HOCKENBERY** Hockenbery, Charles Marion b: 12/15/50, Lacrosse, Wis. BB/TR, 6'1", 195 lbs. Deb: 7/04/75																									
1975 Cal-N	4	0	1.000	16	4	0	0	1	41	48	3	19	15	15.4	5.27	67	.296	.380	0	—	0	-7	-8	-0	-0.8
● **GEORGE HOCKETTE** Hockette, George Edward "Lefty" b: 4/7/08, Perth, Miss. d: 1/20/74, Plantation, Fla. BL/TL, 6', 174 lbs. Deb: 9/17/34																									
1934 Bos-A	2	1	.667	3	3	3	2	0	27¹	22	3	6	14	9.2	1.65	292	.218	.262	3	.273	0	9	10	-0	1.1
1935 Bos-A	2	3	.400	23	4	0	0	0	61	83	6	12	11	14.2	5.16	92	.329	.362	2	.143	-1	-5	-3	3	0.0
Total 2	4	4	.500	26	7	3	2	0	88¹	105	9	18	25	12.6	4.08	117	.297	.333	5	.200	-0	4	7	3	1.1
● **SHOVEL HODGE** Hodge, Clarence Clemet b: 7/6/1893, Mount Andrew, Ala. d: 12/31/67, Ft.Walton Beach, Fla. BL/TR, 6'4", 190 lbs. Deb: 9/06/20																									
1920 Chi-A	1	1	.500	4	2	1	0	0	19²	15	0	12	5	12.4	2.29	165	.224	.342	0	.000	-1	3	3	-1	0.2
1921 Chi-A	6	8	.429	36	10	5	0	2	142²	191	7	54	25	15.8	6.56	65	.335	.397	17	.327	3	-36	-37	3	-2.7
1922 Chi-A	7	6	.538	35	8	2	0	1	139	154	3	65	37	14.3	4.14	98	.300	.381	12	.207	-1	-2	-1	2	-0.1
Total 3	14	15	.483	75	20	8	0	3	301¹	360	10	131	67	14.9	5.17	80	.313	.387	29	.250	1	-34	-35	4	-2.6
● **ED HODGE** Hodge, Ed Oliver b: 4/19/58, Bellflower, Cal. BL/TL, 6'2", 192 lbs. Deb: 5/01/84																									
1984 Min-A	4	3	.571	25	15	0	0	0	100	116	13	29	59	13.1	4.77	88	.291	.340	0	—	0	-9	-6	-2	-0.9
● **ELI HODKEY** Hodkey, Aloysius Joseph b: 11/3/17, Lorain, Ohio BL/TL, 6'4", 185 lbs. Deb: 9/12/46																									
1946 Phi-N	0	1	.000	2	1	0	0	0	4¹	9	0	5	0	29.1	12.46	28	.391	.500	0	.000	-0	-4	-4	-0	-0.4
● **CHARLIE HODNETT** Hodnett, Charles b: 1861, Iowa Deb: 5/03/1883																									
1883 StL-a	2	2	.500	4	4	3	0	0	32	28	1	7	6	9.8	1.41	248	.220	.261	2	.182	-0	7	7	-0	0.7
1884 StL-U	12	2	.857	14	14	12	1	0	121	121	0	16	41	10.2	2.01	147	.243	.267	12	.207	1	14	13	-2	1.0

YEAR	TM/L	W	L	PCT	G	GS	CG	SH	SV	IP	H	HR	BB	SO	RAT	ERA	ERA+	OAV	OOB	BH	AVG	PB	PR	/A	PD	TPI
Total	2	14	4	.778	18	18	15	1	0	153	149	1	23	47	10.1	1.88	163	.238	.266	14	.203	1	20	20	-2	1.7

● GEORGE HODSON
Hodson, George S. b: 6/1870, Pennsylvania Deb: 8/09/1894

YEAR	TM/L	W	L	PCT	G	GS	CG	SH	SV	IP	H	HR	BB	SO	RAT	ERA	ERA+	OAV	OOB	BH	AVG	PB	PR	/A	PD	TPI
1894	Bos-N	4	4	.500	12	11	8	0	0	74	103	4	35	12	17.4	5.84	97	.326	.402	3	.100	-4	-4	-1	-1	-0.5
1895	Phi-N	1	2	.333	4	2	1	0	0	17	27	4	9	6	19.1	9.53	50	.354	.422	0	.000	-1	-9	-9	-1	-0.8
Total	2	5	6	.455	16	13	9	0	0	91	130	8	44	18	17.7	6.53	84	.331	.406	3	.086	-5	-13	-10	-2	-1.3

● BILLY HOEFT
Hoeft, William Frederick b: 5/17/32, Oshkosh, Wis. BL/TL, 6'3", 205 lbs. Deb: 4/18/52

YEAR	TM/L	W	L	PCT	G	GS	CG	SH	SV	IP	H	HR	BB	SO	RAT	ERA	ERA+	OAV	OOB	BH	AVG	PB	PR	/A	PD	TPI
1952	Det-A	2	7	.222	34	10	1	0	4	125	123	14	63	67	13.8	4.32	88	.260	.353	6	.150	-1	-9	-7	1	-0.7
1953	Det-A	9	14	.391	29	27	9	0	2	197^{2}	223	24	58	90	13.0	4.83	84	.283	.335	11	.172	0	-18	-17	-2	-1.7
1954	Det-A	7	15	.318	34	25	10	4	1	175	180	22	59	114	12.5	4.58	81	.266	.328	10	.192	4	-17	-17	-2	-1.5
1955	Det-A☆	16	7	.696	32	29	17	**7**	0	220	187	17	75	133	11.0	2.99	129	.229	.298	17	.207	3	24	21	-3	2.2
1956	Det-A	20	14	.588	38	34	18	4	0	248	276	22	104	172	14.0	4.06	101	.287	.360	20	.250	6	3	1	-3	0.4
1957	Det-A	9	11	.450	34	28	10	1	1	207	188	15	69	111	11.4	3.48	111	.244	.310	10	.149	2	7	9	-2	0.9
1958	Det-A	10	9	.526	36	21	6	0	3	143	148	15	49	94	12.5	4.15	97	.268	.328	12	.273	3	-6	-2	-2	0.0
1959	Det-A	1	1	.500	2	2	0	0	0	9	6	0	4	2	11.0	5.00	81	.188	.297	1	.333	0	-1	-1	0	-0.1
	Bos-A	0	3	.000	5	3	0	0	0	17^{2}	22	1	8	8	15.8	5.60	72	.319	.397	0	.000	-0	-3	-3	0	-0.3
	Bal-A	1	1	.500	16	3	0	0	0	41	50	6	19	30	15.1	5.71	66	.307	.379	3	.250	1	-8	-9	-0	-0.8
	Yr	2	5	.286	23	8	0	0	0	67^{2}	78	7	31	40	14.5	5.59	70	.290	.363	4	.222	0	-13	-13	0	-1.2
1960	Bal-A	2	1	.667	19	0	0	0	0	18^{2}	18	2	14	14	15.4	4.34	88	.240	.360	0	.000	-0	-1	-1	0	-0.1
1961	Bal-A	7	4	.636	35	12	3	1	3	138	106	7	55	100	10.6	2.02	193	.216	.296	7	.179	1	**31**	29	1	3.2
1962	Bal-A	4	8	.333	57	4	0	0	7	113^{2}	103	7	43	73	11.6	4.59	82	.243	.315	3	.158	2	-8	-11	0	-0.8
1963	SF-N	2	0	1.000	23	0	0	0	4	24^{1}	26	5	10	8	13.3	4.44	72	.271	.340	1	1.000	1	-3	-3	-0	-0.3
1964	Mil-N	4	0	1.000	42	0	0	0	4	73^{1}	76	9	18	47	11.7	3.80	93	.271	.318	2	.222	1	-2	-2	0	-0.1
1965	Chi-N	2	2	.500	29	2	1	0	1	51^{1}	41	3	20	44	10.7	2.81	131	.215	.289	3	.273	1	4	5	-1	0.5
1966	Chi-N	1	2	.333	36	0	0	0	3	41	43	4	14	30	12.7	4.61	80	.264	.326	1	.250	0	-5	-4	1	-0.4
	SF-N	0	2	.000	4	0	0	0	0	3^{2}	4	0	3	3	17.2	7.36	50	.250	.368	0	—	0	-2	-2	-0	-0.2
	Yr	1	4	.200	40	0	0	0	3	44^{2}	47	4	17	33	12.9	4.84	76	.261	.325	1	.250	0	-6	-6	0	-0.6
Total	15	97	101	.490	505	200	75	17	33	1847^{1}	1820	173	685	1140	12.4	3.94	98	.259	.327	107	.202	24	-15	-13	-11	0.2

● ART HOELSKOETTER
Hoelskoetter, Arthur "Holley" or "Hoss" (a.k.a. Arthur H. Hostetter)
b: 9/30/1882, St.Louis, Mo. d: 8/3/54, St.Louis, Mo. BR/TR, 6'2", Deb: 9/10/05 ♦

YEAR	TM/L	W	L	PCT	G	GS	CG	SH	SV	IP	H	HR	BB	SO	RAT	ERA	ERA+	OAV	OOB	BH	AVG	PB	PR	/A	PD	TPI
1905	StL-N	0	1	.000	1	1	1	0	0	6	6	1	5	4	16.5	1.50	199	.273	.407	20	.241	0	1	1	0	0.2
1906	StL-N	1	4	.200	12	3	2	0	0	58^{1}	53	1	34	20	13.6	4.63	57	.240	.344	71	.224	1	-13	-13	-1	-1.3
1907	StL-N	0	0	—	2	0	0	0	0	11	9	0	10	8	17.2	5.73	44	.209	.382	98	.247	0	-4	-4	-1	-0.4
Total	3	1	5	.167	15	4	3	0	0	75^{1}	68	2	49	32	14.3	4.54	58	.238	.355	225	.236	1	-16	-16	-1	-1.5

● JOE HOERNER
Hoerner, Joseph Walter b: 11/12/36, Dubuque, Iowa BR/TL, 6'1", 200 lbs. Deb: 9/27/63

YEAR	TM/L	W	L	PCT	G	GS	CG	SH	SV	IP	H	HR	BB	SO	RAT	ERA	ERA+	OAV	OOB	BH	AVG	PB	PR	/A	PD	TPI
1963	Hou-N	0	0	—	1	0	0	0	0	3	2	0	0	2	6.0	0.00	—	.182	.182	0	.000	-0	1	1	0	0.1
1964	Hou-N	0	0	—	7	0	0	0	0	11	13	3	6	4	15.5	4.91	70	.310	.396	0	.000	-0	-2	-2	0	-0.2
1966	StL-N	5	1	.833	57	0	0	0	13	76	57	5	21	63	9.7	1.54	233	.212	.279	1	.125	1	17	17	-1	1.9
1967	*StL-N	4	4	.500	57	0	0	0	15	66	52	5	20	50	10.0	2.59	127	.225	.290	2	.182	0	6	5	-0	0.5
1968	*StL-N	8	2	.800	47	0	0	0	17	48^{2}	34	2	12	42	8.5	1.48	196	.192	.243	0	.000	-1	8	8	-0	0.8
1969	StL-N	2	3	.400	45	0	0	0	15	53^{1}	44	5	9	35	9.1	2.87	125	.230	.269	0	.000	-1	4	4	0	0.4
1970	Phi-N☆	9	5	.643	44	0	0	0	9	57^{2}	53	5	20	39	11.5	2.65	150	.247	.314	2	.200	1	9	9	-2	0.8
1971	Phi-N	4	5	.444	49	0	0	0	9	73	57	6	21	57	9.7	1.97	179	.215	.275	1	.100	-1	12	13	-0	1.3
1972	Phi-N	0	2	.000	15	0	0	0	3	21^{2}	21	2	5	12	11.2	2.08	173	.259	.310	0	.000	-0	3	4	-1	0.3
	Atl-N	1	3	.250	25	0	0	0	2	23^{1}	34	4	8	19	16.6	6.56	58	.351	.406	0	.000	-0	-8	-7	-0	-0.8
	Yr	1	5	.167	40	0	0	0	5	45	55	6	13	31	13.8	4.40	84	.301	.350	0	.000	-1	-5	-4	-1	-0.5
1973	Atl-N	2	2	.500	20	0	0	0	2	12^{2}	17	1	4	10	14.9	6.39	61	.333	.382	0	—	0	-4	-3	-0	-0.4
	KC-A	2	0	1.000	22	0	0	0	4	19^{1}	28	0	13	15	19.1	5.12	80	.329	.418	0	—	0	-3	-2	-0	-0.8
1974	KC-A	2	3	.400	30	0	0	0	2	35^{1}	32	3	12	24	12.2	3.82	100	.244	.327	0	—	0	-1	-0	-1	-0.5
1975	Phi-N	0	0	—	25	0	0	0	0	21	25	3	8	20	14.6	2.57	145	.298	.366	0	.000	-0	2	3	-1	0.2
1976	Tex-A	0	4	.000	41	0	0	0	8	35	41	3	19	15	15.4	5.14	70	.315	.403	0	—	0	-6	-6	-1	-0.8
1977	Cin-N	0	0	—	8	0	0	0	0	5^{2}	9	3	3	5	23.8	12.71	31	.375	.500	0	—	0	-6	-6	-0	-0.6
Total	14	39	34	.534	493	0	0	0	99	562^{2}	519	50	181	412	11.5	2.99	119	.249	.314	6	.102	-1	35	36	-7	2.2

● LEFTY HOERST
Hoerst, Frank Joseph b: 8/11/17, Philadelphia, Pa. BL/TL, 6'3", 192 lbs. Deb: 4/26/40

YEAR	TM/L	W	L	PCT	G	GS	CG	SH	SV	IP	H	HR	BB	SO	RAT	ERA	ERA+	OAV	OOB	BH	AVG	PB	PR	/A	PD	TPI
1940	Phi-N	1	0	1.000	6	0	0	0	0	12	12	1	8	3	15.0	5.25	74	.250	.357	0	.000	-0	-2	-2	1	-0.1
1941	Phi-N	3	10	.231	37	11	1	0	0	105^{2}	111	7	50	33	13.8	5.20	71	.275	.357	4	.182	0	-18	-18	2	-1.6
1942	Phi-N	4	16	.200	33	22	5	0	1	150^{2}	162	11	78	52	14.4	5.20	64	.271	.357	7	.152	-0	-32	-32	2	-3.0
1946	Phi-N	1	6	.143	18	7	2	0	0	68^{1}	77	4	36	17	15.0	4.61	74	.288	.375	1	.059	-1	-9	-9	-1	-1.1
1947	Phi-N	1	1	.500	4	1	0	0	0	11^{1}	19	1	3	0	17.5	7.94	50	.358	.393	2	.500	1	-5	-5	0	-0.4
Total	5	10	33	.233	98	41	8	0	1	348	381	24	175	105	14.5	5.17	68	.279	.362	14	.154	-1	-66	-65	4	-6.2

● RED HOFF
Hoff, Chester Cornelius b: 5/8/1891, Ossining, N.Y. BL/TL, 5'9", 162 lbs. Deb: 9/06/11

YEAR	TM/L	W	L	PCT	G	GS	CG	SH	SV	IP	H	HR	BB	SO	RAT	ERA	ERA+	OAV	OOB	BH	AVG	PB	PR	/A	PD	TPI
1911	NY-A	0	1	.000	5	1	0	0	0	20^{2}	21	0	7	10	12.2	2.18	165	.262	.322	2	.286	0	3	3	1	0.4
1912	NY-A	0	1	.000	5	1	0	0	0	15^{2}	20	0	6	14	14.9	6.89	52	.303	.361	1	.200	-0	-6	-6	-0	-0.6
1913	NY-A	0	0	—	2	0	0	0	0	3	0	0	1	2	3.0	0.00	—	.000	.111	0	.000	-0	1	1	-0	0.1
1915	StL-A	2	2	.500	11	3	2	0	0	43^{2}	26	0	24	23	10.5	1.24	232	.169	.285	3	.176	-1	8	8	1	0.9
Total	4	2	4	.333	23	5	2	0	0	83	67	0	38	49	11.5	2.49	127	.218	.305	6	.200	-1	6	6	1	0.8

● BILL HOFFER
Hoffer, William Leopold "Chick" or "Wizard"
b: 11/8/1870, Cedar Rapids, Iowa d: 7/21/59, Cedar Rapids, Ia. BR/TR, 5'9", 155 lbs. Deb: 4/26/1895

YEAR	TM/L	W	L	PCT	G	GS	CG	SH	SV	IP	H	HR	BB	SO	RAT	ERA	ERA+	OAV	OOB	BH	AVG	PB	PR	/A	PD	TPI
1895	*Bal-N	31	6	**.838**	41	38	32	**4**	0	314	296	9	124	80	12.6	3.21	148	.245	.325	27	.214	-4	55	54	-2	4.0
1896	*Bal-N	25	7	**.781**	35	35	32	3	0	309	317	1	95	93	12.3	3.38	127	.263	.323	38	.304	10	34	31	2	3.8
1897	*Bal-N	22	11	.667	38	33	29	1	0	303^{1}	350	5	104	62	14.0	4.30	97	.287	.351	33	.237	1	0	-4	0	-0.3
1898	Bal-N	0	4	.000	4	4	4	0	0	34^{1}	62	0	16	5	20.7	7.34	49	.386	.445	5	.208	0	-14	-14	-0	-1.2
	Pit-N	3	0	1.000	4	3	3	0	0	31	26	0	15	11	11.9	1.74	204	.226	.316	1	.091	-1	6	6	-0	0.6
	Yr	3	4	.429	8	7	7	0	0	65^{1}	88	0	31	16	16.4	4.68	76	.318	.387	6	.171	-0	-8	-8	-0	-0.6
1899	Pit-N	8	10	.444	23	19	15	2	0	163^{2}	169	5	64	44	13.4	3.63	105	.266	.343	18	.198	-2	4	3	-0	0.2
1901	Cle-A	3	8	.273	16	10	10	0	**3**	99	113	2	35	19	13.5	4.55	78	.283	.343	6	.136	-1	-10	-11	0	-1.0
Total	6	92	46	.667	161	142	125	10	3	1254^{1}	1333	22	453	314	13.2	3.75	112	.270	.339	128	.229	2	76	65	-1	6.1

● DANNY HOFFMAN
Hoffman, Daniel John b: 3/2/1880, Canaan, Conn. d: 3/14/22, Manchester, Conn. BL/TL, 5'9", 175 lbs. Deb: 4/20/03 ♦

YEAR	TM/L	W	L	PCT	G	GS	CG	SH	SV	IP	H	HR	BB	SO	RAT	ERA	ERA+	OAV	OOB	BH	AVG	PB	PR	/A	PD	TPI
1903	Phi-A	0	0	—	1	0	0	0	0	3	2	0	2	0	12.0	3.00	102	.189	.319	61	.246	0	-0	0	-0	0.0

● FRANK HOFFMAN
Hoffman, Frank J. "The Texas Wonder" b: Houston, Tex. Deb: 8/13/1888

YEAR	TM/L	W	L	PCT	G	GS	CG	SH	SV	IP	H	HR	BB	SO	RAT	ERA	ERA+	OAV	OOB	BH	AVG	PB	PR	/A	PD	TPI
1888	KC-a	3	9	.250	12	12	12	0	0	104	102	3	42	38	13.0	2.77	124	.247	.326	6	.154	-2	3	8	0	0.7

● GUY HOFFMAN
Hoffman, Guy Alan b: 7/9/56, Ottawa, Ill. BL/TL, 5'9", 185 lbs. Deb: 7/04/79

YEAR	TM/L	W	L	PCT	G	GS	CG	SH	SV	IP	H	HR	BB	SO	RAT	ERA	ERA+	OAV	OOB	BH	AVG	PB	PR	/A	PD	TPI
1979	Chi-A	0	5	.000	24	0	0	0	2	30^{1}	30	0	23	18	16.0	5.34	80	.261	.388	0	—	0	-4	-4	0	-0.3
1980	Chi-A	1	0	1.000	23	1	0	0	1	37^{2}	38	1	17	24	13.1	2.63	153	.268	.346	0	—	0	6	6	-1	0.5
1983	Chi-A	1	0	1.000	11	0	0	0	0	6	14	1	2	2	24.0	7.50	56	.483	.516	0	—	0	-2	-2	-0	-0.4
1986	Chi-N	6	2	.750	32	8	1	0	0	84	92	6	29	47	13.2	3.86	105	.288	.351	1	.067	-1	-1	2	-1	0.0

YEAR	TM/L	W	L	PCT	G	GS	CG	SH	SV	IP	H	HR	BB	SO	RAT	ERA	ERA+	OAV	OOB	BH	AVG	PB	PR	/A	PD	TPI
1987	Cin-N	9	10	.474	36	22	0	0	0	158^2	160	20	49	87	12.1	4.37	97	.265	.325	5	.111	-2	-5	-2	-2	-0.5
1988	Tex-A	0	0	—	11	0	0	0	0	22^1	22	5	8	9	12.5	5.24	78	.247	.316	0	—	0	-3	-3	0	-0.3
Total	6	17	17	.500	137	31	1	0	3	339	356	33	128	187	13.1	4.25	98	.274	.343	6	.100	-2	-10	-3	-4	-1.0
● BILL HOFFMAN Hoffman, William Joseph b: 3/3/18, Philadelphia, Pa. BL/TL, 5'9", 170 lbs. Deb: 8/13/39																										
1939	Phi-N	0	0	—	3	0	0	0	0	6	8	2	7	1	27.0	13.50	30	.333	.529	0	.000	-0	-6	-6	-0	-0.6
● JOHN HOFFORD Hofford, John William b: 5/25/1863, Philadelphia, Pa. d: 12/16/15, Philadelphia, Pa. Deb: 9/26/1885																										
1885	Pit-a	0	3	.000	3	3	3	0	0	25	28	1	9	21	13.3	3.60	89	.275	.333	1	.125	-1	-1	-1	0	-0.1
1886	Pit-a	3	6	.333	9	9	9	0	0	81	88	1	40	25	14.4	4.33	78	.261	.343	10	.294	3	-8	-9	1	-0.4
Total	2	3	9	.250	12	12	12	0	0	106	116	2	49	46	14.2	4.16	80	.264	.341	11	.262	2	-9	-10	1	-0.5
● GEORGE HOGAN Hogan, George A. b: 9/25/1885, Marion, Ohio d: 2/22/22, Bartlesville, Okla BR/TR, 6', 160 lbs. Deb: 4/18/14 F																										
1914	KC-F	0	1	.000	4	1	0	0	0	13	12	1	7	7	13.8	4.15	74	.255	.364	0	.000	-1	-1	-2	0	-0.2
● EDDIE HOGAN Hogan, Robert Edward b: 4/1860, St.Louis, Mo. BR , 5'7", 153 lbs. Deb: 7/05/1882 ♦																										
1882	StL-a	0	1	.000	1	1	1	0	0	8	10	0	0	4	11.3	1.13	249	.287	.287	1	.333	0	1	1	-1	0.1
● BRAD HOGG Hogg, Carter Bradley b: 3/26/1888, Buena Vista, Ga. d: 4/2/35, Buena Vista, Ga. BR/TR, 6', 185 lbs. Deb: 9/01/11																										
1911	Bos-N	0	3	.000	8	3	2	0	1	25^2	33	0	14	8	16.8	6.66	57	.337	.425	4	.444	1	-9	-8	0	-0.6
1912	Bos-N	1	1	.500	10	1	0	0	1	31	37	2	16	12	16.0	6.97	51	.308	.399	1	.091	-1	-12	-12	-1	-1.2
1915	Chi-N	1	0	1.000	2	2	1	1	0	13	12	1	6	0	13.2	2.08	134	.245	.339	0	.000	-0	1	1	0	0.1
1918	Phi-N	13	13	.500	29	25	17	3	1	228	201	3	61	81	10.6	2.53	119	.245	.302	18	.228	3	6	12	2	2.0
1919	Phi-N	5	12	.294	22	19	13	0	0	150^1	163	7	55	48	13.4	4.43	73	.292	.360	17	.283	3	-25	-20	-2	-2.0
Total	5	20	29	.408	71	50	33	4	3	448	446	13	152	149	12.3	3.70	85	.271	.338	40	.247	6	-40	-27	-0	-1.7
● BILL HOGG Hogg, William "Buffalo Bill" b: 1880, Port Huron, Mich. d: 12/8/09, New Orleans, La. BR/TR, 6', Deb: 4/25/05																										
1905	NY-A	9	13	.409	39	22	9	3	1	205	178	1	101	125	12.7	3.20	92	.235	.333	4	.060	-6	-12	-6	-5	-1.9
1906	NY-A	14	13	.519	28	25	15	3	0	206	171	5	72	107	11.1	2.93	101	.229	.307	9	.125	-5	-5	1	-5	-1.0
1907	NY-A	10	8	.556	25	21	13	0	0	166^2	173	3	83	64	14.2	3.08	91	.269	.359	11	.183	-0	-10	-5	-1	-0.7
1908	NY-A	4	16	.200	24	21	6	0	0	152^1	155	4	63	72	13.1	3.01	82	.262	.337	4	.093	-3	-10	-9	-2	-1.5
Total	4	37	50	.425	116	89	43	6	1	730	677	13	319	368	12.7	3.06	92	.247	.333	28	.116	-15	-38	-20	-12	-5.1
● CHIEF HOGSETT Hogsett, Elon Chester b: 11/2/03, Brownell, Kan. BL/TL, 6', 190 lbs. Deb: 9/18/29																										
1929	Det-A	1	2	.333	4	4	2	1	0	28^2	34	0	9	9	13.8	2.83	152	.312	.370	2	.200	-0	5	5	0	0.5
1930	Det-A	9	8	.529	33	17	4	0	1	146	174	9	63	54	15.2	5.42	88	.300	.377	17	.293	3	-13	-10	2	-0.5
1931	Det-A	3	9	.250	22	12	5	0	2	112^1	150	8	33	47	15.1	5.93	77	.324	.375	11	.234	0	-19	-17	0	-1.5
1932	Det-A	11	9	.550	47	15	7	0	7	178	201	8	66	56	13.8	3.54	133	.286	.351	14	.246	3	19	23	2	2.7
1933	Det-A	6	10	.375	45	2	0	0	9	116	137	7	56	39	15.3	4.50	96	.296	.377	8	.211	-0	-3	-2	1	-0.2
1934	*Det-A	3	2	.600	26	0	0	0	3	50^1	61	4	19	23	14.5	4.29	102	.303	.367	3	.231	-0	1	1	1	0.1
1935	*Det-A	6	6	.500	40	0	0	0	5	96^2	109	1	49	39	15.2	3.54	118	.288	.377	6	.261	2	10	7	3	1.1
1936	Det-A	0	1	.000	3	0	0	0	0	4	8	1	1	1	20.3	9.00	55	.400	.429	0	—	0	-2	-2	0	-0.1
	StL-A	13	15	.464	39	29	10	0	1	215^1	278	15	90	67	16.0	5.52	97	.310	.383	10	.143	-2	-11	-3	1	-0.4
	Yr	13	16	.448	42	29	10	0	1	219^1	286	16	91	68	16.1	5.58	96	.312	.384	10	.143	-2	-13	-5	1	-0.5
1937	StL-A	6	19	.240	37	26	8	1	2	177^1	245	19	75	68	16.5	6.29	77	.328	.393	13	.210	0	-33	-29	-1	-2.6
1938	Was-A	5	6	.455	31	9	1	0	3	91	107	12	36	33	14.9	6.03	75	.292	.368	7	.304	3	-13	-15	0	-1.1
1944	Det-A	0	0	—	3	0	0	0	0	6^1	7	1	4	5	18.5	0.00	—	.250	.382	0	.000	-0	2	3	-0	0.2
Total	11	63	87	.420	330	114	37	2	33	1222	1511	85	501	441	15.3	5.02	94	.305	.376	91	.226	8	-57	-42	9	-1.8
● CAL HOGUE Hogue, Calvin Grey b: 10/24/27, Dayton, Ohio BR/TR, 6', 185 lbs. Deb: 7/15/52																										
1952	Pit-N	1	8	.111	19	12	3	0	0	83^2	79	7	68	34	16.2	4.84	82	.258	.399	6	.250	1	-10	-8	-2	-0.8
1953	Pit-N	1	1	.500	3	2	2	0	0	19	19	4	16	10	17.1	5.21	86	.250	.387	0	.000	-1	-2	-2	0	-0.2
1954	Pit-N	0	1	.000	3	2	0	0	0	11	11	1	12	7	18.8	4.91	85	.282	.451	0	.000	-0	-1	-1	0	-0.1
Total	3	2	10	.167	25	16	5	0	0	113^2	109	12	96	51	16.6	4.91	83	.259	.402	6	.188	0	-13	-10	-1	-1.1
● BOBBY HOGUE Hogue, Robert Clinton b: 4/5/21, Miami, Fla. d: 12/22/87, Miami, Fla. BR/TR, 5'10", 195 lbs. Deb: 4/24/48																										
1948	Bos-N	8	2	.800	40	1	0	0	2	86^1	88	4	19	43	11.4	3.23	119	.265	.309	2	.095	-1	7	6	-1	0.4
1949	Bos-N	2	2	.500	33	0	0	0	3	72	78	4	25	23	13.1	3.13	121	.280	.343	6	.286	1	7	5	2	0.8
1950	Bos-N	3	5	.375	36	1	0	0	7	62^2	69	8	31	15	14.9	5.03	77	.280	.370	3	.231	1	-6	-8	1	-0.7
1951	Bos-N	0	0	—	3	0	0	0	0	5	4	1	3	0	12.6	5.40	68	.235	.350	1	.500	0	-1	-1	-0	-0.1
	StL-A	1	1	.500	18	0	0	0	1	29^2	31	1	23	11	16.4	5.16	85	.279	.403	2	.667	1	-3	-3	1	0.0
	*NY-A	1	0	1.000	7	0	0	0	0	7^1	4	0	3	2	8.6	0.00	—	.174	.269	0	—	0	3	3	0	0.3
	Yr	2	1	.667	25	0	0	0	1	37	35	1	26	13	14.8	4.14	104	.261	.381	2	.667	1	-0	1	1	0.3
1952	NY-A	3	5	.375	27	0	0	0	4	47^1	52	6	25	12	14.8	5.32	62	.294	.384	3	.273	0	-9	-11	-1	-1.1
	StL-A	0	1	.000	8	1	0	0	0	16^1	10	1	13	2	12.7	2.76	142	.179	.333	0	.000	-0	2	2	0	0.2
	Yr	3	6	.333	35	1	0	0	4	63^2	62	7	38	14	14.1	4.66	74	.265	.368	3	.231	0	-7	-8	-1	-0.9
Total	5	18	16	.529	172	3	0	0	17	326^2	336	25	142	108	13.4	3.97	96	.271	.350	17	.233	3	0	-6	1	-0.2
● WALLY HOLBOROW Holborow, Walter Albert b: 11/30/13, New York, N.Y. d: 7/14/86, Ft.Lauderdale, Fla. BR/TR, 5'11", 187 lbs. Deb: 9/27/44																										
1944	Was-A	0	0	—	1	0	0	0	0	3	0	0	2	1	6.0	0.00	—	.000	.182	0	—	0	1	1	0	0.1
1945	Was-A	1	1	.500	15	1	1	1	0	31^1	20	0	16	14	10.3	2.30	135	.189	.295	0	.000	-0	4	3	-1	0.2
1948	Phi-A	1	2	.333	5	1	1	0	0	17^1	32	1	7	3	20.3	5.71	75	.421	.470	2	.500	1	-3	-3	1	-0.1
Total	3	2	3	.400	21	2	2	1	0	51^2	52	1	25	18	13.4	3.31	106	.272	.356	2	.333	1	2	1	-0	0.2
● KEN HOLCOMBE Holcombe, Kenneth Edward b: 8/23/18, Burnsville, N.C. BR/TR, 5'11.5", 169 lbs. Deb: 4/27/45																										
1945	NY-A	3	3	.500	23	2	0	0	0	55^1	43	2	27	20	11.4	1.79	194	.226	.323	2	.133	-1	10	10	-0	1.0
1948	Cin-N	0	0	—	2	0	0	0	0	2^1	3	0	0	2	11.6	7.71	51	.300	.300	0	—	0	-1	-1	-0	-0.1
1950	Chi-A	3	10	.231	24	15	5	0	1	96	122	10	45	37	15.7	4.59	98	.307	.378	5	.156	-2	-0	-1	-0	-0.3
1951	Chi-A	11	12	.478	28	23	12	2	0	159^1	142	9	68	39	11.9	3.78	107	.241	.321	11	.250	1	6	4	2	0.8
1952	Chi-A	0	5	.000	7	7	1	0	0	35	38	3	18	12	14.9	6.17	59	.286	.379	0	.000	-1	-10	-10	0	-1.0
	StL-A	0	2	.000	12	1	0	0	0	21	20	1	9	7	12.4	3.86	101	.263	.341	1	.333	0	-0	0	0	0.1
	Yr	0	7	.000	19	8	1	0	0	56	58	4	27	19	13.7	5.30	71	.275	.357	1	.077	-1	-10	-10	1	-0.9
1953	Bos-A	1	0	1.000	3	0	0	0	1	6	9	0	3	1	18.0	6.00	70	.333	.400	0	.000	-0	-1	-1	0	-0.1
Total	6	18	32	.360	99	48	18	2	2	375	377	25	170	118	13.2	3.98	101	.265	.345	19	.179	-3	3	2	3	0.4
● FRED HOLDSWORTH Holdsworth, Fredrick William b: 5/29/52, Detroit, Mich. BR/TR, 6'1", 190 lbs. Deb: 7/27/72																										
1972	Det-A	0	1	.000	2	2	0	0	0	7	13	0	2	5	19.3	12.86	24	.419	.455	1	.333	0	-8	-8	-0	-0.7
1973	Det-A	0	1	.000	5	2	0	0	0	14^2	13	3	6	9	11.7	6.75	61	.236	.311	0	—	0	-5	-4	-0	-0.9
1974	Det-A	0	3	.000	8	5	0	0	0	35^2	40	4	14	16	13.9	4.29	89	.286	.355	0	—	0	-3	-2	-1	-0.5
1976	Bal-A	4	1	.800	16	0	0	0	2	39^2	24	0	13	24	8.4	2.04	160	.179	.252	0	—	0	7	5	-0	0.8
1977	Bal-A	0	1	.000	12	0	0	0	0	14^1	17	0	16	4	21.3	6.28	60	.333	.500	0	—	0	-4	-4	-0	0.0
	Mon-N	3	3	.500	14	6	0	0	0	42^1	35	6	18	21	11.3	3.19	119	.230	.312	0	.000	-1	3	3	0	0.2
1978	Mon-N	0	0	—	6	0	0	0	0	8^2	16	3	8	3	24.9	7.27	48	.381	.480	0	—	0	-4	-4	-0	-0.4
1980	Mil-A	0	0	—	9	0	0	0	0	19^2	24	2	9	12	15.1	4.58	85	.286	.355	0	—	0	-1	-2	0	0.0
Total	7	7	10	.412	72	15	0	0	2	182	182	18	86	94	13.4	4.40	84	.264	.347	1	.077	-1	-13	-15	-2	-1.5

YEAR	TM/L	W	L	PCT	G	GS	CG	SH	SV	IP	H	HR	BB	SO	RAT	ERA	ERA+	OAV	OOB	BH	AVG	PB	PR	/A	PD	TPI

● WALTER HOLKE Holke, Walter Henry "Union Man" b: 12/25/1892, St.Louis, Mo. d: 10/12/54, St.Louis, Mo. BB/TL, 6'1.5", 185 lbs. Deb: 10/06/14 C♦

YEAR	TM/L	W	L	PCT	G	GS	CG	SH	SV	IP	H	HR	BB	SO	RAT	ERA	ERA+	OAV	OOB	BH	AVG	PB	PR	/A	PD	TPI
1923	Phi-N	0	0	—	1	0	0	0	0	0^1	1	0	0	0	27.0	0.00	—	.500	.500	175	.311	0	0	0	0	0.0

● AL HOLLAND Holland, Alfred Willis b: 8/16/52, Roanoke, Va. BR/TL, 5'11", 207 lbs. Deb: 9/05/77

YEAR	TM/L	W	L	PCT	G	GS	CG	SH	SV	IP	H	HR	BB	SO	RAT	ERA	ERA+	OAV	OOB	BH	AVG	PB	PR	/A	PD	TPI
1977	Pit-N	0	0	—	2	0	0	0	0	2^1	4	0	0	1	15.4	7.71	52	.400	.400	0	—	0	-1	-1	0	-0.1
1979	SF-N	0	0	—	3	0	0	0	0	7	3	0	5	7	10.3	0.00	—	.125	.276	0	—	0	3	3	-0	0.3
1980	SF-N	5	3	.625	54	0	0	0	7	82^1	71	2	34	65	11.6	1.75	202	.233	.312	1	.200	1	17	16	0	1.9
1981	SF-N	7	5	.583	47	3	0	0	7	100^2	87	4	44	78	11.9	2.41	142	.233	.317	1	.063	-1	12	11	-1	1.1
1982	SF-N	7	3	.700	58	7	0	0	5	129^2	115	12	40	97	10.8	3.33	108	.231	.289	2	.059	-3	4	4	0	0.1
1983	*Phi-N	8	4	.667	68	0	0	0	25	91^2	63	8	30	100	9.1	2.26	158	.188	.255	0	.000	-1	14	13	-2	1.2
1984	Phi-N☆	5	10	.333	68	0	0	0	29	98^1	82	14	30	61	10.3	3.39	107	.225	.286	0	.000	-1	2	3	-2	0.0
1985	Phi-N	0	1	.000	3	0	0	0	1	4	5	0	4	1	20.3	4.50	82	.333	.474	0	—	0	-0	-0	0	0.0
	Pit-N	1	3	.250	38	0	0	0	4	58^2	48	5	17	47	10.0	3.38	106	.227	.285	2	.400	2	1	1	-1	0.2
	Yr	1	4	.200	41	0	0	0	5	62^2	53	5	21	48	10.6	3.45	104	.233	.298	2	.400	2	1	1	-1	0.2
	Cal-A	0	1	.000	15	0	0	0	0	24^1	17	4	10	14	10.0	1.48	278	.193	.276	0	—	0	7	7	-0	0.7
1986	NY-A	1	0	1.000	25	1	0	0	0	40^2	44	5	9	37	11.7	5.09	80	.268	.306	0	—	0	-4	-5	-1	-0.5
1987	NY-A	0	0	—	3	0	0	0	0	6^1	9	1	9	5	25.6	14.21	31	.321	.486	0	—	0	-7	-7	0	-0.6
Total	10	34	30	.531	384	11	0	0	78	646	548	55	232	513	10.9	2.98	121	.227	.296	6	.083	-2	48	46	-6	4.3

● MUL HOLLAND Holland, Howard Arthur b: 1/6/03, Franklin, Va. d: 2/16/69, Winchester, Va. BR/TR, 6'4", 185 lbs. Deb: 5/25/26

YEAR	TM/L	W	L	PCT	G	GS	CG	SH	SV	IP	H	HR	BB	SO	RAT	ERA	ERA+	OAV	OOB	BH	AVG	PB	PR	/A	PD	TPI
1926	Cin-N	0	0	—	3	0	0	0	0	6^2	3	0	5	0	10.8	1.35	273	.136	.296	1	.500	0	2	2	1	0.3
1927	NY-N	1	0	1.000	2	0	0	0	0	2	0	0	3	0	13.5	0.00	—	.000	.333	0	—	0	1	1	-0	0.1
1929	StL-N	0	1	.000	8	0	0	0	0	14^1	13	3	7	5	13.2	9.42	50	.232	.328	1	.250	1	-7	-8	-0	-0.6
Total	3	1	1	.500	13	0	0	0	0	23	16	3	15	5	12.5	6.26	69	.190	.320	2	.333	1	-5	-5	0	-0.2

● BILL HOLLAND Holland, William David "Dutch" b: 6/4/15, Varina, N.C. BL/TL, 6'1", 190 lbs. Deb: 9/17/39

YEAR	TM/L	W	L	PCT	G	GS	CG	SH	SV	IP	H	HR	BB	SO	RAT	ERA	ERA+	OAV	OOB	BH	AVG	PB	PR	/A	PD	TPI
1939	Was-A	0	1	.000	3	0	0	0	0	4	6	1	5	2	24.8	11.25	39	.400	.550	0	—	0	-3	-3	0	-0.3

● ED HOLLEY Holley, Edward Edgar b: 7/23/1899, Benton, Ky. d: 10/26/86, Paducah, Ky. BR/TR, 6'1.5", 195 lbs. Deb: 5/24/28

YEAR	TM/L	W	L	PCT	G	GS	CG	SH	SV	IP	H	HR	BB	SO	RAT	ERA	ERA+	OAV	OOB	BH	AVG	PB	PR	/A	PD	TPI
1928	Chi-N	0	0	—	13	1	0	0	0	31	31	1	16	10	14.2	3.77	102	.265	.363	0	.000	-0	1	0	-1	-0.1
1932	Phi-N	11	14	.440	34	30	16	2	0	228	247	15	55	87	12.2	3.95	112	.273	.319	12	.132	-6	-2	12	-2	0.4
1933	Phi-N	13	15	.464	30	28	12	3	0	206^2	219	18	62	56	12.8	3.53	108	.273	.335	12	.162	-2	-4	7	-3	0.2
1934	Phi-N	1	8	.111	15	13	2	0	0	72^2	85	10	31	14	14.9	7.18	66	.294	.370	5	.208	-1	-25	-20	-1	-2.0
	Pit-N	0	3	.000	5	4	0	0	0	9^1	20	1	6	2	27.0	15.43	27	.426	.509	2	1.000	2	-12	-12	0	-0.9
	Yr	1	11	.083	20	17	2	0	0	82	105	11	37	16	15.8	8.12	57	.309	.380	7	.269	1	-37	-32	-1	-2.9
Total	4	25	40	.385	97	76	30	5	0	547^2	602	45	170	169	13.1	4.40	95	.279	.339	31	.158	-8	-42	-13	-6	-2.4

● BUG HOLLIDAY Holliday, James Wear b: 2/8/1867, St.Louis, Mo. d: 2/15/10, Cincinnati, Ohio BR/TR, 5'11", 151 lbs. Deb: 4/17/1889 U♦

YEAR	TM/L	W	L	PCT	G	GS	CG	SH	SV	IP	H	HR	BB	SO	RAT	ERA	ERA+	OAV	OOB	BH	AVG	PB	PR	/A	PD	TPI
1892	Cin-N	0	0	—	1	0	0	0	0	4	13	0	1	0	31.5	11.25	29	.520	.539	176	.292	0	-4	-4	0	-0.3
1896	Cin-N	0	0	—	1	0	0	0	0	1	4	0	2	0	63.0	0.00	—	.582	.709	27	.321	0	0	1	-0	0.0
Total	2	0	0	—	2	0	0	0	0	5	17	0	3	0	37.8	9.00	39	.533	.585	1134	.311	1	-3	-3	-0	-0.3

● CARL HOLLING Holling, Carl b: 7/9/1896, Dana, Cal. d: 7/18/62, Santa Rosa, Cal. BR/TR, 6'1", 172 lbs. Deb: 4/19/21

YEAR	TM/L	W	L	PCT	G	GS	CG	SH	SV	IP	H	HR	BB	SO	RAT	ERA	ERA+	OAV	OOB	BH	AVG	PB	PR	/A	PD	TPI
1921	Det-A	3	7	.300	35	11	4	0	4	136	162	8	58	38	14.8	4.30	99	.305	.378	13	.271	1	-0	-0	2	0.2
1922	Det-A	1	1	.500	5	1	0	0	0	9^1	21	1	5	2	27.0	15.43	25	.525	.596	0	.000	-0	-12	-12	0	-1.1
Total	2	4	8	.333	40	12	4	0	4	145^1	183	9	63	40	15.6	5.02	85	.320	.394	13	.260	1	-12	-12	2	-0.9

● AL HOLLINGSWORTH Hollingsworth, Albert Wayne "Boots" b: 2/25/08, St.Louis, Mo. BL/TL, 6', 174 lbs. Deb: 4/16/35 C

YEAR	TM/L	W	L	PCT	G	GS	CG	SH	SV	IP	H	HR	BB	SO	RAT	ERA	ERA+	OAV	OOB	BH	AVG	PB	PR	/A	PD	TPI
1935	Cin-N	6	13	.316	38	22	8	0	0	173^1	165	5	76	89	12.6	3.89	102	.243	.321	8	.148	-2	2	2	1	0.0
1936	Cin-N	9	10	.474	29	25	9	0	0	184	204	4	66	76	13.5	4.16	92	.281	.345	23	.315	7	-3	-7	-2	-0.2
1937	Cin-N	9	15	.375	43	24	11	1	5	202^1	224	8	73	74	13.3	3.91	95	.278	.339	19	.250	3	0	-4	1	0.0
1938	Cin-N	2	2	.500	9	4	1	0	0	34	43	2	12	13	14.6	7.15	51	.307	.362	3	.250	1	-13	-13	0	-1.2
	Phi-N	5	16	.238	24	21	11	1	0	174^1	177	4	77	80	13.1	3.82	102	.264	.340	15	.224	-0	-1	1	-2	-0.1
	Yr	7	18	.280	33	25	12	1	0	208^1	220	6	89	93	13.3	4.36	88	.272	.344	18	.228	1	-13	-12	-2	-1.3
1939	Phi-N	1	9	.100	15	10	3	0	0	60	78	2	27	24	15.8	5.85	69	.317	.385	2	.100	-1	-13	-12	-0	-1.3
	Bro-N	1	2	.333	8	5	1	0	0	27^1	33	1	11	11	14.8	5.27	76	.311	.381	1	.125	-1	-4	-4	1	-0.3
	Yr	2	11	.154	23	15	4	0	0	87^1	111	3	38	35	15.5	5.67	71	.315	.384	3	.107	-2	-17	-16	1	-1.6
1940	Was-A	1	0	1.000	3	2	0	0	0	18	18	0	11	7	14.5	5.50	76	.261	.363	1	.167	0	-2	-3	1	-0.2
1942	StL-A	10	6	.625	33	18	7	1	4	161	173	4	52	60	12.7	2.96	125	.272	.329	10	.179	0	12	13	0	1.4
1943	StL-A	6	13	.316	35	20	9	1	3	154	169	7	51	63	13.0	4.21	79	.281	.339	7	.140	-1	-16	-15	-1	-1.8
1944	*StL-A	5	7	.417	26	10	3	2	1	92^2	108	3	37	22	14.2	4.47	81	.291	.357	2	.071	-2	-11	-9	-1	-1.2
1945	StL-A	12	9	.571	26	22	15	1	1	173^1	164	4	68	64	12.0	2.70	130	.251	.322	12	.197	1	13	16	2	2.0
1946	StL-A	0	0	—	5	0	0	0	0	11	23	1	4	3	22.1	6.55	57	.411	.450	0	.000	-0	-4	-3	-1	-0.4
	Chi-A	3	2	.600	21	2	0	0	1	55	63	2	22	22	13.9	4.58	74	.288	.353	0	.000	-1	-7	-7	-0	-0.9
	Yr	3	2	.600	26	2	0	0	1	66	86	3	26	25	15.3	4.91	71	.313	.372	0	.000	-1	-10	-11	-1	-1.3
Total	11	70	104	.402	315	185	78	7	15	1520^1	1642	47	587	608	13.3	3.99	93	.275	.341	103	.196	3	-44	-44	-2	-4.2

● BONNIE HOLLINGSWORTH Hollingsworth, John Burnette
b: 12/26/1895, Jacksboro, Tenn. d: 1/4/90, Knoxville, Tenn. BR/TR, 5'10", 170 lbs. Deb: 5/30/22

YEAR	TM/L	W	L	PCT	G	GS	CG	SH	SV	IP	H	HR	BB	SO	RAT	ERA	ERA+	OAV	OOB	BH	AVG	PB	PR	/A	PD	TPI
1922	Pit-N	0	0	—	9	0	0	0	0	13^2	17	0	8	7	17.1	7.90	52	.315	.413	0	—	0	-6	-6	-0	-0.6
1923	Was-A	3	7	.300	17	8	1	0	0	72^2	72	3	50	26	15.5	4.09	92	.272	.393	2	.091	-1	-1	-3	-1	-0.4
1924	Bro-N	1	0	1.000	3	1	1	0	0	8^2	8	0	10	7	18.7	6.23	60	.267	.450	0	.000	-0	-2	-2	0	-0.3
1928	Bos-N	0	2	.000	7	2	0	0	0	22^1	30	2	13	10	17.3	5.24	75	.341	.426	1	.167	-0	-3	-3	0	-0.3
Total	4	4	9	.308	36	11	2	0	0	117^1	127	5	81	50	16.3	4.91	78	.291	.406	3	.097	-2	-12	-14	-1	-1.6

● JESSIE HOLLINS Hollins, Jessie Edward b: 1/27/70, Conroe, Tex. BR/TR, 6'3", 190 lbs. Deb: 9/19/92

YEAR	TM/L	W	L	PCT	G	GS	CG	SH	SV	IP	H	HR	BB	SO	RAT	ERA	ERA+	OAV	OOB	BH	AVG	PB	PR	/A	PD	TPI
1992	Chi-N	0	0	—	4	0	0	0	0	4^2	8	1	5	0	25.1	13.50	27	.400	.520	0	—	0	-5	-5	-0	-0.5

● JOHN HOLLISON Hollison, John Henry "Swede" b: 5/3/1870, Chicago, Ill. d: 8/19/69, Chicago, Ill. BR/TL, 5'8", 162 lbs. Deb: 8/13/1892

YEAR	TM/L	W	L	PCT	G	GS	CG	SH	SV	IP	H	HR	BB	SO	RAT	ERA	ERA+	OAV	OOB	BH	AVG	PB	PR	/A	PD	TPI
1892	Chi-N	0	0	—	1	0	0	0	0	4	1	1	0	2	2.3	2.25	148	.077	.077	0	.000	-0	0	0	0	0.0

● BOBO HOLLOMAN Holloman, Alva Lee b: 3/7/25, Thomaston, Ga. d: 5/1/87, Athens, Ga. BR/TR, 6'2", 207 lbs. Deb: 4/18/53

YEAR	TM/L	W	L	PCT	G	GS	CG	SH	SV	IP	H	HR	BB	SO	RAT	ERA	ERA+	OAV	OOB	BH	AVG	PB	PR	/A	PD	TPI
1953	StL-A	3	7	.300	22	10	1	1	0	65^1	69	2	50	25	16.5	5.23	80	.275	.397	2	.105	-2	-9	-8	-0	-0.9

● JIM HOLLOWAY Holloway, James Madison b: 9/22/08, Plaquemine, La. BR/TR, 6'1", 165 lbs. Deb: 5/17/29

YEAR	TM/L	W	L	PCT	G	GS	CG	SH	SV	IP	H	HR	BB	SO	RAT	ERA	ERA+	OAV	OOB	BH	AVG	PB	PR	/A	PD	TPI
1929	Phi-N	0	0	—	3	0	0	0	0	4^2	10	2	5	1	28.9	13.50	38	.455	.556	1	1.000	0	-5	-4	-0	-0.3

● KEN HOLLOWAY Holloway, Kenneth Eugene (b: Kenneth Eugene Hollaway)
b: 8/8/1897, Thomas County, Ga. d: 9/25/68, Thomasville, Ga. BR/TR, 6', 185 lbs. Deb: 8/27/22

YEAR	TM/L	W	L	PCT	G	GS	CG	SH	SV	IP	H	HR	BB	SO	RAT	ERA	ERA+	OAV	OOB	BH	AVG	PB	PR	/A	PD	TPI
1922	Det-A	0	0	—	1	0	0	0	0	1	1	0	0	1	9.0	0.00	—	.250	.250	0	—	0	0	0	0	0.0
1923	Det-A	11	10	.524	42	24	7	1	1	194	232	12	75	55	14.7	4.45	87	.302	.372	8	.123	-5	-10	-13	1	-1.5
1924	Det-A	14	6	.700	49	14	5	0	3	181^1	209	6	61	46	13.7	4.07	101	.299	.361	11	.190	-1	3	1	2	0.2
1925	Det-A	13	4	.765	38	14	6	0	2	157^2	170	8	67	29	13.6	4.62	93	.282	.356	11	.229	-0	-4	-6	-2	-0.8
1926	Det-A	4	6	.400	36	12	3	0	2	139	192	2	42	43	15.7	5.12	79	.343	.397	11	.239	0	-17	-16	0	-1.5
1927	Det-A	11	12	.478	36	23	11	1	6	183^1	210	10	61	36	13.5	4.07	103	.299	.359	8	.129	-5	1	3	2	-0.1
1928	Det-A	4	8	.333	30	11	5	0	2	120^1	137	2	32	32	13.0	4.34	95	.291	.343	4	.121	-2	-4	-3	1	-0.4

YEAR	TM/L	W	L	PCT	G	GS	CG	SH	SV	IP	H	HR	BB	SO	RAT	ERA	ERA+	OAV	OOB	BH	AVG	PB	PR	/A	PD	TPI
1929	Cle-A	6	5	.545	25	11	6	2	0	119	118	2	37	32	11.9	3.03	147	.264	.323	7	.171	-2	16	19	-2	1.5
1930	Cle-A	1	1	.500	12	2	0	0	2	30	49	5	14	8	18.9	8.40	57	.374	.434	0	.000	-2	-13	-12	1	-1.1
	NY-A	0	0	—	16	0	0	0	0	34^1	52	3	8	11	15.7	5.24	82	.374	.408	3	.231	-0	-2	-4	-0	-0.4
	Yr	1	1	.500	28	2	0	0	2	64^1	101	8	22	19	17.2	6.72	68	.374	.421	3	.120	-3	-15	-16	1	-1.5
Total	9	64	52	.552	285	111	43	4	18	1160	1370	50	397	293	14.0	4.40	95	.303	.364	63	.167	-18	-29	-30	4	-4.1
● JEFF HOLLY	Holly, Jeffrey Owen b: 3/1/53, San Pedro, Cal. BL/TL, 6'5", 210 lbs. Deb: 5/01/77																									
1977	Min-A	2	3	.400	18	5	0	0	0	48^1	57	8	12	32	13.0	6.89	58	.300	.345	0	—	0	-15	-16	-1	-1.4
1978	Min-A	1	1	.500	15	1	0	0	0	35^1	28	1	18	12	11.7	3.57	107	.222	.319	0	—	0	1	1	0	0.0
1979	Min-A	0	0	—	6	0	0	0	0	6^1	10	0	3	5	18.5	7.11	62	.385	.448	0	—	0	-2	-2	0	-0.2
Total	3	3	4	.429	39	6	0	0	0	90	95	9	33	49	12.9	5.60	70	.278	.343	0	—	0	-16	-17	-0	-1.6
● BRIAN HOLMAN	Holman, Brian Scott b: 1/25/65, Denver, Colo. BR/TR, 6'4", 185 lbs. Deb: 6/25/88																									
1988	Mon-N	4	8	.333	18	16	1	1	0	100^1	101	3	34	58	12.1	3.23	111	.264	.324	3	.107	-1	2	4	-1	0.2
1989	Mon-N	1	2	.333	10	3	0	0	0	31^2	34	2	15	23	14.2	4.83	73	.270	.352	1	.125	-0	-5	-5	-0	-0.5
	Sea-A	8	10	.444	23	22	6	2	0	159^2	160	9	62	82	12.9	3.44	117	.261	.335	0	—	0	8	10	1	1.2
1990	Sea-A	11	11	.500	28	28	3	0	0	189^2	188	17	66	121	12.3	4.03	98	.260	.327	0	.000	0	-3	-2	-1	-0.3
1991	Sea-A	13	14	.481	30	30	5	3	0	195^1	199	16	77	108	13.2	3.69	112	.268	.345	0	—	0	9	9	2	1.1
Total	4	37	45	.451	109	99	15	6	0	676^2	682	47	254	392	12.8	3.71	106	.263	.335	4	.108	-1	12	18	-0	1.7
● SCOTT HOLMAN	Holman, Randy Scott b: 9/18/58, Santa Paula, Cal. BR/TR, 6'1", 190 lbs. Deb: 9/20/80																									
1980	NY-N	0	0	—	4	0	0	0	0	7	6	0	1	3	9.0	1.29	276	.250	.280	0	—	0	2	2	-0	0.2
1982	NY-N	2	1	.667	4	4	1	0	0	26^2	23	2	7	11	10.1	2.36	154	.232	.283	2	.222	0	4	4	1	0.5
1983	NY-N	1	7	.125	35	10	0	0	0	101	90	7	52	44	12.7	3.74	97	.242	.336	5	.217	0	-1	-1	2	0.1
Total	3	3	8	.273	43	14	1	0	0	134^2	119	9	60	58	12.0	3.34	108	.240	.324	7	.219	1	4	4	2	0.8
● SHAWN HOLMAN	Holman, Shawn Leroy b: 11/10/64, Sewickley, Pa. BR/TR, 6'2", 185 lbs. Deb: 9/05/89																									
1989	Det-A	0	0	—	5	0	0	0	0	10	8	0	11	9	17.1	1.80	212	.211	.388	0	—	0	2	2	-0	0.2
● DARREN HOLMES	Holmes, Darren Lee b: 4/25/66, Asheville, N.C. BR/TR, 6', 199 lbs. Deb: 9/01/90																									
1990	LA-N	0	1	.000	14	0	0	0	0	17^1	15	1	11	19	13.5	5.19	70	.238	.351	0	—	0	-3	-3	-0	-0.3
1991	Mil-A	1	4	.200	40	0	0	0	3	76^1	90	6	27	59	13.9	4.72	84	.295	.354	0	—	0	-5	-6	1	-0.4
1992	Mil-A	4	4	.500	41	0	0	0	6	42^1	35	1	11	31	10.2	2.55	149	.224	.284	0	—	0	7	6	0	0.7
Total	3	5	9	.357	95	0	0	0	9	136	140	8	49	109	12.7	4.10	95	.267	.333	0	—	0	-1	-3	1	-0.0
● CHICK HOLMES	Holmes, Elwood Marter b: 3/22/1896, Beverly, N.J. d: 4/15/54, Camden, N, J. TR , Deb: 6/27/18																									
1918	Phi-A	0	0	—	2	0	0	0	0	2	4	0	1	0	27.0	13.50	22	.400	.500	0	—	0	-2	-2	-0	-0.3
● JIM HOLMES	Holmes, James Scott b: 8/2/1882, Lawrenceburg, Ky. d: 3/10/60, Jacksonville, Fla. Deb: 9/08/06																									
1906	Phi-A	0	1	.000	3	1	0	0	0	9	10	0	8	1	19.0	4.00	68	.284	.430	3	.600	1	-1	-1	0	0.0
1908	Bro-N	1	4	.200	13	1	1	0	0	40	37	0	20	10	13.5	3.37	69	.270	.375	1	.077	-1	-4	-5	-2	-0.8
Total	2	1	5	.167	16	2	1	0	0	49	47	0	28	11	14.5	3.49	69	.273	.387	4	.222	0	-6	-6	-2	-0.8
● DUCKY HOLMES	Holmes, James William b: 1/28/1869, Des Moines, Iowa d: 8/6/32, Truro, Iowa BL/TR, 5'6", 170 lbs. Deb: 8/08/1895 ♦																									
1895	Lou-N	1	0	1.000	2	1	1	0	0	14	16	1	4	0	13.5	5.79	80	.283	.341	60	.373	1	-2	-2	0	-0.1
1896	Lou-N	0	1	.000	2	1	0	0	0	12	26	0	8	3	25.5	7.50	58	.430	.497	38	.270	0	-4	-4	0	-0.3
Total	2	1	1	.500	4	2	1	0	0	26	42	1	12	3	19.0	6.58	68	.359	.423	1014	.282	1	-6	-6	0	-0.4
● HERM HOLSHOUSER	Holshouser, Herman Alexander b: 1/20/07, Rockwell, N.C. BR/TR, 6', 170 lbs. Deb: 4/15/30																									
1930	StL-A	0	1	.000	25	1	0	0	1	62^1	103	8	28	37	19.3	7.80	63	.376	.439	2	.125	-1	-22	-20	-0	-1.8
● VERN HOLTGRAVE	Holtgrave, Lavern George "Woody" b: 10/18/42, Aviston, Ill. BR/TR, 6'1", 183 lbs. Deb: 9/26/65																									
1965	Det-A	0	0	—	1	0	0	0	0	3	4	0	2	2	18.0	6.00	58	.308	.400	0	—	0	-1	-1	-0	-0.1
● BRIAN HOLTON	Holton, Brian John b: 11/29/59, McKeesport, Pa. BR/TR, 6', 193 lbs. Deb: 9/09/85																									
1985	LA-N	1	1	.500	3	0	0	0	0	4	9	0	1	1	22.5	9.00	39	.450	.476	0	—	0	-2	-2	0	-0.2
1986	LA-N	2	3	.400	12	3	0	0	0	24^1	28	1	6	24	12.9	4.44	78	.292	.340	0	.000	-0	-2	-3	0	-0.3
1987	LA-N	3	2	.600	53	1	0	0	2	83^1	87	11	32	58	12.9	3.89	102	.269	.335	1	.200	0	2	1	1	0.2
1988	*LA-N	7	3	.700	45	0	0	0	1	84^2	69	1	26	49	10.2	1.70	196	.228	.292	0	.000	-1	16	15	-0	1.6
1989	Bal-A	5	7	.417	39	12	0	0	0	116^1	140	11	39	51	13.9	4.02	94	.300	.355	0	—	0	-2	-3	-0	-0.3
1990	Bal-A	2	3	.400	33	0	0	0	0	58	68	7	21	27	13.8	4.50	84	.292	.350	0	—	0	-4	-5	1	-0.4
Total	6	20	19	.513	185	16	0	0	3	370^2	401	31	125	210	12.8	3.62	102	.278	.337	1	.050	-1	8	3	1	0.6
● KEN HOLTZMAN	Holtzman, Kenneth Dale b: 11/3/45, St.Louis, Mo. BR/TL, 6'2", 175 lbs. Deb: 9/04/65																									
1965	Chi-N	0	0	—	3	0	0	0	0	4	2	1	3	3	11.3	2.25	164	.143	.294	0	—	0	1	1	0	0.1
1966	Chi-N	11	16	.407	34	33	9	0	0	220^2	194	27	68	171	10.8	3.79	97	.235	.296	9	.123	-3	-5	-3	-2	-0.8
1967	Chi-N	9	0	1.000	12	12	3	0	0	92^2	76	11	44	62	11.8	2.53	140	.222	.314	7	.200	1	9	10	0	1.3
1968	Chi-N	11	14	.440	34	32	6	3	1	215	201	17	76	151	11.8	3.35	94	.248	.317	10	.125	-2	-9	-4	1	-0.7
1969	Chi-N	17	13	.567	39	39	12	6	0	261^1	248	18	93	176	11.9	3.58	112	.247	.314	15	.150	-1	0	13	-1	1.1
1970	Chi-N	17	11	.607	39	38	15	1	0	287^2	271	30	94	202	11.5	3.38	133	.248	.309	21	.200	2	21	36	0	3.9
1971	Chi-N	9	15	.375	30	29	9	3	0	195	213	18	64	143	12.9	4.48	88	.276	.333	9	.130	-1	-22	-12	-1	-1.4
1972	*Oak-A☆	19	11	.633	39	37	16	4	0	265^1	232	23	52	134	9.8	2.51	113	.236	.278	16	.178	1	16	10	0	1.3
1973	*Oak-A★	21	13	.618	40	40	16	4	0	297^1	275	22	66	157	10.4	2.97	120	.243	.287	0	—	0	28	19	-1	1.9
1974	*Oak-A	19	17	.528	39	38	9	3	0	255^1	273	14	51	117	11.5	3.07	108	.272	.309	0	—	0	16	7	0	0.8
1975	*Oak-A	18	14	.563	39	38	13	2	0	266^1	217	16	108	122	11.2	3.14	115	.222	.303	0	.000	0	19	14	3	1.8
1976	Bal-A	5	4	.556	13	13	6	1	0	97^2	100	4	35	25	12.5	2.86	115	.271	.336	0	—	0	7	5	1	0.6
	NY-A	9	7	.563	21	21	10	2	0	149	165	14	35	41	12.1	4.17	82	.283	.323	0	—	0	-11	-12	-1	-1.3
	Yr	14	11	.560	34	34	16	3	0	246^2	265	18	70	66	12.2	3.65	92	.277	.326	0	—	0	-4	-8	1	-0.7
1977	NY-A	2	3	.400	18	11	0	0	0	71^2	105	7	24	14	16.3	5.78	68	.362	.413	0	—	0	-14	-15	2	-1.1
1978	NY-A	1	0	1.000	5	3	0	0	0	17^2	21	2	9	3	15.3	4.08	89	.313	.395	0	—	0	-1	-1	1	0.1
	Chi-N	0	3	.000	23	6	0	0	2	53	61	10	35	36	16.5	6.11	66	.286	.390	2	.200	1	-15	-12	-0	-1.3
1979	Chi-N	6	9	.400	23	20	3	2	0	117^2	133	15	53	44	14.7	4.59	90	.287	.368	10	.233	2	-11	-6	-2	-0.6
Total	15	174	150	.537	451	410	127	31	3	2867^1	2787	249	910	1601	11.8	3.49	104	.255	.315	99	.163	-0	31	48	1	5.7
● RICK HONEYCUTT	Honeycutt, Frederick Wayne b: 6/29/52, Chattanooga, Tenn. BL/TL, 5'11", 190 lbs. Deb: 8/24/77																									
1977	Sea-A	0	1	.000	10	3	0	0	0	29	26	7	11	17	12.4	4.34	95	.239	.325	0	—	0	-1	-1	-1	-0.1
1978	Sea-A	5	11	.313	26	24	4	1	0	134^1	150	12	49	50	13.5	4.89	78	.285	.349	0	—	0	-17	-16	1	-1.4
1979	Sea-A	11	12	.478	33	28	8	1	0	194	201	22	67	83	12.7	4.04	108	.268	.333	0	—	0	4	7	-1	0.6
1980	Sea-A☆	10	17	.370	30	30	9	1	0	203^1	221	22	60	79	12.6	3.94	105	.280	.333	0	—	0	2	4	-0	0.4
1981	Tex-A	11	6	.647	20	20	8	2	0	127^2	120	12	17	40	9.7	3.31	105	.246	.272	0	—	0	5	2	1	0.5
1982	Tex-A	5	17	.227	30	26	4	1	0	164	201	20	54	64	14.2	5.27	73	.305	.360	0	—	0	-22	-25	1	-2.0
1983	Tex-A★	14	8	.636	25	25	5	2	0	174^2	168	9	37	56	10.9	**2.42**	**165**	.262	.308	0	—	0	**32**	31	3	3.8
	*LA-N	2	3	.400	9	7	1	0	0	39	46	6	13	18	14.1	5.77	62	.297	.359	1	.083	-1	-9	-9	2	-0.8
1984	LA-N	10	9	.526	29	28	6	2	0	183^2	180	11	51	75	11.4	2.84	124	.258	.310	8	.143	-0	15	14	2	1.7
1985	*LA-N	8	12	.400	31	25	1	0	1	142	141	9	49	67	12.1	3.42	102	.261	.323	5	.132	0	3	1	3	0.4
1986	LA-N	11	9	.550	32	28	0	0	0	171	164	9	45	100	11.2	3.32	104	.249	.300	3	.070	0	8	3	2	0.5

YEAR	TM/L	W	L	PCT	G	GS	CG	SH	SV	IP	H	HR	BB	SO	RAT	ERA	ERA+	OAV	OOB	BH	AVG	PB	PR	/A	PD	TPI
1987	LA-N	2	12	.143	27	20	1	1	0	115^2	133	10	45	92	14.0	4.59	86	.278	.343	7	.233	2	-7	-8	-0	-0.6
	Oak-A	1	4	.200	7	4	0	0	0	23^2	25	3	9	10	13.7	5.32	77	.275	.353	0	—	0	-2	-3	-0	-0.3
1988	*Oak-A	3	2	.600	55	0	0	0	7	79^2	74	6	25	47	11.5	3.50	108	.253	.318	0	—	0	4	2	1	0.5
1989	*Oak-A	2	2	.500	64	0	0	0	12	76^2	56	5	26	52	9.7	2.35	157	.207	.279	0	—	0	13	11	1	1.3
1990	*Oak-A	2	2	.500	63	0	0	0	7	63^1	46	2	22	38	9.8	2.70	138	.204	.278	0	.000	0	8	7	1	0.8
1991	Oak-A	2	4	.333	43	0	0	0	0	37^2	37	3	20	26	14.1	3.58	107	.261	.360	0	—	0	2	1	0	0.4
1992	*Oak-A	1	4	.200	54	0	0	0	3	39	41	2	10	32	12.5	3.69	102	.272	.329	0	—	0	1	0	-1	0.2
Total	16	100	135	.426	588	268	47	11	30	1998^1	2030	170	610	946	12.1	3.72	102	.265	.323	24	.133	2	39	20	15	5.9

● DON HOOD Hood, Donald Harris b: 10/16/49, Florence, S.C. BL/TL, 6'2", 180 lbs. Deb: 7/16/73

YEAR	TM/L	W	L	PCT	G	GS	CG	SH	SV	IP	H	HR	BB	SO	RAT	ERA	ERA+	OAV	OOB	BH	AVG	PB	PR	/A	PD	TPI
1973	Bal-A	3	2	.600	8	4	1	1	1	32^1	31	1	6	18	10.6	3.90	96	.256	.297	0	—	0	-0	-1	-1	-0.1
1974	Bal-A	1	1	.500	20	2	0	0	1	57^1	47	1	20	26	10.5	3.45	100	.223	.290	0	—	0	1	-0	-0	0.0
1975	Cle-A	6	10	.375	29	19	2	0	0	135^1	136	16	57	51	12.8	4.39	86	.268	.342	0	—	0	-9	-9	-2	-1.1
1976	Cle-A	3	5	.375	33	6	0	0	1	77^2	89	5	41	32	15.5	4.87	72	.296	.387	0	—	0	-12	-12	0	-1.2
1977	Cle-A	2	1	.667	41	5	1	0	0	105	87	3	49	62	12.0	3.00	131	.224	.317	0	—	0	12	11	-2	1.2
1978	Cle-A	5	6	.455	36	19	1	0	0	154^2	166	13	77	73	14.2	4.48	83	.278	.361	0	—	0	-12	-13	0	-1.2
1979	Cle-A	1	0	1.000	13	0	0	0	1	22	13	1	14	7	11.5	3.68	116	.169	.304	0	—	0	1	1	0	0.2
	NY-A	3	1	.750	27	6	0	0	1	67^1	62	3	30	22	12.6	3.07	132	.252	.338	0	—	0	9	7	1	0.8
	Yr	4	1	.800	40	6	0	0	2	89^1	75	4	44	29	12.2	3.22	128	.231	.327	0	—	0	10	9	1	1.0
1980	StL-N	4	6	.400	33	8	1	0	0	82^1	90	2	34	35	13.8	3.39	109	.288	.362	4	.200	-0	2	3	1	0.3
1982	KC-A	4	0	1.000	30	3	0	0	1	66^2	71	7	22	31	12.8	3.51	116	.276	.338	0	—	0	4	4	0	0.5
1983	KC-A	2	3	.400	27	0	0	0	0	47^2	48	5	14	17	12.1	2.27	180	.273	.333	0	—	0	10	10	1	1.1
Total	10	34	35	.493	297	72	6	1	6	848^1	840	57	364	374	13.0	3.79	101	.263	.342	4	.200	-0	5	2	-0	0.5

● WALLY HOOD Hood, Wallace James Jr. b: 9/24/25, Los Angeles, Cal. BR/TR, 6'1", 190 lbs. Deb: 9/23/49 F

YEAR	TM/L	W	L	PCT	G	GS	CG	SH	SV	IP	H	HR	BB	SO	RAT	ERA	ERA+	OAV	OOB	BH	AVG	PB	PR	/A	PD	TPI
1949	NY-A	0	0	—	2	0	0	0	0	2^1	0	0	1	2	3.9	0.00	—	.000	.143	0	—	0	1	1	-0	0.1

● JAY HOOK Hook, James Wesley b: 11/18/36, Waukegan, Ill. BL/TR, 6'2", 182 lbs. Deb: 9/03/57

YEAR	TM/L	W	L	PCT	G	GS	CG	SH	SV	IP	H	HR	BB	SO	RAT	ERA	ERA+	OAV	OOB	BH	AVG	PB	PR	/A	PD	TPI
1957	Cin-N	0	1	.000	3	2	0	0	0	10	6	0	8	6	12.6	4.50	91	.176	.333	0	.000	-0	-1	-0	0	-0.1
1958	Cin-N	0	1	.000	1	1	0	0	0	3	3	2	2	5	15.0	12.00	35	.250	.357	0	.000	-0	-3	-3	-0	-0.2
1959	Cin-N	5	5	.500	17	15	4	0	0	79	79	11	39	37	13.8	5.13	79	.266	.357	3	.125	-1	-10	-9	-1	-1.1
1960	Cin-N	11	18	.379	36	33	10	2	0	222	222	31	73	103	12.2	4.50	85	.263	.325	6	.083	-3	-18	-17	-1	-2.1
1961	Cin-N	1	3	.250	22	5	0	0	0	62^2	83	14	22	36	15.8	7.76	52	.322	.386	2	.133	-1	-26	-26	-1	-2.5
1962	NY-N	8	19	.296	37	34	13	0	0	213^2	230	31	71	113	13.0	4.84	86	.273	.335	14	.203	2	-21	-16	-0	-1.3
1963	NY-N	4	14	.222	41	20	3	0	1	152^2	168	21	53	89	13.6	5.48	64	.281	.348	9	.237	2	-37	-34	-1	-3.4
1964	NY-N	0	1	.000	3	2	0	0	0	9^2	17	2	7	5	22.3	9.31	38	.395	.480	0	.000	-0	-6	-6	0	-0.6
Total	8	29	62	.319	160	112	30	2	1	752^2	808	112	275	394	13.3	5.23	75	.276	.344	34	.151	-1	-123	-110	-4	-11.3

● BUCK HOOKER Hooker, William Edward b: 8/28/1880, Richmond, Va. d: 7/2/29, Richmond, Va. TR , 5'6", Deb: 9/05/02

YEAR	TM/L	W	L	PCT	G	GS	CG	SH	SV	IP	H	HR	BB	SO	RAT	ERA	ERA+	OAV	OOB	BH	AVG	PB	PR	/A	PD	TPI
1902	Cin-N	0	1	.000	1	1	1	0	0	8	11	1	0	0	12.4	4.50	67	.326	.326	0	.000	-0	-2	-1	-0	-0.2
1903	Cin-N	0	0	—	1	0	0	0	0	2^1	2	0	2	0	15.4	0.00	—	.250	.400	0	.000	-0	1	1	-0	0.1
Total	2	0	1	.000	2	1	1	0	0	10^1	13	1	2	0	13.1	3.48	90	.311	.343	0	.000	-1	-1	-0	-1	-0.1

● HARRY HOOPER Hooper, Harry Bartholomew b: 8/24/1887, Bell Station, Cal. d: 12/18/74, Santa Cruz, Cal. BL/TR, 5'10", 168 lbs. Deb: 4/16/09 H♦

YEAR	TM/L	W	L	PCT	G	GS	CG	SH	SV	IP	H	HR	BB	SO	RAT	ERA	ERA+	OAV	OOB	BH	AVG	PB	PR	/A	PD	TPI
1913	Bos-A	0	0	—	1	0	0	0	0	2	2	0	1	0	13.5	0.00	—	.333	.429	169	.288	0	1	1	-0	0.1

● BOB HOOPER Hooper, Robert Nelson b: 5/30/22, Leamington, Ont., Canada d: 3/17/80, New Brunswick, N.J BR/TR, 5'11", 195 lbs. Deb: 4/19/50

YEAR	TM/L	W	L	PCT	G	GS	CG	SH	SV	IP	H	HR	BB	SO	RAT	ERA	ERA+	OAV	OOB	BH	AVG	PB	PR	/A	PD	TPI
1950	Phi-A	15	10	.600	45	20	3	0	5	170^1	181	15	91	58	14.4	5.02	91	.272	.361	7	.125	-2	-8	-9	3	-0.7
1951	Phi-A	12	10	.545	38	23	9	0	5	189	192	13	61	64	12.2	4.38	98	.267	.327	15	.208	-1	-5	-2	1	-0.2
1952	Phi-A	8	15	.348	43	14	4	0	6	144^1	158	13	68	40	14.3	5.18	76	.279	.361	8	.195	1	-24	-20	3	-1.6
1953	Cle-A	5	4	.556	43	0	0	0	7	69^1	50	4	38	16	11.7	4.02	93	.206	.318	1	.083	-1	-0	-2	1	-0.2
1954	Cle-A	0	0	—	17	0	0	0	2	34^2	39	3	16	12	14.5	4.93	74	.289	.368	0	.000	-1	-5	-5	-0	-0.6
1955	Cin-N	0	2	.000	8	0	0	0	0	13	20	2	6	6	18.0	7.62	56	.357	.419	0	.000	-0	-5	-5	0	-0.5
Total	6	40	41	.494	194	57	16	0	25	620^2	640	50	280	196	13.5	4.80	87	.268	.348	31	.166	-3	-48	-42	8	-3.8

● LEON HOOTEN Hooten, Michael Leon b: 4/4/48, Downey, Cal. BR/TR, 5'11", 180 lbs. Deb: 4/13/74

YEAR	TM/L	W	L	PCT	G	GS	CG	SH	SV	IP	H	HR	BB	SO	RAT	ERA	ERA+	OAV	OOB	BH	AVG	PB	PR	/A	PD	TPI
1974	Oak-A	0	0	—	6	0	0	0	0	8^1	6	1	4	1	11.9	3.24	102	.207	.324	0	—	0	0	0	0	0.0

● BURT HOOTON Hooton, Burt Carlton b: 2/17/50, Greenville, Tex. BR/TR, 6'1", 210 lbs. Deb: 6/17/71

YEAR	TM/L	W	L	PCT	G	GS	CG	SH	SV	IP	H	HR	BB	SO	RAT	ERA	ERA+	OAV	OOB	BH	AVG	PB	PR	/A	PD	TPI
1971	Chi-N	2	0	1.000	3	3	2	1	0	21^1	8	2	10	22	7.6	2.11	186	.111	.220	0	.000	-1	3	4	-0	0.4
1972	Chi-N	11	14	.440	33	31	9	3	0	218^1	201	13	81	132	11.7	2.80	136	.246	.315	9	.125	-1	16	24	1	2.7
1973	Chi-N	14	17	.452	42	34	9	2	0	239^2	248	12	73	134	12.2	3.68	107	.270	.327	9	.129	-0	-1	7	-1	0.6
1974	Chi-N	7	11	.389	48	21	3	1	1	176^1	214	16	51	94	13.7	4.80	79	.299	.348	3	.060	-4	-23	-19	3	-2.0
1975	Chi-N	0	2	.000	3	3	0	0	0	11	18	2	4	5	18.0	8.18	47	.383	.431	0	.000	-0	-6	-5	1	-0.5
	LA-N	18	7	.720	31	30	12	4	0	223^2	172	16	64	148	9.5	2.82	121	.210	.267	9	.129	1	20	14	-2	1.4
	Yr	18	9	.667	34	33	12	4	0	234^2	190	18	68	153	9.9	3.07	111	.219	.276	9	.123	0	14	9	-1	0.9
1976	LA-N	11	15	.423	33	33	8	4	0	226^2	203	16	60	116	10.5	3.26	104	.241	.292	6	.097	-2	6	3	-2	0.0
1977	*LA-N	12	7	.632	32	31	6	2	1	223^1	184	14	60	153	10.0	2.62	146	.225	.281	11	.164	-0	32	30	0	3.1
1978	*LA-N	19	10	.655	32	32	10	3	0	236	196	17	61	104	9.8	2.71	130	.226	.277	10	.149	1	23	21	-1	2.3
1979	LA-N	11	10	.524	29	29	12	1	0	212	191	11	63	129	10.9	2.97	122	.244	.302	11	.147	-1	18	16	-0	1.5
1980	LA-N	14	8	.636	34	33	4	2	1	206^2	194	22	64	118	11.2	3.66	96	.249	.306	4	.063	-3	-1	-4	-0	-0.7
1981	*LA-N★	11	6	.647	23	23	5	4	0	142^1	124	3	33	74	10.1	2.28	146	.237	.285	8	.190	2	19	16	-1	2.0
1982	LA-N	4	7	.364	21	21	2	2	0	120^2	130	5	33	51	12.3	4.03	86	.275	.325	3	.086	-1	-6	-8	0	-0.8
1983	LA-N	9	8	.529	33	27	2	0	0	160	156	21	59	87	12.2	4.22	85	.254	.321	8	.160	1	-11	-11	-0	-1.1
1984	LA-N	3	6	.333	54	6	0	0	4	110	109	5	43	62	12.4	3.44	103	.263	.333	1	.071	-1	2	1	-0	0.0
1985	Tex-A	5	8	.385	29	20	2	0	0	124	149	18	40	62	13.7	5.23	81	.297	.349	0	—	0	-15	-14	-1	-1.5
Total	15	151	136	.526	480	377	86	29	7	2652	2497	193	799	1491	11.3	3.38	108	.250	.306	92	.123	-9	77	77	-4	7.4

● JOHN HOOVER Hoover, John Nicklaus b: 11/22/62, Fresno, Cal. BR/TR, 6'2", 190 lbs. Deb: 5/23/90

YEAR	TM/L	W	L	PCT	G	GS	CG	SH	SV	IP	H	HR	BB	SO	RAT	ERA	ERA+	OAV	OOB	BH	AVG	PB	PR	/A	PD	TPI
1990	Tex-A	0	0	—	2	0	0	0	0	4^2	8	0	3	0	21.2	11.57	34	.364	.440	0	—	0	-4	-4	-0	-0.4

● DICK HOOVER Hoover, Richard Lloyd b: 12/11/25, Columbus, Ohio d: 4/12/81, Lake Placid, Fla. BL/TL, 6', 170 lbs. Deb: 4/16/52

YEAR	TM/L	W	L	PCT	G	GS	CG	SH	SV	IP	H	HR	BB	SO	RAT	ERA	ERA+	OAV	OOB	BH	AVG	PB	PR	/A	PD	TPI
1952	Bos-N	0	0	—	2	0	0	0	0	4^2	8	1	3	0	21.2	7.71	47	.348	.423	0	—	0	-2	-2	-0	-0.2

● SAM HOPE Hope, Samuel b: 12/4/1878, Brooklyn, N.Y. d: 6/30/46, Greenport, N.Y. BR/TR, 5'10", Deb: 8/05/07

YEAR	TM/L	W	L	PCT	G	GS	CG	SH	SV	IP	H	HR	BB	SO	RAT	ERA	ERA+	OAV	OOB	BH	AVG	PB	PR	/A	PD	TPI
1907	Phi-A	0	0	—	1	0	0	0	0	0^1	3	0	0	0	81.0	0.00	—	.762	.762	0	—	0	0	0	0	0.0

● PAUL HOPKINS Hopkins, Paul Henry b: 9/25/04, Chester, Conn. BR/TR, 6', 175 lbs. Deb: 9/29/27

YEAR	TM/L	W	L	PCT	G	GS	CG	SH	SV	IP	H	HR	BB	SO	RAT	ERA	ERA+	OAV	OOB	BH	AVG	PB	PR	/A	PD	TPI
1927	Was-A	1	0	1.000	2	1	0	0	0	9	13	1	4	5	17.0	5.00	81	.361	.425	2	.667	1	-1	-1	0	0.0
1929	Was-A	0	1	.000	7	0	0	0	0	16^1	15	1	9	5	13.2	2.20	192	.250	.348	0	.000	-1	4	4	-0	0.3
	StL-A	0	0	—	2	0	0	0	0	2	0	0	2	1	9.0	0.00	—	.000	.286	0	—	0	1	1	-0	0.1
	Yr	0	1	.000	9	0	0	0	0	18^1	15	1	11	6	12.8	1.96	217	.231	.342	0	.000	-1	5	5	-0	0.4
Total	2	1	1	.500	11	1	0	0	0	27^1	28	2	15	11	14.2	2.96	142	.277	.371	2	.333	1	4	4	-0	0.4

● LEFTY HOPPER Hopper, Clarence F. b: 5/27/1874, Jersey City, N.J. TL , Deb: 10/10/1898

YEAR	TM/L	W	L	PCT	G	GS	CG	SH	SV	IP	H	HR	BB	SO	RAT	ERA	ERA+	OAV	OOB	BH	AVG	PB	PR	/A	PD	TPI
1898	Bro-N	0	2	.000	2	2	2	0	0	11	14	0	5	5	15.5	4.91	73	.307	.376	0	.000	-1	-2	-2	0	-0.2

YEAR TM/L	W	L	PCT	G	GS	CG	SH	SV	IP	H	HR	BB	SO	RAT	ERA	ERA+	OAV	OOB	BH	AVG	PB	PR	/A	PD	TPI

● **JIM HOPPER**   Hopper, James McDaniel   b: 9/1/19, Charlotte, N.C.   d: 1/23/82, Charlotte, N.C.   BR/TR, 6'1", 175 lbs.   Deb: 4/21/46

| 1946 Pit-N | 0 | 1 | .000 | 2 | 1 | 0 | 0 | 0 | 4 | 6 | 1 | 3 | 1 | 20.3 | 11.25 | 31 | .316 | .409 | — | | 0 | -3 | -3 | 0 | -0.3 |

● **BILL HOPPER**   Hopper, William Booth "Bird Dog"   b: 10/26/1890, Jackson, Tenn.   d: 1/14/65, Allen Park, Mich.   BR/TR, 6', 175 lbs.   Deb: 9/11/13

1913 StL-N	0	3	.000	3	3	2	0	0	24	20	2	8	3	11.6	3.75	86	.230	.316	3	.375	1	-1	-1	-0	0.0
1914 StL-N	0	0	—	3	0	0	0	0	5	6	0	5	1	19.8	3.60	78	.286	.423	0	—	0	-0	-0	0	0.0
1915 Was-A	0	1	.000	13	0	0	0	1	31¹	39	0	16	8	16.1	4.60	65	.348	.434	1	.200	0	-6	-6	1	-0.5
Total 3	0	4	.000	19	3	2	0	1	60¹	65	2	29	12	14.6	4.18	73	.295	.387	4	.308	1	-8	-7	1	-0.5

● **JOHN HORAN**   Horan, John J.   b: 1863, Ireland   d: 12/21/05, Chicago, Ill.   Deb: 5/17/1884

| 1884 CP-U | 3 | 6 | .333 | 13 | 10 | 9 | 0 | 0 | 98 | 94 | 2 | 55 | 10 | — | 3.49 | 86 | .236 | .279 | 6 | .088 | -5 | -5 | -5 | -1 | -0.9 |

● **JOE HORLEN**   Horlen, Joel Edward   b: 8/14/37, San Antonio, Tex.   BR/TR, 6', 175 lbs.   Deb: 9/04/61

1961 Chi-A	1	3	.250	5	4	0	0	0	17²	25	2	13	11	19.4	6.62	59	.338	.437	0	.000	-1	-5	-5	0	-0.5
1962 Chi-A	7	6	.538	20	19	5	1	0	108²	108	10	43	63	12.7	4.89	80	.262	.335	2	.053	-3	-11	-12	2	-1.2
1963 Chi-A	11	7	.611	33	21	3	0	0	124	122	10	55	61	13.0	3.27	107	.261	.341	9	.225	1	5	3	1	0.6
1964 Chi-A	13	9	.591	32	28	9	2	0	210²	142	11	55	138	**8.6**	1.88	184	**.190**	**.250**	11	.159	-1	41	37	3	4.5
1965 Chi-A	13	13	.500	34	34	7	4	0	219	203	16	39	125	10.1	2.88	111	.245	.281	9	.132	0	14	8	-0	0.8
1966 Chi-A	10	13	.435	37	29	4	2	1	211	185	24	53	124	10.4	2.43	130	.233	.286	4	.067	-3	24	17	6	2.3
1967 Chi-A☆	19	7	**.731**	35	35	13	**6**	0	258	188	13	58	103	**8.7**	2.06	151	.203	**.253**	14	.169	1	**34**	**30**	3	**3.9**
1968 Chi-A	12	14	.462	35	35	4	1	0	223²	197	16	70	102	11.3	2.37	127	.238	.308	7	.104	-1	15	16	2	0.0
1969 Chi-A	13	16	.448	36	35	7	2	0	235²	237	20	77	121	12.2	3.78	102	.261	.323	14	.182	-1	-4	2	-1	0.0
1970 Chi-A	6	16	.273	28	26	4	0	0	172¹	198	18	41	77	12.7	4.86	80	.287	.331	6	.115	-2	-22	-18	4	-1.6
1971 Chi-A	8	9	.471	34	18	3	0	2	137¹	150	12	30	82	12.1	4.26	84	.284	.329	4	.100	-2	-12	-10	1	-1.2
1972 *Oak-A	3	4	.429	32	6	0	0	1	84	74	3	20	58	10.5	3.00	95	.236	.291	3	.176	-0	1	-1	1	-0.1
Total 12	116	117	.498	361	290	59	18	4	2002	1829	145	554	1065	11.0	3.11	109	.243	.300	83	.134	-12	78	66	22	9.5

● **TRADER HORNE**   Horne, Berlyn Dale "Sonny"   b: 4/12/1899, Bachman, Ohio   d: 2/3/83, Franklin, Ohio   BB/TR, 5'9", 155 lbs.   Deb: 4/24/29

| 1929 Chi-N | 1 | 1 | .500 | 11 | 1 | 0 | 0 | 0 | 23 | 24 | 3 | 21 | 6 | 17.6 | 5.09 | 91 | .273 | .413 | 2 | .400 | 0 | -1 | -1 | 0 | 0.0 |

● **JACK HORNER**   Horner, William Frank   b: 9/21/1863, Baltimore, Md.   d: 7/14/10, New Orleans, La.   Deb: 5/07/1894

| 1894 Bal-N | 0 | 1 | .000 | 2 | 1 | 1 | 0 | 1 | 11 | 15 | 0 | 7 | 2 | 18.8 | 9.00 | 61 | .321 | .421 | 1 | .167 | -0 | -4 | -4 | 0 | -0.3 |

● **JOE HORNUNG**   Hornung, Michael Joseph "Ubbo Ubbo"   b: 6/12/1857, Carthage, N.Y.   d: 10/30/31, Howard Beach, N.Y.   BR/TR, 5'8.5", 164 lbs.   Deb: 5/01/1879   U◆

| 1880 Buf-N | 0 | 0 | — | 1 | 0 | 0 | 0 | 0 | 3 | 2 | 0 | 1 | 0 | 9.0 | 6.00 | 41 | .167 | .231 | 91 | .266 | 0 | -1 | -1 | 0 | -0.1 |

● **HANSON HORSEY**   Horsey, Hanson   b: 11/26/1889, Galena, Md.   d: 12/1/49, Millington, Md.   BR/TR, 5'11", 165 lbs.   Deb: 4/27/12

| 1912 Cin-N | 0 | 0 | — | 1 | 0 | 0 | 0 | 0 | 4 | 14 | 0 | 3 | 0 | 38.3 | 22.50 | 15 | .609 | .654 | 0 | .000 | -0 | -8 | -9 | -0 | -0.6 |

● **VINCE HORSMAN**   Horsman, Vincent Stanley Joseph   b: 3/9/67, Halifax, N.S., Can.   BR/TL, 6'2", 175 lbs.   Deb: 9/05/91

1991 Tor-A	0	0	—	4	0	0	0	0	4	2	0	3	2	11.3	0.00	—	.167	.333	0	—	0	2	2	-0	0.0
1992 Oak-A	2	1	.667	58	0	0	0	1	43¹	39	3	21	18	12.5	2.49	152	.252	.341	0	—	0	7	6	-0	0.7
Total 2	2	1	.667	62	0	0	0	1	47¹	41	3	24	20	12.4	2.28	167	.246	.340	0	—	0	9	8	-0	0.7

● **OSCAR HORSTMANN**   Horstmann, Oscar Theodore   b: 6/2/1891, Alma, Mo.   d: 5/11/77, Salina, Kan.   BR/TR, 5'11", 165 lbs.   Deb: 4/18/17

1917 StL-N	9	4	.692	35	11	4	1	0	138²	111	5	54	50	11.0	3.44	78	.225	.307	9	.196	-1	-11	-12	-0	-1.2
1918 StL-N	0	2	.000	9	2	0	0	0	23	29	0	14	6	16.8	5.48	49	.349	.443	0	.000	-0	-7	-7	1	-0.7
1919 StL-N	0	1	.000	6	2	0	0	0	15	14	0	12	5	15.6	3.00	93	.264	.400	1	.500	-0	-0	-0	0	-0.0
Total 3	9	7	.563	50	15	4	1	1	176²	154	5	80	61	12.1	3.67	74	.245	.334	10	.192	1	-18	-19	1	-1.9

● **ELMER HORTON**   Horton, Elmer E. "Herky Jerky"   b: 9/4/1869, Hamilton, Ohio   d: 8/12/20, Vienna, N.Y.   Deb: 9/24/1896

1896 Pit-N	0	2	.000	2	2	2	0	0	15	22	0	9	3	19.2	9.60	44	.338	.426	0	.000	-1	-9	-9	-1	-0.8
1898 Bro-N	0	1	.000	1	1	1	0	0	9	16	0	6	0	22.0	10.00	36	.383	.460	1	.250	-0	-6	-6	-0	-0.5
Total 2	0	3	.000	3	3	3	0	0	24	38	0	15	3	20.3	9.75	41	.356	.439	1	.091	-1	-15	-15	-1	-1.3

● **RICKY HORTON**   Horton, Ricky Neal   b: 7/30/59, Poughkeepsie, N.Y.   BL/TL, 6'2", 195 lbs.   Deb: 4/07/84

1984 StL-N	9	4	.692	37	18	1	1	1	125²	140	14	39	76	12.9	3.44	101	.285	.339	2	.065	-2	2	0	3	0.2
1985 *StL-N	3	2	.600	49	3	0	0	1	89²	84	5	34	59	12.1	2.91	121	.251	.326	1	.063	0	7	6	2	0.8
1986 StL-N	4	3	.571	42	9	1	0	3	100¹	77	7	26	49	9.3	2.24	162	.218	.273	1	.056	0	16	16	2	1.8
1987 *StL-N	8	3	.727	67	6	0	0	7	125	127	15	42	55	12.2	3.82	109	.263	.323	5	.172	0	4	5	2	0.8
1988 Chi-A	6	10	.375	52	9	1	0	2	109¹	120	6	36	28	13.3	4.86	82	.291	.355	0	—	0	-11	-11	1	-1.0
*LA-N	1	1	.500	12	0	0	0	0	9	11	2	2	8	13.0	5.00	67	.306	.342	0	—	0	-2	-2	1	-0.1
1989 LA-N	0	0	—	23	0	0	0	0	26²	35	1	11	12	15.9	5.06	67	.343	.412	0	.000	-0	-5	-5	0	-0.5
StL-N	0	3	.000	11	8	0	0	0	45²	50	2	10	14	12.4	4.73	77	.282	.332	3	.273	1	-6	-6	0	-0.5
Yr	0	3	.000	34	8	0	0	0	72¹	85	3	21	26	13.6	4.85	73	.301	.356	3	.250	1	-11	-10	1	-1.0
1990 StL-N	1	1	.500	32	0	0	0	1	42	52	3	22	18	16.1	4.93	77	.315	.399	0	.000	0	-5	-5	2	-0.4
Total 7	32	27	.542	325	53	3	1	15	673¹	696	55	222	319	12.5	3.76	100	.273	.334	12	.109	-1	0	-1	12	1.1

● **DAVE HOSKINS**   Hoskins, David Taylor   b: 8/3/25, Greenwood, Miss.   d: 4/2/70, Flint, Mich.   BL/TR, 6'1", 180 lbs.   Deb: 4/18/53

1953 Cle-A	9	3	.750	26	7	3	0	1	112²	102	9	38	55	11.5	3.99	94	.243	.312	15	.259	4	0	-3	0	0.1
1954 Cle-A	0	1	.000	14	1	0	0	0	26²	29	3	10	9	13.2	3.04	121	.284	.348	0	.000	-1	2	2	0	0.1
Total 2	9	4	.692	40	8	3	0	1	139¹	131	12	48	64	11.8	3.81	98	.251	.319	15	.227	3	2	-1	0	0.2

● **GENE HOST**   Host, Eugene Earl "Twinkles" or "Slick"   b: 1/1/33, Leeper, Pa.   BB/TL, 5'11", 190 lbs.   Deb: 9/16/56

1956 Det-A	0	0	—	1	1	0	0	0	4²	9	2	2	5	21.2	7.71	53	.409	.458	0	.000	-0	-2	-2	-0	-0.2
1957 KC-A	0	2	.000	11	2	0	0	0	23²	29	5	14	9	16.4	7.23	55	.315	.406	0	.000	-1	-9	-9	-0	-0.9
Total 2	0	2	.000	12	3	0	0	0	28¹	38	7	16	14	17.2	7.31	55	.333	.415	0	.000	-1	-11	-10	-0	-1.1

● **BYRON HOUCK**   Houck, Byron Simon "Duke"   b: 8/28/1891, Prosper, Minn.   d: 6/17/69, Santa Cruz, Cal.   BR/TR, 6', 175 lbs.   Deb: 5/15/12

1912 Phi-A	8	8	.500	30	21	10	0	1	180²	148	1	74	75	11.7	2.94	105	.234	.326	4	.065	-6	8	3	-1	-0.4
1913 Phi-A	14	6	.700	41	19	4	1	0	176	147	3	122	71	14.1	4.14	67	.214	.337	5	.083	-4	-24	-27	-2	-3.3
1914 Phi-A	0	0	—	3	3	0	0	0	11	14	0	6	4	16.4	3.27	80	.318	.400	1	.333	-0	-1	-1	-0	-0.1
Bro-F	2	6	.250	17	9	3	0	0	92	95	4	43	45	13.7	3.13	102	.272	.355	7	.233	2	1	1	-3	0.0
1918 StL-A	2	4	.333	27	2	0	0	2	71²	58	0	29	29	10.9	2.39	115	.225	.303	3	.150	-1	**3**	**3**	-1	0.2
Total 4	26	24	.520	118	50	17	1	3	531¹	462	8	274	224	12.8	3.30	89	.234	.334	20	.114	-8	-13	-21	-6	-3.6

● **CHARLIE HOUGH**   Hough, Charles Oliver   b: 1/5/48, Honolulu, Hawaii   BR/TR, 6'2", 190 lbs.   Deb: 8/12/70

1970 LA-N	0	0	—	8	0	0	0	0	17	18	7	11	8	15.4	5.29	72	.265	.367	1	.333	0	-2	-3	0	-0.2
1971 LA-N	0	0	—	4	0	0	0	0	4¹	3	1	3	4	12.5	4.15	78	.200	.333	0	—	0	-0	-0	0	0.0
1972 LA-N	0	0	—	2	0	0	0	0	2²	2	0	2	4	16.9	3.38	99	.200	.385	0	—	0	-0	-0	0	0.0
1973 LA-N	4	2	.667	37	0	0	0	5	71²	52	3	45	70	12.9	2.76	124	.207	.341	3	.214	0	7	5	0	0.6
1974 *LA-N	9	4	.692	49	0	0	0	1	96	65	12	40	63	10.2	3.75	91	.196	.291	0	.000	-1	-1	5	-0	-0.5
1975 LA-N	3	7	.300	38	0	0	0	4	61	43	3	34	34	12.5	2.95	115	.195	.323	2	.333	1	5	3	-1	0.4
1976 LA-N	12	8	.600	77	0	0	0	18	142²	102	9	77	81	11.8	2.21	153	.200	.314	6	.286	1	**20**	**19**	-1	2.1
1977 *LA-N	6	12	.333	70	0	0	0	22	127¹	98	10	70	105	12.4	3.32	115	.213	.326	4	.182	1	8	7	-1	0.8
1978 *LA-N	5	5	.500	55	0	0	0	7	93¹	69	6	48	66	11.8	3.28	107	.205	.313	4	.333	1	3	2	-0	0.4

YEAR	TM/L	W	L	PCT	G	GS	CG	SH	SV	IP	H	HR	BB	SO	RAT	ERA	ERA+	OAV	OOB	BH	AVG	PB	PR	/A	PD	TPI
1979	LA-N	7	5	.583	42	14	0	0	0	151^1	152	16	66	76	13.4	4.76	76	.264	.348	6	.158	-0	-17	-19	0	-1.9
1980	LA-N	1	3	.250	19	1	0	0	1	32^1	37	4	21	25	16.7	5.57	63	.291	.400	1	.500	0	-7	-7	-1	-0.8
	Tex-A	2	2	.500	16	2	2	1	0	61^1	54	2	37	47	13.8	3.96	98	.240	.355	0	—	0	0	-0	-0	0.0
1981	Tex-A	4	1	.800	21	5	2	0	1	82	61	4	31	69	10.4	2.96	117	.207	.290	0	—	0	6	5	-1	0.4
1982	Tex-A	16	13	.552	34	34	12	2	0	228	217	21	72	128	11.7	3.95	98	.251	.314	0	—	0	3	-2	1	0.2
1983	Tex-A	15	13	.536	34	33	11	3	0	252	219	22	95	152	11.3	3.18	126	.238	.311	0	—	0	25	23	4	2.9
1984	Tex-A	16	14	.533	36	36	**17**	1	0	266	260	26	94	164	12.3	3.76	110	.255	.324	0	—	0	7	12	3	1.4
1985	Tex-A	14	16	.467	34	34	14	1	0	250^1	198	23	83	141	10.4	3.31	128	.215	.285	0	—	0	23	26	1	2.7
1986	Tex-A★	17	10	.630	33	33	7	2	0	230^1	188	32	89	146	11.2	3.79	113	.221	.302	0	—	0	10	13	1	1.4
1987	Tex-A	18	13	.581	40	40	13	0	0	**285**^{1}	238	36	124	223	12.0	3.79	118	.223	.314	0	—	0	21	22	3	2.5
1988	Tex-A	15	16	.484	34	34	10	0	0	252	202	20	126	174	12.1	3.32	123	.221	.324	0	—	0	18	21	4	2.6
1989	Tex-A	10	13	.435	30	30	5	1	0	182	168	28	95	94	13.3	4.35	91	.245	.342	0	—	0	-9	-8	-2	-0.9
1990	Tex-A	12	12	.500	32	32	5	0	0	218^2	190	24	119	114	13.2	4.07	96	.235	.342	0	—	0	-4	-4	-0	-0.4
1991	Chi-A	9	10	.474	31	29	4	1	0	199^1	167	21	94	107	12.3	4.02	99	.229	.326	0	—	0	2	-1	0	0.0
1992	Chi-A	7	12	.368	27	27	4	0	0	176^1	160	19	66	76	11.9	3.93	97	.239	.314	0	—	0	0	-2	-1	-0.3
Total	23	202	191	.514	803	385	106	12	61	3483^1	2963	346	1542	2171	12.0	3.67	107	.230	.320	27	.208	4	118	106	11	13.3

● PAT HOUSE House, Patrick Lory b: 9/1/40, Boise, Idaho BL/TL, 6'3", 185 lbs. Deb: 9/06/67

YEAR	TM/L	W	L	PCT	G	GS	CG	SH	SV	IP	H	HR	BB	SO	RAT	ERA	ERA+	OAV	OOB	BH	AVG	PB	PR	/A	PD	TPI
1967	Hou-N	1	0	1.000	6	0	0	0	1	4	3	0	0	2	9.0	4.50	74	.214	.267	0	—	0	-1	-1	0	0.0
1968	Hou-N	1	1	.500	18	0	0	0	0	16^1	21	0	6	6	16.0	7.71	38	.323	.397	0	—	0	-9	-9	-0	-1.0
Total	2	2	1	.667	24	0	0	0	1	20^1	24	0	6	8	14.6	7.08	43	.304	.375	0	—	0	-9	-9	0	-1.0

● TOM HOUSE House, Thomas Ross b: 4/29/47, Seattle, Wash. BL/TL, 5'11", 190 lbs. Deb: 6/23/71 C

YEAR	TM/L	W	L	PCT	G	GS	CG	SH	SV	IP	H	HR	BB	SO	RAT	ERA	ERA+	OAV	OOB	BH	AVG	PB	PR	/A	PD	TPI
1971	Atl-N	1	0	1.000	11	1	0	0	0	20^2	20	2	3	11	10.5	3.05	122	.263	.300	2	.400	1	1	2	0	0.2
1972	Atl-N	0	0	—	8	0	0	0	2	9^1	7	1	6	7	13.5	2.89	131	.226	.368	0	.000	-0	1	1	0	0.1
1973	Atl-N	4	2	.667	52	0	0	0	4	67^1	58	13	31	42	12.2	4.68	84	.243	.335	2	.200	0	-8	-6	-0	-0.6
1974	Atl-N	6	2	.750	56	0	0	0	11	102^2	74	5	27	64	9.1	1.93	196	.203	.264	4	.400	1	19	21	1	2.5
1975	Atl-N	7	7	.500	58	0	0	0	11	79^1	79	2	36	36	13.3	3.18	119	.262	.344	1	.111	-0	4	5	1	0.6
1976	Bos-A	1	3	.250	36	0	0	0	4	43^2	39	4	19	27	12.4	4.33	90	.241	.328	0	—	0	-4	-2	1	-0.2
1977	Bos-A	1	0	1.000	8	0	0	0	0	7^2	15	0	6	6	24.7	12.91	35	.405	.488	0	—	0	-8	-7	-0	-0.8
	Sea-A	4	5	.444	26	11	1	0	1	89^1	94	12	19	39	11.8	3.93	105	.268	.313	0	—	0	1	2	-1	0.1
	Yr	5	5	.500	34	11	1	0	1	97	109	12	25	45	12.8	4.64	89	.281	.331	0	—	0	-6	-5	-1	-0.7
1978	Sea-A	5	4	.556	34	9	3	0	0	116	130	10	35	29	13.2	4.66	82	.289	.347	0	—	0	-12	-11	-0	-1.1
Total	8	29	23	.558	289	21	4	0	33	536	516	49	182	261	12.1	3.79	102	.256	.324	9	.257	2	-5	5	1	0.8

● FRED HOUSE House, Willard Edwin b: 10/3/1890, Cabool, Mo. d: 11/16/23, Kansas City, Mo. BR/TR, 6'3", 190 lbs. Deb: 4/22/13

YEAR	TM/L	W	L	PCT	G	GS	CG	SH	SV	IP	H	HR	BB	SO	RAT	ERA	ERA+	OAV	OOB	BH	AVG	PB	PR	/A	PD	TPI
1913	Det-A	1	2	.333	19	2	0	0	0	53^2	64	1	17	16	13.9	5.20	56	.325	.384	0	.000	-1	-14	-14	1	-1.4

● CHARLIE HOUSEHOLDER Householder, Charles F. b: 1856, Harrisburg, Pa. BR/TR, 5'7", 150 lbs. Deb: 4/20/1884 ♦

YEAR	TM/L	W	L	PCT	G	GS	CG	SH	SV	IP	H	HR	BB	SO	RAT	ERA	ERA+	OAV	OOB	BH	AVG	PB	PR	/A	PD	TPI
1884	CP-U	0	0	—	2	0	0	0	0	3	4	0	0	3	12.0	3.00	101	.300	.300	74	.239	0	0	0	-0	0.0

● FRANK HOUSEMAN Houseman, Frank b: Holland Deb: 9/02/1886

YEAR	TM/L	W	L	PCT	G	GS	CG	SH	SV	IP	H	HR	BB	SO	RAT	ERA	ERA+	OAV	OOB	BH	AVG	PB	PR	/A	PD	TPI
1886	Bal-a	0	1	.000	1	1	1	0	0	8	6	0	1	5	9.0	3.38	101	.182	.229	1	.250	-0	0	0	0	0.0

● JOE HOUSER Houser, Joseph William b: 7/3/1891, Steubenville, Ohio d: 1/3/53, Orlando, Fla. BL/TL, 5'9.5", 160 lbs. Deb: 4/24/14

YEAR	TM/L	W	L	PCT	G	GS	CG	SH	SV	IP	H	HR	BB	SO	RAT	ERA	ERA+	OAV	OOB	BH	AVG	PB	PR	/A	PD	TPI
1914	Buf-F	0	1	.000	7	2	0	0	0	23	21	1	20	6	16.0	5.48	60	.250	.394	1	.143	-0	-6	-6	1	-0.5

● ART HOUTTEMAN Houtteman, Arthur Joseph b: 8/7/27, Detroit, Mich. BR/TR, 6'2", 188 lbs. Deb: 4/29/45

YEAR	TM/L	W	L	PCT	G	GS	CG	SH	SV	IP	H	HR	BB	SO	RAT	ERA	ERA+	OAV	OOB	BH	AVG	PB	PR	/A	PD	TPI
1945	Det-A	0	2	.000	13	0	0	0	0	25^1	27	1	11	9	13.9	5.33	66	.270	.348	0	.000	-1	-6	-5	1	-0.5
1946	Det-A	0	1	.000	1	1	0	0	0	8	15	1	0	2	16.9	9.00	41	.385	.385	1	.500	0	-5	-5	-0	-0.4
1947	Det-A	7	2	.778	23	9	7	2	0	110^2	106	6	36	58	11.6	3.42	110	.247	.306	12	.300	2	4	4	-0	0.6
1948	Det-A	2	16	.111	43	20	4	0	10	164^1	186	11	52	74	13.1	4.66	94	.287	.342	11	.196	-2	-7	-5	4	-0.3
1949	Det-A	15	10	.600	34	25	13	2	0	203^2	227	19	59	85	12.9	3.71	112	.282	.335	19	.244	1	11	10	5	1.6
1950	Det-A★	19	12	.613	41	34	21	**4**	4	274^2	257	29	99	88	11.9	3.54	132	.251	.322	14	.151	-3	32	35	3	3.4
1952	Det-A	8	20	.286	35	28	10	2	1	221	218	19	65	109	11.7	4.36	87	.253	.309	7	.101	-5	-17	-14	1	-1.7
1953	Det-A	2	6	.250	16	9	3	1	1	68^2	87	11	29	28	15.7	5.90	69	.309	.381	3	.158	0	-15	-14	-0	-1.3
	Cle-A	7	7	.500	22	13	6	1	3	109	113	4	25	40	11.8	3.80	99	.269	.318	5	.147	-1	2	-1	0	-0.2
	Yr	9	13	.409	38	22	9	2	4	177^2	200	15	54	68	13.1	4.61	84	.283	.339	8	.151	-1	-12	-15	-0	-1.5
1954	*Cle-A	15	7	.682	32	25	11	1	0	188	198	14	59	68	12.4	3.35	110	.273	.330	18	.277	5	8	7	2	1.4
1955	Cle-A	10	6	.625	35	12	3	1	0	124^1	126	15	44	53	12.5	3.98	100	.265	.330	6	.158	-1	-0	0	2	0.2
1956	Cle-A	2	2	.500	22	4	0	0	1	46^2	60	5	31	19	18.3	6.56	64	.317	.424	2	.167	-1	-12	-12	0	-1.2
1957	Cle-A	0	0	—	3	0	0	0	0	4	6	1	3	3	20.3	6.75	55	.353	.450	0	—	0	-1	-1	-0	-0.1
	Bal-A	0	0	—	5	1	0	0	0	6^2	20	0	3	3	31.1	17.55	20	.513	.548	1	.500	0	-10	-10	0	-0.9
	Yr	0	0	—	8	1	0	0	0	10^2	26	1	6	6	27.0	13.50	27	.464	.516	1	.500	0	-12	-12	0	-1.0
Total	12	87	91	.489	325	181	78	14	20	1555	1646	136	516	639	12.7	4.14	99	.272	.333	99	.193	-4	-16	-11	17	0.6

● ED HOVLIK Hovlik, Edward Charles b: 8/20/1891, Cleveland, Ohio d: 3/19/55, Painesville, Ohio BR/TR, 6', 180 lbs. Deb: 7/14/18 F

YEAR	TM/L	W	L	PCT	G	GS	CG	SH	SV	IP	H	HR	BB	SO	RAT	ERA	ERA+	OAV	OOB	BH	AVG	PB	PR	/A	PD	TPI
1918	Was-A	2	1	.667	8	2	1	0	0	28	25	0	10	10	11.3	1.29	212	.272	.343	1	.125	-1	5	4	-1	0.4
1919	Was-A	0	0	—	3	0	0	0	0	5^2	12	0	9	3	33.4	12.71	25	.480	.618	0	.000	-0	-6	-6	0	-0.6
Total	2	2	1	.667	11	2	1	0	0	33^2	37	0	19	13	15.0	3.21	88	.316	.412	1	.100	-1	-1	-1	-0	-0.2

● JOE HOVLIK Hovlik, Joseph b: 8/16/1884, Czechoslovakia d: 11/3/51, Oxford Junction, Ia BR/TR, 5'10.5", 194 lbs. Deb: 7/10/09 F

YEAR	TM/L	W	L	PCT	G	GS	CG	SH	SV	IP	H	HR	BB	SO	RAT	ERA	ERA+	OAV	OOB	BH	AVG	PB	PR	/A	PD	TPI
1909	Was-A	0	0	—	3	0	0	0	0	6	13	0	3	1	25.5	4.50	54	.419	.486	0	.000	0	-1	-1	0	-0.1
1910	Was-A	0	0	—	1	0	0	0	0	1^2	6	0	0	0	37.8	16.20	15	.500	.538	0	—	0	-3	-3	-0	-0.2
1911	Chi-A	2	0	1.000	12	3	1	1	0	47	47	1	20	24	12.8	3.06	105	.257	.330	1	.077	-0	1	1	1	0.1
Total	3	2	0	1.000	16	3	1	1	0	54^2	66	1	23	25	15.0	3.62	86	.292	.363	1	.067	-0	-2	-3	1	-0.2

● BRUCE HOWARD Howard, Bruce Ernest b: 3/23/43, Salisbury, Md. BB/TR, 6'2", 180 lbs. Deb: 9/04/63 F

YEAR	TM/L	W	L	PCT	G	GS	CG	SH	SV	IP	H	HR	BB	SO	RAT	ERA	ERA+	OAV	OOB	BH	AVG	PB	PR	/A	PD	TPI
1963	Chi-A	2	1	.667	7	0	0	0	1	17	12	0	14	9	13.8	2.65	132	.207	.361	1	.250	0	2	2	-0	0.1
1964	Chi-A	2	1	.667	3	3	1	1	0	22^1	10	0	8	17	7.7	0.81	429	.139	.235	0	.000	-1	7	7	-0	0.7
1965	Chi-A	9	8	.529	30	22	1	1	0	148	123	13	72	120	11.9	3.47	92	.224	.316	6	.146	2	-0	-4	-1	-0.4
1966	Chi-A	9	5	.643	27	21	4	2	0	149	110	14	44	85	9.4	2.30	138	.202	.263	3	.070	-0	19	14	0	1.5
1967	Chi-A	3	10	.231	30	17	1	0	0	112^2	102	9	52	76	12.5	3.43	90	.240	.327	5	.179	1	-3	-4	1	-0.2
1968	Bal-A	0	2	.000	10	5	0	0	0	31	30	2	26	19	16.8	3.77	78	.268	.414	2	.286	2	-3	-3	0	-0.1
	Was-A	1	4	.200	13	7	0	0	0	48^2	62	7	23	23	15.7	5.36	54	.330	.403	0	.000	-2	-13	-13	1	-1.5
	Yr	1	6	.143	23	12	0	0	0	79^2	92	9	49	42	15.9	4.74	62	.302	.398	2	.087	0	-16	-16	1	-1.6
Total	6	26	31	.456	120	75	7	4	1	528^2	449	45	239	349	11.8	3.18	99	.231	.317	17	.116	2	9	-2	1	0.1

● EARL HOWARD Howard, Earl Nycum b: 6/25/1893, Everett, Pa. d: 4/4/37, Everett, Pa. BR/TR, 6'1", 160 lbs. Deb: 4/18/18

YEAR	TM/L	W	L	PCT	G	GS	CG	SH	SV	IP	H	HR	BB	SO	RAT	ERA	ERA+	OAV	OOB	BH	AVG	PB	PR	/A	PD	TPI
1918	StL-N	0	0	—	1	0	0	0	0	2	0	0	2	0	9.0	0.00	—	.000	.286	0	—	0	1	1	1	0.1

● FRED HOWARD Howard, Fred Irving b: 9/2/56, Portland, Maine BR/TR, 6'3", 190 lbs. Deb: 5/26/79

YEAR	TM/L	W	L	PCT	G	GS	CG	SH	SV	IP	H	HR	BB	SO	RAT	ERA	ERA+	OAV	OOB	BH	AVG	PB	PR	/A	PD	TPI
1979	Chi-A	1	5	.167	28	6	0	0	0	68	73	5	32	36	14.0	3.57	119	.283	.364	0	—	0	5	5	-1	0.4

● DEL HOWARD Howard, George Elmer b: 12/24/1877, Kenney, Ill. d: 12/24/56, Seattle, Wash. BL/TR, 6', 180 lbs. Deb: 4/15/05 F♦

YEAR	TM/L	W	L	PCT	G	GS	CG	SH	SV	IP	H	HR	BB	SO	RAT	ERA	ERA+	OAV	OOB	BH	AVG	PB	PR	/A	PD	TPI
1905	Pit-N	0	0	—	1	0	0	0	0	6	4	1	1	0	9.0	0.00	—	.200	.273	127	.292	0	2	2	0	0.3

YEAR	TM/L	W	L	PCT	G	GS	CG	SH	SV	IP	H	HR	BB	SO	RAT	ERA	ERA+	OAV	OOB	BH	AVG	PB	PR	/A	PD	TPI
● **LEE HOWARD** Howard, Lee Vincent b: 11/11/23, Staten Island, N.Y BL/TL, 6'2", 175 lbs. Deb: 9/22/46																										
1946	Pit-N	0	1	.000	3	2	1	0	0	13^1	14	0	9	6	15.5	2.03	174	.286	.397	0	.000	-1	2	2	-0	0.2
1947	Pit-N	0	0	—	2	0	0	0	0	2^2	4	1	0	2	13.5	3.38	125	.333	.333	0	—	0	0	0	-0	0.0
Total	2	0	1	.000	5	2	1	0	0	16	18	1	9	8	15.2	2.25	162	.295	.386	0	.000	-1	2	2	-0	0.2
● **CAL HOWE** Howe, Calvin Earl b: 11/27/24, Rock Falls, Ill. BL/TL, 6'3", 205 lbs. Deb: 9/26/52																										
1952	Chi-N	0	0	—	1	0	0	0	0	2	0	0	1	2	4.5	0.00	—	.000	.143	0	—	0	1	1	-0	0.1
● **LES HOWE** Howe, Lester Curtis "Lucky" b: 8/24/1895, Brooklyn, N.Y. d: 7/16/76, Woodmere, N.Y. BR/TR, 5'11.5", 170 lbs. Deb: 8/18/23																										
1923	Bos-A	1	0	1.000	12	2	0	0	0	30	23	0	7	7	9.3	2.40	171	.211	.265	0	.000	-1	5	6	0	0.5
1924	Bos-A	1	0	1.000	4	0	0	0	0	7^1	11	1	2	3	17.2	7.36	59	.423	.483	1	.500	0	-3	-2	0	-0.2
Total	2	2	0	1.000	16	2	0	0	0	37^1	34	1	9	10	10.8	3.38	123	.252	.308	1	.125	-1	3	3	0	0.3
● **STEVE HOWE** Howe, Steven Roy b: 3/10/58, Pontiac, Mich. BL/TL, 6'1", 180 lbs. Deb: 4/11/80																										
1980	LA-N	7	9	.438	59	0	0	0	17	84^2	83	1	22	39	11.4	2.66	132	.256	.307	1	.091	-1	9	8	1	0.9
1981	*LA-N	5	3	.625	41	0	0	0	8	54	51	2	18	32	11.5	2.50	133	.254	.315	0	.000	0	6	5	-1	0.5
1982	LA-N★	7	5	.583	66	0	0	0	13	99^1	87	3	17	49	9.4	2.08	166	.240	.274	0	.000	-1	17	15	-0	1.5
1983	LA-N	4	7	.364	46	0	0	0	18	68^2	55	2	12	52	8.9	1.44	249	.217	.256	1	.125	0	17	16	1	1.9
1985	LA-N	1	1	.500	19	0	0	0	3	22	30	2	5	11	14.7	4.91	71	.319	.360	0	—	0	-3	-4	0	-0.3
	Min-A	2	3	.400	13	0	0	0	0	19	28	1	7	10	16.6	6.16	72	.333	.385	0	—	0	-4	-4	-0	-0.6
1987	Tex-A	3	3	.500	24	0	0	0	1	31^1	33	2	8	19	12.6	4.31	104	.280	.341	0	—	0	1	1	0	0.1
1991	NY-A	3	1	.750	37	0	0	0	3	48^1	39	1	7	34	9.1	1.68	247	.222	.263	0	—	0	13	13	0	1.3
1992	NY-A	3	0	1.000	20	0	0	0	6	22	9	1	3	12	4.9	2.45	165	.122	.156	0	—	0	4	4	1	0.4
Total	8	35	32	.522	325	0	0	0	69	449^1	415	15	99	258	10.5	2.58	142	.246	.292	2	.074	-1	58	55	2	5.7
● **HARRY HOWELL** Howell, Henry Harry b: 11/14/1876, New Jersey d: 5/22/56, Spokane, Wash. BR/TR, 5'9", Deb: 10/10/1898 U♦																										
1898	Bro-N	2	0	1.000	2	2	2	0	0	18	15	0	11	2	13.5	5.00	72	.225	.343	2	.250	0	-3	-3	0	-0.2
1899	Bal-N	13	8	.619	28	25	21	0	1	209^1	248	1	69	58	14.1	3.91	101	.294	.355	12	.146	-4	-1	1	1	-0.2
1900	*Bro-N	6	5	.545	21	10	7	2	0	110^1	131	4	36	26	13.9	3.75	102	.294	.351	12	.286	4	-1	1	1	0.5
1901	Bal-A	14	21	.400	37	34	32	1	0	294^2	333	5	79	93	12.8	3.67	106	.281	.330	41	.218	1	0	7	-1	0.6
1902	Bal-A	9	15	.375	26	23	19	1	0	199	243	5	48	33	13.5	4.12	92	.301	.346	93	.268	6	-12	-8	4	0.2
1903	NY-A	9	6	.600	25	15	13	0	0	155^2	140	4	44	62	11.0	3.53	89	.240	.300	23	.217	2	-10	-7	3	-0.2
1904	StL-A	13	21	.382	34	33	32	2	0	299^2	254	1	60	122	9.8	2.19	113	.231	.278	25	.221	4	14	10	9	2.8
1905	StL-A	15	22	.405	38	37	**35**	4	0	323	252	2	101	198	10.1	1.98	129	.216	.284	26	.193	2	25	20	18	**4.8**
1906	StL-A	15	14	.517	35	33	30	6	1	276^2	233	1	61	140	9.9	2.11	122	.231	.282	13	.126	-3	18	14	7	2.2
1907	StL-A	16	15	.516	42	35	26	2	3	316^1	258	3	88	118	10.1	1.93	130	.225	.285	27	.237	6	22	21	8	4.0
1908	StL-A	18	18	.500	41	32	27	2	1	324^1	279	1	70	117	10.2	1.89	127	.240	.293	22	.183	1	18	18	0	2.3
1909	StL-A	1	1	.500	10	3	0	0	0	37^1	42	0	8	16	12.8	3.13	77	.294	.344	6	.176	0	-3	-3	-0	-0.3
1910	StL-A	0	0	—	1	0	0	0	0	3^1	7	0	2	1	24.3	10.80	23	.467	.529	0	.000	-0	-3	-3	0	-0.3
Total	13	131	146	.473	340	282	244	20	6	2567^2	2435	27	677	986	11.2	2.74	108	.252	.307	302	.217	19	64	64	51	16.2
● **JAY HOWELL** Howell, Jay Canfield b: 11/26/55, Miami, Fla. BR/TR, 6'3", 205 lbs. Deb: 8/10/80																										
1980	Cin-N	0	0	—	5	0	0	0	0	3^1	8	0	0	1	24.3	13.50	26	.471	.500	0	—	0	-4	-4	-0	-0.4
1981	Chi-N	2	0	1.000	10	2	0	0	0	22^1	23	3	10	10	14.1	4.84	76	.277	.368	0	.000	0	-3	-3	1	-0.2
1982	NY-A	2	3	.400	6	6	0	0	0	28	42	1	13	21	17.7	7.71	52	.341	.404	0	—	0	-11	-12	-0	-1.0
1983	NY-A	1	5	.167	19	12	2	0	0	82	89	7	35	61	13.9	5.38	72	.275	.351	0	—	0	-12	-14	0	-1.2
1984	NY-A	9	4	.692	61	1	0	0	7	103^2	86	5	34	109	10.4	2.69	141	.223	.286	0	—	0	15	13	2	1.5
1985	Oak-A☆	9	8	.529	63	0	0	0	29	98	98	5	31	68	11.9	2.85	135	.261	.319	0	—	0	14	11	0	1.2
1986	Oak-A	3	6	.333	38	0	0	0	16	53^1	53	3	23	42	13.0	3.38	115	.262	.341	0	—	0	5	3	-0	0.4
1987	Oak-A★	3	4	.429	36	0	0	0	16	44^1	48	6	21	35	14.2	5.89	70	.277	.359	0	—	0	-7	-9	-0	-0.4
1988	*LA-N	5	3	.625	50	0	0	0	21	65	44	1	21	70	9.1	2.08	160	.188	.258	0	.000	-0	10	9	-0	0.9
1989	LA-N★	5	3	.625	56	0	0	0	28	79^2	60	3	22	55	9.3	1.58	216	.211	.268	0	.000	-0	17	16	-0	1.7
1990	LA-N	5	5	.500	45	0	0	0	16	66	59	5	20	59	11.6	2.18	168	.242	.315	0	.000	-0	12	11	-0	1.1
1991	LA-N	6	5	.545	44	0	0	0	16	51	39	3	11	40	9.0	3.18	113	.213	.262	0	—	0	3	2	0	0.2
1992	LA-N	1	3	.250	41	0	0	0	4	46^2	41	2	18	36	11.6	1.54	224	.230	.305	0	—	0	10	10	0	1.1
Total	13	51	49	.510	474	21	2	0	153	743^1	690	44	259	607	11.7	3.29	113	.246	.314	0	.000	-1	48	35	2	4.9
● **KEN HOWELL** Howell, Kenneth b: 11/28/60, Detroit, Mich. BR/TR, 6'3", 228 lbs. Deb: 6/25/84																										
1984	LA-N	5	5	.500	32	1	0	0	6	51^1	51	1	9	54	10.7	3.33	106	.267	.303	0	.000	-1	1	1	0	0.1
1985	*LA-N	4	7	.364	56	0	0	0	12	86	66	8	35	85	10.6	3.77	92	.208	.287	0	.000	-0	-2	-3	0	-0.3
1986	LA-N	6	12	.333	62	0	0	0	12	97^2	86	7	63	104	14.0	3.87	89	.239	.357	0	.000	-0	-2	-5	-1	-0.6
1987	LA-N	3	4	.429	40	2	0	0	1	55	54	7	29	60	13.6	4.91	81	.265	.356	1	.250	0	-5	-6	-0	-0.6
1988	LA-N	0	1	.000	4	1	0	0	0	12^2	16	0	4	12	14.2	6.39	52	.320	.370	0	.000	-0	-4	-4	-0	-0.5
1989	Phi-N	12	12	.500	33	32	1	1	0	204	155	11	86	164	10.7	3.44	103	.215	.300	6	.092	-2	1	2	-1	-0.1
1990	Phi-N	8	7	.533	18	18	2	0	0	106^2	106	12	49	70	13.3	4.64	82	.260	.343	2	.067	-1	-10	-10	-1	-1.2
Total	7	38	48	.442	245	54	3	1	31	613^1	534	46	275	549	12.0	3.95	91	.237	.323	9	.079	-5	-20	-24	-3	-3.2
● **DIXIE HOWELL** Howell, Millard b: 1/7/20, Bowman, Ky. d: 3/18/60, Hollywood, Fla. BL/TR, 6'2", 210 lbs. Deb: 9/14/40																										
1940	Cle-A	0	0	—	3	0	0	0	0	5	2	0	4	2	10.8	1.80	234	.143	.333	0	—	0	1	1	0	0.1
1949	Cin-N	0	1	.000	5	1	0	0	0	13^1	21	3	8	7	19.6	8.10	52	.362	.439	1	.111	-0	-6	-6	0	-0.6
1955	Chi-A	8	3	.727	35	0	0	0	9	73^2	70	1	25	25	11.6	2.93	135	.250	.311	8	.381	2	8	8	1	1.2
1956	Chi-A	5	6	.455	34	1	0	0	4	64^1	79	3	36	28	16.4	4.62	89	.309	.398	4	.235	2	-3	-4	0	-0.1
1957	Chi-A	6	5	.545	37	0	0	0	6	68^1	64	6	30	37	12.4	3.29	113	.255	.335	5	.185	4	4	3	1	0.8
1958	Chi-A	0	0	—	1	0	0	0	0	1^2	0	0	0	0	0.0	0.00	—	.000	.000	0	—	0	1	1	0	0.1
Total	6	19	15	.559	115	2	0	0	19	226^1	236	13	103	99	13.6	3.78	104	.273	.352	18	.243	8	5	4	2	1.5
● **ROLAND HOWELL** Howell, Roland Boatner "Billiken" b: 1/3/1892, Napoleonville, La. d: 3/31/73, Baton Rouge, La. BR/TR, 6'4", 210 lbs. Deb: 6/14/12																										
1912	StL-N	0	0	—	3	0	0	0	0	1^2	5	0	5	0	54.0	27.00	13	.556	.714	0	—	0	-4	-4	-0	-0.4
● **PETER HOY** Hoy, Peter Alexander b: 6/29/66, Brockville, Ont., Canada BL/TR, 6'7", 220 lbs. Deb: 4/11/92																										
1992	Bos-A	0	0	—	5	0	0	0	0	3^2	8	0	2	2	24.5	7.36	56	.471	.526	0	—	0	-1	-1	0	-0.1
● **TEX HOYLE** Hoyle, Roland Edison b: 7/17/21, Carbondale, Pa. BR/TR, 6'4", 170 lbs. Deb: 4/18/52																										
1952	Phi-A	0	0	—	3	0	0	0	0	2^1	9	2	1	1	38.6	27.00	15	.563	.588	0	—	0	-6	-6	0	-0.5
● **LA MARR HOYT** Hoyt, Dewey La Marr b: 1/1/55, Columbia, S.C. BR/TR, 6'1", 222 lbs. Deb: 9/14/79																										
1979	Chi-A	0	0	—	2	0	0	0	0	3	2	0	0	0	6.0	0.00	—	.200	.200	0	—	0	1	1	-0	0.1
1980	Chi-A	9	3	.750	24	13	3	1	0	112^1	123	8	41	55	13.3	4.57	88	.281	.345	0	—	0	-7	-7	-2	-0.8
1981	Chi-A	9	3	.750	43	1	0	0	10	90^2	80	10	28	60	11.0	3.57	100	.240	.305	0	—	0	1	0	-1	0.0
1982	Chi-A	**19**	15	.559	39	32	14	2	0	239^2	248	17	48	124	11.2	3.53	114	.266	.303	0	—	0	14	13	-1	1.3
1983	*Chi-A	**24**	10	.706	36	36	11	1	0	260^2	236	27	31	148	**9.3**	3.66	114	.238	**.262**	0	—	0	12	15	5	2.0
1984	Chi-A	13	18	.419	34	34	11	1	0	235^2	244	31	43	126	11.2	4.47	93	.266	.302	0	—	0	-13	-8	1	-0.8
1985	SD-N★	16	8	.667	31	31	8	3	0	210^1	210	20	20	83	9.9	3.47	102	.261	.281	4	.063	-4	3	2	1	-0.1
1986	SD-N	8	11	.421	35	25	1	0	0	159	170	27	68	85	13.6	5.15	71	.276	.351	6	.130	-1	-25	-26	-2	-2.9
Total	8	98	68	.590	244	172	48	8	10	1311^1	1313	140	279	681	11.0	3.99	98	.260	.302	10	.091	-5	-13	-10	1	-1.2

● WAITE HOYT
Hoyt, Waite Charles "Schoolboy" b: 9/9/1899, Brooklyn, N.Y. d: 8/25/84, Cincinnati, Ohio BR/TR, 6', 180 lbs. Deb: 7/24/18 H

YEAR	TM/L	W	L	PCT	G	GS	CG	SH	SV	IP	H	HR	BB	SO	RAT	ERA	ERA+	OAV	OOB	BH	AVG	PB	PR	/A	PD	TPI
1918	NY-N	0	0	—	1	0	0	0	0	1	0	0	0	2	0.0	0.00	—	.000	.000	0	.000	-0	0	0	0	0.0
1919	Bos-A	4	6	.400	13	11	6	1	0	105^{1}	99	1	22	28	10.3	3.25	93	.262	.303	5	.132	-2	-0	-3	1	-0.4
1920	Bos-A	6	6	.500	22	11	6	2	1	121^{1}	123	2	47	45	12.7	4.38	83	.270	.339	5	.116	-3	-8	-10	1	-1.1
1921	*NY-A	19	13	.594	43	32	21	1	3	282^{1}	301	3	81	102	12.3	3.09	137	.276	.329	22	.222	-2	37	36	-1	3.2
1922	*NY-A	19	12	.613	37	31	17	3	0	265	271	13	76	95	12.1	3.43	117	.269	.326	20	.217	1	18	17	-2	1.6
1923	*NY-A	17	9	.654	37	28	19	1	1	238^{2}	227	9	66	60	11.2	3.02	131	.253	.307	16	.190	-2	26	24	-1	2.1
1924	NY-A	18	13	.581	46	32	14	2	4	247	295	8	76	71	13.6	3.79	110	.300	.352	10	.133	-5	12	10	-0	0.5
1925	NY-A	11	14	.440	46	30	17	1	6	243	283	14	78	86	13.4	4.00	107	.292	.346	24	.304	5	11	7	3	1.3
1926	*NY-A	16	12	.571	40	28	12	1	4	217^{2}	224	4	62	79	11.9	3.85	100	.264	.316	16	.211	-0	4	0	-3	-0.3
1927	*NY-A	**22**	7	**.759**	36	32	23	3	1	256^{1}	242	10	54	86	10.5	2.63	146	.251	.294	22	.222	0	43	35	-0	3.4
1928	*NY-A	23	7	.767	42	31	19	3	**8**	273	279	16	60	67	11.2	3.36	112	.272	.313	28	.257	2	21	12	-1	1.2
1929	NY-A	10	9	.526	30	25	12	0	1	201^{2}	219	9	69	57	13.0	4.24	91	.279	.339	17	.224	1	0	-9	-2	-0.8
1930	NY-A	2	2	.500	8	7	2	0	0	47^{2}	64	7	9	10	13.8	4.53	95	.317	.346	1	.063	-2	1	-1	-0	-0.3
	Det-A	9	8	.529	26	20	8	1	4	135^{2}	176	7	47	25	14.9	4.78	100	.313	.368	9	.196	-2	-2	0	-3	-0.5
	Yr	11	10	.524	34	27	10	1	4	183^{1}	240	14	56	35	14.6	4.71	99	.314	.363	10	.161	-4	-1	-1	-3	-0.8
1931	Det-A	3	8	.273	16	12	5	0	0	92	124	2	32	10	15.5	5.87	78	.319	.374	4	.133	-2	-15	-13	-0	-1.4
	*Phi-A	10	5	.667	16	14	9	2	0	111	130	9	37	30	13.5	4.22	107	.298	.353	13	.302	3	2	3	1	0.6
	Yr	13	13	.500	32	26	14	2	0	203	254	11	69	40	14.3	4.97	91	.307	.360	17	.233	0	-13	-10	0	-0.8
1932	Bro-N	1	3	.250	8	4	0	0	1	26^{2}	38	3	12	7	16.9	7.76	49	.342	.407	0	.000	-1	-12	-12	1	-1.0
	NY-N	5	7	.417	18	12	3	0	0	97^{1}	103	6	25	29	12.3	3.42	109	.275	.328	3	.097	-2	5	3	1	0.2
	Yr	6	10	.375	26	16	3	0	1	124	141	9	37	36	13.3	4.35	86	.290	.347	3	.081	-3	-7	-9	2	-0.8
1933	Pit-N	5	7	.417	36	8	4	1	4	117	118	3	19	44	10.6	2.92	114	.262	.293	5	.156	-1	5	5	1	0.5
1934	Pit-N	15	6	.714	48	15	8	3	5	190^{2}	184	6	43	105	10.8	2.93	141	.252	.296	10	.179	-1	24	25	-1	2.4
1935	Pit-N	7	11	.389	39	11	5	0	6	164	187	8	27	63	11.8	3.40	121	.285	.315	14	.259	2	11	13	-0	1.4
1936	Pit-N	7	5	.583	22	9	6	0	1	116^{2}	115	5	20	37	10.6	2.70	150	.255	.291	6	.154	-1	17	18	1	1.7
1937	Pit-N	1	2	.333	11	0	0	0	2	28	31	3	6	21	11.9	4.50	86	.270	.306	1	.083	-1	-2	-2	-1	-0.4
	Bro-N	7	7	.500	27	19	10	1	0	167	180	5	30	44	11.3	3.23	125	.270	.301	4	.083	-2	13	15	-1	1.2
	Yr	8	9	.471	38	19	10	1	2	195	211	8	36	65	11.4	3.42	117	.270	.302	5	.083	-3	11	13	-2	0.8
1938	Bro-N	0	3	.000	6	1	0	0	0	16^{1}	24	1	5	3	16.0	4.96	79	.333	.377	0	.000	-0	-2	-2	-0	-0.2
Total	21	237	182	.566	674	423	226	26	52	3762^{1}	4037	154	1003	1206	12.2	3.59	112	.276	.325	255	.198	-16	210	173	-7	14.9

● AL HRABOSKY
Hrabosky, Alan Thomas b: 7/21/49, Oakland, Cal. BR/TL, 5'11", 185 lbs. Deb: 6/16/70

YEAR	TM/L	W	L	PCT	G	GS	CG	SH	SV	IP	H	HR	BB	SO	RAT	ERA	ERA+	OAV	OOB	BH	AVG	PB	PR	/A	PD	TPI
1970	StL-N	2	1	.667	16	1	0	0	0	19	22	2	7	12	13.7	4.74	87	.286	.345	0	.000	-0	-1	-1	-1	-0.2
1971	StL-N	0	0	—	1	0	0	0	0	2	2	0	0	2	9.0	0.00	—	.250	.250	0	—	0	1	1	-0	0.1
1972	StL-N	1	0	1.000	5	0	0	0	0	7	2	0	3	9	6.4	0.00	—	.087	.192	0	.000	-0	3	3	-0	0.3
1973	StL-N	2	4	.333	44	0	0	0	5	56	45	2	21	57	10.9	2.09	174	.220	.298	0	.000	-0	10	10	-1	0.9
1974	StL-N	8	1	.889	65	0	0	0	9	88^{1}	71	3	38	82	11.2	2.95	121	.221	.306	4	.308	1	7	6	-1	0.6
1975	StL-N	13	3	.813	65	0	0	0	**22**	97^{1}	72	3	33	82	9.8	1.66	226	.205	.275	3	.200	1	**21**	**23**	-2	2.3
1976	StL-N	8	6	.571	68	0	0	0	13	95^{1}	89	5	39	73	12.5	3.30	107	.252	.333	0	.000	0	2	2	-0	0.2
1977	StL-N	6	5	.545	65	0	0	0	10	86^{1}	82	12	41	68	13.1	4.38	88	.256	.346	0	.000	-1	-5	-5	-1	-0.7
1978	*KC-A	8	7	.533	58	0	0	0	20	75	52	6	35	60	10.6	2.88	133	.200	.297	0	—	0	7	8	-0	0.6
1979	KC-A	9	4	.692	58	0	0	0	11	65	67	3	41	39	15.1	3.74	114	.272	.378	0	—	0	3	4	-2	0.1
1980	Atl-N	4	2	.667	45	0	0	0	3	59^{2}	50	8	31	31	12.2	3.62	103	.223	.318	0	.000	-0	-0	1	-2	-0.1
1981	Atl-N	1	1	.500	24	0	0	0	1	33^{2}	24	1	9	13	8.8	1.07	335	.207	.264	0	.000	-0	9	9	-1	0.9
1982	Atl-N	2	1	.667	31	0	0	0	3	37^{1}	41	5	17	20	14.0	5.54	67	.285	.360	1	.333	0	-8	-8	-1	-0.8
Total	13	64	35	.646	545	1	0	0	97	722	619	50	315	548	11.8	3.10	121	.234	.318	8	.143	0	49	52	-11	4.2

● CARL HUBBELL
Hubbell, Carl Owen "King Carl" or "The Mealticket"
b: 6/22/03, Carthage, Mo. d: 11/21/88, Scottsdale, Ariz. BR/TL, 6', 170 lbs. Deb: 7/26/28 H

YEAR	TM/L	W	L	PCT	G	GS	CG	SH	SV	IP	H	HR	BB	SO	RAT	ERA	ERA+	OAV	OOB	BH	AVG	PB	PR	/A	PD	TPI
1928	NY-N	10	6	.625	20	14	8	1	1	124	117	7	21	37	10.2	2.83	138	.248	.284	5	.106	-3	16	15	2	1.4
1929	NY-N	18	11	.621	39	35	19	1	1	268	273	17	67	106	11.6	3.69	124	.265	.313	12	.129	-6	30	26	5	2.3
1930	NY-N	17	12	.586	37	32	17	3	2	241^{2}	263	11	58	117	12.4	3.87	122	.278	.327	13	.151	-5	29	23	-1	1.5
1931	NY-N	14	12	.538	36	30	21	4	3	248	211	14	67	155	**10.2**	2.65	139	**.227**	**.282**	20	.241	4	34	29	-2	3.2
1932	NY-N	18	11	.621	40	32	22	0	2	284	260	20	40	137	**9.6**	2.50	148	.238	**.268**	26	.241	4	43	38	6	**5.1**
1933	*NY-N★	**23**	12	.657	45	33	22	**10**	5	**308^{2}**	256	6	47	156	**8.9**	**1.66**	**193**	.227	**.260**	20	.183	1	**58**	**53**	7	**7.1**
1934	NY-N★	21	12	.636	49	34	**25**	5	**8**	313	286	17	37	118	**9.3**	**2.30**	**168**	.239	**.263**	23	.197	-1	**61**	**54**	4	6.0
1935	NY-N☆	23	12	.657	42	35	24	1	0	302^{2}	314	27	49	150	10.9	3.27	118	.263	.294	26	.239	4	25	20	4	2.8
1936	*NY-N★	**26**	6	**.813**	42	34	25	3	3	304	265	7	57	123	**9.7**	**2.31**	**169**	.236	**.276**	25	.227	1	**58**	**54**	1	**5.7**
1937	*NY-N★	**22**	8	**.733**	39	32	18	4	4	261^{2}	261	18	55	**159**	11.0	3.20	122	.257	.298	21	.216	1	21	20	-1	2.0
1938	NY-N☆	13	10	.565	24	22	13	1	1	179	171	16	33	104	**10.4**	3.07	123	.249	**.285**	9	.155	-2	14	14	-1	1.1
1939	NY-N	11	9	.550	29	18	10	0	2	154	150	11	24	62	**10.3**	2.75	143	.249	**.280**	8	.151	-1	20	20	1	2.1
1940	NY-N★	11	12	.478	31	27	11	2	0	214^{1}	220	22	59	86	11.8	3.65	106	.259	.309	15	.185	-0	5	5	1	0.7
1941	NY-N☆	11	9	.550	26	22	11	1	1	164	169	10	53	75	12.3	3.57	104	.266	.325	8	.140	-2	1	2	-3	-0.2
1942	NY-N☆	11	8	.579	24	20	11	0	0	157^{1}	158	17	34	61	11.0	3.95	85	.259	.299	11	.183	-0	-11	-10	-1	-1.2
1943	NY-N	4	4	.500	12	11	3	0	0	66	87	7	24	31	15.1	4.91	70	.322	.378	4	.200	-0	-11	-11	-1	-1.2
Total	16	253	154	.622	535	431	260	36	33	3590^{1}	3461	227	725	1677	10.6	2.98	130	.251	.291	246	.191	-5	393	355	22	38.4

● BILL HUBBELL
Hubbell, Wilbert William b: 6/17/1897, San Francisco, Cal. d: 8/3/80, Lakewood, Colo. BR/TR, 6'1.5", 195 lbs. Deb: 9/24/19

YEAR	TM/L	W	L	PCT	G	GS	CG	SH	SV	IP	H	HR	BB	SO	RAT	ERA	ERA+	OAV	OOB	BH	AVG	PB	PR	/A	PD	TPI
1919	NY-N	1	1	.500	2	2	2	0	0	18^{1}	19	0	2	3	11.3	1.96	143	.260	.299	1	.125	-1	2	2	-0	0.1
1920	NY-N	0	1	.000	14	0	0	0	2	30	26	2	15	8	12.6	2.10	143	.239	.336	1	.200	-0	3	3	1	0.4
	Phi-N	9	9	.500	24	20	9	1	2	150	176	3	42	26	13.3	3.84	89	.301	.352	7	.132	-4	-12	-7	-2	-1.3
	Yr	9	10	.474	38	20	9	1	4	180	202	5	57	34	13.1	3.55	94	.291	.348	8	.138	-4	-8	-4	-1	-0.9
1921	Phi-N	9	16	.360	36	30	15	1	2	220^{1}	269	18	38	43	12.7	4.33	98	.306	.337	12	.160	-2	-13	-2	-1	-0.4
1922	Phi-N	7	15	.318	35	24	11	1	1	189	257	14	41	33	14.4	5.00	93	.317	.353	12	.171	-2	-19	-7	0	-0.8
1923	Phi-N	1	6	.143	22	5	1	0	0	55	102	13	17	8	19.8	8.35	55	.394	.435	4	.235	0	-27	-23	0	-2.1
1924	Phi-N	10	9	.526	36	22	9	2	2	179	233	9	45	30	14.1	4.83	92	.324	.365	13	.220	-1	-19	-7	0	-0.7
1925	Phi-N	0	0	—	2	0	0	0	0	2^{2}	5	0	1	0	20.3	0.00	—	.385	.429	0	.000	-0	1	1	1	0.2
	Bro-N	3	6	.333	33	5	3	0	1	86^{2}	120	8	24	16	15.2	5.30	79	.337	.382	3	.150	0	-10	-11	1	-0.9
	Yr	3	6	.333	35	5	3	0	1	89^{1}	125	8	25	16	15.3	5.14	82	.339	.384	3	.143	0	-9	-9	2	-0.7
Total	7	40	63	.388	204	108	50	5	10	931	1207	67	225	167	14.0	4.68	89	.317	.359	53	.172	-8	-93	-52	0	-5.5

● EARL HUCKLEBERRY
Huckleberry, Earl Eugene b: 5/23/10, Konawa, Okla. BR/TR, 5'11", 165 lbs. Deb: 9/13/35

YEAR	TM/L	W	L	PCT	G	GS	CG	SH	SV	IP	H	HR	BB	SO	RAT	ERA	ERA+	OAV	OOB	BH	AVG	PB	PR	/A	PD	TPI
1935	Phi-A	1	0	1.000	1	1	0	0	0	6^{2}	8	1	4	2	16.2	9.45	48	.296	.387	0	.000	-0	-4	-4	-0	-0.3

● WILLIS HUDLIN
Hudlin, George Willis "Ace" b: 5/23/06, Wagoner, Okla. BR/TR, 6', 190 lbs. Deb: 8/15/26 C

YEAR	TM/L	W	L	PCT	G	GS	CG	SH	SV	IP	H	HR	BB	SO	RAT	ERA	ERA+	OAV	OOB	BH	AVG	PB	PR	/A	PD	TPI
1926	Cle-A	1	3	.250	8	2	1	0	0	32^{1}	25	1	13	6	11.1	2.78	146	.227	.320	1	.125	0	4	5	2	0.6
1927	Cle-A	18	12	.600	43	30	18	1	0	264^{2}	291	3	83	65	13.1	4.01	105	.283	.343	24	.250	2	4	6	3	1.1
1928	*Cle-A	14	14	.500	42	26	10	0	7	220^{1}	231	7	90	62	13.4	4.04	103	.279	.355	14	.194	-0	0	2	2	0.4
1929	Cle-A	17	15	.531	40	33	22	2	1	280^{1}	299	7	73	60	12.0	3.34	133	.272	.318	19	.196	-3	28	34	7	3.8
1930	Cle-A	13	16	.448	37	33	13	1	1	216^{2}	255	12	76	60	13.8	4.57	106	.293	.351	16	.219	-1	2	6	5	0.9
1931	Cle-A	15	14	.517	44	34	15	1	4	254^{1}	313	14	88	83	14.2	4.60	100	.301	.356	20	.200	1	-6	1	4	0.5
1932	Cle-A	12	8	.600	33	21	12	0	2	181^{2}	204	10	59	65	13.1	4.71	101	.278	.332	13	.203	1	-5	1	1	0.2
1933	Cle-A	5	13	.278	34	17	6	0	1	147^{1}	161	7	61	44	13.7	3.97	112	.275	.346	6	.146	-1	5	8	4	1.0

YEAR	TM/L	W	L	PCT	G	GS	CG	SH	SV	IP	H	HR	BB	SO	RAT	ERA	ERA+	OAV	OOB	BH	AVG	PB	PR	/A	PD	TPI
1934	Cle-A	15	10	.600	36	26	15	1	4	195	210	8	65	58	12.9	4.75	96	.277	.338	14	.206	3	-6	-4	5	0.3
1935	Cle-A	15	11	.577	36	29	14	3	5	231^{2}	252	8	61	45	12.3	3.69	122	.277	.324	24	.279	6	20	21	0	2.6
1936	Cle-A	1	5	.167	27	7	1	0	0	64	112	1	31	20	20.4	9.00	56	.397	.460	2	.111	-1	-28	-28	1	-2.4
1937	Cle-A	12	11	.522	35	23	10	2	2	175^{2}	213	8	43	31	13.2	4.10	112	.295	.337	10	.169	-1	10	10	3	1.1
1938	Cle-A	8	8	.500	29	15	8	0	1	127	158	13	45	27	14.5	4.89	95	.303	.361	5	.116	-2	-1	-4	1	-0.4
1939	Cle-A	9	10	.474	27	20	7	0	3	143	175	6	42	28	13.7	4.91	90	.303	.352	9	.188	1	-5	-8	5	-0.2
1940	Cle-A	2	1	.667	4	4	2	0	0	23^{2}	31	3	2	8	12.5	4.94	85	.316	.330	1	.125	-0	-1	-2	-0	-0.2
	Was-A	1	2	.333	8	6	1	0	0	37^{1}	50	9	5	9	13.7	6.51	64	.314	.343	1	.100	-1	-9	-10	0	-0.9
	StL-A	0	1	.000	6	1	0	0	0	11^{1}	19	0	8	4	21.4	11.12	41	.358	.443	1	.500	0	-8	-8	0	-0.7
	Yr	3	4	.429	18	11	3	0	0	72^{1}	100	12	15	21	14.3	6.72	63	.321	.352	3	.150	-1	-19	-20	0	-1.8
	NY-N	0	1	.000	1	1	0	0	0	5	9	1	1	1	18.0	10.80	36	.409	.435	0	.000	-0	-4	-4	0	-0.3
1944	StL-A	0	1	.000	1	0	0	0	0	2	3	0	0	1	13.5	4.50	80	.300	.300	0	—	0	-0	-0	-0	0.0
Total	16	158	156	.503	491	328	155	11	31	2613^{1}	3011	118	846	677	13.4	4.41	102	.289	.345	180	.201	4	-0	26	42	7.4

● CHARLIE HUDSON
Hudson, Charles b: 8/18/49, Ada, Okla. BL/TL, 6'3", 185 lbs. Deb: 5/21/72

YEAR	TM/L	W	L	PCT	G	GS	CG	SH	SV	IP	H	HR	BB	SO	RAT	ERA	ERA+	OAV	OOB	BH	AVG	PB	PR	/A	PD	TPI
1972	StL-N	1	0	1.000	12	0	0	0	0	12^{1}	10	0	7	4	13.1	5.11	67	.233	.353	0	—	0	-2	-2	0	-0.2
1973	Tex-A	4	2	.667	25	4	1	1	1	62^{1}	59	3	31	34	13.0	4.62	81	.254	.342	0	—	0	-6	-6	0	-0.6
1975	Cal-A	0	1	.000	3	1	0	0	0	5^{2}	7	0	4	0	17.5	9.53	37	.304	.407	0	—	0	-4	-4	0	0.0
Total	3	5	3	.625	40	5	1	1	1	80^{1}	76	3	42	38	13.3	5.04	73	.255	.349	0	—	0	-11	-12	0	-0.8

● CHARLES HUDSON
Hudson, Charles Lynn b: 3/16/59, Ennis, Tex. BB/TR, 6'3", 185 lbs. Deb: 5/31/83

YEAR	TM/L	W	L	PCT	G	GS	CG	SH	SV	IP	H	HR	BB	SO	RAT	ERA	ERA+	OAV	OOB	BH	AVG	PB	PR	/A	PD	TPI
1983	*Phi-N	8	8	.500	26	26	3	0	0	169^{1}	158	13	53	101	11.2	3.35	106	.248	.305	5	.093	-2	5	4	-1	0.2
1984	Phi-N	9	11	.450	30	30	1	1	0	173^{2}	181	12	52	94	12.2	4.04	90	.265	.319	5	.089	-2	-9	-8	-2	-1.3
1985	Phi-N	8	13	.381	38	26	3	0	0	193	188	23	74	122	12.3	3.78	97	.252	.320	8	.140	-1	-4	-2	-2	-0.5
1986	Phi-N	7	10	.412	33	23	0	0	0	144	165	20	58	82	13.9	4.94	78	.291	.357	2	.047	-3	-20	-17	-0	-2.1
1987	NY-A	11	7	.611	35	16	6	2	0	154^{2}	137	19	57	100	11.5	3.61	122	.239	.311	0	—	0	15	13	-2	1.2
1988	NY-A	6	6	.500	28	12	1	0	2	106^{1}	93	9	36	58	11.3	4.49	88	.235	.306	0	—	0	-6	-6	-0	-0.7
1989	Det-A	1	5	.167	18	7	0	0	0	66^{2}	75	14	31	23	14.6	6.35	60	.288	.369	0	—	0	-18	-19	-1	-1.8
Total	7	50	60	.455	208	140	14	3	2	1007^{2}	997	110	361	580	12.2	4.14	92	.258	.324	20	.095	-8	-37	-35	-8	-5.0

● HAL HUDSON
Hudson, Hal Campbell "Bud" or "Lefty" b: 5/4/27, Grosse Point, Mich. BL/TL, 5'10", 175 lbs. Deb: 4/20/52

YEAR	TM/L	W	L	PCT	G	GS	CG	SH	SV	IP	H	HR	BB	SO	RAT	ERA	ERA+	OAV	OOB	BH	AVG	PB	PR	/A	PD	TPI
1952	StL-A	0	0	—	3	0	0	0	0	5^{2}	9	0	6	0	23.8	12.71	31	.360	.484	0	.000	-0	-6	-6	-0	-0.6
	Chi-A	0	0	—	2	0	0	0	0	4	7	0	1	4	18.0	2.25	162	.389	.421	0	—	0	1	1	-0	0.1
	Yr	0	0	—	5	0	0	0	0	9^{2}	16	0	7	4	21.4	8.38	45	.372	.460	0	.000	-0	-5	-5	-0	-0.5
1953	Chi-A	0	0	—	1	0	0	0	0	0^{2}	0	0	0	0	0.0	0.00	—	.000	.000	0	—	0	0	0	0	0.0
Total	2	0	0	—	6	0	0	0	0	10^{1}	16	0	7	4	20.0	7.84	49	.364	.451	0	.000	-0	-5	-5	-0	-0.5

● JESSE HUDSON
Hudson, Jesse James b: 7/22/48, Mansfield, La. BL/TL, 6'2", 165 lbs. Deb: 9/19/69

YEAR	TM/L	W	L	PCT	G	GS	CG	SH	SV	IP	H	HR	BB	SO	RAT	ERA	ERA+	OAV	OOB	BH	AVG	PB	PR	/A	PD	TPI
1969	NY-N	0	0	—	1	0	0	0	0	2	2	0	2	3	18.0	4.50	81	.250	.400	0	—	0	-0	-0	0	0.0

● NAT HUDSON
Hudson, Nathaniel P. b: 1/12/1859, Chicago, Ill. d: 3/14/28, Chicago, Ill. TR , Deb: 4/18/1886

YEAR	TM/L	W	L	PCT	G	GS	CG	SH	SV	IP	H	HR	BB	SO	RAT	ERA	ERA+	OAV	OOB	BH	AVG	PB	PR	/A	PD	TPI
1886	*StL-a	16	10	.615	29	27	25	0	**1**	234^{1}	224	3	62	100	11.1	3.03	113	.243	.293	35	.233	1	11	11	-1	0.9
1887	StL-a	4	4	.500	9	9	7	0	0	67	91	2	20	15	15.4	4.97	91	.305	.357	12	.250	0	-5	-3	-2	-0.4
1888	StL-a	25	10	**.714**	39	37	36	5	0	333	283	8	59	130	9.6	2.54	128	.222	.264	50	.255	5	19	27	-1	2.9
1889	StL-a	3	2	.600	9	5	4	0	0	60	71	2	15	13	13.5	4.20	101	.285	.336	13	.250	0	-2	0	-1	0.0
Total	4	48	26	.649	86	78	72	5	1	694^{1}	669	15	156	258	11.0	3.08	114	.244	.291	110	.247	7	23	34	-4	3.4

● REX HUDSON
Hudson, Rex Haughton b: 8/11/53, Tulsa, Okla. BB/TR, 5'11", 165 lbs. Deb: 7/27/74

YEAR	TM/L	W	L	PCT	G	GS	CG	SH	SV	IP	H	HR	BB	SO	RAT	ERA	ERA+	OAV	OOB	BH	AVG	PB	PR	/A	PD	TPI
1974	LA-N	0	0	—	1	0	0	0	0	2	6	2	0	0	27.0	22.50	15	.500	.500	0	—	0	-4	-4	-0	-0.4

● SID HUDSON
Hudson, Sidney Charles b: 1/3/17, Coalfield, Tenn. BR/TR, 6'4", 180 lbs. Deb: 4/18/40 C

YEAR	TM/L	W	L	PCT	G	GS	CG	SH	SV	IP	H	HR	BB	SO	RAT	ERA	ERA+	OAV	OOB	BH	AVG	PB	PR	/A	PD	TPI
1940	Was-A	17	16	.515	38	31	19	3	1	252	272	20	81	96	12.7	4.57	91	.274	.330	22	.237	2	-5	-11	1	-0.8
1941	Was-A★	13	14	.481	33	33	17	3	0	249^{2}	242	12	97	108	12.3	3.46	117	.253	.322	16	.186	-0	19	16	2	1.9
1942	Was-A☆	10	17	.370	35	31	19	1	2	239^{1}	266	9	70	72	12.8	4.36	84	.276	.328	19	.213	1	-19	-19	3	-1.4
1946	Was-A	8	11	.421	31	15	6	1	1	142^{1}	160	9	37	35	12.7	3.60	93	.280	.328	12	.279	3	-2	-4	2	0.0
1947	Was-A	6	9	.400	20	17	5	1	0	106	113	8	58	37	14.6	5.60	66	.272	.363	12	.308	2	-22	-22	1	-1.8
1948	Was-A	4	16	.200	39	29	4	0	1	182	217	11	107	53	16.3	5.88	74	.299	.394	14	.237	2	-32	-31	3	-2.4
1949	Was-A	8	17	.320	40	27	11	2	1	209	234	11	91	54	14.2	4.22	101	.283	.357	16	.239	2	-1	1	4	0.6
1950	Was-A	14	14	.500	30	30	17	0	0	237^{2}	261	17	98	75	13.8	4.09	110	.284	.356	20	.215	-1	13	11	3	1.2
1951	Was-A	5	12	.294	23	19	8	0	0	138^{2}	168	8	52	43	14.5	5.13	80	.302	.365	12	.273	2	-15	-16	3	-1.1
1952	Was-A	3	4	.429	7	7	6	0	0	62^{2}	59	4	29	24	12.6	2.73	130	.257	.340	4	.167	-0	7	6	2	0.8
	Bos-A	7	9	.438	21	18	7	0	0	134^{1}	145	9	36	50	12.6	3.62	109	.276	.330	8	.174	-1	1	5	4	0.8
	Yr	10	13	.435	28	25	13	0	0	197	204	13	65	74	12.6	3.34	114	.270	.333	12	.171	-1	7	11	6	1.6
1953	Bos-A	6	9	.400	30	17	4	0	2	156	164	13	49	60	12.5	3.52	120	.269	.327	7	.140	-2	8	12	1	1.0
1954	Bos-A	3	4	.429	33	5	0	0	5	71^{1}	83	5	30	27	14.5	4.42	93	.296	.369	2	.154	-1	-5	-2	0	-0.3
Total	12	104	152	.406	380	279	123	11	13	2181	2384	136	835	734	13.5	4.28	95	.278	.345	164	.220	9	-54	-55	28	-1.5

● AL HUENKE
Huenke, Albert A. b: 6/26/1891, New Bremen, Ohio d: 9/20/74, St.Mary's, Ohio BR/TR, 6', 175 lbs. Deb: 10/06/14

YEAR	TM/L	W	L	PCT	G	GS	CG	SH	SV	IP	H	HR	BB	SO	RAT	ERA	ERA+	OAV	OOB	BH	AVG	PB	PR	/A	PD	TPI
1914	NY-N	0	0	—	1	0	0	0	0	2	2	0	0	2	9.0	4.50	59	.250	.250	0	.000	-0	-0	-0	-0	-0.1

● PHIL HUFFMAN
Huffman, Phillip Lee b: 6/20/58, Freeport, Tex. BR/TR, 6'2", 180 lbs. Deb: 4/10/79

YEAR	TM/L	W	L	PCT	G	GS	CG	SH	SV	IP	H	HR	BB	SO	RAT	ERA	ERA+	OAV	OOB	BH	AVG	PB	PR	/A	PD	TPI
1979	Tor-A	6	18	.250	31	31	2	1	0	173	220	25	68	56	15.0	5.77	75	.304	.364	0	—	0	-30	-28	0	-2.6
1985	Bal-A	0	0	—	2	1	0	0	0	4^{2}	7	1	5	2	23.1	15.43	26	.350	.480	0	—	0	-6	-6	0	-0.5
Total	2	6	18	.250	33	32	2	1	0	177^{2}	227	26	73	58	15.2	6.03	72	.305	.367	0	—	0	-36	-33	0	-3.1

● ED HUGHES
Hughes, Edward J. b: 10/5/1880, Chicago, Ill. d: 10/11/27, McHenry, Ill. BR/TR, 6'1", 180 lbs. Deb: 8/29/02 F♦

YEAR	TM/L	W	L	PCT	G	GS	CG	SH	SV	IP	H	HR	BB	SO	RAT	ERA	ERA+	OAV	OOB	BH	AVG	PB	PR	/A	PD	TPI
1905	Bos-A	3	2	.600	6	4	2	0	0	33^{1}	38	0	9	8	13.0	4.59	59	.288	.338	3	.214	-0	-7	-7	-2	-0.9
1906	Bos-A	0	0	—	2	0	0	0	0	10	15	0	3	3	16.2	5.40	51	.349	.392	0	.000	-0	-3	-3	-0	-0.4
Total	2	3	2	.600	8	4	2	0	0	43^{1}	53	0	12	11	13.7	4.78	57	.303	.351	4	.190	-1	-10	-10	-2	-1.3

● JIM HUGHES
Hughes, James Jay "Jay" b: 1/22/1874, Sacramento, Cal. d: 6/2/24, Sacramento, Cal. BR/TR, Deb: 4/18/1898 F

YEAR	TM/L	W	L	PCT	G	GS	CG	SH	SV	IP	H	HR	BB	SO	RAT	ERA	ERA+	OAV	OOB	BH	AVG	PB	PR	/A	PD	TPI
1898	Bal-N	23	12	.657	38	35	31	5	0	300^{2}	268	4	100	81	11.6	3.20	112	.237	.309	37	.226	4	14	13	2	1.8
1899	Bro-N	**28**	6	**.824**	35	35	30	3	0	291^{2}	250	6	119	99	11.8	2.68	146	.232	.316	27	.252	5	38	40	2	4.5
1901	Bro-N	17	12	.586	31	29	24	0	0	250^{2}	265	3	102	96	13.6	3.27	103	.269	.346	16	.176	-1	2	2	1	0.2
1902	Bro-N	15	11	.577	31	30	27	0	0	254	228	3	55	94	10.3	2.87	96	.240	.288	20	.213	4	-3	-3	2	0.4
Total	4	83	41	.669	135	129	112	8	0	1097	1011	16	376	370	11.8	3.00	114	.244	.315	100	.219	12	51	52	8	6.9

● JIM HUGHES
Hughes, James Michael b: 7/2/51, Los Angeles, Cal. BR/TR, 6'3", 190 lbs. Deb: 9/14/74

YEAR	TM/L	W	L	PCT	G	GS	CG	SH	SV	IP	H	HR	BB	SO	RAT	ERA	ERA+	OAV	OOB	BH	AVG	PB	PR	/A	PD	TPI
1974	Min-A	0	2	.000	2	2	1	0	0	10^{1}	8	2	4	8	10.5	5.23	72	.216	.293	0	—	0	-2	-2	0	-0.2
1975	Min-A	16	14	.533	37	34	12	2	0	249^{2}	241	17	127	130	13.7	3.82	101	.255	.351	0	—	0	-1	1	1	0.0
1976	Min-A	9	14	.391	37	26	3	0	0	177	190	17	73	87	13.8	4.98	72	.281	.358	0	—	0	-29	-27	-1	-3.0
1977	Min-A	0	0	—	2	0	0	0	0	4^{1}	4	0	1	1	10.4	2.08	192	.250	.294	0	—	0	1	1	-0	0.2
Total	4	25	30	.455	78	62	16	2	0	441^{1}	443	36	205	226	13.6	4.30	87	.265	.352	0	—	0	-31	-27	-1	-3.0

● JIM HUGHES
Hughes, James Robert b: 3/21/23, Chicago, Ill. BR/TR, 6'1", 200 lbs. Deb: 9/13/52

YEAR	TM/L	W	L	PCT	G	GS	CG	SH	SV	IP	H	HR	BB	SO	RAT	ERA	ERA+	OAV	OOB	BH	AVG	PB	PR	/A	PD	TPI
1952	Bro-N	2	1	.667	6	0	0	0	0	18^{2}	16	0	11	8	13.0	1.45	252	.235	.342	0	.000	-0	5	5	-1	0.4

YEAR	TM/L	W	L	PCT	G	GS	CG	SH	SV	IP	H	HR	BB	SO	RAT	ERA	ERA+	OAV	OOB	BH	AVG	PB	PR	/A	PD	TPI
1953	*Bro-N	4	3	.571	48	0	0	0	9	85^{2}	80	6	41	49	12.8	3.47	123	.245	.332	4	.286	1	8	8	-1	0.7
1954	Bro-N	8	4	.667	**60**	0	0	0	**24**	86^{2}	76	7	44	58	12.5	3.22	127	.239	.331	3	.188	-0	8	8	-1	0.7
1955	Bro-N	0	2	.000	24	0	0	0	6	42^{2}	41	10	19	20	12.7	4.22	96	.256	.335	0	.000	-2	-1	-1	0	-0.2
1956	Bro-N	0	0	—	5	0	0	0	0	12	10	3	4	8	10.5	5.25	76	.233	.298	0	.000	-0	-2	-2	-0	-0.2
	Chi-N	1	3	.250	25	1	0	0	0	45^{1}	43	4	30	20	15.3	5.16	73	.259	.385	2	.286	1	-7	-7	-1	-0.7
	Yr	1	3	.250	30	1	0	0	0	57^{1}	53	7	34	28	14.3	5.18	74	.254	.368	2	.222	0	-9	-9	-1	-0.9
1957	Chi-A	0	0	—	4	0	0	0	0	5	12	0	3	2	27.0	10.80	35	.462	.517	0	—	0	-4	-4	0	-0.4
Total	6	15	13	.536	172	1	0	0	39	296	278	30	152	165	13.2	3.83	106	.251	.344	9	.170	-1	7	7	-3	0.3

● MICKEY HUGHES Hughes, Michael J. b: 10/25/1866, New York, N.Y. d: 4/10/31, Jersey City, N.J. TR, 5'6", 165 lbs. Deb: 4/22/1888 F

YEAR	TM/L	W	L	PCT	G	GS	CG	SH	SV	IP	H	HR	BB	SO	RAT	ERA	ERA+	OAV	OOB	BH	AVG	PB	PR	/A	PD	TPI
1888	Bro-a	25	13	.658	40	40	40	2	0	363	281	5	98	159	9.5	2.13	140	.206	.262	19	.137	-6	38	34	-1	2.6
1889	*Bro-a	9	8	.529	20	17	13	0	0	153	172	6	86	54	15.6	4.35	86	.275	.369	12	.176	-3	-9	-11	-0	-1.2
1890	Bro-N	4	4	.500	9	8	6	0	0	66^{1}	77	1	30	22	15.1	5.16	67	.282	.361	1	.038	-4	-12	-13	0	-1.3
	Phi-a	1	3	.250	6	5	4	0	0	41^{1}	64	0	21	15	19.6	5.44	70	.343	.424	2	.125	-1	-7	-7	-1	-0.7
Total	3	39	28	.582	75	70	63	2	0	623^{2}	594	12	235	250	12.3	3.22	102	.242	.314	34	.137	-13	10	4	-1	-0.6

● DICK HUGHES Hughes, Richard Henry b: 2/13/38, Stephens, Ark. BR/TR, 6'3", 195 lbs. Deb: 9/11/66

YEAR	TM/L	W	L	PCT	G	GS	CG	SH	SV	IP	H	HR	BB	SO	RAT	ERA	ERA+	OAV	OOB	BH	AVG	PB	PR	/A	PD	TPI
1966	StL-N	2	1	.667	6	2	1	1	1	21	12	0	7	20	9.0	1.71	209	.162	.253	2	.400	1	4	4	0	0.6
1967	*StL-N	16	6	**.727**	37	27	12	3	3	222^{1}	164	22	48	161	**8.8**	2.67	123	**.203**	**.252**	10	.128	-1	17	15	-2	1.3
1968	*StL-N	2	2	.500	25	5	0	0	4	64	45	7	21	49	9.3	3.52	82	.202	.270	0	.000	-1	-4	-4	1	-0.6
Total	3	20	9	.690	68	34	13	4	8	307^{1}	221	29	76	230	8.9	2.78	116	.200	.256	12	.122	-2	18	15	-1	1.3

● TOM HUGHES Hughes, Thomas Edward b: 9/13/34, Ancon, C.Z., Pan. BL/TR, 6'2", 180 lbs. Deb: 9/13/59

YEAR	TM/L	W	L	PCT	G	GS	CG	SH	SV	IP	H	HR	BB	SO	RAT	ERA	ERA+	OAV	OOB	BH	AVG	PB	PR	/A	PD	TPI
1959	StL-N	0	2	.000	2	2	0	0	0	4	9	2	2	2	24.8	15.75	27	.409	.458	0	.000	-0	-5	-5	-0	-0.5

● TOM HUGHES Hughes, Thomas James "Long Tom" b: 11/29/1878, Chicago, Ill. d: 2/8/56, Chicago, Ill. BR/TR, 6'1", Deb: 9/07/00 F

YEAR	TM/L	W	L	PCT	G	GS	CG	SH	SV	IP	H	HR	BB	SO	RAT	ERA	ERA+	OAV	OOB	BH	AVG	PB	PR	/A	PD	TPI
1900	Chi-N	1	1	.500	3	3	3	0	0	21	31	0	7	12	16.3	5.14	70	.341	.389	0	.000	-0	-3	-4	0	-0.3
1901	Chi-N	10	23	.303	37	35	32	1	0	308^{1}	309	4	115	225	12.8	3.24	100	.259	.331	14	.119	-8	3	-0	-2	-1.0
1902	Bal-A	7	5	.583	13	13	12	1	0	108^{1}	120	2	32	45	12.8	3.90	97	.281	.334	6	.140	-2	-4	-2	1	-0.3
	Bos-A	3	3	.500	9	8	4	0	0	49^{1}	51	0	24	15	13.9	3.28	109	.267	.352	11	.367	2	2	2	-0	0.3
	Yr	10	8	.556	22	21	16	1	0	157^{2}	171	2	56	60	13.0	3.71	100	.276	.337	17	.233	-0	-2	0	1	0.0
1903	*Bos-A	20	7	.741	33	31	25	5	0	244^{2}	232	4	60	112	11.0	2.57	118	.250	.301	26	.280	7	11	13	-4	1.6
1904	NY-A	7	11	.389	19	18	12	1	0	136^{1}	141	3	48	75	12.9	3.70	73	.268	.336	13	.241	1	-17	-15	-3	-1.7
	Was-A	2	13	.133	16	14	14	0	1	124^{1}	133	4	34	48	12.5	3.47	77	.274	.330	13	.228	3	-12	-11	-1	-0.9
	Yr	9	24	.273	35	32	26	1	1	260^{2}	274	7	82	123	12.5	3.59	75	.269	.327	26	.234	4	-29	-26	-3	-2.6
1905	Was-A	17	20	.459	39	35	26	6	0	291^{1}	239	3	79	149	10.2	2.35	113	.225	.286	22	.212	4	10	10	-4	1.1
1906	Was-A	7	17	.292	30	24	18	1	0	204	230	5	81	90	13.9	3.62	73	.287	.356	14	.212	3	-21	-22	-4	-2.5
1907	Was-A	7	14	.333	34	23	18	2	**4**	211	206	1	47	102	11.3	3.11	78	.258	.309	19	.237	3	-13	-16	-1	-1.4
1908	Was-A	18	15	.545	43	31	24	3	4	276^{1}	224	3	77	165	10.0	2.21	103	.227	.287	17	.195	2	6	2	1	0.6
1909	Was-A	4	7	.364	22	13	7	2	1	120^{1}	113	1	33	77	11.3	2.69	90	.246	.303	3	.083	-2	-3	-3	-0	-0.6
1911	Was-A	11	17	.393	34	27	17	2	0	223	251	7	77	86	13.4	3.47	95	.288	.348	15	.185	-1	-3	-5	-2	-0.8
1912	Was-A	13	10	.565	31	26	11	1	0	196	201	8	78	108	13.1	2.94	113	.270	.344	13	.194	1	8	9	0	1.0
1913	Was-A	4	12	.250	36	12	4	0	6	129^{2}	129	6	61	59	14.2	4.30	69	.253	.350	4	.111	-1	-20	-19	1	-2.0
Total	13	131	175	.428	399	313	227	25	16	2644	2610	51	853	1368	12.1	3.09	93	.259	.323	190	.198	12	-57	-64	-18	-6.9

● TOM HUGHES Hughes, Thomas L. "Salida Tom" b: 1/28/1884, Coal Creek, Colo. d: 11/1/61, Los Angeles, Cal. BR/TR, 6'2", 175 lbs. Deb: 9/18/06

YEAR	TM/L	W	L	PCT	G	GS	CG	SH	SV	IP	H	HR	BB	SO	RAT	ERA	ERA+	OAV	OOB	BH	AVG	PB	PR	/A	PD	TPI
1906	NY-A	1	0	1.000	3	1	1	0	0	15	11	2	1	5	7.2	4.20	71	.208	.222	1	.200	0	-3	-2	-1	-0.2
1907	NY-A	2	0	1.000	4	3	2	0	0	27	16	0	11	10	9.7	2.67	105	.174	.276	1	.143	-0	-0	0	-1	-0.1
1909	NY-A	7	8	.467	24	16	9	2	1	118^{2}	109	3	37	69	11.4	2.65	95	.249	.313	5	.128	1	-2	-2	-1	-0.2
1910	NY-A	7	9	.438	23	15	11	0	1	151^{2}	153	2	37	64	11.5	3.50	76	.271	.320	9	.164	-1	-17	-14	1	-1.5
1914	Bos-N	2	0	1.000	2	2	1	0	0	17	14	0	4	11	9.5	2.65	104	.226	.273	0	.000	-1	0	0	1	0.0
1915	Bos-N	16	14	.533	**50**	25	17	4	**9**	280^{1}	208	4	58	171	8.9	2.12	122	.213	.265	9	.100	-3	20	15	-2	1.0
1916	Bos-N	16	3	**.842**	40	14	7	1	5	161	121	2	51	97	10.1	2.35	106	.215	.290	10	.192	2	5	2	-1	0.3
1917	Bos-N	5	3	.625	11	8	6	2	0	74	54	1	30	40	10.6	1.95	131	.216	.307	0	.000	-2	6	5	-0	0.2
1918	Bos-N	0	2	.000	3	3	1	0	0	18^{1}	17	0	6	9	11.3	3.44	78	.250	.311	2	.333	1	-1	-2	0	0.0
Total	9	56	39	.589	160	87	55	9	16	863	703	14	235	476	10.1	2.56	102	.229	.291	37	.130	-4	8	4	-4	-0.5

● TOMMY HUGHES Hughes, Thomas Owen b: 10/7/19, Wilkes-Barre, Pa. d: 11/28/90, Wilkse-Barre, Pa. BR/TR, 6'1", 190 lbs. Deb: 4/19/41

YEAR	TM/L	W	L	PCT	G	GS	CG	SH	SV	IP	H	HR	BB	SO	RAT	ERA	ERA+	OAV	OOB	BH	AVG	PB	PR	/A	PD	TPI
1941	Phi-N	9	14	.391	34	24	5	2	0	170	187	12	82	59	14.5	4.45	83	.280	.362	11	.200	0	-15	-14	1	-1.3
1942	Phi-N	12	18	.400	40	31	19	0	1	253	224	8	99	77	11.5	3.06	108	.238	.310	8	.100	-5	7	7	3	0.5
1946	Phi-N	6	9	.400	29	13	3	2	1	111	123	5	44	34	13.6	4.38	78	.281	.349	3	.097	-1	-12	-12	-1	-1.5
1947	Phi-N	4	11	.267	29	15	4	1	1	127	121	5	59	44	12.8	3.47	115	.265	.350	2	.050	-4	8	8	0	0.4
1948	Cin-N	0	4	.000	12	4	0	0	0	27	43	3	24	7	22.3	9.00	43	.364	.472	1	.143	-0	-15	-15	-0	-1.5
Total	5	31	56	.356	144	87	31	5	3	688	698	33	308	221	13.2	3.92	91	.266	.344	25	.117	-10	-27	-26	2	-3.4

● VERN HUGHES Hughes, Vernon Alexander "Lefty" b: 4/15/1893, Etna, Pa. d: 9/26/61, Sewickley, Pa. BL/TL, 5'10", 155 lbs. Deb: 7/06/14

YEAR	TM/L	W	L	PCT	G	GS	CG	SH	SV	IP	H	HR	BB	SO	RAT	ERA	ERA+	OAV	OOB	BH	AVG	PB	PR	/A	PD	TPI
1914	Bal-F	0	0	—	3	0	0	0	0	5^{2}	5	0	3	0	12.7	3.18	106	.250	.348	0	.000	-0	0	0	-0	0.0

● BILL HUGHES Hughes, William Nesbert b: 11/18/1896, Philadelphia, Pa. d: 2/25/63, Birmingham, Ala. BR/TR, 5'10.5", 155 lbs. Deb: 9/15/21

YEAR	TM/L	W	L	PCT	G	GS	CG	SH	SV	IP	H	HR	BB	SO	RAT	ERA	ERA+	OAV	OOB	BH	AVG	PB	PR	/A	PD	TPI
1921	Pit-N	0	0	—	1	0	0	0	0	2	3	0	1	2	22.5	4.50	85	.375	.500	0	—	0	-0	-0	0	0.0

● BILL HUGHES Hughes, William R. b: 11/25/1866, Bladensville, Ill. d: 8/25/43, Santa Ana, Cal. BL/TL, Deb: 9/28/1884 ♦

YEAR	TM/L	W	L	PCT	G	GS	CG	SH	SV	IP	H	HR	BB	SO	RAT	ERA	ERA+	OAV	OOB	BH	AVG	PB	PR	/A	PD	TPI
1885	Phi-a	0	2	.000	2	2	2	0	0	16^{2}	18	0	10	4	16.2	4.86	71	.269	.380	3	.188	0	-3	-3	-0	-0.2

● JIM HUGHEY Hughey, James Ulysses "Coldwater Jim" b: 3/8/1869, Wakashma, Mich. d: 3/29/45, Coldwater, Mich. TR, 6', Deb: 9/29/1891

YEAR	TM/L	W	L	PCT	G	GS	CG	SH	SV	IP	H	HR	BB	SO	RAT	ERA	ERA+	OAV	OOB	BH	AVG	PB	PR	/A	PD	TPI
1891	Mil-a	1	0	1.000	2	1	1	0	0	15	18	0	3	9	12.6	3.00	146	.287	.320	1	.143	-1	1	2	0	0.2
1893	Chi-N	0	1	.000	2	2	1	0	0	9	14	0	3	4	18.0	11.00	42	.345	.403	0	.000	-0	-6	-6	0	-0.4
1896	Pit-N	6	8	.429	25	14	11	0	0	155	171	3	67	48	14.2	4.99	84	.278	.355	14	.215	-1	-11	-14	-3	-1.5
1897	Pit-N	6	10	.375	25	17	13	0	1	149^{1}	193	3	45	38	14.8	5.06	82	.310	.364	8	.127	-5	-12	-15	-2	-1.7
1898	StL-N	7	24	.226	35	33	31	0	0	283^{2}	325	2	71	74	12.9	3.93	96	.285	.333	11	.113	-6	-10	-5	-1	-1.0
1899	Cle-N	4	30	.118	36	34	32	0	0	283	403	9	88	54	16.3	5.41	68	.334	.389	18	.162	-5	-49	-54	-4	-5.3
1900	StL-N	5	7	.417	20	12	11	0	0	112^{2}	147	4	40	23	15.4	5.19	70	.314	.376	7	.171	0	-19	-19	-2	-1.8
Total	7	29	80	.266	145	113	100	0	1	1007^{2}	1271	21	317	250	14.7	4.87	80	.306	.363	59	.153	-18	-106	-110	-11	-11.5

● TEX HUGHSON Hughson, Cecil Carlton b: 2/9/16, Kyle, Tex. BR/TR, 6'3", 198 lbs. Deb: 4/16/41

YEAR	TM/L	W	L	PCT	G	GS	CG	SH	SV	IP	H	HR	BB	SO	RAT	ERA	ERA+	OAV	OOB	BH	AVG	PB	PR	/A	PD	TPI
1941	Bos-A	5	3	.625	12	8	4	0	0	61	70	3	13	22	12.4	4.13	101	.289	.328	1	.059	-1	0	0	0	-0.1
1942	Bos-A☆	**22**	6	.786	38	30	**22**	4	4	**281**	258	10	75	**113**	10.7	2.59	144	.245	.296	18	.176	1	33	**35**	1	**4.1**
1943	Bos-A★	12	15	.444	35	32	**20**	4	2	266	242	23	73	114	10.7	2.64	126	.247	.300	9	.105	-4	19	20	1	1.9
1944	Bos-A★	18	5	**.783**	28	23	19	2	5	203^{1}	172	4	41	112	**9.5**	2.26	151	.225	**.267**	10	.152	-1	26	26	-0	2.8
1946	*Bos-A	20	11	.645	39	35	21	6	3	278	252	15	51	172	9.9	2.75	133	.238	.274	12	.132	-2	23	28	-2	2.6
1947	Bos-A	12	11	.522	29	26	13	3	0	189^{1}	173	17	71	119	11.7	3.33	117	.244	.314	2	.033	-6	8	12	-0	0.6
1948	Bos-A	3	1	.750	15	0	0	0	0	19^{1}	21	0	7	6	13.0	5.12	86	.276	.337	0	.000	-0	-2	-2	-1	-0.2
1949	Bos-A	4	2	.667	29	2	0	0	3	77^{2}	82	5	41	35	14.4	5.33	82	.268	.356	1	.045	-3	-10	-8	-2	-1.2
Total	8	96	54	.640	225	156	99	19	17	1375^{2}	1270	77	372	693	10.8	2.94	125	.245	.297	53	.119	-16	99	111	-3	10.5

● **MARK HUISMANN** Huismann, Mark Lawrence b: 5/11/58, Littleton, Colo. BR/TR, 6'3", 195 lbs. Deb: 8/16/83

YEAR	TM/L	W	L	PCT	G	GS	CG	SH	SV	IP	H	HR	BB	SO	RAT	ERA	ERA+	OAV	OOB	BH	AVG	PB	PR	/A	PD	TPI
1983	KC-A	2	1	.667	13	0	0	0	0	30^{2}	29	1	17	20	13.5	5.58	73	.250	.346	0	—	0	-5	-5	-1	-0.5
1984	*KC-A	3	3	.500	38	0	0	0	3	75	84	7	21	54	12.7	4.20	96	.286	.335	0	—	0	-2	-1	0	-0.1
1985	KC-A	1	0	1.000	9	0	0	0	0	18^{2}	14	1	3	9	8.2	1.93	216	.219	.254	0	—	0	5	5	0	0.5
1986	KC-A	0	1	.000	10	0	0	0	1	17^{1}	18	1	6	13	12.5	4.15	102	.269	.329	0	—	0	0	0	0	0.1
	Sea-A	3	3	.500	36	1	0	0	4	80	80	18	19	59	11.2	3.71	114	.256	.301	0	—	0	4	5	0	0.5
	Yr	3	4	.429	46	1	0	0	5	97^{1}	98	19	25	72	11.5	3.79	112	.258	.305	0	—	0	4	5	0	0.6
1987	Sea-A	0	0	—	6	0	0	0	0	14^{2}	10	1	4	15	9.8	4.91	96	.196	.281	0	—	0	-1	-0	0	0.0
	Cle-A	2	3	.400	20	0	0	0	2	35^{1}	38	6	8	23	11.7	5.09	89	.271	.311	0	—	0	-3	-2	-0	-0.2
	Yr	2	3	.400	26	0	0	0	2	50	48	7	12	38	10.8	5.04	91	.247	.291	0	—	0	-3	-3	0	-0.2
1988	Det-A	1	0	1.000	5	0	0	0	0	5^{1}	6	0	2	6	13.5	5.06	75	.286	.348	0	—	0	-1	-1	0	0.0
1989	Bal-A	0	0	—	8	0	0	0	1	11^{1}	13	0	0	13	10.3	6.35	60	.277	.277	0	—	0	-3	-3	1	-0.2
1990	Pit-N	1	0	1.000	2	0	0	0	0	3	6	2	1	2	24.0	9.00	40	.462	.533	0	—	0	-2	-2	-0	-0.2
1991	Pit-N	0	0	—	5	0	0	0	0	5	7	0	2	5	16.2	7.20	50	.304	.360	0	—	0	-2	-2	0	-0.2
Total	9	13	11	.542	152	1	0	0	11	296^{1}	305	37	83	219	11.9	4.40	95	.266	.318	0	—	0	-9	-7	1	-0.3

● **HARRY HULIHAN** Hulihan, Harry Joseph b: 4/18/1899, Rutland, Vt. d: 9/11/80, Rutland, Vt. BR/TL, 5'11", 170 lbs. Deb: 8/16/22

YEAR	TM/L	W	L	PCT	G	GS	CG	SH	SV	IP	H	HR	BB	SO	RAT	ERA	ERA+	OAV	OOB	BH	AVG	PB	PR	/A	PD	TPI
1922	Bos-N	2	3	.400	7	6	2	0	0	40	40	0	26	16	15.7	3.15	127	.274	.398	2	.154	-0	4	4	-1	0.3

● **HANK HULVEY** Hulvey, James Hensel b: 7/18/1897, Mt.Sidney, Va. d: 4/9/82, Mount Sydney, Va. BB/TR, 6', 180 lbs. Deb: 9/05/23

YEAR	TM/L	W	L	PCT	G	GS	CG	SH	SV	IP	H	HR	BB	SO	RAT	ERA	ERA+	OAV	OOB	BH	AVG	PB	PR	/A	PD	TPI
1923	Phi-A	0	1	.000	1	1	0	0	0	7	10	1	2	2	15.4	7.71	53	.357	.400	1	.500	0	-3	-3	0	-0.2

● **TOM HUME** Hume, Thomas Hubert b: 3/29/53, Cincinnati, Ohio BR/TR, 6'1", 185 lbs. Deb: 5/25/77

YEAR	TM/L	W	L	PCT	G	GS	CG	SH	SV	IP	H	HR	BB	SO	RAT	ERA	ERA+	OAV	OOB	BH	AVG	PB	PR	/A	PD	TPI
1977	Cin-N	3	3	.500	14	5	0	0	0	43	54	5	17	22	14.9	7.12	55	.305	.366	2	.200	1	-15	-15	-0	-1.4
1978	Cin-N	8	11	.421	42	23	3	0	1	174	198	12	50	90	13.0	4.14	86	.289	.341	3	.067	-3	-11	-11	0	-1.4
1979	*Cin-N	10	9	.526	57	12	2	0	17	163	162	12	33	80	10.8	2.76	**135**	.262	.300	8	.174	0	18	18	0	1.9
1980	Cin-N	9	10	.474	78	0	0	0	25	137	121	6	38	68	10.6	2.56	140	.240	.297	3	.188	0	16	15	3	2.0
1981	Cin-N	9	4	.692	51	0	0	0	13	67^{2}	63	7	31	27	12.6	3.46	103	.259	.345	0	.000	-0	0	1	-0	0.0
1982	Cin-N★	2	6	.250	46	0	0	0	17	63^{2}	57	2	21	22	11.2	3.11	119	.245	.310	0	.000	-1	3	4	-1	0.3
1983	Cin-N	3	5	.375	48	0	0	0	9	66	66	8	41	34	15.0	4.77	80	.264	.374	0	.000	-1	-8	-7	1	-0.7
1984	Cin-N	4	13	.235	54	8	0	0	3	113^{1}	142	14	41	59	14.6	5.64	67	.309	.367	3	.136	-0	-26	-23	1	-2.4
1985	Cin-N	3	5	.375	56	0	0	0	3	80	65	7	35	50	11.6	3.26	116	.224	.314	0	.000	-1	3	5	-0	0.4
1986	Phi-N	4	1	.800	48	1	0	0	4	94^{1}	89	5	34	51	12.0	2.77	139	.252	.323	0	.000	-1	10	11	1	1.2
1987	Phi-N	1	4	.200	38	6	0	0	0	70^{2}	75	10	41	29	15.3	5.60	76	.277	.380	3	.200	0	-12	-11	0	-1.0
	Cin-N	1	0	1.000	11	0	0	0	0	13^{1}	14	0	2	4	11.5	4.05	105	.292	.333	0	—	0	0	0	-0	0.0
	Yr	2	4	.333	49	6	0	0	0	84	89	10	43	33	14.3	5.36	79	.274	.360	3	.200	0	-12	-10	0	-1.0
Total	11	57	71	.445	543	55	5	0	92	1086	1106	88	384	536	12.5	3.85	97	.268	.334	22	.120	-5	-22	-14	5	-1.1

● **BILL HUMPHREY** Humphrey, Byron William b: 6/17/11, Vienna, Mo. d: 2/13/92, Springfield, Mo. BR/TR, 6', 180 lbs. Deb: 4/24/38

YEAR	TM/L	W	L	PCT	G	GS	CG	SH	SV	IP	H	HR	BB	SO	RAT	ERA	ERA+	OAV	OOB	BH	AVG	PB	PR	/A	PD	TPI
1938	Bos-A	0	0	—	2	0	0	0	0	2	5	0	1	0	27.0	9.00	55	.500	.545	0	—	0	-1	-1	-0	-0.1

● **BOB HUMPHREYS** Humphreys, Robert William b: 8/18/35, Covington, Va. BR/TR, 5'11", 170 lbs. Deb: 9/08/62

YEAR	TM/L	W	L	PCT	G	GS	CG	SH	SV	IP	H	HR	BB	SO	RAT	ERA	ERA+	OAV	OOB	BH	AVG	PB	PR	/A	PD	TPI
1962	Det-A	0	1	.000	4	0	0	0	1	5	8	3	2	3	18.0	7.20	57	.381	.435	0	—	0	-2	-2	0	-0.2
1963	StL-N	0	1	.000	9	0	0	0	0	10^{2}	11	4	7	8	16.0	5.06	70	.282	.404	0	—	0	-2	-2	0	-0.2
1964	*StL-N	2	0	1.000	28	0	0	0	2	42^{2}	32	3	15	36	10.1	2.53	150	.213	.289	1	.250	1	5	6	-0	0.7
1965	Chi-N	2	0	1.000	41	0	0	0	0	65^{2}	59	6	27	38	12.1	3.15	117	.244	.325	0	.000	-0	3	4	-1	0.3
1966	Was-A	7	3	.700	58	1	0	0	3	111^{2}	91	6	28	88	9.9	2.82	123	.229	.287	2	.167	1	8	8	-0	0.9
1967	Was-A	6	2	.750	48	2	0	0	4	105^{2}	93	13	41	54	11.6	4.17	76	.238	.314	2	.133	1	-11	-12	-1	-1.4
1968	Was-A	5	7	.417	56	0	0	0	2	92^{2}	78	13	30	56	10.5	3.69	79	.233	.296	2	.400	1	-7	-8	1	-0.7
1969	Was-A	3	3	.500	47	0	0	0	5	79^{2}	69	3	38	43	12.2	3.05	114	.233	.322	1	.077	-1	5	4	0	0.4
1970	Was-A	0	0	—	5	0	0	0	0	6^{2}	4	1	9	6	17.6	1.35	263	.200	.448	0	—	0	2	2	0	0.2
	Mil-A	2	4	.333	23	1	0	0	3	45^{2}	37	3	22	32	12.0	3.15	120	.222	.319	0	.000	-1	3	3	-0	0.3
	Yr	2	4	.333	28	1	0	0	3	52^{1}	41	4	31	38	12.7	2.92	129	.219	.336	0	.000	-1	5	5	0	0.5
Total	9	27	21	.563	319	4	0	0	20	566	482	55	219	364	11.4	3.36	101	.234	.312	8	.131	1	3	3	-2	0.3

● **BERT HUMPHRIES** Humphries, Albert b: 9/26/1880, California, Pa. d: 9/21/45, Orlando, Fla. BR/TR, 5'11.5", 182 lbs. Deb: 4/16/10

YEAR	TM/L	W	L	PCT	G	GS	CG	SH	SV	IP	H	HR	BB	SO	RAT	ERA	ERA+	OAV	OOB	BH	AVG	PB	PR	/A	PD	TPI
1910	Phi-N	0	0	—	5	0	0	0	2	9^{2}	13	0	3	3	15.8	4.66	67	.317	.378	0	.000	0	-2	-2	0	-0.1
1911	Phi-N	3	1	.750	11	5	2	0	1	41	56	1	10	13	15.8	4.17	83	.339	.398	5	.333	3	-4	-3	-1	-0.1
	Cin-N	4	3	.571	14	7	3	0	0	65	62	3	18	16	11.9	2.35	141	.266	.335	1	.063	-1	8	7	0	0.7
	Yr	7	4	.636	25	12	5	0	1	106	118	4	28	29	12.9	3.06	110	.292	.347	6	.194	2	4	4	-0	0.6
1912	Cin-N	9	11	.450	30	15	9	2	2	158^{2}	162	6	36	58	11.7	3.23	104	.270	.319	7	.137	-2	3	2	-1	-0.1
1913	Chi-N	16	4	**.800**	28	20	13	2	1	181	169	10	24	61	9.7	2.69	118	.250	.277	12	.194	1	10	10	-2	0.9
1914	Chi-N	10	11	.476	34	22	8	2	0	171	162	5	37	62	10.6	2.68	104	.250	.293	13	.236	2	2	2	2	0.6
1915	Chi-N	8	13	.381	31	22	10	4	3	171^{2}	183	6	23	45	11.1	2.31	120	.280	.309	8	.174	0	8	9	-2	0.8
Total	6	50	43	.538	153	91	45	10	9	798	807	31	151	258	11.1	2.79	110	.267	.309	46	.186	3	26	25	-3	2.7

● **JOHNNY HUMPHRIES** Humphries, John William b: 6/23/15, Clifton Forge, Va d: 6/24/65, New Orleans, La. BR/TR, 6'1", 185 lbs. Deb: 5/08/38

YEAR	TM/L	W	L	PCT	G	GS	CG	SH	SV	IP	H	HR	BB	SO	RAT	ERA	ERA+	OAV	OOB	BH	AVG	PB	PR	/A	PD	TPI
1938	Cle-A	9	8	.529	**45**	6	1	0	6	103^{1}	105	6	63	56	14.7	5.23	89	.264	.367	3	.103	-1	-5	-7	-1	-0.8
1939	Cle-A	2	4	.333	15	1	0	0	2	28^{1}	30	0	32	12	20.0	8.26	53	.294	.467	0	.000	-1	-11	-12	-0	-1.2
1940	Cle-A	0	2	.000	19	1	1	0	1	33^{2}	35	5	29	17	17.6	8.29	51	.269	.410	0	.000	-1	-15	-15	-1	-1.5
1941	Chi-A	4	2	.667	14	6	4	4	1	73^{1}	63	2	22	25	10.6	1.84	223	.230	.290	2	.087	-1	19	18	-1	1.6
1942	Chi-A	12	12	.500	28	28	17	2	0	228^{1}	227	9	59	71	11.5	2.68	134	.257	.309	18	.225	4	25	23	-2	2.9
1943	Chi-A	11	11	.500	28	27	8	2	0	188^{1}	198	7	54	51	12.3	3.30	101	.268	.322	20	.290	5	-0	1	-2	0.6
1944	Chi-A	8	10	.444	30	20	8	0	1	169	170	9	57	42	12.3	3.67	93	.267	.331	10	.189	0	-5	-5	-3	-0.8
1945	Chi-A	6	14	.300	22	21	10	1	1	153	172	11	48	33	13.1	4.24	78	.282	.337	8	.148	-3	-15	-16	-4	-2.2
1946	Phi-N	0	0	—	10	1	0	0	0	24^{2}	24	1	9	10	12.4	4.01	85	.258	.330	2	.250	0	-2	-2	-1	-0.3
Total	9	52	63	.452	211	111	49	9	12	1002	1024	50	373	317	12.8	3.78	97	.265	.334	63	.191	4	-9	-13	-14	-1.7

● **BEN HUNT** Hunt, Benjamin Franklin "High Pockets" b: 11/10/1888, Eufaula, Okla. d: 9/27/27, Greybull, Wyo. BL/TL, 6'5", 190 lbs. Deb: 8/24/10

YEAR	TM/L	W	L	PCT	G	GS	CG	SH	SV	IP	H	HR	BB	SO	RAT	ERA	ERA+	OAV	OOB	BH	AVG	PB	PR	/A	PD	TPI
1910	Bos-A	2	3	.400	7	7	3	0	0	46^{2}	45	4	20	19	12.5	4.05	63	.266	.344	1	.056	-2	-8	-8	-1	-1.0
1913	StL-N	0	1	.000	2	1	0	0	0	8	6	0	9	6	18.0	3.38	96	.240	.457	0	.000	-0	-0	-0	1	0.0
Total	2	2	4	.333	9	8	3	0	0	54^{2}	51	4	29	25	13.3	3.95	67	.263	.362	1	.050	-2	-8	-8	-0	-1.0

● **KEN HUNT** Hunt, Kenneth Raymond b: 12/14/38, Ogden, Utah BR/TR, 6'4", 200 lbs. Deb: 4/16/61

YEAR	TM/L	W	L	PCT	G	GS	CG	SH	SV	IP	H	HR	BB	SO	RAT	ERA	ERA+	OAV	OOB	BH	AVG	PB	PR	/A	PD	TPI
1961	*Cin-N	9	10	.474	29	22	4	0	0	136^{1}	130	13	66	75	13.3	3.96	103	.257	.349	7	.179	0	1	2	-1	0.1

● **GEORGE HUNTER** Hunter, George Henry b: 7/8/1887, Buffalo, N.Y. d: 1/11/68, Harrisburg, Pa. BB/TL, 5'8.5", 165 lbs. Deb: 5/04/09 F♦

YEAR	TM/L	W	L	PCT	G	GS	CG	SH	SV	IP	H	HR	BB	SO	RAT	ERA	ERA+	OAV	OOB	BH	AVG	PB	PR	/A	PD	TPI
1909	Bro-N	4	10	.286	16	13	10	0	0	113^{1}	104	2	38	43	11.5	2.46	105	.254	.322	28	.228	2	2	2	0	0.5

● **CATFISH HUNTER** Hunter, James Augustus "Jim" b: 4/8/46, Hertford, N.C. BR/TR, 6', 195 lbs. Deb: 5/13/65 H

YEAR	TM/L	W	L	PCT	G	GS	CG	SH	SV	IP	H	HR	BB	SO	RAT	ERA	ERA+	OAV	OOB	BH	AVG	PB	PR	/A	PD	TPI
1965	KC-A	8	8	.500	32	20	3	2	0	133	124	21	46	82	11.6	4.26	82	.246	.311	6	.150	-1	-12	-11	-2	-1.4
1966	KC-A☆	9	11	.450	30	25	4	0	0	176^{2}	158	17	64	103	11.4	4.02	84	.239	.308	9	.153	1	-12	-12	-3	-1.5
1967	KC-A★	13	17	.433	35	35	13	5	0	259^{2}	209	16	84	196	10.2	2.81	113	.219	.284	18	.196	4	12	11	-5	1.2
1968	Oak-A	13	13	.500	36	34	11	2	1	234	210	29	69	172	10.9	3.35	84	.238	.296	19	.232	5	-10	-14	-3	-1.3
1969	Oak-A	12	15	.444	38	35	10	3	0	247	210	34	85	150	10.9	3.35	103	.234	.304	19	.224	4	7	2	-1	0.6

YEAR	TM/L	W	L	PCT	G	GS	CG	SH	SV	IP	H	HR	BB	SO	RAT	ERA	ERA+	OAV	OOB	BH	AVG	PB	PR	/A	PD	TPI
1970	Oak-A★	18	14	.563	40	40	9	1	0	262^1	253	32	74	178	11.5	3.81	93	.250	.307	18	.200	4	-3	-8	-2	-0.6
1971	*Oak-A	21	11	.656	37	37	16	4	0	273^2	225	27	80	181	10.2	2.96	113	.223	.282	36	.350	12	15	11	-4	2.3
1972	*Oak-A☆	21	7	**.750**	38	37	16	5	0	295^1	200	21	70	191	8.3	2.04	139	.189	.242	23	.219	2	33	26	-3	3.1
1973	*Oak-A★	21	5	**.808**	36	36	11	3	0	256^1	222	39	69	124	10.3	3.34	106	.232	.284	1	1.000	0	14	6	-4	0.3
1974	*Oak-A★	**25**	12	.676	41	41	23	6	0	318^1	268	25	46	143	**9.0**	**2.49**	133	.229	**.260**	0	—	0	**40**	29	-4	2.9
1975	NY-A★	**23**	14	.622	39	39	**30**	7	0	**328**	248	25	83	177	**9.2**	2.58	141	**.208**	**.263**	0	—	0	44	39	-4	3.7
1976	*NY-A★	17	15	.531	36	36	21	2	0	298^2	268	28	68	173	10.2	3.53	97	.241	.286	0	.000	0	-0	-4	-2	-0.6
1977	*NY-A	9	9	.500	22	22	8	1	0	143^1	137	29	47	52	11.7	4.71	84	.250	.313	0	—	0	-10	-12	-3	-1.4
1978	*NY-A	12	6	.667	21	20	5	1	0	118	98	16	35	56	10.2	3.58	101	.226	.286	0	—	0	2	0	-1	0.0
1979	NY-A	2	9	.182	19	19	1	0	0	105	128	15	34	34	14.0	5.31	77	.312	.366	0	—	0	-13	-14	-1	-1.5
Total	15	224	166	.574	500	476	181	42	1	3449^1	2958	374	954	2012	10.3	3.26	104	.231	.287	149	.226	32	109	50	-40	5.8

● JIM HUNTER Hunter, James Mac Gregor b: 6/22/64, Jersey City, N.J. BR/TR, 6'3", 205 lbs. Deb: 5/17/91

YEAR	TM/L	W	L	PCT	G	GS	CG	SH	SV	IP	H	HR	BB	SO	RAT	ERA	ERA+	OAV	OOB	BH	AVG	PB	PR	/A	PD	TPI
1991	Mil-A	0	5	.000	8	6	0	0	0	31	45	3	17	14	19.2	7.26	55	.349	.440	0	—	0	-11	-11	1	-1.0

● LEM HUNTER Hunter, Robert Lemuel b: 1/16/1863, Warren, Ohio d: 11/9/56, W.Lafayette, Ohio Deb: 9/01/1883 ♦

YEAR	TM/L	W	L	PCT	G	GS	CG	SH	SV	IP	H	HR	BB	SO	RAT	ERA	ERA+	OAV	OOB	BH	AVG	PB	PR	/A	PD	TPI
1883	Cle-N	0	0	—	1	0	0	0	0	6^1	10	0	2	4	17.1	1.42	222	.370	.414	1	.250	-0	1	1	0	0.1

● WILLARD HUNTER Hunter, Willard Mitchell b: 3/8/34, Newark, N.J. BR/TL, 6'2", 180 lbs. Deb: 4/16/62

YEAR	TM/L	W	L	PCT	G	GS	CG	SH	SV	IP	H	HR	BB	SO	RAT	ERA	ERA+	OAV	OOB	BH	AVG	PB	PR	/A	PD	TPI
1962	LA-N	0	0	—	1	0	0	0	0	2	6	1	4	1	45.0	40.50	9	.545	.667	0	—	0	-8	-8	0	-0.6
	NY-N	1	6	.143	27	6	1	0	0	63	67	9	34	40	14.6	5.57	75	.270	.360	3	.231	0	-11	-10	-1	-1.0
	Yr	1	6	.143	28	6	1	0	0	65	73	10	38	41	15.5	6.65	63	.281	.375	3	.231	0	-20	-18	-1	-1.6
1964	NY-N	3	3	.500	41	0	0	0	5	49	54	4	9	22	11.9	4.41	81	.284	.323	1	1.000	0	-5	-5	-0	-0.5
Total	2	4	9	.308	69	6	1	0	5	114	127	14	47	63	14.0	5.68	69	.283	.355	4	.286	1	-24	-22	-1	-2.1

● WALT HUNTZINGER Huntzinger, Walter Henry "Shakes" b: 2/6/1899, Pottsville, Pa. d: 8/11/81, Upper Darby, Pa. BR/TR, 6', 150 lbs. Deb: 9/29/23

YEAR	TM/L	W	L	PCT	G	GS	CG	SH	SV	IP	H	HR	BB	SO	RAT	ERA	ERA+	OAV	OOB	BH	AVG	PB	PR	/A	PD	TPI
1923	NY-N	0	1	.000	2	1	0	0	0	8	9	0	1	2	11.3	7.88	49	.290	.313	0	.000	-0	-3	-4	-0	-0.4
1924	NY-N	1	1	.500	12	2	0	0	1	32^1	41	3	9	6	13.9	4.45	82	.318	.362	4	.500	1	-2	-3	-0	-0.2
1925	NY-N	5	1	.833	26	1	0	0	0	64^1	68	3	17	19	11.9	3.50	115	.281	.328	1	.091	-1	**6**	**4**	-1	0.2
1926	StL-N	0	4	.000	9	4	2	0	0	34	35	4	14	9	13.0	4.24	92	.267	.338	0	.000	-1	-2	-1	0	-0.2
	Chi-N	1	1	.500	11	0	0	0	2	28^2	26	0	8	4	11.6	0.94	408	.260	.333	1	.143	-1	9	9	0	0.9
	Yr	1	5	.167	20	4	2	0	2	62^2	61	4	22	13	12.4	2.73	142	.264	.336	1	.067	-2	8	8	1	0.7
Total	4	7	8	.467	60	8	2	0	3	167^1	179	10	49	40	12.4	3.60	108	.283	.337	6	.167	-1	8	6	-1	0.3

● TOM HURD Hurd, Thomas Carr "Whitey" b: 5/27/24, Danville, Va. d: 9/5/82, Waterloo, Iowa BR/TR, 5'9", 155 lbs. Deb: 7/30/54

YEAR	TM/L	W	L	PCT	G	GS	CG	SH	SV	IP	H	HR	BB	SO	RAT	ERA	ERA+	OAV	OOB	BH	AVG	PB	PR	/A	PD	TPI
1954	Bos-A	2	0	1.000	16	0	0	0	1	29^2	21	2	12	14	10.0	3.03	135	.198	.280	1	.333	0	2	4	0	0.5
1955	Bos-A	8	6	.571	43	0	0	0	5	80^2	72	7	38	48	12.4	3.01	142	.242	.330	1	.071	-1	8	11	-0	1.0
1956	Bos-A	3	4	.429	40	0	0	0	5	76	84	5	47	34	15.9	5.33	87	.289	.393	6	.500	2	-10	-6	-1	-0.5
Total	3	13	10	.565	99	0	0	0	11	186^1	177	14	97	96	13.4	3.96	111	.255	.350	8	.276	1	1	9	-1	1.0

● BRUCE HURST Hurst, Bruce Vee b: 3/24/58, St.George, Utah BL/TL, 6'3", 215 lbs. Deb: 4/12/80

YEAR	TM/L	W	L	PCT	G	GS	CG	SH	SV	IP	H	HR	BB	SO	RAT	ERA	ERA+	OAV	OOB	BH	AVG	PB	PR	/A	PD	TPI
1980	Bos-A	2	2	.500	12	7	0	0	0	30^2	39	4	16	16	16.7	9.10	46	.307	.393	0	—	0	-17	-17	-0	-1.8
1981	Bos-A	2	0	1.000	5	5	0	0	0	23	23	1	12	11	14.1	4.30	90	.258	.353	0	—	0	-2	-1	-1	-0.2
1982	Bos-A	3	7	.300	28	19	0	0	0	117	161	16	40	53	15.7	5.77	75	.333	.388	0	—	0	-22	-19	1	-2.1
1983	Bos-A	12	12	.500	33	32	6	2	0	211^1	241	22	62	115	13.0	4.09	106	.290	.342	0	—	0	-1	6	1	0.7
1984	Bos-A	12	12	.500	33	33	9	2	0	218	232	25	88	136	13.5	3.92	106	.271	.343	0	—	0	2	6	0	0.6
1985	Bos-A	11	13	.458	35	31	6	1	0	229^1	243	31	70	189	12.4	4.51	95	.273	.328	0	—	0	-9	-6	0	-0.6
1986	*Bos-A	13	8	.619	25	25	11	4	0	174^1	169	18	50	167	11.5	2.99	139	.256	.311	0	—	0	23	23	-1	2.2
1987	Bos-A☆	15	13	.536	33	33	15	3	0	238^2	239	35	76	190	11.9	4.41	103	.262	.320	0	—	0	1	3	0	0.3
1988	*Bos-A	18	6	.750	33	32	7	1	0	216^2	222	21	65	166	12.0	3.66	113	.264	.318	0	—	0	7	11	0	1.1
1989	SD-N	15	11	.577	33	33	**10**	2	0	244^2	214	16	66	179	10.3	2.69	130	.237	.289	5	.071	-2	22	22	1	2.4
1990	SD-N	11	9	.550	33	33	9	**4**	0	223^2	188	21	63	162	10.1	3.14	122	.228	.284	6	.090	-2	16	17	0	1.6
1991	SD-N	15	8	.652	31	31	4	0	0	221^2	201	17	59	141	10.7	3.29	115	.241	.293	9	.134	-1	10	13	-1	1.2
1992	SD-N	14	9	.609	32	32	6	4	0	217^1	223	22	51	131	11.3	3.85	94	.267	.309	11	.159	1	-8	-5	-1	-0.5
Total	13	143	110	.565	366	346	83	23	0	2366^1	2395	249	718	1656	11.9	3.85	105	.264	.319	31	.114	-3	22	52	2	4.9

● JONATHAN HURST Hurst, Jonathan b: 10/20/66, New York, N.Y. BR/TR, 6'3", 175 lbs. Deb: 6/09/92

YEAR	TM/L	W	L	PCT	G	GS	CG	SH	SV	IP	H	HR	BB	SO	RAT	ERA	ERA+	OAV	OOB	BH	AVG	PB	PR	/A	PD	TPI
1992	Mon-N	1	1	.500	3	3	0	0	0	16^1	18	1	7	4	14.3	5.51	63	.281	.361	0	.000	-0	-4	-4	-0	-0.4

● BILL HUSTED Husted, William J. b: 10/11/1866, Gloucester, N.J. d: 5/17/41, Gloucester, N.J. Deb: 4/29/1890

YEAR	TM/L	W	L	PCT	G	GS	CG	SH	SV	IP	H	HR	BB	SO	RAT	ERA	ERA+	OAV	OOB	BH	AVG	PB	PR	/A	PD	TPI
1890	Phi-P	5	10	.333	18	17	12	0	0	129	148	2	67	33	15.3	4.88	88	.276	.361	6	.107	-6	-9	-9	-2	-1.3

● BERT HUSTING Husting, Berthold Juneau "Pete" b: 3/6/1878, Fond Du Lac, Wis. d: 9/3/48, Milwaukee, Wis. BR/TR, Deb: 8/16/00

YEAR	TM/L	W	L	PCT	G	GS	CG	SH	SV	IP	H	HR	BB	SO	RAT	ERA	ERA+	OAV	OOB	BH	AVG	PB	PR	/A	PD	TPI
1900	Pit-N	0	0	—	2	0	0	0	0	8	10	2	5	7	16.9	5.63	65	.305	.397	0	.000	-1	-2	-2	1	-0.2
1901	Mil-A	10	15	.400	34	26	19	0	1	217^1	234	5	95	67	14.2	4.27	84	.272	.354	19	.202	-1	-14	-16	5	-1.1
1902	Bos-A	0	1	.000	1	1	1	0	0	8	15	0	8	4	25.9	9.00	40	.398	.504	1	.250	1	-5	-5	0	-0.3
	Phi-A	14	5	.737	32	27	17	1	0	204	240	7	91	44	15.1	3.79	97	.293	.372	13	.159	-3	-5	-3	2	-0.4
	Yr	14	6	.700	33	28	18	1	0	212	255	7	99	48	15.5	3.99	92	.298	.378	14	.163	-3	-10	-8	3	-0.7
Total	3	24	21	.533	69	54	37	1	1	437^1	499	14	199	122	14.9	4.16	87	.285	.366	33	.180	-5	-26	-26	8	-2.0

● JOHNNY HUTCHINGS Hutchings, John Richard Joseph b: 4/14/16, Chicago, Ill. d: 4/27/63, Indianapolis, Ind. BB/TR, 6'2", 250 lbs. Deb: 4/26/40

YEAR	TM/L	W	L	PCT	G	GS	CG	SH	SV	IP	H	HR	BB	SO	RAT	ERA	ERA+	OAV	OOB	BH	AVG	PB	PR	/A	PD	TPI
1940	*Cin-N	2	1	.667	19	4	0	0	0	54	53	3	18	18	12.0	3.50	108	.260	.323	2	.154	0	2	2	-1	0.1
1941	Cin-N	0	0	—	8	0	0	0	0	11	12	0	4	5	13.1	4.09	88	.279	.340	0	—	0	-1	-1	0	0.0
	Bos-N	1	6	.143	36	7	1	1	2	95^2	110	6	22	36	12.8	4.14	86	.287	.333	4	.148	0	-5	-6	0	-0.6
	Yr	1	6	.143	44	7	1	1	2	106^2	122	6	26	41	12.8	4.13	86	.286	.333	4	.148	0	-6	-7	0	-0.6
1942	Bos-N	1	0	1.000	20	3	0	0	0	65^2	66	2	34	27	14.0	4.39	76	.260	.352	1	.050	-2	-8	-8	-1	-1.1
1944	Bos-N	1	4	.200	14	7	1	0	1	56^2	55	3	26	26	13.0	3.97	96	.252	.335	1	.067	-1	-2	-1	-1	-0.2
1945	Bos-N	7	6	.538	57	12	3	2	3	185	173	21	75	99	12.3	3.75	102	.244	.320	13	.241	2	1	2	0	0.4
1946	Bos-N	0	1	.000	1	1	0	0	0	3	5	1	1	1	18.0	9.00	38	.357	.400	0	.000	-0	-2	-2	-0	-0.2
Total	6	12	18	.400	155	34	5	3	6	471	474	36	180	212	12.7	3.96	93	.260	.330	21	.162	-1	-15	-14	-2	-1.6

● FRED HUTCHINSON Hutchinson, Frederick Charles b: 8/12/19, Seattle, Wash. d: 11/12/64, Bradenton, Fla. BL/TR, 6'2", 200 lbs. Deb: 5/02/39 M♦

YEAR	TM/L	W	L	PCT	G	GS	CG	SH	SV	IP	H	HR	BB	SO	RAT	ERA	ERA+	OAV	OOB	BH	AVG	PB	PR	/A	PD	TPI
1939	Det-A	3	6	.333	13	12	3	0	0	84^2	95	9	51	22	15.5	5.21	94	.287	.382	13	.382	3	-6	-3	-0	0.0
1940	*Det-A	3	7	.300	17	10	1	0	0	76	85	6	26	32	13.4	5.68	84	.281	.342	8	.267	0	-11	-8	0	-0.7
1946	Det-A	14	11	.560	28	26	16	3	2	207	184	14	66	138	10.9	3.09	118	.236	.295	28	.315	8	10	13	3	2.6
1947	Det-A	18	10	.643	33	25	18	3	2	219^2	211	14	61	113	11.2	3.03	124	.251	.304	32	.302	11	16	18	2	3.4
1948	Det-A	13	11	.542	33	28	15	0	0	221	223	32	48	92	**11.1**	4.32	101	.258	**.297**	23	.205	5	-1	1	3	0.9
1949	Det-A	15	7	.682	33	21	9	4	1	188^2	167	18	52	54	**10.5**	2.96	141	.237	**.290**	18	.247	4	26	25	2	3.2
1950	Det-A	17	8	.680	39	26	10	1	0	231^2	269	18	48	71	12.5	3.96	118	.290	.329	31	.326	10	16	19	2	3.0
1951	Det-A★	10	10	.500	31	20	9	2	2	188^1	204	11	27	53	11.1	3.68	113	.275	.302	16	.188	-2	9	10	2	1.0
1952	Det-A	2	1	.667	12	1	0	0	0	37^1	40	4	9	12	12.1	3.38	113	.276	.323	1	.056	-1	1	2	2	0.3
1953	Det-A	0	0	—	3	0	0	0	0	9^2	9	0	0	4	8.4	2.79	146	.243	.243	1	.167	0	1	1	-0	0.2
Total	10	95	71	.572	242	169	81	13	7	1464	1487	126	388	591	11.6	3.73	113	.262	.311	171	.263	40	62	79	15	13.9

● IRA HUTCHINSON Hutchinson, Ira Kendall b: 8/31/10, Chicago, Ill. d: 8/21/73, Chicago, Ill. BR/TR, 5'10.5", 180 lbs. Deb: 9/24/33

YEAR	TM/L	W	L	PCT	G	GS	CG	SH	SV	IP	H	HR	BB	SO	RAT	ERA	ERA+	OAV	OOB	BH	AVG	PB	PR	/A	PD	TPI
1933	Chi-A	0	0	—	1	1	0	0	0	4	7	1	3	2	22.5	13.50	31	.368	.455	1	.500	0	-4	-4	-0	-0.3

YEAR	TM/L	W	L	PCT	G	GS	CG	SH	SV	IP	H	HR	BB	SO	RAT	ERA	ERA+	OAV	OOB	BH	AVG	PB	PR	/A	PD	TPI
1937	Bos-N	4	6	.400	31	8	1	0	0	91^{2}	99	4	35	29	13.3	3.73	96	.286	.353	3	.115	-1	2	-1	1	-0.2
1938	Bos-N	9	8	.529	36	12	4	1	4	151	150	3	61	38	12.8	2.74	125	.258	.332	9	.173	-1	18	12	1	1.2
1939	Bro-N	5	2	.714	41	1	0	0	1	105^{2}	103	9	51	46	13.2	4.34	93	.265	.352	1	.037	-3	-5	-4	1	-0.6
1940	StL-N	4	2	.667	20	2	1	0	1	63^{1}	68	3	19	19	12.4	3.13	128	.271	.322	4	.222	0	5	6	0	0.7
1941	StL-N	1	5	.167	29	0	0	0	5	46^{2}	32	3	19	19	10.2	3.86	98	.196	.288	2	.250	0	-1	-0	0	0.0
1944	Bos-N	9	7	.563	40	8	1	1	1	119^{2}	136	8	53	22	14.4	4.21	91	.296	.373	4	.138	-1	-8	-5	1	-0.6
1945	Bos-N	2	3	.400	11	0	0	0	1	28^{2}	33	2	8	4	13.2	5.02	76	.277	.328	0	.000	-1	-4	-4	1	-0.4
Total	8	34	33	.507	209	32	7	2	13	610^{2}	628	33	249	179	13.1	3.76	100	.270	.344	24	.140	-7	2	-1	5	-0.2

● BILL HUTCHISON Hutchison, William Forrest "Wild Bill" b: 12/17/1859, New Haven, Conn. d: 3/19/26, Kansas City, Mo. BR/TR, 5'9", 175 lbs. Deb: 6/10/1884

YEAR	TM/L	W	L	PCT	G	GS	CG	SH	SV	IP	H	HR	BB	SO	RAT	ERA	ERA+	OAV	OOB	BH	AVG	PB	PR	/A	PD	TPI
1884	KC-U	1	1	.500	2	2	2	0	0	17	14	0	1	5	7.9	2.65	104	.209	.221	2	.250	-0	1	0	2	0.2
1889	Chi-N	16	17	.485	37	36	33	3	0	318	306	11	117	136	12.2	3.54	118	.245	.314	21	.158	-5	17	22	5	1.9
1890	Chi-N	**42**	25	.627	**71**	66	**65**	5	**2**	**603**	505	20	199	289	10.7	2.70	135	.220	.286	53	.203	-4	58	64	5	5.9
1891	Chi-N	**44**	19	.698	**66**	58	**56**	4	1	**561**	508	26	178	261	11.1	2.81	119	.232	.292	45	.185	-1	34	33	-2	2.7
1892	Chi-N	**37**	36	.507	**75**	71	**67**	5	0	**627**	572	11	187	**316**	11.1	2.74	121	.233	.291	57	.217	4	38	41	4	4.6
1893	Chi-N	16	24	.400	44	40	38	2	0	348^{1}	420	9	156	80	15.2	4.75	97	.289	.364	41	.253	2	-3	-5	-3	-0.5
1894	Chi-N	14	16	.467	36	34	28	0	0	277^{2}	373	9	140	59	17.2	6.06	93	.318	.399	42	.309	6	-23	-14	-2	-0.7
1895	Chi-N	13	21	.382	38	35	30	2	0	291	371	13	129	85	15.9	4.73	108	.305	.378	25	.198	-7	2	12	-0	0.3
1897	StL-N	1	4	.200	6	5	2	0	0	40	55	5	22	5	17.8	6.07	73	.324	.408	5	.278	1	-8	-7	-1	-0.6
Total	9	184	163	.530	375	347	321	21	3	3083	3124	104	1129	1236	12.7	3.58	112	.255	.322	291	.216	-4	115	142	7	13.8

● HERB HUTSON Hutson, George Herbert b: 7/17/49, Savannah, Ga. BR/TR, 6'2", 205 lbs. Deb: 4/10/74

YEAR	TM/L	W	L	PCT	G	GS	CG	SH	SV	IP	H	HR	BB	SO	RAT	ERA	ERA+	OAV	OOB	BH	AVG	PB	PR	/A	PD	TPI
1974	Chi-N	0	2	.000	20	2	0	0	0	28^{2}	24	3	15	22	12.6	3.45	110	.233	.336	0	.000	-0	1	1	-1	0.0

● TOM HUTTON Hutton, Thomas George b: 4/20/46, Los Angeles, Cal. BL/TL, 5'11", 180 lbs. Deb: 9/16/66 ♦

YEAR	TM/L	W	L	PCT	G	GS	CG	SH	SV	IP	H	HR	BB	SO	RAT	ERA	ERA+	OAV	OOB	BH	AVG	PB	PR	/A	PD	TPI
1980	Mon-N	0	0	—	1	0	0	0	0	1	3	1	1	1	36.0	27.00	13	.500	.571	12	.218	0	-3	-3	0	-0.2

● DICK HYDE Hyde, Richard Elde b: 8/3/28, Hindsboro, Ill. BR/TR, 5'11", 170 lbs. Deb: 4/23/55

YEAR	TM/L	W	L	PCT	G	GS	CG	SH	SV	IP	H	HR	BB	SO	RAT	ERA	ERA+	OAV	OOB	BH	AVG	PB	PR	/A	PD	TPI
1955	Was-A	0	0	—	3	0	0	0	0	2	2	0	1	1	13.5	4.50	85	.286	.375	0	—	0	-0	-0	-0	0.0
1957	Was-A	4	3	.571	52	2	0	0	1	109^{1}	104	4	56	46	13.7	4.12	95	.261	.361	3	.167	-0	-4	-3	1	-0.2
1958	Was-A	10	3	.769	53	0	0	0	18	103	82	1	35	49	10.4	1.75	218	.220	.291	0	.000	-2	**23**	**24**	2	2.5
1959	Was-A	2	5	.286	37	0	0	0	4	54^{1}	56	5	27	29	14.1	4.97	79	.269	.359	0	.000	-1	-7	-6	2	-0.5
1960	Was-A	0	1	.000	9	0	0	0	0	8^{2}	11	2	5	4	17.7	4.15	94	.355	.459	0	—	0	-0	-0	-0	0.0
1961	Bal-A	1	2	.333	15	0	0	0	0	21	18	1	13	15	13.7	5.57	70	.228	.344	1	1.000	0	-4	-4	1	-0.2
Total	6	17	14	.548	169	2	0	0	23	298^{1}	273	13	137	144	12.8	3.56	109	.249	.339	4	.093	-3	8	10	6	1.6

● JIM HYNDMAN Hyndman, James William b: 7/1865, Ontario Deb: 7/23/1886 ♦

YEAR	TM/L	W	L	PCT	G	GS	CG	SH	SV	IP	H	HR	BB	SO	RAT	ERA	ERA+	OAV	OOB	BH	AVG	PB	PR	/A	PD	TPI
1886	Phi-a	0	1	.000	1	1	0	0	0	2	5	1	5	1	49.5	27.00	13	.455	.647	0	.000	-1	-5	-5	0	-0.4

● PAT HYNES Hynes, Patrick J. b: 3/12/1884, St.Louis, Mo. d: 3/12/07, St.Louis, Mo. TL , Deb: 9/27/03 ♦

YEAR	TM/L	W	L	PCT	G	GS	CG	SH	SV	IP	H	HR	BB	SO	RAT	ERA	ERA+	OAV	OOB	BH	AVG	PB	PR	/A	PD	TPI
1903	StL-N	0	1	.000	1	1	1	0	0	9	10	0	6	1	16.0	4.00	82	.294	.400	0	.000	-0	-1	-1	-1	-0.2
1904	StL-A	1	0	1.000	5	2	1	0	0	26	35	1	7	6	14.5	6.23	40	.322	.363	60	.236	0	-10	-11	-1	-1.1
Total	2	1	1	.500	6	3	2	0	0	35	45	1	13	7	14.9	5.66	47	.316	.373	60	.233	0	-11	-12	-2	-1.3

● HAM IBURG Iburg, Herman Edward b: 10/29/1877, San Francisco, Cal d: 2/11/45, San Francisco, Cal BR/TR, 5'11", 165 lbs. Deb: 4/17/02

YEAR	TM/L	W	L	PCT	G	GS	CG	SH	SV	IP	H	HR	BB	SO	RAT	ERA	ERA+	OAV	OOB	BH	AVG	PB	PR	/A	PD	TPI
1902	Phi-N	11	18	.379	30	30	20	1	0	236	286	1	62	106	13.7	3.89	72	.299	.348	12	.138	-5	-29	-28	0	-3.2

● GARY IGNASIAK Ignasiak, Gary Raymond b: 9/1/49, Anchorville, Mich. BR/TL, 5'11", 185 lbs. Deb: 9/20/73 F

YEAR	TM/L	W	L	PCT	G	GS	CG	SH	SV	IP	H	HR	BB	SO	RAT	ERA	ERA+	OAV	OOB	BH	AVG	PB	PR	/A	PD	TPI
1973	Det-A	0	0	—	3	0	0	0	0	4^{2}	5	0	3	4	15.4	3.86	106	.278	.381	0	—	0	-0	0	0	0.0

● MIKE IGNASIAK Ignasiak, Michael James b: 3/12/66, Mt.Clemens, Mich. BB/TR, 5'11", 175 lbs. Deb: 8/22/91 F

YEAR	TM/L	W	L	PCT	G	GS	CG	SH	SV	IP	H	HR	BB	SO	RAT	ERA	ERA+	OAV	OOB	BH	AVG	PB	PR	/A	PD	TPI
1991	Mil-A	2	1	.667	4	1	0	0	0	12^{2}	7	2	8	10	10.7	5.68	70	.163	.294	0	—	0	-2	-2	-0	-0.2

● DOC IMLAY Imlay, Harry Miller b: 1/12/1889, Allentown, N.J. d: 10/7/48, Bordentown, N.J. BR/TR, 5'11", 168 lbs. Deb: 7/07/13

YEAR	TM/L	W	L	PCT	G	GS	CG	SH	SV	IP	H	HR	BB	SO	RAT	ERA	ERA+	OAV	OOB	BH	AVG	PB	PR	/A	PD	TPI
1913	Phi-N	0	0	—	9	0	0	0	0	13^{2}	19	1	7	7	17.1	7.24	46	.358	.433	0	.000	-0	-6	-6	0	-0.6

● BOB INGERSOLL Ingersoll, Robert Randolph b: 1/8/1883, Rapid City, S.D. d: 1/13/27, Minneapolis, Minn. BR/TR, 5'11.5", 175 lbs. Deb: 4/23/14

YEAR	TM/L	W	L	PCT	G	GS	CG	SH	SV	IP	H	HR	BB	SO	RAT	ERA	ERA+	OAV	OOB	BH	AVG	PB	PR	/A	PD	TPI
1914	Cin-N	0	0	—	4	0	0	0	0	6	5	0	5	2	16.5	3.00	98	.250	.423	1	1.000	0	-0	-0	-0	0.0

● BERT INKS Inks, Albert Preston (b: Albert Preston Inkstein) b: 1/27/1871, Ligonier, Ind. d: 10/3/41, Ligonier, Ind. BL/TL, 6'3", 175 lbs. Deb: 9/02/1891

YEAR	TM/L	W	L	PCT	G	GS	CG	SH	SV	IP	H	HR	BB	SO	RAT	ERA	ERA+	OAV	OOB	BH	AVG	PB	PR	/A	PD	TPI
1891	Bro-N	3	10	.231	13	13	11	1	0	96^{1}	99	2	43	47	13.8	4.02	82	.256	.339	10	.286	2	-7	-8	-0	-0.6
1892	Bro-N	4	2	.667	9	8	4	1	0	58	48	0	33	25	13.2	3.88	82	.216	.328	10	.400	3	-4	-5	0	-0.1
	Was-N	1	2	.333	3	3	3	0	0	21	29	0	10	11	17.6	5.14	63	.315	.394	3	.300	1	-4	-4	-0	-0.3
	Yr	5	4	.556	12	11	7	1	0	79	77	0	43	36	13.9	4.22	76	.242	.336	13	.371	4	-8	-9	-0	-0.4
1894	Bal-N	9	4	.692	22	14	10	0	1	133	181	4	54	30	16.6	5.55	98	.321	.391	18	.316	2	-3	-1	-1	-0.1
	Lou-N	2	6	.250	8	8	8	0	0	59^{2}	87	2	34	8	18.4	6.49	79	.336	.415	12	.444	3	-8	-9	0	-0.5
	Yr	11	10	.524	30	22	18	0	1	192^{2}	268	6	88	38	16.7	5.84	92	.321	.387	30	.357	4	-11	-11	-1	-0.6
1895	Lou-N	7	20	.259	28	27	21	0	0	205^{1}	294	3	78	42	17.0	6.40	72	.331	.394	21	.250	-0	-37	-40	1	-3.0
1896	Phi-N	0	1	.000	3	1	0	0	0	10^{1}	21	1	5	2	23.5	7.84	55	.415	.477	1	.200	-0	-4	-4	-1	-0.4
	Cin-N	1	1	.500	3	3	2	0	0	20	21	0	9	2	13.9	4.50	102	.268	.351	0	.000	-1	-0	0	-1	-0.1
	Yr	1	2	.333	6	4	2	0	0	30^{1}	42	1	14	4	16.9	5.64	80	.323	.393	1	.083	-1	-4	-4	-1	-0.5
Total	5	27	46	.370	89	77	59	2	1	603^{2}	780	12	266	167	16.2	5.52	81	.307	.382	75	.300	9	-68	-72	-2	-5.1

● JEFF INNIS Innis, Jeffrey David b: 7/5/62, Decatur, Ill. BR/TR, 6'1", 170 lbs. Deb: 5/16/87

YEAR	TM/L	W	L	PCT	G	GS	CG	SH	SV	IP	H	HR	BB	SO	RAT	ERA	ERA+	OAV	OOB	BH	AVG	PB	PR	/A	PD	TPI
1987	NY-N	0	1	.000	17	1	0	0	0	25^{2}	29	5	4	28	11.9	3.16	120	.279	.312	0	.000	-0	3	2	-0	0.1
1988	NY-N	1	1	.500	12	0	0	0	0	19	19	0	2	14	9.9	1.89	170	.250	.269	0	—	0	3	3	-1	0.2
1989	NY-N	0	1	.000	29	0	0	0	0	39^{2}	38	2	8	16	10.7	3.18	103	.255	.297	0	.000	-0	1	0	1	0.1
1990	NY-N	1	3	.250	18	0	0	0	1	26^{1}	19	4	10	12	10.3	2.39	156	.209	.294	0	—	0	4	4	0	0.4
1991	NY-N	0	2	.000	69	0	0	0	0	84^{2}	66	2	23	47	9.5	2.66	137	.219	.274	0	.000	-0	10	9	3	1.3
1992	NY-N	6	9	.400	76	0	0	0	1	88	85	4	36	39	13.0	2.86	122	.266	.351	0	.000	-0	6	6	2	0.9
Total	6	8	17	.320	221	1	0	0	2	283^{1}	256	17	83	156	11.1	2.76	128	.246	.307	0	.000	-1	27	24	6	3.0

● DANE IORG Iorg, Dane Charles b: 5/11/50, Eureka, Cal. BL/TR, 6', 180 lbs. Deb: 4/09/77 F♦

YEAR	TM/L	W	L	PCT	G	GS	CG	SH	SV	IP	H	HR	BB	SO	RAT	ERA	ERA+	OAV	OOB	BH	AVG	PB	PR	/A	PD	TPI
1986	SD-N	0	0	—	2	0	0	0	0	3	5	2	1	2	18.0	12.00	30	.357	.400	24	.226	0	-3	-3	-0	-0.3

● HOOKS IOTT Iott, Clarence Eugene b: 12/3/19, Mountain Grove, Mo. d: 8/17/80, St.Petersburg, Fla BB/TL, 6'2", 200 lbs. Deb: 9/06/41

YEAR	TM/L	W	L	PCT	G	GS	CG	SH	SV	IP	H	HR	BB	SO	RAT	ERA	ERA+	OAV	OOB	BH	AVG	PB	PR	/A	PD	TPI
1941	StL-A	0	0	—	2	0	0	0	0	2	2	0	1	1	13.5	9.00	48	.250	.333	0	—	0	-1	-1	0	-0.1
1947	StL-A	0	1	.000	4	0	0	0	0	8^{1}	15	4	14	6	31.3	16.20	24	.375	.537	0	.000	-0	-12	-11	0	-1.0
	NY-N	3	8	.273	20	9	2	1	0	71^{1}	67	3	52	46	15.1	5.93	69	.251	.375	3	.143	1	-15	-15	-0	-1.3
Total	2	3	9	.250	26	9	2	1	0	81^{2}	84	7	67	53	16.8	7.05	58	.267	.397	3	.130	1	-27	-27	0	-2.4

● DARYL IRVINE Irvine, Daryl Keith b: 11/15/64, Harrisonburg, Va. BR/TR, 6'3", 195 lbs. Deb: 4/28/90

YEAR	TM/L	W	L	PCT	G	GS	CG	SH	SV	IP	H	HR	BB	SO	RAT	ERA	ERA+	OAV	OOB	BH	AVG	PB	PR	/A	PD	TPI
1990	Bos-A	1	1	.500	11	0	0	0	0	17^{1}	15	0	10	9	13.0	4.67	87	.246	.352	0	—	0	-1	-1	0	-0.4
1991	Bos-A	0	0	—	9	0	0	0	0	18	25	2	9	8	18.0	6.00	72	.321	.404	0	—	0	-4	-3	0	-0.5
1992	Bos-A	3	4	.429	21	0	0	0	0	28	31	1	14	10	15.1	6.11	68	.287	.379	0	—	0	-7	-6	0	-0.8
Total	3	4	5	.444	41	0	0	0	0	63^{1}	71	3	33	27	15.3	5.68	73	.287	.380	0	—	0	-12	-11	1	-1.7

YEAR	TM/L	W	L	PCT	G	GS	CG	SH	SV	IP	H	HR	BB	SO	RAT	ERA	ERA+	OAV	OOB	BH	AVG	PB	PR	/A	PD	TPI
● ARTHUR IRWIN	Irwin, Arthur Albert "Doc" or "Sandy" b: 2/14/1858, Toronto, Ont., Can. d: 7/16/21, Atlantic Ocean BL/TR, 5'8.5", 158 lbs. Deb: 5/01/1880 FMU♦																									
1884	*Pro-N	0	0	—	1	0	0	0	0	3	5	0	1	0	18.0	3.00	94	.357	.400	97	.240	0	-0	-0	0	0.0
1889	Was-N	0	0	—	1	0	0	0	0	1	1	0	0	0	9.0	0.00	—	.252	.252	73	.233	0	0	0	-0	0.0
Total	2	0	0	—	2	0	0	0	0	4	6	0	1	0	15.8	2.25	138	.334	.369	934	.241	0	0	0	-0	0.0
● BILL IRWIN	Irwin, William Franklin "Phil" b: 9/16/1859, Neville, Ohio d: 8/7/33, Ft.Thomas, Ky. BR/TR, 6', 195 lbs. Deb: 8/30/1886																									
1886	Cin-a	0	2	.000	2	2	2	0	0	17	18	2	8	6	13.8	5.82	60	.247	.321	0	.000	-1	-4	-4	0	-0.4
● FRANK ISBELL	Isbell, William Frank "Bald Eagle" b: 8/21/1875, Delevan, N.Y. d: 7/15/41, Wichita, Kan. BL/TR, 5'11", 190 lbs. Deb: 5/01/1898 ♦																									
1898	Chi-N	4	7	.364	13	9	7	0	0	81	86	0	42	16	15.0	3.56	101	.270	.367	37	.233	-0	0	0	-0	0.0
1901	Chi-A	0	0	—	1	0	0	0	0	1	2	0	0	0	18.0	9.00	39	.409	.409	143	.257	0	-1	-1	0	0.0
1902	Chi-A	0	0	—	1	1	0	0	0	1	3	0	1	1	36.0	9.00	38	.514	.585	130	.252	0	-1	-1	1	0.0
1906	*Chi-A	0	0	—	1	0	0	0	0	2	1	0	0	2	4.5	0.00	—	.152	.152	153	.279	0	1	1	-0	0.1
1907	Chi-A	0	0	—	1	0	0	0	1	0^1	0	0	0	0	0.0	0.00	—	.000	.000	118	.243	0	0	0	0	0.0
Total	5	4	7	.364	17	10	7	0	1	85^1	92	0	43	19	15.0	3.59	99	.273	.367	1056	.250	0	-0	-0	1	0.1
● AL JACKSON	Jackson, Alvin Neil b: 12/25/35, Waco, Tex. BL/TL, 5'10", 169 lbs. Deb: 6/01/59 C																									
1959	Pit-N	0	0	—	8	3	0	0	0	18	30	1	8	13	19.0	6.50	60	.405	.463	1	.200	0	-5	-5	-0	-0.5
1961	Pit-N	1	0	1.000	3	2	1	0	0	23^2	20	2	4	15	9.1	3.42	117	.233	.267	0	.000	-1	2	1	1	0.1
1962	NY-N	8	20	.286	36	33	12	4	0	231^1	244	16	78	118	12.7	4.40	95	.273	.335	5	.068	-5	-12	-5	4	-0.6
1963	NY-N	13	17	.433	37	34	11	0	1	227	237	25	84	142	13.2	3.96	88	.267	.338	16	.203	2	-17	-12	2	-0.9
1964	NY-N	11	16	.407	40	31	11	3	1	213^1	229	18	60	112	12.4	4.26	84	.272	.323	11	.153	2	-17	-16	0	-1.4
1965	NY-N	8	20	.286	37	31	7	3	1	205^1	217	17	61	120	12.5	4.34	81	.271	.329	7	.117	-1	-18	-18	2	-1.8
1966	StL-N	13	15	.464	36	30	11	3	0	232^2	222	18	45	90	10.4	2.51	143	.250	.288	13	.176	2	28	28	4	3.9
1967	StL-N	9	4	.692	38	11	1	1	1	107	117	7	29	43	12.4	3.95	83	.279	.327	8	.258	2	-7	-8	2	-0.4
1968	NY-N	3	7	.300	25	9	0	0	3	92^2	88	5	17	59	10.4	3.69	82	.249	.287	7	.250	1	-7	-7	1	-0.5
1969	NY-N	0	0	—	9	0	0	0	0	11	18	1	4	10	18.8	10.64	34	.353	.411	0	.000	-0	-9	-9	0	-0.8
	Cin-N	1	0	1.000	33	0	0	0	3	27^1	27	5	17	16	15.5	5.27	71	.260	.379	1	.250	0	-5	-5	-0	-0.5
	Yr	1	0	1.000	42	0	0	0	3	38^1	45	6	21	26	16.2	6.81	55	.285	.379	1	.200	0	-14	-13	-0	-1.3
Total	10	67	99	.404	302	184	54	14	10	1389^1	1449	115	407	738	12.3	3.98	91	.268	.324	69	.159	3	-67	-56	16	-3.4
● CHARLIE JACKSON	Jackson, Charles Bernard b: 8/4/1876, Versailles, Ohio d: 11/23/57, Scottsbluff, Neb. TR , Deb: 8/11/05																									
1905	Det-A	0	2	.000	2	2	1	0	0	11	14	1	7	3	17.2	5.73	48	.311	.403	1	.250	0	-4	-4	-0	-0.4
● DANNY JACKSON	Jackson, Danny Lynn b: 1/5/62, San Antonio, Tex. BR/TL, 6', 205 lbs. Deb: 9/11/83																									
1983	KC-A	1	1	.500	4	3	0	0	0	19	26	1	6	9	15.2	5.21	78	.325	.372	0	—	0	-2	-2	0	-0.2
1984	KC-A	2	6	.250	15	11	1	0	0	76	84	4	35	40	14.7	4.26	94	.285	.370	0	—	0	-2	-2	-0	-0.3
1985	*KC-A	14	12	.538	32	32	4	3	0	208	209	7	76	114	12.6	3.42	122	.261	.329	0	—	0	17	17	-1	1.6
1986	KC-A	11	12	.478	32	27	4	1	1	185^2	177	13	79	115	12.6	3.20	133	.256	.335	0	—	0	20	22	-1	2.1
1987	KC-A	9	18	.333	36	34	11	2	0	224	219	11	109	152	13.5	4.02	113	.258	.347	0	—	0	11	13	-2	1.0
1988	Cin-N☆	**23**	8	.742	35	35	**15**	6	0	260^2	206	13	71	161	9.6	2.73	131	.218	.275	13	.144	-0	21	25	2	2.9
1989	Cin-N	6	11	.353	20	20	1	0	0	115^2	122	10	57	70	14.0	5.60	64	.271	.354	8	.222	1	-27	-26	-1	-2.5
1990	*Cin-N	6	6	.500	22	21	0	0	0	117^1	119	11	40	76	12.3	3.61	109	.266	.329	2	.054	-2	2	4	-1	0.1
1991	Chi-N	1	5	.167	17	14	0	0	0	70^2	89	8	48	31	17.6	6.75	58	.309	.409	2	.087	-1	-24	-23	-1	-2.4
1992	Chi-N	4	9	.308	19	19	0	0	0	113	117	5	48	51	13.4	4.22	85	.270	.346	3	.083	-2	-9	-8	-1	-1.2
	*Pit-N	4	4	.500	15	15	0	0	0	88^1	94	1	29	46	12.6	3.36	101	.276	.334	2	.083	-1	1	0	0	0.0
	Yr	8	13	.381	34	34	0	0	0	201^1	211	6	77	97	12.9	3.84	92	.269	.336	5	.083	-3	-8	-7	-1	-1.2
Total	10	81	92	.468	247	231	36	12	1	1478^1	1462	84	598	865	12.7	3.83	103	.260	.335	30	.122	-6	8	22	-6	1.1
● DARRELL JACKSON	Jackson, Darrell Preston b: 4/3/56, Los Angeles, Cal. BB/TL, 5'10", 150 lbs. Deb: 6/16/78																									
1978	Min-A	4	6	.400	19	15	1	1	0	92^1	89	9	48	54	13.5	4.48	85	.256	.350	0	—	0	-7	-7	-1	-0.8
1979	Min-A	4	4	.500	24	8	1	0	0	69^1	89	5	26	43	15.1	4.28	102	.319	.379	0	—	0	-1	1	1	0.0
1980	Min-A	9	9	.500	32	25	1	0	1	172	161	15	69	90	12.1	3.87	113	.250	.325	0	—	0	3	9	-0	0.9
1981	Min-A	3	3	.500	14	5	0	0	0	32^2	35	1	19	26	15.2	4.41	90	.282	.382	0	—	0	-3	-2	-1	-0.2
1982	Min-A	0	5	.000	13	7	0	0	0	44^2	51	6	24	16	15.3	6.25	68	.297	.386	0	—	0	-11	-10	-0	-1.1
Total	5	20	27	.426	102	60	3	1	1	411	425	36	186	229	13.5	4.38	96	.272	.352	0	—	0	-18	-8	-2	-1.2
● DARRIN JACKSON	Jackson, Darrin Jay b: 8/22/62, Los Angeles, Cal. BR/TR, 6'1", 170 lbs. Deb: 6/17/85 ♦																									
1991	SD-N	0	0	—	1	0	0	0	0	2	3	0	2	0	22.5	9.00	42	.375	.500	94	.262	0	-1	-1	-0	-0.1
● GRANT JACKSON	Jackson, Grant Dwight "Buck" b: 9/28/42, Fostoria, Ohio BB/TL, 6', 190 lbs. Deb: 9/03/65 C																									
1965	Phi-N	1	1	.500	6	2	0	0	0	13^2	17	4	5	15	14.5	7.24	48	.304	.361	0	.000	-0	-6	-6	0	-0.6
1966	Phi-N	0	0	—	2	0	0	0	0	1^2	2	0	3	0	27.0	5.40	67	.333	.556	0	—	0	-0	-0	0	0.0
1967	Phi-N	2	3	.400	43	4	0	0	1	84^1	86	3	43	83	14.0	3.84	89	.267	.357	2	.133	-0	-4	-4	-2	-0.6
1968	Phi-N	1	6	.143	33	6	1	0	1	61	59	4	20	49	11.7	2.95	102	.248	.306	3	.300	1	0	0	0	0.2
1969	Phi-N☆	14	18	.438	38	35	13	4	1	253	237	16	92	180	11.9	3.34	106	.249	.318	12	.140	-0	7	6	-2	0.4
1970	Phi-N	5	15	.250	32	23	1	0	0	149^2	170	17	61	104	14.0	5.29	75	.288	.356	4	.091	-2	-21	-22	0	-2.3
1971	*Bal-A	4	3	.571	29	9	0	0	0	77^2	72	7	20	51	10.9	3.13	107	.249	.302	2	.091	0	3	2	-0	0.2
1972	Bal-A	1	1	.500	32	0	0	0	8	41	33	1	9	34	9.2	2.63	117	.217	.261	0	.000	-0	2	2	0	0.2
1973	*Bal-A	8	0	1.000	45	0	0	0	9	80^1	54	5	24	47	8.7	1.90	196	.198	.263	0	—	0	17	16	-0	1.7
1974	*Bal-A	6	4	.600	49	0	0	0	12	66^2	48	7	22	56	9.6	2.57	135	.198	.268	0	—	0	8	7	-1	0.6
1975	Bal-A	4	3	.571	41	0	0	0	7	48^1	42	3	21	39	11.9	3.35	105	.241	.327	0	—	0	2	1	-0	0.1
1976	Bal-A	1	1	.500	13	0	0	0	3	19^1	19	1	9	14	14.0	5.12	64	.268	.366	0	—	0	-3	-4	-0	-0.4
	*NY-A	6	0	1.000	21	2	1	1	1	58^2	38	1	16	25	8.4	1.69	202	.186	.249	0	—	0	12	11	-1	1.1
	Yr	7	1	.875	34	2	1	1	4	78	57	2	25	39	9.6	2.54	133	.205	.273	0	—	0	8	7	-2	0.7
1977	Pit-N	5	3	.625	49	2	0	0	4	91	81	11	39	41	12.0	3.86	103	.240	.321	6	.333	2	1	1	-1	0.2
1978	Pit-N	7	5	.583	60	0	0	0	5	77^1	89	5	32	45	14.2	3.26	114	.298	.367	3	.250	1	3	4	0	0.5
1979	*Pit-N	8	5	.615	72	0	0	0	14	82	67	9	35	39	11.4	2.96	131	.230	.317	0	.000	-1	7	8	-1	0.7
1980	Pit-N	8	4	.667	61	0	0	0	9	71	71	4	20	31	11.5	2.92	125	.275	.327	0	.000	-1	5	6	-0	0.5
1981	Pit-N	1	2	.333	35	0	0	0	4	32^1	30	1	10	17	11.1	2.51	143	.248	.305	0	.000	-0	4	4	-1	0.3
	Mon-N	1	0	1.000	10	0	0	0	0	10^2	14	2	9	4	19.4	7.59	46	.333	.451	0	—	0	-5	-5	0	-0.5
	Yr	2	2	.500	45	0	0	0	4	43	44	3	19	21	13.2	3.77	95	.267	.342	0	.000	-0	-1	-1	-1	-0.2
1982	KC-A	3	1	.750	20	0	0	0	0	38^1	42	7	21	15	15.3	5.17	79	.271	.365	0	—	0	-5	-5	-0	-0.5
	Pit-N	0	0	—	1	0	0	0	0	0^2	1	1	0	0	13.5	13.50	27	.333	.333	0	—	0	-1	-1	-0	-0.1
Total	18	86	75	.534	692	83	16	5	79	1358^2	1272	109	511	889	11.9	3.46	104	.251	.322	32	.136	-2	26	22	-9	1.7
● JOHN JACKSON	Jackson, John Lewis b: 7/15/09, Wynnefield, Pa. d: 10/22/56, Somers Point, N.J. BR/TR, 6'2", 180 lbs. Deb: 6/20/33																									
1933	Phi-N	2	2	.500	10	7	1	0	0	54	74	3	35	11	19.0	6.00	64	.329	.430	3	.143	-1	-16	-13	-2	-1.6
● LARRY JACKSON	Jackson, Lawrence Curtis b: 6/2/31, Nampa, Idaho d: 8/28/90, Boise, Idaho BR/TR, 6'2", 190 lbs. Deb: 4/17/55																									
1955	StL-N	9	14	.391	37	25	4	1	2	177^1	189	25	72	88	13.7	4.31	94	.277	.353	3	.053	-6	-5	-5	0	-1.0
1956	StL-N	2	2	.500	51	1	0	0	9	85^1	75	5	45	50	12.8	4.11	92	.240	.337	1	.091	-0	-3	-3	2	-0.2
1957	StL-N★	15	9	.625	41	22	6	2	1	210^1	196	21	57	96	11.0	3.47	114	.248	.302	13	.181	0	10	12	4	1.6
1958	StL-N★	13	13	.500	49	23	11	1	8	198	211	21	51	124	12.4	3.68	112	.272	.325	9	.150	-2	6	10	-2	0.5

YEAR	TM/L	W	L	PCT	G	GS	CG	SH	SV	IP	H	HR	BB	SO	RAT	ERA	ERA+	OAV	OOB	BH	AVG	PB	PR	/A	PD	TPI
1959	StL-N	14	13	.519	40	37	12	3	0	256	271	13	64	145	11.9	3.30	128	.270	.316	9	.112	-4	18	27	-0	2.4
1960	StL-N★	18	13	.581	43	38	14	3	0	**282**	277	22	70	171	11.2	3.48	118	.257	.304	20	.211	2	9	19	-2	2.1
1961	StL-N	14	11	.560	33	28	12	3	0	211	203	20	56	113	11.2	3.75	117	.252	.303	13	.176	0	7	15	2	1.7
1962	StL-N	16	11	.593	36	35	11	2	0	252^1	267	25	64	112	12.0	3.75	114	.269	.318	15	.169	2	6	15	1	1.8
1963	Chi-N★	14	18	.438	37	37	13	4	0	275	256	11	54	153	10.3	2.55	137	.245	.286	17	.195	3	22	29	2	3.9
1964	Chi-N	**24**	11	.686	40	38	19	3	0	297^2	265	17	58	148	9.8	3.14	118	.235	.273	20	.175	1	13	19	7	2.8
1965	Chi-N	14	21	.400	39	39	12	4	0	257^1	268	28	57	131	11.5	3.85	96	.267	.310	11	.128	1	-9	-5	3	-0.1
1966	Chi-N	0	2	.000	3	2	0	0	0	8	14	3	4	5	20.3	13.50	27	.368	.429	0	.000	-0	-9	-9	0	-0.8
	Phi-N	15	13	.536	35	33	12	5	0	247	243	22	58	107	11.1	2.99	120	.259	.306	13	.146	-0	17	17	1	2.0
	Yr	15	15	.500	38	35	12	**5**	0	255	257	25	62	112	11.4	3.32	108	.264	.311	13	.141	-1	8	8	2	1.2
1967	Phi-N	13	15	.464	40	37	11	4	0	261^2	242	17	54	139	10.4	3.10	110	.241	.284	14	.161	0	8	9	4	1.5
1968	Phi-N	13	17	.433	34	34	12	2	0	243^2	229	9	60	127	10.8	2.77	109	.248	.297	12	.141	-0	6	6	2	0.8
Total	14	194	183	.515	558	429	149	37	20	3262^2	3206	259	824	1709	11.3	3.40	113	.256	.306	170	.156	-5	95	155	25	19.0

● MIKE JACKSON Jackson, Michael Ray b: 12/22/64, Houston, Tex. BR/TR, 6'1", 185 lbs. Deb: 8/11/86

YEAR	TM/L	W	L	PCT	G	GS	CG	SH	SV	IP	H	HR	BB	SO	RAT	ERA	ERA+	OAV	OOB	BH	AVG	PB	PR	/A	PD	TPI
1986	Phi-N	0	0	—	9	0	0	0	0	13^1	12	2	4	3	12.2	3.38	114	.250	.333	0	—	0	1	1	-0	0.0
1987	Phi-N	3	10	.231	55	7	0	0	1	109^1	88	16	56	93	12.1	4.20	101	.219	.319	2	.118	-0	-1	0	-1	-0.1
1988	Sea-A	6	5	.545	62	0	0	0	4	99^1	74	10	43	76	10.8	2.63	158	.209	.298	0	—	0	15	17	-0	1.7
1989	Sea-A	4	6	.400	65	0	0	0	7	99^1	81	8	54	94	12.8	3.17	127	.223	.333	0	—	0	8	9	-1	0.9
1990	Sea-A	5	7	.417	63	0	0	0	3	77^1	64	8	44	69	12.8	4.54	87	.229	.338	0	—	0	-5	-5	1	-0.5
1991	Sea-A	7	7	.500	72	0	0	0	14	88^2	64	5	34	74	10.6	3.25	127	.201	.290	0	—	0	8	9	-1	0.8
1992	SF-N	6	6	.500	67	0	0	0	2	82	76	7	33	80	12.4	3.73	90	.252	.333	0	.000	-0	-2	-3	-0	-0.4
Total	7	31	41	.431	393	7	0	0	31	569^1	459	56	268	489	11.9	3.56	112	.222	.319	2	.105	-1	23	27	-2	2.4

● MIKE JACKSON Jackson, Michael Warren b: 3/27/46, Paterson, N.J. BL/TL, 6'3", 190 lbs. Deb: 5/10/70

YEAR	TM/L	W	L	PCT	G	GS	CG	SH	SV	IP	H	HR	BB	SO	RAT	ERA	ERA+	OAV	OOB	BH	AVG	PB	PR	/A	PD	TPI
1970	Phi-N	1	1	.500	5	0	0	0	0	6^1	6	0	4	4	14.2	1.42	281	.286	.400	1	1.000	0	2	2	0	0.2
1971	StL-N	0	0	—	1	0	0	0	0	0^2	1	0	1	0	27.0	0.00	—	.333	.500	0	.000	-0	0	0	0	0.0
1972	KC-A	1	2	.333	7	3	0	0	0	19^2	24	0	14	15	17.4	6.41	47	.320	.427	0	.000	-1	-7	-7	1	-0.8
1973	KC-A	0	0	—	9	0	0	0	0	22^1	25	3	20	13	18.5	6.85	60	.301	.442	0	—	0	-8	-7	-0	-0.7
	Cle-A	0	0	—	1	0	0	0	0	0^2	1	0	0	1	13.5	0.00	—	.333	.333	0	—	0	0	0	0	0.0
	Yr	0	0	—	10	0	0	0	0	23	26	3	20	14	18.0	6.65	62	.295	.426	0	—	0	-7	-7	-0	-0.7
Total	4	2	3	.400	23	3	0	0	0	49^2	57	3	39	33	17.6	5.80	63	.308	.431	1	.143	-0	-12	-12	1	-1.3

● ROY LEE JACKSON Jackson, Roy Lee b: 5/1/54, Opelika, Ala. BR/TR, 6'2", 194 lbs. Deb: 9/13/77

YEAR	TM/L	W	L	PCT	G	GS	CG	SH	SV	IP	H	HR	BB	SO	RAT	ERA	ERA+	OAV	OOB	BH	AVG	PB	PR	/A	PD	TPI
1977	NY-N	0	2	.000	4	4	0	0	0	24	25	2	15	13	16.1	6.00	62	.263	.381	0	.000	-1	-6	-6	-1	-0.7
1978	NY-N	0	0	—	4	2	0	0	0	12^2	21	2	6	6	20.6	9.24	38	.429	.509	2	.667	1	-8	-8	0	-0.7
1979	NY-N	1	0	1.000	8	0	0	0	0	16^1	11	1	5	10	9.4	2.20	165	.200	.279	1	1.000	0	3	3	0	0.3
1980	NY-N	1	7	.125	24	8	1	0	1	70^2	78	4	20	58	12.5	4.20	84	.287	.336	3	.188	1	-5	-5	-1	-0.6
1981	Tor-A	1	2	.333	39	0	0	0	7	62	65	5	25	27	13.2	2.61	151	.275	.347	0	—	0	7	9	0	0.9
1982	Tor-A	8	8	.500	48	2	0	0	6	97	77	7	31	71	10.2	3.06	146	.218	.284	0	—	0	11	15	0	1.4
1983	Tor-A	8	3	.727	49	0	0	0	7	92	92	6	41	48	13.3	4.50	96	.267	.351	0	—	0	-4	-2	0	-0.4
1984	Tor-A	7	8	.467	54	0	0	0	10	86	73	12	31	58	11.0	3.56	115	.230	.301	0	—	0	4	5	0	0.5
1985	SD-N	2	3	.400	22	2	0	0	2	40	32	4	13	28	10.3	2.70	131	.224	.293	0	.000	-1	4	4	0	0.3
1986	Min-A	0	1	.000	28	0	0	0	1	58^1	57	7	16	32	11.7	3.86	112	.256	.314	0	—	0	2	3	-1	0.1
Total	10	28	34	.452	280	18	1	0	34	559	531	50	203	351	12.1	3.77	107	.254	.325	6	.194	1	8	17	-1	1.1

● TONY JACOBS Jacobs, Anthony Robert b: 8/5/25, Dixmoor, Ill. d: 12/21/80, Nashville, Tenn. BB/TR, 5'9", 150 lbs. Deb: 9/19/48

YEAR	TM/L	W	L	PCT	G	GS	CG	SH	SV	IP	H	HR	BB	SO	RAT	ERA	ERA+	OAV	OOB	BH	AVG	PB	PR	/A	PD	TPI
1948	Chi-N	0	0	—	1	0	0	0	0	2	3	1	0	2	13.5	4.50	87	.333	.333	0	—	0	-0	-0	0	0.0
1955	StL-N	0	0	—	1	0	0	0	0	2	6	1	1	1	31.5	18.00	23	.500	.538	0	.000	-0	-3	-3	0	-0.3
Total	2	0	0	—	2	0	0	0	0	4	9	2	1	3	22.5	11.25	35	.429	.455	0	.000	-0	-3	-3	0	-0.3

● ART JACOBS Jacobs, Arthur Edward b: 8/28/02, Luckey, Ohio d: 6/8/67, Inglewood, Cal. BL/TL, 5'10", 170 lbs. Deb: 6/18/39

YEAR	TM/L	W	L	PCT	G	GS	CG	SH	SV	IP	H	HR	BB	SO	RAT	ERA	ERA+	OAV	OOB	BH	AVG	PB	PR	/A	PD	TPI
1939	Cin-N	0	0	—	1	0	0	0	1	1	2	0	1	0	27.0	9.00	43	.400	.500	0	—	0	-1	-1	-0	-0.1

● BUCKY JACOBS Jacobs, Newton Smith b: 3/21/13, Altavista, Va. d: 6/15/90, Richmond, Va. BR/TR, 5'11", 155 lbs. Deb: 6/27/37

YEAR	TM/L	W	L	PCT	G	GS	CG	SH	SV	IP	H	HR	BB	SO	RAT	ERA	ERA+	OAV	OOB	BH	AVG	PB	PR	/A	PD	TPI
1937	Was-A	1	1	.500	11	1	0	0	0	22^1	26	0	11	8	14.9	4.84	92	.295	.374	0	.000	-1	-1	-1	0	-0.1
1939	Was-A	0	0	—	2	0	0	0	0	3	1	0	0	1	3.0	0.00	—	.100	.100	0	—	0	2	1	-0	0.1
1940	Was-A	0	1	.000	9	0	0	0	0	15	16	1	9	6	16.2	6.00	69	.271	.386	0	.000	-0	-3	-3	1	-0.2
Total	3	1	2	.333	22	1	0	0	0	40^1	43	1	20	15	14.5	4.91	88	.274	.363	0	.000	-1	-2	-3	2	-0.2

● ELMER JACOBS Jacobs, William Elmer b: 8/10/1892, Salem, Mo. d: 2/10/58, Salem, Mo. BR/TR, 6', 165 lbs. Deb: 4/23/14

YEAR	TM/L	W	L	PCT	G	GS	CG	SH	SV	IP	H	HR	BB	SO	RAT	ERA	ERA+	OAV	OOB	BH	AVG	PB	PR	/A	PD	TPI
1914	Phi-N	1	3	.250	14	7	1	0	0	50^2	65	2	20	17	15.6	4.80	61	.342	.413	0	.000	-2	-11	-10	0	-1.2
1916	Pit-N	6	10	.375	34	17	8	0	0	153	151	2	38	46	11.4	2.94	91	.258	.308	3	.075	-2	-5	-4	-2	-0.8
1917	Pit-N	6	19	.240	38	25	10	1	2	227^1	214	3	76	58	11.7	2.81	101	.262	.329	12	.179	-1	-2	1	2	0.1
1918	Pit-N	0	1	.000	8	4	0	0	0	23^1	31	0	14	2	17.4	5.79	50	.344	.433	2	.286	0	-8	-8	1	-0.7
	Phi-N	9	5	.643	18	14	12	4	1	123	91	3	42	33	10.0	2.41	124	.210	.285	6	.158	-1	5	8	-2	0.6
	Yr	9	6	.600	26	18	12	4	1	146^1	122	3	56	35	11.2	2.95	101	.233	.312	8	.178	-1	-3	0	-1	-0.1
1919	Phi-N	6	10	.375	17	15	13	0	0	128^2	150	5	44	37	14.0	3.85	84	.304	.368	8	.178	-1	-13	-9	1	-1.0
	StL-N	3	6	.333	17	8	4	1	1	85^1	81	2	25	31	11.7	2.53	110	.264	.329	8	.348	3	4	2	-0	0.6
	Yr	9	16	.360	34	23	17	1	1	214	231	7	69	68	12.8	3.32	92	.287	.347	16	.235	2	-10	-6	1	-0.4
1920	StL-N	4	8	.333	23	9	1	0	1	77^2	91	2	33	21	14.9	5.21	57	.296	.374	5	.192	-0	-18	-19	1	-1.9
1924	Chi-N	11	12	.478	38	22	13	1	1	190^1	181	9	72	50	12.1	3.74	104	.258	.329	6	.111	-4	3	4	1	0.0
1925	Chi-N	2	3	.400	18	4	1	1	1	55^2	63	9	22	19	13.9	5.17	84	.274	.340	3	.231	-0	-6	-5	0	-0.5
1927	Chi-A	2	4	.333	25	8	2	1	0	74^1	105	3	37	22	17.7	4.60	88	.354	.432	3	.150	-1	-4	-5	2	-0.4
Total	9	50	81	.382	250	133	65	9	7	1189^1	1223	40	423	336	12.8	3.55	91	.275	.343	56	.161	-9	-57	-44	5	-5.2

● BEANY JACOBSON Jacobson, Albert L. (b: Albin L. Jacobson) b: 6/5/1881, Port Washington, Wis. d: 1/31/33, Decatur, Ill. BL/TL, 6', 170 lbs. Deb: 4/30/04

YEAR	TM/L	W	L	PCT	G	GS	CG	SH	SV	IP	H	HR	BB	SO	RAT	ERA	ERA+	OAV	OOB	BH	AVG	PB	PR	/A	PD	TPI
1904	Was-A	6	23	.207	33	30	23	1	0	253^2	276	6	57	75	12.0	3.55	75	.278	.320	8	.091	-6	-27	-25	2	-3.0
1905	Was-A	7	8	.467	22	17	12	0	0	144^1	139	1	35	50	11.1	3.30	80	.254	.304	7	.159	1	-10	-10	-2	-1.2
1906	StL-A	9	9	.500	24	15	12	0	0	155	146	3	27	53	10.3	2.50	103	.252	.291	5	.091	-4	3	1	0	-0.2
1907	StL-A	1	6	.143	7	7	6	0	0	57^1	55	1	26	16	12.7	2.98	84	.254	.334	4	.222	-0	-3	-3	-0	-0.4
	Bos-A	0	0	—	2	1	0	0	0	2	2	0	3	1	22.5	9.00	29	.262	.470	0	—	0	-1	-1	0	-0.1
	Yr	1	6	.143	9	8	6	0	0	59^1	57	1	29	17	13.0	3.19	79	.255	.340	4	.222	-0	-4	-4	-0	-0.5
Total	4	23	46	.333	88	70	53	1	0	612^1	618	11	148	195	11.5	3.19	82	.264	.311	24	.117	-9	-38	-38	-0	-4.9

● LARRY JACOBUS Jacobus, Stuart Louis b: 12/18/1893, Cincinnati, Ohio d: 8/19/65, N.College Hill, O. BB/TR, 6'2", 186 lbs. Deb: 7/15/18

YEAR	TM/L	W	L	PCT	G	GS	CG	SH	SV	IP	H	HR	BB	SO	RAT	ERA	ERA+	OAV	OOB	BH	AVG	PB	PR	/A	PD	TPI
1918	Cin-N	0	1	.000	5	0	0	0	0	17^1	25	0	1	8	13.5	5.71	47	.368	.377	0	.000	-1	-6	-6	-0	-0.7

● PAT JACQUEZ Jacquez, Patrick Thomas b: 4/23/47, Stockton, Cal. BR/TR, 6', 200 lbs. Deb: 4/18/71

YEAR	TM/L	W	L	PCT	G	GS	CG	SH	SV	IP	H	HR	BB	SO	RAT	ERA	ERA+	OAV	OOB	BH	AVG	PB	PR	/A	PD	TPI
1971	Chi-A	0	0	—	2	0	0	0	0	2	4	0	2	1	27.0	4.50	80	.444	.545	0	.000	-0	-0	-0	0	0.0

● JAKE JAECKEL Jaeckel, Paul Henry b: 4/1/42, E.Los Angeles, Cal. BR/TR, 5'10", 170 lbs. Deb: 9/19/64

YEAR	TM/L	W	L	PCT	G	GS	CG	SH	SV	IP	H	HR	BB	SO	RAT	ERA	ERA+	OAV	OOB	BH	AVG	PB	PR	/A	PD	TPI
1964	Chi-N	1	0	1.000	4	0	0	0	1	8	4	0	3	2	7.9	0.00	—	.160	.250	0	.000	-0	3	3	-0	0.3

● CHARLIE JAEGER Jaeger, Charles Thomas b: 4/17/1875, Ottawa, Ill. d: 9/27/42, Ottawa, Ill. BR/TR, Deb: 9/09/04

YEAR	TM/L	W	L	PCT	G	GS	CG	SH	SV	IP	H	HR	BB	SO	RAT	ERA	ERA+	OAV	OOB	BH	AVG	PB	PR	/A	PD	TPI
1904	Det-A	3	3	.500	8	6	5	0	0	49	49	0	15	13	12.9	2.57	99	.261	.335	1	.059	-2	0	-0	-1	-0.2

YEAR	TM/L	W	L	PCT	G	GS	CG	SH	SV	IP	H	HR	BB	SO	RAT	ERA	ERA+	OAV	OOB	BH	AVG	PB	PR	/A	PD	TPI
● **JOE JAEGER**	Jaeger, Joseph Peter "Zip" b: 3/3/1895, St.Cloud, Minn. d: 12/13/63, Hampton, Iowa BR/TR, 6'1", 190 lbs. Deb: 7/28/20																									
1920	Chi-N	0	0	—	2	0	0	0	0	3	6	0	4	0	30.0	12.00	27	.500	.625	0	.000	-0	-3	-3	0	-0.3
● **SIG JAKUCKI**	Jakucki, Sigmund "Jack" b: 8/20/09, Camden, N.J. d: 5/28/79, Galveston, Tex. BR/TR, 6'2.5", 198 lbs. Deb: 8/30/36																									
1936	StL-A	0	3	.000	7	2	0	0	0	20^2	32	2	12	9	19.6	8.71	62	.348	.429	0	.000	-1	-8	-8	0	-0.7
1944	*StL-A	13	9	.591	35	24	12	4	3	198	211	17	54	67	12.2	3.55	101	.268	.318	11	.151	-2	-3	1	1	0.1
1945	StL-A	12	10	.545	30	24	15	1	2	192^1	188	9	65	55	11.9	3.51	100	.257	.318	13	.186	0	-3	0	0	0.1
Total	3	25	22	.532	72	50	27	5	5	411	431	28	131	131	12.4	3.79	96	.268	.325	24	.161	-2	-14	-6	1	-0.5
● **LEFTY JAMERSON**	Jamerson, Charles Dewey "Charlie" b: 1/26/1900, Enfield, Ill. d: 8/4/80, Mockville, N.C. BL/TL, 6'1", 195 lbs. Deb: 8/16/24																									
1924	Bos-A	0	0	—	1	0	0	0	0	1	1	0	3	0	36.0	18.00	24	.250	.571	0	—	0	-2	-2	-0	-0.1
● **JEFF JAMES**	James, Jeffrey Lynn "Jesse" b: 9/29/41, Indianapolis, Ind. BR/TR, 6'3", 195 lbs. Deb: 4/13/68																									
1968	Phi-N	4	4	.500	29	13	1	1	0	116	112	8	46	83	12.6	4.27	70	.256	.332	4	.121	-1	-17	-16	0	-1.9
1969	Phi-N	2	2	.500	6	5	1	0	0	31^2	36	5	14	21	14.2	5.40	66	.288	.360	2	.182	-0	-6	-7	-0	-0.7
Total	2	6	6	.500	35	18	2	1	0	147^2	148	13	60	104	12.9	4.51	69	.263	.338	6	.136	-1	-23	-23	-0	-2.6
● **JOHNNY JAMES**	James, John Phillip b: 7/23/33, Bonner's Ferry, Idaho BL/TR, 5'10", 160 lbs. Deb: 9/06/58																									
1958	NY-A	0	0	—	1	0	0	0	0	3	2	0	4	1	18.0	0.00	—	.250	.500	0	.000	-0	1	1	0	0.1
1960	NY-A	5	1	.833	28	0	0	0	2	43^1	38	3	26	29	13.9	4.36	82	.248	.368	0	.000	-0	-2	-4	0	-0.4
1961	NY-A	0	0	—	1	0	0	0	0	1^1	1	0	0	2	6.8	0.00	—	.250	.250	0	—	0	1	1	0	0.1
	LA-A	0	2	.000	36	3	0	0	0	71^1	66	12	54	41	15.4	5.30	85	.246	.377	0	.000	-2	-10	-6	-0	-0.8
	Yr	0	2	.000	37	3	0	0	0	72^2	67	12	54	43	15.2	5.20	86	.246	.375	0	.000	-2	-10	-6	-0	-0.7
Total	3	5	3	.625	66	3	0	0	2	119	107	15	84	73	14.8	4.76	87	.247	.375	0	.000	-2	-11	-8	0	-1.0
● **RICK JAMES**	James, Richard Lee b: 10/11/47, Sheffield, Ala. BR/TR, 6'2.5", 205 lbs. Deb: 9/20/67																									
1967	Chi-N	0	1	.000	3	1	0	0	0	4^2	9	1	2	2	21.2	13.50	26	.529	.579	0	.000	-0	-5	-5	-0	-0.5
● **BOB JAMES**	James, Robert Harvey b: 8/15/58, Glendale, Cal. BR/TR, 6'4", 230 lbs. Deb: 9/07/78																									
1978	Mon-N	0	1	.000	4	1	0	0	0	4	4	1	4	3	18.0	9.00	39	.267	.421	0	—	0	-2	-2	0	-0.2
1979	Mon-N	0	0	—	2	0	0	0	0	2	2	0	3	1	22.5	13.50	27	.250	.455	0	—	0	-2	-2	-0	-0.2
1982	Mon-N	0	0	—	7	0	0	0	0	9	10	0	8	11	18.0	6.00	61	.294	.429	0	—	0	-2	-2	-0	-0.3
	Det-A	0	2	.000	12	1	0	0	0	19^2	22	4	8	20	13.7	5.03	81	.278	.345	0	—	0	-2	-2	-0	-0.2
1983	Det-A	0	0	—	4	0	0	0	0	4	5	2	3	4	18.0	11.25	35	.313	.421	0	—	0	-3	-3	-0	-0.3
	Mon-N	1	0	1.000	27	0	0	0	7	50	37	3	23	56	11.3	2.88	125	.210	.312	2	.286	0	4	4	1	0.6
1984	Mon-N	6	6	.500	62	0	0	0	10	96	92	6	45	91	13.2	3.66	94	.251	.339	2	.143	-0	-1	-2	-1	-0.4
1985	Chi-A	8	7	.533	69	0	0	0	32	110	90	5	23	88	9.4	2.13	203	.226	.271	0	—	0	25	**27**	-1	2.6
1986	Chi-A	5	4	.556	49	0	0	0	14	58^1	61	8	23	32	13.6	5.25	82	.268	.345	0	—	0	-7	-6	-1	-0.9
1987	Chi-A	4	6	.400	43	0	0	0	10	54	54	10	17	34	12.5	4.67	98	.256	.323	0	—	0	-1	-1	0	-0.2
Total	8	24	26	.480	279	2	0	0	73	407	377	39	157	340	12.2	3.80	105	.246	.323	4	.190	0	8	9	-2	0.5
● **LEFTY JAMES**	James, William A. b: 7/1/1889, Glenroy, Ohio d: 5/3/33, Portsmouth, Ohio BL/TL, 5'11.5", 175 lbs. Deb: 4/13/12																									
1912	Cle-A	0	1	.000	3	1	0	0	1	6	8	0	4	2	21.0	7.50	45	.348	.483	0	.000	-1	-3	-3	-0	-0.3
1913	Cle-A	2	2	.500	11	4	3	0	0	39	42	0	9	18	12.5	3.00	101	.273	.325	3	.231	-0	-0	0	-1	-0.1
1914	Cle-A	0	3	.000	17	6	1	0	0	50^2	44	0	32	16	13.9	3.20	90	.251	.373	0	.000	-1	-3	-2	1	-0.2
Total	3	2	6	.250	31	11	4	0	1	95^2	94	0	45	36	13.7	3.39	88	.267	.361	3	.107	-1	-6	-4	0	-0.6
● **BILL JAMES**	James, William Henry "Big Bill" b: 1/20/1887, Detroit, Mich. d: 5/24/42, Venice, Cal. BB/TR, 6'4", 195 lbs. Deb: 6/12/11																									
1911	Cle-A	2	4	.333	8	6	4	0	0	51^2	58	1	32	21	16.0	4.88	70	.284	.387	1	.059	-2	-9	-8	-1	-1.0
1912	Cle-A	0	0	—	3	0	0	0	0	13^2	15	0	9	5	15.8	4.61	74	.288	.393	0	.000	-0	-2	-2	-1	-0.3
1914	StL-A	15	14	.517	44	35	20	3	1	284	269	4	109	109	12.2	2.85	95	.257	.330	10	.112	-3	-3	-5	5	-0.4
1915	StL-A	7	10	.412	34	23	8	0	1	170^1	155	2	92	58	13.4	3.59	80	.255	.359	8	.190	1	-12	-14	2	-1.2
	Det-A	7	3	.700	11	9	3	1	0	67	57	1	33	24	12.1	2.42	125	.243	.336	6	.286	2	4	5	1	0.8
	Yr	14	13	.519	45	32	11	1	1	237^1	212	3	125	82	12.8	3.26	89	.249	.345	14	.222	3	-9	-9	3	-0.4
1916	Det-A	8	12	.400	30	20	8	0	1	151^2	141	1	79	61	13.7	3.68	78	.255	.360	3	.068	-3	-14	-14	-0	-1.9
1917	Det-A	13	10	.565	34	23	10	2	1	198	163	2	96	62	12.3	2.09	127	.229	.330	12	.211	2	13	12	-0	1.6
1918	Det-A	6	11	.353	19	18	8	1	0	122	127	3	68	42	14.8	3.76	71	.279	.379	5	.109	-3	-13	-15	2	-1.7
1919	Det-A	1	0	1.000	2	1	0	0	0	9^1	12	0	7	3	18.3	5.79	55	.324	.432	1	.250	0	-3	-3	0	-0.3
	Bos-A	3	5	.375	13	7	4	0	0	72^2	74	2	39	12	14.4	4.09	74	.280	.379	3	.143	-1	-7	-9	0	-0.9
	*Chi-A	3	2	.600	5	5	3	2	0	39^1	39	0	14	11	12.6	2.52	126	.281	.355	2	.143	-1	3	3	-1	0.1
	Yr	7	7	.500	20	13	7	2	0	121^1	125	2	60	26	13.9	3.71	83	.282	.370	6	.154	-1	-6	-8	-0	-1.1
Total	8	65	71	.478	203	147	68	9	4	1179^2	1110	16	578	408	13.2	3.20	88	.258	.352	51	.142	-8	-44	-49	8	-5.2
● **BILL JAMES**	James, William Lawrence "Seattle Bill" b: 3/12/1892, Iowa Hill, Cal. d: 3/10/71, Oroville, Cal. BR/TR, 6'3", 196 lbs. Deb: 4/17/13																									
1913	Bos-N	6	10	.375	24	14	10	1	0	135^2	134	4	57	73	13.1	2.79	118	.264	.347	12	.255	1	6	8	0	1.0
1914	*Bos-N	26	7	**.788**	46	37	30	4	2	332^1	261	7	118	156	10.6	1.90	145	.225	.304	33	.256	4	**33**	**32**	-1	**4.0**
1915	Bos-N	5	4	.556	13	10	4	0	0	68^1	68	3	22	23	12.1	3.03	86	.269	.332	1	.048	-2	-2	-3	1	-0.4
1919	Bos-N	0	0	—	1	0	0	0	0	5^1	6	0	2	1	13.5	3.38	85	.273	.333	0	.000	-0	-0	-0	0	0.0
Total	4	37	21	.638	84	61	44	5	2	541^2	469	14	199	253	11.5	2.28	126	.242	.319	46	.231	4	37	35	1	4.6
● **CHARLIE JAMIESON**	Jamieson, Charles Devine "Cuckoo" b: 2/7/1893, Paterson, N.J. d: 10/27/69, Paterson, N.J. BL/TL, 5'8.5", 165 lbs. Deb: 9/20/15 ♦																									
1916	Was-A	0	0	—	1	0	0	0	0	4	2	0	3	2	11.3	4.50	62	.143	.294	36	.248	0	-1	-1	0	-0.1
1917	Was-A	0	0	—	1	0	0	0	0	2^1	10	0	2	1	46.3	38.57	7	.625	.667	6	.171	0	-9	-9	-0	-0.7
1918	Phi-A	2	1	.667	5	2	1	0	0	23	24	0	13	2	15.3	4.30	68	.261	.364	84	.202	0	-4	-4	-0	-0.4
1919	Cle-A	0	0	—	4	1	0	0	0	13	12	0	8	0	13.8	5.54	60	.250	.357	6	.353	0	-3	-3	-0	-0.2
1922	Cle-A	0	0	—	2	0	0	0	0	5^2	7	0	4	2	17.5	3.18	126	.318	.423	183	.323	1	1	1	-0	0.0
Total	5	2	1	.667	13	3	1	0	0	48	55	0	30	7	16.3	6.19	51	.286	.388	1990	.303	2	-17	-16	-1	-1.4
● **JERRY JANESKI**	Janeski, Gerard Joseph b: 4/18/46, Pasadena, Cal. BR/TR, 6'4", 205 lbs. Deb: 4/10/70																									
1970	Chi-A	10	17	.370	35	35	4	1	0	205^2	247	22	63	79	13.8	4.77	82	.300	.353	5	.076	-4	-24	-20	1	-2.3
1971	Was-A	1	5	.167	23	10	0	0	1	61^2	72	5	34	19	15.9	4.96	67	.304	.398	3	.214	1	-10	-11	1	-1.1
1972	Tex-A	0	1	.000	4	1	0	0	0	12^2	11	0	7	7	12.8	2.84	106	.229	.327	0	.000	-0	0	0	0	0.0
Total	3	11	23	.324	62	46	4	1	1	280	330	27	104	105	14.2	4.72	79	.298	.362	8	.098	-4	-34	-31	2	-3.4
● **LARRY JANSEN**	Jansen, Lawrence Joseph b: 7/16/20, Verboort, Ore. BR/TR, 6'2", 190 lbs. Deb: 4/17/47 C																									
1947	NY-N	21	5	**.808**	42	30	20	1	1	248	241	23	57	104	10.9	3.16	129	.262	.306	16	.186	-0	25	25	-0	2.6
1948	NY-N	18	12	.600	42	36	15	4	2	277	283	25	54	126	11.0	3.61	109	.265	.303	13	.137	-2	11	10	2	1.0
1949	NY-N	15	16	.484	37	35	17	3	0	259^2	271	36	62	113	11.6	3.85	104	.263	.306	16	.165	-0	6	4	3	0.6
1950	NY-N★	19	13	.594	40	35	21	**5**	3	275	238	31	55	161	**9.6**	3.01	136	.232	**.271**	16	.167	-0	35	33	2	3.5
1951	*NY-N☆	**23**	11	.676	39	34	18	3	0	278^2	254	26	56	145	10.1	3.04	129	.239	.279	9	.094	-5	29	27	3	2.6
1952	NY-N	11	11	.500	34	27	8	1	2	167^1	183	16	47	74	12.7	4.09	91	.281	.335	8	.178	3	-7	-7	2	-0.3
1953	NY-N	11	16	.407	36	26	6	0	1	184^2	185	24	55	88	11.8	4.14	104	.256	.311	8	.133	-1	3	3	-1	0.1
1954	NY-N	2	2	.500	13	7	0	0	0	40^2	57	5	15	15	16.2	5.98	68	.337	.395	4	.286	1	-9	-9	1	-0.6
1956	Cin-N	2	3	.400	8	7	2	0	1	34^2	39	5	9	16	12.7	5.19	77	.281	.329	0	.000	-1	-5	-5	-0	-0.6
Total	9	122	89	.578	291	237	107	17	10	1765^2	1751	191	410	842	11.1	3.58	112	.258	.302	90	.150	-6	87	82	11	8.9

YEAR	TM/L	W	L	PCT	G	GS	CG	SH	SV	IP	H	HR	BB	SO	RAT	ERA	ERA+	OAV	OOB	BH	AVG	PB	PR	/A	PD	TPI
● **RAY JARVIS**	Jarvis, Raymond Arnold b: 5/10/46, Providence, R.I. BR/TR, 6'2", 198 lbs. Deb: 4/15/69																									
1969	Bos-A	5	6	.455	29	12	2	0	1	100^{1}	105	8	43	36	13.5	4.75	80	.274	.352	2	.069	-2	-13	-11	1	-1.2
1970	Bos-A	0	1	.000	15	0	0	0	0	16	17	1	14	8	18.6	3.94	101	.274	.423	0	—	0	-0	0	0	0.0
Total	2	5	7	.417	44	12	2	0	1	116^{1}	122	9	57	44	14.2	4.64	82	.274	.363	2	.069	-2	-13	-11	1	-1.2
● **PAT JARVIS**	Jarvis, Robert Patrick b: 3/18/41, Carlyle, Ill. BR/TR, 5'10.5", 180 lbs. Deb: 8/04/66																									
1966	Atl-N	6	2	.750	10	9	3	1	0	62^{1}	46	1	12	41	8.5	2.31	157	.206	.250	0	.000	-2	9	9	-1	0.7
1967	Atl-N	15	10	.600	32	30	7	1	0	194	195	15	62	118	12.1	3.66	91	.260	.320	6	.085	-3	-6	-7	-2	-1.3
1968	Atl-N	16	12	.571	34	34	14	1	0	256	202	15	50	157	8.9	2.60	115	.214	.255	12	.141	0	11	11	-3	1.0
1969	*Atl-N	13	11	.542	37	33	4	1	0	217^{1}	204	25	73	123	11.5	4.43	81	.246	.308	8	.113	-3	-20	-20	-0	-2.3
1970	Atl-N	16	16	.500	36	34	11	1	0	254	240	21	72	173	11.1	3.61	119	.247	.299	15	.183	-0	12	19	2	2.1
1971	Atl-N	6	14	.300	35	23	3	3	1	162^{1}	162	16	51	68	12.0	4.10	90	.261	.320	5	.106	-2	-12	-7	1	-0.9
1972	Atl-N	11	7	.611	37	6	0	0	2	98^{2}	94	7	44	56	12.6	4.10	92	.260	.341	3	.125	-0	-7	-3	1	-0.3
1973	Mon-N	2	1	.667	28	0	0	0	0	39^{1}	37	6	16	19	12.4	3.20	119	.250	.327	0	.000	-0	2	3	-0	0.2
Total	8	85	73	.538	249	169	42	8	3	1284	1180	106	380	755	11.0	3.58	101	.243	.300	49	.121	-10	-11	3	-3	-0.8
● **HI JASPER**	Jasper, Henry W. b: 11/15/1880, St.Louis, Mo. d: 5/22/37, St.Louis, Mo. BR/TR, 5'11", 180 lbs. Deb: 4/19/14																									
1914	Chi-A	1	0	1.000	16	0	0	0	0	32^{1}	22	0	20	19	12.0	3.34	80	.210	.341	0	.000	-1	-2	-2	1	-0.2
1915	Chi-A	0	1	.000	3	2	1	0	0	15^{2}	8	2	9	15	9.8	4.60	65	.157	.283	2	.286	0	-3	-3	1	-0.1
1916	StL-N	5	6	.455	21	11	2	0	1	107	97	0	42	37	12.3	3.28	81	.254	.339	7	.212	1	-8	-8	2	-0.6
1919	Cle-A	4	5	.444	12	10	5	0	0	82^{2}	83	1	28	25	12.1	3.59	93	.269	.330	3	.103	-2	-3	-2	1	-0.4
Total	4	10	12	.455	52	23	8	0	1	237^{2}	210	3	99	96	12.0	3.48	84	.248	.333	12	.162	-2	-16	-15	5	-1.3
● **LARRY JASTER**	Jaster, Larry Edward b: 1/13/44, Midland, Mich. BL/TL, 6'3.5", 205 lbs. Deb: 9/17/65																									
1965	StL-N	3	0	1.000	4	3	3	0	0	28	21	1	7	10	9.0	1.61	239	.206	.257	2	.200	0	6	7	-1	0.8
1966	StL-N	11	5	.688	26	21	6	**5**	0	151^{2}	124	17	45	92	10.3	3.26	110	.227	.291	8	.178	1	6	5	-1	0.6
1967	*StL-N	9	7	.563	34	23	2	1	3	152^{1}	141	12	44	87	11.0	3.01	109	.244	.300	5	.100	-1	6	5	-2	0.1
1968	*StL-N	9	13	.409	31	21	3	1	0	154^{1}	153	13	38	70	11.5	3.50	83	.262	.313	6	.140	0	-9	-10	-2	-1.3
1969	Mon-N	1	6	.143	24	11	1	0	0	77	95	17	28	39	14.6	5.49	67	.302	.362	8	.421	3	-16	-16	-2	-1.4
1970	Atl-N	1	1	.500	14	0	0	0	0	22^{1}	33	5	8	9	16.5	6.85	63	.359	.410	0	.000	-0	-7	-6	1	-0.6
1972	Atl-N	1	1	.500	5	1	0	0	0	12^{1}	12	4	8	6	14.6	5.11	74	.267	.377	0	.000	-0	-2	-2	-0	-0.2
Total	7	35	33	.515	138	80	15	7	3	598	579	69	178	313	11.6	3.64	93	.256	.314	29	.170	4	-16	-17	-7	-2.0
● **AL JAVERY**	Javery, Alva William "Beartracks" b: 6/5/18, Worcester, Mass. d: 9/13/77, Woodstock, Conn. BR/TR, 6'3", 183 lbs. Deb: 4/23/40																									
1940	Bos-N	2	4	.333	29	4	1	0	1	83^{1}	99	2	36	42	14.8	5.51	68	.293	.364	2	.087	-1	-15	-17	-2	-1.9
1941	Bos-N	10	11	.476	34	23	9	1	1	160^{2}	181	5	65	54	14.1	4.31	83	.283	.355	6	.103	-4	-12	-13	1	-1.6
1942	Bos-N	12	16	.429	42	37	19	5	0	261	251	8	78	85	11.4	3.03	110	.251	.307	9	.105	-5	8	9	2	0.7
1943	Bos-N★	17	16	.515	41	35	19	5	0	**303**	288	13	99	134	11.6	3.21	106	.248	.309	17	.163	-3	6	7	2	0.7
1944	Bos-N☆	10	19	.345	40	33	11	3	3	254	248	12	118	137	13.0	3.54	108	.262	.345	12	.152	-3	2	8	-2	0.3
1945	Bos-N	2	7	.222	17	14	2	1	0	77^{1}	92	4	51	18	16.6	6.28	61	.295	.394	6	.207	-0	-21	-21	1	-1.9
1946	Bos-N	0	1	.000	2	1	0	0	0	3^{1}	5	0	5	0	27.0	13.50	25	.417	.588	0	.000	-0	-4	-4	-0	-0.4
Total	7	53	74	.417	205	147	61	15	5	1142^{2}	1164	44	452	470	12.9	3.80	94	.264	.335	52	.137	-16	-37	-31	2	-4.1
● **JOEY JAY**	Jay, Joseph Richard b: 8/15/35, Middletown, Conn. BB/TR, 6'4", 228 lbs. Deb: 7/21/53																									
1953	Mil-N	1	0	1.000	3	1	1	1	0	10	6	0	5	4	9.9	0.00	—	.188	.297	0	.000	-0	5	4	-0	0.4
1954	Mil-N	1	0	1.000	15	1	0	0	0	18	21	2	16	13	19.0	6.50	57	.304	.442	0	—	0	-5	-6	-0	-0.5
1955	Mil-N	0	0	—	12	1	0	0	0	19	23	2	13	3	17.1	4.74	79	.324	.429	2	.667	1	-1	-2	-1	-0.2
1957	Mil-N	0	0	—	1	0	0	0	1	0^{2}	0	0	0	0	0.0	0.00	—	.000	.000	0	—	0	0	0	0	0.0
1958	Mil-N	7	5	.583	18	12	6	3	0	96^{2}	60	8	43	74	9.7	2.14	164	.177	.272	3	.094	-1	19	15	0	1.5
1959	Mil-N	6	11	.353	34	19	4	1	0	136^{1}	130	11	64	88	13.1	4.09	87	.248	.336	3	.086	-1	-2	-8	2	-0.8
1960	Mil-N	9	8	.529	32	11	3	0	1	133^{1}	128	10	59	90	13.0	3.24	106	.254	.339	7	.156	0	8	3	-0	0.3
1961	*Cin-N☆	**21**	10	.677	34	34	14	**4**	0	247^{1}	217	25	92	157	11.4	3.53	115	.236	.309	8	.090	-6	14	15	-1	0.8
1962	Cin-N	21	14	.600	39	37	16	4	0	273	269	26	100	155	12.3	3.76	107	.260	.327	15	.167	3	6	8	-2	0.9
1963	Cin-N	7	18	.280	30	22	4	1	1	170	172	19	73	116	13.1	4.29	78	.266	.343	8	.160	0	-19	-18	-0	-1.9
1964	Cin-N	11	11	.500	34	23	10	0	2	183	167	17	36	134	10.1	3.39	107	.245	.285	3	.057	-3	3	5	-2	0.0
1965	Cin-N	9	8	.529	37	24	4	1	1	155^{2}	150	21	63	102	12.5	4.22	89	.252	.328	2	.041	-3	-12	-8	-0	-1.2
1966	Cin-N	6	2	.750	12	10	1	1	0	73^{2}	78	8	23	44	12.7	3.91	100	.275	.335	3	.115	-1	-2	-0	-1	-0.2
	Atl-N	0	4	.000	9	8	0	0	1	29^{2}	39	4	20	19	18.2	7.89	46	.315	.414	1	.125	-0	-14	-14	-0	-1.4
	Yr	6	6	.500	21	18	1	1	1	103^{1}	117	12	43	63	14.0	5.05	76	.285	.354	4	.118	-1	-17	-14	-1	-1.6
Total	13	99	91	.521	310	203	63	16	7	1546^{1}	1460	153	607	999	12.2	3.77	99	.251	.325	55	.114	-10	-1	-5	-6	-2.3
● **TEX JEANES**	Jeanes, Ernest Lee b: 12/19/1900, Maypearl, Tex. d: 4/5/73, Longview, Tex. BR/TR, 6', 176 lbs. Deb: 4/20/21 ♦																									
1922	Cle-A	0	0	—	1	0	0	0	0	0	0	0	1	0	—	—	—	—	1.000	0	.000	0	0	0	0	0.0
1927	NY-N	0	0	—	1	0	0	0	0	1	2	0	2	0	36.0	9.00	43	.400	.571	6	.300	0	-1	-1	-0	-0.1
Total	2	0	0	—	2	0	0	0	0	1	2	0	3	0	45.0	9.00	43	.400	.625	20	.274	0	-1	-1	-0	-0.1
● **GEORGE JEFFCOAT**	Jeffcoat, George Edward b: 12/24/13, New Brookland, S.C d: 10/13/78, Leesville, S.C. BR/TR, 5'11.5", 175 lbs. Deb: 4/20/36 F																									
1936	Bro-N	5	6	.455	40	5	3	0	3	95^{2}	84	7	63	46	14.6	4.52	92	.239	.366	3	.130	-1	-5	-4	-1	-0.6
1937	Bro-N	1	3	.250	21	3	1	1	0	54^{1}	58	4	27	29	14.2	5.13	79	.274	.358	0	.000	-2	-7	-7	-0	-0.9
1939	Bro-N	0	0	—	1	0	0	0	0	2	2	0	0	1	9.0	0.00	—	.286	.286	0	—	0	1	1	-0	0.1
1943	Bos-N	1	2	.333	8	1	0	0	0	17^{2}	15	1	10	10	12.7	3.06	112	.217	.316	2	.500	1	1	1	0	0.2
Total	4	7	11	.389	70	9	4	1	3	169^{2}	159	12	100	86	14.2	4.51	89	.248	.358	5	.128	-2	-11	-9	-1	-1.2
● **HAL JEFFCOAT**	Jeffcoat, Harold Bentley b: 9/6/24, W.Columbia, S.C. BR/TR, 5'10.5", 185 lbs. Deb: 4/20/48 F♦																									
1954	Chi-N	5	6	.455	43	3	1	0	7	104	110	12	58	35	14.9	5.19	81	.276	.373	8	.258	2	-13	-11	1	-0.7
1955	Chi-N	8	6	.571	50	1	0	0	6	100^{2}	107	5	53	32	14.7	2.95	139	.276	.369	4	.174	1	12	13	1	1.4
1956	Cin-N	8	2	.800	38	16	2	0	2	171	189	12	55	55	13.1	3.84	104	.281	.340	8	.148	-1	-1	3	3	0.5
1957	Cin-N	12	13	.480	37	31	10	1	0	207	236	29	46	63	12.6	4.52	91	.294	.338	14	.203	6	-15	-9	-1	-0.4
1958	Cin-N	6	8	.429	49	0	0	0	9	75	76	8	26	35	12.5	3.72	111	.268	.333	5	.556	2	2	4	2	0.8
1959	Cin-N	0	1	.000	17	0	0	0	0	21^{2}	21	3	10	12	12.9	3.32	122	.253	.333	1	1.000	1	2	2	0	0.3
	StL-N	0	1	.000	11	0	0	0	0	17^{2}	33	4	9	7	21.4	9.17	46	.402	.462	0	.000	-0	-10	-10	0	-1.0
	Yr	0	2	.000	28	0	0	0	1	39^{1}	54	7	19	19	16.7	5.95	70	.327	.397	1	.250	0	-9	-8	0	-0.7
Total	6	39	37	.513	245	51	13	1	25	697	772	73	257	239	13.6	4.22	97	.285	.352	487	.248	11	-24	-10	5	0.9
● **MIKE JEFFCOAT**	Jeffcoat, James Michael b: 8/3/59, Pine Bluff, Ark. BL/TL, 6'2", 187 lbs. Deb: 8/21/83																									
1983	Cle-A	1	3	.250	11	2	0	0	0	32^{2}	32	1	13	9	12.7	3.31	128	.256	.331	0	—	0	3	3	-0	0.3
1984	Cle-A	5	2	.714	63	1	0	0	1	75^{1}	82	7	24	41	12.8	2.99	137	.281	.338	0	—	0	8	9	1	1.0
1985	Cle-A	0	0	—	9	0	0	0	0	9^{2}	8	1	6	4	13.0	2.79	148	.235	.350	0	—	0	1	1	1	0.2
	SF-N	0	2	.000	19	1	0	0	0	22	27	4	6	10	14.3	5.32	65	.307	.365	0	.000	0	-4	-5	1	-0.4
1987	Tex-A	0	1	.000	2	2	0	0	0	7	11	4	4	1	19.3	12.86	35	.355	.429	0	—	0	-7	-7	-0	-0.6
1988	Tex-A	0	2	.000	5	2	0	0	0	10	19	1	5	5	23.4	11.70	35	.432	.510	0	—	0	-9	-8	0	-0.9
1989	Tex-A	9	6	.600	22	22	2	2	0	130^{2}	139	7	33	64	12.1	3.58	111	.270	.319	0	—	0	4	6	0	0.5
1990	Tex-A	5	6	.455	44	12	1	0	5	110^{2}	122	12	28	58	12.4	4.47	88	.283	.330	0	—	0	-7	-7	-1	-0.8
1991	Tex-A	5	3	.625	70	0	0	0	5	79^{2}	104	8	25	43	15.0	4.63	87	.320	.376	1	1.000	1	-5	-5	0	-0.5
1992	Tex-A	0	1	.000	6	3	0	0	0	19^{2}	28	2	5	6	15.1	7.32	52	.350	.388	0	—	0	-7	-8	0	-0.7

YEAR TM/L	W	L	PCT	G	GS	CG	SH	SV	IP	H	HR	BB	SO	RAT	ERA	ERA+	OAV	OOB	BH	AVG	PB	PR	/A	PD	TPI
Total 9	25	26	.490	251	45	3	2	7	497^1	572	47	149	241	13.3	4.34	92	.291	.346	1	.500	1	-22	-20	1	-1.9

● JESSE JEFFERSON Jefferson, Jesse Harrison b: 3/3/49, Midlothian, Va. BR/TR, 6'3", 195 lbs. Deb: 6/23/73

YEAR TM/L	W	L	PCT	G	GS	CG	SH	SV	IP	H	HR	BB	SO	RAT	ERA	ERA+	OAV	OOB	BH	AVG	PB	PR	/A	PD	TPI
1973 Bal-A	6	5	.545	18	15	3	0	0	100^2	104	15	46	52	13.4	4.11	91	.267	.345	0	—	0	-3	-4	1	-0.3
1974 Bal-A	1	0	1.000	20	2	0	0	0	57^1	55	2	38	31	14.6	4.40	79	.261	.373	0	—	0	-5	-6	0	-0.4
1975 Bal-A	0	2	.000	4	0	0	0	0	7^2	5	0	8	4	15.3	2.35	149	.227	.433	0	—	0	1	1	0	0.2
Chi-A	5	9	.357	22	21	1	0	0	107^2	100	10	94	67	16.4	5.10	76	.249	.394	0	—	0	-16	-15	0	-1.4
Yr	5	11	.313	26	21	1	0	0	115^1	105	10	102	71	16.3	4.92	78	.248	.397	0	—	0	-15	-14	1	-1.2
1976 Chi-A	2	5	.286	19	9	0	0	0	62^1	86	3	42	30	18.8	8.52	42	.339	.436	0	—	0	-35	-34	1	-3.2
1977 Tor-A	9	17	.346	33	33	8	0	0	217	224	23	83	114	12.8	4.31	97	.269	.336	0	—	0	-6	-3	0	-0.3
1978 Tor-A	7	16	.304	31	30	9	2	0	211^2	214	28	86	97	12.9	4.38	90	.267	.340	0	—	0	-15	-11	0	-1.2
1979 Tor-A	2	10	.167	34	10	2	0	1	116	150	19	45	43	15.3	5.51	79	.328	.390	0	—	0	-17	-15	1	-1.4
1980 Tor-A	4	13	.235	29	18	2	2	0	121^2	130	12	52	53	13.6	5.47	79	.281	.357	0	—	0	-19	-16	1	-1.7
Pit-N	1	0	1.000	1	1	0	0	0	6^2	3	0	2	4	6.8	1.35	270	.143	.217	0	.000	-0	2	2	0	0.2
1981 Cal-A	2	4	.333	26	5	0	0	0	77	80	4	24	27	12.4	3.62	101	.269	.328	0	—	0	0	0	-1	-0.1
Total 9	39	81	.325	237	144	25	4	1	1085^2	1151	116	520	522	14.0	4.81	83	.277	.360	0	.000	-0	-112	-101	3	-9.6

● FERGIE JENKINS Jenkins, Ferguson Arthur b: 12/13/43, Chatham, Ont., Can. BR/TR, 6'5", 210 lbs. Deb: 9/10/65 H

YEAR TM/L	W	L	PCT	G	GS	CG	SH	SV	IP	H	HR	BB	SO	RAT	ERA	ERA+	OAV	OOB	BH	AVG	PB	PR	/A	PD	TPI
1965 Phi-N	2	1	.667	7	0	0	0	1	12^1	7	2	2	10	6.6	2.19	158	.159	.196	0	.000	-0	2	2	-0	0.1
1966 Phi-N	0	0	—	1	0	0	0	0	2^1	3	0	1	2	15.4	3.86	93	.273	.333	0	—	0	-0	-0	-0	0.0
Chi-N	6	8	.429	60	12	2	1	5	182	147	24	51	148	9.9	3.31	111	.219	.277	7	.137	1	6	7	-2	0.7
Yr	6	8	.429	61	12	2	1	5	184^1	150	24	52	150	10.0	3.32	111	.220	.278	7	.137	1	6	7	-2	0.7
1967 Chi-N★	20	13	.606	38	38	**20**	3	0	289^1	230	30	83	236	9.9	2.80	127	.217	.277	14	.151	1	19	24	2	3.1
1968 Chi-N	20	15	.571	40	40	20	3	0	308	255	26	65	260	9.4	2.63	120	.222	.266	16	.160	3	12	18	-1	2.3
1969 Chi-N	21	15	.583	43	42	23	7	1	311^1	284	27	71	**273**	10.5	3.21	125	.242	.290	15	.139	-1	13	28	0	3.0
1970 Chi-N	22	16	.579	40	39	**24**	3	0	313	265	30	60	274	**9.5**	3.39	133	.224	**.265**	14	.124	-3	23	39	-1	3.6
1971 Chi-N★	**24**	13	.649	39	39	**30**	3	0	**325**	304	29	37	263	9.6	2.77	142	.246	.271	28	.243	12	25	42	2	6.5
1972 Chi-N☆	20	12	.625	36	36	23	5	0	289^1	253	32	62	184	10.0	3.20	119	.234	.280	20	.183	2	8	19	3	2.7
1973 Chi-N	14	16	.467	38	38	7	2	0	271	267	35	57	170	10.9	3.89	101	.259	.301	10	.119	-2	-7	2	3	0.4
1974 Tex-A	**25**	12	.676	41	41	**29**	6	0	328^1	286	27	45	225	9.3	2.82	126	.232	.264	1	.500	1	29	27	-0	3.0
1975 Tex-A	17	18	.486	37	37	22	4	0	270	261	37	56	157	10.9	3.93	95	.251	.295	0	—	0	-5	-5	1	-0.5
1976 Bos-A	12	11	.522	30	29	12	2	0	209	201	20	43	142	10.7	3.27	119	.253	.296	0	—	0	6	15	-1	0.9
1977 Bos-A	10	10	.500	28	28	11	1	0	193	190	30	36	105	10.5	3.68	122	.257	.291	0	—	0	8	17	1	1.4
1978 Tex-A	18	8	.692	34	30	16	4	0	249	228	21	41	157	9.8	3.04	123	.245	.279	0	—	0	20	20	2	2.3
1979 Tex-A	16	14	.533	37	37	10	3	0	259	252	40	81	164	11.7	4.07	102	.256	.314	0	—	0	4	2	4	0.7
1980 Tex-A	12	12	.500	29	29	12	0	0	198	190	22	52	129	11.2	3.77	103	.250	.301	0	—	0	6	3	1	0.5
1981 Tex-A	5	8	.385	19	16	1	0	0	106	122	14	40	63	13.8	4.50	77	.290	.351	0	—	0	-10	-12	2	-1.0
1982 Chi-N	14	15	.483	34	34	4	1	0	217^1	221	19	68	134	12.2	3.15	119	.264	.323	10	.149	-1	11	14	-0	1.3
1983 Chi-N	6	9	.400	33	29	1	1	0	167^1	176	19	46	96	12.3	4.30	88	.275	.329	13	.245	3	-13	-10	-1	-0.7
Total 19	284	226	.557	664	594	267	49	7	4500^2	4142	484	997	3192	10.4	3.34	115	.243	.289	148	.165	15	157	254	14	30.3

● JACK JENKINS Jenkins, Warren Washington b: 12/22/42, Covington, Va. BR/TR, 6'2", 195 lbs. Deb: 9/13/62

YEAR TM/L	W	L	PCT	G	GS	CG	SH	SV	IP	H	HR	BB	SO	RAT	ERA	ERA+	OAV	OOB	BH	AVG	PB	PR	/A	PD	TPI
1962 Was-A	0	1	.000	3	1	1	0	0	13^1	12	4	7	10	12.8	4.05	100	.245	.339	0	.000	-0	-0	-0	-0	-0.1
1963 Was-A	0	2	.000	4	2	0	0	0	12^1	16	2	12	5	20.4	5.84	64	.340	.475	1	.333	0	-3	-3	0	-0.3
1969 LA-N	0	0	—	1	0	0	0	0	1	0	0	0	1	0.0	0.00	—	.000	.000	0	—	0	0	0	0	0.0
Total 3	0	3	.000	8	3	1	0	0	26^2	28	6	19	16	15.9	4.73	82	.283	.398	1	.143	-0	-3	-3	0	-0.4

● WILLIE JENSEN Jensen, William Christian b: 11/17/1889, Philadelphia, Pa. d: 3/27/17, Philadelphia, Pa. BL/TR, 5'11.5", 170 lbs. Deb: 9/10/12

YEAR TM/L	W	L	PCT	G	GS	CG	SH	SV	IP	H	HR	BB	SO	RAT	ERA	ERA+	OAV	OOB	BH	AVG	PB	PR	/A	PD	TPI
1912 Det-A	1	2	.333	5	4	1	0	0	33	43	1	18	8	17.2	4.91	66	.339	.429	0	.000	-2	-6	-6	-0	-0.7
1914 Phi-A	0	1	.000	1	1	1	0	0	9	7	1	2	1	9.0	2.00	131	.226	.273	0	.000	0	1	1	0	0.1
Total 2	1	3	.250	6	5	2	0	0	42	50	2	20	9	15.4	4.29	73	.316	.400	0	.000	-2	-5	-5	-0	-0.6

● VIRGIL JESTER Jester, Virgil Milton b: 7/23/27, Denver, Colo. BR/TR, 5'11", 188 lbs. Deb: 6/18/52

YEAR TM/L	W	L	PCT	G	GS	CG	SH	SV	IP	H	HR	BB	SO	RAT	ERA	ERA+	OAV	OOB	BH	AVG	PB	PR	/A	PD	TPI
1952 Bos-N	3	5	.375	19	8	4	1	0	73	80	5	23	25	12.8	3.33	108	.283	.339	4	.211	1	3	2	-1	0.2
1953 Mil-N	0	0	—	2	0	0	0	0	2	4	1	4	0	36.0	22.50	17	.400	.571	0	—	0	-4	-4	0	-0.4
Total 2	3	5	.375	21	8	4	1	0	75	84	6	27	25	13.4	3.84	94	.287	.349	4	.211	1	-1	-2	-1	-0.2

● GERMAN JIMENEZ Jimenez, German (Camarena) b: 12/5/62, Santiago, Mex. BL/TL, 5'11", 200 lbs. Deb: 6/28/88

YEAR TM/L	W	L	PCT	G	GS	CG	SH	SV	IP	H	HR	BB	SO	RAT	ERA	ERA+	OAV	OOB	BH	AVG	PB	PR	/A	PD	TPI
1988 Atl-N	1	6	.143	15	9	0	0	0	55^2	65	4	12	26	12.6	5.01	73	.294	.333	1	.059	-1	-10	-8	-1	-1.1

● JUAN JIMENEZ Jimenez, Juan Antonio (Martes) b: 3/8/49, LaTorre, La Vega, D.R. BR/TR, 6'1", 165 lbs. Deb: 9/09/74

YEAR TM/L	W	L	PCT	G	GS	CG	SH	SV	IP	H	HR	BB	SO	RAT	ERA	ERA+	OAV	OOB	BH	AVG	PB	PR	/A	PD	TPI
1974 Pit-N	0	0	—	4	0	0	0	0	4	6	0	2	2	18.0	6.75	51	.353	.421	0	—	0	-1	-1	-0	-0.2

● TOMMY JOHN John, Thomas Edward b: 5/22/43, Terre Haute, Ind. BR/TL, 6'3", 185 lbs. Deb: 9/06/63

YEAR TM/L	W	L	PCT	G	GS	CG	SH	SV	IP	H	HR	BB	SO	RAT	ERA	ERA+	OAV	OOB	BH	AVG	PB	PR	/A	PD	TPI
1963 Cle-A	0	2	.000	6	3	0	0	0	20^1	23	1	6	9	12.8	2.21	164	.284	.333	0	.000	-1	3	3	-0	0.3
1964 Cle-A	2	9	.182	25	14	2	1	0	94^1	97	10	35	65	12.6	3.91	92	.262	.326	5	.208	0	-3	-3	1	-0.3
1965 Chi-A	14	7	.667	39	27	6	1	3	183^2	162	12	58	126	10.9	3.09	103	.237	.298	10	.169	2	8	2	3	0.8
1966 Chi-A	14	11	.560	34	33	10	**5**	0	223	195	13	57	138	10.5	2.62	121	.235	.290	10	.145	2	20	14	1	1.8
1967 Chi-A	10	13	.435	31	29	9	**6**	0	178^1	143	12	47	110	9.8	2.47	126	.219	.277	8	.157	-0	15	13	6	2.1
1968 Chi-A★	10	5	.667	25	25	5	1	0	177^1	135	10	49	117	9.9	1.98	153	.212	.280	12	.194	2	20	21	6	3.5
1969 Chi-A	9	11	.450	33	33	6	2	0	232^1	230	16	90	128	12.4	3.25	119	.261	.330	9	.114	-2	9	16	7	2.3
1970 Chi-A	12	17	.414	37	37	10	3	0	269^1	253	19	101	138	12.1	3.27	119	.251	.324	17	.202	1	13	19	4	2.6
1971 Chi-A	13	16	.448	38	35	10	3	0	229^1	244	17	58	131	12.0	3.61	99	.274	.321	10	.145	-1	-4	-1	-1	-0.3
1972 LA-N	11	5	.688	29	29	4	1	0	186^2	172	14	40	117	10.4	2.89	115	.244	.287	10	.159	-1	12	9	4	1.3
1973 LA-N	16	7	**.696**	36	31	4	2	0	218	202	16	50	116	10.6	3.10	111	.246	.293	15	.203	2	14	8	7	1.8
1974 LA-N	13	3	.813	22	22	5	3	0	153	133	4	42	78	10.4	2.59	131	.235	.289	6	.118	-1	18	14	2	1.6
1976 LA-N	10	10	.500	31	31	6	2	0	207	207	7	61	91	11.7	3.09	110	.261	.314	7	.109	-2	10	7	-1	0.4
1977 *LA-N	20	7	.741	31	31	11	3	0	220^1	225	12	50	123	11.4	2.78	138	.267	.311	14	.177	1	28	26	2	3.1
1978 *LA-N☆	17	10	.630	33	30	7	0	1	213	230	11	53	124	12.2	3.30	106	.271	.318	8	.121	-1	7	5	2	0.6
1979 NY-A☆	21	9	.700	37	36	17	3	0	276^1	268	9	65	111	11.0	2.96	137	.260	.306	0	—	0	**38**	34	2	3.9
1980 *NY-A★	22	9	.710	36	36	16	**6**	0	265^1	270	13	56	78	11.3	3.43	114	.268	.311	0	—	0	18	15	1	1.7
1981 *NY-A	9	8	.529	20	20	7	0	0	140^1	135	10	39	50	11.4	2.63	136	.256	.311	0	—	0	16	15	1	1.8
1982 NY-A	10	10	.500	30	26	9	2	0	186^2	190	11	34	54	10.9	3.66	109	.266	.302	0	—	0	8	7	2	0.9
*Cal-A	4	2	.667	7	7	1	0	0	35	49	4	5	14	13.9	3.86	105	.336	.358	0	—	0	1	1	1	0.1
Yr	14	12	.538	37	33	10	2	0	221^2	239	15	39	68	11.3	3.69	108	.274	.305	0	—	0	9	7	2	1.0
1983 Cal-A	11	13	.458	34	34	9	0	0	234^2	287	20	49	65	13.0	4.33	93	.304	.340	0	—	0	-7	-8	1	-0.7
1984 Cal-A	7	13	.350	32	29	4	1	0	181^1	223	15	56	47	14.0	4.52	88	.306	.359	0	—	0	-11	-11	0	-1.0
1985 Cal-A	2	4	.333	12	6	0	0	0	38^1	51	3	15	17	15.7	4.70	87	.329	.392	0	—	0	-2	-3	1	-0.1
Oak-A	2	6	.250	11	11	0	0	0	48	66	6	13	8	15.0	6.19	62	.332	.376	0	—	0	-11	-12	1	-1.0
Yr	4	10	.286	23	17	0	0	0	86^1	117	9	28	25	15.2	5.53	72	.328	.378	0	—	0	-13	-15	2	-1.1
1986 NY-A	5	3	.625	13	10	1	0	0	70^2	73	8	15	28	11.5	2.93	140	.275	.319	0	—	0	10	9	1	1.0
1987 NY-A	13	6	.684	33	33	3	1	0	187^2	212	12	47	63	12.7	4.03	109	.288	.336	0	—	0	9	7	-1	0.6
1988 NY-A	9	8	.529	35	32	0	0	0	176^1	221	11	46	81	13.9	4.49	88	.308	.355	0	—	0	-10	-11	2	-0.9
1989 NY-A	2	7	.222	10	10	0	0	0	63^2	87	6	22	18	15.8	5.80	67	.336	.394	0	—	0	-14	-14	2	-1.1
Total 26	288	231	.555	760	700	162	46	4	4710^1	4783	302	1259	2245	11.7	3.34	110	.265	.316	141	.157	1	214	179	55	26.8

YEAR TM/L	W	L	PCT	G	GS	CG	SH	SV	IP	H	HR	BB	SO	RAT	ERA	ERA+	OAV	OOB	BH	AVG	PB	PR	/A	PD	TPI
● **AUGIE JOHNS** Johns, Augustus Francis "Lefty" b: 9/10/1899, St.Louis, Mo. d: 9/12/75, San Antonio, Tex. BL/TL, 5'8.5", 170 lbs. Deb: 4/16/26																									
1926 Det-A	6	4	.600	35	14	3	1	1	112^2	117	6	69	40	15.3	5.35	76	.271	.377	4	.143	-1	-17	-16	-2	-1.8
1927 Det-A	0	0	—	1	0	0	0	0	1	1	0	1	1	18.0	9.00	47	.333	.500	0	—	0	-1	-1	0	0.0
Total 2	6	4	.600	36	14	3	1	1	113^2	118	6	70	41	15.3	5.38	75	.271	.378	4	.143	-1	-17	-17	-2	-1.8
● **OLLIE JOHNS** Johns, Oliver Tracy b: 8/21/1879, Trenton, Ohio d: 6/17/61, Hamilton, Ohio BL/TL, Deb: 9/24/05																									
1905 Cin-N	1	0	1.000	4	1	1	0	1	18	31	1	4	8	17.5	3.50	94	.369	.398	1	.200	-0	-1	-0	-0	-0.1
● **ABE JOHNSON** Johnson, Abraham b: London, Ont., Can. Deb: 7/16/1893																									
1893 Chi-N	0	0	—	1	0	0	0	1	1	2	0	2	0	45.0	36.00	13	.403	.628	0	—	0	-3	-3	-0	-0.3
● **RANKIN JOHNSON** Johnson, Adam Rankin Jr. b: 3/1/17, Hayden, Ariz. BR/TR, 6'3", 177 lbs. Deb: 4/17/41 F																									
1941 Phi-A	1	0	1.000	7	0	0	0	0	10	14	0	3	0	15.3	3.60	116	.326	.370	0	.000	-0	1	1	0	0.1
● **RANKIN JOHNSON** Johnson, Adam Rankin Sr. "Tex" b: 2/4/1888, Burnet, Tex. d: 7/2/72, Williamsport, Pa. BR/TR, 6'1.5", 185 lbs. Deb: 4/20/14 F																									
1914 Bos-A	4	9	.308	16	13	4	2	0	99^1	92	2	34	24	11.7	3.08	87	.265	.336	4	.133	-1	-4	-4	-2	-0.8
Chi-F	9	5	.643	16	14	12	2	0	120	88	5	29	60	9.1	1.58	187	.209	.267	4	.108	-2	22	18	-1	1.6
1915 Chi-F	2	4	.333	11	6	3	0	1	57	58	2	23	19	12.9	4.42	63	.270	.343	1	.045	-2	-9	-10	-2	-1.5
Bal-F	7	11	.389	23	19	12	2	1	150^2	143	3	58	62	12.1	3.35	95	.255	.326	8	.157	-1	-5	-3	-3	-0.7
Yr	9	15	.375	34	25	15	2	2	207^2	201	5	81	81	12.3	3.64	85	.259	.330	9	.123	-3	-14	-13	-5	-2.2
1918 StL-N	1	1	.500	6	1	0	0	0	23	20	0	7	4	10.6	2.74	99	.263	.325	1	.250	0	0	-0	1	0.1
Total 3	23	30	.434	72	53	31	6	2	450	401	12	151	169	11.2	2.92	101	.248	.315	18	.125	-7	4	1	-7	-1.3
● **ART JOHNSON** Johnson, Arthur Gilbert b: 2/15/1897, Warren, Pa. d: 6/7/82, Sarasota, Fla. BB/TL, 6'1", 167 lbs. Deb: 9/18/27																									
1927 NY-N	0	0	—	1	0	0	0	0	3	1	0	1	0	6.0	0.00	—	.125	.222	0	—	0	1	1	-0	0.1
● **ART JOHNSON** Johnson, Arthur Henry "Lefty" b: 7/16/16, Winchester, Mass. BL/TL, 6'2", 185 lbs. Deb: 9/22/40																									
1940 Bos-N	0	1	.000	2	1	0	0	0	6	10	0	3	1	21.0	10.50	35	.345	.424	0	.000	-0	-4	-5	0	-0.4
1941 Bos-N	7	15	.318	43	18	6	0	1	183^1	189	7	71	70	13.0	3.53	101	.270	.342	8	.145	-2	2	1	0	-0.1
1942 Bos-N	0	0	—	4	0	0	0	0	6^1	4	0	5	0	14.2	1.42	235	.190	.370	0	.000	-0	1	1	-0	0.1
Total 3	7	16	.304	49	19	6	0	1	195^2	203	7	79	71	13.3	3.68	97	.271	.346	8	.140	-2	-1	-2	1	-0.4
● **BEN JOHNSON** Johnson, Benjamin Franklin b: 5/16/31, Greenwood, S.C. BR/TR, 6'2", 190 lbs. Deb: 9/06/59																									
1959 Chi-N	0	0	—	4	2	0	0	0	16^2	17	1	4	6	11.3	2.16	183	.262	.304	0	.000	-0	3	3	-0	0.3
1960 Chi-N	2	1	.667	17	0	0	0	1	29^1	39	3	11	9	15.6	4.91	77	.355	.418	0	.000	-0	-4	-4	1	-0.3
Total 2	2	1	.667	21	2	0	0	1	46	56	4	15	15	14.1	3.91	98	.320	.377	0	.000	-1	-0	-0	0	0.0
● **CHET JOHNSON** Johnson, Chester Lillis "Chesty Chet" b: 8/1/17, Redmond, Wash. d: 4/10/83, Seattle, Wash. BL/TL, 6', 175 lbs. Deb: 9/12/46 F																									
1946 StL-A	0	0	—	5	3	0	0	0	18	20	0	13	8	16.5	5.00	75	.286	.398	0	.000	-1	-3	-3	-1	-0.4
● **BART JOHNSON** Johnson, Clair Barth b: 1/3/50, Torrance, Cal. BR/TR, 6'95", 215 lbs. Deb: 9/08/69																									
1969 Chi-A	1	3	.250	4	3	0	0	0	22^1	22	2	6	18	11.3	3.22	120	.259	.308	1	.167	0	1	2	-0	0.2
1970 Chi-A	4	7	.364	18	15	2	1	0	89^2	92	11	46	71	14.1	4.82	81	.268	.358	8	.276	2	-11	-9	-0	-0.7
1971 Chi-A	12	10	.545	53	16	4	0	14	178	148	9	111	153	13.4	2.93	122	.227	.345	11	.193	0	10	13	-1	1.3
1972 Chi-A	0	3	.000	9	0	0	0	1	13^2	18	2	13	9	21.1	9.22	34	.327	.464	0	.000	-0	-9	-9	0	-1.0
1973 Chi-A	3	3	.500	22	9	0	0	0	80^2	76	6	40	56	13.2	4.13	96	.252	.343	0	—	0	-3	-2	-0	-0.4
1974 Chi-A	10	4	.714	18	18	8	2	0	121^2	105	6	32	76	10.2	2.74	136	.229	.281	0	—	0	12	13	-2	1.2
1976 Chi-A	9	16	.360	32	32	8	3	0	211^1	231	20	62	91	12.5	4.73	75	.282	.334	0	—	0	-28	-27	0	-2.8
1977 Chi-A	4	5	.444	29	4	0	0	2	92	114	5	38	46	15.1	4.01	102	.302	.369	0	—	0	0	1	-0	0.1
Total 8	43	51	.457	185	97	22	6	17	809^1	806	61	348	520	13.0	3.94	95	.261	.339	20	.215	3	-28	-19	-4	-2.1
● **CONNIE JOHNSON** Johnson, Clifford b: 12/27/22, Stone Mountain, Ga BR/TR, 6'4", 200 lbs. Deb: 4/17/53																									
1953 Chi-A	4	4	.500	14	10	2	1	0	60^2	55	4	38	44	14.1	3.56	113	.238	.351	1	.050	-2	3	3	-1	0.1
1955 Chi-A	7	4	.636	17	16	5	2	0	99	95	5	52	72	13.5	3.45	114	.251	.343	5	.152	-1	6	5	-1	0.3
1956 Chi-A	0	1	.000	5	2	0	0	0	12^1	11	1	7	6	13.1	3.65	112	.234	.333	0	.000	-0	1	1	0	0.0
Bal-A	9	10	.474	26	25	9	2	0	183^2	165	12	62	130	11.2	3.43	114	.239	.303	15	.259	3	15	10	-3	1.1
Yr	9	11	.450	31	27	9	2	0	196	176	13	69	136	11.3	3.44	114	.239	.305	15	.246	3	16	11	-3	1.1
1957 Bal-A	14	11	.560	35	30	14	3	0	242	212	17	66	177	10.5	3.20	112	.235	.289	12	.135	-4	16	11	-4	0.3
1958 Bal-A	6	9	.400	26	17	4	0	1	118^1	116	13	32	68	11.3	3.88	93	.260	.310	7	.206	1	-1	-4	-2	-0.5
Total 5	40	39	.506	123	100	34	8	1	716	654	52	257	497	11.5	3.44	109	.243	.310	40	.169	-3	38	26	-10	1.3
● **DAVE JOHNSON** Johnson, David Charles b: 10/4/48, Abilene, Tex. BR/TR, 6'1", 183 lbs. Deb: 7/02/74																									
1974 Bal-A	2	2	.500	11	0	0	0	2	15^1	17	1	5	6	12.9	2.93	118	.274	.328	0	—	0	1	1	-0	0.1
1975 Bal-A	0	1	.000	6	0	0	0	0	8^2	8	0	7	4	15.6	4.15	84	.250	.385	0	—	0	-0	-1	0	0.0
1977 Min-A	2	5	.286	30	6	0	0	0	72^2	86	7	23	33	14.1	4.58	87	.299	.361	0	—	0	-4	-5	0	-0.4
1978 Min-A	0	2	.000	6	1	0	0	0	12	15	1	9	7	18.0	7.50	51	.313	.421	0	—	0	-5	-5	0	-0.5
Total 4	4	10	.286	53	7	0	0	2	108^2	126	9	44	50	14.5	4.64	83	.293	.365	0	—	0	-8	-10	-0	-0.8
● **DAVE JOHNSON** Johnson, David Wayne b: 10/24/59, Baltimore, Md. BR/TR, 5'10", 180 lbs. Deb: 5/29/87																									
1987 Pit-N	0	0	—	5	0	0	0	0	6^1	13	1	2	4	21.3	9.95	41	.448	.484	0	—	0	-4	-4	0	-0.4
1989 Bal-A	4	7	.364	14	14	4	0	0	89^1	90	11	28	26	12.3	4.23	90	.265	.328	0	—	0	-3	-4	-2	-0.6
1990 Bal-A	13	9	.591	30	29	3	0	0	180	196	30	43	68	12.1	4.10	93	.280	.324	0	—	0	-4	-6	-3	-0.9
1991 Bal-A	4	8	.333	22	14	0	0	0	84	127	18	24	38	16.6	7.07	56	.349	.395	0	—	0	-28	-29	-1	-2.8
Total 4	21	24	.467	71	57	7	0	0	359^2	426	60	97	136	13.4	4.93	78	.297	.347	0	—	0	-39	-44	-6	-4.7
● **DON JOHNSON** Johnson, Donald Roy b: 11/12/26, Portland, Ore. BR/TR, 6'3", 200 lbs. Deb: 4/20/47																									
1947 NY-A	4	3	.571	15	8	2	0	0	54^1	57	2	23	16	13.4	3.64	97	.270	.345	0	.000	-1	0	-1	-1	-0.3
1950 NY-A	1	0	1.000	8	0	0	0	0	18	35	2	12	9	23.5	10.00	43	.398	.470	0	.000	-0	-11	-11	-0	-1.1
StL-A	5	6	.455	25	12	4	1	1	96	126	14	55	31	17.1	6.09	81	.325	.410	2	.069	-3	-16	-12	-1	-1.5
Yr	6	6	.500	33	12	4	1	1	114	161	16	67	40	18.1	6.71	72	.338	.421	2	.063	-4	-27	-24	-1	-2.6
1951 StL-A	0	1	.000	6	3	0	0	0	15	27	4	18	8	27.6	12.60	35	.391	.523	1	.333	0	-14	-14	0	-1.2
Was-A	7	11	.389	21	20	8	1	0	143^2	138	9	58	52	12.4	3.95	104	.255	.329	4	.085	-5	3	2	-0	-0.3
Yr	7	12	.368	27	23	8	1	0	158^2	165	13	76	60	13.8	4.76	87	.270	.352	5	.100	-5	-11	-11	-0	-1.5
1952 Was-A	0	5	.000	29	6	0	0	2	69	80	4	33	37	15.3	4.43	80	.287	.370	1	.077	-1	-6	-7	-0	-0.8
1954 Chi-A	8	7	.533	46	16	3	3	7	144	129	14	43	68	10.8	3.13	119	.243	.300	1	.029	-3	10	10	0	0.6
1955 Bal-A	2	4	.333	31	5	0	0	1	68	89	4	35	27	16.4	5.82	65	.333	.411	0	.000	-1	-14	-15	0	-1.6
1958 SF-N	0	1	.000	17	0	0	0	1	23	31	2	8	14	16.0	6.26	61	.323	.387	0	.000	-0	-6	-6	-0	-0.7
Total 7	27	38	.415	198	70	17	5	12	631	712	55	285	262	14.4	4.78	84	.288	.364	9	.058	-16	-54	-55	-2	-6.9
● **EARL JOHNSON** Johnson, Earl Douglas "Lefty" b: 4/2/19, Redmond, Was. BL/TL, 6'3", 190 lbs. Deb: 7/20/40 F																									
1940 Bos-A	6	2	.750	17	10	2	0	0	70^1	69	0	39	26	14.1	4.09	110	.260	.359	2	.074	-3	2	3	1	0.1
1941 Bos-A	4	5	.444	17	12	4	0	0	93^2	90	4	51	46	13.8	4.52	92	.247	.344	10	.294	2	-4	-4	2	0.1
1946 *Bos-A	5	4	.556	29	5	0	0	3	80	78	5	39	40	13.4	3.71	99	.250	.337	5	.227	2	-2	-0	-0	0.1
1947 Bos-A	12	11	.522	45	17	6	3	8	142^1	129	7	62	65	12.2	2.97	131	.246	.328	12	.273	1	12	14	2	1.9
1948 Bos-A	10	4	.714	35	3	1	0	5	91^1	98	7	42	45	13.8	4.53	97	.276	.353	3	.097	-3	-2	-1	2	-0.2
1949 Bos-A	3	6	.333	19	3	0	0	0	49^1	65	1	29	20	17.9	7.48	58	.327	.422	0	.000	-1	-18	-17	-1	-1.8

YEAR TM/L	W	L	PCT	G	GS	CG	SH	SV	IP	H	HR	BB	SO	RAT	ERA	ERA+	OAV	OOB	BH	AVG	PB	PR	/A	PD	TPI
1950 Bos-A	0	0	—	11	0	0	0	0	13^2	18	0	8	6	17.8	7.24	68	.333	.429	0	.000	-0	-4	-4	1	-0.3
1951 Det-A	0	0	—	6	0	0	0	1	5^2	9	0	2	2	17.5	6.35	66	.375	.423	0	—	0	-1	-1	0	-0.1
Total 8	40	32	.556	179	50	13	3	17	546^1	556	24	272	250	13.9	4.30	96	.265	.353	32	.187	-2	-18	-10	7	-0.2

● WALT JOHNSON Johnson, Ellis Walter b: 12/8/1892, Minneapolis, Minn. d: 1/4/65, Minneapolis, Minn. BR/TR, 6'0.5", 180 lbs. Deb: 7/06/12

YEAR TM/L	W	L	PCT	G	GS	CG	SH	SV	IP	H	HR	BB	SO	RAT	ERA	ERA+	OAV	OOB	BH	AVG	PB	PR	/A	PD	TPI
1912 Chi-A	0	0	—	3	0	0	0	0	11^2	11	0	7	7	14.7	3.86	83	.262	.380	0	.000	-0	-1	-1	-0	-0.1
1915 Chi-A	0	0	—	1	0	0	0	0	2	3	0	0	3	13.5	9.00	33	.333	.333	0	—	0	-1	-1	-0	-0.1
1917 Phi-A	0	2	.000	4	2	0	0	0	13^2	15	0	5	8	13.2	7.24	38	.294	.357	0	.000	0	-7	-7	0	-0.6
Total 3	0	2	.000	8	2	0	0	0	27^1	29	0	12	18	13.8	5.93	50	.284	.365	0	.000	0	-9	-9	-0	-0.8

● ERNIE JOHNSON Johnson, Ernest Thorwald b: 6/16/24, Brattleboro, Vt. BR/TR, 6'4", 195 lbs. Deb: 4/28/50

YEAR TM/L	W	L	PCT	G	GS	CG	SH	SV	IP	H	HR	BB	SO	RAT	ERA	ERA+	OAV	OOB	BH	AVG	PB	PR	/A	PD	TPI
1950 Bos-N	2	0	1.000	16	1	0	0	0	20^2	37	1	13	15	21.8	6.97	55	.394	.467	1	.500	0	-6	-7	1	-0.5
1952 Bos-N	6	3	.667	29	10	2	1	1	92	100	7	31	45	13.0	4.11	88	.270	.329	2	.091	-0	-4	-5	1	-0.4
1953 Mil-N	4	3	.571	36	1	0	0	0	81	79	4	22	36	11.6	2.67	147	.263	.320	1	.071	-1	15	11	0	1.0
1954 Mil-N	5	2	.714	40	4	1	0	2	99^1	77	11	34	68	10.1	2.81	133	.219	.290	3	.231	0	14	10	1	1.2
1955 Mil-N	5	7	.417	40	2	0	0	4	92	81	5	55	43	13.5	3.42	110	.240	.349	2	.100	-1	6	3	-0	0.2
1956 Mil-N	4	3	.571	36	0	0	0	6	51	54	9	21	26	13.4	3.71	93	.270	.342	1	.250	0	0	-1	0	-0.1
1957 *Mil-N	7	3	.700	30	0	0	0	4	65	67	9	26	44	13.0	3.88	90	.265	.336	6	.353	3	0	-3	1	0.1
1958 Mil-N	3	1	.750	15	0	0	0	1	23^1	35	4	10	13	17.7	8.10	43	.357	.422	0	.000	0	-11	-12	0	-1.1
1959 Bal-A	4	1	.800	31	1	0	0	1	50^1	57	6	19	29	14.1	4.11	92	.286	.357	2	.333	0	-1	-2	0	-0.1
Total 9	40	23	.635	273	19	3	1	19	574^2	587	56	231	319	13.0	3.77	98	.266	.340	18	.180	2	13	-5	5	0.3

● FRED JOHNSON Johnson, Frederick Edward "Deacon" or "Cactus" b: 3/10/1894, Tolar, Tex. d: 6/14/73, Kerrville, Tex. BR/TR, 6', 185 lbs. Deb: 9/27/22

YEAR TM/L	W	L	PCT	G	GS	CG	SH	SV	IP	H	HR	BB	SO	RAT	ERA	ERA+	OAV	OOB	BH	AVG	PB	PR	/A	PD	TPI
1922 NY-N	0	2	.000	2	2	1	0	0	18	20	3	1	8	10.5	4.00	100	.294	.304	0	.000	-1	0	0	-0	-0.1
1923 NY-N	2	0	1.000	3	2	1	0	0	17	11	2	7	5	9.5	4.24	90	.177	.261	0	.000	-1	-0	-1	1	-0.1
1938 StL-A	3	7	.300	17	6	3	0	3	69	91	7	27	24	15.5	5.61	89	.316	.377	6	.240	-0	-6	-5	-2	-0.6
1939 StL-A	0	1	.000	5	2	1	0	0	14	23	0	9	2	20.6	6.43	76	.383	.464	0	.000	-1	-3	-2	1	-0.2
Total 4	5	10	.333	27	12	6	0	3	118	145	12	44	39	14.5	5.26	88	.303	.363	6	.154	-2	-9	-8	0	-1.0

● CHIEF JOHNSON Johnson, George Howard "Murphy" or "Big Murph"
b: 3/30/1886, Winnebago, Neb. d: 6/11/22, Des Moines, Iowa BR/TR, 5'11.5", 190 lbs. Deb: 4/16/13

YEAR TM/L	W	L	PCT	G	GS	CG	SH	SV	IP	H	HR	BB	SO	RAT	ERA	ERA+	OAV	OOB	BH	AVG	PB	PR	/A	PD	TPI
1913 Cin-N	14	16	.467	44	31	13	3	0	269	251	8	86	107	11.5	3.01	108	.256	.320	10	.114	-3	6	7	0	0.5
1914 Cin-N	0	0	—	1	1	0	0	0	4	6	0	2	1	18.0	6.75	43	.333	.400	0	—	0	-2	-2	-0	-0.2
KC-F	9	10	.474	20	19	12	2	0	134	157	2	33	78	13.0	3.16	98	.298	.345	6	.122	-1	1	-1	-3	-0.5
1915 KC-F	17	17	.500	46	34	19	4	2	281^1	253	5	71	118	10.6	2.75	106	.242	.295	11	.126	-2	9	5	2	0.6
Total 3	40	43	.482	111	85	44	9	2	688^1	667	15	192	304	11.5	2.95	104	.259	.315	27	.121	-6	14	10	-1	0.4

● HANK JOHNSON Johnson, Henry Ward b: 5/21/06, Bradenton, Fla. d: 8/20/82, Bradenton, Fla. BR/TR, 5'11.5", 175 lbs. Deb: 4/17/25

YEAR TM/L	W	L	PCT	G	GS	CG	SH	SV	IP	H	HR	BB	SO	RAT	ERA	ERA+	OAV	OOB	BH	AVG	PB	PR	/A	PD	TPI
1925 NY-A	1	3	.250	24	4	2	1	0	67	88	3	37	25	17.9	6.85	62	.319	.414	1	.059	-1	-18	-19	1	-1.8
1926 NY-A	0	0	—	1	0	0	0	1	1	2	0	2	0	36.0	18.00	21	.400	.571	0	—	0	-2	-2	-0	-0.1
1928 NY-A	14	9	.609	31	22	10	1	0	199	188	16	104	110	13.7	4.30	88	.250	.351	19	.241	1	-6	-12	0	-1.0
1929 NY-A	3	3	.500	12	8	2	0	0	42^2	37	5	39	24	16.0	5.06	76	.237	.390	1	.071	-1	-4	-6	-1	-0.7
1930 NY-A	14	11	.560	44	15	7	1	2	175^1	177	12	104	115	14.5	4.67	92	.265	.366	17	.266	5	-0	-7	2	-0.1
1931 NY-A	13	8	.619	40	23	8	0	4	196^1	176	13	102	106	12.8	4.72	84	.234	.326	15	.195	2	-7	-16	-3	-1.7
1932 NY-A	2	2	.500	5	4	2	0	0	31^1	34	7	15	27	14.1	4.88	83	.266	.343	3	.231	0	-1	-3	0	-0.2
1933 Bos-A	8	6	.571	25	21	7	0	1	155^1	156	13	74	65	13.5	4.06	108	.263	.348	12	.231	3	4	6	-2	0.7
1934 Bos-A	6	8	.429	31	14	7	1	1	124^1	162	12	53	66	15.9	5.36	90	.316	.385	10	.233	1	-12	-8	-1	-0.7
1935 Bos-A	2	1	.667	13	2	0	0	1	31	41	3	14	14	16.0	5.52	86	.331	.399	0	.000	-1	-4	-3	-1	-0.5
1936 Phi-A	0	2	.000	3	3	0	0	0	11^2	16	4	10	6	20.8	7.71	66	.296	.415	1	.250	-0	-3	-3	-0	-0.3
1939 Cin-N	0	3	.000	20	0	0	0	1	31^1	30	1	13	10	12.4	2.01	191	.268	.344	2	.400	1	7	6	-1	0.6
Total 12	63	56	.529	249	116	45	4	11	1066^1	1107	89	567	568	14.4	4.75	88	.268	.361	81	.215	9	-47	-67	-6	-5.8

● JIM JOHNSON Johnson, James Brian b: 11/3/45, Muskegon, Mich. BL/TL, 5'11", 175 lbs. Deb: 4/13/70

YEAR TM/L	W	L	PCT	G	GS	CG	SH	SV	IP	H	HR	BB	SO	RAT	ERA	ERA+	OAV	OOB	BH	AVG	PB	PR	/A	PD	TPI
1970 SF-N	1	0	1.000	3	0	0	0	0	6^2	8	0	5	2	17.6	8.10	49	.320	.433	0	.000	0	-3	-3	0	-0.3

● JERRY JOHNSON Johnson, Jerry Michael b: 12/3/43, Miami, Fla. BR/TR, 6'3", 200 lbs. Deb: 7/17/68

YEAR TM/L	W	L	PCT	G	GS	CG	SH	SV	IP	H	HR	BB	SO	RAT	ERA	ERA+	OAV	OOB	BH	AVG	PB	PR	/A	PD	TPI
1968 Phi-N	4	4	.500	16	11	2	0	0	80^2	82	5	29	40	12.6	3.24	93	.264	.330	2	.080	-0	-2	-2	1	-0.2
1969 Phi-N	6	13	.316	33	21	4	2	1	147^1	151	18	57	82	12.9	4.28	83	.268	.338	9	.209	2	-11	-12	-1	-1.1
1970 StL-N	2	0	1.000	7	0	0	0	1	11^1	6	1	3	5	7.1	3.18	130	.146	.205	0	.000	0	1	1	-0	0.1
SF-N	3	4	.429	33	1	0	0	3	65^1	67	5	38	44	14.6	4.27	93	.266	.364	1	.067	-1	-2	-2	-0	-0.4
Yr	5	4	.556	40	1	0	0	4	76^2	73	6	41	49	13.5	4.11	97	.249	.343	1	.063	-1	-1	-1	-1	-0.3
1971 *SF-N	12	9	.571	67	0	0	0	18	109	93	9	48	85	11.7	2.97	114	.230	.313	2	.154	-0	6	5	-0	0.5
1972 SF-N	8	6	.571	48	0	0	0	8	73^1	73	4	40	57	13.9	4.42	79	.261	.353	0	.000	-1	-8	-8	0	-0.9
1973 Cle-A	5	6	.455	39	1	0	0	5	59^2	70	7	39	45	16.4	6.18	63	.299	.399	0	—	0	-16	-15	0	-1.6
1974 Hou-N	2	1	.667	34	0	0	0	0	45	47	2	24	32	14.2	4.80	72	.276	.366	0	.000	-0	-6	-7	0	-0.7
1975 SD-N	3	1	.750	21	4	0	0	0	54	60	3	31	18	15.2	5.17	67	.282	.373	1	.083	-0	-9	-10	-1	-1.1
1976 SD-N	1	3	.250	24	1	0	0	0	39	39	0	26	27	15.0	5.31	62	.260	.369	0	.000	-0	-8	-9	-0	-1.0
1977 Tor-A	2	4	.333	43	0	0	0	5	86	91	9	54	54	15.2	4.60	91	.279	.382	0	—	0	-5	-4	-0	-0.4
Total 10	48	51	.485	365	39	6	2	41	770^2	779	63	389	489	13.7	4.31	83	.265	.352	15	.123	-2	-60	-62	-1	-6.8

● JOHNNY JOHNSON Johnson, John Clifford "Swede" b: 9/29/14, Belmore, Ohio d: 6/26/91, Iron Mountain, Mich. BL/TL, 6', 182 lbs. Deb: 4/19/44

YEAR TM/L	W	L	PCT	G	GS	CG	SH	SV	IP	H	HR	BB	SO	RAT	ERA	ERA+	OAV	OOB	BH	AVG	PB	PR	/A	PD	TPI
1944 NY-A	0	2	.000	22	1	0	0	3	26^2	25	0	24	11	16.9	4.05	86	.243	.391	3	.500	1	-2	-2	-1	-0.1
1945 Chi-A	3	0	1.000	29	0	0	0	4	69^2	85	2	35	38	15.6	4.26	78	.306	.385	4	.286	2	-7	-7	-1	-0.7
Total 2	3	2	.600	51	1	0	0	7	96^1	110	2	59	49	16.0	4.20	80	.289	.387	7	.350	3	-9	-9	-2	-0.8

● YOUNGY JOHNSON Johnson, John Godfred b: 7/22/1877, San Francisco, Cal. d: 8/28/36, Berkeley, Cal. TR , Deb: 4/29/1897

YEAR TM/L	W	L	PCT	G	GS	CG	SH	SV	IP	H	HR	BB	SO	RAT	ERA	ERA+	OAV	OOB	BH	AVG	PB	PR	/A	PD	TPI
1897 Phi-N	1	2	.333	5	2	1	0	0	29	39	0	12	7	16.4	4.66	90	.319	.389	1	.077	-2	-1	-1	-0	-0.3
1899 NY-N	0	0	—	1	0	0	0	0	2	0	0	2	1	9.0	0.00	—	.000	.260	0	.000	-0	1	1	0	0.1
Total 2	1	2	.333	6	2	1	0	0	31	39	0	14	8	16.0	4.35	96	.305	.382	1	.071	-2	-0	-1	-0	-0.2

● JOHN HENRY JOHNSON Johnson, John Henry b: 8/21/56, Houston, Tex. BL/TL, 6'2", 190 lbs. Deb: 4/10/78

YEAR TM/L	W	L	PCT	G	GS	CG	SH	SV	IP	H	HR	BB	SO	RAT	ERA	ERA+	OAV	OOB	BH	AVG	PB	PR	/A	PD	TPI
1978 Oak-A	11	10	.524	33	30	7	2	0	186	164	18	82	91	11.9	3.39	107	.238	.319	0	—	0	8	5	-3	0.3
1979 Oak-A	2	8	.200	14	13	1	0	0	84^2	89	13	36	50	13.4	4.36	93	.269	.342	0	—	0	-1	-3	-1	-0.2
Tex-A	2	6	.250	17	12	1	0	0	82^1	79	12	36	46	12.7	4.92	84	.255	.334	0	—	0	-6	-7	-1	-0.7
Yr	4	14	.222	31	25	2	0	0	167	168	25	72	96	13.0	4.63	88	.261	.336	0	—	0	-8	-10	-1	-0.9
1980 Tex-A	2	2	.500	33	0	0	0	4	38^2	27	2	15	44	10.0	2.33	167	.199	.283	0	—	0	7	7	0	0.7
1981 Tex-A	3	1	.750	24	0	0	0	2	23^2	19	2	6	8	9.9	2.66	130	.232	.292	0	—	0	3	2	1	0.5
1983 Bos-A	3	2	.600	34	1	0	0	1	53^1	58	3	20	51	13.3	3.71	117	.283	.350	0	—	0	2	4	-0	0.3
1984 Bos-A	1	2	.333	30	3	0	0	1	63^2	64	7	27	57	12.9	3.53	118	.260	.333	0	—	0	3	4	-0	0.2
1986 Mil-A	2	1	.667	19	0	0	0	1	44	43	2	10	42	10.8	2.66	163	.251	.293	0	—	0	7	8	-1	0.6
1987 Mil-A	0	1	.000	10	2	0	0	0	26^1	42	1	18	18	20.5	9.57	48	.365	.451	0	—	0	-15	-15	0	-1.3
Total 8	26	33	.441	214	61	9	2	9	602^2	585	60	250	407	12.5	3.90	102	.256	.331	0	—	0	8	6	-5	0.4

● JOHN JOHNSON Johnson, John Louis (b: John Louis Mercer) b: 11/18/1869, Pekin, Ill. d: 1/28/41, Kansas City, Mo. TL , 165 lbs. Deb: 9/11/1894

YEAR TM/L	W	L	PCT	G	GS	CG	SH	SV	IP	H	HR	BB	SO	RAT	ERA	ERA+	OAV	OOB	BH	AVG	PB	PR	/A	PD	TPI
1894 Phi-N	1	1	.500	4	3	2	0	0	32^2	44	3	15	10	16.5	6.06	84	.319	.389	3	.188	-1	-3	-3	0	-0.3

YEAR	TM/L	W	L	PCT	G	GS	CG	SH	SV	IP	H	HR	BB	SO	RAT	ERA	ERA+	OAV	OOB	BH	AVG	PB	PR	/A	PD	TPI
● **JOE JOHNSON** Johnson, Joseph Richard b: 10/30/61, Brookline, Mass. BR/TR, 6'2", 195 lbs. Deb: 7/25/85																										
1985	Atl-N	4	4	.500	15	14	1	0	0	85^2	95	9	24	34	12.8	4.10	94	.285	.339	1	.043	-1	-5	-2	-2	-0.5
1986	Atl-N	6	7	.462	17	15	2	0	0	87	101	8	35	49	14.3	4.97	80	.289	.358	3	.115	-1	-12	-10	2	-0.9
	Tor-A	7	2	.778	16	15	0	0	0	88	94	3	22	39	12.2	3.89	109	.281	.331	0	—	0	3	3	-1	0.1
1987	Tor-A	3	5	.375	14	14	0	0	0	66^2	77	10	18	27	13.1	5.13	88	.289	.339	0	—	0	-5	-5	-0	-0.5
Total	3	20	18	.526	62	58	3	0	0	327^1	367	30	99	149	13.1	4.48	92	.286	.342	4	.082	-2	-19	-13	-2	-1.8
● **KEN JOHNSON** Johnson, Kenneth Travis b: 6/16/33, W.Palm Beach, Fla. BR/TR, 6'4", 210 lbs. Deb: 9/13/58																										
1958	KC-A	0	0	—	2	0	0	0	0	2^1	6	1	3	1	34.7	27.00	14	.429	.529	0	—	0	-6	-6	0	-0.5
1959	KC-A	1	1	.500	2	2	0	0	0	11	11	2	5	8	13.1	4.09	98	.268	.348	0	.000	-0	-0	-0	0	0.0
1960	KC-A	5	10	.333	42	6	2	0	3	120^1	120	16	45	83	12.9	4.26	93	.263	.338	5	.167	-1	-5	-4	2	-0.3
1961	KC-A	0	4	.000	6	1	0	0	0	9^1	11	2	7	4	17.4	10.61	39	.297	.409	0	.000	-0	-7	-7	1	-0.6
	*Cin-N	6	2	.750	15	11	3	1	1	83	71	11	22	42	10.3	3.25	125	.229	.284	6	.240	1	7	7	1	1.0
1962	Hou-N	7	16	.304	33	31	5	1	0	197	195	18	46	178	11.3	3.84	97	.257	.305	4	.077	-3	2	-2	1	-0.4
1963	Hou-N	11	17	.393	37	32	6	1	1	224	204	12	50	148	10.5	2.65	119	.242	.291	5	.068	-4	16	12	2	1.3
1964	Hou-N	11	16	.407	35	35	7	1	0	218	209	15	44	117	10.7	3.63	94	.250	.293	6	.079	-2	-2	-5	1	-0.6
1965	Hou-N	3	2	.600	8	8	1	0	0	51^2	52	4	11	28	11.7	4.18	80	.267	.319	2	.111	-0	-4	-5	1	-0.4
	Mil-N	13	8	.619	29	26	8	1	2	179^2	165	15	37	123	10.3	3.21	110	.240	.282	7	.115	-2	7	6	-3	0.2
	Yr	16	10	.615	37	34	9	1	2	231^1	217	19	48	151	10.4	3.42	102	.244	.285	9	.114	-2	3	2	-2	-0.2
1966	Atl-N	14	8	.636	32	31	11	2	0	215^2	213	24	46	105	10.8	3.30	110	.262	.301	10	.143	0	7	8	0	0.9
1967	Atl-N	13	9	.591	29	29	6	0	0	210^1	191	19	38	85	10.1	2.74	121	.244	.285	9	.127	-0	15	14	-2	1.3
1968	Atl-N	5	8	.385	31	16	1	0	0	135	145	10	25	57	11.9	3.47	86	.279	.324	7	.175	-0	-7	-7	-1	-0.9
1969	Atl-N	0	1	.000	9	2	0	0	1	29	32	4	9	20	12.7	4.97	73	.283	.336	0	.000	-0	-4	-4	0	-0.5
	NY-A	1	2	.333	12	0	0	0	0	26	19	1	11	21	10.4	3.46	100	.202	.286	0	.000	-0	0	0	1	0.1
	Chi-N	1	2	.333	9	1	0	0	1	19	17	2	13	18	14.2	2.84	142	.230	.345	0	.000	-0	2	2	-0	0.2
1970	Mon-N	0	0	—	3	0	0	0	0	6	9	1	1	4	18.0	7.50	55	.321	.387	0	—	0	-2	-2	0	-0.2
Total	13	91	106	.462	334	231	50	7	9	1737^1	1670	157	413	1042	11.1	3.46	101	.253	.302	61	.114	-12	18	8	5	0.6
● **KEN JOHNSON** Johnson, Kenneth Wandersee "Hook" b: 1/14/23, Topeka, Kan. BL/TL, 6'1", 185 lbs. Deb: 9/18/47																										
1947	StL-N	1	0	1.000	2	1	1	0	0	10	2	0	5	8	7.2	0.00	—	.063	.211	2	.500	1	5	5	0	0.6
1948	StL-N	2	4	.333	13	4	0	0	0	45^1	43	1	30	20	14.7	4.76	86	.262	.379	6	.300	2	-4	-3	-0	-0.2
1949	StL-N	0	1	.000	14	2	0	0	0	33^2	29	1	35	18	17.9	6.42	65	.250	.435	2	.250	0	-9	-8	1	-0.7
1950	StL-N	0	0	—	2	0	0	0	0	2	1	0	3	1	18.0	0.00	—	.167	.444	0	—	0	1	1	0	0.1
	*Phi-N	4	1	.800	14	8	3	1	0	60^2	61	3	43	32	15.6	4.01	101	.260	.376	3	.158	-0	1	0	0	0.0
	Yr	4	1	.800	16	8	3	1	0	62^2	62	3	46	33	15.7	3.88	105	.257	.378	3	.158	-0	2	1	0	0.1
1951	Phi-N	5	8	.385	20	18	4	3	0	106^1	103	8	68	58	14.7	4.57	84	.259	.371	5	.143	-1	-7	-9	-0	-1.0
1952	Det-A	0	0	—	9	1	0	0	0	11^1	12	1	11	10	18.3	6.35	60	.273	.418	1	.333	0	-3	-3	0	-0.3
Total	6	12	14	.462	74	34	8	4	0	269^1	251	14	195	147	15.2	4.58	87	.252	.379	19	.213	1	-17	-18	1	-1.5
● **LLOYD JOHNSON** Johnson, Lloyd William "Eppa" b: 12/24/10, Santa Rosa, Cal. d: 10/8/80, Stockton, Cal. BL/TL, 6'4", 204 lbs. Deb: 4/21/34																										
1934	Pit-N	0	0	—	1	0	0	0	0	1	1	0	0	0	9.0	0.00	—	.333	.333	0	—	0	0	0	-0	0.0
● **MIKE JOHNSON** Johnson, Michael Norton b: 3/2/51, Slayton, Minn. BR/TR, 6'1", 185 lbs. Deb: 7/25/74																										
1974	SD-N	0	2	.000	18	0	0	0	0	21^1	29	1	15	15	19.0	4.64	77	.326	.429	0	—	0	-2	-3	-0	-0.3
● **RANDY JOHNSON** Johnson, Randall David b: 9/10/63, Walnut Creek, Cal. BR/TL, 6'10", 225 lbs. Deb: 9/15/88																										
1988	Mon-N	3	0	1.000	4	4	1	0	0	26	23	3	7	25	10.4	2.42	148	.225	.275	1	.111	-0	3	3	-1	0.2
1989	Mon-N	0	4	.000	7	6	0	0	0	29^2	29	2	26	26	16.7	6.67	53	.264	.404	1	.143	-0	-10	-10	-0	-1.0
	Sea-A	7	9	.438	22	22	2	0	0	131	118	11	70	104	13.1	4.40	92	.244	.344	0	—	0	-7	-5	0	-0.6
1990	Sea-A☆	14	11	.560	33	33	5	2	0	219^2	174	26	120	194	12.3	3.65	109	.216	.321	0	—	0	6	8	-1	0.6
1991	Sea-A	13	10	.565	33	33	2	1	0	201^1	151	15	152	228	14.1	3.98	104	.213	.361	0	—	0	3	3	-1	0.2
1992	Sea-A	12	14	.462	31	31	6	2	0	210^1	154	13	144	**241**	13.5	3.77	106	**.206**	.347	0	—	0	4	5	-1	0.4
Total	5	49	48	.505	130	129	16	5	0	818	649	70	519	818	13.3	3.95	101	.219	.343	2	.125	-1	-2	4	-4	-0.2
● **BOB JOHNSON** Johnson, Robert Dale b: 4/25/43, Aurora, Ill. BL/TR, 6'4", 220 lbs. Deb: 9/19/69																										
1969	NY-N	0	0	—	2	0	0	0	1	1^2	1	0	1	1	10.8	0.00	—	.167	.286	0	—	0	1	1	-0	0.1
1970	KC-A	8	13	.381	40	26	10	1	4	214	178	18	82	206	11.4	3.07	122	.228	.310	6	.105	-1	15	16	-1	1.5
1971	*Pit-N	9	10	.474	31	27	7	1	0	174^2	170	19	55	101	12.0	3.45	98	.259	.323	3	.063	-1	0	-1	-1	-0.4
1972	*Pit-N	4	4	.500	31	11	1	0	3	115^2	98	14	46	79	11.5	2.96	112	.231	.312	5	.143	-0	6	5	-2	0.3
1973	Pit-N	4	2	.667	50	2	0	0	4	92	98	12	34	68	13.4	3.62	97	.276	.348	0	.000	-1	0	-1	-2	-0.5
1974	Cle-A	3	4	.429	14	10	0	0	0	72	75	12	37	36	14.4	4.38	83	.273	.365	0	—	0	-6	-6	-0	-0.6
1977	Atl-N	0	1	.000	15	0	0	0	0	22^1	24	7	14	16	16.1	7.25	61	.270	.381	1	.333	0	-8	-7	-1	-0.7
Total	7	28	34	.452	183	76	18	2	12	692^1	644	82	269	507	12.3	3.48	102	.249	.327	15	.096	-3	9	6	-7	-0.3
● **ROY JOHNSON** Johnson, Roy J "Hardrock" b: 10/1/1895, Madill, Okla. d: 1/10/86, Scottsdale, Ariz. BR/TR, 6', 185 lbs. Deb: 8/07/18 MC																										
1918	Phi-A	1	5	.167	10	8	3	0	0	50	47	0	34	12	14.9	3.42	86	.254	.376	1	.067	-2	-4	-3	-0	-0.5
● **JING JOHNSON** Johnson, Russell Conwell b: 10/9/1894, Parker Ford, Pa. d: 12/6/50, Pottstown, Pa. BR/TR, 5'9", 172 lbs. Deb: 6/27/16																										
1916	Phi-A	2	8	.200	12	12	8	0	0	84^1	90	3	39	25	13.8	3.74	76	.288	.368	2	.074	-1	-8	-8	3	-0.7
1917	Phi-A	9	12	.429	34	23	13	0	0	191	184	3	56	55	11.5	2.78	99	.260	.319	12	.203	2	-2	-1	2	0.4
1919	Phi-A	9	15	.375	34	25	12	0	0	202	222	8	62	67	12.8	3.61	95	.291	.346	14	.194	0	-9	-4	5	0.1
1927	Phi-A	4	2	.667	17	3	2	0	0	51^2	42	2	16	16	10.8	3.48	122	.235	.312	2	.167	-1	4	4	1	0.5
1928	Phi-A	0	0	—	3	0	0	0	0	10^2	13	1	5	3	15.2	5.06	79	.310	.383	2	.500	1	-1	-1	0	0.0
Total	5	24	37	.393	100	63	35	0	0	539^2	551	17	178	166	12.4	3.35	95	.275	.338	32	.184	2	-17	-10	10	0.3
● **SI JOHNSON** Johnson, Silas Kenneth b: 10/5/06, Marseilles, Ill. BR/TR, 5'11.5", 185 lbs. Deb: 5/02/28																										
1928	Cin-N	0	0	—	3	0	0	0	0	10^1	9	0	5	1	12.2	4.35	91	.250	.341	1	.250	0	-0	-0	0	0.0
1929	Cin-N	0	0	—	1	0	0	0	0	2	2	0	1	0	13.5	4.50	101	.250	.333	0	—	0	0	0	-0	0.0
1930	Cin-N	3	1	.750	35	3	0	0	0	78^1	86	5	31	47	13.9	4.94	98	.286	.360	4	.235	-0	0	-1	-0	-0.1
1931	Cin-N	11	19	.367	42	33	14	0	0	262^1	273	5	74	95	12.1	3.77	99	.269	.323	13	.149	-3	3	-1	-5	-0.8
1932	Cin-N	13	15	.464	42	27	14	2	2	245	246	8	57	94	11.2	3.27	118	.259	.302	10	.125	-4	17	16	-0	1.2
1933	Cin-N	7	18	.280	34	28	14	4	1	211^1	212	7	54	51	11.5	3.49	97	.263	.312	3	.042	-7	-4	-2	-1	-1.1
1934	Cin-N	7	22	.241	46	31	9	0	3	215^2	264	15	84	89	14.8	5.22	78	.297	.362	10	.139	-3	-28	-27	-3	-3.1
1935	Cin-N	5	11	.313	30	20	4	1	0	130	155	14	59	40	15.0	6.23	64	.293	.367	1	.024	-4	-32	-33	-1	-3.4
1936	Cin-N	0	0	—	2	0	0	0	0	4	7	1	0	2	15.8	13.50	28	.368	.368	0	—	0	-4	-4	-0	-0.4
	StL-N	5	3	.625	12	9	3	1	0	61^2	82	4	11	21	13.7	4.38	90	.314	.344	4	.190	-0	-2	-3	-1	-0.4
	Yr	5	3	.625	14	9	3	1	0	65^2	89	5	11	23	13.8	4.93	80	.318	.346	4	.190	-0	-7	-7	-1	-0.8
1937	StL-N	12	12	.500	38	21	12	1	1	192^1	222	14	43	64	12.4	3.32	120	.292	.330	9	.138	-3	13	14	-2	1.0
1938	StL-N	0	3	.000	6	3	0	0	0	15^2	27	0	6	4	19.0	7.47	53	.380	.429	0	.000	-0	-6	-6	0	-0.6
1940	Phi-N	5	14	.263	37	14	5	0	1	138^1	145	13	42	58	12.3	4.88	80	.268	.323	6	.140	-2	-16	-15	-2	-1.9
1941	Phi-N	5	12	.294	39	21	6	1	2	163^1	207	8	54	80	14.4	4.52	82	.309	.362	7	.149	-2	-16	-15	-1	-1.7
1942	Phi-N	8	19	.296	39	26	10	1	0	195^1	198	6	72	78	12.5	3.69	90	.266	.332	6	.103	-4	-8	-8	-3	-1.5
1943	Phi-N	8	3	.727	21	14	9	1	2	113	110	4	25	46	10.8	3.27	103	.252	.292	6	.182	0	1	1	-0	0.1
1946	Phi-N	0	0	—	1	0	0	0	0	3	7	1	0	2	21.0	3.00	114	.538	.538	1	1.000	0	0	0	-0	0.1
	Bos-N	6	5	.545	28	12	5	1	1	127	134	8	35	41	12.3	2.76	124	.272	.325	5	.135	-2	9	9	-1	0.7

YEAR	TM/L	W	L	PCT	G	GS	CG	SH	SV	IP	H	HR	BB	SO	RAT	ERA	ERA+	OAV	OOB	BH	AVG	PB	PR	/A	PD	TPI
	Yr	6	5	.545	29	12	5	1	1	130	141	9	35	43	12.5	2.77	124	.279	.330	6	.158	-1	9	10	-1	0.8
1947	Bos-N	6	8	.429	36	10	3	0	2	112^2	124	7	34	27	12.7	4.23	92	.275	.327	1	.033	-3	-2	-4	3	-0.4
Total	17	101	165	.380	492	272	108	13	15	2281^1	2510	120	687	840	12.8	4.09	92	.279	.333	87	.123	-37	-76	-79	-17	-12.3

● SYL JOHNSON Johnson, Sylvester W b: 12/31/1900, Portland, Ore. d: 2/20/85, Portland, Ore. BR/TR, 5'11", 180 lbs. Deb: 4/24/22 C

1922	Det-A	7	3	.700	29	8	3	0	1	97	99	7	30	29	12.3	3.71	105	.273	.336	8	.222	0	4	2	-2	0.0
1923	Det-A	12	7	.632	37	18	7	0	0	176^1	181	12	47	93	11.8	3.98	97	.274	.325	10	.161	-1	0	-2	-5	-0.8
1924	Det-A	5	4	.556	29	9	2	0	3	104	117	8	42	55	14.2	4.93	83	.287	.360	7	.206	-0	-8	-9	-1	-1.0
1925	Det-A	0	2	.000	6	0	0	0	0	13	11	1	10	5	14.5	3.46	124	.250	.389	0	.000	-1	1	1	0	0.1
1926	StL-N	0	3	.000	19	6	1	0	1	49	54	3	15	10	13.0	4.22	92	.297	.357	0	.000	-2	-2	-2	-1	-0.4
1927	StL-N	0	0	—	2	0	0	0	0	3	3	1	0	2	9.0	6.00	66	.250	.250	0	—	0	-1	-1	0	-0.1
1928	*StL-N	8	4	.667	34	6	2	0	3	120	117	6	33	66	11.6	3.90	102	.259	.315	6	.158	-0	1	1	-1	0.0
1929	StL-N	13	7	.650	42	19	12	3	3	182^1	186	11	56	80	12.3	3.60	129	.265	.325	7	.117	-2	23	21	-4	1.4
1930	*StL-N	12	10	.545	32	24	9	2	2	187^2	215	13	38	92	12.3	4.65	108	.293	.332	15	.214	-0	7	8	-3	0.3
1931	*StL-N	11	9	.550	32	24	12	2	2	186	186	9	29	82	10.5	3.00	131	.255	.286	14	.233	2	18	19	-3	1.8
1932	StL-N	5	14	.263	32	22	7	0	2	164^2	199	14	35	70	13.0	4.92	80	.299	.338	10	.196	-1	-19	-18	-1	-1.9
1933	StL-N	3	3	.500	35	1	0	0	3	84	89	7	16	28	11.6	4.29	81	.271	.311	5	.238	0	-9	-8	-2	-0.9
1934	Cin-N	0	0	—	2	0	0	0	0	6^2	9	2	0	0	12.2	2.70	151	.310	.310	1	.500	1	1	1	-0	0.2
	Phi-N	5	9	.357	42	10	4	3	3	133^2	122	14	24	54	9.9	3.50	135	.242	.277	8	.195	-1	8	18	-4	1.4
	Yr	5	9	.357	44	10	4	3	3	140^1	131	16	24	54	10.0	3.46	136	.245	.279	9	.209	1	9	19	-4	1.6
1935	Phi-N	10	8	.556	37	18	8	1	6	174^2	182	15	31	89	11.1	3.56	128	.265	.299	14	.241	2	9	19	-3	1.8
1936	Phi-N	5	7	.417	39	8	1	0	7	111	129	10	29	48	13.1	4.30	106	.288	.335	9	.250	-0	-3	3	-2	0.1
1937	Phi-N	4	10	.286	32	15	4	0	3	138	155	20	22	46	11.7	5.02	86	.288	.318	7	.146	-3	-17	-11	-1	-1.4
1938	Phi-N	2	7	.222	22	6	2	0	0	83	87	4	11	21	10.6	4.23	92	.267	.291	1	.034	-3	-4	-3	-2	-0.8
1939	Phi-N	8	8	.500	22	14	6	0	2	111	112	10	15	37	10.4	3.81	105	.264	.291	5	.152	-1	1	2	-1	0.0
1940	Phi-N	2	2	.500	17	2	2	0	2	40^2	37	6	5	13	9.3	4.20	93	.236	.259	0	.000	-1	-2	-1	-0	-0.3
Total	19	112	117	.489	542	210	82	11	43	2165^2	2290	173	488	920	11.7	4.06	104	.273	.316	127	.181	-10	8	43	-36	-0.5

● TOM JOHNSON Johnson, Thomas Raymond b: 4/2/51, St.Paul, Minn. BR/TR, 6'1", 185 lbs. Deb: 9/10/74

1974	Min-A	2	0	1.000	4	0	0	0	1	7	4	0	0	4	5.1	0.00	—	.167	.167	0	—	0	3	3	-0	0.3
1975	Min-A	1	2	.333	18	0	0	0	3	38^2	40	4	21	17	14.7	4.19	92	.263	.360	0	—	0	-2	-1	0	-0.2
1976	Min-A	3	1	.750	18	1	0	0	0	48^1	44	2	8	37	9.7	2.61	138	.243	.275	0	—	0	5	5	0	0.5
1977	Min-A	16	7	.696	71	0	0	0	15	146^2	152	11	47	87	12.5	3.13	127	.272	.334	0	—	0	15	14	1	1.5
1978	Min-A	1	4	.200	18	0	0	0	3	32^2	42	2	17	21	16.8	5.51	69	.318	.404	0	—	0	-6	-6	0	-0.6
Total	5	23	14	.622	129	1	0	0	22	273^1	282	19	93	166	12.6	3.39	114	.269	.334	0	—	0	15	15	1	1.5

● VIC JOHNSON Johnson, Victor Oscar b: 8/3/20, Eau Claire, Wis. BR/TL, 6', 160 lbs. Deb: 5/03/44

1944	Bos-A	0	3	.000	7	5	0	0	0	27^1	42	0	15	7	18.8	6.26	54	.362	.435	0	.000	-1	-9	-9	1	-0.9
1945	Bos-A	6	4	.600	26	9	4	1	2	85^1	90	4	46	21	14.6	4.01	85	.276	.369	5	.167	-1	-6	-6	1	-0.6
1946	Cle-A	0	1	.000	9	1	0	0	0	13^2	20	1	8	3	18.4	9.22	36	.357	.438	0	.000	-0	-9	-9	1	-0.9
Total	3	6	8	.429	42	15	4	1	2	126^1	152	5	69	31	15.9	5.06	67	.305	.392	5	.119	-3	-23	-23	2	-2.4

● WALTER JOHNSON Johnson, Walter Perry "Barney" or "The Big Train"
b: 11/6/1887, Humboldt, Kan. d: 12/10/46, Washington, D.C. BR/TR, 6'1", 200 lbs. Deb: 8/02/07 MH♦

1907	Was-A	5	9	.357	14	12	11	2	0	110^1	100	1	20	71	10.0	1.88	129	.244	.284	4	.111	-2	8	7	-2	0.3
1908	Was-A	14	14	.500	36	30	23	6	1	257^1	194	0	53	160	9.0	1.64	139	.211	.262	13	.165	2	22	18	-4	2.0
1909	Was-A	13	25	.342	40	36	27	4	1	297	247	1	84	164	10.5	2.21	110	.221	.284	13	.129	-2	9	7	-2	0.3
1910	Was-A	25	17	.595	**45**	42	**38**	8	1	**374**	269	1	76	**313**	8.6	1.35	185	.210	.262	24	.175	1	49	**48**	-1	5.7
1911	Was-A	25	13	.658	40	37	**36**	**6**	1	323^1	292	8	70	207	10.3	1.89	174	.238	.283	30	.234	3	**52**	**50**	4	**6.0**
1912	Was-A	33	12	.733	50	37	34	7	2	368	259	2	76	**303**	**8.6**	**1.39**	**239**	**.196**	**.248**	38	.264	9	**79**	**79**	1	**10.0**
1913	Was-A	**36**	7	**.837**	48	36	**29**	**11**	2	**346**	232	9	38	**243**	**7.3**	**1.14**	**258**	**.187**	**.217**	35	.261	10	**69**	**70**	0	**9.7**
1914	Was-A	**28**	18	.609	**51**	40	**33**	**9**	1	**371^2**	287	3	74	**225**	9.0	1.72	164	.217	.265	30	.221	8	42	**45**	2	**6.6**
1915	Was-A	**27**	13	.675	47	39	**35**	**7**	4	**336^2**	258	1	56	**203**	**8.9**	1.55	**192**	.214	**.260**	34	.231	6	**52**	**53**	2	**7.1**
1916	Was-A	**25**	20	.556	48	38	**36**	3	1	**371**	290	0	82	**228**	9.2	1.89	148	.220	.270	32	.225	8	39	**37**	-5	4.7
1917	Was-A	23	16	.590	47	34	30	8	3	328	248	3	68	**188**	9.1	2.20	120	.211	.263	33	.254	10	17	16	-1	2.8
1918	Was-A	**23**	13	.639	39	29	29	**8**	3	325	241	2	70	**162**	**8.8**	**1.27**	**214**	.210	**.260**	40	.267	6	**54**	**53**	-3	**7.4**
1919	Was-A	20	14	.588	39	29	27	**7**	2	290^1	235	0	51	**147**	9.1	**1.49**	**216**	**.219**	**.259**	24	.192	2	**56**	**56**	0	**6.7**
1920	Was-A	8	10	.444	21	15	12	4	3	143^2	135	5	27	78	10.5	3.13	119	.245	.286	17	.266	4	11	10	-1	1.2
1921	Was-A	17	14	.548	35	32	25	1	1	264	265	7	92	**143**	12.2	3.51	117	.263	.326	30	.270	4	23	18	-3	1.8
1922	Was-A	15	16	.484	41	31	23	4	4	280	283	8	99	105	12.5	2.99	129	.267	.334	22	.204	-1	33	27	1	2.7
1923	Was-A	17	12	.586	42	34	18	3	4	261^1	263	9	73	**130**	12.3	3.48	108	.269	.333	18	.194	1	15	8	-2	0.7
1924	*Was-A	**23**	7	**.767**	38	38	20	**6**	0	277^2	233	10	77	**158**	**10.4**	**2.72**	148	**.224**	**.284**	32	.283	6	**47**	41	-1	**4.6**
1925	*Was-A	20	7	.741	30	29	16	3	0	229	211	7	78	108	11.6	3.07	138	**.243**	.311	42	.433	16	34	30	-4	**4.1**
1926	Was-A	15	16	.484	33	33	22	2	0	261^2	259	13	73	125	11.6	3.61	107	.263	.317	20	.194	1	12	7	-5	0.3
1927	Was-A	5	6	.455	18	15	7	1	0	107^2	113	7	26	48	12.2	5.10	80	.278	.332	16	.348	6	-11	-12	0	-0.6
Total	21	417	279	.599	802	666	531	110	34	5923^2	4914	97	1363	3509	9.8	2.16	147	.227	.279	547	.235	97	709	671	-23	84.1

● BILL JOHNSON Johnson, William C. b: 10/6/60, Wilmington, Del. BR/TR, 6'5", 205 lbs. Deb: 9/06/83

1983	Chi-N	1	0	1.000	10	0	0	0	0	12^1	17	0	3	4	14.6	4.38	87	.347	.385	0	—	0	-1	-1	0	0.0
1984	Chi-N	0	0	—	4	0	0	0	0	5^1	4	0	1	3	8.4	1.69	232	.235	.278	0	—	0	1	1	0	0.2
Total	2	1	0	1.000	14	0	0	0	0	17^2	21	0	4	7	12.7	3.57	107	.318	.357	0	—	0	0	1	1	0.2

● JEFF JOHNSON Johnson, William Jeffrey b: 8/4/66, Durham, N.C. BR/TL, 6'3", 200 lbs. Deb: 6/05/91

1991	NY-A	6	11	.353	23	23	0	0	0	127	156	15	33	62	13.8	5.95	70	.305	.354	0	—	0	-26	-26	1	-2.4
1992	NY-A	2	3	.400	13	8	0	0	0	52^2	71	4	23	14	16.4	6.66	61	.329	.398	0	—	0	-16	-15	-0	-1.6
Total	2	8	14	.364	36	31	0	0	0	179^2	227	19	56	76	14.6	6.16	67	.312	.367	0	—	0	-42	-41	1	-4.0

● JOEL JOHNSTON Johnston, Joel Raymond b: 3/8/67, West Chester, Pa. BR/TR, 6'4", 220 lbs. Deb: 9/05/91

1991	KC-A	1	0	1.000	13	0	0	0	0	22^1	9	0	9	21	7.3	0.40	1022	.120	.214	0	—	0	9	9	-0	0.9
1992	KC-A	0	0	—	5	0	0	0	0	2^2	3	2	2	0	16.9	13.50	29	.273	.385	0	—	0	-3	-3	-0	-0.3
Total	2	1	0	1.000	18	0	0	0	0	25	12	2	11	21	8.3	1.80	228	.140	.237	0	—	0	6	6	-0	0.6

● ROY JOINER Joiner, Roy Merrill "Pop" b: 10/30/06, Red Bluff, Cal. d: 12/26/89, Red Bluff, Cal. BL/TL, 6', 170 lbs. Deb: 4/30/34

1934	Chi-N	0	1	.000	20	2	0	0	0	34	61	3	8	9	18.3	8.21	47	.391	.421	2	.200	-0	-16	-16	-0	-1.6
1935	Chi-N	0	0	—	2	0	0	0	0	3^1	6	0	2	0	21.6	5.40	73	.429	.500	0	.000	-0	-1	-1	0	0.0
1940	NY-N	3	2	.600	30	2	0	0	1	53	66	8	17	25	14.9	3.40	114	.308	.373	3	.273	1	3	3	0	0.4
Total	3	3	3	.500	52	4	0	0	1	90^1	133	11	27	34	16.4	5.28	74	.346	.397	5	.227	0	-13	-14	0	-1.2

● DAVE JOLLY Jolly, David "Gabby" b: 10/14/24, Stony Point, N.C. d: 5/27/63, Durham, N.C. BR/TR, 6', 165 lbs. Deb: 5/09/53

1953	Mil-N	0	1	.000	24	0	0	0	0	38^1	34	4	27	23	14.6	3.52	111	.239	.365	1	.500	1	3	2	0	0.2
1954	Mil-N	11	6	.647	47	1	0	0	10	111^1	87	6	64	62	12.4	2.43	154	.215	.326	9	.290	3	20	16	0	2.0
1955	Mil-N	2	3	.400	36	0	0	0	1	58^1	58	6	51	23	17.0	5.71	66	.258	.397	1	.167	0	-11	-13	1	-1.1
1956	Mil-N	2	3	.400	29	0	0	0	7	45^2	39	7	35	20	14.6	3.74	92	.228	.359	0	.000	-0	0	-1	-1	-0.3
1957	Mil-N	1	1	.500	23	0	0	0	1	37^2	37	4	21	27	14.6	5.02	70	.264	.372	3	.600	1	-5	-6	0	-0.5
Total	5	16	14	.533	159	1	0	0	19	291^1	255	27	198	155	14.2	3.77	98	.236	.357	14	.292	5	8	-3	0	0.3

YEAR	TM/L	W	L	PCT	G	GS	CG	SH	SV	IP	H	HR	BB	SO	RAT	ERA	ERA+	OAV	OOB	BH	AVG	PB	PR	/A	PD	TPI
● COWBOY JONES	Jones, Albert Edward "Bronco" b: 8/23/1874, Golden, Colo. d: 2/9/58, Inglewood, Cal. BL/TL, 5'11", 160 lbs. Deb: 6/24/1898																									
1898	Cle-N	4	4	.500	9	9	7	0	0	72	76	0	29	26	13.6	3.00	121	.269	.345	2	.071	-3	5	5	-2	0.1
1899	StL-N	6	5	.545	12	12	9	0	0	85^1	111	1	22	28	14.7	3.59	111	.314	.364	5	.172	0	3	4	2	0.5
1900	StL-N	13	19	.406	39	36	29	3	0	292^2	334	10	82	68	13.4	3.57	102	.286	.343	21	.179	-3	4	2	5	0.4
1901	StL-N	2	6	.250	10	9	7	0	0	76^1	97	4	22	25	14.4	4.48	71	.307	.358	4	.148	0	-10	-11	2	-0.9
Total	4	25	34	.424	70	66	52	3	0	526^1	618	15	155	147	13.8	3.63	100	.292	.349	32	.159	-5	2	-0	6	0.1
● ALEX JONES	Jones, Alexander b: 12/25/1869, Pittsburgh, Pa. d: 4/4/41, Woodville, Pa. BL/TL, 5'6", 135 lbs. Deb: 9/25/1889																									
1889	Pit-N	1	0	1.000	1	1	1	0	0	9	7	0	1	10	8.0	3.00	125	.208	.231	1	.200	0	1	1	0	0.1
1892	Lou-N	5	11	.313	18	16	13	1	0	146^2	130	3	56	44	12.0	3.31	93	.228	.307	8	.145	-1	-0	-4	2	-0.3
	Was-N	0	3	.000	4	4	3	0	0	27	33	0	14	7	16.3	4.00	81	.290	.377	3	.273	0	-2	-2	-1	-0.2
	Yr	5	14	.263	22	20	16	1	0	173^2	163	3	70	51	12.2	3.42	91	.235	.307	11	.167	-1	-3	-6	1	-0.5
1894	Phi-N	1	0	1.000	1	1	1	0	0	9	10	0	0	2	10.0	2.00	255	.278	.278	1	.250	-0	3	3	0	0.2
1903	Det-A	0	1	.000	2	2	0	0	0	8^2	19	0	6	2	26.0	12.46	23	.435	.503	0	.000	-1	-9	-9	-0	-0.8
Total	4	7	15	.318	26	24	18	1	0	200^1	199	3	77	65	12.9	3.73	86	.250	.324	13	.165	-1	-7	-12	1	-1.0
● AL JONES	Jones, Alfornia b: 2/10/59, Charleston, Miss. BR/TR, 6'4", 210 lbs. Deb: 8/06/83																									
1983	Chi-A	0	0	—	2	0	0	0	0	2^1	3	0	2	2	19.3	3.86	109	.375	.500	0	—	0	0	0	-0	0.0
1984	Chi-A	1	1	.500	20	0	0	0	5	20^1	23	3	11	15	15.5	4.43	94	.299	.393	0	—	0	-1	-1	0	-0.3
1985	Chi-A	1	0	1.000	5	0	0	0	0	6	3	0	3	2	9.0	1.50	288	.167	.286	0	—	0	2	2	0	0.2
Total	3	2	1	.667	27	0	0	0	5	28^2	29	3	16	19	14.4	3.77	111	.282	.383	0	—	0	1	1	0	-0.1
● ART JONES	Jones, Arthur Lennox b: 2/7/06, Kershaw, S.C. d: 11/25/80, Columbia, S.C. BR/TR, 6', 165 lbs. Deb: 4/23/32																									
1932	Bro-N	0	0	—	1	0	0	0	0	1	2	0	1	0	27.0	18.00	21	.667	.750	0	—	0	-2	-2	0	-0.1
● BARRY JONES	Jones, Barry Louis b: 2/15/63, Centerville, Ind. BR/TR, 6'4", 225 lbs. Deb: 7/18/86																									
1986	Pit-N	3	4	.429	26	0	0	0	3	37^1	29	3	21	29	12.1	2.89	132	.215	.321	1	.200	0	3	4	1	0.5
1987	Pit-N	2	4	.333	32	0	0	0	1	43^1	55	6	23	28	16.2	5.61	73	.314	.394	0	.000	-0	-7	-7	0	-0.7
1988	Pit-N	1	1	.500	42	0	0	0	2	56^1	57	3	21	31	12.6	3.04	112	.271	.341	0	.000	-0	3	2	0	0.2
	Chi-A	2	2	.500	17	0	0	0	1	26	15	3	17	17	11.1	2.42	164	.170	.305	0	—	0	4	4	0	0.5
1989	Chi-A	3	2	.600	22	0	0	0	1	30^1	22	2	8	17	9.2	2.37	160	.208	.270	0	—	0	5	5	1	0.6
1990	Chi-A	11	4	.733	65	0	0	0	1	74	62	2	33	45	11.7	2.31	165	.235	.322	0	—	0	13	12	2	1.6
1991	Mon-N	4	9	.308	**77**	0	0	0	13	88^2	76	8	33	46	11.2	3.35	108	.246	.321	0	.000	-0	3	3	1	0.4
1992	Phi-N	5	6	.455	44	0	0	0	0	54^1	65	3	24	19	15.1	4.64	75	.305	.381	0	.000	-0	-7	-7	1	-0.7
	NY-N	2	0	1.000	17	0	0	0	1	15^1	20	0	11	11	18.2	9.39	37	.317	.419	0	—	0	-10	-10	0	-1.0
	Yr	7	6	.538	61	0	0	0	1	69^2	85	3	35	30	15.5	5.68	62	.304	.381	0	.000	-0	-17	-17	1	-1.7
Total	7	33	32	.508	342	0	0	0	23	425^2	401	30	191	243	12.6	3.57	104	.257	.340	1	.063	-1	8	6	5	1.4
● CALVIN JONES	Jones, Calvin Douglas b: 9/26/63, Compton, Cal. BR/TR, 6'3", 185 lbs. Deb: 6/14/91																									
1991	Sea-A	2	2	.500	27	0	0	0	2	46^1	33	0	29	42	12.2	2.53	163	.209	.335	0	—	0	8	8	0	0.9
1992	Sea-A	3	5	.375	38	1	0	0	0	61^2	50	8	47	49	14.4	5.69	70	.226	.367	0	—	0	-12	-12	-0	-1.2
Total	2	5	7	.417	65	1	0	0	2	108	83	8	76	91	13.5	4.33	93	.219	.354	0	—	0	-4	-3	0	-0.3
● DEACON JONES	Jones, Carroll Elmer b: 12/20/1892, Arcadia, Kan. d: 12/28/52, Pittsburg, Kan. BR/TR, 6'1", 174 lbs. Deb: 9/23/16																									
1916	Det-A	0	0	—	1	0	0	0	0	7	7	0	5	2	15.4	2.57	111	.269	.387	0	.000	-0	0	0	-0	0.0
1917	Det-A	4	4	.500	24	6	2	0	0	77	69	0	26	28	11.8	2.92	91	.256	.334	0	.000	-1	-2	-2	1	-0.2
1918	Det-A	3	1	.750	21	4	1	0	0	67	60	0	38	15	13.3	3.09	86	.244	.347	5	.185	-1	-2	-3	1	-0.3
Total	3	7	5	.583	46	10	3	0	0	151	136	0	69	45	12.6	2.98	89	.251	.343	5	.114	-2	-4	-5	2	-0.5
● BUMPUS JONES	Jones, Charles Leander b: 1/1/1870, Cedarville, Ohio d: 6/25/38, Xenia, Ohio BR/TR, Deb: 10/15/1892																									
1892	Cin-N	1	0	1.000	1	1	1	0	0	9	0	0	4	3	4.0	0.00	—	.000	.129	0	.000	-0	3	3	-1	0.3
1893	Cin-N	1	3	.250	6	5	2	0	0	28^2	37	1	23	6	20.4	10.05	48	.304	.434	4	.250	1	-17	-17	-1	-1.3
	NY-N	0	1	.000	1	1	0	0	0	4	5	0	10	1	36.0	11.25	41	.297	.575	0	—	0	-3	-3	1	-0.2
	Yr	1	4	.200	7	6	2	0	0	32^2	42	1	33	7	20.9	10.19	47	.292	.428	4	.250	1	-20	-20	-0	-1.5
Total	2	2	4	.333	8	7	3	0	0	41^2	42	1	37	10	18.4	7.99	56	.254	.407	4	.222	1	-17	-16	-1	-1.2
● CHARLEY JONES	Jones, Charles Wesley "Baby" (b: Benjamin Wesley Rippay) b: 4/30/1850, Alamance Co., N.C. BR/TR, 5'11.5", 202 lbs. Deb: 5/04/1875 U♦																									
1887	NY-a	0	0	—	2	0	0	0	0	3	2	0	4	0	18.0	3.00	142	.286	.545	63	.255	0	0	0	-0	0.0
● DALE JONES	Jones, Dale Eldon "Nubs" b: 12/17/18, Marquette, Neb. d: 11/8/80, Orlando, Fla. BR/TR, 6'1", 172 lbs. Deb: 9/07/41																									
1941	Phi-N	0	1	.000	2	1	0	0	0	8^1	13	0	6	2	20.5	7.56	49	.342	.432	1	.333	1	-4	-4	-1	-0.3
● JACK JONES	Jones, Daniel Albion "Jumping Jack" b: 10/23/1860, Litchfield, Conn. d: 10/19/36, Wallingford, Conn. TR , Deb: 7/09/1883																									
1883	Det-N	6	5	.545	12	12	9	1	0	92^2	103	0	19	33	11.8	3.50	89	.259	.293	8	.190	-2	-4	-4	-2	-0.6
	Phi-a	5	2	.714	7	7	7	0	0	65	58	1	6	28	8.9	2.63	133	.223	.241	6	.240	0	5	6	-0	0.5
Total	1	11	7	.611	19	19	16	1	0	157^2	161	1	25	61	10.6	3.14	104	.245	.273	14	.209	-1	1	2	-2	-0.1
● DICK JONES	Jones, Decatur Poindexter b: 5/22/02, Meadville, Miss. BL/TR, 6', 184 lbs. Deb: 9/11/26																									
1926	Was-A	2	1	.667	4	3	1	0	0	21	20	0	11	3	13.3	4.29	90	.263	.356	2	.200	-0	-1	-1	0	-0.1
1927	Was-A	0	0	—	2	0	0	0	0	3^1	8	0	5	1	35.1	21.60	19	.444	.565	0	—	0	-6	-6	-0	-0.5
Total	2	2	1	.667	6	3	1	0	0	24^1	28	0	16	4	16.3	6.66	58	.298	.400	2	.200	-0	-7	-7	-0	-0.6
● DOUG JONES	Jones, Douglas Reid b: 6/24/57, Lebanon, Ind. BR/TR, 6'3", 195 lbs. Deb: 4/09/82																									
1982	Mil-A	0	0	—	4	0	0	0	0	2^2	5	1	1	1	20.3	10.13	37	.385	.429	0	—	0	-2	-2	0	-0.2
1986	Cle-A	1	0	1.000	11	0	0	0	1	18	18	0	6	12	12.5	2.50	166	.257	.325	0	—	0	3	3	0	0.4
1987	Cle-A	6	5	.545	49	0	0	0	8	91^1	101	4	24	87	12.9	3.15	143	.281	.336	0	—	0	13	14	1	1.4
1988	Cle-A★	3	4	.429	51	0	0	0	37	83^1	69	1	16	72	9.4	2.27	181	.218	.260	0	—	0	16	17	0	1.8
1989	Cle-A★	7	10	.412	59	0	0	0	32	80^2	76	4	13	65	10.0	2.34	169	.251	.284	0	—	0	14	14	1	1.5
1990	Cle-A☆	5	5	.500	66	0	0	0	43	84^1	66	5	22	55	9.6	2.56	153	.218	.275	0	—	0	13	13	-1	1.2
1991	Cle-A	4	8	.333	36	4	0	0	7	63^1	87	7	17	48	14.8	5.54	75	.320	.360	0	—	0	-10	-10	1	-0.9
1992	Hou-N★	11	8	.579	80	0	0	0	36	111^2	96	5	17	93	9.5	1.85	180	.235	.274	0	.000	-0	20	18	-1	1.9
Total	8	37	40	.481	356	4	0	0	164	535^1	518	27	116	433	10.9	2.82	140	.253	.299	0	.000	-0	67	68	0	7.1
● EARL JONES	Jones, Earl Leslie "Lefty" b: 6/11/19, Fresno, Cal. d: 1/24/89, Fresno, Cal. BL/TL, 5'10.5", 190 lbs. Deb: 7/06/45																									
1945	StL-A	0	0	—	10	0	0	0	1	28^1	18	0	18	13	11.4	2.54	139	.184	.310	2	.200	1	3	3	-1	0.4
● ELIJAH JONES	Jones, Elijah Albert "Bumpus" b: 1/27/1882, Oxford, Mich. d: 4/29/43, Pontiac, Mich. BR/TR, Deb: 4/13/07																									
1907	Det-A	0	1	.000	4	1	1	0	1	16	23	0	4	9	15.8	5.06	52	.338	.383	0	.000	-1	-4	-4	-0	-0.5
1909	Det-A	1	1	.500	2	2	0	0	0	10	10	0	0	2	9.0	2.70	93	.278	.278	1	.250	0	-0	-0	-0	-0.1
Total	2	1	2	.333	6	3	1	0	1	26	33	0	4	11	13.2	4.15	62	.317	.349	1	.125	-0	-5	-5	-1	-0.6
● GARY JONES	Jones, Gareth Howell b: 6/12/45, Huntington Park, Cal. BL/TL, 6', 191 lbs. Deb: 9/25/70 F																									
1970	NY-A	0	0	—	2	0	0	0	0	2	3	0	1	2	18.0	0.00	—	.375	.444	0	—	0	1	1	-0	0.1
1971	NY-A	0	0	—	12	0	0	0	0	14	19	1	7	10	16.7	9.00	36	.317	.388	0	.000	-0	-9	-9	-0	-1.0
Total	2	0	0	—	14	0	0	0	0	16	22	1	8	12	16.9	7.88	41	.324	.395	0	.000	-0	-8	-8	-0	-0.9

YEAR TM/L	W	L	PCT	G	GS	CG	SH	SV	IP	H	HR	BB	SO	RAT	ERA	ERA+	OAV	OOB	BH	AVG	PB	PR	/A	PD	TPI

● **GORDON JONES**   Jones, Gordon Bassett b: 4/2/30, Portland, Ore.   BR/TR, 6′, 190 lbs.   Deb: 8/06/54 C

1954 StL-N	4	4	.500	11	10	4	2	0	81	78	3	19	48	10.9	2.00	206	.248	.293	3	.125	-1	19	19	-0	2.0
1955 StL-N	1	4	.200	15	9	0	0	0	57	66	10	28	46	15.0	5.84	70	.286	.365	1	.071	-1	-11	-11	-1	-1.3
1956 StL-N	0	2	.000	5	1	0	0	0	11¹	14	2	5	6	15.1	5.56	68	.311	.380	0	.000	-0	-2	-2	-0	-0.3
1957 NY-N	0	1	.000	10	0	0	0	0	11²	16	1	3	5	15.4	6.17	64	.320	.370	1	.500	0	-3	-3	-1	-0.3
1958 SF-N	3	1	.750	11	1	0	0	1	30¹	33	2	5	8	11.6	2.37	161	.284	.320	0	.000	-1	5	5	1	0.5
1959 SF-N	3	2	.600	31	0	0	0	2	43²	45	6	19	29	13.4	4.33	88	.280	.359	0	.000	-0	-2	-3	-0	-0.3
1960 Bal-A	1	1	.500	29	0	0	0	2	55	59	9	13	30	11.9	4.42	86	.281	.326	2	.400	1	-3	-4	-0	-0.3
1961 Bal-A	0	0	—	3	0	0	0	1	5	5	3	0	4	9.0	5.40	72	.250	.250	0	—	0	-1	-1	-0	-0.1
1962 KC-A	3	2	.600	21	0	0	0	6	32²	31	10	14	28	12.4	6.34	66	.252	.328	0	.000	-1	-9	-8	-0	-0.9
1964 Hou-N	0	1	.000	34	0	0	0	0	50	58	3	14	28	13.0	4.14	83	.290	.336	1	.250	0	-3	-4	-0	-0.4
1965 Hou-N	0	0	—	1	0	0	0	0	1	0	0	0	0	0.0	0.00	—	.000	.000	0	—	0	0	0	-0	0.0
Total 11	15	18	.455	171	21	4	2	12	378²	405	49	120	232	12.6	4.16	94	.275	.332	8	.119	-3	-10	-11	-2	-1.4

● **HENRY JONES**   Jones, Henry M. "Baldy" b: Cadillac, Mich.   Deb: 8/20/1884 ♦

| 1890 Pit-N | 2 | 1 | .667 | 5 | 4 | 2 | 0 | 0 | 31 | 35 | 1 | 14 | 13 | 14.2 | 3.48 | 95 | .276 | .348 | 2 | .222 | -0 | 0 | -1 | -1 | -0.1 |

● **JIMMY JONES**   Jones, James Condia b: 4/20/64, Dallas, Tex.   BR/TR, 6′2″, 190 lbs.   Deb: 9/21/86

1986 SD-N	2	0	1.000	3	3	1	1	0	18	10	1	3	15	6.5	2.50	146	.164	.203	1	.167	-0	2	2	-0	0.2
1987 SD-N	9	7	.563	30	22	2	1	0	145²	154	14	54	51	13.2	4.14	96	.270	.339	8	.163	1	-1	-3	1	0.0
1988 SD-N	9	14	.391	29	29	3	0	0	179	192	14	44	82	12.0	4.12	82	.277	.323	9	.164	2	-13	-14	1	-1.2
1989 NY-A	2	1	.667	11	6	0	0	0	48	56	7	16	25	13.9	5.25	74	.293	.354	0	—	0	-7	-7	-0	-0.6
1990 NY-A	1	2	.333	17	7	0	0	0	50	72	8	23	25	17.3	6.30	63	.344	.412	0	—	0	-13	-13	-1	-1.3
1991 Hou-N	6	8	.429	26	22	1	1	0	135¹	143	9	51	88	13.1	4.39	80	.270	.337	7	.184	2	-11	-13	1	-1.1
1992 Hou-N	10	6	.625	25	23	0	0	0	139¹	135	13	39	69	11.6	4.07	82	.258	.315	6	.167	1	-9	-11	-1	-1.0
Total 7	39	38	.506	141	112	7	3	0	715¹	762	66	230	355	12.7	4.35	83	.274	.334	31	.168	7	-52	-60	4	-5.0

● **JIM JONES**   Jones, James Tilford "Sheriff" b: 12/25/1876, London, Ky.   d: 5/6/53, London, Ky.   BR/TR, 5′10″, 162 lbs.   Deb: 6/29/1897 ♦

1897 Lou-N	0	0	—	1	0	0	0	0	6²	19	1	5	0	35.1	18.90	23	.498	.576	1	.250	1	-11	-11	-0	-0.7
1901 NY-N	0	1	.000	1	1	1	0	0	5	6	0	2	3	14.4	10.80	31	.295	.358	19	.209	0	-4	-4	0	-0.3
Total 2	0	1	.000	2	1	1	0	0	11²	25	1	7	3	26.2	15.43	25	.428	.504	79	.230	1	-15	-15	-0	-1.0

● **JEFF JONES**   Jones, Jeffrey Allen b: 7/29/56, Detroit, Mich.   BR/TR, 6′3″, 210 lbs.   Deb: 4/10/80

1980 Oak-A	1	3	.250	35	0	0	0	5	44¹	32	2	26	34	12.0	2.84	133	.204	.321	0	—	0	6	5	1	0.6
1981 *Oak-A	4	1	.800	33	0	0	0	3	61	51	7	40	43	13.9	3.39	102	.233	.359	0	—	0	2	1	-1	0.0
1982 Oak-A	3	1	.750	18	2	0	0	0	37	44	6	26	18	17.3	5.11	76	.306	.415	0	—	0	-4	-5	-0	-0.5
1983 Oak-A	1	1	.500	13	1	0	0	0	29²	43	7	8	14	16.1	5.76	67	.339	.387	0	—	0	-6	-6	-0	-0.6
1984 Oak-A	0	3	.000	13	0	0	0	0	33	31	4	12	19	11.7	3.55	106	.258	.326	0	—	0	2	1	0	0.4
Total 5	9	9	.500	112	3	0	0	8	205	201	26	112	128	14.0	3.95	94	.262	.361	0	—	0	-1	-5	-0	-0.1

● **BROADWAY JONES**   Jones, Jesse Frank b: 11/15/1898, Millsboro, Del.   d: 9/7/77, Lewes, Del.   BR/TR, 5′9″, 154 lbs.   Deb: 7/04/23

| 1923 Phi-N | 0 | 0 | — | 3 | 0 | 0 | 0 | 0 | 8 | 5 | 0 | 7 | 1 | 13.5 | 9.00 | 51 | .185 | .353 | 1 | .500 | 0 | -4 | -4 | -0 | -0.3 |

● **JOHNNY JONES**   Jones, John Paul "Admiral" b: 8/25/1892, Arcadia, La.   d: 6/5/80, Ruston, La.   BR/TR, 6′1″, 151 lbs.   Deb: 4/24/19

1919 NY-N	0	0	—	2	0	0	0	1	6²	9	0	3	3	17.6	5.40	52	.310	.394	0	.000	-0	-2	-2	0	-0.2
1920 Bos-N	1	0	1.000	3	1	0	0	0	9²	16	1	5	6	19.6	6.52	47	.372	.438	1	.250	1	-4	-4	0	-0.3
Total 2	1	0	1.000	5	1	0	0	1	16¹	25	1	8	9	18.7	6.06	49	.347	.420	1	.143	0	-5	-6	0	-0.5

● **STACY JONES**   Jones, Joseph Stacy b: 5/26/67, Gadsden, Ala.   BR/TR, 6′6″, 225 lbs.   Deb: 7/30/91

| 1991 Bal-A | 0 | 0 | — | 4 | 0 | 0 | 0 | 0 | 11 | 11 | 1 | 5 | 10 | 13.1 | 4.09 | 97 | .256 | .333 | 0 | — | 0 | 0 | -0 | 0 | 0.3 |

● **KEN JONES**   Jones, Kenneth Frederick "Broadway" b: 4/13/03, Dover, N.J.   d: 5/15/91, Hartford, Conn.   BR/TR, 6′3″, 193 lbs.   Deb: 5/19/24

1924 Det-A	0	0	—	1	0	0	0	0	2	1	0	4	0	9.0	0.00	—	.143	.250	0	—	0	1	1	-0	0.1
1930 Bos-N	0	1	.000	8	1	0	0	0	19²	28	1	4	4	14.6	5.95	83	.359	.390	1	.200	-0	-2	-2	0	-0.2
Total 2	0	1	.000	9	1	0	0	0	21²	29	1	8	4	14.1	5.40	90	.341	.378	1	.200	0	-1	-1	0	-0.1

● **MIKE JONES**   Jones, Michael b: Hamilton, Ont., Canada   d: 3/24/1894, Hamilton, Ont., Can   BL/TL,   Deb: 8/12/1890

| 1890 Lou-a | 2 | 0 | 1.000 | 3 | 3 | 2 | 0 | 0 | 29 | 29 | 9 | 6 | 12.3 | 3.27 | 118 | .244 | .315 | 4 | .444 | 2 | 1 | 1 | -0 | 0.3 |

● **MIKE JONES**   Jones, Michael Carl b: 7/30/59, Penfield, N.Y.   BL/TL, 6′6″, 215 lbs.   Deb: 9/06/80

1980 KC-A	0	1	.000	3	1	0	0	0	4²	6	0	5	2	21.2	11.57	35	.333	.478	0	—	0	-4	-4	-0	-0.4
1981 *KC-A	6	3	.667	12	11	0	0	0	75²	74	7	28	29	12.4	3.21	112	.256	.326	0	—	0	4	3	0	0.4
1984 *KC-A	2	3	.400	23	12	0	0	0	81	86	10	36	43	13.7	4.89	82	.270	.346	0	—	0	-8	-8	-1	-0.9
1985 KC-A	3	3	.500	33	1	0	0	0	64	62	6	39	32	14.2	4.78	87	.257	.361	0	—	0	-5	-4	-0	-0.4
Total 4	11	10	.524	71	25	0	0	0	225¹	228	23	108	106	13.5	4.43	88	.263	.347	0	—	0	-13	-13	-1	-1.3

● **ODELL JONES**   Jones, Odell b: 1/13/53, Tulare, Cal.   BR/TR, 6′3″, 175 lbs.   Deb: 9/11/75

1975 Pit-N	0	0	—	2	0	0	0	0	3	1	0	0	2	3.0	0.00	—	.100	.100	0	—	0	1	1	0	0.1
1977 Pit-N	3	7	.300	34	15	1	0	0	108	118	14	31	66	12.7	5.08	78	.278	.332	4	.143	-1	-14	-13	-2	-1.6
1978 Pit-N	2	0	1.000	3	1	0	0	0	10	10	1	0	11	11.0	2.00	185	.206	.289	0	.000	-0	2	2	-0	0.2
1979 Sea-A	3	11	.214	25	19	3	0	0	118²	151	16	58	72	16.1	6.07	72	.317	.395	0	—	0	-24	-23	-2	-2.3
1981 Pit-N	4	5	.444	13	8	0	0	0	54¹	51	3	23	30	12.3	3.31	108	.250	.326	2	.200	-0	1	2	0	0.2
1983 Tex-A	3	6	.333	42	0	0	0	10	67	56	4	22	50	10.7	3.09	130	.223	.291	0	—	0	7	7	-1	0.6
1984 Tex-A	2	4	.333	33	0	0	0	2	59¹	62	7	23	28	13.2	3.64	114	.281	.354	0	—	0	2	3	1	0.4
1986 Bal-A	2	2	.500	21	0	0	0	0	49¹	58	4	23	32	14.8	3.83	108	.305	.380	0	—	0	0	0	0	0.1
1988 Mil-A	5	0	1.000	28	2	0	0	1	80²	75	8	29	48	11.7	4.35	91	.251	.319	0	—	0	-3	-3	-1	-0.4
Total 9	24	35	.407	201	45	4	0	13	549¹	579	56	213	338	13.2	4.42	92	.275	.344	6	.154	-1	-27	-23	-5	-2.7

● **OSCAR JONES**   Jones, Oscar Winfield "Flip Flap" b: 1/21/1879, London Grove, Pa.   d: 10/8/46, Perkasie, Pa.   BR/TR, 5′7″, 163 lbs.   Deb: 4/20/03

1903 Bro-N	19	14	.576	38	36	31	4	0	324¹	320	4	77	95	11.5	2.94	109	.260	.313	32	.256	2	12	9	-3	0.8
1904 Bro-N	17	25	.405	46	41	38	0	0	377	387	7	92	96	11.8	2.75	100	.270	.321	24	.175	-1	-0	0	-7	-0.9
1905 Bro-N	8	15	.348	29	20	14	0	1	174	197	6	56	66	13.6	4.66	62	.285	.347	13	.200	-0	-32	-34	-4	-3.7
Total 3	44	54	.449	113	97	83	4	1	875¹	904	17	225	257	12.1	3.20	92	.269	.324	69	.211	1	-20	-25	-14	-3.7

● **PERCY JONES**   Jones, Percy Lee b: 10/28/1899, Harwood, Tex.   d: 3/18/79, Dallas, Tex.   BR/TL, 5′11.5″, 175 lbs.   Deb: 8/06/20

1920 Chi-N	0	0	—	4	0	0	0	0	7	15	1	3	0	24.4	11.57	28	.455	.514	0	.000	-0	-7	-7	-0	-0.7
1921 Chi-N	3	5	.375	32	5	1	0	0	98²	116	2	39	46	14.5	4.56	84	.295	.365	6	.222	-0	-9	-8	-2	-1.0
1922 Chi-N	8	9	.471	44	26	7	2	1	162	197	10	68	45	15.0	4.78	88	.310	.381	4	.085	-4	-12	-10	-1	-1.3
1925 Chi-N	6	6	.500	28	13	6	1	0	124	123	12	71	60	14.4	4.65	93	.263	.366	6	.154	-3	-5	-4	2	-0.5
1926 Chi-N	12	7	.632	30	20	10	2	2	160¹	151	9	90	53	13.8	3.09	125	.260	.359	13	.260	3	13	13	-1	1.5
1927 Chi-N	7	8	.467	30	11	5	1	0	112²	123	3	72	37	16.1	4.07	95	.285	.394	14	.350	3	-2	-3	-2	-0.2
1928 Chi-N	10	6	.625	39	18	9	1	1	154	167	4	56	41	13.4	4.03	95	.288	.358	11	.196	-0	-1	-3	-0	-0.4
1929 Bos-N	7	15	.318	35	22	11	1	0	188¹	219	15	84	69	14.7	4.64	101	.298	.373	9	.148	-0	2	1	1	-0.1
1930 Pit-N	0	1	.000	9	2	0	0	0	19	26	3	11	3	18.9	6.63	75	.329	.430	0	—	-0	-4	-3	-1	-0.4
Total 9	53	57	.482	251	117	49	8	6	1026	1137	53	494	381	14.7	4.34	95	.288	.373	63	.194	-5	-24	-24	1	-2.7

YEAR TM/L	W	L	PCT	G	GS	CG	SH	SV	IP	H	HR	BB	SO	RAT	ERA	ERA+	OAV	OOB	BH	AVG	PB	PR	/A	PD	TPI
● **RANDY JONES** Jones, Randall Leo b: 1/12/50, Fullerton, Cal. BR/TL, 6', 178 lbs. Deb: 6/16/73																									
1973 SD-N	7	6	.538	20	19	6	1	0	139^2	129	13	37	77	10.8	3.16	110	.241	.291	8	.167	0	8	5	0	0.5
1974 SD-N	8	22	.267	40	34	4	1	2	208^1	217	16	78	124	13.0	4.45	80	.270	.339	10	.154	-1	-19	-21	2	-2.0
1975 SD-N★	20	12	.625	37	36	18	6	0	285	242	17	56	103	**9.4**	**2.24**	**155**	.232	.271	11	.133	-1	44	39	5	**4.9**
1976 SD-N★	**22**	14	.611	40	40	**25**	5	0	**315^1**	274	15	50	93	**9.4**	2.74	119	.234	**.267**	6	.058	-6	27	19	8	2.3
1977 SD-N	6	12	.333	27	25	1	0	0	147^1	173	12	36	44	12.8	4.58	77	.291	.332	5	.116	-1	-11	-17	4	-1.4
1978 SD-N	13	14	.481	37	36	7	2	0	253	263	6	64	71	11.6	2.88	115	.272	.317	15	.183	1	20	12	2	1.7
1979 SD-N	11	12	.478	39	39	6	0	0	263	257	17	64	112	11.1	3.63	97	.259	.306	15	.174	0	3	-3	4	0.1
1980 SD-N	5	13	.278	24	24	4	3	0	154^1	165	14	29	53	11.3	3.91	88	.276	.310	3	.067	-3	-5	-8	3	-0.8
1981 NY-N	1	8	.111	13	12	0	0	0	59^1	65	8	38	14	15.8	4.85	72	.274	.377	2	.118	-1	-9	-9	2	-0.9
1982 NY-N	7	10	.412	28	20	2	1	0	107^2	130	11	51	44	15.5	4.60	79	.304	.384	4	.148	0	-12	-12	3	-0.9
Total 10	100	123	.448	305	285	73	19	2	1933	1915	129	503	735	11.3	3.42	101	.260	.309	79	.132	-11	44	6	32	3.5
● **SAM JONES** Jones, Samuel "Toothpick Sam" b: 12/14/25, Stewartsville, Ohio d: 11/5/71, Morgantown, W.Va. BR/TR, 6'4", 200 lbs. Deb: 9/22/51																									
1951 Cle-A	0	1	.000	2	1	0	0	0	8^2	4	0	5	4	9.3	2.08	182	.143	.273	0	.000	-0	2	2	-0	0.1
1952 Cle-A	2	3	.400	14	4	0	0	1	36	38	6	37	28	19.8	7.25	46	.270	.434	1	.100	-1	-14	-16	-1	-1.6
1955 Chi-N★	14	20	.412	36	34	12	4	0	241^2	175	22	185	**198**	13.9	4.10	100	**.206**	.357	14	.182	-2	-2	-0	-0	-0.2
1956 Chi-N	9	14	.391	33	28	8	2	0	188^2	155	21	115	**176**	13.3	3.91	96	.221	.338	10	.175	0	-3	-3	-1	-0.4
1957 StL-N	12	9	.571	28	27	10	2	0	182^2	164	17	71	154	11.9	3.60	110	.239	.316	10	.159	-1	6	7	0	0.7
1958 StL-N	14	13	.519	35	35	14	2	0	250	204	23	107	**225**	11.4	2.88	143	.223	.309	9	.100	-6	30	**35**	-0	3.0
1959 SF-N★	**21**	15	.583	50	35	16	**4**	4	270^2	232	18	109	209	11.6	**2.83**	135	**.228**	.307	11	.129	-2	**34**	30	-2	2.7
1960 SF-N	18	14	.563	39	35	13	3	0	234	200	18	91	190	11.3	3.19	109	.230	.306	16	.200	1	15	7	-2	0.7
1961 SF-N	8	8	.500	37	17	2	0	1	128^1	134	12	57	105	14.0	4.49	85	.264	.348	5	.139	-1	-7	-10	-2	-1.2
1962 Det-A	2	4	.333	30	6	1	0	1	81^1	77	13	35	73	12.6	3.65	111	.254	.335	2	.095	-1	3	4	-0	0.3
1963 StL-N	2	0	1.000	11	0	0	0	2	11	15	0	5	8	16.4	9.00	39	.319	.385	0	.000	0	-7	-7	-0	-0.7
1964 Bal-A	0	0	—	7	0	0	0	0	10^1	5	1	5	6	8.7	2.61	137	.152	.263	0	—	0	1	1	-0	0.1
Total 12	102	101	.502	322	222	76	17	9	1643^1	1403	151	822	1376	12.5	3.59	108	.230	.328	78	.149	-11	58	50	-8	3.5
● **SAM JONES** Jones, Samuel Pond "Sad Sam" b: 7/26/1892, Woodsfield, Ohio d: 7/6/66, Barnesville, Ohio BR/TR, 6', 170 lbs. Deb: 6/13/14																									
1914 Cle-A	0	0	—	1	0	0	0	0	3^1	2	0	2	0	10.8	2.70	107	.200	.333	1	.500	0	0	0	0	0.0
1915 Cle-A	4	9	.308	48	9	2	0	4	145^2	131	0	63	42	12.0	3.65	84	.252	.334	5	.156	-0	-11	-10	0	-1.0
1916 Bos-A	0	1	.000	12	0	0	0	1	27	25	0	10	7	11.7	3.67	76	.272	.343	2	.333	0	-3	-3	-0	-0.3
1917 Bos-A	0	1	.000	9	1	0	0	1	16^1	15	1	6	5	11.6	4.41	59	.259	.328	0	.000	-1	-3	-3	1	-0.4
1918 *Bos-A	16	5	**.762**	24	21	16	5	0	184	151	1	70	44	11.2	2.25	119	.230	.312	10	.175	2	11	9	-1	1.1
1919 Bos-A	12	20	.375	35	31	21	5	1	245	258	4	95	67	13.2	3.75	81	.278	.350	11	.136	-0	-14	-20	3	-1.8
1920 Bos-A	13	16	.448	37	33	21	3	0	274	302	9	79	86	12.6	3.94	93	.288	.340	20	.217	1	-4	-9	-1	-0.9
1921 Bos-A	23	16	.590	40	38	25	**5**	1	298^2	318	1	78	98	12.1	3.22	131	.279	.329	24	.240	5	35	33	-3	3.4
1922 *NY-A	13	13	.500	45	28	20	0	**8**	260	270	16	76	81	12.1	3.67	109	.275	.329	23	.264	8	11	10	-1	1.6
1923 *NY-A	21	8	.724	39	27	18	3	4	243	239	11	69	68	11.6	3.63	109	.257	.312	19	.224	2	10	8	1	1.1
1924 NY-A	9	6	.600	36	21	8	3	3	178^2	187	6	76	53	13.3	3.63	115	.276	.350	9	.176	-0	12	11	-1	0.9
1925 NY-A	15	21	.417	43	31	14	1	2	246^2	267	14	104	92	13.6	4.63	92	.281	.354	13	.162	-3	-7	-10	0	-1.2
1926 *NY-A	9	8	.529	39	23	6	1	5	161	186	6	80	69	15.1	4.98	77	.298	.381	10	.204	1	-17	-20	-1	-2.0
1927 StL-A	8	14	.364	30	26	11	0	0	189^2	211	13	102	72	15.0	4.32	101	.282	.371	6	.109	-2	-4	1	-2	-0.3
1928 Was-A	17	7	.708	30	27	19	4	0	224^2	209	5	78	63	11.6	2.84	141	.252	.319	20	.253	6	30	29	1	3.6
1929 Was-A	9	9	.500	24	24	8	1	0	153^2	156	5	49	36	12.2	3.92	108	.264	.324	8	.157	0	5	5	-1	0.4
1930 Was-A	15	7	.682	25	25	14	1	0	183^1	195	4	61	60	12.7	4.07	113	.277	.337	9	.148	-1	12	11	-1	0.7
1931 Was-A	9	10	.474	25	24	8	1	1	148	185	10	47	58	14.4	4.32	99	.304	.358	15	.313	4	1	-0	-0	0.3
1932 Chi-A	10	15	.400	30	28	10	0	0	200^1	217	9	75	64	13.3	4.22	102	.270	.335	11	.193	2	6	2	3	0.7
1933 Chi-A	10	12	.455	27	25	11	2	0	176^2	181	13	65	60	12.7	3.36	126	.265	.333	9	.155	-0	18	17	-1	1.6
1934 Chi-A	8	12	.400	27	26	11	1	0	183^1	217	16	60	60	13.7	5.11	93	.289	.343	12	.200	2	-12	-8	-2	-0.7
1935 Chi-A	8	7	.533	21	19	7	0	0	140	162	8	51	38	13.8	4.05	114	.284	.343	8	.167	0	6	9	0	0.9
Total 22	229	217	.513	647	487	250	36	31	3883	4084	152	1396	1223	12.9	3.84	104	.274	.339	245	.197	25	81	61	-8	7.7
● **SHELDON JONES** Jones, Sheldon Leslie "Available" b: 2/2/22, Tecumseh, Neb. d: 4/18/91, Greenville, N.C. BR/TR, 6', 180 lbs. Deb: 9/09/46																									
1946 NY-N	1	2	.333	6	4	1	0	0	28	21	4	17	24	12.5	3.21	107	.208	.328	2	.250	0	1	1	-0	0.1
1947 NY-N	2	2	.500	15	6	0	0	0	55^2	51	2	29	24	13.4	3.88	105	.250	.352	2	.125	-1	1	1	-1	-0.1
1948 NY-N	16	8	.667	55	21	8	1	5	201^1	204	16	90	82	13.4	3.35	117	.263	.344	13	.203	1	14	13	0	1.5
1949 NY-N	15	12	.556	42	27	11	1	0	207^1	198	19	88	79	12.8	3.34	119	.248	.331	8	.121	-3	16	15	-0	1.1
1950 NY-N	13	16	.448	40	28	11	2	2	199	188	26	90	97	12.9	4.61	89	.249	.335	6	.105	-2	-10	-11	-2	-1.6
1951 *NY-N	6	11	.353	41	12	2	0	4	120^1	119	12	52	58	13.1	4.26	92	.260	.340	3	.097	-1	-4	-5	0	-0.5
1952 Bos-N	1	4	.200	39	1	0	0	1	70	81	8	31	40	14.5	4.76	76	.286	.359	1	.125	-0	-8	-9	0	-0.9
1953 Chi-N	0	2	.000	22	2	0	0	0	38^1	47	3	16	9	16.0	5.40	82	.299	.382	0	.000	-1	-5	-4	0	-0.5
Total 8	54	57	.486	260	101	33	4	12	920	909	90	413	413	13.3	3.96	100	.258	.342	35	.136	-7	4	1	-3	-0.9
● **SHERMAN JONES** Jones, Sherman Jarvis "Roadblock" b: 2/10/35, Winton, N.C. BL/TR, 6'4", 205 lbs. Deb: 8/02/60																									
1960 SF-N	1	1	.500	16	0	0	0	1	32	37	3	11	10	13.8	3.09	112	.291	.353	2	.286	0	2	1	-1	0.1
1961 *Cin-N	1	1	.500	24	2	0	0	2	55	51	6	27	32	13.1	4.42	92	.256	.351	2	.182	0	-2	-2	-0	-0.2
1962 NY-N	0	4	.000	8	3	0	0	0	23^1	31	3	8	11	15.8	7.71	54	.326	.390	3	.429	1	-10	-9	0	-0.7
Total 3	2	6	.250	48	5	0	0	3	110^1	119	12	46	53	13.9	4.73	83	.283	.360	7	.280	1	-10	-10	-1	-0.8
● **STEVE JONES** Jones, Steven Howell b: 4/22/41, Huntington Park, Cal. BL/TL, 5'10", 175 lbs. Deb: 8/15/67 F																									
1967 Chi-A	2	2	.500	11	3	0	0	0	25^2	21	1	12	17	11.6	4.21	74	.223	.311	1	.250	0	-3	-3	-0	-0.3
1968 Was-A	1	2	.333	7	0	0	0	0	10^2	8	3	7	11	12.7	5.91	49	.205	.326	0	.000	-0	-3	-4	-0	-0.4
1969 KC-A	2	3	.400	20	4	0	0	0	44^2	45	3	24	31	14.5	4.23	87	.260	.360	1	.125	0	-3	-3	0	-0.2
Total 3	5	7	.417	38	7	0	0	0	81	74	7	43	59	13.3	4.44	76	.242	.341	2	.154	1	-9	-9	-1	-0.9
● **RICK JONES** Jones, Thomas Fredrick b: 4/16/55, Jacksonville, Fla. BL/TL, 6'5", 190 lbs. Deb: 4/18/76																									
1976 Bos-A	5	3	.625	24	14	1	0	0	104^1	133	6	26	45	13.8	3.36	116	.311	.352	0	—	0	2	6	-0	0.6
1977 Sea-A	1	4	.200	10	10	0	0	0	42^1	47	10	37	16	17.9	5.10	81	.283	.414	0	—	0	-5	-5	0	-0.4
1978 Sea-A	0	2	.000	3	2	0	0	0	12^1	17	1	7	11	17.5	5.84	65	.315	.393	0	—	0	-3	-3	-0	-0.2
Total 3	6	9	.400	37	26	1	0	0	159	197	17	70	72	15.2	4.02	99	.304	.373	0	—	0	-6	-1	-0	0.0
● **TIM JONES** Jones, Timmothy Byron b: 1/24/54, Sacramento, Cal. BB/TR, 6'5", 220 lbs. Deb: 9/04/77																									
1977 Pit-N	1	0	1.000	3	1	0	0	0	10	4	0	3	5	6.3	0.00	—	.118	.189	0	.000	-0	4	4	-0	0.4
● **TIM JONES** Jones, William Timothy b: 12/1/62, Sumter, S.C. BL/TR, 5'10", 172 lbs. Deb: 7/26/88 ♦																									
1990 StL-N	0	0	—	1	0	0	0	0	1^1	1	0	2	0	20.3	6.75	57	.167	.375	28	.219	0	-0	-0	0	0.0
● **CLAUDE JONNARD** Jonnard, Claude Alfred b: 11/23/1897, Nashville, Tenn. d: 8/27/59, Nashville, Tenn. BR/TR, 6'1", 165 lbs. Deb: 10/01/21 F																									
1921 NY-N	0	0	—	1	0	0	0	1	4	4	0	0	7	9.0	0.00	—	.267	.267	0	.000	-0	2	2	-0	0.1
1922 NY-N	6	1	.857	33	0	0	0	**5**	96	96	7	28	44	11.9	3.84	104	.272	.331	1	.042	-3	3	2	-2	-0.2
1923 *NY-N	4	3	.571	**45**	1	1	0	**5**	96	105	6	35	45	13.1	3.28	116	.279	.340	1	.038	-3	8	6	-1	0.2
1924 *NY-N	4	5	.444	34	3	1	0	5	89^2	80	2	24	40	10.6	2.41	152	.229	.282	1	.045	-3	**15**	**13**	-0	1.0
1926 StL-A	0	2	.000	12	3	0	0	1	36	46	1	24	13	17.5	6.00	71	.313	.409	0	.000	-1	-8	-7	1	-0.6
1929 Chi-N	0	1	.000	12	2	0	0	0	27^2	41	4	11	11	17.2	7.48	62	.320	.379	2	.200	1	-9	-9	0	-0.7

YEAR TM/L	W	L	PCT	G	GS	CG	SH	SV	IP	H	HR	BB	SO	RAT	ERA	ERA+	OAV	OOB	BH	AVG	PB	PR	/A	PD	TPI
Total 6	14	12	.538	137	9	2	0	17	349^{1}	372	20	122	160	12.9	3.79	104	.272	.334	5	.056	-8	10	6	-1	-0.2
● CHARLIE JORDAN	Jordan, Charles T. "Kid" b: 10/4/1871, Baltimore, Md. d: 6/1/28, Hazleton, Pa. Deb: 7/31/1896																								
1896 Phi-N	0	0	—	2	0	0	0	0	4^{2}	9	0	2	3	21.2	7.71	56	.402	.451	1	.500	0	-2	-2	0	-0.1
● HARRY JORDAN	Jordan, Harry J. b: 2/14/1873, Pittsburgh, Pa. d: 3/1/20, Pittsburgh, Pa. Deb: 9/25/1894																								
1894 Pit-N	1	0	1.000	1	1	1	0	0	9	10	0	2	1	13.0	4.00	131	.278	.334	0	.000	-0	1	1	-0	0.1
1895 Pit-N	0	2	.000	2	2	2	0	0	17	24	0	6	4	16.4	4.24	107	.327	.386	2	.286	-0	1	1	-0	0.0
Total 2	1	2	.333	3	3	3	0	0	26	34	0	8	5	15.2	4.15	115	.311	.369	2	.200	-0	2	2	-1	0.1
● MILT JORDAN	Jordan, Milton Mignot b: 5/24/27, Mineral Springs, Pa. BR/TR, 6'2.5", 207 lbs. Deb: 4/16/53																								
1953 Det-A	0	1	.000	8	1	0	0	0	17	26	3	5	4	16.4	5.82	70	.366	.408	1	.500	0	-3	-3	0	-0.3
● NILES JORDAN	Jordan, Niles Chapman b: 12/1/25, Lyman, Wash. BL/TL, 5'11", 180 lbs. Deb: 8/26/51																								
1951 Phi-N	2	3	.400	5	5	2	1	0	36^{2}	35	4	8	11	10.6	3.19	121	.250	.291	1	.077	-1	3	3	-1	0.1
1952 Cin-N	0	1	.000	3	1	0	0	0	6^{1}	14	1	3	2	24.2	9.95	38	.452	.500	0	.000	-0	-4	-4	0	-0.4
Total 2	2	4	.333	8	6	2	1	0	43	49	5	11	13	12.6	4.19	92	.287	.330	1	.071	-1	-1	-2	-1	-0.3
● RIP JORDAN	Jordan, Raymond Willis "Lanky" b: 9/28/1889, Portland, Me. d: 6/5/60, Meriden, Conn. BL/TR, 6', 172 lbs. Deb: 6/25/12																								
1912 Chi-A	0	0	—	4	0	0	0	0	12^{1}	13	2	3	1	12.4	5.11	63	.289	.347	0	.000	-1	-2	-3	-0	-0.3
1919 Was-A	0	0	—	1	1	0	0	0	4	6	1	2	2	18.0	11.25	29	.353	.421	0	.000	-0	-4	-4	-0	-0.3
Total 2	0	0	—	5	1	0	0	0	16^{1}	19	3	5	3	13.8	6.61	48	.306	.368	0	.000	-1	-6	-6	-1	-0.6
● ORVILLE JORGENS	Jorgens, Orville Edward b: 6/4/08, Rockford, Ill. BR/TR, 6'1", 180 lbs. Deb: 4/19/35 F																								
1935 Phi-N	10	15	.400	**53**	24	6	0	2	188^{1}	216	12	96	57	15.3	4.83	94	.283	.370	6	.097	-5	-17	-6	3	-0.8
1936 Phi-N	8	8	.500	39	21	4	0	0	167^{1}	196	16	69	58	14.6	4.79	95	.290	.361	12	.200	-1	-14	-5	1	-0.5
1937 Phi-N	3	4	.429	52	11	1	0	3	140^{2}	159	12	68	34	14.8	4.41	98	.298	.383	5	.143	-1	-8	-1	2	-0.1
Total 3	21	27	.438	144	56	11	0	5	496^{1}	571	40	233	149	14.9	4.70	95	.290	.370	23	.146	-8	-39	-12	5	-1.4
● ADDIE JOSS	Joss, Adrian b: 4/12/1880, Woodland, Wis. d: 4/14/11, Toledo, Ohio BR/TR, 6'3", 185 lbs. Deb: 4/26/02 H																								
1902 Cle-A	17	13	.567	32	29	28	**5**	0	269^{1}	225	2	75	106	10.4	2.77	124	.228	.290	12	.117	-5	24	20	6	2.1
1903 Cle-A	18	13	.581	32	31	31	3	0	283^{2}	232	3	37	120	**8.9**	2.19	130	.223	**.256**	22	.193	0	24	21	4	2.7
1904 Cle-A	14	10	.583	25	24	20	5	0	192^{1}	160	0	30	83	9.2	**1.59**	160	.227	.265	10	.132	-3	22	20	0	1.9
1905 Cle-A	20	12	.625	33	32	31	3	0	286	246	4	46	132	9.6	2.01	131	.233	.273	13	.134	-0	21	20	5	2.7
1906 Cle-A	21	9	.700	34	31	28	9	1	282	220	3	43	106	8.5	1.72	152	.218	.252	21	.210	2	30	28	2	**3.8**
1907 Cle-A	**27**	11	.711	42	38	34	6	2	338^{2}	279	3	54	127	9.0	1.83	137	.226	.263	13	.114	-5	27	26	9	3.3
1908 Cle-A	24	11	.686	42	35	29	9	2	325	232	2	30	130	**7.3**	**1.16**	**206**	**.197**	**.218**	15	.155	2	45	44	2	6.1
1909 Cle-A	14	13	.519	33	28	24	4	0	242^{2}	198	0	31	67	8.6	1.71	150	.226	.255	8	.100	-3	21	23	0	2.4
1910 Cle-A	5	5	.500	13	12	9	1	0	107^{1}	96	2	18	49	9.7	2.26	114	.245	.282	4	.111	-1	3	4	2	0.5
Total 9	160	97	.623	286	260	234	45	5	2327	1888	19	364	920	8.9	1.89	142	.223	.260	118	.144	-14	216	207	30	25.5
● MIKE JOYCE	Joyce, Michael Lewis b: 2/12/41, Detroit, Mich. BR/TR, 6'2", 193 lbs. Deb: 7/02/62																								
1962 Chi-A	2	1	.667	25	1	0	0	2	43^{1}	40	2	14	9	11.2	3.32	118	.247	.307	3	.429	1	3	3	0	0.4
1963 Chi-A	0	0	—	6	0	0	0	0	10^{2}	13	1	8	7	17.7	8.44	42	.289	.396	0	—	0	-6	-6	-0	-0.6
Total 2	2	1	.667	31	1	0	0	2	54	53	3	22	16	12.5	4.33	88	.256	.328	3	.429	1	-3	-3	0	-0.2
● DICK JOYCE	Joyce, Richard Edward b: 11/18/43, Portland, Me. BL/TL, 6'5", 225 lbs. Deb: 9/03/65																								
1965 KC-A	0	1	.000	5	3	0	0	0	13	12	0	4	7	11.1	2.77	126	.240	.296	0	.000	-0	1	1	-0	0.1
● BOB JOYCE	Joyce, Robert Emmett b: 1/14/15, Stockton, Cal. d: 12/10/81, San Francisco, Cal BR/TR, 6'1", 180 lbs. Deb: 5/04/39																								
1939 Phi-A	3	5	.375	30	6	1	0	0	107^{2}	156	13	37	25	16.2	6.69	70	.337	.387	3	.086	-3	-25	-24	1	-2.3
1946 NY-N	3	4	.429	14	7	2	0	0	60^{2}	79	3	20	24	14.7	5.34	64	.315	.365	3	.158	0	-13	-13	1	-1.2
Total 2	6	9	.400	44	13	3	0	0	168^{1}	235	16	57	49	15.7	6.20	69	.329	.380	6	.111	-3	-38	-37	2	-3.5
● RALPH JUDD	Judd, Ralph Wesley b: 12/7/01, Perrysburg, Ohio d: 5/6/57, Lapeer, Mich. BL/TR, 5'10", 170 lbs. Deb: 10/02/27																								
1927 Was-A	0	0	—	1	0	0	0	1	4	8	0	2	2	22.5	6.75	60	.400	.455	0	.000	-0	-1	-1	-0	-0.1
1929 NY-N	3	0	1.000	18	0	0	0	0	50^{2}	49	4	11	21	10.7	2.66	172	.261	.302	0	.000	-2	12	11	0	0.8
1930 NY-N	0	0	—	2	0	0	0	0	7^{2}	13	0	3	0	18.8	5.87	81	.390	.441	0	.000	-1	-1	-1	-0	-0.1
Total 3	3	0	1.000	21	0	0	0	1	62^{1}	70	4	16	23	12.4	3.32	138	.290	.334	0	.000	-3	10	9	0	0.6
● OSCAR JUDD	Judd, Thomas William Oscar "Ossie" b: 2/14/08, London, Ont., Can. BL/TL, 6'0.5", 180 lbs. Deb: 4/16/41																								
1941 Bos-A	0	0	—	7	0	0	0	1	12^{1}	15	1	10	5	18.2	8.76	48	.300	.417	2	.500	2	-6	-6	0	-0.4
1942 Bos-A	8	10	.444	31	19	11	0	2	150^{1}	135	3	90	70	13.6	3.89	96	.239	.346	18	.269	6	-4	-3	-0	0.3
1943 Bos-A☆	11	6	.647	23	20	8	1	0	155^{1}	131	2	69	53	11.8	2.90	114	.230	.317	14	.259	4	7	7	2	1.4
1944 Bos-A	1	1	.500	9	6	1	0	0	30	30	1	15	9	13.5	3.60	94	.261	.346	2	.182	1	-1	-1	-0	0.0
1945 Bos-A	0	1	.000	2	1	0	0	0	6^{1}	10	1	3	5	18.5	8.53	40	.333	.394	1	.500	0	-4	-4	0	-0.3
Phi-N	5	4	.556	23	9	3	1	2	82^{2}	80	3	40	36	13.2	3.81	101	.254	.340	8	.267	3	-0	0	1	0.4
1946 Phi-N	11	12	.478	30	24	12	1	2	173^{1}	169	6	90	65	13.5	3.53	97	.260	.350	25	.316	8	-2	-2	4	1.1
1947 Phi-N	4	15	.211	32	19	8	1	0	146^{2}	155	6	69	54	13.9	4.60	87	.279	.361	12	.188	2	-9	-10	1	-0.6
1948 Phi-N	0	2	.000	4	1	0	0	0	14^{1}	19	1	11	7	18.8	6.91	57	.317	.423	1	.167	0	-5	-5	-0	-0.4
Total 8	40	51	.440	161	99	43	4	7	771^{1}	744	24	397	304	13.4	3.90	93	.256	.347	83	.262	26	-23	-22	8	1.5
● JEFF JUDEN	Juden, Jeffrey Daniel b: 1/19/71, Salem, Mass. BR/TR, 6'7", 245 lbs. Deb: 9/15/91																								
1991 Hou-N	0	2	.000	4	3	0	0	0	18	19	3	7	11	13.0	6.00	58	.275	.342	0	.000	-0	-5	-5	-1	-0.6
● HOWIE JUDSON	Judson, Howard Kolls b: 2/16/26, Hebron, Ill. BR/TR, 6'1", 195 lbs. Deb: 4/22/48																								
1948 Chi-A	4	5	.444	40	5	1	0	8	107^{1}	102	7	56	38	13.5	4.78	89	.255	.351	3	.103	-2	-6	-6	0	-0.7
1949 Chi-A	1	14	.067	26	12	3	0	1	108	114	13	70	36	15.4	4.58	91	.274	.380	2	.065	-3	-5	-5	0	-0.7
1950 Chi-A	2	3	.400	46	3	1	0	0	112	105	10	63	34	13.7	3.94	114	.252	.353	2	.100	-1	**8**	**7**	-2	0.4
1951 Chi-A	5	6	.455	27	14	3	0	1	121^{2}	124	9	55	43	13.4	3.77	107	.264	.343	4	.121	-2	5	4	0	0.1
1952 Chi-A	0	1	.000	21	0	0	0	1	34	30	4	22	15	13.8	4.24	86	.244	.359	0	.000	-0	-2	-2	-0	-0.3
1953 Cin-N	0	1	.000	10	6	0	0	0	38^{2}	58	8	11	11	16.1	5.59	78	.341	.381	1	.111	1	-6	-5	0	-0.4
1954 Cin-N	5	7	.417	37	8	0	0	3	93^{1}	86	9	42	27	12.6	3.95	106	.251	.338	2	.083	-2	1	2	-2	-0.1
Total 7	17	37	.315	207	48	8	0	14	615	619	60	319	204	13.9	4.29	98	.265	.356	14	.093	-9	-4	-6	-3	-1.7
● KEN JUNGELS	Jungels, Kenneth Peter "Curly" b: 6/23/16, Aurora, Ill. d: 9/9/75, West Bend, Wis. BR/TR, 6'1", 180 lbs. Deb: 9/15/37																								
1937 Cle-A	0	0	—	2	0	0	0	0	3	3	0	1	0	12.0	0.00		.273	.333	0	—	0	2	2	0	0.1
1938 Cle-A	1	0	1.000	9	0	0	0	0	15^{1}	21	1	18	7	24.1	8.80	53	.339	.500	0	.000	-1	-7	-7	-0	-0.7
1940 Cle-A	0	0	—	2	0	0	0	0	3^{1}	3	0	1	1	10.8	2.70	156	.273	.333	0	.000	-0	1	1	0	0.0
1941 Cle-A	0	0	—	6	0	0	0	0	13^{2}	17	4	8	6	17.1	7.24	54	.293	.388	0	.000	-0	-5	-5	-0	-0.5
1942 Pit-N	0	0	—	6	0	0	0	0	13^{2}	12	0	4	7	10.5	6.59	51	.235	.291	1	.500	0	-5	-5	0	-0.5
Total 5	1	0	1.000	25	0	0	0	0	49	56	5	32	21	16.7	6.80	60	.290	.399	1	.100	-1	-14	-15	-0	-1.6
● MIKE JUREWICZ	Jurewicz, Michael Allen b: 9/20/45, Buffalo, N.Y. BB/TL, 6'3", 205 lbs. Deb: 9/07/65																								
1965 NY-A	0	0	—	2	0	0	0	0	2^{1}	5	0	1	2	23.1	7.71	44	.417	.462	0	—	0	-1	-1	-0	-0.1

● AL JURISICH Jurisich, Alvin Joseph b: 8/25/21, New Orleans, La. d: 11/3/81, New Orleans, La. BR/TR, 6'2", 193 lbs. Deb: 4/26/44

YEAR	TM/L	W	L	PCT	G	GS	CG	SH	SV	IP	H	HR	BB	SO	RAT	ERA	ERA+	OAV	OOB	BH	AVG	PB	PR	/A	PD	TPI
1944	*StL-N	7	9	.438	30	14	5	2	1	130	102	7	65	53	11.9	3.39	104	.221	.323	8	.178	-1	3	2	-1	0.0
1945	StL-N	3	3	.500	27	6	1	0	0	71^2	61	7	41	42	12.9	5.15	73	.232	.338	2	.087	-2	-11	-11	-1	-1.4
1946	Phi-N	4	3	.571	13	10	2	1	1	68^1	71	9	31	34	13.6	3.69	93	.263	.341	3	.130	-0	-2	-2	-1	-0.4
1947	Phi-N	1	7	.125	34	12	5	0	3	118^1	110	15	52	48	12.4	4.94	81	.258	.340	1	.032	-3	-12	-12	-2	-1.6
Total	4	15	22	.405	104	42	13	3	5	388^1	344	38	189	177	12.5	4.24	87	.242	.334	14	.115	-6	-21	-24	-5	-3.4

● WALT JUSTIS Justis, Walter Newton "Smoke" b: 8/17/1883, Moores Hill, Ind. d: 10/4/41, Lawrenceburg, Ind. BR/TR, 5'11.5", 195 lbs. Deb: 8/01/05

YEAR	TM/L	W	L	PCT	G	GS	CG	SH	SV	IP	H	HR	BB	SO	RAT	ERA	ERA+	OAV	OOB	BH	AVG	PB	PR	/A	PD	TPI
1905	Det-A	0	0	—	2	0	0	0	0	3^1	4	0	6	0	29.7	8.10	34	.298	.539	0	—	0	-2	-2	-0	-0.2

● HEROLD JUUL Juul, Earl Herold b: 5/21/1893, Chicago, Ill. d: 1/4/42, Chicago, Ill. BR/TR, 5'9.5", 150 lbs. Deb: 4/24/14

YEAR	TM/L	W	L	PCT	G	GS	CG	SH	SV	IP	H	HR	BB	SO	RAT	ERA	ERA+	OAV	OOB	BH	AVG	PB	PR	/A	PD	TPI
1914	Bro-F	0	3	.000	9	3	0	0	0	29	26	0	31	16	18.0	6.21	51	.248	.423	2	.222	-0	-10	-10	-0	-1.0

● HERB JUUL Juul, Herbert Victor b: 2/2/1886, Chicago, Ill. d: 11/14/28, Chicago, Ill. BL/TL, 5'11", 150 lbs. Deb: 7/11/11 ♦

YEAR	TM/L	W	L	PCT	G	GS	CG	SH	SV	IP	H	HR	BB	SO	RAT	ERA	ERA+	OAV	OOB	BH	AVG	PB	PR	/A	PD	TPI
1911	Cin-N	0	0	—	1	0	0	0	0	4	3	0	4	2	15.8	4.50	74	.231	.412	0	.000	-0	-0	-1	-0	-0.1

● JIM KAAT Kaat, James Lee b: 11/7/38, Zeeland, Mich. BL/TL, 6'4", 217 lbs. Deb: 8/02/59 C♦

YEAR	TM/L	W	L	PCT	G	GS	CG	SH	SV	IP	H	HR	BB	SO	RAT	ERA	ERA+	OAV	OOB	BH	AVG	PB	PR	/A	PD	TPI
1959	Was-A	0	2	.000	3	2	0	0	0	5	7	1	4	2	23.4	12.60	31	.350	.500	0	.000	-0	-5	-5	0	-0.5
1960	Was-A	1	5	.167	13	9	0	0	0	50	48	8	31	25	15.1	5.58	70	.255	.375	2	.143	-1	-9	-9	0	-0.9
1961	Min-A	9	17	.346	36	29	8	1	0	200^2	188	12	82	122	12.6	3.90	109	.248	.331	15	.238	4	3	8	3	1.4
1962	Min-A☆	18	14	.563	39	35	16	**5**	1	269	243	23	75	173	11.2	3.14	130	.243	.307	18	.180	3	25	28	6	**3.9**
1963	Min-A	10	10	.500	31	27	7	1	1	178^1	195	24	38	105	12.2	4.19	87	.274	.319	8	.131	-0	-11	-11	4	-0.7
1964	Min-A	17	11	.607	36	34	13	0	1	243	231	23	60	171	11.1	3.22	111	.251	.304	14	.169	5	11	10	3	1.8
1965	*Min-A	18	11	.621	45	42	7	2	2	264^1	267	25	63	154	11.4	2.83	126	.258	.304	23	.247	6	19	21	3	3.5
1966	Min-A★	**25**	13	.658	41	41	**19**	3	0	**304**^{2}	271	29	55	205	9.7	2.75	131	.235	.271	23	.195	4	23	**29**	0	3.7
1967	Min-A	16	13	.552	42	38	13	2	0	263^1	269	21	42	211	10.9	3.04	114	.260	.295	17	.172	3	6	12	1	1.8
1968	Min-A	14	12	.538	30	29	9	2	0	208	192	16	40	130	10.2	2.94	105	.243	.282	12	.156	0	1	3	-0	0.4
1969	Min-A	14	13	.519	40	32	10	0	1	242^1	252	23	75	139	12.5	3.49	105	.265	.325	18	.207	6	3	4	-3	0.8
1970	*Min-A	14	10	.583	45	34	4	1	0	230^1	244	26	58	120	11.9	3.56	105	.273	.319	15	.197	3	4	4	2	1.0
1971	Min-A	13	14	.481	39	38	15	4	0	260^1	275	16	47	137	11.3	3.32	107	.268	.304	15	.161	-0	4	7	-0	0.7
1972	Min-A	10	2	.833	15	15	5	0	0	113^1	94	6	20	64	9.1	2.06	155	.227	.263	13	.289	5	13	14	-0	2.4
1973	Min-A	11	12	.478	29	28	7	2	0	181^2	206	26	39	93	12.3	4.41	90	.282	.322	0	—	0	-12	-9	-1	-1.0
	Chi-A	4	1	.800	7	7	3	1	0	42^2	44	4	4	16	10.1	4.22	94	.260	.277	0	—	0	-2	-1	-1	-0.2
	Yr	15	13	.536	36	35	10	3	0	224^1	250	30	43	109	11.8	4.37	90	.276	.309	0	—	0	-14	-10	-2	-1.2
1974	Chi-A	21	13	.618	42	39	15	3	0	277^1	263	18	63	142	10.8	2.92	128	.250	.296	0	.000	0	21	25	-2	2.5
1975	Chi-A★	20	14	.588	43	41	12	1	0	303^2	321	20	77	142	12.1	3.11	124	.274	.324	0	—	0	22	26	-2	2.5
1976	*Phi-N	12	14	.462	38	35	7	1	0	227^2	241	21	32	83	10.8	3.48	102	.274	.300	14	.177	2	1	2	-3	0.1
1977	Phi-N	6	11	.353	35	27	2	0	0	160^1	211	20	40	55	14.2	5.39	74	.320	.361	10	.189	1	-26	-25	-2	-2.5
1978	Phi-N	8	5	.615	26	24	2	1	0	140^1	150	9	32	48	12.0	4.10	87	.280	.326	7	.146	-1	-8	-8	-2	-1.1
1979	Phi-N	1	0	1.000	3	1	0	0	0	8^1	9	1	5	2	15.1	4.32	89	.281	.378	0	.000	0	-1	-0	-0	0.0
	NY-A	2	3	.400	40	1	0	0	2	58^1	64	4	14	23	12.3	3.86	106	.287	.335	0	—	0	2	1	-1	0.1
1980	NY-A	0	1	.000	4	0	0	0	0	5	8	0	4	1	21.6	7.20	54	.381	.480	0	—	0	-2	-2	1	-0.1
	StL-N	8	7	.533	49	14	6	1	4	129^2	140	6	33	36	12.0	3.82	97	.281	.325	5	.143	1	-3	-2	-2	-0.3
1981	StL-N	6	6	.500	41	1	0	0	4	53	60	2	17	8	13.1	3.40	105	.299	.353	3	.375	1	1	1	1	0.3
1982	*StL-N	5	3	.625	62	2	0	0	2	75	79	6	23	35	12.5	4.08	89	.276	.334	0	.000	-1	-4	-4	1	-0.5
1983	StL-N	0	0	—	24	0	0	0	0	34^2	48	5	10	19	15.1	3.89	93	.327	.369	0	.000	-0	-1	-1	0	-0.2
Total	25	283	237	.544	898	625	180	31	18	4530^1	4620	395	1083	2461	11.6	3.45	107	.264	.311	232	.185	43	74	119	6	18.9

● GEORGE KAHLER Kahler, George Runnells "Krum" b: 9/6/1889, Athens, Ohio d: 2/7/24, Battle Creek, Va. BR/TR, 6', 183 lbs. Deb: 8/13/10

YEAR	TM/L	W	L	PCT	G	GS	CG	SH	SV	IP	H	HR	BB	SO	RAT	ERA	ERA+	OAV	OOB	BH	AVG	PB	PR	/A	PD	TPI
1910	Cle-A	6	4	.600	12	12	8	2	0	95^1	80	0	46	38	12.3	1.60	161	.237	.335	5	.143	-2	10	10	-1	0.9
1911	Cle-A	9	8	.529	30	17	10	0	1	154^1	153	1	66	97	13.5	3.27	105	.270	.360	9	.167	-2	1	3	-1	-0.1
1912	Cle-A	12	19	.387	41	32	17	3	1	246^1	263	1	121	104	14.4	3.69	92	.291	.382	9	.112	-6	-10	-8	-4	-1.6
1913	Cle-A	5	11	.313	24	15	5	0	0	117^2	118	1	32	43	11.8	3.14	97	.266	.322	2	.061	-3	-3	-1	-4	-0.9
1914	Cle-A	0	1	.000	2	1	1	0	0	14	17	0	7	3	15.4	3.86	75	.309	.387	0	.000	-0	-2	-2	-0	-0.2
Total	5	32	43	.427	109	77	41	5	2	627^2	631	3	272	285	13.4	3.17	101	.274	.358	25	.121	-14	-4	3	-9	-1.9

● DON KAINER Kainer, Donald Wayne b: 9/3/55, Houston, Tex. BR/TR, 6'3", 205 lbs. Deb: 9/06/80

YEAR	TM/L	W	L	PCT	G	GS	CG	SH	SV	IP	H	HR	BB	SO	RAT	ERA	ERA+	OAV	OOB	BH	AVG	PB	PR	/A	PD	TPI
1980	Tex-A	0	0	—	4	3	0	0	0	19^2	22	0	9	10	15.6	1.83	213	.289	.386	0	—	0	5	5	1	0.6

● DON KAISER Kaiser, Clyde Donald "Tiger" b: 2/3/35, Byng, Okla. BR/TR, 6'5", 195 lbs. Deb: 7/20/55

YEAR	TM/L	W	L	PCT	G	GS	CG	SH	SV	IP	H	HR	BB	SO	RAT	ERA	ERA+	OAV	OOB	BH	AVG	PB	PR	/A	PD	TPI
1955	Chi-N	0	0	—	11	0	0	0	0	18^1	20	2	5	11	12.8	5.40	76	.274	.329	0	.000	-0	-3	-3	-0	-0.3
1956	Chi-N	4	9	.308	27	22	5	1	0	150^1	144	15	52	74	11.8	3.59	105	.247	.310	2	.043	-5	3	3	-0	-0.2
1957	Chi-N	2	6	.250	20	13	1	0	0	72	91	4	28	23	14.9	5.00	77	.316	.377	2	.105	-1	-9	-9	2	-0.8
Total	3	6	15	.286	58	35	6	1	0	240^2	255	21	85	108	12.8	4.15	92	.270	.332	4	.059	-6	-9	-9	1	-1.3

● JEFF KAISER Kaiser, Jeffrey Patrick b: 7/24/60, Wyandotte, Mich. BR/TL, 6'3", 195 lbs. Deb: 4/11/85

YEAR	TM/L	W	L	PCT	G	GS	CG	SH	SV	IP	H	HR	BB	SO	RAT	ERA	ERA+	OAV	OOB	BH	AVG	PB	PR	/A	PD	TPI
1985	Oak-A	0	0	—	15	0	0	0	0	16^2	25	6	20	10	24.8	14.58	26	.342	.489	0	—	0	-19	-20	1	-1.8
1987	Cle-A	0	0	—	2	0	0	0	0	3^1	4	1	3	2	21.6	16.20	28	.286	.444	0	—	0	-4	-4	0	-0.4
1988	Cle-A	0	0	—	3	0	0	0	0	2^2	2	0	1	0	10.1	0.00	—	.286	.375	0	—	0	1	1	0	0.2
1989	Cle-A	0	1	.000	6	0	0	0	0	3^2	5	1	5	4	24.5	7.36	54	.313	.476	0	—	0	-1	-1	-0	-0.3
1990	Cle-A	0	0	—	5	0	0	0	0	12^2	16	2	7	9	16.3	3.55	110	.308	.390	0	—	0	0	1	0	0.1
1991	Det-A	0	1	.000	10	0	0	0	2	5	6	1	5	4	19.8	9.00	46	.286	.423	0	—	0	-3	-3	0	-0.4
Total	6	0	2	.000	41	0	0	0	2	44	58	11	41	29	20.7	9.41	42	.317	.447	0	—	0	-26	-27	1	-2.6

● BOB KAISER Kaiser, Robert Thomas b: 4/29/50, Cincinnati, Ohio BB/TL, 5'10", 175 lbs. Deb: 9/03/71

YEAR	TM/L	W	L	PCT	G	GS	CG	SH	SV	IP	H	HR	BB	SO	RAT	ERA	ERA+	OAV	OOB	BH	AVG	PB	PR	/A	PD	TPI
1971	Cle-A	0	0	—	5	0	0	0	0	6	8	2	3	4	19.5	4.50	85	.333	.448	0	—	0	-1	-0	0	-0.1

● GEORGE KAISERLING Kaiserling, George b: 5/12/1893, Steubenville, Ohio d: 3/2/18, Steubenville, Ohio BR/TR, 6', 175 lbs. Deb: 4/20/14

YEAR	TM/L	W	L	PCT	G	GS	CG	SH	SV	IP	H	HR	BB	SO	RAT	ERA	ERA+	OAV	OOB	BH	AVG	PB	PR	/A	PD	TPI
1914	Ind-F	17	10	.630	37	33	20	1	0	275^1	288	8	72	75	12.3	3.11	112	.274	.330	11	.112	-6	3	11	-3	0.2
1915	New-F	15	15	.500	41	29	16	5	2	261^1	246	1	73	75	11.3	2.24	127	.257	.316	12	.152	-2	23	18	-1	1.6
Total	2	32	25	.561	78	62	36	6	2	536^2	534	9	145	150	11.8	2.68	118	.266	.323	23	.130	-7	26	28	-5	1.8

● BILL KALFASS Kalfass, William Philip "Lefty" b: 3/3/16, New York, N.Y. d: 9/8/68, Brooklyn, N.Y. BR/TL, 6'3.5", 190 lbs. Deb: 9/15/37

YEAR	TM/L	W	L	PCT	G	GS	CG	SH	SV	IP	H	HR	BB	SO	RAT	ERA	ERA+	OAV	OOB	BH	AVG	PB	PR	/A	PD	TPI
1937	Phi-A	1	0	1.000	3	1	1	0	0	12	10	0	10	9	15.0	3.00	157	.233	.377	0	.000	-1	2	2	-0	0.1

● RUDY KALLIO Kallio, Rudolph b: 12/14/1892, Portland, Ore. d: 4/6/79, Newport, Ore. BR/TR, 5'10", 160 lbs. Deb: 4/25/18

YEAR	TM/L	W	L	PCT	G	GS	CG	SH	SV	IP	H	HR	BB	SO	RAT	ERA	ERA+	OAV	OOB	BH	AVG	PB	PR	/A	PD	TPI
1918	Det-A	8	14	.364	30	22	10	2	0	181^1	178	0	76	70	12.7	3.62	73	.261	.336	9	.161	-1	-17	-19	-0	-2.2
1919	Det-A	0	0	—	12	1	0	0	1	22^1	28	0	8	3	14.9	5.64	57	.326	.389	0	.000	-1	-6	-6	-0	-0.7
1925	Bos-A	1	4	.200	7	4	0	0	0	18^2	28	0	9	2	18.3	7.71	59	.364	.437	2	.333	0	-7	-7	-0	-0.6
Total	3	9	18	.333	49	27	10	2	1	222^1	234	0	93	75	13.4	4.17	69	.277	.351	11	.167	-1	-30	-32	-1	-3.5

● SCOTT KAMIENIECKI Kamieniecki, Scott Andrew b: 4/19/64, Mt.Clemens, Mich. BR/TR, 6', 195 lbs. Deb: 6/18/91

YEAR	TM/L	W	L	PCT	G	GS	CG	SH	SV	IP	H	HR	BB	SO	RAT	ERA	ERA+	OAV	OOB	BH	AVG	PB	PR	/A	PD	TPI
1991	NY-A	4	4	.500	9	9	0	0	0	55^1	54	8	22	34	12.8	3.90	106	.256	.335	0	—	0	1	1	1	0.2
1992	NY-A	6	14	.300	28	28	4	0	0	188	193	13	74	88	13.0	4.36	93	.269	.342	0	—	0	-9	-6	-1	-0.9
Total	2	10	18	.357	37	37	4	0	0	243^1	247	21	96	122	13.0	4.25	96	.266	.340	0	—	0	-8	-5	0	-0.7

YEAR TM/L	W	L	PCT	G	GS	CG	SH	SV	IP	H	HR	BB	SO	RAT	ERA	ERA+	OAV	OOB	BH	AVG	PB	PR	/A	PD	TPI
● BOB KAMMEYER Kammeyer, Robert Lynn b: 12/2/50, Kansas City, Kan. BR/TR, 6'4", 210 lbs. Deb: 7/03/78																									
1978 NY-A	0	0	—	7	0	0	0	0	21^{2}	24	1	6	11	13.3	5.82	62	.276	.337	0	—	0	-5	-5	1	-0.4
1979 NY-A	0	0	—	1	0	0	0	0	0	7	2	0	0	—	∞	—	1.000	1.000	0	—	0	-8	-8	0	-0.6
Total 2	0	0	—	8	0	0	0	0	21^{2}	31	3	6	11	16.6	9.14	40	.330	.388	0	—	0	-13	-13	1	-1.0
● IKE KAMP Kamp, Alphonse Francis b: 9/5/1900, Roxbury, Mass. d: 2/25/55, Boston, Mass. BB/TL, 6', 170 lbs. Deb: 9/16/24																									
1924 Bos-N	0	1	.000	1	1	0	0	0	7	9	0	5	4	18.0	5.14	74	.360	.467	0	.000	-0	-1	-1	0	-0.1
1925 Bos-N	2	4	.333	24	4	1	0	0	58^{1}	68	0	35	20	15.9	5.09	79	.301	.395	2	.167	-0	-5	-7	0	-0.6
Total 2	2	5	.286	25	5	1	0	0	65^{1}	77	0	40	24	16.1	5.10	78	.307	.402	2	.154	-0	-6	-8	1	-0.7
● HARRY KANE Kane, Harry "Klondike" (b: Harry Cohen) b: 7/27/1883, Hamburg, Ark. d: 9/15/32, Portland, Ore. BL/TL, Deb: 8/08/02																									
1902 StL-A	0	1	.000	4	1	1	0	0	23	34	2	16	7	19.6	5.48	64	.343	.434	1	.111	-1	-5	-5	-0	-0.5
1903 Det-A	0	2	.000	3	3	2	0	0	18	26	0	8	10	17.5	8.50	34	.336	.405	1	.143	-0	-11	-11	-1	-1.0
1905 Phi-N	1	1	.500	2	2	2	1	0	17	12	0	8	12	10.6	1.59	184	.203	.299	1	.167	-0	3	3	-0	0.2
1906 Phi-N	1	3	.250	6	3	2	0	0	28	28	0	18	14	15.8	3.86	68	.255	.374	0	.000	-1	-4	-4	0	-0.5
Total 4	2	7	.222	15	9	7	1	0	86	100	2	50	43	16.1	4.81	62	.289	.385	3	.100	-2	-17	-17	-1	-1.8
● ERV KANTLEHNER Kantlehner, Erving Leslie "Peanuts" b: 7/31/1892, San Jose, Cal. d: 2/3/90, Santa Barbara, Cal. BL/TL, 6', 190 lbs. Deb: 4/17/14																									
1914 Pit-N	3	2	.600	21	5	3	2	0	67	51	0	39	26	12.5	3.09	86	.218	.337	1	.067	-0	-2	-3	-0	-0.4
1915 Pit-N	5	12	.294	29	18	10	1	3	163	135	1	58	64	10.9	2.26	121	.230	.304	15	.288	3	9	8	1	1.4
1916 Pit-N	5	15	.250	34	21	7	2	2	165	151	1	57	49	11.6	3.16	85	.249	.317	8	.174	-0	-10	-9	1	-0.8
Phi-N	0	0	—	3	0	0	0	0	4	7	0	3	2	22.5	9.00	29	.500	.588	0	—	0	-3	-3	0	-0.3
Yr	5	15	.250	37	21	7	2	2	169	158	1	60	51	11.6	3.30	81	.253	.318	8	.174	-0	-13	-12	1	-1.1
Total 3	13	29	.310	87	44	20	5	5	399	344	2	157	141	11.5	2.84	95	.239	.318	24	.212	2	-6	-6	2	-0.1
● PAUL KARDOW Kardow, Paul Otto "Tex" b: 9/19/15, Humble, Tex. d: 4/27/68, San Antonio, Tex. BR/TR, 6'6", 210 lbs. Deb: 7/01/36																									
1936 Cle-A	0	0	—	2	0	0	0	0	2	1	0	2	0	13.5	4.50	112	.167	.375	0	—	0	0	0	-0	0.0
● ED KARGER Karger, Edwin "Loose" b: 5/6/1883, San Angelo, Tex. d: 9/9/57, Delta, Colo. BR/TL, 5'11", 185 lbs. Deb: 4/15/06																									
1906 Pit-N	2	3	.400	6	2	0	0	0	28	21	0	9	8	10.3	1.93	139	.204	.281	1	.091	-1	2	2	1	0.3
StL-N	5	16	.238	25	20	17	0	1	191^{2}	193	0	43	73	11.4	2.72	97	.271	.319	17	.233	4	-2	-2	3	0.6
Yr	7	19	.269	31	22	17	0	1	219^{2}	214	0	52	81	11.2	2.62	100	.262	.312	18	.214	3	0	0	4	0.9
1907 StL-N	15	19	.441	39	32	29	6	1	314	257	2	65	137	9.5	2.04	123	.223	.270	20	.179	1	15	16	4	2.6
1908 StL-N	4	9	.308	22	15	9	1	0	141^{1}	148	1	50	34	12.7	3.06	77	.260	.322	13	.241	2	-11	-11	-1	-1.0
1909 Cin-N	1	3	.250	9	5	1	0	0	34^{1}	26	0	30	8	15.2	4.46	58	.217	.382	3	.273	2	-7	-7	-0	-0.6
Bos-A	5	2	.714	12	6	3	0	0	68	71	0	22	17	12.7	3.18	79	.273	.337	3	.125	-0	-5	-5	-0	-0.6
1910 Bos-A	11	7	.611	27	25	16	1	1	183^{1}	162	5	53	81	10.8	3.19	80	.230	.289	20	.294	6	-14	-13	-2	-1.0
1911 Bos-A	5	8	.385	25	18	6	1	0	131	134	4	42	57	12.4	3.37	97	.272	.334	11	.234	3	-0	-1	-0	0.1
Total 6	48	67	.417	165	123	81	9	3	1091^{2}	1012	12	314	415	11.2	2.79	94	.246	.305	88	.220	17	-22	-20	5	0.4
● ANDY KARL Karl, Anton Andrew b: 4/8/14, Mt.Vernon, N.Y. d: 4/8/89, LaJolla, Cal. BR/TR, 6'1.5", 175 lbs. Deb: 4/24/43																									
1943 Bos-A	1	1	.500	11	0	0	0	1	26	31	0	13	6	15.2	3.46	96	.310	.389	2	.286	0	-0	-0	1	0.1
Phi-N	1	2	.333	9	2	0	0	0	26^{2}	44	0	11	4	18.6	7.09	48	.383	.437	2	.250	1	-11	-11	0	-1.0
1944 Phi-N	3	2	.600	38	0	0	0	2	89	76	1	21	26	9.9	2.33	155	.237	.287	3	.200	1	**13**	**13**	1	1.5
1945 Phi-N	8	8	.500	**67**	2	1	0	**15**	180^{2}	175	7	50	51	11.4	2.99	128	.253	.306	7	.143	-2	**16**	**17**	1	1.7
1946 Phi-N	3	7	.300	39	0	0	0	5	65^{1}	84	6	22	15	14.7	4.96	69	.321	.375	1	.100	-0	-11	-11	1	-1.1
1947 Bos-N	2	3	.400	27	0	0	0	3	35	41	2	13	5	13.9	3.86	101	.318	.380	1	.167	-0	1	0	2	0.2
Total 5	18	23	.439	191	4	1	0	26	422^{2}	451	16	130	107	12.5	3.51	104	.279	.334	16	.168	-0	7	7	6	1.4
● BILL KARNS Karns, William Arthur b: 12/28/1875, Richmond, Iowa d: 11/15/41, Seattle, Wash. BL/TL, Deb: 8/14/01																									
1901 Bal-A	1	0	1.000	3	1	1	0	0	17	30	0	9	5	20.6	6.35	61	.379	.443	1	.143	-1	-5	-5	-0	-0.5
● HERB KARPEL Karpel, Herbert "Lefty" b: 12/27/17, Brooklyn, N.Y. BL/TL, 5'9.5", 180 lbs. Deb: 4/19/46																									
1946 NY-A	0	0	—	2	0	0	0	0	1^{2}	4	0	0	0	21.6	10.80	32	.500	.500	0	—	0	-1	-1	-0	-0.1
● BENN KARR Karr, Benjamin Joyce "Baldy" b: 11/28/1893, Mt.Pleasant, Miss. d: 12/8/68, Memphis, Tenn. BL/TR, 6', 175 lbs. Deb: 4/20/20																									
1920 Bos-A	3	8	.273	26	2	0	0	1	91^{2}	109	3	24	21	13.2	4.81	76	.304	.349	21	.280	5	-10	-12	-1	-0.8
1921 Bos-A	8	7	.533	26	7	5	0	0	117^{2}	123	8	38	37	12.4	3.67	115	.283	.342	16	.258	1	8	7	-0	0.8
1922 Bos-A	5	12	.294	41	13	7	0	1	183^{1}	212	10	45	41	12.9	4.47	92	.302	.348	21	.214	-1	-9	-7	-1	-0.8
1925 Cle-A	11	12	.478	32	24	12	1	0	197^{2}	248	8	80	41	15.2	4.78	92	.317	.385	24	.261	4	-8	-8	2	-0.2
1926 Cle-A	5	6	.455	30	7	4	0	1	113^{1}	137	9	41	23	14.6	5.00	81	.291	.355	10	.222	2	-12	-12	1	-0.9
1927 Cle-A	3	3	.500	22	5	1	0	2	76^{2}	92	5	32	17	14.7	5.05	83	.315	.385	4	.200	1	-8	-7	2	-0.4
Total 6	35	48	.422	177	58	29	1	5	780^{1}	921	43	260	180	13.9	4.60	90	.303	.362	96	.245	12	-40	-39	2	-2.3
● JACK KATOLL Katoll, John "Big Jack" b: 6/24/1872, Germany d: 6/18/55, Hartland, Ill. BR/TR, 5'11", 195 lbs. Deb: 9/09/1898																									
1898 Chi-N	0	1	.000	2	1	1	0	0	11	8	0	1	3	7.4	0.82	438	.202	.222	0	.000	-1	3	3	-0	0.3
1899 Chi-N	1	1	.500	2	2	2	0	0	18	17	0	4	1	11.0	6.00	62	.249	.301	0	.000	-1	-4	-5	0	-0.4
1901 Chi-A	11	10	.524	27	25	19	0	0	208	231	3	53	59	12.6	2.81	124	.278	.327	10	.125	-4	20	15	2	1.2
1902 Chi-A	0	0	—	1	0	0	0	0	1	1	0	0	2	9.0	0.00	—	.261	.261	0	.000	-0	0	0	0	0.0
Bal-A	5	10	.333	15	13	13	0	0	123	175	5	32	25	15.3	4.02	94	.334	.375	10	.175	-0	-6	-3	4	0.0
Yr	5	10	.333	16	13	13	0	0	124	176	5	32	27	15.2	3.99	94	.334	.374	10	.172	-0	-6	-3	4	0.0
Total 4	17	22	.436	47	41	35	0	0	361	432	8	90	90	13.3	3.32	109	.295	.340	20	.134	-6	13	11	6	1.1
● BOB KATZ Katz, Robert Clyde b: 1/30/11, Lancaster, Pa. d: 12/14/62, St.Joseph, Mich. BR/TR, 5'11.5", 190 lbs. Deb: 5/12/44																									
1944 Cin-N	0	1	.000	6	2	0	0	0	18^{1}	17	0	7	4	11.8	3.93	89	.254	.324	0	.000	-1	-1	-1	1	-0.1
● CURT KAUFMAN Kaufman, Curt Gerrard b: 7/19/57, Omaha, Neb. BR/TR, 6'2", 175 lbs. Deb: 9/10/82																									
1982 NY-A	1	0	1.000	7	0	0	0	0	8^{2}	9	2	6	1	15.6	5.19	77	.265	.375	0	—	0	-1	-1	-0	-0.1
1983 NY-A	0	0	—	4	0	0	0	0	8^{2}	10	0	4	8	14.5	3.12	125	.303	.378	0	—	0	1	1	-0	0.2
1984 Cal-A	2	3	.400	29	1	0	0	1	69	68	13	20	41	11.5	4.57	87	.254	.306	0	—	0	-4	-5	0	-0.4
Total 3	3	3	.500	40	1	0	0	1	86^{1}	87	15	30	50	12.2	4.48	88	.260	.321	0	—	0	-5	-5	0	-0.3
● TONY KAUFMANN Kaufmann, Anthony Charles b: 12/16/1900, Chicago, Ill. d: 6/4/82, Elgin, Ill. BR/TR, 5'11", 165 lbs. Deb: 9/23/21 C♦																									
1921 Chi-N	1	0	1.000	2	1	1	0	1	13	12	0	3	6	10.4	4.15	92	.240	.283	2	.400	1	-1	-0	-1	0.0
1922 Chi-N	7	13	.350	37	9	4	1	3	153	161	15	57	45	13.1	4.06	103	.273	.343	9	.200	1	1	2	-1	0.3
1923 Chi-N	14	10	.583	33	24	18	2	3	206^{1}	209	14	67	72	12.5	3.10	129	.264	.330	16	.216	3	21	21	-1	2.3
1924 Chi-N	16	11	.593	34	26	16	3	0	208^{1}	218	21	66	79	12.4	4.02	97	.272	.330	24	.316	6	-3	-3	-1	0.2
1925 Chi-N	13	13	.500	31	23	14	2	2	196	221	9	77	49	14.0	4.50	96	.292	.363	15	.192	1	-5	-4	-0	-0.2
1926 Chi-N	9	7	.563	26	21	14	1	2	169^{2}	169	6	44	52	11.6	3.02	127	.262	.316	15	.250	2	15	15	-2	1.6
1927 Chi-N	3	3	.500	9	6	3	0	0	53^{1}	75	8	19	21	16.5	6.41	60	.338	.400	5	.313	3	-15	-15	2	-1.0
Phi-N	0	3	.000	5	5	1	0	0	18^{2}	37	2	8	4	21.7	10.61	39	.425	.474	1	.143	0	-14	-13	-0	-1.2
StL-N	0	0	—	1	0	0	0	0	0^{1}	4	0	1	0	135.0	81.00	5	1.000	1.000	0	—	0	-3	-3	0	-0.2
Yr	3	6	.333	15	11	4	0	0	72^{1}	116	10	28	25	17.9	7.84	50	.366	.417	6	.261	3	-32	-31	1	-2.4
1928 StL-N	0	0	—	4	1	0	0	0	4^{2}	8	1	4	2	25.1	9.64	41	.444	.565	0	—	0	-3	-3	-0	-0.3
1930 StL-N	0	1	.000	2	1	0	0	0	10^{1}	15	2	4	2	16.5	7.84	64	.357	.413	1	.333	0	-3	-3	-0	-0.3

YEAR	TM/L	W	L	PCT	G	GS	CG	SH	SV	IP	H	HR	BB	SO	RAT	ERA	ERA+	OAV	OOB	BH	AVG	PB	PR	/A	PD	TPI
1931	StL-N	1	1	.500	15	1	0	0	1	49	65	3	17	13	15.2	6.06	65	.319	.374	2	.111	-1	-12	-12	0	-1.2
1935	StL-N	0	0	—	3	0	0	0	0	3^{2}	4	0	1	0	12.3	2.45	167	.286	.333	0	—	0	1	1	0	0.1
Total	11	64	62	.508	202	118	71	9	12	1086^{1}	1198	81	368	345	13.3	4.18	97	.284	.347	91	.220	17	-22	-17	-5	0.1
● STEVE KEALEY	Kealey, Steven William b: 5/13/47, Torrance, Cal. BR/TR, 6', 185 lbs. Deb: 9/09/68																									
1968	Cal-A	0	1	.000	6	0	0	0	0	10	10	0	5	4	13.5	2.70	108	.256	.341	0	—	0	0	0	-1	0.0
1969	Cal-A	2	0	1.000	15	3	1	1	0	36^{2}	48	4	13	17	15.2	3.93	89	.322	.380	0	.000	-1	-1	-2	-1	-0.4
1970	Cal-A	1	0	1.000	17	0	0	0	1	21^{2}	19	2	6	14	10.4	4.15	87	.260	.316	1	.250	0	-1	-1	-1	-0.2
1971	Chi-A	2	2	.500	54	1	0	0	6	77^{1}	69	10	26	50	11.1	3.84	93	.239	.302	2	.200	1	-3	-2	-0	-0.2
1972	Chi-A	3	2	.600	40	0	0	0	4	57^{1}	50	4	12	37	9.7	3.30	95	.234	.274	0	.000	-0	-2	-1	-1	-0.2
1973	Chi-A	0	0	—	7	0	0	0	0	11^{1}	23	2	7	4	23.8	15.09	26	.418	.484	0	—	0	-14	-14	-0	-1.3
Total	6	8	5	.615	139	4	1	1	11	214^{1}	219	22	69	126	12.1	4.28	80	.267	.325	3	.115	-0	-21	-20	-3	-2.3
● ED KEAS	Keas, Edward James b: 2/2/1863, Dubuque, Iowa d: 1/12/40, Dubuque, Iowa Deb: 8/25/1888																									
1888	Cle-a	3	3	.500	6	6	6	0	0	51	53	1	12	18	11.6	2.29	135	.258	.302	2	.087	-2	4	5	1	0.3
● RAY KEATING	Keating, Raymond Herbert b: 7/21/1891, Bridgeport, Conn. d: 12/28/63, Sacramento, Cal. BR/TR, 5'11", 185 lbs. Deb: 9/12/12																									
1912	NY-A	0	3	.000	6	5	3	0	0	35^{2}	36	0	18	21	13.9	5.80	62	.265	.355	6	.375	2	-10	-9	0	-0.6
1913	NY-A	6	12	.333	28	21	9	2	0	151^{1}	147	3	51	83	11.9	3.21	93	.253	.316	3	.070	-3	-5	-4	-2	-0.9
1914	NY-A	7	11	.389	34	25	14	0	1	210	198	1	67	109	11.6	2.96	93	.253	.316	12	.169	-0	-5	-5	2	-0.3
1915	NY-A	3	6	.333	11	10	8	1	0	79^{1}	66	3	45	37	12.9	3.63	81	.228	.337	4	.154	-1	-6	-6	1	-0.6
1916	NY-A	5	6	.455	14	12	6	0	0	91	91	4	37	35	12.9	3.07	94	.272	.349	7	.241	1	-2	-2	2	0.1
1918	NY-A	2	2	.500	15	6	1	0	0	48^{1}	39	0	30	16	13.2	3.91	72	.238	.362	3	.188	-0	-6	-6	0	-0.6
1919	Bos-N	7	11	.389	22	13	9	1	0	136	129	2	45	48	11.6	2.98	96	.261	.325	7	.152	-1	-1	-2	2	-0.1
Total	7	30	51	.370	130	92	50	4	1	751^{2}	706	13	293	349	12.2	3.29	88	.254	.329	42	.170	-2	-35	-33	5	-3.0
● BOB KEATING	Keating, Robert M. b: 9/22/1862, Springfield, Mass d: 1/19/22, Springfield, Mass. BL/TL, 6'4", Deb: 8/27/1887																									
1887	Bal-a	0	1	.000	1	1	1	0	0	9	16	0	6	0	22.0	11.00	37	.372	.449	1	.250	-0	-7	-7	0	-0.4
● CACTUS KECK	Keck, Frank Joseph b: 1/13/1899, St.Louis, Mo. d: 2/6/81, Kirkwood, Mo. BR/TR, 5'11", 170 lbs. Deb: 5/26/22																									
1922	Cin-N	7	6	.538	27	15	5	1	1	131	138	4	29	27	11.8	3.37	119	.276	.322	7	.159	-1	11	9	-3	0.4
1923	Cin-N	3	6	.333	35	6	1	0	2	87	84	5	32	16	12.3	3.72	104	.254	.325	1	.059	-1	3	1	1	0.1
Total	2	10	12	.455	62	21	6	1	3	218	222	9	61	43	12.0	3.51	112	.267	.323	8	.131	-2	13	10	-3	0.5
● DAVE KEEFE	Keefe, David Edwin b: 1/9/1897, Williston, Vt. d: 2/4/78, Kansas City, Mo. BL/TR, 5'9", 165 lbs. Deb: 4/21/17 C																									
1917	Phi-A	1	0	1.000	3	0	0	0	0	5	5	0	4	1	16.2	1.80	153	.278	.409	0	.000	-0	0	1	0	0.1
1919	Phi-A	0	1	.000	1	1	1	0	0	9	8	0	3	5	11.0	4.00	86	.242	.306	0	.000	-0	-1	-1	0	-0.1
1920	Phi-A	6	7	.462	31	13	7	1	0	130^{1}	129	2	30	41	11.4	2.97	136	.262	.313	10	.250	-0	12	15	1	1.6
1921	Phi-A	2	9	.182	44	12	4	0	1	173	214	19	64	68	14.7	4.68	95	.311	.374	10	.175	-3	-8	-4	-2	-0.9
1922	Cle-A	0	0	—	18	1	0	0	0	36^{1}	47	2	12	11	14.6	6.19	65	.333	.386	2	.333	1	-9	-9	-0	-0.8
Total	5	9	17	.346	97	27	12	1	1	353^{2}	403	23	113	126	13.4	4.15	101	.294	.352	22	.206	-3	-5	2	-1	-0.1
● GEORGE KEEFE	Keefe, George W. b: 1/7/1867, Washington, D.C. d: 8/24/35, Washington, D.C. BL/TL, 5'9", 168 lbs. Deb: 7/30/1886																									
1886	Was-N	0	3	.000	4	4	4	0	0	31^{1}	28	0	15	5	12.4	5.17	64	.233	.319	0	.000	-2	-6	-7	-1	-0.8
1887	Was-N	0	1	.000	1	1	1	0	0	8	16	1	4	0	24.8	9.00	45	.364	.440	0	.000	-1	-4	-4	-0	-0.4
1888	Was-N	6	7	.462	13	13	13	1	0	114	87	2	43	52	10.6	2.84	99	.206	.286	9	.214	1	0	-0	1	0.2
1889	Was-N	8	18	.308	30	27	24	0	0	230	266	6	143	90	16.2	5.13	77	.281	.377	16	.163	-2	-28	-30	-2	-2.8
1890	Buf-P	6	16	.273	25	22	22	0	0	196	280	11	138	55	19.4	6.52	63	.322	.417	16	.203	1	-50	-53	-1	-3.9
1891	Was-a	0	3	.000	5	4	4	0	1	37	44	0	17	11	15.1	2.68	140	.286	.360	2	.143	-0	4	4	1	0.4
Total	6	20	48	.294	78	71	68	1	1	616^{1}	721	20	360	213	16.0	5.05	74	.282	.374	43	.172	-3	-85	-90	-4	-7.3
● JOHN KEEFE	Keefe, John Thomas b: 5/5/1867, Fitchburg, Mass. d: 8/9/37, Fitchburg, Mass. TL , Deb: 4/28/1890																									
1890	Syr-a	17	24	.415	43	41	36	2	0	352^{1}	355	9	148	120	13.5	4.32	82	.254	.336	30	.191	-4	-17	-31	0	-2.9
● BOBBY KEEFE	Keefe, Robert Francis b: 6/16/1882, Folsom, Cal. d: 12/7/64, Sacramento, Cal. BR/TR, 5'11", 155 lbs. Deb: 4/15/07																									
1907	NY-A	3	5	.375	19	3	0	0	3	57^{2}	60	1	20	20	12.6	2.50	112	.270	.333	1	.053	-2	0	2	0	0.0
1911	Cin-N	12	13	.480	39	26	15	0	3	234^{1}	196	7	76	105	10.6	2.69	123	.229	.294	6	.086	-2	19	16	-5	0.8
1912	Cin-N	1	3	.250	17	6	0	0	2	68^{2}	78	0	33	29	15.1	5.24	64	.289	.375	3	.167	-1	-14	-14	0	-1.4
Total	3	16	21	.432	75	35	15	0	8	360^{2}	334	8	129	154	11.8	3.14	103	.248	.317	10	.093	-5	5	4	-5	-0.6
● TIM KEEFE	Keefe, Timothy John "Smiling Tim" or "Sir Timothy" b: 1/1/1857, Cambridge, Mass. d: 4/23/33, Cambridge, Mass. BR/TR, 5'10.5", 185 lbs. Deb: 8/06/1880 UH																									
1880	Tro-N	6	6	.500	12	12	12	0	0	105	71	0	17	43	7.5	**0.86**	**294**	**.187**	.222	10	.233	-0	18	19	1	2.2
1881	Tro-N	18	27	.400	45	45	45	4	0	402	442	4	81	103	11.7	3.25	91	.274	.309	35	.230	4	-21	-13	-0	-0.9
1882	Tro-N	17	26	.395	43	42	41	1	0	375	368	4	81	116	10.8	2.50	113	.244	.283	43	.228	5	17	14	5	2.2
1883	NY-a	41	27	.603	**68**	68	**68**	5	0	**619**	486	6	98	**361**	**8.5**	2.41	138	**.202**	**.233**	57	.220	4	61	63	6	**6.6**
1884	*NY-a	37	17	.685	57	57	56	4	0	482^{2}	378	5	75	317	8.7	2.26	138	**.203**	.240	50	.238	11	53	46	-0	5.4
1885	NY-N	32	13	.711	46	46	45	7	0	400	300	6	102	227	9.0	**1.58**	**169**	.203	.255	27	.163	-0	55	49	0	4.7
1886	NY-N	**42**	20	.677	**64**	64	**62**	2	0	**535**	479	9	102	297	9.8	2.56	126	.231	.267	35	.171	1	45	39	1	3.6
1887	NY-N	35	19	.648	56	56	54	2	0	476^{2}	428	11	108	189	**10.3**	3.12	121	**.230**	**.276**	42	.220	8	51	35	3	3.8
1888	*NY-N	**35**	12	**.745**	51	51	48	**8**	0	434^{1}	317	5	90	**335**	**8.7**	**1.74**	**157**	**.196**	.243	23	.127	-6	**54**	**48**	1	4.4
1889	*NY-N	28	13	.683	47	45	39	3	1	364	319	9	151	225	12.1	3.31	119	**.228**	.312	23	.154	-4	28	25	2	2.1
1890	NY-P	17	11	.607	30	30	23	1	0	229	228	6	85	88	12.6	3.38	134	.248	.317	10	.109	-6	22	30	1	2.1
1891	NY-N	2	5	.286	8	7	4	0	0	55	71	1	27	29	16.7	5.24	61	.302	.383	2	.095	-1	-12	-12	0	-1.1
	Phi-N	3	6	.333	11	10	9	0	1	78^{1}	84	2	28	35	13.3	3.91	87	.264	.331	5	.172	0	-5	-4	0	-0.4
	Yr	5	11	.313	19	17	13	0	1	133^{1}	155	3	55	64	14.4	4.45	75	.278	.347	7	.140	-1	-16	-17	1	-1.5
1892	Phi-N	19	16	.543	39	38	31	2	0	313^{1}	264	4	100	127	10.8	2.36	138	.219	.286	10	.085	-7	32	31	-1	2.2
1893	Phi-N	10	7	.588	22	22	17	0	0	178	202	3	79	53	14.9	4.40	104	.277	.358	18	.228	1	5	4	-2	0.2
Total	14	342	225	.603	599	593	554	39	2	5047^{1}	4437	75	1224	2545	10.3	2.62	125	.226	.275	390	.187	12	404	373	18	37.1
● ED KEEGAN	Keegan, Edward Charles b: 7/8/39, Camden, N.J. BR/TR, 6'3", 165 lbs. Deb: 8/24/59																									
1959	Phi-N	0	3	.000	3	3	0	0	0	9	19	2	13	3	33.0	18.00	23	.432	.569	0	.000	-0	-14	-14	-0	-1.2
1961	KC-A	0	0	—	6	0	0	0	1	6	6	0	5	3	16.5	4.50	91	.261	.393	0	—	0	-0	-0	-0	0.0
1962	Phi-N	0	0	—	4	0	0	0	0	8	6	1	5	5	13.5	2.25	172	.214	.353	0	—	0	2	1	-0	0.1
Total	3	0	3	.000	13	3	0	0	1	23	31	3	23	11	21.9	9.00	45	.326	.467	0	.000	-0	-13	-13	-1	-1.1
● BOB KEEGAN	Keegan, Robert Charles "Smiley" b: 8/4/20, Rochester, N.Y. BR/TR, 6'2.5", 207 lbs. Deb: 5/24/53																									
1953	Chi-A	7	5	.583	22	11	4	2	1	98^{2}	80	4	33	32	10.5	2.74	147	.223	.293	9	.321	2	14	14	1	1.7
1954	Chi-A★	16	9	.640	31	27	14	2	2	209^{2}	211	16	82	61	12.6	3.09	121	.266	.336	9	.120	-2	15	15	-1	1.2
1955	Chi-A	2	5	.286	18	11	1	0	0	58^{2}	83	4	28	29	17.2	5.83	68	.336	.406	6	.333	2	-12	-12	0	-1.0
1956	Chi-A	5	7	.417	20	16	4	0	0	105^{1}	119	15	35	32	13.3	3.93	104	.286	.344	4	.125	-1	3	2	-0	0.1
1957	Chi-A	10	8	.556	30	20	6	2	2	142^{2}	131	22	37	36	10.7	3.53	106	.243	.294	4	.103	-1	4	3	-1	0.1
1958	Chi-A	0	2	.000	14	2	0	0	0	29^{2}	44	9	18	8	18.8	6.07	60	.358	.440	0	.000	-1	-8	-8	1	-0.8
Total	6	40	36	.526	135	87	29	6	5	644^{2}	668	70	233	198	12.7	3.66	105	.270	.335	32	.163	-2	16	14	-1	1.3

YEAR	TM/L	W	L	PCT	G	GS	CG	SH	SV	IP	H	HR	BB	SO	RAT	ERA	ERA+	OAV	OOB	BH	AVG	PB	PR	/A	PD	TPI

● BURT KEELEY
Keeley, Burton Elwood "Speed"   b: 11/2/1879, Wilmington, Ill.   d: 5/3/52, Ely, Minn.   BR/TR, 5'9", 170 lbs.   Deb: 4/18/08

1908	Was-A	6	11	.353	28	15	12	1	1	169²	173	3	48	68	11.9	2.97	77	.259	.313	5	.102	-3	-11	-13	2	-1.5
1909	Was-A	0	0	—	2	0	0	0	0	7	12	0	1	0	18.0	11.57	21	.364	.400	1	.500	-0	-7	-7	1	-0.6
Total	2	6	11	.353	30	15	12	1	1	176²	185	3	49	68	12.2	3.31	69	.264	.317	6	.118	-2	-18	-20	2	-2.1

● VIC KEEN
Keen, Howard Victor   b: 3/16/1899, Belair, Md.   d: 12/10/76, Salisbury, Md.   BR/TR, 5'9", 165 lbs.   Deb: 8/13/18

1918	Phi-A	0	1	.000	1	1	0	0	0	8	9	1	1	1	11.3	3.38	87	.300	.323	0	.000	-0	-1	-0	-1	-0.1
1921	Chi-N	0	3	.000	5	4	1	0	0	25	29	0	9	9	14.0	4.68	82	.319	.386	0	.000	-0	-2	-2	0	-0.3
1922	Chi-N	1	2	.333	7	3	2	0	1	34²	36	4	10	11	12.2	3.89	108	.275	.331	4	.333	1	1	1	-0	0.2
1923	Chi-N	12	8	.600	35	17	10	0	1	177	169	8	57	46	11.7	3.00	133	.255	.319	8	.151	-3	20	20	-2	1.5
1924	Chi-N	15	14	.517	40	28	15	0	3	234²	242	17	80	75	12.5	3.80	103	.272	.335	12	.156	-4	2	3	-3	-0.5
1925	Chi-N	2	6	.250	30	8	1	0	1	83¹	125	8	41	19	17.9	6.26	69	.359	.427	6	.240	1	-18	-18	1	-1.5
1926	*StL-N	10	9	.526	26	21	12	1	0	152	179	15	42	29	13.1	4.56	86	.295	.342	3	.057	-6	-12	-11	-2	-1.8
1927	StL-N	2	1	.667	21	0	0	0	0	33²	39	3	8	12	13.1	4.81	82	.293	.343	1	.250	0	-3	-3	0	-0.3
Total	8	42	44	.488	165	82	41	1	6	748¹	828	56	248	202	13.1	4.11	97	.287	.346	34	.148	-13	-15	-11	-6	-2.8

● KID KEENAN
Keenan, Harry Leon   b: 1875, Louisville, Ky.   d: 6/11/03, Covington, Ky.   TR,   Deb: 8/11/1891

| 1891 | Cin-a | 0 | 1 | .000 | 1 | 1 | 1 | 0 | 0 | 8 | 6 | 0 | 4 | 5 | 12.4 | 0.00 | — | .201 | .316 | 2 | .500 | 1 | 3 | 4 | -0 | 0.4 |

● JIM KEENAN
Keenan, James W.   b: 2/10/1858, New Haven, Conn.   d: 9/21/26, Cincinnati, Ohio   BR/TR, 5'10", 186 lbs.   Deb: 5/17/1875 ♦

1884	Ind-a	0	0	—	1	0	0	0	0	3	2	0	0	0	6.0	3.00	110	.182	.182	73	.293	0	0	0	-0	0.0
1885	Cin-a	0	0	—	1	0	0	0	0	8	7	0	1	0	9.0	1.13	290	.233	.258	35	.265	0	2	2	0	0.2
1886	Cin-a	0	1	.000	2	0	0	0	0	8	8	0	3	2	12.4	3.38	104	.258	.324	40	.270	0	0	0	-0	0.0
Total	3	0	1	.000	4	0	0	0	0	19	17	0	4	2	9.9	2.37	142	.236	.276	452	.241	1	2	2	-0	0.2

● JIMMIE KEENAN
Keenan, James William "Sparkplug"   b: 5/25/1898, Avon, N.Y.   d: 6/5/80, Seminole, Fla.   BL/TL, 5'7", 155 lbs.   Deb: 9/09/20

1920	Phi-N	0	0	—	1	0	0	0	0	3	3	0	1	2	12.0	3.00	114	.333	.400	0	.000	-0	0	0	0	0.0
1921	Phi-N	1	2	.333	15	2	0	0	0	32¹	48	3	15	7	17.8	6.68	63	.364	.432	0	.000	-2	-10	-9	-1	-1.0
Total	2	1	2	.333	16	2	0	0	0	35¹	51	3	16	9	17.3	6.37	65	.362	.430	0	.000	-2	-10	-9	-1	-1.0

● JEFF KEENER
Keener, Jeffrey Bruce   b: 1/14/59, Pana, Ill.   BL/TR, 6', 170 lbs.   Deb: 6/08/82

1982	StL-N	1	1	.500	19	0	0	0	0	22¹	19	1	19	25	15.3	1.61	224	.235	.380	0	—	0	5	5	0	0.6
1983	StL-N	0	0	—	4	0	0	0	0	4¹	6	0	1	4	16.6	8.31	44	.333	.400	0	—	0	-2	-2	0	-0.2
Total	2	1	1	.500	23	0	0	0	0	26²	25	1	20	29	15.5	2.70	134	.253	.383	0	—	0	3	3	0	0.4

● JOE KEENER
Keener, Joseph Donald   b: 4/21/53, San Pedro, Cal.   BR/TR, 6'4", 200 lbs.   Deb: 9/18/76

| 1976 | Mon-N | 0 | 1 | .000 | 2 | 0 | 0 | 0 | 0 | 4¹ | 7 | 0 | 8 | 1 | 33.2 | 10.38 | 36 | .389 | .593 | 0 | .000 | -0 | -3 | -3 | 0 | -0.3 |

● HARRY KEENER
Keener, Joshua Harry "Beans"   b: 9/1869, Easton, Pa.   d: 3/5/12, Easton, Pa.   Deb: 6/27/1896

| 1896 | Phi-N | 3 | 11 | .214 | 16 | 13 | 11 | 0 | 0 | 113¹ | 144 | 5 | 39 | 28 | 15.2 | 5.88 | 73 | .307 | .371 | 16 | .314 | 2 | -19 | -20 | 0 | -1.4 |

● RICKEY KEETON
Keeton, Rickey   b: 3/18/57, Cincinnati, Ohio   BR/TR, 6'2", 190 lbs.   Deb: 5/27/80

1980	Mil-A	2	2	.500	5	5	0	0	0	28¹	35	4	9	8	14.0	4.76	81	.307	.358	0	—	0	-2	-3	0	-0.3
1981	Mil-A	1	0	1.000	17	0	0	0	0	35¹	47	4	11	9	14.8	5.09	67	.329	.377	0	—	0	-6	-7	0	-0.7
Total	2	3	2	.600	22	5	0	0	0	63²	82	8	20	17	14.4	4.95	73	.319	.368	0	—	0	-8	-9	0	-1.0

● FRANK KEFFER
Keffer, C. Frank   b: Philadelphia, Pa.   d: 10/1/32, Chicago, Ill.   Deb: 4/19/1890

| 1890 | Syr-a | 1 | 1 | .500 | 2 | 1 | 1 | 0 | 0 | 16 | 15 | 0 | 9 | 4 | 13.5 | 5.63 | 63 | .240 | .336 | 1 | .143 | -0 | -3 | -4 | 0 | -0.3 |

● CHET KEHN
Kehn, Chester Lawrence   b: 10/30/21, San Diego, Cal.   d: 4/5/84, San Diego, Cal.   BR/TR, 5'11", 168 lbs.   Deb: 4/30/42

| 1942 | Bro-N | 0 | 0 | — | 3 | 1 | 0 | 0 | 0 | 7² | 8 | 2 | 4 | 3 | 14.1 | 7.04 | 46 | .267 | .353 | 2 | 1.000 | 1 | -3 | -3 | 0 | -0.2 |

● KATSY KEIFER
Keifer, Sherman Carl   b: 9/3/1891, California, Pa.   d: 2/19/27, Outwood, Ken.   BB/TL,   Deb: 10/08/14

| 1914 | Ind-F | 1 | 0 | 1.000 | 1 | 1 | 1 | 0 | 0 | 9 | 6 | 0 | 2 | 2 | 8.0 | 2.00 | 173 | .194 | .242 | 1 | .333 | 0 | 1 | 1 | 0 | 0.2 |

● MIKE KEKICH
Kekich, Michael Dennis   b: 4/2/45, San Diego, Cal.   BR/TL, 6'1", 200 lbs.   Deb: 6/09/65

1965	LA-N	0	1	.000	5	1	0	0	0	10¹	10	2	13	9	20.0	9.58	34	.263	.451	0	.000	-0	-7	-7	-0	-0.8
1968	LA-N	2	10	.167	25	20	1	1	0	115	116	9	46	84	12.8	3.91	71	.267	.339	3	.081	-1	-12	-15	-1	-1.9
1969	NY-A	4	6	.400	28	13	1	0	1	105	91	11	49	66	12.2	4.54	77	.236	.325	3	.111	-1	-11	-12	-1	-1.5
1970	NY-A	6	3	.667	26	14	1	0	0	98²	103	12	55	63	14.5	4.83	73	.267	.360	3	.094	-1	-12	-14	-1	-1.7
1971	NY-A	10	9	.526	37	24	3	0	0	170¹	167	13	82	93	13.4	4.07	79	.257	.344	8	.154	-1	-11	-16	1	-1.5
1972	NY-A	10	13	.435	29	28	2	0	0	175¹	172	13	76	78	12.9	3.70	80	.263	.344	8	.136	-1	-12	-15	-1	-1.8
1973	NY-A	1	1	.500	5	4	0	0	0	14²	20	1	14	4	22.1	9.20	40	.351	.493	0	—	0	-9	-9	-0	-0.8
	Cle-A	1	4	.200	16	6	0	0	0	50	73	6	35	26	19.4	7.02	56	.349	.443	0	—	0	-18	-17	-1	-1.8
	Yr	2	5	.286	21	10	0	0	0	64²	93	7	49	30	19.8	7.52	51	.346	.447	0	—	0	-27	-26	-2	-2.6
1975	Tex-A	0	0	—	23	0	0	0	2	31¹	33	2	21	19	15.5	3.73	101	.282	.391	0	—	0	0	0	1	0.1
1977	Sea-A	5	4	.556	41	2	0	0	3	90	90	11	51	55	14.4	5.60	73	.265	.365	0	—	0	-15	-15	-0	-1.5
Total	9	39	51	.433	235	112	8	1	6	860²	875	80	442	497	13.9	4.59	72	.268	.358	25	.120	-5	-108	-121	-4	-13.2

● GEORGE KELB
Kelb, George Francis "Pugger" or "Lefty"   b: 7/17/1870, Toledo, Ohio   d: 10/20/36, Toledo, Ohio   BL/TL,   Deb: 4/17/1898

| 1898 | Cle-N | 0 | 1 | .000 | 3 | 1 | 1 | 0 | 0 | 16¹ | 20 | 0 | 1 | 8 | 15.4 | 4.41 | 82 | .329 | .374 | 1 | .200 | -0 | -1 | -1 | 0 | -0.2 |

● HAL KELLEHER
Kelleher, Harold Joseph   b: 6/24/13, Philadelphia, Pa.   d: 8/27/89, Cape May Court House, N.J.   BR/TR, 6', 165 lbs.   Deb: 9/17/35

1935	Phi-N	2	0	1.000	3	2	1	0	0	25	26	0	12	12	14.0	1.80	252	.260	.345	3	.375	1	6	8	0	1.0
1936	Phi-N	0	5	.000	14	4	1	0	0	44	60	2	29	13	18.8	5.32	85	.331	.432	2	.167	-0	-6	-4	0	-0.4
1937	Phi-N	2	4	.333	27	2	1	0	0	58¹	72	3	31	20	17.0	6.63	65	.308	.404	3	.176	-0	-18	-15	-0	-1.5
1938	Phi-N	0	0	—	6	0	0	0	0	7¹	16	0	9	4	30.7	18.41	21	.432	.543	1	.500	-0	-12	-12	0	-1.0
Total	4	4	9	.308	50	9	4	1	0	134²	174	5	81	49	17.8	5.95	74	.315	.413	9	.231	1	-30	-23	-0	-1.9

● RON KELLER
Keller, Ronald Lee   b: 6/3/43, Indianapolis, Ind.   BR/TR, 6'2", 200 lbs.   Deb: 7/09/66

1966	Min-A	0	0	—	2	0	0	0	0	5¹	7	1	1	1	13.5	5.06	71	.318	.348	0	.000	-0	-1	-1	-0	-0.1
1968	Min-A	0	1	.000	7	1	0	0	0	16	18	2	4	11	12.9	2.81	110	.305	.359	0	.000	-0	0	0	0	0.0
Total	2	0	1	.000	9	1	0	0	0	21¹	25	3	5	12	13.1	3.38	95	.309	.356	0	.000	-0	-1	-0	0	-0.1

● AL KELLETT
Kellett, Alfred Henry   b: 10/30/01, Red Bank, N.J.   d: 7/14/60, New York, N.Y.   BR/TR, 6'3", 200 lbs.   Deb: 7/01/23

1923	Phi-A	0	1	.000	5	0	0	0	0	10	11	0	8	1	17.1	6.30	65	.282	.404	1	.333	-0	-3	-3	1	-0.2
1924	Bos-A	0	0	—	1	0	0	0	0	0	0	0	2	0	∞	∞	—	—	1.000	0	—	0	-2	-2	0	-0.2
Total	2	0	1	.000	6	0	0	0	0	10	11	0	10	1	18.9	8.10	51	.282	.429	1	.333	0	-5	-4	1	-0.4

● HARRY KELLEY
Kelley, Harry Leroy   b: 2/13/06, Parkin, Ark.   d: 3/23/58, Parkin, Ark.   BR/TR, 5'9.5", 170 lbs.   Deb: 4/16/25

1925	Was-A	1	1	.500	6	1	0	0	0	16	30	0	12	7	23.6	9.00	47	.405	.488	0	.000	-1	-8	-8	1	-0.8
1926	Was-A	0	0	—	7	1	0	0	0	10	17	0	8	6	23.4	8.10	48	.405	.510	0	—	-0	-5	-5	-0	-0.5
1936	Phi-A	15	12	.556	35	27	20	1	3	235¹	250	21	75	82	12.5	3.86	132	.275	.332	18	.198	-1	31	32	-2	2.7
1937	Phi-A	13	21	.382	41	29	14	0	0	205	267	16	79	68	15.3	5.36	88	.306	.365	16	.225	1	-17	-15	-1	-1.3
1938	Phi-A	0	2	.000	4	3	0	0	0	8	17	0	10	3	30.4	16.88	29	.436	.551	0	.000	-0	-11	-11	-0	-0.9
	Was-A	9	8	.529	38	14	7	2	1	148¹	162	12	46	44	12.7	4.49	100	.276	.330	12	.250	1	5	0	0	0.2

YEAR	TM/L	W	L	PCT	G	GS	CG	SH	SV	IP	H	HR	BB	SO	RAT	ERA	ERA+	OAV	OOB	BH	AVG	PB	PR	/A	PD	TPI
	Yr	9	10	.474	42	17	7	2	1	156^1	179	12	56	47	13.6	5.12	88	.286	.346	12	.240	1	-6	-10	0	-0.7
1939	Was-A	4	3	.571	15	3	2	0	1	53^2	69	2	14	20	14.4	4.70	93	.314	.363	4	.267	1	-0	-2	-0	-0.2
Total	6	42	47	.472	146	78	43	3	5	676^1	812	51	244	230	14.2	4.86	98	.296	.356	50	.216	0	-5	-8	-2	-0.8

● DICK KELLEY Kelley, Richard Anthony b: 1/8/40, Boston, Mass d: 12/12/91, Northridge, Cal. BR/TL, 6', 175 lbs. Deb: 4/15/64

YEAR	TM/L	W	L	PCT	G	GS	CG	SH	SV	IP	H	HR	BB	SO	RAT	ERA	ERA+	OAV	OOB	BH	AVG	PB	PR	/A	PD	TPI
1964	Mil-N	0	0	—	2	0	0	0	0	2	2	0	3	2	22.5	18.00	20	.250	.455	0	—	0	-3	-3	-0	-0.3
1965	Mil-N	1	1	.500	21	4	0	0	0	45	37	5	20	31	11.4	3.00	117	.226	.310	0	.000	-1	3	3	-0	0.2
1966	Atl-N	7	5	.583	20	13	2	2	0	81	75	6	21	50	11.0	3.22	113	.247	.302	1	.036	-3	3	4	-2	-0.1
1967	Atl-N	2	9	.182	39	9	1	1	2	98	88	8	42	75	12.0	3.77	88	.247	.328	4	.250	1	-4	-5	1	-0.3
1968	Atl-N	2	4	.333	31	11	1	1	1	98	86	4	45	73	12.1	2.76	109	.238	.324	1	.043	-1	3	3	1	0.4
1969	SD-N	4	8	.333	27	23	1	1	0	136	113	11	61	96	11.8	3.57	99	.230	.321	5	.106	-2	0	-1	2	-0.1
1971	SD-N	2	3	.400	48	1	0	0	2	59^2	52	5	23	42	11.9	3.47	95	.232	.315	1	.333	0	-0	-1	0	-0.1
Total	7	18	30	.375	188	61	5	5	5	519^2	453	39	215	369	11.8	3.39	100	.237	.319	12	.096	-5	1	-1	2	-0.3

● TOM KELLEY Kelley, Thomas Henry b: 1/5/44, Manchester, Conn. BR/TR, 6', 191 lbs. Deb: 5/05/64

YEAR	TM/L	W	L	PCT	G	GS	CG	SH	SV	IP	H	HR	BB	SO	RAT	ERA	ERA+	OAV	OOB	BH	AVG	PB	PR	/A	PD	TPI
1964	Cle-A	0	0	—	6	0	0	0	0	9^2	9	1	9	7	17.7	5.59	64	.237	.396	0	—	0	-2	-2	0	-0.2
1965	Cle-A	2	1	.667	4	4	1	0	0	30	19	3	13	31	9.6	2.40	145	.186	.278	2	.222	0	4	4	-0	0.4
1966	Cle-A	4	8	.333	31	7	1	0	0	95^1	97	14	42	64	13.1	4.34	79	.264	.340	4	.143	-1	-10	-10	-1	-1.2
1967	Cle-A	0	0	—	1	0	0	0	0	1	0	0	2	0	18.0	0.00	—	.000	.500	0	—	0	0	0	0	0.1
1971	Atl-N	9	5	.643	28	20	5	0	0	143	140	8	69	68	13.2	2.96	125	.262	.347	2	.047	-4	8	12	-1	0.8
1972	Atl-N	5	7	.417	27	14	2	1	0	116^1	122	12	65	59	14.5	4.56	83	.272	.364	3	.088	-2	-14	-10	-3	-1.5
1973	Atl-N	0	1	.000	7	0	0	0	0	12^2	13	0	7	5	14.2	2.84	138	.289	.385	0	.000	-0	1	2	-0	0.1
Total	7	20	22	.476	104	45	9	1	0	408	400	38	207	234	13.4	3.75	97	.260	.349	11	.095	-7	-13	-4	-5	-1.5

● ALEX KELLNER Kellner, Alexander Raymond b: 8/26/24, Tucson, Ariz. BR/TL, 6', 200 lbs. Deb: 4/29/48 F

YEAR	TM/L	W	L	PCT	G	GS	CG	SH	SV	IP	H	HR	BB	SO	RAT	ERA	ERA+	OAV	OOB	BH	AVG	PB	PR	/A	PD	TPI
1948	Phi-A	0	0	—	13	1	0	0	0	23	21	0	16	14	15.3	7.83	55	.239	.368	0	.000	-1	-9	-9	-0	-1.0
1949	Phi-A☆	20	12	.625	38	27	19	0	1	245	243	18	129	94	13.7	3.75	110	.261	.352	20	.217	1	12	10	-0	1.1
1950	Phi-A	8	20	.286	36	29	15	0	2	225^1	253	28	112	85	14.7	5.47	83	.282	.363	16	.200	-1	-22	-23	-2	-2.4
1951	Phi-A	11	14	.440	33	29	11	1	2	209^2	218	20	93	94	13.5	4.46	96	.272	.350	18	.228	-1	-8	-4	-1	-0.6
1952	Phi-A	12	14	.462	34	33	14	2	0	231^1	223	21	86	105	12.2	4.36	91	.252	.321	17	.207	0	-18	-10	-2	-1.2
1953	Phi-A	11	12	.478	25	25	14	2	0	201^2	210	8	51	81	11.8	3.93	109	.269	.317	15	.217	1	2	8	-2	0.7
1954	Phi-A	6	17	.261	27	27	8	1	0	173^2	204	16	88	69	15.4	5.39	72	.301	.387	10	.182	-0	-32	-29	0	-2.8
1955	KC-A	11	8	.579	30	24	6	3	0	162^2	164	18	60	75	12.7	4.20	99	.265	.335	12	.214	2	-4	-1	-0	0.2
1956	KC-A	7	4	.636	20	17	5	0	0	91^2	103	15	33	44	13.5	4.32	100	.289	.353	6	.200	-0	-2	0	0	0.0
1957	KC-A	6	5	.545	28	21	3	0	0	132^2	141	18	41	72	12.5	4.27	93	.278	.335	11	.234	4	-7	-5	0	0.0
1958	KC-A	0	2	.000	7	6	0	0	0	33^2	40	5	8	22	12.8	5.88	66	.315	.356	1	.091	-0	-8	-7	0	-0.7
	Cin-N	7	3	.700	18	7	4	0	0	82	74	8	20	42	10.6	2.30	180	.243	.296	10	.357	3	15	17	-2	1.9
1959	StL-N	2	1	.667	12	4	0	0	0	37	31	9	10	19	10.2	3.16	134	.220	.276	2	.222	0	3	4	-0	0.4
Total	12	101	112	.474	321	250	99	9	5	1849^1	1925	184	747	816	13.2	4.41	95	.270	.343	138	.215	8	-78	-47	-8	-4.4

● WALT KELLNER Kellner, Walter Joseph b: 4/26/29, Tucson, Ariz. BR/TR, 6', 200 lbs. Deb: 9/06/52 F

YEAR	TM/L	W	L	PCT	G	GS	CG	SH	SV	IP	H	HR	BB	SO	RAT	ERA	ERA+	OAV	OOB	BH	AVG	PB	PR	/A	PD	TPI
1952	Phi-A	0	0	—	1	0	0	0	1	4	4	0	3	2	15.8	6.75	59	.250	.368	0	.000	-0	-1	-1	-0	-0.1
1953	Phi-A	0	0	—	2	0	0	0	0	3	1	0	4	4	18.0	6.00	71	.111	.429	0	—	0	-1	-1	0	0.0
Total	2	0	0	—	3	0	0	0	1	7	5	0	7	6	16.7	6.43	64	.200	.394	0	.000	-0	-2	-2	0	-0.1

● AL KELLOGG Kellogg, Albert C. b: 9/9/1886, Providence, R.I. d: 7/21/53, Portland, Ore. TL, 6'3", 208 lbs. Deb: 9/25/08

YEAR	TM/L	W	L	PCT	G	GS	CG	SH	SV	IP	H	HR	BB	SO	RAT	ERA	ERA+	OAV	OOB	BH	AVG	PB	PR	/A	PD	TPI
1908	Phi-A	0	2	.000	3	3	2	0	0	17	20	1	9	8	15.9	5.82	44	.294	.385	1	.125	-1	-6	-6	0	-0.6

● WIN KELLUM Kellum, Winford Ansley b: 4/11/1876, Waterford, Ont., Canada d: 8/10/51, Big Rapids, Mich. BB/TL, 5'10", 190 lbs. Deb: 4/26/01

YEAR	TM/L	W	L	PCT	G	GS	CG	SH	SV	IP	H	HR	BB	SO	RAT	ERA	ERA+	OAV	OOB	BH	AVG	PB	PR	/A	PD	TPI
1901	Bos-A	2	3	.400	6	6	5	0	0	48	61	3	7	8	13.3	6.38	55	.306	.339	3	.167	-1	-14	-15	1	-1.2
1904	Cin-N	15	10	.600	31	24	22	1	2	224^2	206	1	46	70	10.5	2.60	113	.244	.291	13	.159	1	3	8	1	1.1
1905	StL-N	3	3	.500	11	7	5	1	0	74	70	1	10	19	9.9	2.92	102	.255	.283	5	.200	1	1	0	1	0.2
Total	3	20	16	.556	48	37	32	2	2	346^2	337	5	63	97	10.7	3.19	95	.256	.297	21	.168	1	-10	-6	3	0.1

● BRYAN KELLY Kelly, Bryan Keith b: 2/24/59, Silver Spring, Md. BR/TR, 6'2", 195 lbs. Deb: 9/02/86

YEAR	TM/L	W	L	PCT	G	GS	CG	SH	SV	IP	H	HR	BB	SO	RAT	ERA	ERA+	OAV	OOB	BH	AVG	PB	PR	/A	PD	TPI
1986	Det-A	1	2	.333	6	4	0	0	0	20	21	4	10	18	13.9	4.50	92	.269	.352	0	—	0	-1	-1	0	0.0
1987	Det-A	0	1	.000	5	0	0	0	0	10^2	12	2	7	10	16.0	5.06	83	.286	.388	0	—	0	-1	-1	0	-0.1
Total	2	1	3	.250	11	4	0	0	0	30^2	33	6	17	28	14.7	4.70	89	.275	.365	0	—	0	-1	-2	0	-0.1

● ED KELLY Kelly, Edward Leo b: 12/10/1888, Pawtucket, R.I. d: 11/4/28, Red Lodge, Mont. BR/TR, 5'11.5", 173 lbs. Deb: 4/14/14

YEAR	TM/L	W	L	PCT	G	GS	CG	SH	SV	IP	H	HR	BB	SO	RAT	ERA	ERA+	OAV	OOB	BH	AVG	PB	PR	/A	PD	TPI
1914	Bos-A	0	0	—	3	0	0	0	0	2^1	1	0	1	4	7.7	0.00	—	.100	.182	0	.000	-0	1	1	0	0.1

● GEORGE KELLY Kelly, George Lange "Highpockets" b: 9/10/1895, San Francisco, Cal. d: 10/13/84, Burlingame, Cal. BR/TR, 6'4", 190 lbs. Deb: 8/18/15 FCH♦

YEAR	TM/L	W	L	PCT	G	GS	CG	SH	SV	IP	H	HR	BB	SO	RAT	ERA	ERA+	OAV	OOB	BH	AVG	PB	PR	/A	PD	TPI
1917	NY-N	1	0	1.000	1	0	0	0	0	5	4	0	1	2	9.0	0.00	—	.211	.250	0	.000	-0	2	1	-0	0.1

● HERB KELLY Kelly, Herbert Barrett "Moke" b: 6/4/1892, Mobile, Ala. d: 5/18/73, Torrance, Cal. BL/TL, 5'9", 160 lbs. Deb: 9/25/14

YEAR	TM/L	W	L	PCT	G	GS	CG	SH	SV	IP	H	HR	BB	SO	RAT	ERA	ERA+	OAV	OOB	BH	AVG	PB	PR	/A	PD	TPI
1914	Pit-N	0	2	.000	5	2	2	0	0	25^2	24	1	7	6	10.9	2.45	108	.253	.304	2	.222	0	1	1	-0	0.1
1915	Pit-N	1	1	.500	5	1	0	0	0	11	10	0	4	6	12.3	4.09	67	.250	.333	1	.500	1	-2	-2	1	0.0
Total	2	1	3	.250	10	3	2	0	0	36^2	34	1	11	12	11.3	2.95	91	.252	.313	3	.273	1	-1	-1	1	0.1

● MIKE KELLY Kelly, Michael J. b: 11/9/02, St.Louis, Mo. BR/TR, 6'1", 178 lbs. Deb: 9/03/26

YEAR	TM/L	W	L	PCT	G	GS	CG	SH	SV	IP	H	HR	BB	SO	RAT	ERA	ERA+	OAV	OOB	BH	AVG	PB	PR	/A	PD	TPI
1926	Phi-N	0	0	—	4	0	0	0	0	6^2	9	0	4	2	18.9	9.45	44	.346	.452	0	.000	-1	-4	-4	-0	-0.4

● KING KELLY Kelly, Michael Joseph b: 12/31/1857, Troy, N.Y. d: 11/8/1894, Boston, Mass. BR/TR, 5'10", 170 lbs. Deb: 5/01/1878 MH♦

YEAR	TM/L	W	L	PCT	G	GS	CG	SH	SV	IP	H	HR	BB	SO	RAT	ERA	ERA+	OAV	OOB	BH	AVG	PB	PR	/A	PD	TPI
1880	Chi-N	0	0	—	1	0	0	0	0	3	3	0	1	1	12.0	0.00	—	.250	.308	100	.291	0	1	1	-0	0.1
1883	Chi-N	0	0	—	1	0	0	0	0	1	1	0	0	0	9.0	0.00	—	.333	.333	109	.255	0	0	0	0	0.0
1884	Chi-N	0	1	.000	2	0	0	0	0	5^1	12	2	2	1	23.6	8.44	37	.400	.438	160	.354	1	-3	-3	-0	-0.3
1887	Bos-N	1	0	1.000	3	0	0	0	0	13	17	1	14	0	21.5	3.46	117	.298	.437	156	.322	1	1	1	0	0.1
1890	Bos-P	1	0	1.000	1	0	0	0	0	2	1	0	2	2	13.5	4.50	98	.142	.332	111	.326	0	-0	-0	-0	0.0
1891	Cin-a	0	1	.000	3	0	0	0	0	15^1	21	2	7	0	17.0	5.28	78	.315	.389	84	.297	1	-3	-2	0	-0.1
1892	*Bos-N	0	0	—	1	0	0	0	0	6	8	0	4	0	22.5	1.50	234	.308	.455	53	.189	0	1	1	-0	0.1
Total	7	2	2	.500	12	0	0	0	0	45^2	63	5	30	4	19.1	4.14	92	.312	.412	1813	.308	4	-3	-2	-0	-0.1

● REN KELLY Kelly, Reynolds Joseph b: 11/18/1899, San Francisco, Cal d: 8/24/63, Millbrae, Cal. BR/TR, 6', 183 lbs. Deb: 9/18/23 F

YEAR	TM/L	W	L	PCT	G	GS	CG	SH	SV	IP	H	HR	BB	SO	RAT	ERA	ERA+	OAV	OOB	BH	AVG	PB	PR	/A	PD	TPI
1923	Phi-A	0	0	—	1	0	0	0	0	7	7	0	4	1	14.1	2.57	160	.259	.355	0	.000	-1	1	1	-0	0.0

● BOB KELLY Kelly, Robert Edward b: 10/4/27, Cleveland, Ohio BR/TR, 6', 180 lbs. Deb: 5/04/51

YEAR	TM/L	W	L	PCT	G	GS	CG	SH	SV	IP	H	HR	BB	SO	RAT	ERA	ERA+	OAV	OOB	BH	AVG	PB	PR	/A	PD	TPI
1951	Chi-N	7	4	.636	35	11	4	0	0	123^2	130	8	55	48	13.5	4.66	88	.275	.352	5	.161	-1	-10	-8	-0	-0.8
1952	Chi-N	4	9	.308	31	15	3	2	0	125^1	114	7	46	50	11.7	3.59	107	.236	.306	8	.216	0	2	4	1	0.5
1953	Chi-N	0	1	.000	14	0	0	0	0	17	27	2	9	6	19.6	9.53	47	.375	.451	0	.000	-0	-10	-10	0	-0.9
	Cin-N	1	2	.333	28	5	0	0	2	66^1	71	7	26	29	13.2	4.34	100	.276	.343	2	.118	-1	-0	0	0	-0.1
	Yr	1	3	.250	42	5	0	0	2	83^1	98	9	35	35	14.4	5.40	81	.297	.364	2	.111	-1	-10	-9	1	-1.0
1958	Cin-N	0	0	—	2	1	0	0	0	2	3	0	3	1	27.0	4.50	92	.500	.667	0	—	0	-0	-0	0	0.0
	Cle-A	0	2	.000	13	3	0	0	0	27^2	29	4	13	12	14.0	5.20	70	.282	.368	1	.250	0	-4	-5	0	-0.4
Total	4	12	18	.400	123	35	7	2	2	362	374	28	152	146	13.2	4.50	90	.268	.343	16	.178	-1	-22	-18	1	-1.7

● BILL KELSO
Kelso, William Eugene b: 2/19/40, Kansas City, Mo. BR/TR, 6'4", 215 lbs. Deb: 7/31/64

YEAR	TM/L	W	L	PCT	G	GS	CG	SH	SV	IP	H	HR	BB	SO	RAT	ERA	ERA+	OAV	OOB	BH	AVG	PB	PR	/A	PD	TPI
1964	LA-A	2	0	1.000	10	1	1	1	0	23^2	19	3	9	21	11.0	2.28	144	.218	.299	0	.000	-0	4	3	0	0.3
1966	Cal-A	1	1	.500	5	0	0	0	0	11^1	11	1	6	11	14.3	2.38	141	.244	.346	0	.000	-0	1	1	-0	0.1
1967	Cal-A	5	3	.625	69	1	0	0	11	112	85	6	63	91	12.2	2.97	106	.219	.333	2	.105	-1	3	2	1	0.2
1968	Cin-N	4	1	.800	35	0	0	0	1	54	56	6	15	39	12.3	4.00	79	.277	.336	0	.000	-1	-6	-5	-1	-0.7
Total	4	12	5	.706	119	2	1	1	12	201	171	16	93	162	12.2	3.13	102	.237	.331	2	.059	-2	2	1	-0	-0.1

● RUSS KEMMERER
Kemmerer, Russell Paul "Rusty" or "Dutch" b: 11/1/31, Pittsburgh, Pa. BR/TR, 6'3", 200 lbs. Deb: 6/27/54

YEAR	TM/L	W	L	PCT	G	GS	CG	SH	SV	IP	H	HR	BB	SO	RAT	ERA	ERA+	OAV	OOB	BH	AVG	PB	PR	/A	PD	TPI
1954	Bos-A	5	3	.625	19	9	2	1	0	75^1	71	4	41	37	13.6	3.82	108	.257	.357	3	.143	-0	-1	2	0	0.2
1955	Bos-A	1	1	.500	7	2	0	0	0	17^1	18	3	15	13	17.1	7.27	59	.269	.402	0	.000	-0	-6	-6	-0	-0.6
1957	Bos-A	0	0	—	1	0	0	0	0	4	5	0	2	1	15.8	4.50	89	.333	.412	0	.000	-0	-0	-0	-0	-0.1
	Was-A	7	11	.389	39	26	6	0	0	172^1	214	20	71	81	15.0	4.96	79	.309	.375	3	.067	-1	-22	-20	-3	-2.4
	Yr	7	11	.389	40	26	6	0	0	176^1	219	20	73	82	15.0	4.95	79	.309	.375	3	.065	-1	-23	-21	-3	-2.5
1958	Was-A	6	15	.286	40	30	6	0	0	224^1	234	25	74	111	12.5	4.61	83	.270	.330	11	.159	-2	-21	-20	0	-2.2
1959	Was-A	8	17	.320	37	28	8	0	0	206	221	20	71	89	12.9	4.50	87	.276	.338	8	.133	-1	-15	-13	0	-1.4
1960	Was-A	0	2	.000	3	3	0	0	0	17^1	18	2	10	10	15.1	7.79	50	.269	.372	0	.000	0	-8	-8	1	-0.6
	Chi-A	6	3	.667	36	7	2	1	2	120^2	111	5	45	76	11.7	2.98	127	.248	.318	0	.000	-3	12	11	0	0.8
	Yr	6	5	.545	39	10	2	1	2	138	129	7	55	86	12.1	3.59	106	.250	.323	0	.000	-3	4	3	1	0.2
1961	Chi-A	3	3	.500	47	2	0	0	2	96^2	102	10	26	35	11.9	4.38	89	.278	.326	3	.200	1	-4	-5	1	-0.3
1962	Chi-A	2	1	.667	20	0	0	0	0	28	30	3	11	17	13.2	3.86	101	.270	.336	1	.500	1	0	0	1	0.2
	Hou-N	5	3	.625	36	2	0	0	3	68	72	10	15	23	11.9	4.10	91	.272	.318	3	.333	1	-1	-3	0	-0.2
1963	Hou-N	0	0	—	17	0	0	0	1	36^2	48	1	8	12	13.7	5.65	56	.320	.354	2	.286	0	-10	-10	1	-1.0
Total	9	43	59	.422	302	109	24	2	8	1066^2	1144	103	389	505	13.1	4.46	86	.277	.342	34	.128	-5	-76	-72	1	-7.6

● DUTCH KEMNER
Kemner, Herman John b: 3/4/1899, Quincy, Ill. d: 1/16/88, Quincy, Ill. BR/TR, 5'10.5", 175 lbs. Deb: 4/19/29

YEAR	TM/L	W	L	PCT	G	GS	CG	SH	SV	IP	H	HR	BB	SO	RAT	ERA	ERA+	OAV	OOB	BH	AVG	PB	PR	/A	PD	TPI
1929	Cin-N	0	0	—	9	0	0	0	1	15^1	19	0	8	10	15.8	7.63	60	.328	.409	1	.250	0	-5	-5	0	-0.5

● ED KENNA
Kenna, Edward Benninghaus "The Pitching Poet" b: 10/17/1877, Charleston, W.Va. d: 3/22/12, Grant, Fla. TR, 6', 180 lbs. Deb: 5/05/02

YEAR	TM/L	W	L	PCT	G	GS	CG	SH	SV	IP	H	HR	BB	SO	RAT	ERA	ERA+	OAV	OOB	BH	AVG	PB	PR	/A	PD	TPI
1902	Phi-A	1	1	.500	2	1	1	0	0	17	19	1	11	5	16.4	5.29	69	.283	.391	1	.125	-0	-3	-3	0	-0.3

● VERN KENNEDY
Kennedy, Lloyd Vernon b: 3/20/07, Kansas City, Mo. BL/TR, 6', 175 lbs. Deb: 9/18/34

YEAR	TM/L	W	L	PCT	G	GS	CG	SH	SV	IP	H	HR	BB	SO	RAT	ERA	ERA+	OAV	OOB	BH	AVG	PB	PR	/A	PD	TPI
1934	Chi-A	0	2	.000	3	3	1	0	0	19^1	21	1	9	7	14.0	3.72	127	.300	.380	2	.286	0	2	2	1	0.3
1935	Chi-A	11	11	.500	31	25	16	2	1	211^2	211	17	95	65	13.2	3.91	118	.262	.343	18	.247	1	13	17	2	1.9
1936	Chi-A☆	21	9	.700	35	34	20	1	0	274^1	282	13	147	99	14.2	4.63	112	.268	.360	32	.283	5	13	17	1	2.1
1937	Chi-A	14	13	.519	32	30	15	1	0	221	238	16	124	114	14.9	5.09	90	.273	.366	20	.230	2	-12	-12	0	-0.9
1938	Det-A☆	12	9	.571	33	26	11	0	2	190^1	215	13	113	53	15.6	5.06	99	.287	.381	23	.291	3	-6	-1	2	0.3
1939	Det-A	0	3	.000	4	4	1	0	0	21	25	4	9	9	15.0	6.43	76	.301	.376	2	.286	0	-4	-4	1	-0.3
	StL-A	9	17	.346	33	27	12	1	0	191^2	229	18	115	55	16.2	5.73	85	.297	.389	10	.149	-3	-24	-18	-1	-1.9
	Yr	9	20	.310	37	31	13	1	0	212^2	254	22	124	64	16.0	5.80	84	.297	.387	12	.162	-2	-28	-22	0	-2.2
1940	StL-A	12	17	.414	34	32	18	0	0	222^1	263	18	122	70	15.7	5.59	82	.298	.385	25	.298	7	-30	-25	2	-1.4
1941	StL-A	2	4	.333	6	6	2	0	0	45	44	5	27	6	14.2	4.40	98	.259	.360	6	.400	2	-1	-1	0	0.2
	Was-A	1	7	.125	17	7	2	0	0	66^1	77	5	39	22	16.0	5.70	71	.297	.393	3	.143	-1	-11	-12	0	-1.2
	Yr	3	11	.214	23	13	4	0	0	111^1	121	10	66	28	15.3	5.17	80	.282	.380	9	.250	2	-13	-13	0	-1.0
1942	Cle-A	4	8	.333	28	12	4	0	1	108	99	1	50	37	12.5	4.08	84	.244	.328	6	.200	1	-5	-8	0	-0.6
1943	Cle-A	10	7	.588	28	17	8	1	0	146^2	130	4	59	63	11.7	2.45	127	.242	.319	12	.231	1	14	11	1	1.5
1944	Cle-A	2	5	.286	12	10	2	0	0	59	66	0	37	17	15.7	5.03	66	.289	.389	2	.087	-2	-11	-11	1	-1.2
	Phi-N	1	5	.167	12	7	3	0	0	55^1	60	3	20	23	13.0	4.23	85	.269	.329	6	.286	1	-4	-4	0	-0.3
1945	Phi-N	0	3	.000	12	3	0	0	0	36	43	2	14	13	14.3	5.50	70	.297	.358	2	.182	0	-7	-7	1	-0.5
	Cin-N	5	12	.294	24	20	11	1	1	157^2	170	10	69	38	13.8	4.00	94	.280	.356	12	.226	2	-3	-4	1	-0.1
	Yr	5	15	.250	36	23	11	1	1	193^2	213	12	83	51	13.9	4.28	88	.283	.356	14	.219	2	-10	-11	2	-0.6
Total	12	104	132	.441	344	263	126	7	5	2025^2	2173	130	1049	691	14.4	4.67	94	.277	.363	181	.244	19	-77	-63	13	-2.1

● MONTE KENNEDY
Kennedy, Montia Calvin b: 5/11/22, Amelia, Va. BR/TL, 6'2", 185 lbs. Deb: 4/18/46

YEAR	TM/L	W	L	PCT	G	GS	CG	SH	SV	IP	H	HR	BB	SO	RAT	ERA	ERA+	OAV	OOB	BH	AVG	PB	PR	/A	PD	TPI
1946	NY-N	9	10	.474	38	27	10	1	1	186^2	153	14	116	71	13.2	3.42	101	.224	.340	15	.234	2	-0	0	-0	0.3
1947	NY-N	9	12	.429	34	24	9	0	0	148^1	158	8	88	60	15.2	4.85	84	.272	.372	8	.167	-1	-13	-13	-0	-1.3
1948	NY-N	3	9	.250	25	16	7	1	0	114^1	118	10	57	63	14.0	4.01	98	.264	.351	4	.129	-1	-1	-1	-1	-0.3
1949	NY-N	12	14	.462	38	32	14	4	1	223^1	208	13	100	95	12.5	3.43	116	.242	.323	12	.145	-1	15	14	-2	1.0
1950	NY-N	5	4	.556	36	17	5	0	2	114^1	120	14	53	41	13.9	4.72	87	.269	.351	2	.056	-3	-7	-8	-0	-1.1
1951	*NY-N	1	2	.333	29	5	1	0	0	68	68	0	31	22	13.1	2.25	174	.270	.350	3	.200	0	13	13	-0	1.3
1952	NY-N	3	4	.429	31	6	2	1	0	83^1	73	6	31	48	11.4	3.02	122	.230	.303	2	.091	-1	7	6	1	0.6
1953	NY-N	0	0	—	18	0	0	0	0	22^2	30	2	19	11	19.9	7.15	60	.337	.459	0	.000	-0	-7	-7	0	-0.7
Total	8	42	55	.433	249	127	48	7	4	961	928	67	495	411	13.5	3.84	101	.253	.344	46	.153	-5	6	4	-4	-0.2

● TED KENNEDY
Kennedy, Theodore A. b: 2/1865, Henry, Ill. d: 10/31/07, St.Louis, Mo. BL, Deb: 6/12/1885

YEAR	TM/L	W	L	PCT	G	GS	CG	SH	SV	IP	H	HR	BB	SO	RAT	ERA	ERA+	OAV	OOB	BH	AVG	PB	PR	/A	PD	TPI
1885	Chi-N	7	2	.778	9	9	8	0	0	78^2	91	5	28	36	13.6	3.43	88	.288	.346	3	.083	-4	-5	-3	-0	-0.7
1886	Phi-a	5	15	.250	20	19	19	0	0	172^2	196	4	65	68	14.0	4.53	77	.271	.338	3	.044	-9	-21	-20	1	-2.4
	Lou-a	0	4	.000	4	4	4	0	0	32	53	1	16	14	19.7	5.34	68	.351	.417	1	.077	-1	-7	-6	-1	-0.6
	Yr	5	19	.208	24	23	23	0	0	204^2	249	5	81	82	14.6	4.66	76	.282	.343	4	.049	-11	-28	-26	0	-3.0
Total	2	12	21	.364	33	32	31	0	0	283^1	340	10	109	118	14.5	4.32	79	.286	.350	7	.060	-15	-33	-29	-0	-3.7

● BILL KENNEDY
Kennedy, William Aulton "Lefty" b: 3/14/21, Carnesville, Ga. d: 4/9/83, Seattle, Wash. BL/TL, 6'2", 195 lbs. Deb: 4/26/48

YEAR	TM/L	W	L	PCT	G	GS	CG	SH	SV	IP	H	HR	BB	SO	RAT	ERA	ERA+	OAV	OOB	BH	AVG	PB	PR	/A	PD	TPI
1948	Cle-A	1	0	1.000	6	3	0	0	0	11^1	16	0	13	12	23.0	11.12	37	.333	.475	2	.667	1	-9	-9	0	-0.7
	StL-A	7	8	.467	26	20	3	0	0	132	132	10	104	77	16.4	4.70	97	.259	.389	11	.250	1	-6	-2	-1	-0.2
	Yr	8	8	.500	32	23	3	0	0	143^1	148	10	117	89	17.0	5.21	87	.265	.397	13	.277	2	-15	-11	-1	-0.9
1949	StL-A	4	11	.267	48	16	2	0	1	153^2	172	12	73	69	14.5	4.69	97	.285	.365	6	.150	-2	-8	-3	-2	-0.6
1950	StL-A	0	0	—	1	0	0	0	0	2	1	0	2	1	13.5	0.00	—	.143	.333	0	—	0	1	1	-0	0.1
1951	StL-A	1	5	.167	19	5	1	0	0	56	76	4	37	29	18.3	5.79	76	.332	.427	2	.125	0	-10	-9	1	-0.9
1952	Chi-A	2	2	.500	**47**	1	0	0	5	70^2	54	4	38	46	11.8	2.80	130	.213	.318	3	.231	0	7	7	-1	0.6
1953	Bos-A	0	0	—	16	0	0	0	2	24^1	24	2	17	14	15.5	3.70	114	.255	.375	1	.500	0	1	1	-0	0.1
1956	Cin-N	0	0	—	1	0	0	0	0	2	6	1	0	0	27.0	18.00	22	.667	.667	0	—	0	-3	-3	-0	-0.3
1957	Cin-N	0	2	.000	8	0	0	0	3	12^2	16	1	5	8	15.6	6.39	64	.314	.386	0	.000	0	-4	-3	0	-0.3
Total	8	15	28	.349	172	45	6	0	11	464^2	497	34	289	256	15.5	4.73	92	.275	.379	25	.208	-1	-31	-20	-2	-2.2

● BILL KENNEDY
Kennedy, William Gorman b: 12/22/18, Alexandria, Va. BL/TL, 6'1", 175 lbs. Deb: 5/01/42

YEAR	TM/L	W	L	PCT	G	GS	CG	SH	SV	IP	H	HR	BB	SO	RAT	ERA	ERA+	OAV	OOB	BH	AVG	PB	PR	/A	PD	TPI
1942	Was-A	0	1	.000	8	2	1	0	2	18	21	1	10	4	15.5	8.00	46	.296	.383	0	.000	-1	-9	-9	1	-0.8
1946	Was-A	1	2	.333	21	2	0	0	3	39	40	1	29	18	15.9	6.00	56	.270	.390	1	.125	-0	-11	-11	-0	-1.2
1947	Was-A	0	0	—	2	0	0	0	0	6^2	10	1	5	1	20.3	8.10	46	.370	.469	0	.000	-0	-3	-3	0	-0.3
Total	3	1	3	.250	31	4	1	0	5	63^2	71	3	44	23	16.3	6.79	51	.289	.397	1	.071	-1	-23	-23	0	-2.3

● BRICKYARD KENNEDY
Kennedy, William P. b: 10/7/1867, Bellaire, Ohio d: 9/23/15, Bellaire, Ohio BR/TR, 5'11", 160 lbs. Deb: 4/26/1892

YEAR	TM/L	W	L	PCT	G	GS	CG	SH	SV	IP	H	HR	BB	SO	RAT	ERA	ERA+	OAV	OOB	BH	AVG	PB	PR	/A	PD	TPI
1892	Bro-N	13	8	.619	26	21	18	0	1	191	189	3	95	108	13.6	3.86	82	.248	.335	14	.165	-1	-12	-15	-0	-1.4
1893	Bro-N	25	20	.556	46	44	40	2	1	382^2	376	15	168	107	13.0	3.72	119	.249	.327	39	.248	2	40	30	5	3.1
1894	Bro-N	24	20	.545	48	41	34	0	2	360^2	445	15	149	107	15.1	4.92	101	.300	.368	49	.304	4	16	1	3	0.6
1895	Bro-N	19	12	.613	39	33	26	2	1	279^2	335	13	93	39	14.0	5.12	86	.292	.349	39	.307	4	-10	-22	-1	-1.5
1896	Bro-N	17	20	.459	42	38	28	1	1	305^2	334	12	130	76	14.0	4.42	93	.276	.352	23	.189	-6	-2	-10	3	-1.2

YEAR	TM/L	W	L	PCT	G	GS	CG	SH	SV	IP	H	HR	BB	SO	RAT	ERA	ERA+	OAV	OOB	BH	AVG	PB	PR	/A	PD	TPI
1897	Bro-N	18	20	.474	44	40	36	2	1	343^1	370	6	149	81	13.8	3.91	105	.273	.348	40	.272	4	16	8	2	1.1
1898	Bro-N	16	22	.421	40	39	38	0	0	339^1	360	12	123	73	12.9	3.37	107	.270	.334	34	.252	3	9	8	6	1.6
1899	Bro-N	22	9	.710	40	33	27	2	2	277^1	297	11	86	55	12.5	2.79	140	.274	.329	27	.248	4	33	35	0	3.6
1900	Bro-N	20	13	.606	42	35	26	2	0	292	316	5	111	75	13.3	3.91	98	.275	.342	37	.301	7	-7	-2	1	0.5
1901	Bro-N	3	5	.375	14	8	6	0	0	85^1	80	1	24	28	11.1	3.06	110	.246	.300	6	.167	-1	3	3	-0	0.1
1902	NY-N	1	4	.200	6	6	4	1	0	38^2	44	0	16	9	14.0	3.96	71	.286	.353	4	.267	1	-5	-5	-1	-0.5
1903	*Pit-N	9	6	.600	18	15	10	1	0	125^1	130	0	57	39	13.6	3.45	94	.277	.357	21	.362	8	-2	-3	-1	0.3
Total	12	187	159	.540	405	353	293	13	9	3021	3276	93	1201	797	13.5	3.96	102	.273	.343	333	.261	28	78	33	15	6.3

● ART KENNEY Kenney, Arthur Joseph b: 4/29/16, Milford, Mass. BL/TL, 6', 175 lbs. Deb: 7/01/38

YEAR	TM/L	W	L	PCT	G	GS	CG	SH	SV	IP	H	HR	BB	SO	RAT	ERA	ERA+	OAV	OOB	BH	AVG	PB	PR	/A	PD	TPI
1938	Bos-N	0	0	—	2	0	0	0	0	2^1	3	0	8	2	42.4	15.43	22	.300	.611	0	—	0	-3	-3	0	-0.3

● ED KENT Kent, Edward C. b: 1859, New York TL , 5'6.5", 152 lbs. Deb: 8/14/1884

YEAR	TM/L	W	L	PCT	G	GS	CG	SH	SV	IP	H	HR	BB	SO	RAT	ERA	ERA+	OAV	OOB	BH	AVG	PB	PR	/A	PD	TPI
1884	Tol-a	0	1	.000	1	1	1	0	0	9	14	0	3	4	18.0	6.00	57	.298	.353	0	.000	-1	-3	-3	0	-0.2

● MAURY KENT Kent, Maurice Allen b: 9/17/1885, Marshalltown, Ia. d: 4/19/66, Iowa City, Iowa BR/TR, 6', 168 lbs. Deb: 4/15/12

YEAR	TM/L	W	L	PCT	G	GS	CG	SH	SV	IP	H	HR	BB	SO	RAT	ERA	ERA+	OAV	OOB	BH	AVG	PB	PR	/A	PD	TPI
1912	Bro-N	5	5	.500	20	9	2	1	0	93	107	3	46	24	14.9	4.84	69	.296	.377	8	.229	1	-15	-15	1	-1.3
1913	Bro-N	0	0	—	3	0	0	0	0	7^1	5	0	3	1	9.8	2.45	134	.192	.276	0	.000	-0	1	1	-0	0.0
Total	2	5	5	.500	23	9	2	1	0	100^1	112	3	49	25	14.5	4.66	72	.289	.371	8	.211	0	-14	-15	1	-1.3

● MATT KEOUGH Keough, Matthew Lon b: 7/3/55, Pomona, Cal. BR/TR, 6'3", 190 lbs. Deb: 9/03/77 F

YEAR	TM/L	W	L	PCT	G	GS	CG	SH	SV	IP	H	HR	BB	SO	RAT	ERA	ERA+	OAV	OOB	BH	AVG	PB	PR	/A	PD	TPI
1977	Oak-A	1	3	.250	7	6	0	0	0	42^2	39	4	22	23	13.1	4.85	83	.247	.343	0	—	0	-4	-4	-1	-0.4
1978	Oak-A★	8	15	.348	32	32	6	0	0	197^1	178	9	85	108	12.2	3.24	112	.241	.323	0	—	0	11	9	2	1.1
1979	Oak-A	2	17	.105	30	28	7	1	0	176^2	220	18	78	95	15.5	5.04	80	.315	.389	0	—	0	-16	-20	2	-1.3
1980	Oak-A	16	13	.552	34	32	20	2	0	250	218	24	94	121	11.4	2.92	129	.236	.310	0	—	0	31	24	-1	2.9
1981	*Oak-A	10	6	.625	19	19	10	2	0	140^1	125	11	45	60	10.9	3.40	102	.239	.299	0	—	0	4	1	-2	0.2
1982	Oak-A	11	18	.379	34	34	10	2	0	209^1	233	38	101	75	14.6	5.72	68	.284	.366	0	—	0	-38	-42	-3	-3.9
1983	Oak-A	2	3	.400	14	4	0	0	0	44	50	7	31	28	16.6	5.52	70	.284	.391	0	—	0	-7	-8	-1	-0.6
	NY-A	3	4	.429	12	12	0	0	0	55^2	59	12	20	26	13.1	5.17	75	.266	.332	0	—	0	-7	-8	-0	-0.6
	Yr	5	7	.417	26	16	0	0	0	99^2	109	19	51	54	14.6	5.33	73	.273	.358	0	—	0	-14	-16	-1	-1.2
1985	StL-N	0	1	.000	4	1	0	0	0	10	10	0	4	10	13.5	4.50	79	.278	.366	0	.000	-0	-1	-1	0	-0.1
1986	Chi-N	2	2	.500	19	2	0	0	0	29	36	4	12	19	15.2	4.97	81	.316	.386	2	.400	1	-4	-3	-0	-0.2
	Hou-N	3	2	.600	10	5	0	0	0	35	22	5	18	25	10.5	3.09	117	.180	.291	4	.364	1	2	2	-1	0.3
	Yr	5	4	.556	29	7	0	0	0	64	58	9	30	44	12.5	3.94	96	.245	.332	6	.375	2	-2	-1	-1	0.1
Total	9	58	84	.408	215	175	53	7	0	1190	1190	132	510	590	13.1	4.17	91	.262	.341	6	.333	2	-28	-50	-5	-2.6

● KURT KEPSHIRE Kepshire, Kurt David b: 7/3/59, Bridgeport, Conn. BL/TR, 6'1", 180 lbs. Deb: 7/04/84

YEAR	TM/L	W	L	PCT	G	GS	CG	SH	SV	IP	H	HR	BB	SO	RAT	ERA	ERA+	OAV	OOB	BH	AVG	PB	PR	/A	PD	TPI
1984	StL-N	6	5	.545	17	16	2	2	0	109	100	7	44	71	11.9	3.30	105	.249	.323	2	.056	-2	3	2	-2	-0.2
1985	StL-N	10	9	.526	32	29	0	0	0	153^1	155	16	71	67	13.3	4.75	74	.264	.343	6	.118	-1	-20	-21	-2	-2.3
1986	StL-N	0	1	.000	2	1	0	0	0	8	8	2	4	6	13.5	4.50	81	.258	.343	0	.000	-0	-1	-1	0	-0.1
Total	3	16	15	.516	51	46	2	2	0	270^1	263	25	119	144	12.7	4.16	84	.258	.335	8	.091	-3	-17	-20	-3	-2.6

● CHARLIE KERFELD Kerfeld, Charles Patrick b: 9/28/63, Knob Knoster, Mo. BR/TR, 6'6", 225 lbs. Deb: 7/27/85

YEAR	TM/L	W	L	PCT	G	GS	CG	SH	SV	IP	H	HR	BB	SO	RAT	ERA	ERA+	OAV	OOB	BH	AVG	PB	PR	/A	PD	TPI
1985	Hou-N	4	2	.667	11	6	0	0	0	44^1	44	2	25	30	14.0	4.06	85	.268	.365	0	.000	-1	-2	-3	-1	-0.5
1986	*Hou-N	11	2	.846	61	0	0	0	7	93^2	71	5	42	77	11.0	2.69	134	.213	.305	1	.111	-0	11	9	-1	0.9
1987	Hou-N	0	2	.000	21	0	0	0	0	29^2	34	3	21	17	17.0	6.67	59	.309	.424	0	.000	-0	-9	-9	-0	-0.9
1990	Hou-N	0	2	.000	5	0	0	0	0	3^1	9	0	6	4	40.5	16.20	23	.529	.652	0	—	0	-5	-5	-0	-0.5
	Atl-N	3	1	.750	25	0	0	0	2	30^2	31	2	23	27	15.8	5.58	72	.270	.391	0	—	0	-6	-5	-1	-0.6
	Yr	3	3	.500	30	0	0	0	2	34	40	2	29	31	18.3	6.62	60	.303	.429	0	—	0	-11	-10	-1	-1.1
Total	4	18	9	.667	123	6	0	0	9	201^2	189	12	117	155	13.8	4.24	87	.256	.360	1	.038	-2	-11	-12	-2	-1.6

● GUS KERIAZAKOS Keriazakos, Constantine Nicholas b: 7/28/31, W.Orange, N.J. BR/TR, 6'3", 187 lbs. Deb: 10/01/50

YEAR	TM/L	W	L	PCT	G	GS	CG	SH	SV	IP	H	HR	BB	SO	RAT	ERA	ERA+	OAV	OOB	BH	AVG	PB	PR	/A	PD	TPI
1950	Chi-A	0	1	.000	1	1	0	0	0	2^1	7	0	5	1	46.3	19.29	23	.500	.632	1	1.000	0	-4	-4	-0	-0.3
1954	Was-A	2	3	.400	22	3	2	0	0	59^2	59	4	30	33	13.4	3.77	94	.262	.349	1	.067	-1	-0	-1	-0	-0.3
1955	KC-A	0	1	.000	5	1	0	0	0	11^2	15	4	7	8	17.0	12.34	34	.333	.423	0	.000	-0	-11	-11	-0	-1.0
Total	3	2	5	.286	28	5	2	0	0	73^2	81	8	42	42	15.0	5.62	65	.285	.377	2	.105	-1	-15	-16	-0	-1.6

● BILL KERKSIECK Kerksieck, Wayman William b: 12/6/13, Ulm, Ark. d: 3/11/70, Stuttgart, Ark. BR/TR, 6'1", 183 lbs. Deb: 6/21/39

YEAR	TM/L	W	L	PCT	G	GS	CG	SH	SV	IP	H	HR	BB	SO	RAT	ERA	ERA+	OAV	OOB	BH	AVG	PB	PR	/A	PD	TPI
1939	Phi-N	0	2	.000	23	2	1	0	0	62^2	81	13	32	13	16.2	7.18	56	.328	.405	1	.083	-0	-23	-22	-1	-2.2

● JIM KERN Kern, James Lester b: 3/15/49, Gladwin, Mich. BR/TR, 6'5", 205 lbs. Deb: 9/06/74

YEAR	TM/L	W	L	PCT	G	GS	CG	SH	SV	IP	H	HR	BB	SO	RAT	ERA	ERA+	OAV	OOB	BH	AVG	PB	PR	/A	PD	TPI
1974	Cle-A	0	1	.000	4	3	1	0	0	15^1	16	1	14	11	17.6	4.70	77	.262	.400	0	—	0	-2	-2	-0	-0.2
1975	Cle-A	1	2	.333	13	7	0	0	0	71^2	60	5	45	55	13.8	3.77	100	.233	.357	0	—	0	0	0	0	0.0
1976	Cle-A	10	7	.588	50	2	0	0	15	117^2	91	2	50	111	11.2	2.37	147	.222	.314	0	—	0	15	15	-0	1.6
1977	Cle-A★	8	10	.444	60	0	0	0	18	92	85	3	47	91	13.5	3.42	115	.260	.363	0	—	0	6	5	0	0.7
1978	Cle-A★	10	10	.500	58	0	0	0	13	99^1	77	4	58	95	12.5	3.08	121	.224	.342	0	.000	0	8	7	1	0.8
1979	Tex-A★	13	5	.722	71	0	0	0	29	143	99	5	62	136	10.3	1.57	264	.199	.290	0	—	0	**42**	**41**	-1	**4.1**
1980	Tex-A	3	11	.214	38	1	0	0	2	63^1	65	4	45	40	15.9	4.83	81	.279	.400	0	—	0	-6	-7	0	-0.4
1981	Tex-A	1	2	.333	23	0	0	0	6	30	21	0	22	20	13.2	2.70	128	.204	.349	0	—	0	3	3	-0	0.5
1982	Cin-N	3	5	.375	50	0	0	0	2	76	61	3	48	43	13.1	2.84	130	.222	.342	0	.000	-1	6	7	1	0.8
	Chi-A	2	1	.667	13	1	0	0	3	28	20	3	12	23	10.3	5.14	78	.204	.291	0	—	0	-3	-3	0	-0.3
1983	Chi-A	0	0	—	1	0	0	0	0	0^2	1	0	0	0	13.5	0.00	—	.333	.333	0	—	0	0	0	0	-0.1
1984	Phi-N	0	1	.000	8	0	0	0	0	13^1	20	3	10	8	20.3	10.13	36	.339	.435	0	.000	-0	-10	-10	-0	-1.0
	Mil-A	1	0	1.000	6	0	0	0	0	4^2	6	0	3	4	17.4	0.00	—	.300	.391	0	—	0	2	2	-0	0.4
1985	Mil-A	0	1	.000	5	0	0	0	0	11	14	1	5	3	15.5	6.55	64	.318	.388	0	—	0	-3	-3	1	-0.2
1986	Cle-A	1	1	.500	16	0	0	0	0	27^1	34	1	23	11	19.8	7.90	52	.298	.429	0	—	0	-11	-11	0	-1.0
Total	13	53	57	.482	416	14	1	0	88	793^1	670	35	444	651	13.0	3.32	115	.235	.344	0	.000	-0	48	45	1	5.7

● DICKIE KERR Kerr, Richard Henry b: 7/3/1893, St.Louis, Mo. d: 5/4/63, Houston, Tex. BL/TL, 5'7", 155 lbs. Deb: 4/25/19

YEAR	TM/L	W	L	PCT	G	GS	CG	SH	SV	IP	H	HR	BB	SO	RAT	ERA	ERA+	OAV	OOB	BH	AVG	PB	PR	/A	PD	TPI
1919	*Chi-A	13	7	.650	39	17	10	1	0	212^1	208	2	64	79	11.6	2.88	110	.259	.316	17	.250	5	8	7	1	1.4
1920	Chi-A	21	9	.700	45	28	19	3	**5**	253^2	266	7	72	72	12.1	3.37	112	.278	.331	14	.156	-4	12	11	3	1.0
1921	Chi-A	19	17	.528	44	37	25	3	1	308^2	357	12	96	80	13.5	4.72	90	.295	.352	25	.238	5	-15	-17	-0	-1.1
1925	Chi-A	0	1	.000	12	2	0	0	0	36^2	45	3	18	4	15.7	5.15	81	.304	.383	4	.333	1	-3	-4	0	-0.3
Total	4	53	34	.609	140	84	54	7	6	811^1	876	24	250	235	12.7	3.84	99	.281	.338	60	.218	7	2	-2	4	1.0

● JOE KERRIGAN Kerrigan, Joseph Thomas b: 11/30/54, Philadelphia, Pa. BR/TR, 6'5", 205 lbs. Deb: 7/09/76 C

YEAR	TM/L	W	L	PCT	G	GS	CG	SH	SV	IP	H	HR	BB	SO	RAT	ERA	ERA+	OAV	OOB	BH	AVG	PB	PR	/A	PD	TPI
1976	Mon-N	2	6	.250	38	0	0	0	1	56^2	63	3	23	22	14.0	3.81	98	.289	.362	0	.000	-0	-2	-1	1	0.0
1977	Mon-N	3	5	.375	66	0	0	0	11	89^1	80	4	33	43	11.7	3.22	118	.241	.315	0	.000	-1	7	6	1	0.5
1978	Bal-A	3	1	.750	26	2	0	0	3	71^2	75	10	36	41	14.2	4.77	73	.273	.361	0	—	0	-8	-10	2	-0.9
1980	Bal-A	0	0	—	1	0	0	0	0	2^1	3	0	0	1	11.6	3.86	103	.273	.273	0	—	0	0	0	0	0.1
Total	4	8	12	.400	131	2	0	0	15	220	221	17	92	107	13.1	3.89	95	.264	.342	0	.000	-1	-3	-5	3	-0.3

● RICK KESTER Kester, Richard Lee b: 7/7/46, Iola, Kan. BR/TR, 6', 190 lbs. Deb: 8/18/68

YEAR	TM/L	W	L	PCT	G	GS	CG	SH	SV	IP	H	HR	BB	SO	RAT	ERA	ERA+	OAV	OOB	BH	AVG	PB	PR	/A	PD	TPI
1968	Atl-N	0	0	—	5	0	0	0	0	6^1	8	0	3	9	15.6	5.68	53	.308	.379	0	—	0	-2	-2	-0	-0.2
1969	Atl-N	0	0	—	1	0	0	0	0	2	5	1	0	2	22.5	13.50	27	.455	.455	0	—	0	-2	-2	-0	-0.2
1970	Atl-N	0	0	—	15	0	0	0	0	32^1	36	3	19	20	15.3	5.57	77	.283	.377	0	.000	-1	-5	-5	-1	-0.6

YEAR	TM/L	W	L	PCT	G	GS	CG	SH	SV	IP	H	HR	BB	SO	RAT	ERA	ERA+	OAV	OOB	BH	AVG	PB	PR	/A	PD	TPI
Total	3	0	0	—	21	0	0	0	0	40^{2}	49	4	22	31	15.7	5.98	68	.299	.382	0	.000	-1	-10	-9	-1	-1.0

● GUS KETCHUM Ketchum, Augustus Franklin b: 3/21/1897, Royce City, Tex. d: 9/6/80, Oklahoma City, Okla. BR/TR, 5'9.5", 170 lbs. Deb: 8/07/22

YEAR	TM/L	W	L	PCT	G	GS	CG	SH	SV	IP	H	HR	BB	SO	RAT	ERA	ERA+	OAV	OOB	BH	AVG	PB	PR	/A	PD	TPI
1922	Phi-A	0	1	.000	6	0	0	0	0	16	19	2	8	4	15.8	5.63	76	.302	.389	0	.000	-1	-3	-2	-1	-0.4

● HENRY KEUPPER Keupper, Henry J. b: 6/24/1887, Staunton, Ill. d: 8/14/60, Marion, Ill. BL/TL, 6'1", 185 lbs. Deb: 4/19/14

YEAR	TM/L	W	L	PCT	G	GS	CG	SH	SV	IP	H	HR	BB	SO	RAT	ERA	ERA+	OAV	OOB	BH	AVG	PB	PR	/A	PD	TPI
1914	StL-F	8	20	.286	42	25	12	1	0	213	256	3	49	70	13.1	4.27	79	.291	.332	17	.250	2	-25	-21	2	-1.7

● JIMMY KEY Key, James Edward b: 4/22/61, Huntsville, Ala. BR/TL, 6'1", 190 lbs. Deb: 4/06/84

YEAR	TM/L	W	L	PCT	G	GS	CG	SH	SV	IP	H	HR	BB	SO	RAT	ERA	ERA+	OAV	OOB	BH	AVG	PB	PR	/A	PD	TPI
1984	Tor-A	4	5	.444	63	0	0	0	10	62	70	8	32	44	15.0	4.65	88	.286	.371	0	—	0	-5	-4	1	-0.4
1985	*Tor-A★	14	6	.700	35	32	3	0	0	212^{2}	188	22	50	85	10.2	3.00	140	.237	.284	0	—	0	27	28	4	3.4
1986	Tor-A	14	11	.560	36	35	4	2	0	232	222	24	74	141	11.6	3.57	118	.256	.317	0	—	0	16	17	3	1.9
1987	Tor-A	17	8	.680	36	36	8	1	0	261	210	24	66	161	**9.6**	**2.76**	**163**	**.221**	**.273**	0	—	0	**49**	**50**	2	**5.2**
1988	Tor-A	12	5	.706	21	21	2	2	0	131^{1}	127	13	30	65	11.1	3.29	119	.250	.298	0	—	0	10	9	-0	0.9
1989	*Tor-A	13	14	.481	33	33	5	1	0	216	226	18	27	118	10.7	3.88	97	.270	.295	0	—	0	0	-3	2	0.1
1990	Tor-A	13	7	.650	27	27	0	0	0	154^{2}	169	20	22	88	11.2	4.25	93	.281	.307	0	—	0	-6	-5	0	-0.6
1991	*Tor-A★	16	12	.571	33	33	2	2	0	209^{1}	207	12	44	125	10.9	3.05	138	.254	.295	0	—	0	24	27	3	2.8
1992	*Tor-A	13	13	.500	33	33	4	2	0	216^{2}	205	24	59	117	11.1	3.53	116	.248	.301	0	—	0	10	13	0	1.3
Total	9	116	81	.589	317	250	28	10	10	1695^{2}	1624	165	404	944	10.9	3.42	121	.252	.298	0	—	0	126	133	14	14.6

● DANA KIECKER Kiecker, Dana Ervin b: 2/25/61, Sleepy Eye, Minn. BR/TR, 6'3", 180 lbs. Deb: 4/12/90

YEAR	TM/L	W	L	PCT	G	GS	CG	SH	SV	IP	H	HR	BB	SO	RAT	ERA	ERA+	OAV	OOB	BH	AVG	PB	PR	/A	PD	TPI
1990	*Bos-A	8	9	.471	32	25	0	0	0	152	145	7	54	93	12.3	3.97	103	.253	.328	0	—	0	-1	2	2	0.0
1991	Bos-A	2	3	.400	18	5	0	0	0	40^{1}	56	6	23	21	18.1	7.36	58	.344	.431	0	—	0	-15	-14	1	-1.5
Total	2	10	12	.455	50	30	0	0	0	192^{1}	201	13	77	114	13.5	4.68	88	.273	.351	0	—	0	-16	-12	3	-1.5

● JOE KIEFER Kiefer, Joseph William "Harlem Joe" or "Smoke" b: 7/19/1899, W.Leyden, N.Y. d: 7/5/75, Utica, N.Y. BR/TR, 5'11", 190 lbs. Deb: 10/01/20

YEAR	TM/L	W	L	PCT	G	GS	CG	SH	SV	IP	H	HR	BB	SO	RAT	ERA	ERA+	OAV	OOB	BH	AVG	PB	PR	/A	PD	TPI
1920	Chi-A	0	1	.000	2	1	0	0	0	4^{2}	7	0	5	1	25.1	15.43	24	.333	.481	0	.000	-0	-6	-6	-0	-0.6
1925	Bos-A	0	2	.000	2	2	0	0	0	15	20	0	9	4	18.0	6.00	76	.351	.448	0	.000	-1	-3	-2	1	-0.2
1926	Bos-A	0	2	.000	11	1	0	0	0	30	29	2	16	4	14.1	4.80	85	.266	.370	1	.143	-0	-3	-2	0	-0.2
Total	3	0	5	.000	15	4	0	0	0	49^{2}	56	2	30	9	16.3	6.16	68	.299	.407	1	.077	-1	-11	-11	1	-1.0

● JOHN KIELY Kiely, John Francis b: 10/4/64, Boston, Mass. BR/TR, 6'3", 210 lbs. Deb: 7/26/91

YEAR	TM/L	W	L	PCT	G	GS	CG	SH	SV	IP	H	HR	BB	SO	RAT	ERA	ERA+	OAV	OOB	BH	AVG	PB	PR	/A	PD	TPI
1991	Det-A	0	1	.000	7	0	0	0	0	6^{2}	13	0	9	1	31.1	14.85	28	.448	.590	0	—	0	-8	-8	-0	-0.9
1992	Det-A	4	2	.667	39	0	0	0	0	55	44	2	28	18	11.8	2.13	187	.224	.321	0	—	0	11	11	2	1.4
Total	2	4	3	.571	46	0	0	0	0	61^{2}	57	2	37	19	13.9	3.50	114	.253	.361	0	—	0	3	3	2	0.5

● LEO KIELY Kiely, Leo Patrick "Kiki" b: 11/30/29, Hoboken, N.J. d: 1/18/84, Montclair, N.J. BL/TL, 6'2", 180 lbs. Deb: 6/27/51

YEAR	TM/L	W	L	PCT	G	GS	CG	SH	SV	IP	H	HR	BB	SO	RAT	ERA	ERA+	OAV	OOB	BH	AVG	PB	PR	/A	PD	TPI
1951	Bos-A	7	7	.500	17	16	4	0	0	113^{1}	106	9	39	46	11.7	3.34	134	.251	.317	5	.143	-1	10	14	1	1.5
1954	Bos-A	5	8	.385	28	19	4	1	0	131	153	12	58	59	14.6	3.50	117	.295	.367	9	.180	0	3	9	-1	0.8
1955	Bos-A	3	3	.500	33	4	0	0	6	90	91	5	37	36	12.8	2.80	153	.269	.341	5	.192	-0	12	15	1	1.6
1956	Bos-A	2	2	.500	23	0	0	0	3	31^{1}	47	1	14	9	18.1	5.17	89	.362	.432	1	.167	-0	-4	-2	0	-0.2
1958	Bos-A	5	2	.714	47	0	0	0	12	81	77	3	18	26	10.8	3.00	134	.254	.300	0	.000	-2	7	9	1	0.8
1959	Bos-A	3	3	.500	41	0	0	0	7	55^{2}	67	8	18	30	13.9	4.20	97	.299	.354	0	.000	-1	-2	-1	1	-0.1
1960	KC-A	1	2	.333	20	0	0	0	1	20^{2}	21	1	5	6	11.8	1.74	229	.266	.318	0	.000	0	5	5	1	0.7
Total	7	26	27	.491	209	39	8	1	29	523	562	39	189	212	13.1	3.37	125	.279	.343	20	.144	-4	31	49	5	5.1

● DARRYL KILE Kile, Darryl Andrew b: 12/2/68, Garden Grove, Cal. BR/TR, 6'5", 185 lbs. Deb: 4/08/91

YEAR	TM/L	W	L	PCT	G	GS	CG	SH	SV	IP	H	HR	BB	SO	RAT	ERA	ERA+	OAV	OOB	BH	AVG	PB	PR	/A	PD	TPI
1991	Hou-N	7	11	.389	37	22	0	0	0	153^{2}	144	16	84	100	13.7	3.69	95	.246	.347	0	.000	-3	-0	-3	-2	-0.8
1992	Hou-N	5	10	.333	22	22	2	0	0	125^{1}	124	8	63	90	13.7	3.95	85	.261	.352	5	.156	1	-6	-8	-2	-1.0
Total	2	12	21	.364	59	44	2	0	0	279	268	24	147	190	13.7	3.81	90	.253	.349	5	.071	-2	-6	-12	-4	-1.8

● JOHN KILEY Kiley, John Frederick b: 7/1/1859, S.Dedham, Mass. d: 12/18/40, Norwood, Mass. BL/TL, 5'7", 147 lbs. Deb: 5/01/1884 ♦

YEAR	TM/L	W	L	PCT	G	GS	CG	SH	SV	IP	H	HR	BB	SO	RAT	ERA	ERA+	OAV	OOB	BH	AVG	PB	PR	/A	PD	TPI
1891	Bos-N	0	1	.000	1	1	1	0	0	8	13	3	5	1	20.3	6.75	54	.352	.429	0	.000	-0	-3	-3	0	-0.2

● PAUL KILGUS Kilgus, Paul Nelson b: 2/2/62, Bowling Green, Ky. BL/TL, 6'1", 185 lbs. Deb: 6/07/87

YEAR	TM/L	W	L	PCT	G	GS	CG	SH	SV	IP	H	HR	BB	SO	RAT	ERA	ERA+	OAV	OOB	BH	AVG	PB	PR	/A	PD	TPI
1987	Tex-A	2	7	.222	25	12	0	0	0	89^{1}	95	14	31	42	12.9	4.13	108	.271	.334	0	—	0	3	3	-1	0.2
1988	Tex-A	12	15	.444	32	32	5	3	0	203^{1}	190	18	71	88	12.0	4.16	98	.243	.314	0	—	0	-4	-2	1	-0.1
1989	*Chi-N	6	10	.375	35	23	0	0	2	145^{2}	164	9	49	61	13.5	4.39	86	.283	.344	3	.073	-3	-14	-10	0	-1.3
1990	Tor-A	0	0	—	11	0	0	0	0	16^{1}	19	2	7	7	14.9	6.06	65	.306	.386	0	—	0	-4	-4	0	-0.5
1991	Bal-A	0	2	.000	38	0	0	0	1	62	60	8	24	32	12.6	5.08	78	.256	.333	0	—	0	-7	-8	2	-0.3
Total	5	20	34	.370	141	67	5	3	3	516^{2}	528	51	182	230	12.7	4.39	92	.263	.331	3	.073	-3	-26	-20	2	-2.0

● MIKE KILKENNY Kilkenny, Michael David b: 4/11/45, Bradford, Ont., Can. BR/TL, 6'3.5", 175 lbs. Deb: 4/11/69

YEAR	TM/L	W	L	PCT	G	GS	CG	SH	SV	IP	H	HR	BB	SO	RAT	ERA	ERA+	OAV	OOB	BH	AVG	PB	PR	/A	PD	TPI
1969	Det-A	8	6	.571	39	15	6	4	2	128^{1}	99	13	63	97	11.6	3.37	111	.211	.310	2	.054	-3	4	5	-0	0.3
1970	Det-A	7	6	.538	36	21	3	0	0	129	141	10	70	105	14.9	5.16	72	.279	.369	3	.077	-3	-21	-21	0	-2.3
1971	Det-A	4	5	.444	30	11	2	0	1	86^{1}	83	8	44	47	13.4	5.00	72	.247	.338	2	.083	-2	-15	-14	-0	-1.6
1972	Det-A	0	0	—	1	0	0	0	0	1	1	1	0	0	9.0	9.00	35	.250	.250	0	—	0	-1	-1	0	-0.1
	Oak-A	0	0	—	1	0	0	0	0	1	0	0	0	0	0.0	0.00	—	.000	.000	0	—	0	0	0	-0	0.0
	SD-N	0	0	—	5	0	0	0	0	4^{1}	7	1	3	5	20.8	8.31	40	.350	.435	0	—	0	-2	-2	0	-0.2
	Cle-A	4	1	.800	22	7	1	0	1	58	51	5	39	44	14.0	3.41	94	.237	.354	1	.071	-1	-2	-1	1	-0.2
	Yr	4	1	.800	24	7	1	0	1	60	52	6	39	44	13.6	3.45	95	.234	.349	1	.071	-1	-3	-2	1	-0.3
1973	Cle-A	0	0	—	5	0	0	0	0	2	5	1	5	3	49.5	22.50	17	.455	.647	0	—	0	-4	-4	0	-0.4
Total	5	23	18	.561	139	54	12	4	4	410	387	39	224	301	13.6	4.43	82	.248	.345	8	.070	-8	-41	-37	1	-4.5

● EVANS KILLEEN Killeen, Evans Henry b: 2/27/36, Brooklyn, N.Y. BR/TR, 6', 190 lbs. Deb: 9/07/59

YEAR	TM/L	W	L	PCT	G	GS	CG	SH	SV	IP	H	HR	BB	SO	RAT	ERA	ERA+	OAV	OOB	BH	AVG	PB	PR	/A	PD	TPI
1959	KC-A	0	0	—	4	0	0	0	0	5^{2}	4	0	4	1	12.7	4.76	84	.211	.348	0	—	0	-1	-0	-0	-0.1

● HENRY KILLEEN Killeen, Henry b: 1871, Troy, N.Y. 5'9", 150 lbs. Deb: 9/11/1891

YEAR	TM/L	W	L	PCT	G	GS	CG	SH	SV	IP	H	HR	BB	SO	RAT	ERA	ERA+	OAV	OOB	BH	AVG	PB	PR	/A	PD	TPI
1891	Cle-N	0	1	.000	1	1	1	0	0	8^{2}	11	1	8	3	19.7	6.23	56	.298	.423	0	.000	-0	-3	-3	0	-0.2

● FRANK KILLEN Killen, Frank Bissell "Lefty" b: 11/30/1870, Pittsburgh, Pa. d: 12/3/39, Pittsburgh, Pa. BL/TL, 6'1", 200 lbs. Deb: 8/27/1891

YEAR	TM/L	W	L	PCT	G	GS	CG	SH	SV	IP	H	HR	BB	SO	RAT	ERA	ERA+	OAV	OOB	BH	AVG	PB	PR	/A	PD	TPI
1891	Mil-a	7	4	.636	11	11	11	2	0	96^{2}	73	1	51	38	11.8	1.68	262	.202	.306	8	.229	1	22	29	-0	2.9
1892	Was-N	29	26	.527	60	52	46	2	0	459^{2}	448	15	182	147	12.7	3.31	98	.245	.320	37	.199	9	-1	-3	3	1.0
1893	Pit-N	**36**	14	.720	55	48	38	2	0	415	401	12	140	99	12.1	3.64	125	.246	.312	47	.275	14	47	42	1	4.9
1894	Pit-N	14	11	.560	28	28	20	1	0	204	261	3	86	62	15.5	4.50	116	.308	.375	21	.262	-0	19	17	1	1.4
1895	Pit-N	5	5	.500	13	11	6	0	0	95	113	2	57	25	16.2	5.49	82	.291	.383	13	.342	4	-8	-10	1	-0.4
1896	Pit-N	**30**	18	.625	**52**	50	**44**	**5**	0	**432^{1}**	476	7	119	134	12.7	3.41	123	.277	.329	40	.231	8	46	38	2	4.2
1897	Pit-N	17	23	.425	42	41	**38**	1	0	337^{1}	417	4	76	99	13.4	4.46	94	.301	.341	32	.248	4	-5	-10	-1	-0.6
1898	Pit-N	10	11	.476	23	23	17	0	0	177^{2}	201	3	41	48	12.8	3.75	95	.283	.332	17	.262	2	-3	-4	-0	-0.2
	Was-N	6	9	.400	17	16	15	0	0	128^{1}	149	4	29	43	12.6	3.58	102	.288	.328	15	.273	3	0	1	-0	0.5
	Yr	16	20	.444	40	39	32	0	0	306	350	7	70	91	12.4	3.68	98	.283	.322	32	.267	5	-2	-3	-1	0.3
1899	Was-N	0	2	.000	2	2	1	0	0	12	18	0	4	3	17.3	6.00	65	.345	.403	1	.200	-0	-3	-3	-1	-0.3
	Bos-N	7	5	.583	12	12	11	0	0	99^{1}	108	3	26	23	12.4	4.26	98	.277	.327	7	.171	-2	-4	-1	-0	-0.3
	Yr	7	7	.500	14	14	12	0	0	111^{1}	126	3	30	26	12.9	4.45	93	.284	.334	8	.174	-3	-7	-4	-1	-0.6
1900	Chi-N	3	3	.500	6	6	6	0	0	54	65	1	11	4	13.0	4.67	77	.297	.337	3	.150	-1	-6	-6	-0	-0.6
Total	10	164	131	.556	321	300	253	13	0	2511^{1}	2730	55	822	725	13.0	3.78	109	.272	.332	241	.241	42	104	92	5	12.5

YEAR	TM/L	W	L	PCT	G	GS	CG	SH	SV	IP	H	HR	BB	SO	RAT	ERA	ERA+	OAV	OOB	BH	AVG	PB	PR	/A	PD	TPI
● **ED KILLIAN**	Killian, Edwin Henry "Twilight Ed" b: 11/12/1876, Racine, Wis. d: 7/18/28, Detroit, Mich. BL/TL, 5'11", 170 lbs. Deb: 8/25/03																									
1903	Cle-A	3	4	.429	9	8	7	3	0	61^2	61	1	13	18	11.4	2.48	115	.258	.307	5	.179	-1	3	3	-0	0.2
1904	Det-A	14	20	.412	40	34	32	4	1	331^2	293	0	93	124	10.9	2.44	104	.238	.300	18	.143	-3	6	4	-5	-0.4
1905	Det-A	23	14	.622	39	37	33	**8**	0	313^1	263	0	102	110	10.8	2.27	121	.229	.298	32	.271	7	14	16	-4	2.1
1906	Det-A	10	6	.625	21	16	14	0	2	149^2	165	0	54	47	13.5	3.43	81	.283	.349	9	.170	-1	-12	-11	-2	-1.5
1907	*Det-A	25	13	.658	41	34	29	3	1	314	286	2	91	96	11.2	1.78	147	.245	.307	39	.320	10	27	29	-2	4.3
1908	*Det-A	12	9	.571	27	23	15	0	1	180^2	170	3	53	47	11.5	2.99	81	.252	.314	10	.137	-3	-12	-11	3	-1.3
1909	Det-A	11	9	.550	25	19	14	3	1	173^1	150	1	49	54	10.6	1.71	147	.236	.297	10	.161	-1	15	15	-1	1.5
1910	Det-A	4	3	.571	11	9	5	1	0	74	75	2	27	20	13.1	3.04	87	.268	.345	4	.148	-1	-4	-3	-1	-0.6
Total	8	102	78	.567	213	180	149	22	6	1598^1	1463	9	482	516	11.3	2.38	110	.245	.309	127	.209	6	36	42	-12	4.3
● **JACK KILLILAY**	Killilay, John William b: 5/24/1887, Leavenworth, Kan. d: 10/21/68, Tulsa, Okla. BR/TR, 5'11", 165 lbs. Deb: 5/13/11																									
1911	Bos-A	4	2	.667	14	7	1	0	0	61	65	0	36	28	16.4	3.54	93	.302	.425	1	.042	-2	-1	-2	0	-0.4
● **MATT KILROY**	Kilroy, Matthew Aloysius "Matches" b: 6/21/1866, Philadelphia, Pa. d: 3/2/40, Philadelphia, Pa. BL/TL, 5'9", 175 lbs. Deb: 4/17/1886 F																									
1886	Bal-a	29	34	.460	**68**	68	**66**	5	0	583	476	10	182	**513**	10.5	3.37	102	.210	.274	38	.174	-6	5	4	6	0.4
1887	Bal-a	**46**	19	.708	**69**	69	**66**	**6**	0	**589^1**	585	9	157	217	11.6	3.07	134	.253	.306	59	.247	9	**80**	67	10	**7.3**
1888	Bal-a	17	21	.447	40	40	35	2	0	321	347	5	79	135	12.6	4.04	74	.266	.319	26	.179	0	-35	-38	-1	-3.4
1889	Bal-a	29	25	.537	59	56	**55**	5	0	480^2	476	8	142	217	12.1	2.85	139	.250	.312	57	.274	10	54	59	8	**7.0**
1890	Bos-P	9	15	.375	30	27	18	0	0	217^2	268	14	87	48	15.3	4.26	103	.290	.361	20	.215	-0	-1	3	1	0.3
1891	Cin-a	1	4	.200	7	6	4	0	0	45^1	51	1	19	6	15.5	2.98	138	.274	.366	3	.150	-1	4	6	0	0.5
1892	Was-N	1	1	.500	4	3	2	0	0	26^1	20	0	15	1	12.6	2.39	136	.202	.319	2	.200	-0	3	3	2	0.4
1893	Lou-N	3	2	.600	5	5	5	1	0	35	57	2	23	4	21.6	9.00	49	.355	.448	7	.438	3	-17	-18	1	-1.1
1894	Lou-N	0	5	.000	8	7	3	0	0	37	46	2	20	11	16.5	3.89	131	.302	.390	2	.118	-2	6	5	1	0.4
1898	Chi-N	6	7	.462	13	11	10	0	0	100^1	119	2	30	18	14.4	4.31	83	.293	.357	22	.229	2	-8	-8	1	-0.5
Total	10	141	133	.515	303	292	264	19	0	2435^2	2445	53	754	1170	12.3	3.47	109	.252	.314	236	.222	15	92	83	28	11.3
● **MIKE KILROY**	Kilroy, Michael Joseph b: 11/4/1872, Philadelphia, Pa. d: 10/2/60, Philadelphia, Pa. BR/TR, Deb: 9/01/1888 F																									
1888	Bal-a	0	1	.000	1	1	1	0	0	9	12	1	5	1	17.0	8.00	37	.309	.388	0	.000	-1	-5	-5	-0	-0.4
1891	Phi-N	0	2	.000	3	1	0	0	0	10	15	1	4	3	18.9	9.90	34	.334	.413	2	.400	1	-7	-7	-0	-0.5
Total	2	0	3	.000	4	2	1	0	0	19	27	2	9	4	18.0	9.00	36	.322	.401	2	.222	0	-12	-12	-0	-0.9
● **NEWT KIMBALL**	Kimball, Newell W. b: 3/27/15, Logan, Utah BR/TR, 6'2.5", 190 lbs. Deb: 5/07/37																									
1937	Chi-N	0	0	—	2	0	0	0	0	5	12	1	1	0	23.4	10.80	37	.444	.464	0	.000	-0	-4	-4	0	-0.3
1938	Chi-N	0	0	—	1	0	0	0	0	1	3	0	0	1	27.0	9.00	43	.500	.500	0	—	0	-1	-1	0	-0.1
1940	Bro-N	3	1	.750	21	0	0	0	1	33^2	29	2	15	21	11.8	3.21	125	.238	.321	0	.000	-1	2	3	-0	0.2
	StL-N	1	0	1.000	2	1	1	0	0	14	11	1	6	6	10.9	2.57	155	.208	.288	2	.333	1	2	2	-0	0.3
	Yr	4	1	.800	23	1	1	0	1	47^2	40	3	21	27	11.5	3.02	132	.229	.311	2	.182	0	4	5	-1	0.5
1941	Bro-N	3	1	.750	15	5	1	0	1	52	43	0	29	17	12.5	3.63	101	.225	.327	3	.214	0	-0	0	-0	0.0
1942	Bro-N	2	0	1.000	14	1	0	0	0	29^1	27	0	19	8	14.4	3.68	89	.265	.385	1	.200	-0	-1	-1	-2	-0.3
1943	Bro-N	1	1	.500	5	0	0	0	1	11	9	0	5	2	11.5	1.64	205	.214	.298	0	.000	-0	2	2	-0	0.2
	Phi-N	1	6	.143	34	6	2	0	2	89^2	85	4	42	33	12.8	4.12	82	.253	.338	3	.188	1	-7	-7	-2	-0.9
	Yr	2	7	.222	39	6	2	0	3	100^2	94	4	47	35	12.7	3.84	88	.249	.333	3	.158	1	-5	-5	-2	-0.7
Total	6	11	9	.550	94	13	4	0	5	235^2	219	8	117	88	12.9	3.78	94	.249	.339	9	.180	1	-6	-6	-4	-0.9
● **SAM KIMBER**	Kimber, Samuel Jackson b: 10/29/1852, Philadelphia, Pa. d: 11/7/25, Philadelphia, Pa. BR/TR, 5'10.5", 165 lbs. Deb: 5/01/1884																									
1884	Bro-a	18	20	.474	41	41	41	4	0	361^1	364	6	72	122	11.2	3.81	87	.247	.289	21	.148	-5	-23	-20	-1	-2.3
1885	Pro-N	0	1	.000	1	1	1	0	0	8	15	1	5	4	22.5	11.25	24	.405	.476	0	.000	-0	-7	-8	0	-0.5
Total	2	18	21	.462	42	42	42	4	0	369^1	379	7	77	126	11.5	3.97	83	.251	.294	21	.145	-6	-30	-27	-1	-2.8
● **HARRY KIMBERLIN**	Kimberlin, Harry Lydle "Murphy" or "Mule Trader" b: 3/13/09, Sullivan, Mo. BR/TR, 6'3", 175 lbs. Deb: 7/11/36																									
1936	StL-A	0	0	—	13	0	0	0	0	20	24	3	16	4	18.0	5.40	100	.296	.412	0	.000	-0	-1	-0	-0	-0.1
1937	StL-A	0	2	.000	3	2	1	0	0	15^1	16	2	9	5	14.7	2.35	206	.254	.347	1	.200	-0	4	4	-0	0.4
1938	StL-A	0	0	—	1	1	1	0	0	8	8	1	3	1	12.4	3.38	147	.286	.355	0	.000	-0	1	1	-0	0.1
1939	StL-A	1	2	.333	17	3	0	0	0	41	59	6	19	11	17.6	5.49	89	.326	.396	3	.333	0	-4	-3	0	-0.2
Total	4	1	4	.200	34	6	2	0	0	84^1	107	12	47	21	16.6	4.70	106	.303	.388	4	.250	0	0	3	-1	0.2
● **HAL KIME**	Kime, Harold Lee "Lefty" b: 3/15/1899, W.Salem, Ohio d: 5/16/39, Columbus, Ohio BL/TL, 5'9", 160 lbs. Deb: 6/19/20																									
1920	StL-N	0	0	—	4	0	0	0	0	7	9	0	2	1	15.4	2.57	116	.333	.400	0	.000	-0	0	0	0	0.0
● **CHAD KIMSEY**	Kimsey, Clyde Elias b: 8/6/06, Copperhill, Tenn. d: 12/3/42, Pryor, Okla. BL/TR, 6'2", 200 lbs. Deb: 4/21/29																									
1929	StL-A	3	6	.333	24	3	1	0	1	64^1	83	2	19	13	14.3	5.04	88	.340	.388	8	.267	3	-6	-4	3	0.1
1930	StL-A	6	10	.375	42	4	1	0	1	113^1	139	8	45	32	14.8	6.35	77	.312	.377	24	.343	8	-21	-19	1	-0.8
1931	StL-A	4	6	.400	42	1	0	0	7	94^1	121	1	27	27	14.3	4.39	106	.312	.360	10	.270	5	-0	**3**	2	1.0
1932	StL-A	4	2	.667	33	0	0	0	3	78^1	85	3	33	13	13.6	4.02	121	.281	.352	6	.333	1	4	7	1	0.9
	Chi-A	1	1	.500	7	0	0	0	2	11	8	0	5	6	11.5	2.45	176	.211	.318	0	.000	-0	2	2	1	0.3
	Yr	5	3	.625	40	0	0	0	5	89^1	93	3	38	19	13.3	3.83	125	.274	.348	6	.300	1	6	**10**	2	1.2
1933	Chi-A	4	1	.800	28	2	0	0	0	96	124	7	36	19	15.4	5.53	77	.318	.381	5	.152	-2	-13	-14	1	-1.3
1936	Det-A	2	3	.400	22	0	0	0	3	52	58	2	29	11	15.2	4.85	102	.284	.376	5	.313	2	1	1	2	0.4
Total	6	24	29	.453	198	10	2	0	17	509^1	618	23	194	121	14.5	5.07	92	.307	.371	58	.282	16	-33	-24	11	0.6
● **ELLIS KINDER**	Kinder, Ellis Raymond "Old Folks" b: 7/26/14, Atkins, Ark. d: 10/16/68, Jackson, Tenn. BR/TR, 6', 195 lbs. Deb: 4/30/46																									
1946	StL-A	3	3	.500	33	7	1	0	1	86^2	78	8	36	59	11.8	3.32	112	.241	.318	1	.053	-1	2	4	-1	0.2
1947	StL-A	8	15	.348	34	26	10	2	1	194^1	201	11	82	110	13.1	4.49	86	.264	.336	8	.129	-4	-17	-13	-3	-2.0
1948	Bos-A	10	7	.588	28	22	10	1	0	178	183	10	63	53	12.5	3.74	117	.266	.330	6	.097	-4	11	13	-3	0.6
1949	Bos-A	23	6	**.793**	43	30	19	**6**	4	252	251	21	99	138	12.6	3.36	130	.260	.330	12	.130	-4	24	28	-4	1.9
1950	Bos-A	14	12	.538	48	23	11	1	9	207	212	23	78	95	12.7	4.26	115	.263	.328	13	.183	-1	7	15	-2	1.1
1951	Bos-A	11	2	.846	**63**	2	1	0	**14**	127	108	9	46	84	10.9	2.55	175	.230	.298	4	.118	-3	**22**	**27**	-2	2.2
1952	Bos-A	5	6	.455	23	10	4	0	4	97^2	85	11	28	50	10.5	2.58	153	.234	.290	0	.000	-5	12	15	-0	1.1
1953	Bos-A	10	6	.625	**69**	0	0	0	**27**	107	84	8	38	39	10.4	1.85	227	.215	.288	11	.379	3	**26**	**28**	0	3.2
1954	Bos-A	8	8	.500	48	2	0	0	15	107	106	7	36	67	11.9	3.62	114	.260	.321	5	.185	0	1	6	-2	0.5
1955	Bos-A	5	5	.500	43	0	0	0	18	66^2	57	5	15	31	9.9	2.84	151	.229	.275	3	.250	0	8	11	-1	1.0
1956	StL-N	2	0	1.000	22	0	0	0	6	25^2	23	3	9	4	11.2	3.51	108	.245	.311	0	.000	-0	1	1	-1	0.0
	Chi-A	3	1	.750	29	0	0	0	3	29^2	33	2	8	19	12.4	2.73	150	.277	.323	0	.000	-0	5	5	-1	0.4
1957	Chi-A	0	0	—	1	0	0	0	0	1	0	0	1	0	9.0	0.00	—	.000	.250	0	—	0	0	0	-0	0.0
Total	12	102	71	.590	484	122	56	10	102	1479^2	1421	118	539	749	12.0	3.43	125	.252	.318	63	.142	-20	101	139	-17	10.2
● **SILVER KING**	King, Charles Frederick (b: Charles Frederick Koenig) b: 1/11/1868, St.Louis, Mo. d: 5/21/38, St.Louis, Mo. BR/TR, 6', 170 lbs. Deb: 9/02/1886																									
1886	KC-N	1	3	.250	5	5	5	0	0	39	43	1	9	23	12.0	4.85	78	.243	.280	1	.045	-2	-7	-5	1	-0.5
1887	*StL-a	32	12	.727	46	44	43	2	1	390	401	4	109	128	12.2	3.78	120	.260	.316	46	.207	-4	22	33	-3	1.9
1888	*StL-a	**45**	21	.682	**66**	65	**64**	**6**	0	**585^2**	437	6	76	258	**8.3**	**1.64**	**198**	.200	**.237**	43	.208	10	**92**	105	-1	**11.4**
1889	StL-a	35	16	.686	56	53	47	2	1	458	462	15	125	188	11.9	3.14	134	.254	.309	43	.228	1	36	55	-3	4.6
1890	Chi-P	30	22	.577	56	56	48	**4**	0	461	420	5	163	185	11.7	**2.69**	**161**	**.232**	.301	31	.168	-6	**79**	**84**	6	**7.0**
1891	Pit-N	14	29	.326	48	44	40	3	1	384^1	382	7	144	160	12.7	3.11	105	.249	.321	25	.169	-1	10	7	-2	0.5
1892	NY-N	23	24	.489	52	47	46	1	0	419^1	397	15	174	177	12.7	3.24	99	.240	.320	35	.210	6	2	-1	-1	0.4

YEAR	TM/L	W	L	PCT	G	GS	CG	SH	SV	IP	H	HR	BB	SO	RAT	ERA	ERA+	OAV	OOB	BH	AVG	PB	PR	/A	PD	TPI
1893	NY-N	3	4	.429	7	7	4	0	0	49	69	4	26	13	17.8	8.63	54	.322	.401	3	.176	1	-22	-22	-0	-1.6
	Cin-N	5	6	.455	17	15	8	1	1	105	119	2	56	30	15.6	4.89	98	.277	.369	6	.162	-0	-3	-1	-0	-0.1
	Yr	8	10	.444	24	22	12	1	1	154	188	6	82	43	16.2	6.08	78	.291	.377	9	.167	1	-24	-23	-0	-1.7
1896	Was-N	10	7	.588	22	16	12	0	1	145^1	179	3	43	35	14.0	4.09	108	.300	.351	16	.276	4	4	5	-3	0.5
1897	Was-N	6	9	.400	23	19	12	0	1	154	196	7	45	32	14.7	4.79	91	.307	.363	11	.193	0	-8	-8	1	-0.6
Total	10	204	153	.571	398	371	329	19	6	3190^2	3105	69	970	1229	11.9	3.18	122	.247	.308	260	.199	9	207	253	-6	23.5
● **CLYDE KING** King, Clyde Edward b: 5/23/25, Goldsboro, N.C. BB/TR, 6'1", 175 lbs. Deb: 6/21/44 MC																										
1944	Bro-N	2	1	.667	14	3	1	0	0	43^2	42	1	12	14	11.3	3.09	115	.256	.311	2	.200	-0	3	2	-1	0.1
1945	Bro-N	5	5	.500	42	2	0	0	3	112^1	131	8	48	29	14.3	4.09	92	.295	.364	4	.125	-2	-4	-4	1	-0.5
1947	Bro-N	6	5	.545	29	9	2	0	0	87^2	85	11	29	31	11.7	2.77	149	.252	.311	3	.115	-1	13	13	-1	1.1
1948	Bro-N	0	1	.000	9	0	0	0	0	12^1	14	3	6	5	15.3	8.03	50	.286	.375	0	.000	-0	-6	-6	0	-0.5
1951	Bro-N	14	7	.667	48	3	1	0	6	121^1	118	15	50	33	12.7	4.15	94	.263	.341	4	.138	0	-3	-3	0	-0.3
1952	Bro-N	2	0	1.000	23	0	0	0	0	42^2	56	5	12	17	14.6	5.06	72	.318	.365	0	.000	-1	-6	-7	1	-0.7
1953	Cin-N	3	6	.333	35	4	0	0	2	76	78	15	32	21	13.3	5.21	84	.271	.348	0	.000	-1	-8	-7	-0	-0.8
Total	7	32	25	.561	200	21	4	0	11	496	524	58	189	150	13.1	4.14	95	.275	.343	13	.114	-4	-11	-11	-0	-1.6
● **ERIC KING** King, Eric Steven b: 4/10/64, Oxnard, Cal. BR/TR, 6'2", 215 lbs. Deb: 5/15/86																										
1986	Det-A	11	4	.733	33	16	3	1	3	138^1	108	11	63	79	11.6	3.51	117	.216	.313	0	—	0	10	9	0	0.9
1987	*Det-A	6	9	.400	55	4	0	0	9	116	111	15	60	89	13.6	4.89	86	.251	.345	0	—	0	-6	-9	2	-0.5
1988	Det-A	4	1	.800	23	5	0	0	3	68^2	60	5	34	45	13.0	3.41	112	.233	.334	0	—	0	4	3	-1	0.3
1989	Chi-A	9	10	.474	25	25	1	1	0	159^1	144	13	64	72	12.0	3.39	112	.244	.322	0	—	0	9	7	-0	0.7
1990	Chi-A	12	4	.750	25	25	2	2	0	151	135	10	40	70	10.8	3.28	117	.237	.294	0	—	0	11	9	-1	1.0
1991	Cle-A	6	11	.353	25	24	2	1	0	150^2	166	7	44	59	12.7	4.60	90	.279	.332	0	—	0	-8	-7	-2	-0.9
1992	Det-A	4	6	.400	17	14	0	0	1	79^1	90	12	28	45	13.5	5.22	76	.285	.345	0	—	0	-11	-11	-1	-1.2
Total	7	52	45	.536	203	113	8	5	16	863^1	814	73	333	459	12.3	3.97	101	.249	.324	0	—	0	8	2	-3	0.3
● **NELLIE KING** King, Nelson Joseph b: 3/15/28, Shenandoah, Pa. BR/TR, 6'6", 185 lbs. Deb: 4/15/54																										
1954	Pit-N	0	0	—	4	0	0	0	0	7	10	0	1	3	14.1	5.14	81	.400	.423	0	—	0	-1	-1	0	0.0
1955	Pit-N	1	3	.250	17	4	0	0	0	54^1	60	2	14	21	12.6	2.98	138	.286	.336	0	.000	-2	6	7	-0	0.5
1956	Pit-N	4	1	.800	38	0	0	0	5	60	54	8	19	25	11.1	3.15	120	.241	.303	0	.000	-1	4	4	-1	0.3
1957	Pit-N	2	1	.667	36	0	0	0	1	52	69	7	16	23	15.1	4.50	84	.337	.390	0	.000	-1	-4	-4	-0	-0.5
Total	4	7	5	.583	95	4	0	0	6	173^1	193	17	50	72	12.9	3.58	109	.291	.345	0	.000	-3	6	6	-1	0.3
● **BRIAN KINGMAN** Kingman, Brian Paul b: 7/27/54, Los Angeles, Cal. BR/TR, 6'2", 200 lbs. Deb: 6/28/79																										
1979	Oak-A	8	7	.533	18	17	5	1	0	112^2	113	10	33	58	11.9	4.31	94	.258	.314	0	—	0	-1	-3	-2	-0.4
1980	Oak-A	8	20	.286	32	30	10	1	0	211^1	209	21	82	116	12.6	3.83	98	.256	.326	0	—	0	5	-2	-2	-0.2
1981	*Oak-A	3	6	.333	18	15	3	1	0	100^1	112	10	32	52	13.3	3.95	88	.286	.347	0	—	0	-3	-5	-2	-0.5
1982	Oak-A	4	12	.250	23	20	3	0	1	122^2	131	11	57	46	14.3	4.48	87	.279	.365	0	—	0	-5	-8	-3	-0.7
1983	SF-N	0	0	—	3	0	0	0	0	4^2	10	0	1	1	21.2	7.71	46	.417	.440	0	—	0	-2	-2	-0	-0.2
Total	5	23	45	.338	94	82	21	3	1	551^2	575	52	205	273	13.0	4.13	92	.269	.338	0	—	0	-7	-20	-9	-2.0
● **DAVE KINGMAN** Kingman, David Arthur b: 12/21/48, Pendleton, Ore. BR/TR, 6'6", 210 lbs. Deb: 7/30/71 ♦																										
1973	SF-N	0	0	—	2	0	0	0	0	4	3	0	6	4	20.3	9.00	42	.200	.429	62	.203	1	-2	-2	-0	-0.2
● **DENNIS KINNEY** Kinney, Dennis Paul b: 2/26/52, Toledo, Ohio BL/TL, 6'1", 190 lbs. Deb: 4/09/78																										
1978	Cle-A	0	2	.000	18	0	0	0	5	38^2	37	3	14	19	12.1	4.42	84	.259	.329	0	—	0	-3	-3	-0	-0.3
	SD-N	0	1	.000	7	0	0	0	0	7	6	3	4	2	12.9	6.43	52	.222	.323	0	.000	-0	-2	-2	-0	-0.3
1979	SD-N	0	0	—	13	0	0	0	0	18	17	2	8	11	13.0	3.50	101	.250	.338	0	.000	-0	0	0	-0	0.0
1980	SD-N	4	6	.400	50	0	0	0	1	82^2	79	3	37	40	12.7	4.25	81	.252	.333	1	.083	-0	-6	-7	-0	-0.9
1981	Det-A	0	0	—	6	0	0	0	0	3^2	5	0	4	3	22.1	9.82	38	.313	.450	0	—	0	-3	-2	0	-0.4
1982	Oak-A	0	0	—	3	0	0	0	0	4^1	9	1	4	0	27.0	8.31	47	.474	.565	0	—	0	-2	-2	0	0.1
Total	5	4	9	.308	97	0	0	0	6	154^1	153	12	71	75	13.2	4.55	78	.261	.344	1	.071	-1	-15	-17	-1	-1.8
● **WALT KINNEY** Kinney, Walter William b: 9/9/1893, Denison, Tex. d: 7/1/71, Escondido, Cal. BL/TL, 6'2", 186 lbs. Deb: 7/26/18																										
1918	Bos-A	0	0	—	5	0	0	0	0	15	5	0	8	4	9.0	1.80	149	.106	.263	0	.000	-1	2	1	-0	0.1
1919	Phi-A	9	15	.375	43	21	13	0	2	202^2	199	7	91	97	13.2	3.64	94	.262	.347	25	.284	5	-9	-5	3	0.6
1920	Phi-A	2	4	.333	10	8	5	1	0	61	59	3	28	19	13.0	3.10	130	.261	.345	9	.346	2	5	6	0	0.9
1923	Phi-A	0	1	.000	5	1	0	0	0	12	11	0	9	9	15.0	7.50	55	.229	.351	1	.167	1	-5	-5	-0	-0.4
Total	4	11	20	.355	63	30	18	1	2	290^2	274	10	136	129	13.0	3.59	99	.254	.343	35	.280	7	-8	-2	2	1.2
● **MIKE KINNUNEN** Kinnunen, Michael John b: 4/1/58, Seattle, Wash. BL/TL, 6'1", 185 lbs. Deb: 6/12/80																										
1980	Min-A	0	0	—	21	0	0	0	0	24^2	29	1	9	8	14.2	5.11	85	.290	.355	0	—	0	-3	-2	0	-0.4
1986	Bal-A	0	0	—	9	0	0	0	0	7	8	1	5	1	16.7	6.43	64	.308	.419	0	—	0	-2	-2	0	0.0
1987	Bal-A	0	0	—	18	0	0	0	0	20	27	3	16	14	19.3	4.95	89	.338	.448	0	—	0	-1	-1	-0	0.0
Total	3	0	0	—	48	0	0	0	0	51^2	64	5	30	23	16.5	5.23	83	.311	.401	0	—	0	-6	-5	0	-0.4
● **ED KINSELLA** Kinsella, Edward William "Rube" b: 1/15/1882, Lexington, Ill. d: 1/17/76, Bloomington, Ill. BR/TR, 6'1.5", 175 lbs. Deb: 9/16/05																										
1905	Pit-N	0	1	.000	3	2	2	0	0	17	19	0	3	11	12.2	2.65	113	.292	.333	0	.000	-0	1	1	-1	0.0
1910	StL-A	1	3	.250	10	5	2	0	0	50	62	0	16	10	14.4	3.78	65	.321	.379	3	.250	2	-7	-7	1	-0.5
Total	2	1	4	.200	13	7	4	0	0	67	81	0	19	21	13.8	3.49	75	.314	.368	3	.200	2	-6	-7	0	-0.5
● **MATT KINZER** Kinzer, Matthew Roy b: 6/17/63, Indianapolis, Ind. BR/TR, 6'2", 210 lbs. Deb: 5/18/89																										
1989	StL-N	0	2	.000	8	1	0	0	0	13^1	25	3	4	8	19.6	12.83	28	.403	.439	0	.000	-0	-14	-14	-0	-1.4
1990	Det-A	0	0	—	1	0	0	0	0	1^2	3	0	3	1	32.4	16.20	24	.375	.545	0	—	0	-2	-2	-0	-0.3
Total	2	0	2	.000	9	1	0	0	0	15	28	3	7	9	21.0	13.20	28	.400	.455	0	.000	-0	-16	-16	-1	-1.7
● **HARRY KINZY** Kinzy, Henry Hershel "Slim" b: 7/19/10, Hallsville, Tex. BR/TR, 6'4", 185 lbs. Deb: 6/08/34																										
1934	Chi-A	0	1	.000	13	2	1	0	0	34^1	38	1	31	12	19.1	4.98	95	.290	.440	3	.300	1	-2	-1	-0	-0.1
● **FRED KIPP** Kipp, Fred Leo b: 10/1/31, Piqua, Kan. BL/TL, 6'4", 200 lbs. Deb: 9/10/57																										
1957	Bro-N	0	0	—	1	0	0	0	0	4	6	2	0	3	13.5	9.00	46	.333	.333	0	.000	-0	-2	-2	0	-0.2
1958	LA-N	6	6	.500	40	9	0	0	0	102^1	107	16	45	58	13.5	5.01	82	.273	.349	9	.250	1	-12	-10	1	-0.9
1959	LA-N	0	0	—	2	0	0	0	0	2^2	2	0	3	1	16.9	0.00	—	.222	.417	0	—	0	1	1	0	0.2
1960	NY-A	0	1	.000	4	0	0	0	0	4^1	4	0	0	2	8.3	6.23	57	.250	.250	0	—	0	-1	-1	0	-0.1
Total	4	6	7	.462	47	9	0	0	0	113^1	119	18	48	64	13.3	5.08	80	.274	.347	9	.243	1	-14	-13	1	-1.0
● **BOB KIPPER** Kipper, Robert Wayne b: 7/8/64, Aurora, Ill. BR/TL, 6'2", 200 lbs. Deb: 4/12/85																										
1985	Cal-A	0	1	.000	2	1	0	0	0	3^1	7	1	3	0	27.0	21.60	19	.467	.556	0	—	0	-6	-6	0	-0.5
	Pit-N	1	2	.333	5	4	0	0	0	24^2	21	4	7	13	10.2	5.11	70	.221	.275	2	.250	0	-4	-4	0	-0.4
1986	Pit-N	6	8	.429	20	19	0	0	0	114	123	17	34	81	12.6	4.03	95	.271	.324	1	.030	-3	-4	-2	-1	-0.6
1987	Pit-N	5	9	.357	24	20	1	1	0	110^2	117	25	52	83	13.9	5.94	69	.271	.352	8	.242	2	-23	-22	-0	-2.0
1988	Pit-N	2	6	.250	50	0	0	0	0	65	54	7	26	39	11.4	3.74	91	.234	.317	0	.000	-0	-2	-2	1	-0.1
1989	Pit-N	3	4	.429	52	0	0	0	4	83	55	5	33	58	9.5	2.93	115	.188	.270	1	.111	-0	5	4	-1	0.4
1990	Pit-N	5	2	.714	41	1	0	0	3	62^2	44	7	26	35	10.5	3.02	120	.195	.286	1	.143	-0	5	4	-0	0.4
1991	*Pit-N	2	2	.500	52	0	0	0	4	60	66	7	22	38	13.2	4.65	77	.276	.337	0	.000	-0	-6	-7	-1	-0.9

YEAR TM/L	W	L	PCT	G	GS	CG	SH	SV	IP	H	HR	BB	SO	RAT	ERA	ERA+	OAV	OOB	BH	AVG	PB	PR	/A	PD	TPI
1992 Min-A	3	3	.500	25	0	0	0	0	38^2	40	8	14	22	13.3	4.42	91	.268	.343	0	—	0	-2	-2	0	-0.2
Total 8	27	37	.422	271	45	1	1	11	562	527	81	217	369	12.1	4.34	86	.247	.320	13	.137	-1	-37	-39	-2	-3.9
● THORNTON KIPPER	Kipper, Thornton John b: 9/27/28, Bagley, Wis. BR/TR, 6'3", 190 lbs. Deb: 6/07/53																								
1953 Phi-N	3	3	.500	20	3	0	0	0	45^2	59	8	12	15	14.0	4.73	89	.319	.360	1	.091	-1	-2	-3	-0	-0.4
1954 Phi-N	0	0	—	11	0	0	0	1	13^2	22	0	12	5	23.0	7.90	51	.379	.493	0	.000	-0	-6	-6	0	-0.6
1955 Phi-N	0	1	.000	24	0	0	0	0	39^2	47	4	22	15	15.9	4.99	80	.301	.391	1	.333	0	-4	-5	-1	-0.5
Total 3	3	4	.429	55	3	0	0	1	99	128	12	46	35	16.0	5.27	78	.321	.394	2	.125	-1	-12	-13	-1	-1.5
● CLAY KIRBY	Kirby, Clayton Laws b: 6/25/48, Washington, D.C. d: 10/11/91, Arlington, Va. BR/TR, 6'3", 185 lbs. Deb: 4/11/69																								
1969 SD-N	7	20	.259	35	35	2	0	0	215^2	204	18	100	113	12.9	3.80	93	.252	.339	4	.061	-2	-5	-6	-2	-1.1
1970 SD-N	10	16	.385	36	34	6	1	0	214^2	198	29	120	154	13.7	4.53	88	.248	.352	11	.149	-0	-11	-13	-2	-1.5
1971 SD-N	15	13	.536	38	36	13	2	0	267^1	213	20	103	231	10.7	2.83	117	.216	.292	8	.093	-3	19	14	-0	1.2
1972 SD-N	12	14	.462	34	34	9	2	0	238^2	197	21	116	175	11.9	3.13	105	.226	.318	5	.068	-4	9	4	-1	-0.1
1973 SD-N	8	18	.308	34	31	4	2	0	191^2	214	30	66	129	13.2	4.79	72	.282	.341	5	.093	-2	-24	-28	-2	-3.2
1974 Cin-N	12	9	.571	36	35	7	1	0	230^2	210	15	91	160	11.8	3.28	106	.242	.316	7	.095	-3	9	5	-2	0.0
1975 Cin-N	10	6	.625	26	19	1	0	0	110^2	113	13	54	48	14.0	4.72	76	.263	.352	6	.188	1	-13	-14	-2	-1.5
1976 Mon-N	1	8	.111	22	15	0	0	0	78^2	81	10	63	51	16.7	5.72	65	.273	.403	1	.056	-1	-19	-18	-1	-1.9
Total 8	75	104	.419	261	239	42	8	0	1548	1430	156	713	1061	12.6	3.84	92	.246	.331	47	.098	-15	-37	-56	-13	-8.1
● JOHN KIRBY	Kirby, John F. b: 1/13/1865, St.Louis, Mo. d: 10/6/31, St.Louis, Mo. TR, 5'8", 172 lbs. Deb: 8/01/1884																								
1884 KC-U	0	1	.000	2	2	1	0	0	11	13	0	2	1	12.3	4.09	68	.275	.305	1	.143	-1	-1	-2	1	-0.1
1885 StL-N	5	8	.385	14	14	14	0	0	129^1	118	0	44	46	11.3	3.55	77	.241	.303	3	.060	-5	-10	-12	-2	-1.6
1886 StL-N	11	26	.297	41	41	38	1	0	325	329	9	134	129	12.8	3.30	98	.252	.322	15	.110	-9	1	-3	-1	-1.2
1887 Ind-N	1	6	.143	8	8	5	0	0	62	70	3	43	7	16.7	6.10	68	.272	.381	4	.138	-2	-14	-13	-1	-1.3
Cle-a	0	5	.000	5	5	5	0	0	41	62	1	28	6	20.2	9.00	48	.339	.432	3	.167	-1	-21	-21	-0	-1.6
1888 KC-a	1	4	.200	5	5	5	0	0	43	48	0	7	11	11.7	4.19	82	.272	.304	1	.063	-2	-5	-4	-0	-0.5
Total 5	18	50	.265	75	75	68	1	0	611^1	640	13	258	200	13.3	4.09	81	.260	.332	27	.105	-20	-52	-54	-3	-6.3
● LA RUE KIRBY	Kirby, La Rue b: 12/30/1889, Eureka, Mich. d: 6/10/61, Lansing, Mich. BB/TR, 6', 185 lbs. Deb: 8/07/12 ♦																								
1912 NY-N	1	0	1.000	3	1	1	0	0	11	13	1	6	2	16.4	5.73	59	.295	.392	1	.200	0	-3	-3	0	-0.2
1915 StL-F	0	0	—	1	0	0	0	0	7	7	1	2	7	11.6	5.14	62	.269	.321	38	.213	0	-2	-2	-0	-0.2
Total 2	1	0	1.000	4	1	1	0	0	18	20	2	8	9	14.5	5.50	60	.286	.367	87	.230	0	-4	-4	-0	-0.4
● MIKE KIRCHER	Kircher, Michael Andrew (b: Wolfgang Andrew Kerscher) b: 9/30/1897, Rochester, N.Y. d: 6/26/72, Rochester.N.Y. BB/TR, 6', 180 lbs. Deb: 8/08/19																								
1919 Phi-A	0	0	—	2	0	0	0	0	8	15	0	3	2	20.3	7.88	44	.429	.474	0	.000	-0	-4	-4	-1	-0.4
1920 StL-N	2	1	.667	9	3	1	0	0	36^2	50	0	5	5	14.0	5.40	55	.333	.363	3	.273	0	-9	-10	-1	-1.1
1921 StL-N	0	1	.000	3	0	0	0	0	3^1	4	0	1	2	16.2	8.10	45	.364	.462	0	—	0	-2	-2	0	-0.1
Total 3	2	2	.500	14	3	1	0	0	48	69	0	9	9	15.2	6.00	52	.352	.389	3	.214	-0	-15	-15	-2	-1.6
● BILL KIRK	Kirk, William Partlemore b: 7/19/35, Coatesville, Pa. BL/TL, 6', 165 lbs. Deb: 9/23/61																								
1961 KC-A	0	0	—	1	1	0	0	0	3	6	2	1	3	21.0	12.00	34	.375	.412	0	—	0	-3	-3	-0	-0.2
● DON KIRKWOOD	Kirkwood, Donald Paul b: 9/24/49, Pontiac, Mich. BR/TR, 6'3", 188 lbs. Deb: 9/13/74																								
1974 Cal-A	0	0	—	3	0	0	0	0	7^1	12	0	6	4	22.1	8.59	40	.375	.474	0	—	0	-4	-4	-0	-0.2
1975 Cal-A	6	5	.545	44	2	0	0	7	84	85	6	28	49	12.1	3.11	114	.270	.329	0	—	0	6	4	-0	0.7
1976 Cal-A	6	12	.333	28	26	4	0	0	157^2	167	12	57	78	12.8	4.62	72	.278	.341	0	—	0	-19	-23	1	-2.1
1977 Cal-A	1	0	1.000	13	0	0	0	1	17^2	20	3	9	10	14.8	5.09	77	.290	.372	0	—	0	-2	-2	1	-0.1
Chi-A	1	1	.500	16	0	0	0	0	40	49	3	10	24	13.5	5.17	79	.310	.355	0	—	0	-5	-5	0	-0.5
Yr	2	1	.667	29	0	0	0	1	57^2	69	6	19	34	13.9	5.15	78	.304	.360	0	—	0	-7	-7	1	-0.6
1978 Tor-A	4	5	.444	16	9	3	0	0	68	76	6	25	29	13.4	4.24	93	.289	.351	0	—	0	-4	-2	0	-0.3
Total 5	18	23	.439	120	37	7	0	8	374^2	409	30	135	194	13.1	4.37	82	.284	.347	0	—	0	-28	-33	2	-2.5
● HARRY KIRSCH	Kirsch, Harry Louis "Casey" b: 10/17/1887, Pittsburgh, Pa. d: 12/25/25, Overbrook, Pa. BR/TR, 5'11", 170 lbs. Deb: 4/16/10																								
1910 Cle-A	0	0	—	2	0	0	0	0	3	5	0	1	5	18.0	6.00	43	.385	.429	0	—	0	-1	-1	-0	-0.1
● GARLAND KISER	Kiser, Garland Routhard b: 7/8/68, Charlotte, N.C. BL/TL, 6'3", 190 lbs. Deb: 9/09/91																								
1991 Cle-A	0	0	—	7	0	0	0	0	4^2	7	0	4	3	23.1	9.64	43	.368	.500	0	—	0	-3	-3	-0	-0.3
● RUBE KISINGER	Kisinger, Charles Samuel b: 12/13/1876, Adrian, Mich. d: 7/14/41, Huron, Ohio BR/TR, 6', 190 lbs. Deb: 9/10/02																								
1902 Det-A	2	3	.400	5	5	5	0	0	43^1	48	0	14	7	13.5	3.12	117	.281	.346	3	.158	-1	2	3	-0	0.1
1903 Det-A	7	9	.438	16	14	13	2	0	118^2	118	0	27	33	11.1	2.96	98	.259	.303	6	.128	-3	0	-1	1	-0.3
Total 2	9	12	.429	21	19	18	2	0	162	166	0	41	40	11.8	3.00	103	.265	.315	9	.136	-4	2	2	1	-0.2
● BRUCE KISON	Kison, Bruce Eugene b: 2/18/50, Pasco, Wash. BR/TR, 6'4", 178 lbs. Deb: 7/04/71 C																								
1971 *Pit-N	6	5	.545	18	13	2	1	0	95^1	93	6	36	60	12.7	3.40	100	.259	.337	2	.065	-1	1	-0	1	0.0
1972 *Pit-N	9	7	.563	32	18	6	1	3	152	123	11	69	102	11.9	3.26	102	.220	.316	10	.189	2	3	1	-1	0.2
1973 Pit-N	3	0	1.000	7	7	0	0	0	43^2	36	4	24	26	12.6	3.09	114	.232	.339	1	.083	0	3	2	0	0.2
1974 *Pit-N	9	8	.529	40	16	1	0	2	129	123	8	57	71	13.3	3.49	99	.247	.338	4	.108	-0	2	-1	1	0.0
1975 *Pit-N	12	11	.522	33	29	6	0	0	192	160	10	92	89	12.0	3.23	109	.227	.320	7	.119	-2	8	7	2	0.8
1976 Pit-N	14	9	.609	31	29	6	1	1	193	180	10	52	98	11.0	3.08	113	.247	.299	12	.203	4	9	9	1	1.4
1977 Pit-N	9	10	.474	33	32	3	1	0	193	209	25	55	122	12.6	4.90	81	.278	.333	18	.261	5	-21	-20	1	-1.5
1978 Pit-N	6	6	.500	28	11	0	0	0	96	81	3	39	62	11.7	3.19	116	.229	.314	4	.138	1	4	5	1	0.7
1979 *Pit-N	13	7	.650	33	25	3	1	0	172^1	157	13	45	105	10.8	3.19	122	.246	.300	8	.145	0	10	13	1	1.5
1980 Cal-A	3	6	.333	13	13	2	1	0	73^1	73	5	32	28	13.3	4.91	80	.264	.346	0	—	0	-7	-8	-1	-0.8
1981 Cal-A	1	1	.500	11	4	0	0	0	44	40	8	14	19	11.0	3.48	105	.241	.300	0	—	0	1	1	1	0.1
1982 *Cal-A	10	5	.667	33	16	3	1	1	142	120	15	44	86	10.7	3.17	128	.226	.292	0	—	0	14	14	2	1.6
1983 Cal-A	11	5	.688	26	17	4	1	2	126^2	128	13	43	83	12.4	4.05	99	.264	.330	0	—	0	0	-1	1	0.1
1984 Cal-A	4	5	.444	20	7	0	0	2	65^1	72	10	28	66	14.6	5.37	74	.280	.364	0	—	0	-10	-10	-1	-1.0
1985 Bos-A	5	3	.625	22	9	0	0	1	92	98	9	32	56	12.8	4.11	104	.274	.335	0	—	0	0	2	2	0.0
Total 15	115	88	.567	380	246	36	8	12	1809^2	1693	150	662	1073	12.1	3.66	102	.248	.321	66	.163	8	18	14	11	3.3
● BILL KISSINGER	Kissinger, William Francis "Shang" b: 8/15/1871, Dayton, Ky. d: 4/20/29, Cincinnati, Ohio BR/TR, 185 lbs. Deb: 5/30/1895 ♦																								
1895 Bal-N	1	0	1.000	2	2	1	0	0	11^1	18	0	2	3	15.9	3.97	120	.354	.378	1	.200	-0	1	1	-0	0.0
StL-N	4	12	.250	24	14	9	0	0	140^2	222	8	51	31	18.0	6.72	72	.352	.408	24	.247	-2	-30	-29	0	-2.4
Yr	5	12	.294	26	16	10	0	0	152	240	8	53	34	17.8	6.51	74	.353	.406	25	.245	-2	-29	-28	0	-2.4
1896 StL-N	2	9	.182	20	12	11	0	1	136	209	5	55	22	18.0	6.49	67	.349	.411	22	.301	1	-32	-32	2	-2.3
1897 StL-N	0	4	.000	7	4	2	0	0	31^1	51	2	15	5	21.3	11.49	38	.362	.451	13	.333	2	-25	-25	0	-1.7
Total 3	7	25	.219	53	32	23	0	1	319^1	500	15	123	61	18.2	6.99	66	.352	.413	60	.280	1	-86	-85	2	-6.4
● FRANK KITSON	Kitson, Frank L. b: 4/11/1872, Hopkins, Mich. d: 4/14/30, Allegan, Mich. BL/TR, 5'11", 165 lbs. Deb: 5/19/1898																								
1898 Bal-N	8	5	.615	17	13	13	1	0	119^1	123	0	35	32	12.5	3.24	110	.264	.327	27	.314	3	5	4	0	0.8
1899 Bal-N	22	16	.579	40	37	34	2	0	327^2	329	6	65	75	11.2	2.77	143	.261	.303	27	.201	-2	39	43	-2	3.7
1900 *Bro-N	15	13	.536	40	30	21	2	**4**	253^1	283	12	56	55	12.4	4.19	92	.282	.325	32	.294	5	-14	-10	-5	-0.9
1901 Bro-N	19	11	.633	38	32	26	5	2	280^2	312	9	67	127	12.5	2.98	112	.279	.326	35	.263	5	11	12	-3	1.5

YEAR	TM/L	W	L	PCT	G	GS	CG	SH	SV	IP	H	HR	BB	SO	RAT	ERA	ERA+	OAV	OOB	BH	AVG	PB	PR	/A	PD	TPI
1902	Bro-N	19	12	.613	31	30	28	3	0	259^2	251	4	48	107	10.6	2.84	97	.254	.294	31	.274	7	-2	-2	1	0.6
1903	Det-A	15	16	.484	31	28	28	2	0	257^2	277	8	38	102	11.2	2.58	113	.274	.304	21	.181	-1	11	9	-2	0.6
1904	Det-A	8	13	.381	26	24	19	0	1	199^2	211	7	38	69	11.5	3.07	83	.272	.311	15	.208	0	-10	-11	-0	-1.2
1905	Det-A	12	14	.462	33	27	21	3	1	225^2	230	3	57	78	11.8	3.47	79	.265	.318	16	.184	-1	-20	-18	-2	-2.3
1906	Was-A	6	14	.300	30	21	15	1	0	197	196	2	57	59	11.8	3.65	72	.262	.320	22	.244	8	-21	-22	-0	-1.5
1907	Was-A	0	3	.000	5	3	2	0	0	32	41	1	9	11	14.6	3.94	62	.313	.366	1	.100	-0	-5	-5	-1	-0.7
	NY-A	4	0	1.000	12	4	3	0	0	61	75	0	17	14	14.2	3.10	90	.304	.359	7	.280	1	-4	-2	-2	-0.3
	Yr	4	3	.571	17	7	5	0	0	93	116	1	26	25	14.1	3.39	79	.306	.356	8	.229	0	-9	-7	-2	-1.0
Total	10	128	117	.522	303	249	210	19	8	2213^2	2328	52	487	729	11.8	3.18	99	.270	.315	234	.240	25	-10	-4	-16	0.3

● MALACHI KITTRIDGE Kittridge, Malachi Jedediah "Jedediah" b: 10/12/1869, Clinton, Mass. d: 6/23/28, Gary, Ind. BR/TR, 5'7", 170 lbs. Deb: 4/19/1890 M♦

YEAR	TM/L	W	L	PCT	G	GS	CG	SH	SV	IP	H	HR	BB	SO	RAT	ERA	ERA+	OAV	OOB	BH	AVG	PB	PR	/A	PD	TPI
1896	Chi-N	0	0	—	1	0	0	0	0	1^2	2	0	1	0	16.2	5.40	84	.295	.385	48	.223	-0	-0	-0	-0	0.0

● HUGO KLAERNER Klaerner, Hugo Emil "Dutch" b: 10/15/08, Fredericksburg, Tex. d: 2/3/82, Fredericksburg, Tex. BR/TR, 5'11", 190 lbs. Deb: 9/10/34

YEAR	TM/L	W	L	PCT	G	GS	CG	SH	SV	IP	H	HR	BB	SO	RAT	ERA	ERA+	OAV	OOB	BH	AVG	PB	PR	/A	PD	TPI
1934	Chi-A	0	2	.000	3	3	1	0	0	17^1	24	4	16	9	20.8	10.90	43	.329	.449	2	.333	1	-12	-12	1	-0.8

● FRED KLAGES Klages, Frederick Albert Antony b: 10/31/43, Ambridge, Pa. BR/TR, 6'2", 185 lbs. Deb: 9/11/66

YEAR	TM/L	W	L	PCT	G	GS	CG	SH	SV	IP	H	HR	BB	SO	RAT	ERA	ERA+	OAV	OOB	BH	AVG	PB	PR	/A	PD	TPI
1966	Chi-A	1	0	1.000	3	3	0	0	0	15^2	9	0	7	6	9.2	1.72	184	.167	.262	3	.500	1	3	3	0	0.4
1967	Chi-A	4	4	.500	11	9	0	0	0	44^2	43	6	16	17	12.1	3.83	81	.256	.324	0	.000	-1	-3	-4	-1	-0.6
Total	2	5	4	.556	14	12	0	0	0	60^1	52	6	23	23	11.3	3.28	95	.234	.309	3	.167	-0	0	-1	-1	-0.2

● AL KLAWITTER Klawitter, Albert "Dutch" b: 4/12/1888, Wilkes-Barre, Pa. d: 5/2/50, Milwaukee, Wis. BR/TR, 5'11.5", 187 lbs. Deb: 9/20/09

YEAR	TM/L	W	L	PCT	G	GS	CG	SH	SV	IP	H	HR	BB	SO	RAT	ERA	ERA+	OAV	OOB	BH	AVG	PB	PR	/A	PD	TPI
1909	NY-N	1	1	.500	6	3	2	0	1	27	24	1	13	6	12.3	2.00	128	.247	.336	3	.333	1	2	2	1	0.5
1910	NY-N	0	0	—	1	0	0	0	0	1	2	0	2	0	36.0	9.00	33	.400	.571	0	—	0	-1	-1	-0	-0.1
1913	Det-A	1	2	.333	8	3	1	0	0	32	39	0	15	10	15.2	5.91	49	.305	.378	0	.000	-2	-11	-11	0	-1.2
Total	3	2	3	.400	15	6	3	0	1	60	65	1	30	16	14.3	4.20	66	.283	.365	3	.150	-0	-9	-10	1	-0.8

● TOM KLAWITTER Klawitter, Thomas Carl b: 6/24/58, LaCrosse, Wis. BR/TL, 6'2", 190 lbs. Deb: 4/14/85

YEAR	TM/L	W	L	PCT	G	GS	CG	SH	SV	IP	H	HR	BB	SO	RAT	ERA	ERA+	OAV	OOB	BH	AVG	PB	PR	/A	PD	TPI
1985	Min-A	0	0	—	7	2	0	0	0	9^1	7	2	13	5	19.3	6.75	65	.226	.455	0	—	0	-3	-2	0	-0.5

● HAL KLEINE Kleine, Harold John b: 6/8/23, St.Louis, Mo. d: 12/10/57, St.Louis, Mo. BL/TL, 6'2", 193 lbs. Deb: 4/26/44

YEAR	TM/L	W	L	PCT	G	GS	CG	SH	SV	IP	H	HR	BB	SO	RAT	ERA	ERA+	OAV	OOB	BH	AVG	PB	PR	/A	PD	TPI
1944	Cle-A	1	2	.333	11	6	1	0	0	40^2	38	0	36	13	16.4	5.75	57	.248	.392	2	.143	-1	-11	-11	-1	-1.2
1945	Cle-A	0	0	—	3	0	0	0	0	7	8	0	7	5	19.3	3.86	84	.286	.429	1	.333	0	-0	-0	-0	0.0
Total	2	1	2	.333	14	6	1	0	0	47^2	46	0	43	18	16.8	5.48	60	.254	.397	3	.176	-0	-11	-12	-1	-1.2

● TED KLEINHANS Kleinhans, Theodore Otto b: 4/8/1899, Deer Park, Wis. d: 7/24/85, Redington Beach, Fla. BR/TL, 6', 170 lbs. Deb: 4/20/34

YEAR	TM/L	W	L	PCT	G	GS	CG	SH	SV	IP	H	HR	BB	SO	RAT	ERA	ERA+	OAV	OOB	BH	AVG	PB	PR	/A	PD	TPI
1934	Phi-N	0	0	—	5	0	0	0	0	6	11	1	3	2	21.0	9.00	52	.379	.438	0	.000	-0	-3	-3	0	-0.3
	Cin-N	2	6	.250	24	9	0	0	0	80	107	2	38	23	16.4	5.74	71	.321	.392	3	.130	-1	-15	-15	1	-1.4
	Yr	2	6	.250	29	9	0	0	0	86	118	3	41	25	16.7	5.97	69	.326	.396	3	.125	-1	-18	-18	2	-1.7
1936	NY-A	1	1	.500	19	0	0	0	1	29^1	36	0	23	10	18.1	5.83	80	.300	.413	1	.167	-0	-3	-4	-0	-0.4
1937	Cin-N	1	2	.333	7	3	1	0	0	27^1	29	1	12	13	13.8	2.30	162	.271	.350	2	.250	0	5	4	-1	0.4
1938	Cin-N	0	0	—	1	0	0	0	0	1	2	0	0	0	18.0	9.00	41	.400	.400	0	—	0	-1	-1	-0	-0.1
Total	4	4	9	.308	56	12	1	0	1	143^2	185	4	76	48	16.5	5.26	79	.311	.391	6	.158	-1	-16	-17	1	-1.8

● NUB KLEINKE Kleinke, Norbert Georbe b: 5/19/11, Fond Du Lac, Wis. d: 3/16/50, Off Marin Coast, Cal. BR/TR, 6'1", 170 lbs. Deb: 4/25/35

YEAR	TM/L	W	L	PCT	G	GS	CG	SH	SV	IP	H	HR	BB	SO	RAT	ERA	ERA+	OAV	OOB	BH	AVG	PB	PR	/A	PD	TPI
1935	StL-N	0	0	—	4	2	0	0	0	12^2	19	1	3	5	15.6	4.97	82	.358	.393	0	.000	-0	-1	-1	-0	-0.2
1937	StL-N	1	1	.500	5	2	1	0	0	20^2	25	0	7	9	13.9	4.79	83	.321	.376	0	.000	-1	-2	-2	0	-0.3
Total	2	1	1	.500	9	4	1	0	0	33^1	44	1	10	14	14.6	4.86	83	.336	.383	0	.000	-1	-3	-3	0	-0.5

● ED KLEPFER Klepfer, Edward Lloyd "Big Ed" b: 3/17/1888, Summerville, Pa. d: 8/9/50, Tulsa, Okla. BR/TR, 6', 185 lbs. Deb: 7/04/11

YEAR	TM/L	W	L	PCT	G	GS	CG	SH	SV	IP	H	HR	BB	SO	RAT	ERA	ERA+	OAV	OOB	BH	AVG	PB	PR	/A	PD	TPI
1911	NY-A	0	0	—	2	0	0	0	0	4	5	0	2	4	15.8	6.75	53	.250	.318	0	.000	-0	-2	-1	0	-0.1
1913	NY-A	0	1	.000	8	1	0	0	0	24^2	38	2	12	10	19.0	7.66	39	.373	.448	1	.167	0	-13	-13	0	-1.2
1915	Chi-A	1	0	1.000	3	2	1	0	0	12^2	11	0	5	3	11.4	2.84	105	.234	.308	0	.000	-0	0	0	-0	0.0
	Cle-A	1	6	.143	8	7	2	0	0	43	47	0	11	13	12.1	2.09	146	.283	.328	2	.167	-0	4	5	1	0.5
	Yr	2	6	.250	11	9	3	0	0	55^2	58	0	16	16	12.0	2.26	134	.272	.323	2	.133	-0	4	5	0	0.5
1916	Cle-A	6	6	.500	31	13	4	1	2	143	136	0	46	62	11.7	2.52	119	.262	.327	1	.025	-4	5	8	-0	0.4
1917	Cle-A	14	4	.778	41	27	9	0	1	213	208	0	55	66	11.1	2.37	120	.264	.312	2	.032	-7	7	11	-2	0.3
1919	Cle-A	0	0	—	5	0	0	0	0	7^1	12	1	6	7	22.1	7.36	45	.375	.474	0	.000	-0	-3	-3	0	-0.3
Total	6	22	17	.564	98	50	16	1	3	447^2	457	3	137	165	12.1	2.81	104	.273	.330	6	.048	-11	-2	6	-1	-0.4

● ED KLIEMAN Klieman, Edward Frederick "Specs" or "Babe" b: 3/21/18, Norwood, Ohio d: 11/15/79, Homosassa, Fla. BR/TR, 6'1", 190 lbs. Deb: 9/24/43

YEAR	TM/L	W	L	PCT	G	GS	CG	SH	SV	IP	H	HR	BB	SO	RAT	ERA	ERA+	OAV	OOB	BH	AVG	PB	PR	/A	PD	TPI
1943	Cle-A	0	1	.000	1	1	1	0	0	9	8	0	5	2	13.0	1.00	311	.286	.394	0	.000	-0	2	2	-0	0.2
1944	Cle-A	11	13	.458	47	19	5	1	5	178^1	185	4	70	44	13.2	3.38	98	.274	.348	6	.105	-3	1	-2	1	-0.4
1945	Cle-A	5	8	.385	38	12	4	1	4	126^1	123	3	49	33	12.5	3.85	84	.261	.336	8	.200	1	-7	-8	3	-0.5
1946	Cle-A	0	0	—	9	0	0	0	0	15	18	0	10	2	16.8	6.60	50	.290	.389	0	.000	-0	-5	-5	-1	-0.6
1947	Cle-A	5	4	.556	**58**	0	0	0	**17**	92	78	5	39	21	11.6	3.03	115	.231	.315	2	.105	-1	7	5	2	0.6
1948	*Cle-A	3	2	.600	44	0	0	0	4	79^2	62	3	46	18	12.4	2.60	156	.229	.345	2	.143	-0	**15**	**13**	1	1.4
1949	Was-A	0	0	—	2	0	0	0	0	3	8	0	3	1	33.0	18.00	24	.500	.579	1	1.000	0	-5	-5	-0	-0.4
	Chi-A	2	0	1.000	18	0	0	0	3	33	33	2	15	9	13.1	3.00	139	.273	.353	2	.250	0	4	4	1	0.5
	Yr	2	0	1.000	20	0	0	0	3	36	41	2	18	10	14.8	4.25	98	.299	.381	3	.333	1	-0	-0	1	0.1
1950	Phi-A	0	0	—	5	0	0	0	0	5^2	10	0	2	0	22.2	9.53	48	.357	.438	0	.000	-0	-3	-3	-0	-0.3
Total	8	26	28	.481	222	32	10	2	33	542	525	17	239	130	13.0	3.49	100	.261	.345	21	.146	-3	10	1	6	0.5

● RON KLIMKOWSKI Klimkowski, Ronald Bernard b: 3/1/44, Jersey City, N.J. BR/TR, 6'2", 190 lbs. Deb: 9/15/69

YEAR	TM/L	W	L	PCT	G	GS	CG	SH	SV	IP	H	HR	BB	SO	RAT	ERA	ERA+	OAV	OOB	BH	AVG	PB	PR	/A	PD	TPI
1969	NY-A	0	0	—	3	1	0	0	0	14	6	0	5	3	7.1	0.64	541	.130	.216	0	.000	-0	5	4	-0	0.4
1970	NY-A	6	7	.462	45	3	1	1	1	98^1	80	7	33	40	10.6	2.65	132	.223	.294	1	.053	-1	12	9	0	0.9
1971	Oak-A	2	2	.500	26	0	0	0	2	45^1	37	3	23	25	12.1	3.38	99	.220	.318	2	.400	1	0	-0	1	0.2
1972	NY-A	0	3	.000	16	2	0	0	1	31^1	32	3	15	11	13.8	4.02	73	.271	.358	0	.000	-1	-3	-4	0	-0.5
Total	4	8	12	.400	90	6	1	1	4	189	155	13	76	79	11.2	2.90	116	.224	.306	3	.091	-2	13	10	1	1.0

● BOBBY KLINE Kline, John Robert b: 1/27/29, St.Petersburg, Fla BR/TR, 6', 179 lbs. Deb: 4/11/55 ♦

YEAR	TM/L	W	L	PCT	G	GS	CG	SH	SV	IP	H	HR	BB	SO	RAT	ERA	ERA+	OAV	OOB	BH	AVG	PB	PR	/A	PD	TPI
1955	Was-A	0	0	—	1	0	0	0	0	1	4	1	1	0	45.0	27.00	14	.667	.714	31	.221	0	-3	-3	0	-0.2

● BOB KLINE Kline, Robert George "Junior" b: 12/9/09, Enterprise, Ohio d: 3/16/87, Westerville, Ohio BR/TR, 6'3", 200 lbs. Deb: 9/17/30

YEAR	TM/L	W	L	PCT	G	GS	CG	SH	SV	IP	H	HR	BB	SO	RAT	ERA	ERA+	OAV	OOB	BH	AVG	PB	PR	/A	PD	TPI
1930	Bos-A	0	0	—	1	0	0	0	0	1	1	0	0	0	9.0	0.00	—	.333	.333	0	—	0	1	1	-0	0.0
1931	Bos-A	5	5	.500	28	10	3	0	0	98	110	3	35	25	13.6	4.41	98	.298	.364	9	.333	2	-0	-1	2	0.3
1932	Bos-A	11	13	.458	47	19	4	1	2	172	203	10	76	31	14.7	5.28	85	.294	.365	7	.130	-3	-15	-15	3	-1.4
1933	Bos-A	7	8	.467	46	8	1	0	4	127	127	5	67	16	14.2	4.54	97	.265	.362	6	.176	-1	-4	-2	3	0.0
1934	Phi-A	6	2	.750	20	0	0	0	1	39^2	50	6	13	14	14.3	6.35	69	.314	.366	3	.333	1	-8	-9	1	-0.6
	Was-A	1	0	1.000	6	0	0	0	0	4	10	0	4	1	33.8	15.75	27	.500	.600	0	—	0	-5	-5	0	-0.4
	Yr	7	2	.778	26	0	0	0	1	43^2	60	6	17	15	16.1	7.21	61	.335	.396	3	.333	1	-13	-14	2	-1.0
Total	5	30	28	.517	148	37	8	1	7	441^2	501	24	195	87	14.4	5.05	87	.291	.367	25	.202	-1	-32	-32	9	-2.1

● RON KLINE Kline, Ronald Lee b: 3/9/32, Callery, Pa. BR/TR, 6'3", 205 lbs. Deb: 4/21/52

YEAR	TM/L	W	L	PCT	G	GS	CG	SH	SV	IP	H	HR	BB	SO	RAT	ERA	ERA+	OAV	OOB	BH	AVG	PB	PR	/A	PD	TPI
1952	Pit-N	0	7	.000	27	11	0	0	0	78^2	74	3	66	27	16.7	5.49	73	.253	.401	0	.000	-2	-15	-13	-1	-1.7
1955	Pit-N	6	13	.316	36	19	2	1	2	136^2	161	13	53	48	14.4	4.15	99	.298	.366	5	.132	-2	-2	-1	2	0.0

YEAR	TM/L	W	L	PCT	G	GS	CG	SH	SV	IP	H	HR	BB	SO	RAT	ERA	ERA+	OAV	OOB	BH	AVG	PB	PR	/A	PD	TPI
1956	Pit-N	14	18	.438	44	39	9	2	2	264	263	26	81	125	11.9	3.38	112	.263	.321	10	.127	-3	12	12	-0	0.9
1957	Pit-N	9	16	.360	40	31	11	2	0	205	214	28	61	88	12.1	4.04	94	.268	.321	4	.061	-5	-4	-6	-1	-1.2
1958	Pit-N	13	16	.448	32	32	11	2	0	237^{1}	220	25	92	109	11.8	3.53	110	.252	.323	2	.027	-6	11	9	1	0.4
1959	Pit-N	11	13	.458	33	29	7	0	0	186	186	23	70	91	12.5	4.26	91	.263	.331	8	.136	-2	-6	-8	-1	-1.0
1960	StL-N	4	9	.308	34	17	1	0	1	117^{2}	133	21	43	54	13.5	6.04	68	.284	.344	5	.143	-2	-30	-25	1	-2.6
1961	LA-A	3	6	.333	26	12	0	0	1	104^{2}	119	16	44	70	14.1	4.90	92	.288	.358	3	.097	-2	-10	-5	1	-0.6
	Det-A	5	3	.625	10	8	3	1	0	56^{1}	53	3	17	27	11.2	2.72	151	.245	.300	3	.167	0	8	9	-1	0.9
	Yr	8	9	.471	36	20	3	1	1	161	172	19	61	97	13.0	4.14	106	.272	.336	6	.122	-2	-2	4	0	0.3
1962	Det-A	3	6	.333	36	4	0	0	2	77^{1}	88	9	28	47	13.7	4.31	94	.284	.347	2	.125	-1	-3	-2	1	-0.2
1963	Was-A	3	8	.273	62	1	0	0	17	93^{2}	85	3	30	49	11.3	2.79	133	.249	.316	1	.091	-0	9	10	-1	1.0
1964	Was-A	10	7	.588	61	0	0	0	14	81^{1}	81	4	21	40	11.5	2.32	159	.262	.313	1	.167	0	12	12	-0	1.3
1965	Was-A	7	6	.538	74	0	0	0	**29**	99^{1}	106	7	32	52	12.7	2.63	132	.275	.333	0	.000	-1	9	9	-1	0.8
1966	Was-A	6	4	.600	63	0	0	0	23	90^{1}	79	12	17	46	9.6	2.39	145	.237	.274	1	.167	0	10	11	-2	1.0
1967	Min-A	7	1	.875	54	0	0	0	5	71^{2}	71	10	15	36	10.9	3.77	92	.261	.302	0	.000	-1	-4	-2	-1	-0.4
1968	Pit-N	12	5	.706	56	0	0	0	7	112^{2}	94	3	31	48	10.1	1.68	174	.234	.293	0	.000	-1	**16**	**16**	-1	1.5
1969	Pit-N	1	3	.250	20	0	0	0	3	31	37	3	5	15	12.5	5.81	60	.296	.328	0	.000	-1	-8	-8	-0	-0.9
	SF-N	0	2	.000	7	0	0	0	0	11	16	1	6	7	18.0	4.09	86	.364	.440	0	—	0	-1	-1	-0	-0.1
	Yr	1	5	.167	27	0	0	0	3	42	53	4	11	22	13.7	5.36	65	.310	.352	0	.000	-1	-8	-9	-0	-1.0
	Bos-A	0	1	.000	16	0	0	0	1	17	24	4	17	7	21.7	4.76	80	.329	.456	0	—	0	-2	-2	0	-0.2
1970	Atl-N	0	0	—	5	0	0	0	1	6^{1}	9	4	2	3	15.6	7.11	60	.321	.367	0	—	0	-2	-2	-0	-0.2
Total	17	114	144	.442	736	203	44	8	108	2078	2113	218	731	989	12.5	3.75	101	.266	.331	45	.092	-28	1	13	-5	-1.3

● STEVE KLINE Kline, Steven Jack b: 10/6/47, Wenatchee, Wash. BR/TR, 6'3", 205 lbs. Deb: 7/10/70

YEAR	TM/L	W	L	PCT	G	GS	CG	SH	SV	IP	H	HR	BB	SO	RAT	ERA	ERA+	OAV	OOB	BH	AVG	PB	PR	/A	PD	TPI
1970	NY-A	6	6	.500	16	15	5	0	0	100^{1}	99	8	24	49	11.0	3.41	103	.254	.298	5	.179	1	3	1	1	0.3
1971	NY-A	12	13	.480	31	30	15	1	0	222^{1}	206	21	37	81	9.8	2.96	109	.244	.276	9	.136	-0	13	7	3	1.1
1972	NY-A	16	9	.640	32	32	11	4	0	236^{1}	210	11	44	58	10.1	2.40	123	.237	.281	7	.092	-3	17	14	2	1.6
1973	NY-A	4	7	.364	14	13	2	1	0	74	76	5	31	19	13.1	4.01	91	.270	.344	0	—	0	-2	-3	-0	-0.1
1974	NY-A	2	2	.500	4	4	0	0	0	26	26	3	5	6	11.1	3.46	101	.263	.305	0	—	0	0	0	-0	0.1
	Cle-A	3	8	.273	16	11	1	0	0	71	70	9	31	17	13.3	5.07	71	.266	.352	0	—	0	-11	-11	1	-1.0
	Yr	5	10	.333	20	15	1	0	0	97	96	12	36	23	12.6	4.64	77	.264	.337	0	—	0	-11	-11	1	-0.9
1977	Atl-N	0	0	—	16	0	0	0	1	20^{1}	21	4	12	10	14.6	6.64	67	.259	.355	0	—	0	-6	-5	-0	-0.5
Total	6	43	45	.489	129	105	34	6	1	750^{1}	708	61	184	240	10.9	3.26	101	.249	.298	21	.124	-1	14	3	5	1.5

● BILL KLING Kling, William b: 1/14/1867, Kansas City, Mo. d: 8/26/34, Kansas City, Mo. BL/TR, 6', 190 lbs. Deb: 8/13/1891 F

YEAR	TM/L	W	L	PCT	G	GS	CG	SH	SV	IP	H	HR	BB	SO	RAT	ERA	ERA+	OAV	OOB	BH	AVG	PB	PR	/A	PD	TPI
1891	Phi-N	4	2	.667	12	7	4	0	0	75	90	2	32	26	14.9	4.32	79	.286	.356	6	.194	1	-8	-8	-1	-0.7
1892	Bal-N	0	2	.000	2	2	0	0	0	11	17	1	7	7	21.3	11.45	30	.340	.441	1	.250	1	-10	-10	-0	-0.7
1895	Lou-N	0	0	—	1	0	0	0	0	1	0	0	1	0	9.0	0.00	—	.000	.256	0	.000	-0	1	1	-0	0.0
Total	3	4	4	.500	15	9	4	0	0	87	107	3	40	33	15.6	5.17	66	.291	.367	7	.194	2	-18	-17	-1	-1.4

● BOB KLINGER Klinger, Robert Harold b: 6/4/08, Allenton, Mo. d: 8/19/77, Villa Ridge, Mo. BR/TR, 6', 180 lbs. Deb: 4/19/38

YEAR	TM/L	W	L	PCT	G	GS	CG	SH	SV	IP	H	HR	BB	SO	RAT	ERA	ERA+	OAV	OOB	BH	AVG	PB	PR	/A	PD	TPI
1938	Pit-N	12	5	.706	28	21	10	1	1	159^{1}	152	7	42	58	11.3	2.99	127	.253	.308	10	.167	-2	14	14	0	1.3
1939	Pit-N	14	17	.452	37	33	10	2	0	225	251	11	81	64	13.4	4.36	88	.284	.346	17	.202	0	-11	-13	3	-1.0
1940	Pit-N	8	13	.381	39	22	3	0	3	142	196	5	53	48	16.1	5.39	71	.329	.388	6	.143	-2	-24	-25	1	-2.5
1941	Pit-N	9	4	.692	35	9	3	0	4	116^{2}	127	5	30	36	12.2	3.93	92	.276	.322	8	.250	2	-4	-4	0	-0.2
1942	Pit-N	8	11	.421	37	19	8	1	1	152^{2}	151	6	45	58	11.7	3.24	104	.252	.307	8	.200	1	1	2	1	0.5
1943	Pit-N	11	8	.579	33	25	14	3	0	195	185	6	58	65	11.2	2.72	128	.252	.307	16	.246	3	14	16	0	2.1
1946	*Bos-A	3	2	.600	28	1	0	0	**9**	57	49	1	25	16	11.8	2.37	155	.238	.323	5	.313	1	7	8	-0	0.9
1947	Bos-A	1	1	.500	28	0	0	0	5	42	42	5	24	12	14.4	3.86	101	.253	.351	1	.111	-1	-1	0	-0	-0.1
Total	8	66	61	.520	265	130	48	7	23	1089^{2}	1153	46	358	357	12.6	3.68	100	.271	.331	71	.204	3	-3	-0	5	1.0

● JOE KLINK Klink, Joseph Charles b: 2/3/62, Johnstown, Pa. BL/TL, 5'11", 170 lbs. Deb: 4/09/87

YEAR	TM/L	W	L	PCT	G	GS	CG	SH	SV	IP	H	HR	BB	SO	RAT	ERA	ERA+	OAV	OOB	BH	AVG	PB	PR	/A	PD	TPI
1987	Min-A	0	1	.000	12	0	0	0	0	23	37	4	11	17	18.8	6.65	69	.359	.421	0	—	0	-6	-5	-0	-0.6
1990	*Oak-A	0	0	—	40	0	0	0	1	39^{2}	34	1	18	19	11.8	2.04	182	.233	.317	0	—	0	8	7	-1	0.7
1991	Oak-A	10	3	.769	62	0	0	0	2	62	60	4	21	34	12.5	4.35	88	.259	.333	0	—	0	-2	-4	0	-0.3
Total	3	10	4	.714	114	0	0	0	3	124^{2}	131	9	50	70	13.4	4.04	97	.272	.347	0	—	0	1	-2	-1	-0.2

● JOHNNY KLIPPSTEIN Klippstein, John Calvin b: 10/17/27, Washington, D.C. BR/TR, 6'1", 185 lbs. Deb: 5/03/50

YEAR	TM/L	W	L	PCT	G	GS	CG	SH	SV	IP	H	HR	BB	SO	RAT	ERA	ERA+	OAV	OOB	BH	AVG	PB	PR	/A	PD	TPI
1950	Chi-N	2	9	.182	33	11	3	0	1	104^{2}	112	9	64	51	15.5	5.25	80	.279	.383	11	.333	4	-13	-12	-1	-0.8
1951	Chi-N	6	6	.500	35	11	1	1	2	123^{2}	125	10	53	56	13.4	4.29	95	.263	.344	4	.108	-2	-5	-3	0	-0.4
1952	Chi-N	9	14	.391	41	25	7	2	3	202^{2}	208	17	89	110	13.5	4.44	87	.265	.344	11	.175	1	-16	-13	1	-1.1
1953	Chi-N	10	11	.476	48	19	5	0	6	167^{2}	169	15	107	113	15.2	4.83	92	.258	.369	9	.155	-1	-10	-7	-2	-0.9
1954	Chi-N	4	11	.267	36	21	4	0	1	148	155	13	96	69	15.5	5.29	79	.272	.381	6	.133	-2	-20	-18	1	-1.8
1955	Cin-N	9	10	.474	39	14	3	2	0	138	120	13	60	68	12.0	3.39	125	.233	.318	2	.065	-2	10	13	-0	1.1
1956	Cin-N	12	11	.522	37	29	11	0	1	211	219	26	82	86	13.3	4.09	97	.275	.350	7	.099	-4	-8	-3	1	-0.6
1957	Cin-N	8	11	.421	46	18	3	1	3	146	146	17	68	99	13.4	5.05	81	.261	.344	3	.073	-3	-19	-15	-1	-2.0
1958	Cin-N	3	2	.600	12	4	0	0	1	33	37	5	14	22	14.2	4.91	84	.285	.359	1	.125	-0	-4	-3	-1	-0.4
	LA-N	3	5	.375	45	0	0	0	9	90	81	12	44	73	12.7	3.80	108	.248	.341	1	.050	-2	2	3	-0	0.0
	Yr	6	7	.462	57	4	0	0	10	123	118	17	58	95	13.0	4.10	100	.258	.344	2	.071	-3	-2	0	-1	-0.4
1959	*LA-N	4	0	1.000	28	0	0	0	2	45^{2}	48	8	33	30	16.4	5.91	72	.276	.397	1	.143	-0	-10	-9	-0	-0.9
1960	Cle-A	5	5	.500	49	0	0	0	**14**	74^{1}	53	8	35	46	10.8	2.91	129	.205	.303	2	.143	-0	8	7	0	0.7
1961	Was-A	2	2	.500	42	1	0	0	0	71^{2}	83	13	43	41	16.3	6.78	59	.297	.399	1	.143	-0	-22	-22	1	-2.1
1962	Cin-N	7	6	.538	40	7	0	0	4	108^{2}	113	13	64	67	15.0	4.47	90	.278	.381	3	.125	0	-6	-5	0	-0.5
1963	Phi-N	5	6	.455	49	1	0	0	8	112	80	3	46	86	10.4	1.93	168	.204	.293	1	.038	-2	17	16	-1	1.5
1964	Phi-N	2	1	.667	11	0	0	0	1	22^{1}	22	6	8	13	12.9	4.03	86	.250	.327	0	.000	-0	-1	-1	1	-0.1
	Min-A	0	4	.000	33	0	0	0	2	45^{2}	44	4	20	39	12.8	1.97	181	.260	.342	0	.000	0	8	8	1	1.0
1965	*Min-A	9	3	.750	56	0	0	0	5	76^{1}	59	8	31	59	11.0	2.24	159	.217	.304	0	.000	-1	10	11	-1	1.0
1966	Min-A	1	1	.500	26	0	0	0	3	39^{2}	35	2	20	26	12.9	3.40	106	.238	.337	0	.000	-0	0	1	-0	0.0
1967	Det-A	0	0	—	5	0	0	0	0	6^{2}	6	1	1	4	9.5	5.40	60	.250	.280	0	—	0	-2	-2	-0	-0.2
Total	18	101	118	.461	711	161	37	6	66	1967^{2}	1915	203	978	1158	13.6	4.24	94	.258	.350	63	.125	-15	-80	-54	-0	-6.5

● FRED KLOBEDANZ Klobedanz, Frederick Augustus "Duke" b: 6/13/1871, Waterbury, Conn. d: 4/12/40, Waterbury, Conn. BL/TL, 5'11", 190 lbs. Deb: 8/20/1896

YEAR	TM/L	W	L	PCT	G	GS	CG	SH	SV	IP	H	HR	BB	SO	RAT	ERA	ERA+	OAV	OOB	BH	AVG	PB	PR	/A	PD	TPI
1896	Bos-N	6	4	.600	10	9	9	0	0	80^{2}	69	5	31	26	11.9	3.01	151	.230	.316	13	.317	3	12	14	-1	1.4
1897	*Bos-N	26	7	**.788**	38	37	30	2	0	309^{1}	344	13	125	92	14.3	4.60	97	.279	.357	48	.324	8	-10	-4	-4	0.1
1898	Bos-N	19	10	.655	35	33	25	0	0	270^{2}	281	13	99	51	13.0	3.89	95	.266	.335	27	.213	-1	-8	-6	-1	-0.6
1899	Bos-N	1	4	.200	5	5	4	0	0	33^{1}	39	2	9	8	13.5	4.86	86	.291	.345	2	.182	1	-4	-3	1	-0.1
1902	Bos-N	1	0	1.000	1	1	1	0	0	8	9	0	2	4	13.5	1.13	251	.284	.345	1	.500	1	1	2	-0	0.3
Total	5	53	25	.679	89	85	69	2	0	702	742	33	266	181	13.5	4.12	101	.269	.343	91	.277	12	-8	2	-6	1.1

● STAN KLOPP Klopp, Stanley Harold "Betz" b: 12/22/10, Womelsdorf, Pa. d: 3/11/80, Robesonia, Pa. BR/TR, 6'1.5", 180 lbs. Deb: 4/30/44

YEAR	TM/L	W	L	PCT	G	GS	CG	SH	SV	IP	H	HR	BB	SO	RAT	ERA	ERA+	OAV	OOB	BH	AVG	PB	PR	/A	PD	TPI
1944	Bos-N	1	2	.333	24	0	0	0	0	46^{1}	47	1	33	17	15.5	4.27	89	.272	.388	2	.286	0	-3	-2	-1	-0.3

● BRENT KNACKERT Knackert, Brent Bradley b: 8/1/69, Los Angeles, Cal. BR/TR, 6'3", 185 lbs. Deb: 4/10/90

YEAR	TM/L	W	L	PCT	G	GS	CG	SH	SV	IP	H	HR	BB	SO	RAT	ERA	ERA+	OAV	OOB	BH	AVG	PB	PR	/A	PD	TPI
1990	Sea-A	1	1	.500	24	2	0	0	0	37^{1}	50	5	21	28	17.6	6.51	61	.313	.399	0	—	0	-11	-11	-0	-1.1

● **CHRIS KNAPP** Knapp, Robert Christian b: 9/16/53, Cherry Point, N.C. BR/TR, 6'5", 195 lbs. Deb: 9/04/75

YEAR	TM/L	W	L	PCT	G	GS	CG	SH	SV	IP	H	HR	BB	SO	RAT	ERA	ERA+	OAV	OOB	BH	AVG	PB	PR	/A	PD	TPI
1975	Chi-A	0	0	—	2	0	0	0	0	2	2	0	4	3	27.0	4.50	86	.250	.500	0	—	0	-0	-0	0	-0.1
1976	Chi-A	3	1	.750	11	6	1	0	0	52^1	54	5	32	41	15.0	4.82	74	.273	.377	0	—	0	-8	-7	-0	-0.8
1977	Chi-A	12	7	.632	27	26	4	0	0	146^1	166	16	61	103	14.4	4.80	85	.283	.357	0	—	0	-12	-12	-1	-1.2
1978	Cal-A	14	8	.636	30	29	6	0	0	188^1	178	25	67	126	11.8	4.21	86	.250	.317	0	—	0	-9	-13	-2	-1.5
1979	*Cal-A	5	5	.500	20	18	3	0	0	98	109	8	35	36	13.4	5.51	74	.275	.337	0	—	0	-14	-16	-0	-1.4
1980	Cal-A	2	11	.154	32	20	1	0	1	117^1	133	18	51	46	14.7	6.14	64	.289	.369	0	—	0	-27	-29	-1	-2.8
Total	6	36	32	.529	122	99	15	0	1	604^1	642	72	250	355	13.6	4.99	77	.272	.347	0	—	0	-70	-76	-5	-7.8

● **FRANK KNAUSS** Knauss, Frank H. b: 1868, Cleveland, Ohio BL/TL, 170 lbs. Deb: 6/25/1890

YEAR	TM/L	W	L	PCT	G	GS	CG	SH	SV	IP	H	HR	BB	SO	RAT	ERA	ERA+	OAV	OOB	BH	AVG	PB	PR	/A	PD	TPI
1890	Col-a	17	12	.586	37	34	28	3	2	275^2	206	3	106	148	10.9	2.81	128	**.201**	.290	24	.226	5	33	24	-1	2.6
1891	Cle-N	0	3	.000	3	3	1	0	0	15	23	2	8	6	21.0	7.20	48	.339	.438	1	.167	-0	-6	-6	0	-0.5
1892	Cin-N	0	0	—	1	0	0	0	0	8	13	0	5	2	20.3	3.38	97	.351	.429	1	.333	0	-0	-0	0	0.0
1894	Cle-N	0	1	.000	2	2	1	0	0	11	7	0	14	2	19.6	5.73	95	.181	.431	0	.000	-1	-0	-0	1	0.0
1895	NY-N	0	0	—	1	1	0	0	0	3^2	9	0	2	1	27.0	17.18	27	.458	.509	0	.000	-0	-5	-5	-0	-0.4
Total	5	17	16	.515	44	40	30	3	2	313^1	258	5	135	159	12.1	3.30	111	.218	.312	26	.217	4	20	12	-0	1.7

● **RUDY KNEISCH** Kneisch, Rudolph Frank b: 4/10/1899, Baltimore, Md. d: 4/6/65, Baltimore, Md. BR/TL, 5'10.5", 175 lbs. Deb: 9/21/26

YEAR	TM/L	W	L	PCT	G	GS	CG	SH	SV	IP	H	HR	BB	SO	RAT	ERA	ERA+	OAV	OOB	BH	AVG	PB	PR	/A	PD	TPI
1926	Det-A	0	1	.000	2	2	1	0	0	17	18	2	6	4	13.8	2.65	153	.273	.351	0	.000	-1	3	3	0	0.2

● **PHIL KNELL** Knell, Philip Louis b: 3/12/1865, San Francisco, Cal d: 6/5/44, Santa Monica, Cal. BR/TL, 5'7.5", 154 lbs. Deb: 7/06/1888

YEAR	TM/L	W	L	PCT	G	GS	CG	SH	SV	IP	H	HR	BB	SO	RAT	ERA	ERA+	OAV	OOB	BH	AVG	PB	PR	/A	PD	TPI
1888	Pit-N	1	2	.333	3	3	3	0	0	26^1	20	1	18	15	14.7	3.76	71	.217	.374	1	.091	-1	-3	-3	-0	-0.4
1890	Phi-P	22	11	.667	35	31	30	2	0	286^2	287	10	166	99	15.1	3.83	112	.249	.358	29	.220	-1	13	14	0	1.1
1891	Col-a	28	27	.509	58	52	47	**5**	0	462	363	4	226	228	12.5	2.92	118	**.209**	.319	34	.158	-8	41	28	5	2.1
1892	Was-N	9	13	.409	22	21	17	1	0	170	156	4	76	74	12.9	3.65	89	.234	.323	8	.118	-5	-7	-8	-0	-1.1
	Phi-N	5	5	.500	11	9	7	0	0	80	87	0	35	43	15.0	4.05	80	.266	.357	3	.088	-3	-7	-7	-2	-1.0
	Yr	14	18	.438	33	30	24	1	0	250	243	4	111	117	13.1	3.78	86	.242	.324	11	.108	-7	-14	-15	-2	-2.1
1894	Pit-N	0	0	—	1	0	0	0	0	7	11	0	6	0	23.1	11.57	45	.353	.472	0	.000	-1	-5	-5	1	-0.3
	Lou-N	7	21	.250	32	28	25	0	0	247	330	9	104	67	16.3	5.32	96	.317	.386	31	.274	1	0	-6	-2	-0.6
	Yr	7	21	.250	33	28	25	0	0	254	341	9	110	67	16.5	5.49	93	.318	.388	31	.267	-0	-5	-11	-2	-0.9
1895	Lou-N	0	6	.000	10	6	3	0	0	56^2	75	3	21	19	16.2	6.51	71	.313	.383	6	.231	0	-11	-12	1	-0.8
	Cle-N	7	5	.583	20	13	9	0	0	116^2	149	7	53	30	16.0	5.40	92	.306	.381	11	.200	-3	-8	-5	0	-0.7
	Yr	7	11	.389	30	19	12	0	0	173^1	224	10	74	49	15.8	5.76	85	.306	.374	17	.210	-3	-19	-17	1	-1.5
Total	6	79	90	.467	192	163	141	8	0	1452^1	1478	38	705	575	14.4	4.05	99	.256	.351	123	.187	-20	14	-5	2	-1.7

● **CHARLIE KNEPPER** Knepper, Charles b: 2/18/1871, Anderson, Ind. d: 2/6/46, Muncie, Ind. BR/TR, 6'4", 190 lbs. Deb: 5/26/1899

YEAR	TM/L	W	L	PCT	G	GS	CG	SH	SV	IP	H	HR	BB	SO	RAT	ERA	ERA+	OAV	OOB	BH	AVG	PB	PR	/A	PD	TPI
1899	Cle-N	4	22	.154	27	26	26	0	0	219^2	307	11	77	43	16.3	5.78	64	.329	.390	12	.135	-5	-47	-51	-1	-4.7

● **BOB KNEPPER** Knepper, Robert Wesley b: 5/25/54, Akron, Ohio BL/TL, 6'2", 200 lbs. Deb: 9/10/76

YEAR	TM/L	W	L	PCT	G	GS	CG	SH	SV	IP	H	HR	BB	SO	RAT	ERA	ERA+	OAV	OOB	BH	AVG	PB	PR	/A	PD	TPI
1976	SF-N	1	2	.333	4	4	0	0	0	25	26	0	7	11	11.9	3.24	112	.277	.327	1	.111	-0	1	1	0	0.1
1977	SF-N	11	9	.550	27	27	6	2	0	166	151	14	72	100	12.3	3.36	116	.242	.323	10	.182	1	10	10	-1	1.1
1978	SF-N	17	11	.607	36	35	16	**6**	0	260	218	10	85	147	10.6	2.63	131	.229	.295	5	.063	-3	**27**	24	-2	2.0
1979	SF-N	9	12	.429	34	34	6	2	0	207^1	241	30	77	123	13.9	4.64	75	.289	.352	12	.182	3	-21	-27	-1	-2.5
1980	SF-N	9	16	.360	35	33	8	1	0	215^1	242	15	61	103	13.0	4.10	86	.281	.335	10	.152	-0	-12	-13	2	-1.2
1981	*Hou-N★	9	5	.643	22	22	6	5	0	156^2	128	5	38	75	9.8	2.18	151	.226	.280	7	.149	1	23	19	-1	2.3
1982	Hou-N	5	15	.250	33	29	4	0	1	180	193	14	60	108	12.8	4.45	75	.278	.338	3	.058	-2	-17	-23	1	-2.4
1983	Hou-N	6	13	.316	35	29	4	3	0	203	202	12	71	125	12.3	3.19	107	.261	.326	12	.182	3	10	5	1	0.9
1984	Hou-N	15	10	.600	35	34	11	3	0	233^2	223	26	55	140	10.7	3.20	104	.251	.296	13	.171	4	10	3	-1	0.6
1985	Hou-N	15	13	.536	37	37	4	0	0	241	253	21	54	131	11.6	3.55	98	.271	.313	11	.141	0	1	-2	-3	-0.5
1986	*Hou-N	17	12	.586	40	38	8	**5**	0	258	232	19	62	143	10.4	3.14	115	.242	.290	9	.099	-3	17	13	2	1.3
1987	Hou-N	8	17	.320	33	31	1	0	0	177^2	226	26	54	76	14.4	5.27	74	.313	.364	5	.098	-1	-23	-27	2	-2.5
1988	Hou-N★	14	5	.737	27	27	3	2	0	175	156	13	67	103	11.6	3.14	106	.243	.316	6	.125	-0	6	4	2	0.5
1989	Hou-N	4	10	.286	22	20	0	0	0	113	135	12	60	45	15.7	5.89	57	.303	.388	7	.226	5	-30	-31	1	-2.6
	SF-N	3	2	.600	13	6	1	1	0	52	55	4	15	19	12.3	3.46	97	.270	.323	1	.083	1	0	-1	-1	-0.1
	Yr	7	12	.368	35	26	1	1	0	165	190	16	75	64	14.5	5.13	66	.290	.364	8	.186	5	-30	-32	0	-2.7
1990	SF-N	3	3	.500	12	7	0	0	0	44^1	56	7	19	24	15.4	5.68	64	.311	.380	3	.231	1	-9	-10	0	-0.9
Total	15	146	155	.485	445	413	78	30	1	2708	2737	228	857	1473	12.1	3.68	95	.264	.323	115	.137	7	-8	-55	1	-3.9

● **LOU KNERR** Knerr, Wallace Luther b: 8/21/21, Strasburg, Pa. d: 3/23/80, Denver, Pa. BR/TR, 6'1", 210 lbs. Deb: 4/17/45

YEAR	TM/L	W	L	PCT	G	GS	CG	SH	SV	IP	H	HR	BB	SO	RAT	ERA	ERA+	OAV	OOB	BH	AVG	PB	PR	/A	PD	TPI
1945	Phi-A	5	11	.313	27	17	5	0	0	130	142	6	74	41	15.0	4.22	81	.283	.376	9	.191	-1	-12	-11	0	-1.3
1946	Phi-A	3	16	.158	30	22	6	0	0	148^1	171	13	67	58	14.5	5.40	66	.288	.361	9	.180	0	-31	-31	-0	-3.0
1947	Was-A	0	0	—	6	0	0	0	0	9	17	1	8	5	25.0	11.00	34	.405	.500	1	1.000	0	-7	-7	0	-0.6
Total	3	8	27	.229	63	39	11	0	0	287^1	330	20	149	104	15.1	5.04	69	.290	.373	19	.194	-1	-51	-49	0	-4.9

● **ELMER KNETZER** Knetzer, Elmer Ellsworth "Baron" b: 7/22/1885, Carrick, Pa. d: 10/3/75, Pittsburgh, Pa. BR/TR, 5'10", 180 lbs. Deb: 9/11/09

YEAR	TM/L	W	L	PCT	G	GS	CG	SH	SV	IP	H	HR	BB	SO	RAT	ERA	ERA+	OAV	OOB	BH	AVG	PB	PR	/A	PD	TPI
1909	Bro-N	1	3	.250	5	4	3	0	0	35^2	33	2	22	7	13.9	3.03	86	.252	.359	0	.000	-2	-2	-2	1	-0.3
1910	Bro-N	7	5	.583	20	15	10	3	0	132^2	122	1	60	56	12.4	3.19	95	.255	.339	2	.053	-3	-2	-2	-2	-0.7
1911	Bro-N	11	12	.478	35	20	11	3	0	204	202	1	93	66	13.1	3.49	96	.277	.359	6	.097	-3	-2	-3	-1	-0.8
1912	Bro-N	7	9	.438	33	16	4	1	0	140^1	135	6	70	61	13.4	4.55	74	.254	.345	5	.135	-1	-18	-19	-0	-1.9
1914	Pit-F	20	12	.625	37	30	20	3	1	272	257	9	88	146	11.5	2.88	111	.254	.315	9	.099	-7	10	9	2	0.4
1915	Pit-F	18	14	.563	41	33	22	3	3	279	256	5	89	120	11.2	2.58	117	.251	.311	12	.132	-5	14	13	-0	0.9
1916	Bos-N	0	2	.000	2	0	0	0	0	5	11	0	2	2	23.4	7.20	35	.524	.565	0	—	0	-3	-3	1	-0.2
	Cin-N	5	12	.294	36	16	12	0	1	171^1	161	6	48	70	11.1	2.89	90	.252	.307	8	.154	-1	-5	-6	3	-0.5
	Yr	5	14	.263	38	16	12	0	1	176^1	172	6	50	72	11.5	3.01	86	.261	.316	8	.154	-1	-8	-8	3	-0.7
1917	Cin-N	0	0	—	11	0	0	0	1	27^1	29	0	12	7	14.2	2.96	88	.282	.368	0	.000	-0	-1	-1	0	-0.1
Total	8	69	69	.500	220	134	82	13	6	1267^1	1206	30	484	535	12.1	3.15	97	.258	.330	42	.109	-22	-8	-13	2	-3.2

● **LON KNIGHT** Knight, Alonzo P. b: 6/16/1853, Philadelphia, Pa. d: 4/23/32, Philadelphia, Pa. BR/TR, 5'11.5", 165 lbs. Deb: 9/04/1875 MU♦

YEAR	TM/L	W	L	PCT	G	GS	CG	SH	SV	IP	H	HR	BB	SO	RAT	ERA	ERA+	OAV	OOB	BH	AVG	PB	PR	/A	PD	TPI
1875	Ath-n	6	5	.545	13	13	12	0	0	107	114	0	12		10.6	*2.44*	108	.259	.279	6	.128	-4	0	2		-0.1
1876	Phi-N	10	22	.313	34	32	27	0	0	282	383	0	34	12	13.3	2.62	93	.297	.315	60	.250	-1	-10	-6	-1	-0.6
1884	Phi-a	0	1	.000	2	1	1	0	0	14	24	0	4	2	18.6	9.00	38	.348	.392	131	.271	0	-9	-9	0	-0.7
1885	Phi-a	0	0	—	1	0	0	0	0	5	4	0	2	1	10.8	1.80	191	.103	.146	25	.210	-0	1	1	0	0.1
	Pro-N	0	0	—	1	0	0	0	0	4	4	1	4	1	18.0	6.75	39	.235	.381	13	.160	-0	-2	-2	-0	-0.2
Total	3	10	23	.303	38	33	28	0	0	305	415	1	44	16	13.6	2.95	84	.293	.315	549	.245	-1	-20	-16	-1	-1.4

● **JACK KNIGHT** Knight, Elma Russell b: 1/12/1895, Pittsboro, Miss. d: 7/30/76, San Antonio, Tex. BL/TR, 6', 175 lbs. Deb: 9/20/22

YEAR	TM/L	W	L	PCT	G	GS	CG	SH	SV	IP	H	HR	BB	SO	RAT	ERA	ERA+	OAV	OOB	BH	AVG	PB	PR	/A	PD	TPI
1922	StL-N	0	0	—	1	1	0	0	0	4	9	0	3	1	27.0	9.00	43	.474	.545	1	.500	0	-2	-2	0	-0.2
1925	Phi-N	7	6	.538	33	11	4	0	3	105^1	161	14	36	19	16.9	6.84	70	.354	.402	9	.205	-1	-30	-24	-1	-2.3
1926	Phi-N	3	12	.200	35	15	5	0	2	142^2	206	14	48	29	16.0	6.62	63	.347	.396	12	.214	1	-44	-39	5	-3.2
1927	Bos-N	0	0	—	3	0	0	0	0	3	6	0	2	0	24.0	15.00	25	.429	.500	0	—	0	-4	-4	1	-0.3
Total	4	10	18	.357	72	27	9	0	5	255	382	28	89	49	16.7	6.85	64	.353	.403	22	.216	0	-80	-70	4	-6.0

● **GEORGE KNIGHT** Knight, George Henry b: 11/24/1855, Lakeville, Conn. d: 10/4/12, Lakeville, Conn. Deb: 9/28/1875

YEAR	TM/L	W	L	PCT	G	GS	CG	SH	SV	IP	H	HR	BB	SO	RAT	ERA	ERA+	OAV	OOB	BH	AVG	PB	PR	/A	PD	TPI
1875	NH-n	1	0	1.000	1	1	1	0	0	9	12	0	0		12.0	*2.00*	115	.293	.293	0	.000	-1	0	0		0.0

● JOE KNIGHT

Knight, Jonas William "Quiet Joe"
b: 9/28/1859, Point Stanley, Ont., Canada d: 10/18/38, St.Thomas, Ont., Can. BL/TL, 5'11", 185 lbs. Deb: 5/16/1884 ♦

YEAR TM/L	W	L	PCT	G	GS	CG	SH	SV	IP	H	HR	BB	SO	RAT	ERA	ERA+	OAV	OOB	BH	AVG	PB	PR	/A	PD	TPI
1884 Phi-N	2	4	.333	6	6	6	0	0	51	66	2	21	8	15.4	5.47	55	.293	.354	6	.250	1	-14	-14	-0	-1.1

● HUB KNOLLS

Knolls, Oscar Edward b: 12/18/1883, Valparaiso, Ind. d: 7/1/46, Chicago, Ill. TR, 6'2", 190 lbs. Deb: 5/01/06

YEAR TM/L	W	L	PCT	G	GS	CG	SH	SV	IP	H	HR	BB	SO	RAT	ERA	ERA+	OAV	OOB	BH	AVG	PB	PR	/A	PD	TPI
1906 Bro-N	0	0	—	2	0	0	0	0	6^{2}	13	0	2	3	20.3	4.05	62	.382	.417	1	1.000	1	-1	-1	-1	-0.1

● JACK KNOTT

Knott, John Henry b: 3/2/07, Dallas, Tex. d: 10/13/81, Brownwood, Tex. BR/TR, 6'2.5", 200 lbs. Deb: 4/13/33

YEAR TM/L	W	L	PCT	G	GS	CG	SH	SV	IP	H	HR	BB	SO	RAT	ERA	ERA+	OAV	OOB	BH	AVG	PB	PR	/A	PD	TPI
1933 StL-A	1	8	.111	20	9	0	0	0	82^{2}	88	11	33	19	13.4	5.01	93	.269	.340	7	.304	1	-7	-3	-1	-0.3
1934 StL-A	10	3	.769	45	10	2	0	4	138	149	17	67	56	14.2	4.96	101	.278	.359	4	.133	-1	-7	1	1	0.0
1935 StL-A	11	8	.579	48	19	7	2	**7**	187^{2}	219	8	78	45	14.3	4.60	104	.287	.353	7	.115	-6	-3	4	1	0.0
1936 StL-A	9	17	.346	47	23	9	0	6	192^{2}	272	15	93	60	17.2	7.29	74	.330	.401	4	.070	-6	-48	-41	-1	-4.0
1937 StL-A	8	18	.308	38	22	8	0	2	191^{1}	220	25	91	74	14.9	4.89	99	.291	.370	8	.140	-4	-6	-1	-2	-0.7
1938 StL-A	1	2	.333	7	4	0	0	0	30	35	3	15	8	15.0	4.80	104	.285	.362	1	.100	-1	-0	1	-0	-0.1
Chi-A	5	10	.333	20	18	9	0	0	131	135	8	54	35	13.0	4.05	121	.271	.342	5	.125	-2	11	12	1	1.0
Yr	6	12	.333	27	22	9	0	0	161	170	11	69	43	13.4	4.19	117	.273	.346	6	.120	-3	11	13	1	0.9
1939 Chi-A	11	6	.647	25	23	8	0	0	149^{2}	157	13	41	56	12.0	4.15	114	.269	.318	8	.151	-3	8	10	-1	0.5
1940 Chi-A	11	9	.550	25	23	4	2	0	158	166	12	52	44	12.5	4.56	97	.265	.324	5	.088	-4	-3	-2	-1	-0.6
1941 Phi-A	13	11	.542	27	26	11	0	0	194^{1}	212	20	81	54	13.7	4.40	95	.279	.350	5	.077	-3	-5	-5	-3	-1.0
1942 Phi-A	2	10	.167	20	14	4	0	0	95^{1}	127	7	36	31	15.5	5.57	68	.310	.367	4	.138	-1	-20	-19	1	-1.8
1946 Phi-A	0	1	.000	3	1	0	0	0	6^{1}	7	1	1	2	12.8	5.68	62	.280	.333	0	—	0	-2	-2	-0	-0.2
Total 11	82	103	.443	325	192	62	4	19	1557	1787	140	642	484	14.2	4.97	95	.287	.355	58	.120	-30	-83	-46	-5	-7.2

● ED KNOUFF

Knouff, Edward "Fred" b: 6/1868, Philadelphia, Pa. d: 9/14/1900, Philadelphia, Pa. BR/TR, 210 lbs. Deb: 7/01/1885 ♦

YEAR TM/L	W	L	PCT	G	GS	CG	SH	SV	IP	H	HR	BB	SO	RAT	ERA	ERA+	OAV	OOB	BH	AVG	PB	PR	/A	PD	TPI
1885 Phi-a	7	6	.538	14	13	12	0	0	106	103	0	44	43	13.2	3.65	94	.228	.309	9	.188	-2	-5	-2	1	-0.3
1886 Bal-a	0	1	.000	1	1	1	0	0	9	2	0	5	8	10.0	2.00	171	.067	.263	0	.000	-1	1	1	1	0.2
1887 Bal-a	2	6	.250	9	9	6	0	0	63	79	0	41	27	19.0	7.57	54	.295	.413	9	.290	0	-23	-24	0	-1.7
StL-a	4	2	.667	6	6	6	1	0	50	40	0	36	18	14.2	4.50	101	.225	.364	10	.179	-1	-1	0	-0	-0.1
Yr	6	8	.429	15	15	12	1	0	113	119	0	77	45	15.8	6.21	69	.259	.369	19	.218	-1	-24	-24	0	-1.8
1888 StL-a	5	4	.556	9	9	9	0	0	81	66	0	37	25	12.3	2.67	122	.214	.315	3	.097	-2	4	5	-2	0.1
Cle-a	0	1	.000	2	2	1	0	0	9	8	0	3	2	12.0	1.00	309	.230	.309	1	.167	0	2	2	1	0.3
Yr	5	5	.500	11	11	10	0	0	90	74	0	40	27	11.5	2.50	130	.211	.294	4	.108	-2	6	7	-1	0.4
1889 Phi-a	2	0	1.000	3	3	2	0	0	25	37	2	9	5	16.9	3.96	96	.333	.388	3	.250	0	-0	-0	-1	-0.1
Total 5	20	20	.500	44	43	37	1	0	343	335	2	175	128	14.4	4.17	89	.242	.344	35	.187	-5	-22	-18	0	-1.6

● DAROLD KNOWLES

Knowles, Darold Duane b: 12/9/41, Brunswick, Mo. BL/TL, 6', 190 lbs. Deb: 4/18/65 C

YEAR TM/L	W	L	PCT	G	GS	CG	SH	SV	IP	H	HR	BB	SO	RAT	ERA	ERA+	OAV	OOB	BH	AVG	PB	PR	/A	PD	TPI
1965 Bal-A	0	1	.000	5	1	0	0	0	14^{2}	14	2	10	12	16.6	9.20	38	.250	.391	0	.000	-0	-9	-9	0	-0.9
1966 Phi-N	6	5	.545	69	0	0	0	13	100^{1}	98	4	46	88	13.5	3.05	118	.260	.351	4	.250	0	6	6	2	0.9
1967 Was-A	6	8	.429	61	1	0	0	14	113^{1}	91	5	52	85	11.7	2.70	117	.228	.322	1	.063	-1	7	6	2	0.8
1968 Was-A	1	1	.500	32	0	0	0	4	41^{1}	38	0	12	37	11.1	2.18	134	.241	.298	1	.250	1	4	3	0	0.5
1969 Was-A★	9	2	.818	53	0	0	0	13	84^{1}	73	8	31	59	11.5	2.24	155	.236	.314	1	.077	0	13	11	0	1.2
1970 Was-A	2	14	.125	71	0	0	0	27	119^{1}	100	4	58	71	12.2	2.04	175	.231	.328	1	.050	-1	22	20	2	2.2
1971 Was-A	2	2	.500	12	0	0	0	2	15^{1}	17	2	6	16	13.5	3.52	94	.266	.329	0	.000	-0	-0	-0	-0	-0.1
*Oak-A	5	2	.714	43	0	0	0	7	52^{2}	40	3	16	40	10.1	3.59	93	.221	.295	1	.125	-0	-1	-1	1	-0.1
Yr	7	4	.636	55	0	0	0	9	68	57	5	22	56	10.9	3.57	93	.233	.304	1	.100	-1	-1	-2	1	-0.2
1972 Oak-A	5	1	.833	54	0	0	0	11	65^{2}	49	1	37	36	11.8	1.37	207	.212	.321	3	.250	1	12	11	3	1.7
1973 *Oak-A	6	8	.429	52	5	1	1	9	99	87	7	49	46	12.6	3.09	115	.246	.343	0	—	0	8	5	2	0.7
1974 Oak-A	3	3	.500	45	1	0	0	3	53^{1}	61	6	35	18	16.5	4.22	79	.296	.403	0	—	0	-4	-5	1	-0.2
1975 Chi-N	6	9	.400	58	0	0	0	15	88^{1}	107	3	36	63	14.9	5.81	66	.298	.367	1	.067	-1	-21	-19	3	-1.8
1976 Chi-N	5	7	.417	58	0	0	0	9	71^{2}	61	6	22	39	10.7	2.89	134	.242	.308	1	.143	1	5	8	2	1.1
1977 Tex-A	5	2	.714	42	0	0	0	4	50^{1}	50	3	23	14	13.4	3.22	127	.272	.359	0	—	0	5	5	1	0.6
1978 Mon-N	3	3	.500	60	0	0	0	6	72	63	5	30	34	11.6	2.38	148	.250	.330	1	.167	-0	10	9	2	1.1
1979 StL-N	2	5	.286	48	0	0	0	6	48^{2}	54	5	17	22	13.1	4.07	92	.277	.335	0	.000	-0	-2	-2	-1	-0.3
1980 StL-N	0	1	.000	2	0	0	0	0	1^{2}	3	1	0	1	16.2	10.80	34	.375	.375	0	—	0	-1	-1	-0	-0.1
Total 16	66	74	.471	765	8	1	1	143	1092	1006	65	480	681	12.6	3.12	112	.250	.336	15	.120	-1	53	45	20	7.3

● TOM KNOWLSON

Knowlson, Thomas Herbert "Doc" b: 4/23/1895, Pittsburgh, Pa. d: 4/11/43, Miami Shores, Fla. BB/TR, 5'11", 178 lbs. Deb: 7/03/15

YEAR TM/L	W	L	PCT	G	GS	CG	SH	SV	IP	H	HR	BB	SO	RAT	ERA	ERA+	OAV	OOB	BH	AVG	PB	PR	/A	PD	TPI
1915 Phi-A	4	6	.400	18	9	8	0	0	100^{2}	99	1	60	24	14.8	3.49	84	.273	.386	3	.083	-3	-6	-6	-0	-1.0

● BILL KNOWLTON

Knowlton, William Young b: 8/18/1892, Philadelphia, Pa. d: 2/25/44, Philadelphia, Pa. BR/TR, Deb: 9/03/20

YEAR TM/L	W	L	PCT	G	GS	CG	SH	SV	IP	H	HR	BB	SO	RAT	ERA	ERA+	OAV	OOB	BH	AVG	PB	PR	/A	PD	TPI
1920 Phi-A	0	1	.000	1	1	0	0	0	5^{2}	9	0	3	5	23.8	4.76	84	.346	.469	0	.000	-0	-1	-0	0	-0.1

● KURT KNUDSEN

Knudsen, Kurt David b: 2/20/67, Arlington Heights, Ill. BR/TR, 6'3", 200 lbs. Deb: 5/16/92

YEAR TM/L	W	L	PCT	G	GS	CG	SH	SV	IP	H	HR	BB	SO	RAT	ERA	ERA+	OAV	OOB	BH	AVG	PB	PR	/A	PD	TPI
1992 Det-A	2	3	.400	48	1	0	0	5	70^{2}	70	9	41	51	14.3	4.58	87	.264	.365	0	—	0	-5	-5	0	-0.5

● MARK KNUDSON

Knudson, Mark Richard b: 10/28/60, Denver, Colo. BR/TR, 6'5", 215 lbs. Deb: 7/08/85

YEAR TM/L	W	L	PCT	G	GS	CG	SH	SV	IP	H	HR	BB	SO	RAT	ERA	ERA+	OAV	OOB	BH	AVG	PB	PR	/A	PD	TPI
1985 Hou-N	0	2	.000	2	2	0	0	0	11	21	0	3	4	19.6	9.00	38	.429	.462	0	.000	0	-7	-7	-0	-0.6
1986 Hou-N	1	5	.167	9	7	0	0	0	42^{2}	48	5	15	20	13.5	4.22	85	.279	.340	0	.000	-1	-2	-3	-1	-0.4
Mil-A	0	1	.000	4	1	0	0	0	17^{2}	22	7	5	9	13.8	7.64	57	.286	.329	0	—	0	-7	-7	-0	-0.6
1987 Mil-A	4	4	.500	15	8	1	0	0	62	88	7	14	26	14.8	5.37	85	.331	.364	0	—	0	-6	-6	-1	-0.8
1988 Mil-A	0	0	—	5	0	0	0	0	16	17	1	2	7	10.7	1.13	354	.279	.302	0	—	0	5	5	0	0.5
1989 Mil-A	8	5	.615	40	7	1	0	0	123^{2}	110	15	29	47	10.3	3.35	115	.237	.286	0	—	0	7	7	-1	0.6
1990 Mil-A	10	9	.526	30	27	4	2	0	168^{1}	187	14	40	56	12.3	4.12	94	.282	.325	0	—	0	-4	-5	-2	-0.6
1991 Mil-A	1	3	.250	12	7	0	0	0	35	54	8	15	23	18.0	7.97	50	.355	.417	0	—	0	-15	-16	-0	-1.5
Total 7	24	29	.453	117	59	6	2	0	476^{1}	547	57	123	192	12.8	4.52	87	.287	.333	0	.000	-1	-29	-30	-5	-3.4

● KEVIN KOBEL

Kobel, Kevin Richard b: 10/2/53, Buffalo, N.Y. BR/TL, 6'1", 195 lbs. Deb: 9/08/73

YEAR TM/L	W	L	PCT	G	GS	CG	SH	SV	IP	H	HR	BB	SO	RAT	ERA	ERA+	OAV	OOB	BH	AVG	PB	PR	/A	PD	TPI
1973 Mil-A	0	1	.000	2	1	0	0	0	8^{1}	9	2	8	4	18.4	8.64	44	.273	.415	0	—	0	-4	-5	-0	-0.4
1974 Mil-A	6	14	.300	34	24	3	2	0	169^{1}	166	16	54	74	11.8	3.99	91	.258	.317	0	—	0	-7	-7	1	-0.6
1976 Mil-A	0	1	.000	3	0	0	0	0	4	6	3	3	1	22.5	11.25	31	.375	.500	0	—	0	-3	-3	0	-0.3
1978 NY-N	5	6	.455	32	11	1	0	0	108^{1}	95	9	30	51	10.6	2.91	120	.239	.295	4	.160	0	8	7	-1	0.7
1979 NY-N	6	8	.429	30	27	1	1	0	161^{2}	169	14	46	67	12.1	3.51	104	.274	.328	9	.196	0	4	2	0	0.3
1980 NY-N	1	4	.200	14	1	0	0	0	24^{1}	36	5	11	8	17.4	7.03	51	.353	.416	0	.000	-0	-9	-9	0	-1.0
Total 6	18	34	.346	115	64	5	3	0	476	481	49	152	205	12.1	3.88	93	.266	.326	13	.178	0	-12	-15	0	-1.3

● ALAN KOCH

Koch, Alan Goodman b: 3/25/38, Decatur, Ala. BR/TR, 6'4", 195 lbs. Deb: 7/26/63

YEAR TM/L	W	L	PCT	G	GS	CG	SH	SV	IP	H	HR	BB	SO	RAT	ERA	ERA+	OAV	OOB	BH	AVG	PB	PR	/A	PD	TPI
1963 Det-A	1	1	.500	7	1	0	0	0	10	21	3	9	5	27.9	10.80	35	.467	.564	2	.667	1	-8	-8	0	-0.7
1964 Det-A	0	0	—	3	0	0	0	0	4	6	1	3	1	20.3	6.75	54	.375	.474	0	—	0	-1	-1	-0	-0.2
Was-A	3	10	.231	32	14	1	0	0	114	110	18	43	67	12.3	4.89	76	.253	.325	8	.250	2	-16	-15	-2	-1.5
Yr	3	10	.231	35	14	1	0	0	118	116	19	46	68	12.6	4.96	75	.258	.331	8	.250	2	-17	-17	-2	-1.7
Total 2	4	11	.267	42	15	1	0	0	128	137	22	55	73	13.8	5.41	68	.277	.354	10	.286	3	-25	-24	-2	-2.4

● DICK KOECHER

Koecher, Richard Finlay "Highpockets" b: 3/30/26, Philadelphia, Pa. BL/TL, 6'5", 196 lbs. Deb: 9/29/46

YEAR TM/L	W	L	PCT	G	GS	CG	SH	SV	IP	H	HR	BB	SO	RAT	ERA	ERA+	OAV	OOB	BH	AVG	PB	PR	/A	PD	TPI
1946 Phi-N	0	1	.000	1	1	0	0	0	2^{2}	7	0	1	2	27.0	10.13	34	.467	.500	0	.000	-0	-2	-2	-0	-0.2
1947 Phi-N	0	2	.000	3	2	1	0	0	17	20	1	10	4	16.4	4.76	84	.299	.397	0	.000	-1	-1	-1	0	-0.2

YEAR	TM/L	W	L	PCT	G	GS	CG	SH	SV	IP	H	HR	BB	SO	RAT	ERA	ERA+	OAV	OOB	BH	AVG	PB	PR	/A	PD	TPI
1948	Phi-N	0	1	.000	3	0	0	0	0	6	4	0	3	2	10.5	3.00	132	.235	.350	0	—	0	1	1	-0	0.1
Total	3	0	4	.000	7	3	1	0	0	25^{2}	31	1	14	8	16.1	4.91	80	.313	.404	0	.000	-1	-3	-3	0	-0.3

● **MARK KOENIG** Koenig, Mark Anthony b: 7/19/02, San Francisco, Cal. BB/TR, 6', 180 lbs. Deb: 9/08/25 ♦

YEAR	TM/L	W	L	PCT	G	GS	CG	SH	SV	IP	H	HR	BB	SO	RAT	ERA	ERA+	OAV	OOB	BH	AVG	PB	PR	/A	PD	TPI
1930	Det-A	0	1	.000	2	1	0	0	0	9	11	0	8	6	20.0	10.00	48	.314	.455	64	.240	0	-5	-5	-0	-0.4
1931	Det-A	0	0	—	3	0	0	0	0	7	7	0	11	3	23.1	6.43	71	.280	.500	92	.253	0	-2	-1	0	-0.1
Total	2	0	1	.000	5	1	0	0	0	16	18	0	19	9	21.4	8.44	56	.300	.475	1190	.279	0	-7	-7	-0	-0.5

● **WILL KOENIGSMARK** Koenigsmark, William Thomas b: 2/27/1896, Waterloo, Ill. d: 7/1/72, Waterloo, Ill. BR/TR, 6'4", 180 lbs. Deb: 9/10/19

YEAR	TM/L	W	L	PCT	G	GS	CG	SH	SV	IP	H	HR	BB	SO	RAT	ERA	ERA+	OAV	OOB	BH	AVG	PB	PR	/A	PD	TPI
1919	StL-N	0	0	—	1	0	0	0	0	0	2	0	1	0	—	∞	—	1.000	1.000	0	—	0	-2	-2	0	-0.2

● **ELMER KOESTNER** Koestner, Elmer Joseph "Bob" b: 11/30/1885, Piper City, Ill. d: 10/27/59, Fairbury, Ill. BR/TR, 6'1.5", 175 lbs. Deb: 4/23/10

YEAR	TM/L	W	L	PCT	G	GS	CG	SH	SV	IP	H	HR	BB	SO	RAT	ERA	ERA+	OAV	OOB	BH	AVG	PB	PR	/A	PD	TPI
1910	Cle-A	5	10	.333	27	13	8	1	2	145	145	0	63	44	13.3	3.04	85	.282	.367	15	.313	3	-8	-7	-2	-0.7
1914	Chi-N	0	0	—	4	0	0	0	0	6^{1}	6	0	4	6	14.2	2.84	98	.261	.370	0	.000	-0	-0	-0	-0	0.0
	Cin-N	0	0	—	5	1	0	0	0	18^{1}	18	0	9	6	13.3	4.42	66	.265	.351	2	.400	1	-3	-3	0	-0.2
	Yr	0	0	—	9	1	0	0	0	24^{2}	24	0	13	12	13.5	4.01	72	.264	.356	2	.333	1	-3	-3	0	-0.2
Total	2	5	10	.333	36	14	8	1	2	169^{2}	169	0	76	56	13.3	3.18	83	.279	.365	17	.315	3	-12	-10	-2	-0.9

● **JOE KOHLMAN** Kohlman, Joseph James "Blackie" b: 1/28/13, Philadelphia, Pa. d: 3/16/74, Philadelphia, Pa. BR/TR, 6', 160 lbs. Deb: 9/26/37

YEAR	TM/L	W	L	PCT	G	GS	CG	SH	SV	IP	H	HR	BB	SO	RAT	ERA	ERA+	OAV	OOB	BH	AVG	PB	PR	/A	PD	TPI
1937	Was-A	1	0	1.000	2	2	1	0	0	13	15	0	3	3	12.5	4.15	107	.283	.321	1	.200	-0	1	0	-0	0.0
1938	Was-A	0	0	—	7	0	0	0	0	14^{1}	12	1	11	5	14.4	6.28	72	.240	.377	0	.000	-0	-2	-3	0	-0.3
Total	2	1	0	1.000	9	2	1	0	0	27^{1}	27	1	14	8	13.5	5.27	85	.262	.350	1	.125	-1	-2	-2	-0	-0.3

● **EDDIE KOLB** Kolb, Edward William b: 7/20/1880, Cincinnati, Ohio BR/TR, Deb: 10/15/1899

YEAR	TM/L	W	L	PCT	G	GS	CG	SH	SV	IP	H	HR	BB	SO	RAT	ERA	ERA+	OAV	OOB	BH	AVG	PB	PR	/A	PD	TPI
1899	Cle-N	0	1	.000	1	1	1	0	0	8	18	0	5	1	27.0	10.13	36	.442	.513	1	.250	-0	-6	-6	-1	-0.5

● **RAY KOLP** Kolp, Raymond Carl "Jockey" b: 10/1/1894, New Berlin, Ohio d: 7/29/67, New Orleans, La. BR/TR, 5'10.5", 187 lbs. Deb: 4/16/21

YEAR	TM/L	W	L	PCT	G	GS	CG	SH	SV	IP	H	HR	BB	SO	RAT	ERA	ERA+	OAV	OOB	BH	AVG	PB	PR	/A	PD	TPI
1921	StL-A	8	7	.533	37	18	5	1	0	166^{2}	208	12	51	43	14.0	4.97	90	.314	.363	7	.127	-6	-13	-9	1	-1.3
1922	StL-A	14	4	.778	32	18	9	1	0	169^{2}	199	10	36	54	12.7	3.93	106	.292	.332	17	.298	5	2	4	-4	0.4
1923	StL-A	5	12	.294	34	17	11	1	1	171^{1}	178	11	54	44	12.5	3.89	107	.273	.335	6	.111	-4	2	5	-2	-0.1
1924	StL-A	5	7	.417	25	12	5	1	0	96^{2}	131	4	25	29	14.9	5.68	79	.329	.375	6	.200	-0	-16	-13	-1	-1.2
1927	Cin-N	3	3	.500	24	5	2	1	3	82^{1}	86	5	29	28	12.7	3.06	124	.278	.342	6	.200	-0	8	7	0	0.7
1928	Cin-N	13	10	.565	44	24	12	1	3	209	219	9	55	61	12.0	3.19	124	.280	.330	15	.214	3	19	18	1	2.1
1929	Cin-N	8	10	.444	30	16	4	1	0	145^{1}	151	8	39	27	11.8	4.03	113	.278	.328	8	.163	-1	11	9	1	0.8
1930	Cin-N	7	12	.368	37	19	5	2	3	168^{1}	180	10	34	40	11.4	4.22	114	.278	.314	12	.245	1	14	11	-1	1.1
1931	Cin-N	4	9	.308	30	10	2	0	1	107	144	8	39	24	15.7	4.96	75	.332	.392	4	.125	-1	-13	-15	-1	-1.6
1932	Cin-N	6	10	.375	32	19	7	2	1	159^{2}	176	13	27	42	11.6	3.89	99	.280	.313	9	.184	-1	-0	-1	-2	-0.4
1933	Cin-N	6	9	.400	30	14	4	0	3	150^{1}	168	7	23	28	11.5	3.53	96	.290	.318	7	.156	-1	-3	-2	1	-0.2
1934	Cin-N	0	2	.000	28	2	0	0	3	61^{2}	78	1	12	19	13.4	4.52	90	.312	.348	1	.083	-1	-3	-3	2	-0.2
Total	12	79	95	.454	383	174	66	11	18	1688	1918	98	424	439	12.7	4.08	102	.292	.338	98	.184	-8	8	13	-6	0.1

● **HAL KOLSTAD** Kolstad, Harold Everette b: 6/1/35, Rice Lake, Wis. BR/TR, 5'9", 190 lbs. Deb: 4/22/62

YEAR	TM/L	W	L	PCT	G	GS	CG	SH	SV	IP	H	HR	BB	SO	RAT	ERA	ERA+	OAV	OOB	BH	AVG	PB	PR	/A	PD	TPI
1962	Bos-A	0	2	.000	27	2	0	0	2	61^{1}	65	11	35	36	15.0	5.43	76	.269	.366	1	.056	-2	-10	-9	0	-1.0
1963	Bos-A	0	2	.000	7	0	0	0	0	11	16	4	6	6	19.6	13.09	29	.340	.436	0	.000	-0	-12	-11	-0	-1.1
Total	2	0	4	.000	34	2	0	0	2	72^{1}	81	15	41	42	15.7	6.59	62	.280	.377	1	.053	-2	-22	-20	0	-2.1

● **ED KONETCHY** Konetchy, Edward Joseph "Big Ed" b: 9/3/1885, Lacrosse, Wis. d: 5/27/47, Ft.Worth, Tex. BR/TR, 6'2.5", 195 lbs. Deb: 6/29/07 ♦

YEAR	TM/L	W	L	PCT	G	GS	CG	SH	SV	IP	H	HR	BB	SO	RAT	ERA	ERA+	OAV	OOB	BH	AVG	PB	PR	/A	PD	TPI
1910	StL-N	0	0	—	1	0	0	0	0	4	4	0	1	0	11.3	4.50	66	.267	.313	157	.302	0	-1	-1	-0	-0.1
1913	StL-N	1	0	1.000	1	0	0	0	0	4^{2}	1	0	4	3	9.6	0.00	—	.071	.278	139	.276	0	2	2	-0	0.2
1918	Bos-N	0	1	.000	1	1	1	0	0	8	14	1	2	3	18.0	6.75	40	.378	.410	103	.236	0	-4	-4	-0	-0.3
Total	3	1	1	.500	3	1	1	0	0	16^{2}	19	1	7	6	14.0	4.32	67	.288	.356	2150	.281	1	-3	-3	-1	-0.2

● **DOUG KONIECZNY** Konieczny, Douglas James b: 9/27/51, Detroit, Mich. BR/TR, 6'4", 220 lbs. Deb: 9/11/73

YEAR	TM/L	W	L	PCT	G	GS	CG	SH	SV	IP	H	HR	BB	SO	RAT	ERA	ERA+	OAV	OOB	BH	AVG	PB	PR	/A	PD	TPI
1973	Hou-N	0	1	.000	2	2	0	0	0	13	12	0	4	6	11.1	5.54	66	.279	.340	0	.000	-0	-3	-3	-0	-0.3
1974	Hou-N	0	3	.000	6	3	0	0	0	16	18	0	12	8	18.0	7.88	44	.290	.421	0	.000	-0	-8	-8	-0	-0.8
1975	Hou-N	6	13	.316	32	29	4	1	0	171	184	15	87	89	14.3	4.47	75	.280	.365	8	.160	1	-16	-21	-2	-2.2
1977	Hou-N	1	1	.500	4	4	0	0	0	21	26	1	8	7	15.0	6.00	59	.302	.368	1	.143	-0	-5	-6	0	-0.5
Total	4	7	18	.280	44	38	4	1	0	221	240	16	111	110	14.5	4.93	69	.283	.368	9	.138	-0	-31	-37	-2	-3.8

● **ALEX KONIKOWSKI** Konikowski, Alexander James "Whitey" b: 6/8/28, Throop, Pa. BR/TR, 6'1", 187 lbs. Deb: 6/16/48

YEAR	TM/L	W	L	PCT	G	GS	CG	SH	SV	IP	H	HR	BB	SO	RAT	ERA	ERA+	OAV	OOB	BH	AVG	PB	PR	/A	PD	TPI
1948	NY-N	2	3	.400	22	1	0	0	1	33^{1}	46	7	17	9	17.0	7.56	52	.346	.420	0	.000	0	-13	-13	1	-1.2
1951	*NY-N	0	0	—	3	0	0	0	0	4	2	0	0	5	4.5	0.00	—	.154	.154	0	—	0	2	2	0	0.2
1954	NY-N	0	0	—	10	0	0	0	0	12	10	1	12	6	16.5	7.50	54	.244	.415	0	.000	-0	-5	-5	-0	-0.5
Total	3	2	3	.400	35	1	0	0	1	49^{1}	58	8	29	20	15.9	6.93	57	.310	.403	0	.000	0	-16	-16	0	-1.5

● **JIM KONSTANTY** Konstanty, Casimir James b: 3/2/17, Strykersville, N.Y. d: 6/11/76, Oneonta, N.Y. BR/TR, 6'1.5", 202 lbs. Deb: 6/18/44

YEAR	TM/L	W	L	PCT	G	GS	CG	SH	SV	IP	H	HR	BB	SO	RAT	ERA	ERA+	OAV	OOB	BH	AVG	PB	PR	/A	PD	TPI
1944	Cin-N	6	4	.600	20	12	5	1	0	112^{2}	113	11	33	19	11.7	2.80	125	.266	.320	10	.294	2	10	9	1	1.2
1946	Bos-N	0	1	.000	10	1	0	0	0	15^{1}	17	2	7	9	14.1	5.28	65	.283	.358	0	.000	0	-3	-3	1	-0.3
1948	Phi-N	1	0	1.000	6	0	0	0	2	9^{2}	7	0	2	7	8.4	0.93	424	.233	.281	0	.000	-0	3	3	-0	0.3
1949	Phi-N	9	5	.643	53	0	0	0	7	97	98	9	29	43	11.9	3.25	121	.280	.337	3	.176	-0	9	8	1	0.8
1950	*Phi-N★	16	7	.696	**74**	0	0	0	**22**	152	108	11	50	56	9.4	2.66	152	.205	.274	4	.108	-2	**25**	**23**	-1	2.0
1951	Phi-N	4	11	.267	58	1	0	0	9	115^{2}	127	9	31	27	12.3	4.05	95	.282	.328	3	.158	-0	-1	-3	1	-0.1
1952	Phi-N	5	3	.625	42	2	2	1	6	80	87	9	21	16	12.1	3.94	93	.274	.319	1	.071	-0	-2	-3	-0	-0.3
1953	Phi-N	14	10	.583	48	19	7	0	5	170^{2}	198	18	42	45	12.8	4.43	95	.290	.334	11	.220	-0	-3	-4	0	-0.4
1954	Phi-N	2	3	.400	33	1	0	0	3	50^{1}	62	7	12	11	13.2	3.75	108	.316	.356	0	.000	-2	2	2	0	0.0
	NY-A	1	1	.500	9	0	0	0	2	18^{1}	11	0	6	3	8.3	0.98	350	.183	.258	0	.000	-0	6	5	0	0.5
1955	NY-A	7	2	.778	45	0	0	0	11	73^{2}	68	5	24	19	11.2	2.32	161	.247	.308	1	.125	-0	13	12	-0	1.1
1956	NY-A	0	0	—	8	0	0	0	2	11	15	3	6	6	17.2	4.91	79	.319	.396	0	.000	-0	-1	-1	-0	-0.2
	StL-N	1	1	.500	27	0	0	0	5	39^{1}	46	4	6	7	11.9	4.58	83	.301	.327	0	—	0	-4	-3	-1	-0.4
Total	11	66	48	.579	433	36	14	2	74	945^{2}	957	88	269	268	11.7	3.46	112	.268	.320	33	.163	-4	54	44	2	4.2

● **ERNIE KOOB** Koob, Ernest Gerald b: 9/11/1893, Keeler, Mich. d: 11/12/41, Lemay, Mo. BL/TL, 5'10", 160 lbs. Deb: 6/23/15

YEAR	TM/L	W	L	PCT	G	GS	CG	SH	SV	IP	H	HR	BB	SO	RAT	ERA	ERA+	OAV	OOB	BH	AVG	PB	PR	/A	PD	TPI
1915	StL-A	4	5	.444	28	13	6	0	1	133^{2}	119	2	50	37	12.1	2.36	122	.254	.339	5	.135	-1	9	8	-2	0.5
1916	StL-A	11	8	.579	33	20	10	2	2	166^{2}	153	1	56	26	11.6	2.54	108	.252	.321	0	.000	-1	5	4	-4	-0.1
1917	StL-A	6	14	.300	39	18	3	1	1	133^{2}	139	1	57	47	13.6	3.91	67	.280	.361	4	.114	-1	-18	-19	1	-2.1
1919	StL-A	2	3	.400	25	4	0	0	0	66	77	3	23	11	13.9	4.64	72	.296	.358	0	.000	-2	-10	-10	0	-1.2
Total	4	23	30	.434	125	55	19	3	4	500	488	7	186	121	12.6	3.13	90	.266	.342	9	.070	-5	-15	-18	-4	-2.9

● **CAL KOONCE** Koonce, Calvin Lee b: 11/18/40, Fayetteville, N.C. BR/TR, 6'1", 185 lbs. Deb: 4/14/62

YEAR	TM/L	W	L	PCT	G	GS	CG	SH	SV	IP	H	HR	BB	SO	RAT	ERA	ERA+	OAV	OOB	BH	AVG	PB	PR	/A	PD	TPI
1962	Chi-N	10	10	.500	35	30	3	1	0	190^{2}	200	17	86	84	13.8	3.97	105	.271	.353	6	.094	-4	-0	4	-1	-0.1
1963	Chi-N	2	6	.250	21	13	0	0	0	72^{2}	75	9	32	44	13.5	4.58	77	.273	.353	2	.105	-0	-10	-9	1	-0.9
1964	Chi-N	3	0	1.000	6	2	0	0	0	31	30	1	7	17	10.7	2.03	183	.254	.296	0	.000	-1	5	6	2	0.7
1965	Chi-N	7	9	.438	38	23	3	1	0	173	181	17	52	88	12.4	3.69	100	.271	.329	5	.102	-0	-3	-0	-0	0.0
1966	Chi-N	5	5	.500	45	5	0	0	2	108^{2}	113	13	35	65	12.3	3.81	97	.268	.325	3	.130	0	-2	-2	1	0.0
1967	Chi-N	2	2	.500	34	0	0	0	2	51	52	2	21	28	13.1	4.59	77	.268	.343	0	.000	-1	-7	-6	1	-0.6
	NY-N	3	3	.500	11	6	2	1	0	45	45	2	7	24	10.4	2.80	121	.259	.287	2	.154	-0	3	3	1	0.4

YEAR	TM/L	W	L	PCT	G	GS	CG	SH	SV	IP	H	HR	BB	SO	RAT	ERA	ERA+	OAV	OOB	BH	AVG	PB	PR	/A	PD	TPI
	Yr	5	5	.500	45	6	2	1	2	96	97	4	28	52	11.7	3.75	93	.262	.314	2	.100	-1	-4	-3	2	-0.2
1968	NY-N	6	4	.600	55	2	0	0	11	97	80	4	32	50	10.5	2.41	125	.235	.303	0	.000	-1	6	7	-1	0.6
1969	NY-N	6	3	.667	40	0	0	0	7	83	85	8	42	48	14.1	4.99	73	.269	.360	4	.235	0	-13	-12	1	-1.1
1970	NY-N	0	2	.000	13	0	0	0	0	22	25	2	14	10	16.4	3.27	123	.301	.408	0	.000	-0	2	2	0	0.2
	Bos-A	3	4	.429	23	8	1	0	2	76^1	64	7	29	37	11.3	3.54	112	.231	.311	2	.095	-0	2	4	2	0.6
1971	Bos-A	0	1	.000	13	1	0	0	0	21	22	3	11	9	14.1	5.57	66	.278	.367	0	.000	0	-5	-4	1	-0.4
Total	10	47	49	.490	334	90	9	3	24	971^1	972	85	368	504	12.6	3.78	98	.264	.335	24	.100	-6	-23	-9	9	-0.6
● JERRY KOOSMAN	Koosman, Jerome Martin b: 12/23/42, Appleton, Minn. BR/TL, 6'2", 208 lbs. Deb: 4/14/67																									
1967	NY-N	0	2	.000	9	3	0	0	0	22^1	22	3	19	11	16.5	6.04	56	.259	.394	0	.000	0	-7	-7	0	-0.7
1968	NY-N★	19	12	.613	35	34	17	7	0	263^2	221	16	69	178	10.2	2.08	145	.228	.285	7	.077	-3	26	27	-1	2.8
1969	*NY-N★	17	9	.654	32	32	16	6	0	241	187	14	68	180	9.7	2.28	160	.216	.277	4	.048	-7	35	37	-1	3.3
1970	NY-N	12	7	.632	30	29	5	1	0	212	189	22	71	118	11.1	3.14	128	.237	.300	6	.086	-2	21	21	-3	1.6
1971	NY-N	6	11	.353	26	24	4	0	0	165^2	160	12	51	96	11.5	3.04	112	.256	.313	8	.160	0	8	7	-1	0.7
1972	NY-N	11	12	.478	34	24	4	1	1	163	155	14	52	147	11.8	4.14	81	.250	.314	4	.085	-3	-12	-14	0	-1.8
1973	*NY-N	14	15	.483	35	35	12	3	0	263	234	18	76	156	10.7	2.84	127	.242	.300	8	.103	-3	24	23	-1	2.0
1974	NY-N	15	11	.577	35	35	13	0	0	265	258	16	85	188	11.9	3.36	106	.257	.320	16	.186	2	8	6	-0	0.8
1975	NY-N	14	13	.519	36	34	11	4	2	239^2	234	19	98	173	12.6	3.42	101	.261	.337	14	.179	1	5	1	-1	0.2
1976	NY-N	21	10	.677	34	32	17	3	0	247^1	205	19	66	200	9.9	2.69	122	.226	.279	17	.215	3	22	17	0	2.2
1977	NY-N	8	20	.286	32	32	6	1	0	226^2	195	17	81	192	11.1	3.49	107	.232	.302	8	.111	-3	10	6	-2	0.2
1978	NY-N	3	15	.167	38	32	3	0	2	235^1	221	17	84	160	12.0	3.75	93	.255	.327	6	.086	-3	-4	-7	2	-0.9
1979	Min-A	20	13	.606	37	36	10	2	0	263^2	268	19	83	157	12.1	3.38	130	.268	.326	0	—	0	24	29	2	3.2
1980	Min-A	16	13	.552	38	34	8	0	2	243^1	252	24	69	149	12.1	4.03	108	.272	.326	0	—	0	0	9	1	0.8
1981	Min-A	3	9	.250	19	13	2	1	5	94^1	98	8	34	55	12.6	4.20	94	.272	.335	0	—	0	-6	-3	0	-0.3
	Chi-A	1	4	.200	8	3	1	0	0	27	27	2	7	21	11.3	3.33	107	.260	.306	0	—	0	1	1	-0	0.1
	Yr	4	13	.235	27	16	3	1	5	121^1	125	10	41	76	12.3	4.01	96	.267	.325	0	—	0	-5	-2	-0	-0.2
1982	Chi-A	11	7	.611	42	19	3	1	3	173^1	194	9	38	88	12.1	3.84	105	.287	.327	0	—	0	4	4	0	0.4
1983	*Chi-A	11	7	.611	37	24	2	1	2	169^2	176	19	53	90	12.5	4.77	88	.266	.326	0	—	0	-13	-11	0	-1.1
1984	Phi-N	14	15	.483	36	34	3	1	0	224	232	8	60	137	11.9	3.25	112	.267	.317	8	.108	-3	8	9	-1	0.6
1985	Phi-N	6	4	.600	19	18	3	1	0	99^1	107	14	34	60	13.0	4.62	80	.276	.340	3	.088	-2	-11	-10	-0	-1.3
Total	19	222	209	.515	612	527	140	33	17	3839^1	3635	290	1198	2556	11.5	3.36	110	.252	.313	109	.119	-22	145	143	-6	12.8
● HOWIE KOPLITZ	Koplitz, Howard Dean b: 5/4/38, Oshkosh, Wis. BR/TR, 5'11", 195 lbs. Deb: 9/08/61																									
1961	Det-A	2	0	1.000	4	1	1	0	0	12	16	0	8	9	18.0	2.25	182	.327	.421	0	.000	-1	2	2	-0	0.2
1962	Det-A	3	0	1.000	10	6	1	0	0	37^2	54	5	10	10	15.3	5.26	77	.342	.381	3	.231	1	-5	-5	0	-0.4
1964	Was-A	0	0	—	6	1	0	0	0	17	20	3	13	9	17.5	4.76	78	.290	.402	0	.000	-0	-2	-2	0	-0.2
1965	Was-A	4	7	.364	33	11	0	0	1	106^2	97	11	48	59	12.5	4.05	86	.249	.336	3	.100	-1	-7	-7	1	-0.7
1966	Was-A	0	0	—	1	0	0	0	0	2	0	0	1	0	4.5	0.00	—	.000	.200	0	—	0	1	1	0	0.1
Total	5	9	7	.563	54	19	2	0	1	175^1	187	19	80	87	13.9	4.21	87	.280	.359	6	.118	-1	-11	-11	1	-1.0
● GEORGE KORINCE	Korince, George Eugene "Moose" b: 1/10/46, Ottawa, Ont., Canada BR/TR, 6'3", 210 lbs. Deb: 9/10/66																									
1966	Det-A	0	0	—	2	0	0	0	0	3	1	0	3	2	15.0	0.00	—	.091	.333	0	—	0	1	1	-0	0.1
1967	Det-A	1	0	1.000	9	0	0	0	0	14	10	1	11	11	13.5	5.14	63	.204	.350	0	.000	-0	-3	-3	0	-0.3
Total	2	1	0	1.000	11	0	0	0	0	17	11	1	14	13	13.8	4.24	78	.183	.347	0	.000	-0	-2	-2	-0	-0.2
● JIM KORWAN	Korwan, James "Long Jim" b: 3/4/1874, Brooklyn, N.Y. d: 8/1899, Brooklyn, N.Y. BR/TR, 6'1", 181 lbs. Deb: 4/24/1894																									
1894	Bro-N	0	0	—	1	0	0	0	0	5	9	1	5	2	25.2	14.40	34	.385	.493	0	.000	-0	-5	-5	0	-0.4
1897	Chi-N	1	2	.333	5	4	3	0	0	34	47	1	28	12	20.1	5.82	77	.325	.438	0	.000	-2	-6	-5	2	-0.5
Total	2	1	2	.333	6	4	3	0	0	39	56	2	33	14	20.8	6.92	66	.333	.446	0	.000	-3	-11	-10	2	-0.9
● BILL KOSKI	Koski, William John "T-Bone" b: 2/6/32, Madera, Cal. BR/TR, 6'4", 185 lbs. Deb: 4/28/51																									
1951	Pit-N	0	1	.000	13	1	0	0	0	27	26	2	28	6	18.0	6.67	63	.257	.419	0	.000	-1	-8	-7	-1	-0.8
● DAVE KOSLO	Koslo, George Bernard (b: George Bernard Koslowski) b: 3/31/20, Menasha, Wis. d: 12/1/75, Menasha, Wis. BL/TL, 5'11", 180 lbs. Deb: 9/12/41																									
1941	NY-N	1	2	.333	4	3	2	0	0	23^2	17	0	10	12	10.3	1.90	194	.202	.287	1	.111	-1	5	5	-1	0.4
1942	NY-N	3	6	.333	19	11	3	1	0	78	79	7	32	42	12.9	5.08	66	.261	.333	3	.120	-0	-15	-15	-1	-1.6
1946	NY-N	14	19	.424	40	35	17	3	1	265^1	251	15	101	121	12.1	3.63	95	.249	.320	11	.125	-3	-6	-6	2	-0.8
1947	NY-N	15	10	.600	39	31	10	3	0	217^1	223	23	82	86	12.8	4.39	93	.259	.326	10	.128	-1	-8	-8	-1	-0.9
1948	NY-N	8	10	.444	35	18	5	3	3	149	168	7	62	58	14.0	3.87	102	.290	.359	5	.114	-1	2	1	-1	-0.1
1949	NY-N	11	14	.440	38	23	15	0	4	212	193	13	43	64	**10.0**	**2.50**	**159**	.239	**.278**	10	.145	1	**36**	35	0	**3.7**
1950	NY-N	13	15	.464	40	22	7	1	3	186^2	190	18	68	56	12.7	3.91	105	.268	.337	8	.123	-1	5	4	-0	0.3
1951	*NY-N	10	9	.526	39	16	5	2	3	149^2	153	18	45	54	12.0	3.31	118	.258	.313	5	.100	-1	11	10	2	1.1
1952	NY-N	10	7	.588	41	17	8	2	5	166^1	154	10	47	67	11.0	3.19	116	.242	.296	2	.037	-4	10	9	1	0.7
1953	NY-N	6	12	.333	37	12	2	0	2	111^2	135	8	36	36	13.9	4.76	90	.296	.349	1	.033	-3	-6	-6	1	-0.8
1954	Bal-A	0	1	.000	3	1	0	0	0	14^1	20	1	3	3	14.4	3.14	114	.333	.365	0	.000	-0	1	1	-0	0.0
	Mil-N	1	1	.500	12	0	0	0	1	17^1	13	0	9	7	11.4	3.12	120	.228	.333	0	.000	-0	2	1	-1	0.0
1955	Mil-N	0	1	.000	1	0	0	0	0	0	1	1	0	0	—	∞	—	1.000	1.000	0	—	0	-1	-1	0	-0.1
Total	12	92	107	.462	348	189	74	15	22	1591^1	1597	121	538	606	12.2	3.68	105	.260	.321	56	.109	-15	34	32	2	1.9
● JOE KOSTAL	Kostal, Joseph William "Cudgey" b: 3/17/1876, Chicago, Ill. d: 10/17/33, Guelph, Ont., Can. BR/TR, 5'6", 130 lbs. Deb: 7/14/1896																									
1896	Lou-N	0	0	—	2	0	0	0	0	2	4	0	0	0	18.0	0.00	—	.411	.411	0	—	0	1	1	-0	0.1
● SANDY KOUFAX	Koufax, Sanford (b: Sanford Braun) b: 12/30/35, Brooklyn, N.Y. BR/TL, 6'2", 210 lbs. Deb: 6/24/55 H																									
1955	Bro-N	2	2	.500	12	5	2	2	0	41^2	33	2	28	30	13.4	3.02	134	.216	.341	0	.000	-2	5	5	-0	0.3
1956	Bro-N	2	4	.333	16	10	0	0	0	58^2	66	10	29	30	14.6	4.91	81	.286	.365	2	.118	-0	-7	-6	-1	-0.8
1957	Bro-N	5	4	.556	34	13	2	0	0	104^1	83	14	51	122	11.7	3.88	107	.216	.311	0	.000	-3	-0	3	-2	-0.2
1958	LA-N	11	11	.500	40	26	5	0	1	158^2	132	19	105	131	13.5	4.48	91	**.220**	.337	6	.122	-2	-9	-7	-0	-0.9
1959	*LA-N	8	6	.571	35	23	6	1	2	153^1	136	23	92	173	13.4	4.05	104	.235	.340	6	.111	-2	-2	3	-1	0.1
1960	LA-N	8	13	.381	37	26	7	2	1	175	133	20	100	197	12.0	3.91	102	**.207**	.315	7	.123	-2	-3	1	-1	-0.2
1961	LA-N★	18	13	.581	42	35	15	2	1	255^2	212	27	96	**269**	10.9	3.52	123	**.222**	.295	5	.065	-5	15	23	-3	1.5
1962	LA-N☆	14	7	.667	28	26	11	2	1	184^1	134	13	57	216	**9.4**	**2.54**	143	**.197**	**.261**	6	.087	-2	29	22	-2	1.8
1963	*LA-N☆	**25**	5	.833	40	40	20	**11**	0	311	214	18	58	**306**	**8.0**	**1.88**	161	**.189**	**.230**	7	.064	-3	**49**	39	-4	3.7
1964	LA-N☆	19	5	**.792**	29	28	15	**7**	1	223	154	13	53	223	**8.4**	**1.74**	**187**	**.191**	**.241**	7	.095	-1	45	37	-4	3.7
1965	*LA-N★	**26**	8	**.765**	43	41	**27**	8	2	**335^2**	216	26	71	**382**	**7.8**	**2.04**	160	**.179**	**.228**	20	.177	5	**56**	46	-2	5.4
1966	*LA-N★	**27**	9	.750	41	41	**27**	**5**	0	**323**	241	19	77	**317**	8.9	**1.73**	**191**	.205	.253	9	.076	-5	**67**	**56**	-4	5.4
Total	12	165	87	.655	397	314	137	40	9	2324^1	1754	204	817	2396	10.0	2.76	131	.205	.276	75	.097	-24	243	221	-25	19.8
● JOE KOUKALIK	Koukalik, Joseph b: 3/3/1880, Chicago, Ill. d: 12/27/45, Chicago, Ill. 5'8", 160 lbs. Deb: 9/01/04																									
1904	Bro-N	0	1	.000	1	1	1	0	0	8	10	0	4	1	15.8	1.13	244	.333	.412	0	.000	-0	1	1	-0	0.1
● LOU KOUPAL	Koupal, Louis Laddie b: 12/19/1898, Tabor, S.D. d: 12/8/61, San Gabriel, Cal. BR/TR, 5'11", 175 lbs. Deb: 4/17/25																									
1925	Pit-N	0	0	—	6	0	0	0	0	9	14	1	7	0	21.0	9.00	50	.378	.477	0	.000	-0	-5	-5	0	-0.4
1926	Pit-N	0	2	.000	6	2	1	0	0	19^2	22	0	8	7	14.2	3.20	123	.289	.365	1	.250	0	1	2	-0	0.2
1928	Bro-N	1	0	1.000	17	1	1	0	1	37^1	43	0	15	10	14.2	2.41	165	.303	.373	1	.111	-1	7	6	1	0.7
1929	Bro-N	0	1	.000	18	3	0	0	4	40^1	49	3	25	17	16.5	5.36	86	.308	.402	1	.071	-2	-3	-3	-1	-0.5

YEAR	TM/L	W	L	PCT	G	GS	CG	SH	SV	IP	H	HR	BB	SO	RAT	ERA	ERA+	OAV	OOB	BH	AVG	PB	PR	/A	PD	TPI
	Phi-N	5	5	.500	15	12	3	0	2	86^2	106	5	29	18	14.2	4.78	109	.305	.362	4	.125	-2	-1	4	-1	0.1
	Yr	5	6	.455	33	15	3	0	6	127	155	8	54	35	15.0	4.96	101	.306	.375	5	.109	-4	-3	1	-1	-0.4
1930	Phi-N	0	4	.000	13	4	1	0	0	36^2	52	4	17	11	17.2	8.59	64	.344	.414	1	.083	-2	-15	-13	-1	-1.3
1937	StL-A	4	9	.308	26	13	6	0	0	105^2	150	10	55	24	17.5	6.56	74	.339	.412	3	.094	-3	-23	-20	-0	-2.1
Total	6	10	21	.323	101	35	12	0	7	335^1	436	23	156	87	16.0	5.58	86	.322	.394	11	.106	-9	-38	-29	-2	-3.3
● **FABIAN KOWALIK**	Kowalik, Fabian Lorenz b: 4/22/08, Falls City, Tex. d: 8/14/54, Karnes City, Tex. BR/TR, 5'11", 185 lbs. Deb: 9/04/32																									
1932	Chi-A	0	1	.000	2	1	0	0	0	10^1	16	2	4	2	18.3	6.97	62	.340	.404	5	.385	1	-3	-3	-0	-0.2
1935	*Chi-N	2	2	.500	20	2	1	0	1	55	60	2	19	20	12.9	4.42	89	.280	.339	3	.200	-0	-2	-3	1	-0.3
1936	Chi-N	0	2	.000	6	0	0	0	1	16	24	1	7	1	17.4	6.75	59	.358	.419	0	.000	-1	-5	-5	0	-0.5
	Phi-N	1	5	.167	22	8	2	0	0	77	100	5	31	19	15.5	5.38	84	.308	.372	13	.228	-0	-12	-7	-2	-0.9
	Bos-N	0	1	.000	1	1	1	0	0	9	18	0	2	0	20.0	8.00	48	.419	.444	2	.400	1	-4	-4	0	-0.3
	Yr	1	8	.111	29	9	3	0	1	102	142	6	40	20	16.1	5.82	75	.325	.382	15	.224	-0	-20	-16	-1	-1.7
Total	3	3	11	.214	51	12	4	0	2	167^1	218	10	63	42	15.3	5.43	78	.313	.373	23	.242	-0	-26	-22	-1	-2.2
● **JOE KRAEMER**	Kraemer, Joseph Wayne b: 9/10/64, Olympia, Wash. BL/TL, 6'2", 185 lbs. Deb: 8/22/89																									
1989	Chi-N	0	1	.000	1	1	0	0	0	3^2	7	0	2	5	22.1	4.91	77	.368	.429	0	.000	-0	-1	-0	-0	-0.1
1990	Chi-N	0	0	—	18	0	0	0	0	25	31	2	14	16	16.9	7.20	57	.310	.405	0	—	0	-9	-9	0	-0.9
Total	2	0	1	.000	19	1	0	0	0	28^2	38	2	16	21	17.6	6.91	58	.319	.409	0	.000	-0	-10	-9	0	-1.0
● **JOE KRAKAUSKAS**	Krakauskas, Joseph Victor Lawrence b: 3/28/15, Montreal, Que., Can d: 7/8/60, Hamilton, Ont., Can BL/TL, 6'1", 203 lbs. Deb: 9/09/37																									
1937	Was-A	4	1	.800	5	4	3	0	0	40	33	0	22	18	12.4	2.70	164	.226	.327	2	.125	-0	9	8	-1	0.6
1938	Was-A	7	5	.583	29	10	5	1	0	121^1	99	4	88	104	14.1	3.12	145	.220	.352	6	.182	1	23	19	-1	1.8
1939	Was-A	11	17	.393	39	29	12	0	1	217^1	230	13	114	110	14.3	4.60	95	.276	.364	16	.208	3	1	-6	-2	-0.5
1940	Was-A	1	6	.143	32	10	2	0	2	109	137	7	73	68	17.3	6.44	65	.309	.406	8	.250	1	-25	-28	1	-2.3
1941	Cle-A	1	2	.333	12	5	0	0	0	41^2	39	3	29	25	14.7	4.10	96	.245	.362	1	.077	-1	0	-1	1	-0.1
1942	Cle-A	0	0	—	3	0	0	0	0	7	7	1	4	2	14.1	3.86	89	.259	.355	0	.000	-0	-0	-0	1	0.0
1946	Cle-A	2	5	.286	29	5	0	0	1	47^1	60	2	25	20	16.2	5.51	60	.314	.394	0	.000	-1	-11	-12	1	-1.2
Total	7	26	36	.419	149	63	22	1	4	583^2	605	30	355	347	14.9	4.53	93	.269	.369	33	.180	2	-4	-20	-1	-1.7
● **JACK KRALICK**	Kralick, John Francis b: 6/1/35, Youngstown, Ohio BL/TL, 6'2", 180 lbs. Deb: 4/15/59																									
1959	Was-A	0	0	—	6	0	0	0	0	12^1	13	5	6	7	13.9	6.57	60	.289	.373	0	.000	-0	-4	-4	1	-0.3
1960	Was-A	8	6	.571	35	18	7	2	1	151	139	12	45	71	11.2	3.04	128	.245	.305	5	.122	-1	14	14	-1	1.3
1961	Min-A	13	11	.542	33	33	11	2	0	242	257	21	64	137	12.0	3.61	118	.274	.323	13	.151	-2	11	17	2	1.7
1962	Min-A	12	11	.522	39	37	7	1	0	242^2	239	30	61	139	11.2	3.86	106	.258	.305	18	.202	3	3	6	1	1.0
1963	Min-A	1	4	.200	5	5	1	1	0	25^2	28	2	8	13	13.0	3.86	94	.280	.339	1	.167	1	-1	-1	0	0.1
	Cle-A	13	9	.591	28	27	10	3	0	197^1	187	19	41	116	10.4	2.92	124	.249	.288	11	.183	1	16	15	-1	1.7
	Yr	14	13	.519	33	32	11	4	0	223	215	21	49	129	10.7	3.03	120	.252	.293	12	.182	2	15	15	-1	1.8
1964	Cle-A☆	12	7	.632	30	29	8	3	0	190^2	196	17	51	119	12.1	3.21	112	.267	.322	10	.156	-1	9	8	0	0.8
1965	Cle-A	5	11	.313	30	16	1	0	0	86	106	9	21	34	13.5	4.92	71	.298	.340	3	.143	-1	-14	-14	-1	-1.6
1966	Cle-A	3	4	.429	27	4	0	0	0	68^1	69	9	20	31	11.9	3.82	90	.268	.324	1	.077	-1	-3	-3	1	-0.3
1967	Cle-A	0	2	.000	2	0	0	0	0	2	4	0	1	1	22.5	9.00	36	.444	.500	0	—	0	-1	-1	1	-0.1
Total	9	67	65	.508	235	169	45	12	1	1218	1238	124	318	668	11.7	3.56	108	.264	.314	62	.162	0	30	38	3	4.3
● **STEVE KRALY**	Kraly, Steve Charles "Lefty" b: 4/18/29, Whiting, Ind. BL/TL, 5'10", 152 lbs. Deb: 8/09/53																									
1953	NY-A	0	2	.000	5	3	0	0	1	25	19	2	16	8	13.3	3.24	114	.209	.339	0	.000	-1	2	1	0	0.1
● **JACK KRAMER**	Kramer, John Henry b: 1/5/18, New Orleans, La. BR/TR, 6'2", 190 lbs. Deb: 4/25/39																									
1939	StL-A	9	16	.360	40	31	10	2	0	211^2	269	18	127	68	17.0	5.83	84	.318	.409	9	.136	-1	-28	-23	-1	-2.2
1940	StL-A	3	7	.300	16	9	1	0	0	64^2	86	4	26	12	15.6	6.26	73	.327	.388	1	.050	-1	-14	-12	0	-1.1
1941	StL-A	4	3	.571	29	3	0	0	2	59^1	69	5	40	20	16.5	5.16	83	.289	.391	0	.000	1	-7	-6	0	-0.4
1943	StL-A	0	0	—	3	0	0	0	0	9	11	0	8	4	20.0	8.00	42	.297	.435	1	.500	1	-5	-5	-0	-0.4
1944	*StL-A	17	13	.567	33	31	18	1	0	257	233	3	75	124	10.8	2.49	145	.241	.297	14	.165	1	27	32	3	4.1
1945	StL-A†	10	15	.400	29	25	15	3	2	193	190	13	73	99	12.3	3.36	105	.254	.320	9	.148	-0	0	4	1	0.5
1946	StL-A★	13	11	.542	31	28	13	3	0	194^2	190	6	68	69	11.9	3.19	117	.257	.319	8	.136	-1	7	12	-0	1.1
1947	StL-A☆	11	16	.407	33	28	9	1	1	199^1	206	16	89	77	13.4	4.97	78	.270	.348	7	.113	-2	-28	-24	1	-2.5
1948	Bos-A	18	5	**.783**	29	29	14	2	0	205	233	12	64	72	13.0	4.35	101	.284	.336	11	.151	-1	-1	1	-3	-0.3
1949	Bos-A	6	8	.429	21	18	7	2	1	111^2	126	8	49	24	14.2	5.16	85	.286	.358	9	.257	3	-12	-10	-1	-0.7
1950	NY-N	3	6	.333	35	9	1	0	1	86^2	91	6	39	27	13.7	3.53	116	.268	.346	2	.100	1	6	5	0	0.7
1951	NY-N	0	0	—	4	1	0	0	0	4^2	11	0	3	2	27.0	15.43	25	.524	.583	0	—	0	-6	-6	0	-0.5
	NY-A	1	3	.250	19	3	0	0	0	40^2	46	1	21	15	14.8	4.65	82	.280	.362	1	.100	-0	-2	-4	-1	-0.5
Total	12	95	103	.480	322	215	88	14	7	1637^1	1761	92	682	613	13.5	4.24	96	.276	.347	72	.144	0	-63	-35	0	-2.2
● **RANDY KRAMER**	Kramer, Randall John b: 9/20/60, Palo Alto, Cal. BR/TR, 6'2", 170 lbs. Deb: 9/11/88																									
1988	Pit-N	1	2	.333	5	1	0	0	0	10	12	1	1	7	12.6	5.40	63	.316	.350	0	.000	-0	-2	-2	-0	-0.3
1989	Pit-N	5	9	.357	35	15	1	1	2	111^1	90	10	61	52	12.8	3.96	85	.224	.337	5	.152	-0	-6	-7	-1	-0.9
1990	Pit-N	0	1	.000	12	2	0	0	0	25^2	27	3	9	15	13.3	4.91	74	.273	.345	0	.000	-0	-3	-4	1	-0.4
	Chi-N	0	2	.000	10	2	0	0	0	20^1	20	3	12	12	14.6	3.98	102	.253	.359	0	.000	-0	-0	0	-0	0.0
	Yr	0	3	.000	22	4	0	0	0	46	47	6	21	27	13.5	4.50	85	.261	.342	0	.000	-1	-4	-3	0	-0.4
1992	Sea-A	0	1	.000	4	4	0	0	0	16^1	30	2	7	6	20.9	7.71	52	.400	.458	0	—	0	-7	-7	-0	-0.7
Total	4	6	15	.286	66	24	1	1	2	183^2	179	19	90	92	13.8	4.51	78	.259	.354	5	.122	-1	-18	-20	-2	-2.3
● **TOM KRAMER**	Kramer, Thomas Joseph b: 1/9/68, Cincinnati, Ohio BB/TR, 6', 185 lbs. Deb: 9/12/91																									
1991	Cle-A	0	0	—	4	0	0	0	0	4^2	10	1	6	4	30.9	17.36	24	.476	.593	0	—	0	-7	-7	-0	-0.6
● **GENE KRAPP**	Krapp, Eugene Hamley "Rubber Arm" b: 5/12/1887, Rochester, N.Y. d: 4/13/23, Detroit, Mich. BR/TR, 5'5", 165 lbs. Deb: 4/14/11																									
1911	Cle-A	13	9	.591	35	26	14	1	1	222	188	1	138	132	13.7	3.41	100	.232	.353	17	.230	4	-1	0	4	0.8
1912	Cle-A	2	5	.286	9	7	4	0	0	58^2	57	0	42	22	15.8	4.60	74	.273	.404	7	.318	1	-8	-8	2	-0.4
1914	Buf-F	16	14	.533	36	29	18	1	0	252^2	198	4	115	106	11.6	2.49	132	.210	.304	11	.143	-1	20	22	5	2.9
1915	Buf-F	9	19	.321	38	30	14	1	0	231	188	6	123	93	12.3	3.51	89	.230	.333	9	.129	-2	-12	-10	7	-0.5
Total	4	40	47	.460	118	92	50	3	1	764^1	631	11	418	353	12.7	3.23	102	.227	.335	44	.181	2	-2	5	19	2.8
● **JACK KRAUS**	Kraus, John William "Tex" or "Texas Jack" b: 4/26/18, San Antonio, Tex. d: 1/2/76, San Antonio, Tex. BR/TL, 6'4", 190 lbs. Deb: 4/25/43																									
1943	Phi-N	9	15	.375	34	25	10	1	2	199^2	197	7	78	48	12.4	3.16	107	.259	.328	4	.067	-5	5	5	1	0.2
1945	Phi-N	4	9	.308	19	13	0	0	0	81^2	96	3	40	28	15.4	5.40	71	.293	.376	3	.120	-1	-15	-14	0	-1.4
1946	NY-N	2	1	.667	17	1	0	0	0	25	25	4	15	7	14.8	6.12	56	.260	.366	0	.000	-0	-8	-7	1	-0.7
Total	3	15	25	.375	70	39	10	1	2	306^1	318	14	133	83	13.4	4.00	88	.268	.345	7	.080	-6	-17	-17	2	-1.9
● **HARRY KRAUSE**	Krause, Harry William "Hal" b: 7/12/1887, San Francisco, Cal. d: 10/23/40, San Francisco, Cal BB/TL, 5'10", 165 lbs. Deb: 4/20/08																									
1908	Phi-A	1	1	.500	4	2	2	0	0	21	20	0	4	10	11.6	2.57	100	.247	.307	0	.000	-0	-0	-0	-1	-0.2
1909	Phi-A	18	8	.692	32	21	16	7	0	213	151	2	49	139	9.0	**1.39**	**173**	.204	.266	12	.156	-1	26	**24**	-3	2.3
1910	Phi-A	6	6	.500	16	11	9	2	0	112^1	99	4	42	60	11.9	2.88	82	.254	.339	8	.211	1	-5	-6	-2	-0.9
1911	Phi-A	11	8	.579	27	19	12	1	2	169	155	2	47	85	11.2	3.04	104	.251	.313	15	.254	2	6	2	-3	0.1
1912	Phi-A	0	2	.000	4	2	0	0	0	5^1	10	0	2	3	21.9	13.50	23	.435	.500	1	.250	0	-6	-6	0	-0.6
	Cle-A	0	1	.000	2	2	0	0	0	4^2	11	0	2	1	25.1	11.57	29	.500	.542	0	—	0	-4	-4	-0	-0.4

YEAR	TM/L	W	L	PCT	G	GS	CG	SH	SV	IP	H	HR	BB	SO	RAT	ERA	ERA+	OAV	OOB	BH	AVG	PB	PR	/A	PD	TPI
	Yr	0	3	.000	6	4	0	0	0	10	21	0	4	4	22.5	12.60	26	.457	.500	1	.250	0	-10	-10	-0	-1.0
Total	5	36	26	.581	85	57	39	10	2	525^1	446	8	146	298	10.7	2.50	107	.238	.305	36	.195	1	16	10	-9	0.3

● LEW KRAUSSE Krausse, Lewis Bernard Jr. b: 4/25/43, Media, Pa. BR/TR, 5'11", 186 lbs. Deb: 6/16/61 F

YEAR	TM/L	W	L	PCT	G	GS	CG	SH	SV	IP	H	HR	BB	SO	RAT	ERA	ERA+	OAV	OOB	BH	AVG	PB	PR	/A	PD	TPI
1961	KC-A	2	5	.286	12	8	2	1	0	55^2	49	3	46	32	15.5	4.85	85	.243	.386	2	.118	-1	-5	-5	-1	-0.6
1964	KC-A	0	2	.000	5	4	0	0	0	14^2	22	1	9	9	20.3	7.36	52	.349	.446	0	.000	0	-6	-6	-0	-0.6
1965	KC-A	2	4	.333	7	5	0	0	0	25	29	1	8	22	13.3	5.04	69	.284	.336	0	.000	-1	-4	-4	-1	-0.6
1966	KC-A	14	9	.609	36	22	4	1	3	177^2	144	8	63	87	10.8	2.99	114	.222	.297	8	.154	0	9	8	-3	0.6
1967	KC-A	7	17	.292	48	19	0	0	6	160	140	17	67	96	11.9	4.27	75	.236	.317	6	.146	1	-19	-19	-0	-2.0
1968	Oak-A	10	11	.476	36	25	2	0	4	185	147	16	62	105	10.3	3.11	91	.217	.286	9	.161	3	-3	-6	-2	-0.5
1969	Oak-A	7	7	.500	43	16	4	2	7	140	134	23	48	85	12.0	4.44	77	.256	.325	8	.167	4	-13	-16	-1	-1.3
1970	Mil-A	13	18	.419	37	35	8	1	0	216	235	33	67	130	12.8	4.75	80	.275	.330	9	.138	1	-25	-23	-0	-2.3
1971	Mil-A	8	12	.400	43	22	1	0	0	180^1	164	23	62	92	11.5	2.94	118	.239	.307	1	.023	-3	10	11	-1	0.7
1972	Bos-A	1	3	.250	24	7	0	0	1	60^2	74	9	28	35	15.6	6.38	50	.308	.387	2	.125	-0	-22	-21	1	-2.3
1973	StL-N	0	0	—	1	0	0	0	0	2	2	0	1	1	13.5	0.00	—	.250	.333	0	—	0	1	1	0	0.1
1974	Atl-N	4	3	.571	29	4	0	0	0	66^2	65	3	32	27	13.4	4.18	90	.258	.346	2	.333	2	-4	-3	-1	-0.2
Total	12	68	91	.428	321	167	21	5	21	1283^2	1205	137	493	721	12.2	4.00	85	.248	.322	47	.133	6	-81	-84	-9	-9.0

● LEW KRAUSSE Krausse, Lewis Bernard Sr. b: 6/8/12, Media, Pa. d: 9/6/88, Sarasota, Fla. BR/TR, 6'0.5", 167 lbs. Deb: 6/11/31 F

YEAR	TM/L	W	L	PCT	G	GS	CG	SH	SV	IP	H	HR	BB	SO	RAT	ERA	ERA+	OAV	OOB	BH	AVG	PB	PR	/A	PD	TPI
1931	Phi-A	1	0	1.000	3	1	1	0	0	11	6	2	6	1	9.8	4.09	110	.150	.261	0	.000	0	0	0	0	0.1
1932	Phi-A	4	1	.800	20	3	2	1	0	57	64	3	24	16	13.9	4.58	99	.281	.349	2	.133	-0	-1	-0	1	0.0
Total	2	5	1	.833	23	4	3	1	0	68	70	5	30	17	13.2	4.50	100	.261	.336	2	.118	0	-0	0	1	0.1

● KEN KRAVEC Kravec, Kenneth Peter b: 7/29/51, Cleveland, Ohio BL/TL, 6'2", 185 lbs. Deb: 9/04/75

YEAR	TM/L	W	L	PCT	G	GS	CG	SH	SV	IP	H	HR	BB	SO	RAT	ERA	ERA+	OAV	OOB	BH	AVG	PB	PR	/A	PD	TPI
1975	Chi-A	0	1	.000	2	1	0	0	0	4^1	1	0	8	1	18.7	6.23	62	.071	.409	0	—	0	-1	-1	1	-0.1
1976	Chi-A	1	5	.167	9	8	1	0	0	49^2	49	3	32	38	14.9	4.89	73	.257	.366	0	—	0	-8	-7	-0	-0.8
1977	Chi-A	11	8	.579	26	25	6	1	0	166^2	161	12	57	125	12.1	4.10	99	.250	.317	0	—	0	-1	-0	0	0.0
1978	Chi-A	11	16	.407	30	30	7	2	0	203	188	22	95	154	13.0	4.08	93	.245	.336	0	—	0	-7	-6	-1	-0.7
1979	Chi-A	15	13	.536	36	35	10	3	1	250	208	20	111	132	12.0	3.74	113	.233	.327	0	—	0	13	14	-1	1.3
1980	Chi-A	3	6	.333	20	15	0	0	0	81^2	100	13	44	37	16.4	6.94	58	.298	.387	0	—	0	-26	-26	0	-2.4
1981	Chi-N	1	6	.143	24	12	0	0	0	78^1	80	5	39	50	14.1	5.06	73	.268	.361	0	.000	-1	-14	-12	1	-1.3
1982	Chi-N	1	1	.500	13	2	0	0	0	25	27	3	18	20	16.2	6.12	61	.267	.378	0	.000	-0	-7	-7	-0	-0.7
Total	8	43	56	.434	160	128	24	6	1	858^2	814	78	404	557	13.2	4.47	89	.251	.341	0	.000	-1	-51	-46	-0	-4.7

● RAY KRAWCZYK Krawczyk, Raymond Allen b: 10/9/59, Pittsburgh, Pa. BR/TR, 6'1", 186 lbs. Deb: 6/29/84

YEAR	TM/L	W	L	PCT	G	GS	CG	SH	SV	IP	H	HR	BB	SO	RAT	ERA	ERA+	OAV	OOB	BH	AVG	PB	PR	/A	PD	TPI
1984	Pit-N	0	0	—	4	0	0	0	0	5^1	7	0	4	3	18.6	3.38	107	.350	.458	0	—	0	0	0	-0	0.0
1985	Pit-N	0	2	.000	8	0	0	0	0	8^1	20	1	6	9	29.2	14.04	25	.455	.529	0	—	0	-10	-10	0	-0.9
1986	Pit-N	0	1	.000	12	0	0	0	0	12^1	17	3	10	7	19.7	7.30	53	.321	.429	0	—	0	-5	-5	-0	-0.5
1988	Cal-A	0	1	.000	14	1	0	0	1	24^1	29	2	8	17	14.4	4.81	80	.299	.364	0	—	0	-2	-3	1	-0.1
1989	Mil-A	0	0	—	1	0	0	0	0	2	4	0	1	6	22.5	13.50	28	.400	.455	0	—	0	-2	-2	0	-0.2
Total	5	0	4	.000	39	1	0	0	1	52^1	77	6	29	42	18.7	7.05	54	.344	.426	0	—	0	-19	-19	0	-1.7

● RAY KREMER Kremer, Remy Peter "Wiz" b: 3/23/1893, Oakland, Cal. d: 2/8/65, Pinole, Cal. BR/TR, 6'1", 190 lbs. Deb: 4/18/24

YEAR	TM/L	W	L	PCT	G	GS	CG	SH	SV	IP	H	HR	BB	SO	RAT	ERA	ERA+	OAV	OOB	BH	AVG	PB	PR	/A	PD	TPI
1924	Pit-N	18	10	.643	**41**	30	17	**4**	1	259^1	262	7	51	64	11.0	3.19	120	.265	.304	13	.151	-4	19	19	-2	1.3
1925	*Pit-N	17	8	.680	40	27	14	0	2	214^2	232	19	47	62	12.1	3.69	121	.278	.323	14	.197	1	14	18	-3	1.5
1926	Pit-N	**20**	6	**.769**	37	26	18	3	5	231^1	221	9	51	74	10.7	**2.61**	**151**	.252	.296	21	.253	3	**31**	**34**	-3	**3.5**
1927	*Pit-N	19	8	.704	35	28	18	3	2	226	205	9	53	63	10.3	**2.47**	**166**	.244	.289	14	.169	-2	36	41	-3	3.8
1928	Pit-N	15	13	.536	34	31	17	1	0	219	253	15	68	61	13.4	4.64	87	.297	.352	14	.179	0	-16	-14	-4	-1.8
1929	Pit-N	18	10	.643	34	27	14	0	0	221^2	226	21	60	66	11.7	4.26	112	.271	.320	11	.128	-2	11	13	-3	0.7
1930	Pit-N	**20**	12	.625	39	38	18	1	0	**276**	366	29	63	58	14.0	5.02	99	.322	.359	16	.157	-4	-2	-1	-4	-0.9
1931	Pit-N	11	15	.423	30	30	15	1	0	230	246	6	65	58	12.4	3.33	116	.271	.323	17	.227	4	14	13	-6	1.2
1932	Pit-N	4	3	.571	11	10	3	1	0	56^2	61	5	16	6	12.4	4.29	89	.270	.321	2	.105	-1	-3	-3	-2	-0.6
1933	Pit-N	1	0	1.000	7	0	0	0	0	20	36	2	9	4	20.2	10.35	32	.387	.441	0	.000	-1	-16	-16	1	-1.5
Total	10	143	85	.627	308	247	134	14	10	1954^2	2108	122	483	516	12.1	3.76	113	.278	.323	122	.178	-7	90	104	-27	7.2

● JIM KREMMEL Kremmel, James Louis b: 2/28/48, Belleville, Ill. BL/TL, 6', 175 lbs. Deb: 7/04/73

YEAR	TM/L	W	L	PCT	G	GS	CG	SH	SV	IP	H	HR	BB	SO	RAT	ERA	ERA+	OAV	OOB	BH	AVG	PB	PR	/A	PD	TPI
1973	Tex-A	0	2	.000	4	2	0	0	0	9	15	1	6	6	23.0	9.00	41	.366	.469	0	—	0	-5	-5	-0	-0.5
1974	Chi-N	0	2	.000	23	2	0	0	0	31	37	3	18	22	16.3	5.23	73	.303	.397	0	.000	-0	-6	-5	-0	-0.5
Total	2	0	4	.000	27	4	0	0	0	40	52	4	24	28	17.8	6.07	62	.319	.416	0	.000	-0	-11	-10	-0	-1.0

● RED KRESS Kress, Ralph b: 1/2/07, Columbia, Cal. d: 11/29/62, Los Angeles, Cal. BR/TR, 5'11.5", 165 lbs. Deb: 9/24/27 C♦

YEAR	TM/L	W	L	PCT	G	GS	CG	SH	SV	IP	H	HR	BB	SO	RAT	ERA	ERA+	OAV	OOB	BH	AVG	PB	PR	/A	PD	TPI
1935	Was-A	0	0	—	3	0	0	0	0	5^2	8	0	5	5	20.6	12.71	34	.333	.448	75	.298	1	-5	-5	0	-0.4
1946	NY-N	0	0	—	1	0	0	0	0	3^2	5	1	1	1	17.2	12.27	28	.333	.412	0	.000	0	-4	-4	1	-0.2
Total	2	0	0	—	4	0	0	0	0	9^1	13	1	6	6	19.3	12.54	32	.333	.435	1454	.286	1	-9	-9	1	-0.6

● LOU KRETLOW Kretlow, Louis Henry "Lena" b: 6/27/21, Apache, Okla. BR/TR, 6'2", 185 lbs. Deb: 9/26/46

YEAR	TM/L	W	L	PCT	G	GS	CG	SH	SV	IP	H	HR	BB	SO	RAT	ERA	ERA+	OAV	OOB	BH	AVG	PB	PR	/A	PD	TPI
1946	Det-A	1	0	1.000	1	1	1	0	0	9	7	2	2	4	9.0	3.00	122	.206	.250	2	.500	1	1	1	-0	0.2
1948	Det-A	2	1	.667	5	2	1	0	0	23^1	21	1	11	9	12.3	4.63	94	.233	.317	4	.500	1	-1	-1	0	0.1
1949	Det-A	3	2	.600	25	10	1	0	0	76	85	5	69	40	18.4	6.16	68	.290	.427	0	.000	-4	-17	-17	2	-1.8
1950	StL-A	0	2	.000	9	2	0	0	0	14^1	25	2	18	10	28.3	11.93	41	.403	.549	0	.000	-1	-12	-11	-0	-1.0
	Chi-A	0	0	—	11	1	0	0	0	21^1	17	1	27	14	18.6	3.80	118	.221	.423	0	.000	-1	2	2	-1	0.0
	Yr	0	2	.000	20	3	0	0	0	35^2	42	3	45	24	22.0	7.07	66	.298	.468	0	.000	-1	-10	-9	-1	-1.0
1951	Chi-A	6	9	.400	26	18	7	1	0	137	129	7	74	89	13.5	4.20	96	.250	.347	4	.083	-5	-1	-3	-0	-0.8
1952	Chi-A	4	4	.500	19	11	4	2	1	79	52	5	56	63	12.4	2.96	123	.186	.323	1	.050	-1	6	6	-1	0.5
1953	Chi-A	0	0	—	9	3	0	0	0	20^2	12	2	30	15	18.7	3.48	116	.171	.426	0	.000	-0	1	1	0	0.2
	StL-A	1	5	.167	22	11	0	0	0	81	93	5	52	37	16.1	5.11	82	.286	.385	5	.200	-1	-10	-8	-2	-1.0
	Yr	1	5	.167	31	14	0	0	0	101^2	105	7	82	52	16.6	4.78	87	.265	.391	5	.172	-1	-9	-7	-1	-0.8
1954	Bal-A	6	11	.353	32	20	5	0	0	166^2	169	12	82	82	13.6	4.37	82	.269	.354	8	.157	-0	-12	-15	0	-1.5
1955	Bal-A	0	4	.000	15	5	0	0	0	38^1	50	3	27	26	18.3	8.22	46	.316	.419	1	.091	-1	-18	-19	1	-1.7
1956	KC-A	4	9	.308	25	20	3	0	0	118^2	121	17	74	61	14.8	5.31	82	.262	.364	2	.061	-3	-15	-13	-1	-1.5
Total	10	27	47	.365	199	104	22	3	1	785^1	781	62	522	450	15.0	4.87	82	.261	.372	27	.114	-13	-76	-77	-1	-8.3

● RICK KREUGER Kreuger, Richard Allen b: 11/3/48, Grand Rapids, Mich. BR/TL, 6'2", 185 lbs. Deb: 9/06/75

YEAR	TM/L	W	L	PCT	G	GS	CG	SH	SV	IP	H	HR	BB	SO	RAT	ERA	ERA+	OAV	OOB	BH	AVG	PB	PR	/A	PD	TPI
1975	Bos-A	0	0	—	2	0	0	0	0	4	3	0	1	1	9.0	4.50	90	.200	.250	0	—	0	-0	-0	0	-0.1
1976	Bos-A	2	1	.667	8	4	1	0	0	31	31	3	16	12	13.6	4.06	96	.272	.362	0	—	0	-2	-1	1	0.0
1977	Bos-A	0	1	.000	1	0	0	0	0	0	2	0	0	0	—	∞	—	1.000	1.000	0	—	0	-2	-2	0	-0.2
1978	Cle-A	0	0	—	6	0	0	0	0	9^1	6	1	3	7	8.7	3.86	97	.194	.265	0	—	0	-0	-0	0	0.0
Total	4	2	2	.500	17	4	1	0	0	44^1	42	4	20	20	12.6	4.47	87	.259	.341	0	—	0	-4	-3	1	-0.3

● FRANK KREUTZER Kreutzer, Franklin James b: 2/7/39, Buffalo, N.Y. BR/TL, 6'1", 190 lbs. Deb: 9/20/62

YEAR	TM/L	W	L	PCT	G	GS	CG	SH	SV	IP	H	HR	BB	SO	RAT	ERA	ERA+	OAV	OOB	BH	AVG	PB	PR	/A	PD	TPI
1962	Chi-A	0	0	—	1	0	0	0	0	1^1	0	0	1	1	6.8	0.00	—	.000	.200	0	—	0	1	1	0	0.1
1963	Chi-A	1	0	1.000	1	1	0	0	0	5	3	1	1	0	7.2	1.80	195	.188	.235	0	.000	-0	1	1	0	0.1
1964	Chi-A	3	1	.750	17	2	0	0	1	40^1	37	1	18	32	12.3	3.35	103	.239	.318	1	.125	-0	1	0	1	0.1
	Was-A	2	6	.250	13	9	0	0	0	45^1	48	6	23	27	14.3	4.76	78	.267	.353	0	.000	-1	-6	-5	0	-0.7
	Yr	5	7	.417	30	11	0	0	1	85^2	85	7	41	59	13.3	4.10	87	.253	.336	1	.053	-1	-5	-5	1	-0.6

YEAR	TM/L	W	L	PCT	G	GS	CG	SH	SV	IP	H	HR	BB	SO	RAT	ERA	ERA+	OAV	OOB	BH	AVG	PB	PR	/A	PD	TPI
1965	Was-A	2	6	.250	33	14	2	1	0	85^1	73	7	54	65	13.6	4.32	80	.232	.348	1	.045	-1	-8	-8	-2	-1.1
1966	Was-A	0	5	.000	9	6	0	0	0	31^1	30	9	10	24	11.8	6.03	57	.236	.297	2	.250	0	-9	-9	0	-0.9
1969	Was-A	0	0	—	4	0	0	0	0	2	3	0	2	2	22.5	4.50	77	.333	.455	0	—	0	-0	-0	0	0.0
Total	6	8	18	.308	78	32	2	1	1	210^2	194	24	109	151	13.1	4.40	80	.241	.334	4	.078	-2	-20	-21	-1	-2.4

● KRIEGER Krieger Deb: 7/28/1884 ♦

YEAR	TM/L	W	L	PCT	G	GS	CG	SH	SV	IP	H	HR	BB	SO	RAT	ERA	ERA+	OAV	OOB	BH	AVG	PB	PR	/A	PD	TPI
1884	KC-U	0	1	.000	1	1	0	0	0	7	9	0	5	3	18.0	0.00	—	.292	.391	0	.000	-0	2	2	0	0.2

● KURT KRIEGER Krieger, Kurt Ferdinand "Dutch" b: 9/16/26, Traisen, Austria d: 8/16/70, St.Louis, Mo. BR/TR, 6'3", 212 lbs. Deb: 4/21/49

YEAR	TM/L	W	L	PCT	G	GS	CG	SH	SV	IP	H	HR	BB	SO	RAT	ERA	ERA+	OAV	OOB	BH	AVG	PB	PR	/A	PD	TPI
1949	StL-N	0	0	—	1	0	0	0	0	1	0	0	1	0	9.0	0.00	—	.000	.250	0	—	0	0	0	-0	0.0
1951	StL-N	0	0	—	2	0	0	0	0	4	6	1	5	3	24.8	15.75	25	.353	.500	0	—	0	-5	-5	0	-0.5
Total	2	0	0	—	3	0	0	0	0	5	6	1	6	3	21.6	12.60	32	.300	.462	0	—	0	-5	-5	0	-0.5

● HOWIE KRIST Krist, Howard Wilbur "Spud" b: 2/28/16, W.Henrietta, N.Y. d: 4/23/89, Buffalo, N.Y. BL/TR, 6'1", 175 lbs. Deb: 9/12/37

YEAR	TM/L	W	L	PCT	G	GS	CG	SH	SV	IP	H	HR	BB	SO	RAT	ERA	ERA+	OAV	OOB	BH	AVG	PB	PR	/A	PD	TPI
1937	StL-N	3	1	.750	6	4	1	0	0	27^2	34	0	10	6	14.3	4.23	94	.304	.361	0	.000	-1	-1	-1	-1	-0.3
1938	StL-N	0	0	—	2	0	0	0	0	1^1	1	0	0	1	6.8	0.00	—	.250	.250	0	—	0	1	1	0	0.1
1941	StL-N	10	0	1.000	37	8	2	0	2	114	107	10	35	36	11.3	4.03	93	.246	.304	9	.237	1	-5	-3	-1	-0.4
1942	StL-N	13	3	.813	34	8	3	0	1	118^1	103	2	43	47	11.3	2.51	136	.233	.304	6	.143	-1	11	12	-2	0.9
1943	*StL-N	11	5	.688	34	17	9	2	3	164^1	141	5	62	57	11.3	2.90	116	.233	.309	10	.167	-2	9	8	-5	0.1
1946	StL-N	0	2	.000	15	0	0	0	0	18^2	22	3	8	3	14.9	6.75	51	.306	.383	0	—	0	-7	-7	0	-0.7
Total	6	37	11	.771	128	37	15	2	6	444^1	408	20	158	150	11.6	3.32	106	.244	.313	25	.168	-3	7	10	-9	-0.3

● GUS KROCK Krock, August H. b: 5/9/1866, Milwaukee, Wis. d: 3/22/05, Pasadena, Cal. TL, 6', 196 lbs. Deb: 4/24/1888

YEAR	TM/L	W	L	PCT	G	GS	CG	SH	SV	IP	H	HR	BB	SO	RAT	ERA	ERA+	OAV	OOB	BH	AVG	PB	PR	/A	PD	TPI
1888	Chi-N	25	14	.641	39	39	39	4	0	339^2	295	20	45	161	9.2	2.44	124	.227	.258	22	.164	-3	16	22	-3	1.5
1889	Chi-N	3	3	.500	7	7	5	0	0	60^2	86	10	14	16	15.1	4.90	85	.324	.362	4	.167	-1	-6	-5	0	-0.5
	Ind-N	2	2	.500	4	4	3	0	0	32	48	2	14	10	17.4	7.31	57	.336	.396	5	.357	1	-12	-11	-1	-0.8
	Was-N	2	4	.333	6	6	6	0	0	48	65	1	22	17	16.5	5.25	75	.314	.382	2	.087	-2	-7	-7	-0	-0.8
	Yr	7	9	.438	17	17	14	0	0	140^2	199	13	50	43	16.0	5.57	73	.322	.374	11	.180	-2	-24	-23	-1	-2.1
1890	Buf-P	0	3	.000	4	3	3	0	0	25	43	1	15	5	20.9	6.12	67	.363	.435	1	.083	-1	-5	-6	0	-0.5
Total	3	32	26	.552	60	59	56	4	0	505^1	537	34	110	209	11.7	3.49	97	.264	.306	34	.164	-7	-14	-6	-4	-1.1

● RUBE KROH Kroh, Floyd Myron b: 8/25/1886, Friendship, N.Y. d: 3/17/44, New Orleans, La. BL/TL, 6'2", 186 lbs. Deb: 9/30/06

YEAR	TM/L	W	L	PCT	G	GS	CG	SH	SV	IP	H	HR	BB	SO	RAT	ERA	ERA+	OAV	OOB	BH	AVG	PB	PR	/A	PD	TPI
1906	Bos-A	1	0	1.000	1	1	1	1	0	9	2	0	4	5	6.0	0.00	—	.074	.192	0	.000	-0	3	3	0	0.4
1907	Bos-A	1	4	.200	7	5	1	0	0	34^1	33	0	8	8	11.3	2.62	99	.255	.308	3	.273	0	-0	-0	-0	0.0
1908	Chi-N	0	0	—	2	1	0	0	0	12	9	0	4	11	9.8	1.50	157	.200	.265	0	.000	-0	1	1	0	0.1
1909	Chi-N	9	4	.692	17	13	10	2	0	120^1	97	2	30	51	9.6	1.65	155	.224	.276	6	.150	-0	13	12	1	1.5
1910	Chi-N	3	1	.750	6	4	1	0	0	34^1	33	1	15	16	13.1	4.46	65	.254	.340	3	.250	0	-5	-6	1	-0.5
1912	Bos-N	0	0	—	3	1	0	0	0	6^1	8	0	6	1	19.9	5.68	63	.364	.500	1	.500	0	-2	-1	0	-0.1
Total	6	14	9	.609	36	25	13	3	0	216^1	182	3	67	92	10.6	2.29	115	.231	.296	13	.181	-0	9	8	2	1.4

● GARY KROLL Kroll, Gary Melvin b: 7/8/41, Culver City, Cal. BR/TR, 6'6", 220 lbs. Deb: 7/26/64

YEAR	TM/L	W	L	PCT	G	GS	CG	SH	SV	IP	H	HR	BB	SO	RAT	ERA	ERA+	OAV	OOB	BH	AVG	PB	PR	/A	PD	TPI
1964	Phi-N	0	0	—	2	0	0	0	0	3	3	0	2	2	15.0	3.00	116	.250	.357	0	—	0	0	0	-0	0.0
	NY-N	0	1	.000	8	2	0	0	0	21^2	19	1	15	24	14.5	4.15	86	.241	.368	1	.333	0	-1	-1	1	0.0
	Yr	0	1	.000	10	2	0	0	0	24^2	22	1	17	26	14.6	4.01	89	.242	.367	1	.333	0	-1	-1	1	0.0
1965	NY-N	6	6	.500	32	11	1	0	1	87	83	12	41	62	13.4	4.45	79	.249	.342	3	.115	-1	-9	-9	-0	-1.0
1966	Hou-N	0	0	—	10	0	0	0	0	23^2	26	2	11	22	14.1	3.80	90	.280	.356	0	.000	-0	-1	-1	0	-0.1
1969	Cle-A	0	0	—	19	0	0	0	0	24	16	3	22	28	14.3	4.13	91	.188	.355	0	—	0	-1	-1	-0	-0.1
Total	4	6	7	.462	71	13	1	0	1	159^1	147	18	91	138	13.8	4.24	84	.244	.350	4	.125	-1	-12	-12	1	-1.2

● BILL KRUEGER Krueger, William Culp b: 4/24/58, Waukegan, Ill. BL/TL, 6'5", 210 lbs. Deb: 4/10/83

YEAR	TM/L	W	L	PCT	G	GS	CG	SH	SV	IP	H	HR	BB	SO	RAT	ERA	ERA+	OAV	OOB	BH	AVG	PB	PR	/A	PD	TPI
1983	Oak-A	7	6	.538	17	16	2	0	0	109^2	104	7	53	58	13.0	3.61	107	.252	.340	0	—	0	5	3	-2	0.2
1984	Oak-A	10	10	.500	26	24	1	0	0	142	156	9	85	61	15.4	4.75	79	.285	.383	0	—	0	-12	-16	-2	-1.3
1985	Oak-A	9	10	.474	32	23	2	0	0	151^1	165	13	69	56	14.0	4.52	85	.276	.353	0	—	0	-6	-11	-1	-0.8
1986	Oak-A	1	2	.333	11	3	0	0	1	34^1	40	4	13	10	13.9	6.03	64	.301	.363	0	—	0	-7	-8	1	-0.7
1987	Oak-A	0	3	.000	9	0	0	0	0	5^2	9	0	8	2	27.0	9.53	43	.360	.515	0	—	0	-3	-3	-0	-0.3
	LA-N	0	0	—	2	0	0	0	0	2^1	3	0	1	2	15.4	0.00	—	.250	.308	0	—	0	1	1	-0	0.1
1988	LA-N	0	0	—	1	1	0	0	0	2^1	4	0	2	1	27.0	11.57	29	.364	.500	0	—	0	-2	-2	0	-0.2
1989	Mil-A	3	2	.600	34	5	0	0	3	93^2	96	9	33	72	12.4	3.84	100	.264	.325	0	—	0	0	-0	-0	0.0
1990	Mil-A	6	8	.429	30	17	0	0	0	129	137	10	54	64	13.5	3.98	97	.276	.351	0	—	0	-1	-2	-1	-0.2
1991	Sea-A	11	8	.579	35	25	1	0	0	175	194	15	60	91	13.3	3.60	114	.289	.351	0	—	0	10	10	1	1.1
1992	Min-A	10	6	.625	27	27	2	2	0	161^1	166	18	46	86	12.0	4.30	94	.263	.317	0	—	0	-6	-5	-3	-0.9
	Mon-N	0	2	.000	9	2	0	0	0	17^1	23	0	7	13	16.1	6.75	52	.315	.383	0	.000	-0	-6	-6	-0	-0.7
Total	10	57	57	.500	233	143	8	2	4	1024	1097	85	431	516	13.6	4.25	92	.276	.350	0	.000	-0	-28	-39	-8	-3.7

● ABE KRUGER Kruger, Abraham b: 2/14/1885, Morris Run, Pa. d: 7/4/62, Elmira, N.Y. BR/TR, 6'2", 190 lbs. Deb: 10/06/08

YEAR	TM/L	W	L	PCT	G	GS	CG	SH	SV	IP	H	HR	BB	SO	RAT	ERA	ERA+	OAV	OOB	BH	AVG	PB	PR	/A	PD	TPI
1908	Bro-N	0	1	.000	2	1	0	0	0	6^1	5	0	3	2	15.6	4.26	55	.238	.407	0	.000	-0	-1	-1	1	-0.1

● MIKE KRUKOW Krukow, Michael Edward b: 1/21/52, Long Beach, Cal. BR/TR, 6'5", 205 lbs. Deb: 9/06/76

YEAR	TM/L	W	L	PCT	G	GS	CG	SH	SV	IP	H	HR	BB	SO	RAT	ERA	ERA+	OAV	OOB	BH	AVG	PB	PR	/A	PD	TPI
1976	Chi-N	0	0	—	2	0	0	0	0	4^1	6	0	2	1	16.6	8.31	46	.333	.400	0	.000	-0	-2	-2	-0	-0.2
1977	Chi-N	8	14	.364	34	33	1	1	0	172	195	16	61	106	13.6	4.40	100	.281	.341	11	.200	-0	-9	-0	1	0.0
1978	Chi-N	9	3	.750	27	20	3	1	0	138	125	11	53	81	11.9	3.91	103	.243	.320	11	.244	3	-5	2	-0	0.5
1979	Chi-N	9	9	.500	28	28	0	0	0	164^2	172	13	81	119	14.0	4.21	98	.275	.361	16	.314	5	-9	-2	-2	0.2
1980	Chi-N	10	15	.400	34	34	3	0	0	205	200	13	80	130	12.6	4.39	89	.258	.334	16	.246	3	-18	-11	-3	-1.1
1981	Chi-N	9	9	.500	25	25	2	1	0	144^1	146	11	55	101	12.7	3.68	100	.264	.333	9	.180	-0	-3	0	0	0.1
1982	Phi-N	13	11	.542	33	33	7	2	0	208	211	8	82	138	12.8	3.12	118	.268	.339	13	.181	-0	11	13	2	1.5
1983	SF-N	11	11	.500	31	31	2	1	0	184^1	189	17	76	136	13.1	3.95	89	.261	.333	16	.254	5	-7	-9	-2	-0.6
1984	SF-N	11	12	.478	35	33	3	1	1	199^1	234	22	78	141	14.3	4.56	77	.290	.356	10	.139	-1	-22	-23	-2	-2.6
1985	SF-N	8	11	.421	28	28	6	1	0	194^2	176	19	49	150	10.5	3.38	102	.238	.288	12	.218	4	5	1	-0	0.5
1986	SF-N★	20	9	.690	34	34	10	2	0	245	204	24	55	178	9.7	2.94	120	.223	.271	12	.146	0	21	16	-1	1.7
1987	*SF-N	5	6	.455	30	28	3	0	0	163	182	24	46	104	12.7	4.80	80	.288	.338	9	.167	1	-13	-17	1	-1.5
1988	SF-N	7	4	.636	20	20	1	0	0	124^2	111	13	31	75	10.6	3.54	92	.236	.291	3	.073	-0	-1	-4	-0	-0.5
1989	SF-N	4	3	.571	8	8	0	0	0	43	37	5	18	18	11.7	3.98	85	.236	.318	1	.063	-1	-2	-3	0	-0.4
Total	14	124	117	.515	369	355	41	10	1	2190^1	2188	196	767	1478	12.3	3.89	96	.260	.325	139	.193	18	-54	-39	-5	-2.4

● AL KRUMM Krumm, Albert b: Columbus, Ohio TR, Deb: 5/17/1889

YEAR	TM/L	W	L	PCT	G	GS	CG	SH	SV	IP	H	HR	BB	SO	RAT	ERA	ERA+	OAV	OOB	BH	AVG	PB	PR	/A	PD	TPI
1889	Pit-N	0	1	.000	1	1	1	0	0	9	8	0	10	4	18.0	10.00	37	.231	.403	0	.000	-1	-6	-6	-0	-0.5

● JOHNNY KUCAB Kucab, John Albert b: 12/17/19, Olyphant, Pa. d: 5/26/77, Youngstown, Ohio BR/TR, 6'2", 185 lbs. Deb: 9/14/50

YEAR	TM/L	W	L	PCT	G	GS	CG	SH	SV	IP	H	HR	BB	SO	RAT	ERA	ERA+	OAV	OOB	BH	AVG	PB	PR	/A	PD	TPI
1950	Phi-A	1	1	.500	4	2	2	0	0	26	29	4	8	8	12.8	3.46	131	.282	.333	1	.111	-0	3	3	-1	0.2
1951	Phi-A	4	3	.571	30	1	0	0	4	74^2	76	9	23	23	12.1	4.22	101	.265	.322	0	.000	-2	-1	0	-2	-0.3
1952	Phi-A	0	1	.000	25	0	0	0	2	51^1	64	5	20	17	14.9	5.26	75	.312	.376	2	.200	-0	-9	-7	-0	-0.8
Total	3	5	5	.500	59	3	2	0	6	152	169	18	51	48	13.1	4.44	95	.284	.343	3	.086	-2	-7	-4	-2	-0.9

● JACK KUCEK Kucek, John Andrew Charles b: 6/8/53, Warren, Ohio BR/TR, 6'2", 200 lbs. Deb: 8/08/74

YEAR	TM/L	W	L	PCT	G	GS	CG	SH	SV	IP	H	HR	BB	SO	RAT	ERA	ERA+	OAV	OOB	BH	AVG	PB	PR	/A	PD	TPI
1974	Chi-A	1	4	.200	9	7	0	0	0	37^2	48	3	21	25	16.7	5.26	71	.320	.407	0	—	0	-7	-6	1	-0.6
1975	Chi-A	0	0	—	2	0	0	0	0	3^2	9	0	4	2	31.9	4.91	79	.500	.591	0	—	0	-0	-0	-0	-0.1

YEAR	TM/L	W	L	PCT	G	GS	CG	SH	SV	IP	H	HR	BB	SO	RAT	ERA	ERA+	OAV	OOB	BH	AVG	PB	PR	/A	PD	TPI
1976	Chi-A	0	0	—	2	0	0	0	0	4^2	9	2	4	2	25.1	9.64	37	.429	.520	0	—	0	-3	-3	-0	-0.3
1977	Chi-A	0	1	.000	8	3	0	0	0	34^2	35	4	10	25	12.2	3.63	112	.267	.329	0	—	0	2	2	1	0.3
1978	Chi-A	2	3	.400	10	5	3	0	1	52	42	5	27	30	11.9	3.29	116	.220	.317	0	—	0	3	3	-0	0.3
1979	Chi-A	0	0	—	1	0	0	0	0	0^2	0	0	3	0	40.5	0.00	—	.000	.500	0	—	0	0	0	0	0.0
	Phi-N	1	0	1.000	4	0	0	0	0	4^1	6	2	1	2	14.5	8.31	46	.333	.368	0	—	0	-2	-2	-0	-0.2
1980	Tor-A	3	8	.273	23	12	0	0	1	68	83	9	41	35	16.5	6.75	64	.300	.392	0	—	0	-21	-19	-1	-1.9
Total	7	7	16	.304	59	27	3	0	2	205^2	232	25	111	121	15.2	5.12	78	.287	.376	0	—	0	-29	-26	0	-2.5
● JOHNNY KUCKS	Kucks, John Charles b: 7/27/33, Hoboken, N.J. BR/TR, 6'3", 184 lbs. Deb: 4/17/55																									
1955	*NY-A	8	7	.533	29	13	3	1	0	126^2	122	8	44	49	11.9	3.41	110	.252	.317	2	.050	-4	8	5	-0	0.1
1956	*NY-A☆	18	9	.667	34	31	12	3	0	224^1	223	19	72	67	12.2	3.85	100	.261	.326	11	.143	-1	8	0	0	-0.1
1957	*NY-A	8	10	.444	37	23	4	1	2	179^1	169	13	59	78	11.8	3.56	101	.251	.319	6	.109	-2	4	0	3	0.2
1958	*NY-A	8	8	.500	34	15	4	1	4	126	132	14	39	46	12.6	3.93	90	.269	.331	5	.125	-1	-2	-6	1	-0.6
1959	NY-A	0	1	.000	9	1	0	0	0	16^2	21	5	9	9	16.2	8.64	42	.323	.405	0	.000	-0	-9	-9	0	-0.9
	KC-A	8	11	.421	33	23	6	1	1	151^1	163	10	42	51	12.9	3.87	104	.278	.339	4	.085	-3	-0	2	1	0.1
	Yr	8	12	.400	42	24	6	1	1	168	184	15	51	60	13.2	4.34	91	.282	.345	4	.082	-3	-9	-7	2	-0.8
1960	KC-A	4	10	.286	31	17	1	0	0	114	140	22	43	38	14.5	6.00	66	.306	.367	4	.133	-1	-27	-26	-0	-2.6
Total	6	54	56	.491	207	123	30	7	7	938^1	970	91	308	338	12.6	4.10	92	.269	.333	32	.110	-12	-18	-32	5	-3.8
● BERT KUCZYNSKI	Kuczynski, Bernard Carl b: 1/8/20, Philadelphia, Pa. BR/TR, 6', 195 lbs. Deb: 6/02/43																									
1943	Phi-A	0	1	.000	6	1	0	0	0	24^2	36	2	9	8	17.1	4.01	85	.336	.398	0	.000	-0	-2	-2	-0	-0.2
● FRED KUHAULUA	Kuhaulua, Fred Mahele b: 2/23/53, Honolulu, Hawaii BL/TL, 5'11", 175 lbs. Deb: 8/02/77																									
1977	Cal-A	0	0	—	3	1	0	0	0	6^1	15	1	7	3	31.3	15.63	25	.455	.550	0	—	0	-8	-8	0	-0.7
1981	SD-N	1	0	1.000	5	4	0	0	0	29^1	28	1	9	16	11.4	2.45	133	.257	.314	1	.111	-0	3	3	-1	0.1
Total	2	1	0	1.000	8	5	0	0	0	35^2	43	2	16	19	14.9	4.79	70	.303	.373	1	.111	-0	-5	-6	-1	-0.6
● BUB KUHN	Kuhn, Bernard Daniel b: 10/12/1899, Vicksburg, Mich. d: 11/20/56, Detroit, Mich. BL/TR, 6'1.5", 182 lbs. Deb: 9/01/24																									
1924	Cle-A	0	1	.000	1	0	0	0	0	1	4	1	0	0	36.0	27.00	16	.667	.667	0	—	0	-3	-3	0	-0.2
● JOHN KULL	Kull, John A. b: 6/24/1882, Shenandoah, Pa. d: 3/30/36, Schuylkill, Pa. BL/TL, 6'2", 190 lbs. Deb: 10/02/09																									
1909	Phi-A	1	0	1.000	1	0	0	0	0	3	3	0	5	4	27.0	3.00	80	.250	.500	1	1.000	0	-0	-0	0	0.0
● MIKE KUME	Kume, John Michael b: 5/19/26, Premier, W.Va. BR/TR, 6'1", 195 lbs. Deb: 8/26/55																									
1955	KC-A	0	2	.000	6	4	0	0	0	23^2	35	1	15	7	20.2	7.99	52	.354	.453	1	.125	-1	-11	-10	-0	-1.0
● JEFF KUNKEL	Kunkel, Jeffrey William b: 3/25/62, W.Palm Beach, Fla. BR/TR, 6'2", 180 lbs. Deb: 7/23/84 F♦																									
1988	Tex-A	0	0	—	1	0	0	0	0	1	0	0	0	1	0.0	0.00	—	.000	.000	35	.227	1	0	0	0	0.0
1989	Tex-A	0	0	—	1	0	0	0	0	1^2	4	1	3	0	37.8	21.60	18	.444	.583	79	.270	1	-3	-3	0	-0.3
Total	2	0	0	—	2	0	0	0	0	2^2	4	1	3	1	23.6	13.50	30	.333	.467	192	.221	2	-3	-3	0	-0.3
● BILL KUNKEL	Kunkel, William Gustave James b: 7/7/36, Hoboken, N.J. d: 5/4/85, Red Bank, N.J. BR/TR, 6'1", 187 lbs. Deb: 4/15/61 FU																									
1961	KC-A	3	4	.429	58	2	0	0	4	88^2	103	11	32	46	13.7	5.18	80	.289	.348	1	.125	-0	-11	-10	0	-1.0
1962	KC-A	0	0	—	9	0	0	0	0	7^2	8	3	4	6	14.1	3.52	118	.258	.343	0	—	0	0	1	-0	0.0
1963	NY-A	3	2	.600	22	0	0	0	0	46^1	42	3	13	31	10.7	2.72	129	.239	.291	2	.333	1	5	4	-1	0.4
Total	3	6	6	.500	89	2	0	0	4	142^2	153	17	49	83	12.7	4.29	91	.272	.330	3	.214	1	-6	-6	-1	-0.6
● EARL KUNZ	Kunz, Earl Dewey "Pinches" b: 12/25/1899, Sacramento, Cal. d: 4/14/63, Sacramento, Cal. BR/TR, 5'10", 170 lbs. Deb: 4/19/23																									
1923	Pit-N	1	2	.333	21	2	1	0	1	45^2	48	2	24	12	14.2	5.52	73	.293	.383	1	.083	-1	-8	-8	-1	-0.9
● RYAN KUROSAKI	Kurosaki, Ryan Yoshitomo b: 7/3/52, Honolulu, Hawaii BR/TR, 5'10", 160 lbs. Deb: 5/20/75																									
1975	StL-N	0	0	—	7	0	0	0	0	13	15	3	7	6	15.2	7.62	49	.283	.367	0	.000	-0	-6	-6	-0	-0.6
● HAL KURTZ	Kurtz, Harold James "Bud" b: 8/20/43, Washington, D.C. BR/TR, 6'3", 205 lbs. Deb: 4/18/68																									
1968	Cle-A	1	0	1.000	28	0	0	0	1	38	37	2	15	16	13.5	5.21	57	.255	.345	0	.000	-0	-9	-10	-1	-1.2
● ED KUSEL	Kusel, Edward D. b: 2/15/1886, Cleveland, Ohio d: 10/20/48, Cleveland, Ohio TR, 6', 165 lbs. Deb: 9/18/09																									
1909	StL-A	0	3	.000	3	3	3	0	0	24	43	1	1	2	16.5	7.13	34	.384	.389	3	.300	1	-12	-13	-1	-1.1
● EMIL KUSH	Kush, Emil Benedict b: 11/4/16, Chicago, Ill. d: 11/26/69, River Grove, Ill. BR/TR, 5'11", 185 lbs. Deb: 9/21/41																									
1941	Chi-N	0	0	—	2	0	0	0	0	4	2	0	0	2	4.5	2.25	156	.143	.143	0	.000	-0	1	1	-0	0.0
1942	Chi-N	0	0	—	1	0	0	0	0	2	1	0	1	1	9.0	0.00	—	.167	.286	0	.000	-0	1	1	0	0.1
1946	Chi-N	9	2	.818	40	6	1	1	2	129^2	120	4	43	50	11.5	3.05	109	.253	.319	8	.211	0	5	4	2	0.7
1947	Chi-N	8	3	.727	47	1	1	0	5	91	80	8	53	44	13.5	3.36	117	.247	.358	5	.250	1	7	6	1	0.8
1948	Chi-N	1	4	.200	34	1	0	0	3	72	70	5	37	31	13.6	4.38	89	.253	.345	2	.154	0	-3	-4	1	-0.3
1949	Chi-N	3	3	.500	26	0	0	0	2	47^2	51	7	24	22	14.5	3.78	107	.283	.374	3	.333	1	1	1	1	0.4
Total	6	21	12	.636	150	8	2	1	12	346^1	324	24	158	150	12.8	3.48	106	.254	.341	18	.220	2	12	9	5	1.7
● CRAIG KUSICK	Kusick, Craig Robert b: 9/30/48, Milwaukee, Wis. BR/TR, 6'3", 232 lbs. Deb: 9/08/73 ♦																									
1979	Tor-A	0	0	—	1	0	0	0	0	3^2	3	1	0	0	7.4	4.91	88	.214	.214	11	.204	1	-0	-0	-0	0.0
● MARTY KUTYNA	Kutyna, Marion John b: 11/14/32, Philadelphia, Pa. BR/TR, 6', 190 lbs. Deb: 9/19/59																									
1959	KC-A	0	0	—	4	0	0	0	1	7^1	7	0	1	1	9.8	0.00	—	.250	.276	0	—	0	3	3	0	0.4
1960	KC-A	3	2	.600	51	0	0	0	4	61^2	64	7	32	20	14.0	3.94	101	.274	.361	1	.200	-0	-0	0	0	0.0
1961	Was-A	6	8	.429	50	6	0	0	3	143	147	12	48	64	12.4	3.97	101	.271	.332	7	.206	-0	1	1	3	0.4
1962	Was-A	5	6	.455	54	0	0	0	0	78	83	9	27	25	12.7	4.04	100	.275	.334	1	.125	-0	-1	-0	1	0.1
Total	4	14	16	.467	159	6	0	0	8	290	301	28	108	110	12.8	3.88	103	.272	.338	9	.191	-0	3	4	4	0.9
● JERRY KUTZLER	Kutzler, Jerry Scott b: 3/25/65, Waukegan, Ill. BL/TR, 6'1", 175 lbs. Deb: 4/28/90																									
1990	Chi-A	2	1	.667	7	7	0	0	0	31^1	38	2	14	21	14.9	6.03	63	.304	.374	0	—	0	-7	-8	-0	-0.8
● BOB KUZAVA	Kuzava, Robert Leroy "Sarge" b: 5/28/23, Wyandotte, Mich. BB/TL, 6'2", 204 lbs. Deb: 9/21/46																									
1946	Cle-A	1	0	1.000	2	2	0	0	0	12	9	0	11	4	15.8	3.00	110	.191	.356	1	.200	-0	1	0	0	0.1
1947	Cle-A	1	1	.500	4	4	1	1	0	21^2	22	1	9	9	13.3	4.15	84	.265	.344	1	.111	-1	-1	-2	1	-0.1
1949	Chi-A	10	6	.625	29	18	9	1	0	156^2	139	6	91	83	13.3	4.02	104	.240	.344	2	.036	-6	3	3	-2	-0.5
1950	Chi-A	1	3	.250	10	7	1	0	0	44^1	43	5	27	21	14.2	5.68	79	.257	.361	1	.083	-0	-5	-6	0	-0.6
	Was-A	8	7	.533	22	22	8	1	0	155	156	8	75	84	13.5	3.95	114	.263	.346	5	.100	-2	11	9	-1	0.7
	Yr	9	10	.474	32	29	9	1	0	199^1	199	13	102	105	13.6	4.33	104	.261	.350	6	.097	-2	5	3	-1	0.1
1951	Was-A	3	3	.500	8	8	3	0	0	52^1	57	5	28	22	15.0	5.50	74	.284	.377	3	.176	-0	-8	-8	0	-0.8
	*NY-A	8	4	.667	23	8	4	1	5	82^1	76	5	27	50	11.4	2.40	159	.241	.303	3	.136	0	16	13	-1	1.2
	Yr	11	7	.611	31	16	7	1	5	134^2	133	10	55	72	12.6	3.61	109	.257	.329	6	.154	0	8	5	-1	0.4
1952	*NY-A	8	8	.500	28	12	6	1	3	133	115	7	63	67	12.1	3.45	96	.240	.329	4	.093	-1	3	-2	-2	-0.5
1953	*NY-A	6	5	.545	33	6	2	2	4	92^1	92	9	34	48	12.3	3.31	111	.264	.330	1	.048	-1	7	4	-2	0.1
1954	NY-A	1	3	.250	20	3	0	0	1	39^2	46	3	18	22	14.5	5.45	63	.297	.370	0	.000	-0	-8	-9	-1	-1.0
	Bal-A	1	3	.250	4	4	0	0	0	23^2	30	0	11	15	15.6	4.18	86	.323	.394	0	.000	-1	-1	-2	-1	-0.3
	Yr	2	6	.250	24	7	0	0	1	63^1	76	3	29	37	14.9	4.97	70	.304	.376	0	.000	-1	-9	-10	-1	-1.3
1955	Bal-A	0	1	.000	6	1	0	0	0	12^1	10	0	4	5	10.2	3.65	105	.222	.286	0	.000	-0	0	0	-1	0.0

YEAR	TM/L	W	L	PCT	G	GS	CG	SH	SV	IP	H	HR	BB	SO	RAT	ERA	ERA+	OAV	OOB	BH	AVG	PB	PR	/A	PD	TPI
	Phi-N	1	0	1.000	17	4	0	0	0	32^1	47	5	12	13	16.4	7.24	55	.333	.386	1	.143	-0	-11	-12	0	-1.1
1957	Pit-N	0	0	—	4	0	0	0	0	2	3	0	3	1	27.0	9.00	42	.333	.500	0	—	0	-1	-1	-0	-0.1
	StL-N	0	0	—	3	0	0	0	0	2^1	4	0	2	2	23.1	3.86	103	.364	.462	0	—	0	0	0	0	0.0
	Yr	0	0	—	7	0	0	0	0	4^1	7	0	5	3	24.9	6.23	62	.350	.480	0	—	0	-1	-1	0	-0.1
Total	10	49	44	.527	213	99	34	7	13	862	849	54	415	446	13.3	4.05	97	.260	.345	22	.086	-13	5	-12	-8	-2.9

● CLEM LABINE Labine, Clement Walter b: 8/6/26, Lincoln, R.I. BR/TR, 6′, 180 lbs. Deb: 4/18/50

YEAR	TM/L	W	L	PCT	G	GS	CG	SH	SV	IP	H	HR	BB	SO	RAT	ERA	ERA+	OAV	OOB	BH	AVG	PB	PR	/A	PD	TPI
1950	Bro-N	0	0	—	1	0	0	0	0	2	2	0	1	0	13.5	4.50	91	.286	.375	0	—	0	-0	-0	-0	0.0
1951	Bro-N	5	1	.833	14	6	5	2	0	65^1	52	4	20	39	9.9	2.20	178	.223	.285	3	.143	-1	13	12	-1	1.2
1952	Bro-N	8	4	.667	25	9	0	0	0	77	76	3	47	43	14.5	5.14	71	.259	.364	1	.045	-2	-12	-13	1	-1.4
1953	*Bro-N	11	6	.647	37	7	0	0	7	110^1	92	9	30	44	10.0	2.77	154	.225	.278	2	.071	-1	19	18	0	1.7
1954	Bro-N	7	6	.538	47	2	0	0	5	108^1	101	7	56	43	13.1	4.15	98	.247	.339	1	.033	-2	-1	-1	1	-0.2
1955	*Bro-N	13	5	.722	**60**	8	1	0	11	144^1	121	12	55	67	11.0	3.24	125	.229	.301	3	.097	1	13	13	3	1.7
1956	*Bro-N☆	10	6	.625	62	3	1	0	**19**	115^2	111	11	39	75	11.9	3.35	119	.253	.318	2	.087	-1	5	8	1	0.7
1957	Bro-N★	5	7	.417	58	0	0	0	**17**	104^2	104	8	27	67	11.4	3.44	121	.259	.307	2	.100	-1	5	8	2	0.9
1958	LA-N	6	6	.500	52	2	0	0	14	104	112	8	33	43	12.6	4.15	99	.283	.340	1	.056	-1	-2	-1	0	-0.1
1959	*LA-N	5	10	.333	56	0	0	0	9	84^2	91	11	25	37	12.4	3.93	108	.282	.335	0	.000	-2	0	3	1	0.2
1960	LA-N	0	1	.000	13	0	0	0	1	17	26	1	8	15	18.0	5.82	68	.356	.420	1	.500	1	-4	-4	-0	-0.3
	Det-A	0	3	.000	14	0	0	0	2	19^1	19	2	12	6	14.4	5.12	77	.257	.360	0	.000	-0	-3	-2	0	-0.3
	*Pit-N	3	0	1.000	15	0	0	0	3	30^1	29	0	11	21	12.2	1.48	253	.254	.325	0	.000	-0	8	8	0	0.8
1961	Pit-N	4	1	.800	56	1	0	0	8	92^2	102	4	31	49	13.1	3.69	108	.284	.344	1	.100	-0	4	3	-1	0.2
1962	NY-N	0	0	—	3	0	0	0	0	4	5	1	1	2	13.5	11.25	37	.278	.316	0	—	0	-3	-3	0	-0.3
Total	13	77	56	.579	513	38	7	2	96	1079^2	1043	81	396	551	12.1	3.63	112	.256	.323	17	.075	-11	41	50	8	4.8

● BOB LACEY Lacey, Robert Joseph b: 8/25/53, Fredericksburg, Va. BR/TL, 6′5″, 210 lbs. Deb: 5/13/77

YEAR	TM/L	W	L	PCT	G	GS	CG	SH	SV	IP	H	HR	BB	SO	RAT	ERA	ERA+	OAV	OOB	BH	AVG	PB	PR	/A	PD	TPI
1977	Oak-A	6	8	.429	64	0	0	0	7	121^2	100	13	43	69	10.6	3.03	133	.234	.304	0	—	0	14	13	3	1.7
1978	Oak-A	8	9	.471	**74**	0	0	0	5	119^2	126	10	35	60	12.2	3.01	121	.270	.323	0	—	0	10	8	2	1.1
1979	Oak-A	1	5	.167	42	0	0	0	4	47^2	66	7	24	33	17.2	5.85	69	.327	.401	0	—	0	-9	-10	0	-0.9
1980	Oak-A	3	2	.600	47	1	1	1	6	79^2	68	7	21	45	10.2	2.94	128	.234	.288	0	—	0	10	7	-0	0.8
1981	Cle-A	0	0	—	14	0	0	0	0	21^1	36	5	3	11	16.5	7.59	48	.371	.390	0	—	0	-9	-9	-0	-0.9
	Tex-A	0	0	—	1	0	0	0	0	1	1	1	0	0	9.0	9.00	39	.250	.250	0	—	0	-1	-1	0	0.0
	Yr	0	0	—	15	0	0	0	0	22^1	37	6	3	11	16.1	7.66	47	.356	.374	0	—	0	-10	-10	0	-0.9
1983	Cal-A	1	2	.333	8	0	0	0	0	8^2	12	1	0	7	12.5	5.19	77	.343	.343	0	—	0	-1	-1	-0	-0.1
1984	SF-N	1	3	.250	34	1	0	0	0	51	55	5	13	26	12.0	3.88	90	.276	.321	2	.333	1	-2	-2	0	-0.1
Total	7	20	29	.408	284	2	1	1	22	450^2	464	49	139	251	12.1	3.67	103	.269	.325	2	.333	1	12	6	5	1.6

● MARCEL LACHEMANN Lachemann, Marcel Ernest b: 6/13/41, Los Angeles, Cal. BR/TR, 6′, 185 lbs. Deb: 6/04/69 FC

YEAR	TM/L	W	L	PCT	G	GS	CG	SH	SV	IP	H	HR	BB	SO	RAT	ERA	ERA+	OAV	OOB	BH	AVG	PB	PR	/A	PD	TPI
1969	Oak-A	4	1	.800	28	0	0	0	2	43^1	43	1	19	16	13.3	3.95	87	.261	.344	0	.000	-0	-2	-2	1	-0.2
1970	Oak-A	3	3	.500	41	0	0	0	3	58^1	58	6	18	39	12.0	2.78	127	.266	.328	0	.000	-1	6	5	1	0.6
1971	Oak-A	0	0	—	1	0	0	0	0	0^1	2	0	1	0	81.0	54.00	6	1.000	1.000	0	—	0	-2	-2	0	-0.2
Total	3	7	4	.636	70	0	0	0	5	102	103	7	38	55	12.8	3.44	102	.268	.340	0	.000	-1	3	1	2	0.2

● AL LACHOWICZ Lachowicz, Allen Richard b: 9/6/60, Pittsburgh, Pa. BR/TR, 6′3″, 198 lbs. Deb: 9/13/83

YEAR	TM/L	W	L	PCT	G	GS	CG	SH	SV	IP	H	HR	BB	SO	RAT	ERA	ERA+	OAV	OOB	BH	AVG	PB	PR	/A	PD	TPI
1983	Tex-A	0	1	.000	2	1	0	0	0	8	9	0	2	8	12.4	2.25	178	.281	.324	0	—	0	2	2	0	0.2

● GEORGE LaCLAIRE LaClaire, George Lewis "Frenchy" b: 10/18/1886, Milton, Vt. d: 10/10/18, Farnham, Que., Can. BR/TR, 5′9″, 170 lbs. Deb: 6/05/14

YEAR	TM/L	W	L	PCT	G	GS	CG	SH	SV	IP	H	HR	BB	SO	RAT	ERA	ERA+	OAV	OOB	BH	AVG	PB	PR	/A	PD	TPI
1914	Pit-F	5	2	.714	22	7	5	1	0	103^1	99	1	25	49	10.9	4.01	79	.262	.309	5	.147	-1	-9	-9	0	-1.1
1915	Pit-F	1	2	.333	14	3	1	0	1	45^2	43	1	13	10	11.0	3.35	90	.253	.306	2	.154	-1	-2	-2	1	-0.2
	Buf-F	0	0	—	1	0	0	0	0	3	4	0	1	2	15.0	6.00	52	.333	.385	0	—	0	-1	-1	-0	-0.1
	Bal-F	1	8	.111	18	9	6	1	1	84	76	2	22	30	10.5	2.46	129	.246	.296	2	.083	-2	5	7	0	0.6
	Yr	2	10	.167	33	12	7	1	2	132^2	123	3	36	42	10.8	2.85	110	.251	.302	4	.108	-3	3	4	1	0.3
Total	2	7	12	.368	55	19	12	2	2	236	222	4	61	91	10.8	3.36	94	.255	.305	9	.127	-4	-6	-5	1	-0.8

● FRANK LaCORTE LaCorte, Frank Joseph b: 10/13/51, San Jose, Cal. BR/TR, 6′1″, 180 lbs. Deb: 9/08/75

YEAR	TM/L	W	L	PCT	G	GS	CG	SH	SV	IP	H	HR	BB	SO	RAT	ERA	ERA+	OAV	OOB	BH	AVG	PB	PR	/A	PD	TPI
1975	Atl-N	0	3	.000	3	2	0	0	0	13^2	13	1	6	10	12.5	5.27	72	.245	.322	0	.000	-1	-3	-2	0	-0.3
1976	Atl-N	3	12	.200	19	17	1	0	0	105^1	97	6	53	79	13.3	4.70	81	.249	.348	3	.091	-2	-14	-11	-0	-1.4
1977	Atl-N	1	8	.111	14	7	0	0	0	37	67	10	29	28	23.8	11.68	38	.394	.488	2	.200	-0	-32	-30	0	-2.7
1978	Atl-N	0	1	.000	2	2	0	0	0	14^2	9	0	4	7	8.0	3.68	110	.180	.241	0	.000	-1	-0	1	-0	0.0
1979	Atl-N	0	0	—	6	0	0	0	0	8^1	9	2	5	6	15.1	7.56	54	.273	.368	0	.000	-0	-4	-3	-0	-0.4
	Hou-N	1	2	.333	12	3	0	0	0	27	21	3	10	24	10.3	5.00	70	.208	.279	0	.000	-0	-4	-4	-1	-0.5
	Yr	1	2	.333	18	3	0	0	0	35^1	30	5	15	30	11.5	5.60	65	.224	.302	0	.000	-0	-7	-8	-1	-0.9
1980	*Hou-N	8	5	.615	55	0	0	0	11	83	61	4	43	66	11.3	2.82	117	.210	.311	1	.167	0	7	4	-2	0.3
1981	*Hou-N	4	2	.667	37	0	0	0	5	42	41	1	21	40	13.3	3.64	90	.258	.344	1	.333	0	-1	-2	-0	-0.2
1982	Hou-N	1	5	.167	55	0	0	0	7	76^1	71	5	46	51	13.8	4.48	74	.247	.350	0	.000	-1	-7	-10	-2	-1.3
1983	Hou-N	4	4	.500	37	0	0	0	3	53^1	35	8	28	48	11.0	5.06	67	.190	.304	1	.200	0	-9	-10	-0	-1.0
1984	Cal-A	1	2	.333	13	1	0	0	0	29^1	33	9	13	13	14.1	7.06	56	.282	.354	0	—	0	-10	-10	-0	-1.0
Total	10	23	44	.343	253	32	1	0	26	490	457	49	258	372	13.3	5.01	72	.249	.345	8	.104	-4	-75	-77	-7	-8.5

● MIKE LaCOSS LaCoss, Michael James b: 5/30/56, Glendale, Cal. BR/TR, 6′4″, 190 lbs. Deb: 7/18/78

YEAR	TM/L	W	L	PCT	G	GS	CG	SH	SV	IP	H	HR	BB	SO	RAT	ERA	ERA+	OAV	OOB	BH	AVG	PB	PR	/A	PD	TPI
1978	Cin-N	4	8	.333	16	15	2	1	0	96	104	5	46	31	14.2	4.50	79	.288	.370	2	.067	-2	-10	-10	-1	-1.3
1979	*Cin-N★	14	8	.636	35	32	6	1	0	205^2	202	13	79	73	12.4	3.50	107	.263	.333	9	.129	-1	5	5	1	0.5
1980	Cin-N	10	12	.455	34	29	4	2	0	169^1	207	9	68	59	14.7	4.62	77	.303	.367	5	.091	-3	-19	-20	1	-2.2
1981	Cin-N	4	7	.364	20	13	1	1	1	78	102	7	30	22	15.3	6.12	58	.325	.386	0	.000	-2	-23	-22	0	-2.4
1982	Hou-N	6	6	.500	41	8	0	0	0	115	107	3	54	51	12.9	2.90	115	.252	.342	6	.250	2	9	5	-1	0.7
1983	Hou-N	5	7	.417	38	17	2	0	1	138	142	10	56	53	13.0	4.43	77	.273	.346	3	.086	-2	-12	-16	1	-1.7
1984	Hou-N	7	5	.583	39	18	2	1	3	132	132	3	55	86	12.8	4.02	83	.261	.334	4	.129	-0	-6	-10	0	-1.1
1985	KC-A	1	1	.500	21	0	0	0	1	40^2	49	2	29	26	17.3	5.09	82	.304	.411	0	—	0	-4	-4	0	-0.4
1986	SF-N	10	13	.435	37	31	4	1	0	204^1	179	14	70	86	11.2	3.57	99	.240	.310	14	.230	5	3	-1	1	0.5
1987	*SF-N	13	10	.565	39	26	2	1	0	171	184	16	63	79	13.1	3.68	104	.283	.348	3	.060	-2	8	3	4	0.4
1988	SF-N	7	7	.500	19	19	1	1	0	114^1	99	5	47	70	11.6	3.62	90	.234	.312	8	.242	2	-2	-5	3	0.1
1989	*SF-N	10	10	.500	45	18	1	0	6	150^1	143	3	65	78	12.9	3.17	106	.255	.340	3	.073	-1	5	3	-1	0.2
1990	SF-N	6	4	.600	13	12	1	0	0	77^2	75	5	39	39	13.2	3.94	92	.259	.347	1	.043	-1	-1	-3	-1	-0.5
1991	SF-N	1	5	.167	18	5	0	0	0	47^1	61	4	24	30	16.5	7.23	50	.314	.395	2	.222	1	-19	-19	-0	-1.9
Total	14	98	103	.488	415	243	26	9	12	1739^2	1786	99	725	783	13.1	4.02	88	.270	.345	60	.125	-4	-66	-93	8	-9.1

● PETE LADD Ladd, Peter Linwood b: 7/17/56, Portland, Maine BR/TR, 6′3″, 240 lbs. Deb: 8/17/79

YEAR	TM/L	W	L	PCT	G	GS	CG	SH	SV	IP	H	HR	BB	SO	RAT	ERA	ERA+	OAV	OOB	BH	AVG	PB	PR	/A	PD	TPI
1979	Hou-N	1	1	.500	10	0	0	0	0	12^1	8	1	8	6	13.1	2.92	120	.178	.327	0	.000	-0	1	1	0	0.1
1982	*Mil-A	1	3	.250	16	0	0	0	3	18	16	5	6	12	11.0	4.00	95	.239	.301	0	—	0	0	-0	-1	-0.1
1983	Mil-A	3	4	.429	44	0	0	0	25	49^1	30	3	16	41	8.6	2.55	146	.172	.246	0	—	0	8	6	-0	0.7
1984	Mil-A	4	9	.308	54	1	0	0	3	91	94	16	38	75	13.2	5.24	73	.266	.339	0	—	0	-13	-14	-2	-1.5
1985	Mil-A	0	0	—	29	0	0	0	2	45^2	58	5	10	22	13.8	4.53	92	.315	.357	0	—	0	-2	-2	-0	-0.2
1986	Sea-A	8	6	.571	52	0	0	0	6	70^2	69	10	18	53	11.5	3.82	111	.258	.313	0	—	0	3	3	-1	0.2
Total	6	17	23	.425	205	1	0	0	39	287	275	40	96	209	11.9	4.14	96	.252	.318	0	.000	-0	-2	-6	-4	-0.8

YEAR	TM/L	W	L	PCT	G	GS	CG	SH	SV	IP	H	HR	BB	SO	RAT	ERA	ERA+	OAV	OOB	BH	AVG	PB	PR	/A	PD	TPI
● **DOYLE LADE**	Lade, Doyle Marion "Porky" b: 2/17/21, Fairbury, Neb. BR/TR, 5'10", 183 lbs. Deb: 9/18/46																									
1946	Chi-N	0	2	.000	3	2	0	0	0	15^1	15	0	3	8	11.2	4.11	81	.238	.284	1	.200	-0	-1	-1	0	-0.1
1947	Chi-N	11	10	.524	34	25	7	1	0	187^1	202	15	79	62	13.5	3.94	100	.276	.347	13	.217	2	2	0	2	0.5
1948	Chi-N	5	6	.455	19	12	6	0	0	87^1	99	4	31	29	13.5	4.02	97	.283	.343	5	.156	-1	-1	-1	1	0.0
1949	Chi-N	4	5	.444	36	13	5	1	1	129^2	141	14	58	43	14.0	5.00	81	.274	.350	7	.219	2	-14	-14	0	-1.2
1950	Chi-N	5	6	.455	34	12	2	0	2	117^2	126	14	50	36	13.6	4.74	89	.275	.349	10	.286	3	-8	-7	3	-0.1
Total	5	25	29	.463	126	64	20	2	3	537^1	583	47	221	178	13.6	4.39	91	.275	.346	36	.220	6	-21	-23	7	-0.9
● **STEVE LADEW**	Ladew, Stephen b: St.Louis, Mo. Deb: 9/27/1889 ♦																									
1889	KC-a	0	0	—	1	0	0	0	0	2	1	0	3	0	18.0	4.50	93	.144	.403	0	.000	-0	-0	-0	0	0.0
● **FLIP LAFFERTY**	Lafferty, Frank Bernard b: 5/4/1854, Scranton, Pa. d: 2/8/10, Wilmington, Del. TR , Deb: 9/15/1876 ♦																									
1876	Phi-N	0	1	.000	1	1	1	0	0	9	5	0	0	0	5.0	0.00	—	.152	.152	0	.000	-1	2	2	0	0.2
● **ED LAFITTE**	Lafitte, Edward Francis "Doc" b: 4/7/1886, New Orleans, La. d: 4/12/71, Jenkintown, Pa. BR/TR, 6'2", 188 lbs. Deb: 4/16/09																									
1909	Det-A	0	1	.000	3	1	1	0	1	14	22	2	2	11	16.1	3.86	65	.344	.373	1	.250	0	-2	-2	0	-0.2
1911	Det-A	11	8	.579	29	20	15	0	1	172^1	205	2	52	63	13.7	3.92	88	.302	.356	11	.157	-3	-11	-9	-2	-1.3
1912	Det-A	0	0	—	1	0	0	0	0	1^2	2	0	2	0	21.6	16.20	20	.333	.500	0	—	0	-2	-2	0	-0.2
1914	Bro-F	18	15	.545	42	33	23	0	2	290^2	260	7	127	137	12.5	2.63	121	.248	.338	26	.257	4	19	18	3	2.8
1915	Bro-F	6	9	.400	17	16	7	0	0	117^2	126	6	57	34	14.1	3.98	76	.288	.371	14	.264	3	-12	-13	-2	-1.3
	Buf-F	2	2	.500	14	5	1	1	1	50^1	53	1	22	17	13.8	3.40	92	.286	.368	2	.118	-1	-2	-2	0	-0.3
	Yr	8	11	.421	31	21	8	1	1	168	179	7	79	51	13.9	3.80	80	.287	.369	16	.229	2	-14	-14	-2	-1.6
Total	5	37	35	.514	106	75	47	1	5	646^2	668	18	262	262	13.3	3.34	96	.276	.353	54	.220	4	-11	-9	-0	-0.5
● **ED LAGGER**	Lagger, Edwin Joseph b: 7/14/12, Joliet, Ill. d: 11/10/81, Joliet, Ill. BR/TR, 6'3", 200 lbs. Deb: 6/15/34																									
1934	Phi-A	0	0	—	8	0	0	0	0	18	27	1	14	2	21.0	11.00	40	.342	.447	0	.000	-1	-13	-13	1	-1.1
● **LERRIN LaGROW**	LaGrow, Lerrin Harris b: 7/8/48, Phoenix, Ariz. BR/TR, 6'5", 220 lbs. Deb: 7/28/70																									
1970	Det-A	0	1	.000	10	0	0	0	0	12^1	16	2	6	7	16.1	7.30	51	.308	.379	0	.000	-0	-5	-5	-0	-0.5
1972	*Det-A	0	1	.000	16	0	0	0	2	27^1	22	0	6	9	9.2	1.32	239	.222	.267	0	—	0	5	6	-0	0.6
1973	Det-A	1	5	.167	21	3	0	0	3	54	54	8	23	33	13.0	4.33	94	.263	.341	0	—	0	-3	-1	1	-0.1
1974	Det-A	8	19	.296	37	34	11	0	0	216^1	245	21	80	85	13.6	4.66	82	.287	.350	0	—	0	-25	-21	3	-1.9
1975	Det-A	7	14	.333	32	26	7	2	0	164^1	183	15	66	75	13.7	4.38	92	.280	.348	0	—	0	-11	-7	-2	-1.0
1976	StL-N	0	1	.000	8	2	1	0	0	24^1	21	0	7	10	10.7	1.48	239	.241	.305	0	.000	-1	5	6	0	0.6
1977	Chi-A	7	3	.700	66	0	0	0	25	98^2	81	10	35	63	10.7	2.46	166	.230	.302	0	—	0	17	18	1	1.8
1978	Chi-A	6	5	.545	52	0	0	0	16	88	85	9	38	41	12.9	4.40	86	.260	.342	0	—	0	-6	-6	2	-0.5
1979	Chi-A	0	3	.000	11	2	0	0	1	17^2	27	2	16	9	22.4	9.17	46	.346	.463	0	—	0	-10	-10	-0	-0.9
	LA-N	5	1	.833	31	0	0	0	4	37	38	2	18	22	13.6	3.41	107	.270	.352	1	.333	0	1	1	-0	0.1
1980	Phi-N	0	2	.000	25	0	0	0	3	39	42	5	17	21	13.6	4.15	91	.276	.349	1	.250	0	-2	-2	-0	-0.2
Total	10	34	55	.382	309	67	19	2	54	779	814	74	312	375	13.1	4.11	94	.271	.342	2	.154	-0	-33	-21	2	-2.0
● **JEFF LAHTI**	Lahti, Jeffrey Allen b: 10/8/56, Oregon City, Ore. BR/TR, 6', 180 lbs. Deb: 6/27/82																									
1982	*StL-N	5	4	.556	33	1	0	0	0	56^2	53	3	21	22	12.1	3.81	95	.245	.318	1	.077	-1	-1	-1	2	-0.1
1983	StL-N	3	3	.500	53	0	0	0	0	74	64	2	29	26	11.4	3.16	114	.240	.316	0	.000	-1	4	4	1	0.4
1984	StL-N	4	2	.667	63	0	0	0	1	84^2	69	6	34	45	11.2	3.72	93	.225	.306	1	.167	-0	-1	-2	0	-0.2
1985	*StL-N	5	2	.714	52	0	0	0	19	68^1	63	3	26	41	11.7	1.84	192	.251	.321	0	.000	-1	13	13	-0	1.2
1986	StL-N	0	0	—	4	0	0	0	0	2^1	3	0	1	3	15.4	0.00	—	.333	.400	0	—	0	1	1	-0	0.1
Total	5	17	11	.607	205	1	0	0	20	286	252	14	111	137	11.6	3.12	114	.240	.316	2	.053	-3	15	14	2	1.4
● **EDDIE LAKE**	Lake, Edward Erving "Sparky" b: 3/18/16, Antioch, Cal. BR/TR, 5'7", 160 lbs. Deb: 9/26/39 ♦																									
1944	Bos-A	0	0	—	6	0	0	0	0	19^1	20	2	11	7	15.8	4.19	81	.278	.395	26	.206	1	-2	-2	0	-0.1
● **JOE LAKE**	Lake, Joseph Henry b: 1/6/1881, Brooklyn, N.Y. d: 6/30/50, Brooklyn, N.Y. BR/TR, 6', 185 lbs. Deb: 4/21/08																									
1908	NY-A	9	22	.290	38	27	19	2	0	269^1	252	6	77	118	11.2	3.17	78	.242	.298	21	.188	0	-23	-21	-4	-2.7
1909	NY-A	14	11	.560	31	26	17	3	1	215^1	180	2	59	117	10.2	1.88	135	.225	.283	14	.173	1	14	16	5	2.6
1910	StL-A	11	17	.393	35	29	24	1	2	261^1	243	2	77	141	11.1	2.20	112	.248	.304	21	.231	2	9	8	1	1.2
1911	StL-A	10	15	.400	30	25	14	2	0	215^1	245	3	40	69	12.1	3.30	102	.282	.316	21	.262	2	1	2	6	0.9
1912	StL-A	1	7	.125	11	6	4	0	0	57	70	0	16	28	13.7	4.42	75	.314	.363	3	.150	-1	-7	-7	2	-0.6
	Det-A	9	11	.450	26	14	11	0	1	162^2	190	3	39	86	12.8	3.10	105	.296	.340	9	.145	-3	4	3	0	0.0
	Yr	10	18	.357	37	20	15	0	1	219^2	260	3	55	114	13.0	3.44	95	.301	.345	12	.146	-4	-3	-4	2	-0.6
1913	Det-A	8	7	.533	28	12	6	0	1	137	149	3	24	35	11.4	3.28	89	.278	.309	12	.267	4	-5	-6	3	0.2
Total	6	62	90	.408	199	139	95	8	5	1318	1329	19	332	594	11.5	2.85	99	.261	.309	101	.206	4	-7	-5	12	1.6
● **AL LAKEMAN**	Lakeman, Albert Wesley "Moose" b: 12/31/18, Cincinnati, Ohio d: 5/25/76, Spartanburg, S.C. BR/TR, 6'2", 195 lbs. Deb: 4/19/42 C♦																									
1948	Phi-N	0	0	—	1	0	0	0	0	0^2	1	1	0	0	13.5	13.50	29	.333	.333	11	.162	0	-1	-1	-0	-0.1
● **JACK LAMABE**	Lamabe, John Alexander b: 10/3/36, Farmingdale, N.Y. BR/TR, 6'1", 198 lbs. Deb: 4/17/62																									
1962	Pit-N	3	1	.750	46	0	0	0	2	78	70	4	40	56	12.7	2.88	136	.238	.329	0	.000	-1	9	9	1	0.9
1963	Bos-A	7	4	.636	65	2	0	0	6	151^1	139	8	46	93	11.2	3.15	120	.247	.308	3	.094	-1	8	11	1	1.1
1964	Bos-A	9	13	.409	39	25	3	0	1	177^1	235	25	57	109	14.9	5.89	65	.318	.369	6	.115	-1	-45	-40	-0	-4.1
1965	Bos-A	0	3	.000	14	0	0	0	0	25^1	34	5	14	17	18.1	8.17	46	.340	.436	0	.000	-0	-13	-13	0	-1.3
	Hou-N	0	2	.000	3	2	0	0	0	12^2	17	3	3	6	14.2	4.26	79	.315	.351	1	.250	0	-1	-1	-0	-0.1
1966	Chi-A	7	9	.438	34	17	3	2	0	121^1	116	9	35	67	11.3	3.93	81	.251	.305	2	.057	-2	-7	-10	-0	-1.3
1967	Chi-A	1	0	1.000	3	0	0	0	0	5	7	0	1	3	14.4	1.80	172	.318	.348	0	—	0	1	1	0	0.1
	NY-N	0	3	.000	16	2	0	0	1	31^2	24	4	8	23	9.1	3.98	85	.200	.250	0	.000	-0	-2	-2	-0	-0.3
	*StL-N	3	4	.429	23	1	1	1	4	47^2	43	2	10	30	10.0	2.83	116	.244	.285	2	.200	0	3	2	-0	0.3
	Yr	3	7	.300	39	3	1	1	5	79^1	67	6	18	53	9.6	3.29	101	.226	.270	2	.133	-0	1	0	-0	0.0
1968	Chi-N	3	2	.600	42	0	0	0	1	61^1	68	7	24	30	13.6	4.26	74	.289	.358	1	.200	0	-9	-7	-1	-0.8
Total	7	33	41	.446	285	49	7	3	15	711^2	753	67	238	434	12.7	4.24	85	.272	.333	15	.096	-6	-55	-51	0	-5.5
● **AL LaMACCHIA**	LaMacchia, Alfred Anthony b: 7/22/21, St.Louis, Mo. BR/TR, 5'10.5", 190 lbs. Deb: 9/27/43																									
1943	StL-A	0	1	.000	1	1	0	0	0	4	9	0	2	2	24.8	11.25	30	.450	.500	0	.000	-0	-4	-4	-0	-0.3
1945	StL-A	2	0	1.000	5	0	0	0	0	9	6	0	3	2	9.0	2.00	176	.207	.281	0	.000	-0	1	2	0	0.1
1946	StL-A	0	0	—	8	0	0	0	0	15	17	2	7	3	14.4	6.00	62	.279	.353	0	.000	-0	-4	-4	-0	-0.4
	Was-A	0	1	.000	2	0	0	0	0	2^2	6	1	2	0	27.0	16.88	20	.462	.533	0	—	0	-4	-4	-0	-0.4
	Yr	0	1	.000	10	0	0	0	0	17^2	23	3	9	3	16.3	7.64	48	.311	.386	0	.000	-0	-8	-8	-0	-0.8
Total	3	2	2	.500	16	1	0	0	0	30^2	38	3	14	7	15.3	6.46	55	.309	.380	0	.000	-1	-10	-10	-1	-1.0
● **HANK LAMANNA**	Lamanna, Frank b: 8/22/19, Watertown, Pa. d: 9/1/80, Syracuse, N.Y. BR/TR, 6'2.5", 195 lbs. Deb: 4/16/40																									
1940	Bos-N	1	0	1.000	5	1	1	0	0	13^1	13	1	8	3	14.2	4.73	79	.271	.375	1	.200	0	-1	-1	0	-0.1
1941	Bos-N	5	4	.556	35	4	0	0	1	72^2	77	5	56	23	16.6	5.33	67	.285	.410	9	.281	1	-14	-14	1	-1.2
1942	Bos-N	0	1	.000	5	0	0	0	0	6^2	5	1	3	2	10.8	5.40	62	.208	.296	0	.000	-0	-2	-2	-0	-0.2
Total	3	6	5	.545	45	5	1	0	1	92^2	95	7	67	28	15.8	5.24	68	.278	.398	10	.256	1	-17	-17	1	-1.5

YEAR TM/L	W	L	PCT	G	GS	CG	SH	SV	IP	H	HR	BB	SO	RAT	ERA	ERA+	OAV	OOB	BH	AVG	PB	PR	/A	PD	TPI

● **FRANK LAMANSKE**　Lamanske, Frank James "Lefty"　b: 9/30/06, Oglesby, Ill.　d: 8/4/71, Olney, Ill.　BL/TL, 5'11", 170 lbs.　Deb: 4/27/35

| 1935 Bro-N | 0 | 0 | — | 2 | 0 | 0 | 0 | 0 | 3² | 5 | 0 | 1 | 1 | 14.7 | 7.36 | 54 | .313 | .353 | 0 | .000 | -0 | -1 | -1 | 0 | -0.1 |

● **WAYNE LaMASTER**　LaMaster, Noble Wayne　b: 2/13/07, Speed, Ind.　d: 8/4/89, New Albany, Ind.　BL/TL, 5'8", 170 lbs.　Deb: 4/19/37

1937 Phi-N	15	19	.441	50	30	10	1	4	220¹	255	24	82	135	13.8	5.31	82	.290	.352	15	.190	-2	-34	-24	-4	-2.9
1938 Phi-N	4	7	.364	18	12	1	1	0	63²	80	8	31	35	16.1	7.77	50	.301	.380	9	.409	4	-28	-27	1	-2.1
Bro-N	0	1	.000	3	0	0	0	0	11¹	17	0	3	3	15.9	4.76	82	.340	.377	1	.167	-0	-1	-1	-0	-0.1
Yr	4	8	.333	21	12	1	1	0	75	97	8	34	38	15.7	7.32	53	.304	.371	10	.357	4	-29	-29	1	-2.2
Total 2	19	27	.413	71	42	11	2	4	295¹	352	32	116	173	14.4	5.82	72	.295	.360	25	.234	1	-64	-53	-4	-5.1

● **JOHN LAMB**　Lamb, John Andrew　b: 7/20/46, Sharon, Conn.　BR/TR, 6'3", 180 lbs.　Deb: 8/12/70

1970 Pit-N	0	1	.000	23	0	0	0	3	32¹	23	2	13	24	10.6	2.78	140	.209	.304	0	.000	-0	5	4	-1	0.3
1971 Pit-N	0	0	—	2	0	0	0	0	4¹	3	0	1	1	8.3	0.00	—	.188	.235	0	—	-0	2	2	0	0.2
1973 Pit-N	0	1	.000	22	0	0	0	2	29²	37	3	10	11	14.3	6.07	58	.308	.362	0	.000	-0	-8	-8	0	-0.9
Total 3	0	2	.000	47	0	0	0	5	66¹	63	5	24	36	12.1	4.07	91	.256	.327	0	.000	-1	-2	-3	-1	-0.4

● **RAY LAMB**　Lamb, Raymond Richard　b: 12/28/44, Glendale, Cal.　BR/TR, 6'1", 175 lbs.　Deb: 8/01/69

1969 LA-N	0	1	.000	10	0	0	0	1	15	12	2	7	11	11.4	1.80	185	.235	.328	0	.000	-0	3	3	0	0.3
1970 LA-N	6	1	.857	35	0	0	0	0	57	59	4	27	32	14.2	3.79	101	.277	.369	0	.000	-0	2	0	-1	-0.1
1971 Cle-A	6	12	.333	43	21	3	1	1	158¹	147	6	69	91	12.3	3.35	114	.247	.326	4	.093	-2	2	8	-2	0.4
1972 Cle-A	5	6	.455	34	9	0	0	0	107²	101	5	29	64	11.0	3.09	104	.248	.299	0	.000	-1	-0	1	-1	-0.1
1973 Cle-A	3	3	.500	32	1	0	0	2	86	98	7	42	60	14.9	4.60	85	.291	.373	0	—	0	-8	-7	-0	-0.8
Total 5	20	23	.465	154	31	3	1	4	424	417	29	174	258	12.7	3.54	104	.260	.335	4	.058	-4	-1	7	-4	-0.3

● **CLAYTON LAMBERT**　Lambert, Clayton Patrick　b: 3/26/17, Summitt, Ill.　d: 4/3/81, Ogden, Utah　BR/TR, 6'2", 185 lbs.　Deb: 4/22/46

1946 Cin-N	2	2	.500	23	4	2	0	1	52²	48	3	20	20	11.8	4.27	78	.251	.325	2	.154	-1	-5	-5	-1	-0.7
1947 Cin-N	0	0	—	3	0	0	0	0	5²	12	3	6	1	28.6	15.88	26	.444	.545	0	.000	-0	-7	-7	0	-0.6
Total 2	2	2	.500	26	4	2	0	1	58¹	60	6	26	21	13.4	5.40	63	.275	.355	2	.143	-1	-12	-13	-1	-1.3

● **GENE LAMBERT**　Lambert, Eugene Marion　b: 4/26/21, Crenshaw, Miss.　BR/TR, 5'11", 175 lbs.　Deb: 9/14/41

1941 Phi-N	0	1	.000	2	1	0	0	0	9	11	0	2	3	13.0	2.00	185	.297	.333	0	.000	-0	2	2	-0	0.1
1942 Phi-N	0	0	—	1	0	0	0	0	1	3	0	0	1	27.0	9.00	37	.500	.500	0	—	0	-1	-1	0	0.0
Total 2	0	1	.000	3	1	0	0	0	10	14	0	2	4	14.4	2.70	136	.326	.356	0	.000	-0	1	1	0	0.1

● **OTIS LAMBETH**　Lambeth, Otis Samuel　b: 5/13/1890, Berlin, Kan.　d: 6/5/76, Moran, Kan.　BR/TR, 6', 175 lbs.　Deb: 7/16/16

1916 Cle-A	4	3	.571	15	9	3	0	1	74	69	1	38	28	13.4	2.92	103	.256	.354	3	.111	-1	-1	1	-2	-0.3
1917 Cle-A	7	6	.538	26	10	2	0	2	97¹	97	2	30	27	12.8	3.14	90	.274	.349	6	.188	-0	-5	-3	-1	-0.5
1918 Cle-A	0	0	—	2	0	0	0	0	7	10	0	6	3	20.6	6.43	47	.370	.485	1	1.000	0	-3	-3	0	-0.2
Total 3	11	9	.550	43	19	5	0	3	178¹	176	3	74	58	13.3	3.18	92	.270	.357	10	.167	-1	-9	-5	-3	-1.0

● **FRED LAMLINE**　Lamline, Frederick Arthur "Dutch" (b: Frederick Arthur Lamlein)　b: 8/14/1887, Port Huron, Mich.　d: 9/20/70, Port Huron, Mich.　BR/TR, 5'11", 171 lbs.　Deb: 9/18/12

1912 Chi-A	0	0	—	1	0	0	0	0	2	7	0	2	1	40.5	31.50	10	.583	.643	0	—	0	-6	-6	0	-0.5
1915 StL-N	0	0	—	4	0	0	0	0	19	21	0	3	11	12.3	1.42	196	.300	.347	1	.125	-0	3	3	0	0.3
Total 2	0	0	—	5	0	0	0	0	21	28	0	5	12	15.0	4.29	64	.341	.393	1	.125	-0	-3	-3	0	-0.2

● **DENNIS LAMP**　Lamp, Dennis Patrick　b: 9/23/52, Los Angeles, Cal.　BR/TR, 6'3", 210 lbs.　Deb: 8/21/77

1977 Chi-N	0	2	.000	11	3	0	0	0	30	43	3	8	12	15.9	6.30	70	.344	.393	3	.375	1	-8	-6	0	-0.5
1978 Chi-N	7	15	.318	37	36	6	3	0	223²	221	16	56	73	11.3	3.30	122	.258	.307	15	.205	0	7	18	3	2.3
1979 Chi-N	11	10	.524	38	32	6	1	0	200¹	223	14	46	86	12.3	3.50	117	.287	.331	9	.155	-1	5	14	4	1.7
1980 Chi-N	10	14	.417	41	37	2	1	0	202²	259	16	82	83	15.2	5.20	75	.317	.380	6	.098	-3	-36	-29	2	-3.0
1981 Chi-A	7	6	.538	27	10	3	1	0	127	103	4	43	71	10.4	2.41	148	.222	.289	0	—	0	18	16	1	1.9
1982 Chi-A	11	8	.579	44	27	3	2	5	189²	206	9	59	78	12.9	3.99	101	.279	.337	0	—	0	2	1	2	0.3
1983 *Chi-A	7	7	.500	49	5	1	0	15	116¹	123	6	29	44	12.1	3.71	113	.275	.325	0	—	0	5	6	0	0.6
1984 Tor-A	8	8	.500	56	4	0	0	9	85	97	9	38	45	14.4	4.55	90	.285	.359	0	—	0	-5	-4	1	-0.3
1985 *Tor-A	11	0	1.000	53	1	0	0	2	105²	96	7	27	68	10.5	3.32	127	.247	.296	0	—	0	10	10	2	1.2
1986 Tor-A	2	6	.250	40	2	0	0	2	73	93	5	23	30	14.3	5.05	83	.309	.358	0	—	0	-7	-7	0	-0.7
1987 Oak-A	1	3	.250	36	5	0	0	0	56²	76	5	22	36	15.7	5.08	81	.326	.387	0	—	0	-4	-6	-0	-0.3
1988 Bos-A	7	6	.538	46	0	0	0	0	82²	92	3	19	49	12.3	3.48	118	.284	.328	0	—	0	4	6	1	0.7
1989 Bos-A	2	2	.667	42	0	0	0	0	112¹	96	4	27	61	9.9	2.32	176	.235	.283	0	—	0	19	22	2	2.4
1990 *Bos-A	3	5	.375	47	1	0	0	0	105²	114	10	30	49	12.5	4.68	87	.279	.333	0	—	0	-9	-7	-0	-0.7
1991 Bos-A	6	3	.667	51	0	0	0	0	92	100	8	31	57	13.1	4.70	92	.275	.337	0	—	0	-6	-4	-0	-0.4
1992 Pit-N	1	1	.500	21	0	0	0	0	28	33	3	9	15	14.1	5.14	66	.292	.355	0	.000	-0	-5	-5	0	-0.6
Total 16	96	96	.500	639	163	21	7	35	1830²	1975	122	549	857	12.6	3.93	103	.278	.333	33	.164	-3	-11	26	18	4.6

● **HENRY LAMPE**　Lampe, Henry Joseph　b: 9/19/1872, Boston, Mass.　d: 9/16/36, Dorchester, Mass.　BR/TL, 5'11.5", 175 lbs.　Deb: 5/14/1894

1894 Bos-N	0	1	.000	2	1	0	0	0	5¹	17	5	7	1	40.5	11.81	48	.525	.610	0	.000	-0	-4	-4	0	-0.3
1895 Phi-N	0	2	.000	7	3	2	0	0	44	68	3	33	18	20.9	7.57	63	.348	.444	2	.125	-1	-14	-14	-0	-1.1
Total 2	0	3	.000	9	4	2	0	0	49¹	85	8	40	19	23.0	8.03	61	.373	.469	2	.111	-1	-17	-17	0	-1.4

● **DICK LANAHAN**　Lanahan, Richard Anthony　b: 9/27/11, Washington, D.C.　d: 3/12/75, Rochester, Minn.　BL/TL, 6', 186 lbs.　Deb: 9/15/35

1935 Was-A	0	3	.000	3	3	0	0	0	20²	27	2	17	10	20.0	5.66	76	.314	.438	1	.167	-0	-3	-3	-0	-0.3
1937 Was-A	0	1	.000	6	2	0	0	0	11¹	16	2	13	2	23.8	12.71	35	.320	.469	0	.000	0	-10	-10	-0	-0.8
1940 Pit-N	6	8	.429	40	8	4	0	2	108	121	8	42	45	13.7	4.25	90	.279	.345	4	.118	-2	-5	-5	-0	-0.7
1941 Pit-N	0	1	.000	7	0	0	0	0	12	13	1	3	5	13.5	5.25	69	.283	.353	0	.000	-0	-2	-2	-0	-0.2
Total 4	6	13	.316	56	13	4	0	2	152	177	13	75	62	15.3	5.15	76	.288	.371	5	.119	-2	-20	-21	0	-2.0

● **LES LANCASTER**　Lancaster, Lester Wayne　b: 4/21/62, Dallas, Tex.　BR/TR, 6'2", 205 lbs.　Deb: 4/07/87

1987 Chi-N	8	3	.727	27	18	0	0	0	132¹	138	14	51	78	12.9	4.90	87	.268	.335	4	.082	-2	-12	-9	-1	-1.2
1988 Chi-N	4	6	.400	44	3	1	0	5	85²	89	4	34	36	13.0	3.78	95	.273	.343	1	.050	-1	-3	-2	-1	-0.3
1989 *Chi-N	4	2	.667	42	0	0	0	8	72²	60	9	15	56	9.3	1.36	276	.226	.267	2	.182	0	17	**19**	-1	2.1
1990 Chi-N	9	5	.643	55	6	1	1	6	109	121	11	40	65	13.4	4.62	88	.283	.346	1	.050	-1	-10	-7	-1	-0.6
1991 Chi-N	9	7	.563	64	11	1	0	3	156	150	13	49	102	11.7	3.52	110	.256	.317	5	.179	0	3	6	-1	0.6
1992 Det-A	3	4	.429	41	1	0	0	0	86²	101	11	51	35	16.1	6.33	63	.294	.389	0	—	0	-23	-23	-1	-2.3
Total 6	37	27	.578	273	39	3	1	22	642¹	659	55	240	372	12.7	4.16	95	.267	.335	13	.102	-4	-28	-14	-1	-1.7

● **GARY LANCE**　Lance, Gary Dean　b: 9/21/48, Greenville, S.C.　BB/TR, 6'3", 195 lbs.　Deb: 9/28/77

| 1977 KC-A | 0 | 1 | .000 | 1 | 0 | 0 | 0 | 0 | 2 | 2 | 0 | 2 | 0 | 18.0 | 4.50 | 90 | .286 | .444 | 0 | — | 0 | -0 | -0 | -0 | 0.0 |

● **DOC LANDIS**　Landis, Samuel H.　b: 8/16/1854, Philadelphia, Pa.　5'11", 172 lbs.　Deb: 5/02/1882

1882 Phi-a	1	1	.500	2	2	2	0	0	17	16	1	1	13	9.0	3.18	94	.232	.243	2	.167	-0	-1	-0	-0	-0.1
Bal-a	11	27	.289	42	39	35	0	0	341	409	7	46	62	12.0	3.33	83	.278	.300	29	.166	-6	-24	-22	-2	-2.5
Yr	12	28	.300	44	41	37	0	0	358	425	8	47	75	11.9	3.32	83	.276	.298	31	.166	-7	-25	-22	-3	-2.6

● **BILL LANDIS**　Landis, William Henry　b: 10/8/42, Hanford, Cal.　BL/TL, 6'2", 178 lbs.　Deb: 9/28/63

| 1963 KC-A | 0 | 0 | — | 1 | 0 | 0 | 0 | 0 | 1² | 0 | 0 | 1 | 3 | 5.4 | 0.00 | — | .000 | .167 | 0 | — | 0 | 1 | 1 | -0 | 0.1 |

YEAR	TM/L	W	L	PCT	G	GS	CG	SH	SV	IP	H	HR	BB	SO	RAT	ERA	ERA+	OAV	OOB	BH	AVG	PB	PR	/A	PD	TPI
1967	Bos-A	1	0	1.000	18	1	0	0	0	25^2	24	6	11	23	12.3	5.26	66	.253	.330	0	.000	-0	-6	-5	-1	-0.6
1968	Bos-A	3	3	.500	38	1	0	0	3	60	48	4	30	59	12.0	3.15	100	.223	.324	0	.000	-1	-1	0	-1	-0.2
1969	Bos-A	5	5	.500	45	5	0	0	1	82^1	82	7	49	50	14.6	5.25	72	.269	.375	0	.000	-0	-15	-13	0	-1.3
Total	4	9	8	.529	102	7	0	0	4	169^2	154	17	91	135	13.3	4.46	79	.248	.349	0	.000	-1	-21	-17	-2	-2.0

● **LARRY LANDRETH** Landreth, Larry Robert b: 3/11/55, Stratford, Ont., Can BR/TR, 6'1", 175 lbs. Deb: 9/16/76

YEAR	TM/L	W	L	PCT	G	GS	CG	SH	SV	IP	H	HR	BB	SO	RAT	ERA	ERA+	OAV	OOB	BH	AVG	PB	PR	/A	PD	TPI
1976	Mon-N	1	2	.333	3	3	0	0	0	11	13	1	10	7	18.8	4.09	91	.310	.442	0	.000	-0	-1	-0	-0	-0.1
1977	Mon-N	0	2	.000	4	1	0	0	0	9^1	16	0	8	5	23.1	9.64	39	.381	.480	0	.000	-0	-6	-6	-0	-0.6
Total	2	1	4	.200	7	4	0	0	0	20^1	29	1	18	12	20.8	6.64	57	.345	.461	0	.000	-1	-7	-6	-1	-0.7

● **JOE LANDRUM** Landrum, Joseph Butler b: 12/13/28, Columbia, S.C. BR/TR, 5'11", 180 lbs. Deb: 7/13/50 F

YEAR	TM/L	W	L	PCT	G	GS	CG	SH	SV	IP	H	HR	BB	SO	RAT	ERA	ERA+	OAV	OOB	BH	AVG	PB	PR	/A	PD	TPI
1950	Bro-N	0	0	—	7	0	0	0	1	6^2	12	2	1	5	18.9	8.10	51	.414	.452	0	—	0	-3	-3	0	-0.2
1952	Bro-N	1	3	.250	9	5	2	0	0	38	46	3	10	17	13.5	5.21	70	.301	.348	1	.125	-0	-6	-7	-0	-0.7
Total	2	1	3	.250	16	5	2	0	1	44^2	58	5	11	22	14.3	5.64	66	.319	.364	1	.125	-0	-9	-10	0	-0.9

● **BILL LANDRUM** Landrum, Thomas William b: 8/17/57, Columbia, S.C. BR/TR, 6'2", 200 lbs. Deb: 8/31/86 F

YEAR	TM/L	W	L	PCT	G	GS	CG	SH	SV	IP	H	HR	BB	SO	RAT	ERA	ERA+	OAV	OOB	BH	AVG	PB	PR	/A	PD	TPI
1986	Cin-N	0	0	—	10	0	0	0	0	13^1	23	0	4	14	18.2	6.75	57	.390	.429	0	.000	-0	-4	-4	-0	-0.5
1987	Cin-N	3	2	.600	44	2	0	0	2	65	68	3	34	42	14.1	4.71	90	.292	.382	1	.200	0	-5	-3	1	-0.3
1988	Chi-N	1	0	1.000	7	0	0	0	0	12^1	19	1	3	6	16.1	5.84	62	.365	.400	0	.000	-0	-3	-3	-0	-0.4
1989	Pit-N	2	3	.400	56	0	0	0	26	81	60	2	28	51	9.8	1.67	201	.205	.275	0	.000	-0	16	15	-0	1.6
1990	*Pit-N	7	3	.700	54	0	0	0	13	71^2	69	4	21	39	11.3	2.13	169	.262	.317	1	.111	0	13	12	-0	1.2
1991	*Pit-N	4	4	.500	61	0	0	0	17	76^1	76	4	19	45	11.2	3.18	112	.252	.297	0	.000	-0	4	3	-1	0.2
1992	Mon-N	1	1	.500	18	0	0	0	0	20	27	3	9	7	17.1	7.20	48	.325	.404	0	—	0	-8	-8	-0	-0.9
Total	7	18	13	.581	250	2	0	0	58	339^2	342	17	118	204	12.2	3.37	109	.267	.329	2	.080	-1	13	11	-1	0.9

● **JERRY LANE** Lane, Jerald Hal b: 2/7/26, Ashland, N.Y. d: 7/24/88, Chattanooga, Tenn BR/TR, 6'0.5", 205 lbs. Deb: 7/07/53

YEAR	TM/L	W	L	PCT	G	GS	CG	SH	SV	IP	H	HR	BB	SO	RAT	ERA	ERA+	OAV	OOB	BH	AVG	PB	PR	/A	PD	TPI
1953	Was-A	1	4	.200	20	2	0	0	0	56^2	64	3	16	26	12.9	4.92	79	.288	.339	1	.111	0	-6	-6	-0	-0.7
1954	Cin-N	1	0	1.000	3	0	0	0	0	10^2	9	0	3	2	10.1	1.69	248	.237	.293	0	.000	-0	3	3	-1	0.2
1955	Cin-N	0	2	.000	8	0	0	0	1	11	11	2	6	5	13.9	4.91	86	.289	.386	0	—	0	-1	-1	0	-0.1
Total	3	2	6	.250	31	2	0	0	1	78^1	84	5	25	33	12.6	4.48	89	.282	.340	1	.077	0	-4	-4	-1	-0.6

● **SAM LANFORD** Lanford, Lewis Grover b: 1/8/1886, Woodruff, S.C. d: 9/14/70, Woodruff, S.C. BR/TR, 5'9", 155 lbs. Deb: 8/19/07

YEAR	TM/L	W	L	PCT	G	GS	CG	SH	SV	IP	H	HR	BB	SO	RAT	ERA	ERA+	OAV	OOB	BH	AVG	PB	PR	/A	PD	TPI
1907	Was-A	0	1	.000	2	1	0	0	0	7	10	0	5	2	21.9	5.14	47	.337	.463	1	.333	0	-2	-2	-0	-0.2

● **WALT LANFRANCONI** Lanfranconi, Walter Oswald b: 11/9/16, Barre, Vt. d: 8/18/86, Barre, Vt. BR/TR, 5'7.5", 155 lbs. Deb: 9/12/41

YEAR	TM/L	W	L	PCT	G	GS	CG	SH	SV	IP	H	HR	BB	SO	RAT	ERA	ERA+	OAV	OOB	BH	AVG	PB	PR	/A	PD	TPI
1941	Chi-N	0	1	.000	2	1	0	0	0	6	7	0	2	1	13.5	3.00	117	.280	.333	0	.000	-0	0	0	-0	0.0
1947	Bos-N	4	4	.500	36	4	1	0	1	64	65	2	27	18	12.9	2.95	132	.272	.346	0	.000	-1	**8**	**7**	1	0.7
Total	2	4	5	.444	38	5	1	0	1	70	72	2	29	19	13.0	2.96	131	.273	.345	0	.000	-1	8	7	1	0.7

● **MARTY LANG** Lang, Martin John b: 9/27/05, Hooper, Neb. d: 1/13/68, Lakewood, Colo. BR/TL, 5'11", 160 lbs. Deb: 7/04/30

YEAR	TM/L	W	L	PCT	G	GS	CG	SH	SV	IP	H	HR	BB	SO	RAT	ERA	ERA+	OAV	OOB	BH	AVG	PB	PR	/A	PD	TPI
1930	Pit-N	0	0	—	2	0	0	0	0	1^2	9	2	3	2	64.8	54.00	9	.692	.750	0	—	0	-9	-9	-0	-0.7

● **CHIP LANG** Lang, Robert David b: 8/21/52, Pittsburgh, Pa. BR/TR, 6'4", 205 lbs. Deb: 9/08/75

YEAR	TM/L	W	L	PCT	G	GS	CG	SH	SV	IP	H	HR	BB	SO	RAT	ERA	ERA+	OAV	OOB	BH	AVG	PB	PR	/A	PD	TPI
1975	Mon-N	0	0	—	1	1	0	0	0	1^2	2	0	3	2	27.0	10.80	35	.333	.556	0	—	0	-1	-1	-0	-0.1
1976	Mon-N	1	3	.250	29	2	0	0	0	62^1	56	3	34	30	13.4	4.19	89	.242	.347	1	.167	-0	-5	-3	0	-0.3
Total	2	1	3	.250	30	3	0	0	0	64	58	3	37	32	13.8	4.36	85	.245	.354	1	.167	-0	-6	-5	0	-0.4

● **FRANK LANGE** Lange, Frank Herman "Seagan" b: 10/28/1883, Columbia, Wis. d: 12/26/45, Madison, Wis. BR/TR, 5'11", 180 lbs. Deb: 5/16/10

YEAR	TM/L	W	L	PCT	G	GS	CG	SH	SV	IP	H	HR	BB	SO	RAT	ERA	ERA+	OAV	OOB	BH	AVG	PB	PR	/A	PD	TPI
1910	Chi-A	9	4	.692	23	15	6	1	0	130^2	93	2	54	98	10.7	1.65	145	.204	.301	13	.255	3	13	11	-2	1.3
1911	Chi-A	8	8	.500	29	22	8	1	0	161^2	151	3	77	104	12.9	3.23	100	.251	.339	22	.289	8	2	-0	-1	0.7
1912	Chi-A	10	10	.500	31	20	11	2	3	165^1	165	4	68	96	12.9	3.27	98	.270	.347	14	.215	2	1	-1	-1	0.0
1913	Chi-A	1	3	.250	12	3	0	0	0	40^2	46	0	20	20	14.8	4.87	60	.295	.379	3	.167	1	-9	-9	1	-0.7
Total	4	28	25	.528	95	60	25	4	3	498^1	455	9	219	318	12.5	2.96	100	.249	.335	52	.248	13	7	1	-2	1.3

● **ERV LANGE** Lange, Erwin Henry b: 8/12/1887, Forest Park, Ill. d: 4/24/71, Maywood, Ill. BR/TR, 5'10", 170 lbs. Deb: 4/19/14

YEAR	TM/L	W	L	PCT	G	GS	CG	SH	SV	IP	H	HR	BB	SO	RAT	ERA	ERA+	OAV	OOB	BH	AVG	PB	PR	/A	PD	TPI
1914	Chi-F	12	11	.522	36	22	10	2	2	190	162	3	55	87	10.4	2.23	133	.224	.282	9	.176	2	21	15	-3	1.5

● **DICK LANGE** Lange, Richard Otto b: 9/1/48, Harbor Beach, Mich. BR/TR, 5'10", 185 lbs. Deb: 9/09/72

YEAR	TM/L	W	L	PCT	G	GS	CG	SH	SV	IP	H	HR	BB	SO	RAT	ERA	ERA+	OAV	OOB	BH	AVG	PB	PR	/A	PD	TPI
1972	Cal-A	0	0	—	2	1	0	0	0	7^2	7	0	2	8	10.6	4.70	62	.233	.281	0	.000	-0	-1	-2	0	-0.2
1973	Cal-A	2	1	.667	17	4	1	0	0	52^2	61	9	21	27	14.2	4.44	80	.292	.359	0	—	0	-4	-5	0	-0.5
1974	Cal-A	3	8	.273	21	18	1	0	0	113^2	111	10	47	57	12.8	3.80	90	.248	.325	0	—	0	-2	-5	-1	-0.5
1975	Cal-A	4	6	.400	30	8	1	0	1	102	119	12	53	45	15.3	5.21	68	.292	.374	0	—	0	-16	-19	-0	-1.9
Total	4	9	15	.375	70	31	3	0	1	276	298	31	123	137	13.9	4.47	78	.272	.349	0	.000	-0	-24	-30	-1	-3.1

● **RICK LANGFORD** Langford, James Rick b: 3/20/52, Farmville, Va. BR/TR, 6', 180 lbs. Deb: 6/13/76

YEAR	TM/L	W	L	PCT	G	GS	CG	SH	SV	IP	H	HR	BB	SO	RAT	ERA	ERA+	OAV	OOB	BH	AVG	PB	PR	/A	PD	TPI
1976	Pit-N	0	1	.000	12	1	0	0	0	23	27	2	14	17	16.0	6.26	56	.307	.402	1	.200	0	-7	-7	0	-0.7
1977	Oak-A	8	19	.296	37	31	6	1	0	208^1	223	18	73	141	12.9	4.02	100	.273	.334	0	—	0	1	0	1	0.1
1978	Oak-A	7	13	.350	37	24	4	2	0	175^2	169	15	56	92	11.7	3.43	106	.253	.314	0	—	0	6	4	1	0.6
1979	Oak-A	12	16	.429	34	29	14	1	0	218^2	233	22	57	101	12.1	4.28	94	.273	.322	0	—	0	-2	-6	2	0.0
1980	Oak-A	19	12	.613	35	33	**28**	2	0	**290**	276	29	64	102	10.6	3.26	116	.255	.297	0	—	0	25	16	1	2.2
1981	*Oak-A	12	10	.545	24	24	**18**	2	0	195^1	190	14	58	84	11.6	2.99	116	.255	.311	0	—	0	14	10	-2	1.0
1982	Oak-A	11	16	.407	32	31	15	2	0	237^1	265	33	49	79	12.0	4.21	93	.281	.318	0	.000	0	-4	-8	1	-0.7
1983	Oak-A	0	4	.000	7	7	0	0	0	20	43	4	10	2	24.7	12.15	32	.448	.509	0	—	0	-18	-18	-0	-1.6
1984	Oak-A	0	0	—	3	2	0	0	0	8^2	15	2	2	2	17.7	8.31	45	.366	.395	0	—	0	-4	-4	-0	-0.4
1985	Oak-A	3	5	.375	23	3	0	0	0	59	60	8	15	21	11.4	3.51	110	.261	.306	0	—	0	4	2	-0	0.2
1986	Oak-A	1	10	.091	16	11	0	0	0	55	69	13	18	30	14.4	7.36	53	.300	.353	0	—	0	-19	-21	-1	-2.1
Total	11	73	106	.408	260	196	85	10	0	1491	1570	160	416	671	12.1	4.01	95	.271	.322	1	.167	0	-3	-32	3	-1.4

● **MARK LANGSTON** Langston, Mark Edward b: 8/20/60, San Diego, Cal. BR/TL, 6'2", 190 lbs. Deb: 4/07/84

YEAR	TM/L	W	L	PCT	G	GS	CG	SH	SV	IP	H	HR	BB	SO	RAT	ERA	ERA+	OAV	OOB	BH	AVG	PB	PR	/A	PD	TPI
1984	Sea-A	17	10	.630	35	33	5	2	0	225	188	16	118	**204**	12.6	3.40	117	.230	.332	0	—	0	15	15	1	1.6
1985	Sea-A	7	14	.333	24	24	2	0	0	126^2	122	22	91	72	15.3	5.47	77	.255	.376	0	—	0	-19	-18	2	-1.5
1986	Sea-A	12	14	.462	37	36	9	0	0	239^1	234	30	123	**245**	13.6	4.85	87	.255	.346	0	—	0	-18	-16	-1	-1.6
1987	Sea-A★	19	13	.594	35	35	14	3	0	272	242	30	114	**262**	11.9	3.84	123	.238	.318	0	—	0	19	27	1	2.6
1988	Sea-A	15	11	.577	35	35	9	3	0	261^1	222	32	110	235	11.5	3.34	125	.233	.314	0	—	0	18	24	3	2.8
1989	Sea-A	4	5	.444	10	10	2	1	0	73^1	60	3	19	60	10.2	3.56	113	.221	.282	0	—	0	3	4	-0	0.3
	Mon-N	12	9	.571	24	24	6	4	0	176^2	138	13	93	175	11.8	2.39	147	.218	.318	11	.172	0	22	22	-0	2.5
1990	Cal-A	10	17	.370	33	33	5	1	0	223	215	13	104	195	13.1	4.40	87	.259	.345	0	—	0	-12	-14	2	-1.2
1991	Cal-A☆	19	8	.704	34	34	7	0	0	246^1	190	30	96	183	10.5	3.00	137	.215	.293	0	—	0	30	30	1	3.2
1992	Cal-A★	13	14	.481	32	32	9	2	0	229	206	14	74	174	11.2	3.66	107	.242	.307	0	.000	0	7	6	2	0.9
Total	9	128	115	.527	299	296	68	16	0	2072^2	1817	203	942	1805	12.1	3.75	109	.237	.324	11	.167	0	64	79	11	9.6

● **MAX LANIER** Lanier, Hubert Max b: 8/18/15, Denton, N.C. BR/TL, 5'10", 187 lbs. Deb: 4/20/38 F

YEAR	TM/L	W	L	PCT	G	GS	CG	SH	SV	IP	H	HR	BB	SO	RAT	ERA	ERA+	OAV	OOB	BH	AVG	PB	PR	/A	PD	TPI
1938	StL-N	0	3	.000	18	3	1	0	0	45	57	1	28	14	17.4	4.20	94	.317	.414	1	.100	-1	-2	-1	-0	-0.2
1939	StL-N	2	1	.667	7	6	2	0	0	37^2	29	0	13	14	10.3	2.39	172	.220	.295	4	.286	1	6	7	-0	0.8
1940	StL-N	9	6	.600	35	11	4	2	3	105	113	1	38	49	13.0	3.34	119	.276	.339	6	.200	-0	6	8	1	0.8
1941	StL-N	10	8	.556	35	18	8	2	3	153	126	4	59	93	10.9	2.82	133	.225	.300	10	.192	-1	14	16	2	1.8

YEAR TM/L	W	L	PCT	G	GS	CG	SH	SV	IP	H	HR	BB	SO	RAT	ERA	ERA+	OAV	OOB	BH	AVG	PB	PR	/A	PD	TPI
1942 *StL-N	13	8	.619	34	20	8	2	2	161	137	4	60	93	11.1	2.96	116	.234	.308	12	.255	3	6	8	1	1.2
1943 *StL-N☆	15	7	.682	32	25	14	2	3	213^1	195	3	75	123	11.5	**1.90**	**177**	.246	.312	12	.164	-2	**35**	**35**	0	3.7
1944 *StL-N†	17	12	.586	33	30	16	5	0	224^1	192	5	71	141	10.7	2.65	133	.234	.297	14	.182	-0	24	22	-0	2.2
1945 StL-N	2	2	.500	4	3	3	0	0	26	22	0	8	16	10.4	1.73	216	.222	.280	2	.182	-0	6	6	-0	0.6
1946 StL-N	6	0	1.000	6	6	6	2	0	56	45	1	19	36	10.4	1.93	179	.228	.300	5	.200	-0	9	9	-0	1.1
1949 StL-N	5	4	.556	15	15	4	1	0	92	92	5	35	37	12.4	3.82	109	.261	.328	2	.074	-2	2	4	-1	0.1
1950 StL-N	11	9	.550	27	27	10	2	0	181^1	173	13	68	89	12.0	3.13	137	.249	.317	11	.162	-1	20	24	0	2.3
1951 StL-N	11	9	.550	31	23	9	2	1	160	149	14	50	59	11.2	3.26	122	.248	.306	8	.151	-2	12	12	0	1.1
1952 NY-N	7	12	.368	37	16	6	1	5	137	124	11	65	47	12.6	3.94	94	.244	.333	11	.268	3	-3	-4	3	0.2
1953 NY-N	0	0	—	3	0	0	0	0	5^1	8	1	3	2	18.6	6.75	64	.381	.458	0	.000	-0	-1	-1	0	-0.1
StL-A	0	1	.000	10	1	0	0	0	22^1	28	2	19	8	18.9	7.25	58	.322	.443	1	.167	-0	-8	-8	-0	-0.8
Total 14	108	82	.568	327	204	91	21	17	1619^1	1490	65	611	821	11.8	3.01	125	.247	.318	99	.185	-3	127	136	5	14.8

● JOHNNY LANNING Lanning, John Young "Tobacco Chewin' Johnny" b: 9/6/10, Asheville, N.C. d: 11/8/89, Asheville, N.C. BR/TR, 6'1", 185 lbs. Deb: 4/17/36 F

YEAR TM/L	W	L	PCT	G	GS	CG	SH	SV	IP	H	HR	BB	SO	RAT	ERA	ERA+	OAV	OOB	BH	AVG	PB	PR	/A	PD	TPI
1936 Bos-N	7	11	.389	28	20	3	1	0	153	154	9	55	33	12.3	3.65	105	.263	.326	7	.135	-2	6	3	-2	0.0
1937 Bos-N	5	7	.417	32	11	4	1	2	116^2	107	10	40	37	11.4	3.93	91	.236	.300	4	.121	-1	-0	-5	-0	-0.6
1938 Bos-N	8	7	.533	32	18	4	1	0	138	146	5	52	39	13.0	3.72	92	.267	.332	9	.188	-1	1	-4	-1	-0.6
1939 Bos-N	5	6	.455	37	6	3	0	4	129	120	6	53	45	12.2	3.42	108	.252	.329	6	.143	-1	7	4	0	0.3
1940 Pit-N	8	4	.667	38	7	2	0	2	115^2	119	8	39	42	12.3	4.05	94	.268	.327	7	.200	1	-3	-3	-0	-0.2
1941 Pit-N	11	11	.500	34	23	9	0	1	175^2	175	6	47	41	11.4	3.13	116	.256	.304	6	.107	-2	10	9	1	1.0
1942 Pit-N	6	8	.429	34	8	2	1	1	119^1	125	7	26	31	11.5	3.32	102	.274	.314	4	.138	-0	-0	1	-0	0.0
1943 Pit-N	4	1	.800	12	2	0	0	2	27	23	0	9	11	10.7	2.33	149	.223	.286	1	.167	-0	3	3	-1	0.3
1945 Pit-N	0	0	—	1	0	0	0	0	2	8	1	0	0	36.0	36.00	11	.571	.571	0	—	0	-7	-7	0	-0.5
1946 Pit-N	4	5	.444	27	9	3	0	1	91	97	3	31	16	12.8	3.07	115	.269	.329	3	.143	-0	3	5	1	0.5
1947 Bos-N	0	0	—	3	0	0	0	0	3^2	4	0	6	0	24.5	9.82	40	.400	.625	0	—	0	-2	-2	0	-0.2
Total 11	58	60	.492	278	104	30	4	13	1071	1078	55	358	295	12.1	3.58	101	.261	.321	47	.146	-6	19	5	-1	-0.0

● RED LANNING Lanning, Lester Alfred b: 5/13/1895, Harvard, Ill. d: 6/13/62, Bristol, Conn. BL/TL, 5'9", 165 lbs. Deb: 6/20/16 ♦

YEAR TM/L	W	L	PCT	G	GS	CG	SH	SV	IP	H	HR	BB	SO	RAT	ERA	ERA+	OAV	OOB	BH	AVG	PB	PR	/A	PD	TPI
1916 Phi-A	0	3	.000	6	3	1	0	0	24^1	38	1	17	9	21.1	8.14	35	.362	.460	6	.182	1	-14	-14	0	-1.3

● TOM LANNING Lanning, Thomas Newton b: 4/22/07, Asheville, N.C. d: 11/4/67, Marietta, Ga. BL/TL, 6'1", 165 lbs. Deb: 9/14/38 F

YEAR TM/L	W	L	PCT	G	GS	CG	SH	SV	IP	H	HR	BB	SO	RAT	ERA	ERA+	OAV	OOB	BH	AVG	PB	PR	/A	PD	TPI
1938 Phi-N	0	1	.000	3	1	0	0	0	7	9	0	2	2	14.1	6.43	60	.300	.344	1	1.000	0	-2	-2	-0	-0.2

● GENE LANSING Lansing, Eugene Hewitt "Jigger" b: 1/11/1898, Albany, N.Y. d: 1/18/45, Rensselaer, N.Y. BR/TR, 6'1", 185 lbs. Deb: 4/27/22

YEAR TM/L	W	L	PCT	G	GS	CG	SH	SV	IP	H	HR	BB	SO	RAT	ERA	ERA+	OAV	OOB	BH	AVG	PB	PR	/A	PD	TPI
1922 Bos-N	0	1	.000	15	1	0	0	0	40^2	46	1	22	14	15.0	5.98	67	.301	.389	0	.000	-1	-8	-9	-0	-0.9

● PAUL LaPALME LaPalme, Paul Edmore "Lefty" b: 12/14/23, Springfield, Mass. BL/TL, 5'10", 184 lbs. Deb: 5/28/51

YEAR TM/L	W	L	PCT	G	GS	CG	SH	SV	IP	H	HR	BB	SO	RAT	ERA	ERA+	OAV	OOB	BH	AVG	PB	PR	/A	PD	TPI
1951 Pit-N	1	5	.167	22	8	1	1	0	54^1	79	6	31	24	18.4	6.29	67	.333	.413	1	.100	-0	-14	-12	-1	-1.3
1952 Pit-N	1	2	.333	31	2	0	0	0	59^2	56	6	37	25	14.2	3.92	102	.253	.363	1	.100	-0	-1	0	1	0.1
1953 Pit-N	8	16	.333	35	24	7	1	2	176^1	191	20	64	86	13.0	4.59	97	.272	.333	5	.085	-5	-6	-2	-2	-0.9
1954 Pit-N	4	10	.286	33	15	2	0	0	120^2	147	15	54	57	15.0	5.52	76	.302	.372	5	.143	-0	-19	-18	-0	-1.8
1955 StL-N	4	3	.571	56	0	0	0	3	91^2	76	10	34	39	10.9	2.75	148	.228	.301	4	.211	0	13	13	1	1.5
1956 StL-N	0	0	—	1	0	0	0	0	0^2	4	0	2	0	81.0	81.00	5	.667	.750	0	—	0	-6	-6	-0	-0.5
Cin-N	2	4	.333	11	2	0	0	0	27	26	7	4	4	10.0	4.67	85	.257	.286	2	.500	1	-3	-2	-0	-0.1
Yr	2	4	.333	12	2	0	0	0	27^2	30	7	6	4	11.7	6.51	61	.280	.319	2	.500	1	-8	-8	-0	-0.6
Chi-A	3	1	.750	29	0	0	0	2	45^2	31	2	27	23	11.4	2.36	173	.195	.312	0	.000	-1	9	9	1	0.8
1957 Chi-A	1	4	.200	35	0	0	0	7	40^1	35	5	19	19	12.3	3.35	112	.235	.325	2	.500	1	2	2	1	0.4
Total 7	24	45	.348	253	51	10	2	14	616^1	645	71	272	277	13.4	4.42	95	.269	.345	20	.136	-4	-25	-16	-0	-1.8

● ANDY LAPIHUSKA Lapihuska, Andrew "Apples" b: 11/1/22, Delmont, N.J. BL/TR, 5'10.5", 175 lbs. Deb: 9/12/42

YEAR TM/L	W	L	PCT	G	GS	CG	SH	SV	IP	H	HR	BB	SO	RAT	ERA	ERA+	OAV	OOB	BH	AVG	PB	PR	/A	PD	TPI
1942 Phi-N	0	2	.000	3	2	0	0	0	20^2	17	0	13	8	13.9	5.23	63	.221	.348	2	.286	0	-4	-4	0	-0.4
1943 Phi-N	0	0	—	1	0	0	0	0	2^1	5	1	3	0	30.9	23.14	15	.417	.533	0	.000	-0	-5	-5	-0	-0.5
Total 2	0	2	.000	4	2	0	0	0	23	22	1	16	8	15.7	7.04	47	.247	.374	2	.222	0	-10	-10	0	-0.9

● DAVE LaPOINT LaPoint, David Jeffrey b: 7/29/59, Glens Falls, N.Y. BL/TL, 6'3", 215 lbs. Deb: 9/10/80

YEAR TM/L	W	L	PCT	G	GS	CG	SH	SV	IP	H	HR	BB	SO	RAT	ERA	ERA+	OAV	OOB	BH	AVG	PB	PR	/A	PD	TPI
1980 Mil-A	1	0	1.000	5	3	0	0	1	15	17	2	13	5	18.0	6.00	64	.293	.423	0	—	0	-3	-4	-1	-0.2
1981 StL-N	1	0	1.000	3	2	0	0	0	10^2	12	1	2	4	12.7	4.22	84	.293	.341	0	.000	-1	-1	-1	0	-0.1
1982 *StL-N	9	3	.750	42	21	0	0	0	152^2	170	8	52	81	13.3	3.42	106	.290	.350	2	.053	-3	3	3	-3	-0.3
1983 StL-N	12	9	.571	37	29	1	0	0	191^1	191	12	84	113	13.1	3.95	92	.267	.347	9	.153	1	-7	-7	-1	-0.7
1984 StL-N	12	10	.545	33	33	2	1	0	193	205	9	77	130	13.2	3.96	88	.278	.347	4	.068	-3	-8	-11	-2	-1.6
1985 SF-N	7	17	.292	31	31	2	1	0	206^2	215	18	74	122	12.6	3.57	96	.269	.331	10	.167	2	0	-3	-2	-0.3
1986 Det-A	3	6	.333	16	8	0	0	0	67^2	85	11	32	36	15.6	5.72	72	.307	.379	0	—	0	-12	-12	-1	-1.2
SD-N	1	4	.200	24	4	0	0	0	61^1	67	8	24	41	13.5	4.26	86	.276	.343	0	.000	-1	-4	-4	-0	-0.5
1987 StL-N	1	1	.500	6	2	0	0	0	16	26	4	5	8	17.4	6.75	62	.351	.392	0	.000	-0	-5	-5	0	-0.5
Chi-A	6	3	.667	14	12	2	1	0	82^2	69	7	31	43	11.0	2.94	156	.224	.297	0	—	0	14	15	2	1.5
1988 Chi-A	10	11	.476	25	25	1	1	0	161^1	151	10	47	79	11.2	3.40	117	.245	.300	0	—	0	10	10	-2	0.9
Pit-N	4	2	.667	8	8	1	0	0	52	54	4	10	19	11.1	2.77	123	.271	.306	1	.063	-1	4	4	0	0.3
1989 NY-A	6	9	.400	20	20	0	0	0	113^2	146	12	45	51	15.3	5.62	69	.310	.373	0	—	0	-22	-22	-2	-2.2
1990 NY-A	7	10	.412	28	27	2	0	0	157^2	180	11	57	67	13.6	4.11	97	.292	.353	0	—	0	-4	-2	-0	-0.3
1991 Phi-N	0	1	.000	2	2	0	0	0	5	10	0	6	3	30.6	16.20	23	.435	.567	0	.000	-0	-7	-7	0	-0.6
Total 12	80	86	.482	294	227	11	4	1	1486^2	1598	117	559	802	13.2	4.02	93	.277	.343	26	.104	-6	-40	-46	-12	-5.8

● TERRY LARKIN Larkin, Frank S. d: 9/16/1894, Brooklyn, N.Y. BR/TR, Deb: 5/20/1876 ♦

YEAR TM/L	W	L	PCT	G	GS	CG	SH	SV	IP	H	HR	BB	SO	RAT	ERA	ERA+	OAV	OOB	BH	AVG	PB	PR	/A	PD	TPI
1876 NY-N	0	1	.000	1	1	1	0	0	9	9	0	0	0	9.0	3.00	71	.231	.231	0	.000	-1	-1	-1	-0	-0.1
1877 Har-N	29	25	.537	56	56	55	4	0	501	510	2	53	96	10.1	2.14	114	**.245**	.264	52	.228	6	37	16	-1	1.8
1878 Chi-N	29	26	.527	56	56	56	1	0	506	511	4	31	163	9.6	2.24	108	.246	.257	65	.288	14	4	10	-4	1.9
1879 Chi-N	31	23	.574	58	58	57	4	0	513^1	514	5	30	142	9.5	2.44	105	.240	**.250**	50	.219	2	3	7	-7	0.1
1880 Tro-N	0	5	.000	5	5	3	0	0	38	83	1	10	5	22.0	8.76	29	.421	.449	3	.150	-0	-27	-26	0	-2.1
Total 5	89	80	.527	176	176	172	9	0	1567^1	1627	12	124	406	10.1	2.43	102	.249	.263	215	.235	20	17	9	-12	1.6

● PAT LARKIN Larkin, Patrick Clibborn b: 6/14/60, Arcadia, Cal. BL/TL, 6', 180 lbs. Deb: 7/16/83

YEAR TM/L	W	L	PCT	G	GS	CG	SH	SV	IP	H	HR	BB	SO	RAT	ERA	ERA+	OAV	OOB	BH	AVG	PB	PR	/A	PD	TPI
1983 SF-N	0	0	—	5	0	0	0	0	10^1	13	1	3	6	15.7	4.35	81	.317	.391	0	.000	-0	-1	-1	-0	-0.1

● STEVE LARKIN Larkin, Stephen Patrick b: 12/9/10, Cincinnati, Ohio d: 5/2/69, Norristown, Pa. BR/TR, 6'1", 195 lbs. Deb: 5/06/34

YEAR TM/L	W	L	PCT	G	GS	CG	SH	SV	IP	H	HR	BB	SO	RAT	ERA	ERA+	OAV	OOB	BH	AVG	PB	PR	/A	PD	TPI
1934 Det-A	0	0	—	2	1	0	0	0	6	8	0	5	8	19.5	1.50	293	.296	.406	1	.333	0	2	2	0	0.3

● DAVE LaROCHE LaRoche, David Eugene b: 5/14/48, Colorado Springs, Colo. BL/TL, 6'2", 200 lbs. Deb: 5/11/70 C

YEAR TM/L	W	L	PCT	G	GS	CG	SH	SV	IP	H	HR	BB	SO	RAT	ERA	ERA+	OAV	OOB	BH	AVG	PB	PR	/A	PD	TPI
1970 Cal-A	4	1	.800	38	0	0	0	4	49^2	41	6	21	44	12.0	3.44	105	.224	.317	2	.250	1	1	1	0	0.2
1971 Cal-A	5	1	.833	56	0	0	0	9	72	55	3	27	63	10.4	2.50	129	.212	.289	1	.091	-0	8	6	-1	0.5
1972 Min-A	5	7	.417	62	0	0	0	10	95^1	72	9	39	79	11.0	2.83	113	.209	.300	1	.091	0	2	4	0	0.5
1973 Chi-N	4	1	.800	45	0	0	0	4	54^1	55	7	29	34	14.1	5.80	68	.274	.368	2	.500	1	-13	-11	1	-0.9
1974 Chi-N	5	6	.455	49	4	0	0	5	92	103	9	47	49	15.0	4.79	80	.286	.373	9	.333	3	-12	-10	-0	-0.8
1975 Cle-A	5	3	.625	61	0	0	0	17	82^1	61	5	57	94	13.1	2.19	173	.210	.344	0	—	0	15	15	1	1.6
1976 Cle-A☆	1	4	.200	61	0	0	0	21	96^1	57	2	49	104	10.0	2.24	156	.175	.285	0	—	0	14	13	-1	1.4
1977 Cle-A	2	2	.500	13	0	0	0	4	18^2	15	3	7	18	10.6	5.30	74	.234	.310	0	—	0	-3	-3	-0	-0.3

YEAR	TM/L	W	L	PCT	G	GS	CG	SH	SV	IP	H	HR	BB	SO	RAT	ERA	ERA+	OAV	OOB	BH	AVG	PB	PR	/A	PD	TPI
	Cal-A	6	5	.545	46	0	0	0	13	81^1	64	8	37	61	11.4	3.10	126	.218	.310	0	—	0	9	7	-0	0.8
	Yr	8	7	.533	59	0	0	0	17	100	79	11	44	79	11.3	3.51	112	.220	.309	0	—	0	6	5	-0	0.5
1978	Cal-A	10	9	.526	59	0	0	0	25	95^2	73	7	48	70	11.6	2.82	128	.215	.316	0	—	0	10	8	-0	1.1
1979	*Cal-A	7	11	.389	53	1	0	0	10	85^2	107	13	32	59	14.8	5.57	73	.314	.376	0	—	0	-13	-14	1	-1.0
1980	Cal-A	3	5	.375	52	9	1	0	4	128	122	14	39	89	11.5	4.08	96	.256	.317	0	—	0	-1	-2	-1	-0.3
1981	*NY-A	4	1	.800	26	1	0	0	0	47	38	3	16	24	10.5	2.49	144	.229	.301	0	—	0	6	6	-1	0.6
1982	NY-A	4	2	.667	25	0	0	0	0	50	54	4	11	31	11.9	3.42	117	.273	.314	0	—	0	4	3	-1	0.3
1983	NY-A	0	0	—	1	0	0	0	0	1	2	1	0	0	18.0	18.00	22	.400	.400	0	—	0	-2	-2	0	0.0
Total	14	65	58	.528	647	15	1	0	126	1049^1	919	94	459	819	12.1	3.53	105	.239	.325	15	.246	5	26	22	-1	3.7

● JOHN LaROSE LaRose, Henry John b: 10/25/51, Pawtucket, R.I. BL/TL, 6'1", 185 lbs. Deb: 9/20/78

YEAR	TM/L	W	L	PCT	G	GS	CG	SH	SV	IP	H	HR	BB	SO	RAT	ERA	ERA+	OAV	OOB	BH	AVG	PB	PR	/A	PD	TPI
1978	Bos-A	0	0	—	1	0	0	0	0	2	3	1	3	0	27.0	22.50	18	.375	.545	0	—	0	-4	-4	0	-0.7

● DON LARSEN Larsen, Don James b: 8/7/29, Michigan City, Ind. BR/TR, 6'4", 227 lbs. Deb: 4/18/53

YEAR	TM/L	W	L	PCT	G	GS	CG	SH	SV	IP	H	HR	BB	SO	RAT	ERA	ERA+	OAV	OOB	BH	AVG	PB	PR	/A	PD	TPI
1953	StL-A	7	12	.368	38	22	7	2	2	192^2	201	11	64	96	12.6	4.16	101	.267	.328	23	.284	6	-3	1	-1	0.8
1954	Bal-A	3	21	.125	29	28	12	1	0	201^2	213	18	89	80	13.5	4.37	82	.274	.349	22	.250	8	-15	-18	0	-0.9
1955	*NY-A	9	2	.818	19	13	5	1	2	97	81	8	51	44	12.4	3.06	122	.229	.329	6	.146	2	10	7	-1	0.9
1956	*NY-A	11	5	.688	38	20	6	1	1	179^2	133	19	96	107	11.8	3.26	119	.204	.313	19	.241	6	18	12	-1	1.7
1957	*NY-A	10	4	.714	27	20	4	1	0	139^2	113	12	87	81	12.9	3.74	96	.220	.333	14	.250	5	1	-2	-0	0.1
1958	*NY-A	9	6	.600	19	19	5	3	0	114^1	100	4	52	55	12.3	3.07	115	.233	.322	15	.306	8	9	6	-1	1.3
1959	NY-A	6	7	.462	25	18	3	1	3	124^2	122	14	76	69	14.4	4.33	84	.260	.365	12	.255	4	-7	-10	-0	-0.6
1960	KC-A	1	10	.091	22	15	0	0	0	83^2	97	11	42	43	15.0	5.38	74	.293	.373	6	.207	0	-14	-13	-1	-1.4
1961	KC-A	1	0	1.000	8	1	0	0	0	15	21	2	11	13	19.8	4.20	98	.344	.452	6	.300	1	-0	-0	0	0.2
	Chi-A	7	2	.778	25	3	0	0	2	74^1	64	5	29	53	11.4	4.12	95	.231	.306	8	.320	3	-1	-2	0	0.1
	Yr	8	2	.800	33	4	0	0	2	89^1	85	7	40	66	12.7	4.13	96	.251	.332	14	.311	4	-1	-2	1	0.3
1962	*SF-N	5	4	.556	49	0	0	0	11	86^1	83	9	47	58	13.8	4.38	87	.256	.354	5	.200	1	-4	-6	0	-0.4
1963	SF-N	7	7	.500	46	0	0	0	3	62	46	8	30	44	11.0	3.05	105	.203	.296	2	.182	0	2	1	0	0.2
1964	SF-N	0	1	.000	6	0	0	0	0	10^1	10	0	6	6	13.9	4.35	82	.256	.356	0	.000	-0	-1	-1	-0	-0.1
	Hou-N	4	8	.333	30	10	2	1	1	103^1	92	4	20	58	9.8	2.26	151	.233	.272	3	.097	0	15	13	0	1.5
	Yr	4	9	.308	36	10	2	1	1	113^2	102	4	26	64	10.2	2.45	140	.235	.280	3	.094	0	14	12	0	1.4
1965	Hou-N	0	0	—	1	1	0	0	0	5^1	8	0	3	1	18.6	5.06	66	.348	.423	0	.000	-0	-1	-1	1	-0.1
	Bal-A	1	2	.333	27	1	0	0	1	54	53	4	20	40	12.3	2.67	130	.255	.323	3	.273	1	5	5	1	0.7
1967	Chi-N	0	0	—	3	0	0	0	0	4	5	1	2	1	15.8	9.00	39	.333	.412	0	—	0	-3	-2	0	-0.2
Total	14	81	91	.471	412	171	44	11	26	1548	1442	130	725	849	12.8	3.78	99	.247	.332	144	.242	44	10	-9	-1	3.8

● DAN LARSON Larson, Daniel James b: 7/4/54, Los Angeles, Cal. BR/TR, 6', 180 lbs. Deb: 7/18/76

YEAR	TM/L	W	L	PCT	G	GS	CG	SH	SV	IP	H	HR	BB	SO	RAT	ERA	ERA+	OAV	OOB	BH	AVG	PB	PR	/A	PD	TPI
1976	Hou-N	5	8	.385	13	13	5	0	0	92^1	81	3	28	42	10.7	3.02	106	.236	.296	9	.290	3	5	2	0	0.6
1977	Hou-N	1	7	.125	32	10	1	0	1	97^2	108	13	45	44	14.3	5.81	61	.280	.358	6	.214	1	-21	-24	0	-2.3
1978	Phi-N	0	0	—	1	0	0	0	0	1	1	1	1	2	18.0	9.00	40	.250	.400	0	—	0	-1	-1	0	-0.1
1979	Phi-N	1	1	.500	3	3	0	0	0	19	17	1	9	9	12.8	4.26	90	.250	.346	0	.000	-1	-1	-1	0	-0.1
1980	Phi-N	0	5	.000	12	7	0	0	0	45^2	46	4	24	17	13.8	3.15	120	.271	.361	2	.154	0	2	3	-1	0.3
1981	Phi-N	3	0	1.000	5	4	1	0	0	28	27	4	15	15	13.5	4.18	87	.260	.353	1	.111	0	-2	-2	-0	-0.2
1982	Chi-N	0	4	.000	12	6	0	0	0	39^2	51	4	18	22	16.1	5.67	66	.327	.403	3	.273	0	-9	-9	1	-0.7
Total	7	10	25	.286	78	43	7	0	1	323^1	331	30	140	151	13.3	4.40	80	.269	.346	21	.216	4	-26	-31	1	-2.5

● AL LARY Lary, Alfred Allen b: 9/26/29, Northport, Ala. BR/TR, 6'3", 185 lbs. Deb: 9/06/54 F♦

YEAR	TM/L	W	L	PCT	G	GS	CG	SH	SV	IP	H	HR	BB	SO	RAT	ERA	ERA+	OAV	OOB	BH	AVG	PB	PR	/A	PD	TPI
1954	Chi-N	0	0	—	1	1	0	0	0	6	3	0	7	4	15.0	3.00	140	.150	.370	1	.500	0	1	1	0	0.1
1962	Chi-N	0	1	.000	15	3	0	0	0	34	42	5	15	18	15.1	7.15	58	.311	.380	1	.167	0	-12	-11	-0	-1.1
Total	2	0	1	.000	16	4	0	0	0	40	45	5	22	22	15.1	6.52	64	.290	.379	2	.250	1	-11	-11	-0	-1.0

● FRANK LARY Lary, Frank Strong "Mule" or "The Yankee Killer" b: 4/10/30, Northport, Ala. BR/TR, 5'11", 180 lbs. Deb: 9/14/54 F

YEAR	TM/L	W	L	PCT	G	GS	CG	SH	SV	IP	H	HR	BB	SO	RAT	ERA	ERA+	OAV	OOB	BH	AVG	PB	PR	/A	PD	TPI
1954	Det-A	0	0	—	3	0	0	0	0	3^2	4	0	3	5	17.2	2.45	150	.286	.412	0	—	0	1	1	-0	0.0
1955	Det-A	14	15	.483	36	31	16	2	1	235	232	10	89	98	12.5	3.10	124	.262	.334	16	.195	1	22	19	1	2.2
1956	Det-A	**21**	13	.618	41	38	20	3	1	**294**	289	20	116	165	12.8	3.15	131	.257	.333	19	.184	0	33	31	-0	3.2
1957	Det-A	11	16	.407	40	35	12	2	3	237^2	250	23	72	107	12.6	3.98	97	.276	.337	9	.123	-3	-5	-3	0	-0.6
1958	Det-A	16	15	.516	39	34	**19**	3	1	**260**^{1}	249	20	68	131	11.4	2.90	139	.251	.307	15	.170	-1	25	33	-0	3.3
1959	Det-A	17	10	.630	32	32	11	3	0	223	225	23	46	137	11.4	3.55	114	.261	.307	10	.125	-2	8	13	-0	1.0
1960	Det-A★	15	15	.500	38	36	**15**	2	1	**274**^{1}	262	25	62	149	11.3	3.51	113	.249	.302	17	.183	4	11	14	-2	1.6
1961	Det-A★	23	9	.719	36	36	**22**	4	0	275^1	252	24	66	146	10.6	3.24	127	.243	.293	25	.231	4	24	26	4	**3.6**
1962	Det-A	2	6	.250	17	14	2	1	0	80	98	17	21	41	13.8	5.74	71	.297	.346	4	.167	1	-16	-15	-1	-1.5
1963	Det-A	4	9	.308	16	14	6	0	0	107^1	90	15	26	46	10.1	3.27	114	.226	.281	8	.229	1	4	6	1	0.9
1964	Det-A	0	2	.000	6	4	0	0	0	18	24	3	10	6	18.5	7.00	52	.316	.416	0	.000	-1	-7	-7	-1	-0.8
	NY-N	2	3	.400	13	8	3	1	1	57^1	62	7	14	27	12.6	4.55	79	.279	.333	2	.118	1	-6	-6	-0	-0.6
	Mil-N	1	0	1.000	5	2	0	0	0	12^1	15	4	0	4	10.9	4.38	80	.306	.306	0	.000	-0	-1	-1	1	-0.1
	Yr	3	3	.500	18	10	3	1	1	69^2	77	11	14	31	11.8	4.52	79	.279	.314	2	.100	0	-8	-7	0	-0.7
1965	NY-N	1	3	.250	14	7	0	0	1	57^1	48	2	16	23	10.2	2.98	118	.233	.291	4	.211	0	4	3	0	0.5
	Chi-A	1	0	1.000	14	1	0	0	2	26^2	23	4	7	14	10.8	4.05	79	.230	.294	1	.500	0	-2	-3	0	-0.2
Total	12	128	116	.525	350	292	126	21	11	2162^1	2123	197	616	1099	11.8	3.49	113	.257	.316	130	.177	5	95	112	3	12.5

● FRED LASHER Lasher, Frederick Walter b: 8/19/41, Poughkeepsie, N.Y. BR/TR, 6'4", 210 lbs. Deb: 4/12/63

YEAR	TM/L	W	L	PCT	G	GS	CG	SH	SV	IP	H	HR	BB	SO	RAT	ERA	ERA+	OAV	OOB	BH	AVG	PB	PR	/A	PD	TPI
1963	Min-A	0	0	—	11	0	0	0	0	11^1	12	1	11	10	18.3	4.76	76	.286	.434	0	.000	-0	-1	-1	0	-0.1
1967	Det-A	2	1	.667	17	0	0	0	9	30	25	1	11	28	11.1	3.90	84	.221	.296	1	.111	-0	-2	-2	-0	-0.3
1968	*Det-A	5	1	.833	34	0	0	0	5	48^2	37	5	22	32	10.9	3.33	90	.215	.304	1	.111	-0	-2	-2	1	-0.2
1969	Det-A	2	1	.667	32	0	0	0	0	44	34	5	22	26	11.9	3.07	122	.224	.330	0	.000	-0	3	3	0	0.3
1970	Det-A	1	3	.250	12	0	0	0	3	9	10	0	12	8	23.0	5.00	75	.278	.469	0	.000	-0	-1	-1	0	-0.1
	Cle-A	1	7	.125	43	1	0	0	5	57^2	57	6	30	44	14.0	4.06	98	.264	.361	0	.000	-1	-2	-1	-1	-0.3
	Yr	2	10	.167	55	1	0	0	8	66^2	67	6	42	52	15.1	4.18	94	.264	.375	0	.000	-1	-3	-2	-1	-0.4
1971	Cal-A	0	0	—	2	0	0	0	0	1^1	4	0	2	0	40.5	27.00	12	.667	.750	0	—	0	-3	-4	-0	-0.3
Total	6	11	13	.458	151	1	0	0	22	202	179	18	110	148	13.2	3.88	91	.243	.347	2	.063	-2	-10	-8	0	-1.0

● BILL LASKEY Laskey, William Alan b: 12/20/57, Toledo, Ohio BR/TR, 6'5", 190 lbs. Deb: 4/23/82

YEAR	TM/L	W	L	PCT	G	GS	CG	SH	SV	IP	H	HR	BB	SO	RAT	ERA	ERA+	OAV	OOB	BH	AVG	PB	PR	/A	PD	TPI
1982	SF-N	13	12	.520	32	31	7	1	0	189^1	186	14	43	88	11.0	3.14	115	.261	.304	8	.129	-2	10	10	0	0.8
1983	SF-N	13	10	.565	25	25	1	0	0	148^1	151	18	45	81	12.1	4.19	84	.266	.323	5	.106	0	-9	-11	-1	-1.2
1984	SF-N	9	14	.391	35	34	2	0	0	207^2	222	20	50	71	12.0	4.33	81	.273	.320	4	.063	-3	-17	-19	-3	-2.5
1985	SF-N	5	11	.313	19	19	0	0	0	114	110	10	39	42	11.8	3.55	97	.255	.317	4	.133	1	0	-1	0	-0.1
	Mon-N	0	5	.000	11	7	0	0	0	34^1	55	9	14	18	18.6	9.44	36	.362	.423	1	.143	-0	-22	-23	1	-2.1
	Yr	5	16	.238	30	26	0	0	0	148^1	165	19	53	60	13.3	4.91	70	.281	.343	5	.135	0	-22	-25	1	-2.2
1986	SF-N	1	1	.500	20	0	0	0	1	27^1	28	5	13	8	13.5	4.28	82	.275	.357	0	.000	-0	-2	-2	0	-0.2
1988	Cle-A	1	0	1.000	17	0	0	0	1	24^1	32	0	6	17	14.1	5.18	79	.320	.358	0	—	0	-3	-3	0	-0.5
Total	6	42	53	.442	159	116	10	1	2	745^1	784	76	210	325	12.2	4.14	85	.272	.325	22	.105	-4	-44	-50	-2	-5.8

● BILL LASLEY Lasley, Willard Almond b: 7/13/02, Gallipolis, Ohio d: 8/21/90, Seattle, Wash. BB/TR, 6', 175 lbs. Deb: 9/19/24

YEAR	TM/L	W	L	PCT	G	GS	CG	SH	SV	IP	H	HR	BB	SO	RAT	ERA	ERA+	OAV	OOB	BH	AVG	PB	PR	/A	PD	TPI
1924	StL-A	0	0	—	2	0	0	0	0	4	7	0	2	0	20.3	6.75	67	.412	.474	0	.000	-0	-1	-1	-0	-0.1

YEAR	TM/L	W	L	PCT	G	GS	CG	SH	SV	IP	H	HR	BB	SO	RAT	ERA	ERA+	OAV	OOB	BH	AVG	PB	PR	/A	PD	TPI
● TOM LASORDA	Lasorda, Thomas Charles b: 9/22/27, Norristown, Pa. BL/TL, 5'10", 175 lbs. Deb: 8/05/54 MC																									
1954	Bro-N	0	0	—	4	0	0	0	0	9	8	2	5	5	13.0	5.00	82	.242	.342	0	.000	-0	-1	-1	-0	-0.1
1955	Bro-N	0	0	—	4	1	0	0	0	4	5	1	6	4	27.0	13.50	30	.313	.522	0	—	0	-4	-4	-0	-0.4
1956	KC-A	0	4	.000	18	5	0	0	1	45^1	40	6	45	28	17.5	6.15	70	.240	.409	1	.077	-1	-10	-9	0	-1.0
Total	3	0	4	.000	26	6	0	0	1	58^1	53	9	56	37	17.4	6.48	66	.245	.409	1	.071	-2	-15	-14	0	-1.5
● BILL LATHAM	Latham, William Carol b: 8/29/60, Birmingham, Ala. BL/TL, 6'2", 190 lbs. Deb: 4/15/85																									
1985	NY-N	1	3	.250	7	3	0	0	0	22^2	21	1	7	10	11.1	3.97	87	.250	.308	1	.333	1	-1	-1	1	0.0
1986	Min-A	0	1	.000	7	2	0	0	0	16	24	1	6	8	17.4	7.31	59	.358	.419	0	—	0	-6	-5	-1	-0.7
Total	2	1	4	.200	14	5	0	0	0	38^2	45	2	13	18	13.7	5.35	71	.298	.358	1	.333	1	-7	-7	0	-0.7
● BILL LATHROP	Lathrop, William George b: 8/12/1891, Hanover, Wis. d: 11/20/58, Janesville, Wis. BR/TR, 6'2.5", 184 lbs. Deb: 7/29/13																									
1913	Chi-A	0	1	.000	6	0	0	0	0	17	16	0	12	9	15.4	4.24	69	.262	.392	0	.000	-1	-2	-2	0	-0.3
1914	Chi-A	1	2	.333	19	1	0	0	0	47^2	41	0	19	7	11.7	2.64	102	.241	.325	0	.000	-1	1	0	1	0.0
Total	2	1	3	.250	25	1	0	0	0	64^2	57	0	31	16	12.7	3.06	90	.247	.343	0	.000	-2	-2	-2	1	-0.3
● BARRY LATMAN	Latman, Arnold Barry b: 5/21/36, Los Angeles, Cal. BR/TR, 6'3", 210 lbs. Deb: 9/10/57																									
1957	Chi-A	1	2	.333	7	2	0	0	1	12^1	12	2	13	9	19.0	8.03	47	.267	.441	0	.000	-0	-6	-6	0	-0.6
1958	Chi-A	3	0	1.000	13	3	1	1	0	47^2	27	1	17	28	8.5	0.76	481	.162	.243	1	.083	-0	16	15	-1	1.6
1959	Chi-A	8	5	.615	37	21	5	2	0	156	138	15	72	97	12.3	3.75	100	.235	.323	6	.128	-1	2	0	-3	-0.4
1960	Cle-A	7	7	.500	31	20	4	0	0	147^1	146	19	72	94	13.7	4.03	93	.258	.348	9	.220	1	-3	-5	-1	-0.4
1961	Cle-A☆	13	5	.722	45	18	4	2	5	176^2	163	23	54	108	11.3	4.02	98	.244	.306	4	.073	-3	-0	-2	-3	-0.8
1962	Cle-A	8	13	.381	45	21	7	1	5	179^1	179	23	72	117	12.8	4.17	93	.261	.336	10	.189	2	-4	-6	-1	-0.5
1963	Cle-A	7	12	.368	38	21	4	2	2	149^1	146	23	52	133	12.3	4.94	73	.257	.325	8	.182	2	-22	-22	3	-1.8
1964	LA-A	6	10	.375	40	18	2	1	2	138	128	15	52	81	12.2	3.85	85	.244	.321	5	.125	-1	-3	-9	-1	-1.1
1965	Cal-A	1	1	.500	18	0	0	0	0	31^2	30	3	16	18	13.1	2.84	120	.254	.343	0	.000	-0	2	2	-1	0.1
1966	Hou-N	2	7	.222	31	9	1	1	1	103	88	5	35	74	11.4	2.71	126	.233	.310	4	.154	0	10	8	-0	0.9
1967	Hou-N	3	6	.333	39	1	0	0	0	77^2	73	13	34	70	13.1	4.52	73	.252	.342	1	.091	-1	-10	-10	0	-1.2
Total	11	59	68	.465	344	134	28	10	16	1219	1130	142	489	829	12.3	3.91	94	.246	.325	48	.145	-1	-17	-34	-8	-4.2
● BILL LATTIMORE	Lattimore, William Hershel "Slothful Bill" b: 5/25/1884, Roxton, Tex. d: 10/30/19, Colorado Springs, Colo. BL/TL, 5'9", 165 lbs. Deb: 4/17/08																									
1908	Cle-A	1	2	.333	4	4	1	1	0	24	24	0	7	5	11.6	4.50	53	.247	.298	4	.444	1	-6	-6	-1	-0.5
● CHUCK LAUER	Lauer, John Charles b: 1865, Pittsburgh, Pa. TR , Deb: 7/17/1884 ♦																									
1884	Pit-a	0	2	.000	3	3	2	0	0	19	23	0	9	8	16.6	7.58	44	.277	.368	5	.114	-1	-9	-9	-1	-0.8
● GEORGE LAUZERIQUE	Lauzerique, George Albert b: 7/22/47, Havana, Cuba BR/TR, 6'1", 180 lbs. Deb: 9/17/67																									
1967	KC-A	0	2	.000	3	2	0	0	0	16	11	2	6	10	10.1	2.25	142	.193	.281	0	.000	-0	2	2	0	0.2
1968	Oak-A	0	0	—	1	0	0	0	0	1	0	0	1	0	9.0	0.00	—	.000	.333	0	—	0	0	0	0	0.1
1969	Oak-A	3	4	.429	19	8	1	0	0	61^1	58	14	27	39	12.8	4.70	73	.250	.333	2	.100	-1	-7	-9	1	-0.9
1970	Mil-A	1	2	.333	11	4	1	0	0	35	41	7	14	24	14.4	6.94	55	.295	.364	2	.200	1	-13	-12	-0	-1.1
Total	4	4	8	.333	34	14	2	0	0	113^1	110	23	48	73	12.9	5.00	70	.256	.336	4	.121	-0	-18	-19	1	-1.7
● GARY LAVELLE	Lavelle, Gary Robert b: 1/3/49, Scranton, Pa. BB/TL, 6'1", 200 lbs. Deb: 9/10/74																									
1974	SF-N	0	3	.000	10	0	0	0	0	16^2	14	1	10	12	13.0	2.16	176	.222	.329	0	.000	-0	3	3	-0	0.3
1975	SF-N	6	3	.667	65	0	0	0	8	82^1	80	3	48	51	14.3	2.95	129	.260	.365	1	.111	-0	6	8	0	0.8
1976	SF-N	10	6	.625	65	0	0	0	12	110^1	102	6	52	71	12.7	2.69	135	.246	.333	1	.077	-1	10	11	-2	1.0
1977	SF-N★	7	7	.500	73	0	0	0	20	118^1	106	4	37	93	10.9	2.05	190	.239	.298	0	.000	-2	24	24	1	2.4
1978	SF-N	13	10	.565	67	0	0	0	14	97^2	96	3	44	63	13.1	3.32	104	.263	.345	1	.067	-1	3	1	0	0.1
1979	SF-N	7	9	.438	70	0	0	0	20	96^2	86	5	42	80	12.1	2.51	139	.247	.332	1	.250	0	13	11	0	1.1
1980	SF-N	6	8	.429	62	0	0	0	9	100	106	4	36	66	12.8	3.42	103	.275	.336	0	.000	-1	2	1	0	0.0
1981	SF-N	2	6	.250	34	3	0	0	4	65^2	58	3	23	45	11.4	3.84	89	.244	.316	3	.273	1	-3	-3	1	-0.1
1982	SF-N	10	7	.588	68	0	0	0	8	104^2	97	6	29	76	10.9	2.67	135	.247	.300	2	.154	0	11	11	2	1.4
1983	SF-N☆	7	4	.636	56	0	0	0	20	87	73	4	19	68	9.5	2.59	137	.229	.272	0	.000	-1	10	9	2	1.0
1984	SF-N	5	4	.556	77	0	0	0	12	101	92	5	42	71	12.0	2.76	127	.246	.324	0	.000	-0	9	8	-1	0.8
1985	*Tor-A	5	7	.417	69	0	0	0	8	72^2	54	5	36	50	11.1	3.10	136	.214	.313	0	—	0	8	9	-0	0.8
1987	Tor-A	2	3	.400	23	0	0	0	1	27^2	36	2	19	17	17.9	5.53	81	.313	.410	0	—	0	-3	-3	0	-0.3
	Oak-A	0	0	—	6	0	0	0	0	4^1	4	0	3	6	14.5	8.31	50	.267	.389	0	—	0	-2	-2	-0	0.1
	Yr	2	3	.400	29	0	0	0	1	32	40	2	22	23	17.4	5.91	75	.305	.405	0	—	0	-5	-5	0	-0.2
Total	13	80	77	.510	745	3	0	0	136	1085	1004	51	440	769	12.1	2.93	125	.249	.325	9	.081	-6	92	89	4	9.4
● JIMMY LAVENDER	Lavender, James Sanford b: 3/25/1884, Barnesville, Ga. d: 1/12/60, Cartersville, Ga. BR/TR, 5'11", 165 lbs. Deb: 4/23/12																									
1912	Chi-N	16	13	.552	42	31	15	3	3	251^2	240	8	89	109	12.1	3.04	110	.257	.328	13	.149	-3	10	8	1	0.6
1913	Chi-N	10	14	.417	40	20	10	0	2	204	206	6	98	91	14.0	3.66	87	.267	.359	8	.118	-4	-10	-11	-2	-1.7
1914	Chi-N	11	11	.500	37	28	11	2	0	214^1	191	11	87	87	12.1	3.07	91	.247	.331	11	.175	2	-7	-7	3	-0.2
1915	Chi-N	10	16	.385	41	24	13	1	4	220	178	5	67	117	10.4	2.58	108	.228	.298	9	.134	-2	4	5	3	0.7
1916	Chi-N	10	14	.417	36	25	9	4	2	188	163	3	62	91	11.2	2.82	103	.240	.312	8	.151	-2	-4	2	-1	-0.1
1917	Phi-N	6	8	.429	28	14	7	0	1	129^1	119	5	44	52	11.6	3.55	79	.250	.317	5	.139	-1	-12	-11	-2	-1.5
Total	6	63	76	.453	224	142	65	10	12	1207^1	1097	38	447	547	11.9	3.09	97	.249	.325	54	.144	-9	-19	-12	2	-2.2
● RON LAW	Law, Ronald David b: 3/14/46, Hamilton, Ont., Can. BR/TR, 6'2", 165 lbs. Deb: 6/29/69																									
1969	Cle-A	3	4	.429	35	1	0	0	1	52^1	68	2	34	29	17.9	4.99	76	.325	.424	1	.143	-0	-8	-7	0	-0.7
● VANCE LAW	Law, Vance Aaron b: 10/1/56, Boise, Idaho BR/TR, 6'2", 190 lbs. Deb: 6/01/80 F♦																									
1986	Mon-N	0	0	—	3	0	0	0	0	4	3	0	2	0	11.3	2.25	164	.214	.313	81	.225	1	1	1	0	0.1
1987	Mon-N	0	0	—	3	0	0	0	0	3^1	5	0	0	2	13.5	5.40	78	.333	.333	119	.273	1	-0	-0	0	0.0
1991	Oak-A	0	0	—	1	0	0	0	0	0^2	1	0	1	0	27.0	0.00	—	.333	.500	28	.209	1	0	0	0	0.0
Total	3	0	0	—	7	0	0	0	0	8	9	0	3	2	13.5	3.38	116	.281	.343	972	.256	3	0	0	0	0.1
● VERN LAW	Law, Vernon Sanders "Deacon" b: 3/12/30, Meridian, Idaho BR/TR, 6'2", 195 lbs. Deb: 6/11/50 FC																									
1950	Pit-N	7	9	.438	27	17	5	1	0	128	137	11	49	57	13.4	4.92	89	.272	.341	3	.073	-2	-11	-8	-2	-1.1
1951	Pit-N	6	9	.400	28	14	2	1	2	114	109	9	51	41	13.1	4.50	94	.253	.341	11	.344	5	-7	-3	-1	0.1
1954	Pit-N	9	13	.409	39	18	7	0	3	161^2	201	20	56	57	14.5	5.51	76	.311	.368	12	.231	4	-26	-24	-1	-1.9
1955	Pit-N	10	10	.500	43	24	8	1	1	200^2	221	19	61	82	12.7	3.81	108	.280	.333	16	.254	3	5	7	0	1.1
1956	Pit-N	8	16	.333	39	32	6	0	2	195^2	218	24	49	60	12.6	4.32	87	.281	.329	10	.175	1	-12	-12	-1	-1.1
1957	Pit-N	10	8	.556	31	25	9	3	1	172^2	172	18	32	55	10.7	2.87	132	.256	.291	12	.190	1	19	18	-2	1.8
1958	Pit-N	14	12	.538	35	29	6	1	3	202^1	235	16	39	56	12.2	3.96	98	.297	.331	12	.194	6	-0	-2	-0	0.3
1959	Pit-N	18	9	.667	34	33	20	2	1	266	245	25	53	110	10.2	2.98	130	.243	.282	16	.167	1	29	26	1	3.0
1960	*Pit-N★	20	9	.690	35	35	**18**	3	0	271^2	266	25	40	120	10.3	3.08	122	.257	.287	17	.181	3	21	20	1	2.6
1961	Pit-N	3	4	.429	11	10	1	0	0	59^1	72	10	18	20	13.8	4.70	85	.305	.357	5	.263	1	-4	-5	1	-0.3
1962	Pit-N	10	7	.588	23	20	7	2	0	139^1	156	21	27	78	11.9	3.94	100	.276	.310	14	.311	5	0	-0	1	0.6
1963	Pit-N	4	5	.444	18	12	1	1	0	76^2	91	11	13	31	12.2	4.93	67	.296	.325	5	.217	1	-14	-14	1	-1.3
1964	Pit-N	12	13	.480	35	29	7	5	0	192	203	18	32	93	11.1	3.61	97	.270	.300	19	.311	8	-2	-2	1	0.7
1965	Pit-N	17	9	.654	29	28	13	4	0	217^1	182	17	35	101	9.1	2.15	163	.229	.264	20	.244	4	33	33	1	4.3

YEAR	TM/L	W	L	PCT	G	GS	CG	SH	SV	IP	H	HR	BB	SO	RAT	ERA	ERA+	OAV	OOB	BH	AVG	PB	PR	/A	PD	TPI
1966	Pit-N	12	8	.600	31	28	8	4	0	177^2	203	19	24	88	11.7	4.05	88	.292	.320	16	.242	5	-9	-9	2	-0.4
1967	Pit-N	2	6	.250	25	10	1	0	0	97	122	5	18	43	13.1	4.18	81	.308	.340	3	.111	-0	-9	-9	-0	-1.0
Total	16	162	147	.524	483	364	119	28	13	2672	2833	268	597	1092	11.7	3.77	101	.272	.314	191	.216	45	14	15	2	7.4
● **BROOKS LAWRENCE**	Lawrence, Brooks Ulysses "Bull" b: 1/30/25, Springfield, Ohio BR/TR, 6', 205 lbs. Deb: 6/24/54																									
1954	StL-N	15	6	.714	35	18	8	0	1	158^2	141	17	72	72	12.5	3.74	110	.243	.335	10	.189	0	6	6	0	0.7
1955	StL-N	3	8	.273	46	10	2	1	1	96	102	11	58	52	15.7	6.56	62	.278	.387	2	.095	-2	-27	-27	1	-2.6
1956	Cin-N☆	19	10	.655	49	30	11	1	0	218^2	210	26	71	96	11.6	3.99	100	.256	.317	11	.157	-1	-5	-0	3	0.2
1957	Cin-N	16	13	.552	49	32	12	1	4	250^1	234	26	76	121	11.4	3.52	117	.247	.309	14	.171	-0	10	16	-0	1.6
1958	Cin-N	8	13	.381	46	23	6	2	5	181	194	12	55	74	12.6	4.13	100	.275	.331	6	.113	-2	-4	0	-0	-0.2
1959	Cin-N	7	12	.368	43	14	3	0	10	128^1	144	17	45	64	13.5	4.77	85	.281	.344	6	.150	-1	-12	-10	-0	-1.1
1960	Cin-N	1	0	1.000	7	0	0	0	1	7^2	9	1	8	2	20.0	10.57	36	.310	.459	0	—	0	-6	-6	0	-0.5
Total	7	69	62	.527	275	127	42	5	22	1040^2	1034	110	385	481	12.6	4.25	96	.261	.332	49	.154	-5	-38	-20	4	-1.9
● **BOB LAWRENCE**	Lawrence, Robert Andrew "Larry" b: 12/14/1899, Brooklyn, N.Y. d: 11/6/83, Jamaica, N.Y. BR/TR, 5'11", 180 lbs. Deb: 7/19/24																									
1924	Chi-A	0	0	—	1	0	0	0	0	1	1	0	1	1	18.0	9.00	46	.250	.400	0	—	0	-1	-1	0	-0.1
● **AL LAWSON**	Lawson, Alfred William b: 3/24/1869, London, England d: 11/29/54, San Antonio, Tex. BR/TR, 5'11", 161 lbs. Deb: 5/13/1890																									
1890	Bos-N	0	1	.000	1	1	1	0	0	9	12	0	4	1	16.0	4.00	94	.310	.375	0	.000	-0	-0	-0	0	0.0
	Pit-N	0	2	.000	2	2	1	0	0	10	15	0	10	2	22.5	9.00	37	.336	.458	0	.000	-1	-6	-6	0	-0.5
	Yr	0	3	.000	3	3	2	0	0	19	27	0	14	3	19.4	6.63	53	.324	.421	0	.000	-1	-6	-7	0	-0.5
● **ROXIE LAWSON**	Lawson, Alfred Voyle b: 4/13/06, Donnellson, Iowa d: 4/9/77, Stockport, Iowa BR/TR, 6', 170 lbs. Deb: 8/03/30																									
1930	Cle-A	1	2	.333	7	4	2	0	0	33^2	46	1	23	10	18.4	6.15	79	.324	.418	1	.091	-1	-6	-5	-0	-0.5
1931	Cle-A	0	2	.000	17	3	0	0	0	55^2	72	5	36	20	17.5	7.60	61	.304	.396	2	.143	-0	-20	-18	-1	-1.7
1933	Det-A	0	1	.000	4	2	0	0	0	16	17	2	17	6	19.1	7.31	59	.270	.425	0	.000	-1	-5	-5	0	-0.5
1935	Det-A	3	1	.750	7	4	4	2	2	40	34	3	24	16	13.0	1.57	265	.233	.341	4	.308	1	13	12	-1	1.2
1936	Det-A	8	6	.571	41	8	3	0	3	128	139	13	71	34	15.0	5.48	90	.281	.376	10	.222	1	-6	-8	1	-0.5
1937	Det-A	18	7	.720	37	29	15	0	1	217^1	236	17	115	68	14.6	5.26	89	.271	.357	21	.259	3	-15	-14	-1	-1.1
1938	Det-A	8	9	.471	27	16	5	0	1	127	154	13	82	39	16.7	5.46	92	.299	.395	2	.044	-5	-9	-6	1	-1.0
1939	Det-A	1	1	.500	2	1	0	0	0	11^1	7	1	7	4	11.1	4.76	103	.167	.286	0	.000	-1	-0	0	0	0.0
	StL-A	3	7	.300	36	14	5	0	0	150^2	181	10	83	43	15.9	5.32	92	.307	.394	8	.186	-1	-12	-8	-1	-0.8
	Yr	4	8	.333	38	15	5	0	0	162	188	11	90	47	15.6	5.28	92	.297	.387	8	.170	-2	-12	-7	-0	-0.8
1940	StL-A	5	3	.625	30	2	0	0	4	72	77	5	54	18	16.4	5.13	89	.278	.396	1	.045	-3	-6	-4	-0	-0.7
Total	9	47	39	.547	208	83	34	2	11	851^2	963	70	512	258	15.7	5.37	89	.285	.380	49	.173	-7	-67	-57	-2	-5.6
● **BOB LAWSON**	Lawson, Robert Baker b: 8/23/1876, Brookneal, Va. d: 10/28/52, Chapel Hill, N.C. BR/TR, 5'10", 170 lbs. Deb: 5/07/01																									
1901	Bos-N	2	2	.500	6	4	4	0	0	46	45	0	28	12	14.7	3.33	109	.254	.363	4	.148	-0	-0	1	1	0.2
1902	Bal-A	0	2	.000	3	2	1	0	0	13	21	0	3	5	18.0	4.85	78	.363	.414	1	.167	-0	-2	-2	1	-0.1
Total	2	2	4	.333	9	6	5	0	0	59	66	0	31	17	15.4	3.66	100	.281	.374	5	.152	-1	-2	-0	1	0.1
● **STEVE LAWSON**	Lawson, Steven George b: 12/28/50, Oakland, Cal. BR/TL, 6'1", 175 lbs. Deb: 8/03/72																									
1972	Tex-A	0	0	—	13	0	0	0	1	16	13	1	10	13	12.9	2.81	107	.213	.324	1	1.000	0	0	0	-0	0.1
● **BILL LAXTON**	Laxton, William Harry b: 1/5/48, Camden, N.J. BL/TL, 6'1", 190 lbs. Deb: 9/15/70																									
1970	Phi-N	0	0	—	2	0	0	0	0	2	2	2	2	2	22.5	13.50	30	.250	.455	0	—	0	-2	-2	-0	-0.2
1971	SD-N	0	2	.000	18	0	0	0	0	27^2	32	4	26	23	19.2	6.83	48	.305	.447	0	—	0	-10	-11	0	-1.1
1974	SD-N	0	1	.000	30	1	0	0	0	44^2	37	5	38	40	15.7	4.03	88	.226	.380	1	.200	0	-2	-2	-0	-0.3
1976	Det-A	0	5	.000	26	3	0	0	2	94^2	77	13	51	74	12.7	4.09	91	.221	.331	0	—	0	-6	-4	-2	-0.6
1977	Sea-A	3	2	.600	43	0	0	0	3	72^2	62	10	39	49	13.0	4.95	83	.233	.340	0	—	0	-7	-7	-1	-0.8
	Cle-A	0	0	—	2	0	0	0	0	1^2	2	0	2	1	21.6	5.40	73	.286	.444	0	—	0	-0	-0	0	0.0
	Yr	3	2	.600	45	0	0	0	3	74^1	64	10	41	50	12.7	4.96	83	.228	.326	0	—	0	-7	-7	-1	-0.8
Total	5	3	10	.231	121	4	0	0	5	243^1	212	34	158	189	14.2	4.73	79	.236	.359	1	.200	0	-28	-26	-3	-3.0
● **TIM LAYANA**	Layana, Timothy Joseph b: 3/2/64, Inglewood, Cal. BR/TR, 6'2", 195 lbs. Deb: 4/09/90																									
1990	Cin-N	5	3	.625	55	0	0	0	2	80	71	7	44	53	13.2	3.49	113	.244	.347	0	.000	-1	3	4	0	0.4
1991	Cin-N	0	2	.000	22	0	0	0	0	20^2	23	1	11	14	14.8	6.97	55	.277	.362	0	.000	-0	-8	-7	0	-0.7
Total	2	5	5	.500	77	0	0	0	2	100^2	94	8	55	67	13.5	4.20	93	.251	.350	0	.000	-1	-5	-3	1	-0.3
● **DANNY LAZAR**	Lazar, John Dan b: 11/14/43, East Chicago, Ind. BL/TL, 6'1", 190 lbs. Deb: 6/21/68																									
1968	Chi-A	0	1	.000	8	1	0	0	0	13^1	14	1	4	11	12.2	4.05	75	.269	.321	0	.000	0	-2	-2	0	-0.2
1969	Chi-A	0	0	—	9	3	0	0	0	20^2	21	5	11	9	14.4	6.53	59	.280	.379	0	.000	-0	-7	-6	-0	-0.7
Total	2	0	1	.000	17	4	0	0	0	34	35	6	15	20	13.5	5.56	63	.276	.357	0	.000	-0	-8	-8	-0	-0.9
● **JACK LAZORKO**	Lazorko, Jack Thomas b: 3/30/56, Hoboken, N.J. BR/TR, 5'11", 200 lbs. Deb: 6/04/84																									
1984	Mil-A	0	1	.000	15	1	0	0	1	39^2	37	7	22	24	13.6	4.31	89	.245	.345	0	—	0	-1	-2	0	0.0
1985	Sea-A	0	0	—	15	0	0	0	1	20^1	23	1	8	7	15.0	3.54	119	.291	.378	0	—	0	1	2	1	0.2
1986	Det-A	0	0	—	3	0	0	0	0	6^2	8	0	4	3	16.2	4.05	102	.296	.387	0	—	0	0	0	0	0.0
1987	Cal-A	5	6	.455	26	11	2	0	0	117^2	108	20	44	55	11.8	4.59	94	.248	.320	0	—	0	-2	-4	2	-0.1
1988	Cal-A	0	1	.000	10	3	0	0	0	37^2	37	5	16	19	12.9	3.35	115	.255	.333	0	—	0	3	2	0	0.4
Total	5	5	8	.385	69	15	2	0	2	222	213	33	94	108	12.7	4.22	98	.254	.334	0	—	0	1	-2	3	0.5
● **CHARLIE LEA**	Lea, Charles William b: 12/25/56, Orleans, France BR/TR, 6'4", 197 lbs. Deb: 6/12/80																									
1980	Mon-N	7	5	.583	21	19	0	0	0	104	103	5	55	56	13.8	3.72	96	.262	.356	3	.081	-2	-1	-2	-1	-0.5
1981	Mon-N	5	4	.556	16	11	2	2	0	64^1	63	4	26	31	12.6	4.62	76	.268	.344	2	.133	-0	-8	-8	-0	-0.9
1982	Mon-N	12	10	.545	27	27	4	2	0	177^2	145	16	56	115	10.2	3.24	112	.222	.283	8	.123	-1	7	8	-1	0.6
1983	Mon-N	16	11	.593	33	33	8	4	0	222	195	15	84	137	11.4	3.12	115	.238	.309	8	.114	-2	12	11	-1	0.9
1984	Mon-N★	15	10	.600	30	30	8	0	0	224^1	198	19	68	123	10.8	2.89	119	.239	.299	8	.111	-3	17	13	0	1.2
1987	Mon-N	0	1	.000	1	1	0	0	0	1	4	1	2	1	54.0	36.00	12	.571	.667	0	—	0	-4	-4	0	-0.3
1988	Min-A	7	7	.500	24	23	0	0	0	130	156	19	50	72	14.6	4.85	84	.301	.368	0	—	0	-13	-11	-1	-1.3
Total	7	62	48	.564	152	144	22	8	0	923^1	864	79	341	535	11.9	3.54	102	.250	.320	29	.112	-7	11	8	-4	-0.3
● **RICK LEACH**	Leach, Richard Max b: 5/4/57, Ann Arbor, Mich. BL/TL, 6', 195 lbs. Deb: 4/30/81 ♦																									
1984	Tor-A	0	0	—	1	0	0	0	0	1	2	1	2	0	36.0	27.00	15	.400	.571	23	.261	0	-3	-3	0	-0.2
● **TERRY LEACH**	Leach, Terry Hester b: 3/13/54, Selma, Ala. BR/TR, 6', 215 lbs. Deb: 8/12/81																									
1981	NY-N	1	1	.500	21	1	0	0	0	35^1	26	2	12	16	9.7	2.55	137	.205	.273	0	.000	1	4	4	1	0.5
1982	NY-N	2	1	.667	21	1	1	1	3	45^1	46	2	18	30	12.7	4.17	87	.271	.340	1	.125	-0	-3	-3	-0	-0.3
1985	NY-N	3	4	.429	22	4	1	1	1	55^2	48	3	14	30	10.2	2.91	119	.235	.288	2	.167	1	4	3	1	0.5
1986	NY-N	0	0	—	6	0	0	0	0	6^2	6	0	3	4	12.2	2.70	131	.222	.300	0	—	0	1	1	0	0.1
1987	NY-N	11	1	.917	44	12	1	1	0	131^1	132	14	29	61	11.1	3.22	117	.262	.304	2	.061	-1	13	8	1	0.8
1988	*NY-N	7	2	.778	52	0	0	0	3	92	95	5	24	51	11.9	2.54	127	.268	.320	2	.143	0	9	7	2	1.0
1989	NY-N	0	0	—	10	0	0	0	0	21^1	19	1	4	2	10.1	4.22	77	.244	.289	0	.000	-0	-2	-2	1	-0.2
	KC-A	5	6	.455	30	3	0	0	0	73^2	78	4	36	34	14.0	4.15	93	.278	.362	0	—	0	-2	-3	1	-0.1
1990	Min-A	2	5	.286	55	0	0	0	2	81^2	84	2	21	46	11.7	3.20	130	.268	.316	0	—	0	6	9	1	0.9
1991	*Min-A	1	2	.333	50	0	0	0	0	67^1	82	3	14	32	12.8	3.61	118	.299	.333	0	—	0	4	5	1	0.5

YEAR TM/L	W	L	PCT	G	GS	CG	SH	SV	IP	H	HR	BB	SO	RAT	ERA	ERA+	OAV	OOB	BH	AVG	PB	PR	/A	PD	TPI
1992 Chi-A	6	5	.545	51	0	0	0	0	73^2	57	2	20	22	9.9	1.95	195	.215	.280	0	—	0	16	15	1	1.8
Total 10	38	27	.585	362	21	3	3	9	684	673	38	195	328	11.6	3.16	118	.259	.314	7	.097	-1	50	44	9	5.5

● **LUIS LEAL** Leal, Luis Enrique (b: Luis Enrique Albarado (Leal)) b: 3/21/57, Barquisimeto, Venz. BR/TR, 6'3", 205 lbs. Deb: 5/25/80

YEAR TM/L	W	L	PCT	G	GS	CG	SH	SV	IP	H	HR	BB	SO	RAT	ERA	ERA+	OAV	OOB	BH	AVG	PB	PR	/A	PD	TPI
1980 Tor-A	3	4	.429	13	10	1	0	0	59^2	72	6	31	26	15.7	4.53	95	.314	.398	0	—	0	-3	-1	-1	-0.2
1981 Tor-A	7	13	.350	29	19	3	0	1	129^2	127	8	44	71	12.2	3.68	107	.254	.321	0	—	0	-0	4	-1	0.3
1982 Tor-A	12	15	.444	38	38	10	0	0	249^2	250	24	79	111	12.0	3.93	114	.262	.320	0	—	0	4	15	-1	1.2
1983 Tor-A	13	12	.520	35	35	7	1	0	217^1	216	23	65	116	11.9	4.31	100	.257	.315	0	—	0	-6	-0	-1	-0.3
1984 Tor-A	13	8	.619	35	35	6	2	0	222^1	221	27	77	134	12.2	3.89	105	.258	.323	0	—	0	3	5	0	0.5
1985 Tor-A	3	6	.333	15	14	0	0	0	67^1	82	13	24	33	14.6	5.75	73	.303	.366	0	—	0	-12	-12	0	-1.1
Total 6	51	58	.468	165	151	27	3	1	946	968	101	320	491	12.5	4.14	103	.265	.328	0	—	0	-15	11	-2	0.4

● **KING LEAR** Lear, Charles Bernard b: 1/23/1891, Greencastle, Pa. d: 10/31/76, Greencastle, Pa. BR/TR, 6', 175 lbs. Deb: 5/02/14

YEAR TM/L	W	L	PCT	G	GS	CG	SH	SV	IP	H	HR	BB	SO	RAT	ERA	ERA+	OAV	OOB	BH	AVG	PB	PR	/A	PD	TPI
1914 Cin-N	1	2	.333	17	4	3	1	1	55^2	55	3	19	20	12.3	3.07	95	.271	.339	3	.188	1	-2	-1	-0	-0.1
1915 Cin-N	6	10	.375	40	15	9	0	0	167^2	169	7	45	46	11.8	3.01	95	.270	.324	8	.170	-1	-5	-3	-4	-0.8
Total 2	7	12	.368	57	19	12	1	1	223^1	224	10	64	66	11.9	3.02	95	.270	.328	11	.175	-0	-6	-4	-4	-0.9

● **FRANK LEARY** Leary, Francis Patrick b: 2/26/1881, Wayland, Mass. d: 10/4/07, Natick, Mass. TR , Deb: 4/30/07

YEAR TM/L	W	L	PCT	G	GS	CG	SH	SV	IP	H	HR	BB	SO	RAT	ERA	ERA+	OAV	OOB	BH	AVG	PB	PR	/A	PD	TPI
1907 Cin-N	0	1	.000	2	1	0	0	0	8	7	0	6	4	14.6	1.13	231	.269	.406	0	.000	-0	1	1	0	0.2

● **JACK LEARY** Leary, John J. b: 1858, New Haven, Conn. TL , 5'11", 186 lbs. Deb: 8/21/1880 ♦

YEAR TM/L	W	L	PCT	G	GS	CG	SH	SV	IP	H	HR	BB	SO	RAT	ERA	ERA+	OAV	OOB	BH	AVG	PB	PR	/A	PD	TPI
1880 Bos-N	0	1	.000	1	1	0	0	0	3	8	0	0	1	24.0	15.00	15	.727	.727	0	.000	-0	-4	-4	0	-0.3
1881 Det-N	0	2	.000	2	2	1	0	0	13	13	0	2	2	10.4	4.15	70	.255	.283	3	.273	1	-2	-2	-0	-0.1
1882 Pit-a	1	0	1.000	3	2	1	0	0	18^2	28	0	3	5	14.9	6.27	42	.325	.348	75	.292	1	-7	-8	0	-0.6
Bal-a	2	1	.667	3	3	3	0	0	26	29	1	8	2	12.8	1.38	199	.264	.314	4	.222	0	4	4	-0	0.4
Yr	3	1	.750	6	5	4	0	0	44^2	57	1	11	7	13.7	3.43	79	.291	.329	79	.287	1	-4	-4	0	-0.2
1884 Alt-U	0	3	.000	3	3	2	0	0	24	31	0	2	7	12.4	5.25	63	.293	.306	3	.091	-2	-6	-5	-0	-0.5
CP-U	0	2	.000	2	1	1	0	0	10	14	0	5	6	17.1	5.40	56	.310	.379	7	.175	-0	-3	-3	-0	-0.2
Yr	0	5	.000	5	4	3	0	0	34	45	0	7	13	13.8	5.29	61	.298	.330	10	.137	-2	-9	-8	-0	-0.7
Total 4	3	9	.250	14	12	8	0	0	94^2	123	1	20	23	13.6	4.56	63	.301	.334	125	.232	-1	-18	-18	-0	-1.3

● **TIM LEARY** Leary, Timothy James b: 12/23/58, Santa Monica, Cal. BR/TR, 6'3", 205 lbs. Deb: 4/12/81

YEAR TM/L	W	L	PCT	G	GS	CG	SH	SV	IP	H	HR	BB	SO	RAT	ERA	ERA+	OAV	OOB	BH	AVG	PB	PR	/A	PD	TPI
1981 NY-N	0	0	—	1	1	0	0	0	2	0	0	1	3	4.5	0.00	—	.000	.143	0	.000	-0	1	1	0	0.1
1983 NY-N	1	1	.500	2	2	1	0	0	10^2	15	0	4	9	16.0	3.38	107	.319	.373	1	.333	0	0	0	0	0.1
1984 NY-N	3	3	.500	20	7	0	0	0	53^2	61	2	18	29	13.6	4.02	88	.285	.346	3	.300	2	-3	-3	-1	-0.2
1985 Mil-A	1	4	.200	5	5	0	0	0	33^1	40	5	8	29	13.2	4.05	103	.296	.340	0	—	0	0	0	1	0.1
1986 Mil-A	12	12	.500	33	30	3	2	0	188^1	216	20	53	110	13.2	4.21	103	.289	.342	0	—	0	-1	3	1	0.3
1987 LA-N	3	11	.214	39	12	0	0	1	107^2	121	15	36	61	13.3	4.76	83	.285	.344	7	.304	2	-8	-10	1	-0.7
1988 *LA-N	17	11	.607	35	34	9	6	0	228^2	201	13	56	180	10.4	2.91	114	.234	.285	18	.269	5	14	11	2	1.9
1989 LA-N	6	7	.462	19	17	2	0	0	117^1	107	9	37	59	11.2	3.38	101	.247	.309	2	.061	-2	2	1	1	-0.1
Cin-N	2	7	.222	14	14	0	0	0	89^2	98	8	31	64	13.2	3.71	97	.278	.342	5	.192	2	-2	-1	0	0.1
Yr	8	14	.364	33	31	2	0	0	207	205	17	68	123	12.0	3.52	99	.259	.320	7	.119	-0	-1	-1	1	0.0
1990 NY-A	9	19	.321	31	31	6	1	0	208	202	18	78	138	12.4	4.11	97	.257	.330	0	—	0	-5	-3	2	-0.1
1991 NY-A	4	10	.286	28	18	1	0	0	120^2	150	20	57	83	15.7	6.49	64	.312	.389	0	—	0	-32	-31	-0	-3.0
1992 NY-A	5	6	.455	18	15	2	0	0	97	84	9	57	34	13.5	5.57	73	.245	.359	0	—	0	-18	-16	-1	-1.7
Sea-A	3	4	.429	8	8	1	0	0	44	47	3	30	12	16.8	4.91	81	.280	.404	0	—	0	-5	-4	1	-0.4
Yr	8	10	.444	26	23	3	0	0	141	131	12	87	46	14.2	5.36	75	.251	.364	0	—	0	-22	-21	-0	-2.1
Total 11	66	95	.410	253	194	25	9	1	1301	1342	122	466	811	12.8	4.21	91	.269	.336	36	.221	9	-56	-55	5	-3.6

● **RAZOR LEDBETTER** Ledbetter, Ralph Overton b: 12/8/1894, Rutherford College N.C. d: 2/1/69, W.Palm Beach, Fla. BR/TR, 6'3", 190 lbs. Deb: 4/16/15

YEAR TM/L	W	L	PCT	G	GS	CG	SH	SV	IP	H	HR	BB	SO	RAT	ERA	ERA+	OAV	OOB	BH	AVG	PB	PR	/A	PD	TPI
1915 Det-A	0	0	—	1	0	0	0	0	1	1	0	0	0	9.0	0.00	—	.333	.333	0	—	0	0	0	0	0.1

● **DON LEE** Lee, Donald Edward b: 2/26/34, Globe, Ariz. BR/TR, 6'4", 210 lbs. Deb: 4/23/57 F

YEAR TM/L	W	L	PCT	G	GS	CG	SH	SV	IP	H	HR	BB	SO	RAT	ERA	ERA+	OAV	OOB	BH	AVG	PB	PR	/A	PD	TPI
1957 Det-A	1	3	.250	11	6	0	0	0	38^2	48	6	18	19	15.6	4.66	83	.308	.383	2	.167	-0	-4	-3	-0	-0.4
1958 Det-A	0	0	—	1	0	0	0	0	2	1	1	1	0	13.5	9.00	45	.143	.333	0	—	0	-1	-1	-0	-0.1
1960 Was-A	8	7	.533	44	20	1	0	3	165	160	16	64	88	12.4	3.44	113	.258	.330	5	.116	-0	8	8	1	0.9
1961 Min-A	3	6	.333	37	10	4	0	3	115	93	12	35	65	10.3	3.52	120	.221	.288	2	.067	-3	6	9	2	0.8
1962 Min-A	3	3	.500	9	9	1	0	0	52	51	8	24	28	14.2	4.50	91	.256	.357	4	.211	0	-3	-2	0	-0.2
LA-A	8	8	.500	27	22	4	2	2	153^1	153	12	39	74	11.4	3.11	124	.256	.305	9	.184	-0	15	13	-2	1.1
Yr	11	11	.500	36	31	5	2	2	205^1	204	20	63	102	11.8	3.46	113	.254	.310	13	.191	0	12	10	-2	0.9
1963 LA-A	8	11	.421	40	22	3	2	1	154	148	12	51	89	12.2	3.68	93	.251	.320	7	.156	-1	-1	-4	-1	-0.6
1964 LA-A	5	4	.556	33	8	0	0	2	89^1	99	6	25	73	12.6	2.72	121	.279	.328	6	.261	2	9	6	-1	0.8
1965 Cal-A	0	1	.000	10	0	0	0	0	14	21	4	5	12	17.4	6.43	53	.350	.409	1	.333	1	-5	-5	-0	-0.4
Hou-N	0	0	—	7	0	0	0	0	8	8	0	3	3	13.5	3.38	99	.267	.353	0	.000	-0	0	-0	0	0.0
1966 Hou-N	2	0	1.000	9	0	0	0	0	18	17	1	4	9	10.5	2.50	137	.250	.292	1	1.000	0	2	2	1	0.3
Chi-N	2	1	.667	16	0	0	0	0	19	28	3	12	7	18.9	7.11	52	.346	.430	0	—	0	-7	-7	-0	-0.7
Yr	4	1	.800	25	0	0	0	0	37	45	4	16	16	14.8	4.86	73	.302	.370	1	1.000	0	-5	-5	1	-0.4
Total 9	40	44	.476	244	97	13	4	11	828^1	827	81	281	467	12.4	3.61	104	.260	.326	37	.164	-1	20	14	1	1.5

● **MARK LEE** Lee, Mark Linden b: 6/14/53, Inglewood, Cal. BR/TR, 6'4", 225 lbs. Deb: 4/23/78

YEAR TM/L	W	L	PCT	G	GS	CG	SH	SV	IP	H	HR	BB	SO	RAT	ERA	ERA+	OAV	OOB	BH	AVG	PB	PR	/A	PD	TPI
1978 SD-N	5	1	.833	56	0	0	0	2	85	74	2	36	31	11.9	3.28	101	.240	.324	0	.000	-1	3	0	2	0.1
1979 SD-N	2	4	.333	46	1	0	0	5	65	88	3	25	25	15.9	4.29	82	.332	.394	2	.333	1	-4	-6	1	-0.4
1980 Pit-N	0	1	.000	4	0	0	0	0	5^2	5	0	3	2	12.7	4.76	76	.227	.320	0	—	0	-1	-1	0	0.0
1981 Pit-N	0	2	.000	12	0	0	0	2	19^2	17	1	5	5	10.1	2.75	131	.233	.282	1	.500	0	2	2	1	0.4
Total 4	7	8	.467	118	1	0	0	9	175^1	184	6	69	63	13.2	3.64	94	.275	.347	3	.231	1	-0	-4	4	0.1

● **MARK LEE** Lee, Mark Owen b: 7/20/64, Williston, N.Dak. BL/TL, 6'3", 198 lbs. Deb: 9/08/88

YEAR TM/L	W	L	PCT	G	GS	CG	SH	SV	IP	H	HR	BB	SO	RAT	ERA	ERA+	OAV	OOB	BH	AVG	PB	PR	/A	PD	TPI
1988 KC-A	0	0	—	4	0	0	0	0	5	6	0	1	0	12.6	3.60	111	.300	.333	0	—	0	0	0	0	0.0
1990 Mil-A	1	0	1.000	11	0	0	0	0	21^1	20	1	4	14	10.1	2.11	184	.256	.293	0	—	0	4	4	-0	0.4
1991 Mil-A	2	5	.286	62	0	0	0	1	67^2	72	10	31	43	13.8	3.86	103	.283	.364	0	—	0	2	1	1	0.3
Total 3	3	5	.375	77	0	0	0	1	94	98	11	36	57	12.9	3.45	115	.278	.347	0	—	0	6	5	0	0.7

● **MIKE LEE** Lee, Michael Randall b: 5/19/41, Bell, Cal. BL/TL, 6'5", 220 lbs. Deb: 5/06/60

YEAR TM/L	W	L	PCT	G	GS	CG	SH	SV	IP	H	HR	BB	SO	RAT	ERA	ERA+	OAV	OOB	BH	AVG	PB	PR	/A	PD	TPI
1960 Cle-A	0	0	—	7	0	0	0	0	9	6	1	11	6	18.0	2.00	187	.207	.439	0	—	0	2	2	-0	0.1
1963 LA-A	1	1	.500	6	4	0	0	0	26	30	3	14	11	15.6	3.81	90	.300	.391	0	.000	-1	-1	-1	1	-0.1
Total 2	1	1	.500	13	4	0	0	0	35	36	4	25	17	16.2	3.34	105	.279	.404	0	.000	-1	1	1	1	0.0

● **BOB LEE** Lee, Robert Dean "Moose" or "Horse" b: 11/26/37, Ottumwa, Iowa BR/TR, 6'3", 230 lbs. Deb: 4/15/64

YEAR TM/L	W	L	PCT	G	GS	CG	SH	SV	IP	H	HR	BB	SO	RAT	ERA	ERA+	OAV	OOB	BH	AVG	PB	PR	/A	PD	TPI
1964 LA-A	6	5	.545	64	5	0	0	19	137	87	6	58	111	9.6	1.51	217	.182	.272	0	.000	-2	**32**	27	-2	2.5
1965 Cal-A☆	9	7	.563	69	0	0	0	23	131^1	95	11	42	89	9.5	1.92	177	.205	.272	3	.143	1	22	22	-1	2.3
1966 Cal-A	5	4	.556	61	0	0	0	16	101^2	90	8	31	46	10.8	2.74	122	.237	.297	0	.000	-0	8	7	-1	0.7
1967 LA-N	0	0	—	4	0	0	0	0	6^2	6	2	3	2	13.5	5.40	57	.222	.323	0	—	0	-2	-2	-0	-0.2
Cin-N	3	3	.500	27	1	0	0	2	50^2	51	0	25	33	13.5	4.44	84	.262	.345	3	.375	1	-6	-4	-1	-0.4
Yr	3	3	.500	31	1	0	0	2	57^1	57	2	28	35	13.3	4.55	81	.254	.337	3	.375	1	-8	-6	-1	-0.6
1968 Cin-N	2	4	.333	44	1	0	0	3	65^1	73	4	37	34	15.3	5.10	62	.302	.396	1	.200	0	-15	-14	-1	-1.7

YEAR	TM/L	W	L	PCT	G	GS	CG	SH	SV	IP	H	HR	BB	SO	RAT	ERA	ERA+	OAV	OOB	BH	AVG	PB	PR	/A	PD	TPI
Total	5	25	23	.521	269	7	0	0	63	492^2	402	31	196	315	11.0	2.70	125	.225	.304	7	.104	-1	40	36	-6	3.2

● ROY LEE Lee, Roy Edwin b: 9/28/17, Elmira, N.Y. d: 11/11/85, St.Louis, Mo. BL/TL, 5'11.5", 175 lbs. Deb: 9/23/45

YEAR	TM/L	W	L	PCT	G	GS	CG	SH	SV	IP	H	HR	BB	SO	RAT	ERA	ERA+	OAV	OOB	BH	AVG	PB	PR	/A	PD	TPI
1945	NY-N	0	2	.000	3	1	0	0	0	7	8	3	3	0	14.1	11.57	34	.267	.333	0	.000	-0	-6	-6	-0	-0.6

● TOM LEE Lee, Thomas Frank b: 6/8/1862, Philadelphia, Pa. d: 3/4/1886, Milwaukee, Wis. Deb: 6/14/1884

YEAR	TM/L	W	L	PCT	G	GS	CG	SH	SV	IP	H	HR	BB	SO	RAT	ERA	ERA+	OAV	OOB	BH	AVG	PB	PR	/A	PD	TPI
1884	Chi-N	1	4	.200	5	5	5	0	0	45^1	55	12	15	14	13.9	3.77	83	.272	.323	3	.125	-2	-4	-3	-0	-0.5
	Bal-U	5	8	.385	15	14	12	0	0	122	121	1	29	81	11.1	3.39	98	.242	.283	23	.280	1	-5	-1	0	0.0
Total	1	6	12	.333	20	19	17	0	0	167^1	176	13	44	95	11.8	3.50	93	.251	.295	26	.245	-1	-9	-4	0	-0.5

● THORNTON LEE Lee, Thornton Starr "Lefty" b: 9/13/06, Sonoma, Cal. BL/TL, 6'3", 205 lbs. Deb: 9/19/33 F

YEAR	TM/L	W	L	PCT	G	GS	CG	SH	SV	IP	H	HR	BB	SO	RAT	ERA	ERA+	OAV	OOB	BH	AVG	PB	PR	/A	PD	TPI
1933	Cle-A	1	1	.500	3	2	2	0	0	17^1	13	1	11	7	12.5	4.15	107	.203	.320	3	.375	1	0	1	-0	0.2
1934	Cle-A	1	1	.500	24	6	0	0	0	85^2	105	8	44	41	16.0	5.04	90	.308	.392	2	.095	-1	-5	-5	0	-0.5
1935	Cle-A	7	10	.412	32	20	8	1	1	180^2	179	6	71	81	12.7	4.04	112	.259	.331	12	.197	-1	8	9	2	1.0
1936	Cle-A	3	5	.375	43	8	2	0	3	127	138	2	67	49	14.7	4.89	103	.271	.358	5	.122	-2	**2**	2	2	0.2
1937	Chi-A	12	10	.545	30	25	13	2	0	204^2	209	17	60	80	11.9	3.52	131	.260	.312	15	.211	1	25	25	-1	2.3
1938	Chi-A	13	12	.520	33	30	18	1	1	245^1	252	12	94	77	12.8	3.49	140	.263	.331	25	.258	6	36	**38**	-2	**4.1**
1939	Chi-A	15	11	.577	33	29	15	2	3	235	260	14	70	81	12.8	4.21	112	.285	.338	15	.165	-3	11	14	0	1.0
1940	Chi-A	12	13	.480	28	27	24	1	0	228	223	13	56	87	11.1	3.47	127	.254	.300	23	.274	4	23	24	-3	2.5
1941	Chi-A★	22	11	.667	35	34	**30**	3	1	300^1	258	18	92	130	**10.6**	**2.37**	**173**	.232	**.293**	29	.254	5	**59**	**58**	-2	**6.6**
1942	Chi-A	2	6	.250	11	8	6	1	0	76	82	4	31	25	13.6	3.32	109	.278	.351	6	.200	0	3	2	-2	0.1
1943	Chi-A	5	9	.357	19	19	7	1	0	127	129	8	50	35	13.0	4.18	80	.266	.340	3	.071	-4	-12	-12	-3	-1.9
1944	Chi-A	3	9	.250	15	14	6	0	0	113^1	105	3	25	39	10.4	3.02	114	.246	.290	4	.095	-3	5	5	2	0.4
1945	Chi-A	15	12	.556	29	28	19	1	0	228^1	208	6	76	108	11.6	2.44	136	.245	.314	14	.179	-1	23	22	-1	2.2
1946	Chi-A	2	4	.333	7	7	2	0	0	43^1	39	1	23	23	13.1	3.53	97	.244	.342	4	.267	1	-0	-1	-0	0.0
1947	Chi-A	3	7	.300	21	11	2	1	1	86^2	86	5	56	57	15.0	4.47	82	.261	.372	6	.207	0	-7	-8	0	-0.7
1948	NY-N	1	3	.250	11	4	1	0	0	32^2	41	3	12	17	14.9	4.41	89	.304	.365	1	.091	-1	-2	-2	0	-0.2
Total	16	117	124	.485	374	272	155	14	10	2331^1	2327	121	838	937	12.4	3.56	119	.260	.326	167	.200	1	169	172	-7	17.3

● BILL LEE Lee, William Crutcher "Big Bill" b: 10/21/09, Plaquemine, La. d: 6/15/77, Plaquemine, La. BR/TR, 6'3", 195 lbs. Deb: 4/29/34

YEAR	TM/L	W	L	PCT	G	GS	CG	SH	SV	IP	H	HR	BB	SO	RAT	ERA	ERA+	OAV	OOB	BH	AVG	PB	PR	/A	PD	TPI
1934	Chi-N	13	14	.481	35	29	16	4	1	214^1	218	9	74	104	12.3	3.40	114	.263	.325	10	.132	-2	16	11	2	1.0
1935	*Chi-N	20	6	**.769**	39	32	18	3	1	252	241	11	84	100	11.8	2.96	133	.251	.314	24	.235	2	30	27	-0	2.9
1936	Chi-N	18	11	.621	43	33	20	**4**	1	258^2	238	14	93	102	11.6	3.31	121	.246	.314	12	.138	-3	21	19	1	1.7
1937	Chi-N	14	15	.483	42	33	17	2	3	272^1	289	14	73	108	12.0	3.54	113	.273	.320	15	.172	-1	11	13	3	1.5
1938	*Chi-N★	**22**	9	**.710**	44	37	19	**9**	2	291	281	18	74	121	11.0	**2.66**	**144**	.252	.299	20	.198	1	**37**	**38**	1	**4.1**
1939	Chi-N★	19	15	.559	37	36	20	1	0	282^1	295	18	85	105	12.1	3.44	114	.272	.325	13	.126	-4	15	16	5	1.6
1940	Chi-N	9	17	.346	37	30	9	1	0	211^1	246	12	70	70	13.5	5.03	75	.294	.350	10	.132	-2	-28	-30	-1	-3.2
1941	Chi-N	8	14	.364	28	22	12	0	1	167^1	179	6	43	62	12.0	3.76	93	.270	.316	11	.186	1	-2	-5	1	-0.3
1942	Chi-N	13	13	.500	32	30	18	1	0	219^2	221	4	67	75	11.8	3.85	83	.258	.312	11	.159	1	-13	-16	1	-1.4
1943	Chi-N	3	7	.300	13	12	4	0	0	78^1	83	4	27	18	12.6	3.56	94	.273	.332	7	.269	1	-2	-2	-1	-0.2
	Phi-N	1	5	.167	13	7	2	0	3	60^2	70	4	21	17	13.6	4.60	73	.298	.358	1	.059	-2	-8	-8	-1	-1.1
	Yr	4	12	.250	26	19	6	0	3	139	153	8	48	35	13.1	4.01	84	.284	.344	8	.186	-0	-10	-10	-2	-1.3
1944	Phi-N	10	11	.476	31	28	11	3	1	208^1	199	9	57	50	11.2	3.15	115	.248	.300	14	.194	-0	11	11	2	1.3
1945	Phi-N	3	6	.333	13	13	2	0	0	77^1	107	0	30	13	15.9	4.66	82	.318	.374	4	.167	-1	-7	-7	0	-0.7
	Bos-N	6	3	.667	16	13	6	1	0	106^1	112	6	36	12	12.5	2.79	137	.279	.338	4	.129	-1	12	12	1	1.3
	Yr	9	9	.500	29	26	8	1	0	183^2	219	6	66	25	14.0	3.58	107	.297	.354	8	.145	-1	5	5	1	0.6
1946	Bos-N	10	9	.526	25	21	8	0	0	140	148	7	45	32	12.5	4.18	82	.273	.330	8	.170	-1	-12	-12	1	-1.2
1947	Chi-N	0	2	.000	14	2	0	0	0	24	26	2	14	9	15.4	4.50	88	.268	.366	1	.333	0	-1	-1	0	-0.1
Total	14	169	157	.518	462	378	182	29	13	2864	2953	138	893	998	12.2	3.54	106	.266	.322	165	.168	-10	78	66	14	7.2

● BILL LEE Lee, William Francis b: 12/28/46, Burbank, Cal. BL/TL, 6'3", 210 lbs. Deb: 6/25/69

YEAR	TM/L	W	L	PCT	G	GS	CG	SH	SV	IP	H	HR	BB	SO	RAT	ERA	ERA+	OAV	OOB	BH	AVG	PB	PR	/A	PD	TPI
1969	Bos-A	1	3	.250	20	1	0	0	0	52	56	9	28	45	14.9	4.50	84	.281	.376	0	.000	-1	-5	-4	-0	-0.6
1970	Bos-A	2	2	.500	11	5	0	0	1	37	48	3	14	19	15.1	4.62	86	.320	.378	0	.000	-1	-4	-3	1	-0.3
1971	Bos-A	9	2	.818	47	3	0	0	2	102	102	7	46	74	13.1	2.74	135	.256	.335	5	.217	0	8	11	0	1.3
1972	Bos-A	7	4	.636	47	0	0	0	5	84^1	75	5	32	43	11.5	3.20	100	.248	.322	3	.188	1	-1	0	3	0.5
1973	Bos-A☆	17	11	.607	38	33	18	1	1	284^2	275	20	76	120	11.3	2.75	146	.257	.309	0	—	0	34	40	1	4.5
1974	Bos-A	17	15	.531	38	37	16	1	0	282^1	320	25	67	95	12.5	3.51	110	.290	.333	0	—	0	3	11	4	1.3
1975	*Bos-A	17	9	.654	41	34	17	4	0	260	274	20	69	78	12.0	3.95	103	.273	.322	0	—	0	-5	4	2	0.5
1976	Bos-A	5	7	.417	24	14	1	0	3	96	124	13	28	29	14.5	5.63	70	.307	.356	0	—	0	-22	-18	1	-1.8
1977	Bos-A	9	5	.643	27	16	4	0	1	128	155	14	29	31	12.9	4.43	101	.306	.344	0	—	0	-5	1	2	0.1
1978	Bos-A	10	10	.500	28	24	8	1	0	177	198	20	59	44	13.2	3.46	119	.285	.343	0	—	0	6	13	0	0.7
1979	Mon-N	16	10	.615	33	33	6	3	0	222	230	20	46	59	11.2	3.04	121	.265	.303	16	.216	2	17	15	1	1.9
1980	Mon-N	4	6	.400	24	18	2	0	0	118	156	13	22	34	13.8	4.96	72	.319	.352	9	.220	1	-18	-18	-0	-1.8
1981	*Mon-N	5	6	.455	31	7	0	0	6	88^2	90	6	14	34	10.8	2.94	119	.265	.298	8	.364	3	5	5	3	1.3
1982	Mon-N	0	0	—	7	0	0	0	0	12^1	19	1	1	8	14.6	4.38	83	.352	.364	0	—	0	-1	-1	0	-0.1
Total	14	119	90	.569	416	225	72	10	19	1944^1	2122	176	531	713	12.4	3.62	107	.280	.329	41	.208	5	12	55	16	7.5

● WATTY LEE Lee, Wyatt Arnold b: 8/12/1879, Lynch's Station, Va. d: 3/6/36, Washington, D.C. BL/TL, 5'10.5", 171 lbs. Deb: 4/30/01 ♦

YEAR	TM/L	W	L	PCT	G	GS	CG	SH	SV	IP	H	HR	BB	SO	RAT	ERA	ERA+	OAV	OOB	BH	AVG	PB	PR	/A	PD	TPI
1901	Was-A	16	16	.500	36	33	25	2	0	262	328	14	45	63	13.2	4.40	83	.303	.336	33	.256	4	-21	-21	2	-1.3
1902	Was-A	5	7	.417	13	10	10	0	0	98	118	5	20	24	13.4	5.05	73	.298	.345	100	.256	3	-16	-15	1	-1.0
1903	Was-A	8	12	.400	22	20	15	2	0	166^2	169	5	40	70	11.7	3.08	102	.262	.312	48	.208	2	-2	1	3	0.6
1904	Pit-N	1	2	.333	5	3	1	0	0	22^2	34	0	9	5	18.3	8.74	31	.337	.407	4	.333	1	-15	-15	0	-1.3
Total	4	30	37	.448	76	66	51	4	0	549^1	649	24	114	162	13.0	4.29	81	.292	.334	185	.242	9	-55	-50	5	-3.0

● SAM LEEVER Leever, Samuel "Deacon" or "The Goshen Schoolmaster" b: 12/23/1871, Goshen, Ohio d: 5/19/53, Goshen, Ohio BR/TR, 5'10.5", 175 lbs. Deb: 5/26/1898

YEAR	TM/L	W	L	PCT	G	GS	CG	SH	SV	IP	H	HR	BB	SO	RAT	ERA	ERA+	OAV	OOB	BH	AVG	PB	PR	/A	PD	TPI
1898	Pit-N	1	0	1.000	5	3	2	0	0	33	26	0	5	15	8.7	2.45	145	.215	.253	3	.250	0	4	4	-0	0.4
1899	Pit-N	21	23	.477	**51**	39	35	4	**3**	**379**	353	7	122	121	11.5	3.18	120	.247	.311	33	.226	3	28	27	1	2.9
1900	*Pit-N	15	13	.536	30	29	25	3	0	232^2	236	2	48	84	11.4	2.71	134	.263	.307	18	.205	0	26	24	-1	2.2
1901	Pit-N	14	5	.737	21	20	18	2	0	176	182	2	39	82	11.6	2.86	114	.265	.310	13	.183	-1	9	8	2	0.9
1902	Pit-N	15	7	.682	28	26	23	4	2	222	203	2	31	86	9.7	2.39	114	.243	.276	16	.178	-0	10	9	-4	0.5
1903	*Pit-N	25	7	**.781**	36	34	30	**7**	1	284^1	255	2	60	90	10.1	**2.06**	**157**	.238	.282	19	.165	-3	38	37	-0	3.3
1904	Pit-N	18	11	.621	34	32	26	1	0	253^1	224	2	54	63	10.1	2.17	127	.237	.282	26	.263	6	16	16	-1	2.3
1905	Pit-N	20	5	**.800**	33	29	20	3	1	229^2	199	3	54	81	10.4	2.70	111	.231	.286	9	.102	-4	8	8	0	0.4
1906	Pit-N	22	7	.759	36	31	25	6	0	260^1	232	3	48	76	9.9	2.32	115	.243	.284	20	.211	2	9	10	-5	0.8
1907	Pit-N	14	9	.609	31	24	17	5	0	216^2	182	3	46	65	9.8	1.66	147	.229	.278	11	.151	-1	20	19	-5	1.4
1908	Pit-N	15	7	.682	38	20	14	4	2	192^2	179	1	41	28	10.6	2.10	110	.249	.295	9	.148	-0	6	4	-4	0.1
1909	Pit-N	8	1	.889	19	4	2	0	2	70	74	0	14	23	11.8	2.83	96	.276	.322	4	.167	0	-2	-1	0	-0.1
1910	Pit-N	6	5	.545	26	8	4	0	2	111	104	2	25	33	10.9	2.76	112	.259	.313	2	.065	-3	3	4	1	0.2
Total	13	194	100	.660	388	299	241	39	13	2660^2	2449	29	587	847	10.6	2.47	123	.245	.293	183	.184	-1	175	169	-15	15.3

● BILL LeFEBVRE LeFebvre, Wilfrid Henry "Lefty" b: 11/11/15, Natick, R.I. BL/TL, 5'11.5", 180 lbs. Deb: 6/10/38 ♦

YEAR	TM/L	W	L	PCT	G	GS	CG	SH	SV	IP	H	HR	BB	SO	RAT	ERA	ERA+	OAV	OOB	BH	AVG	PB	PR	/A	PD	TPI
1938	Bos-A	0	0	—	1	0	0	0	0	4	8	2	0	0	20.3	13.50	37	.400	.429	1	1.000	1	-4	-4	-0	-0.2
1939	Bos-A	1	1	.500	5	3	0	0	0	26^1	35	2	14	8	16.7	5.81	81	.333	.412	3	.300	1	-3	-3	-1	-0.3
1943	Was-A	2	0	1.000	6	3	1	0	0	32^1	33	3	16	10	13.6	4.45	72	.268	.353	4	.286	2	-4	-4	-0	-0.3

YEAR	TM/L	W	L	PCT	G	GS	CG	SH	SV	IP	H	HR	BB	SO	RAT	ERA	ERA+	OAV	OOB	BH	AVG	PB	PR	/A	PD	TPI
1944	Was-A	2	4	.333	24	4	2	0	3	69^2	86	3	21	18	14.0	4.52	72	.305	.355	16	.258	3	-8	-10	-0	-0.5
Total	4	5	5	.500	36	10	3	0	3	132^1	162	10	51	36	14.6	5.03	71	.306	.369	24	.276	7	-20	-21	-1	-1.3

● CRAIG LEFFERTS Lefferts, Craig Lindsey b: 9/29/57, Munich, W.Germany BL/TL, 6'1", 210 lbs. Deb: 4/07/83

YEAR	TM/L	W	L	PCT	G	GS	CG	SH	SV	IP	H	HR	BB	SO	RAT	ERA	ERA+	OAV	OOB	BH	AVG	PB	PR	/A	PD	TPI
1983	Chi-N	3	4	.429	56	5	0	0	1	89	80	13	29	60	11.2	3.13	121	.243	.308	2	.111	-1	5	6	0	0.6
1984	*SD-N	3	4	.429	62	0	0	0	10	105^2	88	4	24	56	9.6	2.13	167	.229	.276	5	.294	1	17	17	-1	1.8
1985	SD-N	7	6	.538	60	0	0	0	2	83^1	75	7	30	48	11.3	3.35	106	.244	.312	1	.250	0	2	2	-0	0.2
1986	SD-N	9	8	.529	**83**	0	0	0	4	107^2	98	7	44	72	12.0	3.09	118	.253	.331	1	.125	1	7	7	2	0.9
1987	SD-N	2	2	.500	33	0	0	0	2	51^1	56	9	15	39	12.8	4.38	90	.272	.327	1	.333	0	-2	-2	-1	-0.3
	*SF-N	3	3	.500	44	0	0	0	4	47^1	36	4	18	18	10.3	3.23	119	.216	.292	1	.250	0	4	3	-1	0.3
	Yr	5	5	.500	77	0	0	0	6	98^2	92	13	33	57	11.4	3.83	102	.245	.306	2	.286	1	3	1	-1	0.0
1988	SF-N	3	8	.273	64	0	0	0	11	92^1	74	7	23	58	9.6	2.92	112	.225	.278	0	.000	-1	5	3	-1	0.2
1989	*SF-N	2	4	.333	70	0	0	0	20	107	93	11	22	71	9.8	2.69	125	.233	.275	0	.000	-1	10	8	-1	0.7
1990	SD-N	7	5	.583	56	0	0	0	23	78^2	68	10	22	60	10.4	2.52	152	.228	.283	1	.250	0	11	11	0	1.2
1991	SD-N	1	6	.143	54	0	0	0	23	69	74	5	14	48	11.6	3.91	97	.285	.324	0	.000	-1	-2	-1	0	-0.1
1992	SD-N	13	9	.591	27	27	0	0	0	163^1	180	16	35	81	11.8	3.69	98	.285	.322	4	.077	-3	-3	-1	-1	-0.5
	Bal-A	1	3	.250	5	5	1	0	0	33	34	3	6	23	10.9	4.09	95	.268	.301	0	—	0	-1	-1	-1	-0.1
Total	10	54	62	.466	614	37	1	0	100	1027^2	956	96	282	634	10.9	3.17	115	.250	.303	16	.121	-3	55	53	-3	4.9

● REGIS LEHENY Leheny, Regis Francis b: 1/5/08, Pittsburgh, Pa. d: 11/2/76, Pittsburgh, Pa. BL/TL, 6'0.5", 180 lbs. Deb: 5/21/32

YEAR	TM/L	W	L	PCT	G	GS	CG	SH	SV	IP	H	HR	BB	SO	RAT	ERA	ERA+	OAV	OOB	BH	AVG	PB	PR	/A	PD	TPI
1932	Bos-A	0	0	—	2	0	0	0	0	2^2	5	0	3	1	27.0	16.88	27	.417	.533	0	.000	-0	-4	-4	0	-0.3

● JIM LEHEW Lehew, James Anthony b: 8/19/37, Baltimore, Md. BR/TR, 6', 185 lbs. Deb: 9/13/61

YEAR	TM/L	W	L	PCT	G	GS	CG	SH	SV	IP	H	HR	BB	SO	RAT	ERA	ERA+	OAV	OOB	BH	AVG	PB	PR	/A	PD	TPI
1961	Bal-A	0	0	—	2	0	0	0	0	2	1	0	0	0	4.5	0.00	—	.167	.167	0	—	0	1	1	0	0.1
1962	Bal-A	0	0	—	6	0	0	0	0	9^2	10	0	3	2	12.1	1.86	202	.303	.361	0	.000	-0	2	2	0	0.2
Total	2	0	0	—	8	0	0	0	0	11^2	11	0	3	2	10.8	1.54	245	.282	.333	0	.000	-0	3	3	0	0.3

● KEN LEHMAN Lehman, Kenneth Karl b: 6/10/28, Seattle, Wash. BL/TL, 6', 186 lbs. Deb: 9/05/52

YEAR	TM/L	W	L	PCT	G	GS	CG	SH	SV	IP	H	HR	BB	SO	RAT	ERA	ERA+	OAV	OOB	BH	AVG	PB	PR	/A	PD	TPI
1952	*Bro-N	1	2	.333	4	3	0	0	0	15^1	19	1	6	7	14.7	5.28	69	.297	.357	0	.000	0	-3	-3	0	-0.2
1956	Bro-N	2	3	.400	25	4	0	0	0	49^1	65	11	23	29	16.1	5.66	70	.325	.395	3	.300	1	-10	-9	1	-0.8
1957	Bro-N	0	0	—	3	0	0	0	0	7	7	0	1	3	10.3	0.00	—	.259	.286	1	.500	0	3	3	0	0.4
	Bal-A	8	3	.727	30	3	1	0	6	68	57	1	22	32	10.5	2.78	129	.232	.295	4	.200	1	8	6	-1	0.7
1958	Bal-A	2	1	.667	31	1	1	0	0	62	64	5	18	36	12.2	3.48	103	.276	.333	1	.071	-1	2	1	0	0.0
1961	Phi-N	1	1	.500	41	2	0	0	1	63^1	61	6	25	27	12.4	4.26	96	.260	.333	0	.000	-1	-2	-1	1	-0.1
Total	5	14	10	.583	134	13	2	0	7	265	273	24	95	134	12.6	3.91	97	.272	.337	9	.161	1	-2	-3	2	-0.0

● NORM LEHR Lehr, Norman Carl Michael "King" b: 5/28/01, Rochester, N.Y. d: 7/17/68, Livonia, N.Y. BR/TR, 6', 168 lbs. Deb: 5/20/26

YEAR	TM/L	W	L	PCT	G	GS	CG	SH	SV	IP	H	HR	BB	SO	RAT	ERA	ERA+	OAV	OOB	BH	AVG	PB	PR	/A	PD	TPI
1926	Cle-A	0	0	—	4	0	0	0	0	14^2	11	0	4	4	9.2	3.07	132	.216	.273	0	.000	-1	2	2	1	0.2

● HANK LEIBER Leiber, Henry Edward b: 1/17/11, Phoenix, Ariz. BR/TR, 6'1.5", 205 lbs. Deb: 4/16/33 ♦

YEAR	TM/L	W	L	PCT	G	GS	CG	SH	SV	IP	H	HR	BB	SO	RAT	ERA	ERA+	OAV	OOB	BH	AVG	PB	PR	/A	PD	TPI
1942	NY-N	0	1	.000	1	1	1	0	0	9	9	0	5	5	15.0	6.00	56	.290	.405	32	.218	0	-3	-3	0	-0.2

● CHARLIE LEIBRANDT Leibrandt, Charles Louis b: 10/4/56, Chicago, Ill. BR/TL, 6'3", 200 lbs. Deb: 9/17/79

YEAR	TM/L	W	L	PCT	G	GS	CG	SH	SV	IP	H	HR	BB	SO	RAT	ERA	ERA+	OAV	OOB	BH	AVG	PB	PR	/A	PD	TPI
1979	*Cin-N	0	0	—	3	0	0	0	0	4^1	2	0	2	1	8.3	0.00	—	.154	.267	0	—	0	2	2	0	0.2
1980	Cin-N	10	9	.526	36	27	5	2	0	173^2	200	15	54	62	13.3	4.25	84	.292	.346	11	.196	1	-13	-13	1	-1.1
1981	Cin-N	1	1	.500	7	4	1	1	0	30	28	0	15	9	12.9	3.60	99	.262	.352	0	.000	-0	-0	-0	0	0.0
1982	Cin-N	5	7	.417	36	11	0	0	2	107^2	130	4	48	34	15.0	5.10	73	.308	.381	2	.080	-1	-18	-17	-0	-1.9
1984	*KC-A	11	7	.611	23	23	0	0	0	143^2	158	11	38	53	12.5	3.63	111	.277	.326	0	—	0	6	6	-2	0.5
1985	*KC-A	17	9	.654	33	33	8	3	0	237^2	223	17	68	108	11.1	2.69	155	.248	.302	0	—	0	38	39	4	4.6
1986	KC-A	14	11	.560	35	34	8	1	0	231^1	238	18	63	108	11.9	4.09	104	.268	.319	0	—	0	2	4	2	0.6
1987	KC-A	16	11	.593	35	35	8	3	0	240^1	235	23	74	151	11.6	3.41	134	.253	.308	0	—	0	28	31	4	3.5
1988	KC-A	13	12	.520	35	35	7	2	0	243	244	20	62	125	11.5	3.19	125	.264	.313	0	—	0	21	22	2	2.5
1989	KC-A	5	11	.313	33	27	3	1	0	161	196	13	54	73	14.1	5.14	75	.304	.360	0	—	0	-23	-23	-0	-2.3
1990	Atl-N	9	11	.450	24	24	5	2	0	162^1	164	9	35	76	11.3	3.16	128	.261	.304	9	.180	1	11	16	1	1.9
1991	*Atl-N	15	13	.536	36	36	1	1	0	229^2	212	18	56	128	10.7	3.49	111	.245	.294	3	.043	-4	5	10	4	1.0
1992	*Atl-N	15	7	.682	32	31	5	2	0	193	191	9	42	104	11.1	3.36	112	.258	.302	7	.121	-2	3	8	3	1.1
Total	13	131	109	.546	368	320	51	18	2	2157^2	2221	157	611	1032	12.0	3.65	110	.267	.320	32	.120	-5	64	85	20	10.6

● LEFTY LEIFIELD Leifield, Albert Peter b: 9/5/1883, Trenton, Ill. d: 10/10/70, Alexandria, Va. BL/TL, 6'1", 165 lbs. Deb: 9/03/05 C

YEAR	TM/L	W	L	PCT	G	GS	CG	SH	SV	IP	H	HR	BB	SO	RAT	ERA	ERA+	OAV	OOB	BH	AVG	PB	PR	/A	PD	TPI
1905	Pit-N	5	2	.714	8	7	6	1	0	56	52	0	14	10	11.3	2.89	104	.248	.307	7	.350	3	1	1	1	0.5
1906	Pit-N	18	13	.581	37	31	24	8	1	255^2	214	3	68	111	10.4	1.87	143	.231	.294	11	.125	-3	22	23	1	2.4
1907	Pit-N	20	16	.556	40	33	24	6	1	286	270	1	100	112	12.0	2.33	105	.256	.328	15	.147	0	5	3	4	0.8
1908	Pit-N	15	14	.517	34	26	18	5	2	218^2	168	1	86	87	10.9	2.10	110	.212	.299	17	.227	3	6	5	-0	0.8
1909	*Pit-N	19	8	.704	32	27	13	3	0	201^2	172	4	54	43	10.4	2.37	115	.229	.286	14	.192	2	5	8	-2	0.9
1910	Pit-N	15	13	.536	40	30	13	3	2	218^1	197	6	67	64	11.3	2.64	117	.253	.320	11	.183	1	10	11	3	1.5
1911	Pit-N	16	16	.500	42	37	26	2	1	318	301	7	82	111	11.3	2.63	130	.260	.318	24	.235	6	27	28	-1	3.5
1912	Pit-N	1	2	.333	6	1	1	1	0	23^2	29	0	10	8	15.6	4.18	78	.302	.380	1	.143	0	-2	-2	1	-0.1
	Chi-N	7	2	.778	13	9	4	1	0	70^2	68	0	21	23	11.7	2.42	138	.258	.319	3	.115	-1	8	7	1	0.7
	Yr	8	4	.667	19	10	5	2	0	94^1	97	0	31	31	12.5	2.86	116	.268	.331	4	.121	-1	6	5	2	0.6
1913	Chi-N	0	1	.000	6	1	0	0	0	21^1	28	0	5	4	13.9	5.48	58	.329	.367	0	.000	-1	-5	-5	1	-0.6
1918	StL-A	2	6	.250	15	6	3	1	0	67	61	1	19	22	11.0	2.55	107	.252	.312	1	.053	-2	2	1	1	0.1
1919	StL-A	6	4	.600	19	9	6	2	0	92	96	4	25	18	12.2	2.93	113	.270	.325	3	.100	-3	3	4	1	0.2
1920	StL-A	0	0	—	4	0	0	0	0	9	17	0	3	3	20.0	7.00	56	.405	.444	0	.000	-0	-3	-3	-0	-0.3
Total	12	124	97	.561	296	217	138	33	7	1838	1673	27	554	616	11.3	2.47	116	.248	.313	107	.175	6	77	81	10	10.4

● DAVE LEIPER Leiper, David Paul b: 6/18/62, Whittier, Cal. BL/TL, 6'1", 160 lbs. Deb: 9/02/84

YEAR	TM/L	W	L	PCT	G	GS	CG	SH	SV	IP	H	HR	BB	SO	RAT	ERA	ERA+	OAV	OOB	BH	AVG	PB	PR	/A	PD	TPI
1984	Oak-A	1	0	1.000	8	0	0	0	0	7	12	2	5	3	21.9	9.00	42	.353	.436	0	—	0	-4	-4	0	-0.4
1986	Oak-A	2	2	.500	33	0	0	0	1	31^2	28	3	18	15	13.6	4.83	80	.252	.366	0	—	0	-2	-3	0	-0.3
1987	Oak-A	2	1	.667	45	0	0	0	1	52^1	49	6	18	33	11.7	3.78	109	.246	.312	0	—	0	4	2	1	0.4
	SD-N	1	0	1.000	12	0	0	0	1	16	16	2	5	10	11.8	4.50	88	.267	.323	0	—	0	-1	-1	-0	-0.1
1988	SD-N	3	0	1.000	35	0	0	0	1	54	45	1	14	33	9.8	2.17	157	.231	.282	1	.500	0	8	7	0	0.9
1989	SD-N	0	1	.000	22	0	0	0	0	28^2	40	2	20	7	19.5	5.02	70	.333	.437	0	.000	-0	-5	-5	1	-0.5
Total	5	9	4	.692	155	0	0	0	4	189^2	190	16	80	101	13.0	3.94	96	.264	.342	1	.333	0	-0	-4	2	-0.0

● JACK LEIPER Leiper, John Henry Thomas b: 12/23/1867, Chester, Pa. d: 8/23/60, West Goshen, Pa. BL/TL, 5'11", Deb: 9/04/1891

YEAR	TM/L	W	L	PCT	G	GS	CG	SH	SV	IP	H	HR	BB	SO	RAT	ERA	ERA+	OAV	OOB	BH	AVG	PB	PR	/A	PD	TPI
1891	Col-a	2	2	.500	6	5	4	0	0	45	41	3	39	19	16.8	5.40	64	.234	.386	3	.143	-2	-8	-10	-1	-0.9

● JOHN LEISTER Leister, John William b: 1/3/61, San Antonio, Tex. BR/TR, 6'2", 200 lbs. Deb: 5/28/87

YEAR	TM/L	W	L	PCT	G	GS	CG	SH	SV	IP	H	HR	BB	SO	RAT	ERA	ERA+	OAV	OOB	BH	AVG	PB	PR	/A	PD	TPI
1987	Bos-A	0	2	.000	8	6	0	0	0	30^1	49	9	12	16	18.1	9.20	49	.368	.421	0	—	0	-16	-16	-1	-1.4
1990	Bos-A	0	0	—	2	1	0	0	0	5^2	7	0	4	3	17.5	4.76	86	.304	.407	0	—	0	-1	-0	-0	-0.3
Total	2	0	2	.000	10	7	0	0	0	36	56	9	16	19	18.0	8.50	53	.359	.419	0	—	0	-17	-16	-1	-1.7

● AL LEITER Leiter, Alois Terry b: 10/23/65, Toms River, N.J. BL/TL, 6'3", 210 lbs. Deb: 9/15/87 F

YEAR	TM/L	W	L	PCT	G	GS	CG	SH	SV	IP	H	HR	BB	SO	RAT	ERA	ERA+	OAV	OOB	BH	AVG	PB	PR	/A	PD	TPI
1987	NY-A	2	2	.500	4	4	0	0	0	22^2	24	2	15	28	15.5	6.35	69	.273	.379	0	—	0	-5	-5	-0	-0.4
1988	NY-A	4	4	.500	14	14	0	0	0	57^1	49	7	33	60	13.7	3.92	100	.231	.348	0	—	0	0	0	1	0.1
1989	NY-A	1	2	.333	4	4	0	0	0	26^2	23	1	21	22	15.5	6.08	64	.235	.380	0	—	0	-6	-7	-0	-0.6

YEAR	TM/L	W	L	PCT	G	GS	CG	SH	SV	IP	H	HR	BB	SO	RAT	ERA	ERA+	OAV	OOB	BH	AVG	PB	PR	/A	PD	TPI
	Tor-A	0	0	—	1	1	0	0	0	6^2	9	1	2	4	14.9	4.05	93	.310	.355	0	—	0	-0	-0	-0	0.0
	Yr	1	2	.333	5	5	0	0	0	33^1	32	2	23	26	14.9	5.67	68	.246	.359	0	—	0	-7	-7	-1	-0.6
1990	Tor-A	0	0	—	4	0	0	0	0	6^1	1	0	2	5	4.3	0.00	—	.050	.136	0	—	0	3	3	0	0.2
1991	Tor-A	0	0	—	3	0	0	0	0	1^2	3	0	5	1	43.2	27.00	16	.429	.667	0	—	0	-4	-4	0	-0.6
1992	Tor-A	0	0	—	1	0	0	0	0	1	1	0	2	0	27.0	9.00	45	.200	.429	0	—	0	-1	-1	0	-0.3
Total	6	7	8	.467	31	23	0	0	0	122^1	110	11	80	120	14.5	5.00	80	.240	.361	0	—	0	-13	-14	0	-1.6

● **MARK LEITER** Leiter, Mark Edward b: 4/13/63, Joliet, Ill. BR/TR, 6′3″, 200 lbs. Deb: 7/24/90 F

YEAR	TM/L	W	L	PCT	G	GS	CG	SH	SV	IP	H	HR	BB	SO	RAT	ERA	ERA+	OAV	OOB	BH	AVG	PB	PR	/A	PD	TPI
1990	NY-A	1	1	.500	8	3	0	0	0	26^1	33	5	9	21	15.0	6.84	58	.314	.379	0	—	0	-9	-8	1	-0.7
1991	Det-A	9	7	.563	38	15	1	0	1	134^2	125	16	50	103	12.1	4.21	99	.245	.319	0	—	0	-2	-1	-1	-0.2
1992	Det-A	8	5	.615	35	14	1	0	0	112	116	9	43	75	13.0	4.18	95	.277	.348	0	—	0	-3	-2	0	-0.3
Total	3	18	13	.581	81	32	2	0	1	273	274	30	102	199	12.8	4.45	91	.265	.337	0	—	0	-13	-12	1	-1.2

● **BILL LEITH** Leith, William "Shady Bill" b: 5/31/1873, Matteawan, N.Y. d: 7/16/40, Beacon, N.Y. TL , Deb: 9/25/1899

YEAR	TM/L	W	L	PCT	G	GS	CG	SH	SV	IP	H	HR	BB	SO	RAT	ERA	ERA+	OAV	OOB	BH	AVG	PB	PR	/A	PD	TPI
1899	Was-N	0	0	—	1	0	0	0	0	2	4	0	2	1	31.5	18.00	22	.413	.552	0	.000	-0	-3	-3	-0	-0.3

● **DOC LEITNER** Leitner, George Aloysius b: 9/14/1865, Piermont, N.Y. d: 5/18/37, New York, N.Y. BR/TR, 5′11.5″, 185 lbs. Deb: 8/10/1887

YEAR	TM/L	W	L	PCT	G	GS	CG	SH	SV	IP	H	HR	BB	SO	RAT	ERA	ERA+	OAV	OOB	BH	AVG	PB	PR	/A	PD	TPI
1887	Ind-N	2	6	.250	8	8	8	0	0	65	69	6	41	27	15.2	5.68	73	.259	.358	4	.148	-3	-12	-11	-2	-1.2

● **DUMMY LEITNER** Leitner, George Michael b: 6/19/1871, Parkton, Md. d: 2/20/60, Baltimore, Md. BL/TR, 5′7″, 120 lbs. Deb: 6/29/01

YEAR	TM/L	W	L	PCT	G	GS	CG	SH	SV	IP	H	HR	BB	SO	RAT	ERA	ERA+	OAV	OOB	BH	AVG	PB	PR	/A	PD	TPI
1901	Phi-A	0	0	—	1	0	0	0	0	2	1	0	1	1	9.0	0.00	—	.148	.257	0	.000	-0	1	1	-0	0.1
	NY-N	0	2	.000	2	2	2	0	0	18	27	0	4	3	16.0	4.50	73	.344	.383	1	.143	-0	-2	-2	-0	-0.3
1902	Cle-A	0	0	—	1	1	0	0	0	8	11	0	1	0	13.5	4.50	77	.327	.346	1	.250	0	-1	-1	0	-0.1
	Chi-A	0	0	—	1	0	0	0	0	4	9	0	2	0	29.3	13.50	25	.443	.534	0	.000	-0	-4	-4	0	-0.4
	Yr	0	0	—	2	1	0	0	0	12	20	0	3	0	18.8	7.50	46	.370	.424	1	.143	-0	-5	-5	1	-0.5
Total	2	0	2	.000	5	3	2	0	0	32	48	0	8	4	16.6	5.34	63	.344	.392	2	.133	-1	-7	-7	0	-0.7

● **BILL LELIVELT** Lelivelt, William John b: 10/21/1884, Chicago, Ill. d: 2/14/68, Chicago, Ill. BR/TR, 6′, 195 lbs. Deb: 7/19/09 F

YEAR	TM/L	W	L	PCT	G	GS	CG	SH	SV	IP	H	HR	BB	SO	RAT	ERA	ERA+	OAV	OOB	BH	AVG	PB	PR	/A	PD	TPI
1909	Det-A	0	1	.000	4	2	1	0	1	20	27	0	2	4	13.0	4.50	56	.325	.341	2	.333	1	-4	-4	0	-0.4
1910	Det-A	0	1	.000	1	1	1	0	0	9	6	0	3	2	9.0	1.00	263	.207	.281	1	.500	1	2	2	0	0.3
Total	2	0	2	.000	5	3	2	0	1	29	33	0	5	6	11.8	3.41	75	.295	.325	3	.375	2	-3	-3	0	-0.1

● **DAVE LEMANCZYK** Lemanczyk, David Lawrence b: 8/17/50, Syracuse, N.Y. BR/TR, 6′4″, 235 lbs. Deb: 4/15/73

YEAR	TM/L	W	L	PCT	G	GS	CG	SH	SV	IP	H	HR	BB	SO	RAT	ERA	ERA+	OAV	OOB	BH	AVG	PB	PR	/A	PD	TPI
1973	Det-A	0	0	—	1	0	0	0	0	2^1	4	0	0	0	15.4	11.57	35	.364	.364	0	—	0	-2	-2	-0	-0.2
1974	Det-A	2	1	.667	22	3	0	0	0	78^2	79	12	44	52	14.3	4.00	95	.261	.358	0	—	0	-3	-2	1	-0.2
1975	Det-A	2	7	.222	26	6	4	0	0	109	120	8	46	67	14.0	4.46	90	.281	.355	0	—	0	-8	-5	0	-0.8
1976	Det-A	4	6	.400	20	10	1	0	0	81^1	86	7	34	51	13.3	5.09	73	.271	.342	0	—	0	-14	-12	1	-1.5
1977	Tor-A	13	16	.448	34	34	11	0	0	252	278	20	87	105	13.2	4.25	99	.282	.343	0	—	0	-5	-1	0	-0.2
1978	Tor-A	4	14	.222	29	20	3	0	0	136^2	170	16	65	62	15.7	6.26	63	.313	.389	0	—	0	-38	-35	-1	-3.6
1979	Tor-A☆	8	10	.444	22	20	11	3	0	143	137	12	45	63	11.8	3.71	117	.258	.324	0	—	0	8	10	0	0.9
1980	Tor-A	2	5	.286	10	8	0	0	0	43^1	57	4	15	10	15.0	5.40	80	.322	.375	0	—	0	-7	-5	1	-0.5
	Cal-A	2	4	.333	21	2	0	0	0	66^2	81	8	27	19	14.9	4.32	91	.301	.369	0	—	0	-2	-3	-2	-0.4
	Yr	4	9	.308	31	10	0	0	0	110	138	12	42	29	14.9	4.75	86	.308	.370	0	—	0	-9	-8	-1	-0.9
Total	8	37	63	.370	185	103	30	3	0	913	1012	87	363	429	13.8	4.62	88	.284	.354	0	—	0	-72	-56	0	-6.5

● **DENNY LEMASTER** Lemaster, Denver Clayton b: 2/25/39, Corona, Cal. BR/TL, 6′1″, 185 lbs. Deb: 7/15/62

YEAR	TM/L	W	L	PCT	G	GS	CG	SH	SV	IP	H	HR	BB	SO	RAT	ERA	ERA+	OAV	OOB	BH	AVG	PB	PR	/A	PD	TPI
1962	Mil-N	3	4	.429	17	12	4	1	0	86^2	75	11	32	69	11.4	3.01	126	.233	.308	4	.121	-1	9	8	-2	0.5
1963	Mil-N	11	14	.440	46	31	10	1	1	237	199	30	85	190	10.8	3.04	106	.227	.296	14	.189	3	7	5	-3	0.5
1964	Mil-N	17	11	.607	39	35	9	3	1	221	216	27	75	185	12.0	4.15	85	.252	.315	9	.134	0	-15	-15	0	-1.6
1965	Mil-N	7	13	.350	32	23	4	1	0	146^1	140	12	58	111	12.4	4.43	80	.251	.325	4	.089	-1	-14	-15	-0	-1.7
1966	Atl-N	11	8	.579	27	27	10	3	0	171	170	25	41	139	11.2	3.74	97	.258	.303	7	.119	-1	-2	-2	-2	-0.5
1967	Atl-N†	9	9	.500	31	31	8	2	0	215^1	184	20	72	148	10.8	3.34	99	.229	.295	7	.104	-2	1	-1	-1	-0.3
1968	Hou-N	10	15	.400	33	32	7	2	0	224	231	11	72	146	12.3	2.81	105	.262	.321	2	.031	-3	4	4	-3	-0.3
1969	Hou-N	13	17	.433	38	37	11	1	1	244^2	232	20	72	173	11.2	3.16	112	.246	.300	15	.170	3	12	10	-1	1.3
1970	Hou-N	7	12	.368	39	21	3	0	3	162	169	22	65	103	13.1	4.56	85	.268	.338	8	.178	2	-9	-12	-2	-1.1
1971	Hou-N	0	2	.000	42	0	0	0	2	60	59	4	22	28	12.3	3.45	98	.262	.331	1	.167	-0	0	-1	-0	-0.1
1972	Mon-N	2	0	1.000	13	0	0	0	0	19^2	28	2	6	13	16.0	7.78	46	.329	.380	1	.333	1	-9	-9	-1	-0.9
Total	11	90	105	.462	357	249	66	14	8	1787^2	1703	184	600	1305	11.7	3.58	96	.249	.312	72	.130	0	-18	-28	-13	-4.2

● **DICK LeMAY** LeMay, Richard Paul b: 8/28/38, Cincinnati, Ohio BL/TL, 6′3″, 190 lbs. Deb: 6/13/61

YEAR	TM/L	W	L	PCT	G	GS	CG	SH	SV	IP	H	HR	BB	SO	RAT	ERA	ERA+	OAV	OOB	BH	AVG	PB	PR	/A	PD	TPI
1961	SF-N	3	6	.333	27	5	1	0	3	83^1	65	11	36	54	11.3	3.56	107	.217	.309	2	.077	-1	4	2	-0	0.1
1962	SF-N	0	1	.000	9	0	0	0	1	9^1	9	2	9	5	17.4	7.71	49	.265	.419	0	—	0	-4	-4	0	-0.4
1963	Chi-N	0	1	.000	9	1	0	0	0	15^1	26	1	4	10	17.6	5.28	66	.394	.429	0	.000	-0	-3	-3	-0	-0.4
Total	3	3	8	.273	45	6	1	0	4	108	100	14	49	69	12.8	4.17	91	.250	.338	2	.071	-1	-3	-5	-0	-0.7

● **BOB LEMON** Lemon, Robert Granville b: 9/22/20, San Bernardino, Cal. BL/TR, 6′, 185 lbs. Deb: 9/09/41 MCH♦

YEAR	TM/L	W	L	PCT	G	GS	CG	SH	SV	IP	H	HR	BB	SO	RAT	ERA	ERA+	OAV	OOB	BH	AVG	PB	PR	/A	PD	TPI
1946	Cle-A	4	5	.444	32	5	1	0	1	94	77	1	68	39	13.9	2.49	133	.229	.359	16	.180	2	11	9	4	1.4
1947	Cle-A	11	5	.688	37	15	6	1	3	167^1	150	7	97	65	13.5	3.44	101	.242	.348	18	.321	8	5	1	4	1.6
1948	*Cle-A☆	20	14	.588	43	37	**20**	**10**	2	**293^2**	231	12	129	147	11.1	2.82	144	.216	.302	34	.286	13	**48**	40	8	**6.5**
1949	Cle-A☆	22	10	.688	37	33	22	2	1	279^2	211	19	137	138	11.4	2.99	133	.211	.309	29	.269	15	37	31	6	5.5
1950	Cle-A★	**23**	11	.676	44	37	**22**	3	3	**288**	281	28	146	**170**	13.4	3.84	113	.257	.345	37	.272	16	23	16	5	3.5
1951	Cle-A★	17	14	.548	42	34	17	1	2	263^1	244	19	124	132	12.6	3.52	108	.244	.328	21	.206	4	18	8	4	1.6
1952	Cle-A★	22	11	.667	42	36	**28**	5	4	**309^2**	236	15	105	131	10.1	2.50	134	**.208**	.279	28	.226	6	40	29	7	4.6
1953	Cle-A☆	21	15	.583	41	36	23	5	1	**286^2**	283	16	110	98	12.7	3.36	112	.262	.336	26	.232	8	20	13	8	3.0
1954	*Cle-A★	**23**	7	.767	36	33	**21**	2	0	258^1	228	12	92	110	11.3	2.72	135	.237	.307	21	.214	5	29	27	4	**4.0**
1955	Cle-A	**18**	10	.643	35	31	5	0	2	211^1	218	17	74	100	12.6	3.88	103	.266	.330	19	.244	6	2	3	2	1.1
1956	Cle-A	20	14	.588	39	35	**21**	2	3	255^1	230	23	89	94	11.5	3.03	139	.239	.307	18	.194	5	32	33	4	4.4
1957	Cle-A	6	11	.353	21	17	2	0	0	117^1	129	9	64	45	15.3	4.60	81	.287	.385	3	.065	-3	-11	-12	3	-1.2
1958	Cle-A	0	1	.000	11	1	0	0	0	25^1	41	3	16	8	20.6	5.33	68	.376	.460	3	.231	0	-4	-5	1	-0.4
Total	13	207	128	.618	460	350	188	31	22	2850	2559	181	1251	1277	12.2	3.23	119	.241	.324	274	.232	86	251	193	60	35.6

● **DAVE LEMONDS** Lemonds, David Lee b: 7/5/48, Charlotte, N.C. BL/TL, 6′1.5″, 180 lbs. Deb: 6/30/69

YEAR	TM/L	W	L	PCT	G	GS	CG	SH	SV	IP	H	HR	BB	SO	RAT	ERA	ERA+	OAV	OOB	BH	AVG	PB	PR	/A	PD	TPI
1969	Chi-N	0	1	.000	2	1	0	0	0	4^2	5	0	5	0	19.3	3.86	104	.313	.476	0	.000	-0	-0	0	0	0.0
1972	Chi-A	4	7	.364	31	18	0	0	0	94^2	87	6	38	69	12.0	2.95	106	.247	.322	3	.120	-1	1	2	-0	0.1
Total	2	4	8	.333	33	19	0	0	0	99^1	92	6	43	69	12.3	2.99	106	.250	.330	3	.115	-1	1	2	-0	0.1

● **MARK LEMONGELLO** Lemongello, Mark b: 7/21/55, Jersey City, N.J. BR/TR, 6′1″, 180 lbs. Deb: 9/14/76

YEAR	TM/L	W	L	PCT	G	GS	CG	SH	SV	IP	H	HR	BB	SO	RAT	ERA	ERA+	OAV	OOB	BH	AVG	PB	PR	/A	PD	TPI
1976	Hou-N	3	1	.750	4	4	1	0	0	29	26	2	7	9	10.2	2.79	114	.236	.282	0	.000	-1	2	1	1	0.2
1977	Hou-N	9	14	.391	34	30	5	0	0	214^2	237	20	52	83	12.2	3.48	102	.281	.325	6	.087	-3	10	2	-1	-0.2
1978	Hou-N	9	14	.391	33	30	9	1	1	210^1	204	20	66	77	11.9	3.94	84	.259	.323	11	.172	1	-8	-15	-0	-1.4
1979	Tor-A	1	9	.100	18	10	2	0	0	83	97	14	34	40	14.5	6.29	69	.299	.371	0	—	0	-19	-18	1	-1.7
Total	4	22	38	.367	89	74	17	1	1	537	564	56	159	209	12.4	4.06	88	.273	.329	17	.121	-3	-15	-30	1	-3.1

● **ED LENNON** Lennon, Edward Francis b: 8/17/1897, Philadelphia, Pa. d: 9/13/47, Philadelphia, Pa. BR/TR, 5′11″, 170 lbs. Deb: 6/30/28

YEAR	TM/L	W	L	PCT	G	GS	CG	SH	SV	IP	H	HR	BB	SO	RAT	ERA	ERA+	OAV	OOB	BH	AVG	PB	PR	/A	PD	TPI
1928	Phi-N	0	0	—	5	0	0	0	0	12^1	19	0	10	6	21.2	8.76	49	.373	.475	0	.000	-1	-7	-6	-0	-0.7

YEAR	TM/L	W	L	PCT	G	GS	CG	SH	SV	IP	H	HR	BB	SO	RAT	ERA	ERA+	OAV	OOB	BH	AVG	PB	PR	/A	PD	TPI
● DANILO LEON	Leon, Danilo Enrique b: 4/3/67, LaConcepcion, Venez. BR/TR, 6'1", 170 lbs. Deb: 6/06/92																									
1992	Tex-A	1	1	.500	15	0	0	0	0	18^1	18	5	10	15	15.2	5.89	65	.254	.369	0	—	0	-4	-4	0	-0.4
● IZZY LEON	Leon, Isidoro (Becerra) b: 1/4/11, Cruces, Las Villas, Cuba BR/TR, 5'10", 160 lbs. Deb: 6/21/45																									
1945	Phi-N	0	4	.000	14	4	0	0	0	38^2	49	3	19	11	15.8	5.35	72	.312	.386	1	.111	-0	-7	-7	0	-0.7
● MAX LEON	Leon, Maximino (Molino) b: 2/4/50, Pozo Hondo, Aculo, Mexico BR/TR, 6', 170 lbs. Deb: 7/18/73																									
1973	Atl-N	2	2	.500	12	1	1	0	0	27	30	6	9	18	14.0	5.33	74	.278	.350	2	.286	0	-5	-4	-0	-0.4
1974	Atl-N	4	7	.364	34	2	1	1	3	75	68	5	14	38	10.0	2.64	143	.242	.280	2	.133	-1	8	9	1	1.0
1975	Atl-N	2	1	.667	50	1	0	0	6	85	90	5	33	53	13.8	4.13	91	.274	.352	3	.333	1	-5	-3	1	-0.2
1976	Atl-N	2	4	.333	30	0	0	0	3	36	32	2	15	16	12.3	2.75	138	.234	.318	0	.000	-0	3	4	-1	0.4
1977	Atl-N	4	4	.500	31	9	0	0	1	81^2	89	9	25	44	13.6	3.97	112	.280	.349	6	.316	1	-1	4	0	0.6
1978	Atl-N	0	0	—	5	0	0	0	0	5^2	6	1	4	1	17.5	6.35	64	.273	.407	0	—	0	-2	-1	-0	-0.2
Total	6	14	18	.438	162	13	2	1	13	310^1	315	28	100	170	12.7	3.71	107	.264	.332	13	.250	1	-1	9	1	1.2
● DENNIS LEONARD	Leonard, Dennis Patrick b: 5/8/51, Brooklyn, N.Y. BR/TR, 6'1", 190 lbs. Deb: 9/04/74																									
1974	KC-A	0	4	.000	5	4	0	0	0	22	28	0	12	8	17.6	5.32	72	.329	.430	0	—	0	-4	-4	1	-0.3
1975	KC-A	15	7	.682	32	30	8	0	0	212^1	212	18	90	146	13.2	3.77	102	.263	.344	0	—	0	0	2	0	0.2
1976	*KC-A	17	10	.630	35	34	16	2	0	259	247	16	70	150	11.4	3.51	100	.255	.313	0	—	0	0	-0	-4	-0.5
1977	*KC-A	**20**	12	.625	38	37	21	5	1	292^2	246	18	79	244	10.2	3.04	133	.227	.285	0	—	0	33	32	-2	3.1
1978	*KC-A	21	17	.553	40	40	20	4	0	294^2	283	27	78	183	11.3	3.33	115	.254	.308	0	—	0	14	16	0	1.6
1979	KC-A	14	12	.538	32	32	12	**5**	0	236	226	33	56	126	10.8	4.08	104	.253	.299	0	—	0	4	5	0	0.3
1980	*KC-A	20	11	.645	38	38	9	3	0	280^1	271	30	80	155	11.3	3.79	107	.253	.306	0	—	0	8	8	-0	0.8
1981	*KC-A	13	11	.542	26	26	9	2	0	**201^2**	202	15	41	107	11.0	2.99	121	.258	.298	0	—	0	15	14	0	1.6
1982	KC-A	10	6	.625	21	21	2	0	0	130^2	145	20	46	58	13.3	5.10	80	.279	.340	0	—	0	-15	-15	1	-1.4
1983	KC-A	6	3	.667	10	10	1	0	0	63	69	3	19	31	12.6	3.71	110	.277	.328	0	—	0	2	3	0	0.3
1985	KC-A	0	0	—	2	0	0	0	0	2	1	0	0	1	4.5	0.00	—	.143	.143	0	—	0	1	1	-0	0.1
1986	KC-A	8	13	.381	33	30	5	2	0	192^2	207	22	51	114	12.2	4.44	96	.275	.324	0	—	0	-6	-4	0	-0.5
Total	12	144	106	.576	312	302	103	23	1	2187	2137	202	622	1323	11.6	3.70	106	.257	.312	0	—	0	52	58	-3	5.3
● ELMER LEONARD	Leonard, Elmer Ellsworth "Tiny" b: 11/12/1888, Napa, Cal. d: 5/27/81, Napa, Cal. BR/TR, 6'3.5", 210 lbs. Deb: 6/22/11																									
1911	Phi-A	2	2	.500	5	1	1	0	0	19	26	0	10	10	18.0	2.84	111	.329	.418	2	.286	1	1	1	-1	0.1
● DUTCH LEONARD	Leonard, Emil John b: 3/25/09, Auburn, Ill. d: 4/17/83, Springfield, Ill. BR/TR, 6', 175 lbs. Deb: 8/31/33 C																									
1933	Bro-N	2	3	.400	10	3	2	0	0	40	42	0	10	6	11.7	2.93	110	.261	.304	0	.000	-1	2	1	0	0.0
1934	Bro-N	14	11	.560	44	20	11	2	5	183^2	210	12	33	58	12.1	3.28	119	.286	.320	12	.179	-1	16	13	1	1.3
1935	Bro-N	2	9	.182	43	11	4	0	**8**	137^2	152	11	29	41	11.9	3.92	101	.280	.318	1	.026	-4	1	1	-1	-0.4
1936	Bro-N	0	0	—	16	0	0	0	1	32	34	2	5	8	11.0	3.66	113	.262	.289	2	.400	0	1	2	1	0.3
1938	Was-A	12	15	.444	33	31	15	3	0	223^1	221	11	53	68	**11.3**	3.43	132	.256	**.305**	19	.232	3	34	27	0	2.9
1939	Was-A	20	8	.714	34	34	21	2	0	269^1	273	16	59	88	11.3	3.54	123	.262	.305	21	.221	0	32	24	2	2.5
1940	Was-A☆	14	19	.424	35	35	23	2	0	289	328	19	78	124	12.7	3.49	120	.286	.332	16	.158	-4	29	22	5	2.2
1941	Was-A	18	13	.581	34	33	19	4	0	256	271	6	54	91	11.5	3.45	117	.270	.309	9	.102	-5	20	17	-1	1.1
1942	Was-A	2	2	.500	6	5	1	1	0	35	28	1	5	15	8.5	4.11	89	.214	.243	1	.100	-0	-2	-2	-0	-0.2
1943	Was-A★	11	13	.458	31	30	15	2	1	219^2	218	9	46	51	11.0	3.28	98	.257	.298	7	.104	-4	0	-2	2	-0.4
1944	Was-A☆	14	14	.500	32	31	17	3	0	229^1	222	8	37	62	10.3	3.06	106	.252	.284	18	.228	2	9	5	1	0.9
1945	Was-A†	17	7	.708	31	29	12	4	1	216	208	5	35	96	10.2	2.13	146	.248	.279	18	.231	1	30	23	0	2.8
1946	Was-A	10	10	.500	26	23	7	2	0	161^2	182	9	36	62	12.4	3.56	94	.281	.323	9	.170	-1	-1	-4	3	-0.1
1947	Phi-N	17	12	.586	32	29	19	3	0	235	224	14	57	103	10.8	2.68	149	.258	.306	14	.175	-1	36	35	3	3.9
1948	Phi-N	12	17	.414	34	31	16	1	0	225^2	226	9	54	92	11.3	2.51	157	.265	.312	12	.145	-3	36	36	4	3.9
1949	Chi-N	7	16	.304	33	28	10	1	0	180	198	4	43	83	12.4	4.15	97	.272	.319	12	.203	0	-2	-2	1	-0.1
1950	Chi-N	5	1	.833	35	1	0	0	6	74	70	7	27	28	12.0	3.77	111	.248	.318	1	.063	-2	3	4	0	0.2
1951	Chi-N☆	10	6	.625	41	1	0	0	3	81^2	69	3	28	30	10.9	2.64	155	.234	.305	0	.000	-3	12	13	2	1.2
1952	Chi-N	2	2	.500	45	0	0	0	11	66^2	56	3	24	37	11.2	2.16	178	.235	.313	2	.200	-0	12	13	2	1.5
1953	Chi-N	2	3	.400	45	0	0	0	8	62^2	72	9	24	27	13.9	4.60	97	.289	.354	3	.300	1	-2	-1	0	0.0
Total	20	191	181	.513	640	375	192	30	44	3218^1	3304	158	737	1170	11.5	3.25	119	.265	.309	177	.168	-21	267	224	24	23.5
● DUTCH LEONARD	Leonard, Hubert Benjamin b: 4/16/1892, Birmingham, Ohio d: 7/11/52, Fresno, Cal. BL/TL, 5'10.5", 185 lbs. Deb: 4/12/13																									
1913	Bos-A	14	16	.467	42	28	14	3	1	259^1	245	0	94	144	11.9	2.39	123	.253	.321	15	.181	1	16	16	-2	1.6
1914	Bos-A	19	5	.792	36	25	17	7	3	224^2	139	3	60	176	**8.3**	**0.96**	**280**	**.180**	**.246**	10	.147	-1	**44**	43	-3	4.7
1915	*Bos-A	15	7	.682	32	21	10	2	0	183^1	130	3	67	116	10.4	2.36	118	**.208**	.299	14	.264	5	12	9	-4	1.0
1916	*Bos-A	18	12	.600	48	34	17	6	6	274	244	6	66	144	10.4	2.36	117	.247	.300	17	.200	2	14	12	-6	0.9
1917	Bos-A	16	17	.485	37	36	26	4	1	294^1	257	4	72	144	10.2	2.17	119	.236	.286	9	.087	-6	16	13	-5	0.2
1918	Bos-A	8	6	.571	16	16	12	3	0	125^2	119	0	53	47	12.5	2.72	99	.254	.332	8	.186	0	1	-1	-2	-0.2
1919	Det-A	14	13	.519	29	28	18	4	0	217^1	212	7	65	102	11.8	2.77	115	.254	.313	11	.155	-3	11	10	-4	0.3
1920	Det-A	10	17	.370	28	27	10	3	0	191^1	192	8	63	76	12.4	4.33	86	.271	.338	12	.211	2	-11	-13	-1	-1.2
1921	Det-A	11	13	.458	36	32	16	1	1	245	273	15	63	120	12.7	3.75	114	.286	.336	14	.171	-4	15	14	-3	0.7
1924	Det-A	3	2	.600	9	7	3	0	1	51^1	68	1	18	26	15.3	4.56	90	.327	.383	4	.211	-0	-2	-3	-0	-0.3
1925	Det-A	11	4	.733	18	18	9	0	0	125^2	143	7	43	65	13.4	4.51	95	.289	.347	10	.200	-1	-2	-3	-2	-0.5
Total	11	139	112	.554	331	272	152	33	13	2192	2022	54	664	1160	11.3	2.76	115	.249	.311	124	.173	-5	114	98	-32	7.2
● DAVE LEONHARD	Leonhard, David Paul b: 1/22/42, Arlington, Va. BR/TR, 5'11", 165 lbs. Deb: 9/21/67																									
1967	Bal-A	0	0	—	3	2	0	0	1	14^1	11	1	6	9	11.3	3.14	100	.200	.290	0	.000	-1	0	0	0	0.0
1968	Bal-A	7	7	.500	28	18	5	2	1	126^1	95	10	57	61	11.0	3.13	93	.216	.309	4	.129	-1	-2	-3	1	-0.3
1969	*Bal-A	7	4	.636	37	3	1	1	1	94	78	8	38	37	11.1	2.49	143	.228	.305	2	.095	-0	12	11	-1	1.1
1970	Bal-A	0	0	—	23	0	0	0	1	28^1	32	5	18	14	15.9	5.08	72	.294	.394	0	.000	0	-4	-5	1	-0.4
1971	*Bal-A	2	3	.400	12	6	1	1	1	54	51	5	19	18	11.8	2.83	118	.252	.320	5	.278	1	4	3	1	0.5
1972	Bal-A	0	0	—	14	0	0	0	0	20	20	3	12	7	14.4	4.50	68	.260	.360	1	1.000	1	-3	-3	0	-0.2
Total	6	16	14	.533	117	29	7	4	5	337	287	32	150	146	11.8	3.15	103	.234	.320	12	.156	1	6	4	3	0.7
● RUDY LEOPOLD	Leopold, Rudolph Matas b: 7/27/05, Grand Cane, La. d: 9/3/65, Baton Rouge, La. BL/TL, 6', 160 lbs. Deb: 7/04/28																									
1928	Chi-A	0	0	—	2	0	0	0	0	2^1	3	0	0	0	11.6	3.86	105	.273	.273	0	.000	-0	0	0	-0	0.0
● RANDY LERCH	Lerch, Randy Louis b: 10/9/54, Sacramento, Cal. BL/TL, 6'5", 190 lbs. Deb: 9/14/75																									
1975	Phi-N	0	0	—	3	0	0	0	0	7	6	1	1	8	9.0	6.43	58	.231	.259	0	—	0	-2	-2	-0	-0.2
1976	Phi-N	0	0	—	1	0	0	0	1	3	3	0	0	0	9.0	3.00	118	.250	.250	1	1.000	1	0	0	-0	0.1
1977	Phi-N	10	6	.625	32	28	3	0	0	168^2	207	20	75	81	15.1	5.07	79	.312	.383	9	.167	-0	-22	-20	2	-1.8
1978	*Phi-N	11	8	.579	33	28	5	0	0	184	183	15	70	96	12.4	3.96	90	.263	.332	15	.250	7	-8	-8	1	0.0
1979	Phi-N	10	13	.435	37	35	6	1	0	214	228	20	60	92	12.2	3.74	102	.281	.333	11	.153	1	-0	2	2	0.4
1980	Phi-N	4	14	.222	30	22	2	0	0	150	178	15	55	57	14.0	5.16	73	.302	.362	12	.267	4	-26	-23	1	-1.9
1981	*Mil-A	7	9	.438	23	18	1	0	0	110^2	134	8	43	53	14.4	4.31	79	.303	.365	0	—	0	-8	-11	0	-0.9
1982	Mil-A	8	7	.533	21	20	1	1	0	108^2	123	12	51	33	14.7	4.97	76	.286	.366	0	—	0	-11	-14	-1	-1.2
	Mon-N	2	0	1.000	6	4	0	0	0	23^2	26	0	8	4	12.9	3.42	106	.289	.347	2	.250	0	0	1	-0	0.1
1983	Mon-N	1	3	.250	19	5	0	0	0	38^2	45	6	18	24	14.9	6.75	53	.292	.370	2	.222	1	-13	-14	-0	-1.3
	SF-N	1	0	1.000	7	0	0	0	0	10^2	9	1	8	6	14.3	3.38	105	.231	.362	0	—	0	0	0	0	0.0
	Yr	2	3	.400	26	5	0	0	0	49^1	54	7	26	30	14.6	6.02	59	.277	.362	2	.222	1	-13	-13	-0	-1.3

YEAR	TM/L	W	L	PCT	G	GS	CG	SH	SV	IP	H	HR	BB	SO	RAT	ERA	ERA+	OAV	OOB	BH	AVG	PB	PR	/A	PD	TPI
1984	SF-N	5	3	.625	37	4	0	0	2	72^1	80	3	36	48	14.6	4.23	83	.287	.370	2	.133	1	-5	-6	1	-0.5
1986	Phi-N	1	1	.500	4	0	0	0	0	8	10	0	7	5	19.1	7.88	49	.286	.405	1	.333	1	-4	-4	-0	-0.3
Total	11	60	64	.484	253	164	18	2	3	1099^1	1232	101	432	507	13.7	4.53	82	.289	.356	55	.206	15	-98	-98	4	-7.5
● **LOUIS LeROY**	LeRoy, Louis Paul "Chief" b: 2/18/1879, Omro Village, Wis. d: 10/10/44, Shawano, Wis. BR/TR, 5'10", 180 lbs. Deb: 9/22/05																									
1905	NY-A	1	1	.500	3	3	2	0	0	24	26	2	1	8	10.5	3.75	78	.277	.292	1	.125	-0	-3	-2	-0	-0.3
1906	NY-A	2	0	1.000	11	2	1	0	1	44^2	33	0	12	28	9.5	2.22	134	.209	.273	2	.143	-1	2	4	1	0.4
1910	Bos-A	0	0	—	1	0	0	0	0	4	7	1	2	3	20.3	11.25	23	.389	.450	0	.000	-0	-4	-4	0	-0.4
Total	3	3	1	.750	15	5	3	0	1	72^2	66	3	15	39	10.4	3.22	91	.245	.292	3	.130	-1	-4	-2	1	-0.3
● **BARRY LERSCH**	Lersch, Barry Lee b: 9/7/44, Denver, Colo. BB/TR, 6', 180 lbs. Deb: 4/08/69																									
1969	Phi-N	0	3	.000	10	0	0	0	2	17^2	20	6	10	13	15.8	7.13	50	.286	.383	0	.000	-0	-7	-7	1	-0.7
1970	Phi-N	6	3	.667	42	11	3	0	3	138	119	17	47	92	10.9	3.26	122	.232	.297	2	.065	-2	12	11	-1	0.9
1971	Phi-N	5	14	.263	38	30	3	0	0	214^1	203	28	50	113	10.7	3.78	93	.252	.298	10	.169	2	-7	-6	-1	-0.5
1972	Phi-N	4	6	.400	36	8	3	1	0	100^2	86	8	33	48	10.9	3.04	118	.231	.299	0	.000	-2	5	6	-0	0.4
1973	Phi-N	3	6	.333	42	4	0	0	1	98^1	105	10	27	51	12.3	4.39	86	.279	.330	3	.176	0	-8	-7	-0	-0.7
1974	StL-N	0	0	—	1	0	0	0	0	1^1	3	1	5	0	54.0	40.50	9	.429	.667	0	—	0	-5	-5	0	-0.4
Total	6	18	32	.360	169	53	9	1	6	570^1	536	70	172	317	11.3	3.82	97	.250	.308	15	.113	-3	-11	-8	-1	-1.0
● **DON LESHNOCK**	Leshnock, Donald Lee b: 11/25/46, Youngstown, Ohio BR/TL, 6'3", 195 lbs. Deb: 6/07/72																									
1972	Det-A	0	0	—	1	0	0	0	0	1	2	0	0	2	18.0	0.00	—	.400	.400	0	—	0	0	0	0	0.0
● **BRAD LESLEY**	Lesley, Bradley Jay b: 9/11/58, Turlock, Cal. BR/TR, 6'6", 230 lbs. Deb: 7/31/82																									
1982	Cin-N	0	2	.000	28	0	0	0	4	38^1	27	1	13	29	9.4	2.58	143	.197	.267	0	.000	-0	4	5	-0	0.5
1983	Cin-N	0	0	—	5	0	0	0	0	8^1	9	1	0	5	9.7	2.16	176	.290	.290	0	—	0	1	2	-0	0.2
1984	Cin-N	0	1	.000	16	0	0	0	2	19^1	17	3	14	7	14.4	5.12	74	.246	.373	1	.500	0	-3	-3	0	-0.3
1985	Mil-A	1	0	1.000	5	0	0	0	0	6^1	8	2	2	5	14.2	9.95	42	.296	.345	0	—	0	-4	-4	0	-0.4
Total	4	1	3	.250	54	0	0	0	6	72^1	61	7	29	46	11.2	3.86	98	.231	.307	1	.333	0	-2	-1	-0	-0.0
● **WALT LEVERENZ**	Leverenz, Walter Fred "Tiny" b: 7/21/1887, Chicago, Ill. d: 3/19/73, Atascadero, Cal. BL/TL, 5'10", 175 lbs. Deb: 4/18/13																									
1913	StL-A	6	17	.261	30	27	13	2	1	202^2	159	3	89	87	11.5	2.58	114	.222	.318	12	.176	-1	8	8	-1	0.6
1914	StL-A	1	12	.077	27	16	5	0	0	111^1	107	5	63	41	14.1	3.80	71	.264	.368	6	.182	-0	-13	-14	-1	-1.6
1915	StL-A	0	2	.000	5	1	0	0	1	9	11	0	8	3	20.0	8.00	36	.333	.476	0	.000	-0	-5	-5	0	-0.5
Total	3	7	31	.184	62	44	18	2	2	323	277	8	160	131	12.7	3.15	91	.240	.341	18	.176	-1	-10	-11	-3	-1.5
● **DIXIE LEVERETT**	Leverett, Gorham Vance b: 3/29/1894, Georgetown, Tex. d: 2/20/57, Beaverton, Ore. BR/TR, 5'11", 190 lbs. Deb: 5/06/22																									
1922	Chi-A	13	10	.565	33	27	16	4	2	223^2	224	11	79	60	12.3	3.34	122	.264	.329	21	.253	3	18	18	-1	2.0
1923	Chi-A	10	13	.435	38	24	9	0	3	192^2	212	6	64	64	13.2	4.06	97	.280	.341	16	.267	4	-2	-2	-1	0.1
1924	Chi-A	2	3	.400	21	11	4	0	0	99	123	2	41	29	15.2	5.82	71	.314	.383	6	.188	-1	-17	-19	0	-1.7
1926	Chi-A	1	1	.500	6	3	1	0	0	24	31	1	7	12	14.3	6.00	64	.316	.362	1	.143	-0	-5	-6	0	-0.5
1929	Bos-N	3	7	.300	24	12	3	0	1	97^2	135	5	30	28	15.7	6.36	74	.339	.393	6	.188	-0	-18	-18	-0	-1.6
Total	5	29	34	.460	122	77	33	4	6	637	725	25	221	193	13.6	4.51	92	.291	.353	50	.234	6	-25	-27	-1	-1.7
● **HOD LEVERETTE**	Leverette, Horace Wilbur "Levy" b: 2/4/1889, Shreveport, La. d: 4/10/58, St.Petersburg, Fla BR/TR, 6', 180 lbs. Deb: 4/22/20																									
1920	StL-A	0	2	.000	3	2	0	0	0	10^1	9	1	12	0	18.3	5.23	75	.250	.438	0	.000	-1	-2	-1	1	-0.1
● **DUTCH LEVSEN**	Levsen, Emil Henry b: 4/29/1898, Wyoming, Iowa d: 3/12/72, St.Louis Park, Minn. BR/TR, 6', 180 lbs. Deb: 9/28/23																									
1923	Cle-A	0	0	—	3	0	0	0	0	4^1	4	0	0	1	8.3	0.00	—	.267	.267	0	.000	-0	2	2	1	0.3
1924	Cle-A	1	1	.500	4	1	1	0	0	16^1	22	0	4	3	14.3	4.41	97	.333	.371	0	.000	-1	-0	-0	0	-0.1
1925	Cle-A	1	2	.333	4	3	2	0	0	24^1	30	1	16	9	17.4	5.55	80	.313	.416	2	.250	0	-3	-3	-1	-0.3
1926	Cle-A	16	13	.552	33	31	18	2	0	237^1	235	11	85	53	12.4	3.41	119	.261	.330	17	.205	-0	16	17	-1	1.6
1927	Cle-A	3	7	.300	25	13	2	1	0	80^1	96	1	37	15	15.1	5.49	77	.303	.379	5	.200	-1	-12	-11	1	-1.1
1928	Cle-A	0	3	.000	11	3	0	0	0	41^1	39	4	31	7	15.7	5.44	76	.258	.391	0	.000	-2	-6	-6	-0	-0.8
Total	6	21	26	.447	80	51	23	3	0	404	426	17	173	88	13.6	4.17	99	.276	.354	24	.178	-4	-4	-2	1	-0.4
● **DENNIS LEWALLYN**	Lewallyn, Dennis Dale b: 8/11/53, Pensacola, Fla. BR/TR, 6'4", 200 lbs. Deb: 9/21/75																									
1975	LA-N	0	0	—	2	0	0	0	0	3	1	0	0	0	3.0	0.00	—	.100	.100	0	—	0	1	1	0	0.1
1976	LA-N	1	1	.500	4	2	0	0	0	16^2	12	1	6	4	9.7	2.16	157	.207	.281	0	.000	-1	2	2	0	0.2
1977	LA-N	3	1	.750	5	1	0	0	1	17	22	1	4	8	13.8	4.24	90	.306	.342	0	.000	-1	-1	-1	-0	-0.2
1978	LA-N	0	0	—	1	0	0	0	0	2	2	0	0	0	9.0	0.00	—	.250	.250	0	—	0	1	1	-0	0.1
1979	LA-N	0	1	.000	7	0	0	0	0	12^1	19	0	5	1	18.2	5.11	71	.358	.424	1	.500	0	-2	-2	0	-0.1
1980	Tex-A	0	0	—	4	0	0	0	0	5^2	7	0	4	1	17.5	7.94	49	.304	.407	0	—	0	-2	-3	0	-0.2
1981	Cle-A	0	0	—	7	0	0	0	0	13^1	16	1	2	11	12.2	5.40	67	.296	.321	0	—	0	-3	-3	-0	-0.2
1982	Cle-A	0	1	.000	4	0	0	0	0	10^1	13	3	1	3	12.2	6.97	59	.310	.326	0	—	0	-3	-3	-0	-0.3
Total	8	4	4	.500	34	3	0	0	1	80^1	92	6	22	28	12.9	4.48	82	.287	.335	1	.077	-1	-6	-7	0	-0.6
● **DAN LEWANDOWSKI**	Lewandowski, Daniel William b: 1/6/28, Buffalo, N.Y. BR/TR, 6', 180 lbs. Deb: 9/22/51																									
1951	StL-N	0	1	.000	2	0	0	0	0	1	3	0	1	1	36.0	9.00	44	.500	.571	0	—	0	-1	-1	0	-0.1
● **LEWIS**	Lewis b: Brooklyn, N.Y. Deb: 7/12/1890 ♦																									
1890	Buf-P	0	1	.000	1	1	0	0	0	3	13	3	7	1	60.0	60.00	7	.590	.689	1	.200	-0	-19	-19	1	-1.0
● **TED LEWIS**	Lewis, Edward Morgan "Parson" b: 12/25/1872, Machynlleth, Wales d: 5/24/36, Durham, N.H. BR/TR, 5'10.5", 158 lbs. Deb: 7/06/1896																									
1896	Bos-N	1	4	.200	6	5	4	0	0	41^2	37	2	27	12	13.8	3.24	140	.236	.349	2	.111	-2	5	6	1	0.4
1897	*Bos-N	21	12	.636	38	34	30	2	1	290	316	11	125	65	14.0	3.85	116	.275	.351	28	.248	-2	15	20	-5	1.1
1898	Bos-N	26	8	**.765**	41	33	29	1	2	313^1	267	9	109	72	11.1	2.90	127	.229	.300	37	.282	4	25	28	-1	3.0
1899	Bos-N	17	11	.607	29	25	23	2	0	234^2	245	10	73	60	12.5	3.49	119	.269	.328	25	.260	0	10	17	-4	1.2
1900	Bos-N	13	12	.520	30	22	19	1	0	209	215	11	86	66	13.1	4.13	100	.265	.339	10	.137	-4	-10	-0	-3	-0.7
1901	Bos-A	16	17	.485	39	34	31	1	1	316^1	299	14	91	103	11.3	3.53	100	.247	.304	21	.174	-2	5	0	-2	-0.4
Total	6	94	64	.595	183	153	136	7	4	1405	1379	57	511	378	12.4	3.53	113	.255	.324	123	.223	-5	49	71	-13	4.6
● **DUFFY LEWIS**	Lewis, George Edward b: 4/18/1888, San Francisco, Cal d: 6/17/79, Salem, N.H. BL/TL, 5'10.5", 165 lbs. Deb: 4/16/10 C♦																									
1913	Bos-A	0	0	—	1	0	0	0	0	1	3	0	0	1	27.0	18.00	16	.500	.500	164	.298	0	-2	-2	-0	-0.2
● **JIM LEWIS**	Lewis, James Martin b: 10/12/55, Miami, Fla. BR/TR, 6'3", 190 lbs. Deb: 9/12/79																									
1979	Sea-A	0	0	—	2	0	0	0	0	2^1	10	1	1	0	42.4	15.43	28	.625	.647	0	—	0	-3	-3	-0	-0.4
1982	NY-A	0	0	—	1	0	0	0	0	0^2	3	0	3	0	81.0	54.00	7	.500	.667	0	—	0	-4	-4	0	-0.2
1983	Min-A	0	0	—	6	0	0	0	0	18	24	5	7	8	16.0	6.50	65	.324	.390	0	—	0	-5	-5	0	-0.6
1985	Sea-A	0	1	.000	2	1	0	0	0	4^2	8	1	1	1	21.2	7.71	55	.421	.500	0	—	0	-2	-2	-0	-0.2
Total	4	0	1	.000	11	1	0	0	0	25^2	45	7	12	9	21.0	8.77	48	.391	.462	0	—	0	-13	-13	-0	-1.4
● **JIM LEWIS**	Lewis, James Steven b: 7/20/64, Jackson, Mich. BR/TR, 6'2", 200 lbs. Deb: 8/09/91																									
1991	SD-N	0	0	—	12	0	0	0	0	13	14	2	11	10	17.3	4.15	91	.275	.403	0	.000	-0	-1	-1	1	0.0
● **RICHIE LEWIS**	Lewis, Richie Todd b: 1/25/66, Muncie, Ind. BR/TR, 5'10", 170 lbs. Deb: 7/31/92																									
1992	Bal-A	1	1	.500	2	2	0	0	0	6^2	13	1	7	4	27.0	10.80	36	.406	.513	0	—	0	-5	-5	0	-0.4

● SCOTT LEWIS Lewis, Scott Allen b: 12/5/65, Grants Pass, Ore. BR/TR, 6'3", 190 lbs. Deb: 9/25/90

YEAR	TM/L	W	L	PCT	G	GS	CG	SH	SV	IP	H	HR	BB	SO	RAT	ERA	ERA+	OAV	OOB	BH	AVG	PB	PR	/A	PD	TPI
1990	Cal-A	1	1	.500	2	2	1	0	0	16^1	10	2	2	9	6.6	2.20	173	.172	.200	0	—	0	3	3	-0	0.3
1991	Cal-A	3	5	.375	16	11	0	0	0	60^1	81	9	21	37	15.5	6.27	65	.316	.373	0	—	0	-15	-14	-0	-1.4
1992	Cal-A	4	0	1.000	21	2	0	0	0	38^1	36	3	14	18	12.2	3.99	98	.255	.331	0	—	0	-0	-0	1	0.1
Total	3	8	6	.571	39	15	1	0	0	115	127	14	37	64	13.1	4.93	81	.279	.339	0	—	0	-12	-12	0	-1.0

● BERT LEWIS Lewis, William Burton b: 10/3/1895, Tonawanda, N.Y. d: 3/24/50, Tonawanda, N.Y. BR/TR, 6'2", 176 lbs. Deb: 4/19/24

YEAR	TM/L	W	L	PCT	G	GS	CG	SH	SV	IP	H	HR	BB	SO	RAT	ERA	ERA+	OAV	OOB	BH	AVG	PB	PR	/A	PD	TPI
1924	Phi-N	0	0	—	12	0	0	0	0	18	23	1	7	3	15.5	6.00	74	.315	.383	0	.000	-1	-4	-3	0	-0.4

● TERRY LEY Ley, Terrence Richard b: 2/21/47, Portland, Ore. BL/TL, 6', 190 lbs. Deb: 8/20/71

YEAR	TM/L	W	L	PCT	G	GS	CG	SH	SV	IP	H	HR	BB	SO	RAT	ERA	ERA+	OAV	OOB	BH	AVG	PB	PR	/A	PD	TPI
1971	NY-A	0	0	—	6	0	0	0	0	9	9	1	9	7	20.0	5.00	65	.257	.435	0	—	0	-2	-2	0	-0.2

● AL LIBKE Libke, Albert Walter b: 9/12/18, Tacoma, Wash. BL/TR, 6'4", 215 lbs. Deb: 4/19/45 ♦

YEAR	TM/L	W	L	PCT	G	GS	CG	SH	SV	IP	H	HR	BB	SO	RAT	ERA	ERA+	OAV	OOB	BH	AVG	PB	PR	/A	PD	TPI
1945	Cin-N	0	0	—	4	0	0	0	0	4^1	3	0	3	2	12.5	0.00	—	.200	.333	127	.283	1	2	2	0	0.2
1946	Cin-N	0	0	—	1	1	0	0	0	5	4	0	3	2	12.6	3.60	93	.235	.350	109	.253	0	-0	-0	-0	0.0
Total	2	0	0	—	5	1	0	0	0	9^1	7	0	6	4	12.5	1.93	183	.219	.342	236	.268	2	2	2	0	0.2

● DON LIDDLE Liddle, Donald Eugene b: 5/25/25, Mt.Carmel, Ill. BL/TL, 5'10", 165 lbs. Deb: 4/17/53

YEAR	TM/L	W	L	PCT	G	GS	CG	SH	SV	IP	H	HR	BB	SO	RAT	ERA	ERA+	OAV	OOB	BH	AVG	PB	PR	/A	PD	TPI
1953	Mil-N	7	6	.538	31	15	4	0	2	128^2	119	6	55	63	12.3	3.08	127	.248	.328	3	.088	-2	17	12	-1	1.0
1954	*NY-N	9	4	.692	28	19	4	3	0	126^2	100	5	55	44	11.2	3.06	132	.223	.312	7	.189	2	14	14	-1	1.5
1955	NY-N	10	4	.714	33	13	4	0	1	106^1	97	18	61	56	13.7	4.23	95	.246	.353	5	.185	1	-2	-2	-1	-0.2
1956	NY-N	1	2	.333	11	5	1	0	1	41^1	45	5	14	21	13.1	3.92	97	.278	.339	2	.167	-0	-1	-1	0	0.0
	StL-N	1	2	.333	14	2	0	0	0	24^2	36	8	18	14	19.7	8.39	45	.353	.450	0	.000	-0	-13	-13	-0	-1.3
	Yr	2	4	.333	25	7	1	0	1	66	81	13	32	35	15.4	5.59	68	.302	.377	2	.143	-0	-13	-13	0	-1.3
Total	4	28	18	.609	117	54	13	3	4	427^2	397	42	203	198	12.8	3.75	106	.250	.339	17	.152	1	16	10	-2	1.0

● DUTCH LIEBER Lieber, Charles Edwin b: 2/1/10, Alameda, Cal. d: 12/31/61, Sawtelle, Cal. BR/TR, 6'0.5", 180 lbs. Deb: 4/18/35

YEAR	TM/L	W	L	PCT	G	GS	CG	SH	SV	IP	H	HR	BB	SO	RAT	ERA	ERA+	OAV	OOB	BH	AVG	PB	PR	/A	PD	TPI
1935	Phi-A	1	1	.500	18	1	0	0	2	46^2	45	1	19	14	12.5	3.09	147	.263	.340	2	.143	-1	7	8	0	0.6
1936	Phi-A	0	1	.000	3	0	0	0	0	11^2	17	0	6	1	17.7	7.71	66	.362	.434	0	.000	-0	-3	-3	1	-0.3
Total	2	1	2	.333	21	1	0	0	2	58^1	62	1	25	15	13.6	4.01	116	.284	.361	2	.118	-2	4	4	1	0.3

● GLENN LIEBHARDT Liebhardt, Glenn Ignatius "Sandy" b: 7/31/10, Cleveland, Ohio d: 3/14/92, Winston-Salem, N.C. BR/TR, 5'10.5", 170 lbs. Deb: 4/22/30 F

YEAR	TM/L	W	L	PCT	G	GS	CG	SH	SV	IP	H	HR	BB	SO	RAT	ERA	ERA+	OAV	OOB	BH	AVG	PB	PR	/A	PD	TPI
1930	Phi-A	0	1	.000	5	0	0	0	0	9	14	2	8	2	22.0	11.00	42	.359	.468	0	.000	-0	-6	-6	-0	-0.6
1936	StL-A	0	0	—	24	0	0	0	0	55^1	98	4	27	20	20.7	8.78	61	.375	.438	0	.000	-2	-23	-21	-2	-2.0
1938	StL-A	0	0	—	2	0	0	0	0	3	4	1	0	1	12.0	6.00	83	.308	.308	0	—	0	-0	-0	0	0.0
Total	3	0	1	.000	31	0	0	0	0	67^1	116	7	35	23	20.5	8.96	59	.371	.437	0	.000	-2	-30	-28	-2	-2.6

● GLENN LIEBHARDT Liebhardt, Glenn John b: 3/10/1883, Milton, Ind. d: 7/13/56, Cleveland, Ohio BR/TR, 5'10", 175 lbs. Deb: 10/02/06 F

YEAR	TM/L	W	L	PCT	G	GS	CG	SH	SV	IP	H	HR	BB	SO	RAT	ERA	ERA+	OAV	OOB	BH	AVG	PB	PR	/A	PD	TPI
1906	Cle-A	2	0	1.000	2	2	2	0	0	18	13	0	1	9	7.0	1.50	175	.205	.218	0	.000	-1	2	2	0	0.2
1907	Cle-A	18	14	.563	38	34	27	4	1	280^1	254	1	85	110	11.2	2.05	122	.244	.306	14	.161	-1	15	14	1	1.5
1908	Cle-A	15	16	.484	38	26	19	3	0	262	222	2	81	146	10.5	2.20	109	.235	.297	14	.175	0	6	6	1	0.7
1909	Cle-A	1	5	.167	12	4	1	0	1	52^1	54	0	16	15	12.2	2.92	87	.314	.376	0	.000	-2	-3	-2	-2	-0.6
Total	4	36	35	.507	90	66	49	7	2	612^2	543	3	183	280	10.9	2.17	114	.244	.305	28	.147	-4	21	20	0	1.8

● GENE LILLARD Lillard, Robert Eugene b: 11/12/13, Santa Barbara, Cal d: 4/12/91, Goleta, Cal. BR/TR, 5'10.5", 178 lbs. Deb: 5/08/36 F♦

YEAR	TM/L	W	L	PCT	G	GS	CG	SH	SV	IP	H	HR	BB	SO	RAT	ERA	ERA+	OAV	OOB	BH	AVG	PB	PR	/A	PD	TPI
1939	Chi-N	3	5	.375	20	7	2	0	0	55	68	2	36	31	17.5	6.55	60	.309	.413	1	.100	1	-16	-16	0	-1.4
1940	StL-N	0	1	.000	2	1	0	0	0	4^2	8	1	4	2	25.1	13.50	30	.364	.481	0	—	0	-5	-5	0	-0.4
Total	2	3	6	.333	22	8	2	0	0	59^2	76	3	40	33	18.1	7.09	56	.314	.420	8	.182	1	-21	-21	0	-1.8

● JIM LILLIE Lillie, James J. "Grasshopper" (b: James J. Lilly) b: 7/27/1861, New Haven, Conn. d: 11/9/1890, Kansas City, Mo. Deb: 5/17/1883 ♦

YEAR	TM/L	W	L	PCT	G	GS	CG	SH	SV	IP	H	HR	BB	SO	RAT	ERA	ERA+	OAV	OOB	BH	AVG	PB	PR	/A	PD	TPI
1883	Buf-N	0	1	.000	3	0	0	0	0	12	16	0	2	4	13.5	3.00	106	.302	.327	47	.234	0	0	0	0	0.0
1884	Buf-N	0	1	.000	2	1	0	0	0	13	22	0	5	4	18.7	6.23	51	.324	.370	105	.223	-0	-5	-4	0	-0.3
1886	KC-N	0	0	—	1	0	0	0	0	6	8	0	1	0	13.5	4.50	84	.348	.375	73	.175	-0	-1	-0	0	0.0
Total	3	0	2	.000	6	1	0	0	0	31	46	0	8	8	15.7	4.65	71	.319	.355	332	.219	-0	-5	-5	1	-0.3

● DEREK LILLIQUIST Lilliquist, Derek Jansen b: 2/20/66, Winter Park, Fla. BL/TL, 6', 200 lbs. Deb: 4/13/89

YEAR	TM/L	W	L	PCT	G	GS	CG	SH	SV	IP	H	HR	BB	SO	RAT	ERA	ERA+	OAV	OOB	BH	AVG	PB	PR	/A	PD	TPI
1989	Atl-N	8	10	.444	32	30	0	0	0	165^2	202	16	34	79	12.9	3.97	92	.301	.337	12	.190	0	-9	-6	-1	-0.7
1990	Atl-N	2	8	.200	12	11	0	0	0	61^2	75	10	19	34	13.9	6.28	64	.301	.353	8	.348	4	-17	-15	-1	-1.2
	SD-N	3	3	.500	16	7	1	1	0	60^1	61	6	23	29	12.8	4.33	88	.266	.339	3	.150	-0	-4	-3	-2	-0.5
	Yr	5	11	.313	28	18	1	1	0	122	136	16	42	63	13.3	5.31	74	.282	.342	11	.256	4	-21	-19	-3	-1.7
1991	SD-N	0	2	.000	6	2	0	0	0	14^1	25	3	4	7	18.2	8.79	43	.379	.414	0	.000	-0	-8	-8	0	-0.8
1992	Cle-A	5	3	.625	71	0	0	0	6	61^2	39	5	18	47	8.6	1.75	230	.186	.257	0	—	0	15	16	0	1.6
Total	4	18	26	.409	137	50	1	1	6	363^2	402	40	98	196	12.5	4.23	90	.282	.331	23	.213	4	-22	-17	-3	-1.6

● EZRA LINCOLN Lincoln, Ezra Perry b: 11/17/1868, Raynham, Mass. d: 5/7/51, Taunton, Mass. BL/TL, 5'11", 160 lbs. Deb: 5/02/1890

YEAR	TM/L	W	L	PCT	G	GS	CG	SH	SV	IP	H	HR	BB	SO	RAT	ERA	ERA+	OAV	OOB	BH	AVG	PB	PR	/A	PD	TPI
1890	Cle-N	3	11	.214	15	15	13	0	0	118	157	1	53	22	16.1	4.42	81	.310	.376	8	.157	-3	-11	-11	0	-1.2
	Syr-a	0	3	.000	3	3	2	0	0	20	33	1	4	6	17.1	10.35	34	.358	.391	0	.000	-1	-14	-15	-0	-1.2
Total	1	3	14	.176	18	18	15	0	0	138	190	2	57	28	16.2	5.28	68	.317	.379	8	.136	-4	-26	-26	0	-2.4

● VIVE LINDAMAN Lindaman, Vivan Alexander b: 10/28/1877, Charles City, Iowa d: 2/13/27, Charles City, Iowa BR/TR, 6'1", 200 lbs. Deb: 4/14/06

YEAR	TM/L	W	L	PCT	G	GS	CG	SH	SV	IP	H	HR	BB	SO	RAT	ERA	ERA+	OAV	OOB	BH	AVG	PB	PR	/A	PD	TPI
1906	Bos-N	12	23	.343	39	37	32	2	0	307^1	303	4	90	115	11.8	2.43	111	.264	.324	14	.132	-2	7	9	-2	0.7
1907	Bos-N	11	15	.423	34	28	24	2	1	260	252	10	108	90	13.0	3.63	70	.265	.349	11	.122	-2	-34	-31	-2	-3.8
1908	Bos-N	12	16	.429	43	30	21	2	1	270^2	246	7	70	68	10.8	2.36	102	.249	.306	15	.176	0	0	2	-3	-0.2
1909	Bos-N	1	6	.143	15	6	6	1	0	66	75	1	28	13	14.2	4.64	61	.299	.371	6	.273	1	-15	-13	-1	-1.4
Total	4	36	60	.375	131	101	83	7	2	904	876	22	296	286	12.0	2.92	88	.263	.329	46	.152	-3	-41	-34	-8	-4.7

● PAUL LINDBLAD Lindblad, Paul Aaron b: 8/9/41, Chanute, Kan. BL/TL, 6'1", 195 lbs. Deb: 9/15/65

YEAR	TM/L	W	L	PCT	G	GS	CG	SH	SV	IP	H	HR	BB	SO	RAT	ERA	ERA+	OAV	OOB	BH	AVG	PB	PR	/A	PD	TPI
1965	KC-A	0	1	.000	4	0	0	0	0	7^1	12	3	0	12	16.0	11.05	32	.353	.371	0	.000	-0	-6	-6	0	-0.6
1966	KC-A	5	10	.333	38	14	0	0	1	121	138	14	37	69	13.2	4.17	82	.292	.348	5	.147	0	-10	-10	0	-1.0
1967	KC-A	5	8	.385	46	10	1	1	6	115^2	106	15	35	83	11.4	3.58	89	.241	.306	7	.206	2	-4	-5	0	-0.4
1968	Oak-A	4	3	.571	47	1	0	0	2	56^1	51	6	14	42	10.4	2.40	118	.237	.284	3	.375	1	4	3	0	0.5
1969	Oak-A	9	6	.600	60	0	0	0	9	78^1	72	8	33	64	12.3	4.14	83	.240	.319	4	.333	1	-4	-6	-0	-0.5
1970	Oak-A	8	2	.800	62	0	0	0	3	63^1	52	7	28	42	11.4	2.70	131	.222	.305	0	.000	-1	7	6	-0	0.5
1971	Oak-A	1	0	1.000	8	0	0	0	0	16	18	1	2	4	11.8	3.94	85	.295	.328	1	.333	0	-1	-1	0	-0.1
	Was-A	6	4	.600	43	0	0	0	8	83^2	58	6	29	50	9.6	2.58	128	.196	.272	3	.158	0	8	7	1	0.9
	Yr	7	4	.636	51	0	0	0	8	99^2	76	7	31	54	9.8	2.80	118	.212	.279	4	.182	1	7	6	1	0.8
1972	Tex-A	5	8	.385	**66**	0	0	0	9	99^2	95	7	29	51	11.2	2.62	115	.257	.311	3	.200	0	5	4	-1	0.4
1973	*Oak-A	1	5	.167	36	3	0	0	2	78	89	8	28	33	13.8	3.69	96	.292	.357	0	—	0	1	-1	-1	-0.2
1974	Oak-A	4	4	.500	45	2	0	0	6	100^2	85	4	30	46	10.5	2.06	161	.231	.292	0	—	0	17	14	0	1.6
1975	*Oak-A	9	1	.900	68	0	0	0	7	122^1	105	6	43	58	10.9	2.72	133	.237	.305	0	.000	0	14	12	1	1.4
1976	Oak-A	6	5	.545	65	0	0	0	5	114^2	111	5	24	37	10.8	3.06	110	.253	.296	0	—	0	6	4	1	0.7
1977	Tex-A	4	5	.444	42	1	0	0	4	98^2	103	16	29	46	12.1	4.20	97	.270	.324	0	—	0	-2	-1	0	-0.2
1978	Tex-A	1	1	.500	18	0	0	0	2	39^2	41	2	15	25	13.2	3.63	103	.279	.354	0	—	0	1	0	-0	0.0
	*NY-A	0	0	—	7	1	0	0	0	18^1	21	4	8	9	14.2	4.42	82	.284	.354	0	—	0	-1	-2	0	0.0
	Yr	1	1	.500	25	1	0	0	2	58	62	6	23	34	13.2	3.88	95	.276	.343	0	—	0	-1	-1	0	0.0

YEAR	TM/L	W	L	PCT	G	GS	CG	SH	SV	IP	H	HR	BB	SO	RAT	ERA	ERA+	OAV	OOB	BH	AVG	PB	PR	/A	PD	TPI
Total	14	68	63	.519	655	32	1	1	64	1213^{2}	1157	112	384	671	11.6	3.29	104	.253	.314	26	.195	4	35	17	2	3.0
● **LYMAN LINDE** Linde, Lyman Gilbert b: 9/20/20, Beaver Dam, Wis. BR/TR, 5'11", 185 lbs. Deb: 9/11/47																										
1947	Cle-A	0	0	—	1	0	0	0	0	0^{2}	3	0	1	0	54.0	27.00	13	.600	.667	0	—	0	-2	-2	0	-0.2
1948	Cle-A	0	0	—	3	0	0	0	0	10	9	1	4	0	11.7	5.40	75	.243	.317	0	.000	-0	-1	-1	-0	-0.2
Total	2	0	0	—	4	0	0	0	0	10^{2}	12	1	5	0	14.3	6.75	60	.286	.362	0	.000	-0	-3	-3	-0	-0.4
● **JOHNNY LINDELL** Lindell, John Harlan b: 8/30/16, Greeley, Colo. d: 8/27/85, Newport Beach, Cal. BR/TR, 6'4.5", 217 lbs. Deb: 4/18/41 ♦																										
1942	NY-A	2	1	.667	23	2	0	0	1	52^{2}	52	3	22	28	12.8	3.76	92	.254	.329	6	.250	1	-1	-2	-0	-0.1
1953	Pit-N	5	16	.238	27	23	13	1	0	175^{2}	173	17	116	102	15.1	4.71	95	.262	.377	26	.286	7	-8	-5	3	1.2
	Phi-N	1	1	.500	5	3	2	0	0	23^{1}	22	0	23	16	17.4	4.24	99	.259	.417	7	.389	2	0	-0	-0	0.2
	Yr	6	17	.261	32	26	15	1	0	199	195	17	139	118	15.1	4.66	95	.259	.375	33	.303	9	-8	-5	2	1.4
Total	2	8	18	.308	55	28	15	1	1	251^{2}	247	20	161	146	14.8	4.47	95	.260	.371	762	.273	10	-9	-7	2	1.3
● **ERNIE LINDEMANN** Lindemann, Ernest b: 6/10/1883, New York, N.Y. d: 12/27/51, Brooklyn, N.Y. BR/TR, Deb: 6/28/07																										
1907	Bos-N	0	0	—	1	1	0	0	0	6^{1}	6	0	4	3	14.2	5.68	45	.286	.400	1	.500	0	-2	-2	0	-0.2
● **CARL LINDQUIST** Lindquist, Carl Emil b: 5/9/19, Morris Run, Pa. BR/TR, 6'2", 185 lbs. Deb: 9/27/43																										
1943	Bos-N	0	2	.000	2	2	0	0	0	13	17	3	4	1	14.5	6.23	55	.315	.362	0	.000	-1	-4	-4	0	-0.4
1944	Bos-N	0	0	—	5	0	0	0	0	8^{2}	8	1	2	4	10.4	3.12	123	.222	.263	0	.000	-0	0	1	-0	0.0
Total	2	0	2	.000	7	2	0	0	0	21^{2}	25	4	6	5	12.9	4.98	72	.278	.323	0	.000	-1	-4	-3	-0	-0.4
● **JIM LINDSEY** Lindsey, James Kendrick b: 1/24/1898, Greensburg, La. d: 10/25/63, Jackson, La. BR/TR, 6'1", 175 lbs. Deb: 5/01/22																										
1922	Cle-A	4	5	.444	29	5	0	0	1	83^{2}	105	4	24	29	14.2	6.02	67	.324	.376	4	.167	-1	-18	-19	-1	-1.9
1924	Cle-A	0	0	—	3	0	0	0	0	3	8	0	3	0	33.0	21.00	20	.500	.579	0	.000	-1	-6	-6	0	-0.5
1929	StL-N	1	1	.500	2	2	1	0	0	16^{1}	20	1	2	8	12.7	5.51	85	.290	.319	1	.200	-0	-1	-2	-0	-0.2
1930	*StL-N	7	5	.583	39	6	3	0	5	105^{2}	131	6	46	50	15.4	4.43	113	.312	.385	8	.286	1	6	7	-3	0.4
1931	*StL-N	6	4	.600	35	2	1	1	7	74^{2}	77	2	45	32	14.7	2.77	142	.270	.370	1	.111	-0	**9**	**10**	-0	0.9
1932	StL-N	3	3	.500	33	5	0	0	3	89^{1}	96	6	38	31	13.7	4.94	80	.279	.354	3	.143	-1	-10	-10	-1	-1.2
1933	StL-N	0	0	—	1	0	0	0	0	2	2	0	1	1	13.5	4.50	77	.286	.375	0	—	0	-0	-0	-0	0.0
1934	Cin-N	0	0	—	4	0	0	0	0	4	4	0	2	2	15.8	4.50	91	.286	.412	0	—	0	-0	-0	0	0.0
	StL-N	0	1	.000	11	0	0	0	1	14	21	2	3	7	15.4	6.43	66	.328	.358	0	.000	-0	-4	-3	-0	-0.4
	Yr	0	1	.000	15	0	0	0	1	18	25	2	5	9	15.0	6.00	70	.316	.357	0	.000	-0	-4	-4	-0	-0.4
1937	Bro-N	0	1	.000	20	0	0	0	2	38^{1}	43	4	12	15	13.1	3.52	115	.295	.352	1	.167	-0	2	2	-1	0.1
Total	9	21	20	.512	177	20	5	1	19	431	507	25	176	175	14.5	4.70	91	.300	.370	18	.186	-3	-23	-21	-6	-2.8
● **AXEL LINDSTROM** Lindstrom, Axel Olaf b: 8/26/1895, Gustavsberg, Sweden d: 6/24/40, Asheville, N.C. BR/TR, 5'10", 180 lbs. Deb: 10/03/16																										
1916	Phi-A	0	0	—	1	0	0	0	1	4	2	0	0	1	6.8	4.50	63	.182	.250	1	.500	0	-1	-1	-0	0.0
● **DICK LINES** Lines, Richard George b: 8/17/38, Montreal, Que., Can. BR/TL, 6'1", 175 lbs. Deb: 4/16/66																										
1966	Was-A	5	2	.714	53	0	0	0	2	83	63	4	24	49	9.5	2.28	152	.213	.274	0	.000	-1	11	11	2	1.3
1967	Was-A	2	5	.286	54	0	0	0	4	85^{2}	83	6	24	54	11.2	3.36	94	.245	.295	1	.111	1	-1	-2	0	-0.1
Total	2	7	7	.500	107	0	0	0	6	168^{2}	146	10	48	103	10.4	2.83	117	.230	.285	1	.053	-1	9	9	2	1.2
● **FRED LINK** Link, Edward Theodore "Laddie" b: 3/11/1886, Columbus, Ohio d: 5/22/39, Houston, Tex. BL/TL, 6', 170 lbs. Deb: 4/15/10																										
1910	Cle-A	5	6	.455	22	13	6	1	1	127^{2}	121	0	50	55	12.5	3.17	82	.259	.340	7	.167	-1	-9	-8	-1	-1.2
	StL-A	0	1	.000	3	3	0	0	0	17	24	0	13	5	20.1	4.24	58	.375	.487	1	.167	-0	-3	-3	-0	-0.4
	Yr	5	7	.417	25	16	6	1	1	144^{2}	145	0	63	60	13.0	3.30	78	.270	.347	8	.167	-1	-12	-12	-2	-1.6
● **ED LINKE** Linke, Edward Karl "Babe" b: 11/9/11, Chicago, Ill. d: 6/21/88, Chicago, Ill. BR/TR, 5'11", 180 lbs. Deb: 4/27/33																										
1933	Was-A	1	0	1.000	3	2	0	0	0	16	15	0	11	6	14.6	5.06	83	.250	.366	1	.167	0	-1	-2	-0	-0.1
1934	Was-A	2	2	.500	7	4	2	0	0	34^{2}	38	1	9	9	12.2	4.15	104	.277	.322	2	.182	0	1	1	0	0.1
1935	Was-A	11	7	.611	40	22	10	1	3	178	211	6	80	51	14.8	5.01	86	.296	.367	20	.294	6	-11	-14	-1	-0.8
1936	Was-A	1	5	.167	13	6	1	0	0	52	73	4	14	11	15.1	7.10	67	.330	.370	6	.400	4	-12	-13	1	-0.7
1937	Was-A	6	1	.857	36	7	0	0	3	128^{2}	158	11	59	61	15.5	5.60	79	.304	.379	10	.217	1	-14	-17	-0	-1.5
1938	StL-A	1	7	.125	21	2	0	0	0	39^{2}	60	6	33	18	21.1	7.94	63	.357	.463	2	.200	0	-14	-13	1	-1.1
Total	6	22	22	.500	120	43	13	1	6	449	555	28	206	156	15.4	5.61	79	.305	.377	41	.263	12	-51	-58	0	-4.1
● **ROYCE LINT** Lint, Royce James b: 1/1/21, Birmingham, Ala. BL/TL, 6'1", 165 lbs. Deb: 4/13/54																										
1954	StL-N	2	3	.400	30	4	1	1	0	70^{1}	75	9	30	36	13.4	4.86	85	.273	.344	1	.100	1	-6	-6	1	-0.4
● **DOUG LINTON** Linton, Douglas Warren b: 9/7/65, Santa Ana, Cal. BR/TR, 6'1", 185 lbs. Deb: 8/03/92																										
1992	Tor-A	1	3	.250	8	3	0	0	0	24	31	5	17	16	18.0	8.63	47	.323	.425	0	—	0	-12	-12	-0	-1.2
● **FRANK LINZY** Linzy, Frank Alfred b: 9/15/40, Ft.Gibson, Okla BR/TR, 6'1", 190 lbs. Deb: 8/14/63																										
1963	SF-N	0	0	—	8	1	0	0	0	16^{2}	22	0	10	14	17.8	4.86	66	.324	.418	0	.000	-0	-3	-3	0	-0.3
1965	SF-N	9	3	.750	57	0	0	0	21	81^{2}	76	2	23	35	11.2	1.43	251	.250	.309	4	.222	1	**19**	**20**	5	2.8
1966	SF-N	7	11	.389	51	0	0	0	16	100^{1}	107	4	34	57	12.8	2.96	124	.273	.334	3	.150	0	7	8	1	0.9
1967	SF-N	7	7	.500	57	0	0	0	17	95^{2}	67	4	34	38	9.5	1.51	218	.203	.277	0	.000	-2	20	19	3	2.3
1968	SF-N	9	8	.529	57	0	0	0	12	94^{2}	76	1	27	36	9.9	2.09	141	.218	.277	0	.000	-1	9	9	4	1.3
1969	SF-N	14	9	.609	58	0	0	0	11	116^{1}	129	5	38	62	13.2	3.64	96	.283	.342	8	.267	3	-1	-2	3	0.4
1970	SF-N	2	1	.667	20	0	0	0	1	25^{2}	33	2	11	16	15.8	7.01	57	.327	.398	0	.000	-0	-8	-9	0	-0.9
	StL-N	3	5	.375	47	0	0	0	2	61^{1}	66	3	23	19	13.1	3.67	112	.282	.346	0	.000	-1	3	3	1	0.3
	Yr	5	6	.455	67	0	0	0	3	87	99	5	34	35	13.8	4.66	88	.293	.358	0	.000	-1	-6	-6	1	-0.6
1971	StL-N	4	3	.571	50	0	0	0	6	59^{1}	49	2	27	24	11.5	2.12	170	.226	.311	2	.500	1	9	10	1	1.2
1972	Mil-A	2	2	.500	47	0	0	0	12	77^{1}	70	4	27	24	11.5	3.03	100	.248	.318	1	.111	-0	0	0	1	0.1
1973	Mil-A	2	6	.250	42	1	0	0	13	63	68	7	21	21	12.9	3.57	105	.282	.342	0	—	0	2	1	0	0.1
1974	Phi-N	3	2	.600	22	0	0	0	0	24^{2}	27	1	7	12	12.4	3.28	115	.284	.333	0	—	0	1	1	1	0.2
Total	11	62	57	.521	516	2	0	0	111	816^{2}	790	35	282	358	12.0	2.85	122	.257	.323	18	.149	0	58	57	20	8.4
● **ANGELO LiPETRI** LiPetri, Michael Angelo b: 7/6/30, Brooklyn, N.Y. BR/TR, 6'1.5", 180 lbs. Deb: 4/25/56																										
1956	Phi-N	0	0	—	6	0	0	0	0	11	7	2	3	8	9.0	3.27	114	.175	.250	0	.000	-0	1	1	0	0.1
1958	Phi-N	0	0	—	4	0	0	0	0	4	6	1	0	1	15.8	11.25	35	.353	.389	0	—	0	-3	-3	0	-0.3
Total	2	0	0	—	10	0	0	0	0	15	13	3	3	9	10.8	5.40	70	.228	.290	0	.000	-0	-3	-3	0	-0.2
● **TOM LIPP** Lipp, Thomas C. (b: Thomas C. Lieb) b: 6/4/1870, Baltimore, Md. d: 5/30/32, Baltimore, Md. 5'11.5", 170 lbs. Deb: 9/18/1897																										
1897	Phi-N	0	1	.000	1	1	1	0	0	3	8	0	2	1	30.0	15.00	28	.482	.537	1	1.000	0	-4	-4	-0	-0.2
● **NIG LIPSCOMB** Lipscomb, Gerard b: 2/24/11, Rutherfordton, N.C d: 2/27/78, Huntersville, N.C. BR/TR, 6', 175 lbs. Deb: 4/23/37 ♦																										
1937	StL-A	0	0	—	3	0	0	0	0	9^{2}	13	3	5	1	16.8	6.52	74	.333	.409	31	.323	1	-2	-2	-0	-0.2
● **HOD LISENBEE** Lisenbee, Horace Milton b: 9/23/1898, Clarksville, Tenn d: 11/14/87, Clarksville, Tenn. BR/TR, 5'11", 170 lbs. Deb: 4/23/27																										
1927	Was-A	18	9	.667	39	34	17	**4**	0	242	221	6	78	105	11.2	3.57	114	.245	.307	11	.133	-4	15	13	-2	0.6
1928	Was-A	2	6	.250	16	9	3	0	0	77	102	4	32	13	16.2	6.08	66	.326	.397	4	.174	-0	-17	-18	-1	-1.7
1929	Bos-A	0	0	—	5	0	0	0	0	8^{2}	10	1	4	2	14.5	5.19	82	.294	.368	0	.000	-0	-1	-1	0	-0.1
1930	Bos-A	10	17	.370	37	31	15	0	0	237^{1}	254	20	86	47	13.1	4.40	105	.280	.346	20	.267	1	7	6	-4	0.3

YEAR TM/L		W	L	PCT	G	GS	CG	SH	SV	IP	H	HR	BB	SO	RAT	ERA	ERA+	OAV	OOB	BH	AVG	PB	PR	/A	PD	TPI
1931	Bos-A	5	12	.294	41	17	6	0	0	164^2	190	13	49	42	13.2	5.19	83	.281	.332	12	.226	0	-15	-16	-2	-1.6
1932	Bos-A	0	4	.000	19	6	3	0	0	73^1	87	9	25	13	13.9	5.65	80	.296	.353	1	.048	-2	-10	-9	-1	-1.1
1936	Phi-A	1	7	.125	19	7	4	0	0	85^2	115	9	24	17	14.6	6.20	82	.322	.365	3	.120	-1	-11	-10	-1	-1.0
1945	Cin-N	1	3	.250	31	3	0	0	1	80^1	97	12	16	14	12.9	5.49	68	.294	.330	0	.000	-3	-15	-15	-1	-1.9
Total	8	37	58	.389	207	107	48	4	1	969	1076	74	314	253	13.1	4.81	90	.282	.340	51	.169	-10	-47	-51	-11	-6.5

● AD LISKA Liska, Adolph James b: 7/10/06, Dwight, Neb. BR/TR, 5'11.5", 160 lbs. Deb: 4/17/29

YEAR TM/L		W	L	PCT	G	GS	CG	SH	SV	IP	H	HR	BB	SO	RAT	ERA	ERA+	OAV	OOB	BH	AVG	PB	PR	/A	PD	TPI
1929	Was-A	3	9	.250	24	10	4	0	0	94^1	87	1	42	33	12.6	4.77	89	.249	.335	5	.172	-1	-6	-6	3	-0.3
1930	Was-A	9	7	.563	32	16	7	1	1	150^2	140	6	71	40	12.9	3.29	140	.250	.340	5	.096	-4	23	22	6	2.3
1931	Was-A	0	1	.000	2	1	0	0	0	4	9	0	1	2	22.5	6.75	64	.450	.476	0	.000	-0	-1	-1	0	-0.1
1932	Phi-N	2	0	1.000	8	0	0	0	1	26^2	22	0	10	6	11.1	1.69	261	.239	.320	0	.000	-1	6	8	1	0.9
1933	Phi-N	3	1	.750	45	1	0	0	1	75^2	96	5	26	23	14.5	4.52	84	.310	.363	1	.071	-1	-10	-6	4	-0.4
Total	5	17	18	.486	111	28	11	1	3	351^1	354	12	150	104	13.1	3.87	112	.266	.344	11	.107	-7	13	19	14	2.4

● MARK LITTELL Littell, Mark Alan b: 1/17/53, Cape Girardeau, Mo. BL/TR, 6'3", 210 lbs. Deb: 6/14/73

YEAR TM/L		W	L	PCT	G	GS	CG	SH	SV	IP	H	HR	BB	SO	RAT	ERA	ERA+	OAV	OOB	BH	AVG	PB	PR	/A	PD	TPI
1973	KC-A	1	3	.250	8	7	1	0	0	38	44	5	23	16	15.9	5.68	72	.288	.381	0	—	0	-8	-7	-0	-0.9
1975	KC-A	1	2	.333	7	3	1	0	0	24^1	19	1	15	19	12.6	3.70	104	.229	.347	0	—	0	0	0	1	0.1
1976	*KC-A	8	4	.667	60	1	0	0	16	104	68	1	60	92	11.1	2.08	169	.188	.304	0	.000	0	**17**	16	-1	1.7
1977	*KC-A	8	4	.667	48	5	0	0	12	104^2	73	6	55	106	11.1	3.61	112	.198	.304	0	.000	0	5	5	-1	0.4
1978	StL-N	4	8	.333	72	2	0	0	11	106^1	80	8	59	130	12.1	2.79	126	.213	.326	0	.000	-0	9	9	-1	0.8
1979	StL-N	9	4	.692	63	0	0	0	13	82^1	60	2	39	67	10.8	2.19	172	.203	.296	0	.000	-1	14	14	-1	1.3
1980	StL-N	0	2	.000	14	0	0	0	2	10^2	14	2	7	7	17.7	9.28	40	.318	.412	0	.000	-0	-7	-7	-0	-0.7
1981	StL-N	1	3	.250	28	1	0	0	2	41	36	2	31	22	14.7	4.39	81	.237	.366	2	.250	0	-4	-4	-1	-0.4
1982	StL-N	0	1	.000	16	0	0	0	0	20^2	22	1	15	7	16.1	5.23	69	.272	.385	0	.000	-0	-4	-4	-1	-0.5
Total	9	32	31	.508	316	19	2	0	56	532	416	28	304	466	12.3	3.32	112	.217	.326	2	.059	-2	23	24	-4	1.8

● JEFF LITTLE Little, Donald Jeffrey b: 12/25/54, Fremont, Ohio BR/TL, 6'6", 220 lbs. Deb: 9/06/80

YEAR TM/L		W	L	PCT	G	GS	CG	SH	SV	IP	H	HR	BB	SO	RAT	ERA	ERA+	OAV	OOB	BH	AVG	PB	PR	/A	PD	TPI
1980	StL-N	1	1	.500	7	2	0	0	0	18^2	18	0	9	17	13.0	3.86	96	.250	.333	1	.167	-0	-1	-0	-0	-0.1
1982	Min-A	2	0	1.000	33	0	0	0	0	36^1	33	6	27	26	14.9	4.21	101	.244	.370	0	—	0	-1	0	-1	-0.2
Total	2	3	1	.750	40	2	0	0	0	55	51	6	36	43	14.2	4.09	99	.246	.358	1	.167	-0	-1	-0	-1	-0.3

● JOHN LITTLEFIELD Littlefield, John Andrew b: 1/5/54, Covina, Cal. BR/TR, 6'2", 200 lbs. Deb: 6/08/80

YEAR TM/L		W	L	PCT	G	GS	CG	SH	SV	IP	H	HR	BB	SO	RAT	ERA	ERA+	OAV	OOB	BH	AVG	PB	PR	/A	PD	TPI
1980	StL-N	5	5	.500	52	0	0	0	9	66	71	2	20	22	12.5	3.14	118	.282	.337	0	.000	-1	3	4	0	0.3
1981	SD-N	2	3	.400	42	0	0	0	2	64	53	5	28	21	11.5	3.66	89	.235	.322	0	.000	-0	-1	-3	-0	-0.3
Total	2	7	8	.467	94	0	0	0	11	130	124	7	48	43	12.0	3.39	102	.259	.330	0	.000	-1	2	1	-0	0.0

● DICK LITTLEFIELD Littlefield, Richard Bernard b: 3/18/26, Detroit, Mich. BL/TL, 6', 180 lbs. Deb: 7/07/50

YEAR TM/L		W	L	PCT	G	GS	CG	SH	SV	IP	H	HR	BB	SO	RAT	ERA	ERA+	OAV	OOB	BH	AVG	PB	PR	/A	PD	TPI
1950	Bos-A	2	2	.500	15	2	0	0	1	23^1	27	6	24	13	20.1	9.26	53	.297	.448	0	.000	-1	-12	-11	1	-1.0
1951	Chi-A	1	1	.500	4	2	0	0	0	9^2	9	1	17	7	24.2	8.38	48	.243	.481	0	.000	0	-5	-5	-0	-0.4
1952	Det-A	0	3	.000	28	1	0	0	1	47^2	46	4	25	32	13.4	4.34	88	.257	.348	1	.143	-0	-4	-3	-1	-0.4
	StL-A	2	3	.400	7	5	3	0	0	46^1	35	4	17	34	10.1	2.72	144	.205	.277	1	.063	-2	5	6	-1	0.4
	Yr	2	6	.250	35	6	3	0	1	94	81	8	42	66	11.8	3.54	109	.231	.314	2	.087	-2	1	3	-2	0.0
1953	StL-A	7	12	.368	36	22	2	0	0	152^1	153	17	84	104	14.2	5.08	83	.264	.361	8	.190	-1	-18	-15	-1	-1.6
1954	Bal-A	0	0	—	3	0	0	0	0	6	8	0	6	5	22.5	10.50	34	.333	.484	0	.000	-0	-5	-5	-0	-0.5
	Pit-N	10	11	.476	23	21	7	1	0	155	140	10	85	92	13.2	3.60	116	.239	.337	8	.163	0	8	10	-3	0.8
1955	Pit-N	5	12	.294	35	17	4	1	0	130	148	15	68	70	15.1	5.12	80	.290	.375	6	.176	0	-16	-15	-2	-1.6
1956	Pit-N	0	0	—	6	2	0	0	0	12^2	14	2	6	10	14.2	4.26	88	.286	.364	0	.000	-0	-1	-1	-0	-0.1
	StL-N	0	2	.000	3	2	0	0	0	9^2	9	2	4	5	12.1	7.45	51	.237	.310	0	.000	-0	-4	-4	-0	-0.4
	NY-N	4	4	.500	31	7	0	0	2	97	78	16	39	65	10.9	4.08	93	.231	.310	2	.083	-2	-3	-3	0	-0.5
	Yr	4	6	.400	40	11	0	0	2	119^1	101	20	49	80	11.3	4.37	86	.238	.316	2	.071	-2	-8	-8	-1	-1.0
1957	Chi-N	2	3	.400	48	2	0	0	4	65^2	76	12	37	51	15.6	5.35	72	.295	.385	2	.182	0	-11	-11	-1	-1.2
1958	Mil-N	0	1	.000	4	0	0	0	1	6^1	7	2	1	7	12.8	4.26	83	.280	.333	0	—	0	-0	-1	-0	-0.1
Total	9	33	54	.379	243	83	16	2	9	761^2	750	91	413	495	13.9	4.71	86	.260	.355	28	.145	-5	-65	-56	-9	-6.6

● CARLISLE LITTLEJOHN Littlejohn, Charles Carlisle b: 10/6/01, Irene, Tex. d: 10/27/77, Kansas City, Mo. BR/TR, 5'10", 175 lbs. Deb: 5/11/27

YEAR TM/L		W	L	PCT	G	GS	CG	SH	SV	IP	H	HR	BB	SO	RAT	ERA	ERA+	OAV	OOB	BH	AVG	PB	PR	/A	PD	TPI
1927	StL-N	3	1	.750	14	2	1	0	0	42	47	4	14	16	13.1	4.50	88	.292	.349	5	.417	2	-3	-3	-1	-0.2
1928	StL-N	2	1	.667	12	2	1	0	0	32	36	2	14	6	14.1	3.66	109	.286	.357	0	.000	-2	1	1	-0	-0.1
Total	2	5	2	.714	26	4	2	0	0	74	83	6	28	22	13.5	4.14	96	.289	.352	5	.217	-0	-2	-1	-1	-0.3

● GREG LITTON Litton, Jon Gregory b: 7/13/64, New Orleans, La. BR/TR, 6', 175 lbs. Deb: 5/02/89 ♦

YEAR TM/L		W	L	PCT	G	GS	CG	SH	SV	IP	H	HR	BB	SO	RAT	ERA	ERA+	OAV	OOB	BH	AVG	PB	PR	/A	PD	TPI
1991	SF-N	0	0	—	1	0	0	0	0	1	1	0	3	0	36.0	9.00	40	.250	.571	23	.181	0	-1	-1	0	-0.1

● BUDDY LIVELY Lively, Everett Adrian "Red" b: 2/14/25, Birmingham, Ala. BR/TR, 6'0.5", 200 lbs. Deb: 4/17/47 F

YEAR TM/L		W	L	PCT	G	GS	CG	SH	SV	IP	H	HR	BB	SO	RAT	ERA	ERA+	OAV	OOB	BH	AVG	PB	PR	/A	PD	TPI
1947	Cin-N	4	7	.364	38	17	3	1	0	123	126	16	63	52	13.8	4.68	88	.265	.351	6	.188	2	-9	-8	-0	-0.6
1948	Cin-N	0	0	—	10	0	0	0	0	22^2	13	0	11	12	9.9	2.38	164	.165	.275	0	.000	-0	4	4	-1	0.3
1949	Cin-N	4	6	.400	31	10	3	1	1	103^1	91	11	53	30	12.5	3.92	107	.245	.339	4	.154	0	1	3	-1	0.2
Total	3	8	13	.381	79	27	6	2	1	249	230	27	127	94	12.9	4.16	99	.248	.339	10	.167	1	-3	-1	-2	-0.1

● JACK LIVELY Lively, Henry Everett b: 5/29/1885, Joppa, Ala. d: 12/5/67, Arab, Ala. BR/TR, 5'9", 185 lbs. Deb: 4/16/11 F

YEAR TM/L		W	L	PCT	G	GS	CG	SH	SV	IP	H	HR	BB	SO	RAT	ERA	ERA+	OAV	OOB	BH	AVG	PB	PR	/A	PD	TPI
1911	Det-A	7	5	.583	18	14	10	0	0	113^2	143	1	34	45	14.6	4.59	75	.313	.369	11	.256	3	-16	-14	-1	-1.2

● WES LIVENGOOD Livengood, Wesley Amos b: 7/18/10, Salisbury, N.C. BR/TR, 6'2", 172 lbs. Deb: 5/30/39

YEAR TM/L		W	L	PCT	G	GS	CG	SH	SV	IP	H	HR	BB	SO	RAT	ERA	ERA+	OAV	OOB	BH	AVG	PB	PR	/A	PD	TPI
1939	Cin-N	0	0	—	5	0	0	0	0	5^2	9	3	3	4	19.1	9.53	40	.360	.429	0	—	0	-4	-4	0	-0.3

● JAKE LIVINGSTONE Livingstone, Jacob M. b: 1/1/1880, St.Petersburg, Russia d: 3/22/49, Wassaic, N.Y. Deb: 9/06/01

YEAR TM/L		W	L	PCT	G	GS	CG	SH	SV	IP	H	HR	BB	SO	RAT	ERA	ERA+	OAV	OOB	BH	AVG	PB	PR	/A	PD	TPI
1901	NY-N	0	0	—	2	0	0	0	0	12	26	0	7	6	27.0	9.00	37	.430	.511	1	.167	0	-8	-8	-0	-0.7

● CLEM LLEWELLYN Llewellyn, Clement Manley "Lew" b: 8/1/1895, Dobson, N.C. d: 11/26/69, Concord, N.C. BL/TR, 6'2", 195 lbs. Deb: 6/18/22

YEAR TM/L		W	L	PCT	G	GS	CG	SH	SV	IP	H	HR	BB	SO	RAT	ERA	ERA+	OAV	OOB	BH	AVG	PB	PR	/A	PD	TPI
1922	NY-A	0	0	—	1	0	0	0	0	1	1	0	0	0	9.0	0.00	—	.250	.250	0	—	0	0	0	-0	0.0

● HARRY LOCHHEAD Lochhead, Robert Henry b: 3/29/1876, Stockton, Cal. d: 8/22/09, Stockton, Cal. TR , Deb: 4/16/1899 ♦

YEAR TM/L		W	L	PCT	G	GS	CG	SH	SV	IP	H	HR	BB	SO	RAT	ERA	ERA+	OAV	OOB	BH	AVG	PB	PR	/A	PD	TPI
1899	Cle-N	0	0	—	1	0	0	0	0	3^2	4	0	2	0	14.7	0.00	—	.277	.365	129	.238	0	2	2	-0	0.1

● CHUCK LOCKE Locke, Charles Edward b: 5/5/32, Malden, Mo. BR/TR, 5'11", 185 lbs. Deb: 9/16/55

YEAR TM/L		W	L	PCT	G	GS	CG	SH	SV	IP	H	HR	BB	SO	RAT	ERA	ERA+	OAV	OOB	BH	AVG	PB	PR	/A	PD	TPI
1955	Bal-A	0	0	—	2	0	0	0	0	3	0	0	1	1	3.0	0.00	—	.000	.100	0	—	0	1	1	0	0.1

● BOBBY LOCKE Locke, Lawrence Donald b: 3/3/34, Rowes Run, Pa. BR/TR, 5'11", 185 lbs. Deb: 6/18/59

YEAR TM/L		W	L	PCT	G	GS	CG	SH	SV	IP	H	HR	BB	SO	RAT	ERA	ERA+	OAV	OOB	BH	AVG	PB	PR	/A	PD	TPI
1959	Cle-A	3	2	.600	24	7	0	0	2	77^2	66	6	41	40	12.7	3.13	118	.233	.336	8	.333	3	6	5	0	0.8
1960	Cle-A	3	5	.375	32	11	2	2	2	123	121	10	37	53	11.7	3.37	111	.255	.311	9	.237	3	7	5	2	1.0
1961	Cle-A	4	4	.500	37	4	0	0	2	95^1	112	12	40	37	14.5	4.53	87	.300	.371	4	.211	0	-5	-6	1	-0.5
1962	StL-N	0	0	—	1	0	0	0	0	2	1	0	2	1	13.5	0.00	—	.143	.333	0	—	0	1	1	0	0.1
	Phi-N	1	0	1.000	5	0	0	0	0	15^2	16	4	10	9	14.9	5.74	67	.262	.366	2	.286	0	-3	-3	1	-0.2
	Yr	1	0	1.000	6	0	0	0	0	17^2	17	4	12	10	14.8	5.09	77	.250	.363	2	.286	0	-2	-2	1	-0.1
1963	Phi-N	0	0	—	9	0	0	0	0	10^2	10	0	5	7	12.7	5.91	55	.244	.326	0	.000	-0	-3	-3	-0	-0.4
1964	Phi-N	0	0	—	8	0	0	0	0	19^1	21	2	6	11	12.6	2.79	124	.276	.329	0	.000	-0	2	1	0	0.1
1965	Cin-N	0	1	.000	11	0	0	0	0	17^1	20	2	8	8	14.5	5.71	66	.299	.373	0	.000	0	-4	-4	1	-0.3

YEAR	TM/L	W	L	PCT	G	GS	CG	SH	SV	IP	H	HR	BB	SO	RAT	ERA	ERA+	OAV	OOB	BH	AVG	PB	PR	/A	PD	TPI
1967	Cal-A	3	0	1.000	9	1	0	0	2	19^1	14	1	3	7	8.4	2.33	135	.203	.247	2	.667	1	2	2	0	0.3
1968	Cal-A	2	3	.400	29	0	0	0	2	36^1	51	3	13	21	16.1	6.44	45	.331	.387	0	.000	-0	-14	-14	-1	-1.7
Total	9	16	15	.516	165	23	2	2	10	416^2	432	40	165	194	13.1	4.02	91	.269	.340	25	.255	7	-12	-17	4	-0.8

● RON LOCKE Locke, Ronald Thomas b: 4/4/42, Wakefield, R.I. BR/TL, 5'11", 168 lbs. Deb: 4/23/64

YEAR	TM/L	W	L	PCT	G	GS	CG	SH	SV	IP	H	HR	BB	SO	RAT	ERA	ERA+	OAV	OOB	BH	AVG	PB	PR	/A	PD	TPI
1964	NY-N	1	2	.333	25	3	0	0	0	41^1	46	3	22	17	15.0	3.48	103	.289	.379	0	.000	-1	0	0	-0	0.0

● BOB LOCKER Locker, Robert Awtry b: 3/15/38, George, Iowa BB/TR, 6'3", 200 lbs. Deb: 4/14/65

YEAR	TM/L	W	L	PCT	G	GS	CG	SH	SV	IP	H	HR	BB	SO	RAT	ERA	ERA+	OAV	OOB	BH	AVG	PB	PR	/A	PD	TPI
1965	Chi-A	5	2	.714	51	0	0	0	2	91^1	71	6	30	69	10.1	3.15	101	.216	.285	0	.000	-1	3	0	3	0.3
1966	Chi-A	9	8	.529	56	0	0	0	12	95	73	2	23	70	9.6	2.46	129	.206	.264	4	.250	1	10	7	3	1.2
1967	Chi-A	7	5	.583	**77**	0	0	0	20	124^2	102	5	23	80	9.7	2.09	148	.222	.274	0	.000	-1	16	14	5	2.0
1968	Chi-A	5	4	.556	70	0	0	0	10	90^1	78	4	27	62	10.6	2.29	132	.234	.293	0	.000	-1	7	7	2	1.1
1969	Chi-A	2	3	.400	17	0	0	0	4	22	26	6	6	15	13.1	6.55	59	.292	.337	0	.000	-0	-7	-7	0	-0.7
	Sea-A	3	3	.500	51	0	0	0	6	78^1	69	3	26	46	11.3	2.18	166	.234	.302	1	.083	-0	13	13	2	1.5
	Yr	5	6	.455	68	0	0	0	10	100^1	95	9	32	61	11.7	3.14	117	.247	.310	1	.077	-1	5	6	2	0.8
1970	Mil-A	0	1	.000	28	0	0	0	3	31^2	37	1	10	19	14.8	3.41	111	.306	.382	0	.000	-0	1	1	-0	0.1
	Oak-A	3	3	.500	38	0	0	0	4	56^1	49	1	19	33	11.0	2.88	123	.232	.299	1	.167	-0	5	4	1	0.5
	Yr	3	4	.429	66	0	0	0	7	88	86	2	29	52	11.9	3.07	118	.254	.315	1	.143	-0	6	5	0	0.6
1971	*Oak-A	7	2	.778	47	0	0	0	6	72^1	68	3	19	46	10.9	2.86	116	.249	.300	0	.000	-0	5	4	1	0.5
1972	*Oak-A	6	1	.857	56	0	0	0	10	78	69	1	16	47	10.0	2.65	107	.235	.280	0	.000	0	4	2	-1	0.1
1973	Chi-N	10	6	.625	63	0	0	0	18	106^1	96	6	42	76	12.0	2.54	155	.244	.323	1	.067	-1	13	17	2	1.8
1975	Chi-N	0	1	.000	22	0	0	0	0	32^2	38	3	16	14	15.4	4.96	77	.306	.394	0	—	0	-5	-4	1	-0.4
Total	10	57	39	.594	576	0	0	0	95	879	776	41	257	577	10.9	2.75	122	.237	.300	7	.074	-4	64	58	18	8.0

● SKIP LOCKWOOD Lockwood, Claude Edward b: 8/17/46, Boston, Mass. BR/TR, 6', 190 lbs. Deb: 4/23/65 ♦

YEAR	TM/L	W	L	PCT	G	GS	CG	SH	SV	IP	H	HR	BB	SO	RAT	ERA	ERA+	OAV	OOB	BH	AVG	PB	PR	/A	PD	TPI
1969	Sea-A	0	1	.000	6	3	0	0	0	23	24	3	6	10	11.7	3.52	103	.279	.326	0	.000	-1	0	0	0	0.0
1970	Mil-A	5	12	.294	27	26	3	1	0	173^2	173	22	79	93	13.4	4.30	88	.266	.351	12	.226	2	-11	-10	-1	-0.9
1971	Mil-A	10	15	.400	33	32	5	1	0	208	191	13	91	115	12.4	3.33	104	.246	.329	5	.081	-1	3	3	-3	-0.1
1972	Mil-A	8	15	.348	29	27	5	3	0	170	148	11	71	106	11.8	3.60	84	.232	.313	7	.132	-1	-10	-11	-3	-1.6
1973	Mil-A	5	12	.294	37	15	3	0	0	154^2	164	10	59	87	13.3	3.90	96	.280	.352	0	—	0	-1	-2	0	-0.2
1974	Cal-A	2	5	.286	37	2	0	0	1	81^1	81	8	32	39	13.1	4.32	80	.264	.343	0	—	0	-6	-8	-0	-0.8
1975	NY-N	1	3	.250	24	0	0	0	2	48^1	28	3	25	61	10.1	1.49	232	.174	.289	1	.167	-0	11	11	-1	1.1
1976	NY-N	10	7	.588	56	0	0	0	19	94^1	62	6	34	108	9.3	2.67	123	.186	.266	6	.333	3	9	7	-0	0.9
1977	NY-N	4	8	.333	63	0	0	0	20	104	87	5	31	84	10.6	3.38	111	.227	.291	3	.200	0	6	4	-2	0.2
1978	NY-N	7	13	.350	57	0	0	0	15	90^2	78	10	31	73	10.8	3.57	98	.236	.302	2	.182	1	0	-1	-2	-0.1
1979	NY-N	2	5	.286	27	0	0	0	9	42^1	33	3	14	42	10.0	1.49	245	.224	.292	0	.000	-0	11	10	-1	1.0
1980	Bos-A	3	1	.750	24	1	0	0	2	45^2	61	4	17	11	15.4	5.32	79	.321	.377	0	—	0	-7	-6	-1	-0.6
Total	12	57	97	.370	420	106	16	5	68	1236	1130	98	490	829	12.0	3.55	99	.246	.323	40	.154	3	4	-3	-13	-1.1

● MILO LOCKWOOD Lockwood, Milo Hathaway b: 4/7/1858, Solon, Ohio d: 10/9/1897, Economy, Pa. 5'10", 160 lbs. Deb: 4/17/1884 ♦

YEAR	TM/L	W	L	PCT	G	GS	CG	SH	SV	IP	H	HR	BB	SO	RAT	ERA	ERA+	OAV	OOB	BH	AVG	PB	PR	/A	PD	TPI
1884	Was-U	1	9	.100	11	10	6	0	0	67^2	99	4	15	48	15.2	7.45	40	.320	.351	14	.209	0	-33	-34	1	-2.5

● BILLY LOES Loes, William b: 12/13/29, Long Island City, N.Y. BR/TR, 6'1", 170 lbs. Deb: 5/18/50

YEAR	TM/L	W	L	PCT	G	GS	CG	SH	SV	IP	H	HR	BB	SO	RAT	ERA	ERA+	OAV	OOB	BH	AVG	PB	PR	/A	PD	TPI
1950	Bro-N	0	0	—	10	0	0	0	0	12^2	16	5	5	2	14.9	7.82	52	.314	.375	0	.000	0	-5	-5	-0	-0.5
1952	*Bro-N	13	8	.619	39	21	8	4	1	187^1	154	12	71	115	11.0	2.69	135	.224	.299	5	.093	-3	22	20	-0	1.8
1953	*Bro-N	14	8	.636	32	25	9	1	0	162^2	165	21	53	75	12.2	4.54	94	.261	.322	7	.125	-2	-5	-5	3	-0.5
1954	Bro-N	13	5	.722	28	21	6	0	0	147^2	154	14	60	97	13.1	4.14	99	.269	.339	6	.118	-2	-1	-1	-1	-0.4
1955	*Bro-N	10	4	.714	22	19	6	0	0	128	116	16	46	85	11.5	3.59	113	.240	.308	4	.091	-3	6	7	-0	0.4
1956	Bro-N	0	1	.000	1	1	0	0	0	1^1	5	1	1	2	40.5	40.50	10	.556	.600	0	—	0	-5	-5	0	-0.4
	Bal-A	2	7	.222	21	6	1	0	3	56^2	65	4	23	22	14.3	4.76	82	.291	.363	3	.176	-1	-4	-5	1	-0.5
1957	Bal-A★	12	7	.632	31	18	8	3	4	155^1	142	8	37	86	10.6	3.24	111	.245	.295	4	.080	-3	9	6	2	0.5
1958	Bal-A	3	9	.250	32	10	1	0	5	114	106	10	44	44	12.5	3.63	99	.252	.334	2	.067	-2	2	-0	0	-0.3
1959	Bal-A	4	7	.364	37	0	0	0	14	64^1	58	5	25	34	12.0	4.06	93	.239	.317	1	.125	-0	-1	-2	1	-0.1
1960	SF-N	3	2	.600	37	0	0	0	5	45^2	40	9	17	28	12.0	4.93	71	.247	.333	1	.250	0	-6	-7	1	-0.7
1961	SF-N	6	5	.545	26	18	3	1	0	114^2	114	13	39	55	12.4	4.24	90	.258	.325	5	.156	-0	-3	-5	0	-0.6
Total	11	80	63	.559	316	139	42	9	32	1190^1	1135	118	421	645	12.0	3.89	99	.252	.321	38	.110	-17	9	-5	6	-1.3

● FRANK LOFTUS Loftus, Francis Patrick b: 3/10/1898, Scranton, Pa. d: 10/27/80, Belchertown, Mass. BR/TR, 5'9", 190 lbs. Deb: 9/26/26

YEAR	TM/L	W	L	PCT	G	GS	CG	SH	SV	IP	H	HR	BB	SO	RAT	ERA	ERA+	OAV	OOB	BH	AVG	PB	PR	/A	PD	TPI
1926	Was-A	0	0	—	1	0	0	0	0	1	3	0	2	0	45.0	9.00	43	.600	.714	0	—	0	-1	-1	-0	-0.1

● BOB LOGAN Logan, Robert Dean "Lefty" b: 2/10/10, Thompson, Neb. d: 5/20/78, Indianapolis, Ind. BR/TL, 5'10", 170 lbs. Deb: 4/18/35

YEAR	TM/L	W	L	PCT	G	GS	CG	SH	SV	IP	H	HR	BB	SO	RAT	ERA	ERA+	OAV	OOB	BH	AVG	PB	PR	/A	PD	TPI
1935	Bro-N	0	1	.000	2	0	0	0	0	2^2	2	0	1	1	10.1	3.38	118	.182	.250	0	—	0	0	0	0	0.0
1937	Det-A	0	0	—	1	0	0	0	0	0^2	1	0	1	1	27.0	0.00	—	.333	.500	0	—	0	0	0	0	0.0
	Chi-N	0	0	—	4	0	0	0	1	6^1	6	0	4	2	14.2	1.42	280	.261	.370	0	.000	-0	2	2	-0	0.1
1938	Chi-N	0	2	.000	14	0	0	0	2	22^2	18	0	17	10	14.3	2.78	138	.222	.364	0	.000	-0	3	3	-0	0.2
1941	Cin-N	0	1	.000	2	0	0	0	0	3^1	5	0	5	0	27.0	8.10	44	.333	.500	0	—	0	-2	-2	0	-0.1
1945	Bos-N	7	11	.389	34	25	5	1	1	187	213	9	53	53	12.9	3.18	121	.283	.331	13	.213	1	13	14	0	1.5
Total	5	7	15	.318	57	25	5	1	4	222^2	245	9	81	67	13.3	3.15	122	.277	.339	13	.200	1	16	17	0	1.7

● BILL LOHRMAN Lohrman, William Le Roy b: 5/22/13, Brooklyn, N.Y. BR/TR, 6'1", 185 lbs. Deb: 6/19/34

YEAR	TM/L	W	L	PCT	G	GS	CG	SH	SV	IP	H	HR	BB	SO	RAT	ERA	ERA+	OAV	OOB	BH	AVG	PB	PR	/A	PD	TPI
1934	Phi-N	0	1	.000	4	0	0	0	1	6	5	0	1	2	9.0	4.50	105	.217	.250	1	.500	0	-0	0	0	0.1
1937	NY-N	1	0	1.000	2	1	1	0	1	10	5	0	2	3	6.3	0.90	432	.152	.200	0	.000	-0	3	3	0	0.4
1938	NY-N	9	6	.600	31	14	3	0	0	152	152	9	33	52	11.1	3.32	114	.253	.294	4	.082	-4	8	8	2	0.6
1939	NY-N	12	13	.480	38	24	9	1	1	185^2	200	15	45	70	12.0	4.07	96	.282	.327	14	.233	4	-3	-3	-0	0.1
1940	NY-N	10	15	.400	31	28	11	4	1	195	200	19	43	73	11.4	3.78	103	.264	.306	8	.123	-3	1	2	2	0.2
1941	NY-N	9	10	.474	33	20	6	2	3	159	184	7	40	61	12.7	4.02	92	.286	.327	11	.229	4	-7	-6	0	-0.2
1942	StL-N	1	1	.500	5	0	0	0	0	12^2	11	0	2	6	9.2	1.42	241	.244	.277	2	.667	1	3	3	0	0.4
	NY-N	13	4	.765	26	19	12	2	0	158	143	11	33	41	10.1	2.56	131	.240	.282	7	.121	-3	13	14	-1	1.2
	Yr	14	5	.737	31	19	12	2	0	170^2	154	11	35	47	10.1	2.48	136	.240	.281	9	.148	-2	16	17	-1	1.6
1943	NY-N	5	6	.455	17	12	3	0	1	80^1	110	7	25	16	15.3	5.15	67	.324	.374	1	.037	-3	-16	-15	-1	-1.9
	Bro-N	0	2	.000	6	2	2	0	0	27^2	29	2	10	5	13.0	3.58	94	.274	.342	1	.143	0	-1	-1	-0	-0.1
	Yr	5	8	.385	23	14	5	0	1	108	139	9	35	21	14.6	4.75	72	.311	.362	2	.059	-3	-16	-16	-1	-2.0
1944	Bro-N	0	0	—	3	0	0	0	0	2^2	4	0	4	1	27.0	0.00	—	.500	.667	0	—	0	1	1	-0	0.1
	Cin-N	0	1	.000	2	1	0	0	0	1^2	5	0	2	0	37.8	27.00	13	.500	.583	0	—	0	-4	-4	-0	-0.4
	Yr	0	1	.000	5	1	0	0	0	4^1	9	0	6	1	31.2	10.38	34	.500	.625	0	—	0	-3	-3	-0	-0.3
Total	9	60	59	.504	198	121	47	9	8	990^2	1048	70	240	330	11.8	3.69	101	.271	.315	49	.153	-3	-1	2	3	0.5

● MICKEY LOLICH Lolich, Michael Stephen b: 9/12/40, Portland, Ore. BB/TL, 6', 210 lbs. Deb: 5/12/63

YEAR	TM/L	W	L	PCT	G	GS	CG	SH	SV	IP	H	HR	BB	SO	RAT	ERA	ERA+	OAV	OOB	BH	AVG	PB	PR	/A	PD	TPI
1963	Det-A	5	9	.357	33	18	4	0	0	144^1	145	13	56	103	12.8	3.55	105	.265	.338	2	.056	-1	1	3	-1	0.2
1964	Det-A	18	9	.667	44	33	12	6	2	232	196	26	64	192	10.3	3.26	112	.225	.282	7	.109	1	9	10	-2	1.0
1965	Det-A	15	9	.625	43	37	7	3	3	243^2	216	23	72	226	11.1	3.44	101	.236	.301	5	.058	-6	1	1	-2	-0.7
1966	Det-A	14	14	.500	40	33	5	1	3	203^2	204	24	83	173	12.9	4.77	73	.257	.331	9	.141	1	-30	-29	-3	-3.2
1967	Det-A	14	13	.519	31	30	11	**6**	0	204	165	14	56	174	10.1	3.04	107	.221	.282	12	.197	3	4	5	-2	0.6
1968	*Det-A	17	9	.654	39	32	8	4	1	220	178	23	65	197	10.4	3.19	94	.219	.286	8	.114	0	-5	-4	-2	-0.8
1969	Det-A☆	19	11	.633	37	36	15	1	1	280^2	214	22	122	271	11.2	3.14	119	.210	.304	8	.088	-3	15	18	-0	1.6

YEAR TM/L	W	L	PCT	G	GS	CG	SH	SV	IP	H	HR	BB	SO	RAT	ERA	ERA+	OAV	OOB	BH	AVG	PB	PR	/A	PD	TPI
1970 Det-A	14	19	.424	40	39	13	3	0	272^2	272	27	109	230	12.7	3.80	98	.260	.333	11	.134	1	-2	-2	1	0.0
1971 Det-A★	**25**	14	.641	45	45	**29**	4	0	**376**	336	36	92	**308**	10.4	2.92	123	.237	.287	15	.130	1	23	28	-4	2.8
1972 *Det-A★	22	14	.611	41	41	23	4	0	327^1	282	29	74	250	10.1	2.50	126	.234	.284	6	.067	-0	20	23	-4	2.2
1973 Det-A	16	15	.516	42	42	17	3	0	308^2	315	35	79	214	11.6	3.82	107	.266	.315	0	—	0	-0	9	-1	0.8
1974 Det-A	16	21	.432	41	41	27	3	0	308	310	38	78	202	11.4	4.15	92	.268	.316	0	—	0	-18	-12	-4	-1.6
1975 Det-A	12	18	.400	32	32	19	1	0	240^2	260	19	64	139	12.1	3.78	106	.279	.325	0	—	0	-0	6	-2	0.4
1976 NY-N	8	13	.381	31	30	5	2	0	192^2	184	14	52	120	11.0	3.22	102	.252	.302	7	.130	0	6	2	-1	0.1
1978 SD-N	2	1	.667	20	2	0	0	1	34^2	30	0	11	13	10.9	1.56	214	.240	.307	0	.000	-0	8	7	-0	0.7
1979 SD-N	0	2	.000	27	5	0	0	0	49^1	59	4	22	20	14.8	4.74	74	.304	.375	0	.000	-0	-6	-7	0	-0.7
Total 16	217	191	.532	586	496	195	41	11	3638^1	3366	347	1099	2832	11.3	3.44	104	.246	.306	90	.110	-4	25	58	-25	3.4

● TIM LOLLAR Lollar, William Timothy b: 3/17/56, Poplar Bluff, Mo. BL/TL, 6'3", 200 lbs. Deb: 6/28/80

YEAR TM/L	W	L	PCT	G	GS	CG	SH	SV	IP	H	HR	BB	SO	RAT	ERA	ERA+	OAV	OOB	BH	AVG	PB	PR	/A	PD	TPI
1980 NY-A	1	0	1.000	14	1	0	0	2	32^1	33	3	20	13	14.8	3.34	117	.280	.384	0	—	0	2	2	0	0.2
1981 SD-N	2	8	.200	24	11	0	0	1	76^2	87	4	51	38	16.6	6.10	53	.293	.402	3	.167	1	-22	-24	2	-2.1
1982 SD-N	16	9	.640	34	34	4	2	0	232^2	192	20	87	150	10.9	3.13	109	.224	.298	21	.247	8	12	8	0	1.7
1983 SD-N	7	12	.368	30	30	1	0	0	175^2	170	22	85	135	13.3	4.61	76	.258	.347	14	.241	5	-19	-22	-2	-1.8
1984 *SD-N	11	13	.458	31	31	3	2	0	195^2	168	18	105	131	12.6	3.91	91	.234	.333	15	.221	7	-7	-7	-2	-0.3
1985 Chi-A	3	5	.375	18	13	0	0	0	83	83	10	58	61	15.4	4.66	93	.266	.383	0	—	0	-5	-3	-0	-0.4
Bos-A	5	5	.500	16	10	1	0	1	67	57	9	40	44	13.2	4.57	94	.230	.339	0	.000	0	-3	-2	-1	-0.3
Yr	8	10	.444	34	23	1	0	1	150	140	19	98	105	14.3	4.62	93	.248	.360	0	.000	0	-8	-5	-1	-0.7
1986 Bos-A	2	0	1.000	32	1	0	0	0	43	51	7	34	28	18.4	6.91	60	.304	.429	1	1.000	0	-13	-13	1	-1.2
Total 7	47	52	.475	199	131	9	4	4	906	841	93	480	600	13.3	4.27	85	.249	.345	54	.234	23	-55	-63	-3	-4.2

● VIC LOMBARDI Lombardi, Victor Alvin b: 9/20/22, Reedley, Cal. BL/TL, 5'7", 158 lbs. Deb: 4/18/45

YEAR TM/L	W	L	PCT	G	GS	CG	SH	SV	IP	H	HR	BB	SO	RAT	ERA	ERA+	OAV	OOB	BH	AVG	PB	PR	/A	PD	TPI
1945 Bro-N	10	11	.476	38	24	9	0	4	203^2	195	11	86	64	12.6	3.31	113	.252	.331	13	.183	-1	11	10	-1	0.9
1946 Bro-N	13	10	.565	41	25	13	2	3	193	170	10	84	60	11.9	2.89	117	.235	.316	14	.230	2	11	10	0	1.3
1947 *Bro-N	12	11	.522	33	20	7	3	3	174^2	156	12	65	72	11.5	2.99	138	.241	.312	16	.242	2	21	22	1	2.5
1948 Pit-N	10	9	.526	38	17	9	0	4	163	156	9	67	54	12.4	3.70	110	.255	.330	10	.208	1	5	7	1	0.9
1949 Pit-N	5	5	.500	34	12	4	0	1	134	149	14	68	64	14.8	4.57	92	.286	.372	17	.347	5	-8	-5	1	0.1
1950 Pit-N	0	5	.000	39	2	0	0	1	76^1	93	14	48	26	16.9	6.60	66	.310	.409	4	.250	1	-21	-19	0	-1.7
Total 6	50	51	.495	223	100	42	5	16	944^2	919	70	418	340	12.9	3.68	106	.257	.337	74	.238	10	19	25	3	4.0

● LOU LOMBARDO Lombardo, Louis b: 11/18/28, Carlstadt, N.J. BL/TL, 6'2", 210 lbs. Deb: 9/22/48

YEAR TM/L	W	L	PCT	G	GS	CG	SH	SV	IP	H	HR	BB	SO	RAT	ERA	ERA+	OAV	OOB	BH	AVG	PB	PR	/A	PD	TPI
1948 NY-N	0	0	—	2	0	0	0	0	5^1	5	1	5	0	18.6	6.75	58	.250	.423	0	.000	-0	-2	-2	0	-0.2

● JIM LONBORG Lonborg, James Reynold b: 4/16/42, Santa Maria, Cal. BR/TR, 6'5", 210 lbs. Deb: 4/23/65

YEAR TM/L	W	L	PCT	G	GS	CG	SH	SV	IP	H	HR	BB	SO	RAT	ERA	ERA+	OAV	OOB	BH	AVG	PB	PR	/A	PD	TPI
1965 Bos-A	9	17	.346	32	31	7	1	0	185^1	193	20	65	113	12.7	4.47	83	.262	.324	8	.136	0	-21	-15	-2	-1.7
1966 Bos-A	10	10	.500	45	23	3	1	2	181^2	173	18	55	131	11.6	3.86	98	.249	.310	5	.093	-2	-9	-1	-1	-0.4
1967 *Bos-A☆	**22**	9	.710	39	39	15	2	0	273^1	228	23	83	**246**	10.9	3.16	110	.225	.296	14	.141	-1	2	10	-2	0.7
1968 Bos-A	6	10	.375	23	17	4	1	0	113^1	89	11	59	73	12.6	4.29	74	.216	.330	11	.282	4	-16	-14	-2	-1.4
1969 Bos-A	7	11	.389	29	23	4	0	1	143^2	148	15	65	100	13.8	4.51	84	.270	.355	4	.098	-1	-14	-11	-0	-1.3
1970 Bos-A	4	1	.800	9	4	0	0	0	34	33	3	9	21	11.1	3.18	125	.260	.309	4	.444	2	2	3	0	0.6
1971 Bos-A	10	7	.588	27	26	5	1	0	167^2	167	15	67	100	13.3	4.13	89	.259	.342	9	.170	0	-13	-8	1	-0.8
1972 Mil-A	14	12	.538	33	30	11	2	1	223	197	17	76	143	11.5	2.83	107	.238	.311	10	.145	-1	6	5	-2	0.3
1973 Phi-N	13	16	.448	38	30	6	0	0	199^1	218	25	80	106	13.9	4.88	78	.279	.353	8	.136	0	-27	-24	-1	-2.5
1974 Phi-N	17	13	.567	39	39	16	3	0	283	280	22	70	121	11.3	3.21	118	.261	.310	9	.096	-4	13	18	-4	1.0
1975 Phi-N	8	6	.571	27	26	6	2	0	159^1	161	12	45	72	11.9	4.12	90	.257	.312	1	.023	-3	-9	-7	0	-1.0
1976 *Phi-N	18	10	.643	33	32	8	1	1	222	210	18	50	118	10.7	3.08	115	.249	.294	11	.164	1	10	11	-3	1.0
1977 *Phi-N	11	4	.733	25	25	4	1	0	157^2	157	15	50	76	12.1	4.11	97	.261	.323	5	.104	-2	-4	-2	-1	-0.6
1978 Phi-N	8	10	.444	22	22	1	0	0	113^2	132	16	45	48	14.2	5.23	68	.293	.359	6	.176	1	-21	-21	-0	-2.1
1979 Phi-N	0	1	.000	4	1	0	0	0	7^1	14	3	4	7	23.3	11.05	35	.389	.463	0	.000	-0	-6	-6	-0	-0.6
Total 15	157	137	.534	425	368	90	15	4	2464^1	2400	233	823	1475	12.2	3.86	94	.255	.322	105	.136	-5	-106	-63	-18	-8.8

● LEP LONG Long, Lester b: 7/12/1888, Summit, N.J. d: 10/21/58, Birmingham, Ala. BR/TR, 5'10", 153 lbs. Deb: 6/29/11

YEAR TM/L	W	L	PCT	G	GS	CG	SH	SV	IP	H	HR	BB	SO	RAT	ERA	ERA+	OAV	OOB	BH	AVG	PB	PR	/A	PD	TPI
1911 Phi-A	0	0	—	4	0	0	0	0	8	15	0	5	4	22.5	4.50	70	.405	.476	0	.000	-0	-1	-1	0	-0.2

● RED LONG Long, Nelson b: 9/28/1876, Burlington, Ont., Canada d: 8/11/29, Hamilton, Ont., Can BR/TR, 6'1", 190 lbs. Deb: 9/11/02

YEAR TM/L	W	L	PCT	G	GS	CG	SH	SV	IP	H	HR	BB	SO	RAT	ERA	ERA+	OAV	OOB	BH	AVG	PB	PR	/A	PD	TPI
1902 Bos-N	0	0	—	1	1	1	0	0	8	4	0	3	5	9.0	1.13	251	.150	.260	0	.000	-0	1	2	-0	0.1

● BOB LONG Long, Robert Earl b: 11/11/54, Jasper, Tenn. BR/TR, 6'3", 178 lbs. Deb: 9/02/81

YEAR TM/L	W	L	PCT	G	GS	CG	SH	SV	IP	H	HR	BB	SO	RAT	ERA	ERA+	OAV	OOB	BH	AVG	PB	PR	/A	PD	TPI
1981 Pit-N	1	2	.333	5	3	0	0	0	19^2	23	2	10	8	15.1	5.95	60	.299	.379	0	.000	-0	-5	-5	-1	-0.6
1985 Sea-A	0	0	—	28	0	0	0	0	38^1	30	7	17	29	11.5	3.76	112	.210	.302	0	—	0	2	2	-0	0.2
Total 2	1	2	.333	33	3	0	0	0	58	53	9	27	37	12.7	4.50	89	.241	.329	0	.000	-0	-4	-3	-1	-0.4

● TOM LONG Long, Thomas Francis "Little Hawk" b: 4/22/1898, Memphis, Tenn. d: 9/16/73, Louisville, Ky. BL/TL, 5'9", 154 lbs. Deb: 4/26/24

YEAR TM/L	W	L	PCT	G	GS	CG	SH	SV	IP	H	HR	BB	SO	RAT	ERA	ERA+	OAV	OOB	BH	AVG	PB	PR	/A	PD	TPI
1924 Bro-N	0	0	—	1	0	0	0	0	2	2	0	2	0	18.0	9.00	42	.333	.500	0	—	0	-1	-1	-0	-0.1

● BILL LONG Long, William Douglas b: 2/29/60, Cincinnati, Ohio BR/TR, 6', 185 lbs. Deb: 7/21/85

YEAR TM/L	W	L	PCT	G	GS	CG	SH	SV	IP	H	HR	BB	SO	RAT	ERA	ERA+	OAV	OOB	BH	AVG	PB	PR	/A	PD	TPI
1985 Chi-A	0	1	.000	4	3	0	0	0	14	25	4	5	13	19.3	10.29	42	.391	.435	0	—	0	-10	-9	0	-0.8
1987 Chi-A	8	8	.500	29	23	5	2	1	169	179	20	28	72	11.2	4.37	105	.272	.304	0	—	0	2	4	0	0.2
1988 Chi-A	8	11	.421	47	18	3	0	2	174	187	21	43	77	12.1	4.03	98	.280	.327	0	—	0	-1	-1	-0	-0.1
1989 Chi-A	5	5	.500	30	8	0	0	1	98^2	101	8	37	51	13.0	3.92	97	.265	.336	0	—	0	-0	-1	0	0.0
1990 Chi-A	0	1	.000	4	0	0	0	0	5^2	6	2	2	2	12.7	6.35	60	.261	.320	0	—	0	-2	-2	0	-0.1
Chi-N	6	1	.857	42	0	0	0	5	55^2	66	8	21	32	14.2	4.37	93	.301	.365	0	.000	-0	-4	-2	0	-0.2
1991 Mon-N	0	0	—	3	0	0	0	0	1^2	4	0	4	0	43.2	10.80	33	.500	.667	0	—	0	-1	-1	-0	-0.1
Total 6	27	27	.500	159	52	8	2	9	518^2	568	63	140	247	12.5	4.37	95	.281	.331	0	.000	-0	-16	-13	1	-1.1

● PETE LOOS Loos, Ivan b: 3/23/1878, Philadelphia, Pa. d: 2/23/56, Darby, Pa. TR, Deb: 5/02/01

YEAR TM/L	W	L	PCT	G	GS	CG	SH	SV	IP	H	HR	BB	SO	RAT	ERA	ERA+	OAV	OOB	BH	AVG	PB	PR	/A	PD	TPI
1901 Phi-A	0	1	.000	1	1	0	0	0	1	2	0	4	0	54.0	27.00	14	.409	.675	0	—	0	-3	-3	0	-0.2

● ED LOPAT Lopat, Edmund Walter (b: Edmund Walter Lopatynski) b: 6/21/18, New York, N.Y. d: 6/15/92, Darien, Conn. BL/TL, 5'10", 185 lbs. Deb: 4/30/44 MC

YEAR TM/L	W	L	PCT	G	GS	CG	SH	SV	IP	H	HR	BB	SO	RAT	ERA	ERA+	OAV	OOB	BH	AVG	PB	PR	/A	PD	TPI
1944 Chi-A	11	10	.524	27	25	13	1	0	210	217	12	59	75	11.9	3.26	105	.265	.316	25	.309	6	4	4	1	1.3
1945 Chi-A	10	13	.435	26	24	17	1	1	199^1	226	8	56	74	13.0	4.11	81	.285	.336	24	.293	5	-16	-17	-1	-1.4
1946 Chi-A	13	13	.500	29	29	20	2	0	231	216	18	48	89	10.3	2.73	125	.248	.288	22	.253	6	20	18	1	2.8
1947 Chi-A	16	13	.552	31	31	22	3	0	252^2	241	17	73	109	11.3	2.81	130	.253	.307	19	.198	0	25	24	-1	2.5
1948 NY-A	17	11	.607	33	31	13	3	0	226^2	246	16	66	83	12.5	3.65	112	.284	.336	14	.173	-1	16	11	2	1.1
1949 *NY-A	15	10	.600	31	30	14	4	1	215^1	222	19	69	70	12.4	3.26	124	.269	.330	20	.263	7	22	19	0	2.6
1950 *NY-A	18	8	.692	35	32	15	3	1	236^1	244	19	65	72	11.9	3.47	124	.266	.317	19	.232	7	29	22	1	2.9
1951 *NY-A★	21	9	.700	31	31	20	4	0	234^2	209	12	71	93	**10.9**	2.91	131	.239	**.298**	15	.179	1	31	24	2	2.6
1952 *NY-A	10	5	.667	20	19	10	2	0	149^1	127	11	53	56	11.1	2.53	131	.234	.307	9	.173	1	19	13	0	1.5
1953 *NY-A	16	4	**.800**	25	24	9	3	0	178^1	169	13	32	50	10.3	**2.42**	**152**	.250	.288	12	.190	1	31	25	1	2.9
1954 NY-A	12	4	.750	26	23	7	0	0	170	189	14	33	54	12.1	3.55	97	.288	.328	1	.018	-5	3	-2	-1	-0.8
1955 NY-A	4	8	.333	16	12	3	1	0	86^2	101	12	16	24	12.3	3.74	100	.294	.328	4	.138	-1	2	0	-1	-0.2
Bal-A	3	4	.429	10	7	1	0	0	49	57	8	9	10	12.7	4.22	90	.294	.335	3	.176	0	-1	-2	1	-0.1
Yr	7	12	.368	26	19	4	1	0	135^2	158	20	25	34	12.3	3.91	96	.293	.328	7	.152	-1	1	-2	-0	-0.3

YEAR	TM/L	W	L	PCT	G	GS	CG	SH	SV	IP	H	HR	BB	SO	RAT	ERA	ERA+	OAV	OOB	BH	AVG	PB	PR	/A	PD	TPI
Total	12	166	112	.597	340	318	164	27	3	2439^{1}	2464	179	650	859	11.6	3.21	116	.264	.315	187	.211	28	186	138	4	17.7
● ART LOPATKA Lopatka, Arthur Joseph b: 5/28/19, Chicago, Ill. BB/TL, 5'10", 170 lbs. Deb: 9/12/45																										
1945	StL-N	1	0	1.000	4	1	1	0	0	11^{2}	7	0	3	5	8.5	1.54	243	.159	.229	1	.250	0	3	3	-0	0.3
1946	Phi-N	0	1	.000	4	1	0	0	0	5^{1}	13	1	4	4	28.7	16.88	20	.448	.515	0	—	0	-8	-8	0	-0.8
Total	2	1	1	.500	8	2	1	0	0	17	20	1	7	9	14.8	6.35	57	.274	.346	1	.250	0	-5	-5	-0	-0.5
● AURELIO LOPEZ Lopez, Aurelio Alejandro (Rios) b: 9/21/48, Tecamachalco Puebla, Mexico d: 9/22/92, Matehuala, Mex. BR/TR, 6', 220 lbs. Deb: 9/01/74																										
1974	KC-A	0	0	—	8	1	0	0	0	16	21	0	10	5	17.4	5.63	68	.344	.437	0	—	0	-4	-3	0	-0.3
1978	StL-N	4	2	.667	25	4	0	0	0	65	52	4	32	46	11.8	4.29	82	.218	.313	3	.214	0	-5	-6	-1	-0.7
1979	Det-A	10	5	.667	61	0	0	0	21	127	95	12	51	106	10.6	2.41	179	.210	.294	0	—	0	25	27	-0	2.5
1980	Det-A	13	6	.684	67	1	0	0	21	124	125	15	45	97	12.6	3.77	109	.263	.330	0	—	0	4	5	-1	0.3
1981	Det-A	5	2	.714	29	3	0	0	3	81^{2}	70	8	31	53	11.4	3.64	104	.233	.309	0	—	0	0	1	-0	0.1
1982	Det-A	3	1	.750	19	0	0	0	3	41	41	8	19	26	13.2	5.27	77	.268	.349	0	—	0	-5	-5	0	-0.6
1983	Det-A☆	9	8	.529	57	0	0	0	18	115^{1}	87	12	49	90	10.7	2.81	139	.210	.295	0	—	0	16	14	-1	1.5
1984	*Det-A	10	1	.909	71	0	0	0	14	137^{2}	109	16	52	94	10.7	2.94	133	.221	.298	0	—	0	16	15	-2	1.4
1985	Det-A	3	7	.300	51	0	0	0	5	86^{1}	82	15	41	53	12.9	4.80	85	.250	.335	0	—	0	-6	-7	-0	-0.7
1986	*Hou-N	3	3	.500	45	0	0	0	7	78	64	6	25	44	10.3	3.46	104	.221	.283	0	.000	-1	2	1	-2	-0.2
1987	Hou-N	2	1	.667	26	0	0	0	1	38	39	6	12	21	12.6	4.50	87	.273	.338	0	.000	-0	-2	-2	-0	-0.3
Total	11	62	36	.633	459	9	0	0	93	910	785	102	367	635	11.5	3.56	111	.234	.313	3	.125	-1	41	39	-8	3.0
● RAMON LOPEZ Lopez, Jose Ramon (Hevia) b: 5/26/33, Las Villas, Cuba d: 9/4/82, Miami, Fla. BR/TR, 6', 175 lbs. Deb: 8/21/66																										
1966	Cal-A	0	1	.000	4	1	0	0	0	7	4	1	4	2	10.3	5.14	65	.154	.267	0	—	0	-1	-1	-0	-0.2
● MARCELINO LOPEZ Lopez, Marcelino Pons b: 9/23/43, Havana, Cuba BR/TL, 6'3", 210 lbs. Deb: 4/14/63																										
1963	Phi-N	1	0	1.000	4	2	0	0	0	6	8	0	7	2	22.5	6.00	54	.333	.484	0	.000	-0	-2	-2	0	-0.2
1965	Cal-A	14	13	.519	35	32	8	1	1	215^{1}	185	12	82	122	11.3	2.93	116	.230	.305	14	.203	3	13	11	4	2.1
1966	Cal-A	7	14	.333	37	32	6	2	1	199	188	20	68	132	12.0	3.93	85	.251	.321	11	.190	2	-11	-13	2	-1.0
1967	Cal-A	0	2	.000	4	3	0	0	0	9	11	1	9	6	20.0	9.00	35	.324	.465	1	.500	0	-6	-6	-0	-0.6
	Bal-A	1	0	1.000	4	4	0	0	0	17^{2}	15	1	10	15	12.7	2.55	124	.227	.329	0	.000	-0	1	1	-1	0.0
	Yr	1	2	.333	8	7	0	0	0	26^{2}	26	2	19	21	15.2	4.73	67	.257	.375	1	.143	0	-4	-5	-1	-0.6
1969	*Bal-A	5	3	.625	27	4	0	0	0	69^{1}	65	3	34	57	13.1	4.41	81	.252	.344	3	.214	1	-6	-7	-1	-0.7
1970	*Bal-A	1	1	.500	25	3	0	0	0	60^{2}	47	2	37	49	12.5	2.08	176	.217	.331	1	.077	0	11	11	-1	1.0
1971	Mil-A	2	7	.222	31	11	0	0	0	67^{2}	64	5	60	42	16.5	4.66	75	.251	.394	1	.059	-1	-9	-9	1	-1.0
1972	Cle-A	0	0	—	4	2	0	0	0	8^{1}	8	0	10	1	19.4	5.40	60	.276	.462	0	.000	-0	-2	-2	-0	-0.2
Total	8	31	40	.437	171	93	14	3	2	653	591	44	317	426	12.7	3.62	94	.243	.334	31	.171	4	-11	-15	4	-0.6
● BRIS LORD Lord, Bristol Robotham "The Human Eyeball" b: 9/21/1883, Upland, Pa. d: 11/13/64, Annapolis, Md. BR/TR, 5'9", 185 lbs. Deb: 4/21/05 ♦																										
1907	Phi-A	0	0	—	1	0	0	0	0	1	3	0	0	0	27.0	9.00	29	.516	.516	31	.182	0	-1	-1	-0	-0.1
● LEFTY LORENZEN Lorenzen, Adolph Andreas b: 1/12/1893, Davenport, Iowa d: 3/5/63, Davenport, Iowa BL/TL, 5'10", 164 lbs. Deb: 9/12/13																										
1913	Det-A	0	0	—	1	0	0	0	0	2	4	0	3	0	31.5	18.00	16	.667	.778	1	.500	0	-3	-3	1	-0.2
● JOE LOTZ Lotz, Joseph Peter "Smokey" b: 1/2/1891, Remsen, Iowa d: 1/1/71, Castro Valley, Cal. BR/TR, 5'8.5", 175 lbs. Deb: 7/15/16																										
1916	StL-N	0	3	.000	12	3	1	0	0	40	31	1	17	18	11.0	4.27	62	.225	.314	4	.333	1	-7	-7	-1	-0.7
● ART LOUDELL Loudell, Arthur (b: Arthur Laudel) b: 4/10/1882, Latham, Mo. d: 2/19/61, Kansas City, Mo. BR/TR, 5'11", 173 lbs. Deb: 8/13/10																										
1910	Det-A	1	1	.500	5	2	1	0	0	21^{1}	23	0	14	12	15.6	3.38	78	.284	.389	1	.143	-0	-2	-2	-1	-0.3
● LARRY LOUGHLIN Loughlin, Larry John b: 8/16/41, Tacoma, Wash. BL/TL, 6'1", 190 lbs. Deb: 5/27/67																										
1967	Phi-N	0	0	—	3	0	0	0	0	5^{1}	9	1	4	5	21.9	15.19	22	.375	.464	1	1.000	1	-7	-7	-0	-0.6
● DON LOUN Loun, Donald Nelson b: 11/9/40, Frederick, Md. BR/TL, 6'2", 185 lbs. Deb: 9/23/64																										
1964	Was-A	1	1	.500	2	2	1	1	0	13	13	0	3	3	11.1	2.08	178	.250	.291	0	.000	-0	2	2	0	0.3
● SLIM LOVE Love, Edward Haughton b: 8/1/1890, Love, Miss. d: 11/30/42, Memphis, Tenn. BL/TL, 6'7", 195 lbs. Deb: 9/08/13																										
1913	Was-A	1	0	1.000	5	1	0	0	1	16^{2}	14	0	6	5	10.8	1.62	182	.226	.294	1	.200	0	2	2	-1	0.2
1916	NY-A	2	0	1.000	20	1	0	0	0	47^{2}	46	2	23	21	13.0	4.91	59	.274	.361	0	.000	-2	-11	-11	-0	-1.3
1917	NY-A	6	5	.545	33	9	2	0	1	130^{1}	115	0	57	82	11.9	2.35	114	.251	.335	6	.167	-1	5	5	-2	0.2
1918	NY-A	13	12	.520	38	29	13	1	1	228^{2}	207	3	116	95	13.1	3.07	92	.253	.353	17	.230	2	-7	-6	-5	-0.9
1919	Det-A	6	4	.600	22	8	4	0	1	89^{2}	92	3	40	46	13.9	3.01	106	.275	.363	6	.222	0	2	2	-2	0.0
1920	Det-A	0	0	—	1	0	0	0	0	4^{1}	6	0	4	2	20.8	8.31	45	.375	.500	0	—	0	-2	-2	0	-0.2
Total	6	28	21	.571	119	48	19	1	4	517^{1}	480	8	246	251	12.9	3.04	94	.259	.351	30	.192	-0	-11	-10	-9	-2.0
● VANCE LOVELACE Lovelace, Vance Odell b: 8/9/63, Tampa, Fla. BL/TL, 6'5", 205 lbs. Deb: 9/10/88																										
1988	Cal-A	0	0	—	3	0	0	0	0	1^{1}	2	1	3	0	33.8	13.50	29	.400	.625	0	—	0	-1	-1	0	0.0
1989	Cal-A	0	0	—	1	0	0	0	0	1	0	0	1	1	9.0	0.00	—	.000	.250	0	—	0	0	0	0	0.2
1990	Sea-A	0	0	—	5	0	0	0	0	2^{1}	3	0	6	1	38.6	3.86	103	.300	.588	0	—	0	0	0	-0	0.0
Total	3	0	0	—	9	0	0	0	0	4^{2}	5	1	10	2	30.9	5.79	67	.278	.552	0	—	0	-1	-1	-0	0.2
● LYNN LOVENGUTH Lovenguth, Lynn Richard b: 11/29/22, Camden, N.Y. BL/TR, 5'10.5", 170 lbs. Deb: 4/18/55																										
1955	Phi-N	0	1	.000	14	0	0	0	0	18	17	1	10	14	14.5	4.50	88	.258	.372	0	.000	-0	-1	-1	-0	-0.2
1957	StL-N	0	1	.000	2	1	0	0	0	9	6	0	6	6	12.0	2.00	198	.182	.308	0	.000	-0	2	2	-0	0.1
Total	2	0	2	.000	16	1	0	0	0	27	23	1	16	20	13.7	3.67	108	.232	.350	0	.000	-1	1	1	-1	-0.1
● JOHN LOVETT Lovett, John b: 5/6/1877, Monday, Ohio d: 12/5/37, Murray City, Ohio Deb: 5/22/03																										
1903	StL-N	0	0	—	3	1	0	0	0	5	6	0	5	3	21.6	5.40	60	.300	.462	1	.333	0	-1	-1	-0	-0.1
● LEN LOVETT Lovett, Leonard Walker b: 7/17/1852, Lancaster Co., Pa d: 11/18/22, Newark, Del. BR/TR, Deb: 8/04/1873 ♦																										
1873	Res-n	0	1	.000	1	1	1	0	0	9	22	0	1	1	23.0	7.00	48	.400	.411	2	.400	0	-4	-4		-0.2
● TOM LOVETT Lovett, Thomas Joseph b: 12/7/1863, Providence, R.I. d: 3/19/28, Providence, R.I. BR , 5'8", 162 lbs. Deb: 6/04/1885																										
1885	Phi-a	7	8	.467	16	16	15	1	0	138^{2}	130	3	38	56	11.2	3.70	93	.236	.291	13	.224	0	-7	-4	-1	-0.5
1889	*Bro-a	17	10	.630	29	28	23	1	0	229	234	3	65	92	12.1	4.32	86	.256	.311	19	.190	-1	-12	-15	-0	-1.4
1890	*Bro-N	30	11	**.732**	44	41	39	4	0	372	327	14	141	124	11.7	2.78	124	.229	.306	33	.201	-1	33	27	-0	2.3
1891	Bro-N	23	19	.548	44	43	39	3	0	365^{2}	361	14	129	129	12.6	3.69	90	.248	.318	25	.163	-5	-14	-16	-2	-2.0
1893	Bro-N	3	5	.375	14	8	6	0	1	96	134	2	35	15	16.4	6.56	67	.321	.381	9	.180	-2	-20	-23	-1	-2.0
1894	Bos-N	8	6	.571	15	13	10	0	0	104	155	12	36	23	16.8	5.97	95	.341	.393	7	.143	-5	-7	-3	-1	-0.7
Total	6	88	59	.599	162	149	132	9	1	1305^{1}	1341	48	444	439	12.7	3.94	94	.257	.322	106	.185	-13	-28	-34	-5	-4.3
● PETE LOVRICH Lovrich, Peter b: 10/16/42, Blue Island, Ill. BR/TR, 6'4", 200 lbs. Deb: 4/26/63																										
1963	KC-A	1	1	.500	20	1	0	0	0	20^{2}	25	5	10	16	15.7	7.84	49	.291	.371	0	—	0	-10	-9	-1	-1.0
● GROVER LOWDERMILK Lowdermilk, Grover Cleveland "Slim" b: 1/15/1885, Sandborn, Ind. d: 3/31/68, Odin, Ill. BR/TR, 6'4", 190 lbs. Deb: 7/03/09 F																										
1909	StL-N	0	2	.000	7	3	1	0	0	29	28	0	30	14	18.9	6.21	41	.292	.473	1	.100	-1	-12	-12	-0	-1.3
1911	StL-N	0	1	.000	11	2	1	1	0	33^{1}	37	1	33	15	19.4	7.29	46	.301	.456	1	.111	-1	-14	-14	0	-1.4
1912	Chi-N	0	1	.000	2	1	1	0	0	13	17	1	14	8	21.5	9.69	34	.304	.443	0	.000	-1	-9	-9	-0	-0.8

YEAR TM/L	W	L	PCT	G	GS	CG	SH	SV	IP	H	HR	BB	SO	RAT	ERA	ERA+	OAV	OOB	BH	AVG	PB	PR	/A	PD	TPI
1915 StL-A	9	17	.346	38	29	14	1	0	222^1	183	1	133	130	13.4	3.12	92	.234	.357	9	.125	-2	-4	-6	0	-0.9
Det-A	4	1	.800	7	5	0	0	0	28	17	0	24	18	13.5	4.18	73	.185	.359	1	.125	-0	-4	-4	0	-0.4
Yr	13	18	.419	45	34	14	1	0	250^1	200	1	157	148	12.9	3.24	89	.225	.342	10	.125	-3	-8	-10	0	-1.3
1916 Det-A	0	0	—	1	0	0	0	0	0^1	0	0	3	0	81.0	0.00	—	.000	.750	0	—	0	0	0	0	0.0
Cle-A	1	5	.167	10	9	2	0	0	51^1	52	0	45	28	17.5	3.16	95	.277	.424	3	.167	-0	-2	-1	0	-0.1
Yr	1	5	.167	11	9	2	0	0	51^2	52	0	48	28	17.9	3.14	96	.275	.429	3	.167	-0	-2	-1	0	-0.1
1917 StL-A	2	1	.667	3	2	2	1	0	19	16	0	4	9	9.5	1.42	183	.225	.267	0	.000	-1	3	2	0	0.2
1918 StL-A	2	6	.250	13	11	4	0	0	80	74	1	38	25	12.9	3.15	87	.255	.347	7	.250	1	-3	-4	2	0.0
1919 StL-A	0	0	—	7	0	0	0	0	12	6	0	4	6	11.3	0.75	442	.176	.349	0	.000	-0	3	3	-0	0.3
*Chi-A	5	5	.500	20	11	5	0	0	96^2	95	0	43	43	13.2	2.79	114	.268	.353	3	.088	-3	5	4	1	0.2
Yr	5	5	.500	27	11	5	0	0	108^2	101	0	47	49	12.6	2.57	125	.256	.342	3	.086	-3	8	8	1	0.5
1920 Chi-A	0	0	—	3	0	0	0	0	5^1	9	0	5	0	23.6	6.75	56	.409	.519	0	—	0	-2	-2	1	-0.1
Total 9	23	39	.371	122	73	30	3	0	590^1	534	4	376	296	14.4	3.58	82	.253	.375	25	.131	-8	-40	-41	5	-4.3

● LOU LOWDERMILK

Lowdermilk, Louis Bailey b: 2/23/1887, Sandborn, Ind. d: 12/27/75, Centralia, Ill. BR/TL, 6'1", 180 lbs. Deb: 4/20/11 F

YEAR TM/L	W	L	PCT	G	GS	CG	SH	SV	IP	H	HR	BB	SO	RAT	ERA	ERA+	OAV	OOB	BH	AVG	PB	PR	/A	PD	TPI
1911 StL-N	3	4	.429	16	3	3	0	0	65	72	0	29	20	14.7	3.46	98	.304	.391	2	.111	-1	-0	-1	-2	-0.3
1912 StL-N	1	1	.500	4	1	1	0	1	15	14	0	9	2	13.8	3.00	114	.246	.348	1	.250	0	1	1	0	0.1
Total 2	4	5	.444	20	4	4	0	1	80	86	0	38	22	14.5	3.37	100	.293	.383	3	.136	-1	0	0	-2	-0.2

● GEORGE LOWE

Lowe, George Wesley "Doc" b: 4/25/1895, Ridgefield Park, N.J. d: 9/2/81, Somers Point, N.J. BR/TR, 6'2", 180 lbs. Deb: 7/28/20

YEAR TM/L	W	L	PCT	G	GS	CG	SH	SV	IP	H	HR	BB	SO	RAT	ERA	ERA+	OAV	OOB	BH	AVG	PB	PR	/A	PD	TPI
1920 Cin-N	0	0	—	1	0	0	0	0	2	1	0	1	0	9.0	0.00	—	.167	.286	0	—	0	1	1	-0	0.1

● BOBBY LOWE

Lowe, Robert Lincoln "Link" b: 7/10/1868, Pittsburgh, Pa. d: 12/8/51, Detroit, Mich. BR/TR, 5'10", 150 lbs. Deb: 4/19/1890 M♦

YEAR TM/L	W	L	PCT	G	GS	CG	SH	SV	IP	H	HR	BB	SO	RAT	ERA	ERA+	OAV	OOB	BH	AVG	PB	PR	/A	PD	TPI
1891 Bos-N	0	0	—	1	0	0	0	0	1	3	0	1	0	36.0	9.00	41	.501	.572	129	.260	0	-1	-1	-0	-0.1

● TURK LOWN

Lown, Omar Joseph b: 5/30/24, Brooklyn, N.Y. BR/TR, 6'1", 185 lbs. Deb: 4/24/51

YEAR TM/L	W	L	PCT	G	GS	CG	SH	SV	IP	H	HR	BB	SO	RAT	ERA	ERA+	OAV	OOB	BH	AVG	PB	PR	/A	PD	TPI
1951 Chi-N	4	9	.308	31	18	3	1	0	127	125	14	90	39	15.3	5.46	75	.260	.378	8	.205	1	-21	-19	0	-1.7
1952 Chi-N	4	11	.267	33	19	5	0	0	156^2	154	13	93	73	14.4	4.37	88	.257	.359	7	.140	-0	-11	-9	1	-0.8
1953 Chi-N	8	7	.533	49	12	2	0	3	148^1	166	20	84	76	15.3	5.16	86	.282	.373	6	.125	-2	-14	-12	2	-1.1
1954 Chi-N	0	2	.000	15	0	0	0	0	22	23	1	15	16	15.5	6.14	68	.261	.369	0	—	0	-5	-5	1	-0.4
1956 Chi-N	9	8	.529	61	0	0	0	13	110^2	95	10	78	74	14.2	3.58	105	.240	.366	5	.217	2	2	2	-1	0.4
1957 Chi-N	5	7	.417	**67**	0	0	0	12	93	74	10	51	51	12.1	3.77	103	.221	.324	2	.200	0	1	1	2	0.3
1958 Chi-N	0	0	—	4	0	0	0	0	4	2	0	3	4	11.3	4.50	87	.154	.313	0	—	0	-0	-0	-0	0.0
Cin-N	0	2	.000	11	0	0	0	0	11^2	12	2	12	9	18.5	5.40	77	.273	.429	0	.000	-0	-2	-2	-0	-0.2
Yr	0	2	.000	15	0	0	0	0	15^2	14	2	15	13	16.7	5.17	79	.246	.403	0	.000	-0	-2	-2	-0	-0.2
Chi-A	3	3	.500	27	0	0	0	8	40^2	49	1	28	40	17.0	3.98	91	.308	.412	3	.333	1	-1	-2	0	-0.1
1959 *Chi-A	9	2	.818	60	0	0	0	**15**	93^1	73	12	42	63	11.3	2.89	130	.215	.305	3	.250	1	10	9	1	1.0
1960 Chi-A	2	3	.400	45	0	0	0	5	67^1	60	6	34	39	12.6	3.88	98	.239	.330	1	.200	1	-0	-1	0	0.0
1961 Chi-A	7	5	.583	59	0	0	0	11	101	87	13	35	50	10.9	2.76	142	.238	.304	0	.000	-2	14	13	-1	1.1
1962 Chi-A	4	2	.667	42	0	0	0	6	56^1	58	3	25	40	13.4	3.04	129	.269	.347	0	.000	-0	6	5	1	0.7
Total 11	55	61	.474	504	49	10	1	73	1032	978	105	590	574	13.8	4.12	96	.252	.352	35	.164	1	-21	-18	7	-0.8

● SAM LOWRY

Lowry, Samuel Joseph b: 3/25/20, Philadelphia, Pa. BR/TR, 5'11", 170 lbs. Deb: 9/19/42

YEAR TM/L	W	L	PCT	G	GS	CG	SH	SV	IP	H	HR	BB	SO	RAT	ERA	ERA+	OAV	OOB	BH	AVG	PB	PR	/A	PD	TPI
1942 Phi-A	0	0	—	1	0	0	0	0	3	3	0	1	0	12.0	6.00	63	.250	.308	0	.000	-0	-1	-1	-0	-0.1
1943 Phi-A	0	0	—	5	0	0	0	0	18	18	1	9	3	13.5	5.00	68	.269	.355	1	.167	-0	-3	-3	0	-0.3
Total 2	0	0	—	6	0	0	0	0	21	21	1	10	3	13.3	5.14	67	.266	.348	1	.143	-0	-4	-4	0	-0.4

● MIKE LOYND

Loynd, Michael Wallace b: 3/26/64, St.Louis, Mo. BR/TR, 6'4", 210 lbs. Deb: 7/24/86

YEAR TM/L	W	L	PCT	G	GS	CG	SH	SV	IP	H	HR	BB	SO	RAT	ERA	ERA+	OAV	OOB	BH	AVG	PB	PR	/A	PD	TPI
1986 Tex-A	2	2	.500	9	8	0	0	1	42	49	4	19	33	15.0	5.36	80	.290	.368	0	—	0	-6	-5	0	-0.5
1987 Tex-A	1	5	.167	26	8	0	0	1	69^1	82	14	38	48	15.7	6.10	73	.287	.372	0	—	0	-13	-13	-1	-1.2
Total 2	3	7	.300	35	16	0	0	2	111^1	131	18	57	81	15.4	5.82	76	.288	.371	0	—	0	-18	-17	-1	-1.7

● PAT LUBY

Luby, John Perkins b: 1868, Charleston, S.C. d: 4/24/1899, Charleston, S.C. TR, 6', 185 lbs. Deb: 6/16/1890

YEAR TM/L	W	L	PCT	G	GS	CG	SH	SV	IP	H	HR	BB	SO	RAT	ERA	ERA+	OAV	OOB	BH	AVG	PB	PR	/A	PD	TPI
1890 Chi-N	20	9	.690	34	31	26	0	1	267^2	226	6	95	85	11.3	3.19	115	.222	.298	31	.267	8	11	14	-2	1.8
1891 Chi-N	8	11	.421	30	24	18	0	1	206	221	11	94	52	14.6	4.76	70	.264	.352	24	.245	7	-32	-33	-0	-2.2
1892 Chi-N	10	16	.385	31	26	24	1	1	247^1	247	10	106	64	13.2	3.13	106	.250	.329	31	.190	1	4	5	1	0.6
1895 Lou-N	1	5	.167	11	6	5	0	0	71^1	115	5	19	12	17.8	6.81	68	.357	.405	15	.283	2	-16	-17	1	-1.1
Total 4	39	41	.488	106	87	73	1	3	792^1	809	32	314	213	13.3	3.91	91	.255	.332	101	.235	17	-33	-31	-1	-0.9

● RED LUCAS

Lucas, Charles Frederick "The Nashville Narcissus" b: 4/28/02, Columbia, Tenn. d: 7/9/86, Nashville, Tenn. BL/TR, 5'9.5", 170 lbs. Deb: 4/19/23 ♦

YEAR TM/L	W	L	PCT	G	GS	CG	SH	SV	IP	H	HR	BB	SO	RAT	ERA	ERA+	OAV	OOB	BH	AVG	PB	PR	/A	PD	TPI
1923 NY-N	0	0	—	3	0	0	0	1	5^1	9	0	4	3	21.9	0.00	—	.346	.433	0	.000	-0	2	2	1	0.2
1924 Bos-N	1	4	.200	27	4	1	0	0	83^2	112	5	18	30	14.6	5.16	74	.332	.377	11	.333	2	-12	-12	1	-0.9
1926 Cin-N	8	5	.615	39	11	7	1	2	154	161	6	30	34	11.3	3.68	100	.277	.314	23	.303	6	2	0	-1	0.9
1927 Cin-N	18	11	.621	37	23	19	4	2	239^2	231	6	39	51	10.1	3.38	112	.256	.287	47	.313	6	14	11	-1	2.2
1928 Cin-N	13	9	.591	27	19	13	**4**	1	167^1	164	9	42	35	11.1	3.39	117	.258	.304	23	.315	6	11	10	-0	1.7
1929 Cin-N	19	12	.613	32	32	**28**	2	0	270	267	14	58	72	**10.9**	3.60	127	**.257**	**.297**	41	.293	10	33	29	0	3.9
1930 Cin-N	14	16	.467	33	28	18	1	1	210^2	270	15	44	53	13.5	5.38	90	.315	.349	38	.336	14	-10	-13	-3	-0.1
1931 Cin-N	14	13	.519	29	29	**24**	3	0	238	261	10	39	56	11.3	3.59	104	.280	.309	43	.281	10	7	4	1	1.6
1932 Cin-N	13	17	.433	31	31	**28**	0	0	269^1	261	10	35	63	9.9	2.94	131	.249	.274	43	.287	13	28	27	-0	4.4
1933 Cin-N	10	16	.385	29	29	21	3	0	219^2	248	13	18	40	11.0	3.40	100	.289	.305	35	.287	12	-2	-0	0	1.4
1934 Pit-N	10	9	.526	29	21	12	1	0	172^2	198	14	40	44	12.5	4.38	94	.283	.324	23	.219	3	-6	-5	-3	-0.5
1935 Pit-N	8	6	.571	20	19	8	2	0	125^2	136	10	23	29	11.5	3.44	119	.272	.307	21	.318	8	8	9	-1	1.6
1936 Pit-N	15	4	.789	27	22	12	0	0	175^2	178	7	26	53	10.6	3.18	128	.257	.287	26	.241	4	16	17	-1	2.1
1937 Pit-N	8	10	.444	20	20	9	1	0	126^1	150	12	23	20	12.4	4.27	90	.290	.322	22	.268	5	-5	-6	-2	-0.2
1938 Pit-N	6	3	.667	13	13	4	0	0	84	90	5	16	19	11.5	3.54	107	.283	.319	5	.109	-2	2	2	-1	-0.1
Total 15	157	135	.538	396	301	204	22	7	2542	2736	136	455	602	11.4	3.72	107	.275	.308	404	.281	97	92	77	-9	18.2

● GARY LUCAS

Lucas, Gary Paul b: 11/8/54, Riverside, Cal. BL/TL, 6'5", 200 lbs. Deb: 4/16/80

YEAR TM/L	W	L	PCT	G	GS	CG	SH	SV	IP	H	HR	BB	SO	RAT	ERA	ERA+	OAV	OOB	BH	AVG	PB	PR	/A	PD	TPI
1980 SD-N	5	8	.385	46	18	0	0	3	150	138	8	43	85	10.9	3.24	106	.250	.306	6	.171	-0	6	3	1	0.4
1981 SD-N	7	7	.500	**57**	0	0	0	13	90	78	1	36	53	11.7	2.00	163	.247	.330	1	.100	-0	**15**	13	0	1.3
1982 SD-N	1	10	.091	65	0	0	0	16	97^1	89	5	29	64	11.0	3.24	106	.245	.303	0	.000	-1	4	2	1	0.2
1983 SD-N	5	8	.385	62	0	0	0	17	91	85	9	34	60	11.8	2.87	122	.245	.312	0	.000	-1	8	6	-1	0.4
1984 Mon-N	0	3	.000	55	0	0	0	8	53	54	4	20	42	12.6	2.72	126	.267	.333	0	.000	-0	5	4	2	0.6
1985 Mon-N	6	2	.750	49	0	0	0	1	67^2	63	6	24	31	11.6	3.19	106	.251	.316	0	.000	-1	3	1	-0	0.1
1986 *Cal-A	4	1	.800	27	0	0	0	2	45^2	45	1	6	31	10.1	3.15	130	.253	.277	0	—	0	5	5	1	0.6
1987 Cal-A	1	5	.167	48	0	0	0	3	74^1	66	7	35	44	12.5	3.63	118	.241	.331	0	—	0	7	6	1	0.6
Total 8	29	44	.397	409	18	0	0	63	669	618	41	227	410	11.5	3.01	118	.249	.314	7	.087	-4	53	40	4	4.2

● RAY LUCAS

Lucas, Ray Wesley "Luke" b: 10/2/08, Springfield, Ohio d: 10/9/69, Harrison, Mich. BR/TR, 6'2", 175 lbs. Deb: 9/28/29

YEAR TM/L	W	L	PCT	G	GS	CG	SH	SV	IP	H	HR	BB	SO	RAT	ERA	ERA+	OAV	OOB	BH	AVG	PB	PR	/A	PD	TPI
1929 NY-N	0	0	—	3	0	0	0	1	8	3	0	3	1	6.8	0.00	—	.111	.200	1	.500	0	4	4	0	0.5
1930 NY-N	0	0	—	6	0	0	0	0	10^1	9	2	10	1	17.4	6.97	68	.265	.444	0	.000	-0	-2	-3	1	-0.2
1931 NY-N	0	0	—	1	0	0	0	0	2	1	1	1	0	9.0	4.50	82	.143	.250	0	—	0	-0	-0	-0	0.0
1933 Bro-N	0	0	—	2	0	0	0	0	5	6	0	4	0	19.8	7.20	45	.316	.458	0	—	0	-2	-2	0	-0.2
1934 Bro-N	1	1	.500	10	2	0	0	0	30^2	39	2	14	3	16.4	6.75	58	.328	.412	2	.333	1	-9	-10	1	-0.7
Total 5	1	1	.500	22	2	0	0	1	56	58	5	32	5	15.3	5.79	71	.282	.391	3	.333	1	-10	-11	2	-0.6

YEAR	TM/L	W	L	PCT	G	GS	CG	SH	SV	IP	H	HR	BB	SO	RAT	ERA	ERA+	OAV	OOB	BH	AVG	PB	PR	/A	PD	TPI
● JOE LUCEY	Lucey, Joseph Earl "Scootch" b: 3/27/1897, Holyoke, Mass. d: 7/30/80, Holyoke, Mass. BR/TR, 6', 168 lbs. Deb: 7/06/20 ♦																									
1925	Bos-A	0	1	.000	7	2	0	0	0	11	18	0	14	2	26.2	9.00	50	.360	.500	2	.133	-1	-6	-5	1	-0.5
● CON LUCID	Lucid, Cornelius Cecil b: 2/24/1874, Dublin, Ireland d: 6/25/31, Houston, Tex. Deb: 5/01/1893																									
1893	Lou-N	0	1	.000	2	1	0	0	0	6	10	0	10	0	31.5	15.00	29	.360	.542	1	.333	0	-7	-7	-0	-0.5
1894	Bro-N	5	3	.625	10	9	7	0	0	71^{1}	87	6	44	15	17.7	6.56	75	.298	.405	7	.212	-2	-10	-13	-2	-1.2
1895	Bro-N	10	7	.588	21	19	12	2	0	137	164	4	72	24	16.0	5.52	80	.292	.380	13	.245	2	-11	-17	-1	-1.2
	Phi-N	6	3	.667	10	10	7	1	0	69^{2}	80	3	35	19	16.0	5.94	81	.284	.380	10	.345	3	-9	-9	-2	-0.6
	Yr	16	10	.615	31	29	19	3	0	206^{2}	244	7	107	43	15.7	5.66	80	.287	.373	23	.280	5	-20	-26	-2	-1.8
1896	Phi-N	1	4	.200	5	5	5	0	0	42	75	2	17	3	20.1	8.36	52	.384	.438	2	.125	-2	-19	-19	-1	-1.6
1897	StL-N	1	5	.167	6	6	5	0	0	49	66	0	26	4	16.9	3.67	120	.319	.395	3	.176	-0	3	4	1	0.4
Total	5	23	23	.500	54	50	36	3	0	375	482	15	204	65	17.1	6.02	76	.308	.397	36	.238	2	-52	-60	-5	-4.7
● LOU LUCIER	Lucier, Louis Joseph b: 3/23/18, Northbridge, Mass. BR/TR, 5'8", 160 lbs. Deb: 4/23/43																									
1943	Bos-A	3	4	.429	16	9	3	0	0	74	94	1	33	23	15.7	3.89	85	.322	.394	4	.200	-0	-5	-5	3	-0.2
1944	Bos-A	0	0	—	3	0	0	0	0	5^{1}	7	0	7	2	23.6	5.06	67	.292	.452	0	.000	-0	-1	-1	-0	-0.1
	Phi-N	0	0	—	1	0	0	0	0	2	3	0	2	1	22.5	13.50	27	.333	.455	0	—	0	-2	-2	-0	-0.2
1945	Phi-N	0	1	.000	13	0	0	0	1	20^{1}	14	1	5	5	8.4	2.21	173	.194	.247	1	.250	0	4	4	1	0.5
Total	3	3	5	.375	33	9	3	0	1	101^{2}	118	2	47	31	14.8	3.81	90	.297	.374	5	.200	-0	-4	-4	4	0.0
● HOWARD LUCKEY	Luckey, Howard J. b: Philadelphia, Pa. Deb: 10/02/1890																									
1890	Phi-a	0	0	—	1	0	0	0	0	2	1	0	3	1	18.0	9.00	43	.144	.403	0	.000	-0	-1	-1	-0	-0.1
● WILLIE LUDOLPH	Ludolph, William Francis "Wee Willie" b: 1/21/1900, San Francisco, Cal d: 4/8/52, Oakland, Cal. BR/TR, 6'1.5", 170 lbs. Deb: 5/28/24																									
1924	Det-A	0	0	—	3	0	0	0	0	5^{2}	5	0	2	1	12.7	4.76	86	.250	.348	0	.000	-0	-0	-0	0	0.0
● STEVE LUEBBER	Luebber, Stephen Lee b: 7/9/49, Clinton, Mo. BR/TR, 6'3", 195 lbs. Deb: 6/27/71																									
1971	Min-A	2	5	.286	18	12	0	0	1	68	73	7	37	35	15.1	5.03	71	.278	.375	1	.053	-2	-12	-11	0	-1.3
1972	Min-A	0	0	—	2	0	0	0	0	2^{1}	3	0	2	1	19.3	0.00	—	.333	.455	0	—	0	1	1	0	0.1
1976	Min-A	4	5	.444	38	12	2	1	2	119^{1}	109	9	62	45	13.0	4.00	90	.248	.342	0	—	0	-6	-5	-1	-0.7
1979	Tor-A	0	0	—	1	0	0	0	0	0	2	0	1	0	—	∞	—	1.000	1.000	0	—	0	-1	-1	0	-0.1
1981	Bal-A	0	0	—	7	0	0	0	0	16^{2}	26	3	4	12	16.7	7.56	48	.366	.408	0	—	0	-7	-7	0	-0.7
Total	5	6	10	.375	66	24	2	1	3	206^{1}	213	19	106	93	14.2	4.62	77	.271	.362	1	.053	-2	-26	-24	-1	-2.7
● DICK LUEBKE	Luebke, Richard Raymond b: 4/8/35, Chicago, Ill. d: 12/4/74, San Diego, Cal. BR/TL, 6'4", 200 lbs. Deb: 8/11/62																									
1962	Bal-A	0	1	.000	10	0	0	0	0	13^{1}	12	0	6	7	12.2	2.70	139	.250	.333	0	—	0	2	2	-0	0.1
● RICK LUECKEN	Luecken, Richard Fred b: 11/15/60, McAllen, Tex. BR/TR, 6'6", 210 lbs. Deb: 6/06/89																									
1989	KC-A	2	1	.667	19	0	0	0	1	23^{2}	23	3	13	16	13.7	3.42	112	.258	.353	0	—	0	1	1	-0	0.1
1990	Atl-N	1	4	.200	36	0	0	0	1	53	73	5	30	35	18.0	5.77	70	.336	.424	1	.333	1	-12	-10	0	-1.0
	Tor-A	0	0	—	1	0	0	0	0	1	2	1	1	0	27.0	9.00	44	.500	.600	0	—	0	-1	-1	0	-0.1
Total	2	3	5	.375	56	0	0	0	2	77^{2}	98	9	44	51	16.8	5.10	78	.316	.406	1	.333	1	-11	-10	-0	-1.0
● HENRY LUFF	Luff, Henry T. b: 9/14/1856, Philadelphia, Pa. d: 10/11/16, Philadelphia, Pa. 5'11", 175 lbs. Deb: 4/21/1875 ♦																									
1875	NH-n	1	6	.143	10	7	5	0	0	69^{2}	100	2	3		13.3	*4.78*	48	.297	.303	46	.279	3	-18	-19		-1.3
● URBANO LUGO	Lugo, Rafael Urbano (Colina) b: 8/12/62, Punto Fijo, Venez. BR/TR, 6', 190 lbs. Deb: 4/28/85																									
1985	Cal-A	3	4	.429	20	10	1	0	0	83	86	10	29	42	12.9	3.69	111	.274	.343	0	—	0	4	4	0	0.4
1986	Cal-A	1	1	.500	6	3	0	0	0	21^{1}	21	4	6	9	11.4	3.80	108	.266	.318	0	—	0	1	1	-0	0.1
1987	Cal-A	0	2	.000	7	5	0	0	0	28	42	8	18	24	19.3	9.32	46	.339	.423	0	—	0	-15	-16	-0	-1.4
1988	Cal-A	0	0	—	1	0	0	0	0	2	2	1	1	1	13.5	9.00	43	.250	.333	0	—	0	-1	-1	-0	-0.1
1989	Mon-N	0	0	—	3	0	0	0	0	4	4	1	0	3	9.0	6.75	52	.250	.250	0	—	0	-1	-1	0	-0.2
1990	Det-A	2	0	1.000	13	1	0	0	0	24^{1}	30	9	13	12	17.0	7.03	56	.313	.411	0	—	0	-8	-8	1	-0.8
Total	6	6	7	.462	50	19	1	0	0	162^{2}	185	33	67	91	14.3	5.31	77	.290	.364	0	—	0	-21	-22	0	-2.0
● WILD BILL LUHRSEN	Luhrsen, William Ferdinand b: 4/14/1884, Buckley, Ill. d: 8/15/73, Little Rock, Ark. BR/TR, 5'9", 165 lbs. Deb: 8/23/13																									
1913	Pit-N	3	1	.750	5	3	2	0	0	29	25	3	16	11	13.3	2.48	121	.248	.361	0	.000	-1	2	2	1	0.1
● AL LUKENS	Lukens, Albert P. b: 11/1868, Pennsylvania 5'9", 168 lbs. Deb: 6/23/1894																									
1894	Phi-N	0	1	.000	3	2	1	0	0	15	26	0	10	0	23.4	10.20	50	.376	.474	0	.000	-2	-8	-8	-0	-0.7
● RALPH LUMENTI	Lumenti, Raphael Anthony b: 12/21/36, Milford, Mass. BL/TL, 6'3", 185 lbs. Deb: 9/07/57																									
1957	Was-A	0	1	.000	3	2	0	0	0	9^{1}	9	1	5	8	14.5	6.75	58	.250	.357	0	.000	-0	-3	-3	0	-0.3
1958	Was-A	1	2	.333	8	4	0	0	0	21	21	2	36	20	24.9	8.57	44	.266	.500	2	.250	0	-11	-11	0	-1.0
1959	Was-A	0	0	—	2	0	0	0	0	3	2	0	1	2	9.0	0.00	—	.200	.273	0	—	0	1	1	-0	0.1
Total	3	1	3	.250	13	6	0	0	0	33^{1}	32	3	42	30	20.5	7.29	53	.256	.450	2	.200	-0	-13	-13	0	-1.2
● MEMO LUNA	Luna, Guillermo Romero b: 6/25/30, Tacubaya, Mexico BL/TL, 6', 168 lbs. Deb: 4/20/54																									
1954	StL-N	0	1	.000	1	1	0	0	0	0^{2}	2	0	2	0	54.0	27.00	15	.667	.800	0	—	0	-2	-2	-0	-0.2
● JACK LUNDBOM	Lundbom, John Frederick b: 3/10/1877, Manistee, Mich. d: 10/31/49, Manistee, Mich. BR/TR, 6'2", 187 lbs. Deb: 5/09/02																									
1902	Cle-A	1	1	.500	8	3	1	0	0	34	48	1	16	7	17.2	6.62	52	.332	.403	4	.267	1	-11	-12	-0	-1.1
● CARL LUNDGREN	Lundgren, Carl Leonard b: 2/16/1880, Marengo, Ill. d: 8/21/34, Marengo, Ill. BR/TR, 5'11", 175 lbs. Deb: 6/19/02																									
1902	Chi-N	9	9	.500	18	18	17	1	0	160	158	2	45	68	11.8	1.97	137	.258	.315	7	.106	-4	14	13	-3	0.7
1903	Chi-N	11	9	.550	27	20	16	0	**3**	193	191	1	60	67	12.0	2.94	107	.262	.323	7	.115	-1	7	4	-2	0.0
1904	Chi-N	17	9	.654	31	27	25	2	1	242	203	2	77	106	10.6	2.60	102	.226	.290	20	.222	4	4	2	-1	0.4
1905	Chi-N	13	5	.722	23	19	16	3	0	169^{1}	132	3	53	69	10.3	2.23	134	.220	.293	11	.180	1	15	14	1	1.7
1906	Chi-N	17	6	.739	27	24	21	5	2	207^{2}	160	3	89	103	11.1	2.21	119	.221	.313	12	.179	2	10	10	-1	1.2
1907	Chi-N	18	7	.720	28	25	21	7	0	207	130	0	92	84	9.7	1.17	212	**.185**	.282	7	.106	-3	**30**	30	-0	3.2
1908	Chi-N	6	9	.400	23	15	9	1	0	138^{2}	149	5	56	38	13.3	4.22	56	.284	.353	7	.149	-2	-29	-29	-2	-3.4
1909	Chi-N	0	1	.000	2	1	0	0	0	4^{1}	6	0	4	0	20.8	4.15	61	.353	.476	1	.500	0	-1	-1	-0	-0.1
Total	8	91	55	.623	179	149	125	19	6	1322	1129	16	476	535	11.2	2.42	113	.235	.308	72	.157	-2	50	44	-8	3.7
● DEL LUNDGREN	Lundgren, Ebin Delmar b: 9/21/1899, Lindsborg, Kan. d: 10/19/84, Lindsborg, Kan. BR/TR, 5'8", 160 lbs. Deb: 4/27/24																									
1924	Pit-N	0	1	.000	8	1	0	0	0	16^{2}	25	0	3	4	15.7	6.48	59	.403	.439	0	.000	-1	-5	-5	0	-0.5
1926	Bos-A	0	2	.000	18	1	0	0	0	31	35	2	28	11	19.2	7.55	54	.307	.455	0	.000	-0	-12	-12	0	-1.1
1927	Bos-A	5	12	.294	30	17	5	2	0	136^{1}	160	7	87	39	16.6	6.27	67	.302	.405	7	.159	-2	-32	-31	-2	-3.1
Total	3	5	15	.250	56	19	5	2	0	184	220	9	118	54	16.9	6.51	64	.312	.416	7	.137	-3	-49	-48	-2	-4.7
● DOLF LUQUE	Luque, Adolfo Domingo De Guzman "The Pride Of Havana" b: 8/4/1890, Havana, Cuba d: 7/3/57, Havana, Cuba BR/TR, 5'7", 160 lbs. Deb: 5/20/14 C																									
1914	Bos-N	0	1	.000	2	1	1	0	0	8^{2}	5	0	4	1	9.3	4.15	66	.167	.265	0	.000	-0	-1	-1	-1	-0.2
1915	Bos-N	0	0	—	2	1	0	0	0	5	6	0	4	3	18.0	3.60	72	.286	.400	0	.000	-0	-0	-1	0	-0.1
1918	Cin-N	6	3	.667	12	10	9	1	0	83	84	1	32	26	12.7	3.80	70	.277	.348	9	.321	4	-10	-10	-0	-0.7
1919	*Cin-N	10	3	.769	30	9	6	2	3	106	89	2	36	40	10.8	2.63	105	.237	.308	4	.125	-0	3	2	1	0.3
1920	Cin-N	13	9	.591	37	23	10	1	1	207^{2}	168	5	60	72	10.1	2.51	121	**.225**	.286	17	.266	4	14	12	-2	1.6

YEAR	TM/L	W	L	PCT	G	GS	CG	SH	SV	IP	H	HR	BB	SO	RAT	ERA	ERA+	OAV	OOB	BH	AVG	PB	PR	/A	PD	TPI
1921	Cin-N	17	19	.472	41	36	25	**3**	3	304	318	13	64	102	11.3	3.38	106	.273	.312	30	.270	6	14	7	1	1.3
1922	Cin-N	13	23	.361	39	32	18	0	0	261	266	7	72	79	11.7	3.31	121	.268	.318	18	.209	1	23	20	0	2.1
1923	Cin-N	**27**	8	**.771**	41	37	28	**6**	2	322	279	2	88	151	10.4	**1.93**	**200**	**.235**	.291	21	.202	2	**74**	**69**	1	**7.5**
1924	Cin-N	10	15	.400	31	28	13	2	0	219^1	229	5	53	86	11.7	3.16	119	.271	.316	13	.178	-1	17	15	1	1.5
1925	Cin-N	16	18	.471	36	36	22	**4**	0	291	263	7	78	140	**10.6**	**2.63**	**156**	**.239**	**.291**	26	.255	5	**53**	**48**	4	**5.8**
1926	Cin-N	13	16	.448	34	30	16	1	0	233^2	231	7	77	83	11.9	3.43	108	.260	.321	27	.346	8	10	7	2	1.7
1927	Cin-N	13	12	.520	29	27	17	2	0	230^2	225	10	56	76	11.0	3.20	118	.260	.305	18	.217	2	18	15	4	2.1
1928	Cin-N	11	10	.524	33	29	11	1	1	234^1	254	12	84	72	13.1	3.57	111	.284	.347	8	.119	-1	11	10	-2	0.7
1929	Cin-N	5	16	.238	32	22	8	1	0	176	213	7	56	43	13.9	4.50	101	.310	.364	15	.278	4	4	1	0	0.5
1930	Bro-N	14	8	.636	31	24	16	2	2	199	221	18	58	62	12.6	4.30	114	.287	.337	18	.240	1	15	14	1	1.5
1931	Bro-N	7	6	.538	19	15	5	0	0	102^2	122	6	27	25	13.1	4.56	84	.297	.342	4	.133	0	-8	-9	-1	-0.9
1932	NY-N	6	7	.462	38	5	1	0	5	110	128	4	32	32	13.1	4.01	93	.290	.338	1	.040	-2	-2	-4	1	-0.4
1933	*NY-N	8	2	.800	35	0	0	0	4	80^1	75	4	19	23	10.5	2.69	119	.251	.296	5	.263	1	6	5	0	0.6
1934	NY-N	4	3	.571	26	0	0	0	7	42^1	54	3	17	12	15.3	3.83	101	.316	.381	2	.286	1	1	0	1	0.2
1935	NY-N	1	0	1.000	2	0	0	0	0	3^2	1	0	1	2	4.9	0.00	—	.077	.143	1	1.000	0	2	2	-0	0.2
Total	20	194	179	.520	550	365	206	26	28	3220^1	3231	113	918	1130	11.7	3.24	117	.265	.318	237	.227	35	245	200	13	25.3
● **JOHNNY LUSH**	Lush, John Charles b: 10/8/1885, Williamsport, Pa. d: 11/18/46, Beverly Hills, Cal BL/TL, 5'9.5", 165 lbs. Deb: 4/22/04 ♦																									
1904	Phi-N	0	6	.000	7	6	3	0	0	42^2	52	0	27	27	18.1	3.59	75	.301	.415	102	.276	2	-4	-4	1	-0.2
1905	Phi-N	2	0	1.000	2	2	1	0	0	17	12	0	8	8	11.1	1.59	184	.194	.296	5	.313	0	3	3	0	0.4
1906	Phi-N	18	15	.545	37	35	24	5	0	281	254	2	119	151	12.5	2.37	110	.236	.321	56	.264	7	8	8	3	2.0
1907	Phi-N	3	5	.375	8	8	5	2	0	57^1	48	0	21	20	11.3	2.98	81	.227	.306	8	.200	1	-3	-4	1	-0.3
	StL-N	7	10	.412	20	19	15	3	0	144	132	2	42	71	11.4	2.50	100	.246	.311	23	.280	5	-0	0	-0	0.8
	Yr	10	15	.400	28	27	20	5	0	201^1	180	2	63	91	11.2	2.64	94	.240	.306	31	.254	6	-4	-4	0	0.5
1908	StL-N	11	18	.379	38	32	23	3	1	250^2	221	6	57	93	10.4	2.12	111	.231	.283	15	.169	1	7	7	0	0.9
1909	StL-N	11	18	.379	34	28	21	2	0	221^1	215	1	69	66	12.0	3.13	81	.260	.324	22	.239	4	-13	-15	-1	-1.1
1910	StL-N	14	13	.519	36	24	13	1	1	225^1	235	6	70	54	12.5	3.20	93	.276	.336	21	.226	4	-4	-5	-2	-0.4
Total	7	66	85	.437	182	154	105	16	2	1239^1	1169	17	413	490	11.9	2.68	97	.249	.318	252	.254	24	-7	-11	1	2.1
● **SPARKY LYLE**	Lyle, Albert Walter b: 7/22/44, DuBois, Pa. BL/TL, 6'1", 192 lbs. Deb: 7/04/67																									
1967	Bos-A	1	2	.333	27	0	0	0	5	43^1	33	3	14	42	10.2	2.28	153	.213	.287	2	.250	1	5	6	-0	0.7
1968	Bos-A	6	1	.857	49	0	0	0	11	65^2	67	6	14	52	11.1	2.74	115	.261	.299	1	.125	-0	2	3	-1	0.2
1969	Bos-A	8	3	.727	71	0	0	0	17	102^2	91	8	48	93	12.3	2.54	150	.240	.327	2	.118	-1	12	14	1	1.6
1970	Bos-A	1	7	.125	63	0	0	0	20	67^1	62	5	34	51	13.0	3.88	102	.244	.336	0	.000	-1	-1	1	-1	-0.1
1971	Bos-A	6	4	.600	50	0	0	0	16	52^1	41	5	23	37	11.0	2.75	134	.228	.315	3	1.000	1	4	5	0	0.8
1972	NY-A	9	5	.643	59	0	0	0	**35**	107^2	84	3	29	75	9.4	1.92	153	.216	.271	4	.190	1	**14**	**12**	-1	1.4
1973	NY-A★	5	9	.357	51	0	0	0	27	82^1	66	4	18	63	9.2	2.51	146	.216	.259	0	—	0	12	11	0	1.2
1974	NY-A	9	3	.750	66	0	0	0	15	114	93	6	43	89	10.8	1.66	210	.226	.300	0	.000	0	**25**	23	-1	2.4
1975	NY-A	5	7	.417	49	0	0	0	6	89^1	94	1	36	65	13.3	3.12	117	.275	.347	0	—	0	6	5	0	0.6
1976	*NY-A☆	7	8	.467	64	0	0	0	**23**	103^2	82	5	42	61	10.8	2.26	151	.225	.305	0	—	0	15	13	-1	1.3
1977	*NY-A★	13	5	.722	**72**	0	0	0	26	137	131	7	33	68	10.9	2.17	182	.257	.305	0	—	0	**29**	**27**	-1	2.7
1978	*NY-A	9	3	.750	59	0	0	0	9	111^2	116	6	33	33	12.3	3.47	104	.278	.337	0	—	0	4	2	0	0.3
1979	Tex-A	5	8	.385	67	0	0	0	13	95	78	9	28	48	10.0	3.13	133	.226	.284	0	—	0	11	11	-1	1.0
1980	Tex-A	3	2	.600	49	0	0	0	8	80^2	97	9	28	43	13.9	4.69	83	.306	.362	0	—	0	-6	-7	-0	-0.7
	Phi-N	0	0	—	10	0	0	0	2	14	11	0	6	6	10.9	1.93	196	.220	.304	0	—	0	3	3	-1	0.3
1981	*Phi-N	9	6	.600	48	0	0	0	2	75	85	4	33	29	14.3	4.44	82	.301	.377	2	.400	1	-8	-7	1	-0.5
1982	Phi-N	3	3	.500	34	0	0	0	2	36^2	50	3	12	12	15.2	5.15	71	.327	.376	1	.500	1	-6	-6	1	-0.5
	Chi-A	0	0	—	11	0	0	0	1	12	11	0	7	6	13.5	3.00	134	.262	.367	0	—	0	1	1	-0	0.1
Total	16	99	76	.566	899	0	0	0	238	1390^1	1292	84	481	873	11.6	2.88	127	.251	.316	15	.192	2	121	119	-4	12.8
● **JIM LYLE**	Lyle, James Charles b: 7/24/1900, Lake, Miss. d: 10/10/77, Williamsport, Pa. BR/TR, 6'1", 180 lbs. Deb: 10/02/25																									
1925	Was-A	0	0	—	1	0	0	0	0	3	5	0	1	3	18.0	6.00	70	.333	.375	0	—	0	-1	-1	-0	-0.1
● **ADRIAN LYNCH**	Lynch, Adrian Ryan b: 2/9/1897, Laurens, Iowa d: 3/16/34, Davenport, Iowa BB/TR, 6'1.5", 185 lbs. Deb: 8/04/20																									
1920	StL-A	2	0	1.000	5	3	1	0	0	22^1	23	1	17	8	16.5	5.24	75	.277	.406	2	.222	0	-4	-3	-1	-0.4
● **ED LYNCH**	Lynch, Edward Francis b: 2/25/56, Brooklyn, N.Y. BR/TR, 6'6", 230 lbs. Deb: 8/31/80																									
1980	NY-N	1	1	.500	5	4	0	0	0	19^1	24	0	5	9	14.0	5.12	69	.304	.353	2	.333	0	-3	-3	0	-0.3
1981	NY-N	4	5	.444	17	13	0	0	0	80^1	79	6	21	27	11.3	2.91	120	.254	.303	3	.143	1	5	5	-1	0.6
1982	NY-N	4	8	.333	43	12	0	0	2	139^1	145	6	40	51	12.0	3.55	102	.273	.325	0	.000	-3	1	1	-1	-0.4
1983	NY-N	10	10	.500	30	27	1	0	0	174^2	208	17	41	44	13.0	4.28	85	.302	.344	8	.154	-1	-13	-13	-1	-1.5
1984	NY-N	9	8	.529	40	13	0	0	2	124	169	14	24	62	14.3	4.50	79	.324	.359	6	.222	1	-13	-13	-1	-1.4
1985	NY-N	10	8	.556	31	29	6	1	0	191	188	19	27	65	10.2	3.44	100	.256	.283	4	.077	-2	3	0	-4	-0.6
1986	NY-N	0	0	—	1	0	0	0	0	1^2	2	0	0	1	10.8	0.00	—	.286	.286	0	—	0	1	1	-0	0.1
	Chi-N	7	5	.583	23	13	1	1	0	99^2	105	10	23	57	11.6	3.79	107	.279	.322	1	.033	-2	-1	3	-1	0.0
	Yr	7	5	.583	24	13	1	1	0	101^1	107	10	23	58	11.6	3.73	108	.279	.321	1	.033	-2	-0	3	-1	0.1
1987	Chi-N	2	9	.182	58	8	0	0	4	110^1	130	17	48	80	14.7	5.38	79	.295	.367	3	.188	-0	-16	-14	1	-1.3
Total	8	47	54	.465	248	119	8	2	8	940^1	1050	89	229	396	12.4	4.00	92	.284	.329	27	.114	-6	-35	-33	-8	-4.8
● **JACK LYNCH**	Lynch, John H. b: 2/5/1857, New York, N.Y d: 4/20/23, Bronx, N.Y. BR/TR, 5'8", 185 lbs. Deb: 5/02/1881																									
1881	Buf-N	10	9	.526	20	19	17	0	0	165^2	203	2	29	32	12.6	3.59	77	.297	.325	13	.167	-3	-15	-15	1	-1.5
1883	NY-a	13	15	.464	29	29	29	1	0	255	263	6	25	119	10.2	4.09	81	.249	.267	20	.187	-3	-22	-22	-1	-2.2
1884	NY-a	37	15	.712	55	54	54	5	0	496	420	10	42	292	8.6	2.67	117	.215	.236	30	.152	-6	32	25	-5	1.2
1885	NY-a	23	21	.523	44	43	43	1	0	379	410	17	42	177	10.8	3.61	82	.263	.283	30	.196	2	-15	-27	-5	-2.7
1886	NY-a	20	30	.400	51	50	50	1	0	432^2	485	10	116	193	12.8	3.95	86	.271	.320	27	.160	-6	-24	-26	-3	-2.9
1887	NY-a	7	14	.333	21	21	21	0	0	187	245	8	36	45	13.7	5.10	83	.305	.338	14	.169	-4	-17	-18	2	-1.5
1890	Bro-a	0	1	.000	1	1	1	0	0	9	22	1	5	1	27.0	12.00	32	.452	.503	3	.750	2	-8	-8	1	-0.4
Total	7	110	105	.512	221	217	215	8	0	1924^1	2048	54	295	859	11.1	3.69	88	.260	.289	137	.173	-17	-69	-92	-10	-10.0
● **MIKE LYNCH**	Lynch, Michael Joseph b: 6/28/1880, Holyoke, Mass. d: 4/2/27, Garrison, N.Y. BR/TR, 5'10", 155 lbs. Deb: 6/21/04																									
1904	Pit-N	15	11	.577	27	24	24	1	0	222^2	200	1	91	95	12.4	2.71	101	.243	.330	20	.230	4	1	1	-2	0.2
1905	Pit-N	17	8	.680	33	22	13	0	2	206^1	191	3	107	106	13.2	3.79	79	.254	.351	11	.136	-1	-18	-18	0	-2.0
1906	Pit-N	6	5	.545	18	12	7	0	0	119	101	2	31	48	10.6	2.42	110	.232	.295	8	.205	-0	3	3	-1	0.3
1907	Pit-N	2	2	.500	7	4	2	0	0	36	37	0	22	9	15.0	2.25	108	.282	.390	3	.250	1	1	1	1	0.3
	NY-N	3	6	.333	12	10	7	0	1	72	68	3	30	34	12.3	3.38	73	.249	.323	8	.296	2	-7	-7	0	-0.5
	Yr	5	8	.385	19	14	9	0	1	108	105	3	52	43	13.1	3.00	82	.259	.344	11	.282	3	-6	-6	2	-0.2
Total	4	43	32	.573	97	72	53	1	3	656	597	9	281	292	12.4	3.05	91	.248	.333	50	.203	5	-21	-20	-1	-1.7
● **TOM LYNCH**	Lynch, Thomas S. b: 1863, Peru, Ill. d: 5/13/03, Peru, Ill. BL , 5'11", 175 lbs. Deb: 8/05/1884																									
1884	Chi-N	0	0	—	1	1	0	0	0	7	7	1	3	2	12.9	2.57	122	.241	.313	0	.000	-1	0	0	0	0.0
● **RED LYNN**	Lynn, Japhet Monroe b: 12/27/13, Kenney, Tex. d: 10/27/77, Bellville, Tex. BR/TR, 6', 162 lbs. Deb: 4/25/39																									
1939	Det-A	0	1	.000	4	0	0	0	0	8^1	11	2	3	3	16.2	8.64	57	.324	.395	0	.000	-0	-4	-3	0	-0.3
	NY-N	1	0	1.000	26	0	0	0	1	49^2	44	3	21	22	12.1	3.08	127	.240	.325	0	.000	-1	5	5	-1	0.3
1940	NY-N	4	3	.571	33	0	0	0	3	42^1	40	3	24	25	13.8	3.83	101	.247	.348	0	.000	-1	0	0	-1	-0.1

YEAR	TM/L	W	L	PCT	G	GS	CG	SH	SV	IP	H	HR	BB	SO	RAT	ERA	ERA+	OAV	OOB	BH	AVG	PB	PR	/A	PD	TPI
1944	Chi-N	5	4	.556	22	7	4	1	1	84^1	80	4	37	35	12.6	4.06	87	.251	.331	6	.207	0	-4	-5	1	-0.3
Total	3	10	8	.556	85	7	4	1	5	184^2	175	12	85	85	12.9	3.95	96	.251	.336	6	.146	-1	-3	-4	-1	-0.4

● **AL LYONS** Lyons, Albert Harold b: 7/18/18, St.Joseph, Mo. d: 12/20/65, Inglewood, Cal. BR/TR, 6'2", 195 lbs. Deb: 4/19/44

YEAR	TM/L	W	L	PCT	G	GS	CG	SH	SV	IP	H	HR	BB	SO	RAT	ERA	ERA+	OAV	OOB	BH	AVG	PB	PR	/A	PD	TPI
1944	NY-A	0	0	—	11	0	0	0	0	39^2	43	2	24	14	15.7	4.54	77	.291	.397	9	.346	2	-5	-5	-1	-0.3
1946	NY-A	0	1	.000	2	1	0	0	0	8^1	11	0	6	4	19.4	5.40	64	.314	.429	0	.000	-1	-2	-2	0	-0.2
1947	NY-A	1	0	1.000	6	0	0	0	0	11	18	2	9	7	22.1	9.00	39	.367	.466	4	.667	1	-6	-7	0	-0.5
	Pit-N	1	2	.333	13	0	0	0	0	28^1	36	4	12	16	15.6	7.31	58	.300	.368	2	.200	1	-10	-10	1	-0.7
1948	Bos-N	1	0	1.000	7	0	0	0	0	12^2	17	1	8	5	17.8	7.82	49	.309	.397	2	.167	0	-5	-6	1	-0.4
Total	4	3	3	.500	39	1	0	0	0	100	125	9	59	46	16.9	6.30	59	.307	.400	17	.293	5	-29	-28	2	-2.1

● **GEORGE LYONS** Lyons, George Tony "Smooth" b: 1/25/1891, Bible Grove, Ill. d: 8/12/81, Nevada, Mo. BR/TR, 5'11", 180 lbs. Deb: 9/06/20

YEAR	TM/L	W	L	PCT	G	GS	CG	SH	SV	IP	H	HR	BB	SO	RAT	ERA	ERA+	OAV	OOB	BH	AVG	PB	PR	/A	PD	TPI
1920	StL-N	2	1	.667	7	2	1	0	0	23^1	21	2	9	5	12.0	3.09	97	.262	.344	1	.143	-0	0	-0	1	0.0
1924	StL-A	3	2	.600	26	6	2	0	0	77^2	97	2	45	25	17.0	5.21	87	.323	.420	5	.250	-0	-8	-6	1	-0.5
Total	2	5	3	.625	33	8	3	0	0	101	118	4	54	30	15.9	4.72	88	.311	.405	6	.222	-0	-8	-7	2	-0.5

● **HARRY LYONS** Lyons, Harry P. b: 3/25/1866, Chester, Pa. d: 6/30/12, Mauricetown, N.J. BR/TR, 5'10.5", 157 lbs. Deb: 8/29/1887 ♦

YEAR	TM/L	W	L	PCT	G	GS	CG	SH	SV	IP	H	HR	BB	SO	RAT	ERA	ERA+	OAV	OOB	BH	AVG	PB	PR	/A	PD	TPI
1890	Roc-a	0	0	—	1	0	0	0	0	3^2	8	0	1	2	22.1	12.27	29	.424	.453	152	.260	0	-3	-4	0	-0.3

● **HERSH LYONS** Lyons, Herschel Englebert b: 7/23/15, Fresno, Cal. BR/TR, 5'11", 195 lbs. Deb: 4/17/41

YEAR	TM/L	W	L	PCT	G	GS	CG	SH	SV	IP	H	HR	BB	SO	RAT	ERA	ERA+	OAV	OOB	BH	AVG	PB	PR	/A	PD	TPI
1941	StL-N	0	0	—	1	0	0	0	0	1^1	1	0	3	1	27.0	0.00	—	.200	.500	0	—	0	1	1	0	0.1

● **STEVE LYONS** Lyons, Stephen John b: 6/3/60, Tacoma, Wash. BL/TR, 6'3", 192 lbs. Deb: 4/15/85 ♦

YEAR	TM/L	W	L	PCT	G	GS	CG	SH	SV	IP	H	HR	BB	SO	RAT	ERA	ERA+	OAV	OOB	BH	AVG	PB	PR	/A	PD	TPI
1990	Chi-A	0	0	—	1	0	0	0	0	2	2	0	4	1	27.0	4.50	85	.250	.500	28	.192	0	-0	-0	0	0.0
1991	Bos-A	0	0	—	1	0	0	0	0	1	2	0	0	1	18.0	0.00	—	.400	.400	51	.241	0	0	0	0	0.1
Total	2	0	0	—	2	0	0	0	0	3	4	0	4	2	24.0	3.00	133	.308	.471	542	.253	0	0	0	0	0.1

● **TED LYONS** Lyons, Theodore Amar b: 12/28/1900, Lake Charles, La. d: 7/25/86, Sulphur, La. BB/TR, 5'11", 200 lbs. Deb: 7/02/23 MCH♦

YEAR	TM/L	W	L	PCT	G	GS	CG	SH	SV	IP	H	HR	BB	SO	RAT	ERA	ERA+	OAV	OOB	BH	AVG	PB	PR	/A	PD	TPI
1923	Chi-A	2	1	.667	9	1	0	0	0	22^2	30	2	15	6	18.3	6.35	62	.323	.422	1	.200	0	-6	-6	1	-0.5
1924	Chi-A	12	11	.522	41	22	12	0	3	216^1	279	10	72	52	14.7	4.87	85	.322	.375	17	.221	0	-15	-18	-3	-1.9
1925	Chi-A	**21**	11	.656	43	32	19	**5**	3	262^2	274	7	83	45	12.3	3.26	128	.278	.335	18	.186	-3	33	26	2	2.4
1926	Chi-A	18	16	.529	39	31	24	3	2	283^2	268	6	106	51	11.9	3.01	128	.252	.320	22	.212	-0	32	27	4	3.0
1927	Chi-A	**22**	14	.611	39	34	**30**	2	2	**307^2**	291	7	67	71	10.5	2.84	143	.251	.292	28	.255	5	**45**	**41**	0	**4.8**
1928	Chi-A	15	14	.517	39	27	21	0	6	240	276	11	68	60	13.0	3.98	102	.295	.344	23	.253	1	2	2	2	0.4
1929	Chi-A	14	20	.412	37	31	21	1	2	259^1	276	11	76	57	12.3	4.10	105	.278	.331	20	.220	1	4	5	3	0.9
1930	Chi-A	22	15	.595	42	36	**29**	1	1	**297^2**	331	12	57	69	11.8	3.78	122	.285	.319	38	.311	8	29	28	3	3.7
1931	Chi-A	4	6	.400	22	12	7	0	0	101	117	6	33	16	13.4	4.01	106	.296	.350	5	.152	-1	4	3	-1	0.1
1932	Chi-A	10	15	.400	33	26	19	1	2	230^2	243	10	71	58	12.4	3.28	132	.272	.327	19	.260	5	31	27	-1	3.0
1933	Chi-A	10	21	.323	36	27	14	2	1	228	260	10	74	74	13.2	4.38	97	.280	.333	26	.286	6	-3	-4	0	0.2
1934	Chi-A	11	13	.458	30	24	21	0	1	205^1	249	15	66	53	13.9	4.87	97	.293	.345	20	.206	1	-8	-3	2	0.0
1935	Chi-A	15	8	.652	23	22	19	3	0	190^2	194	15	56	54	11.9	3.02	153	.262	.317	18	.220	-0	30	34	-1	3.3
1936	Chi-A	10	13	.435	26	24	15	1	0	182	227	21	45	48	13.6	5.14	101	.305	.347	11	.157	-3	-2	1	1	0.0
1937	Chi-A	12	7	.632	22	22	11	0	0	169^1	182	21	45	45	12.1	4.15	111	.278	.326	12	.211	1	9	9	0	1.0
1938	Chi-A	9	11	.450	23	23	17	1	0	194^2	238	13	52	54	13.4	3.70	132	.299	.342	14	.194	-1	24	26	2	2.5
1939	Chi-A☆	14	6	.700	21	21	16	0	0	172^2	162	7	26	65	**9.9**	2.76	171	.247	**.276**	18	.295	4	36	38	-1	4.1
1940	Chi-A	12	8	.600	22	22	17	**4**	0	186^1	188	17	37	72	10.9	3.24	137	.252	.287	18	.240	2	24	25	-2	2.4
1941	Chi-A	12	10	.545	22	22	19	2	0	187^1	199	9	37	63	11.5	3.70	111	.269	.308	20	.270	4	9	8	1	1.3
1942	Chi-A	14	6	.700	20	20	20	1	0	180^1	167	11	26	50	9.7	**2.10**	**172**	.245	.275	16	.239	4	31	30	1	4.0
1946	Chi-A	1	4	.200	5	5	5	0	0	42^2	38	2	9	10	9.9	2.32	147	.235	.275	0	.000	-1	6	5	0	0.5
Total	21	260	230	.531	594	484	356	27	23	4161	4489	223	1121	1073	12.2	3.67	118	.276	.324	364	.233	32	313	302	12	35.2

● **TOBY LYONS** Lyons, Thomas A. b: 3/27/1869, Cambridge, Mass. d: 8/27/20, Boston, Mass. Deb: 4/18/1890

YEAR	TM/L	W	L	PCT	G	GS	CG	SH	SV	IP	H	HR	BB	SO	RAT	ERA	ERA+	OAV	OOB	BH	AVG	PB	PR	/A	PD	TPI
1890	Syr-a	0	2	.000	3	3	2	0	0	22^1	40	1	21	6	25.0	10.48	34	.377	.484	4	.333	1	-16	-17	0	-1.2

● **RICK LYSANDER** Lysander, Richard Eugene b: 2/21/53, Huntington Park, Cal. BR/TR, 6'2", 190 lbs. Deb: 4/12/80

YEAR	TM/L	W	L	PCT	G	GS	CG	SH	SV	IP	H	HR	BB	SO	RAT	ERA	ERA+	OAV	OOB	BH	AVG	PB	PR	/A	PD	TPI
1980	Oak-A	0	0	—	5	0	0	0	0	13^2	24	3	4	5	18.4	7.90	48	.381	.418	0	—	0	-6	-6	0	-0.2
1983	Min-A	5	12	.294	61	4	1	1	3	125	132	8	43	58	12.7	3.38	126	.275	.337	0	—	0	9	12	1	1.0
1984	Min-A	4	3	.571	36	0	0	0	5	56^2	62	2	27	22	14.1	3.49	120	.283	.362	0	—	0	3	4	0	0.1
1985	Min-A	0	2	.000	35	1	0	0	3	61	72	3	22	26	13.9	6.05	73	.305	.364	0	—	0	-13	-11	-1	-1.4
Total	4	9	17	.346	137	5	1	1	11	256^1	290	16	96	111	13.6	4.28	99	.291	.354	0	—	0	-6	-1	0	-0.5

● **BILL LYSTON** Lyston, William Edward b: 1863, Near Baltimore, Md. d: 8/4/44, Baltimore, Md. TR , Deb: 8/29/1891

YEAR	TM/L	W	L	PCT	G	GS	CG	SH	SV	IP	H	HR	BB	SO	RAT	ERA	ERA+	OAV	OOB	BH	AVG	PB	PR	/A	PD	TPI
1891	Col-a	0	1	.000	1	1	1	0	0	6	10	0	6	1	25.5	10.50	33	.359	.488	0	.000	-0	-5	-5	-0	-0.4
1894	Cle-N	0	0	—	1	1	0	0	0	3^2	5	1	4	0	22.1	9.82	56	.321	.460	0	.000	-0	-2	-2	-0	-0.2
Total	2	0	1	.000	2	2	1	0	0	9^2	15	1	10	1	24.2	10.24	41	.346	.478	0	.000	-0	-6	-7	-0	-0.6

● **DUKE MAAS** Maas, Duane Fredrick b: 1/31/29, Utica, Mich. d: 12/7/76, Mt.Clemens, Mich. BR/TR, 5'10", 170 lbs. Deb: 4/21/55

YEAR	TM/L	W	L	PCT	G	GS	CG	SH	SV	IP	H	HR	BB	SO	RAT	ERA	ERA+	OAV	OOB	BH	AVG	PB	PR	/A	PD	TPI
1955	Det-A	5	6	.455	18	16	5	2	0	86^2	91	7	50	42	14.8	4.88	79	.271	.369	5	.167	0	-9	-10	0	-0.9
1956	Det-A	0	7	.000	26	7	0	0	0	63^1	81	9	32	34	16.9	6.54	63	.313	.401	3	.188	0	-17	-17	-0	-1.7
1957	Det-A	10	14	.417	45	26	8	2	6	219^1	210	23	65	116	11.4	3.28	118	.252	.309	6	.085	-4	12	14	0	1.1
1958	KC-A	4	5	.444	10	7	3	1	1	55^1	49	3	13	19	10.2	3.90	100	.241	.290	3	.176	0	-1	0	0	0.1
	*NY-A	7	3	.700	22	13	2	1	0	101^1	93	9	36	50	11.6	3.82	92	.242	.310	3	.088	-2	-1	-3	-1	-0.6
	Yr	11	8	.579	32	20	5	2	1	156^2	142	12	49	69	11.1	3.85	95	.241	.302	6	.118	-1	-1	-3	-1	-0.5
1959	NY-A	14	8	.636	38	21	3	1	4	138	149	14	53	67	13.3	4.43	82	.278	.345	5	.125	-1	-9	-12	1	-1.3
1960	*NY-A	5	1	.833	35	1	0	0	4	70^1	70	6	35	28	13.6	4.09	87	.265	.353	0	.000	-1	-2	-4	1	-0.4
1961	NY-A	0	0	—	1	0	0	0	0	0^1	2	0	0	0	54.0	54.00	7	1.000	1.000	0	—	0	-2	-2	0	-0.2
Total	7	45	44	.506	195	91	21	7	15	734^2	745	71	284	356	12.8	4.19	90	.264	.336	25	.117	-7	-27	-34	0	-3.9

● **BOB MABE** Mabe, Robert Lee b: 10/8/29, Danville, Va. BR/TR, 5'11", 165 lbs. Deb: 4/18/58

YEAR	TM/L	W	L	PCT	G	GS	CG	SH	SV	IP	H	HR	BB	SO	RAT	ERA	ERA+	OAV	OOB	BH	AVG	PB	PR	/A	PD	TPI
1958	StL-N	3	9	.250	31	13	4	0	0	111^2	113	11	41	74	12.7	4.51	91	.260	.330	1	.042	-2	-7	-5	0	-0.7
1959	Cin-N	4	2	.667	18	1	0	0	3	29^2	29	6	19	8	14.6	5.46	74	.254	.361	0	.000	-1	-5	-5	-0	-0.6
1960	Bal-A	0	0	—	2	0	0	0	0	0^2	4	0	1	0	67.5	27.00	14	.571	.625	0	—	0	-2	-2	-0	-0.2
Total	3	7	11	.389	51	14	4	0	3	142	146	17	61	82	13.4	4.82	85	.263	.340	1	.032	-3	-14	-11	-0	-1.5

● **MAC MacARTHUR** MacArthur, Malcolm b: 1/19/1862, Glasgow, Scotland d: 10/18/32, Detroit, Mich. TR , Deb: 5/02/1884

YEAR	TM/L	W	L	PCT	G	GS	CG	SH	SV	IP	H	HR	BB	SO	RAT	ERA	ERA+	OAV	OOB	BH	AVG	PB	PR	/A	PD	TPI
1884	Ind-a	1	5	.167	6	6	6	0	0	52	57	1	21	19	13.8	5.02	66	.263	.333	2	.095	-2	-10	-10	0	-1.0

● **FRANK MacCORMACK** MacCormack, Frank Louis b: 9/21/54, Jersey City, N.J. BR/TR, 6'4", 210 lbs. Deb: 6/14/76

YEAR	TM/L	W	L	PCT	G	GS	CG	SH	SV	IP	H	HR	BB	SO	RAT	ERA	ERA+	OAV	OOB	BH	AVG	PB	PR	/A	PD	TPI
1976	Det-A	0	5	.000	9	8	0	0	0	32^2	35	1	34	14	19.3	5.79	64	.294	.455	0	.000	0	-8	-8	-0	-0.8
1977	Sea-A	0	0	—	3	3	0	0	0	7	4	0	12	4	24.4	3.86	107	.174	.500	0	—	0	0	0	0	0.1
Total	2	0	5	.000	12	11	0	0	0	39^2	39	1	46	18	20.2	5.45	69	.275	.464	0	.000	0	-8	-7	-0	-0.7

● **ROB MacDONALD** MacDonald, Robert Joseph b: 4/27/65, East Orange, N.J. BL/TL, 6'3", 200 lbs. Deb: 8/14/90

YEAR	TM/L	W	L	PCT	G	GS	CG	SH	SV	IP	H	HR	BB	SO	RAT	ERA	ERA+	OAV	OOB	BH	AVG	PB	PR	/A	PD	TPI
1990	Tor-A	0	0	—	4	0	0	0	0	2^1	0	0	2	0	7.7	0.00	—	.000	.250	0	—	0	1	1	-0	0.0
1991	*Tor-A	3	3	.500	45	0	0	0	0	53^2	51	5	25	24	12.7	2.85	148	.252	.335	0	—	0	7	8	-1	0.5
1992	Tor-A	1	0	1.000	27	0	0	0	0	47^1	50	4	16	26	12.7	4.37	93	.270	.332	0	—	0	-2	-2	-1	-0.4

YEAR	TM/L	W	L	PCT	G	GS	CG	SH	SV	IP	H	HR	BB	SO	RAT	ERA	ERA+	OAV	OOB	BH	AVG	PB	PR	/A	PD	TPI
Total	3	4	3	.571	76	0	0	0	0	103^1	101	9	43	50	12.6	3.48	119	.257	.332	0	—	0	6	8	-2	0.1

● BILL MacDONALD MacDonald, William Paul b: 3/28/29, Alameda, Cal. BR/TR, 5'10", 170 lbs. Deb: 5/06/50

YEAR	TM/L	W	L	PCT	G	GS	CG	SH	SV	IP	H	HR	BB	SO	RAT	ERA	ERA+	OAV	OOB	BH	AVG	PB	PR	/A	PD	TPI
1950	Pit-N	8	10	.444	32	20	6	2	1	153	138	17	88	60	13.4	4.29	102	.243	.346	6	.122	-2	-3	2	-3	-0.3
1953	Pit-N	0	1	.000	4	1	0	0	0	7^1	12	0	8	4	25.8	12.27	36	.400	.538	0	—	0	-7	-6	-0	-0.6
Total	2	8	11	.421	36	21	6	2	1	160^1	150	17	96	64	13.9	4.66	94	.251	.356	6	.122	-2	-9	-5	-3	-0.9

● JIMMY MACE Mace, Harry L. b: Washington, D.C. 5'11", 185 lbs. Deb: 5/05/1891

YEAR	TM/L	W	L	PCT	G	GS	CG	SH	SV	IP	H	HR	BB	SO	RAT	ERA	ERA+	OAV	OOB	BH	AVG	PB	PR	/A	PD	TPI
1891	Was-a	0	1	.000	3	1	1	0	0	16	18	0	8	3	15.2	7.31	51	.274	.362	0	.000	-1	-6	-6	-0	-0.6

● DANNY MacFAYDEN MacFayden, Daniel Knowles "Deacon Danny" b: 6/10/05, N.Truro, Mass. d: 8/26/72, Brunswick, Me. BR/TR, 5'11", 170 lbs. Deb: 8/25/26

YEAR	TM/L	W	L	PCT	G	GS	CG	SH	SV	IP	H	HR	BB	SO	RAT	ERA	ERA+	OAV	OOB	BH	AVG	PB	PR	/A	PD	TPI
1926	Bos-A	0	1	.000	3	1	1	0	0	13	10	0	7	1	11.8	4.85	84	.217	.321	1	.333	0	-1	-1	1	0.0
1927	Bos-A	5	8	.385	34	16	6	1	2	160^1	176	9	59	42	13.5	4.27	99	.294	.363	13	.283	4	-2	-1	-2	0.2
1928	Bos-A	9	15	.375	33	28	9	0	0	195	215	12	78	61	13.8	4.75	87	.289	.361	9	.143	-1	-15	-14	-1	-1.5
1929	Bos-A	10	18	.357	32	26	14	**4**	0	221	225	8	81	61	12.7	3.62	118	.271	.340	13	.176	-3	15	16	2	1.5
1930	Bos-A	11	14	.440	36	33	18	1	2	269^1	293	9	93	76	13.1	4.21	109	.281	.343	13	.141	-4	13	12	2	0.9
1931	Bos-A	16	12	.571	35	32	17	2	0	230^2	263	4	79	74	13.6	4.02	107	.281	.341	10	.123	-5	9	7	2	0.5
1932	Bos-A	1	10	.091	12	11	6	0	0	77^2	91	3	33	29	14.5	5.10	88	.289	.358	3	.120	-2	-5	-5	0	-0.6
	NY-A	7	5	.583	17	15	9	0	1	121^1	137	11	37	33	13.1	3.93	104	.281	.334	5	.102	-2	7	2	-2	-0.2
	Yr	8	15	.348	29	26	15	0	1	199	228	14	70	62	13.6	4.39	97	.284	.342	8	.108	-4	2	-3	-1	-0.8
1933	NY-A	3	2	.600	25	6	2	0	0	90^1	120	8	37	28	15.8	5.88	66	.319	.383	1	.029	-4	-16	-20	-0	-2.2
1934	NY-A	4	3	.571	22	11	4	0	0	96	110	5	31	41	13.4	4.50	90	.288	.345	4	.103	-2	-0	-5	-1	-0.7
1935	Cin-N	1	2	.333	7	4	1	0	0	36	39	1	13	13	13.0	4.75	84	.281	.342	1	.091	-1	-3	-3	1	-0.3
	Bos-N	5	13	.278	28	20	7	1	0	151^2	200	8	34	46	14.2	5.10	74	.314	.354	8	.157	-1	-18	-22	2	-2.0
	Yr	6	15	.286	35	24	8	1	0	187^2	239	9	47	59	14.0	5.04	76	.308	.352	9	.145	-2	-21	-25	3	-2.3
1936	Bos-N	17	13	.567	37	31	21	2	0	266^2	268	5	66	86	11.4	2.87	134	.259	.307	8	.096	-5	34	29	3	2.8
1937	Bos-N	14	14	.500	32	32	16	2	0	246	250	5	60	70	11.4	2.93	123	.268	.313	13	.157	-2	27	18	1	1.8
1938	Bos-N	14	9	.609	29	29	19	5	0	219^2	208	6	64	58	11.3	2.95	116	.247	.304	9	.117	-4	20	12	-1	0.7
1939	Bos-N	8	14	.364	33	28	8	0	2	191^2	221	11	59	46	13.3	3.90	95	.291	.345	12	.179	-1	0	-4	1	-0.4
1940	Pit-N	5	4	.556	35	8	0	0	2	91^1	112	5	27	24	14.1	3.55	107	.302	.356	5	.179	-0	3	3	1	0.3
1941	Was-A	0	1	.000	5	0	0	0	0	7	12	1	5	3	21.9	10.29	39	.375	.459	0	—	0	-5	-5	0	-0.4
1943	Bos-N	2	1	.667	10	1	0	0	0	21^1	31	1	9	5	17.3	5.91	58	.344	.410	1	.250	0	-6	-6	-0	-0.6
Total	17	132	159	.454	465	332	158	18	9	2706	2981	112	872	797	13.0	3.96	101	.281	.340	129	.142	-32	58	11	10	-0.2

● JULIO MACHADO Machado, Julio Segundo (Rondon) b: 12/1/65, Zulia, Venezuela BR/TR, 5'9", 165 lbs. Deb: 9/07/89

YEAR	TM/L	W	L	PCT	G	GS	CG	SH	SV	IP	H	HR	BB	SO	RAT	ERA	ERA+	OAV	OOB	BH	AVG	PB	PR	/A	PD	TPI
1989	NY-N	0	1	.000	10	0	0	0	0	11	9	0	3	14	9.8	3.27	100	.214	.267	0	—	0	0	-0	-0	0.0
1990	NY-N	4	1	.800	27	0	0	0	0	34^1	32	4	17	27	13.4	3.15	119	.248	.345	0	—	0	2	2	-0	0.2
	Mil-A	0	0	—	10	0	0	0	3	13	9	0	8	12	11.8	0.69	559	.191	.309	0	—	0	5	5	-0	0.5
1991	Mil-A	3	3	.500	54	0	0	0	3	88^2	65	12	55	98	12.5	3.45	115	.211	.336	0	—	0	6	5	-1	0.5
Total	3	7	5	.583	101	0	0	0	6	147	115	16	83	151	12.4	3.12	123	.219	.331	0	—	0	14	12	-1	1.2

● CHUCK MACHEMEHL Machemehl, Charles Walter b: 4/20/47, Brenham, Tex. BR/TR, 6'4", 200 lbs. Deb: 4/06/71

YEAR	TM/L	W	L	PCT	G	GS	CG	SH	SV	IP	H	HR	BB	SO	RAT	ERA	ERA+	OAV	OOB	BH	AVG	PB	PR	/A	PD	TPI
1971	Cle-A	0	2	.000	14	0	0	0	3	18^1	16	2	15	9	15.2	6.38	60	.246	.387	1	.500	0	-6	-5	0	-0.5

● DENNY MACK Mack, Dennis Joseph (b: Dennis Joseph McGee) b: 1851, Easton, Pa. d: 4/10/1888, Wilkes-Barre, Pa. BR/TR, 5'7", 164 lbs. Deb: 5/06/1871 MU♦

YEAR	TM/L	W	L	PCT	G	GS	CG	SH	SV	IP	H	HR	BB	SO	RAT	ERA	ERA+	OAV	OOB	BH	AVG	PB	PR	/A	PD	TPI
1871	Rok-n	0	1	.000	3	1	1	0	0	13	20	0	3	1	15.9	3.46	118	.299	.329	30	.246	-0	1	1		0.1

● FRANK MACK Mack, Frank George "Stubby" b: 2/2/1900, Okahoma City, Okla. d: 7/2/71, Clearwater, Fla. BR/TR, 6'1.5", 180 lbs. Deb: 8/16/22

YEAR	TM/L	W	L	PCT	G	GS	CG	SH	SV	IP	H	HR	BB	SO	RAT	ERA	ERA+	OAV	OOB	BH	AVG	PB	PR	/A	PD	TPI
1922	Chi-A	2	2	.500	8	4	1	1	0	34^1	36	2	16	11	13.6	3.67	111	.281	.361	3	.250	1	1	2	-1	0.1
1923	Chi-A	0	1	.000	11	0	0	0	0	23^1	23	0	11	6	13.1	4.24	93	.284	.370	0	.000	-1	-1	-1	0	-0.1
1925	Chi-A	0	0	—	8	0	0	0	0	13^1	24	1	13	6	25.0	9.45	44	.444	.552	1	.333	0	-7	-8	-0	-0.7
Total	3	2	3	.400	27	4	1	1	0	71	83	3	40	23	15.6	4.94	82	.316	.406	4	.190	0	-7	-7	-1	-0.7

● TONY MACK Mack, Tony Lynn b: 4/30/61, Lexington, Ky. BR/TR, 5'10", 177 lbs. Deb: 7/27/85

YEAR	TM/L	W	L	PCT	G	GS	CG	SH	SV	IP	H	HR	BB	SO	RAT	ERA	ERA+	OAV	OOB	BH	AVG	PB	PR	/A	PD	TPI
1985	Cal-A	0	1	.000	1	1	0	0	0	2^1	8	0	0	0	30.9	15.43	27	.571	.571	0	—	0	-3	-3	-0	-0.2

● BILL MACK Mack, William Francis b: 2/12/1885, Elmira, N.Y. d: 9/30/71, Elmira, N.Y. BL/TL, 6'1", 155 lbs. Deb: 7/14/08

YEAR	TM/L	W	L	PCT	G	GS	CG	SH	SV	IP	H	HR	BB	SO	RAT	ERA	ERA+	OAV	OOB	BH	AVG	PB	PR	/A	PD	TPI
1908	Chi-N	0	0	—	2	0	0	0	0	6	5	1	1	2	10.5	3.00	78	.263	.333	2	.667	1	-0	-0	-0	0.1

● KEN MacKENZIE MacKenzie, Kenneth Purvis b: 3/10/34, Gore Bay, Ont., Can. BR/TL, 6', 185 lbs. Deb: 5/02/60

YEAR	TM/L	W	L	PCT	G	GS	CG	SH	SV	IP	H	HR	BB	SO	RAT	ERA	ERA+	OAV	OOB	BH	AVG	PB	PR	/A	PD	TPI
1960	Mil-N	0	1	.000	9	0	0	0	0	8^1	9	2	3	9	13.0	6.48	53	.281	.343	0	.000	-0	-3	-3	-0	-0.3
1961	Mil-N	0	1	.000	5	0	0	0	0	7	8	1	2	5	14.1	5.14	73	.296	.367	0	.000	-0	-1	-1	0	-0.1
1962	NY-N	5	4	.556	42	1	0	0	1	80	87	10	34	51	13.9	4.95	84	.280	.356	1	.083	-1	-9	-7	1	-0.7
1963	NY-N	3	1	.750	34	0	0	0	3	58	63	11	12	41	11.9	4.97	70	.267	.308	0	.000	-1	-11	-10	-1	-1.2
	StL-N	0	0	—	8	0	0	0	0	9	9	1	3	7	12.0	4.00	89	.250	.308	0	—	0	-1	-0	-0	-0.1
	Yr	3	1	.750	42	0	0	0	3	67	72	12	15	48	11.7	4.84	72	.262	.300	0	.000	-1	-12	-10	-1	-1.3
1964	SF-N	0	0	—	10	0	0	0	1	9	9	1	3	3	12.0	5.00	71	.265	.324	0	—	0	-1	-1	0	-0.1
1965	Hou-N	0	3	.000	21	0	0	0	0	37	46	7	6	26	12.6	3.89	86	.299	.325	3	.273	1	-1	-2	-0	-0.2
Total	6	8	10	.444	129	1	0	0	5	208^1	231	33	63	142	13.0	4.80	78	.278	.334	4	.111	-2	-27	-24	-1	-2.7

● JOHN MACKINSON Mackinson, John Joseph b: 10/29/23, Orange, N.J. d: 10/17/89, Reseda, Cal. BR/TR, 5'10.5", 160 lbs. Deb: 4/16/53

YEAR	TM/L	W	L	PCT	G	GS	CG	SH	SV	IP	H	HR	BB	SO	RAT	ERA	ERA+	OAV	OOB	BH	AVG	PB	PR	/A	PD	TPI
1953	Phi-A	0	0	—	1	0	0	0	0	1^1	1	0	2	0	20.3	0.00	—	.200	.429	0	—	0	1	1	0	0.1
1955	StL-N	0	1	.000	8	1	0	0	0	20^2	24	3	10	8	15.2	7.84	52	.296	.380	0	.000	-0	-9	-9	-0	-0.8
Total	2	0	1	.000	9	1	0	0	0	22	25	3	12	8	15.5	7.36	55	.291	.384	0	.000	-0	-8	-8	-0	-0.7

● BILLY MacLEOD MacLeod, William Daniel b: 5/13/42, Gloucester, Mass. BL/TL, 6'2", 190 lbs. Deb: 9/13/62

YEAR	TM/L	W	L	PCT	G	GS	CG	SH	SV	IP	H	HR	BB	SO	RAT	ERA	ERA+	OAV	OOB	BH	AVG	PB	PR	/A	PD	TPI
1962	Bos-A	0	1	.000	2	0	0	0	0	1^2	4	0	1	2	27.0	5.40	76	.444	.500	0	—	0	-0	-0	-0	0.0

● MAX MACON Macon, Max Cullen b: 10/14/15, Pensacola, Fla. d: 8/5/89, Jupiter, Fla. BL/TL, 6'3", 175 lbs. Deb: 4/21/38 ♦

YEAR	TM/L	W	L	PCT	G	GS	CG	SH	SV	IP	H	HR	BB	SO	RAT	ERA	ERA+	OAV	OOB	BH	AVG	PB	PR	/A	PD	TPI
1938	StL-N	4	11	.267	38	12	5	1	2	129^1	133	9	61	39	13.8	4.11	96	.268	.352	11	.306	2	-5	-2	1	0.1
1940	Bro-N	1	0	1.000	2	0	0	0	0	2	5	2	0	1	22.5	22.50	18	.455	.455	1	1.000	0	-4	-4	-0	-0.3
1942	Bro-N	5	3	.625	14	8	4	1	1	84	67	3	33	27	10.9	1.93	169	.220	.300	12	.279	4	13	12	-0	1.8
1943	Bro-N	7	5	.583	25	9	0	0	0	77	91	4	32	21	14.8	5.96	56	.291	.364	9	.164	-1	-22	-22	1	-2.4
1944	Bos-N	0	0	—	1	0	0	0	0	3	10	2	1	1	33.0	21.00	18	.556	.579	100	.273	0	-6	-6	0	-0.4
1947	Bos-N	0	0	—	1	0	0	0	0	2	1	0	1	1	9.0	0.00	—	.167	.286	0	.000	-0	1	1	0	0.1
Total	6	17	19	.472	81	29	9	2	3	297^1	307	20	128	90	13.5	4.24	85	.267	.345	133	.265	5	-23	-21	1	-1.1

● HARRY MacPHERSON MacPherson, Harry William b: 7/10/26, N.Andover, Mass. BR/TR, 5'10", 150 lbs. Deb: 8/14/44

YEAR	TM/L	W	L	PCT	G	GS	CG	SH	SV	IP	H	HR	BB	SO	RAT	ERA	ERA+	OAV	OOB	BH	AVG	PB	PR	/A	PD	TPI
1944	Bos-N	0	0	—	1	0	0	0	0	1	0	0	1	1	9.0	0.00	—	.000	.250	0	—	0	0	0	0	0.0

● JIMMY MACULLAR Macullar, James F. "Little Mac" b: 1/16/1855, Boston, Mass. d: 4/8/24, Baltimore, Md. BR/TL, 5'6", 155 lbs. Deb: 5/05/1879 MU♦

YEAR	TM/L	W	L	PCT	G	GS	CG	SH	SV	IP	H	HR	BB	SO	RAT	ERA	ERA+	OAV	OOB	BH	AVG	PB	PR	/A	PD	TPI
1885	Bal-a	0	0	—	1	0	0	0	0	1	0	0	0	0	0.0	0.00	—	.000	.000	61	.191	0	0	0	0	0.0
1886	Bal-a	0	0	—	1	0	0	0	0	2	4	0	0	1	18.0	9.00	38	.400	.400	55	.205	0	-1	-1	-0	-0.1
Total	2	0	0	—	2	0	0	0	0	3	4	0	0	1	12.0	6.00	56	.308	.308	319	.207	0	-1	-1	-0	-0.1

YEAR TM/L	W	L	PCT	G	GS	CG	SH	SV	IP	H	HR	BB	SO	RAT	ERA	ERA+	OAV	OOB	BH	AVG	PB	PR	/A	PD	TPI

● KEITH MacWHORTER MacWhorter, Keith b: 12/30/55, Worcester, Mass. BR/TR, 6'4", 190 lbs. Deb: 5/10/80

| 1980 Bos-A | 0 | 3 | .000 | 14 | 2 | 0 | 0 | 0 | 42¹ | 46 | 3 | 18 | 21 | 14.0 | 5.53 | 76 | .280 | .359 | 0 | — | 0 | -7 | -6 | 0 | -0.8 |

● LEN MADDEN Madden, Leonard Joseph "Lefty" b: 7/2/1890, Toledo, Ohio d: 9/9/49, Toledo, Ohio BL/TL, 6'2", 165 lbs. Deb: 8/31/12

| 1912 Chi-N | 0 | 1 | .000 | 6 | 2 | 0 | 0 | 0 | 12¹ | 16 | 1 | 9 | 5 | 19.0 | 2.92 | 114 | .302 | .413 | 1 | .250 | 0 | 1 | 1 | -0 | 0.0 |

● MIKE MADDEN Madden, Michael Anthony b: 1/13/58, Denver, Colo. BL/TL, 6'1", 190 lbs. Deb: 4/05/83

1983 Hou-N	9	5	.643	28	13	0	0	0	94²	76	4	45	44	11.6	3.14	108	.231	.325	1	.045	-1	5	3	0	0.2
1984 Hou-N	2	3	.400	17	7	0	0	0	40²	46	1	35	29	17.9	5.53	60	.297	.426	2	.333	1	-9	-10	-1	-1.0
1985 Hou-N	0	0	—	13	0	0	0	0	19	29	1	11	16	18.9	4.26	81	.363	.440	0	—	0	-1	-2	-0	-0.2
1986 Hou-N	1	2	.333	13	6	0	0	0	39²	47	3	22	30	15.7	4.08	88	.297	.383	0	.000	-1	-2	-2	-0	-0.3
Total 4	12	10	.545	71	26	0	0	0	194	198	9	113	119	14.5	3.94	87	.274	.373	3	.081	-1	-7	-11	-1	-1.3

● KID MADDEN Madden, Michael Joseph b: 10/22/1866, Portland, Me. d: 3/16/1896, Portland, Maine TL, 5'7.5", 130 lbs. Deb: 5/06/1887

1887 Bos-N	21	14	.600	37	37	36	3	0	321	317	20	122	81	12.9	3.79	107	.251	.327	32	.242	3	10	10	-2	0.9
1888 Bos-N	7	11	.389	20	18	17	1	0	165	142	6	24	53	9.9	2.95	97	.228	.273	11	.164	2	-2	-1	-3	-0.2
1889 Bos-N	10	10	.500	22	19	18	1	1	178	194	7	71	64	14.2	4.40	95	.269	.348	25	.291	3	-8	-5	0	-0.2
1890 Bos-P	3	2	.600	10	7	5	1	0	62	85	2	25	24	17.1	4.79	92	.313	.387	7	.184	-1	-4	-3	1	-0.3
1891 Bos-a	0	1	.000	1	1	1	0	0	8	10	2	6	6	21.4	6.75	52	.296	.444	2	.667	1	-3	-3	0	-0.1
Bal-a	13	12	.520	32	27	20	1	1	224	239	4	88	56	14.1	4.10	91	.264	.345	29	.271	5	-9	-9	4	-0.2
Yr	13	13	.500	33	28	21	1	1	232	249	6	94	62	14.2	4.19	89	.264	.346	31	.282	5	-12	-12	4	-0.0
Total 5	54	50	.519	122	109	97	7	2	958	987	41	336	284	13.2	3.92	97	.259	.332	106	.245	8	-15	-11	4	-0.0

● MORRIS MADDEN Madden, Morris De Wayne b: 8/31/60, Laurens, S.C. BL/TL, 6' ", 155 lbs. Deb: 6/11/87

1987 Det-A	0	0	—	2	0	0	0	0	1²	4	0	3	0	37.8	16.20	26	.444	.583	0	—	0	-2	-2	-0	-0.2
1988 Pit-N	0	0	—	5	0	0	0	0	5²	5	0	7	3	19.1	0.00	—	.294	.500	0	—	0	2	2	0	0.3
1989 Pit-N	2	2	.500	9	3	0	0	0	14	17	0	13	6	19.3	7.07	47	.327	.462	0	.000	-0	-6	-6	-1	-0.7
Total 3	2	2	.500	16	3	0	0	0	21¹	26	0	23	9	20.7	5.91	58	.333	.485	0	.000	-0	-6	-6	-1	-0.6

● NICK MADDOX Maddox, Nicholas b: 11/9/1886, Govans, Md. d: 11/27/54, Pittsburgh, Pa. BL/TR, 6', 175 lbs. Deb: 9/13/07

1907 Pit-N	5	1	.833	6	6	6	1	0	54	32	0	13	38	8.2	0.83	292	.178	.249	5	.250	2	10	10	-0	1.5
1908 Pit-N	23	8	.742	36	32	22	4	1	260²	209	5	90	70	10.7	2.28	101	.223	.283	25	.266	8	2	1	-1	0.9
1909 *Pit-N	13	8	.619	31	27	17	4	0	203¹	173	2	39	56	11.0	2.21	123	.232	.283	15	.224	4	9	12	-1	1.6
1910 Pit-N	2	3	.400	20	7	2	0	0	87¹	73	0	28	29	10.9	3.40	91	.246	.321	6	.214	1	-4	-3	-0	-0.2
Total 4	43	20	.683	93	72	47	9	1	605¹	487	7	170	193	10.3	2.29	112	.225	.292	51	.244	15	17	19	-2	3.8

● GREG MADDUX Maddux, Gregory Alan b: 4/14/66, San Angelo, Tex. BR/TR, 6', 150 lbs. Deb: 9/03/86 F

1986 Chi-N	2	4	.333	6	5	1	0	0	31	44	3	11	20	16.3	5.52	73	.336	.392	4	.333	1	-6	-5	0	-0.4
1987 Chi-N	6	14	.300	30	27	1	1	0	155²	181	17	74	101	15.0	5.61	76	.294	.374	5	.119	-2	-26	-23	6	-1.8
1988 Chi-N☆	18	8	.692	34	34	9	3	0	249	230	13	81	140	11.6	3.18	113	.244	.309	19	.198	2	7	12	2	1.8
1989 *Chi-N	19	12	.613	35	35	7	1	0	238¹	222	13	82	135	11.7	2.95	128	.249	.317	17	.210	2	15	21	3	3.0
1990 Chi-N	15	15	.500	35	35	8	2	0	237	242	11	71	144	12.0	3.46	118	.265	.321	12	.145	-2	9	16	8	2.4
1991 Chi-N	15	11	.577	37	37	7	2	0	263	232	18	66	198	10.4	3.35	116	.237	.289	18	.205	3	10	15	5	2.6
1992 Chi-N★	20	11	.645	35	35	9	4	0	268	201	7	70	199	9.6	2.18	165	.210	.273	15	.170	2	39	42	6	6.0
Total 7	95	75	.559	212	208	42	13	0	1442	1352	82	455	937	11.6	3.35	115	.249	.312	90	.184	5	47	79	31	13.6

● MIKE MADDUX Maddux, Michael Ausley b: 8/27/61, Dayton, Ohio BL/TR, 6'2", 180 lbs. Deb: 6/03/86 F

1986 Phi-N	3	7	.300	16	16	0	0	0	78	88	6	34	44	14.4	5.42	71	.286	.362	1	.045	-2	-15	-14	-1	-1.6
1987 Phi-N	2	0	1.000	7	2	0	0	0	17	17	0	5	11	11.6	2.65	160	.254	.306	0	.000	-0	3	3	-0	0.2
1988 Phi-N	4	3	.571	25	11	0	0	0	88²	91	6	34	59	13.2	3.76	95	.275	.351	3	.130	-0	-3	-2	1	-0.1
1989 Phi-N	1	3	.250	16	4	2	1	1	43²	52	3	14	26	14.0	5.15	69	.304	.364	0	.000	-1	-8	-8	2	-0.7
1990 LA-N	0	1	.000	11	2	0	0	0	20²	24	3	4	11	12.6	6.53	58	.293	.333	0	—	-0	-6	-7	-0	-0.7
1991 SD-N	7	2	.778	64	1	0	0	5	98²	78	4	27	57	9.7	2.46	154	.221	.278	1	.077	-0	13	15	1	1.6
1992 SD-N	2	2	.500	50	1	0	0	5	79²	71	2	24	60	10.7	2.37	153	.236	.292	1	.111	-0	10	11	2	1.4
Total 7	19	18	.514	189	37	2	1	11	426¹	421	24	142	272	12.1	3.74	99	.261	.325	6	.073	-3	-6	-1	4	0.1

● TONY MADIGAN Madigan, William "Tice" b: 7/1868, Washington, D.C. d: 12/4/54, Washington, D.C. TR, 5'5.5", 126 lbs. Deb: 7/10/1886

| 1886 Was-N | 1 | 13 | .071 | 14 | 14 | 13 | 0 | 0 | 115² | 159 | 3 | 44 | 29 | 15.8 | 5.06 | 65 | .320 | .375 | 4 | .083 | -4 | -22 | -23 | 0 | -2.2 |

● DAVE MADISON Madison, David Pledger b: 2/1/21, Boroksville, Miss. d: 12/8/85, Macon, Miss. BR/TR, 6'3", 190 lbs. Deb: 9/26/50

1950 NY-A				1	0	0	0	0	3	3	1	1	1	12.0	6.00	72	.273	.333	0	—	0	-0	-1	-0	0.0
1952 StL-A	4	2	.667	31	4	0	0	0	78	78	7	48	35	15.0	4.38	89	.264	.374	2	.118	-1	-6	-4	-0	-0.5
Det-A	1	1	.500	10	1	0	0	0	15	16	1	10	7	16.2	7.80	49	.291	.409	0	.000	0	-7	-7	-0	-0.7
Yr	5	3	.625	41	5	0	0	0	93	94	8	58	42	14.8	4.94	79	.265	.370	2	.105	-1	-13	-11	-0	-1.2
1953 Det-A	3	4	.429	32	1	0	0	0	62	76	7	44	27	17.9	6.82	60	.303	.413	1	.091	-1	-19	-19	0	-1.9
Total 3	8	7	.533	74	6	0	0	0	158	173	16	103	70	16.2	5.70	70	.282	.392	3	.100	-2	-33	-30	0	-3.1

● ALEX MADRID Madrid, Alexander b: 4/18/63, Springerville, Ariz BR/TR, 6'3", 200 lbs. Deb: 7/20/87

1987 Mil-A	0	0	—	3	0	0	0	0	5¹	11	1	1	1	20.3	15.19	30	.440	.462	0	—	0	-6	-6	-0	-0.7
1988 Phi-N	1	1	.500	5	2	1	0	0	16¹	15	0	6	2	11.6	2.76	129	.246	.313	0	.000	-0	1	1	-0	0.1
1989 Phi-N	1	2	.333	6	3	0	0	0	24²	32	3	14	13	17.1	5.47	65	.314	.402	0	.000	-0	-5	-5	-1	-0.6
Total 3	2	3	.400	14	5	1	0	0	46¹	58	4	21	16	15.5	5.63	65	.309	.381	0	.000	-1	-11	-10	-1	-1.2

● HECTOR MAESTRI Maestri, Hector Anibal (Garcia) b: 4/19/35, Havana, Cuba BR/TR, 5'10", 158 lbs. Deb: 9/24/60

1960 Was-A	0	0	—	1	0	0	0	0	2	1	0	1	1	9.0	0.00	—	.167	.286	0	—	0	1	1	-0	0.1
1961 Was-A	0	1	.000	1	1	0	0	0	6	6	1	2	2	12.0	1.50	268	.250	.308	0	.000	-0	2	2	-0	0.2
Total 2	0	1	.000	2	1	0	0	0	8	7	1	3	3	11.3	1.13	354	.233	.303	0	.000	-0	3	3	-0	0.3

● BILL MAGEE Magee, William J. b: 1875, Canada BR/TR, 5'10", 154 lbs. Deb: 5/18/1897

1897 Lou-N	4	12	.250	22	16	13	1	0	155¹	186	6	99	44	17.1	5.39	79	.294	.398	13	.210	-2	-19	-19	1	-1.7
1898 Lou-N	16	15	.516	38	33	29	3	0	295¹	294	6	129	55	13.5	4.05	88	.258	.343	14	.126	-9	-15	-16	-2	-2.4
1899 Lou-N	3	7	.300	12	10	6	1	0	71	91	1	28	13	16.2	5.20	74	.311	.388	3	.111	-2	-11	-11	1	-1.0
Phi-N	3	5	.375	9	9	7	0	0	70	82	0	32	4	15.6	5.66	65	.292	.378	5	.161	-2	-14	-15	-1	-1.5
Was-N	1	4	.200	8	7	4	0	0	42	54	3	28	11	19.1	8.57	46	.311	.427	5	.333	1	-22	-22	1	-1.6
Yr	7	16	.304	29	26	17	1	0	183	227	4	88	28	15.8	6.15	62	.297	.375	13	.178	-2	-47	-48	1	-4.1
1901 StL-N	0	0	—	1	1	0	0	0	8	8	0	4	3	13.5	4.50	71	.259	.344	2	.500	1	-1	-1	-0	0.0
NY-N	0	4	.000	6	5	4	0	0	42¹	56	4	11	14	14.7	5.95	56	.316	.362	2	.143	-1	-12	-12	-0	-1.1
Yr	0	4	.000	7	6	4	0	0	50¹	64	4	15	17	14.5	5.72	57	.307	.360	4	.222	1	-13	-14	-0	-1.1
1902 NY-N	0	0	—	2	1	0	0	0	5	5	0	1	2	10.8	3.60	78	.260	.297	0	.000	-0	-0	-0	-0	-0.1
Phi-N	2	4	.333	8	6	6	0	0	53²	61	1	18	15	13.8	3.69	76	.286	.350	4	.211	-0	-5	-5	-0	-0.6
Yr	2	4	.333	10	7	6	0	0	58²	66	1	19	17	13.5	3.68	76	.284	.345	4	.200	-1	-6	-6	-0	-0.7
Total 5	29	51	.363	106	88	69	5	0	742²	837	23	350	161	15.1	4.93	75	.283	.369	48	.169	-13	-99	-102	-0	-10.0

● SAL MAGLIE Maglie, Salvatore Anthony "The Barber" b: 4/26/17, Niagara Falls, N.Y BR/TR, 6'2", 180 lbs. Deb: 8/09/45 C

| 1945 NY-N | 5 | 4 | .556 | 13 | 10 | 7 | 3 | 0 | 84¹ | 72 | 2 | 22 | 32 | 10.2 | 2.35 | 167 | .231 | .286 | 5 | .167 | -1 | 14 | 15 | 0 | 1.5 |

YEAR	TM/L	W	L	PCT	G	GS	CG	SH	SV	IP	H	HR	BB	SO	RAT	ERA	ERA+	OAV	OOB	BH	AVG	PB	PR	/A	PD	TPI
1950	NY-N	18	4	**.818**	47	16	12	**5**	1	206	169	14	86	96	11.6	**2.71**	**151**	.226	.314	8	.121	-1	33	32	3	3.4
1951	*NY-N★	**23**	6	.793	42	37	22	3	4	298	254	27	86	146	10.4	2.93	**134**	**.230**	.289	17	.152	-3	**34**	**33**	1	**3.3**
1952	NY-N☆	18	8	.692	35	31	12	5	1	216	199	16	75	112	11.7	2.92	127	.244	.312	5	.072	-3	20	19	1	1.7
1953	NY-N	8	9	.471	27	24	9	3	0	145^1	158	19	47	80	12.8	4.15	103	.278	.334	13	.271	2	2	2	-2	0.3
1954	*NY-N	14	6	.700	34	32	9	1	2	218^1	222	21	70	117	12.2	3.26	124	.262	.320	8	.127	-2	20	19	0	1.7
1955	NY-N	9	5	.643	23	21	6	0	0	129^2	142	18	48	71	13.4	3.75	107	.278	.344	5	.125	-2	4	4	-2	0.0
	Cle-A	0	2	.000	10	2	0	0	2	25^2	26	0	7	11	11.9	3.86	103	.252	.306	0	.000	-0	0	0	-1	-0.1
1956	Cle-A	0	0	—	2	0	0	0	0	5	6	1	2	2	14.4	3.60	117	.300	.364	0	—	0	0	0	-0	0.0
	*Bro-N	13	5	.722	28	26	9	3	0	191	154	21	52	108	9.9	2.87	**138**	.222	.281	9	.129	-4	19	23	-2	1.9
1957	Bro-N	6	6	.500	19	17	4	1	1	101^1	94	12	26	50	11.0	2.93	142	.245	.300	1	.034	-3	11	14	-1	1.0
	NY-A	2	0	1.000	6	3	1	1	3	26	22	1	7	9	10.4	1.73	207	.227	.286	2	.250	0	6	5	-0	0.6
1958	NY-A	1	1	.500	7	3	0	0	0	23^1	27	3	9	7	13.9	4.63	76	.300	.364	1	.143	1	-2	-3	0	-0.2
	StL-N	2	6	.250	10	10	2	0	0	53	46	14	25	21	12.4	4.75	87	.232	.324	2	.125	-1	-5	-4	-1	-0.5
Total	10	119	62	.657	303	232	93	25	14	1723	1591	169	562	862	11.5	3.15	127	.245	.309	76	.135	-17	156	160	-2	14.6

● MIKE MAGNANTE Magnante, Michael Anthony b: 6/17/65, Glendale, Cal. BL/TL, 6′1″, 180 lbs. Deb: 4/22/91

YEAR	TM/L	W	L	PCT	G	GS	CG	SH	SV	IP	H	HR	BB	SO	RAT	ERA	ERA+	OAV	OOB	BH	AVG	PB	PR	/A	PD	TPI
1991	KC-A	0	1	.000	38	0	0	0	0	55	55	3	23	42	12.8	2.45	168	.262	.335	0	—	0	10	10	-0	1.0
1992	KC-A	4	9	.308	44	12	0	0	0	89^1	115	5	35	31	15.3	4.94	81	.325	.389	0	—	0	-10	-9	2	-0.8
Total	2	4	10	.286	82	12	0	0	0	144^1	170	8	58	73	14.3	3.99	101	.301	.369	0	—	0	0	1	2	0.2

● JIM MAGNUSON Magnuson, James Robert b: 8/18/46, Marinette, Wis. d: 5/30/91, Green Bay, Wis. BR/TL, 6′2″, 190 lbs. Deb: 6/28/70

YEAR	TM/L	W	L	PCT	G	GS	CG	SH	SV	IP	H	HR	BB	SO	RAT	ERA	ERA+	OAV	OOB	BH	AVG	PB	PR	/A	PD	TPI
1970	Chi-A	1	5	.167	13	6	0	0	0	44^2	45	7	16	20	12.5	4.84	81	.263	.330	0	.000	-1	-6	-5	-0	-0.6
1971	Chi-A	1	1	.500	15	4	0	0	0	30	30	0	16	11	14.4	4.50	80	.265	.366	0	.000	-0	-3	-3	-0	-0.4
1973	NY-A	0	1	.000	8	0	0	0	0	27^1	38	2	9	9	15.5	4.28	86	.342	.392	0	—	0	-1	-2	0	-0.1
Total	3	2	7	.222	36	10	0	0	0	102	113	9	41	40	13.9	4.59	82	.286	.358	0	.000	-2	-10	-10	0	-1.1

● JOE MAGRANE Magrane, Joseph David b: 7/2/64, Des Moines, Iowa BR/TL, 6′6″, 225 lbs. Deb: 4/25/87

YEAR	TM/L	W	L	PCT	G	GS	CG	SH	SV	IP	H	HR	BB	SO	RAT	ERA	ERA+	OAV	OOB	BH	AVG	PB	PR	/A	PD	TPI
1987	*StL-N	9	7	.563	27	26	4	2	0	170^1	157	9	60	101	12.0	3.54	117	.245	.320	7	.135	1	10	12	-0	1.3
1988	StL-N	5	9	.357	24	24	4	3	0	165^1	133	6	51	100	10.1	**2.18**	**160**	.217	.280	8	.167	1	23	24	2	3.2
1989	StL-N	18	9	.667	34	33	9	3	0	234^2	219	5	72	127	11.4	2.91	124	.251	.313	11	.138	1	15	19	-1	2.0
1990	StL-N	10	17	.370	31	31	3	2	0	203^1	204	10	59	100	12.0	3.59	106	.264	.322	7	.127	-0	5	5	1	0.7
1992	StL-N	1	2	.333	5	5	0	0	0	31^1	34	2	15	20	14.6	4.02	86	.279	.367	2	.200	1	-2	-2	-0	-0.1
Total	5	43	44	.494	121	119	20	10	0	805	747	32	257	448	11.5	3.11	121	.247	.312	35	.143	4	52	57	2	7.1

● PETE MAGRINI Magrini, Peter Alexander b: 6/8/42, San Francisco, Cal. BR/TR, 6′, 195 lbs. Deb: 4/13/66

YEAR	TM/L	W	L	PCT	G	GS	CG	SH	SV	IP	H	HR	BB	SO	RAT	ERA	ERA+	OAV	OOB	BH	AVG	PB	PR	/A	PD	TPI
1966	Bos-A	0	1	.000	3	1	0	0	0	7^1	8	0	8	3	20.9	9.82	39	.308	.486	0	.000	-0	-5	-5	-0	-0.5

● ART MAHAFFEY Mahaffey, Arthur b: 6/4/38, Cincinnati, Ohio BR/TR, 6′2″, 200 lbs. Deb: 7/30/60

YEAR	TM/L	W	L	PCT	G	GS	CG	SH	SV	IP	H	HR	BB	SO	RAT	ERA	ERA+	OAV	OOB	BH	AVG	PB	PR	/A	PD	TPI
1960	Phi-N	7	3	.700	14	12	5	1	0	93^1	78	9	34	56	10.9	2.31	168	.229	.301	3	.100	-2	15	16	-1	1.5
1961	Phi-N★	11	19	.367	36	32	12	3	0	219^1	205	27	70	158	11.6	4.10	99	.249	.314	8	.127	-2	-2	-1	-2	-0.4
1962	Phi-N★	19	14	.576	41	39	20	2	0	274	253	36	81	177	11.4	3.94	98	.246	.309	13	.141	1	0	-2	-4	-0.5
1963	Phi-N	7	10	.412	26	22	6	1	0	149	143	18	48	97	11.8	3.99	81	.255	.319	10	.200	2	-12	-12	-1	-1.1
1964	Phi-N	12	9	.571	34	29	2	2	0	157^1	161	17	82	80	14.2	4.52	77	.269	.362	6	.120	0	-17	-18	-2	-2.1
1965	Phi-N	2	5	.286	22	9	1	0	0	71	82	11	32	52	15.3	6.21	56	.294	.381	2	.095	-1	-21	-22	-1	-2.4
1966	StL-N	1	4	.200	12	5	0	0	1	35	37	7	21	19	15.2	6.43	56	.276	.378	0	.000	-1	-11	-11	-1	-1.2
Total	7	59	64	.480	185	148	46	9	1	999	959	125	368	639	12.3	4.17	89	.255	.328	42	.134	-2	-47	-50	-11	-6.2

● ROY MAHAFFEY Mahaffey, Lee Roy "Popeye" b: 2/9/03, Belton, S.C. d: 7/23/69, Anderson, S.C. BR/TR, 6′, 180 lbs. Deb: 8/31/26

YEAR	TM/L	W	L	PCT	G	GS	CG	SH	SV	IP	H	HR	BB	SO	RAT	ERA	ERA+	OAV	OOB	BH	AVG	PB	PR	/A	PD	TPI
1926	Pit-N	0	0	—	4	0	0	0	0	4^2	5	0	1	3	13.5	0.00	—	.294	.368	0	.000	-0	2	2	-0	0.1
1927	Pit-N	1	0	1.000	2	1	0	0	0	9^1	9	0	9	4	20.3	7.71	53	.300	.500	2	.400	0	-4	-4	-0	-0.3
1930	Phi-A	9	5	.643	33	16	6	0	0	152^2	186	16	53	38	14.3	5.01	93	.298	.357	7	.119	-5	-6	-6	-1	-1.1
1931	*Phi-A	15	4	.789	30	20	8	0	2	162^1	161	9	82	59	13.6	4.21	107	.258	.347	12	.190	1	3	5	-3	0.2
1932	Phi-A	13	13	.500	37	28	13	0	0	222^2	245	27	96	106	14.0	5.09	89	.274	.348	15	.172	-2	-15	-14	-2	-1.6
1933	Phi-A	13	10	.565	33	23	9	0	0	179^1	198	5	74	66	13.9	5.17	83	.275	.346	14	.215	-0	-18	-18	-2	-1.8
1934	Phi-A	6	7	.462	37	14	3	0	2	129	142	10	55	37	13.8	5.37	82	.276	.347	13	.271	2	-13	-14	-2	-1.2
1935	Phi-A	8	4	.667	27	17	5	0	0	136	153	11	42	39	13.2	3.90	116	.283	.341	9	.176	-2	8	10	-1	0.6
1936	StL-A	2	6	.250	21	9	1	0	1	60	82	6	40	13	18.5	8.10	66	.315	.409	1	.063	-1	-20	-18	-2	-1.8
Total	9	67	49	.578	224	128	45	0	5	1056	1181	84	452	365	14.1	5.01	90	.280	.353	73	.184	-7	-63	-57	-13	-6.9

● LOU MAHAFFEY Mahaffey, Louis Wood b: 1/3/1874, Kentucky d: 10/26/49, Torrance, Cal. 5′9″, 170 lbs. Deb: 4/26/1898

YEAR	TM/L	W	L	PCT	G	GS	CG	SH	SV	IP	H	HR	BB	SO	RAT	ERA	ERA+	OAV	OOB	BH	AVG	PB	PR	/A	PD	TPI
1898	Lou-N	0	1	.000	1	1	1	0	0	9	10	0	5	1	15.0	3.00	119	.279	.367	0	.000	-0	1	1	-0	0.0

● ART MAHAN Mahan, Arthur Leo b: 6/8/13, Somerville, Mass. BL/TL, 5′11″, 178 lbs. Deb: 4/30/40 ♦

YEAR	TM/L	W	L	PCT	G	GS	CG	SH	SV	IP	H	HR	BB	SO	RAT	ERA	ERA+	OAV	OOB	BH	AVG	PB	PR	/A	PD	TPI
1940	Phi-N	0	0	—	1	0	0	0	0	1	1	0	0	0	9.0	0.00	—	.333	.333	133	.244	0	0	0	-0	0.0

● MICKEY MAHLER Mahler, Michael James b: 7/30/52, Montgomery, Ala. BB/TL, 6′3″, 189 lbs. Deb: 9/13/77 F

YEAR	TM/L	W	L	PCT	G	GS	CG	SH	SV	IP	H	HR	BB	SO	RAT	ERA	ERA+	OAV	OOB	BH	AVG	PB	PR	/A	PD	TPI
1977	Atl-N	1	2	.333	5	5	0	0	0	23	31	4	9	14	16.0	6.26	71	.326	.390	3	.500	2	-6	-5	-0	-0.3
1978	Atl-N	4	11	.267	34	21	1	0		134^2	130	16	66	92	13.6	4.68	87	.255	.349	4	.098	-3	-16	-9	-1	-1.4
1979	Atl-N	5	11	.313	26	18	1	0	0	100	123	11	47	71	15.6	5.85	69	.304	.381	3	.111	-1	-24	-20	-0	-2.1
1980	Pit-N	0	0	—	2	0	0	0	0	1	4	1	3	1	63.0	63.00	6	.571	.700	0	—	0	-7	-7	0	-0.6
1981	Cal-A	0	0	—	6	0	0	0	0	6^1	1	0	2	5	4.3	0.00	—	.056	.150	0	—	0	3	3	0	0.3
1982	Cal-A	2	0	1.000	6	0	0	0	0	8	9	0	6	5	16.9	1.13	360	.300	.417	0	—	0	3	3	-0	0.3
1985	Mon-N	1	4	.200	9	7	1	1	1	48^1	40	3	24	32	12.1	3.54	96	.229	.325	3	.188	1	0	-1	-1	-0.1
	Det-A	1	2	.333	3	2	0	0	0	20^2	19	2	4	14	10.0	1.74	234	.241	.277	0	—	0	6	5	-0	0.6
1986	Tex-A	0	2	.000	29	5	0	0	3	63	71	3	29	28	14.7	4.14	104	.295	.377	0	—	0	0	1	-0	0.1
	Tor-A	0	0	—	2	0	0	0	0	1	1	0	0	0	18.0	0.00	—	.200	.333	0	—	0	0	0	0	0.1
	Yr	0	2	.000	31	5	0	0	3	64	72	3	29	28	14.3	4.08	105	.285	.360	0	—	0	1	2	0	0.2
Total	8	14	32	.304	122	58	3	1	4	406	429	40	190	262	14.1	4.68	86	.274	.359	13	.144	-1	-41	-29	-3	-3.1

● RICK MAHLER Mahler, Richard Keith b: 8/5/53, Austin, Tex. BR/TR, 6′1″, 202 lbs. Deb: 4/20/79 F

YEAR	TM/L	W	L	PCT	G	GS	CG	SH	SV	IP	H	HR	BB	SO	RAT	ERA	ERA+	OAV	OOB	BH	AVG	PB	PR	/A	PD	TPI
1979	Atl-N	0	0	—	15	0	0	0	0	22	28	4	11	12	16.0	6.14	66	.311	.386	1	.500	0	-6	-5	-0	-0.5
1980	Atl-N	0	0	—	2	0	0	0	0	3^2	2	0	0	1	4.9	2.45	152	.154	.154	0	—	0	0	1	0	0.1
1981	Atl-N	8	6	.571	34	14	1	0	2	112^1	109	5	43	54	12.3	2.80	128	.258	.328	4	.148	-1	9	10	1	1.0
1982	*Atl-N	9	10	.474	39	33	5	2	0	205^1	213	18	62	105	12.1	4.21	89	.272	.327	11	.190	2	-14	-11	2	-0.8
1983	Atl-N	0	0	—	10	0	0	0	0	14^1	16	0	9	7	15.7	5.02	77	.296	.397	0	.000	-0	-2	-2	-0	-0.2
1984	Atl-N	13	10	.565	38	29	9	1	0	222	209	13	62	106	11.1	3.12	123	.251	.305	21	.296	5	12	18	2	2.8
1985	Atl-N	17	15	.531	39	39	6	1	0	266^2	272	24	79	107	11.9	3.48	111	.268	.322	14	.156	-1	3	11	1	1.2
1986	Atl-N	14	18	.438	39	39	7	1	0	237^2	283	25	95	137	14.4	4.88	81	.301	.367	16	.193	2	-31	-24	2	-2.1
1987	Atl-N	8	13	.381	39	28	3	1	0	197	212	24	85	95	13.7	4.98	87	.283	.357	11	.169	1	-20	-14	2	-1.0
1988	Atl-N	9	16	.360	39	34	5	0	0	249	279	17	42	131	11.9	3.69	100	.282	.317	9	.125	-2	-7	-0	1	-0.1
1989	Cin-N	9	13	.409	40	31	5	2	0	220^2	242	15	51	102	12.4	3.83	94	.282	.329	11	.177	2	-8	-6	-0	-0.5
1990	*Cin-N	7	6	.538	35	16	2	1	4	134^2	134	16	39	68	11.8	4.28	92	.261	.317	4	.114	-1	-7	-5	-0	-0.6
1991	Mon-N	1	3	.250	10	6	0	0	0	37^1	37	2	15	17	12.5	3.62	100	.268	.340	1	.111	-0	0	0	1	0.0
	Atl-N	1	1	.500	13	2	0	0	0	28^2	33	2	13	10	15.1	5.65	69	.282	.364	1	.200	0	-6	-6	0	-0.5
	Yr	2	4	.333	23	8	0	0	0	66	70	4	28	27	13.6	4.50	83	.273	.350	2	.143	-0	-6	-6	1	-0.5

YEAR	TM/L	W	L	PCT	G	GS	CG	SH	SV	IP	H	HR	BB	SO	RAT	ERA	ERA+	OAV	OOB	BH	AVG	PB	PR	/A	PD	TPI
Total	13	96	111	.464	392	271	43	9	6	1951^1	2069	165	606	952	12.5	3.99	96	.275	.332	104	.179	8	-77	-33	10	-1.2
● PAT MAHOMES	Mahomes, Patrick Lavon b: 8/9/70, Bryan, Tex. BR/TR, 6'1", 175 lbs. Deb: 4/12/92																									
1992	Min-A	3	4	.429	14	13	0	0	0	69^2	73	5	37	44	14.2	5.04	80	.279	.368	0	—	0	-9	-8	-1	-1.1
● AL MAHON	Mahon, Alfred Gwinn "Lefty" b: 9/23/09, Albion, Neb. d: 12/26/77, New Haven, Conn. BL/TL, 5'11", 160 lbs. Deb: 4/22/30																									
1930	Phi-A	0	0	—	3	0	0	0	0	4^1	11	0	7	0	37.4	22.85	20	.579	.692	0	.000	0	-9	-9	0	-0.7
● CHRIS MAHONEY	Mahoney, Christopher John b: 6/11/1885, Milton, Mass. d: 7/15/54, Visalia, Cal. BR/TR, 5'9", 160 lbs. Deb: 7/12/10																									
1910	Bos-A	0	1	.000	2	1	0	0	1	11	16	1	5	6	17.2	3.27	78	.327	.389	1	.143	-0	-1	-1	1	-0.1
● MIKE MAHONEY	Mahoney, George W. "Big Mike" b: 12/5/1873, Boston, Mass. d: 1/3/40, Boston, Mass. BR, 6'4", 220 lbs. Deb: 5/18/1897 ♦																									
1897	Bos-N	0	0	—	1	0	0	0	0	1	3	0	1	1	36.0	18.00	25	.511	.582	1	.500	0	-2	-2	0	-0.1
● BOB MAHONEY	Mahoney, Robert Paul b: 6/20/28, LeRoy, Minn. BR/TR, 6'1", 185 lbs. Deb: 5/03/51																									
1951	Chi-A	0	0	—	3	0	0	0	0	6^2	5	1	5	3	13.5	5.40	75	.208	.345	0	—	0	-1	-1	-0	-0.1
	StL-A	2	5	.286	30	4	0	0	0	81	86	7	41	30	14.1	4.44	99	.274	.358	4	.222	-0	-3	-0	-1	-0.1
	Yr	2	5	.286	33	4	0	0	0	87^2	91	8	46	33	14.1	4.52	97	.269	.357	4	.222	-0	-4	-1	-1	-0.2
1952	StL-A	0	0	—	3	0	0	0	0	3	8	0	4	1	36.0	18.00	22	.500	.600	0	—	0	-5	-5	-0	-0.5
Total	2	2	5	.286	36	4	0	0	0	90^2	99	8	50	34	14.8	4.96	88	.280	.369	4	.222	-0	-9	-6	-1	-0.7
● DUSTER MAILS	Mails, John Walter "Walter" or "The Great" b: 10/1/1894, San Quentin, Cal. d: 7/5/74, San Francisco, Cal BL/TL, 6', 195 lbs. Deb: 9/28/15																									
1915	Bro-N	0	1	.000	2	0	0	0	0	5	6	2	5	3	19.8	3.60	77	.333	.478	0	.000	-0	-0	-0	0	0.0
1916	Bro-N	0	1	.000	11	0	0	0	0	17^1	15	1	9	13	12.5	3.63	74	.242	.338	1	.250	0	-2	-2	-0	-0.2
1920	*Cle-A	7	0	1.000	9	8	6	2	0	63^1	54	1	18	25	10.2	1.85	206	.230	.285	4	.200	0	14	14	-1	1.3
1921	Cle-A	14	8	.636	34	24	10	2	2	194^1	210	4	89	87	13.9	3.94	108	.283	.361	6	.094	-4	8	7	-3	-0.1
1922	Cle-A	4	7	.364	26	13	4	1	0	104	122	8	40	54	14.4	5.28	76	.291	.359	5	.161	-0	-14	-15	0	-1.4
1925	StL-N	7	7	.500	21	14	9	0	0	131	145	11	58	49	14.4	4.60	94	.279	.360	6	.133	-2	-5	-4	-1	-0.7
1926	StL-N	0	1	.000	1	0	0	0	0	1	2	0	1	1	27.0	0.00	—	.400	.500	0	—	0	0	0	0	0.1
Total	7	32	25	.561	104	59	29	5	2	516	554	27	220	232	13.7	4.10	100	.277	.352	22	.133	-7	0	0	-5	-1.0
● WOODY MAIN	Main, Forrest Harry b: 2/12/22, Delano, Cal. BR/TR, 6'3.5", 195 lbs. Deb: 4/21/48																									
1948	Pit-N	1	1	.500	17	0	0	0	0	27	35	4	19	12	18.0	8.33	49	.324	.425	0	.000	-0	-13	-13	0	-1.2
1950	Pit-N	1	0	1.000	12	0	0	0	1	20^1	21	2	11	12	14.6	4.87	90	.256	.351	2	.400	1	-2	-1	0	0.0
1952	Pit-N	2	12	.143	48	11	2	0	2	153^1	149	14	52	79	11.8	4.46	90	.253	.314	2	.054	-3	-12	-8	-3	-1.4
1953	Pit-N	0	0	—	2	0	0	0	0	4	5	1	2	4	15.8	11.25	40	.294	.368	0	—	0	-3	-3	-0	-0.3
Total	4	4	13	.235	79	11	2	0	3	204^2	210	21	84	107	13.0	5.14	79	.264	.335	4	.091	-3	-30	-25	-3	-2.9
● ALEX MAIN	Main, Miles Grant b: 5/13/1884, Montrose, Mich. d: 12/29/65, Royal Oak, Mich. BL/TR, 6'5", 195 lbs. Deb: 4/18/14																									
1914	Det-A	6	6	.500	32	12	5	1	3	138^1	131	2	59	55	12.6	2.67	105	.259	.340	4	.100	-2	1	2	4	0.4
1915	KC-F	13	14	.481	35	28	18	2	3	230	181	4	75	91	10.2	2.54	115	.222	.291	15	.197	1	13	10	3	1.5
1918	Phi-N	2	2	.500	8	4	1	1	0	35	30	1	16	14	13.1	4.63	65	.240	.349	1	.091	-1	-7	-6	0	-0.7
Total	3	21	22	.488	75	44	24	4	6	403^1	342	7	150	160	11.3	2.77	105	.236	.313	20	.157	-2	6	6	7	1.2
● JIM MAINS	Mains, James Royal b: 6/12/22, Bridgton, Maine d: 3/17/69, Bridgton, Maine BR/TR, 6'2", 190 lbs. Deb: 8/22/43																									
1943	Phi-A	0	1	.000	1	1	1	0	0	8	9	0	3	4	13.5	5.63	60	.281	.343	0	.000	0	-2	-2	-0	-0.2
● WILLARD MAINS	Mains, Willard Eben "Grasshopper" b: 7/7/1868, N.Windham, Maine d: 5/23/23, Bridgton, Maine TR, 6'2", 190 lbs. Deb: 8/03/1888																									
1888	Chi-N	1	1	.500	2	2	1	0	0	11	8	0	6	5	12.3	4.91	62	.211	.333	1	.143	-0	-3	-2	-0	-0.2
1891	Cin-a	12	12	.500	30	23	19	0	0	204	196	3	107	76	13.9	2.69	153	.244	.342	22	.244	1	23	32	3	3.4
	Mil-a	0	2	.000	2	2	1	0	0	10	14	1	10	2	21.6	10.80	41	.320	.447	3	.600	1	-8	-7	0	-0.5
	Yr	12	14	.462	32	25	20	0	0	214	210	4	117	78	13.8	3.07	135	.245	.335	25	.263	2	16	25	3	2.9
1896	Bos-N	3	2	.600	8	5	3	0	1	42^2	43	1	31	13	16.0	5.48	83	.260	.383	6	.273	-0	-5	-4	-0	-0.4
Total	3	16	17	.485	42	32	24	0	1	267^2	261	5	154	96	14.5	3.53	118	.249	.353	32	.258	2	8	19	3	2.3
● FRANK MAKOSKY	Makosky, Frank b: 1/20/10, Boonton, N.J. d: 1/10/87, Stroudsburg, Pa. BR/TR, 6'1", 185 lbs. Deb: 4/30/37																									
1937	NY-A	5	2	.714	26	1	1	0	3	58	64	6	24	27	13.7	4.97	90	.277	.345	5	.313	1	-2	-3	2	0.0
● TOM MAKOWSKI	Makowski, Thomas Anthony b: 12/22/50, Buffalo, N.Y. BR/TL, 5'11", 185 lbs. Deb: 5/01/75																									
1975	Det-A	0	0	—	3	0	0	0	0	9^1	10	2	9	3	18.3	4.82	83	.278	.422	0	—	0	-1	-1	0	-0.2
● JOHN MALARKEY	Malarkey, John S. "Liz" b: 5/4/1872, Springfield, Ohio d: 10/29/49, Cincinnati, Ohio TR, 5'11", 155 lbs. Deb: 9/21/1894																									
1894	Was-N	2	1	.667	3	3	3	0	0	26	42	1	5	3	16.3	4.15	127	.359	.386	1	.071	-2	3	3	-1	0.0
1895	Was-N	0	8	.000	22	8	5	0	2	100^2	135	3	60	32	18.1	5.99	80	.316	.410	5	.135	-4	-14	-13	-1	-1.5
1896	Was-N	0	1	.000	1	1	0	0	0	7	9	1	3	0	15.4	1.29	343	.309	.374	1	.500	1	2	2	0	0.3
1899	Chi-N	0	1	.000	1	1	1	0	0	9	19	0	5	7	25.0	13.00	29	.426	.494	1	.200	0	-9	-9	0	-0.6
1902	Bos-N	8	10	.444	21	19	17	1	1	170^1	158	0	58	39	11.4	2.59	109	.246	.308	13	.210	2	4	4	2	1.0
1903	Bos-N	11	16	.407	32	27	25	2	0	253	266	5	96	98	13.3	3.09	104	.272	.344	14	.161	-0	5	3	2	0.6
Total	6	21	37	.362	80	59	51	3	3	566	629	10	227	179	13.9	3.64	96	.281	.353	35	.169	-3	-8	-9	2	-0.2
● BILL MALARKEY	Malarkey, William John b: 11/26/1878, Port Byron, Ill. d: 12/12/56, Phoenix, Ariz. BR/TR, 5'10", 185 lbs. Deb: 4/16/08																									
1908	NY-N	0	2	.000	15	0	0	0	2	35	31	1	10	12	10.8	2.57	94	.242	.302	0	.000	-1	-1	-1	-0	-0.2
● CARLOS MALDONADO	Maldonado, Carlos Cesar (Delgado) b: 10/18/66, Chepo, Panama BB/TR, 6'2", 210 lbs. Deb: 9/16/90																									
1990	KC-A	0	0	—	4	0	0	0	0	6	9	0	4	9	19.5	9.00	43	.346	.433	0	—	0	-3	-3	-0	-0.2
1991	KC-A	0	0	—	5	0	0	0	0	7^2	11	0	9	1	23.5	8.22	50	.333	.476	0	—	0	-4	-3	-0	-0.4
Total	2	0	0	—	9	0	0	0	0	13^2	20	0	13	10	21.7	8.56	47	.339	.458	0	—	0	-7	-7	-1	-0.6
● CY MALIS	Malis, Cyrus Sol b: 2/26/07, Philadelphia, Pa. d: 1/12/71, N.Hollywood, Cal. BR/TR, 5'11", 175 lbs. Deb: 8/17/34																									
1934	Phi-N	0	0	—	1	0	0	0	0	3^2	4	0	2	1	14.7	4.91	96	.267	.353	0	—	0	-0	-0	-0	0.0
● MAL MALLETTE	Mallette, Malcolm Francis b: 1/30/22, Syracuse, N.Y. BL/TL, 6'2", 200 lbs. Deb: 9/25/50																									
1950	Bro-N	0	0	—	2	0	0	0	0	1^1	2	0	1	2	20.3	0.00	—	.333	.429	0	—	0	1	1	0	0.1
● ROB MALLICOAT	Mallicoat, Robbin Dale b: 11/16/64, St.Helens, Ore. BL/TL, 6'3", 180 lbs. Deb: 9/11/87																									
1987	Hou-N	0	0	—	4	1	0	0	0	6^2	8	0	6	4	18.9	6.75	58	.320	.452	0	—	0	-2	-2	0	-0.2
1991	Hou-N	0	2	.000	24	0	0	0	1	23^1	22	2	13	18	14.3	3.86	91	.259	.370	0	.000	-0	-0	-1	-1	-0.2
1992	Hou-N	0	0	—	23	0	0	0	0	23^2	26	2	19	20	19.0	7.23	46	.283	.431	0	.000	-0	-10	-10	-0	-1.1
Total	3	0	2	.000	51	1	0	0	1	53^2	56	4	38	42	16.9	5.70	61	.277	.409	0	.000	-0	-12	-13	-1	-1.5
● ALEX MALLOY	Malloy, Archibald Alexander "Lick" b: 10/31/1886, Laurinburg, N.C. d: 3/1/61, Ferris, Tex. BR/TR, 6'2", 180 lbs. Deb: 9/10/10																									
1910	StL-A	0	6	.000	7	6	4	0	0	52^2	47	0	17	27	11.3	2.56	97	.261	.332	1	.063	-1	-0	-1	0	-0.2
● HERM MALLOY	Malloy, Herman "Tug" b: 6/1/1885, Massillon, Ohio d: 5/9/42, Nimishillen, Ohio BR/TR, 6', Deb: 10/06/07																									
1907	Det-A	0	1	.000	1	1	1	0	0	8	13	1	5	6	20.3	5.63	46	.366	.444	1	.250	0	-3	-3	-0	-0.2
1908	Det-A	0	2	.000	3	2	2	0	0	17	20	1	4	8	13.8	3.71	65	.278	.333	3	.333	1	-2	-2	1	-0.1
Total	2	0	3	.000	4	3	3	0	0	25	33	2	9	14	15.8	4.32	57	.307	.371	4	.308	1	-5	-5	1	-0.3

YEAR TM/L	W	L	PCT	G	GS	CG	SH	SV	IP	H	HR	BB	SO	RAT	ERA	ERA+	OAV	OOB	BH	AVG	PB	PR	/A	PD	TPI

● BOB MALLOY Malloy, Robert Paul b: 5/28/18, Canonsburg, Pa. BR/TR, 5'11", 185 lbs. Deb: 5/04/43

1943 Cin-N	0	0	—	6	0	0	0	0	10	14	1	8	4	19.8	6.30	53	.778	.846	2	.667	1	-3	-3	-0	-0.3
1944 Cin-N	1	1	.500	9	0	0	0	0	23¹	22	0	11	4	12.7	3.09	113	.265	.351	0	.000	-1	1	1	0	0.0
1946 Cin-N	2	5	.286	27	3	1	0	2	72	71	2	26	24	12.4	2.75	122	.265	.334	5	.278	1	5	5	-1	0.5
1947 Cin-N	0	0	—	1	0	0	0	0	1	3	1	0	1	27.0	18.00	23	.600	.600	0	—	0	-2	-2	0	-0.1
1949 StL-A	1	1	.500	5	0	0	0	0	9²	6	0	7	2	12.1	2.79	162	.200	.351	0	.000	-0	2	2	0	0.1
Total 5	4	7	.364	48	3	1	0	2	116	116	4	52	35	13.2	3.26	106	.287	.371	7	.226	1	3	3	-1	0.2

● BOB MALLOY Malloy, Robert William b: 11/24/64, Arlington, Va. BR/TR, 6'5", 200 lbs. Deb: 5/26/87

1987 Tex-A	0	0	—	2	2	0	0	0	11	13	6	3	8	13.1	6.55	68	.271	.314	0	—	0	-3	-3	-0	-0.2
1990 Mon-N	0	0	—	1	0	0	0	0	2	1	0	1	1	9.0	0.00	—	.143	.250	0	—	0	1	1	-0	0.1
Total 2	0	0	—	3	2	0	0	0	13	14	6	4	9	12.5	5.54	78	.255	.305	0	—	0	-2	-2	-0	-0.1

● MALONE Malone Deb: 6/20/1872

| 1872 Eck-n | 0 | 3 | .000 | 3 | 3 | 3 | 0 | 0 | 27 | 98 | 1 | 0 | 0 | 32.7 | 11.33 | 31 | .516 | .516 | 5 | .313 | 0 | -23 | -24 | | -1.3 |

● CHUCK MALONE Malone, Charles Ray b: 7/8/65, Harrisburg, Ark. BR/TR, 6'7", 250 lbs. Deb: 9/06/90

| 1990 Phi-N | 1 | 0 | 1.000 | 7 | 0 | 0 | 0 | 0 | 7¹ | 3 | 1 | 11 | 7 | 17.2 | 3.68 | 104 | .130 | .412 | 0 | — | 0 | 0 | 0 | -0 | 0.0 |

● PAT MALONE Malone, Perce Leigh b: 9/25/02, Altoona, Pa. d: 5/13/43, Altoona, Pa. BL/TR, 6', 200 lbs. Deb: 4/12/28

1928 Chi-N	18	13	.581	42	25	16	2	2	250²	218	15	99	155	11.6	2.84	136	.236	.314	18	.189	1	32	28	0	2.9
1929 *Chi-N	22	10	.688	40	30	19	5	2	267	283	12	102	166	13.2	3.57	129	.276	.345	22	.210	2	34	31	-3	2.7
1930 Chi-N	20	9	.690	45	35	22	1	4	271²	290	14	96	142	13.0	3.94	124	.271	.334	26	.248	5	31	28	-2	2.8
1931 Chi-N	16	9	.640	36	30	12	2	0	228¹	229	9	88	112	12.7	3.90	99	.258	.328	17	.215	2	-1	-1	0	0.0
1932 *Chi-N	15	17	.469	37	33	17	2	0	237	222	13	78	120	11.6	3.38	111	.244	.308	14	.179	0	13	10	-3	0.7
1933 Chi-N	10	14	.417	31	26	13	2	0	186¹	186	10	59	72	12.1	3.91	84	.258	.318	10	.159	-2	-12	-13	-1	-1.7
1934 Chi-N	14	7	.667	34	21	8	1	0	191	200	14	55	111	12.2	3.53	110	.270	.322	11	.172	-2	11	7	-1	0.4
1935 NY-A	3	5	.375	29	2	0	0	3	56¹	53	7	33	25	13.9	5.43	75	.252	.357	0	.000	-2	-6	-9	-0	-1.0
1936 *NY-A	12	4	.750	35	9	5	0	9	134²	144	6	60	72	13.9	3.81	122	.273	.352	10	.196	-0	18	13	-2	0.9
1937 NY-A	4	4	.500	28	9	3	0	6	92	109	5	35	49	14.5	5.48	81	.291	.357	1	.030	-4	-9	-11	-2	-1.6
Total 10	134	92	.593	357	220	115	15	26	1915	1934	103	705	1024	12.6	3.74	111	.262	.330	129	.188	-2	112	85	-14	6.1

● CHARLIE MALONEY Maloney, Charles Michael b: 5/22/1886, Cambridge, Mass. d: 1/17/67, Arlington, Mass. BR/TR, 5'8", 155 lbs. Deb: 8/10/08

| 1908 Bos-N | 0 | 0 | — | 1 | 0 | 0 | 0 | 0 | 2 | 3 | 0 | 1 | 0 | 18.0 | 4.50 | 54 | .429 | .500 | 0 | — | -0 | -0 | 0 | 0.0 |

● JIM MALONEY Maloney, James William b: 6/2/40, Fresno, Cal. BL/TR, 6'2", 207 lbs. Deb: 7/27/60

1960 Cin-N	2	6	.250	11	10	2	1	0	63²	61	5	37	48	14.1	4.66	82	.255	.360	2	.111	-0	-6	-6	-0	-0.7
1961 *Cin-N	6	7	.462	27	11	1	0	2	94²	86	16	59	57	13.9	4.37	93	.242	.352	11	.379	4	-4	-3	-1	0.0
1962 Cin-N	9	7	.563	22	17	3	0	1	115¹	90	11	66	105	12.3	3.51	115	.214	.323	8	.186	0	6	7	-1	0.5
1963 Cin-N	23	7	.767	33	33	13	6	0	250¹	183	17	88	265	10.0	2.77	121	.202	.276	15	.169	1	14	16	-2	1.7
1964 Cin-N	15	10	.600	31	31	11	2	0	216	175	16	83	214	10.8	2.71	133	.222	.297	11	.151	1	20	22	-2	2.3
1965 Cin-N★	20	9	.690	33	33	14	5	0	255¹	189	13	110	244	10.7	2.54	148	.206	.295	20	.225	7	28	34	-1	4.6
1966 Cin-N	16	8	.667	32	32	10	5	0	224²	174	18	90	216	11.0	2.80	139	.214	.300	18	.222	3	20	27	-0	3.4
1967 Cin-N	15	11	.577	30	29	6	3	0	196¹	181	8	72	153	11.7	3.25	115	.247	.317	11	.159	-0	3	11	-1	1.1
1968 Cin-N	16	10	.615	33	32	8	5	0	207	183	17	80	181	11.5	3.61	88	.239	.313	18	.243	6	-14	-10	-2	-0.7
1969 Cin-N	12	5	.706	30	27	6	3	0	178²	135	11	86	102	11.2	2.77	136	.208	.302	11	.200	6	16	20	-1	2.7
1970 Cin-N	0	1	.000	7	3	0	0	0	16²	26	3	15	7	23.2	11.34	36	.366	.489	0	.000	-0	-14	-14	-0	-1.2
1971 Cal-A	0	3	.000	13	4	0	0	0	30¹	35	3	24	13	17.8	5.04	64	.294	.417	1	.200	0	-5	-6	-0	-0.6
Total 12	134	84	.615	302	262	74	30	4	1849	1518	138	810	1605	11.5	3.19	115	.224	.310	126	.201	28	64	98	-10	13.1

● PAUL MALOY Maloy, Paul Augustus "Biff" b: 6/4/1892, Bascom, Ohio d: 3/18/76, Sandusky, Ohio BR/TR, 5'11", 185 lbs. Deb: 7/11/13

| 1913 Bos-A | 0 | 0 | — | 2 | 0 | 0 | 0 | 0 | 2 | 2 | 0 | 1 | 0 | 22.5 | 9.00 | 33 | .286 | .500 | 0 | — | 0 | -1 | -1 | -0 | -0.2 |

● GORDON MALTZBERGER Maltzberger, Gordon Ralph "Maltzy" b: 9/4/12, Utopia, Tex. d: 12/11/74, Rialto, Cal. BR/TR, 6', 170 lbs. Deb: 4/27/43 C

1943 Chi-A	7	4	.636	37	0	0	0	14	98²	86	8	24	48	10.2	2.46	136	.236	.287	3	.120	0	9	10	-1	1.1
1944 Chi-A	10	5	.667	46	0	0	0	12	91¹	81	2	19	49	10.0	2.96	116	.235	.277	3	.136	-1	5	5	-1	0.4
1946 Chi-A	2	0	1.000	19	0	0	0	2	39²	30	3	6	17	8.4	1.59	215	.205	.242	0	.000	-0	8	8	-1	0.8
1947 Chi-A	1	4	.200	33	0	0	0	5	63²	61	4	25	22	12.3	3.39	108	.257	.331	1	.143	1	2	2	1	0.3
Total 4	20	13	.606	135	0	0	0	33	293¹	258	17	74	136	10.3	2.70	128	.236	.288	7	.117	0	25	24	0	2.6

● AL MAMAUX Mamaux, Albert Leon b: 5/30/1894, Pittsburgh, Pa. d: 1/2/63, Santa Monica, Cal. BR/TR, 6'0.5", 168 lbs. Deb: 9/23/13

1913 Pit-N	0	0	—	1	0	0	0	0	3	2	0	2	2	12.0	3.00	100	.167	.286	0	.000	-0	0	0	0	0.0
1914 Pit-N	5	2	.714	13	6	4	2	0	63	41	1	24	30	9.6	1.71	155	.186	.272	5	.250	1	8	7	1	1.0
1915 Pit-N	21	8	.724	38	31	17	8	0	251²	182	3	96	152	10.3	2.04	134	.208	.293	15	.163	-2	20	19	-3	1.4
1916 Pit-N	21	15	.583	45	38	26	1	2	310	264	3	136	163	11.9	2.53	106	.239	.327	21	.191	1	3	5	0	0.8
1917 Pit-N	2	11	.154	16	13	5	0	0	85²	92	1	50	22	15.2	5.25	54	.278	.378	7	.226	1	-24	-23	-1	-2.5
1918 Bro-N	0	1	.000	2	1	0	0	0	8	14	0	2	2	18.0	6.75	41	.438	.471	0	.000	-0	-4	-4	1	-0.3
1919 Bro-N	10	12	.455	30	24	16	2	0	199¹	174	2	66	80	11.0	2.66	112	.245	.312	11	.175	0	6	7	-1	0.7
1920 *Bro-N	12	8	.600	41	18	9	2	4	190²	172	9	63	101	11.3	2.69	119	.255	.322	10	.167	-0	9	11	-1	1.0
1921 Bro-N	3	3	.500	12	1	0	0	1	43	36	1	13	21	10.5	3.14	124	.240	.305	2	.182	-0	3	4	1	0.4
1922 Bro-N	1	4	.200	37	7	1	0	3	87²	97	7	33	35	13.6	3.70	110	.290	.358	4	.235	3	4	4	0	0.7
1923 Bro-N	2	0	1.000	5	1	0	0	0	13	20	0	6	5	18.0	8.31	47	.385	.448	1	.500	0	-6	-6	0	-0.5
1924 NY-A	1	1	.500	14	2	0	0	0	38	44	2	20	12	15.4	5.68	73	.308	.396	1	.077	-1	-6	-6	-1	-0.7
Total 12	76	67	.531	254	140	78	15	10	1293	1138	22	511	625	11.7	2.90	104	.245	.325	77	.182	2	13	17	-3	1.9

● HAL MANDERS Manders, Harold Carl b: 6/14/17, Waukee, Iowa BR/TR, 6', 187 lbs. Deb: 8/12/41

1941 Det-A	1	0	1.000	8	0	0	0	0	15¹	13	0	8	7	12.9	2.35	194	.236	.344	0	.000	-1	3	4	-0	0.3
1942 Det-A	2	0	1.000	18	0	0	0	0	33	39	4	15	14	15.0	4.09	97	.307	.385	1	.250	-0	-2	-1	-0	0.0
1946 Det-A	0	0	—	2	0	0	0	0	6	8	1	2	3	16.5	10.50	35	.364	.440	1	.500	-0	-5	-5	-0	-0.4
Chi-N	0	1	.000	2	1	0	0	0	6	11	1	3	4	22.5	9.00	37	.423	.500	0	.000	-0	-4	-4	-0	-0.4
Total 3	3	1	.750	30	1	0	0	0	60¹	71	6	28	28	15.4	4.77	84	.309	.393	2	.167	-0	-7	-5	-1	-0.5

● LEO MANGUM Mangum, Leo Allan "Blackie" b: 5/24/1896, Durham, N.C. d: 7/9/74, Lima, Ohio BR/TR, 6'1", 187 lbs. Deb: 7/11/24

1924 Chi-A	1	4	.200	13	7	1	0	0	47	69	3	25	12	18.2	7.09	58	.359	.436	1	.071	-1	-15	-15	0	-1.5
1925 Chi-A	1	0	1.000	7	0	0	0	0	15	25	0	6	6	18.6	7.80	53	.373	.425	2	.500	1	-6	-6	-0	-0.5
1928 NY-N	0	0	—	1	1	0	0	0	3	6	0	5	1	33.0	15.00	26	.500	.647	1	1.000	0	-4	-4	1	-0.2
1932 Bos-N	0	0	—	7	0	0	0	0	10¹	17	1	0	3	14.8	5.23	72	.333	.333	0	.000	-0	-2	-2	1	-0.1
1933 Bos-N	4	3	.571	25	5	2	1	0	84	93	2	11	28	11.1	3.32	92	.280	.303	2	.091	-2	0	-2	-2	-0.2
1934 Bos-N	5	3	.625	29	3	1	0	0	94¹	127	6	23	28	14.3	5.72	67	.315	.352	9	.281	2	-17	-20	1	-1.6
1935 Bos-N	0	0	—	3	0	0	0	0	4²	6	0	2	0	15.4	3.86	98	.300	.364	0	—	-0	0	-0	0	0.0
Total 7	11	10	.524	85	16	4	1	0	258¹	343	15	72	78	14.5	5.37	68	.318	.362	15	.200	0	-43	-49	4	-4.1

● ERNIE MANNING Manning, Ernest Devon "Ed" b: 10/9/1890, Florala, Ala. d: 4/28/73, Pensacola, Fla. BL/TR, 6', 175 lbs. Deb: 5/03/14

| 1914 StL-A | 0 | 0 | — | 4 | 0 | 0 | 0 | 0 | 10 | 11 | 0 | 3 | 3 | 12.6 | 3.60 | 75 | .297 | .350 | 0 | .000 | -0 | -1 | -1 | 0 | -0.1 |

YEAR TM/L	W	L	PCT	G	GS	CG	SH	SV	IP	H	HR	BB	SO	RAT	ERA	ERA+	OAV	OOB	BH	AVG	PB	PR	/A	PD	TPI

● **JIM MANNING**   Manning, James Benjamin   b: 7/21/43, L'Anse, Mich.   BR/TR, 6'1", 185 lbs.   Deb: 4/15/62

| 1962 Min-A | 0 | 0 | — | 5 | 1 | 0 | 0 | 0 | 7 | 14 | 0 | 1 | 3 | 20.6 | 5.14 | 79 | .389 | .421 | 0 | .000 | -0 | -1 | -1 | 0 | -0.1 |

● **JACK MANNING**   Manning, John E.   b: 12/20/1853, Braintree, Mass.   d: 8/15/29, Boston, Mass.   BR/TR, 5'8.5", 158 lbs.   Deb: 4/23/1873   M♦

1874 Bal-n	4	16	.200	22	20	18	0	0	179²	231	3	10		12.1	3.41	89	.272	.281	59	.351	7	-8	-7		-0.1
1875 Bos-n	15	2	.882	27	17	8	1	7	139²	153	1	14		10.8	2.19	108	.258	.275	94	.274	4	4	3		0.4
1876 Bos-N	18	5	.783	34	20	13	0	5	197¹	213	1	32	24	11.2	2.14	105	.252	.279	76	.264	3	4	2	0	0.3
1877 Cin-N	0	4	.000	10	4	2	0	1	44	81	1	7	6	18.4	6.95	38	.379	.398	80	.317	4	-20	-21	0	-1.6
1878 Bos-N	1	0	1.000	3	1	1	0	0	11¹	24	1	5	2	23.0	14.29	17	.393	.439	63	.254	0	-15	-15	0	-1.1
Total 2 n	19	18	.514	49	37	26	1	7	319¹	384	4	24		11.5	2.87	95	.266	.278	197	.292	11	-4	-5		0.3
Total 3	19	9	.679	47	25	16	0	6	252²	320	3	44	32	13.0	3.53	66	.284	.311	725	.257	11	-32	-34	1	-2.4

● **RUBE MANNING**   Manning, Walter S.   b: 4/29/1883, Chambersburg, Pa.   d: 4/23/30, Williamsport, Pa.   BR/TR, 6', 180 lbs.   Deb: 9/25/07

1907 NY-A	0	1	.000	1	1	1	0	0	9	8	0	3	3	12.0	3.00	93	.240	.321	0	—	-0	-0	-0	-0	-0.1
1908 NY-A	13	16	.448	41	26	19	2	1	245	228	4	86	113	12.2	2.94	84	.256	.334	17	.187	0	-15	-12	-1	-1.5
1909 NY-A	7	11	.389	26	21	11	2	1	173	167	2	48	71	11.7	3.17	80	.265	.326	11	.183	-0	-13	-12	-1	-1.4
1910 NY-A	2	4	.333	16	9	4	0	0	75	80	4	25	25	13.1	3.72	71	.283	.349	5	.192	-0	-10	-9	-1	-1.0
Total 4	22	32	.407	84	57	35	4	2	502	483	10	162	212	12.1	3.14	81	.263	.333	33	.183	-0	-39	-34	-3	-4.0

● **RAMON MANON**   Manon, Ramon (Reyes)   b: 1/20/68, Santo Domingo, D.R.   BR/TR, 6', 150 lbs.   Deb: 4/19/90

| 1990 Tex-A | 0 | 0 | — | 2 | 0 | 0 | 0 | 0 | 2 | 3 | 0 | 3 | 3 | 27.0 | 13.50 | 29 | .333 | .500 | 0 | | 0 | -2 | -2 | 0 | -0.2 |

● **TOM MANSELL**   Mansell, Thomas E. "Brick"   b: 1/1/1855, Auburn, N.Y.   d: 10/6/34, Auburn, N.Y.   BL/TL, 5'8", 160 lbs.   Deb: 5/01/1879   F♦

| 1883 Det-N | 0 | 0 | — | 1 | 1 | 0 | 0 | 0 | 6² | 21 | 2 | 5 | 0 | 35.1 | 18.90 | 16 | .553 | .605 | 29 | .221 | -0 | -12 | -12 | -0 | -0.7 |

● **LOU MANSKE**   Manske, Louis Hugo   b: 7/4/1884, Milwaukee, Wis.   d: 4/27/63, Milwaukee, Wis.   BL/TL, 6',   Deb: 8/31/06

| 1906 Pit-N | 0 | 0 | — | 2 | 1 | 0 | 0 | 0 | 8 | 12 | 0 | 5 | 6 | 19.1 | 5.63 | 48 | .387 | .472 | 0 | .000 | -1 | -3 | -3 | -0 | -0.4 |

● **BARRY MANUEL**   Manuel, Barry Paul   b: 8/12/65, Mamou, La.   BR/TR, 5'11", 180 lbs.   Deb: 9/06/91

1991 Tex-A	1	0	1.000	8	0	0	0	0	16	7	0	6	5	7.3	1.13	358	.143	.236	0	—	0	5	5	1	0.6
1992 Tex-A	1	0	1.000	3	0	0	0	0	5²	6	2	1	9	12.7	4.76	80	.261	.320	0	—	0	-1	-1	-0	0.1
Total 2	2	0	1.000	11	0	0	0	0	21²	13	2	7	14	8.7	2.08	191	.181	.262	0	—	0	5	5	1	0.7

● **MOXIE MANUEL**   Manuel, Mark Garfield   b: 10/16/1881, Metropolis, Ill.   d: 4/26/24, Memphis, Tenn.   BR/TB, 5'11", 170 lbs.   Deb: 9/25/05

1905 Was-A	0	0	—	3	1	1	0	0	10	9	0	3	3	11.7	5.40	49	.242	.315	1	.250	-0	-3	-3	0	-0.3
1908 Chi-A	3	4	.429	18	6	3	0	1	60¹	52	0	25	25	11.8	3.28	71	.251	.338	1	.063	-1	-6	-6	0	-0.8
Total 2	3	4	.429	21	7	4	0	1	70¹	61	0	28	28	11.8	3.58	66	.250	.334	2	.100	-1	-9	-10	0	-1.1

● **DICK MANVILLE**   Manville, Richard Wesley   b: 12/25/26, Des Moines, Iowa   BR/TR, 6'4", 192 lbs.   Deb: 4/30/50

1950 Bos-N	0	0	—	1	0	0	0	0	2	0	0	3	2	13.5	0.00	—	.000	.300	0	—	0	1	1	-0	0.1
1952 Chi-N	0	0	—	11	0	0	0	0	17	25	2	12	6	19.6	7.94	48	.362	.457	1	.500	0	-8	-8	0	-0.7
Total 2	0	0	—	12	0	0	0	0	19	25	2	15	8	18.9	7.11	54	.329	.440	1	.500	0	-7	-7	0	-0.6

● **JOSIAS MANZANILLO**   Manzanillo, Josias (Adams)   b: 10/16/67, San Pedro De Macoris, D.R.   BR/TR, 6', 190 lbs.   Deb: 10/05/91   F

| 1991 Bos-A | 0 | 0 | — | 1 | 0 | 0 | 0 | 0 | 1 | 2 | 0 | 3 | 1 | 45.0 | 18.00 | 24 | .400 | .625 | 0 | — | 0 | -2 | -2 | 0 | -0.2 |

● **RAVELO MANZANILLO**   Manzanillo, Ravelo (Adams)   b: 10/17/63, San Pedro De Macoris, D.R.   BL/TL, 6', 210 lbs.   Deb: 9/25/88   F

| 1988 Chi-A | 0 | 1 | .000 | 2 | 2 | 0 | 0 | 0 | 9¹ | 7 | 1 | 12 | 10 | 19.3 | 5.79 | 69 | .212 | .435 | 0 | — | 0 | -2 | -2 | 0 | -0.2 |

● **ROLLA MAPEL**   Mapel, Rolla Hamilton "Lefty"   b: 3/9/1890, Lee's Summitt, Mo.   d: 4/6/66, San Diego, Cal.   BL/TL, 5'11.5", 165 lbs.   Deb: 8/31/19

| 1919 StL-A | 0 | 3 | .000 | 4 | 3 | 2 | 0 | 0 | 20 | 17 | 0 | 17 | 2 | 16.6 | 4.50 | 74 | .262 | .435 | 1 | .167 | -0 | -3 | -3 | 1 | -0.2 |

● **PAUL MARAK**   Marak, Paul Patrick   b: 8/2/65, Lakenheath, England   BR/TR, 6'2", 175 lbs.   Deb: 9/01/90

| 1990 Atl-N | 1 | 2 | .333 | 7 | 7 | 1 | 1 | 0 | 39 | 39 | 2 | 19 | 15 | 14.1 | 3.69 | 109 | .267 | .363 | 1 | .091 | -0 | 0 | 1 | 1 | 0.2 |

● **GEORGES MARANDA**   Maranda, Georges Henri   b: 1/15/32, Levis, Que., Can.   BR/TR, 6'2", 195 lbs.   Deb: 4/26/60

1960 SF-N	1	4	.200	17	4	0	0	0	50²	50	6	30	28	14.2	4.62	75	.254	.352	2	.167	-0	-5	-6	2	-0.5
1962 Min-A	1	3	.250	32	4	0	0	0	72²	69	11	36	36	13.4	4.46	92	.252	.345	4	.250	-1	-4	-3	1	-0.1
Total 2	2	7	.222	49	8	0	0	0	123¹	119	17	65	64	13.7	4.52	85	.253	.348	6	.214	1	-9	-10	2	-0.6

● **FIRPO MARBERRY**   Marberry, Fredrick   b: 11/30/1898, Streetman, Tex.   d: 6/30/76, Mexia, Tex.   BR/TR, 6'1", 190 lbs.   Deb: 8/11/23   U

1923 Was-A	4	0	1.000	11	4	2	0	0	44²	42	1	17	18	12.5	2.82	133	.258	.339	2	.143	-1	6	5	-0	0.4
1924 *Was-A	11	12	.478	**50**	15	6	0	15	195¹	190	3	70	68	12.4	3.09	131	.262	.335	8	.136	-4	25	21	-1	1.5
1925 *Was-A	9	5	.643	**55**	0	0	0	15	93¹	84	4	45	53	12.8	3.47	122	.246	.341	5	.263	1	**10**	8	1	0.9
1926 Was-A	12	7	.632	**64**	5	3	0	22	138	120	4	66	43	12.3	3.00	129	.243	.336	6	.176	-1	16	13	-1	1.2
1927 Was-A	10	7	.588	56	10	2	0	9	155¹	177	4	68	74	14.4	4.64	88	.296	.371	5	.122	-3	-9	-10	-1	-1.4
1928 Was-A	13	13	.500	**48**	11	7	1	3	161¹	160	4	42	76	11.4	3.85	104	.268	.319	5	.109	-4	3	3	-1	-0.2
1929 Was-A	19	12	.613	**49**	26	16	0	11	250¹	233	6	69	121	**11.1**	3.06	139	.252	**.308**	19	.235	2	33	33	-2	3.1
1930 Was-A	15	5	.750	33	22	9	2	1	185	190	15	53	56	11.8	4.09	113	.270	.321	24	.329	5	12	11	-1	1.3
1931 Was-A	16	4	.800	45	25	11	1	7	219	211	13	63	88	11.4	3.45	124	.252	.307	19	.232	1	23	20	-2	1.9
1932 Was-A	8	4	.667	**54**	15	8	1	13	197²	202	13	72	66	12.6	4.01	108	.268	.333	11	.167	-2	10	7	1	0.6
1933 Det-A	16	11	.593	37	32	15	1	2	238¹	232	13	61	84	**11.1**	3.29	131	.254	**.302**	11	.122	-5	26	27	-3	1.8
1934 *Det-A	15	5	.750	38	19	6	1	3	155²	174	12	46	64	12.8	4.57	96	.276	.327	12	.218	2	-1	-3	-2	-0.2
1935 Det-A	0	1	.000	5	2	1	0	0	19	22	2	9	7	14.7	4.26	98	.289	.365	1	.200	0	-0	-0	0	0.1
1936 NY-N	0	0	—	1	0	0	0	0	0¹	1	0	0	0	27.0	0.00	—	.500	.500	0	.000	-0	0	0	0	0.1
Was-A	0	2	.000	5	1	0	0	1	14	11	2	3	4	9.6	3.86	124	.208	.263	0	.000	-0	2	1	0	0.1
Total 14	148	88	.627	551	187	86	7	101	2067¹	2049	96	686	822	12.1	3.63	116	.262	.325	128	.192	-8	156	136	-12	11.0

● **WALT MARBET**   Marbet, Walter William   b: 9/13/1890, Plymouth Co., Ia.   d: 9/24/56, Hohenwald, Tenn.   BR/TR, 6'1", 175 lbs.   Deb: 6/17/13

| 1913 StL-N | 0 | 1 | .000 | 3 | 1 | 0 | 0 | 0 | 3¹ | 9 | 0 | 4 | 1 | 35.1 | 16.20 | 20 | .500 | .591 | 0 | — | 0 | -5 | -5 | -0 | -0.5 |

● **PHIL MARCHILDON**   Marchildon, Philip Joseph "Babe"   b: 10/25/13, Penetanguishene, Ont., Canada   BR/TR, 5'11", 175 lbs.   Deb: 9/22/40

1940 Phi-A	0	2	.000	2	2	1	0	0	10	12	1	8	4	18.0	7.20	62	.286	.400	0	.000	-0	-3	-3	0	-0.3
1941 Phi-A	10	15	.400	30	27	14	1	0	204¹	188	15	118	74	13.6	3.57	117	.245	.348	11	.167	1	13	14	-3	1.2
1942 Phi-A	17	14	.548	38	31	18	1	1	244	215	14	140	110	13.2	4.20	90	.235	.339	20	.238	3	-15	-12	-3	-1.2
1945 Phi-A	0	1	.000	3	2	0	0	0	9	5	0	11	2	16.0	4.00	86	.179	.410	1	.500	1	-1	-1	0	0.0
1946 Phi-A	13	16	.448	36	29	16	1	1	226²	197	14	114	95	12.5	3.49	101	.237	.332	5	.067	-6	0	1	-2	-0.6
1947 Phi-A	19	9	.679	35	35	21	2	0	276²	228	15	141	128	12.2	3.22	118	.224	.323	15	.153	-2	15	18	-3	1.5
1948 Phi-A	9	15	.375	33	30	12	1	0	226¹	214	19	131	66	13.9	4.53	95	.251	.353	5	.069	-5	-6	-6	-1	-1.2
1949 Phi-A	0	3	.000	7	6	0	0	0	16	24	3	19	2	24.8	11.81	35	.358	.506	1	.167	-0	-14	-14	-0	-1.2
1950 Bos-A	0	0	—	1	0	0	0	0	1¹	1	0	2	0	20.3	6.75	73	.200	.429	0	—	0	-0	-0	0	0.0
Total 9	68	75	.476	185	162	82	6	2	1214¹	1084	81	684	481	13.3	3.93	100	.240	.342	58	.143	-9	-11	-1	-11	-1.8

● **JOHNNY MARCUM**   Marcum, John Alfred "Footsie"   b: 9/9/09, Campbellsburg, Ky.   d: 9/10/84, Louisville, Ky.   BL/TR, 5'11", 197 lbs.   Deb: 9/07/33   ♦

| 1933 Phi-A | 3 | 2 | .600 | 5 | 5 | 4 | 2 | 0 | 37 | 28 | 0 | 20 | 14 | 11.7 | 1.95 | 220 | .200 | .300 | 2 | .167 | 0 | 10 | 10 | 0 | 1.1 |
| 1934 Phi-A | 14 | 11 | .560 | 37 | 31 | 17 | 2 | 0 | 232 | 257 | 13 | 88 | 92 | 13.5 | 4.50 | 97 | .280 | .346 | 30 | .268 | 6 | -3 | -0 | -0 | 0.2 |

YEAR	TM/L	W	L	PCT	G	GS	CG	SH	SV	IP	H	HR	BB	SO	RAT	ERA	ERA+	OAV	OOB	BH	AVG	PB	PR	/A	PD	TPI
1935	Phi-A	17	12	.586	39	27	19	2	3	242^2	256	9	83	99	12.6	4.08	111	.268	.328	37	.311	9	10	13	-3	1.8
1936	Bos-A	8	13	.381	31	23	9	1	1	174	194	14	52	57	12.7	4.81	110	.281	.332	18	.205	1	4	10	0	0.9
1937	Bos-A	13	11	.542	37	23	9	1	3	183^2	230	17	47	59	13.7	4.85	98	.306	.348	23	.267	5	-5	-2	1	0.4
1938	Bos-A	5	6	.455	15	11	7	0	0	92^1	113	11	25	25	13.5	4.09	120	.298	.342	5	.135	-1	7	9	-1	0.7
1939	StL-A	2	5	.286	12	6	2	0	0	47^2	66	12	10	14	14.5	7.74	63	.332	.367	10	.455	3	-17	-15	-0	-1.1
	Chi-A	3	3	.500	19	6	2	0	0	90	125	15	19	32	14.4	6.00	79	.326	.357	16	.281	2	-14	-13	-1	-1.0
	Yr	5	8	.385	31	12	4	0	0	137^2	191	27	29	46	14.4	6.60	72	.327	.359	26	.329	6	-30	-28	-1	-2.1
Total	7	65	63	.508	195	132	69	8	7	1099^1	1269	91	344	392	13.3	4.66	101	.287	.340	141	.265	26	-4	7	-4	3.0

● LEO MARENTETTE Marentette, Leo John b: 2/18/41, Detroit, Mich. BR/TR, 6'2", 200 lbs. Deb: 9/26/65

YEAR	TM/L	W	L	PCT	G	GS	CG	SH	SV	IP	H	HR	BB	SO	RAT	ERA	ERA+	OAV	OOB	BH	AVG	PB	PR	/A	PD	TPI
1965	Det-A	0	0	—	2	0	0	0	0	3	1	0	1	3	6.0	0.00	—	.111	.200	0	—	0	1	1	0	0.1
1969	Mon-N	0	0	—	3	0	0	0	0	5^1	9	1	1	4	16.9	6.75	54	.391	.417	0	.000	-0	-2	-2	0	-0.2
Total	2	0	0	—	5	0	0	0	0	8^1	10	1	2	7	13.0	4.32	83	.313	.353	0	.000	-0	-1	-1	0	-0.1

● JOE MARGONERI Margoneri, Joseph Emanuel b: 1/13/30, Somerset, Pa. BL/TL, 6', 185 lbs. Deb: 4/25/56

YEAR	TM/L	W	L	PCT	G	GS	CG	SH	SV	IP	H	HR	BB	SO	RAT	ERA	ERA+	OAV	OOB	BH	AVG	PB	PR	/A	PD	TPI
1956	NY-N	6	6	.500	23	13	2	0	0	91^2	88	12	49	49	13.5	3.93	96	.254	.346	3	.103	-1	-2	-1	-0	-0.3
1957	NY-N	1	1	.500	13	2	1	0	0	34^1	44	1	21	18	17.3	5.24	75	.314	.407	0	.000	-1	-5	-5	-0	-0.6
Total	2	7	7	.500	36	15	3	0	0	126	132	13	70	67	14.5	4.29	89	.271	.364	3	.081	-2	-7	-6	-1	-0.9

● JUAN MARICHAL Marichal, Juan Antonio (Sanchez) "Manito" b: 10/20/37, Laguna Verde, D.R. BR/TR, 6', 185 lbs. Deb: 7/19/60 H

YEAR	TM/L	W	L	PCT	G	GS	CG	SH	SV	IP	H	HR	BB	SO	RAT	ERA	ERA+	OAV	OOB	BH	AVG	PB	PR	/A	PD	TPI
1960	SF-N	6	2	.750	11	11	6	1	0	81^1	59	5	28	58	9.6	2.66	131	.200	.269	4	.129	0	10	7	0	0.8
1961	SF-N	13	10	.565	29	27	9	3	0	185	183	24	48	124	11.3	3.89	98	.257	.306	7	.119	-2	3	-2	-1	-0.5
1962	*SF-N★	18	11	.621	37	36	18	3	1	262^2	233	34	90	153	11.2	3.36	113	.234	.300	21	.236	4	17	13	-1	1.6
1963	SF-N☆	**25**	8	.758	41	40	18	5	0	**321^1**	259	27	61	248	9.0	2.41	133	.216	.256	20	.179	3	31	28	-3	3.1
1964	SF-N★	21	8	.724	33	33	**22**	4	0	269	241	18	52	206	9.8	2.48	144	.236	.273	14	.144	-1	32	33	1	3.5
1965	SF-N★	22	13	.629	39	37	24	**10**	1	295^1	224	27	46	240	8.3	2.13	**169**	.205	.240	17	.173	1	46	**48**	-0	**5.6**
1966	SF-N★	25	6	**.806**	37	36	25	4	0	307^1	228	32	36	222	**7.9**	2.23	165	**.202**	**.230**	28	.250	6	47	49	0	**6.4**
1967	SF-N★	14	10	.583	26	26	18	2	0	202^1	195	20	42	166	10.6	2.76	119	.249	.288	14	.177	3	14	12	-2	1.4
1968	SF-N★	**26**	9	.743	38	38	**30**	5	0	**326**	295	21	46	218	9.6	2.43	121	.238	.269	20	.163	1	20	19	3	2.8
1969	SF-N☆	21	11	.656	37	36	27	**8**	0	299^2	244	15	54	205	**9.1**	**2.10**	**167**	.222	.263	15	.138	-1	**50**	47	4	5.7
1970	SF-N	12	10	.545	34	33	14	1	0	242^2	269	28	48	123	11.8	4.12	97	.277	.312	5	.059	-6	-2	-4	2	-0.8
1971	*SF-N★	18	11	.621	37	37	18	4	0	279	244	27	56	159	9.8	2.94	116	.233	.274	14	.133	0	16	14	3	1.9
1972	SF-N	6	16	.273	25	24	6	0	0	165	176	15	46	72	12.3	3.71	94	.277	.329	10	.196	1	-5	-4	0	-0.3
1973	SF-N	11	15	.423	34	32	9	2	0	207^1	231	22	37	87	11.7	3.82	100	.277	.309	13	.188	1	-4	-0	4	0.5
1974	Bos-A	5	1	.833	11	9	0	0	0	57^1	61	3	14	21	12.1	4.87	79	.270	.318	0	—	0	-8	-7	-0	-1.0
1975	LA-N	0	1	.000	2	2	0	0	0	6	11	2	5	1	24.0	13.50	25	.407	.500	0	.000	-0	-7	-7	0	-0.6
Total	16	243	142	.631	471	457	244	52	2	3507^1	3153	320	709	2303	10.0	2.89	122	.237	.278	202	.165	11	262	247	9	30.1

● DAN MARION Marion, Donald G. "Rube" b: 7/31/1890, Cleveland, Ohio d: 1/18/33, Milwaukee, Wis. BR/TR, 6'1", 187 lbs. Deb: 4/23/14

YEAR	TM/L	W	L	PCT	G	GS	CG	SH	SV	IP	H	HR	BB	SO	RAT	ERA	ERA+	OAV	OOB	BH	AVG	PB	PR	/A	PD	TPI
1914	Bro-F	3	2	.600	17	9	4	0	0	89^1	97	1	38	41	14.2	3.93	81	.281	.362	7	.194	-1	-7	-7	-1	-1.0
1915	Bro-F	12	9	.571	35	25	15	2	0	208^1	193	1	64	46	11.2	3.20	94	.248	.308	13	.176	-1	-4	-4	-1	-0.6
Total	2	15	11	.577	52	34	19	2	0	297^2	290	2	102	87	12.1	3.42	90	.258	.325	20	.182	-2	-11	-11	-2	-1.6

● DUKE MARKELL Markell, Harry Duquesne (b: Harry Duquesne Makowsky)
b: 8/17/23, Paris, France d: 6/14/84, Ft.Lauderdale, Fla. BR/TR, 6'1.5", 209 lbs. Deb: 9/06/51

YEAR	TM/L	W	L	PCT	G	GS	CG	SH	SV	IP	H	HR	BB	SO	RAT	ERA	ERA+	OAV	OOB	BH	AVG	PB	PR	/A	PD	TPI
1951	StL-A	1	1	.500	5	2	1	0	0	21^1	25	3	20	10	19.0	6.33	69	.298	.433	1	.167	-0	-5	-5	-1	-0.5

● CLIFF MARKLE Markle, Clifford Monroe b: 5/3/1894, Dravosburg, Pa. d: 5/24/74, Temple City, Cal. BR/TR, 5'9", 163 lbs. Deb: 9/18/15

YEAR	TM/L	W	L	PCT	G	GS	CG	SH	SV	IP	H	HR	BB	SO	RAT	ERA	ERA+	OAV	OOB	BH	AVG	PB	PR	/A	PD	TPI
1915	NY-A	2	0	1.000	3	2	2	0	0	23	15	1	6	12	8.2	0.39	749	.185	.241	0	.000	0	7	6	-1	0.7
1916	NY-A	4	3	.571	11	7	3	1	0	45^2	41	0	31	14	15.0	4.53	64	.256	.390	0	.000	-2	-9	-8	-0	-1.1
1921	Cin-N	2	6	.250	10	6	5	0	0	67	75	0	20	23	12.8	3.76	95	.291	.342	3	.125	-1	0	-1	-1	-0.4
1922	Cin-N	4	5	.444	25	3	2	1	0	75^2	75	3	33	34	12.8	3.81	105	.268	.345	3	.150	-0	2	2	-0	0.1
1924	NY-A	0	3	.000	7	3	0	0	0	23^1	29	5	20	7	18.9	8.87	47	.333	.458	0	.000	-1	-12	-12	-1	-1.2
Total	5	12	17	.414	56	21	12	2	0	234^2	235	9	110	90	13.4	4.10	87	.271	.356	6	.087	-4	-12	-14	-3	-1.9

● DICK MARLOWE Marlowe, Richard Burton b: 6/27/29, Hickory, N.C. d: 12/30/68, Toledo, Ohio BR/TR, 6'2", 170 lbs. Deb: 9/19/51

YEAR	TM/L	W	L	PCT	G	GS	CG	SH	SV	IP	H	HR	BB	SO	RAT	ERA	ERA+	OAV	OOB	BH	AVG	PB	PR	/A	PD	TPI
1951	Det-A	0	1	.000	2	1	0	0	0	1^2	5	0	2	1	37.8	32.40	13	.500	.583	0	—	0	-5	-5	-0	-0.5
1952	Det-A	0	2	.000	4	1	0	0	0	11	21	1	3	3	19.6	7.36	52	.420	.453	0	.000	-0	-5	-4	-0	-0.5
1953	Det-A	6	7	.462	42	11	2	0	0	119^2	152	13	42	52	14.7	5.26	77	.319	.377	7	.219	-0	-17	-16	-1	-1.6
1954	Det-A	5	4	.556	38	2	0	0	2	84	76	11	40	39	12.4	4.18	88	.244	.330	3	.167	0	-4	-5	-1	-0.5
1955	Det-A	1	0	1.000	4	1	1	0	1	15	12	1	4	9	9.6	1.80	213	.218	.271	0	.000	-0	4	3	-0	0.3
1956	Det-A	1	1	.500	7	1	0	0	0	11	12	1	9	4	17.2	5.73	72	.279	.404	0	.000	-0	-2	-2	0	-0.2
	Chi-A	0	0	—	1	0	0	0	0	1	2	1	1	0	27.0	9.00	46	.500	.600	0	—	0	-1	-1	-0	-0.1
	Yr	1	1	.500	8	1	0	0	0	12	14	2	10	4	18.0	6.00	69	.298	.421	0	.000	-0	-2	-3	-0	-0.3
Total	6	13	15	.464	98	17	3	0	3	243^1	280	28	101	108	14.2	4.99	78	.295	.364	10	.175	-1	-30	-29	-2	-3.1

● LOU MARONE Marone, Louis Stephen b: 12/3/45, San Diego, Cal. BR/TL, 5'11", 185 lbs. Deb: 5/30/69

YEAR	TM/L	W	L	PCT	G	GS	CG	SH	SV	IP	H	HR	BB	SO	RAT	ERA	ERA+	OAV	OOB	BH	AVG	PB	PR	/A	PD	TPI
1969	Pit-N	1	1	.500	29	0	0	0	0	35^1	24	2	13	25	9.9	2.55	137	.195	.283	0	—	0	4	4	-1	0.3
1970	Pit-N	0	0	—	1	0	0	0	0	2^1	2	1	0	0	7.7	3.86	101	.222	.222	0	—	0	0	0	-0	0.0
Total	2	1	1	.500	30	0	0	0	0	37^2	26	3	13	25	9.8	2.63	134	.197	.279	0	—	0	4	4	-1	0.3

● RUBE MARQUARD Marquard, Richard William b: 10/9/1889, Cleveland, Ohio d: 6/1/80, Baltimore, Md. BB/TL, 6'3", 180 lbs. Deb: 9/25/08 H

YEAR	TM/L	W	L	PCT	G	GS	CG	SH	SV	IP	H	HR	BB	SO	RAT	ERA	ERA+	OAV	OOB	BH	AVG	PB	PR	/A	PD	TPI
1908	NY-N	0	1	.000	1	1	0	0	0	5	6	0	2	2	16.2	3.60	67	.316	.409	0	.000	-0	-1	-1	-0	-0.1
1909	NY-N	5	13	.278	29	21	8	0	1	173	155	2	73	109	12.3	2.60	98	.248	.335	8	.148	-1	-0	-1	-0	-0.3
1910	NY-N	4	4	.500	13	8	2	0	0	70^2	65	2	40	52	13.9	4.46	67	.254	.363	3	.111	-1	-11	-12	-0	-1.4
1911	*NY-N	24	7	**.774**	45	33	22	5	3	277^2	221	9	106	**237**	10.7	2.50	135	.219	.296	17	.163	-1	28	27	-4	2.2
1912	*NY-N	**26**	11	.703	43	38	22	1	1	294^2	286	9	80	175	11.3	2.57	132	.255	.306	21	.219	2	28	27	-3	2.5
1913	*NY-N	23	10	.697	42	33	20	4	3	288	248	10	49	151	9.4	2.50	125	.237	.273	23	.219	2	23	20	-6	1.6
1914	NY-N	12	22	.353	39	33	15	4	2	268	261	9	47	92	10.4	3.06	87	.262	.297	15	.179	-1	-8	-12	1	-1.3
1915	NY-N	9	8	.529	27	20	10	2	2	169	178	8	33	79	11.3	3.73	69	.272	.308	6	.109	-2	-18	-22	-0	-2.6
	Bro-N	2	2	.500	6	3	0	0	1	24^2	29	0	5	13	12.4	6.20	45	.276	.309	1	.125	-0	-9	-9	-0	-1.0
	Yr	11	10	.524	33	23	10	2	3	193^2	207	8	38	92	11.4	4.04	64	.272	.307	7	.111	-3	-28	-31	-0	-3.6
1916	*Bro-N	13	6	.684	36	20	15	2	5	205	169	2	38	107	9.1	1.58	170	.229	.267	9	.143	-1	24	25	-4	2.4
1917	Bro-N	19	12	.613	37	29	14	2	0	232^2	200	5	60	117	10.1	2.55	110	.232	.282	15	.200	0	4	6	-4	0.3
1918	Bro-N	9	18	.333	34	29	19	4	0	239	231	7	59	89	11.0	2.64	106	.260	.307	13	.171	-2	3	4	-2	0.0
1919	Bro-N	3	3	.500	8	7	3	0	0	59	54	1	10	29	9.8	2.29	130	.244	.277	6	.261	1	4	4	-1	0.5
1920	*Bro-N	10	7	.588	28	26	10	1	0	189^2	181	5	35	89	10.3	3.23	99	.251	.287	10	.169	-1	-2	-0	-4	-0.6
1921	Cin-N	17	14	.548	39	35	18	2	0	265^2	291	8	50	88	11.8	3.39	106	.285	.323	19	.200	-1	12	6	-3	0.1
1922	Bos-N	11	15	.423	39	24	7	0	1	198	255	12	66	57	14.6	5.09	79	.322	.374	14	.222	-1	-22	-24	1	-2.2
1923	Bos-N	11	14	.440	38	29	11	3	0	239	265	10	65	78	12.5	3.73	107	.288	.337	12	.140	-6	7	7	0	0.1
1924	Bos-N	1	2	.333	6	6	1	0	0	36	33	3	13	10	11.8	3.00	127	.254	.326	3	.273	0	3	3	-0	0.4
1925	Bos-N	2	8	.200	26	8	0	0	0	72	105	5	27	19	16.5	5.75	70	.341	.394	3	.136	-1	-12	-14	-2	-1.6
Total	18	201	177	.532	536	403	197	30	19	3306^2	3233	107	858	1593	11.2	3.08	103	.260	.310	198	.179	-16	53	36	-31	-1.0

YEAR TM/L	W	L	PCT	G	GS	CG	SH	SV	IP	H	HR	BB	SO	RAT	ERA	ERA+	OAV	OOB	BH	AVG	PB	PR	/A	PD	TPI
● **JIM MARQUIS** Marquis, James Milburn b: 11/18/1900, Yoakum, Tex. d: 8/5/92, Jackson, Cal. BR/TR, 5'11", 174 lbs. Deb: 8/08/25																									
1925 NY-A	0	0	—	2	0	0	0	0	7^1	12	1	6	0	22.1	9.82	43	.414	.514	0	.000	-0	-4	-5	0	-0.4
● **CONNIE MARRERO** Marrero, Conrado Eugenio (Ramos) b: 4/25/11, Las Villas, Cuba BR/TR, 5'7", 158 lbs. Deb: 4/21/50																									
1950 Was-A	6	10	.375	27	19	8	1	1	152	159	17	55	63	12.9	4.50	100	.269	.335	6	.122	-1	1	-0	-3	-0.4
1951 Was-A☆	11	9	.550	25	25	16	2	0	187	198	8	71	66	13.1	3.90	105	.268	.335	10	.164	-2	5	4	-2	0.1
1952 Was-A	11	8	.579	22	22	16	2	0	184^1	175	9	53	77	11.3	2.88	123	.249	.305	5	.079	-5	16	14	-3	0.6
1953 Was-A	8	7	.533	22	20	10	2	2	145^2	130	14	48	65	11.3	3.03	129	.241	.309	6	.125	-2	16	14	-1	1.1
1954 Was-A	3	6	.333	22	8	1	0	0	66^1	74	12	22	26	13.0	4.75	75	.287	.343	0	.000	-1	-8	-9	-1	-1.1
Total 5	39	40	.494	118	94	51	7	3	735^1	736	60	249	297	12.3	3.67	108	.260	.323	27	.114	-11	30	23	-10	0.3
● **BUCK MARROW** Marrow, Charles Kennon b: 8/29/09, Tarboro, N.C. d: 11/21/82, Newport News, Va. BR/TR, 6'4", 200 lbs. Deb: 7/03/32																									
1932 Det-A	2	5	.286	18	7	2	0	1	63^2	70	6	29	31	14.8	4.81	98	.278	.366	3	.158	-0	-2	-1	1	0.0
1937 Bro-N	1	2	.333	6	3	1	0	0	16^1	19	2	9	2	15.4	6.61	61	.284	.368	0	.000	-1	-5	-5	0	-0.5
1938 Bro-N	0	1	.000	15	0	0	0	0	19^2	23	1	11	6	16.9	4.58	85	.291	.398	0	.000	-0	-2	-1	0	-0.1
Total 3	3	8	.273	39	10	3	0	1	99^2	112	9	49	39	15.4	5.06	88	.281	.373	3	.120	-1	-9	-7	1	-0.6
● **ED MARS** Mars, Edward M. b: 12/4/1866, Chicago, Ill. d: 12/9/41, Chicago, Ill. 5'9", 166 lbs. Deb: 8/12/1890																									
1890 Syr-a	9	5	.643	16	14	14	0	0	121^1	132	2	49	59	13.8	4.67	76	.269	.341	14	.275	4	-11	-15	1	-0.9
● **CUDDLES MARSHALL** Marshall, Clarence Westly b: 4/28/25, Bellingham, Wash. BR/TR, 6'3", 200 lbs. Deb: 4/24/46																									
1946 NY-A	3	4	.429	23	11	1	0	0	81	96	4	56	32	16.9	5.33	65	.308	.413	4	.143	-1	-16	-17	1	-1.7
1948 NY-A	0	0	—	1	0	0	0	0	1	0	0	3	0	27.0	0.00	—	.000	.500	0	—	0	0	0	-0	0.0
1949 NY-A	3	0	1.000	21	2	0	0	3	49^1	48	3	48	13	17.9	5.11	79	.259	.417	1	.111	-0	-5	-6	1	-0.5
1950 StL-A	1	3	.250	28	2	0	0	1	53^2	72	1	51	24	20.8	7.88	63	.321	.449	4	.333	0	-20	-17	-1	-1.7
Total 4	7	7	.500	73	15	1	0	4	185	216	8	158	69	18.3	5.98	67	.298	.426	9	.184	-0	-41	-40	0	-3.9
● **MIKE MARSHALL** Marshall, Michael Grant b: 1/15/43, Adrian, Mich. BR/TR, 5'10", 180 lbs. Deb: 5/31/67																									
1967 Det-A	1	3	.250	37	0	0	0	10	59	51	6	20	41	11.1	1.98	165	.233	.303	2	.222	0	8	8	1	1.0
1969 Sea-A	3	10	.231	20	14	3	1	0	87^2	99	8	35	47	14.0	5.13	71	.281	.350	7	.259	3	-15	-15	3	-0.9
1970 Hou-N	0	1	.000	4	0	0	0	0	5^1	8	0	4	5	21.9	8.44	46	.400	.520	0	—	0	-3	-3	1	-0.2
Mon-N	3	7	.300	24	5	0	0	3	64^2	56	4	29	38	11.8	3.48	118	.225	.306	1	.091	0	4	5	2	0.6
Yr	3	8	.273	28	5	0	0	3	70	64	4	33	43	12.5	3.86	106	.237	.320	1	.091	0	1	2	2	0.4
1971 Mon-N	5	8	.385	66	0	0	0	23	111^1	100	9	50	85	12.4	4.28	82	.247	.336	3	.188	0	-10	-9	3	-0.6
1972 Mon-N	14	8	.636	**65**	0	0	0	18	116	82	3	47	95	10.2	1.78	199	.202	.289	3	.136	0	**22**	**23**	0	2.5
1973 Mon-N	14	11	.560	**92**	0	0	0	**31**	179	163	10	75	124	12.2	2.66	143	.252	.333	8	.242	1	20	**23**	3	2.9
1974 *LA-N★	15	12	.556	**106**	0	0	0	**21**	208^1	191	9	56	143	10.7	2.42	141	.247	.299	8	.235	1	**28**	**23**	1	2.5
1975 LA-N☆	9	14	.391	57	0	0	0	13	109^1	98	8	39	64	11.6	3.29	103	.242	.315	1	.067	-1	4	1	2	0.2
1976 LA-N	4	3	.571	30	0	0	0	8	62^2	64	2	25	39	12.9	4.45	76	.270	.342	0	.000	0	-7	-7	2	-0.6
Atl-N	2	1	.667	24	0	0	0	6	36^2	35	4	14	17	12.3	3.19	119	.259	.333	1	.167	0	1	2	0	0.3
Yr	6	4	.600	54	0	0	0	14	99^1	99	6	39	56	12.6	3.99	89	.264	.335	1	.091	1	-5	-5	2	-0.3
1977 Atl-N	1	0	1.000	4	0	0	0	0	6	12	1	2	6	21.0	9.00	49	.400	.438	1	1.000	0	-3	-3	-0	-0.3
Tex-A	2	2	.500	12	4	0	0	1	35^2	42	0	13	18	14.4	4.04	101	.304	.373	0	—	0	0	0	0	0.0
1978 Min-A	10	12	.455	54	0	0	0	21	99	80	3	37	56	10.7	2.45	156	.225	.300	0	—	0	14	15	1	1.6
1979 Min-A	10	15	.400	**90**	1	0	0	**32**	142^2	132	8	48	81	11.6	2.65	165	.254	.322	0	—	0	25	27	3	2.7
1980 Min-A	1	3	.250	18	0	0	0	1	32^1	42	2	12	13	15.6	6.12	71	.323	.389	0	—	0	-8	-6	1	-1.0
1981 NY-N	3	2	.600	20	0	0	0	0	31	26	2	8	8	9.9	2.61	133	.224	.274	0	—	0	3	3	-0	0.4
Total 14	97	112	.464	723	24	3	1	188	1386^2	1281	79	514	880	11.9	3.14	118	.249	.321	35	.196	6	84	87	20	11.1
● **RUBE MARSHALL** Marshall, Roy De Verne "Cy" b: 1/19/1890, Salineville, Ohio d: 6/11/80, Dover, Ohio BR/TR, 5'11", 170 lbs. Deb: 9/28/12																									
1912 Phi-N	0	1	.000	2	1	0	0	0	3	12	0	1	2	39.0	21.00	17	.632	.650	0	—	0	-6	-6	0	-0.5
1913 Phi-N	0	1	.000	14	3	0	0	1	45^1	54	2	22	18	15.3	4.57	73	.297	.376	1	.091	-1	-7	-6	0	-0.7
1914 Phi-N	6	7	.462	27	19	7	0	1	134^1	144	2	50	49	13.3	3.75	78	.279	.349	6	.140	-2	-14	-12	1	-1.4
1915 Buf-F	2	1	.667	21	4	2	0	0	59^1	62	1	33	21	14.7	3.94	79	.281	.379	5	.294	1	-6	-5	-1	-0.6
Total 4	8	10	.444	64	27	9	0	2	242	272	5	106	90	14.4	4.17	74	.290	.367	12	.169	-2	-33	-30	-0	-3.2
● **PHONNEY MARTIN** Martin, Alphonse Case b: 8/4/1845, New York, N.Y. d: 5/24/33, Hollis, N.Y. 5'7", 148 lbs. Deb: 4/26/1872 ♦																									
1872 Tro-n	1	2	.333	8	3	0	0	0	37^1	73	0	2	1	18.1	5.79	64	.365	.371	34	.283	0	-9	-9		-0.6
Eck-n	2	7	.222	10	9	9	0	0	85	142	1	4	2	15.5	4.45	78	.318	.324	14	.177	-2	-7	-9		-0.7
Yr	3	9	.250	18	12	9	0	0	122^1	215	1	6	3	16.3	4.86	73	.332	.338	48	.241	-2	-15	-18		-1.3
1873 Mut-n	0	1	.000	6	1	1	0	0	34	50	0	7	1	15.1	3.44	92	.294	.322	30	.216	-1	-1	-1		-0.1
Total 2 n	3	10	.231	24	13	10	0	0	156^1	265	1	13	4	16.0	4.55	70	.324	.335	78	.231	-2	-23	-24		-1.4
● **BARNEY MARTIN** Martin, Barnes Robertson b: 3/3/23, Columbia, S.C. BR/TR, 5'11", 170 lbs. Deb: 4/22/53 F																									
1953 Cin-N	0	0	—	1	0	0	0	0	2	3	0	1	1	18.0	9.00	48	.333	.400	0	—	0	-1	-1	-0	-0.1
● **RENIE MARTIN** Martin, Donald Renie b: 8/30/55, Dover, Del. BR/TR, 6'4", 190 lbs. Deb: 5/09/79																									
1979 KC-A	0	3	.000	25	0	0	0	5	34^2	32	1	14	25	12.2	5.19	82	.248	.326	0	—	0	-4	-4	1	-0.4
1980 *KC-A	10	10	.500	32	20	2	0	2	137^1	133	18	70	68	13.4	4.39	92	.255	.345	0	—	0	-5	-5	-0	-0.6
1981 *KC-A	4	5	.444	29	0	0	0	4	61^2	55	2	29	25	12.3	2.77	130	.244	.331	0	—	0	6	6	1	0.7
1982 SF-N	7	10	.412	29	25	1	0	0	141^1	148	14	64	63	13.5	4.65	77	.274	.350	13	.265	3	-16	-17	1	-1.3
1983 SF-N	2	4	.333	37	6	0	0	1	94^1	95	11	51	43	14.2	4.20	84	.268	.365	9	.346	4	-6	-7	1	-0.1
1984 SF-N	1	1	.500	12	0	0	0	0	23^1	29	2	16	8	17.4	3.86	91	.305	.405	3	.500	1	-1	-1	1	0.1
Phi-N	0	2	.000	9	0	0	0	0	15^2	17	2	12	5	16.7	4.60	79	.274	.392	0	.000	-0	-2	-2	1	-0.1
Yr	1	3	.250	21	0	0	0	0	39	46	4	28	13	17.1	4.15	86	.293	.400	3	.375	1	-2	-3	2	0.0
Total 6	24	35	.407	173	51	3	0	12	508^1	509	50	256	237	13.6	4.27	88	.264	.352	25	.301	8	-28	-29	5	-1.7
● **SPEED MARTIN** Martin, Elwood Good b: 9/15/1893, Wawawai, Wash. d: 6/14/83, Lemon Grove, Cal. BR/TR, 6', 165 lbs. Deb: 7/05/17																									
1917 StL-A	0	2	.000	9	2	0	0	0	15^2	20	0	5	5	14.4	5.74	45	.339	.391	0	.000	-0	-5	-5	1	-0.5
1918 Chi-N	5	2	.714	9	5	4	1	1	53^2	47	0	14	16	10.4	1.84	151	.246	.301	3	.188	-0	5	6	1	0.7
1919 Chi-N	8	8	.500	35	14	7	2	2	163^2	158	2	52	54	11.8	2.47	116	.259	.321	8	.182	-1	8	7	2	0.9
1920 Chi-N	4	15	.211	35	13	6	0	2	136	165	2	50	44	14.3	4.83	66	.305	.365	7	.159	-1	-26	-25	1	-2.4
1921 Chi-N	11	15	.423	37	28	13	1	1	217^1	245	12	68	86	13.0	4.35	88	.298	.353	17	.233	1	-14	-13	2	-0.9
1922 Chi-N	1	0	1.000	1	1	0	0	0	6	10	0	2	2	18.0	7.50	56	.385	.429	0	.000	0	-2	-2	-0	-0.2
Total 6	29	42	.408	126	63	30	4	6	592^1	645	16	191	207	12.8	3.78	87	.287	.344	35	.194	-0	-33	-32	7	-2.4
● **FRED MARTIN** Martin, Fred Turner b: 6/27/15, Williams, Okla. d: 6/11/79, Chicago, Ill. BR/TR, 6'1", 185 lbs. Deb: 4/21/46 C																									
1946 StL-N	2	1	.667	6	3	2	0	0	28^2	29	0	8	19	11.6	4.08	85	.254	.303	3	.273	0	-2	-2	0	-0.1
1949 StL-N	6	0	1.000	21	5	3	0	0	70	65	3	20	30	10.9	2.44	170	.243	.295	6	.300	1	12	13	0	1.5
1950 StL-N	4	2	.667	30	2	0	0	0	63^1	87	4	30	19	16.8	5.12	84	.331	.401	4	.267	1	-7	-6	1	-0.4
Total 3	12	3	.800	57	10	5	0	0	162	181	7	58	68	13.3	3.78	108	.281	.341	13	.283	2	3	6	1	1.0
● **DOC MARTIN** Martin, Harold Winthrop b: 9/23/1887, Roxbury, Mass. d: 4/14/35, Milton, Mass. BR/TR, 5'11", 165 lbs. Deb: 10/07/08																									
1908 Phi-A	0	1	.000	1	1	0	0	0	2	2	0	3	2	27.0	13.50	19	.286	.545	0	.000	-0	-2	-2	-0	-0.3
1911 Phi-A	1	1	.500	11	3	1	0	0	38	40	1	17	21	14.7	4.50	70	.272	.367	3	.214	0	-5	-6	0	-0.5

YEAR	TM/L	W	L	PCT	G	GS	CG	SH	SV	IP	H	HR	BB	SO	RAT	ERA	ERA+	OAV	OOB	BH	AVG	PB	PR	/A	PD	TPI
1912	Phi-A	0	0	—	2	0	0	0	0	4^1	5	0	5	4	22.8	10.38	30	.333	.524	0	.000	-0	-3	-4	0	-0.3
Total	3	1	2	.333	14	4	1	0	0	44^1	47	1	25	27	16.0	5.48	57	.278	.393	3	.167	-0	-11	-12	1	-1.1

● PEPPER MARTIN Martin, John Leonard Roosevelt "The Wild Horse Of The Osage"
b: 2/29/04, Temple, Okla. d: 3/5/65, McAlester, Okla. BR/TR, 5'8", 170 lbs. Deb: 4/16/28 C♦

YEAR	TM/L	W	L	PCT	G	GS	CG	SH	SV	IP	H	HR	BB	SO	RAT	ERA	ERA+	OAV	OOB	BH	AVG	PB	PR	/A	PD	TPI
1934	*StL-N★	0	0	—	1	0	0	0	0	2	1	0	0	0	4.5	4.50	94	.167	.167	131	.289	0	-0	-0	0	0.0
1936	StL-N	0	0	—	1	0	0	0	0	2	1	0	2	0	13.5	0.00	—	.200	.429	177	.309	0	1	1	-0	0.1
Total	2	0	0	—	2	0	0	0	0	4	2	0	2	0	9.0	2.25	181	.182	.308	1227	.298	1	1	1	0	0.1

● JOHN MARTIN Martin, John Robert b: 4/11/56, Wyandotte, Mich. BB/TL, 6', 190 lbs. Deb: 8/27/80

YEAR	TM/L	W	L	PCT	G	GS	CG	SH	SV	IP	H	HR	BB	SO	RAT	ERA	ERA+	OAV	OOB	BH	AVG	PB	PR	/A	PD	TPI
1980	StL-N	2	3	.400	9	5	1	0	0	42	39	1	9	23	10.3	4.29	86	.247	.287	3	.273	1	-3	-3	-1	-0.3
1981	StL-N	8	5	.615	17	15	4	0	0	102^2	85	10	26	36	9.9	3.42	104	.228	.283	7	.212	2	1	2	0	0.4
1982	StL-N	4	5	.444	24	7	0	0	0	66	56	6	30	21	11.7	4.23	86	.230	.314	1	.091	-0	-5	-4	-1	-0.6
1983	StL-N	3	1	.750	26	5	0	0	0	66^1	60	6	26	29	11.9	3.53	103	.242	.319	4	.222	1	1	1	1	0.2
	Det-A	0	0	—	15	0	0	0	1	13^1	15	2	4	11	12.8	7.43	53	.294	.345	0	—	0	-5	-5	0	-0.5
Total	4	17	14	.548	91	32	5	0	1	290^1	255	25	95	120	11.0	3.94	92	.238	.302	15	.205	3	-11	-10	-1	-0.8

● MORRIE MARTIN Martin, Morris Webster "Lefty" b: 9/3/22, Dixon, Mo. BL/TL, 6', 180 lbs. Deb: 4/25/49

YEAR	TM/L	W	L	PCT	G	GS	CG	SH	SV	IP	H	HR	BB	SO	RAT	ERA	ERA+	OAV	OOB	BH	AVG	PB	PR	/A	PD	TPI
1949	Bro-N	1	3	.250	10	4	0	0	0	30^2	39	5	15	15	16.4	7.04	58	.320	.403	2	.200	-0	-10	-10	0	-1.0
1951	Phi-A	11	4	.733	35	13	3	1	0	138	139	13	63	35	13.5	3.78	113	.259	.343	11	.220	-1	5	8	2	0.8
1952	Phi-A	0	2	.000	5	5	0	0	0	25^1	32	1	15	13	17.4	6.39	62	.302	.398	1	.111	-1	-8	-7	-0	-0.8
1953	Phi-A	10	12	.455	58	11	2	0	7	156^1	158	12	59	64	13.0	4.43	97	.262	.336	4	.095	-4	-8	-3	-0	-0.7
1954	Phi-A	2	4	.333	13	6	2	0	0	52^2	57	9	19	24	13.3	5.47	71	.278	.345	4	.235	0	-10	-9	-0	-0.9
	Chi-A	5	4	.556	35	2	1	0	5	70	52	5	24	31	9.9	2.06	182	.210	.282	2	.133	-0	13	13	-1	1.3
	Yr	7	8	.467	48	8	3	0	5	122^2	109	14	43	55	11.2	3.52	108	.237	.304	6	.188	-0	3	4	-1	0.4
1955	Chi-A	2	3	.400	37	0	0	0	2	52	50	4	20	22	12.5	3.63	109	.259	.335	3	.300	0	2	2	1	0.3
1956	Chi-A	1	0	1.000	10	0	0	0	0	18^1	21	1	7	9	13.7	4.91	84	.292	.354	1	.200	0	-2	-2	0	-0.1
	Bal-A	1	1	.500	9	0	0	0	0	5	10	1	2	3	23.4	10.80	36	.400	.464	0	—	0	-4	-4	-0	-0.4
	Yr	2	1	.667	19	0	0	0	0	23^1	31	2	9	12	15.8	6.17	66	.316	.380	1	.200	0	-5	-5	0	-0.5
1957	StL-N	0	0	—	4	1	0	0	0	10^2	5	0	4	7	8.4	2.53	157	.143	.250	0	.000	-0	2	2	0	0.2
1958	StL-N	3	1	.750	17	0	0	0	0	24^2	19	3	12	16	12.0	4.74	87	.211	.317	0	.000	-1	-2	-2	-0	-0.3
	Cle-A	2	0	1.000	14	0	0	0	1	18^2	20	0	8	5	13.5	2.41	151	.294	.368	0	—	0	3	3	-0	0.2
1959	Chi-N	0	0	—	3	0	0	0	0	2^1	5	2	1	1	27.0	19.29	20	.455	.538	0	—	0	-4	-4	0	-0.4
Total	10	38	34	.528	250	42	8	1	15	604^2	607	56	249	245	13.1	4.29	95	.262	.341	28	.170	-6	-23	-13	1	-1.8

● PAT MARTIN Martin, Patrick Francis b: 4/13/1892, Brooklyn, N.Y. d: 2/4/49, Brooklyn, N.Y. BL/TL, 5'11.5", 170 lbs. Deb: 9/20/19

YEAR	TM/L	W	L	PCT	G	GS	CG	SH	SV	IP	H	HR	BB	SO	RAT	ERA	ERA+	OAV	OOB	BH	AVG	PB	PR	/A	PD	TPI
1919	Phi-A	0	2	.000	2	2	1	0	0	11	11	0	8	6	15.5	4.09	84	.256	.373	0	.000	-0	-1	-1	-0	-0.2
1920	Phi-A	1	4	.200	8	5	2	0	0	32^1	48	2	25	14	21.4	6.12	66	.364	.478	4	.400	1	-8	-8	-1	-0.7
Total	2	1	6	.143	10	7	3	0	0	43^1	59	2	33	20	19.9	5.61	69	.337	.453	4	.308	1	-9	-8	-1	-0.9

● PAUL MARTIN Martin, Paul Charles b: 3/10/32, Brownstone, Pa. BR/TR, 6'6", 235 lbs. Deb: 7/02/55

YEAR	TM/L	W	L	PCT	G	GS	CG	SH	SV	IP	H	HR	BB	SO	RAT	ERA	ERA+	OAV	OOB	BH	AVG	PB	PR	/A	PD	TPI
1955	Pit-N	0	1	.000	7	1	0	0	0	7	13	0	17	3	39.9	14.14	29	.464	.674	0	—	0	-8	-8	-0	-0.7

● RAY MARTIN Martin, Raymond Joseph b: 3/13/25, Norwood, Mass. BR/TR, 6'2", 177 lbs. Deb: 8/15/43

YEAR	TM/L	W	L	PCT	G	GS	CG	SH	SV	IP	H	HR	BB	SO	RAT	ERA	ERA+	OAV	OOB	BH	AVG	PB	PR	/A	PD	TPI
1943	Bos-N	0	0	—	2	0	0	0	0	3^1	3	0	1	1	10.8	8.10	42	.231	.286	0	.000	-0	-2	-2	0	-0.2
1947	Bos-N	1	0	1.000	1	1	1	0	0	9	7	0	4	2	11.0	1.00	389	.212	.297	0	.000	-0	3	3	0	0.4
1948	Bos-N	0	0	—	2	0	0	0	0	2^1	0	0	1	0	3.9	0.00	—	.000	.125	0	—	0	1	1	-0	0.1
Total	3	1	0	1.000	5	1	1	0	0	14^2	10	0	6	3	9.8	2.45	154	.189	.271	0	.000	-0	2	2	1	0.3

● JOE MARTINA Martina, Joseph John "Oyster Joe" b: 7/8/1889, New Orleans, La. d: 3/22/62, New Orleans, La. BR/TR, 6', 183 lbs. Deb: 4/19/24

YEAR	TM/L	W	L	PCT	G	GS	CG	SH	SV	IP	H	HR	BB	SO	RAT	ERA	ERA+	OAV	OOB	BH	AVG	PB	PR	/A	PD	TPI
1924	*Was-A	6	8	.429	24	13	8	0	0	125^1	129	7	56	57	13.7	4.67	86	.271	.355	14	.326	3	-6	-9	-2	-0.7

● ALFREDO MARTINEZ Martinez, Alfredo b: 3/15/57, Los Angeles, Cal. BR/TR, 6'3", 185 lbs. Deb: 4/20/80

YEAR	TM/L	W	L	PCT	G	GS	CG	SH	SV	IP	H	HR	BB	SO	RAT	ERA	ERA+	OAV	OOB	BH	AVG	PB	PR	/A	PD	TPI
1980	Cal-A	7	9	.438	30	23	4	1	0	149^1	150	14	59	57	12.7	4.52	87	.259	.328	0	—	0	-8	-10	-2	-1.0
1981	Cal-A	0	0	—	2	0	0	0	0	6	5	1	3	4	12.0	3.00	122	.227	.320	0	—	0	0	0	0	0.1
Total	2	7	9	.438	32	23	4	1	0	155^1	155	15	62	61	12.6	4.46	88	.257	.328	0	—	0	-8	-9	-2	-0.9

● DAVE MARTINEZ Martinez, David b: 9/26/64, New York, N.Y. BL/TL, 5'10", 150 lbs. Deb: 6/15/86 ♦

YEAR	TM/L	W	L	PCT	G	GS	CG	SH	SV	IP	H	HR	BB	SO	RAT	ERA	ERA+	OAV	OOB	BH	AVG	PB	PR	/A	PD	TPI
1990	Mon-N	0	0	—	1	0	0	0	0	0^1	2	0	2	0	108.0	54.00	7	.667	.800	109	.279	0	-2	-2	0	-0.2

● TIPPY MARTINEZ Martinez, Felix Anthony b: 5/31/50, LaJunta, Colo. BL/TL, 5'10", 180 lbs. Deb: 8/09/74

YEAR	TM/L	W	L	PCT	G	GS	CG	SH	SV	IP	H	HR	BB	SO	RAT	ERA	ERA+	OAV	OOB	BH	AVG	PB	PR	/A	PD	TPI
1974	NY-A	0	0	—	10	0	0	0	0	12^2	14	0	9	10	17.1	4.26	82	.286	.407	0	—	0	-1	-1	-0	0.0
1975	NY-A	1	2	.333	23	2	0	0	8	37	27	2	32	20	14.6	2.68	136	.208	.368	0	—	0	5	4	-1	0.3
1976	NY-A	2	0	1.000	11	0	0	0	2	28	18	1	14	14	10.3	1.93	177	.191	.296	0	—	0	5	5	1	0.6
	Bal-A	3	1	.750	28	0	0	0	8	41^2	32	0	28	31	13.2	2.59	126	.222	.353	0	—	0	4	3	1	0.5
	Yr	5	1	.833	39	0	0	0	10	69^2	50	1	42	45	12.0	2.33	143	.210	.331	0	—	0	9	8	2	1.1
1977	Bal-A	5	1	.833	41	0	0	0	9	50	47	2	27	29	13.3	2.70	140	.266	.363	0	—	0	8	6	1	0.9
1978	Bal-A	3	3	.500	42	0	0	0	5	69	77	4	40	57	15.4	4.83	72	.281	.375	0	—	0	-8	-10	1	-0.5
1979	*Bal-A	10	3	.769	39	0	0	0	3	78	59	0	31	61	10.5	2.88	139	.210	.291	0	—	0	12	10	1	1.3
1980	Bal-A	4	4	.500	53	0	0	0	10	80^2	69	5	34	68	11.6	3.01	131	.240	.322	0	—	0	9	8	2	1.0
1981	Bal-A	3	3	.500	37	0	0	0	11	59	48	4	32	50	12.2	2.90	125	.231	.333	0	—	0	5	5	1	0.6
1982	Bal-A	8	8	.500	76	0	0	0	16	95	81	6	37	78	11.3	3.41	118	.240	.317	0	—	0	7	7	-0	0.7
1983	*Bal-A☆	9	3	.750	65	0	0	0	21	103^1	76	10	37	81	9.8	2.35	168	.211	.284	0	—	0	20	18	2	2.1
1984	Bal-A	4	9	.308	55	0	0	0	17	89^2	88	9	51	72	14.0	3.91	99	.260	.356	0	—	0	1	-0	0	0.0
1985	Bal-A	3	3	.500	49	0	0	0	4	70	70	8	37	47	13.8	5.40	75	.261	.351	0	—	0	-10	-11	1	-0.9
1986	Bal-A	0	2	.000	14	0	0	0	1	16	18	1	12	11	16.9	5.63	73	.295	.411	0	—	0	-3	-3	0	-0.2
1988	Min-A	0	0	—	3	0	0	0	0	4	8	1	4	3	29.3	18.00	23	.471	.591	0	—	0	-6	-6	-0	-0.6
Total	14	55	42	.567	546	2	0	0	115	834	732	53	425	632	12.6	3.45	111	.242	.337	0	—	0	47	34	9	5.8

● BUCK MARTINEZ Martinez, John Albert b: 11/7/48, Redding, Cal. BR/TR, 5'10", 190 lbs. Deb: 6/18/69 ♦

YEAR	TM/L	W	L	PCT	G	GS	CG	SH	SV	IP	H	HR	BB	SO	RAT	ERA	ERA+	OAV	OOB	BH	AVG	PB	PR	/A	PD	TPI
1979	Mil-A	0	0	—	1	0	0	0	0	1	1	0	1	0	18.0	9.00	46	.250	.400	53	.270	1	-1	-1	0	-0.1

● DENNIS MARTINEZ Martinez, Jose Dennis (Emilia) b: 5/14/55, Granada, Nicaragua BR/TR, 6'1", 185 lbs. Deb: 9/14/76

YEAR	TM/L	W	L	PCT	G	GS	CG	SH	SV	IP	H	HR	BB	SO	RAT	ERA	ERA+	OAV	OOB	BH	AVG	PB	PR	/A	PD	TPI
1976	Bal-A	1	2	.333	4	2	1	0	0	27^2	23	1	8	18	10.1	2.60	126	.237	.295	0	—	0	3	2	0	0.5
1977	Bal-A	14	7	.667	42	13	5	0	4	166^2	157	10	64	107	12.4	4.10	92	.253	.330	0	—	0	-1	-6	0	-0.5
1978	Bal-A	16	11	.593	40	38	15	2	0	276^1	257	20	93	142	11.5	3.52	99	.250	.314	0	—	0	8	-1	4	0.5
1979	*Bal-A	15	16	.484	40	39	**18**	3	0	**292^1**	279	28	78	132	11.0	3.66	109	.253	.303	0	—	0	18	11	3	1.5
1980	Bal-A	6	4	.600	25	12	2	0	1	99^2	103	12	44	42	13.5	3.97	100	.272	.351	0	—	0	1	-0	0	0.0
1981	Bal-A	**14**	5	.737	25	24	9	2	0	179	173	10	62	88	11.9	3.32	109	.254	.318	0	—	0	7	6	4	1.1
1982	Bal-A	16	12	.571	40	39	10	2	0	252	262	30	87	111	12.7	4.21	96	.267	.331	0	—	0	-4	-5	0	-0.5
1983	Bal-A	7	16	.304	32	25	4	0	0	153	209	21	45	71	15.1	5.53	71	.330	.376	0	—	0	-25	-27	5	-2.0
1984	Bal-A	6	9	.400	34	20	2	0	0	141^2	145	26	37	77	11.9	5.02	77	.263	.315	0	—	0	-16	-18	1	-1.6
1985	Bal-A	13	11	.542	33	31	3	1	0	180	203	29	63	68	13.8	5.15	78	.288	.353	0	—	0	-20	-22	0	-2.1
1986	Bal-A	0	0	—	4	0	0	0	0	6^2	11	0	2	2	17.6	6.75	61	.367	.406	0	—	0	-2	-2	0	-0.1
	Mon-N	3	6	.333	19	15	1	1	0	98	103	11	28	63	12.3	4.59	80	.274	.329	3	.100	-0	-10	-10	1	-0.9
1987	Mon-N	11	4	.733	22	22	2	1	0	144^2	133	9	40	84	11.1	3.30	127	.244	.302	3	.065	-2	13	15	0	1.3

YEAR	TM/L	W	L	PCT	G	GS	CG	SH	SV	IP	H	HR	BB	SO	RAT	ERA	ERA+	OAV	OOB	BH	AVG	PB	PR	/A	PD	TPI
1988	Mon-N	15	13	.536	34	34	9	2	0	235^1	215	21	55	120	10.6	2.72	132	.239	.287	15	.192	2	19	23	0	2.8
1989	Mon-N	16	7	.696	34	33	5	2	0	232	227	21	49	142	11.0	3.18	111	.257	.301	9	.125	-1	8	9	3	1.3
1990	Mon-N★	10	11	.476	32	32	7	2	0	226	191	16	49	156	9.8	2.95	124	.228	.275	7	.103	-2	21	18	1	1.8
1991	Mon-N★	14	11	.560	31	31	**9**	**5**	0	222	187	9	62	123	10.3	**2.39**	151	.226	.283	11	.153	1	**32**	30	4	3.9
1992	Mon-N★	16	11	.593	32	32	6	0	0	226^1	172	12	60	147	9.6	2.47	141	.211	.273	14	.189	1	26	26	3	3.3
Total	17	193	156	.553	523	442	108	23	5	3159^1	3050	286	926	1693	11.6	3.62	104	.254	.312	62	.141	-3	77	50	31	10.3
● **MARTY MARTINEZ**	Martinez, Orlando (Oliva) b: 8/23/41, Havana, Cuba BB/TR, 6'1", 175 lbs. Deb: 5/02/62 MC♦																									
1969	Hou-N	0	0	—	1	0	0	0	0	0^2	1	1	0	0	13.5	13.50	26	.333	.333	61	.308	0	-1	-1	-0	-0.1
● **PEDRO MARTINEZ**	Martinez, Pedro Jamie b: 7/25/71, Manoguayabo, D.R. BR/TR, 5'11", 150 lbs. Deb: 9/24/92 F																									
1992	LA-N	0	1	.000	2	1	0	0	0	8	6	0	1	8	7.9	2.25	154	.200	.226	0	.000	-0	1	1	-0	0.1
● **RAMON MARTINEZ**	Martinez, Ramon Jaime (b: Ramon Jaime (Martinez) b: 3/22/68, Santo Domingo, D.R. BR/TR, 6'4", 165 lbs. Deb: 8/13/88 F																									
1988	LA-N	1	3	.250	9	6	0	0	0	35^2	27	0	22	23	12.4	3.79	88	.216	.333	0	.000	-1	-1	-2	-0	-0.3
1989	LA-N	6	4	.600	15	15	2	2	0	98^2	79	11	41	89	11.4	3.19	107	.219	.308	6	.162	0	3	2	1	0.4
1990	LA-N★	20	6	.769	33	33	**12**	3	0	234^1	191	22	67	223	10.1	2.92	125	.220	.279	10	.125	-2	23	19	0	1.9
1991	LA-N	17	13	.567	33	33	6	4	0	220^1	190	18	69	150	10.9	3.27	110	.229	.294	9	.117	-1	10	8	-1	0.6
1992	LA-N	8	11	.421	25	25	1	1	0	150^2	141	11	69	101	12.8	4.00	86	.245	.331	6	.120	-2	-8	-9	-1	-1.2
Total	5	52	37	.584	115	112	21	10	0	739^2	628	62	268	586	11.2	3.32	107	.228	.301	31	.124	-5	27	19	-1	1.4
● **ROGELIO MARTINEZ**	Martinez, Rogelio (Ulloa) "Limonar" b: 11/5/18, Cidra, Cuba BR/TR, 6', 180 lbs. Deb: 7/13/50																									
1950	Was-A	0	1	.000	2	1	0	0	0	1^1	4	0	2	0	40.5	27.00	17	.500	.600	0	—	0	-3	-3	-0	-0.3
● **SILVIO MARTINEZ**	Martinez, Silvio Ramon (Cabrera) b: 8/19/55, Santiago, D.R. BR/TR, 5'10", 170 lbs. Deb: 4/09/77																									
1977	Chi-A	0	1	.000	10	0	0	0	1	21	28	4	12	10	17.1	5.57	73	.337	.421	0	—	0	-4	-3	0	-0.3
1978	StL-N	9	8	.529	22	22	5	2	0	138^1	114	11	71	45	12.2	3.64	96	.228	.326	8	.170	0	-1	-2	-1	-0.3
1979	StL-N	15	8	.652	32	29	7	2	0	206^2	204	14	67	102	11.8	3.27	115	.259	.317	8	.129	-2	11	11	-3	0.7
1980	StL-N	5	10	.333	25	20	2	0	0	119^2	127	8	48	39	13.3	4.81	77	.273	.343	3	.086	-2	-16	-15	-2	-1.9
1981	StL-N	2	5	.286	18	16	0	0	0	97	95	4	39	34	12.5	3.99	89	.260	.333	7	.200	1	-5	-5	-1	-0.5
Total	5	31	32	.492	107	87	14	4	1	582^2	568	41	237	230	12.5	3.88	95	.258	.331	26	.145	-3	-15	-14	-7	-2.3
● **WEDO MARTINI**	Martini, Guido Joe "Southern" b: 7/1/13, Birmingham, Ala. d: 10/28/70, Philadelphia, Pa. BR/TR, 5'10", 165 lbs. Deb: 7/28/35																									
1935	Phi-A	0	2	.000	3	2	0	0	0	6^1	8	0	11	1	27.0	17.05	27	.333	.543	0	.000	-0	-9	-9	1	-0.7
● **JOE MARTY**	Marty, Joseph Anton b: 9/1/13, Sacramento, Cal. d: 10/4/84, Sacramento, Cal. BR/TR, 6', 182 lbs. Deb: 4/22/37 ♦																									
1939	Phi-N	0	0	—	1	0	0	0	0	4	2	0	3	1	11.3	4.50	89	.154	.313	76	.254	0	-0	-0	-0	0.0
● **RANDY MARTZ**	Martz, Randy Carl b: 5/28/56, Harrisburg, Pa. BL/TR, 6'4", 210 lbs. Deb: 9/06/80																									
1980	Chi-N	1	2	.333	6	6	0	0	0	30^1	28	1	11	5	11.6	2.08	188	.241	.307	1	.111	-1	5	6	1	0.7
1981	Chi-N	5	7	.417	33	14	1	0	6	107^2	103	6	49	32	12.8	3.68	100	.256	.338	6	.214	1	-2	0	0	0.1
1982	Chi-N	11	10	.524	28	24	1	0	1	147^2	157	17	36	40	11.9	4.21	89	.272	.318	6	.143	1	-10	-8	1	-0.6
1983	Chi-A	0	0	—	1	1	0	0	0	5	4	0	4	1	14.4	3.60	116	.211	.348	0	—	0	0	0	-0	-0.1
Total	4	17	19	.472	68	45	2	0	7	290^2	292	24	100	78	12.3	3.78	99	.262	.325	13	.165	2	-7	-1	1	0.1
● **DEL MASON**	Mason, Adelbert William b: 10/29/1883, Newfane, N.Y. d: 12/31/62, Winter Park, Fla. BR/TR, 6', 160 lbs. Deb: 4/23/04																									
1904	Was-A	0	3	.000	5	3	2	0	0	33	45	1	13	16	16.4	6.00	44	.325	.391	0	.000	-2	-12	-12	-1	-1.4
1906	Cin-N	0	1	.000	2	1	1	0	0	12	10	1	6	4	12.8	4.50	61	.250	.362	0	.000	-1	-2	-2	-0	-0.3
1907	Cin-N	5	12	.294	25	17	13	1	0	146	144	2	55	45	12.6	3.14	83	.277	.353	8	.182	-0	-11	-9	1	-0.9
Total	3	5	16	.238	32	21	16	1	0	191	199	4	74	65	13.3	3.72	70	.285	.361	8	.125	-3	-26	-23	0	-2.6
● **CHARLIE MASON**	Mason, Charles E. b: 6/25/1853, New Orleans, La. d: 10/21/36, Philadelphia, Pa. TR , 175 lbs. Deb: 4/26/1875 M♦																									
1875	Was-n	0	0	—	1	0	0	0	0	2	3	0	1		18.0	*4.50*	58	.300	.364	3	.088	-0	-0	-0		0.0
● **ERNIE MASON**	Mason, Ernest b: New Orleans, La. d: 7/30/04, Covington, La. Deb: 7/17/1894																									
1894	StL-N	0	3	.000	4	2	2	0	0	22^2	34	1	10	3	17.5	7.15	76	.342	.403	3	.250	-0	-5	-4	-1	-0.4
● **HANK MASON**	Mason, Henry b: 6/19/31, Marshall, Mo. BR/TR, 6', 185 lbs. Deb: 9/12/58																									
1958	Phi-N	0	0	—	1	0	0	0	0	5	7	0	2	3	18.0	10.80	37	.368	.455	0	.000	-0	-4	-4	-0	-0.4
1960	Phi-N	0	0	—	3	0	0	0	0	5^2	9	1	5	3	22.2	9.53	41	.375	.483	0	.000	-0	-4	-4	-0	-0.4
Total	2	0	0	—	4	0	0	0	0	10^2	16	1	7	6	20.3	10.13	39	.372	.471	0	.000	-0	-7	-7	-0	-0.8
● **MIKE MASON**	Mason, Michael Paul b: 11/21/58, Faribault, Minn. BL/TL, 6'2", 205 lbs. Deb: 9/13/82																									
1982	Tex-A	1	2	.333	4	4	0	0	0	23	21	3	9	8	11.7	5.09	76	.244	.316	0	—	0	-3	-3	0	-0.1
1983	Tex-A	0	2	.000	5	0	0	0	0	10^2	10	0	6	9	14.3	5.91	68	.244	.354	0	—	0	-2	-2	0	-0.1
1984	Tex-A	9	13	.409	36	24	4	0	0	184^1	159	18	51	113	10.4	3.61	115	.233	.288	0	—	0	8	11	-1	0.9
1985	Tex-A	8	15	.348	38	30	1	1	0	179	212	22	73	92	14.5	4.83	88	.299	.366	0	—	0	-14	-12	-0	-1.2
1986	Tex-A	7	3	.700	27	22	2	1	0	135	135	11	56	85	12.7	4.33	99	.257	.329	0	—	0	-2	-0	0	-0.1
1987	Tex-A	0	2	.000	8	6	0	0	0	29	37	6	22	21	19.6	5.59	80	.322	.447	0	—	0	-4	-4	0	-0.3
	Chi-N	4	1	.800	17	4	0	0	0	38	43	4	23	28	15.9	5.68	75	.303	.404	2	.222	0	-7	-6	-0	-0.5
1988	Min-A	0	1	.000	5	0	0	0	0	6^2	8	1	9	7	23.0	10.80	38	.286	.459	0	—	0	-5	-5	-0	-0.5
Total	7	29	39	.426	140	90	7	2	0	605^2	625	65	249	363	13.2	4.53	93	.268	.342	2	.222	0	-28	-21	-1	-1.9
● **ROGER MASON**	Mason, Roger Le Roy b: 9/18/58, Bellaire, Mich. BR/TR, 6'6", 215 lbs. Deb: 9/04/84																									
1984	Det-A	1	1	.500	5	2	0	0	1	22	23	1	10	15	13.5	4.50	87	.271	.347	0	—	0	-1	-1	0	-0.1
1985	SF-N	1	3	.250	5	5	1	1	0	29^2	28	1	11	26	11.8	2.12	162	.243	.310	1	.091	-0	5	4	-0	0.4
1986	SF-N	3	4	.429	11	11	1	0	0	60	56	5	30	43	13.4	4.80	73	.250	.346	1	.048	-2	-7	-9	-1	-1.1
1987	SF-N	1	1	.500	5	5	0	0	0	26	30	4	10	18	13.8	4.50	85	.303	.367	1	.125	0	-1	-2	0	-0.2
1989	Hou-N	0	0	—	2	0	0	0	0	1^1	2	0	2	3	27.0	20.25	17	.333	.500	0	—	0	-2	-2	0	-0.2
1991	*Pit-N	3	2	.600	24	0	0	0	3	29^2	21	2	6	21	8.5	3.03	118	.200	.250	0	—	0	2	2	0	0.2
1992	*Pit-N	5	7	.417	65	0	0	0	8	88	80	11	33	56	12.0	4.09	83	.246	.323	0	.000	-1	-6	-7	-1	-0.9
Total	7	14	18	.438	117	23	2	1	12	256^2	240	24	102	182	12.3	4.07	87	.250	.327	3	.060	-2	-11	-15	-2	-1.9
● **WALT MASTERS**	Masters, Walter Thomas b: 3/28/07, Pen Argyl, Pa. d: 7/10/92, BR/TR, 5'10.5", 180 lbs. Deb: 7/09/31																									
1931	Was-A	0	0	—	3	0	0	0	1	9	7	0	4	1	11.0	2.00	215	.226	.314	0	.000	-0	2	2	1	0.2
1937	Phi-N	0	0	—	1	0	0	0	0	1	5	0	1	0	54.0	36.00	12	.714	.750	0	—	0	-4	-4	-0	-0.3
1939	Phi-A	0	0	—	4	0	0	0	0	11	15	0	8	2	18.8	6.55	72	.306	.404	0	.000	-0	-2	-2	0	-0.2
Total	3	0	0	—	8	0	0	0	1	21	27	0	13	3	17.1	6.00	75	.310	.400	0	.000	-1	-4	-3	1	-0.3
● **PAUL MASTERSON**	Masterson, Paul Nickalis "Lefty" b: 10/16/15, Chicago, Ill. BL/TL, 5'11", 165 lbs. Deb: 9/15/40																									
1940	Phi-N	0	0	—	2	0	0	0	0	5	5	0	2	3	12.6	7.20	54	.263	.333	0	.000	-0	-2	-2	0	-0.2
1941	Phi-N	1	0	1.000	2	1	1	0	0	11^1	11	0	6	8	13.5	4.76	78	.250	.340	0	.000	-1	-1	-1	0	-0.2
1942	Phi-N	0	0	—	4	0	0	0	0	8^1	10	1	5	3	16.2	6.48	51	.303	.395	0	—	0	-3	-3	0	-0.3
Total	3	1	0	1.000	8	1	1	0	0	24^2	26	1	13	14	14.2	5.84	62	.271	.358	0	.000	-1	-6	-6	0	-0.7
● **WALT MASTERSON**	Masterson, Walter Edward b: 6/22/20, Philadelphia, Pa. BR/TR, 6'2", 189 lbs. Deb: 5/08/39																									
1939	Was-A	2	2	.500	24	5	1	0	0	58^1	66	2	48	12	17.9	5.55	78	.293	.422	2	.154	-0	-6	-8	-1	-0.8

YEAR	TM/L	W	L	PCT	G	GS	CG	SH	SV	IP	H	HR	BB	SO	RAT	ERA	ERA+	OAV	OOB	BH	AVG	PB	PR	/A	PD	TPI
1940	Was-A	3	13	.188	31	19	3	0	2	130^{1}	128	6	88	68	15.1	4.90	85	.257	.371	7	.184	0	-8	-11	-1	-1.1
1941	Was-A	4	3	.571	34	6	1	0	3	78^{1}	101	3	53	40	17.8	5.97	68	.321	.420	2	.105	-1	-16	-17	1	-1.6
1942	Was-A	5	9	.357	25	15	8	4	2	142^{2}	138	6	54	63	12.2	3.34	109	.251	.321	7	.156	-0	5	5	-2	0.3
1945	Was-A	1	2	.333	4	2	1	1	0	25	21	1	10	14	11.2	1.08	287	.228	.304	1	.111	-1	6	6	0	0.6
1946	Was-A	5	6	.455	29	9	2	0	1	91^{1}	105	8	67	61	17.2	6.01	56	.295	.411	2	.080	-1	-25	-27	0	-2.8
1947	Was-A★	12	16	.429	35	31	14	4	1	253	215	11	97	135	11.2	3.13	119	.234	.309	11	.133	-3	16	17	3	1.8
1948	Was-A★	8	15	.348	33	27	9	2	2	188	171	12	122	72	14.2	3.83	113	.247	.363	11	.193	-0	10	11	-2	0.9
1949	Was-A	3	2	.600	10	7	3	0	0	53	42	4	21	17	11.2	3.23	132	.216	.303	1	.056	-2	6	6	1	0.6
	Bos-A	3	4	.429	18	5	1	0	4	55	58	2	35	19	15.2	4.25	102	.283	.387	2	.118	-0	-0	1	-1	-0.1
	Yr	6	6	.500	28	12	4	0	4	108	100	6	56	36	13.0	3.75	115	.249	.341	3	.086	-2	5	7	-0	0.5
1950	Bos-A	8	6	.571	33	15	6	0	1	129^{1}	145	15	82	60	15.9	5.64	87	.287	.387	6	.136	-3	-15	-11	1	-1.1
1951	Bos-A	3	0	1.000	30	1	0	0	2	59^{1}	53	1	32	39	12.9	3.34	134	.228	.322	2	.182	-1	5	7	0	0.7
1952	Bos-A	1	1	.500	5	1	0	0	0	9^{1}	18	1	11	3	28.0	11.57	34	.400	.518	0	.000	0	-8	-8	0	-0.8
	Was-A	9	8	.529	24	21	11	0	2	160^{2}	153	11	72	89	12.8	3.70	96	.253	.336	6	.120	-1	-0	-2	1	-0.3
	Yr	10	9	.526	29	22	11	0	2	170	171	12	83	92	13.6	4.13	87	.263	.350	6	.115	-1	-9	-10	1	-1.1
1953	Was-A	10	12	.455	29	20	10	4	0	166^{1}	145	16	62	95	11.4	3.63	107	.232	.304	7	.137	-1	7	5	0	0.4
1956	Det-A	1	1	.500	35	0	0	0	0	49^{2}	54	2	32	28	15.8	4.17	99	.289	.395	1	.250	0	-0	-0	-0	-0.1
Total	14	78	100	.438	399	184	70	15	20	1649^{2}	1613	101	886	815	13.8	4.15	96	.258	.353	68	.140	-14	-24	-27	0	-3.4

● LEN MATARAZZO

Matarazzo, Leonard b: 9/12/28, New Castle, Pa. BR/TR, 6'4", 195 lbs. Deb: 9/06/52

YEAR	TM/L	W	L	PCT	G	GS	CG	SH	SV	IP	H	HR	BB	SO	RAT	ERA	ERA+	OAV	OOB	BH	AVG	PB	PR	/A	PD	TPI
1952	Phi-A	0	0	—	1	0	0	0	0	1	1	0	1	0	18.0	0.00	—	.250	.400	0	—	0	0	0	-0	0.0

● GREG MATHEWS

Mathews, Gregory Inman b: 5/17/62, Harbor City, Cal. BR/TL, 6'2", 180 lbs. Deb: 6/03/86

YEAR	TM/L	W	L	PCT	G	GS	CG	SH	SV	IP	H	HR	BB	SO	RAT	ERA	ERA+	OAV	OOB	BH	AVG	PB	PR	/A	PD	TPI
1986	StL-N	11	8	.579	23	22	1	0	0	145^{1}	139	15	44	67	11.5	3.65	100	.259	.317	2	.047	-3	1	-0	-2	-0.5
1987	*StL-N	11	11	.500	32	32	2	1	0	197^{2}	184	17	71	108	11.6	3.73	111	.249	.314	13	.191	1	8	9	-1	0.9
1988	StL-N	4	6	.400	13	13	1	0	0	68	61	4	33	31	12.7	4.24	82	.247	.340	4	.174	0	-6	-6	0	-0.6
1990	StL-N	0	5	.000	11	10	0	0	0	50^{2}	53	2	30	18	15.1	5.33	72	.277	.381	3	.214	1	-9	-9	1	-0.6
1992	Phi-N	2	3	.400	14	7	0	0	0	52^{1}	54	7	24	27	13.6	5.16	68	.270	.351	0	.000	-1	-10	-10	-1	-1.2
Total	5	28	33	.459	93	84	4	1	0	514	491	45	202	251	12.3	4.08	94	.256	.330	22	.136	-1	-16	-15	-3	-2.0

● BOBBY MATHEWS

Mathews, Robert T. b: 11/21/1851, Baltimore, Md. d: 4/17/1898, Baltimore, Md. BR/TR, 5'5.5", 140 lbs. Deb: 5/04/1871 U♦

YEAR	TM/L	W	L	PCT	G	GS	CG	SH	SV	IP	H	HR	BB	SO	RAT	ERA	ERA+	OAV	OOB	BH	AVG	PB	PR	/A	PD	TPI
1871	Kek-n	6	11	.353	19	19	19	**1**	0	169	261	5	21	17	15.0	5.17	88	.305	.322	24	.270	-3	-18	-11		-0.8
1872	Bal-n	25	18	.581	49	47	39	0	0	405^{1}	477	3	52	**55**	11.7	3.15	119	.256	.277	50	.226	-7	25	27		1.3
1873	Mut-n	29	23	.558	52	52	47	2	0	443	489	5	62	**75**	11.2	2.56	124	.251	.274	43	.193	-2	34	30		1.9
1874	Mut-n	42	22	.656	65	65	62	**4**	0	578	647	3	39		10.7	**2.30**	**133**	.258	.270	70	.236	-3	**44**	**49**		3.6
1875	Mut-n	29	38	.433	70	70	**69**	2	0	**626^{2}**	709	3	23		10.5	*2.41*	107	.259	.265	47	.175	-12	3	12		-0.1
1876	NY-N	21	34	.382	56	56	55	2	0	516	693	8	24	37	12.5	2.86	75	.301	.308	40	.183	-9	-32	-41	-3	-4.3
1877	Cin-N	3	12	.200	15	15	13	0	0	129^{1}	208	0	17	9	15.7	4.04	66	.339	.357	10	.169	-3	-18	-20	-1	-2.0
1879	Pro-N	12	6	.667	27	25	15	1	**1**	189	194	4	26	90	10.5	2.29	103	.258	.282	35	.202	-0	4	1	0	0.1
1881	Pro-N	4	8	.333	14	14	10	1	0	102^{1}	121	2	21	28	12.5	3.17	84	.268	.300	11	.193	-2	-4	-6	-1	-0.7
	Bos-N	1	0	1.000	5	1	1	0	2	23	22	0	11	5	12.9	2.35	113	.239	.320	12	.169	-1	1	1	-0	0.0
	Yr	5	8	.385	19	15	11	1	**2**	125^{1}	143	2	32	33	12.6	3.02	88	.263	.304	23	.180	-3	-3	-5	-2	-0.7
1882	Bos-N	19	15	.559	34	32	31	0	0	285	278	5	22	153	9.5	2.87	100	.232	.246	38	.225	-2	1	-0	-4	-0.6
1883	Phi-a	30	13	.698	44	44	41	1	0	381	396	11	31	203	10.1	2.46	142	.251	.265	31	.186	-8	36	44	-1	3.2
1884	Phi-a	30	18	.625	49	49	48	3	0	430^{2}	401	10	49	286	9.7	3.32	102	.232	.258	34	.185	-5	-4	4	-2	-0.4
1885	Phi-a	30	17	.638	48	48	46	2	0	422^{1}	394	3	57	286	10.0	2.43	142	.233	.267	30	.168	-7	38	47	0	3.8
1886	Phi-a	13	9	.591	24	24	22	0	0	197^{2}	226	3	53	93	13.3	3.96	88	.267	.320	21	.239	-0	-11	-10	0	-0.9
1887	Phi-a	3	4	.429	7	7	7	0	0	58	75	4	25	9	16.0	6.67	64	.298	.368	5	.200	-0	-15	-15	0	-1.2
Total	5 n	131	112	.539	255	253	236	9	0	2222	2583	19	197	147	11.3	*2.76*	116	.261	.275	234	.213	-27	89	107		5.9
Total	10	166	136	.550	323	315	289	10	3	2734^{1}	3008	50	336	1199	11.2	3.00	100	.261	.285	267	.192	-27	-3	-2	-11	-3.0

● TERRY MATHEWS

Mathews, Terry Alan b: 10/5/64, Alexandria, La. BL/TR, 6'2", 200 lbs. Deb: 6/21/91

YEAR	TM/L	W	L	PCT	G	GS	CG	SH	SV	IP	H	HR	BB	SO	RAT	ERA	ERA+	OAV	OOB	BH	AVG	PB	PR	/A	PD	TPI
1991	Tex-A	4	0	1.000	34	2	0	0	1	57^{1}	54	5	18	51	11.5	3.61	112	.251	.312	0	—	0	3	3	0	0.3
1992	Tex-A	2	4	.333	40	0	0	0	0	42^{1}	48	4	31	26	17.0	5.95	64	.294	.410	0	—	0	-9	-10	0	-1.0
Total	2	6	4	.600	74	2	0	0	1	99^{2}	102	9	49	77	13.8	4.61	86	.270	.357	0	—	0	-6	-7	0	-0.7

● CHRISTY MATHEWSON

Mathewson, Christopher "Matty" or "Big Six"
b: 8/12/1880, Factoryville, Pa. d: 10/7/25, Saranac Lake, N.Y. BR/TR, 6'1.5", 195 lbs. Deb: 7/17/00 FMCH

YEAR	TM/L	W	L	PCT	G	GS	CG	SH	SV	IP	H	HR	BB	SO	RAT	ERA	ERA+	OAV	OOB	BH	AVG	PB	PR	/A	PD	TPI
1900	NY-N	0	3	.000	6	1	1	0	0	33^{2}	37	1	20	15	16.3	5.08	71	.278	.389	2	.182	0	-5	-5	0	-0.4
1901	NY-N	20	17	.541	40	38	36	5	0	336	288	3	97	221	10.6	2.41	137	.230	.291	28	.215	-1	34	33	8	4.2
1902	NY-N	14	17	.452	34	32	29	**8**	0	276^{2}	241	3	73	159	10.5	2.11	133	.235	.291	26	.205	1	20	21	4	3.0
1903	NY-N	30	13	.698	45	42	37	3	2	366^{1}	321	4	100	**267**	10.6	2.26	148	.231	.287	28	.226	3	**41**	44	2	**4.9**
1904	NY-N	33	12	.733	48	46	33	4	1	367^{2}	306	7	78	**212**	9.5	2.03	134	.226	.270	30	.226	6	29	28	6	4.4
1905	*NY-N	**31**	9	.775	43	37	32	**8**	2	338^{2}	252	4	64	**206**	**8.4**	**1.28**	**230**	.205	**.245**	30	.236	8	**65**	**62**	6	**9.0**
1906	NY-N	22	12	.647	38	35	22	6	1	266^{2}	262	3	77	128	11.5	2.97	88	.259	.313	24	.264	7	-10	-11	4	0.0
1907	NY-N	**24**	12	.667	41	36	31	**8**	2	315	250	6	53	**178**	**8.7**	2.00	124	.212	**.247**	20	.187	2	17	17	1	2.3
1908	NY-N	**37**	11	.771	**56**	44	**34**	**11**	**5**	**390^{2}**	285	5	42	**259**	**7.6**	**1.43**	**169**	.200	**.225**	20	.155	1	**41**	**43**	10	**6.6**
1909	NY-N	25	6	**.806**	37	33	26	8	2	275^{1}	192	2	36	149	**7.5**	**1.14**	**224**	.200	**.228**	25	.263	7	45	43	6	**6.9**
1910	NY-N	**27**	9	.750	38	35	**27**	2	0	318^{1}	292	5	60	184	10.0	1.89	157	.248	.286	25	.234	7	**40**	**38**	7	**5.9**
1911	*NY-N	26	13	.667	45	37	29	5	3	307	303	5	38	141	10.0	**1.99**	**169**	.259	.283	22	.196	0	**48**	**47**	7	**5.8**
1912	*NY-N	23	12	.657	43	34	27	0	4	310	311	6	34	134	10.1	2.12	159	.260	**.281**	29	.264	5	**44**	**43**	0	**5.0**
1913	*NY-N	25	11	.694	40	35	25	4	2	306	291	8	21	93	**9.2**	**2.06**	**152**	.252	**.266**	19	.184	-0	**39**	**36**	4	**4.3**
1914	NY-N	24	13	.649	41	35	29	5	2	312	314	16	23	80	9.8	3.00	88	.263	.278	23	.219	6	-7	-12	2	-0.5
1915	NY-N	8	14	.364	27	24	11	1	0	186	199	9	20	57	10.6	3.58	72	.277	.298	8	.157	2	-17	-21	1	-2.0
1916	NY-N	3	4	.429	12	6	4	1	2	65^{2}	59	3	7	16	9.0	2.33	104	.243	.264	0	.000	-1	2	1	2	0.2
	Cin-N	1	0	1.000	1	1	1	0	0	9	15	1	1	3	16.0	8.00	32	.366	.381	3	.600	1	-5	-5	0	-0.3
	Yr	4	4	.500	13	7	5	1	2	74^{2}	74	4	8	19	9.9	3.01	81	.261	.281	3	.136	1	-3	-5	2	-0.1
Total	17	373	188	.665	635	551	434	79	28	4780^{2}	4218	91	844	2502	9.6	2.13	136	.236	.273	362	.215	55	420	403	68	59.3

● HENRY MATHEWSON

Mathewson, Henry b: 12/24/1886, Factoryville, Pa. d: 7/1/17, Factoryville, Pa. BR/TR, 6'3", 175 lbs. Deb: 9/28/06 F

YEAR	TM/L	W	L	PCT	G	GS	CG	SH	SV	IP	H	HR	BB	SO	RAT	ERA	ERA+	OAV	OOB	BH	AVG	PB	PR	/A	PD	TPI
1906	NY-N	0	1	.000	2	1	1	0	1	10	7	0	14	2	19.8	5.40	48	.194	.431	0	.000	-0	-3	-3	0	-0.3
1907	NY-N	0	0	—	1	0	0	0	1	1	1	0	0	0	9.0	0.00	—	.250	.250	0	—	0	0	0	-0	0.0
Total	2	0	1	.000	3	1	1	0	2	11	8	0	14	2	18.8	4.91	53	.200	.418	0	.000	-0	-3	-3	0	-0.3

● CARL MATHIAS

Mathias, Carl Lynwood "Stubby" b: 6/13/36, Bechtelsville, Pa BB/TL, 5'11", 195 lbs. Deb: 7/31/60

YEAR	TM/L	W	L	PCT	G	GS	CG	SH	SV	IP	H	HR	BB	SO	RAT	ERA	ERA+	OAV	OOB	BH	AVG	PB	PR	/A	PD	TPI
1960	Cle-A	0	1	.000	7	0	0	0	0	15^{1}	14	2	8	13	12.9	3.52	106	.233	.324	0	.000	-0	1	0	0	0.0
1961	Was-A	0	1	.000	4	3	0	0	0	13^{2}	22	3	4	7	17.8	11.20	36	.361	.409	1	.200	-0	-11	-11	-0	-1.0
Total	2	0	2	.000	11	3	0	0	0	29	36	5	12	20	15.2	7.14	54	.298	.366	1	.167	-0	-10	-11	0	-1.0

● RON MATHIS

Mathis, Ronald Vance b: 9/25/58, Kansas City, Mo. BR/TR, 6', 175 lbs. Deb: 4/13/85

YEAR	TM/L	W	L	PCT	G	GS	CG	SH	SV	IP	H	HR	BB	SO	RAT	ERA	ERA+	OAV	OOB	BH	AVG	PB	PR	/A	PD	TPI
1985	Hou-N	3	5	.375	23	8	0	0	1	70	83	7	27	34	14.3	6.04	57	.293	.357	1	.071	-1	-19	-20	-0	-2.1
1987	Hou-N	0	1	.000	8	0	0	0	0	12	10	2	11	8	15.8	5.25	75	.233	.389	0	.000	-0	-2	-2	0	-0.2
Total	2	3	6	.333	31	8	0	0	1	82	93	9	38	42	14.5	5.93	60	.285	.362	1	.063	-1	-21	-22	-0	-2.3

YEAR	TM/L	W	L	PCT	G	GS	CG	SH	SV	IP	H	HR	BB	SO	RAT	ERA	ERA+	OAV	OOB	BH	AVG	PB	PR	/A	PD	TPI
● JON MATLACK	Matlack, Jonathan Trumpbour b: 1/19/50, West Chester, Pa. BL/TL, 6'3", 205 lbs. Deb: 7/11/71																									
1971	NY-N	0	3	.000	7	6	0	0	0	37	31	2	15	24	11.2	4.14	82	.228	.305	3	.273	1	-3	-3	-1	-0.3
1972	NY-N	15	10	.600	34	32	8	4	0	244	215	14	71	169	10.6	2.32	145	.234	.291	10	.128	1	31	28	-1	3.2
1973	*NY-N	14	16	.467	34	34	14	3	0	242	210	16	99	205	11.6	3.20	113	.236	.314	9	.138	2	12	11	1	1.5
1974	NY-N★	13	15	.464	34	34	14	**7**	0	265^1	221	8	76	195	10.2	2.41	148	.226	.285	8	.101	-4	36	34	-0	3.3
1975	NY-N★	16	12	.571	33	32	8	3	0	228^2	224	15	58	154	11.1	3.38	102	.254	.300	7	.100	0	6	2	-2	0.0
1976	NY-N☆	17	10	.630	35	35	16	**6**	0	262	236	18	57	153	10.2	2.95	112	.242	.286	17	.193	4	16	10	-1	1.3
1977	NY-N	7	15	.318	26	26	5	3	0	169	175	19	43	123	11.7	4.21	89	.273	.321	3	.060	-2	-6	-9	0	-1.0
1978	Tex-A	15	13	.536	35	33	18	2	1	270	252	14	51	157	10.2	2.27	165	.245	.284	0	—	0	45	44	0	5.0
1979	Tex-A	5	4	.556	13	13	2	0	0	85	98	9	15	35	12.1	4.13	100	.293	.325	0	—	0	1	0	0	0.1
1980	Tex-A	10	10	.500	35	34	8	1	1	234^2	265	17	48	142	12.0	3.68	106	.287	.323	0	—	0	9	6	-3	0.3
1981	Tex-A	4	7	.364	17	16	1	1	0	104^1	101	8	41	43	12.3	4.14	84	.258	.330	0	—	0	-6	-8	-0	-0.7
1982	Tex-A	7	7	.500	33	14	1	0	1	147^2	158	14	37	78	12.0	3.53	109	.275	.321	0	—	0	9	6	0	0.8
1983	Tex-A	2	4	.333	25	9	2	0	0	73^1	90	7	27	38	14.7	4.66	86	.307	.372	0	—	0	-5	-5	1	-0.4
Total	13	125	126	.498	361	318	97	30	3	2363	2276	161	638	1516	11.2	3.18	114	.254	.305	57	.129	2	145	115	-5	13.1
● AL MATTERN	Mattern, Alonzo Albert b: 6/16/1883, W.Rush, N.Y. d: 11/6/58, West Rush, N.Y. BL/TR, 5'10", 165 lbs. Deb: 9/16/08																									
1908	Bos-N	1	2	.333	5	3	1	1	0	30^1	30	0	6	8	10.7	2.08	116	.265	.303	1	.125	-0	1	1	-0	0.1
1909	Bos-N	15	21	.417	47	32	24	2	3	316^1	322	4	108	98	12.3	2.85	99	.268	.330	17	.168	-1	-9	-1	3	0.1
1910	Bos-N	16	19	.457	**51**	37	17	**6**	1	305	288	5	121	94	12.2	2.98	112	.257	.332	16	.163	-5	2	12	1	0.8
1911	Bos-N	4	15	.211	33	21	11	0	0	186^1	228	13	63	51	14.1	4.97	77	.320	.376	11	.175	-2	-33	-24	2	-2.3
1912	Bos-N	0	1	.000	2	1	0	0	0	6^1	10	0	1	3	15.6	7.11	50	.313	.333	0	.000	-0	-3	-2	0	-0.2
Total	5	36	58	.383	138	94	53	9	4	844^1	878	22	299	254	12.7	3.37	95	.276	.340	45	.165	-9	-41	-15	5	-1.5
● C. V. MATTERSON	Matterson, C. V. b: Ohio Deb: 6/13/1884 ♦																									
1884	StL-U	1	0	1.000	1	1	0	0	0	6	9	1	3	3	18.0	9.00	33	.325	.391	0	.000	-1	-4	-4	-0	-0.4
● EDDIE MATTESON	Matteson, Henry Edson "Matty" b: 9/7/1884, Guys Mills, Pa. d: 9/1/43, Westfield, N.Y. BR/TR, 5'10.5", 160 lbs. Deb: 5/30/14																									
1914	Phi-N	3	2	.600	15	3	2	0	0	58	58	1	23	28	12.7	3.10	95	.278	.352	4	.182	-0	-2	-1	-2	-0.3
1918	Was-A	5	3	.625	14	6	2	0	0	67^2	57	2	15	17	9.7	1.73	158	.238	.286	2	.105	-2	8	8	-1	0.5
Total	2	8	5	.615	29	9	4	0	0	125^2	115	3	38	45	11.1	2.36	120	.257	.318	6	.146	-2	6	6	-3	0.2
● JOE MATTHEWS	Matthews, John Joseph "Lefty" b: 9/29/1898, Baltimore, Md. d: 2/8/68, Hagerstown, Md. BB/TL, 6', 170 lbs. Deb: 9/18/22																									
1922	Bos-N	0	1	.000	3	1	0	0	0	10	5	1	6	0	10.8	3.60	111	.143	.286	0	.000	-0	1	0	-0	0.0
● WILLIAM MATTHEWS	Matthews, William Calvin b: 1/12/1878, Mahanoy City, Pa. d: 1/23/46, Mahanoy City, Pa. TR , Deb: 8/28/09																									
1909	Bos-A	0	0	—	5	1	0	0	0	16^2	16	1	10	6	14.0	3.24	77	.271	.377	0	.000	-1	-1	-1	-0	-0.3
● DALE MATTHEWSON	Matthewson, Dale Wesley b: 5/15/23, Catasaqua, Pa. d: 2/20/84, Blairsville, Ga. BR/TR, 5'11.5", 145 lbs. Deb: 7/03/43																									
1943	Phi-N	0	3	.000	11	1	0	0	0	26	26	1	8	8	11.8	4.85	70	.271	.327	0	.000	-0	-4	-4	-0	-0.5
1944	Phi-N	0	0	—	17	1	0	0	0	32	27	1	16	8	12.1	3.94	92	.237	.331	1	.333	0	-1	-1	-0	-0.1
Total	2	0	3	.000	28	2	0	0	0	58	53	2	24	16	11.9	4.34	81	.252	.329	1	.200	-0	-5	-5	-0	-0.6
● MIKE MATTIMORE	Mattimore, Michael Joseph b: 1859, Renovo, Pa. d: 4/28/31, Butte, Mont. BL/TL, 5'8.5", 160 lbs. Deb: 5/03/1887 ♦																									
1887	NY-N	3	3	.500	7	7	6	1	0	57^1	47	2	28	12	12.4	2.35	160	.218	.319	8	.250	-0	11	9	-1	0.7
1888	Phi-a	15	10	.600	26	24	24	4	0	221	221	6	65	80	12.2	3.38	88	.251	.312	38	.268	7	-8	-10	4	0.0
1889	Phi-a	2	1	.667	5	1	1	0	1	31	43	0	13	6	16.5	5.81	65	.319	.383	17	.233	1	-7	-7	-0	-0.5
	KC-a	0	0	—	1	0	0	0	0	3	3	1	2	1	15.0	3.00	139	.252	.360	12	.160	-0	0	0	-0	0.0
	Yr	2	1	.667	6	1	1	0	1	34	46	1	15	7	16.1	5.56	69	.311	.375	29	.196	0	-6	-7	-0	-0.5
1890	Bro-a	6	13	.316	19	19	19	0	0	178^1	201	3	76	33	14.6	4.54	86	.276	.354	17	.132	-3	-13	-13	-0	-1.3
Total	4	26	27	.491	58	51	50	5	1	490^2	515	12	184	132	13.4	3.83	90	.261	.334	92	.204	4	-17	-20	2	-1.1
● EARL MATTINGLY	Mattingly, Laurence Earl b: 11/4/04, Newport, Md. BR/TR, 5'10.5", 164 lbs. Deb: 4/15/31																									
1931	Bro-N	0	1	.000	8	0	0	0	0	14^1	15	0	10	6	17.0	2.51	152	.268	.397	0	.000	-0	2	2	1	0.2
● RICK MATULA	Matula, Richard Carlton b: 11/22/53, Wharton, Tex. BR/TR, 6', 190 lbs. Deb: 4/08/79																									
1979	Atl-N	8	10	.444	28	28	1	0	0	171^1	193	14	64	67	13.7	4.15	98	.286	.350	5	.094	-3	-8	-2	1	-0.5
1980	Atl-N	11	13	.458	33	30	3	1	0	176^2	195	17	60	62	13.0	4.58	82	.286	.343	6	.105	-3	-19	-17	1	-1.9
1981	Atl-N	0	0	—	5	0	0	0	0	7	8	1	2	0	12.9	6.43	56	.286	.333	0	.000	-0	-2	-2	0	-0.2
Total	3	19	23	.452	66	58	4	1	0	355	396	32	126	129	13.3	4.41	88	.286	.347	11	.099	-6	-30	-21	2	-2.6
● HARRY MATUZAK	Matuzak, Harry George "Matty" b: 1/27/10, Omer, Mich. d: 11/16/78, Fair Hope, Ala. BR/TR, 5'11.5", 185 lbs. Deb: 4/19/34																									
1934	Phi-A	0	3	.000	11	0	0	0	0	24	28	2	10	9	14.6	4.88	90	.292	.364	1	.167	0	-1	-1	0	-0.1
1936	Phi-A	0	1	.000	6	1	0	0	0	15	21	0	4	8	15.0	7.20	71	.318	.357	0	.000	-0	-4	-3	-0	-0.3
Total	2	0	4	.000	17	1	0	0	0	39	49	2	14	17	14.8	5.77	81	.302	.362	1	.111	-0	-5	-5	0	-0.4
● HAL MAUCK	Mauck, Alfred Maris b: 3/6/1869, Princeton, Ind. d: 4/27/21, Princeton, Ind. BR/TR, 5'11", 185 lbs. Deb: 4/29/1893																									
1893	Chi-N	8	10	.444	23	18	12	1	0	143	168	2	60	23	14.9	4.41	105	.284	.359	9	.148	-5	4	4	-1	-0.2
● AL MAUL	Maul, Albert Joseph "Smiling Al" b: 10/9/1865, Philadelphia, Pa. d: 5/3/58, Philadelphia, Pa. BR/TR, 6', 175 lbs. Deb: 6/20/1884 ♦																									
1884	Phi-U	0	1	.000	1	1	1	0	0	8	10	0	1	7	12.4	4.50	64	.287	.306	0	.000	-1	-1	-1	-0	-0.2
1887	Phi-N	4	2	.667	7	5	4	0	0	50^1	72	2	15	18	15.9	5.54	76	.326	.374	17	.304	3	-8	-7	0	-0.4
1888	Pit-N	0	2	.000	3	1	1	0	0	17	26	0	5	12	16.4	6.35	42	.342	.383	54	.208	0	-7	-7	0	-0.6
1889	Pit-N	1	4	.200	6	4	4	0	0	42	64	3	28	11	19.9	9.86	38	.340	.428	71	.276	2	-27	-29	1	-1.9
1890	Pit-P	16	12	.571	30	28	26	2	0	246^2	258	13	104	81	13.6	3.79	103	.258	.335	42	.259	6	12	3	5	1.1
1891	Pit-N	1	2	.333	8	3	3	0	1	39	44	0	16	13	14.5	2.31	142	.274	.351	28	.188	1	5	4	-0	0.4
1893	Was-N	12	21	.364	37	33	29	1	0	297	355	17	144	72	15.7	5.30	87	.288	.370	34	.254	10	-21	-22	0	-1.0
1894	Was-N	11	15	.423	29	27	21	0	0	204^2	275	12	73	34	15.7	5.94	89	.318	.378	30	.240	1	-14	-15	2	-0.8
1895	Was-N	10	5	.667	16	16	14	0	0	135^2	136	5	37	34	11.7	**2.45**	**196**	.257	.309	18	.250	1	35	35	1	3.4
1896	Was-N	5	2	.714	8	8	7	0	0	62	75	0	20	18	14.4	3.63	121	.296	.357	8	.286	2	5	5	-1	0.5
1897	Was-N	0	1	.000	1	1	0	0	0	2	4	0	1	0	22.5	9.00	48	.411	.465	0	.000	-0	-1	-1	0	-0.1
	Bal-N	0	0	—	2	2	0	0	0	7^2	9	0	8	2	24.7	7.04	59	.290	.488	1	.333	0	-2	-2	-0	-0.2
	Yr	0	1	.000	3	3	0	0	0	9^2	13	0	9	2	24.2	7.45	56	.319	.484	1	.250	-0	-3	-3	-0	-0.3
1898	Bal-N	20	7	.741	28	28	26	1	0	239^2	207	3	49	31	9.8	2.10	170	.231	.274	19	.204	3	40	39	-5	3.8
1899	Bro-N	2	0	1.000	4	4	2	0	0	26	35	1	6	2	14.9	4.50	87	.321	.368	3	.273	0	-2	-2	0	-0.1
1900	Phi-N	2	3	.400	5	4	3	0	0	38	53	2	3	6	13.7	6.16	59	.329	.349	3	.200	0	-10	-11	0	-0.9
1901	NY-N	0	3	.000	3	3	2	0	0	19	39	1	8	5	22.7	11.37	29	.417	.468	3	.375	1	-17	-17	0	-1.2
Total	15	84	80	.512	188	168	143	4	1	1434^2	1662	59	518	346	14.1	4.43	96	.284	.348	331	.240	30	-14	-28	4	1.8
● ERNIE MAUN	Maun, Ernest Gerald b: 2/3/01, Clearwater, Kan. d: 1/1/87, Corpus Christi, Tex. BR/TR, 6', 165 lbs. Deb: 5/16/24																									
1924	NY-N	1	1	.500	22	0	0	0	1	35	46	2	10	5	14.7	5.91	62	.326	.375	2	.667	1	-8	-9	-1	-0.8
1926	Phi-N	1	4	.200	14	5	0	0	0	37^2	57	4	18	9	18.2	6.45	64	.339	.406	3	.250	-0	-11	-10	-0	-0.9
Total	2	2	5	.286	36	5	0	0	1	72^2	103	6	28	14	16.5	6.19	63	.333	.392	5	.333	1	-19	-18	-1	-1.7
● DICK MAUNEY	Mauney, Richard b: 1/26/20, Concord, N.C. d: 2/6/70, Albermarle, N.C. BR/TR, 5'11.5", 164 lbs. Deb: 6/13/45																									
1945	Phi-N	6	10	.375	20	16	6	2	1	122^2	127	7	27	35	11.4	3.08	124	.268	.310	6	.146	-0	10	10	1	1.1

YEAR TM/L	W	L	PCT	G	GS	CG	SH	SV	IP	H	HR	BB	SO	RAT	ERA	ERA+	OAV	OOB	BH	AVG	PB	PR	/A	PD	TPI
1946 Phi-N	6	4	.600	24	7	3	1	2	90	98	4	18	31	11.9	2.70	127	.279	.320	4	.167	-1	7	7	0	0.8
1947 Phi-N	0	0	—	9	1	0	0	1	16^1	15	1	7	6	12.7	3.86	104	.288	.383	0	.000	-0	0	0	1	0.1
Total 3	12	14	.462	53	24	9	3	4	229	240	12	52	72	11.7	2.99	123	.274	.319	10	.149	-1	17	18	2	2.0
● **HARRY MAUPIN** Maupin, Henry Carr b: 7/11/1872, Wellesville, Mo. d: 8/23/52, Deb: 10/05/1898																									
1898 StL-N	0	2	.000	2	2	2	0	0	18	22	0	3	3	14.0	5.50	69	.299	.352	3	.429	1	-4	-3	-1	-0.3
1899 Cle-N	0	3	.000	5	3	2	0	0	25	55	0	7	3	22.7	12.60	29	.436	.470	0	.000	-2	-24	-25	-1	-2.0
Total 2	0	5	.000	7	5	4	0	0	43	77	0	10	6	19.0	9.63	39	.385	.426	3	.176	-1	-28	-28	-2	-2.3
● **RALPH MAURIELLO** Mauriello, Ralph "Tami" b: 8/25/34, Brooklyn, N.Y. BR/TR, 6'3", 195 lbs. Deb: 9/13/58																									
1958 LA-N	1	1	.500	3	2	0	0	0	11^2	10	1	8	11	13.9	4.63	89	.238	.360	0	.000	-1	-1	-1	-0	-0.1
● **TIM MAUSER** Mauser, Timothy Edward b: 10/4/66, Fort Worth, Tex. BR/TR, 6', 185 lbs. Deb: 7/07/91																									
1991 Phi-N	0	0	—	3	0	0	0	0	10^2	18	3	3	6	17.7	7.59	48	.367	.404	0	.000	-0	-5	-5	-0	-0.5
● **LARRY MAXIE** Maxie, Larry Hans b: 10/10/40, Upland, Cal. BR/TR, 6'4", 220 lbs. Deb: 8/30/69																									
1969 Atl-N	0	0	—	2	0	0	0	0	3	1	0	1	1	9.0	3.00	120	.111	.273	0	—	0	0	0	0	0.1
● **BERT MAXWELL** Maxwell, James Albert b: 10/17/1886, Texarkana, Ark. d: 12/10/61, Brady, Tex. BB/TR, 6', 180 lbs. Deb: 9/12/06																									
1906 Pit-N	0	1	.000	1	1	0	0	0	8	8	0	2	1	11.3	5.63	48	.286	.333	0	.000	-0	-3	-3	0	-0.3
1908 Phi-A	0	0	—	4	0	0	0	0	13	23	0	9	7	23.5	11.08	23	.348	.442	0	.000	-1	-13	-12	-0	-1.2
1911 NY-N	1	2	.333	4	3	3	0	0	31	37	0	7	8	13.4	2.90	116	.311	.359	1	.111	-0	2	2	1	0.2
1914 Bro-F	3	4	.429	12	8	6	1	1	71^1	76	0	24	19	12.7	3.28	97	.276	.337	2	.087	-2	-1	-1	1	-0.2
Total 4	4	7	.364	21	12	9	1	1	123^1	144	0	42	35	13.9	4.16	76	.295	.357	3	.075	-3	-14	-14	1	-1.5
● **JAKIE MAY** May, Frank Spruiell b: 11/25/1895, Youngville, N.C. d: 6/3/70, Wendell, N.C. BR/TL, 5'8", 178 lbs. Deb: 6/26/17																									
1917 StL-N	0	0	—	15	1	0	0	0	29^1	29	0	11	18	13.2	3.38	80	.302	.391	0	.000	-1	-2	-2	2	-0.1
1918 StL-N	5	6	.455	29	16	6	0	0	152^2	149	2	69	61	13.6	3.83	71	.264	.358	3	.067	-1	-18	-19	-2	-2.4
1919 StL-N	3	12	.200	28	19	8	1	0	125^2	99	1	87	58	14.3	3.22	87	.230	.377	6	.162	-1	-4	-6	-1	-0.9
1920 StL-N	1	4	.200	16	5	3	0	0	70^2	65	0	37	33	13.9	3.06	98	.251	.360	5	.227	1	1	-1	-2	-0.1
1921 StL-N	1	3	.250	5	5	1	0	0	21	29	0	12	5	17.6	4.71	78	.333	.414	2	.333	1	-2	-2	-1	-0.2
1924 Cin-N	3	3	.500	38	4	2	0	**6**	99	104	2	29	59	12.6	3.00	126	.276	.337	3	.111	-2	10	8	-0	0.7
1925 Cin-N	8	9	.471	36	12	7	1	2	137^1	146	3	45	74	13.0	3.87	106	.272	.337	8	.186	0	6	4	0	0.4
1926 Cin-N	13	9	.591	45	15	9	1	3	167^2	175	4	44	103	12.1	3.22	115	.276	.329	7	.146	-1	11	9	-1	0.6
1927 Cin-N	15	12	.556	44	28	17	2	1	235^2	242	4	70	121	12.4	3.51	108	.274	.337	14	.184	0	11	7	1	0.8
1928 Cin-N	3	5	.375	21	11	1	1	1	79^1	99	1	35	39	15.3	4.42	89	.315	.386	8	.296	1	-4	-4	-1	-0.4
1929 Cin-N	10	14	.417	41	24	10	0	3	199	219	7	75	92	13.5	4.61	99	.285	.352	13	.203	-1	2	-1	-0	-0.2
1930 Cin-N	3	11	.214	26	18	5	1	0	112^1	147	6	41	44	15.5	5.77	84	.320	.383	5	.128	-1	-10	-12	0	-1.1
1931 Chi-N	5	5	.500	31	4	1	0	2	79	81	2	43	38	14.5	3.87	100	.275	.372	5	.227	1	-0	-0	0	0.1
1932 *Chi-N	2	2	.500	35	0	0	0	1	53^2	61	3	19	20	13.8	4.36	86	.281	.345	1	.125	-0	-3	-4	-0	-0.4
Total 14	72	95	.431	410	162	70	7	19	1562^1	1645	35	617	765	13.5	3.88	97	.278	.355	80	.171	-4	-3	-23	-6	-3.2
● **RUDY MAY** May, Rudolph b: 7/18/44, Coffeyville, Kan. BL/TL, 6'3", 207 lbs. Deb: 4/18/65																									
1965 Cal-A	4	9	.308	30	19	2	1	0	124	111	7	78	76	14.0	3.92	87	.245	.361	6	.200	3	-6	-7	-2	-0.6
1969 Cal-A	10	13	.435	43	25	4	0	2	180^1	142	20	66	133	10.5	3.44	101	.220	.296	4	.082	-2	4	1	-1	-0.2
1970 Cal-A	7	13	.350	38	34	2	2	0	208^2	190	20	81	164	11.8	4.01	90	.245	.319	6	.087	-2	-7	-9	0	-1.2
1971 Cal-A	11	12	.478	32	31	7	2	0	208^1	160	12	87	156	10.8	3.02	107	.213	.297	10	.147	0	10	5	-1	0.5
1972 Cal-A	12	11	.522	35	30	10	3	1	205^1	162	15	82	169	10.7	2.94	99	.215	.293	7	.113	-1	3	-1	-2	-0.4
1973 Cal-A	7	17	.292	34	28	10	4	0	185	177	20	80	134	12.6	4.38	81	.254	.333	0	—	0	-12	-17	2	-1.5
1974 Cal-A	0	1	.000	18	3	0	0	2	27	29	2	10	12	13.3	7.00	49	.274	.342	0	—	0	-10	-11	1	-0.6
NY-A	8	4	.667	17	15	8	2	0	114^1	75	5	48	90	10.0	2.28	153	.188	.282	0	—	0	17	15	-2	1.7
Yr	8	5	.615	35	18	8	2	2	141^1	104	7	58	102	10.6	3.18	109	.204	.291	0	—	0	7	5	-0	1.1
1975 NY-A	14	12	.538	32	31	13	1	0	212	179	9	99	145	11.9	3.06	119	.231	.320	0	—	0	17	14	-1	1.5
1976 NY-A	4	3	.571	11	11	2	1	0	68	49	5	28	38	10.3	3.57	96	.206	.292	0	—	0	-0	-1	0	-0.1
Bal-A	11	7	.611	24	21	5	1	0	152^1	156	11	42	71	11.7	3.78	87	.267	.316	0	—	0	-4	-9	-1	-0.9
Yr	15	10	.600	35	32	7	2	0	220^1	205	16	70	109	11.2	3.72	89	.249	.308	0	—	0	-5	-10	-1	-1.0
1977 Bal-A	18	14	.563	37	37	11	4	0	251^2	243	25	78	105	11.7	3.61	105	.255	.315	0	—	0	13	5	-3	0.5
1978 Mon-N	8	10	.444	27	23	4	1	0	144	141	15	42	87	11.8	3.88	91	.255	.315	6	.143	0	-5	-6	-2	-0.7
1979 Mon-N	10	3	.769	33	7	2	1	0	93^2	88	4	31	67	11.8	2.31	159	.255	.324	3	.143	-0	15	14	1	1.5
1980 *NY-A	15	5	.750	41	17	3	1	3	175^1	144	14	39	133	**9.4**	**2.46**	**159**	.224	**.268**	0	—	0	31	28	0	3.0
1981 *NY-A	6	11	.353	27	22	4	0	1	147^2	137	10	41	79	11.0	4.14	86	.246	.300	0	—	0	-8	-9	1	-0.8
1982 NY-A	6	6	.500	41	6	0	0	3	106	109	4	14	85	10.5	2.89	138	.267	.292	0	—	0	14	13	1	1.4
1983 NY-A	1	5	.167	15	0	0	0	0	18^1	22	1	12	16	17.2	6.87	57	.293	.398	0	—	0	-6	-6	0	-0.5
Total 16	152	156	.494	535	360	87	24	12	2622	2314	199	958	1760	11.4	3.46	102	.238	.310	42	.123	-2	64	20	-7	2.6
● **SCOTT MAY** May, Scott Francis b: 11/11/61, West Bend, Wis. BR/TR, 6'1", 185 lbs. Deb: 9/02/88																									
1988 Tex-A	0	0	—	3	1	0	0	0	7^1	8	3	4	4	14.7	8.59	48	.296	.387	0	—	0	-4	-4	0	-0.5
1991 Chi-N	0	0	—	2	0	0	0	0	2	6	0	1	1	31.5	18.00	22	.545	.583	0	—	0	-3	-3	-0	-0.3
Total 2	0	0	—	5	1	0	0	0	9^1	14	3	5	5	18.3	10.61	38	.368	.442	0	—	0	-7	-7	-0	-0.8
● **BUCKSHOT MAY** May, William Herbert b: 12/13/1899, Bakersfield, Cal. d: 3/15/84, Bakersfield, Cal. BR/TR, 6'2", 169 lbs. Deb: 5/09/24																									
1924 Pit-N	0	0	—	1	0	0	0	0	1	2	0	0	1	18.0	0.00	—	.500	.500	0	—	0	0	0	0	0.0
● **ED MAYER** Mayer, Edwin David b: 11/30/31, San Francisco, Cal BL/TL, 6'2", 185 lbs. Deb: 9/15/57																									
1957 Chi-N	0	0	—	3	1	0	0	0	7^2	8	2	2	3	12.9	5.87	66	.258	.324	1	.500	0	-2	-2	0	-0.1
1958 Chi-N	2	2	.500	19	0	0	0	1	23^2	15	0	16	14	12.9	3.80	103	.190	.347	1	.200	-0	0	0	-0	0.0
Total 2	2	2	.500	22	1	0	0	1	31^1	23	2	18	17	12.9	4.31	91	.209	.341	2	.286	0	-1	-1	0	-0.1
● **ERSKINE MAYER** Mayer, Erskine John (b: James Erskine) b: 1/16/1889, Atlanta, Ga. d: 3/10/57, Los Angeles, Cal. BR/TR, 6', 168 lbs. Deb: 9/04/12 F																									
1912 Phi-N	0	1	.000	7	1	0	0	0	21^1	27	1	7	5	14.8	6.33	57	.318	.376	0	.000	-0	-7	-6	0	-0.6
1913 Phi-N	9	9	.500	39	20	7	2	1	170^2	172	6	46	51	12.0	3.11	107	.272	.330	6	.120	-2	2	4	0	0.2
1914 Phi-N	21	19	.525	48	39	24	4	2	321	308	8	91	116	11.6	2.58	114	.256	.315	21	.194	2	8	13	4	2.1
1915 *Phi-N	21	15	.583	43	33	20	2	2	274^2	240	9	59	114	10.3	2.36	116	.243	.295	21	.239	5	12	12	1	2.0
1916 Phi-N	7	7	.500	28	16	7	2	0	140	148	7	33	62	11.9	3.15	84	.281	.328	5	.132	-1	-8	-8	3	-0.6
1917 Phi-N	11	6	.647	28	18	11	1	0	160	160	6	33	64	11.1	2.76	102	.268	.310	10	.196	-0	-1	1	-0	0.0
1918 Phi-N	7	4	.636	13	13	7	0	0	104	108	2	26	16	11.9	3.12	96	.276	.328	8	.216	1	-4	-1	-0	-0.1
Pit-N	9	3	.750	15	14	11	1	0	123^1	122	1	27	25	11.2	2.26	127	.268	.314	7	.167	2	7	8	-2	0.9
Yr	16	7	.696	28	27	18	1	0	227^1	230	3	53	41	11.4	2.65	110	.270	.316	15	.190	2	3	7	-2	0.8
1919 Pit-N	5	3	.625	18	10	6	0	1	88^1	100	2	12	20	11.6	4.48	67	.267	.294	6	.207	0	-15	-14	-1	-1.6
*Chi-A	1	3	.250	6	2	0	0	0	23^2	30	1	11	9	15.6	8.37	38	.316	.387	0	.000	-1	-14	-14	-0	-1.4
Total 8	91	70	.565	245	166	93	12	6	1427	1415	43	345	482	11.4	2.96	99	.264	.316	84	.185	6	-21	-5	4	0.9
● **SAM MAYER** Mayer, Samuel Frankel (b: Samuel Frankel Erskine) b: 2/28/1893, Atlanta, Ga. d: 7/1/62, Atlanta, Ga. BR/TL, 5'10", 164 lbs. Deb: 9/14/15 F♦																									
1915 Was-A	0	0	—	1	0	0	0	0	0	0	0	2	0	—	—	—	—	1.000	7	.241	0	0	0	0	0.0

YEAR	TM/L	W	L	PCT	G	GS	CG	SH	SV	IP	H	HR	BB	SO	RAT	ERA	ERA+	OAV	OOB	BH	AVG	PB	PR	/A	PD	TPI
● **AL MAYS**	Mays, Albert C. b: 5/17/1865, Canal Dover, Ohio d: 5/7/05, Parkersburg, W.Va. BR , Deb: 5/10/1885																									
1885	Lou-a	6	11	.353	17	17	17	0	0	150	129	3	43	61	10.8	2.76	117	.219	.282	13	.213	0	8	8	-0	0.7
1886	NY-a	11	28	.282	41	41	39	1	0	350	330	7	140	163	12.4	3.39	101	.240	.317	16	.119	-10	2	1	-1	-0.7
1887	NY-a	17	34	.333	52	52	50	0	0	441^1	551	11	136	124	14.4	4.73	90	.298	.353	45	.204	-1	-21	-24	6	-1.4
1888	Bro-a	9	9	.500	18	18	17	1	0	160^2	150	1	32	67	10.8	2.80	107	.238	.287	5	.079	-4	5	3	2	0.1
1889	Col-a	10	7	.588	21	19	13	1	0	140	167	4	56	52	14.6	4.82	75	.287	.354	7	.130	-1	-15	-19	1	-1.5
1890	Col-a	0	1	.000	1	1	1	0	0	9	14	0	8	2	23.0	8.00	45	.344	.463	0	.000	-0	-4	-4	-1	-0.4
Total	6	53	90	.371	150	148	137	3	0	1251	1341	26	415	469	13.1	3.91	94	.265	.328	86	.160	-16	-26	-35	7	-3.2
● **CARL MAYS**	Mays, Carl William "Sub" b: 11/12/1891, Liberty, Ky. d: 4/4/71, ElCajon, Cal. BL/TR, 5'11.5", 195 lbs. Deb: 4/15/15																									
1915	Bos-A	6	5	.545	38	6	2	0	**7**	131^2	119	0	21	65	9.9	2.60	107	.244	.282	9	.237	2	5	3	2	0.6
1916	*Bos-A	18	13	.581	44	24	14	2	3	245	208	3	74	76	10.7	2.39	116	.234	.299	18	.234	7	12	10	9	3.0
1917	Bos-A	22	9	.710	35	33	27	2	0	289	230	1	74	91	9.9	1.74	148	.221	.282	27	.252	6	30	27	8	4.9
1918	*Bos-A	21	13	.618	35	33	**30**	**8**	0	293^1	230	2	81	114	9.9	2.21	121	.221	.284	30	.288	9	19	15	9	4.0
1919	Bos-A	5	11	.313	21	16	14	2	2	146	131	3	40	53	10.8	2.47	123	.247	.306	8	.151	-2	12	9	3	1.1
	NY-A	9	3	.750	13	13	12	1	0	120	96	2	37	54	10.4	1.65	193	.216	.283	14	.311	3	21	21	1	2.9
	Yr	14	14	.500	34	29	26	3	2	266	227	5	77	107	10.5	2.10	148	.231	.291	22	.224	1	33	30	4	4.0
1920	NY-A	26	11	.703	45	37	26	**6**	2	312	310	13	84	92	11.6	3.06	125	.263	.316	26	.239	2	26	26	6	3.4
1921	*NY-A	**27**	9	**.750**	**49**	38	30	1	**7**	**336^2**	332	11	76	70	11.1	3.05	139	.257	.303	49	.343	12	46	44	3	5.8
1922	*NY-A	12	14	.462	34	29	21	1	2	240	257	12	50	41	11.8	3.60	111	.285	.327	23	.250	1	12	11	6	1.7
1923	NY-A	5	2	.714	23	7	2	0	0	81^1	119	8	32	16	17.2	6.20	64	.357	.420	4	.148	1	-20	-20	3	-1.6
1924	Cin-N	20	9	.690	37	27	15	2	0	226	238	3	36	63	11.1	3.15	120	.270	.302	24	.289	7	18	16	8	3.2
1925	Cin-N	3	5	.375	12	5	3	0	2	51^2	60	0	13	10	13.1	3.31	124	.294	.342	4	.250	1	6	5	1	0.6
1926	Cin-N	19	12	.613	39	33	**24**	3	1	281	286	3	53	58	11.0	3.14	118	.269	.306	22	.224	2	21	17	10	3.0
1927	Cin-N	3	7	.300	14	9	6	0	0	82	89	1	10	17	11.0	3.51	108	.276	.300	13	.406	5	4	2	4	1.2
1928	Cin-N	4	1	.800	14	7	4	1	1	62^2	67	3	22	10	12.8	3.88	102	.275	.335	8	.296	1	1	1	0	0.2
1929	NY-N	7	2	.778	37	8	1	0	4	123	140	8	31	32	12.7	4.32	106	.287	.333	12	.353	4	5	4	2	0.9
Total	15	207	126	.622	490	325	231	29	31	3021^1	2912	73	734	862	11.1	2.92	119	.257	.307	291	.268	62	217	189	74	34.9
● **MATT MAYSEY**	Maysey, Matthew Samuel b: 1/8/67, Hamilton, Ont., Canada BR/TR, 6'4", 225 lbs. Deb: 7/08/92																									
1992	Mon-N	0	0	—	2	0	0	0	0	2^1	4	1	0	1	19.3	3.86	90	.364	.417	0	—	0	-0	-0	-0	0.0
● **JACK McADAMS**	McAdams, George D. b: 12/17/1886, Benton, Ark. d: 5/21/37, San Francisco, Cal BR/TR, 6'1.5", 170 lbs. Deb: 7/22/11																									
1911	StL-N	0	0	—	6	0	0	0	0	9^2	7	0	5	4	13.0	3.72	91	.226	.368	0	.000	-0	-0	-0	0	0.0
● **BILL McAFEE**	McAfee, William Fort b: 9/7/07, Smithville, Ga. d: 7/8/58, Culpepper, Va. BR/TR, 6'2", 186 lbs. Deb: 5/12/30																									
1930	Chi-N	0	0	—	2	0	0	0	0	1	3	0	2	0	45.0	0.00	—	.375	.500	0	—	0	1	1	-0	0.0
1931	Bos-N	0	1	.000	18	1	0	0	0	29^2	39	2	10	9	14.9	6.37	59	.333	.386	0	.000	-0	-8	-9	0	-0.8
1932	Was-A	6	1	.857	8	5	2	0	0	41^1	47	3	22	10	15.0	3.92	110	.287	.371	2	.111	-1	3	2	1	0.1
1933	Was-A	3	2	.600	27	1	0	0	5	53	64	3	21	14	14.6	6.62	63	.296	.361	4	.267	2	-14	-14	0	-1.1
1934	StL-A	1	0	1.000	28	0	0	0	0	61^2	84	4	26	11	16.5	5.84	86	.332	.401	3	.188	-0	-9	-6	-1	-0.6
Total	5	10	4	.714	83	7	2	0	5	186^2	237	12	81	44	15.5	5.69	78	.313	.382	9	.173	0	-28	-26	1	-2.4
● **JIMMY McALEER**	McAleer, James Robert "Loafer" b: 7/10/1864, Youngstown, Ohio d: 4/29/31, Youngstown, Ohio BR/TR, 6', 175 lbs. Deb: 4/24/1889 M♦																									
1901	Cle-A	0	0	—	1	0	0	0	0	0^1	2	0	3	0	135.0	0.00	—	.675	.839	1	.143	-0	0	0	0	0.0
● **JACK McALEESE**	McAleese, John James b: 1877, Sharon, Pa. d: 11/15/50, New York, N.Y. BR/TR, 5'8", Deb: 8/10/01 ♦																									
1901	Chi-A	0	0	—	1	0	0	0	0	3	7	0	1	1	24.0	9.00	39	.447	.480	0	.000	-0	-2	-2	0	-0.2
● **SPORT McALLISTER**	McAllister, Lewis William b: 7/23/1874, Austin, Miss. d: 7/17/62, Wyandotte, Mich. BB/TR, 5'11", 180 lbs. Deb: 8/07/1896 ♦																									
1896	Cle-N	0	0	—	1	0	0	0	0	4	9	0	2	0	24.8	6.75	67	.439	.489	6	.222	-0	-1	-1	0	-0.1
1897	Cle-N	1	2	.333	4	3	3	0	0	28	29	3	9	10	12.2	4.50	100	.265	.321	30	.219	-0	-1	-0	1	0.0
1898	Cle-N	3	4	.429	9	7	6	0	0	65^1	73	2	23	9	13.6	4.55	80	.280	.346	13	.228	1	-7	-7	-1	-0.6
1899	Cle-N	0	1	.000	3	1	1	0	0	16	29	0	10	2	24.2	9.56	39	.389	.486	99	.237	0	-10	-10	-0	-0.8
Total	4	4	7	.364	17	11	10	0	0	113^1	140	5	44	21	15.2	5.32	73	.301	.370	358	.247	1	-19	-18	0	-1.5
● **ERNIE McANALLY**	McAnally, Ernest Lee b: 8/15/46, Pittsburg, Tex. BR/TR, 6'1", 190 lbs. Deb: 4/11/71																									
1971	Mon-N	11	12	.478	31	25	8	2	0	177^2	150	9	87	98	12.4	3.90	90	.228	.326	7	.117	-2	-9	-7	0	-1.0
1972	Mon-N	6	15	.286	29	27	4	2	0	170	165	13	71	102	12.7	3.81	93	.259	.337	6	.113	-2	-7	-5	3	-0.4
1973	Mon-N	7	9	.438	27	24	4	0	0	147	158	13	54	72	13.2	4.04	94	.274	.340	9	.184	-1	-6	-4	-0	-0.5
1974	Mon-N	6	13	.316	25	21	5	2	0	128^2	126	10	56	79	13.0	4.48	86	.256	.336	5	.119	-2	-12	-9	1	-1.1
Total	4	30	49	.380	112	97	21	6	0	623^1	599	45	268	351	12.8	4.03	91	.253	.334	27	.132	-6	-34	-25	3	-3.0
● **JIM McANDREW**	McAndrew, James Clement b: 1/11/44, Lost Nation, Iowa BR/TR, 6'2", 185 lbs. Deb: 7/21/68																									
1968	NY-N	4	7	.364	12	12	2	1	0	79	66	5	17	46	9.9	2.28	133	.230	.282	1	.045	-1	6	7	-1	0.5
1969	NY-N	6	7	.462	27	21	4	2	0	135	112	12	44	90	10.5	3.47	105	.225	.291	5	.135	0	2	3	-1	0.1
1970	NY-N	10	14	.417	32	27	9	3	2	184^1	166	18	38	111	10.1	3.56	113	.239	.281	8	.148	1	10	9	-2	0.8
1971	NY-N	2	5	.286	24	10	0	0	0	90^1	78	10	32	42	11.1	4.38	78	.227	.294	1	.043	-1	-9	-10	1	-1.1
1972	NY-N	11	8	.579	28	23	4	0	1	160^2	133	12	38	81	9.9	2.80	120	.225	.278	2	.047	-2	12	10	-1	0.7
1973	NY-N	3	8	.273	23	12	0	0	1	80^1	109	9	31	38	16.0	5.38	67	.330	.393	2	.133	2	-15	-16	-1	-1.5
1974	SD-N	1	4	.200	15	5	1	0	0	41^2	48	7	13	16	13.2	5.62	63	.284	.335	1	.143	0	-9	-10	-1	-1.0
Total	7	37	53	.411	161	110	20	6	4	771^1	712	73	213	424	11.0	3.65	98	.245	.300	20	.100	-2	-4	-6	-6	-1.5
● **DIXIE McARTHUR**	McArthur, Oland Alexander b: 2/1/1892, Vernon, Ala. d: 5/31/86, West Point, Miss. BR/TR, 6'1", 185 lbs. Deb: 7/10/14																									
1914	Pit-N	0	0	—	1	0	0	0	0	1	1	0	0	1	9.0	0.00	—	.250	.250	0	—	0	0	0	0	0.0
● **WICKEY McAVOY**	McAvoy, James Eugene b: 10/22/1894, Rochester, N.Y. d: 7/6/73, Rochester, N.Y. BR/TR, 5'11", 172 lbs. Deb: 9/29/13 ♦																									
1918	Phi-A	0	0	—	1	0	0	0	0	0^2	1	1	0	0	13.5	13.50	22	.500	.500	66	.244	0	-1	-1	0	-0.1
● **TOM McAVOY**	McAvoy, Thomas John b: 8/12/36, Brooklyn, N.Y. BL/TL, 6'3", 200 lbs. Deb: 9/27/59																									
1959	Was-A	0	0	—	1	0	0	0	0	2^2	1	0	2	0	10.1	0.00	—	.125	.300	0	.000	-0	1	1	0	0.1
● **AL McBEAN**	McBean, Alvin O'Neal b: 5/15/38, Charlotte Amalie, V.I. BR/TR, 6', 180 lbs. Deb: 7/02/61																									
1961	Pit-N	3	2	.600	27	2	0	0	0	74^1	72	4	42	49	14.3	3.75	106	.263	.369	4	.267	1	2	2	2	0.5
1962	Pit-N	15	10	.600	33	29	6	2	0	189^2	212	11	65	119	13.5	3.70	106	.285	.348	14	.209	2	5	5	0	0.7
1963	Pit-N	13	3	.813	55	7	2	1	11	122^1	100	5	39	74	10.4	2.57	128	.222	.287	6	.194	2	10	10	2	1.4
1964	Pit-N	8	3	.727	58	0	0	0	22	89^2	76	4	17	41	9.7	1.91	184	.234	.280	1	.083	-1	**16**	**16**	4	2.1
1965	Pit-N	6	6	.500	62	1	0	0	18	114	111	5	42	54	12.3	2.29	153	.260	.331	6	.222	1	16	15	1	1.9
1966	Pit-N	4	3	.571	47	0	0	0	3	86^2	95	9	24	54	12.6	3.22	111	.280	.332	1	.100	-1	4	3	1	0.4
1967	Pit-N	7	4	.636	51	8	5	0	4	131	118	6	43	54	11.1	2.54	132	.248	.312	6	.207	2	12	12	0	1.6
1968	Pit-N	9	12	.429	36	28	9	2	0	198^1	204	10	63	100	12.3	3.58	82	.269	.330	13	.194	2	-13	-15	4	-0.9
1969	SD-N	0	1	.000	1	1	0	0	0	7	10	1	2	1	15.4	5.14	69	.345	.387	1	.500	0	-1	-1	-0	-0.1
	LA-N	2	6	.250	31	0	0	0	4	48^1	46	6	21	26	12.8	3.91	85	.258	.343	0	.000	0	-2	-3	-1	-0.5
	Yr	2	7	.222	32	1	0	0	4	55^1	56	7	23	27	13.2	4.07	82	.271	.349	1	.200	0	-3	-4	-1	-0.6
1970	LA-N	0	0	—	1	0	0	0	0	1	1	0	0	0	9.0	0.00	—	.333	.333	0	—	0	0	0	-0	0.0

YEAR TM/L	W	L	PCT	G	GS	CG	SH	SV	IP	H	HR	BB	SO	RAT	ERA	ERA+	OAV	OOB	BH	AVG	PB	PR	/A	PD	TPI
Pit-N	0	0	—	7	0	0	0	1	10	13	2	7	3	18.0	8.10	48	.317	.417	0	.000	-0	-5	-5	0	-0.5
Yr	0	0	—	8	0	0	0	1	11	14	2	7	3	17.2	7.36	53	.318	.412	0	.000	-0	-4	-4	0	-0.5
Total 10	67	50	.573	409	76	22	5	63	1072^{1}	1058	63	365	575	12.2	3.13	111	.262	.327	52	.197	9	45	40	13	6.6

● PRYOR McBEE McBee, Pryor Edward "Lefty" b: 6/20/01, Blanco, Okla. d: 4/19/63, Roseville, Cal. BR/TL, 6'1", 190 lbs. Deb: 5/22/26

YEAR TM/L	W	L	PCT	G	GS	CG	SH	SV	IP	H	HR	BB	SO	RAT	ERA	ERA+	OAV	OOB	BH	AVG	PB	PR	/A	PD	TPI
1926 Chi-A	0	0	—	1	0	0	0	0	1^{1}	1	0	3	1	27.0	6.75	57	.250	.571	0	—	0	-0	-0	0	0.0

● DICK McBRIDE McBride, James Dickson b: 1845, Philadelphia, Pa. d: 10/10/16, Philadelphia, Pa. TR, 5'9", 150 lbs. Deb: 5/20/1871 M

YEAR TM/L	W	L	PCT	G	GS	CG	SH	SV	IP	H	HR	BB	SO	RAT	ERA	ERA+	OAV	OOB	BH	AVG	PB	PR	/A	PD	TPI
1871 Ath-n	18	5	**.783**	25	25	25	0	0	222	285	3	40	15	13.2	4.58	88	.280	.307	31	.235	-4	-9	-14		-1.2
1872 Ath-n	30	14	.682	47	47	47	1	0	419	513	3	26	44	11.6	3.01	121	.268	.278	73	.281	3	33	29		2.2
1873 Ath-n	24	19	.558	46	46	38	**3**	0	382^{2}	453	3	47	25	11.8	3.32	103	.263	.282	71	.281	3	-3	4		0.4
1874 Ath-n	33	22	.600	55	55	55	0	0	487	514	5	29		**10.0**	*2.55*	124	**.241**	**.251**	57	.216	-8	24	33		1.8
1875 Ath-n	44	14	.759	60	60	59	6	0	538	602	4	25		10.5	*1.97*	134	.266	.274	73	.271	4	29	40		3.8
1876 Bos-N	0	4	.000	4	4	3	0	0	33	53	1	5	2	15.8	2.73	83	.353	.374	3	.188	-1	-2	-2	-0	-0.3
Total 5 n	149	74	.668	233	233	224	10	0	2048^{2}	2367	18	167	<u>84</u>	11.1	*2.86*	115	.261	.275	305	.259	-2	75	98		7.0

● KEN McBRIDE McBride, Kenneth Faye b: 8/12/35, Huntsville, Ala. BR/TR, 6', 195 lbs. Deb: 8/04/59 C

YEAR TM/L	W	L	PCT	G	GS	CG	SH	SV	IP	H	HR	BB	SO	RAT	ERA	ERA+	OAV	OOB	BH	AVG	PB	PR	/A	PD	TPI
1959 Chi-A	0	1	.000	11	2	0	0	1	22^{2}	20	1	17	12	14.7	3.18	118	.230	.356	1	.167	-0	2	1	1	0.2
1960 Chi-A	0	1	.000	5	0	0	0	0	4^{2}	6	0	3	4	19.3	3.86	98	.333	.455	0	—	0	0	-0	-0	0.0
1961 LA-A☆	12	15	.444	38	36	11	1	1	241^{2}	229	28	102	180	12.6	3.65	124	.252	.332	7	.084	-6	10	23	4	2.2
1962 LA-A†	11	5	.688	24	23	6	4	0	149^{1}	136	9	70	83	13.0	3.50	110	.249	.344	9	.164	0	8	6	5	1.1
1963 LA-A★	13	12	.520	36	36	11	2	0	251	198	22	82	147	10.5	3.26	105	.218	.293	15	.172	2	10	5	3	1.0
1964 LA-A	4	13	.235	29	21	0	0	1	116^{1}	104	14	75	66	15.1	5.26	62	.239	.370	6	.214	3	-21	-26	3	-2.0
1965 Cal-A	0	3	.000	8	4	0	0	0	22	24	1	14	11	16.4	6.14	55	.270	.381	0	.000	-0	-7	-7	-0	-0.7
Total 7	40	50	.444	151	122	28	7	3	807^{2}	717	75	363	503	12.6	3.79	101	.240	.332	38	.144	-1	2	2	15	1.8

● PETE McBRIDE McBride, Peter William b: 7/9/1875, Adams, Mass. d: 7/3/44, N.Adams, Mass. BR/TR, 5'10", 170 lbs. Deb: 9/20/1898

YEAR TM/L	W	L	PCT	G	GS	CG	SH	SV	IP	H	HR	BB	SO	RAT	ERA	ERA+	OAV	OOB	BH	AVG	PB	PR	/A	PD	TPI
1898 Cle-N	0	1	.000	1	1	1	0	0	7	9	0	4	6	18.0	6.43	56	.309	.411	2	1.000	1	-2	-2	-0	-0.1
1899 StL-N	2	4	.333	11	6	4	0	0	64	65	4	40	26	15.3	4.08	98	.263	.375	5	.185	0	-2	-1	-1	-0.1
Total 2	2	5	.286	12	7	5	0	0	71	74	4	44	32	15.6	4.31	92	.268	.378	7	.241	1	-4	-3	-1	-0.2

● RALPH McCABE McCabe, Ralph Herbert "Mack" b: 10/21/18, Napanee, Ont., Can. d: 5/3/74, Windsor, Ont., Can. BR/TR, 6'4", 195 lbs. Deb: 9/18/46

YEAR TM/L	W	L	PCT	G	GS	CG	SH	SV	IP	H	HR	BB	SO	RAT	ERA	ERA+	OAV	OOB	BH	AVG	PB	PR	/A	PD	TPI
1946 Cle-A	0	1	.000	1	1	0	0	0	4	5	3	2	3	18.0	11.25	29	.313	.421	0	.000	-0	-3	-4	0	-0.3

● DICK McCABE McCabe, Richard James b: 2/21/1896, Mamaroneck, N.Y. d: 4/11/50, Buffalo, N.Y. BR/TR, 5'10.5", 159 lbs. Deb: 5/30/18

YEAR TM/L	W	L	PCT	G	GS	CG	SH	SV	IP	H	HR	BB	SO	RAT	ERA	ERA+	OAV	OOB	BH	AVG	PB	PR	/A	PD	TPI
1918 Bos-A	0	1	.000	3	1	0	0	0	9^{2}	13	0	2	3	14.0	2.79	96	.351	.385	0	.000	-0	-0	-0	0	0.0
1922 Chi-A	1	0	1.000	3	0	0	0	0	3^{1}	4	0	0	1	10.8	5.40	75	.308	.308	0	—	0	-1	-0	-0	-0.1
Total 2	1	1	.500	6	1	0	0	0	13	17	0	2	4	13.2	3.46	88	.340	.365	0	.000	-0	-1	-1	-0	-0.1

● TIM McCABE McCabe, Timothy J. b: 10/19/1894, Ironton, Mo. d: 4/12/77, Ironton, Mo. BR/TR, 6', 190 lbs. Deb: 8/16/15

YEAR TM/L	W	L	PCT	G	GS	CG	SH	SV	IP	H	HR	BB	SO	RAT	ERA	ERA+	OAV	OOB	BH	AVG	PB	PR	/A	PD	TPI
1915 StL-A	3	1	.750	7	4	4	1	0	41^{2}	25	1	9	17	7.6	1.30	221	.177	.232	1	.067	-1	8	7	-1	0.7
1916 StL-A	2	0	1.000	13	0	0	0	0	25^{2}	29	0	7	7	13.3	3.16	87	.282	.339	0	.000	-0	-1	-1	1	0.0
1917 StL-A	0	0	—	1	0	0	0	0	2^{1}	4	1	4	2	30.9	23.14	11	.400	.571	0	—	0	-5	-5	0	-0.4
1918 StL-A	0	0	—	1	0	0	0	0	1^{1}	2	0	1	0	20.3	13.50	20	.333	.429	0	—	0	-2	-2	-0	-0.2
Total 4	5	1	.833	22	4	4	1	0	71	60	2	21	26	10.6	2.92	96	.231	.296	1	.053	-1	-0	-1	1	0.1

● HARRY McCAFFERY McCaffery, Harry Charles b: 11/25/1858, St.Louis, Mo. d: 4/19/28, St.Louis, Mo. BR/TR, 5'10.5", 185 lbs. Deb: 6/15/1882 U♦

YEAR TM/L	W	L	PCT	G	GS	CG	SH	SV	IP	H	HR	BB	SO	RAT	ERA	ERA+	OAV	OOB	BH	AVG	PB	PR	/A	PD	TPI
1885 Cin-a	1	0	1.000	1	1	1	0	0	9	13	1	2	2	17.0	6.00	54	.342	.405	0	.000	-1	-3	-3	-0	-0.3

● BILL McCAHAN McCahan, William Glenn b: 6/7/21, Philadelphia, Pa. d: 7/3/86, Fort Worth, Tex. BR/TR, 5'11", 200 lbs. Deb: 9/15/46

YEAR TM/L	W	L	PCT	G	GS	CG	SH	SV	IP	H	HR	BB	SO	RAT	ERA	ERA+	OAV	OOB	BH	AVG	PB	PR	/A	PD	TPI
1946 Phi-A	1	1	.500	4	2	2	1	0	18	16	0	9	6	12.5	1.00	355	.246	.338	2	.400	1	5	5	0	0.7
1947 Phi-A	10	5	.667	29	19	10	1	0	165^{1}	160	7	62	47	12.1	3.32	115	.252	.318	9	.164	-1	7	9	1	1.0
1948 Phi-A	4	7	.364	17	15	5	0	0	86^{2}	98	8	65	20	16.9	5.71	75	.284	.398	8	.258	1	-14	-14	-1	-1.3
1949 Phi-A	1	1	.500	7	4	0	0	0	20^{2}	23	0	9	3	13.9	2.61	157	.291	.364	1	.200	-0	4	3	-0	0.3
Total 4	16	14	.533	57	40	17	2	0	290^{2}	297	15	145	76	13.7	3.84	103	.264	.348	20	.208	1	2	4	-1	0.7

● WINDY McCALL McCall, John William b: 7/18/25, San Francisco, Cal. BL/TL, 6', 180 lbs. Deb: 4/25/48

YEAR TM/L	W	L	PCT	G	GS	CG	SH	SV	IP	H	HR	BB	SO	RAT	ERA	ERA+	OAV	OOB	BH	AVG	PB	PR	/A	PD	TPI
1948 Bos-A	0	1	.000	1	1	0	0	0	1^{1}	6	1	1	0	47.3	20.25	22	.600	.636	0	—	0	-2	-2	0	-0.2
1949 Bos-A	0	0	—	5	0	0	0	0	9^{1}	13	2	10	8	22.2	11.57	38	.333	.469	2	.667	1	-8	-7	-0	-0.6
1950 Pit-N	0	0	—	2	0	0	0	0	6^{2}	12	2	4	5	21.6	9.45	46	.387	.457	0	.000	0	-4	-4	0	-0.3
1954 NY-N	2	5	.286	33	4	0	0	2	61	50	5	29	38	12.1	3.25	124	.219	.315	0	.000	-1	6	5	-1	0.3
1955 NY-N	6	5	.545	42	6	4	0	3	95	86	8	37	50	12.2	3.69	109	.244	.326	2	.118	-1	4	3	1	0.3
1956 NY-N	3	4	.429	46	4	0	0	7	77^{1}	74	7	20	41	11.1	3.61	105	.252	.302	3	.200	-0	1	1	-2	0.0
1957 NY-N	0	0	—	5	0	0	0	0	3	8	1	2	2	33.0	15.00	26	.533	.611	0	—	0	-4	-4	-0	-0.4
Total 7	11	15	.423	134	15	4	0	12	253^{2}	249	26	103	144	12.9	4.22	94	.257	.335	7	.146	-1	-7	-7	-3	-0.9

● LARRY McCALL McCall, Larry Stephen b: 9/8/52, Asheville, N.C. BL/TR, 6'2", 195 lbs. Deb: 9/10/77

YEAR TM/L	W	L	PCT	G	GS	CG	SH	SV	IP	H	HR	BB	SO	RAT	ERA	ERA+	OAV	OOB	BH	AVG	PB	PR	/A	PD	TPI
1977 NY-A	0	1	.000	2	0	0	0	0	6	12	1	1	0	19.5	7.50	53	.375	.394	0	—	0	-2	-2	-0	-0.2
1978 NY-A	1	1	.500	5	1	0	0	0	16	20	2	6	7	15.2	5.63	64	.323	.391	0	—	0	-3	-4	0	-0.2
1979 Tex-A	1	0	1.000	2	1	0	0	0	8^{1}	7	0	3	3	10.8	2.16	192	.226	.294	0	—	0	2	2	0	0.3
Total 3	2	2	.500	9	2	0	0	0	30^{1}	39	3	10	10	14.8	5.04	76	.312	.368	0	—	0	-4	-4	0	-0.1

● DUTCH McCALL McCall, Robert Leonard b: 12/27/20, Columbia, Tenn. BL/TL, 6'1", 184 lbs. Deb: 4/27/48

YEAR TM/L	W	L	PCT	G	GS	CG	SH	SV	IP	H	HR	BB	SO	RAT	ERA	ERA+	OAV	OOB	BH	AVG	PB	PR	/A	PD	TPI
1948 Chi-N	4	13	.235	30	20	5	0	0	151^{1}	158	14	85	89	14.5	4.82	81	.268	.361	9	.170	1	-14	-15	1	-1.3

● RANDY McCAMENT McCament, Larry Randall b: 7/29/62, Albuquerque, N.Mex. BR/TR, 6'3", 195 lbs. Deb: 6/28/89

YEAR TM/L	W	L	PCT	G	GS	CG	SH	SV	IP	H	HR	BB	SO	RAT	ERA	ERA+	OAV	OOB	BH	AVG	PB	PR	/A	PD	TPI
1989 SF-N	1	1	.500	25	0	0	0	0	36^{2}	32	4	23	12	13.7	3.93	86	.241	.357	1	.333	0	-2	-2	0	-0.2
1990 SF-N	0	0	—	3	0	0	0	0	6	8	0	5	5	19.5	3.00	121	.333	.448	0	.000	-0	1	0	-0	0.0
Total 2	1	1	.500	28	0	0	0	0	42^{2}	40	4	28	17	14.6	3.80	90	.255	.371	1	.250	0	-1	-2	0	-0.2

● GENE McCANN McCann, Henry Eugene "Mike" b: 6/13/1876, Baltimore, Md. d: 4/26/43, New York, N.Y. TR, 5'10", Deb: 4/19/01

YEAR TM/L	W	L	PCT	G	GS	CG	SH	SV	IP	H	HR	BB	SO	RAT	ERA	ERA+	OAV	OOB	BH	AVG	PB	PR	/A	PD	TPI
1901 Bro-N	2	3	.400	6	5	3	0	0	34	34	1	16	9	14.3	3.44	97	.259	.357	0	.000	-1	-0	-0	0	-0.1
1902 Bro-N	1	2	.333	3	3	3	0	0	30	32	0	12	9	13.2	2.40	115	.273	.340	1	.083	-1	1	1	1	0.1
Total 2	3	5	.375	9	8	6	0	0	64	66	1	28	18	13.8	2.95	104	.265	.349	1	.045	-2	1	1	1	0.0

● ARCH McCARTHY McCarthy, Archibald Joseph b: Ypsilanti, Mich. Deb: 8/14/02

YEAR TM/L	W	L	PCT	G	GS	CG	SH	SV	IP	H	HR	BB	SO	RAT	ERA	ERA+	OAV	OOB	BH	AVG	PB	PR	/A	PD	TPI
1902 Det-A	2	7	.222	10	8	8	0	0	72	90	2	31	10	15.6	6.13	60	.306	.380	2	.071	-3	-20	-20	-2	-2.1

● JOHNNY McCARTHY McCarthy, John Joseph b: 1/7/10, Chicago, Ill. d: 9/13/73, Mundelein, Ill. BL/TL, 6'1.5", 185 lbs. Deb: 9/02/34 ♦

YEAR TM/L	W	L	PCT	G	GS	CG	SH	SV	IP	H	HR	BB	SO	RAT	ERA	ERA+	OAV	OOB	BH	AVG	PB	PR	/A	PD	TPI
1939 NY-N	0	0	—	1	0	0	0	0	5	8	1	2	0	18.0	7.20	55	.364	.417	21	.262	0	-2	-2	0	-0.1

● TOMMY McCARTHY McCarthy, Thomas Francis Michael b: 7/24/1863, Boston, Mass. d: 8/5/22, Boston, Mass. BR/TR, 5'7", 170 lbs. Deb: 7/10/1884 MH♦

YEAR TM/L	W	L	PCT	G	GS	CG	SH	SV	IP	H	HR	BB	SO	RAT	ERA	ERA+	OAV	OOB	BH	AVG	PB	PR	/A	PD	TPI
1884 Bos-U	0	7	.000	7	6	5	0	0	56	73	2	14	18	14.0	4.82	61	.295	.333	45	.215	-0	-11	-12	1	-0.9
1886 Phi-N	0	0	—	1	0	0	0	0	1	0	0	1	1	9.0	0.00	—	.000	.250	5	.185	0	0	0	0	0.0
1888 *StL-a	0	0	—	2	0	0	0	0	4^{1}	3	1	2	1	10.4	4.15	79	.188	.279	140	.274	0	-1	-0	-0	-0.1
1889 StL-a	0	0	—	1	0	0	0	0	5	4	0	6	1	18.0	7.20	59	.213	.403	176	.291	0	-2	-2	-0	-0.1
1891 StL-a	0	0	—	1	0	0	0	0	1	2	0	0	0	18.0	9.00	47	.402	.402	179	.310	0	-1	-1	-0	0.0

YEAR	TM/L	W	L	PCT	G	GS	CG	SH	SV	IP	H	HR	BB	SO	RAT	ERA	ERA+	OAV	OOB	BH	AVG	PB	PR	/A	PD	TPI
1894	Bos-N	0	0	—	1	0	0	0	0	2	1	0	3	0	18.0	4.50	126	.148	.410	188	.349	0	0	0	-0	0.0
Total	6	0	7	.000	13	6	5	0	0	69^1	83	3	26	21	14.1	4.93	64	.280	.338	1496	.292	1	-14	-14	1	-1.1
● **TOM McCARTHY**	McCarthy, Thomas Michael b: 6/18/61, Lundstahl, W.Ger. BR/TR, 6', 180 lbs. Deb: 7/05/85																									
1985	Bos-A	0	0	—	3	0	0	0	0	5	7	1	4	2	19.8	10.80	40	.350	.458	0	—	0	-4	-4	-0	-0.4
1988	Chi-A	2	0	1.000	6	0	0	0	1	13	9	0	2	5	9.0	1.38	287	.191	.255	0	—	0	4	4	0	0.5
1989	Chi-A	1	2	.333	31	0	0	0	0	66^2	72	8	20	27	12.7	3.51	108	.280	.337	0	—	0	3	2	1	0.3
Total	3	3	2	.600	40	0	0	0	1	84^2	88	9	26	34	12.5	3.61	107	.272	.333	0	—	0	3	2	1	0.4
● **TOM McCARTHY**	McCarthy, Thomas Patrick b: 5/22/1884, Ft.Wayne, Ind. d: 3/28/33, Mishawaka, Ind. TR , 5'7", 170 lbs. Deb: 5/10/08																									
1908	Cin-N	0	1	.000	1	1	0	0	0	3^2	6	0	3	3	22.1	9.82	23	.300	.391	0	.000	-0	-3	-3	0	-0.3
	Pit-N	0	0	—	2	1	0	0	0	6	3	0	6	1	13.5	0.00	—	.176	.391	0	.000	-0	2	2	1	0.2
	Bos-N	7	3	.700	14	11	7	2	0	94	77	0	28	27	10.1	1.63	148	.235	.298	6	.171	-0	8	8	0	1.1
	Yr	7	4	.636	17	13	7	2	0	103^2	86	0	37	31	10.8	1.82	132	.236	.308	6	.146	-1	6	7	1	1.0
1909	Bos-N	0	5	.000	8	7	3	0	0	46^1	47	3	28	11	15.0	3.50	81	.272	.379	2	.125	-0	-5	-3	0	-0.4
Total	2	7	9	.438	25	20	10	2	0	150	133	3	65	42	12.1	2.34	108	.248	.332	8	.140	-1	2	3	1	0.6
● **BILL McCARTHY**	McCarthy, William Thomas b: 4/11/1882, Ashland, Mass. d: 5/29/39, Boston, Mass. BR/TR, 5'11", 180 lbs. Deb: 4/21/06																									
1906	Bos-N	0	0	—	1	0	0	0	0	2	2	0	3	0	22.5	9.00	30	.182	.357	0	.000	-0	-1	-1	-0	-0.2
● **JOHN McCARTY**	McCarty, John A. b: St.Louis, Mo. TR , Deb: 4/18/1889																									
1889	KC-a	8	6	.571	15	14	13	0	0	119^2	147	4	61	36	16.1	3.91	107	.293	.376	18	.228	-2	-1	4	-0	0.1
● **KIRK McCASKILL**	McCaskill, Kirk Edward b: 4/9/61, Kapuskasing, Ont.Can BR/TR, 6'1", 200 lbs. Deb: 5/01/85																									
1985	Cal-A	12	12	.500	30	29	6	1	0	189^2	189	23	64	102	12.2	4.70	87	.258	.321	0	—	0	-12	-12	-0	-1.2
1986	*Cal-A	17	10	.630	34	33	10	2	0	246^1	207	19	92	202	11.1	3.36	122	.229	.303	0	—	0	22	20	-0	2.2
1987	Cal-A	4	6	.400	14	13	1	1	0	74^2	84	14	34	56	14.5	5.67	76	.286	.364	0	—	0	-10	-11	1	-1.0
1988	Cal-A	8	6	.571	23	23	4	2	0	146^1	155	9	61	98	13.3	4.31	90	.274	.346	0	—	0	-6	-7	0	-0.5
1989	Cal-A	15	10	.600	32	32	6	4	0	212	202	16	59	107	11.2	2.93	130	.254	.308	0	—	0	22	21	2	2.5
1990	Cal-A	12	11	.522	29	29	2	1	0	174^1	161	9	72	78	12.1	3.25	117	.244	.320	0	—	0	13	11	2	1.3
1991	Cal-A	10	19	.345	30	30	1	0	0	177^2	193	19	66	71	13.3	4.26	96	.283	.349	0	—	0	-3	-3	1	-0.2
1992	Chi-A	12	13	.480	34	34	0	0	0	209	193	11	95	109	12.7	4.18	91	.242	.328	0	—	0	-6	-8	2	-0.6
Total	8	90	87	.508	226	223	30	11	0	1430	1384	120	543	823	12.3	3.91	102	.255	.326	0	—	0	22	10	6	2.5
● **STEVE McCATTY**	McCatty, Steven Earl b: 3/20/54, Detroit, Mich. BR/TR, 6'3", 205 lbs. Deb: 9/17/77																									
1977	Oak-A	0	0	—	4	2	0	0	0	14^1	16	1	7	9	15.1	5.02	80	.276	.364	0	—	0	-2	-2	-1	-0.2
1978	Oak-A	0	0	—	9	0	0	0	0	20	26	1	9	10	15.7	4.50	81	.310	.376	0	—	0	-2	-2	-0	0.1
1979	Oak-A	11	12	.478	31	23	8	0	0	185^2	207	17	80	87	14.4	4.22	96	.284	.363	0	—	0	-0	-4	-2	-0.2
1980	Oak-A	14	14	.500	33	31	11	1	0	221^2	202	27	99	114	12.5	3.86	98	.240	.325	0	—	0	4	-2	-1	0.1
1981	*Oak-A	**14**	7	.667	22	22	16	**4**	0	185^2	140	12	61	91	9.8	2.33	149	.211	.279	0	—	0	**27**	**24**	-1	**2.8**
1982	Oak-A	6	3	.667	21	20	2	0	0	128^2	124	16	70	66	13.8	3.99	98	.255	.354	0	—	0	1	-1	-1	-0.1
1983	Oak-A	6	9	.400	38	24	3	2	5	167	156	16	82	65	12.9	3.99	97	.247	.334	0	—	0	1	-2	-2	-0.5
1984	Oak-A	8	14	.364	33	30	4	0	0	179^2	206	24	71	63	13.9	4.76	79	.289	.355	0	—	0	-15	-20	-2	-1.7
1985	Oak-A	4	4	.500	30	9	1	0	0	85^2	95	10	41	36	14.7	5.57	69	.286	.371	0	—	0	-14	-16	0	-1.4
Total	9	63	63	.500	221	161	45	7	5	1188^1	1172	124	520	541	13.0	3.99	95	.258	.339	0	—	0	2	-26	-9	-1.1
● **AL McCAULEY**	McCauley, Allen A. b: 3/4/1863, Indianapolis, Ind. d: 8/24/17, Wayne Twnshp., Ind BL/TL, 6', 180 lbs. Deb: 6/21/1884 ♦																									
1884	Ind-a	2	7	.222	10	9	9	0	0	76	87	2	25	34	13.3	5.09	65	.261	.313	10	.189	1	-16	-15	2	-1.0
● **JOE McCLAIN**	McClain, Joseph Fred b: 5/5/33, Johnson City, Tenn. BR/TR, 6', 183 lbs. Deb: 4/14/61																									
1961	Was-A	8	18	.308	33	29	7	2	1	212	221	22	48	76	11.6	3.86	104	.270	.313	14	.206	1	4	4	-3	0.2
1962	Was-A	0	4	.000	10	4	0	0	0	24	33	8	11	6	17.3	9.38	43	.327	.404	1	.143	-0	-14	-14	0	-1.3
Total	2	8	22	.267	43	33	7	2	1	236	254	30	59	82	12.2	4.42	91	.276	.324	15	.200	1	-11	-11	-3	-1.1
● **PAUL McCLELLAN**	McClellan, Paul William b: 2/8/66, San Mateo, Cal. BR/TR, 6'2", 180 lbs. Deb: 9/02/90																									
1990	SF-N	0	1	.000	4	1	0	0	0	7^2	14	3	6	2	24.7	11.74	31	.389	.488	1	.500	0	-7	-7	0	-0.6
1991	SF-N	3	6	.333	13	12	1	0	0	71	68	12	25	44	11.9	4.56	78	.252	.318	3	.143	-0	-7	-8	-1	-0.9
Total	2	3	7	.300	17	13	1	0	0	78^2	82	15	31	46	13.2	5.26	68	.268	.339	4	.174	0	-14	-15	-1	-1.5
● **JIM McCLOSKEY**	McCloskey, James Ellwood "Irish" b: 5/26/10, Danville, Pa. d: 8/18/71, Jersey City, N.J. BL/TL, 5'9.5", 180 lbs. Deb: 4/21/36																									
1936	Bos-N	0	0	—	4	1	0	0	0	8	14	1	3	2	20.3	11.25	34	.378	.439	0	.000	-0	-6	-7	0	-0.6
● **JOHN McCLOSKEY**	McCloskey, James John b: 8/20/1882, Wyoming, Pa. d: 6/5/19, Wilkes-Barre, Pa. Deb: 5/03/06																									
1906	Phi-N	3	2	.600	9	4	3	0	0	41	46	2	9	6	12.3	2.85	92	.280	.322	3	.200	0	-1	-1	-1	-0.2
1907	Phi-N	0	0	—	3	0	0	0	0	9	15	0	6	3	22.0	7.00	35	.417	.512	0	.000	-0	-5	-5	0	-0.5
Total	2	3	2	.600	12	4	3	0	0	50	61	2	15	9	14.0	3.60	72	.305	.359	3	.158	-0	-6	-6	-1	-0.7
● **BOB McCLURE**	McClure, Robert Craig b: 4/29/52, Oakland, Cal. BR/TL, 5'11", 170 lbs. Deb: 8/13/75																									
1975	KC-A	1	0	1.000	12	0	0	0	1	15^1	4	0	14	15	10.6	0.00	—	.077	.273	0	—	0	6	7	-0	0.6
1976	KC-A	0	0	—	8	0	0	0	0	4	3	0	8	3	24.8	9.00	39	.214	.500	0	—	0	-2	-2	-0	-0.3
1977	Mil-A	2	1	.667	68	0	0	0	6	71^1	64	2	34	57	12.5	2.52	161	.249	.339	0	—	0	12	12	2	1.4
1978	Mil-A	2	6	.250	44	0	0	0	9	65	53	8	30	47	12.3	3.74	101	.223	.325	0	—	0	0	0	-1	-0.1
1979	Mil-A	5	2	.714	36	0	0	0	5	51	53	6	24	37	14.1	3.88	107	.269	.357	0	—	0	2	2	-0	0.1
1980	Mil-A	5	8	.385	52	5	2	1	10	90^2	83	6	37	47	12.1	3.08	126	.241	.318	0	—	0	10	8	-1	0.9
1981	*Mil-A	0	0	—	4	0	0	0	0	7^2	7	1	4	6	12.9	3.52	97	.233	.324	0	—	0	0	-0	-0	0.2
1982	*Mil-A	12	7	.632	34	26	5	0	0	172^2	160	21	74	99	12.4	4.22	90	.248	.329	0	—	0	-3	-8	-1	-0.8
1983	Mil-A	9	9	.500	24	23	4	0	0	142	152	11	68	68	14.3	4.50	83	.277	.362	0	—	0	-7	-12	-1	-1.2
1984	Mil-A	4	8	.333	39	18	1	0	1	139^2	154	9	52	68	13.4	4.38	88	.282	.347	0	—	0	-6	-8	-0	-0.5
1985	Mil-A	4	1	.800	38	1	0	0	3	85^2	91	10	30	57	13.0	4.31	97	.274	.340	0	—	0	-2	-1	-0	-0.1
1986	Mil-A	2	1	.667	13	0	0	0	0	16^1	18	2	10	11	15.4	3.86	112	.286	.384	0	—	0	1	1	-0	-0.2
	Mon-N	2	5	.286	52	0	0	0	6	62^2	53	2	23	42	11.1	3.02	122	.232	.306	1	.250	0	5	5	0	0.5
1987	Mon-N	6	1	.857	52	0	0	0	5	52^1	47	8	20	33	11.5	3.44	122	.241	.312	0	.000	-0	4	4	0	0.4
1988	Mon-N	1	3	.250	19	0	0	0	2	19	23	3	6	12	14.2	6.16	58	.307	.366	0	.000	-0	-6	-5	0	-0.6
	NY-N	1	0	1.000	14	0	0	0	1	11	12	1	2	7	12.3	4.09	79	.279	.326	0	—	0	-1	-1	-0	-0.1
	Yr	2	3	.400	33	0	0	0	3	30	35	4	8	19	13.2	5.40	64	.289	.338	0	.000	-0	-7	-6	-0	-0.7
1989	Cal-A	6	1	.857	48	0	0	0	3	52^1	39	2	15	36	9.5	1.55	246	.212	.275	0	—	0	14	13	-1	1.3
1990	Cal-A	2	0	1.000	11	0	0	0	0	7	7	0	3	6	12.9	6.43	59	.269	.345	0	—	0	-2	-2	0	-0.2
1991	Cal-A	0	0	—	13	0	0	0	0	9^2	13	3	5	5	17.7	9.31	44	.317	.404	0	—	0	-6	-6	0	-0.5
	StL-N	1	1	.500	32	0	0	0	0	23	24	1	8	15	12.9	3.13	119	.282	.351	1	1.000	0	1	1	-0	0.2
1992	StL-N	2	2	.500	71	0	0	0	0	54	52	6	25	24	13.2	3.17	109	.261	.350	0	—	0	2	2	-0	0.1
Total	18	67	56	.545	684	73	12	1	52	1152^1	1112	102	492	695	12.8	3.79	102	.256	.336	2	.222	0	23	8	-4	1.1
● **HARRY McCLUSKEY**	McCluskey, Harry Robert b: 3/29/1892, Clay Center, Ohio d: 6/7/62, Toledo, Ohio BL/TL, 5'11.5", 173 lbs. Deb: 7/29/15																									
1915	Cin-N	0	0	—	3	0	0	0	0	5	4	0	0	2	7.2	5.40	53	.182	.182	0	.000	-0	-1	-1	-0	-0.2

YEAR TM/L	W	L	PCT	G	GS	CG	SH	SV	IP	H	HR	BB	SO	RAT	ERA	ERA+	OAV	OOB	BH	AVG	PB	PR	/A	PD	TPI
● ALEX McCOLL McColl, Alexander Boyd "Red" b: 3/29/1894, Eagleville, Ohio d: 2/6/91, Kingsville, Ohio BB/TR, 6'1", 178 lbs. Deb: 8/27/33																									
1933 *Was-A	1	0	1.000	4	1	1	0	0	17	13	0	7	5	10.6	2.65	158	.210	.290	2	.333	1	3	3	-0	0.3
1934 Was-A	3	4	.429	42	2	1	0	1	112	129	6	36	29	13.3	3.86	112	.291	.345	3	.097	-2	8	6	2	0.6
Total 2	4	4	.500	46	3	2	0	1	129	142	6	43	34	13.0	3.70	116	.281	.338	5	.135	-1	11	9	2	0.9
● RALPH McCONNAUGHEY McConnaughey, Ralph James b: 8/5/1889, Pennsylvania d: 6/4/66, Detroit, Mich. BR/TR, 5'8.5", 166 lbs. Deb: 7/08/14																									
1914 Ind-F	0	2	.000	7	2	1	0	0	26	23	3	16	7	13.8	4.85	72	.245	.360	1	.125	-0	-5	-4	-0	-0.5
● GEORGE McCONNELL McConnell, George Neely "Slats" b: 9/16/1877, Shelbyville, Tenn d: 5/10/64, Chattanooga, Tenn. BR/TR, 6'3", 190 lbs. Deb: 4/13/09 ♦																									
1909 NY-A	0	1	.000	2	1	0	0	0	4	3	0	3	4	13.5	2.25	112	.231	.375	9	.209	0	0	0	1	0.1
1912 NY-A	8	12	.400	23	20	19	0	0	176^{2}	172	3	52	91	11.6	2.75	131	.269	.328	27	.297	3	11	17	5	2.9
1913 NY-A	4	15	.211	35	20	8	0	3	180	162	2	60	72	11.4	3.20	93	.245	.314	12	.179	-1	-5	-4	5	-0.1
1914 Chi-N	0	1	.000	1	1	0	0	0	7	3	0	3	3	7.7	1.29	216	.125	.222	0	.000	-0	1	1	0	0.1
1915 Chi-F	**25**	10	**.714**	44	35	23	4	1	303	262	8	89	151	10.7	2.20	127	.232	.292	31	.248	6	28	20	3	3.2
1916 Chi-N	4	12	.250	28	20	8	1	0	171^{1}	137	8	35	82	9.3	2.57	113	.223	.271	9	.158	-2	1	6	2	0.7
Total 6	41	51	.446	133	97	58	5	4	842	739	21	242	403	10.7	2.60	117	.240	.300	88	.229	6	36	40	15	6.9
● BILLY McCOOL McCool, William John b: 7/14/44, Batesville, Ind. BR/TL, 6'2", 203 lbs. Deb: 4/24/64																									
1964 Cin-N	6	5	.545	40	3	0	0	7	89^{1}	66	3	29	87	9.7	2.42	150	.206	.274	0	.000	-2	11	12	-2	0.9
1965 Cin-N	9	10	.474	62	2	0	0	21	105^{1}	93	9	47	120	12.3	4.27	88	.237	.324	1	.037	-2	-9	-6	-0	-0.9
1966 Cin-N☆	8	8	.500	57	0	0	0	18	105^{1}	76	5	41	104	10.3	2.48	157	.205	.290	3	.167	-0	13	17	2	2.0
1967 Cin-N	3	7	.300	31	11	0	0	2	97^{1}	92	8	56	83	14.1	3.42	110	.246	.352	2	.077	-1	-1	4	-1	0.2
1968 Cin-N	3	4	.429	30	4	0	0	2	50^{2}	59	4	41	30	17.8	4.97	64	.294	.413	1	.125	-0	-11	-10	-1	-1.3
1969 SD-N	3	5	.375	54	0	0	0	7	58^{2}	59	2	42	35	16.4	4.30	82	.266	.396	0	.000	-0	-5	-5	-0	-0.6
1970 StL-N	0	3	.000	18	0	0	0	1	21^{2}	20	0	16	12	15.0	6.23	66	.250	.375	0	.000	-0	-5	-5	0	-0.5
Total 7	32	42	.432	292	20	0	0	58	528^{1}	465	31	272	471	12.9	3.59	103	.237	.336	7	.069	-6	-6	6	-1	-0.2
● JIM McCORMICK McCormick, James b: 1856, Glasgow, Scotland d: 3/10/18, Paterson, N.J. BR/TR, 5'10.5", 215 lbs. Deb: 5/20/1878 M																									
1878 Ind-N	5	8	.385	14	14	12	1	0	117	128	0	15	36	11.0	1.69	120	.269	.292	8	.143	-2	8	4	2	0.4
1879 Cle-N	20	40	.333	62	60	59	3	0	546^{1}	582	4	74	197	10.8	2.42	103	.259	.282	62	.220	-1	4	5	4	0.7
1880 Cle-N	**45**	28	.616	**74**	74	**72**	7	0	**657^{2}**	585	2	75	260	9.0	1.85	127	.226	.247	71	.246	1	38	**37**	1	**4.0**
1881 Cle-N	26	30	.464	59	58	**57**	2	0	526	484	4	84	178	9.7	2.45	107	.235	.265	79	.256	6	19	10	-3	1.2
1882 Cle-N	**36**	30	.545	**68**	67	**65**	4	0	**595^{2}**	550	14	103	200	9.9	2.37	118	.238	.271	57	.218	-4	35	28	-2	2.0
1883 Cle-N	28	12	**.700**	43	41	36	1	1	342	316	1	65	145	10.0	**1.84**	**171**	.233	.268	37	.236	-1	49	50	7	5.2
1884 Cle-N	19	22	.463	42	41	39	3	0	359	357	17	75	182	10.8	2.86	110	.247	.285	50	.263	2	5	12	0	1.3
Cin-U	21	3	**.875**	24	24	24	**7**	0	210	151	3	14	161	**7.1**	**1.54**	**205**	**.188**	**.202**	27	.245	-1	34	38	2	3.5
1885 Pro-N	1	3	.250	4	4	4	0	0	37	34	1	20	8	13.1	2.43	109	.234	.327	3	.214	0	2	1	3	0.4
*Chi-N	20	4	.833	24	24	24	3	0	215	187	8	40	88	9.5	2.43	125	.224	.260	23	.223	0	9	15	3	1.6
Yr	21	7	.750	28	28	28	3	0	252	221	9	60	96	10.0	2.43	123	.226	.271	26	.222	1	11	15	5	2.0
1886 *Chi-N	31	11	.738	42	42	38	2	0	347^{2}	341	18	100	172	11.4	2.82	129	.253	.304	41	.236	2	19	32	2	3.2
1887 Pit-N	13	23	.361	36	36	36	0	0	322^{1}	377	12	84	77	13.2	4.30	90	.285	.334	33	.243	-0	-8	-15	5	-0.9
Total 10	265	214	.553	492	485	466	33	1	4275^{2}	4092	84	749	1704	10.2	2.43	119	.242	.274	491	.236	2	215	215	22	22.6
● JERRY McCORMICK McCormick, John b: Philadelphia, Pa. d: 9/19/05, Philadelphia, Pa. Deb: 5/01/1883 ♦																									
1884 Phi-U	0	0	—	1	0	0	0	0	2	5	1	0	3	22.5	9.00	32	.446	.446	84	.285	0	-1	-1	-0	-0.1
● MIKE McCORMICK McCormick, Michael Francis b: 9/29/38, Pasadena, Cal. BL/TL, 6'2", 195 lbs. Deb: 9/03/56																									
1956 NY-N	0	1	.000	3	2	0	0	0	6^{2}	7	1	10	4	23.0	9.45	40	.269	.472	0	.000	-0	-4	-4	-0	-0.4
1957 NY-N	3	1	.750	24	5	1	0	0	74^{2}	79	7	32	50	13.7	4.10	96	.280	.360	6	.273	1	-2	-1	-1	-0.1
1958 SF-N	11	8	.579	42	28	8	2	1	178^{1}	192	19	60	82	12.9	4.59	83	.276	.336	12	.222	1	-13	-15	2	-1.2
1959 SF-N	12	16	.429	47	31	7	3	4	225^{2}	213	24	86	151	12.0	3.99	96	.248	.317	7	.106	-2	-1	-4	1	-0.6
1960 SF-N★	15	12	.556	40	34	15	4	3	253	228	15	65	154	10.5	**2.70**	129	.241	.291	16	.182	1	**30**	22	3	2.7
1961 SF-N★	13	16	.448	40	35	13	3	0	250	235	33	75	163	11.2	3.20	119	.249	.306	15	.188	1	23	17	-2	1.6
1962 SF-N	5	5	.500	28	15	1	0	0	98^{2}	112	18	45	42	14.4	5.38	71	.286	.361	3	.107	0	-16	-17	-1	-1.7
1963 Bal-A	6	8	.429	25	21	2	0	0	136	132	18	66	75	13.1	4.30	82	.256	.340	8	.174	1	-10	-12	-0	-1.2
1964 Bal-A	0	2	.000	4	2	0	0	0	17^{1}	21	1	8	13	15.1	5.19	69	.288	.358	1	.167	-0	-3	-3	-0	-0.3
1965 Was-A	8	8	.500	44	21	3	1	1	158	158	17	36	88	11.1	3.36	103	.260	.301	3	.073	-1	2	2	-1	0.0
1966 Was-A	11	14	.440	41	32	8	3	0	216	193	23	51	101	10.3	3.46	100	.236	.282	14	.212	4	-1	0	-1	0.3
1967 SF-N	**22**	10	.688	40	35	14	5	0	262^{1}	220	25	81	150	10.5	2.85	115	.226	.289	10	.119	0	15	13	-2	1.2
1968 SF-N	12	14	.462	38	28	9	2	1	198^{1}	196	17	49	121	11.2	3.58	82	.254	.300	6	.103	1	-13	-14	-2	-1.7
1969 SF-N	11	9	.550	32	28	9	0	0	196^{2}	175	20	77	76	11.6	3.34	105	.237	.310	9	.136	1	6	3	-1	0.3
1970 SF-N	3	4	.429	23	11	1	0	2	78^{1}	80	15	36	37	13.7	6.20	64	.262	.346	4	.160	0	-19	-19	1	-1.8
NY-A	2	0	1.000	9	4	0	0	0	20^{2}	26	2	13	12	17.0	6.10	58	.295	.386	1	.200	0	-5	-6	-1	-0.6
1971 KC-A	0	0	—	4	1	0	0	0	9^{2}	14	0	5	2	17.7	9.31	37	.350	.422	0	.000	-0	-6	-6	1	-0.5
Total 16	134	128	.511	484	333	91	23	12	2380^{1}	2281	255	795	1321	11.7	3.73	95	.251	.313	115	.156	9	-18	-45	-5	-4.0
● HARRY McCORMICK McCormick, Patrick Henry b: 10/25/1855, Syracuse, N.Y. d: 8/8/1889, Syracuse, N.Y. BR/TR, 5'9", 155 lbs. Deb: 5/01/1879																									
1879 Syr-N	18	33	.353	54	54	49	5	0	457^{1}	517	3	31	96	10.8	2.99	79	.266	.277	51	.222	-0	-25	-32	-7	-3.3
1881 Wor-N	1	8	.111	9	9	9	1	0	78^{1}	89	1	15	7	11.9	3.56	85	.275	.307	6	.133	-2	-7	-5	-1	-0.7
1882 Cin-a	14	11	.560	25	25	24	3	0	219^{2}	177	4	42	33	9.0	1.52	174	.206	.243	12	.129	-5	29	27	0	2.0
1883 Cin-a	8	6	.571	15	15	14	1	0	128^{2}	139	1	27	21	11.6	2.87	113	.258	.294	17	.309	4	6	5	1	0.8
Total 4	41	58	.414	103	103	96	10	0	884	922	9	115	157	10.6	2.66	98	.251	.274	86	.203	-4	3	-4	-7	-1.2
● BILL McCORRY McCorry, William Charles b: 7/9/1887, Saranac Lake, N.Y. d: 3/22/73, Augusta, Ga. BL/TR, 5'9", 157 lbs. Deb: 9/17/09																									
1909 StL-A	0	2	.000	2	2	2	0	0	15	29	1	6	10	21.0	9.00	27	.397	.443	0	.000	-0	-11	-11	-1	-1.0
● LES McCRABB McCrabb, Lester William "Buster" b: 11/4/14, Wakefield, Pa. BR/TR, 5'11", 175 lbs. Deb: 9/07/39 C																									
1939 Phi-A	1	2	.333	5	4	2	0	0	35^{2}	42	4	10	11	13.4	4.04	117	.290	.340	0	.000	-2	2	3	-0	0.1
1940 Phi-A	0	0	—	4	0	0	0	0	11^{2}	19	2	2	4	17.0	6.94	64	.365	.400	1	.250	0	-3	-3	0	-0.3
1941 Phi-A	9	13	.409	26	23	11	1	2	157^{1}	188	16	49	40	13.7	5.49	76	.293	.346	8	.143	-2	-24	-23	-2	-2.4
1942 Phi-A	0	0	—	1	0	0	0	0	4	14	2	2	0	38.3	31.50	12	.560	.607	0	.000	-0	-12	-12	0	-0.8
1950 Phi-A	0	0	—	2	0	0	0	0	1^{1}	7	0	0	2	47.3	27.00	17	.636	.636	0	—	0	-3	-3	0	-0.3
Total 5	10	15	.400	38	27	13	1	2	210	270	24	63	57	14.5	5.96	72	.309	.359	9	.122	-4	-40	-39	-1	-3.7
● ED McCREERY McCreery, Esley Porterfield "Big Ed" b: 12/24/1889, Cripple Creek, Colo. d: 10/19/60, Sacramento, Cal. BR/TR, 6', 190 lbs. Deb: 8/16/14																									
1914 Det-A	1	0	1.000	3	1	0	0	0	4	6	0	3	4	20.3	11.25	25	.316	.409	0	.000	-0	-4	-4	0	-0.4
● TOM McCREERY McCreery, Thomas Livingston b: 10/19/1874, Beaver, Pa. d: 7/3/41, Beaver, Pa. BB/TR, 5'11", 180 lbs. Deb: 6/08/1895 ♦																									
1895 Lou-N	3	1	.750	8	4	3	1	1	48^{2}	51	0	38	14	17.4	5.36	86	.265	.400	35	.324	1	-3	-4	1	-0.1
1896 Lou-N	0	1	.000	1	1	0	0	0	1	4	1	5	0	81.0	36.00	12	.582	.758	155	.351	0	-4	-4	0	-0.3
1900 Pit-N	0	0	—	1	0	0	0	0	3	3	2	1	0	12.0	12.00	30	.260	.319	29	.220	0	-3	-3	0	-0.2
Total 3	3	2	.600	10	5	3	1	1	52^{2}	58	3	44	14	18.3	6.32	72	.276	.412	855	.290	2	-9	-10	1	-0.6
● LANCE McCULLERS McCullers, Lance Graye b: 3/8/64, Tampa, Fla. BB/TR, 6'1", 218 lbs. Deb: 8/12/85																									
1985 SD-N	0	2	.000	21	0	0	0	5	35	23	3	16	27	10.3	2.31	153	.195	.296	0	.000	-0	5	5	0	0.5

YEAR	TM/L	W	L	PCT	G	GS	CG	SH	SV	IP	H	HR	BB	SO	RAT	ERA	ERA+	OAV	OOB	BH	AVG	PB	PR	/A	PD	TPI
1986	SD-N	10	10	.500	70	7	0	0	5	136	103	12	58	92	10.9	2.78	131	.216	.306	2	.091	0	14	13	-1	1.3
1987	SD-N	8	10	.444	78	0	0	0	16	123^1	115	11	59	126	12.8	3.72	106	.244	.331	1	.071	-1	5	3	1	0.3
1988	SD-N	3	6	.333	60	0	0	0	10	97^2	70	8	55	81	11.5	2.49	136	.205	.315	2	.250	1	10	10	0	1.1
1989	NY-A	4	3	.571	52	1	0	0	3	84^2	83	9	37	82	13.1	4.57	85	.255	.337	0	—	0	-6	-7	-0	-0.7
1990	NY-A	1	0	1.000	11	0	0	0	0	15	14	2	6	11	12.0	3.60	110	.241	.313	0	—	0	1	1	0	0.1
	Det-A	1	0	1.000	9	1	0	0	0	29^2	18	2	13	20	9.4	2.73	145	.170	.261	0	—	0	4	4	-1	0.4
	Yr	2	0	1.000	20	1	0	0	0	44^2	32	4	19	31	10.3	3.02	131	.194	.277	0	—	0	4	5	-1	0.5
1992	Tex-A	1	0	1.000	5	0	0	0	0	5	1	0	8	3	16.2	5.40	71	.067	.391	0	—	0	-1	-1	0	0.0
Total	7	28	31	.475	306	9	0	0	39	526^1	427	47	252	442	11.8	3.25	115	.223	.317	5	.104	0	32	28	-1	3.0

● CHARLIE McCULLOUGH McCullough, Charles F. b: 1867, Dublin, Ireland Deb: 4/23/1890

YEAR	TM/L	W	L	PCT	G	GS	CG	SH	SV	IP	H	HR	BB	SO	RAT	ERA	ERA+	OAV	OOB	BH	AVG	PB	PR	/A	PD	TPI
1890	Bro-a	4	21	.160	26	25	24	0	0	215^2	247	5	102	61	15.2	4.59	85	.279	.364	2	.023	-12	-17	-17	-2	-2.6
	Syr-a	1	2	.333	3	3	3	0	0	26	29	1	14	8	14.9	7.27	49	.274	.358	1	.111	0	-10	-11	-0	-0.8
	Yr	5	23	.179	29	28	27	0	0	241^2	276	6	116	69	14.6	4.88	79	.274	.349	3	.032	-12	-27	-27	-3	-3.4

● PAUL McCULLOUGH McCullough, Paul Willard b: 7/28/1898, New Castle, Pa. d: 11/7/70, New Castle, Pa. BR/TR, 5'9.5", 190 lbs. Deb: 7/02/29

YEAR	TM/L	W	L	PCT	G	GS	CG	SH	SV	IP	H	HR	BB	SO	RAT	ERA	ERA+	OAV	OOB	BH	AVG	PB	PR	/A	PD	TPI
1929	Was-A	0	0	—	3	0	0	0	0	7^1	7	1	2	3	11.0	8.59	49	.250	.300	0	.000	-0	-4	-4	-0	-0.4

● PHIL McCULLOUGH McCullough, Pinson Lamar b: 7/22/17, Stockbridge, Ga. BR/TR, 6'4", 204 lbs. Deb: 4/22/42

YEAR	TM/L	W	L	PCT	G	GS	CG	SH	SV	IP	H	HR	BB	SO	RAT	ERA	ERA+	OAV	OOB	BH	AVG	PB	PR	/A	PD	TPI
1942	Was-A	0	0	—	1	0	0	0	0	3	5	0	2	2	21.0	6.00	61	.333	.412	0	.000	-0	-1	-1	0	-0.1

● LINDY McDANIEL McDaniel, Lyndall Dale b: 12/13/35, Hollis, Okla. BR/TR, 6'3", 195 lbs. Deb: 9/02/55 F

YEAR	TM/L	W	L	PCT	G	GS	CG	SH	SV	IP	H	HR	BB	SO	RAT	ERA	ERA+	OAV	OOB	BH	AVG	PB	PR	/A	PD	TPI
1955	StL-N	0	0	—	4	2	0	0	0	19	22	4	7	7	13.7	4.74	86	.293	.354	1	.200	-0	-1	-1	0	-0.1
1956	StL-N	7	6	.538	39	7	1	0	0	116^1	121	7	42	59	12.6	3.40	111	.273	.335	7	.219	2	5	5	1	0.8
1957	StL-N	15	9	.625	30	26	10	1	0	191	196	13	53	75	11.9	3.49	114	.266	.317	19	.257	4	8	10	-0	1.5
1958	StL-N	5	7	.417	26	17	2	1	0	108^2	139	17	31	47	14.2	5.80	71	.305	.352	2	.067	-3	-22	-20	1	-2.1
1959	StL-N	14	12	.538	62	7	1	0	**15**	132	144	11	41	86	12.7	3.82	111	.283	.338	1	.034	-2	2	6	2	0.6
1960	StL-N★	12	4	.750	65	2	1	0	**26**	116^1	85	8	24	105	8.5	2.09	196	.207	.253	6	.231	1	**22**	**26**	1	2.9
1961	StL-N	10	6	.625	55	0	0	0	9	94^1	117	11	31	65	14.3	4.87	90	.305	.361	4	.235	-0	-9	-5	1	-0.4
1962	StL-N	3	10	.231	55	2	0	0	14	107	96	12	29	79	10.6	4.12	104	.239	.292	2	.095	-1	-2	2	2	0.3
1963	Chi-N	13	7	.650	57	0	0	0	**22**	88	82	9	27	75	11.1	2.86	123	.251	.308	2	.091	-0	4	6	0	0.7
1964	Chi-N	1	7	.125	63	0	0	0	15	95	104	4	23	71	12.1	3.88	96	.276	.319	2	.125	-1	-4	-2	0	-0.2
1965	Chi-N	5	6	.455	71	0	0	0	2	128^2	115	12	47	92	11.3	2.59	142	.241	.309	0	.000	-1	14	16	2	1.8
1966	SF-N	10	5	.667	64	0	0	0	6	121^2	103	5	35	93	10.2	2.66	138	.228	.284	2	.091	-1	13	14	1	1.4
1967	SF-N	2	6	.250	41	3	0	0	3	72^2	69	5	24	48	11.8	3.72	88	.248	.313	1	.091	-1	-3	-3	2	-0.3
1968	SF-N	0	0	—	12	0	0	0	0	19^1	30	2	5	9	16.3	7.45	40	.357	.393	0	.000	-0	-10	-10	0	-1.0
	NY-A	4	1	.800	24	0	0	0	10	51^1	30	5	12	43	7.5	1.75	165	.166	.222	0	.000	-1	7	7	2	0.9
1969	NY-A	5	6	.455	51	0	0	0	5	83^2	84	4	23	60	11.5	3.55	98	.261	.310	0	.000	-1	1	-1	1	0.0
1970	NY-A	9	5	.643	62	0	0	0	29	111^2	88	7	23	81	8.9	2.01	174	.217	.259	4	.167	0	21	19	1	2.0
1971	NY-A	5	10	.333	44	0	0	0	4	69^2	82	12	24	39	13.7	5.04	64	.296	.352	1	.111	-0	-12	-14	0	-1.5
1972	NY-A	3	1	.750	37	0	0	0	0	68	54	4	25	47	10.5	2.25	131	.217	.288	2	.286	1	6	5	1	0.9
1973	NY-A	12	6	.667	47	3	1	0	10	160^1	148	11	49	93	11.1	2.86	128	.250	.309	0	.000	0	17	14	3	1.8
1974	KC-A	1	4	.200	38	5	2	0	1	106^2	109	6	24	47	11.2	3.46	110	.265	.306	0	—	0	2	4	1	0.5
1975	KC-A	5	1	.833	40	0	0	0	1	78	81	3	24	40	12.1	4.15	93	.273	.327	0	—	0	-3	-3	-0	-0.3
Total	21	141	119	.542	987	74	18	2	172	2139^1	2099	172	623	1361	11.5	3.45	109	.258	.312	56	.148	-3	55	74	23	10.2

● VON McDANIEL McDaniel, Max Von b: 4/18/39, Hollis, Okla. BR/TR, 6'2.5", 180 lbs. Deb: 6/13/57 F

YEAR	TM/L	W	L	PCT	G	GS	CG	SH	SV	IP	H	HR	BB	SO	RAT	ERA	ERA+	OAV	OOB	BH	AVG	PB	PR	/A	PD	TPI
1957	StL-N	7	5	.583	17	13	4	2	0	86^2	71	7	31	45	10.7	3.22	123	.225	.296	0	.000	-3	6	7	-1	0.3
1958	StL-N	0	0	—	2	1	0	0	0	2	5	0	5	0	45.0	13.50	31	.500	.667	0	—	0	-2	-2	-0	-0.2
Total	2	7	5	.583	19	14	4	2	0	88^2	76	7	36	45	11.5	3.45	115	.233	.311	0	.000	-3	4	5	-1	0.1

● JOE McDERMOTT McDermott, Joseph Deb: 5/04/1871 ♦

YEAR	TM/L	W	L	PCT	G	GS	CG	SH	SV	IP	H	HR	BB	SO	RAT	ERA	ERA+	OAV	OOB	BH	AVG	PB	PR	/A	PD	TPI
1872	Eck-n	0	7	.000	7	7	7	0	0	63	142	3	12	1	22.0	8.29	42	.374	.393	9	.273	1	-32	-34		-2.0

● MICKEY McDERMOTT McDermott, Maurice Joseph "Maury" b: 8/29/28, Poughkeepsie, N.Y. BL/TL, 6'2", 170 lbs. Deb: 4/24/48 C♦

YEAR	TM/L	W	L	PCT	G	GS	CG	SH	SV	IP	H	HR	BB	SO	RAT	ERA	ERA+	OAV	OOB	BH	AVG	PB	PR	/A	PD	TPI
1948	Bos-A	0	0	—	7	0	0	0	0	23^1	16	2	35	17	20.1	6.17	71	.208	.460	3	.375	1	-5	-5	1	-0.3
1949	Bos-A	5	4	.556	12	12	6	2	0	80	63	5	52	50	13.3	4.05	108	.220	.345	7	.212	1	1	3	-0	0.3
1950	Bos-A	7	3	.700	38	15	4	0	5	130	119	8	124	96	17.0	5.19	94	.249	.406	16	.364	7	-9	-4	1	0.3
1951	Bos-A	8	8	.500	34	19	9	1	3	172	141	10	92	127	12.5	3.35	133	.226	.330	18	.273	3	15	21	1	2.5
1952	Bos-A	10	9	.526	30	21	7	2	0	162	139	14	92	117	13.0	3.72	106	.234	.340	14	.226	3	-1	4	-0	0.7
1953	Bos-A	18	10	.643	32	30	8	4	0	206^1	169	9	109	92	12.2	3.01	140	.224	.323	28	.301	7	23	27	1	**3.7**
1954	Was-A	7	15	.318	30	26	11	1	1	196^1	172	8	110	95	13.1	3.44	103	.239	.342	19	.200	3	6	3	1	0.6
1955	Was-A	10	10	.500	31	20	8	1	1	156	140	9	100	78	14.4	3.75	102	.243	.364	25	.263	7	4	1	0	1.0
1956	*NY-A	2	6	.250	23	9	1	0	0	87	85	10	47	38	13.7	4.24	91	.261	.354	11	.212	3	-1	-4	-0	-0.1
1957	KC-A	1	4	.200	29	4	0	0	0	69	68	9	50	29	15.4	5.48	72	.266	.386	12	.245	4	-13	-12	1	-0.4
1958	Det-A	0	0	—	2	0	0	0	0	2	6	0	2	0	36.0	9.00	45	.500	.571	1	.333	0	-1	-1	-0	-0.1
1961	StL-N	1	0	1.000	19	0	0	0	4	27	29	3	15	15	14.7	3.67	120	.271	.361	1	.071	-1	1	2	-0	0.1
	KC-A	0	0	—	4	0	0	0	0	5^2	14	0	10	3	38.1	14.29	29	.452	.585	1	.200	1	-6	-6	-0	-0.6
Total	12	69	69	.500	291	156	54	11	14	1316^2	1161	87	838	757	13.9	3.91	105	.240	.355	156	.252	37	14	29	4	7.7

● MIKE McDERMOTT McDermott, Michael Joseph b: 9/7/1862, St.Louis, Mo. d: 6/30/43, St.Louis, Mo. TR , 5'8", 145 lbs. Deb: 9/02/1889

YEAR	TM/L	W	L	PCT	G	GS	CG	SH	SV	IP	H	HR	BB	SO	RAT	ERA	ERA+	OAV	OOB	BH	AVG	PB	PR	/A	PD	TPI
1889	Lou-a	1	8	.111	9	9	9	0	0	84^1	108	4	34	22	15.4	4.16	92	.302	.366	6	.182	-1	-3	-3	-0	-0.3
1895	Lou-N	4	19	.174	33	26	18	0	0	207^1	258	8	103	42	16.1	5.99	77	.300	.382	13	.159	-2	-28	-31	1	-2.4
1896	Lou-N	2	7	.222	12	10	4	1	0	65	87	4	44	12	19.0	7.34	59	.318	.423	8	.296	1	-21	-22	1	-1.6
1897	Cle-N	4	5	.444	9	7	4	0	0	62	75	2	25	12	15.0	4.50	100	.296	.367	8	.320	1	-1	-0	1	0.2
	StL-N	1	2	.333	4	4	1	0	0	21^1	23	2	19	3	18.6	9.28	47	.273	.418	2	.222	-0	-12	-12	1	-0.8
	Yr	5	7	.417	13	11	5	0	0	83^1	98	4	44	15	15.6	5.72	78	.288	.373	10	.294	1	-13	-12	2	-0.6
Total	4	12	41	.226	67	56	36	1	0	440	551	20	225	91	16.4	5.79	76	.301	.385	37	.210	-1	-65	-67	4	-4.9

● DANNY McDEVITT McDevitt, Daniel Eugene b: 11/18/32, New York, N.Y. BL/TL, 5'10", 175 lbs. Deb: 6/17/57

YEAR	TM/L	W	L	PCT	G	GS	CG	SH	SV	IP	H	HR	BB	SO	RAT	ERA	ERA+	OAV	OOB	BH	AVG	PB	PR	/A	PD	TPI
1957	Bro-N	7	4	.636	22	17	5	2	0	119	105	5	72	90	13.8	3.25	128	.238	.353	6	.154	-0	8	12	2	1.4
1958	LA-N	2	6	.250	13	10	2	0	0	48^1	71	6	31	26	19.0	7.45	55	.355	.442	2	.133	-0	-19	-18	-1	-1.8
1959	LA-N	10	8	.556	39	22	6	2	4	145	149	16	51	106	13.3	3.97	106	.263	.339	5	.109	-2	-0	4	0	0.2
1960	LA-N	0	4	.000	24	7	0	0	0	53	51	7	42	30	16.8	4.25	93	.260	.406	2	.200	0	-3	-2	-0	-0.2
1961	NY-A	1	2	.333	8	2	0	0	1	13	18	2	8	8	18.7	7.62	49	.353	.450	0	.000	0	-5	-6	0	-0.5
	Min-A	1	0	1.000	16	1	0	0	0	26^2	20	1	19	15	14.5	2.36	179	.213	.368	0	.000	-0	5	6	0	0.6
	Yr	2	2	.500	24	3	0	0	1	39^2	38	3	27	23	15.7	4.08	100	.259	.388	0	.000	-0	-0	-0	0	0.1
1962	KC-A	0	3	.000	33	1	0	0	2	51	47	5	41	28	15.7	5.82	71	.250	.387	2	.222	0	-11	-9	1	-0.9
Total	6	21	27	.438	155	60	13	4	7	456	461	42	264	303	14.9	4.40	94	.265	.372	17	.138	-3	-25	-13	2	-1.2

● HANK McDONALD McDonald, Henry Monroe b: 1/16/11, Santa Monica, Cal. d: 10/17/82, Hemet, Cal. BR/TR, 6'3", 200 lbs. Deb: 4/16/31

YEAR	TM/L	W	L	PCT	G	GS	CG	SH	SV	IP	H	HR	BB	SO	RAT	ERA	ERA+	OAV	OOB	BH	AVG	PB	PR	/A	PD	TPI
1931	Phi-A	2	4	.333	19	10	1	1	0	70^1	62	3	41	23	13.3	3.71	121	.239	.346	2	.095	-1	5	6	-1	0.4
1933	Phi-A	1	1	.500	4	1	0	0	0	12^1	14	0	4	1	13.1	5.11	84	.264	.316	0	.000	-0	-1	-1	-0	-0.1
	StL-A	0	4	.000	25	5	0	0	0	58^1	83	6	34	22	18.5	8.64	54	.332	.418	2	.143	-1	-28	-26	-0	-2.4
	Yr	1	5	.167	29	6	0	0	0	70^2	97	6	38	23	17.6	8.02	57	.320	.401	2	.111	-1	-29	-27	-0	-2.5

YEAR	TM/L	W	L	PCT	G	GS	CG	SH	SV	IP	H	HR	BB	SO	RAT	ERA	ERA+	OAV	OOB	BH	AVG	PB	PR	/A	PD	TPI
Total	2	3	9	.250	48	16	1	1	0	141	159	9	79	46	15.4	5.87	77	.283	.375	4	.103	-2	-24	-21	-1	-2.1
● **JIM McDONALD**	McDonald, Jimmie Le Roy "Hot Rod" b: 5/17/27, Grants Pass, Ore. BR/TR, 5'10.5", 185 lbs. Deb: 7/27/50																									
1950	Bos-A	1	0	1.000	9	0	0	0	0	19	23	1	10	5	16.1	3.79	129	.329	.420	1	.333	1	2	2	1	0.4
1951	StL-A	4	7	.364	16	11	5	0	1	84	84	5	46	28	14.1	4.07	108	.260	.356	6	.207	-0	0	3	1	0.3
1952	NY-A	3	4	.429	26	5	1	0	0	69^1	71	1	40	20	14.7	3.50	95	.268	.368	6	.316	3	1	-1	3	0.4
1953	*NY-A	9	7	.563	27	18	6	2	0	129^2	128	4	39	43	11.7	3.82	97	.260	.316	4	.098	-3	3	-2	2	-0.3
1954	NY-A	4	1	.800	16	10	3	1	0	71	54	3	45	20	12.7	3.17	108	.213	.334	4	.211	2	4	2	1	0.5
1955	Bal-A	3	5	.375	21	8	0	0	0	51^2	76	5	30	20	18.5	7.14	53	.345	.424	2	.182	1	-18	-19	1	-1.6
1956	Chi-A	0	2	.000	8	3	0	0	0	18^2	29	2	7	10	17.8	8.68	47	.377	.435	0	.000	-0	-9	-9	-0	-0.9
1957	Chi-A	0	1	.000	10	0	0	0	0	22^1	18	2	10	12	11.3	2.01	185	.234	.322	0	.000	0	4	4	-0	0.5
1958	Chi-A	0	0	—	3	0	0	0	0	2^1	6	1	4	0	38.6	19.29	19	.429	.556	0	—	0	-4	-4	0	-0.4
Total	9	24	27	.471	136	55	15	3	1	468	489	24	231	158	14.0	4.27	89	.273	.359	23	.180	4	-17	-25	8	-1.1
● **JOHN McDONALD**	McDonald, John Joseph (b: John Joseph McDonnell) b: 1/27/1883, Throop, Pa. d: 4/9/50, Roselle, N.J. BR/TR, 6'1", 170 lbs. Deb: 9/13/07																									
1907	Was-A	0	0	—	1	0	0	0	0	6	12	0	2	3	21.0	9.00	27	.415	.453	1	.333	1	-4	-4	-0	-0.4
● **BEN McDONALD**	McDonald, Larry Benard b: 11/14/67, Baton Rouge, La. BR/TR, 6'7", 212 lbs. Deb: 9/06/89																									
1989	Bal-A	1	0	1.000	6	0	0	0	0	7^1	8	2	4	3	14.7	8.59	44	.286	.375	0	—	0	-4	-4	0	-0.3
1990	Bal-A	8	5	.615	21	15	3	2	0	118^2	88	9	35	65	9.3	2.43	156	.205	.265	0	—	0	20	18	0	2.0
1991	Bal-A	6	8	.429	21	21	1	0	0	126^1	126	16	43	85	12.1	4.84	82	.261	.323	0	—	0	-11	-13	-1	-1.3
1992	Bal-A	13	13	.500	35	35	4	2	0	227	213	32	74	158	11.7	4.24	92	.247	.313	0	—	0	-8	-9	1	-0.7
Total	4	28	26	.519	83	71	8	4	0	479^1	435	59	156	311	11.3	4.02	97	.241	.305	0	—	0	-3	-7	0	-0.3
● **McDOOLAN**	McDoolan Deb: 4/14/1873																									
1873	Mar-n	0	1	.000	1	1	1	0	0	9	18	0	0	0	18.0	3.00	108	.305	.305	0	.000	-1	0	0		0.0
● **SANDY McDOUGAL**	McDougal, John Auchanbolt b: 5/21/1874, Buffalo, N.Y. d: 10/2/10, Buffalo, N.Y. BR/TR, 5'10", 155 lbs. Deb: 6/12/1895																									
1895	Bro-N	0	0	—	1	0	0	0	1	3	3	0	5	2	24.0	12.00	37	.256	.479	0	.000	-0	-2	-3	-0	-0.2
1905	StL-N	1	4	.200	5	5	5	0	0	44^2	50	0	12	10	12.5	3.43	87	.301	.348	2	.133	-1	-2	-2	3	0.0
Total	2	1	4	.200	6	5	5	0	1	47^2	53	0	17	12	13.2	3.97	78	.298	.360	2	.125	-1	-5	-5	3	-0.2
● **DEWEY McDOUGAL**	McDougal, John H. b: 9/19/1871, Aledo, Ill. d: 4/28/36, Galesburg, Ill. TR , 170 lbs. Deb: 4/24/1895																									
1895	StL-N	3	10	.231	18	14	10	0	0	114^2	187	11	46	23	19.1	8.32	58	.360	.422	6	.146	-2	-45	-44	-1	-3.5
1896	StL-N	0	1	.000	3	1	0	0	0	10	13	2	4	0	16.2	8.10	54	.312	.385	0	.000	-1	-4	-4	1	-0.3
Total	2	3	11	.214	21	15	10	0	0	124^2	200	13	50	23	18.8	8.30	58	.356	.420	6	.136	-3	-49	-49	-1	-3.8
● **JACK McDOWELL**	McDowell, Jack Burns b: 1/16/66, Van Nuys, Cal. BR/TR, 6'5", 180 lbs. Deb: 9/15/87																									
1987	Chi-A	3	0	1.000	4	4	0	0	0	28	16	1	6	15	7.7	1.93	237	.168	.233	0	—	0	8	8	0	0.9
1988	Chi-A	5	10	.333	26	26	1	0	0	158^2	147	12	68	84	12.6	3.97	100	.245	.329	0	—	0	-0	-0	-1	-0.1
1990	Chi-A	14	9	.609	33	33	4	0	0	205	189	20	77	165	12.0	3.82	100	.244	.317	0	—	0	2	0	-0	0.0
1991	Chi-A★	17	10	.630	35	35	**15**	3	0	253^2	212	19	82	191	10.6	3.41	117	.228	.293	0	—	0	19	16	0	1.7
1992	Chi-A★	20	10	.667	34	34	**13**	1	0	260^2	247	21	75	178	11.4	3.18	120	.251	.309	0	—	0	22	19	-1	1.9
Total	5	59	39	.602	132	132	33	4	0	906	811	73	308	633	11.4	3.49	112	.240	.308	0	—	0	51	43	-2	4.4
● **ROGER McDOWELL**	McDowell, Roger Alan b: 12/21/60, Cincinnati, Ohio BR/TR, 6'1", 175 lbs. Deb: 4/11/85																									
1985	NY-N	6	5	.545	62	2	0	0	17	127^1	108	9	37	70	10.3	2.83	122	.230	.287	3	.158	0	11	9	2	1.2
1986	*NY-N	14	9	.609	75	0	0	0	22	128	107	4	42	65	10.7	3.02	117	.228	.296	5	.278	1	10	7	3	1.2
1987	NY-N	7	5	.583	56	0	0	0	25	88^2	95	7	28	32	12.7	4.16	91	.276	.334	3	.231	1	-1	-4	1	-0.2
1988	*NY-N	5	5	.500	62	0	0	0	16	89	80	1	31	46	11.5	2.63	122	.238	.308	3	.333	2	8	6	2	1.0
1989	NY-N	1	5	.167	25	0	0	0	4	35^1	34	1	16	15	13.2	3.31	99	.254	.342	1	.500	0	1	-0	2	0.3
	Phi-N	3	3	.500	44	0	0	0	19	56^2	45	2	22	32	10.8	1.11	319	.220	.298	0	.000	-0	15	15	1	1.8
	Yr	4	8	.333	69	0	0	0	23	92	79	3	38	47	11.5	1.96	176	.231	.310	1	.333	0	16	15	3	2.1
1990	Phi-N	6	8	.429	72	0	0	0	22	86^1	92	2	35	39	13.4	3.86	99	.286	.359	0	.000	-0	-1	-0	1	0.1
1991	Phi-N	3	6	.333	38	0	0	0	3	59	61	1	32	28	14.5	3.20	114	.266	.361	0	.000	-0	3	3	2	0.5
	LA-N	6	3	.667	33	0	0	0	7	42^1	39	3	16	22	11.7	2.55	141	.257	.327	0	—	0	5	5	1	0.5
	Yr	9	9	.500	71	0	0	0	10	101^1	100	4	48	50	13.1	2.93	124	.260	.343	0	.000	-0	8	8	2	1.0
1992	LA-N	6	10	.375	65	0	0	0	14	83^2	103	3	42	50	15.7	4.09	85	.306	.384	0	.000	1	-5	-6	2	-0.4
Total	8	57	59	.491	532	2	0	0	149	796^1	764	33	301	399	12.2	3.14	113	.255	.326	15	.217	5	46	35	16	6.0
● **SAM McDOWELL**	McDowell, Samuel Edward Thomas "Sudden Sam" b: 9/21/42, Pittsburgh, Pa. BL/TL, 6'5", 218 lbs. Deb: 9/15/61																									
1961	Cle-A	0	0	—	1	1	0	0	0	6^1	3	0	5	5	11.4	0.00	—	.136	.296	0	.000	-0	3	3	0	0.3
1962	Cle-A	3	7	.300	25	13	0	0	1	87^2	81	9	70	70	15.9	6.06	64	.243	.381	4	.154	-1	-20	-21	-0	-2.1
1963	Cle-A	3	5	.375	14	12	3	1	0	65	63	6	44	63	14.8	4.85	75	.256	.369	4	.211	0	-9	-9	-0	-0.9
1964	Cle-A	11	6	.647	31	24	6	2	1	173^1	148	8	100	177	13.0	2.70	133	.229	.336	8	.143	0	18	17	-1	1.8
1965	Cle-A★	17	11	.607	42	35	14	3	4	273	178	9	132	**325**	10.4	**2.18**	**160**	**.185**	.287	12	.126	-3	**39**	**40**	1	**4.3**
1966	Cle-A†	9	8	.529	35	28	8	**5**	3	194^1	130	12	102	**225**	11.0	2.87	120	**.188**	.298	12	.200	1	12	12	1	1.6
1967	Cle-A	13	15	.464	37	37	10	1	0	236^1	201	21	123	236	12.6	3.85	85	.233	.333	15	.183	1	-16	-15	-1	-1.6
1968	Cle-A★	15	14	.517	38	37	11	3	0	269	181	13	110	**283**	10.1	1.81	164	.189	.279	13	.153	0	35	34	-1	4.2
1969	Cle-A★	18	14	.563	39	38	18	4	1	285	222	13	102	**279**	10.5	2.94	128	.213	.288	16	.174	-1	22	26	-0	2.7
1970	Cle-A★	20	12	.625	39	39	19	1	0	**305**	236	25	131	**304**	11.0	2.92	136	.213	.300	13	.124	-4	27	**35**	-2	3.2
1971	Cle-A†	13	17	.433	35	31	8	2	1	214^2	160	22	153	192	13.2	3.40	113	.207	.340	13	.178	-1	2	10	-2	0.8
1972	SF-N	10	8	.556	28	25	4	0	0	164^1	155	12	86	122	13.5	4.33	81	.253	.350	7	.119	-1	-16	-15	-0	-1.8
1973	SF-N	1	2	.333	18	3	0	0	3	40	45	4	29	35	16.6	4.50	85	.285	.396	2	.167	-0	-4	-3	0	-0.3
	NY-A	5	8	.385	16	15	2	1	0	95^2	73	4	64	75	12.9	3.95	93	.212	.335	0	—	0	-1	-3	0	-0.3
1974	NY-A	1	6	.143	13	7	0	0	0	48	42	6	41	33	15.6	4.69	74	.236	.379	0	—	0	-6	-6	-1	-0.7
1975	Pit-N	2	1	.667	14	1	0	0	0	34^2	30	0	20	29	13.0	2.86	124	.242	.347	0	.000	-1	3	3	0	0.2
Total	15	141	134	.513	425	346	103	23	14	2492^1	1948	164	1312	2453	12.0	3.17	112	.215	.318	119	.154	-8	88	107	-5	11.4
● **CHUCK McELROY**	McElroy, Charles Dwayne b: 10/1/67, Galveston, Tex. BL/TL, 6', 160 lbs. Deb: 9/04/89																									
1989	Phi-N	0	0	—	11	0	0	0	0	10^1	12	1	4	8	13.9	1.74	203	.286	.348	0	—	0	2	2	-0	0.2
1990	Phi-N	0	1	.000	16	0	0	0	0	14	24	0	10	16	21.9	7.71	50	.369	.453	0	—	0	-6	-6	-0	-0.6
1991	Chi-N	6	2	.750	71	0	0	0	3	101^1	73	7	57	92	11.5	1.95	199	.210	.322	3	.300	1	**19**	**22**	1	2.4
1992	Chi-N	4	7	.364	72	0	0	0	6	83^2	73	5	51	83	13.3	3.55	102	.237	.345	4	.667	3	-0	1	-1	0.3
Total	4	10	10	.500	170	0	0	0	9	209^1	182	13	122	199	13.1	2.97	126	.239	.344	7	.438	4	15	18	-1	2.3
● **JIM McELROY**	McElroy, James D. b: 1863, San Francisco, Cal. d: 7/24/1889, Needles, Cal. 5'10", 170 lbs. Deb: 5/26/1884																									
1884	Phi-N	1	12	.077	13	13	13	0	0	111	115	1	54	45	13.7	4.86	61	.254	.333	7	.146	-3	-23	-23	-0	-2.2
	Wil-U	0	1	.000	1	1	0	0	0	5	10	0	0	3	18.0	10.80	30	.391	.391	0	.000	-0	-4	-4	0	-0.3
Total	1	1	13	.071	14	14	13	0	0	116	125	1	54	48	13.9	5.12	59	.261	.336	7	.140	-4	-28	-27	0	-2.5
● **WILL McENANEY**	McEnaney, William Henry b: 2/14/52, Springfield, Ohio BL/TL, 6', 180 lbs. Deb: 7/03/74																									
1974	Cin-N	2	1	.667	24	0	0	0	2	27	24	4	9	13	11.0	4.33	80	.250	.314	0	—	0	-2	-3	-1	-0.3
1975	*Cin-N	5	2	.714	70	0	0	0	15	91	92	6	23	48	11.6	2.47	145	.264	.314	0	.000	-2	12	11	-1	0.9
1976	Cin-N	2	6	.250	55	0	0	0	7	72^1	97	3	23	28	15.1	4.85	72	.323	.373	1	.167	1	-11	-11	0	-1.1
1977	Mon-N	3	5	.375	69	0	0	0	3	86^2	92	6	22	38	12.0	3.95	96	.271	.319	0	.000	-1	-0	-1	-0	-0.2

YEAR	TM/L	W	L	PCT	G	GS	CG	SH	SV	IP	H	HR	BB	SO	RAT	ERA	ERA+	OAV	OOB	BH	AVG	PB	PR	/A	PD	TPI
1978	Pit-N	0	0	—	6	0	0	0	0	8^2	15	3	2	6	18.7	10.38	36	.395	.439	0	—	0	-7	-6	0	-0.6
1979	StL-N	0	3	.000	45	0	0	0	2	64	60	3	16	15	11.0	2.95	127	.251	.304	0	.000	-0	6	6	2	0.7
Total	6	12	17	.414	269	0	0	0	29	349^2	380	25	95	148	12.4	3.76	97	.279	.330	1	.032	-2	-3	-4	-1	-0.6

● LOU McEVOY McEvoy, Louis Anthony b: 5/30/02, Williamsburg, Kan. d: 12/17/53, Webster Groves, Mo BR/TR, 6'2.5", 203 lbs. Deb: 4/28/30

YEAR	TM/L	W	L	PCT	G	GS	CG	SH	SV	IP	H	HR	BB	SO	RAT	ERA	ERA+	OAV	OOB	BH	AVG	PB	PR	/A	PD	TPI
1930	NY-A	1	3	.250	28	1	0	0	3	52^1	64	4	29	14	16.3	6.71	64	.288	.375	2	.125	-1	-12	-14	-1	-1.4
1931	NY-A	0	0	—	6	0	0	0	1	12^1	19	1	12	3	23.4	12.41	32	.358	.485	0	.000	-1	-11	-12	0	-1.0
Total	2	1	3	.250	34	1	0	0	4	64^2	83	5	41	17	17.7	7.79	54	.302	.398	2	.100	-1	-23	-26	-1	-2.4

● BARNEY McFADDEN McFadden, Bernard Joseph b: 2/22/1874, Eckley, Pa. d: 4/28/24, Mauch Chunk, Pa. BR/TR, 6'1", 195 lbs. Deb: 4/24/01

YEAR	TM/L	W	L	PCT	G	GS	CG	SH	SV	IP	H	HR	BB	SO	RAT	ERA	ERA+	OAV	OOB	BH	AVG	PB	PR	/A	PD	TPI
1901	Cin-N	3	4	.429	8	5	4	0	0	46	54	2	40	11	19.6	6.07	53	.291	.431	3	.150	-1	-14	-15	1	-1.3
1902	Phi-N	0	1	.000	1	1	1	0	0	9	14	0	7	3	21.0	8.00	35	.354	.451	0	.000	-0	-5	-5	0	-0.5
Total	2	3	5	.375	9	6	5	0	0	55	68	2	47	14	19.8	6.38	49	.302	.435	3	.130	-2	-19	-20	1	-1.8

● DAN McFARLAN McFarlan, Anderson Daniel b: 11/1/1873, Gainesville, Tex. d: 9/23/24, Louisville, Ky. Deb: 9/02/1895 F

YEAR	TM/L	W	L	PCT	G	GS	CG	SH	SV	IP	H	HR	BB	SO	RAT	ERA	ERA+	OAV	OOB	BH	AVG	PB	PR	/A	PD	TPI
1895	Lou-N	0	7	.000	7	7	6	0	0	46	80	4	15	10	19.6	6.65	70	.375	.429	5	.238	-1	-10	-10	1	-0.8
1899	Bro-N	0	0	—	1	0	0	0	0	6	6	1	3	0	13.5	1.50	261	.260	.345	0	.000	-0	2	2	0	0.2
	Was-N	8	18	.308	32	28	22	1	0	211^2	268	5	64	41	14.6	4.76	82	.308	.363	16	.186	-1	-21	-20	-1	-1.8
	Yr	8	18	.308	33	28	22	1	0	217^2	274	6	67	41	14.6	4.67	84	.307	.362	16	.182	-1	-20	-18	-0	-1.6
Total	2	8	25	.242	40	35	28	1	0	263^2	354	10	82	51	15.4	5.02	81	.320	.375	21	.193	-2	-29	-29	1	-2.4

● CHAPPIE McFARLAND McFarland, Charles A. b: 3/13/1875, White Hill, Ill. d: 12/14/24, Houston, Tex. TR, 6'1", Deb: 9/15/02 F

YEAR	TM/L	W	L	PCT	G	GS	CG	SH	SV	IP	H	HR	BB	SO	RAT	ERA	ERA+	OAV	OOB	BH	AVG	PB	PR	/A	PD	TPI
1902	StL-N	0	1	.000	2	1	1	0	0	11	11	1	3	3	11.5	5.73	48	.260	.309	0	.000	-1	-4	-4	0	-0.4
1903	StL-N	9	19	.321	28	26	25	1	0	229	253	2	48	76	12.1	3.07	106	.284	.325	8	.108	-4	5	5	2	0.4
1904	StL-N	14	18	.438	32	31	28	1	0	269^1	266	7	56	111	10.9	3.21	84	.248	.288	13	.131	-3	-14	-15	7	-1.1
1905	StL-N	8	18	.308	31	28	22	3	1	250^1	281	3	65	85	12.7	3.81	78	.284	.332	14	.165	1	-22	-23	1	-2.2
1906	StL-N	2	1	.667	6	4	2	0	1	37^1	33	1	8	16	9.9	1.93	136	.219	.258	2	.133	-1	3	3	1	0.3
	Pit-N	1	3	.250	6	5	2	1	0	35^1	39	0	7	11	12.2	2.55	105	.298	.343	5	.385	1	0	0	0	0.2
	Bro-N	0	1	.000	1	1	1	0	0	9	10	1	5	5	15.0	8.00	32	.286	.375	0	.000	-0	-5	-5	-0	-0.5
	Yr	3	5	.375	13	10	5	1	1	81^2	82	2	20	32	11.2	2.87	92	.257	.301	7	.226	0	-2	-2	1	0.0
Total	5	34	61	.358	106	96	81	6	2	841^1	893	15	192	307	11.8	3.35	87	.270	.313	42	.143	-6	-37	-39	11	-3.3

● CHRIS McFARLAND McFarland, Christopher b: 8/17/1861, Fall River, Mass. d: 5/24/18, New Bedford, Mass. 5'9", 170 lbs. Deb: 4/19/1884 ♦

YEAR	TM/L	W	L	PCT	G	GS	CG	SH	SV	IP	H	HR	BB	SO	RAT	ERA	ERA+	OAV	OOB	BH	AVG	PB	PR	/A	PD	TPI
1884	Bal-U	0	1	.000	1	1	0	0	0	3	9	1	1	3	30.0	15.00	22	.491	.517	3	.214	-0	-4	-4	-0	-0.3

● MONTE McFARLAND McFarland, La Mont A. b: 1873, Illinois d: 11/15/13, Peoria, Ill. Deb: 9/14/1895 F

YEAR	TM/L	W	L	PCT	G	GS	CG	SH	SV	IP	H	HR	BB	SO	RAT	ERA	ERA+	OAV	OOB	BH	AVG	PB	PR	/A	PD	TPI
1895	Chi-N	2	0	1.000	2	2	2	0	0	14	21	0	5	5	16.7	5.14	99	.341	.390	1	.143	-1	-1	-0	0	-0.1
1896	Chi-N	0	4	.000	4	3	2	0	0	25	32	0	21	3	19.8	7.20	63	.308	.434	0	.000	-2	-8	-7	0	-0.7
Total	2	2	4	.333	6	5	4	0	0	39	53	0	26	8	18.7	6.46	73	.321	.419	1	.053	-3	-8	-7	1	-0.8

● JACK McFETRIDGE McFetridge, John Reed b: 8/25/1869, Philadelphia, Pa. d: 1/10/17, Philadelphia, Pa. 6', 175 lbs. Deb: 6/07/1890

YEAR	TM/L	W	L	PCT	G	GS	CG	SH	SV	IP	H	HR	BB	SO	RAT	ERA	ERA+	OAV	OOB	BH	AVG	PB	PR	/A	PD	TPI
1890	Phi-N	1	0	1.000	1	1	1	0	0	9	5	0	2	4	7.0	1.00	366	.158	.208	3	.750	1	3	3	-0	0.4
1903	Phi-N	1	11	.083	14	13	11	0	0	103	120	2	49	31	15.0	4.89	67	.299	.379	6	.176	0	-19	-19	-1	-1.7
Total	2	2	11	.154	15	14	12	0	0	112	125	2	51	35	14.4	4.58	72	.288	.367	9	.237	2	-16	-16	-1	-1.3

● ANDY McGAFFIGAN McGaffigan, Andrew Joseph b: 10/25/56, W.Palm Beach, Fla. BR/TR, 6'3", 195 lbs. Deb: 9/22/81

YEAR	TM/L	W	L	PCT	G	GS	CG	SH	SV	IP	H	HR	BB	SO	RAT	ERA	ERA+	OAV	OOB	BH	AVG	PB	PR	/A	PD	TPI
1981	NY-A	0	0	—	2	0	0	0	0	7	5	1	3	2	10.3	2.57	139	.200	.286	0	—	0	1	1	-0	0.1
1982	SF-N	1	0	1.000	4	0	0	0	0	8	5	0	1	4	7.9	0.00	—	.179	.233	0	.000	-0	3	3	-0	0.3
1983	SF-N	3	9	.250	43	16	0	0	2	134^1	131	17	39	93	11.5	4.29	82	.255	.309	2	.067	-1	-10	-11	-3	-1.6
1984	Mon-N	3	4	.429	21	3	0	0	1	46	37	2	15	39	10.2	2.54	135	.220	.284	0	.000	-1	5	4	-0	0.4
	Cin-N	0	2	.000	9	3	0	0	0	23	23	2	8	18	12.1	5.48	69	.261	.323	0	.000	-0	-5	-4	-1	-0.5
	Yr	3	6	.333	30	6	0	0	1	69	60	4	23	57	10.8	3.52	101	.233	.296	0	.000	-1	1	0	-1	-0.1
1985	Cin-N	3	3	.500	15	15	2	0	0	94^1	88	4	30	83	11.4	3.72	102	.247	.309	1	.034	-2	-1	1	0	-0.1
1986	Mon-N	10	5	.667	48	14	1	1	2	142^2	114	9	55	104	10.8	2.65	139	.223	.301	2	.061	-2	17	17	-2	1.4
1987	Mon-N	5	2	.714	69	0	0	0	12	120^1	105	5	42	100	11.2	2.39	176	.235	.305	0	.000	-1	23	24	-0	2.3
1988	Mon-N	6	0	1.000	63	0	0	0	4	91^1	81	4	37	71	11.8	2.76	130	.233	.311	0	.000	-0	7	8	-1	0.8
1989	Mon-N	3	5	.375	57	0	0	0	2	75	85	3	30	40	14.2	4.68	75	.293	.365	1	1.000	0	-10	-10	-1	-1.1
1990	SF-N	0	0	—	4	0	0	0	0	4^2	10	2	4	4	27.0	17.36	21	.455	.538	0	—	0	-7	-7	-0	-0.7
	KC-A	4	3	.571	24	11	0	0	1	78^2	75	6	28	49	12.0	3.09	124	.248	.315	0	—	0	7	6	-1	0.6
1991	KC-A	0	0	—	4	0	0	0	0	8	14	0	2	3	18.0	4.50	92	.389	.421	0	—	0	-0	-0	-0	-0.1
Total	11	38	33	.535	363	62	3	1	24	833^1	773	55	294	610	11.7	3.38	110	.247	.314	6	.048	-7	30	32	-10	1.8

● JACK McGEACHEY McGeachey, John Charles b: 5/23/1864, Clinton, Mass. d: 4/5/30, Cambridge, Mass. BR/TR, 5'8", 165 lbs. Deb: 6/17/1886 ♦

YEAR	TM/L	W	L	PCT	G	GS	CG	SH	SV	IP	H	HR	BB	SO	RAT	ERA	ERA+	OAV	OOB	BH	AVG	PB	PR	/A	PD	TPI
1887	Ind-N	0	1	.000	1	0	0	0	0	6^1	13	2	4	3	24.2	11.37	36	.351	.415	109	.269	0	-5	-5	0	-0.4
1888	Ind-N	0	0	—	1	0	0	0	0	5	5	1	3	0	14.4	7.20	41	.238	.333	99	.219	0	-2	-2	-0	-0.2
1889	Ind-N	0	0	—	3	0	0	0	0	4^2	7	2	6	3	25.1	11.57	36	.336	.485	142	.267	0	-4	-4	-0	-0.3
Total	3	0	1	.000	5	0	0	0	0	16	25	5	13	6	21.4	10.13	37	.317	.414	604	.245	0	-11	-11	-0	-0.9

● BILL McGEE McGee, William Henry "Fiddler Bill" b: 11/16/09, Batchtown, Ill. d: 2/11/87, St.Louis, Mo. BR/TR, 6'1", 215 lbs. Deb: 9/29/35

YEAR	TM/L	W	L	PCT	G	GS	CG	SH	SV	IP	H	HR	BB	SO	RAT	ERA	ERA+	OAV	OOB	BH	AVG	PB	PR	/A	PD	TPI
1935	StL-N	1	0	1.000	1	1	1	0	0	9	3	0	1	2	4.0	1.00	410	.103	.133	1	.333	0	3	3	-0	0.3
1936	StL-N	1	1	.500	7	2	0	0	0	16	23	3	4	8	15.2	7.88	50	.359	.397	1	.250	0	-7	-7	0	-0.6
1937	StL-N	1	0	1.000	4	1	1	0	0	14	13	1	4	9	11.6	2.57	155	.255	.321	1	.200	-0	2	2	0	0.2
1938	StL-N	7	12	.368	47	25	10	1	5	216	216	4	78	104	12.3	3.21	123	.257	.321	14	.209	1	14	18	-0	1.9
1939	StL-N	12	5	.706	43	17	5	4	0	156	155	14	59	56	12.3	3.81	108	.261	.328	8	.145	-3	2	5	0	0.3
1940	StL-N	16	10	.615	38	31	11	3	0	218	222	13	96	78	13.2	3.80	105	.263	.340	13	.178	-1	1	5	-3	0.1
1941	StL-N	0	1	.000	4	3	0	0	0	14	17	1	13	2	19.9	5.14	73	.298	.437	0	.000	-1	-2	-2	-0	-0.3
	NY-N	2	9	.182	22	14	1	0	0	106	117	9	54	41	14.5	4.92	75	.285	.368	5	.161	-1	-15	-14	-2	-1.7
	Yr	2	10	.167	26	17	1	0	0	120	134	10	67	43	15.1	4.95	75	.286	.375	5	.143	-2	-18	-17	-2	-2.0
1942	NY-N	6	3	.667	31	8	2	1	1	104	95	8	46	40	12.3	2.94	114	.244	.326	3	.103	-2	4	5	-1	0.2
Total	8	46	41	.529	197	102	31	9	6	853	861	53	355	340	12.9	3.74	104	.263	.336	46	.170	-6	2	14	-5	0.4

● CONNY McGEEHAN McGeehan, Cornelius Bernard b: 8/25/1882, Drifton, Pa. d: 7/4/07, Hazleton, Pa. Deb: 7/15/03 F

YEAR	TM/L	W	L	PCT	G	GS	CG	SH	SV	IP	H	HR	BB	SO	RAT	ERA	ERA+	OAV	OOB	BH	AVG	PB	PR	/A	PD	TPI
1903	Phi-A	1	0	1.000	3	0	0	0	0	10	9	0	1	4	9.9	4.50	68	.240	.278	0	.000	-1	-2	-2	0	-0.2

● PAT McGEHEE McGehee, Patrick Henry b: 7/2/1888, Meadville, Miss. d: 12/30/46, Paducah, Ky. BL/TR, 6'2.5", 180 lbs. Deb: 8/23/12

YEAR	TM/L	W	L	PCT	G	GS	CG	SH	SV	IP	H	HR	BB	SO	RAT	ERA	ERA+	OAV	OOB	BH	AVG	PB	PR	/A	PD	TPI
1912	Det-A	0	0	—	1	1	0	0	0	0	1	0	1	0	—	—	—	1.000	1.000	0	—	0	0	0	0	0.0

● RANDY McGILBERRY McGilberry, Randall Kent b: 10/29/53, Mobile, Ala. BB/TR, 6'1", 195 lbs. Deb: 9/06/77

YEAR	TM/L	W	L	PCT	G	GS	CG	SH	SV	IP	H	HR	BB	SO	RAT	ERA	ERA+	OAV	OOB	BH	AVG	PB	PR	/A	PD	TPI
1977	KC-A	0	1	.000	3	0	0	0	0	7	7	1	1	1	10.3	5.14	78	.280	.308	0	—	0	-1	-1	0	-0.1
1978	KC-A	0	1	.000	18	0	0	0	0	25^2	27	2	18	12	15.8	4.21	91	.276	.388	0	—	0	-1	-1	0	-0.3
Total	2	0	2	.000	21	0	0	0	0	32^2	34	3	19	13	14.6	4.41	88	.276	.373	0	—	0	-2	-2	0	-0.4

● BILL McGILL McGill, William John "Parson" b: 6/29/1880, Galva, Kan. d: 8/7/59, Alva, Okla. BR/TR, 6'2", Deb: 9/16/07

YEAR	TM/L	W	L	PCT	G	GS	CG	SH	SV	IP	H	HR	BB	SO	RAT	ERA	ERA+	OAV	OOB	BH	AVG	PB	PR	/A	PD	TPI
1907	StL-A	1	0	1.000	2	2	1	0	0	18^1	22	0	2	8	11.8	3.44	73	.299	.318	0	.000	-1	-2	-2	-0	-0.3

● WILLIE McGILL McGill, William Vaness "Kid" b: 11/10/1873, Atlanta, Ga. d: 8/29/44, Indianapolis, Ind. TL, 5'6.5", 170 lbs. Deb: 5/08/1890

YEAR	TM/L	W	L	PCT	G	GS	CG	SH	SV	IP	H	HR	BB	SO	RAT	ERA	ERA+	OAV	OOB	BH	AVG	PB	PR	/A	PD	TPI
1890	Cle-P	11	9	.550	24	20	19	0	0	183^{2}	222	5	96	82	16.2	4.12	97	.286	.373	10	.147	2	2	-3	1	0.1
1891	Cin-a	2	5	.286	8	8	6	0	0	65	69	1	37	19	15.1	4.98	83	.263	.360	2	.100	0	-9	-6	-1	-0.6
	StL-a	19	10	.655	35	31	22	1	1	249	225	10	131	154	13.4	2.93	144	.233	.333	14	.161	1	22	35	-4	2.9
	Yr	21	15	.583	43	39	28	1	1	314	294	11	168	173	13.6	3.35	125	.239	.337	16	.150	1	13	29	-5	2.3
1892	Cin-N	1	1	.500	3	3	1	0	0	17	18	0	5	7	12.2	5.29	62	.261	.311	2	.286	0	-4	-4	0	-0.3
1893	Chi-N	17	18	.486	39	34	26	1	0	302^{2}	311	6	181	91	15.0	4.61	101	.258	.361	29	.234	2	2	1	-5	-0.1
1894	Chi-N	7	19	.269	27	23	22	0	0	208	272	2	117	58	17.3	5.84	96	.312	.400	20	.244	0	-12	-5	-2	-0.5
1895	Phi-N	10	8	.556	20	20	13	0	0	146	177	2	81	70	16.2	5.55	86	.295	.382	14	.222	-0	-12	-12	0	-1.0
1896	Phi-N	5	4	.556	12	11	7	0	0	79^{2}	87	0	53	29	16.3	5.31	81	.276	.386	6	.207	-0	-8	-9	0	-0.7
Total	7	72	74	.493	168	150	116	2	1	1251	1381	26	701	510	15.4	4.59	100	.273	.368	97	.202	6	-19	-1	-11	-0.2

● JOHN McGILLEN McGillen, John Joseph b: 8/6/17, Eddystone, Pa. d: 8/11/87, Upland, Pa. BL/TL, 6'1", 175 lbs. Deb: 4/20/44

YEAR	TM/L	W	L	PCT	G	GS	CG	SH	SV	IP	H	HR	BB	SO	RAT	ERA	ERA+	OAV	OOB	BH	AVG	PB	PR	/A	PD	TPI
1944	Phi-A	0	0	—	2	0	0	0	0	1	1	0	2	0	27.0	18.00	19	.333	.600	0	—	0	-2	-2	-0	-0.2

● JIM McGINLEY McGinley, James William b: 10/2/1878, Groveland, Mass. d: 9/20/61, Haverhill, Mass. BR/TR, 5'9.5", 165 lbs. Deb: 9/22/04

YEAR	TM/L	W	L	PCT	G	GS	CG	SH	SV	IP	H	HR	BB	SO	RAT	ERA	ERA+	OAV	OOB	BH	AVG	PB	PR	/A	PD	TPI
1904	StL-N	2	1	.667	3	3	3	0	0	27	28	0	6	6	12.3	2.00	135	.267	.325	1	.091	-1	2	2	-1	0.0
1905	StL-N	0	1	.000	1	1	0	0	0	3	5	1	2	0	21.0	15.00	20	.333	.412	1	1.000	0	-4	-4	-0	-0.3
Total	2	2	2	.500	4	4	3	0	0	30	33	1	8	6	13.2	3.30	83	.275	.336	2	.167	-0	-2	-2	-2	-0.3

● DAN McGINN McGinn, Daniel Michael b: 11/29/43, Omaha, Neb. BL/TL, 6', 190 lbs. Deb: 9/03/68

YEAR	TM/L	W	L	PCT	G	GS	CG	SH	SV	IP	H	HR	BB	SO	RAT	ERA	ERA+	OAV	OOB	BH	AVG	PB	PR	/A	PD	TPI
1968	Cin-N	0	1	.000	14	0	0	0	0	12	13	1	11	16	18.8	5.25	60	.271	.417	0	.000	-0	-3	-3	0	-0.3
1969	Mon-N	7	10	.412	74	1	0	0	6	132^{1}	123	8	65	112	13.1	3.94	93	.245	.337	5	.172	1	-5	-4	1	-0.2
1970	Mon-N	7	10	.412	52	19	3	2	0	130^{2}	154	13	78	83	16.5	5.44	76	.296	.395	4	.114	-2	-20	-19	2	-1.9
1971	Mon-N	1	4	.200	28	6	1	0	0	71	74	7	42	40	14.8	5.96	59	.274	.374	4	.235	0	-20	-19	1	-1.8
1972	Chi-N	0	5	.000	42	2	0	0	4	62^{2}	78	5	29	42	15.9	5.89	65	.301	.380	2	.250	1	-17	-14	-1	-1.5
Total	5	15	30	.333	210	28	4	2	10	408^{2}	442	34	225	293	15.1	5.11	74	.276	.372	15	.165	-0	-65	-59	3	-5.7

● GUS McGINNIS McGinnis, August b: 1870, Painesville, Ohio TL, 5'11", 168 lbs. Deb: 4/27/1893

YEAR	TM/L	W	L	PCT	G	GS	CG	SH	SV	IP	H	HR	BB	SO	RAT	ERA	ERA+	OAV	OOB	BH	AVG	PB	PR	/A	PD	TPI
1893	Chi-N	2	5	.286	13	5	3	0	0	67^{1}	85	2	31	13	15.9	5.35	87	.299	.374	6	.240	2	-5	-5	0	-0.3
	Phi-N	1	3	.250	5	4	4	1	0	37^{1}	39	0	17	12	14.0	4.34	105	.261	.344	3	.200	-1	1	1	0	0.1
	Yr	3	8	.273	18	9	7	1	0	104^{2}	124	2	48	25	15.0	4.99	92	.284	.357	9	.225	1	-4	-4	1	-0.2

● JUMBO McGINNIS McGinnis, George Washington b: 2/22/1864, Alton, Mo. d: 5/18/34, St.Louis, Mo. 5'10", 197 lbs. Deb: 5/02/1882

YEAR	TM/L	W	L	PCT	G	GS	CG	SH	SV	IP	H	HR	BB	SO	RAT	ERA	ERA+	OAV	OOB	BH	AVG	PB	PR	/A	PD	TPI
1882	StL-a	25	18	.581	45	45	43	3	0	388^{1}	391	2	53	134	10.3	2.60	108	.245	.269	44	.217	1	4	9	-5	0.5
1883	StL-a	28	16	.636	45	45	41	**6**	0	382^{2}	325	3	69	128	9.3	2.33	150	.215	.249	36	.200	-6	41	49	1	4.0
1884	StL-a	24	16	.600	40	40	39	5	0	354^{1}	331	4	35	141	9.6	2.84	115	.233	.258	34	.233	3	16	16	-1	1.6
1885	StL-a	6	6	.500	13	13	12	3	0	112	98	1	19	41	9.9	3.38	97	.225	.267	11	.220	0	-2	-1	-1	-0.3
1886	StL-a	5	5	.500	10	10	10	1	0	87^{2}	107	2	27	30	14.5	3.80	91	.288	.347	7	.189	-0	-3	-3	0	-0.4
	Bal-a	11	13	.458	26	25	24	0	0	209^{1}	235	6	48	70	12.8	3.48	98	.280	.329	16	.188	-1	-1	-1	-0	-0.2
	Yr	16	18	.471	36	35	34	1	0	297	342	8	75	100	13.1	3.58	96	.281	.330	23	.189	-1	-4	-5	-0	-0.6
1887	Cin-a	3	5	.375	8	8	8	0	0	69^{1}	85	3	43	18	17.7	5.45	80	.296	.402	6	.194	-1	-9	-9	-0	-0.7
Total	6	102	79	.564	187	186	177	18	0	1603^{2}	1572	21	294	562	10.7	2.95	112	.243	.281	154	.210	-4	47	61	-7	4.5

● JOE McGINNITY McGinnity, Joseph Jerome "Iron Man" (b: Joseph Jerome McGinty)
b: 3/19/1871, Rock Island, Ill. d: 11/14/29, Brooklyn, N.Y. BR/TR, 5'11", 206 lbs. Deb: 4/18/1899 CH

YEAR	TM/L	W	L	PCT	G	GS	CG	SH	SV	IP	H	HR	BB	SO	RAT	ERA	ERA+	OAV	OOB	BH	AVG	PB	PR	/A	PD	TPI
1899	Bal-N	**28**	16	.636	48	41	38	4	2	366^{1}	358	3	93	74	11.7	2.68	148	.256	.314	28	.193	-6	48	52	1	4.5
1900	*Bro-N	**28**	8	**.778**	44	37	32	1	0	**343**	350	5	113	93	13.2	2.94	131	.264	.340	28	.193	-5	29	34	-2	2.5
1901	Bal-A	26	20	.565	**48**	43	**39**	1	1	**382**	412	7	96	75	12.5	3.56	109	.272	.324	31	.209	-5	5	13	-1	0.7
1902	Bal-A	13	10	.565	25	23	19	0	0	198^{2}	219	3	46	39	12.4	3.44	110	.280	.326	25	.287	5	3	7	-2	1.0
	NY-N	8	8	.500	19	16	16	1	0	153	122	1	32	67	9.5	2.06	136	.219	.271	8	.121	-4	12	13	1	1.0
1903	NY-N	**31**	20	.608	**55**	48	**44**	3	2	**434**	391	4	109	171	10.8	2.43	138	.236	.291	34	.206	-3	41	**44**	-4	3.7
1904	NY-N	**35**	8	**.814**	**51**	44	38	**9**	**5**	**408**	307	8	86	144	9.0	**1.61**	**169**	.206	.256	25	.176	-1	**51**	**51**	3	**5.7**
1905	*NY-N	21	15	.583	**46**	38	26	2	3	320^{1}	289	6	71	125	10.5	2.87	102	.240	.290	28	.233	6	5	2	2	1.0
1906	NY-N	**27**	12	.692	**45**	37	32	3	2	339^{2}	316	1	71	105	10.4	2.25	116	.246	.289	15	.130	-4	14	14	1	1.2
1907	NY-N	18	18	.500	**47**	34	23	3	**4**	310^{1}	320	6	58	120	11.4	3.16	78	.266	.308	18	.175	-1	-24	-24	2	-2.4
1908	NY-N	11	7	.611	37	20	7	5	**5**	186	192	8	37	55	11.4	2.27	106	.267	.310	11	.180	-0	2	3	-1	0.2
Total	10	246	142	.634	465	381	314	32	24	3441^{1}	3276	52	812	1068	11.2	2.66	120	.249	.302	251	.194	-18	186	207	-0	19.1

● LYNN McGLOTHEN McGlothen, Lynn Everatt b: 3/27/50, Monroe, La. d: 8/14/84, Dubach, La. BL/TR, 6'2", 195 lbs. Deb: 6/25/72

YEAR	TM/L	W	L	PCT	G	GS	CG	SH	SV	IP	H	HR	BB	SO	RAT	ERA	ERA+	OAV	OOB	BH	AVG	PB	PR	/A	PD	TPI
1972	Bos-A	8	7	.533	22	22	4	1	0	145	135	9	59	112	12.5	3.41	94	.247	.328	10	.189	1	-6	-3	3	0.1
1973	Bos-A	1	2	.333	6	3	0	0	0	23	39	6	8	16	18.8	8.22	49	.386	.436	0	—	0	-11	-11	-0	-1.0
1974	StL-N★	16	12	.571	31	31	8	3	0	237^{1}	212	12	89	142	11.5	2.69	133	.241	.312	15	.181	-1	24	23	1	2.6
1975	StL-N	15	13	.536	35	34	9	2	0	239	231	21	97	146	12.5	3.92	96	.254	.329	7	.087	-5	-8	-4	-2	-1.2
1976	StL-N	13	15	.464	33	32	10	4	0	205	209	10	68	106	12.3	3.91	90	.268	.330	15	.211	2	-9	-8	-2	-0.8
1977	SF-N	2	9	.182	21	15	2	0	0	80	94	9	52	42	16.5	5.62	69	.299	.401	2	.105	-1	-15	-15	-2	-1.7
1978	SF-N	0	0	—	5	1	0	0	0	12^{2}	15	0	4	9	13.5	4.97	69	.313	.365	0	.000	-0	-2	-2	-0	-0.3
	Chi-N	5	3	.625	49	1	0	0	0	80	77	7	39	60	13.0	3.04	133	.257	.342	3	.231	1	5	9	-2	0.8
	Yr	5	3	.625	54	2	0	0	0	92^{2}	92	7	43	69	13.1	3.30	120	.264	.344	3	.188	0	3	7	-2	0.5
1979	Chi-N	13	14	.481	42	29	6	1	2	212	236	27	55	147	12.5	4.12	100	.283	.330	16	.225	2	-9	-0	-2	-0.1
1980	Chi-N	12	14	.462	39	27	2	2	0	182^{1}	211	24	64	119	13.6	4.79	82	.293	.352	10	.196	2	-24	-18	-2	-1.9
1981	Chi-N	1	4	.200	20	6	0	0	0	54^{2}	71	1	28	26	16.5	4.77	77	.317	.395	1	.083	-1	-8	-7	1	-0.7
	Chi-A	0	0	—	11	0	0	0	0	21^{2}	14	0	7	12	9.1	4.15	86	.189	.268	0	—	0	-1	-1	-0	-0.1
1982	NY-A	0	0	—	4	0	0	0	0	5	9	1	2	2	19.8	10.80	37	.375	.423	0	—	0	-4	-4	0	-0.3
Total	11	86	93	.480	318	201	41	13	2	1497^{2}	1553	127	572	939	12.9	3.98	94	.270	.339	79	.173	-0	-68	-42	-7	-4.6

● PAT McGLOTHIN McGlothin, Ezra Mac b: 10/20/20, Coalfield, Tenn. BL/TR, 6'3.5", 180 lbs. Deb: 4/25/49

YEAR	TM/L	W	L	PCT	G	GS	CG	SH	SV	IP	H	HR	BB	SO	RAT	ERA	ERA+	OAV	OOB	BH	AVG	PB	PR	/A	PD	TPI
1949	Bro-N	1	1	.500	7	0	0	0	0	15^{2}	13	2	5	11	10.3	4.60	89	.224	.286	0	.000	-0	-1	-1	1	-0.1
1950	Bro-N	0	0	—	1	0	0	0	0	2	5	0	1	2	27.0	13.50	30	.455	.500	0	—	0	-2	-2	-0	-0.2
Total	2	1	1	.500	8	0	0	0	0	17^{2}	18	2	6	13	12.2	5.60	73	.261	.320	0	.000	-0	-3	-3	1	-0.3

● JIM McGLOTHLIN McGlothlin, James Milton "Red" b: 10/6/43, Los Angeles, Cal. d: 12/23/75, Union, Ky. BR/TR, 6'1", 185 lbs. Deb: 9/20/65

YEAR	TM/L	W	L	PCT	G	GS	CG	SH	SV	IP	H	HR	BB	SO	RAT	ERA	ERA+	OAV	OOB	BH	AVG	PB	PR	/A	PD	TPI
1965	Cal-A	0	3	.000	3	3	1	0	0	18	18	1	7	9	12.5	3.50	97	.261	.329	0	.000	-1	-0	-0	-0	-0.1
1966	Cal-A	3	1	.750	19	11	0	0	0	67^{2}	79	9	19	41	13.2	4.52	74	.292	.340	1	.059	-0	-8	-9	-0	-0.9
1967	Cal-A★	12	8	.600	32	29	9	**6**	3	197^{1}	163	13	56	137	10.2	2.96	106	.226	.286	8	.140	-0	6	4	1	0.5
1968	Cal-A	10	15	.400	40	32	8	0	3	208^{1}	187	19	60	135	11.0	3.54	82	.244	.305	7	.111	-1	-13	-15	2	-1.6
1969	Cal-A	8	16	.333	37	35	4	1	0	201	188	19	58	96	11.2	3.18	110	.249	.307	7	.121	-1	10	7	2	0.8
1970	*Cin-N	14	10	.583	35	34	5	3	0	210^{2}	192	19	86	97	12.0	3.59	112	.245	.322	8	.121	1	11	10	5	1.7
1971	Cin-N	8	12	.400	30	26	6	0	0	170^{2}	151	15	47	93	10.7	3.22	104	.243	.301	7	.137	1	5	3	1	0.5
1972	*Cin-N	9	8	.529	31	21	3	1	0	145	165	15	49	69	13.3	3.91	82	.287	.343	8	.174	3	-7	-11	-0	-0.9
1973	Cin-N	3	3	.500	24	9	0	0	0	63^{1}	91	13	23	18	16.2	6.68	51	.340	.392	2	.125	0	-21	-23	1	-2.1
	Chi-A	0	1	.000	5	1	0	0	0	18^{1}	13	2	13	14	12.8	3.93	101	.203	.338	0	—	0	-0	0	0	0.0
Total	9	67	77	.465	256	201	36	11	3	1300^{1}	1247	125	418	709	11.7	3.61	93	.255	.317	48	.126	2	-19	-34	11	-2.1

YEAR TM/L	W	L	PCT	G	GS	CG	SH	SV	IP	H	HR	BB	SO	RAT	ERA	ERA+	OAV	OOB	BH	AVG	PB	PR	/A	PD	TPI
● **STONEY McGLYNN** McGlynn, Ulysses Simpson Grant b: 5/26/1872, Lancaster, Pa. d: 8/26/41, Manitowoc, Wis. BR/TR, 5'11", 185 lbs. Deb: 9/20/06																									
1906 StL-N	2	2	.500	6	6	6	0	0	48	43	0	15	25	11.1	2.44	108	.249	.312	1	.059	-1	1	1	2	0.2
1907 StL-N	14	25	.359	45	39	**33**	3	1	**352**^{1}	329	6	112	109	11.4	2.91	86	.251	.312	25	.200	3	-17	-16	-1	-1.6
1908 StL-N	1	6	.143	16	6	4	0	1	75^2	76	0	17	23	11.3	3.45	68	.256	.301	2	.077	-1	-9	-9	1	-1.0
Total 3	17	33	.340	67	51	43	3	2	476	448	6	144	157	11.3	2.95	85	.252	.310	28	.167	1	-25	-24	2	-2.4
● **MICKEY McGOWAN** McGowan, Tullis Earl b: 11/26/21, Dothan, Ala. BL/TL, 6'2", 200 lbs. Deb: 4/22/48																									
1948 NY-N	0	0	—	3	0	0	0	0	3^2	3	1	4	2	17.2	7.36	53	.231	.412	0	.000	-0	-1	-1	0	-0.1
● **HOWARD McGRANER** McGraner, Howard "Muck" b: 9/11/1889, Hanley Run, Ohio d: 10/22/52, Zaleski, Ohio BL/TL, 5'7", 155 lbs. Deb: 9/12/12																									
1912 Cin-N	1	0	1.000	4	0	0	0	0	19	22	2	7	5	14.2	7.11	47	.293	.361	2	.250	1	-8	-8	1	-0.6
● **TUG McGRAW** McGraw, Frank Edwin b: 8/30/44, Martinez, Cal. BR/TL, 6', 185 lbs. Deb: 4/18/65																									
1965 NY-N	2	7	.222	37	9	2	0	1	97^2	88	8	48	57	12.8	3.32	106	.249	.344	3	.130	-1	2	2	-1	0.1
1966 NY-N	2	9	.182	15	12	1	0	0	62^1	72	11	25	34	14.0	5.34	68	.294	.359	4	.235	1	-12	-12	-0	-1.1
1967 NY-N	0	3	.000	4	4	0	0	0	17^1	13	3	13	18	13.5	7.79	44	.206	.342	1	.250	0	-9	-8	0	-0.7
1969 *NY-N	9	3	.750	42	4	1	0	12	100^1	89	6	47	92	12.2	2.24	163	.243	.329	4	.167	0	**15**	**16**	1	1.8
1970 NY-N	4	6	.400	57	0	0	0	10	90^2	77	6	49	81	12.6	3.28	123	.231	.332	4	.308	1	8	8	1	1.0
1971 NY-N	11	4	.733	51	1	0	0	8	111	73	4	41	109	9.5	1.70	200	.189	.271	4	.222	2	**22**	**21**	-1	2.4
1972 NY-N★	8	6	.571	54	0	0	0	27	106	71	3	40	92	9.7	1.70	198	.197	.282	2	.100	-0	21	20	-0	2.1
1973 *NY-N	5	6	.455	60	2	0	0	25	118^2	106	11	55	81	12.4	3.87	93	.243	.331	4	.167	1	-3	-3	0	-0.2
1974 NY-N	6	11	.353	41	4	1	1	3	88^2	96	12	32	54	13.0	4.16	86	.279	.340	1	.071	-0	-5	-6	-1	-0.7
1975 Phi-N☆	9	6	.600	56	0	0	0	14	102^2	84	6	36	55	10.8	2.98	125	.226	.299	2	.154	-0	7	9	-0	0.8
1976 *Phi-N	7	6	.538	58	0	0	0	11	97^1	81	4	42	76	11.4	2.50	142	.226	.307	1	.143	0	11	11	-1	1.2
1977 *Phi-N	7	3	.700	45	0	0	0	9	79	62	6	24	58	9.9	2.62	153	.221	.284	4	.400	2	11	12	0	1.5
1978 *Phi-N	8	7	.533	55	1	0	0	9	89^2	82	6	23	63	10.5	3.21	111	.245	.293	0	.000	-0	4	4	0	0.3
1979 Phi-N	4	3	.571	65	1	0	0	16	83^2	83	9	29	57	12.3	5.16	74	.259	.324	1	.167	-0	-13	-12	-1	-1.4
1980 *Phi-N	5	4	.556	57	0	0	0	20	92^1	62	3	23	75	8.5	1.46	259	.194	.253	2	.250	0	**22**	24	0	2.6
1981 *Phi-N	2	4	.333	34	0	0	0	10	44	35	2	14	26	10.0	2.66	136	.219	.282	0	.000	-0	4	5	-1	0.4
1982 Phi-N	3	3	.500	34	0	0	0	5	39^2	50	3	12	25	14.3	4.31	85	.305	.356	0	.000	-0	-3	-3	0	-0.3
1983 Phi-N	2	1	.667	34	1	0	0	0	55^2	58	4	19	30	12.4	3.56	100	.271	.330	1	.333	0	0	0	0	0.0
1984 Phi-N	2	0	1.000	25	0	0	0	0	38	36	1	10	26	10.9	3.79	96	.245	.293	1	.333	0	-1	-1	0	0.0
Total 19	96	92	.511	824	39	5	1	180	1514^2	1318	108	582	1109	11.4	3.14	116	.237	.312	39	.182	5	81	85	-1	9.8
● **JOHN McGRAW** McGraw, John b: 1890, d: 11/14/18, Cleveland, Ohio BR/TR, 190 lbs. Deb: 7/29/14																									
1914 Bro-F	0	0	—	1	0	0	0	0	2	0	0	0	2	4.5	0.00	—	.000	.143	0	—	0	1	1	-0	0.1
● **BOB McGRAW** McGraw, Robert Emmett b: 4/10/1895, LaVeta, Colo. d: 6/2/78, Boise, Idaho BR/TR, 6'2", 160 lbs. Deb: 9/25/17																									
1917 NY-A	0	1	.000	2	2	1	0	0	11	9	0	3	3	9.8	0.82	328	.257	.316	0	.000	-0	2	2	-0	0.2
1918 NY-A	0	1	.000	1	1	0	0	0	0	0	0	4	0	—	∞	—	—	1.000	0	—	0	-4	-4	0	-0.4
1919 NY-A	1	0	1.000	6	0	0	0	0	16^1	11	1	10	3	12.1	3.31	97	.216	.355	0	.000	-0	-0	-0	-0	-0.1
Bos-A	0	2	.000	10	1	0	0	0	26^2	33	0	17	6	17.9	6.75	45	.347	.461	1	.100	-1	-10	-11	-1	-1.2
Yr	1	2	.333	16	1	0	0	0	43	44	1	27	9	15.5	5.44	57	.299	.418	1	.077	-1	-11	-11	-1	-1.3
1920 NY-A	0	0	—	15	0	0	0	0	27	24	1	20	11	15.0	4.67	82	.240	.372	0	.000	-1	-3	-3	-1	-0.4
1925 Bro-N	0	2	.000	2	2	2	0	0	19^2	14	0	13	3	12.4	3.20	130	.222	.355	1	.167	-0	2	2	-1	0.1
1926 Bro-N	9	13	.409	33	21	10	0	1	174^1	197	12	67	49	13.7	4.59	83	.292	.358	8	.145	-2	-15	-15	-1	-1.7
1927 Bro-N	0	1	.000	1	1	0	0	0	4	5	1	2	2	15.8	9.00	44	.313	.389	0	.000	-0	-2	-2	0	-0.2
StL-N	4	5	.444	18	12	4	1	0	94	121	3	30	37	14.5	5.07	78	.323	.373	6	.182	1	-12	-12	1	-1.0
Yr	4	6	.400	19	13	4	1	0	98	126	4	32	39	14.5	5.23	75	.322	.374	6	.176	1	-14	-14	1	-1.2
1928 Phi-N	7	8	.467	39	3	0	0	1	132	150	7	56	28	14.1	4.64	92	.326	.400	4	.111	-2	-10	-5	-1	-0.8
1929 Phi-N	5	5	.500	41	4	0	0	4	86^1	113	6	43	22	16.5	5.73	91	.324	.401	4	.200	0	-10	-5	1	-0.3
Total 9	26	38	.406	168	47	17	1	6	591^1	677	31	265	164	14.5	4.89	83	.305	.382	24	.138	-6	-61	-54	-2	-5.8
● **SCOTT McGREGOR** McGregor, Scott Houston b: 1/18/54, Inglewood, Cal. BB/TL, 6'1", 190 lbs. Deb: 9/19/76																									
1976 Bal-A	0	1	.000	3	2	0	0	0	14^2	17	0	5	6	13.5	3.68	89	.293	.349	0	—	0	-0	-1	0	0.0
1977 Bal-A	3	5	.375	29	5	1	0	4	114	119	8	30	55	12.3	4.42	86	.275	.333	0	—	0	-5	-8	-1	-0.9
1978 Bal-A	15	13	.536	35	32	13	4	1	233	217	19	47	94	10.2	3.32	105	.248	.287	0	—	0	11	4	0	0.9
1979 *Bal-A	13	6	.684	27	23	7	2	0	174^2	165	19	23	81	**9.8**	3.35	120	.248	**.275**	0	—	0	17	13	-1	1.4
1980 Bal-A	20	8	.714	36	36	12	4	0	252	254	16	58	119	11.2	3.32	119	.265	.308	0	—	0	20	18	-3	1.5
1981 Bal-A☆	13	5	.722	24	22	8	3	0	160	167	13	40	82	11.6	3.26	111	.273	.318	0	—	0	7	6	1	0.8
1982 Bal-A	14	12	.538	37	37	7	1	0	226^1	238	31	52	84	11.6	4.61	87	.267	.308	0	—	0	-14	-15	-1	-1.5
1983 *Bal-A	18	7	.720	36	36	12	2	0	260	271	24	45	86	11.0	3.18	124	.269	.301	0	—	0	25	22	-1	2.2
1984 Bal-A	15	12	.556	30	30	10	3	0	196^1	216	18	54	67	12.6	3.94	98	.280	.331	0	—	0	1	-2	2	0.2
1985 Bal-A	14	14	.500	35	34	8	1	0	204	226	34	65	86	12.9	4.81	84	.283	.337	0	—	0	-15	-18	-1	-1.6
1986 Bal-A	11	15	.423	34	33	4	2	0	203	216	35	57	95	12.2	4.52	91	.270	.321	0	—	0	-8	-9	-1	-0.8
1987 Bal-A	2	7	.222	26	15	1	1	0	85^1	112	15	35	39	15.8	6.64	66	.326	.393	0	—	0	-21	-21	3	-1.6
1988 Bal-A	0	3	.000	4	4	0	0	0	17^1	27	3	7	10	17.7	8.83	44	.370	.425	0	—	0	-9	-9	1	-0.7
Total 13	138	108	.561	356	309	83	23	5	2140^2	2245	235	518	904	11.7	3.99	98	.271	.316	0	—	0	10	-19	-2	-0.1
● **SLIM McGREW** McGrew, Walter Howard b: 8/5/1899, Yoakum, Tex. d: 8/21/67, Houston, Tex. BR/TR, 6'7.5", 235 lbs. Deb: 4/18/22																									
1922 Was-A	0	0	—	1	0	0	0	0	1^2	4	0	2	1	32.4	10.80	36	.500	.600	0	.000	-0	-1	-1	0	-0.1
1923 Was-A	0	0	—	3	0	0	0	0	5	11	0	3	1	25.2	12.60	30	.440	.500	0	.000	-0	-5	-5	0	-0.4
1924 Was-A	0	1	.000	6	2	0	0	0	23^1	25	1	12	8	14.3	5.01	80	.281	.366	0	.000	-1	-2	-3	-1	-0.4
Total 3	0	1	.000	10	2	0	0	0	30	40	1	17	10	17.1	6.60	60	.328	.410	0	.000	-2	-8	-9	0	-0.9
● **MC GUIRE** McGuire Deb: 6/16/1894																									
1894 Cin-N	0	0	—	1	0	0	0	0	6	15	0	5	1	30.0	10.50	53	.465	.537	1	.250	-0	-3	-3	0	-0.2
● **DEACON McGUIRE** McGuire, James Thomas b: 11/18/1863, Youngstown, Ohio d: 10/31/36, Albion, Mich. BR/TR, 6'1", 185 lbs. Deb: 6/21/1884 MC♦																									
1890 Roc-a	0	0	—	1	0	0	0	0	4	10	0	1	1	24.8	6.75	53	.458	.481	99	.299	0	-1	-1	0	-0.1
● **TOM McGUIRE** McGuire, Thomas Patrick "Elmer" b: 2/1/1892, Chicago, Ill. d: 12/7/59, Phoenix, Ariz. BR/TR, 6', 175 lbs. Deb: 4/18/14																									
1914 Chi-F	5	6	.455	24	12	7	0	0	131^1	143	7	57	37	14.0	3.70	80	.288	.366	19	.271	4	-7	-11	0	-0.5
1919 Chi-A	0	0	—	1	0	0	0	0	3	5	0	3	0	24.0	9.00	35	.500	.615	0	.000	-0	-2	-2	0	-0.2
Total 2	5	6	.455	25	12	7	0	0	134^1	148	7	60	37	14.2	3.82	77	.292	.371	19	.268	4	-9	-13	1	-0.7
● **BILL McGUNNIGLE** McGunnigle, William Henry "Gunner" b: 1/1/1855, Boston, Mass. d: 3/9/1899, Brockton, Mass. BR/TR, 5'9", 155 lbs. Deb: 5/02/1879 M♦																									
1879 Buf-N	9	5	.643	14	13	13	2	0	120	113	0	16	62	9.7	2.63	99	**.235**	.260	30	.175	-2	-2	-0	1	-0.1
1880 Buf-N	2	3	.400	5	5	4	1	0	37	43	0	8	3	12.4	3.41	72	.279	.315	4	.182	-1	-4	-4	-1	-0.5
Total 2	11	8	.579	19	18	17	3	0	157	156	0	24	65	10.3	2.81	92	.246	.274	35	.173	-3	-6	-4	0	-0.6
● **MARTY McHALE** McHale, Martin Joseph b: 10/30/1888, Stoneham, Mass. d: 5/7/79, Hempstead, N.Y. BR/TR, 5'11.5", 174 lbs. Deb: 9/28/10																									
1910 Bos-A	0	2	.000	2	2	1	0	0	13^2	15	0	6	14	14.5	4.61	55	.259	.338	0	.000	-1	-3	-3	-0	-0.4
1911 Bos-A	0	0	—	4	1	0	0	0	9^1	19	1	3	3	22.2	9.64	34	.475	.523	0	.000	-0	-7	-7	0	-0.6
1913 NY-A	2	4	.333	7	6	4	1	0	48^2	49	1	10	11	11.1	2.96	101	.266	.308	0	.000	-1	-0	0	-1	-0.2

YEAR	TM/L	W	L	PCT	G	GS	CG	SH	SV	IP	H	HR	BB	SO	RAT	ERA	ERA+	OAV	OOB	BH	AVG	PB	PR	/A	PD	TPI
1914	NY-A	7	16	.304	31	23	12	0	1	191	195	3	33	75	10.9	2.97	93	.268	.303	12	.200	2	-5	-4	-3	-0.6
1915	NY-A	3	7	.300	13	11	6	0	0	78^1	86	1	19	25	12.1	4.25	69	.277	.318	3	.143	1	-11	-11	0	-1.1
1916	Bos-A	0	1	.000	2	1	0	0	0	6	7	0	4	1	18.0	3.00	92	.280	.400	0	—	0	-0	-0	0	0.1
	Cle-A	0	0	—	5	0	0	0	0	11^1	10	1	6	2	12.7	5.56	54	.270	.372	0	.000	-0	-3	-3	-0	-0.4
	Yr	0	1	.000	7	1	0	0	0	17^1	17	1	10	3	14.0	4.67	63	.270	.370	0	.000	0	-4	-3	0	-0.3
Total	6	12	30	.286	64	44	23	1	1	358^1	381	7	81	131	11.8	3.57	80	.275	.319	15	.140	-0	-30	-29	-4	-3.2

● VANCE McILREE McIlree, Vance Elmer b: 10/14/1897, Riverside, Iowa d: 5/6/59, Kansas City, Mo. BR/TR, 6′, 160 lbs. Deb: 9/13/21

YEAR	TM/L	W	L	PCT	G	GS	CG	SH	SV	IP	H	HR	BB	SO	RAT	ERA	ERA+	OAV	OOB	BH	AVG	PB	PR	/A	PD	TPI
1921	Was-A	0	0	—	1	0	0	0	0	1	1	0	0	0	9.0	9.00	46	.200	.200	0	—	0	-1	-1	-0	-0.1

● IRISH McILVEEN McIlveen, Henry Cooke b: 7/27/1880, Belfast, Ireland d: 10/18/60, Lorain, Ohio BL/TL, 5′11.5″, 180 lbs. Deb: 7/10/06 ♦

YEAR	TM/L	W	L	PCT	G	GS	CG	SH	SV	IP	H	HR	BB	SO	RAT	ERA	ERA+	OAV	OOB	BH	AVG	PB	PR	/A	PD	TPI
1906	Pit-N	0	1	.000	2	1	0	0	0	7	10	1	2	3	15.4	7.71	35	.357	.400	2	.400	1	-4	-4	0	-0.3

● STOVER McILWAIN McIlwain, Stover William "Smokey" b: 9/22/39, Savannah, Ga. d: 1/15/66, Buffalo, N.Y. BR/TR, 6′2″, 195 lbs. Deb: 9/25/57

YEAR	TM/L	W	L	PCT	G	GS	CG	SH	SV	IP	H	HR	BB	SO	RAT	ERA	ERA+	OAV	OOB	BH	AVG	PB	PR	/A	PD	TPI
1957	Chi-A	0	0	—	1	0	0	0	0	1	2	0	1	0	27.0	0.00	—	.500	.600	0	—	0	0	0	-0	0.0
1958	Chi-A	0	0	—	1	1	0	0	0	4	4	1	0	4	9.0	2.25	162	.250	.250	0	.000	-0	1	1	0	0.0
Total	2	0	0	—	2	1	0	0	0	5	6	1	1	4	12.6	1.80	203	.300	.333	0	.000	-0	1	1	-0	0.0

● HARRY McINTIRE McIntire, John Reid b: 1/11/1879, Dayton, Ohio d: 1/9/49, Daytona Beach, Fla. BR/TR, 5′11″, 180 lbs. Deb: 4/14/05

YEAR	TM/L	W	L	PCT	G	GS	CG	SH	SV	IP	H	HR	BB	SO	RAT	ERA	ERA+	OAV	OOB	BH	AVG	PB	PR	/A	PD	TPI
1905	Bro-N	8	25	.242	40	35	29	1	1	308^2	340	6	101	135	13.4	3.70	78	.285	.351	34	.246	6	-24	-28	-3	-2.4
1906	Bro-N	13	21	.382	39	31	25	4	3	276	254	2	89	121	11.6	2.97	85	.247	.316	18	.175	1	-10	-14	-1	-1.4
1907	Bro-N	7	15	.318	28	22	19	3	0	199^2	178	6	79	49	11.9	2.39	98	.248	.329	15	.217	4	2	-1	-1	0.3
1908	Bro-N	11	20	.355	40	35	26	4	2	288	259	5	90	108	11.5	2.69	87	.252	.324	20	.200	2	-10	-11	-2	-1.3
1909	Bro-N	7	17	.292	32	26	20	2	1	228	200	5	91	84	12.3	3.63	71	.246	.337	13	.171	1	-26	-26	-0	-2.7
1910	*Chi-N	13	9	.591	28	19	10	2	0	176	152	5	50	65	10.8	3.07	94	.240	.305	17	.258	3	-1	-4	-1	-0.1
1911	Chi-N	11	7	.611	25	17	9	1	0	149	147	5	33	56	11.1	4.11	81	.257	.302	14	.264	4	-12	-13	-0	-0.9
1912	Chi-N	1	2	.333	4	3	2	0	0	23^2	22	0	6	8	10.6	3.80	88	.256	.304	3	.300	1	-1	-1	-0	0.0
1913	Cin-N	0	1	.000	1	0	0	0	0	1	3	0	0	0	27.0	27.00	12	.600	.600	0	—	0	-3	-3	-0	-0.2
Total	9	71	117	.378	237	188	140	17	7	1650	1555	34	539	626	11.9	3.22	83	.256	.326	134	.218	23	-85	-100	-7	-8.7

● JOE McINTOSH McIntosh, Joseph Anthony b: 8/4/51, Billings, Mont. BB/TR, 6′2″, 185 lbs. Deb: 4/05/74

YEAR	TM/L	W	L	PCT	G	GS	CG	SH	SV	IP	H	HR	BB	SO	RAT	ERA	ERA+	OAV	OOB	BH	AVG	PB	PR	/A	PD	TPI
1974	SD-N	0	4	.000	10	5	0	0	0	37^1	36	3	17	22	13.0	3.62	98	.250	.333	0	.000	-1	0	-0	-0	-0.2
1975	SD-N	8	15	.348	37	28	4	1	0	183	195	14	60	71	12.6	3.69	94	.273	.332	9	.188	2	-1	-4	-0	-0.3
Total	2	8	19	.296	47	33	4	1	0	220^1	231	17	77	93	12.7	3.68	95	.270	.332	9	.155	1	-1	-5	-1	-0.5

● FRANK McINTYRE McIntyre, Frank W. b: Detroit d: 7/8/1887, Detroit, Mich. Deb: 5/16/1883

YEAR	TM/L	W	L	PCT	G	GS	CG	SH	SV	IP	H	HR	BB	SO	RAT	ERA	ERA+	OAV	OOB	BH	AVG	PB	PR	/A	PD	TPI
1883	Det-N	1	0	1.000	1	1	1	0	0	11	11	0	1	0	9.8	0.82	380	.234	.250	0	.000	-0	3	3	0	0.3
	Col-a	1	1	.500	2	2	2	0	0	19	20	0	7	6	12.8	5.21	59	.253	.314	0	.000	-0	-4	-5	-1	-0.5
Total	1	2	1	.667	3	3	3	0	0	30	31	0	8	6	11.7	3.60	86	.246	.291	0	.000	-1	-1	-2	-1	-0.2

● DOC McJAMES McJames, James McCutchen (b: James Mc Cutchen James) b: 8/27/1873, Williamsburg, S.C. d: 9/23/01, Charleston, S.C. TR , Deb: 9/24/1895

YEAR	TM/L	W	L	PCT	G	GS	CG	SH	SV	IP	H	HR	BB	SO	RAT	ERA	ERA+	OAV	OOB	BH	AVG	PB	PR	/A	PD	TPI
1895	Was-N	1	1	.500	2	2	2	0	0	17	17	0	16	9	17.5	1.59	302	.256	.401	1	.143	-1	6	6	0	0.5
1896	Was-N	12	20	.375	37	33	29	0	1	280^1	310	2	135	103	14.5	4.27	103	.278	.359	18	.162	-9	3	4	-0	-0.4
1897	Was-N	15	23	.395	44	39	33	**3**	2	323^2	361	7	137	**156**	14.4	3.61	120	.280	.358	21	.169	-7	25	26	0	1.7
1898	Bal-N	27	15	.643	45	42	40	2	0	374	327	5	113	178	10.9	2.36	152	.234	.296	27	.181	-4	52	51	-3	4.2
1899	Bro-N	19	15	.559	37	34	27	1	1	275^1	295	4	122	105	14.0	3.50	112	.274	.353	19	.170	-5	11	13	3	0.9
1901	Bro-N	5	6	.455	13	12	6	0	0	91	104	1	40	42	14.9	4.75	71	.285	.367	1	.029	-4	-14	-14	-2	-1.8
Total	6	79	80	.497	178	162	137	6	4	1361^1	1414	19	563	593	13.4	3.43	117	.266	.343	87	.162	-30	83	86	-1	5.1

● ARCHIE McKAIN McKain, Archie Richard "Happy" b: 5/12/11, Delphos, Kan. d: 5/21/85, Salina, Kan. BB/TL, 5′10″, 175 lbs. Deb: 4/25/37

YEAR	TM/L	W	L	PCT	G	GS	CG	SH	SV	IP	H	HR	BB	SO	RAT	ERA	ERA+	OAV	OOB	BH	AVG	PB	PR	/A	PD	TPI
1937	Bos-A	8	8	.500	36	18	3	0	2	137	152	7	64	66	14.2	4.66	102	.273	.348	13	.265	3	-1	1	0	0.4
1938	Bos-A	5	4	.556	37	5	1	0	6	99^2	119	6	44	27	14.9	4.52	109	.297	.369	2	.065	-2	3	**5**	2	0.4
1939	Det-A	5	6	.455	32	11	4	1	4	129^2	120	6	54	49	12.1	3.68	133	.247	.322	9	.220	4	14	17	-2	1.9
1940	*Det-A	5	0	1.000	27	0	0	0	3	51	48	2	25	24	12.9	2.82	168	.247	.333	1	.143	0	9	11	1	1.2
1941	Det-A	2	1	.667	15	0	0	0	0	43	58	3	11	14	14.4	5.02	90	.330	.369	0	.000	-1	-4	-2	2	-0.1
	StL-A	0	1	.000	8	0	0	0	1	10	16	2	4	2	18.9	8.10	53	.364	.429	0	.000	-0	-4	-4	1	-0.4
	Yr	2	2	.500	23	0	0	0	1	53	74	5	15	16	15.3	5.60	80	.336	.381	0	.000	-2	-9	-7	3	-0.5
1943	StL-A	1	1	.500	10	0	0	0	0	16	16	0	6	6	12.4	3.94	84	.242	.306	0	.000	-0	-1	-1	0	-0.1
Total	6	26	21	.553	165	34	8	1	16	486^1	529	26	208	188	13.7	4.26	112	.275	.347	25	.176	3	15	27	4	3.3

● HAL McKAIN McKain, Harold Le Roy b: 7/10/06, Logan, Iowa d: 1/24/70, Sacramento, Cal. BL/TR, 5′11″, 185 lbs. Deb: 9/22/27

YEAR	TM/L	W	L	PCT	G	GS	CG	SH	SV	IP	H	HR	BB	SO	RAT	ERA	ERA+	OAV	OOB	BH	AVG	PB	PR	/A	PD	TPI
1927	Cle-A	0	1	.000	2	1	0	0	0	11	18	0	4	5	18.0	4.09	103	.391	.440	0	.000	-1	0	0	0	0.0
1929	Chi-A	6	9	.400	34	10	4	1	1	158	158	10	85	33	14.4	3.65	117	.275	.378	10	.227	2	11	11	4	1.7
1930	Chi-A	6	4	.600	32	5	0	0	5	89	108	0	42	52	15.5	5.56	83	.299	.377	13	.419	7	-9	-9	1	-0.1
1931	Chi-A	6	9	.400	27	8	3	0	0	112	134	10	57	39	15.6	5.71	75	.295	.377	5	.119	-1	-16	-18	2	-1.5
1932	Chi-A	0	0	—	8	0	0	0	0	11^1	17	1	5	7	17.5	11.12	39	.340	.400	0	.000	-0	-8	-9	0	-0.7
Total	5	18	23	.439	103	24	7	1	6	381^1	435	21	193	136	15.2	4.93	88	.293	.380	28	.230	8	-23	-24	7	-0.6

● REEVE McKAY McKay, Reeve Stewart "Rip" b: 11/16/1881, Morgan, Tex. d: 1/18/46, Dallas, Tex. TR , 6′1.5″, 168 lbs. Deb: 10/02/15

YEAR	TM/L	W	L	PCT	G	GS	CG	SH	SV	IP	H	HR	BB	SO	RAT	ERA	ERA+	OAV	OOB	BH	AVG	PB	PR	/A	PD	TPI
1915	StL-A	0	0	—	1	0	0	0	0	1	1	0	0	0	9.0	9.00	32	.500	.500	0	—	0	-1	-1	0	-0.1

● JIM McKEE McKee, James Marion b: 2/1/47, Columbus, Ohio BR/TR, 6′7″, 215 lbs. Deb: 9/15/72

YEAR	TM/L	W	L	PCT	G	GS	CG	SH	SV	IP	H	HR	BB	SO	RAT	ERA	ERA+	OAV	OOB	BH	AVG	PB	PR	/A	PD	TPI
1972	Pit-N	1	0	1.000	2	0	0	0	0	5	2	0	1	4	5.4	0.00	—	.125	.176	0	—	0	2	2	-0	0.2
1973	Pit-N	0	1	.000	15	1	0	0	0	27	31	2	17	13	16.3	5.67	62	.287	.389	0	.000	-0	-6	-6	-0	-0.7
Total	2	1	1	.500	17	1	0	0	0	32	33	2	18	17	14.6	4.78	73	.266	.364	0	.000	-0	-4	-5	-1	-0.5

● ROGERS McKEE McKee, Rogers Hornsby b: 9/16/26, Shelby, N.C. BL/TL, 6′1″, 160 lbs. Deb: 8/18/43

YEAR	TM/L	W	L	PCT	G	GS	CG	SH	SV	IP	H	HR	BB	SO	RAT	ERA	ERA+	OAV	OOB	BH	AVG	PB	PR	/A	PD	TPI
1943	Phi-N	1	0	1.000	4	1	1	0	0	13^1	12	0	5	1	11.5	6.08	56	.226	.293	1	.200	0	-4	-4	0	-0.4
1944	Phi-N	0	0	—	1	0	0	0	0	2	2	1	1	0	13.5	4.50	80	.250	.333	0	—	0	-0	-0	0	0.0
Total	2	1	0	1.000	5	1	1	0	0	15^1	14	1	6	1	11.7	5.87	58	.230	.299	1	.200	0	-4	-4	0	-0.4

● TIM McKEITHAN McKeithan, Emmett James b: 11/2/06, Lawndale, N.C. d: 8/20/69, Forest City, N.C. BR/TR, 6′2″, 182 lbs. Deb: 7/21/32

YEAR	TM/L	W	L	PCT	G	GS	CG	SH	SV	IP	H	HR	BB	SO	RAT	ERA	ERA+	OAV	OOB	BH	AVG	PB	PR	/A	PD	TPI
1932	Phi-A	0	1	.000	4	2	0	0	0	12^2	18	0	5	0	16.3	7.11	64	.340	.397	0	.000	0	-4	-4	0	-0.3
1933	Phi-A	1	0	1.000	3	1	0	0	0	9	10	0	4	3	14.0	4.00	107	.278	.350	1	.333	0	0	0	0	0.1
1934	Phi-A	0	0	—	3	0	0	0	0	4	7	2	5	0	27.0	15.75	28	.389	.522	0	.000	-0	-5	-5	-0	-0.5
Total	3	1	1	.500	10	3	0	0	0	25^2	35	2	14	3	17.2	7.36	60	.327	.405	1	.143	0	-8	-8	0	-0.7

● RUSS McKELVY McKelvy, Russell Errett b: 9/8/1856, Meadville, Pa. d: 10/19/15, Omaha, Neb. BR/TR, Deb: 5/01/1878 ♦

YEAR	TM/L	W	L	PCT	G	GS	CG	SH	SV	IP	H	HR	BB	SO	RAT	ERA	ERA+	OAV	OOB	BH	AVG	PB	PR	/A	PD	TPI
1878	Ind-N	0	2	.000	4	1	1	0	0	25	38	1	3	3	14.8	2.16	94	.322	.339	57	.225	0	0	-0	1	0.0

● KIT McKENNA McKenna, James William b: 2/10/1873, Lynchburg, Va. d: 3/31/41, Lynchburg, Va. Deb: 7/07/1898

YEAR	TM/L	W	L	PCT	G	GS	CG	SH	SV	IP	H	HR	BB	SO	RAT	ERA	ERA+	OAV	OOB	BH	AVG	PB	PR	/A	PD	TPI
1898	Bro-N	2	6	.250	14	9	7	0	0	100^2	118	4	57	27	17.2	5.63	64	.290	.399	9	.225	0	-23	-23	2	-1.8
1899	Bal-N	2	3	.400	8	4	4	0	1	45	66	1	19	7	17.6	4.60	86	.340	.407	1	.059	-1	-4	-3	-0	-0.4
Total	2	4	9	.308	22	13	11	0	1	145^2	184	5	76	34	17.3	5.31	70	.306	.402	10	.175	-1	-26	-26	1	-2.2

YEAR TM/L	W	L	PCT	G	GS	CG	SH	SV	IP	H	HR	BB	SO	RAT	ERA	ERA+	OAV	OOB	BH	AVG	PB	PR	/A	PD	TPI

● LIMB McKENRY   McKenry, Frank Gordon "Big Pete" b: 8/13/1888, Piney Flats, Tenn. d: 11/1/56, Fresno, Cal. BR/TR, 6'4", 205 lbs. Deb: 8/27/15

1915 Cin-N	5	5	.500	21	11	5	0	0	110¹	94	2	39	37	11.1	2.94	97	.238	.311	5	.152	0	-2	-1	1	0.1
1916 Cin-N	1	1	.500	6	1	0	0	0	14²	14	0	8	2	14.7	4.30	60	.259	.375	2	.400	2	-3	-3	-0	-0.1
Total 2	6	6	.500	27	12	5	0	0	125	108	2	47	39	11.5	3.10	91	.241	.319	7	.184	2	-5	-4	1	0.0

● JOEL McKEON   McKeon, Joel Jacob b: 2/25/63, Covington, Ky. BL/TL, 6', 185 lbs. Deb: 5/06/86

1986 Chi-A	3	1	.750	30	0	0	0	1	33	18	2	17	18	9.5	2.45	176	.165	.278	0	—	0	6	7	-1	0.6
1987 Chi-A	1	2	.333	13	0	0	0	0	21	27	8	15	14	18.0	9.43	49	.318	.420	0	—	0	-12	-11	-0	-1.2
Total 2	4	3	.571	43	0	0	0	1	54	45	10	32	32	12.8	5.17	85	.232	.341	0	—	0	-5	-5	-1	-0.6

● LARRY McKEON   McKeon, Lawrence G. b: 3/25/1866, New York d: 7/18/15, Indianapolis, Ind 5'10", 168 lbs. Deb: 5/01/1884

1884 Ind-a	18	41	.305	61	60	59	2	0	512	488	20	94	308	10.5	3.50	94	.235	.275	53	.212	-3	-14	-12	8	-0.6
1885 Cin-a	20	13	.606	33	33	32	2	0	290	273	5	50	117	10.4	2.86	114	.241	.281	20	.165	-5	13	13	-0	0.7
1886 Cin-a	8	8	.500	19	19	16	0	0	156	174	6	54	46	13.3	5.08	69	.276	.336	19	.253	1	-28	-27	1	-2.1
KC-N	0	2	.000	3	3	3	0	0	21	44	0	8	3	22.3	10.71	35	.411	.452	0	.000	-2	-17	-16	0	-1.3
Total 3	46	64	.418	116	115	110	4	0	979	979	31	206	474	11.2	3.71	90	.248	.291	92	.202	-8	-47	-42	8	-3.3

● DENNY McLAIN   McLain, Dennis Dale b: 3/29/44, Chicago, Ill. BR/TR, 6'1", 185 lbs. Deb: 9/21/63

1963 Det-A	2	1	.667	3	3	2	0	0	21	20	2	16	22	15.4	4.29	87	.253	.379	1	.200	1	-2	-1	1	0.0
1964 Det-A	4	5	.444	19	16	3	0	0	100	84	16	37	70	11.0	4.05	90	.225	.297	5	.135	-1	-5	-4	-2	-0.8
1965 Det-A	16	6	.727	33	29	13	4	1	220¹	174	25	62	192	9.7	2.61	133	.216	.273	4	.054	-4	21	21	-0	1.9
1966 Det-A★	20	14	.588	38	38	14	4	0	264¹	205	42	104	192	10.6	3.92	89	.214	.294	17	.183	2	-14	-13	-1	-1.3
1967 Det-A★	17	16	.515	37	37	10	3	0	235	209	35	73	161	10.9	3.79	86	.237	.297	10	.118	-3	-15	-14	-2	-2.0
1968 *Det-A★	**31**	6	**.838**	41	41	**28**	6	0	**336**	241	31	63	280	8.3	1.96	154	.200	.243	18	.162	0	38	**39**	1	**4.9**
1969 Det-A★	**24**	9	.727	42	41	23	**9**	0	**325**	288	25	67	181	9.9	2.80	133	.237	.279	17	.160	-1	30	34	-5	3.0
1970 Det-A	3	5	.375	14	14	1	0	0	91¹	100	19	28	52	12.9	4.63	80	.273	.330	2	.065	-2	-9	-9	-0	-1.1
1971 Was-A	10	22	.313	33	32	9	3	0	216²	233	31	72	103	12.8	4.28	77	.281	.341	6	.103	-1	-20	-23	-1	-2.5
1972 Oak-A	1	2	.333	5	5	0	0	0	22¹	32	4	8	8	16.1	6.04	47	.323	.374	0	.000	-0	-7	-8	0	-0.7
Atl-N	3	5	.375	15	8	2	0	1	54	60	12	18	21	13.2	6.50	58	.279	.338	2	.167	0	-18	-16	-1	-1.7
Total 10	131	91	.590	280	264	105	29	2	1886	1646	242	548	1282	10.6	3.39	101	.234	.292	82	.133	-9	-1	5	-10	-0.4

● BARNEY McLAUGHLIN   McLaughlin, Bernard b: 1857, Ireland d: 2/13/21, Lowell, Mass. BR/TR, Deb: 8/02/1884 F♦

| 1884 KC-U | 1 | 3 | .250 | 7 | 4 | 4 | 0 | 0 | 48² | 62 | 2 | 15 | 14 | 14.2 | 5.36 | 51 | .291 | .337 | 37 | .228 | 1 | -13 | -14 | 0 | -1.1 |

● BYRON McLAUGHLIN   McLaughlin, Byron Scott b: 9/29/55, Van Nuys, Cal. BR/TR, 6'1", 185 lbs. Deb: 9/18/77

1977 Sea-A	0	0	—	1	0	0	0	0	1¹	5	1	0	1	33.8	27.00	15	.625	.625	0	—	0	-3	-3	0	-0.3
1978 Sea-A	4	8	.333	20	17	4	0	0	107	97	15	39	87	11.9	4.37	87	.238	.314	0	—	0	-7	-7	-2	-0.8
1979 Sea-A	7	7	.500	47	7	1	0	14	123²	114	13	60	74	12.8	4.22	103	.251	.340	0	—	0	-0	2	-2	0.0
1980 Sea-A	3	6	.333	45	4	0	0	2	90²	124	15	50	41	17.5	6.85	60	.331	.412	0	—	0	-28	-27	-2	-2.8
1983 Cal-A	2	4	.333	16	7	0	0	0	55²	63	3	22	45	14.1	5.17	78	.286	.357	0	—	0	-7	-7	-0	-0.7
Total 5	16	25	.390	129	35	5	0	16	378¹	403	47	171	248	13.9	5.11	80	.275	.356	0	—	0	-46	-43	-5	-4.6

● FRANK McLAUGHLIN   McLaughlin, Francis Edward b: 6/19/1856, Lowell, Mass. d: 4/5/17, Lowell, Mass. BR/TR, 5'9", 160 lbs. Deb: 8/09/1882 F♦

1883 Pit-a	0	0	—	2	0	0	0	0	9	14	0	3	1	17.0	13.00	25	.334	.378	25	.219	-1	-10	-10	-0	-0.7
1884 KC-U	0	0	—	2	1	0	0	0	10	15	0	2	3	15.3	5.40	51	.325	.353	28	.228	0	-3	-3	-1	-0.3
Total 2	0	0	—	4	1	0	0	0	19	29	0	5	4	16.1	9.00	33	.329	.365	97	.228	0	-12	-13	-1	-1.0

● JIM McLAUGHLIN   McLaughlin, James Thomas b: 11/18/1860, Cleveland, Ohio d: 11/16/1895, Cleveland, Ohio TL , Deb: 5/30/1884

| 1884 Bal-a | 1 | 2 | .333 | 3 | 2 | 2 | 0 | 0 | 22 | 27 | 2 | 11 | 8 | 15.5 | 3.68 | 94 | .300 | .376 | 5 | .227 | 0 | -1 | -1 | 0 | 0.0 |

● JOEY McLAUGHLIN   McLaughlin, Joey Richard b: 7/11/56, Tulsa, Okla. BR/TR, 6'2", 205 lbs. Deb: 6/11/77

1977 Atl-N	0	0	—	3	2	0	0	0	6	10	3	3	3	19.5	15.00	30	.385	.448	0	.000	-0	-7	-7	0	-0.6
1979 Atl-N	5	3	.625	37	0	0	0	5	69	54	3	34	40	11.6	2.48	163	.224	.322	2	.182	0	10	12	-1	1.2
1980 Tor-A	6	9	.400	55	10	0	0	4	135²	159	16	53	70	14.3	4.51	95	.302	.370	0	—	0	-7	-3	-0	-0.5
1981 Tor-A	1	5	.167	40	0	0	0	10	60	55	2	21	38	11.4	2.85	138	.249	.314	0	—	0	5	7	-0	0.6
1982 Tor-A	8	6	.571	44	0	0	0	9	70	54	7	30	49	10.9	3.21	139	.212	.297	0	—	0	7	10	1	0.8
1983 Tor-A	7	4	.636	50	0	0	0	9	64²	71	8	37	47	13.9	4.45	95	.259	.357	0	—	0	-3	-1	-0	-0.1
1984 Tor-A	0	0	—	6	0	0	0	0	10²	12	0	7	3	16.0	2.53	162	.286	.388	0	—	0	2	2	-0	-0.1
Tex-A	2	1	.667	15	0	0	0	0	32²	33	4	13	21	12.7	4.41	94	.260	.329	0	—	0	-2	-1	-0	-0.4
Yr	2	1	.667	21	0	0	0	0	43¹	45	4	20	24	13.5	3.95	105	.265	.342	0	—	0	0	0	-0	-0.5
Total 7	29	28	.509	250	12	0	0	36	448²	440	46	198	268	12.9	3.85	110	.262	.341	2	.167	-0	5	19	-0	0.9

● JUD McLAUGHLIN   McLaughlin, Justin Theodore b: 3/24/12, Brighton, Mass. d: 9/27/64, Cambridge, Mass. BL/TL, 5'11", 155 lbs. Deb: 6/23/31

1931 Bos-A	0	0	—	9	0	0	0	0	12	23	1	8	3	23.3	12.00	36	.397	.470	0	—	0	-10	-10	0	-0.9
1932 Bos-A	0	0	—	1	0	0	0	0	3	5	0	4	0	27.0	15.00	30	.385	.529	0	.000	-0	-4	-4	0	-0.3
1933 Bos-A	0	0	—	6	0	0	0	0	8²	14	1	5	1	19.7	6.23	70	.359	.432	0	—	0	-2	-2	0	-0.2
Total 3	0	0	—	16	0	0	0	0	23²	42	2	17	4	22.4	10.27	42	.382	.465	0	.000	-0	-16	-16	0	-1.4

● BO McLAUGHLIN   McLaughlin, Michael Duane b: 10/23/53, Oakland, Cal. BR/TR, 6'5", 210 lbs. Deb: 7/20/76

1976 Hou-N	4	5	.444	17	11	4	2	1	79	71	6	17	32	10.3	2.85	112	.244	.290	0	.000	-1	6	3	0	0.2
1977 Hou-N	4	7	.364	46	6	0	0	5	84²	81	6	34	59	12.9	4.25	84	.260	.344	0	.000	-1	-3	-6	1	-0.6
1978 Hou-N	0	1	.000	12	0	0	0	2	23¹	30	2	16	10	18.5	5.01	66	.313	.421	0	.000	-0	-4	-4	-0	-0.5
1979 Hou-N	1	2	.333	12	0	0	0	0	16¹	22	2	4	12	14.3	5.51	64	.314	.351	0	.000	-0	-3	-4	0	-0.4
Atl-N	1	1	.500	37	1	0	0	0	49²	63	2	16	45	14.7	4.89	83	.303	.358	0	.000	-0	-6	-5	-1	-0.6
Yr	2	3	.400	49	1	0	0	0	66	85	4	20	57	14.6	5.05	78	.305	.355	0	.000	-0	-10	-8	-1	-1.0
1981 Oak-A	0	0	—	11	0	0	0	1	11²	17	1	9	3	20.8	11.57	30	.333	.443	0	—	0	-10	-10	0	-0.9
1982 Oak-A	0	4	.000	21	2	0	0	0	48¹	51	3	27	27	14.7	4.84	85	.267	.361	0	—	0	-4	-5	0	-0.3
Total 6	10	20	.333	156	21	5	2	9	313	335	22	123	188	13.6	4.49	80	.275	.348	0	.000	-2	-25	-32	0	-3.1

● PAT McLAUGHLIN   McLaughlin, Patrick Elmer b: 8/17/10, Taylor, Tex. BR/TR, 6'2", 175 lbs. Deb: 4/25/37

1937 Det-A	0	2	.000	10	3	0	0	0	32²	39	3	16	8	15.2	6.34	74	.291	.367	1	.100	-1	-6	-6	-1	-0.7
1940 Phi-A	0	0	—	1	0	0	0	0	1²	4	1	1	0	27.0	16.20	27	.444	.500	0	—	0	-2	-2	0	-0.2
1945 Det-A	0	0	—	1	0	0	0	0	1	2	0	0	0	18.0	9.00	39	.400	.400	0	—	0	-1	-1	-0	-0.1
Total 3	0	2	.000	12	3	0	0	0	35¹	45	4	17	8	15.8	6.88	67	.304	.376	1	.100	-1	-9	-9	-1	-0.9

● WARREN McLAUGHLIN   McLaughlin, Warren A. b: 1/22/1876, N.Plainfield, N.J. d: 10/22/23, Plainfield, N.J. TL , Deb: 7/07/00

1900 Phi-N	0	0	—	1	0	0	0	0	6	4	0	6	1	15.0	4.50	80	.190	.369	1	.500	1	-1	-1	0	0.0
1902 Pit-N	3	0	1.000	3	3	3	0	0	26	27	0	9	13	12.8	2.77	99	.268	.334	4	.364	1	0	-0	-1	0.0
1903 Phi-N	0	3	.000	3	2	2	0	0	23	38	0	11	3	19.6	7.04	46	.376	.442	2	.200	0	-10	-10	-0	-0.8
Total 3	3	3	.500	7	5	5	0	0	55	69	0	26	17	15.9	4.75	64	.309	.386	7	.304	2	-10	-10	-2	-0.8

● AL McLEAN   McLean, Albert Eldon "Elrod" b: 9/20/12, Chicago, Ill. d: 9/29/90, Asheboro, N.C. BR/TR, 6', 175 lbs. Deb: 7/16/35

| 1935 Was-A | 0 | 0 | — | 4 | 0 | 0 | 0 | 0 | 8² | 12 | 0 | 5 | 3 | 17.7 | 7.27 | 59 | .324 | .405 | 0 | .000 | -0 | -3 | -3 | 0 | -0.3 |

● WAYNE McLELAND   McLeland, Wayne Gaffney "Nubbin" b: 8/29/24, Milton, Iowa BR/TR, 6', 180 lbs. Deb: 4/20/51

| 1951 Det-A | 0 | 1 | .000 | 6 | 1 | 0 | 0 | 0 | 11 | 20 | 1 | 4 | 0 | 20.5 | 8.18 | 51 | .400 | .455 | 0 | .000 | -0 | -5 | -5 | 0 | -0.5 |

YEAR	TM/L	W	L	PCT	G	GS	CG	SH	SV	IP	H	HR	BB	SO	RAT	ERA	ERA+	OAV	OOB	BH	AVG	PB	PR	/A	PD	TPI
1952	Det-A	0	0	—	4	0	0	0	0	2^2	4	0	6	0	33.8	10.13	38	.444	.667	0	—	0	-2	-2	-0	-0.2
Total	2	0	1	.000	10	1	0	0	0	13^2	24	1	10	0	23.0	8.56	48	.407	.500	0	.000	-0	-7	-7	0	-0.7

● CAL McLISH McLish, Calvin Coolidge Julius Caesar Tuskahoma "Buster" b: 12/1/25, Anadarko, Okla. BB/TR, 6'1", 200 lbs. Deb: 5/13/44 C

YEAR	TM/L	W	L	PCT	G	GS	CG	SH	SV	IP	H	HR	BB	SO	RAT	ERA	ERA+	OAV	OOB	BH	AVG	PB	PR	/A	PD	TPI
1944	Bro-N	3	10	.231	23	13	3	0	0	84	110	10	48	24	17.0	7.82	45	.321	.406	7	.219	0	-39	-40	-2	-3.8
1946	Bro-N	0	0	—	1	0	0	0	0	0	1	0	0	0	—	∞	—	1.000	1.000	0	—	0	-2	-2	0	-0.2
1947	Pit-N	0	0	—	1	0	0	0	0	1	2	0	0	0	27.0	18.00	23	.400	.500	0	—	0	-2	-2	0	-0.1
1948	Pit-N	0	0	—	2	1	0	0	0	5	8	0	2	1	18.0	9.00	45	.400	.455	0	.000	-0	-3	-3	0	-0.3
1949	Chi-N	1	1	.500	8	2	0	0	0	23	31	5	12	6	16.8	5.87	69	.341	.417	3	.333	2	-5	-5	1	-0.3
1951	Chi-N	4	10	.286	30	17	5	1	0	145^2	159	16	52	46	13.2	4.45	92	.283	.347	5	.119	-1	-8	-6	-0	-0.7
1956	Cle-A	2	4	.333	37	2	0	0	1	61^2	67	5	32	27	14.4	4.96	85	.282	.367	1	.111	1	-6	-5	1	-0.3
1957	Cle-A	9	7	.563	42	7	2	0	1	144^1	118	11	67	88	11.7	2.74	135	.220	.309	8	.186	3	17	16	1	2.1
1958	Cle-A	16	8	.667	39	30	13	0	1	225^2	214	25	70	97	11.4	2.99	122	.251	.309	6	.094	-1	19	16	0	1.7
1959	Cle-A★	19	8	.704	35	32	130		1	235^1	253	26	72	113	12.6	3.63	101	.270	.326	14	.189	1	6	1	3	0.6
1960	Cin-N	4	14	.222	37	21	2	1	0	151^1	170	16	48	56	13.4	4.16	92	.287	.348	2	.049	-4	-7	-6	1	-0.8
1961	Chi-A	10	13	.435	31	27	4	0	1	162^1	178	21	47	80	12.5	4.38	89	.280	.330	9	.167	-1	-6	-8	2	-0.7
1962	Phi-N	11	5	.688	32	24	5	1	1	154^2	184	15	45	71	13.4	4.25	91	.293	.343	4	.078	-2	-5	-6	-1	-0.8
1963	Phi-N	13	11	.542	32	32	10	2	0	209^2	184	14	56	98	10.5	3.26	99	.239	.294	14	.203	4	1	-1	2	0.5
1964	Phi-N	0	1	.000	2	1	0	0	0	5^1	6	0	1	6	11.8	3.38	103	.261	.292	0	.000	-0	0	0	0	0.0
Total	15	92	92	.500	352	209	57	5	6	1609	1685	164	552	713	12.7	4.01	93	.270	.332	73	.149	4	-39	-50	9	-3.1

● SAM McMACKIN McMackin, Samuel b: 1872, Cleveland, Ohio d: 2/11/03, Columbus, Ohio BR/TL, Deb: 9/04/02

YEAR	TM/L	W	L	PCT	G	GS	CG	SH	SV	IP	H	HR	BB	SO	RAT	ERA	ERA+	OAV	OOB	BH	AVG	PB	PR	/A	PD	TPI
1902	Chi-A	0	0	—	1	0	0	0	0	3	1	0	0	2	3.0	0.00	—	.105	.105	0	.000	-0	1	1	0	0.1
	Det-A	0	1	.000	1	1	1	0	0	8^1	9	0	4	2	15.1	3.24	113	.276	.372	2	.500	1	0	0	0	0.1
	Yr	0	1	.000	2	1	1	0	0	11^1	10	0	4	4	11.9	2.38	150	.237	.318	2	.400	0	2	2	1	0.2

● JACK McMAHAN McMahan, Jack Wally b: 7/22/32, Hot Springs, Ark. BR/TL, 6', 175 lbs. Deb: 4/18/56

YEAR	TM/L	W	L	PCT	G	GS	CG	SH	SV	IP	H	HR	BB	SO	RAT	ERA	ERA+	OAV	OOB	BH	AVG	PB	PR	/A	PD	TPI
1956	Pit-N	0	0	—	11	0	0	0	0	13^1	18	1	9	9	18.2	6.08	62	.340	.435	0	.000	-0	-3	-3	0	-0.3
	KC-A	0	5	.000	23	9	0	0	0	61^2	69	7	31	13	14.9	4.82	90	.290	.376	0	.000	-2	-5	-3	-0	-0.6
Total	1	0	5	.000	34	9	0	0	0	75	87	8	40	22	15.5	5.04	84	.299	.387	0	.000	-2	-8	-7	0	-0.9

● DON McMAHON McMahon, Donald John b: 1/4/30, Brooklyn, N.Y. d: 7/22/87, Los Angeles, Cal. BR/TR, 6'2", 222 lbs. Deb: 6/30/57 C

YEAR	TM/L	W	L	PCT	G	GS	CG	SH	SV	IP	H	HR	BB	SO	RAT	ERA	ERA+	OAV	OOB	BH	AVG	PB	PR	/A	PD	TPI
1957	*Mil-N	2	3	.400	32	0	0	0	9	46^2	33	0	29	46	12.0	1.54	227	.196	.315	2	.250	1	12	10	-0	1.1
1958	*Mil-N☆	7	2	.778	38	0	0	0	8	58^2	50	4	29	37	12.4	3.68	96	.235	.332	1	.111	0	2	-1	-0	-0.1
1959	Mil-N	5	3	.625	60	0	0	0	**15**	80^2	81	5	37	55	13.3	2.57	138	.259	.339	2	.222	1	12	9	-1	0.9
1960	Mil-N	3	6	.333	48	0	0	0	10	63^2	66	9	32	50	14.1	5.94	58	.263	.351	0	.000	-1	-15	-18	0	-1.9
1961	Mil-N	6	4	.600	53	0	0	0	8	92	84	4	51	55	13.4	2.84	132	.249	.351	3	.188	0	12	9	1	1.1
1962	Mil-N	0	1	.000	2	0	0	0	0	3	3	1	0	3	9.0	6.00	63	.250	.250	0	—	0	-1	-1	-0	-0.1
	Hou-N	5	5	.500	51	0	0	0	8	76^2	53	4	33	69	10.2	1.53	245	.201	.292	1	.083	-1	21	19	-0	1.8
	Yr	5	6	.455	53	0	0	0	8	79^2	56	5	33	72	10.2	1.69	221	.203	.290	1	.083	-1	20	18	-0	1.7
1963	Hou-N	1	5	.167	49	2	0	0	5	80	83	10	26	51	12.3	4.05	78	.270	.327	1	.083	0	-7	-8	-0	-0.8
1964	Cle-A	6	4	.600	70	0	0	0	16	101	67	7	52	92	10.8	2.41	150	.189	.297	2	.143	-0	14	13	-1	1.3
1965	Cle-A	3	3	.500	58	0	0	0	11	85	79	8	37	60	12.4	3.28	106	.248	.329	2	.222	0	2	2	1	0.3
1966	Cle-A	1	1	.500	12	0	0	0	1	12^1	8	1	6	5	10.2	2.92	118	.190	.292	0	.000	-0	1	1	-0	0.0
	Bos-A	8	7	.533	49	0	0	0	9	78	65	7	38	57	12.2	2.65	143	.232	.330	1	.091	-0	7	10	-1	1.0
	Yr	9	8	.529	61	0	0	0	10	90^1	73	8	44	62	12.0	2.69	140	.226	.324	1	.077	-0	7	11	-1	1.0
1967	Bos-A	1	2	.333	11	0	0	0	2	17^2	14	4	13	10	13.8	3.57	98	.215	.346	0	.000	-0	-1	-0	0	0.0
	Chi-A	5	0	1.000	52	0	0	0	3	91^2	54	5	27	74	8.5	1.67	186	.173	.252	2	.182	0	16	15	-0	1.6
	Yr	6	2	.750	63	0	0	0	5	109^1	68	9	40	84	9.4	1.98	160	.180	.270	2	.154	-0	15	14	-0	1.6
1968	Chi-A	2	1	.667	25	0	0	0	0	46	31	2	20	32	10.6	1.96	155	.190	.290	1	.333	0	5	5	-1	0.6
	*Det-A	3	1	.750	20	0	0	0	1	35^2	22	2	10	33	8.1	2.02	149	.180	.242	0	.000	-0	4	4	-0	0.4
	Yr	5	2	.714	45	0	0	0	1	81^2	53	4	30	65	9.1	1.98	152	.183	.259	1	.143	-0	9	9	-1	1.0
1969	Det-A	3	5	.375	34	0	0	0	11	37	25	2	18	38	10.7	3.89	96	.192	.295	0	.000	-1	-1	-1	0	-0.1
	SF-N	3	1	.750	13	0	0	0	2	23^2	13	1	9	21	8.4	3.04	115	.157	.239	1	.333	0	1	1	0	0.2
1970	SF-N	9	5	.643	61	0	0	0	19	94^1	70	9	45	74	11.2	2.96	134	.202	.297	2	.143	0	11	11	-1	1.0
1971	*SF-N	10	6	.625	61	0	0	0	4	82	73	9	37	71	12.8	4.06	84	.242	.338	0	.000	-1	-5	-6	1	-0.6
1972	SF-N	3	3	.500	44	0	0	0	5	63	46	8	21	45	9.7	3.71	94	.206	.278	1	.250	0	-2	-2	-0	-0.2
1973	SF-N	4	0	1.000	22	0	0	0	6	30^1	21	1	7	20	8.3	1.48	257	.189	.237	1	1.000	0	7	8	0	0.9
1974	SF-N	0	0	—	9	0	0	0	0	11^2	13	2	2	5	11.6	3.09	123	.283	.313	0	—	0	1	1	-0	0.1
Total	18	90	68	.570	874	2	0	0	153	1310^2	1054	105	579	1003	11.4	2.96	119	.221	.310	23	.137	-1	96	83	-1	8.5

● DOC McMAHON McMahon, Henry John b: 12/19/1886, Woburn, Mass. d: 12/11/29, Woburn, Mass. Deb: 10/06/08

YEAR	TM/L	W	L	PCT	G	GS	CG	SH	SV	IP	H	HR	BB	SO	RAT	ERA	ERA+	OAV	OOB	BH	AVG	PB	PR	/A	PD	TPI
1908	Bos-A	1	0	1.000	1	1	1	0	0	9	14	0	0	3	14.0	3.00	82	.350	.350	2	.400	1	-1	-1	-0	0.0

● SADIE McMAHON McMahon, John Joseph b: 9/19/1867, Wilmington, Del. d: 2/20/54, Delaware City, Del BR/TR, 5'9.5", 165 lbs. Deb: 7/05/1889

YEAR	TM/L	W	L	PCT	G	GS	CG	SH	SV	IP	H	HR	BB	SO	RAT	ERA	ERA+	OAV	OOB	BH	AVG	PB	PR	/A	PD	TPI
1889	Phi-a	14	12	.538	28	27	27	2	0	242	230	5	102	117	12.9	3.53	107	.243	.325	16	.154	-5	8	7	4	0.4
1890	Phi-a	29	18	.617	48	46	44	0	1	410	414	5	133	225	12.4	3.34	115	.254	.318	40	.229	3	24	23	9	3.2
	Bal-a	7	3	.700	12	11	11	1	0	99	84	1	33	66	11.2	3.00	135	.223	.296	4	.103	-4	10	12	2	0.9
	Yr	**36**	21	.632	**60**	57	**55**	1	1	**509**	498	6	166	**291**	11.8	3.27	118	.246	.305	44	.206	-1	34	34	11	4.1
1891	Bal-a	**35**	24	.593	61	58	**53**	**5**	1	**503**	493	13	149	219	11.8	2.81	133	.248	.306	43	.205	-3	51	52	5	4.8
1892	Bal-N	19	25	.432	48	46	44	2	1	397	430	9	145	118	13.2	3.24	106	.265	.329	25	.141	-10	2	8	0	0.0
1893	Bal-N	23	18	.561	43	40	35	0	1	346^1	378	6	156	79	14.1	4.37	109	.269	.346	36	.243	-4	12	15	-1	0.9
1894	Bal-N	25	8	.758	35	33	26	0	0	275^2	317	7	111	60	14.3	4.21	130	.285	.355	36	.286	1	34	38	3	3.2
1895	*Bal-N	10	4	.714	15	15	15	**4**	0	122^1	110	1	32	37	10.7	2.94	162	.237	.292	16	.314	1	25	25	-1	2.2
1896	Bal-N	11	9	.550	22	22	19	0	0	175^2	195	4	55	33	13.0	3.48	123	.279	.334	9	.123	-7	17	16	0	0.7
1897	Bro-N	0	6	.000	9	7	5	0	0	63	75	1	29	13	15.3	5.86	70	.293	.372	5	.200	-1	-11	-12	0	-1.1
Total	9	173	127	.577	321	305	279	14	4	2634	2726	52	945	967	12.9	3.51	118	.260	.326	230	.204	-29	172	182	21	15.2

● JOHN McMAKIN McMakin, John Weaver "Spartanburg John" b: 3/6/1878, Spartanburg, S.C. d: 9/25/56, Lyman, S.C. BR/TL, 5'11", 165 lbs. Deb: 4/19/02

YEAR	TM/L	W	L	PCT	G	GS	CG	SH	SV	IP	H	HR	BB	SO	RAT	ERA	ERA+	OAV	OOB	BH	AVG	PB	PR	/A	PD	TPI
1902	Bro-N	2	2	.500	4	4	4	0	0	32	34	0	11	6	13.5	3.09	89	.272	.345	2	.182	0	-1	-1	-0	-0.1

● JOE McMANUS McManus, Joab Logan b: 9/7/1887, Palmyra, Ill. d: 12/23/55, Beckley, W.Va. BR/TR, 5'11", 180 lbs. Deb: 4/12/13

YEAR	TM/L	W	L	PCT	G	GS	CG	SH	SV	IP	H	HR	BB	SO	RAT	ERA	ERA+	OAV	OOB	BH	AVG	PB	PR	/A	PD	TPI
1913	Cin-N	0	0	—	1	0	0	0	0	2	3	0	4	1	31.5	18.00	18	.375	.583	0	—	0	-3	-3	0	-0.3

● PAT McMANUS McManus, Patrick b: Ireland d: 10/6/17, Brooklyn, N.Y. Deb: 5/22/1879

YEAR	TM/L	W	L	PCT	G	GS	CG	SH	SV	IP	H	HR	BB	SO	RAT	ERA	ERA+	OAV	OOB	BH	AVG	PB	PR	/A	PD	TPI
1879	Tro-N	0	2	.000	2	2	2	0	0	21	24	1	1	6	10.7	3.00	83	.258	.266	1	.125	-1	-1	-1	0	-0.1

● GEORGE McMULLEN McMullen, George b: California Deb: 7/02/1887

YEAR	TM/L	W	L	PCT	G	GS	CG	SH	SV	IP	H	HR	BB	SO	RAT	ERA	ERA+	OAV	OOB	BH	AVG	PB	PR	/A	PD	TPI
1887	NY-a	2	1	.667	3	3	2	0	0	21	25	2	19	2	18.9	7.71	55	.269	.393	1	.083	-2	-8	-8	0	-0.7

● JOHN McMULLIN McMullin, John F. "Lefty" b: 1848, Philadelphia, Pa. d: 4/11/1881, Philadelphia, Pa. BR/TL, 5'9", 160 lbs. Deb: 5/09/1871 ♦

YEAR	TM/L	W	L	PCT	G	GS	CG	SH	SV	IP	H	HR	BB	SO	RAT	ERA	ERA+	OAV	OOB	BH	AVG	PB	PR	/A	PD	TPI
1871	Tro-n	12	15	.444	29	29	28	0	0	249	430	4	75	12	18.3	5.53	76	.342	.379	38	.279	1	-36	-36		-2.3
1872	Mut-n	1	0	1.000	3	1	1	0	0	15	18	0	2	1	12.0	3.60	96	.247	.267	60	.253	0	0	-0		0.0
1873	Ath-n	1	0	1.000	1	1	1	0	0	8	10	0	1	2	12.4	2.25	152	.303	.324	62	.273	0	1	1		0.1
1875	Phi-n	0	0	—	4	0	0	0	0	12^2	31	0	1		22.7	6.39	39	.425	.432	56	.251	1	-6	-5		-0.4

YEAR	TM/L	W	L	PCT	G	GS	CG	SH	SV	IP	H	HR	BB	SO	RAT	ERA	ERA+	OAV	OOB	BH	AVG	PB	PR	/A	PD	TPI
Total	4 n	14	15	.483	37	31	30	0	0	284^2	489	4	79	15	18.0	*5.37*	47	.340	.374	305	.281	2	-92	-90		-2.6

● **CRAIG McMURTRY** McMurtry, Joe Craig b: 11/5/59, Troy, Tex. BR/TR, 6'5", 195 lbs. Deb: 4/10/83

YEAR	TM/L	W	L	PCT	G	GS	CG	SH	SV	IP	H	HR	BB	SO	RAT	ERA	ERA+	OAV	OOB	BH	AVG	PB	PR	/A	PD	TPI
1983	Atl-N	15	9	.625	36	35	6	3	0	224^2	204	13	88	105	11.7	3.08	126	.243	.315	6	.086	-4	14	20	3	2.1
1984	Atl-N	9	17	.346	37	30	0	0	0	183^1	184	16	102	99	14.1	4.32	89	.268	.363	6	.115	-1	-15	-10	4	-0.7
1985	Atl-N	0	3	.000	17	6	0	0	1	45	56	6	27	28	16.8	6.60	58	.306	.398	1	.071	-1	-15	-14	1	-1.4
1986	Atl-N	1	6	.143	37	5	0	0	0	79^2	82	7	43	50	14.3	4.74	84	.265	.359	2	.125	-0	-9	-7	0	-0.7
1988	Tex-A	3	3	.500	32	0	0	0	3	60	37	5	24	35	9.3	2.25	181	.180	.270	0	—	0	11	12	1	1.3
1989	Tex-A	0	0	—	19	0	0	0	0	23	29	3	13	14	17.2	7.43	53	.312	.407	0	—	0	-9	-9	0	-0.9
1990	Tex-A	0	3	.000	23	3	0	0	0	41^2	43	4	30	14	16.0	4.32	91	.281	.402	0	—	0	-2	-2	1	-0.1
Total	7	28	41	.406	201	79	6	3	4	657^1	635	54	327	345	13.3	4.03	97	.257	.346	15	.099	-6	-25	-9	10	-0.4

● **EDGAR McNABB** McNabb, Edgar J. "Texas" b: 10/24/1865, Cochocton, Ohio d: 2/28/1894, Pittsburgh, Pa. BR/TR, 5'11.5", 170 lbs. Deb: 5/12/1893

YEAR	TM/L	W	L	PCT	G	GS	CG	SH	SV	IP	H	HR	BB	SO	RAT	ERA	ERA+	OAV	OOB	BH	AVG	PB	PR	/A	PD	TPI
1893	Bal-N	8	7	.533	21	14	12	0	0	142	167	5	53	18	14.5	4.12	115	.284	.352	13	.194	-3	9	10	0	0.7

● **DAVE McNALLY** McNally, David Arthur b: 10/31/42, Billings, Mont. BR/TL, 5'11", 190 lbs. Deb: 9/26/62

YEAR	TM/L	W	L	PCT	G	GS	CG	SH	SV	IP	H	HR	BB	SO	RAT	ERA	ERA+	OAV	OOB	BH	AVG	PB	PR	/A	PD	TPI
1962	Bal-A	1	0	1.000	1	1	1	1	0	9	2	0	3	4	5.0	0.00	—	.071	.161	0	.000	-0	4	4	0	0.4
1963	Bal-A	7	8	.467	29	20	2	0	1	125^2	133	9	55	78	13.8	4.58	77	.276	.356	2	.053	-2	-13	-15	-1	-1.8
1964	Bal-A	9	11	.450	30	23	5	3	0	159^1	157	15	51	88	12.3	3.67	97	.260	.327	7	.137	0	-1	-2	0	-0.2
1965	Bal-A	11	6	.647	35	29	6	2	0	198^2	163	15	73	116	11.0	2.85	122	.222	.298	6	.092	-3	13	14	0	1.2
1966	*Bal-A	13	6	.684	34	33	5	1	0	213	212	22	64	158	11.8	3.17	105	.256	.313	15	.195	3	6	4	0	0.7
1967	Bal-A	7	7	.500	24	22	3	1	0	119	134	13	39	70	13.2	4.54	69	.295	.354	6	.158	0	-17	-18	-2	-2.1
1968	Bal-A	22	10	.688	35	35	18	5	0	273	175	24	55	202	**7.9**	1.95	150	.182	.234	11	.128	4	31	30	-3	3.7
1969	*Bal-A★	20	7	.741	41	40	11	4	0	268^2	232	21	84	166	10.8	3.22	111	.234	.297	8	.085	-2	12	10	-4	0.5
1970	*Bal-A☆	**24**	9	.727	40	40	16	1	0	296	277	29	78	185	11.0	3.22	113	.250	.304	14	.133	4	16	14	-2	1.6
1971	*Bal-A	21	5	**.808**	30	30	11	1	0	224^1	188	24	58	91	10.1	2.89	116	.229	.284	12	.162	3	14	12	-0	1.5
1972	Bal-A★	13	17	.433	36	36	12	6	0	241	220	15	68	120	10.8	2.95	104	.247	.302	12	.152	2	3	3	1	0.6
1973	*Bal-A	17	17	.500	38	38	17	4	0	266	247	16	81	87	11.3	3.21	116	.251	.312	0	—	0	18	15	1	1.7
1974	*Bal-A	16	10	.615	39	37	13	4	1	259	260	19	81	111	12.1	3.58	96	.270	.331	0	—	0	1	-4	2	-0.2
1975	Mon-N	3	6	.333	12	12	0	0	0	77^1	88	8	36	36	14.9	5.24	73	.280	.362	4	.190	2	-14	-12	-1	-1.1
Total	14	184	119	.607	424	396	120	33	2	2730	2488	230	826	1512	11.2	3.24	106	.245	.306	97	.133	9	74	55	-8	6.5

● **TIM McNAMARA** McNamara, Timothy Augustine b: 11/20/1898, Millville, Mass. BR/TR, 5'11", 170 lbs. Deb: 4/27/22

YEAR	TM/L	W	L	PCT	G	GS	CG	SH	SV	IP	H	HR	BB	SO	RAT	ERA	ERA+	OAV	OOB	BH	AVG	PB	PR	/A	PD	TPI
1922	Bos-N	3	4	.429	24	5	4	2	0	70^2	55	2	26	16	10.4	2.42	165	.225	.303	2	.118	-1	**13**	**12**	-0	1.1
1923	Bos-N	3	13	.188	32	16	3	0	0	139^1	185	8	29	32	14.1	4.91	81	.320	.357	7	.179	1	-14	-14	-2	-1.4
1924	Bos-N	8	12	.400	35	21	6	2	0	179	242	9	31	35	13.9	5.18	74	.334	.364	6	.140	-1	-26	-27	1	-2.6
1925	Bos-N	0	0	—	1	0	0	0	0	0^2	6	0	2	1	108.0	81.00	5	.857	.889	0	—	0	-6	-6	0	-0.4
1926	NY-N	0	0	—	6	0	0	0	0	6	7	0	4	4	16.5	9.00	42	.304	.407	0	—	0	-3	-3	0	-0.3
Total	5	14	29	.326	98	42	13	4	0	395^2	495	19	92	88	13.6	4.78	82	.314	.355	15	.152	-1	-36	-38	-2	-3.6

● **GORDON McNAUGHTON** McNaughton, Gordon Joseph b: 7/31/10, Chicago, Ill. d: 8/6/42, Chicago, Ill. BR/TR, 6'1", 190 lbs. Deb: 8/13/32

YEAR	TM/L	W	L	PCT	G	GS	CG	SH	SV	IP	H	HR	BB	SO	RAT	ERA	ERA+	OAV	OOB	BH	AVG	PB	PR	/A	PD	TPI
1932	Bos-A	0	1	.000	6	2	0	0	0	21	21	1	22	6	19.7	6.43	70	.259	.434	2	.250	0	-5	-5	1	-0.3

● **HARRY McNEAL** McNeal, John Harley b: 8/11/1877, Iberia, Ohio d: 1/11/45, Cleveland, Ohio BR/TR, 6'3", 175 lbs. Deb: 8/05/01

YEAR	TM/L	W	L	PCT	G	GS	CG	SH	SV	IP	H	HR	BB	SO	RAT	ERA	ERA+	OAV	OOB	BH	AVG	PB	PR	/A	PD	TPI
1901	Cle-A	5	5	.500	12	10	9	0	0	85^1	120	4	30	15	16.6	4.43	80	.328	.389	6	.162	-2	-7	-8	-2	-1.1

● **ED McNICHOL** McNichol, Edwin Briggs b: 1/10/1879, Martins Ferry, O. d: 11/1/52, Salineville, O. BR/TR, 5'5", 170 lbs. Deb: 7/09/04

YEAR	TM/L	W	L	PCT	G	GS	CG	SH	SV	IP	H	HR	BB	SO	RAT	ERA	ERA+	OAV	OOB	BH	AVG	PB	PR	/A	PD	TPI
1904	Bos-N	2	12	.143	17	15	12	1	0	122	120	3	74	39	14.7	4.28	64	.262	.371	4	.093	-4	-21	-21	-2	-2.5

● **FRANK McPARTLIN** McPartlin, Frank b: 2/16/1872, Hoosick Falls, N.Y d: 11/13/43, New York, N.Y. TR, 6', 180 lbs. Deb: 8/22/1899

YEAR	TM/L	W	L	PCT	G	GS	CG	SH	SV	IP	H	HR	BB	SO	RAT	ERA	ERA+	OAV	OOB	BH	AVG	PB	PR	/A	PD	TPI
1899	NY-N	0	0	—	1	0	0	0	0	4	4	0	3	2	20.3	4.50	83	.260	.442	0	.000	-0	-0	-0	0	0.0

● **JOHN McPHERSON** McPherson, John Jacob b: 3/9/1869, Easton, Pa. d: 9/30/41, Easton, Pa. Deb: 7/12/01

YEAR	TM/L	W	L	PCT	G	GS	CG	SH	SV	IP	H	HR	BB	SO	RAT	ERA	ERA+	OAV	OOB	BH	AVG	PB	PR	/A	PD	TPI
1901	Phi-A	0	1	.000	1	1	0	0	0	4	7	0	4	0	27.0	11.25	34	.377	.510	0	.000	-0	-3	-3	0	-0.3
1904	Phi-N	1	12	.077	15	12	11	1	0	128	130	1	46	32	12.8	3.66	73	.264	.334	3	.064	-4	-13	-14	0	-1.7
Total	2	1	13	.071	16	13	11	1	0	132	137	1	50	32	13.2	3.89	70	.268	.341	3	.063	-4	-16	-17	1	-2.0

● **HERB McQUAID** McQuaid, Herbert George b: 3/29/1899, San Francisco, Cal d: 4/4/66, Richmond, Cal. BR/TR, 6'2", 185 lbs. Deb: 6/22/23

YEAR	TM/L	W	L	PCT	G	GS	CG	SH	SV	IP	H	HR	BB	SO	RAT	ERA	ERA+	OAV	OOB	BH	AVG	PB	PR	/A	PD	TPI
1923	Cin-N	1	0	1.000	12	1	0	0	0	34^1	31	0	10	9	11.5	2.36	164	.238	.308	0	.000	-1	6	6	1	0.5
1926	NY-A	1	0	1.000	17	1	0	0	0	38^1	48	5	13	6	14.8	6.10	63	.329	.391	0	.000	-1	-9	-10	0	-1.0
Total	2	2	0	1.000	29	2	0	0	0	72^2	79	5	23	15	13.3	4.33	89	.286	.352	0	.000	-2	-3	-4	1	-0.5

● **MIKE McQUEEN** McQueen, Michael Robert b: 8/30/50, Oklahoma City, Okla BL/TL, 5'11", 190 lbs. Deb: 10/02/69

YEAR	TM/L	W	L	PCT	G	GS	CG	SH	SV	IP	H	HR	BB	SO	RAT	ERA	ERA+	OAV	OOB	BH	AVG	PB	PR	/A	PD	TPI
1969	Atl-N	0	0	—	1	1	0	0	0	3	2	0	3	3	15.0	3.00	120	.182	.357	0	—	0	0	0	-0	0.0
1970	Atl-N	1	5	.167	22	8	1	0	1	66	67	10	31	54	13.5	5.59	77	.266	.349	6	.300	2	-11	-10	-1	-0.8
1971	Atl-N	4	1	.800	17	3	0	0	1	56	47	7	23	38	11.6	3.54	105	.228	.312	4	.211	0	-0	1	-1	0.0
1972	Atl-N	0	5	.000	23	7	1	0	1	78^1	79	11	44	40	14.2	4.60	82	.260	.355	2	.087	-2	-10	-7	-1	-1.0
1974	Cin-N	0	0	—	10	0	0	0	0	15	17	4	11	5	16.8	5.40	65	.288	.400	1	1.000	0	-3	-3	-1	-0.3
Total	5	5	11	.313	73	19	2	0	3	218^1	212	32	112	140	13.5	4.66	84	.255	.346	13	.206	1	-24	-18	-4	-2.1

● **GEORGE McQUILLAN** McQuillan, George Watt b: 5/1/1885, Brooklyn, N.Y. d: 3/30/40, Columbus, Ohio BR/TR, 5'11.5", 175 lbs. Deb: 5/08/07

YEAR	TM/L	W	L	PCT	G	GS	CG	SH	SV	IP	H	HR	BB	SO	RAT	ERA	ERA+	OAV	OOB	BH	AVG	PB	PR	/A	PD	TPI
1907	Phi-N	4	0	1.000	6	5	5	3	0	41	21	0	11	28	7.2	0.66	368	.158	.228	4	.364	3	8	8	-2	1.2
1908	Phi-N	23	17	.575	48	42	32	7	2	359^2	263	1	91	114	9.0	1.53	159	.207	.263	18	.151	-2	33	36	-3	3.9
1909	Phi-N	13	16	.448	41	28	16	4	2	247^2	202	5	54	96	9.3	2.14	121	.226	.271	9	.118	-3	13	13	-2	0.7
1910	Phi-N	9	6	.600	24	17	13	3	1	152^1	109	2	50	71	9.6	1.60	196	.204	.276	7	.149	-1	24	26	-0	2.7
1911	Cin-N	2	6	.250	19	5	2	0	0	77	92	2	31	28	14.8	4.68	71	.308	.380	2	.091	-1	-11	-12	-1	-1.4
1913	Pit-N	8	6	.571	25	16	7	0	1	141^2	144	1	35	59	11.4	3.43	88	.273	.319	4	.103	-1	-4	-7	-1	-0.9
1914	Pit-N	13	17	.433	45	28	15	0	4	259^1	248	8	60	96	11.0	2.98	89	.261	.310	5	.068	-4	-6	-10	0	-1.4
1915	Pit-N	8	10	.444	30	20	9	0	1	149	160	1	39	56	12.1	2.84	96	.284	.332	4	.091	-3	-1	-2	0	-0.5
	Phi-N	4	3	.571	9	8	5	0	0	63^2	60	1	11	13	10.2	2.12	129	.247	.282	1	.043	-2	4	4	-1	0.2
	Yr	12	13	.480	39	28	14	0	1	212^2	220	2	50	69	11.5	2.62	104	.272	.315	5	.075	-5	3	3	-1	-0.3
1916	Phi-N	1	7	.125	21	3	1	0	2	62	58	2	15	22	11.0	2.76	96	.251	.305	1	.091	-1	-1	-1	-0	-0.2
1918	Cle-A	0	1	.000	5	1	0	0	1	23	25	0	4	7	11.3	2.35	128	.284	.315	0	.000	-0	1	2	0	0.2
Total	10	85	89	.489	273	173	105	17	14	1576^1	1382	23	401	590	10.4	2.38	114	.241	.294	55	.117	-15	62	59	-9	4.5

● **HUGH McQUILLAN** McQuillan, Hugh A. "Handsome Hugh" b: 9/15/1897, New York, N.Y. d: 8/26/47, New York, N.Y. BR/TR, 6', 170 lbs. Deb: 7/26/18

YEAR	TM/L	W	L	PCT	G	GS	CG	SH	SV	IP	H	HR	BB	SO	RAT	ERA	ERA+	OAV	OOB	BH	AVG	PB	PR	/A	PD	TPI
1918	Bos-N	1	0	1.000	1	1	1	0	0	9	7	0	5	1	12.0	3.00	90	.219	.324	1	.250	0	-0	-0	0	0.0
1919	Bos-N	2	3	.400	16	7	2	0	1	60	66	3	14	13	12.2	3.45	83	.288	.332	4	.222	0	-4	-4	-1	-0.5
1920	Bos-N	11	15	.423	38	27	17	1	5	225^2	230	3	70	53	12.0	3.55	86	.273	.330	19	.257	6	-10	-13	2	-0.5
1921	Bos-N	13	17	.433	45	31	13	2	5	250	284	9	90	94	13.5	4.00	91	.291	.352	18	.205	1	-6	-10	0	-0.8
1922	Bos-N	5	10	.333	28	17	7	0	0	136	154	3	56	33	14.0	4.24	94	.299	.369	7	.167	-1	-2	-4	1	-0.4
	*NY-N	6	5	.545	15	13	5	0	1	94^1	111	7	34	24	13.8	3.82	105	.301	.360	7	.189	-1	3	2	-1	0.0
	Yr	11	15	.423	43	30	12	0	1	230^1	265	10	90	57	13.9	4.06	98	.299	.364	14	.177	-2	1	-2	-0	-0.4
1923	*NY-N	15	14	.517	38	32	15	5	0	229^2	224	12	66	75	11.6	3.41	112	.259	.315	14	.171	-2	15	11	-1	0.7
1924	*NY-N	14	8	.636	27	23	14	1	3	184	179	8	43	49	11.0	2.69	136	.259	.304	14	.209	-1	24	20	-2	1.7
1925	NY-N	2	3	.400	14	11	2	0	1	70	95	9	23	23	15.3	6.04	67	.343	.395	3	.143	-1	-14	-16	1	-1.4

YEAR	TM/L	W	L	PCT	G	GS	CG	SH	SV	IP	H	HR	BB	SO	RAT	ERA	ERA+	OAV	OOB	BH	AVG	PB	PR	/A	PD	TPI
1926	NY-N	11	10	.524	33	22	12	1	0	167	171	7	42	47	11.5	3.72	101	.271	.318	7	.132	-3	2	1	2	0.0
1927	NY-N	5	4	.556	11	9	5	0	0	58	73	4	22	17	14.9	4.50	86	.309	.371	4	.211	1	-4	-4	0	-0.3
	Bos-N	3	5	.375	13	11	2	0	0	78	109	2	24	17	15.6	5.54	67	.332	.381	5	.227	0	-14	-16	0	-1.4
	Yr	8	9	.471	24	20	7	0	0	136	182	6	46	34	15.2	5.10	74	.322	.375	9	.220	1	-18	-20	1	-1.7
Total	10	88	94	.484	279	204	95	10	16	1561^2	1703	67	489	446	12.7	3.83	95	.284	.340	103	.195	0	-10	-32	1	-2.9

● NORM McRAE McRae, Norman b: 9/26/47, Elizabeth, N.J. BR/TR, 6'1", 195 lbs. Deb: 9/13/69

YEAR	TM/L	W	L	PCT	G	GS	CG	SH	SV	IP	H	HR	BB	SO	RAT	ERA	ERA+	OAV	OOB	BH	AVG	PB	PR	/A	PD	TPI
1969	Det-A	0	0	—	3	0	0	0	0	3	2	0	1	3	9.0	6.00	62	.200	.273	0	—	0	-1	-1	-0	-0.1
1970	Det-A	0	0	—	19	0	0	0	0	31^1	26	1	25	16	14.9	2.87	130	.226	.369	0	.000	-0	3	3	1	0.3
Total	2	0	0	—	22	0	0	0	0	34^1	28	1	26	19	14.4	3.15	118	.224	.362	0	.000	-0	2	2	0	0.2

● TRICK McSORLEY McSorley, John Bernard b: 12/6/1858, St.Louis, Mo. d: 2/9/36, St.Louis, Mo. TR , 5'4", 142 lbs. Deb: 5/06/1875 ♦

YEAR	TM/L	W	L	PCT	G	GS	CG	SH	SV	IP	H	HR	BB	SO	RAT	ERA	ERA+	OAV	OOB	BH	AVG	PB	PR	/A	PD	TPI
1884	Tol-a	0	0	—	1	0	0	0	0	2	5	0	0	1	22.5	4.50	76	.556	.556	17	.250	0	-0	-0	-0	0.0

● BILL McTIGUE McTigue, William Patrick "Rebel" b: 1/3/1891, Nashville, Tenn. d: 5/8/20, Nashville, Tenn. BL/TL, 6'1.5", 175 lbs. Deb: 5/02/11 ♦

YEAR	TM/L	W	L	PCT	G	GS	CG	SH	SV	IP	H	HR	BB	SO	RAT	ERA	ERA+	OAV	OOB	BH	AVG	PB	PR	/A	PD	TPI
1911	Bos-N	0	5	.000	14	8	0	0	0	37	37	3	49	23	21.4	7.05	54	.280	.481	1	.083	-1	-15	-13	-1	-1.4
1912	Bos-N	2	0	1.000	10	1	1	0	0	34^2	39	0	18	17	14.8	5.45	66	.289	.373	1	.077	-1	-8	-7	1	-0.7
1916	Det-A	0	0	—	3	0	0	0	0	5^1	5	0	5	1	16.9	5.06	57	.278	.435	0	.000	-0	-1	-1	0	-0.1
Total	3	2	5	.286	27	9	1	0	0	77	81	3	72	41	18.1	6.19	59	.284	.432	2	.077	-2	-24	-22	0	-2.2

● CAL McVEY McVey, Calvin Alexander b: 8/30/1850, Montrose, Iowa d: 8/20/26, San Francisco, Cal BR/TR, 5'9", 170 lbs. Deb: 5/05/1871 M♦

YEAR	TM/L	W	L	PCT	G	GS	CG	SH	SV	IP	H	HR	BB	SO	RAT	ERA	ERA+	OAV	OOB	BH	AVG	PB	PR	/A	PD	TPI
1875	Bos-n	1	0	1.000	3	2	0	0	1	11	15	0	1		13.1	3.27	72	.294	.308	137	.352	2	-1	-1		0.0
1876	Chi-N	5	2	.714	11	6	5	0	2	59^1	57	0	2	9	8.9	1.52	161	.235	.241	107	.347	3	5	6	0	0.7
1877	Chi-N	4	8	.333	17	10	6	0	**2**	92	129	2	11	20	13.7	4.50	66	.301	.319	98	.368	7	-17	-16	-1	-1.1
1879	Cin-N	0	2	.000	3	1	1	0	0	14	34	1	2	7	23.1	8.36	28	.453	.468	105	.297	1	-9	-9	0	-0.7
Total	3	9	12	.429	31	17	12	0	4	165^1	220	3	15	36	12.8	3.76	73	.295	.309	393	.328	11	-21	-19	-1	-1.1

● DOUG McWEENY McWeeny, Douglas Lawrence "Buzz" b: 8/17/1896, Chicago, Ill. d: 1/1/53, Melrose Park, Ill. BR/TR, 6'2", 190 lbs. Deb: 4/24/21

YEAR	TM/L	W	L	PCT	G	GS	CG	SH	SV	IP	H	HR	BB	SO	RAT	ERA	ERA+	OAV	OOB	BH	AVG	PB	PR	/A	PD	TPI
1921	Chi-A	3	6	.333	27	8	3	0	2	97^2	127	7	45	46	15.8	6.08	70	.325	.394	1	.032	-4	-20	-20	-1	-2.2
1922	Chi-A	0	1	.000	4	1	0	0	0	10^2	13	0	7	5	16.9	5.91	69	.325	.426	0	.000	0	-2	-2	-0	-0.2
1924	Chi-A	1	3	.250	13	5	2	0	0	43^1	47	2	17	18	13.7	4.57	90	.294	.369	0	.000	-0	-2	-2	3	0.0
1926	Bro-N	11	13	.458	42	24	10	1	1	216^1	213	6	84	96	12.7	3.04	126	.258	.333	7	.109	-4	19	19	-1	1.3
1927	Bro-N	4	8	.333	34	22	6	0	1	164^1	167	13	70	73	13.4	3.56	111	.266	.347	2	.043	-4	7	7	1	0.4
1928	Bro-N	14	14	.500	42	32	12	**4**	1	244	218	11	114	79	12.4	3.17	125	.235	.322	14	.173	-1	22	22	3	2.4
1929	Bro-N	4	10	.286	36	24	4	0	1	146	167	17	93	59	16.2	6.10	76	.288	.390	5	.104	-2	-22	-24	-2	-2.5
1930	Cin-N	0	2	.000	8	2	0	0	0	25^2	28	0	20	10	16.8	7.36	66	.283	.403	1	.143	-0	-7	-7	0	-0.6
Total	8	37	57	.394	206	118	37	5	6	948	980	56	450	386	13.8	4.17	98	.269	.353	30	.104	-16	-5	-8	2	-1.4

● LARRY McWILLIAMS McWilliams, Larry Dean b: 2/10/54, Wichita, Kan. BL/TL, 6'5", 180 lbs. Deb: 7/17/78

YEAR	TM/L	W	L	PCT	G	GS	CG	SH	SV	IP	H	HR	BB	SO	RAT	ERA	ERA+	OAV	OOB	BH	AVG	PB	PR	/A	PD	TPI
1978	Atl-N	9	3	.750	15	15	3	1	0	99^1	84	11	35	42	11.0	2.81	144	.224	.294	2	.063	-2	8	14	1	1.4
1979	Atl-N	3	2	.600	13	13	1	0	0	66^1	69	4	22	32	12.9	5.56	73	.272	.339	5	.208	1	-13	-11	1	-0.9
1980	Atl-N	9	14	.391	30	30	4	1	0	163^2	188	27	39	77	12.9	4.95	76	.285	.332	8	.157	-0	-25	-22	-0	-2.3
1981	Atl-N	2	1	.667	6	5	2	1	0	37^2	31	2	8	23	9.3	3.11	115	.230	.273	1	.100	-0	2	2	1	0.3
1982	Atl-N	2	3	.400	27	2	0	0	0	37^2	52	3	20	24	17.7	6.21	60	.327	.409	1	.167	0	-11	-10	2	-0.9
	Pit-N	6	5	.545	19	18	2	2	1	121^2	106	9	24	94	9.9	3.11	119	.232	.276	6	.188	-0	7	8	2	1.0
	Yr	8	8	.500	46	20	2	2	1	159^1	158	12	44	118	11.6	3.84	97	.255	.309	7	.184	-0	-4	-2	4	0.1
1983	Pit-N	15	8	.652	35	35	8	4	0	238	205	19	87	199	11.2	3.25	114	.230	.300	9	.114	-3	10	12	1	1.1
1984	Pit-N	12	11	.522	34	32	7	2	1	227^1	226	18	78	149	12.1	2.93	123	.263	.326	9	.122	-3	17	17	0	1.5
1985	Pit-N	7	9	.438	30	19	2	0	0	126^1	139	9	62	52	14.8	4.70	76	.283	.371	5	.125	-1	-16	-16	-0	-1.7
1986	Pit-N	3	11	.214	49	15	0	0	0	122^1	129	16	49	80	13.6	5.15	74	.268	.345	4	.138	0	-19	-18	-0	-1.8
1987	Atl-N	0	1	.000	9	2	0	0	0	20^1	25	2	7	13	15.0	5.75	76	.301	.370	1	.200	0	-4	-3	0	-0.3
1988	StL-N	6	9	.400	42	17	2	1	1	136	130	10	45	70	11.8	3.90	89	.253	.319	6	.162	1	-7	-6	-0	-0.6
1989	Phi-N	2	11	.154	40	16	2	1	0	120^2	123	3	49	54	13.1	4.10	86	.265	.340	3	.111	-1	-8	-7	1	-0.8
	KC-A	2	2	.500	8	5	1	0	0	32^2	31	2	8	24	11.6	4.13	93	.254	.316	0	—	0	-1	-1	-0	-0.1
1990	KC-A	0	0	—	13	0	0	0	0	8^1	10	2	9	7	21.6	9.72	39	.313	.476	0	—	0	-5	-5	0	-0.5
Total	13	78	90	.464	370	224	34	13	3	1558^1	1548	137	542	940	12.4	3.99	93	.259	.326	60	.135	-8	-66	-48	8	-4.6

● RUSTY MEACHAM Meacham, Russell Loren b: 1/27/68, Stuart, Fla. BR/TR, 6'2", 166 lbs. Deb: 6/29/91

YEAR	TM/L	W	L	PCT	G	GS	CG	SH	SV	IP	H	HR	BB	SO	RAT	ERA	ERA+	OAV	OOB	BH	AVG	PB	PR	/A	PD	TPI
1991	Det-A	2	1	.667	10	4	0	0	0	27^2	35	4	11	14	15.0	5.20	80	.315	.377	0	—	0	-3	-3	0	-0.4
1992	KC-A	10	4	.714	64	0	0	0	2	101^2	88	5	21	64	9.7	2.74	145	.233	.275	0	—	0	13	14	2	1.6
Total	2	12	5	.706	74	4	0	0	2	129^1	123	9	32	78	10.9	3.27	123	.252	.299	0	—	0	10	11	2	1.2

● JOHNNY MEADOR Meador, John Davis b: 12/4/1892, Madison, N.C. d: 4/11/70, Winston-Salem, N.C BR/TR, 5'10.5", 165 lbs. Deb: 4/24/20

YEAR	TM/L	W	L	PCT	G	GS	CG	SH	SV	IP	H	HR	BB	SO	RAT	ERA	ERA+	OAV	OOB	BH	AVG	PB	PR	/A	PD	TPI
1920	Pit-N	0	2	.000	12	2	0	0	0	36^1	48	1	7	5	13.6	4.21	76	.340	.372	1	.167	-0	-4	-4	1	-0.4

● LEE MEADOWS Meadows, Henry Lee "Specs" b: 7/12/1894, Oxford, N.C. d: 1/29/63, Daytona Beach, Fla BL/TR, 5'9", 190 lbs. Deb: 4/19/15

YEAR	TM/L	W	L	PCT	G	GS	CG	SH	SV	IP	H	HR	BB	SO	RAT	ERA	ERA+	OAV	OOB	BH	AVG	PB	PR	/A	PD	TPI
1915	StL-N	13	11	.542	39	26	14	1	0	244	232	5	88	104	12.0	2.99	93	.259	.329	8	.096	-4	-6	-5	-3	-1.3
1916	StL-N	12	23	.343	**51**	36	11	1	2	289	261	3	119	120	12.3	2.58	102	.247	.332	15	.158	-1	1	2	1	0.2
1917	StL-N	15	9	.625	43	37	18	4	2	265^2	253	5	90	100	11.8	3.08	87	.262	.328	9	.101	-6	-11	-12	-3	-2.2
1918	StL-N	8	14	.364	30	21	12	0	1	165^1	176	1	56	49	13.2	3.59	75	.280	.348	7	.127	-2	-15	-16	-2	-2.1
1919	StL-N	4	10	.286	22	12	3	1	0	92	100	3	30	28	12.9	3.03	92	.292	.352	3	.103	-2	-1	-2	3	-0.2
	Phi-N	8	10	.444	18	17	15	3	0	158^1	128	2	49	88	10.5	2.33	138	.229	.300	6	.118	-4	10	16	-1	1.3
	Yr	12	20	.375	40	29	18	4	0	250^1	228	5	79	116	11.3	2.59	118	.252	.317	9	.112	-5	9	13	2	1.1
1920	Phi-N	16	14	.533	35	33	19	3	0	247	249	5	90	95	12.6	2.84	120	.270	.341	14	.171	-3	8	16	0	1.4
1921	Phi-N	11	16	.407	28	27	15	2	0	194^1	226	10	62	52	13.5	4.31	98	.288	.343	13	.210	2	-11	-2	4	0.4
1922	Phi-N	12	18	.400	33	33	19	2	0	237	264	8	71	62	13.1	4.03	116	.288	.346	27	.314	4	2	17	3	2.4
1923	Phi-N	1	3	.250	8	5	0	0	1	19^2	40	0	15	10	25.2	13.27	35	.430	.509	4	.400	2	-20	-19	0	-1.5
	Pit-N	16	10	.615	31	25	17	1	0	227	250	3	44	66	11.7	3.01	133	.284	.319	22	.250	3	25	25	2	3.0
	Yr	17	13	.567	39	30	17	1	1	246^2	290	3	59	76	12.8	3.83	106	.298	.339	26	.265	5	5	6	2	1.5
1924	Pit-N	13	12	.520	36	30	15	3	0	229^1	240	7	51	61	11.6	3.26	118	.278	.322	16	.195	-1	16	15	-1	1.2
1925	*Pit-N	19	10	.655	35	31	20	1	1	255^1	272	11	67	87	12.2	3.67	122	.273	.323	17	.175	-1	17	23	1	2.1
1926	Pit-N	**20**	9	.690	36	31	15	1	0	226^2	254	10	52	54	12.3	3.97	99	.287	.329	20	.227	-1	-4	-1	3	0.1
1927	*Pit-N	19	10	.655	40	38	**25**	2	0	299^1	315	11	66	84	11.7	3.40	121	.273	.317	18	.157	-5	17	24	-1	1.7
1928	Pit-N	1	1	.500	4	2	1	0	0	10	18	0	5	3	20.7	8.10	50	.383	.442	2	.500	1	-5	-4	-0	-0.4
1929	Pit-N	0	0	—	1	0	0	0	0	0^2	2	0	1	0	40.5	13.50	35	.500	.600	0	.000	-0	-1	-1	-0	-0.1
Total	15	188	180	.511	490	404	219	25	7	3160^2	3280	84	956	1063	12.3	3.37	106	.274	.332	201	.180	-19	22	71	6	6.0

● RUFUS MEADOWS Meadows, Rufus Rivers b: 8/25/07, Chase City, Va. d: 5/10/70, Wichita, Kan. BL/TL, 5'11", 175 lbs. Deb: 4/23/26

YEAR	TM/L	W	L	PCT	G	GS	CG	SH	SV	IP	H	HR	BB	SO	RAT	ERA	ERA+	OAV	OOB	BH	AVG	PB	PR	/A	PD	TPI
1926	Cin-N	0	0	—	1	0	0	0	0	0^1	0	0	0	0	0.0	0.00	—	.000	.000	0	.000	-0	0	0	0	0.0

● DAVE MEADS Meads, David Donald b: 1/7/64, Montclair, N.J. BL/TL, 6' ", 175 lbs. Deb: 4/13/87

YEAR	TM/L	W	L	PCT	G	GS	CG	SH	SV	IP	H	HR	BB	SO	RAT	ERA	ERA+	OAV	OOB	BH	AVG	PB	PR	/A	PD	TPI
1987	Hou-N	5	3	.625	45	0	0	0	0	48^2	60	8	16	32	14.2	5.55	71	.321	.377	1	.333	1	-8	-9	-1	-0.9
1988	Hou-N	3	1	.750	22	2	0	0	0	39^2	37	4	14	27	11.6	3.18	105	.240	.304	1	.250	1	1	1	-0	0.2
Total	2	8	4	.667	67	2	0	0	0	88^1	97	12	30	59	13.0	4.48	81	.284	.344	2	.286	1	-7	-8	-1	-0.7

● **GEORGE MEAKIM** Meakim, George Clinton b: 7/11/1865, Brooklyn, N.Y. d: 2/17/23, Queens, N.Y. BR/TR, 5'7.5", 154 lbs. Deb: 5/02/1890

YEAR	TM/L	W	L	PCT	G	GS	CG	SH	SV	IP	H	HR	BB	SO	RAT	ERA	ERA+	OAV	OOB	BH	AVG	PB	PR	/A	PD	TPI
1890	*Lou-a	12	7	.632	28	21	16	3	1	192	173	4	63	123	11.3	2.91	132	.233	.298	11	.153	-2	21	20	-1	1.6
1891	Phi-a	1	4	.200	6	6	4	0	0	35	51	1	22	13	19.0	6.94	55	.329	.415	3	.200	0	-13	-12	2	-0.8
1892	Chi-N	0	1	.000	1	1	1	0	0	9	18	0	2	0	20.0	11.00	30	.400	.426	2	.400	0	-8	-8	-0	-0.5
	Cin-N	1	1	.500	3	3	1	0	0	13^2	19	1	9	4	19.8	8.56	38	.317	.423	0	.000	-1	-8	-8	0	-0.7
	Yr	1	2	.333	4	4	2	0	0	22^2	37	1	11	4	19.9	9.53	35	.352	.424	2	.200	-0	-16	-16	-0	-1.2
1895	Lou-N	1	0	1.000	1	1	1	0	0	7	7	0	4	2	14.1	2.57	180	.256	.352	1	.333	0	2	2	0	0.1
Total	4	15	13	.536	39	32	23	3	1	256^2	268	6	100	142	13.2	4.03	95	.260	.331	17	.170	-2	-6	-6	1	-0.3

● **DOC MEDICH** Medich, George Francis b: 12/9/48, Aliquippa, Pa. BR/TR, 6'5", 227 lbs. Deb: 9/05/72

YEAR	TM/L	W	L	PCT	G	GS	CG	SH	SV	IP	H	HR	BB	SO	RAT	ERA	ERA+	OAV	OOB	BH	AVG	PB	PR	/A	PD	TPI
1972	NY-A	0	0	—	1	1	0	0	0	0	2	0	2	0	—	∞	—	1.000	1.000	0	—	0	-2	-2	0	-0.2
1973	NY-A	14	9	.609	34	32	11	3	0	235	217	20	74	145	11.3	2.95	124	.241	.300	0	—	0	23	19	-2	1.9
1974	NY-A	19	15	.559	38	38	17	4	0	279^2	275	24	91	154	12.0	3.60	97	.259	.323	0	—	0	0	-4	-1	-0.3
1975	NY-A	16	16	.500	38	37	15	2	0	272^1	271	25	72	132	11.4	3.50	104	.264	.313	0	—	0	8	4	-3	0.3
1976	Pit-N	8	11	.421	29	26	3	0	0	179	193	10	48	86	12.2	3.52	99	.281	.330	5	.096	-2	-0	-1	1	-0.1
1977	Oak-A	10	6	.625	26	25	1	0	0	147^2	155	19	49	74	12.6	4.69	86	.265	.325	0	—	0	-10	-11	-1	-1.1
	Sea-A	2	0	1.000	3	3	1	0	0	22^1	26	1	4	3	12.9	3.63	113	.286	.330	0	—	0	1	1	-1	0.1
	Yr	12	6	.667	29	28	2	0	0	170	181	20	53	77	12.5	4.55	89	.265	.319	0	—	0	-9	-10	-2	-1.0
	NY-N	0	1	.000	1	1	0	0	0	7	6	0	1	3	9.0	3.86	97	.261	.292	0	.000	-0	0	-0	-0	0.0
1978	Tex-A	9	8	.529	28	22	6	2	2	171	166	10	52	71	11.6	3.74	100	.255	.313	0	—	0	0	0	1	0.1
1979	Tex-A	10	7	.588	29	19	4	1	0	149	156	9	49	58	12.6	4.17	100	.269	.330	0	—	0	1	-0	1	0.2
1980	Tex-A	14	11	.560	34	32	6	0	0	204^1	230	13	56	91	12.7	3.92	99	.285	.334	0	—	0	3	-1	-1	-0.2
1981	Tex-A	10	6	.625	20	20	4	**4**	0	143^1	136	8	33	65	10.7	3.08	113	.252	.297	0	—	0	9	6	1	1.1
1982	Tex-A	7	11	.389	21	21	2	0	0	122^2	146	8	61	37	15.4	5.06	76	.307	.390	0	—	0	-13	-16	0	-1.2
	*Mil-A	5	4	.556	10	10	1	0	0	63	57	4	32	36	12.9	5.00	76	.242	.335	0	—	0	-6	-9	-1	-0.4
	Yr	12	15	.444	31	31	3	0	0	185^2	203	12	93	73	14.4	5.04	76	.281	.364	0	—	0	-20	-25	-0	-1.6
Total	11	124	105	.541	312	287	71	16	2	1996^1	2036	151	624	955	12.1	3.78	98	.266	.324	5	.093	-2	13	-13	-5	0.2

● **IRV MEDLINGER** Medlinger, Irving John b: 6/18/27, Chicago, Ill. d: 9/3/75, Wheeling, Ill. BL/TL, 5'11", 185 lbs. Deb: 4/20/49

YEAR	TM/L	W	L	PCT	G	GS	CG	SH	SV	IP	H	HR	BB	SO	RAT	ERA	ERA+	OAV	OOB	BH	AVG	PB	PR	/A	PD	TPI
1949	StL-A	0	0	—	3	0	0	0	0	4	11	1	3	4	31.5	27.00	17	.478	.538	0	—	0	-10	-10	-0	-0.8
1951	StL-A	0	0	—	6	0	0	0	0	9^2	10	1	12	5	20.5	8.38	52	.270	.449	0	—	0	-5	-4	-0	-0.4
Total	2	0	0	—	9	0	0	0	0	13^2	21	2	15	9	23.7	13.83	32	.350	.480	0	—	0	-15	-14	-0	-1.2

● **SCOTT MEDVIN** Medvin, Scott Howard b: 9/16/61, North Olmstead, O. BR/TR, 6'1", 195 lbs. Deb: 5/11/88

YEAR	TM/L	W	L	PCT	G	GS	CG	SH	SV	IP	H	HR	BB	SO	RAT	ERA	ERA+	OAV	OOB	BH	AVG	PB	PR	/A	PD	TPI
1988	Pit-N	3	0	1.000	17	0	0	0	0	27^2	23	1	9	16	10.7	4.88	70	.230	.300	0	.000	-0	-4	-5	0	-0.5
1989	Pit-N	0	1	.000	6	0	0	0	0	6^1	6	0	5	4	15.6	5.68	59	.240	.367	0	—	0	-2	-2	0	-0.1
1990	Sea-A	0	1	.000	5	0	0	0	0	4^1	7	0	2	1	20.8	6.23	64	.368	.455	0	—	0	-1	-1	0	-0.1
Total	3	3	2	.600	28	0	0	0	0	38^1	36	1	16	21	12.7	5.17	67	.250	.333	0	.000	-0	-7	-7	1	-0.7

● **PETE MEEGAN** Meegan, Peter J. "Steady Pete" b: 11/13/1863, San Francisco, Cal d: 3/15/05, San Francisco, Cal Deb: 8/12/1884

YEAR	TM/L	W	L	PCT	G	GS	CG	SH	SV	IP	H	HR	BB	SO	RAT	ERA	ERA+	OAV	OOB	BH	AVG	PB	PR	/A	PD	TPI
1884	Ric-a	7	12	.368	22	22	22	1	0	179	177	7	29	106	11.1	4.32	77	.246	.288	12	.160	-2	-21	-20	2	-1.8
1885	Pit-a	7	8	.467	18	16	14	1	0	146	146	1	38	58	12.0	3.39	95	.247	.303	13	.194	-1	-2	-3	-1	-0.4
Total	2	14	20	.412	40	38	36	2	0	325	323	8	67	164	11.5	3.90	84	.246	.295	25	.176	-3	-24	-23	1	-2.2

● **BILL MEEHAN** Meehan, William Thomas b: 9/4/1889, Osceola Mills, Pa. d: 10/8/82, Douglas, Wyo. BR/TR, 5'9", 155 lbs. Deb: 9/17/15

YEAR	TM/L	W	L	PCT	G	GS	CG	SH	SV	IP	H	HR	BB	SO	RAT	ERA	ERA+	OAV	OOB	BH	AVG	PB	PR	/A	PD	TPI
1915	Phi-A	0	1	.000	1	1	0	0	0	4	7	0	3	4	22.5	11.25	26	.389	.476	1	1.000	0	-4	-4	0	-0.3

● **ROY MEEKER** Meeker, Charles Roy b: 9/15/1900, Lead Mines, Mo. d: 3/25/29, Orlando, Fla. BL/TL, 5'9", 175 lbs. Deb: 9/22/23

YEAR	TM/L	W	L	PCT	G	GS	CG	SH	SV	IP	H	HR	BB	SO	RAT	ERA	ERA+	OAV	OOB	BH	AVG	PB	PR	/A	PD	TPI
1923	Phi-A	3	0	1.000	5	2	2	0	0	25	24	0	13	12	13.3	3.60	114	.253	.343	1	.111	-1	1	1	-0	0.1
1924	Phi-A	5	12	.294	30	14	5	1	0	146	166	7	81	37	15.5	4.68	91	.288	.381	11	.229	-0	-7	-6	-1	-0.7
1926	Cin-N	0	2	.000	7	1	1	0	0	21	24	1	9	5	14.1	6.43	57	.324	.398	0	.000	-1	-6	-6	0	-0.7
Total	3	8	14	.364	42	17	8	1	0	192	214	8	103	54	15.1	4.73	89	.287	.377	12	.190	-2	-12	-11	-1	-1.3

● **JOUETT MEEKIN** Meekin, Jouett b: 2/21/1867, New Albany, Ind. d: 12/14/44, New Albany, Ind. BR/TR, 6'1", 180 lbs. Deb: 6/13/1891

YEAR	TM/L	W	L	PCT	G	GS	CG	SH	SV	IP	H	HR	BB	SO	RAT	ERA	ERA+	OAV	OOB	BH	AVG	PB	PR	/A	PD	TPI
1891	Lou-a	10	16	.385	29	26	25	2	0	228	227	2	113	144	13.7	4.30	85	.251	.338	21	.216	4	-15	-16	-2	-1.2
1892	Lou-N	7	10	.412	19	18	17	0	0	156^1	168	3	78	67	14.5	4.03	76	.264	.350	5	.078	-4	-13	-17	0	-1.8
	Was-N	3	10	.231	14	14	13	1	0	112	112	2	48	58	13.2	3.46	94	.250	.328	6	.133	-1	-2	-3	-0	-0.3
	Yr	10	20	.333	33	32	30	1	0	268^1	280	5	126	125	13.8	3.79	83	.257	.336	11	.101	-5	-15	-19	0	-2.1
1893	Was-N	10	15	.400	31	28	24	1	0	245	289	6	140	91	16.0	4.96	93	.285	.376	29	.257	3	-8	-9	1	-0.4
1894	*NY-N	33	9	**.786**	52	48	40	1	2	409	404	13	171	133	12.9	3.70	142	.255	.332	48	.282	7	74	70	-3	5.9
1895	NY-N	16	11	.593	29	29	24	1	0	225^2	296	10	73	76	15.1	5.30	88	.311	.366	28	.292	4	-13	-17	-1	-1.1
1896	NY-N	26	14	.650	42	41	34	0	0	334^1	378	8	127	110	14.0	3.82	110	.283	.351	43	.299	12	20	14	-3	2.0
1897	NY-N	20	11	.645	37	34	30	2	0	303^2	328	9	99	83	12.9	3.76	110	.273	.333	41	.299	5	19	13	-3	1.4
1898	NY-N	16	18	.471	38	37	34	1	0	320	329	9	108	82	12.6	3.77	92	.264	.328	27	.209	1	-6	-10	-5	-1.4
1899	NY-N	5	11	.313	18	18	16	0	0	148^1	169	4	70	30	15.0	4.37	86	.286	.369	12	.207	1	-8	-10	-3	-1.1
	Bos-N	7	6	.538	13	13	12	0	0	108	111	0	23	23	11.3	2.83	147	.265	.307	7	.171	-2	12	16	-2	1.1
	Yr	12	17	.414	31	31	28	0	0	256^1	280	4	93	53	13.2	3.72	105	.275	.337	19	.192	-1	4	6	-5	0.0
1900	Pit-N	0	2	.000	2	2	1	0	0	13	20	1	8	3	20.1	6.92	52	.351	.439	0	.000	-1	-5	-5	-1	-0.5
Total	10	153	133	.535	324	308	270	9	2	2603^1	2831	67	1058	900	13.8	4.07	102	.273	.345	267	.243	29	55	27	-22	2.6

● **PHIL MEELER** Meeler, Charles Phillip b: 7/3/48, South Boston, Va. BR/TR, 6'5", 215 lbs. Deb: 5/10/72

YEAR	TM/L	W	L	PCT	G	GS	CG	SH	SV	IP	H	HR	BB	SO	RAT	ERA	ERA+	OAV	OOB	BH	AVG	PB	PR	/A	PD	TPI
1972	Det-A	0	1	.000	7	0	0	0	0	8^1	10	0	7	5	18.4	4.32	73	.303	.425	0	.000	-0	-1	-1	0	-0.1

● **RUSS MEERS** Meers, Russell Harlan "Babe" b: 11/28/18, Tilton, Ill. BL/TL, 5'10", 170 lbs. Deb: 9/28/41

YEAR	TM/L	W	L	PCT	G	GS	CG	SH	SV	IP	H	HR	BB	SO	RAT	ERA	ERA+	OAV	OOB	BH	AVG	PB	PR	/A	PD	TPI
1941	Chi-N	0	1	.000	1	1	1	0	0	8	5	0	0	5	6.8	1.13	312	.172	.200	0	.000	-0	2	2	-0	0.2
1946	Chi-N	1	2	.333	7	2	0	0	0	11^1	10	0	10	2	15.9	3.18	104	.238	.385	1	1.000	0	0	0	0	0.1
1947	Chi-N	2	0	1.000	35	1	0	0	0	64^1	61	5	38	28	14.1	4.48	88	.263	.371	2	.143	-1	-3	-4	-0	-0.4
Total	3	3	3	.500	43	4	0	0	0	83^2	76	5	48	35	13.7	3.98	96	.251	.359	3	.176	-0	-0	-1	-0	-0.1

● **HEINIE MEINE** Meine, Henry William "The Count Of Luxemburg" b: 5/1/1896, St.Louis, Mo. d: 3/18/68, St.Louis, Mo. BR/TR, 5'11", 180 lbs. Deb: 8/16/22

YEAR	TM/L	W	L	PCT	G	GS	CG	SH	SV	IP	H	HR	BB	SO	RAT	ERA	ERA+	OAV	OOB	BH	AVG	PB	PR	/A	PD	TPI
1922	StL-A	0	0	—	1	0	0	0	0	4	5	1	2	0	15.8	4.50	92	.313	.389	0	.000	-0	-0	-0	0	0.0
1929	Pit-N	7	6	.538	22	13	7	1	1	108	120	4	34	19	13.4	4.50	106	.291	.355	4	.103	-2	3	3	-2	0.0
1930	Pit-N	6	8	.429	20	16	4	0	1	117^1	168	6	44	18	16.6	6.14	81	.346	.406	5	.122	-3	-15	-15	3	-1.3
1931	Pit-N	**19**	13	.594	36	35	22	3	0	**284**	278	8	87	58	11.8	2.98	129	.254	.313	14	.146	-2	28	27	-0	2.6
1932	Pit-N	12	9	.571	28	25	13	1	1	172^1	193	6	45	32	12.6	3.86	99	.278	.324	10	.164	-2	0	-1	-1	-0.4
1933	Pit-N	15	8	.652	32	29	12	2	0	207^1	227	10	50	50	12.1	3.65	91	.278	.321	13	.173	-1	-7	-8	-3	-1.2
1934	Pit-N	7	6	.538	26	14	2	0	0	106^1	134	12	25	22	13.5	4.32	95	.306	.345	3	.107	-1	-3	-2	-1	-0.4
Total	7	66	50	.569	165	132	60	7	3	999^1	1125	47	287	199	12.9	3.95	101	.284	.337	49	.144	-12	5	4	-4	-0.7

● **FRANK MEINKE** Meinke, Frank Louis b: 10/18/1863, Chicago, Ill. d: 11/8/31, Chicago, Ill. 5'10.5", 172 lbs. Deb: 5/01/1884 F♦

YEAR	TM/L	W	L	PCT	G	GS	CG	SH	SV	IP	H	HR	BB	SO	RAT	ERA	ERA+	OAV	OOB	BH	AVG	PB	PR	/A	PD	TPI
1884	Det-N	8	23	.258	35	31	31	1	0	289	341	10	63	124	12.6	3.18	91	.275	.310	56	.164	-3	-6	-9	-2	-1.1
1885	Det-N	0	1	.000	1	1	0	0	0	5	13	0	4	0	30.6	3.60	79	.433	.500	0	.000	-0	-0	-0	0	-0.1
Total	2	8	24	.250	36	32	31	1	0	294	354	10	67	124	12.9	3.18	91	.279	.315	56	.163	-3	-7	-9	-2	-1.2

YEAR TM/L	W	L	PCT	G	GS	CG	SH	SV	IP	H	HR	BB	SO	RAT	ERA	ERA+	OAV	OOB	BH	AVG	PB	PR	/A	PD	TPI

● SAM MEJIAS Mejias, Samuel Elias b: 5/9/52, Santiago, D.R. BR/TR, 6', 170 lbs. Deb: 9/06/76 ♦

| 1978 Mon-N | 0 | 0 | — | 1 | 0 | 0 | 0 | 0 | 1 | 0 | 0 | 0 | 0 | 9.0 | 0.00 | — | .000 | .250 | 13 | .232 | 0 | 0 | 0 | 0 | 0.0 |

● JOSE MELENDEZ Melendez, Jose Luis (Garcia) b: 9/2/65, Naguabo, P.R. BR/TR, 6'2", 175 lbs. Deb: 9/11/90

1990 Sea-A	0	0	—	3	0	0	0	0	5¹	8	2	3	7	20.3	11.81	33	.333	.429	0	—	0	-5	-5	-0	-0.5
1991 SD-N	8	5	.615	31	9	0	0	3	93²	77	11	24	60	9.8	3.27	116	.221	.273	2	.100	-0	4	6	-1	0.4
1992 SD-N	6	7	.462	56	3	0	0	0	89¹	82	9	20	82	10.6	2.92	124	.249	.298	0	.000	-1	6	7	-1	0.6
Total 3	14	12	.538	90	12	0	0	3	188¹	167	22	47	149	10.5	3.35	111	.238	.291	2	.080	-1	5	8	-2	0.5

● STEVE MELTER Melter, Stephen Blazius b: 1/2/1886, Cherokee, Iowa d: 1/28/62, Mishawaka, Ind. BR/TR, 6'2", 180 lbs. Deb: 6/27/09

| 1909 StL-N | 0 | 1 | .000 | 23 | 1 | 0 | 0 | 3 | 64¹ | 79 | 1 | 20 | 24 | 14.1 | 3.50 | 72 | .322 | .378 | 2 | .133 | -0 | -6 | -7 | 1 | -0.6 |

● CLIFF MELTON Melton, Clifford George "Mickey Mouse" or "Mountain Music" b: 1/3/12, Brevard, N.C. d: 7/28/86, Baltimore, Md. BL/TL, 6'5.5", 203 lbs. Deb: 4/25/37

1937 *NY-N	20	9	.690	46	27	14	2	7	248	216	9	55	142	10.1	2.61	149	.233	.280	10	.122	-5	36	35	4	3.5
1938 NY-N	14	14	.500	36	31	10	1	0	243	266	19	61	101	12.1	3.89	97	.276	.319	14	.175	-1	-3	-3	2	-0.2
1939 NY-N	12	15	.444	41	23	9	2	5	207¹	214	7	65	95	12.3	3.56	110	.269	.327	12	.182	-1	8	8	1	0.8
1940 NY-N	10	11	.476	37	21	4	1	2	166²	185	9	68	91	13.8	4.91	79	.285	.355	12	.222	2	-20	-19	2	-1.6
1941 NY-N	8	11	.421	42	22	9	3	1	194¹	181	14	61	100	11.3	3.01	123	.246	.305	7	.115	-3	13	15	4	1.6
1942 NY-N†	11	5	.688	23	17	12	2	1	143²	122	9	33	61	9.8	2.63	128	.229	.276	11	.234	2	11	12	3	1.8
1943 NY-N	9	13	.409	34	28	6	2	0	186¹	184	7	69	69	12.4	3.19	108	.257	.325	8	.148	0	4	5	3	1.0
1944 NY-N	2	2	.500	13	10	1	0	0	64¹	78	5	19	15	13.7	4.06	90	.294	.344	3	.120	-2	-3	-3	1	-0.3
Total 8	86	80	.518	272	179	65	13	16	1453²	1446	79	431	660	11.8	3.42	109	.259	.314	77	.164	-9	47	50	20	6.6

● RUBE MELTON Melton, Reuben Franklin b: 2/27/17, Cramerton, N.C. d: 9/11/71, Greer, S.C. BR/TR, 6'5", 205 lbs. Deb: 4/17/41

1941 Phi-N	1	5	.167	25	5	2	0	0	83²	81	7	47	57	13.8	4.73	78	.258	.355	2	.105	-1	-10	-10	-1	-1.2
1942 Phi-N	9	20	.310	42	29	10	1	4	209¹	180	7	114	107	12.8	3.70	89	.234	.335	8	.123	-1	-9	-9	-2	-1.2
1943 Bro-N	5	8	.385	30	17	4	2	0	119¹	106	3	79	63	14.3	3.92	86	.243	.365	4	.105	-2	-7	-7	-1	-1.2
1944 Bro-N	9	13	.409	37	23	6	1	0	187¹	178	1	96	91	13.3	3.46	103	.254	.345	7	.123	-3	3	2	0	0.0
1946 Bro-N	6	3	.667	24	12	3	2	1	99²	72	3	52	44	11.5	1.99	170	.206	.314	3	.107	-2	16	15	0	1.5
1947 Bro-N	0	1	.000	4	1	0	0	0	4²	7	1	7	1	27.0	13.50	31	.350	.519	1	1.000	0	-5	-5	-0	-0.4
Total 6	30	50	.375	162	87	25	6	5	704	624	22	395	363	13.2	3.62	95	.241	.344	25	.120	-9	-12	-14	-5	-2.5

● MARIO MENDOZA Mendoza, Mario (Aizpuru) b: 12/26/50, Chihuahua, Mex. BR/TR, 5'11", 187 lbs. Deb: 4/26/74 C♦

| 1977 Pit-N | 0 | 0 | — | 1 | 0 | 0 | 0 | 0 | 2 | 3 | 1 | 2 | 0 | 22.5 | 13.50 | 30 | .375 | .500 | 16 | .198 | 0 | -2 | -2 | 0 | -0.2 |

● MIKE MENDOZA Mendoza, Michael Joseph b: 11/26/55, Inglewood, Cal. BR/TR, 6'5", 215 lbs. Deb: 9/07/79 ♦

| 1979 Hou-N | 0 | 0 | — | 1 | 0 | 0 | 0 | 0 | 1 | 0 | 0 | 0 | 0 | 0.0 | 0.00 | — | .000 | .000 | 0 | — | 0 | 0 | 0 | 0 | 0.0 |

● JOCK MENEFEE Menefee, John b: 1/15/1868, West Virginia d: 3/11/53, Belle Vernon, Pa. BR/TR, 6', 165 lbs. Deb: 8/17/1892 ♦

1892 Pit-N	0	0	—	1	0	0	0	0	4	10	0	2	0	27.0	11.25	29	.455	.500	0	.000	-0	-4	-4	0	-0.3
1893 Lou-N	8	7	.533	15	15	14	1	0	129¹	150	3	40	30	13.4	4.24	104	.282	.335	20	.274	3	6	2	2	0.6
1894 Lou-N	8	17	.320	28	24	20	1	0	211²	258	3	50	43	13.5	4.29	119	.297	.342	13	.165	-5	24	19	2	1.2
Pit-N	5	8	.385	13	13	13	0	0	111²	159	4	39	33	16.1	5.40	97	.331	.383	12	.255	0	-1	-2	2	0.0
Yr	13	25	.342	41	37	33	1	0	323¹	417	7	89	76	14.1	4.68	110	.307	.351	25	.198	-5	23	17	4	1.2
1895 Pit-N	0	1	.000	2	1	0	0	0	1²	2	0	7	0	54.0	16.20	28	.293	.674	0	—	0	-2	-2	0	-0.2
1898 NY-N	0	1	.000	1	1	0	0	0	9¹	11	0	2	3	14.5	4.82	74	.291	.359	0	.000	-1	-1	-1	0	-0.2
1900 Chi-N	9	4	.692	16	13	11	0	0	117	140	4	35	30	14.2	3.85	94	.296	.356	5	.109	-4	-2	-3	-2	-0.7
1901 Chi-N	8	12	.400	21	20	19	0	0	182¹	201	4	34	55	11.9	3.80	85	.278	.316	39	.257	3	-10	-11	-1	-0.7
1902 Chi-N	12	10	.545	22	21	20	4	0	197¹	202	2	26	60	10.7	2.42	112	.265	.294	50	.231	2	8	6	-1	0.9
1903 Chi-N	8	10	.444	22	17	13	1	0	147	157	3	38	39	12.3	3.00	105	.275	.327	13	.203	1	4	2	3	0.5
Total 9	58	70	.453	139	125	111	7	0	1111¹	1290	20	273	293	13.0	3.81	101	.288	.335	152	.222	-1	23	6	6	1.1

● TONY MENENDEZ Menendez, Anthony b: 2/20/65, Havana, Cuba BR/TR, 6'2", 190 lbs. Deb: 6/22/92

| 1992 Cin-N | 1 | 0 | 1.000 | 3 | 0 | 0 | 0 | 0 | 4² | 1 | 1 | 0 | 5 | 1.9 | 1.93 | 190 | .067 | .067 | 0 | — | 0 | 1 | 1 | -0 | 0.1 |

● MIKE MEOLA Meola, Emile Michael b: 10/19/05, New York, N.Y. d: 9/1/76, Fair Lawn, N.J. BR/TR, 5'11", 175 lbs. Deb: 4/24/33

1933 Bos-A	0	0	—	3	0	0	0	0	2¹	5	0	2	1	27.0	23.14	19	.417	.500	0	—	0	-5	-5	-0	-0.4
1936 StL-A	0	1	.000	9	0	0	0	0	19¹	29	0	13	6	20.0	9.31	58	.358	.453	1	.500	1	-9	-8	0	-0.6
Bos-A	0	2	.000	6	3	1	0	1	21¹	29	0	10	8	16.9	5.48	97	.326	.400	1	.143	-1	-1	-0	1	0.0
Yr	0	3	.000	15	3	1	0	1	40²	58	0	23	14	18.1	7.30	73	.339	.421	2	.222	0	-10	-9	1	-0.6
Total 2	0	3	.000	18	3	1	0	1	43	63	0	25	15	18.8	8.16	65	.346	.431	2	.222	0	-15	-14	1	-1.0

● WIN MERCER Mercer, George Barclay b: 6/20/1874, Chester, W.Va. d: 1/12/03, San Francisco, Cal. BR/TR, 5'7", 140 lbs. Deb: 4/21/1894 ♦

1894 Was-N	17	23	.425	50	38	29	0	3	336¹	442	9	126	72	15.6	3.85	137	.313	.375	48	.293	3	55	53	2	4.6
1895 Was-N	13	23	.361	43	38	32	0	2	311	430	17	96	84	15.7	4.46	108	.323	.376	50	.255	0	11	12	-1	1.0
1896 Was-N	25	18	.581	46	45	38	2	0	366¹	456	10	117	94	14.6	4.13	107	.302	.361	38	.244	-1	10	11	1	1.1
1897 Was-N	20	20	.500	46	42	34	3	3	333	397	5	103	88	14.3	3.24	134	.293	.356	43	.319	7	40	41	-1	4.3
1898 Was-N	12	18	.400	33	30	24	0	0	233²	309	3	71	52	15.3	4.81	76	.316	.373	80	.321	8	-31	-30	-1	-2.1
1899 Was-N	7	14	.333	23	21	21	0	0	186	234	2	53	60	14.6	4.60	85	.307	.356	112	.299	5	-15	-14	3	-0.5
1900 NY-N	13	17	.433	33	29	26	1	0	242²	303	5	58	90	14.1	3.86	94	.305	.355	73	.294	6	-4	-7	2	0.1
1901 Was-A	9	13	.409	24	22	19	1	1	179²	217	8	50	31	13.9	4.56	80	.295	.348	42	.300	6	-18	-18	1	-0.9
1902 Det-A	15	18	.455	35	33	28	4	1	281²	282	5	80	40	11.9	3.04	120	.261	.318	18	.180	-2	17	19	4	2.0
Total 9	131	164	.444	333	298	251	11	10	2470¹	3070	64	754	528	14.5	3.99	106	.302	.359	504	.286	33	64	68	8	9.6

● JACK MERCER Mercer, Harry Vernon b: 3/10/1889, Zanesville, Ohio d: 6/25/45, Dayton Ohio Deb: 8/02/10

| 1910 Pit-N | 0 | 0 | — | 1 | 0 | 0 | 0 | 0 | 2 | 1 | 0 | 2 | 1 | 18.0 | 0.00 | — | .000 | .500 | 0 | — | 0 | 0 | 0 | 0 | 0.0 |

● MARK MERCER Mercer, Mark Kenneth b: 5/22/54, Fort Bragg, N.C. BL/TL, 6'5", 220 lbs. Deb: 9/01/81

| 1981 Tex-A | 0 | 1 | .000 | 7 | 0 | 0 | 0 | 2 | 7² | 7 | 1 | 7 | 8 | 16.4 | 4.70 | 74 | .241 | .389 | 0 | — | 0 | -1 | -1 | 0 | 0.1 |

● KENT MERCKER Mercker, Kent Franklin b: 2/1/68, Indianapolis, Ind. BL/TL, 6'1", 175 lbs. Deb: 9/22/89

1989 Atl-N	0	0	—	2	1	0	0	0	4¹	8	0	6	4	29.1	12.46	29	.400	.538	0	.000	-0	-4	-4	-0	-0.4
1990 Atl-N	4	7	.364	36	0	0	0	7	48¹	43	6	24	39	12.8	3.17	127	.236	.332	0	.000	-0	3	5	-1	0.3
1991 *Atl-N	5	5	.625	50	4	0	0	6	73¹	56	5	35	62	11.4	2.58	151	.211	.305	1	.100	-0	9	11	-1	1.0
1992 *Atl-N	3	2	.600	53	0	0	0	6	68¹	51	4	35	49	11.7	3.42	109	.207	.313	0	.000	-1	2	2	-2	0.0
Total 4	12	12	.500	141	5	0	0	19	194¹	158	15	100	154	12.2	3.24	119	.221	.322	1	.053	-1	9	14	-4	0.9

● SPIKE MERENA Merena, John Joseph b: 11/18/09, Paterson, N.J. d: 3/9/77, Bridgeport, Conn. BL/TL, 6', 185 lbs. Deb: 9/16/34

| 1934 Bos-A | 1 | 2 | .333 | 4 | 3 | 2 | 1 | 0 | 24² | 20 | 2 | 16 | 7 | 13.5 | 2.92 | 165 | .222 | .346 | 1 | .143 | -0 | 4 | 5 | -1 | 0.4 |

● RON MERIDITH Meridith, Ronald Knox b: 11/26/56, San Pedro, Cal. BL/TL, 6', 175 lbs. Deb: 9/16/84

1984 Chi-N	0	0	—	3	0	0	0	0	5¹	6	1	2	4	13.5	3.38	116	.273	.333	0	—	0	0	0	-0	0.0
1985 Chi-N	3	2	.600	32	0	0	0	1	46¹	53	3	24	31	15.2	4.47	89	.301	.388	1	.250	0	-5	-2	0	-0.2
1986 Tex-A	0	0	—	5	0	0	0	0	9	3	0	1	2	9.0	3.00	143	.086	.375	0	—	0	0	0	0	0.0
1987 Tex-A	1	0	1.000	11	0	0	0	0	20²	25	7	12	17	16.1	6.10	73	.298	.385	0	—	0	-4	-4	0	-0.3

YEAR	TM/L	W	L	PCT	G	GS	CG	SH	SV	IP	H	HR	BB	SO	RAT	ERA	ERA+	OAV	OOB	BH	AVG	PB	PR	/A	PD	TPI
Total	4	5	2	.714	51	0	0	0	1	75^1	86	11	39	46	15.1	4.78	87	.298	.383	1	.250	0	-8	-5	1	-0.5
● **GEORGE MERRITT**	Merritt, George Washington b: 4/14/1880, Paterson, N.J. d: 2/21/38, Memphis, Tenn. TR , 6′, 160 lbs. Deb: 9/06/01 ♦																									
1901	Pit-N	3	0	1.000	3	3	3	0	0	24	28	0	5	5	13.1	4.88	67	.289	.337	3	.273	1	-4	-4	-0	-0.3
1903	Pit-N	0	0	—	1	0	0	0	0	4	4	0	1	2	11.3	2.25	144	.267	.313	4	.148	-0	0	0	-0	0.0
Total	2	3	0	1.000	4	3	3	0	0	28	32	0	6	7	12.9	4.50	73	.286	.334	10	.213	1	-4	-4	-0	-0.3
● **JIM MERRITT**	Merritt, James Joseph b: 12/9/43, Altadena, Cal. BL/TL, 6′2″, 180 lbs. Deb: 8/02/65																									
1965	*Min-A	5	4	.556	16	9	1	0	2	76^2	68	11	20	61	10.3	3.17	112	.239	.289	3	.136	0	2	3	-0	0.4
1966	Min-A	7	14	.333	31	18	5	1	3	144	112	17	33	124	9.1	3.38	107	.212	.258	4	.103	-1	1	4	-0	0.3
1967	Min-A	13	7	.650	37	28	11	4	0	227^2	196	21	30	161	9.2	2.53	137	.230	.262	10	.135	0	18	24	-2	2.5
1968	Min-A	12	16	.429	38	34	11	1	1	238^1	207	21	52	181	10.0	3.25	95	.232	.279	10	.141	0	-7	-4	1	-0.5
1969	Cin-N	17	9	.654	42	36	8	1	0	251	269	33	61	144	12.0	4.37	86	.273	.318	11	.143	0	-22	-17	-3	-2.0
1970	*Cin-N★	20	12	.625	35	35	12	1	0	234	248	21	53	136	11.6	4.08	99	.270	.311	14	.169	3	-1	-1	-2	-0.1
1971	Cin-N	1	11	.083	28	11	0	0	0	107	115	14	31	38	12.5	4.37	77	.279	.334	4	.138	0	-11	-12	-2	-1.4
1972	Cin-N	1	0	1.000	4	1	0	0	0	8	13	1	2	4	16.9	4.50	71	.361	.395	0	.000	-0	-1	-1	-0	-0.2
1973	Tex-A	5	13	.278	35	19	8	1	1	160	191	18	34	65	12.7	4.05	92	.296	.332	0	—	0	-4	-6	-1	-0.5
1974	Tex-A	0	0	—	26	1	0	0	0	32^2	46	3	6	18	14.3	4.13	86	.329	.356	0	—	0	-2	-2	-1	-0.2
1975	Tex-A	0	0	—	5	0	0	0	0	3^2	3	0	0	0	9.8	0.00	—	.214	.267	0	—	0	2	2	-0	0.1
Total	11	81	86	.485	297	192	56	9	7	1483	1468	160	322	932	11.0	3.65	98	.257	.300	56	.141	3	-25	-11	-10	-1.6
● **LLOYD MERRITT**	Merritt, Lloyd Wesley b: 4/8/33, St.Louis, Mo. BR/TR, 6′, 189 lbs. Deb: 4/22/57																									
1957	StL-N	1	2	.333	44	0	0	0	7	65^1	60	7	28	35	12.7	3.31	120	.251	.339	0	.000	-0	4	5	0	0.5
● **SAM MERTES**	Mertes, Samuel Blair "Sandow" b: 8/6/1872, San Francisco, Cal. d: 3/11/45, San Francisco, Cal BR/TR, 5′10″, 185 lbs. Deb: 6/30/1896 ♦																									
1902	Chi-A	1	0	1.000	1	0	0	0	0	8	6	0	0	0	6.8	1.13	301	.209	.209	140	.282	0	2	2	-1	0.2
● **JIM MERTZ**	Mertz, James Verlin b: 8/10/16, Lima, Ohio BR/TR, 5′10.5″, 170 lbs. Deb: 5/01/43																									
1943	Was-A	5	7	.417	33	10	2	0	3	116^2	109	7	58	53	12.9	4.63	69	.251	.339	7	.184	0	-17	-18	0	-1.9
● **JOSE MESA**	Mesa, Jose Ramon b: 5/22/66, Pueblo Viejo, D.R. BR/TR, 6′3″, 220 lbs. Deb: 9/10/87																									
1987	Bal-A	1	3	.250	6	5	0	0	0	31^1	38	7	15	17	15.2	6.03	73	.297	.371	0	—	0	-5	-6	-1	-0.6
1990	Bal-A	3	2	.600	7	7	0	0	0	46^2	37	2	27	24	12.5	3.86	98	.218	.328	0	—	0	0	-0	-0	0.1
1991	Bal-A	6	11	.353	23	23	2	1	0	123^2	151	11	62	64	15.7	5.97	66	.307	.388	0	—	0	-26	-28	1	-2.5
1992	Bal-A	3	8	.273	13	12	0	0	0	67^2	77	9	27	22	14.1	5.19	75	.287	.357	0	—	0	-9	-10	0	-0.9
	Cle-A	4	4	.500	15	15	1	1	0	93	92	5	43	40	13.3	4.16	97	.262	.346	0	—	0	-2	-1	-1	-0.2
	Yr	7	12	.368	28	27	1	1	0	160^2	169	14	70	62	13.5	4.59	87	.271	.346	0	—	0	-12	-11	-0	-1.1
Total	4	17	28	.378	64	62	3	2	0	362^1	395	34	174	167	14.3	5.09	78	.280	.363	0	—	0	-43	-45	-1	-4.1
● **BUD MESSENGER**	Messenger, Andrew Warren b: 2/1/1898, Grand Blanc, Mich. d: 11/4/71, Lansing, Mich. BR/TR, 6′, 175 lbs. Deb: 7/31/24																									
1924	Cle-A	2	0	1.000	5	2	1	0	0	25	28	4	14	4	15.1	4.32	99	.283	.372	1	.125	-0	-0	-0	-0	-0.1
● **ANDY MESSERSMITH**	Messersmith, John Alexander b: 8/6/45, Toms River, N.J. BR/TR, 6′1″, 200 lbs. Deb: 7/04/68																									
1968	Cal-A	4	2	.667	28	5	2	1	4	81^1	44	3	35	74	8.9	2.21	132	.157	.253	2	.100	-1	7	6	0	0.7
1969	Cal-A	16	11	.593	40	33	10	2	2	250	169	17	100	211	9.9	2.52	138	**.190**	.276	12	.156	2	31	27	-1	3.0
1970	Cal-A	11	10	.524	37	26	6	1	5	194^2	144	21	78	162	10.5	3.01	120	**.205**	.290	11	.157	0	15	13	-1	1.4
1971	Cal-A☆	20	13	.606	38	38	14	4	0	276^2	224	16	121	179	11.5	2.99	108	.218	.304	16	.172	4	14	8	1	1.3
1972	Cal-A	8	11	.421	25	21	10	3	2	169^2	125	5	68	142	10.3	2.81	104	.207	.290	10	.189	2	5	2	0	0.5
1973	LA-N	14	10	.583	33	33	10	3	0	249^2	196	24	77	177	10.1	2.70	127	.214	.279	15	.169	2	27	20	-0	2.3
1974	*LA-N★	**20**	6	**.769**	39	39	13	3	0	292^1	227	24	94	221	**10.0**	2.59	132	.212	**.278**	23	.240	9	34	26	0	3.9
1975	LA-N☆	19	14	.576	42	40	**19**	**7**	1	**321^2**	244	22	96	213	9.7	2.29	148	**.213**	.276	17	.157	2	**47**	**40**	-2	4.4
1976	Atl-N†	11	11	.500	29	28	12	3	1	207^1	166	14	74	135	10.5	3.04	125	.219	.290	12	.179	0	11	17	1	2.0
1977	Atl-N	5	4	.556	16	16	1	0	0	102^1	101	12	39	69	12.5	4.40	101	.256	.326	4	.118	0	-6	1	-0	0.1
1978	NY-A	0	3	.000	6	5	0	0	0	22^1	24	7	15	16	16.1	5.64	64	.267	.377	0	—	0	-5	-5	-0	-0.3
1979	LA-N	2	4	.333	11	11	1	0	0	62^1	55	9	34	26	12.9	4.91	74	.244	.344	2	.091	-1	-8	-9	0	-0.9
Total	12	130	99	.568	344	295	98	27	15	2230^1	1719	174	831	1625	10.5	2.86	121	.212	.289	124	.170	19	172	145	-1	18.4
● **TOM METCALF**	Metcalf, Thomas John b: 7/16/40, Amherst, Wis. BR/TR, 6′2.5″, 174 lbs. Deb: 8/04/63																									
1963	NY-A	1	0	1.000	8	0	0	0	0	13	12	1	3	3	10.4	2.77	127	.250	.294	0	—	0	1	1	-0	0.1
● **DEWEY METIVIER**	Metivier, George Dewey b: 5/6/1898, Cambridge, Mass. d: 3/2/47, Cambridge, Mass. BL/TR, 5′11″, 175 lbs. Deb: 9/15/22																									
1922	Cle-A	2	0	1.000	2	2	2	0	0	18	18	1	3	1	11.0	4.50	89	.265	.306	1	.167	-0	-1	-1	-1	-0.1
1923	Cle-A	4	2	.667	26	5	1	0	1	73^1	111	1	38	9	19.0	6.50	61	.368	.448	3	.150	-0	-21	-21	0	-1.9
1924	Cle-A	1	5	.167	26	6	1	0	3	76^1	110	3	34	14	17.0	5.31	81	.358	.422	3	.125	-2	-9	-9	-1	-1.1
Total	3	7	7	.500	54	13	4	0	4	167^2	239	5	75	24	17.2	5.74	72	.353	.423	7	.140	-3	-31	-30	-1	-3.1
● **BUTCH METZGER**	Metzger, Clarence Edward b: 5/23/52, Lafayette, Ind. BR/TR, 6′1″, 185 lbs. Deb: 9/08/74																									
1974	SF-N	1	0	1.000	10	0	0	0	0	12^2	11	0	12	5	16.3	3.55	107	.239	.397	0	—	0	0	0	-0	0.0
1975	SD-N	1	0	1.000	4	0	0	0	0	4^2	6	1	4	6	19.3	7.71	45	.316	.435	0	—	0	-2	-2	0	-0.2
1976	SD-N	11	4	.733	77	0	0	0	16	123^1	119	5	52	89	12.7	2.92	112	.258	.337	0	.000	-0	8	5	-0	0.5
1977	SD-N	0	0	—	17	1	0	0	0	22^2	27	5	12	6	15.9	5.56	64	.307	.396	0	.000	-0	-4	-5	-0	-0.6
	StL-N	4	2	.667	58	0	0	0	7	92^2	78	8	38	48	11.4	3.11	124	.228	.307	0	.000	-0	8	8	-1	0.6
	Yr	4	2	.667	75	1	0	0	7	115^1	105	13	50	54	12.2	3.59	105	.242	.322	0	.000	-1	4	3	-1	0.0
1978	NY-N	1	3	.250	25	0	0	0	0	37^1	48	4	22	21	17.1	6.51	54	.324	.415	0	—	0	-12	-13	-1	-1.3
Total	5	18	9	.667	191	1	0	0	23	293^1	289	23	140	175	13.3	3.74	94	.262	.348	0	.000	-1	-2	-7	-2	-1.0
● **BRIAN MEYER**	Meyer, Brian Scott b: 1/29/63, Camden, N.J. BR/TR, 6′, 190 lbs. Deb: 9/03/88																									
1988	Hou-N	0	0	—	8	0	0	0	0	12^1	9	2	4	10	9.5	1.46	227	.225	.295	0	—	0	3	3	1	0.3
1989	Hou-N	0	1	.000	12	0	0	0	1	18	16	0	13	13	15.0	4.50	75	.239	.370	0	—	0	-2	-2	0	-0.2
1990	Hou-N	0	4	.000	14	0	0	0	1	20^1	16	3	6	6	9.7	2.21	168	.211	.268	0	.000	-0	4	3	1	0.4
Total	3	0	5	.000	34	0	0	0	2	50^2	41	5	23	29	11.5	2.84	123	.224	.314	0	.000	-0	4	4	1	0.5
● **JACK MEYER**	Meyer, John Robert b: 3/23/32, Philadelphia, Pa. d: 3/9/67, Philadelphia, Pa. BR/TR, 6′1″, 175 lbs. Deb: 4/16/55																									
1955	Phi-N	6	11	.353	50	5	0	0	**16**	110^1	75	14	66	97	11.7	3.43	116	.190	.310	2	.100	0	8	7	-1	0.6
1956	Phi-N	7	11	.389	41	7	2	0	2	96	86	8	51	66	13.2	4.41	84	.242	.343	4	.200	1	-7	-7	0	-0.6
1957	Phi-N	0	2	.000	19	2	0	0	0	37^2	44	7	28	34	17.4	5.73	66	.297	.412	1	.167	0	-8	-8	0	-0.7
1958	Phi-N	3	6	.333	37	5	1	0	2	90^1	77	8	33	87	11.1	3.59	110	.232	.303	5	.278	1	4	4	-1	0.3
1959	Phi-N	5	3	.625	47	1	1	0	1	93^2	76	9	53	71	12.5	3.36	122	.222	.328	1	.071	-1	6	8	0	0.7
1960	Phi-N	3	1	.750	7	4	0	0	0	25	25	2	11	18	13.0	4.32	90	.272	.350	1	.125	-0	-2	-1	-0	-0.1
1961	Phi-N	0	0	—	1	0	0	0	0	2	2	1	2	2	18.0	9.00	45	.286	.444	0	—	0	-1	-1	-0	-0.1
Total	7	24	34	.414	202	24	4	0	21	455	385	49	244	375	12.6	3.92	100	.230	.332	14	.163	1	0	0	-1	0.1
● **BOB MEYER**	Meyer, Robert Bernard b: 8/4/39, Toledo, Ohio BR/TL, 6′2″, 185 lbs. Deb: 4/20/64																									
1964	NY-A	0	3	.000	7	1	0	0	0	18^1	16	1	12	12	13.7	4.91	74	.235	.350	0	.000	-0	-3	-3	1	-0.3
	LA-A	1	1	.500	6	5	0	0	0	18	25	2	13	13	19.5	5.00	66	.333	.438	0	.000	-1	-3	-3	0	-0.4
	KC-A	1	4	.200	9	7	2	0	0	42	37	2	33	30	15.0	3.86	99	.248	.385	0	.000	-1	-1	-0	-1	-0.2

YEAR	TM/L	W	L	PCT	G	GS	CG	SH	SV	IP	H	HR	BB	SO	RAT	ERA	ERA+	OAV	OOB	BH	AVG	PB	PR	/A	PD	TPI
	Yr	2	8	.200	22	13	2	0	0	78^1	78	5	58	55	15.6	4.37	84	.266	.387	0	.000	-2	-6	-6	-0	-0.9
1969	Sea-A	0	3	.000	6	5	1	0	0	32^2	30	4	10	17	11.6	3.31	110	.252	.321	1	.091	-1	1	1	-1	0.0
1970	Mil-A	0	1	.000	10	0	0	0	0	18^1	24	3	12	20	17.7	6.38	59	.329	.424	1	.333	0	-5	-5	0	-0.5
Total	3	2	12	.143	38	18	3	0	0	129^1	132	12	80	92	15.0	4.38	84	.273	.379	2	.057	-3	-11	-10	-1	-1.4

● **RUSS MEYER** Meyer, Russell Charles "Rowdy" or "The Mad Monk" b: 10/25/23, Peru, Ill. BB/TR, 6'1", 185 lbs. Deb: 9/13/46 C

YEAR	TM/L	W	L	PCT	G	GS	CG	SH	SV	IP	H	HR	BB	SO	RAT	ERA	ERA+	OAV	OOB	BH	AVG	PB	PR	/A	PD	TPI
1946	Chi-N	0	0	—	4	1	0	0	1	17	21	2	10	10	16.4	3.18	104	.309	.397	1	.200	0	0	0	0	0.1
1947	Chi-N	3	2	.600	23	2	1	0	0	45	43	4	14	22	11.6	3.40	116	.257	.319	3	.250	0	3	3	-0	0.3
1948	Chi-N	10	10	.500	29	26	8	3	0	164^2	157	8	77	89	12.8	3.66	107	.254	.338	6	.107	-3	5	4	-0	0.2
1949	Phi-N	17	8	.680	37	28	14	2	1	213	199	14	70	78	11.4	3.08	128	.250	.311	10	.143	-1	23	20	-2	1.8
1950	*Phi-N	9	11	.450	32	25	3	0	1	159^2	193	21	67	74	14.8	5.30	76	.304	.373	7	.140	-1	-21	-22	1	-2.1
1951	Phi-N	8	9	.471	28	24	7	2	0	168	172	13	55	65	12.3	3.48	111	.263	.322	5	.104	-2	9	7	-3	0.2
1952	Phi-N	13	14	.481	37	32	14	1	1	232^1	235	10	65	92	11.7	3.14	116	.260	.311	7	.089	-2	15	13	-2	0.9
1953	*Bro-N	15	5	.750	34	32	10	2	0	191^1	201	25	63	106	12.5	4.56	93	.269	.327	11	.147	-2	-6	-6	-0	-0.9
1954	Bro-N	11	6	.647	36	28	6	2	0	180^1	193	17	49	70	12.2	3.99	102	.275	.324	2	.043	-3	2	2	-2	-0.4
1955	*Bro-N	6	2	.750	18	11	2	1	0	73	86	8	31	26	14.4	5.42	75	.300	.368	1	.037	-3	-11	-11	1	-1.2
1956	Chi-N	1	6	.143	20	9	0	0	0	57	71	11	26	28	15.6	6.32	60	.313	.388	1	.083	-1	-16	-16	2	-1.5
	Cin-N	0	0	—	1	0	0	0	0	1	1	0	0	1	9.0	0.00	—	.250	.250	0	—	0	0	0	0	0.1
	Yr	1	6	.143	21	9	0	0	0	58	72	11	26	29	15.2	6.21	61	.305	.374	1	.083	-1	-16	-16	2	-1.4
1957	Bos-A	0	0	—	2	1	0	0	0	5	10	0	3	1	23.4	5.40	74	.417	.481	1	1.000	0	-1	-1	1	0.0
1959	KC-A	1	0	1.000	18	0	0	0	1	24	24	3	11	10	13.5	4.50	89	.261	.346	0	.000	-0	-2	-1	-0	-0.2
Total	13	94	73	.563	319	219	65	13	5	1531^1	1606	136	541	672	12.7	3.99	99	.271	.334	55	.114	-18	2	-8	-5	-2.7

● **LEVI MEYERLE** Meyerle, Levi Samuel "Long Levi" b: 7/1845, Philadelphia, Pa. d: 11/4/21, Philadelphia, Pa. BR/TR, 6'1", 177 lbs. Deb: 5/20/1871 ♦

YEAR	TM/L	W	L	PCT	G	GS	CG	SH	SV	IP	H	HR	BB	SO	RAT	ERA	ERA+	OAV	OOB	BH	AVG	PB	PR	/A	PD	TPI
1871	Ath-n	0	0	—	1	0	0	0	0	1	1	0	2	0	27.0	9.00	45	.250	.500	64	.492	1	-1	-1		0.0
1876	Phi-N	0	2	.000	2	2	2	0	0	18	28	0	1	0	14.5	5.00	48	.337	.345	87	.340	1	-5	-5	-0	-0.4

● **GENE MICHAEL** Michael, Eugene Richard "Stick" b: 6/2/38, Kent, Ohio BB/TR, 6'2", 183 lbs. Deb: 7/15/66 MC♦

YEAR	TM/L	W	L	PCT	G	GS	CG	SH	SV	IP	H	HR	BB	SO	RAT	ERA	ERA+	OAV	OOB	BH	AVG	PB	PR	/A	PD	TPI
1968	NY-A	0	0	—	1	0	0	0	0	3	5	0	0	3	18.0	0.00	—	.357	.400	23	.198	0	1	1	0	0.1

● **JOHN MICHAELS** Michaels, John Joseph b: 7/10/07, Bridgeport, Conn. BL/TL, 5'10.5", 154 lbs. Deb: 4/16/32

YEAR	TM/L	W	L	PCT	G	GS	CG	SH	SV	IP	H	HR	BB	SO	RAT	ERA	ERA+	OAV	OOB	BH	AVG	PB	PR	/A	PD	TPI
1932	Bos-A	1	6	.143	28	8	2	0	0	80^2	101	4	27	16	14.6	5.13	88	.304	.362	3	.143	-1	-6	-6	1	-0.5

● **JOHN MICHAELSON** Michaelson, John August "Mike" b: 8/12/1893, Tivalkoski, Finland d: 4/16/68, Woodruff, Wis. BR/TR, 5'9", 165 lbs. Deb: 8/28/21

YEAR	TM/L	W	L	PCT	G	GS	CG	SH	SV	IP	H	HR	BB	SO	RAT	ERA	ERA+	OAV	OOB	BH	AVG	PB	PR	/A	PD	TPI
1921	Chi-A	0	0	—	2	0	0	0	0	2^2	4	0	1	1	16.9	10.13	42	.400	.455	0	—	0	-2	-2	-0	-0.2

● **GLENN MICKENS** Mickens, Glenn Roger b: 7/26/30, Wilmar, Cal. BR/TR, 6', 175 lbs. Deb: 7/19/53

YEAR	TM/L	W	L	PCT	G	GS	CG	SH	SV	IP	H	HR	BB	SO	RAT	ERA	ERA+	OAV	OOB	BH	AVG	PB	PR	/A	PD	TPI
1953	Bro-N	0	1	.000	4	2	0	0	0	6^1	11	2	4	5	21.3	11.37	37	.393	.469	0	.000	-0	-5	-5	0	-0.5

● **JIM MIDDLETON** Middleton, James Blaine "Rifle Jim" b: 5/28/1889, Argos, Ind. d: 1/12/74, Argos, Ind. BR/TR, 5'11.5", 165 lbs. Deb: 4/18/17

YEAR	TM/L	W	L	PCT	G	GS	CG	SH	SV	IP	H	HR	BB	SO	RAT	ERA	ERA+	OAV	OOB	BH	AVG	PB	PR	/A	PD	TPI
1917	NY-N	1	1	.500	13	0	0	0	1	36	35	1	8	9	11.0	2.75	93	.255	.301	0	.000	-1	-0	-1	1	-0.2
1921	Det-A	6	11	.353	38	10	2	0	**7**	121^2	149	5	44	31	14.4	5.03	85	.302	.361	5	.147	-2	-10	-10	1	-1.0
Total	2	7	12	.368	51	10	2	0	8	157^2	184	6	52	40	13.6	4.51	86	.292	.348	5	.119	-3	-10	-11	2	-1.2

● **JOHN MIDDLETON** Middleton, John Wayne "Lefty" b: 4/11/1900, Mt.Calm, Tex. d: 11/3/86, Amarillo, Tex. BL/TL, 6'1", 185 lbs. Deb: 9/06/22

YEAR	TM/L	W	L	PCT	G	GS	CG	SH	SV	IP	H	HR	BB	SO	RAT	ERA	ERA+	OAV	OOB	BH	AVG	PB	PR	/A	PD	TPI
1922	Cle-A	0	1	.000	2	1	0	0	0	7^1	8	1	6	2	17.2	7.36	54	.286	.412	1	.333	0	-3	-3	0	-0.2

● **DICK MIDKIFF** Midkiff, Richard b: 9/28/14, Gonzales, Tex. d: 10/30/56, Temple, Tex. BR/TR, 6'2", 185 lbs. Deb: 4/24/38

YEAR	TM/L	W	L	PCT	G	GS	CG	SH	SV	IP	H	HR	BB	SO	RAT	ERA	ERA+	OAV	OOB	BH	AVG	PB	PR	/A	PD	TPI
1938	Bos-A	1	1	.500	13	2	0	0	0	35^1	43	5	21	10	16.3	5.09	97	.305	.395	2	.200	0	-1	-1	0	-0.1

● **GARY MIELKE** Mielke, Gary Roger b: 1/28/63, St.James, Minn. BR/TR, 6'3", 185 lbs. Deb: 8/19/87

YEAR	TM/L	W	L	PCT	G	GS	CG	SH	SV	IP	H	HR	BB	SO	RAT	ERA	ERA+	OAV	OOB	BH	AVG	PB	PR	/A	PD	TPI
1987	Tex-A	0	0	—	3	0	0	0	0	3	3	2	1	3	12.0	6.00	75	.250	.308	0	—	0	-1	-1	-0	-0.1
1989	Tex-A	1	0	1.000	43	0	0	0	1	49^2	52	4	25	26	14.3	3.26	122	.280	.371	0	—	0	3	4	-0	0.3
1990	Tex-A	0	3	.000	33	0	0	0	0	41	42	4	15	13	13.0	3.73	105	.271	.343	0	—	0	1	1	0	0.1
Total	3	1	3	.250	79	0	0	0	1	93^2	97	10	41	42	13.6	3.56	111	.275	.357	0	—	0	4	4	-0	0.3

● **PETE MIKKELSEN** Mikkelsen, Peter James b: 10/25/39, Staten Island, N.Y. BR/TR, 6'2", 220 lbs. Deb: 4/17/64

YEAR	TM/L	W	L	PCT	G	GS	CG	SH	SV	IP	H	HR	BB	SO	RAT	ERA	ERA+	OAV	OOB	BH	AVG	PB	PR	/A	PD	TPI
1964	*NY-A	7	4	.636	50	0	0	0	12	86	79	3	41	63	13.0	3.56	102	.247	.340	1	.063	-1	1	1	1	0.1
1965	NY-A	4	9	.308	41	3	0	0	1	82^1	78	10	36	69	12.8	3.28	104	.249	.332	1	.100	-0	2	1	1	0.2
1966	Pit-N	9	8	.529	71	0	0	0	14	126	106	8	51	76	11.6	3.07	116	.234	.318	3	.150	-0	7	7	-0	0.7
1967	Pit-N	1	2	.333	32	0	0	0	2	56^1	50	7	19	30	11.5	4.31	78	.237	.309	0	.000	-0	-6	-6	-1	-0.8
	Chi-N	0	0	—	7	0	0	0	0	7	9	1	5	0	19.3	6.43	55	.333	.455	0	—	0	-2	-2	-0	-0.2
	Yr	1	2	.333	39	0	0	0	2	63^1	59	8	24	30	11.9	4.55	74	.244	.315	0	.000	-0	-8	-8	-1	-1.0
1968	Chi-N	0	0	—	3	0	0	0	0	4^2	7	3	1	5	15.4	7.71	41	.350	.381	1	1.000	0	-2	-2	0	-0.2
	StL-N	0	0	—	5	0	0	0	0	16	10	0	7	8	9.6	1.13	257	.179	.270	0	.000	-0	3	3	-1	0.3
	Yr	0	0	—	8	0	0	0	0	20^2	17	3	8	13	10.9	2.61	113	.224	.298	1	.250	0	1	1	-1	0.1
1969	LA-N	7	5	.583	48	0	0	0	4	81^1	57	9	30	51	10.1	2.77	120	.193	.277	1	.167	-0	7	5	1	0.6
1970	LA-N	4	2	.667	33	0	0	0	6	62	48	5	20	47	10.5	2.76	139	.211	.287	2	.333	1	9	7	0	0.8
1971	LA-N	8	5	.615	41	0	0	0	5	74	67	10	17	46	10.3	3.65	89	.242	.288	2	.200	0	-2	-3	1	-0.3
1972	LA-N	5	5	.500	33	0	0	0	5	57^2	65	3	23	41	14.5	4.06	82	.283	.360	0	.000	-0	-4	-5	-0	-0.6
Total	9	45	40	.529	364	3	0	0	49	653^1	576	59	250	436	11.8	3.38	102	.237	.316	11	.133	-2	13	6	2	0.6

● **HANK MIKLOS** Miklos, John Joseph b: 11/27/10, Chicago, Ill. BL/TL, 5'11", 175 lbs. Deb: 4/23/44

YEAR	TM/L	W	L	PCT	G	GS	CG	SH	SV	IP	H	HR	BB	SO	RAT	ERA	ERA+	OAV	OOB	BH	AVG	PB	PR	/A	PD	TPI
1944	Chi-N	0	0	—	2	0	0	0	0	7	9	1	3	0	15.4	7.71	46	.333	.400	0	.000	-0	-3	-3	1	-0.3

● **BOB MILACKI** Milacki, Robert b: 7/28/64, Trenton, N.J. BR/TR, 6'4", 220 lbs. Deb: 9/18/88

YEAR	TM/L	W	L	PCT	G	GS	CG	SH	SV	IP	H	HR	BB	SO	RAT	ERA	ERA+	OAV	OOB	BH	AVG	PB	PR	/A	PD	TPI
1988	Bal-A	2	0	1.000	3	3	1	1	0	25	9	1	9	18	6.5	0.72	542	.110	.198	0	—	0	9	9	0	1.3
1989	Bal-A	14	12	.538	37	36	3	2	0	243	233	21	88	113	12.0	3.74	101	.254	.320	0	—	0	4	1	-0	0.2
1990	Bal-A	5	8	.385	27	24	1	1	0	135^1	143	18	61	60	13.6	4.46	85	.273	.349	0	—	0	-8	-10	1	-0.9
1991	Bal-A	10	9	.526	31	26	3	1	0	184	175	17	53	108	11.2	4.01	99	.253	.307	0	—	0	2	-1	1	0.1
1992	Bal-A	6	8	.429	23	20	0	0	1	115^2	140	16	44	51	14.5	5.84	67	.296	.358	0	—	0	-24	-25	-1	-2.4
Total	5	37	37	.500	121	109	8	5	1	703	700	73	255	350	12.3	4.19	92	.260	.326	0	—	0	-18	-26	1	-1.7

● **CARL MILES** Miles, Carl Thomas b: 3/22/18, Trenton, Mo. BB/TL, 5'11", 178 lbs. Deb: 6/08/40

YEAR	TM/L	W	L	PCT	G	GS	CG	SH	SV	IP	H	HR	BB	SO	RAT	ERA	ERA+	OAV	OOB	BH	AVG	PB	PR	/A	PD	TPI
1940	Phi-A	0	0	—	2	0	0	0	0	8	9	2	8	6	19.1	13.50	33	.281	.425	3	.750	2	-8	-8	-0	-0.5

● **JIM MILES** Miles, James Charlie b: 8/8/43, Grenada, Miss. BR/TR, 6'2", 210 lbs. Deb: 9/07/68

YEAR	TM/L	W	L	PCT	G	GS	CG	SH	SV	IP	H	HR	BB	SO	RAT	ERA	ERA+	OAV	OOB	BH	AVG	PB	PR	/A	PD	TPI
1968	Was-A	0	0	—	3	0	0	0	0	4^1	8	0	2	5	20.8	12.46	23	.421	.476	0	—	0	-5	-5	-0	-0.5
1969	Was-A	0	1	.000	10	1	0	0	0	20^1	19	2	15	15	16.8	6.20	56	.257	.409	1	.333	0	-6	-6	1	-0.5
Total	2	0	1	.000	13	1	0	0	0	24^2	27	2	17	20	17.5	7.30	46	.290	.421	1	.333	0	-10	-11	1	-1.0

● **SAM MILITELLO** Militello, Sam Salvatore b: 11/26/69, Tampa, Fla. BR/TR, 6'3", 200 lbs. Deb: 8/09/92

YEAR	TM/L	W	L	PCT	G	GS	CG	SH	SV	IP	H	HR	BB	SO	RAT	ERA	ERA+	OAV	OOB	BH	AVG	PB	PR	/A	PD	TPI
1992	NY-A	3	3	.500	9	9	0	0	0	60	43	6	32	42	11.6	3.45	117	.195	.302	0	—	0	3	4	-1	0.3

● **JOHNNY MILJUS** Miljus, John Kenneth "Jovo" or "Big Serb" b: 6/30/1895, Pittsburgh, Pa. d: 2/11/76, Poulson, Montana BR/TR, 6'1", 178 lbs. Deb: 10/02/15

YEAR	TM/L	W	L	PCT	G	GS	CG	SH	SV	IP	H	HR	BB	SO	RAT	ERA	ERA+	OAV	OOB	BH	AVG	PB	PR	/A	PD	TPI
1915	Pit-F	0	0	—	1	0	0	0	0	1	1	0	0	0	9.0	0.00	—	.250	.250	0	—	0	0	0	0	0.1
1917	Bro-N	0	1	.000	4	1	1	0	0	15	14	0	8	9	15.0	0.60	466	.250	.373	0	.000	-1	4	4	-0	0.3

YEAR	TM/L	W	L	PCT	G	GS	CG	SH	SV	IP	H	HR	BB	SO	RAT	ERA	ERA+	OAV	OOB	BH	AVG	PB	PR	/A	PD	TPI
1920	Bro-N	1	0	1.000	9	0	0	0	0	23^1	24	2	4	9	10.8	3.09	104	.267	.298	2	.333	1	0	0	1	0.2
1921	Bro-N	6	3	.667	28	9	3	0	1	93^2	115	1	27	37	13.8	4.23	92	.312	.362	5	.167	-2	-5	-4	2	-0.4
1927	*Pit-N	8	3	.727	19	6	3	2	0	75^2	62	0	17	24	9.4	1.90	216	.228	.273	5	.179	-1	17	19	2	2.0
1928	Pit-N	5	7	.417	21	10	3	0	1	69^2	90	2	33	26	16.3	5.30	77	.313	.389	8	.308	1	-10	-10	-0	-0.8
	Cle-A	1	4	.200	11	4	1	0	1	50^2	46	1	20	19	11.7	2.66	156	.243	.316	3	.200	-0	8	8	-0	0.8
1929	Cle-A	8	8	.500	34	15	4	0	2	128^1	174	10	64	42	16.9	5.19	86	.331	.406	11	.256	1	-13	-11	0	-0.9
Total	7	29	26	.527	127	45	15	2	5	457^1	526	16	173	166	14.0	3.92	104	.293	.359	34	.222	0	0	7	4	1.3

● BURT MILLER Miller, Burt b: Kalamazoo, Mich. Deb: 7/15/1897

YEAR	TM/L	W	L	PCT	G	GS	CG	SH	SV	IP	H	HR	BB	SO	RAT	ERA	ERA+	OAV	OOB	BH	AVG	PB	PR	/A	PD	TPI
1897	Lou-N	0	1	.000	4	1	1	0	0	17	32	0	3	3	18.5	7.94	54	.396	.418	1	.167	-1	-7	-7	0	-0.6

● DYAR MILLER Miller, Dyar K b: 5/29/46, Batesville, Ind. BR/TR, 6'1", 195 lbs. Deb: 6/09/75 C

YEAR	TM/L	W	L	PCT	G	GS	CG	SH	SV	IP	H	HR	BB	SO	RAT	ERA	ERA+	OAV	OOB	BH	AVG	PB	PR	/A	PD	TPI
1975	Bal-A	6	3	.667	30	0	0	0	8	46^1	32	3	16	33	9.3	2.72	129	.199	.271	0	—	0	5	4	0	0.6
1976	Bal-A	2	4	.333	49	0	0	0	7	88^2	79	5	36	37	11.8	2.94	111	.246	.324	0	—	0	6	3	-1	0.2
1977	Bal-A	2	2	.500	12	0	0	0	1	22^1	25	6	10	9	14.1	5.64	67	.278	.350	0	—	0	-4	-5	-0	-0.3
	Cal-A	4	4	.500	41	0	0	0	4	92^1	81	10	30	49	10.8	3.02	129	.242	.304	0	—	0	11	9	-1	1.0
	Yr	6	6	.500	53	0	0	0	5	114^2	106	16	40	58	11.5	3.53	110	.249	.314	0	—	0	7	5	-1	0.7
1978	Cal-A	6	2	.750	41	0	0	0	1	84^2	85	3	41	34	13.9	2.66	136	.264	.356	0	—	0	10	9	-2	0.8
1979	Cal-A	1	0	1.000	14	1	0	0	0	35^1	44	2	13	16	15.0	3.31	123	.319	.386	0	—	0	4	3	-1	0.4
	Tor-A	0	0	—	10	0	0	0	0	15^1	27	3	5	7	18.8	10.57	41	.391	.432	0	—	0	-11	-11	-0	-1.0
	Yr	1	0	1.000	24	1	0	0	0	50^2	71	5	18	23	15.8	5.51	75	.333	.385	0	—	0	-7	-8	-1	-0.6
1980	NY-N	1	2	.333	31	0	0	0	1	42	37	1	11	28	10.3	1.93	184	.242	.293	0	.000	-0	8	8	-1	0.7
1981	NY-N	1	0	1.000	23	0	0	0	0	38^1	49	2	15	22	15.3	3.29	106	.327	.392	1	.333	0	1	1	-1	0.0
Total	7	23	17	.575	251	1	0	0	22	465^1	459	35	177	235	12.5	3.23	113	.264	.335	1	.250	0	30	22	-7	2.4

● ELMER MILLER Miller, Elmer Joseph "Lefty" b: 4/17/03, Detroit, Mich. d: 1/8/87, Corona, Cal. BL/TL, 5'11", 189 lbs. Deb: 6/21/29 ♦

YEAR	TM/L	W	L	PCT	G	GS	CG	SH	SV	IP	H	HR	BB	SO	RAT	ERA	ERA+	OAV	OOB	BH	AVG	PB	PR	/A	PD	TPI
1929	Phi-N	0	1	.000	8	2	0	0	0	11^1	12	1	21	5	28.6	11.12	47	.279	.537	9	.237	0	-8	-7	-0	-0.6

● FRANK MILLER Miller, Frank Lee "Bullet" b: 5/13/1886, Allegan, Mich. d: 2/19/74, Allegan, Mich. BR/TR, 6', 188 lbs. Deb: 7/12/13

YEAR	TM/L	W	L	PCT	G	GS	CG	SH	SV	IP	H	HR	BB	SO	RAT	ERA	ERA+	OAV	OOB	BH	AVG	PB	PR	/A	PD	TPI
1913	Chi-A	0	1	.000	1	1	0	0	0	1^2	4	0	3	2	37.8	27.00	11	.571	.700	0	—	0	-4	-4	0	-0.4
1916	Pit-N	7	10	.412	30	20	10	2	1	173	135	4	49	88	9.9	2.29	117	.226	.292	7	.137	-1	6	8	-1	0.7
1917	Pit-N	10	19	.345	38	28	14	5	1	224	216	1	60	92	11.3	3.13	91	.251	.304	9	.118	-5	-11	-7	1	-1.3
1918	Pit-N	11	8	.579	23	23	14	2	0	170^1	152	1	37	47	10.4	2.38	121	.250	.301	6	.105	-4	7	9	-0	0.6
1919	Pit-N	13	12	.520	32	26	16	3	0	201^2	170	6	34	59	9.3	3.03	100	.234	.272	7	.106	-5	-3	-0	1	-0.5
1922	Bos-N	11	13	.458	31	23	14	2	1	200	213	7	60	65	12.4	3.51	114	.279	.333	8	.118	-5	13	11	1	0.7
1923	Bos-N	0	3	.000	8	6	0	0	1	39^1	54	2	11	6	15.6	4.58	87	.335	.389	1	.143	-0	-3	-3	-1	-0.3
Total	7	52	66	.441	163	127	68	14	4	1010	944	21	254	359	10.9	3.01	104	.253	.306	38	.117	-19	7	15	1	-0.5

● FRED MILLER Miller, Frederick Holman "Speedy" b: 6/28/1886, Fairfield, Ind. d: 5/2/53, Brookville, Ind. BL/TL, 6'2", 190 lbs. Deb: 7/08/10

YEAR	TM/L	W	L	PCT	G	GS	CG	SH	SV	IP	H	HR	BB	SO	RAT	ERA	ERA+	OAV	OOB	BH	AVG	PB	PR	/A	PD	TPI
1910	Bro-N	1	1	.500	6	2	0	0	0	21	25	1	13	2	17.6	4.71	64	.309	.423	2	.250	0	-4	-4	0	-0.3

● JAKE MILLER Miller, Jacob Walter b: 2/28/1898, Wagram, Ohio d: 8/20/75, Venice, Fla. BL/TL, 6'2", 170 lbs. Deb: 9/11/24 F

YEAR	TM/L	W	L	PCT	G	GS	CG	SH	SV	IP	H	HR	BB	SO	RAT	ERA	ERA+	OAV	OOB	BH	AVG	PB	PR	/A	PD	TPI
1924	Cle-A	0	1	.000	2	2	1	0	0	12	13	0	5	4	13.5	3.00	142	.265	.333	0	.000	-1	2	2	0	0.1
1925	Cle-A	10	13	.435	32	22	13	0	2	190^1	207	4	62	51	13.1	3.31	133	.279	.340	13	.183	-4	23	23	0	1.9
1926	Cle-A	7	4	.636	18	11	5	3	1	82^2	99	1	18	24	13.0	3.27	124	.307	.348	2	.083	-2	7	7	-1	0.4
1927	Cle-A	10	8	.556	34	23	11	0	0	185^1	189	4	48	53	11.8	3.21	131	.271	.324	8	.138	-4	19	21	1	1.7
1928	Cle-A	8	9	.471	25	24	8	0	0	158	203	6	43	37	14.3	4.44	93	.332	.381	7	.135	-4	-7	-5	1	-0.9
1929	Cle-A	14	12	.538	29	29	14	2	0	206	227	7	60	58	12.8	3.58	124	.279	.334	15	.200	-3	15	20	1	1.8
1930	Cle-A	4	4	.500	24	9	1	0	0	88^1	147	6	38	31	19.3	7.13	68	.373	.433	10	.303	1	-24	-23	2	-1.7
1931	Cle-A	2	1	.667	10	5	1	1	0	41^1	45	2	19	17	13.9	4.35	106	.273	.348	1	.077	-2	0	1	1	0.0
1933	Chi-A	5	6	.455	26	14	4	2	0	105^2	130	3	47	30	15.6	5.62	75	.297	.373	7	.189	-1	-16	-16	1	-1.5
Total	9	60	58	.508	200	139	58	8	3	1069^2	1260	33	340	305	13.8	4.09	106	.298	.355	63	.171	-19	19	30	6	1.8

● OX MILLER Miller, John Anthony b: 5/4/15, Gause, Tex. BR/TR, 6'1", 190 lbs. Deb: 8/07/43

YEAR	TM/L	W	L	PCT	G	GS	CG	SH	SV	IP	H	HR	BB	SO	RAT	ERA	ERA+	OAV	OOB	BH	AVG	PB	PR	/A	PD	TPI
1943	Was-A	0	0	—	3	0	0	0	0	6	10	1	5	1	22.5	10.50	31	.370	.469	0	.000	-0	-5	-5	1	-0.4
	StL-A	0	0	—	2	0	0	0	0	6	7	2	3	3	18.0	12.00	28	.304	.429	0	.000	-0	-6	-6	1	-0.5
	Yr	0	0	—	5	0	0	0	0	12	17	3	8	4	20.3	11.25	29	.340	.450	0	.000	-0	-11	-11	1	-0.9
1945	StL-A	2	1	.667	4	3	3	0	0	28^1	23	2	5	4	8.9	1.59	222	.219	.255	2	.182	-0	6	6	-1	0.5
1946	StL-A	1	3	.250	11	3	0	0	1	35^1	52	5	15	12	17.1	6.88	54	.338	.396	2	.286	1	-13	-12	1	-1.1
1947	Chi-N	1	2	.333	4	4	1	0	0	16	31	2	5	7	20.3	10.13	39	.397	.434	3	.429	2	-11	-11	-0	-0.8
Total	4	4	6	.400	24	10	4	0	1	91^2	123	12	33	27	15.5	6.38	57	.318	.374	7	.259	2	-29	-28	0	-2.3

● JOHN MILLER Miller, John Ernest b: 5/30/41, Baltimore, Md. BR/TR, 6'2", 210 lbs. Deb: 9/22/62

YEAR	TM/L	W	L	PCT	G	GS	CG	SH	SV	IP	H	HR	BB	SO	RAT	ERA	ERA+	OAV	OOB	BH	AVG	PB	PR	/A	PD	TPI
1962	Bal-A	1	1	.500	2	1	0	0	0	10	2	0	5	4	6.3	0.90	418	.065	.194	0	.000	-0	3	3	0	0.3
1963	Bal-A	1	1	.500	3	2	0	0	0	17	12	0	14	16	13.8	3.18	111	.194	.342	0	.000	-1	1	1	-0	0.0
1965	Bal-A	6	4	.600	16	16	1	0	0	93^1	75	4	58	71	12.9	3.18	109	.223	.338	3	.100	-1	3	3	0	0.3
1966	Bal-A	4	8	.333	23	16	0	0	0	100^2	92	15	58	81	13.4	4.74	70	.241	.342	4	.118	-1	-15	-16	1	-1.7
1967	Bal-A	0	0	—	2	0	0	0	0	6	7	1	3	6	18.0	7.50	42	.304	.429	0	—	0	-3	-3	0	-0.3
Total	5	12	14	.462	46	35	1	0	0	227	188	20	138	178	13.0	3.89	88	.225	.337	7	.096	-3	-10	-12	1	-1.4

● CYCLONE MILLER Miller, Joseph H. b: 9/24/1859, Springfield, Mass d: 10/13/16, New London, Conn. TL, 5'9.5", 165 lbs. Deb: 7/11/1884

YEAR	TM/L	W	L	PCT	G	GS	CG	SH	SV	IP	H	HR	BB	SO	RAT	ERA	ERA+	OAV	OOB	BH	AVG	PB	PR	/A	PD	TPI
1884	CP-U	1	0	1.000	1	1	1	0	0	9	4	0	0	13	4.0	1.00	302	.125	.125	1	.250	-0	2	2	1	0.3
	Pro-N	3	2	.600	6	5	2	0	0	34^2	36	0	11	12	12.2	2.08	136	.259	.313	1	.043	-3	3	3	-1	0.0
	Phi-N	0	1	.000	1	1	1	0	0	9	17	5	6	1	23.0	10.00	30	.386	.460	0	.000	-1	-7	-7	0	-0.5
	Yr	3	3	.500	7	6	3	0	0	43^2	53	5	17	13	14.4	3.71	77	.290	.350	1	.037	-3	-4	-4	-1	-0.5
1886	Phi-a	10	8	.556	19	19	19	1	0	169^2	158	6	59	99	11.7	2.97	118	.239	.305	9	.136	-1	9	10	1	0.9
Total	2	14	11	.560	27	26	23	1	0	222^1	215	11	76	125	11.9	3.04	110	.245	.308	11	.113	-5	8	8	1	0.7

● WHITEY MILLER Miller, Kenneth Albert b: 5/2/15, St.Louis, Mo. d: 4/3/91, St.Louis, Mo. BR/TR, 6'1", 195 lbs. Deb: 9/15/44

YEAR	TM/L	W	L	PCT	G	GS	CG	SH	SV	IP	H	HR	BB	SO	RAT	ERA	ERA+	OAV	OOB	BH	AVG	PB	PR	/A	PD	TPI
1944	NY-N	0	1	.000	4	0	0	0	0	5	1	0	4	2	9.0	0.00	—	.059	.238	0	.000	-0	2	2	0	0.2

● LARRY MILLER Miller, Larry Don b: 6/19/37, Topeka, Kan. BL/TL, 6', 195 lbs. Deb: 6/21/64

YEAR	TM/L	W	L	PCT	G	GS	CG	SH	SV	IP	H	HR	BB	SO	RAT	ERA	ERA+	OAV	OOB	BH	AVG	PB	PR	/A	PD	TPI
1964	LA-N	4	8	.333	16	14	1	0	0	79^2	87	1	28	50	13.2	4.18	78	.275	.338	7	.269	2	-6	-8	-1	-0.8
1965	NY-N	1	4	.200	28	5	0	0	0	57^1	66	6	25	36	14.4	5.02	70	.289	.362	2	.182	0	-9	-10	-0	-1.0
1966	NY-N	0	2	.000	4	1	0	0	0	8^1	9	3	4	7	14.0	7.56	48	.273	.351	1	.500	0	-4	-4	-0	-0.4
Total	3	5	14	.263	48	20	1	0	0	145^1	162	10	57	93	13.7	4.71	72	.281	.349	10	.256	2	-19	-21	-1	-2.2

● RED MILLER Miller, Leo Alphonso b: 2/11/1897, Philadelphia, Pa. d: 10/20/73, Orlando, Fla. BR/TR, 5'11", 195 lbs. Deb: 4/13/23

YEAR	TM/L	W	L	PCT	G	GS	CG	SH	SV	IP	H	HR	BB	SO	RAT	ERA	ERA+	OAV	OOB	BH	AVG	PB	PR	/A	PD	TPI
1923	Phi-N	0	0	—	1	0	0	0	0	1^2	6	0	1	0	37.8	32.40	14	.545	.583	0	.000	-0	-5	-5	-0	-0.4

● PAUL MILLER Miller, Paul Robert b: 4/27/65, Burlington, Wis. BR/TR, 6'5", 215 lbs. Deb: 7/30/91

YEAR	TM/L	W	L	PCT	G	GS	CG	SH	SV	IP	H	HR	BB	SO	RAT	ERA	ERA+	OAV	OOB	BH	AVG	PB	PR	/A	PD	TPI
1991	Pit-N	0	0	—	1	1	0	0	0	5	4	0	3	2	12.6	5.40	66	.222	.333	0	.000	-0	-1	-1	-0	-0.1
1992	Pit-N	1	0	1.000	6	0	0	0	0	11^1	11	0	1	5	9.5	2.38	143	.256	.273	0	.000	-0	1	1	-0	0.1
Total	2	1	0	1.000	7	1	0	0	0	16^1	15	0	4	7	10.5	3.31	105	.246	.292	0	.000	-1	0	0	-0	0.0

YEAR	TM/L	W	L	PCT	G	GS	CG	SH	SV	IP	H	HR	BB	SO	RAT	ERA	ERA+	OAV	OOB	BH	AVG	PB	PR	/A	PD	TPI
● **RALPH MILLER**	Miller, Ralph Darwin b: 3/15/1873, Cincinnati, Ohio d: 5/8/73, Cincinnati, Ohio BR/TR, 5'11", 170 lbs. Deb: 5/04/1898																									
1898	Bro-N	4	14	.222	23	21	16	0	0	151^2	161	4	86	43	15.4	5.34	67	.270	.374	12	.194	-1	-29	-30	3	-2.5
1899	Bal-N	1	3	.250	6	4	3	0	0	36	42	0	14	3	15.0	4.50	88	.291	.369	2	.182	1	-3	-2	-1	-0.1
Total	2	5	17	.227	29	25	19	0	0	187^2	203	4	100	46	15.3	5.18	71	.274	.373	14	.192	-0	-32	-32	2	-2.6
● **RALPH MILLER**	Miller, Ralph Henry "Moose" or "Lefty" b: 1/14/1899, Vinton, Iowa d: 2/18/67, White Bear Lake, Minn. BR/TL, 6'1.5", 190 lbs. Deb: 9/16/21 F																									
1921	Was-A	0	0	—	1	0	0	0	0	1	0	0	0	0	0.0	0.00	—	.000	.000	0	—	0	0	0	-0	0.0
● **RANDY MILLER**	Miller, Randall Scott b: 3/18/53, Oxnard, Cal. BR/TR, 6'1", 180 lbs. Deb: 9/07/77																									
1977	Bal-A	0	0	—	1	0	0	0	0	0^2	4	0	0	0	54.0	40.50	9	.800	.800	0	—	0	-3	-3	-0	-0.2
1978	Mon-N	0	1	.000	5	0	0	0	0	7	11	1	3	6	18.0	10.29	34	.393	.452	0	.000	-0	-5	-5	0	-0.5
Total	2	0	1	.000	6	0	0	0	0	7^2	15	1	3	6	21.1	12.91	27	.455	.500	0	.000	-0	-8	-8	0	-0.7
● **BOB MILLER**	Miller, Robert Gerald b: 7/15/35, Berwyn, Ill. BR/TL, 6'1", 185 lbs. Deb: 6/25/53																									
1953	Det-A	1	2	.333	13	1	0	0	0	36^1	43	2	21	9	16.1	5.94	68	.289	.380	1	.125	-1	-8	-8	0	-0.7
1954	Det-A	1	1	.500	32	1	0	0	1	69^2	62	1	26	27	11.4	2.45	150	.244	.314	2	.133	-0	10	10	-1	0.9
1955	Det-A	2	1	.667	7	3	1	0	0	25^1	26	4	12	11	13.5	2.49	154	.263	.342	2	.222	0	4	4	-0	0.4
1956	Det-A	0	2	.000	11	3	0	0	0	31^2	37	5	22	16	16.8	5.68	72	.308	.415	1	.143	0	-5	-6	-1	-0.6
1962	Cin-N	0	0	—	6	0	0	0	0	5^1	14	1	3	4	32.1	21.94	18	.538	.613	0	.000	-0	-11	-11	0	-1.0
	NY-N	2	2	.500	17	0	0	0	1	20^1	24	2	8	8	14.6	7.08	59	.312	.384	0	.000	-0	-7	-7	0	-0.6
	Yr	2	2	.500	23	0	0	0	1	25^2	38	3	11	12	17.5	10.17	41	.355	.420	0	.000	-0	-18	-17	0	-1.6
Total	5	6	8	.429	86	8	1	0	2	188^2	206	15	92	75	14.4	4.72	83	.284	.368	6	.146	-1	-17	-17	-1	-1.6
● **BOB MILLER**	Miller, Robert John b: 6/16/26, Detroit, Mich. BR/TR, 6'3", 190 lbs. Deb: 9/16/49																									
1949	Phi-N	0	0	—	3	0	0	0	0	2^2	2	0	2	0	13.5	0.00	—	.200	.333	0	—	0	1	1	0	0.1
1950	*Phi-N	11	6	.647	35	22	7	2	1	174	190	9	57	44	13.0	3.57	113	.277	.337	11	.180	-1	11	9	2	1.0
1951	Phi-N	2	1	.667	17	3	0	0	0	34^1	47	2	18	10	17.3	6.82	56	.331	.410	3	.429	1	-11	-11	-1	-1.1
1952	Phi-N	0	1	.000	3	1	0	0	0	9	13	2	1	2	14.0	6.00	61	.351	.368	0	.000	-0	-2	-2	0	-0.2
1953	Phi-N	8	9	.471	35	20	8	3	2	157^1	169	14	42	63	12.2	4.00	105	.271	.319	10	.182	-1	5	4	-1	0.2
1954	Phi-N	7	9	.438	30	16	5	0	0	150	176	14	39	42	13.1	4.56	89	.300	.347	8	.160	0	-8	-9	1	-0.7
1955	Phi-N	8	4	.667	40	0	0	0	1	89^2	80	6	28	28	10.9	2.41	165	.242	.304	5	.278	1	16	16	0	1.7
1956	Phi-N	3	6	.333	49	6	3	1	5	122^1	115	14	34	53	11.2	3.24	115	.248	.303	2	.091	-1	7	7	-0	0.5
1957	Phi-N	2	5	.286	32	1	0	0	6	60^1	61	4	17	12	11.8	2.69	142	.265	.319	2	.250	2	8	8	-1	0.9
1958	Phi-N	1	1	.500	17	0	0	0	0	22^1	36	7	9	9	18.1	11.69	34	.360	.413	0	.000	-0	-19	-19	-0	-1.9
Total	10	42	42	.500	261	69	23	6	15	822	889	72	247	263	12.6	3.96	101	.277	.332	41	.184	1	8	2	1	0.5
● **BOB MILLER**	Miller, Robert Lane b: 2/18/39, St.Louis, Mo. BR/TR, 6'1", 182 lbs. Deb: 6/26/57 C																									
1957	StL-N	0	0	—	5	0	0	0	0	9	13	2	5	7	18.0	7.00	57	.325	.400	0	—	0	-3	-3	0	-0.3
1959	StL-N	4	3	.571	11	10	3	0	0	70^2	66	2	21	43	11.2	3.31	128	.248	.306	5	.208	0	5	7	1	0.9
1960	StL-N	4	3	.571	15	7	0	0	0	52^2	53	2	17	33	12.1	3.42	120	.262	.323	2	.143	-1	2	4	0	0.4
1961	StL-N	1	3	.250	34	5	0	0	3	74^1	82	6	46	39	15.5	4.24	104	.290	.389	5	.357	2	-2	1	1	0.4
1962	NY-N	1	12	.077	33	21	1	0	0	143^2	146	20	62	91	13.4	4.89	86	.259	.339	5	.122	-1	-15	-11	2	-1.0
1963	LA-N	10	8	.556	42	23	2	0	1	187	171	7	65	125	11.5	2.89	105	.244	.311	4	.070	-2	8	3	5	0.6
1964	LA-N	7	7	.500	**74**	2	0	0	9	137^2	115	1	63	94	11.8	2.62	124	.226	.314	3	.158	1	14	10	2	1.3
1965	*LA-N	6	7	.462	61	1	0	0	9	103	82	9	26	77	9.7	2.97	110	.225	.282	0	.000	-1	7	3	2	0.4
1966	*LA-N	4	2	.667	46	0	0	0	5	84^1	70	5	29	58	10.7	2.77	119	.230	.299	1	.077	-1	8	5	-1	0.3
1967	LA-N	2	9	.182	52	4	0	0	0	85^2	88	9	27	32	12.4	4.31	72	.273	.335	1	.125	-0	-9	-12	1	-1.2
1968	Min-A	0	3	.000	45	0	0	0	2	72^1	65	1	24	41	11.7	2.74	113	.239	.312	1	.143	-0	2	3	1	0.4
1969	*Min-A	5	5	.500	48	11	1	0	3	119^1	118	9	32	57	11.3	3.02	121	.264	.313	0	.000	-3	8	8	1	0.7
1970	Cle-A	2	2	.500	15	2	0	0	1	28	35	1	15	15	16.1	4.18	95	.310	.391	1	.200	0	-1	-1	-1	-0.1
	Chi-A	4	6	.400	15	12	0	0	0	70	88	11	33	36	16.1	5.01	78	.315	.396	4	.174	0	-10	-9	2	-0.6
	Yr	6	8	.429	30	14	0	0	1	98	123	12	48	51	16.1	4.78	82	.313	.393	5	.179	1	-12	-9	1	-0.7
	Chi-N	0	0	—	7	1	0	0	2	9	6	3	6	4	12.0	5.00	90	.194	.324	0	—	0	-1	-0	0	0.0
1971	Chi-N	0	0	—	2	0	0	0	0	7	10	0	1	2	14.1	5.14	76	.357	.379	0	.000	-0	-1	-1	0	-0.1
	SD-N	7	3	.700	38	0	0	0	7	63^2	53	0	26	36	11.3	1.41	233	.227	.308	0	.000	-1	15	13	1	1.4
	*Pit-N	1	2	.333	16	0	0	0	3	28	20	1	13	13	10.6	1.29	263	.200	.292	0	.000	0	7	7	0	0.8
	Yr	8	5	.615	56	0	0	0	10	98^2	83	1	40	51	11.2	1.64	205	.229	.305	0	.000	-1	20	19	2	2.1
1972	*Pit-N	5	2	.714	36	0	0	0	3	54^1	54	3	24	18	13.1	2.65	125	.263	.343	0	.000	-0	5	4	-0	0.4
1973	SD-N	0	0	—	18	0	0	0	0	30^2	29	4	12	15	12.0	4.11	84	.244	.313	0	.000	-0	-2	-2	-1	-0.3
	NY-N	0	0	—	1	0	0	0	0	1	0	0	0	1	0.0	0.00	—	.000	.000	0	—	0	0	0	0	0.0
	Yr	0	0	—	19	0	0	0	0	31^2	29	4	12	16	11.7	3.98	87	.236	.304	0	.000	-0	-1	-2	-1	-0.3
	Det-A	4	2	.667	22	0	0	0	1	42	34	3	22	23	12.0	3.43	119	.230	.329	0	—	0	2	3	0	-0.1
1974	NY-N	2	2	.500	58	0	0	0	2	78	89	2	39	35	14.9	3.58	100	.296	.378	1	.111	-0	0	-0	0	0.0
Total	17	69	81	.460	694	99	7	0	51	1551^1	1487	101	608	895	12.3	3.37	105	.255	.328	33	.110	-8	38	31	18	4.3
● **BOB MILLER**	Miller, Robert W. b: 1862, Deb: 8/30/1890																									
1890	Roc-a	3	7	.300	13	12	11	0	1	92^1	89	2	26	20	11.5	4.29	83	.246	.301	6	.150	-1	-4	-7	0	-0.7
1891	Was-a	2	5	.286	7	7	3	0	0	42	53	3	24	13	17.8	4.29	87	.298	.399	2	.111	-2	-3	-3	1	-0.3
Total	2	5	12	.294	20	19	14	0	1	134^1	142	5	50	33	13.5	4.29	84	.263	.335	8	.138	-3	-7	-10	1	-1.0
● **ROGER MILLER**	Miller, Roger Wesley b: 8/1/54, Connellsville, Pa. BR/TR, 6'3", 200 lbs. Deb: 9/08/74																									
1974	Mil-A	0	0	—	2	0	0	0	0	2^1	3	1	0	2	15.4	11.57	31	.300	.364	0	—	0	-2	-2	-0	-0.2
● **RONNIE MILLER**	Miller, Roland Arthur b: 8/28/18, Mason City, Iowa BB/TR, 5'11", 167 lbs. Deb: 9/10/41																									
1941	Was-A	0	0	—	1	0	0	0	0	2	2	0	1	0	13.5	4.50	90	.333	.429	0	—	0	-0	-0	-0	0.0
● **ROSCOE MILLER**	Miller, Roscoe Clyde "Roxy" or "Rubberlegs" b: 12/2/1876, Greenville, Ind. d: 4/18/13, Corydon, Ind. BR/TR, 6'2", 190 lbs. Deb: 4/25/01																									
1901	Det-A	23	13	.639	38	36	35	3	1	332	339	1	98	79	12.2	2.95	130	.261	.320	27	.208	0	26	33	4	3.6
1902	Det-A	6	12	.333	20	18	15	1	1	148^2	158	3	57	39	13.6	3.69	99	.273	.347	11	.183	-2	-2	-1	1	-0.1
	NY-N	1	8	.111	10	9	7	0	0	72^2	77	1	11	15	11.5	4.58	61	.272	.310	1	.048	-3	-15	-14	-1	-1.7
1903	NY-N	2	5	.286	15	8	6	0	**3**	85	101	1	24	30	13.3	4.13	81	.302	.351	5	.161	-1	-8	-7	-1	-0.9
1904	Pit-N	7	7	.500	19	17	11	2	0	134^1	133	4	39	35	11.8	3.35	82	.256	.313	2	.043	-4	-9	-9	-1	-1.4
Total	4	39	45	.464	102	88	74	6	5	772^2	808	10	229	198	12.5	3.45	100	.268	.326	46	.160	-9	-7	1	2	-0.5
● **RUSS MILLER**	Miller, Russell Lewis b: 3/25/1900, Etna, Ohio d: 4/30/62, Bucyrus, Ohio BR/TR, 5'11", 165 lbs. Deb: 9/24/27 F																									
1927	Phi-N	1	1	.500	2	2	1	0	0	15^1	21	2	3	4	14.7	5.28	78	.339	.379	1	.333	0	-2	-2	-0	-0.2
1928	Phi-N	0	12	.000	33	12	1	0	1	108	137	14	34	19	14.3	5.42	79	.315	.365	4	.148	-1	-17	-14	0	-1.4
Total	2	1	13	.071	35	14	2	0	1	123^1	158	16	37	23	14.3	5.40	79	.318	.366	5	.167	-1	-19	-16	0	-1.6
● **STU MILLER**	Miller, Stuart Leonard b: 12/26/27, Northampton, Mass. BR/TR, 5'11.5", 165 lbs. Deb: 8/12/52																									
1952	StL-N	6	3	.667	12	11	6	2	0	88	63	3	26	64	9.3	2.05	182	.197	.262	3	.120	-1	16	16	3	2.0
1953	StL-N	7	8	.467	40	18	8	2	4	137^2	161	19	47	79	13.7	5.56	77	.293	.351	8	.186	1	-19	-20	5	-1.4
1954	StL-N	2	3	.400	19	4	0	0	2	46^2	55	5	29	22	16.8	5.79	71	.307	.412	4	.308	1	-9	-9	2	-0.5
1956	StL-N	0	1	.000	3	0	0	0	1	7^1	12	3	5	5	20.9	4.91	77	.387	.472	0	.000	-0	-1	-1	0	-0.1
	Phi-N	5	8	.385	24	15	2	0	0	106^2	109	16	51	55	13.8	4.47	83	.263	.349	4	.160	2	-8	-9	0	-0.7

YEAR	TM/L	W	L	PCT	G	GS	CG	SH	SV	IP	H	HR	BB	SO	RAT	ERA	ERA+	OAV	OOB	BH	AVG	PB	PR	/A	PD	TPI
	Yr	5	9	.357	27	15	2	0	1	114	121	19	56	60	14.3	4.50	83	.271	.357	4	.154	2	-9	-10	0	-0.8
1957	NY-N	7	9	.438	38	13	0	0	1	124	110	15	45	60	11.5	3.63	108	.242	.315	2	.057	-3	3	4	2	0.2
1958	SF-N	6	9	.400	41	20	4	1	0	182	160	16	49	119	10.4	**2.47**	**154**	.233	**.286**	6	.120	-0	30	27	1	3.0
1959	SF-N	8	7	.533	59	9	2	0	8	167^{2}	164	15	57	95	12.1	2.84	134	.260	.326	2	.044	-3	**21**	18	3	1.8
1960	SF-N	7	6	.538	47	3	2	0	2	101^{2}	100	9	31	65	11.9	3.90	89	.256	.315	5	.200	1	-2	-5	2	-0.3
1961	SF-N★	14	5	.737	63	0	0	0	**17**	122	95	4	37	89	9.8	2.66	143	.215	.277	4	.200	1	**19**	16	2	1.9
1962	*SF-N	5	8	.385	59	0	0	0	19	107	107	8	42	78	12.7	4.12	92	.268	.341	2	.125	-0	-2	-4	0	-0.4
1963	Bal-A	5	8	.385	**71**	0	0	0	**27**	112^{1}	93	5	53	114	11.9	2.24	157	.232	.326	5	.313	2	17	16	2	2.1
1964	Bal-A	7	7	.500	66	0	0	0	23	97	77	7	34	87	10.6	3.06	117	.222	.297	1	.111	-0	6	5	1	0.6
1965	Bal-A	14	7	.667	67	0	0	0	24	119^{1}	87	5	32	104	9.1	1.89	184	.207	.265	1	.063	-1	21	21	1	2.3
1966	Bal-A	9	4	.692	51	0	0	0	18	92	65	5	22	67	8.9	2.25	148	.201	.260	2	.105	-1	12	11	-1	1.0
1967	Bal-A	3	10	.231	42	0	0	0	8	81^{1}	63	5	36	60	11.1	2.55	124	.220	.309	0	.000	-1	6	5	-0	0.5
1968	Atl-N	0	0	—	2	0	0	0	0	1^{1}	1	0	4	1	33.8	27.00	11	.500	.833	0	—	0	-4	-4	0	-0.3
Total	16	105	103	.505	704	93	24	5	154	1694	1522	140	600	1164	11.5	3.24	115	.242	.312	49	.133	-2	107	90	22	11.7

● WALT MILLER Miller, Walter W. b: 10/19/1884, Gas City, Ind. d: 3/1/56, Marion, Ind. BR/TR, 5′11.5″, 180 lbs. Deb: 9/20/11

YEAR	TM/L	W	L	PCT	G	GS	CG	SH	SV	IP	H	HR	BB	SO	RAT	ERA	ERA+	OAV	OOB	BH	AVG	PB	PR	/A	PD	TPI
1911	Bro-N	0	1	.000	3	2	0	0	0	11	16	0	6	0	18.8	6.55	51	.356	.442	0	.000	-1	-4	-4	-0	-0.4

● BILL MILLER Miller, William Francis "Wild Bill" b: 4/12/10, Hannibal, Mo. d: 2/26/82, Hannibal, Mo. BR/TR, 6′, 180 lbs. Deb: 10/02/37

YEAR	TM/L	W	L	PCT	G	GS	CG	SH	SV	IP	H	HR	BB	SO	RAT	ERA	ERA+	OAV	OOB	BH	AVG	PB	PR	/A	PD	TPI
1937	StL-A	0	1	.000	1	1	0	0	0	4	7	1	4	1	27.0	13.50	36	.389	.522	0	.000	-0	-4	-4	0	-0.3

● BILL MILLER Miller, William Paul "Lefty" or "Hooks" b: 7/26/27, Minersville, Pa. BL/TL, 6′, 175 lbs. Deb: 4/20/52

YEAR	TM/L	W	L	PCT	G	GS	CG	SH	SV	IP	H	HR	BB	SO	RAT	ERA	ERA+	OAV	OOB	BH	AVG	PB	PR	/A	PD	TPI
1952	NY-A	4	6	.400	21	13	5	2	0	88	78	4	49	45	13.2	3.48	96	.241	.345	6	.214	1	2	-2	-0	-0.1
1953	NY-A	2	1	.667	13	3	0	0	1	34	46	3	19	17	17.5	4.76	77	.324	.407	2	.200	0	-3	-4	1	-0.3
1954	NY-A	0	1	.000	2	1	0	0	0	5^{2}	9	0	1	6	15.9	6.35	54	.375	.400	0	.000	-0	-2	-2	-0	-0.2
1955	Bal-A	0	1	.000	5	1	0	0	0	4	3	0	10	4	29.3	13.50	28	.200	.520	1	1.000	0	-4	-4	0	-0.4
Total	4	6	9	.400	41	18	5	2	1	131^{2}	136	7	79	72	14.9	4.24	81	.270	.372	9	.225	1	-7	-12	0	-1.0

● JOHN MILLIGAN Milligan, John Alexander b: 1/22/04, Schuylerville, N.Y. d: 5/15/72, Fort Pierce, Fla. BR/TL, 5′10″, 172 lbs. Deb: 8/11/28

YEAR	TM/L	W	L	PCT	G	GS	CG	SH	SV	IP	H	HR	BB	SO	RAT	ERA	ERA+	OAV	OOB	BH	AVG	PB	PR	/A	PD	TPI
1928	Phi-N	2	5	.286	13	7	3	0	0	68	69	2	32	22	13.5	4.37	98	.274	.358	1	.050	-2	-3	-1	1	-0.2
1929	Phi-N	0	1	.000	8	3	0	0	0	9^{2}	29	0	10	2	38.2	16.76	31	.527	.612	1	.333	0	-13	-12	0	-1.0
1930	Phi-N	1	2	.333	9	2	1	0	0	28^{1}	26	0	21	7	15.6	3.18	172	.255	.392	1	.111	-1	6	7	1	0.7
1931	Phi-N	0	0	—	3	0	0	0	0	8	11	0	4	6	18.0	3.38	126	.324	.410	0	.000	-0	0	1	-0	0.0
1934	Was-A	0	0	—	2	0	0	0	0	2^{2}	6	0	0	1	20.3	10.13	43	.500	.500	0	—	0	-2	-2	0	-0.1
Total	5	3	8	.273	35	12	4	0	0	116^{2}	141	2	67	38	16.5	5.17	90	.310	.405	3	.088	-4	-11	-7	2	-0.6

● BILLY MILLIGAN Milligan, William Joseph b: 8/19/1878, Buffalo, N.Y. d: 10/14/28, Buffalo, N.Y. BR/TL, 5′7″, Deb: 4/30/01

YEAR	TM/L	W	L	PCT	G	GS	CG	SH	SV	IP	H	HR	BB	SO	RAT	ERA	ERA+	OAV	OOB	BH	AVG	PB	PR	/A	PD	TPI
1901	Phi-A	0	3	.000	6	3	2	0	0	33	43	1	14	5	16.1	4.36	86	.311	.383	5	.333	2	-3	-2	-0	0.0
1904	NY-N	0	1	.000	5	1	1	0	2	25	36	2	4	6	14.8	5.40	51	.310	.339	1	.111	0	-7	-7	-0	-0.7
Total	2	0	4	.000	11	4	3	0	2	58	79	3	18	11	15.5	4.81	69	.311	.363	6	.250	2	-10	-10	-1	-0.7

● BOB MILLIKEN Milliken, Robert Fogle "Bobo" b: 8/25/26, Majorsville, W.Va. BR/TR, 6′, 195 lbs. Deb: 4/22/53 C

YEAR	TM/L	W	L	PCT	G	GS	CG	SH	SV	IP	H	HR	BB	SO	RAT	ERA	ERA+	OAV	OOB	BH	AVG	PB	PR	/A	PD	TPI
1953	*Bro-N	8	4	.667	37	10	3	0	2	117^{2}	94	13	42	65	10.4	3.37	127	.214	.283	4	.118	-1	12	12	-2	0.8
1954	Bro-N	5	2	.714	24	3	0	0	2	62^{2}	58	12	18	25	11.2	4.02	102	.246	.305	3	.176	-0	0	0	-1	-0.1
Total	2	13	6	.684	61	13	3	0	4	180^{1}	152	25	60	90	10.7	3.59	117	.225	.290	7	.137	-2	12	12	-3	0.7

● ALAN MILLS Mills, Alan Bernard b: 10/18/66, Lakeland, Fla. BR/TR, 6′1″, 190 lbs. Deb: 4/14/90

YEAR	TM/L	W	L	PCT	G	GS	CG	SH	SV	IP	H	HR	BB	SO	RAT	ERA	ERA+	OAV	OOB	BH	AVG	PB	PR	/A	PD	TPI
1990	NY-A	1	5	.167	36	0	0	0	0	41^{2}	48	4	33	24	17.7	4.10	97	.298	.421	0	—	0	-1	-1	1	0.0
1991	NY-A	1	1	.500	6	2	0	0	0	16^{1}	16	1	8	11	13.2	4.41	94	.254	.338	0	—	0	-1	-0	1	0.0
1992	Bal-A	10	4	.714	35	3	0	0	2	103^{1}	78	5	54	60	11.6	2.61	149	.215	.319	0	—	0	15	15	1	1.7
Total	3	12	10	.545	77	5	0	0	2	161^{1}	142	10	95	95	13.3	3.18	124	.242	.350	0	—	0	14	14	2	1.7

● ART MILLS Mills, Arthur Grant b: 3/2/03, Utica, N.Y. d: 7/23/75, Utica, N.Y. BR/TR, 5′10″, 155 lbs. Deb: 4/16/27 FC

YEAR	TM/L	W	L	PCT	G	GS	CG	SH	SV	IP	H	HR	BB	SO	RAT	ERA	ERA+	OAV	OOB	BH	AVG	PB	PR	/A	PD	TPI
1927	Bos-N	0	1	.000	15	1	0	0	0	37^{2}	41	1	18	7	14.8	3.82	97	.287	.378	0	.000	-1	0	-0	1	0.0
1928	Bos-N	0	0	—	4	0	0	0	0	7^{2}	17	3	8	0	31.7	12.91	30	.472	.587	0	.000	-0	-8	-8	-0	-0.7
Total	2	0	1	.000	19	1	0	0	0	45^{1}	58	4	26	7	17.7	5.36	70	.324	.424	0	.000	-1	-7	-8	1	-0.7

● LEFTY MILLS Mills, Howard Robinson b: 5/12/10, Dedham, Mass. d: 9/23/82, Riverside, Cal. BL/TL, 6′1″, 187 lbs. Deb: 6/10/34

YEAR	TM/L	W	L	PCT	G	GS	CG	SH	SV	IP	H	HR	BB	SO	RAT	ERA	ERA+	OAV	OOB	BH	AVG	PB	PR	/A	PD	TPI
1934	StL-A	0	0	—	4	0	0	0	0	8^{2}	10	0	11	2	21.8	4.15	120	.303	.477	1	.333	0	0	1	-0	0.1
1937	StL-A	1	1	.500	2	2	1	0	0	12^{2}	16	1	10	10	18.5	6.39	75	.286	.394	0	.000	-1	-2	-2	0	-0.3
1938	StL-A	10	12	.455	30	27	15	1	0	210^{1}	216	16	116	134	14.5	5.31	94	.262	.358	6	.091	-3	-12	-8	-2	-1.1
1939	StL-A	4	11	.267	34	14	4	0	2	144^{1}	147	16	113	103	16.7	6.55	74	.264	.395	11	.234	1	-31	-27	-1	-2.4
1940	StL-A	0	6	.000	26	5	1	0	0	59	64	7	52	18	18.2	7.78	59	.275	.413	2	.154	-0	-22	-21	0	-1.9
Total	5	15	30	.333	96	48	21	1	2	435	453	40	302	267	16.0	6.06	81	.266	.382	20	.149	-3	-67	-57	-3	-5.6

● DICK MILLS Mills, Richard Alan b: 1/29/45, Boston, Mass. BR/TR, 6′3″, 195 lbs. Deb: 9/07/70

YEAR	TM/L	W	L	PCT	G	GS	CG	SH	SV	IP	H	HR	BB	SO	RAT	ERA	ERA+	OAV	OOB	BH	AVG	PB	PR	/A	PD	TPI
1970	Bos-A	0	0	—	2	0	0	0	0	3^{2}	6	0	3	3	24.5	2.45	161	.353	.476	0	—	0	1	1	0	0.1

● WILLIE MILLS Mills, William Grant "Wee Willie" b: 8/15/1877, Schenevus, N.Y. d: 7/5/14, Norwood, N.Y. BR/TR, 5′7″, 150 lbs. Deb: 7/13/01 F

YEAR	TM/L	W	L	PCT	G	GS	CG	SH	SV	IP	H	HR	BB	SO	RAT	ERA	ERA+	OAV	OOB	BH	AVG	PB	PR	/A	PD	TPI
1901	NY-N	0	2	.000	2	2	2	0	0	16	21	2	4	3	14.6	8.44	39	.314	.362	1	.167	0	-9	-9	-0	-0.8

● AL MILNAR Milnar, Albert Joseph "Happy" b: 12/26/13, Cleveland, Ohio BL/TL, 6′2″, 195 lbs. Deb: 4/30/36

YEAR	TM/L	W	L	PCT	G	GS	CG	SH	SV	IP	H	HR	BB	SO	RAT	ERA	ERA+	OAV	OOB	BH	AVG	PB	PR	/A	PD	TPI
1936	Cle-A	1	2	.333	4	3	1	0	0	22	26	0	18	9	18.0	7.36	68	.286	.404	3	.300	0	-6	-6	0	-0.4
1938	Cle-A	3	1	.750	23	5	2	0	1	68^{1}	90	5	26	29	15.3	5.00	93	.320	.378	4	.154	-0	-2	-3	0	-0.3
1939	Cle-A	14	12	.538	37	26	12	2	3	209	212	11	99	76	13.4	3.79	116	.264	.345	20	.253	3	19	14	0	1.7
1940	Cle-A☆	18	10	.643	37	33	15	**4**	3	242^{1}	242	14	99	99	12.7	3.27	129	.257	.328	17	.181	-1	30	26	-5	1.9
1941	Cle-A	12	19	.387	35	30	9	1	0	229^{1}	236	9	116	82	13.9	4.36	90	.266	.352	14	.171	2	-5	-11	-3	-1.0
1942	Cle-A	6	8	.429	28	19	8	2	0	157	146	3	85	35	13.5	4.13	84	.251	.350	12	.171	2	-8	-12	1	-0.9
1943	Cle-A	1	3	.250	16	6	0	0	0	39	51	0	35	12	20.1	8.08	38	.329	.455	4	.211	0	-21	-22	0	-2.1
	StL-A	1	2	.333	3	2	1	0	0	14^{2}	23	0	9	7	19.6	5.52	60	.354	.432	2	.333	1	-4	-4	0	-0.2
	Yr	2	5	.286	19	8	1	0	0	53^{2}	74	0	44	19	19.8	7.38	43	.335	.445	6	.240	1	-24	-25	0	-2.3
1946	StL-A	1	1	.500	4	2	1	1	0	14^{2}	15	1	6	1	12.9	2.45	152	.278	.350	3	.750	1	2	2	-0	0.4
	Phi-N	0	0	—	1	1	0	0	0	0	2	0	2	0	—	∞	—	1.000	1.000	0	—	0	-4	-4	0	-0.3
Total	8	57	58	.496	188	127	49	10	7	996^{1}	1043	43	495	350	14.0	4.22	96	.270	.354	79	.203	9	2	-18	-6	-1.2

● GEORGE MILSTEAD Milstead, George Earl "Cowboy" b: 6/26/03, Cleburne, Tex. d: 8/9/77, Cleburne, Tex. BL/TL, 5′10″, 144 lbs. Deb: 6/27/24

YEAR	TM/L	W	L	PCT	G	GS	CG	SH	SV	IP	H	HR	BB	SO	RAT	ERA	ERA+	OAV	OOB	BH	AVG	PB	PR	/A	PD	TPI
1924	Chi-N	1	1	.500	13	2	1	0	0	29^{2}	41	3	13	6	16.7	6.07	64	.328	.396	1	.167	0	-7	-7	0	-0.6
1925	Chi-N	1	1	.500	5	3	1	0	0	21	26	0	8	7	14.6	3.00	144	.310	.370	0	.000	-1	3	3	0	0.2
1926	Chi-N	1	5	.167	18	4	0	0	2	55^{1}	63	0	24	14	14.3	3.58	107	.309	.384	1	.053	-2	2	2	2	0.2
Total	3	3	7	.300	36	9	2	0	2	106	130	3	45	27	15.0	4.16	95	.315	.385	2	.063	-3	-3	-2	3	-0.2

● LARRY MILTON Milton, Samuel Lawrence "Tug" b: 5/4/1879, Owensboro, Ky. d: 5/16/42, Hannibal, Mo. TR , Deb: 5/07/03

YEAR	TM/L	W	L	PCT	G	GS	CG	SH	SV	IP	H	HR	BB	SO	RAT	ERA	ERA+	OAV	OOB	BH	AVG	PB	PR	/A	PD	TPI
1903	StL-N	0	0	—	1	0	0	0	0	4	3	0	1	0	9.0	2.25	145	.200	.250	1	.500	0	0	0	0	0.1

● COTTON MINAHAN Minahan, Edmund Joseph b: 12/10/1882, Springfield, Ohio d: 5/20/58, E.Orange, N.J. BR/TR, 6′, 190 lbs. Deb: 4/21/07

YEAR	TM/L	W	L	PCT	G	GS	CG	SH	SV	IP	H	HR	BB	SO	RAT	ERA	ERA+	OAV	OOB	BH	AVG	PB	PR	/A	PD	TPI
1907	Cin-N	0	2	.000	2	2	1	0	0	14	12	0	13	4	16.7	1.29	202	.261	.433	0	.000	-1	2	2	-1	0.1

YEAR	TM/L	W	L	PCT	G	GS	CG	SH	SV	IP	H	HR	BB	SO	RAT	ERA	ERA+	OAV	OOB	BH	AVG	PB	PR	/A	PD	TPI
● **RUDY MINARCIN**	Minarcin, Rudy Anthony "Buster" b: 3/25/30, N.Vandergrift, Pa. BR/TR, 6', 195 lbs. Deb: 4/11/55																									
1955	Cin-N	5	9	.357	41	12	3	1	1	115^2	116	17	51	45	13.2	4.90	86	.261	.341	5	.179	-1	-11	-9	2	-0.7
1956	Bos-A	1	0	1.000	3	1	0	0	0	9^2	9	2	8	5	16.8	2.79	165	.250	.400	1	.500	1	1	2	0	0.3
1957	Bos-A	0	0	—	26	0	0	0	2	44^2	44	5	30	20	15.1	4.43	90	.267	.383	0	.000	0	-3	-2	-0	-0.2
Total	3	6	9	.400	70	13	3	1	3	170	169	24	89	70	13.9	4.66	90	.262	.356	6	.188	0	-13	-9	2	-0.6
● **RAY MINER**	Miner, Raymond Theadore "Lefty" b: 4/4/1897, Glens Falls, N.Y. d: 9/15/63, Glenridge, N.Y. BR/TL, 5'11", 160 lbs. Deb: 9/15/21																									
1921	Phi-A	0	0	—	1	0	0	0	0	1	2	0	3	0	45.0	36.00	12	.400	.625	0	—	0	-4	-4	-0	-0.3
● **CRAIG MINETTO**	Minetto, Craig Stephen b: 4/25/54, Stockton, Cal. BL/TL, 6', 185 lbs. Deb: 7/04/78																									
1978	Oak-A	0	0	—	4	1	0	0	0	12	13	1	7	3	16.5	3.75	97	.283	.400	0	—	0	0	-0	-0	0.0
1979	Oak-A	1	5	.167	36	13	0	0	0	118^1	131	16	58	64	14.6	5.55	73	.282	.365	0	—	0	-18	-20	-2	-1.7
1980	Oak-A	0	2	.000	7	1	0	0	1	8	11	2	3	5	15.8	7.88	48	.324	.378	0	—	0	-3	-4	-0	0.0
1981	Oak-A	0	0	—	8	0	0	0	0	6^2	7	0	4	4	16.2	2.70	129	.280	.400	0	—	0	1	1	-0	0.2
Total	4	1	7	.125	55	15	0	0	1	145	162	19	72	76	14.9	5.40	73	.284	.370	0	—	0	-20	-23	-2	-1.5
● **STEVE MINGORI**	Mingori, Stephen Bernard b: 2/29/44, Kansas City, Mo. BL/TL, 5'10", 170 lbs. Deb: 8/05/70																									
1970	Cle-A	1	0	1.000	21	0	0	0	1	20^1	17	2	12	16	13.3	2.66	149	.227	.341	0	.000	-0	2	3	0	0.3
1971	Cle-A	1	2	.333	54	0	0	0	4	56^2	31	2	24	45	8.9	1.43	268	.166	.264	1	.500	0	13	15	1	1.8
1972	Cle-A	0	6	.000	41	0	0	0	10	57	67	4	36	47	16.6	3.95	81	.293	.393	1	.125	-0	-6	-5	1	-0.5
1973	Cle-A	0	0	—	5	0	0	0	0	11^2	10	3	10	4	15.4	6.17	64	.233	.377	0	—	0	-3	-3	1	-0.3
	KC-A	3	3	.500	19	1	0	0	1	56^1	59	6	23	46	13.6	3.04	135	.267	.344	0	—	0	5	7	-0	0.2
	Yr	3	3	.500	24	1	0	0	1	68	69	9	33	50	13.9	3.57	114	.261	.350	0	—	0	2	4	1	-0.1
1974	KC-A	2	3	.400	36	0	0	0	2	67^1	53	4	23	43	10.4	2.81	136	.212	.284	0	—	0	6	8	2	0.8
1975	KC-A	0	3	.000	36	0	0	0	2	50^1	42	2	20	25	11.3	2.50	154	.226	.304	0	.000	0	7	8	0	0.8
1976	*KC-A	5	5	.500	55	0	0	0	10	85^1	73	3	25	38	10.7	2.32	151	.238	.301	0	—	0	11	11	3	1.5
1977	*KC-A	2	4	.333	43	0	0	0	4	64	59	4	19	19	11.1	3.09	130	.254	.313	0	—	0	7	7	1	0.7
1978	*KC-A	1	4	.200	45	0	0	0	7	69	64	5	16	28	10.8	2.74	140	.242	.292	0	—	0	8	8	0	0.9
1979	KC-A	3	3	.500	30	1	0	0	1	46^2	69	10	17	18	16.8	5.79	74	.348	.403	0	—	0	-8	-8	-1	-0.9
Total	10	18	33	.353	385	2	0	0	42	584^2	544	45	225	329	12.1	3.03	126	.248	.323	2	.167	0	43	51	7	5.3
● **PAUL MINNER**	Minner, Paul Edison "Lefty" b: 7/30/23, New Wilmington, Pa. BL/TL, 6'5", 210 lbs. Deb: 9/12/46																									
1946	Bro-N	0	1	.000	3	0	0	0	0	4	6	1	3	3	20.3	6.75	50	.333	.429	0	—	0	-1	-1	-0	-0.2
1948	Bro-N	4	3	.571	28	2	0	0	1	62^2	61	5	26	23	12.5	2.44	164	.257	.331	4	.190	1	11	11	0	1.3
1949	*Bro-N	3	1	.750	27	1	0	0	2	47^1	49	7	18	17	12.9	3.80	108	.272	.342	3	.214	-0	1	2	0	0.2
1950	Chi-N	8	13	.381	39	24	9	1	4	190^1	217	18	72	99	13.7	4.11	102	.287	.350	14	.215	3	1	2	3	0.7
1951	Chi-N	6	17	.261	33	28	14	3	1	201^2	219	20	64	68	12.6	3.79	108	.277	.331	18	.254	5	4	7	3	1.6
1952	Chi-N	14	9	.609	28	27	12	2	0	180^2	180	13	54	61	11.7	3.74	103	.258	.312	15	.234	6	-0	2	2	1.0
1953	Chi-N	12	15	.444	31	27	9	2	1	201	227	15	40	64	12.1	4.21	106	.283	.320	15	.221	2	2	5	4	1.1
1954	Chi-N	11	11	.500	32	29	12	0	1	218	236	19	50	79	11.8	3.96	106	.280	.321	13	.171	3	3	6	1	1.0
1955	Chi-N	9	9	.500	22	22	7	1	0	157^2	173	15	47	53	12.6	3.48	117	.283	.335	13	.232	2	10	11	2	1.5
1956	Chi-N	2	5	.286	10	9	1	0	0	47	60	9	19	14	15.5	6.89	55	.324	.393	3	.250	2	-16	-16	0	-1.4
Total	10	69	84	.451	253	169	64	9	10	1310^1	1428	122	393	481	12.6	3.94	105	.279	.332	98	.219	23	12	27	15	6.8
● **DON MINNICK**	Minnick, Donald Athey b: 4/14/31, Lynchburg, Va. BR/TR, 6'3", 195 lbs. Deb: 9/23/57																									
1957	Was-A	0	1	.000	2	1	0	0	0	9^1	14	1	2	7	15.4	4.82	81	.341	.372	0	.000	-0	-1	-1	-0	-0.1
● **BLAS MINOR**	Minor, Blas b: 3/20/66, Merced, Cal. BR/TR, 6'3", 195 lbs. Deb: 7/28/92																									
1992	Pit-N	0	0	—	1	0	0	0	0	2	3	0	0	0	13.5	4.50	76	.333	.333	0	—	0	-0	-0	0	0.0
● **JIM MINSHALL**	Minshall, James Edward b: 7/4/47, Covington, Ky. BR/TR, 6'6", 215 lbs. Deb: 9/14/74																									
1974	Pit-N	0	1	.000	5	0	0	0	0	4^1	1	0	2	3	6.2	0.00	—	.083	.214	0	—	0	2	2	-0	0.2
1975	Pit-N	0	0	—	1	0	0	0	0	1	0	0	2	2	18.0	0.00	—	.000	.400	0	—	0	0	0	0	0.0
Total	2	0	1	.000	6	0	0	0	0	5^1	1	0	4	5	8.4	0.00	—	.067	.263	0	—	0	2	2	-0	0.2
● **GREG MINTON**	Minton, Gregory Brian b: 7/29/51, Lubbock, Tex. BB/TR, 6'2", 190 lbs. Deb: 9/07/75																									
1975	SF-N	1	1	.500	4	2	0	0	0	17	19	1	11	6	16.4	6.88	55	.288	.397	0	.000	-1	-6	-6	1	-0.6
1976	SF-N	0	3	.000	10	2	0	0	0	25^2	32	0	12	7	15.8	4.91	74	.317	.395	1	.200	-0	-4	-4	-0	-0.4
1977	SF-N	1	1	.500	2	2	0	0	0	14	14	0	4	5	11.6	4.50	87	.264	.316	1	.333	1	-1	-1	0	0.0
1978	SF-N	0	1	.000	11	0	0	0	0	15^2	22	3	8	6	17.8	8.04	43	.338	.419	0	.000	-0	-8	-8	0	-0.8
1979	SF-N	4	3	.571	46	0	0	0	4	79^2	59	0	27	33	9.9	1.81	193	.215	.289	0	.000	-0	17	15	2	1.8
1980	SF-N	4	6	.400	68	0	0	0	19	91^1	81	0	34	42	11.3	2.46	144	.243	.313	1	.125	-0	12	11	2	1.3
1981	SF-N	4	5	.444	55	0	0	0	21	84^1	84	0	36	29	12.8	2.88	119	.267	.342	0	.000	-1	6	5	3	0.7
1982	SF-N★	10	4	.714	78	0	0	0	30	123	108	5	42	58	11.1	1.83	196	.244	.313	3	.176	0	**24**	**24**	1	2.7
1983	SF-N	7	11	.389	73	0	0	0	22	106^2	117	6	47	38	13.8	3.54	100	.283	.356	6	.545	4	1	-0	-0	0.4
1984	SF-N	4	9	.308	74	1	0	0	19	124^1	130	6	57	48	13.5	3.76	93	.267	.344	1	.048	-1	-2	-4	2	-0.3
1985	SF-N	5	4	.556	68	0	0	0	4	96^2	98	6	54	37	14.2	3.54	97	.272	.367	0	.000	-1	1	-1	2	0.1
1986	SF-N	4	4	.500	48	0	0	0	5	68^2	63	4	34	34	12.8	3.93	90	.251	.343	2	.400	2	-2	-3	2	0.0
1987	SF-N	1	0	1.000	15	0	0	0	1	23^1	30	2	10	9	15.8	3.47	111	.323	.394	0	.000	-0	2	1	0	0.1
	Cal-A	5	4	.556	41	0	0	0	10	76	71	4	29	35	12.0	3.08	140	.257	.330	0	—	0	12	10	2	1.2
1988	Cal-A	4	5	.444	44	0	0	0	7	79	67	1	34	46	11.8	2.85	135	.233	.320	0	—	0	10	9	2	1.1
1989	Cal-A	4	3	.571	62	0	0	0	8	90	76	4	37	42	11.5	2.20	173	.230	.311	0	—	0	17	16	2	1.9
1990	Cal-A	1	1	.500	11	0	0	0	0	15^1	11	1	7	4	11.2	2.35	163	.212	.317	0	—	0	3	3	0	0.4
Total	16	59	65	.476	710	7	0	0	150	1130^2	1082	43	483	479	12.6	3.10	117	.257	.336	15	.146	2	80	68	19	9.6
● **GINO MINUTELLI**	Minutelli, Gino Michael b: 5/23/64, Wilmington, Del. BL/TL, 6', 180 lbs. Deb: 9/18/90																									
1990	Cin-N	0	0	—	2	0	0	0	0	1	0	0	2	0	27.0	9.00	44	.000	.500	0	—	0	-1	-1	0	-0.1
1991	Cin-N	0	2	.000	16	3	0	0	0	25^1	30	5	18	21	17.1	6.04	63	.288	.393	0	.000	-0	-7	-6	0	-0.6
Total	2	0	2	.000	18	3	0	0	0	26^1	30	5	20	21	17.4	6.15	62	.280	.398	0	.000	-0	-7	-7	0	-0.7
● **PAUL MIRABELLA**	Mirabella, Paul Thomas b: 3/20/54, Belleville, N.J. BL/TL, 6'2", 196 lbs. Deb: 7/28/78																									
1978	Tex-A	3	2	.600	10	4	0	0	1	28	30	2	17	23	15.1	5.79	65	.286	.385	0	—	0	-6	-6	-0	-0.7
1979	NY-A	0	4	.000	10	1	0	0	0	14^1	16	3	10	4	17.0	8.79	46	.276	.391	0	—	0	-7	-8	-0	-0.6
1980	Tor-A	5	12	.294	33	22	3	1	0	130^2	151	11	66	53	15.2	4.34	99	.294	.378	0	—	0	-4	-1	0	-0.1
1981	Tor-A	0	0	—	8	1	0	0	0	14^2	20	2	7	9	17.2	7.36	53	.313	.389	0	—	0	-6	-6	-0	-0.8
1982	Tex-A	1	1	.500	40	0	0	0	3	50^2	46	4	22	29	12.4	4.80	81	.241	.326	0	—	0	-4	-5	-0	-0.3
1983	Bal-A	0	0	—	3	2	0	0	0	9^2	9	1	7	4	14.9	5.59	71	.243	.364	0	—	0	-2	-2	-0	-0.1
1984	Sea-A	2	5	.286	52	1	0	0	3	68	74	6	32	41	14.2	4.37	91	.282	.363	0	—	0	-3	-3	1	-0.2
1985	Sea-A	0	0	—	10	0	0	0	0	13^2	9	0	4	8	9.9	1.32	320	.188	.278	0	—	0	4	4	-0	0.4
1986	Sea-A	0	0	—	8	0	0	0	0	6^1	13	1	3	6	22.7	8.53	50	.419	.471	0	—	0	-3	-3	0	-0.3
1987	Mil-A	2	1	.667	29	0	0	0	2	29^1	30	0	16	14	14.1	4.91	93	.268	.359	0	—	0	-1	-1	1	-0.1
1988	Mil-A	2	2	.500	38	0	0	0	4	60	44	3	21	33	9.8	1.65	241	.204	.274	0	—	0	15	16	1	1.7
1989	Mil-A	0	0	—	13	0	0	0	0	15^1	18	1	7	6	15.3	7.63	50	.290	.371	0	—	0	-6	-6	0	-0.5
1990	Mil-A	4	2	.667	44	2	0	0	0	59	66	9	27	28	14.5	3.97	98	.281	.360	0	—	0	-0	-1	-0	0.0
Total	13	19	29	.396	298	33	3	1	13	499^2	526	43	239	258	14.0	4.45	91	.272	.356	0	—	0	-24	-21	0	-1.6

● **ROY MITCHELL** Mitchell, Albert Roy b: 4/19/1885, Belton, Tex. d: 9/8/59, Temple, Tex. BR/TR, 5'9.5", 170 lbs. Deb: 9/10/10

YEAR	TM/L	W	L	PCT	G	GS	CG	SH	SV	IP	H	HR	BB	SO	RAT	ERA	ERA+	OAV	OOB	BH	AVG	PB	PR	/A	PD	TPI
1910	StL-A	4	2	.667	6	6	6	0	0	52	43	0	12	23	9.9	2.60	95	.244	.300	4	.211	0	-0	-1	1	0.0
1911	StL-A	4	8	.333	28	12	8	1	0	133^1	134	4	45	40	12.5	3.85	88	.273	.341	11	.224	2	-7	-7	-0	-0.5
1912	StL-A	3	4	.429	13	7	5	0	0	62	81	2	17	22	14.8	4.65	71	.323	.375	6	.316	3	-9	-9	-1	-0.7
1913	StL-A	13	16	.448	33	27	21	4	1	245^1	265	6	47	59	11.6	3.01	98	.280	.318	13	.148	-1	-2	-2	-1	-0.4
1914	StL-A	4	5	.444	28	9	4	0	**4**	103^1	134	1	38	38	15.5	4.35	62	.320	.384	7	.206	1	-19	-19	0	-1.9
1918	Chi-A	0	1	.000	2	2	0	0	0	12	18	1	4	3	16.5	7.50	36	.346	.393	0	.000	-0	-6	-6	0	-0.6
	Cin-N	4	0	1.000	5	3	3	2	0	36^1	27	0	5	9	7.9	0.74	359	.208	.237	3	.214	0	8	8	-0	1.0
1919	Cin-N	0	1	.000	7	1	0	0	0	31	32	0	9	10	11.9	2.32	119	.276	.328	0	.000	-1	2	2	1	0.1
Total	7	32	37	.464	122	67	47	7	5	675^1	734	14	177	204	12.4	3.42	86	.284	.336	44	.187	3	-34	-35	-1	-3.0

● **CHARLIE MITCHELL** Mitchell, Charles Ross b: 6/24/62, Dickson, Tenn. BR/TR, 6'3", 170 lbs. Deb: 8/09/84 F

YEAR	TM/L	W	L	PCT	G	GS	CG	SH	SV	IP	H	HR	BB	SO	RAT	ERA	ERA+	OAV	OOB	BH	AVG	PB	PR	/A	PD	TPI
1984	Bos-A	0	0	—	10	0	0	0	0	16^1	14	1	6	7	12.1	2.76	151	.226	.314	0	—	0	2	3	0	0.2
1985	Bos-A	0	0	—	2	0	0	0	0	1^2	5	1	0	2	27.0	16.20	26	.500	.500	0	—	0	-2	-2	0	-0.2
Total	2	0	0	—	12	0	0	0	0	18	19	2	6	9	13.5	4.00	104	.264	.338	0	—	0	0	0	0	0.0

● **CLARENCE MITCHELL** Mitchell, Clarence Elmer b: 2/22/1891, Franklin, Neb. d: 11/6/63, Grand Island, Neb. BL/TL, 5'11.5", 190 lbs. Deb: 6/02/11 C♦

YEAR	TM/L	W	L	PCT	G	GS	CG	SH	SV	IP	H	HR	BB	SO	RAT	ERA	ERA+	OAV	OOB	BH	AVG	PB	PR	/A	PD	TPI
1911	Det-A	1	0	1.000	5	1	0	0	0	14^1	20	1	7	4	17.0	8.16	42	.351	.422	2	.500	1	-8	-7	-1	-0.6
1916	Cin-N	11	10	.524	29	24	17	1	0	194^2	211	4	45	52	12.3	3.14	83	.285	.334	28	.239	2	-11	-12	1	-0.9
1917	Cin-N	9	15	.375	32	20	10	2	1	159^1	166	4	34	37	11.4	3.22	81	.268	.308	25	.278	4	-9	-11	0	-0.8
1918	Bro-N	0	1	.000	1	1	0	0	0	0^1	4	0	0	0	108.0	108.00	3	1.000	1.000	6	.250	0	-4	-4	0	-0.4
1919	Bro-N	7	5	.583	23	11	9	0	0	108^2	123	0	23	43	12.1	3.06	97	.297	.334	18	.367	6	-2	-1	1	0.7
1920	*Bro-N	5	2	.714	19	7	3	1	1	78^2	85	1	23	18	12.4	3.09	104	.288	.340	25	.234	1	0	1	1	0.4
1921	Bro-N	11	9	.550	37	18	13	**3**	2	190	206	7	46	39	12.2	2.89	135	.280	.327	24	.264	3	19	21	3	2.8
1922	Bro-N	0	3	.000	5	3	0	0	0	12^2	28	0	7	1	25.6	14.21	29	.467	.529	45	.290	2	-14	-14	1	-1.1
1923	Phi-N	9	10	.474	29	19	8	1	0	139^1	170	8	46	41	14.2	4.72	98	.299	.355	21	.269	4	-11	-2	-3	-0.1
1924	Phi-N	6	13	.316	30	26	9	1	1	165	223	10	58	36	15.7	5.62	79	.321	.379	26	.255	-1	-32	-21	3	-1.8
1925	Phi-N	10	17	.370	32	26	12	1	1	199^1	245	23	51	46	13.6	5.28	90	.302	.347	18	.196	-2	-22	-11	4	-0.8
1926	Phi-N	9	14	.391	28	25	12	0	1	178^2	232	7	55	52	14.7	4.58	90	.318	.369	19	.244	1	-15	-9	4	-0.3
1927	Phi-N	6	3	.667	13	12	8	1	0	94^2	99	7	28	17	12.3	4.09	101	.271	.327	10	.238	2	-2	0	1	0.3
1928	Phi-N	0	0	—	3	0	0	0	0	5^2	13	0	2	0	23.8	9.53	45	.542	.577	1	.250	0	-3	-3	0	-0.3
	*StL-N	8	9	.471	19	18	9	1	0	150	149	8	38	31	11.4	3.30	121	.265	.315	7	.125	-3	11	12	2	1.0
	Yr	8	9	.471	22	18	9	1	0	155^2	162	8	40	31	11.9	3.53	114	.276	.326	8	.133	-3	8	8	3	0.7
1929	StL-N	8	11	.421	25	22	16	0	0	173	221	13	60	39	14.9	4.27	109	.320	.379	18	.273	4	9	8	-1	1.0
1930	StL-N	1	0	1.000	1	1	0	0	0	3	5	0	2	1	21.0	6.00	84	.357	.438	1	.500	0	-0	-0	-0	0.0
	NY-N	10	3	.769	24	16	5	0	0	129	151	10	36	40	13.1	3.98	119	.298	.346	12	.255	0	14	11	2	1.2
	Yr	11	3	.786	25	17	5	0	0	132	156	10	38	41	13.3	4.02	118	.300	.349	13	.265	1	14	11	2	1.2
1931	NY-N	13	11	.542	27	25	13	0	0	190^1	221	12	52	39	13.1	4.07	91	.285	.332	16	.219	2	-4	-8	-2	-0.8
1932	NY-N	1	3	.250	8	3	1	0	2	30^1	41	1	11	7	15.7	4.15	89	.325	.384	2	.200	0	-1	-1	-1	-0.2
Total	18	125	139	.473	390	278	145	12	9	2217	2613	116	624	543	13.4	4.12	95	.297	.347	324	.252	27	-86	-54	17	-0.7

● **CRAIG MITCHELL** Mitchell, Craig Seton b: 4/14/54, Santa Rosa, Cal. BR/TR, 6'3", 180 lbs. Deb: 9/25/75

YEAR	TM/L	W	L	PCT	G	GS	CG	SH	SV	IP	H	HR	BB	SO	RAT	ERA	ERA+	OAV	OOB	BH	AVG	PB	PR	/A	PD	TPI
1975	Oak-A	0	1	.000	1	1	0	0	0	3^2	6	0	2	2	19.6	12.27	30	.375	.444	0	—	0	-3	-4	0	-0.3
1976	Oak-A	0	0	—	1	0	0	0	0	3^1	3	0	0	0	8.1	2.70	124	.231	.231	0	—	0	0	0	0	0.0
1977	Oak-A	0	1	.000	3	1	0	0	0	5^2	9	1	2	1	17.5	7.94	51	.346	.393	0	—	0	-2	-2	-0	-0.2
Total	3	0	2	.000	5	2	0	0	0	12^2	18	1	4	3	15.6	7.82	48	.327	.373	0	—	0	-6	-6	0	-0.5

● **FRED MITCHELL** Mitchell, Frederick Francis (b: Frederick Francis Yapp)
b: 6/5/1878, Cambridge, Mass. d: 10/13/70, Newton, Mass. BR/TR, 5'9.5", 185 lbs. Deb: 4/27/01 M♦

YEAR	TM/L	W	L	PCT	G	GS	CG	SH	SV	IP	H	HR	BB	SO	RAT	ERA	ERA+	OAV	OOB	BH	AVG	PB	PR	/A	PD	TPI
1901	Bos-A	6	6	.500	17	13	10	0	0	108^2	115	2	51	34	14.7	3.81	93	.268	.362	7	.159	-1	-2	-3	0	-0.4
1902	Bos-A	0	1	.000	1	0	0	0	0	4	8	1	5	2	29.3	11.25	32	.414	.534	0	.000	-0	-3	-3	0	-0.3
	Phi-A	5	7	.417	18	14	9	0	1	107^2	120	4	59	22	15.8	3.59	102	.282	.382	9	.188	-1	-0	1	2	0.2
	Yr	5	8	.385	19	14	9	0	1	111^2	128	5	64	24	16.3	3.87	95	.288	.390	9	.184	-1	-4	-3	3	-0.1
1903	Phi-N	11	16	.407	28	28	24	1	0	227	250	4	102	69	14.7	4.48	73	.284	.370	19	.200	-1	-31	-30	-3	-3.1
1904	Phi-N	4	7	.364	13	13	11	0	0	108^2	133	3	25	29	13.7	3.40	79	.306	.353	17	.207	1	-8	-9	3	-0.5
	Bro-N	2	5	.286	8	8	8	1	0	66	73	0	23	16	13.5	3.82	72	.291	.357	7	.292	2	-8	-8	1	-0.4
	Yr	6	12	.333	21	21	19	1	0	174^2	206	3	48	45	13.2	3.56	76	.297	.345	24	.226	3	-16	-17	4	-0.9
1905	Bro-N	3	7	.300	12	10	9	0	0	96^1	107	2	38	44	14.0	4.76	61	.285	.358	15	.190	0	-19	-20	1	-1.8
Total	5	31	49	.387	97	86	71	2	1	718^1	806	16	303	216	14.6	4.10	78	.286	.367	120	.210	0	-71	-73	5	-6.3

● **JOHN MITCHELL** Mitchell, John Kyle b: 8/11/65, Dickson, Tenn. BR/TR, 6'2", 195 lbs. Deb: 9/08/86 F

YEAR	TM/L	W	L	PCT	G	GS	CG	SH	SV	IP	H	HR	BB	SO	RAT	ERA	ERA+	OAV	OOB	BH	AVG	PB	PR	/A	PD	TPI
1986	NY-N	0	1	.000	4	1	0	0	0	10	10	1	4	2	12.6	3.60	98	.278	.350	0	.000	-0	0	-0	0	0.0
1987	NY-N	3	6	.333	20	19	1	0	0	111^2	124	6	36	57	13.1	4.11	92	.279	.336	4	.114	-1	-0	-4	1	-0.4
1988	NY-N	0	0	—	1	0	0	0	0	1	2	0	1	1	27.0	0.00	—	.500	.600	0	.000	-0	0	0	0	0.0
1989	NY-N	0	1	.000	2	0	0	0	0	3	3	0	4	4	21.0	6.00	54	.231	.412	0	—	0	-1	-1	-0	-0.1
1990	Bal-A	6	6	.500	24	17	0	0	0	114^1	133	7	48	43	14.5	4.64	82	.300	.372	0	—	0	-9	-11	1	-0.9
Total	5	9	14	.391	51	37	1	0	0	240	272	14	93	107	13.9	4.35	87	.289	.356	4	.105	-1	-10	-16	2	-1.4

● **MONROE MITCHELL** Mitchell, Monroe Barr b: 9/11/01, Starkville, Miss. d: 9/4/76, Valdosta, Ga. BR/TL, 6'1.5", 170 lbs. Deb: 7/11/23

YEAR	TM/L	W	L	PCT	G	GS	CG	SH	SV	IP	H	HR	BB	SO	RAT	ERA	ERA+	OAV	OOB	BH	AVG	PB	PR	/A	PD	TPI
1923	Was-A	2	4	.333	10	6	3	1	2	41^2	57	0	22	8	17.3	6.48	58	.350	.430	3	.250	1	-12	-13	-1	-1.1

● **PAUL MITCHELL** Mitchell, Paul Michael b: 8/19/49, Worcester, Mass. BR/TR, 6'1", 195 lbs. Deb: 7/01/75

YEAR	TM/L	W	L	PCT	G	GS	CG	SH	SV	IP	H	HR	BB	SO	RAT	ERA	ERA+	OAV	OOB	BH	AVG	PB	PR	/A	PD	TPI
1975	Bal-A	3	0	1.000	11	4	1	0	0	57	41	8	19	31	9.5	3.63	97	.204	.273	0	—	0	1	-1	-1	-0.2
1976	Oak-A	9	7	.563	26	26	4	1	0	142	169	15	30	67	12.7	4.25	79	.294	.331	0	—	0	-11	-14	-1	-1.6
1977	Oak-A	0	3	.000	5	3	0	0	0	13^2	21	3	7	5	18.4	10.54	38	.339	.406	0	—	0	-10	-10	0	-0.8
	Sea-A	3	3	.500	9	9	0	0	0	39^2	50	7	16	20	15.2	4.99	82	.311	.376	0	—	0	-4	-4	0	-0.3
	Yr	3	6	.333	14	12	0	0	0	53^1	71	10	23	25	16.0	6.41	64	.318	.385	0	—	0	-14	-14	1	-1.1
1978	Sea-A	8	14	.364	29	29	4	2	0	168	173	21	79	75	13.6	4.18	91	.270	.352	0	—	0	-8	-7	-1	-0.8
1979	Sea-A	1	4	.200	10	6	1	0	0	36^2	46	4	15	18	15.0	4.42	99	.309	.372	0	—	0	-1	-0	-0	-0.1
	Mil-A	3	3	.500	18	8	0	0	0	75	81	11	10	32	11.3	5.76	72	.276	.307	0	—	0	-13	-13	-1	-1.3
	Yr	4	7	.364	28	14	1	0	0	111^2	127	15	25	50	12.5	5.32	79	.287	.329	0	—	0	-14	-14	-1	-1.4
1980	Mil-A	5	5	.500	17	11	1	1	1	89^1	92	7	15	29	10.9	3.53	110	.267	.300	0	—	0	5	3	0	0.4
Total	6	32	39	.451	125	96	11	4	1	621^1	673	76	191	277	12.6	4.45	85	.278	.332	0	—	0	-41	-46	-3	-4.7

● **BOBBY MITCHELL** Mitchell, Robert McKasha b: 2/6/1856, Cincinnati, Ohio d: 5/1/33, Springfield, Ohio BL/TL, 5'5", 135 lbs. Deb: 9/06/1877 ♦

YEAR	TM/L	W	L	PCT	G	GS	CG	SH	SV	IP	H	HR	BB	SO	RAT	ERA	ERA+	OAV	OOB	BH	AVG	PB	PR	/A	PD	TPI
1877	Cin-N	6	5	.545	12	12	11	1	0	100	123	0	11	41	12.1	3.51	75	.281	.299	10	.204	-0	-8	-10	-0	-0.8
1878	Cin-N	7	2	.778	9	9	9	1	0	80	69	1	18	51	9.8	2.14	100	**.223**	.265	12	.245	1	2	-0	0	0.1
1879	Cle-N	7	15	.318	23	22	20	0	0	194^2	236	0	42	90	12.9	3.28	76	.283	.317	16	.147	-4	-17	-17	-4	-2.1
1882	StL-a	0	1	.000	1	1	0	0	0	7	12	0	2	2	18.0	7.71	36	.355	.391	0	.000	-1	-4	-4	-0	-0.3
Total	4	20	23	.465	45	44	40	2	0	381^2	440	1	73	184	12.1	3.18	77	.272	.304	38	.180	-5	-27	-30	-4	-3.1

● **WILLIE MITCHELL** Mitchell, William b: 12/1/1889, Pleasant Grove, Miss. d: 11/23/73, Sardis, Miss. BR/TL, 6', 176 lbs. Deb: 9/22/09

YEAR	TM/L	W	L	PCT	G	GS	CG	SH	SV	IP	H	HR	BB	SO	RAT	ERA	ERA+	OAV	OOB	BH	AVG	PB	PR	/A	PD	TPI
1909	Cle-A	1	2	.333	3	3	3	0	0	23	18	0	10	8	12.5	1.57	163	.225	.340	2	.286	1	2	3	0	0.4
1910	Cle-A	12	8	.600	35	18	11	1	0	183^2	155	2	55	102	11.0	2.60	100	.236	.310	10	.159	-3	-2	-0	-2	-0.6
1911	Cle-A	7	14	.333	30	22	9	0	0	177^1	190	1	60	78	13.3	3.76	91	.284	.354	7	.109	-5	-8	-7	-1	-1.2

YEAR	TM/L	W	L	PCT	G	GS	CG	SH	SV	IP	H	HR	BB	SO	RAT	ERA	ERA+	OAV	OOB	BH	AVG	PB	PR	/A	PD	TPI
1912	Cle-A	5	8	.385	29	15	8	0	1	163^2	149	0	56	94	11.7	2.80	122	.240	.309	6	.113	-4	9	11	-3	0.4
1913	Cle-A	14	8	.636	35	22	14	4	0	217	153	1	88	141	10.3	1.91	159	.199	.288	10	.143	-2	25	27	-3	2.5
1914	Cle-A	12	17	.414	39	32	16	3	1	257	228	3	124	179	12.6	3.19	91	.238	.330	7	.086	-4	-13	-9	-5	-1.9
1915	Cle-A	11	14	.440	36	30	12	1	1	236	210	1	84	149	11.3	2.82	108	.241	.309	10	.127	-5	3	6	-4	-0.3
1916	Cle-A	2	5	.286	12	6	1	0	1	43^2	55	1	19	24	15.3	5.15	58	.309	.376	0	.000	-1	-11	-10	-1	-1.3
	Det-A	7	5	.583	23	17	7	2	0	127^2	119	1	48	60	12.1	3.31	86	.253	.329	9	.250	2	-7	-6	-3	-0.8
	Yr	9	10	.474	35	23	8	2	1	171^1	174	2	67	84	12.9	3.78	77	.269	.342	9	.191	1	-18	-17	-4	-2.1
1917	Det-A	12	8	.600	30	22	12	5	0	185^1	172	2	46	80	11.2	2.19	121	.250	.309	7	.119	-3	10	9	-2	0.4
1918	Det-A	0	1	.000	1	1	0	0	0	4	3	0	5	2	18.0	9.00	30	.200	.400	0	.000	-0	-3	-3	0	-0.3
1919	Det-A	1	2	.333	3	2	0	0	0	13^2	12	2	10	4	15.1	5.27	61	.255	.397	1	.200	0	-3	-3	0	-0.3
Total	11	84	92	.477	276	190	93	16	4	1632	1464	14	605	921	11.8	2.88	103	.243	.320	69	.130	-24	3	18	-23	-3.0

● VINEGAR BEND MIZELL Mizell, Wilmer David b: 8/13/30, Leakesville, Miss. BR/TL, 6'3.5", 205 lbs. Deb: 4/22/52

YEAR	TM/L	W	L	PCT	G	GS	CG	SH	SV	IP	H	HR	BB	SO	RAT	ERA	ERA+	OAV	OOB	BH	AVG	PB	PR	/A	PD	TPI
1952	StL-N	10	8	.556	30	30	7	2	0	190	171	12	103	146	13.0	3.65	102	.237	.333	3	.044	-5	2	1	-2	-0.6
1953	StL-N	13	11	.542	33	33	10	1	0	224^1	193	12	114	173	12.5	3.49	122	.227	.321	7	.084	-4	20	19	-0	1.5
1956	StL-N	14	14	.500	33	33	11	3	0	208^2	172	20	92	153	11.7	3.62	104	.222	.310	8	.107	-3	3	4	0	0.1
1957	StL-N	8	10	.444	33	21	7	2	0	149^1	136	18	51	87	11.3	3.74	106	.241	.305	4	.089	-2	2	4	1	0.3
1958	StL-N	10	14	.417	30	29	8	2	0	189^2	178	17	91	80	12.9	3.42	121	.252	.339	7	.115	-3	11	15	-1	1.1
1959	StL-N	13	10	.565	31	30	8	1	0	201^1	196	21	89	108	13.1	4.20	101	.252	.334	14	.187	1	-6	1	-2	-0.1
1960	StL-N	1	3	.250	9	9	0	0	0	55^1	64	7	28	42	15.0	4.55	90	.291	.371	2	.111	-1	-5	-3	0	-0.3
	*Pit-N	13	5	.722	23	23	8	3	0	155^2	141	7	46	71	11.0	3.12	120	.247	.306	7	.137	-1	11	11	-3	0.8
	Yr	14	8	.636	32	32	8	3	0	211	205	14	74	113	12.0	3.50	110	.259	.325	9	.130	-1	6	8	-2	0.5
1961	Pit-N	7	10	.412	25	17	2	1	0	100	120	16	31	37	13.6	5.04	79	.299	.350	3	.130	-1	-11	-12	-3	-1.4
1962	Pit-N	1	1	.500	4	3	0	0	0	16^1	15	3	10	6	14.3	4.96	79	.254	.371	0	.000	-0	-2	-2	0	-0.2
	NY-N	0	2	.000	17	2	0	0	0	38	48	10	25	15	17.5	7.34	57	.324	.425	2	.250	0	-14	-13	-1	-1.3
	Yr	1	3	.250	21	5	0	0	0	54^1	63	13	35	21	16.4	6.63	62	.301	.404	2	.143	-0	-16	-15	-0	-1.5
Total	9	90	88	.506	268	230	61	15	0	1528^2	1434	143	680	918	12.6	3.85	104	.247	.329	57	.111	-19	12	25	-9	-0.1

● DAVE MLICKI Mlicki, David John b: 6/8/68, Cleveland, Ohio BR/TR, 6'4", 185 lbs. Deb: 9/12/92

YEAR	TM/L	W	L	PCT	G	GS	CG	SH	SV	IP	H	HR	BB	SO	RAT	ERA	ERA+	OAV	OOB	BH	AVG	PB	PR	/A	PD	TPI
1992	Cle-A	0	2	.000	4	4	0	0	0	21^2	23	3	16	16	16.6	4.98	81	.280	.404	0	—	0	-3	-2	1	-0.2

● KEVIN MMAHAT Mmahat, Kevin Paul b: 11/9/64, Memphis, Tenn. BL/TL, 6'5", 220 lbs. Deb: 9/09/89

YEAR	TM/L	W	L	PCT	G	GS	CG	SH	SV	IP	H	HR	BB	SO	RAT	ERA	ERA+	OAV	OOB	BH	AVG	PB	PR	/A	PD	TPI
1989	NY-A	0	2	.000	4	2	0	0	0	7^2	13	2	8	3	25.8	12.91	30	.406	.537	0	—	0	-8	-8	-0	-0.7

● MIKE MODAK Modak, Michael b: 5/18/22, Campbell, Ohio BR/TR, 5'10.5", 195 lbs. Deb: 7/04/45

YEAR	TM/L	W	L	PCT	G	GS	CG	SH	SV	IP	H	HR	BB	SO	RAT	ERA	ERA+	OAV	OOB	BH	AVG	PB	PR	/A	PD	TPI
1945	Cin-N	1	2	.333	20	3	1	1	1	42^1	52	0	23	7	15.9	5.74	65	.308	.391	1	.100	-1	-9	-9	-1	-1.1

● DENNIS MOELLER Moeller, Dennis Michael b: 9/15/67, Tarzana, Cal. BR/TL, 6'2", 195 lbs. Deb: 7/28/92

YEAR	TM/L	W	L	PCT	G	GS	CG	SH	SV	IP	H	HR	BB	SO	RAT	ERA	ERA+	OAV	OOB	BH	AVG	PB	PR	/A	PD	TPI
1992	KC-A	0	3	.000	5	4	0	0	0	18	24	5	11	6	17.5	7.00	57	.333	.422	0	—	0	-6	-6	0	-0.6

● JOE MOELLER Moeller, Joseph Douglas b: 2/15/43, Blue Island, Ill. BR/TR, 6'5", 208 lbs. Deb: 4/12/62

YEAR	TM/L	W	L	PCT	G	GS	CG	SH	SV	IP	H	HR	BB	SO	RAT	ERA	ERA+	OAV	OOB	BH	AVG	PB	PR	/A	PD	TPI
1962	LA-N	6	5	.545	19	15	1	0	1	85^2	87	10	58	46	15.2	5.25	69	.266	.377	7	.212	1	-12	-15	1	-1.4
1964	LA-N	7	13	.350	27	24	1	0	0	145^1	153	14	31	97	11.6	4.21	77	.265	.307	3	.067	-2	-11	-16	-0	-1.8
1966	*LA-N	2	4	.333	29	8	0	0	0	78^2	73	4	14	31	10.3	2.52	131	.244	.285	2	.167	1	10	7	1	0.9
1967	LA-N	0	0	—	6	0	0	0	0	5	9	1	3	2	21.6	9.00	34	.409	.480	0	—	0	-3	-3	0	-0.3
1968	LA-N	1	1	.500	3	3	0	0	0	16	17	1	2	11	11.3	5.06	55	.270	.303	0	.000	-1	-4	-4	0	-0.5
1969	LA-N	1	0	1.000	23	4	0	0	1	51^1	54	4	13	25	11.7	3.33	100	.278	.324	2	.200	0	1	-0	1	0.1
1970	LA-N	7	9	.438	31	19	2	1	4	135^1	131	16	43	63	11.6	3.92	98	.248	.306	6	.154	0	2	-1	-2	-0.3
1971	LA-N	2	4	.333	28	1	0	0	1	66^1	72	5	12	32	11.4	3.80	85	.279	.311	0	.000	-0	-2	-4	1	-0.4
Total	8	26	36	.419	166	74	4	1	7	583^2	596	55	176	307	12.0	4.01	86	.263	.318	20	.129	-2	-20	-37	2	-3.7

● RON MOELLER Moeller, Ronald Ralph "The Kid" b: 10/13/38, Cincinnati, Ohio BL/TL, 6', 180 lbs. Deb: 9/08/56

YEAR	TM/L	W	L	PCT	G	GS	CG	SH	SV	IP	H	HR	BB	SO	RAT	ERA	ERA+	OAV	OOB	BH	AVG	PB	PR	/A	PD	TPI
1956	Bal-A	0	1	.000	4	1	0	0	0	8^2	10	0	3	2	13.5	4.15	94	.286	.342	0	.000	-0	0	-0	-0	-0.1
1958	Bal-A	0	0	—	4	0	0	0	0	4^1	6	0	3	3	18.7	4.15	87	.333	.429	0	—	0	-0	-0	0	0.0
1961	LA-A	4	8	.333	33	18	1	1	0	112^2	122	15	83	87	16.5	5.83	77	.275	.392	6	.207	2	-23	-17	1	-1.3
1963	LA-A	0	0	—	3	0	0	0	0	2^2	5	1	1	2	20.3	6.75	51	.385	.429	0	—	0	-1	-1	0	-0.1
	Was-A	2	0	1.000	8	3	0	0	0	24^1	31	4	10	10	15.5	6.29	59	.316	.385	2	.222	0	-7	-7	-1	-0.8
	Yr	2	0	1.000	11	3	0	0	0	27	36	5	11	12	16.0	6.33	58	.324	.390	2	.222	0	-8	-8	-1	-0.9
Total	4	6	9	.400	52	22	1	1	0	152^2	174	20	100	104	16.3	5.78	74	.287	.390	8	.205	2	-31	-25	0	-2.3

● SAM MOFFETT Moffett, Samuel R. b: 3/14/1857, Wheeling, W.Va. d: 5/5/07, Butte, Mont. TR, 6', 175 lbs. Deb: 5/15/1884 F♦

YEAR	TM/L	W	L	PCT	G	GS	CG	SH	SV	IP	H	HR	BB	SO	RAT	ERA	ERA+	OAV	OOB	BH	AVG	PB	PR	/A	PD	TPI
1884	Cle-N	3	19	.136	24	22	21	0	0	197^2	236	9	58	84	13.4	3.87	81	.284	.330	47	.184	-3	-20	-16	2	-1.4
1887	Ind-N	1	5	.167	6	6	6	0	0	50	47	1	23	3	13.3	3.78	110	.242	.335	5	.122	-2	2	2	-0	-0.1
1888	Ind-N	2	5	.286	7	7	6	1	0	56	62	3	17	7	13.0	4.66	64	.278	.335	4	.114	-1	-11	-11	-2	-1.2
Total	3	6	29	.171	37	35	33	1	0	303^2	345	13	98	94	13.3	4.00	82	.276	.332	56	.169	-6	-29	-24	-0	-2.7

● RANDY MOFFITT Moffitt, Randall James b: 10/13/48, Long Beach, Cal. BR/TR, 6'3", 190 lbs. Deb: 6/11/72

YEAR	TM/L	W	L	PCT	G	GS	CG	SH	SV	IP	H	HR	BB	SO	RAT	ERA	ERA+	OAV	OOB	BH	AVG	PB	PR	/A	PD	TPI
1972	SF-N	1	5	.167	40	0	0	0	4	70^2	72	5	30	37	13.2	3.69	94	.266	.343	0	.000	-1	-2	-2	0	-0.3
1973	SF-N	4	4	.500	60	0	0	0	14	100^1	86	9	31	65	10.6	2.42	158	.225	.285	1	.059	-1	14	16	-1	1.4
1974	SF-N	5	7	.417	61	1	0	0	15	102	99	9	29	49	11.5	4.50	84	.256	.311	5	.313	2	-10	-8	1	-0.6
1975	SF-N	4	5	.444	55	0	0	0	11	74	73	6	32	39	13.1	3.89	98	.257	.339	3	.214	1	-2	-1	-0	-0.1
1976	SF-N	6	6	.500	58	0	0	0	14	103	92	6	35	50	11.2	2.27	160	.238	.303	2	.143	-0	14	16	-0	1.6
1977	SF-N	4	9	.308	64	0	0	0	11	87^2	91	4	39	68	13.7	3.59	109	.273	.355	0	.000	-0	3	3	1	0.4
1978	SF-N	8	4	.667	70	0	0	0	12	81^2	79	5	33	52	12.7	3.31	104	.258	.336	1	.143	0	2	1	-1	0.0
1979	SF-N	2	5	.286	28	0	0	0	2	35	53	5	14	16	17.7	7.71	45	.356	.418	0	.000	-0	-15	-16	-0	-1.7
1980	SF-N	1	1	.500	13	0	0	0	0	16^2	18	2	4	10	12.4	4.86	73	.281	.333	0	.000	-0	-2	-2	0	-0.3
1981	SF-N	0	0	—	10	0	0	0	0	11^1	15	2	2	11	13.5	7.94	43	.313	.340	0	—	0	-6	-6	-0	-0.6
1982	Hou-N	2	4	.333	30	0	0	0	3	41^2	36	3	13	20	11.7	3.02	110	.228	.307	0	.000	-0	3	1	-1	0.0
1983	Tor-A	6	2	.750	45	0	0	0	10	57^1	52	5	24	38	12.1	3.77	114	.243	.322	0	—	0	2	3	0	0.2
Total	12	43	52	.453	534	1	0	0	96	781^1	766	61	286	455	12.4	3.65	102	.257	.327	12	.140	-1	0	5	-3	-0.0

● HERB MOFORD Moford, Herbert b: 8/6/28, Brooksville, Ky. BR/TR, 6'1", 175 lbs. Deb: 4/12/55

YEAR	TM/L	W	L	PCT	G	GS	CG	SH	SV	IP	H	HR	BB	SO	RAT	ERA	ERA+	OAV	OOB	BH	AVG	PB	PR	/A	PD	TPI
1955	StL-N	1	1	.500	14	1	0	0	2	24	29	5	15	8	16.9	7.88	52	.299	.398	0	.000	-0	-10	-10	1	-0.9
1958	Det-A	4	9	.308	25	11	6	0	1	109^2	83	10	42	58	11.0	3.61	112	.214	.305	1	.027	-4	2	5	1	0.2
1959	Bos-A	0	2	.000	4	2	0	0	0	8^2	10	3	6	7	16.6	11.42	36	.286	.390	0	.000	-0	-7	-7	0	-0.7
1962	NY-N	0	1	.000	7	0	0	0	0	15	21	3	1	5	13.2	7.20	58	.318	.328	1	.250	0	-5	-5	-0	-0.5
Total	4	5	13	.278	50	14	6	0	3	157^1	143	21	64	78	12.4	5.03	81	.244	.329	2	.045	-5	-21	-17	2	-1.9

● GEORGE MOGRIDGE Mogridge, George Anthony b: 2/18/1889, Rochester, N.Y. d: 3/4/62, Rochester, N.Y. BL/TL, 6'2", 165 lbs. Deb: 8/17/11

YEAR	TM/L	W	L	PCT	G	GS	CG	SH	SV	IP	H	HR	BB	SO	RAT	ERA	ERA+	OAV	OOB	BH	AVG	PB	PR	/A	PD	TPI
1911	Chi-A	0	2	.000	4	1	0	0	0	12^2	12	1	1	5	9.2	4.97	65	.255	.271	2	.400	0	-2	-2	-0	-0.2
1912	Chi-A	3	4	.429	17	8	2	0	3	64^2	69	2	15	31	11.8	4.04	79	.264	.307	2	.125	-0	-5	-6	-1	-0.7
1915	NY-A	2	3	.400	6	5	3	1	0	41	33	0	11	11	10.3	1.76	167	.219	.285	1	.083	-1	5	5	-1	0.5
1916	NY-A	6	12	.333	30	21	10	2	0	194^2	174	3	45	66	10.4	2.31	125	.252	.305	14	.212	1	11	13	1	1.7
1917	NY-A	9	11	.450	29	25	15	1	0	196^1	185	5	39	46	10.7	2.98	90	.255	.301	11	.159	-1	-7	-6	1	-0.7
1918	NY-A	16	13	.552	**45**	19	13	1	**7**	239^1	232	6	43	62	10.6	2.18	130	.263	.304	15	.190	-0	16	17	3	2.2

YEAR	TM/L	W	L	PCT	G	GS	CG	SH	SV	IP	H	HR	BB	SO	RAT	ERA	ERA+	OAV	OOB	BH	AVG	PB	PR	/A	PD	TPI
1919	NY-A	10	7	.588	35	18	13	3	0	169	159	6	46	58	11.3	2.77	115	.250	.307	6	.125	-1	9	8	1	0.8
1920	NY-A	5	9	.357	26	15	7	0	1	125^{1}	146	4	36	35	13.3	4.31	89	.287	.338	7	.167	-1	-7	-7	1	-0.7
1921	Was-A	18	14	.563	38	36	21	4	0	288	301	12	66	101	11.7	3.00	137	.269	.313	15	.153	-5	41	36	2	3.1
1922	Was-A	18	13	.581	34	32	18	3	0	251^{2}	300	12	72	61	13.7	3.58	108	.304	.358	21	.244	4	13	8	-1	1.1
1923	Was-A	13	13	.500	33	30	17	3	1	211	228	10	56	62	12.2	3.11	121	.285	.334	17	.227	1	20	15	1	1.8
1924	*Was-A	16	11	.593	30	30	13	2	0	213	217	2	61	48	12.0	3.76	107	.270	.327	13	.176	-2	11	7	0	0.4
1925	Was-A	3	4	.429	10	8	3	0	0	53	58	2	18	12	13.6	4.08	104	.291	.362	2	.105	-2	2	1	-0	-0.1
	StL-A	1	1	.500	2	2	1	0	0	15^{1}	17	2	5	8	13.5	5.87	80	.279	.343	0	.000	-0	-3	-2	0	-0.2
	Yr	4	5	.444	12	10	4	0	0	68^{1}	75	4	23	20	13.0	4.48	97	.284	.344	2	.087	-2	-1	-1	0	-0.3
1926	Bos-N	6	10	.375	39	10	2	0	3	142	173	6	36	46	13.4	4.50	79	.311	.356	8	.174	-1	-11	-15	2	-1.3
1927	Bos-N	6	4	.600	20	1	0	0	5	48^{2}	48	4	15	26	12.0	3.70	100	.257	.319	3	.200	0	1	0	1	0.1
Total	15	132	131	.502	398	261	138	20	20	2265^{2}	2352	77	565	678	11.9	3.23	109	.273	.323	137	.182	-8	95	75	11	7.8

● GEORGE MOHART Mohart, George Benjamin b: 3/6/1892, Buffalo, N.Y. d: 10/2/70, Silver Creek, N.Y. BR/TR, 5'9", 165 lbs. Deb: 4/15/20

YEAR	TM/L	W	L	PCT	G	GS	CG	SH	SV	IP	H	HR	BB	SO	RAT	ERA	ERA+	OAV	OOB	BH	AVG	PB	PR	/A	PD	TPI
1920	Bro-N	0	1	.000	13	1	0	0	0	35^{2}	33	0	7	13	10.9	1.77	181	.250	.303	1	.125	-0	5	6	1	0.7
1921	Bro-N	0	0	—	2	0	0	0	0	7	8	0	1	1	12.9	3.86	101	.296	.345	1	.500	0	-0	0	-0	0.0
Total	2	0	1	.000	15	1	0	0	0	42^{2}	41	0	8	14	11.2	2.11	157	.258	.310	2	.200	0	5	6	1	0.7

● DALE MOHORCIC Mohorcic, Dale Robert b: 1/25/56, Cleveland, Ohio BL/TL, 6'3", 220 lbs. Deb: 5/31/86

YEAR	TM/L	W	L	PCT	G	GS	CG	SH	SV	IP	H	HR	BB	SO	RAT	ERA	ERA+	OAV	OOB	BH	AVG	PB	PR	/A	PD	TPI
1986	Tex-A	2	4	.333	58	0	0	0	7	79	86	5	15	29	11.6	2.51	172	.279	.315	0	—	0	15	16	0	1.6
1987	Tex-A	7	6	.538	74	0	0	0	16	99^{1}	88	11	19	48	9.9	2.99	150	.244	.286	0	—	0	16	16	2	1.8
1988	Tex-A	2	6	.250	43	0	0	0	5	52	62	6	20	25	15.1	4.85	84	.295	.370	0	—	0	-5	-4	0	-0.4
	NY-A	2	2	.500	13	0	0	0	1	22^{2}	21	1	9	19	13.1	2.78	142	.239	.330	0	—	0	3	3	-1	0.3
	Yr	4	8	.333	56	0	0	0	6	74^{2}	83	7	29	44	13.9	4.22	96	.269	.338	0	—	0	-2	-2	-0	-0.1
1989	NY-A	2	1	.667	32	0	0	0	2	57^{2}	65	8	18	24	13.9	4.99	77	.286	.355	0	—	0	-7	-7	1	-0.6
1990	Mon-N	1	2	.333	34	0	0	0	2	53	56	6	18	29	13.2	3.23	113	.286	.358	1	.125	-0	3	2	0	0.3
Total	5	16	21	.432	254	0	0	0	33	363^{2}	378	37	99	174	12.3	3.49	118	.272	.330	1	.125	-0	25	26	3	3.0

● BILL MOISAN Moisan, William Joseph b: 7/30/25, Bradford, Mass. BL/TR, 6'1", 170 lbs. Deb: 9/17/53

YEAR	TM/L	W	L	PCT	G	GS	CG	SH	SV	IP	H	HR	BB	SO	RAT	ERA	ERA+	OAV	OOB	BH	AVG	PB	PR	/A	PD	TPI
1953	Chi-N	0	0	—	3	0	0	0	0	5	5	0	2	1	14.4	5.40	82	.278	.381	0	—	0	-1	-1	0	-0.1

● CARLTON MOLESWORTH Molesworth, Carlton b: 2/15/1876, Frederick, Md. d: 7/25/61, Frederick, Md. BL/TL, 5'6", 200 lbs. Deb: 9/14/1895

YEAR	TM/L	W	L	PCT	G	GS	CG	SH	SV	IP	H	HR	BB	SO	RAT	ERA	ERA+	OAV	OOB	BH	AVG	PB	PR	/A	PD	TPI
1895	Was-N	0	2	.000	4	3	1	0	0	16	33	1	15	7	29.3	14.63	33	.416	.529	1	.143	-1	-17	-17	-0	-1.3

● RICHIE MOLONEY Moloney, Richard Henry b: 6/7/50, Brookline, Mass. BR/TR, 6'3", 185 lbs. Deb: 9/20/70

YEAR	TM/L	W	L	PCT	G	GS	CG	SH	SV	IP	H	HR	BB	SO	RAT	ERA	ERA+	OAV	OOB	BH	AVG	PB	PR	/A	PD	TPI
1970	Chi-A	0	0	—	1	0	0	0	0	1	2	0	0	1	18.0	0.00	—	.400	.400	0	—	0	0	0	0	0.0

● VINCE MOLYNEAUX Molyneaux, Vincent Leo b: 8/17/1888, Lewiston, N.Y. d: 5/4/50, Stamford, Conn. BR/TR, 6', 180 lbs. Deb: 7/05/17

YEAR	TM/L	W	L	PCT	G	GS	CG	SH	SV	IP	H	HR	BB	SO	RAT	ERA	ERA+	OAV	OOB	BH	AVG	PB	PR	/A	PD	TPI
1917	StL-A	0	0	—	7	0	0	0	0	22	18	0	20	4	15.5	4.91	53	.237	.396	0	.000	-1	-5	-6	0	-0.6
1918	Bos-A	1	0	1.000	6	0	0	0	0	10^{2}	3	0	8	1	9.3	3.38	80	.086	.256	0	.000	-0	-1	-1	0	-0.1
Total	2	1	0	1.000	13	0	0	0	0	32^{2}	21	0	28	5	13.5	4.41	60	.189	.353	0	.000	-1	-6	-6	1	-0.7

● RINTY MONAHAN Monahan, Edward Francis b: 4/28/28, Brooklyn, N.Y. BR/TR, 6'1.5", 195 lbs. Deb: 8/09/53

YEAR	TM/L	W	L	PCT	G	GS	CG	SH	SV	IP	H	HR	BB	SO	RAT	ERA	ERA+	OAV	OOB	BH	AVG	PB	PR	/A	PD	TPI
1953	Phi-A	0	0	—	4	0	0	0	0	10^{2}	11	0	7	2	15.2	4.22	102	.275	.383	0	.000	-0	-0	0	-0	0.0

● BILL MONBOUQUETTE Monbouquette, William Charles b: 8/11/36, Medford, Mass. BR/TR, 5'11", 195 lbs. Deb: 7/18/58 C

YEAR	TM/L	W	L	PCT	G	GS	CG	SH	SV	IP	H	HR	BB	SO	RAT	ERA	ERA+	OAV	OOB	BH	AVG	PB	PR	/A	PD	TPI
1958	Bos-A	3	4	.429	10	8	3	0	0	54^{1}	52	4	20	30	11.9	3.31	121	.251	.317	3	.176	-1	3	4	-1	0.3
1959	Bos-A	7	7	.500	34	17	4	0	0	151^{2}	165	15	33	87	11.9	4.15	98	.285	.327	3	.065	-4	-5	-2	-0	-0.6
1960	Bos-A★	14	11	.560	35	30	12	3	0	215	217	18	68	134	12.0	3.64	111	.263	.320	6	.092	-3	6	10	-0	0.7
1961	Bos-A	14	14	.500	32	32	12	1	0	236^{1}	233	24	100	161	12.7	3.39	123	.254	.327	9	.130	-1	17	20	-1	1.9
1962	Bos-A☆	15	13	.536	35	35	11	4	0	235^{1}	227	22	65	153	11.3	3.33	124	.251	.303	7	.096	-3	17	21	-4	1.4
1963	Bos-A☆	20	10	.667	37	36	13	1	0	266^{2}	258	31	42	174	10.1	3.81	99	.250	.280	10	.114	-4	-5	-1	1	-0.4
1964	Bos-A	13	14	.481	36	35	7	5	1	234	258	34	40	120	11.5	4.04	95	.277	.308	6	.083	-2	-11	-5	0	-0.7
1965	Bos-A	10	18	.357	35	35	10	2	0	228^{2}	239	32	40	110	11.0	3.70	101	.269	.301	4	.059	-3	-6	1	0	-0.2
1966	Det-A	7	8	.467	30	14	2	1	0	102^{2}	120	14	22	61	12.7	4.73	74	.293	.333	4	.154	-0	-15	-14	-1	-1.6
1967	Det-A	0	0	—	2	0	0	0	0	2	1	0	0	2	4.5	0.00	—	.143	.143	0	—	0	1	1	0	0.1
	NY-A	6	5	.545	33	10	2	1	1	133^{1}	122	6	17	53	9.7	2.36	132	.246	.277	5	.156	-0	13	11	-1	1.2
	Yr	6	5	.545	35	10	2	1	1	135^{1}	123	6	17	55	9.6	2.33	134	.245	.275	5	.156	-0	14	12	-1	1.3
1968	NY-A	5	7	.417	17	11	2	0	0	89^{1}	92	7	13	32	10.9	4.43	65	.264	.296	3	.115	0	-14	-15	1	-1.5
	SF-N	0	1	.000	7	0	0	0	1	12^{1}	11	4	2	5	9.5	3.65	81	.239	.271	0	—	0	-1	-1	0	-0.1
Total	11	114	112	.504	343	263	78	18	3	1961^{2}	1995	211	462	1122	11.4	3.68	104	.263	.307	60	.103	-21	-2	29	-6	0.5

● SID MONGE Monge, Isidro Pedroza b: 4/11/51, Agua Preita, Mexico BB/TL, 6'2", 195 lbs. Deb: 9/12/75

YEAR	TM/L	W	L	PCT	G	GS	CG	SH	SV	IP	H	HR	BB	SO	RAT	ERA	ERA+	OAV	OOB	BH	AVG	PB	PR	/A	PD	TPI
1975	Cal-A	0	2	.000	4	2	2	0	0	23^{2}	22	3	10	17	12.5	4.18	85	.242	.324	0	—	0	-1	-2	-0	0.2
1976	Cal-A	6	7	.462	32	13	2	0	0	117^{2}	108	10	49	53	12.1	3.37	99	.248	.326	0	—	0	2	-1	-1	0.2
1977	Cal-A	0	1	.000	4	0	0	0	1	12^{1}	14	2	6	4	14.6	2.92	134	.304	.385	0	—	0	2	1	0	0.5
	Cle-A	1	2	.333	33	0	0	0	3	39	47	6	27	25	17.1	6.23	63	.309	.413	0	—	0	-9	-10	-1	-0.8
	Yr	1	3	.250	37	0	0	0	4	51^{1}	61	8	33	29	16.5	5.44	72	.307	.405	0	—	0	-8	-9	-1	-0.3
1978	Cle-A	4	3	.571	48	2	0	0	6	84^{2}	71	4	51	54	13.0	2.76	135	.225	.332	0	—	0	9	9	-0	1.0
1979	Cle-A☆	12	10	.545	76	0	0	0	19	131	96	9	64	108	11.1	2.40	177	.209	.307	0	—	0	26	27	-0	2.6
1980	Cle-A	3	5	.375	67	0	0	0	14	94^{1}	80	12	40	61	11.7	3.53	115	.227	.311	0	—	0	5	6	-2	0.4
1981	Cle-A	3	5	.375	31	0	0	0	4	58	58	9	21	41	12.3	4.34	83	.266	.331	0	—	0	-4	-5	-1	-0.5
1982	Phi-N	7	1	.875	47	0	0	0	2	72	70	8	22	43	11.8	3.75	98	.256	.316	1	.111	-0	-1	-1	1	0.0
1983	Phi-N	3	0	1.000	14	0	0	0	0	11^{2}	20	4	6	7	20.1	6.94	51	.377	.441	0	.000	-0	-4	-4	-0	-0.5
	SD-N	7	3	.700	47	0	0	0	7	68^{2}	65	4	31	32	12.7	3.15	111	.257	.340	1	.100	-0	4	3	-0	0.2
	Yr	10	3	.769	61	0	0	0	7	80^{1}	85	8	37	39	13.8	3.70	95	.277	.357	1	.091	-1	-1	-2	-1	-0.3
1984	SD-N	2	1	.667	13	0	0	0	0	15	17	3	17	7	20.4	4.80	74	.293	.453	0	.000	-0	-2	-2	-0	-0.3
	Det-A	1	0	1.000	19	0	0	0	0	36	40	5	12	19	13.5	4.25	92	.282	.346	0	—	0	-1	-1	-1	-0.2
Total	10	49	40	.551	435	17	4	0	56	764	708	79	356	471	12.7	3.53	107	.248	.334	2	.095	-1	25	20	-6	2.8

● ED MONROE Monroe, Edward Oliver "Peck" b: 2/22/1895, Louisville, Ky. d: 4/29/69, Louisville, Ky. BR/TR, 6'5", 187 lbs. Deb: 5/29/17

YEAR	TM/L	W	L	PCT	G	GS	CG	SH	SV	IP	H	HR	BB	SO	RAT	ERA	ERA+	OAV	OOB	BH	AVG	PB	PR	/A	PD	TPI
1917	NY-A	1	0	1.000	9	1	1	0	1	28^{2}	35	1	6	12	13.5	3.45	78	.310	.355	2	.167	-0	-3	-2	-0	-0.3
1918	NY-A	0	0	—	1	0	0	0	0	2	1	0	2	1	13.5	4.50	63	.143	.333	0	—	0	-0	-0	0	0.0
Total	2	1	0	1.000	10	1	1	0	1	30^{2}	36	1	8	13	13.5	3.52	77	.300	.354	2	.167	-0	-3	-3	0	-0.3

● LARRY MONROE Monroe, Lawrence James b: 6/20/56, Detroit, Mich. BR/TR, 6'4", 200 lbs. Deb: 8/23/76

YEAR	TM/L	W	L	PCT	G	GS	CG	SH	SV	IP	H	HR	BB	SO	RAT	ERA	ERA+	OAV	OOB	BH	AVG	PB	PR	/A	PD	TPI
1976	Chi-A	0	1	.000	8	2	0	0	0	21^{2}	23	0	13	9	15.0	4.15	86	.284	.383	0	—	0	-2	-1	-0	-0.2

● ZACH MONROE Monroe, Zachary Charles b: 7/8/31, Peoria, Ill. BR/TR, 6', 198 lbs. Deb: 6/27/58

YEAR	TM/L	W	L	PCT	G	GS	CG	SH	SV	IP	H	HR	BB	SO	RAT	ERA	ERA+	OAV	OOB	BH	AVG	PB	PR	/A	PD	TPI
1958	*NY-A	4	2	.667	21	6	1	0	1	58	57	8	27	18	13.0	3.26	108	.263	.344	2	.118	-1	3	2	0	0.1
1959	NY-A	0	0	—	3	0	0	0	0	3^{1}	3	2	2	1	13.5	5.40	67	.231	.333	0	—	0	-1	-1	0	-0.1
Total	2	4	2	.667	24	6	1	0	1	61^{1}	60	10	29	19	13.1	3.38	105	.261	.344	2	.118	-1	3	1	1	0.0

● JOHN MONTAGUE Montague, John Evans b: 9/12/47, Newport News, Va. BR/TR, 6'2", 213 lbs. Deb: 9/09/73

YEAR	TM/L	W	L	PCT	G	GS	CG	SH	SV	IP	H	HR	BB	SO	RAT	ERA	ERA+	OAV	OOB	BH	AVG	PB	PR	/A	PD	TPI
1973	Mon-N	0	0	—	4	0	0	0	0	7^{2}	8	0	2	7	12.9	3.52	108	.286	.355	0	.000	-0	0	0	-0	0.0
1974	Mon-N	3	4	.429	46	1	0	0	3	82^{2}	73	5	38	43	12.5	3.16	122	.241	.333	1	.100	-0	4	6	-2	0.5

YEAR	TM/L	W	L	PCT	G	GS	CG	SH	SV	IP	H	HR	BB	SO	RAT	ERA	ERA+	OAV	OOB	BH	AVG	PB	PR	/A	PD	TPI
1975	Mon-N	0	1	.000	12	0	0	0	2	17^2	23	4	6	9	15.8	5.60	68	.324	.392	0	.000	-0	-4	-3	-0	-0.4
	Phi-N	0	0	—	3	0	0	0	0	5	8	1	4	1	21.6	9.00	41	.400	.500	0	—	0	-3	-3	0	-0.3
	Yr	0	1	.000	15	0	0	0	2	22^2	31	5	10	10	16.3	6.35	60	.326	.390	0	.000	-0	-7	-6	0	-0.7
1977	Sea-A	8	12	.400	47	15	2	0	4	182^1	193	20	75	98	13.4	4.29	96	.272	.345	0	—	0	-5	-4	1	-0.2
1978	Sea-A	1	3	.250	19	0	0	0	2	43^2	52	2	24	14	15.7	6.18	62	.308	.394	0	—	0	-12	-12	-1	-1.2
1979	Sea-A	6	4	.600	41	1	0	0	1	116^1	125	14	47	60	13.5	5.57	78	.284	.356	0	—	0	-18	-16	1	-1.5
	*Cal-A	2	0	1.000	14	0	0	0	6	17^2	16	3	9	6	12.7	5.09	80	.242	.333	0	—	0	-2	-2	-1	-0.1
	Yr	8	4	.667	55	1	0	0	7	134	141	17	56	66	13.2	5.51	78	.273	.344	0	—	0	-19	-18	-0	-1.6
1980	Cal-A	4	2	.667	37	0	0	0	3	73^2	97	8	21	22	14.5	5.13	77	.324	.371	0	—	0	-9	-10	0	-0.8
Total	7	24	26	.480	223	17	2	0	21	546^2	595	57	226	260	13.7	4.76	85	.283	.356	1	.083	-0	-47	-42	-1	-4.0

● RAFAEL MONTALVO Montalvo, Rafael Edgardo (Torres) b: 3/31/64, Rio Piedras, P.R. BR/TR, 6', 185 lbs. Deb: 4/13/86

YEAR	TM/L	W	L	PCT	G	GS	CG	SH	SV	IP	H	HR	BB	SO	RAT	ERA	ERA+	OAV	OOB	BH	AVG	PB	PR	/A	PD	TPI
1986	Hou-N	0	0	—	1	0	0	0	0	1	1	0	2	0	27.0	9.00	40	.250	.500	0	—	0	-1	-1	0	0.0

● AURELIO MONTEAGUDO Monteagudo, Aurelio Faustino (Cintra) b: 11/19/43, Caibarien, Cuba d: 11/10/90, Saltillo, Mexico BR/TR, 5'11", 185 lbs. Deb: 9/01/63 F

YEAR	TM/L	W	L	PCT	G	GS	CG	SH	SV	IP	H	HR	BB	SO	RAT	ERA	ERA+	OAV	OOB	BH	AVG	PB	PR	/A	PD	TPI
1963	KC-A	0	0	—	4	0	0	0	0	7	4	0	3	3	9.0	2.57	149	.182	.280	0	—	0	1	1	0	0.1
1964	KC-A	0	4	.000	11	6	0	0	0	31^1	40	11	10	14	14.6	8.90	43	.317	.372	2	.286	1	-18	-18	-0	-1.6
1965	KC-A	0	0	—	4	0	0	0	0	7	5	1	4	5	11.6	3.86	90	.185	.290	0	—	0	-0	-0	-0	-0.1
1966	KC-A	0	0	—	6	0	0	0	0	12^2	12	0	7	3	13.5	2.84	120	.261	.358	0	—	0	1	1	-0	0.1
	Hou-N	0	0	—	10	0	0	0	1	15^1	14	1	11	7	14.7	4.70	73	.241	.362	0	.000	-0	-2	-2	-0	-0.2
1967	Chi-A	0	1	.000	1	1	0	0	0	1^1	4	1	2	0	40.5	20.25	15	.500	.600	0	—	0	-3	-3	-0	-0.2
1970	KC-A	1	1	.500	21	0	0	0	0	27^1	20	2	9	18	9.9	2.96	126	.200	.273	0	.000	-0	2	2	-1	0.2
1973	Cal-A	2	1	.667	15	0	0	0	3	30	23	2	16	8	12.9	4.20	84	.215	.339	0	—	0	-1	-2	0	0.3
Total	7	3	7	.300	72	7	0	0	4	132	122	18	62	58	13.0	5.05	72	.247	.338	2	.200	1	-20	-21	-1	-1.4

● RENE MONTEAGUDO Monteagudo, Rene (Miranda) b: 3/12/16, Havana, Cuba d: 9/14/73, Hialeah, Fla. BL/TL, 5'7", 165 lbs. Deb: 9/06/38 F♦

YEAR	TM/L	W	L	PCT	G	GS	CG	SH	SV	IP	H	HR	BB	SO	RAT	ERA	ERA+	OAV	OOB	BH	AVG	PB	PR	/A	PD	TPI
1938	Was-A	1	1	.500	5	3	2	0	0	22	26	3	15	13	16.8	5.73	79	.286	.387	3	.500	1	-2	-3	-1	-0.2
1940	Was-A	2	6	.250	27	8	3	0	2	100^2	128	7	52	64	16.4	6.08	69	.316	.398	6	.182	0	-19	-21	-1	-2.0
1945	Phi-N	0	0	—	14	0	0	0	0	45^2	67	1	28	16	19.1	7.49	51	.347	.435	58	.301	2	-19	-19	-1	-1.6
Total	3	3	7	.300	46	11	5	0	2	168^1	221	11	95	93	17.2	6.42	64	.321	.407	78	.289	4	-40	-43	-3	-3.8

● JOHN MONTEFUSCO Montefusco, John Joseph "Count" b: 5/25/50, Long Branch, N.J. BR/TR, 6'1", 180 lbs. Deb: 9/03/74

YEAR	TM/L	W	L	PCT	G	GS	CG	SH	SV	IP	H	HR	BB	SO	RAT	ERA	ERA+	OAV	OOB	BH	AVG	PB	PR	/A	PD	TPI
1974	SF-N	3	2	.600	7	5	1	1	0	39^1	41	3	19	34	13.7	4.81	79	.256	.335	4	.286	3	-5	-4	-0	-0.2
1975	SF-N	15	9	.625	35	34	10	4	0	243^2	210	11	86	215	11.2	2.88	132	.233	.305	7	.087	-3	20	25	-1	2.3
1976	SF-N★	16	14	.533	37	36	11	**6**	0	253^1	224	11	74	172	10.7	2.84	128	.238	.296	8	.103	-2	19	22	-4	1.8
1977	SF-N	7	12	.368	26	25	4	0	0	157^1	170	10	46	110	12.5	3.49	112	.273	.326	6	.122	-1	7	7	-2	0.5
1978	SF-N	11	9	.550	36	36	3	0	0	238^2	233	25	68	177	11.5	3.81	91	.255	.310	4	.057	-3	-6	-10	-2	-1.4
1979	SF-N	3	8	.273	22	22	0	0	0	137	145	15	51	76	13.0	3.94	89	.279	.346	7	.167	1	-3	-7	0	-0.6
1980	SF-N	4	8	.333	22	17	1	0	0	113^1	120	15	39	85	12.8	4.37	81	.265	.327	1	.033	-2	-10	-10	-1	-1.4
1981	Atl-N	2	3	.400	26	9	0	0	1	77^1	75	9	27	34	11.9	3.49	103	.260	.324	1	.067	-1	-0	1	0	0.0
1982	SD-N	10	11	.476	32	32	1	0	0	184^1	177	17	41	83	10.8	4.00	86	.251	.295	5	.086	-2	-8	-12	-1	-1.5
1983	SD-N	9	4	.692	31	10	1	0	4	95^1	94	6	32	52	12.0	3.30	105	.265	.327	1	.053	-1	3	2	-1	0.0
	NY-A	5	0	1.000	6	6	0	0	0	38	39	3	10	15	11.8	3.32	117	.271	.323	0	—	0	3	2	-1	0.2
1984	NY-A	5	3	.625	11	11	0	0	0	55^1	55	5	13	23	11.2	3.58	106	.253	.299	0	—	0	3	1	-1	0.1
1985	NY-A	0	0	—	3	1	0	0	0	7	12	3	2	2	18.0	10.29	39	.387	.424	0	—	0	-5	-5	0	-0.3
1986	NY-A	0	0	—	4	0	0	0	0	12^1	9	2	5	3	10.2	2.19	187	.200	.280	0	—	0	3	3	0	0.4
Total	13	90	83	.520	298	244	32	11	5	1652^1	1604	135	513	1081	11.7	3.54	102	.255	.314	44	.097	-10	20	16	-12	-0.1

● MANNY MONTEJO Montejo, Manuel (Bofill) b: 10/16/35, Caibarien, Cuba BR/TR, 5'11", 150 lbs. Deb: 7/25/61

YEAR	TM/L	W	L	PCT	G	GS	CG	SH	SV	IP	H	HR	BB	SO	RAT	ERA	ERA+	OAV	OOB	BH	AVG	PB	PR	/A	PD	TPI
1961	Det-A	0	0	—	12	0	0	0	0	16^1	13	2	6	15	11.6	3.86	106	.217	.309	0	—	0	0	0	-1	0.0

● RICH MONTELEONE Monteleone, Richard b: 3/22/63, Tampa, Fla. BR/TR, 6'2", 220 lbs. Deb: 4/15/87

YEAR	TM/L	W	L	PCT	G	GS	CG	SH	SV	IP	H	HR	BB	SO	RAT	ERA	ERA+	OAV	OOB	BH	AVG	PB	PR	/A	PD	TPI
1987	Sea-A	0	0	—	3	0	0	0	0	7	10	2	4	2	19.3	6.43	73	.345	.441	0	—	0	-2	-1	0	-0.4
1988	Cal-A	0	0	—	3	0	0	0	0	4^1	4	0	1	3	12.5	0.00	—	.222	.300	0	—	0	2	2	0	0.4
1989	Cal-A	2	2	.500	24	0	0	0	0	39^2	39	3	13	27	12.0	3.18	120	.255	.317	0	—	0	3	3	1	0.5
1990	NY-A	0	1	.000	5	0	0	0	0	7^1	8	0	2	8	12.3	6.14	65	.276	.323	0	—	0	-2	-2	0	-0.2
1991	NY-A	3	1	.750	26	0	0	0	0	47	42	5	19	34	11.7	3.64	114	.236	.310	0	—	0	2	3	1	0.3
1992	NY-A	7	3	.700	47	0	0	0	0	92^2	82	7	27	62	10.6	3.30	123	.235	.290	0	—	0	7	8	-1	0.5
Total	6	12	7	.632	108	0	0	0	0	198	185	17	66	136	11.5	3.50	115	.245	.308	0	—	0	11	12	1	1.1

● JEFF MONTGOMERY Montgomery, Jeffrey Thomas b: 1/7/62, Wellston, Ohio BR/TR, 5'11", 180 lbs. Deb: 8/01/87

YEAR	TM/L	W	L	PCT	G	GS	CG	SH	SV	IP	H	HR	BB	SO	RAT	ERA	ERA+	OAV	OOB	BH	AVG	PB	PR	/A	PD	TPI
1987	Cin-N	2	2	.500	14	1	0	0	0	19^1	25	2	9	13	15.8	6.52	65	.313	.382	0	.000	-0	-5	-5	0	-0.5
1988	KC-A	7	2	.778	45	0	0	0	1	62^2	54	6	30	47	12.4	3.45	116	.231	.323	0	—	0	4	4	0	0.3
1989	KC-A	7	3	.700	63	0	0	0	18	92	66	3	25	94	9.1	1.37	281	.198	.258	0	—	0	**26**	**25**	-1	2.6
1990	KC-A	6	5	.545	73	0	0	0	24	94^1	81	6	34	94	11.4	2.39	161	.227	.303	0	—	0	16	15	0	1.7
1991	KC-A	4	4	.500	67	0	0	0	33	90	83	6	28	77	11.3	2.90	142	.246	.307	0	—	0	12	12	-0	1.2
1992	KC-A★	1	6	.143	65	0	0	0	39	82^2	61	5	27	69	9.9	2.18	183	.205	.278	0	—	0	16	17	2	1.8
Total	6	27	22	.551	327	1	0	0	115	441	370	28	153	394	11.0	2.57	154	.226	.297	0	.000	-0	68	68	2	7.1

● MONTY MONTGOMERY Montgomery, Monty Bryson b: 9/1/46, Albermarle, N.C. BR/TR, 6'3", 200 lbs. Deb: 9/14/71

YEAR	TM/L	W	L	PCT	G	GS	CG	SH	SV	IP	H	HR	BB	SO	RAT	ERA	ERA+	OAV	OOB	BH	AVG	PB	PR	/A	PD	TPI
1971	KC-A	3	0	1.000	3	2	0	0	0	21^1	16	0	3	12	8.0	2.11	163	.205	.235	0	.000	-0	3	3	0	0.3
1972	KC-A	3	3	.500	9	8	1	1	0	56^1	55	2	17	24	11.5	3.04	100	.263	.319	3	.176	0	0	-0	-0	0.0
Total	2	6	3	.667	12	10	1	1	0	77^2	71	2	20	36	10.5	2.78	113	.247	.296	3	.125	0	3	3	-0	0.3

● RAMON MONZANT Monzant, Ramon Segundo (Espina) b: 1/4/33, Maracaibo, Venez. BR/TR, 6', 165 lbs. Deb: 7/02/54

YEAR	TM/L	W	L	PCT	G	GS	CG	SH	SV	IP	H	HR	BB	SO	RAT	ERA	ERA+	OAV	OOB	BH	AVG	PB	PR	/A	PD	TPI
1954	NY-N	0	0	—	6	1	0	0	0	7^2	8	0	11	5	22.3	4.70	86	.276	.475	0	.000	-0	-1	-1	-0	-0.1
1955	NY-N	4	8	.333	28	12	3	0	0	94^2	98	11	43	54	13.7	3.99	101	.278	.361	3	.125	-1	0	0	-1	-0.2
1956	NY-N	1	0	1.000	4	1	1	0	0	13	8	4	7	11	10.4	4.15	91	.170	.278	0	.000	-1	-1	-1	-0	-0.1
1957	NY-N	3	2	.600	24	2	0	0	0	49^2	55	6	16	37	13.2	3.99	99	.286	.348	3	.300	1	-1	-0	-1	-0.1
1958	SF-N	8	11	.421	43	16	4	1	1	150^2	160	21	57	93	13.3	4.72	81	.273	.344	8	.163	-1	-13	-15	1	-1.5
1960	SF-N	0	0	—	1	0	0	0	0	1	1	1	0	1	9.0	9.00	39	.250	.250	0	—	0	-1	-1	0	0.0
Total	6	16	21	.432	106	32	8	1	1	316^2	330	43	134	201	13.5	4.38	89	.273	.350	14	.157	-2	-15	-17	-1	-2.0

● LEO MOON Moon, Leo "Lefty" b: 6/22/1899, Belmont, N.C. d: 8/25/70, New Orleans, La. BR/TL, 5'11", 165 lbs. Deb: 7/09/32

YEAR	TM/L	W	L	PCT	G	GS	CG	SH	SV	IP	H	HR	BB	SO	RAT	ERA	ERA+	OAV	OOB	BH	AVG	PB	PR	/A	PD	TPI
1932	Cle-A	0	0	—	1	0	0	0	0	5^2	11	0	7	1	28.6	11.12	43	.379	.500	1	.500	0	-4	-4	0	-0.3

● JIM MOONEY Mooney, Jim Irving b: 9/4/06, Mooresburg, Tenn. d: 4/27/79, Johnson City, Tenn BR/TL, 5'11", 168 lbs. Deb: 8/14/31

YEAR	TM/L	W	L	PCT	G	GS	CG	SH	SV	IP	H	HR	BB	SO	RAT	ERA	ERA+	OAV	OOB	BH	AVG	PB	PR	/A	PD	TPI
1931	NY-N	7	1	.875	10	8	6	2	0	71^2	71	1	16	38	11.1	2.01	184	.262	.306	4	.160	-1	15	13	-1	1.2
1932	NY-N	6	10	.375	29	18	4	1	0	124^2	154	18	42	37	14.1	5.05	73	.299	.352	5	.122	-2	-16	-19	-2	-2.1
1933	StL-N	2	5	.286	21	8	2	0	1	77^1	87	1	26	14	13.2	3.72	93	.296	.353	1	.050	-2	-3	-2	1	-0.4
1934	*StL-N	2	4	.333	32	7	1	0	1	82^1	114	3	49	27	18.3	5.47	77	.326	.414	1	.053	-2	-13	-11	-1	-1.4
Total	4	17	20	.459	92	41	13	3	2	356	426	23	133	116	14.3	4.25	89	.298	.360	11	.105	-7	-18	-19	-3	-2.7

● BILL MOONEYHAM Mooneyham, William Craig b: 8/16/60, Livermore, Cal. BR/TR, 6', 175 lbs. Deb: 4/19/86

YEAR	TM/L	W	L	PCT	G	GS	CG	SH	SV	IP	H	HR	BB	SO	RAT	ERA	ERA+	OAV	OOB	BH	AVG	PB	PR	/A	PD	TPI
1986	Oak-A	4	5	.444	45	6	0	0	2	99^2	103	4	67	75	15.6	4.52	86	.270	.384	0	—	0	-4	-7	1	-0.2

● BALOR MOORE Moore, Balor Lilbon b: 1/25/51, Smithville, Tex. BL/TL, 6'2", 184 lbs. Deb: 5/21/70

YEAR	TM/L	W	L	PCT	G	GS	CG	SH	SV	IP	H	HR	BB	SO	RAT	ERA	ERA+	OAV	OOB	BH	AVG	PB	PR	/A	PD	TPI
1970	Mon-N	0	2	.000	6	2	0	0	0	9^2	14	0	8	6	20.5	7.45	55	.368	.478	1	.333	0	-4	-4	0	-0.3
1972	Mon-N	9	9	.500	22	22	6	3	0	147^2	122	15	59	161	11.3	3.47	102	.226	.307	8	.145	-0	-0	1	0	0.1
1973	Mon-N	7	16	.304	35	32	3	1	0	176^1	151	18	109	151	13.4	4.49	85	.233	.346	3	.057	-3	-16	-13	-1	-1.7
1974	Mon-N	0	2	.000	8	2	0	0	0	13^2	13	1	15	16	18.4	3.95	97	.245	.412	0	.000	-0	-1	-0	-0	-0.1
1977	Cal-A	0	2	.000	7	3	0	0	0	22^2	28	7	10	14	16.3	3.97	99	.298	.383	0	—	0	0	-0	-1	0.0
1978	Tor-A	6	9	.400	37	18	2	0	0	144^1	165	16	54	75	14.1	4.93	80	.294	.363	0	—	0	-19	-16	1	-1.5
1979	Tor-A	5	7	.417	34	16	5	0	0	139^1	135	17	79	51	14.3	4.84	90	.262	.369	0	—	0	-10	-8	-1	-0.8
1980	Tor-A	1	1	.500	31	3	0	0	1	64^2	76	6	31	22	15.4	5.29	81	.309	.395	0	—	0	-9	-7	-0	-0.8
Total	8	28	48	.368	180	98	16	4	1	718^1	704	80	365	496	13.8	4.52	87	.261	.355	12	.106	-4	-58	-47	-1	-5.1

● BRAD MOORE Moore, Bradley Alan b: 6/21/64, Loveland, Colo. BR/TR, 6'1", 185 lbs. Deb: 6/14/88

YEAR	TM/L	W	L	PCT	G	GS	CG	SH	SV	IP	H	HR	BB	SO	RAT	ERA	ERA+	OAV	OOB	BH	AVG	PB	PR	/A	PD	TPI
1988	Phi-N	0	0	—	5	0	0	0	0	5^2	4	0	4	2	12.7	0.00	—	.267	.421	0	—	0	2	2	0	0.3
1990	Phi-N	0	0	—	3	0	0	0	0	2^2	4	0	2	1	20.3	3.38	113	.400	.500	0	—	0	0	0	0	0.0
Total	2	0	0	—	8	0	0	0	0	8^1	8	0	6	3	15.1	1.08	338	.320	.452	0	—	0	2	2	0	0.3

● CARLOS MOORE Moore, Carlos Whitman b: 8/13/06, Clinton, Tenn. d: 7/2/58, New Orleans, La. BR/TR, 6'1.5", 180 lbs. Deb: 5/04/30

YEAR	TM/L	W	L	PCT	G	GS	CG	SH	SV	IP	H	HR	BB	SO	RAT	ERA	ERA+	OAV	OOB	BH	AVG	PB	PR	/A	PD	TPI
1930	Was-A	0	0	—	4	0	0	0	0	11^2	9	0	4	2	10.0	2.31	199	.225	.295	0	.000	-1	3	3	-0	0.2

● DEE MOORE Moore, D C b: 4/6/14, Hedley, Tex. BR/TR, 5'11", 190 lbs. Deb: 9/12/36 ♦

YEAR	TM/L	W	L	PCT	G	GS	CG	SH	SV	IP	H	HR	BB	SO	RAT	ERA	ERA+	OAV	OOB	BH	AVG	PB	PR	/A	PD	TPI
1936	Cin-N	0	0	—	2	1	0	0	0	7	3	0	2	3	6.4	0.00	—	.120	.185	4	.400	1	3	3	0	0.4

● DONNIE MOORE Moore, Donnie Ray b: 2/13/54, Lubbock, Tex. d: 7/18/89, Anaheim, Cal. BL/TR, 6', 185 lbs. Deb: 9/14/75

YEAR	TM/L	W	L	PCT	G	GS	CG	SH	SV	IP	H	HR	BB	SO	RAT	ERA	ERA+	OAV	OOB	BH	AVG	PB	PR	/A	PD	TPI
1975	Chi-N	0	0	—	4	1	0	0	0	8^2	12	1	4	8	16.6	4.15	92	.316	.381	0	.000	-0	-1	-0	-0	-0.1
1977	Chi-N	4	2	.667	27	1	0	0	0	48^2	51	1	18	34	12.8	4.07	108	.285	.350	3	.300	1	-1	2	1	0.4
1978	Chi-N	9	7	.563	71	1	0	0	4	103	117	7	31	50	13.1	4.11	98	.287	.340	4	.267	1	-6	-1	0	0.1
1979	Chi-N	1	4	.200	39	1	0	0	1	73	95	8	25	43	15.0	5.18	79	.321	.378	2	.154	0	-12	-9	1	-0.8
1980	StL-N	1	1	.500	11	0	0	0	0	21^2	25	1	5	10	12.9	6.23	59	.298	.344	3	.750	2	-6	-6	-1	-0.5
1981	Mil-A	0	0	—	3	0	0	0	0	4	4	0	4	2	18.0	6.75	51	.286	.444	0	—	0	-1	-1	0	0.0
1982	*Atl-N	3	1	.750	16	0	0	0	1	27^2	32	1	7	17	13.3	4.23	88	.294	.347	0	.000	-0	-2	-2	0	-0.1
1983	Atl-N	2	3	.400	43	0	0	0	6	68^2	72	6	10	41	10.7	3.67	106	.279	.306	4	.500	1	-0	2	-1	0.2
1984	Atl-N	4	5	.444	47	0	0	0	16	64^1	63	3	18	47	11.5	2.94	131	.258	.312	0	.000	-0	5	7	0	0.7
1985	Cal-A★	8	8	.500	65	0	0	0	31	103	91	9	21	72	9.8	1.92	214	.237	.277	0	—	0	**25**	25	-1	2.5
1986	*Cal-A	4	5	.444	49	0	0	0	21	72^2	60	10	22	53	10.2	2.97	138	.228	.288	0	—	0	10	9	-1	0.9
1987	Cal-A	2	2	.500	14	0	0	0	5	26^2	28	2	13	17	13.8	2.70	159	.259	.339	0	—	0	5	5	-1	0.5
1988	Cal-A	5	2	.714	27	0	0	0	4	33	48	4	8	22	15.3	4.91	79	.343	.378	0	—	0	-3	-4	0	-0.2
Total	13	43	40	.518	416	4	0	0	89	655	698	53	186	416	12.3	3.67	110	.276	.328	16	.281	5	12	27	-1	3.6

● EARL MOORE Moore, Earl Alonzo "Big Ebbie" or "Crossfire" b: 7/29/1879, Pickerington, O. d: 11/28/61, Columbus, Ohio BR/TR, 6', 195 lbs. Deb: 4/25/01

YEAR	TM/L	W	L	PCT	G	GS	CG	SH	SV	IP	H	HR	BB	SO	RAT	ERA	ERA+	OAV	OOB	BH	AVG	PB	PR	/A	PD	TPI
1901	Cle-A	16	14	.533	31	30	28	4	0	251^1	234	4	107	99	12.5	2.90	122	.244	.325	16	.162	-5	21	18	-4	0.8
1902	Cle-A	17	17	.500	36	34	29	4	1	293	304	8	101	84	12.7	2.95	117	.268	.332	24	.212	-0	20	16	-1	1.4
1903	Cle-A	19	9	.679	29	27	27	3	1	247^2	196	0	62	148	9.6	**1.74**	**164**	**.217**	.271	8	.092	-5	**34**	31	-3	2.5
1904	Cle-A	12	11	.522	26	24	22	1	0	227^2	186	2	61	139	10.1	2.25	113	.224	.284	12	.140	-2	9	7	-7	-0.2
1905	Cle-A	15	15	.500	31	30	28	3	0	269	232	6	92	131	11.3	2.64	100	.234	.308	10	.104	-4	1	-0	-2	-0.8
1906	Cle-A	1	1	.500	5	4	2	0	0	29^2	27	1	18	8	14.3	3.94	66	.246	.362	0	.000	-1	-4	-4	-1	-0.7
1907	Cle-A	1	1	.500	3	2	1	0	0	19^1	18	0	8	7	12.6	4.66	54	.249	.332	0	.000	-1	-5	-5	0	-0.5
	NY-A	2	6	.250	12	9	3	0	1	64	72	1	30	28	14.8	3.94	71	.286	.368	6	.273	1	-10	-8	-0	-0.8
	Yr	3	7	.300	15	11	4	0	1	83^1	90	1	38	35	14.1	4.10	67	.276	.357	6	.207	0	-14	-13	-0	-1.3
1908	Phi-N	2	1	.667	3	3	3	1	0	26	20	0	8	16	10.4	0.00	—	.217	.294	2	.222	0	7	7	-1	1.0
1909	Phi-N	18	12	.600	38	34	24	4	0	299^2	238	7	108	173	10.7	2.10	124	.210	.283	9	.094	-4	17	17	-5	0.8
1910	Phi-N	22	15	.595	46	35	18	**6**	0	283	228	5	121	**185**	11.4	2.58	121	.228	.318	20	.230	2	14	17	-4	1.7
1911	Phi-N	15	19	.441	42	36	21	5	1	308^1	265	11	164	174	12.9	2.63	131	.240	.345	11	.109	-6	27	28	-3	1.9
1912	Phi-N	9	14	.391	31	24	10	1	0	182^1	186	3	77	79	13.3	3.31	110	.275	.355	6	.107	-4	2	7	-2	-0.1
1913	Phi-N	1	3	.250	12	4	0	0	1	52	50	3	40	24	15.8	5.02	66	.254	.382	0	.000	-2	-10	-10	1	-1.1
	Chi-N	1	1	.500	7	2	0	0	0	28^1	34	3	12	12	14.6	4.45	72	.321	.390	1	.125	-0	-4	-4	1	-0.4
	Yr	2	4	.333	19	6	0	0	1	80^1	84	6	52	36	15.2	4.82	68	.276	.382	1	.042	-3	-14	-14	2	-1.5
1914	Buf-F	11	15	.423	36	27	14	2	2	194^2	184	3	99	96	13.5	4.30	77	.263	.362	9	.161	-1	-24	-22	-2	-2.5
Total	14	162	154	.513	388	325	230	34	7	2776	2474	57	1108	1403	11.9	2.78	111	.241	.321	134	.141	-33	95	95	-33	3.0

● EUEL MOORE Moore, Euel Walton "Chief" b: 5/27/08, Reagan, Okla. d: 2/12/89, Tishomingo, Okla. BR/TR, 6'2", 185 lbs. Deb: 7/08/34

YEAR	TM/L	W	L	PCT	G	GS	CG	SH	SV	IP	H	HR	BB	SO	RAT	ERA	ERA+	OAV	OOB	BH	AVG	PB	PR	/A	PD	TPI
1934	Phi-N	5	7	.417	20	16	3	0	1	122^1	145	9	41	38	13.7	4.05	117	.288	.342	5	.109	-5	0	9	-1	0.3
1935	Phi-N	1	6	.143	15	8	1	0	1	40^1	63	5	20	15	19.0	7.81	58	.354	.425	6	.400	1	-17	-15	0	-1.2
	NY-N	1	0	1.000	6	0	0	0	0	8	9	0	4	3	14.6	5.63	69	.281	.361	0	.000	-0	-1	-2	0	-0.2
	Yr	2	6	.250	21	8	1	0	1	48^1	72	5	24	18	17.9	7.45	59	.340	.407	6	.353	1	-18	-16	0	-1.4
1936	Phi-N	2	3	.400	20	5	1	0	1	54^1	76	4	12	19	14.7	6.96	65	.311	.346	4	.222	-0	-18	-15	-1	-1.5
Total	3	9	16	.360	61	29	5	0	3	225	293	18	77	75	14.9	5.48	84	.306	.360	15	.185	-4	-36	-22	-3	-2.6

● GENE MOORE Moore, Eugene Sr. "Blue Goose" b: 11/9/1885, Lancaster, Tex. d: 8/31/38, Dallas, Tex. BL/TL, 6'2", 185 lbs. Deb: 9/28/09 F

YEAR	TM/L	W	L	PCT	G	GS	CG	SH	SV	IP	H	HR	BB	SO	RAT	ERA	ERA+	OAV	OOB	BH	AVG	PB	PR	/A	PD	TPI
1909	Pit-N	0	0	—	1	0	0	0	0	2	4	0	3	2	31.5	18.00	15	.364	.500	0	.000	-0	-3	-3	-0	-0.3
1910	Pit-N	2	1	.667	4	1	0	0	0	17^1	19	1	7	9	13.5	3.12	99	.268	.333	0	.000	-1	-0	-0	0	-0.1
1912	Cin-N	1	0	1.000	5	2	0	0	1	14^2	17	0	11	6	18.4	4.91	68	.304	.435	0	.000	-1	-2	-3	-0	-0.3
Total	3	2	2	.500	10	3	0	0	1	34	40	1	21	17	16.7	4.76	67	.290	.391	0	.000	-2	-6	-6	0	-0.7

● GEORGE MOORE Moore, George Raymond b: 11/25/1872, Cambridge, Mass. d: 11/17/48, Barnstable, Mass. BB/TR, 5'10", 165 lbs. Deb: 6/14/05

YEAR	TM/L	W	L	PCT	G	GS	CG	SH	SV	IP	H	HR	BB	SO	RAT	ERA	ERA+	OAV	OOB	BH	AVG	PB	PR	/A	PD	TPI
1905	Pit-N	0	0	—	1	0	0	0	0	3	2	0	0	1	6.0	0.00	—	.200	.200	0	.000	-0	1	1	-0	0.1

● JIM MOORE Moore, James Stanford b: 12/14/03, Prescott, Ark. d: 5/19/73, Seattle, Wash. BR/TR, 6', 165 lbs. Deb: 9/21/28

YEAR	TM/L	W	L	PCT	G	GS	CG	SH	SV	IP	H	HR	BB	SO	RAT	ERA	ERA+	OAV	OOB	BH	AVG	PB	PR	/A	PD	TPI
1928	Cle-A	0	1	.000	1	1	1	0	0	9	5	0	5	1	10.0	2.00	207	.161	.278	0	.000	-0	2	2	-0	0.1
1929	Cle-A	0	0	—	2	0	0	0	0	5^2	6	1	4	0	15.9	9.53	47	.273	.385	0	.000	-0	-3	-3	0	-0.3
1930	Chi-A	2	1	.667	9	5	2	0	1	40	42	0	12	11	12.1	3.60	128	.268	.320	3	.231	-0	5	5	-0	0.4
1931	Chi-A	0	2	.000	33	4	0	0	0	83^2	93	3	27	15	13.0	4.95	86	.282	.338	1	.063	-1	-5	-6	1	-0.6
1932	Chi-A	0	0	—	1	0	0	0	0	1	1	0	1	2	18.0	0.00	—	.250	.400	0	.000	-0	0	0	0	0.0
Total	5	2	4	.333	46	10	3	0	1	139^1	147	4	49	29	12.7	4.52	97	.270	.332	4	.114	-2	-1	-2	1	-0.4

● WHITEY MOORE Moore, Lloyd Albert b: 6/10/12, Tuscarawas, Ohio d: 12/10/87, Ulrichsville, O. BR/TR, 6'1", 195 lbs. Deb: 9/27/36

YEAR	TM/L	W	L	PCT	G	GS	CG	SH	SV	IP	H	HR	BB	SO	RAT	ERA	ERA+	OAV	OOB	BH	AVG	PB	PR	/A	PD	TPI
1936	Cin-N	1	0	1.000	1	0	0	0	0	5	3	0	3	4	10.8	5.40	71	.167	.286	0	.000	-0	-1	-1	-0	-0.1
1937	Cin-N	0	3	.000	13	6	0	0	0	38^2	32	1	39	27	17.5	4.89	76	.239	.424	0	.000	-1	-4	-5	-0	-0.6
1938	Cin-N	6	4	.600	19	11	3	1	0	90^1	66	4	42	38	11.1	3.49	105	.205	.302	2	.077	-2	3	2	-1	-0.2
1939	*Cin-N	13	12	.520	42	24	9	2	3	187^2	177	10	95	81	13.3	3.45	111	.254	.348	6	.098	-4	10	8	-1	0.3
1940	*Cin-N	8	8	.500	25	15	5	1	1	116^2	100	8	56	60	12.6	3.63	104	.231	.329	5	.128	-1	3	2	-3	-0.3
1941	Cin-N	2	1	.667	23	4	1	0	0	61^2	62	2	45	17	16.1	4.38	82	.256	.379	3	.167	-1	-5	-5	-1	-0.7
1942	Cin-N	0	0	—	1	0	0	0	0	1	0	0	1	0	9.0	0.00	—	.000	.250	0	—	0	0	0	-0	0.0
	StL-N	0	1	.000	9	0	0	0	0	12^1	10	0	11	1	16.1	4.38	78	.217	.379	0	.000	-0	-1	-1	-1	-0.2
	Yr	0	1	.000	10	0	0	0	0	13^1	10	0	12	1	15.5	4.05	84	.204	.371	0	.000	-0	-1	-1	-1	-0.2
Total	7	30	29	.508	133	60	18	4	4	513^1	450	25	292	228	13.4	3.75	100	.237	.346	16	.103	-10	4	-0	-7	-1.8

● MIKE MOORE Moore, Michael Wayne b: 11/26/59, Eakly, Okla. BR/TR, 6'4", 205 lbs. Deb: 4/11/82

YEAR	TM/L	W	L	PCT	G	GS	CG	SH	SV	IP	H	HR	BB	SO	RAT	ERA	ERA+	OAV	OOB	BH	AVG	PB	PR	/A	PD	TPI
1982	Sea-A	7	14	.333	28	27	1	1	0	144^1	159	21	79	73	15.0	5.36	79	.285	.376	0	—	0	-21	-18	1	-1.6
1983	Sea-A	6	8	.429	22	21	3	2	0	128	130	10	60	108	13.6	4.71	90	.267	.352	0	—	0	-9	-6	2	-0.5
1984	Sea-A	7	17	.292	34	33	6	0	0	212	236	16	85	158	13.8	4.97	80	.282	.352	0	—	0	-23	-23	3	-1.9
1985	Sea-A	17	10	.630	35	34	14	2	0	247	230	18	70	155	11.1	3.46	122	.247	.302	0	—	0	19	21	2	2.3
1986	Sea-A	11	13	.458	38	37	11	1	1	266	279	28	94	146	13.0	4.30	99	.273	.341	0	—	0	-4	-2	-1	-0.2
1987	Sea-A	9	19	.321	33	33	12	0	0	231	268	29	84	115	13.7	4.71	100	.292	.351	0	.000	0	-7	0	1	0.1
1988	Sea-A	9	15	.375	37	32	9	3	1	228^2	196	24	63	182	10.3	3.78	110	.232	.287	0	—	0	5	10	1	0.7
1989	*Oak-A★	19	11	.633	35	35	6	3	0	241^2	193	14	83	172	10.4	2.61	141	.219	.288	0	—	0	34	29	2	3.6
1990	*Oak-A	13	15	.464	33	33	3	0	0	199^1	204	14	84	73	13.1	4.65	80	.267	.342	0	—	0	-16	-21	1	-1.7
1991	Oak-A	17	8	.680	33	33	3	1	0	210	176	11	105	153	12.3	2.96	130	.229	.326	0	—	0	27	20	2	2.4
1992	*Oak-A	17	12	.586	36	36	2	0	0	223	229	20	103	117	13.7	4.12	92	.268	.353	0	—	0	-4	-8	-1	-0.6
Total	11	132	142	.482	364	354	70	13	2	2331	2300	205	910	1452	12.6	4.07	100	.259	.332	0	.000	0	0	0	15	2.6

● RAY MOORE Moore, Raymond Leroy "Farmer" b: 6/1/26, Meadows, Md. BR/TR, 6'1", 205 lbs. Deb: 8/01/52

YEAR	TM/L	W	L	PCT	G	GS	CG	SH	SV	IP	H	HR	BB	SO	RAT	ERA	ERA+	OAV	OOB	BH	AVG	PB	PR	/A	PD	TPI
1952	Bro-N	1	2	.333	14	2	0	0	0	28^1	29	3	26	11	18.1	4.76	76	.274	.425	0	.000	-0	-3	-4	-0	-0.4
1953	Bro-N	0	1	.000	1	1	1	0	0	8	6	1	4	4	11.3	3.38	126	.214	.313	0	.000	-0	1	1	-0	0.0
1955	Bal-A	10	10	.500	46	14	3	1	6	151^2	128	14	80	80	12.6	3.92	97	.229	.329	6	.136	-2	1	-2	-2	-0.5
1956	Bal-A	12	7	.632	32	27	9	1	0	185	161	12	99	105	12.7	4.18	94	.238	.336	19	.271	5	-1	-5	-2	-0.2
1957	Bal-A	11	13	.458	34	32	7	1	0	227^1	196	17	112	117	12.3	3.72	97	.236	.328	18	.214	3	2	-3	-2	-0.2
1958	Chi-A	9	7	.563	32	20	4	2	2	136^2	107	10	70	73	11.7	3.82	95	.220	.318	9	.205	2	-1	-3	-1	-0.2
1959	*Chi-A	3	6	.333	29	8	0	0	0	89^2	86	10	46	49	13.3	4.12	91	.261	.354	2	.087	-1	-3	-4	-1	-0.5
1960	Chi-A	1	1	.500	14	0	0	0	0	20^2	19	5	11	3	13.1	5.66	67	.253	.349	0	.000	-0	-4	-4	-0	-0.5
	Was-A	3	2	.600	37	0	0	0	13	65^2	49	5	27	29	10.6	2.88	135	.213	.298	1	.071	-1	7	7	-2	0.5
	Yr	4	3	.571	51	0	0	0	13	86^1	68	10	38	32	11.2	3.54	109	.222	.310	1	.063	-1	3	3	-2	0.0
1961	Min-A	4	4	.500	46	0	0	0	14	56^1	49	8	38	45	14.1	3.67	115	.233	.353	0	.000	0	2	4	-0	0.3
1962	Min-A	8	3	.727	49	0	0	0	9	64^2	55	8	30	58	12.1	4.73	86	.231	.322	0	.000	-1	-5	-5	-1	-0.6
1963	Min-A	1	3	.250	31	1	0	0	2	38^2	50	8	17	38	15.8	6.98	52	.309	.378	1	.333	0	-14	-14	0	-1.4
Total	11	63	59	.516	365	105	24	5	46	1072^2	935	101	560	612	12.7	4.06	93	.238	.335	56	.187	5	-18	-32	-10	-3.7

● BARRY MOORE Moore, Robert Barry b: 4/3/43, Statesville, N.C. BL/TL, 6'1", 190 lbs. Deb: 5/29/65

YEAR	TM/L	W	L	PCT	G	GS	CG	SH	SV	IP	H	HR	BB	SO	RAT	ERA	ERA+	OAV	OOB	BH	AVG	PB	PR	/A	PD	TPI
1965	Was-A	0	0	—	1	0	0	0	0	1	1	0	1	0	18.0	0.00	—	.333	.500	0	—	0	0	0	-0	0.0
1966	Was-A	3	3	.500	12	11	1	0	0	62^1	55	3	39	28	13.7	3.75	92	.240	.353	2	.105	-1	-2	-2	0	-0.3
1967	Was-A	7	11	.389	27	26	3	1	0	143^2	127	15	71	74	12.6	3.76	84	.240	.333	6	.130	-0	-8	-10	1	-0.9
1968	Was-A	4	6	.400	32	18	0	0	3	117^2	116	8	42	56	12.2	3.37	87	.261	.327	3	.097	-1	-5	-6	1	-0.7
1969	Was-A	9	8	.529	31	25	4	0	0	134	123	12	67	51	12.9	4.30	81	.246	.338	9	.209	1	-10	-12	-2	-1.3
1970	Cle-A	3	5	.375	13	12	0	0	0	70^1	70	8	46	35	15.0	4.22	94	.262	.373	2	.095	-1	-4	-2	1	-0.3
	Chi-A	0	4	.000	24	7	0	0	0	70^2	85	12	34	34	16.2	6.37	61	.302	.393	5	.263	1	-21	-19	1	-1.8
	Yr	3	9	.250	37	19	0	0	0	141	155	20	80	69	15.5	5.30	74	.281	.380	7	.175	-0	-25	-21	1	-2.1
Total	6	26	37	.413	140	99	8	1	3	599^2	577	58	300	278	13.4	4.16	82	.256	.348	27	.151	-1	-50	-51	2	-5.3

● BOBBY MOORE Moore, Robert Devell b: 11/8/58, Sweetwater, La. BR/TR, 6'4", 200 lbs. Deb: 9/11/85

YEAR	TM/L	W	L	PCT	G	GS	CG	SH	SV	IP	H	HR	BB	SO	RAT	ERA	ERA+	OAV	OOB	BH	AVG	PB	PR	/A	PD	TPI
1985	SF-N	0	0	—	11	0	0	0	0	16^2	18	1	10	10	15.1	3.24	106	.269	.364	0	.000	-0	1	0	-1	0.0

● ROY MOORE Moore, Roy Daniel b: 10/26/1898, Austin, Tex. d: 4/5/51, Seattle, Wash. BB/TL, 6', 185 lbs. Deb: 4/15/20

YEAR	TM/L	W	L	PCT	G	GS	CG	SH	SV	IP	H	HR	BB	SO	RAT	ERA	ERA+	OAV	OOB	BH	AVG	PB	PR	/A	PD	TPI
1920	Phi-A	1	13	.071	24	14	5	0	0	132^2	161	6	64	45	15.5	4.68	86	.314	.393	10	.200	-1	-13	-10	2	-0.9
1921	Phi-A	10	10	.500	29	26	12	0	0	191^2	206	4	122	64	15.6	4.51	99	.280	.385	19	.257	3	-5	-1	2	0.5
1922	Phi-A	0	3	.000	15	6	0	0	0	50^2	65	1	32	29	17.8	7.64	56	.319	.418	5	.263	1	-20	-19	-0	-1.7
	Det-A	0	0	—	9	0	0	0	2	19^2	29	0	10	9	20.1	5.95	65	.367	.468	3	.429	1	-4	-5	0	-0.3
	Yr	0	3	.000	24	6	0	0	2	70^1	94	1	42	38	18.0	7.17	58	.329	.423	8	.308	2	-24	-24	-0	-2.0
1923	Det-A	0	0	—	3	0	0	0	1	12	15	0	11	7	19.5	3.00	129	.288	.413	0	.000	-0	1	1	1	0.1
Total	4	11	26	.297	80	46	17	0	3	406^2	476	11	239	154	16.2	4.98	85	.300	.397	37	.239	4	-41	-33	4	-2.3

● TERRY MOORE Moore, Terry Bluford b: 5/27/12, Vernon, Ala. BR/TR, 5'11", 195 lbs. Deb: 4/16/35 MC♦

YEAR	TM/L	W	L	PCT	G	GS	CG	SH	SV	IP	H	HR	BB	SO	RAT	ERA	ERA+	OAV	OOB	BH	AVG	PB	PR	/A	PD	TPI
1939	StL-N★	0	0	—	1	0	0	0	0	1	0	0	0	1	0.0	0.00	—	.000	.000	123	.295	0	0	0	0	0.1

● TOMMY MOORE Moore, Tommy Joe b: 7/7/48, Lynwood, Cal. BR/TR, 5'11", 175 lbs. Deb: 9/15/72

YEAR	TM/L	W	L	PCT	G	GS	CG	SH	SV	IP	H	HR	BB	SO	RAT	ERA	ERA+	OAV	OOB	BH	AVG	PB	PR	/A	PD	TPI
1972	NY-N	0	0	—	3	1	0	0	0	12^1	12	1	1	5	9.5	2.92	115	.273	.289	1	.333	0	1	1	0	0.1
1973	NY-N	0	1	.000	3	1	0	0	0	3^1	6	1	3	1	24.3	10.80	33	.400	.500	0	—	0	-3	-3	-0	-0.3
1975	StL-N	0	0	—	10	0	0	0	0	18^2	15	2	12	6	13.0	3.86	97	.203	.314	1	.500	0	-0	-0	0	0.1
	Tex-A	0	2	.000	12	0	0	0	0	21	31	1	12	15	18.9	8.14	46	.352	.436	0	—	0	-10	-10	0	-1.0
1977	Sea-A	2	1	.667	14	1	0	0	0	33	36	1	21	13	16.4	4.91	84	.281	.395	0	—	0	-3	-3	-1	-0.3
Total	4	2	4	.333	42	3	0	0	0	88^1	100	6	49	40	15.6	5.40	71	.287	.381	2	.400	1	-16	-15	-0	-1.4

● CY MOORE Moore, William Austin b: 2/7/05, Elberton, Ga. d: 3/28/72, Augusta, Ga. BR/TR, 6'1", 178 lbs. Deb: 6/07/29

YEAR	TM/L	W	L	PCT	G	GS	CG	SH	SV	IP	H	HR	BB	SO	RAT	ERA	ERA+	OAV	OOB	BH	AVG	PB	PR	/A	PD	TPI
1929	Bro-N	3	3	.500	32	4	0	0	2	68	87	3	31	17	15.6	5.56	83	.320	.389	3	.188	-0	-6	-7	-1	-0.7
1930	Bro-N	0	0	—	1	0	0	0	0	0	2	0	0	0	—	—	—	1.000	1.000	0	—	0	0	0	0	0.0
1931	Bro-N	1	2	.333	23	1	1	0	0	61^2	62	5	13	35	11.5	3.79	100	.262	.311	2	.154	-1	0	0	0	0.0
1932	Bro-N	0	3	.000	20	2	0	0	0	48^2	56	3	17	21	13.7	4.81	79	.293	.354	3	.214	0	-5	-5	0	-0.5
1933	Phi-N	8	9	.471	36	18	9	3	1	161^1	177	7	42	53	12.4	3.74	102	.279	.326	3	.063	-5	-7	1	0	-0.3
1934	Phi-N	4	9	.308	35	15	3	0	0	126^2	163	11	65	55	16.3	6.47	73	.309	.387	6	.143	-3	-34	-25	-1	-2.7
Total	6	16	26	.381	147	40	13	3	3	466^1	547	29	168	181	14.0	4.86	86	.293	.355	17	.128	-9	-52	-34	-2	-4.2

● BILL MOORE Moore, William Christopher b: 9/3/02, Corning, N.Y. d: 1/24/84, Corning, N.Y. BR/TR, 6'3", 195 lbs. Deb: 4/15/25

YEAR	TM/L	W	L	PCT	G	GS	CG	SH	SV	IP	H	HR	BB	SO	RAT	ERA	ERA+	OAV	OOB	BH	AVG	PB	PR	/A	PD	TPI
1925	Det-A	0	0	—	1	0	0	0	0	0	0	0	3	0	—	∞	—	—	1.000	0	—	0	-2	-2	0	-0.2

● WILCY MOORE Moore, William Wilcy "Cy" b: 5/20/1897, Bonita, Tex. d: 3/29/63, Hollis, Okla. BR/TR, 6', 195 lbs. Deb: 4/14/27

YEAR	TM/L	W	L	PCT	G	GS	CG	SH	SV	IP	H	HR	BB	SO	RAT	ERA	ERA+	OAV	OOB	BH	AVG	PB	PR	/A	PD	TPI
1927	*NY-A	19	7	.731	50	12	6	1	**13**	213	185	2	59	75	**10.4**	**2.28**	**169**	**.234**	**.289**	6	.080	-6	44	37	8	3.9
1928	NY-A	4	4	.500	35	2	0	0	2	60^1	71	4	31	18	15.2	4.18	90	.286	.366	2	.143	-1	-1	-3	1	-0.2
1929	NY-A	6	4	.600	41	0	0	0	8	61	64	4	19	21	12.2	4.13	93	.268	.322	1	.067	-2	**1**	-2	2	-0.1
1931	Bos-A	11	13	.458	53	15	8	1	**10**	185^1	195	7	55	37	12.2	3.88	111	.269	.322	9	.161	-3	10	9	6	1.1
1932	Bos-A	4	10	.286	37	2	0	0	4	84^1	98	5	42	28	15.0	5.23	86	.284	.363	1	.045	-3	-7	-7	3	-0.6
	*NY-A	2	0	1.000	10	1	0	0	4	25	27	1	6	8	11.9	2.52	162	.273	.314	0	.000	-1	5	4	-0	0.3
	Yr	6	10	.375	47	3	0	0	8	109^1	125	6	48	36	14.2	4.61	95	.281	.351	1	.033	-4	-2	-3	3	-0.3
1933	NY-A	5	6	.455	35	0	0	0	8	62	92	1	20	17	16.3	5.52	70	.333	.378	2	.133	-1	-9	-11	0	-1.1
Total	6	51	44	.537	261	32	14	2	49	691	732	24	232	204	12.6	3.70	110	.269	.327	21	.102	-16	44	27	20	3.3

● BOB MOORHEAD Moorhead, Charles Robert b: 1/23/38, Chambersburg, Pa. d: 12/3/86, Lemoyne, Pa. BR/TR, 6'1", 208 lbs. Deb: 4/11/62

YEAR	TM/L	W	L	PCT	G	GS	CG	SH	SV	IP	H	HR	BB	SO	RAT	ERA	ERA+	OAV	OOB	BH	AVG	PB	PR	/A	PD	TPI
1962	NY-N	0	2	.000	38	7	0	0	0	105^1	118	13	42	63	14.0	4.53	92	.289	.361	1	.045	-1	-7	-4	2	-0.2
1965	NY-N	0	1	.000	9	0	0	0	0	14^1	16	0	5	5	13.2	4.40	80	.271	.328	0	—	0	-1	-1	0	-0.1
Total	2	0	3	.000	47	7	0	0	0	119^2	134	13	47	68	13.9	4.51	91	.287	.357	1	.045	-1	-8	-5	3	-0.3

● BOB MOOSE Moose, Robert Ralph b: 10/9/47, Export, Pa. d: 10/9/76, Martins Ferry, Ohio BR/TR, 6', 200 lbs. Deb: 9/19/67

YEAR	TM/L	W	L	PCT	G	GS	CG	SH	SV	IP	H	HR	BB	SO	RAT	ERA	ERA+	OAV	OOB	BH	AVG	PB	PR	/A	PD	TPI
1967	Pit-N	1	0	1.000	2	2	1	0	0	14^2	14	1	4	7	11.7	3.68	91	.259	.322	2	.333	1	-1	-1	-0	0.1
1968	Pit-N	8	12	.400	38	22	3	3	3	171^1	136	5	41	126	9.5	2.73	107	.218	.269	5	.093	-2	5	4	2	0.4

YEAR TM/L	W	L	PCT	G	GS	CG	SH	SV	IP	H	HR	BB	SO	RAT	ERA	ERA+	OAV	OOB	BH	AVG	PB	PR	/A	PD	TPI
1969 Pit-N	14	3	.824	44	19	6	1	4	170	149	9	62	165	11.4	2.91	120	.231	.303	4	.075	-1	13	11	1	1.1
1970 *Pit-N	11	10	.524	28	27	9	2	0	189^2	186	14	64	119	12.0	3.99	98	.262	.326	12	.182	3	1	-2	-1	-0.1
1971 *Pit-N	11	7	.611	30	18	3	1	1	140	169	12	35	68	13.2	4.11	82	.301	.344	4	.103	-1	-10	-11	0	-1.2
1972 *Pit-N	13	10	.565	31	30	6	3	1	226	213	11	47	144	10.5	2.91	114	.248	.290	12	.169	2	14	10	1	1.5
1973 Pit-N	12	13	.480	33	29	6	3	0	201^1	219	11	70	111	13.1	3.53	100	.280	.342	9	.134	-0	3	-0	2	0.1
1974 Pit-N	1	5	.167	7	6	0	0	0	35^2	59	4	7	15	17.2	7.57	45	.386	.420	2	.182	0	-16	-16	2	-1.3
1975 Pit-N	2	2	.500	23	5	1	0	0	67^2	63	4	25	34	12.0	3.72	95	.246	.318	3	.167	0	-1	-1	2	0.0
1976 Pit-N	3	9	.250	53	2	0	0	10	88	100	4	32	38	13.9	3.68	95	.294	.362	3	.250	2	-2	-2	-0	0.0
Total 10	76	71	.517	289	160	35	13	19	1304^1	1308	75	387	827	11.9	3.50	98	.262	.319	56	.141	4	7	-9	8	0.6

● **JAKE MOOTY** Mooty, J T b: 4/13/13, Bennett, Tex. d: 4/20/70, Fort Worth, Tex. BR/TR, 5'10.5", 170 lbs. Deb: 9/09/36

YEAR TM/L	W	L	PCT	G	GS	CG	SH	SV	IP	H	HR	BB	SO	RAT	ERA	ERA+	OAV	OOB	BH	AVG	PB	PR	/A	PD	TPI
1936 Cin-N	0	0	—	8	0	0	0	1	13^2	10	0	4	11	9.2	3.95	97	.204	.264	0	.000	-0	0	-0	-0	-0.1
1937 Cin-N	0	3	.000	14	2	0	0	1	39	54	2	22	11	17.5	8.31	45	.327	.406	0	.000	-1	-19	-20	-0	-1.9
1940 Chi-N	6	6	.500	20	12	6	0	1	114	101	11	49	42	11.9	2.92	128	.243	.325	10	.263	1	12	10	-2	1.1
1941 Chi-N	8	9	.471	33	14	7	1	4	153^1	143	9	56	45	11.8	3.35	105	.251	.320	10	.200	1	5	3	1	0.4
1942 Chi-N	2	5	.286	19	10	1	0	1	84^1	89	11	44	28	14.2	4.70	68	.265	.350	6	.214	0	-13	-14	0	-1.4
1943 Chi-N	0	0	—	2	0	0	0	0	1	2	0	1	1	27.0	0.00	—	.400	.500	0	—	0	0	0	0	0.0
1944 Det-A	0	0	—	15	0	0	0	0	28^1	35	0	18	7	17.2	4.45	80	.310	.409	1	.143	-0	-3	-3	-0	-0.4
Total 7	16	23	.410	111	38	14	1	8	433^2	434	33	194	145	13.1	4.03	88	.263	.341	27	.205	1	-18	-23	-1	-2.3

● **HIKER MORAN** Moran, Albert Thomas b: 1/1/12, Rochester, N.Y. BR/TR, 6'4.5", 185 lbs. Deb: 9/29/38

YEAR TM/L	W	L	PCT	G	GS	CG	SH	SV	IP	H	HR	BB	SO	RAT	ERA	ERA+	OAV	OOB	BH	AVG	PB	PR	/A	PD	TPI
1938 Bos-N	0	0	—	1	0	0	0	0	3	1	0	1	0	6.0	0.00	—	.111	.200	0	.000	-0	1	1	-0	0.1
1939 Bos-N	1	1	.500	6	2	1	0	0	20	21	3	11	4	14.4	4.50	82	.276	.368	1	.200	1	-1	-2	-0	-0.2
Total 2	1	1	.500	7	2	1	0	0	23	22	3	12	4	13.3	3.91	94	.259	.351	1	.167	0	-0	-1	-1	-0.1

● **BILL MORAN** Moran, Carl William "Bugs" b: 9/26/50, Portsmouth, Va. BR/TR, 6'4", 210 lbs. Deb: 4/12/74

YEAR TM/L	W	L	PCT	G	GS	CG	SH	SV	IP	H	HR	BB	SO	RAT	ERA	ERA+	OAV	OOB	BH	AVG	PB	PR	/A	PD	TPI
1974 Chi-A	1	3	.250	15	5	0	0	0	46^1	57	5	23	17	16.7	4.66	80	.302	.394	0	—	0	-5	-5	-1	-0.6

● **CHARLIE MORAN** Moran, Charles Barthell "Uncle Charlie" b: 2/22/1878, Nashville, Tenn. d: 6/14/49, Horse Cave, Ky. BR/TR, 5'8", 180 lbs. Deb: 9/09/03 U♦

YEAR TM/L	W	L	PCT	G	GS	CG	SH	SV	IP	H	HR	BB	SO	RAT	ERA	ERA+	OAV	OOB	BH	AVG	PB	PR	/A	PD	TPI
1903 StL-N	0	1	.000	3	2	2	0	0	24	30	0	19	7	18.8	5.25	62	.297	.413	6	.429	1	-5	-5	-1	-0.4

● **HARRY MORAN** Moran, Harry Edwin b: 4/2/1889, Slater, W.Va. d: 11/28/62, Beckley, W.Va. BL/TL, 6'1", 165 lbs. Deb: 6/23/12

YEAR TM/L	W	L	PCT	G	GS	CG	SH	SV	IP	H	HR	BB	SO	RAT	ERA	ERA+	OAV	OOB	BH	AVG	PB	PR	/A	PD	TPI
1912 Det-A	0	1	.000	5	2	1	0	0	14^2	19	1	12	3	20.3	4.91	66	.339	.471	1	.200	-0	-3	-3	-0	-0.3
1914 Buf-F	10	7	.588	34	16	7	2	2	154	159	7	53	73	13.0	4.27	77	.276	.348	10	.196	1	-18	-17	-1	-1.8
1915 New-F	13	9	.591	34	23	13	2	0	205^2	193	2	66	87	12.1	2.54	112	.262	.337	11	.180	0	11	7	1	1.0
Total 3	23	17	.575	73	41	21	4	2	374^1	371	10	131	163	12.8	3.34	91	.271	.348	22	.188	1	-9	-13	-0	-1.1

● **SAM MORAN** Moran, Samuel b: 9/16/1870, Rochester, N.Y. d: 8/29/1897, Rochester, N.Y. TL , 160 lbs. Deb: 8/28/1895

YEAR TM/L	W	L	PCT	G	GS	CG	SH	SV	IP	H	HR	BB	SO	RAT	ERA	ERA+	OAV	OOB	BH	AVG	PB	PR	/A	PD	TPI
1895 Pit-N	2	4	.333	10	6	6	0	0	62^2	78	2	51	19	19.0	7.47	61	.300	.421	4	.154	-1	-19	-21	0	-1.6

● **FORREST MORE** More, Forrest b: 9/30/1883, Hayden, Ind. d: 8/17/68, Columbus, Ind. BR/TR, 6', 180 lbs. Deb: 4/15/09

YEAR TM/L	W	L	PCT	G	GS	CG	SH	SV	IP	H	HR	BB	SO	RAT	ERA	ERA+	OAV	OOB	BH	AVG	PB	PR	/A	PD	TPI
1909 StL-N	1	5	.167	15	3	1	0	0	50	48	0	20	17	12.8	5.04	50	.258	.340	2	.154	1	-14	-14	1	-1.3
Bos-N	1	5	.167	10	4	3	0	0	48^2	47	0	20	10	13.1	4.44	64	.270	.359	1	.067	-1	-10	-9	0	-1.0
Yr	2	10	.167	25	7	4	0	0	98^2	95	0	40	27	12.7	4.74	56	.262	.342	3	.107	-1	-23	-23	1	-2.3

● **DAVE MOREHEAD** Morehead, David Michael "Moe" b: 9/5/42, San Diego, Cal. BR/TR, 6'1", 185 lbs. Deb: 4/13/63

YEAR TM/L	W	L	PCT	G	GS	CG	SH	SV	IP	H	HR	BB	SO	RAT	ERA	ERA+	OAV	OOB	BH	AVG	PB	PR	/A	PD	TPI
1963 Bos-A	10	13	.435	29	29	6	1	0	174^2	137	20	99	136	12.2	3.81	99	.211	.316	6	.105	-3	-4	-1	1	-0.3
1964 Bos-A	8	15	.348	32	30	3	1	0	166^2	156	14	112	139	14.7	4.97	78	.248	.365	5	.093	-2	-25	-21	-1	-2.4
1965 Bos-A	10	18	.357	34	33	5	2	0	192^2	157	18	113	163	12.8	4.06	92	.217	.326	8	.131	0	-13	-7	-2	-0.9
1966 Bos-A	1	2	.333	12	5	0	0	0	28	31	7	7	20	12.2	5.46	70	.274	.317	3	.500	1	-6	-5	-0	-0.5
1967 *Bos-A	5	4	.556	10	9	1	1	0	47^2	48	0	22	40	13.6	4.34	80	.264	.350	1	.083	-0	-6	-5	-1	-0.6
1968 Bos-A	1	4	.200	11	9	3	1	0	55	52	3	20	28	12.1	2.45	129	.249	.320	2	.125	-0	3	4	-1	0.3
1969 KC-A	2	3	.400	21	2	0	0	0	33	28	7	28	32	15.3	5.73	64	.239	.386	0	.000	-0	-8	-7	-0	-0.8
1970 KC-A	3	5	.375	28	17	1	0	1	121^2	121	9	62	69	13.6	3.62	103	.261	.349	6	.167	-0	1	2	-2	0.0
Total 8	40	64	.385	177	134	19	6	1	819^1	730	78	463	627	13.2	4.15	90	.237	.338	31	.127	-5	-57	-39	-7	-5.2

● **SETH MOREHEAD** Morehead, Seth Marvin "Moe" b: 8/15/34, Houston, Tex. BL/TL, 6'0.5", 195 lbs. Deb: 4/27/57

YEAR TM/L	W	L	PCT	G	GS	CG	SH	SV	IP	H	HR	BB	SO	RAT	ERA	ERA+	OAV	OOB	BH	AVG	PB	PR	/A	PD	TPI
1957 Phi-N	1	1	.500	34	1	1	0	1	58^2	57	1	20	36	12.1	3.68	103	.254	.321	0	.000	-1	1	1	-1	-0.1
1958 Phi-N	1	6	.143	27	11	0	0	0	92^1	121	8	26	54	14.4	5.85	68	.319	.365	4	.182	0	-19	-19	-2	-2.0
1959 Phi-N	0	2	.000	3	3	0	0	0	10	15	3	3	8	17.1	9.90	41	.333	.388	0	.000	-0	-7	-6	0	-0.6
Chi-N	0	1	.000	11	2	0	0	0	18^2	25	1	8	9	15.9	4.82	82	.313	.375	1	.500	1	-2	-2	-1	-0.2
Yr	0	3	.000	14	5	0	0	0	28^2	40	4	11	17	16.0	6.59	61	.317	.372	1	.200	0	-8	-8	-1	-0.8
1960 Chi-N	2	9	.182	45	7	2	0	4	123^1	123	17	46	64	12.5	3.94	96	.258	.326	4	.138	-1	-2	-2	-0	-0.3
1961 Mil-N	1	0	1.000	12	0	0	0	0	15^1	16	4	7	13	14.1	6.46	58	.271	.358	0	—	0	-4	-5	-0	-0.5
Total 5	5	19	.208	132	24	3	0	5	318^1	357	34	110	184	13.4	4.81	80	.282	.343	9	.145	-1	-33	-34	-4	-3.7

● **LEW MOREN** Moren, Lewis Howard "Hicks" b: 8/4/1883, Pittsburgh, Pa. d: 11/2/66, Pittsburgh, Pa. BR/TR, 5'11", 150 lbs. Deb: 9/21/03

YEAR TM/L	W	L	PCT	G	GS	CG	SH	SV	IP	H	HR	BB	SO	RAT	ERA	ERA+	OAV	OOB	BH	AVG	PB	PR	/A	PD	TPI
1903 Pit-N	0	1	.000	1	1	1	0	0	6	9	0	2	2	18.0	9.00	36	.346	.414	0	.000	-0	-4	-4	-0	-0.3
1904 Pit-N	0	0	—	1	0	0	0	0	4	7	1	4	0	27.0	9.00	30	.412	.545	0	.000	-0	-3	-3	0	-0.3
1907 Phi-N	11	18	.379	37	31	21	3	1	255	202	3	101	98	11.0	2.54	95	.226	.311	6	.081	-2	-2	-3	-0	-0.7
1908 Phi-N	8	9	.471	28	16	9	4	0	154	146	1	49	72	11.5	2.92	83	.258	.320	12	.245	2	-10	-8	0	-0.8
1909 Phi-N	16	15	.516	40	31	19	2	1	257^2	226	6	93	110	11.3	2.65	98	.239	.309	10	.111	-3	-2	-2	-5	-1.0
1910 Phi-N	13	14	.481	34	26	12	1	1	205^1	207	6	82	74	13.1	3.55	88	.269	.347	11	.149	-1	-12	-10	-0	-1.2
Total 6	48	57	.457	141	105	62	10	3	882	797	17	331	356	11.8	2.95	90	.248	.323	39	.134	-5	-31	-30	-5	-4.3

● **ANGEL MORENO** Moreno, Angel (Veneroso) b: 6/6/55, LaMendosa Soledad Mex. BL/TL, 5'9", 165 lbs. Deb: 8/15/81

YEAR TM/L	W	L	PCT	G	GS	CG	SH	SV	IP	H	HR	BB	SO	RAT	ERA	ERA+	OAV	OOB	BH	AVG	PB	PR	/A	PD	TPI
1981 Cal-A	1	3	.250	8	4	1	0	0	31^1	27	2	14	12	11.8	2.87	127	.233	.315	0	—	0	3	3	-0	0.3
1982 Cal-A	3	7	.300	13	8	2	0	1	49^1	55	7	23	22	14.4	4.74	85	.288	.367	0	—	0	-4	-4	-0	-0.4
Total 2	4	10	.286	21	12	3	0	1	80^2	82	9	37	34	13.4	4.02	97	.267	.348	0	—	0	-1	-1	-0	-0.1

● **JULIO MORENO** Moreno, Julio (Gonzalez) b: 1/28/21, Guines, Cuba d: 1/2/87, Miami, Fla. BR/TR, 5'8", 165 lbs. Deb: 9/08/50

YEAR TM/L	W	L	PCT	G	GS	CG	SH	SV	IP	H	HR	BB	SO	RAT	ERA	ERA+	OAV	OOB	BH	AVG	PB	PR	/A	PD	TPI
1950 Was-A	1	1	.500	4	3	1	0	0	21^1	22	1	12	7	14.8	4.64	97	.268	.368	1	.125	-1	-0	-0	0	-0.1
1951 Was-A	5	11	.313	31	18	5	0	2	132^2	132	18	80	37	14.4	4.88	84	.256	.357	7	.175	-1	-11	-12	0	-1.2
1952 Was-A	9	9	.500	26	22	7	0	0	147^1	154	10	52	62	12.9	3.97	90	.270	.337	6	.122	-2	-5	-7	-1	-1.0
1953 Was-A	3	1	.750	12	2	1	0	0	35^1	41	2	13	13	13.8	2.80	139	.291	.351	0	.000	-1	5	4	-0	0.3
Total 4	18	22	.450	73	45	14	0	2	336^2	349	31	157	119	13.7	4.25	91	.267	.349	14	.132	-5	-12	-15	-1	-2.0

● **ROGER MORET** Moret, Rogelio (Torres) b: 9/16/49, Guayama, P.R. BB/TL, 6'4", 175 lbs. Deb: 9/13/70

YEAR TM/L	W	L	PCT	G	GS	CG	SH	SV	IP	H	HR	BB	SO	RAT	ERA	ERA+	OAV	OOB	BH	AVG	PB	PR	/A	PD	TPI
1970 Bos-A	1	0	1.000	3	1	0	0	0	8^1	7	0	4	2	11.9	3.24	122	.226	.314	0	.000	-0	0	1	-0	0.0
1971 Bos-A	4	3	.571	13	7	4	1	0	71	50	5	40	47	11.7	2.92	127	.205	.322	2	.087	-1	4	6	-0	0.5
1972 Bos-A	0	0	—	3	0	0	0	0	5	5	0	6	4	19.8	3.60	89	.263	.440	0	.000	-0	-0	-0	-0	-0.1
1973 Bos-A	13	2	.867	30	15	5	2	3	156^1	138	19	67	90	12.0	3.17	127	.238	.320	0	—	0	11	15	-0	1.5
1974 Bos-A	9	10	.474	31	21	10	1	2	173^1	158	15	79	111	12.4	3.74	103	.243	.327	0	—	0	-2	2	-2	-0.2
1975 *Bos-A	14	3	.824	36	16	4	1	1	145	132	8	76	80	13.0	3.60	113	.248	.344	0	—	0	3	8	-1	0.7
1976 Atl-N	3	5	.375	27	12	1	0	1	77^1	84	7	27	30	13.0	5.00	76	.280	.341	3	.130	-1	-13	-10	-0	-1.2
1977 Tex-A	3	3	.500	18	8	0	0	4	72^1	59	6	38	39	12.1	3.73	109	.220	.317	0	—	0	3	3	-1	0.1

YEAR TM/L	W	L	PCT	G	GS	CG	SH	SV	IP	H	HR	BB	SO	RAT	ERA	ERA+	OAV	OOB	BH	AVG	PB	PR	/A	PD	TPI
1978 Tex-A	0	1	.000	7	2	0	0	1	14^2	23	1	2	5	16.0	4.91	76	.390	.419	0	—	0	-2	-2	-0	-0.2
Total 9	47	27	.635	168	82	24	5	12	723^1	656	61	339	408	12.5	3.66	107	.245	.332	5	.100	-3	4	22	-6	1.1
● DAVE MOREY	Morey, David Beale b: 2/25/1889, Malden, Mass. d: 1/4/86, Oak Bluff, Mass. BL/TR, 6', 185 lbs. Deb: 7/04/13																								
1913 Phi-A	0	0	—	2	0	0	0	0	4	2	0	2	1	11.3	4.50	61	.182	.357	0	.000	-0	-1	-1	0	-0.1
● CY MORGAN	Morgan, Cyril Arlon b: 11/11/1895, Lakeville, Mass. d: 9/11/46, Lakeville, Mass. BR/TR, 6', 170 lbs. Deb: 6/08/21																								
1921 Bos-N	1	1	.500	17	0	0	0	1	30^1	37	0	17	8	16.3	6.53	56	.314	.404	0	.000	-1	-9	-10	1	-0.9
1922 Bos-N	0	0	—	2	0	0	0	0	1^1	8	0	2	0	67.5	27.00	15	.667	.714	0	—	0	-3	-3	-0	-0.3
Total 2	1	1	.500	19	0	0	0	1	31^2	45	0	19	8	18.5	7.39	50	.346	.433	0	.000	-1	-13	-13	1	-1.2
● CY MORGAN	Morgan, Harry Richard b: 11/10/1878, Pomeroy, Ohio d: 6/28/62, Wheeling, W.Va. BR/TR, 6', 175 lbs. Deb: 9/18/03																								
1903 StL-A	0	2	.000	2	1	1	0	0	13	12	0	6	6	13.8	4.15	70	.245	.350	1	.250	0	-2	-2	-0	-0.2
1904 StL-A	0	2	.000	8	3	2	0	0	51	51	3	10	24	11.1	3.71	67	.261	.304	1	.056	-2	-6	-7	1	-0.8
1905 StL-A	2	5	.286	13	8	5	1	0	77^1	82	1	37	44	14.3	3.61	71	.273	.360	8	.258	2	-8	-9	2	-0.6
1907 StL-A	2	5	.286	10	6	4	0	0	55	77	3	17	14	15.9	6.05	42	.332	.385	2	.100	-1	-21	-22	1	-2.1
Bos-A	6	6	.500	16	13	9	2	0	114^1	77	1	34	50	9.1	1.97	131	.193	.263	2	.057	-4	7	8	-1	0.3
Yr	8	11	.421	26	19	13	2	0	169^1	154	4	51	64	11.1	3.30	78	.243	.304	4	.073	-5	-14	-14	1	-1.8
1908 Bos-A	14	13	.519	30	26	17	2	1	205	166	7	90	99	11.7	2.46	100	.226	.319	8	.127	-3	-1	0	1	-0.3
1909 Bos-A	2	6	.250	12	10	5	0	1	64^2	52	0	31	30	12.4	2.37	106	.240	.350	1	.050	-2	1	1	2	0.2
Phi-A	16	11	.593	28	26	21	5	0	228^2	152	3	71	81	9.4	1.65	146	.191	.271	8	.108	-3	21	19	-2	1.7
Yr	18	17	.514	40	36	26	5	1	293^1	204	3	102	111	9.9	1.81	134	**.200**	.283	9	.096	-4	22	20	1	1.9
1910 Phi-A	18	12	.600	36	34	23	3	0	290^2	214	0	117	134	10.8	1.55	153	.216	.310	14	.141	-3	31	27	1	2.8
1911 Phi-A	15	7	.682	38	30	15	2	1	249^2	217	0	113	136	12.7	2.70	117	.243	.341	15	.160	-5	18	12	3	1.0
1912 Phi-A	3	8	.273	16	14	5	0	0	93^2	75	0	51	47	12.6	3.75	82	.226	.338	1	.033	-3	-4	-7	2	-0.7
1913 Cin-N	0	1	.000	1	1	0	0	0	2^1	5	0	1	2	27.0	15.43	21	.500	.583	0	.000	-0	-3	-3	0	-0.3
Total 10	78	78	.500	210	172	107	15	3	1445^1	1180	18	578	667	11.5	2.51	105	.229	.318	61	.125	-24	32	19	12	1.0
● BILL MORGAN	Morgan, Henry William b: 10/1857, Washington, D.C. Deb: 5/04/1875 ♦																								
1875 RS-n	1	3	.250	7	4	4	1	0	42	38	0	1		8.4	*3.43*	71	.200	.204	18	.261	1	-5	-5		-0.3
● MIKE MORGAN	Morgan, Michael Thomas b: 10/8/59, Tulare, Cal. BR/TR, 6'3", 195 lbs. Deb: 6/11/78																								
1978 Oak-A	0	3	.000	3	3	1	0	0	12^1	19	1	8	0	19.7	7.30	50	.373	.458	0	—	0	-5	-5	1	-0.3
1979 Oak-A	2	10	.167	13	13	2	0	0	77^1	102	7	50	17	18.0	5.94	68	.332	.431	0	—	0	-15	-16	1	-1.1
1982 NY-A	7	11	.389	30	23	2	0	0	150^1	167	15	67	71	14.1	4.37	91	.285	.360	0	—	0	-5	-6	1	-0.6
1983 Tor-A	0	3	.000	16	4	0	0	0	45^1	48	6	21	22	13.7	5.16	83	.273	.350	0	—	0	-6	-4	1	-0.5
1985 Sea-A	1	1	.500	2	2	0	0	0	6	11	2	5	2	24.0	12.00	35	.393	.485	0	—	0	-5	-5	0	-0.5
1986 Sea-A	11	17	.393	37	33	9	1	1	216^1	243	24	86	116	13.9	4.53	94	.286	.354	0	—	0	-9	-7	-0	-0.7
1987 Sea-A	12	17	.414	34	31	8	2	0	207	245	25	53	85	13.2	4.65	101	.296	.342	0	—	0	-5	2	1	0.3
1988 Bal-A	1	6	.143	22	10	2	0	1	71^1	70	6	23	29	11.9	5.43	72	.255	.315	0	—	0	-12	-12	0	-0.9
1989 LA-N	8	11	.421	40	19	0	0	0	152^2	130	6	33	72	9.7	2.53	135	.234	.280	3	.083	-2	16	15	4	1.9
1990 LA-N	11	15	.423	33	33	6	**4**	0	211	216	19	60	106	12.0	3.75	97	.266	.321	8	.113	-2	1	-2	3	-0.1
1991 LA-N★	14	10	.583	34	33	5	1	1	236^1	197	12	61	140	9.9	2.78	129	.226	.279	7	.092	-3	24	21	2	2.2
1992 Chi-N	16	8	.667	34	34	6	1	0	240	203	14	79	123	10.7	2.55	141	.234	.300	8	.108	-2	25	28	2	3.1
Total 12	83	112	.426	298	238	41	9	3	1626	1651	137	546	783	12.3	3.87	101	.266	.328	26	.101	-9	6	7	15	2.8
● TOM MORGAN	Morgan, Tom Stephen "Plowboy" b: 5/20/30, ElMonte, Cal. d: 1/13/87, Anaheim, Cal. BR/TR, 6'2", 195 lbs. Deb: 4/20/51 C																								
1951 *NY-A	9	3	.750	27	16	4	2	2	124^2	119	11	36	57	11.4	3.68	104	.253	.310	12	.273	2	6	2	2	0.5
1952 NY-A	5	4	.556	16	12	2	1	2	93^2	86	8	33	35	11.8	3.07	108	.252	.325	6	.182	1	6	3	3	0.7
1954 NY-A	11	5	.688	32	17	7	4	1	143	149	8	40	34	12.2	3.34	103	.274	.330	7	.143	0	6	2	3	0.4
1955 *NY-A	7	3	.700	40	1	0	0	10	72	72	3	24	17	12.6	3.25	115	.267	.338	4	.222	0	6	4	2	0.7
1956 *NY-A	6	7	.462	41	0	0	0	11	71^1	74	2	27	20	13.1	4.16	93	.284	.357	2	.154	-0	-0	-2	1	-0.2
1957 KC-A	9	7	.563	46	13	5	0	7	143^2	160	19	61	32	14.0	4.64	85	.299	.373	3	.091	-2	-14	-11	4	-1.0
1958 Det-A	2	5	.286	39	1	0	0	1	62^2	70	7	4	32	10.8	3.16	128	.286	.300	2	.200	-0	4	6	-0	0.6
1959 Det-A	1	4	.200	46	1	0	0	9	92^2	94	11	18	39	11.5	3.98	102	.265	.311	9	.391	4	-1	1	-0	0.5
1960 Det-A	3	2	.600	22	0	0	0	1	29	33	6	10	12	13.3	4.66	85	.295	.352	0	—	0	-3	-2	0	-0.2
Was-A	1	3	.250	14	0	0	0	0	24	36	6	5	11	15.8	3.75	104	.343	.378	0	.000	-1	0	0	-0	0.0
Yr	4	5	.444	36	0	0	0	1	53	69	12	15	23	14.4	4.25	92	.315	.362	0	.000	-1	-2	-2	0	-0.2
1961 LA-A	8	2	.800	59	0	0	0	10	91^2	74	7	17	39	9.4	2.36	191	.224	.272	1	.083	-1	17	**22**	1	2.2
1962 LA-A	5	2	.714	48	0	0	0	9	58^2	53	6	19	29	11.2	2.91	132	.247	.311	0	.000	-1	7	6	-1	0.4
1963 LA-A	0	0	—	13	0	0	0	1	16^1	20	1	6	7	16.0	5.51	62	.313	.397	0	.000	-0	-3	-4	-0	-0.4
Total 12	67	47	.588	443	61	18	7	64	1023^1	1040	95	300	364	12.1	3.61	106	.270	.329	46	.186	2	32	26	13	4.2
● GENE MORIARITY	Moriarity, Eugene John b: Holyoke, Mass. BL/TL, 5'8", 130 lbs. Deb: 6/18/1884 ♦																								
1884 Ind-a	0	2	.000	2	2	2	0	0	13^2	16	0	7	4	15.8	5.27	62	.267	.353	8	.216	0	-3	-3	0	-0.2
1885 Det-N	0	0	—	1	0	0	0	0	2	3	0	1	1	18.0	9.00	32	.300	.364	1	.026	-0	-1	-1	-0	-0.1
Total 2	0	2	.000	3	2	2	0	0	15^2	19	0	8	5	16.1	5.74	56	.271	.354	41	.152	-0	-4	-4	0	-0.3
● JOHN MORLAN	Morlan, John Glen b: 11/22/47, Columbus, Ohio BR/TR, 6', 178 lbs. Deb: 7/20/73																								
1973 Pit-N	2	2	.500	10	7	1	0	0	41	42	4	23	23	14.3	3.95	89	.276	.371	2	.182	1	-1	-2	-1	-0.2
1974 Pit-N	0	3	.000	39	0	0	0	0	65	54	2	48	38	14.5	4.29	80	.227	.363	0	.000	-1	-5	-6	-1	-0.8
Total 2	2	5	.286	49	7	1	0	0	106	96	6	71	61	14.4	4.16	83	.246	.366	2	.111	0	-6	-8	-1	-1.0
● DAN MOROGIELLO	Morogiello, Daniel Joseph b: 3/26/55, Brooklyn, N.Y. BL/TL, 6'1", 200 lbs. Deb: 5/20/83																								
1983 Bal-A	0	1	.000	22	0	0	0	1	37^2	39	1	10	15	11.9	2.39	165	.265	.316	0	—	0	7	7	-1	0.6
● JIM MORONEY	Moroney, James Francis b: 12/4/1885, Boston, Mass. d: 2/26/29, Philadelphia, Pa. BL/TL, 6'1", 175 lbs. Deb: 4/24/06																								
1906 Bos-N	0	3	.000	3	3	3	0	0	27	28	1	12	11	15.3	5.33	50	.259	.365	1	.100	-1	-8	-8	0	-0.8
1910 Phi-N	1	2	.333	12	2	1	0	1	42	43	1	11	13	12.4	2.14	146	.295	.360	0	.000	-1	4	5	-0	0.3
1912 Chi-N	1	1	.500	10	3	1	0	1	23^2	25	0	17	5	17.5	4.56	73	.316	.460	3	.500	1	-3	-3	-0	-0.2
Total 3	2	6	.250	25	8	5	0	2	92^2	96	2	40	29	14.6	3.69	83	.288	.388	4	.154	-1	-7	-7	-1	-0.7
● BILL MORRELL	Morrell, Willard Blackmer b: 4/9/1900, Boston, Mass. d: 8/5/75, Birmingham, Ala. BR/TR, 6', 172 lbs. Deb: 4/20/26																								
1926 Was-A	3	3	.500	26	2	1	0	1	69^2	83	5	29	16	14.7	5.30	73	.311	.383	4	.235	1	-10	-11	-1	-1.1
1930 NY-N	0	0	—	2	0	0	0	0	8	6	0	1	3	7.9	1.13	421	.214	.241	0	.000	-0	3	3	0	0.3
1931 NY-N	5	3	.625	20	7	2	0	1	66	83	4	27	16	15.0	4.36	85	.306	.369	2	.111	-0	-4	-5	-0	-0.6
Total 3	8	6	.571	48	9	3	0	2	143^2	172	9	57	35	14.5	4.64	83	.304	.370	6	.162	0	-10	-13	-1	-1.4
● JOHN MORRILL	Morrill, John Francis "Honest John" b: 2/19/1855, Boston, Mass. d: 4/2/32, Boston, Mass. BR/TR, 5'10.5", 155 lbs. Deb: 4/24/1876 M♦																								
1880 Bos-N	0	0	—	3	0	0	0	0	10^2	9	0	1	0	8.4	0.84	269	.273	.294	81	.237	0	2	2	0	0.2
1881 Bos-N	0	1	.000	3	0	0	0	1	5^2	9	0	1	0	15.9	6.35	42	.333	.357	90	.289	1	-2	-2	-0	-0.2
1882 Bos-N	0	0	—	1	0	0	0	0	2	3	0	0	2	13.5	0.00	—	.375	.375	101	.289	0	1	1	0	0.1
1883 Bos-N	1	0	1.000	2	1	1	0	0	13	15	0	4	5	13.2	2.77	112	.268	.317	129	.319	1	1	0	-0	0.1
1884 Bos-N	0	1	.000	7	1	1	0	**2**	23	34	0	6	13	15.7	7.43	39	.315	.351	114	.260	1	-11	-12	0	-0.9
1886 Bos-N	0	0	—	1	0	0	0	0	4	5	0	0	2	11.3	0.00	—	.313	.313	106	.247	0	1	1	0	0.2
1889 Was-N	0	0	—	1	0	0	0	0	0^1	0	0	0	0	0.0	0.00	—	.000	.000	27	.185	0	0	0	0	0.0

YEAR TM/L	W	L	PCT	G	GS	CG	SH	SV	IP	H	HR	BB	SO	RAT	ERA	ERA+	OAV	OOB	BH	AVG	PB	PR	/A	PD	TPI
Total 7	1	2	.333	18	2	2	0	3	58^2	75	0	12	22	13.3	4.30	66	.301	.333	1275	.260	4	-9	-10	0	-0.5

● DANNY MORRIS Morris, Danny Walker b: 6/11/46, Greenville, Ky. BR/TR, 6'1", 200 lbs. Deb: 9/10/68

YEAR TM/L	W	L	PCT	G	GS	CG	SH	SV	IP	H	HR	BB	SO	RAT	ERA	ERA+	OAV	OOB	BH	AVG	PB	PR	/A	PD	TPI
1968 Min-A	0	1	.000	3	2	0	0	0	10^2	11	0	4	6	12.7	1.69	183	.262	.326	0	.000	-0	2	2	0	0.2
1969 Min-A	0	1	.000	3	1	0	0	0	5^1	5	1	4	1	15.2	5.06	72	.238	.360	0	—	0	-1	-1	0	-0.1
Total 2	0	2	.000	6	3	0	0	0	16	16	1	8	7	13.5	2.81	117	.254	.338	0	.000	-0	1	1	0	0.1

● E. MORRIS Morris, E. b: Trenton, N.J. Deb: 9/11/1884 ♦

YEAR TM/L	W	L	PCT	G	GS	CG	SH	SV	IP	H	HR	BB	SO	RAT	ERA	ERA+	OAV	OOB	BH	AVG	PB	PR	/A	PD	TPI
1884 Bal-U	0	0	—	1	0	0	0	0	1	2	0	2	0	36.0	9.00	37	.391	.562	0	.000	-1	-1	-1	-0	-0.1

● ED MORRIS Morris, Edward "Cannonball" b: 9/29/1862, Brooklyn, N.Y. d: 4/12/37, Pittsburgh, Pa. BR/TL, 165 lbs. Deb: 5/01/1884

YEAR TM/L	W	L	PCT	G	GS	CG	SH	SV	IP	H	HR	BB	SO	RAT	ERA	ERA+	OAV	OOB	BH	AVG	PB	PR	/A	PD	TPI
1884 Col-a	34	13	**.723**	52	52	47	3	0	429^2	335	3	51	302	8.4	2.18	139	.204	.234	37	.186	1	51	41	2	4.2
1885 Pit-a	39	24	.619	**63**	63	**63**	**7**	0	**581**	459	5	101	**298**	**8.9**	2.35	137	**.208**	**.247**	44	.186	-5	58	56	-1	4.7
1886 Pit-a	**41**	20	.672	64	63	63	**12**	**1**	555^1	455	5	118	326	**9.4**	2.45	138	.214	**.258**	38	.167	-7	62	58	-1	4.5
1887 Pit-N	14	22	.389	38	38	37	1	0	317^2	375	13	71	91	12.9	4.31	90	.286	.326	25	.198	-4	-8	-15	-2	-1.8
1888 Pit-N	29	23	.558	**55**	55	**54**	5	0	480	470	7	74	135	10.4	2.31	116	.245	.276	19	.101	-10	29	19	1	0.9
1889 Pit-N	6	13	.316	21	21	18	0	0	170	196	4	48	40	13.2	4.13	91	.280	.332	7	.097	-5	-2	-7	-2	-1.1
1890 Pit-P	8	7	.533	18	15	15	1	0	144^1	178	5	35	25	13.5	4.86	80	.290	.332	9	.143	-3	-10	-15	-3	-1.6
Total 7	171	122	.584	311	307	297	29	1	2678	2468	42	498	1217	10.2	2.82	116	.235	.273	179	.161	-33	179	137	-5	9.8

● JACK MORRIS Morris, John Scott b: 5/16/55, St.Paul, Minn. BR/TR, 6'3", 200 lbs. Deb: 7/26/77

YEAR TM/L	W	L	PCT	G	GS	CG	SH	SV	IP	H	HR	BB	SO	RAT	ERA	ERA+	OAV	OOB	BH	AVG	PB	PR	/A	PD	TPI
1977 Det-A	1	1	.500	7	6	1	0	0	45^2	38	4	23	28	12.0	3.74	114	.235	.330	0	—	0	2	3	0	0.1
1978 Det-A	3	5	.375	28	7	0	0	0	106	107	8	49	48	13.5	4.33	89	.268	.352	0	—	0	-7	-5	-0	-0.7
1979 Det-A	17	7	.708	27	27	9	1	0	197^2	179	19	59	113	11.0	3.28	132	.244	.304	0	—	0	21	23	-1	2.3
1980 Det-A	16	15	.516	36	36	11	2	0	250	252	20	87	112	12.3	4.18	98	.262	.326	0	—	0	-4	-2	3	0.1
1981 Det-A★	**14**	7	.667	25	25	15	1	0	198	153	14	78	97	10.6	3.05	124	.218	.298	0	—	0	13	16	-0	1.7
1982 Det-A	17	16	.515	37	37	17	3	0	266^1	247	37	96	135	11.6	4.06	100	.247	.312	0	—	0	1	0	-0	0.0
1983 Det-A	20	13	.606	37	37	20	1	0	**293^2**	257	30	83	**232**	10.5	3.34	117	.233	.289	0	—	0	24	19	-1	1.8
1984 *Det-A★	19	11	.633	35	35	9	1	0	240^1	221	20	87	148	11.6	3.60	109	.241	.308	0	—	0	11	9	2	1.0
1985 Det-A★	16	11	.593	35	35	13	4	0	257	212	21	110	191	11.5	3.33	122	.225	.309	0	—	0	23	21	-1	2.1
1986 Det-A	21	8	.724	35	35	15	**6**	0	267	229	40	82	223	10.5	3.27	126	.229	.287	0	—	0	27	25	0	2.6
1987 *Det-A★	18	11	.621	34	34	13	0	0	266	227	39	93	208	10.9	3.38	125	.228	.294	0	.000	0	32	25	-2	2.3
1988 Det-A	15	13	.536	34	34	10	2	0	235	225	20	83	168	11.9	3.94	97	.251	.318	0	—	0	1	-3	0	-0.3
1989 Det-A	6	14	.300	24	24	10	0	0	170^1	189	23	59	115	13.2	4.86	79	.283	.342	0	—	0	-19	-20	1	-1.8
1990 Det-A	15	18	.455	36	36	**11**	3	0	249^2	231	26	97	162	12.0	4.51	88	.242	.316	0	—	0	-17	-15	-1	-1.7
1991 *Min-A★	18	12	.600	35	35	10	2	0	246^2	226	18	92	163	11.8	3.43	124	.245	.317	0	—	0	18	23	-1	2.3
1992 *Tor-A	**21**	6	.778	34	34	6	1	0	240^2	222	18	80	132	11.7	4.04	101	.246	.314	0	—	0	-3	1	-1	0.0
Total 16	237	168	.585	499	477	170	27	0	3530	3215	357	1258	2275	11.5	3.73	108	.242	.311	0	.000	0	123	120	-3	11.8

● JOHN MORRIS Morris, John Wallace b: 8/23/41, Lewes, Del. BR/TL, 6'1", 198 lbs. Deb: 7/19/66

YEAR TM/L	W	L	PCT	G	GS	CG	SH	SV	IP	H	HR	BB	SO	RAT	ERA	ERA+	OAV	OOB	BH	AVG	PB	PR	/A	PD	TPI
1966 Phi-N	1	1	.500	13	0	0	0	0	13^2	15	2	3	8	12.5	5.27	68	.278	.328	0	—	0	-3	-3	0	-0.2
1968 Bal-A	2	0	1.000	19	0	0	0	0	31^2	19	4	17	22	11.4	2.56	114	.173	.305	0	.000	-1	1	1	0	0.1
1969 Sea-A	0	0	—	6	0	0	0	0	12^2	16	2	8	8	17.1	6.39	57	.308	.400	1	1.000	1	-4	-4	1	-0.2
1970 Mil-A	4	3	.571	20	9	2	0	0	73^1	70	4	22	40	11.5	3.93	96	.253	.312	3	.176	0	-2	-1	1	0.0
1971 Mil-A	2	2	.500	43	1	0	0	1	67^2	69	4	27	42	12.9	3.72	93	.270	.342	1	.200	0	-2	-2	1	-0.1
1972 SF-N	0	0	—	7	0	0	0	0	6^1	9	2	2	5	15.6	4.26	82	.310	.355	0	—	0	-1	-1	0	-0.1
1973 SF-N	1	0	1.000	7	0	0	0	0	6^1	12	0	3	3	21.3	8.53	45	.429	.484	0	.000	-0	-3	-3	0	-0.3
1974 SF-N	1	1	.500	17	0	0	0	1	20^2	17	1	4	9	9.1	3.05	125	.215	.253	1	1.000	0	1	2	-1	0.2
Total 8	11	7	.611	132	10	2	0	2	232^1	227	19	86	137	12.4	3.95	90	.256	.328	6	.194	1	-11	-10	3	-0.6

● BUGS MORRIS Morris, Joseph Harley (a.k.a. Joseph Harley Bennett In 1918)
b: 4/19/1892, Kansas City, Mo. d: 11/21/57, Noel, Mo. BR/TR, 5'9.5", 163 lbs. Deb: 7/20/18

YEAR TM/L	W	L	PCT	G	GS	CG	SH	SV	IP	H	HR	BB	SO	RAT	ERA	ERA+	OAV	OOB	BH	AVG	PB	PR	/A	PD	TPI
1918 StL-A	0	2	.000	4	2	0	0	0	10^1	12	1	7	0	16.5	3.48	79	.308	.413	1	.250	0	-1	-1	0	-0.1
1921 Chi-A	0	3	.000	3	2	1	0	0	17^2	19	1	16	2	17.8	6.11	69	.297	.438	2	.333	0	-4	-4	1	-0.3
StL-A	0	0	—	3	1	0	0	0	5^2	11	1	6	3	30.2	14.29	31	.407	.543	1	1.000	0	-6	-6	-0	-0.5
Yr	0	3	.000	6	3	1	0	0	23^1	30	2	22	5	20.8	8.10	53	.330	.470	3	.429	1	-10	-10	0	-0.8
Total 2	0	5	.000	10	5	1	0	0	33^2	42	3	29	5	19.5	6.68	57	.323	.453	4	.364	1	-11	-11	1	-0.9

● ED MORRIS Morris, Walter Edward "Big Ed" b: 12/7/1899, Foshee, Ala. d: 3/3/32, Century, Fla. BR/TR, 6'2", 185 lbs. Deb: 8/05/22

YEAR TM/L	W	L	PCT	G	GS	CG	SH	SV	IP	H	HR	BB	SO	RAT	ERA	ERA+	OAV	OOB	BH	AVG	PB	PR	/A	PD	TPI
1922 Chi-N	0	0	—	5	0	0	0	0	12	22	1	6	5	21.0	8.25	51	.386	.444	1	.250	-0	-6	-5	-0	-0.5
1928 Bos-A	19	15	.559	47	29	20	0	5	257^2	255	7	80	104	11.9	3.53	117	.264	.323	14	.154	-4	15	17	-2	1.1
1929 Bos-A	14	14	.500	33	26	17	2	1	208^1	227	7	95	73	14.0	4.45	96	.282	.360	16	.232	2	-5	-4	-2	-0.3
1930 Bos-A	4	9	.308	18	9	3	0	0	65^1	67	1	38	28	14.5	4.13	112	.260	.355	6	.316	2	4	3	-0	0.4
1931 Bos-A	5	7	.417	37	14	3	0	0	130^2	131	4	74	46	14.5	4.75	91	.260	.361	6	.158	-2	-5	-6	0	-0.7
Total 5	42	45	.483	140	78	43	2	6	674	702	20	293	256	13.4	4.19	101	.271	.348	43	.195	-1	3	4	-4	0.0

● BILL MORRISETTE Morrisette, William Lee b: 1/17/1893, Baltimore, Md. d: 3/25/66, Virginia Beach, Va BR/TR, 6', 176 lbs. Deb: 9/19/15

YEAR TM/L	W	L	PCT	G	GS	CG	SH	SV	IP	H	HR	BB	SO	RAT	ERA	ERA+	OAV	OOB	BH	AVG	PB	PR	/A	PD	TPI
1915 Phi-A	2	0	1.000	4	1	1	0	0	20	15	0	5	11	9.0	1.35	217	.195	.244	2	.286	0	4	4	0	0.4
1916 Phi-A	0	0	—	1	0	0	0	0	4	6	0	5	2	24.8	6.75	42	.429	.579	0	.000	0	-2	-2	1	-0.1
1920 Det-A	1	1	.500	8	3	1	0	0	27	25	0	19	15	15.7	4.33	86	.245	.379	0	.000	-1	-2	-2	-0	-0.3
Total 3	3	1	.750	13	4	2	0	0	51	46	0	29	28	13.8	3.35	100	.238	.347	2	.125	-1	0	-0	0	0.0

● JIM MORRISON Morrison, James Forrest b: 9/23/52, Pensacola, Fla. BR/TR, 5'11", 182 lbs. Deb: 9/18/77 ♦

YEAR TM/L	W	L	PCT	G	GS	CG	SH	SV	IP	H	HR	BB	SO	RAT	ERA	ERA+	OAV	OOB	BH	AVG	PB	PR	/A	PD	TPI
1988 Atl-N	0	0	—	3	0	0	0	0	3^2	3	0	2	1	12.3	0.00	—	.214	.313	14	.152	0	1	1	-0	0.2

● JOHNNY MORRISON Morrison, John Dewey "Jughandle Johnny" b: 10/22/1895, Pellville, Ky. d: 3/20/66, Louisville, Ky. BR/TR, 5'11", 188 lbs. Deb: 9/28/20 F

YEAR TM/L	W	L	PCT	G	GS	CG	SH	SV	IP	H	HR	BB	SO	RAT	ERA	ERA+	OAV	OOB	BH	AVG	PB	PR	/A	PD	TPI
1920 Pit-N	1	0	1.000	2	1	1	1	0	7	4	0	1	3	6.4	0.00	—	.167	.200	0	.000	-0	2	3	0	0.2
1921 Pit-N	9	7	.563	21	17	11	**3**	0	144	131	3	33	52	10.3	2.88	133	.258	.305	5	.119	-1	15	15	-0	1.4
1922 Pit-N	17	11	.607	45	33	20	**5**	1	286^1	315	10	87	104	12.8	3.43	119	.286	.341	20	.198	-2	21	21	0	1.7
1923 Pit-N	25	13	.658	42	37	27	2	2	301^2	287	6	110	114	12.0	3.49	115	.253	.321	21	.183	-3	17	17	-0	1.3
1924 Pit-N	11	16	.407	**41**	25	10	0	2	237^2	213	7	73	85	11.0	3.75	102	.245	.307	13	.169	-2	3	2	-2	-0.2
1925 *Pit-N	17	14	.548	**44**	26	10	0	**4**	211	245	12	60	60	13.3	3.88	115	.291	.343	13	.178	-2	9	14	-2	0.8
1926 Pit-N	6	8	.429	26	13	6	2	2	122^1	119	2	44	39	12.1	3.38	116	.267	.335	3	.077	-4	6	7	-2	0.1
1927 Pit-N	3	2	.600	21	2	1	0	3	53^2	63	2	21	21	14.1	4.19	98	.304	.368	2	.154	-0	-2	-0	-1	-0.2
1929 Bro-N	13	7	.650	39	10	4	0	**8**	136^2	150	11	61	57	14.1	4.48	103	.279	.355	7	.163	-2	4	2	-3	-0.3
1930 Bro-N	1	2	.333	16	0	0	0	1	34^2	47	4	16	11	16.4	5.45	90	.346	.414	0	.000	-1	-2	-2	-0	-0.3
Total 10	103	80	.563	297	164	90	13	23	1535	1574	57	506	546	12.4	3.65	113	.271	.332	84	.164	-19	74	79	-11	4.5

● MIKE MORRISON Morrison, Michael b: 2/6/1867, Erie, Pa. d: 6/16/55, Erie, Pa. BR/TR, 5'8.5", 156 lbs. Deb: 4/19/1887

YEAR TM/L	W	L	PCT	G	GS	CG	SH	SV	IP	H	HR	BB	SO	RAT	ERA	ERA+	OAV	OOB	BH	AVG	PB	PR	/A	PD	TPI
1887 Cle-a	12	25	.324	40	40	35	0	0	316^2	385	13	205	158	17.4	4.92	88	.294	.398	27	.191	-4	-22	-20	10	-1.1
1888 Cle-a	1	3	.250	4	4	4	0	0	35	40	3	19	14	15.4	5.40	57	.277	.365	4	.235	-0	-9	-9	0	-0.8
1890 Syr-a	6	9	.400	17	14	13	1	0	127	131	4	81	69	15.9	5.88	60	.258	.374	29	.242	3	-28	-33	2	-2.3
Bal-a	1	2	.333	4	4	3	0	0	26	15	0	20	13	12.8	3.81	107	.163	.325	1	.111	-1	0	1	1	0.1
Yr	7	11	.389	21	18	16	1	0	153	146	4	101	82	14.6	5.53	66	.238	.348	30	.233	2	-28	-32	3	-2.2
Total 3	20	39	.339	65	62	55	1	0	504^2	571	20	325	254	16.7	5.14	78	.278	.387	61	.213	-2	-59	-62	12	-4.1

YEAR TM/L	W	L	PCT	G	GS	CG	SH	SV	IP	H	HR	BB	SO	RAT	ERA	ERA+	OAV	OOB	BH	AVG	PB	PR	/A	PD	TPI

● **PHIL MORRISON** Morrison, Philip Melvin b: 10/18/1894, Rockport, Ind. d: 1/18/55, Lexington, Ky. BB/TR, 6'2", 190 lbs. Deb: 9/30/21 F

| 1921 Pit-N | 0 | 0 | — | 1 | 0 | 0 | 0 | 0 | 0² | 1 | 0 | 0 | 1 | 13.5 | 0.00 | — | .333 | .333 | 0 | — | 0 | 0 | 0 | 0 | 0.0 |

● **HANK MORRISON** Morrison, Stephen Henry b: 5/22/1866, Olneyville, R.I. d: 9/30/27, Attleboro, Mass. BR/TR, 5'10", 180 lbs. Deb: 5/28/1887

| 1887 Ind-N | 3 | 4 | .429 | 7 | 7 | 5 | 0 | 0 | 57 | 79 | 2 | 27 | 13 | 16.9 | 7.58 | 55 | .307 | .375 | 3 | .115 | -2 | -22 | -22 | -1 | -1.9 |

● **GUY MORRISON** Morrison, Walter Guy b: 8/29/1895, Hinton, W.Va. d: 8/14/34, Grand Rapids, Mich BR/TR, 5'11", 185 lbs. Deb: 8/31/27

1927 Bos-N	1	2	.333	11	3	1	0	0	34¹	40	1	15	6	14.4	4.46	83	.296	.367	1	.125	1	-2	-3	1	-0.1
1928 Bos-N	0	0	—	1	0	0	0	0	3	4	1	3	0	21.0	12.00	33	.308	.438	0	—	0	-3	-3	0	-0.2
Total 2	1	2	.333	12	3	1	0	0	37¹	44	2	18	6	14.9	5.06	74	.297	.373	1	.125	1	-5	-6	1	-0.3

● **FRANK MORRISSEY** Morrissey, Michael Joseph "Deacon" b: 5/5/1876, Baltimore, Md. d: 2/22/39, Baltimore, Md. TR, 5'4", 140 lbs. Deb: 7/13/01

1901 Bos-A	0	0	—	1	0	0	0	0	4¹	5	0	2	1	16.6	2.08	170	.286	.390	0	.000	-1	1	1	0	0.0
1902 Chi-N	1	3	.250	5	5	5	0	0	40	40	0	8	13	10.8	2.25	120	.260	.297	2	.091	-1	2	2	0	0.2
Total 2	1	3	.250	6	5	5	0	0	44¹	45	0	10	14	11.4	2.23	125	.263	.307	2	.080	-1	3	3	1	0.2

● **CARL MORTON** Morton, Carl Wendle b: 1/18/44, Kansas City, Mo. d: 4/12/83, Tulsa, Okla. BR/TR, 6', 200 lbs. Deb: 4/11/69

1969 Mon-N	0	3	.000	8	5	0	0	0	29¹	29	2	18	16	15.0	4.60	80	.264	.377	0	.000	-0	-3	-3	1	-0.3
1970 Mon-N	18	11	.621	43	37	10	4	0	284²	281	27	125	154	13.0	3.60	114	.262	.341	15	.161	2	14	16	1	2.0
1971 Mon-N	10	18	.357	36	35	9	0	1	213²	252	22	83	84	14.3	4.80	73	.295	.360	14	.182	1	-32	-30	2	-2.6
1972 Mon-N	7	13	.350	27	27	3	1	0	172	170	16	53	51	11.8	3.92	90	.258	.316	7	.135	1	-9	-7	1	-0.6
1973 Atl-N	15	10	.600	38	37	10	4	0	256¹	254	18	70	112	11.5	3.41	115	.259	.311	17	.181	4	7	15	0	2.0
1974 Atl-N	16	12	.571	38	38	7	1	0	274²	293	16	89	113	12.6	3.15	120	.277	.334	10	.112	-4	14	19	-1	1.6
1975 Atl-N	17	16	.515	39	39	11	2	0	277²	302	19	82	78	12.5	3.50	108	.278	.330	15	.160	-1	4	8	0	0.8
1976 Atl-N	4	9	.308	26	24	1	1	0	140¹	172	6	45	42	14.2	4.17	91	.306	.362	8	.178	-0	-10	-6	2	-0.4
Total 8	87	92	.486	255	242	51	13	1	1648²	1753	120	565	650	12.8	3.73	102	.276	.338	86	.156	4	-15	13	6	2.5

● **CHARLIE MORTON** Morton, Charles Hazen b: 10/12/1854, Kingsville, Ohio d: 12/9/21, Massillon, Ohio TR , Deb: 5/02/1882 MU♦

| 1884 Tol-a | 0 | 1 | .000 | 3 | 1 | 1 | 0 | 0 | 23¹ | 18 | 0 | 5 | 7 | 9.3 | 3.09 | 111 | .209 | .261 | 18 | .162 | -0 | 0 | 1 | -1 | 0.0 |

● **GUY MORTON** Morton, Guy Sr. "The Alabama Blossom" b: 6/1/1893, Vernon, Ala. d: 10/18/34, Sheffield, Ala. BR/TR, 6'1", 175 lbs. Deb: 6/20/14 F

1914 Cle-A	1	13	.071	25	13	5	0	1	128	116	1	55	80	12.2	3.02	95	.257	.341	1	.029	-4	-4	-2	-1	-0.8
1915 Cle-A	16	15	.516	34	27	15	6	1	240	189	5	60	134	9.4	2.14	143	.216	.268	12	.146	-4	21	24	-0	2.1
1916 Cle-A	12	8	.600	27	18	9	0	0	149²	139	1	42	88	11.1	2.89	104	.246	.302	12	.211	-1	-1	2	-1	0.0
1917 Cle-A	10	10	.500	35	18	6	1	2	161	158	3	59	62	12.2	2.74	103	.266	.335	4	.085	-5	-1	2	-2	-0.5
1918 Cle-A	14	8	.636	30	28	13	1	0	214²	189	1	77	123	11.3	2.64	114	.240	.310	12	.156	-2	3	9	-1	0.7
1919 Cle-A	9	9	.500	26	20	9	3	0	147¹	128	3	47	64	10.7	2.81	119	.233	.293	9	.161	-2	7	9	-1	0.6
1920 Cle-A	8	6	.571	29	17	6	1	1	137	140	2	57	72	13.0	4.47	85	.270	.344	10	.211	-1	-10	-10	-2	-1.3
1921 Cle-A	8	3	.727	30	7	3	2	0	107²	98	1	32	45	11.0	2.76	155	.244	.303	6	.171	-2	18	18	-2	1.4
1922 Cle-A	14	9	.609	38	23	13	3	0	202²	218	7	85	102	13.6	4.00	100	.277	.351	13	.191	-2	1	0	3	0.2
1923 Cle-A	6	6	.500	33	14	3	2	1	129¹	133	3	56	54	13.3	4.24	93	.276	.354	7	.159	-2	-4	-4	-1	-0.7
1924 Cle-A	0	1	.000	10	0	0	0	0	12¹	12	0	13	6	18.2	6.57	65	.250	.410	0	.000	-0	-3	-3	-0	-0.3
Total 11	98	88	.527	317	185	82	19	6	1629²	1520	27	583	830	11.7	3.13	108	.251	.319	86	.157	-24	27	48	-7	1.4

● **KEVIN MORTON** Morton, Kevin Joseph b: 8/3/68, Norwalk, Conn. BR/TL, 6'2", 185 lbs. Deb: 7/05/91

| 1991 Bos-A | 6 | 5 | .545 | 16 | 15 | 1 | 0 | 0 | 86¹ | 93 | 9 | 40 | 45 | 14.0 | 4.59 | 94 | .284 | .363 | 0 | — | 0 | -5 | -3 | 1 | -0.2 |

● **SPARROW MORTON** Morton, William P. TL , Deb: 7/15/1884

| 1884 Phi-N | 0 | 2 | .000 | 2 | 2 | 2 | 0 | 0 | 17 | 16 | 0 | 11 | 5 | 14.3 | 5.29 | 56 | .222 | .325 | 3 | .375 | 1 | -4 | -4 | -0 | -0.3 |

● **EARL MOSELEY** Moseley, Earl Victor "Vic" b: 9/7/1884, Middleburg, Ohio d: 7/1/63, Alliance, Ohio BR/TR, 5'9.5", 168 lbs. Deb: 6/17/13

1913 Bos-A	8	5	.615	24	15	7	3	0	120²	105	1	49	62	11.5	3.13	94	.245	.322	3	.081	-2	-3	-3	1	-0.4
1914 Ind-F	19	18	.514	43	38	29	4	1	316²	303	5	123	205	12.2	3.47	100	.258	.330	12	.110	-7	-9	-0	-0	-0.8
1915 New-F	15	15	.500	38	32	22	5	1	268	222	2	99	142	10.8	1.91	149	.229	.302	13	.148	-2	33	28	-4	2.4
1916 Cin-N	7	10	.412	31	15	7	0	1	150¹	145	5	69	60	12.8	3.89	67	.257	.338	4	.087	-2	-21	-22	-2	-2.8
Total 4	49	48	.505	136	100	65	12	3	855²	775	13	340	469	11.8	3.01	101	.247	.322	32	.114	-14	0	3	-5	-1.6

● **WALTER MOSER** Moser, Walter Fredrick b: 2/27/1881, Concord, N.C. d: 12/10/46, Philadelphia, Pa. BR/TR, 5'9", 170 lbs. Deb: 9/03/06

1906 Phi-N	0	4	.000	6	4	4	0	0	42²	49	0	15	17	13.7	3.59	73	.295	.357	0	.000	-2	-5	-5	-1	-0.7
1911 Bos-A	0	1	.000	6	3	1	0	0	24²	37	0	11	11	17.9	4.01	82	.366	.434	0	.000	-1	-2	-2	0	-0.3
StL-A	0	2	.000	2	2	0	0	0	3¹	11	0	4	2	40.5	21.60	16	.478	.556	1	1.000	0	-7	-7	0	-0.5
Yr	0	3	.000	8	5	1	0	0	28	48	0	15	13	20.3	6.11	54	.384	.450	1	.125	-1	-9	-9	0	-0.8
Total 2	0	7	.000	14	9	5	0	0	70²	97	0	30	30	16.4	4.58	63	.334	.401	1	.045	-2	-13	-13	-1	-1.5

● **JOHN MOSES** Moses, John William b: 8/9/57, Los Angeles, Cal. BB/TL, 5'10", 170 lbs. Deb: 8/23/82 ♦

1989 Min-A	0	0	—	1	0	0	0	0	1	0	0	0	0	9.0	0.00	—	.000	.333	68	.281	1	0	0	0	0.0
1990 Min-A	0	0	—	2	0	0	0	0	2	5	0	3	0	31.5	13.50	31	.455	.538	38	.221	1	-2	-2	-0	-0.2
Total 2	0	0	—	3	0	0	0	0	3	5	0	3	0	24.0	9.00	46	.385	.500	438	.254	1	-2	-2	-0	-0.2

● **PAUL MOSKAU** Moskau, Paul Richard b: 12/20/53, St.Joseph, Mo. BR/TR, 6'2", 210 lbs. Deb: 6/21/77

1977 Cin-N	6	6	.500	20	19	2	2	0	108	116	10	40	71	13.1	4.00	98	.278	.342	7	.184	2	-1	-1	1	0.2
1978 Cin-N	6	4	.600	26	25	2	1	1	145	139	17	57	88	12.4	3.97	89	.255	.329	10	.204	3	-6	-7	-2	-0.6
1979 Cin-N	5	4	.556	21	15	1	0	0	106¹	107	9	51	58	13.4	3.89	96	.263	.345	2	.081	-2	-2	-2	1	-0.3
1980 Cin-N	9	7	.563	33	19	2	1	2	152²	147	13	41	94	11.1	4.01	89	.257	.308	7	.159	-0	-7	-7	0	-0.8
1981 Cin-N	2	1	.667	27	1	0	0	2	54²	54	4	32	32	14.3	4.94	72	.258	.360	0	.000	-0	-9	-8	1	-0.9
1982 Pit-N	1	3	.250	13	5	0	0	0	35	43	7	8	15	13.1	4.37	85	.303	.340	1	.091	-1	-3	-3	-0	-0.4
1983 Chi-N	3	2	.600	8	8	0	0	0	32	44	7	14	16	16.3	6.75	56	.331	.395	2	.182	0	-11	-11	0	-1.0
Total 7	32	27	.542	148	92	7	4	5	633²	650	67	243	374	12.8	4.22	87	.268	.336	30	.153	2	-39	-39	-0	-3.8

● **JIM MOSOLF** Mosolf, James Frederick b: 8/21/05, Puyallup, Wash. d: 12/28/79, Dallas, Ore. BL/TR, 5'10", 186 lbs. Deb: 9/09/29 ♦

| 1930 Pit-N | 0 | 0 | — | 1 | 0 | 0 | 0 | 0 | 0¹ | 1 | 0 | 0 | 1 | 27.0 | 27.00 | 18 | .500 | .500 | 17 | .333 | 0 | -1 | -1 | 0 | -0.1 |

● **MAL MOSS** Moss, Charles Malcolm b: 4/18/05, Sullivan, Ind. d: 2/5/83, Savannah, Ga. BR/TL, 6', 175 lbs. Deb: 4/29/30

| 1930 Chi-N | 0 | 0 | — | 12 | 1 | 0 | 0 | 1 | 18² | 18 | 0 | 14 | 4 | 15.4 | 6.27 | 78 | .254 | .376 | 3 | .273 | 0 | -3 | -3 | 0 | -0.2 |

● **RAY MOSS** Moss, Raymond Earl b: 12/5/01, Chattanooga, Tenn. BR/TR, 6'1", 185 lbs. Deb: 4/17/26

1926 Bro-N	0	0	—	1	0	0	0	0	1	3	0	0	0	27.0	9.00	42	.600	.600	0	.000	-0	-1	-1	-0	-0.1
1927 Bro-N	1	0	1.000	1	1	0	0	0	8¹	11	0	1	3	13.0	3.24	122	.333	.353	1	.333	1	1	1	-0	0.1
1928 Bro-N	0	3	.000	22	5	1	1	1	60¹	62	5	35	5	14.5	4.92	81	.279	.377	8	.320	2	-6	-6	-0	-0.4
1929 Bro-N	11	6	.647	39	20	7	2	0	182	214	9	81	59	14.9	5.04	92	.296	.373	5	.076	-5	-7	-9	-2	-1.4
1930 Bro-N	9	6	.600	36	11	5	0	1	118¹	127	13	55	30	14.1	5.10	96	.270	.352	6	.154	-2	-2	-2	-2	-0.5
1931 Bro-N	0	0	—	1	0	0	0	0	1	0	0	1	0	18.0	0.00	—	.333	.502	0	0	0	0	0	0	0.1
Bos-N	1	3	.250	12	6	0	0	0	45	56	2	16	14	14.4	4.60	82	.306	.362	2	.133	-1	-4	-4	0	-0.5
Yr	1	3	.250	13	6	0	0	0	46	57	2	17	14	14.5	4.50	84	.306	.365	2	.133	-1	-3	-4	0	-0.4
Total 6	22	18	.550	112	42	13	3	2	416	474	29	189	109	14.6	4.95	91	.289	.367	22	.148	-5	-18	-21	-4	-2.7

YEAR	TM/L	W	L	PCT	G	GS	CG	SH	SV	IP	H	HR	BB	SO	RAT	ERA	ERA+	OAV	OOB	BH	AVG	PB	PR	/A	PD	TPI
● **DON MOSSI**	Mossi, Donald Louis "The Sphinx" b: 1/11/29, St.Helena, Cal. BL/TL, 6'1", 195 lbs. Deb: 4/17/54																									
1954	*Cle-A	6	1	.857	40	5	2	0	7	93	56	5	39	55	9.3	1.94	190	.176	.268	3	.158	0	**18**	**18**	-1	1.8
1955	Cle-A	4	3	.571	57	1	0	0	9	81^{2}	81	4	18	69	11.0	2.42	164	.253	.295	1	.111	0	14	14	2	1.6
1956	Cle-A	6	5	.545	48	3	0	0	11	87^{2}	79	6	33	59	11.6	3.59	117	.240	.311	3	.150	0	6	6	0	0.6
1957	Cle-A★	11	10	.524	36	22	6	1	2	159	165	16	57	97	12.7	4.13	90	.265	.329	12	.218	2	-6	-7	-1	-0.7
1958	Cle-A	7	8	.467	43	5	0	0	3	101^{2}	106	6	30	55	12.4	3.90	94	.269	.327	3	.115	-2	-1	-3	0	-0.4
1959	Det-A	17	9	.654	34	30	15	3	0	228	210	20	49	125	10.3	3.36	121	.243	.286	13	.169	0	13	18	0	1.9
1960	Det-A	9	8	.529	23	22	9	2	0	158^{1}	158	17	32	69	10.9	3.47	114	.258	.296	5	.116	-0	7	9	-1	0.8
1961	Det-A	15	7	.682	35	34	12	1	1	240^{1}	237	29	47	137	10.6	2.96	139	.258	.294	13	.165	1	28	**30**	0	3.3
1962	Det-A	11	13	.458	35	27	8	1	1	180^{1}	195	24	36	121	11.6	4.19	97	.270	.305	9	.164	1	-4	-2	-2	-0.3
1963	Det-A	7	7	.500	24	16	3	0	2	122^{2}	110	20	17	68	9.6	3.74	100	.236	.269	8	.205	2	-2	0	-0	0.2
1964	Chi-A	3	1	.750	34	0	0	0	7	40	37	9	7	36	10.1	2.93	118	.240	.278	1	.167	-0	3	2	-0	0.2
1965	KC-A	5	8	.385	51	0	0	0	7	55^{1}	59	0	20	41	12.8	3.74	93	.278	.341	0	.000	-1	-2	-2	-0	-0.3
Total	12	101	80	.558	460	165	55	8	50	1548	1493	156	385	932	11.0	3.43	114	.252	.299	71	.163	4	74	83	-2	8.7
● **EARL MOSSOR**	Mossor, Earl Dalton b: 7/21/25, Forbes, Tenn. d: 12/29/88, Batavia, Ohio BL/TR, 6'1", 175 lbs. Deb: 4/30/51																									
1951	Bro-N	0	0	—	3	0	0	0	0	1^{2}	2	1	7	1	48.6	32.40	12	.333	.692	1	1.000	0	-5	-5	-0	-0.5
● **GLEN MOULDER**	Moulder, Glen Hubert b: 9/28/17, Cleveland, Okla. BR/TR, 6', 180 lbs. Deb: 4/28/46																									
1946	Bro-N	0	0	—	1	0	0	0	0	2	2	1	1	1	13.5	4.50	75	.286	.375	0	—	0	-0	-0	-0	0.0
1947	StL-A	4	2	.667	32	2	0	0	2	73	78	4	43	23	14.9	3.82	101	.283	.379	4	.235	-0	-1	0	1	0.1
1948	Chi-A	3	6	.333	33	9	0	0	2	85^{2}	108	8	54	26	17.1	6.41	66	.316	.411	6	.300	2	-20	-20	-0	-1.8
Total	3	7	8	.467	66	11	0	0	4	160^{2}	188	13	98	50	16.1	5.21	78	.301	.396	10	.270	1	-21	-20	1	-1.7
● **FRANK MOUNTAIN**	Mountain, Frank Henry b: 5/17/1860, Ft.Edward, N.Y. d: 11/19/39, Schenectady, N.Y. BR/TR, 5'11", 185 lbs. Deb: 7/19/1880 ♦																									
1880	Tro-N	1	1	.500	2	2	2	0	0	17	23	0	6	2	15.4	5.29	48	.307	.358	2	.222	-0	-6	-5	0	-0.5
1881	Det-N	3	4	.429	7	7	7	0	0	60	80	2	18	13	14.7	5.25	56	.292	.336	4	.160	-0	-17	-16	-1	-1.4
1882	Wor-N	0	5	.000	5	5	5	0	0	42	47	0	11	5	12.4	3.00	104	.255	.297	1	.063	-3	-0	1	-1	-0.2
	Phi-a	2	6	.250	8	8	8	0	0	69	72	1	11	15	10.8	3.91	76	.251	.279	12	.333	3	-9	-7	1	-0.3
	Wor-N	2	11	.154	13	13	11	0	0	102	138	4	24	24	14.3	3.97	78	.299	.334	19	.271	2	-12	-10	-1	-0.7
1883	Col-a	26	33	.441	59	59	57	4	0	503	546	8	123	159	12.0	3.60	86	.259	.300	60	.217	7	-16	-29	1	-1.8
1884	Col-a	23	17	.575	42	41	40	5	**1**	360^{2}	289	7	78	156	9.4	2.45	124	.209	.257	50	.238	8	32	23	4	3.4
1885	Pit-a	1	4	.200	5	5	5	0	0	46	56	1	24	7	16.0	4.30	75	.320	.408	2	.100	-1	-5	-6	0	-0.5
1886	Pit-a	0	2	.000	2	2	2	0	0	16	22	0	14	2	23.1	7.88	43	.319	.466	8	.145	0	-8	-8	0	-0.6
Total	7	58	83	.411	143	142	137	9	1	1215^{2}	1273	23	309	383	11.8	3.47	88	.254	.299	158	.220	15	-41	-54	4	-2.6
● **BILL MOUNTJOY**	Mountjoy, William R. "Medicine Bill" b: 1857, Port Huron, Mich. d: 5/19/34, London, Ont., Can. TR , Deb: 9/29/1883																									
1883	Cin-a	0	1	.000	1	1	1	0	0	8	9	0	2	3	12.4	2.25	144	.266	.307	0	.000	-0	1	1	-0	0.0
1884	Cin-a	19	12	.613	33	33	32	3	0	289	274	5	43	96	10.4	2.93	114	.238	.275	18	.151	-4	10	13	-0	0.9
1885	Cin-a	10	7	.588	17	17	17	1	0	153^{2}	149	5	52	50	12.2	3.16	103	.247	.314	10	.167	-1	1	2	-1	0.1
	Bal-a	2	4	.333	6	6	6	1	0	53	72	1	13	15	15.1	5.43	60	.316	.363	1	.056	-0	-13	-13	1	-1.0
	Yr	12	11	.522	23	23	23	2	0	206^{2}	221	6	65	65	12.6	3.75	87	.264	.320	11	.141	-1	-11	-11	-0	-0.9
Total	3	31	24	.564	57	57	56	5	0	503^{2}	504	11	110	164	11.5	3.25	102	.250	.297	29	.145	-5	-0	3	-1	0.0
● **ED MOYER**	Moyer, Charles Edward b: 8/15/1885, Andover, Ohio d: 11/18/62, Jacksonville, Fla. Deb: 7/20/10																									
1910	Was-A	0	3	.000	6	3	2	0	0	25	22	1	13	3	13.7	3.24	77	.253	.369	1	.125	-1	-2	-2	1	-0.1
● **JAMIE MOYER**	Moyer, Jamie b: 11/18/62, Sellersville, Pa. BL/TL, 6', 170 lbs. Deb: 6/16/86																									
1986	Chi-N	7	4	.636	16	16	1	1	0	87^{1}	107	10	42	45	15.7	5.05	80	.311	.391	2	.091	-0	-13	-10	1	-0.9
1987	Chi-N	12	15	.444	35	33	1	0	0	201	210	28	97	147	14.0	5.10	84	.271	.355	14	.230	3	-23	-19	2	-1.3
1988	Chi-N	9	15	.375	34	30	3	1	0	202	212	20	55	121	12.1	3.48	104	.272	.324	5	.083	-2	-1	3	3	0.4
1989	Tex-A	4	9	.308	15	15	1	0	0	76	84	10	33	44	14.1	4.86	82	.283	.358	0	—	0	-8	-8	1	-0.7
1990	Tex-A	2	6	.250	33	10	1	0	0	102^{1}	115	6	39	58	13.9	4.66	84	.290	.360	0	—	0	-9	-8	0	-0.8
1991	StL-N	0	5	.000	8	7	0	0	0	31^{1}	38	5	16	20	15.8	5.74	65	.319	.404	0	.000	-1	-7	-7	-0	-0.8
Total	6	34	54	.386	141	111	7	2	0	700	766	79	282	435	13.7	4.56	86	.283	.354	21	.139	1	-60	-48	7	-4.1
● **RON MROZINSKI**	Mrozinski, Ronald Frank b: 9/16/30, White Haven, Pa. BR/TL, 5'11", 160 lbs. Deb: 6/20/54																									
1954	Phi-N	1	1	.500	15	4	1	0	0	48	49	10	25	26	13.9	4.50	90	.261	.347	1	.083	-1	-2	-2	-1	-0.4
1955	Phi-N	0	2	.000	22	1	0	0	1	34^{1}	38	2	19	18	16.0	6.55	61	.299	.407	0	.000	-1	-10	-10	-0	-1.0
Total	2	1	3	.250	37	5	1	0	1	82^{1}	87	12	44	44	14.8	5.36	75	.276	.372	1	.063	-2	-12	-12	-1	-1.4
● **PHIL MUDROCK**	Mudrock, Philip Ray b: 6/12/37, Louisville, Colo. BR/TR, 6'1", 190 lbs. Deb: 4/19/63																									
1963	Chi-N	0	0	—	1	0	0	0	0	1	2	0	0	0	18.0	9.00	39	.400	.400	0	—	0	-1	-1	-0	-0.1
● **GORDIE MUELLER**	Mueller, Joseph Gordon b: 12/10/22, Baltimore, Md. BR/TR, 6'4", 200 lbs. Deb: 4/19/50																									
1950	Bos-A	0	0	—	8	0	0	0	0	7	11	1	13	1	30.9	10.29	48	.344	.533	0	.000	-0	-4	-4	0	-0.4
● **LES MUELLER**	Mueller, Leslie Clyde b: 3/4/19, Belleville, Ill. BR/TR, 6'3", 190 lbs. Deb: 8/15/41																									
1941	Det-A	0	0	—	4	0	0	0	0	13	9	1	10	8	13.2	4.85	94	.205	.352	0	.000	-0	-1	-0	0	-0.1
1945	*Det-A	6	8	.429	26	18	6	2	1	134^{2}	117	8	58	42	11.8	3.68	96	.234	.316	8	.182	1	-5	-2	-2	-0.4
Total	2	6	8	.429	30	18	6	2	1	147^{2}	126	9	68	50	11.9	3.78	95	.231	.319	8	.170	0	-6	-3	-2	-0.5
● **WILLIE MUELLER**	Mueller, Willard Lawrence b: 8/30/56, West Bend, Wis. BR/TR, 6'4", 220 lbs. Deb: 8/12/78																									
1978	Mil-A	1	0	1.000	5	0	0	0	0	12^{2}	16	1	6	6	15.6	6.39	59	.291	.361	0	—	0	-4	-4	0	-0.4
1981	Mil-A	0	0	—	1	0	0	0	0	2	4	0	0	1	18.0	4.50	76	.400	.400	0	—	0	-0	-0	0	0.1
Total	2	1	0	1.000	6	0	0	0	0	14^{2}	20	1	6	7	16.0	6.14	60	.308	.366	0	—	0	-4	-4	0	-0.3
● **BILLY MUFFETT**	Muffett, Billy Arnold "Muff" b: 9/21/30, Hammond, Ind. BR/TR, 6'1", 198 lbs. Deb: 8/03/57 C																									
1957	StL-N	3	2	.600	23	0	0	0	8	44	35	1	13	21	9.8	2.25	176	.222	.281	0	.000	-1	8	8	-1	0.7
1958	StL-N	4	6	.400	35	6	1	0	5	84	107	11	42	41	16.5	4.93	84	.316	.399	4	.200	0	-9	-7	-1	-0.8
1959	SF-N	0	0	—	5	0	0	0	0	6^{2}	11	2	3	3	18.9	5.40	71	.407	.467	0	—	0	-1	-1	-0	-0.1
1960	Bos-A	6	4	.600	23	14	4	1	0	125	116	6	36	75	11.3	3.24	125	.242	.301	11	.268	2	9	11	-0	1.4
1961	Bos-A	3	11	.214	38	11	2	0	2	112^{2}	130	18	36	47	13.4	5.67	73	.291	.346	5	.217	2	-21	-19	-0	-1.7
1962	Bos-A	0	0	—	1	1	0	0	0	4	8	0	2	1	22.5	9.00	46	.471	.526	0	.000	-0	-2	-2	-0	-0.2
Total	6	16	23	.410	125	32	7	1	15	376^{1}	407	38	132	188	13.2	4.33	94	.277	.342	20	.217	4	-16	-10	-2	-0.7
● **JOE MUICH**	Muich, Ignatius Andrew b: 11/23/03, St.Louis, Mo. BR/TR, 6'2", 175 lbs. Deb: 9/04/24																									
1924	Bos-N	0	0	—	3	0	0	0	0	9	19	1	5	1	24.0	11.00	35	.432	.490	0	.000	-0	-7	-7	-0	-0.7
● **JOE MUIR**	Muir, Joseph Allen b: 11/26/22, Oriole, Md. d: 6/25/80, Baltimore, Md. BL/TL, 6'1", 172 lbs. Deb: 4/21/51																									
1951	Pit-N	0	2	.000	9	1	0	0	0	16^{1}	11	2	7	5	9.9	2.76	153	.180	.265	0	.000	-0	2	3	1	0.3
1952	Pit-N	2	3	.400	12	5	1	0	0	35^{2}	42	3	18	17	15.1	6.31	63	.288	.366	1	.111	-0	-10	-9	-0	-0.9
Total	2	2	5	.286	21	6	1	0	0	52	53	5	25	22	13.5	5.19	78	.256	.336	1	.100	-0	-8	-7	1	-0.6
● **HUGH MULCAHY**	Mulcahy, Hugh Noyes "Losing Pitcher" b: 9/9/13, Brighton, Mass. BR/TR, 6'2", 190 lbs. Deb: 7/24/35 C																									
1935	Phi-N	1	5	.167	18	5	0	0	1	52^{2}	62	2	25	11	15.7	4.78	95	.295	.383	0	.000	-3	-4	-1	1	-0.3

YEAR	TM/L	W	L	PCT	G	GS	CG	SH	SV	IP	H	HR	BB	SO	RAT	ERA	ERA+	OAV	OOB	BH	AVG	PB	PR	/A	PD	TPI
1936	Phi-N	1	1	.500	3	2	2	0	0	22^2	20	0	12	2	13.5	3.18	143	.238	.347	2	.250	0	2	3	0	0.4
1937	Phi-N	8	18	.308	**56**	25	9	1	3	215^2	256	17	97	54	15.0	5.13	84	.296	.372	11	.151	-3	-29	-19	3	-1.8
1938	Phi-N	10	20	.333	46	34	15	0	1	267^1	294	14	120	90	14.1	4.61	84	.278	.354	16	.170	-2	-24	-22	1	-2.2
1939	Phi-N	9	16	.360	38	31	14	1	4	225^2	246	19	93	59	14.0	4.99	80	.282	.359	12	.158	-3	-27	-25	0	-2.6
1940	Phi-N☆	13	22	.371	36	36	21	3	0	280	283	12	91	82	12.1	3.60	108	.261	.320	19	.202	1	8	9	3	1.4
1945	Phi-N	1	3	.250	5	4	1	0	0	28^1	33	1	9	2	13.3	3.81	101	.295	.347	0	.000	-1	-0	0	1	0.0
1946	Phi-N	2	4	.333	16	5	1	0	0	62^2	69	3	33	12	15.4	4.45	77	.295	.393	3	.188	1	-7	-7	1	-0.5
1947	Pit-N	0	0	—	2	1	0	0	0	6^2	8	1	7	2	20.3	4.05	104	.333	.484	1	.333	0	0	0	1	0.1
Total	9	45	89	.336	220	143	63	5	9	1161^2	1271	69	487	314	13.9	4.49	89	.280	.355	64	.165	-9	-82	-61	11	-5.5

● **TERRY MULHOLLAND** Mulholland, Terence John b: 3/9/63, Uniontown, Pa. BR/TL, 6'3", 200 lbs. Deb: 6/08/86

YEAR	TM/L	W	L	PCT	G	GS	CG	SH	SV	IP	H	HR	BB	SO	RAT	ERA	ERA+	OAV	OOB	BH	AVG	PB	PR	/A	PD	TPI
1986	SF-N	1	7	.125	15	10	0	0	0	54^2	51	3	35	27	14.3	4.94	71	.251	.364	1	.053	-1	-7	-9	-1	-1.0
1988	SF-N	2	1	.667	9	6	2	1	0	46	50	3	7	18	11.3	3.72	88	.281	.312	0	.000	-1	-1	-2	0	-0.3
1989	SF-N	0	0	—	5	1	0	0	0	11	15	0	4	6	15.5	4.09	82	.319	.373	0	.000	-0	-1	-1	0	-0.1
	Phi-N	4	7	.364	20	17	2	1	0	104^1	122	8	32	60	13.6	5.00	71	.292	.348	2	.059	-2	-17	-17	1	-1.9
	Yr	4	7	.364	25	18	2	1	0	115^1	137	8	36	66	13.8	4.92	72	.295	.350	2	.056	-2	-18	-18	1	-2.0
1990	Phi-N	9	10	.474	33	26	6	1	0	180^2	172	15	42	75	10.8	3.34	115	.252	.297	6	.097	-2	9	10	-3	0.4
1991	Phi-N	16	13	.552	34	34	8	3	0	232	231	15	49	142	11.0	3.61	102	.260	.301	7	.087	-4	2	1	-2	-0.4
1992	Phi-N	13	11	.542	32	32	**12**	2	0	229	227	14	46	125	10.8	3.81	92	.261	.300	8	.096	-3	-8	-8	1	-1.0
Total	6	45	49	.479	148	126	30	8	0	857^2	868	58	215	453	11.5	3.87	93	.264	.312	24	.082	-13	-24	-26	-3	-4.3

● **TONY MULLANE** Mullane, Anthony John "Count" or "The Apollo Of The Box" b: 1/20/1859, Cork, Ireland d: 4/25/44, Chicago, Ill. BB/TB, 5'10.5", 165 lbs. Deb: 8/27/1881 ♦

YEAR	TM/L	W	L	PCT	G	GS	CG	SH	SV	IP	H	HR	BB	SO	RAT	ERA	ERA+	OAV	OOB	BH	AVG	PB	PR	/A	PD	TPI
1881	Det-N	1	4	.200	5	5	5	0	0	44	55	2	17	7	14.7	4.91	59	.302	.362	5	.263	-0	-10	-10	0	-0.8
1882	Lou-a	30	24	.556	**55**	55	51	5	0	460^1	418	4	78	**170**	9.7	1.88	132	.226	.257	78	.257	11	41	31	11	4.9
1883	StL-a	35	15	**.700**	53	49	49	3	**1**	460^2	372	3	74	191	8.7	2.19	**159**	.206	.238	69	.225	1	57	66	1	6.3
1884	Tol-a	36	26	.581	67	65	64	**7**	0	567	481	5	89	325	9.6	2.52	135	.214	.255	97	.276	16	46	56	10	7.9
1886	Cin-a	33	27	.550	63	56	55	1	0	529^2	501	11	166	250	11.6	3.70	95	.242	.303	73	.225	2	-15	-11	2	-0.6
1887	Cin-a	31	17	.646	48	48	47	**6**	0	416^1	414	11	121	97	12.3	3.24	134	.257	.322	44	.221	1	49	51	-1	4.4
1888	Cin-a	26	16	.619	44	42	41	4	**1**	380^1	341	9	75	186	10.5	2.84	112	.231	.282	44	.251	5	9	14	-0	1.8
1889	Cin-a	11	9	.550	33	24	17	0	**5**	220	218	4	89	112	13.1	2.99	131	.251	.329	58	.296	9	21	22	-1	2.6
1890	Cin-N	12	10	.545	25	21	21	0	1	209	175	7	96	91	12.0	2.24	159	.220	.311	79	.276	6	31	31	0	3.5
1891	Cin-N	23	26	.469	51	47	42	1	0	426^1	390	15	187	124	12.6	3.23	104	.234	.318	31	.148	-5	6	7	1	0.3
1892	Cin-N	21	13	.618	37	34	30	3	1	295	222	12	127	109	11.0	2.59	126	**.201**	.290	20	.169	-2	23	22	6	2.6
1893	Cin-N	6	6	.500	15	13	11	0	1	122^1	130	4	65	24	15.0	4.41	108	.264	.360	15	.288	2	3	5	0	0.6
	Bal-N	12	16	.429	34	26	23	0	1	244^2	277	4	124	71	15.0	4.45	107	.277	.360	26	.228	-3	6	8	3	0.7
	Yr	18	22	.450	49	39	34	0	**2**	367	407	8	189	95	14.8	4.44	107	.271	.355	41	.247	-1	9	13	3	1.3
1894	Bal-N	6	9	.400	21	15	9	0	4	122^2	155	4	90	43	18.5	6.31	87	.305	.416	21	.396	5	-13	-12	-1	-0.5
	Cle-N	1	2	.333	4	4	3	0	0	33	46	3	10	3	15.3	7.64	72	.326	.371	1	.077	-1	-8	-8	2	-0.5
	Yr	7	11	.389	25	19	12	0	**4**	155^2	201	7	100	46	17.4	6.59	83	.306	.398	22	.333	4	-22	-20	1	-1.0
Total	13	284	220	.563	555	504	468	30	15	4531^1	4195	98	1408	1803	11.5	3.05	118	.235	.298	661	.243	47	245	270	33	33.2

● **JOE MULLIGAN** Mulligan, Joseph Ignatius "Big Joe" b: 7/31/13, Weymouth, Mass. d: 6/5/86, W.Roxbury, Mass. BR/TR, 6'4", 210 lbs. Deb: 6/28/34

YEAR	TM/L	W	L	PCT	G	GS	CG	SH	SV	IP	H	HR	BB	SO	RAT	ERA	ERA+	OAV	OOB	BH	AVG	PB	PR	/A	PD	TPI
1934	Bos-A	1	0	1.000	14	2	1	0	0	44^2	46	1	27	13	15.1	3.63	132	.279	.387	0	.000	-2	4	6	0	0.4

● **DICK MULLIGAN** Mulligan, Richard Charles b: 3/18/18, Wilkes-Barre, Pa. BL/TL, 6', 167 lbs. Deb: 9/24/41

YEAR	TM/L	W	L	PCT	G	GS	CG	SH	SV	IP	H	HR	BB	SO	RAT	ERA	ERA+	OAV	OOB	BH	AVG	PB	PR	/A	PD	TPI
1941	Was-A	0	1	.000	1	1	1	0	0	9	11	0	2	2	13.0	5.00	81	.306	.342	0	.000	-0	-1	-1	0	-0.1
1946	Phi-N	2	2	.500	19	5	1	0	1	54^2	61	0	27	16	15.1	4.77	72	.289	.380	0	.000	-1	-8	-8	0	-0.9
	Bos-N	1	0	1.000	4	0	0	0	0	15^1	6	1	9	4	8.8	2.35	146	.122	.259	0	.000	0	2	2	-0	0.2
	Yr	3	2	.600	23	5	1	0	1	70	67	1	36	20	13.2	4.24	81	.254	.343	0	.000	-1	-6	-6	-0	-0.7
1947	Bos-N	0	0	—	1	0	0	0	0	2	4	0	1	1	22.5	9.00	43	.400	.455	0	—	0	-1	-1	-0	-0.1
Total	3	3	3	.500	25	6	2	0	1	81	82	1	39	23	13.9	4.44	79	.268	.358	0	.000	-1	-8	-8	-0	-0.9

● **GEORGE MULLIN** Mullin, George Joseph "Wabash George" b: 7/4/1880, Toledo, Ohio d: 1/7/44, Wabash, Ind. BR/TR, 5'11", 188 lbs. Deb: 5/04/02 ♦

YEAR	TM/L	W	L	PCT	G	GS	CG	SH	SV	IP	H	HR	BB	SO	RAT	ERA	ERA+	OAV	OOB	BH	AVG	PB	PR	/A	PD	TPI
1902	Det-A	13	16	.448	35	30	25	0	0	260	282	4	95	78	13.2	3.67	99	.277	.341	39	.325	9	-3	-1	2	1.1
1903	Det-A	19	15	.559	41	36	31	6	**2**	320^2	284	4	106	170	11.2	2.25	130	.237	.303	35	.278	8	26	24	5	4.2
1904	Det-A	17	23	.425	45	44	42	7	0	382^1	345	1	131	161	11.4	2.40	106	.242	.310	45	.290	11	8	6	8	3.2
1905	Det-A	21	21	.500	44	41	**35**	1	0	**347^2**	303	4	138	168	11.6	2.51	109	.236	.314	35	.259	6	6	9	7	2.6
1906	Det-A	21	18	.538	40	40	35	2	0	330	315	3	108	123	11.9	2.78	99	.254	.322	32	.225	4	-3	-1	3	0.7
1907	*Det-A	20	20	.500	46	42	35	5	3	357^1	346	1	106	146	11.8	2.59	101	.256	.317	34	.217	3	-2	1	4	1.0
1908	*Det-A	17	13	.567	39	30	26	1	0	290^2	301	1	71	121	11.7	3.10	78	.271	.319	32	.256	7	-23	-22	3	-1.3
1909	*Det-A	**29**	8	**.784**	40	35	29	3	1	303^2	258	1	78	124	10.2	2.22	113	.234	.289	27	.214	5	9	10	1	1.9
1910	Det-A	21	12	.636	38	32	27	5	0	289	260	7	102	98	11.7	2.87	92	.254	.330	33	.256	6	-11	-8	1	0.0
1911	Det-A	18	10	.643	30	29	25	2	0	234^1	245	7	61	87	12.2	3.07	113	.276	.331	28	.286	8	7	10	-2	1.6
1912	Det-A	12	17	.414	30	29	22	2	0	226	214	3	92	88	12.5	3.54	92	.255	.335	25	.278	9	-6	-7	0	0.3
1913	Det-A	1	6	.143	7	7	4	0	0	52^1	53	1	18	16	12.6	2.75	106	.268	.335	7	.350	3	1	1	1	0.5
	Was-A	3	5	.375	11	9	3	0	0	57^1	69	1	25	14	15.5	5.02	59	.283	.361	4	.190	0	-13	-13	1	-1.2
	Yr	4	11	.267	18	16	7	0	0	109^2	122	2	43	30	14.0	3.94	75	.275	.346	11	.268	3	-12	-12	1	-0.7
1914	Ind-F	14	10	.583	36	20	11	1	2	203	202	4	91	74	13.4	2.70	128	.261	.346	24	.312	9	11	17	-4	2.5
1915	New-F	2	2	.500	5	4	3	0	0	32^1	41	0	16	14	15.9	5.85	49	.318	.393	1	.100	-0	-10	-11	-1	-1.1
Total	14	228	196	.538	487	428	353	35	8	3686^2	3518	42	1238	1482	11.9	2.82	101	.254	.321	401	.262	89	-3	16	28	16.0

● **DOMINIC MULRENAN** Mulrenan, Dominic Joseph b: 12/18/1893, Woburn, Mass. d: 7/27/64, Melrose, Mass. BR/TR, 5'11", 170 lbs. Deb: 4/24/21

YEAR	TM/L	W	L	PCT	G	GS	CG	SH	SV	IP	H	HR	BB	SO	RAT	ERA	ERA+	OAV	OOB	BH	AVG	PB	PR	/A	PD	TPI
1921	Chi-A	2	8	.200	12	10	3	0	0	56	84	2	36	10	19.6	7.23	59	.359	.449	3	.150	-1	-18	-19	0	-1.7

● **FRANK MULRONEY** Mulroney, Francis Joseph b: 4/8/03, Mallard, Iowa d: 11/11/85, Aberdeen, Wash. BR/TR, 6', 170 lbs. Deb: 4/15/30

YEAR	TM/L	W	L	PCT	G	GS	CG	SH	SV	IP	H	HR	BB	SO	RAT	ERA	ERA+	OAV	OOB	BH	AVG	PB	PR	/A	PD	TPI
1930	Bos-A	0	1	.000	2	0	0	0	0	3	3	0	0	2	9.0	3.00	154	.273	.273	0	—	0	1	1	0	0.1

● **BOB MUNCRIEF** Muncrief, Robert Cleveland b: 1/28/16, Madill, Okla. BR/TR, 6'2", 190 lbs. Deb: 9/30/37

YEAR	TM/L	W	L	PCT	G	GS	CG	SH	SV	IP	H	HR	BB	SO	RAT	ERA	ERA+	OAV	OOB	BH	AVG	PB	PR	/A	PD	TPI
1937	StL-A	0	0	—	1	1	0	0	0	2	3	1	2	0	22.5	4.50	107	.300	.417	0	—	0	0	0	-0	0.0
1939	StL-A	0	0	—	2	0	0	0	0	3	7	1	3	1	30.0	15.00	32	.500	.588	0	—	0	-3	-3	-0	-0.3
1941	StL-A	13	9	.591	36	24	12	2	1	214^1	221	18	53	67	11.7	3.65	118	.266	.314	18	.237	2	12	15	-1	1.6
1942	StL-A	6	8	.429	24	18	7	1	0	134^1	149	11	31	39	12.1	3.89	95	.280	.319	5	.111	-1	-3	-3	-0	-0.4
1943	StL-A	13	12	.520	35	27	12	3	1	205	211	13	48	80	11.5	2.81	118	.264	.307	10	.152	-2	11	12	-3	0.8
1944	*StL-A★	13	8	.619	33	27	12	3	1	219^1	216	11	50	88	11.0	3.08	117	.258	.302	18	.231	1	9	13	-1	1.4
1945	StL-A	13	4	.765	27	15	10	0	1	145^2	132	8	44	54	11.0	2.72	130	.239	.297	3	.067	-4	10	13	-1	0.8
1946	StL-A	3	12	.200	29	14	4	1	0	115^1	149	6	31	49	14.0	4.99	75	.314	.356	1	.031	-3	-19	-16	-1	-2.1
1947	StL-A	8	14	.364	31	23	7	0	0	176^1	210	14	51	74	13.4	4.90	79	.299	.348	6	.105	-4	-23	-20	0	-2.3
1948	*Cle-A	5	4	.556	21	9	1	1	0	72^1	76	8	31	24	13.3	3.98	102	.279	.353	2	.111	-1	2	1	-0	-0.1
1949	Pit-N	1	5	.167	13	4	1	0	3	35^2	44	8	13	11	14.4	6.31	67	.310	.368	1	.143	-0	-9	-8	1	-0.7
	Chi-N	5	6	.455	34	3	1	0	2	75	80	9	31	36	13.4	4.56	88	.276	.348	4	.286	1	-4	-4	-0	-0.3
	Yr	6	11	.353	47	7	2	0	5	110^2	124	17	44	47	13.7	5.12	80	.287	.354	5	.238	1	-13	-13	1	-1.0
1951	NY-A	0	0	—	2	0	0	0	0	3	5	0	4	2	27.0	9.00	43	.417	.563	0	—	0	-2	-2	0	-0.1
Total	12	80	82	.494	288	165	67	11	9	1401^1	1503	108	392	525	12.3	3.80	100	.275	.325	68	.155	-10	-20	-3	-7	-1.7

YEAR	TM/L	W	L	PCT	G	GS	CG	SH	SV	IP	H	HR	BB	SO	RAT	ERA	ERA+	OAV	OOB	BH	AVG	PB	PR	/A	PD	TPI
● **RED MUNGER** Munger, George David b: 10/4/18, Houston, Tex. BR/TR, 6'2", 200 lbs. Deb: 5/01/43																										
1943	StL-N	9	5	.643	32	9	5	0	2	93^1	101	2	42	45	13.8	3.95	85	.281	.357	6	.214	1	-6	-6	1	-0.5
1944	StL-N†	11	3	.786	21	12	7	2	2	121	92	2	41	55	10.0	1.34	263	.212	.284	5	.114	-3	31	29	3	3.3
1946	*StL-N	2	2	.500	10	7	2	0	1	48^2	47	0	12	28	10.9	3.33	104	.255	.301	4	.250	1	0	1	2	0.3
1947	StL-N☆	16	5	.762	40	31	13	6	3	224^1	218	12	76	123	11.9	3.37	123	.255	.318	15	.185	1	17	19	3	2.2
1948	StL-N	10	11	.476	39	25	7	2	0	166	179	13	74	72	13.8	4.50	91	.272	.347	8	.160	0	-10	-8	2	-0.6
1949	StL-N★	15	8	.652	35	28	12	2	2	188^1	179	13	87	82	12.8	3.87	108	.255	.339	17	.258	4	4	6	1	1.1
1950	StL-N	7	8	.467	32	20	5	1	0	154^2	158	15	70	61	13.4	3.90	110	.262	.342	7	.137	-2	4	7	0	0.5
1951	StL-N	4	6	.400	23	11	3	0	0	94^2	106	13	46	44	14.5	5.32	74	.286	.365	5	.172	-0	-14	-14	2	-1.2
1952	StL-N	0	1	.000	1	1	0	0	0	4^1	7	2	1	1	18.7	12.46	30	.389	.450	0	.000	-0	-4	-4	0	-0.3
	Pit-N	0	3	.000	5	4	0	0	0	26^1	30	6	10	8	13.7	7.18	56	.283	.345	0	.000	-1	-10	-9	1	-0.9
	Yr	0	4	.000	6	5	0	0	0	30^2	37	8	11	9	14.1	7.92	50	.296	.353	0	.000	-1	-14	-14	1	-1.2
1956	Pit-N	3	4	.429	35	13	0	0	2	107	126	8	41	45	14.0	4.04	93	.299	.361	3	.107	-0	-3	-3	-1	-0.4
Total	10	77	56	.579	273	161	54	13	12	1228^2	1243	86	500	564	12.8	3.83	103	.264	.336	70	.174	1	8	17	13	3.5
● **VAN MUNGO** Mungo, Van Lingle b: 6/8/11, Pageland, S.C. d: 2/12/85, Pageland, S.C. BR/TR, 6'2", 185 lbs. Deb: 9/07/31																										
1931	Bro-N	3	1	.750	5	4	2	1	0	31	27	0	13	12	11.9	2.32	164	.241	.325	3	.250	1	5	5	-1	0.6
1932	Bro-N	13	11	.542	39	33	11	1	2	223^1	224	9	115	107	13.9	4.43	86	.260	.351	16	.203	0	-14	-15	2	-1.3
1933	Bro-N	16	15	.516	41	28	18	3	0	248	223	7	84	110	11.1	2.72	118	.236	.298	15	.179	-0	17	14	1	1.6
1934	Bro-N★	18	16	.529	45	38	22	3	3	**315^1**	300	15	104	184	11.6	3.37	116	.249	.310	30	.248	4	24	19	2	2.5
1935	Bro-N	16	10	.615	37	26	18	**4**	2	214^1	205	13	90	143	12.5	3.65	109	.252	.328	26	.289	5	9	8	1	1.3
1936	Bro-N☆	18	19	.486	45	37	22	2	3	311^2	275	8	118	**238**	11.4	3.35	123	**.234**	.305	22	.179	-4	23	27	2	2.5
1937	Bro-N★	9	11	.450	25	21	14	0	3	161	136	3	56	122	10.9	2.91	139	**.229**	.298	16	.250	2	18	20	3	2.7
1938	Bro-N	4	11	.267	24	18	6	2	0	133^1	133	11	72	72	14.0	3.92	100	.259	.353	9	.191	1	-2	-0	1	0.2
1939	Bro-N	4	5	.444	14	10	1	0	0	77^1	70	7	33	34	12.3	3.26	124	.239	.322	10	.345	2	6	7	-1	1.0
1940	Bro-N	1	0	1.000	7	0	0	0	1	22	24	1	10	9	13.9	2.45	163	.282	.358	0	.000	-1	3	4	-0	0.2
1941	Bro-N	0	0	—	2	0	0	0	0	2	1	0	2	0	13.5	4.50	81	.143	.333	0	—	0	-0	-0	0	0.0
1942	NY-N	1	2	.333	9	5	0	0	0	36^1	38	4	21	27	14.6	5.94	57	.273	.369	3	.214	-0	-11	-10	0	-1.0
1943	NY-N	3	7	.300	45	13	2	2	2	154^1	140	7	79	83	13.1	3.91	88	.243	.341	7	.159	-1	-9	-8	1	-0.8
1945	NY-N	14	7	.667	26	26	7	2	0	183	161	4	71	101	11.6	3.20	122	.238	.314	17	.233	4	12	15	-0	1.9
Total	14	120	115	.511	364	259	123	20	16	2113	1957	89	868	1242	12.2	3.47	110	.245	.321	174	.221	13	83	83	11	11.4
● **MANNY MUNIZ** Muniz, Manuel (Rodriguez) b: 12/31/47, Caguas, P.R. BR/TR, 5'11", 190 lbs. Deb: 9/03/71																										
1971	Phi-N	0	1	.000	5	0	0	0	0	10^1	9	2	8	6	14.8	6.97	51	.225	.354	0	.000	-0	-4	-4	-0	-0.4
● **SCOTT MUNNINGHOFF** Munninghoff, Scott Andrew b: 12/5/58, Cincinnati, Ohio BR/TR, 6', 175 lbs. Deb: 4/13/80																										
1980	Phi-N	0	0	—	4	0	0	0	0	6	8	0	5	2	19.5	4.50	84	.320	.433	1	1.000	1	-1	-0	0	0.1
● **LES MUNNS** Munns, Leslie Ernest "Big Ed" or "Nemo" b: 12/1/08, Fort Bragg, Cal. BR/TR, 6'5", 212 lbs. Deb: 4/22/34																										
1934	Bro-N	3	7	.300	33	9	4	0	0	99^1	106	7	60	41	15.0	4.71	83	.280	.378	7	.241	2	-7	-9	2	-0.5
1935	Bro-N	1	3	.250	21	5	0	0	1	58^1	74	5	33	13	17.1	5.55	72	.319	.413	3	.188	-0	-10	-10	-2	-1.2
1936	StL-N	0	3	.000	7	1	0	0	1	24	23	2	12	4	13.1	3.00	131	.240	.324	1	.111	-1	3	3	1	0.3
Total	3	4	13	.235	61	15	4	0	2	181^2	203	14	105	58	15.5	4.76	83	.287	.382	11	.204	1	-14	-17	1	-1.4
● **MIKE MUNOZ** Munoz, Michael Anthony b: 7/12/65, Baldwin Park, Cal. BL/TL, 6'2", 190 lbs. Deb: 9/06/89																										
1989	LA-N	0	0	—	3	0	0	0	0	2^2	5	1	2	3	23.6	16.88	20	.417	.500	0	—	0	-4	-4	0	-0.4
1990	LA-N	0	1	.000	8	0	0	0	0	5^2	6	0	3	2	14.3	3.18	115	.300	.391	0	.000	-0	0	0	-0	0.0
1991	Det-A	0	0	—	6	0	0	0	0	9^1	14	0	5	3	18.3	9.64	43	.350	.422	0	—	0	-6	-6	0	-0.6
1992	Det-A	1	2	.333	65	0	0	0	2	48	44	3	25	23	12.9	3.00	133	.246	.338	0	—	0	5	5	2	0.7
Total	4	1	3	.250	82	0	0	0	2	65^2	69	4	35	31	14.3	4.52	87	.275	.364	0	.000	-0	-4	-4	2	-0.3
● **STEVE MURA** Mura, Stephen Andrew b: 2/12/55, New Orleans, La. BR/TR, 6'2", 190 lbs. Deb: 9/05/78																										
1978	SD-N	0	2	.000	5	2	0	0	0	7^2	15	1	5	5	23.5	11.74	28	.441	.513	0	.000	-0	-7	-7	-0	-0.7
1979	SD-N	4	4	.500	38	5	0	0	2	73	57	6	37	59	11.7	3.08	114	.217	.316	0	.000	-1	5	4	-0	0.2
1980	SD-N	8	7	.533	37	23	3	1	2	168^2	149	9	86	109	12.7	3.68	93	.246	.343	7	.137	-0	-2	-5	0	-0.5
1981	SD-N	5	14	.263	23	22	2	0	0	138^2	156	10	50	70	13.4	4.28	76	.285	.344	6	.136	-0	-12	-16	1	-1.5
1982	StL-N	12	11	.522	35	30	7	1	0	184^1	196	16	80	84	13.5	4.05	89	.278	.352	3	.057	-4	-9	-9	-1	-1.4
1983	Chi-A	0	0	—	6	0	0	0	0	12^1	13	1	6	4	13.9	4.38	96	.260	.339	0	—	0	-0	-0	-0	-0.2
1985	Oak-A	1	1	.500	23	1	0	0	1	48	41	3	25	29	12.4	4.13	93	.225	.319	0	—	0	0	-1	-0	0.2
Total	7	30	39	.435	167	83	12	2	5	632^2	627	46	289	360	13.1	4.00	88	.263	.343	16	.101	-5	-25	-35	-1	-3.9
● **MASANORI MURAKAMI** Murakami, Masanori b: 5/6/44, Otsuki, Japan BL/TL, 6', 180 lbs. Deb: 9/01/64																										
1964	SF-N	1	0	1.000	9	0	0	0	1	15	8	1	1	15	5.4	1.80	198	.163	.180	0	.000	-0	3	3	-1	0.2
1965	SF-N	4	1	.800	45	1	0	0	8	74^1	57	9	22	85	9.9	3.75	96	.205	.271	2	.154	-0	-2	-1	-2	-0.3
Total	2	5	1	.833	54	1	0	0	9	89^1	65	10	23	100	9.2	3.43	105	.199	.258	2	.125	-1	1	2	-2	-0.1
● **TIM MURCHISON** Murchison, Thomas Malcolm b: 10/8/1896, Liberty, N.C. d: 10/20/62, Liberty, N.C. BR/TL, 6', 185 lbs. Deb: 6/21/17																										
1917	StL-N	0	0	—	1	0	0	0	0	1	0	0	2	2	18.0	0.00	—	.000	.400	0	—	0	0	0	0	0.0
1920	Cle-A	0	0	—	2	0	0	0	0	5	3	0	4	0	12.6	0.00	—	.200	.368	0	.000	-0	2	2	1	0.3
Total	2	0	0	—	3	0	0	0	0	6	3	0	6	2	13.5	0.00	—	.167	.375	0	.000	-0	2	2	1	0.3
● **RED MURFF** Murff, John Robert b: 4/1/21, Burlington, Tex. BR/TR, 6'3", 195 lbs. Deb: 4/21/56																										
1956	Mil-N	0	0	—	14	1	0	0	1	24^1	25	3	7	18	11.8	4.44	78	.272	.323	1	.200	0	-2	-3	0	-0.2
1957	Mil-N	2	2	.500	12	1	0	0	2	26	31	3	11	13	14.5	4.85	72	.301	.368	0	.000	-1	-3	-4	0	-0.4
Total	2	2	2	.500	26	2	0	0	3	50^1	56	6	18	31	13.2	4.65	75	.287	.347	1	.091	-1	-5	-7	1	-0.6
● **CON MURPHY** Murphy, Cornelius B. "Monk" or "Razzle Dazzle" b: 10/15/1863, Worcester, Mass. d: 8/1/14, Worcester, Mass. TR, 5'9", 130 lbs. Deb: 9/11/1884																										
1884	Phi-N	0	3	.000	3	3	3	0	0	26	37	1	6	10	14.9	6.58	45	.319	.352	0	.000	-1	-10	-10	0	-0.9
1890	Bro-P	4	10	.286	20	14	11	0	2	139	168	2	82	29	16.6	4.79	93	.286	.379	15	.217	-1	-9	-5	-1	-0.6
Total	2	4	13	.235	23	17	14	0	2	165	205	3	88	39	16.3	5.07	83	.292	.375	15	.190	-3	-19	-16	-0	-1.5
● **DANNY MURPHY** Murphy, Daniel Francis b: 8/23/42, Beverly, Mass. BL/TR, 5'11", 185 lbs. Deb: 6/18/60 ♦																										
1969	Chi-A	2	1	.667	17	0	0	0	4	31^1	28	2	10	16	11.5	2.01	192	.252	.325	0	.000	0	6	6	-0	0.7
1970	Chi-A	2	3	.400	51	0	0	0	5	80^2	82	11	49	42	15.1	5.69	68	.273	.382	2	.333	2	-18	-16	-1	-1.5
Total	2	4	4	.500	68	0	0	0	9	112	110	13	59	58	14.1	4.66	83	.268	.368	23	.177	2	-12	-10	-1	-0.8
● **DAN MURPHY** Murphy, Daniel Lee b: 9/18/64, Artesia, Cal. BR/TR, 6'2", 195 lbs. Deb: 8/10/89																										
1989	SD-N	0	0	—	7	0	0	0	0	6^1	6	1	4	1	14.2	5.68	61	.231	.333	0	—	0	-2	-2	-0	-0.2
● **ED MURPHY** Murphy, Edward J. b: 1/22/1877, Auburn, N.Y. d: 1/29/35, Weedsport, N.Y. TR, 6'1", 186 lbs. Deb: 4/23/1898																										
1898	Phi-N	1	2	.333	7	3	2	0	0	30	41	3	10	8	15.6	5.10	67	.323	.377	5	.357	1	-5	-6	1	-0.3
1901	StL-N	10	9	.526	23	21	16	0	0	165	201	5	32	42	12.8	4.20	76	.298	.331	16	.250	3	-16	-19	2	-1.3
1902	StL-N	10	6	.625	23	17	12	1	1	164	187	7	31	37	12.1	3.02	91	.286	.321	16	.262	1	-4	-5	2	-0.2
1903	StL-N	4	8	.333	15	12	9	0	0	106	108	2	38	16	12.9	3.31	99	.262	.333	13	.203	-1	-0	-1	0	-0.1
Total	4	25	25	.500	68	53	39	1	1	465	537	17	111	103	12.7	3.64	84	.288	.331	50	.246	5	-26	-30	5	-1.9

● JOHN MURPHY
Murphy, John H. b: 3/8/1867, Philadelphia, Pa. Deb: 4/17/1884

YEAR	TM/L	W	L	PCT	G	GS	CG	SH	SV	IP	H	HR	BB	SO	RAT	ERA	ERA+	OAV	OOB	BH	AVG	PB	PR	/A	PD	TPI
1884	Wil-U	0	6	.000	7	6	5	0	0	48	52	3	2	27	10.1	3.00	110	.258	.266	2	.065	-3	0	2	-1	-0.1
	Alt-U	5	6	.455	14	10	10	0	0	111^{2}	141	3	9	46	12.1	3.87	85	.289	.302	14	.149	-5	-11	-7	1	-0.8
	Yr	5	12	.294	21	16	15	0	0	159^{2}	193	6	11	73	11.5	3.61	91	.280	.291	16	.128	-7	-10	-6	0	-0.9

● JOHNNY MURPHY
Murphy, John Joseph "Grandma" "Fireman" Or "Fordham Johnny"
b: 7/14/08, New York, N.Y. d: 1/14/70, New York, N.Y. BR/TR, 6'2", 190 lbs. Deb: 5/19/32

YEAR	TM/L	W	L	PCT	G	GS	CG	SH	SV	IP	H	HR	BB	SO	RAT	ERA	ERA+	OAV	OOB	BH	AVG	PB	PR	/A	PD	TPI
1932	NY-A	0	0	—	2	0	0	0	0	3^{1}	7	0	3	2	27.0	16.20	25	.438	.526	1	1.000	0	-4	-4	0	-0.3
1934	NY-A	14	10	.583	40	20	10	0	4	207^{2}	193	11	76	70	11.7	3.12	130	.250	.317	7	.099	-3	32	22	1	1.9
1935	NY-A	10	5	.667	40	8	4	0	5	117	110	7	55	28	12.7	4.08	99	.243	.325	5	.156	2	5	-0	-1	0.1
1936	*NY-A	9	3	.750	27	5	2	0	5	88	90	5	36	34	13.0	3.38	138	.262	.334	13	.361	4	16	13	1	1.6
1937	*NY-A☆	13	4	.765	39	4	0	0	10	110	121	7	50	36	14.1	4.17	107	.277	.352	8	.229	2	5	3	4	0.8
1938	*NY-A☆	8	2	.800	32	2	1	0	**11**	91^{1}	90	5	41	43	13.0	4.24	107	.256	.336	2	.063	-3	**6**	3	1	0.1
1939	*NY-A☆	3	6	.333	38	0	0	0	**19**	61^{1}	57	2	28	30	12.5	4.40	99	.252	.335	2	.182	1	1	-0	1	0.1
1940	NY-A	8	4	.667	35	1	0	0	9	63^{1}	58	5	15	23	10.4	3.69	109	.247	.292	1	.077	0	5	2	1	0.3
1941	*NY-A	8	3	.727	35	0	0	0	**15**	77^{1}	68	1	40	29	12.6	1.98	199	.237	.330	1	.056	-1	**19**	**17**	-1	1.4
1942	NY-A	4	10	.286	31	0	0	0	**11**	58	66	2	23	24	14.1	3.41	101	.293	.364	2	.154	0	2	0	0	0.1
1943	*NY-A	12	4	.750	37	0	0	0	8	68	44	2	30	31	9.8	2.51	128	.183	.273	1	.053	-2	6	5	-0	0.3
1946	NY-A	4	2	.667	27	0	0	0	7	45	40	4	19	19	11.8	3.40	102	.240	.317	0	.000	-0	1	0	1	0.1
1947	Bos-A	0	0	—	32	0	0	0	3	54^{2}	41	1	28	9	11.4	2.80	139	.206	.304	3	.273	1	6	7	0	0.8
Total	13	93	53	.637	415	40	17	0	107	1045	985	52	444	378	12.4	3.50	117	.249	.326	46	.154	0	98	68	8	7.3

● JOE MURPHY
Murphy, Joseph Akin b: 9/7/1866, St.Louis, Mo. d: 3/28/51, Coral Gables, Fla. 5'11", 160 lbs. Deb: 4/28/1886

YEAR	TM/L	W	L	PCT	G	GS	CG	SH	SV	IP	H	HR	BB	SO	RAT	ERA	ERA+	OAV	OOB	BH	AVG	PB	PR	/A	PD	TPI
1886	Cin-a	2	3	.400	5	5	5	0	0	46	50	0	21	11	14.1	4.89	72	.256	.332	0	.000	-3	-7	-7	-1	-0.9
	StL-N	0	4	.000	4	4	3	0	0	33	45	3	16	11	16.6	8.18	39	.319	.389	3	.214	0	-18	-18	-0	-1.4
	StL-a	1	0	1.000	1	1	1	0	0	7	5	0	3	3	10.3	3.86	89	.179	.258	0	.000	-1	-0	-0	-0	-0.1
1887	StL-a	1	0	1.000	1	1	1	0	0	9	13	0	4	5	17.0	5.00	91	.317	.378	1	.167	-1	-1	-0	0	-0.1
Total	2	4	7	.364	11	11	10	0	0	95	113	3	44	30	15.0	5.97	59	.279	.351	4	.098	-4	-26	-26	-2	-2.5

● ROB MURPHY
Murphy, Robert Albert b: 5/26/60, Miami, Fla. BL/TL, 6'2", 205 lbs. Deb: 9/13/85

YEAR	TM/L	W	L	PCT	G	GS	CG	SH	SV	IP	H	HR	BB	SO	RAT	ERA	ERA+	OAV	OOB	BH	AVG	PB	PR	/A	PD	TPI
1985	Cin-N	0	0	—	2	0	0	0	0	3	2	1	2	1	12.0	6.00	63	.200	.333	0	—	0	-1	-1	-0	-0.1
1986	Cin-N	6	0	1.000	34	0	0	0	1	50^{1}	26	0	21	36	8.4	0.72	541	.155	.249	0	.000	-0	17	18	0	1.9
1987	Cin-N	8	5	.615	87	0	0	0	3	100^{2}	91	7	32	99	11.0	3.04	140	.239	.299	1	.200	0	12	13	0	1.4
1988	Cin-N	0	6	.000	**76**	0	0	0	3	84^{2}	69	3	38	74	11.5	3.08	116	.229	.318	0	—	0	3	5	1	0.6
1989	Bos-A	5	7	.417	74	0	0	0	9	105	97	7	41	107	11.9	2.74	149	.251	.325	0	—	0	13	16	1	1.5
1990	*Bos-A	0	6	.000	68	0	0	0	7	57	85	10	32	54	18.6	6.32	65	.348	.426	0	—	0	-15	-14	0	-1.4
1991	Sea-A	0	1	.000	57	0	0	0	4	48	47	4	19	34	12.6	3.00	137	.250	.322	0	—	0	6	6	0	0.6
1992	Hou-N	3	1	.750	59	0	0	0	0	55^{2}	56	2	21	42	12.4	4.04	83	.260	.326	0	.000	-0	-3	-4	1	-0.4
Total	8	22	26	.458	457	0	0	0	27	504^{1}	473	34	206	447	12.2	3.25	121	.250	.325	1	.111	-0	32	38	3	4.1

● BOB MURPHY
Murphy, Robert J. b: 12/26/1866, Dutchess Co., N.Y. Deb: 5/27/1890

YEAR	TM/L	W	L	PCT	G	GS	CG	SH	SV	IP	H	HR	BB	SO	RAT	ERA	ERA+	OAV	OOB	BH	AVG	PB	PR	/A	PD	TPI
1890	NY-N	1	0	1.000	3	2	1	0	0	18	23	0	10	8	16.5	5.50	64	.301	.382	1	.111	-1	-4	-4	-0	-0.4
	Bro-a	3	9	.250	12	12	10	0	0	96	121	6	46	26	16.1	5.72	68	.299	.377	9	.180	-0	-20	-19	2	-1.4
Total	1	4	9	.308	15	14	11	0	0	114	144	6	56	34	16.2	5.68	67	.299	.378	10	.169	-1	-24	-23	2	-1.8

● TOM MURPHY
Murphy, Thomas Andrew b: 12/30/45, Cleveland, Ohio BR/TR, 6'3", 185 lbs. Deb: 6/13/68

YEAR	TM/L	W	L	PCT	G	GS	CG	SH	SV	IP	H	HR	BB	SO	RAT	ERA	ERA+	OAV	OOB	BH	AVG	PB	PR	/A	PD	TPI
1968	Cal-A	5	6	.455	15	15	3	0	0	99^{1}	67	5	28	56	9.1	2.17	134	.191	.261	0	.000	-2	9	8	-1	0.5
1969	Cal-A	10	16	.385	36	35	4	0	0	215^{2}	213	12	69	100	12.6	4.21	83	.260	.333	10	.141	-0	-14	-18	1	-1.7
1970	Cal-A	16	13	.552	39	38	5	2	0	227	223	32	81	99	12.3	4.24	85	.261	.330	14	.184	2	-13	-16	-1	-1.4
1971	Cal-A	6	17	.261	37	36	7	0	0	243^{1}	228	24	82	89	11.8	3.77	86	.256	.325	13	.173	1	-8	-14	1	-1.3
1972	Cal-A	0	0	—	6	0	0	0	0	10	13	0	8	2	18.9	5.40	54	.342	.457	0	.000	-0	-3	-3	1	-0.3
	KC-A	4	4	.500	18	9	1	1	1	70^{1}	77	3	16	34	12.7	3.07	99	.287	.341	0	.000	-1	-0	-0	1	-0.1
	Yr	4	4	.500	24	9	1	1	1	80^{1}	90	3	24	36	13.4	3.36	90	.293	.356	0	.000	-1	-3	-3	1	-0.4
1973	StL-N	3	7	.300	19	13	2	0	0	88^{2}	89	5	22	42	11.6	3.76	97	.269	.320	4	.174	0	-1	-1	1	0.0
1974	Mil-A	10	10	.500	70	0	0	0	20	123	97	6	51	47	11.0	1.90	190	.224	.309	1	.500	1	23	**23**	2	2.8
1975	Mil-A	1	9	.100	52	0	0	0	20	72^{1}	85	5	27	32	14.6	4.60	83	.295	.366	0	—	0	-7	-6	0	-0.6
1976	Mil-A	0	1	.000	15	0	0	0	1	18^{1}	25	2	9	7	17.7	7.36	47	.313	.396	0	—	0	-8	-8	0	-0.6
	Bos-A	4	5	.444	37	0	0	0	8	81	91	5	25	32	13.1	3.44	114	.290	.346	0	—	0	1	4	-0	-0.5
	Yr	4	6	.400	52	0	0	0	9	99^{1}	116	7	34	39	13.8	4.17	92	.293	.352	0	—	0	-7	-4	0	-1.1
1977	Bos-A	0	1	.000	16	0	0	0	0	30^{2}	44	6	12	13	16.4	6.75	67	.338	.394	0	—	0	-9	-8	0	-1.5
	Tor-A	2	1	.667	19	1	0	0	2	52	63	6	18	26	14.2	3.63	115	.304	.363	0	—	0	2	3	-0	0.2
	Yr	2	2	.500	35	1	0	0	2	82^{2}	107	12	30	39	15.0	4.79	90	.317	.374	0	—	0	-7	-4	0	-1.3
1978	Tor-A	6	9	.400	50	0	0	0	7	94	87	11	37	36	11.9	3.93	100	.256	.329	0	—	0	-2	-0	2	0.2
1979	Tor-A	1	2	.333	10	0	0	0	0	18^{1}	23	1	8	6	15.2	5.40	80	.311	.378	0	—	0	-2	-2	1	-0.2
Total	12	68	101	.402	439	147	22	3	59	1444	1425	123	493	621	12.3	3.78	94	.263	.332	42	.145	0	-32	-38	7	-4.5

● WALTER MURPHY
Murphy, Walter Joseph b: 9/27/07, New York, N.Y. BR/TR, 6'1.5", 180 lbs. Deb: 4/19/31

YEAR	TM/L	W	L	PCT	G	GS	CG	SH	SV	IP	H	HR	BB	SO	RAT	ERA	ERA+	OAV	OOB	BH	AVG	PB	PR	/A	PD	TPI
1931	Bos-A	0	0	—	2	0	0	0	0	2	4	0	1	0	22.5	9.00	48	.444	.500	0	—	0	-1	-1	-0	-0.1

● DALE MURRAY
Murray, Dale Albert b: 2/2/50, Cuero, Tex. BR/TR, 6'4", 205 lbs. Deb: 7/07/74

YEAR	TM/L	W	L	PCT	G	GS	CG	SH	SV	IP	H	HR	BB	SO	RAT	ERA	ERA+	OAV	OOB	BH	AVG	PB	PR	/A	PD	TPI
1974	Mon-N	1	1	.500	32	0	0	0	10	69^{2}	46	1	23	31	8.9	1.03	371	.187	.257	0	.000	-1	20	22	0	2.3
1975	Mon-N	15	8	.652	63	0	0	0	9	111^{1}	134	0	39	43	14.2	3.96	97	.305	.365	3	.214	1	-4	-2	3	0.1
1976	Mon-N	4	9	.308	**81**	0	0	0	13	113^{1}	117	1	37	35	12.2	3.26	114	.277	.336	0	.000	-1	3	6	4	1.0
1977	Cin-N	7	2	.778	61	1	0	0	4	102	125	13	46	42	15.3	4.94	80	.314	.388	2	.167	-0	-12	-11	0	-1.2
1978	Cin-N	1	1	.500	15	0	0	0	2	32^{2}	34	1	17	25	14.3	4.13	86	.272	.364	0	.000	-0	-2	-2	1	-0.2
	NY-N	8	5	.615	53	0	0	0	5	86^{1}	85	4	36	37	12.8	3.65	96	.266	.345	0	.000	-0	-1	-2	2	0.0
	Yr	9	6	.600	68	0	0	0	7	119	119	5	53	62	13.2	3.78	93	.266	.346	0	.000	-1	-3	-4	2	-0.2
1979	NY-N	4	8	.333	58	0	0	0	4	97	105	6	52	37	14.6	4.82	75	.287	.376	0	.000	-0	-12	-13	1	-1.2
	Mon-N	1	2	.333	9	0	0	0	1	13^{1}	14	1	3	4	11.5	2.70	136	.292	.333	0	.000	-0	2	1	-1	0.1
	Yr	5	10	.333	67	0	0	0	5	110^{1}	119	7	55	41	14.2	4.57	80	.285	.369	0	.000	-1	-10	-11	0	-1.1
1980	Mon-N	0	1	.000	16	0	0	0	0	29^{1}	39	3	12	16	15.6	6.14	58	.315	.375	0	.000	-0	-8	-8	-1	-0.9
1981	Tor-A	1	0	1.000	11	0	0	0	0	15^{1}	12	0	5	12	10.0	1.17	336	.211	.274	0	—	0	4	5	1	0.2
1982	Tor-A	8	7	.533	56	0	0	0	11	111	115	3	32	60	12.2	3.16	142	.268	.323	0	—	0	11	16	3	1.2
1983	NY-A	2	4	.333	40	0	0	0	1	94^{1}	113	5	22	45	13.0	4.48	87	.297	.337	0	—	0	-4	-6	0	-0.4
1984	NY-A	1	2	.333	19	0	0	0	0	23^{2}	30	2	5	13	14.1	4.94	77	.306	.352	0	—	0	-3	-3	-0	0.0
1985	NY-A	0	0	—	3	0	0	0	0	2	4	0	0	0	18.0	13.50	30	.400	.400	0	—	0	-2	-2	-0	0.0
	Tex-A	0	0	—	1	0	0	0	0	1	3	0	0	0	27.0	18.00	23	.750	.750	0	—	0	-2	-2	0	-0.2
	Yr	0	0	—	4	0	0	0	0	3	7	0	0	0	21.0	15.00	27	.500	.500	0	—	0	-4	-4	0	-0.2
Total	12	53	50	.515	518	1	0	0	60	902^{1}	976	40	329	400	13.2	3.85	100	.282	.346	5	.077	-3	-9	-1	13	0.8

● GEORGE MURRAY
Murray, George King "Smiler" b: 9/23/1898, Charlotte, N.C. d: 10/18/55, Memphis, Tenn. BR/TR, 6'2", 200 lbs. Deb: 5/08/22

YEAR	TM/L	W	L	PCT	G	GS	CG	SH	SV	IP	H	HR	BB	SO	RAT	ERA	ERA+	OAV	OOB	BH	AVG	PB	PR	/A	PD	TPI
1922	NY-A	4	2	.667	22	2	0	0	0	56^{2}	53	0	26	14	12.7	3.97	101	.255	.340	5	.278	2	**0**	**0**	-0	0.2
1923	Bos-A	7	11	.389	39	18	5	0	0	177^{2}	190	9	87	40	14.4	4.91	84	.291	.380	9	.164	-3	-18	-16	-2	-1.9
1924	Bos-A	2	9	.182	28	7	0	0	0	80^{1}	97	6	32	27	15.2	6.72	65	.307	.383	4	.182	-1	-22	-21	0	-2.0

YEAR	TM/L	W	L	PCT	G	GS	CG	SH	SV	IP	H	HR	BB	SO	RAT	ERA	ERA+	OAV	OOB	BH	AVG	PB	PR	/A	PD	TPI
1926	Was-A	6	3	.667	12	12	5	0	0	81^{1}	89	1	37	28	14.6	5.64	69	.287	.374	5	.139	-2	-15	-16	-1	-1.7
1927	Was-A	1	1	.500	7	3	0	0	0	18	18	1	15	5	17.5	7.00	58	.265	.412	1	.167	-0	-6	-6	-1	-0.6
1933	Chi-A	0	0	—	2	0	0	0	0	2^{1}	3	0	2	0	19.3	7.71	55	.375	.500	0	—	0	-1	-1	0	-0.1
Total	6	20	26	.435	110	42	10	0	0	416^{1}	450	17	199	114	14.5	5.38	76	.288	.376	24	.175	-4	-61	-59	-3	-6.1
● **JIM MURRAY**	Murray, James Francis "Big Jim" b: 12/31/1900, Scranton, Pa. d: 7/15/73, New York, N.Y. BB/TL, 6'2", 210 lbs. Deb: 7/03/22																									
1922	Bro-N	0	0	—	4	0	0	0	1	6	8	0	3	3	16.5	4.50	90	.320	.393	1	.500	0	-0	-0	-0	0.0
● **AMBY MURRAY**	Murray, Joseph Ambrose b: 6/4/13, Fall River, Mass. BL/TL, 5'7", 150 lbs. Deb: 7/05/36																									
1936	Bos-N	0	0	—	4	1	0	0	0	11	15	1	3	2	14.7	4.09	94	.319	.360	1	.250	0	-0	-0	0	0.0
● **JOE MURRAY**	Murray, Joseph Ambrose b: 11/11/20, Wilkes-Barre, Pa. BL/TL, 6', 165 lbs. Deb: 8/17/50																									
1950	Phi-A	0	3	.000	8	2	0	0	0	30	34	1	21	8	16.5	5.70	80	.283	.390	0	.000	-2	-4	-4	1	-0.5
● **PAT MURRAY**	Murray, Patrick Joseph b: 7/18/1897, Scottsville, N.Y. d: 11/5/83, Rochester, N.Y. BR/TL, 6', 175 lbs. Deb: 7/01/19																									
1919	Phi-N	0	2	.000	8	2	1	0	0	34^{1}	50	0	12	11	17.3	6.29	51	.347	.412	0	.000	-2	-13	-12	-0	-1.4
● **DENNIS MUSGRAVES**	Musgraves, Dennis Eugene b: 12/25/43, Indianapolis, Ind. BR/TR, 6'4", 188 lbs. Deb: 7/09/65																									
1965	NY-N	0	0	—	5	1	0	0	0	16	11	0	7	11	11.3	0.56	627	.200	.313	0	.000	-0	5	5	-0	0.6
● **STAN MUSIAL**	Musial, Stanley Frank "Stan The Man" b: 11/21/20, Donora, Pa. BL/TL, 6', 175 lbs. Deb: 9/17/41 H♦																									
1952	StL-N★	0	0	—	1	0	0	0	0	0	0	0	0	0	—	—	—	.000	.000	194	.336	1	0	0	0	0.0
● **JEFF MUSSELMAN**	Musselman, Jeffrey Joseph b: 6/21/63, Doylestown, Pa. BL/TL, 6', 180 lbs. Deb: 9/02/86																									
1986	Tor-A	0	0	—	6	0	0	0	0	5^{1}	8	1	5	4	21.9	10.13	42	.333	.448	0	—	0	-4	-4	0	-0.5
1987	Tor-A	12	5	.706	68	1	0	0	3	89	75	7	54	54	13.3	4.15	108	.237	.354	0	—	0	3	3	1	0.3
1988	Tor-A	8	5	.615	15	15	0	0	0	85	80	4	30	39	12.0	3.18	124	.252	.322	0	—	0	7	7	-1	0.6
1989	Tor-A	0	1	.000	5	3	0	0	0	11	19	2	9	3	22.9	10.64	35	.404	.500	0	—	0	-8	-8	-0	-0.7
	NY-N	3	2	.600	20	0	0	0	0	26^{1}	27	1	14	11	14.0	3.08	106	.267	.357	0	—	0	1	1	2	0.3
1990	NY-N	0	2	.000	28	0	0	0	0	32	40	3	11	14	14.6	5.63	67	.310	.369	0	.000	-0	-7	-7	0	-0.7
Total	5	23	15	.605	142	19	0	0	3	248^{2}	249	18	123	125	13.7	4.31	94	.266	.356	0	.000	0	-7	-8	2	-0.7
● **RON MUSSELMAN**	Musselman, Ralph Ronald b: 11/11/54, Wilmington, N.C. BR/TR, 6'2", 185 lbs. Deb: 8/18/82																									
1982	Sea-A	1	0	1.000	12	0	0	0	0	15^{2}	18	2	6	9	14.4	3.45	123	.300	.373	0	—	0	1	1	0	0.0
1984	Tor-A	0	2	.000	11	0	0	0	1	21^{1}	18	2	10	9	11.8	2.11	194	.225	.311	0	—	0	4	5	-0	0.2
1985	Tor-A	3	0	1.000	25	4	0	0	0	52^{1}	59	2	24	29	14.3	4.47	94	.284	.358	0	—	0	-2	-2	-1	-0.4
Total	3	4	2	.667	48	4	0	0	1	89^{1}	95	6	40	47	13.7	3.73	112	.273	.350	0	—	0	4	5	-1	-0.2
● **PAUL MUSSER**	Musser, Paul b: 6/24/1889, Millheim, Pa. d: 7/7/73, State College, Pa. BR/TR, 6', 175 lbs. Deb: 6/06/12																									
1912	Was-A	0	0	—	7	2	0	0	2	20^{2}	16	0	16	10	14.8	2.61	127	.225	.382	0	.000	-1	2	2	0	0.1
1919	Bos-A	0	2	.000	5	4	1	0	0	19^{2}	26	0	8	14	15.6	4.12	73	.342	.405	0	.000	-1	-2	-2	-0	-0.4
Total	2	0	2	.000	12	6	1	0	2	40^{1}	42	0	24	24	15.2	3.35	95	.286	.393	0	.000	-2	-0	-1	0	-0.3
● **BARNEY MUSSILL**	Mussill, Bernard James b: 10/1/19, Bowerhill, Pa. BR/TL, 6'1", 200 lbs. Deb: 4/20/44																									
1944	Phi-N	0	1	.000	16	0	0	0	0	19^{1}	20	1	13	5	15.4	6.05	60	.267	.375	0	.000	-0	-5	-5	-0	-0.5
● **MIKE MUSSINA**	Mussina, Michael Cole b: 12/8/68, Williamsport, Pa. BR/TR, 6'2", 185 lbs. Deb: 8/04/91																									
1991	Bal-A	4	5	.444	12	12	2	0	0	87^{2}	77	7	21	52	10.2	2.87	137	.239	.288	0	—	0	12	10	-0	1.2
1992	Bal-A★	18	5	**.783**	32	32	8	4	0	241	212	16	48	130	**9.8**	2.54	154	.239	**.279**	0	—	0	37	37	-0	4.0
Total	2	22	10	.688	44	44	10	4	0	328^{2}	289	23	69	182	9.9	2.63	149	.239	.282	0	—	0	49	47	-1	5.2
● **ALEX MUSTAIKIS**	Mustaikis, Alexander Dominick b: 3/26/09, Chelsea, Mass. d: 1/17/70, Scranton, Pa. BR/TR, 6'3", 180 lbs. Deb: 7/07/40																									
1940	Bos-A	0	1	.000	6	1	0	0	0	15	15	1	15	6	18.0	9.00	50	.254	.405	2	.333	1	-8	-8	1	-0.5
● **JEFF MUTIS**	Mutis, Jeffrey Thomas b: 12/20/66, Allentown, Pa. BL/TL, 6'2", 185 lbs. Deb: 6/15/91																									
1991	Cle-A	0	3	.000	3	3	0	0	0	12^{1}	23	1	7	6	21.9	11.68	36	.397	.462	0	—	0	-10	-10	-0	-0.9
1992	Cle-A	0	2	.000	3	2	0	0	0	11^{1}	24	4	6	8	23.8	9.53	42	.429	.484	0	—	0	-7	-7	0	-0.7
Total	2	0	5	.000	6	5	0	0	0	23^{2}	47	5	13	14	22.8	10.65	38	.412	.472	0	—	0	-17	-17	0	-1.6
● **ELMER MYERS**	Myers, Elmer Glenn b: 3/2/1894, York Springs, Pa. d: 7/29/76, Collingwood, N.J. BR/TR, 6'2", 185 lbs. Deb: 10/06/15																									
1915	Phi-A	1	0	1.000	1	1	1	1	0	9	2	0	5	12	7.0	0.00	—	.074	.219	0	.000	-0	3	3	-0	0.2
1916	Phi-A	14	23	.378	44	35	31	2	1	315	280	7	168	182	13.2	3.66	78	.248	.353	27	.214	2	-29	-28	5	-2.1
1917	Phi-A	9	16	.360	38	23	13	2	3	201^{2}	221	2	79	88	13.6	4.42	62	.283	.353	18	.247	2	-39	-37	1	-3.6
1918	Phi-A	4	8	.333	18	15	5	1	1	95^{1}	101	4	42	17	13.9	4.63	63	.283	.365	5	.143	-2	-20	-18	2	-1.9
1919	Cle-A	8	7	.533	23	15	6	1	1	134^{2}	134	3	43	38	12.5	3.74	89	.264	.334	11	.239	2	-8	-6	1	-0.3
1920	Cle-A	2	4	.333	16	7	2	0	1	71^{2}	93	1	23	16	15.1	4.77	80	.316	.374	6	.240	0	-8	-8	0	-0.7
	Bos-A	9	1	.900	12	10	9	1	0	97	90	1	24	34	10.8	2.13	171	.249	.299	12	.316	3	18	16	-1	1.9
	Yr	11	5	.688	28	17	11	1	1	168^{2}	183	2	47	50	12.4	3.25	114	.277	.327	18	.286	3	10	9	-1	1.2
1921	Bos-A	8	12	.400	30	20	11	0	0	172	217	11	53	40	14.7	4.87	87	.315	.373	14	.215	-2	-11	-12	0	-1.3
1922	Bos-A	0	1	.000	3	1	0	0	0	5^{2}	10	1	3	1	23.8	17.47	24	.370	.469	0	.000	-0	-8	-8	0	-0.7
Total	8	55	72	.433	185	127	78	8	7	1102	1148	30	440	428	13.4	4.06	80	.275	.352	93	.226	4	-102	-97	8	-8.5
● **HENRY MYERS**	Myers, Henry C. b: 5/1858, Philadelphia, Pa. d: 4/18/1895, Philadelphia, Pa. BR/TR, 5'9", 159 lbs. Deb: 8/20/1881 M♦																									
1882	Bal-a	0	2	.000	6	2	1	0	0	26	30	2	4	7	11.8	6.58	42	.271	.296	53	.180	-1	-11	-11	-0	-1.0
● **JOSEPH MYERS**	Myers, Joseph William b: 3/18/1882, Wilmington, Del. d: 2/11/56, Delaware City, Del BR/TR, 5'10.5", 205 lbs. Deb: 10/07/05																									
1905	Phi-A	0	0	—	1	1	1	0	0	5	3	0	3	5	12.6	3.60	74	.175	.331	0	.000	-0	-1	-1	-0	-0.1
● **RANDY MYERS**	Myers, Randall Kirk b: 9/19/62, Vancouver, Wash. BL/TL, 6'1", 190 lbs. Deb: 10/06/85																									
1985	NY-N	0	0	—	1	0	0	0	0	2	0	0	1	2	4.5	0.00	—	.000	.143	0	—	0	1	1	0	0.1
1986	NY-N	0	0	—	10	0	0	0	0	10^{2}	11	1	9	13	17.7	4.22	84	.256	.396	0	—	0	-1	-1	0	-0.1
1987	NY-N	3	6	.333	54	0	0	0	6	75	61	6	30	92	10.9	3.96	95	.225	.302	2	.286	0	1	-2	0	-0.1
1988	*NY-N	7	3	.700	55	0	0	0	26	68	45	5	17	69	8.5	1.72	187	.190	.250	1	.250	1	13	11	-1	1.2
1989	NY-N	7	4	.636	65	0	0	0	24	84^{1}	62	4	40	88	10.9	2.35	139	.206	.299	0	.000	-1	11	9	0	0.9
1990	*Cin-N★	4	6	.400	66	0	0	0	31	86^{2}	59	6	38	98	10.4	2.08	190	.193	.288	1	.250	0	17	18	0	1.9
1991	Cin-N	6	13	.316	58	12	1	0	6	132	116	8	80	108	13.4	3.55	107	.242	.351	5	.172	0	2	4	-1	0.3
1992	SD-N	3	6	.333	66	0	0	0	38	79^{2}	84	7	34	66	13.4	4.29	85	.279	.354	1	.143	-0	-7	-6	-0	-0.7
Total	8	30	38	.441	375	12	1	0	131	538^{1}	438	37	249	536	11.6	3.06	119	.225	.316	10	.179	1	37	34	-2	3.5
● **BOB MYRICK**	Myrick, Robert Howard b: 10/1/52, Hattiesburg, Miss. BR/TL, 6'1", 195 lbs. Deb: 5/28/76																									
1976	NY-N	1	1	.500	21	1	0	0	0	27^{2}	34	2	13	11	15.3	3.25	101	.306	.379	0	.000	-0	1	0	0	0.0
1977	NY-N	2	2	.500	44	4	0	0	2	87^{1}	86	5	33	49	12.4	3.61	104	.265	.334	2	.182	-0	3	1	0	0.1
1978	NY-N	0	3	.000	17	0	0	0	0	24^{2}	18	3	13	13	11.3	3.28	106	.207	.310	0	.000	-0	1	1	0	0.1
Total	3	3	6	.333	82	5	0	0	2	139^{2}	138	10	59	73	12.8	3.48	104	.264	.340	2	.125	-1	4	2	1	0.2
● **CHRIS NABHOLZ**	Nabholz, Christopher William b: 1/5/67, Harrisburg, Pa. BL/TL, 6'5", 210 lbs. Deb: 6/11/90																									
1990	Mon-N	6	2	.750	11	11	1	1	0	70	43	6	32	53	9.9	2.83	129	.176	.276	0	.000	-2	7	6	-0	0.5

YEAR	TM/L	W	L	PCT	G	GS	CG	SH	SV	IP	H	HR	BB	SO	RAT	ERA	ERA+	OAV	OOB	BH	AVG	PB	PR	/A	PD	TPI
1991	Mon-N	8	7	.533	24	24	1	0	0	153^2	134	5	57	99	11.3	3.63	100	.237	.309	6	.115	-1	1	-0	1	0.0
1992	Mon-N	11	12	.478	32	32	1	1	0	195	176	11	74	130	11.8	3.32	105	.244	.318	8	.123	-1	4	4	3	0.6
Total	3	25	21	.543	67	67	3	2	0	418^2	353	22	163	282	11.3	3.35	106	.230	.308	14	.101	-3	12	10	4	1.1
● **JACK NABORS**	Nabors, Herman John b: 11/19/1887, Montevallo, Ala. d: 11/20/23, Wilton, Ala. BR/TR, 6'3", 185 lbs. Deb: 8/09/15																									
1915	Phi-A	0	5	.000	10	7	2	0	0	54	58	1	35	18	16.3	5.50	53	.304	.424	2	.125	-1	-15	-15	-0	-1.6
1916	Phi-A	1	20	.048	40	30	11	0	1	212^2	206	2	95	74	12.9	3.47	82	.266	.349	7	.101	-4	-15	-14	-2	-2.2
1917	Phi-A	0	0	—	2	0	0	0	0	3	2	0	1	2	9.0	3.00	92	.200	.273	0	—	0	-0	-0	0	0.0
Total	3	1	25	.038	52	37	13	0	1	269^2	266	3	131	94	13.5	3.87	74	.273	.364	9	.106	-6	-31	-30	-2	-3.8
● **BILL NAGEL**	Nagel, William Taylor b: 8/19/15, Memphis, Tenn. d: 10/8/81, Freehold, N.J. BR/TR, 6'1", 190 lbs. Deb: 4/20/39 ♦																									
1939	Phi-A	0	0	—	1	0	0	0	0	3	7	1	1	0	24.0	12.00	39	.438	.471	86	.252	0	-2	-2	-0	-0.2
● **JUDGE NAGLE**	Nagle, Walter Harold "Lucky" b: 3/10/1880, Santa Rosa, Cal. d: 5/26/71, Santa Rosa, Cal. BR/TR, 6', 176 lbs. Deb: 4/26/11																									
1911	Pit-N	4	2	.667	8	3	1	0	1	27^1	33	3	6	11	13.2	3.62	95	.324	.367	1	.143	-0	-1	-1	0	-0.1
	Bos-A	1	1	.500	5	1	0	0	0	27	27	2	6	12	11.0	3.33	98	.262	.303	1	.100	-1	0	-0	-1	-0.2
Total	1	5	3	.625	13	4	1	0	1	54^1	60	5	12	23	12.1	3.48	96	.293	.335	2	.118	-1	-1	-1	-1	-0.3
● **CHARLES NAGY**	Nagy, Charles Harrison b: 5/5/67, Bridgeport, Conn. BL/TR, 6'3", 200 lbs. Deb: 6/29/90																									
1990	Cle-A	2	4	.333	9	8	0	0	0	45^2	58	7	21	26	15.8	5.91	66	.315	.388	0	—	0	-10	-10	1	-0.9
1991	Cle-A	10	15	.400	33	33	6	1	0	211^1	228	15	66	109	12.8	4.13	101	.275	.333	0	—	0	-1	1	-1	-0.1
1992	Cle-A★	17	10	.630	33	33	10	3	0	252	245	11	57	169	10.9	2.96	136	.260	.303	0	—	0	27	30	3	3.5
Total	3	29	29	.500	75	74	16	4	0	509	531	33	144	304	12.1	3.71	110	.271	.324	0	—	0	16	20	2	2.5
● **STEVE NAGY**	Nagy, Stephen b: 5/28/19, Franklin, N.J. BL/TL, 5'9", 174 lbs. Deb: 4/20/47																									
1947	Pit-N	1	3	.250	6	1	0	0	0	14	18	1	9	4	17.4	5.79	73	.310	.403	1	.250	0	-3	-2	0	-0.2
1950	Was-A	2	5	.286	9	9	2	0	0	53^1	69	5	29	17	16.5	6.58	68	.307	.386	5	.227	2	-12	-12	-0	-0.9
Total	2	3	8	.273	15	10	2	0	0	67^1	87	6	38	21	16.7	6.42	69	.307	.389	6	.231	2	-15	-15	-0	-1.1
● **MIKE NAGY**	Nagy, Michael Timothy b: 3/25/48, Bronx, N.Y. BR/TR, 6'3", 200 lbs. Deb: 4/21/69																									
1969	Bos-A	12	2	.857	33	28	7	1	0	196^2	183	10	106	84	13.7	3.11	122	.245	.347	5	.077	-2	11	15	0	1.4
1970	Bos-A	6	5	.545	23	20	4	0	0	128^2	138	16	64	56	14.3	4.48	88	.275	.359	11	.250	2	-11	-7	-1	-0.6
1971	Bos-A	1	3	.250	12	7	0	0	0	38	46	4	20	9	15.6	6.63	56	.315	.398	1	.083	-1	-13	-12	-0	-1.3
1972	Bos-A	0	0	—	1	0	0	0	0	2	3	0	0	2	18.0	9.00	36	.375	.444	0	—	0	-1	-1	-0	-0.1
1973	StL-N	0	2	.000	9	7	0	0	0	40^2	44	4	15	14	13.3	4.20	87	.282	.349	1	.091	-1	-2	-3	-0	-0.4
1974	Hou-N	1	1	.500	9	0	0	0	0	12^2	17	3	5	5	16.3	8.53	41	.309	.377	0	.000	-0	-7	-7	-0	-0.7
Total	6	20	13	.606	87	62	11	1	0	418^2	431	37	210	170	14.1	4.15	92	.267	.357	18	.135	-2	-24	-16	-1	-1.7
● **SAM NAHEM**	Nahem, Samuel Ralph "Subway Sam" b: 10/19/15, New York, N.Y. BR/TR, 6'1.5", 190 lbs. Deb: 10/02/38																									
1938	Bro-N	1	0	1.000	1	1	1	0	0	9	6	0	4	2	10.0	3.00	130	.194	.286	2	.400	1	1	1	-0	0.1
1941	StL-N	5	2	.714	26	8	2	0	1	81^2	76	2	38	31	12.8	2.98	126	.243	.329	4	.174	-1	6	7	1	0.7
1942	Phi-N	1	3	.250	35	2	0	0	0	74^2	72	2	40	38	13.7	4.94	67	.254	.350	2	.100	-1	-13	-14	1	-1.4
1948	Phi-N	3	3	.500	28	1	0	0	0	59	68	4	45	30	17.7	7.02	56	.288	.408	2	.154	-0	-20	-20	-1	-2.1
Total	4	10	8	.556	90	12	3	0	1	224^1	222	8	127	101	14.3	4.69	78	.257	.357	10	.164	-2	-27	-26	1	-2.7
● **PETE NAKTENIS**	Naktenis, Peter Ernest b: 6/12/14, Aberdeen, Wash. BL/TL, 6'1", 185 lbs. Deb: 6/13/36																									
1936	Phi-A	0	1	.000	7	1	0	0	0	18^2	24	2	27	18	25.6	12.54	41	.324	.515	1	.200	-0	-16	-15	-1	-1.3
1939	Cin-N	0	0	—	3	0	0	0	0	4	2	0	0	1	9.0	2.25	170	.154	.267	0	—	0	1	1	0	0.1
Total	2	0	1	.000	10	1	0	0	0	22^2	26	2	27	19	22.6	10.72	45	.299	.483	1	.200	-0	-15	-15	-0	-1.2
● **BUDDY NAPIER**	Napier, Skelton Le Roy b: 12/18/1889, Byronville, Ga. d: 3/29/68, Hutchins, Tex. BR/TR, 5'11", 165 lbs. Deb: 8/14/12																									
1912	StL-A	1	2	.333	7	2	0	0	0	25^1	33	0	5	10	14.6	4.97	67	.317	.366	0	.000	-1	-5	-5	-0	-0.6
1918	Chi-N	0	0	—	1	0	0	0	0	6^2	10	0	4	2	18.9	5.40	52	.357	.438	1	.333	0	-2	-2	-0	-0.2
1920	Cin-N	4	2	.667	9	5	5	1	0	49	47	0	7	17	10.1	1.29	236	.254	.285	3	.214	1	10	10	0	1.2
1921	Cin-N	0	2	.000	22	6	1	0	1	56^2	72	2	13	14	13.5	5.56	64	.329	.366	2	.143	1	-11	-12	1	-1.0
Total	4	5	6	.455	39	13	6	1	1	137^2	162	2	29	43	12.7	3.92	84	.302	.343	6	.158	1	-8	-9	1	-0.6
● **GONZALO NARANJO**	Naranjo, Lazaro Ramon Gonzalo b: 11/25/34, Havana, Cuba BL/TR, 5'11.5", 165 lbs. Deb: 7/08/56																									
1956	Pit-N	1	2	.333	17	3	0	0	0	34^1	37	7	17	26	14.4	4.46	85	.282	.369	1	.143	0	-3	-3	1	-0.1
● **RAY NARLESKI**	Narleski, Raymond Edmond b: 11/25/28, Camden, N.J. BR/TR, 6'1", 175 lbs. Deb: 4/17/54 F																									
1954	*Cle-A	3	3	.500	42	2	1	0	13	89	59	8	44	52	10.6	2.22	165	.189	.293	0	.000	-2	15	14	-1	1.2
1955	Cle-A	9	1	.900	**60**	1	1	0	**19**	111^2	91	11	52	94	11.5	3.71	108	.220	.308	7	.292	1	3	3	-2	0.3
1956	Cle-A†	3	2	.600	32	0	0	0	4	59^1	36	5	19	42	8.5	1.52	277	.170	.241	2	.250	0	**17**	**18**	-1	1.7
1957	Cle-A	11	5	.688	46	15	7	1	16	154^1	136	14	70	93	12.2	3.09	120	.235	.322	4	.093	-2	12	11	-4	0.5
1958	Cle-A★	13	10	.565	44	24	7	0	1	183^1	179	21	91	102	13.4	4.07	90	.255	.343	11	.204	1	-6	-9	-3	-1.1
1959	Det-A	4	12	.250	42	10	1	0	5	104^1	105	21	59	71	14.2	5.78	70	.254	.348	2	.095	-1	-22	-20	-2	-2.3
Total	6	43	33	.566	266	52	17	1	58	702	606	80	335	454	12.2	3.60	106	.230	.320	26	.157	-2	19	18	-12	0.3
● **BUSTER NARUM**	Narum, Leslie Ferdinand b: 11/16/40, Philadelphia, Pa. BR/TR, 6'1", 200 lbs. Deb: 4/14/63																									
1963	Bal-A	0	0	—	7	0	0	0	0	9	8	0	5	5	13.0	3.00	118	.242	.342	1	1.000	1	1	1	0	0.2
1964	Was-A	9	15	.375	38	32	7	2	0	199	195	31	73	121	12.3	4.30	86	.259	.328	4	.061	-5	-15	-13	-3	-2.1
1965	Was-A	4	12	.250	46	24	2	0	0	173^2	176	16	91	86	14.2	4.46	78	.267	.361	2	.043	-2	-19	-19	2	-2.0
1966	Was-A	0	0	—	3	0	0	0	0	3^1	11	2	4	0	40.5	21.60	16	.579	.652	0	—	0	-7	-7	-0	-0.6
1967	Was-A	1	0	1.000	2	2	0	0	0	11^2	8	1	4	8	9.3	3.09	103	.195	.267	0	.000	-1	0	0	-0	-0.1
Total	5	14	27	.341	96	58	9	2	0	396^2	398	50	177	220	13.3	4.45	80	.264	.346	7	.059	-6	-40	-38	-1	-4.6
● **JIM NASH**	Nash, James Edwin b: 2/9/45, Hawthorne, Nev. BR/TR, 6'5", 230 lbs. Deb: 7/03/66																									
1966	KC-A	12	1	.923	18	17	5	0	1	127	95	6	47	98	10.1	2.06	165	.204	.277	5	.102	-2	19	19	-3	1.6
1967	KC-A	12	17	.414	37	34	8	2	0	222^1	200	21	87	186	11.8	3.76	85	.242	.317	7	.100	-2	-13	-14	-2	-2.0
1968	Oak-A	13	13	.500	34	33	12	6	0	228^2	185	18	55	169	9.6	2.28	123	.219	.270	5	.068	-2	18	14	-3	1.0
1969	Oak-A	8	8	.500	26	19	3	1	0	115^1	112	17	30	75	11.2	3.67	94	.247	.296	4	.111	-1	-1	-3	-1	-0.5
1970	Atl-N	13	9	.591	34	33	6	2	0	212^1	211	22	90	153	13.0	4.07	105	.257	.334	7	.087	-3	-1	5	0	0.2
1971	Atl-N	9	7	.563	32	19	2	0	2	133	166	17	50	65	14.6	4.94	75	.314	.374	7	.149	-1	-22	-18	-1	-2.1
1972	Atl-N	1	1	.500	11	4	0	0	1	31^1	35	2	25	10	17.2	5.46	69	.307	.432	2	.222	0	-7	-6	-0	-0.6
	Phi-N	0	8	.000	9	8	0	0	0	37^1	46	5	17	15	15.9	6.27	57	.311	.393	1	.100	-0	-12	-11	0	-1.1
	Yr	1	9	.100	20	12	0	0	1	68^2	81	7	42	25	16.5	5.90	62	.305	.405	3	.158	-0	-19	-17	-0	-1.7
Total	7	68	64	.515	201	167	36	11	4	1107^1	1050	108	401	771	11.9	3.58	96	.250	.318	38	.101	-11	-18	-16	-10	-3.5
● **BILLY NASH**	Nash, William Mitchell b: 6/24/1865, Richmond, Va. d: 11/15/29, E.Orange, N.J. BR/TR, 5'8.5", 167 lbs. Deb: 8/05/1884 MU♦																									
1889	Bos-N	0	0	—	1	0	0	0	0	1	0	0	1	0	9.0	0.00	—	.000	.252	132	.274	0	0	0	-0	0.0
1890	Bos-P	0	0	—	1	0	0	0	0	0^1	1	0	0	0	27.0	0.00	—	.499	.499	130	.266	0	0	0	0	0.0
Total	2	0	0	—	2	0	0	0	0	1^1	1	0	1	0	13.5	0.00	—	.201	.335	1606	.275	1	1	1	-0	0.0
● **PHILIP NASTU**	Nastu, Philip b: 3/8/55, Bridgeport, Conn. BL/TL, 6'2", 180 lbs. Deb: 9/15/78																									
1978	SF-N	0	1	.000	3	1	0	0	0	8	8	1	2	5	11.3	5.63	61	.258	.303	0	.000	-0	-2	-2	-0	-0.2

YEAR	TM/L	W	L	PCT	G	GS	CG	SH	SV	IP	H	HR	BB	SO	RAT	ERA	ERA+	OAV	OOB	BH	AVG	PB	PR	/A	PD	TPI
1979	SF-N	3	4	.429	25	14	1	0	0	100	105	14	41	47	13.3	4.32	81	.272	.345	1	.042	-1	-7	-9	0	-1.0
1980	SF-N	0	0	—	6	0	0	0	0	6	10	1	5	1	22.5	6.00	59	.357	.455	0	—	0	-2	-2	0	-0.1
Total	3	3	5	.375	34	15	1	0	0	114	123	16	48	53	13.7	4.50	78	.276	.349	1	.040	-1	-10	-13	0	-1.3

● JAIME NAVARRO Navarro, Jaime (Cintron) b: 3/27/67, Bayamon, P.R. BR/TR, 6'4", 210 lbs. Deb: 6/20/89 F

YEAR	TM/L	W	L	PCT	G	GS	CG	SH	SV	IP	H	HR	BB	SO	RAT	ERA	ERA+	OAV	OOB	BH	AVG	PB	PR	/A	PD	TPI
1989	Mil-A	7	8	.467	19	17	1	0	0	109^2	119	6	32	56	12.5	3.12	123	.277	.328	0	—	0	9	9	-0	0.9
1990	Mil-A	8	7	.533	32	22	3	0	1	149^1	176	11	41	75	13.3	4.46	87	.293	.343	0	—	0	-9	-10	-0	-1.0
1991	Mil-A	15	12	.556	34	34	10	2	0	234	237	18	73	114	12.2	3.92	101	.261	.320	0	—	0	4	1	-1	0.0
1992	Mil-A	17	11	.607	34	34	5	3	0	246	224	14	64	100	10.8	3.33	115	.246	.299	0	—	0	17	13	-3	1.1
Total	4	47	38	.553	119	107	19	5	1	739	756	49	210	345	12.0	3.71	104	.265	.319	0	—	0	21	14	-5	1.0

● JULIO NAVARRO Navarro, Julio (Ventura) "Whiplash" b: 1/9/36, Vieques, P.R. BR/TR, 5'11", 190 lbs. Deb: 9/03/62 F

YEAR	TM/L	W	L	PCT	G	GS	CG	SH	SV	IP	H	HR	BB	SO	RAT	ERA	ERA+	OAV	OOB	BH	AVG	PB	PR	/A	PD	TPI
1962	LA-A	1	1	.500	9	0	0	0	0	15^1	20	2	4	11	14.1	4.70	82	.317	.358	1	.500	0	-1	-1	-0	-0.1
1963	LA-A	4	5	.444	57	0	0	0	12	90^1	75	7	32	53	10.9	2.89	119	.228	.300	3	.200	1	7	5	1	0.8
1964	LA-A	0	0	—	5	0	0	0	1	9^1	5	0	5	8	11.6	1.93	170	.167	.324	0	.000	-0	2	1	0	0.1
	Det-A	2	1	.667	26	0	0	0	2	41	40	9	16	36	12.7	3.95	93	.250	.326	0	.000	-1	-1	-1	-0	-0.2
	Yr	2	1	.667	31	0	0	0	3	50^1	45	9	21	44	12.2	3.58	100	.234	.316	0	.000	-1	0	0	0	-0.1
1965	Det-A	0	2	.000	15	1	0	0	1	30	25	5	12	22	11.1	4.20	83	.238	.316	0	.000	-0	-2	-2	0	-0.3
1966	Det-A	0	0	—	1	0	0	0	0	0	2	2	0	0	—	∞	—	1.000	1.000	0	—	0	-3	-3	0	-0.3
1970	Atl-N	0	0	—	17	0	0	0	1	26^1	24	7	1	21	8.9	4.10	105	.233	.248	1	.167	-0	-0	1	0	0.0
Total	6	7	9	.438	130	1	0	0	17	212^1	191	32	70	151	11.4	3.65	99	.241	.309	5	.147	-0	1	-1	1	0.0

● EARL NAYLOR Naylor, Earl Eugene b: 5/19/19, Kansas City, Mo. d: 1/16/90, Winter Haven, Fla. BR/TR, 6', 190 lbs. Deb: 4/15/42 ♦

YEAR	TM/L	W	L	PCT	G	GS	CG	SH	SV	IP	H	HR	BB	SO	RAT	ERA	ERA+	OAV	OOB	BH	AVG	PB	PR	/A	PD	TPI
1942	Phi-N	0	5	.000	20	4	1	0	0	60^1	68	5	29	19	14.5	6.12	54	.286	.363	33	.196	1	-19	-19	-0	-1.9

● ROLLIE NAYLOR Naylor, Roleine Cecil b: 2/4/1892, Crum, Tex. d: 6/18/66, Fort Worth, Tex. BR/TR, 6'1.5", 180 lbs. Deb: 9/14/17

YEAR	TM/L	W	L	PCT	G	GS	CG	SH	SV	IP	H	HR	BB	SO	RAT	ERA	ERA+	OAV	OOB	BH	AVG	PB	PR	/A	PD	TPI
1917	Phi-A	2	2	.500	5	5	3	0	0	33	30	1	11	11	11.5	1.64	168	.265	.336	1	.091	-1	4	4	1	0.5
1919	Phi-A	5	18	.217	31	23	17	0	0	204^2	210	2	64	68	12.2	3.34	103	.280	.339	12	.169	-2	-3	2	-0	-0.1
1920	Phi-A	10	23	.303	42	36	20	0	0	251^1	306	7	86	90	14.3	3.47	116	.312	.371	14	.163	-6	9	15	2	1.1
1921	Phi-A	3	13	.188	32	19	6	0	0	169^1	214	10	55	39	14.5	4.84	92	.315	.369	6	.115	-4	-10	-7	-2	-1.1
1922	Phi-A	10	15	.400	35	26	11	0	0	171^1	212	7	51	37	14.0	4.73	90	.309	.359	11	.200	1	-13	-9	1	-0.7
1923	Phi-A	12	7	.632	26	20	9	2	0	143	149	5	59	27	13.1	3.46	119	.273	.344	11	.244	1	8	10	-2	1.0
1924	Phi-A	0	5	.000	10	7	1	0	0	38^1	53	2	20	10	17.1	6.34	68	.333	.408	3	.375	1	-9	-9	0	-0.7
Total	7	42	83	.336	181	136	67	2	0	1011	1174	34	346	282	13.7	3.93	102	.300	.359	58	.177	-11	-14	7	1	0.0

● MIKE NAYMICK Naymick, Michael John b: 9/6/17, Berlin, Pa. BR/TR, 6'8", 225 lbs. Deb: 9/24/39

YEAR	TM/L	W	L	PCT	G	GS	CG	SH	SV	IP	H	HR	BB	SO	RAT	ERA	ERA+	OAV	OOB	BH	AVG	PB	PR	/A	PD	TPI
1939	Cle-A	0	1	.000	2	1	1	0	0	4^2	3	0	5	3	15.4	1.93	228	.188	.381	0	.000	-0	1	1	-0	0.1
1940	Cle-A	1	2	.333	13	4	0	0	0	30	36	1	17	15	16.8	5.10	83	.290	.389	1	.167	0	-2	-3	1	-0.2
1943	Cle-A	4	4	.500	29	4	0	0	2	62^2	32	3	47	41	11.8	2.30	135	.160	.328	3	.188	-0	7	6	1	0.6
1944	Cle-A	0	0	—	7	0	0	0	0	13	16	1	10	4	18.0	9.69	34	.314	.426	0	.000	-0	-9	-9	0	-0.9
	StL-N	0	0	—	1	0	0	0	0	2	2	0	1	1	13.5	4.50	78	.333	.429	0	—	0	-0	-0	0	0.0
Total	4	5	7	.417	52	9	1	0	2	112^1	89	5	80	64	14.0	3.93	89	.224	.362	4	.154	-1	-3	-6	1	-0.4

● DENNY NEAGLE Neagle, Dennis Edward b: 9/13/68, Gambrills, Md. BL/TL, 6'4", 200 lbs. Deb: 7/27/91

YEAR	TM/L	W	L	PCT	G	GS	CG	SH	SV	IP	H	HR	BB	SO	RAT	ERA	ERA+	OAV	OOB	BH	AVG	PB	PR	/A	PD	TPI
1991	Min-A	0	1	.000	7	3	0	0	0	20	28	3	7	14	15.7	4.05	105	.329	.380	0	—	0	0	0	-0	0.0
1992	*Pit-N	4	6	.400	55	6	0	0	2	86^1	81	9	43	77	13.1	4.48	76	.247	.338	0	.000	-1	-9	-10	-0	-1.3
Total	2	4	7	.364	62	9	0	0	2	106^1	109	12	50	91	13.6	4.40	81	.264	.346	0	.000	-1	-9	-10	-1	-1.3

● JACK NEAGLE Neagle, John Henry b: 1/2/1858, Syracuse, N.Y. d: 9/20/04, Syracuse, N.Y. BR/TR, 5'6", 155 lbs. Deb: 7/08/1879 ♦

YEAR	TM/L	W	L	PCT	G	GS	CG	SH	SV	IP	H	HR	BB	SO	RAT	ERA	ERA+	OAV	OOB	BH	AVG	PB	PR	/A	PD	TPI
1879	Cin-N	0	1	.000	2	2	1	0	0	13	13	0	5	4	12.5	3.46	67	.241	.305	2	.167	-0	-1	-2	-0	-0.2
1883	Phi-N	1	7	.125	8	7	6	0	0	61^1	88	0	21	13	16.0	6.90	45	.315	.363	12	.164	-2	-26	-26	-1	-2.2
	Bal-a	1	4	.200	6	5	4	0	0	46	48	1	20	9	13.3	4.89	71	.252	.323	10	.286	1	-8	-7	-0	-0.5
	Pit-a	3	12	.200	16	16	12	0	0	114	156	9	25	41	14.3	5.84	55	.306	.338	19	.188	-1	-32	-33	-1	-2.8
	Yr	4	16	.200	22	21	16	0	0	160	204	10	45	50	14.0	5.57	59	.291	.334	29	.213	0	-40	-41	-1	-3.3
1884	Pit-a	11	26	.297	38	38	37	2	0	326	354	6	70	85	12.2	3.73	90	.255	.300	22	.149	-6	-17	-13	-3	-1.9
Total	3	16	50	.242	70	68	60	2	0	560^1	659	16	141	152	13.1	4.59	72	.272	.317	65	.176	-8	-85	-81	-5	-7.6

● JOE NEALE Neale, Joseph Hunt b: 5/7/1866, Wadsworth, Ohio d: 12/30/13, Akron, Ohio BR/TR, 5'8", 153 lbs. Deb: 6/21/1886 ♦

YEAR	TM/L	W	L	PCT	G	GS	CG	SH	SV	IP	H	HR	BB	SO	RAT	ERA	ERA+	OAV	OOB	BH	AVG	PB	PR	/A	PD	TPI
1886	Lou-a	0	1	.000	1	1	0	0	0	7	11	0	7	0	24.4	7.71	47	.393	.528	0	.000	-0	-3	-3	1	-0.2
1887	Lou-a	1	4	.200	5	4	4	0	0	41^1	60	4	15	11	16.8	6.97	63	.326	.383	1	.053	-2	-12	-12	0	-1.0
1890	StL-a	5	3	.625	10	9	8	0	0	69	53	4	15	23	9.4	3.39	127	.206	.261	2	.067	-3	4	7	-2	0.2
1891	StL-a	6	4	.600	15	11	9	1	1	110^1	109	4	36	24	12.4	4.24	99	.249	.317	6	.118	-4	-6	-0	2	-0.2
Total	4	12	12	.500	31	25	21	1	1	227^2	233	12	73	58	12.7	4.59	93	.257	.322	9	.086	-9	-18	-8	1	-1.2

● RON NECCIAI Necciai, Ronald Andrew b: 6/18/32, Manown, Pa. BR/TR, 6'5", 185 lbs. Deb: 8/10/52

YEAR	TM/L	W	L	PCT	G	GS	CG	SH	SV	IP	H	HR	BB	SO	RAT	ERA	ERA+	OAV	OOB	BH	AVG	PB	PR	/A	PD	TPI
1952	Pit-N	1	6	.143	12	9	0	0	0	54^2	63	5	32	31	15.8	7.08	56	.296	.390	1	.059	-1	-20	-19	-0	-1.9

● RON NEGRAY Negray, Ronald Alvin b: 2/26/30, Akron, Ohio BR/TR, 6'1", 185 lbs. Deb: 9/14/52

YEAR	TM/L	W	L	PCT	G	GS	CG	SH	SV	IP	H	HR	BB	SO	RAT	ERA	ERA+	OAV	OOB	BH	AVG	PB	PR	/A	PD	TPI
1952	Bro-N	0	0	—	4	1	0	0	0	13	15	0	5	5	13.8	3.46	105	.294	.357	0	.000	-0	0	0	-0	0.0
1955	Phi-N	4	3	.571	19	10	2	0	0	71^2	71	13	21	30	11.6	3.52	113	.257	.310	0	.000	-3	4	4	-0	0.0
1956	Phi-N	2	3	.400	39	4	0	0	3	66^2	72	6	24	44	13.1	4.18	89	.280	.344	3	.429	1	-3	-3	0	-0.2
1958	LA-N	0	0	—	4	0	0	0	0	11^1	12	4	7	2	15.1	7.15	57	.279	.380	0	.000	-0	-4	-4	-0	-0.4
Total	4	6	6	.500	66	15	2	0	3	162^2	170	23	57	81	12.6	4.04	95	.271	.333	3	.086	-3	-3	-3	-1	-0.6

● JIM NEHER Neher, James Gilmore b: 2/5/1889, Rochester, N.Y. d: 11/11/51, Buffalo, N.Y. BR/TR, 5'11", 185 lbs. Deb: 9/10/12

YEAR	TM/L	W	L	PCT	G	GS	CG	SH	SV	IP	H	HR	BB	SO	RAT	ERA	ERA+	OAV	OOB	BH	AVG	PB	PR	/A	PD	TPI
1912	Cle-A	0	0	—	1	0	0	0	0	1	0	0	0	0	0.0	0.00	—	.000	.000	0	—	0	0	0	-0	0.0

● ART NEHF Nehf, Arthur Neukom b: 7/31/1892, Terre Haute, Ind. d: 12/18/60, Phoenix, Ariz. BL/TL, 5'9.5", 176 lbs. Deb: 8/13/15

YEAR	TM/L	W	L	PCT	G	GS	CG	SH	SV	IP	H	HR	BB	SO	RAT	ERA	ERA+	OAV	OOB	BH	AVG	PB	PR	/A	PD	TPI
1915	Bos-N	5	4	.556	12	10	6	4	0	78^1	60	0	21	39	9.7	2.53	103	.214	.276	4	.143	-1	2	1	0	0.0
1916	Bos-N	7	5	.583	22	12	6	1	0	121	110	1	20	36	9.9	2.01	124	.244	.281	5	.125	-0	8	6	-1	0.6
1917	Bos-N	17	8	.680	38	23	17	5	0	233^1	197	4	39	101	9.3	2.16	118	.231	.268	12	.171	5	14	10	-0	1.7
1918	Bos-N	15	15	.500	32	31	**28**	2	0	284^1	274	2	76	96	11.3	2.69	100	.259	.312	16	.168	1	2	-0	3	0.5
1919	Bos-N	8	9	.471	22	19	13	1	0	168^2	151	6	40	53	10.5	3.09	92	.242	.294	13	.206	2	-3	-4	1	-0.1
	NY-N	9	2	.818	13	12	9	2	0	102	70	2	19	24	8.0	1.50	187	.196	.240	8	.229	3	16	15	-1	2.1
	Yr	17	11	.607	35	31	22	3	0	270^2	221	8	59	77	9.4	2.49	114	.224	.269	21	.214	5	13	10	0	2.0
1920	NY-N	21	12	.636	40	33	22	4	0	280^2	273	8	45	79	10.2	3.08	97	.260	.291	26	.268	5	2	-3	3	0.5
1921	*NY-N	20	10	.667	41	34	18	2	1	260^2	266	18	55	67	11.2	3.63	101	.271	.311	18	.202	0	5	1	3	0.4
1922	*NY-N	19	13	.594	37	35	20	2	1	268^1	286	15	64	60	11.9	3.29	122	.276	.321	25	.255	4	24	21	1	2.3
1923	*NY-N	13	10	.565	34	27	7	1	2	196	219	14	49	50	12.4	4.50	85	.281	.326	12	.190	1	-11	-15	1	-1.2
1924	*NY-N	14	4	.778	30	20	11	0	2	171^2	167	14	42	72	11.1	3.62	101	.254	.301	13	.228	5	5	1	2	0.9
1925	NY-N	11	9	.550	29	20	8	1	1	155	193	7	50	63	14.2	3.77	107	.308	.360	11	.216	1	9	5	2	0.7
1926	NY-N	0	0	—	2	0	0	0	0	1^2	2	0	1	0	16.2	10.80	35	.286	.375	0	.000	-0	-1	-1	0	-0.1
	Cin-N	0	1	.000	7	0	0	0	0	17	25	0	5	4	16.4	3.71	100	.379	.431	1	.200	-0	0	-0	1	0.0
	Yr	0	1	.000	9	0	0	0	0	18^2	27	0	6	4	16.4	4.34	85	.370	.425	1	.167	-0	-1	-1	1	-0.1
1927	Cin-N	3	5	.375	21	5	1	0	4	45^1	59	2	14	21	14.5	5.56	68	.319	.367	1	.077	-1	-8	-9	1	-0.9
	Chi-N	1	1	.500	8	2	2	1	1	26^1	25	0	9	12	11.6	1.37	283	.260	.324	3	.429	1	7	7	-0	0.9

YEAR TM/L	W	L	PCT	G	GS	CG	SH	SV	IP	H	HR	BB	SO	RAT	ERA	ERA+	OAV	OOB	BH	AVG	PB	PR	/A	PD	TPI
Yr	4	6	.400	29	7	3	1	5	71^{2}	84	2	23	33	13.4	4.02	95	.299	.352	4	.200	0	-1	-2	1	0.0
1928 Chi-N	13	7	.650	31	21	10	2	0	176^{2}	190	3	52	40	12.4	2.65	145	.281	.334	11	.190	2	26	23	1	2.7
1929 *Chi-N	8	5	.615	32	15	4	0	1	120^{2}	148	11	39	27	14.1	5.59	83	.310	.365	13	.289	4	-12	-13	1	-0.8
Total 15	184	120	.605	451	319	182	28	13	2707^{2}	2715	107	640	844	11.3	3.20	105	.265	.310	192	.210	33	85	45	17	10.2

● GARY NEIBAUER Neibauer, Gary Wayne b: 10/29/44, Billings, Mont. BR/TR, 6'3", 200 lbs. Deb: 4/12/69

YEAR TM/L	W	L	PCT	G	GS	CG	SH	SV	IP	H	HR	BB	SO	RAT	ERA	ERA+	OAV	OOB	BH	AVG	PB	PR	/A	PD	TPI
1969 *Atl-N	1	2	.333	29	0	0	0	0	57^{2}	42	9	31	42	11.5	3.90	92	.204	.311	0	.000	-1	-2	-2	-0	-0.3
1970 Atl-N	0	3	.000	7	0	0	0	0	12^{2}	11	0	8	9	13.5	4.97	86	.239	.352	0	.000	-0	-1	-1	-0	-0.1
1971 Atl-N	1	0	1.000	6	1	0	0	1	21	14	3	9	6	10.3	2.14	173	.187	.282	0	.000	-1	3	4	0	0.3
1972 Atl-N	0	0	—	8	0	0	0	0	17^{1}	27	6	6	8	17.7	7.27	52	.360	.415	0	.000	-0	-7	-7	-0	-0.8
Phi-N	0	2	.000	9	2	0	0	0	18^{2}	17	1	14	7	15.4	5.30	68	.239	.372	1	.250	0	-4	-4	-0	-0.4
Yr	0	2	.000	17	2	0	0	0	36	44	7	20	15	16.3	6.25	59	.297	.385	1	.125	-0	-11	-10	-1	-1.2
1973 Atl-N	2	1	.667	16	1	0	0	0	21^{1}	24	3	19	9	19.0	7.17	55	.282	.425	1	.250	1	-8	-8	-1	-0.7
Total 5	4	8	.333	75	4	0	0	1	148^{2}	135	22	87	81	13.8	4.78	78	.242	.350	2	.069	-1	-20	-17	-2	-2.0

● JIM NEIDLINGER Neidlinger, James Llewellyn b: 9/24/64, Vallejo, Cal. BB/TR, 6'4", 180 lbs. Deb: 8/01/90

YEAR TM/L	W	L	PCT	G	GS	CG	SH	SV	IP	H	HR	BB	SO	RAT	ERA	ERA+	OAV	OOB	BH	AVG	PB	PR	/A	PD	TPI
1990 LA-N	5	3	.625	12	12	0	0	0	74	67	4	15	46	10.1	3.28	111	.241	.282	3	.120	-0	4	3	-1	0.2

● AL NEIGER Neiger, Alvin Edward b: 3/26/39, Wilmington, Del. BL/TL, 6', 195 lbs. Deb: 7/30/60

YEAR TM/L	W	L	PCT	G	GS	CG	SH	SV	IP	H	HR	BB	SO	RAT	ERA	ERA+	OAV	OOB	BH	AVG	PB	PR	/A	PD	TPI
1960 Phi-N	0	0	—	6	0	0	0	0	12^{2}	16	2	4	3	15.6	5.68	68	.340	.415	1	.500	0	-3	-3	-0	-0.2

● ERNIE NEITZKE Neitzke, Ernest Fredrich b: 11/13/1894, Toledo, Ohio d: 4/27/77, Sylvania, Ohio BR/TR, 5'10", 180 lbs. Deb: 6/02/21 ♦

YEAR TM/L	W	L	PCT	G	GS	CG	SH	SV	IP	H	HR	BB	SO	RAT	ERA	ERA+	OAV	OOB	BH	AVG	PB	PR	/A	PD	TPI
1921 Bos-A	0	0	—	2	0	0	0	0	7^{1}	8	0	4	1	14.7	6.14	69	.333	.429	6	.240	0	-2	-2	0	-0.1

● BOTS NEKOLA Nekola, Francis Joseph b: 12/10/06, New York, N.Y. d: 3/11/87, Rockville Ctr., Md BL/TL, 5'11.5", 175 lbs. Deb: 7/19/29

YEAR TM/L	W	L	PCT	G	GS	CG	SH	SV	IP	H	HR	BB	SO	RAT	ERA	ERA+	OAV	OOB	BH	AVG	PB	PR	/A	PD	TPI
1929 NY-A	0	0	—	9	1	0	0	0	18^{2}	21	0	15	2	17.4	4.34	89	.296	.419	2	.500	1	-0	-1	1	0.1
1933 Det-A	0	0	—	2	0	0	0	0	1^{1}	4	1	1	0	33.8	27.00	16	.500	.556	0	—	0	-3	-3	-0	-0.3
Total 2	0	0	—	11	1	0	0	0	20	25	1	16	2	18.4	5.85	66	.316	.432	2	.500	1	-4	-4	1	-0.2

● RED NELSON Nelson, Albert Francis (b: Albert W. Horazdovsky)
b: 5/19/1886, Cleveland, Ohio d: 10/26/56, St.Petersburg, Fla BR/TR, 5'11", 190 lbs. Deb: 9/09/10

YEAR TM/L	W	L	PCT	G	GS	CG	SH	SV	IP	H	HR	BB	SO	RAT	ERA	ERA+	OAV	OOB	BH	AVG	PB	PR	/A	PD	TPI
1910 StL-A	5	1	.833	7	6	6	1	0	60	57	0	14	30	11.3	2.55	97	.261	.318	6	.261	2	-0	-1	4	0.6
1911 StL-A	3	9	.250	16	13	6	0	0	81	103	1	44	24	17.1	5.22	65	.324	.417	3	.111	-2	-17	-17	-1	-1.8
1912 StL-A	0	2	.000	8	3	0	0	1	18	21	0	13	9	17.0	7.00	47	.318	.430	1	.333	1	-7	-7	-1	-0.7
Phi-N	2	0	1.000	4	2	1	0	0	19^{1}	25	2	6	2	15.4	3.72	97	.305	.367	1	.100	-1	-1	-0	-0	-0.1
1913 Phi-N	0	0	—	2	0	0	0	0	8^{1}	9	0	4	3	14.0	2.16	154	.290	.371	1	.333	0	1	1	0	0.2
Cin-N	0	0	—	2	0	0	0	0	1^{2}	6	1	4	0	59.4	37.80	9	.667	.786	0	—	0	-6	-6	-0	-0.6
Yr	0	0	—	4	0	0	0	0	10	15	1	8	3	21.6	8.10	41	.375	.490	1	.333	0	-5	-5	0	-0.4
Total 4	10	12	.455	39	24	13	1	1	188^{1}	221	4	85	68	15.3	4.54	68	.305	.389	12	.182	0	-31	-30	2	-2.4

● ANDY NELSON Nelson, Andrew "Peaches" TL , Deb: 5/26/08

YEAR TM/L	W	L	PCT	G	GS	CG	SH	SV	IP	H	HR	BB	SO	RAT	ERA	ERA+	OAV	OOB	BH	AVG	PB	PR	/A	PD	TPI
1908 Chi-A	0	0	—	2	1	0	0	0	9	11	0	4	1	16.0	2.00	116	.282	.364	0	.000	0	0	0	-1	0.0

● EMMETT NELSON Nelson, George Emmett "Ramrod" b: 2/26/05, Viborg, S.Dak. d: 8/25/67, Sioux Falls, S.D. BR/TR, 6'3", 180 lbs. Deb: 6/24/35

YEAR TM/L	W	L	PCT	G	GS	CG	SH	SV	IP	H	HR	BB	SO	RAT	ERA	ERA+	OAV	OOB	BH	AVG	PB	PR	/A	PD	TPI
1935 Cin-N	4	4	.500	19	7	3	1	1	60^{1}	70	2	23	14	14.2	4.33	92	.295	.363	2	.133	-1	-2	-2	1	-0.2
1936 Cin-N	1	0	1.000	6	1	0	0	0	17	24	1	4	3	15.4	3.18	120	.333	.377	1	.167	-0	2	1	-0	0.1
Total 2	5	4	.556	25	8	3	1	1	77^{1}	94	3	27	17	14.4	4.07	97	.304	.366	3	.143	-1	-0	-1	1	-0.1

● JIM NELSON Nelson, James Lorin b: 7/4/47, Birmingham, Ala. BR/TR, 6', 180 lbs. Deb: 5/30/70

YEAR TM/L	W	L	PCT	G	GS	CG	SH	SV	IP	H	HR	BB	SO	RAT	ERA	ERA+	OAV	OOB	BH	AVG	PB	PR	/A	PD	TPI
1970 Pit-N	4	2	.667	15	10	1	1	0	68^{1}	64	5	38	42	13.8	3.42	114	.255	.360	4	.200	0	5	4	-1	0.3
1971 Pit-N	2	2	.500	17	2	0	0	0	34^{2}	27	0	26	11	15.1	2.34	145	.225	.384	3	.500	2	4	4	-0	0.6
Total 2	6	4	.600	32	12	1	1	0	103	91	5	64	53	14.2	3.06	122	.245	.368	7	.269	2	9	8	-1	0.9

● JEFF NELSON Nelson, Jeffrey Allan b: 11/17/66, Baltimore, Md. BR/TR, 6'8", 225 lbs. Deb: 4/16/92

YEAR TM/L	W	L	PCT	G	GS	CG	SH	SV	IP	H	HR	BB	SO	RAT	ERA	ERA+	OAV	OOB	BH	AVG	PB	PR	/A	PD	TPI
1992 Sea-A	1	7	.125	66	0	0	0	6	81	71	7	44	46	13.4	3.44	116	.245	.356	0	—	0	4	5	0	0.5

● LUKE NELSON Nelson, Luther Martin b: 12/4/1893, Cable, Ill. d: 11/14/85, Moline, Ill. BR/TR, 6', 180 lbs. Deb: 5/25/19

YEAR TM/L	W	L	PCT	G	GS	CG	SH	SV	IP	H	HR	BB	SO	RAT	ERA	ERA+	OAV	OOB	BH	AVG	PB	PR	/A	PD	TPI
1919 NY-A	3	0	1.000	9	1	0	0	0	24^{1}	22	1	11	11	12.6	2.96	108	.244	.333	1	.143	-0	1	1	-0	0.0

● LYNN NELSON Nelson, Lynn Bernard "Line Drive" b: 2/24/05, Sheldon, N.Dak. d: 2/15/55, Kansas City, Mo. BL/TR, 5'10.5", 170 lbs. Deb: 4/18/30 ♦

YEAR TM/L	W	L	PCT	G	GS	CG	SH	SV	IP	H	HR	BB	SO	RAT	ERA	ERA+	OAV	OOB	BH	AVG	PB	PR	/A	PD	TPI
1930 Chi-N	3	2	.600	37	3	0	0	0	81^{1}	97	10	28	29	14.5	5.09	96	.300	.367	4	.222	0	-1	-2	1	0.0
1933 Chi-N	5	5	.500	24	3	3	0	1	75^{2}	65	2	30	20	11.3	3.21	102	.232	.306	5	.238	2	1	1	1	0.3
1934 Chi-N	0	1	.000	2	1	0	0	0	1	4	1	1	0	45.0	36.00	11	.667	.714	0	—	0	-4	-4	-0	-0.3
1937 Phi-A	4	9	.308	30	4	1	0	2	116	140	12	51	49	15.0	5.90	80	.300	.371	40	.354	6	-16	-15	-2	-0.5
1938 Phi-A	10	11	.476	32	23	13	0	2	191	215	29	79	75	14.1	5.65	85	.277	.347	31	.277	4	-18	-17	-0	-1.1
1939 Phi-A	10	13	.435	35	24	12	2	1	197^{2}	233	27	64	75	13.7	4.78	98	.292	.347	15	.188	-2	-4	-2	-1	-0.4
1940 Det-A	1	1	.500	6	2	0	0	0	14	23	5	9	7	20.6	10.93	44	.371	.451	8	.348	2	-10	-10	0	-0.7
Total 7	33	42	.440	166	60	29	2	6	676^{2}	777	86	262	255	14.0	5.25	88	.287	.353	103	.281	13	-52	-49	-1	-2.7

● MEL NELSON Nelson, Melvin Frederick b: 5/30/36, San Diego, Cal. BR/TL, 6', 185 lbs. Deb: 9/27/60

YEAR TM/L	W	L	PCT	G	GS	CG	SH	SV	IP	H	HR	BB	SO	RAT	ERA	ERA+	OAV	OOB	BH	AVG	PB	PR	/A	PD	TPI
1960 StL-N	0	1	.000	2	1	0	0	0	8	7	1	2	7	10.1	3.38	121	.226	.273	1	.500	0	0	1	-0	0.1
1963 LA-A	2	3	.400	36	3	0	0	1	52^{2}	55	7	32	41	15.2	5.30	65	.263	.366	1	.091	-1	-10	-11	1	-1.1
1965 Min-A	0	4	.000	28	3	0	0	3	54^{2}	57	7	23	31	13.5	4.12	86	.261	.337	1	.111	-0	-4	-3	-0	-0.5
1967 Min-A	0	0	—	1	0	0	0	0	0^{1}	3	1	0	0	81.0	54.00	6	.750	.750	0	—	0	-2	-2	0	-0.2
1968 *StL-N	2	1	.667	18	4	1	0	1	52^{2}	49	3	9	16	9.9	2.91	100	.254	.287	2	.167	0	0	-0	-0	0.0
1969 StL-N	0	1	.000	8	0	0	0	0	5^{1}	13	0	3	3	27.0	11.81	30	.520	.571	0	—	0	-5	-5	-0	-0.5
Total 6	4	10	.286	93	11	1	0	5	173^{2}	184	19	69	98	13.3	4.40	76	.271	.341	5	.147	-0	-20	-21	0	-2.2

● ROGER NELSON Nelson, Roger Eugene "Spider" b: 6/7/44, Altadena, Cal. BR/TR, 6'3", 205 lbs. Deb: 9/09/67

YEAR TM/L	W	L	PCT	G	GS	CG	SH	SV	IP	H	HR	BB	SO	RAT	ERA	ERA+	OAV	OOB	BH	AVG	PB	PR	/A	PD	TPI
1967 Chi-A	0	1	.000	5	0	0	0	0	7	4	1	0	4	7.7	1.29	241	.182	.250	0	—	0	2	1	0	0.2
1968 Bal-A	4	3	.571	19	6	0	0	1	71	49	3	26	70	9.6	2.41	121	.192	.270	1	.063	-0	5	4	-0	0.4
1969 KC-A	7	13	.350	29	29	8	1	0	193^{1}	170	12	65	82	11.2	3.31	112	.243	.313	8	.138	-1	7	8	-1	0.7
1970 KC-A	0	2	.000	4	2	0	0	0	9	18	3	0	3	19.0	10.00	37	.419	.432	0	—	0	-6	-6	0	-0.5
1971 KC-A	0	1	.000	13	1	0	0	0	34	35	1	5	29	10.6	5.29	65	.269	.296	2	.333	1	-7	-7	1	-0.6
1972 KC-A	11	6	.647	34	19	10	6	3	173^{1}	120	13	31	120	**7.9**	2.08	146	.196	**.236**	5	.093	-2	19	18	1	2.1
1973 *Cin-N	3	2	.600	14	8	1	0	0	54^{2}	49	4	24	17	12.5	3.46	98	.246	.336	2	.111	-1	1	-0	1	0.0
1974 Cin-N	4	4	.500	14	12	1	0	1	85^{1}	67	7	35	42	10.9	3.38	103	.213	.293	5	.179	0	2	1	-1	0.1
1976 KC-A	0	0	—	3	0	0	0	0	8^{2}	4	0	4	4	10.4	2.08	169	.138	.286	0	—	0	1	1	0	0.1
Total 9	29	32	.475	135	77	20	7	5	636^{1}	516	44	190	371	10.2	3.06	110	.224	.288	23	.128	-3	23	21	2	2.5

● GENE NELSON Nelson, Wayland Eugene b: 12/3/60, Tampa, Fla. BR/TR, 6', 174 lbs. Deb: 5/04/81

YEAR TM/L	W	L	PCT	G	GS	CG	SH	SV	IP	H	HR	BB	SO	RAT	ERA	ERA+	OAV	OOB	BH	AVG	PB	PR	/A	PD	TPI
1981 NY-A	3	1	.750	8	7	0	0	0	39^{1}	40	5	23	16	14.6	4.81	74	.261	.362	0	—	0	-5	-5	-0	-0.5
1982 Sea-A	6	9	.400	22	19	2	1	0	122^{2}	133	16	60	71	14.3	4.62	92	.279	.362	0	—	0	-7	-5	1	-0.4
1983 Sea-A	0	3	.000	10	5	1	0	0	32	38	6	21	11	16.9	7.88	54	.295	.397	0	—	0	-14	-13	1	-1.3
1984 Chi-A	3	5	.375	20	9	2	0	1	74^{2}	72	9	17	36	10.8	4.46	93	.254	.299	0	—	0	-4	-3	0	-0.2
1985 Chi-A	10	10	.500	46	18	1	0	2	145^{2}	144	23	67	101	13.5	4.26	101	.258	.345	0	.000	0	-2	1	0	0.1

YEAR TM/L	W	L	PCT	G	GS	CG	SH	SV	IP	H	HR	BB	SO	RAT	ERA	ERA+	OAV	OOB	BH	AVG	PB	PR	/A	PD	TPI
1986 Chi-A	6	6	.500	54	1	0	0	6	114^2	118	7	41	70	12.7	3.85	112	.271	.338	0	—	0	4	6	1	0.6
1987 Oak-A	6	5	.545	54	6	0	0	3	123^2	120	12	35	94	11.6	3.93	105	.249	.307	0	—	0	7	3	-1	0.2
1988 *Oak-A	9	6	.600	54	1	0	0	3	111^2	93	9	38	67	10.8	3.06	123	.228	.298	0	—	0	11	9	-1	0.8
1989 *Oak-A	3	5	.375	50	0	0	0	3	80	60	5	30	70	10.3	3.26	113	.203	.280	0	—	0	6	4	-1	0.2
1990 *Oak-A	3	3	.500	51	0	0	0	5	74^2	55	5	17	38	9.0	1.57	237	.208	.263	0	—	0	19	18	-1	1.8
1991 Oak-A	1	5	.167	44	0	0	0	0	48^2	60	12	23	23	15.9	6.84	56	.306	.387	0	—	0	-15	-16	-1	-1.6
1992 Oak-A	3	1	.750	28	2	0	0	0	51^2	68	5	22	23	15.7	6.45	59	.335	.400	0	—	0	-14	-15	-1	-1.6
Total 12	53	59	.473	441	68	6	1	23	1019^1	1001	114	394	620	12.6	4.19	96	.258	.331	0	.000	0	-14	-18	-3	-1.9
● BILL NELSON Nelson, William F. b: 9/28/1863, Terre Haute, Ind. d: 6/23/41, Terre Haute, Ind. TR , Deb: 9/03/1884																									
1884 Pit-a	1	2	.333	3	3	3	0	0	26	26	1	8	6	13.2	4.50	75	.252	.330	2	.167	-1	-4	-3	-0	-0.4
● HAL NEUBAUER Neubauer, Harold Charles b: 5/13/02, Hoboken, N.J. d: 9/9/49, Barrington, R.I. BR/TR, 6'0.5", 185 lbs. Deb: 6/12/25																									
1925 Bos-A	1	0	1.000	7	0	0	0	0	10^1	17	2	11	4	24.4	12.19	37	.378	.500	0	—	0	-9	-9	0	-0.8
● TEX NEUER Neuer, John S. b: 6/8/1877, Fremont, Ohio d: 1/14/66, Northumberland, Pa TL , Deb: 8/28/07																									
1907 NY-A	4	2	.667	7	6	6	3	0	54	40	1	19	22	9.8	2.17	129	.208	.280	2	.095	-2	2	4	-1	0.1
● DAN NEUMEIER Neumeier, Daniel George b: 3/9/48, Shawano, Wis. BR/TR, 6'5", 205 lbs. Deb: 9/08/72																									
1972 Chi-A	0	0	—	3	0	0	0	0	3	2	0	3	0	15.0	9.00	35	.200	.385	0	.000	-0	-2	-2	-0	-0.2
● ERNIE NEVEL Nevel, Ernie Wyre b: 8/17/19, Charleston, Mo. d: 7/10/88, Springfield, Mo. BR/TR, 5'11", 190 lbs. Deb: 9/26/50																									
1950 NY-A	0	1	.000	3	1	0	0	0	6^1	10	0	6	3	22.7	9.95	43	.345	.457	0	.000	-0	-4	-4	0	-0.3
1951 NY-A	0	0	—	1	0	0	0	1	4	1	0	1	1	4.5	0.00	—	.083	.154	0	.000	-0	2	2	-0	0.1
1953 Cin-N	0	0	—	10	0	0	0	0	10^1	16	0	1	5	14.8	6.10	71	.390	.405	0	—	0	-2	-2	0	-0.2
Total 3	0	1	.000	14	1	0	0	1	20^2	27	0	8	9	15.2	6.10	69	.329	.389	0	.000	-0	-4	-4	0	-0.4
● ERNIE NEVERS Nevers, Ernest Alonzo b: 6/11/02, Willow River, Minn. d: 5/3/76, San Rafael, Cal. BR/TR, 6', 205 lbs. Deb: 4/26/26																									
1926 StL-A	2	4	.333	11	7	4	0	0	74^2	82	4	24	16	12.9	4.46	96	.290	.347	5	.185	-1	-4	-1	2	0.0
1927 StL-A	3	8	.273	27	5	2	0	2	94^2	105	8	35	22	13.5	4.94	88	.311	.379	7	.219	-1	-8	-6	1	-0.5
1928 StL-A	1	0	1.000	6	0	0	0	0	9	9	1	2	1	11.0	3.00	140	.281	.324	0	.000	-0	1	1	0	0.1
Total 3	6	12	.333	44	12	6	0	2	178^1	196	13	61	39	13.1	4.64	93	.300	.363	12	.200	-2	-11	-6	3	-0.4
● DON NEWCOMBE Newcombe, Donald "Newk" b: 6/14/26, Madison, N.J. BL/TR, 6'4", 225 lbs. Deb: 5/20/49 ♦																									
1949 *Bro-N★	17	8	.680	38	31	19	**5**	1	244^1	223	17	73	149	11.0	3.17	129	.243	.301	22	.229	3	24	25	1	3.0
1950 Bro-N★	19	11	.633	40	35	20	4	3	267^1	258	22	75	130	11.3	3.70	111	.254	.306	24	.247	7	13	12	-0	1.8
1951 Bro-N★	20	9	.690	40	36	18	3	0	272	235	19	91	**164**	11.0	3.28	120	.230	.297	23	.223	5	21	20	1	2.6
1954 Bro-N	9	8	.529	29	25	6	0	0	144^1	158	24	49	82	13.2	4.55	90	.274	.337	15	.319	4	-8	-8	-1	-0.5
1955 *Bro-N★	20	5	**.800**	34	31	17	1	0	233^2	222	35	38	143	**10.1**	3.20	127	.249	.280	42	.359	20	22	22	-2	**4.3**
1956 *Bro-N	**27**	7	**.794**	38	36	18	5	0	268	219	33	46	139	**9.0**	3.06	130	**.221**	**.257**	26	.234	9	21	**27**	0	**3.9**
1957 Bro-N	11	12	.478	28	28	12	4	0	198^2	199	28	33	90	10.6	3.49	119	.258	.290	17	.230	5	9	15	1	2.2
1958 LA-N	0	6	.000	11	8	1	0	0	34^1	53	11	8	16	16.0	7.86	52	.346	.379	5	.417	2	-15	-14	0	-1.2
Cin-N	7	7	.500	20	18	7	0	1	133^1	159	20	28	53	12.7	3.85	108	.298	.335	21	.350	8	2	4	-2	1.1
Yr	7	13	.350	31	26	8	0	1	167^2	212	31	36	69	13.4	4.67	89	.309	.344	26	.361	10	-13	-10	-2	-0.1
1959 Cin-N	13	8	.619	30	29	17	2	1	222	216	25	27	100	10.1	3.16	128	.253	.280	32	.305	15	19	22	-1	**3.9**
1960 Cin-N	4	6	.400	16	15	1	0	0	82^2	99	12	14	36	12.6	4.57	84	.304	.338	5	.139	-0	-7	-7	-1	-0.8
Cle-A	2	3	.400	20	2	0	0	1	54	61	6	8	27	11.5	4.33	86	.289	.315	6	.300	2	-3	-4	-1	-0.3
Total 10	149	90	.623	344	294	136	24	7	2154^2	2102	252	490	1129	11.0	3.56	114	.254	.299	238	.271	81	97	116	-6	20.0
● TOM NEWELL Newell, Thomas Dean b: 5/17/63, Monrovia, Cal. BR/TR, 6'1", 185 lbs. Deb: 9/09/87																									
1987 Phi-N	0	0	—	2	0	0	0	0	1	4	1	3	1	63.0	36.00	12	.571	.700	0	—	0	-4	-4	0	-0.3
● DON NEWHAUSER Newhauser, Donald Louis b: 11/7/47, Miami, Fla. BR/TR, 6'4", 200 lbs. Deb: 6/15/72																									
1972 Bos-A	4	2	.667	31	0	0	0	4	37	30	2	25	27	13.9	2.43	132	.226	.356	0	.000	-0	3	3	-0	0.3
1973 Bos-A	0	0	—	9	0	0	0	1	12	9	0	13	8	17.3	0.00	—	.205	.397	0	—	0	5	5	-0	0.1
1974 Bos-A	0	1	.000	2	0	0	0	0	3^2	5	0	4	2	22.1	9.82	39	.357	.500	0	—	0	-3	-2	0	-0.4
Total 3	4	3	.571	42	0	0	0	5	52^2	44	2	42	37	15.2	2.39	144	.230	.377	0	.000	-0	5	6	-0	0.0
● HAL NEWHOUSER Newhouser, Harold b: 5/20/21, Detroit, Mich. BL/TL, 6'2", 192 lbs. Deb: 9/29/39 H																									
1939 Det-A	0	1	.000	1	1	1	0	0	5	3	0	4	4	12.6	5.40	91	.188	.350	0	.000	-0	-0	-0	0	0.0
1940 Det-A	9	9	.500	28	20	7	0	0	133^1	149	12	76	89	15.3	4.86	98	.282	.374	8	.200	-1	-7	-2	2	0.0
1941 Det-A	9	11	.450	33	27	5	1	0	173	166	6	137	106	15.8	4.79	95	.249	.378	9	.150	-2	-12	-5	2	-0.5
1942 Det-A☆	8	14	.364	38	23	11	1	5	183^2	137	4	114	103	12.4	2.45	161	**.207**	.325	8	.154	-1	25	31	2	3.5
1943 Det-A★	8	17	.320	37	25	10	1	1	195^2	163	3	111	144	12.6	3.04	116	.224	.327	12	.185	-1	6	11	3	1.4
1944 Det-A★	**29**	9	.763	47	34	25	6	2	312^1	264	6	102	**187**	10.6	2.22	161	.230	.293	29	.242	4	42	47	1	5.9
1945 *Det-A†	**25**	9	**.735**	40	36	**29**	**8**	2	**313^1**	239	5	110	**212**	10.0	**1.81**	**194**	**.211**	.281	28	.257	5	**54**	**59**	3	**8.0**
1946 Det-A★	**26**	9	.743	37	34	29	6	1	292^2	215	10	98	275	**9.7**	**1.94**	**189**	**.201**	**.269**	13	.126	-1	51	**56**	2	**6.5**
1947 Det-A★	17	17	.500	40	36	**24**	3	2	285	268	9	110	176	12.0	2.87	131	.249	.320	19	.198	2	26	**28**	3	**3.7**
1948 Det-A★	**21**	12	.636	39	35	19	2	1	272^1	249	10	99	143	11.5	3.01	145	.242	.309	19	.207	1	39	41	2	4.5
1949 Det-A	18	11	.621	38	35	22	3	1	292	277	19	111	144	12.0	3.36	124	.251	.319	18	.198	2	27	26	3	3.0
1950 Det-A	15	13	.536	35	30	15	1	3	213^2	232	23	81	87	13.4	4.34	108	.279	.346	13	.176	-2	6	8	-0	0.6
1951 Det-A	6	6	.500	15	14	7	1	0	96^1	98	10	19	37	11.2	3.92	106	.268	.310	9	.310	2	2	3	1	0.6
1952 Det-A	9	9	.500	25	19	8	0	0	154	148	13	47	57	11.4	3.74	102	.254	.310	10	.217	3	-1	1	1	0.5
1953 Det-A	0	1	.000	7	4	0	0	1	21^2	31	4	8	6	17.0	7.06	58	.348	.414	4	.500	2	-7	-7	0	-0.5
1954 *Cle-A	7	2	.778	26	1	0	0	7	46^2	34	3	18	25	10.0	2.51	147	.209	.287	2	.154	-0	6	6	-0	0.6
1955 Cle-A	0	0	—	2	0	0	0	0	2^1	1	0	4	1	19.3	0.00	—	.125	.417	0	—	0	1	1	-0	0.1
Total 17	207	150	.580	488	374	212	33	26	2993	2674	137	1249	1796	11.9	3.06	130	.239	.316	201	.201	12	257	305	22	37.9
● FLOYD NEWKIRK Newkirk, Floyd Elmo "Three-Finger" b: 7/16/08, Norris City, Ill. d: 4/15/76, Clayton, Mo. BR/TR, 5'11", 178 lbs. Deb: 8/21/34 F																									
1934 NY-A	0	0	—	1	0	0	0	0	1	1	0	1	0	18.0	0.00	—	.333	.500	0	—	0	0	0	0	0.1
● JOEL NEWKIRK Newkirk, Joel Inez "Sailor" b: 5/1/1896, Kyana, Ind. d: 1/22/66, Eldorado, Ill. BR/TR, 6', 180 lbs. Deb: 8/20/19 F																									
1919 Chi-N	0	0	—	1	0	0	0	0	2	2	0	3	1	27.0	13.50	21	.286	.545	0	.000	-0	-2	-2	0	-0.2
1920 Chi-N	0	1	.000	2	1	0	0	0	6^2	8	1	6	2	18.9	5.40	59	.333	.467	0	.000	-0	-2	-2	-1	-0.3
Total 2	0	1	.000	3	1	0	0	0	8^2	10	1	9	3	20.8	7.27	43	.323	.488	0	.000	-1	-4	-4	-0	-0.5
● MAURY NEWLIN Newlin, Maurice Milton b: 6/22/14, Bloomingdale, Ind d: 8/14/78, Houston, Tex. BR/TR, 6', 176 lbs. Deb: 9/20/40																									
1940 StL-A	1	0	1.000	1	1	0	0	0	6	4	1	2	3	9.0	6.00	76	.190	.261	1	.500	0	-1	-1	-0	-0.1
1941 StL-A	0	2	.000	14	0	0	0	1	27^2	43	4	12	10	17.9	6.51	66	.361	.420	0	.000	-1	-7	-7	1	-0.7
Total 2	1	2	.333	15	1	0	0	1	33^2	47	5	14	13	16.3	6.42	68	.336	.396	1	.125	-1	-8	-8	0	-0.8
● FRED NEWMAN Newman, Frederick William b: 2/21/42, Boston, Mass. d: 6/24/87, Framingham, Mass. BR/TR, 6'3", 190 lbs. Deb: 9/16/62																									
1962 LA-A	0	1	.000	4	1	0	0	0	6^1	11	0	3	4	19.9	9.95	39	.393	.452	0	.000	-0	-4	-4	-0	-0.4
1963 LA-A	1	5	.167	12	8	0	0	0	44	56	6	15	16	14.9	5.32	64	.316	.376	4	.250	1	-8	-9	-0	-0.9
1964 LA-A	13	10	.565	32	28	7	2	0	190	177	9	39	83	10.6	2.75	120	.246	.291	11	.180	2	19	11	4	1.9
1965 Cal-A	14	16	.467	36	36	10	2	0	260^2	225	15	64	109	10.0	2.93	116	.234	.282	7	.095	-0	15	13	8	2.4

YEAR	TM/L	W	L	PCT	G	GS	CG	SH	SV	IP	H	HR	BB	SO	RAT	ERA	ERA+	OAV	OOB	BH	AVG	PB	PR	/A	PD	TPI
1966	Cal-A	4	7	.364	21	19	1	0	0	102^{2}	112	7	31	42	13.1	4.73	71	.289	.351	6	.200	1	-15	-16	1	-1.4
1967	Cal-A	1	0	1.000	3	1	0	0	0	6^{1}	8	1	2	0	15.6	1.42	221	.320	.393	0	.000	-0	1	1	-0	0.1
Total	6	33	39	.458	108	93	18	4	0	610	589	38	154	254	11.2	3.41	99	.256	.308	28	.153	3	8	-3	12	1.7

● JEFF NEWMAN Newman, Jeffrey Lynn b: 9/11/48, Fort Worth, Tex. BR/TR, 6'2", 218 lbs. Deb: 6/30/76 MC♦

YEAR	TM/L	W	L	PCT	G	GS	CG	SH	SV	IP	H	HR	BB	SO	RAT	ERA	ERA+	OAV	OOB	BH	AVG	PB	PR	/A	PD	TPI
1977	Oak-A	0	0	—	1	0	0	0	0	1	1	0	0	0	18.0	0.00	—	.250	.400	36	.222	0	0	0	0	0.0

● RAY NEWMAN Newman, Raymond Francis b: 6/20/45, Evansville, Ind. BL/TL, 6'5", 205 lbs. Deb: 5/16/71

YEAR	TM/L	W	L	PCT	G	GS	CG	SH	SV	IP	H	HR	BB	SO	RAT	ERA	ERA+	OAV	OOB	BH	AVG	PB	PR	/A	PD	TPI
1971	Chi-N	1	2	.333	30	0	0	0	2	38^{1}	30	4	17	35	11.0	3.52	112	.219	.305	0	.000	-1	-0	2	0	0.1
1972	Mil-A	0	0	—	4	0	0	0	1	7	4	0	2	1	7.7	0.00	—	.182	.250	1	1.000	0	2	2	0	0.4
1973	Mil-A	2	1	.667	11	0	0	0	1	18^{1}	19	2	5	10	11.8	2.95	128	.260	.308	0	—	0	2	2	1	0.4
Total	3	3	3	.500	45	0	0	0	4	63^{2}	53	6	24	46	10.9	2.97	128	.228	.301	1	.143	-0	4	6	1	0.9

● BOBO NEWSOM Newsom, Louis Norman "Buck" b: 8/11/07, Hartsville, S.C. d: 12/7/62, Orlando, Fla. BR/TR, 6'3", 200 lbs. Deb: 9/11/29

YEAR	TM/L	W	L	PCT	G	GS	CG	SH	SV	IP	H	HR	BB	SO	RAT	ERA	ERA+	OAV	OOB	BH	AVG	PB	PR	/A	PD	TPI
1929	Bro-N	0	3	.000	3	2	0	0	0	9^{1}	15	0	5	6	19.3	10.61	44	.375	.444	0	.000	-0	-6	-6	0	-0.5
1930	Bro-N	0	0	—	2	0	0	0	0	3	2	0	2	1	12.0	0.00	—	.167	.286	0	—	0	2	2	-0	0.1
1932	Chi-N	0	0	—	1	0	0	0	0	1	1	0	0	0	9.0	0.00	—	.333	.333	0	—	0	0	0	0	0.1
1934	StL-A	16	20	.444	47	32	15	2	5	262^{1}	259	15	149	135	14.0	4.01	124	.261	.358	17	.183	-3	14	29	0	2.4
1935	StL-A	0	6	.000	7	6	1	0	1	42^{2}	54	2	13	22	14.1	4.85	99	.303	.351	1	.091	-1	-2	-0	0	-0.1
	Was-A	11	12	.478	28	23	17	2	2	198^{1}	222	9	84	65	14.1	4.45	97	.288	.361	22	.301	4	0	-3	-3	-0.1
	Yr	11	18	.379	35	29	18	2	3	241	276	11	97	87	14.1	4.52	97	.291	.359	23	.274	3	-2	-3	-2	-0.2
1936	Was-A	17	15	.531	43	38	24	4	2	285^{2}	294	13	146	156	14.0	4.32	111	.268	.355	23	.213	0	23	15	1	1.4
1937	Was-A	3	4	.429	11	10	3	0	0	67^{2}	76	4	48	39	16.9	5.85	76	.287	.402	3	.120	-1	-9	-11	0	-1.0
	Bos-A	13	10	.565	30	27	14	1	0	207^{2}	193	14	119	127	13.7	4.46	106	.243	.344	19	.253	2	4	6	-2	0.7
	Yr	16	14	.533	41	37	17	1	0	275^{1}	269	18	167	166	14.3	4.81	97	.253	.356	22	.220	2	-6	-4	-1	-0.3
1938	StL-A★	20	16	.556	44	40	**31**	0	1	**329^{2}**	334	30	192	226	14.5	5.08	98	.265	.364	31	.250	2	-11	-4	-3	-0.4
1939	StL-A	3	1	.750	6	6	3	0	0	45^{2}	50	5	22	28	14.4	4.73	103	.266	.346	4	.222	-0	-1	1	0	0.1
	Det-A	17	10	.630	35	31	21	3	2	246	222	14	104	164	12.0	3.37	145	.238	.316	18	.186	-4	34	42	-1	3.5
	Yr	20	11	.645	41	37	**24**	3	2	291^{2}	272	19	126	192	12.3	3.58	136	.243	.320	22	.191	-4	34	42	-1	3.6
1940	*Det-A★	21	5	.808	36	34	20	3	0	264	235	19	100	164	11.5	2.83	**168**	.238	.310	23	.215	-1	46	56	-3	5.3
1941	Det-A	12	20	.375	43	36	12	2	2	250^{1}	265	15	118	175	13.9	4.60	99	.264	.343	9	.102	-6	-13	-2	-2	-0.9
1942	Was-A	11	17	.393	30	29	15	2	0	213^{2}	236	5	92	**113**	13.9	4.93	74	.280	.353	12	.160	-2	-30	-30	-3	-3.3
	Bro-N	2	2	.500	6	5	2	1	0	32	28	1	14	21	12.1	3.38	97	.235	.321	0	.000	-1	-0	-0	-1	-0.3
1943	Bro-N	9	4	.692	22	12	6	1	1	125	113	4	57	75	12.4	3.02	111	.244	.329	11	.250	1	5	5	0	0.6
	StL-A	1	6	.143	10	9	0	0	0	52^{1}	69	7	35	37	18.1	7.39	45	.318	.415	5	.333	1	-24	-24	-1	-2.2
	Was-A	3	3	.500	6	6	2	0	0	40	38	1	21	11	13.7	3.82	84	.247	.345	2	.133	-1	-2	-3	-1	-0.5
	Yr	4	9	.308	16	15	2	0	0	92^{1}	107	8	56	48	16.1	5.85	56	.288	.384	7	.233	0	-26	-26	-2	-2.7
1944	Phi-A★	13	15	.464	37	33	18	2	1	265	243	11	82	142	11.2	2.82	123	.244	.304	10	.114	-6	18	19	-1	1.4
1945	Phi-A	8	20	.286	36	34	16	3	0	257^{1}	255	12	103	127	12.6	3.29	104	.260	.332	14	.163	-4	2	4	-4	-0.4
1946	Phi-A	3	5	.375	10	9	3	1	0	58^{2}	61	2	30	32	14.7	3.38	105	.266	.364	2	.105	-1	1	1	-1	0.0
	Was-A	11	8	.579	24	22	14	2	1	178	163	5	60	82	11.4	2.78	120	.242	.306	10	.161	-2	14	11	-3	0.7
	Yr	14	13	.519	34	31	17	3	1	236^{2}	224	7	90	114	12.0	2.93	116	.247	.316	12	.148	-3	15	12	-4	0.7
1947	Was-A	4	6	.400	14	13	1	0	0	83^{2}	99	2	37	40	14.7	4.09	91	.296	.368	7	.241	1	-4	-3	-2	-0.4
	*NY-A	7	5	.583	17	15	6	2	0	115^{2}	109	8	30	42	11.0	2.80	126	.250	.301	4	.095	-3	12	9	-2	0.5
	Yr	11	11	.500	31	28	7	2	0	199^{1}	208	10	67	82	12.5	3.34	108	.270	.330	11	.155	-3	8	6	-3	0.1
1948	NY-N	0	4	.000	11	4	0	0	0	25^{2}	35	1	13	9	16.8	4.21	94	.330	.403	3	.429	1	-1	-1	-0	0.0
1952	Was-A	1	1	.500	10	0	0	0	2	12^{2}	16	2	9	5	17.8	4.97	72	.302	.403	0	.000	-0	-2	-2	0	-0.2
	Phi-A	3	3	.500	14	5	1	0	1	47^{2}	38	2	23	22	11.9	3.59	110	.220	.318	2	.133	-1	0	2	0	0.1
	Yr	4	4	.500	24	5	1	0	3	60^{1}	54	4	32	27	13.1	3.88	100	.239	.338	2	.118	-1	-1	-0	1	-0.1
1953	Phi-A	2	1	.667	17	2	1	0	0	38^{2}	44	3	24	16	17.0	4.89	88	.282	.395	1	.167	-0	-4	-3	0	-0.3
Total	20	211	222	.487	600	483	246	31	21	3759^{1}	3769	206	1732	2082	13.3	3.98	107	.261	.342	253	.189	-27	67	109	-29	6.3

● DICK NEWSOME Newsome, Heber Hampton b: 12/13/09, Ahoskie, N.C. d: 12/15/65, Ahoskie, N.C. BR/TR, 6', 185 lbs. Deb: 4/25/41

YEAR	TM/L	W	L	PCT	G	GS	CG	SH	SV	IP	H	HR	BB	SO	RAT	ERA	ERA+	OAV	OOB	BH	AVG	PB	PR	/A	PD	TPI
1941	Bos-A	19	10	.655	36	29	17	2	0	213^{2}	235	13	79	58	13.5	4.13	101	.277	.344	19	.244	3	0	1	3	0.7
1942	Bos-A	8	10	.444	24	23	11	0	0	158	174	11	67	40	13.7	5.01	74	.278	.348	13	.236	2	-24	-23	1	-2.0
1943	Bos-A	8	13	.381	25	22	8	2	0	154^{1}	166	8	68	40	13.9	4.49	74	.274	.352	7	.146	-1	-20	-20	-2	-2.3
Total	3	35	33	.515	85	74	36	4	0	526	575	32	214	138	13.7	4.50	84	.276	.347	39	.215	3	-44	-42	2	-3.6

● DOC NEWTON Newton, Eustace James b: 10/26/1877, Indianapolis, Ind. d: 5/14/31, Memphis, Tenn. BL/TL, 6', 185 lbs. Deb: 4/27/00

YEAR	TM/L	W	L	PCT	G	GS	CG	SH	SV	IP	H	HR	BB	SO	RAT	ERA	ERA+	OAV	OOB	BH	AVG	PB	PR	/A	PD	TPI
1900	Cin-N	9	15	.375	35	27	22	1	0	234^{2}	255	4	100	88	14.1	4.14	89	.276	.355	17	.198	-1	-12	-12	-2	-1.4
1901	Cin-N	4	13	.235	20	18	17	0	0	168^{1}	190	6	59	65	14.0	4.12	78	.282	.352	9	.130	-4	-15	-17	1	-1.9
	Bro-N	6	5	.545	13	12	9	0	0	105	110	1	30	45	12.6	2.83	119	.268	.328	9	.220	1	6	6	-0	0.6
	Yr	10	18	.357	33	30	26	0	0	273^{1}	300	7	89	110	13.0	3.62	90	.274	.332	18	.164	-3	-9	-11	1	-1.3
1902	Bro-N	15	14	.517	31	28	26	4	2	264^{1}	208	2	87	107	10.4	2.42	114	**.217**	.288	19	.174	-1	11	10	-2	0.7
1905	NY-A	2	2	.500	11	7	2	0	0	59^{2}	61	1	24	15	13.1	2.11	139	.266	.340	3	.136	-1	4	5	-1	0.3
1906	NY-A	7	5	.583	21	15	6	2	0	125	118	3	33	52	11.4	3.17	94	.252	.313	9	.220	-0	-7	-3	2	-0.2
1907	NY-A	7	10	.412	19	15	10	0	0	133	132	0	31	70	11.4	3.18	88	.261	.311	4	.108	-1	-9	-6	1	-0.7
1908	NY-A	4	5	.444	23	13	6	1	1	88^{1}	78	0	41	49	12.8	2.95	84	.242	.341	4	.160	-0	-5	-5	0	-0.5
1909	NY-A	0	3	.000	4	4	1	0	0	22^{1}	27	0	11	11	16.5	2.82	90	.300	.394	1	.167	0	-1	-1	1	0.0
Total	8	54	72	.429	177	139	99	8	3	1200^{2}	1179	17	416	502	12.5	3.22	95	.257	.328	75	.172	-9	-29	-19	-2	-3.1

● KID NICHOLS Nichols, Charles Augustus b: 9/14/1869, Madison, Wis. d: 4/11/53, Kansas City, Mo. BB/TR, 5'10.5", 175 lbs. Deb: 4/23/1890 MH

YEAR	TM/L	W	L	PCT	G	GS	CG	SH	SV	IP	H	HR	BB	SO	RAT	ERA	ERA+	OAV	OOB	BH	AVG	PB	PR	/A	PD	TPI
1890	Bos-N	27	19	.587	48	47	47	**7**	0	424	374	8	112	222	10.5	2.23	168	.229	.284	43	.247	1	63	**72**	0	**6.9**
1891	Bos-N	30	17	.638	52	48	45	5	**3**	425^{1}	413	15	103	240	11.3	2.39	**153**	.245	.295	36	.197	-3	**45**	**60**	6	**5.8**
1892	*Bos-N	35	16	.686	53	51	49	5	0	453	404	15	121	187	10.6	2.84	124	.229	.283	39	.198	1	22	34	-1	3.2
1893	Bos-N	34	14	.708	52	44	43	1	1	425	426	15	118	94	11.8	3.52	140	.253	.308	39	.220	-2	54	67	-2	5.4
1894	Bos-N	32	13	.711	50	46	40	**3**	0	407	488	23	121	113	13.7	4.75	120	.294	.345	50	.294	3	26	42	0	3.5
1895	Bos-N	26	16	.619	47	42	42	1	**3**	379^{2}	417	15	86	140	12.0	3.41	149	.275	.316	37	.236	-4	58	**71**	-0	5.7
1896	Bos-N	**30**	14	.682	49	43	37	3	1	372^{1}	387	14	101	102	12.0	2.83	161	.266	.317	28	.190	-3	**63**	**71**	2	6.2
1897	*Bos-N	**31**	11	.738	**46**	40	37	2	**3**	**368**	362	9	68	127	**10.6**	2.64	**169**	.255	**.291**	39	.265	3	**68**	**75**	-2	**7.0**
1898	Bos-N	**31**	12	.721	**50**	42	40	5	**4**	388	316	7	85	138	**9.6**	2.13	173	**.221**	**.272**	38	.241	2	**64**	**67**	-2	**6.8**
1899	Bos-N	21	19	.525	42	37	37	4	1	343^{1}	326	11	82	108	10.9	2.99	139	.250	.298	26	.191	-5	33	45	-1	3.7
1900	Bos-N	13	16	.448	29	27	25	**4**	0	231^{1}	215	11	72	53	11.6	3.07	134	.246	.311	18	.200	-2	16	27	-1	2.3
1901	Bos-N	19	16	.543	38	34	33	4	0	321	306	8	90	143	11.3	3.22	112	.250	.305	46	.282	10	4	14	-1	2.5
1904	StL-N	21	13	.618	36	35	35	3	1	317	268	3	50	134	9.2	2.02	134	.222	.256	17	.156	-1	25	24	-1	2.5
1905	StL-N	1	5	.167	7	7	5	0	0	51^{2}	64	1	18	16	14.3	5.40	55	.296	.350	5	.227	0	-14	-14	-1	-1.4
	Phi-N	10	6	.625	17	16	15	1	0	138^{2}	129	1	28	50	10.4	2.27	129	.250	.294	10	.189	0	11	10	-4	0.7
	Yr	11	11	.500	24	23	20	1	0	190^{1}	193	2	46	66	11.5	3.12	94	.264	.311	15	.200	0	-2	-4	-5	-0.7
1906	Phi-N	0	1	.000	4	2	1	0	0	11	17	0	13	1	26.2	9.82	27	.386	.542	0	.000	-0	-9	-9	-1	-0.9
Total	15	361	208	.634	620	561	531	48	17	5056^{1}	4912	156	1268	1868	11.2	2.95	139	.250	.300	471	.226	-0	531	653	-9	59.9

● CHET NICHOLS Nichols, Chester Raymond Jr. b: 2/22/31, Pawtucket, R.I. BB/TL, 6'1.5", 195 lbs. Deb: 4/19/51 F

YEAR	TM/L	W	L	PCT	G	GS	CG	SH	SV	IP	H	HR	BB	SO	RAT	ERA	ERA+	OAV	OOB	BH	AVG	PB	PR	/A	PD	TPI
1951	Bos-N	11	8	.579	33	19	12	3	2	156	142	4	69	71	12.2	**2.88**	127	.246	.327	7	.137	-2	19	14	2	1.4
1954	Mil-N	9	11	.450	35	20	5	1	1	122^{1}	132	5	65	55	14.8	4.41	84	.286	.379	3	.086	-2	-5	-9	1	-1.1

YEAR	TM/L	W	L	PCT	G	GS	CG	SH	SV	IP	H	HR	BB	SO	RAT	ERA	ERA+	OAV	OOB	BH	AVG	PB	PR	/A	PD	TPI
1955	Mil-N	9	8	.529	34	21	6	0	1	144	139	20	67	44	12.9	4.00	94	.253	.335	8	.154	-2	1	-4	2	-0.4
1956	Mil-N	0	1	.000	2	0	0	0	0	4	9	1	3	2	27.0	6.75	51	.563	.632	0	.000	-0	-1	-1	0	-0.1
1960	Bos-A	0	2	.000	6	1	0	0	0	12^{2}	12	0	4	11	11.4	4.26	95	.240	.296	0	.000	-0	-1	-0	0	0.0
1961	Bos-A	3	2	.600	26	2	0	0	3	51^{2}	40	3	26	20	11.5	2.09	199	.221	.319	1	.111	-0	11	12	3	1.5
1962	Bos-A	1	1	.500	29	1	0	0	3	57	61	3	22	33	13.1	3.00	138	.276	.342	0	.000	-1	6	7	1	0.8
1963	Bos-A	1	3	.250	21	7	0	0	0	52^{2}	61	8	24	27	14.5	4.78	79	.298	.371	3	.231	0	-7	-6	-0	-0.6
1964	Cin-N	0	0	—	3	0	0	0	0	3	4	1	0	3	12.0	6.00	60	.308	.308	0	—	0	-1	-1	-0	-0.1
Total	9	34	36	.486	189	71	23	4	10	603^{1}	600	45	280	266	13.2	3.64	105	.264	.346	22	.127	-8	22	11	8	1.4

● CHET NICHOLS Nichols, Chester Raymond Sr. "Nick" b: 7/3/1897, Woonsocket, R.I. d: 7/11/82, Pawtucket, R.I. BR/TR, 5'11", 160 lbs. Deb: 7/30/26 F

YEAR	TM/L	W	L	PCT	G	GS	CG	SH	SV	IP	H	HR	BB	SO	RAT	ERA	ERA+	OAV	OOB	BH	AVG	PB	PR	/A	PD	TPI
1926	Pit-N	0	0	—	3	0	0	0	0	7^{2}	13	0	5	2	21.1	8.22	48	.342	.419	1	.333	0	-4	-4	0	-0.3
1927	Pit-N	0	3	.000	8	0	0	0	0	27^{2}	34	1	17	9	16.9	5.86	70	.309	.406	1	.111	-0	-6	-5	-0	-0.6
1928	NY-N	0	0	—	3	0	0	0	0	2^{2}	11	0	3	1	50.6	23.63	17	.611	.682	0	—	0	-6	-6	0	-0.5
1930	Phi-N	1	2	.333	16	5	1	0	0	59^{2}	76	8	16	15	14.2	6.79	80	.306	.353	6	.300	0	-12	-9	1	-0.7
1931	Phi-N	0	1	.000	3	0	0	0	0	5^{2}	10	0	1	1	17.5	9.53	45	.435	.458	0	.000	-0	-4	-3	0	-0.3
1932	Phi-N	0	2	.000	11	0	0	0	1	19^{1}	23	2	14	5	17.2	6.98	63	.299	.407	0	.000	-1	-7	-6	0	-0.6
Total	6	1	8	.111	44	5	1	0	1	122^{2}	167	11	56	33	16.7	7.19	67	.325	.395	8	.211	-1	-38	-33	1	-3.0

● DOLAN NICHOLS Nichols, Dolan Levon "Nick" b: 2/28/30, Tishomingo, Miss. d: 11/20/89, Tupelo, Miss. BR/TR, 6', 195 lbs. Deb: 4/15/58

YEAR	TM/L	W	L	PCT	G	GS	CG	SH	SV	IP	H	HR	BB	SO	RAT	ERA	ERA+	OAV	OOB	BH	AVG	PB	PR	/A	PD	TPI
1958	Chi-N	0	4	.000	24	0	0	0	1	41^{1}	46	1	16	9	13.7	5.01	78	.295	.364	0	.000	-1	-5	-5	1	-0.5

● TRICKY NICHOLS Nichols, Frederick C. b: 7/26/1850, Bridgeport, Conn. d: 8/22/1897, Bridgeport, Conn. BR/TR, 5'7.5", 150 lbs. Deb: 4/21/1875

YEAR	TM/L	W	L	PCT	G	GS	CG	SH	SV	IP	H	HR	BB	SO	RAT	ERA	ERA+	OAV	OOB	BH	AVG	PB	PR	/A	PD	TPI
1875	NH-n	4	29	.121	34	33	30	0	0	288	319	2	10		10.3	3.03	76	.243	.248	23	.192	-2	-18	-24		-2.0
1876	Bos-N	1	0	1.000	1	1	1	0	0	9	7	0	0	0	7.0	1.00	226	.200	.200	0	.000	-1	1	1	0	0.1
1877	StL-N	18	23	.439	42	39	35	1	0	350	376	2	53	80	11.0	2.60	100	.263	.289	31	.167	-6	8	0	-0	-0.6
1878	Pro-N	4	7	.364	11	10	10	0	0	98	157	0	8	21	15.2	4.22	52	.344	.356	9	.184	-0	-21	-22	2	-1.8
1880	Wor-N	0	2	.000	2	2	2	0	0	17^{2}	29	0	4	4	16.8	4.08	64	.358	.388	0	.000	-1	-3	-3	-1	-0.4
1882	Bal-a	1	12	.077	16	13	12	0	0	118^{1}	155	2	17	21	13.1	5.02	55	.296	.319	15	.158	-2	-31	-30	-2	-2.7
Total	5	24	44	.353	72	65	60	1	0	593	724	4	82	126	12.2	3.37	76	.287	.309	55	.161	-10	-45	-53	-1	-5.4

● ROD NICHOLS Nichols, Rodney Lea b: 12/29/64, Burlington, Iowa BR/TR, 6'2", 190 lbs. Deb: 7/30/88

YEAR	TM/L	W	L	PCT	G	GS	CG	SH	SV	IP	H	HR	BB	SO	RAT	ERA	ERA+	OAV	OOB	BH	AVG	PB	PR	/A	PD	TPI
1988	Cle-A	1	7	.125	11	10	3	0	0	69^{1}	73	5	23	31	12.7	5.06	81	.272	.334	0	—	0	-8	-7	-0	-0.7
1989	Cle-A	4	6	.400	15	11	0	0	0	71^{2}	81	9	24	42	13.4	4.40	90	.285	.345	0	—	0	-4	-3	-0	-0.5
1990	Cle-A	0	3	.000	4	2	0	0	0	16	24	5	6	3	18.0	7.88	50	.343	.410	0	—	0	-7	-7	0	-0.6
1991	Cle-A	2	11	.154	31	16	3	1	1	137^{1}	145	6	30	76	11.9	3.54	117	.273	.319	0	—	0	8	9	-1	0.9
1992	Cle-A	4	3	.571	30	9	0	0	0	105^{1}	114	13	31	56	12.6	4.53	89	.273	.327	0	—	0	-7	-6	-0	-0.6
Total	5	11	30	.268	91	48	6	1	1	399^{2}	437	38	114	208	12.7	4.39	93	.278	.333	0	—	0	-18	-14	-1	-1.5

● FRANK NICHOLSON Nicholson, Frank Collins b: 8/29/1889, Berlin, Pa. d: 11/10/72, Jersey Shore, Pa. BR/TR, 6'2", 175 lbs. Deb: 9/06/12

YEAR	TM/L	W	L	PCT	G	GS	CG	SH	SV	IP	H	HR	BB	SO	RAT	ERA	ERA+	OAV	OOB	BH	AVG	PB	PR	/A	PD	TPI
1912	Phi-N	0	0	—	2	0	0	0	0	4	8	1	2	1	22.5	6.75	54	.471	.526	0	—	0	-1	-1	0	-0.1

● GEORGE NICOL Nicol, George Edward b: 10/17/1870, Barry, Ill. d: 8/10/24, Milwaukee, Wis. TL, 5'7", 155 lbs. Deb: 9/23/1890 ♦

YEAR	TM/L	W	L	PCT	G	GS	CG	SH	SV	IP	H	HR	BB	SO	RAT	ERA	ERA+	OAV	OOB	BH	AVG	PB	PR	/A	PD	TPI
1890	StL-a	2	1	.667	3	3	2	0	0	17	11	1	19	16	16.9	4.76	91	.179	.389	2	.286	1	-2	-1	-0	0.0
1891	Chi-N	0	1	.000	3	2	0	0	0	11	14	0	10	12	20.5	4.91	68	.299	.432	2	.333	1	-2	-2	-1	-0.1
1894	Pit-N	3	4	.429	8	5	3	0	0	44^{1}	57	2	33	11	19.3	6.50	81	.309	.427	9	.450	2	-6	-6	-1	-0.4
	Lou-N	0	1	.000	1	1	1	0	0	9	19	2	5	3	25.0	15.00	34	.423	.491	38	.352	0	-10	-10	0	-0.6
	Yr	3	5	.375	9	6	4	0	0	53^{1}	76	4	38	14	19.4	7.93	66	.324	.420	47	.367	2	-15	-16	-1	-1.0
Total	3	5	7	.417	15	11	6	0	0	81^{1}	101	5	67	42	19.6	6.86	70	.299	.428	51	.362	5	-19	-19	-2	-1.1

● DAVID NIED Nied, David Glen b: 12/22/68, Dallas, Texas BR/TR, 6'2", 175 lbs. Deb: 9/01/92

YEAR	TM/L	W	L	PCT	G	GS	CG	SH	SV	IP	H	HR	BB	SO	RAT	ERA	ERA+	OAV	OOB	BH	AVG	PB	PR	/A	PD	TPI
1992	Atl-N	3	0	1.000	6	2	0	0	0	23	10	0	5	19	5.9	1.17	319	.130	.183	2	.286	0	6	7	-0	0.8

● TOM NIEDENFUER Niedenfuer, Thomas Edward b: 8/13/59, St.Louis Park, Minn. BR/TR, 6'5", 225 lbs. Deb: 8/15/81

YEAR	TM/L	W	L	PCT	G	GS	CG	SH	SV	IP	H	HR	BB	SO	RAT	ERA	ERA+	OAV	OOB	BH	AVG	PB	PR	/A	PD	TPI
1981	*LA-N	3	1	.750	17	0	0	0	2	26	25	1	6	12	11.1	3.81	87	.258	.308	0	—	0	-1	-1	-0	-0.2
1982	LA-N	3	4	.429	55	0	0	0	9	69^{2}	71	3	25	60	12.7	2.71	128	.269	.337	0	.000	-0	7	6	-1	0.5
1983	*LA-N	8	3	.727	66	0	0	0	11	94^{2}	55	6	29	66	8.1	1.90	189	.170	.240	0	.000	-0	18	18	-1	1.7
1984	LA-N	2	5	.286	33	0	0	0	11	47^{1}	39	3	23	45	12.2	2.47	143	.227	.325	0	.000	-0	6	6	-0	0.5
1985	*LA-N	7	9	.438	64	0	0	0	19	106^{1}	86	6	24	102	9.4	2.71	128	.223	.270	1	.111	-0	10	9	-1	0.8
1986	LA-N	6	6	.500	60	0	0	0	11	80	86	11	29	55	13.0	3.71	93	.280	.344	2	.500	1	0	-2	0	-0.2
1987	LA-N	1	0	1.000	15	0	0	0	1	16^{1}	13	1	9	10	12.7	2.76	144	.220	.333	0	—	0	2	2	0	0.3
	Bal-A	3	5	.375	45	0	0	0	13	52^{1}	55	11	22	37	13.4	4.99	88	.266	.339	0	—	0	-3	-3	-1	-0.4
1988	Bal-A	3	4	.429	52	0	0	0	18	59	59	8	19	40	12.2	3.51	111	.259	.321	0	—	0	3	3	-1	0.2
1989	Sea-A	0	3	.000	25	0	0	0	0	36^{1}	46	7	15	15	15.4	6.69	60	.309	.376	0	—	0	-11	-11	0	-1.2
1990	StL-N	0	6	.000	52	0	0	0	2	65	66	3	25	32	12.6	3.46	110	.269	.337	0	.000	-0	2	3	-1	0.1
Total	10	36	46	.439	484	0	0	0	97	653	601	60	226	474	11.6	3.29	112	.247	.314	3	.115	-1	34	28	-5	2.1

● DICK NIEHAUS Niehaus, Richard J. b: 10/24/1892, Covington, Ky. d: 3/12/57, Atlanta, Ga. BL/TL, 5'11", 165 lbs. Deb: 9/09/13

YEAR	TM/L	W	L	PCT	G	GS	CG	SH	SV	IP	H	HR	BB	SO	RAT	ERA	ERA+	OAV	OOB	BH	AVG	PB	PR	/A	PD	TPI
1913	StL-N	0	2	.000	3	3	2	0	0	24	20	1	13	4	12.4	4.13	78	.241	.344	2	.286	1	-2	-2	0	-0.1
1914	StL-N	1	0	1.000	8	1	1	0	0	17^{1}	18	1	8	6	13.5	3.12	90	.269	.347	1	.250	1	-1	-1	-1	0.0
1915	StL-N	2	1	.667	15	2	0	0	0	45^{1}	48	1	22	21	14.1	3.97	70	.281	.366	1	.071	-1	-6	-6	0	-0.7
1920	Cle-A	1	2	.333	19	3	0	0	2	40	42	0	16	12	13.3	3.60	106	.269	.341	4	.444	2	1	1	-1	0.1
Total	4	4	5	.444	45	9	3	0	2	126^{2}	128	4	59	43	13.4	3.77	85	.268	.351	8	.235	2	-8	-8	-1	-0.7

● JOE NIEKRO Niekro, Joseph Franklin b: 11/7/44, Martins Ferry, Ohio BR/TR, 6'1", 190 lbs. Deb: 4/16/67 F

YEAR	TM/L	W	L	PCT	G	GS	CG	SH	SV	IP	H	HR	BB	SO	RAT	ERA	ERA+	OAV	OOB	BH	AVG	PB	PR	/A	PD	TPI
1967	Chi-N	10	7	.588	36	22	7	2	0	169^{2}	171	15	32	77	10.9	3.34	106	.257	.293	9	.196	1	1	4	-1	0.5
1968	Chi-N	14	10	.583	34	29	2	1	2	177	204	18	59	65	13.5	4.32	73	.294	.351	6	.100	-2	-26	-23	0	-2.7
1969	Chi-N	0	1	.000	4	3	0	0	0	19^{1}	24	3	6	7	14.0	3.72	108	.304	.353	1	.200	0	-0	1	1	0.2
	SD-N	8	17	.320	37	31	8	3	0	202	213	15	45	55	11.5	3.70	96	.273	.312	6	.118	0	-2	-4	-1	-0.5
	Yr	8	18	.308	41	34	8	3	0	221^{1}	237	18	51	62	11.7	3.70	97	.275	.316	7	.125	0	-3	-3	-1	-0.3
1970	Det-A	12	13	.480	38	34	6	2	0	213	221	28	72	101	12.5	4.06	92	.266	.327	13	.197	4	-8	-8	1	-0.4
1971	Det-A	6	7	.462	31	15	0	0	1	122^{1}	136	13	49	43	13.8	4.49	80	.283	.352	4	.133	-0	-14	-12	1	-1.2
1972	Det-A	3	2	.600	18	7	1	0	1	47	62	3	8	24	13.6	3.83	82	.330	.360	3	.250	1	-4	-4	-0	-0.3
1973	Atl-N	2	4	.333	20	0	0	0	3	24	23	2	11	12	12.8	4.13	95	.277	.362	1	.333	0	-1	-1	1	0.0
1974	Atl-N	3	2	.600	27	2	0	0	0	43	36	5	18	31	11.7	3.56	106	.237	.326	0	.000	-1	0	1	1	0.1
1975	Hou-N	6	4	.600	40	4	1	1	4	88	79	3	39	54	12.3	3.07	110	.240	.324	3	.214	1	5	3	0	0.4
1976	Hou-N	4	8	.333	36	13	0	0	0	118	107	8	56	77	12.5	3.36	95	.238	.324	5	.185	2	2	-2	-1	-0.1
1977	Hou-N	13	8	.619	44	14	9	2	5	180^{2}	155	14	64	101	11.0	3.04	117	.237	.306	7	.140	-1	17	11	1	1.1
1978	Hou-N	14	14	.500	35	29	10	1	0	202^{2}	190	13	73	97	12.1	3.86	86	.248	.321	9	.138	-1	-6	-13	-1	-1.5
1979	Hou-N☆	**21**	11	.656	38	38	11	**5**	0	263^{2}	221	17	107	119	11.4	3.00	117	.228	.309	10	.120	-2	21	15	0	1.4
1980	*Hou-N	20	12	.625	37	36	11	2	0	256	268	12	79	127	12.3	3.55	93	.270	.326	22	.275	7	1	-8	-1	-0.1
1981	*Hou-N	9	9	.500	24	24	5	2	0	166	150	8	47	77	10.7	2.82	117	.243	.297	9	.176	1	12	9	-1	1.0
1982	Hou-N	17	12	.586	35	35	16	5	0	270	224	12	64	130	9.8	2.47	134	.229	.279	8	.090	-4	34	25	0	2.4
1983	Hou-N	15	14	.517	38	38	9	1	0	263^{2}	238	15	101	152	11.7	3.48	98	.241	.313	8	.094	-3	4	-2	-2	-0.8
1984	Hou-N	16	12	.571	38	38	6	1	0	248^{1}	223	16	89	127	11.5	3.04	109	.241	.310	11	.133	-1	15	8	1	0.8
1985	Hou-N	9	12	.429	32	32	4	1	0	213	197	21	99	117	12.7	3.72	93	.247	.333	17	.250	3	-3	-6	0	-0.3

YEAR	TM/L	W	L	PCT	G	GS	CG	SH	SV	IP	H	HR	BB	SO	RAT	ERA	ERA+	OAV	OOB	BH	AVG	PB	PR	/A	PD	TPI
	NY-A	2	1	.667	3	3	0	0	0	12^1	14	3	8	4	16.1	5.84	69	.280	.379	0	—	0	-2	-3	0	-0.2
1986	NY-A	9	10	.474	25	25	0	0	0	125^2	139	15	63	59	14.5	4.87	84	.275	.356	0	—	0	-10	-11	-1	-1.1
1987	NY-A	3	4	.429	8	8	1	0	0	50^2	40	4	19	30	11.2	3.55	123	.215	.301	0	—	0	5	5	-0	0.4
	*Min-A	4	9	.308	19	18	0	0	0	96^1	115	11	45	54	15.5	6.26	74	.296	.378	0	—	0	-19	-18	-1	-1.7
	Yr	7	13	.350	27	26	1	0	0	147	155	15	64	84	13.8	5.33	85	.268	.347	0	—	0	-14	-13	-1	-1.3
1988	Min-A	1	1	.500	5	2	0	0	0	11^2	16	2	9	7	19.3	10.03	41	.320	.424	0	—	0	-8	-8	1	-0.7
Total	22	221	204	.520	702	500	107	29	16	3584	3466	276	1262	1747	12.0	3.59	97	.255	.321	152	.156	6	14	-38	-3	-3.3

● **PHIL NIEKRO** Niekro, Philip Henry b: 4/1/39, Blaine, Ohio BR/TR, 6'1", 180 lbs. Deb: 4/15/64 F

YEAR	TM/L	W	L	PCT	G	GS	CG	SH	SV	IP	H	HR	BB	SO	RAT	ERA	ERA+	OAV	OOB	BH	AVG	PB	PR	/A	PD	TPI
1964	Mil-N	0	0	—	10	0	0	0	0	15	15	1	7	8	13.8	4.80	73	.273	.365	0	—	0	-2	-2	-0	-0.2
1965	Mil-N	2	3	.400	41	1	0	0	6	74^2	73	5	26	49	12.3	2.89	122	.258	.327	1	.100	-0	5	5	1	0.6
1966	Atl-N	4	3	.571	28	0	0	0	2	50^1	48	4	23	17	13.1	4.11	88	.249	.335	0	.000	-1	-3	-3	2	-0.2
1967	Atl-N	11	9	.550	46	20	10	1	9	207	164	9	55	129	9.8	**1.87**	**178**	.218	.277	7	.123	-0	35	33	1	3.9
1968	Atl-N	14	12	.538	37	34	15	5	2	257	228	16	45	140	9.7	2.59	116	.239	.277	8	.104	-1	11	11	3	1.6
1969	*Atl-N★	23	13	.639	40	35	21	4	1	284^1	235	21	57	193	9.4	2.56	141	.221	.264	20	.211	3	33	33	2	4.2
1970	Atl-N	12	18	.400	34	32	10	3	0	229^2	222	40	68	168	11.6	4.27	100	.248	.305	12	.152	-1	-6	0	2	0.1
1971	Atl-N	15	14	.517	42	36	18	4	2	268^2	248	27	70	173	10.8	2.98	124	.245	.296	14	.152	-3	14	22	2	2.3
1972	Atl-N	16	12	.571	38	36	17	1	0	282^1	254	22	53	164	9.9	3.06	124	.236	.275	18	.194	1	12	23	1	2.8
1973	Atl-N	13	10	.565	42	30	9	1	4	245	214	21	89	131	11.3	3.31	119	.234	.306	10	.122	-2	10	17	2	1.9
1974	Atl-N	**20**	13	.606	41	39	**18**	6	1	**302^1**	249	19	88	195	10.2	2.38	159	.225	.286	20	.192	-0	**42**	**47**	0	**5.3**
1975	Atl-N☆	15	15	.500	39	37	13	1	0	275^2	285	29	72	144	12.0	3.20	118	.269	.322	17	.172	-0	13	18	1	1.9
1976	Atl-N	17	11	.607	38	37	10	2	0	270^2	249	18	101	173	11.9	3.29	115	.242	.315	18	.191	1	6	15	1	1.8
1977	Atl-N	16	20	.444	44	43	**20**	2	0	**330^1**	315	26	164	**262**	13.3	4.03	110	.255	.346	19	.174	-3	-5	15	2	1.4
1978	Atl-N★	19	18	.514	44	42	**22**	4	1	**334^1**	295	16	102	248	11.0	2.88	141	.235	.299	27	.225	3	26	**43**	4	**5.7**
1979	Atl-N	**21**	20	.512	44	44	**23**	1	0	**342**	311	41	113	208	11.4	3.39	119	.241	.307	24	.195	2	13	25	3	**3.2**
1980	Atl-N	15	18	.455	40	38	11	3	1	275	256	30	85	176	11.3	3.63	103	.249	.308	12	.133	-2	-1	3	1	0.2
1981	Atl-N	7	7	.500	22	22	3	3	0	139^1	120	6	56	62	11.4	3.10	115	.233	.310	4	.077	-4	6	7	0	0.4
1982	*Atl-N☆	17	4	**.810**	35	35	4	2	0	234^1	225	23	73	144	11.6	3.61	103	.255	.314	17	.195	2	-0	3	1	0.6
1983	Atl-N	11	10	.524	34	33	2	0	0	201^2	212	18	105	128	14.2	3.97	98	.276	.364	12	.185	0	-8	-2	0	-0.2
1984	NY-A☆	16	8	.667	32	31	5	1	0	215^2	219	15	76	136	12.4	3.09	123	.267	.331	0	—	0	22	17	2	2.0
1985	NY-A	16	12	.571	33	33	7	1	0	220	203	29	120	149	13.3	4.09	98	.245	.342	0	—	0	1	-2	-2	-0.4
1986	Cle-A	11	11	.500	34	32	5	0	0	210^1	241	24	95	81	14.6	4.32	96	.287	.363	0	—	0	-3	-4	-1	-0.4
1987	Tor-A	0	2	.000	3	3	0	0	0	12	15	4	7	7	16.5	8.25	54	.306	.393	0	—	0	-5	-5	-0	-0.5
	Cle-A	7	11	.389	22	22	2	0	0	123^2	142	18	53	57	14.5	5.89	77	.286	.359	0	—	0	-20	-19	0	-1.7
	Yr	7	13	.350	25	25	2	0	0	135^2	157	22	60	64	14.7	6.10	74	.288	.362	0	—	0	-25	-24	-0	-2.2
	Atl-N	0	0	—	1	1	0	0	0	3	6	0	6	0	36.0	15.00	29	.429	.600	0	.000	-0	-4	-4	-0	-0.3
Total	24	318	274	.537	864	716	245	45	29	5404^1	5044	482	1809	3342	11.6	3.35	115	.247	.312	260	.169	-5	192	299	28	36.0

● **JERRY NIELSEN** Nielsen, Gerald Arthur b: 8/5/66, Sacramento, Cal. BL/TL, 6'3", 185 lbs. Deb: 7/12/92

YEAR	TM/L	W	L	PCT	G	GS	CG	SH	SV	IP	H	HR	BB	SO	RAT	ERA	ERA+	OAV	OOB	BH	AVG	PB	PR	/A	PD	TPI
1992	NY-A	1	0	1.000	20	0	0	0	0	19^2	17	1	18	12	16.0	4.58	88	.243	.398	0	—	0	-1	-1	0	-0.1

● **SCOTT NIELSEN** Nielsen, Jeffrey Scott b: 12/18/58, Salt Lake City, Ut. BR/TR, 6'1", 190 lbs. Deb: 7/07/86

YEAR	TM/L	W	L	PCT	G	GS	CG	SH	SV	IP	H	HR	BB	SO	RAT	ERA	ERA+	OAV	OOB	BH	AVG	PB	PR	/A	PD	TPI
1986	NY-A	4	4	.500	10	9	2	2	0	56	66	12	12	20	12.9	4.02	102	.299	.340	0	—	0	1	0	-1	0.0
1987	Chi-A	3	5	.375	19	7	1	1	2	66^1	83	9	25	23	14.8	6.24	73	.307	.368	0	—	0	-13	-12	-1	-1.2
1988	NY-A	1	2	.333	7	2	0	0	0	19^2	27	5	13	4	18.3	6.86	57	.333	.426	0	—	0	-6	-6	0	-0.6
1989	NY-A	1	0	1.000	2	0	0	0	0	0^2	2	0	1	0	40.5	13.50	29	.500	.600	0	—	0	-1	-1	0	0.0
Total	4	9	11	.450	38	18	3	3	2	142^2	178	26	51	47	14.6	5.49	78	.309	.368	0	—	0	-19	-19	-1	-1.8

● **RANDY NIEMANN** Niemann, Randal Harold b: 11/15/55, Scotia, Cal. BL/TL, 6'4", 200 lbs. Deb: 5/20/79

YEAR	TM/L	W	L	PCT	G	GS	CG	SH	SV	IP	H	HR	BB	SO	RAT	ERA	ERA+	OAV	OOB	BH	AVG	PB	PR	/A	PD	TPI
1979	Hou-N	3	2	.600	26	7	3	2	1	67	68	1	22	24	12.2	3.76	93	.272	.333	2	.133	-0	-0	-2	-1	-0.3
1980	Hou-N	0	1	.000	22	1	0	0	1	33	40	2	12	18	14.2	5.45	60	.299	.356	2	.333	1	-7	-8	1	-0.7
1982	Pit-N	1	1	.500	20	0	0	0	1	35^1	34	1	17	26	13.5	5.09	73	.254	.346	2	1.000	1	-6	-5	1	-0.4
1983	Pit-N	0	1	.000	8	1	0	0	0	13^2	20	2	7	8	18.4	9.22	40	.357	.438	0	.000	-0	-8	-8	0	-0.8
1984	Chi-A	0	0	—	5	0	0	0	0	5^1	5	0	5	5	16.9	1.69	246	.263	.417	0	—	0	1	1	0	0.1
1985	NY-N	0	0	—	4	0	0	0	0	4^2	5	0	0	2	9.6	0.00	—	.278	.278	0	—	0	2	2	0	0.2
1986	NY-N	2	3	.400	31	1	0	0	0	35^2	44	2	12	18	14.1	3.79	93	.308	.361	2	.333	1	-0	-1	1	0.1
1987	Min-A	1	0	1.000	6	0	0	0	0	5^1	3	0	7	1	20.3	8.44	55	.158	.429	0	—	0	-2	-2	0	-0.2
Total	8	7	8	.467	122	10	3	2	3	200	219	8	82	102	13.8	4.64	77	.283	.357	8	.267	2	-21	-24	2	-2.0

● **JACK NIEMES** Niemes, Jacob Leland b: 10/19/19, Cincinnati, Ohio d: 3/4/66, Hamilton, Ohio BR/TL, 6'1", 180 lbs. Deb: 5/30/43

YEAR	TM/L	W	L	PCT	G	GS	CG	SH	SV	IP	H	HR	BB	SO	RAT	ERA	ERA+	OAV	OOB	BH	AVG	PB	PR	/A	PD	TPI
1943	Cin-N	0	0	—	3	0	0	0	0	3	5	0	2	1	21.0	6.00	55	.385	.467	0	—	0	-1	-1	-0	-0.1

● **CHUCK NIESON** Nieson, Charles Bassett b: 9/24/42, Hanford, Cal. BR/TR, 6'2", 185 lbs. Deb: 9/18/64

YEAR	TM/L	W	L	PCT	G	GS	CG	SH	SV	IP	H	HR	BB	SO	RAT	ERA	ERA+	OAV	OOB	BH	AVG	PB	PR	/A	PD	TPI
1964	Min-A	0	0	—	2	0	0	0	0	2	1	1	1	5	9.0	4.50	79	.143	.250	0	—	0	-0	-0	0	0.0

● **JUAN NIEVES** Nieves, Juan Manuel (Cruz) b: 1/5/65, Las Lomas, P.R. BL/TL, 6'3", 175 lbs. Deb: 4/10/86

YEAR	TM/L	W	L	PCT	G	GS	CG	SH	SV	IP	H	HR	BB	SO	RAT	ERA	ERA+	OAV	OOB	BH	AVG	PB	PR	/A	PD	TPI
1986	Mil-A	11	12	.478	35	33	4	3	0	184^2	224	17	77	116	14.7	4.92	88	.299	.366	0	—	0	-15	-12	-2	-1.4
1987	Mil-A	14	8	.636	34	33	3	1	0	195^2	199	24	100	163	13.8	4.88	94	.264	.351	0	—	0	-9	-7	-1	-0.8
1988	Mil-A	7	5	.583	25	15	1	1	1	110^1	84	13	50	73	11.0	4.08	98	.208	.297	0	—	0	-1	-1	-0	-0.2
Total	3	32	25	.561	94	81	8	5	1	490^2	507	54	227	352	13.5	4.71	92	.266	.345	0	—	0	-26	-20	-4	-2.4

● **JOHNNY NIGGELING** Niggeling, John Arnold b: 7/10/03, Remsen, Iowa d: 9/16/63, LeMars, Iowa BR/TR, 6', 170 lbs. Deb: 4/30/38

YEAR	TM/L	W	L	PCT	G	GS	CG	SH	SV	IP	H	HR	BB	SO	RAT	ERA	ERA+	OAV	OOB	BH	AVG	PB	PR	/A	PD	TPI
1938	Bos-N	1	0	1.000	2	0	0	0	0	2	4	0	1	1	22.5	9.00	38	.400	.455	0	—	0	-1	-1	-0	-0.1
1939	Cin-N	2	1	.667	10	5	2	1	0	40^1	51	2	13	20	14.7	5.80	66	.309	.367	2	.154	-0	-8	-9	-0	-0.9
1940	StL-A	7	11	.389	28	20	10	1	0	153^2	148	9	69	82	13.0	4.45	103	.250	.333	9	.176	-1	-1	2	-0	0.1
1941	StL-A	7	9	.438	24	20	13	1	0	168^1	168	17	63	68	12.4	3.80	113	.255	.320	10	.167	-1	7	9	-1	0.7
1942	StL-A	15	11	.577	28	27	16	3	0	206^1	173	10	93	107	12.1	2.66	139	.226	.319	10	.139	-2	23	24	-2	2.2
1943	StL-A	6	8	.429	20	20	7	0	0	150^1	122	7	57	73	11.1	3.17	105	.220	.299	3	.061	-4	2	3	-0	-0.3
	Was-A	4	2	.667	6	6	5	3	0	51	27	0	17	24	7.8	0.88	363	.153	.227	5	.278	1	14	13	0	1.9
	Yr	10	10	.500	26	26	12	3	0	201^1	149	7	74	97	10.0	2.59	127	.202	.275	8	.119	-3	16	16	0	1.6
1944	Was-A	10	8	.556	24	24	14	2	0	206	164	5	88	121	11.2	2.32	141	.221	.307	9	.130	-2	25	21	-1	2.0
1945	Was-A	7	12	.368	26	25	8	2	0	176^2	161	7	73	90	12.1	3.16	98	.240	.318	7	.119	-3	4	-1	-2	-0.7
1946	Was-A	3	2	.600	8	6	3	0	0	38	39	1	21	10	14.4	4.03	83	.265	.361	2	.182	0	-2	-3	-0	-0.3
	Bos-N	2	5	.286	8	8	3	0	0	58	54	2	21	24	11.8	3.26	105	.243	.311	2	.111	-1	1	1	0	0.0
Total	9	64	69	.481	184	161	81	12	0	1250^2	1111	60	516	620	12.0	3.22	113	.236	.316	59	.140	-14	63	58	-7	4.6

● **AL NIPPER** Nipper, Albert Samuel b: 4/2/59, San Diego, Cal. BR/TR, 6', 194 lbs. Deb: 9/06/83

YEAR	TM/L	W	L	PCT	G	GS	CG	SH	SV	IP	H	HR	BB	SO	RAT	ERA	ERA+	OAV	OOB	BH	AVG	PB	PR	/A	PD	TPI
1983	Bos-A	1	1	.500	3	2	1	0	0	16	17	0	7	5	14.1	2.25	193	.293	.379	0	—	0	3	4	-0	0.1
1984	Bos-A	11	6	.647	29	24	6	0	0	182^2	183	18	52	84	11.9	3.89	107	.257	.313	0	—	0	2	5	3	0.7
1985	Bos-A	9	12	.429	25	25	5	0	0	162	157	14	82	85	13.8	4.06	106	.256	.352	0	—	0	2	4	2	0.6
1986	*Bos-A	10	12	.455	26	26	3	0	0	159	186	24	47	79	13.4	5.38	77	.290	.342	0	—	0	-21	-21	3	-1.7
1987	Bos-A	11	12	.478	30	30	6	0	0	174	196	30	62	89	13.7	5.43	84	.284	.349	0	—	0	-19	-17	1	-1.5
1988	Chi-N	2	4	.333	22	12	0	0	1	80	72	9	34	27	12.3	3.04	119	.238	.322	2	.087	-1	4	5	-2	0.3
1990	Cle-A	2	3	.400	9	5	0	0	0	24	35	2	19	12	21.0	6.75	58	.354	.467	0	—	0	-8	-8	-0	-0.7
Total	7	46	50	.479	144	124	21	0	1	797^2	846	97	303	381	13.3	4.52	93	.271	.342	2	.087	-1	-37	-28	7	-2.2

YEAR TM/L	W	L	PCT	G	GS	CG	SH	SV	IP	H	HR	BB	SO	RAT	ERA	ERA+	OAV	OOB	BH	AVG	PB	PR	/A	PD	TPI
● MERLIN NIPPERT	Nippert, Merlin Lee b: 9/1/38, Mangum, Okla. BR/TR, 6'1", 175 lbs. Deb: 9/12/62																								
1962 Bos-A	0	0	—	4	0	0	0	0	6	4	1	4	3	12.0	4.50	92	.200	.333	0	—	0	-0	-0	-0	0.0
● RON NISCHWITZ	Nischwitz, Ronald Lee b: 7/1/37, Dayton, Ohio BB/TL, 6'3", 205 lbs. Deb: 9/04/61																								
1961 Det-A	0	1	.000	6	1	0	0	0	11^{1}	13	2	8	8	16.7	5.56	74	.295	.404	0	.000	-0	-2	-2	-0	-0.2
1962 Det-A	4	5	.444	48	0	0	0	4	64^{2}	73	5	26	28	13.9	3.90	104	.285	.353	5	.417	2	1	1	0	0.4
1963 Cle-A	0	2	.000	14	0	0	0	1	16^{2}	17	3	8	10	13.5	6.48	56	.262	.342	0	.000	-0	-5	-5	0	-0.5
1965 Det-A	1	0	1.000	20	0	0	0	1	22^{2}	21	2	6	12	10.7	2.78	125	.259	.310	0	.000	-0	2	2	-0	0.1
Total 4	5	8	.385	88	1	0	0	6	115^{1}	124	12	48	58	13.5	4.21	92	.278	.349	5	.278	1	-5	-4	0	-0.2
● OTHO NITCHOLAS	Nitcholas, Otho James b: 9/13/08, McKinney, Tex. d: 9/11/86, McKinney, Tex. BR/TR, 6', 190 lbs. Deb: 4/18/45																								
1945 Bro-N	1	0	1.000	7	0	0	0	0	18^{2}	19	4	1	4	9.6	5.30	71	.257	.267	1	.250	0	-3	-3	-0	-0.3
● WILLARD NIXON	Nixon, Willard Lee b: 6/17/28, Taylorsville, Ga. BL/TR, 6'2", 195 lbs. Deb: 7/07/50																								
1950 Bos-A	8	6	.571	22	15	2	0	2	101^{1}	126	8	58	57	16.5	6.04	81	.310	.398	5	.139	-1	-16	-13	-0	-1.3
1951 Bos-A	7	4	.636	33	14	2	1	1	125	136	12	56	70	14.3	4.90	91	.285	.368	13	.289	3	-11	-6	-0	-0.3
1952 Bos-A	5	4	.556	23	13	5	0	0	103^{2}	115	12	61	50	15.6	4.86	81	.290	.390	11	.208	1	-14	-11	1	-0.9
1953 Bos-A	4	8	.333	23	15	5	1	0	116^{2}	114	6	59	57	13.4	3.93	107	.254	.343	8	.190	0	1	4	-0	0.4
1954 Bos-A	11	12	.478	31	30	8	2	0	199^{2}	182	16	87	102	12.5	4.06	101	.248	.335	18	.265	5	-7	1	1	0.8
1955 Bos-A	12	10	.545	31	31	7	3	0	208	207	10	85	95	12.8	4.07	105	.259	.333	18	.261	5	-2	5	2	1.3
1956 Bos-A	9	8	.529	23	22	9	1	0	145^{1}	142	9	57	74	12.8	4.21	110	.255	.333	11	.204	-1	-1	7	2	0.7
1957 Bos-A	12	13	.480	29	29	11	1	0	191	207	10	56	96	12.7	3.68	108	.280	.337	22	.293	5	2	7	-1	1.1
1958 Bos-A	1	7	.125	10	8	2	0	0	43^{1}	48	7	11	15	12.3	6.02	67	.281	.324	5	.294	1	-11	-10	0	-0.9
Total 9	69	72	.489	225	177	51	9	3	1234	1277	90	530	616	13.5	4.39	97	.270	.349	111	.242	19	-59	-16	5	0.9
● JUNIOR NOBOA	Noboa, Miliciades Arturo (Diaz) b: 11/10/64, Azua, D.R. BR/TR, 5'10", 160 lbs. Deb: 8/22/84 ♦																								
1990 Mon-N	0	0	—	1	0	0	0	0	0^{2}	0	0	1	0	13.5	0.00	—	.000	.500	42	.266	0	0	0	0	0.0
● THE ONLY NOLAN	Nolan, Edward Sylvester b: 11/7/1857, Paterson, N.J. d: 5/18/13, Paterson, N.J. BL/TR, 5'8", 171 lbs. Deb: 5/01/1878																								
1878 Ind-N	13	22	.371	38	38	37	1	0	347	357	1	56	125	10.7	2.57	79	.253	.281	37	.243	5	-10	-21	2	-1.2
1881 Cle-N	8	14	.364	22	21	20	0	0	180	183	3	38	54	11.1	3.05	86	.251	.288	41	.244	1	-6	-9	-1	-0.8
1883 Pit-a	0	7	.000	7	7	6	0	0	55	81	0	10	23	14.9	4.25	75	.322	.348	8	.308	1	-6	-6	-0	-0.4
1884 Wil-U	1	4	.200	5	5	5	0	0	40	44	1	7	52	11.5	2.93	113	.261	.291	9	.273	1	0	2	1	0.3
1885 Phi-N	1	5	.167	7	7	6	0	0	54	55	1	24	20	13.2	4.17	67	.256	.331	2	.077	-2	-8	-8	-1	-0.9
Total 5	23	52	.307	79	78	74	1	0	676	720	6	135	274	11.4	2.98	81	.259	.293	97	.240	7	-29	-43	1	-3.0
● GARY NOLAN	Nolan, Gary Lynn b: 5/27/48, Herlong, Cal. BR/TR, 6'2.5", 197 lbs. Deb: 4/15/67																								
1967 Cin-N	14	8	.636	33	32	8	5	0	226^{2}	193	18	62	206	10.3	2.58	145	.228	.284	7	.104	-2	20	29	-1	3.1
1968 Cin-N	9	4	.692	23	22	4	2	0	150	105	10	49	111	9.4	2.40	132	.196	.267	6	.130	2	10	13	-2	1.5
1969 Cin-N	8	8	.500	16	15	2	1	0	108^{2}	102	11	40	83	11.8	3.56	106	.247	.313	8	.229	3	0	2	-2	0.5
1970 *Cin-N	18	7	.720	37	37	4	2	0	250^{2}	226	25	96	181	11.6	3.27	123	.240	.311	13	.159	1	22	21	-1	2.1
1971 Cin-N	12	15	.444	35	35	9	0	0	244^{2}	208	12	59	146	9.9	3.16	106	.227	.275	11	.147	-1	8	5	1	0.6
1972 *Cin-N†	15	5	**.750**	25	25	6	2	0	176	147	13	30	90	9.1	1.99	161	.227	.262	7	.117	-1	29	24	-1	2.5
1973 Cin-N	0	1	.000	2	2	0	0	0	10^{1}	6	1	7	3	11.3	3.48	98	.167	.302	0	.000	0	0	-0	-0	0.0
1975 *Cin-N	15	9	.625	32	32	5	1	0	210^{2}	202	18	29	74	9.9	3.16	114	.251	.278	12	.176	2	11	10	-2	1.0
1976 *Cin-N	15	9	.625	34	34	7	1	0	239^{1}	232	28	27	113	9.8	3.46	101	.254	.276	8	.101	-3	1	1	-4	-0.6
1977 Cin-N	4	1	.800	8	8	0	0	0	39^{1}	53	5	12	28	14.9	4.81	82	.321	.367	1	.067	-1	-4	-4	-0	-0.5
Cal-A	0	3	.000	5	5	0	0	0	18^{1}	31	5	2	4	16.2	8.84	44	.365	.379	0	—	0	-10	-10	-0	-0.9
Total 10	110	70	.611	250	247	45	14	0	1674^{2}	1505	146	413	1039	10.4	3.08	116	.239	.287	73	.138	1	87	93	-12	9.3
● DICK NOLD	Nold, Richard Louis b: 5/4/43, San Francisco, Cal. BR/TR, 6'2", 190 lbs. Deb: 8/19/67																								
1967 Was-A	0	2	.000	7	3	0	0	0	20^{1}	19	1	13	10	14.2	4.87	65	.241	.348	0	.000	-0	-4	-4	-0	-0.4
● DICKIE NOLES	Noles, Dickie Ray b: 11/19/56, Charlotte, N.C. BR/TR, 6'2", 190 lbs. Deb: 7/05/79																								
1979 Phi-N	3	4	.429	14	14	0	0	0	90	80	6	38	42	12.0	3.80	101	.246	.329	3	.100	-1	-1	0	1	0.0
1980 *Phi-N	1	4	.200	48	3	0	0	6	81	80	5	42	57	13.7	3.89	97	.254	.344	4	.308	1	-3	-1	-0	0.0
1981 *Phi-N	2	2	.500	13	8	0	0	0	58^{1}	57	2	23	34	12.8	4.17	87	.260	.339	2	.105	-1	-4	-4	-1	-0.6
1982 Chi-N	10	13	.435	31	30	2	2	0	171	180	11	61	85	12.9	4.42	84	.274	.340	6	.107	-2	-16	-13	-0	-1.5
1983 Chi-N	5	10	.333	24	18	1	1	0	116^{1}	133	9	37	59	13.2	4.72	80	.287	.341	9	.237	2	-14	-12	-0	-1.1
1984 Chi-N	2	2	.500	21	1	0	0	0	50^{2}	60	4	16	14	13.7	5.15	76	.305	.360	0	.000	-1	-9	-7	-1	-0.9
Tex-A	2	3	.400	18	6	0	0	0	57^{2}	60	6	30	39	14.8	5.15	80	.262	.360	0	—	0	-7	-6	-1	-0.8
1985 Tex-A	4	8	.333	28	13	0	0	1	110^{1}	129	11	33	59	13.7	5.06	84	.289	.346	0	—	0	-11	-10	1	-0.9
1986 Cle-A	3	2	.600	32	0	0	0	0	54^{2}	56	9	30	32	15.0	5.10	81	.269	.374	0	—	0	-6	-6	0	-0.5
1987 Chi-N	4	2	.667	41	1	0	0	2	64^{1}	59	1	27	33	12.7	3.50	122	.239	.326	0	.000	-1	4	6	1	0.5
Det-A	0	0	—	4	0	0	0	2	2	2	0	1	0	13.5	4.50	94	.250	.333	0	—	0	-0	-0	0	0.3
1988 Bal-A	0	2	.000	2	2	0	0	0	3^{1}	11	2	0	1	32.4	24.30	16	.500	.522	0	—	0	-8	-8	-0	-0.5
1990 Phi-N	0	1	.000	1	0	0	0	0	0^{1}	2	0	0	0	54.0	27.00	14	.667	.667	0	—	0	-1	-1	0	-0.1
Total 11	36	53	.404	277	96	3	3	11	860	909	66	338	455	13.4	4.56	86	.272	.345	24	.136	-4	-75	-61	-2	-6.1
● ERIC NOLTE	Nolte, Eric Carl b: 4/28/64, Canoga Park, Cal. BL/TL, 6'3", 205 lbs. Deb: 8/01/87																								
1987 SD-N	2	6	.250	12	12	1	0	0	67^{1}	57	6	36	44	12.7	3.21	123	.226	.328	2	.095	-1	7	6	-1	0.5
1988 SD-N	0	0	—	2	0	0	0	0	3	3	1	2	1	15.0	6.00	57	.273	.385	0	—	0	-1	-1	-0	-0.1
1989 SD-N	0	0	—	3	1	0	0	0	9	15	1	7	8	22.0	11.00	32	.375	.468	0	.000	-0	-8	-8	-0	-0.7
1991 SD-N	3	2	.600	6	6	0	0	0	22	37	6	10	15	19.2	11.05	34	.378	.435	1	.111	-0	-18	-18	-0	-1.6
Tex-A	0	0	—	3	0	0	0	0	2^{2}	3	0	3	1	20.3	3.38	119	.273	.429	0	—	0	0	0	-0	0.1
Total 4	5	8	.385	26	19	1	0	0	104	115	14	58	69	15.1	5.63	69	.279	.371	3	.094	-1	-20	-20	-1	-1.8
● JERRY NOPS	Nops, Jeremiah H. b: 6/23/1875, Toledo, Ohio d: 3/26/37, Camden, N.J. BL/TL, 5'8.5", 168 lbs. Deb: 9/07/1896																								
1896 Phi-N	1	0	1.000	1	1	1	0	0	7	11	0	1	1	15.4	5.14	84	.354	.374	0	.000	-1	-1	-1	-0	-0.1
Bal-N	2	1	.667	3	3	3	0	0	22	29	0	2	8	12.7	6.14	70	.315	.329	1	.111	-1	-4	-5	-0	-0.4
Yr	3	1	.750	4	4	4	0	0	29	40	0	3	9	13.3	5.90	73	.325	.341	1	.077	-2	-5	-5	-0	-0.5
1897 *Bal-N	20	6	.769	30	25	23	1	0	220^{2}	235	5	52	69	12.1	2.81	148	.271	.318	18	.196	-3	37	33	-2	2.5
1898 Bal-N	16	9	.640	33	29	23	2	0	235	241	5	78	91	12.8	3.56	101	.263	.332	20	.220	2	1	0	-4	-0.2
1899 Bal-N	17	11	.607	33	33	26	2	0	259	296	1	71	60	13.1	4.03	98	.287	.339	29	.276	1	-5	-2	-3	-0.3
1900 Bro-N	4	4	.500	9	8	6	1	0	68	79	1	18	22	13.1	3.84	100	.290	.338	4	.160	-1	-1	0	-1	-0.2
1901 Bal-A	12	10	.545	27	23	17	1	1	176^{2}	192	5	59	43	13.4	4.08	95	.274	.341	13	.220	-0	-8	-4	-4	-0.8
Total 6	72	41	.637	136	122	99	7	1	988^{1}	1083	17	281	294	12.9	3.70	106	.277	.333	85	.221	-3	19	23	-15	0.5
● WAYNE NORDHAGEN	Nordhagen, Wayne Oren b: 7/4/48, Thief River Falls, Minn. BR/TR, 6'2", 205 lbs. Deb: 7/16/76 ♦																								
1979 Chi-A	0	0	—	2	0	0	0	0	2	2	0	1	2	13.5	9.00	47	.286	.375	54	.280	2	-1	-1	-0	-0.1
● JOHN NORIEGA	Noriega, John Alan b: 12/20/43, Ogden, Utah BR/TR, 6'4", 185 lbs. Deb: 5/01/69																								
1969 Cin-N	0	0	—	5	0	0	0	0	7^{2}	12	1	3	4	17.6	5.87	64	.400	.455	0	—	0	-2	-2	-0	-0.2
1970 Cin-N	0	0	—	8	0	0	0	0	18	25	0	10	6	18.5	8.00	50	.333	.425	1	.250	0	-8	-8	1	-0.7
Total 2	0	0	—	13	0	0	0	0	25^{2}	37	1	13	10	18.2	7.36	54	.352	.433	1	.250	0	-10	-10	1	-0.9

● FRED NORMAN Norman, Fredie Hubert b: 8/20/42, San Antonio, Tex. BB/TL, 5'8", 160 lbs. Deb: 9/21/62

YEAR	TM/L	W	L	PCT	G	GS	CG	SH	SV	IP	H	HR	BB	SO	RAT	ERA	ERA+	OAV	OOB	BH	AVG	PB	PR	/A	PD	TPI
1962	KC-A	0	0	—	2	0	0	0	0	4	4	0	1	2	11.3	2.25	185	.250	.294	0	—	0	1	1	-0	0.1
1963	KC-A	0	1	.000	2	2	0	0	0	6^1	9	1	7	6	22.7	11.37	34	.346	.485	0	.000	-0	-5	-5	0	-0.5
1964	Chi-N	0	4	.000	8	5	0	0	0	31^2	34	9	21	20	15.9	6.54	57	.279	.389	1	.091	-1	-11	-10	-0	-1.0
1966	Chi-N	0	0	—	2	0	0	0	0	4	5	0	2	6	15.8	4.50	82	.313	.389	0	—	0	-0	-0	-0	0.0
1967	Chi-N	0	0	—	1	0	0	0	0	1	0	0	0	3	0.0	0.00	—	.000	.000	0	—	0	0	0	0	0.0
1970	LA-N	2	0	1.000	30	0	0	0	1	62	65	8	33	47	14.5	5.23	73	.273	.366	1	.143	0	-8	-10	-1	-1.0
	StL-N	0	0	—	1	0	0	0	0	1	1	0	0	0	9.0	0.00	—	.333	.333	0	—	0	0	0	0	0.1
	Yr	2	0	1.000	31	0	0	0	1	63	66	8	33	47	14.1	5.14	75	.269	.356	1	.143	0	-8	-9	-1	-0.9
1971	StL-N	0	0	—	4	0	0	0	0	3^2	7	1	7	4	34.4	12.27	29	.438	.609	0	—	0	-4	-4	-0	-0.4
	SD-N	3	12	.200	20	18	5	0	0	127^1	114	7	56	77	12.2	3.32	99	.240	.323	9	.237	2	2	-0	-1	0.1
	Yr	3	12	.200	24	18	5	0	0	131	121	8	63	81	12.8	3.57	92	.246	.334	9	.237	2	-2	-4	-1	-0.3
1972	SD-N	9	11	.450	42	28	10	6	2	211^2	195	18	88	167	12.1	3.44	95	.244	.321	8	.125	1	0	-4	-1	-0.4
1973	SD-N	1	7	.125	12	11	1	0	0	74	72	9	29	49	12.4	4.26	82	.262	.334	3	.136	-0	-5	-6	1	-0.6
	*Cin-N	12	6	.667	24	24	7	3	0	166^1	136	18	72	112	11.3	3.30	103	.224	.307	3	.052	-4	7	2	-1	-0.3
	Yr	13	13	.500	36	35	8	3	0	240^1	208	27	101	161	11.6	3.60	95	.235	.314	6	.075	-4	2	-5	-0	-0.9
1974	Cin-N	13	12	.520	35	26	8	2	0	186^1	170	15	68	141	11.6	3.14	111	.241	.309	8	.131	-2	10	7	-3	0.2
1975	*Cin-N	12	4	.750	34	26	2	0	0	188	163	23	84	119	11.8	3.73	96	.235	.318	7	.117	-2	-2	-3	-2	-0.7
1976	*Cin-N	12	7	.632	33	24	8	3	0	180^1	153	10	70	126	11.3	3.09	113	.231	.308	7	.140	-1	8	8	-3	0.4
1977	Cin-N	14	13	.519	35	34	8	1	0	221^1	200	28	98	160	12.2	3.38	116	.241	.324	8	.110	-2	13	14	-0	1.1
1978	Cin-N	11	9	.550	36	31	0	0	1	177^1	173	19	82	111	13.1	3.70	96	.255	.338	7	.140	-1	-3	-3	-1	-0.5
1979	*Cin-N	11	13	.458	34	31	5	0	0	195^1	193	14	57	95	11.5	3.64	103	.258	.311	9	.153	0	2	2	-2	0.1
1980	Mon-N	4	4	.500	48	8	2	0	4	98	96	8	40	58	12.8	4.13	86	.259	.337	1	.050	-2	-6	-6	-1	-1.0
Total	16	104	103	.502	403	268	56	15	8	1939^2	1790	188	815	1303	12.2	3.64	98	.246	.324	72	.125	-11	-0	-17	-15	-4.3

● MIKE NORRIS Norris, Michael Kelvin b: 3/19/55, San Francisco, Cal. BR/TR, 6'2", 175 lbs. Deb: 4/10/75

YEAR	TM/L	W	L	PCT	G	GS	CG	SH	SV	IP	H	HR	BB	SO	RAT	ERA	ERA+	OAV	OOB	BH	AVG	PB	PR	/A	PD	TPI
1975	Oak-A	1	0	1.000	4	3	1	1	0	16^2	6	0	8	5	7.6	0.00	—	.107	.219	0	—	0	7	7	0	0.8
1976	Oak-A	4	5	.444	24	19	1	1	0	96	91	10	56	44	14.0	4.78	70	.250	.353	0	—	0	-13	-15	3	-1.2
1977	Oak-A	2	7	.222	16	12	1	1	0	77^1	77	14	31	35	13.0	4.77	84	.260	.338	0	.000	0	-6	-6	1	-0.5
1978	Oak-A	0	5	.000	14	5	1	0	0	49	46	2	35	36	15.4	5.51	66	.249	.377	0	—	0	-10	-10	-0	-0.8
1979	Oak-A	5	8	.385	29	18	3	0	0	146^1	146	11	94	96	15.3	4.80	84	.265	.381	0	—	0	-9	-12	-1	-1.0
1980	Oak-A	22	9	.710	33	33	24	1	0	284^1	215	18	83	180	9.6	2.53	149	**.209**	.272	0	—	0	**47**	**39**	3	**4.8**
1981	*Oak-A★	12	9	.571	23	23	12	2	0	172^2	145	17	63	78	11.4	3.75	93	.228	.308	0	—	0	-2	-5	-0	-0.6
1982	Oak-A	7	11	.389	28	28	7	1	0	166^1	154	25	84	83	13.2	4.76	82	.242	.336	0	—	0	-13	-16	1	-1.5
1983	Oak-A	4	5	.444	16	16	2	0	0	88^2	68	11	36	63	10.9	3.76	103	.213	.299	0	—	0	3	1	-2	0.1
1990	Oak-A	1	0	1.000	14	0	0	0	0	27	24	0	9	16	11.7	3.00	124	.242	.318	0	—	0	3	2	0	0.3
Total	10	58	59	.496	201	157	52	7	0	1124^1	972	108	499	636	12.1	3.89	97	.233	.322	0	.000	0	7	-16	5	0.4

● LOU NORTH North, Louis Alexander b: 6/15/1891, Elgin, Ill. d: 5/16/74, Shelton, Conn. BR/TR, 5'11", 175 lbs. Deb: 8/22/13

YEAR	TM/L	W	L	PCT	G	GS	CG	SH	SV	IP	H	HR	BB	SO	RAT	ERA	ERA+	OAV	OOB	BH	AVG	PB	PR	/A	PD	TPI
1913	Det-A	0	1	.000	1	1	0	0	0	6	10	1	9	3	28.5	15.00	19	.357	.514	0	.000	-0	-8	-8	-0	-0.6
1917	StL-N	0	0	—	5	0	0	0	0	11^1	14	1	4	4	14.3	3.97	68	.350	.409	0	.000	-0	-2	-2	0	-0.2
1920	StL-N	3	2	.600	24	6	3	0	1	88	90	3	32	37	12.7	3.27	91	.278	.346	7	.226	0	-1	-3	-1	-0.4
1921	StL-N	4	4	.500	40	0	0	0	**7**	86^1	81	5	32	28	11.9	3.54	103	.256	.327	3	.158	-1	**2**	**1**	-2	-0.2
1922	StL-N	10	3	.769	**53**	11	4	0	4	149^2	164	4	64	84	14.1	4.45	87	.283	.361	11	.234	2	-6	-10	4	-0.3
1923	StL-N	3	4	.429	34	3	0	0	1	71^2	90	8	31	24	15.6	5.15	76	.308	.380	4	.182	-1	-9	-10	1	-1.0
1924	StL-N	0	0	—	6	0	0	0	0	14^2	15	1	9	8	14.7	6.75	56	.273	.375	1	.250	-0	-5	-5	-0	-0.5
	Bos-N	1	2	.333	9	4	1	0	0	35^1	45	1	19	11	16.3	5.35	71	.321	.403	1	.111	-1	-6	-6	-1	-0.7
	Yr	1	2	.333	15	4	1	0	0	50	60	2	28	19	15.8	5.76	66	.308	.395	2	.154	-1	-11	-11	-1	-1.2
Total	7	21	16	.568	172	25	8	0	13	463	509	24	200	199	14.0	4.43	82	.287	.363	27	.197	-1	-34	-42	0	-3.9

● JAKE NORTHROP Northrop, George Howard "Jerky" b: 3/5/1888, Monroeton, Pa. d: 11/16/45, Monroeton, Pa. BL/TR, 5'11", 170 lbs. Deb: 7/29/18

YEAR	TM/L	W	L	PCT	G	GS	CG	SH	SV	IP	H	HR	BB	SO	RAT	ERA	ERA+	OAV	OOB	BH	AVG	PB	PR	/A	PD	TPI
1918	Bos-N	5	1	.833	7	4	4	1	0	40	26	0	3	4	6.5	1.35	199	.183	.200	2	.154	-1	6	6	0	0.6
1919	Bos-N	1	5	.167	11	3	2	0	0	37^1	43	2	10	9	13.0	4.58	62	.301	.351	4	.500	3	-7	-7	1	-0.4
Total	2	6	6	.500	18	7	6	1	0	77^1	69	2	13	13	9.7	2.91	95	.242	.278	6	.286	2	-1	-1	1	0.2

● EFFIE NORTON Norton, Elisha Strong "Leiter" b: 8/17/1873, Conneaut, Ohio d: 3/5/50, Aspinwall, Pa. BR/TR, Deb: 8/08/1896

YEAR	TM/L	W	L	PCT	G	GS	CG	SH	SV	IP	H	HR	BB	SO	RAT	ERA	ERA+	OAV	OOB	BH	AVG	PB	PR	/A	PD	TPI
1896	Was-N	3	1	.750	8	5	2	0	0	44	49	2	14	13	14.1	3.07	144	.280	.353	4	.211	-0	6	7	-0	0.5
1897	Was-N	2	1	.667	4	2	1	0	0	17	31	0	11	3	22.2	6.88	63	.388	.463	5	.278	1	-5	-5	-0	-0.4
Total	2	5	2	.714	12	7	3	0	0	61	80	2	25	16	16.4	4.13	106	.314	.388	9	.243	0	1	2	-1	0.1

● TOM NORTON Norton, Thomas John b: 4/26/50, Elyria, Ohio BR/TR, 6'1", 200 lbs. Deb: 4/18/72

YEAR	TM/L	W	L	PCT	G	GS	CG	SH	SV	IP	H	HR	BB	SO	RAT	ERA	ERA+	OAV	OOB	BH	AVG	PB	PR	/A	PD	TPI
1972	Min-A	0	1	.000	21	0	0	0	0	32^1	31	1	14	22	12.8	2.78	115	.252	.333	0	—	0	1	2	1	0.3

● RANDY NOSEK Nosek, Randall William b: 1/8/67, Omaha, Neb. BR/TR, 6'4", 215 lbs. Deb: 5/27/89

YEAR	TM/L	W	L	PCT	G	GS	CG	SH	SV	IP	H	HR	BB	SO	RAT	ERA	ERA+	OAV	OOB	BH	AVG	PB	PR	/A	PD	TPI
1989	Det-A	0	2	.000	2	2	0	0	0	5^1	7	2	10	4	28.7	13.50	28	.333	.548	0	—	0	-6	-6	-0	-0.5
1990	Det-A	1	1	.500	3	2	0	0	0	7	7	1	9	3	20.6	7.71	51	.280	.471	0	—	0	-3	-3	-0	-0.3
Total	2	1	3	.250	5	4	0	0	0	12^1	14	3	19	7	24.1	10.22	38	.304	.508	0	—	0	-9	-9	-0	-0.8

● DON NOTTEBART Nottebart, Donald Edward b: 1/23/36, West Newton, Mass. BR/TR, 6'1", 190 lbs. Deb: 7/01/60

YEAR	TM/L	W	L	PCT	G	GS	CG	SH	SV	IP	H	HR	BB	SO	RAT	ERA	ERA+	OAV	OOB	BH	AVG	PB	PR	/A	PD	TPI
1960	Mil-N	1	0	1.000	5	1	0	0	1	15^1	14	0	15	8	17.0	4.11	83	.233	.387	0	.000	-1	-1	-1	1	-0.1
1961	Mil-N	6	7	.462	38	11	2	0	3	126^1	117	11	48	66	11.9	4.06	92	.251	.323	7	.184	0	-0	-4	2	-0.2
1962	Mil-N	2	2	.500	39	0	0	0	2	64	64	4	20	36	12.4	3.23	117	.258	.324	2	.333	1	5	4	2	0.6
1963	Hou-N	11	8	.579	31	27	9	2	0	193	170	10	39	118	9.8	3.17	99	.234	.275	11	.167	0	3	-0	-0	0.0
1964	Hou-N	6	11	.353	28	24	2	0	0	157	165	12	37	90	11.6	3.90	88	.275	.319	3	.064	-2	-6	-8	4	-0.7
1965	Hou-N	4	15	.211	29	25	3	0	0	158	166	14	55	77	12.9	4.67	72	.273	.338	5	.104	-1	-20	-23	2	-2.2
1966	Cin-N	5	4	.556	59	1	0	0	11	111^1	97	11	43	69	11.5	3.07	127	.235	.311	4	.167	-0	7	10	1	1.1
1967	Cin-N	0	3	.000	47	0	0	0	4	79^1	75	4	19	48	10.9	1.93	194	.253	.303	0	.000	-0	13	16	1	1.8
1969	NY-A	0	0	—	4	0	0	0	0	6	6	1	0	5	10.5	4.50	77	.261	.292	0	—	0	-1	-1	0	-0.1
	Chi-N	1	1	.500	16	0	0	0	0	18	28	2	7	8	17.5	7.00	58	.350	.402	0	.000	0	-7	-6	0	-0.6
Total	9	36	51	.414	296	89	16	2	21	928^1	902	69	283	525	11.7	3.65	96	.256	.315	32	.134	-3	-8	-13	11	-0.4

● CHET NOURSE Nourse, Chester Linwood b: 8/7/1887, Ipswich, Mass. d: 4/20/58, Clearwater, Fla. BR/TR, 6'3", 185 lbs. Deb: 7/27/09

YEAR	TM/L	W	L	PCT	G	GS	CG	SH	SV	IP	H	HR	BB	SO	RAT	ERA	ERA+	OAV	OOB	BH	AVG	PB	PR	/A	PD	TPI
1909	Bos-A	0	0	—	3	0	0	0	0	5	5	0	5	3	18.0	7.20	35	.263	.417	0	.000	-0	-3	-3	0	-0.3

● RAFAEL NOVOA Novoa, Rafael Angel b: 10/26/67, New York, N.Y. BL/TL, 6', 180 lbs. Deb: 7/31/90

YEAR	TM/L	W	L	PCT	G	GS	CG	SH	SV	IP	H	HR	BB	SO	RAT	ERA	ERA+	OAV	OOB	BH	AVG	PB	PR	/A	PD	TPI
1990	SF-N	0	1	.000	7	2	0	0	1	18^2	21	3	13	14	16.4	6.75	54	.284	.391	1	.200	0	-6	-6	-1	-0.7

● WIN NOYES Noyes, Winfield Charles b: 6/16/1889, Pleasanton, Neb. d: 4/8/69, Cashmere, Wash. BR/TR, 6', 180 lbs. Deb: 5/19/13

YEAR	TM/L	W	L	PCT	G	GS	CG	SH	SV	IP	H	HR	BB	SO	RAT	ERA	ERA+	OAV	OOB	BH	AVG	PB	PR	/A	PD	TPI
1913	Bos-N	0	0	—	11	0	0	0	0	20^2	22	1	6	5	13.9	4.79	69	.289	.372	1	.250	0	-4	-3	0	-0.4
1917	Phi-A	10	10	.500	27	22	11	1	1	171	156	5	77	64	12.5	2.95	93	.258	.345	6	.115	-2	-5	-4	-1	-0.7
1919	Phi-A	1	5	.167	10	6	3	0	0	49	66	1	15	20	15.1	5.69	60	.332	.381	2	.125	-1	-13	-12	0	-1.3
	Chi-A	0	0	—	1	1	0	0	0	6	10	0	0	4	15.0	7.50	42	.385	.385	1	.500	0	-3	-3	-0	-0.2
	Yr	1	5	.167	11	7	3	0	0	55	76	1	15	24	14.9	5.89	58	.336	.378	3	.167	-1	-16	-15	0	-1.5
Total	3	11	15	.423	49	29	14	1	1	246^2	254	7	98	93	13.2	3.76	78	.280	.356	10	.135	-3	-25	-22	-1	-2.6

● EDWIN NUNEZ Nunez, Edwin (Martinez) b: 5/27/63, Humacao, P.R. BR/TR, 6'5", 237 lbs. Deb: 4/07/82

YEAR	TM/L	W	L	PCT	G	GS	CG	SH	SV	IP	H	HR	BB	SO	RAT	ERA	ERA+	OAV	OOB	BH	AVG	PB	PR	/A	PD	TPI
1982	Sea-A	1	2	.333	8	5	0	0	0	35^1	36	7	16	27	13.2	4.58	92	.269	.347	0	—	0	-2	-1	0	-0.1
1983	Sea-A	0	4	.000	14	5	0	0	0	37	40	3	22	35	15.8	4.38	97	.278	.385	0	—	0	-1	-0	0	-0.1
1984	Sea-A	2	2	.500	37	0	0	0	7	67^2	55	8	21	57	10.5	3.19	125	.218	.286	0	—	0	6	6	-1	0.6
1985	Sea-A	7	3	.700	70	0	0	0	16	90^1	79	13	34	58	11.3	3.09	136	.234	.305	0	—	0	11	11	0	1.1
1986	Sea-A	1	2	.333	14	1	0	0	0	21^2	25	5	5	17	12.5	5.82	73	.284	.323	0	—	0	-4	-4	-0	-0.4
1987	Sea-A	3	4	.429	48	0	0	0	12	47^1	45	7	18	34	12.2	3.80	124	.262	.335	0	—	0	3	5	-0	0.1
1988	Sea-A	1	4	.200	14	3	0	0	0	29^1	45	4	14	19	18.7	7.98	52	.366	.439	0	—	0	-13	-12	1	-1.3
	NY-N	1	0	1.000	10	0	0	0	0	14	21	1	3	8	15.4	4.50	72	.339	.369	0	—	0	-2	-2	-0	-0.2
1989	Det-A	3	4	.429	27	0	0	0	1	54	49	6	36	41	14.2	4.17	92	.254	.371	0	—	0	-2	-2	1	-0.1
1990	Det-A	3	1	.750	42	0	0	0	6	80^1	65	4	37	66	11.7	2.24	177	.218	.309	0	—	0	15	15	-1	1.5
1991	Mil-A	2	1	.667	23	0	0	0	8	25^1	28	6	13	24	14.6	6.04	66	.277	.360	0	—	0	-5	-6	-0	-0.5
1992	Mil-A	1	1	.500	10	0	0	0	0	13^2	12	1	6	10	11.9	2.63	145	.231	.310	0	—	0	2	2	-0	0.3
	Tex-A	0	2	.000	39	0	0	0	3	45^2	51	5	16	39	13.6	5.52	69	.279	.343	0	—	0	-8	-9	-1	-0.8
	Yr	1	3	.250	49	0	0	0	3	59^1	63	6	22	49	13.2	4.85	79	.268	.336	0	—	0	-6	-7	-1	-0.5
Total	11	25	30	.455	356	14	0	0	53	561^2	551	70	241	435	12.9	4.04	101	.258	.336	0	—	0	-0	2	-1	0.1

● JOSE NUNEZ Nunez, Jose (Jimenez) b: 1/13/64, Jarabacoa, D.R. BR/TR, 6'3", 175 lbs. Deb: 4/09/87

YEAR	TM/L	W	L	PCT	G	GS	CG	SH	SV	IP	H	HR	BB	SO	RAT	ERA	ERA+	OAV	OOB	BH	AVG	PB	PR	/A	PD	TPI
1987	Tor-A	5	2	.714	37	9	0	0	0	97	91	12	58	99	13.8	5.01	90	.256	.360	0	—	0	-6	-6	-1	-0.6
1988	Tor-A	0	1	.000	13	2	0	0	0	29^1	28	3	17	18	14.1	3.07	128	.259	.365	0	—	0	3	3	0	0.3
1989	Tor-A	0	0	—	6	1	0	0	0	10^2	8	0	2	14	8.4	2.53	149	.200	.238	0	—	0	2	1	-0	0.2
1990	Chi-N	4	7	.364	21	10	0	0	0	60^2	61	5	34	40	14.1	6.53	62	.270	.365	0	.000	-1	-18	-17	0	-1.7
Total	4	9	10	.474	77	22	0	0	0	197^2	188	20	111	171	13.7	5.05	84	.258	.356	0	.000	-1	-20	-18	-1	-1.8

● HOWIE NUNN Nunn, Howard Ralph b: 10/18/35, Westfield, N.C. BR/TR, 6', 173 lbs. Deb: 4/11/59

YEAR	TM/L	W	L	PCT	G	GS	CG	SH	SV	IP	H	HR	BB	SO	RAT	ERA	ERA+	OAV	OOB	BH	AVG	PB	PR	/A	PD	TPI
1959	StL-N	2	2	.500	16	0	0	0	0	21^1	23	3	15	20	16.0	7.59	56	.291	.404	0	.000	-0	-9	-8	1	-0.7
1961	Cin-N	2	1	.667	24	0	0	0	0	37^2	35	0	24	26	14.3	3.58	113	.252	.366	2	.250	0	2	2	-0	0.2
1962	Cin-N	0	0	—	6	0	0	0	0	9^2	15	0	3	4	16.8	5.59	72	.375	.419	0	.000	-0	-2	-2	0	-0.2
Total	3	4	3	.571	46	0	0	0	0	68^2	73	3	42	50	15.2	5.11	80	.283	.385	2	.200	-0	-9	-8	1	-0.7

● JOE NUXHALL Nuxhall, Joseph Henry b: 7/30/28, Hamilton, Ohio BL/TL, 6'3", 219 lbs. Deb: 6/10/44

YEAR	TM/L	W	L	PCT	G	GS	CG	SH	SV	IP	H	HR	BB	SO	RAT	ERA	ERA+	OAV	OOB	BH	AVG	PB	PR	/A	PD	TPI
1944	Cin-N	0	0	—	1	0	0	0	0	0^2	2	0	5	0	94.5	67.50	5	.500	.778	0	—	0	-5	-5	-0	-0.4
1952	Cin-N	1	4	.200	37	5	2	0	1	92^1	83	4	42	52	12.5	3.22	117	.246	.334	2	.087	-2	5	6	2	0.6
1953	Cin-N	9	11	.450	30	17	5	1	2	141^2	136	13	69	52	13.5	4.32	101	.252	.345	16	.327	8	-1	1	-2	0.6
1954	Cin-N	12	5	.706	35	14	5	1	0	166^2	188	11	59	85	13.7	3.89	108	.292	.357	9	.173	4	3	6	0	0.9
1955	Cin-N★	17	12	.586	50	33	14	**5**	3	257	240	25	78	98	11.3	3.47	122	.249	.309	17	.198	4	16	22	-2	2.4
1956	Cin-N☆	13	11	.542	44	32	10	2	3	200^2	196	18	87	120	13.0	3.72	107	.257	.338	11	.186	3	1	6	-1	0.8
1957	Cin-N	10	10	.500	39	28	6	2	1	174^1	192	24	53	99	13.0	4.75	87	.275	.332	14	.237	3	-17	-12	-2	-1.2
1958	Cin-N	12	11	.522	36	26	5	0	0	175^2	169	15	63	111	11.9	3.79	109	.257	.323	13	.210	0	3	7	-0	0.6
1959	Cin-N	9	9	.500	28	21	6	1	1	131^2	155	10	35	75	13.1	4.24	96	.292	.337	11	.250	3	-4	-3	-1	-0.1
1960	Cin-N	1	8	.111	38	6	0	0	0	112	130	8	27	72	12.9	4.42	86	.297	.344	2	.077	-1	-8	-7	2	-0.7
1961	KC-A	5	8	.385	37	13	1	0	1	128	135	12	65	81	14.3	5.34	77	.268	.355	19	.292	8	-19	-17	-1	-1.0
1962	LA-A	0	0	—	5	0	0	0	0	5^1	7	0	5	2	21.9	10.13	38	.304	.448	0	—	0	-4	-4	0	-0.3
	Cin-N	5	0	1.000	12	9	1	0	1	66	59	4	25	57	11.6	2.45	164	.240	.313	7	.269	3	11	12	-0	1.5
1963	Cin-N	15	8	.652	35	29	14	2	2	217^1	194	14	39	169	9.9	2.61	128	.237	.277	12	.158	0	16	18	-1	1.8
1964	Cin-N	9	8	.529	32	22	7	4	2	154^2	146	19	51	111	11.8	4.07	89	.250	.317	7	.130	-1	-9	-8	-2	-1.0
1965	Cin-N	11	4	.733	32	16	5	1	2	148^2	142	18	31	117	10.7	3.45	109	.252	.295	8	.178	1	1	5	-3	0.3
1966	Cin-N	6	8	.429	35	16	2	1	0	130	136	14	42	71	12.9	4.50	87	.270	.338	4	.100	-2	-13	-9	-1	-1.2
Total	16	135	117	.536	526	287	83	20	19	2302^2	2310	209	776	1372	12.3	3.90	102	.262	.327	152	.198	29	-21	16	-12	3.6

● RICH NYE Nye, Richard Raymond b: 8/4/44, Oakland, Cal. BL/TL, 6'4", 185 lbs. Deb: 9/16/66

YEAR	TM/L	W	L	PCT	G	GS	CG	SH	SV	IP	H	HR	BB	SO	RAT	ERA	ERA+	OAV	OOB	BH	AVG	PB	PR	/A	PD	TPI
1966	Chi-N	0	2	.000	3	2	0	0	0	17	16	1	7	9	12.2	2.12	174	.254	.329	1	.250	0	3	3	-1	0.3
1967	Chi-N	13	10	.565	35	30	7	0	0	205	179	15	52	119	10.2	3.20	111	.234	.284	16	.213	3	4	8	-0	1.2
1968	Chi-N	7	12	.368	27	20	6	1	1	132^2	145	16	34	74	12.2	3.80	83	.276	.321	8	.182	-0	-12	-9	-0	-1.1
1969	Chi-N	3	5	.375	34	5	1	0	3	68^2	72	13	21	39	12.3	5.11	79	.271	.326	1	.063	-1	-12	-8	-1	-1.1
1970	StL-N	0	0	—	6	0	0	0	0	8	13	2	6	5	21.4	4.50	91	.371	.463	1	.500	1	-0	-0	0	0.0
	Mon-N	3	2	.600	8	6	2	0	0	46^1	47	3	20	21	13.0	4.08	101	.260	.333	3	.176	0	-0	0	0	0.0
	Yr	3	2	.600	14	6	2	0	0	54^1	60	5	26	26	14.2	4.14	99	.276	.354	4	.211	1	-1	-0	0	0.0
Total	5	26	31	.456	113	63	16	1	4	477^2	472	50	140	267	11.6	3.71	96	.257	.311	30	.190	2	-17	-7	-2	-0.7

● JERRY NYMAN Nyman, Gerald Smith b: 11/23/42, Logan, Utah BL/TL, 5'10", 165 lbs. Deb: 8/24/68

YEAR	TM/L	W	L	PCT	G	GS	CG	SH	SV	IP	H	HR	BB	SO	RAT	ERA	ERA+	OAV	OOB	BH	AVG	PB	PR	/A	PD	TPI
1968	Chi-A	2	1	.667	8	7	1	1	0	40^1	38	1	16	27	12.0	2.01	151	.247	.318	2	.154	-0	4	5	-0	0.5
1969	Chi-A	4	4	.500	20	10	2	1	0	64^2	58	7	39	40	13.5	5.29	73	.244	.350	1	.050	-1	-12	-10	-1	-1.2
1970	SD-N	0	2	.000	2	2	0	0	0	5^1	8	1	2	2	16.9	15.19	26	.364	.417	0	—	0	-7	-7	-0	-0.6
Total	3	6	7	.462	30	19	3	2	0	110^1	104	9	57	69	13.1	4.57	78	.251	.342	3	.091	-1	-14	-12	-1	-1.3

● PRINCE OANA Oana, Henry Kauhane b: 1/22/08, Waipahu, Hawaii d: 6/19/76, Austin, Tex. BR/TR, 6'2", 193 lbs. Deb: 4/22/34 ♦

YEAR	TM/L	W	L	PCT	G	GS	CG	SH	SV	IP	H	HR	BB	SO	RAT	ERA	ERA+	OAV	OOB	BH	AVG	PB	PR	/A	PD	TPI
1943	Det-A	3	2	.600	10	0	0	0	0	34	34	4	19	15	14.6	4.50	78	.262	.364	10	.385	5	-5	-4	-0	0.1
1945	Det-A	0	0	—	3	1	0	0	1	11^1	3	0	7	3	7.9	1.59	221	.086	.238	1	.200	-0	2	2	-0	0.2
Total	2	3	2	.600	13	1	0	0	1	45^1	37	4	26	18	12.9	3.77	93	.224	.337	16	.308	5	-2	-1	-1	0.3

● HENRY OBERBECK Oberbeck, Henry A. b: 5/17/1858, Missouri d: 8/26/21, St.Louis, Mo. Deb: 5/07/1883 ♦

YEAR	TM/L	W	L	PCT	G	GS	CG	SH	SV	IP	H	HR	BB	SO	RAT	ERA	ERA+	OAV	OOB	BH	AVG	PB	PR	/A	PD	TPI
1884	Bal-U	0	0	—	2	1	0	0	0	6	9	0	2	1	16.5	3.00	110	.325	.371	23	.184	-0	0	0	-0	0.0
	KC-U	0	5	.000	6	4	3	0	0	29^2	47	0	3	6	15.2	5.76	48	.337	.351	17	.189	-0	-9	-10	-1	-0.9
	Yr	0	5	.000	8	5	3	0	0	35^2	56	0	5	7	15.4	5.30	54	.335	.355	40	.186	-1	-9	-10	-1	-0.9

● DOC OBERLANDER Oberlander, Hartman Louis b: 5/12/1864, Waukegan, Ill. d: 11/14/22, Pryor, Montana TL, Deb: 5/16/1888

YEAR	TM/L	W	L	PCT	G	GS	CG	SH	SV	IP	H	HR	BB	SO	RAT	ERA	ERA+	OAV	OOB	BH	AVG	PB	PR	/A	PD	TPI
1888	Cle-a	1	2	.333	3	3	3	0	0	25^2	27	2	18	23	16.1	5.26	59	.261	.375	3	.214	0	-6	-6	-0	-0.5

● FRANK OBERLIN Oberlin, Frank Rufus "Flossie" b: 3/29/1876, Elsie, Mich. d: 1/6/52, Ashley, Ind. BR/TR, 6'1", 165 lbs. Deb: 9/20/06

YEAR	TM/L	W	L	PCT	G	GS	CG	SH	SV	IP	H	HR	BB	SO	RAT	ERA	ERA+	OAV	OOB	BH	AVG	PB	PR	/A	PD	TPI
1906	Bos-A	1	3	.250	4	4	4	0	0	34	38	0	13	13	14.0	3.18	87	.286	.358	2	.154	-0	-2	-2	1	-0.1
1907	Bos-A	1	5	.167	12	4	2	0	0	46	48	2	24	18	14.3	4.30	60	.271	.361	2	.154	-0	-9	-9	-1	-1.0
	Was-A	2	6	.250	11	8	3	0	0	48^2	57	0	12	18	13.1	4.62	52	.294	.341	1	.056	-2	-11	-12	-1	-1.5
	Yr	3	11	.214	23	12	5	0	0	94^2	105	2	36	36	13.6	4.47	56	.282	.348	3	.097	-2	-20	-21	-2	-2.5
1909	Was-A	1	4	.200	9	4	1	0	0	41	41	1	16	13	13.8	3.73	65	.266	.358	2	.143	-1	-6	-6	-1	-0.8
1910	Was-A	0	6	.000	8	6	6	0	0	57^1	52	0	23	18	12.1	2.98	84	.259	.341	1	.053	-2	-3	-3	-1	-0.6
Total	4	5	24	.172	44	26	16	0	0	227	236	3	88	80	13.4	3.77	67	.275	.351	8	.104	-4	-31	-31	-3	-4.0

● DAN O'BRIEN O'Brien, Daniel Jogues b: 4/22/54, St.Petersburg, Fla. BR/TR, 6'4", 215 lbs. Deb: 9/04/78

YEAR	TM/L	W	L	PCT	G	GS	CG	SH	SV	IP	H	HR	BB	SO	RAT	ERA	ERA+	OAV	OOB	BH	AVG	PB	PR	/A	PD	TPI
1978	StL-N	0	2	.000	7	2	0	0	0	18	22	1	8	12	16.0	4.50	78	.301	.386	0	.000	-0	-2	-2	-0	-0.3
1979	StL-N	1	1	.500	6	0	0	0	0	11	21	0	3	5	19.6	8.18	46	.420	.453	0	.000	-0	-5	-5	-0	-0.6
Total	2	1	3	.250	13	2	0	0	0	29	43	1	11	17	17.4	5.90	61	.350	.412	0	.000	-1	-7	-7	-1	-0.9

● EDDIE O'BRIEN O'Brien, Edward Joseph b: 12/11/30, S.Amboy, N.J. BR/TR, 5'9", 165 lbs. Deb: 4/25/53 FC♦

YEAR	TM/L	W	L	PCT	G	GS	CG	SH	SV	IP	H	HR	BB	SO	RAT	ERA	ERA+	OAV	OOB	BH	AVG	PB	PR	/A	PD	TPI
1956	Pit-N	0	0	—	1	0	0	0	0	2	1	0	0	0	9.0	0.00	—	.167	.286	14	.264	0	1	1	-0	0.1

YEAR	TM/L	W	L	PCT	G	GS	CG	SH	SV	IP	H	HR	BB	SO	RAT	ERA	ERA+	OAV	OOB	BH	AVG	PB	PR	/A	PD	TPI
1957	Pit-N	1	0	1.000	3	1	1	0	0	12^1	11	2	3	10	10.2	2.19	173	.229	.275	0	.000	-0	2	2	0	0.2
1958	Pit-N	0	0	—	1	0	0	0	0	2	4	1	1	1	22.5	13.50	29	.444	.500	0	—	0	-2	-2	-0	-0.2
Total	3	1	0	1.000	5	1	1	0	0	16^1	16	3	4	11	11.6	3.31	115	.254	.309	131	.236	-0	1	1	-0	0.1
● DARBY O'BRIEN O'Brien, John F. b: 4/15/1867, Troy, N.Y. d: 3/11/1892, W.Troy, N.Y. BR/TR, 5'10", 165 lbs. Deb: 6/23/1888																										
1888	Cle-a	11	19	.367	30	30	30	1	0	259	245	5	99	135	12.4	3.30	94	.241	.315	20	.183	-3	-7	-6	2	-0.6
1889	Cle-N	22	17	.564	41	41	39	1	0	346^2	345	9	167	122	13.9	4.15	97	.252	.343	35	.250	4	-5	-5	2	0.1
1890	Cle-P	8	16	.333	25	25	22	0	0	206^1	229	9	93	54	14.9	3.40	117	.269	.354	15	.156	-5	19	13	-1	0.5
1891	Bos-a	18	13	.581	40	30	22	0	**2**	268^2	300	13	127	87	15.0	3.65	96	.273	.359	30	.234	1	2	-5	-3	-0.6
Total	4	59	65	.476	136	126	113	2	2	1080^2	1119	36	486	398	14.0	3.68	100	.258	.343	100	.211	-4	9	-2	0	-0.6
● JOHNNY O'BRIEN O'Brien, John Thomas b: 12/11/30, S.Amboy, N.J. BR/TR, 5'9", 170 lbs. Deb: 4/19/53 F♦																										
1956	Pit-N	1	0	1.000	8	0	0	0	0	19	8	2	9	9	9.0	2.84	133	.133	.268	18	.173	-0	2	2	-1	0.1
1957	Pit-N	0	3	.000	16	1	0	0	0	40	46	7	24	19	16.0	6.07	62	.293	.390	11	.314	2	-10	-10	-1	-0.9
1958	StL-N	0	0	—	1	0	0	0	0	2	7	0	2	2	40.5	22.50	18	.538	.600	0	.000	0	-4	-4	-0	-0.3
Total	3	1	3	.250	25	1	0	0	0	61	61	9	35	30	14.6	5.61	68	.265	.369	204	.250	2	-12	-12	-2	-1.1
● BOB O'BRIEN O'Brien, Robert Allen b: 4/23/49, Pittsburgh, Pa. BL/TL, 5'10", 170 lbs. Deb: 4/11/71																										
1971	LA-N	2	2	.500	14	4	1	1	0	42	42	4	13	15	12.0	3.00	108	.262	.322	1	.111	-0	2	1	-1	0.0
● TOM O'BRIEN O'Brien, Thomas H. b: 6/22/1860, Salem, Mass. d: 4/21/21, Worcester, Mass. BR/TR, Deb: 6/14/1882 ♦																										
1887	NY-a	0	0	—	1	0	0	0	0	3^2	4	0	5	0	22.1	7.36	58	.211	.375	25	.194	-0	-1	-1	-0	-0.1
● BUCK O'BRIEN O'Brien, Thomas Joseph b: 5/9/1882, Brockton, Mass. d: 7/25/59, Boston, Mass. BR/TR, 5'10", 188 lbs. Deb: 9/09/11																										
1911	Bos-A	5	1	.833	6	5	5	2	0	47^2	30	0	21	31	9.8	0.38	868	.180	.275	2	.125	-1	16	15	1	1.7
1912	*Bos-A	20	13	.606	37	34	25	2	0	275^2	237	3	90	115	11.0	2.58	132	.237	.306	13	.138	-5	23	25	0	2.2
1913	Bos-A	4	9	.308	15	12	6	0	0	90^1	103	0	35	54	13.7	3.69	80	.305	.370	5	.167	0	-8	-7	1	-0.7
	Chi-A	0	2	.000	6	3	0	0	0	18^1	21	0	13	4	16.7	3.93	74	.318	.430	0	.000	-0	-2	-2	-0	-0.3
	Yr	4	11	.267	21	15	6	0	0	108^2	124	0	48	58	14.2	3.73	79	.307	.381	5	.152	-0	-10	-10	0	-1.0
Total	3	29	25	.537	64	54	36	4	0	432	391	3	159	204	11.7	2.63	125	.249	.322	20	.140	-6	29	31	1	2.9
● DARBY O'BRIEN O'Brien, William D. b: 9/1/1863, Peoria, Ill. d: 6/15/1893, Peoria, Ill. BR/TR, 6'1", 186 lbs. Deb: 4/16/1887 ♦																										
1887	NY-a	0	0	—	1	0	0	0	0	1	1	0	1	0	18.0	0.00	—	.333	.500	157	.301	0	0	0	-0	0.0
● BILLY O'BRIEN O'Brien, William Smith b: 3/14/1860, Albany, N.Y. d: 5/26/11, Kansas City, Mo. BR , 6', 185 lbs. Deb: 9/27/1884 ♦																										
1884	StP-U	1	0	1.000	2	0	0	0	0	10	8	0	3	7	9.9	1.80	91	.205	.261	7	.233	1	1	-0	0	0.0
● WALTER OCKEY Ockey, Walter Andrew "Footie" (b: Walter Andrew Okpych) b: 1/4/20, New York, N.Y. d: 12/4/71, Staten Island, N.Y. BR/TR, 6', 175 lbs. Deb: 5/03/44																										
1944	NY-N	0	0	—	2	0	0	0	0	2^2	2	1	2	1	13.5	3.38	109	.200	.333	0	—	0	0	0	0	0.0
● PAT O'CONNELL O'Connell, Patrick H. b: 6/10/1861, Bangor, Me. d: 1/24/43, Lewiston, Maine BR/TR, 5'10", 175 lbs. Deb: 7/22/1886 ♦																										
1886	Bal-a	0	0	—	1	0	0	0	0	3	4	0	2	1	18.0	6.00	57	.333	.429	30	.181	-0	-1	-1	-0	-0.1
● ANDY O'CONNOR O'Connor, Andrew James b: 9/14/1884, Roxbury, Mass. d: 9/26/80, Norwood, Mass. BR/TR, 6', 160 lbs. Deb: 10/06/08																										
1908	NY-A	0	1	.000	1	1	1	0	0	8	15	0	7	5	28.1	10.13	25	.429	.556	0	.000	-0	-7	-7	-0	-0.6
● FRANK O'CONNOR O'Connor, Frank Henry b: 9/15/1870, Keeseville, N.Y. d: 12/26/13, Brattleboro, Vt. BL/TL, 6', 185 lbs. Deb: 8/03/1893																										
1893	Phi-N	0	0	—	3	1	0	0	1	4	2	0	9	0	24.8	11.25	41	.145	.482	2	1.000	2	-3	-3	0	-0.1
● JACK O'CONNOR O'Connor, Jack William b: 6/2/58, Twenty-Nine Palms, Cal. BL/TL, 6'3", 215 lbs. Deb: 4/09/81																										
1981	Min-A	3	2	.600	28	0	0	0	0	35^1	46	3	30	16	19.9	5.86	67	.336	.462	0	—	0	-9	-8	1	-0.7
1982	Min-A	8	9	.471	23	19	6	1	0	126	122	13	57	56	12.9	4.29	99	.255	.337	0	—	0	-3	-1	-3	-0.4
1983	Min-A	2	3	.400	27	8	0	0	0	83	107	13	36	56	15.5	5.86	73	.315	.380	0	—	0	-17	-15	-1	-1.8
1984	Min-A	0	0	—	2	0	0	0	0	4^2	1	1	4	0	9.6	1.93	218	.067	.263	0	—	0	1	1	-0	-0.2
1985	Mon-N	0	2	.000	20	1	0	0	0	23^2	21	1	13	16	12.9	4.94	69	.239	.337	0	—	0	-4	-4	-1	-0.5
1987	Bal-A	1	1	.500	29	0	0	0	2	46	46	5	23	33	13.5	4.30	102	.263	.348	0	—	0	1	0	-1	0.2
Total	6	14	17	.452	129	28	6	1	2	318^2	343	36	163	177	14.4	4.89	85	.278	.364	0	—	0	-30	-25	-5	-3.4
● HANK O'DAY O'Day, Henry Francis b: 7/8/1862, Chicago, Ill. d: 7/2/35, Chicago, Ill. TR , Deb: 5/02/1884 MU																										
1884	Tol-a	9	28	.243	41	40	35	2	**1**	326^2	335	6	66	163	11.5	3.75	91	.252	.297	51	.211	-1	-18	-12	4	-0.8
1885	Pit-a	5	7	.417	12	12	10	0	0	103	110	4	16	36	11.6	3.67	88	.258	.296	12	.245	1	-5	-5	0	-0.3
1886	Was-N	2	2	.500	6	6	6	0	0	49	41	1	17	47	10.7	1.65	199	.219	.284	1	.053	-2	9	9	1	0.8
1887	Was-N	8	20	.286	30	30	29	0	0	254^2	255	15	109	86	13.2	4.17	97	.254	.332	23	.198	-3	-3	-3	1	-0.5
1888	Was-N	16	29	.356	46	46	46	3	0	403	359	19	117	186	11.0	3.10	90	.232	.293	23	.139	-6	-11	-13	-3	-2.2
1889	Was-N	2	10	.167	13	13	11	0	0	108	117	7	57	23	15.0	4.33	91	.268	.360	8	.182	-1	-4	-5	0	-0.4
	*NY-N	9	1	.900	10	10	8	0	0	78	83	2	35	28	14.4	4.27	92	.264	.351	3	.097	-2	-2	-3	-1	-0.4
	Yr	11	11	.500	23	23	19	0	0	186	200	9	92	51	14.5	4.31	92	.264	.349	11	.147	-2	-6	-8	-0	-0.8
1890	NY-P	22	13	.629	43	35	32	1	**3**	329	356	11	163	94	14.7	4.21	108	.264	.351	34	.227	-2	1	12	-4	0.4
Total	7	73	110	.399	201	192	177	6	4	1651^1	1656	65	580	663	12.6	3.74	97	.251	.320	155	.190	-16	-33	-22	-0	-3.4
● PAUL O'DEA O'Dea, Paul "Lefty" b: 7/3/20, Cleveland, Ohio d: 12/11/78, Cleveland, Ohio BL/TL, 6', 200 lbs. Deb: 4/19/44 ♦																										
1944	Cle-A	0	0	—	3	0	0	0	0	4^1	5	0	6	0	22.8	2.08	159	.333	.524	55	.318	1	1	1	-0	0.1
1945	Cle-A	0	0	—	1	0	0	0	0	2	4	0	2	0	27.0	13.50	24	.400	.500	52	.235	0	-2	-2	0	-0.2
Total	2	0	0	—	4	0	0	0	0	6^1	9	0	8	0	24.2	5.68	58	.360	.515	107	.272	1	-2	-2	-0	-0.1
● BILLY O'DELL O'Dell, William Oliver b: 2/10/33, Whitmire, S.C. BB/TL, 5'11", 170 lbs. Deb: 6/20/54																										
1954	Bal-A	1	1	.500	7	2	1	0	0	16^1	15	0	5	6	11.0	2.76	130	.242	.299	0	.000	-0	2	1	0	0.2
1956	Bal-A	0	0	—	4	1	0	0	0	8	6	0	6	6	13.5	1.13	349	.222	.364	0	.000	-0	3	2	-0	0.2
1957	Bal-A	4	10	.286	35	15	2	1	4	140^1	107	12	39	97	9.7	2.69	133	.212	.276	5	.147	-1	17	14	-2	1.2
1958	Bal-A★	14	11	.560	41	25	12	3	8	221^1	201	13	51	137	10.4	2.97	121	.241	.288	8	.111	-1	20	15	-0	1.6
1959	Bal-A★	10	12	.455	38	24	6	2	1	199^1	163	18	67	88	10.4	2.93	129	.220	.286	5	.083	-3	21	19	1	1.8
1960	SF-N	8	13	.381	43	24	6	1	2	202^2	198	16	72	145	12.1	3.20	109	.252	.317	6	.107	1	13	6	-1	0.6
1961	SF-N	7	5	.583	46	14	4	1	2	130^1	132	10	33	110	11.5	3.59	106	.260	.306	4	.103	-2	6	3	-1	0.0
1962	*SF-N	19	14	.576	43	39	20	2	0	280^2	282	18	66	195	11.4	3.53	108	.258	.304	12	.133	-1	13	8	-2	0.5
1963	SF-N	14	10	.583	36	33	10	3	1	222^1	218	14	70	116	11.9	3.16	101	.253	.314	16	.205	4	3	1	-4	0.0
1964	SF-N	8	7	.533	36	8	1	0	2	85	82	10	35	54	12.8	5.40	66	.252	.332	0	.000	-2	-18	-17	-1	-2.1
1965	Mil-N	10	6	.625	62	1	0	0	18	111^1	87	10	30	78	9.6	2.18	161	.215	.272	4	.174	1	17	17	-0	1.8
1966	Atl-N	2	3	.400	24	0	0	0	6	41^1	44	3	18	20	13.9	2.40	152	.272	.352	2	.250	0	6	6	-0	0.6
	Pit-N	3	2	.600	37	2	0	0	4	71^1	74	3	23	47	12.7	2.78	129	.275	.341	1	.063	-1	7	6	-1	0.5
	Yr	5	5	.500	61	2	0	0	10	112^2	118	6	41	67	13.0	2.64	136	.273	.341	3	.125	-1	12	12	-1	1.1
1967	Pit-N	5	6	.455	27	11	1	0	0	86^2	88	10	41	34	13.7	5.82	58	.265	.351	3	.115	-0	-24	-24	-1	-2.5
Total	13	105	100	.512	479	199	63	13	48	1817	1697	137	556	1133	11.4	3.29	109	.246	.306	66	.125	-7	85	59	-12	4.4
● TED ODENWALD Odenwald, Theodore Joseph "Lefty" b: 1/4/02, Hudson, Wis. d: 10/23/65, Shakopee, Minn. BR/TL, 5'10", 147 lbs. Deb: 4/13/21																										
1921	Cle-A	1	0	1.000	10	0	0	0	0	17^1	16	0	6	4	11.9	1.56	274	.262	.338	0	.000	-1	5	5	0	0.4
1922	Cle-A	0	0	—	1	0	0	0	0	1^1	6	0	2	2	54.0	40.50	10	.600	.667	0	—	0	-5	-5	0	-0.4

YEAR TM/L	W	L	PCT	G	GS	CG	SH	SV	IP	H	HR	BB	SO	RAT	ERA	ERA+	OAV	OOB	BH	AVG	PB	PR	/A	PD	TPI
Total 2	1	0	1.000	11	0	0	0	0	18^2	22	0	8	6	14.9	4.34	98	.310	.387	0	.000	-1	-0	-0	0	0.0

● **DAVE ODOM** Odom, David Everett "Blimp" or "Porky" b: 6/5/18, Dinuba, Cal. d: 11/19/87, Myrtle Beach, Fla. BR/TR, 6'1", 220 lbs. Deb: 5/31/43

YEAR TM/L	W	L	PCT	G	GS	CG	SH	SV	IP	H	HR	BB	SO	RAT	ERA	ERA+	OAV	OOB	BH	AVG	PB	PR	/A	PD	TPI
1943 Bos-N	0	3	.000	22	3	1	0	2	54^2	54	3	30	17	14.5	5.27	65	.269	.374	0	.000	-2	-11	-11	-1	-1.5

● **BLUE MOON ODOM** Odom, Johnny Lee b: 5/29/45, Macon, Ga. BR/TR, 6', 185 lbs. Deb: 9/05/64 ♦

YEAR TM/L	W	L	PCT	G	GS	CG	SH	SV	IP	H	HR	BB	SO	RAT	ERA	ERA+	OAV	OOB	BH	AVG	PB	PR	/A	PD	TPI
1964 KC-A	1	2	.333	5	5	1	1	0	17	29	5	11	10	21.2	10.06	38	.363	.440	0	.000	-0	-12	-12	0	-1.1
1965 KC-A	0	0	—	1	0	0	0	0	1	2	0	2	0	36.0	9.00	39	.400	.571	0	—	0	-1	-1	0	0.0
1966 KC-A	5	5	.500	14	14	4	2	0	90^1	70	1	53	47	12.5	2.49	136	.215	.328	3	.097	-1	9	9	2	1.1
1967 KC-A	3	8	.273	29	17	0	0	0	103^2	94	9	68	67	14.3	5.04	63	.243	.360	8	.286	2	-21	-21	0	-2.0
1968 Oak-A★	16	10	.615	32	31	9	4	0	231^1	179	9	98	143	11.0	2.45	115	.216	.304	17	.218	6	14	9	1	2.0
1969 Oak-A★	15	6	.714	32	32	10	3	0	231^1	179	15	112	150	11.6	2.92	118	.215	.312	21	.266	11	18	13	1	2.7
1970 Oak-A	9	8	.529	29	29	4	1	0	156^1	128	14	100	88	13.6	3.80	93	.227	.351	13	.241	6	-1	-5	2	0.4
1971 Oak-A	10	12	.455	25	25	3	1	0	140^2	147	13	71	69	13.9	4.29	78	.271	.355	8	.160	1	-13	-15	-1	-1.5
1972 *Oak-A	15	6	.714	31	30	4	2	0	194^1	164	10	87	86	11.8	2.50	114	.234	.321	8	.121	0	12	7	0	0.9
1973 *Oak-A	5	12	.294	30	24	3	0	0	150^1	153	14	67	83	13.3	4.49	79	.263	.341	0	.000	0	-11	-16	-1	-1.7
1974 *Oak-A	1	5	.167	34	5	1	0	1	87^1	85	4	52	52	14.4	3.81	87	.267	.375	0	—	0	-2	-5	1	-0.4
1975 Oak-A	0	2	.000	7	2	0	0	0	11	19	1	11	4	25.4	12.27	30	.422	.544	0	—	0	-10	-11	0	-1.0
Cle-A	1	0	1.000	3	1	1	1	0	10^1	4	1	8	10	10.5	2.61	145	.118	.286	0	—	0	1	1	-0	0.1
Yr	1	2	.333	10	3	1	1	0	21^1	23	2	19	14	17.7	7.59	49	.284	.420	0	—	0	-9	-9	-0	-0.9
Atl-N	1	7	.125	15	10	0	0	0	56	78	5	28	30	17.0	7.07	53	.342	.414	1	.077	-1	-21	-21	0	-2.0
1976 Chi-A	2	2	.500	8	4	0	0	0	28	31	2	20	18	16.7	5.79	62	.282	.397	0	—	0	-7	-7	-1	-0.8
Total 13	84	85	.497	295	229	40	15	1	1509	1362	103	788	857	13.0	3.70	89	.244	.341	79	.195	25	-45	-71	5	-3.3

● **GEORGE O'DONNELL** O'Donnell, George Dana b: 5/27/29, Winchester, Ill. BR/TR, 6'3", 175 lbs. Deb: 4/18/54

YEAR TM/L	W	L	PCT	G	GS	CG	SH	SV	IP	H	HR	BB	SO	RAT	ERA	ERA+	OAV	OOB	BH	AVG	PB	PR	/A	PD	TPI
1954 Pit-N	3	9	.250	21	10	3	0	1	87^1	105	4	21	8	13.2	4.53	92	.315	.360	2	.087	-1	-4	-3	1	-0.3

● **JOHN O'DONOGHUE** O'Donoghue, John Eugene b: 10/7/39, Kansas City, Mo. BR/TL, 6'3", 210 lbs. Deb: 9/29/63

YEAR TM/L	W	L	PCT	G	GS	CG	SH	SV	IP	H	HR	BB	SO	RAT	ERA	ERA+	OAV	OOB	BH	AVG	PB	PR	/A	PD	TPI
1963 KC-A	0	1	.000	1	1	0	0	0	6	6	0	2	1	12.0	1.50	256	.286	.348	0	.000	-0	1	2	-0	0.1
1964 KC-A	10	14	.417	39	32	2	1	0	173^2	202	24	65	79	14.0	4.92	78	.286	.349	13	.236	2	-25	-21	-1	-2.0
1965 KC-A☆	9	18	.333	34	30	4	1	0	177^2	183	15	66	82	12.7	3.95	88	.267	.332	12	.218	3	-10	-9	0	-0.6
1966 Cle-A	6	8	.429	32	13	2	0	0	108	109	13	23	49	11.2	3.83	90	.264	.306	5	.152	-0	-5	-5	1	-0.5
1967 Cle-A	8	9	.471	33	17	5	2	2	130^2	120	10	33	81	10.7	3.24	101	.247	.298	4	.100	-0	-0	0	3	0.4
1968 Bal-A	0	0	—	16	0	0	0	2	22	34	2	7	11	16.8	6.14	48	.374	.418	0	.000	-0	-8	-8	0	-0.9
1969 Sea-A	2	2	.500	55	0	0	0	6	70	58	5	37	48	12.6	2.96	123	.230	.336	1	.077	-1	5	5	-0	0.5
1970 Mil-A	2	0	1.000	25	0	0	0	0	23^1	29	4	9	13	14.7	5.01	76	.299	.358	0	.000	-0	-3	-3	1	-0.3
Mon-N	2	3	.400	9	3	0	0	0	22^1	20	2	11	6	13.3	5.24	78	.263	.371	0	.000	-0	-3	-3	0	-0.3
1971 Mon-N	0	0	—	13	0	0	0	0	17^1	19	3	7	7	13.5	4.67	75	.271	.338	0	—	0	-2	-2	-0	-0.2
Total 9	39	55	.415	257	96	13	4	10	751	780	78	260	377	12.6	4.07	87	.269	.332	35	.170	2	-49	-44	4	-3.8

● **LEFTY O'DOUL** O'Doul, Francis Joseph b: 3/4/1897, San Francisco, Cal. d: 12/7/69, San Francisco, Cal. BL/TL, 6', 180 lbs. Deb: 4/29/19 ♦

YEAR TM/L	W	L	PCT	G	GS	CG	SH	SV	IP	H	HR	BB	SO	RAT	ERA	ERA+	OAV	OOB	BH	AVG	PB	PR	/A	PD	TPI
1919 NY-A	0	0	—	3	0	0	0	0	5	7	0	4	2	19.8	3.60	89	.304	.407	4	.250	0	-0	-0	-0	0.0
1920 NY-A	0	0	—	2	0	0	0	0	3^2	4	0	2	2	17.2	4.91	78	.286	.412	2	.167	-0	-0	-0	-0	-0.1
1922 NY-A	0	0	—	6	0	0	0	0	16	24	0	12	5	20.3	3.38	119	.353	.450	3	.333	1	1	1	0	0.2
1923 Bos-A	1	1	.500	23	1	0	0	0	53	69	2	31	10	17.7	5.43	76	.337	.433	5	.143	-1	-9	-8	1	-0.8
Total 4	1	1	.500	34	1	0	0	0	77^2	104	2	49	19	18.3	4.87	83	.335	.434	1140	.349	-1	-8	-7	1	-0.7

● **BRYAN OELKERS** Oelkers, Bryan Alois b: 3/11/61, Zaragoza, Spain BL/TL, 6'3", 192 lbs. Deb: 4/09/83

YEAR TM/L	W	L	PCT	G	GS	CG	SH	SV	IP	H	HR	BB	SO	RAT	ERA	ERA+	OAV	OOB	BH	AVG	PB	PR	/A	PD	TPI
1983 Min-A	0	5	.000	10	8	0	0	0	34^1	56	7	17	13	19.1	8.65	49	.376	.440	0	—	0	-18	-17	-1	-1.8
1986 Cle-A	3	3	.500	35	4	0	0	1	69	70	13	40	33	15.1	4.70	88	.262	.371	0	—	0	-4	-4	-1	-0.4
Total 2	3	8	.273	45	12	0	0	1	103^1	126	20	57	46	16.5	6.01	70	.303	.395	0	—	0	-21	-21	-2	-2.2

● **JOE OESCHGER** Oeschger, Joseph Carl b: 5/24/1892, Chicago, Ill. d: 7/28/86, Rohnert Park, Cal BR/TR, 6' ", 190 lbs. Deb: 4/21/14

YEAR TM/L	W	L	PCT	G	GS	CG	SH	SV	IP	H	HR	BB	SO	RAT	ERA	ERA+	OAV	OOB	BH	AVG	PB	PR	/A	PD	TPI
1914 Phi-N	4	8	.333	32	10	5	0	1	124	129	5	54	47	14.0	3.77	78	.279	.366	3	.075	-4	-14	-11	-1	-1.7
1915 Phi-N	1	0	1.000	6	1	1	0	0	23^2	21	1	9	8	11.4	3.42	80	.247	.319	0	.000	-1	-2	-2	-0	-0.3
1916 Phi-N	1	0	1.000	14	0	0	0	0	30^1	18	2	14	17	9.8	2.37	112	.184	.292	0	.000	-1	1	1	1	0.1
1917 Phi-N	15	14	.517	42	30	18	5	1	262	241	7	72	123	11.0	2.75	102	.249	.305	10	.114	-4	-1	2	-3	-0.7
1918 Phi-N	6	18	.250	30	23	13	2	**3**	184	159	3	83	60	12.2	3.03	99	.238	.328	5	.083	-4	-6	-1	-2	-0.7
1919 Phi-N	0	1	.000	5	4	2	0	0	38	52	1	16	5	16.6	5.92	54	.340	.409	0	.000	-2	-13	-11	-0	-1.3
NY-N	0	1	.000	5	1	0	0	0	8	12	0	2	3	15.8	4.50	62	.400	.438	0	.000	-0	-1	-2	0	-0.2
Bos-N	4	2	.667	7	7	4	1	0	56^2	63	0	21	16	13.5	2.54	112	.300	.366	2	.091	-1	2	2	-1	-0.1
Yr	4	4	.500	17	12	6	1	0	102^2	127	1	39	24	14.6	3.94	76	.322	.384	2	.053	-4	-12	-11	-2	-1.6
1920 Bos-N	15	13	.536	38	30	20	5	0	299	294	10	99	80	12.1	3.46	88	.265	.329	18	.178	-3	-11	-14	-3	-2.0
1921 Bos-N	20	14	.588	46	36	19	**3**	0	299	303	11	97	68	12.5	3.52	104	.274	.341	28	.255	2	9	4	2	0.9
1922 Bos-N	6	21	.222	46	23	10	1	1	195^2	234	8	81	51	14.9	5.06	79	.303	.375	12	.190	-0	-21	-23	1	-2.0
1923 Bos-N	5	15	.250	44	19	6	1	2	166^1	227	4	54	33	15.5	5.68	70	.330	.383	12	.231	-0	-31	-31	0	-2.9
1924 NY-N	2	0	1.000	10	2	0	0	0	29	35	1	14	10	15.2	3.10	118	.287	.360	3	.429	1	2	2	-1	0.2
Phi-N	2	7	.222	19	8	0	0	0	65^1	88	6	16	8	14.7	4.41	101	.333	.378	5	.250	-1	-4	0	-0	0.0
Yr	4	7	.364	29	10	0	0	0	94^1	123	7	30	18	14.9	4.01	105	.319	.372	8	.296	0	-1	2	-1	0.2
1925 Bro-N	1	2	.333	21	3	1	0	0	37	60	2	19	6	19.5	6.08	69	.382	.452	1	.125	-0	-7	-8	-0	-0.8
Total 12	82	116	.414	365	197	99	18	8	1818	1936	61	651	535	13.1	3.81	88	.281	.349	99	.165	-19	-96	-89	-8	-11.5

● **JACK OGDEN** Ogden, John Mahlon b: 11/5/1897, Ogden, Pa. d: 11/9/77, Philadelphia, Pa. BR/TR, 6', 190 lbs. Deb: 6/22/18 F

YEAR TM/L	W	L	PCT	G	GS	CG	SH	SV	IP	H	HR	BB	SO	RAT	ERA	ERA+	OAV	OOB	BH	AVG	PB	PR	/A	PD	TPI
1918 NY-N	0	0	—	5	0	0	0	0	8^2	8	0	3	1	13.5	3.12	84	.296	.406	0	.000	-0	-0	-0	-0	-0.1
1928 StL-A	15	16	.484	38	31	18	1	2	242^2	257	23	80	67	12.5	4.15	101	.274	.331	17	.200	-1	-3	1	-4	-0.3
1929 StL-A	4	8	.333	34	14	7	0	0	131^1	154	8	44	32	13.6	4.93	90	.301	.357	11	.244	0	-10	-7	0	-0.7
1931 Cin-N	4	8	.333	22	9	3	1	1	89	79	3	32	24	11.2	2.93	127	.242	.310	4	.148	-1	9	8	-1	0.6
1932 Cin-N	2	2	.500	24	3	1	0	0	57	72	5	22	20	14.8	5.21	74	.310	.370	2	.167	0	-8	-9	1	-0.8
Total 5	25	34	.424	123	57	29	2	3	528^2	570	39	181	144	12.8	4.24	97	.280	.340	34	.200	-1	-13	-8	-4	-1.3

● **CURLY OGDEN** Ogden, Warren Harvey b: 1/24/01, Ogden, Pa. d: 8/6/64, Chester, Pa. BR/TR, 6'1.5", 180 lbs. Deb: 7/18/22 F

YEAR TM/L	W	L	PCT	G	GS	CG	SH	SV	IP	H	HR	BB	SO	RAT	ERA	ERA+	OAV	OOB	BH	AVG	PB	PR	/A	PD	TPI
1922 Phi-A	1	4	.200	15	6	4	0	0	72^1	59	4	33	20	12.1	3.11	137	.237	.338	7	.241	-0	8	9	-0	0.9
1923 Phi-A	1	2	.333	18	2	0	0	0	46^1	63	2	32	14	19.0	5.63	73	.330	.434	5	.294	1	-8	-8	0	-0.7
1924 Phi-A	0	3	.000	5	1	0	0	0	12^2	14	1	7	4	15.6	4.97	86	.275	.373	0	.000	-1	-1	-1	-0	-0.2
*Was-A	9	5	.643	16	16	9	3	0	108	83	3	51	23	11.3	2.58	156	.221	.317	13	.277	2	20	17	-0	1.9
Yr	9	8	.529	21	17	9	3	0	120^2	97	4	58	27	11.7	2.83	143	.227	.322	13	.260	1	19	16	-1	1.7
1925 Was-A	3	1	.750	17	4	2	1	0	42	45	1	18	6	13.9	4.50	94	.288	.369	3	.250	-0	-0	-1	-0	-0.2
1926 Was-A	4	4	.500	22	9	4	0	0	96^1	114	2	45	21	15.3	4.30	90	.305	.387	5	.185	-1	-3	-5	-1	-0.6
Total 5	18	19	.486	93	38	19	4	0	377^2	378	13	186	88	13.9	3.79	108	.271	.364	33	.244	1	14	12	-2	1.1

● **JOE OGRODOWSKI** Ogrodowski, Joseph Anthony b: 11/20/06, Hoytville, Pa. d: 6/24/59, Elmira, N.Y. BR/TR, 5'11", 165 lbs. Deb: 4/27/25

YEAR TM/L	W	L	PCT	G	GS	CG	SH	SV	IP	H	HR	BB	SO	RAT	ERA	ERA+	OAV	OOB	BH	AVG	PB	PR	/A	PD	TPI
1925 Bos-N	0	0	—	1	0	0	0	0	1	6	0	3	0	81.0	54.00	7	.600	.692	0	—	0	-6	-6	-0	-0.4

● **BILL O'HARA** O'Hara, William Alexander b: 8/14/1883, Toronto, Ont., Can. d: 6/15/31, Jersey City, N.J. BL/TR, 5'10", Deb: 4/15/09 ♦

YEAR TM/L	W	L	PCT	G	GS	CG	SH	SV	IP	H	HR	BB	SO	RAT	ERA	ERA+	OAV	OOB	BH	AVG	PB	PR	/A	PD	TPI
1910 StL-N	0	0	—	1	0	0	0	0	1	0	0	0	0	0.0	0.00	—	.000	.000	3	.150	-0	0	0	-0	0.0

YEAR TM/L	W	L	PCT	G	GS	CG	SH	SV	IP	H	HR	BB	SO	RAT	ERA	ERA+	OAV	OOB	BH	AVG	PB	PR	/A	PD	TPI

● JOE OHL   Ohl, Joseph Earl b: 1/10/1888, Jobstown, N.J.   d: 12/18/51, Camden, N.J.   BL/TL,   Deb: 7/29/09

| 1909 Was-A | 0 | 0 | — | 4 | 0 | 0 | 0 | 0 | 8² | 7 | 0 | 1 | 2 | 9.3 | 2.08 | 117 | .194 | .237 | 0 | .000 | -0 | 0 | 0 | -0 | 0.0 |

● BOB OJEDA   Ojeda, Robert Michael b: 12/17/57, Los Angeles, Cal.   BL/TL, 6'1", 190 lbs.   Deb: 7/13/80

1980 Bos-A	1	1	.500	7	7	0	0	0	26	39	2	14	12	18.3	6.92	61	.361	.434	0	—	0	-8	-8	-0	-1.1
1981 Bos-A	6	2	.750	10	10	2	0	0	66¹	50	6	25	28	10.4	3.12	124	.212	.293	0	—	0	4	6	-0	0.2
1982 Bos-A	4	6	.400	22	14	0	0	0	78¹	95	13	29	52	14.4	5.63	76	.296	.356	0	—	0	-14	-12	-1	-1.6
1983 Bos-A	12	7	.632	29	28	5	0	0	173²	173	15	73	94	12.9	4.04	108	.265	.342	0	—	0	0	6	0	0.2
1984 Bos-A	12	12	.500	33	32	8	**5**	0	216²	211	17	96	137	12.8	3.99	104	.259	.338	0	—	0	0	4	1	0.2
1985 Bos-A	9	11	.450	39	22	5	0	1	157²	166	11	48	102	12.3	4.00	107	.273	.328	0	—	0	3	5	0	0.3
1986 *NY-N	18	5	**.783**	32	30	7	2	0	217¹	185	15	52	148	9.9	2.57	138	.230	.279	8	.113	-2	28	23	1	2.3
1987 NY-N	3	5	.375	10	7	0	0	0	46¹	45	5	10	21	10.7	3.88	97	.253	.293	1	.071	-0	1	-1	0	-0.1
1988 NY-N	10	13	.435	29	29	5	5	0	190¹	158	6	33	133	9.2	2.88	112	.225	.264	10	.164	1	12	7	2	1.1
1989 NY-N	13	11	.542	31	31	5	2	0	192	179	16	78	95	12.1	3.47	94	.245	.319	7	.106	-2	1	-4	2	-0.4
1990 NY-N	7	6	.538	38	12	0	0	0	118	123	10	40	62	12.6	3.66	102	.272	.334	4	.133	-0	2	1	3	0.3
1991 LA-N	12	9	.571	31	31	2	1	0	189¹	181	15	70	120	12.1	3.18	113	.257	.326	9	.161	1	11	9	1	1.2
1992 LA-N	6	9	.400	29	29	2	1	0	166¹	169	8	81	94	13.6	3.63	95	.268	.352	5	.102	-1	-2	-3	2	-0.3
Total 13	113	97	.538	340	282	41	16	1	1838¹	1774	139	649	1098	12.0	3.60	104	.255	.321	44	.127	-3	36	31	9	2.3

● FRANK OKRIE   Okrie, Frank Anthony "Lefty" b: 10/28/1896, Detroit, Mich.   d: 10/16/59, Detroit, Mich.   BL/TL, 5'11", 175 lbs.   Deb: 4/20/20   F

| 1920 Det-A | 1 | 2 | .333 | 21 | 1 | 1 | 0 | 0 | 41 | 44 | 2 | 18 | 9 | 14.7 | 5.27 | 71 | .295 | .390 | 1 | .200 | -0 | -7 | -7 | 6 | -0.1 |

● RED OLDHAM   Oldham, John Cyrus b: 7/15/1893, Zion, Md.   d: 1/28/61, Costa Mesa, Cal.   BB/TL, 6' ", 176 lbs.   Deb: 8/19/14

1914 Det-A	2	4	.333	9	7	3	0	0	45¹	42	1	8	23	10.5	3.38	83	.243	.288	4	.267	1	-3	-3	-1	-0.3
1915 Det-A	3	0	1.000	17	2	1	0	4	57²	52	1	17	17	11.4	2.81	108	.243	.311	2	.143	-0	1	1	0	0.1
1920 Det-A	8	13	.381	39	22	10	1	1	215¹	248	5	91	62	14.4	3.85	97	.302	.376	12	.174	-1	-1	-3	4	-0.1
1921 Det-A	11	14	.440	40	28	12	1	1	229¹	258	11	81	67	13.5	4.24	101	.288	.351	19	.224	2	1	1	1	0.4
1922 Det-A	10	13	.435	43	27	9	0	3	212	256	14	59	72	13.8	4.67	83	.305	.363	19	.260	4	-15	-19	1	-1.3
1925 *Pit-N	3	2	.600	11	4	3	0	1	53	66	2	18	10	14.6	3.91	114	.313	.372	6	.333	2	3	3	0	0.0
1926 Pit-N	2	2	.500	17	2	0	0	2	41²	56	1	18	16	16.2	5.62	70	.359	.429	2	.222	0	-8	-8	0	-0.7
Total 7	39	48	.448	176	92	38	2	12	854¹	978	35	292	267	13.7	4.15	93	.295	.358	64	.226	9	-23	-26	4	-1.3

● STEVE OLIN   Olin, Steven Robert b: 10/10/65, Portland, Ore.   BR/TR, 6'3", 185 lbs.   Deb: 7/29/89

1989 Cle-A	1	4	.200	25	0	0	0	1	36	35	1	14	24	12.3	3.75	106	.255	.325	0	—	0	1	1	0	0.1
1990 Cle-A	4	4	.500	50	0	0	0	1	92¹	96	3	26	64	12.5	3.41	115	.270	.331	0	—	0	5	5	2	0.8
1991 Cle-A	3	6	.333	48	0	0	0	17	56¹	61	2	23	38	13.6	3.36	124	.274	.344	0	—	0	5	5	0	0.5
1992 Cle-A	8	5	.615	72	0	0	0	29	88¹	80	8	27	47	11.3	2.34	172	.248	.314	0	—	0	16	17	1	1.7
Total 4	16	19	.457	195	1	0	0	48	273	272	14	90	173	12.3	3.10	129	.262	.328	0	—	0	26	28	3	3.1

● OMAR OLIVARES   Olivares, Omar (Palqu) b: 7/6/67, Mayaguez, P.R.   BR/TR, 6'1", 185 lbs.   Deb: 8/18/90   F

1990 StL-N	1	1	.500	9	6	0	0	0	49¹	45	2	17	20	11.7	2.92	131	.249	.320	3	.176	1	5	5	1	0.7
1991 StL-N	11	7	.611	28	24	0	0	1	167¹	148	13	61	91	11.5	3.71	100	.243	.317	12	.226	3	-1	0	2	0.5
1992 StL-N	9	9	.500	32	30	1	0	0	197	189	20	63	124	11.7	3.84	90	.257	.319	16	.235	4	-7	-9	3	-0.2
Total 3	21	17	.553	69	60	1	0	1	413²	382	35	141	235	11.6	3.68	98	.250	.318	31	.225	8	-3	-4	5	1.0

● FRANCISCO OLIVERAS   Oliveras, Francisco Javier (Noa) b: 1/31/63, Santurce, P.R.   BR/TR, 5'10", 170 lbs.   Deb: 5/03/89

1989 Min-A	3	4	.429	12	8	1	0	0	55²	64	8	15	24	12.9	4.53	91	.288	.336	0	—	0	-4	-2	-1	-0.3
1990 SF-N	2	2	.500	33	2	0	0	0	55¹	47	5	21	41	11.4	2.77	132	.230	.308	0	.000	-0	6	5	-1	0.5
1991 SF-N	6	6	.500	55	1	0	0	3	79¹	69	12	22	48	10.4	3.86	93	.242	.299	2	.200	0	-2	-2	-0	-0.3
1992 SF-N	0	3	.000	16	7	0	0	0	44²	44	11	10	17	10.5	3.63	92	.250	.297	1	.143	0	-1	-1	-0	-0.1
Total 4	11	15	.423	116	18	1	0	5	235	221	36	68	130	11.3	3.71	99	.253	.310	3	.136	-0	-1	-2	-2	-0.2

● DIOMEDES OLIVO   Olivo, Diomedes Antonio (Maldonado) b: 1/22/19, Guayubin, D.R.   d: 2/15/77, Santo Domingo, D.R.   BL/TL, 6'1", 195 lbs.   Deb: 9/05/60   F

1960 Pit-N	0	0	—	4	0	0	0	0	9²	8	1	5	10	12.1	2.79	134	.216	.310	0	.000	-0	1	1	-0	0.1
1962 Pit-N	5	1	.833	62	1	0	0	7	84¹	88	5	25	66	12.1	2.77	142	.277	.329	3	.188	1	11	11	-1	1.1
1963 StL-N	0	5	.000	19	0	0	0	0	13¹	16	1	9	9	17.6	5.40	66	.296	.406	0	—	0	-3	-3	0	-0.3
Total 3	5	6	.455	85	1	0	0	7	107¹	112	7	39	85	12.7	3.10	125	.274	.339	3	.176	-0	9	9	-0	0.9

● CHI-CHI OLIVO   Olivo, Federico Emilio (Maldonado) b: 3/18/28, Guayubin, D.R.   d: 2/3/77, Guayubin, D.R.   BR/TR, 6'2", 215 lbs.   Deb: 6/05/61   F

1961 Mil-N	0	0	—	3	0	0	0	0	2	3	1	5	3	36.0	18.00	21	.500	.727	0	—	0	-3	-3	-0	-0.1
1964 Mil-N	2	1	.667	38	0	0	0	5	60	55	7	21	45	11.4	3.75	94	.247	.311	1	.250	0	-1	-2	1	-0.1
1965 Mil-N	0	1	.000	8	0	0	0	0	13	12	1	5	11	11.8	1.38	254	.267	.340	0	—	0	3	3	-0	0.3
1966 Atl-N	5	4	.556	47	0	0	0	7	66	59	4	19	41	10.8	4.23	86	.240	.297	1	.111	-0	-5	-4	-1	-0.6
Total 4	7	6	.538	96	0	0	0	12	141	129	13	50	98	11.5	3.96	90	.248	.315	2	.154	-0	-6	-6	-1	-0.7

● JIM OLLOM   Ollom, James Donald b: 7/8/45, Snohomish, Wash.   BR/TL, 6'4", 210 lbs.   Deb: 9/03/66

1966 Min-A	0	0	—	3	1	0	0	0	10	6	1	11	11	7.2	3.60	100	.167	.211	0	.000	0	-0	-0	-0	0.0
1967 Min-A	0	1	.000	21	2	0	0	0	35	33	4	11	17	12.3	5.40	64	.258	.336	1	.200	0	-8	-8	-0	-0.8
Total 2	0	1	.000	24	3	0	0	0	45	39	5	12	28	11.2	5.00	70	.238	.309	1	.143	0	-9	-8	-0	-0.8

● FRED OLMSTEAD   Olmstead, Frederic William b: 7/3/1881, Grand Rapids, Mich.   d: 10/22/36, Muskogee, Okla.   BR/TR, 5'11", 170 lbs.   Deb: 7/02/08

1908 Chi-A	0	0	—	1	0	0	0	0	2	6	0	1	1	31.5	13.50	47	.600	.636	0	.000	0	-2	-2	-0	-0.2
1909 Chi-A	3	2	.600	8	6	5	0	0	54²	52	1	12	21	10.7	1.81	129	.277	.323	2	.095	-1	4	3	-0	0.2
1910 Chi-A	10	12	.455	32	20	14	4	0	184¹	174	1	50	68	11.1	1.95	123	.260	.316	10	.154	-2	12	9	1	0.9
1911 Chi-A	6	6	.500	25	11	7	1	2	117²	146	3	30	45	13.9	4.21	77	.309	.358	7	.189	-0	-11	-13	-1	-1.3
Total 4	19	20	.487	66	37	26	5	2	358²	378	5	93	135	12.1	2.74	97	.283	.334	19	.153	-3	2	-3	-0	-0.4

● AL OLMSTED   Olmsted, Alan Ray b: 3/18/57, St.Louis, Mo.   BR/TL, 6'2", 195 lbs.   Deb: 9/12/80

| 1980 StL-N | 1 | 1 | .500 | 5 | 5 | 0 | 0 | 0 | 34² | 32 | 2 | 14 | 14 | 12.2 | 2.86 | 129 | .244 | .322 | 2 | .182 | -0 | 3 | 3 | 1 | 0.4 |

● HANK OLMSTED   Olmsted, Henry Theodore b: 1/12/1879, Saginaw Bay, Mich.   d: 1/6/69, Bradenton, Fla.   BR/TR, 5'8.5", 147 lbs.   Deb: 7/15/05

| 1905 Bos-A | 1 | 2 | .333 | 3 | 3 | 3 | 0 | 0 | 25 | 18 | 0 | 12 | 6 | 10.8 | 3.24 | 83 | .203 | .298 | 1 | .125 | -0 | -2 | -1 | -0 | -0.2 |

● OLE OLSEN   Olsen, Arthur b: 9/12/1894, S.Norwalk, Conn.   d: 9/12/80, Norwalk, Conn.   BR/TR, 5'10", 163 lbs.   Deb: 4/12/22

1922 Det-A	7	6	.538	37	15	5	0	0	137	147	8	40	52	13.2	4.53	86	.281	.348	7	.179	-1	-7	-10	1	-1.0
1923 Det-A	1	1	.500	17	2	1	0	0	41¹	42	1	17	12	13.9	6.31	61	.290	.383	1	.125	-1	-11	-11	-1	-1.2
Total 2	8	7	.533	54	17	6	0	3	178¹	189	9	57	64	13.4	4.95	78	.283	.356	8	.170	-1	-18	-21	-0	-2.2

● VERN OLSEN   Olsen, Vern Jarl b: 3/16/18, Hillsboro, Ore.   d: 7/13/89, Maywood, Ill.   BR/TL, 6'0.5", 175 lbs.   Deb: 9/08/39

1939 Chi-N	1	0	1.000	4	0	0	0	0	7²	2	0	7	3	10.6	0.00	—	.087	.300	0	.000	0	3	3	-0	0.4
1940 Chi-N	13	9	.591	34	20	9	4	0	172²	172	5	62	71	12.3	2.97	126	.260	.325	15	.263	3	17	15	4	2.1
1941 Chi-N	10	8	.556	37	23	10	2	1	185²	202	7	59	73	12.7	3.15	111	.276	.331	15	.238	3	10	7	2	1.3
1942 Chi-N	6	9	.400	32	17	4	1	0	140¹	161	6	55	46	13.9	4.49	71	.283	.347	9	.188	1	-18	-20	1	-1.8
1946 Chi-N	0	0	—	5	0	0	0	0	9²	10	0	9	8	17.7	2.79	119	.294	.442	0	—	0	1	1	0	0.1
Total 5	30	26	.536	112	60	23	7	2	516	547	18	192	201	13.0	3.40	103	.271	.335	39	.231	8	12	6	7	2.3

YEAR TM/L	W	L	PCT	G	GS	CG	SH	SV	IP	H	HR	BB	SO	RAT	ERA	ERA+	OAV	OOB	BH	AVG	PB	PR	/A	PD	TPI

● GREGG OLSON
Olson, Greggory William b: 10/11/66, Scribner, Neb. BR/TR, 6'4", 210 lbs. Deb: 9/02/88

1988 Bal-A	1	1	.500	10	0	0	0	0	11	10	1	10	9	16.4	3.27	119	.244	.392	0	—	0	1	1	0	0.3
1989 Bal-A	5	2	.714	64	0	0	0	27	85	57	1	46	90	11.0	1.69	224	.188	.296	0	—	0	21	20	0	2.1
1990 Bal-A☆	6	5	.545	64	0	0	0	37	74¹	57	3	31	74	11.0	2.42	157	.213	.301	0	—	0	12	11	-1	1.2
1991 Bal-A	4	6	.400	72	0	0	0	31	73²	74	1	29	72	12.7	3.18	124	.261	.332	0	—	0	8	6	0	0.9
1992 Bal-A	1	5	.167	60	0	0	0	36	61¹	46	3	24	58	10.3	2.05	190	.211	.289	0	—	0	13	13	1	1.4
Total 5	17	19	.472	270	0	0	0	131	305¹	244	9	140	303	11.5	2.36	164	.219	.309	0	—	0	54	51	1	5.9

● TED OLSON
Olson, Theodore Otto b: 8/27/12, Quincy, Mass. d: 12/9/80, Weymouth, Mass. BR/TR, 6'2.5", 185 lbs. Deb: 6/21/36

1936 Bos-A	1	1	.500	5	3	1	0	0	18¹	24	3	8	5	15.7	7.36	72	.324	.390	1	.143	-0	-5	-4	0	-0.4
1937 Bos-A	0	0	—	11	0	0	0	0	32¹	42	4	15	11	15.9	7.24	66	.318	.388	3	.300	1	-9	-9	1	-0.6
1938 Bos-A	0	0	—	2	0	0	0	0	7	9	0	2	2	14.1	6.43	77	.310	.355	0	.000	-0	-1	-1	-0	-0.1
Total 3	1	1	.500	18	3	1	0	0	57²	75	7	25	18	15.6	7.18	69	.319	.385	4	.222	1	-15	-14	1	-1.1

● ED OLWINE
Olwine, Edward R. b: 5/28/58, Greenville, Ohio BL/TL, 6'2", 165 lbs. Deb: 6/02/86

1986 Atl-N	0	0	—	37	0	0	0	1	47²	35	5	17	37	10.0	3.40	117	.207	.283	1	.333	1	2	3	-0	0.3
1987 Atl-N	0	1	.000	27	0	0	0	1	23¹	25	4	8	12	13.1	5.01	87	.269	.333	0	—	0	-2	-2	-0	-0.2
1988 Atl-N	0	0	—	16	0	0	0	1	18²	22	4	4	5	13.0	6.75	54	.286	.329	0	—	0	-7	-6	-1	-0.7
Total 3	0	1	.000	80	0	0	0	3	89²	82	13	29	54	11.4	4.52	89	.242	.307	1	.333	1	-8	-5	-1	-0.6

● SKINNY O'NEAL
O'Neal, Oran Herbert b: 5/2/1899, Gatewood, Mo. d: 6/2/81, Springfield, Mo. BR/TR, 5'11", 160 lbs. Deb: 4/18/25

1925 Phi-N	0	0	—	11	1	0	0	0	20¹	35	2	12	6	20.8	9.30	51	.407	.480	1	.167	-0	-11	-10	-0	-1.0
1927 Phi-N	0	0	—	2	0	0	0	0	5	9	0	2	2	19.8	9.00	46	.409	.458	0	.000	-0	-3	-3	1	-0.2
Total 2	0	0	—	13	1	0	0	0	25¹	44	2	14	8	20.6	9.24	50	.407	.475	1	.143	-0	-14	-13	0	-1.2

● RANDY O'NEAL
O'Neal, Randall Jeffrey b: 8/30/60, Ashland, Ky. BR/TR, 6'2", 195 lbs. Deb: 9/12/84

1984 Det-A	2	1	.667	4	3	0	0	0	18²	16	0	6	12	10.6	3.38	116	.222	.282	0	—	0	1	1	-0	0.1
1985 Det-A	5	5	.500	28	12	1	0	1	94¹	82	8	36	52	11.4	3.24	126	.240	.316	0	—	0	9	9	1	1.0
1986 Det-A	3	7	.300	37	11	1	0	2	122²	121	13	44	68	12.3	4.33	95	.260	.327	2	—	0	-2	-3	1	-0.2
1987 Atl-N	4	2	.667	16	10	0	0	0	61	79	12	24	33	15.5	5.61	78	.316	.380	-1	2 .105	-1	-10	-9	1	-0.8
StL-N	0	0	—	1	1	0	0	0	5	2	0	2	4	7.2	1.80	231	.111	.200	1	1.000	0	1	1	0	0.2
Yr	4	2	.667	17	11	0	0	0	66	81	12	26	37	14.6	5.32	81	.298	.359	3	.150	0	-9	-7	1	-0.6
1988 StL-N	2	3	.400	10	8	0	0	0	53	57	7	10	20	11.7	4.58	76	.274	.314	0	—	0	-7	-7	1	-0.8
1989 Phi-N	0	1	.000	20	1	0	0	0	39	46	5	9	29	12.7	6.23	57	.301	.340	0	.000	-1	-12	-12	1	-1.2
1990 SF-N	1	0	1.000	26	0	0	0	0	47	58	3	18	30	14.6	3.83	95	.314	.374	1	.167	-0	-0	-1	-0	-0.1
Total 7	17	19	.472	142	46	2	0	3	440²	461	48	149	248	12.6	4.35	91	.272	.334	4	.080	-3	-19	-19	5	-1.8

● ED O'NEIL
O'Neil, Edward J. b: 3/11/1859, Fall River, Mass. d: 9/30/1892, Fall River, Mass. TR, 5'11", 180 lbs. Deb: 6/20/1890

1890 Tol-a	0	2	.000	2	2	2	0	0	16	27	0	13	2	22.5	7.88	50	.363	.458	0	.000	-2	-7	-7	0	-0.6
Phi-a	0	6	.000	6	6	6	0	0	52	84	0	32	17	21.3	9.69	40	.353	.444	5	.161	-1	-34	-34	1	-2.4
Yr	0	8	.000	8	8	8	0	0	68	111	0	45	19	21.6	9.26	42	.355	.447	5	.125	-2	-41	-41	1	-3.0

● J. O'NEILL
O'Neill, J. b: Bedford, Pa. Deb: 8/20/1875

| 1875 Atl-n | 0 | 4 | .000 | 5 | 4 | 3 | 0 | 0 | 34 | 56 | 2 | 0 | | 14.8 | 4.76 | 48 | .324 | .324 | 3 | .115 | -1 | -9 | -9 | | -0.8 |

● TIP O'NEILL
O'Neill, James Edward b: 5/25/1858, Woodstock, Ont., Canada d: 12/31/15, Montreal, Que., Can BR/TR, 6'1.5", 167 lbs. Deb: 5/05/1883 ◆

1883 NY-N	5	12	.294	19	19	15	0	0	148	182	5	64	55	15.0	4.07	76	.289	.354	15	.197	-1	-15	-16	-1	-1.5
1884 StL-a	11	4	.733	17	14	14	0	0	141	125	3	51	36	11.5	2.68	122	.219	.288	82	.276	5	9	9	0	1.3
Total 2	16	16	.500	36	33	29	0	0	289	307	8	115	91	13.3	3.39	94	.256	.323	1386	.326	3	-6	-7	-1	-0.2

● HARRY O'NEILL
O'Neill, Joseph Henry b: 2/20/1897, Ridgetown, Ont., Canada d: 9/5/69, Ridgetown, Ont., Can. BR/TR, 6', 180 lbs. Deb: 9/15/22

1922 Phi-A	0	0	—	1	0	0	0	0	3	2	0	1	0	12.0	3.00	142	.200	.333	0	.000	-0	0	0	0	0.0
1923 Phi-A	0	0	—	3	0	0	0	0	2	1	0	3	2	18.0	0.00	—	.167	.444	0	—	-0	1	1	-0	0.1
Total 2	0	0	—	4	0	0	0	0	5	3	0	4	2	14.4	1.80	233	.188	.381	0	.000	-0	1	1	0	0.1

● MIKE O'NEILL
O'Neill, Michael Joyce (a.k.a. Michael Joyce in 1901) b: 9/7/1877, Galway, Ireland d: 8/12/59, Scranton, Pa. BR/TR, 5'11", 185 lbs. Deb: 9/20/01 F◆

1901 StL-N	2	2	.500	5	4	4	1	0	41	29	2	10	16	9.4	1.32	242	.198	.268	6	.400	2	9	8	-1	1.1
1902 StL-N	16	15	.516	36	32	29	2	2	288¹	297	3	66	105	11.7	2.90	94	.266	.314	43	.319	9	-4	-5	0	0.8
1903 StL-N	4	13	.235	19	17	12	0	0	145	184	2	43	39	14.5	3.79	86	.304	.356	25	.227	2	-8	-8	-0	-0.6
1904 StL-N	10	14	.417	25	24	23	1	0	220	229	1	50	68	11.5	2.09	129	.262	.304	21	.231	4	16	15	1	2.4
Total 4	32	44	.421	85	77	68	4	2	694¹	739	8	169	228	12.1	2.73	105	.269	.318	97	.255	17	13	10	-0	3.7

● PAUL O'NEILL
O'Neill, Paul Andrew b: 2/25/63, Columbus, Ohio BL/TL, 6'4", 205 lbs. Deb: 9/03/85 ◆

| 1987 Cin-N | 0 | 0 | — | 1 | 0 | 0 | 0 | 0 | 2 | 2 | 1 | 4 | 2 | 27.0 | 13.50 | 31 | .286 | .545 | 41 | .256 | 0 | -2 | -2 | -0 | -0.2 |

● EMMETT O'NEILL
O'Neill, Robert Emmett "Pinky" b: 1/13/18, San Mateo, Cal. BR/TR, 6'3", 185 lbs. Deb: 8/03/43

1943 Bos-A	1	4	.200	11	5	1	0	0	57²	56	3	46	20	16.1	4.53	73	.256	.387	3	.188	1	-8	-8	0	-0.7
1944 Bos-A	6	11	.353	28	22	8	1	0	151²	154	6	89	68	14.5	4.63	73	.265	.365	10	.182	-0	-20	-21	-2	-2.3
1945 Bos-A	8	11	.421	24	22	10	1	0	141²	134	5	117	55	16.3	5.15	66	.258	.399	9	.180	2	-28	-27	1	-2.5
1946 Chi-N	0	0	—	1	0	0	0	0	1	0	0	3	1	27.0	0.00	—	.000	.500	0	—	0	0	0	0	0.0
Chi-A	0	0	—	2	0	0	0	0	3²	4	0	5	0	22.1	0.00	—	.333	.529	0	.000	-0	1	1	0	0.1
Total 4	15	26	.366	66	49	19	2	0	355²	348	14	260	144	15.6	4.76	71	.261	.385	22	.180	2	-54	-54	-2	-5.4

● STEVE ONTIVEROS
Ontiveros, Steven b: 3/5/61, Tularosa, N.Mex. BR/TR, 6', 180 lbs. Deb: 6/14/85

1985 Oak-A	1	3	.250	39	0	0	0	8	74²	45	4	19	36	8.0	1.93	200	.174	.236	0	—	0	18	16	1	1.7
1986 Oak-A	2	2	.500	46	0	0	0	10	72²	72	10	25	54	12.1	4.71	82	.265	.329	0	—	0	-4	-7	-0	-0.7
1987 Oak-A	10	8	.556	35	22	2	1	1	150²	141	19	50	97	11.6	4.00	103	.242	.306	0	—	0	8	2	2	0.5
1988 Oak-A	3	4	.429	10	10	0	0	0	54²	57	4	21	30	12.8	4.61	82	.265	.331	0	—	0	-4	-5	1	-0.4
1989 Phi-N	2	1	.667	6	5	0	0	0	30²	34	2	15	12	14.4	3.82	93	.288	.368	1	.083	-0	-1	-1	1	0.0
1990 Phi-N	0	0	—	5	0	0	0	0	10	9	1	3	6	10.8	2.70	142	.225	.279	0	—	0	1	1	1	0.2
Total 6	18	18	.500	141	37	2	1	19	393¹	358	40	133	235	11.4	3.78	104	.241	.306	1	.083	-0	18	7	6	1.3

● JOSE OQUENDO
Oquendo, Jose Manuel (Contreras) b: 7/4/63, Rio Piedras, P.R. BB/TR, 5'10", 160 lbs. Deb: 5/02/83 ◆

1987 *StL-N	0	0	—	1	0	0	0	0	1	1	0	2	0	54.0	27.00	15	.571	.667	71	.286	0	-3	-3	-0	-0.2
1988 StL-N	0	1	.000	1	0	0	0	0	4	4	0	6	1	22.5	4.50	77	.267	.476	125	.277	0	-0	-0	-0	0.0
1991 StL-N	0	0	—	1	0	0	0	0	1	2	0	2	1	36.0	27.00	14	.400	.571	88	.240	0	-3	-3	-0	-0.2
Total 3	0	1	.000	3	0	0	0	0	6	10	0	9	2	30.0	12.00	30	.370	.541	726	.261	1	-6	-6	-0	-0.4

● DON O'RILEY
O'Riley, Donald Lee b: 3/12/45, Topeka, Kan. BR/TR, 6'3", 205 lbs. Deb: 6/20/69

1969 KC-A	1	1	.500	18	1	0	0	0	23¹	32	6	15	10	18.1	6.94	53	.311	.398	0	.000	-0	-9	-8	-0	-0.9
1970 KC-A	0	0	—	9	2	0	0	0	23¹	26	5	9	13	13.9	5.40	69	.277	.346	0	.000	-0	-4	-4	-0	-0.5
Total 2	1	1	.500	27	3	0	0	0	46²	58	5	24	23	16.0	6.17	60	.294	.374	0	.000	-0	-13	-13	-1	-1.4

● JESSE OROSCO
Orosco, Jesse Russell b: 4/21/57, Santa Barbara, Cal. BR/TL, 6'2", 185 lbs. Deb: 4/05/79

| 1979 NY-N | 1 | 2 | .333 | 18 | 2 | 0 | 0 | 0 | 35 | 33 | 4 | 22 | 22 | 14.7 | 4.89 | 74 | .260 | .377 | 0 | .000 | -1 | -4 | -5 | 1 | -0.5 |

YEAR TM/L	W	L	PCT	G	GS	CG	SH	SV	IP	H	HR	BB	SO	RAT	ERA	ERA+	OAV	OOB	BH	AVG	PB	PR	/A	PD	TPI
1981 NY-N	0	1	.000	8	0	0	0	1	17^1	13	2	6	18	9.9	1.56	224	.213	.284	0	.000	-0	4	4	0	0.4
1982 NY-N	4	10	.286	54	2	0	0	4	109^1	92	7	40	89	11.0	2.72	134	.230	.303	2	.143	-0	11	11	0	1.1
1983 NY-N★	13	7	.650	62	0	0	0	17	110	76	3	38	84	9.4	1.47	246	.197	.271	4	.333	1	**26**	**26**	1	3.0
1984 NY-N☆	10	6	.625	60	0	0	0	31	87	58	7	34	85	9.7	2.59	137	.185	.269	1	.250	1	10	9	-0	1.1
1985 NY-N	8	6	.571	54	0	0	0	17	79	66	6	34	68	11.4	2.73	126	.224	.304	3	.429	1	8	6	-1	0.7
1986 *NY-N	8	6	.571	58	0	0	0	21	81	64	6	35	62	11.3	2.33	151	.217	.306	0	.000	0	12	11	-1	1.1
1987 NY-N	3	9	.250	58	0	0	0	16	77	78	5	31	78	13.0	4.44	85	.266	.340	0	.000	-1	-3	-6	-0	-0.6
1988 *LA-N	3	2	.600	55	0	0	0	9	53	41	4	30	43	12.4	2.72	123	.215	.327	0	.000	-0	4	4	0	0.4
1989 Cle-A	3	4	.429	69	0	0	0	3	78	54	7	26	79	9.5	2.08	191	.198	.272	0	—	0	16	16	1	1.8
1990 Cle-A	5	4	.556	55	0	0	0	2	64^2	58	9	38	55	13.4	3.90	101	.239	.342	0	—	0	0	0	1	0.1
1991 Cle-A	2	0	1.000	47	0	0	0	0	45^2	52	4	15	36	13.4	3.74	111	.286	.343	0	—	0	2	2	-1	0.1
1992 Mil-A	3	1	.750	59	0	0	0	1	39	33	5	13	40	10.8	3.23	118	.232	.301	0	—	0	3	3	-0	0.4
Total 13	63	58	.521	657	4	0	0	122	876	718	69	362	759	11.3	2.84	130	.224	.307	10	.172	1	88	82	2	9.1
● O'ROURKE																									
O'Rourke Deb: 7/09/1872																									
1872 Eck-n	0	1	.000	1	1	1	0	0	9	16	0	2	0	18.0	6.00	58	.327	.353	0	.000	-1	-2	-3		-0.2
● JIM O'ROURKE																									
O'Rourke, James Henry "Orator Jim" b: 9/1/1850, Bridgeport, Conn. d: 1/8/19, Bridgeport, Conn. BR/TR, 5'8", 185 lbs. Deb: 4/26/1872 FMUH♦																									
1883 Buf-N	0	0	—	2	0	0	0	1	7	10	0	1	1	14.1	6.43	49	.357	.379	143	.328	1	-3	-3	-0	-0.2
1884 Buf-N	0	1	.000	4	0	0	0	1	12^2	7	0	1	3	5.7	2.84	111	.175	.195	162	.347	2	0	0	-0	0.1
Total 2	0	1	.000	6	0	0	0	2	19^2	17	0	2	4	8.7	4.12	77	.250	.271	2304	.310	3	-2	-2	-1	-0.1
● MIKE O'ROURKE																									
O'Rourke, Michael J. Deb: 9/01/1890																									
1890 Bal-a	1	2	.333	5	5	5	0	0	41	45	0	10	8	12.7	3.95	103	.270	.323	3	.115	-0	-0	0	1	0.0
● DAVE ORR																									
Orr, David L. b: 9/29/1859, New York, N.Y. d: 6/3/15, Brooklyn, N.Y. BR/TR, 5'11", 250 lbs. Deb: 5/17/1883 M♦																									
1885 NY-a	0	0	—	3	0	0	0	0	10	11	2	5	1	14.4	7.20	41	.229	.302	152	.342	2	-4	-5	-0	-0.4
● JOE ORRELL																									
Orrell, Forrest Gordon b: 10/6/17, National City, Cal. BR/TR, 6'4", 210 lbs. Deb: 8/12/43																									
1943 Det-A	0	0	—	10	0	0	0	1	19^1	18	0	11	2	14.4	3.72	95	.257	.373	1	.250	0	-1	-0	-0	-0.1
1944 Det-A	2	1	.667	10	2	0	0	0	22^1	26	0	11	10	15.3	2.42	147	.286	.369	1	.250	0	3	3	1	0.4
1945 Det-A	2	3	.400	12	5	1	0	0	48	46	1	24	14	13.5	3.00	117	.260	.355	2	.133	-1	2	3	-0	0.1
Total 3	4	4	.500	32	7	1	0	1	89^2	90	1	46	26	14.2	3.01	117	.266	.362	4	.174	-1	4	5	0	0.4
● PHIL ORTEGA																									
Ortega, Filomeno Coronado "Kemo" b: 10/7/39, Gilbert, Ariz. BR/TR, 6'2", 175 lbs. Deb: 9/10/60																									
1960 LA-N	0	0	—	3	1	0	0	0	6^1	12	1	5	4	24.2	17.05	23	.400	.486	0	.000	-0	-9	-9	0	-0.8
1961 LA-N	0	2	.000	4	2	1	0	0	13	10	6	2	15	8.3	5.54	78	.208	.240	1	.250	0	-2	-2	-0	-0.2
1962 LA-N	0	2	.000	24	3	0	0	1	53^2	60	8	39	30	17.1	6.88	53	.276	.394	0	.000	-1	-17	-19	-1	-2.0
1963 LA-N	0	0	—	1	0	0	0	0	1	2	1	0	1	18.0	18.00	17	.400	.400	0	—	0	-2	-2	0	-0.2
1964 LA-N	7	9	.438	34	25	4	3	1	157^1	149	22	56	107	12.1	4.00	81	.249	.320	6	.136	-0	-8	-13	-2	-1.6
1965 Was-A	12	15	.444	35	29	4	2	0	179^2	176	33	97	88	13.9	5.11	68	.262	.359	11	.208	4	-33	-33	-1	-3.0
1966 Was-A	12	12	.500	33	31	5	1	0	197^1	158	29	53	121	9.9	3.92	88	.218	.276	3	.056	-2	-11	-10	-1	-1.4
1967 Was-A	10	10	.500	34	34	5	2	0	219^2	189	16	57	122	10.3	3.03	104	.231	.286	4	.061	-3	5	3	-1	0.0
1968 Was-A	5	12	.294	31	16	1	1	0	115^2	115	12	62	57	14.2	4.98	59	.263	.361	4	.167	1	-26	-27	-0	-2.7
1969 Cal-A	0	0	—	5	0	0	0	0	8	13	3	7	4	22.5	10.13	34	.333	.435	0	—	0	-6	-6	0	-0.6
Total 10	46	62	.426	204	141	20	9	2	951^2	884	131	378	549	12.2	4.43	75	.246	.323	29	.115	-1	-109	-117	-6	-12.5
● AL ORTH																									
Orth, Albert Lewis "Smiling Al" or "The Curveless Wonder" b: 9/5/1872, Tipton, Ind. d: 10/8/48, Lynchburg, Va. BL/TR, 6', 200 lbs. Deb: 8/15/1895 U♦																									
1895 Phi-N	8	1	.889	11	10	9	0	1	88	103	0	22	25	13.0	3.89	123	.288	.332	16	.356	4	9	9	-2	0.9
1896 Phi-N	15	10	.600	25	23	19	0	0	196	244	10	46	23	13.5	4.41	98	.303	.342	21	.256	3	-1	-2	1	0.1
1897 Phi-N	14	19	.424	36	34	29	2	0	282^1	349	12	82	64	13.9	4.62	91	.301	.350	50	.329	7	-10	-13	1	-0.3
1898 Phi-N	15	13	.536	32	28	25	1	0	250	290	2	53	52	12.6	3.02	114	.288	.329	36	.293	7	16	11	0	1.9
1899 Phi-N	14	3	.824	21	15	13	3	1	144^2	149	0	19	35	10.6	2.49	148	.266	.294	13	.210	1	22	19	-4	1.5
1900 Phi-N	14	14	.500	33	30	24	2	1	262	302	4	60	68	12.9	3.78	96	.288	.335	40	.310	6	-2	-5	1	0.3
1901 Phi-N	20	12	.625	35	33	30	**6**	1	281^2	250	3	32	92	**9.3**	2.27	150	.236	**.264**	36	.281	5	33	35	3	**4.6**
1902 Was-A	19	18	.514	38	37	36	1	0	324	367	18	40	76	11.5	3.97	93	.286	.311	38	.217	2	-14	-10	1	-0.6
1903 Was-A	10	22	.313	36	32	30	2	**2**	279^2	326	8	62	88	12.7	4.34	72	.290	.331	49	.302	9	-43	-38	-0	-2.6
1904 Was-A	3	4	.429	10	7	7	0	0	73^2	88	2	15	23	13.0	4.76	56	.297	.337	22	.216	0	-18	-17	0	-1.7
NY-A	11	6	.647	20	18	11	2	0	137^2	122	0	19	47	9.3	2.68	101	.238	.267	19	.297	3	-1	0	1	0.5
Yr	14	10	.583	30	25	18	2	0	211^1	210	2	34	70	10.4	3.41	79	.259	.290	41	.247	3	-19	-17	1	-1.2
1905 NY-A	18	16	.529	40	37	26	6	0	305^1	273	8	61	121	10.1	2.86	103	.240	.284	24	.183	-1	-7	3	-0	0.1
1906 NY-A	**27**	17	.614	45	39	**36**	3	0	**338**^{2}	317	2	66	133	10.2	2.34	127	.251	.288	37	.274	6	13	24	-1	3.3
1907 NY-A	14	21	.400	36	33	21	2	0	248^2	244	2	53	78	11.0	2.61	107	.259	.302	34	.324	7	-2	5	3	1.9
1908 NY-A	2	13	.133	21	17	8	1	0	139^1	134	4	30	22	10.9	3.42	72	.255	.300	20	.290	5	-16	-15	-1	-1.2
1909 NY-A	0	0	—	1	1	0	0	0	3	6	0	1	1	21.0	12.00	21	.429	.467	9	.265	0	-3	-3	-0	-0.3
Total 15	204	189	.519	440	394	324	31	6	3354^2	3564	75	661	948	11.6	3.37	101	.272	.311	464	.273	64	-23	15	2	8.4
● BABY ORTIZ																									
Ortiz, Oliverio (Nunez) b: 12/5/19, Camaguey, Cuba d: 3/27/84, Central Senado, Camaguey, Cuba BR/TR, 6', 190 lbs. Deb: 9/23/44 F																									
1944 Was-A	0	2	.000	2	2	1	0	0	13	13	0	6	4	13.2	6.23	52	.255	.333	1	.167	-0	-4	-4	-1	-0.5
● OSSIE ORWOLL																									
Orwoll, Oswald Christian b: 11/17/1900, Portland, Ore. d: 5/8/67, Decorah, Iowa BL/TL, 6', 174 lbs. Deb: 4/13/28 ♦																									
1928 Phi-A	6	5	.545	27	8	3	0	2	106	110	7	50	53	13.8	4.58	87	.274	.358	52	.306	7	-6	-7	-0	-0.3
1929 Phi-A	0	2	.000	12	0	0	0	1	30	32	6	6	12	11.4	4.80	88	.278	.314	13	.255	1	-2	-2	-0	-0.1
Total 2	6	7	.462	39	8	3	0	3	136	142	13	56	65	13.2	4.63	88	.275	.348	65	.294	7	-8	-9	-1	-0.4
● OZZIE OSBORN																									
Osborn, Danny Leon b: 6/19/46, Springfield, Mo. BR/TR, 6'2", 195 lbs. Deb: 4/26/75																									
1975 Chi-A	3	0	1.000	24	0	0	0	0	58	57	2	37	38	14.9	4.50	86	.265	.378	0	—	0	-5	-4	-1	-0.6
● BOB OSBORN																									
Osborn, John Bode b: 4/17/03, San Diego, Tex. d: 4/19/60, Paris, Ark. BR/TR, 6'1", 175 lbs. Deb: 9/16/25																									
1925 Chi-N	0	0	—	1	0	0	0	0	2	6	0	0	0	27.0	0.00	—	.600	.600	0	—	0	1	1	0	0.1
1926 Chi-N	6	5	.545	31	15	6	0	1	136^1	157	3	58	43	14.2	3.63	106	.301	.371	6	.146	-3	3	3	2	0.2
1927 Chi-N	5	5	.500	24	12	2	0	0	107^2	125	2	48	45	14.5	4.18	92	.294	.367	8	.205	-0	-3	-4	-1	-0.5
1929 Chi-N	0	0	—	3	1	0	0	0	9	8	0	2	1	10.0	3.00	154	.242	.286	1	.250	0	2	2	-0	0.1
1930 Chi-N	10	6	.625	35	13	3	0	1	126^2	147	9	53	42	14.3	4.97	98	.300	.369	4	.095	-5	-0	-1	2	-0.3
1931 Pit-N	6	1	.857	27	2	0	0	0	64^2	85	3	20	9	14.8	5.01	77	.316	.366	3	.167	-0	-8	-8	-1	-0.9
Total 6	27	17	.614	121	43	11	0	2	446^1	528	17	181	140	14.4	4.32	97	.302	.368	22	.153	-8	-6	-7	2	-1.3
● PAT OSBORN																									
Osborn, Larry Patrick b: 5/4/49, Murray, Ky. BL/TL, 6'4", 195 lbs. Deb: 4/13/74																									
1974 Cin-N	0	0	—	6	0	0	0	0	9	11	2	4	4	15.0	8.00	44	.297	.366	0	.000	-0	-4	-5	0	-0.4
1975 Mil-A	0	1	.000	6	1	0	0	0	11^2	19	2	9	1	23.1	5.40	71	.404	.517	0	—	0	-2	-2	0	-0.2
Total 2	0	1	.000	12	1	0	0	0	20^2	30	4	13	5	19.6	6.53	56	.357	.455	0	.000	-0	-6	-7	1	-0.6
● DONOVAN OSBORNE																									
Osborne, Donovan Alan b: 6/21/69, Roseville, Cal. BB/TL, 6'2", 195 lbs. Deb: 4/09/92																									
1992 StL-N	11	9	.550	34	29	0	0	0	179	193	14	38	104	11.7	3.77	91	.275	.314	7	.121	-1	-5	-6	-3	-1.1

YEAR	TM/L	W	L	PCT	G	GS	CG	SH	SV	IP	H	HR	BB	SO	RAT	ERA	ERA+	OAV	OOB	BH	AVG	PB	PR	/A	PD	TPI
● TINY OSBORNE	Osborne, Earnest Preston b: 4/9/1893, Porterdale, Ga. d: 1/5/69, Atlanta, Ga. BL/TR, 6'4.5", 215 lbs. Deb: 4/15/22 F																									
1922	Chi-N	9	5	.643	41	14	7	1	3	184	183	7	95	81	14.2	4.50	93	.271	.370	9	.134	-4	-8	-6	-3	-1.2
1923	Chi-N	8	15	.348	37	25	8	1	1	179^2	174	14	89	69	13.3	4.56	88	.255	.342	12	.200	-1	-11	-11	-1	-1.3
1924	Chi-N	0	0	—	2	0	0	0	1	3	3	0	2	2	15.0	3.00	130	.300	.417	0	—	0	0	0	0	0.0
	Bro-N	6	5	.545	21	13	6	0	0	104^1	123	1	54	52	15.6	5.09	74	.298	.384	9	.250	1	-14	-16	-1	-1.5
	Yr	6	5	.545	23	13	6	0	1	107^1	126	1	56	54	15.6	5.03	75	.298	.385	9	.250	1	-14	-15	-1	-1.5
1925	Bro-N	8	15	.348	41	22	10	0	1	175	210	9	75	59	14.9	4.94	85	.304	.375	14	.246	1	-13	-15	-2	-1.4
Total	4	31	40	.437	142	74	31	2	6	646	693	31	315	263	14.3	4.72	86	.280	.367	44	.200	-3	-46	-47	-6	-5.4
● FRED OSBORNE	Osborne, Frederick W. b: Hampton, Iowa TL , Deb: 7/14/1890 ♦																									
1890	Pit-N	0	5	.000	8	5	5	0	0	58	82	6	45	14	20.8	8.38	39	.323	.438	40	.238	1	-31	-33	-0	-2.5
● WAYNE OSBORNE	Osborne, Wayne Harold "Ossie" or "Fish Hook" b: 10/11/12, Watsonville, Cal. d: 3/13/87, Camas, Wash. BL/TR, 6'2.5", 172 lbs. Deb: 4/18/35																									
1935	Pit-N	0	0	—	2	0	0	0	0	1^1	1	0	0	1	6.8	6.75	61	.250	.250	0	—	0	-0	-0	0	0.0
1936	Bos-N	1	1	.500	5	3	0	0	0	20	31	1	9	8	18.0	5.85	66	.352	.412	2	.250	0	-4	-4	0	-0.4
Total	2	1	1	.500	7	3	0	0	0	21^1	32	1	9	9	17.3	5.91	65	.348	.406	2	.250	0	-4	-5	0	-0.4
● CHARLIE OSGOOD	Osgood, Charles Benjamin b: 11/23/26, Somerville, Mass. BR/TR, 5'10", 180 lbs. Deb: 6/18/44																									
1944	Bro-N	0	0	—	1	0	0	0	0	3	2	0	3	0	18.0	3.00	118	.222	.462	0	—	0	0	0	-0	0.0
● DAN OSINSKI	Osinski, Daniel b: 11/17/33, Chicago, Ill. BR/TR, 6'2", 195 lbs. Deb: 4/11/62																									
1962	KC-A	0	0	—	4	0	0	0	0	4^2	8	1	8	4	30.9	17.36	24	.381	.552	0	—	0	-7	-7	0	-0.6
	LA-A	6	4	.600	33	0	0	0	4	54^1	45	3	30	44	12.4	2.82	137	.223	.323	0	.000	-1	7	6	0	0.6
	Yr	6	4	.600	37	0	0	0	4	59	53	4	38	48	13.9	3.97	98	.237	.347	0	.000	-1	0	-1	0	0.0
1963	LA-A	8	8	.500	47	16	4	1	0	159^1	145	15	80	100	12.8	3.28	105	.242	.333	5	.111	-2	6	3	-1	0.0
1964	LA-A	3	3	.500	47	4	1	1	2	93	87	8	39	88	12.4	3.48	94	.244	.322	1	.056	-1	1	-2	1	-0.2
1965	Mil-N	0	3	.000	61	0	0	0	6	83	81	4	40	54	13.2	2.82	125	.261	.348	1	.167	-0	7	6	-0	0.6
1966	Bos-A	4	3	.571	44	1	0	0	2	67^1	68	8	28	44	13.0	3.61	105	.274	.350	2	.333	0	-1	1	-1	0.1
1967	*Bos-A	3	1	.750	34	0	0	0	2	63^2	61	5	14	38	10.6	2.54	137	.243	.283	3	.333	1	5	7	-0	0.8
1969	Chi-A	5	5	.500	51	0	0	0	2	60^2	56	3	23	27	11.7	3.56	108	.251	.321	0	.000	-0	0	2	2	0.4
1970	Hou-N	0	1	.000	3	0	0	0	0	3^2	5	0	2	1	17.2	9.82	39	.357	.438	0	—	0	-2	-2	-0	-0.2
Total	8	29	28	.509	324	21	5	2	18	589^2	556	47	264	400	12.6	3.34	107	.250	.331	12	.122	-3	16	15	1	1.5
● CLAUDE OSTEEN	Osteen, Claude Wilson b: 8/9/39, Caney Springs, Tenn. BL/TL, 5'11", 173 lbs. Deb: 7/06/57 C																									
1957	Cin-N	0	0	—	3	0	0	0	0	4	4	0	3	3	15.8	2.25	183	.250	.368	0	.000	-0	1	1	-0	0.1
1959	Cin-N	0	0	—	2	0	0	0	0	7^2	11	1	9	3	23.5	7.04	58	.333	.476	0	.000	-0	-3	-3	-0	-0.3
1960	Cin-N	0	1	.000	20	3	0	0	0	48^1	53	5	30	15	15.6	5.03	76	.293	.396	1	.083	-1	-7	-6	0	-0.7
1961	Cin-N	0	0	—	1	0	0	0	0	0^1	0	0	0	0	0.0	0.00	—	.000	.000	0	—	0	0	0	0	0.0
	Was-A	1	1	.500	3	3	0	0	0	18^1	14	3	9	14	11.8	4.91	82	.219	.324	1	.143	-0	-2	-2	0	-0.2
1962	Was-A	8	13	.381	28	22	7	2	1	150^1	140	12	47	59	11.4	3.65	111	.246	.309	10	.208	1	5	6	0	0.8
1963	Was-A	9	14	.391	40	29	8	2	0	212^1	222	23	60	109	12.0	3.35	111	.270	.320	12	.171	1	7	9	-1	0.9
1964	Was-A	15	13	.536	37	36	13	0	0	257	256	20	64	133	11.3	3.33	111	.259	.306	14	.156	1	8	11	2	1.5
1965	*LA-N	15	15	.500	40	40	9	1	0	287	253	19	78	162	10.5	2.79	117	.236	.290	12	.121	-1	24	15	6	2.2
1966	*LA-N	17	14	.548	39	38	8	3	0	240^1	238	6	65	137	11.4	2.85	116	.261	.312	16	.211	5	20	12	1	2.0
1967	LA-N☆	17	17	.500	39	39	14	5	0	288^1	298	19	52	152	11.0	3.22	96	.270	.304	18	.178	5	5	-4	-0	0.2
1968	LA-N	12	18	.400	39	36	5	3	0	253^2	267	14	54	119	11.6	3.09	90	.275	.316	15	.179	2	-3	-9	1	-0.7
1969	LA-N	20	15	.571	41	41	16	7	0	321	293	17	74	183	10.5	2.66	125	.245	.293	24	.216	6	33	24	3	3.5
1970	LA-N★	16	14	.533	37	37	11	4	0	258^2	280	24	52	114	11.7	3.83	100	.276	.313	19	.204	5	6	0	-1	0.4
1971	LA-N	14	11	.560	38	38	11	4	0	259	262	25	63	109	11.4	3.51	92	.266	.312	16	.186	2	-1	-8	6	0.0
1972	LA-N	20	11	.645	33	33	14	4	0	252	232	16	69	100	10.9	2.64	126	.245	.299	24	.273	9	23	19	-0	3.2
1973	LA-N★	16	11	.593	33	33	12	3	0	236^2	227	20	61	86	11.0	3.31	104	.258	.307	12	.154	-1	9	3	2	0.5
1974	Hou-N	9	9	.500	23	21	7	2	0	138^1	158	8	47	45	13.5	3.71	93	.292	.351	13	.283	3	-1	-4	0	0.0
	StL-N	0	2	.000	8	2	0	0	0	22^2	26	1	11	6	14.7	4.37	82	.286	.363	0	.000	-1	-2	-2	0	-0.3
	Yr	9	11	.450	31	23	7	2	0	161	184	9	58	51	13.5	3.80	92	.288	.347	13	.245	2	-3	-6	0	-0.3
1975	Chi-A	7	16	.304	37	37	5	0	0	204^1	237	16	92	63	14.6	4.36	89	.294	.367	0	—	0	-13	-11	1	-1.1
Total	18	196	195	.501	541	488	140	40	1	3460^1	3471	249	940	1612	11.6	3.30	104	.263	.314	207	.188	37	110	50	20	12.0
● DARRELL OSTEEN	Osteen, Milton Darrell b: 2/14/43, Oklahoma City, Okla. BR/TR, 6'1", 170 lbs. Deb: 9/02/65																									
1965	Cin-N	0	0	—	3	0	0	0	0	3	2	0	4	1	18.0	0.00	—	.200	.429	0	—	0	1	1	0	0.1
1966	Cin-N	0	2	.000	13	0	0	0	1	15	26	3	9	17	21.0	12.00	33	.371	.443	1	.500	0	-14	-13	-0	-1.3
1967	Cin-N	0	2	.000	10	0	0	0	2	14^1	10	1	13	13	16.3	6.28	60	.196	.388	0	.000	-0	-5	-4	0	-0.4
1970	Oak-A	1	0	1.000	3	1	0	0	0	5^2	9	0	3	3	19.1	6.35	56	.346	.414	0	.000	-0	-2	-2	-0	-0.2
Total	4	1	4	.200	29	1	0	0	3	38	47	4	29	34	18.7	8.05	47	.299	.418	1	.200	0	-19	-18	-0	-1.8
● FRED OSTENDORF	Ostendorf, Frederick K. b: 8/5/1890, Baltimore, Md. d: 3/2/65, Keoughtan, Va. BL/TL, 6'0.5", 169 lbs. Deb: 7/16/14																									
1914	Ind-F	0	0	—	1	0	0	0	0	2	5	0	2	0	36.0	22.50	15	.500	.615	0	.000	-0	-4	-4	0	-0.4
● BILL OSTER	Oster, William Charles b: 1/2/33, New York, N.Y. BL/TL, 6'3", 198 lbs. Deb: 8/23/54																									
1954	Phi-A	0	1	.000	8	1	0	0	0	15^2	19	2	12	5	17.8	6.32	62	.311	.425	1	.333	0	-5	-4	-0	-0.4
● FRITZ OSTERMUELLER	Ostermueller, Frederick Raymond b: 9/15/07, Quincy, Ill. d: 12/17/57, Quincy, Ill. BL/TL, 5'11", 175 lbs. Deb: 4/21/34																									
1934	Bos-A	10	13	.435	33	23	10	0	3	198^2	200	7	99	75	13.6	3.49	138	.262	.348	13	.167	-2	22	29	3	2.9
1935	Bos-A	7	8	.467	22	19	10	0	1	137^2	135	0	78	41	14.1	3.92	121	.257	.356	14	.286	1	8	13	-0	1.3
1936	Bos-A	10	16	.385	43	23	7	1	2	180^2	210	8	84	90	14.8	4.88	109	.288	.364	15	.234	0	3	9	3	1.0
1937	Bos-A	3	7	.300	25	7	2	0	1	86^2	101	2	44	29	15.2	4.98	95	.286	.367	11	.333	3	-4	-2	0	0.1
1938	Bos-A	13	5	.722	31	18	10	1	2	176^2	199	15	58	46	13.2	4.58	108	.275	.331	16	.216	2	4	7	-0	0.7
1939	Bos-A	11	7	.611	34	20	8	0	4	159^1	173	6	58	61	13.2	4.24	112	.277	.341	9	.161	-2	7	9	-1	0.6
1940	Bos-A	5	9	.357	31	16	5	0	0	143^2	166	7	70	80	14.8	4.95	91	.284	.361	17	.315	4	-9	-7	-1	-0.4
1941	StL-A	0	3	.000	15	2	0	0	0	46	45	3	23	20	13.3	4.50	96	.257	.343	3	.214	0	-2	-1	0	-0.1
1942	StL-A	3	1	.750	10	4	2	0	0	43^2	46	4	17	21	13.0	3.71	100	.266	.332	3	.188	-0	-0	-0	-1	-0.1
1943	StL-A	0	2	.000	11	3	0	0	0	28^2	36	1	13	4	15.4	5.02	66	.321	.392	2	.286	0	-5	-5	0	-0.5
	Bro-N	1	1	.500	7	1	0	0	0	27^1	21	0	12	15	10.9	3.29	102	.212	.297	0	.000	-1	0	0	-0	-0.1
1944	Bro-N	2	1	.667	10	4	3	0	1	41^2	46	3	12	17	12.5	3.24	110	.267	.315	2	.154	-0	2	1	-0	0.1
	Pit-N	11	7	.611	28	24	14	1	1	204^2	201	7	65	80	11.7	2.73	136	.260	.318	20	.250	2	20	23	-1	2.6
	Yr	13	8	.619	38	28	17	1	2	246^1	247	10	77	97	11.9	2.81	131	.261	.317	22	.237	2	22	24	-1	2.7
1945	Pit-N	5	4	.556	14	11	4	1	0	80^2	74	6	37	29	12.6	4.57	86	.236	.321	9	.321	2	-7	-6	0	-0.3
1946	Pit-N	13	10	.565	27	25	16	2	0	193^1	193	5	56	57	11.7	2.84	124	.263	.318	21	.328	7	12	15	-2	2.2
1947	Pit-N	12	10	.545	26	24	12	3	0	183	181	18	68	66	12.3	3.84	110	.254	.320	12	.188	0	5	8	-1	0.7
1948	Pit-N	8	11	.421	23	22	10	2	0	134^1	143	13	41	43	12.4	4.42	92	.262	.315	8	.182	-0	-7	-5	-1	-0.7
Total	15	114	115	.498	390	246	113	11	15	2066^2	2170	105	835	774	13.2	3.99	109	.268	.337	175	.234	17	49	85	-3	10.0
● JOE OSTROWSKI	Ostrowski, Joseph Paul "Professor" or "Specs" b: 11/15/16, W.Wyoming, Pa. BL/TL, 6', 180 lbs. Deb: 7/18/48																									
1948	StL-A	4	6	.400	26	9	3	0	3	78^1	108	6	17	20	14.4	5.97	76	.333	.367	4	.222	1	-15	-12	2	-0.9
1949	StL-A	8	8	.500	40	13	4	0	2	141	185	16	27	34	13.5	4.79	95	.307	.337	7	.189	2	-9	-4	-1	-0.2
1950	StL-A	2	4	.333	9	7	2	0	0	57^1	57	2	7	15	10.0	2.51	197	.251	.274	4	.222	2	13	16	-1	1.7

YEAR	TM/L	W	L	PCT	G	GS	CG	SH	SV	IP	H	HR	BB	SO	RAT	ERA	ERA+	OAV	OOB	BH	AVG	PB	PR	/A	PD	TPI
	NY-A	1	1	.500	21	4	1	0	3	43^2	50	11	15	15	13.4	5.15	83	.294	.351	1	.111	-0	-3	-4	0	-0.4
	Yr	3	5	.375	30	11	3	0	3	101	107	13	22	30	11.5	3.65	128	.270	.308	5	.185	1	10	11	-1	1.3
1951	*NY-A	6	4	.600	34	3	2	0	5	95^1	103	4	18	30	11.5	3.49	110	.279	.314	3	.107	-2	7	4	-1	0.1
1952	NY-A	2	2	.500	20	1	0	0	2	40	56	5	14	17	16.0	5.62	59	.327	.382	0	.000	-1	-9	-10	-1	-1.2
Total	5	23	25	.479	150	37	12	0	15	455^2	559	44	98	131	13.0	4.54	95	.300	.336	19	.161	2	-16	-12	-1	-0.9

● AL OSUNA Osuna, Alfonso b: 8/10/65, Inglewood, Cal. BR/TL, 6'3", 200 lbs. Deb: 9/02/90

YEAR	TM/L	W	L	PCT	G	GS	CG	SH	SV	IP	H	HR	BB	SO	RAT	ERA	ERA+	OAV	OOB	BH	AVG	PB	PR	/A	PD	TPI
1990	Hou-N	2	0	1.000	12	0	0	0	0	11^1	10	1	6	6	15.1	4.76	78	.270	.413	0	—	0	-1	-1	-0	-0.1
1991	Hou-N	7	6	.538	71	0	0	0	12	81^2	59	5	46	68	11.9	3.42	103	.201	.316	0	.000	-0	2	1	-0	0.1
1992	Hou-N	6	3	.667	66	0	0	0	0	61^2	52	8	38	37	13.3	4.23	79	.236	.351	0	—	0	-5	-6	0	-0.6
Total	3	15	9	.625	149	0	0	0	12	154^2	121	14	90	111	12.7	3.84	90	.220	.337	0	.000	-0	-4	-7	-0	-0.6

● BILL OTEY Otey, William Tilford "Steamboat Bill" b: 12/16/1886, Dayton, Ohio d: 4/23/31, Dayton, Ohio BL/TL, 6'2", 181 lbs. Deb: 9/27/07

YEAR	TM/L	W	L	PCT	G	GS	CG	SH	SV	IP	H	HR	BB	SO	RAT	ERA	ERA+	OAV	OOB	BH	AVG	PB	PR	/A	PD	TPI
1907	Pit-N	0	1	.000	3	2	1	0	0	16^1	23	1	4	5	15.4	4.41	55	.319	.364	1	.250	0	-4	-4	-0	-0.4
1910	Was-A	0	1	.000	9	1	1	0	0	34^2	40	1	6	12	12.2	3.38	74	.301	.336	5	.385	2	-3	-3	-1	-0.3
1911	Was-A	1	3	.250	12	2	0	0	0	49^2	68	2	15	16	15.6	6.34	52	.333	.387	1	.059	-2	-17	-17	1	-1.6
Total	3	1	5	.167	24	5	2	0	0	100^2	131	4	25	33	14.4	5.01	57	.320	.367	7	.206	0	-23	-24	-1	-2.3

● HARRY OTIS Otis, Harry George "Cannonball" b: 10/5/1886, W.New York, N.J. d: 1/29/76, Teaneck, N.J. BR/TL, 6' ", 180 lbs. Deb: 9/05/09

YEAR	TM/L	W	L	PCT	G	GS	CG	SH	SV	IP	H	HR	BB	SO	RAT	ERA	ERA+	OAV	OOB	BH	AVG	PB	PR	/A	PD	TPI
1909	Cle-A	2	2	.500	5	3	0	0	0	26^1	26	0	18	6	16.1	1.37	187	.283	.416	1	.111	-0	3	3	-0	0.4

● DENNIS O'TOOLE O'Toole, Dennis Joseph b: 3/13/49, Chicago, Ill. BR/TR, 6'3", 195 lbs. Deb: 9/08/69 F

YEAR	TM/L	W	L	PCT	G	GS	CG	SH	SV	IP	H	HR	BB	SO	RAT	ERA	ERA+	OAV	OOB	BH	AVG	PB	PR	/A	PD	TPI
1969	Chi-A	0	0	—	2	0	0	0	0	4	5	0	2	4	15.8	6.75	57	.333	.412	0	—	0	-1	-1	-0	-0.1
1970	Chi-A	0	0	—	3	0	0	0	0	3^1	5	0	2	3	18.9	2.70	144	.357	.438	0	—	0	0	0	-0	0.0
1971	Chi-A	0	0	—	1	0	0	0	0	2	0	0	1	2	4.5	0.00	—	.000	.143	0	—	0	1	1	-0	0.1
1972	Chi-A	0	0	—	3	0	0	0	0	5	10	0	2	5	21.6	5.40	58	.417	.462	0	—	0	-1	-1	0	-0.1
1973	Chi-A	0	0	—	6	0	0	0	0	16	23	3	3	8	14.6	5.63	70	.329	.356	0	—	0	-3	-3	0	-0.5
Total	5	0	0	—	15	0	0	0	0	30^1	43	3	10	22	15.7	5.04	75	.333	.381	0	—	0	-5	-4	-0	-0.6

● JIM O'TOOLE O'Toole, James Jerome b: 1/10/37, Chicago, Ill. BB/TL, 6', 198 lbs. Deb: 9/26/58 F

YEAR	TM/L	W	L	PCT	G	GS	CG	SH	SV	IP	H	HR	BB	SO	RAT	ERA	ERA+	OAV	OOB	BH	AVG	PB	PR	/A	PD	TPI
1958	Cin-N	0	1	.000	1	1	0	0	0	7	4	0	5	4	11.6	1.29	322	.154	.290	0	.000	-0	2	2	-0	0.2
1959	Cin-N	5	8	.385	28	19	3	1	0	129^1	144	14	73	68	15.4	5.15	79	.287	.382	5	.135	-0	-17	-16	1	-1.5
1960	Cin-N	12	12	.500	34	31	7	2	1	196^1	198	14	66	124	12.3	3.80	100	.263	.325	7	.106	-3	-1	0	-3	-0.6
1961	*Cin-N	19	9	.679	39	35	11	3	2	252^2	229	16	93	178	11.6	3.10	131	.240	.310	16	.172	-1	26	27	-0	2.7
1962	Cin-N	16	13	.552	36	34	11	3	0	251^2	222	20	87	170	11.2	3.50	115	.238	.307	10	.110	-5	12	15	-2	0.8
1963	Cin-N★	17	14	.548	33	32	12	5	0	234^1	208	13	57	146	10.3	2.88	116	.239	.288	11	.149	-1	11	12	-3	1.0
1964	Cin-N	17	7	.708	30	30	9	3	0	220	194	8	51	145	10.0	2.66	136	.235	.279	7	.100	-1	21	23	-2	2.2
1965	Cin-N	3	10	.231	29	22	2	0	1	127^2	154	14	47	71	14.4	5.92	63	.294	.355	4	.089	-2	-34	-31	-2	-3.4
1966	Cin-N	5	7	.417	25	24	2	0	0	142	139	16	49	96	12.1	3.55	110	.254	.318	6	.128	-2	1	6	-1	0.3
1967	Chi-A	4	3	.571	15	10	1	1	0	54^1	53	4	18	37	11.9	2.82	110	.251	.313	1	.077	-1	3	2	-1	0.1
Total	10	98	84	.538	270	238	58	18	4	1615^1	1545	119	546	1039	11.8	3.57	106	.251	.315	67	.125	-16	24	40	-12	1.8

● MARTY O'TOOLE O'Toole, Martin James b: 11/27/1888, Wm.Penn, Pa. d: 2/18/49, Aberdeen, Wash. BR/TR, 5'11", 175 lbs. Deb: 9/21/08

YEAR	TM/L	W	L	PCT	G	GS	CG	SH	SV	IP	H	HR	BB	SO	RAT	ERA	ERA+	OAV	OOB	BH	AVG	PB	PR	/A	PD	TPI
1908	Cin-N	1	0	1.000	3	2	1	0	0	15	15	0	7	5	13.2	2.40	96	.273	.355	1	.200	-0	-0	-0	-0	0.0
1911	Pit-N	3	2	.600	5	5	3	0	0	38	28	1	20	34	11.4	2.37	145	.215	.320	5	.357	2	4	4	0	0.7
1912	Pit-N	15	17	.469	37	36	17	5	0	275^1	237	4	159	150	13.0	2.71	120	.241	.348	22	.222	1	21	17	1	1.9
1913	Pit-N	6	8	.429	26	16	7	0	1	144^2	148	3	55	58	12.8	3.30	91	.271	.341	7	.132	-2	-1	-5	-0	-0.7
1914	Pit-N	1	8	.111	19	9	1	0	1	92^1	92	3	47	36	13.5	4.68	57	.270	.358	5	.167	0	-19	-21	-1	-2.2
	NY-N	1	1	.500	10	5	2	0	0	34	34	0	12	13	12.2	4.24	63	.262	.324	3	.300	1	-5	-6	-0	-0.6
	Yr	2	9	.182	29	14	3	0	1	126^1	126	3	59	49	13.2	4.56	58	.268	.349	8	.200	1	-25	-27	-1	-2.8
Total	5	27	36	.429	100	73	31	5	2	599^1	554	11	300	296	12.9	3.21	95	.254	.345	43	.204	2	-1	-10	-0	-0.9

● JIM OTTEN Otten, James Edward b: 7/1/51, Lewiston, Mont. BR/TR, 6'2", 195 lbs. Deb: 7/31/74

YEAR	TM/L	W	L	PCT	G	GS	CG	SH	SV	IP	H	HR	BB	SO	RAT	ERA	ERA+	OAV	OOB	BH	AVG	PB	PR	/A	PD	TPI
1974	Chi-A	0	1	.000	5	1	0	0	0	16^1	22	0	12	11	19.3	5.51	68	.324	.432	0	—	0	-3	-3	-0	-0.5
1975	Chi-A	0	0	—	2	0	0	0	0	5^1	4	1	7	3	18.6	6.75	57	.235	.458	0	—	0	-2	-2	0	-0.2
1976	Chi-A	0	0	—	2	0	0	0	0	6	9	0	2	3	16.5	4.50	79	.333	.379	0	—	0	-1	-1	-0	-0.1
1980	StL-N	0	5	.000	31	4	0	0	0	55^1	71	3	26	38	16.1	5.53	67	.323	.399	1	.200	-0	-12	-11	1	-1.1
1981	StL-N	1	0	1.000	24	0	0	0	0	35^2	44	3	20	20	16.1	5.30	67	.321	.408	0	.000	-0	-7	-7	-1	-0.8
Total	5	1	6	.143	64	5	0	0	0	118^2	150	7	67	75	16.7	5.46	67	.320	.408	1	.143	-0	-25	-24	-1	-2.7

● DAVE OTTO Otto, David Alan b: 11/12/64, Chicago, Ill. BL/TL, 6'7", 210 lbs. Deb: 9/08/87

YEAR	TM/L	W	L	PCT	G	GS	CG	SH	SV	IP	H	HR	BB	SO	RAT	ERA	ERA+	OAV	OOB	BH	AVG	PB	PR	/A	PD	TPI
1987	Oak-A	0	0	—	3	0	0	0	0	6	7	1	1	3	12.0	9.00	46	.304	.333	0	—	0	-3	-3	-0	-0.3
1988	Oak-A	0	0	—	3	2	0	0	0	10	9	0	6	7	13.5	1.80	210	.243	.349	0	—	0	2	2	0	0.4
1989	Oak-A	0	0	—	1	1	0	0	0	6^2	6	0	2	4	10.8	2.70	136	.261	.320	0	—	0	1	1	-0	0.1
1990	Oak-A	0	0	—	2	0	0	0	0	2^1	3	0	3	2	23.1	7.71	48	.300	.462	0	—	0	-1	-1	0	0.0
1991	Cle-A	2	8	.200	18	14	1	0	0	100	108	7	27	47	12.5	4.23	98	.283	.337	0	—	0	-2	-1	-0	-0.1
1992	Cle-A	5	9	.357	18	16	0	0	0	80^1	110	12	33	32	16.1	7.06	57	.333	.396	0	—	0	-28	-27	0	-2.5
Total	6	7	17	.292	45	33	1	0	0	205^1	243	20	72	95	14.0	5.35	76	.302	.363	0	—	0	-30	-29	0	-2.4

● ORVAL OVERALL Overall, Orval b: 2/2/1881, Farmersville, Cal. d: 7/14/47, Fresno, Cal. BB/TR, 6'2", 214 lbs. Deb: 4/16/05

YEAR	TM/L	W	L	PCT	G	GS	CG	SH	SV	IP	H	HR	BB	SO	RAT	ERA	ERA+	OAV	OOB	BH	AVG	PB	PR	/A	PD	TPI
1905	Cin-N	18	23	.439	42	39	32	2	0	318	290	4	147	173	12.8	2.86	116	.252	.343	17	.145	-3	5	16	-1	1.2
1906	Cin-N	4	5	.444	13	10	6	0	0	82^1	77	1	46	33	13.9	4.26	65	.253	.359	6	.194	0	-15	-14	-1	-1.6
	*Chi-N	12	3	.800	18	14	13	2	1	144	116	1	51	94	10.7	1.88	141	.217	.290	9	.170	-1	12	12	0	1.3
	Yr	16	8	.667	31	24	19	2	1	226^1	193	2	97	127	11.7	2.74	98	.229	.311	15	.179	-1	-3	-2	-1	-0.3
1907	*Chi-N	23	7	.767	36	30	26	**8**	3	268^1	201	3	69	141	9.4	1.68	149	.208	.268	20	.213	4	24	24	2	3.5
1908	*Chi-N	15	11	.577	37	27	16	4	4	225	165	3	78	167	9.8	1.92	123	.208	.280	9	.129	-1	11	11	-1	1.0
1909	Chi-N	20	11	.645	38	32	23	**9**	3	285	204	1	80	**205**	9.2	1.42	179	**.198**	.262	22	.229	8	37	36	0	5.2
1910	*Chi-N	12	6	.667	23	21	11	4	1	144^2	106	2	54	92	10.0	2.68	108	.212	.291	5	.122	-1	6	3	1	0.4
1913	Chi-N	4	5	.444	11	9	6	1	0	68	73	1	26	30	13.2	3.31	96	.284	.352	6	.250	2	-1	-1	1	0.2
Total	7	108	71	.603	218	182	133	30	12	1535^1	1232	16	551	935	10.7	2.23	123	.223	.298	94	.179	8	79	87	1	11.2

● STUBBY OVERMIRE Overmire, Frank b: 5/16/19, Moline, Mich. d: 3/3/77, Lakeland, Fla. BR/TL, 5'7", 170 lbs. Deb: 4/25/43 C

YEAR	TM/L	W	L	PCT	G	GS	CG	SH	SV	IP	H	HR	BB	SO	RAT	ERA	ERA+	OAV	OOB	BH	AVG	PB	PR	/A	PD	TPI
1943	Det-A	7	6	.538	29	18	8	3	1	147	135	5	38	48	10.7	3.18	111	.243	.293	7	.167	0	2	6	-1	0.5
1944	Det-A	11	11	.500	32	28	11	3	1	199^2	214	2	41	57	11.6	3.07	116	.271	.309	11	.175	1	8	11	2	1.4
1945	*Det-A	9	9	.500	31	22	9	0	4	162^1	189	6	42	36	13.0	3.88	91	.294	.341	10	.189	0	-9	-7	0	-0.7
1946	Det-A	5	7	.417	24	13	3	0	1	97^1	106	6	29	34	12.5	4.62	79	.274	.325	5	.152	-1	-12	-10	1	-1.0
1947	Det-A	11	5	.688	28	17	7	3	0	140^2	142	9	44	33	12.0	3.77	100	.259	.315	7	.149	-1	-1	-0	-0	-0.1
1948	Det-A	3	4	.429	37	4	0	0	3	66^1	89	5	31	14	16.3	5.97	73	.326	.395	1	.071	-1	-12	-12	1	-1.1
1949	Det-A	1	3	.250	14	1	0	0	0	17^1	29	2	9	3	20.3	9.87	42	.377	.448	1	.333	0	-11	-11	0	-1.0
1950	StL-A	9	12	.429	31	19	8	2	0	161	200	11	45	39	13.8	4.19	118	.298	.343	8	.167	1	7	14	-2	1.2
1951	StL-A	1	6	.143	8	7	3	0	0	53^1	61	5	21	13	13.8	3.54	124	.281	.345	1	.071	-1	3	5	-1	0.3
	NY-A	1	1	.500	15	4	1	0	0	44^2	50	2	18	14	14.1	4.63	83	.287	.361	1	.143	0	-3	-4	0	-0.4
	Yr	2	7	.222	23	11	4	0	0	98	111	7	39	27	14.0	4.04	102	.284	.352	2	.095	-1	1	1	-1	-0.1
1952	StL-A	0	3	.000	17	4	0	0	0	41	44	3	7	10	11.2	3.73	105	.270	.300	2	.182	-0	-0	1	1	0.1
Total	10	58	67	.464	266	137	50	11	10	1130^2	1259	56	325	301	12.7	3.96	98	.280	.330	54	.161	-0	-28	-8	1	-0.8

● MIKE OVERY Overy, Harry Michael b: 1/27/51, Clinton, Ill. BR/TR, 6'2", 190 lbs. Deb: 8/14/76

YEAR	TM/L	W	L	PCT	G	GS	CG	SH	SV	IP	H	HR	BB	SO	RAT	ERA	ERA+	OAV	OOB	BH	AVG	PB	PR	/A	PD	TPI
1976	Cal-A	0	2	.000	5	0	0	0	0	7^1	6	1	3	8	12.3	6.14	54	.214	.313	0	—	0	-2	-2	0	0.2

● ERNIE OVITZ Ovitz, Ernest Gayheart b: 10/7/1885, Mineral Point, Wis. d: 9/11/80, Green Bay, Wis. BR/TR, 5'8.5", 156 lbs. Deb: 6/22/11

YEAR	TM/L	W	L	PCT	G	GS	CG	SH	SV	IP	H	HR	BB	SO	RAT	ERA	ERA+	OAV	OOB	BH	AVG	PB	PR	/A	PD	TPI
1911	Chi-N	0	0	—	1	0	0	0	0	2	3	0	3	0	27.0	4.50	74	.375	.545	0	—	0	-0	-0	-0	0.0

● BOB OWCHINKO Owchinko, Robert Dennis b: 1/1/55, Detroit, Mich. BL/TL, 6'2", 195 lbs. Deb: 9/25/76

YEAR	TM/L	W	L	PCT	G	GS	CG	SH	SV	IP	H	HR	BB	SO	RAT	ERA	ERA+	OAV	OOB	BH	AVG	PB	PR	/A	PD	TPI
1976	SD-N	0	2	.000	2	2	0	0	0	4^1	11	0	3	4	29.1	16.62	20	.478	.538	0	.000	-0	-6	-6	0	-0.6
1977	SD-N	9	12	.429	30	28	3	2	0	170	191	20	67	101	13.7	4.45	80	.287	.352	4	.082	-2	-10	-17	-2	-2.0
1978	SD-N	10	13	.435	36	33	4	1	0	202^1	198	14	78	94	12.3	3.56	93	.263	.333	11	.175	1	0	-5	-1	-0.5
1979	SD-N	6	12	.333	42	20	2	0	0	149^1	144	16	55	66	12.1	3.74	94	.259	.328	4	.121	-0	-0	-3	-0	-0.4
1980	Cle-A	2	9	.182	29	14	1	1	0	114^1	138	13	47	66	14.7	5.27	77	.301	.368	0	—	0	-16	-15	-0	-1.5
1981	*Oak-A	4	3	.571	29	0	0	0	2	39^1	34	2	19	26	12.4	3.20	109	.245	.340	0	—	0	2	1	-0	0.3
1982	Oak-A	2	4	.333	54	0	0	0	3	102	111	11	52	67	14.4	5.21	75	.275	.358	0	—	0	-13	-15	-1	-1.3
1983	Pit-N	0	0	—	1	0	0	0	0	0	2	1	0	0	—	∞	—	1.000	1.000	0	—	0	-1	-1	0	-0.1
1984	Cin-N	3	5	.375	49	4	0	0	2	94	91	10	39	60	12.4	4.12	92	.253	.327	2	.167	1	-6	-4	-1	-0.3
1986	Mon-N	1	0	1.000	3	3	0	0	0	15	17	1	3	6	12.0	3.60	103	.288	.323	1	.200	0	0	0	-0	0.0
Total	10	37	60	.381	275	104	10	4	7	890^2	937	88	363	490	13.2	4.28	85	.274	.345	22	.135	0	-49	-66	-5	-6.4

● FRANK OWEN Owen, Frank Malcolm "Yip" b: 12/23/1879, Ypsilanti, Mich. d: 11/24/42, Dearborn, Mich. BL/TR, Deb: 4/29/01

YEAR	TM/L	W	L	PCT	G	GS	CG	SH	SV	IP	H	HR	BB	SO	RAT	ERA	ERA+	OAV	OOB	BH	AVG	PB	PR	/A	PD	TPI
1901	Det-A	1	3	.250	8	5	3	0	0	56	70	1	30	17	16.7	4.34	89	.302	.392	1	.050	-2	-4	-3	2	-0.3
1903	Chi-A	8	12	.400	26	20	15	1	1	167^1	167	1	44	66	11.7	3.50	80	.259	.314	7	.123	-1	-10	-13	4	-1.0
1904	Chi-A	21	15	.583	37	36	34	4	1	315	243	2	61	103	9.0	1.94	126	.214	.261	23	.215	5	23	18	6	3.4
1905	Chi-A	21	13	.618	42	38	32	3	0	334	276	6	56	125	9.2	2.10	118	.226	.265	18	.145	-3	21	14	3	1.4
1906	*Chi-A	22	13	.629	42	36	27	7	0	293	289	4	54	66	10.7	2.33	109	.261	.297	14	.136	-2	12	7	4	0.9
1907	Chi-A	2	3	.400	11	4	2	0	0	47	43	1	13	15	10.7	2.49	96	.245	.297	4	.250	0	0	-0	1	0.0
1908	Chi-A	6	7	.462	25	14	5	1	0	140	142	2	37	48	11.7	3.41	68	.260	.310	9	.180	1	-16	-17	2	-1.6
1909	Chi-A	1	1	.500	3	2	1	0	0	16	19	0	3	3	12.9	4.50	52	.279	.319	1	.167	-0	-4	-4	-0	-0.4
Total	8	82	67	.550	194	155	119	16	2	1368^1	1249	17	298	443	10.4	2.55	100	.244	.290	77	.159	-3	22	1	21	2.4

● JIM OWENS Owens, James Philip "Bear" b: 1/16/34, Gifford, Pa. BR/TR, 5'11", 190 lbs. Deb: 4/19/55 C

YEAR	TM/L	W	L	PCT	G	GS	CG	SH	SV	IP	H	HR	BB	SO	RAT	ERA	ERA+	OAV	OOB	BH	AVG	PB	PR	/A	PD	TPI
1955	Phi-N	0	2	.000	3	2	0	0	0	8^2	13	2	7	6	20.8	8.31	48	.382	.488	0	.000	-0	-4	-4	-0	-0.4
1956	Phi-N	0	4	.000	10	5	0	0	0	29^2	35	3	22	22	17.9	7.28	51	.313	.434	1	.167	0	-12	-12	0	-1.1
1958	Phi-N	1	0	1.000	1	1	0	0	0	7	4	1	5	3	11.6	2.57	154	.154	.290	0	.000	0	1	1	-0	0.1
1959	Phi-N	12	12	.500	31	30	11	1	1	221^1	203	14	73	135	11.4	3.21	128	.244	.308	9	.120	-1	18	22	-0	2.1
1960	Phi-N	4	14	.222	31	22	6	0	0	150	182	21	64	83	14.8	5.04	77	.299	.367	3	.068	-3	-21	-19	-1	-2.3
1961	Phi-N	5	10	.333	20	17	3	0	0	106^2	119	8	32	38	12.7	4.47	91	.287	.339	2	.074	-1	-5	-5	-2	-0.7
1962	Phi-N	2	4	.333	23	12	1	0	0	69^2	90	12	33	21	15.9	6.33	61	.318	.389	2	.143	0	-18	-19	-1	-1.9
1963	Cin-N	0	2	.000	19	3	0	0	4	42^1	42	6	24	29	14.0	5.31	63	.259	.355	1	.125	0	-10	-9	1	-0.9
1964	Hou-N	8	7	.533	48	11	0	0	6	118	115	7	32	88	11.2	3.28	104	.262	.312	3	.103	-1	3	2	-1	0.0
1965	Hou-N	6	5	.545	50	0	0	0	8	71^1	64	4	29	53	11.7	3.28	102	.238	.312	1	.125	-0	2	1	-0	0.0
1966	Hou-N	4	7	.364	40	0	0	0	2	50	53	5	17	32	12.8	4.68	73	.273	.335	0	.000	-0	-6	-7	1	-0.7
1967	Hou-N	0	1	.000	10	0	0	0	0	10^2	12	1	2	6	11.8	4.22	78	.308	.341	0	—	0	-1	-1	-0	-0.2
Total	12	42	68	.382	286	103	21	1	21	885^1	932	84	340	516	13.0	4.31	88	.273	.340	22	.101	-7	-53	-51	-5	-6.0

● RICK OWNBEY Ownbey, Richard Wayne b: 10/20/57, Corona, Cal. BR/TR, 6'3", 185 lbs. Deb: 8/17/82

YEAR	TM/L	W	L	PCT	G	GS	CG	SH	SV	IP	H	HR	BB	SO	RAT	ERA	ERA+	OAV	OOB	BH	AVG	PB	PR	/A	PD	TPI
1982	NY-N	1	2	.333	8	8	2	0	0	50^1	44	3	43	28	15.6	3.75	97	.242	.387	3	.200	1	-1	-1	-1	-0.1
1983	NY-N	1	3	.250	10	4	0	0	0	34^2	31	4	21	19	13.8	4.67	78	.240	.351	1	.111	-0	-4	-4	0	-0.4
1984	StL-N	0	3	.000	4	4	0	0	0	19	23	1	8	11	14.7	4.74	73	.303	.369	0	.000	-0	-2	-3	-0	-0.3
1986	StL-N	1	3	.250	17	3	0	0	0	42^2	47	4	19	25	14.3	3.80	96	.294	.376	0	.000	-1	-0	-1	-1	-0.2
Total	4	3	11	.214	39	19	2	0	0	146^2	145	12	91	83	14.7	4.11	88	.265	.373	4	.114	-1	-8	-8	-2	-1.0

● DOC OZMER Ozmer, Horace Robert b: 5/25/01, Atlanta, Ga. d: 12/28/70, Atlanta, Ga. BR/TR, 5'10.5", 185 lbs. Deb: 5/11/23

YEAR	TM/L	W	L	PCT	G	GS	CG	SH	SV	IP	H	HR	BB	SO	RAT	ERA	ERA+	OAV	OOB	BH	AVG	PB	PR	/A	PD	TPI
1923	Phi-A	0	0	—	1	0	0	0	0	2	1	0	1	1	9.0	4.50	91	.167	.286	0	—	0	-0	-0	0	0.0

● CHARLIE PABOR Pabor, Charles Henry b: 9/24/1846, New York, N.Y. d: 4/22/13, New Haven, Conn. BL/TL, 5'8", 155 lbs. Deb: 5/04/1871 M♦

YEAR	TM/L	W	L	PCT	G	GS	CG	SH	SV	IP	H	HR	BB	SO	RAT	ERA	ERA+	OAV	OOB	BH	AVG	PB	PR	/A	PD	TPI
1871	Cle-n	0	2	.000	7	1	1	0	0	29^1	50	4	6	0	17.2	6.75	61	.325	.350	42	.296	0	-8	-9		-0.5
1872	Cle-n	1	1	.500	2	2	2	0	0	18	20	0	3	0	11.5	3.00	121	.253	.280	19	.211	-0	1	1		0.1
1875	Atl-n	0	1	.000	1	1	0	0	0	4	11	0	1		27.0	*9.00*	26	.440	.462	36	.235	0	-3	-3		-0.2
Total	3 n	1	4	.200	10	4	3	0	0	51^1	81	4	10	0	16.0	*5.61*	41	.314	.340	205	.288	-0	-18	-19		-0.6

● JOHN PACELLA Pacella, John Lewis b: 9/15/56, Brooklyn, N.Y. BR/TR, 6'3", 195 lbs. Deb: 9/15/77

YEAR	TM/L	W	L	PCT	G	GS	CG	SH	SV	IP	H	HR	BB	SO	RAT	ERA	ERA+	OAV	OOB	BH	AVG	PB	PR	/A	PD	TPI
1977	NY-N	0	0	—	3	0	0	0	0	4	2	0	2	1	9.0	0.00	—	.133	.235	0	—	0	2	2	-0	0.1
1979	NY-N	0	2	.000	4	3	0	0	0	16^1	16	0	4	12	11.0	4.41	83	.246	.290	0	.000	-0	-1	-1	-0	-0.2
1980	NY-N	3	4	.429	32	15	0	0	0	84	89	5	59	68	16.1	5.14	69	.280	.396	2	.100	-1	-14	-15	-0	-1.7
1982	NY-A	0	1	.000	3	1	0	0	0	10	13	0	9	2	20.7	7.20	55	.342	.479	0	—	0	-3	-4	-0	-0.3
	Min-A	1	2	.333	21	1	0	0	2	51^2	61	14	37	20	17.1	7.32	58	.299	.407	0	—	0	-19	-18	-1	-2.0
	Yr	1	3	.250	24	2	0	0	2	61^2	74	14	46	22	17.5	7.30	58	.301	.411	0	—	0	-22	-21	-2	-2.3
1984	Bal-A	0	1	.000	6	1	0	0	0	14^2	15	2	9	8	14.7	6.75	57	.268	.369	0	—	0	-4	-5	-0	-0.3
1986	Det-A	0	0	—	5	0	0	0	1	11	10	0	13	5	18.8	4.09	101	.294	.489	0	—	0	0	0	1	0.1
Total	6	4	10	.286	74	21	0	0	3	191^2	206	21	133	116	16.1	5.73	67	.282	.395	2	.083	-1	-40	-41	-2	-4.3

● PAT PACILLO Pacillo, Patrick Michael b: 7/23/63, Jersey City, N.J. BR/TR, 6'2", 205 lbs. Deb: 5/23/87

YEAR	TM/L	W	L	PCT	G	GS	CG	SH	SV	IP	H	HR	BB	SO	RAT	ERA	ERA+	OAV	OOB	BH	AVG	PB	PR	/A	PD	TPI
1987	Cin-N	3	3	.500	12	7	0	0	0	39^2	41	7	19	23	13.8	6.13	69	.270	.355	1	.091	-0	-9	-8	-0	-0.8
1988	Cin-N	1	0	1.000	6	0	0	0	0	10^2	14	2	4	11	15.2	5.06	71	.318	.375	0	.000	-0	-2	-2	-0	-0.2
Total	2	4	3	.571	18	7	0	0	0	50^1	55	9	23	34	14.1	5.90	70	.281	.359	1	.083	-0	-11	-10	-1	-1.0

● GENE PACKARD Packard, Eugene Milo b: 7/13/1887, Colorado Springs, Colorado d: 5/19/59, Riverside, Cal. BL/TL, 5'10", 155 lbs. Deb: 9/27/12

YEAR	TM/L	W	L	PCT	G	GS	CG	SH	SV	IP	H	HR	BB	SO	RAT	ERA	ERA+	OAV	OOB	BH	AVG	PB	PR	/A	PD	TPI
1912	Cin-N	1	0	1.000	1	1	1	0	0	9	7	0	4	2	11.0	3.00	112	.206	.289	1	.250	1	0	0	0	0.1
1913	Cin-N	7	11	.389	39	21	9	2	0	190^2	208	2	64	73	13.2	2.97	109	.286	.350	11	.180	-0	5	6	-1	0.5
1914	KC-F	20	14	.588	42	34	24	4	5	302	282	5	88	154	11.1	2.89	107	.246	.301	28	.241	4	11	7	9	2.0
1915	KC-F	20	12	.625	42	31	21	5	2	281^2	250	3	74	108	10.6	2.68	109	.242	.298	22	.232	3	11	7	7	1.9
1916	Chi-N	10	6	.625	37	15	5	2	5	155^1	154	4	38	36	11.3	2.78	105	.256	.304	7	.130	-1	-3	2	5	0.7
1917	Chi-N	0	0	—	2	0	0	0	0	1^2	3	1	0	1	16.2	10.80	27	.375	.375	0	—	0	-1	-1	0	-0.1
	StL-N	9	6	.600	34	11	6	0	2	153^1	138	4	25	44	9.7	2.47	109	.246	.281	15	.288	3	4	4	-1	0.8
	Yr	9	6	.600	36	11	6	0	2	155	141	5	25	45	9.8	2.55	105	.247	.283	15	.288	3	3	2	-0	0.7
1918	StL-N	12	12	.500	30	23	10	1	2	182^1	184	6	33	46	11.0	3.50	77	.266	.304	12	.174	-1	-15	-16	-1	-1.9
1919	Phi-N	6	8	.429	21	16	10	1	1	134^1	167	3	30	24	13.5	4.15	78	.321	.363	7	.137	-2	-19	-14	-0	-1.7
Total	8	85	69	.552	248	152	86	15	17	1410^1	1393	28	356	488	11.4	3.01	99	.262	.312	103	.205	7	-7	-4	17	2.3

● JOE PACTWA Pactwa, Joseph Martin b: 6/2/48, Hammond, Ind. BL/TL, 5'11", 185 lbs. Deb: 9/15/75

YEAR	TM/L	W	L	PCT	G	GS	CG	SH	SV	IP	H	HR	BB	SO	RAT	ERA	ERA+	OAV	OOB	BH	AVG	PB	PR	/A	PD	TPI
1975	Cal-A	1	0	1.000	4	3	0	0	0	16^1	23	0	10	3	18.2	3.86	92	.343	.429	0	—	0	-0	-1	-0	0.4

● DAVE PAGAN Pagan, David Percy b: 9/15/49, Nipawin, Sask., Canada BR/TR, 6'2", 175 lbs. Deb: 7/01/73

YEAR	TM/L	W	L	PCT	G	GS	CG	SH	SV	IP	H	HR	BB	SO	RAT	ERA	ERA+	OAV	OOB	BH	AVG	PB	PR	/A	PD	TPI
1973	NY-A	0	0	—	4	1	0	0	0	12^2	16	1	1	9	12.1	2.84	129	.320	.333	0	—	0	1	1	0	0.4

YEAR	TM/L	W	L	PCT	G	GS	CG	SH	SV	IP	H	HR	BB	SO	RAT	ERA	ERA+	OAV	OOB	BH	AVG	PB	PR	/A	PD	TPI
1974	NY-A	1	3	.250	16	6	1	0	0	49^1	49	1	28	39	14.0	5.11	68	.265	.362	0	—	0	-8	-9	-0	-0.9
1975	NY-A	0	0	—	13	0	0	0	1	31	30	2	13	18	13.1	4.06	90	.256	.341	0	—	0	-1	-1	-1	0.0
1976	NY-A	1	1	.500	7	2	1	0	0	23^2	18	0	4	13	8.4	2.28	150	.222	.259	0	—	0	3	3	-1	0.4
	Bal-A	1	4	.200	20	5	0	0	1	46^2	54	2	23	34	15.0	5.98	55	.298	.380	0	—	0	-13	-14	-1	-1.1
	Yr	2	5	.286	27	7	1	0	1	70^1	72	2	27	47	12.8	4.73	70	.273	.342	0	—	0	-9	-11	-2	-0.7
1977	Sea-A	1	1	.500	24	4	1	1	2	66	86	3	26	30	15.5	6.14	67	.323	.388	0	—	0	-15	-15	-0	-1.4
	Pit-N	0	0	—	1	0	0	0	0	3	1	0	0	4	3.0	0.00	—	.100	.100	0	—	0	1	1	0	0.2
Total	5	4	9	.308	85	18	3	1	4	232^1	254	9	95	147	13.7	4.96	74	.285	.358	0	—	0	-31	-34	-2	-2.4

● JOE PAGE Page, Joseph Francis "Fireman" b: 10/28/17, Cherry Valley, Pa. d: 4/21/80, Latrobe, Pa. BL/TL, 6'2", 205 lbs. Deb: 4/19/44

YEAR	TM/L	W	L	PCT	G	GS	CG	SH	SV	IP	H	HR	BB	SO	RAT	ERA	ERA+	OAV	OOB	BH	AVG	PB	PR	/A	PD	TPI
1944	NY-A☆	5	7	.417	19	16	4	0	0	102^2	100	3	52	63	13.6	4.56	76	.258	.351	5	.156	-0	-13	-12	-1	-1.4
1945	NY-A	6	3	.667	20	9	4	0	0	102	95	1	46	50	12.4	2.82	123	.246	.326	9	.250	1	6	7	-2	0.7
1946	NY-A	9	8	.529	31	17	6	1	3	136	126	7	72	77	13.4	3.57	97	.252	.351	7	.163	-0	-1	-2	-1	-0.3
1947	*NY-A★	14	8	.636	56	2	0	0	**17**	141^1	105	5	72	116	11.3	2.48	142	.208	.308	10	.217	1	**19**	**17**	-1	1.8
1948	NY-A☆	7	8	.467	**55**	1	0	0	16	107^2	116	6	66	77	15.3	4.26	96	.275	.374	7	.292	3	0	-2	-1	0.0
1949	*NY-A	13	8	.619	**60**	0	0	0	**27**	135^1	103	8	75	99	12.2	2.59	156	.215	.328	7	.175	-1	**24**	**22**	-2	1.9
1950	NY-A	3	7	.300	37	0	0	0	13	55^1	66	8	31	33	15.8	5.04	85	.295	.380	2	.250	1	-3	-5	-1	-0.4
1954	Pit-N	0	0	—	7	0	0	0	0	9^2	16	4	7	4	22.3	11.17	37	.364	.462	0	—	0	-8	-8	0	-0.7
Total	8	57	49	.538	285	45	14	1	76	790	727	42	421	519	13.2	3.53	106	.247	.344	47	.205	5	25	18	-7	1.6

● PHIL PAGE Page, Philippe Rausac b: 8/23/05, Springfield, Mass. d: 7/27/58, Springfield, Mass BR/TL, 6'2", 175 lbs. Deb: 9/18/28 C

YEAR	TM/L	W	L	PCT	G	GS	CG	SH	SV	IP	H	HR	BB	SO	RAT	ERA	ERA+	OAV	OOB	BH	AVG	PB	PR	/A	PD	TPI
1928	Det-A	2	0	1.000	3	2	2	0	0	22	21	1	10	3	12.7	2.45	167	.256	.337	2	.222	-0	4	4	1	0.5
1929	Det-A	0	2	.000	10	4	1	0	0	25^1	29	1	19	6	17.4	8.17	53	.296	.415	1	.125	-1	-11	-11	-1	-1.1
1930	Det-A	0	1	.000	12	0	0	0	0	12	23	1	9	2	24.0	9.75	49	.434	.516	0	—	0	-7	-7	0	-0.6
1934	Bro-N	1	0	1.000	6	0	0	0	0	10	13	1	6	4	17.1	5.40	72	.342	.432	0	.000	-0	-1	-2	1	-0.1
Total	4	3	3	.500	31	6	3	0	0	69^1	86	4	44	15	17.0	6.23	68	.317	.415	3	.167	-1	-15	-15	1	-1.3

● SAM PAGE Page, Samuel Walter b: 2/11/16, Woodruff, S.C. BL/TR, 6', 172 lbs. Deb: 9/11/39

YEAR	TM/L	W	L	PCT	G	GS	CG	SH	SV	IP	H	HR	BB	SO	RAT	ERA	ERA+	OAV	OOB	BH	AVG	PB	PR	/A	PD	TPI
1939	Phi-A	0	3	.000	4	3	1	0	0	22	34	1	15	11	20.0	6.95	68	.343	.430	3	.429	1	-6	-5	1	-0.3

● VANCE PAGE Page, Vance Linwood b: 9/15/05, Elm City, N.C. d: 7/14/51, Wilson, N.C. BR/TR, 6', 180 lbs. Deb: 8/06/38

YEAR	TM/L	W	L	PCT	G	GS	CG	SH	SV	IP	H	HR	BB	SO	RAT	ERA	ERA+	OAV	OOB	BH	AVG	PB	PR	/A	PD	TPI
1938	*Chi-N	5	4	.556	13	9	3	0	1	68	90	4	13	18	13.6	3.84	100	.323	.353	4	.154	-1	-0	-0	3	0.1
1939	Chi-N	7	7	.500	27	17	8	1	1	139^1	169	8	37	43	13.4	3.88	102	.298	.342	12	.255	3	1	1	1	0.4
1940	Chi-N	1	3	.250	30	1	0	0	2	59	65	1	26	22	13.9	4.42	85	.271	.342	4	.308	2	-4	-4	0	-0.2
1941	Chi-N	2	2	.500	25	3	1	0	1	48^1	48	2	30	17	14.9	4.28	82	.254	.362	2	.286	1	-3	-4	0	-0.3
Total	4	15	16	.484	95	30	12	1	5	314^2	372	15	106	100	13.8	4.03	95	.292	.348	22	.237	4	-7	-8	4	0.0

● PAT PAIGE Paige, George Lynn "Piggy" b: 5/5/1883, Paw Paw, Mich. d: 6/8/39, Berlin, Wis. BL/TR, 5'10", 175 lbs. Deb: 5/20/11

YEAR	TM/L	W	L	PCT	G	GS	CG	SH	SV	IP	H	HR	BB	SO	RAT	ERA	ERA+	OAV	OOB	BH	AVG	PB	PR	/A	PD	TPI
1911	Cle-A	1	0	1.000	2	1	1	0	0	16	21	0	7	6	15.8	4.50	76	.339	.406	1	.143	-0	-2	-2	1	-0.1

● SATCHEL PAIGE Paige, Leroy Robert b: 7/7/06, Mobile, Ala. d: 6/8/82, Kansas City, Mo. BR/TR, 6'3.5", 180 lbs. Deb: 7/09/48 CH

YEAR	TM/L	W	L	PCT	G	GS	CG	SH	SV	IP	H	HR	BB	SO	RAT	ERA	ERA+	OAV	OOB	BH	AVG	PB	PR	/A	PD	TPI
1948	*Cle-A	6	1	.857	21	7	3	2	1	72^2	61	2	25	45	10.8	2.48	164	.228	.297	2	.087	-2	15	13	-0	1.0
1949	Cle-A	4	7	.364	31	5	1	0	5	83	70	4	33	54	11.3	3.04	131	.230	.308	1	.063	-1	11	9	-1	0.7
1951	StL-A	3	4	.429	23	3	0	0	5	62	67	6	29	48	14.1	4.79	92	.276	.355	2	.125	-2	-5	-3	-1	-0.5
1952	StL-A☆	12	10	.545	46	6	3	2	10	138	116	5	57	91	11.5	3.07	128	.226	.307	5	.128	-2	9	13	0	1.2
1953	StL-A★	3	9	.250	57	4	0	0	11	117^1	114	12	39	51	11.8	3.53	119	.257	.319	2	.069	-3	6	9	-2	0.4
1965	KC-A	0	0	—	1	1	0	0	0	3	1	0	0	1	3.0	0.00	—	.100	.100	0	.000	-0	1	1	-0	0.1
Total	6	28	31	.475	179	26	7	4	32	476	429	29	183	290	11.7	3.29	124	.241	.314	12	.097	-10	37	42	-3	2.9

● PHIL PAINE Paine, Phillips Steere "Flip" b: 6/8/30, Chepachet, R.I. d: 2/19/78, Lebanon, Pa. BR/TR, 6'2", 181 lbs. Deb: 7/14/51

YEAR	TM/L	W	L	PCT	G	GS	CG	SH	SV	IP	H	HR	BB	SO	RAT	ERA	ERA+	OAV	OOB	BH	AVG	PB	PR	/A	PD	TPI
1951	Bos-N	2	0	1.000	21	0	0	0	0	35^1	36	2	20	17	15.3	3.06	120	.271	.382	0	.000	-0	4	2	-0	0.2
1954	Mil-N	1	0	1.000	11	0	0	0	0	14	14	1	12	11	17.4	3.86	97	.292	.443	0	—	0	0	-0	-0	-0.1
1955	Mil-N	2	0	1.000	15	0	0	0	0	25^1	20	2	14	26	12.1	2.49	151	.225	.330	1	.333	0	4	4	0	0.4
1956	Mil-N	0	0	—	1	0	0	0	0	0	3	0	0	0	—	∞	—	1.000	1.000	0	—	0	-2	-2	0	-0.2
1957	Mil-N	0	0	—	1	0	0	0	0	2	1	0	3	2	18.0	0.00	—	.143	.400	0	—	0	1	1	0	0.1
1958	StL-N	5	1	.833	46	0	0	0	1	73^1	70	7	31	45	13.0	3.56	116	.256	.343	2	.286	0	3	5	0	0.5
Total	6	10	1	.909	95	0	0	0	1	150	144	12	80	101	14.0	3.36	116	.260	.364	3	.214	-0	10	9	-0	0.9

● VICENTE PALACIOS Palacios, Vicente (Diaz) b: 7/19/63, Verzcruz, Mex. BR/TR, 6'3", 165 lbs. Deb: 9/04/87

YEAR	TM/L	W	L	PCT	G	GS	CG	SH	SV	IP	H	HR	BB	SO	RAT	ERA	ERA+	OAV	OOB	BH	AVG	PB	PR	/A	PD	TPI
1987	Pit-N	2	1	.667	6	4	0	0	0	29^1	27	1	9	13	11.4	4.30	96	.250	.314	1	.111	-0	-1	-1	-1	-0.2
1988	Pit-N	1	2	.333	7	3	0	0	0	24^1	28	3	15	15	15.9	6.66	51	.295	.391	0	.000	-0	-9	-9	0	-0.9
1990	Pit-N	0	0	—	7	0	0	0	3	15	4	0	2	8	3.6	0.00	—	.083	.120	0	.000	-0	6	6	-0	0.6
1991	Pit-N	6	3	.667	36	7	1	1	3	81^2	69	12	38	64	11.9	3.75	95	.228	.316	1	.071	-1	-1	-2	-1	-0.3
1992	Pit-N	3	2	.600	20	8	0	0	0	53	56	1	27	33	14.1	4.25	80	.280	.366	1	.071	-1	-4	-5	-0	-0.6
Total	5	12	8	.600	76	22	1	1	6	203^1	184	17	91	133	12.3	4.03	89	.244	.327	3	.061	-3	-8	-10	-1	-1.4

● MIKE PALAGYI Palagyi, Michael Raymond b: 7/4/17, Conneaut, Ohio BR/TR, 6'2", 185 lbs. Deb: 8/18/39

YEAR	TM/L	W	L	PCT	G	GS	CG	SH	SV	IP	H	HR	BB	SO	RAT	ERA	ERA+	OAV	OOB	BH	AVG	PB	PR	/A	PD	TPI
1939	Was-A	0	0	—	1	0	0	0	0	0	0	0	3	0	—	∞	—	—	1.000	0	—	0	-3	-3	0	-0.2

● ERV PALICA Palica, Ervin Martin (b: Ervin Martin Pavliecivich)
b: 2/9/28, Lomita, Cal. d: 5/29/82, Huntington Beach, Cal. BR/TR, 6'1.5", 180 lbs. Deb: 4/21/45 ♦

YEAR	TM/L	W	L	PCT	G	GS	CG	SH	SV	IP	H	HR	BB	SO	RAT	ERA	ERA+	OAV	OOB	BH	AVG	PB	PR	/A	PD	TPI
1947	Bro-N	0	1	.000	3	0	0	0	0	3	2	0	2	1	15.0	3.00	138	.182	.357	0	—	0	0	0	-0	0.0
1948	Bro-N	6	6	.500	41	10	3	0	3	125^1	111	13	58	74	12.4	4.45	90	.239	.327	5	.128	0	-7	-6	-1	-0.7
1949	*Bro-N	8	9	.471	49	1	0	0	6	97	93	6	49	44	13.3	3.62	113	.261	.352	3	.158	0	5	5	-0	0.5
1950	Bro-N	13	8	.619	43	19	10	2	1	201^1	176	13	98	131	12.3	3.58	115	.237	.327	15	.221	2	13	12	-4	1.0
1951	Bro-N	2	6	.250	19	8	0	0	0	53	55	10	20	15	12.7	4.75	83	.259	.323	2	.154	0	-5	-5	1	-0.4
1953	Bro-N	0	0	—	4	0	0	0	0	6	10	1	8	3	27.0	12.00	36	.370	.514	1	1.000	0	-5	-5	0	-0.4
1954	Bro-N	3	3	.500	25	3	0	0	0	67^2	77	9	31	25	14.5	5.32	77	.285	.361	4	.250	1	-9	-9	-2	-1.0
1955	Bal-A	5	11	.313	33	25	5	1	0	169^2	165	10	83	68	13.3	4.14	92	.260	.348	13	.236	2	-3	-6	-1	-0.4
1956	Bal-A	4	11	.267	29	14	2	0	0	116^1	117	10	50	62	13.0	4.49	87	.264	.339	5	.156	-2	-4	-7	-0	-0.9
Total	9	41	55	.427	246	80	20	3	10	839^1	806	72	399	423	13.0	4.22	94	.255	.340	48	.198	5	-16	-22	-7	-2.3

● DONN PALL Pall, Donn Steven b: 1/11/62, Chicago, Ill. BR/TR, 6'2", 185 lbs. Deb: 8/01/88

YEAR	TM/L	W	L	PCT	G	GS	CG	SH	SV	IP	H	HR	BB	SO	RAT	ERA	ERA+	OAV	OOB	BH	AVG	PB	PR	/A	PD	TPI
1988	Chi-A	0	2	.000	17	0	0	0	0	28^2	39	1	8	16	14.8	3.45	115	.328	.370	0	—	0	2	2	1	0.2
1989	Chi-A	4	5	.444	53	0	0	0	6	87	90	9	19	58	12.1	3.31	115	.270	.325	0	—	0	6	5	-1	0.4
1990	Chi-A	3	5	.375	56	0	0	0	2	76	63	7	24	39	10.8	3.32	115	.232	.303	0	—	0	5	4	-0	0.4
1991	Chi-A	7	2	.778	51	0	0	0	0	71	59	7	20	40	10.4	2.41	165	.231	.295	0	—	0	13	12	-1	1.3
1992	Chi-A	5	2	.714	39	0	0	0	1	73	79	9	27	27	13.3	4.93	77	.272	.339	0	—	0	-8	-9	-1	-0.9
Total	5	19	16	.543	216	0	0	0	9	335^2	330	33	98	180	11.9	3.49	111	.260	.322	0	—	0	17	14	-2	1.4

● MIKE PALM Palm, Richard Paul b: 2/13/25, Boston, Mass. BR/TR, 6'3.5", 190 lbs. Deb: 7/11/48

YEAR	TM/L	W	L	PCT	G	GS	CG	SH	SV	IP	H	HR	BB	SO	RAT	ERA	ERA+	OAV	OOB	BH	AVG	PB	PR	/A	PD	TPI
1948	Bos-A	0	0	—	3	0	0	0	0	3	6	0	5	1	33.0	6.00	73	.400	.550	0	.000	-0	-1	-1	-0	-0.1

● PALMER Palmer b: St.Louis, Mo. Deb: 5/28/1885

YEAR	TM/L	W	L	PCT	G	GS	CG	SH	SV	IP	H	HR	BB	SO	RAT	ERA	ERA+	OAV	OOB	BH	AVG	PB	PR	/A	PD	TPI
1885	StL-N	0	4	.000	4	4	4	0	0	34	46	2	20	9	17.5	3.44	80	.311	.393	1	.091	-0	-2	-3	-1	-0.4

● DAVID PALMER Palmer, David William b: 10/19/57, Glens Falls, N.Y. BR/TR, 6'1", 205 lbs. Deb: 9/09/78

YEAR	TM/L	W	L	PCT	G	GS	CG	SH	SV	IP	H	HR	BB	SO	RAT	ERA	ERA+	OAV	OOB	BH	AVG	PB	PR	/A	PD	TPI
1978	Mon-N	0	1	.000	5	1	0	0	0	9^2	9	1	2	7	10.2	2.79	126	.243	.282	0	.000	-0	1	1	1	0.1
1979	Mon-N	10	2	.833	36	11	2	1	2	122^2	110	10	30	72	10.4	2.64	139	.237	.286	1	.032	-3	15	14	-0	1.2
1980	Mon-N	8	6	.571	24	19	3	1	0	129^2	124	11	30	73	10.8	2.98	119	.255	.301	9	.200	1	9	8	1	1.2
1982	Mon-N	6	4	.600	13	13	1	0	0	73^2	60	3	36	46	12.0	3.18	115	.224	.320	1	.042	-2	3	4	0	0.2
1984	Mon-N	7	3	.700	20	19	1	1	0	105^1	101	5	44	66	12.4	3.84	89	.256	.331	5	.152	1	-3	-5	1	-0.3
1985	Mon-N	7	10	.412	24	23	0	0	0	135^2	128	5	67	106	13.1	3.71	91	.250	.341	4	.111	-1	-2	-5	2	-0.5
1986	Atl-N	11	10	.524	35	35	2	0	0	209^2	181	17	102	170	12.4	3.65	109	.234	.327	12	.182	2	2	8	2	1.1
1987	Atl-N	8	11	.421	28	28	0	0	0	152^1	169	17	64	111	14.2	4.90	89	.281	.357	6	.125	-0	-14	-9	1	-0.9
1988	Phi-N	7	9	.438	22	22	1	1	0	129	129	8	48	85	12.3	4.47	80	.261	.327	10	.256	5	-15	-13	-1	-0.9
1989	Det-A	0	3	.000	5	5	0	0	0	17^1	25	1	11	12	18.7	7.79	49	.342	.429	0	—	0	-8	-8	-0	-0.6
Total	10	64	59	.520	212	176	10	4	2	1085	1036	78	434	748	12.4	3.78	99	.252	.327	48	.149	2	-11	-6	5	0.6

● JIM PALMER Palmer, James Alvin b: 10/15/45, New York, N.Y. BR/TR, 6'3", 196 lbs. Deb: 4/17/65 H

YEAR	TM/L	W	L	PCT	G	GS	CG	SH	SV	IP	H	HR	BB	SO	RAT	ERA	ERA+	OAV	OOB	BH	AVG	PB	PR	/A	PD	TPI
1965	Bal-A	5	4	.556	27	6	0	0	1	92	75	6	56	75	13.0	3.72	93	.229	.345	5	.192	1	-3	-3	0	-0.1
1966	*Bal-A	15	10	.600	30	30	6	0	0	208^1	176	21	91	147	11.5	3.46	96	.231	.313	7	.096	-2	-0	-3	-1	-0.6
1967	Bal-A	3	1	.750	9	9	2	1	0	49	34	6	20	23	9.9	2.94	107	.199	.283	1	.077	0	2	1	0	0.2
1969	*Bal-A	16	4	**.800**	26	23	11	6	0	181	131	11	64	123	9.7	2.34	152	.200	.272	13	.203	2	26	25	-4	2.6
1970	*Bal-A★	20	10	.667	39	39	17	**5**	0	**305**	263	21	100	199	10.7	2.71	134	.231	.294	17	.150	-1	**34**	32	-0	**3.3**
1971	*Bal-A★	20	9	.690	37	37	20	3	0	282	231	19	106	184	10.9	2.68	125	.221	.295	20	.196	2	24	21	0	2.6
1972	Bal-A★	21	10	.677	36	36	18	3	0	274^1	219	21	70	184	9.5	2.07	149	.217	.269	22	.224	4	30	31	-1	4.1
1973	*Bal-A	22	9	.710	38	37	19	6	1	296^1	225	16	113	158	10.4	**2.40**	156	.211	.289	0	—	0	47	44	-1	4.7
1974	*Bal-A	7	12	.368	26	26	5	2	0	178^2	176	12	69	84	12.5	3.27	105	.257	.328	0	—	0	7	4	2	0.6
1975	Bal-A☆	**23**	11	.676	39	38	25	**10**	1	323	253	20	80	193	9.3	**2.09**	**168**	.216	.267	0	—	0	**61**	**51**	2	**6.4**
1976	Bal-A	**22**	13	.629	40	40	23	6	0	**315**	255	20	84	159	9.9	2.51	130	.224	.282	0	—	0	35	27	1	3.6
1977	Bal-A★	**20**	11	.645	39	39	**22**	3	0	**319**	263	24	99	193	10.3	2.91	130	.229	.292	0	—	0	41	31	0	3.8
1978	Bal-A★	21	12	.636	38	38	19	6	0	**296**	246	19	97	138	10.5	2.46	142	.227	.291	0	—	0	43	34	1	4.3
1979	*Bal-A	10	6	.625	23	22	7	0	0	155^2	144	12	43	67	10.8	3.30	122	.246	.297	0	—	0	16	12	-0	1.5
1980	Bal-A	16	10	.615	34	33	4	0	0	224	238	26	74	109	12.7	3.98	99	.275	.334	0	—	0	1	-1	1	0.1
1981	Bal-A	7	8	.467	22	22	5	0	0	127^1	117	14	46	35	11.7	3.75	97	.247	.316	0	—	0	-1	-2	1	0.0
1982	Bal-A	15	5	**.750**	36	32	8	2	1	227	195	22	63	103	**10.4**	3.13	129	.231	**.287**	0	—	0	24	23	1	2.5
1983	*Bal-A	5	4	.556	14	11	0	0	0	76^2	86	11	19	34	12.3	4.23	94	.281	.323	0	—	0	-1	-2	-1	-0.3
1984	Bal-A	0	3	.000	5	3	0	0	0	17^2	22	2	17	4	19.9	9.17	42	.319	.453	0	—	0	-10	-10	0	-0.9
Total	19	268	152	.638	558	521	211	53	4	3948	3349	303	1311	2212	10.7	2.86	125	.230	.296	85	.174	7	374	315	3	38.4

● LOWELL PALMER Palmer, Lowell Raymond b: 8/18/47, Sacramento, Cal. BR/TR, 6'1", 190 lbs. Deb: 6/21/69

YEAR	TM/L	W	L	PCT	G	GS	CG	SH	SV	IP	H	HR	BB	SO	RAT	ERA	ERA+	OAV	OOB	BH	AVG	PB	PR	/A	PD	TPI
1969	Phi-N	2	8	.200	26	9	1	1	0	90	91	12	47	68	14.4	5.20	68	.264	.362	3	.136	1	-16	-17	-0	-1.6
1970	Phi-N	1	2	.333	38	5	0	0	0	102	98	15	55	85	13.9	5.47	73	.255	.355	4	.148	1	-16	-17	-1	-1.6
1971	Phi-N	0	0	—	3	1	0	0	0	15	13	3	13	6	18.0	6.00	59	.236	.417	1	.200	-0	-4	-4	-0	-0.4
1972	StL-N	0	3	.000	16	2	0	0	0	34^2	30	2	26	25	14.8	3.89	87	.244	.380	0	.000	-1	-2	-2	0	-0.3
	Cle-A	0	0	—	1	0	0	0	0	2	2	0	2	3	18.0	4.50	71	.222	.364	0	—	0	-0	-0	-0	0.0
1974	SD-N	2	5	.286	22	8	1	0	0	73	68	9	59	52	16.5	5.67	63	.256	.404	2	.087	-1	-17	-17	-1	-1.9
Total	5	5	18	.217	106	25	2	1	0	316^2	302	41	202	239	15.0	5.29	69	.255	.374	10	.122	-0	-55	-57	-1	-5.8

● EMILIO PALMERO Palmero, Emilio Antonio "Pal" b: 6/13/1895, Guanabacoa, Cuba d: 7/15/70, Toledo, Ohio BL/TL, 5'11", 157 lbs. Deb: 9/21/15

YEAR	TM/L	W	L	PCT	G	GS	CG	SH	SV	IP	H	HR	BB	SO	RAT	ERA	ERA+	OAV	OOB	BH	AVG	PB	PR	/A	PD	TPI
1915	NY-N	0	2	.000	3	2	1	0	0	11^2	10	0	9	8	17.0	3.09	83	.233	.400	1	.250	0	-0	-1	0	0.0
1916	NY-N	0	3	.000	4	1	0	0	0	15^2	17	2	8	8	14.9	8.04	30	.288	.382	0	.000	-0	-9	-10	1	-0.9
1921	StL-A	4	7	.364	24	9	4	0	0	90	109	1	49	26	16.4	5.00	90	.319	.413	8	.216	1	-7	-5	1	-0.3
1926	Was-A	2	2	.500	7	3	0	0	0	17	22	1	15	6	20.1	4.76	81	.344	.475	1	.333	0	-1	-2	-0	-0.2
1928	Bos-N	0	1	.000	3	1	0	0	0	6^2	14	0	2	0	21.6	5.40	72	.452	.485	0	.000	-0	-1	-1	-0	-0.1
Total	5	6	15	.286	41	16	5	0	0	141	172	4	83	48	17.0	5.17	77	.319	.420	10	.208	1	-19	-19	2	-1.5

● ED PALMQUIST Palmquist, Edwin Lee b: 6/10/33, Los Angeles, Cal. BR/TR, 6'3", 195 lbs. Deb: 6/10/60

YEAR	TM/L	W	L	PCT	G	GS	CG	SH	SV	IP	H	HR	BB	SO	RAT	ERA	ERA+	OAV	OOB	BH	AVG	PB	PR	/A	PD	TPI
1960	LA-N	0	1	.000	22	0	0	0	0	39	34	6	16	23	11.8	2.54	156	.243	.325	0	.000	-1	5	6	0	0.6
1961	LA-N	0	1	.000	5	0	0	0	1	8^2	10	0	7	5	19.7	6.23	70	.333	.487	0	—	0	-2	-2	-0	-0.2
	Min-A	1	1	.500	9	2	0	0	0	21	33	7	13	13	21.0	9.43	45	.359	.454	0	.000	-0	-13	-12	0	-1.1
Total	2	1	3	.250	36	2	0	0	1	68^2	77	13	36	41	15.6	5.11	80	.294	.391	0	.000	-1	-9	-8	0	-0.7

● JIM PANTHER Panther, James Edward b: 3/1/45, Burlington, Iowa BR/TR, 6'1", 190 lbs. Deb: 4/05/71

YEAR	TM/L	W	L	PCT	G	GS	CG	SH	SV	IP	H	HR	BB	SO	RAT	ERA	ERA+	OAV	OOB	BH	AVG	PB	PR	/A	PD	TPI
1971	Oak-A	0	1	.000	4	0	0	0	0	5^2	10	1	5	4	23.8	11.12	30	.385	.484	0	.000	-0	-5	-5	0	-0.5
1972	Tex-A	5	9	.357	58	4	0	0	0	93^2	101	8	46	44	14.6	4.13	73	.277	.365	1	.125	0	-11	-12	0	-1.3
1973	Atl-N	2	3	.400	23	0	0	0	0	30^2	45	3	9	8	15.8	7.63	52	.363	.406	0	—	0	-14	-13	-1	-1.4
Total	3	7	13	.350	85	4	0	0	0	130	156	12	60	56	15.3	5.26	61	.303	.381	1	.111	-0	-30	-29	-1	-3.2

● JOHN PAPA Papa, John Paul b: 12/5/40, Bridgeport, Conn. BR/TR, 5'11", 190 lbs. Deb: 4/11/61

YEAR	TM/L	W	L	PCT	G	GS	CG	SH	SV	IP	H	HR	BB	SO	RAT	ERA	ERA+	OAV	OOB	BH	AVG	PB	PR	/A	PD	TPI
1961	Bal-A	0	0	—	2	0	0	0	0	1	2	1	3	3	45.0	18.00	22	.400	.625	0	—	0	-2	-2	0	-0.1
1962	Bal-A	0	0	—	1	0	0	0	0	1	3	0	1	0	36.0	27.00	14	.600	.667	0	—	0	-3	-3	-0	-0.2
Total	2	0	0	—	3	0	0	0	0	2	5	1	4	3	40.5	22.50	17	.500	.643	0	—	0	-4	-4	-0	-0.3

● AL PAPAI Papai, Alfred Thomas b: 5/7/19, Divernon, Ill. BR/TR, 6'3", 185 lbs. Deb: 4/24/48

YEAR	TM/L	W	L	PCT	G	GS	CG	SH	SV	IP	H	HR	BB	SO	RAT	ERA	ERA+	OAV	OOB	BH	AVG	PB	PR	/A	PD	TPI
1948	StL-N	0	1	.000	10	0	0	0	0	16	14	3	7	8	11.8	5.06	81	.241	.323	0	.000	-0	-2	-2	0	-0.2
1949	StL-A	4	11	.267	42	15	6	0	2	142^1	175	8	81	31	16.3	5.06	90	.298	.384	3	.079	-2	-14	-8	3	-0.7
1950	Bos-A	4	2	.667	16	3	2	0	2	50^2	61	5	28	19	15.8	6.75	73	.293	.377	3	.176	-0	-12	-10	-1	-1.0
	StL-N	1	0	1.000	13	0	0	0	0	19	21	0	14	7	16.6	5.21	82	.300	.417	0	.000	-0	-2	-2	0	-0.2
1955	Chi-A	0	0	—	7	0	0	0	0	11^2	10	1	8	5	13.9	3.86	102	.244	.367	0	.000	-0	0	0	1	0.1
Total	4	9	14	.391	88	18	8	0	4	239^2	281	17	138	70	15.8	5.37	84	.291	.381	6	.097	-3	-30	-22	4	-2.0

● LARRY PAPE Pape, Laurence Albert b: 7/21/1883, Norwood, Ohio d: 7/21/18, Swissvale, Pa. BR/TR, 5'11", 175 lbs. Deb: 7/06/09

YEAR	TM/L	W	L	PCT	G	GS	CG	SH	SV	IP	H	HR	BB	SO	RAT	ERA	ERA+	OAV	OOB	BH	AVG	PB	PR	/A	PD	TPI
1909	Bos-A	2	0	1.000	11	3	2	1	2	58^1	46	0	12	18	9.7	2.01	125	.218	.276	3	.143	-1	3	3	-3	0.0
1911	Bos-A	10	8	.556	27	19	10	1	0	176^1	167	3	63	49	11.9	2.45	134	.264	.335	13	.203	-1	18	16	5	2.0
1912	Bos-A	1	1	.500	13	2	1	0	1	48^2	74	0	16	17	17.0	4.99	68	.366	.418	4	.235	1	-9	-9	0	-0.7
Total	3	13	9	.591	51	24	13	2	3	283^1	287	3	91	84	12.4	2.80	112	.275	.339	20	.196	-1	12	11	2	1.3

● FRANK PAPISH Papish, Frank Richard "Pap" b: 10/21/17, Pueblo, Colo. d: 8/30/65, Pueblo, Colo. BR/TL, 6'2", 192 lbs. Deb: 5/08/45

YEAR	TM/L	W	L	PCT	G	GS	CG	SH	SV	IP	H	HR	BB	SO	RAT	ERA	ERA+	OAV	OOB	BH	AVG	PB	PR	/A	PD	TPI
1945	Chi-A	4	4	.500	19	5	3	0	1	84^1	75	3	40	45	12.3	3.74	89	.241	.328	6	.231	1	-3	-4	1	-0.2
1946	Chi-A	7	5	.583	31	15	6	2	0	138	122	7	63	66	12.1	2.74	125	.243	.328	8	.186	0	12	10	0	1.1
1947	Chi-A	12	12	.500	38	26	6	1	3	199	185	6	98	79	12.9	3.26	112	.245	.333	5	.086	-5	10	9	-1	0.3
1948	Chi-A	2	8	.200	32	14	2	0	4	95^1	97	7	75	41	16.5	5.00	85	.265	.394	5	.185	-1	-8	-8	-1	-0.9
1949	Cle-A	1	0	1.000	25	3	1	0	1	62	54	2	39	23	13.5	3.19	125	.240	.352	1	.125	0	7	5	0	0.6
1950	Pit-N	0	0	—	4	1	0	0	0	2^1	8	1	4	1	46.3	27.00	16	.533	.632	0	—	0	-6	-6	0	-0.5
Total	6	26	29	.473	149	64	18	3	9	581	541	26	319	255	13.4	3.58	103	.249	.346	25	.154	-5	12	7	0	0.4

● JOHN PAPPALAU Pappalau, John Joseph b: 4/3/1875, Albany, N.Y. d: 5/12/44, Albany, N.Y. BR/TR, 6', 175 lbs. Deb: 6/09/1897

YEAR	TM/L	W	L	PCT	G	GS	CG	SH	SV	IP	H	HR	BB	SO	RAT	ERA	ERA+	OAV	OOB	BH	AVG	PB	PR	/A	PD	TPI
1897	Cle-N	0	1	.000	2	1	1	0	0	12	22	0	6	3	22.5	10.50	43	.390	.465	0	.000	-0	-8	-8	0	-0.6

YEAR TM/L	W	L	PCT	G	GS	CG	SH	SV	IP	H	HR	BB	SO	RAT	ERA	ERA+	OAV	OOB	BH	AVG	PB	PR	/A	PD	TPI
● MILT PAPPAS Pappas, Milton Stephen "Gimpy" (b: Miltiades Stergios Papastegios) b: 5/11/39, Detroit, Mich. BR/TR, 6'3", 190 lbs. Deb: 8/10/57																									
1957 Bal-A	0	0	—	4	0	0	0	0	9	6	0	3	3	9.0	1.00	359	.200	.273	0	.000	-0	3	3	0	0.3
1958 Bal-A	10	10	.500	31	21	3	0	0	135^1	135	8	48	72	12.3	4.06	89	.262	.327	6	.143	-0	-4	-7	1	-0.6
1959 Bal-A	15	9	.625	33	27	15	4	3	209^1	175	8	75	120	10.9	3.27	116	.226	.298	11	.139	-3	14	12	-1	0.8
1960 Bal-A	15	11	.577	30	27	11	3	0	205^2	184	15	83	126	11.9	3.37	113	.243	.323	3	.043	-5	12	10	1	0.6
1961 Bal-A	13	9	.591	26	23	11	4	1	177^2	134	16	78	89	11.1	3.04	129	.208	.301	9	.136	1	19	17	2	2.1
1962 Bal-A★	12	10	.545	35	32	9	1	0	205^1	200	31	75	130	12.1	4.03	93	.257	.324	6	.087	-0	-1	-6	2	-0.5
1963 Bal-A	16	9	.640	34	32	11	4	0	216^2	186	21	69	120	10.8	3.03	116	.233	.298	9	.127	-1	14	12	3	1.5
1964 Bal-A	16	7	.696	37	36	13	7	0	251^2	225	21	48	157	10.0	2.97	120	.239	.281	12	.129	-2	18	17	-1	1.5
1965 Bal-A★	13	9	.591	34	34	9	3	0	221^1	192	22	52	127	10.0	2.60	133	.233	.281	5	.071	-3	21	21	-3	1.6
1966 Cin-N	12	11	.522	33	32	6	2	0	209^2	224	23	39	133	11.4	4.29	91	.275	.310	8	.107	-2	-16	-9	0	-1.2
1967 Cin-N	16	13	.552	34	32	5	3	0	217^2	218	19	38	129	10.8	3.35	112	.259	.295	7	.097	-2	1	10	0	0.8
1968 Cin-N	2	5	.286	15	11	0	0	0	62^2	70	9	10	43	11.8	5.60	56	.275	.307	1	.063	-1	-18	-17	-0	-1.9
Atl-N	10	8	.556	22	19	3	1	0	121^1	111	8	22	75	10.1	2.37	126	.246	.285	6	.162	2	8	8	-1	1.1
Yr	12	13	.480	37	30	3	1	0	184	181	17	32	118	10.6	3.47	88	.255	.290	7	.132	1	-10	-9	-1	-0.8
1969 *Atl-N	6	10	.375	26	24	1	0	0	144	149	14	44	72	12.3	3.63	99	.267	.325	7	.156	3	-0	-0	-0	0.2
1970 Atl-N	2	2	.500	11	3	1	0	0	35^2	44	6	7	25	13.4	6.06	71	.293	.333	0	.000	-1	-8	-7	0	-0.8
Chi-N	10	8	.556	21	20	6	2	0	144^2	135	14	36	80	10.6	2.68	168	.248	.294	12	.240	5	22	29	-1	3.6
Yr	12	10	.545	32	23	7	2	0	180^1	179	20	43	105	11.1	3.34	133	.256	.300	12	.200	3	14	22	-1	2.8
1971 Chi-N	17	14	.548	35	35	14	**5**	0	261^1	279	25	62	99	11.9	3.51	112	.274	.319	14	.154	-1	-1	12	-2	1.0
1972 Chi-N	17	7	.708	29	28	10	3	0	195	187	18	29	80	10.3	2.77	138	.251	.287	13	.191	2	15	23	0	2.8
1973 Chi-N	7	12	.368	30	29	1	1	0	162	192	20	40	48	13.1	4.28	92	.299	.344	3	.063	-3	-11	-6	-1	-0.9
Total 17	209	164	.560	520	465	129	43	4	3186	3046	298	858	1728	11.2	3.40	110	.252	.306	132	.123	-14	86	123	0	12.0
● JIM PARK Park, James b: 11/10/1892, Richmond, Ky. d: 12/17/70, Lexington, Ky. BR/TR, 6'2", 175 lbs. Deb: 9/07/15																									
1915 StL-A	2	0	1.000	3	3	1	0	0	22^2	18	1	9	5	10.7	1.19	240	.214	.290	4	.400	1	4	4	-1	0.6
1916 StL-A	1	4	.200	26	6	1	0	0	79	69	2	25	26	10.8	2.62	105	.244	.307	2	.100	-1	2	1	-2	-0.2
1917 StL-A	1	1	.500	13	0	0	0	0	20^1	27	1	12	9	17.3	6.64	39	.333	.419	0	.000	-0	-9	-9	0	-1.0
Total 3	4	5	.444	42	9	2	0	0	122	114	4	46	40	11.9	3.02	91	.254	.325	6	.188	-0	-3	-4	-2	-0.6
● DOC PARKER Parker, Harley Park b: 6/14/1872, Theresa, N.Y. d: 3/3/41, Chicago, Ill. BR/TR, 6'2", 200 lbs. Deb: 7/11/1893 F																									
1893 Chi-N	0	0	—	1	0	0	0	1	2	5	0	1	0	27.0	13.50	34	.458	.503	0	.000	-0	-2	-2	-0	-0.2
1895 Chi-N	4	2	.667	7	6	5	1	0	51^1	65	1	9	9	13.5	3.68	138	.304	.341	7	.318	1	6	8	0	0.8
1896 Chi-N	1	5	.167	9	7	7	0	0	73	100	3	27	15	16.0	6.16	74	.323	.383	10	.278	0	-15	-13	1	-1.0
1901 Cin-N	0	1	.000	1	1	1	0	0	8	26	1	2	0	31.5	15.75	20	.531	.550	0	.000	-0	-11	-11	-0	-0.8
Total 4	5	8	.385	18	14	13	1	1	134^1	196	5	39	24	16.1	5.90	79	.336	.384	17	.274	0	-21	-18	1	-1.2
● HARRY PARKER Parker, Harry William b: 9/14/47, Highland, Ill. BR/TR, 6'3", 190 lbs. Deb: 8/08/70																									
1970 StL-N	1	1	.500	7	4	0	0	0	22^1	24	0	15	9	15.7	3.22	128	.276	.382	2	.250	0	2	2	0	0.3
1971 StL-N	0	0	—	4	0	0	0	0	5	6	2	2	2	14.4	7.20	50	.286	.348	0	—	0	-2	-2	-0	-0.2
1973 *NY-N	8	4	.667	38	9	0	0	5	96^2	79	7	36	63	11.0	3.35	108	.217	.293	4	.174	-0	3	3	-0	0.2
1974 NY-N	4	12	.250	40	16	1	0	4	131	145	10	46	58	13.3	3.92	91	.281	.343	0	.000	-4	-4	-5	-2	-1.1
1975 NY-N	2	3	.400	18	1	0	0	2	34^2	37	2	19	22	14.5	4.41	78	.272	.361	0	.000	1	-3	-4	-0	-0.3
StL-N	0	1	.000	14	0	0	0	1	18^2	21	3	10	13	14.9	6.27	60	.288	.373	0	.000	0	-5	-5	1	-0.5
Yr	2	4	.333	32	1	0	0	3	53^1	58	5	29	35	14.7	5.06	70	.278	.366	0	.000	1	-9	-9	0	-0.8
1976 Cle-A	0	0	—	3	0	0	0	0	7	3	0	0	5	3.9	0.00	—	.136	.136	0	—	0	3	3	0	0.3
Total 6	15	21	.417	124	30	1	0	12	315^1	315	24	128	172	12.8	3.85	94	.258	.332	6	.086	-3	-7	-8	-1	-1.3
● CLAY PARKER Parker, James Clayton b: 12/19/62, Columbia, La. BR/TR, 6'1", 185 lbs. Deb: 9/14/87																									
1987 Sea-A	0	0	—	3	1	0	0	0	7^2	15	2	4	8	23.5	10.57	45	.405	.476	0	—	0	-5	-5	0	-0.7
1989 NY-A	4	5	.444	22	17	2	0	0	120	123	12	31	53	11.7	3.68	105	.264	.313	0	—	0	3	3	0	0.4
1990 NY-A	1	1	.500	5	2	0	0	0	22	19	5	7	20	10.6	4.50	88	.229	.289	0	—	0	-1	-1	-0	-0.2
Det-A	2	2	.500	24	1	0	0	0	51	45	6	25	20	12.5	3.18	125	.242	.335	0	—	0	4	4	0	0.4
Yr	3	3	.500	29	3	0	0	0	73	64	11	32	40	12.0	3.58	111	.237	.320	0	—	0	3	3	0	0.2
1992 Sea-A	0	2	.000	8	6	0	0	0	33^1	47	6	11	20	16.2	7.56	53	.338	.395	0	—	0	-13	-13	-0	-1.3
Total 4	7	10	.412	62	27	2	0	0	234	249	31	78	121	12.8	4.42	89	.273	.335	0	—	0	-13	-13	0	-1.4
● JAY PARKER Parker, Jay b: 7/8/1874, Theresa, N.Y. d: 6/8/35, Hartford, Mich. BR/TR, 5'11", 185 lbs. Deb: 9/27/1899 F																									
1899 Pit-N	0	0	—	1	1	0	0	0	0	0	0	2	0	—	∞	—	—	1.000	0	—	0	-2	-2	0	-0.2
● ROY PARKER Parker, Roy William b: 2/29/1896, Union, Mo. d: 5/17/54, Tulsa, Okla. BR/TR, 6'3", 200 lbs. Deb: 9/10/19																									
1919 StL-N	0	0	—	2	0	0	0	0	2	6	0	1	0	36.0	31.50	9	.333	.400	0	—	0	-6	-6	0	-0.6
● SLICKER PARKS Parks, Vernon Henry b: 11/10/1895, Dallas, Mich. d: 2/21/78, Royal Oak, Mich. BR/TR, 5'10", 158 lbs. Deb: 7/11/21																									
1921 Det-A	3	2	.600	10	1	0	0	0	25^1	33	2	16	10	17.8	5.68	75	.306	.400	1	.111	-1	-4	-4	-1	-0.5
● BILL PARKS Parks, William Robert b: 6/4/1849, Easton, Pa. d: 10/10/11, Easton, Pa. BR/TR, 5'8", 150 lbs. Deb: 4/26/1875 M♦																									
1875 Was-n	4	8	.333	14	11	9	0	0	106^2	146	5	6		12.8	*4.05*	65	.281	.289	20	.179	-3	-19	-17		-1.5
Phi-n	0	0	—	2	0	0	0	0	5^1	13	0	1		23.6	*6.75*	37	.419	.438	1	.167	-0	-3	-3		-0.2
Yr	4	8	.333	16	11	9	0	0	112	159	5	7		13.3	*4.18*	63	.289	.297	21	.178	-4	-21	-19		-1.7
● ROY PARMELEE Parmelee, Le Roy Earl "Tarzan" b: 4/25/07, Lambertville, Mich d: 8/31/81, Monroe, Mich. BR/TR, 6'1", 190 lbs. Deb: 9/28/29																									
1929 NY-N	1	0	1.000	2	1	0	0	0	7	13	1	3	1	21.9	9.00	51	.481	.548	1	.500	0	-3	-3	0	-0.3
1930 NY-N	0	1	.000	11	1	0	0	0	21	18	3	26	19	18.9	9.43	50	.228	.419	1	.250	1	-10	-11	0	-0.9
1931 NY-N	2	2	.500	13	5	4	0	0	58^2	47	1	33	30	12.7	3.68	100	.223	.336	4	.200	-0	1	0	0	0.0
1932 NY-N	0	3	.000	8	3	0	0	0	25^1	25	0	14	23	14.6	3.91	95	.250	.353	2	.400	1	-0	-1	0	0.1
1933 NY-N	13	8	.619	32	32	14	3	0	218^1	191	9	77	132	11.6	3.17	101	.232	.309	19	.235	4	4	1	0	0.5
1934 NY-N	10	6	.625	22	20	7	2	0	152^2	134	6	60	83	11.8	3.42	113	**.238**	.318	11	.200	2	11	8	2	1.1
1935 NY-N	14	10	.583	34	31	13	0	0	226	214	20	97	79	12.7	4.22	91	.249	.332	18	.209	3	-5	-9	2	-0.5
1936 StL-N	11	11	.500	37	28	9	0	2	221	226	13	107	79	14.0	4.56	86	.270	.360	15	.197	-0	-13	-15	-1	-1.5
1937 Chi-N	7	8	.467	33	18	8	0	0	145^2	165	13	79	55	15.5	5.13	78	.286	.379	9	.173	0	-20	-19	1	-1.7
1939 Phi-A	1	6	.143	14	5	0	0	1	44^2	42	2	35	13	16.1	6.45	73	.235	.369	2	.133	-1	-9	-9	0	-0.8
Total 10	59	55	.518	206	144	55	5	3	1120^1	1075	68	531	514	13.3	4.27	89	.253	.343	82	.207	9	-45	-58	5	-4.0
● MEL PARNELL Parnell, Melvin Lloyd "Dusty" b: 6/13/22, New Orleans, La. BL/TL, 6', 180 lbs. Deb: 4/20/47																									
1947 Bos-A	2	3	.400	15	5	1	0	0	50^2	60	1	27	23	15.6	6.39	61	.296	.381	1	.056	-2	-15	-14	-1	-1.6
1948 Bos-A	15	8	.652	35	27	16	1	0	212	205	7	90	77	12.7	3.14	140	.252	.330	13	.162	-4	27	29	2	2.7
1949 Bos-A★	**25**	7	.781	39	33	**27**	4	2	**295**^{1}	258	8	134	122	12.1	2.77	157	.237	.324	29	.254	2	**47**	**52**	-0	**5.6**
1950 Bos-A	18	10	.643	40	31	21	2	3	249	244	17	106	93	12.9	3.61	136	.259	.338	19	.194	-1	27	36	5	3.8
1951 Bos-A★	18	11	.621	36	29	11	3	2	221	229	11	77	77	12.5	3.26	137	.272	.333	25	.309	4	21	30	-0	**3.5**
1952 Bos-A	12	12	.500	33	29	15	3	2	214	207	13	89	107	12.7	3.62	109	.255	.332	8	.095	-4	1	8	1	0.5
1953 Bos-A	21	8	.724	38	34	12	5	0	241	217	15	116	136	12.6	3.06	137	.239	.328	21	.223	1	25	31	-2	3.1
1954 Bos-A	3	7	.300	19	15	4	1	0	92^1	104	7	35	38	13.6	3.70	111	.287	.352	3	.088	-2	0	4	0	0.2
1955 Bos-A	2	3	.400	13	9	0	0	1	46	62	12	25	18	17.2	7.83	55	.318	.398	6	.316	1	-20	-18	0	-1.6
1956 Bos-A	7	6	.538	21	20	6	1	0	131^1	129	13	59	41	12.9	3.77	123	.256	.335	7	.152	-2	6	12	-1	0.9

YEAR	TM/L	W	L	PCT	G	GS	CG	SH	SV	IP	H	HR	BB	SO	RAT	ERA	ERA+	OAV	OOB	BH	AVG	PB	PR	/A	PD	TPI
Total	10	123	75	.621	289	232	113	20	10	1752^{2}	1715	104	758	732	12.8	3.50	125	.257	.336	132	.198	-7	119	170	3	17.1
● RUBE PARNHAM	Parnham, James Arthur b: 2/1/1894, Heidelberg, Pa. d: 11/25/63, McKeesport, Pa. BR/TR, 6'3", 185 lbs. Deb: 9/20/16																									
1916	Phi-A	2	1	.667	4	3	2	0	0	24^{2}	27	0	13	8	14.6	4.01	71	.300	.388	3	.273	1	-3	-3	1	-0.2
1917	Phi-A	0	1	.000	2	2	0	0	0	11	12	1	9	4	17.2	4.09	67	.316	.447	0	.000	-0	-2	-2	0	-0.2
Total	2	2	2	.500	6	5	2	0	0	35^{2}	39	1	22	12	15.4	4.04	70	.305	.407	3	.214	0	-5	-5	1	-0.4
● JEFF PARRETT	Parrett, Jeffrey Dale b: 8/26/61, Indianapolis, Ind. BR/TR, 6'3", 200 lbs. Deb: 4/11/86																									
1986	Mon-N	0	1	.000	12	0	0	0	0	20^{1}	19	3	13	21	14.2	4.87	76	.247	.356	1	.500	0	-3	-3	0	-0.2
1987	Mon-N	7	6	.538	45	0	0	0	6	62	53	8	30	56	12.0	4.21	100	.229	.318	0	.000	-1	-1	-0	0	-0.1
1988	Mon-N	12	4	.750	61	0	0	0	6	91^{2}	66	8	45	62	11.0	2.65	136	.214	.316	0	—	0	8	10	-1	1.0
1989	Phi-N	12	6	.667	72	0	0	0	6	105^{2}	90	6	44	98	11.4	2.98	119	.232	.310	0	.000	-1	6	7	-1	0.5
1990	Phi-N	4	9	.308	47	5	0	0	1	81^{2}	92	10	36	69	14.2	5.18	74	.293	.368	0	.000	-1	-13	-12	-0	-1.4
	Atl-N	1	1	.500	20	0	0	0	1	27	27	1	19	17	15.7	3.00	134	.281	.405	1	1.000	0	2	3	0	0.4
	Yr	5	10	.333	67	5	0	0	2	108^{2}	119	11	55	86	14.5	4.64	84	.289	.374	1	.091	-1	-10	-9	0	-1.0
1991	Atl-N	1	2	.333	18	0	0	0	1	21^{1}	31	2	12	14	18.1	6.33	61	.326	.402	0	—	0	-6	-6	1	-0.5
1992	*Oak-A	9	1	.900	66	0	0	0	0	98^{1}	81	7	42	78	11.4	3.02	125	.226	.311	0	—	0	10	8	-1	0.8
Total	7	46	30	.605	341	5	0	0	21	508	459	45	241	415	12.5	3.65	103	.246	.334	2	.087	-1	4	7	-2	0.5
● MIKE PARROTT	Parrott, Michael Everett Arch b: 12/6/54, Oxnard, Cal. BR/TR, 6'4", 210 lbs. Deb: 9/05/77																									
1977	Bal-A	0	0	—	3	0	0	0	0	4^{1}	4	0	2	2	12.5	2.08	183	.250	.333	0	—	0	1	1	-0	0.1
1978	Sea-A	1	5	.167	27	10	0	0	1	82^{1}	108	8	32	41	15.6	5.14	74	.316	.379	0	—	0	-13	-12	0	-1.2
1979	Sea-A	14	12	.538	38	30	13	2	0	229^{1}	231	17	86	127	12.7	3.77	116	.267	.338	0	—	0	11	15	3	1.6
1980	Sea-A	1	16	.059	27	16	1	0	3	94	136	16	42	53	17.1	7.28	57	.348	.412	0	—	0	-34	-33	4	-2.8
1981	Sea-A	3	6	.333	24	12	0	0	1	85	102	3	28	43	13.9	5.08	76	.299	.354	0	—	0	-13	-12	0	-1.3
Total	5	19	39	.328	119	68	14	2	5	495	581	44	190	266	14.2	4.87	85	.297	.363	0	—	0	-48	-41	6	-3.6
● TOM PARROTT	Parrott, Thomas William "Tacky Tom" b: 4/10/1868, Portland, Ore. d: 1/1/32, Dundee, Ore. BR/TR, 5'10.5", 170 lbs. Deb: 6/18/1893 F♦																									
1893	Chi-N	0	3	.000	4	3	2	0	0	27	35	1	17	7	17.3	6.67	69	.305	.394	7	.259	-0	-6	-6	-1	-0.5
	Cin-N	10	7	.588	22	17	11	1	0	154	174	1	70	33	14.8	4.09	117	.276	.357	13	.191	-3	10	12	2	0.9
	Yr	10	10	.500	26	20	13	1	0	181	209	2	87	40	15.2	4.48	106	.281	.363	20	.211	-3	4	6	1	0.4
1894	Cin-N	17	19	.472	41	36	31	1	1	308^{2}	402	19	126	61	15.7	5.60	99	.311	.377	74	.323	8	-9	-1	3	0.7
1895	Cin-N	11	18	.379	41	31	23	0	**3**	263^{1}	382	8	76	57	15.8	5.47	91	.333	.378	69	.343	11	-20	-14	3	-0.1
1896	StL-N	1	1	.500	7	2	2	0	0	42	62	4	18	8	17.8	6.21	70	.340	.408	138	.291	1	-9	-9	-0	-0.7
Total	4	39	48	.448	115	89	69	2	4	795	1055	33	307	166	15.7	5.33	96	.314	.376	301	.301	18	-34	-19	6	0.3
● JIGGS PARSON	Parson, William Edwin b: 12/28/1885, Parker, S.Dak. d: 5/19/67, Los Angeles, Cal. BR/TR, 6'2", 180 lbs. Deb: 5/16/10																									
1910	Bos-N	0	2	.000	10	4	0	0	0	35^{1}	35	2	26	7	16.0	3.82	87	.278	.409	1	.083	-1	-3	-2	-0	-0.3
1911	Bos-N	0	1	.000	7	0	0	0	0	25	36	2	15	7	19.8	6.48	59	.375	.478	2	.200	-0	-9	-7	-1	-0.8
Total	2	0	3	.000	17	4	0	0	0	60^{1}	71	4	41	14	17.6	4.92	72	.320	.439	3	.136	-2	-12	-9	-1	-1.1
● CHARLIE PARSONS	Parsons, Charles James b: 7/18/1863, Cherry Flats, Pa. d: 3/24/36, Mansfield, Pa. BL/TL, 5'10", 160 lbs. Deb: 5/29/1886																									
1886	Bos-N	0	2	.000	2	2	2	0	0	16	20	0	4	5	13.5	3.94	81	.308	.348	3	.375	1	-1	-1	-1	-0.1
1887	NY-a	1	1	.500	4	4	4	0	0	34	51	0	6	5	15.4	4.50	94	.319	.347	3	.200	-1	-1	-1	0	-0.1
1890	Cle-N	0	1	.000	2	1	0	0	0	9	12	0	6	2	22.0	6.00	60	.310	.452	3	.750	1	-2	-2	0	-0.1
Total	3	1	4	.200	8	7	6	0	0	59	83	0	16	12	15.9	4.58	84	.315	.365	9	.333	2	-4	-5	-1	-0.3
● TOM PARSONS	Parsons, Thomas Anthony b: 9/13/39, Lakeville, Conn. BR/TR, 6'7", 210 lbs. Deb: 9/05/63																									
1963	Pit-N	0	1	.000	1	1	0	0	0	4^{1}	7	1	2	2	18.7	8.31	40	.368	.429	0	.000	-0	-2	-2	0	-0.2
1964	NY-N	1	2	.333	4	2	1	0	0	19^{1}	20	1	6	10	12.1	4.19	85	.274	.329	0	.000	-1	-1	-1	-0	-0.2
1965	NY-N	1	10	.091	35	11	1	1	1	90^{2}	108	17	17	58	12.4	4.67	76	.290	.321	1	.056	-1	-11	-11	1	-1.1
Total	3	2	13	.133	40	14	2	1	1	114^{1}	135	19	25	70	12.6	4.72	75	.291	.327	1	.037	-2	-15	-15	1	-1.5
● BILL PARSONS	Parsons, William Raymond b: 8/17/48, Riverside, Cal. BR/TR, 6'6", 195 lbs. Deb: 4/13/71																									
1971	Mil-A	13	17	.433	36	35	12	4	0	244^{2}	219	19	93	139	11.6	3.20	108	.241	.315	12	.167	3	7	7	0	1.2
1972	Mil-A	13	13	.500	33	30	10	2	0	214	194	27	68	111	11.1	3.91	77	.240	.301	11	.164	0	-20	-21	-3	-2.5
1973	Mil-A	3	6	.333	20	17	0	0	0	59^{2}	59	6	67	30	19.0	6.79	55	.257	.424	0	—	0	-20	-20	-0	-1.9
1974	Oak-A	0	0	—	4	0	0	0	0	2	1	0	3	2	18.0	0.00	—	.143	.400	0	—	0	1	1	-0	0.1
Total	4	29	36	.446	93	82	22	6	0	520^{1}	473	52	231	282	12.3	3.89	85	.242	.325	23	.165	3	-32	-33	-3	-3.1
● STAN PARTENHEIMER	Partenheimer, Stanwood Wendell "Party" b: 10/21/22, Chicopee Falls, Mass. d: 1/28/89, Wilson, N.C. BR/TL, 5'11", 175 lbs. Deb: 5/27/44 F																									
1944	Bos-A	0	0	—	1	1	0	0	0	1	3	0	2	0	45.0	18.00	19	.500	.625	0	.000	-0	-2	-2	-0	-0.2
1945	StL-N	0	0	—	8	2	0	0	0	13^{1}	12	2	16	6	18.9	6.08	62	.250	.438	0	.000	-0	-3	-3	0	-0.4
Total	2	0	0	—	9	3	0	0	0	14^{1}	15	2	18	6	20.7	6.91	54	.278	.458	0	.000	-1	-5	-5	0	-0.6
● BILL PASCHALL	Paschall, William Herbert b: 4/22/54, Norfolk, Va. BR/TR, 6', 175 lbs. Deb: 9/20/78																									
1978	KC-A	0	1	.000	2	0	0	0	1	8	6	0	0	5	7.9	3.38	113	.207	.233	0	—	0	0	0	-0	-0.1
1979	KC-A	0	1	.000	7	0	0	0	0	13^{2}	18	2	5	3	16.5	6.59	65	.300	.373	0	—	0	-4	-4	-0	-0.5
1981	KC-A	0	0	—	2	0	0	0	0	2	2	0	0	1	9.0	4.50	80	.286	.286	0	—	0	-0	-0	-0	0.0
Total	3	0	2	.000	11	0	0	0	1	23^{2}	26	2	5	9	12.9	5.32	76	.271	.327	0	—	0	-3	-3	-1	-0.6
● CAMILO PASCUAL	Pascual, Camilo Alberto (Lus) "Little Potato" b: 1/20/34, Havana, Cuba BR/TR, 5'11", 185 lbs. Deb: 4/15/54 FC																									
1954	Was-A	4	7	.364	48	4	1	0	3	119^{1}	126	7	61	60	14.6	4.22	84	.276	.368	4	.133	-0	-7	-9	3	-0.6
1955	Was-A	2	12	.143	43	16	1	0	3	129	158	5	70	82	16.3	6.14	62	.311	.401	7	.219	0	-31	-33	2	-2.9
1956	Was-A	6	18	.250	39	27	6	0	2	188^{2}	194	33	89	162	13.8	5.87	74	.261	.345	8	.138	-2	-36	-32	1	-3.1
1957	Was-A	8	17	.320	29	26	8	2	0	175^{2}	168	11	76	113	12.7	4.10	95	.258	.338	7	.140	-2	-6	-4	2	-0.4
1958	Was-A	8	12	.400	31	27	6	2	0	177^{1}	166	14	60	146	11.6	3.15	121	.248	.313	9	.158	-1	12	13	1	1.4
1959	Was-A†	17	10	.630	32	30	**17**	**6**	0	238^{2}	202	10	69	185	10.3	2.64	148	.226	.284	26	.302	6	32	34	5	**5.0**
1960	Was-A†	12	8	.600	26	22	8	3	2	151^{2}	139	11	53	143	11.5	3.03	128	.240	.306	9	.176	3	14	15	0	1.8
1961	Min-A★	15	16	.484	35	33	15	**8**	0	252^{1}	205	26	100	**221**	11.0	3.46	123	.217	.294	14	.165	-0	16	22	1	2.3
1962	Min-A★	20	11	.645	34	33	**18**	**5**	0	257^{2}	236	25	59	**206**	10.4	3.32	123	.241	.286	26	.268	8	19	22	0	3.2
1963	Min-A	21	9	.700	31	31	**18**	3	0	248^{1}	205	21	81	**202**	10.5	2.46	148	.224	.289	23	.250	6	32	**33**	-1	4.3
1964	Min-A★	15	12	.556	36	36	14	1	0	267^{1}	245	30	98	213	11.6	3.30	108	.241	.309	17	.181	4	10	8	0	1.3
1965	*Min-A	9	3	.750	27	27	5	1	0	156	126	12	63	96	11.2	3.35	106	.217	.299	12	.200	3	2	4	2	0.9
1966	Min-A	8	6	.571	21	19	2	0	0	103	113	9	30	56	12.7	4.89	73	.278	.330	8	.216	1	-17	-15	2	-1.2
1967	Was-A	12	10	.545	28	27	5	1	0	164^{2}	147	15	43	106	10.5	3.28	96	.237	.289	9	.176	1	-1	-2	-0	-0.1
1968	Was-A	13	12	.520	31	31	8	4	0	201	181	11	59	111	10.9	2.69	109	.239	.298	12	.185	1	7	5	1	0.9
1969	Was-A	2	5	.286	14	13	0	0	0	55^{1}	49	12	38	34	15.0	6.83	51	.239	.371	4	.235	0	-20	-21	-0	-2.0
	Cin-N	0	0	—	5	1	0	0	0	7^{1}	14	2	4	3	22.1	8.59	44	.424	.486	0	—	0	-4	-4	-0	-0.4
1970	LA-N	0	0	—	10	0	0	0	0	14	12	2	5	8	11.6	2.57	149	.231	.310	0	—	0	2	2	0	0.2
1971	Cle-A	2	2	.500	9	1	0	0	0	23^{1}	17	0	11	20	11.2	3.09	124	.205	.305	3	.600	1	1	2	1	0.4
Total	18	174	170	.506	529	404	132	36	10	2930^{2}	2703	256	1069	2167	11.8	3.63	103	.244	.314	198	.205	30	26	38	18	11.0
● CARLOS PASCUAL	Pascual, Carlos Alberto (Lus) b: 3/13/31, Havana, Cuba BR/TR, 5'6", 165 lbs. Deb: 9/24/50 F																									
1950	Was-A	1	1	.500	2	2	2	0	0	17	12	0	8	3	11.1	2.12	212	.194	.296	1	.250	0	5	4	-1	0.4

● LARRY PASHNICK
Pashnick, Larry John b: 4/25/56, Lincoln Park, Mich. BR/TR, 6'3", 205 lbs. Deb: 4/10/82

YEAR TM/L	W	L	PCT	G	GS	CG	SH	SV	IP	H	HR	BB	SO	RAT	ERA	ERA+	OAV	OOB	BH	AVG	PB	PR	/A	PD	TPI
1982 Det-A	4	4	.500	28	13	1	0	0	94^1	110	17	25	19	13.0	4.01	101	.297	.343	0	—	0	1	1	-1	0.0
1983 Det-A	1	3	.250	12	6	0	0	0	37^2	48	5	18	17	16.5	5.26	74	.308	.390	0	—	0	-5	-6	1	-0.5
1984 Min-A	2	1	.667	13	1	0	0	0	38^1	38	3	11	10	12.0	3.52	119	.260	.321	0	—	0	2	3	0	0.3
Total 3	7	8	.467	53	20	1	0	0	170^1	196	25	54	46	13.5	4.17	97	.292	.350	0	—	0	-2	-2	0	-0.2

● CLAUDE PASSEAU
Passeau, Claude William b: 4/9/09, Wayensboro, Miss. BR/TR, 6'3", 198 lbs. Deb: 9/29/35

YEAR TM/L	W	L	PCT	G	GS	CG	SH	SV	IP	H	HR	BB	SO	RAT	ERA	ERA+	OAV	OOB	BH	AVG	PB	PR	/A	PD	TPI
1935 Pit-N	0	1	.000	1	1	0	0	0	3	7	0	2	1	27.0	12.00	34	.500	.563	0	.000	-0	-3	-3	0	-0.2
1936 Phi-N	11	15	.423	49	21	8	2	3	217^1	247	7	55	85	12.7	3.48	130	.280	.325	22	.282	4	13	26	1	3.1
1937 Phi-N	14	18	.438	50	34	18	1	2	**292^1**	348	16	79	135	13.3	4.34	100	.296	.343	21	.196	-0	-14	-0	0	0.0
1938 Phi-N	11	18	.379	44	33	15	0	1	239	281	8	93	100	14.4	4.52	86	.287	.354	13	.162	-2	-19	-17	3	-1.6
1939 Phi-N	2	4	.333	8	8	4	1	0	53^1	54	1	25	29	13.5	4.22	95	.263	.346	4	.200	-0	-2	-1	0	-0.2
Chi-N	13	9	.591	34	27	13	1	3	221	215	8	48	108	10.9	3.05	129	.254	.297	12	.156	-1	21	22	1	2.2
Yr	15	13	.536	42	35	17	2	3	274^1	269	9	73	**137**	11.4	3.28	120	.255	.306	16	.165	-2	19	20	1	2.0
1940 Chi-N	20	13	.606	46	31	20	4	5	280^2	259	8	59	124	10.3	2.50	150	.237	.278	20	.204	6	42	39	1	4.9
1941 Chi-N★	14	14	.500	34	30	20	3	0	231	262	10	52	80	12.3	3.35	105	.281	.320	19	.221	4	7	4	-1	0.8
1942 Chi-N★	19	14	.576	35	34	24	3	0	278^1	284	13	74	89	11.7	2.68	119	.260	.309	19	.181	1	20	16	1	1.9
1943 Chi-N☆	15	12	.556	35	31	18	1	1	257	245	10	66	93	11.0	2.91	115	.249	.299	19	.198	1	14	12	1	1.6
1944 Chi-N	15	9	.625	34	27	18	2	3	227	234	8	50	89	11.3	2.89	122	.266	.306	13	.162	-1	18	16	1	1.7
1945 *Chi-N†	17	9	.654	34	27	19	**5**	1	227	205	4	59	98	10.5	2.46	149	.238	.289	17	.187	1	34	**30**	3	**3.6**
1946 Chi-N★	9	8	.529	21	21	10	2	0	129^1	118	5	42	47	11.2	3.13	106	.237	.298	10	.204	3	4	3	1	0.7
1947 Chi-N	2	6	.250	19	6	1	1	2	63^1	97	7	24	26	17.3	6.25	63	.353	.407	0	.000	-2	-15	-16	-1	-1.8
Total 13	162	150	.519	444	331	188	26	21	2719^2	2856	105	728	1104	12.0	3.32	113	.267	.316	189	.192	13	120	128	11	16.7

● FRANK PASTORE
Pastore, Frank Enrico b: 8/21/57, Alhambra, Cal. BR/TR, 6'3", 205 lbs. Deb: 4/04/79

YEAR TM/L	W	L	PCT	G	GS	CG	SH	SV	IP	H	HR	BB	SO	RAT	ERA	ERA+	OAV	OOB	BH	AVG	PB	PR	/A	PD	TPI
1979 *Cin-N	6	7	.462	30	9	2	1	4	95^1	102	8	23	63	11.9	4.25	88	.271	.315	4	.160	-0	-5	-5	0	-0.6
1980 Cin-N	13	7	.650	27	27	9	2	0	184^2	161	13	42	110	9.9	3.27	109	.233	.277	10	.156	-1	7	6	-1	0.5
1981 Cin-N	4	9	.308	22	22	2	1	0	132	125	11	35	81	11.1	4.02	88	.247	.300	5	.114	-2	-8	-7	-2	-1.1
1982 Cin-N	8	13	.381	31	29	3	2	0	188^1	210	13	57	94	13.0	3.97	93	.286	.341	10	.172	1	-8	-6	-2	-0.7
1983 Cin-N	9	12	.429	36	29	4	1	0	184^1	207	20	64	93	13.3	4.88	78	.290	.349	11	.186	2	-26	-22	-1	-2.2
1984 Cin-N	3	8	.273	24	16	1	0	0	98^1	110	10	40	53	14.0	6.50	58	.285	.357	2	.071	-2	-32	-30	0	-3.0
1985 Cin-N	2	1	.667	17	6	1	0	0	54	60	1	16	29	12.8	3.83	99	.287	.341	2	.143	-0	-1	-0	0	0.0
1986 Min-A	3	1	.750	33	1	0	0	2	49^1	54	4	24	18	14.2	4.01	107	.283	.363	0	—	0	1	2	-1	0.0
Total 8	48	58	.453	220	139	22	7	6	986^1	1029	80	301	541	12.3	4.29	87	.270	.326	44	.151	-2	-72	-62	-5	-7.1

● JIM PASTORIUS
Pastorius, James W. "Sunny Jim" b: 7/12/1881, Pittsburgh, Pa. d: 5/10/41, Pittsburgh, Pa. BL/TL, 5'9", 165 lbs. Deb: 4/15/06

YEAR TM/L	W	L	PCT	G	GS	CG	SH	SV	IP	H	HR	BB	SO	RAT	ERA	ERA+	OAV	OOB	BH	AVG	PB	PR	/A	PD	TPI
1906 Bro-N	10	14	.417	29	24	16	3	0	211^2	225	4	69	58	12.6	3.61	70	.274	.333	10	.141	-0	-23	-26	-1	-2.8
1907 Bro-N	16	12	.571	28	26	20	4	0	222	218	2	77	70	12.2	2.35	100	.264	.331	15	.205	2	3	-0	-1	0.2
1908 Bro-N	4	20	.167	28	25	16	2	0	213^2	171	5	74	54	10.6	2.44	96	.216	.288	8	.129	-0	-2	-2	0	-0.3
1909 Bro-N	1	9	.100	12	9	5	1	0	79^2	91	4	58	23	16.9	5.76	45	.313	.429	2	.080	-1	-28	-28	1	-2.7
Total 4	31	55	.360	97	84	57	10	0	727	705	15	278	205	12.4	3.12	78	.258	.330	35	.152	1	-50	-56	-1	-5.6

● JOE PATE
Pate, Joseph William b: 6/6/1892, Alice, Tex. d: 12/26/48, Fort Worth, Tex. BL/TL, 5'10", 184 lbs. Deb: 4/15/26

YEAR TM/L	W	L	PCT	G	GS	CG	SH	SV	IP	H	HR	BB	SO	RAT	ERA	ERA+	OAV	OOB	BH	AVG	PB	PR	/A	PD	TPI
1926 Phi-A	9	0	1.000	47	2	0	0	6	113	109	3	51	24	12.9	2.71	154	.262	.345	4	.148	-0	**16**	**18**	3	2.1
1927 Phi-A	0	3	.000	32	0	0	0	6	53^2	67	3	21	14	14.9	5.20	82	.318	.382	3	.300	1	-6	-6	0	-0.4
Total 2	9	3	.750	79	2	0	0	12	166^2	176	6	72	38	13.6	3.51	120	.281	.358	7	.189	1	10	13	4	1.7

● CASE PATTEN
Patten, Case Lyman "Casey" b: 5/7/1876, Westport, N.Y. d: 5/31/35, Rochester, N.Y. BB/TL, 6', 175 lbs. Deb: 5/04/01

YEAR TM/L	W	L	PCT	G	GS	CG	SH	SV	IP	H	HR	BB	SO	RAT	ERA	ERA+	OAV	OOB	BH	AVG	PB	PR	/A	PD	TPI
1901 Was-A	18	10	.643	32	30	26	4	0	254^1	285	8	74	109	13.3	3.93	93	.280	.339	13	.135	-5	-7	-7	0	-1.1
1902 Was-A	17	16	.515	36	34	33	1	1	299^2	331	11	89	92	12.9	4.05	91	.280	.337	12	.096	-10	-16	-12	-1	-2.1
1903 Was-A	11	22	.333	36	34	32	0	1	300	313	11	80	133	11.9	3.60	87	.268	.317	14	.132	-6	-21	-16	1	-2.1
1904 Was-A	14	23	.378	45	39	37	2	**3**	357^2	367	2	79	150	11.7	3.07	87	.266	.315	16	.127	-6	-19	-16	1	-2.2
1905 Was-A	14	22	.389	42	36	29	2	0	309^2	300	3	86	113	11.5	3.14	85	.255	.312	16	.155	-3	-16	-17	-2	-2.3
1906 Was-A	19	16	.543	38	32	28	7	0	282^2	253	2	79	96	10.8	2.17	122	.242	.299	11	.117	-5	17	15	-1	1.1
1907 Was-A	12	16	.429	36	29	20	1	0	237^1	272	3	63	58	12.9	3.56	68	.289	.337	11	.126	-3	-27	-30	-5	-3.9
1908 Was-A	0	2	.000	4	3	1	0	0	18	25	0	6	6	15.5	3.50	65	.333	.383	1	.200	-0	-2	-2	-0	-0.3
Bos-A	0	1	.000	1	1	0	0	0	3	8	0	1	0	27.0	15.00	16	.533	.563	0	.000	-0	-4	-4	0	-0.4
Yr	0	3	.000	5	4	1	0	0	21	33	0	7	6	17.1	5.14	45	.367	.412	1	.167	-0	-6	-7	-0	-0.7
Total 8	105	128	.451	270	238	206	17	5	2062^1	2154	40	557	757	12.2	3.36	88	.269	.323	94	.127	-39	-96	-91	-7	-13.3

● DARYL PATTERSON
Patterson, Daryl Alan b: 11/21/43, Coalinga, Cal. BL/TR, 6'4", 195 lbs. Deb: 4/10/68

YEAR TM/L	W	L	PCT	G	GS	CG	SH	SV	IP	H	HR	BB	SO	RAT	ERA	ERA+	OAV	OOB	BH	AVG	PB	PR	/A	PD	TPI
1968 *Det-A	2	3	.400	38	1	0	0	7	68	53	3	27	49	11.1	2.12	142	.213	.300	0	.000	-1	7	7	-0	0.6
1969 Det-A	0	2	.000	18	0	0	0	0	22^1	15	2	19	12	13.7	2.82	132	.205	.370	0	.000	-0	2	2	-1	0.2
1970 Det-A	7	1	.875	43	0	0	0	2	78	81	9	39	55	14.4	4.85	77	.269	.362	0	.000	-1	-10	-10	-1	-1.2
1971 Det-A	0	1	.000	12	0	0	0	0	9^1	14	1	6	5	20.3	4.82	74	.359	.457	0	—	0	-1	-1	-0	-0.1
Oak-A	0	0	—	4	0	0	0	0	5^2	5	2	4	2	15.9	7.94	42	.238	.385	0	.000	-0	-3	-3	-0	-0.3
Yr	0	1	.000	16	0	0	0	0	15	19	3	10	7	18.0	6.00	58	.311	.417	0	.000	-0	-4	-4	-0	-0.4
StL-N	0	1	.000	13	2	0	0	1	26^2	20	3	15	11	11.8	4.39	82	.211	.318	0	.000	-0	-3	-2	-1	-0.3
1974 Pit-N	2	1	.667	14	0	0	0	1	21	35	3	9	8	18.9	7.29	47	.376	.431	0	.000	-0	-9	-9	0	-0.9
Total 5	11	9	.550	142	3	0	0	11	231	223	23	119	142	13.8	4.09	85	.256	.353	0	.000	-3	-17	-16	-3	-2.0

● DAVE PATTERSON
Patterson, David Glenn b: 7/25/56, Springfield, Mo. BR/TR, 6', 170 lbs. Deb: 6/09/79

YEAR TM/L	W	L	PCT	G	GS	CG	SH	SV	IP	H	HR	BB	SO	RAT	ERA	ERA+	OAV	OOB	BH	AVG	PB	PR	/A	PD	TPI
1979 LA-N	4	1	.800	36	0	0	0	6	53	62	5	22	34	14.3	5.26	69	.292	.359	1	.143	-0	-9	-10	-0	-1.1

● GIL PATTERSON
Patterson, Gilbert Thomas b: 9/5/55, Philadelphia, Pa. BR/TR, 6'1", 185 lbs. Deb: 4/19/77

YEAR TM/L	W	L	PCT	G	GS	CG	SH	SV	IP	H	HR	BB	SO	RAT	ERA	ERA+	OAV	OOB	BH	AVG	PB	PR	/A	PD	TPI
1977 NY-A	1	2	.333	10	6	0	0	1	33^1	38	3	20	29	16.5	5.40	73	.290	.396	0	—	0	-5	-5	1	-0.4

● KEN PATTERSON
Patterson, Kenneth Brian b: 7/8/64, Costa Mesa, Cal. BL/TL, 6'4", 210 lbs. Deb: 7/09/88

YEAR TM/L	W	L	PCT	G	GS	CG	SH	SV	IP	H	HR	BB	SO	RAT	ERA	ERA+	OAV	OOB	BH	AVG	PB	PR	/A	PD	TPI
1988 Chi-A	0	2	.000	9	2	0	0	1	20^2	25	2	7	8	13.9	4.79	83	.294	.348	0	—	0	-2	-2	-0	-0.2
1989 Chi-A	6	1	.857	50	1	0	0	0	65^2	64	11	28	43	12.9	4.52	84	.257	.337	0	—	0	-5	-5	-1	-0.6
1990 Chi-A	2	1	.667	43	0	0	0	2	66^1	58	6	34	40	12.8	3.39	113	.242	.341	0	—	0	4	3	0	0.5
1991 Chi-A	3	0	1.000	43	0	0	0	1	63^2	48	5	35	32	11.9	2.83	140	.214	.323	0	—	0	9	8	-1	0.8
1992 Chi-N	2	3	.400	32	1	0	0	0	41^2	41	7	27	23	14.9	3.89	93	.268	.381	0	.000	-0	-2	-1	-0	-0.2
Total 5	13	7	.650	177	4	0	0	4	258	236	31	131	146	13.0	3.73	103	.248	.343	0	.000	-0	4	3	-2	0.3

● REGGIE PATTERSON
Patterson, Reginald Allen b: 11/7/58, Birmingham, Ala. BR/TR, 6'4", 180 lbs. Deb: 8/13/81

YEAR TM/L	W	L	PCT	G	GS	CG	SH	SV	IP	H	HR	BB	SO	RAT	ERA	ERA+	OAV	OOB	BH	AVG	PB	PR	/A	PD	TPI
1981 Chi-A	0	1	.000	6	1	0	0	0	7^1	14	1	6	2	24.5	13.50	26	.412	.500	0	—	0	-8	-8	0	-0.8
1983 Chi-N	1	2	.333	5	2	0	0	0	18^2	17	3	6	10	12.1	4.82	79	.246	.325	0	.000	-1	-2	-2	-0	-0.3
1984 Chi-N	0	1	.000	3	1	0	0	0	6	10	1	2	5	18.0	10.50	37	.357	.400	0	.000	-0	-5	-4	0	-0.4
1985 Chi-N	3	0	1.000	8	5	1	0	0	39	36	2	10	17	10.6	3.00	133	.250	.299	1	.100	-0	3	4	-0	0.4
Total 4	4	4	.500	22	9	1	0	0	71	77	7	24	34	13.1	5.20	75	.280	.342	1	.056	-1	-13	-10	0	-1.1

● BOB PATTERSON
Patterson, Robert Chandler b: 5/16/59, Jacksonville, Fla. BR/TL, 6'2", 195 lbs. Deb: 9/02/85

YEAR TM/L	W	L	PCT	G	GS	CG	SH	SV	IP	H	HR	BB	SO	RAT	ERA	ERA+	OAV	OOB	BH	AVG	PB	PR	/A	PD	TPI
1985 SD-N	0	0	—	3	0	0	0	0	4	13	2	3	1	36.0	24.75	14	.565	.615	0	—	0	-9	-9	-0	-0.9
1986 Pit-N	2	3	.400	11	5	0	0	0	36^1	49	0	5	20	13.4	4.95	77	.322	.344	1	.125	-0	-5	-5	1	-0.4

YEAR	TM/L	W	L	PCT	G	GS	CG	SH	SV	IP	H	HR	BB	SO	RAT	ERA	ERA+	OAV	OOB	BH	AVG	PB	PR	/A	PD	TPI
1987	Pit-N	1	4	.200	15	7	0	0	0	43	49	5	22	27	15.1	6.70	61	.290	.375	1	.083	-1	-13	-12	-0	-1.3
1989	Pit-N	4	3	.571	12	3	0	0	1	26^2	23	3	8	20	10.5	4.05	83	.232	.290	0	.000	0	-2	-2	-0	-0.3
1990	*Pit-N	8	5	.615	55	5	0	0	5	94^2	88	9	21	70	10.6	2.95	123	.249	.296	1	.053	-1	9	7	-0	0.6
1991	*Pit-N	4	3	.571	54	1	0	0	2	65^2	67	7	15	57	11.2	4.11	87	.267	.308	1	.250	0	-3	-4	0	-0.4
1992	*Pit-N	6	3	.667	60	0	0	0	9	64^2	59	7	23	43	11.4	2.92	117	.246	.312	2	.333	1	4	3	-1	0.4
Total	7	25	21	.543	210	21	0	0	17	335	348	33	97	238	12.1	4.22	86	.270	.323	6	.115	-1	-19	-22	-1	-2.3

● ROY PATTERSON Patterson, Roy Lewis "Boy Wonder" b: 12/17/1876, Stoddard, Wis. d: 4/14/53, St.Croix Falls, Wis. BR/TR, 6', 185 lbs. Deb: 4/24/01

YEAR	TM/L	W	L	PCT	G	GS	CG	SH	SV	IP	H	HR	BB	SO	RAT	ERA	ERA+	OAV	OOB	BH	AVG	PB	PR	/A	PD	TPI
1901	Chi-A	20	16	.556	41	35	30	4	0	312^1	345	11	62	127	12.0	3.37	103	.277	.316	26	.222	1	10	4	0	0.4
1902	Chi-A	19	14	.576	34	30	26	2	0	268	262	5	67	61	11.1	3.06	111	.256	.304	20	.190	-2	15	10	1	0.9
1903	Chi-A	15	15	.500	34	30	26	2	1	293	275	5	69	89	10.9	2.70	104	.248	.298	11	.105	-6	8	3	2	0.0
1904	Chi-A	9	9	.500	22	17	14	4	0	165	148	1	24	64	9.8	2.29	107	.241	.278	6	.103	-4	6	3	-1	-0.2
1905	Chi-A	4	6	.400	13	9	7	0	0	88^2	73	0	16	29	9.3	1.83	135	.226	.269	8	.267	2	8	6	1	1.0
1906	Chi-A	10	7	.588	21	18	12	3	1	142	119	1	17	45	8.9	2.09	121	.231	.261	3	.061	-4	9	7	0	0.3
1907	Chi-A	4	6	.400	19	13	4	1	0	96	105	0	18	27	11.7	2.63	92	.280	.316	3	.097	-2	-1	-2	1	-0.4
Total	7	81	73	.526	184	152	119	16	2	1365	1327	23	273	442	10.8	2.75	107	.255	.297	77	.156	-15	57	31	5	2.0

● MARTY PATTIN Pattin, Martin William b: 4/6/43, Charleston, Ill. BR/TR, 5'11", 180 lbs. Deb: 5/14/68 C

YEAR	TM/L	W	L	PCT	G	GS	CG	SH	SV	IP	H	HR	BB	SO	RAT	ERA	ERA+	OAV	OOB	BH	AVG	PB	PR	/A	PD	TPI
1968	Cal-A	4	4	.500	52	4	0	0	3	84	67	7	37	66	11.4	2.79	104	.221	.310	1	.083	-1	2	1	-1	-0.1
1969	Sea-A	7	12	.368	34	27	2	1	0	158^2	166	29	71	126	13.6	5.62	65	.268	.345	9	.155	-1	-35	-35	-1	-3.7
1970	Mil-A	14	12	.538	37	29	11	0	0	233^1	204	20	71	161	10.8	3.39	112	.235	.298	9	.129	-2	8	10	2	1.1
1971	Mil-A☆	14	14	.500	36	36	9	5	0	264^2	225	29	73	169	10.3	3.13	111	.235	.292	7	.084	-3	10	10	-1	0.7
1972	Bos-A	17	13	.567	38	35	13	4	0	253	232	19	65	168	10.9	3.24	99	.243	.297	12	.140	0	-5	-1	1	0.0
1973	Bos-A	15	15	.500	34	30	11	2	1	219^1	238	31	69	119	12.9	4.31	93	.277	.337	0	—	0	-12	-7	1	-1.0
1974	KC-A	3	7	.300	25	11	2	0	0	117^1	121	10	28	50	11.6	3.99	96	.264	.309	0	—	0	-5	-2	-1	-0.7
1975	KC-A	10	10	.500	44	15	5	1	5	177	173	13	45	89	11.2	3.25	118	.253	.302	0	—	0	10	12	-1	1.0
1976	*KC-A	8	14	.364	44	15	4	1	5	141	114	9	38	65	9.9	2.49	141	.216	.273	0	—	0	16	16	-0	1.6
1977	*KC-A	10	3	.769	31	10	4	0	0	128^1	115	16	37	55	10.8	3.58	113	.242	.300	0	—	0	7	7	-1	0.5
1978	*KC-A	3	3	.500	32	5	2	0	4	78^2	72	8	25	30	11.3	3.32	115	.248	.312	0	—	0	4	4	-2	0.1
1979	KC-A	5	2	.714	31	7	1	0	3	94^1	109	11	21	41	12.5	4.58	93	.293	.332	0	—	0	-4	-3	-1	-0.5
1980	*KC-A	4	0	1.000	37	0	0	0	4	89	97	7	23	40	12.2	3.64	111	.277	.324	0	—	0	4	4	-1	0.3
Total	13	114	109	.511	475	224	64	14	25	2038^2	1933	209	603	1179	11.4	3.62	102	.250	.309	38	.123	-7	0	16	-6	-0.7

● JIMMY PATTISON Pattison, James Wells b: 12/18/08, Bronx, N.Y. d: 2/22/91, Melbourne, Fla. BL/TL, 6', 185 lbs. Deb: 4/18/29

YEAR	TM/L	W	L	PCT	G	GS	CG	SH	SV	IP	H	HR	BB	SO	RAT	ERA	ERA+	OAV	OOB	BH	AVG	PB	PR	/A	PD	TPI
1929	Bro-N	0	1	.000	6	0	0	0	0	11^2	9	1	4	5	10.0	4.63	100	.231	.302	1	.500	0	0	-0	-0	0.0

● HARRY PATTON Patton, Harry Claude b: 6/29/1884, Gillespie, Ill. d: 6/9/30, St.Louis, Mo. Deb: 8/22/10

YEAR	TM/L	W	L	PCT	G	GS	CG	SH	SV	IP	H	HR	BB	SO	RAT	ERA	ERA+	OAV	OOB	BH	AVG	PB	PR	/A	PD	TPI
1910	StL-N	0	0	—	1	0	0	0	0	4	4	0	2	2	13.5	2.25	132	.267	.353	0	—	0	0	0	0	0.1

● MIKE PAUL Paul, Michael George b: 4/18/45, Detroit, Mich. BL/TL, 6', 183 lbs. Deb: 5/27/68 C

YEAR	TM/L	W	L	PCT	G	GS	CG	SH	SV	IP	H	HR	BB	SO	RAT	ERA	ERA+	OAV	OOB	BH	AVG	PB	PR	/A	PD	TPI
1968	Cle-A	5	8	.385	36	7	0	0	3	91^2	72	11	35	87	11.0	3.93	75	.213	.296	4	.167	0	-10	-10	-1	-1.2
1969	Cle-A	5	10	.333	47	12	0	0	2	117^1	104	12	54	98	12.3	3.61	104	.241	.328	0	.000	-3	0	2	-1	-0.2
1970	Cle-A	2	8	.200	30	15	1	0	0	88	91	13	45	70	13.9	4.81	82	.271	.357	4	.154	-1	-11	-8	-2	-1.1
1971	Cle-A	2	7	.222	17	12	1	0	0	62	78	8	14	33	14.1	5.95	64	.318	.367	1	.053	-1	-17	-15	-1	-1.7
1972	Tex-A	8	9	.471	49	20	2	1	1	161^2	149	4	52	108	11.3	2.17	139	.246	.308	8	.167	1	16	15	-1	1.7
1973	Tex-A	5	4	.556	36	10	1	0	2	87^1	104	9	36	49	14.9	4.95	75	.295	.368	0	—	0	-11	-12	1	-1.1
	Chi-N	0	1	.000	11	1	0	0	0	18^1	17	2	9	6	12.8	3.44	115	.258	.347	0	.000	-0	0	1	0	0.1
1974	Chi-N	0	1	.000	2	0	0	0	0	1^1	4	1	1	1	33.8	27.00	14	.500	.556	0	—	0	-3	-3	0	-0.3
Total	7	27	48	.360	228	77	5	1	8	627^2	619	60	246	452	12.7	3.91	89	.260	.334	17	.115	-5	-35	-30	-4	-3.8

● GENE PAULETTE Paulette, Eugene Edward b: 5/26/1891, Centralia, Ill. d: 2/8/66, Little Rock, Ark. BR/TR, 6', 150 lbs. Deb: 6/16/11 ♦

YEAR	TM/L	W	L	PCT	G	GS	CG	SH	SV	IP	H	HR	BB	SO	RAT	ERA	ERA+	OAV	OOB	BH	AVG	PB	PR	/A	PD	TPI
1918	StL-N	0	0	—	1	0	0	0	0	0^1	1	0	0	0	27.0	0.00	—	.500	.500	126	.273	0	0	0	0	0.0

● GIL PAULSEN Paulsen, Guilford Paul Hans b: 11/14/02, Graettinger, Iowa BR/TR, 6'2.5", 190 lbs. Deb: 10/03/25

YEAR	TM/L	W	L	PCT	G	GS	CG	SH	SV	IP	H	HR	BB	SO	RAT	ERA	ERA+	OAV	OOB	BH	AVG	PB	PR	/A	PD	TPI
1925	StL-N	0	0	—	1	0	0	0	0	2	1	0	0	1	4.5	0.00	—	.125	.125	0	—	0	1	1	0	0.1

● DAVE PAVLAS Pavlas, David Lee b: 8/12/62, Frankfurt, W.Germany BR/TR, 6'7", 180 lbs. Deb: 8/21/90

YEAR	TM/L	W	L	PCT	G	GS	CG	SH	SV	IP	H	HR	BB	SO	RAT	ERA	ERA+	OAV	OOB	BH	AVG	PB	PR	/A	PD	TPI
1990	Chi-N	2	0	1.000	13	0	0	0	0	21^1	23	2	6	12	12.2	2.11	193	.271	.319	0	.000	0	4	5	-0	0.5
1991	Chi-N	0	0	—	1	0	0	0	0	1	3	1	0	0	27.0	18.00	22	.750	.750	0	—	0	-2	-2	-0	-0.2
Total	2	2	0	1.000	14	0	0	0	0	22^1	26	3	6	12	12.9	2.82	144	.292	.337	0	.000	0	2	3	-0	0.3

● ROGER PAVLIK Pavlik, Roger Allen b: 10/4/67, Houston, Tex. BB/TR, 6'3", 220 lbs. Deb: 5/02/92

YEAR	TM/L	W	L	PCT	G	GS	CG	SH	SV	IP	H	HR	BB	SO	RAT	ERA	ERA+	OAV	OOB	BH	AVG	PB	PR	/A	PD	TPI
1992	Tex-A	4	4	.500	13	12	1	0	0	62	66	3	34	45	15.0	4.21	91	.280	.377	0	—	0	-2	-3	-1	-0.2

● JOHN PAWLOWSKI Pawlowski, John b: 9/6/63, Johnson City, N.Y. BR/TR, 6'2", 175 lbs. Deb: 9/19/87

YEAR	TM/L	W	L	PCT	G	GS	CG	SH	SV	IP	H	HR	BB	SO	RAT	ERA	ERA+	OAV	OOB	BH	AVG	PB	PR	/A	PD	TPI
1987	Chi-A	0	0	—	2	0	0	0	0	3^2	7	0	3	2	24.5	4.91	93	.438	.526	0	—	0	-0	-0	-0	-0.1
1988	Chi-A	1	0	1.000	6	0	0	0	0	14	20	2	3	10	14.8	8.36	48	.328	.359	0	—	0	-7	-7	0	-0.6
Total	2	1	0	1.000	8	0	0	0	0	17^2	27	2	6	12	16.8	7.64	54	.351	.398	0	—	0	-7	-7	-0	-0.7

● MIKE PAXTON Paxton, Michael De Wayne b: 9/3/53, Memphis, Tenn. BR/TR, 5'11", 190 lbs. Deb: 5/25/77

YEAR	TM/L	W	L	PCT	G	GS	CG	SH	SV	IP	H	HR	BB	SO	RAT	ERA	ERA+	OAV	OOB	BH	AVG	PB	PR	/A	PD	TPI
1977	Bos-A	10	5	.667	29	12	2	1	0	108	134	7	25	58	13.5	3.83	117	.311	.353	0	—	0	3	8	-0	0.0
1978	Cle-A	12	11	.522	33	27	5	2	1	191	179	13	63	96	11.8	3.86	97	.247	.314	0	—	0	-2	-3	-1	-0.3
1979	Cle-A	8	8	.500	33	24	3	0	0	159^2	210	14	52	70	14.9	5.92	72	.315	.366	0	—	0	-30	-30	0	-2.8
1980	Cle-A	0	0	—	4	0	0	0	0	7^2	13	4	6	6	22.3	12.91	32	.394	.487	0	—	0	-8	-8	-0	-0.7
Total	4	30	24	.556	99	63	10	3	1	466^1	536	38	146	230	13.4	4.71	87	.289	.345	0	—	0	-37	-32	-2	-3.8

● GEORGE PAYNE Payne, George Washington b: 5/23/1890, Mt.Vernon, Ky. d: 1/24/59, Bellflower, Cal. BR/TR, 5'11", 172 lbs. Deb: 5/08/20

YEAR	TM/L	W	L	PCT	G	GS	CG	SH	SV	IP	H	HR	BB	SO	RAT	ERA	ERA+	OAV	OOB	BH	AVG	PB	PR	/A	PD	TPI
1920	Chi-A	1	1	.500	12	0	0	0	0	29^2	39	2	9	7	14.6	5.46	69	.312	.358	1	.125	-0	-5	-6	-1	-0.7

● HARLEY PAYNE Payne, Harley Fenwick "Lady" b: 1/9/1868, Windsor, Ont., Can. d: 12/29/35, Orwell, Ohio BB/TL, 6', 160 lbs. Deb: 4/18/1896

YEAR	TM/L	W	L	PCT	G	GS	CG	SH	SV	IP	H	HR	BB	SO	RAT	ERA	ERA+	OAV	OOB	BH	AVG	PB	PR	/A	PD	TPI
1896	Bro-N	14	16	.467	34	28	24	2	0	241^2	284	4	58	52	13.0	3.39	122	.290	.335	21	.214	0	26	20	3	2.0
1897	Bro-N	14	17	.452	40	38	30	1	0	280	350	8	71	86	14.1	4.63	89	.303	.353	26	.236	-0	-10	-16	1	-1.3
1898	Bro-N	1	0	1.000	1	1	1	0	0	9	11	0	3	2	14.0	4.00	90	.299	.352	3	.750	1	-0	-0	0	0.1
1899	Pit-N	1	3	.250	5	5	2	0	0	26^1	33	2	4	8	13.3	3.76	101	.306	.342	1	.100	-1	0	0	2	0.1
Total	4	30	36	.455	80	72	57	3	0	557	678	14	136	148	13.6	4.04	101	.298	.345	51	.230	0	16	3	7	0.9

● MIKE PAYNE Payne, Michael Earl b: 11/15/61, Woonsocket, R.I. BR/TR, 5'11", 165 lbs. Deb: 8/22/84

YEAR	TM/L	W	L	PCT	G	GS	CG	SH	SV	IP	H	HR	BB	SO	RAT	ERA	ERA+	OAV	OOB	BH	AVG	PB	PR	/A	PD	TPI
1984	Atl-N	0	1	.000	3	1	0	0	0	5^2	7	0	3	3	15.9	6.35	61	.333	.417	0	.000	-0	-2	-2	0	-0.2

● MIKE PAZIK Pazik, Michael Joseph b: 1/26/50, Lynn, Mass. BL/TL, 6'2", 195 lbs. Deb: 5/11/75

YEAR	TM/L	W	L	PCT	G	GS	CG	SH	SV	IP	H	HR	BB	SO	RAT	ERA	ERA+	OAV	OOB	BH	AVG	PB	PR	/A	PD	TPI
1975	Min-A	0	4	.000	5	3	0	0	0	19^2	28	5	10	8	17.4	8.24	47	.329	.400	0	—	0	-10	-10	-1	-1.1
1976	Min-A	0	0	—	5	0	0	0	0	9	13	0	4	6	18.0	7.00	51	.342	.419	0	—	0	-3	-3	-0	-0.5
1977	Min-A	1	0	1.000	3	3	0	0	0	18	18	1	6	6	12.0	2.50	159	.265	.324	0	—	0	3	3	0	0.4
Total	3	1	4	.200	13	6	0	0	0	46^2	59	6	20	20	15.4	5.79	67	.309	.377	0	—	0	-10	-10	-1	-1.2

YEAR TM/L	W	L	PCT	G	GS	CG	SH	SV	IP	H	HR	BB	SO	RAT	ERA	ERA+	OAV	OOB	BH	AVG	PB	PR	/A	PD	TPI
● FRANK PEARCE Pearce, Frank b: Louisville, Ky. Deb: 10/04/1876																									
1876 Lou-N	0	0	—	1	0	0	0	0	4	5	0	1	1	13.5	4.50	60	.263	.300	0	.000	-0	-1	-1	-0	-0.1
● FRANK PEARCE Pearce, Franklin Thomas b: 8/31/05, Middletown, Ky. d: 9/3/50, Van Buren, N.Y. BR/TR, 6', 170 lbs. Deb: 4/20/33																									
1933 Phi-N	5	4	.556	20	7	3	1	0	82	78	5	29	18	11.7	3.62	105	.251	.315	5	.192	-1	-3	2	0	0.1
1934 Phi-N	0	2	.000	7	1	0	0	0	20	25	4	5	4	13.5	7.20	66	.301	.341	2	.667	1	-7	-6	-1	-0.5
1935 Phi-N	0	0	—	5	0	0	0	0	13	22	0	6	7	19.4	8.31	55	.361	.418	2	.500	1	-6	-5	0	-0.4
Total 3	5	6	.455	32	8	3	1	0	115	125	9	40	29	12.9	4.77	85	.275	.333	9	.273	1	-16	-9	-0	-0.8
● GEORGE PEARCE Pearce, George Thomas "Filbert" b: 1/10/1888, Aurora, Ill. d: 10/11/35, Joliet, Ill. BL/TL, 5'10.5", 175 lbs. Deb: 4/16/12																									
1912 Chi-N	0	0	—	3	2	0	0	0	14^2	15	0	12	9	16.6	5.52	60	.185	.290	1	.167	0	-3	-4	1	-0.3
1913 Chi-N	13	5	.722	25	21	15	3	0	163^1	137	4	59	73	11.0	2.31	137	.234	.308	4	.073	-3	16	16	-0	1.3
1914 Chi-N	9	12	.429	30	16	4	0	1	141	122	3	65	78	12.1	3.51	79	.239	.327	4	.089	-3	-11	-11	2	-1.4
1915 Chi-N	13	9	.591	36	20	8	2	0	176	158	1	77	96	12.2	3.32	84	.244	.328	11	.196	1	-11	-11	-0	-1.1
1916 Chi-N	0	0	—	4	1	0	0	0	4^1	6	0	1	0	14.5	2.08	140	.300	.333	0	—	0	0	0	-0	0.0
1917 StL-N	1	1	.500	5	0	0	0	0	10^1	7	0	3	4	9.6	3.48	77	.184	.262	0	.000	-1	-1	-1	0	-0.1
Total 6	36	27	.571	103	60	27	5	1	509^2	445	8	217	260	11.9	3.11	94	.236	.318	20	.120	-6	-10	-10	2	-1.6
● JIM PEARCE Pearce, James Madison b: 6/9/25, Zebulon, N.C. BR/TR, 6'6", 180 lbs. Deb: 9/08/49																									
1949 Was-A	0	1	.000	2	1	0	0	0	5^1	9	1	5	1	23.6	8.44	50	.375	.483	0	.000	-0	-3	-2	1	-0.2
1950 Was-A	2	1	.667	20	3	1	0	0	56^2	58	2	37	18	15.2	6.04	74	.270	.379	2	.154	-1	-9	-10	-0	-1.0
1953 Was-A	0	1	.000	4	1	0	0	0	9^1	15	3	6	0	20.3	7.71	51	.405	.488	0	.000	-0	-4	-4	-0	-0.4
1954 Cin-N	1	0	1.000	2	1	1	0	0	11	7	0	5	3	10.6	0.00	—	.194	.310	0	.000	-0	5	5	0	0.5
1955 Cin-N	0	1	.000	2	1	0	0	0	3^1	8	0	0	0	21.6	10.80	39	.471	.471	0	—	0	-3	-2	0	-0.2
Total 5	3	4	.429	30	7	2	0	0	85^2	97	6	53	22	16.0	5.78	76	.295	.396	2	.105	-2	-13	-13	0	-1.3
● DICKEY PEARCE Pearce, Richard J. b: 2/29/1836, Brooklyn, N.Y. d: 10/12/08, Wareham, Mass. BR/TR, 5'3.5", 161 lbs. Deb: 5/18/1871 MU♦																									
1875 StL-n	0	0	—	2	0	0	0	0	5^1	10	0	0		16.9	*6.75*	33	.357	.357	77	.247	0	-3	-3		-0.2
● FRANK PEARS Pears, Frank H. b: 8/30/1866, Kentucky d: 11/29/23, St.Louis, Mo. TR , Deb: 10/06/1889 U																									
1889 KC-a	0	2	.000	3	2	2	0	0	22	21	2	9	5	12.7	4.91	85	.244	.322	1	.091	-1	-3	-2	-0	-0.3
1893 StL-N	0	0	—	1	0	0	0	0	4	9	0	2	0	27.0	13.50	35	.432	.503	0	.000	-0	-4	-4	0	-0.3
Total 2	0	2	.000	4	2	2	0	0	26	30	2	11	5	14.9	6.23	69	.280	.358	1	.077	-2	-7	-6	-0	-0.6
● ALEX PEARSON Pearson, Alexander Franklin b: 3/9/1877, Greensboro, Pa. d: 10/30/66, Rochester, Pa. BR/TR, 5'10.5", 160 lbs. Deb: 8/01/02																									
1902 StL-N	2	6	.250	11	10	8	0	0	82	90	0	22	24	12.6	3.95	69	.279	.330	9	.265	0	-11	-11	-0	-1.1
1903 Cle-A	1	2	.333	4	3	2	0	0	30^1	34	1	3	12	11.3	3.56	80	.282	.305	1	.083	-1	-2	-2	0	-0.3
Total 2	3	8	.273	15	13	10	0	0	112^1	124	1	25	36	12.3	3.85	72	.280	.324	10	.217	-1	-13	-13	-0	-1.4
● IKE PEARSON Pearson, Issac Overton b: 3/1/17, Grenada, Miss. d: 3/17/85, Sarasota, Fla. BR/TR, 6'1", 180 lbs. Deb: 6/06/39																									
1939 Phi-N	2	13	.133	26	13	4	0	0	125	144	15	56	29	14.8	5.76	70	.296	.374	2	.054	-3	-26	-24	1	-2.5
1940 Phi-N	3	14	.176	29	20	5	1	1	145^1	160	13	57	43	13.6	5.45	72	.275	.343	9	.205	1	-26	-25	1	-2.2
1941 Phi-N	4	14	.222	46	10	0	0	6	136	139	8	70	38	14.4	3.57	104	.266	.361	5	.125	-2	1	2	0	0.0
1942 Phi-N	1	6	.143	35	7	0	0	0	85^1	87	4	50	21	14.9	4.54	73	.271	.376	1	.043	-2	-12	-12	-0	-1.5
1946 Phi-N	1	0	1.000	5	2	1	1	0	14^1	16	1	8	6	15.7	3.77	91	.271	.368	1	.200	1	-1	-1	0	0.0
1948 Chi-A	2	3	.400	23	2	0	0	1	53	62	8	27	12	15.5	4.92	87	.292	.378	2	.200	-0	-4	-4	1	-0.3
Total 6	13	50	.206	164	54	10	2	8	559	608	49	268	149	14.5	4.83	79	.279	.363	20	.126	-6	-66	-64	2	-6.5
● MONTE PEARSON Pearson, Montgomery Marcellus "Hoot" b: 9/2/09, Oakland, Cal. d: 1/27/78, Fresno, Cal. BR/TR, 6', 175 lbs. Deb: 4/22/32																									
1932 Cle-A	0	0	—	8	0	0	0	0	8	10	1	11	5	23.6	10.13	47	.323	.500	0	—	0	-5	-5	1	-0.4
1933 Cle-A	10	5	.667	19	16	10	0	0	135^1	111	5	55	54	11.0	2.33	191	.221	.297	13	.260	1	29	32	-1	3.3
1934 Cle-A	18	13	.581	39	33	19	0	2	254^2	257	16	130	140	13.7	4.52	101	.260	.346	25	.272	6	-1	1	1	0.7
1935 Cle-A	8	13	.381	30	24	10	1	0	181^2	199	9	103	90	15.0	4.90	92	.279	.371	11	.177	-0	-9	-8	2	-0.6
1936 *NY-A☆	19	7	**.731**	33	31	15	1	1	223	191	13	135	118	13.3	3.71	125	**.233**	.343	23	.253	6	33	23	1	2.7
1937 *NY-A	9	3	.750	22	20	7	1	1	144^2	145	6	64	71	13.1	3.17	140	.261	.339	11	.216	1	23	20	-1	2.0
1938 *NY-A	16	7	.696	28	27	17	1	0	202	198	12	113	98	13.9	3.97	114	.258	.354	13	.171	1	18	13	2	1.4
1939 *NY-A	12	5	.706	22	20	8	0	0	146^1	151	9	70	76	13.7	4.49	97	.272	.354	17	.321	6	2	-2	1	0.4
1940 NY-A☆	7	5	.583	16	16	7	1	0	109^2	108	8	44	43	12.5	3.69	109	.262	.333	4	.121	-1	8	4	2	0.5
1941 Cin-N	1	3	.250	7	4	1	0	0	24^1	22	3	15	8	13.7	5.18	69	.242	.349	0	.000	-1	-4	-4	-0	-0.5
Total 10	100	61	.621	224	191	94	5	4	1429^2	1392	82	740	703	13.5	4.00	112	.256	.346	117	.228	18	95	75	8	9.5
● MARV PEASLEY Peasley, Marvin Warren b: 7/16/1888, Jonesport, Me. d: 12/27/48, San Francisco, Cal. BL/TL, 6'1", 175 lbs. Deb: 9/27/10																									
1910 Det-A	0	1	.000	2	1	0	0	0	10	13	0	11	4	22.5	8.10	32	.295	.446	0	.000	0	-6	-6	-0	-0.6
● GEORGE PECHINEY Pechiney, George Adolphe "Pisch" b: 9/20/1861, Cincinnati, Ohio d: 7/14/43, Cincinnati, Ohio BR/TR, 5'9", 184 lbs. Deb: 8/04/1885																									
1885 Cin-a	7	4	.636	11	11	11	1	0	98	95	1	30	49	12.0	2.02	161	.247	.311	6	.150	-2	13	13	1	1.2
1886 Cin-a	15	21	.417	40	40	35	2	0	330^1	355	4	133	110	13.7	4.14	85	.266	.339	30	.208	-1	-25	-23	-3	-2.3
1887 Cle-a	1	9	.100	10	10	10	0	0	86	118	8	44	24	17.3	7.12	61	.303	.378	9	.250	-0	-27	-27	0	-2.0
Total 3	23	34	.404	61	61	56	3	0	514^1	568	13	207	183	14.0	4.23	85	.269	.341	45	.205	-3	-39	-36	-2	-3.1
● BILL PECOTA Pecota, William Joseph b: 2/16/60, Redwood City, Cal. BR/TR, 6'2", 195 lbs. Deb: 9/19/86 ♦																									
1991 KC-A	0	0	—	1	0	0	0	0	2	4	0	0	0	18.0	4.50	92	.444	.444	114	.286	0	-0	-0	-0	0.0
1992 NY-N	0	0	—	1	0	0	0	0	1	1	1	0	0	9.0	9.00	39	.250	.250	61	.227	0	-1	-1	-0	-0.1
Total 2	0	0	—	2	0	0	0	0	3	5	1	0	0	15.0	6.00	65	.385	.385	336	.248	0	-1	-1	-0	-0.1
● STEVE PEEK Peek, Stephen George b: 7/30/14, Springfield, Mass d: 9/20/91, Syracuse, N.Y. BB/TR, 6'2", 195 lbs. Deb: 4/16/41																									
1941 NY-A	4	2	.667	17	8	2	0	0	80	85	6	39	18	13.9	5.06	78	.276	.357	1	.036	-3	-8	-10	0	-1.2
● RED PEERY Peery, George Allan b: 8/15/06, Payson, Utah d: 5/6/85, Salt Lake City, Ut. BL/TL, 5'11", 160 lbs. Deb: 9/22/27																									
1927 Pit-N	0	0	—	1	0	0	0	0	1	0	0	1	0	9.0	0.00	—	.000	.200	0	—	0	0	0	0	0.1
1929 Bos-N	0	1	.000	9	1	0	0	0	44	53	1	9	3	12.7	5.11	91	.305	.339	3	.214	1	-2	-2	-0	-0.1
Total 2	0	1	.000	10	1	0	0	0	45	53	1	10	3	12.6	5.00	93	.298	.335	3	.214	1	-2	-2	0	0.0
● HEINIE PEITZ Peitz, Henry Clement b: 11/28/1870, St.Louis, Mo. d: 10/23/43, Cincinnati, Ohio BR/TR, 5'11", 165 lbs. Deb: 10/15/1892 FC♦																									
1894 StL-N	0	0	—	1	0	0	0	0	3	7	0	2	0	30.0	9.00	60	.448	.537	89	.263	0	-1	-1	-0	-0.1
1897 Cin-N	0	1	.000	2	1	1	0	0	8	9	0	4	0	16.9	7.88	58	.282	.395	78	.293	0	-3	-3	1	-0.2
1899 Cin-N	0	0	—	1	0	0	0	0	5	6	0	1	3	12.6	5.40	73	.297	.330	79	.272	0	-1	-1	0	0.0
Total 3	0	1	.000	4	1	1	0	0	16	22	0	7	3	18.0	7.31	62	.324	.411	1117	.271	1	-5	-5	1	-0.3
● BARNEY PELTY Pelty, Barney b: 9/10/1880, Farmington, Mo. d: 5/24/39, Farmington, Mo. BR/TR, 5'9", 175 lbs. Deb: 8/20/03																									
1903 StL-A	3	3	.500	7	6	5	0	1	48^2	49	1	15	20	12.2	2.40	121	.261	.322	3	.150	-0	3	3	-1	0.2
1904 StL-A	15	18	.455	39	35	31	2	0	301	270	7	77	126	10.9	2.84	87	.241	.300	15	.127	-7	-8	-12	-1	-2.1
1905 StL-A	14	14	.500	31	28	27	1	0	258^2	222	3	68	114	10.2	2.75	93	.233	.286	15	.153	-4	-3	-6	3	-0.7
1906 StL-A	16	11	.593	34	30	25	4	2	260^2	189	1	59	92	9.2	1.59	163	**.206**	.268	15	.163	-3	**32**	29	5	3.7
1907 StL-A	12	21	.364	36	31	29	5	1	273	234	1	64	85	10.5	2.57	98	.233	.292	16	.168	-2	-1	-2	2	-0.2
1908 StL-A	7	4	.636	20	13	7	2	0	122	104	0	32	36	10.8	1.99	120	.241	.309	5	.119	-3	5	5	1	0.4

YEAR	TM/L	W	L	PCT	G	GS	CG	SH	SV	IP	H	HR	BB	SO	RAT	ERA	ERA+	OAV	OOB	BH	AVG	PB	PR	/A	PD	TPI
1909	StL-A	11	11	.500	27	23	17	5	0	199^1	158	2	53	88	9.8	2.30	105	.222	.281	15	.165	0	4	3	4	0.8
1910	StL-A	5	11	.313	27	19	13	3	0	165^1	157	3	70	48	12.8	3.48	71	.263	.348	5	.089	-4	-18	-19	4	-2.0
1911	StL-A	7	15	.318	28	22	18	1	0	197	197	4	69	59	12.3	2.97	114	.265	.331	9	.138	-3	8	9	1	0.7
1912	StL-A	1	5	.167	6	6	2	0	0	38^2	43	0	15	10	14.2	5.59	59	.297	.374	0	.000	-2	-10	-10	0	-1.0
	Was-A	1	4	.200	11	4	1	0	0	43^2	40	0	10	15	11.1	3.30	101	.250	.310	2	.222	0	0	0	-1	0.0
	Yr	2	9	.182	17	10	3	0	0	82^1	83	0	25	25	12.2	4.37	76	.269	.332	2	.095	-2	-10	-10	-1	-1.0
Total	10	92	117	.440	266	217	175	23	4	1908	1663	22	532	693	10.8	2.63	100	.239	.301	100	.143	-26	14	0	17	-0.2

● ALEJANDRO PENA Pena, Alejandro (Vasquez) b: 6/25/59, Cambiaso, D.R. BR/TR, 6'1", 205 lbs. Deb: 9/14/81

YEAR	TM/L	W	L	PCT	G	GS	CG	SH	SV	IP	H	HR	BB	SO	RAT	ERA	ERA+	OAV	OOB	BH	AVG	PB	PR	/A	PD	TPI
1981	*LA-N	1	1	.500	14	0	0	0	2	25^1	18	2	11	14	10.3	2.84	117	.194	.279	0	.000	-1	2	1	0	0.1
1982	LA-N	0	2	.000	29	0	0	0	0	35^2	37	2	21	20	14.9	4.79	72	.272	.373	0	—	0	-5	-5	1	-0.4
1983	*LA-N	12	9	.571	34	26	4	3	1	177	152	7	51	120	10.4	2.75	131	.229	.285	6	.100	-2	17	17	2	1.7
1984	LA-N	12	6	.667	28	28	8	**4**	0	199^1	186	7	46	135	10.6	**2.48**	**142**	.246	.292	8	.121	-1	**24**	23	-1	2.3
1985	LA-N	0	1	.000	2	1	0	0	0	4^1	7	1	3	2	20.8	8.31	42	.350	.435	0	.000	-0	-2	-2	-0	-0.2
1986	LA-N	1	2	.333	24	10	0	0	1	70	74	6	30	46	13.5	4.89	71	.270	.344	3	.176	0	-9	-11	-1	-1.2
1987	LA-N	2	7	.222	37	7	0	0	11	87^1	82	9	37	76	12.5	3.50	113	.251	.331	1	.077	-1	6	4	-2	0.1
1988	*LA-N	6	7	.462	60	0	0	0	12	94^1	75	4	27	83	9.8	1.91	175	.218	.277	0	.000	-1	16	15	-0	1.5
1989	LA-N	4	3	.571	53	0	0	0	5	76	62	6	18	75	9.7	2.13	160	.220	.272	1	1.000	0	12	11	-1	1.1
1990	NY-N	3	3	.500	52	0	0	0	5	76	71	4	22	76	11.1	3.20	117	.245	.300	1	.167	0	5	5	-1	0.4
1991	NY-N	6	1	.857	44	0	0	0	4	63	63	5	19	49	11.7	2.71	134	.267	.322	0	—	0	7	6	-0	0.7
	*Atl-N	2	0	1.000	15	0	0	0	11	19^1	11	1	3	13	6.5	1.40	278	.167	.203	0	.000	-0	5	5	-0	0.6
	Yr	8	1	.889	59	0	0	0	15	82^1	74	6	22	62	10.5	2.40	154	.242	.293	0	.000	-0	12	12	-0	1.3
1992	Atl-N	1	6	.143	41	0	0	0	15	42	40	7	13	34	11.4	4.07	92	.255	.312	0	.000	-0	-3	-2	-1	-0.3
Total	12	50	48	.510	433	72	12	7	67	969^2	878	61	301	743	11.1	2.95	121	.241	.301	20	.112	-4	75	68	-6	6.4

● HIPOLITO PENA Pena, Hipolito (Concepcion) b: 1/30/64, Fantino, D.R. BL/TL, 6'3", 165 lbs. Deb: 9/01/86

YEAR	TM/L	W	L	PCT	G	GS	CG	SH	SV	IP	H	HR	BB	SO	RAT	ERA	ERA+	OAV	OOB	BH	AVG	PB	PR	/A	PD	TPI
1986	Pit-N	0	3	.000	10	1	0	0	1	8^1	7	3	3	6	11.9	8.64	44	.206	.289	0	—	0	-5	-4	-0	-0.5
1987	Pit-N	0	3	.000	16	1	0	0	1	25^2	16	2	26	16	14.7	4.56	90	.184	.372	1	.167	-0	-1	-1	-0	-0.1
1988	NY-A	1	1	.500	16	0	0	0	0	14^1	10	1	9	10	11.9	3.14	125	.192	.311	0	—	0	1	1	0	0.2
Total	3	1	7	.125	42	2	0	0	2	48^1	33	6	38	32	13.4	4.84	83	.191	.340	1	.167	-0	-5	-4	0	-0.4

● JIM PENA Pena, James Patrick b: 9/17/64, Los Angeles, Cal. BL/TL, 6', 175 lbs. Deb: 7/07/92

YEAR	TM/L	W	L	PCT	G	GS	CG	SH	SV	IP	H	HR	BB	SO	RAT	ERA	ERA+	OAV	OOB	BH	AVG	PB	PR	/A	PD	TPI
1992	SF-N	1	1	.500	25	2	0	0	0	44	49	4	20	32	14.3	3.48	96	.282	.359	1	.200	0	0	-1	1	0.0

● JOSE PENA Pena, Jose (Gutierrez) b: 12/3/42, Ciudad Juarez, Mex. BR/TR, 6'2", 190 lbs. Deb: 6/01/69

YEAR	TM/L	W	L	PCT	G	GS	CG	SH	SV	IP	H	HR	BB	SO	RAT	ERA	ERA+	OAV	OOB	BH	AVG	PB	PR	/A	PD	TPI
1969	Cin-N	1	1	.500	6	0	0	0	0	5	10	0	5	3	27.0	18.00	21	.400	.500	0	—	0	-8	-8	0	-0.8
1970	LA-N	4	3	.571	29	0	0	0	4	57	51	8	29	31	13.1	4.42	87	.241	.340	1	.125	0	-2	-4	1	-0.3
1971	LA-N	2	0	1.000	21	0	0	0	1	43	32	7	18	44	10.7	3.56	91	.211	.298	2	.667	1	-0	-2	-1	-0.1
1972	LA-N	0	0	—	5	0	0	0	0	7^1	13	1	6	4	23.3	8.59	39	.371	.463	0	—	0	-4	-4	-0	-0.5
Total	4	7	4	.636	61	0	0	0	5	112^1	106	16	58	82	13.5	4.97	72	.250	.346	3	.273	1	-15	-18	0	-1.7

● ORLANDO PENA Pena, Orlando Gregorio (Quevara) b: 11/17/33, Victoria De Las Tunas, Cuba BR/TR, 5'11", 154 lbs. Deb: 8/24/58

YEAR	TM/L	W	L	PCT	G	GS	CG	SH	SV	IP	H	HR	BB	SO	RAT	ERA	ERA+	OAV	OOB	BH	AVG	PB	PR	/A	PD	TPI
1958	Cin-N	1	0	1.000	9	0	0	0	3	15	10	0	4	11	8.4	0.60	691	.185	.241	0	—	0	6	6	-0	0.6
1959	Cin-N	5	9	.357	46	8	1	0	5	136	150	26	39	76	12.5	4.76	85	.280	.329	3	.088	-0	-12	-11	-1	-1.2
1960	Cin-N	0	1	.000	4	0	0	0	0	9^1	8	0	3	9	10.6	2.89	132	.222	.282	0	.000	-0	1	1	-0	0.1
1962	KC-A	6	4	.600	13	12	6	1	0	89^2	71	9	27	56	9.9	3.01	138	.213	.274	5	.161	-0	10	11	-1	1.0
1963	KC-A	12	20	.375	35	33	9	3	0	217	218	24	53	128	11.4	3.69	104	.260	.308	9	.145	0	-1	4	-2	0.2
1964	KC-A	12	14	.462	40	32	5	0	0	219^1	231	40	73	184	12.8	4.43	86	.268	.331	12	.160	0	-20	-15	-2	-1.7
1965	KC-A	0	6	.000	12	5	0	0	0	35^1	42	4	13	24	14.5	6.88	51	.302	.370	1	.111	-0	-13	-13	-0	-1.4
	Det-A	4	6	.400	30	0	0	0	4	57^1	54	5	20	55	11.8	2.51	138	.252	.319	2	.250	1	6	6	-1	0.6
	Yr	4	12	.250	42	5	0	0	4	92^2	96	9	33	79	12.6	4.18	83	.270	.333	3	.176	1	-7	-7	-1	-0.8
1966	Det-A	4	2	.667	54	0	0	0	7	108	105	16	35	79	12.1	3.08	113	.252	.317	2	.111	-1	4	5	2	0.7
1967	Det-A	0	1	.000	2	0	0	0	0	2	5	0	0	2	27.0	13.50	24	.500	.545	0	—	0	-2	-2	-0	-0.2
	Cle-A	0	3	.000	48	1	0	0	8	88^1	67	8	22	72	9.2	3.36	97	.208	.261	0	.000	-1	-1	-1	-0	-0.2
	Yr	0	4	.000	50	1	0	0	8	90^1	72	8	22	74	9.5	3.59	91	.216	.266	0	.000	-1	-4	-3	-1	-0.4
1970	Pit-N	2	1	.667	23	0	0	0	2	37^2	38	6	7	25	11.0	4.78	82	.268	.307	0	.000	-1	-3	-4	1	-0.4
1971	Bal-A	0	1	.000	5	0	0	0	0	14^2	16	0	5	4	12.9	3.07	109	.281	.339	0	.000	-0	1	0	0	0.0
1973	Bal-A	1	1	.500	11	2	0	0	1	44^2	36	10	8	23	9.3	4.03	93	.218	.263	0	—	0	-1	-1	-0	-0.2
	StL-N	4	4	.500	42	0	0	0	6	62	60	3	14	38	10.7	2.18	167	.251	.292	1	.143	-0	10	10	0	1.1
1974	StL-N	5	2	.714	42	0	0	0	1	45	45	0	20	23	13.2	2.60	137	.269	.351	1	.500	0	5	5	-0	0.5
	Cal-A	0	0	—	4	0	0	0	3	8	6	0	1	5	7.9	0.00	—	.214	.241	0	—	0	3	3	0	0.9
1975	Cal-A	0	2	.000	7	0	0	0	0	12^2	13	0	8	4	14.9	2.13	166	.283	.389	0	—	0	2	2	-1	0.6
Total	14	56	77	.421	427	93	21	4	40	1202	1175	151	352	818	11.6	3.71	101	.255	.312	36	.136	-3	-7	6	-6	1.0

● RAMON PENA Pena, Ramon Arturo (Padilla) b: 5/5/62, Santiago, D.R. BR/TR, 5'10", 155 lbs. Deb: 4/27/89 F

YEAR	TM/L	W	L	PCT	G	GS	CG	SH	SV	IP	H	HR	BB	SO	RAT	ERA	ERA+	OAV	OOB	BH	AVG	PB	PR	/A	PD	TPI
1989	Det-A	0	0	—	8	0	0	0	0	18	26	0	8	12	18.0	6.00	64	.338	.414	0	—	0	-4	-4	1	-0.4

● RUSTY PENCE Pence, Russell William b: 3/11/1900, Marine, Ill. d: 8/11/71, Hot Srpings, Ark. BR/TR, 6', 185 lbs. Deb: 5/13/21

YEAR	TM/L	W	L	PCT	G	GS	CG	SH	SV	IP	H	HR	BB	SO	RAT	ERA	ERA+	OAV	OOB	BH	AVG	PB	PR	/A	PD	TPI
1921	Chi-A	0	0	—	4	0	0	0	0	5^1	6	0	7	2	23.6	8.44	50	.286	.483	0	.000	-0	-2	-2	0	-0.2

● KEN PENNER Penner, Kenneth William b: 4/24/1896, Booneville, Ind. d: 5/28/59, Sacramento, Cal. BL/TR, 5'11.5", 170 lbs. Deb: 9/11/16

YEAR	TM/L	W	L	PCT	G	GS	CG	SH	SV	IP	H	HR	BB	SO	RAT	ERA	ERA+	OAV	OOB	BH	AVG	PB	PR	/A	PD	TPI
1916	Cle-A	1	0	1.000	4	2	0	0	0	12^2	14	0	4	5	12.8	4.26	71	.304	.360	0	.000	-0	-2	-2	1	-0.2
1929	Chi-N	0	1	.000	5	0	0	0	0	12^2	14	1	6	3	14.2	2.84	162	.280	.357	1	.250	0	3	2	-0	0.2
Total	2	1	1	.500	9	2	0	0	0	25^1	28	1	10	8	13.5	3.55	108	.292	.358	1	.167	-0	1	1	1	0.0

● KEWPIE PENNINGTON Pennington, George Louis b: 9/24/1896, New York, N.Y. d: 5/3/53, Newark, N.J. BR/TR, 5'8.5", 168 lbs. Deb: 4/14/17

YEAR	TM/L	W	L	PCT	G	GS	CG	SH	SV	IP	H	HR	BB	SO	RAT	ERA	ERA+	OAV	OOB	BH	AVG	PB	PR	/A	PD	TPI
1917	StL-A	0	0	—	1	0	0	0	0	1	1	0	0	0	9.0	0.00	—	.250	.250	0	—	0	0	0	-0	0.0

● HERB PENNOCK Pennock, Herbert Jefferis "The Knight Of Kennett Square"
b: 2/10/1894, Kennett Square, Pa d: 1/30/48, New York, N.Y. BB/TL, 6', 160 lbs. Deb: 5/14/12 CH

YEAR	TM/L	W	L	PCT	G	GS	CG	SH	SV	IP	H	HR	BB	SO	RAT	ERA	ERA+	OAV	OOB	BH	AVG	PB	PR	/A	PD	TPI
1912	Phi-A	1	2	.333	17	2	1	0	2	50	48	1	30	38	14.6	4.50	68	.262	.375	2	.133	-1	-7	-8	1	-0.8
1913	Phi-A	2	1	.667	14	3	1	0	0	33^1	30	4	22	17	14.0	5.13	54	.221	.329	1	.111	-0	-8	-9	-0	-0.9
1914	*Phi-A	11	4	.733	28	14	8	3	3	151^2	136	1	65	90	12.0	2.79	94	.248	.330	12	.214	2	-1	-3	-1	-0.1
1915	Phi-A	3	6	.333	11	8	3	1	1	44	46	2	29	24	15.8	5.32	55	.266	.377	5	.278	1	-12	-12	1	-1.0
	Bos-A	0	0	—	5	1	0	0	0	14	23	0	10	7	21.2	9.64	29	.390	.478	1	.167	0	-10	-11	-1	-1.1
	Yr	3	6	.333	16	9	3	1	1	58	69	2	39	31	16.8	6.36	45	.295	.396	6	.250	1	-22	-22	-0	-2.1
1916	Bos-A	0	2	.000	9	2	0	0	1	26^2	23	0	8	12	10.8	3.04	91	.245	.311	1	.125	-0	-1	-1	-1	-0.2
1917	Bos-A	5	5	.500	24	5	4	1	1	100^2	90	2	23	35	10.4	3.31	78	.243	.292	4	.167	2	-7	-8	-0	-0.8
1919	Bos-A	16	8	.667	32	26	16	5	0	219	223	2	48	70	11.3	2.71	111	.274	.316	13	.173	1	13	8	-2	0.7
1920	Bos-A	16	13	.552	37	31	19	4	2	242^1	244	9	61	68	11.5	3.68	99	.264	.312	20	.260	4	3	-1	-3	0.1
1921	Bos-A	12	14	.462	32	32	15	1	0	222^2	268	7	59	91	13.3	4.04	105	.307	.352	18	.212	2	6	5	1	0.7
1922	Bos-A	10	17	.370	32	26	15	1	1	202	230	7	74	59	13.6	4.32	95	.297	.359	9	.138	-3	-6	-5	1	-0.6
1923	*NY-A	19	6	**.760**	35	27	21	1	3	238^1	235	11	68	93	11.5	3.13	126	.261	.314	16	.193	0	23	21	1	2.2
1924	NY-A	21	9	.700	40	34	25	4	3	286^1	302	13	64	101	11.5	2.83	147	.273	.314	16	.158	-2	45	**42**	-1	3.9
1925	NY-A	16	17	.485	47	31	21	2	2	**277**	267	11	71	88	**11.0**	2.96	144	.254	**.303**	20	.202	-3	**44**	**40**	-3	3.3

YEAR TM/L	W	L	PCT	G	GS	CG	SH	SV	IP	H	HR	BB	SO	RAT	ERA	ERA+	OAV	OOB	BH	AVG	PB	PR	/A	PD	TPI
1926 *NY-A	23	11	.676	40	33	19	1	2	266^1	294	11	43	78	**11.5**	3.62	107	.282	**.313**	18	.212	3	12	7	1	1.0
1927 *NY-A	19	8	.704	34	26	18	1	2	209^2	225	5	48	51	11.8	3.00	128	.283	.325	15	.217	0	26	20	-2	1.7
1928 NY-A	17	6	.739	28	24	18	**5**	3	211	215	2	40	53	10.9	2.56	147	.267	.302	15	.203	-1	35	28	2	2.9
1929 NY-A	9	11	.450	27	23	8	1	2	157^1	205	11	28	49	13.5	4.92	78	.318	.349	9	.176	-1	-12	-19	-1	-1.8
1930 NY-A	11	7	.611	25	19	11	1	0	156^1	194	8	20	46	12.3	4.32	100	.301	.322	11	.183	-2	6	-0	-2	-0.4
1931 NY-A	11	6	.647	25	25	12	1	0	189^1	247	7	30	65	13.2	4.28	93	.315	.342	10	.152	1	2	-7	-1	-0.6
1932 *NY-A	9	5	.643	22	21	9	1	0	146^2	191	8	38	54	14.1	4.60	89	.310	.350	8	.151	0	-2	-9	-1	-0.8
1933 NY-A	7	4	.636	23	5	2	1	4	65	96	4	21	22	16.2	5.54	70	.342	.387	5	.238	0	-9	-12	-0	-1.1
1934 Bos-A	2	0	1.000	30	2	1	0	1	62	68	2	16	16	12.2	3.05	158	.276	.321	3	.214	-0	**10**	**12**	-1	1.0
Total 22	240	162	.597	617	420	247	35	33	3571^2	3900	128	916	1227	12.2	3.60	106	.281	.328	232	.191	3	150	81	-11	7.3

● PAUL PENSON Penson, Paul Eugene b: 7/12/31, Kansas City, Kan. BR/TR, 6'1", 185 lbs. Deb: 4/21/54

YEAR TM/L	W	L	PCT	G	GS	CG	SH	SV	IP	H	HR	BB	SO	RAT	ERA	ERA+	OAV	OOB	BH	AVG	PB	PR	/A	PD	TPI
1954 Phi-N	1	1	.500	5	3	0	0	0	16	14	1	14	3	15.8	4.50	90	.237	.384	0	.000	-1	-1	-1	-1	-0.2

● GENE PENTZ Pentz, Eugene David b: 6/21/53, Johnstown, Pa. BR/TR, 6'1", 200 lbs. Deb: 7/29/75

YEAR TM/L	W	L	PCT	G	GS	CG	SH	SV	IP	H	HR	BB	SO	RAT	ERA	ERA+	OAV	OOB	BH	AVG	PB	PR	/A	PD	TPI
1975 Det-A	0	4	.000	13	0	0	0	0	25^1	27	0	20	21	16.7	3.20	126	.293	.420	0	—	0	2	2	-0	-0.1
1976 Hou-N	3	3	.500	40	0	0	0	5	63^2	62	5	31	36	13.3	2.97	108	.259	.347	1	.200	0	4	2	1	0.3
1977 Hou-N	5	2	.714	41	4	0	0	2	87	76	8	44	51	12.5	3.83	93	.236	.330	0	.000	-1	1	-3	0	-0.4
1978 Hou-N	0	0	—	10	0	0	0	0	15	12	1	13	8	15.6	6.00	55	.214	.371	0	.000	-0	-4	-4	1	-0.4
Total 4	8	9	.471	104	4	0	0	7	191	177	14	108	116	13.6	3.63	96	.250	.351	1	.053	-1	2	-3	1	-0.6

● JIMMY PEOPLES Peoples, James Elsworth b: 10/8/1863, Big Beaver, Mich. d: 8/29/20, Detroit, Mich. TR , 5'8", 200 lbs. Deb: 5/29/1884 U♦

YEAR TM/L	W	L	PCT	G	GS	CG	SH	SV	IP	H	HR	BB	SO	RAT	ERA	ERA+	OAV	OOB	BH	AVG	PB	PR	/A	PD	TPI
1885 Cin-a	0	2	.000	2	2	1	0	0	15	30	0	2	4	21.0	12.00	27	.390	.427	4	.182	-0	-15	-15	1	-1.0

● LAURIN PEPPER Pepper, Hugh McLaurin b: 1/18/31, Vaughan, Miss. BR/TR, 5'11", 190 lbs. Deb: 7/04/54

YEAR TM/L	W	L	PCT	G	GS	CG	SH	SV	IP	H	HR	BB	SO	RAT	ERA	ERA+	OAV	OOB	BH	AVG	PB	PR	/A	PD	TPI
1954 Pit-N	1	5	.167	14	8	0	0	0	50^2	63	4	43	17	18.8	7.99	52	.315	.436	4	.235	0	-22	-21	1	-1.8
1955 Pit-N	0	1	.000	14	1	0	0	0	20	30	5	25	7	25.6	10.35	40	.370	.528	0	.000	-0	-14	-14	-0	-1.4
1956 Pit-N	1	1	.500	11	7	0	0	0	30	30	1	25	12	16.5	3.00	126	.256	.387	0	.000	-0	3	3	-1	0.2
1957 Pit-N	0	1	.000	5	1	0	0	0	9	11	1	5	4	16.0	8.00	47	.297	.381	0	—	0	-4	-4	-0	-0.4
Total 4	2	8	.200	44	17	0	0	0	109^2	134	11	98	40	19.2	7.06	57	.308	.437	4	.160	-0	-38	-37	0	-3.4

● BOB PEPPER Pepper, Robert Ernest b: 5/3/1895, Rosston, Pa. d: 4/8/68, Fort Cliff, Pa. BR/TR, 6'2", 178 lbs. Deb: 7/23/15

YEAR TM/L	W	L	PCT	G	GS	CG	SH	SV	IP	H	HR	BB	SO	RAT	ERA	ERA+	OAV	OOB	BH	AVG	PB	PR	/A	PD	TPI
1915 Phi-A	0	0	—	1	0	0	0	0	5	6	0	4	0	19.8	1.80	163	.333	.478	0	.000	-0	1	1	-0	0.0

● HARRISON PEPPERS Peppers, Harrison (b: William Harrison Pepper) b: 9/1866, Kentucky d: 11/5/03, Webb City, Mo. BL , Deb: 6/30/1894

YEAR TM/L	W	L	PCT	G	GS	CG	SH	SV	IP	H	HR	BB	SO	RAT	ERA	ERA+	OAV	OOB	BH	AVG	PB	PR	/A	PD	TPI
1894 Lou-N	0	1	.000	2	1	0	0	0	8	10	0	4	0	15.8	6.75	75	.303	.378	0	.000	-1	-1	-1	-0	-0.2

● LUIS PERAZA Peraza, Luis (Rios) b: 6/17/42, Rio Piedras, P.R. BR/TR, 5'11", 185 lbs. Deb: 4/09/69

YEAR TM/L	W	L	PCT	G	GS	CG	SH	SV	IP	H	HR	BB	SO	RAT	ERA	ERA+	OAV	OOB	BH	AVG	PB	PR	/A	PD	TPI
1969 Phi-N	0	0	—	8	0	0	0	0	9	12	1	2	7	14.0	6.00	59	.364	.400	0	.000	-0	-2	-2	-0	-0.3

● OSWALDO PERAZA Peraza, Oswald Jose b: 10/19/62, Puerto Cabello, Venez. BR/TR, 6'4", 172 lbs. Deb: 4/04/88

YEAR TM/L	W	L	PCT	G	GS	CG	SH	SV	IP	H	HR	BB	SO	RAT	ERA	ERA+	OAV	OOB	BH	AVG	PB	PR	/A	PD	TPI
1988 Bal-A	5	7	.417	19	15	1	0	0	86	98	10	37	61	14.3	5.55	70	.282	.355	0	—	0	-15	-16	0	-1.4

● HUB PERDUE Perdue, Herbert Rodney "The Gallatin Squash" b: 6/7/1882, Bethpage, Tenn. d: 10/31/68, Gallatin, Tex. BR/TR, 5'10.5", 192 lbs. Deb: 4/19/11

YEAR TM/L	W	L	PCT	G	GS	CG	SH	SV	IP	H	HR	BB	SO	RAT	ERA	ERA+	OAV	OOB	BH	AVG	PB	PR	/A	PD	TPI
1911 Bos-N	6	10	.375	24	19	9	0	1	137^1	180	10	41	40	14.7	4.98	77	.321	.372	10	.208	-1	-24	-18	-0	-1.8
1912 Bos-N	13	16	.448	37	30	20	1	3	249	295	11	54	101	12.7	3.80	94	.303	.341	12	.138	-6	-11	-6	-4	-1.5
1913 Bos-N	16	13	.552	38	32	16	3	1	212^1	201	7	39	91	10.3	3.26	101	.249	.287	7	.104	-5	-1	0	-7	-1.1
1914 Bos-N	2	5	.286	9	9	2	0	0	51	60	5	11	13	13.1	5.82	47	.311	.357	1	.071	-0	-17	-17	0	-1.7
StL-N	8	8	.500	22	19	12	0	1	153^1	160	3	35	43	11.7	2.82	99	.290	.338	8	.167	-1	-0	-0	-4	-0.6
Yr	10	13	.435	31	28	14	0	1	204^1	220	8	46	56	11.9	3.57	78	.295	.340	9	.145	-1	-18	-18	-4	-2.3
1915 StL-N	6	12	.333	31	13	5	1	1	115^1	141	7	19	29	12.6	4.21	66	.311	.341	4	.111	-1	-19	-18	-0	-2.1
Total 5	51	64	.443	161	122	64	5	7	918^1	1037	43	199	317	12.3	3.85	85	.293	.334	42	.140	-14	-73	-60	-15	-8.8

● GEORGE PEREZ Perez, George Thomas b: 12/29/37, San Fernando, Cal. BR/TR, 6'2.5", 200 lbs. Deb: 4/17/58

YEAR TM/L	W	L	PCT	G	GS	CG	SH	SV	IP	H	HR	BB	SO	RAT	ERA	ERA+	OAV	OOB	BH	AVG	PB	PR	/A	PD	TPI
1958 Pit-N	0	1	.000	4	0	0	0	1	8^1	9	1	4	2	14.0	5.40	72	.300	.382	0	.000	-0	-1	-1	-0	-0.2

● MELIDO PEREZ Perez, Melido Turpen Gross (b: Melido Turpen Gross (Perez)) b: 2/15/66, San Cristobal, D.R. BR/TR, 6'4", 180 lbs. Deb: 9/04/87 F

YEAR TM/L	W	L	PCT	G	GS	CG	SH	SV	IP	H	HR	BB	SO	RAT	ERA	ERA+	OAV	OOB	BH	AVG	PB	PR	/A	PD	TPI
1987 KC-A	1	1	.500	3	3	0	0	0	10^1	18	2	5	5	20.0	7.84	58	.375	.434	0	—	0	-4	-4	-1	-0.4
1988 Chi-A	12	10	.545	32	32	3	1	0	197	186	26	72	138	11.9	3.79	105	.248	.316	0	—	0	4	4	-2	0.2
1989 Chi-A	11	14	.440	31	31	2	0	0	183^1	187	23	90	141	13.7	5.01	76	.264	.350	0	—	0	-23	-25	-1	-2.5
1990 Chi-A	13	14	.481	35	35	3	3	0	197	177	14	86	161	12.1	4.61	83	.241	.322	0	—	0	-16	-17	-2	-1.7
1991 Chi-A	8	7	.533	49	8	0	0	1	135^2	111	15	52	128	10.9	3.12	127	.224	.299	0	—	0	15	13	1	1.5
1992 NY-A	13	16	.448	33	33	10	1	0	247^2	212	16	93	218	11.3	2.87	141	.235	.310	0	—	0	29	32	-1	3.3
Total 6	58	62	.483	183	142	18	5	1	971	891	96	398	791	12.1	3.90	101	.245	.322	0	—	0	6	3	-5	0.4

● MIKE PEREZ Perez, Michael Irvin (Ortega) b: 10/19/64, Yauco, P.R. BR/TR, 6', 185 lbs. Deb: 9/05/90

YEAR TM/L	W	L	PCT	G	GS	CG	SH	SV	IP	H	HR	BB	SO	RAT	ERA	ERA+	OAV	OOB	BH	AVG	PB	PR	/A	PD	TPI
1990 StL-N	1	0	1.000	13	0	0	0	1	13^2	12	0	3	5	9.9	3.95	97	.240	.283	0	.000	-0	-0	-0	0	0.0
1991 StL-N	0	2	.000	14	0	0	0	0	17	19	1	7	7	14.3	5.82	64	.288	.365	0	—	0	-4	-4	-0	-0.4
1992 StL-N	9	3	.750	77	0	0	0	0	93	70	4	32	46	10.0	1.84	187	.210	.281	0	.000	-0	17	17	0	1.8
Total 3	10	5	.667	104	0	0	0	1	123^2	101	5	42	58	10.6	2.62	134	.225	.294	0	.000	-0	13	12	0	1.4

● PASCUAL PEREZ Perez, Pascual Gross (b: Pascual Gross (Perez)) b: 5/17/57, San Cristobal, D.R. BR/TR, 6'2", 163 lbs. Deb: 5/07/80 F

YEAR TM/L	W	L	PCT	G	GS	CG	SH	SV	IP	H	HR	BB	SO	RAT	ERA	ERA+	OAV	OOB	BH	AVG	PB	PR	/A	PD	TPI
1980 Pit-N	0	1	.000	2	2	0	0	0	12	15	0	2	7	14.3	3.75	97	.341	.396	1	.250	0	-0	-0	-0	0.0
1981 Pit-N	2	7	.222	17	13	2	0	0	86^1	92	5	34	46	13.4	3.96	91	.273	.345	3	.136	-0	-5	-4	-0	-0.4
1982 *Atl-N	4	4	.500	16	11	0	0	0	79^1	85	4	17	29	11.6	3.06	122	.276	.314	3	.167	1	5	6	0	0.8
1983 Atl-N★	15	8	.652	33	33	7	1	0	215^1	213	20	51	144	11.2	3.43	113	.260	.307	12	.160	-1	5	11	1	1.2
1984 Atl-N	14	8	.636	30	30	4	1	0	211^2	208	26	51	145	11.1	3.74	103	.260	.307	5	.076	-2	-4	3	3	0.4
1985 Atl-N	1	13	.071	22	22	0	0	0	95^1	115	10	57	57	16.3	6.14	63	.297	.389	3	.120	-0	-27	-24	-1	-2.5
1987 Mon-N	7	0	1.000	10	10	2	0	0	70^1	52	5	16	58	8.8	2.30	182	.206	.257	1	.042	-2	14	15	1	1.5
1988 Mon-N	12	8	.600	27	27	4	2	0	188	133	15	44	131	**8.8**	2.44	147	.196	**.253**	2	.037	-3	21	24	2	2.6
1989 Mon-N	9	13	.409	33	28	2	0	0	198^1	178	15	45	152	10.3	3.31	107	.237	.283	11	.204	2	4	5	0	0.8
1990 NY-A	1	2	.333	3	3	0	0	0	14	8	0	3	12	7.1	1.29	309	.163	.212	0	—	0	4	4	-0	0.4
1991 NY-A	2	4	.333	14	14	0	0	0	73^2	68	7	24	41	11.2	3.18	130	.250	.311	0	—	0	8	8	-0	0.8
Total 11	67	68	.496	207	193	21	4	0	1244^1	1167	107	344	822	11.1	3.44	110	.249	.303	41	.120	-5	25	47	6	5.6

● YORKIS PEREZ Perez, Yorkis Miguel b: 9/30/67, Bajos De Haina, D.R. BL/TL, 6', 180 lbs. Deb: 9/30/91

YEAR TM/L	W	L	PCT	G	GS	CG	SH	SV	IP	H	HR	BB	SO	RAT	ERA	ERA+	OAV	OOB	BH	AVG	PB	PR	/A	PD	TPI
1991 Chi-N	1	0	1.000	3	0	0	0	0	4^1	2	0	2	3	8.3	2.08	187	.167	.286	0	—	0	1	1	0	0.1

● CECIL PERKINS Perkins, Cecil Boyce b: 12/1/40, Baltimore, Md. BR/TR, 6', 175 lbs. Deb: 7/05/67

YEAR TM/L	W	L	PCT	G	GS	CG	SH	SV	IP	H	HR	BB	SO	RAT	ERA	ERA+	OAV	OOB	BH	AVG	PB	PR	/A	PD	TPI
1967 NY-A	0	1	.000	2	1	0	0	0	5	6	1	2	1	14.4	9.00	35	.316	.381	0	.000	-0	-3	-3	0	-0.3

● CHARLIE PERKINS Perkins, Charles Sullivan "Lefty" b: 9/9/05, Ensley, Ala. d: 5/25/88, Salem, Ore. BR/TL, 6'1", 175 lbs. Deb: 5/01/30

YEAR TM/L	W	L	PCT	G	GS	CG	SH	SV	IP	H	HR	BB	SO	RAT	ERA	ERA+	OAV	OOB	BH	AVG	PB	PR	/A	PD	TPI
1930 Phi-A	0	0	—	8	1	0	0	0	23^2	25	0	15	15	15.2	6.46	72	.313	.421	1	.125	-1	-5	-5	0	-0.5
1934 Bro-N	0	3	.000	11	2	0	0	0	24^1	37	3	14	5	19.6	8.51	46	.336	.421	2	.286	0	-12	-12	-1	-1.2
Total 2	0	3	.000	19	3	0	0	0	48	62	3	29	20	17.4	7.50	57	.326	.421	3	.200	-1	-17	-17	-1	-1.7

YEAR	TM/L	W	L	PCT	G	GS	CG	SH	SV	IP	H	HR	BB	SO	RAT	ERA	ERA+	OAV	OOB	BH	AVG	PB	PR	/A	PD	TPI
● JOHN PERKOVICH	Perkovich, John Joseph "Perky" b: 3/10/24, Chicago, Ill. BR/TR, 5'11", 170 lbs. Deb: 5/06/50																									
1950	Chi-A	0	0	—	1	0	0	0	0	5	7	3	1	3	14.4	7.20	62	.318	.348	0	.000	-0	-1	-2	-0	-0.2
● HARRY PERKOWSKI	Perkowski, Harry Walter b: 9/6/22, Dante, Va. BL/TL, 6'2.5", 196 lbs. Deb: 9/13/47																									
1947	Cin-N	0	0	—	3	1	0	0	0	7^1	12	1	3	2	18.4	3.68	111	.375	.429	0	.000	0	0	0	-0	0.0
1949	Cin-N	1	1	.500	5	3	2	0	0	23^2	21	2	14	3	13.3	4.56	92	.236	.340	3	.333	1	-1	-1	-1	-0.1
1950	Cin-N	0	0	—	22	0	0	0	0	34^1	36	6	23	19	15.7	5.24	81	.286	.400	7	.318	2	-4	-4	1	-0.1
1951	Cin-N	3	6	.333	35	7	1	0	1	102	96	2	46	56	12.6	2.82	144	.251	.333	1	.040	-3	13	14	1	1.2
1952	Cin-N	12	10	.545	33	24	11	1	0	194	197	9	89	86	13.4	3.80	99	.265	.347	12	.160	-0	-2	-1	1	0.0
1953	Cin-N	12	11	.522	33	25	7	2	2	193	204	26	62	70	12.5	4.52	96	.271	.327	14	.203	1	-5	-4	-0	-0.2
1954	Cin-N	2	8	.200	28	12	3	1	0	95^2	100	16	62	32	15.3	6.11	69	.276	.384	4	.160	0	-22	-20	-1	-2.0
1955	Chi-N	3	4	.429	25	4	0	0	2	47^2	53	3	25	28	14.7	5.29	77	.283	.368	2	.154	-0	-7	-6	1	-0.5
Total	8	33	40	.452	184	76	24	4	5	697^2	719	65	324	296	13.5	4.37	94	.269	.350	43	.180	1	-27	-21	2	-1.7
● JON PERLMAN	Perlman, Jonathan Samuel b: 12/13/56, Dallas, Tex. BL/TR, 6'3", 185 lbs. Deb: 9/06/85																									
1985	Chi-N	1	0	1.000	6	0	0	0	0	8^2	10	3	8	4	18.7	11.42	35	.313	.450	0	.000	-0	-8	-7	0	-0.7
1987	SF-N	0	0	—	10	0	0	0	0	11^1	11	1	4	3	12.7	3.97	97	.256	.333	0	—	0	0	-0	-0	0.0
1988	Cle-A	0	2	.000	10	0	0	0	0	19^2	25	0	11	10	16.5	5.49	75	.309	.391	0	—	0	-3	-3	1	-0.3
Total	3	1	2	.333	26	0	0	0	0	39^2	46	4	23	17	15.9	6.35	63	.295	.389	0	.000	-0	-11	-10	1	-1.0
● LEN PERME	Perme, Leonard John b: 11/25/17, Cleveland, Ohio BL/TL, 6', 170 lbs. Deb: 9/08/42																									
1942	Chi-A	0	1	.000	4	1	1	0	0	13	5	0	4	4	6.9	1.38	260	.119	.213	1	.333	0	3	3	-0	0.4
1946	Chi-A	0	0	—	4	0	0	0	0	4^1	6	0	7	2	27.0	8.31	41	.316	.500	0	—	0	-2	-2	0	-0.2
Total	2	0	1	.000	8	1	1	0	0	17^1	11	0	11	6	11.9	3.12	114	.180	.315	1	.333	0	1	1	0	0.2
● HUB PERNOLL	Pernoll, Henry Hubbard b: 3/14/1888, Grant's Pass, Ore. d: 2/18/44, Grant's Pass, Ore. BR/TL, 5'8", 175 lbs. Deb: 4/25/10																									
1910	Det-A	4	3	.571	11	5	4	0	0	54^2	54	1	14	25	12.0	2.96	89	.270	.333	1	.063	-2	-3	-2	3	-0.1
1912	Det-A	0	0	—	3	0	0	0	0	9	9	0	4	3	13.0	6.00	54	.265	.342	0	.000	-0	-3	-3	0	-0.3
Total	2	4	3	.571	14	5	4	0	0	63^2	63	1	18	28	12.2	3.39	80	.269	.335	1	.053	-2	-5	-5	3	-0.4
● RON PERRANOSKI	Perranoski, Ronald Peter (b: Ronald Peter Perzanowski) b: 4/1/36, Paterson, N.J. BL/TL, 6', 192 lbs. Deb: 4/14/61 C																									
1961	LA-N	7	5	.583	53	1	0	0	6	91^2	82	5	41	56	12.5	2.65	164	.244	.333	1	.083	-0	14	**17**	0	1.7
1962	LA-N	6	6	.500	**70**	0	0	0	20	107^1	103	1	36	68	11.7	2.85	127	.255	.316	1	.071	-1	13	9	-1	0.8
1963	*LA-N	16	3	**.842**	**69**	0	0	0	21	129	112	7	43	75	11.1	1.67	180	.231	.299	3	.125	0	**23**	19	0	2.1
1964	LA-N	5	7	.417	72	0	0	0	14	125^1	128	5	46	79	12.6	3.09	105	.263	.328	2	.105	-0	6	2	2	0.4
1965	*LA-N	6	6	.500	59	0	0	0	17	104^2	85	2	40	53	11.0	2.24	146	.226	.305	3	.158	1	15	12	-1	1.2
1966	*LA-N	6	7	.462	55	0	0	0	7	82	82	4	31	50	12.5	3.18	104	.269	.338	2	.250	1	4	1	2	0.5
1967	LA-N	6	7	.462	**70**	0	0	0	16	110	97	4	45	75	11.9	2.45	126	.240	.320	1	.100	-0	11	8	1	1.0
1968	Min-A	8	7	.533	66	0	0	0	6	87	86	5	38	65	12.8	3.10	100	.252	.327	0	.000	-1	-1	-0	-0	-0.1
1969	*Min-A	9	10	.474	75	0	0	0	**31**	119^2	85	4	52	62	10.4	2.11	173	.205	.295	2	.083	-1	20	**21**	1	2.1
1970	*Min-A	7	8	.467	67	0	0	0	**34**	111	108	7	42	55	12.2	2.43	153	.259	.328	1	.042	-2	16	16	-1	1.3
1971	Min-A	1	4	.200	36	0	0	0	5	42^2	60	2	28	21	19.2	6.75	53	.337	.435	0	.000	-0	-16	-15	-0	-1.6
	Det-A	0	1	.000	11	0	0	0	2	18	16	2	3	8	10.0	2.50	144	.254	.299	0	.000	-0	2	2	-0	0.2
	Yr	1	5	.167	47	0	0	0	7	60^2	76	4	31	29	16.0	5.49	65	.309	.388	0	.000	-1	-14	-13	-1	-1.4
1972	Det-A	0	1	.000	17	0	0	0	0	18^2	23	2	8	10	15.4	7.71	41	.307	.381	0	.000	-0	-10	-9	-1	-1.1
	LA-N	2	0	1.000	9	0	0	0	0	16^2	19	0	8	5	14.6	2.70	123	.292	.370	0	—	0	1	1	-0	0.1
1973	Cal-A	0	2	.000	8	0	0	0	0	11	11	0	7	5	15.5	4.09	87	.282	.404	0	—	0	-0	-1	0	0.0
Total	13	79	74	.516	737	1	0	0	179	1174^2	1097	50	468	687	12.2	2.79	123	.250	.325	16	.096	-4	99	83	2	8.6
● BILL PERRIN	Perrin, William Joseph "Lefty" b: 6/23/10, New Orleans, La. d: 6/30/74, New Orleans, La. BR/TL, 5'11", 172 lbs. Deb: 9/30/34																									
1934	Cle-A	0	1	.000	1	1	0	0	0	5	13	0	2	3	28.8	14.40	32	.520	.571	0	.000	-0	-6	-5	0	-0.4
● GEORGE PERRING	Perring, George Wilson b: 8/13/1884, Sharon, Wis. d: 8/20/60, Beloit, Wis. BR/TR, 6', 190 lbs. Deb: 4/25/08 ♦																									
1914	KC-F	0	0	—	1	0	0	0	0	0^2	2	0	1	0	40.5	13.50	23	1.000	1.000	138	.278	0	-1	-1	-0	-0.1
● POL PERRITT	Perritt, William Dayton b: 8/30/1892, Arcadia, La. d: 10/15/47, Shreveport, La. BR/TR, 6'2", 168 lbs. Deb: 9/07/12																									
1912	StL-N	1	1	.500	6	3	1	0	0	31	25	0	10	13	10.2	3.19	107	.243	.310	2	.222	-0	1	1	0	0.1
1913	StL-N	6	14	.300	36	21	8	0	0	175	205	9	64	64	14.2	5.25	62	.300	.367	12	.203	-1	-40	-39	1	-3.9
1914	StL-N	16	13	.552	41	32	18	3	2	286	248	7	93	115	11.2	2.36	118	.245	.318	13	.141	-2	14	14	-3	1.0
1915	NY-N	12	18	.400	35	30	16	4	0	220	226	6	59	91	12.1	2.66	96	.266	.323	11	.162	-0	2	-2	-5	-0.9
1916	NY-N	18	11	.621	40	28	17	5	2	251	243	11	56	115	11.0	2.62	93	.257	.304	7	.084	-4	0	-5	-2	-1.2
1917	*NY-N	17	7	.708	35	26	14	5	1	215	186	3	45	72	10.0	1.88	135	.237	.284	11	.157	-2	20	16	1	1.7
1918	NY-N	18	13	.581	35	31	19	6	0	233	212	5	38	60	9.7	2.74	96	.246	.278	14	.175	-1	1	-3	-3	-0.8
1919	NY-N	1	1	.500	11	3	0	0	1	19	27	0	12	2	19.4	7.11	39	.386	.488	0	.000	-1	-9	-9	0	-1.0
1920	NY-N	0	0	—	8	0	0	0	2	15	9	0	4	3	7.8	1.80	167	.167	.224	0	.000	-1	2	2	0	0.2
1921	NY-N	2	0	1.000	5	1	0	0	0	11^2	17	0	2	5	14.7	3.86	95	.321	.345	0	.000	-0	-0	-0	-1	-0.1
	Det-A	1	0	1.000	4	2	0	0	0	13	18	0	7	3	18.0	4.85	88	.383	.473	2	.400	0	-1	-1	-0	-0.1
Total	10	92	78	.541	256	177	93	23	8	1469^2	1416	41	390	543	11.4	2.89	94	.259	.315	72	.151	-12	-10	-28	-11	-5.0
● GAYLORD PERRY	Perry, Gaylord Jackson b: 9/15/38, Williamston, N.C. BR/TR, 6'4", 215 lbs. Deb: 4/14/62 FH																									
1962	SF-N	3	1	.750	13	7	1	0	0	43	54	3	14	20	14.2	5.23	73	.310	.362	3	.231	0	-6	-7	-1	-0.7
1963	SF-N	1	6	.143	31	4	0	0	2	76	84	10	29	52	13.6	4.03	79	.279	.346	4	.222	1	-6	-7	-0	-0.7
1964	SF-N	12	11	.522	44	19	5	2	5	206^1	179	16	43	155	9.9	2.75	130	.232	.278	3	.054	-3	18	19	-2	1.5
1965	SF-N	8	12	.400	47	26	6	0	1	195^2	194	21	70	170	12.4	4.19	86	.256	.324	10	.156	-0	-14	-13	3	-1.0
1966	SF-N★	21	8	.724	36	35	13	3	0	255^2	242	15	40	201	10.1	2.99	123	.247	.280	16	.186	-0	17	19	1	2.1
1967	SF-N	15	17	.469	39	37	18	3	1	293	231	20	84	230	9.8	2.61	126	.214	.274	13	.143	-1	25	22	4	2.8
1968	SF-N	16	15	.516	39	38	19	3	1	291	240	10	59	173	9.4	2.44	120	.222	.265	11	.113	-3	18	16	4	2.1
1969	SF-N	19	14	.576	40	39	26	3	0	**325^1**	290	23	91	233	10.8	2.49	141	.237	.295	14	.120	-2	40	37	3	4.3
1970	SF-N★	**23**	13	.639	41	41	23	**5**	0	**328^2**	292	27	84	214	10.5	3.20	124	.237	.290	14	.117	-3	31	28	5	3.1
1971	*SF-N	16	12	.571	37	37	14	2	0	280	255	20	67	158	10.5	2.76	123	.242	.290	10	.102	-3	22	20	0	1.8
1972	Cle-A★	**24**	16	.600	41	40	**29**	5	1	342^2	253	17	82	234	9.1	1.92	168	.205	.261	17	.155	1	**44**	**49**	2	**6.6**
1973	Cle-A	19	19	.500	41	41	**29**	7	0	344	315	34	115	238	11.4	3.38	116	.246	.311	0	—	0	17	21	1	2.3
1974	Cle-A★	21	13	.618	37	37	28	4	0	322^1	230	25	99	216	9.4	2.51	**144**	.204	.272	0	—	0	40	**39**	1	**4.6**
1975	Cle-A	6	9	.400	15	15	10	1	0	121^2	120	16	34	85	11.5	3.55	106	.256	.308	0	—	0	3	3	1	0.5
	Tex-A	12	8	.600	22	22	15	4	0	184	157	12	36	148	9.6	3.03	124	.227	.268	0	—	0	15	15	-1	1.6
	Yr	18	17	.514	37	37	25	5	0	305^2	277	28	70	233	10.3	3.24	116	.238	.283	0	—	0	18	18	1	2.1
1976	Tex-A	15	14	.517	32	32	21	2	0	250^1	232	14	52	143	10.2	3.24	111	.247	.287	0	—	0	8	10	-3	0.6
1977	Tex-A	15	12	.556	34	34	13	4	0	238	239	21	56	177	11.3	3.37	121	.262	.308	0	—	0	18	19	-1	1.8
1978	SD-N	**21**	6	**.778**	37	37	5	2	0	260^2	241	9	66	154	10.7	2.73	122	.248	.298	8	.092	-3	25	17	0	1.6
1979	SD-N★	12	11	.522	32	32	10	0	0	232^2	225	12	67	140	11.4	3.06	115	.257	.313	6	.085	-2	17	12	1	1.2
1980	Tex-A	6	9	.400	24	24	6	2	0	155	159	12	46	107	12.3	3.43	114	.268	.328	0	—	0	10	8	1	1.2
	NY-A	4	4	.500	10	8	0	0	0	50^2	65	2	18	28	14.9	4.44	88	.320	.378	0	—	0	-2	-3	-0	-0.2
	Yr	10	13	.435	34	32	6	2	0	205^2	224	14	64	135	12.6	3.68	106	.278	.332	0	—	0	8	5	1	1.0
1981	Atl-N	8	9	.471	23	23	3	0	0	150^2	182	9	24	60	12.5	3.94	91	.304	.335	12	.250	3	-8	-6	-1	-0.5
1982	Sea-A	10	12	.455	32	32	6	0	0	216^2	245	27	54	116	12.6	4.40	96	.287	.332	0	—	0	-8	-4	0	-0.4

YEAR TM/L	W	L	PCT	G	GS	CG	SH	SV	IP	H	HR	BB	SO	RAT	ERA	ERA+	OAV	OOB	BH	AVG	PB	PR	/A	PD	TPI
1983 Sea-A	3	10	.231	16	16	2	0	0	102	116	18	23	42	12.5	4.94	86	.286	.329	0	—	0	-10	-8	0	-0.8
KC-A	4	4	.500	14	14	1	1	0	84^1	98	6	26	40	13.3	4.27	95	.292	.344	0	—	0	-2	-2	0	-0.1
Yr	7	14	.333	30	30	3	1	0	186^1	214	24	49	82	12.8	4.64	90	.286	.331	0	—	0	-12	-10	1	-0.9
Total 22	314	265	.542	777	690	303	53	11	5350^1	4938	399	1379	3534	10.8	3.11	117	.245	.297	141	.131	-16	311	305	21	35.3
● SCOTT PERRY Perry, Herbert Scott b: 4/17/1891, Dennison, Tex. d: 10/27/59, Kansas City, Mo. BR/TR, 6'1", 195 lbs. Deb: 5/13/15																									
1915 StL-A	0	0	—	1	1	0	0	0	2	5	0	1	0	31.5	13.50	21	.455	.538	0	—	0	-2	-2	-0	-0.2
1916 Chi-N	2	1	.667	4	3	2	1	0	28^1	30	0	3	10	10.5	2.54	115	.291	.311	3	.273	1	0	1	0	0.2
1917 Cin-N	0	0	—	4	1	0	0	0	13^1	17	0	8	4	17.6	6.75	39	.321	.419	0	.000	-1	-6	-6	-0	-0.7
1918 Phi-A	20	19	.513	44	36	**30**	3	2	**332^1**	295	1	111	81	11.0	1.98	148	.247	.312	15	.134	-6	30	35	2	3.6
1919 Phi-A	4	17	.190	25	21	12	0	1	183^2	193	4	72	38	13.1	3.58	96	.282	.352	8	.136	-3	-7	-3	6	0.1
1920 Phi-A	11	25	.306	42	34	20	1	1	263^2	310	14	65	79	13.0	3.62	111	.300	.345	13	.157	-4	5	12	0	0.8
1921 Phi-A	3	6	.333	12	8	5	0	1	70	77	4	24	19	13.1	4.11	108	.288	.349	1	.038	-4	1	3	1	0.0
Total 7	40	68	.370	132	104	69	5	5	893^1	927	23	284	231	12.3	3.07	113	.277	.336	40	.135	-17	21	40	9	3.8
● JIM PERRY Perry, James Evan b: 10/30/36, Williamston, N.C. BB/TR, 6'4", 200 lbs. Deb: 4/23/59 F																									
1959 Cle-A	12	10	.545	44	13	8	2	4	153	122	10	55	79	10.5	2.65	139	.225	.298	15	.300	3	21	18	-0	2.2
1960 Cle-A	**18**	10	**.643**	41	36	10	**4**	1	261^1	257	35	91	120	12.1	3.62	103	.260	.324	22	.242	3	7	4	0	0.6
1961 Cle-A☆	10	17	.370	35	35	6	1	0	223^2	238	28	87	90	13.3	4.71	84	.273	.343	12	.164	-1	-17	-19	-0	-1.9
1962 Cle-A	12	12	.500	35	27	7	3	0	193^2	213	21	59	74	12.7	4.14	94	.285	.339	11	.183	0	-4	-6	1	-0.4
1963 Cle-A	0	0	—	5	0	0	0	0	10^1	12	0	2	7	12.2	5.23	69	.293	.326	0	.000	-0	-2	-2	0	-0.2
Min-A	9	9	.500	35	25	5	1	1	168^1	167	17	57	65	12.1	3.74	97	.256	.318	11	.216	3	-2	-2	-1	0.0
Yr	9	9	.500	40	25	5	1	1	178^2	179	17	59	72	12.1	3.83	95	.258	.318	11	.208	3	-4	-4	-1	-0.2
1964 Min-A	6	3	.667	42	1	0	0	2	65^1	61	7	23	55	11.7	3.44	104	.245	.311	2	.154	-0	1	1	-0	0.1
1965 *Min-A	12	7	.632	36	19	4	2	0	167^2	142	18	47	88	10.3	2.63	135	.232	.290	9	.170	1	15	17	-1	1.9
1966 Min-A	11	7	.611	33	25	8	1	0	184^1	149	17	53	122	10.1	2.54	142	.222	.284	13	.220	5	18	22	-2	2.8
1967 Min-A	8	7	.533	37	11	3	2	0	130^2	123	8	50	94	12.1	3.03	114	.255	.328	8	.190	1	3	6	-1	0.7
1968 Min-A	8	6	.571	32	18	3	2	1	139	113	8	26	69	9.3	2.27	136	.219	.263	6	.143	2	11	13	1	1.8
1969 *Min-A	20	6	.769	46	36	12	3	0	261^2	244	18	66	153	11.0	2.82	129	.247	.300	16	.172	1	23	24	-2	2.5
1970 *Min-A★	**24**	12	.667	40	40	13	4	0	278^2	258	20	57	168	10.5	3.04	123	.243	.287	24	.247	5	21	21	1	2.9
1971 Min-A☆	17	17	.500	40	39	8	0	1	270	263	39	102	126	12.3	4.23	84	.259	.329	17	.185	1	-23	-20	0	-2.0
1972 Min-A	13	16	.448	35	35	5	2	0	217^2	191	14	60	85	10.7	3.35	96	.236	.295	11	.155	-1	-7	-3	-1	-0.6
1973 Det-A	14	13	.519	35	34	7	1	0	203	225	22	55	66	12.6	4.03	101	.282	.331	0	—	0	-5	1	-0	0.1
1974 Cle-A	17	12	.586	36	36	8	3	0	252	242	11	64	71	11.1	2.96	122	.254	.304	0	—	0	18	18	-1	2.0
1975 Cle-A	1	6	.143	8	6	0	0	0	37^2	46	8	18	11	15.3	6.69	57	.309	.383	0	—	0	-12	-12	0	-1.1
Oak-A	3	4	.429	15	11	2	1	0	67^2	61	7	26	33	12.5	4.66	78	.237	.324	0	—	0	-7	-8	-1	-0.7
Yr	4	10	.286	23	17	2	1	0	105^1	107	15	44	44	13.5	5.38	68	.264	.346	0	—	0	-19	-20	-1	-1.8
Total 17	215	174	.553	630	447	109	32	10	3285^2	3127	308	998	1576	11.5	3.45	106	.252	.312	177	.199	24	61	75	-7	10.7
● PAT PERRY Perry, William Patrick b: 2/4/59, Taylorsville, Ill. BL/TL, 6'1", 170 lbs. Deb: 9/12/85																									
1985 StL-N	1	0	1.000	6	0	0	0	0	12^1	3	0	3	6	4.4	0.00	—	.077	.143	1	.500	0	5	5	-0	0.5
1986 StL-N	2	3	.400	46	0	0	0	2	68^2	59	5	34	29	12.2	3.80	96	.239	.331	0	.000	-1	-1	-1	1	-0.1
1987 StL-N	4	2	.667	45	0	0	0	1	65^2	54	7	21	33	10.6	4.39	95	.222	.289	1	.143	-0	-2	-2	0	-0.1
Cin-N	1	0	1.000	12	0	0	0	1	15^1	6	0	4	6	6.5	0.00	—	.122	.204	0	—	0	7	7	0	0.8
Yr	5	2	.714	57	0	0	0	2	81	60	7	25	39	9.6	3.56	117	.203	.268	1	.143	-0	5	6	1	0.7
1988 Cin-N	2	2	.500	12	0	0	0	0	20^2	21	4	9	11	13.1	5.66	63	.262	.337	0	.000	-0	-5	-5	-0	-0.5
Chi-N	2	2	.500	35	0	0	0	1	38	40	5	7	24	11.4	3.32	109	.270	.308	1	1.000	1	1	1	-0	0.3
Yr	4	4	.500	47	0	0	0	1	58^2	61	9	16	35	12.0	4.14	87	.264	.315	1	.333	1	-5	-4	-0	-0.2
1989 Chi-N	0	1	.000	19	0	0	0	1	35^2	23	2	16	20	9.8	1.77	213	.187	.281	1	.167	-0	7	8	-1	0.8
1990 LA-N	0	0	—	7	0	0	0	0	6^2	9	0	5	2	20.3	8.10	45	.310	.429	0	.000	-0	-3	-3	-0	-0.4
Total 6	12	10	.545	182	0	0	0	6	263	215	23	99	131	10.9	3.46	110	.224	.300	4	.148	0	8	10	-0	1.3
● PARSON PERRYMAN Perryman, Emmett Key b: 10/24/1888, Everett Springs, Ga. d: 9/12/66, Starke, Fla. BR/TR, 6'4.5", 193 lbs. Deb: 4/14/15																									
1915 StL-A	2	4	.333	24	3	0	0	0	50^1	52	2	16	19	12.3	3.93	73	.281	.342	0	.000	-1	-6	-6	1	-0.6
● BILL PERTICA Pertica, William Andrew b: 3/5/1897, Santa Barbara, Cal. d: 12/28/67, Los Angeles, Cal. BR/TR, 5'9", 165 lbs. Deb: 8/07/18																									
1918 Bos-A	0	0	—	1	0	0	0	0	3	3	0	0	1	9.0	3.00	89	.273	.273	0	.000	-0	-0	-0	0	0.0
1921 StL-N	14	10	.583	38	31	15	2	2	208^1	212	9	70	67	12.6	3.37	109	.267	.334	10	.143	-3	10	7	-3	0.1
1922 StL-N	8	8	.500	34	14	2	0	0	117^1	153	5	65	30	17.0	5.91	65	.333	.419	6	.182	-0	-24	-27	1	-2.4
1923 StL-N	0	0	—	1	1	0	0	0	2^1	2	0	3	0	23.1	3.86	101	.250	.500	0	.000	-0	0	0	0	0.0
Total 4	22	18	.550	74	46	17	2	2	331	370	14	138	98	14.2	4.27	87	.291	.367	16	.152	-4	-14	-20	-2	-2.3
● STAN PERZANOWSKI Perzanowski, Stanley b: 8/25/50, East Chicago, Ind. BB/TR, 6'2", 170 lbs. Deb: 6/20/71																									
1971 Chi-A	0	1	.000	5	0	0	0	1	6	14	1	3	5	25.5	12.00	30	.412	.459	0	.000	-0	-6	-6	-0	-0.6
1974 Chi-A	0	0	—	2	1	0	0	0	2^1	8	1	2	2	38.6	19.29	19	.533	.588	0	—	0	-4	-4	0	-0.5
1975 Tex-A	3	3	.500	12	8	1	0	0	66	59	1	25	26	12.1	3.00	125	.246	.330	0	—	0	6	6	1	0.8
1976 Tex-A	0	0	—	5	0	0	0	0	11^2	20	3	4	6	20.1	10.03	36	.385	.448	0	—	0	-8	-8	0	-0.9
1978 Min-A	2	7	.222	13	7	1	0	1	56^2	59	1	26	31	14.1	5.24	73	.276	.365	0	—	0	-9	-9	1	-0.8
Total 5	5	11	.313	37	16	2	0	2	142^2	160	7	60	70	14.6	5.11	74	.288	.369	0	.000	-0	-22	-21	2	-2.0
● JEFF PETEREK Peterek, Jeffrey Allen b: 9/22/63, Michigan City, Ind. BR/TR, 6'2", 195 lbs. Deb: 8/14/89																									
1989 Mil-A	0	2	.000	7	4	0	0	0	31^1	31	3	14	16	12.9	4.02	95	.252	.328	0	—	0	-0	-1	0	-0.1
● GARY PETERS Peters, Gary Charles b: 4/21/37, Grove City, Pa. BL/TL, 6'2", 200 lbs. Deb: 9/10/59																									
1959 Chi-A	0	0	—	2	0	0	0	0	1	2	0	2	1	36.0	0.00	—	.400	.571	0	—	0	0	0	0	0.0
1960 Chi-A	0	0	—	2	0	0	0	0	3^1	4	0	1	4	13.5	2.70	140	.286	.333	0	—	0	0	0	-0	0.0
1961 Chi-A	0	0	—	3	0	0	0	1	10^1	10	0	2	6	10.5	1.74	225	.270	.308	1	.333	0	3	2	1	0.4
1962 Chi-A	0	1	.000	5	0	0	0	0	6^1	8	0	1	4	14.2	5.68	69	.308	.357	0	—	0	-1	-1	0	-0.1
1963 Chi-A	19	8	.704	41	30	13	4	1	243	192	9	68	189	9.9	**2.33**	**150**	.216	.278	21	.259	9	**35**	32	-1	**4.4**
1964 Chi-A☆	**20**	8	.714	37	36	11	3	0	273^2	217	20	104	205	10.8	2.50	138	.219	.297	25	.208	8	34	29	0	4.1
1965 Chi-A	10	12	.455	33	30	1	0	0	176^1	181	19	63	95	12.7	3.62	88	.265	.331	13	.181	2	-3	-8	0	-0.7
1966 Chi-A	12	10	.545	30	27	11	4	0	204^2	156	11	45	129	**9.0**	**1.98**	**160**	.212	**.261**	19	.235	6	**33**	27	1	**4.0**
1967 Chi-A★	16	11	.593	38	36	11	3	0	260	187	15	91	215	10.0	2.28	136	**.199**	.277	21	.212	6	27	24	3	3.8
1968 Chi-A	4	13	.235	31	25	6	1	1	162^2	146	7	60	110	11.8	3.76	80	.242	.318	15	.208	7	-14	-13	-0	-0.8
1969 Chi-A	10	15	.400	36	32	7	3	0	218^2	238	21	78	140	13.2	4.53	85	.283	.347	12	.169	2	-22	-16	-2	-1.6
1970 Bos-A	16	11	.593	34	34	10	4	0	221^2	221	20	83	155	12.6	4.06	98	.257	.328	20	.244	7	-9	-2	-1	0.3
1971 Bos-A	14	11	.560	34	32	9	1	1	214	241	25	70	100	13.3	4.37	84	.288	.347	26	.271	9	-22	-16	-2	-1.0
1972 Bos-A	3	3	.500	33	4	0	0	1	85^1	91	10	38	67	13.9	4.32	74	.279	.360	6	.200	1	-12	-11	-1	-1.1
Total 14	124	103	.546	359	286	79	23	5	2081	1894	157	706	1420	11.5	3.25	106	.243	.311	179	.222	57	50	46	-1	11.7
● JOHN PETERS Peters, John Paul b: 4/8/1850, Louisiana, Mo. d: 1/4/24, St.Louis, Mo. BR/TR, 5'7", 180 lbs. Deb: 5/23/1874 ♦																									
1876 Chi-N	0	0	—	1	0	0	0	1	1	1	0	1	0	18.0	0.00	—	.250	.400	111	.351	0	0	0	0	0.0
● RUBE PETERS Peters, Oscar Casper b: 3/15/1885, Grandfork, Ill. d: 2/7/65, Pequannock, N.J. BR/TR, 6'1", 195 lbs. Deb: 4/13/12																									
1912 Chi-A	5	6	.455	28	11	4	0	0	108^2	134	2	33	39	14.3	4.14	77	.309	.366	6	.194	-1	-10	-11	4	-0.7

YEAR TM/L	W	L	PCT	G	GS	CG	SH	SV	IP	H	HR	BB	SO	RAT	ERA	ERA+	OAV	OOB	BH	AVG	PB	PR	/A	PD	TPI
1914 Bro-F	2	2	.500	11	3	1	0	0	37^{2}	52	1	16	13	16.2	3.82	84	.335	.398	1	.091	-1	-3	-3	0	-0.3
Total 2	7	8	.467	39	14	5	0	0	146^{1}	186	3	49	52	14.8	4.06	79	.316	.374	7	.167	-1	-13	-14	4	-1.0
● **RAY PETERS**	Peters, Raymond James b: 8/27/46, Buffalo, N.Y. BR/TR, 6'5.5", 210 lbs. Deb: 6/04/70																								
1970 Mil-A	0	2	.000	2	2	0	0	0	2	7	0	5	1	54.0	31.50	12	.583	.706	0	—	0	-6	-6	0	-0.5
● **STEVE PETERS**	Peters, Steven Bradley b: 11/14/62, Oklahoma City, Okla BL/TL, 5'10", 170 lbs. Deb: 8/11/87																								
1987 StL-N	0	0	—	12	0	0	0	1	15	17	1	6	11	13.8	1.80	231	.298	.365	0	.000	-0	4	4	1	0.4
1988 StL-N	3	3	.500	44	0	0	0	0	45	57	8	22	30	15.8	6.40	54	.313	.387	0	.000	-0	-15	-15	-1	-1.6
Total 2	3	3	.500	56	0	0	0	1	60	74	9	28	41	15.3	5.25	69	.310	.382	0	.000	-1	-11	-11	0	-1.2
● **ADAM PETERSON**	Peterson, Adam Charles b: 12/11/65, Long Beach, Cal. BR/TR, 6'3", 190 lbs. Deb: 9/19/87																								
1987 Chi-A	0	0	—	1	1	0	0	0	4	8	1	3	1	24.8	13.50	34	.444	.524	0	—	0	-4	-4	-0	-0.4
1988 Chi-A	0	1	.000	2	2	0	0	0	6	6	0	6	5	18.0	13.50	29	.240	.387	0	—	0	-6	-6	-0	-0.6
1989 Chi-A	0	1	.000	3	2	0	0	0	5^{1}	13	1	2	3	25.3	15.19	25	.464	.500	0	—	0	-7	-7	-0	-0.6
1990 Chi-A	2	5	.286	20	11	2	0	0	85	90	12	26	29	12.5	4.55	84	.278	.335	0	—	0	-6	-7	-1	-0.7
1991 SD-N	3	4	.429	13	11	0	0	0	54^{2}	50	10	28	37	12.8	4.45	85	.242	.332	0	.000	-1	-5	-4	-0	-0.5
Total 5	5	11	.313	39	27	2	0	0	155	167	24	65	75	13.6	5.46	70	.277	.350	0	.000	-1	-28	-28	-2	-2.8
● **FRITZ PETERSON**	Peterson, Fritz Fred (b: Fred Ingels Peterson) b: 2/8/42, Chicago, Ill. BB/TL, 6', 200 lbs. Deb: 4/15/66																								
1966 NY-A	12	11	.522	34	32	11	2	0	215	196	15	40	96	10.0	3.31	101	.241	.279	15	.224	4	3	0	-0	0.4
1967 NY-A	8	14	.364	36	30	6	1	0	181^{1}	179	11	43	102	11.2	3.47	90	.256	.302	7	.146	1	-5	-7	1	-0.5
1968 NY-A	12	11	.522	36	27	6	2	0	212^{1}	187	13	29	115	9.3	2.63	110	.241	.272	5	.079	-2	8	6	4	1.0
1969 NY-A	17	16	.515	37	37	16	4	0	272	228	15	43	150	**9.1**	2.55	136	.229	.263	9	.112	-0	32	28	2	3.4
1970 NY-A★	20	11	.645	39	37	8	2	0	260^{1}	247	24	40	127	**10.0**	2.90	121	.248	**.280**	20	.222	5	23	18	2	2.7
1971 NY-A	15	13	.536	37	35	16	4	1	274	269	25	42	139	10.3	3.05	106	.258	.289	7	.082	-3	12	5	2	0.5
1972 NY-A	17	15	.531	35	35	12	3	0	250^{1}	270	17	44	100	11.5	3.24	91	.276	.310	19	.232	3	-5	-8	1	-0.4
1973 NY-A	8	15	.348	31	31	6	0	0	184^{1}	207	18	49	59	12.8	3.95	93	.286	.337	0	—	0	-3	-6	0	-0.6
1974 NY-A	0	0	—	3	1	0	0	0	7^{2}	13	1	2	5	17.6	4.70	74	.361	.395	0	—	0	-1	-1	-0	0.1
Cle-A	9	14	.391	29	29	3	0	0	152^{2}	187	16	37	52	13.4	4.36	83	.305	.349	0	—	0	-13	-13	1	-1.1
Yr	9	14	.391	32	30	3	0	0	160^{1}	200	17	39	57	13.6	4.38	82	.308	.351	0	—	0	-14	-14	1	-1.0
1975 Cle-A	14	8	.636	25	25	6	2	0	146^{1}	154	15	40	47	12.3	3.94	96	.275	.331	0	—	0	-3	-3	1	-0.2
1976 Cle-A	0	3	.000	9	9	0	0	0	47	59	3	10	19	13.2	5.55	63	.309	.343	0	—	0	-11	-11	-0	-1.0
Tex-A	1	0	1.000	4	2	0	0	0	15	21	0	7	4	16.8	3.60	100	.344	.412	0	—	0	-0	-0	0	-0.1
Yr	1	3	.250	13	11	0	0	0	62	80	3	17	23	14.1	5.08	69	.316	.359	0	—	0	-11	-11	0	-1.1
Total 11	133	131	.504	355	330	90	20	1	2218^{1}	2217	173	426	1015	10.9	3.30	101	.261	.300	82	.159	8	40	10	15	4.2
● **JIM PETERSON**	Peterson, James Niels b: 8/18/08, Philadelphia, Pa. d: 4/8/75, Palm Beach, Fla. BR/TR, 6'0.5", 200 lbs. Deb: 7/09/31																								
1931 Phi-A	0	1	.000	6	1	1	0	0	13	18	0	4	7	15.2	6.23	72	.321	.367	1	.500	1	-3	-3	-0	-0.2
1933 Phi-A	2	5	.286	32	5	0	0	0	90^{2}	114	6	36	18	14.9	4.96	86	.305	.366	4	.148	-1	-7	-7	2	-0.5
1937 Bro-N	0	0	—	3	0	0	0	0	5^{2}	8	3	2	4	15.9	7.94	51	.333	.385	0	—	0	-3	-2	1	-0.2
Total 3	2	6	.250	41	6	1	0	0	109^{1}	140	9	42	29	15.0	5.27	82	.308	.367	5	.172	0	-12	-12	3	-0.9
● **KENT PETERSON**	Peterson, Kent Franklin "Pete" b: 12/21/25, Goshen, Utah BR/TL, 5'10", 175 lbs. Deb: 7/15/44																								
1944 Cin-N	0	0	—	1	0	0	0	0	1	0	0	0	0	0.0	0.00	—	.000	.000	0	—	0	0	0	-0	0.0
1947 Cin-N	6	13	.316	37	17	3	1	2	152^{1}	156	8	62	78	13.1	4.25	96	.265	.338	3	.068	-3	-3	-3	-2	-0.8
1948 Cin-N	2	15	.118	43	17	2	0	1	137	146	10	59	64	13.9	4.60	85	.271	.350	5	.139	-2	-10	-10	0	-1.2
1949 Cin-N	4	5	.444	30	7	2	0	0	66^{1}	66	8	46	28	15.7	6.24	67	.261	.383	1	.056	-2	-16	-15	-1	-1.7
1950 Cin-N	0	3	.000	9	2	0	0	0	20	25	4	17	6	18.9	7.20	59	.305	.424	1	.333	0	-7	-7	-1	-0.7
1951 Cin-N	1	1	.500	9	0	0	0	0	9^{2}	13	0	8	5	20.5	6.52	63	.317	.440	0	.000	-0	-3	-3	0	-0.3
1952 Phi-N	0	0	—	3	0	0	0	2	7	2	0	2	7	5.1	0.00	—	.091	.167	0	.000	-0	3	3	-0	0.3
1953 Phi-N	0	1	.000	15	0	0	0	0	27	26	3	21	20	16.0	6.67	63	.252	.384	0	.000	-1	-7	-7	-0	-0.8
Total 8	13	38	.255	147	43	7	1	5	420^{1}	434	33	215	208	14.2	4.95	82	.266	.357	10	.091	-8	-43	-42	-4	-5.2
● **SID PETERSON**	Peterson, Sidney Herbert b: 1/31/18, Havelock, N.Dak. BR/TR, 6'3", 200 lbs. Deb: 5/04/43																								
1943 StL-A	2	0	1.000	3	0	0	0	0	10	15	0	3	0	17.1	2.70	123	.341	.396	0	.000	-0	1	1	-0	0.0
● **MARK PETKOVSEK**	Petkovsek, Mark Joseph b: 11/18/65, Beaumont, Tex. BR/TR, 6', 185 lbs. Deb: 6/08/91																								
1991 Tex-A	0	1	.000	4	1	0	0	0	9^{1}	21	4	4	6	24.1	14.46	28	.438	.481	0	—	0	-11	-11	-0	-1.0
● **DAN PETRY**	Petry, Daniel Joseph b: 11/13/58, Palo Alto, Cal. BR/TR, 6'4", 200 lbs. Deb: 7/08/79																								
1979 Det-A	6	5	.545	15	15	2	0	0	98	90	11	33	43	11.7	3.95	110	.254	.325	0	—	0	3	4	-1	0.3
1980 Det-A	10	9	.526	27	25	4	3	0	164^{2}	156	9	83	88	13.1	3.94	104	.253	.342	0	—	0	2	3	2	0.4
1981 Det-A	10	9	.526	23	22	7	2	0	141	115	10	57	79	11.0	3.00	126	.224	.302	0	—	0	10	12	2	1.4
1982 Det-A	15	9	.625	35	35	8	1	0	246	220	15	100	132	11.9	3.22	126	.241	.319	0	—	0	23	23	4	2.9
1983 Det-A	19	11	.633	38	38	9	2	0	266^{1}	256	37	99	122	12.2	3.92	100	.256	.327	0	—	0	4	-0	3	0.3
1984 *Det-A	18	8	.692	35	35	7	2	0	233^{1}	231	21	66	144	11.6	3.24	121	.259	.312	0	—	0	19	18	3	2.2
1985 Det-A★	15	13	.536	34	34	8	0	0	238^{2}	190	24	81	109	10.3	3.36	121	.217	.285	0	—	0	21	19	0	2.0
1986 Det-A	5	10	.333	20	20	2	0	0	116	122	15	53	56	14.0	4.66	89	.268	.350	0	—	0	-6	-7	1	-0.5
1987 *Det-A	9	7	.563	30	21	0	0	0	134^{2}	148	22	76	93	15.6	5.61	75	.279	.379	0	—	0	-17	-21	1	-1.7
1988 Cal-A	3	9	.250	22	22	4	1	0	139^{2}	139	18	59	64	13.1	4.38	88	.263	.344	0	—	0	-6	-8	2	-0.5
1989 Cal-A	3	2	.600	19	4	0	0	0	51	53	8	23	21	13.6	5.47	70	.275	.355	0	—	0	-9	-9	0	-0.9
1990 Det-A	10	9	.526	32	23	1	0	0	149^{2}	148	14	77	73	13.6	4.45	89	.263	.353	0	—	0	-9	-8	2	-0.7
1991 Det-A	2	3	.400	17	6	0	0	0	54^{2}	66	9	19	18	14.0	4.94	84	.300	.356	0	—	0	-5	-5	2	-0.4
Atl-N	0	0	—	10	0	0	0	0	24^{1}	29	2	14	9	16.3	5.55	70	.296	.389	1	.200	0	-5	-4	0	-0.4
Bos-A	0	0	—	13	0	0	0	1	22^{1}	21	3	12	12	13.7	4.43	97	.250	.351	0	—	0	-1	-0	0	-0.1
Total 13	125	104	.546	370	300	52	11	1	2080^{1}	1984	218	852	1063	12.5	3.95	102	.253	.330	1	.200	0	24	16	22	4.3
● **JAY PETTIBONE**	Pettibone, Harry Jonathan b: 6/21/57, Mt.Clemens, Mich. BR/TR, 6'4", 182 lbs. Deb: 9/11/83																								
1983 Min-A	0	4	.000	4	4	1	0	0	27	28	8	8	10	12.7	5.33	80	.280	.345	0	—	0	-4	-3	0	-0.3
● **PAUL PETTIT**	Pettit, George William Paul "Lefty" b: 11/29/31, Los Angeles, Cal. BL/TL, 6'2", 195 lbs. Deb: 5/04/51																								
1951 Pit-N	0	0	—	2	0	0	0	0	2^{2}	2	1	1	0	10.1	3.38	125	.200	.273	0	.000	-0	0	0	-0	0.0
1953 Pit-N	1	2	.333	10	5	0	0	0	28	33	1	20	14	17.0	7.71	58	.297	.405	2	.250	1	-11	-10	0	-0.8
Total 2	1	2	.333	12	5	0	0	0	30^{2}	35	2	21	14	16.4	7.34	61	.289	.394	2	.222	1	-10	-10	0	-0.8
● **LEON PETTIT**	Pettit, Leon Arthur "Lefty" b: 6/23/02, Waynesburg, Pa. d: 11/21/74, Columbia, Tenn. BL/TL, 5'10.5", 165 lbs. Deb: 4/18/35																								
1935 Was-A	8	5	.615	41	7	1	0	3	109	129	6	58	45	15.8	4.95	87	.301	.390	2	.080	0	-6	-8	-0	-0.7
1937 Phi-N	0	1	.000	3	1	0	0	0	4	6	1	4	0	22.5	11.25	39	.353	.476	0	—	0	-3	-3	0	-0.3
Total 2	8	6	.571	44	8	1	0	3	113	135	7	62	45	16.0	5.18	84	.303	.393	2	.080	0	-9	-11	-0	-1.0
● **BOB PETTIT**	Pettit, Robert Henry b: 7/19/1861, Williamstown, Mass. d: 11/1/10, Derby, Conn. BL/TR, 5'9", 160 lbs. Deb: 9/03/1887 ♦																								
1887 Chi-N	0	0	—	1	0	0	0	**1**	1	3	0	2	0	45.0	0.00	—	.375	.500	36	.261	0	0	0	0	0.0
● **CHARLIE PETTY**	Petty, Charles E. b: 6/28/1866, Nashville, Tenn. TR , Deb: 7/30/1889																								
1889 Cin-a	2	3	.400	5	5	5	0	0	44	44	3	20	10	14.3	5.52	71	.252	.349	6	.300	1	-8	-8	0	-0.6

YEAR TM/L	W	L	PCT	G	GS	CG	SH	SV	IP	H	HR	BB	SO	RAT	ERA	ERA+	OAV	OOB	BH	AVG	PB	PR	/A	PD	TPI
1893 NY-N	5	2	.714	9	6	4	0	0	54	66	0	28	12	15.8	3.33	140	.292	.373	7	.318	2	8	8	-0	0.9
1894 Was-N	3	8	.273	16	12	8	0	0	103	156	4	32	14	17.2	5.59	94	.345	.399	8	.195	-2	-3	-4	-1	-0.5
Cle-N	0	2	.000	4	3	2	0	0	27	42	4	14	4	19.7	8.67	63	.351	.431	1	.083	-2	-10	-10	-1	-0.9
Yr	3	10	.231	20	15	10	0	0	130	198	8	46	18	17.1	6.23	85	.341	.392	9	.170	-4	-13	-13	-1	-1.4
Total 3	10	15	.400	34	26	19	0	0	228	308	11	94	40	16.6	5.41	90	.317	.388	22	.232	-0	-13	-13	-2	-1.1

● JESSE PETTY

Petty, Jesse Lee "The Silver Fox" b: 11/23/1894, Orr, Okla. d: 10/23/71, St.Paul, Minn. BR/TL, 6', 195 lbs. Deb: 4/14/21

YEAR TM/L	W	L	PCT	G	GS	CG	SH	SV	IP	H	HR	BB	SO	RAT	ERA	ERA+	OAV	OOB	BH	AVG	PB	PR	/A	PD	TPI
1921 Cle-A	0	0	—	4	0	0	0	0	9	10	0	0	0	10.0	2.00	213	.345	.345	0	.000	-0	2	2	1	0.3
1925 Bro-N	9	9	.500	28	22	7	0	0	153	188	15	47	39	13.9	4.88	86	.304	.355	7	.140	-3	-10	-12	-2	-1.5
1926 Bro-N	17	17	.500	38	33	23	1	1	275^2	246	9	79	101	10.7	2.84	135	**.240**	.296	17	.175	-3	30	30	-4	2.4
1927 Bro-N	13	18	.419	42	33	19	2	1	271^2	263	13	53	101	10.6	2.98	133	.254	.293	9	.099	-7	28	30	-3	2.0
1928 Bro-N	15	15	.500	40	31	15	2	1	234	264	18	56	74	12.5	4.04	98	.289	.334	9	.111	-5	-1	-2	-4	-1.1
1929 Pit-N	11	10	.524	36	25	12	1	0	184^1	197	12	42	58	11.7	3.71	129	.277	.317	7	.104	-6	21	22	-2	1.3
1930 Pit-N	1	6	.143	10	7	0	0	1	41^1	67	8	13	16	17.9	8.27	60	.362	.410	1	.083	-1	-15	-15	-0	-1.4
Chi-N	1	3	.250	9	3	0	0	0	39^1	51	2	6	18	13.0	2.97	164	.317	.341	3	.231	0	9	8	-0	0.8
Yr	2	9	.182	19	10	0	0	1	80^2	118	10	19	34	15.3	5.69	87	.339	.373	4	.160	-1	-6	-7	-0	-0.6
Total 7	67	78	.462	207	154	76	6	4	1208^1	1286	77	296	407	11.9	3.68	113	.275	.320	53	.128	-25	63	63	-14	2.8

● PRETZEL PEZZULLO

Pezzullo, John b: 12/10/10, Bridgeport, Conn. d: 5/16/90, Dallas, Tex. BL/TL, 5'11.5", 180 lbs. Deb: 4/18/35

YEAR TM/L	W	L	PCT	G	GS	CG	SH	SV	IP	H	HR	BB	SO	RAT	ERA	ERA+	OAV	OOB	BH	AVG	PB	PR	/A	PD	TPI
1935 Phi-N	3	5	.375	41	7	2	0	1	84^1	115	5	45	24	17.8	6.40	71	.321	.407	6	.250	1	-22	-18	-2	-1.8
1936 Phi-N	0	0	—	1	0	0	0	0	2	1	0	6	0	31.5	4.50	101	.167	.583	0	—	0	-0	0	-0	0.0
Total 2	3	5	.375	42	7	2	0	1	86^1	116	5	51	24	18.1	6.36	71	.319	.412	6	.250	1	-22	-18	-2	-1.8

● JEFF PFEFFER

Pfeffer, Edward Joseph b: 3/4/1888, Seymour, Ill. d: 8/15/72, Chicago, Ill. BR/TR, 6'3", 210 lbs. Deb: 4/16/11 F

YEAR TM/L	W	L	PCT	G	GS	CG	SH	SV	IP	H	HR	BB	SO	RAT	ERA	ERA+	OAV	OOB	BH	AVG	PB	PR	/A	PD	TPI
1911 StL-A	0	0	—	2	0	0	0	0	10	11	0	4	4	13.5	7.20	47	.297	.366	0	.000	-1	-4	-4	-0	-0.4
1913 Bro-N	0	1	.000	5	2	1	0	0	24^1	28	0	13	13	16.6	3.33	99	.311	.421	0	.000	-1	-0	-0	0	-0.1
1914 Bro-N	23	12	.657	43	34	27	3	4	315	264	9	91	135	10.3	1.97	145	.232	.293	23	.198	-1	29	31	-4	3.0
1915 Bro-N	19	14	.576	40	34	26	6	3	291^2	243	8	76	84	10.4	2.10	132	.231	.293	27	.255	5	21	22	-4	2.5
1916 *Bro-N	25	11	.694	41	37	30	6	1	328^2	274	5	63	128	9.7	1.92	140	.230	.278	34	.279	7	26	28	-5	3.7
1917 Bro-N	11	15	.423	30	30	24	3	0	266	225	4	66	115	10.4	2.23	125	.234	.294	13	.130	-5	14	17	-2	1.1
1918 Bro-N	1	0	1.000	1	1	1	1	0	9	2	0	3	1	5.0	0.00	—	.071	.161	1	.250	0	3	3	0	0.5
1919 Bro-N	17	13	.567	30	30	26	4	0	267	270	7	49	92	11.2	2.66	112	.267	.308	20	.206	1	7	9	1	1.2
1920 *Bro-N	16	9	.640	30	28	20	2	0	215	225	5	45	80	11.5	3.01	106	.273	.314	18	.243	1	3	5	-3	0.2
1921 Bro-N	1	5	.167	6	5	2	0	0	31^2	36	0	9	8	13.1	4.55	86	.310	.365	0	.000	-2	-3	-2	0	-0.4
StL-N	9	3	.750	18	13	7	1	0	98^2	115	3	28	22	13.5	4.29	86	.305	.361	4	.138	-1	-6	-7	-2	-0.9
Yr	10	8	.556	24	18	9	1	0	130^1	151	3	37	30	13.3	4.35	86	.306	.360	4	.100	-2	-8	-9	-1	-1.3
1922 StL-N	19	12	.613	44	32	19	1	2	261^1	286	12	58	83	12.2	3.58	108	.279	.324	24	.245	4	15	8	1	1.2
1923 StL-N	8	9	.471	26	18	7	1	0	152^1	171	8	40	32	13.0	4.02	97	.287	.341	7	.127	-4	-0	-2	-1	-0.7
1924 StL-N	4	5	.444	16	12	3	0	0	78	102	3	30	20	15.3	5.31	71	.318	.378	3	.115	-2	-12	-13	-1	-1.5
Pit-N	5	3	.625	15	4	1	0	0	58^2	68	3	17	19	13.0	3.07	125	.293	.341	6	.240	-0	5	5	-1	0.3
Yr	9	8	.529	31	16	4	0	0	136^2	170	6	47	39	14.3	4.35	88	.307	.361	9	.176	-3	-7	-8	-2	-1.2
Total 13	158	112	.585	347	280	194	28	10	2407^1	2320	67	592	836	11.3	2.77	114	.258	.311	180	.206	2	97	103	-21	9.7

● BIG JEFF PFEFFER

Pfeffer, Francis Xavier b: 3/31/1882, Champaign, Ill. d: 12/19/54, Kankakee, Ill. BR/TR, 6'1", 185 lbs. Deb: 4/15/05 F

YEAR TM/L	W	L	PCT	G	GS	CG	SH	SV	IP	H	HR	BB	SO	RAT	ERA	ERA+	OAV	OOB	BH	AVG	PB	PR	/A	PD	TPI
1905 Chi-N	4	4	.500	15	11	9	0	0	101	84	2	36	56	11.0	2.50	120	.240	.318	8	.200	1	6	5	-1	0.5
1906 Bos-N	13	22	.371	35	35	33	4	0	302^1	270	4	114	158	11.9	2.95	91	.246	.325	31	.196	2	-11	-9	2	-0.3
1907 Bos-N	6	8	.429	19	16	12	1	0	144	129	3	61	65	12.3	3.00	85	.253	.341	15	.250	3	-8	-7	-0	-0.5
1908 Bos-N	0	0	—	4	0	0	0	0	10	18	1	8	3	23.4	12.60	19	.383	.473	0	.000	-0	-11	-11	-0	-1.2
1910 Chi-N	1	0	1.000	13	1	1	0	0	41^1	43	1	16	11	13.1	3.27	88	.281	.353	3	.176	1	-1	-2	-1	-0.2
1911 Bos-N	7	5	.583	26	6	4	1	2	97	116	3	57	24	16.1	4.73	81	.301	.391	9	.196	1	-14	-10	0	-0.8
Total 6	31	39	.443	112	69	59	6	2	695^2	660	14	292	317	12.7	3.30	87	.260	.342	66	.204	7	-40	-34	-0	-2.5

● FRED PFEFFER

Pfeffer, Nathaniel Frederick "Fritz" or "Dandelion"
b: 3/17/1860, Louisville, Ky. d: 4/10/32, Chicago, Ill. BR/TR, 5'10.5", 184 lbs. Deb: 5/01/1882 M♦

YEAR TM/L	W	L	PCT	G	GS	CG	SH	SV	IP	H	HR	BB	SO	RAT	ERA	ERA+	OAV	OOB	BH	AVG	PB	PR	/A	PD	TPI
1884 Chi-N	0	0	—	1	0	0	0	0	1	3	0	1	0	36.0	9.00	35	.333	.400	135	.289	0	-1	-1	-0	-0.1
1885 *Chi-N	2	1	.667	5	2	2	0	**2**	31^2	26	1	8	13	9.7	2.56	119	.222	.272	113	.241	1	1	2	-0	0.2
1892 Lou-N	0	0	—	1	0	0	0	0	5	4	0	5	0	16.2	1.80	170	.211	.375	121	.257	0	1	1	0	0.1
1894 Lou-N	0	0	—	1	0	0	0	0	7	8	0	6	0	19.3	2.57	198	.284	.427	126	.308	0	2	2	-0	0.2
Total 4	2	1	.667	8	2	2	0	2	44^2	41	1	20	13	12.5	2.62	130	.237	.319	1671	.255	2	3	4	-1	0.4

● JACK PFIESTER

Pfiester, John Albert "Jack The Giant Killer" (b: John Albert Hagenbush)
b: 5/24/1878, Cincinnati, Ohio d: 9/3/53, Loveland, Ohio BR/TL, 5'11", 180 lbs. Deb: 9/08/03

YEAR TM/L	W	L	PCT	G	GS	CG	SH	SV	IP	H	HR	BB	SO	RAT	ERA	ERA+	OAV	OOB	BH	AVG	PB	PR	/A	PD	TPI
1903 Pit-N	0	3	.000	3	3	2	0	0	19	26	0	10	15	18.0	6.16	53	.321	.409	0	.000	-1	-6	-6	-0	-0.6
1904 Pit-N	1	1	.500	3	2	1	0	0	20	28	0	9	6	16.6	7.20	38	.318	.381	2	.286	1	-10	-10	0	-0.8
1906 *Chi-N	20	8	.714	31	29	20	4	0	250^2	173	3	63	153	8.9	1.51	175	.194	.258	4	.048	-8	31	32	-1	2.7
1907 *Chi-N	14	9	.609	30	22	13	3	0	195	143	1	48	90	9.0	**1.15**	**216**	.207	.263	6	.094	-3	29	29	-2	2.8
1908 *Chi-N	12	10	.545	33	29	18	3	0	252	204	1	70	117	10.2	2.00	118	.223	.287	8	.101	-4	10	10	-3	0.3
1909 Chi-N	17	6	.739	29	25	13	5	0	196^2	179	1	49	73	10.7	2.43	105	.240	.291	11	.169	0	4	3	3	0.6
1910 *Chi-N	6	3	.667	14	13	5	2	0	100^1	82	0	26	34	9.8	1.79	161	.225	.279	3	.091	-2	14	12	-0	1.0
1911 Chi-N	1	4	.200	6	5	3	0	0	33^2	34	0	18	15	14.4	4.01	83	.262	.360	2	.182	0	-2	-3	1	-0.2
Total 8	71	44	.617	149	128	75	17	0	1067^1	869	6	293	503	10.1	2.02	128	.223	.284	36	.103	-15	69	67	-3	5.8

● DAN PFISTER

Pfister, Daniel Albin b: 12/20/36, Plainfield, N.J. BR/TR, 6', 187 lbs. Deb: 9/09/61

YEAR TM/L	W	L	PCT	G	GS	CG	SH	SV	IP	H	HR	BB	SO	RAT	ERA	ERA+	OAV	OOB	BH	AVG	PB	PR	/A	PD	TPI
1961 KC-A	0	0	—	2	0	0	0	0	2^1	5	2	4	3	34.7	15.43	27	.417	.563	0	—	0	-3	-3	-0	-0.3
1962 KC-A	4	14	.222	41	25	2	0	1	196^1	175	27	106	123	13.3	4.54	92	.238	.341	12	.185	-1	-12	-8	1	-0.8
1963 KC-A	1	0	1.000	3	1	0	0	0	9^1	8	1	3	9	11.6	1.93	199	.229	.308	0	.000	-0	2	2	0	0.2
1964 KC-A	1	5	.167	19	3	0	0	0	41^1	50	10	29	21	18.5	6.53	58	.311	.434	0	.000	-0	-13	-12	-0	-1.3
Total 4	6	19	.240	65	29	2	0	1	249^1	238	40	142	156	14.3	4.87	84	.252	.359	12	.162	-2	-27	-22	1	-2.2

● BILL PFLANN

Pflann, William F. b: Brooklyn, N.Y. 6', 205 lbs. Deb: 6/16/1894

YEAR TM/L	W	L	PCT	G	GS	CG	SH	SV	IP	H	HR	BB	SO	RAT	ERA	ERA+	OAV	OOB	BH	AVG	PB	PR	/A	PD	TPI
1894 Cin-N	0	1	.000	1	1	0	0	0	3	10	1	4	0	42.0	27.00	21	.537	.618	0	.000	-0	-7	-7	0	-0.5

● LEE PFUND

Pfund, Le Roy Herbert b: 10/10/18, Oak Park, Ill. BR/TR, 6'1", 185 lbs. Deb: 4/21/45

YEAR TM/L	W	L	PCT	G	GS	CG	SH	SV	IP	H	HR	BB	SO	RAT	ERA	ERA+	OAV	OOB	BH	AVG	PB	PR	/A	PD	TPI
1945 Bro-N	3	2	.600	15	10	2	0	0	62^1	69	4	35	27	15.7	5.20	72	.274	.373	4	.182	0	-10	-10	1	-0.9

● BILL PHEBUS

Phebus, Raymond William b: 8/9/09, Cherryvale, Kan. d: 10/11/89, Bartow, Fla. BR/TR, 5'9", 170 lbs. Deb: 9/06/36

YEAR TM/L	W	L	PCT	G	GS	CG	SH	SV	IP	H	HR	BB	SO	RAT	ERA	ERA+	OAV	OOB	BH	AVG	PB	PR	/A	PD	TPI
1936 Was-A	0	0	—	2	1	0	0	0	7^1	4	1	4	4	11.0	2.45	195	.114	.225	0	.000	0	2	2	-0	0.2
1937 Was-A	3	2	.600	6	5	4	1	1	40^2	33	2	24	12	13.1	2.21	200	.232	.351	0	.000	1	11	10	-1	1.0
1938 Was-A	0	0	—	5	0	0	0	1	6^1	9	1	7	2	22.7	11.37	40	.346	.485	0	.000	-0	-5	-5	0	-0.4
Total 3	3	2	.600	13	6	4	1	2	54^1	46	4	35	18	13.9	3.31	135	.227	.349	0	.000	1	8	7	-1	0.8

● RAY PHELPS

Phelps, Raymond Clifford b: 12/11/03, Dunlap, Tenn. d: 7/7/71, Fort Pierce, Fla. BR/TR, 6'2", 200 lbs. Deb: 4/23/30

YEAR TM/L	W	L	PCT	G	GS	CG	SH	SV	IP	H	HR	BB	SO	RAT	ERA	ERA+	OAV	OOB	BH	AVG	PB	PR	/A	PD	TPI
1930 Bro-N	14	7	.667	36	24	11	2	0	179^2	198	21	52	64	12.7	4.11	120	.280	.332	10	.147	-2	17	16	2	1.4
1931 Bro-N	7	9	.438	28	26	3	1	0	149^1	184	3	44	50	14.0	5.00	76	.306	.357	8	.157	-1	-19	-20	0	-2.0
1932 Bro-N	4	5	.444	20	8	4	1	0	79^1	101	5	27	21	14.9	5.90	65	.323	.382	2	.087	-1	-18	-18	0	-1.8
1935 Chi-A	4	8	.333	27	17	4	0	1	125	126	10	55	38	13.2	4.82	96	.262	.341	5	.122	-4	-5	-3	2	-0.5

YEAR	TM/L	W	L	PCT	G	GS	CG	SH	SV	IP	H	HR	BB	SO	RAT	ERA	ERA+	OAV	OOB	BH	AVG	PB	PR	/A	PD	TPI
1936	Chi-A	4	6	.400	15	4	2	0	0	68^{2}	91	9	42	17	17.7	6.03	86	.331	.423	6	.231	1	-8	-6	1	-0.4
Total	5	33	35	.485	126	79	24	4	1	602	700	48	220	190	14.0	4.93	90	.294	.358	31	.148	-8	-32	-31	5	-3.3
● **DEACON PHILLIPPE**	Phillippe, Charles Louis b: 5/23/1872, Rural Retreat, Va. d: 3/30/52, Avalon, Pa. BR/TR, 6'0.5", 180 lbs. Deb: 4/21/1899																									
1899	Lou-N	21	17	.553	42	38	33	2	1	321	331	10	64	68	11.3	3.17	122	.266	.306	26	.203	-2	24	25	-0	2.1
1900	*Pit-N	20	13	.606	38	33	29	1	0	279	274	7	42	75	**10.5**	2.84	128	.256	**.290**	19	.181	-4	27	25	-2	1.8
1901	Pit-N	22	12	.647	37	32	30	1	2	296	274	7	38	103	9.8	2.22	147	.244	.275	26	.230	5	**36**	34	3	4.3
1902	Pit-N	20	9	.690	31	30	29	5	0	272	265	1	26	122	9.7	2.05	133	.255	.275	25	.221	2	22	21	-2	2.2
1903	*Pit-N	25	9	.735	36	33	31	4	2	289^{1}	269	4	29	123	**9.4**	2.43	133	.241	**.263**	26	.210	2	27	26	-2	2.5
1904	Pit-N	10	10	.500	21	19	17	3	1	166^{2}	183	1	26	82	11.4	3.24	85	.272	.302	8	.123	-4	-9	-9	-0	-1.3
1905	Pit-N	20	13	.606	38	33	25	5	0	279	235	0	48	133	9.5	2.19	137	.233	.274	9	.093	-5	25	25	-1	2.1
1906	Pit-N	15	10	.600	33	24	19	3	0	218^{2}	216	3	26	90	10.0	2.47	108	.252	.276	20	.244	3	4	5	-1	0.7
1907	Pit-N	14	11	.560	35	26	17	1	2	214	214	2	36	61	10.7	2.61	93	.264	.300	12	.185	1	-3	-4	-2	-0.5
1908	Pit-N	0	0	—	5	0	0	0	0	12	20	0	3	1	17.3	11.25	20	.357	.390	1	.250	0	-12	-12	-1	-1.2
1909	*Pit-N	8	3	.727	22	12	7	1	0	131^{2}	121	2	14	38	9.5	2.32	117	.253	.280	3	.071	-3	4	6	-2	0.0
1910	Pit-N	14	2	.875	31	8	5	1	4	121^{2}	111	4	9	30	9.1	2.29	135	.239	.258	9	.220	1	10	11	-3	0.9
1911	Pit-N	0	0	—	3	0	0	0	0	6	5	0	2	3	10.5	7.50	46	.238	.304	1	1.000	1	-3	-3	0	-0.1
Total	13	189	109	.634	372	288	242	27	12	2607	2518	41	363	929	10.1	2.59	120	.253	.283	185	.189	-2	153	150	-14	13.5
● **BUZ PHILLIPS**	Phillips, Albert Abernathy b: 5/25/04, Newton, N.C. d: 11/6/64, Baltimore, Md. BR/TR, 5'11.5", 185 lbs. Deb: 8/05/30																									
1930	Phi-N	0	0	—	14	1	0	0	0	43^{2}	68	6	18	9	17.9	8.04	68	.354	.412	6	.462	3	-15	-12	-1	-0.9
● **RED PHILLIPS**	Phillips, Clarence Lemuel b: 11/3/08, Pauls Valley, Okla. d: 2/1/88, Wichita, Kan. BR/TR, 6'3.5", 195 lbs. Deb: 7/24/34																									
1934	Det-A	2	0	1.000	7	1	1	0	1	23^{1}	31	1	16	3	18.1	6.17	71	.316	.412	3	.250	1	-4	-5	-1	-0.4
1936	Det-A	2	4	.333	22	6	3	0	0	87^{1}	124	12	22	15	15.0	6.49	76	.332	.370	10	.303	2	-14	-15	-0	-1.2
Total	2	4	4	.500	29	7	4	0	1	110^{2}	155	13	38	18	15.7	6.42	75	.329	.379	13	.289	3	-18	-20	-1	-1.6
● **JACK PHILLIPS**	Phillips, Jack Dorn "Stretch" b: 9/6/21, Clarence, N.Y. BR/TR, 6'4", 193 lbs. Deb: 8/22/47 ♦																									
1950	Pit-N	0	0	—	1	0	0	0	0	5	7	0	1	2	14.4	7.20	61	.333	.364	61	.293	0	-2	-2	0	-0.1
● **JACK PHILLIPS**	Phillips, John Stephen b: 5/24/19, St.Louis, Mo. d: 6/16/58, St.Louis, Mo. BR/TR, 6'1", 185 lbs. Deb: 7/13/45 ♦																									
1945	NY-N	0	0	—	1	0	0	0	0	4^{1}	5	1	5	0	22.8	10.38	38	.313	.500	1	.500	0	-3	-3	-0	-0.3
● **ED PHILLIPS**	Phillips, Norman Edwin b: 9/20/44, Ardmore, Okla. BR/TR, 6'1", 190 lbs. Deb: 4/09/70																									
1970	Bos-A	0	2	.000	18	0	0	0	0	23^{2}	29	4	10	23	15.6	5.32	74	.312	.390	0	.000	-0	-4	-4	-1	-0.5
● **TOM PHILLIPS**	Phillips, Thomas Gerald b: 4/5/1889, Phillipsburg, Pa. d: 4/12/29, Phillipsburg, Pa. BR/TR, 6'2", 190 lbs. Deb: 9/13/15																									
1915	StL-A	1	3	.250	5	4	1	0	0	27^{1}	28	0	12	5	13.8	2.96	97	.283	.372	1	.111	-1	-0	-0	-1	-0.2
1919	Cle-A	3	2	.600	22	3	2	0	0	55	55	2	34	18	15.1	2.95	114	.272	.385	4	.364	1	**2**	**2**	-1	0.2
1921	Was-A	1	0	1.000	1	1	1	0	0	9	9	0	3	2	12.0	2.00	206	.290	.353	0	.000	-1	2	2	-0	0.1
1922	Was-A	3	7	.300	17	7	2	1	0	70	72	2	22	19	12.6	4.89	79	.273	.338	3	.150	-1	-7	-8	-1	-0.9
Total	4	8	12	.400	45	15	6	1	0	161^{1}	164	4	71	44	13.6	3.74	95	.275	.361	8	.186	-1	-3	-3	-3	-0.8
● **BILL PHILLIPS**	Phillips, William Corcoran "Whoa Bill" or "Silver Bill" b: 11/9/1868, Allenport, Pa. d: 10/25/41, Charleroi, Pa. BR/TR, 5'11", 180 lbs. Deb: 8/11/1890 M																									
1890	Pit-N	1	9	.100	10	10	9	0	0	82	123	8	29	25	16.8	7.57	44	.336	.386	11	.239	1	-36	-39	0	-2.9
1895	Cin-N	6	7	.462	18	9	6	0	2	109	126	6	44	15	14.6	6.03	83	.285	.359	15	.313	2	-15	-13	1	-0.8
1899	Cin-N	17	9	.654	33	27	18	1	1	227^{2}	234	3	71	43	12.6	3.32	118	.265	.330	12	.130	-5	14	15	-0	0.9
1900	Cin-N	9	11	.450	29	24	17	3	0	208^{1}	229	5	67	51	13.3	4.28	86	.279	.342	13	.165	-4	-13	-14	6	-1.0
1901	Cin-N	14	18	.438	37	36	29	1	0	281^{1}	364	7	67	109	14.1	4.64	69	.311	.353	22	.202	2	-41	-45	5	-3.5
1902	Cin-N	16	16	.500	33	33	30	0	0	269	267	3	55	85	11.0	2.51	119	.259	.301	39	.342	10	8	15	3	3.1
1903	Cin-N	7	6	.538	16	13	11	1	0	118^{1}	134	0	30	46	13.0	3.35	106	.279	.330	10	.175	-2	-1	3	2	0.3
Total	7	70	76	.479	176	152	120	6	3	1295^{2}	1477	32	363	374	13.2	4.09	87	.284	.338	122	.224	3	-85	-77	16	-3.9
● **TAYLOR PHILLIPS**	Phillips, William Taylor "Tay" b: 6/18/33, Atlanta, Ga. BL/TL, 5'11", 185 lbs. Deb: 6/08/56																									
1956	Mil-N	5	3	.625	23	6	3	0	2	87^{2}	69	6	33	36	11.2	2.26	153	.223	.311	0	.000	-2	15	12	2	1.3
1957	Mil-N	3	2	.600	27	6	0	0	2	73	82	3	40	36	15.2	5.55	63	.300	.392	2	.100	-1	-14	-17	0	-1.7
1958	Chi-N	7	10	.412	39	27	5	1	1	170^{1}	178	22	79	102	13.9	4.76	82	.266	.349	3	.056	-4	-15	-16	1	-1.8
1959	Chi-N	0	2	.000	7	2	0	0	0	16^{2}	22	3	11	5	18.9	7.56	52	.319	.427	0	.000	-0	-7	-7	0	-0.7
	Phi-N	1	4	.200	32	3	1	0	1	63	72	4	31	35	15.3	5.00	82	.303	.392	1	.091	-1	-7	-6	0	-0.6
	Yr	1	6	.143	39	5	1	0	1	79^{2}	94	7	42	40	15.8	5.54	74	.303	.393	1	.067	-1	-14	-13	1	-1.3
1960	Phi-N	0	1	.000	10	1	0	0	0	14	21	2	4	6	16.7	8.36	46	.356	.406	0	.000	-0	-7	-7	-0	-0.7
1963	Chi-A	0	0	—	9	0	0	0	0	14	16	2	13	13	19.3	10.29	34	.302	.448	0	.000	-0	-10	-11	0	-1.1
Total	6	16	22	.421	147	45	9	1	6	438^{2}	460	42	211	233	14.2	4.82	78	.275	.364	6	.053	-9	-46	-51	4	-5.3
● **TOM PHOEBUS**	Phoebus, Thomas Harold b: 4/7/42, Baltimore, Md. BR/TR, 5'8", 185 lbs. Deb: 9/15/66																									
1966	Bal-A	2	1	.667	3	3	2	2	0	22	16	0	6	17	9.0	1.23	271	.213	.272	1	.167	0	5	5	-0	0.6
1967	Bal-A	14	9	.609	33	33	7	4	0	208	177	16	114	179	12.6	3.33	95	.227	.326	11	.145	1	-2	-4	-2	-0.6
1968	Bal-A	15	15	.500	36	36	9	3	0	240^{2}	186	10	105	193	11.0	2.62	112	.212	.299	15	.183	3	10	8	-0	1.3
1969	Bal-A	14	7	.667	35	33	6	2	0	202	180	23	87	117	12.1	3.52	101	.241	.324	15	.200	2	2	1	-1	0.2
1970	*Bal-A	5	5	.500	27	21	3	0	0	135	106	11	62	72	11.6	3.07	119	.219	.315	7	.163	-0	10	9	0	0.9
1971	SD-N	3	11	.214	29	21	2	0	0	133^{1}	144	14	64	80	14.2	4.45	74	.280	.363	6	.167	1	-15	-17	-1	-1.7
1972	SD-N	0	1	.000	1	1	0	0	0	5^{2}	3	2	6	8	14.3	7.94	41	.150	.346	0	.000	-0	-3	-3	0	-0.3
	Chi-N	3	3	.500	37	1	0	0	6	83^{1}	76	9	45	59	13.3	3.78	101	.247	.346	2	.133	-1	-3	0	1	0.0
	Yr	3	4	.429	38	2	0	0	6	89	79	11	51	67	13.3	4.04	93	.241	.346	2	.118	-1	-6	-3	1	-0.3
Total	7	56	52	.519	201	149	29	11	6	1030	888	85	489	725	12.2	3.33	100	.233	.324	57	.170	5	4	-1	-3	0.4
● **BILL PHYLE**	Phyle, William Joseph b: 6/25/1875, Duluth, Minn. d: 8/6/53, Los Angeles, Cal. TR , Deb: 9/17/1898 ♦																									
1898	Chi-N	2	1	.667	3	3	3	2	0	23	24	0	6	4	12.5	0.78	458	.267	.327	1	.111	-0	7	7	-1	0.7
1899	Chi-N	1	8	.111	10	9	9	0	1	83^{2}	92	2	29	10	13.4	4.20	89	.279	.344	6	.176	-2	-3	-4	1	-0.5
1901	NY-N	7	10	.412	24	19	16	0	1	168^{2}	208	2	54	62	14.2	4.27	77	.301	.356	12	.182	-1	-18	-18	1	-1.7
Total	3	10	19	.345	37	31	28	2	2	275^{1}	324	4	89	76	13.9	3.96	88	.292	.350	32	.176	-3	-14	-15	2	-1.5
● **DOUG PIATT**	Piatt, Douglas William b: 9/26/65, Beaver, Pa. BL/TR, 6'1", 185 lbs. Deb: 6/11/91																									
1991	Mon-N	0	0	—	21	0	0	0	0	34^{2}	29	3	17	29	11.9	2.60	139	.230	.322	0	.000	-0	4	4	0	0.4
● **WILEY PIATT**	Piatt, Wiley Harold "Iron Man" b: 7/13/1874, Blue Creek, Ohio d: 9/20/46, Cincinnati, Ohio BL/TL, 5'10", 175 lbs. Deb: 4/22/1898																									
1898	Phi-N	24	14	.632	39	37	33	**6**	0	306	285	2	97	121	11.8	3.18	108	.245	.314	32	.262	3	15	9	-2	1.0
1899	Phi-N	23	15	.605	39	38	31	2	0	305	323	6	86	89	12.7	3.45	107	.271	.332	33	.270	4	14	8	-5	0.7
1900	Phi-N	9	10	.474	22	20	16	1	0	160^{2}	194	5	71	47	15.7	4.71	77	.298	.380	17	.250	1	-18	-19	-3	-1.8
1901	Phi-A	5	12	.294	18	16	15	0	1	140	176	4	60	45	15.5	4.63	82	.303	.374	13	.224	0	-15	-13	-4	-1.5
	Chi-A	4	2	.667	7	6	4	1	0	51^{2}	42	2	14	19	10.3	2.79	125	.220	.284	2	.118	-1	5	4	-1	0.1
	Yr	9	14	.391	25	22	19	1	1	191^{2}	218	6	74	64	13.9	4.13	89	.281	.346	15	.200	-1	-10	-9	-5	-1.4
1902	Chi-A	12	12	.500	32	30	22	2	0	246	263	3	66	96	12.3	3.51	96	.274	.326	17	.200	1	2	-3	-3	-0.5
1903	Bos-N	9	14	.391	25	23	18	0	0	181	198	5	61	100	13.1	3.18	101	.280	.340	16	.225	1	2	1	-3	0.0
Total	6	86	79	.521	182	170	139	12	1	1390^{1}	1481	27	455	517	13.0	3.61	97	.272	.337	130	.239	10	4	-15	-20	-2.0

YEAR TM/L	W	L	PCT	G	GS	CG	SH	SV	IP	H	HR	BB	SO	RAT	ERA	ERA+	OAV	OOB	BH	AVG	PB	PR	/A	PD	TPI
● **HIPOLITO PICHARDO**	Pichardo, Hipolito b: 8/22/69, Jicome Esperanza, D.R. BR/TR, 6'1", 160 lbs. Deb: 4/21/92																								
1992 KC-A	9	6	.600	31	24	1	1	0	143^{2}	148	9	49	59	12.5	3.95	101	.267	.330	0	—	0	-0	1	0	0.0
● **RON PICHE**	Piche, Ronald Jacques b: 5/22/35, Verdun, Que., Canada BR/TR, 5'11", 165 lbs. Deb: 5/30/60 C																								
1960 Mil-N	3	5	.375	37	0	0	0	9	48	48	3	23	38	13.9	3.56	96	.258	.349	0	.000	-0	1	-1	-1	-0.1
1961 Mil-N	2	2	.500	12	1	1	0	1	23^{1}	20	1	16	16	13.9	3.47	108	.238	.360	0	.000	-1	1	1	0	0.0
1962 Mil-N	3	2	.600	14	8	2	0	0	52	54	6	29	28	14.9	4.85	78	.273	.374	1	.056	-1	-5	-6	1	-0.7
1963 Mil-N	1	1	.500	37	1	0	0	0	53	53	4	25	40	13.2	3.40	95	.256	.336	0	.000	-1	-1	-1	1	0.0
1965 Cal-A	0	3	.000	14	1	0	0	0	19^{2}	20	5	12	14	14.6	6.86	50	.267	.368	0	.000	-0	-7	-8	0	-0.8
1966 StL-N	1	3	.250	20	0	0	0	2	25^{1}	21	4	18	21	14.2	4.26	84	.214	.342	0	.000	-0	-2	-2	-0	-0.3
Total 6	10	16	.385	134	11	3	0	12	221^{1}	216	23	123	157	14.1	4.19	84	.255	.354	1	.024	-3	-13	-16	1	-1.9
● **CHARLIE PICKETT**	Pickett, Charles Albert b: 3/1/1883, Delaware, Ohio d: 5/20/69, Springfield, Ohio BR/TR, 6'1", 175 lbs. Deb: 6/21/10																								
1910 StL-N	0	0	—	2	0	0	0	0	6	7	0	2	2	13.5	1.50	199	.280	.333	0	—	0	1	1	-0	0.1
● **CLARENCE PICKREL**	Pickrel, Clarence Douglas b: 3/28/11, Grenta, Va. d: 11/4/83, Rocky Mount, Va. BR/TR, 6'1", 180 lbs. Deb: 4/22/33																								
1933 Phi-N	1	0	1.000	9	0	0	0	0	13^{2}	20	0	3	6	15.8	3.95	97	.357	.400	0	.000	-0	-1	-0	-1	-0.1
1934 Bos-N	0	0	—	10	1	0	0	0	16	24	0	7	9	17.4	5.06	76	.333	.392	0	.000	-0	-2	-2	-1	-0.3
Total 2	1	0	1.000	19	1	0	0	0	29^{2}	44	0	10	15	16.7	4.55	85	.344	.396	0	.000	-0	-3	-2	-1	-0.4
● **JEFF PICO**	Pico, Jeffrey Mark b: 2/12/66, Antioch, Cal. BR/TR, 6'1", 190 lbs. Deb: 5/31/88																								
1988 Chi-N	6	7	.462	29	13	3	2	1	112^{2}	108	6	37	57	11.6	4.15	87	.252	.312	5	.147	-0	-9	-7	-0	-0.8
1989 Chi-N	3	1	.750	53	5	0	0	2	90^{2}	99	8	31	38	12.9	3.77	100	.278	.336	1	.100	-1	-3	-0	1	0.1
1990 Chi-N	4	4	.500	31	8	0	0	2	92	120	7	37	37	15.5	4.79	85	.321	.383	6	.273	2	-10	-7	1	-0.4
Total 3	13	12	.520	113	26	3	2	5	295^{1}	327	21	105	132	13.2	4.24	90	.282	.343	12	.182	1	-22	-14	2	-1.1
● **MARIO PICONE**	Picone, Mario Peter "Babe" b: 7/5/26, Brooklyn, N.Y. BR/TR, 5'11", 180 lbs. Deb: 9/27/47																								
1947 NY-N	0	0	—	2	1	0	0	0	7	10	1	2	1	15.4	7.71	53	.345	.387	1	.500	1	-3	-3	0	-0.2
1952 NY-N	0	1	.000	2	1	0	0	0	9	11	2	5	3	16.0	7.00	53	.306	.390	0	.000	-0	-3	-3	0	-0.3
1954 NY-N	0	0	—	5	0	0	0	0	13^{2}	13	1	11	6	15.8	5.27	77	.283	.421	0	.000	0	-2	-2	-0	-0.2
Cin-N	0	1	.000	4	1	0	0	0	10^{1}	9	3	7	1	13.9	6.10	69	.243	.364	0	.000	0	-2	-2	0	-0.2
Yr	0	1	.000	9	1	0	0	0	24	22	4	18	7	15.0	5.63	73	.265	.396	0	.000	0	-4	-4	0	-0.4
Total 3	0	2	.000	13	3	0	0	0	40	43	7	25	11	15.3	6.30	64	.291	.393	1	.167	1	-10	-10	1	-0.9
● **AL PIECHOTA**	Piechota, Aloysius Edward "Pie" b: 1/19/14, Chicago, Ill. BR/TR, 6', 195 lbs. Deb: 5/07/40																								
1940 Bos-N	2	5	.286	21	8	2	0	0	61	68	6	41	18	16.1	5.75	65	.278	.381	4	.200	1	-13	-14	-0	-1.3
1941 Bos-N	0	0	—	1	0	0	0	0	1	0	0	1	0	9.0	0.00	—	.000	.250	0	—	0	0	0	-0	0.0
Total 2	2	5	.286	22	8	2	0	0	62	68	6	42	18	16.0	5.66	66	.274	.379	4	.200	1	-13	-13	-0	-1.3
● **CY PIEH**	Pieh, Edwin John b: 9/29/1886, Waunakee, Wis. d: 9/12/45, Jacksonville, Fla BR/TR, 6'2", 190 lbs. Deb: 9/06/13																								
1913 NY-A	1	0	1.000	4	0	0	0	0	10^{1}	10	0	7	6	14.8	4.35	69	.250	.362	1	.250	0	-2	-2	1	0.0
1914 NY-A	4	4	.500	18	4	1	0	0	62^{1}	68	6	29	24	14.0	5.05	55	.289	.367	2	.118	-0	-16	-16	-1	-1.8
1915 NY-A	4	5	.444	21	8	3	2	0	94	78	2	39	46	11.7	2.87	102	.234	.324	2	.067	-3	1	1	0	-0.3
Total 3	9	9	.500	43	12	4	2	0	166^{2}	156	8	75	76	12.7	3.78	76	.257	.343	5	.098	-3	-17	-17	-0	-2.1
● **ED PIERCE**	Pierce, Edward John b: 10/6/68, Arcadia, Cal. BL/TL, 6'1", 185 lbs. Deb: 9/06/92																								
1992 KC-A	0	0	—	2	1	0	0	0	5^{1}	9	1	4	3	21.9	3.38	118	.429	.520	0	—	0	0	0	0	0.0
● **RAY PIERCE**	Pierce, Raymond Lester "Lefty" b: 6/6/1897, Emporia, Kan. d: 5/4/63, Denver, Colo. BL/TL, 5'7", 156 lbs. Deb: 5/12/24																								
1924 Chi-N	0	0	—	6	0	0	0	0	7^{1}	7	2	4	2	13.5	7.36	53	.269	.367	0	—	0	-3	-3	-0	-0.3
1925 Phi-N	5	4	.556	23	8	4	0	0	90	134	7	24	18	15.9	5.50	87	.356	.397	5	.179	-0	-12	-7	0	-0.7
1926 Phi-N	2	7	.222	37	7	1	0	0	84^{2}	128	3	35	18	17.4	5.63	74	.348	.406	3	.125	-2	-17	-14	-1	-1.6
Total 3	7	11	.389	66	15	5	0	0	182	269	12	63	38	16.5	5.64	79	.349	.400	8	.154	-2	-32	-24	-1	-2.6
● **TONY PIERCE**	Pierce, Tony Michael b: 1/29/46, Brunswick, Ga. BR/TL, 6'1", 190 lbs. Deb: 4/14/67																								
1967 KC-A	3	4	.429	49	6	0	0	7	97^{2}	79	6	30	61	10.5	3.04	105	.221	.290	0	.000	-2	2	2	-1	-0.2
1968 Oak-A	1	2	.333	17	3	0	0	1	32^{2}	39	3	10	16	13.8	3.86	73	.295	.350	0	.000	-1	-3	-4	1	-0.4
Total 2	4	6	.400	66	9	0	0	8	130^{1}	118	9	40	77	11.3	3.25	95	.241	.306	0	.000	-3	-1	-2	-1	-0.6
● **BILLY PIERCE**	Pierce, Walter William b: 4/2/27, Detroit, Mich. BL/TL, 5'10", 160 lbs. Deb: 6/01/45																								
1945 Det-A	0	0	—	5	0	0	0	0	10	6	1	10	10	15.3	1.80	195	.182	.386	0	.000	-0	2	2	0	0.2
1948 Det-A	3	0	1.000	22	5	0	0	0	55^{1}	47	5	51	36	16.1	6.34	69	.234	.391	5	.294	2	-13	-12	0	-1.0
1949 Chi-A	7	15	.318	32	26	8	0	0	171^{2}	145	11	112	95	13.5	3.88	108	.228	.344	9	.176	-1	6	6	1	0.6
1950 Chi-A	12	16	.429	33	29	15	1	1	219^{1}	189	11	137	118	13.5	3.98	113	.228	.339	20	.260	4	15	12	-2	1.4
1951 Chi-A	15	14	.517	37	28	18	1	2	240^{1}	237	14	73	113	11.6	3.03	133	.258	.313	16	.203	-0	29	27	-1	2.6
1952 Chi-A	15	12	.556	33	32	14	4	1	255^{1}	214	12	79	144	10.4	2.57	142	.227	.289	17	.187	0	31	31	0	3.3
1953 Chi-A★	18	12	.600	40	33	19	7	3	271^{1}	216	20	102	**186**	10.6	2.72	148	**.218**	.292	11	.126	-4	**38**	**39**	-2	3.4
1954 Chi-A	9	10	.474	36	26	12	4	3	188^{2}	179	15	86	148	12.8	3.48	107	.249	.332	11	.193	0	5	5	-2	0.4
1955 Chi-A★	15	10	.600	33	26	16	6	1	205^{2}	162	16	64	157	**10.0**	**1.97**	**200**	.213	**.277**	12	.171	-1	**45**	**45**	-1	**4.7**
1956 Chi-A★	20	9	.690	35	33	**21**	1	1	276^{1}	261	24	100	192	11.9	3.32	123	.249	.316	16	.157	-4	26	24	-3	1.7
1957 Chi-A★	**20**	12	.625	37	34	**16**	4	2	257	228	18	71	171	10.5	3.26	115	.234	.287	17	.172	-2	15	14	0	1.2
1958 Chi-A☆	17	11	.607	35	32	**19**	3	2	245	204	33	66	144	10.0	2.68	136	.227	.280	17	.205	2	30	26	-3	2.7
1959 *Chi-A☆	14	15	.483	34	33	12	2	0	224	217	26	62	114	11.3	3.62	104	.253	.306	13	.191	3	6	4	0	0.6
1960 Chi-A	14	7	.667	32	30	8	1	0	196^{1}	201	24	46	108	11.3	3.62	104	.266	.308	12	.179	1	5	3	-1	0.3
1961 Chi-A☆	10	9	.526	39	28	5	1	3	180	190	17	54	106	12.3	3.80	103	.275	.328	8	.143	-2	4	2	-0	0.0
1962 *SF-N	16	6	.727	30	23	7	2	1	162^{1}	147	19	35	76	10.3	3.49	109	.239	.284	12	.214	2	8	5	-1	0.6
1963 SF-N	3	11	.214	38	13	3	1	8	99	106	12	20	52	11.5	4.27	75	.272	.309	4	.129	-0	-11	-12	0	-1.2
1964 SF-N	3	0	1.000	34	1	0	0	4	49	40	6	10	29	9.2	2.20	162	.222	.263	3	.333	1	7	7	-1	0.8
Total 18	211	169	.555	585	432	193	38	32	3306^{2}	2989	284	1178	1999	11.4	3.27	119	.240	.307	203	.184	0	250	229	-15	22.3
● **BILL PIERCY**	Piercy, William Benton "Wild Bill" b: 5/2/1896, ElMonte, Cal. d: 8/28/51, Long Beach, Cal. BR/TR, 6'1.5", 170 lbs. Deb: 10/03/17																								
1917 NY-A	0	1	.000	1	1	1	0	0	9	9	0	2	4	11.0	3.00	90	.257	.297	0	.000	0	-0	-0	-0	0.0
1921 *NY-A	5	4	.556	14	10	5	1	0	81^{2}	82	4	28	35	12.9	2.98	142	.263	.337	6	.214	0	12	11	-0	1.1
1922 Bos-A	3	9	.250	29	12	7	1	0	121^{1}	140	2	62	24	15.4	4.67	88	.304	.394	5	.147	-1	-8	-8	2	-0.6
1923 Bos-A	8	17	.320	30	24	11	0	0	187^{1}	193	5	73	51	13.5	3.41	121	.277	.357	7	.132	-3	12	15	3	1.5
1924 Bos-A	5	7	.417	23	18	3	0	0	121	156	4	66	20	17.3	5.95	73	.335	.429	6	.154	-2	-23	-21	1	-2.0
1926 Chi-N	6	5	.545	19	5	1	0	0	90^{1}	96	1	37	31	13.8	4.48	86	.280	.360	9	.257	1	-7	-6	0	-0.5
Total 6	27	43	.386	116	70	28	2	0	610^{2}	676	16	268	165	14.5	4.26	97	.292	.376	33	.173	-5	-15	-10	7	-0.5
● **MARINO PIERETTI**	Pieretti, Marino Paul "Chick" b: 9/23/20, Lucca, Italy d: 1/30/81, San Francisco, Cal. BR/TR, 5'7", 158 lbs. Deb: 4/19/45																								
1945 Was-A	14	13	.519	44	27	14	3	2	233^{1}	235	3	91	66	12.6	3.32	94	.257	.325	18	.222	2	1	-6	1	-0.3
1946 Was-A	2	2	.500	30	2	1	0	0	62	70	9	40	20	16.3	5.95	56	.292	.397	3	.214	0	-17	-18	1	-1.7
1947 Was-A	2	4	.333	23	10	2	1	0	83^{1}	97	3	47	32	15.8	4.21	88	.287	.377	6	.231	-0	-5	-5	-0	-0.5
1948 Was-A	0	2	.000	8	1	0	0	0	11^{2}	18	1	7	6	19.3	10.80	40	.375	.455	0	.000	-0	-8	-8	-0	-0.8
Chi-A	8	10	.444	21	18	4	0	1	120	117	6	52	28	12.7	4.95	86	.262	.339	7	.179	-1	-9	-9	1	-0.8

YEAR TM/L	W	L	PCT	G	GS	CG	SH	SV	IP	H	HR	BB	SO	RAT	ERA	ERA+	OAV	OOB	BH	AVG	PB	PR	/A	PD	TPI
Yr	8	12	.400	29	19	4	0	1	131^2	135	7	59	34	13.3	5.47	78	.273	.351	7	.171	-1	-17	-18	1	-1.6
1949 Chi-A	4	6	.400	39	9	0	0	4	116	131	10	54	25	14.4	5.51	76	.289	.364	9	.237	1	-17	-17	2	-1.4
1950 Cle-A	0	1	.000	29	1	0	0	1	47^1	45	2	30	11	14.3	4.18	104	.253	.361	2	.286	0	2	1	1	0.2
Total 6	30	38	.441	194	68	21	4	8	673^2	713	34	321	188	13.9	4.53	81	.272	.353	45	.217	2	-52	-63	5	-5.3
● AL PIEROTTI	Pierotti, Albert Felix b: 10/24/1895, Boston, Mass. d: 2/12/64, Everett, Mass. BR/TR, 5'10.5", 195 lbs. Deb: 8/09/20																								
1920 Bos-N	1	1	.500	6	2	2	0	0	25	23	2	9	12	11.5	2.88	106	.250	.317	2	.250	0	1	0	-0	0.0
1921 Bos-N	0	1	.000	2	0	0	0	0	1^2	3	0	3	1	32.4	21.60	17	.375	.545	0	.000	-0	-3	-3	0	-0.3
Total 2	1	2	.333	8	2	2	0	0	26^2	26	2	12	13	12.8	4.05	76	.260	.339	2	.222	-0	-3	-3	-0	-0.3
● BILL PIERRO	Pierro, William Leonard "Wild Bill" b: 4/15/26, Brooklyn, N.Y. BR/TR, 6'1", 155 lbs. Deb: 7/17/50																								
1950 Pit-N	0	2	.000	12	3	0	0	0	29	33	2	28	13	19.6	10.55	42	.289	.438	2	.222	-0	-21	-20	-1	-1.8
● DAVE PIERSON	Pierson, David P. b: 8/20/1855, Wilkes-Barre, Pa. d: 11/11/22, Trenton, N.J. BR/TR, 5'7", 142 lbs. Deb: 4/25/1876 F♦																								
1876 Cin-N	0	1	.000	1	1	0	0	0	0	2	1	0	0	—	∞	—	1.000	1.000	55	.236	-0	-2	-2	0	-0.2
● WILLIAM PIERSON	Pierson, William Morris b: 6/14/1899, Atlantic City, N.J. d: 2/20/59, Atlantic City, N.J BL/TL, 6'2", 180 lbs. Deb: 7/04/18																								
1918 Phi-A	0	1	.000	8	1	0	0	0	21^2	20	0	20	6	17.4	3.32	88	.286	.457	1	.250	-0	-1	-1	-1	-0.2
1919 Phi-A	0	0	—	2	1	0	0	0	7^2	9	0	8	4	20.0	3.52	97	.333	.486	1	.333	0	-0	-0	0	0.0
1924 Phi-A	0	0	—	1	0	0	0	0	2^2	3	0	3	0	20.3	3.38	127	.300	.462	0	—	0	0	0	0	0.0
Total 3	0	1	.000	11	2	0	0	0	32	32	0	31	10	18.3	3.38	94	.299	.464	2	.286	0	-1	-1	-1	-0.2
● GEORGE PIKTUZIS	Piktuzis, George Richard b: 1/3/32, Chicago, Ill. BR/TL, 6'2", 200 lbs. Deb: 4/25/56																								
1956 Chi-N	0	0	—	2	0	0	0	0	5	6	1	2	3	14.4	7.20	52	.333	.400	0	—	0	-2	-2	-0	-0.2
● DUANE PILLETTE	Pillette, Duane Xavier "Dee" b: 7/24/22, Detroit, Mich. BR/TR, 6'3", 205 lbs. Deb: 7/19/49 F																								
1949 NY-A	2	4	.333	12	3	2	0	0	37^1	43	6	19	9	14.9	4.34	93	.299	.380	0	.000	-1	-1	-1	1	-0.1
1950 NY-A	0	0	—	4	0	0	0	0	7	9	0	3	4	15.4	1.29	334	.321	.387	0	—	0	3	2	-0	0.2
StL-A	3	5	.375	24	7	1	0	2	73^2	104	6	44	18	18.3	7.09	70	.337	.423	3	.136	-1	-21	-17	-0	-1.7
Yr	3	5	.375	28	7	1	0	2	80^2	113	6	47	22	18.1	6.58	74	.335	.420	3	.136	-1	-18	-15	-1	-1.5
1951 StL-A	6	14	.300	35	24	6	1	0	191	205	14	115	65	15.3	4.99	88	.276	.376	8	.136	-4	-19	-13	-1	-1.6
1952 StL-A	10	13	.435	30	30	9	1	0	205^1	222	14	55	62	12.4	3.59	109	.274	.325	12	.182	0	2	7	-2	0.6
1953 StL-A	7	13	.350	31	25	5	1	0	166^2	181	16	62	58	13.2	4.48	94	.277	.341	7	.132	-1	-9	-5	-1	-0.7
1954 Bal-A	10	14	.417	25	25	11	1	0	179	158	9	67	66	11.4	3.12	115	.234	.305	7	.132	-1	12	9	3	1.2
1955 Bal-A	0	3	.000	7	5	0	0	0	20^2	31	0	14	13	19.6	6.53	58	.344	.433	1	.167	0	-6	-6	0	-0.6
1956 Phi-N	0	0	—	20	0	0	0	0	23^1	32	2	12	10	17.0	6.56	57	.330	.404	0	.000	-0	-7	-7	-0	-0.8
Total 8	38	66	.365	188	119	34	4	2	904	985	67	391	305	13.9	4.40	93	.277	.352	38	.140	-7	-45	-32	-1	-3.5
● HERMAN PILLETTE	Pillette, Herman Polycarp "Old Folks" b: 12/26/1895, St.Paul, Ore. d: 4/30/60, Sacramento, Cal. BR/TR, 6'2", 190 lbs. Deb: 7/30/17 F																								
1917 Cin-N	0	0	—	1	0	0	0	0	1	4	0	0	0	36.0	18.00	15	.571	.571	0	—	0	-2	-2	-0	-0.2
1922 Det-A	19	12	.613	40	37	18	4	1	274^2	270	6	95	71	12.5	2.85	136	.258	.328	17	.172	-3	36	31	3	3.1
1923 Det-A	14	19	.424	47	36	14	0	1	250^1	280	7	83	64	13.3	3.85	100	.288	.347	21	.247	4	4	0	4	0.8
1924 Det-A	1	1	.500	19	3	1	0	1	37^2	46	1	14	13	15.1	4.78	86	.297	.366	4	.364	1	-2	-3	0	-0.2
Total 4	34	32	.515	107	76	33	4	3	563^2	600	14	192	148	13.0	3.45	113	.275	.340	42	.215	2	36	27	7	3.5
● SQUIZ PILLION	Pillion, Cecil Randolph b: 4/13/1894, Hartford, Conn. d: 9/30/62, Pittsburgh, Pa. BL/TL, 6', 178 lbs. Deb: 8/20/15																								
1915 Phi-A	0	0	—	2	0	0	0	0	5^1	10	0	2	0	21.9	6.75	43	.400	.464	0	.000	-0	-2	-2	0	-0.2
● HORACIO PINA	Pina, Horacio (Garcia) b: 3/12/45, Coahuila, Mexico BR/TR, 6'2", 177 lbs. Deb: 8/14/68																								
1968 Cle-A	1	1	.500	12	3	0	0	2	31^1	24	0	15	24	11.5	1.72	172	.218	.317	0	.000	-1	4	4	-0	0.4
1969 Cle-A	4	2	.667	31	4	0	0	1	46^2	44	6	27	32	14.7	5.21	72	.256	.373	3	.500	1	-8	-7	0	-0.6
1970 Was-A	5	3	.625	61	0	0	0	6	71	66	4	35	41	13.2	2.79	127	.250	.344	0	.000	-0	7	6	1	0.7
1971 Was-A	1	1	.500	56	0	0	0	2	57^2	47	2	31	38	12.8	3.59	92	.227	.339	0	.000	-0	-1	-2	1	-0.1
1972 Tex-A	2	7	.222	60	0	0	0	15	76	61	3	43	60	13.3	3.20	94	.228	.352	1	.200	0	-1	-2	3	0.2
1973 *Oak-A	6	3	.667	47	0	0	0	8	88	58	8	34	41	10.2	2.76	128	.193	.292	0	—	0	10	8	3	1.3
1974 Chi-N	3	4	.429	34	0	0	0	4	47^1	49	4	28	32	15.0	3.99	96	.268	.371	1	.200	-0	-2	-1	1	-0.1
Cal-A	1	2	.333	11	0	0	0	0	11^2	9	1	3	6	9.3	2.31	149	.209	.261	0	—	0	2	1	1	0.6
1978 Phi-N	0	0	—	2	0	0	0	0	2^1	0	0	0	4	0.0	0.00	—	.000	.000	0	.000	-0	1	1	0	0.1
Total 8	23	23	.500	314	7	0	0	38	432	358	28	216	278	12.6	3.25	106	.231	.336	5	.185	0	12	9	9	2.5
● ED PINKHAM	Pinkham, Edward b: 1849, Brooklyn, N.Y. TL, 5'7", 142 lbs. Deb: 5/08/1871 ♦																								
1871 Chi-n	1	0	1.000	3	0	0	0	1	10^1	10	0	3	0	11.3	3.48	132	.208	.255	25	.263	1	**1**	**1**		0.1
● GEORGE PINKNEY	Pinkney, George Burton b: 1/11/1862, Orange Prairie, Ill. d: 11/10/26, Peoria, Ill. BR/TR, 5'7", 160 lbs. Deb: 8/16/1884 ♦																								
1886 Bro-a	0	0	—	1	0	0	0	0	2	2	0	0	0	9.0	4.50	78	.400	.400	156	.261	0	-0	-0	-0	0.0
● ED PINNANCE	Pinnance, Edward D. "Peanuts" b: 10/22/1879, Walpole Island, Ont., Canada d: 12/12/44, Walpole Island, Ontario, Canada BL/TR, 6'1", 180 lbs. Deb: 9/14/03																								
1903 Phi-A	0	0	—	2	1	0	0	1	7	5	0	2	2	9.0	2.57	119	.200	.260	0	.000	-0	0	0	-0	0.0
● LERTON PINTO	Pinto, William Lerton b: 4/8/1899, Chillcothe, Ohio d: 5/13/83, Oxnard, Cal. BL/TL, 6', 190 lbs. Deb: 5/23/22																								
1922 Phi-N	0	1	.000	9	0	0	0	0	24^2	31	1	14	4	16.4	5.11	91	.320	.405	1	.111	-1	-3	-1	-1	-0.2
1924 Phi-N	0	0	—	3	0	0	0	0	4	7	1	0	1	15.8	9.00	50	.467	.467	0	.000	-0	-2	-2	0	-0.2
Total 2	0	1	.000	12	0	0	0	0	28^2	38	2	14	5	16.3	5.65	82	.339	.413	1	.100	-1	-5	-3	-1	-0.4
● ED PIPGRAS	Pipgras, Edward John b: 6/15/04, Schleswig, Iowa d: 4/13/64, Currie, Minn. BR/TR, 6'2.5", 175 lbs. Deb: 8/25/32 F																								
1932 Bro-N	0	1	.000	5	1	0	0	0	10	16	2	6	5	19.8	5.40	71	.348	.423	0	.000	-0	-2	-2	0	-0.2
● GEORGE PIPGRAS	Pipgras, George William b: 12/20/1899, Ida Grove, Iowa d: 10/19/86, Gainesville, Fla. BR/TR, 6'1.5", 185 lbs. Deb: 6/09/23 FU																								
1923 NY-A	1	3	.250	8	2	2	0	0	33^1	34	2	25	12	16.2	5.94	66	.276	.403	0	.000	-1	-7	-7	-0	-0.8
1924 NY-A	0	1	.000	9	1	0	0	1	15^1	20	0	18	4	24.7	9.98	42	.351	.532	1	.333	0	-10	-10	1	-0.8
1927 *NY-A	10	3	.769	29	21	9	1	0	166^1	148	2	77	81	12.2	4.11	94	.247	.334	16	.239	2	1	-5	-1	-0.4
1928 *NY-A	**24**	13	.649	46	38	22	4	3	**300^2**	314	4	103	139	12.6	3.38	111	.272	.333	18	.157	-3	22	13	-4	0.4
1929 NY-A	18	12	.600	39	33	13	3	0	225^1	229	16	95	125	13.1	4.23	91	.264	.340	12	.143	-3	0	-9	-3	-1.5
1930 NY-A	15	15	.500	44	30	15	**3**	4	221	230	9	70	111	12.5	4.11	105	.263	.324	12	.150	-2	13	5	-2	-0.1
1931 NY-A	7	6	.538	36	14	6	1	3	137^2	134	8	58	59	12.7	3.79	105	.251	.327	1	.024	-5	9	3	-2	-0.4
1932 *NY-A	16	9	.640	32	27	14	2	0	219	235	15	87	111	13.5	4.19	97	.269	.340	18	.220	1	7	-3	-2	-0.4
1933 NY-A	2	2	.500	4	4	3	0	0	33	32	1	12	14	12.0	3.27	119	.252	.317	1	.091	-1	4	2	1	0.2
Bos-A	9	8	.529	22	17	9	2	1	128^1	140	5	45	56	13.1	4.07	108	.276	.337	9	.196	-1	3	4	-2	0.2
Yr	11	10	.524	26	21	12	2	1	161^1	172	6	57	70	12.9	3.90	110	.271	.333	10	.175	-1	7	7	-1	0.4
1934 Bos-A	0	0	—	2	1	0	0	0	3^1	4	1	3	0	18.9	8.10	59	.308	.438	0	.000	-0	-1	-1	0	-0.1
1935 Bos-A	0	1	.000	5	1	0	0	0	5	9	3	5	2	27.0	14.40	33	.391	.517	0	—	0	-6	-5	0	-0.5
Total 11	102	73	.583	276	189	93	16	12	1488^1	1529	66	598	714	13.1	4.09	98	.266	.339	88	.163	-13	35	-14	-15	-4.2
● COTTON PIPPEN	Pippen, Henry Harold b: 4/2/11, Cisco, Tex. d: 2/15/81, Williams, Cal. BR/TR, 6'2", 180 lbs. Deb: 8/28/36																								
1936 StL-N	0	2	.000	6	3	0	0	0	21	37	5	8	8	20.1	7.71	51	.402	.461	1	.167	0	-9	-9	1	-0.7
1939 Phi-A	4	11	.267	25	17	5	0	1	118^2	169	13	40	33	15.9	5.99	79	.329	.378	3	.086	-2	-18	-17	2	-1.6

YEAR	TM/L	W	L	PCT	G	GS	CG	SH	SV	IP	H	HR	BB	SO	RAT	ERA	ERA+	OAV	OOB	BH	AVG	PB	PR	/A	PD	TPI
	Det-A	0	1	.000	3	2	0	0	0	14	18	1	6	5	15.4	7.07	69	.310	.375	2	.400	0	-4	-3	-0	-0.3
	Yr	4	12	.250	28	19	5	0	1	132^2	187	14	46	38	15.8	6.11	77	.326	.376	5	.125	-2	-22	-20	1	-1.9
1940	Det-A	1	2	.333	4	3	0	0	0	21^1	29	3	10	9	16.9	6.75	70	.326	.400	0	.000	-1	-6	-5	0	-0.5
Total	3	5	16	.238	38	25	5	0	1	175	253	22	64	55	16.5	6.38	73	.336	.391	6	.111	-3	-36	-34	2	-3.1
● **GERRY PIRTLE**	Pirtle, Gerald Eugene b: 12/3/47, Tulsa, Okla. BR/TR, 6'1", 185 lbs. Deb: 7/02/78																									
1978	Mon-N	0	2	.000	19	0	0	0	0	25^2	33	5	23	14	20.3	5.96	59	.314	.446	0	—	0	-7	-7	-0	-0.7
● **SKIP PITLOCK**	Pitlock, Lee Patrick Thomas b: 11/6/47, Hillside, Ill. BL/TL, 6'2", 180 lbs. Deb: 6/12/70																									
1970	SF-N	5	5	.500	18	15	1	0	0	87	92	13	48	56	14.9	4.66	85	.274	.371	2	.080	-0	-6	-7	0	-0.6
1974	Chi-A	3	3	.500	40	5	0	0	1	105^2	103	7	55	68	14.1	4.43	84	.257	.356	0	—	0	-10	-8	-1	-1.1
1975	Chi-A	0	0	—	1	0	0	0	0	0	1	0	0	0	—	—	—	1.000	1.000	0	—	0	0	0	0	-0.1
Total	3	8	8	.500	59	20	1	0	1	192^2	196	20	103	124	14.5	4.53	85	.266	.364	2	.080	-0	-15	-15	-1	-1.8
● **TOGIE PITTINGER**	Pittinger, Charles Reno b: 1/12/1872, Greencastle, Pa. d: 1/14/09, Greencastle, Pa. BL/TR, 6'2", 175 lbs. Deb: 4/26/00																									
1900	Bos-N	2	9	.182	18	13	8	0	0	114	135	7	54	27	15.6	5.13	80	.294	.378	6	.130	-5	-18	-13	-1	-1.6
1901	Bos-N	13	16	.448	34	33	27	1	0	281^1	288	7	76	129	11.9	3.01	120	.263	.315	11	.110	-9	10	19	3	1.3
1902	Bos-N	27	16	.628	46	40	36	7	0	389^1	360	4	128	174	11.7	2.52	112	.245	.313	20	.136	-9	11	13	-2	0.2
1903	Bos-N	18	22	.450	44	39	35	3	1	351^2	396	12	143	140	14.2	3.48	92	.294	.369	14	.109	-9	-8	-11	-3	-2.0
1904	Bos-N	15	21	.417	38	38	35	5	0	335^1	298	1	144	146	12.2	2.66	104	.242	.329	13	.107	-9	3	4	5	0.0
1905	Phi-N	23	14	.622	**46**	37	29	4	2	337^1	311	3	104	136	11.5	3.09	94	.247	.313	19	.156	-3	-3	-6	-3	-1.3
1906	Phi-N	8	10	.444	20	16	9	2	0	129^2	128	2	50	43	13.2	3.40	77	.252	.334	4	.091	-2	-11	-11	-1	-1.5
1907	Phi-N	9	5	.643	16	12	8	1	0	102	101	3	35	37	12.4	3.00	81	.261	.330	5	.139	-0	-6	-7	-1	-0.9
Total	8	115	113	.504	262	228	187	23	3	2040^2	2017	39	734	832	12.6	3.10	98	.260	.332	92	.124	-46	-23	-13	-3	-5.8
● **STAN PITULA**	Pitula, Stanley b: 3/23/31, Hackensack, N.J. d: 8/15/65, Hackensack, N.J. BR/TR, 5'10", 170 lbs. Deb: 4/24/57																									
1957	Cle-A	2	2	.500	23	5	1	0	0	59^2	67	8	32	17	15.2	4.98	75	.296	.388	3	.200	0	-8	-8	-1	-0.9
● **JUAN PIZARRO**	Pizarro, Juan Ramon (Cordova) b: 2/7/37, Santurce, P.R. BL/TL, 5'11", 190 lbs. Deb: 5/04/57																									
1957	*Mil-N	5	6	.455	24	10	3	0	0	99^1	99	16	51	68	13.7	4.62	76	.261	.350	9	.250	3	-8	-12	-1	-1.0
1958	*Mil-N	6	4	.600	16	10	7	1	1	96^2	75	12	47	84	11.7	2.70	130	.212	.312	8	.250	3	13	9	1	1.3
1959	Mil-N	6	2	.750	29	14	6	2	0	133^2	117	13	70	126	13.1	3.77	94	.237	.342	5	.122	0	3	-3	0	-0.3
1960	Mil-N	6	7	.462	21	17	3	0	0	114^2	105	13	72	88	14.2	4.55	75	.244	.357	11	.275	3	-10	-14	-1	-1.2
1961	Chi-A	14	7	.667	39	25	12	1	2	194^2	164	17	89	188	11.9	3.05	128	.226	.314	17	.246	5	21	19	-1	2.3
1962	Chi-A	12	14	.462	36	32	9	1	1	203^1	182	16	97	173	12.4	3.81	103	.236	.322	11	.159	-0	4	2	-2	0.0
1963	Chi-A★	16	8	.667	32	28	10	3	1	214^2	177	14	63	163	10.2	2.39	147	.224	.284	13	.178	3	30	27	-3	2.9
1964	Chi-A☆	19	9	.679	33	33	11	4	0	239	193	23	55	162	9.5	2.56	135	.219	.267	19	.211	4	28	24	-1	2.9
1965	Chi-A	6	3	.667	18	18	2	1	0	97	96	9	37	65	12.4	3.43	93	.254	.322	8	.235	3	0	-3	-0	0.0
1966	Chi-A	8	6	.571	34	9	1	0	3	88^2	91	9	39	42	13.3	3.76	84	.269	.347	4	.154	0	-3	-6	1	-0.5
1967	Pit-N	8	10	.444	50	9	1	1	9	107	99	10	52	96	12.9	3.95	85	.245	.334	7	.259	2	-7	-7	-1	-0.7
1968	Pit-N	1	1	.500	12	0	0	0	0	11	14	2	10	6	20.5	3.27	89	.311	.446	0	.000	-0	-0	-0	-0	-0.1
	Bos-A	6	8	.429	19	12	6	0	2	107^2	97	15	44	84	11.8	3.59	88	.242	.317	5	.161	1	-7	-5	2	-0.3
1969	Bos-A	0	1	.000	6	0	0	0	2	9	14	2	6	4	20.0	6.00	63	.359	.444	1	.333	0	-2	-2	0	-0.2
	Cle-A	3	3	.500	48	4	1	0	4	82^2	67	6	49	44	12.8	3.16	119	.229	.343	3	.200	0	4	6	0	0.6
	Oak-A	1	1	.500	3	0	0	0	1	7^2	3	1	3	4	7.0	2.35	146	.125	.222	1	.500	0	1	1	-0	0.1
	Yr	4	5	.444	57	4	1	0	7	99^1	84	9	58	52	12.9	3.35	112	.230	.335	5	.250	1	3	4	0	0.5
1970	Chi-N	0	0	—	12	0	0	0	1	15^2	16	2	9	14	14.9	4.60	98	.262	.366	0	.000	-0	-1	-0	0	0.0
1971	Chi-N	7	6	.538	16	14	6	3	0	101^1	78	10	40	67	10.7	3.46	114	.209	.289	6	.176	1	0	5	0	0.7
1972	Chi-N	4	5	.444	16	7	1	0	1	59^1	66	7	32	24	15.0	3.94	97	.293	.384	3	.143	-1	-3	-1	1	0.0
1973	Chi-N	0	1	.000	2	0	0	0	0	4	6	1	1	3	18.0	11.25	35	.353	.421	0	.000	-0	-3	-3	0	-0.3
	Hou-N	2	2	.500	15	1	0	0	0	23^1	28	1	11	10	15.4	6.56	55	.301	.381	0	.000	-0	-8	-8	1	-0.7
	Yr	2	3	.400	17	1	0	0	0	27^1	34	2	12	13	15.5	7.24	51	.304	.376	0	.000	-0	-11	-11	1	-1.0
1974	*Pit-N	1	1	.500	7	2	0	0	0	24	20	2	11	7	11.6	1.88	184	.220	.304	2	.333	0	5	4	-0	0.5
Total	18	131	105	.555	488	245	79	17	28	2034^1	1807	201	888	1522	12.1	3.43	104	.237	.320	133	.202	28	55	33	-5	6.0
● **GORDIE PLADSON**	Pladson, Gordon Cecil b: 7/31/56, New Westminster, B.C., Canada BR/TR, 6'4", 210 lbs. Deb: 9/07/79																									
1979	Hou-N	0	0	—	4	0	0	0	0	4	9	1	2	2	24.8	4.50	78	.450	.500	0	—	0	-0	-0	-0	-0.1
1980	Hou-N	0	4	.000	12	6	0	0	0	41^1	38	3	16	13	11.8	4.35	75	.244	.314	0	.000	-1	-3	-5	0	-0.6
1981	Hou-N	0	0	—	2	0	0	0	0	4	9	0	3	3	27.0	9.00	37	.429	.500	0	—	0	-2	-3	-0	-0.3
1982	Hou-N	0	0	—	2	0	0	0	0	1^1	10	0	2	0	81.0	54.00	6	.769	.800	0	—	0	-7	-8	-0	-0.7
Total	4	0	4	.000	20	6	0	0	0	50^2	66	4	23	18	15.8	6.04	55	.314	.382	0	.000	-1	-14	-15	-0	-1.7
● **EMIL PLANETA**	Planeta, Emil Joseph b: 1/31/09, Higganum, Conn. d: 2/2/63, Rocky Hill, Conn. BR/TR, 6', 190 lbs. Deb: 9/20/31																									
1931	NY-N	0	0	—	2	0	0	0	0	5^1	7	0	4	0	18.6	10.13	36	.292	.393	0	.000	-0	-4	-4	-0	-0.4
● **ED PLANK**	Plank, Edward Arthur b: 4/9/52, Chicago, Ill. BR/TR, 6'1", 205 lbs. Deb: 9/06/78																									
1978	SF-N	0	0	—	5	0	0	0	0	6^2	6	1	2	1	10.8	4.05	85	.273	.333	0	—	0	-0	-0	-0	-0.1
1979	SF-N	0	0	—	4	0	0	0	0	3^2	9	0	2	1	27.0	7.36	47	.450	.500	0	—	0	-1	-2	-0	-0.2
Total	2	0	0	—	9	0	0	0	0	10^1	15	1	4	2	16.5	5.23	66	.357	.413	0	—	0	-2	-2	-1	-0.3
● **EDDIE PLANK**	Plank, Edward Stewart "Gettysburg Eddie" b: 8/31/1875, Gettysburg, Pa. d: 2/24/26, Gettysburg, Pa. BL/TL, 5'11.5", 175 lbs. Deb: 5/13/01 H																									
1901	Phi-A	17	13	.567	33	32	28	1	0	260^2	254	2	68	90	11.4	3.31	114	.252	.305	18	.182	-5	10	13	-2	0.7
1902	Phi-A	20	15	.571	36	32	31	1	0	300	319	5	61	107	11.9	3.30	111	.273	.318	35	.292	6	9	12	-2	1.6
1903	Phi-A	23	16	.590	**43**	40	33	3	0	336	317	5	65	176	10.8	2.38	128	.249	.297	25	.187	-1	22	25	-1	2.4
1904	Phi-A	26	17	.605	44	43	37	7	0	357^1	311	2	86	201	10.5	2.17	124	.235	.291	31	.240	2	17	20	-0	2.6
1905	*Phi-A	24	12	.667	41	41	**35**	4	0	346^2	287	3	75	210	10.0	2.26	118	.227	.282	29	.230	3	15	15	-3	1.7
1906	Phi-A	19	6	**.760**	26	25	21	5	0	211^2	173	1	51	108	10.2	2.25	121	.226	.288	17	.233	1	10	11	-2	1.2
1907	Phi-A	24	16	.600	43	40	33	**8**	0	343^2	282	5	85	183	10.0	2.20	119	.226	.283	26	.211	2	13	16	-1	1.9
1908	Phi-A	14	16	.467	34	28	21	4	1	244^2	202	1	46	135	9.5	2.17	118	.224	.269	16	.180	-1	6	11	-4	0.6
1909	Phi-A	19	10	.655	34	33	24	3	0	265^1	215	1	62	132	9.7	1.76	136	.224	.277	21	.219	4	21	19	1	2.7
1910	Phi-A	16	10	.615	38	32	22	1	2	250^1	218	3	55	123	10.1	2.01	118	.237	.286	11	.128	-3	14	10	-3	0.4
1911	*Phi-A	23	8	.742	40	30	24	**6**	**4**	256^2	237	2	77	149	11.5	2.10	150	.255	.322	18	.191	-1	35	30	1	3.0
1912	Phi-A	26	6	.813	37	30	23	5	2	259^2	234	1	83	110	11.2	2.22	139	.245	.309	24	.267	4	32	25	-2	2.9
1913	*Phi-A	18	10	.643	41	30	18	7	4	242^2	211	3	57	151	10.1	2.60	106	.234	.283	8	.105	-0	9	4	-1	0.2
1914	*Phi-A	15	7	.682	34	22	12	4	3	185^1	178	2	42	110	11.0	2.87	91	.266	.315	9	.150	0	-3	-5	-3	-0.9
1915	StL-F	21	11	.656	42	31	23	6	3	268^1	212	1	54	147	**9.0**	2.08	**154**	.218	**.262**	24	.258	5	28	33	-3	4.0
1916	StL-A	16	15	.516	37	26	17	3	3	235^2	203	2	67	88	10.5	2.33	118	.237	.297	15	.185	-0	13	11	-4	0.8
1917	StL-A	5	6	.455	20	14	8	1	1	131	105	2	38	26	10.0	1.79	145	.225	.287	4	.105	-1	13	12	-2	1.0
Total	17	326	194	.627	623	529	410	69	23	4495^2	3958	41	1072	2246	10.4	2.35	122	.239	.292	331	.206	15	267	263	-32	26.8
● **BILL PLEIS**	Pleis, William b: 8/5/37, St.Louis, Mo. BL/TL, 5'10", 175 lbs. Deb: 4/16/61																									
1961	Min-A	4	2	.667	37	0	0	0	2	56^1	59	4	34	32	15.5	4.95	86	.266	.373	1	.111	-1	-6	-4	-1	-0.6
1962	Min-A	2	5	.286	21	4	0	0	3	45	46	7	14	31	12.2	4.40	93	.264	.323	4	.286	1	-2	-2	-1	-0.1
1963	Min-A	6	2	.750	36	4	1	0	0	68	67	10	16	37	11.0	4.37	83	.258	.301	2	.125	0	-6	-5	-0	-0.6
1964	Min-A	4	1	.800	47	0	0	0	4	50^2	43	6	31	42	13.3	3.91	92	.232	.346	1	.250	0	-2	-2	0	-0.1

YEAR TM/L	W	L	PCT	G	GS	CG	SH	SV	IP	H	HR	BB	SO	RAT	ERA	ERA+	OAV	OOB	BH	AVG	PB	PR	/A	PD	TPI
1965 *Min-A	4	4	.500	41	2	0	0	4	51^1	49	3	27	33	13.3	2.98	119	.250	.341	0	.000	-1	3	3	-0	0.2
1966 Min-A	1	2	.333	8	0	0	0	0	9^1	5	1	4	9	8.7	1.93	186	.152	.243	0	—	0	2	2	-0	0.2
Total 6	21	16	.568	190	10	1	0	13	280^2	269	31	126	184	12.9	4.07	93	.251	.334	8	.160	0	-11	-8	-3	-1.0
● DAN PLESAC Plesac, Daniel Thomas b: 2/4/62, Gary, Ind. BL/TL, 6'5", 210 lbs. Deb: 4/11/86																									
1986 Mil-A	10	7	.588	51	0	0	0	14	91	81	5	29	75	10.9	2.97	146	.240	.301	0	—	0	12	14	-1	1.3
1987 Mil-A★	5	6	.455	57	0	0	0	23	79^1	63	8	23	89	10.1	2.61	175	.213	.276	0	—	0	16	17	0	1.7
1988 Mil-A★	1	2	.333	50	0	0	0	30	52^1	46	2	12	52	10.0	2.41	165	.234	.278	0	—	0	9	9	-0	0.9
1989 Mil-A★	3	4	.429	52	0	0	0	33	61^1	47	6	17	52	9.4	2.35	163	.213	.269	0	—	0	10	10	-0	1.1
1990 Mil-A	3	7	.300	66	0	0	0	24	69	67	5	31	65	13.2	4.43	87	.257	.342	0	—	0	-4	-4	-0	-0.5
1991 Mil-A	2	7	.222	45	10	0	0	8	92^1	92	12	39	61	13.1	4.29	93	.263	.342	0	—	0	-2	-3	-2	-0.5
1992 Mil-A	5	4	.556	44	4	0	0	1	79	64	5	35	54	11.6	2.96	129	.229	.321	0	—	0	9	7	-1	0.8
Total 7	29	37	.439	365	14	0	0	133	524^1	460	43	186	448	11.3	3.21	127	.237	.307	0	—	0	51	50	-3	4.8
● NORMAN PLITT Plitt, Norman William b: 2/21/1893, York, Pa. d: 2/1/54, New York, N.Y. BR/TR, 5'11", 180 lbs. Deb: 4/26/18																									
1918 Bro-N	0	0	—	1	0	0	0	0	2	3	0	1	0	18.0	4.50	62	.429	.500	1	1.000	0	-0	-0	-0	0.0
1927 Bro-N	2	6	.250	19	8	1	0	0	62^1	73	3	36	9	15.9	4.91	81	.303	.396	4	.222	-0	-7	-7	0	-0.6
NY-N	1	0	1.000	3	0	0	0	0	7^1	9	0	1	0	13.5	3.68	105	.310	.355	0	.000	-0	0	0	0	0.0
Yr	3	6	.333	22	8	1	0	0	69^2	82	3	37	9	15.5	4.78	83	.303	.388	4	.211	-0	-7	-6	1	-0.6
Total 2	3	6	.333	23	8	1	0	0	71^2	85	3	38	9	15.7	4.77	82	.307	.394	5	.250	0	-7	-7	1	-0.6
● TIM PLODINEC Plodinec, Timothy Alfred b: 1/27/47, Aliquippa, Pa. BR/TR, 6'4", 190 lbs. Deb: 6/02/72																									
1972 StL-N	0	0	—	1	0	0	0	0	0^1	3	0	0	0	81.0	27.00	13	.750	.750	0	—	0	-1	-1	0	-0.1
● ERIC PLUNK Plunk, Eric Vaughn b: 9/3/63, Wilmington, Cal. BR/TR, 6'5", 210 lbs. Deb: 5/12/86																									
1986 Oak-A	4	7	.364	26	15	0	0	0	120^1	91	14	102	98	14.8	5.31	73	.214	.372	0	—	0	-15	-19	-2	-2.0
1987 Oak-A	4	6	.400	32	11	0	0	2	95	91	8	62	90	14.7	4.74	87	.253	.366	0	—	0	-3	-6	-1	-0.7
1988 *Oak-A	7	2	.778	49	0	0	0	5	78	62	6	39	79	11.8	3.00	126	.217	.313	0	—	0	8	7	-1	0.7
1989 Oak-A	1	1	.500	23	0	0	0	1	28^2	17	1	12	24	9.4	2.20	167	.172	.268	0	—	0	5	5	-0	0.7
NY-A	7	5	.583	27	7	0	0	0	75^2	65	9	52	61	13.9	3.69	105	.237	.359	0	—	0	2	2	-2	0.1
Yr	8	6	.571	50	7	0	0	1	104^1	82	10	64	85	12.6	3.28	116	.219	.333	0	—	0	7	6	-2	0.8
1990 NY-A	6	3	.667	47	0	0	0	0	72^2	58	6	43	67	12.8	2.72	146	.225	.340	0	—	0	10	10	2	1.2
1991 NY-A	2	5	.286	43	8	0	0	0	111^2	128	18	62	103	15.4	4.76	87	.286	.374	0	—	0	-8	-8	-2	-0.9
1992 Cle-A	9	6	.600	58	0	0	0	4	71^2	61	5	38	50	12.4	3.64	111	.229	.326	0	—	0	2	3	-0	0.2
Total 7	40	35	.533	305	41	0	0	12	653^2	573	67	410	572	13.7	4.06	98	.237	.351	0	—	0	1	-7	-6	-0.7
● JEFF PLYMPTON Plympton, Jeffrey Hunter b: 11/24/65, Framingham, Mass. BR/TR, 6'2", 205 lbs. Deb: 6/15/91																									
1991 Bos-A	0	0	—	4	0	0	0	0	5^1	5	0	4	2	15.2	0.00	—	.263	.391	0	—	0	2	3	-0	0.1
● RAY POAT Poat, Raymond Willis b: 12/19/17, Chicago, Ill. d: 4/29/90, Oak Lawn, Ill. BR/TR, 6'2", 200 lbs. Deb: 4/15/42																									
1942 Cle-A	1	3	.250	4	4	1	1	0	18^1	24	1	9	8	16.7	5.40	64	.296	.374	0	.000	-0	-4	-4	0	-0.4
1943 Cle-A	2	5	.286	17	4	1	0	0	45	44	3	20	31	12.8	4.40	71	.259	.337	2	.154	-0	-6	-6	-0	-0.7
1944 Cle-A	4	8	.333	36	6	1	0	1	80^2	82	9	37	40	13.3	5.13	64	.265	.343	0	.000	-2	-15	-16	-0	-1.9
1947 NY-N	4	3	.571	7	7	5	0	0	60	53	8	13	25	9.9	2.55	160	.238	.280	4	.190	2	10	10	-0	1.3
1948 NY-N	11	10	.524	39	24	7	3	0	157^2	162	21	67	57	13.2	4.34	91	.262	.337	7	.125	-1	-7	-7	-2	-1.0
1949 NY-N	0	0	—	2	0	0	0	0	2^1	8	0	1	0	34.7	19.29	21	.615	.643	0	—	0	-4	-4	-0	-0.4
Pit-N	0	1	.000	11	2	0	0	0	36	52	6	15	17	16.8	6.25	67	.335	.394	1	.100	-1	-9	-8	-0	-0.9
Yr	0	1	.000	13	2	0	0	0	38^1	60	6	16	17	17.8	7.04	59	.357	.413	1	.100	-1	-13	-12	-0	-1.3
Total 6	22	30	.423	116	47	15	4	1	400	425	48	162	178	13.3	4.55	82	.271	.340	14	.115	-3	-34	-36	-3	-4.0
● BUD PODBIELAN Podbielan, Clarence Anthony b: 3/6/24, Curlew, Wash. d: 10/26/82, Syracuse, N.Y. BR/TR, 6'1.5", 170 lbs. Deb: 4/25/49																									
1949 Bro-N	0	1	.000	7	1	0	0	0	12^1	9	1	9	5	13.9	3.65	112	.205	.352	0	.000	-0	1	1	1	0.1
1950 Bro-N	5	4	.556	20	10	2	0	1	72^2	93	10	29	28	15.4	5.33	77	.307	.371	3	.107	-1	-10	-10	1	-1.0
1951 Bro-N	2	2	.500	27	5	1	0	0	79^2	67	9	36	26	11.9	3.50	112	.233	.322	7	.304	1	4	4	0	0.5
1952 Bro-N	0	0	—	3	0	0	0	0	2	4	1	3	1	31.5	18.00	20	.444	.583	0	—	0	-3	-3	-0	-0.3
Cin-N	4	5	.444	24	7	4	1	1	86^2	78	8	26	22	10.9	2.80	135	.245	.304	4	.160	0	9	9	-1	0.9
Yr	4	5	.444	27	7	4	1	1	88^2	82	9	29	23	11.4	3.15	120	.251	.314	4	.160	0	6	6	-1	0.6
1953 Cin-N	6	16	.273	36	24	8	1	1	186^1	214	21	67	74	14.0	4.73	92	.290	.356	7	.125	-3	-9	-8	-0	-1.0
1954 Cin-N	7	10	.412	27	24	4	0	0	131	157	20	58	42	14.9	5.36	78	.300	.372	6	.143	-1	-19	-17	-2	-1.8
1955 Cin-N	1	2	.333	17	2	0	0	0	42	36	4	11	26	10.3	3.21	132	.234	.289	2	.400	1	4	5	0	0.6
1957 Cin-N	0	1	.000	5	3	1	0	0	16	18	4	4	13	12.4	6.19	66	.290	.333	0	.000	-1	-4	-4	-1	-0.5
1959 Cle-A	0	1	.000	6	0	0	0	0	12^1	17	1	2	5	13.9	5.84	63	.354	.380	0	.000	-0	-3	-3	0	-0.3
Total 9	25	42	.373	172	76	20	2	3	641	693	79	245	242	13.4	4.49	92	.279	.348	29	.154	-4	-30	-26	-2	-2.8
● JOHNNY PODGAJNY Podgajny, John Sigmund "Specs" b: 6/10/20, Chester, Pa. d: 3/2/71, Chester, Pa. BR/TR, 6'2", 173 lbs. Deb: 9/15/40																									
1940 Phi-N	1	3	.250	4	4	3	0	0	35	33	0	1	12	9.0	2.83	138	.250	.261	2	.167	-0	4	4	0	0.4
1941 Phi-N	9	12	.429	34	24	8	0	0	181^1	191	8	70	53	13.2	4.62	80	.270	.339	8	.129	-3	-20	-18	1	-2.0
1942 Phi-N	6	14	.300	43	23	6	0	0	186^2	191	9	63	40	12.8	3.91	85	.268	.337	11	.183	-0	-12	-12	-1	-1.4
1943 Phi-N	4	4	.500	13	5	3	0	0	64	77	4	16	13	13.1	4.22	80	.310	.352	5	.250	1	-6	-6	1	-0.4
Pit-N	0	4	.000	15	5	0	0	0	34^1	37	1	13	7	13.1	4.72	74	.266	.329	1	.143	-0	-5	-5	2	-0.4
Yr	4	8	.333	28	10	3	0	0	98^1	114	5	29	20	13.1	4.39	78	.295	.344	6	.222	0	-11	-11	3	-0.8
1946 Cle-A	0	0	—	6	0	0	0	0	9	13	0	2	4	15.0	5.00	66	.302	.333	0	—	0	-1	-2	0	-0.2
Total 5	20	37	.351	115	61	20	0	0	510^1	542	22	165	129	12.8	4.20	84	.273	.334	27	.168	-3	-41	-39	3	-4.0
● JOHNNY PODRES Podres, John Joseph b: 9/30/32, Witherbee, N.Y. BL/TL, 5'11", 192 lbs. Deb: 4/17/53 C																									
1953 *Bro-N	9	4	.692	33	18	3	1	0	115	126	12	64	82	14.9	4.23	101	.282	.373	11	.306	2	1	0	-0	0.2
1954 Bro-N	11	7	.611	29	21	6	2	0	151^2	147	13	53	79	11.9	4.27	96	.255	.319	17	.283	5	-3	-3	-2	0.0
1955 *Bro-N	9	10	.474	27	24	5	2	0	159^1	160	15	57	114	12.5	3.95	103	.259	.326	11	.183	-0	1	2	-1	0.0
1957 Bro-N	12	9	.571	31	27	10	**6**	3	196	168	15	44	109	**9.8**	**2.66**	**156**	.230	**.274**	15	.208	1	26	33	-0	3.6
1958 LA-N☆	13	15	.464	39	31	10	2	1	210^1	208	27	78	143	12.3	3.72	110	.261	.328	9	.127	-3	5	9	-2	0.4
1959 *LA-N	14	9	.609	34	29	6	2	0	195	192	23	74	145	12.4	4.11	103	.261	.331	16	.246	4	-3	3	1	0.8
1960 LA-N★	14	12	.538	34	33	8	1	0	227^2	217	25	71	159	11.4	3.08	129	.250	.308	9	.136	-1	17	22	-2	2.0
1961 LA-N	18	5	**.783**	32	29	6	1	0	182^2	192	27	51	124	12.2	3.74	116	.271	.324	16	.232	1	6	12	-2	1.2
1962 LA-N★	15	13	.536	40	40	8	0	0	255	270	20	71	178	12.1	3.81	95	.272	.323	14	.159	1	4	-5	-4	-0.8
1963 *LA-N	14	12	.538	37	34	10	5	1	198^1	196	16	64	134	11.9	3.54	85	.257	.316	9	.141	1	-6	-11	-1	-1.2
1964 LA-N	0	2	.000	2	2	0	0	0	2^2	5	1	3	0	27.0	16.88	19	.417	.533	0	—	0	-4	-4	-0	-0.4
1965 LA-N	7	6	.538	27	22	2	1	1	134	126	17	39	63	11.2	3.43	95	.247	.303	8	.178	1	2	-2	-3	-0.5
1966 LA-N	0	0	—	1	0	0	0	0	1^2	2	0	1	1	16.2	0.00	—	.400	.500	0	—	0	1	1	0	0.1
Det-A	4	5	.444	36	13	2	1	4	107^2	106	12	34	53	11.8	3.43	102	.259	.317	7	.233	2	0	1	-1	0.2
1967 Det-A	3	1	.750	21	8	0	0	1	63^1	58	12	11	34	9.9	3.84	85	.244	.280	2	.100	-1	-4	-4	-1	-0.6
1969 SD-N	5	6	.455	17	9	1	0	0	64^2	66	7	28	17	13.2	4.31	82	.264	.341	1	.063	-1	-5	-6	-1	-0.8
Total 15	148	116	.561	440	340	77	24	11	2265	2239	242	743	1435	12.0	3.68	105	.259	.319	145	.190	12	37	45	-17	4.2
● JOE POETZ Poetz, Joseph Frank "Bull Montana" b: 6/22/1900, St.Louis, Mo. d: 2/7/42, St.Louis, Mo. BR/TR, 5'10.5", 175 lbs. Deb: 9/14/26																									
1926 NY-N	0	1	.000	2	1	0	0	0	8	5	2	8	0	15.8	3.38	111	.192	.400	0	.000	0	0	0	0	0.1

YEAR	TM/L	W	L	PCT	G	GS	CG	SH	SV	IP	H	HR	BB	SO	RAT	ERA	ERA+	OAV	OOB	BH	AVG	PB	PR	/A	PD	TPI
● **BOOTS POFFENBERGER**	Poffenberger, Cletus Elwood b: 7/1/15, Williamsport, Md. BR/TR, 5'10", 178 lbs. Deb: 6/11/37																									
1937	Det-A	10	5	.667	29	16	5	0	3	137^1	147	8	79	35	15.1	4.65	100	.277	.375	11	.216	-0	-1	0	1	0.1
1938	Det-A	6	7	.462	25	15	8	1	1	125	147	8	66	28	15.5	4.82	104	.297	.382	8	.182	-1	-1	2	-2	0.0
1939	Bro-N	0	0	—	3	1	0	0	0	5	7	1	4	2	19.8	5.40	75	.318	.423	0	.000	-0	-1	-1	0	-0.1
Total	3	16	12	.571	57	32	13	1	4	267^1	301	17	149	65	15.4	4.75	101	.287	.379	19	.198	-2	-2	2	-0	0.0
● **TOM POHOLSKY**	Poholsky, Thomas George b: 8/26/29, Detroit, Mich. BR/TR, 6'3", 205 lbs. Deb: 4/20/50																									
1950	StL-N	0	0	—	5	1	0	0	0	14^2	16	2	3	2	11.7	3.68	117	.281	.317	0	.000	-0	1	1	-0	0.0
1951	StL-N	7	13	.350	38	26	10	1	1	195	204	15	68	70	12.6	4.43	89	.271	.331	14	.209	0	-10	-10	1	-0.8
1954	StL-N	5	7	.417	25	13	4	0	0	106	101	11	20	55	10.6	3.06	135	.254	.296	4	.148	-1	12	12	0	1.2
1955	StL-N	9	11	.450	30	24	8	2	0	151	143	26	35	66	10.7	3.81	106	.244	.289	8	.182	-0	4	4	-1	0.3
1956	StL-N	9	14	.391	33	29	7	2	0	203	210	27	44	95	11.5	3.59	105	.268	.311	11	.159	-1	4	4	0	0.4
1957	Chi-N	1	7	.125	28	11	1	0	0	84	117	9	22	28	15.1	4.93	79	.330	.372	2	.105	-1	-10	-10	0	-1.0
Total	6	31	52	.373	159	104	30	5	1	753^2	791	90	192	316	11.9	3.93	101	.270	.317	39	.171	-3	1	2	1	0.1
● **JENNINGS POINDEXTER**	Poindexter, Chester Jennings "Jinx" b: 9/30/10, Pauls Valley, Okla. d: 3/3/83, Norman, Okla. BL/TL, 5'10", 165 lbs. Deb: 9/15/36																									
1936	Bos-A	0	2	.000	3	3	0	0	0	10^2	13	0	16	2	24.5	6.75	79	.302	.492	0	.000	-1	-2	-2	-0	-0.2
1939	Phi-N	0	0	—	11	1	0	0	0	30^1	29	0	15	12	13.1	4.15	96	.250	.336	2	.200	-0	-1	-0	-0	-0.1
Total	2	0	2	.000	14	4	0	0	0	41	42	0	31	14	16.0	4.83	90	.264	.384	2	.143	-1	-3	-2	-0	-0.3
● **LOU POLCHOW**	Polchow, Louis William b: 3/14/1881, Mankato, Minn. d: 8/15/12, Good Thunder, Minn 5'9", Deb: 9/14/02																									
1902	Cle-A	0	1	.000	1	1	1	0	0	8	9	0	4	2	14.6	5.63	61	.284	.364	0	.000	-1	-2	-2	-0	-0.2
● **DICK POLE**	Pole, Richard Henry b: 10/13/50, Trout Creek, Mich. BR/TR, 6'3", 210 lbs. Deb: 8/03/73 C																									
1973	Bos-A	3	2	.600	12	7	0	0	0	54^2	70	4	18	24	14.5	5.60	72	.318	.370	0	—	0	-11	-10	-0	-1.3
1974	Bos-A	1	1	.500	15	2	0	0	1	45	55	6	13	32	13.8	4.20	91	.304	.354	0	—	0	-3	-2	1	-0.2
1975	*Bos-A	4	6	.400	18	11	2	1	0	89^2	102	11	32	42	13.7	4.42	92	.290	.352	0	—	0	-6	-3	0	-0.4
1976	Bos-A	6	5	.545	31	15	1	0	0	120^2	131	8	48	49	13.5	4.33	90	.279	.348	0	.000	0	-11	-6	-1	-0.7
1977	Sea-A	7	12	.368	25	24	3	0	0	122^1	127	16	57	51	14.0	5.15	80	.270	.356	0	—	0	-15	-14	-3	-1.6
1978	Sea-A	4	11	.267	21	18	2	0	0	98^2	122	16	41	41	15.1	6.48	59	.306	.375	0	—	0	-30	-29	-1	-2.9
Total	6	25	37	.403	122	77	8	1	1	531	607	61	209	239	14.1	5.05	79	.290	.359	0	.000	0	-76	-63	-5	-7.1
● **KEN POLIVKA**	Polivka, Kenneth Lyle "Soup" b: 1/21/21, Chicago, Ill. d: 7/23/88, Aurora, Ill. BL/TL, 5'10.5", 175 lbs. Deb: 4/18/47																									
1947	Cin-N	0	0	—	2	0	0	0	0	3	3	0	3	1	18.0	3.00	137	.250	.400	0	—	0	0	0	-0	0.0
● **HOWIE POLLET**	Pollet, Howard Joseph b: 6/26/21, New Orleans, La. d: 8/8/74, Houston, Tex. BL/TL, 6'1.5", 175 lbs. Deb: 8/20/41 C																									
1941	StL-N	5	2	.714	9	8	6	2	0	70	55	1	27	37	10.7	1.93	195	.212	.289	5	.179	-0	13	14	1	1.7
1942	*StL-N	7	5	.583	27	13	5	2	0	109^1	102	7	39	42	11.8	2.88	119	.242	.309	7	.226	3	5	7	-2	0.8
1943	StL-N†	8	4	.667	16	14	12	5	0	118^1	83	2	32	61	8.9	1.75	192	.200	.261	7	.163	-1	21	21	-2	2.1
1946	*StL-N☆	**21**	10	.677	40	32	22	4	5	**266**	228	12	86	107	10.8	**2.10**	**165**	.234	.300	14	.161	-0	**39**	**40**	1	4.6
1947	StL-N	9	11	.450	37	24	9	0	2	176^1	195	11	87	73	14.5	4.34	95	.286	.369	15	.231	2	-5	-4	0	-0.2
1948	StL-N	13	8	.619	36	26	11	0	0	186^1	216	10	67	80	13.8	4.54	90	.289	.349	8	.118	-3	-12	-9	2	-1.1
1949	StL-N★	20	9	.690	39	28	17	**5**	1	230^2	228	9	59	108	11.3	2.77	150	.256	.304	16	.195	1	33	**36**	-2	3.7
1950	StL-N	14	13	.519	37	30	14	2	2	232^1	228	19	68	117	11.5	3.29	130	.256	.310	12	.143	-2	22	26	0	2.4
1951	StL-N	0	3	.000	6	2	0	0	1	12^1	10	1	8	10	13.1	4.38	91	.208	.321	0	.000	1	-1	-1	0	0.0
	Pit-N	6	10	.375	21	21	4	1	0	128^2	149	24	51	47	14.1	5.04	84	.294	.360	5	.139	-0	-15	-12	-0	-1.2
	Yr	6	13	.316	27	23	4	1	1	141	159	25	59	57	14.0	4.98	84	.287	.357	5	.135	0	-16	-12	0	-1.2
1952	Pit-N	7	16	.304	31	30	9	1	0	214	217	22	71	90	12.2	4.12	97	.266	.327	13	.191	2	-9	-3	1	0.0
1953	Pit-N	1	1	.500	5	2	0	0	0	12^2	27	2	6	8	23.4	10.66	42	.482	.532	1	.333	0	-9	-9	-0	-0.8
	Chi-N	5	6	.455	25	17	2	0	1	111^1	120	6	44	45	13.3	4.12	108	.271	.338	4	.129	-1	2	4	-1	0.2
	Yr	6	7	.462	30	19	2	0	1	124	147	8	50	53	14.4	4.79	93	.295	.360	5	.147	-1	-7	-5	-1	-0.6
1954	Chi-N	8	10	.444	20	20	4	2	0	128^1	131	4	54	58	13.0	3.58	117	.263	.335	13	.277	2	7	9	-0	1.2
1955	Chi-N	4	3	.571	24	7	1	1	5	61	62	11	27	27	13.1	5.61	73	.265	.341	6	.400	3	-11	-10	1	-0.6
1956	Chi-A	3	1	.750	11	4	0	0	0	26^1	27	2	11	14	13.0	4.10	100	.252	.322	3	.375	1	0	-0	0	0.1
	Pit-N	0	4	.000	19	0	0	0	3	23^1	18	3	8	10	10.0	3.09	122	.212	.280	0	.000	0	2	2	0	0.2
Total	14	131	116	.530	403	278	116	25	20	2107^1	2096	146	745	934	12.2	3.51	113	.260	.324	129	.185	7	82	111	0	13.1
● **LOU POLLI**	Polli, Louis Americo "Crip" b: 7/9/01, Barre, Vt. BR/TR, 5'10.5", 165 lbs. Deb: 4/18/32																									
1932	StL-A	0	0	—	5	0	0	0	0	6^2	13	0	3	5	21.6	5.40	90	.406	.457	1	.500	0	-1	-0	-0	0.0
1944	NY-N	0	2	.000	19	0	0	0	3	35^2	42	3	20	6	15.6	4.54	81	.294	.380	0	.000	-1	-4	-3	-0	-0.5
Total	2	0	2	.000	24	0	0	0	3	42^1	55	3	23	11	16.6	4.68	82	.314	.394	1	.125	-1	-4	-4	-1	-0.5
● **JOHN POLONI**	Poloni, John Paul b: 2/28/54, Dearborn, Mich. BL/TL, 6'5", 210 lbs. Deb: 9/16/77																									
1977	Tex-A	1	0	1.000	2	1	0	0	0	7	8	1	1	5	11.6	6.43	63	.286	.310	0	—	0	-2	-2	-0	-0.2
● **JOHN POMORSKI**	Pomorski, John Leon b: 12/30/05, Brooklyn, N.Y. d: 12/6/77, Brampton, Ont., Can. BR/TR, 6', 178 lbs. Deb: 4/17/34																									
1934	Chi-A	0	0	—	3	0	0	0	0	1^2	1	0	2	0	16.2	5.40	88	.143	.333	0	—	0	-0	-0	0	0.0
● **ARLIE POND**	Pond, Erasmus Arlington b: 1/19/1872, Rutland, Vt. d: 9/19/30, Cebu, Philippines BR/TR, 5'10", 160 lbs. Deb: 7/04/1895																									
1895	Bal-N	0	1	.000	6	1	1	0	2	13^2	10	0	12	13	15.1	5.93	80	.202	.367	2	.333	1	-2	-2	0	-0.1
1896	Bal-N	16	8	.667	28	26	21	2	0	214^1	232	4	57	80	12.4	3.49	123	.274	.324	19	.235	0	21	19	-2	1.5
1897	Bal-N	18	9	.667	32	28	23	0	0	248	267	4	72	59	12.8	3.52	119	.273	.332	22	.244	2	22	18	-1	1.7
1898	Bal-N	1	1	.500	3	2	1	1	0	20	8	0	9	4	8.5	0.45	796	.122	.249	2	.286	1	7	7	-1	0.7
Total	4	35	19	.648	69	57	46	3	2	496	517	8	150	156	12.5	3.45	122	.266	.327	45	.245	3	48	42	-3	3.8
● **ELMER PONDER**	Ponder, Charles Elmer b: 6/26/1893, Reed, Okla. d: 4/20/74, Albuquerque, N.Mex BR/TR, 6', 178 lbs. Deb: 9/18/17																									
1917	Pit-N	1	1	.500	3	2	1	1	0	21^1	12	0	6	11	8.0	1.69	168	.167	.241	0	.000	-1	2	3	-1	0.1
1919	Pit-N	0	5	.000	9	5	0	0	0	47^1	55	0	6	6	12.2	3.99	76	.297	.330	2	.133	-1	-6	-5	-1	-0.7
1920	Pit-N	11	15	.423	33	23	13	2	0	196	182	3	40	62	10.3	2.62	123	.246	.286	7	.119	-4	11	13	1	1.0
1921	Pit-N	2	0	1.000	8	1	1	0	0	24^2	29	1	3	3	11.7	2.19	175	.305	.327	0	.000	-2	4	5	0	0.3
	Chi-N	3	6	.333	16	11	5	0	0	89^1	117	7	17	31	13.8	4.74	81	.321	.356	4	.121	-2	-9	-9	2	-0.9
	Yr	5	6	.455	24	12	6	0	0	114	146	8	20	34	13.3	4.18	91	.317	.350	4	.093	-4	-5	-5	2	-0.6
Total	4	17	27	.386	69	42	20	3	0	378^2	395	11	72	113	11.3	3.21	105	.271	.309	13	.105	-10	3	6	0	-0.2
● **ED POOLE**	Poole, Edward I. b: 9/7/1874, Canton, Ohio d: 3/11/19, Malvern, Ohio BR/TR, 5'10", 175 lbs. Deb: 10/06/00 ♦																									
1900	Pit-N	1	0	1.000	1	0	0	0	0	7	4	0	0	3	5.1	1.29	283	.167	.167	2	.500	1	2	2	0	0.4
1901	Pit-N	5	4	.556	12	10	8	1	0	80	78	3	30	26	12.9	3.60	91	.254	.334	16	.205	1	-2	-3	0	-0.2
1902	Pit-N	0	0	—	1	0	0	0	0	8	7	0	3	2	11.3	1.13	243	.235	.305	1	.250	0	1	1	-0	0.1
	Cin-N	12	4	.750	16	16	16	2	0	138	129	2	54	55	12.5	2.15	139	.247	.327	7	.115	-5	10	13	-0	0.9
	Yr	12	4	.750	17	16	16	2	0	146	136	2	57	57	12.4	2.10	142	.247	.326	8	.123	-5	11	14	-0	1.0
1903	Cin-N	7	13	.350	25	21	18	1	0	184	188	4	77	73	13.5	3.28	109	.270	.352	17	.243	0	-0	6	2	0.8
1904	Bro-N	8	14	.364	25	23	19	1	1	178	178	4	74	67	13.1	3.39	81	.268	.349	8	.129	-3	-13	-13	3	-1.3
Total	5	33	35	.485	80	70	61	5	1	595	584	13	238	226	13.0	3.04	103	.260	.341	51	.183	-6	-2	6	6	0.7

● **JIM POOLE** Poole, James Richard b: 4/28/66, Rochester, N.Y. BL/TL, 6'2", 190 lbs. Deb: 6/15/90

YEAR	TM/L	W	L	PCT	G	GS	CG	SH	SV	IP	H	HR	BB	SO	RAT	ERA	ERA+	OAV	OOB	BH	AVG	PB	PR	/A	PD	TPI
1990	LA-N	0	0	—	16	0	0	0	0	10^{2}	7	1	8	6	12.7	4.22	87	.184	.326	0	—	0	-1	-1	-0	-0.1
1991	Tex-A	0	0	—	5	0	0	0	1	6	10	0	3	4	19.5	4.50	90	.370	.433	0	—	0	-0	-0	-0	0.1
	Bal-A	3	2	.600	24	0	0	0	0	36	19	3	9	34	7.0	2.00	198	.157	.215	0	—	0	8	8	0	1.2
	Yr	3	2	.600	29	0	0	0	1	42	29	3	12	38	8.8	2.36	168	.195	.255	0	—	0	8	7	0	1.3
1992	Bal-A	0	0	—	6	0	0	0	0	3^{1}	3	0	1	3	10.8	0.00	—	.231	.286	0	—	0	1	1	0	0.2
Total	3	3	2	.600	51	0	0	0	1	56	39	4	21	47	9.6	2.57	152	.196	.273	0	—	0	9	8	0	1.4

● **TOM POORMAN** Poorman, Thomas Iverson b: 10/14/1857, Lock Haven, Pa. d: 2/18/05, Lock Haven, Pa. BL/TR, 5'7", 135 lbs. Deb: 5/05/1880 ♦

YEAR	TM/L	W	L	PCT	G	GS	CG	SH	SV	IP	H	HR	BB	SO	RAT	ERA	ERA+	OAV	OOB	BH	AVG	PB	PR	/A	PD	TPI
1880	Buf-N	1	8	.111	11	9	9	0	1	85	117	3	19	13	14.4	4.13	59	.307	.340	11	.157	-3	-17	-16	1	-1.6
	Chi-N	2	0	1.000	2	1	0	0	0	15	12	0	8	0	12.0	2.40	101	.203	.299	5	.200	0	-0	0	-1	-0.1
	Yr	3	8	.273	13	10	9	0	1	100	129	3	27	13	14.0	3.87	63	.293	.334	16	.168	-3	-17	-16	0	-1.7
1884	Tol-a	0	1	.000	1	1	1	0	0	9	13	1	2	0	15.0	3.00	114	.310	.341	89	.233	0	0	0	0	0.0
1887	Phi-a	0	0	—	1	0	0	0	0	0^{2}	5	1	1	1	81.0	40.50	11	1.250	1.200	155	.265	0	-3	-3	0	-0.2
Total	3	3	9	.250	15	11	10	0	1	109^{2}	147	5	30	14	14.5	4.02	63	.302	.343	498	.244	-3	-19	-18	0	-1.9

● **BILL POPP** Popp, William Peter b: 6/7/1877, St.Louis, Mo. d: 9/5/09, St.Louis, Mo. TR, 5'10.5", 170 lbs. Deb: 4/19/02

YEAR	TM/L	W	L	PCT	G	GS	CG	SH	SV	IP	H	HR	BB	SO	RAT	ERA	ERA+	OAV	OOB	BH	AVG	PB	PR	/A	PD	TPI
1902	StL-N	2	6	.250	9	7	5	0	0	60^{1}	87	2	26	20	17.6	4.92	56	.337	.408	1	.048	-3	-14	-15	1	-1.6

● **ED PORRAY** Porray, Edmund Joseph b: 12/5/1888, AtSea On Atlantic Ocean d: 7/13/54, Lackawaxen, Pa. BR/TR, 5'11", 170 lbs. Deb: 4/17/14

YEAR	TM/L	W	L	PCT	G	GS	CG	SH	SV	IP	H	HR	BB	SO	RAT	ERA	ERA+	OAV	OOB	BH	AVG	PB	PR	/A	PD	TPI
1914	Buf-F	0	1	.000	3	3	0	0	0	10^{1}	18	2	7	0	21.8	4.35	76	.391	.472	0	.000	-1	-1	-1	1	-0.1

● **CHUCK PORTER** Porter, Charles William b: 1/12/56, Baltimore, Md. BR/TR, 6'3", 188 lbs. Deb: 9/14/81

YEAR	TM/L	W	L	PCT	G	GS	CG	SH	SV	IP	H	HR	BB	SO	RAT	ERA	ERA+	OAV	OOB	BH	AVG	PB	PR	/A	PD	TPI
1981	Mil-A	0	0	—	3	0	0	0	0	4^{1}	6	0	1	1	14.5	4.15	82	.316	.350	0	—	0	-0	-0	-0	0.0
1982	Mil-A	0	0	—	3	0	0	0	0	3^{2}	3	0	1	3	9.8	4.91	77	.250	.308	0	—	0	-0	-0	-0	0.0
1983	Mil-A	7	9	.438	25	21	6	1	0	134	162	9	38	76	13.6	4.50	83	.298	.346	0	—	0	-7	-11	0	-0.9
1984	Mil-A	6	4	.600	17	12	1	0	0	81^{1}	92	8	12	48	11.5	3.87	99	.284	.310	0	—	0	1	-0	0	0.0
1985	Mil-A	0	0	—	6	1	0	0	0	13^{2}	15	1	2	8	11.2	1.98	211	.273	.298	0	—	0	3	3	-0	0.3
Total	5	13	13	.500	54	34	7	1	0	237	278	18	54	136	12.7	4.14	92	.291	.331	0	—	0	-3	-9	-0	-0.6

● **HENRY PORTER** Porter, Henry b: 6/1858, Vergennes, Vt. d: 12/30/06, Brockton, Mass. BR/TR, Deb: 9/27/1884

YEAR	TM/L	W	L	PCT	G	GS	CG	SH	SV	IP	H	HR	BB	SO	RAT	ERA	ERA+	OAV	OOB	BH	AVG	PB	PR	/A	PD	TPI
1884	Mil-U	3	3	.500	6	6	6	1	0	51	32	1	9	71	7.2	3.00	55	.168	.205	11	.275	2	0	-8	1	-0.4
1885	Bro-a	33	21	.611	54	54	53	2	0	481^{2}	427	11	107	197	10.3	2.78	118	.223	.270	40	.205	-2	25	27	3	2.6
1886	Bro-a	27	19	.587	48	48	48	1	0	424	439	8	120	163	12.0	3.42	102	.252	.303	33	.179	-9	2	3	-2	-0.7
1887	Bro-a	15	24	.385	40	40	38	1	0	339^{2}	416	7	96	74	13.8	4.21	102	.297	.345	29	.199	-2	3	3	-2	-0.1
1888	KC-a	18	37	.327	55	54	53	4	0	474	527	16	120	145	12.7	4.16	83	.271	.321	28	.144	-13	-58	-38	4	-4.1
1889	KC-a	0	3	.000	4	4	3	0	0	23	52	0	14	9	26.2	12.52	33	.433	.496	1	.100	-1	-22	-21	0	-1.6
Total	6	96	107	.473	207	206	201	9	0	1793^{1}	1893	43	466	659	12.1	3.70	96	.259	.308	142	.184	-26	-50	-32	3	-4.3

● **NED PORTER** Porter, Ned Swindell b: 5/6/05, Apalachicola, Fla. d: 6/30/68, Gainesville, Fla. BR/TR, 6', 173 lbs. Deb: 8/07/26

YEAR	TM/L	W	L	PCT	G	GS	CG	SH	SV	IP	H	HR	BB	SO	RAT	ERA	ERA+	OAV	OOB	BH	AVG	PB	PR	/A	PD	TPI
1926	NY-N	0	0	—	2	0	0	0	0	2	2	1	0	1	9.0	4.50	83	.250	.250	0	—	0	-0	-0	-0	0.0
1927	NY-N	0	0	—	1	0	0	0	0	2	3	0	1	0	18.0	0.00	—	.333	.400	0	—	0	1	1	-0	0.1
Total	2	0	0	—	3	0	0	0	0	4	5	1	1	1	13.5	2.25	169	.294	.333	0	—	0	1	1	-0	0.1

● **ODIE PORTER** Porter, Odie Oscar b: 5/24/1877, Borden, Ind. d: 5/2/03, Borden, Ind. TL, Deb: 6/16/02

YEAR	TM/L	W	L	PCT	G	GS	CG	SH	SV	IP	H	HR	BB	SO	RAT	ERA	ERA+	OAV	OOB	BH	AVG	PB	PR	/A	PD	TPI
1902	Phi-A	0	1	.000	1	1	1	0	0	8	12	0	5	2	19.1	3.38	109	.346	.428	0	.000	-0	0	0	0	0.0

● **BOB PORTERFIELD** Porterfield, Erwin Coolidge b: 8/10/23, Newport, Va. d: 4/28/80, Sealy, Tex. BR/TR, 6', 190 lbs. Deb: 8/08/48

YEAR	TM/L	W	L	PCT	G	GS	CG	SH	SV	IP	H	HR	BB	SO	RAT	ERA	ERA+	OAV	OOB	BH	AVG	PB	PR	/A	PD	TPI
1948	NY-A	5	3	.625	16	12	2	1	0	78	85	5	34	30	13.7	4.50	91	.273	.345	6	.250	0	-2	-4	-1	-0.4
1949	NY-A	2	5	.286	12	8	3	0	0	57^{2}	53	3	29	25	13.0	4.06	100	.251	.344	1	.053	-2	1	-0	-1	-0.2
1950	NY-A	1	1	.500	10	2	0	0	1	19^{2}	28	2	8	9	16.5	8.69	49	.341	.400	1	.333	0	-9	-10	-0	-0.8
1951	NY-A	0	0	—	2	0	0	0	0	3	5	0	3	2	24.0	15.00	26	.385	.500	0	—	0	-4	-4	-0	-0.3
	Was-A	9	8	.529	19	19	10	3	0	133^{1}	109	8	54	53	11.0	3.24	126	.224	.302	6	.130	-3	13	13	-0	1.0
	Yr	9	8	.529	21	19	10	3	0	136^{1}	114	8	57	55	11.3	3.50	117	.228	.308	6	.130	-3	9	9	-0	0.7
1952	Was-A	13	14	.481	31	29	15	3	0	231^{1}	222	7	85	80	12.1	2.72	131	.254	.323	15	.190	0	24	21	-3	2.0
1953	Was-A	**22**	10	.688	34	32	**24**	**9**	0	255	243	19	73	77	11.2	3.35	116	.257	.310	25	.255	8	18	15	2	2.7
1954	Was-A★	13	15	.464	32	31	**21**	2	0	244	249	14	77	82	12.1	3.32	107	.266	.324	9	.102	-3	11	6	3	0.7
1955	Was-A	10	17	.370	30	27	8	2	0	178	197	14	54	74	12.8	4.45	86	.282	.335	12	.190	1	-10	-12	-1	-1.2
1956	Bos-A	3	12	.200	25	18	4	1	0	126	127	21	64	53	13.7	5.14	90	.260	.347	14	.326	3	-14	-7	-2	-0.6
1957	Bos-A	4	4	.500	28	9	3	1	1	102^{1}	107	8	30	28	12.1	4.05	99	.272	.325	5	.172	-0	-3	-1	1	0.0
1958	Bos-A	0	0	—	2	0	0	0	0	4	3	1	0	1	6.8	4.50	89	.214	.214	0	—	0	-0	-0	-0	0.0
	Pit-N	4	6	.400	37	6	2	1	5	87^{2}	78	7	19	39	10.1	3.29	118	.241	.285	1	.050	-1	6	6	-0	0.5
1959	Pit-N	0	0	—	6	0	0	0	0	5^{1}	6	1	2	1	13.5	1.69	229	.286	.348	0	—	0	1	1	-0	0.1
	Chi-N	0	0	—	4	0	0	0	0	6^{1}	14	1	3	0	24.2	11.37	35	.424	.472	0	.000	-0	-5	-5	0	-0.5
	Pit-N	1	2	.333	30	0	0	0	1	36	45	2	17	18	15.5	4.75	81	.321	.395	0	.000	-0	-3	-4	1	-0.3
	Yr	1	2	.333	40	0	0	0	1	47^{2}	65	4	22	19	16.4	5.29	73	.335	.403	0	.000	-0	-7	-7	1	-0.7
Total	12	87	97	.473	318	193	92	23	8	1567^{2}	1571	113	552	572	12.3	3.79	102	.263	.327	95	.184	4	26	16	0	2.7

● **AL PORTO** Porto, Alfred "Lefty" b: 6/27/26, Heilwood, Pa. BL/TL, 5'11", 176 lbs. Deb: 4/22/48

YEAR	TM/L	W	L	PCT	G	GS	CG	SH	SV	IP	H	HR	BB	SO	RAT	ERA	ERA+	OAV	OOB	BH	AVG	PB	PR	/A	PD	TPI
1948	Phi-N	0	0	—	3	0	0	0	0	4	2	0	1	1	6.8	0.00	—	.143	.200	0	—	0	2	2	-0	0.2

● **ARNIE PORTOCARRERO** Portocarrero, Arnold Mario b: 7/5/31, New York, N.Y. d: 6/21/86, Kansas City, Kan. BR/TR, 6'3", 196 lbs. Deb: 4/18/54

YEAR	TM/L	W	L	PCT	G	GS	CG	SH	SV	IP	H	HR	BB	SO	RAT	ERA	ERA+	OAV	OOB	BH	AVG	PB	PR	/A	PD	TPI
1954	Phi-A	9	18	.333	34	33	16	1	0	248	233	25	114	132	12.8	4.06	96	.249	.334	8	.107	-2	-9	-4	-4	-1.0
1955	KC-A	5	9	.357	24	20	4	1	0	111^{1}	109	12	67	34	14.6	4.77	88	.259	.366	4	.108	-2	-10	-7	-1	-0.9
1956	KC-A	0	1	.000	3	1	0	0	0	8	9	2	7	2	18.0	10.13	43	.300	.432	0	.000	-0	-5	-5	-0	-0.5
1957	KC-A	4	9	.308	33	17	1	0	0	114^{2}	103	10	34	42	11.0	3.92	101	.240	.300	3	.107	-1	-2	0	-1	-0.2
1958	Bal-A	15	11	.577	32	27	10	3	2	204^{2}	173	17	57	90	10.2	3.25	110	.229	.286	11	.164	0	12	8	-3	0.5
1959	Bal-A	2	7	.222	27	14	1	0	0	90	107	10	32	23	14.1	6.80	56	.294	.354	0	.000	-2	-29	-30	1	-3.1
1960	Bal-A	3	2	.600	13	5	1	0	0	40^{2}	44	6	9	15	11.7	4.43	86	.275	.314	0	.000	-1	-2	-3	-1	-0.5
Total	7	38	57	.400	166	117	33	5	2	817^{1}	778	82	320	338	12.3	4.32	89	.252	.325	26	.108	-9	-47	-42	-9	-5.7

● **MARK PORTUGAL** Portugal, Mark Steven b: 10/30/62, Los Angeles, Cal. BR/TR, 6', 190 lbs. Deb: 8/14/85

YEAR	TM/L	W	L	PCT	G	GS	CG	SH	SV	IP	H	HR	BB	SO	RAT	ERA	ERA+	OAV	OOB	BH	AVG	PB	PR	/A	PD	TPI
1985	Min-A	1	3	.250	6	4	0	0	0	24^{1}	24	3	14	12	14.1	5.55	79	.270	.369	0	—	0	-4	-3	1	-0.2
1986	Min-A	6	10	.375	27	15	3	0	1	112^{2}	112	10	50	67	13.0	4.31	100	.265	.345	0	—	0	-2	-0	-0	-0.1
1987	Min-A	1	3	.250	13	7	0	0	0	44	58	13	24	28	17.0	7.77	59	.326	.409	0	—	0	-16	-15	0	-1.5
1988	Min-A	3	3	.500	26	0	0	0	3	57^{2}	60	11	17	31	12.2	4.53	90	.274	.329	0	—	0	-4	-3	-2	-0.6
1989	Hou-N	7	1	.875	20	15	2	1	0	108	91	7	37	86	10.8	2.75	123	.232	.302	7	.206	3	9	8	0	1.2
1990	Hou-N	11	10	.524	32	32	1	0	0	196^{2}	187	21	67	136	11.8	3.62	103	.250	.315	9	.136	-1	4	2	-0	0.1
1991	Hou-N	10	12	.455	32	27	1	0	1	168^{1}	163	19	59	120	12.0	4.49	78	.256	.321	9	.196	2	-15	-18	-1	-1.7
1992	Hou-N	6	3	.667	18	16	1	1	0	101^{1}	76	7	41	62	10.5	2.66	125	.213	.296	3	.107	-1	9	8	0	0.8
Total	8	45	45	.500	174	116	8	2	5	813	771	91	309	542	12.1	4.01	94	.254	.325	28	.161	3	-18	-23	-2	-2.0

● **BILL POSEDEL** Posedel, William John "Sailor Bill" or "Barnacle Bill"
b: 8/2/06, San Francisco, Cal. d: 11/28/89, Livermore, Cal. BR/TR, 5'11", 175 lbs. Deb: 4/23/38 C

YEAR	TM/L	W	L	PCT	G	GS	CG	SH	SV	IP	H	HR	BB	SO	RAT	ERA	ERA+	OAV	OOB	BH	AVG	PB	PR	/A	PD	TPI
1938	Bro-N	8	9	.471	33	17	6	1	1	140	178	14	46	49	14.5	5.66	69	.311	.365	10	.227	1	-29	-27	-1	-2.7

YEAR	TM/L	W	L	PCT	G	GS	CG	SH	SV	IP	H	HR	BB	SO	RAT	ERA	ERA+	OAV	OOB	BH	AVG	PB	PR	/A	PD	TPI
1939	Bos-N	15	13	.536	33	29	18	5	0	220^2	221	8	78	73	12.2	3.92	94	.268	.331	8	.110	-3	0	-5	-1	-1.0
1940	Bos-N	12	17	.414	35	32	18	0	1	233	263	16	81	86	13.3	4.13	90	.288	.346	14	.171	1	-7	-11	-0	-1.0
1941	Bos-N	4	4	.500	18	9	3	0	0	57^1	61	6	30	10	14.4	4.87	73	.279	.368	8	.320	2	-8	-8	-0	-0.6
1946	Bos-N	2	0	1.000	19	0	0	0	4	28^1	34	4	13	9	14.9	6.99	49	.304	.376	0	.000	-0	-11	-11	-0	-1.2
Total	5	41	43	.488	138	87	45	6	6	679^1	757	48	248	227	13.4	4.56	82	.286	.349	40	.176	0	-55	-63	-4	-6.5
● **BOB POSER**	Poser, John Falk b: 3/16/10, Columbus, Wis. BL/TR, 6', 173 lbs. Deb: 4/17/32																									
1932	Chi-A	0	0	—	1	0	0	0	0	0^2	3	0	2	1	67.5	27.00	16	.600	.714	0	.000	-0	-2	-2	0	-0.2
1935	StL-A	1	1	.500	4	1	0	0	0	13^2	26	0	4	1	19.8	9.22	52	.400	.435	1	.250	0	-7	-7	-1	-0.6
Total	2	1	1	.500	5	1	0	0	0	14^1	29	0	6	2	22.0	10.05	47	.414	.461	1	.143	0	-9	-8	-1	-0.8
● **LOU POSSEHL**	Possehl, Louis Thomas b: 4/12/26, Chicago, Ill. BR/TR, 6'2", 180 lbs. Deb: 8/25/46 F																									
1946	Phi-N	1	2	.333	4	4	0	0	0	13^2	19	0	10	4	19.8	5.93	58	.339	.448	0	.000	-0	-4	-4	0	-0.4
1947	Phi-N	0	0	—	2	0	0	0	0	4^1	5	0	0	1	12.5	4.15	96	.385	.429	0	—	0	-0	-0	0	0.1
1948	Phi-N	1	1	.500	3	2	1	0	0	14^2	17	3	4	7	12.9	4.91	80	.304	.350	1	.250	0	-2	-2	0	-0.1
1951	Phi-N	0	1	.000	2	1	0	0	0	6	9	0	3	6	18.0	6.00	64	.333	.400	0	.000	-0	-1	-1	0	-0.1
1952	Phi-N	0	1	.000	4	1	0	0	0	12^2	12	3	7	4	13.5	4.97	73	.235	.328	0	.000	-0	-2	-2	-0	-0.2
Total	5	2	5	.286	15	8	1	0	0	51^1	62	6	24	22	15.4	5.26	71	.305	.384	1	.100	-0	-9	-9	0	-0.7
● **NELLIE POTT**	Pott, Nelson Adolph "Lefty" b: 7/16/1899, Cincinnati, Ohio d: 12/3/63, Cincinnati, Ohio BL/TL, 6', 185 lbs. Deb: 4/19/22																									
1922	Cle-A	0	0	—	2	0	0	0	0	2	7	1	2	0	40.5	31.50	13	.583	.643	0	—	0	-6	-6	-0	-0.5
● **DYKES POTTER**	Potter, Maryland Dykes b: 9/7/10, Ashland, Ky. BR/TR, 6', 185 lbs. Deb: 4/26/38 F																									
1938	Bro-N	0	0	—	2	0	0	0	0	2	4	1	0	1	18.0	4.50	87	.400	.400	0	—	0	-0	-0	-0	0.0
● **NELS POTTER**	Potter, Nelson Thomas "Nellie" b: 8/23/11, Mt.Morris, Ill. d: 9/30/90, Mt.Morris, Ill. BL/TR, 5'11", 180 lbs. Deb: 4/25/36																									
1936	StL-N	0	0	—	1	0	0	0	0	1	0	0	0	0	0.0	0.00	—	.000	.000	0	—	0	0	0	-0	0.0
1938	Phi-A	2	12	.143	35	9	4	0	5	111^1	139	15	49	43	15.4	6.47	75	.306	.376	10	.256	1	-21	-20	-1	-1.7
1939	Phi-A	8	12	.400	41	25	9	0	2	196^1	258	26	88	60	16.1	6.60	71	.321	.391	12	.179	-1	-43	-41	-0	-3.7
1940	Phi-A	9	14	.391	31	25	13	0	0	200^2	213	18	71	73	12.8	4.44	100	.269	.330	18	.254	2	-1	0	-0	0.2
1941	Phi-A	1	1	.500	10	3	1	0	2	23^1	35	3	16	7	19.7	9.26	45	.337	.425	1	.167	0	-13	-13	0	-1.2
	Bos-A	2	0	1.000	10	0	0	0	0	20	21	0	16	6	16.6	4.50	93	.284	.411	0	.000	-0	-1	-1	-0	-0.1
	Yr	3	1	.750	20	3	1	0	2	43^1	56	3	32	13	18.3	7.06	59	.315	.419	1	.111	0	-14	-14	-0	-1.3
1943	StL-A	10	5	.667	33	13	8	0	1	168^1	146	11	54	80	10.9	2.78	120	.235	.299	8	.145	-1	10	10	1	1.1
1944	*StL-A	19	7	.731	32	29	16	3	0	232	211	6	70	91	10.9	2.83	127	.244	.301	13	.159	-2	15	20	2	2.1
1945	StL-A	15	11	.577	32	32	21	3	0	255^1	212	10	68	129	9.9	2.47	143	.226	.279	28	.304	4	25	30	-1	3.8
1946	StL-A	8	9	.471	23	19	10	0	0	145	152	9	59	72	13.3	3.72	100	.268	.340	12	.231	2	-4	0	-1	0.2
1947	StL-A	4	10	.286	32	10	3	0	2	122^2	130	13	44	65	12.9	4.04	96	.277	.342	9	.257	3	-5	-2	1	0.2
1948	StL-A	1	1	.500	2	2	0	0	0	10^1	11	1	4	4	14.8	5.23	87	.262	.354	2	.500	1	-1	-1	1	0.0
	Phi-A	2	2	.500	8	0	0	0	1	18	17	1	5	13	11.0	4.00	107	.250	.301	1	.250	0	1	1	-0	0.1
	Yr	3	3	.500	10	2	0	0	1	28^1	28	2	9	17	11.8	4.45	99	.250	.306	3	.375	1	-0	-0	0	0.1
	*Bos-N	5	2	.714	18	7	3	0	2	85	77	4	8	47	9.0	2.33	165	.245	.264	11	.379	3	15	14	1	1.9
1949	Bos-N	6	11	.353	41	3	1	0	7	96^2	99	6	30	57	12.1	4.19	90	.265	.321	3	.130	-0	-2	-4	1	-0.4
Total	12	92	97	.487	349	177	89	6	22	1686	1721	123	582	747	12.4	3.99	99	.265	.328	128	.228	12	-23	-6	3	2.5
● **SQUIRE POTTER**	Potter, Squire b: 3/18/02, Flatwoods, Ky. d: 1/27/83, Ashland, Ky. BR/TR, 6'1", 185 lbs. Deb: 8/07/23 F																									
1923	Was-A	0	0	—	1	0	0	0	0	3	11	0	4	1	45.0	21.00	18	.688	.750	0	—	0	-6	-6	-0	-0.5
● **BILL POUNDS**	Pounds, Jeared Wells b: 3/11/1878, Paterson, N.J. d: 7/7/36, Paterson, N.J. BR/TR, 5'10.5", 178 lbs. Deb: 5/02/03																									
1903	Cle-A	0	0	—	1	0	0	0	0	5	8	0	0	2	14.4	10.80	26	.359	.359	1	.500	0	-4	-4	-0	-0.3
	Bro-N	0	0	—	1	0	0	0	0	6	8	1	2	2	15.0	6.00	53	.348	.400	2	.667	1	-2	-2	0	-0.1
Total	1	0	0	—	2	0	0	0	0	11	16	1	2	4	14.7	8.18	37	.354	.381	3	.600	1	-6	-6	0	-0.4
● **ABNER POWELL**	Powell, Charles Abner "Ab" b: 12/15/1860, Shenandoah, Pa. d: 8/7/53, New Orleans, La. BR/TR, 5'7", 160 lbs. Deb: 8/04/1884 ♦																									
1884	Was-U	6	12	.333	18	17	14	1	0	134	135	3	19	78	10.3	3.43	87	.245	.270	54	.283	3	-6	-7	2	-0.2
1886	Bal-a	2	5	.286	7	7	7	0	0	60	66	2	26	15	14.0	5.10	67	.264	.336	7	.179	-1	-11	-11	2	-0.8
	Cin-a	0	1	.000	4	1	1	0	0	15^1	16	0	9	4	14.7	4.70	75	.271	.368	17	.230	-0	-2	-2	-0	-0.2
	Yr	2	6	.250	11	8	8	0	0	75^1	82	2	35	19	14.0	5.02	69	.265	.339	24	.212	-1	-13	-13	1	-1.0
Total	2	8	18	.308	29	25	22	1	0	209^1	217	5	54	97	11.7	4.00	78	.252	.297	78	.257	3	-19	-20	3	-1.2
● **DENNIS POWELL**	Powell, Dennis Clay b: 8/13/63, Moultrie, Ga. BR/TL, 6'3", 200 lbs. Deb: 7/07/85																									
1985	LA-N	1	1	.500	16	2	0	0	1	29^1	30	7	13	19	13.5	5.22	67	.263	.344	0	.000	-0	-5	-6	0	-0.6
1986	LA-N	2	7	.222	27	6	0	0	0	65^1	65	5	25	31	12.5	4.27	81	.272	.343	3	.214	1	-4	-6	-1	-0.5
1987	Sea-A	1	3	.250	16	3	0	0	0	34^1	32	3	15	17	12.3	3.15	150	.250	.329	0	—	0	5	6	0	0.5
1988	Sea-A	1	3	.250	12	2	0	0	0	18^2	29	2	11	15	20.3	8.68	48	.363	.452	0	—	0	-10	-9	0	-1.0
1989	Sea-A	2	2	.500	43	1	0	0	2	45	49	6	21	27	14.4	5.00	81	.285	.369	0	—	0	-6	-5	1	-0.5
1990	Sea-A	0	0	—	2	0	0	0	0	3	5	0	2	0	24.0	9.00	44	.357	.471	0	—	0	-2	-2	-0	-0.2
	Mil-A	0	4	.000	9	7	0	0	0	39^1	59	0	19	23	18.1	6.86	56	.341	.409	0	—	0	-13	-13	1	-1.1
	Yr	0	4	.000	11	7	0	0	0	42^1	64	0	21	23	18.3	7.02	55	.340	.410	0	—	0	-15	-15	1	-1.3
1992	Sea-A	4	2	.667	49	0	0	0	0	57	49	5	29	35	12.8	4.58	87	.238	.340	0	—	0	-4	-4	-0	-0.5
Total	7	11	22	.333	174	21	0	0	3	292	318	28	135	167	14.3	5.09	77	.282	.365	3	.176	1	-38	-39	1	-3.9
● **GROVER POWELL**	Powell, Grover David b: 10/10/40, Sayre, Pa. d: 5/21/85, Raleigh, N.C. BL/TL, 5'10", 175 lbs. Deb: 7/13/63																									
1963	NY-N	1	1	.500	20	4	1	1	0	49^2	37	2	32	39	12.7	2.72	128	.202	.324	2	.200	1	3	4	0	0.6
● **JACK POWELL**	Powell, John Joseph "Red" b: 7/9/1874, Bloomington, Ill. d: 10/17/44, Chicago, Ill. BR/TR, 5'11", 195 lbs. Deb: 6/23/1897																									
1897	Cle-N	15	10	.600	27	26	24	2	0	225	245	2	62	61	12.6	3.16	142	.275	.329	20	.206	-4	29	33	-1	2.5
1898	Cle-N	23	15	.605	42	41	36	**6**	0	342	328	8	112	93	12.0	3.00	121	.251	.317	18	.132	-7	23	24	-2	1.4
1899	StL-N	23	19	.548	48	43	**40**	2	0	373	433	15	85	87	12.9	3.52	113	.290	.334	27	.201	-1	14	19	-3	1.4
1900	StL-N	17	16	.515	38	37	28	3	0	287^2	325	9	77	77	12.7	4.44	82	.284	.331	31	.284	9	-24	-26	0	-1.5
1901	StL-N	19	19	.500	**45**	37	33	2	**3**	338^1	351	14	50	133	10.9	3.54	90	.266	.296	21	.176	1	-8	-13	-5	-1.6
1902	StL-A	22	17	.564	42	39	36	3	**2**	328^1	320	12	93	137	11.6	3.21	110	.256	.312	26	.205	3	13	12	-5	0.9
1903	StL-A	15	19	.441	38	34	33	4	**2**	306^1	294	11	58	169	10.5	2.91	100	.252	.291	25	.208	2	2	0	-1	0.1
1904	NY-A	23	19	.548	47	45	38	3	0	390^1	340	15	92	202	10.2	2.44	111	.235	.286	26	.178	-3	7	12	-6	0.4
1905	NY-A	8	13	.381	37	23	13	1	1	203	214	4	57	84	12.3	3.50	84	.272	.326	12	.185	-0	-19	-13	-6	-2.1
	StL-A	2	1	.667	3	3	3	0	0	28	22	0	5	12	8.7	1.61	159	.218	.255	1	.100	-0	3	3	-1	0.2
	Yr	10	14	.417	40	26	16	1	1	231	236	4	62	96	11.6	3.27	88	.264	.312	13	.173	-0	-16	-10	-7	-1.9
1906	StL-A	13	14	.481	28	26	25	3	1	244	196	2	55	132	9.5	1.77	146	.223	.274	21	.233	3	25	22	-3	2.5
1907	StL-A	13	16	.448	32	31	27	4	1	255^2	229	4	62	96	10.4	2.68	94	.241	.291	12	.132	-3	-4	-4	-3	-1.2
1908	StL-A	16	13	.552	33	32	23	5	1	256	208	1	47	85	9.2	2.11	114	.231	.274	21	.236	3	8	8	-6	0.5
1909	StL-A	12	16	.429	34	27	18	4	3	239	221	1	42	82	10.1	2.11	115	.250	.287	14	.179	0	10	8	-4	0.5
1910	StL-A	7	11	.389	21	18	8	3	0	129^1	121	0	28	52	10.4	2.30	108	.250	.292	7	.163	-1	3	3	-3	-0.2
1911	StL-A	8	19	.296	31	27	18	1	1	207^2	224	7	44	52	11.9	3.29	102	.262	.304	12	.164	-3	1	2	-5	-0.5
1912	StL-A	9	17	.346	32	27	19	0	0	235^1	248	5	52	67	11.6	3.10	107	.276	.318	15	.183	0	6	6	-4	0.3
Total	16	245	254	.491	578	516	422	46	15	4389	4319	110	1021	1621	11.2	2.97	106	.258	.305	309	.192	-3	90	94	-58	3.6

YEAR TM/L	W	L	PCT	G	GS	CG	SH	SV	IP	H	HR	BB	SO	RAT	ERA	ERA+	OAV	OOB	BH	AVG	PB	PR	/A	PD	TPI
● **JACK POWELL** Powell, Reginald Bertrand b: 8/17/1891, Holcomb, Mo. d: 3/12/30, Memphis, Tenn. TR , 6'2", Deb: 6/14/13																									
1913 StL-A	0	0	—	2	0	0	0	0	2	1	0	2	0	13.5	0.00	—	.143	.333	0	—	0	1	1	1	0.1
● **BILL POWELL** Powell, William Burris "Big Bill" b: 5/8/1885, Richmond, Va. d: 9/28/67, E.Liverpool, Ohio BR/TR, 6'2.5", 182 lbs. Deb: 4/16/09																									
1909 Pit-N	0	1	.000	3	1	0	0	0	7^1	7	0	6	2	17.2	3.68	74	.292	.452	1	.333	0	-1	-1	0	-0.1
1910 Pit-N	4	6	.400	12	9	4	2	0	75	65	0	34	23	12.5	2.40	129	.242	.338	6	.261	1	5	6	2	0.9
1912 Chi-N	0	0	—	1	0	0	0	0	2	2	0	1	0	13.5	9.00	37	.250	.333	0	—	0	-1	-1	0	-0.1
1913 Cin-N	0	1	.000	1	1	0	0	0	0^1	2	0	2	0	108.0	54.00	6	1.000	1.000	0	—	0	-2	-2	0	-0.2
Total 4	4	8	.333	17	11	4	2	0	84^2	76	0	43	25	13.3	2.87	107	.251	.355	7	.269	1	1	2	2	0.5
● **TED POWER** Power, Ted Henry b: 1/31/55, Guthrie, Okla. BR/TR, 6'4", 225 lbs. Deb: 9/09/81																									
1981 LA-N	1	3	.250	5	2	0	0	0	14^1	16	0	7	7	15.1	3.14	106	.286	.375	0	.000	-0	1	0	-1	-0.1
1982 LA-N	1	1	.500	12	4	0	0	0	33^2	38	4	23	15	16.3	6.68	52	.288	.394	0	.000	-1	-12	-12	-0	-1.3
1983 Cin-N	5	6	.455	49	6	1	0	2	111	120	10	49	57	13.8	4.54	84	.286	.362	0	.000	-2	-11	-9	-2	-1.3
1984 Cin-N	9	7	.563	**78**	0	0	0	11	108^2	93	4	46	81	11.5	2.82	134	.237	.317	0	.000	-0	9	12	0	1.2
1985 Cin-N	8	6	.571	64	0	0	0	27	80	65	2	45	42	12.5	2.70	140	.227	.334	0	—	0	8	10	-2	0.8
1986 Cin-N	10	6	.625	56	10	0	0	1	129	115	13	52	95	11.7	3.70	105	.245	.322	3	.125	0	0	2	-0	0.3
1987 Cin-N	10	13	.435	34	34	2	1	0	204	213	28	71	133	12.7	4.50	94	.267	.329	7	.119	0	-10	-6	-3	-0.9
1988 KC-A	5	6	.455	22	12	2	2	0	80^1	98	7	30	44	14.7	5.94	67	.305	.370	0	—	0	-18	-17	-0	-1.8
Det-A	1	1	.500	4	2	0	0	0	18^2	23	1	8	13	14.9	5.79	66	.307	.373	0	—	0	-4	-4	0	-0.3
Yr	6	7	.462	26	14	2	2	0	99	121	8	38	57	14.5	5.91	67	.300	.361	0	—	0	-21	-22	-0	-2.1
1989 StL-N	7	7	.500	23	15	0	0	0	97	96	7	21	43	10.9	3.71	98	.255	.296	3	.091	-2	-2	-1	-2	-0.5
1990 *Pit-N	1	3	.250	40	0	0	0	7	51^2	50	5	17	42	11.7	3.66	99	.255	.315	1	.125	0	1	-0	-1	-0.1
1991 Cin-N	5	3	.625	68	0	0	0	3	87	87	6	31	51	12.4	3.62	105	.265	.332	0	.000	-0	1	2	-0	0.2
1992 Cle-A	3	3	.500	64	0	0	0	6	99^1	88	7	35	51	11.5	2.54	159	.248	.322	0	—	0	15	16	0	1.6
Total 12	66	65	.504	519	85	5	3	57	1114^2	1102	94	435	674	12.5	3.94	99	.262	.334	14	.089	-4	-21	-7	-11	-2.2
● **JIM POWERS** Powers, James T. b: 1868, New York, N.Y. 5'10", 150 lbs. Deb: 4/18/1890																									
1890 Bro-a	1	2	.333	4	2	2	0	0	30	38	1	16	3	16.5	5.70	68	.300	.382	2	.154	-1	-6	-6	-0	-0.5
● **IKE POWERS** Powers, John Lloyd b: 3/13/06, Hancock, Md. d: 12/22/68, Hancock, Md. BR/TR, 6'0.5", 188 lbs. Deb: 7/26/27																									
1927 Phi-A	1	1	.500	11	1	0	0	0	26	26	1	7	3	11.4	4.50	95	.271	.320	2	.400	1	-1	-1	-0	0.0
1928 Phi-A	1	0	1.000	9	0	0	0	2	12	8	1	10	4	14.3	4.50	89	.222	.404	0	—	0	-1	-1	1	0.0
Total 2	2	1	.667	20	1	0	0	2	38	34	2	17	7	12.3	4.50	93	.258	.347	2	.400	1	-2	-1	1	0.0
● **WILLIE PRALL** Prall, Wilfred Anthony b: 4/20/50, Hackensack, N.J. BL/TL, 6'3", 200 lbs. Deb: 9/03/75																									
1975 Chi-N	0	2	.000	3	3	0	0	0	14^2	21	1	8	7	17.8	8.59	45	.339	.414	0	.000	-0	-8	-8	0	-0.7
● **AL PRATT** Pratt, Albert George "Uncle Al" b: 11/19/1848, Allegheny, Pa. d: 11/21/37, Pittsburgh, Pa. TR , 5'7", 140 lbs. Deb: 5/04/1871 MU																									
1871 Cle-n	10	17	.370	28	28	22	0	0	224^2	296	9	47	**34**	13.7	3.77	110	.277	.307	34	.262	2	11	9		0.8
1872 Cle-n	2	9	.182	15	12	8	0	0	104^2	150	3	14	7	14.1	4.39	83	.288	.307	18	.281	1	-8	-9		-0.5
Total 2 n	12	26	.316	43	40	30	0	0	329^1	446	12	61	41	13.9	3.96	92	.280	.307	52	.268	3	-9	-12		0.3
● **JOHN PREGENZER** Pregenzer, John Arthur b: 8/2/35, Burlington, Wis. BR/TR, 6'5", 220 lbs. Deb: 4/20/63																									
1963 SF-N	0	0	—	6	0	0	0	1	9^1	8	0	8	5	16.4	4.82	66	.242	.405	0	—	0	-2	-2	0	-0.2
1964 SF-N	2	0	1.000	13	0	0	0	0	18^1	21	1	11	8	16.2	4.91	73	.296	.398	0	—	0	-3	-3	-0	-0.3
Total 2	2	0	1.000	19	0	0	0	1	27^2	29	1	19	13	16.3	4.88	70	.279	.400	0	—	0	-4	-4	-0	-0.5
● **JIM PRENDERGAST** Prendergast, James Bartholomew b: 8/23/17, Brooklyn, N.Y. BL/TL, 6'1", 208 lbs. Deb: 4/25/48																									
1948 Bos-N	1	1	.500	10	2	0	0	1	16^2	30	1	5	3	18.9	10.26	37	.380	.417	0	.000	-1	-12	-12	0	-1.1
● **MIKE PRENDERGAST** Prendergast, Michael Thomas b: 12/15/1888, Arlington, Ill. d: 11/18/67, Omaha, Neb. BR/TR, 5'9.5", 165 lbs. Deb: 4/26/14																									
1914 Chi-F	5	9	.357	30	19	7	1	0	136	131	6	40	71	11.5	2.38	124	.255	.313	4	.108	-2	12	9	-2	0.5
1915 Chi-F	14	12	.538	42	30	16	3	0	253^2	220	6	67	95	10.3	2.48	112	.240	.295	6	.075	-7	15	9	-3	-0.1
1916 Chi-N	6	11	.353	35	10	4	2	2	152	127	5	23	56	8.9	2.31	126	.228	.260	7	.152	-2	5	10	-1	0.9
1917 Chi-N	3	6	.333	35	8	1	0	1	99^1	112	6	21	43	12.1	3.35	86	.302	.339	7	.250	1	-7	-5	-1	-0.5
1918 Phi-N	13	14	.481	33	30	20	0	1	252^1	257	6	46	41	10.8	2.89	104	.273	.308	7	.082	-8	-4	3	-2	-0.8
1919 Phi-N	0	1	.000	5	0	0	0	0	15	20	0	10	5	18.6	8.40	38	.351	.456	1	.333	0	-9	-9	0	-0.8
Total 6	41	53	.436	180	97	48	6	4	908^1	867	29	207	311	10.7	2.74	107	.258	.304	32	.115	-17	13	18	-8	-0.8
● **GEORGE PRENTISS** Prentiss, George Pepper (a.k.a. George Pepper Wilson In 1901) b: 6/10/1876, Wilmington, Del. d: 9/8/02, Wilmington, Del. BB/TR, 5'11", 175 lbs. Deb: 9/23/01																									
1901 Bos-A	1	0	1.000	2	1	1	0	0	10	7	0	6	0	11.7	1.80	196	.195	.311	1	.333	1	2	2	-0	0.3
1902 Bos-A	2	2	.500	7	4	3	0	0	41	55	0	10	9	14.3	5.27	68	.321	.359	5	.313	1	-8	-8	-0	-0.7
Bal-A	0	1	.000	2	2	0	0	0	6^2	14	1	5	1	25.7	10.80	35	.426	.501	0	.000	-1	-5	-5	-0	-0.5
Yr	2	3	.400	9	6	3	0	0	47^2	69	1	15	10	15.9	6.04	60	.338	.383	5	.250	-0	-13	-13	-0	-1.2
Total 2	3	3	.500	11	7	4	0	0	57^2	76	1	21	10	15.1	5.31	68	.317	.372	6	.261	1	-11	-11	-0	-0.9
● **JOE PRESKO** Presko, Joseph Edward "Little Joe" b: 10/7/28, Kansas City, Mo. BR/TR, 6', 170 lbs. Deb: 5/03/51																									
1951 StL-N	7	4	.636	15	12	5	0	2	88^2	86	9	20	38	11.0	3.45	115	.251	.296	6	.162	-1	5	5	-1	0.3
1952 StL-N	7	10	.412	28	18	5	1	0	146^2	140	15	57	63	12.1	4.05	92	.247	.317	4	.093	-2	-5	-5	-1	-0.8
1953 StL-N	6	13	.316	34	25	4	0	1	161^2	165	19	65	56	13.1	5.01	85	.261	.335	13	.220	1	-13	-14	-1	-1.3
1954 StL-N	4	9	.308	37	6	1	1	0	71^2	97	14	41	36	18.0	6.91	60	.327	.417	4	.250	0	-23	-22	-0	-2.1
1957 Det-A	1	1	.500	7	0	0	0	0	11	10	0	4	3	12.3	1.64	236	.278	.366	0	.000	-0	3	3	-0	0.2
1958 Det-A	0	0	—	7	0	0	0	2	10^2	13	0	1	6	11.8	3.38	120	.317	.333	0	—	0	0	1	-0	0.1
Total 6	25	37	.403	128	61	15	2	5	490^1	511	57	188	202	13.1	4.61	87	.267	.337	27	.173	-1	-33	-33	-4	-3.6
● **TOT PRESSNELL** Pressnell, Forest Charles b: 8/8/06, Findlay, Ohio BR/TR, 5'10", 175 lbs. Deb: 4/21/38																									
1938 Bro-N	11	14	.440	43	19	6	1	3	192	209	11	56	57	12.8	3.56	110	.276	.332	9	.143	-1	5	7	-1	0.5
1939 Bro-N	9	7	.563	31	18	10	2	2	156^2	171	8	33	43	11.8	4.02	100	.273	.311	10	.196	-1	-2	0	0	-0.1
1940 Bro-N	6	5	.545	24	4	1	1	2	68^1	58	4	17	21	10.1	3.69	108	.221	.274	0	.000	-2	1	2	-1	-0.1
1941 Chi-N	5	3	.625	29	1	0	0	1	70	69	2	23	27	12.3	3.09	114	.253	.320	3	.200	0	**4**	**3**	-1	0.3
1942 Chi-N	1	1	.500	27	0	0	0	4	39^1	40	5	5	9	11.4	5.49	58	.260	.305	2	.667	1	-10	-10	-0	-0.9
Total 5	32	30	.516	154	42	17	4	12	526^1	547	30	134	157	12.0	3.80	101	.264	.315	24	.161	-3	-1	3	-3	-0.3
● **JOE PRICE** Price, Joseph Walter b: 11/29/56, Inglewood, Cal. BR/TL, 6'4", 220 lbs. Deb: 6/14/80																									
1980 Cin-N	7	3	.700	24	13	2	0	0	111^1	95	10	37	44	10.8	3.56	101	.236	.302	5	.128	-2	1	0	-1	-0.2
1981 Cin-N	6	1	.857	41	0	0	0	4	53^2	42	3	18	41	10.1	2.52	141	.222	.290	0	.000	-0	6	6	1	0.7
1982 Cin-N	3	4	.429	59	1	0	0	3	72^2	73	7	32	71	13.5	2.85	130	.263	.347	1	.333	0	6	7	-1	0.7
1983 Cin-N	10	6	.625	21	21	5	0	0	144	118	12	46	83	10.3	2.88	132	.225	.287	4	.098	-1	12	15	-0	1.4
1984 Cin-N	7	13	.350	30	30	3	1	0	171^2	176	19	61	129	12.5	4.19	90	.261	.324	7	.146	-1	-12	-8	-3	-1.1
1985 Cin-N	2	2	.500	26	8	0	0	1	64^2	59	10	23	52	11.4	3.90	97	.242	.307	0	.000	-1	-2	-1	-1	-0.3
1986 Cin-N	1	2	.333	25	2	0	0	0	41^2	49	5	22	30	15.3	5.40	72	.293	.376	1	.143	0	-8	-7	-1	-0.8
1987 *SF-N	2	2	.500	20	0	0	0	1	35	19	5	13	42	8.5	2.57	149	.154	.241	1	.167	-0	6	5	-1	0.4
1988 SF-N	1	6	.143	38	3	0	0	4	61^2	59	5	27	49	12.7	3.94	83	.249	.328	0	.000	-0	-3	-5	-0	-0.6
1989 SF-N	1	1	.500	7	1	0	0	0	14	16	3	4	10	12.9	5.79	58	.314	.364	0	.000	-0	-4	-4	0	-0.4

YEAR	TM/L	W	L	PCT	G	GS	CG	SH	SV	IP	H	HR	BB	SO	RAT	ERA	ERA+	OAV	OOB	BH	AVG	PB	PR	/A	PD	TPI
	Bos-A	2	5	.286	31	5	0	0	0	70^1	71	8	30	52	12.9	4.35	94	.262	.336	0	—	0	-4	-2	-1	-0.6
1990	Bal-A	3	4	.429	50	0	0	0	0	65^1	62	8	24	54	11.8	3.58	106	.253	.320	0	—	0	2	2	-0	0.3
Total	11	45	49	.479	372	84	10	1	13	906	839	95	337	657	11.8	3.65	102	.246	.316	19	.111	-5	0	8	-8	-0.5

● BILL PRICE Price, William b: Philadelphia, Pa. Deb: 4/27/1890

YEAR	TM/L	W	L	PCT	G	GS	CG	SH	SV	IP	H	HR	BB	SO	RAT	ERA	ERA+	OAV	OOB	BH	AVG	PB	PR	/A	PD	TPI
1890	Phi-a	1	0	1.000	1	1	1	0	0	9	6	0	7	1	14.0	2.00	192	.184	.344	1	.250	-0	2	2	0	0.2

● BOB PRIDDY Priddy, Robert Simpson b: 12/10/39, Pittsburgh, Pa. BR/TR, 6'1", 200 lbs. Deb: 9/20/62

YEAR	TM/L	W	L	PCT	G	GS	CG	SH	SV	IP	H	HR	BB	SO	RAT	ERA	ERA+	OAV	OOB	BH	AVG	PB	PR	/A	PD	TPI
1962	Pit-N	1	0	1.000	2	0	0	0	0	3	4	0	1	1	15.0	3.00	131	.308	.357	0	—	0	0	0	-0	0.0
1964	Pit-N	1	2	.333	19	0	0	0	1	34^1	35	2	15	23	13.4	3.93	89	.282	.364	0	.000	0	-2	-2	-1	-0.3
1965	SF-N	1	0	1.000	8	0	0	0	0	10^1	6	1	2	7	7.0	1.74	207	.176	.222	0	.000	-0	2	2	0	0.2
1966	SF-N	6	3	.667	38	3	0	0	1	91	88	8	28	51	11.8	3.96	93	.259	.321	3	.176	0	-4	-3	-1	-0.4
1967	Was-A	3	7	.300	46	8	1	0	4	110	98	12	33	57	10.7	3.44	92	.240	.297	4	.182	1	-3	-3	1	-0.1
1968	Chi-A	3	11	.214	35	18	2	0	0	114	106	14	41	66	11.9	3.63	83	.244	.315	1	.042	-1	-8	-8	-2	-1.1
1969	Chi-A	0	0	—	4	0	0	0	0	8	10	2	2	5	13.5	4.50	86	.303	.343	0	—	0	-1	-1	0	0.0
	Cal-A	0	1	.000	15	0	0	0	0	26^1	24	4	7	15	10.6	4.78	73	.242	.292	0	.000	0	-3	-4	0	-0.4
	Yr	0	1	.000	19	0	0	0	0	34^1	34	6	9	20	11.3	4.72	76	.258	.305	0	.000	0	-4	-4	0	-0.4
	Atl-N	0	0	—	1	0	0	0	0	2	1	0	1	1	9.0	0.00	—	.143	.250	0	—	0	1	1	-0	0.1
1970	Atl-N	5	5	.500	41	0	0	0	8	73	75	9	24	32	12.6	5.42	79	.269	.333	3	.200	0	-11	-9	1	-0.8
1971	Atl-N	4	9	.308	40	0	0	0	4	64	71	8	44	36	16.3	4.22	88	.289	.399	2	.182	0	-5	-4	1	-0.3
Total	9	24	38	.387	249	29	3	0	18	536	518	60	198	294	12.2	4.00	87	.257	.327	13	.137	1	-33	-30	-2	-3.1

● RAY PRIM Prim, Raymond Lee "Pop" b: 12/30/06, Salitpa, Ala. BR/TL, 6', 178 lbs. Deb: 9/24/33

YEAR	TM/L	W	L	PCT	G	GS	CG	SH	SV	IP	H	HR	BB	SO	RAT	ERA	ERA+	OAV	OOB	BH	AVG	PB	PR	/A	PD	TPI
1933	Was-A	0	1	.000	2	1	0	0	0	14^1	13	0	2	6	9.4	3.14	133	.232	.259	0	.000	-1	2	2	1	0.2
1934	Was-A	0	2	.000	8	1	0	0	0	14^2	19	1	8	3	16.6	6.75	64	.339	.422	0	.000	-0	-4	-4	0	-0.3
1935	Phi-N	3	4	.429	29	6	1	0	0	73^1	110	4	15	27	15.3	5.77	79	.340	.369	2	.083	-3	-14	-10	-0	-1.2
1943	Chi-N	4	3	.571	29	5	0	0	1	60	67	2	14	27	12.2	2.55	131	.282	.321	2	.167	-0	6	5	2	0.8
1945	*Chi-N	13	8	.619	34	19	9	2	2	165^1	142	9	23	88	**9.0**	**2.40**	**153**	**.228**	**.256**	13	.255	3	26	23	-1	2.6
1946	Chi-N	2	3	.400	14	2	0	0	1	23^1	28	5	10	10	14.7	5.79	57	.289	.355	1	.200	0	-6	-6	1	-0.6
Total	6	22	21	.512	116	34	10	2	4	351	379	21	72	161	11.6	3.56	107	.272	.308	18	.180	-0	9	9	3	1.5

● DON PRINCE Prince, Donald Mark b: 4/5/38, Clarkton, N.C. BR/TR, 6'4", 200 lbs. Deb: 9/21/62

YEAR	TM/L	W	L	PCT	G	GS	CG	SH	SV	IP	H	HR	BB	SO	RAT	ERA	ERA+	OAV	OOB	BH	AVG	PB	PR	/A	PD	TPI
1962	Chi-N	0	0	—	1	0	0	0	0	1	0	0	1	0	18.0	0.00	—	.000	.500	0	—	0	0	0	0	0.1

● JIM PROCTOR Proctor, James Arthur b: 9/9/35, Brandywine, Md. BR/TR, 6', 165 lbs. Deb: 9/14/59

YEAR	TM/L	W	L	PCT	G	GS	CG	SH	SV	IP	H	HR	BB	SO	RAT	ERA	ERA+	OAV	OOB	BH	AVG	PB	PR	/A	PD	TPI
1959	Det-A	0	1	.000	2	1	0	0	0	2^2	8	0	3	0	37.1	16.88	24	.533	.611	0	—	0	-4	-4	0	-0.3

● RED PROCTOR Proctor, Noah Richard b: 10/27/1900, Williamsburg, Va. d: 12/17/54, Richmond, Va. BR/TR, 6'1", 165 lbs. Deb: 8/06/23

YEAR	TM/L	W	L	PCT	G	GS	CG	SH	SV	IP	H	HR	BB	SO	RAT	ERA	ERA+	OAV	OOB	BH	AVG	PB	PR	/A	PD	TPI
1923	Chi-A	0	0	—	2	0	0	0	0	4	11	0	2	0	29.3	13.50	29	.550	.591	0	—	0	-4	-4	-0	-0.4

● GEORGE PROESER Proeser, George "Yatz" b: 5/30/1864, Cincinnati, Ohio d: 10/13/41, New Burlington, O. BL/TL, 5'10", 190 lbs. Deb: 9/15/1888 ♦

YEAR	TM/L	W	L	PCT	G	GS	CG	SH	SV	IP	H	HR	BB	SO	RAT	ERA	ERA+	OAV	OOB	BH	AVG	PB	PR	/A	PD	TPI
1888	Cle-a	3	4	.429	7	7	7	1	0	59	53	4	30	20	13.7	3.81	81	.231	.338	7	.304	2	-5	-5	-1	-0.3

● MIKE PROLY Proly, Michael James b: 12/15/50, Jamaica, N.Y. BR/TR, 6', 185 lbs. Deb: 4/10/76

YEAR	TM/L	W	L	PCT	G	GS	CG	SH	SV	IP	H	HR	BB	SO	RAT	ERA	ERA+	OAV	OOB	BH	AVG	PB	PR	/A	PD	TPI
1976	StL-N	1	0	1.000	14	0	0	0	0	17	21	0	6	4	14.3	3.71	95	.328	.386	0	—	0	-0	-0	0	0.0
1978	Chi-A	5	2	.714	14	6	2	0	1	65^2	63	4	12	19	10.3	2.74	139	.250	.284	0	—	0	7	8	-1	0.7
1979	Chi-A	3	8	.273	38	6	0	0	9	88^1	89	6	40	32	13.2	3.87	110	.260	.339	0	—	0	3	4	1	0.4
1980	Chi-A	5	10	.333	62	3	0	0	8	146^2	136	7	58	56	12.1	3.07	131	.253	.329	0	—	0	16	16	2	1.8
1981	Phi-N	2	1	.667	35	2	0	0	2	63	66	6	19	19	12.3	3.86	94	.282	.339	0	.000	-1	-3	-2	1	-0.2
1982	Chi-N	5	3	.625	44	1	0	0	1	82	77	5	22	24	11.1	2.30	162	.257	.312	4	.286	1	12	13	0	1.6
1983	Chi-N	1	5	.167	60	0	0	0	1	83	79	5	38	31	12.8	3.58	106	.259	.343	1	.091	-0	0	2	0	0.2
Total	7	22	29	.431	267	18	2	0	22	545^2	531	33	195	185	12.1	3.23	121	.261	.328	5	.156	-0	36	40	4	4.5

● BILL PROUGH Prough, Herschel Clinton "Clint" b: 11/28/1887, Markle, Ind. d: 12/29/36, Richmond, Ind. BR/TR, 6'3", 185 lbs. Deb: 4/27/12

YEAR	TM/L	W	L	PCT	G	GS	CG	SH	SV	IP	H	HR	BB	SO	RAT	ERA	ERA+	OAV	OOB	BH	AVG	PB	PR	/A	PD	TPI
1912	Cin-N	0	0	—	1	0	0	0	0	3	7	0	1	0	24.0	6.00	56	.538	.571	0	.000	-0	-1	-1	-0	-0.1

● AUGIE PRUDHOMME Prudhomme, John Olgus b: 11/20/02, Frierson, La. BR/TR, 6'2", 186 lbs. Deb: 4/19/29

YEAR	TM/L	W	L	PCT	G	GS	CG	SH	SV	IP	H	HR	BB	SO	RAT	ERA	ERA+	OAV	OOB	BH	AVG	PB	PR	/A	PD	TPI
1929	Det-A	1	6	.143	34	6	2	0	1	94	119	7	53	26	16.7	6.22	69	.322	.410	5	.238	1	-21	-20	1	-1.7

● HUB PRUETT Pruett, Hubert Shelby "Shucks" b: 9/1/1900, Malden, Mo. d: 1/28/82, Ladue, Mo. BL/TL, 5'10.5", 165 lbs. Deb: 4/26/22

YEAR	TM/L	W	L	PCT	G	GS	CG	SH	SV	IP	H	HR	BB	SO	RAT	ERA	ERA+	OAV	OOB	BH	AVG	PB	PR	/A	PD	TPI
1922	StL-A	7	7	.500	39	8	4	0	7	119^2	99	2	59	70	12.3	2.33	178	.235	.336	5	.147	-1	23	24	2	2.5
1923	StL-A	4	7	.364	32	8	3	0	2	104^1	109	3	64	59	15.2	4.31	97	.279	.385	3	.130	-1	-4	-2	1	-0.1
1924	StL-A	3	4	.429	33	1	0	0	0	65	64	1	42	27	15.2	4.57	99	.270	.389	3	.200	-1	-2	-0	1	0.0
1927	Phi-N	7	17	.292	31	28	12	1	1	186	238	6	89	90	16.4	6.05	68	.314	.395	13	.217	1	-44	-40	3	-3.3
1928	Phi-N	2	4	.333	13	9	4	0	0	71^1	78	2	49	35	16.4	4.54	94	.291	.406	5	.208	-0	-4	-2	0	-0.2
1930	NY-N	5	4	.556	45	8	1	0	3	135^2	152	11	63	49	14.5	4.78	99	.287	.367	5	.135	-1	3	-1	1	-0.1
1932	Bos-N	1	5	.167	18	7	4	0	0	63	76	3	30	27	16.0	5.14	73	.308	.396	2	.105	-1	-9	-10	2	-0.8
Total	7	29	48	.377	211	69	28	1	13	745	816	28	396	357	15.1	4.63	92	.286	.380	36	.170	-3	-38	-29	9	-2.0

● TEX PRUIETT Pruiett, Charles Le Roy b: 4/10/1883, Osgood, Ind. d: 3/6/53, Ventura, Cal. BL/TR, Deb: 4/26/07

YEAR	TM/L	W	L	PCT	G	GS	CG	SH	SV	IP	H	HR	BB	SO	RAT	ERA	ERA+	OAV	OOB	BH	AVG	PB	PR	/A	PD	TPI
1907	Bos-A	3	11	.214	35	17	6	2	3	173^2	166	1	59	54	12.2	3.11	83	.254	.326	8	.157	-1	-11	-10	1	-1.1
1908	Bos-A	1	7	.125	13	6	1	1	2	58^2	55	1	21	28	12.0	1.99	124	.257	.329	1	.063	-2	3	3	0	0.2
Total	2	4	18	.182	48	23	7	3	5	232^1	221	2	80	82	12.2	2.83	90	.254	.327	9	.134	-2	-8	-7	1	-0.9

● TROY PUCKETT Puckett, Troy Levi b: 12/10/1889, Winchester, Ind. d: 4/13/71, Winchester, Ind. BL/TR, 6'2", 186 lbs. Deb: 10/04/11

YEAR	TM/L	W	L	PCT	G	GS	CG	SH	SV	IP	H	HR	BB	SO	RAT	ERA	ERA+	OAV	OOB	BH	AVG	PB	PR	/A	PD	TPI
1911	Phi-N	0	0	—	1	0	0	0	0	2	4	0	2	1	31.5	13.50	26	.444	.583	0	—	0	-2	-2	0	-0.2

● MIGUEL PUENTE Puente, Miguel Antonio (Aguilar) b: 5/8/48, San Luis Potosi, Mex BR/TR, 6', 160 lbs. Deb: 5/03/70

YEAR	TM/L	W	L	PCT	G	GS	CG	SH	SV	IP	H	HR	BB	SO	RAT	ERA	ERA+	OAV	OOB	BH	AVG	PB	PR	/A	PD	TPI
1970	SF-N	1	3	.250	6	4	1	0	0	18^2	25	5	11	14	17.4	8.20	48	.325	.409	0	.000	-1	-9	-9	0	-0.9

● TIM PUGH Pugh, Timothy Dean b: 1/26/67, Lake Tahoe, Cal. BR/TR, 6'6", 225 lbs. Deb: 9/01/92

YEAR	TM/L	W	L	PCT	G	GS	CG	SH	SV	IP	H	HR	BB	SO	RAT	ERA	ERA+	OAV	OOB	BH	AVG	PB	PR	/A	PD	TPI
1992	Cin-N	4	2	.667	7	7	0	0	0	45^1	47	2	13	18	12.1	2.58	142	.276	.332	1	.077	-0	5	5	-0	0.5

● CHARLIE PULEO Puleo, Charles Michael b: 2/7/55, Glen Ridge, N.J. BR/TR, 6'3", 200 lbs. Deb: 9/16/81

YEAR	TM/L	W	L	PCT	G	GS	CG	SH	SV	IP	H	HR	BB	SO	RAT	ERA	ERA+	OAV	OOB	BH	AVG	PB	PR	/A	PD	TPI
1981	NY-N	0	0	—	4	1	0	0	0	13^1	8	0	8	8	10.8	0.00	—	.182	.308	0	.000	-0	5	5	0	0.6
1982	NY-N	9	9	.500	36	24	1	1	1	171	179	13	90	98	14.3	4.47	81	.275	.364	6	.125	-1	-17	-16	3	-1.4
1983	Cin-N	6	12	.333	27	24	0	0	0	143^2	145	18	91	71	15.1	4.89	78	.269	.379	5	.100	-2	-20	-17	-2	-2.0
1984	Cin-N	1	2	.333	5	4	0	0	0	22	27	2	15	6	17.2	5.73	66	.297	.396	1	.200	0	-5	-5	-1	-0.5
1986	Atl-N	1	2	.333	5	3	1	0	0	24^1	13	4	12	18	9.6	2.96	134	.160	.277	2	.333	0	2	3	-0	0.3
1987	Atl-N	6	8	.429	35	16	1	0	0	123^1	122	11	40	99	12.0	4.23	103	.262	.325	5	.179	1	-2	2	-2	0.1
1988	Atl-N	5	5	.500	53	3	0	0	1	106^1	101	9	47	70	12.8	3.47	106	.251	.333	3	.231	0	-0	2	-0	0.2
1989	Atl-N	1	1	.500	15	1	0	0	0	29	26	2	16	17	13.0	4.66	78	.245	.344	0	.000	-0	-4	-3	-1	-0.4
Total	8	29	39	.426	180	76	3	1	2	633	621	59	319	387	13.6	4.25	90	.261	.351	22	.144	-1	-41	-30	-2	-3.1

● ALFONSO PULIDO Pulido, Alfonso (Manzo) b: 1/23/57, Veracruz, Mexico BL/TL, 5'11", 170 lbs. Deb: 9/05/83

YEAR	TM/L	W	L	PCT	G	GS	CG	SH	SV	IP	H	HR	BB	SO	RAT	ERA	ERA+	OAV	OOB	BH	AVG	PB	PR	/A	PD	TPI
1983	Pit-N	0	0	—	1	1	0	0	0	2	4	2	1	1	22.5	9.00	41	.400	.455	0	—	0	-1	-1	-0	-0.1
1984	Pit-N	0	0	—	1	0	0	0	0	2	3	0	1	2	18.0	9.00	40	.333	.400	0	—	0	-1	-1	-0	-0.1

YEAR	TM/L	W	L	PCT	G	GS	CG	SH	SV	IP	H	HR	BB	SO	RAT	ERA	ERA+	OAV	OOB	BH	AVG	PB	PR	/A	PD	TPI
1986	NY-A	1	1	.500	10	3	0	0	1	30^{2}	38	8	9	13	13.8	4.70	87	.306	.353	0	—	0	-2	-2	-0	-0.1
Total	3	1	1	.500	12	4	0	0	1	34^{2}	45	10	11	16	14.5	5.19	78	.315	.364	0	—	0	-4	-4	-0	-0.3

● SPENCER PUMPELLY Pumpelly, Spencer Armstrong b: 4/11/1893, Owego, N.Y. d: 12/5/73, Sayre, Pa. Deb: 7/11/25

YEAR	TM/L	W	L	PCT	G	GS	CG	SH	SV	IP	H	HR	BB	SO	RAT	ERA	ERA+	OAV	OOB	BH	AVG	PB	PR	/A	PD	TPI
1925	Was-A	0	0	—	1	0	0	0	0	1	1	1	1	0	18.0	9.00	47	.333	.500	0	—	0	-1	-1	-0	-0.1

● BLONDIE PURCELL Purcell, William Aloysius b: Paterson, N.J. BR/TR, 5'9.5", 159 lbs. Deb: 5/01/1879 M♦

YEAR	TM/L	W	L	PCT	G	GS	CG	SH	SV	IP	H	HR	BB	SO	RAT	ERA	ERA+	OAV	OOB	BH	AVG	PB	PR	/A	PD	TPI
1879	Syr-N	4	15	.211	22	17	15	0	0	179^{2}	245	1	19	28	13.2	3.76	63	.303	.319	72	.260	3	-25	-28	-3	-2.4
	Cin-N	0	2	.000	2	2	2	0	0	18	27	0	2	3	14.5	4.00	58	.355	.372	11	.220	-0	-3	-3	0	-0.3
	Yr	4	17	.190	24	19	17	0	0	197^{2}	272	1	21	31	13.3	3.78	63	.308	.324	83	.254	3	-28	-31	-2	-2.7
1880	Cin-N	3	17	.150	25	21	21	0	0	196	235	1	32	47	12.3	3.21	77	.271	.297	95	.292	4	-18	-16	-0	-1.1
1881	Buf-N	4	1	.800	9	5	5	0	0	61^{2}	62	2	9	15	10.4	2.77	100	.248	.274	33	.292	2	0	0	1	0.2
1882	Buf-N	2	1	.667	6	3	2	0	0	31	44	2	4	9	13.9	4.94	59	.338	.358	105	.276	1	-7	-7	1	-0.5
1883	Phi-N	2	6	.250	11	9	7	0	0	80	110	0	12	30	13.7	4.39	70	.306	.329	114	.268	2	-11	-12	1	-0.7
1884	Phi-N	0	0	—	1	0	0	0	0	4	3	1	0	1	6.8	2.25	133	.188	.188	108	.252	0	0	0	-0	0.0
1885	Phi-a	0	1	.000	1	0	0	0	0	6	11	0	2	3	19.5	6.00	57	.423	.464	90	.296	0	-2	-2	0	-0.1
1886	Bal-a	0	0	—	1	0	0	0	0	1	1	0	0	0	9.0	9.00	38	.200	.200	19	.224	0	-1	-1	0	-0.1
1887	Bal-a	0	0	—	1	0	0	0	0	4	8	0	4	2	29.3	15.75	26	.381	.500	142	.250	0	-5	-5	-0	-0.4
Total	9	15	43	.259	79	57	52	0	0	581^{1}	746	7	84	138	12.9	3.73	70	.292	.314	1217	.267	12	-72	-73	-1	-5.4

● JOHN PURDIN Purdin, John Nolan b: 7/16/42, Lynx, Ohio BR/TR, 6'2", 185 lbs. Deb: 9/16/64

YEAR	TM/L	W	L	PCT	G	GS	CG	SH	SV	IP	H	HR	BB	SO	RAT	ERA	ERA+	OAV	OOB	BH	AVG	PB	PR	/A	PD	TPI
1964	LA-N	2	0	1.000	3	2	1	1	0	16	6	1	6	8	6.8	0.56	576	.115	.207	1	.200	0	5	5	-0	0.5
1965	LA-N	2	1	.667	11	2	0	0	0	22^{2}	26	8	13	16	15.5	6.75	48	.283	.371	0	.000	-0	-8	-9	-1	-1.0
1968	LA-N	2	3	.400	35	1	0	0	2	55^{2}	42	2	21	38	10.2	3.07	90	.206	.280	3	.500	1	-1	-2	-0	-0.1
1969	LA-N	0	0	—	9	0	0	0	0	16^{1}	19	7	12	6	17.1	6.06	55	.292	.403	0	.000	-0	-4	-5	0	-0.5
Total	4	6	4	.600	58	5	1	1	2	110^{2}	93	18	52	68	11.8	3.90	77	.225	.312	4	.250	1	-8	-11	-1	-1.1

● BOB PURKEY Purkey, Robert Thomas b: 7/14/29, Pittsburgh, Pa. BR/TR, 6'2", 195 lbs. Deb: 4/14/54

YEAR	TM/L	W	L	PCT	G	GS	CG	SH	SV	IP	H	HR	BB	SO	RAT	ERA	ERA+	OAV	OOB	BH	AVG	PB	PR	/A	PD	TPI
1954	Pit-N	3	8	.273	36	11	0	0	0	131^{1}	145	3	62	38	14.7	5.07	83	.293	.379	2	.077	-1	-15	-13	5	-0.9
1955	Pit-N	2	7	.222	14	10	2	0	1	67^{2}	77	5	25	24	13.8	5.32	77	.287	.353	6	.316	2	-10	-9	1	-0.6
1956	Pit-N	0	0	—	2	0	0	0	0	4	2	1	0	1	4.5	2.25	168	.143	.143	0	—	0	1	1	0	0.1
1957	Pit-N	11	14	.440	48	21	6	1	2	179^{2}	194	10	38	51	12.0	3.86	98	.278	.322	5	.111	-0	0	-1	-1	-0.2
1958	Cin-N☆	17	11	.607	37	34	17	3	0	250	259	25	49	70	11.2	3.60	115	.268	.306	9	.111	-2	10	15	2	1.5
1959	Cin-N	13	18	.419	38	33	9	1	1	218	241	25	43	78	12.0	4.25	95	.279	.318	11	.167	3	-7	-5	-0	-0.2
1960	Cin-N	17	11	.607	41	33	11	1	0	252^{2}	259	23	59	97	11.6	3.60	106	.265	.312	11	.133	-2	5	6	2	0.7
1961	*Cin-N★	16	12	.571	36	34	13	1	1	246^{1}	245	27	51	116	11.0	3.73	109	.255	.297	8	.100	-3	8	9	6	1.2
1962	Cin-N★	23	5	**.821**	37	37	18	2	0	288^{1}	260	28	64	141	10.6	2.81	143	.240	.291	11	.103	-3	36	**39**	3	4.1
1963	Cin-N	6	10	.375	21	21	4	1	0	137	143	12	33	55	11.7	3.55	94	.272	.318	4	.098	-1	-4	-3	1	-0.3
1964	Cin-N	11	9	.550	34	25	9	2	1	195^{2}	181	16	49	78	10.9	3.04	119	.246	.299	3	.052	-4	11	13	2	1.1
1965	StL-N	10	9	.526	32	17	3	1	2	124^{1}	148	20	33	39	13.6	5.79	66	.294	.346	1	.029	-3	-31	-27	1	-2.9
1966	Pit-N	0	1	.000	10	0	0	0	1	19^{2}	16	0	4	5	9.2	1.37	260	.235	.278	0	.000	-0	5	5	1	0.6
Total	13	129	115	.529	386	276	92	13	9	2114^{2}	2170	195	510	793	11.7	3.79	103	.266	.315	71	.110	-13	9	30	21	4.2

● OSCAR PURNER Purner, Oscar E. b: 1873, Washington, D.C. Deb: 9/02/1895

YEAR	TM/L	W	L	PCT	G	GS	CG	SH	SV	IP	H	HR	BB	SO	RAT	ERA	ERA+	OAV	OOB	BH	AVG	PB	PR	/A	PD	TPI
1895	Was-N	0	0	—	1	0	0	0	0	2	4	1	3	0	31.5	9.00	53	.408	.547	0	.000	-0	-1	-1	-0	-0.1

● AMBROSE PUTTMANN Puttmann, Ambrose Nicholas "Putty" or "Brose"
b: 9/9/1880, Cincinnati, Ohio d: 6/21/36, Jamaica, N.Y. TL, 6'4", 185 lbs. Deb: 9/04/03

YEAR	TM/L	W	L	PCT	G	GS	CG	SH	SV	IP	H	HR	BB	SO	RAT	ERA	ERA+	OAV	OOB	BH	AVG	PB	PR	/A	PD	TPI
1903	NY-A	2	0	1.000	3	2	1	0	0	19	16	0	4	8	9.9	0.95	330	.228	.279	1	.143	-0	4	5	1	0.6
1904	NY-A	2	0	1.000	9	3	2	1	0	49^{1}	40	0	17	26	10.4	2.74	99	.223	.290	5	.278	2	-1	-0	0	0.2
1905	NY-A	2	7	.222	17	9	5	1	1	86^{1}	79	2	37	39	12.6	4.27	69	.245	.332	10	.313	3	-15	-13	-0	-1.1
1906	StL-N	2	2	.500	4	4	0	0	0	18^{2}	23	2	9	12	16.4	5.30	50	.303	.391	2	.333	0	-6	-6	0	-0.5
Total	4	8	9	.471	33	18	8	2	1	173^{1}	158	4	67	85	12.1	3.58	80	.244	.322	18	.286	5	-18	-14	1	-0.8

● JOHN PYECHA Pyecha, John Nicholas b: 11/25/31, Aliquippa, Pa. BR/TR, 6'5", 200 lbs. Deb: 4/24/54

YEAR	TM/L	W	L	PCT	G	GS	CG	SH	SV	IP	H	HR	BB	SO	RAT	ERA	ERA+	OAV	OOB	BH	AVG	PB	PR	/A	PD	TPI
1954	Chi-N	0	1	.000	1	0	0	0	0	2^{2}	4	1	2	2	20.3	10.13	41	.333	.429	0	.000	-0	-2	-2	-0	-0.2

● HARLAN PYLE Pyle, Harlan Albert "Firpo" b: 11/29/05, Burchard, Neb. BR/TR, 6'2", 180 lbs. Deb: 9/21/28

YEAR	TM/L	W	L	PCT	G	GS	CG	SH	SV	IP	H	HR	BB	SO	RAT	ERA	ERA+	OAV	OOB	BH	AVG	PB	PR	/A	PD	TPI
1928	Cin-N	0	0	—	2	1	0	0	0	1^{1}	1	0	4	1	33.8	20.25	20	.143	.455	0	.000	-0	-2	-2	0	-0.2

● SHADOW PYLE Pyle, Harry Thomas b: 11/29/1861, Reading, Pa. d: 12/26/08, Reading, Pa. 5'8", 136 lbs. Deb: 10/15/1884

YEAR	TM/L	W	L	PCT	G	GS	CG	SH	SV	IP	H	HR	BB	SO	RAT	ERA	ERA+	OAV	OOB	BH	AVG	PB	PR	/A	PD	TPI
1884	Phi-N	0	1	.000	1	1	1	0	0	9	9	0	6	4	15.0	4.00	75	.257	.366	0	.000	-1	-1	-1	-0	-0.2
1887	Chi-N	1	3	.250	4	4	3	0	0	26^{2}	32	1	21	5	18.6	4.73	95	.291	.414	3	.188	-0	-2	-1	1	0.0
Total	2	1	4	.200	5	5	4	0	0	35^{2}	41	1	27	9	17.7	4.54	90	.283	.402	3	.150	-1	-3	-2	1	-0.2

● EWALD PYLE Pyle, Herbert Ewald "Lefty" b: 8/27/10, St.Louis, Mo. BL/TL, 6'0.5", 175 lbs. Deb: 4/23/39

YEAR	TM/L	W	L	PCT	G	GS	CG	SH	SV	IP	H	HR	BB	SO	RAT	ERA	ERA+	OAV	OOB	BH	AVG	PB	PR	/A	PD	TPI
1939	StL-A	0	2	.000	6	1	0	0	0	8^{1}	17	3	11	5	30.2	12.96	38	.405	.528	0	.000	-0	-8	-7	1	-0.6
1942	StL-A	0	0	—	2	0	0	0	0	5^{1}	6	0	4	1	16.9	6.75	55	.286	.400	0	.000	-0	-2	-2	-0	-0.2
1943	Was-A	4	8	.333	18	11	2	1	1	72^{2}	70	0	45	25	14.4	4.09	78	.254	.360	2	.100	-1	-6	-7	-1	-0.9
1944	NY-N	7	10	.412	31	21	3	0	0	164	152	12	68	79	12.4	4.34	85	.241	.321	8	.157	-0	-13	-12	0	-1.2
1945	NY-N	0	0	—	6	1	0	0	0	6^{1}	16	0	4	2	28.4	17.05	23	.457	.513	0	.000	-0	-9	-9	1	-0.8
	Bos-N	0	1	.000	4	2	0	0	0	13^{2}	16	1	18	10	22.4	7.24	53	.302	.479	2	.333	1	-5	-5	-0	-0.4
	Yr	0	1	.000	10	3	0	0	0	20	32	1	22	12	24.3	10.35	37	.364	.491	2	.250	0	-15	-14	0	-1.2
Total	5	11	21	.344	67	36	5	1	1	270^{1}	277	16	150	122	14.4	5.03	71	.262	.357	12	.143	-2	-44	-43	-0	-4.1

● TOM QUALTERS Qualters, Thomas Francis "Money Bags" b: 4/1/35, McKeesport, Pa. BR/TR, 6'0.5", 190 lbs. Deb: 9/13/53

YEAR	TM/L	W	L	PCT	G	GS	CG	SH	SV	IP	H	HR	BB	SO	RAT	ERA	ERA+	OAV	OOB	BH	AVG	PB	PR	/A	PD	TPI
1953	Phi-N	0	0	—	1	0	0	0	0	0^{1}	4	1	1	0	162.0	162.00	3	.800	.857	0	—	0	-6	-6	0	-0.4
1957	Phi-N	0	0	—	6	0	0	0	0	7^{1}	12	0	4	6	19.6	7.36	52	.400	.471	0	—	0	-3	-3	0	-0.3
1958	Phi-N	0	0	—	1	0	0	0	0	2	2	0	1	0	13.5	4.50	88	.222	.300	0	—	0	-0	-0	-0	0.0
	Chi-A	0	0	—	26	0	0	0	0	43	45	1	20	14	13.6	4.19	87	.281	.361	0	.000	0	-2	-3	1	-0.2
Total	3	0	0	—	34	0	0	0	0	52^{2}	63	2	26	20	15.4	5.64	65	.309	.390	0	.000	0	-11	-11	1	-0.9

● PAUL QUANTRILL Quantrill, Paul John b: 11/3/68, London, Ont., Canada BL/TR, 6'1", 175 lbs. Deb: 7/20/92

YEAR	TM/L	W	L	PCT	G	GS	CG	SH	SV	IP	H	HR	BB	SO	RAT	ERA	ERA+	OAV	OOB	BH	AVG	PB	PR	/A	PD	TPI
1992	Bos-A	2	3	.400	27	0	0	0	1	49^{1}	55	1	15	24	13.0	2.19	189	.288	.343	0	—	0	10	11	-0	1.1

● BILL QUARLES Quarles, William H. b: 1869, Petersburg, Va. d: 3/25/1897, Petersburg, Va. 6'3", Deb: 5/21/1891

YEAR	TM/L	W	L	PCT	G	GS	CG	SH	SV	IP	H	HR	BB	SO	RAT	ERA	ERA+	OAV	OOB	BH	AVG	PB	PR	/A	PD	TPI
1891	Was-a	1	1	.500	3	2	2	0	0	22	32	1	12	10	18.8	8.18	46	.328	.413	0	.000	-2	-11	-11	-0	-1.0
1893	Bos-N	2	1	.667	3	3	3	0	0	27	31	2	5	6	12.7	4.67	106	.280	.322	2	.222	-0	-0	1	-0	0.1
Total	2	3	2	.600	6	5	5	0	0	49	63	3	17	16	15.4	6.24	70	.302	.366	2	.100	-2	-11	-10	-1	-0.9

● MEL QUEEN Queen, Melvin Douglas b: 3/26/42, Johnson City, N.Y. BL/TR, 6'1", 197 lbs. Deb: 4/13/64 FC♦

YEAR	TM/L	W	L	PCT	G	GS	CG	SH	SV	IP	H	HR	BB	SO	RAT	ERA	ERA+	OAV	OOB	BH	AVG	PB	PR	/A	PD	TPI
1966	Cin-N	0	0	—	7	0	0	0	1	7	11	0	6	9	21.9	6.43	61	.367	.472	7	.127	0	-2	-2	0	-0.2
1967	Cin-N	14	8	.636	31	24	6	2	0	195^{2}	155	17	52	154	9.8	2.76	136	.215	.273	17	.210	3	13	22	-2	2.6
1968	Cin-N	0	1	.000	5	4	0	0	0	18^{1}	25	7	6	20	15.2	5.89	54	.333	.383	1	.125	0	-6	-6	0	-0.6
1969	Cin-N	1	0	1.000	2	2	0	0	0	12	7	2	3	7	8.3	2.25	167	.163	.234	1	.167	-0	2	2	-0	0.2
1970	Cal-A	3	6	.333	34	3	0	0	9	60	58	5	28	44	13.7	4.20	86	.261	.357	4	.250	1	-3	-4	-1	-0.4

YEAR TM/L	W	L	PCT	G	GS	CG	SH	SV	IP	H	HR	BB	SO	RAT	ERA	ERA+	OAV	OOB	BH	AVG	PB	PR	/A	PD	TPI
1971 Cal-A	2	2	.500	44	0	0	0	4	65^2	49	3	29	53	11.8	1.78	182	.212	.321	0	.000	-1	12	11	-1	1.0
1972 Cal-A	0	0	—	17	0	0	0	0	31	31	2	19	19	15.4	4.35	67	.265	.381	0	.000	0	-4	-5	-0	-0.6
Total 7	20	17	.541	140	33	6	2	14	389^2	336	36	143	306	11.6	3.14	113	.233	.313	49	.179	3	12	18	-4	2.0

● MEL QUEEN Queen, Melvin Joseph b: 3/4/18, Maxwell, Pa. d: 4/4/82, Fort Smith, Ark. BR/TR, 6'0.5", 204 lbs. Deb: 4/18/42 F

YEAR TM/L	W	L	PCT	G	GS	CG	SH	SV	IP	H	HR	BB	SO	RAT	ERA	ERA+	OAV	OOB	BH	AVG	PB	PR	/A	PD	TPI
1942 NY-A	1	0	1.000	4	0	0	0	0	5^2	6	0	3	0	17.5	0.00	—	.300	.440	0	—	0	2	2	0	0.2
1944 NY-A	6	3	.667	10	10	4	1	0	81^2	68	7	34	30	11.4	3.31	105	.227	.308	6	.194	0	1	2	-2	0.0
1946 NY-A	1	1	.500	14	3	1	0	0	30^1	40	2	21	26	18.1	6.53	53	.315	.412	1	.143	-0	-10	-10	-0	-1.1
1947 NY-A	0	0	—	5	0	0	0	0	6^2	9	2	4	2	18.9	9.45	37	.321	.424	0	.000	-0	-4	-4	-0	-0.5
Pit-N	3	7	.300	14	12	2	0	0	74	70	8	51	34	14.8	4.01	105	.244	.360	2	.077	-2	0	2	-1	-0.2
1948 Pit-N	4	4	.500	25	8	0	0	1	66^1	82	8	40	34	17.0	6.65	61	.308	.405	1	.059	-2	-20	-19	-1	-2.0
1950 Pit-N	5	14	.263	33	21	4	1	0	120^1	135	18	73	76	15.7	5.98	73	.284	.381	2	.057	-3	-25	-21	-1	-2.4
1951 Pit-N	7	9	.438	39	21	4	1	0	168^1	149	21	99	123	13.3	4.44	95	.233	.337	5	.106	-3	-9	-4	-3	-1.0
1952 Pit-N	0	2	.000	2	2	0	0	0	3^1	8	2	4	3	32.4	29.70	13	.381	.480	0	—	0	-10	-10	-0	-0.8
Total 8	27	40	.403	146	77	15	3	1	556^2	567	68	329	328	14.7	5.09	80	.262	.362	17	.104	-11	-74	-63	-9	-7.8

● EDDIE QUICK Quick, Edward b: Baltimore, Md. d: 6/19/13, Rocky Ford, Colo. TR , 5'11", Deb: 9/28/03

YEAR TM/L	W	L	PCT	G	GS	CG	SH	SV	IP	H	HR	BB	SO	RAT	ERA	ERA+	OAV	OOB	BH	AVG	PB	PR	/A	PD	TPI
1903 NY-A	0	0	—	1	1	0	0	0	2	5	0	1	0	27.0	9.00	35	.467	.513	0	.000	-0	-1	-1	0	-0.1

● TAD QUINN Quinn, Clarence Carr b: 9/21/1882, Torrington, Conn. d: 8/6/46, Waterbury, Conn. TR , 6'1", Deb: 9/27/02

YEAR TM/L	W	L	PCT	G	GS	CG	SH	SV	IP	H	HR	BB	SO	RAT	ERA	ERA+	OAV	OOB	BH	AVG	PB	PR	/A	PD	TPI
1902 Phi-A	0	1	.000	1	1	1	0	0	8	12	1	1	3	14.6	4.50	82	.346	.364	0	.000	-0	-1	-1	-0	-0.1
1903 Phi-A	0	0	—	2	0	0	0	0	9	11	0	5	1	16.0	5.00	61	.300	.384	2	.667	1	-2	-2	1	0.0
Total 2	0	1	.000	3	1	1	0	0	17	23	1	6	4	15.4	4.76	70	.322	.375	2	.333	1	-3	-3	0	-0.1

● FRANK QUINN Quinn, Frank William b: 11/27/27, Springfield, Mass. BR/TR, 6'2", 180 lbs. Deb: 5/29/49

YEAR TM/L	W	L	PCT	G	GS	CG	SH	SV	IP	H	HR	BB	SO	RAT	ERA	ERA+	OAV	OOB	BH	AVG	PB	PR	/A	PD	TPI
1949 Bos-A	0	0	—	8	0	0	0	0	22	18	2	9	4	11.5	2.86	152	.222	.308	1	.167	-0	3	4	-0	0.3
1950 Bos-A	0	0	—	1	0	0	0	0	2	2	0	1	0	13.5	9.00	54	.250	.333	0	—	0	-1	-1	0	-0.1
Total 2	0	0	—	9	0	0	0	0	24	20	2	10	4	11.6	3.38	131	.225	.310	1	.167	-0	2	3	0	0.2

● JACK QUINN Quinn, John Picus (b: John Quinn Picus) b: 7/5/1883, Janesville, Pa. d: 4/17/46, Pottsville, Pa. BR/TR, 6' ", 196 lbs. Deb: 4/15/09

YEAR TM/L	W	L	PCT	G	GS	CG	SH	SV	IP	H	HR	BB	SO	RAT	ERA	ERA+	OAV	OOB	BH	AVG	PB	PR	/A	PD	TPI
1909 NY-A	9	5	.643	23	11	8	0	1	118^2	110	1	24	36	10.5	1.97	128	.252	.297	7	.156	0	7	7	3	1.2
1910 NY-A	18	12	.600	35	31	20	0	0	235^2	214	2	58	82	10.6	2.37	112	.247	.299	19	.232	4	4	8	7	2.1
1911 NY-A	8	10	.444	40	16	7	0	2	174^2	203	2	41	71	12.8	3.76	96	.297	.341	10	.164	-1	-8	-3	3	-0.1
1912 NY-A	5	7	.417	18	11	7	0	0	102^2	139	4	23	47	14.6	5.79	62	.325	.365	8	.205	-1	-28	-25	2	-2.2
1913 Bos-N	4	3	.571	8	7	6	1	0	56^1	55	1	7	33	10.1	2.40	137	.261	.288	4	.200	1	5	6	2	1.0
1914 Bal-F	26	14	.650	46	42	27	4	1	342^2	335	3	65	164	10.7	2.60	130	.266	.307	33	.273	8	23	29	1	4.2
1915 Bal-F	9	22	.290	44	31	21	0	1	273^2	289	9	63	118	11.8	3.45	92	.278	.325	29	.264	4	-13	-8	3	0.1
1918 Chi-A	5	1	.833	6	5	5	0	0	51	38	0	7	22	7.9	2.29	119	.216	.246	4	.222	1	3	3	0	0.5
1919 NY-A	15	14	.517	38	31	18	4	0	266	242	8	65	97	10.6	2.61	123	.244	.295	19	.209	1	18	17	1	2.0
1920 NY-A	18	10	.643	41	32	17	2	3	253^1	271	8	48	101	11.4	3.20	119	.273	.308	8	.091	-5	17	18	3	1.4
1921 *NY-A	8	7	.533	33	13	6	0	0	119	158	2	32	44	14.7	3.78	112	.327	.375	9	.220	1	7	6	1	0.7
1922 Bos-A	13	16	.448	40	32	16	4	0	256	263	9	59	67	11.4	3.48	118	.267	.311	9	.099	-5	16	18	5	1.8
1923 Bos-A	13	17	.433	42	28	16	1	7	243	302	6	53	71	13.4	3.89	106	.316	.356	18	.225	0	3	6	-1	0.5
1924 Bos-A	12	13	.480	44	25	13	2	7	228^2	241	10	52	64	12.0	3.27	134	.273	.322	14	.179	-4	24	28	4	2.7
1925 Bos-A	7	8	.467	19	15	8	0	0	105	140	3	26	24	14.5	4.37	104	.315	.357	3	.094	-2	0	2	2	0.2
Phi-A	6	3	.667	18	14	4	0	0	99^2	119	3	16	19	12.5	3.88	120	.296	.328	3	.097	-3	6	8	1	0.6
Yr	13	11	.542	37	29	12	0	0	204^2	259	6	42	43	13.4	4.13	111	.305	.340	6	.095	-5	6	11	3	0.8
1926 Phi-A	10	11	.476	31	21	8	3	1	163^2	191	4	36	58	12.5	3.41	122	.296	.334	8	.174	-0	11	14	1	1.4
1927 Phi-A	15	10	.600	34	25	11	3	1	201^1	211	8	37	43	11.3	3.26	131	.278	.315	6	.091	-7	20	22	-1	1.4
1928 Phi-A	18	7	.720	31	28	18	4	1	211^1	239	3	34	43	11.9	2.90	139	.286	.320	13	.165	-3	27	26	1	2.4
1929 *Phi-A	11	9	.550	35	18	7	0	2	161	182	8	39	41	12.4	3.97	107	.290	.332	8	.133	-4	5	5	0	0.0
1930 *Phi-A	9	7	.563	35	7	0	0	6	89^2	109	6	22	28	13.2	4.42	106	.302	.344	9	.265	1	**2**	**3**	2	0.5
1931 Bro-N	5	4	.556	39	1	0	0	**15**	64^1	65	1	24	25	12.6	2.66	143	.266	.335	3	.200	0	9	8	1	0.9
1932 Bro-N	3	7	.300	42	0	0	0	**8**	87^1	102	1	24	28	13.1	3.30	116	.296	.343	4	.200	0	**6**	**5**	0	0.5
1933 Cin-N	0	1	.000	14	0	0	0	1	15^2	20	0	5	3	14.4	4.02	84	.323	.373	0	.000	-0	-1	-1	1	-0.1
Total 23	247	218	.531	756	444	243	28	57	3920^1	4238	102	860	1329	11.9	3.29	114	.280	.323	248	.184	-13	162	204	40	23.7

● WIMPY QUINN Quinn, Wellington Hunt b: 5/12/18, Birmingham, Ala. d: 9/1/54, Santa Monica, Cal. BR/TR, 6'2", 187 lbs. Deb: 6/08/41

YEAR TM/L	W	L	PCT	G	GS	CG	SH	SV	IP	H	HR	BB	SO	RAT	ERA	ERA+	OAV	OOB	BH	AVG	PB	PR	/A	PD	TPI
1941 Chi-N	0	0	—	3	0	0	0	0	5	3	0	3	2	10.8	7.20	49	.158	.273	1	.500	0	-2	-2	-0	-0.2

● LUIS QUINTANA Quintana, Luis Joaquin (Santos) b: 12/25/51, Vega Baja, P.R. BL/TL, 6'2", 175 lbs. Deb: 7/09/74

YEAR TM/L	W	L	PCT	G	GS	CG	SH	SV	IP	H	HR	BB	SO	RAT	ERA	ERA+	OAV	OOB	BH	AVG	PB	PR	/A	PD	TPI
1974 Cal-A	2	1	.667	18	0	0	0	0	12^2	17	0	14	11	22.0	4.26	81	.327	.470	0	—	0	-1	-1	-0	0.1
1975 Cal-A	0	2	.000	4	0	0	0	0	7	13	2	6	5	24.4	6.43	55	.394	.487	0	—	0	-2	-2	-0	-0.2
Total 2	2	3	.400	22	0	0	0	0	19^2	30	2	20	16	22.9	5.03	69	.353	.476	0	—	0	-3	-3	-0	-0.1

● ART QUIRK Quirk, Arthur Lincoln b: 4/11/38, Providence, R.I. BR/TL, 5'11", 170 lbs. Deb: 4/17/62

YEAR TM/L	W	L	PCT	G	GS	CG	SH	SV	IP	H	HR	BB	SO	RAT	ERA	ERA+	OAV	OOB	BH	AVG	PB	PR	/A	PD	TPI
1962 Bal-A	2	2	.500	7	5	0	0	0	27^1	36	3	18	18	17.8	5.93	63	.308	.400	1	.143	0	-6	-7	1	-0.6
1963 Was-A	1	0	1.000	7	3	0	0	0	21	23	3	8	12	13.3	4.29	87	.280	.344	1	.250	0	-2	-1	-0	-0.1
Total 2	3	2	.600	14	8	0	0	0	48^1	59	6	26	30	15.8	5.21	72	.296	.378	2	.182	0	-7	-8	0	-0.7

● DAN QUISENBERRY Quisenberry, Daniel Raymond b: 2/7/53, Santa Monica, Cal. BR/TR, 6'2", 180 lbs. Deb: 7/08/79

YEAR TM/L	W	L	PCT	G	GS	CG	SH	SV	IP	H	HR	BB	SO	RAT	ERA	ERA+	OAV	OOB	BH	AVG	PB	PR	/A	PD	TPI
1979 KC-A	3	2	.600	32	0	0	0	5	40	42	5	7	13	11.0	3.15	135	.278	.310	0	—	0	5	5	1	0.5
1980 *KC-A	12	7	.632	**75**	0	0	0	**33**	128^1	129	5	27	37	11.0	3.09	131	.265	.305	0	—	0	14	14	3	1.7
1981 *KC-A	1	4	.200	40	0	0	0	18	62^1	59	1	15	20	10.8	1.73	208	.258	.306	0	—	0	13	13	3	1.7
1982 KC-A★	9	7	.563	72	0	0	0	**35**	136^2	126	12	12	46	9.1	2.57	159	.252	.270	0	—	0	23	23	6	3.0
1983 KC-A★	5	3	.625	**69**	0	0	0	**45**	139	118	6	11	48	8.4	1.94	210	.229	.245	0	—	0	**33**	**33**	2	3.5
1984 *KC-A☆	6	3	.667	72	0	0	0	**44**	129^1	121	10	12	41	9.3	2.64	152	.247	.265	0	—	0	19	20	3	2.3
1985 *KC-A	8	9	.471	**84**	0	0	0	**37**	129	142	8	16	54	11.1	2.37	175	.280	.303	0	—	0	25	26	1	2.7
1986 KC-A	3	7	.300	62	0	0	0	12	81^1	92	2	24	36	13.2	2.77	154	.291	.347	0	—	0	13	13	2	1.5
1987 KC-A	4	1	.800	47	0	0	0	8	49	58	3	10	17	12.7	2.76	165	.287	.324	0	—	0	9	10	2	1.0
1988 KC-A	0	1	.000	20	0	0	0	1	25^1	32	0	5	9	13.1	3.55	112	.305	.336	0	—	0	1	1	1	0.2
StL-N	2	0	1.000	33	0	0	0	0	38	54	4	6	19	14.2	6.16	56	.344	.368	0	.000	0	-11	-11	0	-1.1
1989 StL-N	3	1	.750	63	0	0	0	6	78^1	78	2	14	37	10.6	2.64	137	.261	.294	1	.250	0	7	9	2	1.2
1990 SF-N	0	1	.000	5	0	0	0	0	6^2	13	1	3	2	21.6	13.50	27	.419	.471	0	.000	-0	-7	-7	-0	-0.7
Total 12	56	46	.549	674	0	0	0	244	1043^1	1064	59	162	379	10.6	2.76	146	.267	.297	1	.167	0	144	147	25	17.5

● CHARLIE RABE Rabe, Charles Henry b: 5/6/32, Boyce, Tex. BL/TL, 6'1", 180 lbs. Deb: 9/21/57

YEAR TM/L	W	L	PCT	G	GS	CG	SH	SV	IP	H	HR	BB	SO	RAT	ERA	ERA+	OAV	OOB	BH	AVG	PB	PR	/A	PD	TPI
1957 Cin-N	0	1	.000	2	1	0	0	0	8^1	5	2	0	6	5.4	2.16	190	.167	.167	0	.000	-0	2	2	-0	0.1
1958 Cin-N	0	3	.000	9	1	0	0	0	18^2	25	3	9	10	16.4	4.34	96	.321	.391	0	.000	-1	-1	-0	0	-0.1
Total 2	0	4	.000	11	2	0	0	0	27	30	5	9	16	13.0	3.67	113	.278	.333	0	.000	-1	1	1	0	0.0

● STEVE RACHUNOK Rachunok, Stephen Stepanovich "The Mad Russian" b: 12/5/16, Rittman, Ohio BR/TR, 6'4.5", 205 lbs. Deb: 9/17/40

YEAR TM/L	W	L	PCT	G	GS	CG	SH	SV	IP	H	HR	BB	SO	RAT	ERA	ERA+	OAV	OOB	BH	AVG	PB	PR	/A	PD	TPI
1940 Bro-N	0	1	.000	2	1	1	0	0	10	9	0	5	10	12.6	4.50	89	.243	.333	0	.000	0	-1	-1	0	0.0

● MIKE RACZKA Raczka, Michael b: 11/16/62, New Britain, Conn. BL/TL, 6', 200 lbs. Deb: 8/15/92

YEAR TM/L	W	L	PCT	G	GS	CG	SH	SV	IP	H	HR	BB	SO	RAT	ERA	ERA+	OAV	OOB	BH	AVG	PB	PR	/A	PD	TPI
1992 Oak-A	0	0	—	8	0	0	0	0	6^1	8	0	5	2	18.5	8.53	44	.308	.419	0	—	0	-3	-3	-0	-0.3

● DICK RADATZ Radatz, Richard Raymond "The Monster" b: 4/2/37, Detroit, Mich. BR/TR, 6'5", 235 lbs. Deb: 4/10/62

YEAR	TM/L	W	L	PCT	G	GS	CG	SH	SV	IP	H	HR	BB	SO	RAT	ERA	ERA+	OAV	OOB	BH	AVG	PB	PR	/A	PD	TPI
1962	Bos-A	9	6	.600	**62**	0	0	0	**24**	124^2	95	9	40	144	10.0	2.24	184	.211	.281	3	.097	-2	**24**	**26**	-2	2.3
1963	Bos-A★	15	6	.714	66	0	0	0	25	132^1	94	9	51	162	10.2	1.97	192	.201	.286	2	.069	-2	**24**	**27**	-2	2.5
1964	Bos-A★	16	9	.640	79	0	0	0	**29**	157	103	13	58	181	9.6	2.29	168	.186	.271	6	.162	-0	23	**27**	-2	2.7
1965	Bos-A	9	11	.450	63	0	0	0	22	124^1	104	11	53	121	11.7	3.91	95	.227	.314	5	.185	1	-6	-3	-1	-0.2
1966	Bos-A	0	2	.000	16	0	0	0	4	19	24	3	11	19	16.6	4.74	80	.304	.389	0	.000	-0	-3	-2	-1	-0.3
	Cle-A	0	3	.000	39	0	0	0	10	56^2	49	6	34	49	13.7	4.61	75	.233	.348	1	.111	-0	-7	-7	-1	-0.9
	Yr	0	5	.000	55	0	0	0	14	75^2	73	9	45	68	14.4	4.64	76	.253	.359	1	.091	-1	-10	-9	-2	-1.2
1967	Cle-A	0	0	—	3	0	0	0	0	3	5	1	2	1	21.0	6.00	54	.357	.438	0	—	0	-1	-1	0	-0.1
	Chi-N	1	0	1.000	20	0	0	0	5	23^1	12	4	24	18	15.8	6.56	54	.154	.383	1	.250	0	-8	-8	-0	-0.8
1969	Det-A	2	2	.500	11	0	0	0	0	18^2	14	3	5	18	9.2	3.38	111	.212	.268	0	.000	-0	1	1	0	0.1
	Mon-N	0	4	.000	22	0	0	0	3	34^2	32	6	18	32	13.2	5.71	64	.244	.340	1	.250	0	-8	-8	-1	-0.8
Total	7	52	43	.547	381	0	0	0	122	693^2	532	65	296	745	11.1	3.13	122	.212	.303	19	.131	-3	38	53	-9	4.5

● CHARLEY RADBOURN Radbourn, Charles Gardner "Old Hoss" b: 12/11/1854, Rochester, N.Y. d: 2/5/1897, Bloomington, Ill. BR/TR, 5'9", 168 lbs. Deb: 5/05/1880 H♦

YEAR	TM/L	W	L	PCT	G	GS	CG	SH	SV	IP	H	HR	BB	SO	RAT	ERA	ERA+	OAV	OOB	BH	AVG	PB	PR	/A	PD	TPI
1881	Pro-N	25	11	**.694**	41	36	34	3	0	325^1	309	1	64	117	10.3	2.43	109	**.235**	.270	59	.219	-1	12	8	3	0.9
1882	Pro-N	33	20	.623	55	52	51	**6**	0	474	429	6	51	**201**	9.1	2.09	135	.226	.246	78	.239	-1	**43**	**38**	1	**3.4**
1883	Pro-N	**48**	25	.658	**76**	68	66	4	1	632^1	563	7	56	315	**8.8**	2.05	151	.227	**.244**	108	.283	14	**76**	**73**	5	**8.1**
1884	*Pro-N	**59**	12	**.831**	**75**	73	**73**	11	1	**678^2**	528	18	98	**441**	8.3	**1.38**	**205**	.205	.234	83	.230	6	121	109	-4	**10.4**
1885	Pro-N	28	21	.571	49	49	49	2	0	445^2	423	4	83	154	10.2	2.20	120	.241	.275	58	.233	11	31	22	4	3.5
1886	Bos-N	27	31	.466	58	58	57	3	0	509^1	521	18	111	218	11.2	3.00	106	.254	.292	60	.237	8	17	11	2	1.8
1887	Bos-N	24	23	.511	50	50	48	1	0	425	505	20	133	87	13.8	4.55	89	.286	.340	40	.229	2	-23	-23	-3	-2.1
1888	Bos-N	7	16	.304	24	24	24	1	0	207	187	8	45	64	10.4	2.87	99	.234	.282	17	.215	1	-0	-0	-1	-0.1
1889	Bos-N	20	11	.645	33	31	28	1	0	277	282	14	72	99	11.8	3.67	113	.256	.306	23	.189	-2	11	15	2	1.4
1890	Bos-P	27	12	.692	41	38	36	1	0	343	352	8	100	80	12.1	3.31	133	.254	.309	39	.253	0	35	42	2	3.6
1891	Cin-N	11	13	.458	26	24	23	2	0	218	236	13	62	54	12.8	4.25	79	.266	.323	17	.177	-1	-22	-21	-3	-2.1
Total	11	309	195	.613	528	503	489	35	2	4535^1	4335	117	875	1830	10.4	2.67	120	.241	.278	585	.235	37	302	267	7	28.8

● GEORGE RADBOURN Radbourn, George B. "Dordy" b: 4/8/1856, Bloomington, Ill. d: 1/1/04, Bloomington, Ill. Deb: 5/30/1883

YEAR	TM/L	W	L	PCT	G	GS	CG	SH	SV	IP	H	HR	BB	SO	RAT	ERA	ERA+	OAV	OOB	BH	AVG	PB	PR	/A	PD	TPI
1883	Det-N	1	2	.333	3	3	2	0	0	22	38	1	7	2	18.4	6.55	47	.345	.385	2	.167	-1	-8	-8	-0	-0.7

● ROY RADEBAUGH Radebaugh, Roy b: 2/22/1884, Champaign, Ill. d: 1/17/45, Cedar Rapids, Iowa BR/TR, 5'7", 160 lbs. Deb: 9/22/11

YEAR	TM/L	W	L	PCT	G	GS	CG	SH	SV	IP	H	HR	BB	SO	RAT	ERA	ERA+	OAV	OOB	BH	AVG	PB	PR	/A	PD	TPI
1911	StL-N	0	0	—	2	1	0	0	0	10	6	0	4	1	9.0	2.70	125	.176	.263	0	.000	-0	1	1	0	0.1

● DREW RADER Rader, Drew Leon "Lefty" b: 5/14/01, Elmira, N.Y. d: 6/5/75, Catskill, N.Y. BR/TL, 6'2", 187 lbs. Deb: 7/18/21

YEAR	TM/L	W	L	PCT	G	GS	CG	SH	SV	IP	H	HR	BB	SO	RAT	ERA	ERA+	OAV	OOB	BH	AVG	PB	PR	/A	PD	TPI
1921	Pit-N	0	0	—	1	0	0	0	0	2	2	0	0	0	9.0	0.00	—	.286	.286	0	.000	-0	1	1	-0	0.1

● PAUL RADFORD Radford, Paul Revere "Shorty" b: 10/14/1861, Roxbury, Mass. d: 2/21/45, Boston, Mass. BR/TR, 5'6", 148 lbs. Deb: 5/01/1883 ♦

YEAR	TM/L	W	L	PCT	G	GS	CG	SH	SV	IP	H	HR	BB	SO	RAT	ERA	ERA+	OAV	OOB	BH	AVG	PB	PR	/A	PD	TPI
1884	*Pro-N	0	2	.000	2	2	1	0	0	13	27	0	3	2	20.8	7.62	37	.403	.429	70	.197	0	-7	-7	-0	-0.6
1885	Pro-N	0	2	.000	3	2	2	0	0	18^1	34	1	8	3	20.6	7.85	34	.378	.429	90	.243	1	-10	-11	0	-0.8
1887	NY-a	0	0	—	2	0	0	0	0	5	15	1	3	4	32.4	18.00	24	.789	.818	129	.265	1	-8	-8	-0	-0.5
1890	Cle-P	0	0	—	1	0	0	0	0	5	7	1	1	3	14.4	3.60	110	.317	.347	136	.292	0	0	0	1	0.1
1891	Bos-a	0	0	—	1	0	0	0	0	1	0	0	0	0	0.0	0.00	—	.000	.000	118	.259	0	0	0	-0	0.0
1893	Was-N	0	0	—	1	0	0	0	0	1	2	2	2	1	36.0	18.00	26	.403	.575	106	.228	0	-1	-1	0	-0.1
Total	6	0	4	.000	10	4	3	0	0	43^1	85	5	17	13	21.2	8.52	36	.413	.457	1206	.242	2	-25	-26	0	-1.9

● SCOTT RADINSKY Radinsky, Scott David b: 3/3/68, Glendale, Cal. BL/TL, 6'3", 190 lbs. Deb: 4/09/90

YEAR	TM/L	W	L	PCT	G	GS	CG	SH	SV	IP	H	HR	BB	SO	RAT	ERA	ERA+	OAV	OOB	BH	AVG	PB	PR	/A	PD	TPI
1990	Chi-A	6	1	.857	62	0	0	0	4	52^1	47	1	36	46	14.6	4.82	79	.241	.365	0	—	0	-5	-6	0	-0.6
1991	Chi-A	5	5	.500	67	0	0	0	8	71^1	53	4	23	49	9.7	2.02	197	.206	.274	0	—	0	16	15	1	1.7
1992	Chi-A	3	7	.300	68	0	0	0	15	59^1	54	3	34	48	13.7	2.73	140	.243	.349	0	—	0	8	7	0	0.8
Total	3	14	13	.519	197	0	0	0	27	183	154	8	93	143	12.4	3.05	127	.228	.326	0	—	0	19	17	1	1.9

● HAL RAETHER Raether, Harold Herman "Bud" b: 10/10/32, Lake Mills, Wis. BR/TR, 6'1", 185 lbs. Deb: 7/04/54

YEAR	TM/L	W	L	PCT	G	GS	CG	SH	SV	IP	H	HR	BB	SO	RAT	ERA	ERA+	OAV	OOB	BH	AVG	PB	PR	/A	PD	TPI
1954	Phi-A	0	0	—	1	0	0	0	0	2	1	0	4	0	22.5	4.50	87	.200	.556	0	—	0	-0	-0	0	0.0
1957	KC-A	0	0	—	1	0	0	0	0	2	2	1	0	0	9.0	9.00	44	.250	.250	0	—	0	-1	-1	-0	-0.1
Total	2	0	0	—	2	0	0	0	0	4	3	1	4	0	15.8	6.75	58	.231	.412	0	—	0	-1	-1	0	-0.1

● KEN RAFFENSBERGER Raffensberger, Kenneth David b: 8/8/17, York, Pa. BR/TL, 6'2", 185 lbs. Deb: 4/25/39

YEAR	TM/L	W	L	PCT	G	GS	CG	SH	SV	IP	H	HR	BB	SO	RAT	ERA	ERA+	OAV	OOB	BH	AVG	PB	PR	/A	PD	TPI
1939	StL-N	0	0	—	1	0	0	0	0	1	2	0	0	1	18.0	0.00	—	.400	.400	0	—	0	0	0	0	0.0
1940	Chi-N	7	9	.438	43	10	3	0	3	114^2	120	10	29	55	11.9	3.38	111	.271	.319	5	.167	-1	6	5	-1	0.3
1941	Chi-N	0	1	.000	10	1	0	0	0	18	17	0	7	5	12.0	4.50	78	.262	.333	0	.000	-1	-2	-2	1	-0.2
1943	Phi-N	0	1	.000	1	1	1	0	0	8	7	0	2	3	10.1	1.13	300	.241	.290	0	.000	-0	2	2	-0	0.2
1944	Phi-N★	13	20	.394	37	31	18	3	0	258^2	257	9	45	136	10.6	3.06	118	.252	.285	11	.138	-3	16	16	-3	1.0
1945	Phi-N	0	3	.000	5	4	1	0	0	24^1	28	3	14	6	15.5	4.44	86	.283	.372	0	.000	-1	-2	-2	0	-0.3
1946	Phi-N	8	15	.348	39	23	14	2	**6**	196	203	10	39	73	11.2	3.63	95	.265	.302	10	.167	-1	-5	-4	-3	-0.8
1947	Phi-N	2	6	.250	10	7	3	1	0	41	50	4	8	16	13.0	5.49	73	.307	.343	4	.267	0	-7	-7	1	-0.5
	Cin-N	6	5	.545	19	15	7	0	1	106^2	132	11	29	38	13.6	4.13	99	.305	.348	6	.162	-1	-1	-0	-1	-0.2
	Yr	8	11	.421	29	22	10	1	1	147^2	182	15	37	54	13.3	4.51	90	.305	.345	10	.192	-0	-7	-7	0	-0.7
1948	Cin-N	11	12	.478	40	24	7	4	0	180^1	187	15	37	57	11.2	3.84	102	.259	.296	7	.113	-3	2	1	-2	-0.3
1949	Cin-N	18	17	.514	41	38	20	**5**	0	284	289	23	80	103	11.8	3.39	123	.264	.315	16	.178	0	21	25	-3	2.3
1950	Cin-N	14	19	.424	38	35	18	4	0	239	271	34	40	87	11.8	4.26	100	.279	.308	11	.134	-2	-3	-1	-2	-0.4
1951	Cin-N	16	17	.485	42	33	14	5	5	248^2	232	30	38	81	**10.0**	3.44	119	.246	.279	10	.122	-3	14	18	-4	1.1
1952	Cin-N	17	13	.567	38	33	18	**6**	1	247	247	18	45	93	10.7	2.81	134	.261	.295	8	.107	-2	25	27	-2	2.4
1953	Cin-N	7	14	.333	26	26	9	1	0	174	200	23	33	47	12.1	3.93	111	.289	.322	8	.140	-1	7	8	2	0.8
1954	Cin-N	0	2	.000	6	1	0	0	0	10^1	15	2	3	5	15.7	7.84	53	.333	.375	1	.500	0	-4	-4	-0	-0.4
Total	15	119	154	.436	396	282	133	31	16	2151^2	2257	192	449	806	11.4	3.60	110	.267	.306	97	.141	-17	71	82	-18	5.0

● AL RAFFO Raffo, Albert Martin b: 11/27/41, San Francisco, Cal. BR/TR, 6'5", 210 lbs. Deb: 4/29/69

YEAR	TM/L	W	L	PCT	G	GS	CG	SH	SV	IP	H	HR	BB	SO	RAT	ERA	ERA+	OAV	OOB	BH	AVG	PB	PR	/A	PD	TPI
1969	Phi-N	1	3	.250	45	0	0	0	1	72^1	81	6	25	38	13.7	4.11	86	.286	.353	1	.167	0	-4	-5	1	-0.4

● PAT RAGAN Ragan, Don Carlos Patrick b: 11/15/1888, Blanchard, Iowa d: 9/4/56, Los Angeles, Cal. BR/TR, 5'10.5", 185 lbs. Deb: 4/21/09 C

YEAR	TM/L	W	L	PCT	G	GS	CG	SH	SV	IP	H	HR	BB	SO	RAT	ERA	ERA+	OAV	OOB	BH	AVG	PB	PR	/A	PD	TPI
1909	Cin-N	0	1	.000	2	0	0	0	0	8	7	0	4	2	12.4	3.38	77	.259	.355	1	.500	0	-1	-1	-0	-0.1
	Chi-N	0	0	—	2	0	0	0	0	3^2	4	0	1	2	12.3	2.45	104	.286	.333	0	.000	-0	0	0	-0	0.0
	Yr	0	1	.000	4	0	0	0	0	11^2	11	0	5	4	12.3	3.09	84	.268	.348	1	.250	0	-1	-1	-0	-0.1
1911	Bro-N	4	3	.571	22	7	5	1	1	93^2	81	0	31	39	11.0	2.11	158	.252	.321	4	.138	-1	13	13	-1	1.1
1912	Bro-N	7	18	.280	36	26	12	1	1	208	211	7	65	101	12.1	3.63	92	.270	.329	4	.060	-7	-5	-7	-1	-1.4
1913	Bro-N	15	18	.455	44	32	14	0	0	264^2	284	10	64	109	12.0	3.77	87	.281	.327	15	.165	-2	-17	-14	2	-1.5
1914	Bro-N	10	15	.400	38	26	14	1	3	208^1	214	5	85	106	13.0	2.98	96	.270	.343	10	.133	-3	-4	-3	0	-0.6
1915	Bro-N	1	0	1.000	5	0	0	0	0	19^2	11	0	8	7	8.7	0.92	304	.164	.253	1	.167	-0	4	4	0	0.4
	Bos-N	16	12	.571	33	26	13	3	0	227	208	2	59	81	10.9	2.46	105	.255	.311	12	.150	-0	7	3	-2	0.0
	Yr	17	12	.586	38	26	13	3	0	246^2	219	2	67	88	10.7	2.34	112	.248	.306	13	.151	-1	11	7	-2	0.4
1916	Bos-N	9	9	.500	28	23	14	3	0	182	143	3	47	94	9.4	2.08	120	.218	.270	13	.217	3	11	8	1	1.4
1917	Bos-N	6	9	.400	30	13	5	1	1	147^2	138	6	35	61	10.6	2.93	87	.250	.295	6	.125	-1	-4	-6	0	-0.8
1918	Bos-N	8	17	.320	30	25	15	2	0	206^1	212	4	54	68	11.8	3.23	83	.270	.320	13	.183	-2	-11	-12	-0	-1.5

YEAR	TM/L	W	L	PCT	G	GS	CG	SH	SV	IP	H	HR	BB	SO	RAT	ERA	ERA+	OAV	OOB	BH	AVG	PB	PR	/A	PD	TPI
1919	Bos-N	0	2	.000	4	3	0	0	0	12^2	16	0	3	3	13.5	7.11	40	.281	.317	1	.250	0	-6	-6	0	-0.6
	NY-N	1	0	1.000	7	1	1	0	0	22^2	19	0	14	7	13.1	1.59	177	.247	.363	3	.429	1	3	3	0	0.5
	Yr	1	2	.333	11	4	1	0	0	35^1	35	0	17	10	13.2	3.57	79	.261	.344	4	.364	1	-3	-3	0	-0.1
	Chi-A	0	0	—	1	0	0	0	0	1	1	0	0	0	9.0	0.00	—	.250	.250	0	—	0	0	0	0	0.1
1923	Phi-N	0	0	—	1	0	0	0	0	3	6	1	0	0	18.0	6.00	77	.400	.400	1	.500	0	-1	-0	-0	0.0
Total	11	77	104	.425	283	182	93	12	6	1608^1	1555	38	470	680	11.5	2.99	97	.260	.317	84	.154	-12	-8	-18	-2	-3.0

● FRANK RAGLAND Ragland, Frank Roland b: 5/26/04, Water Valley, Miss. d: 7/28/59, Paris, Miss. BR/TR, 6′1″, 186 lbs. Deb: 4/17/32

YEAR	TM/L	W	L	PCT	G	GS	CG	SH	SV	IP	H	HR	BB	SO	RAT	ERA	ERA+	OAV	OOB	BH	AVG	PB	PR	/A	PD	TPI
1932	Was-A	1	0	1.000	12	1	0	0	0	37^2	54	5	21	11	18.6	7.41	58	.346	.433	3	.273	1	-12	-13	0	-1.1
1933	Phi-N	0	4	.000	11	5	0	0	0	38^1	51	1	10	4	14.6	6.81	56	.317	.360	2	.200	0	-15	-13	1	-1.2
Total	2	1	4	.200	23	6	0	0	0	76	105	6	31	15	16.6	7.11	58	.331	.398	5	.238	1	-27	-25	1	-2.3

● ERIC RAICH Raich, Eric James b: 11/1/51, Detroit, Mich. BR/TR, 6′4″, 225 lbs. Deb: 5/24/75

YEAR	TM/L	W	L	PCT	G	GS	CG	SH	SV	IP	H	HR	BB	SO	RAT	ERA	ERA+	OAV	OOB	BH	AVG	PB	PR	/A	PD	TPI
1975	Cle-A	7	8	.467	18	17	2	0	0	92^2	118	12	31	34	14.6	5.54	68	.320	.374	0	—	0	-18	-18	-1	-1.8
1976	Cle-A	0	0	—	1	0	0	0	0	2^2	7	1	0	1	23.6	16.88	21	.467	.467	0	—	0	-4	-4	-0	-0.3
Total	2	7	8	.467	19	17	2	0	0	95^1	125	13	31	35	14.8	5.85	64	.326	.377	0	—	0	-22	-22	-1	-2.1

● CHUCK RAINEY Rainey, Charles David b: 7/14/54, San Diego, Cal. BR/TR, 5′11″, 190 lbs. Deb: 4/08/79

YEAR	TM/L	W	L	PCT	G	GS	CG	SH	SV	IP	H	HR	BB	SO	RAT	ERA	ERA+	OAV	OOB	BH	AVG	PB	PR	/A	PD	TPI
1979	Bos-A	8	5	.615	20	16	4	1	1	103^2	97	7	41	41	12.2	3.82	116	.250	.326	0	—	0	5	7	1	0.7
1980	Bos-A	8	3	.727	16	13	2	1	0	87	92	7	41	43	14.0	4.86	87	.273	.355	0	—	0	-8	-6	-1	-0.8
1981	Bos-A	0	1	.000	11	2	0	0	0	40	39	2	13	20	11.7	2.70	143	.252	.310	0	—	0	4	5	1	0.5
1982	Bos-A	7	5	.583	27	25	3	3	0	129	146	14	63	57	14.7	5.02	86	.294	.376	0	—	0	-14	-10	1	-1.0
1983	Chi-N	14	13	.519	34	34	1	1	0	191	219	17	74	84	13.9	4.48	85	.295	.361	9	.161	1	-18	-15	3	-1.2
1984	Chi-N	5	7	.417	17	16	0	0	0	88^1	102	4	38	45	14.5	4.28	91	.290	.362	3	.097	-1	-7	-4	1	-0.4
	Oak-A	1	1	.500	16	0	0	0	1	30^2	43	2	17	10	17.6	6.75	55	.333	.411	0	—	0	-9	-10	-0	-1.0
Total	6	43	35	.551	141	106	10	6	2	669^2	738	53	287	300	13.9	4.50	90	.284	.358	12	.138	-1	-47	-33	5	-3.2

● DAVE RAJSICH Rajsich, David Christopher b: 9/28/51, Youngstown, Ohio BL/TL, 6′5″, 175 lbs. Deb: 7/02/78 F

YEAR	TM/L	W	L	PCT	G	GS	CG	SH	SV	IP	H	HR	BB	SO	RAT	ERA	ERA+	OAV	OOB	BH	AVG	PB	PR	/A	PD	TPI
1978	NY-A	0	0	—	4	2	0	0	0	13^1	16	0	6	9	14.9	4.05	89	.320	.393	0	—	0	-0	-1	-0	-0.1
1979	Tex-A	1	3	.250	27	3	0	0	0	53^2	56	7	18	32	12.4	3.52	118	.267	.325	0	—	0	4	4	1	0.5
1980	Tex-A	2	1	.667	24	1	0	0	2	48^1	56	7	22	35	15.1	5.96	65	.295	.377	0	—	0	-10	-11	0	-1.0
Total	3	3	4	.429	55	6	0	0	2	115^1	128	14	46	76	13.8	4.60	86	.284	.355	0	—	0	-7	-8	1	-0.6

● ED RAKOW Rakow, Edward Charles "Rock" b: 5/30/36, Pittsburgh, Pa. BB/TR, 5′11″, 178 lbs. Deb: 4/22/60

YEAR	TM/L	W	L	PCT	G	GS	CG	SH	SV	IP	H	HR	BB	SO	RAT	ERA	ERA+	OAV	OOB	BH	AVG	PB	PR	/A	PD	TPI
1960	LA-N	0	1	.000	9	2	0	0	0	22	30	5	11	9	16.8	7.36	54	.323	.394	2	.333	0	-9	-8	-0	-0.8
1961	KC-A	2	8	.200	45	11	1	0	1	124^2	131	14	49	81	13.6	4.76	86	.269	.346	3	.103	-2	-10	-9	1	-1.0
1962	KC-A	14	17	.452	42	35	11	2	1	235^1	232	31	98	159	12.8	4.25	98	.260	.336	8	.098	-5	-7	-2	2	-0.5
1963	KC-A	9	10	.474	34	26	7	1	0	174^1	173	18	61	104	12.3	3.92	98	.261	.328	6	.105	-2	-6	-2	1	-0.2
1964	Det-A	8	9	.471	42	13	1	0	3	152^1	155	14	59	96	13.0	3.72	98	.266	.340	0	.000	-4	-2	-1	2	-0.3
1965	Det-A	0	0	—	6	0	0	0	0	13^1	14	2	11	10	16.9	6.08	57	.280	.410	0	.000	-0	-4	-4	-1	-0.5
1967	Atl-N	3	2	.600	17	3	0	0	0	39^1	36	4	15	25	11.9	5.26	63	.240	.313	0	.000	-1	-8	-8	-1	-1.0
Total	7	36	47	.434	195	90	20	3	5	761^1	771	88	304	484	13.0	4.33	91	.264	.339	19	.084	-13	-46	-35	4	-4.3

● JOHN RALEIGH Raleigh, John Austin b: 4/21/1890, Elkhorn, Wis. d: 8/24/55, Escondido, Cal. BR/TL, Deb: 8/04/09

YEAR	TM/L	W	L	PCT	G	GS	CG	SH	SV	IP	H	HR	BB	SO	RAT	ERA	ERA+	OAV	OOB	BH	AVG	PB	PR	/A	PD	TPI
1909	StL-N	1	10	.091	15	10	3	0	0	80^2	85	0	21	26	12.2	3.79	67	.285	.339	2	.087	-2	-11	-11	0	-1.4
1910	StL-N	0	0	—	3	1	0	0	0	5	8	0	0	2	14.4	9.00	33	.364	.364	0	.000	-0	-3	-3	0	-0.3
Total	2	1	10	.091	18	11	3	0	0	85^2	93	0	21	28	12.3	4.10	62	.291	.340	2	.083	-2	-14	-15	0	-1.7

● PEP RAMBERT Rambert, Elmer Donald b: 8/1/16, Cleveland, Ohio d: 11/16/74, W.Palm Beach, Fla. BR/TR, 6′, 175 lbs. Deb: 9/23/39

YEAR	TM/L	W	L	PCT	G	GS	CG	SH	SV	IP	H	HR	BB	SO	RAT	ERA	ERA+	OAV	OOB	BH	AVG	PB	PR	/A	PD	TPI
1939	Pit-N	0	0	—	2	0	0	0	0	3^2	7	0	1	4	19.6	9.82	39	.389	.421	0	—	0	-2	-2	0	-0.2
1940	Pit-N	0	1	.000	3	1	0	0	0	8^1	12	0	4	0	20.5	7.56	50	.333	.442	0	.000	0	-3	-3	0	-0.3
Total	2	0	1	.000	5	1	0	0	0	12	19	0	5	4	20.3	8.25	46	.352	.435	0	.000	0	-6	-6	0	-0.5

● PETE RAMBO Rambo, Warren Dawson b: 11/1/06, Thorofare, N.J. d: 6/19/91, Camden, N.J. BR/TR, 5′9″, 150 lbs. Deb: 9/16/26

YEAR	TM/L	W	L	PCT	G	GS	CG	SH	SV	IP	H	HR	BB	SO	RAT	ERA	ERA+	OAV	OOB	BH	AVG	PB	PR	/A	PD	TPI
1926	Phi-N	0	0	—	1	0	0	0	0	3^2	6	0	4	4	24.5	14.73	28	.353	.476	1	1.000	0	-4	-4	0	-0.3

● ALLAN RAMIREZ Ramirez, Daniel Allan b: 5/1/57, Victoria, Tex. BR/TR, 5′10″, 180 lbs. Deb: 6/08/83

YEAR	TM/L	W	L	PCT	G	GS	CG	SH	SV	IP	H	HR	BB	SO	RAT	ERA	ERA+	OAV	OOB	BH	AVG	PB	PR	/A	PD	TPI
1983	Bal-A	4	4	.500	11	10	1	0	0	57	46	6	30	20	12.0	3.47	114	.229	.329	0	—	0	4	3	0	0.4

● PEDRO RAMOS Ramos, Pedro (Guerra) "Pete" b: 4/28/35, Pinar Del Rio, Cuba BB/TR, 6′, 185 lbs. Deb: 4/11/55 ♦

YEAR	TM/L	W	L	PCT	G	GS	CG	SH	SV	IP	H	HR	BB	SO	RAT	ERA	ERA+	OAV	OOB	BH	AVG	PB	PR	/A	PD	TPI
1955	Was-A	5	11	.313	45	9	3	1	5	130	121	13	39	34	11.8	3.88	99	.253	.323	3	.079	-2	1	-1	-1	-0.4
1956	Was-A	12	10	.545	37	18	4	0	0	152	178	23	76	54	15.2	5.27	82	.299	.381	9	.205	1	-19	-16	-0	-1.5
1957	Was-A	12	16	.429	43	30	7	1	0	231	251	43	69	91	12.7	4.79	81	.271	.327	13	.171	-1	-26	-23	-0	-2.4
1958	Was-A	14	18	.438	43	37	10	4	3	259^1	277	38	77	132	12.5	4.23	90	.273	.327	21	.239	1	-13	-12	-1	-1.1
1959	Was-A☆	13	19	.406	37	35	11	0	0	233^2	233	29	52	95	11.3	4.16	94	.257	.304	11	.147	-0	-8	-6	-1	-0.7
1960	Was-A	11	18	.379	43	36	14	1	2	274	254	24	99	160	11.8	3.45	113	.245	.315	10	.116	-2	13	13	0	1.2
1961	Min-A	11	20	.355	42	34	9	3	2	264^1	265	39	79	174	11.8	3.95	107	.258	.313	16	.172	2	2	9	-3	0.7
1962	Cle-A	10	12	.455	37	27	7	2	1	201^1	189	28	85	96	12.5	3.71	104	.246	.326	10	.147	2	6	4	0	0.6
1963	Cle-A	9	8	.529	36	22	5	0	0	184^2	156	29	41	169	9.8	3.12	116	.226	.273	6	.109	1	10	10	-2	1.0
1964	Cle-A	7	10	.412	36	19	3	1	0	133	144	18	26	98	11.8	5.14	70	.273	.312	7	.179	2	-22	-23	-1	-2.2
	NY-A	1	0	1.000	13	0	0	0	8	21^2	13	1	0	21	5.4	1.25	291	.183	.183	0	.000	-1	6	6	-1	0.5
	Yr	8	10	.444	49	19	3	1	8	154^2	157	19	26	119	10.6	4.60	78	.259	.290	7	.159	1	-17	-17	-2	-1.7
1965	NY-A	5	5	.500	65	0	0	0	19	92^1	80	7	27	68	10.5	2.92	116	.237	.296	1	.083	-1	5	5	-1	0.4
1966	NY-A	3	9	.250	52	1	0	0	13	89^2	98	10	18	58	11.7	3.61	92	.283	.321	2	.154	-0	-2	-3	-0	-0.3
1967	Phi-N	0	0	—	6	0	0	0	0	8	14	1	8	1	27.0	9.00	38	.412	.545	0	.000	-0	-5	-5	1	-0.5
1969	Pit-N	0	1	.000	5	0	0	0	0	6	8	2	0	4	12.0	6.00	58	.320	.320	0	.000	-0	-2	-2	0	-0.2
	Cin-N	4	3	.571	38	0	0	0	2	66^1	73	8	24	40	13.8	5.16	73	.284	.357	0	.000	-1	-12	-10	-0	-1.1
	Yr	4	4	.500	43	0	0	0	2	72^1	81	10	24	44	13.7	5.23	72	.287	.354	0	.000	-1	-13	-12	-0	-1.3
1970	Was-A	0	0	—	4	0	0	0	0	8^1	10	2	4	10	15.1	7.56	47	.294	.368	0	.000	0	-4	-4	0	-0.3
Total	15	117	160	.422	582	268	73	13	55	2355^2	2364	315	724	1305	12.1	4.08	95	.261	.320	109	.155	-0	-68	-58	-9	-6.3

● WILLIE RAMSDELL Ramsdell, James Willard "The Knuck" b: 4/4/16, Williamsburg, Kan. d: 10/8/69, Wichita, Kan. BR/TR, 5′10″, 180 lbs. Deb: 9/24/47

YEAR	TM/L	W	L	PCT	G	GS	CG	SH	SV	IP	H	HR	BB	SO	RAT	ERA	ERA+	OAV	OOB	BH	AVG	PB	PR	/A	PD	TPI
1947	Bro-N	1	1	.500	2	0	0	0	0	2^2	4	0	3	3	27.0	6.75	61	.333	.500	1	1.000	0	-1	-1	0	0.0
1948	Bro-N	4	4	.500	27	1	0	0	4	50^1	48	6	41	34	16.5	5.19	77	.251	.391	1	.091	-1	-7	-7	1	-0.6
1950	Bro-N	1	2	.333	5	0	0	0	1	6^1	7	0	2	2	14.2	2.84	144	.292	.370	0	.000	-0	1	1	0	0.1
	Cin-N	7	12	.368	27	22	8	1	0	157^1	151	17	75	83	13.0	3.72	114	.255	.341	10	.200	1	7	9	-1	0.9
	Yr	8	14	.364	32	22	8	1	1	163^2	158	17	77	85	13.0	3.68	115	.256	.341	10	.189	0	8	10	-1	1.0
1951	Cin-N	9	17	.346	31	31	10	1	0	196	204	18	70	88	12.9	4.04	101	.266	.333	9	.155	-1	-2	1	-2	-0.2
1952	Chi-N	2	3	.400	19	4	0	0	0	67	41	5	24	30	9.4	2.42	159	.173	.263	1	.056	-1	10	11	-1	1.0
Total	5	24	39	.381	111	58	18	2	5	479^2	455	46	215	240	12.9	3.83	107	.250	.335	22	.156	-2	9	14	-2	1.2

● TOAD RAMSEY Ramsey, Thomas A. b: 8/8/1864, Indianapolis, Ind. d: 3/27/06, Indianapolis, Ind. BR/TL, Deb: 9/05/1885

YEAR	TM/L	W	L	PCT	G	GS	CG	SH	SV	IP	H	HR	BB	SO	RAT	ERA	ERA+	OAV	OOB	BH	AVG	PB	PR	/A	PD	TPI
1885	Lou-a	3	6	.333	9	9	9	0	0	79	44	1	28	83	8.3	1.94	167	.150	.227	4	.129	-2	12	11	-0	0.8
1886	Lou-a	38	27	.585	67	67	**66**	3	0	**588^2**	447	3	207	499	10.2	2.45	149	**.198**	.269	58	.241	-2	66	**78**	-3	6.6
1887	Lou-a	37	27	.578	65	64	61	0	0	561	544	9	167	**355**	11.7	3.43	128	.242	.299	43	.191	-9	54	60	-9	3.4
1888	Lou-a	8	30	.211	40	40	37	1	0	342^1	362	10	86	228	12.1	3.42	90	.262	.310	17	.120	-7	-13	-13	-4	-2.1

YEAR	TM/L	W	L	PCT	G	GS	CG	SH	SV	IP	H	HR	BB	SO	RAT	ERA	ERA+	OAV	OOB	BH	AVG	PB	PR	/A	PD	TPI
1889	Lou-a	1	16	.059	18	18	15	0	0	140	175	7	71	60	15.9	5.59	69	.297	.374	15	.263	0	-27	-27	-2	-2.3
	StL-a	3	1	.750	5	3	3	0	0	41	44	0	10	33	12.1	3.95	107	.266	.312	5	.294	1	-0	1	-1	0.1
	Yr	4	17	.190	23	21	18	0	0	181	219	7	81	93	15.0	5.22	75	.289	.359	20	.270	1	-28	-26	-2	-2.2
1890	StL-a	24	17	.585	44	40	34	1	0	348^2	325	10	102	257	11.2	3.69	117	.239	.296	33	.228	-1	7	24	-7	1.4
Total	6	114	124	.479	248	241	225	5	0	2100^2	1941	40	671	1515	11.4	3.29	117	.234	.295	175	.204	-22	97	134	-25	7.9

● RIBS RANEY

Raney, Frank Robert Donald (b: Frank Robert Donald Raniszewski) b: 2/16/23, Detroit, Mich. BR/TR, 6'4", 190 lbs. Deb: 9/18/49

YEAR	TM/L	W	L	PCT	G	GS	CG	SH	SV	IP	H	HR	BB	SO	RAT	ERA	ERA+	OAV	OOB	BH	AVG	PB	PR	/A	PD	TPI
1949	StL-A	1	2	.333	3	3	1	0	0	16^1	23	2	12	5	19.3	7.71	59	.333	.432	0	.000	-1	-6	-6	-0	-0.6
1950	StL-A	0	1	.000	1	0	0	0	0	2	2	0	2	2	18.0	4.50	110	.250	.400	0	.000	-0	0	0	0	0.0
Total	2	1	3	.250	4	3	1	0	0	18^1	25	2	14	7	19.1	7.36	62	.325	.429	0	.000	-1	-6	-6	-0	-0.6

● PAT RAPP

Rapp, Patrick Leland b: 7/13/67, Jennings, La. BR/TR, 6'3", 195 lbs. Deb: 7/10/92

YEAR	TM/L	W	L	PCT	G	GS	CG	SH	SV	IP	H	HR	BB	SO	RAT	ERA	ERA+	OAV	OOB	BH	AVG	PB	PR	/A	PD	TPI
1992	SF-N	0	2	.000	3	2	0	0	0	10	8	0	6	3	13.5	7.20	47	.235	.366	0	.000	-0	-4	-4	0	-0.4

● VIC RASCHI

Raschi, Victor John Angelo b: 3/28/19, W.Springfield, Mass. d: 10/14/88, Groveland, N.Y. BR/TR, 6'1", 205 lbs. Deb: 9/23/46

YEAR	TM/L	W	L	PCT	G	GS	CG	SH	SV	IP	H	HR	BB	SO	RAT	ERA	ERA+	OAV	OOB	BH	AVG	PB	PR	/A	PD	TPI
1946	NY-A	2	0	1.000	2	2	2	0	0	16	14	0	5	11	10.7	3.94	88	.230	.288	1	.250	0	-1	-1	0	-0.1
1947	*NY-A	7	2	.778	15	14	6	1	0	104^2	89	11	38	51	11.0	3.87	91	.226	.296	10	.250	2	-2	-4	-0	-0.3
1948	NY-A★	19	8	.704	36	31	18	6	1	222^2	208	15	74	124	11.5	3.84	106	.247	.310	19	.235	2	11	6	-1	0.6
1949	*NY-A★	21	10	.677	38	37	21	3	0	274^2	247	16	138	124	12.8	3.34	121	.241	.334	13	.157	1	26	21	1	2.3
1950	*NY-A★	21	8	**.724**	33	32	17	2	1	256^2	232	19	116	155	12.3	4.00	107	.243	.327	17	.198	1	17	8	-3	0.7
1951	*NY-A	21	10	.677	35	34	15	4	0	258^1	233	20	103	**164**	11.9	3.27	117	.242	.319	15	.176	-2	24	16	-3	1.1
1952	*NY-A★	16	6	.727	31	31	13	4	0	223	174	13	91	127	10.9	2.78	119	.216	.300	13	.188	3	22	13	-4	1.3
1953	*NY-A	13	6	.684	28	26	7	4	1	181	150	11	55	76	**10.2**	3.33	111	.224	**.283**	9	.143	-2	13	7	-2	0.3
1954	StL-N	8	9	.471	30	29	6	2	0	179	182	24	71	73	12.7	4.73	87	.268	.337	9	.141	-2	-13	-12	1	-1.3
1955	StL-N	0	1	.000	1	1	0	0	0	1^2	5	0	1	1	32.4	21.60	19	.556	.600	0	—	0	-3	-3	-0	-0.3
	KC-A	4	6	.400	20	18	1	0	0	101^1	132	10	35	38	14.9	5.42	77	.312	.366	6	.182	-0	-16	-14	1	-1.3
Total	10	132	66	.667	269	255	106	26	3	1819	1666	139	727	944	12.0	3.72	105	.244	.319	112	.184	3	78	38	-9	3.0

● DENNIS RASMUSSEN

Rasmussen, Dennis Lee b: 4/18/59, Los Angles, Cal. BL/TL, 6'7", 230 lbs. Deb: 9/16/83 F

YEAR	TM/L	W	L	PCT	G	GS	CG	SH	SV	IP	H	HR	BB	SO	RAT	ERA	ERA+	OAV	OOB	BH	AVG	PB	PR	/A	PD	TPI
1983	SD-N	0	0	—	4	1	0	0	0	13^2	10	1	8	13	11.9	1.98	176	.200	.310	0	.000	-0	3	2	1	0.3
1984	NY-A	9	6	.600	24	24	1	0	0	147^2	127	16	60	110	11.6	4.57	83	.234	.315	0	—	0	-10	-13	-1	-1.1
1985	NY-A	3	5	.375	22	16	2	0	0	101^2	97	10	42	63	12.4	3.98	100	.255	.331	0	—	0	2	0	0	0.2
1986	NY-A	18	6	.750	31	31	3	1	0	202	160	28	74	131	10.5	3.88	105	.217	.290	0	—	0	7	5	-1	0.5
1987	NY-A	9	7	.563	26	25	2	0	0	146	145	31	55	89	12.6	4.75	92	.260	.331	0	—	0	-5	-6	-0	-0.5
	Cin-N	4	1	.800	7	7	0	0	0	45^1	39	5	12	39	10.3	3.97	107	.229	.284	1	.067	-1	1	1	0	0.1
1988	Cin-N	2	6	.250	11	11	1	1	0	56^1	68	8	22	27	14.7	5.75	62	.300	.367	5	.227	1	-14	-14	0	-1.3
	SD-N	14	4	.778	20	20	6	0	0	148^1	131	9	36	85	10.3	2.55	133	.238	.287	9	.188	2	15	14	2	2.0
	Yr	16	10	.615	31	31	7	1	0	204^2	199	17	58	112	11.4	3.43	100	.254	.308	14	.200	3	0	0	2	0.7
1989	SD-N	10	10	.500	33	33	1	0	0	183^2	190	18	72	87	13.0	4.26	82	.270	.340	11	.169	1	-16	-16	-1	-1.6
1990	SD-N	11	15	.423	32	32	3	1	0	187^2	217	28	62	86	13.5	4.51	85	.292	.349	18	.290	5	-15	-14	0	-0.9
1991	SD-N	6	13	.316	24	24	1	1	0	146^2	155	12	49	75	12.6	3.74	101	.271	.331	6	.136	1	-1	1	2	0.3
1992	Chi-N	0	0	—	3	1	0	0	0	5	7	2	2	0	18.0	10.80	33	.350	.435	0	—	0	-4	-4	0	-0.4
	KC-A	4	1	.800	5	5	1	1	0	37^2	25	0	6	12	7.4	1.43	278	.197	.233	0	—	0	10	11	1	1.3
Total	10	90	74	.549	242	230	21	5	0	1421^2	1371	168	500	817	12.0	4.05	95	.255	.321	50	.193	8	-27	-32	2	-1.1

● ERIC RASMUSSEN

Rasmussen, Eric Ralph (Born Harold Ralph Rasmussen) b: 3/22/52, Racine, Wis. BR/TR, 6'3", 205 lbs. Deb: 7/21/75

YEAR	TM/L	W	L	PCT	G	GS	CG	SH	SV	IP	H	HR	BB	SO	RAT	ERA	ERA+	OAV	OOB	BH	AVG	PB	PR	/A	PD	TPI
1975	StL-N	5	5	.500	14	13	2	1	0	81	86	8	20	59	11.8	3.78	99	.264	.306	4	.154	-0	-1	-0	-0	-0.1
1976	StL-N	6	12	.333	43	17	2	1	0	150^1	139	10	54	76	11.7	3.53	100	.247	.315	4	.105	-1	-1	0	3	0.2
1977	StL-N	11	17	.393	34	34	11	3	0	233	223	24	63	120	11.2	3.48	111	.254	.308	10	.139	0	11	10	-1	0.9
1978	StL-N	2	5	.286	10	10	2	1	0	60^1	61	4	20	32	12.1	4.18	84	.270	.329	2	.111	-1	-4	-4	0	-0.5
	SD-N	12	10	.545	27	24	3	2	0	146^1	154	16	43	59	12.2	4.06	82	.277	.331	7	.152	-1	-8	-12	1	-1.2
	Yr	14	15	.483	37	34	5	3	0	206^2	215	20	63	91	12.1	4.09	83	.274	.329	9	.141	-2	-12	-16	1	-1.7
1979	SD-N	6	9	.400	45	20	5	3	3	156^2	142	9	42	54	10.6	3.27	108	.244	.295	2	.056	-2	8	4	-1	0.2
1980	SD-N	4	11	.267	40	14	0	0	1	111^1	130	9	33	50	13.4	4.37	79	.295	.349	2	.095	-1	-9	-12	-0	-1.3
1982	StL-N	1	2	.333	8	3	0	0	0	18^1	21	2	8	15	14.2	4.42	82	.288	.358	0	.000	-0	-2	-2	0	-0.2
1983	StL-N	0	0	—	6	0	0	0	1	7^2	16	1	4	6	23.5	11.74	31	.444	.500	0	—	0	-7	-7	0	-0.7
	KC-A	3	6	.333	11	9	2	1	0	52^2	61	4	22	18	14.2	4.78	85	.289	.356	0	—	0	-4	-4	-0	-0.4
Total	8	50	77	.394	238	144	27	12	5	1017^2	1033	87	309	489	12.0	3.85	94	.266	.321	31	.119	-5	-17	-27	2	-3.1

● HANS RASMUSSEN

Rasmussen, Henry Florian b: 4/18/1895, Chicago, Ill. d: 1/1/49, Chicago, Ill. BR/TR, 6'6", 220 lbs. Deb: 8/11/15

YEAR	TM/L	W	L	PCT	G	GS	CG	SH	SV	IP	H	HR	BB	SO	RAT	ERA	ERA+	OAV	OOB	BH	AVG	PB	PR	/A	PD	TPI
1915	Chi-F	0	0	—	2	0	0	0	0	2	3	0	2	2	22.5	13.50	21	.600	.714	0	.000	-0	-2	-2	0	-0.2

● FRED RATH

Rath, Frederick Helsher b: 9/1/43, Little Rock, Ark. BR/TR, 6'3", 200 lbs. Deb: 9/10/68

YEAR	TM/L	W	L	PCT	G	GS	CG	SH	SV	IP	H	HR	BB	SO	RAT	ERA	ERA+	OAV	OOB	BH	AVG	PB	PR	/A	PD	TPI
1968	Chi-A	0	0	—	5	0	0	0	0	11^1	8	0	3	3	9.5	1.59	191	.182	.250	0	—	0	2	2	0	0.2
1969	Chi-A	0	2	.000	3	2	0	0	0	11^2	11	4	8	4	14.7	7.71	50	.256	.373	0	.000	-0	-5	-5	0	-0.5
Total	2	0	2	.000	8	2	0	0	0	23	19	4	11	7	12.1	4.70	73	.218	.313	0	.000	-0	-4	-3	0	-0.3

● STEVE RATZER

Ratzer, Steven Wayne b: 9/9/53, Paterson, N.J. BR/TR, 6'1", 192 lbs. Deb: 10/05/80

YEAR	TM/L	W	L	PCT	G	GS	CG	SH	SV	IP	H	HR	BB	SO	RAT	ERA	ERA+	OAV	OOB	BH	AVG	PB	PR	/A	PD	TPI
1980	Mon-N	0	0	—	1	1	0	0	0	4	9	0	2	0	24.8	11.25	32	.450	.500	0	.000	-0	-3	-3	0	-0.3
1981	Mon-N	1	1	.500	12	0	0	0	0	17^1	23	2	7	4	15.6	6.23	56	.311	.370	0	.000	-0	-5	-5	1	-0.5
Total	2	1	1	.500	13	1	0	0	0	21^1	32	2	9	4	17.3	7.17	49	.340	.398	0	.000	-0	-9	-9	1	-0.8

● DOUG RAU

Rau, Douglas James b: 12/15/48, Columbus, Tex. BL/TL, 6'2", 175 lbs. Deb: 9/02/72

YEAR	TM/L	W	L	PCT	G	GS	CG	SH	SV	IP	H	HR	BB	SO	RAT	ERA	ERA+	OAV	OOB	BH	AVG	PB	PR	/A	PD	TPI
1972	LA-N	2	2	.500	7	3	2	0	0	32^2	18	1	11	19	8.3	2.20	151	.159	.240	1	.143	1	5	4	0	0.6
1973	LA-N	4	2	.667	31	3	0	0	3	63^2	64	5	28	51	13.1	3.96	87	.259	.337	1	.091	-1	-2	-4	-0	-0.5
1974	*LA-N	13	11	.542	36	35	3	1	0	198^1	191	20	70	126	12.0	3.72	91	.251	.318	9	.141	-1	-2	-7	-0	-0.8
1975	LA-N	15	9	.625	38	38	8	2	0	257^2	227	18	61	151	10.2	3.11	109	.236	.283	17	.195	2	15	8	-1	1.0
1976	LA-N	16	12	.571	34	32	8	3	0	231	221	18	69	98	11.6	2.57	132	.258	.318	9	.150	1	24	21	-0	2.3
1977	*LA-N	14	8	.636	32	32	4	2	0	212^1	232	15	49	126	12.2	3.43	111	.282	.327	10	.141	-0	11	9	-1	0.7
1978	*LA-N	15	9	.625	30	30	7	2	0	199	219	17	68	95	13.1	3.26	108	.284	.344	9	.143	-1	7	6	-2	0.3
1979	LA-N	1	5	.167	11	11	1	1	0	56	73	3	22	28	15.9	5.30	69	.320	.390	2	.143	1	-10	-10	0	-0.9
1981	Cal-A	1	2	.333	3	3	0	0	0	10^1	14	2	4	3	15.7	8.71	42	.341	.400	0	—	0	-6	-6	-0	-0.6
Total	9	81	60	.574	222	187	33	11	3	1261	1259	99	382	697	11.9	3.35	104	.262	.320	58	.154	2	41	21	-6	2.1

● BOB RAUCH

Rauch, Robert John b: 6/16/49, Brookings, S.D. BR/TR, 6'4", 200 lbs. Deb: 6/29/72

YEAR	TM/L	W	L	PCT	G	GS	CG	SH	SV	IP	H	HR	BB	SO	RAT	ERA	ERA+	OAV	OOB	BH	AVG	PB	PR	/A	PD	TPI
1972	NY-N	0	1	.000	19	0	0	0	1	27	27	3	21	23	16.0	5.00	67	.273	.400	0	.000	-0	-5	-5	0	-0.5

● LANCE RAUTZHAN

Rautzhan, Clarence George b: 8/20/52, Pottsville, Pa. BR/TL, 6'1", 195 lbs. Deb: 7/23/77

YEAR	TM/L	W	L	PCT	G	GS	CG	SH	SV	IP	H	HR	BB	SO	RAT	ERA	ERA+	OAV	OOB	BH	AVG	PB	PR	/A	PD	TPI
1977	*LA-N	4	1	.800	25	0	0	0	2	20^2	25	0	7	13	13.9	4.35	88	.313	.368	0	.000	-0	-1	-1	0	-0.1
1978	*LA-N	2	1	.667	43	0	0	0	4	61^1	61	1	19	25	11.9	2.93	120	.263	.321	0	.000	-0	4	4	2	0.5
1979	LA-N	0	2	.000	12	0	0	0	1	9^2	9	0	11	5	19.6	7.45	49	.273	.467	0	—	0	-4	-4	0	-0.4
	Mil-A	0	0	—	3	0	0	0	0	3	3	0	10	2	39.0	9.00	46	.300	.650	0	—	0	-2	-2	0	-0.1
Total	3	6	4	.600	83	0	0	0	7	94^2	98	1	47	45	14.0	3.90	93	.276	.364	0	.000	-1	-2	-3	2	-0.1

● SHANE RAWLEY

Rawley, Shane William b: 7/27/55, Racine, Wis. BR/TL, 6', 180 lbs. Deb: 4/06/78

YEAR	TM/L	W	L	PCT	G	GS	CG	SH	SV	IP	H	HR	BB	SO	RAT	ERA	ERA+	OAV	OOB	BH	AVG	PB	PR	/A	PD	TPI
1978	Sea-A	4	9	.308	52	2	0	0	4	111^1	114	7	51	66	13.7	4.12	92	.275	.362	0	—	0	-4	-4	1	-0.3

YEAR	TM/L	W	L	PCT	G	GS	CG	SH	SV	IP	H	HR	BB	SO	RAT	ERA	ERA+	OAV	OOB	BH	AVG	PB	PR	/A	PD	TPI
1979	Sea-A	5	9	.357	48	3	0	0	11	84^{1}	88	2	40	48	13.8	3.84	113	.278	.361	0	—	0	3	5	1	0.4
1980	Sea-A	7	7	.500	59	0	0	0	13	113^{2}	103	3	63	68	13.4	3.33	124	.257	.363	0	—	0	9	10	2	1.2
1981	Sea-A	4	6	.400	46	0	0	0	8	68^{1}	64	1	38	35	13.6	3.95	97	.257	.358	0	—	0	-2	-1	0	-0.2
1982	NY-A	11	10	.524	47	17	3	0	3	164	165	10	54	111	12.1	4.06	98	.267	.328	0	—	0	0	-1	1	0.1
1983	NY-A	14	14	.500	34	33	13	2	1	238^{1}	246	19	79	124	12.4	3.78	103	.269	.329	0	—	0	8	3	0	0.5
1984	NY-A	2	3	.400	11	10	0	0	0	42	46	0	27	24	15.6	6.21	61	.272	.372	0	—	0	-10	-11	-0	-0.8
	Phi-N	10	6	.625	18	18	3	0	0	120^{1}	117	13	27	58	10.8	3.81	95	.257	.300	5	.116	-2	-3	-2	-1	-0.5
1985	Phi-N	13	8	.619	36	31	6	2	0	198^{2}	188	16	81	106	12.3	3.31	111	.249	.323	8	.138	0	6	8	1	1.0
1986	Phi-N☆	11	7	.611	23	23	7	1	0	157^{2}	166	13	50	73	12.4	3.54	109	.270	.326	9	.173	0	3	5	-0	0.6
1987	Phi-N	17	11	.607	36	36	4	1	0	229^{2}	250	23	86	123	13.4	4.39	97	.279	.346	12	.152	-0	-8	-4	-1	-0.5
1988	Phi-N	8	16	.333	32	32	4	1	0	198	220	27	78	87	13.7	4.18	85	.286	.355	6	.105	-1	-16	-14	-0	-1.6
1989	Min-A	5	12	.294	27	25	1	0	0	145	167	19	60	68	14.1	5.21	79	.293	.361	0	—	0	-21	-17	-1	-1.8
Total	12	111	118	.485	469	230	41	7	40	1871^{1}	1934	153	734	991	13.0	4.02	97	.271	.341	40	.138	-3	-36	-22	2	-1.9

● CARL RAY Ray, Carl Grady b: 1/31/1889, Danbury, N.C. d: 4/3/70, Walnut Cove, N.C. BL/TL, 5′11″, 170 lbs. Deb: 9/25/15

YEAR	TM/L	W	L	PCT	G	GS	CG	SH	SV	IP	H	HR	BB	SO	RAT	ERA	ERA+	OAV	OOB	BH	AVG	PB	PR	/A	PD	TPI
1915	Phi-A	0	1	.000	2	1	0	0	0	7^{1}	11	0	6	6	25.8	4.91	60	.333	.488	0	.000	0	-2	-2	-0	-0.2
1916	Phi-A	0	1	.000	3	1	0	0	0	9^{1}	9	0	14	5	23.1	4.82	59	.257	.480	0	.000	-0	-2	-2	-0	-0.3
Total	2	0	2	.000	5	2	0	0	0	16^{2}	20	0	20	11	24.3	4.86	59	.294	.484	0	.000	-0	-4	-4	-1	-0.5

● JIM RAY Ray, James Francis "Sting" b: 12/1/44, Rock Hill, S.C. BR/TR, 6′1″, 195 lbs. Deb: 9/16/65

YEAR	TM/L	W	L	PCT	G	GS	CG	SH	SV	IP	H	HR	BB	SO	RAT	ERA	ERA+	OAV	OOB	BH	AVG	PB	PR	/A	PD	TPI
1965	Hou-N	0	2	.000	3	2	0	0	0	7^{2}	11	1	6	7	20.0	10.57	32	.355	.459	0	.000	-0	-6	-6	0	-0.6
1966	Hou-N	0	0	—	1	0	0	0	0	0	0	0	1	0	—	∞	—	—	1.000	0	—	0	-1	-1	0	-0.1
1968	Hou-N	2	3	.400	41	2	1	0	1	80^{2}	65	5	25	71	10.2	2.68	110	.220	.283	1	.067	-1	3	2	-1	0.1
1969	Hou-N	8	2	.800	40	13	0	0	0	115	105	11	48	115	12.1	3.91	90	.245	.324	3	.115	-1	-4	-5	-1	-0.7
1970	Hou-N	6	3	.667	52	2	0	0	5	105	97	13	49	67	12.5	3.26	119	.251	.336	5	.185	-0	9	7	0	0.7
1971	Hou-N	10	4	.714	47	1	0	0	3	97^{2}	72	3	31	46	9.7	2.12	159	.211	.281	3	.167	0	15	14	-2	1.3
1972	Hou-N	10	9	.526	54	0	0	0	8	90^{1}	77	10	44	50	12.4	4.28	79	.227	.321	1	.063	-1	-8	-9	-1	-1.2
1973	Hou-N	6	4	.600	42	0	0	0	6	69	65	5	38	25	13.8	4.43	82	.253	.356	3	.231	0	-6	-6	-1	-0.7
1974	Det-A	1	3	.250	28	0	0	0	2	52^{1}	49	4	29	26	13.6	4.47	85	.254	.354	0	—	0	-5	-4	0	-0.6
Total	9	43	30	.589	308	20	1	0	25	617^{2}	541	52	271	407	12.0	3.61	97	.238	.323	16	.137	-3	-4	-8	-6	-1.8

● FARMER RAY Ray, Robert Henry b: 9/17/1886, Ft.Lyon, Colo. d: 3/11/63, Electra, Tex. BL/TR, 5′11″, 160 lbs. Deb: 6/13/10

YEAR	TM/L	W	L	PCT	G	GS	CG	SH	SV	IP	H	HR	BB	SO	RAT	ERA	ERA+	OAV	OOB	BH	AVG	PB	PR	/A	PD	TPI
1910	StL-A	4	10	.286	21	16	11	0	0	140^{2}	146	3	49	35	12.9	3.58	69	.285	.356	7	.175	0	-17	-17	-3	-2.1

● CURT RAYDON Raydon, Curtis Lowell b: 11/18/33, Bloomington, Ill. BR/TR, 6′4″, 190 lbs. Deb: 4/15/58

YEAR	TM/L	W	L	PCT	G	GS	CG	SH	SV	IP	H	HR	BB	SO	RAT	ERA	ERA+	OAV	OOB	BH	AVG	PB	PR	/A	PD	TPI
1958	Pit-N	8	4	.667	31	20	2	1	1	134^{1}	118	18	61	85	12.3	3.62	107	.236	.326	1	.026	-2	5	4	-3	-0.1

● BUGS RAYMOND Raymond, Arthur Lawrence b: 2/24/1882, Chicago, Ill. d: 9/7/12, Chicago, Ill. BR/TR, 5′10″, 180 lbs. Deb: 9/23/04

YEAR	TM/L	W	L	PCT	G	GS	CG	SH	SV	IP	H	HR	BB	SO	RAT	ERA	ERA+	OAV	OOB	BH	AVG	PB	PR	/A	PD	TPI
1904	Det-A	0	1	.000	5	2	1	0	0	14^{2}	14	0	6	7	13.5	3.07	83	.252	.346	0	.000	-1	-1	-1	1	0.0
1907	StL-N	2	4	.333	8	6	6	1	0	64^{2}	56	3	21	34	10.9	1.67	150	.230	.294	2	.091	-0	6	6	0	0.7
1908	StL-N	15	25	.375	48	37	23	5	2	324^{1}	236	2	95	145	9.6	2.03	116	.207	.277	17	.189	1	12	12	3	2.0
1909	NY-N	18	12	.600	39	31	18	2	0	270	239	7	87	121	11.1	2.47	104	.245	.311	13	.146	0	4	3	2	0.5
1910	NY-N	4	11	.267	19	11	6	0	0	99^{1}	106	2	40	55	14.0	3.81	78	.280	.362	5	.156	-1	-9	-9	2	-0.8
1911	NY-N	6	4	.600	17	9	4	1	0	81^{2}	73	1	33	39	11.9	3.31	102	.248	.328	5	.200	-0	1	1	1	0.1
Total	6	45	57	.441	136	96	58	9	2	854^{2}	724	15	282	401	10.9	2.49	105	.235	.306	42	.160	-0	14	11	9	2.5

● HARRY RAYMOND Raymond, Harry H. "Jack" b: 2/20/1862, Utica, N.Y. d: 3/21/25, San Diego, Cal. 5′9″, 179 lbs. Deb: 9/09/1888 ♦

YEAR	TM/L	W	L	PCT	G	GS	CG	SH	SV	IP	H	HR	BB	SO	RAT	ERA	ERA+	OAV	OOB	BH	AVG	PB	PR	/A	PD	TPI
1889	Lou-a	1	0	1.000	1	1	1	0	0	9	8	0	11	1	19.0	1.00	385	.231	.416	123	.239	0	3	3	-0	0.2

● CLAUDE RAYMOND Raymond, Joseph Claude Marc "Frenchy" b: 5/7/37, St.Jean, Que., Canada BR/TR, 5′10″, 175 lbs. Deb: 4/15/59

YEAR	TM/L	W	L	PCT	G	GS	CG	SH	SV	IP	H	HR	BB	SO	RAT	ERA	ERA+	OAV	OOB	BH	AVG	PB	PR	/A	PD	TPI
1959	Chi-A	0	0	—	3	0	0	0	0	4	5	2	2	1	15.8	9.00	42	.333	.412	0	—	0	-2	-2	0	-0.2
1961	Mil-N	1	0	1.000	13	0	0	0	2	20^{1}	22	2	9	13	14.2	3.98	94	.275	.356	0	.000	-0	0	-1	0	-0.1
1962	Mil-N	5	5	.500	26	0	0	0	10	42^{2}	37	5	15	40	11.4	2.74	138	.236	.310	0	.000	-1	6	5	-1	0.3
1963	Mil-N	4	6	.400	45	0	0	0	5	53^{1}	57	12	27	44	14.9	5.40	60	.268	.361	2	.500	2	-13	-13	1	-1.1
1964	Hou-N	5	5	.500	38	0	0	0	0	79^{2}	64	3	22	56	10.1	2.82	121	.229	.292	1	.071	-0	6	5	1	0.7
1965	Hou-N	7	4	.636	33	7	2	0	5	96^{1}	87	6	16	79	10.1	2.90	116	.244	.286	3	.115	-0	7	5	-0	0.4
1966	Hou-N☆	7	5	.583	62	0	0	0	16	92	85	10	25	73	11.2	3.13	109	.242	.300	1	.111	-0	5	3	-2	0.1
1967	Hou-N	0	4	.000	21	0	0	0	5	31	31	5	7	17	11.6	3.19	104	.256	.308	1	.200	0	1	0	-0	0.0
	Atl-N	4	1	.800	28	0	0	0	5	34^{1}	33	2	11	14	11.5	2.62	127	.260	.319	0	.000	-0	3	3	0	0.3
	Yr	4	5	.444	49	0	0	0	10	65^{1}	64	7	18	31	11.3	2.89	115	.255	.305	1	.143	0	4	3	-0	0.3
1968	Atl-N	3	5	.375	36	0	0	0	10	60^{1}	56	4	18	37	11.2	2.83	106	.256	.315	1	.143	-0	1	1	0	0.1
1969	Atl-N	2	2	.500	33	0	0	0	1	48	56	4	13	15	13.3	5.25	69	.298	.350	2	.286	0	-9	-9	-1	-0.9
	Mon-N	1	2	.333	15	0	0	0	1	22	21	2	8	11	12.7	4.09	90	.256	.337	0	.000	-0	-1	-1	1	-0.1
	Yr	3	4	.429	48	0	0	0	2	70	77	6	21	26	12.9	4.89	74	.281	.337	2	.182	-0	-10	-10	-0	-1.0
1970	Mon-N	6	7	.462	59	0	0	0	23	83^{1}	76	13	27	68	11.3	4.43	93	.240	.303	0	.000	-1	-4	-3	-1	-0.5
1971	Mon-N	1	7	.125	37	0	0	0	0	53^{2}	81	5	25	29	17.8	4.70	75	.373	.438	0	.000	-0	-7	-7	1	-0.6
Total	12	46	53	.465	449	7	2	0	83	721	711	75	225	497	12.0	3.66	96	.261	.324	11	.109	-2	-7	-13	-0	-1.6

● BARRY RAZIANO Raziano, Barry John b: 2/5/47, New Orleans, La. BB/TR, 5′10″, 175 lbs. Deb: 8/18/73

YEAR	TM/L	W	L	PCT	G	GS	CG	SH	SV	IP	H	HR	BB	SO	RAT	ERA	ERA+	OAV	OOB	BH	AVG	PB	PR	/A	PD	TPI
1973	KC-A	0	0	—	2	0	0	0	0	5	6	1	1	0	14.4	5.40	76	.316	.381	0	—	0	-1	-1	0	-0.1
1974	Cal-A	1	2	.333	13	0	0	0	1	16^{2}	15	1	8	9	12.4	6.48	53	.246	.333	0	—	0	-5	-6	-0	-0.2
Total	2	1	2	.333	15	0	0	0	1	21^{2}	21	2	9	9	12.9	6.23	58	.262	.344	0	—	0	-6	-6	-0	-0.3

● RIP REAGAN Reagan, Arthur (b: Arthur Edgar Ragan) b: 6/5/1878, Lincoln, Ill. d: 6/8/53, Kansas City, Mo. BR/TR, 5′11″, 170 lbs. Deb: 9/19/03

YEAR	TM/L	W	L	PCT	G	GS	CG	SH	SV	IP	H	HR	BB	SO	RAT	ERA	ERA+	OAV	OOB	BH	AVG	PB	PR	/A	PD	TPI
1903	Cin-N	0	2	.000	3	2	2	0	0	18	40	0	7	7	24.0	6.00	59	.455	.500	2	.250	0	-5	-5	-0	-0.4

● JIM REARDON Reardon, James Matthew b: 1866, Hoosick Falls, N.Y. d: 2/25/1891, Hoosick Falls, N.Y Deb: 7/17/1886

YEAR	TM/L	W	L	PCT	G	GS	CG	SH	SV	IP	H	HR	BB	SO	RAT	ERA	ERA+	OAV	OOB	BH	AVG	PB	PR	/A	PD	TPI
1886	StL-N	0	1	.000	1	1	1	0	0	8	10	1	5	0	16.9	6.75	48	.323	.417	1	.250	0	-3	-3	-0	-0.3
	Cin-a	0	1	.000	1	1	0	0	0	2	5	0	4	0	40.5	18.00	20	.500	.643	0	.000	-1	-3	-3	0	-0.3
Total	1	0	2	.000	2	2	1	0	0	10	15	1	9	0	21.6	9.00	36	.366	.480	1	.143	-1	-6	-6	-0	-0.6

● JEFF REARDON Reardon, Jeffrey James b: 10/1/55, Dalton, Mass. BR/TR, 6′1″, 195 lbs. Deb: 8/25/79

YEAR	TM/L	W	L	PCT	G	GS	CG	SH	SV	IP	H	HR	BB	SO	RAT	ERA	ERA+	OAV	OOB	BH	AVG	PB	PR	/A	PD	TPI
1979	NY-N	1	2	.333	18	0	0	0	2	20^{2}	12	2	9	10	9.1	1.74	209	.174	.269	0	—	0	5	4	-0	0.4
1980	NY-N	8	7	.533	61	0	0	0	6	110^{1}	96	10	47	101	11.7	2.61	136	.231	.310	0	.000	-1	12	12	-2	0.9
1981	NY-N	1	0	1.000	18	0	0	0	2	28^{2}	27	2	12	28	12.6	3.45	101	.245	.325	0	.000	-0	0	0	-1	-0.1
	*Mon-N	2	0	1.000	25	0	0	0	6	41^{2}	21	3	9	21	6.7	1.30	269	.148	.204	0	.000	-0	10	10	-1	0.9
	Yr	3	0	1.000	43	0	0	0	8	70^{1}	48	5	21	49	9.0	2.18	160	.189	.254	0	.000	-1	10	10	-2	0.8
1982	Mon-N	7	4	.636	75	0	0	0	26	109	87	6	36	86	10.3	2.06	176	.221	.289	1	.100	-0	19	19	-1	1.9
1983	Mon-N	7	9	.438	66	0	0	0	21	92	87	7	44	78	12.9	3.03	118	.250	.336	1	.125	-0	6	6	-2	0.3
1984	Mon-N	7	7	.500	68	0	0	0	23	87	70	5	37	79	11.4	2.90	118	.220	.307	0	.000	-1	7	5	-2	0.3
1985	Mon-N★	2	8	.200	63	0	0	0	**41**	87^{2}	68	7	26	67	9.8	3.18	107	.209	.270	2	.286	0	4	2	-1	0.2
1986	Mon-N☆	7	9	.438	62	0	0	0	35	89	83	12	26	67	11.1	3.94	94	.251	.307	1	.125	-0	-2	-3	-0	-0.3
1987	*Min-A	8	8	.500	63	0	0	0	31	80^{1}	70	14	28	83	11.3	4.48	103	.232	.303	0	—	0	-0	1	-1	0.0
1988	Min-A☆	2	4	.333	63	0	0	0	42	73	68	6	15	56	10.5	2.47	165	.245	.289	0	—	0	12	13	-2	0.9
1989	Min-A	5	4	.556	65	0	0	0	31	73	68	8	12	46	10.2	4.07	102	.246	.285	0	—	0	-2	1	-2	-0.6

YEAR TM/L	W	L	PCT	G	GS	CG	SH	SV	IP	H	HR	BB	SO	RAT	ERA	ERA+	OAV	OOB	BH	AVG	PB	PR	/A	PD	TPI
1990 *Bos-A	5	3	.625	47	0	0	0	21	51^{1}	39	5	19	33	10.3	3.16	129	.206	.282	0	—	0	4	5	-1	0.2
1991 Bos-A★	1	4	.200	57	0	0	0	40	59^{1}	54	9	16	44	10.8	3.03	142	.236	.289	0	—	0	7	8	-2	0.4
1992 Bos-A	2	2	.500	46	0	0	0	27	42^{1}	53	6	7	32	13.0	4.25	98	.308	.339	0	—	0	-1	-0	-0	-0.2
*Atl-N	3	0	1.000	14	0	0	0	3	15^{2}	14	0	2	7	9.8	1.15	326	.241	.279	0	—	0	4	5	-0	0.4
Total 14	68	71	.489	811	0	0	0	357	1061	917	102	345	838	10.9	3.05	124	.232	.297	5	.091	-2	84	87	-18	5.6

● **FRANK REBERGER** Reberger, Frank Beall "Crane" b: 6/7/44, Caldwell, Idaho BL/TR, 6'5", 200 lbs. Deb: 6/06/68 C

YEAR TM/L	W	L	PCT	G	GS	CG	SH	SV	IP	H	HR	BB	SO	RAT	ERA	ERA+	OAV	OOB	BH	AVG	PB	PR	/A	PD	TPI
1968 Chi-N	0	1	.000	3	1	0	0	0	6	9	1	2	3	16.5	4.50	70	.346	.393	0	—	0	-1	-1	0	0.0
1969 SD-N	1	2	.333	67	0	0	0	6	87^{2}	83	6	41	65	12.9	3.59	98	.258	.345	1	.200	0	0	-1	2	0.2
1970 SF-N	7	8	.467	45	18	3	0	2	152	178	13	98	117	16.8	5.57	71	.293	.397	11	.234	1	-26	-27	-0	-2.5
1971 SF-N	3	0	1.000	13	7	0	0	0	43^{2}	37	5	19	21	12.0	3.92	87	.228	.317	3	.231	0	-2	-3	0	-0.2
1972 SF-N	3	4	.429	20	11	2	0	0	99^{1}	97	10	37	52	12.6	3.99	87	.257	.332	8	.229	2	-6	-6	1	-0.3
Total 5	14	15	.483	148	37	5	0	8	388^{2}	404	35	197	258	14.3	4.52	81	.270	.361	23	.230	4	-35	-36	4	-2.8

● **JOHN RECCIUS** Reccius, John b: 6/7/1862, Louisville, Ky. d: 9/1/30, Louisville, Ky. 5'6.5", Deb: 5/02/1882 F♦

YEAR TM/L	W	L	PCT	G	GS	CG	SH	SV	IP	H	HR	BB	SO	RAT	ERA	ERA+	OAV	OOB	BH	AVG	PB	PR	/A	PD	TPI
1882 Lou-a	4	6	.400	13	10	9	1	0	95	106	3	22	31	12.1	3.03	82	.264	.302	63	.237	3	-4	-6	-1	-0.5
1883 Lou-a	0	0	—	1	0	0	0	0	4	10	0	0	0	22.5	2.25	133	.446	.446	9	.143	-0	0	0	0	0.1
Total 2	4	6	.400	14	10	9	1	0	99	116	3	22	31	12.5	3.00	83	.274	.310	72	.219	3	-3	-6	-1	-0.4

● **PHIL RECCIUS** Reccius, Phillip b: 6/7/1862, Louisville, Ky. d: 2/15/03, Louisville, Ky. 5'9", 163 lbs. Deb: 9/25/1882 F♦

YEAR TM/L	W	L	PCT	G	GS	CG	SH	SV	IP	H	HR	BB	SO	RAT	ERA	ERA+	OAV	OOB	BH	AVG	PB	PR	/A	PD	TPI
1884 Lou-a	6	7	.462	18	11	11	0	0	129^{1}	118	2	19	46	9.8	2.71	114	.228	.261	63	.240	2	8	5	0	0.7
1885 Lou-a	0	4	.000	7	5	4	0	1	40	46	0	11	10	13.0	3.82	84	.253	.299	97	.241	1	-3	-3	1	-0.1
1886 Lou-a	0	1	.000	1	1	0	0	0	3	7	0	3	0	30.0	9.00	40	.467	.556	4	.308	0	-2	-2	-0	-0.1
1887 Cle-a	0	0	—	1	0	0	0	0	7	8	0	5	0	16.7	7.71	56	.320	.433	47	.205	-0	-3	-3	0	-0.2
Total 4	6	12	.333	27	17	15	0	1	179^{1}	179	2	38	56	11.1	3.26	97	.242	.284	225	.231	3	1	-2	1	0.3

● **PHIL REDDING** Redding, Philip Hayden b: 1/25/1890, Crystal Springs, Miss. d: 3/30/29, Greenwood, Miss. BL/TR, 5'11.5", 190 lbs. Deb: 9/14/12

YEAR TM/L	W	L	PCT	G	GS	CG	SH	SV	IP	H	HR	BB	SO	RAT	ERA	ERA+	OAV	OOB	BH	AVG	PB	PR	/A	PD	TPI
1912 StL-N	2	1	.667	3	3	2	0	0	25^{1}	31	2	11	9	14.9	4.97	69	.313	.382	0	.000	-1	-4	-4	-0	-0.5
1913 StL-N	0	0	—	1	0	0	0	0	2^{2}	2	0	1	1	10.1	6.75	48	.286	.375	0	.000	-0	-1	-1	0	-0.1
Total 2	2	1	.667	4	3	2	0	0	28	33	2	12	10	14.5	5.14	66	.311	.381	0	.000	-1	-5	-5	-0	-0.6

● **PETE REDFERN** Redfern, Peter Irvine b: 8/25/54, Glendale, Cal. BR/TR, 6'2", 195 lbs. Deb: 5/15/76

YEAR TM/L	W	L	PCT	G	GS	CG	SH	SV	IP	H	HR	BB	SO	RAT	ERA	ERA+	OAV	OOB	BH	AVG	PB	PR	/A	PD	TPI
1976 Min-A	8	8	.500	23	23	1	1	0	118	105	6	63	74	13.0	3.51	103	.241	.341	0	—	0	0	1	-1	-0.1
1977 Min-A	6	9	.400	30	28	1	0	0	137^{1}	164	13	66	73	15.3	5.18	77	.304	.384	0	—	0	-17	-18	1	-1.6
1978 Min-A	0	2	.000	3	2	0	0	0	9^{2}	10	2	6	4	14.9	6.52	59	.294	.400	0	—	0	-3	-3	0	-0.4
1979 Min-A	7	3	.700	40	6	0	0	1	108^{1}	106	8	35	85	11.8	3.49	126	.258	.318	0	—	0	9	11	-1	0.7
1980 Min-A	7	7	.500	23	16	2	0	2	104^{2}	117	11	33	73	12.9	4.56	96	.283	.336	0	—	0	-6	-2	-1	-0.3
1981 Min-A	9	8	.529	24	23	3	0	0	141^{2}	140	12	52	77	12.3	4.07	97	.261	.328	0	—	0	-6	-2	-1	-0.6
1982 Min-A	5	11	.313	27	13	2	0	0	94^{1}	122	16	51	40	16.6	6.58	64	.322	.404	0	—	0	-26	-25	0	-2.3
Total 7	42	48	.467	170	111	9	1	3	714	764	68	306	426	13.6	4.54	89	.278	.353	0	—	0	-50	-38	-2	-4.6

● **HOWIE REED** Reed, Howard Dean "Diz" b: 12/21/36, Dallas, Tex. d: 12/7/84, Corpus Christi, Tex. BR/TR, 6'1", 210 lbs. Deb: 9/13/58

YEAR TM/L	W	L	PCT	G	GS	CG	SH	SV	IP	H	HR	BB	SO	RAT	ERA	ERA+	OAV	OOB	BH	AVG	PB	PR	/A	PD	TPI
1958 KC-A	1	0	1.000	3	1	1	0	0	10^{1}	5	0	4	5	7.8	0.87	449	.132	.214	0	.000	0	3	3	-0	0.4
1959 KC-A	0	3	.000	6	3	0	0	0	20^{2}	26	3	10	11	15.7	7.40	54	.313	.387	0	.000	-0	-8	-8	-1	-0.8
1960 KC-A	0	0	—	1	0	0	0	0	1^{2}	2	1	0	1	10.8	0.00	—	.286	.286	0	—	0	1	1	-0	0.1
1964 LA-N	3	4	.429	26	7	0	0	1	90	79	4	36	52	11.5	3.20	101	.236	.310	2	.100	-0	3	0	1	0.1
1965 *LA-N	7	5	.583	38	5	0	0	1	78	73	6	27	47	11.9	3.12	105	.243	.312	0	.000	0	4	1	1	0.2
1966 LA-N	0	0	—	1	0	0	0	0	1^{2}	1	0	0	0	5.4	0.00	—	.167	.167	0	.000	-0	1	1	0	0.1
Cal-A	0	1	.000	19	1	0	0	1	43	39	5	15	17	11.3	2.93	115	.247	.312	0	.000	-1	2	2	-0	0.1
1967 Hou-N	1	1	.500	4	2	0	0	0	18^{1}	19	0	2	9	10.3	3.44	96	.268	.288	0	.000	-0	-0	-0	-0	-0.1
1969 Mon-N	6	7	.462	31	15	2	1	1	106	119	7	50	59	14.5	4.84	76	.290	.369	4	.125	1	-15	-14	2	-1.1
1970 Mon-N	6	5	.545	57	1	0	0	5	89	81	7	40	42	12.4	3.13	131	.252	.339	0	.000	-0	9	10	0	1.0
1971 Mon-N	2	3	.400	43	0	0	0	0	56^{2}	66	8	24	25	14.3	4.29	82	.296	.364	0	.000	-0	-5	-5	0	-0.5
Total 10	26	29	.473	229	35	3	1	9	515^{1}	510	41	208	268	12.7	3.72	96	.261	.334	6	.066	-1	-5	-9	3	-0.5

● **JERRY REED** Reed, Jerry Maxwell b: 10/8/55, Bryson City, N.C. BR/TR, 6'1", 190 lbs. Deb: 9/11/81

YEAR TM/L	W	L	PCT	G	GS	CG	SH	SV	IP	H	HR	BB	SO	RAT	ERA	ERA+	OAV	OOB	BH	AVG	PB	PR	/A	PD	TPI
1981 Phi-N	0	1	.000	4	0	0	0	0	4^{2}	7	0	6	5	25.1	7.71	47	.333	.481	0	—	0	-2	-2	0	-0.2
1982 Phi-N	1	0	1.000	7	0	0	0	0	8^{2}	11	0	3	1	15.6	5.19	71	.324	.395	0	—	0	-2	-1	-0	-0.2
Cle-A	1	1	.500	6	1	0	0	0	15^{2}	15	1	3	10	10.3	3.45	118	.250	.286	0	—	0	1	1	0	0.1
1983 Cle-A	0	0	—	7	0	0	0	0	21^{1}	26	4	9	11	14.8	7.17	59	.310	.376	0	—	0	-7	-7	1	-0.6
1985 Cle-A	3	5	.375	33	5	0	0	8	72^{1}	67	12	19	37	11.1	4.11	101	.245	.302	0	—	0	0	0	1	0.1
1986 Sea-A	4	0	1.000	11	4	0	0	0	34^{2}	38	3	13	16	13.2	3.12	136	.273	.336	0	—	0	4	4	-0	0.4
1987 Sea-A	1	2	.333	39	1	0	0	7	81^{2}	79	7	24	51	11.7	3.42	138	.255	.315	0	—	0	9	12	-0	0.8
1988 Sea-A	1	1	.500	46	0	0	0	1	86^{1}	82	8	33	48	12.2	3.96	105	.256	.330	0	—	0	0	2	1	0.1
1989 Sea-A	7	7	.500	52	1	0	0	0	101^{2}	89	10	43	50	11.8	3.19	126	.235	.314	0	—	0	8	9	-0	0.7
1990 Sea-A	0	1	.000	4	0	0	0	0	7^{1}	8	1	3	2	13.5	4.91	81	.286	.355	0	—	0	-1	-1	0	-0.1
Bos-A	2	1	.667	29	0	0	0	2	45	55	1	16	17	14.2	4.80	85	.302	.359	0	—	0	-4	-4	-0	-0.6
Yr	2	2	.500	33	0	0	0	2	52^{1}	63	2	19	19	14.1	4.82	84	.300	.358	0	—	0	-5	-4	0	-0.7
Total 9	20	19	.513	238	12	0	0	18	479^{1}	477	47	172	248	12.4	3.94	107	.261	.328	0	—	0	6	14	2	0.5

● **RICK REED** Reed, Richard Allen b: 8/16/64, Huntington, W.Va. BR/TR, 6', 195 lbs. Deb: 8/08/88

YEAR TM/L	W	L	PCT	G	GS	CG	SH	SV	IP	H	HR	BB	SO	RAT	ERA	ERA+	OAV	OOB	BH	AVG	PB	PR	/A	PD	TPI
1988 Pit-N	1	0	1.000	2	2	0	0	0	12	10	1	2	6	9.0	3.00	113	.233	.267	0	.000	-0	1	1	0	0.0
1989 Pit-N	1	4	.200	15	7	0	0	0	54^{2}	62	5	11	34	12.3	5.60	60	.290	.330	1	.077	-0	-13	-14	-0	-1.4
1990 Pit-N	2	3	.400	13	8	1	1	1	53^{2}	62	6	12	27	12.6	4.36	83	.279	.319	4	.250	1	-3	-4	-1	-0.4
1991 Pit-N	0	0	—	1	1	0	0	0	4^{1}	8	1	1	2	18.7	10.38	34	.400	.429	1	.500	1	-3	-3	-0	-0.2
1992 KC-A	3	7	.300	19	18	1	1	0	100^{1}	105	10	20	49	11.7	3.68	108	.271	.316	0	—	0	3	3	1	0.4
Total 5	7	14	.333	50	36	2	2	1	225	247	23	46	118	12.0	4.40	84	.279	.320	6	.171	1	-16	-17	-0	-1.6

● **BOB REED** Reed, Robert Edward b: 1/12/45, Boston, Mass. BR/TR, 5'10", 175 lbs. Deb: 9/05/69

YEAR TM/L	W	L	PCT	G	GS	CG	SH	SV	IP	H	HR	BB	SO	RAT	ERA	ERA+	OAV	OOB	BH	AVG	PB	PR	/A	PD	TPI
1969 Det-A	0	0	—	8	1	0	0	0	14^{2}	9	0	8	9	10.4	1.84	203	.184	.298	1	.500	0	3	3	0	0.4
1970 Det-A	2	4	.333	16	4	0	0	2	46^{1}	54	5	14	26	13.2	4.86	77	.292	.342	1	.083	-0	-6	-6	-1	-0.7
Total 2	2	4	.333	24	5	0	0	2	61	63	5	22	35	12.5	4.13	90	.269	.332	2	.143	-0	-3	-3	-0	-0.3

● **RON REED** Reed, Ronald Lee b: 11/2/42, LaPorte, Ind. BR/TR, 6'6", 215 lbs. Deb: 9/26/66

YEAR TM/L	W	L	PCT	G	GS	CG	SH	SV	IP	H	HR	BB	SO	RAT	ERA	ERA+	OAV	OOB	BH	AVG	PB	PR	/A	PD	TPI
1966 Atl-N	1	1	.500	2	2	0	0	0	8^{1}	7	1	4	6	11.9	2.16	168	.226	.314	0	.000	-0	1	1	-0	0.1
1967 Atl-N	1	1	.500	3	3	0	0	0	21^{1}	21	1	3	11	11.0	2.95	112	.262	.306	0	.000	-1	1	1	1	0.1
1968 Atl-N★	11	10	.524	35	28	6	1	0	201^{2}	189	10	49	111	10.9	3.35	89	.246	.297	10	.161	1	-8	-8	0	-0.8
1969 *Atl-N	18	10	.643	36	33	7	1	0	241^{1}	227	24	56	160	10.8	3.47	104	.246	.294	10	.125	-2	3	4	-1	0.1
1970 Atl-N	7	10	.412	21	18	6	0	0	134^{2}	140	16	39	68	12.1	4.41	97	.266	.319	4	.091	-3	-5	-2	-1	-0.3
1971 Atl-N	13	14	.481	32	32	8	1	0	222^{1}	221	26	54	129	11.2	3.72	100	.261	.306	11	.149	-3	-6	-0	-1	-0.4
1972 Atl-N	11	15	.423	31	30	11	1	0	213	222	18	60	111	12.2	3.93	96	.270	.325	13	.178	-1	-11	-3	1	-0.3
1973 Atl-N	4	11	.267	20	19	2	0	1	116^{1}	133	7	31	64	12.9	4.41	89	.287	.335	9	.200	0	-10	-6	1	-0.5
1974 Atl-N	10	11	.476	28	28	6	2	0	186	171	16	41	78	10.4	3.39	112	.243	.286	6	.105	-3	5	8	-2	0.3
1975 Atl-N	4	5	.444	10	10	1	0	0	74^{2}	93	1	16	40	13.1	4.22	89	.304	.339	6	.231	1	-5	-4	-0	-0.3
StL-N	9	8	.529	24	24	7	2	0	175^{2}	181	4	37	99	11.4	3.23	116	.263	.305	9	.161	-0	8	10	-1	1.0

YEAR	TM/L	W	L	PCT	G	GS	CG	SH	SV	IP	H	HR	BB	SO	RAT	ERA	ERA+	OAV	OOB	BH	AVG	PB	PR	/A	PD	TPI
	Yr	13	13	.500	34	34	8	2	0	250^1	274	5	53	139	11.9	3.52	107	.275	.314	15	.183	1	3	7	-1	0.7
1976	*Phi-N	8	7	.533	59	4	1	0	14	128	88	8	32	96	8.6	2.46	144	.193	.249	4	.167	-0	15	15	-1	1.5
1977	*Phi-N	7	5	.583	60	3	0	0	15	124^1	101	9	37	84	10.1	2.75	145	.223	.283	2	.111	-0	16	17	-1	1.7
1978	*Phi-N	3	4	.429	66	0	0	0	17	108^2	87	6	23	85	9.5	2.24	160	.223	.275	0	.000	-0	16	16	-2	1.5
1979	Phi-N	13	8	.619	61	0	0	0	5	102	110	9	32	58	12.7	4.15	92	.278	.335	3	.300	1	-5	-4	-0	-0.3
1980	*Phi-N	7	5	.583	55	0	0	0	9	91^1	88	4	30	54	11.7	4.04	94	.253	.314	3	.300	1	-4	-3	1	-0.1
1981	*Phi-N	5	3	.625	39	0	0	0	8	61^1	54	6	17	40	10.6	3.08	118	.237	.293	3	.500	1	3	4	-1	0.5
1982	Phi-N	5	5	.500	57	2	0	0	14	98	85	4	24	57	10.3	2.66	138	.235	.289	4	.333	2	10	11	2	1.5
1983	*Phi-N	9	1	.900	61	0	0	0	8	95^2	89	5	34	73	11.7	3.48	102	.248	.315	1	.167	-0	2	1	-2	-0.1
1984	Chi-A	0	6	.000	51	0	0	0	12	73	67	7	14	57	10.1	3.08	135	.248	.288	0	.000	0	7	9	0	0.9
Total	19	146	140	.510	751	236	55	8	103	2477^2	2374	182	633	1481	11.1	3.46	107	.252	.303	98	.158	-6	32	68	-3	6.1

● STEVE REED Reed, Steven Vincent b: 3/11/66, Los Angeles, Cal. BR/TR, 6'2", 200 lbs. Deb: 8/30/92

YEAR	TM/L	W	L	PCT	G	GS	CG	SH	SV	IP	H	HR	BB	SO	RAT	ERA	ERA+	OAV	OOB	BH	AVG	PB	PR	/A	PD	TPI
1992	SF-N	1	0	1.000	18	0	0	0	0	15^2	13	2	3	11	9.8	2.30	146	.220	.270	0	—	0	2	2	1	0.3

● BILL REEDER Reeder, William Edgar b: 2/20/22, Dike, Texas BR/TR, 6'5", 205 lbs. Deb: 4/23/49

YEAR	TM/L	W	L	PCT	G	GS	CG	SH	SV	IP	H	HR	BB	SO	RAT	ERA	ERA+	OAV	OOB	BH	AVG	PB	PR	/A	PD	TPI
1949	StL-N	1	1	.500	21	1	0	0	0	33^2	33	2	30	21	17.1	5.08	82	.270	.418	0	.000	-0	-4	-3	-0	-0.4

● STAN REES Rees, Stanley Milton "Nellie" b: 2/25/1899, Cynthiana, Ky. d: 8/30/37, Lexington, Ky. BL/TL, 6'3", 190 lbs. Deb: 6/12/18

YEAR	TM/L	W	L	PCT	G	GS	CG	SH	SV	IP	H	HR	BB	SO	RAT	ERA	ERA+	OAV	OOB	BH	AVG	PB	PR	/A	PD	TPI
1918	Was-A	1	0	1.000	2	0	0	0	0	2	3	0	4	1	31.5	0.00	—	.500	.700	0	—	0	1	1	0	0.1

● BOBBY REEVES Reeves, Robert Edwin "Gunner" b: 6/24/04, Hill City, Tenn. BR/TR, 5'11", 170 lbs. Deb: 6/09/26 ♦

YEAR	TM/L	W	L	PCT	G	GS	CG	SH	SV	IP	H	HR	BB	SO	RAT	ERA	ERA+	OAV	OOB	BH	AVG	PB	PR	/A	PD	TPI
1931	Bos-A	0	0	—	1	0	0	0	0	7^1	6	0	1	0	8.6	3.68	117	.214	.241	14	.167	0	1	1	0	0.1

● MIKE REGAN Regan, Michael Joseph b: 11/19/1887, Phoenix, N.Y. d: 5/22/61, Albany, N.Y. BR/TR, 5'11", 165 lbs. Deb: 5/13/17

YEAR	TM/L	W	L	PCT	G	GS	CG	SH	SV	IP	H	HR	BB	SO	RAT	ERA	ERA+	OAV	OOB	BH	AVG	PB	PR	/A	PD	TPI
1917	Cin-N	11	10	.524	32	26	16	1	0	216	228	4	41	50	11.4	2.71	97	.273	.310	15	.200	1	0	-2	3	0.2
1918	Cin-N	5	5	.500	22	6	4	3	2	80	77	0	29	15	11.9	3.26	82	.262	.328	8	.296	2	-4	-5	-1	-0.4
1919	Cin-N	0	0	—	1	0	0	0	0	2^1	1	0	0	1	3.9	0.00	—	.143	.143	0	.000	-0	1	1	-0	0.1
Total	3	16	15	.516	55	32	20	4	2	298^1	306	4	70	66	11.5	2.84	93	.269	.314	23	.223	3	-4	-7	2	-0.1

● PHIL REGAN Regan, Philip Raymond "The Vulture" b: 4/6/37, Otsego, Mich. BR/TR, 6'3", 200 lbs. Deb: 7/19/60 C

YEAR	TM/L	W	L	PCT	G	GS	CG	SH	SV	IP	H	HR	BB	SO	RAT	ERA	ERA+	OAV	OOB	BH	AVG	PB	PR	/A	PD	TPI
1960	Det-A	0	4	.000	17	7	0	0	1	68	70	11	25	38	12.8	4.50	88	.267	.336	1	.059	-1	-5	-4	-1	-0.6
1961	Det-A	10	7	.588	32	16	6	0	2	120	134	19	41	46	13.2	5.25	78	.281	.339	3	.075	-2	-16	-15	-3	-1.9
1962	Det-A	11	9	.550	35	23	6	0	0	171^1	169	23	64	87	12.3	4.04	101	.254	.320	13	.206	1	-1	0	-2	-0.1
1963	Det-A	15	9	.625	38	27	5	1	1	189	179	33	59	115	11.7	3.86	97	.245	.308	9	.143	-1	-5	-2	-3	-0.6
1964	Det-A	5	10	.333	32	21	2	0	1	146^2	162	21	49	91	13.3	5.03	73	.282	.344	13	.317	5	-23	-22	-0	-1.8
1965	Det-A	1	5	.167	16	7	1	0	0	51^2	57	6	20	37	13.4	5.05	69	.282	.347	1	.083	-0	-9	-9	-0	-1.0
1966	*LA-N☆	14	1	.933	65	0	0	0	**21**	116^2	85	6	24	88	8.4	1.62	203	.207	.251	3	.143	0	**26**	**22**	1	2.4
1967	LA-N	6	9	.400	55	3	0	0	6	96^1	108	2	32	53	13.3	2.99	104	.284	.343	1	.100	-0	4	1	1	0.2
1968	LA-N	2	0	1.000	5	0	0	0	0	7^2	10	1	1	7	12.9	3.52	78	.313	.333	0	.000	-0	-0	-1	-0	-0.1
	Chi-N	10	5	.667	68	0	0	0	25	127	109	9	24	60	9.6	2.20	144	.232	.272	3	.150	0	11	14	0	1.6
	Yr	12	5	.706	73	0	0	0	**25**	134^2	119	10	25	67	9.8	2.27	138	.237	.276	3	.143	0	11	13	-0	1.5
1969	Chi-N	12	6	.667	71	0	0	0	17	112	120	6	35	56	12.6	3.70	109	.282	.339	1	.067	-0	-1	4	0	0.5
1970	Chi-N	5	9	.357	54	0	0	0	12	75^2	81	8	32	31	13.6	4.76	95	.287	.362	0	.000	-1	-6	-2	2	-0.1
1971	Chi-N	5	5	.500	48	1	0	0	6	73^1	84	4	33	28	14.6	3.93	100	.301	.379	0	.000	-1	-4	0	1	0.0
1972	Chi-N	0	1	.000	5	0	0	0	0	4	6	0	2	2	18.0	2.25	169	.400	.471	0	—	0	1	1	-0	0.1
	Chi-A	0	1	.000	10	0	0	0	0	13^1	18	1	6	4	16.9	4.05	77	.346	.424	1	1.000	0	-1	-1	0	-0.1
Total	13	96	81	.542	551	105	20	1	92	1372^2	1392	150	447	743	12.2	3.84	97	.265	.325	49	.153	1	-31	-16	-4	-1.5

● EARL REID Reid, Earl Percy b: 6/8/13, Bangor, Ala. d: 5/11/84, Cullman, Ala. BL/TR, 6'3", 190 lbs. Deb: 5/08/46

YEAR	TM/L	W	L	PCT	G	GS	CG	SH	SV	IP	H	HR	BB	SO	RAT	ERA	ERA+	OAV	OOB	BH	AVG	PB	PR	/A	PD	TPI
1946	Bos-N	1	0	1.000	2	0	0	0	0	3	4	0	3	2	21.0	3.00	114	.308	.438	0	—	0	0	0	-0	0.0

● BILL REIDY Reidy, William Joseph b: 10/9/1873, Cleveland, Ohio d: 10/14/15, Cleveland, Ohio BR/TR, 5'10", 175 lbs. Deb: 7/21/1896

YEAR	TM/L	W	L	PCT	G	GS	CG	SH	SV	IP	H	HR	BB	SO	RAT	ERA	ERA+	OAV	OOB	BH	AVG	PB	PR	/A	PD	TPI
1896	NY-N	0	1	.000	2	1	1	0	0	13	24	0	2	1	20.1	7.62	55	.391	.437	0	.000	-1	-5	-5	0	-0.4
1899	Bro-N	1	0	1.000	2	1	1	0	1	7	9	0	2	2	14.1	2.57	152	.311	.356	0	.000	-1	1	1	0	0.1
1901	Mil-A	16	20	.444	37	33	28	2	0	301^1	364	14	62	50	13.0	4.21	85	.295	.333	16	.143	-7	-18	-21	-3	-2.6
1902	StL-A	3	5	.375	12	9	7	0	0	95	111	0	13	16	12.4	4.45	79	.292	.327	8	.195	-0	-9	-10	1	-0.8
1903	StL-A	1	4	.200	5	5	5	1	0	43	53	1	7	8	13.2	3.98	73	.302	.339	1	.067	-2	-5	-5	-1	-0.8
	Bro-N	6	7	.462	15	13	11	0	0	104	130	0	14	21	13.0	3.46	92	.315	.346	9	.243	1	-2	-3	-1	-0.3
1904	Bro-N	0	4	.000	6	4	2	0	1	38^1	49	0	6	11	13.4	4.46	62	.293	.326	5	.156	-0	-7	-7	-1	-0.8
Total	6	27	41	.397	79	66	55	3	2	601^2	740	15	106	109	13.1	4.17	82	.301	.337	39	.159	-9	-46	-50	-5	-5.6

● ART REINHART Reinhart, Arthur Conrad b: 5/29/1899, Ackley, Iowa d: 11/11/46, Houston, Tex. BL/TL, 6'1", 170 lbs. Deb: 4/26/19

YEAR	TM/L	W	L	PCT	G	GS	CG	SH	SV	IP	H	HR	BB	SO	RAT	ERA	ERA+	OAV	OOB	BH	AVG	PB	PR	/A	PD	TPI
1919	StL-N	0	0	—	1	0	0	0	0	0	0	0	0	0	—	—	—	—	1.000	0	—	0	0	0	0	0.0
1925	StL-N	11	5	.688	20	16	15	1	0	144^2	149	7	47	26	12.4	3.05	142	.278	.341	22	.328	5	20	20	-0	2.5
1926	*StL-N	10	5	.667	27	11	9	0	0	143	159	5	47	26	13.2	4.22	93	.295	.355	20	.317	4	-6	-5	1	0.0
1927	StL-N	5	2	.714	21	9	4	2	1	81^2	82	5	36	15	13.0	4.19	94	.267	.344	10	.313	2	-2	-2	-1	-0.1
1928	StL-N	4	6	.400	23	9	3	1	2	75^1	80	3	27	12	12.8	2.87	139	.272	.333	4	.167	-0	9	9	-1	0.8
Total	5	30	18	.625	92	45	31	4	3	444^2	470	20	157	79	12.9	3.60	113	.280	.345	56	.301	11	20	23	-1	3.2

● JACK REIS Reis, Harrie Crane b: 6/14/1890, Cincinnati, Ohio d: 7/20/39, Cincinnati, Ohio BR/TR, 5'10.5", 160 lbs. Deb: 9/09/11

YEAR	TM/L	W	L	PCT	G	GS	CG	SH	SV	IP	H	HR	BB	SO	RAT	ERA	ERA+	OAV	OOB	BH	AVG	PB	PR	/A	PD	TPI
1911	StL-N	0	0	—	3	0	0	0	0	9^1	5	0	8	4	12.5	0.96	350	.156	.325	0	.000	-0	3	3	0	0.3

● LAURIE REIS Reis, Lawrence P. b: 11/20/1858, Illinois d: 1/24/21, Chicago, Ill. BR/TR, 160 lbs. Deb: 10/01/1877

YEAR	TM/L	W	L	PCT	G	GS	CG	SH	SV	IP	H	HR	BB	SO	RAT	ERA	ERA+	OAV	OOB	BH	AVG	PB	PR	/A	PD	TPI
1877	Chi-N	3	1	.750	4	4	4	1	0	36	29	1	6	11	8.8	0.75	396	.213	.246	2	.125	-2	8	9	-0	0.6
1878	Chi-N	1	3	.250	4	4	4	0	0	36	55	0	4	8	14.8	3.25	75	.335	.351	3	.150	-1	-4	-3	-1	-0.5
Total	2	4	4	.500	8	8	8	1	0	72	84	1	10	19	11.8	2.00	135	.280	.303	5	.139	-2	4	6	-2	0.1

● BOBBY REIS Reis, Robert Joseph Thomas b: 1/2/09, Woodside, N.Y. d: 5/1/73, St.Paul, Minn. BR/TR, 6'1", 175 lbs. Deb: 9/19/31 ♦

YEAR	TM/L	W	L	PCT	G	GS	CG	SH	SV	IP	H	HR	BB	SO	RAT	ERA	ERA+	OAV	OOB	BH	AVG	PB	PR	/A	PD	TPI
1935	Bro-N	3	2	.600	14	2	1	0	2	41^1	46	0	24	7	15.5	2.83	140	.277	.372	21	.247	1	5	5	1	0.7
1936	Bos-N	6	5	.545	35	5	3	0	0	138^2	152	7	74	25	15.0	4.48	86	.283	.375	13	.217	1	-7	-10	4	-0.5
1937	Bos-N	0	0	—	4	0	0	0	0	5	3	0	5	0	14.4	1.80	199	.158	.333	21	.244	1	1	1	-0	0.1
1938	Bos-N	1	6	.143	16	2	1	0	0	57^2	61	5	41	20	16.9	4.99	69	.271	.397	9	.184	-0	-8	-10	0	-1.0
Total	4	10	13	.435	69	9	5	0	2	242^2	262	12	144	52	15.5	4.27	88	.277	.379	70	.233	3	-8	-14	5	-0.7

● TOMMY REIS Reis, Thomas Edward b: 8/6/14, Newport, Ky. BR/TR, 6'2", 180 lbs. Deb: 4/27/38

YEAR	TM/L	W	L	PCT	G	GS	CG	SH	SV	IP	H	HR	BB	SO	RAT	ERA	ERA+	OAV	OOB	BH	AVG	PB	PR	/A	PD	TPI
1938	Phi-N	0	1	.000	4	0	0	0	0	4^2	8	0	8	2	30.9	19.29	20	.364	.533	0	.000	-0	-8	-8	0	-0.7
	Bos-N	0	0	—	4	0	0	0	0	6^1	8	1	1	4	12.8	7.11	48	.296	.321	0	—	0	-2	-3	-0	-0.3
	Yr	0	1	.000	8	0	0	0	0	11	16	1	9	6	20.5	12.27	30	.327	.431	0	.000	-0	-10	-11	-0	-1.0

● BUGS REISIGL Reisigl, Jacob b: 12/12/1887, Brooklyn, N.Y. d: 2/24/57, Amsterdam, N.Y. BR/TR, 5'10.5", 175 lbs. Deb: 9/20/11

YEAR	TM/L	W	L	PCT	G	GS	CG	SH	SV	IP	H	HR	BB	SO	RAT	ERA	ERA+	OAV	OOB	BH	AVG	PB	PR	/A	PD	TPI
1911	Cle-A	0	1	.000	2	1	1	0	0	13	13	1	3	6	11.1	6.23	55	.271	.314	0	.000	-1	-4	-4	-0	-0.4

● DOC REISLING Reisling, Frank Carl b: 7/25/1874, Martins Ferry, O. d: 3/4/55, Tulsa, Okla. BR/TR, 5'10", 180 lbs. Deb: 9/10/04

YEAR	TM/L	W	L	PCT	G	GS	CG	SH	SV	IP	H	HR	BB	SO	RAT	ERA	ERA+	OAV	OOB	BH	AVG	PB	PR	/A	PD	TPI
1904	Bro-N	3	4	.429	7	7	6	1	0	51	45	0	10	19	11.3	2.12	130	.238	.308	2	.154	-0	4	4	0	0.4
1905	Bro-N	0	1	.000	2	0	0	0	0	3	3	0	4	2	21.0	3.00	96	.273	.467	0	.000	0	0	-0	0	0.0

YEAR	TM/L	W	L	PCT	G	GS	CG	SH	SV	IP	H	HR	BB	SO	RAT	ERA	ERA+	OAV	OOB	BH	AVG	PB	PR	/A	PD	TPI
1909	Was-A	2	4	.333	10	6	6	1	0	66^2	70	0	17	22	11.7	2.43	100	.270	.315	4	.167	0	0	0	-1	-0.1
1910	Was-A	10	10	.500	30	20	13	2	1	191	185	3	44	57	11.0	2.54	98	.264	.312	12	.200	2	-1	-1	0	0.1
Total	4	15	19	.441	49	33	25	4	1	311^2	303	3	75	100	11.3	2.45	103	.261	.314	18	.184	2	3	2	-1	0.4

● MIKE REMLINGER Remlinger, Michael John b: 3/23/66, Middletown, N.Y. BL/TL, 6′, 195 lbs. Deb: 6/15/91

YEAR	TM/L	W	L	PCT	G	GS	CG	SH	SV	IP	H	HR	BB	SO	RAT	ERA	ERA+	OAV	OOB	BH	AVG	PB	PR	/A	PD	TPI
1991	SF-N	2	1	.667	8	6	1	1	0	35	36	5	20	19	14.4	4.37	82	.271	.366	0	.000	-0	-3	-3	-0	-0.4

● WIN REMMERSWAAL Remmerswaal, Wilhelmus Abraham b: 3/8/54, The Hague, Holland BR/TR, 6′2″, 160 lbs. Deb: 8/03/79

YEAR	TM/L	W	L	PCT	G	GS	CG	SH	SV	IP	H	HR	BB	SO	RAT	ERA	ERA+	OAV	OOB	BH	AVG	PB	PR	/A	PD	TPI
1979	Bos-A	1	0	1.000	8	0	0	0	0	20^1	26	1	12	16	17.3	7.08	62	.317	.411	0	—	0	-6	-6	-0	-1.0
1980	Bos-A	2	1	.667	14	0	0	0	0	35^1	39	4	9	20	12.2	4.58	92	.295	.340	0	—	0	-2	-1	-1	-0.2
Total	2	3	1	.750	22	0	0	0	0	55^2	65	5	21	36	14.1	5.50	78	.304	.369	0	—	0	-9	-7	-1	-1.2

● ALEX REMNEAS Remneas, Alexander Norman b: 2/21/1886, Minneapolis, Minn. d: 8/27/75, Phoenix, Ariz. BR/TR, 6′1″, 180 lbs. Deb: 4/15/12

YEAR	TM/L	W	L	PCT	G	GS	CG	SH	SV	IP	H	HR	BB	SO	RAT	ERA	ERA+	OAV	OOB	BH	AVG	PB	PR	/A	PD	TPI
1912	Det-A	0	0	—	1	0	0	0	0	1^2	5	0	0	0	27.0	27.00	12	.455	.455	0	—	0	-4	-4	0	-0.3
1915	StL-A	0	0	—	2	0	0	0	0	6	3	0	3	5	10.5	1.50	191	.136	.269	0	.000	-0	1	1	0	0.1
Total	2	0	0	—	3	0	0	0	0	7^2	8	0	3	5	14.1	7.04	42	.242	.324	0	.000	0	-3	-3	0	-0.2

● ERWIN RENFER Renfer, Erwin Arthur b: 12/11/1891, Elgin, Ill. d: 10/26/57, Sycamore, Ill. BR/TR, 6′, 180 lbs. Deb: 9/18/13

YEAR	TM/L	W	L	PCT	G	GS	CG	SH	SV	IP	H	HR	BB	SO	RAT	ERA	ERA+	OAV	OOB	BH	AVG	PB	PR	/A	PD	TPI
1913	Det-A	0	1	.000	1	1	0	0	0	6	5	0	3	1	13.5	6.00	49	.227	.346	0	.000	-0	-2	-2	0	-0.2

● LADDIE RENFROE Renfroe, Cohen Williams b: 5/9/62, Natchez, Miss. BB/TR, 5′11″, 200 lbs. Deb: 7/03/91

YEAR	TM/L	W	L	PCT	G	GS	CG	SH	SV	IP	H	HR	BB	SO	RAT	ERA	ERA+	OAV	OOB	BH	AVG	PB	PR	/A	PD	TPI
1991	Chi-N	0	1	.000	4	0	0	0	0	4^2	11	1	2	4	25.1	13.50	29	.440	.481	0	.000	-0	-5	-5	0	-0.5

● MARSHALL RENFROE Renfroe, Marshall Daniel b: 5/25/36, Century, Fla. d: 12/10/70, Pensacola, Fla. BL/TL, 6′, 180 lbs. Deb: 9/27/59

YEAR	TM/L	W	L	PCT	G	GS	CG	SH	SV	IP	H	HR	BB	SO	RAT	ERA	ERA+	OAV	OOB	BH	AVG	PB	PR	/A	PD	TPI
1959	SF-N	0	0	—	1	1	0	0	0	2	3	1	3	3	27.0	27.00	14	.333	.500	0	.000	-0	-5	-5	-0	-0.4

● HAL RENIFF Reniff, Harold Eugene "Porky" b: 7/2/38, Warren, Ohio BR/TR, 6′, 215 lbs. Deb: 6/08/61

YEAR	TM/L	W	L	PCT	G	GS	CG	SH	SV	IP	H	HR	BB	SO	RAT	ERA	ERA+	OAV	OOB	BH	AVG	PB	PR	/A	PD	TPI
1961	NY-A	2	0	1.000	25	0	0	0	2	45^1	31	1	31	21	12.3	2.58	144	.197	.330	0	.000	-1	7	6	-1	0.5
1962	NY-A	0	0	—	2	0	0	0	0	3^2	6	0	5	1	29.5	7.36	51	.400	.571	0	—	0	-1	-1	-0	-0.2
1963	*NY-A	4	3	.571	48	0	0	0	18	89^1	63	3	42	56	10.8	2.62	134	.202	.301	0	.000	-1	10	9	3	1.1
1964	*NY-A	6	4	.600	41	0	0	0	9	69^1	47	3	30	38	10.0	3.12	116	.199	.289	1	.100	-1	4	4	0	0.4
1965	NY-A	3	4	.429	51	0	0	0	3	85^1	74	4	48	74	13.4	3.80	90	.232	.341	0	.000	-0	-3	-4	-0	-0.5
1966	NY-A	3	7	.300	56	0	0	0	9	95^1	80	2	49	79	12.7	3.21	104	.229	.333	4	.286	1	2	1	-1	0.1
1967	NY-A	0	2	.000	24	0	0	0	0	40	40	0	14	24	12.8	4.27	73	.256	.329	0	.000	-0	-5	-5	-1	-0.6
	NY-N	3	3	.500	29	0	0	0	4	43	42	1	23	21	13.8	3.35	101	.266	.363	0	.000	-0	0	0	-1	-0.1
Total	7	21	23	.477	276	0	0	0	45	471^1	383	14	242	314	12.3	3.27	106	.225	.327	5	.096	-2	14	10	-0	0.7

● JIM RENINGER Reninger, James David b: 3/7/13, Aurora, Ill. BR/TR, 6′3″, 210 lbs. Deb: 9/17/38

YEAR	TM/L	W	L	PCT	G	GS	CG	SH	SV	IP	H	HR	BB	SO	RAT	ERA	ERA+	OAV	OOB	BH	AVG	PB	PR	/A	PD	TPI
1938	Phi-A	0	2	.000	4	4	1	0	0	22^2	28	3	14	9	16.7	7.15	68	.295	.385	0	.000	-0	-6	-6	0	-0.5
1939	Phi-A	0	2	.000	4	2	0	0	0	16^1	24	3	12	3	19.8	7.71	61	.369	.468	1	.167	-0	-6	-5	0	-0.5
Total	2	0	4	.000	8	6	1	0	0	39	52	6	26	12	18.0	7.38	65	.325	.419	1	.077	-1	-12	-11	0	-1.0

● STEVE RENKO Renko, Steven b: 12/10/44, Kansas City, Kan. BR/TR, 6′5″, 230 lbs. Deb: 6/27/69

YEAR	TM/L	W	L	PCT	G	GS	CG	SH	SV	IP	H	HR	BB	SO	RAT	ERA	ERA+	OAV	OOB	BH	AVG	PB	PR	/A	PD	TPI
1969	Mon-N	6	7	.462	18	15	4	0	0	103^1	94	14	50	68	12.7	4.01	92	.243	.333	6	.167	1	-5	-4	-1	-0.4
1970	Mon-N	13	11	.542	41	33	7	1	1	222^2	203	27	104	142	12.7	4.32	95	.241	.329	16	.200	2	-7	-5	-0	-0.3
1971	Mon-N	15	14	.517	40	37	9	3	0	275^2	256	24	135	129	12.9	3.75	94	.247	.336	21	.210	4	-9	-7	-2	-0.4
1972	Mon-N	1	10	.091	30	12	0	0	0	97	96	11	67	66	15.1	5.20	68	.262	.376	7	.292	1	-19	-18	1	-1.6
1973	Mon-N	15	11	.577	36	34	9	0	1	249^2	201	26	108	164	11.2	2.81	136	.218	.300	24	.273	8	24	28	-2	3.8
1974	Mon-N	12	16	.429	37	35	8	1	0	227^2	222	17	81	138	12.0	4.03	95	.257	.321	17	.210	3	-10	-5	3	0.2
1975	Mon-N	6	12	.333	31	25	3	1	1	170^1	175	20	76	99	13.3	4.07	94	.265	.341	15	.278	5	-8	-5	-0	0.0
1976	Mon-N	0	1	.000	5	1	0	0	0	13	15	2	3	4	12.5	5.54	67	.288	.327	1	.333	0	-3	-3	-1	-0.3
	Chi-N	8	11	.421	28	27	4	1	0	163^1	164	12	43	112	11.4	3.86	100	.258	.305	5	.094	-4	-6	0	-1	-0.5
	Yr	8	12	.400	33	28	4	1	0	176^1	179	14	46	116	11.5	3.98	97	.260	.307	6	.107	-3	-9	-3	-2	-0.8
1977	Chi-N	2	2	.500	13	8	0	0	1	51^1	51	10	21	34	12.8	4.56	96	.258	.332	2	.167	0	-4	-1	-1	-0.2
	Chi-A	5	0	1.000	8	8	0	0	0	53^1	55	3	17	36	12.3	3.54	115	.274	.333	0	—	0	3	3	0	0.3
1978	Oak-A	6	12	.333	27	25	3	1	0	151	152	10	67	89	13.2	4.29	85	.265	.344	0	—	0	-9	-11	-0	-0.7
1979	Bos-A	11	9	.550	27	27	4	1	0	171	174	22	53	99	12.1	4.11	107	.260	.317	0	—	0	2	6	-1	0.3
1980	Bos-A	9	9	.500	32	23	1	0	0	165^1	180	17	56	90	12.9	4.19	101	.281	.340	0	—	0	-3	0	-1	-0.2
1981	Cal-A	8	4	.667	22	15	0	0	1	102	93	7	42	50	12.0	3.44	106	.250	.328	0	—	0	2	2	-2	0.1
1982	Cal-A	11	6	.647	31	23	4	0	0	156	163	17	51	81	12.4	4.44	91	.269	.327	0	—	0	-6	-7	-2	-0.8
1983	KC-A	6	11	.353	25	17	1	0	1	121^1	144	9	36	54	13.4	4.30	95	.293	.341	0	—	0	-3	-3	-1	-0.4
Total	15	134	146	.479	451	365	57	9	6	2494	2438	248	1010	1455	12.5	3.99	98	.256	.329	114	.215	21	-62	-27	-9	-1.1

● ANDY REPLOGLE Replogle, Andrew David b: 10/7/53, South Bend, Ind. BR/TR, 6′5″, 205 lbs. Deb: 4/11/78

YEAR	TM/L	W	L	PCT	G	GS	CG	SH	SV	IP	H	HR	BB	SO	RAT	ERA	ERA+	OAV	OOB	BH	AVG	PB	PR	/A	PD	TPI
1978	Mil-A	9	5	.643	32	18	3	2	0	149^1	177	14	47	41	13.6	3.92	96	.301	.353	0	—	0	-3	-3	-2	-0.5
1979	Mil-A	0	0	—	3	0	0	0	0	8	13	0	2	2	16.9	5.63	74	.382	.417	0	—	0	-1	-1	0	-0.1
Total	2	9	5	.643	35	18	3	2	0	157^1	190	14	49	43	13.7	4.00	94	.305	.357	0	—	0	-4	-4	-2	-0.6

● XAVIER RESCIGNO Rescigno, Xavier Frederick "Mr. X" b: 10/13/13, New York, N.Y. BR/TR, 5′10.5″, 175 lbs. Deb: 4/22/43

YEAR	TM/L	W	L	PCT	G	GS	CG	SH	SV	IP	H	HR	BB	SO	RAT	ERA	ERA+	OAV	OOB	BH	AVG	PB	PR	/A	PD	TPI
1943	Pit-N	6	9	.400	37	14	5	1	2	132^2	125	6	45	41	11.7	2.98	117	.252	.317	5	.143	0	6	7	-2	0.6
1944	Pit-N	10	8	.556	48	6	2	0	5	124	146	9	34	45	13.1	4.35	85	.291	.337	2	.091	-1	-10	-9	-0	-1.0
1945	Pit-N	3	5	.375	44	1	0	0	9	78^2	95	6	34	29	14.9	5.72	69	.303	.372	2	.133	-0	-17	-16	-0	-1.6
Total	3	19	22	.463	129	21	7	1	16	335^1	366	21	113	115	13.0	4.13	89	.279	.338	9	.125	-1	-21	-17	-3	-2.0

● GEORGE RETTGER Rettger, George Edward b: 7/29/1868, Cleveland, Ohio d: 6/5/21, Lakewood, Ohio BR/TR, 5′11″, 175 lbs. Deb: 8/13/1891

YEAR	TM/L	W	L	PCT	G	GS	CG	SH	SV	IP	H	HR	BB	SO	RAT	ERA	ERA+	OAV	OOB	BH	AVG	PB	PR	/A	PD	TPI
1891	StL-a	7	3	.700	14	12	10	1	1	92^2	85	4	51	49	14.0	3.40	124	.236	.343	3	.071	-4	3	8	-1	0.4
1892	Cle-N	1	3	.250	6	5	3	0	0	38	32	2	31	12	15.2	4.26	80	.219	.360	2	.133	-0	-4	-4	-0	-0.4
	Cin-N	1	0	1.000	1	1	1	0	0	9	8	0	10	1	19.0	4.00	82	.229	.413	1	.125	-0	-1	-1	-0	-0.1
	Yr	2	3	.400	7	6	4	0	0	47	40	2	41	13	15.7	4.21	80	.220	.366	3	.130	-0	-5	-4	-0	-0.5
Total	2	9	6	.600	21	18	14	1	1	139^2	125	6	92	62	14.6	3.67	107	.231	.353	6	.092	-4	-1	4	-1	-0.1

● OTTO RETTIG Rettig, Adolph John b: 1/29/1894, New York, N.Y. d: 6/16/77, Stuart, Fla. BR/TR, 5′11″, 165 lbs. Deb: 7/19/22

YEAR	TM/L	W	L	PCT	G	GS	CG	SH	SV	IP	H	HR	BB	SO	RAT	ERA	ERA+	OAV	OOB	BH	AVG	PB	PR	/A	PD	TPI
1922	Phi-A	1	2	.333	4	4	1	0	0	18^1	18	0	12	3	15.2	4.91	87	.265	.383	0	.000	-1	-2	-1	0	-0.2

● ED REULBACH Reulbach, Edward Marvin "Big Ed" b: 12/1/1882, Detroit, Mich. d: 7/17/61, Glens Falls, N.Y. BR/TR, 6′1″, 190 lbs. Deb: 5/16/05

YEAR	TM/L	W	L	PCT	G	GS	CG	SH	SV	IP	H	HR	BB	SO	RAT	ERA	ERA+	OAV	OOB	BH	AVG	PB	PR	/A	PD	TPI
1905	Chi-N	18	14	.563	34	29	28	5	1	291^2	208	1	73	152	9.2	1.42	210	**.201**	.266	14	.127	-5	51	51	-1	4.8
1906	*Chi-N	19	4	**.826**	33	24	20	6	3	218	129	2	92	94	9.7	1.65	160	**.175**	.278	13	.157	-2	24	24	3	2.8
1907	*Chi-N	17	4	**.810**	27	22	16	4	0	192	147	1	64	96	10.3	1.69	148	.217	.294	11	.175	0	17	17	1	2.1
1908	*Chi-N	24	7	**.774**	46	35	25	7	1	297^2	227	4	106	133	10.4	2.03	116	.214	.292	23	.232	7	11	11	-1	1.8
1909	Chi-N	19	10	.655	35	32	23	6	0	262^2	194	1	82	105	9.8	1.78	143	.212	.285	12	.140	-1	24	22	4	2.9
1910	*Chi-N	12	8	.600	24	23	14	1	0	173^1	162	1	49	56	11.4	3.12	92	.251	.313	6	.107	-3	-2	-5	1	-0.8
1911	Chi-N	16	9	.640	33	29	15	2	0	221^2	191	3	103	79	12.1	2.96	112	.236	.325	6	.090	-1	11	9	3	1.0
1912	Chi-N	10	6	.625	39	19	8	0	4	169	161	7	60	75	12.2	3.78	88	.259	.332	6	.109	-3	-7	-8	4	-0.7
1913	Chi-N	1	3	.250	10	3	1	0	0	38^2	41	1	21	10	14.7	4.42	72	.281	.375	3	.250	0	-5	-5	0	-0.5
	Bro-N	7	6	.538	15	12	8	2	0	110	77	3	34	46	9.4	2.05	161	.202	.274	3	.103	0	14	15	-1	1.6
	Yr	8	9	.471	25	15	9	2	0	148^2	118	4	55	56	10.7	2.66	123	.223	.301	6	.146	0	9	10	-1	1.1

YEAR	TM/L	W	L	PCT	G	GS	CG	SH	SV	IP	H	HR	BB	SO	RAT	ERA	ERA+	OAV	OOB	BH	AVG	PB	PR	/A	PD	TPI
1914	Bro-N	11	18	.379	44	29	14	3	3	256	228	5	83	119	11.3	2.64	108	.242	.310	9	.122	-0	4	6	1	0.8
1915	New-F	21	10	.677	33	30	23	4	1	270	233	3	69	117	10.2	2.23	127	.236	.287	18	.196	-0	24	18	1	2.2
1916	Bos-N	7	6	.538	21	11	6	0	0	109^1	99	1	41	47	11.9	2.47	101	.251	.328	3	.091	-1	2	0	5	0.5
1917	Bos-N	0	1	.000	5	2	0	0	0	22^1	21	0	15	9	14.9	2.82	90	.256	.378	0	.000	1	-0	-1	1	0.1
Total	13	182	106	.632	399	300	201	40	13	2632^1	2118	33	892	1138	10.7	2.28	123	.224	.299	127	.147	-9	168	155	22	18.6
● **PAUL REUSCHEL** Reuschel, Paul Richard b: 1/12/47, Quincy, Ill. BR/TR, 6'4", 225 lbs. Deb: 7/25/75 F																										
1975	Chi-N	1	3	.250	28	0	0	0	5	36	44	1	13	12	14.5	3.50	110	.312	.374	0	.000	-0	0	1	0	0.1
1976	Chi-N	4	2	.667	50	2	0	0	3	87	94	12	33	55	13.2	4.55	85	.278	.344	2	.154	-0	-10	-7	1	-0.6
1977	Chi-N	5	6	.455	69	0	0	0	4	107	105	9	40	62	12.2	4.37	100	.262	.329	0	.000	-2	-6	0	2	0.1
1978	Chi-N	2	0	1.000	16	0	0	0	0	28	29	4	13	13	13.8	5.14	78	.269	.352	0	.000	-1	-5	-3	-0	-0.4
	Cle-A	2	4	.333	18	6	1	0	0	89^2	95	5	22	24	11.9	3.11	120	.271	.318	0	—	0	6	6	1	0.7
1979	Cle-A	2	1	.667	17	1	0	0	1	45^1	73	7	11	22	16.7	7.94	54	.365	.398	0	—	0	-19	-19	1	-1.7
Total	5	16	16	.500	198	9	1	0	13	393	440	38	132	188	13.2	4.51	89	.286	.344	2	.063	-2	-32	-21	5	-1.8
● **RICK REUSCHEL** Reuschel, Rickey Eugene b: 5/16/49, Quincy, Ill. BR/TR, 6'3", 235 lbs. Deb: 6/19/72 F																										
1972	Chi-N	10	8	.556	21	18	5	4	0	129	127	3	29	87	11.0	2.93	130	.259	.303	6	.136	-1	7	13	-0	1.2
1973	Chi-N	14	15	.483	36	36	7	3	0	237	244	15	62	168	11.8	3.00	131	.263	.312	9	.123	-3	17	25	4	2.7
1974	Chi-N	13	12	.520	41	38	8	2	0	240^2	262	18	83	160	13.1	4.30	89	.276	.338	19	.221	2	-18	-13	5	-0.7
1975	Chi-N	11	17	.393	38	37	6	0	1	234	244	17	67	155	12.2	3.73	103	.268	.323	16	.208	2	-3	3	3	0.8
1976	Chi-N	14	12	.538	38	37	9	2	1	260	260	17	64	146	11.5	3.46	111	.265	.315	19	.229	4	1	11	3	2.1
1977	Chi-N★	20	10	.667	39	37	8	4	1	252	233	13	74	166	11.1	2.79	157	.247	.305	18	.207	2	31	**45**	3	5.5
1978	Chi-N	14	15	.483	35	35	9	1	0	242^2	235	16	54	115	10.9	3.41	118	.254	.299	10	.137	-1	4	17	2	1.9
1979	Chi-N	18	12	.600	36	36	5	1	0	239	251	16	75	125	12.7	3.62	114	.274	.335	13	.165	1	3	13	5	2.0
1980	Chi-N	11	13	.458	38	38	6	0	0	257	281	13	76	140	12.6	3.40	115	.286	.340	13	.159	-1	6	15	5	2.0
1981	Chi-N	4	7	.364	13	13	1	0	0	85^2	87	4	23	53	12.0	3.47	107	.267	.323	2	.080	-2	0	2	2	0.2
	*NY-A	4	4	.500	12	11	3	0	0	70^2	75	4	10	22	11.0	2.67	134	.280	.308	0	—	0	8	7	1	0.9
1983	Chi-N	1	1	.500	4	4	0	0	0	20^2	18	1	10	9	12.2	3.92	97	.234	.322	1	.143	-0	-1	-0	1	0.1
1984	Chi-N	5	5	.500	19	14	1	0	0	92^1	123	7	23	43	14.5	5.17	76	.339	.383	7	.241	2	-16	-13	1	-1.0
1985	Pit-N	14	8	.636	31	26	9	1	1	194	153	7	52	138	9.6	2.27	157	.215	.272	10	.169	2	28	28	4	3.9
1986	Pit-N	9	16	.360	35	34	4	2	0	215^2	232	20	57	125	12.4	3.96	97	.274	.326	11	.157	0	-6	-3	3	0.0
1987	Pit-N★	8	6	.571	25	25	9	3	0	177	163	12	35	80	10.4	2.75	150	.246	.290	9	.150	2	26	27	1	3.2
	*SF-N	5	3	.625	9	8	3	1	0	50	44	1	7	27	9.5	4.32	89	.230	.265	2	.105	-0	-1	-3	0	-0.2
	Yr	13	9	.591	34	33	**12**	**4**	0	227	207	13	42	107	**10.0**	3.09	131	.239	.276	11	.139	2	25	24	1	3.0
1988	SF-N	19	11	.633	36	36	7	2	0	245	242	11	42	92	10.7	3.12	104	.260	.297	8	.110	-1	9	4	-2	0.0
1989	*SF-N★	17	8	.680	32	32	2	0	0	208^1	195	18	54	111	10.8	2.94	115	.247	.297	10	.164	1	13	10	-0	1.2
1990	SF-N	3	6	.333	15	13	0	0	1	87	102	8	31	49	13.9	3.93	93	.297	.357	4	.154	0	-1	-3	0	-0.2
1991	SF-N	0	2	.000	4	1	0	0	0	10^2	17	0	7	4	20.3	4.22	85	.370	.453	0	.000	-0	-1	-1	-0	-0.1
Total	19	214	191	.528	557	529	102	26	5	3548^1	3588	221	935	2015	11.7	3.37	114	.264	.316	187	.168	9	108	183	39	25.5
● **JERRY REUSS** Reuss, Jerry b: 6/19/49, St.Louis, Mo. BL/TL, 6'5", 217 lbs. Deb: 9/27/69																										
1969	StL-N	1	0	1.000	1	1	0	0	0	7	2	0	3	3	9.0	0.00	—	.091	.259	1	.333	0	3	3	0	0.4
1970	StL-N	7	8	.467	20	20	5	2	0	127^1	132	9	49	74	12.9	4.10	100	.271	.339	2	.050	-3	-1	0	-0	-0.3
1971	StL-N	14	14	.500	36	35	7	2	0	211	228	15	109	131	14.7	4.78	75	.279	.368	8	.123	0	-31	-28	-2	-3.0
1972	Hou-N	9	13	.409	33	30	4	1	1	192	177	14	83	174	12.7	4.17	81	.246	.332	7	.106	-1	-15	-17	-1	-2.0
1973	Hou-N	16	13	.552	41	40	12	3	0	279^1	271	17	117	177	12.6	3.74	97	.256	.332	13	.137	-1	-2	-3	-2	-0.7
1974	*Pit-N	16	11	.593	35	35	14	1	0	260	259	20	101	105	12.5	3.50	99	.261	.329	13	.151	0	4	-1	-2	-0.4
1975	*Pit-N★	18	11	.621	32	32	15	6	0	237^1	224	10	78	131	11.5	2.54	139	.253	.314	14	.197	2	28	26	2	3.4
1976	Pit-N	14	9	.609	31	29	11	3	2	209^1	209	16	51	108	11.3	3.53	99	.256	.301	16	.242	6	-1	-1	-2	0.3
1977	Pit-N	10	13	.435	33	33	8	2	0	208	225	11	71	116	13.0	4.11	97	.280	.341	12	.171	1	-5	-3	1	-0.1
1978	Pit-N	3	2	.600	23	12	3	1	0	82^2	97	5	23	42	13.4	4.90	76	.297	.348	5	.185	0	-12	-11	-0	-1.1
1979	LA-N	7	14	.333	39	21	4	1	3	160	178	4	60	83	13.6	3.54	103	.282	.347	7	.167	1	3	2	1	0.4
1980	LA-N★	18	6	.750	37	29	10	**6**	3	229^1	193	12	40	111	9.1	2.51	139	.227	.261	6	.088	-1	28	25	1	2.8
1981	*LA-N	10	4	.714	22	22	8	2	0	152^2	138	6	27	51	10.0	2.30	144	.243	.282	10	.196	0	20	17	3	2.3
1982	LA-N	18	11	.621	39	37	8	4	0	254^2	232	11	50	138	10.0	3.11	111	.240	.278	17	.221	3	14	10	2	1.6
1983	*LA-N	12	11	.522	32	31	7	0	0	223^1	233	12	50	143	11.5	2.94	122	.271	.313	20	.282	5	17	16	4	2.8
1984	LA-N	5	7	.417	30	15	2	0	1	99	102	4	31	44	12.1	3.82	92	.266	.321	4	.167	1	-3	-3	-0	-0.3
1985	*LA-N	14	10	.583	34	33	5	3	0	212^2	210	13	58	84	11.5	2.92	119	.260	.312	10	.135	-1	16	13	-2	1.0
1986	LA-N	2	6	.250	19	13	0	0	1	74	96	13	17	29	14.0	5.84	59	.313	.353	5	.250	2	-17	-20	1	-1.7
1987	LA-N	0	0	—	1	0	0	0	0	2	2	0	0	2	9.0	4.50	88	.333	.333	0	—	0	-0	-0	-0	0.0
	Cin-N	0	5	.000	7	7	0	0	0	34^2	52	2	12	10	16.9	7.79	54	.351	.404	1	.125	0	-14	-14	-1	-1.3
	Yr	0	5	.000	8	7	0	0	0	36^2	54	2	12	12	16.4	7.61	56	.348	.399	1	.125	0	-14	-14	-1	-1.3
	Cal-A	4	5	.444	17	16	1	1	0	82^1	112	16	17	37	14.3	5.25	82	.327	.362	0	—	0	-7	-9	2	-0.7
1988	Chi-A	13	9	.591	32	29	2	0	0	183	183	15	43	73	11.3	3.44	115	.263	.309	0	—	0	11	11	0	1.1
1989	Chi-A	8	5	.615	23	19	1	1	0	106^2	135	12	21	27	13.4	5.06	75	.308	.344	0	—	0	-14	-15	-2	-1.7
	Mil-A	1	4	.200	7	7	0	0	0	33^2	36	7	13	13	13.4	5.35	72	.273	.342	0	—	0	-5	-6	-0	-0.6
	Yr	9	9	.500	30	26	1	1	0	140^1	171	19	34	40	13.2	5.13	74	.295	.336	0	—	0	-19	-21	-2	-2.3
1990	Pit-N	0	0	—	4	1	0	0	0	7^2	8	1	3	1	12.9	3.52	103	.267	.333	0	—	0	0	0	0	0.0
Total	22	220	191	.535	628	547	127	39	11	3669^2	3734	245	1127	1907	12.1	3.64	100	.265	.322	171	.167	15	16	-7	2	2.2
● **TODD REVENIG** Revenig, Todd Michael b: 6/28/69, Brainerd, Minn. BR/TR, 6'1", 185 lbs. Deb: 8/24/92																										
1992	Oak-A	0	0	—	2	0	0	0	0	2	2	0	0	1	9.0	0.00	—	.286	.286	0	—	0	1	1	-0	0.4
● **ALLIE REYNOLDS** Reynolds, Allie Pierce "Superchief" b: 2/10/15, Bethany, Okla. BR/TR, 6', 195 lbs. Deb: 9/17/42																										
1942	Cle-A	0	0	—	2	0	0	0	0	5	5	0	4	2	16.2	0.00	—	.250	.375	0	.000	-0	2	2	-0	0.2
1943	Cle-A	11	12	.478	34	21	11	3	3	198^2	140	3	109	**151**	11.6	2.99	104	**.202**	.316	10	.149	-1	7	3	-0	0.1
1944	Cle-A	11	8	.579	28	21	5	1	1	158	141	2	91	84	13.4	3.30	100	.240	.346	7	.123	-3	2	-0	-1	-0.4
1945	Cle-A	18	12	.600	44	30	16	2	4	247^1	227	7	130	112	13.2	3.20	101	.247	.343	8	.094	-7	5	1	-1	-0.7
1946	Cle-A	11	15	.423	31	28	9	3	0	183^1	180	10	108	107	14.2	3.88	85	.259	.359	14	.222	1	-8	-12	-1	-1.2
1947	*NY-A	19	8	**.704**	34	30	17	4	2	241^2	207	23	123	129	12.4	3.20	110	.227	.322	13	.146	-2	13	9	-2	0.5
1948	NY-A	16	7	.696	39	31	11	1	3	236^1	240	17	111	101	13.5	3.77	108	.268	.351	16	.193	0	14	8	-3	0.5
1949	*NY-A☆	17	6	.739	35	31	4	2	1	213^2	200	15	123	105	13.8	4.00	101	.250	.353	17	.218	5	5	1	-0	0.6
1950	*NY-A★	16	12	.571	35	29	14	2	2	240^2	215	12	138	160	13.5	3.74	115	.242	.349	15	.185	1	22	15	-1	1.4
1951	*NY-A	17	8	.680	40	26	16	**7**	7	221	171	12	100	126	11.2	3.05	125	**.213**	.304	14	.184	0	26	19	-3	1.6
1952	*NY-A☆	20	8	.714	35	29	24	**6**	6	244^1	194	10	97	**160**	11.0	**2.06**	**161**	.218	.300	13	.153	-0	**44**	34	-1	3.6
1953	*NY-A★	13	7	.650	41	15	5	1	13	145	140	9	61	86	12.8	3.41	108	.253	.333	5	.122	1	9	4	-2	0.3
1954	NY-A†	13	4	.765	36	18	5	4	7	157^1	133	13	66	100	11.6	3.32	104	.233	.316	8	.160	-0	7	2	-0	0.1
Total	13	182	107	.630	434	309	137	36	49	2492^1	2193	133	1261	1423	12.7	3.30	110	.238	.333	140	.163	-4	149	87	-16	6.6
● **ARCHIE REYNOLDS** Reynolds, Archie Edward b: 1/3/46, Glendale, Cal. BR/TR, 6'2", 205 lbs. Deb: 8/15/68																										
1968	Chi-N	0	1	.000	7	1	0	0	0	13^1	14	1	7	6	14.9	6.75	47	.259	.355	1	.500	1	-6	-5	-0	-0.6
1969	Chi-N	0	1	.000	2	2	0	0	0	7^1	11	1	7	4	22.1	2.45	164	.379	.500	0	.000	0	1	1	0	0.2
1970	Chi-N	0	2	.000	7	1	0	0	0	15	17	2	9	9	16.2	6.60	68	.298	.403	0	.000	0	-4	-3	-0	-0.4
1971	Cal-A	0	3	.000	15	1	0	0	0	27^1	32	2	18	15	16.5	4.61	70	.305	.407	0	.000	-0	-3	-4	0	-0.4

YEAR	TM/L	W	L	PCT	G	GS	CG	SH	SV	IP	H	HR	BB	SO	RAT	ERA	ERA+	OAV	OOB	BH	AVG	PB	PR	/A	PD	TPI
1972	Mil-A	0	1	.000	5	2	0	0	0	18^2	26	2	8	13	16.4	7.23	42	.338	.400	2	.500	1	-9	-9	-1	-0.9
Total	5	0	8	.000	36	7	0	0	0	81^2	100	8	49	47	16.6	5.73	61	.311	.405	3	.273	2	-21	-21	-1	-2.1
● **CHARLIE REYNOLDS** Reynolds, Charles E. b: 7/31/1857, Allegany, N.Y. d: 5/1/13, Buffalo, N.Y. Deb: 5/18/1882																										
1882	Phi-a	1	1	.500	2	2	1	0	0	12	18	0	3	4	15.8	5.25	57	.325	.360	1	.125	-1	-3	-3	-1	-0.4
● **CRAIG REYNOLDS** Reynolds, Gordon Craig b: 12/27/52, Houston, Tex. BL/TR, 6'1", 175 lbs. Deb: 8/01/75 ♦																										
1986	*Hou-N	0	0	—	1	0	0	0	0	1	3	0	2	1	45.0	27.00	13	.500	.625	78	.249	0	-3	-3	0	-0.2
1989	Hou-N	0	0	—	1	0	0	0	0	1	3	0	1	0	45.0	27.00	13	.500	.625	38	.201	0	-3	-3	0	-0.2
Total	2	0	0	—	2	0	0	0	0	2	6	0	3	1	45.0	27.00	13	.500	.625	1142	.256	0	-5	-5	0	-0.4
● **KEN REYNOLDS** Reynolds, Kenneth Lee b: 1/4/47, Trevose, Pa. BL/TL, 6', 180 lbs. Deb: 9/05/70																										
1970	Phi-N	0	0	—	4	0	0	0	0	2^1	3	0	4	1	27.0	0.00	—	.333	.538	0	—	0	1	1	0	0.1
1971	Phi-N	5	9	.357	35	25	2	1	0	162^1	163	11	82	81	13.9	4.49	78	.269	.361	10	.200	2	-19	-17	-1	-1.7
1972	Phi-N	2	15	.118	33	23	2	0	0	154^1	149	17	60	87	12.2	4.26	84	.258	.329	8	.200	1	-14	-11	-0	-1.1
1973	Mil-A	0	1	.000	2	1	0	0	0	7^1	5	1	10	3	19.6	7.36	51	.200	.444	0	—	0	-3	-3	1	-0.1
1975	StL-N	0	1	.000	10	0	0	0	0	17	12	0	11	7	12.2	1.59	236	.214	.343	0	.000	-0	4	4	1	0.5
1976	SD-N	0	3	.000	19	2	0	0	1	32^1	38	0	29	18	18.6	6.40	51	.309	.441	0	.000	-1	-10	-11	-0	-1.2
Total	6	7	29	.194	103	51	4	1	1	375^2	370	29	196	197	13.8	4.46	80	.265	.358	18	.186	2	-41	-38	0	-3.5
● **SHANE REYNOLDS** Reynolds, Richard Shane b: 3/26/68, Bastrop, La. BR/TR, 6'3", 210 lbs. Deb: 7/20/92																										
1992	Hou-N	1	3	.250	8	5	0	0	0	25^1	42	2	6	10	17.1	7.11	47	.385	.417	2	.500	1	-10	-11	0	-0.9
● **BOB REYNOLDS** Reynolds, Robert Allen b: 1/21/47, Seattle, Wash. BR/TR, 6', 205 lbs. Deb: 9/19/69																										
1969	Mon-N	0	0	—	1	1	0	0	0	1^1	3	0	3	2	40.5	20.25	18	.429	.600	0	—	0	-2	-2	0	-0.2
1971	StL-N	0	0	—	4	0	0	0	0	7	15	2	6	4	28.3	10.29	35	.441	.537	0	.000	-0	-5	-5	-0	-0.5
	Mil-A	0	1	.000	3	0	0	0	0	6	4	0	3	4	10.5	3.00	116	.222	.333	0	.000	-0	0	0	0	0.0
1972	Bal-A	0	0	—	3	0	0	0	0	9^2	8	0	7	5	14.0	1.86	165	.258	.395	0	.000	-0	1	1	-0	0.1
1973	*Bal-A	7	5	.583	42	1	0	0	9	111	88	3	31	77	9.6	1.95	192	.219	.275	0	—	0	23	22	-2	2.1
1974	*Bal-A	7	5	.583	54	0	0	0	7	69^1	75	4	14	43	11.7	2.73	127	.278	.316	0	—	0	7	6	-0	0.6
1975	Bal-A	0	1	.000	7	0	0	0	0	6	11	1	1	1	18.0	9.00	39	.423	.444	0	—	0	-3	-4	-0	0.1
	Det-A	0	2	.000	21	0	0	0	3	34^2	40	8	14	26	14.3	4.67	86	.288	.357	0	—	0	-3	-3	0	-0.5
	Cle-A	0	2	.000	5	0	0	0	2	9^2	11	0	3	5	13.0	4.66	81	.289	.341	0	—	0	-1	-1	-0	-0.1
	Yr	0	5	.000	33	0	0	0	5	50^1	62	9	18	32	14.3	5.19	75	.301	.357	0	—	0	-8	-7	-0	-0.5
Total	6	14	16	.467	140	2	0	0	21	254^2	255	18	82	167	12.0	3.15	116	.264	.324	0	.000	-0	16	14	-3	1.6
● **ROSS REYNOLDS** Reynolds, Ross Ernest "Doc" b: 8/20/1887, Barksdale, Tex. d: 6/23/70, Ada, Okla. BR/TR, 6'2", 185 lbs. Deb: 5/02/14																										
1914	Det-A	5	3	.625	26	7	3	1	0	78	62	0	39	31	12.3	2.08	135	.230	.340	1	.048	-2	6	6	-1	0.4
1915	Det-A	0	1	.000	4	2	0	0	0	11^1	17	0	5	2	18.3	6.35	48	.378	.451	0	.000	-0	-4	-4	0	-0.4
Total	2	5	4	.556	30	9	3	1	0	89^1	79	0	44	33	13.1	2.62	108	.251	.355	1	.042	-3	1	2	-1	0.0
● **ARMANDO REYNOSO** Reynoso, Armando Martin (Gutierrez) b: 5/1/66, San Luis Potosi, Mex. BR/TR, 6', 186 lbs. Deb: 8/11/91																										
1991	Atl-N	2	1	.667	6	5	0	0	0	23^1	26	4	10	10	15.0	6.17	63	.299	.390	0	.000	-0	-6	-6	2	-0.5
1992	Atl-N	1	0	1.000	3	1	0	0	1	7^2	11	2	2	2	16.4	4.70	80	.393	.452	0	.000	-0	-1	-1	0	-0.1
Total	2	3	1	.750	9	6	0	0	1	31	37	6	12	12	15.4	5.81	66	.322	.405	0	.000	-1	-7	-7	2	-0.6
● **FLINT RHEM** Rhem, Charles Flint "Shad" b: 1/24/01, Rhems, S.C. d: 7/30/69, Columbia, S.C. BR/TR, 6'2", 180 lbs. Deb: 9/06/24																										
1924	StL-N	2	2	.500	6	3	3	0	1	32^1	31	1	17	20	13.4	4.45	85	.254	.345	2	.167	-0	-2	-2	0	-0.2
1925	StL-N	8	13	.381	30	23	8	1	1	170	204	16	58	66	14.1	4.92	88	.299	.357	14	.237	1	-12	-11	0	-0.9
1926	*StL-N	**20**	7	.741	34	34	20	1	0	258	241	12	75	72	11.1	3.21	122	.250	.305	18	.188	-2	18	20	1	1.9
1927	StL-N	10	12	.455	27	26	9	2	0	169^1	189	6	54	51	13.1	4.41	90	.285	.342	4	.068	-6	-9	-9	-3	-1.6
1928	*StL-N	11	8	.579	28	22	9	0	3	169^2	199	13	71	47	14.5	4.14	97	.296	.365	11	.164	-1	-3	-3	2	-0.3
1930	*StL-N	12	8	.600	26	19	9	0	0	139^2	173	11	37	47	13.7	4.45	113	.306	.352	12	.231	-1	8	9	-3	0.5
1931	*StL-N	11	10	.524	33	26	10	2	1	207^1	214	17	60	72	12.0	3.56	111	.268	.321	9	.130	-4	7	9	-2	0.3
1932	StL-N	4	2	.667	6	6	5	1	0	50	48	3	10	18	10.4	3.06	129	.257	.294	3	.188	0	5	5	0	0.5
	Phi-N	11	7	.611	26	20	10	0	1	168^2	177	13	49	35	12.1	3.74	118	.269	.319	7	.113	-5	3	13	-0	0.7
	Yr	15	9	.625	32	26	15	1	1	218^2	225	16	59	53	11.7	3.58	120	.266	.314	10	.128	-5	7	18	-0	1.2
1933	Phi-N	5	14	.263	28	19	3	0	2	125	182	10	33	27	15.6	6.62	58	.340	.381	4	.087	-4	-46	-39	-0	-4.2
1934	StL-N	1	0	1.000	5	1	0	0	1	15^2	26	0	7	6	19.0	4.60	92	.394	.452	0	.000	-0	-1	-1	-0	-0.1
	Bos-N	8	8	.500	25	20	5	1	0	152^2	164	5	38	56	11.9	3.60	106	.273	.317	3	.058	-5	8	4	1	0.0
	Yr	9	8	.529	30	21	5	1	1	168^1	190	5	45	62	12.6	3.69	105	.285	.331	3	.056	-5	7	3	1	-0.1
1935	Bos-N	0	5	.000	10	6	0	0	0	40^1	61	4	11	10	16.1	5.36	71	.341	.379	0	.000	-1	-6	-7	0	-0.8
1936	StL-N	2	1	.667	10	4	0	0	0	26^2	49	2	9	7	19.6	6.75	58	.405	.446	1	.125	-0	-8	-8	-1	-0.9
Total	12	105	97	.520	294	229	91	8	10	1725^1	1958	113	529	534	13.1	4.20	98	.287	.340	88	.144	-29	-39	-20	-3	-5.1
● **BILLY RHINES** Rhines, William Pearl "Bunker" b: 3/14/1869, Ridgway, Pa. d: 1/30/22, Ridgway, Pa. BR/TR, 5'11", 168 lbs. Deb: 4/22/1890																										
1890	Cin-N	28	17	.622	46	45	45	6	0	401^1	337	6	113	182	**10.4**	**1.95**	**182**	.221	**.281**	29	.188	-5	**72**	72	1	6.4
1891	Cin-N	17	24	.415	48	43	40	1	1	372^2	364	4	124	138	12.3	2.87	117	.246	.314	18	.122	-9	20	21	3	1.4
1892	Cin-N	4	7	.364	12	10	7	0	0	83^2	113	0	36	12	16.5	5.06	65	.310	.379	5	.167	1	-16	-17	-1	-1.5
1893	Lou-N	1	4	.200	5	5	3	0	0	31	49	3	19	0	20.6	8.71	51	.348	.436	1	.091	-1	-14	-15	0	-1.2
1895	Cin-N	19	10	.655	38	33	25	0	0	267^2	322	4	76	72	14.1	4.81	103	.293	.351	25	.221	-4	-1	5	-0	0.1
1896	Cin-N	8	6	.571	19	17	11	3	0	143	128	1	48	32	**11.6**	**2.45**	**188**	**.238**	**.311**	10	.192	-3	30	34	0	2.9
1897	Cin-N	21	15	.583	41	32	26	1	0	288^2	311	4	86	65	12.9	4.08	112	.273	.333	17	.159	-7	7	15	-2	0.5
1898	Pit-N	12	16	.429	31	29	27	2	0	258	289	0	61	48	12.7	3.52	101	.281	.329	15	.150	-5	2	1	5	0.2
1899	Pit-N	4	4	.500	9	9	4	0	0	54	59	3	13	6	12.7	6.00	64	.278	.331	10	.435	4	-13	-13	-1	-0.9
Total	9	114	103	.525	249	223	188	13	1	1900	1972	25	576	555	12.6	3.47	114	.262	.323	130	.176	-28	88	101	4	7.9
● **BOB RHOADS** Rhoads, Robert Barton "Dusty" b: 10/4/1879, Wooster, Ohio d: 2/12/67, San Bernardino, Cal. BR/TR, 6'1", 215 lbs. Deb: 4/19/02																										
1902	Chi-N	4	8	.333	16	12	12	1	1	118	131	1	42	43	13.7	3.20	84	.281	.348	10	.222	0	-6	-7	-1	-0.7
1903	StL-N	5	8	.385	17	13	12	1	0	129	154	3	47	52	14.2	4.60	71	.303	.366	7	.140	-2	-19	-19	-1	-2.0
	Cle-A	2	3	.400	5	5	5	0	0	41	55	2	3	21	13.4	5.27	54	.320	.343	2	.118	-1	-10	-11	-0	-1.1
1904	Cle-A	10	9	.526	22	19	18	0	0	175^1	175	1	48	72	11.7	2.87	88	.261	.314	18	.196	0	-5	-7	-1	-0.8
1905	Cle-A	16	9	.640	28	26	24	4	0	235	219	4	55	61	10.5	2.83	93	.248	.293	21	.221	4	-5	-5	0	-0.1
1906	Cle-A	22	10	.688	38	34	31	7	0	315	259	5	92	89	10.2	1.80	146	.227	.288	19	.161	-3	31	29	-2	2.7
1907	Cle-A	15	14	.517	35	31	23	5	1	275	258	0	84	76	11.7	2.29	110	.250	.315	17	.185	-1	8	7	-1	0.4
1908	Cle-A	18	12	.600	37	30	20	1	0	270	229	2	73	62	10.3	1.77	135	.239	.298	20	.222	4	19	19	2	2.9
1909	Cle-A	5	9	.357	20	15	9	2	0	133^1	124	1	50	46	12.2	2.90	88	.281	.361	7	.163	-0	-6	-5	1	-0.6
Total	8	97	82	.542	218	185	154	21	2	1691^2	1604	19	494	522	11.4	2.61	100	.256	.315	121	.188	-0	7	1	-3	0.7
● **RICK RHODEN** Rhoden, Richard Alan b: 5/16/53, Boynton Beach, Fla. BR/TR, 6'3", 195 lbs. Deb: 7/05/74																										
1974	LA-N	1	0	1.000	4	0	0	0	0	9	5	1	4	7	9.0	2.00	170	.161	.257	1	.500	0	2	1	-0	0.2
1975	LA-N	3	3	.500	26	11	1	0	0	99^1	94	8	32	40	11.5	3.08	110	.253	.314	2	.071	-2	6	4	0	0.2
1976	LA-N★	12	3	.800	27	26	10	3	0	181	165	17	53	77	10.9	2.98	113	.242	.298	20	.308	7	10	8	-2	1.4
1977	*LA-N	16	10	.615	31	31	4	1	0	216^1	223	20	63	122	12.0	3.74	102	.270	.323	18	.231	5	4	2	-3	0.4
1978	*LA-N	10	8	.556	30	23	6	3	0	164^2	160	13	51	79	11.7	3.66	96	.255	.314	7	.135	-0	-2	-3	-1	-0.5

YEAR	TM/L	W	L	PCT	G	GS	CG	SH	SV	IP	H	HR	BB	SO	RAT	ERA	ERA+	OAV	OOB	BH	AVG	PB	PR	/A	PD	TPI
1979	Pit-N	0	1	.000	1	1	0	0	0	5	5	0	2	2	12.6	7.20	54	.263	.333	1	1.000	0	-2	-2	0	-0.1
1980	Pit-N	7	5	.583	20	19	2	0	0	126^{2}	133	9	40	70	12.5	3.84	95	.273	.332	15	.375	6	-3	-3	0	0.4
1981	Pit-N	9	4	.692	21	21	4	2	0	136^{1}	147	6	53	76	13.3	3.89	92	.283	.352	9	.188	1	-6	-5	1	-0.3
1982	Pit-N	11	14	.440	35	35	6	1	0	230^{1}	239	14	70	128	12.2	4.14	89	.267	.321	22	.265	9	-14	-11	2	0.0
1983	Pit-N	13	13	.500	36	35	7	2	1	244^{1}	256	13	68	153	12.0	3.09	120	.276	.327	13	.151	-2	14	17	1	1.7
1984	Pit-N	14	9	.609	33	33	6	3	0	238^{1}	216	13	62	136	10.5	2.72	132	.243	.293	28	.333	10	23	**23**	2	**3.9**
1985	Pit-N	10	15	.400	35	35	2	0	0	213^{1}	254	18	69	128	13.9	4.47	80	.296	.352	14	.189	2	-21	-21	-0	-2.0
1986	Pit-N☆	15	12	.556	34	34	12	1	0	253^{2}	211	17	76	159	10.3	2.84	135	.228	.288	25	.278	9	25	28	1	4.2
1987	NY-A	16	10	.615	30	29	4	0	0	181^{2}	184	22	61	107	12.3	3.86	113	.268	.330	0	—	0	12	10	-0	1.1
1988	NY-A	12	12	.500	30	30	5	1	0	197	206	20	56	94	12.3	4.29	92	.269	.325	0	.000	0	-7	-8	-1	-0.8
1989	Hou-N	2	6	.250	20	17	0	0	0	96^{2}	108	7	41	41	14.2	4.28	79	.289	.364	6	.207	1	-8	-10	1	-0.8
Total	16	151	125	.547	413	380	69	17	1	2593^{2}	2606	198	801	1419	12.0	3.59	103	.264	.321	181	.238	46	33	32	1	9.0

● ARTHUR LEE RHODES Rhodes, Arthur Lee b: 10/24/69, Waco, Tex. BL/TL, 6'2", 190 lbs. Deb: 8/21/91

YEAR	TM/L	W	L	PCT	G	GS	CG	SH	SV	IP	H	HR	BB	SO	RAT	ERA	ERA+	OAV	OOB	BH	AVG	PB	PR	/A	PD	TPI
1991	Bal-A	0	3	.000	8	8	0	0	0	36	47	4	23	23	17.5	8.00	49	.320	.412	0	—	0	-16	-16	-1	-1.3
1992	Bal-A	7	5	.583	15	15	2	1	0	94^{1}	87	6	38	77	12.0	3.63	108	.249	.325	0	—	0	3	3	0	0.3
Total	2	7	8	.467	23	23	2	1	0	130^{1}	134	10	61	100	13.5	4.83	81	.270	.351	0	—	0	-12	-13	-1	-1.0

● CHARLIE RHODES Rhodes, Charles Anderson "Dusty" b: 4/7/1885, Caney, Kan. d: 10/26/18, Caney, Kan. BR/TR, 5'7", 180 lbs. Deb: 7/26/06

YEAR	TM/L	W	L	PCT	G	GS	CG	SH	SV	IP	H	HR	BB	SO	RAT	ERA	ERA+	OAV	OOB	BH	AVG	PB	PR	/A	PD	TPI
1906	StL-N	3	4	.429	9	6	3	0	0	45	37	0	20	32	12.6	3.40	77	.223	.328	3	.188	-0	-4	-4	0	-0.4
1908	Cin-N	0	0	—	1	0	0	0	0	4	1	0	2	4	9.0	0.00	—	.077	.250	0	.000	-0	1	1	0	0.2
	StL-N	1	2	.333	4	4	3	0	0	33	23	2	12	15	9.8	3.00	79	.200	.281	3	.250	1	-2	-2	1	-0.1
	Yr	1	2	.333	5	4	3	0	0	37	24	2	14	19	9.5	2.68	88	.186	.271	3	.231	1	-1	-1	1	0.1
1909	StL-N	3	5	.375	12	10	4	0	0	61	55	0	33	25	13.3	3.98	64	.256	.360	4	.211	1	-9	-10	2	-0.7
Total	3	7	11	.389	26	20	10	0	0	143	116	2	67	76	12.1	3.46	73	.228	.329	10	.208	2	-14	-15	4	-1.0

● GORDON RHODES Rhodes, John Gordon "Dusty" b: 8/11/07, Winnemucca, Nev. d: 3/24/60, Long Beach, Cal. BR/TR, 6', 187 lbs. Deb: 4/29/29

YEAR	TM/L	W	L	PCT	G	GS	CG	SH	SV	IP	H	HR	BB	SO	RAT	ERA	ERA+	OAV	OOB	BH	AVG	PB	PR	/A	PD	TPI
1929	NY-A	0	4	.000	10	4	0	0	0	42^{2}	57	3	16	13	15.8	4.85	80	.333	.397	3	.300	1	-3	-5	-1	-0.4
1930	NY-A	0	0	—	3	0	0	0	0	2	3	0	4	1	31.5	9.00	48	.500	.700	0	—	0	-1	-1	0	-0.1
1931	NY-A	6	3	.667	18	11	4	0	0	87	82	3	52	36	13.9	3.41	116	.235	.334	6	.214	1	9	5	0	0.6
1932	NY-A	1	2	.333	10	2	1	0	0	24	25	0	21	15	17.3	7.88	52	.275	.411	2	.286	0	-9	-10	1	-0.7
	Bos-A	1	8	.111	12	11	4	0	0	79^{1}	79	5	31	22	12.5	5.11	88	.261	.329	2	.074	-2	-6	-5	-0	-0.7
	Yr	2	10	.167	22	13	5	0	0	103^{1}	104	5	52	37	13.6	5.75	76	.264	.350	4	.118	-2	-15	-16	1	-1.4
1933	Bos-A	12	15	.444	34	29	14	0	0	232	242	13	93	85	13.0	4.03	109	.265	.334	23	.267	5	6	9	-1	1.2
1934	Bos-A	12	12	.500	44	31	10	0	2	219	247	10	98	79	14.3	4.56	105	.285	.360	10	.133	-4	-2	6	1	0.2
1935	Bos-A	2	10	.167	34	19	1	0	2	146^{1}	195	14	60	44	15.7	5.41	88	.324	.387	7	.146	-4	-16	-11	-1	-1.4
1936	Phi-A	9	20	.310	35	28	13	1	1	216^{1}	266	26	102	61	15.4	5.74	89	.304	.378	16	.213	-2	-17	-15	-3	-1.7
Total	8	43	74	.368	200	135	47	1	5	1048^{2}	1196	74	477	356	14.4	4.85	95	.286	.361	69	.194	-5	-37	-28	-3	-3.0

● BILL RHODES Rhodes, William Clarence b: Pottstown, Pa. Deb: 6/14/1893

YEAR	TM/L	W	L	PCT	G	GS	CG	SH	SV	IP	H	HR	BB	SO	RAT	ERA	ERA+	OAV	OOB	BH	AVG	PB	PR	/A	PD	TPI
1893	Lou-N	5	12	.294	20	19	17	0	0	151^{2}	244	10	66	22	19.0	7.60	58	.352	.416	9	.129	-3	-49	-54	-2	-4.4

● DENNIS RIBANT Ribant, Dennis Joseph b: 9/20/41, Detroit, Mich. BR/TR, 5'11", 175 lbs. Deb: 8/09/64

YEAR	TM/L	W	L	PCT	G	GS	CG	SH	SV	IP	H	HR	BB	SO	RAT	ERA	ERA+	OAV	OOB	BH	AVG	PB	PR	/A	PD	TPI
1964	NY-N	1	5	.167	14	7	1	1	1	57^{2}	65	8	9	35	11.5	5.15	69	.281	.308	2	.100	-0	-10	-10	-1	-1.1
1965	NY-N	1	3	.250	19	1	0	0	3	35^{1}	29	5	6	13	8.9	3.82	92	.228	.263	0	.000	-1	-1	-1	-0	-0.2
1966	NY-N	11	9	.550	39	26	10	1	3	188^{1}	184	20	40	84	10.8	3.20	114	.254	.294	12	.197	0	8	9	0	1.1
1967	Pit-N	9	8	.529	38	22	2	0	0	172	186	16	40	75	12.0	4.08	82	.280	.324	16	.267	5	-14	-14	2	-0.7
1968	Det-A	2	2	.500	14	0	0	0	1	24^{1}	20	1	10	7	11.5	2.22	136	.217	.301	1	.200	0	2	2	-1	0.2
	Chi-A	0	2	.000	17	0	0	0	1	31^{1}	42	3	17	20	17.5	6.03	50	.318	.404	0	.000	-1	-11	-10	0	-1.2
	Yr	2	4	.333	31	0	0	0	2	55^{2}	62	4	27	27	14.7	4.37	69	.276	.358	1	.083	-0	-9	-8	-0	-1.0
1969	StL-N	0	0	—	1	0	0	0	0	1^{1}	4	1	1	0	33.8	13.50	26	.571	.625	0	—	0	-1	-1	-0	-0.1
	Cin-N	0	0	—	7	0	0	0	0	8^{1}	6	1	3	7	9.7	1.08	348	.188	.257	0	—	0	2	2	-0	0.2
	Yr	0	0	—	8	0	0	0	0	9^{2}	10	2	4	7	13.0	2.79	134	.250	.318	0	—	0	1	1	-0	0.1
Total	6	24	29	.453	149	56	13	2	9	518^{2}	536	55	126	241	11.6	3.87	90	.267	.312	31	.195	4	-24	-23	0	-1.8

● FRANK RICCELLI Riccelli, Frank Joseph b: 2/24/53, Syracuse, N.Y. BL/TL, 6'3", 205 lbs. Deb: 9/11/76

YEAR	TM/L	W	L	PCT	G	GS	CG	SH	SV	IP	H	HR	BB	SO	RAT	ERA	ERA+	OAV	OOB	BH	AVG	PB	PR	/A	PD	TPI
1976	SF-N	1	1	.500	4	3	0	0	0	16	16	1	5	11	11.8	5.63	64	.258	.313	1	.167	-0	-4	-4	-0	-0.4
1978	Hou-N	0	0	—	2	0	0	0	0	3	1	0	0	1	3.0	0.00	—	.100	.100	0	—	0	1	1	-0	0.1
1979	Hou-N	2	2	.500	11	2	0	0	0	22	22	0	18	20	16.4	4.09	86	.262	.392	2	.333	1	-1	-1	1	0.0
Total	3	3	3	.500	17	5	0	0	0	41	39	1	23	32	13.6	4.39	81	.250	.346	3	.250	1	-3	-4	0	-0.3

● SAM RICE Rice, Edgar Charles b: 2/20/1890, Morocco, Ind. d: 10/13/74, Rossmor, Md. BL/TR, 5'9", 150 lbs. Deb: 8/07/15 H♦

YEAR	TM/L	W	L	PCT	G	GS	CG	SH	SV	IP	H	HR	BB	SO	RAT	ERA	ERA+	OAV	OOB	BH	AVG	PB	PR	/A	PD	TPI
1915	Was-A	1	0	1.000	4	2	1	0	0	18	13	0	9	9	11.0	2.00	148	.213	.314	3	.375	1	2	2	0	0.3
1916	Was-A	0	1	.000	5	1	0	0	0	21^{1}	18	0	10	3	11.8	2.95	95	.237	.326	59	.299	2	-0	-0	-0	0.0
Total	2	1	1	.500	9	3	1	0	0	39^{1}	31	0	19	12	11.4	2.52	114	.226	.321	2987	.322	2	2	2	0	0.3

● PAT RICE Rice, Patrick Edward b: 11/2/63, Rapid City, S.Dak. BR/TR, 6'2", 200 lbs. Deb: 5/18/91

YEAR	TM/L	W	L	PCT	G	GS	CG	SH	SV	IP	H	HR	BB	SO	RAT	ERA	ERA+	OAV	OOB	BH	AVG	PB	PR	/A	PD	TPI
1991	Sea-A	1	1	.500	7	2	0	0	0	21	18	3	10	12	12.4	3.00	137	.234	.330	0	—	0	3	3	-0	0.2

● WOODY RICH Rich, Woodrow Earl b: 3/9/16, Morganton, N.C. d: 4/18/83, Morganton, N.C. BL/TR, 6'2", 185 lbs. Deb: 4/22/39

YEAR	TM/L	W	L	PCT	G	GS	CG	SH	SV	IP	H	HR	BB	SO	RAT	ERA	ERA+	OAV	OOB	BH	AVG	PB	PR	/A	PD	TPI
1939	Bos-A	4	3	.571	21	12	3	0	1	77	78	2	35	24	13.8	4.91	96	.264	.352	7	.259	0	-2	-2	1	0.0
1940	Bos-A	1	0	1.000	3	1	1	0	0	11^{2}	9	2	1	8	7.7	0.77	583	.214	.233	0	.000	-1	5	5	-0	0.4
1941	Bos-A	0	0	—	2	1	0	0	0	3^{2}	8	1	2	4	24.5	17.18	24	.421	.476	0	—	0	-5	-5	0	-0.4
1944	Bos-N	1	1	.500	7	2	1	0	0	25	32	3	12	6	16.9	5.76	66	.327	.416	1	.125	-1	-6	-5	0	-0.6
Total	4	6	4	.600	33	16	5	0	1	117^{1}	127	8	50	42	14.2	5.06	89	.280	.361	8	.205	-1	-9	-7	2	-0.6

● J.R. RICHARD Richard, James Rodney b: 3/7/50, Vienna, La. BR/TR, 6'8", 222 lbs. Deb: 9/05/71

YEAR	TM/L	W	L	PCT	G	GS	CG	SH	SV	IP	H	HR	BB	SO	RAT	ERA	ERA+	OAV	OOB	BH	AVG	PB	PR	/A	PD	TPI
1971	Hou-N	2	1	.667	4	4	1	0	0	21	17	1	16	29	14.1	3.43	98	.215	.347	0	.000	-1	0	-0	0	-0.1
1972	Hou-N	1	0	1.000	4	1	0	0	0	6	10	0	8	8	30.0	13.50	25	.385	.556	0	—	0	-7	-7	0	-0.6
1973	Hou-N	6	2	.750	16	10	2	1	0	72	54	2	38	75	11.6	4.00	91	.210	.314	5	.179	-0	-3	-3	-1	-0.4
1974	Hou-N	2	3	.400	15	9	0	0	0	64^{2}	58	3	36	42	13.2	4.18	83	.243	.344	3	.143	0	-4	-5	-1	-0.6
1975	Hou-N	12	10	.545	33	31	7	1	0	203	178	8	138	176	14.2	4.39	77	.238	.359	15	.203	4	-17	-23	-2	-2.1
1976	Hou-N	20	15	.571	39	39	14	3	0	291	221	14	151	214	11.6	2.75	116	**.212**	.314	14	.140	0	24	14	-1	1.5
1977	Hou-N	18	12	.600	36	36	13	3	0	267	212	18	104	214	10.7	2.97	120	.218	.293	20	.230	6	28	18	3	2.8
1978	Hou-N	18	11	.621	36	36	16	3	0	275^{1}	192	12	141	**303**	11.0	3.11	107	**.196**	.299	18	.178	1	14	6	2	1.0
1979	Hou-N	18	13	.581	38	38	19	4	0	292^{1}	220	13	98	**313**	9.9	**2.71**	130	**.209**	.278	12	.126	-0	**33**	**26**	-1	2.7
1980	Hou-N★	10	4	.714	17	17	4	4	0	113^{2}	65	2	40	119	8.3	1.90	173	.166	.244	6	.154	1	21	18	-1	2.0
Total	10	107	71	.601	238	221	76	19	0	1606	1227	73	770	1493	11.3	3.15	108	.212	.306	93	.168	11	91	44	0	6.2

● DUANE RICHARDS Richards, Duane Lee b: 12/16/36, Spartanburg, Ind. BR/TR, 6'3", 200 lbs. Deb: 9/25/60

YEAR	TM/L	W	L	PCT	G	GS	CG	SH	SV	IP	H	HR	BB	SO	RAT	ERA	ERA+	OAV	OOB	BH	AVG	PB	PR	/A	PD	TPI
1960	Cin-N	0	0	—	2	0	0	0	0	3	5	0	2	2	21.0	9.00	42	.385	.467	0	—	0	-2	-2	0	-0.2

● RUSTY RICHARDS Richards, Russell Earl b: 1/27/65, Houston, Tex. BL/TR, 6'4", 200 lbs. Deb: 9/20/89

YEAR	TM/L	W	L	PCT	G	GS	CG	SH	SV	IP	H	HR	BB	SO	RAT	ERA	ERA+	OAV	OOB	BH	AVG	PB	PR	/A	PD	TPI
1989	Atl-N	0	0	—	2	2	0	0	0	9^{1}	10	2	6	4	16.4	4.82	76	.278	.395	0	.000	-0	-1	-1	0	-0.1
1990	Atl-N	0	0	—	1	0	0	0	0	1	2	1	1	0	27.0	27.00	15	.400	.500	0	—	0	-3	-3	0	-0.2
Total	2	0	0	—	3	2	0	0	0	10^{1}	12	3	7	4	17.4	6.97	53	.293	.408	0	.000	-0	-4	-4	0	-0.3

YEAR	TM/L	W	L	PCT	G	GS	CG	SH	SV	IP	H	HR	BB	SO	RAT	ERA	ERA+	OAV	OOB	BH	AVG	PB	PR	/A	PD	TPI
● HARDY RICHARDSON Richardson, Abram Harding "Old True Blue" b: 4/21/1855, Clarksboro, N.J. d: 1/14/31, Utica, N.Y. BR/TR, 5'9.5", 170 lbs. Deb: 5/01/1879 ♦																										
1885	Buf-N	0	0	—	1	0	0	0	0	4	5	0	3	1	18.0	2.25	132	.294	.400	136	.319	0	0	0	0	0.1
1886	Det-N	3	0	1.000	4	0	0	0	0	12	11	1	10	5	15.8	4.50	74	.208	.333	189	.351	2	-2	-2	-0	-0.1
Total	2	3	0	1.000	5	0	0	0	0	16	16	1	13	6	16.3	3.94	82	.229	.349	1688	.299	3	-1	-1	0	0.0
● DANNY RICHARDSON Richardson, Daniel b: 1/25/1863, Elmira, N.Y. d: 9/12/26, New York, N.Y. BR/TR, 5'8", 165 lbs. Deb: 5/22/1884 M♦																										
1885	NY-N	7	1	.875	9	8	7	1	0	75	58	0	18	21	9.1	2.40	111	.205	.252	52	.263	2	4	2	-1	0.3
1886	NY-N	0	2	.000	5	1	1	0	0	25	33	1	11	17	15.8	5.76	56	.320	.386	55	.232	1	-7	-7	1	-0.5
1887	NY-N	0	0	—	1	0	0	0	0	0	0	0	1	0	—	—	—	—	1.000	125	.278	0	0	0	0	0.0
Total	3	7	3	.700	15	9	8	1	0	100	91	1	30	38	10.9	3.24	86	.236	.291	1129	.254	3	-3	-5	-0	-0.2
● GORDIE RICHARDSON Richardson, Gordon Clark b: 7/19/38, Colquitt, Ga. BR/TL, 6', 185 lbs. Deb: 7/26/64																										
1964	*StL-N	4	2	.667	19	6	1	0	1	47	40	2	15	28	10.7	2.30	166	.231	.296	1	.077	-0	6	8	-1	0.7
1965	NY-N	2	2	.500	35	0	0	0	2	52^1	41	5	16	43	10.1	3.78	93	.224	.294	0	.000	-1	-1	-1	-0	-0.3
1966	NY-N	0	2	.000	15	1	0	0	1	18^2	24	7	6	15	14.5	9.16	40	.312	.361	0	.000	-0	-12	-11	-0	-1.2
Total	3	6	6	.500	69	7	1	0	4	118	105	14	37	86	11.1	4.04	90	.242	.307	1	.048	-1	-6	-5	-2	-0.8
● JEFF RICHARDSON Richardson, Jeffrey Scott b: 8/29/63, Wichita, Kan. BR/TR, 6'3", 185 lbs. Deb: 9/19/90																										
1990	Cal-A	0	0	—	1	0	0	0	0	0^1	1	0	0	0	27.0	0.00	—	.500	.500	0	—	0	0	0	0	0.2
● JACK RICHARDSON Richardson, John William b: 10/3/1891, Central City, Ill. d: 1/18/70, Marion, Ill. BB/TR, 6'3", 197 lbs. Deb: 9/17/15																										
1915	Phi-A	0	1	.000	3	3	2	0	0	24	21	0	14	11	13.5	2.63	111	.253	.367	0	.000	-1	1	1	-0	-0.1
1916	Phi-A	0	0	—	1	0	0	0	0	0^2	2	0	1	1	40.5	40.50	7	.667	.750	0	—	0	-3	-3	-0	-0.3
Total	2	0	1	.000	4	3	2	0	0	24^2	23	0	15	12	14.2	3.65	80	.267	.382	0	.000	-1	-2	-2	-0	-0.4
● PETE RICHERT Richert, Peter Gerard b: 10/29/39, Floral Park, N.Y. BL/TL, 6', 184 lbs. Deb: 4/12/62																										
1962	LA-N	5	4	.556	19	12	1	0	0	81^1	77	6	45	75	13.6	3.87	94	.249	.346	2	.080	-1	1	-2	1	-0.3
1963	LA-N	5	3	.625	20	12	1	0	0	78	80	7	28	54	12.6	4.50	67	.262	.326	4	.182	1	-11	-13	-1	-1.4
1964	LA-N	2	3	.400	8	6	1	1	0	34^2	38	2	18	25	15.1	4.15	78	.271	.363	1	.091	-0	-2	-4	1	-0.3
1965	Was-A★	15	12	.556	34	29	6	0	0	194	146	18	84	161	10.8	2.60	134	.210	.297	10	.156	-0	19	19	-0	2.0
1966	Was-A★	14	14	.500	36	34	7	0	0	245^2	196	36	69	195	9.7	3.37	103	.215	.271	14	.163	2	2	2	-2	0.2
1967	Was-A	2	6	.250	11	10	1	1	0	54^1	49	5	15	41	10.8	4.64	68	.237	.291	1	.059	-1	-8	-9	-1	-1.2
	Bal-A	7	10	.412	26	19	5	1	2	132^1	107	11	41	90	10.1	2.99	105	.220	.282	4	.108	-1	4	2	1	0.2
	Yr	9	16	.360	37	29	6	2	2	186^2	156	16	56	131	10.3	3.47	91	.223	.282	5	.093	-2	-5	-7	-1	-1.0
1968	Bal-A	6	3	.667	36	0	0	0	6	62^1	51	7	12	47	9.5	3.47	84	.225	.273	2	.200	0	-3	-4	1	-0.3
1969	*Bal-A	7	4	.636	44	0	0	0	12	57^1	42	7	14	54	8.8	2.20	162	.202	.252	1	.125	-0	9	9	-1	0.9
1970	Bal-A	7	2	.778	50	0	0	0	13	54^2	36	5	24	66	10.0	1.98	185	.194	.289	0	.000	-0	11	10	0	1.1
1971	Bal-A	3	5	.375	35	0	0	0	4	36^1	26	3	22	35	12.1	3.47	97	.205	.327	0	.000	-0	-0	-0	0	0.0
1972	LA-N	2	3	.400	37	0	0	0	6	52	42	3	18	38	10.6	2.25	148	.219	.289	3	.500	1	7	6	-0	0.8
1973	LA-N	3	3	.500	39	0	0	0	7	51	44	5	19	31	11.3	3.18	108	.234	.308	1	.200	0	3	1	1	0.2
1974	StL-N	0	0	—	13	0	0	0	1	11^1	10	1	11	4	16.7	2.38	150	.244	.404	0	—	0	2	2	-0	0.1
	Phi-N	2	1	.667	21	0	0	0	0	20^1	15	0	4	9	8.4	2.21	171	.205	.247	0	—	0	3	4	-0	0.4
	Yr	2	1	.667	34	0	0	0	1	31^2	25	1	15	13	11.4	2.27	163	.216	.305	0	—	0	5	5	-1	0.5
Total	13	80	73	.523	429	122	22	3	51	1165^2	959	116	424	925	10.8	3.19	106	.223	.295	43	.145	-1	34	24	-3	2.4
● LEW RICHIE Richie, Lewis A. b: 8/23/1883, Ambler, Pa. d: 8/15/36, South Montain, Pa. BR/TR, 5'8", 165 lbs. Deb: 5/08/06																										
1906	Phi-N	9	11	.450	33	22	14	3	0	205^2	170	3	79	65	11.2	2.41	109	.230	.309	3	.050	-3	5	5	-3	-0.1
1907	Phi-N	6	6	.500	25	12	9	2	0	117	88	0	38	40	10.1	1.77	137	.215	.290	7	.163	0	9	8	-1	0.8
1908	Phi-N	7	10	.412	25	15	13	2	1	157^2	125	1	49	58	10.3	1.83	133	.233	.304	11	.212	2	9	10	-1	1.3
1909	Phi-N	1	1	.500	11	1	0	0	1	45	40	0	18	11	12.0	2.00	130	.263	.349	4	.250	1	3	3	-1	0.4
	Bos-N	7	7	.500	22	13	9	2	2	131^2	118	2	44	42	11.1	2.32	121	.247	.312	5	.114	-2	4	7	-3	0.2
	Yr	8	8	.500	33	14	9	2	3	176^2	158	2	62	53	11.3	2.24	123	.250	.318	9	.150	-1	7	10	-4	0.6
1910	Bos-N	0	3	.000	4	2	0	0	0	16^1	20	0	9	7	16.0	2.76	121	.317	.403	0	.000	-1	1	1	1	0.1
	*Chi-N	11	4	.733	30	11	8	3	4	130	117	1	51	52	11.8	2.70	107	.257	.336	9	.225	3	5	3	1	0.6
	Yr	11	7	.611	34	13	8	3	4	146^1	137	1	60	59	12.3	2.71	108	.264	.344	9	.205	2	5	4	1	0.7
1911	Chi-N	15	11	.577	36	28	18	4	1	253	213	6	103	78	11.3	2.31	143	.235	.315	14	.154	-3	31	28	0	2.6
1912	Chi-N	16	8	.667	39	27	15	4	0	238	222	5	74	69	11.4	2.95	113	.261	.324	10	.132	-3	12	10	-2	0.4
1913	Chi-N	2	4	.333	16	5	0	0	0	65	77	3	30	15	15.0	5.82	55	.304	.380	2	.118	-0	-19	-19	-1	-2.0
Total	8	74	65	.532	241	136	86	20	9	1359^1	1190	21	495	437	11.4	2.54	115	.246	.320	65	.147	-7	60	58	-11	4.3
● BERYL RICHMOND Richmond, Beryl Justice b: 8/24/07, Glen Easton, W.Va. d: 4/24/80, Cameron, W.Va. BB/TL, 6'1", 185 lbs. Deb: 4/21/33																										
1933	Chi-N	0	0	—	4	0	0	0	0	4^2	10	0	2	2	23.1	1.93	170	.455	.500	0	.000	-0	1	1	-0	0.0
1934	Cin-N	1	2	.333	6	2	1	0	0	19^1	23	0	10	9	15.4	3.72	110	.303	.384	0	.000	-1	1	1	-0	0.0
Total	2	1	2	.333	10	2	1	0	0	24	33	0	12	11	16.9	3.38	116	.337	.409	0	.000	-1	1	1	-0	0.0
● LEE RICHMOND Richmond, J. Lee b: 5/5/1857, Sheffield, Ohio d: 10/1/29, Toledo, Ohio TL, 5'10", 142 lbs. Deb: 9/27/1879 ♦																										
1879	Bos-N	1	0	1.000	1	1	1	0	0	9	4	0	1	11	5.0	2.00	124	.114	.139	2	.333	0	0	0	0	0.1
1880	Wor-N	32	32	.500	**74**	66	57	5	**3**	590^2	541	7	74	243	9.4	2.15	121	.232	.255	70	.227	-4	15	29	-6	2.0
1881	Wor-N	25	26	.490	53	52	50	3	0	462^1	547	7	68	156	12.0	3.39	89	.284	.309	63	.250	-1	-31	-19	2	-1.5
1882	Wor-N	14	33	.298	48	46	44	0	0	411	525	11	88	123	13.4	3.74	83	.294	.327	64	.281	8	-39	-29	3	-1.6
1883	Pro-N	3	7	.300	12	12	8	0	0	92	122	2	27	13	14.6	3.33	93	.314	.358	55	.284	3	-2	-2	-0	0.0
1886	Cin-a	0	2	.000	3	2	1	0	0	18	24	0	11	6	18.5	8.00	44	.308	.407	8	.276	0	-9	-9	-0	-0.7
Total	6	75	100	.429	191	179	161	8	3	1583	1763	27	269	552	11.6	3.06	95	.269	.298	262	.257	7	-66	-28	-1	-1.7
● RAY RICHMOND Richmond, Raymond Sinclair b: 6/15/1896, Fillmore, Ill. d: 10/21/69, DeSoto, Mo. BR/TR, 6', 175 lbs. Deb: 9/25/20																										
1920	StL-A	2	0	1.000	2	2	1	0	0	17	18	0	9	4	14.3	6.35	62	.273	.360	1	.167	-0	-5	-5	0	-0.4
1921	StL-A	0	1	.000	6	2	0	0	0	14^1	21	1	13	6	23.2	11.30	40	.362	.500	0	.000	-1	-11	-11	0	-1.0
Total	2	2	1	.667	8	4	1	0	0	31^1	39	1	22	10	18.4	8.62	48	.315	.430	1	.100	-1	-16	-15	0	-1.4
● REGGIE RICHTER Richter, Emil Henry b: 9/14/1888, Dusseldorf, Germany d: 8/2/34, Winfield, Ill. BR/TR, 6'2", 180 lbs. Deb: 5/30/11																										
1911	Chi-N	1	3	.250	22	5	0	0	2	54^2	62	1	20	34	14.0	3.13	106	.307	.378	1	.100	-1	**2**	**1**	-0	0.0
● DICK RICKETTS Ricketts, Richard James b: 12/4/33, Pottstown, Pa. d: 3/6/88, Rochester, N.Y. BL/TR, 6'7", 215 lbs. Deb: 6/14/59 F																										
1959	StL-N	1	6	.143	12	9	0	0	0	55^2	68	7	30	25	15.8	5.82	73	.301	.383	1	.056	-2	-12	-10	-2	-1.3
● ELMER RIDDLE Riddle, Elmer Ray b: 7/31/14, Columbus, Ga. d: 5/14/84, Columbus, Ga. BR/TR, 5'11.5", 170 lbs. Deb: 10/01/39 F																										
1939	Cin-N	0	0	—	1	0	0	0	0	2	1	0	0	0	4.5	0.00	—	.143	.143	0	—	0	1	1	-0	0.1
1940	*Cin-N	1	2	.333	15	1	1	0	2	33^2	30	0	17	9	12.6	1.87	202	.250	.343	1	.143	0	7	7	0	0.7
1941	Cin-N	19	4	**.826**	33	22	15	4	1	216^2	180	8	59	80	10.1	**2.24**	**160**	.224	.282	16	.225	3	33	33	-1	3.8
1942	Cin-N	7	11	.389	29	19	7	1	0	158^1	157	7	79	78	13.6	3.69	89	.260	.349	15	.259	3	-7	-7	-1	-0.6
1943	Cin-N	**21**	11	.656	36	33	19	5	3	260^1	235	6	107	69	11.9	2.63	126	.245	.322	18	.194	1	22	20	-1	2.2
1944	Cin-N	2	2	.500	4	4	2	0	0	26^2	25	0	12	6	12.5	4.05	86	.250	.330	1	.125	-0	-1	-2	1	-0.1
1945	Cin-N	1	4	.200	12	3	0	0	0	29^2	39	4	27	5	20.0	8.19	46	.333	.458	3	.273	1	-14	-15	0	-1.3
1947	Cin-N	1	0	1.000	16	3	0	0	0	30^1	42	5	31	8	22.0	8.31	49	.333	.468	0	.000	-0	-14	-14	-1	-1.4

YEAR	TM/L	W	L	PCT	G	GS	CG	SH	SV	IP	H	HR	BB	SO	RAT	ERA	ERA+	OAV	OOB	BH	AVG	PB	PR	/A	PD	TPI
1948	Pit-N☆	12	10	.545	28	27	12	3	1	191	184	20	81	63	12.6	3.49	117	.250	.327	12	.188	1	10	12	0	1.4
1949	Pit-N	1	8	.111	16	12	1	0	1	74^1	81	9	45	24	15.7	5.33	79	.281	.386	3	.136	-1	-11	-9	-2	-1.1
Total	10	65	52	.556	190	124	57	13	8	1023	974	59	458	342	12.8	3.40	107	.252	.335	69	.204	7	26	25	-4	3.7

● DENNY RIDDLEBERGER Riddleberger, Dennis Michael b: 11/22/45, Clifton Forge, Va. BR/TL, 6′3″, 195 lbs. Deb: 9/15/70

YEAR	TM/L	W	L	PCT	G	GS	CG	SH	SV	IP	H	HR	BB	SO	RAT	ERA	ERA+	OAV	OOB	BH	AVG	PB	PR	/A	PD	TPI
1970	Was-A	0	0	—	8	0	0	0	0	9^1	7	1	2	5	8.7	0.96	369	.219	.265	0	—	0	3	3	-0	0.2
1971	Was-A	3	1	.750	57	0	0	0	1	69^2	67	9	32	56	12.9	3.23	102	.260	.344	0	.000	0	2	1	-0	0.1
1972	Cle-A	1	3	.250	38	0	0	0	0	54	45	5	22	34	11.5	2.50	129	.237	.322	0	.000	-0	3	4	-0	0.4
Total	3	4	4	.500	103	0	0	0	1	133	119	15	56	95	12.0	2.77	119	.248	.330	0	.000	-0	8	8	-1	0.7

● DORSEY RIDDLEMOSER Riddlemoser, Dorsey Lee b: 3/25/1875, Frederick, Md. d: 5/11/54, Frederick, Md. BR/TR, Deb: 8/22/1899

YEAR	TM/L	W	L	PCT	G	GS	CG	SH	SV	IP	H	HR	BB	SO	RAT	ERA	ERA+	OAV	OOB	BH	AVG	PB	PR	/A	PD	TPI
1899	Was-N	0	0	—	1	0	0	0	0	2	7	0	2	0	40.5	18.00	22	.552	.613	0	.000	-0	-3	-3	0	-0.3

● JACK RIDGWAY Ridgway, Jacob A. b: 7/23/1889, Philadelphia, Pa. d: 2/23/28, Philadelphia, Pa. BL/TR, 5′11″, 174 lbs. Deb: 5/20/14

YEAR	TM/L	W	L	PCT	G	GS	CG	SH	SV	IP	H	HR	BB	SO	RAT	ERA	ERA+	OAV	OOB	BH	AVG	PB	PR	/A	PD	TPI
1914	Bal-F	0	1	.000	4	1	0	0	0	9	20	1	3	2	24.0	11.00	31	.444	.490	0	.000	-0	-8	-8	0	-0.7

● STEVE RIDZIK Ridzik, Stephen George b: 4/29/29, Yonkers, N.Y. BR/TR, 5′11″, 170 lbs. Deb: 9/04/50

YEAR	TM/L	W	L	PCT	G	GS	CG	SH	SV	IP	H	HR	BB	SO	RAT	ERA	ERA+	OAV	OOB	BH	AVG	PB	PR	/A	PD	TPI
1950	Phi-N	0	0	—	1	0	0	0	0	3	3	1	1	2	12.0	6.00	67	.300	.364	0	—	0	-1	-1	-0	-0.1
1952	Phi-N	4	2	.667	24	9	2	0	0	92^2	74	10	37	43	10.9	3.01	121	.218	.297	3	.136	0	7	7	-2	0.5
1953	Phi-N	9	6	.600	42	12	1	0	0	124	119	15	48	53	12.5	3.77	112	.256	.332	7	.194	2	7	6	-1	0.7
1954	Phi-N	4	5	.444	35	6	0	0	0	80^2	72	7	44	45	12.9	4.13	98	.233	.329	5	.227	1	-1	-1	0	0.0
1955	Phi-N	0	1	.000	3	1	0	0	0	11	7	1	8	6	14.7	2.45	162	.179	.360	0	.000	-1	2	2	-0	0.1
	Cin-N	0	3	.000	13	2	0	0	0	30	35	4	14	6	15.0	4.50	94	.299	.379	1	.167	-0	-2	-1	-1	-0.2
	Yr	0	4	.000	16	3	0	0	0	41	42	5	22	12	14.3	3.95	105	.264	.357	1	.100	-1	0	1	-1	-0.1
1956	NY-N	6	2	.750	41	5	1	1	0	92^1	80	7	65	53	14.6	3.80	99	.240	.371	7	.250	1	-0	-0	-0	0.0
1957	NY-N	0	2	.000	15	0	0	0	0	26^2	19	3	19	13	13.5	4.73	83	.213	.364	1	.200	-0	-3	-2	0	-0.2
1958	Cle-A	0	2	.000	6	0	0	0	0	8^2	9	1	5	6	14.5	2.08	176	.257	.350	0	.000	-0	2	2	0	0.2
1963	Was-A	5	6	.455	20	10	0	0	1	89^2	82	16	35	47	12.2	4.82	77	.240	.319	5	.172	0	-12	-11	-0	-1.1
1964	Was-A	5	5	.500	49	3	0	0	2	112	96	10	31	60	10.8	2.89	128	.236	.301	6	.222	1	9	10	-1	1.1
1965	Was-A	6	4	.600	63	0	0	0	8	109^2	108	18	43	72	13.0	4.02	86	.257	.335	3	.167	0	-7	-7	0	-0.6
1966	Phi-N	0	0	—	2	0	0	0	0	2^1	5	0	1	0	23.1	7.71	47	.455	.500	0	—	0	-1	-1	-0	-0.1
Total	12	39	38	.506	314	48	4	1	11	782^2	709	93	351	406	12.6	3.79	101	.243	.332	38	.192	4	2	3	-4	0.3

● ELMER RIEGER Rieger, Elmer Jay b: 2/25/1889, Perris, Cal. d: 10/21/59, Los Angeles, Cal. BB/TR, 6′, 175 lbs. Deb: 4/20/10

YEAR	TM/L	W	L	PCT	G	GS	CG	SH	SV	IP	H	HR	BB	SO	RAT	ERA	ERA+	OAV	OOB	BH	AVG	PB	PR	/A	PD	TPI
1910	StL-N	0	2	.000	13	2	0	0	0	21^1	26	1	7	9	14.3	5.48	54	.325	.386	0	.000	0	-6	-6	0	-0.6

● DAVE RIGHETTI Righetti, David Allan b: 11/28/58, San Jose, Cal. BL/TL, 6′3″, 198 lbs. Deb: 9/16/79

YEAR	TM/L	W	L	PCT	G	GS	CG	SH	SV	IP	H	HR	BB	SO	RAT	ERA	ERA+	OAV	OOB	BH	AVG	PB	PR	/A	PD	TPI
1979	NY-A	0	1	.000	3	3	0	0	0	17^1	10	2	10	13	10.4	3.63	112	.182	.308	0	—	0	1	1	0	0.3
1981	*NY-A	8	4	.667	15	15	2	0	0	105^1	75	1	38	89	9.7	**2.05**	**174**	**.196**	.269	0	—	0	19	18	-1	2.0
1982	NY-A	11	10	.524	33	27	4	0	1	183	155	11	108	163	13.2	3.79	105	.229	.340	0	—	0	6	4	-2	0.3
1983	NY-A	14	8	.636	31	31	7	2	0	217	194	12	67	169	10.9	3.44	113	.237	.297	0	—	0	15	11	-1	1.0
1984	NY-A	5	6	.455	64	0	0	0	31	96^1	79	5	37	90	10.8	2.34	162	.223	.296	0	—	0	18	16	-0	1.6
1985	NY-A	12	7	.632	74	0	0	0	29	107	96	5	45	92	11.9	2.78	144	.241	.318	0	—	0	16	15	-1	1.6
1986	NY-A★	8	8	.500	74	0	0	0	**46**	106^2	88	4	35	83	10.5	2.45	167	.226	.293	0	—	0	20	19	-1	1.9
1987	NY-A★	8	6	.571	60	0	0	0	31	95	95	9	44	77	13.4	3.51	125	.262	.346	0	—	0	10	9	-0	0.9
1988	NY-A	5	4	.556	60	0	0	0	25	87	86	5	37	70	12.8	3.52	112	.257	.332	0	—	0	4	4	-1	0.4
1989	NY-A	2	6	.250	55	0	0	0	25	69	73	3	26	51	13.0	3.00	129	.277	.344	0	—	0	7	7	-0	0.6
1990	NY-A	1	1	.500	53	0	0	0	36	53	48	8	26	43	12.9	3.57	111	.234	.326	0	—	0	2	2	-1	0.1
1991	SF-N	2	7	.222	61	0	0	0	24	71^2	64	4	28	51	11.9	3.39	106	.240	.319	0	.000	-0	2	2	1	0.2
1992	SF-N	2	7	.222	54	4	0	0	3	78^1	79	4	36	47	13.2	5.06	66	.269	.348	1	.143	-0	-14	-15	-2	-1.8
Total	13	78	75	.510	637	80	13	2	251	1286^2	1142	73	537	1038	11.9	3.25	120	.238	.317	1	.100	-0	107	92	-9	9.1

● JOHNNY RIGNEY Rigney, John Dungan b: 10/28/14, Oak Park, Ill. d: 10/21/84, Lombard, Ill. BR/TR, 6′2″, 190 lbs. Deb: 4/21/37

YEAR	TM/L	W	L	PCT	G	GS	CG	SH	SV	IP	H	HR	BB	SO	RAT	ERA	ERA+	OAV	OOB	BH	AVG	PB	PR	/A	PD	TPI
1937	Chi-A	2	5	.286	22	4	0	0	1	90^2	107	10	46	38	15.5	4.96	93	.290	.373	5	.167	-0	-3	-4	-1	-0.4
1938	Chi-A	9	9	.500	38	12	7	1	1	167	164	16	72	84	12.8	3.56	138	.256	.333	8	.145	-3	23	25	0	2.1
1939	Chi-A	15	8	.652	35	29	11	2	0	218^2	208	10	84	119	12.1	3.70	128	.247	.316	16	.200	-1	22	25	-2	2.1
1940	Chi-A	14	18	.438	39	33	19	2	3	280^2	240	22	90	141	10.6	3.11	142	.230	.292	20	.215	1	40	41	-1	4.0
1941	Chi-A	13	13	.500	30	29	18	3	0	237	224	21	92	119	12.1	3.84	107	.249	.320	17	.202	2	8	7	-0	0.8
1942	Chi-A	3	3	.500	7	7	6	0	0	59	40	2	16	34	8.7	3.20	112	.185	.245	1	.053	-1	3	3	0	0.1
1946	Chi-A	5	5	.500	15	11	3	2	0	82^2	76	6	35	51	12.3	4.03	85	.240	.319	4	.154	-1	-5	-6	-1	-0.7
1947	Chi-A	2	3	.400	11	7	2	0	0	50^2	42	3	15	19	10.1	1.95	187	.228	.286	0	.000	-2	10	10	1	1.0
Total	8	63	64	.496	197	132	66	10	5	1186^1	1101	90	450	605	11.9	3.59	121	.244	.314	71	.177	-6	98	100	-3	9.0

● JOSE RIJO Rijo, Jose Antonio (Abreu) b: 5/13/65, San Cristobal, D.R. BR/TR, 6′1″, 200 lbs. Deb: 4/05/84

YEAR	TM/L	W	L	PCT	G	GS	CG	SH	SV	IP	H	HR	BB	SO	RAT	ERA	ERA+	OAV	OOB	BH	AVG	PB	PR	/A	PD	TPI
1984	NY-A	2	8	.200	24	5	0	0	2	62^1	74	5	33	47	15.6	4.76	80	.298	.383	0	—	0	-5	-7	1	-0.6
1985	Oak-A	6	4	.600	12	9	0	0	0	63^2	57	6	28	65	12.2	3.53	109	.239	.322	0	—	0	4	2	-1	0.7
1986	Oak-A	9	11	.450	39	26	4	0	1	193^2	172	24	108	176	13.2	4.65	83	.237	.339	0	—	0	-10	-17	-1	-1.1
1987	Oak-A	2	7	.222	21	14	1	0	0	82^1	106	10	41	67	16.3	5.90	70	.305	.381	0	—	0	-13	-16	0	-1.1
1988	Cin-N	13	8	.619	49	19	0	0	0	162	120	7	63	160	10.3	2.39	150	.209	.291	2	.054	-2	19	21	0	2.2
1989	Cin-N	7	6	.538	19	19	1	1	0	111	101	6	48	86	12.2	2.84	127	.249	.332	8	.211	1	8	9	-0	1.2
1990	*Cin-N	14	8	.636	29	29	7	1	0	197	151	10	78	152	10.6	2.70	146	.212	.292	10	.161	0	24	27	1	3.1
1991	Cin-N	15	6	**.714**	30	30	3	1	0	204^1	165	8	55	172	**9.8**	2.51	151	.219	**.274**	14	.209	1	27	29	-0	3.3
1992	Cin-N	15	10	.600	33	33	2	0	0	211	185	15	44	171	9.9	2.56	143	.238	.282	14	.194	1	22	26	1	3.2
Total	9	83	68	.550	256	184	18	3	3	1287^1	1131	91	498	1096	11.5	3.26	117	.237	.311	48	.174	2	76	78	0	10.9

● GEORGE RILEY Riley, George Michael b: 10/6/56, Philadelphia, Pa. BL/TL, 6′2″, 210 lbs. Deb: 9/15/79

YEAR	TM/L	W	L	PCT	G	GS	CG	SH	SV	IP	H	HR	BB	SO	RAT	ERA	ERA+	OAV	OOB	BH	AVG	PB	PR	/A	PD	TPI
1979	Chi-N	0	1	.000	4	1	0	0	0	13	16	1	6	5	16.6	5.54	74	.320	.414	0	.000	-0	-3	-2	0	-0.2
1980	Chi-N	0	4	.000	22	0	0	0	0	36	41	2	20	18	15.8	5.75	68	.293	.389	0	.000	-0	-9	-7	1	-0.7
1984	SF-N	1	0	1.000	5	4	0	0	0	29^1	39	1	7	12	14.7	3.99	88	.315	.361	1	.100	-0	-1	-2	-0	-0.2
1986	Mon-N	0	0	—	10	0	0	0	0	8^2	7	0	8	5	16.6	4.15	89	.212	.381	0	—	0	-0	-0	-0	-0.1
Total	4	1	5	.167	41	5	0	0	0	87	103	4	41	40	15.6	4.97	76	.297	.382	1	.077	-1	-13	-11	1	-1.2

● ANDY RINCON Rincon, Andrew John b: 3/5/59, Monterey Park, Cal. BR/TR, 6′3″, 195 lbs. Deb: 9/15/80

YEAR	TM/L	W	L	PCT	G	GS	CG	SH	SV	IP	H	HR	BB	SO	RAT	ERA	ERA+	OAV	OOB	BH	AVG	PB	PR	/A	PD	TPI
1980	StL-N	3	1	.750	4	4	1	0	0	31	23	1	7	22	8.7	2.61	141	.215	.263	3	.250	0	3	4	0	0.5
1981	StL-N	3	1	.750	5	5	1	1	0	35^2	27	0	5	13	8.6	1.77	201	.214	.256	3	.231	1	7	7	-0	0.9
1982	StL-N	2	3	.400	11	6	1	0	0	40	35	1	25	11	13.5	4.72	77	.241	.353	1	.100	-0	-5	-5	-1	-0.6
Total	3	8	5	.615	20	15	3	1	0	106^2	85	2	37	46	10.5	3.12	116	.225	.297	7	.200	1	5	6	-1	0.8

● JEFF RINEER Rineer, Jeffrey Alan b: 7/3/55, Lancaster, Pa. BL/TL, 6′4″, 205 lbs. Deb: 9/30/79

YEAR	TM/L	W	L	PCT	G	GS	CG	SH	SV	IP	H	HR	BB	SO	RAT	ERA	ERA+	OAV	OOB	BH	AVG	PB	PR	/A	PD	TPI
1979	Bal-A	0	0	—	1	0	0	0	0	1	0	0	0	0	0.0	0.00	—	.000	.000	0	—	0	0	0	0	0.4

● JIMMY RING Ring, James Joseph b: 2/15/1895, Brooklyn, N.Y. d: 7/6/65, New York, N.Y. BR/TR, 6′1″, 170 lbs. Deb: 4/13/17

YEAR	TM/L	W	L	PCT	G	GS	CG	SH	SV	IP	H	HR	BB	SO	RAT	ERA	ERA+	OAV	OOB	BH	AVG	PB	PR	/A	PD	TPI
1917	Cin-N	3	7	.300	24	7	3	0	2	88	90	2	35	33	12.9	4.40	60	.272	.343	2	.077	-2	-16	-17	0	-2.0
1918	Cin-N	9	5	.643	21	18	13	4	0	142^1	130	5	48	26	11.4	2.85	94	.247	.314	6	.120	-3	-1	-3	-3	-1.0
1919	*Cin-N	10	9	.526	32	18	12	2	3	183	150	1	51	61	10.0	2.26	123	.232	.291	6	.097	-5	13	10	3	1.0
1920	Cin-N	17	16	.515	42	33	18	1	1	266^2	268	4	92	73	12.3	3.54	86	.264	.329	19	.198	-0	-12	-15	1	-1.6

YEAR	TM/L	W	L	PCT	G	GS	CG	SH	SV	IP	H	HR	BB	SO	RAT	ERA	ERA+	OAV	OOB	BH	AVG	PB	PR	/A	PD	TPI
1921	Phi-N	10	19	.345	34	30	21	0	1	246	258	8	88	88	12.8	4.24	100	.274	.340	12	.145	-5	-13	-0	3	-0.2
1922	Phi-N	12	18	.400	40	33	17	0	1	249^1	292	19	103	116	14.4	4.58	102	.297	.365	13	.148	-5	-13	2	4	0.2
1923	Phi-N	18	16	.529	39	36	23	0	0	304^1	336	13	115	112	13.4	3.87	119	.283	.347	12	.106	-10	4	25	3	1.7
1924	Phi-N	10	12	.455	32	31	16	1	0	215^1	236	9	108	72	14.5	3.97	112	.286	.371	17	.230	-1	-2	12	2	1.4
1925	Phi-N	14	16	.467	38	37	21	1	0	270	325	14	119	93	14.8	4.37	109	.297	.367	11	.109	-8	-3	12	2	0.6
1926	NY-N	11	10	.524	39	23	5	0	2	183^1	207	12	74	76	13.8	4.57	82	.290	.357	8	.143	-3	-15	-17	-1	-2.0
1927	StL-N	0	4	.000	13	3	1	0	0	33	39	3	17	13	15.5	6.55	60	.300	.385	3	.375	1	-10	-10	1	-0.7
1928	Phi-N	4	17	.190	35	25	4	0	1	173	214	14	103	72	16.6	6.40	67	.316	.407	11	.183	-2	-46	-41	1	-3.9
Total	12	118	149	.442	389	294	154	9	11	2354^1	2545	104	953	835	13.5	4.12	95	.281	.351	120	.147	-42	-115	-50	16	-6.5

● ALLEN RIPLEY Ripley, Allen Stevens b: 10/18/52, Norwood, Mass. BR/TR, 6′3″, 190 lbs. Deb: 4/10/78 F

YEAR	TM/L	W	L	PCT	G	GS	CG	SH	SV	IP	H	HR	BB	SO	RAT	ERA	ERA+	OAV	OOB	BH	AVG	PB	PR	/A	PD	TPI
1978	Bos-A	2	5	.286	15	11	1	0	0	73	92	10	22	26	14.4	5.55	74	.311	.364	0	—	0	-14	-12	-1	-2.0
1979	Bos-A	3	1	.750	16	3	0	0	1	64^2	77	9	25	34	14.6	5.15	86	.295	.363	0	—	0	-7	-5	-1	-1.0
1980	SF-N	9	10	.474	23	20	2	0	0	112^2	119	10	36	65	12.7	4.15	85	.274	.335	6	.150	-0	-7	-8	0	-0.8
1981	SF-N	4	4	.500	19	14	1	0	0	90^2	103	5	27	47	13.2	4.07	84	.289	.345	4	.133	-1	-6	-6	1	-0.7
1982	Chi-N	5	7	.417	28	19	0	0	0	122^2	130	12	38	57	12.5	4.18	89	.285	.343	5	.132	-2	-8	-6	1	-0.7
Total	5	23	27	.460	101	67	4	0	1	463^2	521	46	148	229	13.3	4.50	84	.289	.348	15	.139	-3	-42	-37	-0	-5.2

● WALT RIPLEY Ripley, Walter Franklin b: 11/26/16, Worcester, Mass. d: 10/7/90, Attleboro, Mass. BR/TR, 6′, 168 lbs. Deb: 8/17/35 F

YEAR	TM/L	W	L	PCT	G	GS	CG	SH	SV	IP	H	HR	BB	SO	RAT	ERA	ERA+	OAV	OOB	BH	AVG	PB	PR	/A	PD	TPI
1935	Bos-A	0	0	—	2	0	0	0	0	4	7	0	3	0	22.5	9.00	53	.412	.500	0	—	0	-2	-2	-0	-0.2

● RAY RIPPELMEYER Rippelmeyer, Raymond Roy b: 7/9/33, Valmeyer, Ill. BR/TR, 6′3″, 200 lbs. Deb: 4/14/62 C

YEAR	TM/L	W	L	PCT	G	GS	CG	SH	SV	IP	H	HR	BB	SO	RAT	ERA	ERA+	OAV	OOB	BH	AVG	PB	PR	/A	PD	TPI
1962	Was-A	1	2	.333	18	1	0	0	0	39^1	47	7	17	17	14.6	5.49	74	.294	.362	3	.500	2	-7	-6	2	-0.2

● CHARLIE RIPPLE Ripple, Charles Dawson b: 12/1/21, Bolton, N.C. d: 5/6/79, Wilmington, N.C. BL/TL, 6′2″, 210 lbs. Deb: 9/25/44

YEAR	TM/L	W	L	PCT	G	GS	CG	SH	SV	IP	H	HR	BB	SO	RAT	ERA	ERA+	OAV	OOB	BH	AVG	PB	PR	/A	PD	TPI
1944	Phi-N	0	0	—	1	1	0	0	0	2^1	6	0	4	2	38.6	15.43	23	.500	.625	1	1.000	0	-3	-3	-0	-0.2
1945	Phi-N	0	1	.000	4	0	0	0	0	7^2	7	0	10	5	20.0	7.04	54	.241	.436	0	.000	-0	-3	-3	-0	-0.3
1946	Phi-N	1	0	1.000	6	0	0	0	0	3^1	5	0	6	3	29.7	10.80	32	.385	.579	0	—	0	-3	-3	-0	-0.3
Total	3	1	1	.500	11	1	0	0	0	13^1	18	0	20	10	25.7	9.45	39	.333	.514	1	.500	0	-9	-9	-0	-0.8

● BILL RISLEY Risley, William Charles b: 5/29/67, Chicago, Ill. BR/TR, 6′2″, 215 lbs. Deb: 7/08/92

YEAR	TM/L	W	L	PCT	G	GS	CG	SH	SV	IP	H	HR	BB	SO	RAT	ERA	ERA+	OAV	OOB	BH	AVG	PB	PR	/A	PD	TPI
1992	Mon-N	1	0	1.000	1	1	0	0	0	5	4	0	1	2	9.0	1.80	194	.235	.278	0	.000	-0	1	1	0	0.1

● JAY RITCHIE Ritchie, Jay Seay b: 11/20/36, Salisbury, N.C. BR/TR, 6′4″, 190 lbs. Deb: 8/04/64

YEAR	TM/L	W	L	PCT	G	GS	CG	SH	SV	IP	H	HR	BB	SO	RAT	ERA	ERA+	OAV	OOB	BH	AVG	PB	PR	/A	PD	TPI
1964	Bos-A	1	1	.500	21	0	0	0	0	46	43	4	14	35	11.2	2.74	141	.249	.305	1	.111	-1	5	6	-0	0.5
1965	Bos-A	1	2	.333	44	0	0	0	2	71	83	3	26	55	13.9	3.17	118	.302	.364	1	.200	0	2	4	0	0.5
1966	Atl-N	0	1	.000	22	0	0	0	4	35^1	32	3	12	33	11.2	4.08	89	.241	.303	2	.500	1	-2	-2	0	-0.1
1967	Atl-N	4	6	.400	52	0	0	0	2	82^1	75	6	29	57	11.8	3.17	105	.245	.319	3	.300	1	2	1	1	0.4
1968	Cin-N	2	3	.400	28	2	0	0	0	56^2	68	7	13	32	13.0	4.61	69	.293	.333	0	.000	-1	-10	-9	-1	-1.2
Total	5	8	13	.381	167	2	0	0	8	291^1	301	23	94	212	12.4	3.49	101	.269	.329	7	.200	1	-3	1	0	0.1

● WALLY RITCHIE Ritchie, Wallace Reid b: 7/12/65, Glendale, Cal. BL/TL, 6′2″, 180 lbs. Deb: 5/01/87

YEAR	TM/L	W	L	PCT	G	GS	CG	SH	SV	IP	H	HR	BB	SO	RAT	ERA	ERA+	OAV	OOB	BH	AVG	PB	PR	/A	PD	TPI
1987	Phi-N	3	2	.600	49	0	0	0	3	62^1	60	8	29	45	13.0	3.75	113	.254	.338	1	.250	0	2	3	-0	0.3
1988	Phi-N	0	0	—	19	0	0	0	0	26	19	1	17	8	12.8	3.12	114	.207	.336	0	—	0	1	1	-0	0.1
1991	Phi-N	1	2	.333	39	0	0	0	0	50^1	44	4	17	26	11.3	2.50	146	.234	.304	0	.000	-0	7	7	-0	0.6
1992	Phi-N	2	1	.667	40	0	0	0	1	39	44	3	17	19	14.1	3.00	117	.288	.359	0	.000	0	2	2	-0	0.2
Total	4	6	5	.545	147	0	0	0	4	177^2	167	16	80	98	12.7	3.14	121	.250	.333	1	.125	0	12	13	-1	1.2

● REGGIE RITTER Ritter, Reggie Blake b: 1/23/60, Malvern, Ark. BL/TR, 6′2″, 195 lbs. Deb: 5/17/86

YEAR	TM/L	W	L	PCT	G	GS	CG	SH	SV	IP	H	HR	BB	SO	RAT	ERA	ERA+	OAV	OOB	BH	AVG	PB	PR	/A	PD	TPI
1986	Cle-A	0	0	—	5	0	0	0	0	10	14	1	4	6	17.1	6.30	66	.341	.413	0	—	0	-2	-2	0	0.0
1987	Cle-A	1	1	.500	14	0	0	0	0	26^2	33	5	16	11	16.5	6.08	74	.300	.389	0	—	0	-5	-5	0	-0.4
Total	2	1	1	.500	19	0	0	0	0	36^2	47	6	20	17	16.7	6.14	72	.311	.395	0	—	0	-7	-7	1	-0.4

● HANK RITTER Ritter, William Herbert b: 10/12/1893, McCoysville, Pa. d: 9/3/64, Akron, Ohio BR/TR, 6′, 180 lbs. Deb: 8/03/12

YEAR	TM/L	W	L	PCT	G	GS	CG	SH	SV	IP	H	HR	BB	SO	RAT	ERA	ERA+	OAV	OOB	BH	AVG	PB	PR	/A	PD	TPI
1912	Phi-N	0	0	—	3	0	0	0	0	6	5	0	5	1	15.0	4.50	81	.192	.323	0	.000	-0	-1	-1	-0	-0.1
1914	NY-N	1	0	1.000	1	0	0	0	0	8	4	0	4	4	9.0	1.13	236	.160	.276	0	.000	-0	1	1	-0	0.1
1915	NY-N	2	1	.667	22	2	0	0	2	58^1	66	4	15	35	13.3	4.63	55	.291	.348	2	.125	-1	-12	-13	-0	-1.6
1916	NY-N	1	0	1.000	3	0	0	0	0	5	3	0	0	3	7.2	0.00	—	.200	.250	0	—	0	1	1	0	0.2
Total	4	4	1	.800	29	2	0	0	2	77^1	78	4	24	43	12.6	3.96	67	.266	.334	2	.100	-1	-10	-11	-1	-1.4

● JIM RITTWAGE Rittwage, James Michael b: 10/23/44, Cleveland, Ohio BR/TR, 6′3″, 190 lbs. Deb: 9/07/70

YEAR	TM/L	W	L	PCT	G	GS	CG	SH	SV	IP	H	HR	BB	SO	RAT	ERA	ERA+	OAV	OOB	BH	AVG	PB	PR	/A	PD	TPI
1970	Cle-A	1	1	.500	8	3	1	0	0	26	18	0	21	16	13.5	4.15	95	.194	.342	3	.375	1	-1	-1	0	0.1

● KEVIN RITZ Ritz, Kevin D b: 6/8/65, Eatonstown, N.J. BR/TR, 6′4″, 195 lbs. Deb: 7/15/89

YEAR	TM/L	W	L	PCT	G	GS	CG	SH	SV	IP	H	HR	BB	SO	RAT	ERA	ERA+	OAV	OOB	BH	AVG	PB	PR	/A	PD	TPI
1989	Det-A	4	6	.400	12	12	1	0	0	74	75	2	44	56	14.6	4.38	87	.265	.366	0	—	0	-4	-5	0	-0.4
1990	Det-A	0	4	.000	4	4	0	0	0	7^1	14	0	14	3	34.4	11.05	36	.400	.571	0	—	0	-6	-6	1	-0.5
1991	Det-A	0	3	.000	11	5	0	0	0	15^1	17	1	22	9	24.1	11.74	35	.288	.494	0	—	0	-13	-13	0	-1.2
1992	Det-A	2	5	.286	23	11	0	0	0	80^1	88	4	44	57	15.1	5.60	71	.278	.372	0	—	0	-15	-14	0	-1.5
Total	4	6	18	.250	50	32	1	0	0	177	194	7	124	125	16.5	5.85	67	.280	.394	0	—	0	-38	-38	1	-3.6

● BEN RIVERA Rivera, Bienvenido Santana b: 1/11/69, San Pedro De Macoris, D.R. BR/TR, 6′6″, 210 lbs. Deb: 4/09/92

YEAR	TM/L	W	L	PCT	G	GS	CG	SH	SV	IP	H	HR	BB	SO	RAT	ERA	ERA+	OAV	OOB	BH	AVG	PB	PR	/A	PD	TPI
1992	Atl-N	0	1	.000	8	0	0	0	0	15^1	21	1	13	11	21.1	4.70	80	.339	.468	0	.000	-0	-2	-2	0	-0.2
	Phi-N	7	3	.700	20	14	4	1	0	102	78	8	32	66	9.9	2.82	124	.211	.278	3	.094	-1	8	8	-0	0.7
	Yr	7	4	.636	28	14	4	1	0	117^1	99	9	45	77	11.2	3.07	115	.228	.304	3	.091	-1	6	6	0	0.5

● TINK RIVIERE Riviere, Arthur Bernard b: 8/2/1899, Liberty, Tex. d: 9/27/65, Liberty, Tex. BR/TR, 5′10″, 167 lbs. Deb: 4/15/21

YEAR	TM/L	W	L	PCT	G	GS	CG	SH	SV	IP	H	HR	BB	SO	RAT	ERA	ERA+	OAV	OOB	BH	AVG	PB	PR	/A	PD	TPI
1921	StL-N	1	0	1.000	18	2	0	0	0	38^1	45	2	20	15	15.7	6.10	60	.280	.366	3	.375	2	-10	-10	-2	-1.0
1925	Chi-A	0	0	—	3	0	0	0	0	4^2	6	0	7	1	27.0	13.50	31	.429	.636	0	.000	-0	-5	-5	1	-0.4
Total	2	1	0	1.000	21	2	0	0	0	43	51	2	27	16	17.0	6.91	54	.291	.395	3	.333	2	-15	-15	-1	-1.4

● EPPA RIXEY Rixey, Eppa "Jeptha" b: 5/3/1891, Culpeper, Va. d: 2/28/63, Cincinnati, Ohio BR/TL, 6′5″, 210 lbs. Deb: 6/21/12 H

YEAR	TM/L	W	L	PCT	G	GS	CG	SH	SV	IP	H	HR	BB	SO	RAT	ERA	ERA+	OAV	OOB	BH	AVG	PB	PR	/A	PD	TPI
1912	Phi-N	10	10	.500	23	20	10	3	0	162	147	2	54	59	11.3	2.50	145	.256	.322	9	.170	-2	16	20	-1	1.8
1913	Phi-N	9	5	.643	35	19	9	1	2	155^2	148	4	56	75	12.1	3.12	107	.258	.331	9	.191	-0	1	4	-0	0.3
1914	Phi-N	2	11	.154	24	15	2	0	0	103	124	0	45	41	15.0	4.37	67	.313	.387	1	.038	-1	-18	-16	0	-1.8
1915	*Phi-N	11	12	.478	29	22	10	2	1	176^2	163	2	64	88	11.7	2.39	115	.250	.319	9	.164	-0	7	7	0	0.8
1916	Phi-N	22	10	.688	38	33	20	3	0	287	239	2	74	134	10.0	1.85	143	.229	.284	15	.155	-2	25	26	3	3.2
1917	Phi-N	16	21	.432	39	36	23	4	1	281^1	249	1	67	121	10.3	2.27	124	.241	.290	18	.191	-2	14	17	4	2.2
1919	Phi-N	6	12	.333	23	18	11	1	0	154	160	4	50	63	12.4	3.97	81	.278	.339	7	.149	-2	-18	-13	2	-1.4
1920	Phi-N	11	22	.333	41	33	25	0	2	284^1	288	5	69	109	11.4	3.48	98	.274	.321	25	.248	2	-11	-2	3	0.3
1921	Cin-N	19	18	.514	40	36	21	2	1	301	324	1	66	76	11.8	2.78	129	.282	.324	13	.129	-5	**34**	27	3	2.5
1922	Cin-N	**25**	13	.658	40	38	26	2	0	**313**^{1}	337	13	45	80	11.1	3.53	113	.275	.303	21	.193	-1	20	16	-0	1.4
1923	Cin-N	20	15	.571	42	37	23	3	1	309	334	3	65	97	11.7	2.80	138	.280	.320	17	.159	-4	41	37	2	3.3
1924	Cin-N	15	14	.517	35	29	15	**4**	1	238^1	219	3	47	57	10.1	2.76	137	.246	.285	18	.214	1	29	27	-1	2.8
1925	Cin-N	21	11	.656	39	36	22	2	1	287^1	302	8	47	69	11.2	2.88	143	.273	.307	22	.214	-1	44	39	-2	3.6
1926	Cin-N	14	8	.636	37	29	14	3	0	233	231	12	58	61	11.2	3.40	109	.265	.313	19	.226	0	11	8	-2	0.6
1927	Cin-N	12	10	.545	34	29	11	1	1	219^2	240	3	43	42	11.7	3.48	109	.287	.325	20	.247	4	11	7	-1	1.0

YEAR TM/L		W	L	PCT	G	GS	CG	SH	SV	IP	H	HR	BB	SO	RAT	ERA	ERA+	OAV	OOB	BH	AVG	PB	PR	/A	PD	TPI
1928	Cin-N	19	18	.514	43	37	17	3	2	291^1	317	4	67	58	12.0	3.43	115	.288	.330	18	.173	-1	18	17	-0	1.5
1929	Cin-N	10	13	.435	35	24	11	0	1	201	235	6	60	37	13.3	4.16	110	.296	.348	15	.231	0	12	9	-1	0.8
1930	Cin-N	9	13	.409	32	21	5	0	0	164	207	11	47	37	14.3	5.10	95	.317	.370	11	.200	-1	-2	-5	0	-0.5
1931	Cin-N	4	7	.364	22	17	4	0	0	126^2	143	4	30	22	12.3	3.91	96	.291	.332	6	.150	-1	-1	-2	4	0.0
1932	Cin-N	5	5	.500	25	11	6	2	0	111^2	108	3	16	14	10.3	2.66	145	.254	.288	9	.265	1	15	15	1	1.7
1933	Cin-N	6	3	.667	16	12	5	1	0	94^1	118	1	12	10	12.4	3.15	108	.298	.319	9	.257	2	2	3	1	0.6
Total	21	266	251	.515	692	552	290	37	14	4494^2	4633	92	1082	1350	11.6	3.15	116	.272	.318	291	.191	-14	250	248	16	24.7

● **JOHN ROACH** Roach, John F. b: Farrensville, Pa. d: 3/1/15, Sandusky, Ohio BR/TL, 5'9", 175 lbs. Deb: 5/14/1887

YEAR TM/L		W	L	PCT	G	GS	CG	SH	SV	IP	H	HR	BB	SO	RAT	ERA	ERA+	OAV	OOB	BH	AVG	PB	PR	/A	PD	TPI
1887	NY-N	0	1	.000	1	1	1	0	0	8	18	0	4	3	25.9	11.25	33	.419	.479	1	.250	-0	-6	-7	-0	-0.5

● **SKEL ROACH** Roach, Skel (b: Rudolph Charles Weichbrodt) b: 10/20/1871, Germany d: 3/9/58, Oak Park, Ill. BR/TR, Deb: 8/09/1899

YEAR TM/L		W	L	PCT	G	GS	CG	SH	SV	IP	H	HR	BB	SO	RAT	ERA	ERA+	OAV	OOB	BH	AVG	PB	PR	/A	PD	TPI
1899	Chi-N	1	0	1.000	1	1	1	0	0	9	13	0	1	0	14.0	3.00	125	.337	.354	0	.000	-1	1	1	-0	0.0

● **BRUCE ROBBINS** Robbins, Bruce Duane b: 9/10/59, Portland, Ind. BL/TL, 6'1", 190 lbs. Deb: 7/28/79

YEAR TM/L		W	L	PCT	G	GS	CG	SH	SV	IP	H	HR	BB	SO	RAT	ERA	ERA+	OAV	OOB	BH	AVG	PB	PR	/A	PD	TPI
1979	Det-A	3	3	.500	10	8	0	0	0	46	45	3	21	22	12.9	3.91	111	.265	.346	0	—	0	2	2	-1	0.1
1980	Det-A	4	2	.667	15	6	0	0	0	51^2	60	12	28	23	15.3	6.62	62	.287	.371	0	—	0	-15	-14	0	-1.5
Total	2	7	5	.583	25	14	0	0	0	97^2	105	15	49	45	14.2	5.34	79	.277	.360	0	—	0	-13	-12	-0	-1.4

● **BERT ROBERGE** Roberge, Bertrand Roland b: 10/3/54, Lewiston, Maine BR/TR, 6'4", 190 lbs. Deb: 5/28/79

YEAR TM/L		W	L	PCT	G	GS	CG	SH	SV	IP	H	HR	BB	SO	RAT	ERA	ERA+	OAV	OOB	BH	AVG	PB	PR	/A	PD	TPI
1979	Hou-N	3	0	1.000	26	0	0	0	4	32	20	0	17	13	10.4	1.69	208	.196	.311	0	.000	-0	7	6	-0	0.6
1980	Hou-N	2	0	1.000	14	0	0	0	0	24^1	24	2	10	9	13.3	5.92	56	.261	.346	0	.000	-0	-6	-7	0	-0.7
1982	Hou-N	1	2	.333	22	0	0	0	3	25^2	29	0	6	18	12.3	4.21	79	.284	.324	0	.000	-0	-2	-3	0	-0.3
1984	Chi-A	3	3	.500	21	0	0	0	0	40^2	36	2	15	25	12.0	3.76	111	.240	.321	0	—	0	1	2	1	0.1
1985	Mon-N	3	3	.500	42	0	0	0	2	68	58	5	22	34	10.9	3.44	99	.232	.299	0	.000	-0	1	-0	0	0.0
1986	Mon-N	0	4	.000	21	0	0	0	1	28^2	33	2	10	20	13.8	6.28	59	.295	.358	0	.000	-0	-8	-8	-0	-0.9
Total	6	12	12	.500	146	0	0	0	10	219^1	200	11	80	119	11.8	3.98	90	.248	.321	0	.000	-1	-7	-10	1	-1.2

● **DALE ROBERTS** Roberts, Dale "Mountain Man" b: 4/12/42, Owenton, Ky. BR/TL, 6'4", 180 lbs. Deb: 9/09/67

YEAR TM/L		W	L	PCT	G	GS	CG	SH	SV	IP	H	HR	BB	SO	RAT	ERA	ERA+	OAV	OOB	BH	AVG	PB	PR	/A	PD	TPI
1967	NY-A	0	0	—	2	0	0	0	0	2	3	0	2	0	31.5	9.00	35	.429	.636	0	—	0	-1	-1	0	-0.1

● **DAVE ROBERTS** Roberts, David Arthur b: 9/11/44, Gallipolis, Ohio BL/TL, 6'2", 197 lbs. Deb: 7/06/69

YEAR TM/L		W	L	PCT	G	GS	CG	SH	SV	IP	H	HR	BB	SO	RAT	ERA	ERA+	OAV	OOB	BH	AVG	PB	PR	/A	PD	TPI
1969	SD-N	0	3	.000	22	5	0	0	1	48^2	65	5	19	19	16.1	4.81	74	.322	.388	4	.267	1	-7	-7	0	-0.6
1970	SD-N	8	14	.364	43	21	3	2	1	181^2	182	16	43	102	11.2	3.81	104	.261	.305	9	.153	1	5	3	-0	0.4
1971	SD-N	14	17	.452	37	34	14	2	0	269^2	238	9	61	135	10.1	2.10	157	.240	.288	19	.221	2	41	36	1	4.4
1972	Hou-N	12	7	.632	35	28	7	3	2	192	227	18	57	111	13.4	4.50	75	.296	.346	16	.239	5	-22	-24	-1	-2.1
1973	Hou-N	17	11	.607	39	36	12	6	0	249^1	264	15	62	119	11.8	2.85	127	.271	.316	11	.129	-3	22	22	-1	2.0
1974	Hou-N	10	12	.455	34	30	8	2	1	204	216	6	65	72	12.5	3.40	102	.276	.333	16	.219	5	5	1	2	0.9
1975	Hou-N	8	14	.364	32	27	7	0	1	198^1	182	16	73	101	11.7	4.27	79	.244	.313	9	.143	0	-14	-20	1	-1.8
1976	Det-A	16	17	.485	36	36	18	4	0	252	254	16	63	79	11.5	4.00	93	.264	.312	0	—	0	-13	-8	2	-0.9
1977	Det-A	4	10	.286	22	22	5	0	0	129^1	143	20	41	46	12.9	5.15	83	.274	.330	0	—	0	-16	-12	-0	-1.6
	Chi-N	1	1	.500	17	6	1	0	1	53	55	1	12	23	11.5	3.23	136	.275	.319	1	.059	-2	4	7	2	0.7
1978	Chi-N	6	8	.429	35	20	2	1	1	142^1	159	17	56	54	13.8	5.25	77	.288	.357	17	.327	7	-26	-19	1	-1.2
1979	SF-N	0	2	.000	26	1	0	0	3	42	42	3	18	23	13.1	2.57	136	.262	.341	0	.000	-1	5	4	1	0.4
	*Pit-N	5	2	.714	21	3	0	0	1	38^2	47	1	12	15	14.0	3.26	119	.318	.373	0	.000	-1	2	3	0	0.3
	Yr	5	4	.556	47	4	0	0	4	80^2	89	4	30	38	13.4	2.90	127	.287	.352	0	.000	-1	7	7	1	0.7
1980	Pit-N	0	1	.000	2	0	0	0	0	2^1	2	0	1	1	11.6	3.86	94	.250	.333	0	—	0	-0	-0	-0	0.0
	Sea-A	2	3	.400	37	4	0	0	3	80^1	86	7	27	47	12.8	4.37	95	.270	.329	0	—	0	-3	-2	-1	-0.4
1981	NY-N	0	3	.000	7	4	0	0	0	15^1	26	5	5	10	18.2	9.39	37	.366	.408	1	.250	0	-10	-10	0	-1.0
Total	13	103	125	.452	445	277	77	20	15	2099	2188	155	615	957	12.2	3.78	97	.270	.324	103	.194	15	-27	-28	7	-0.5

● **JIM ROBERTS** Roberts, James Newson "Big Jim" b: 10/13/1895, Artesia, Miss. d: 6/24/84, Columbus, Miss. BR/TR, 6'3", 205 lbs. Deb: 7/27/24

YEAR TM/L		W	L	PCT	G	GS	CG	SH	SV	IP	H	HR	BB	SO	RAT	ERA	ERA+	OAV	OOB	BH	AVG	PB	PR	/A	PD	TPI
1924	Bro-N	0	3	.000	11	5	0	0	0	25^1	41	1	8	10	18.1	7.46	50	.360	.411	1	.143	-0	-10	-10	-0	-1.0
1925	Bro-N	0	0	—	1	0	0	0	0	1	1	0	0	0	9.0	0.00	—	.500	.500	0	—	0	0	0	0	0.0
Total	2	0	3	.000	12	5	0	0	0	26^1	42	1	8	10	17.8	7.18	52	.362	.413	1	.143	-0	-10	-10	-0	-1.0

● **LEON ROBERTS** Roberts, Leon Kauffman b: 1/22/51, Vicksburg, Mich. BR/TR, 6'3", 200 lbs. Deb: 9/03/74 ♦

YEAR TM/L		W	L	PCT	G	GS	CG	SH	SV	IP	H	HR	BB	SO	RAT	ERA	ERA+	OAV	OOB	BH	AVG	PB	PR	/A	PD	TPI
1984	KC-A	0	0	—	1	0	0	0	0	1	4	1	1	1	45.0	27.00	15	.571	.625	10	.222	0	-3	-3	0	-0.2

● **RAY ROBERTS** Roberts, Raymond b: 8/25/1895, Cruger, Miss. d: 1/30/62, Cruger, Miss. BL/TR, 5'11", 180 lbs. Deb: 9/12/19

YEAR TM/L		W	L	PCT	G	GS	CG	SH	SV	IP	H	HR	BB	SO	RAT	ERA	ERA+	OAV	OOB	BH	AVG	PB	PR	/A	PD	TPI
1919	Phi-A	0	2	.000	3	2	0	0	0	14	21	0	3	2	15.4	7.71	44	.368	.400	1	.250	-0	-7	-7	-0	-0.6

● **ROBIN ROBERTS** Roberts, Robin Evan b: 9/30/26, Springfield, Ill. BB/TR, 6', 190 lbs. Deb: 6/18/48 H

YEAR TM/L		W	L	PCT	G	GS	CG	SH	SV	IP	H	HR	BB	SO	RAT	ERA	ERA+	OAV	OOB	BH	AVG	PB	PR	/A	PD	TPI
1948	Phi-N	7	9	.438	20	20	9	0	0	146^2	148	10	61	84	13.1	3.19	124	.278	.356	11	.250	4	12	12	-2	1.5
1949	Phi-N	15	15	.500	43	31	11	3	4	226^2	229	15	75	95	12.3	3.69	107	.273	.337	5	.075	-3	9	6	-3	0.0
1950	*Phi-N★	20	11	.645	40	39	21	**5**	1	304^1	282	29	77	146	10.7	3.02	134	.248	.297	12	.118	-3	**38**	35	0	3.2
1951	Phi-N★	21	15	.583	44	39	22	6	2	**315**	284	20	64	127	10.0	3.03	127	.237	**.278**	15	.172	5	33	29	-3	3.2
1952	Phi-N☆	**28**	7	.800	39	37	**30**	3	2	**330**	292	22	45	148	9.3	2.59	141	.234	.263	14	.125	2	**42**	**39**	-3	4.1
1953	Phi-N★	**23**	16	.590	44	41	**33**	5	2	**346^2**	324	30	61	**198**	10.0	2.75	153	.242	.276	22	.179	2	59	**56**	-1	5.9
1954	Phi-N★	**23**	15	.605	45	38	**29**	4	4	**336^2**	289	35	56	**185**	**9.4**	2.97	136	.231	**.267**	15	.123	-3	41	40	-4	3.5
1955	Phi-N★	**23**	14	.622	41	38	**26**	1	3	**305**	292	41	53	160	10.2	3.28	121	.246	**.280**	27	.252	14	26	24	-5	3.4
1956	Phi-N☆	19	18	.514	43	37	**22**	1	3	297^1	328	46	40	157	11.2	4.45	84	.282	.307	20	.200	4	-22	-24	-0	-2.0
1957	Phi-N	10	22	.313	39	32	14	2	2	249^2	246	40	43	128	10.5	4.07	93	.252	.284	13	.162	0	-5	-7	0	-0.7
1958	Phi-N	17	14	.548	35	34	21	1	0	269^2	270	30	51	130	10.8	3.24	122	.259	.294	20	.202	4	21	22	-2	2.4
1959	Phi-N	15	17	.469	35	35	19	2	0	257^1	267	34	35	137	10.7	4.27	96	.263	.291	17	.191	3	-9	-5	0	-0.1
1960	Phi-N	12	16	.429	35	33	13	2	1	237^1	256	31	34	122	11.1	4.02	97	.275	.302	12	.152	-1	-7	-4	-3	-0.7
1961	Phi-N	1	10	.091	26	18	2	0	0	117	154	19	23	54	13.8	5.85	70	.326	.360	3	.091	-2	-24	-23	-2	-2.5
1962	Bal-A	10	9	.526	27	25	6	0	0	191^1	176	17	41	102	10.4	2.78	135	.244	.289	10	.192	2	25	21	-1	2.3
1963	Bal-A	14	13	.519	35	35	9	2	0	251^1	230	35	40	124	9.8	3.33	106	.240	**.272**	16	.203	2	8	6	-2	0.6
1964	Bal-A	13	7	.650	31	31	8	4	0	204	203	18	52	109	11.4	2.91	123	.261	.310	9	.132	-1	16	15	-2	1.3
1965	Bal-A	5	7	.417	20	15	5	1	0	114^2	110	17	20	63	10.3	3.38	103	.252	.286	6	.171	1	1	1	-1	0.1
	Hou-N	5	2	.714	10	10	3	2	0	76	61	1	10	34	8.4	1.89	177	.216	.243	5	.238	3	14	12	-2	1.6
1966	Hou-N	3	5	.375	13	12	1	1	1	63^2	79	7	10	26	12.7	3.82	90	.307	.336	1	.063	-1	-1	-3	-1	-0.4
	Chi-N	2	3	.400	11	9	1	0	0	48^1	62	8	11	28	13.6	6.14	60	.313	.349	2	.200	1	-14	-13	0	-1.2
	Yr	5	8	.385	24	21	2	1	1	112	141	15	21	54	13.0	4.82	73	.307	.337	3	.115	0	-15	-16	-0	-1.6
Total	19	286	245	.539	676	609	305	45	25	4688^2	4582	505	902	2357	10.6	3.41	113	.255	.293	255	.167	34	264	239	-35	25.5

● **CHARLIE ROBERTSON** Robertson, Charles Culbertson b: 1/31/1896, Dexter, Tex. d: 8/23/84, Fort Worth, Tex. BL/TR, 6', 175 lbs. Deb: 5/13/19

YEAR TM/L		W	L	PCT	G	GS	CG	SH	SV	IP	H	HR	BB	SO	RAT	ERA	ERA+	OAV	OOB	BH	AVG	PB	PR	/A	PD	TPI
1919	Chi-A	0	1	.000	1	1	0	0	0	2	5	0	0	1	22.5	9.00	35	.556	.556	0	—	0	-1	-1	-0	-0.1
1922	Chi-A	14	15	.483	37	34	21	3	0	272	294	9	89	83	12.8	3.64	112	.286	.345	16	.184	-2	12	13	-5	0.7
1923	Chi-A	13	18	.419	38	34	18	1	0	255	262	8	104	91	13.1	3.81	104	.272	.346	21	.247	0	5	4	-2	0.2
1924	Chi-A	4	10	.286	17	14	5	0	0	97^1	108	2	54	29	15.0	4.99	83	.293	.383	6	.182	-1	-8	-9	-2	-1.1
1925	Chi-A	8	12	.400	24	23	6	2	0	137	181	8	47	27	15.1	5.26	79	.327	.381	10	.222	0	-13	-17	-2	-1.6
1926	StL-A	1	2	.333	8	7	1	0	0	28	38	4	21	13	19.6	8.36	51	.333	.445	3	.300	1	-13	-13	0	-1.1
1927	Bos-N	7	17	.292	28	22	6	0	0	154^1	188	2	46	49	13.9	4.72	79	.308	.360	12	.240	1	-14	-17	-1	-1.7

YEAR TM/L	W	L	PCT	G	GS	CG	SH	SV	IP	H	HR	BB	SO	RAT	ERA	ERA+	OAV	OOB	BH	AVG	PB	PR	/A	PD	TPI
1928 Bos-N	2	5	.286	13	7	3	0	1	59^1	73	5	16	17	13.5	5.31	74	.308	.352	0	.000	-1	-9	-9	-1	-1.0
Total 8	49	80	.380	166	142	60	6	1	1005	1149	38	377	310	13.8	4.44	90	.296	.361	68	.208	-2	-42	-49	-13	-5.7

● JERRY ROBERTSON Robertson, Jerry Lee b: 10/13/43, Winchester, Kan. BB/TR, 6'2", 205 lbs. Deb: 4/08/69

YEAR TM/L	W	L	PCT	G	GS	CG	SH	SV	IP	H	HR	BB	SO	RAT	ERA	ERA+	OAV	OOB	BH	AVG	PB	PR	/A	PD	TPI
1969 Mon-N	5	16	.238	38	27	3	0	1	179^2	186	17	81	133	13.6	3.96	93	.272	.352	5	.089	-3	-7	-6	-3	-1.1
1970 Det-A	0	0	—	11	0	0	0	0	14^2	19	1	5	11	14.7	3.68	101	.306	.358	0	—	0	0	0	-0	0.0
Total 2	5	16	.238	49	27	3	0	1	194^1	205	18	86	144	13.7	3.94	93	.274	.352	5	.089	-3	-7	-6	-3	-1.1

● DICK ROBERTSON Robertson, Preston b: 1891, Washington, D.C. d: 10/2/44, New Orleans, La. BR/TR, 5'9", 160 lbs. Deb: 9/16/13

YEAR TM/L	W	L	PCT	G	GS	CG	SH	SV	IP	H	HR	BB	SO	RAT	ERA	ERA+	OAV	OOB	BH	AVG	PB	PR	/A	PD	TPI
1913 Cin-N	0	1	.000	2	1	1	0	0	10	13	0	9	1	19.8	7.20	45	.342	.468	0	.000	-0	-4	-4	-0	-0.5
1918 Bro-N	3	6	.333	13	9	7	1	0	87	87	0	28	18	11.9	2.59	108	.272	.330	9	.300	2	2	2	-0	0.4
1919 Was-A	0	1	.000	7	4	0	0	0	27^2	25	1	9	7	11.1	2.28	141	.253	.315	0	.000	-1	3	3	0	0.2
Total 3	3	8	.273	22	14	8	1	0	124^2	125	1	46	26	12.3	2.89	101	.274	.340	9	.225	0	0	0	-1	0.1

● RICH ROBERTSON Robertson, Richard Paul b: 10/14/44, Albany, Cal. BR/TR, 6'2", 210 lbs. Deb: 9/10/66

YEAR TM/L	W	L	PCT	G	GS	CG	SH	SV	IP	H	HR	BB	SO	RAT	ERA	ERA+	OAV	OOB	BH	AVG	PB	PR	/A	PD	TPI
1966 SF-N	0	0	—	1	0	0	0	0	2^1	3	0	2	2	19.3	7.71	48	.300	.417	0	—	0	-1	-1	-0	-0.1
1967 SF-N	0	0	—	1	0	0	0	0	2	3	0	0	1	13.5	4.50	73	.333	.333	0	—	0	-0	-0	0	0.0
1968 SF-N	2	0	1.000	3	1	0	0	0	9	9	0	3	8	12.0	6.00	49	.265	.324	1	.500	0	-3	-3	0	-0.3
1969 SF-N	1	3	.250	17	7	1	1	0	44^1	53	4	21	20	15.2	5.48	64	.298	.375	0	.000	-1	-9	-10	0	-1.0
1970 SF-N	8	9	.471	41	26	6	0	1	183^2	199	22	96	121	14.5	4.85	82	.277	.363	6	.102	-0	-16	-18	-0	-1.8
1971 SF-N	2	2	.500	23	6	1	0	1	61	66	5	31	32	14.6	4.57	74	.267	.354	1	.067	-1	-8	-8	-1	-1.1
Total 6	13	14	.481	86	40	8	1	2	302^1	333	31	153	184	14.6	4.94	76	.278	.362	8	.093	-2	-38	-40	-1	-4.3

● DEWEY ROBINSON Robinson, Dewey Everett b: 4/28/55, Evanston, Ill. BR/TR, 6', 180 lbs. Deb: 4/06/79

YEAR TM/L	W	L	PCT	G	GS	CG	SH	SV	IP	H	HR	BB	SO	RAT	ERA	ERA+	OAV	OOB	BH	AVG	PB	PR	/A	PD	TPI
1979 Chi-A	0	1	.000	11	0	0	0	0	14^1	11	1	9	5	12.6	6.28	68	.212	.328	0	—	0	-3	-3	-0	-0.3
1980 Chi-A	1	1	.500	15	0	0	0	0	35	26	2	16	28	10.8	3.09	131	.215	.307	0	—	0	4	4	0	0.4
1981 Chi-A	1	0	1.000	4	0	0	0	0	4	5	1	3	2	18.0	4.50	79	.357	.471	0	—	0	-0	-0	-0	0.0
Total 3	2	2	.500	30	0	0	0	0	53^1	42	4	28	35	11.8	4.05	100	.225	.326	0	—	0	0	0	-0	0.1

● DON ROBINSON Robinson, Don Allen b: 6/8/57, Ashland, Ky. BR/TR, 6'4", 231 lbs. Deb: 4/10/78

YEAR TM/L	W	L	PCT	G	GS	CG	SH	SV	IP	H	HR	BB	SO	RAT	ERA	ERA+	OAV	OOB	BH	AVG	PB	PR	/A	PD	TPI
1978 Pit-N	14	6	.700	35	32	9	1	1	228^1	203	20	57	135	10.4	3.47	107	.236	.286	20	.235	2	3	6	-1	0.8
1979 *Pit-N	8	8	.500	29	25	4	0	0	160^2	171	12	52	96	12.7	3.87	100	.277	.337	10	.204	1	-2	0	-3	-0.2
1980 Pit-N	7	10	.412	29	24	3	2	1	160^1	157	14	45	103	11.6	3.99	91	.257	.314	19	.333	7	-7	-6	0	0.0
1981 Pit-N	0	3	.000	16	2	0	0	2	38^1	47	4	23	17	16.4	5.87	61	.313	.405	3	.250	1	-10	-10	1	-0.8
1982 Pit-N	15	13	.536	38	30	6	0	0	227	213	26	103	165	12.6	4.28	87	.250	.333	24	.282	9	-17	-15	-2	-0.8
1983 Pit-N	2	2	.500	9	6	0	0	0	36^1	43	5	21	28	15.9	4.46	83	.297	.386	2	.154	1	-3	-3	0	-0.2
1984 Pit-N	5	6	.455	51	1	0	0	10	122	99	6	49	110	10.9	3.02	119	.226	.304	9	.290	4	8	8	1	1.3
1985 Pit-N	5	11	.313	44	6	0	0	3	95^1	95	6	42	65	13.1	3.87	92	.255	.334	5	.238	3	-3	-3	-0	-0.1
1986 Pit-N	3	4	.429	50	0	0	0	14	69^1	61	5	27	53	11.7	3.38	114	.237	.315	4	.667	2	3	4	0	0.6
1987 Pit-N	6	6	.500	42	0	0	0	12	65^1	66	6	22	53	12.1	3.86	107	.267	.327	1	.143	0	2	2	0	0.2
*SF-N	5	1	.833	25	0	0	0	7	42^2	39	1	18	26	12.0	2.74	140	.239	.315	3	.273	2	6	5	-1	0.7
Yr	11	7	.611	67	0	0	0	19	108	105	7	40	79	12.1	3.42	117	.255	.322	4	.222	2	8	7	-1	0.9
1988 SF-N	10	5	.667	51	19	3	2	6	176^2	152	11	49	122	10.4	2.45	133	.231	.287	9	.173	2	20	16	-2	1.9
1989 *SF-N	12	11	.522	34	32	5	1	0	197	184	22	37	96	10.2	3.43	98	.248	.285	15	.185	4	2	-1	-4	-0.2
1990 SF-N	10	7	.588	26	25	4	0	0	157^2	173	18	41	78	12.3	4.57	80	.280	.326	9	.143	1	-14	-16	-2	-1.7
1991 SF-N	5	9	.357	34	16	0	0	1	121^1	123	12	50	78	12.9	4.38	82	.265	.337	6	.150	0	-9	-11	-0	-1.1
1992 Cal-A	1	0	1.000	3	3	0	0	0	16^1	19	1	3	9	12.1	2.20	177	.292	.324	0	—	0	3	3	-1	0.3
Phi-N	1	4	.200	8	8	0	0	0	43^2	49	6	4	17	11.1	6.18	57	.290	.310	7	.389	3	-13	-13	-1	-1.1
Total 15	109	106	.507	524	229	34	6	57	1958^1	1894	175	643	1251	11.8	3.79	96	.255	.317	146	.231	41	-34	-34	-14	-0.4

● HUMBERTO ROBINSON Robinson, Humberto Valentino b: 6/25/30, Colon, Panama BR/TR, 6'1", 155 lbs. Deb: 4/20/55

YEAR TM/L	W	L	PCT	G	GS	CG	SH	SV	IP	H	HR	BB	SO	RAT	ERA	ERA+	OAV	OOB	BH	AVG	PB	PR	/A	PD	TPI
1955 Mil-N	3	1	.750	13	2	1	0	2	38	31	1	25	19	14.2	3.08	122	.235	.373	1	.077	-1	4	3	0	0.2
1956 Mil-N	0	0	—	1	0	0	0	0	2	1	0	2	0	13.5	0.00	—	.167	.375	0	—	0	1	1	0	0.1
1958 Mil-N	2	4	.333	19	0	0	0	1	41^2	30	4	13	26	9.7	3.02	116	.203	.276	1	.167	1	4	2	1	0.4
1959 Cle-A	1	0	1.000	5	0	0	0	0	8^2	9	0	4	6	13.5	4.15	89	.281	.361	0	—	0	-0	-0	0	0.0
Phi-N	2	4	.333	31	4	1	0	1	73	70	6	24	32	11.6	3.33	123	.251	.310	3	.231	1	5	6	0	0.8
1960 Phi-N	0	4	.000	33	1	0	0	0	49^2	48	6	22	31	12.7	3.44	113	.255	.333	1	.167	-0	2	2	0	0.2
Total 5	8	13	.381	102	7	2	0	4	213	189	17	90	114	12.0	3.25	119	.241	.323	6	.158	0	16	14	2	1.7

● JEFF ROBINSON Robinson, Jeffrey Daniel b: 12/13/60, Santa Ana, Cal. BR/TR, 6'4", 200 lbs. Deb: 4/07/84

YEAR TM/L	W	L	PCT	G	GS	CG	SH	SV	IP	H	HR	BB	SO	RAT	ERA	ERA+	OAV	OOB	BH	AVG	PB	PR	/A	PD	TPI
1984 SF-N	7	15	.318	34	33	1	1	0	171^2	195	12	52	102	13.3	4.56	77	.288	.345	7	.115	-2	-19	-20	0	-2.2
1985 SF-N	0	0	—	8	0	0	0	0	12^1	16	2	10	8	19.0	5.11	67	.333	.448	0	—	0	-2	-2	-0	-0.3
1986 SF-N	6	3	.667	64	1	0	0	8	104^1	92	8	32	90	10.8	3.36	105	.234	.293	1	.067	-1	4	2	-1	0.0
1987 SF-N	6	8	.429	63	0	0	0	10	96^2	69	10	48	82	11.0	2.79	138	.207	.309	2	.111	-1	14	11	1	1.2
Pit-N	2	1	.667	18	0	0	0	4	26^2	20	1	6	19	8.8	3.04	135	.215	.263	1	.250	1	3	3	0	0.5
Yr	8	9	.471	81	0	0	0	14	123^1	89	11	54	101	10.4	2.85	137	.206	.295	3	.136	0	17	14	1	1.7
1988 Pit-N	11	5	.688	75	0	0	0	9	124^2	113	6	39	87	11.2	3.03	112	.244	.307	3	.188	0	6	5	0	0.6
1989 Pit-N	7	13	.350	50	19	0	0	4	141^1	161	14	59	95	14.1	4.58	73	.283	.351	8	.229	2	-17	-19	1	-1.7
1990 NY-A	3	6	.333	54	4	1	0	0	88^2	82	8	34	43	11.9	3.45	115	.248	.320	0	—	0	4	5	2	0.7
1991 Cal-A	0	3	.000	39	0	0	0	3	57	56	9	29	57	13.7	5.37	76	.259	.352	0	—	0	-8	-8	0	-0.8
1992 Chi-N	4	3	.571	49	5	0	0	1	78	76	5	40	46	13.6	3.00	120	.263	.356	0	.000	-1	4	5	1	0.5
Total 9	46	57	.447	454	62	2	1	39	901^1	880	75	349	629	12.5	3.79	95	.258	.330	22	.137	-1	-10	-18	4	-1.5

● JEFF ROBINSON Robinson, Jeffrey Mark b: 12/14/61, Ventura, Cal. BR/TR, 6'6", 240 lbs. Deb: 4/12/87

YEAR TM/L	W	L	PCT	G	GS	CG	SH	SV	IP	H	HR	BB	SO	RAT	ERA	ERA+	OAV	OOB	BH	AVG	PB	PR	/A	PD	TPI
1987 *Det-A	9	6	.600	29	21	2	1	0	127^1	132	16	54	98	13.6	5.37	79	.262	.342	0	—	0	-13	-16	-1	-1.6
1988 Det-A	13	6	.684	24	23	6	2	0	172	121	19	72	114	10.3	2.98	128	**.197**	.284	0	—	0	19	16	-0	1.7
1989 Det-A	4	5	.444	16	16	1	1	0	78	76	10	46	40	14.2	4.73	81	.259	.361	0	—	0	-7	-8	-1	-0.9
1990 Det-A	10	9	.526	27	27	1	1	0	145	141	23	88	76	14.6	5.96	66	.255	.364	0	—	0	-33	-32	-1	-3.1
1991 Bal-A	4	9	.308	21	19	0	0	0	104^1	119	12	51	65	15.2	5.18	76	.289	.375	0	—	0	-13	-14	-1	-1.3
1992 Tex-A	4	4	.500	16	4	0	0	0	45^2	50	6	21	18	14.0	5.72	67	.281	.357	0	—	0	-9	-10	-0	-0.9
Pit-N	3	1	.750	8	7	0	0	0	36^1	33	2	15	14	12.1	4.46	76	.244	.325	1	.091	-1	-4	-4	0	-0.5
Total 6	47	40	.540	141	117	10	5	0	708^2	672	88	347	425	13.2	4.79	82	.250	.341	1	.091	-1	-60	-68	-4	-6.6

● JACK ROBINSON Robinson, John Edward b: 2/20/21, Orange, N.J. BR/TR, 6', 175 lbs. Deb: 5/04/49

YEAR TM/L	W	L	PCT	G	GS	CG	SH	SV	IP	H	HR	BB	SO	RAT	ERA	ERA+	OAV	OOB	BH	AVG	PB	PR	/A	PD	TPI
1949 Bos-A	0	0	—	3	0	0	0	0	4	4	0	1	1	13.5	2.25	194	.267	.353	0	—	0	1	1	0	0.1

● HANK ROBINSON Robinson, John Henry "Rube" (b: John Henry Roberson)
b: 8/16/1889, Floyd, Ark. d: 7/3/65, N.Little Rock, Ark BR/TL, 5'11.5", 160 lbs. Deb: 9/02/11

YEAR TM/L	W	L	PCT	G	GS	CG	SH	SV	IP	H	HR	BB	SO	RAT	ERA	ERA+	OAV	OOB	BH	AVG	PB	PR	/A	PD	TPI
1911 Pit-N	0	1	.000	5	0	0	0	0	13	13	0	5	8	13.2	2.77	124	.283	.365	0	.000	-0	1	1	1	0.1
1912 Pit-N	12	7	.632	33	16	11	0	2	175	146	3	30	79	**9.6**	2.26	144	.237	.284	15	.254	2	22	19	-1	2.1
1913 Pit-N	14	9	.609	43	23	8	1	0	196^1	184	1	41	50	10.6	2.38	126	.255	.301	11	.180	-1	18	14	-2	1.2
1914 StL-N	7	8	.467	26	16	6	1	0	126	128	1	32	30	11.7	3.00	93	.274	.325	6	.171	-0	-3	-3	2	-0.1
1915 StL-N	7	8	.467	32	15	6	1	0	143	128	1	35	57	10.7	2.45	114	.245	.301	5	.106	-2	5	5	1	0.5
1918 NY-A	2	4	.333	11	3	1	0	0	48	47	0	16	14	12.4	3.00	94	.269	.340	0	.000	-2	-1	-1	-0	-0.3
Total 6	42	37	.532	150	73	32	3	2	701^1	646	6	159	238	10.7	2.53	118	.253	.305	37	.170	-3	42	36	1	3.5

YEAR TM/L	W	L	PCT	G	GS	CG	SH	SV	IP	H	HR	BB	SO	RAT	ERA	ERA+	OAV	OOB	BH	AVG	PB	PR	/A	PD	TPI

● **RON ROBINSON** Robinson, Ronald Dean b: 3/24/62, Exeter, Cal. BR/TR, 6'4", 235 lbs. Deb: 8/14/84

1984 Cin-N	1	2	.333	12	5	1	0	0	39²	35	3	13	24	10.9	2.72	139	.232	.293	0	.000	-1	4	5	0	0.4
1985 Cin-N	7	7	.500	33	12	0	0	1	108¹	107	11	32	76	11.6	3.99	95	.259	.314	2	.091	-1	-5	-2	1	-0.3
1986 Cin-N	10	3	.769	70	0	0	0	14	116²	110	10	43	117	12.0	3.24	119	.253	.323	1	.071	-1	6	8	1	0.9
1987 Cin-N	7	5	.583	48	18	0	0	4	154	148	14	43	99	11.2	3.68	115	.256	.308	7	.194	0	7	10	-2	0.4
1988 Cin-N	3	7	.300	17	16	0	0	0	78²	88	5	26	38	13.3	4.12	87	.285	.344	5	.200	1	-6	-5	-0	-0.5
1989 Cin-N	5	3	.625	15	15	0	0	0	83¹	80	8	28	36	11.9	3.35	108	.252	.317	6	.214	1	1	2	-0	0.3
1990 Cin-N	2	2	.500	6	5	0	0	0	31¹	36	2	14	14	14.4	4.88	81	.295	.368	1	.091	-1	-4	-3	-0	-0.4
Mil-A	12	5	.706	22	22	7	2	0	148¹	158	5	37	57	12.2	2.91	133	.275	.326	0	—	0	16	16	-0	1.7
1991 Mil-A	0	1	.000	1	1	0	0	0	4¹	6	0	3	0	20.8	6.23	64	.353	.476	0	—	0	-1	-1	0	0.1
1992 Mil-A	1	4	.200	8	8	0	0	0	35¹	51	3	14	12	17.1	5.86	65	.331	.394	0	—	0	-8	-8	-0	-0.7
Total 9	48	39	.552	232	102	8	2	19	800	819	61	253	473	12.3	3.63	107	.267	.326	22	.153	-2	12	21	-1	2.3

● **BILL ROBINSON** Robinson, William (b: William Anderson) b: Taylorsville, Ky. Deb: 8/12/1889

| 1889 Lou-a | 0 | 1 | .000 | 1 | 1 | 1 | 0 | 0 | 8 | 10 | 2 | 6 | 2 | 18.0 | 10.13 | 38 | .297 | .403 | 1 | .333 | 0 | -6 | -6 | -0 | -0.4 |

● **YANK ROBINSON** Robinson, William H. b: 9/19/1859, Philadelphia, Pa. d: 8/25/1894, St.Louis, Mo. BR/TR, 5'6.5", 170 lbs. Deb: 8/24/1882 ♦

1882 Det-N	0	0	—	1	0	0	0	0	2	0	0	1	0	4.5	0.00	—	.000	.125	7	.179	-0	1	1	0	0.1
1884 Bal-U	3	3	.500	11	3	3	0	0	75	96	1	18	61	13.7	3.48	95	.291	.328	111	.267	2	-4	-1	-3	-0.3
1886 *StL-a	1	1	.000	1	1	1	0	0	9	10	0	7	1	17.0	3.00	115	.286	.405	132	.274	0	0	-0	-0	0.1
1887 *StL-a	0	0	—	1	0	0	0	1	3	3	0	3	0	21.0	3.00	151	.333	.538	131	.305	0	0	1	-0	0.0
Total 4	3	4	.429	14	4	4	0	1	89	109	1	29	62	14.1	3.34	101	.287	.339	825	.241	2	-2	0	-3	-0.1

● **CHICK ROBITAILLE** Robitaille, Joseph Anthony b: 3/2/1879, Whitehall, N.Y. d: 7/30/47, Waterford, N.Y. BR/TR, 5'8", 150 lbs. Deb: 9/02/04

1904 Pit-N	4	3	.571	9	8	8	0	0	66	52	1	13	34	9.0	1.91	144	.208	.250	2	.095	-2	6	6	-1	0.3
1905 Pit-N	8	5	.615	17	12	10	0	0	120¹	126	1	28	32	11.7	2.92	103	.276	.322	6	.133	-2	1	1	-0	-0.1
Total 2	12	8	.600	26	20	18	0	0	186¹	178	2	41	66	10.8	2.56	114	.252	.297	8	.121	-4	7	7	-1	0.2

● **ARMANDO ROCHE** Roche, Armando (Baez) b: 12/7/26, Havana, Cuba BR/TR, 6', 190 lbs. Deb: 5/10/45

| 1945 Was-A | 0 | 0 | — | 2 | 0 | 0 | 0 | 0 | 6 | 10 | 0 | 2 | 0 | 18.0 | 6.00 | 52 | .400 | .444 | 0 | .000 | -0 | -2 | -2 | 0 | -0.2 |

● **MIKE ROCHFORD** Rochford, Michael Joseph b: 3/14/63, Methuen, Mass. BL/TL, 6'4", 205 lbs. Deb: 9/03/88

1988 Bos-A	0	0	—	2	0	0	0	0	2¹	4	0	1	1	19.3	0.00	—	.364	.417	0	—	0	1	1	0	0.1
1989 Bos-A	0	0	—	4	0	0	0	0	4	4	1	4	1	18.0	6.75	61	.267	.421	0	—	0	-1	-1	-0	-0.2
1990 Bos-A	0	1	.000	2	1	0	0	0	4	10	1	4	0	31.5	18.00	23	.526	.609	0	—	0	-6	-6	-0	-0.6
Total 3	0	1	.000	8	1	0	0	0	10¹	18	2	9	2	23.5	9.58	43	.400	.500	0	—	0	-7	-6	-0	-0.7

● **RICH RODAS** Rodas, Richard Martin b: 11/7/59, Roseville, Cal. BL/TL, 6'1", 180 lbs. Deb: 9/06/83

1983 LA-N	0	0	—	7	0	0	0	0	4²	4	0	3	5	13.5	1.93	186	.222	.333	0	—	0	1	1	-0	0.1
1984 LA-N	0	0	—	3	0	0	0	0	5	5	2	1	1	10.8	5.40	65	.250	.286	0	.000	-0	-1	-1	0	-0.1
Total 2	0	0	—	10	0	0	0	0	9²	9	2	4	6	12.1	3.72	96	.237	.310	0	.000	-0	-0	-0	0	0.0

● **EDUARDO RODRIGUEZ** Rodriguez, Eduardo (Reyes) b: 3/6/52, Barceloneta, P.R. BR/TR, 6', 185 lbs. Deb: 6/20/73

1973 Mil-A	9	7	.563	30	6	2	0	5	76¹	71	6	47	49	14.1	3.30	114	.247	.357	1	1.000	1	4	4	-0	0.5
1974 Mil-A	7	4	.636	43	6	0	0	4	111²	97	7	51	58	12.3	3.63	100	.241	.333	0	—	0	-0	-0	-0	0.0
1975 Mil-A	7	0	1.000	43	1	0	0	7	87²	77	9	44	65	12.9	3.49	110	.235	.334	0	—	0	3	3	-2	0.2
1976 Mil-A	5	13	.278	45	12	3	0	8	136	124	10	65	77	12.7	3.64	96	.249	.339	0	—	0	-2	-2	-1	-0.2
1977 Mil-A	5	6	.455	42	5	1	1	4	142²	126	15	56	104	11.7	4.35	93	.236	.311	0	—	0	-5	-5	-1	-0.5
1978 Mil-A	5	5	.500	32	8	0	0	2	105¹	107	9	26	51	11.5	3.93	96	.262	.310	0	—	0	-2	-2	-0	-0.3
1979 KC-A	4	1	.800	29	1	1	0	2	74¹	79	9	34	26	14.0	4.84	88	.276	.359	0	—	0	-5	-5	-1	-0.7
Total 7	42	36	.538	264	39	7	1	32	734	681	65	323	430	12.6	3.89	98	.248	.332	1	1.000	1	-7	-7	-5	-1.0

● **FREDDY RODRIGUEZ** Rodriguez, Fernando Pedro (Borrego) b: 4/29/24, Havana, Cuba BR/TR, 6', 180 lbs. Deb: 4/18/58

1958 Chi-N	0	0	—	7	0	0	0	2	7¹	8	2	5	5	17.2	7.36	53	.267	.389	0	.000	-0	-3	-3	-0	-0.3
1959 Phi-N	0	0	—	1	0	0	0	0	2	4	1	0	1	22.5	13.50	30	.400	.455	0	—	0	-2	-2	-0	-0.2
Total 2	0	0	—	8	0	0	0	2	9¹	12	3	5	6	18.3	8.68	46	.300	.404	0	.000	-0	-5	-5	-0	-0.5

● **RICK RODRIGUEZ** Rodriguez, Ricardo b: 9/21/60, Oakland, Cal. BR/TR, 6'3", 190 lbs. Deb: 9/17/86

1986 Oak-A	1	2	.333	3	3	0	0	0	16¹	17	4	7	2	13.2	6.61	58	.262	.333	0	—	0	-4	-5	0	-0.3
1987 Oak-A	1	0	1.000	15	0	0	0	0	24¹	32	1	15	9	17.8	2.96	139	.337	.432	0	—	0	4	3	1	0.4
1988 Cle-A	1	2	.333	10	5	0	0	0	33	43	4	17	9	16.6	7.09	58	.323	.404	0	—	0	-11	-11	1	-1.0
1990 SF-N	0	0	—	3	0	0	0	0	3¹	5	0	2	2	18.9	8.10	45	.357	.438	0	—	0	-2	-0	0	-0.2
Total 4	3	4	.429	31	8	0	0	0	77	97	9	41	22	16.4	5.73	71	.316	.400	0	—	0	-13	-14	2	-1.1

● **RICH RODRIGUEZ** Rodriguez, Richard Anthony b: 3/1/63, Downey, Cal. BL/TL, 5'10", 194 lbs. Deb: 6/30/90

1990 SD-N	1	1	.500	32	0	0	0	0	47²	52	2	16	22	13.0	2.83	135	.287	.348	0	.000	-0	5	5	1	0.6
1991 SD-N	3	1	.750	64	1	0	0	0	80	66	8	44	40	12.4	3.26	116	.234	.337	0	.000	-0	4	5	-0	0.4
1992 SD-N	6	3	.667	61	1	0	0	0	91	77	4	29	64	10.5	2.37	153	.229	.290	0	.000	-1	11	13	1	1.4
Total 3	10	5	.667	157	2	0	0	1	218²	195	14	89	126	11.7	2.80	133	.244	.321	0	.000	-1	20	23	1	2.4

● **ROSARIO RODRIGUEZ** Rodriguez, Rosario Isabel (Echavarria) b: 7/8/69, Los Mochis, Mexico BR/TL, 6', 185 lbs. Deb: 9/01/89

1989 Cin-N	1	1	.500	7	0	0	0	0	4¹	3	0	3	0	12.5	4.15	87	.188	.316	0	—	0	-0	-0	0	0.0
1990 Cin-N	0	0	—	9	0	0	0	0	10¹	15	3	2	8	15.7	6.10	65	.357	.400	0	—	0	-3	-2	0	-0.2
1991 *Pit-N	1	1	.500	18	0	0	0	6	15¹	14	1	8	10	13.5	4.11	87	.246	.348	0	.000	-0	-1	-1	0	-0.1
Total 3	2	2	.500	34	0	0	0	6	30	32	4	13	18	14.1	4.80	77	.278	.362	0	.000	-0	-4	-4	1	-0.3

● **ROBERTO RODRIQUEZ** Rodriquez, Roberto (Munoz) b: 11/29/41, Caracas, Venez. BR/TR, 6'3", 185 lbs. Deb: 5/13/67

1967 KC-A	1	1	.500	15	5	0	0	2	40¹	42	4	14	29	12.7	3.57	89	.268	.331	0	.000	-1	-2	-2	-0	-0.3
1970 Oak-A	0	0	—	6	0	0	0	0	12¹	10	2	3	8	9.5	2.92	121	.227	.277	0	.000	-0	1	1	-0	0.1
SD-N	0	0	—	10	0	0	0	3	16¹	26	1	5	18	17.1	6.61	60	.366	.408	0	.000	-0	-5	-5	0	-0.5
Chi-N	3	2	.600	26	0	0	0	2	43¹	50	6	15	46	13.5	5.82	77	.289	.346	1	.125	1	-9	-6	-0	-0.5
Yr	3	2	.600	36	0	0	0	5	59²	76	7	20	54	14.5	6.03	72	.311	.364	1	.091	0	-13	-11	-0	-1.0
Total 3	4	3	.571	57	5	0	0	7	112¹	128	13	37	91	13.3	4.81	80	.288	.344	1	.048	-1	-14	-12	-0	-1.2

● **PREACHER ROE** Roe, Elwin Charles b: 2/26/15, Ash Flat, Ark. BR/TL, 6'2", 170 lbs. Deb: 8/22/38

1938 StL-N	0	0	—	1	0	0	0	0	2	6	0	2	2	27.0	13.50	29	.429	.500	0	.000	-0	-3	-3	-0	-0.3
1944 Pit-N	13	11	.542	39	25	7	1	1	185¹	182	7	59	88	11.8	3.11	120	.253	.311	7	.132	-2	10	13	-1	0.9
1945 Pit-N†	14	13	.519	33	31	15	3	1	235	228	11	46	**148**	10.5	2.87	137	.259	.296	8	.107	-4	24	28	1	2.6
1946 Pit-N	3	8	.273	21	10	1	0	2	70	83	5	25	28	14.1	5.14	69	.294	.356	1	.067	-1	-13	-13	-0	-1.4
1947 Pit-N	4	15	.211	38	22	4	1	2	144	156	19	63	59	13.7	5.25	80	.276	.348	5	.125	-2	-19	-16	-1	-1.9
1948 Bro-N	12	8	.600	34	22	8	2	2	177²	156	14	33	86	9.7	2.63	152	.233	.271	5	.098	-2	26	27	-1	2.5
1949 *Bro-N★	15	6	**.714**	30	27	13	3	1	212¹	201	25	44	109	10.5	2.79	147	.252	.293	8	.114	-2	29	31	-2	2.7
1950 Bro-N☆	19	11	.633	36	32	16	2	1	250²	245	24	66	125	11.3	3.30	124	.258	.308	14	.154	-3	23	22	-1	1.7
1951 Bro-N☆	22	3	**.880**	34	33	19	2	0	257²	247	30	64	113	10.9	3.04	129	.258	.304	10	.112	-5	26	25	-1	2.0
1952 *Bro-N†	11	2	.846	27	25	8	2	0	158²	163	16	39	83	11.6	3.12	117	.270	.317	4	.070	-3	11	9	-1	0.5

YEAR	TM/L	W	L	PCT	G	GS	CG	SH	SV	IP	H	HR	BB	SO	RAT	ERA	ERA+	OAV	OOB	BH	AVG	PB	PR	/A	PD	TPI
1953	*Bro-N	11	3	.786	25	24	9	1	0	157	171	27	40	85	12.2	4.36	98	.278	.323	3	.053	-4	-1	-2	1	-0.5
1954	Bro-N	3	4	.429	15	10	1	0	0	63	69	11	23	31	13.1	5.00	82	.279	.341	3	.143	-0	-7	-6	-0	-0.7
Total	12	127	84	.602	333	261	101	17	10	1914^1	1907	199	504	956	11.4	3.43	116	.261	.310	68	.110	-27	108	115	-9	8.1
● **CLAY ROE**	Roe, James Clay "Shad" b: 1/7/04, Green Briar, Tenn. d: 4/4/56, Cleveland, Miss. BL/TL, 6'1", 180 lbs. Deb: 10/03/23																									
1923	Was-A	0	1	.000	1	1	0	0	0	1^2	0	0	6	2	32.4	0.00	—	.000	.500	0	—	0	1	1	-0	0.1
● **ED ROEBUCK**	Roebuck, Edward Jack b: 7/3/31, East Millsboro, Pa. BR/TR, 6'2", 185 lbs. Deb: 4/18/55																									
1955	*Bro-N	5	6	.455	47	0	0	0	12	84	96	14	24	33	13.2	4.71	86	.288	.342	2	.111	-1	-6	-6	1	-0.6
1956	*Bro-N	5	4	.556	43	0	0	0	1	89^1	83	15	29	60	11.5	3.93	101	.251	.315	6	.333	2	-2	0	1	0.3
1957	Bro-N	8	2	.800	44	1	0	0	8	96^1	70	9	46	73	11.0	2.71	154	.205	.303	5	.238	3	13	**16**	2	2.2
1958	LA-N	0	1	.000	32	0	0	0	5	44	45	9	15	26	12.7	3.48	118	.271	.339	2	.500	1	2	3	-0	0.4
1960	LA-N	8	3	.727	58	0	0	0	8	116^2	109	13	38	77	11.3	2.78	143	.256	.317	4	.167	-0	13	15	2	1.8
1961	LA-N	2	0	1.000	5	0	0	0	0	9	12	1	2	9	14.0	5.00	87	.324	.359	0	.000	-0	-1	-1	0	-0.1
1962	LA-N	10	2	.833	64	0	0	0	9	119^1	102	11	54	72	12.2	3.09	117	.232	.325	6	.214	1	11	7	0	0.8
1963	LA-N	2	4	.333	29	0	0	0	0	40^1	54	4	21	26	17.2	4.24	71	.321	.403	1	.250	0	-4	-5	1	-0.5
	Was-A	2	1	.667	26	0	0	0	4	57^1	63	5	29	25	14.8	3.30	113	.284	.372	2	.182	0	2	3	1	0.3
1964	Was-A	0	0	—	2	0	0	0	0	1	0	0	2	0	18.0	9.00	41	.000	.333	0	—	0	-1	-1	0	-0.1
	Phi-N	5	3	.625	60	0	0	0	12	77^1	55	7	25	42	9.8	2.21	157	.196	.272	0	.000	-1	11	11	1	1.2
1965	Phi-N	5	3	.625	44	0	0	0	3	50^1	55	2	15	29	13.4	3.40	102	.288	.355	0	.000	-0	1	0	-1	-0.1
1966	Phi-N	0	2	.000	6	0	0	0	0	6	9	0	2	5	16.5	6.00	60	.333	.379	0	—	0	-2	-2	-0	-0.2
Total	11	52	31	.627	460	1	0	0	62	791	753	90	302	477	12.3	3.35	114	.254	.329	28	.204	4	38	41	7	5.4
● **MIKE ROESLER**	Roesler, Michael Joseph b: 9/12/63, Fort Wayne, Ind. BR/TR, 6'5", 195 lbs. Deb: 8/09/89																									
1989	Cin-N	0	1	.000	17	0	0	0	0	25	22	4	9	14	11.2	3.96	91	.239	.307	0	—	0	-1	-1	-1	-0.2
1990	Pit-N	1	0	1.000	5	0	0	0	0	6	5	1	2	4	10.5	3.00	121	.217	.280	0	.000	-0	1	0	-0	0.0
Total	2	1	1	.500	22	0	0	0	0	31	27	5	11	18	11.0	3.77	96	.235	.302	0	.000	-0	-1	-1	-1	-0.2
● **OSCAR ROETTGER**	Roettger, Oscar Frederick Louis "Okkie" b: 2/19/1900, St.Louis, Mo. d: 7/4/86, St.Louis, Mo. BR/TR, 6', 170 lbs. Deb: 7/07/23 F♦																									
1923	NY-A	0	0	—	5	0	0	0	1	11^2	16	3	12	7	22.4	8.49	46	.340	.483	0	.000	-0	-6	-6	0	-0.6
1924	NY-A	0	0	—	1	0	0	0	0	0	1	0	2	0	—	—	—	1.000	1.000	0	—	0	0	0	0	0.0
Total	2	0	0	—	6	0	0	0	1	11^2	17	3	14	7	24.7	8.49	46	.354	.508	14	.212	-0	-6	-6	0	-0.6
● **JOE ROGALSKI**	Rogalski, Joseph Anthony b: 7/15/12, Ashland, Wis. d: 11/20/51, Ashland, Wis. BR/TR, 6'2", 187 lbs. Deb: 9/14/38																									
1938	Det-A	0	0	—	2	0	0	0	0	7	12	0	0	2	15.4	2.57	194	.400	.400	0	.000	-0	2	2	-0	0.1
● **KEVIN ROGERS**	Rogers, Charles Kevin b: 8/20/68, Cleveland, Miss. BB/TL, 6'2", 190 lbs. Deb: 9/04/92																									
1992	SF-N	0	2	.000	6	6	0	0	0	34	37	4	13	26	13.5	4.24	79	.280	.349	2	.222	0	-3	-3	-1	-0.4
● **KENNY ROGERS**	Rogers, Kenneth Scott b: 11/10/64, Savannah, Ga. BL/TL, 6'1", 200 lbs. Deb: 4/06/89																									
1989	Tex-A	3	4	.429	73	0	0	0	2	73^2	60	2	42	63	13.0	2.93	135	.232	.348	0	—	0	8	8	2	1.1
1990	Tex-A	10	6	.625	69	3	0	0	15	97^2	93	6	42	74	12.5	3.13	125	.249	.326	0	—	0	8	9	2	1.1
1991	Tex-A	10	10	.500	63	9	0	0	5	109^2	121	14	61	73	15.4	5.42	74	.281	.378	0	—	0	-16	-17	-0	-1.6
1992	Tex-A	3	6	.333	**81**	0	0	0	6	78^2	80	7	26	70	12.1	3.09	124	.261	.319	0	—	0	7	6	1	1.0
Total	4	26	26	.500	286	12	0	0	28	359^2	354	29	171	280	13.4	3.78	104	.259	.346	0	—	0	7	6	5	1.6
● **LEE ROGERS**	Rogers, Lee Otis "Buck" b: 10/8/13, Tuscaloosa, Ala. BR/TL, 5'11", 170 lbs. Deb: 4/27/38																									
1938	Bos-A	1	1	.500	14	2	0	0	0	27^2	32	4	18	7	16.3	6.51	76	.302	.403	0	.000	-0	-5	-5	1	-0.4
	Bro-N	0	2	.000	12	2	0	0	0	23^2	23	0	10	11	12.9	5.70	68	.256	.337	0	.000	0	-5	-5	1	-0.3
Total	1	1	3	.250	26	4	0	0	0	51^1	55	4	28	18	14.7	6.14	73	.281	.373	0	.000	0	-10	-10	2	-0.7
● **BUCK ROGERS**	Rogers, Orlin Woodrow "Lefty" b: 11/5/12, Spring Garden, Va. BR/TL, 5'8.5", 164 lbs. Deb: 9/15/35																									
1935	Was-A	0	1	.000	2	1	0	0	0	10	16	0	6	7	19.8	7.20	60	.340	.415	0	.000	-0	-3	-3	-0	-0.3
● **STEVE ROGERS**	Rogers, Stephen Douglas b: 10/26/49, Jefferson City, Mo. BR/TR, 6'1", 182 lbs. Deb: 7/18/73																									
1973	Mon-N	10	5	.667	17	17	7	3	0	134	93	5	49	64	9.6	1.54	247	.199	.276	4	.098	-1	31	34	1	4.1
1974	Mon-N☆	15	22	.405	38	38	11	1	0	253^2	255	19	80	154	12.1	4.47	86	.265	.324	11	.139	-1	-24	-18	3	-1.7
1975	Mon-N	11	12	.478	35	35	12	3	0	251^2	248	13	88	137	12.2	3.29	116	.260	.325	13	.169	1	9	15	0	1.8
1976	Mon-N	7	17	.292	33	32	8	4	1	230	212	10	69	150	11.2	3.21	116	.250	.309	11	.149	-2	7	13	5	1.8
1977	Mon-N	17	16	.515	40	40	17	4	0	301^2	272	16	81	206	10.7	3.10	123	.242	.296	10	.104	-4	27	24	4	2.4
1978	Mon-N★	13	10	.565	30	29	11	1	1	219	186	12	64	126	10.4	2.47	143	.235	.294	8	.113	-2	27	26	1	2.8
1979	Mon-N★	13	12	.520	37	37	13	**5**	0	248^2	232	14	78	143	11.4	3.00	122	.251	.312	12	.156	1	20	18	2	2.3
1980	Mon-N	16	11	.593	37	37	**14**	4	0	281	247	16	85	147	10.7	2.98	120	.238	.298	13	.160	1	19	18	-1	2.0
1981	*Mon-N	12	8	.600	22	22	7	3	0	160^2	149	7	41	87	10.8	3.42	102	.248	.298	8	.145	-1	1	1	-1	0.0
1982	Mon-N★	19	8	.704	35	35	14	4	0	277	245	12	65	179	10.3	**2.40**	**151**	.237	.286	11	.129	0	**37**	**38**	0	**4.3**
1983	Mon-N☆	17	12	.586	36	36	13	**5**	0	273	258	14	78	146	11.2	3.23	111	.252	.308	12	.146	-1	12	11	-2	0.9
1984	Mon-N	6	15	.286	31	28	1	0	0	169^1	171	12	78	64	13.3	4.31	80	.267	.348	7	.143	1	-13	-17	0	-1.6
1985	Mon-N	2	4	.333	8	7	1	0	0	38	51	1	20	18	16.8	5.68	60	.329	.406	2	.143	0	-9	-10	1	-0.8
Total	13	158	152	.510	399	393	129	37	2	2837^2	2619	151	876	1621	11.2	3.17	115	.248	.308	122	.138	-8	146	154	14	18.3
● **TOM ROGERS**	Rogers, Thomas Andrew "Shotgun" b: 2/12/1892, Sparta, Tenn. d: 3/7/36, Nashville, Tenn. BR/TR, 6'0.5", 180 lbs. Deb: 4/14/17																									
1917	StL-A	3	6	.333	24	8	3	0	0	108^2	112	2	44	27	13.2	3.89	67	.277	.352	5	.172	-1	-15	-16	-0	-1.8
1918	StL-A	8	10	.444	29	16	11	0	2	154	148	3	49	29	11.7	3.27	84	.267	.330	13	.245	2	-8	-9	2	-0.7
1919	StL-A	0	1	.000	2	0	0	0	0	1	7	0	0	1	63.0	27.00	12	.700	.700	0	—	0	-3	-3	0	-0.3
	Phi-A	4	12	.250	23	18	7	1	0	140	152	9	60	37	13.8	4.31	80	.292	.369	11	.224	-0	-17	-14	4	-1.0
	Yr	4	13	.235	25	18	7	1	0	141	159	9	60	38	14.2	4.47	77	.300	.374	11	.224	-0	-19	-16	4	-1.3
1921	*NY-A	0	1	.000	5	0	0	0	1	11	12	1	9	0	18.0	7.36	58	.300	.440	1	.333	0	-4	-4	1	-0.3
Total	4	15	30	.333	83	42	21	1	3	414^2	431	15	162	94	13.1	3.95	75	.282	.354	30	.224	1	-46	-45	6	-4.1
● **CLINT ROGGE**	Rogge, Francis Clinton b: 7/19/1889, Memphis, Mich. d: 1/6/69, Mt.Clemens, Mich. BL/TR, 5'10", 185 lbs. Deb: 4/11/15																									
1915	Pit-F	17	11	.607	37	31	17	5	0	254^1	240	6	93	93	12.1	2.55	118	.257	.330	14	.173	-0	14	13	1	1.6
1921	Cin-N	1	2	.333	6	3	0	0	0	35^1	43	2	9	12	13.2	4.08	88	.307	.349	1	.100	0	-1	-2	0	-0.1
Total	2	18	13	.581	43	34	17	5	0	289^2	283	8	102	105	12.2	2.73	113	.264	.332	15	.165	0	13	11	1	1.5
● **GARRY ROGGENBURK**	Roggenburk, Garry Earl b: 4/16/40, Cleveland, Ohio BR/TL, 6'6", 195 lbs. Deb: 4/20/63																									
1963	Min-A	2	4	.333	36	2	0	0	4	50	47	3	22	24	13.3	2.16	169	.253	.347	1	.143	0	8	8	1	0.9
1965	Min-A	1	0	1.000	12	0	0	0	2	21	21	1	12	6	14.1	3.43	104	.266	.363	0	.000	-0	0	0	-1	0.0
1966	Min-A	1	2	.333	12	0	0	0	1	12^1	14	4	10	3	17.5	5.84	62	.292	.414	0	—	0	-3	-3	0	-0.3
	Bos-A	0	0	—	1	0	0	0	0	0^1	1	0	1	0	54.0	0.00	—	.500	.667	0	—	0	0	0	0	0.0
	Yr	1	2	.333	13	0	0	0	1	12^2	15	4	11	3	18.5	5.68	63	.300	.426	0	—	0	-3	-3	0	-0.3
1968	Bos-A	0	0	—	4	0	0	0	0	8^1	9	0	3	4	13.0	2.16	146	.257	.316	0	—	0	1	1	-0	0.1
1969	Bos-A	0	1	.000	7	0	0	0	0	9^2	13	1	5	8	17.7	8.38	45	.342	.432	0	.000	-0	-5	-5	0	-0.5
	Sea-A	2	2	.500	7	4	1	0	0	24^1	27	6	11	11	14.4	4.44	82	.276	.355	1	.125	-0	-2	-2	-0	-0.3
	Yr	2	3	.400	14	4	1	0	0	34	40	7	16	19	15.1	5.56	66	.292	.370	1	.100	-1	-7	-7	0	-0.8
Total	5	6	9	.400	79	6	1	0	7	126	132	15	64	56	14.5	3.64	99	.272	.364	2	.100	-1	-1	-1	0	-0.1

YEAR	TM/L	W	L	PCT	G	GS	CG	SH	SV	IP	H	HR	BB	SO	RAT	ERA	ERA+	OAV	OOB	BH	AVG	PB	PR	/A	PD	TPI
● SAUL ROGOVIN Rogovin, Saul Walter b: 10/10/23, Brooklyn, N.Y. BR/TR, 6'2", 205 lbs. Deb: 4/28/49																										
1949	Det-A	0	1	.000	5	0	0	0	0	5^2	13	1	7	2	31.8	14.29	29	.464	.571	0	—	0	-6	-6	-0	-0.6
1950	Det-A	2	1	.667	11	5	1	0	0	40	39	5	26	11	15.1	4.50	104	.258	.374	3	.188	0	0	1	-1	0.0
1951	Det-A	1	1	.500	5	4	0	0	0	24	23	4	7	5	11.3	5.25	80	.247	.300	2	.286	1	-3	-3	0	-0.1
	Chi-A	11	7	.611	22	22	17	3	0	192^2	166	11	67	77	10.9	2.48	163	.234	.301	15	.203	-0	35	33	-1	3.5
	Yr	12	8	.600	27	26	17	3	0	216^2	189	15	74	82	11.0	**2.78**	**146**	.235	.301	17	.210	1	32	**31**	-0	3.4
1952	Chi-A	14	9	.609	33	30	12	3	1	231^2	224	14	79	121	11.9	3.85	95	.255	.318	17	.202	3	-4	-5	-0	-0.3
1953	Chi-A	7	12	.368	22	19	4	1	1	131	151	17	48	62	13.8	5.22	77	.289	.351	5	.135	-0	-18	-17	-0	-1.7
1955	Bal-A	1	8	.111	14	12	1	0	0	71	79	5	27	35	13.7	4.56	84	.288	.356	2	.091	-1	-5	-6	-0	-0.8
	Phi-N	5	3	.625	12	11	5	2	0	73	60	3	17	27	9.5	3.08	129	.230	.277	6	.250	2	8	7	-1	0.9
1956	Phi-N	7	6	.538	22	18	3	0	0	106^2	122	22	27	48	12.6	4.98	75	.282	.325	4	.111	-2	-14	-15	-1	-1.8
1957	Phi-N	0	0	—	4	0	0	0	0	8	11	1	3	0	15.8	9.00	42	.333	.389	0	—	0	-5	-5	-0	-0.5
Total	8	48	48	.500	150	121	43	9	2	883^2	888	83	308	388	12.3	4.06	96	.262	.326	54	.180	2	-12	-16	-4	-1.4
● LES ROHR Rohr, Leslie Norvin b: 3/5/46, Lowestoft, England BL/TL, 6'5", 205 lbs. Deb: 9/19/67																										
1967	NY-N	2	1	.667	3	3	0	0	0	17	13	1	9	15	11.6	2.12	160	.224	.328	0	.000	-1	2	2	-1	0.1
1968	NY-N	0	2	.000	2	1	0	0	0	6	9	0	7	5	24.0	4.50	67	.333	.471	0	—	0	-1	-1	0	-0.1
1969	NY-N	0	0	—	1	0	0	0	0	1^1	5	0	1	0	40.5	20.25	18	.625	.667	0	—	0	-2	-2	-0	-0.2
Total	3	2	3	.400	6	4	0	0	0	24^1	27	1	17	20	16.3	3.70	90	.290	.400	0	.000	-0	-1	-1	-1	-0.2
● BILLY ROHR Rohr, William Joseph b: 7/1/45, San Diego, Cal. BL/TL, 6'3", 170 lbs. Deb: 4/14/67																										
1967	Bos-A	2	3	.400	10	8	2	1	0	42^1	43	4	22	16	14.2	5.10	68	.256	.349	0	.000	-1	-9	-8	-0	-0.9
1968	Cle-A	1	0	1.000	17	0	0	0	1	18^1	18	5	10	5	13.7	6.87	43	.265	.359	0	.000	-0	-8	-8	0	-0.9
Total	2	3	3	.500	27	8	2	1	1	60^2	61	9	32	21	14.1	5.64	59	.258	.352	0	.000	-1	-17	-16	-0	-1.8
● MEL ROJAS Rojas, Melquiades (Medrano) b: 12/10/66, Haina, D.R. BR/TR, 5'11", 175 lbs. Deb: 8/01/90																										
1990	Mon-N	3	1	.750	23	0	0	0	1	40	34	5	24	26	13.5	3.60	101	.234	.351	0	.000	-0	1	0	-0	-0.1
1991	Mon-N	3	3	.500	37	0	0	0	6	48	42	4	13	37	10.5	3.75	96	.228	.283	0	.000	-0	-0	-1	-0	-0.2
1992	Mon-N	7	1	.875	68	0	0	0	10	100^2	71	2	34	70	9.6	1.43	244	.199	.272	1	.067	-1	**23**	**23**	-0	2.4
Total	3	13	5	.722	128	0	0	0	17	188^2	147	11	71	133	10.6	2.48	143	.214	.293	1	.045	-2	24	23	-1	2.1
● MINNIE ROJAS Rojas, Minervino Alejandro (Landin) b: 11/26/38, Remidios, Las Villas, Cuba BR/TR, 6'1", 170 lbs. Deb: 5/30/66																										
1966	Cal-A	7	4	.636	47	2	0	0	10	84^1	83	9	15	37	10.6	2.88	117	.262	.297	1	.071	-0	5	4	-1	0.3
1967	Cal-A	12	9	.571	72	0	0	0	**27**	121^2	106	7	38	83	10.9	2.52	125	.232	.296	1	.059	-1	10	8	-2	0.6
1968	Cal-A	4	3	.571	38	0	0	0	6	55	55	11	15	33	11.5	4.25	68	.252	.300	1	.100	-0	-8	-8	-1	-1.1
Total	3	23	16	.590	157	2	0	0	43	261	244	27	68	153	10.9	3.00	105	.246	.297	3	.073	-2	7	5	-4	-0.2
● COOKIE ROJAS Rojas, Octavio Victor (Rivas) b: 3/6/39, Havana, Cuba BR/TR, 5'10", 170 lbs. Deb: 4/10/62 MC♦																										
1967	Phi-N	0	0	—	1	0	0	0	0	1	1	0	0	0	9.0	0.00	—	.200	.200	137	.259	0	0	0	-0	0.0
● JIM ROLAND Roland, James Ivan b: 12/14/42, Franklin, N.C. BR/TL, 6'3", 190 lbs. Deb: 9/20/62																										
1962	Min-A	0	0	—	1	0	0	0	0	2	1	0	0	1	4.5	0.00	—	.143	.143	0	—	0	1	1	-0	0.1
1963	Min-A	4	1	.800	10	7	2	1	0	49	32	4	27	34	10.8	2.57	142	.185	.295	0	.000	-2	6	6	0	0.5
1964	Min-A	2	6	.250	30	13	1	0	3	94^1	76	12	55	63	12.9	4.10	87	.218	.332	4	.148	-1	-5	-6	-1	-0.8
1966	Min-A	0	0	—	1	0	0	0	0	2	0	0	0	1	0.0	0.00	—	.000	.000	0	—	0	1	1	-0	0.1
1967	Min-A	0	1	.000	25	0	0	0	2	35^2	33	3	17	16	12.6	3.03	114	.244	.329	0	.000	-0	1	2	-0	0.1
1968	Min-A	4	1	.800	28	4	1	0	0	61^2	55	3	24	36	11.8	3.50	88	.238	.315	0	.000	-1	-4	-3	1	-0.3
1969	Oak-A	5	1	.833	39	3	2	0	1	86^1	59	2	46	48	11.6	2.19	157	.197	.316	2	.095	-1	14	12	0	1.2
1970	Oak-A	3	3	.500	28	2	0	0	2	43^1	28	2	23	26	10.6	2.70	131	.181	.287	0	.000	-0	5	4	1	0.4
1971	Oak-A	1	3	.250	31	0	0	0	1	45^1	34	4	19	30	11.5	3.18	105	.214	.317	0	.000	-0	1	1	-1	0.0
1972	Oak-A	0	0	—	2	0	0	0	0	2^1	5	0	0	0	19.3	3.86	74	.455	.455	0	—	0	-0	-0	0	0.0
	NY-A	0	1	.000	16	0	0	0	0	25	27	3	16	13	15.8	5.04	58	.287	.396	0	.000	-0	-6	-6	-0	-0.7
	Tex-A	0	0	—	5	0	0	0	0	3^1	7	1	2	4	27.0	8.10	37	.412	.500	0	—	0	-2	-2	-0	-0.2
	Yr	0	1	.000	23	0	0	0	0	30^2	39	4	18	17	17.0	5.28	56	.317	.408	0	.000	-0	-8	-8	-0	-0.9
Total	10	19	17	.528	216	29	6	1	9	450^1	357	34	229	272	12.1	3.22	106	.218	.321	6	.071	-5	12	10	-1	0.4
● JOSE ROMAN Roman, Jose Rafael (Sarita) b: 5/21/63, Santo Domingo, D.R. BR/TR, 6', 175 lbs. Deb: 9/05/84																										
1984	Cle-A	0	2	.000	3	2	0	0	0	6	9	1	11	3	30.0	18.00	23	.391	.588	0	—	0	-9	-9	-0	-0.9
1985	Cle-A	0	4	.000	5	3	0	0	0	16^1	13	3	14	12	14.9	6.61	63	.200	.342	0	—	0	-4	-4	-0	-0.4
1986	Cle-A	1	2	.333	6	5	0	0	0	22	23	3	17	9	16.8	6.55	63	.280	.410	0	—	0	-6	-6	-1	-0.6
Total	3	1	8	.111	14	10	0	0	0	44^1	45	7	42	24	17.9	8.12	51	.265	.413	0	—	0	-20	-20	-1	-1.9
● RON ROMANICK Romanick, Ronald James b: 11/6/60, Burley, Idaho BR/TR, 6'4", 195 lbs. Deb: 4/05/84																										
1984	Cal-A	12	12	.500	33	33	8	2	0	229^2	240	23	61	87	12.0	3.76	105	.270	.320	0	—	0	6	5	-2	0.4
1985	Cal-A	14	9	.609	31	31	6	1	0	195	210	29	62	64	12.7	4.11	100	.280	.338	0	—	0	1	0	-3	-0.3
1986	Cal-A	5	8	.385	18	18	1	1	0	106^1	124	13	44	38	14.2	5.50	75	.297	.364	0	—	0	-16	-16	-1	-1.6
Total	3	31	29	.517	82	82	15	4	0	531	574	65	167	189	12.7	4.24	96	.279	.336	0	—	0	-9	-11	-6	-1.5
● JIM ROMANO Romano, James King b: 4/6/27, Brooklyn, N.Y. d: 9/12/90, New York, N.Y. BR/TR, 6'4", 190 lbs. Deb: 9/21/50																										
1950	Bro-N	0	0	—	3	1	0	0	0	6^1	8	0	2	8	14.2	5.68	72	.296	.345	0	.000	-0	-1	-1	0	-0.1
● DUTCH ROMBERGER Romberger, Allen Isaiah b: 5/26/27, Klingerstown, Pa. d: 5/26/83, Weikert, Pa. BR/TR, 6', 185 lbs. Deb: 5/31/54																										
1954	Phi-A	1	1	.500	10	0	0	0	0	15^2	28	3	12	6	23.0	11.49	34	.406	.494	0	.000	0	-14	-13	-0	-1.3
● RAMON ROMERO Romero, Ramon (De Los Santos) b: 1/8/59, San Pedro De Macoris, D.R. BL/TL, 6'4", 170 lbs. Deb: 9/18/84																										
1984	Cle-A	0	0	—	1	0	0	0	0	3	0	0	0	3	3.0	0.00	—	.000	.111	0	—	0	1	1	-0	0.1
1985	Cle-A	2	3	.400	19	10	0	0	0	64^1	69	13	38	38	15.7	6.58	63	.276	.382	0	—	0	-17	-17	-1	-1.7
Total	2	2	3	.400	20	10	0	0	0	67^1	69	13	38	41	15.1	6.28	66	.267	.374	0	—	0	-16	-16	-1	-1.6
● EDDIE ROMMEL Rommel, Edwin Americus b: 9/13/1897, Baltimore, Md. d: 8/26/70, Baltimore, Md. BR/TR, 6'2", 197 lbs. Deb: 4/19/20 CU																										
1920	Phi-A	7	7	.500	33	12	8	2	1	173^2	165	5	43	43	11.0	2.85	141	.259	.309	11	.216	-0	18	23	5	2.8
1921	Phi-A	16	23	.410	46	32	20	0	3	285^1	312	21	87	71	12.6	3.94	113	.284	.337	18	.191	-2	11	16	3	1.6
1922	Phi-A	**27**	13	.675	**51**	33	22	3	2	294	294	21	63	54	11.1	3.28	130	.267	.309	17	.181	-3	25	32	3	3.2
1923	Phi-A	18	19	.486	**56**	31	19	3	5	297^2	306	14	108	76	12.6	3.27	126	.271	.336	24	.238	1	24	28	6	**3.5**
1924	Phi-A	18	15	.545	43	34	21	3	1	278	302	8	94	72	12.9	3.95	108	.284	.344	15	.158	-6	9	10	8	1.1
1925	Phi-A	**21**	10	.677	52	28	14	1	3	261	285	10	95	67	13.3	3.69	126	.281	.346	15	.185	-1	20	28	5	3.0
1926	Phi-A	11	11	.500	37	26	12	3	0	219	225	10	54	52	11.5	3.08	135	.268	.314	6	.098	-4	23	26	2	2.5
1927	Phi-A	11	3	.786	30	17	8	2	1	146^2	166	6	48	33	13.3	4.36	98	.286	.343	8	.157	-3	-4	-2	3	-0.1
1928	Phi-A	13	5	.722	43	11	6	0	4	173^2	177	11	26	37	10.6	3.06	131	.266	.295	12	.255	3	19	18	3	2.4
1929	*Phi-A	12	2	.857	32	6	4	0	4	113^2	135	10	34	25	13.5	2.85	148	.294	.344	8	.205	-0	18	17	1	1.7
1930	Phi-A	9	4	.692	35	9	5	0	3	130^1	142	11	27	35	11.7	4.28	109	.277	.315	10	.263	3	5	6	1	0.9
1931	*Phi-A	7	5	.583	25	10	8	1	0	118	136	5	27	18	12.5	2.97	151	.291	.331	14	.259	2	18	20	-0	2.1
1932	Phi-A	1	2	.333	17	0	0	0	2	65^1	84	6	18	16	14.1	5.51	82	.315	.358	6	.300	2	-7	-7	2	-0.3
Total	13	171	119	.590	500	249	147	18	29	2556^1	2729	138	724	599	12.3	3.54	122	.277	.329	164	.199	-8	179	217	42	24.4

YEAR	TM/L	W	L	PCT	G	GS	CG	SH	SV	IP	H	HR	BB	SO	RAT	ERA	ERA+	OAV	OOB	BH	AVG	PB	PR	/A	PD	TPI
● **ENRIQUE ROMO**	Romo, Enrique (Navarro) b: 7/15/47, Santa Rosalia, Mex BR/TR, 5'11", 185 lbs. Deb: 4/07/77 F																									
1977	Sea-A	8	10	.444	58	3	0	0	16	114^{1}	93	8	39	105	10.8	2.83	145	.227	.302	0	—	0	16	16	1	1.7
1978	Sea-A	11	7	.611	56	0	0	0	10	107^{1}	88	12	39	62	11.1	3.69	103	.227	.306	0	—	0	1	1	-1	0.0
1979	*Pit-N	10	5	.667	84	0	0	0	5	129^{1}	122	11	43	106	11.7	2.99	130	.253	.318	2	.167	-0	11	13	2	1.5
1980	Pit-N	5	5	.500	74	0	0	0	11	123^{2}	117	10	28	82	10.6	3.27	111	.252	.296	5	.455	3	4	5	1	0.9
1981	Pit-N	1	3	.250	33	0	0	0	9	41^{2}	47	5	18	23	14.0	4.54	79	.288	.359	0	.000	-0	-5	-4	-0	-0.6
1982	Pit-N	9	3	.750	45	0	0	0	1	86^{2}	81	11	36	58	12.3	4.36	85	.245	.322	3	.300	1	-7	-6	-0	-0.6
Total	6	44	33	.571	350	3	0	0	52	603	548	57	203	436	11.4	3.45	111	.245	.312	10	.270	4	19	25	2	2.9
● **VICENTE ROMO**	Romo, Vicente (Navarro) "Huevo" b: 4/12/43, Santa Rosalia, Mex. BR/TR, 6'1", 195 lbs. Deb: 4/11/68 F																									
1968	LA-N	0	0	—	1	0	0	0	0	1	1	0	0	0	9.0	0.00	—	.250	.250	0	—	0	0	0	-0	0.0
	Cle-A	5	3	.625	40	1	0	0	12	83^{1}	43	5	32	54	8.3	1.62	183	.154	.245	2	.143	-0	13	12	-0	1.4
1969	Cle-A	1	1	.500	3	0	0	0	0	8	7	0	3	7	11.3	2.25	167	.233	.303	1	.500	0	1	1	-0	0.2
	Bos-A	7	9	.438	52	11	4	1	11	127^{1}	116	14	50	89	11.8	3.18	120	.247	.321	4	.129	-1	6	9	0	0.9
	Yr	8	10	.444	55	11	4	1	11	135^{1}	123	14	53	96	11.8	3.13	122	.246	.319	5	.152	-0	7	10	0	1.1
1970	Bos-A	7	3	.700	48	10	0	0	6	108	115	14	43	71	13.2	4.08	97	.273	.340	4	.148	0	-4	-1	1	-0.1
1971	Chi-A	1	7	.125	45	2	0	0	5	72	52	5	37	48	11.1	3.38	106	.202	.303	4	.364	1	1	2	1	0.5
1972	Chi-A	3	0	1.000	28	0	0	0	1	51^{2}	47	5	18	46	11.5	3.31	94	.246	.314	0	.000	-1	-1	-1	1	-0.1
1973	SD-N	2	3	.400	49	1	0	0	7	87^{2}	85	11	46	51	13.4	3.70	94	.260	.351	2	.125	-0	-0	-2	0	-0.2
1974	SD-N	5	5	.500	54	1	0	0	9	71	78	6	37	26	14.8	4.56	78	.290	.380	0	.000	-1	-7	-8	2	-0.7
1982	LA-N	1	2	.333	15	6	0	0	1	35^{2}	25	1	14	24	10.3	3.03	114	.195	.285	1	.200	0	2	2	1	0.2
Total	8	32	33	.492	335	32	4	1	52	645^{2}	569	61	280	416	11.9	3.36	106	.239	.322	18	.149	-1	10	13	5	2.1
● **JOHN ROMONOSKY**	Romonosky, John b: 7/7/29, Harrisburg, Ill. BR/TR, 6'2", 195 lbs. Deb: 9/06/53																									
1953	StL-N	0	0	—	2	2	0	0	0	7^{2}	9	1	4	3	16.4	4.70	91	.281	.378	0	.000	-0	-0	-0	-0	-0.1
1958	Was-A	2	4	.333	18	5	1	0	0	55^{1}	52	6	28	38	13.0	6.51	59	.243	.331	4	.308	2	-17	-17	0	-1.4
1959	Was-A	1	0	1.000	12	2	0	0	0	38^{1}	36	4	19	22	13.6	3.29	119	.254	.354	2	.182	0	2	3	-0	0.3
Total	3	3	4	.429	32	9	1	0	0	101^{1}	97	11	51	63	13.5	5.15	75	.250	.343	6	.231	2	-15	-14	-0	-1.2
● **GILBERTO RONDON**	Rondon, Gilberto b: 11/18/53, Bronx, N.Y. BR/TR, 6'2", 200 lbs. Deb: 4/10/76 F																									
1976	Hou-N	2	2	.500	19	7	0	0	0	53^{2}	70	6	39	21	18.3	5.70	56	.315	.418	4	.286	1	-13	-15	-1	-1.5
1979	Chi-A	0	0	—	4	0	0	0	0	9^{2}	11	2	6	3	15.8	3.72	114	.282	.378	0	—	0	1	1	-0	0.0
Total	2	2	2	.500	23	7	0	0	0	63^{1}	81	8	45	24	17.9	5.40	62	.310	.412	4	.286	1	-13	-14	-1	-1.5
● **JIM ROOKER**	Rooker, James Phillip b: 9/23/41, Lakeview, Ore. BR/TL, 6', 201 lbs. Deb: 6/30/68																									
1968	Det-A	0	0	—	2	0	0	0	0	4^{2}	4	0	1	4	9.6	3.86	78	.235	.278	0	.000	-0	-0	-0	0	0.0
1969	KC-A	4	16	.200	28	22	8	1	0	158^{1}	136	13	73	108	11.9	3.75	98	.229	.315	16	.281	8	-2	-1	-1	0.7
1970	KC-A	10	15	.400	38	29	6	3	1	203^{2}	190	11	102	117	12.9	3.54	106	.252	.341	14	.200	3	4	5	-0	0.8
1971	KC-A	2	7	.222	20	7	1	1	0	54	59	2	24	31	14.0	5.33	64	.284	.361	0	.000	-0	-11	-11	-1	-1.3
1972	KC-A	5	6	.455	18	10	4	2	0	72	78	3	24	44	12.9	4.38	69	.280	.339	2	.100	-1	-11	-11	1	-1.2
1973	Pit-N	10	6	.625	41	18	6	3	5	170^{1}	143	12	52	122	10.4	2.85	123	.229	.290	12	.245	3	15	13	1	1.7
1974	*Pit-N	15	11	.577	33	33	15	1	0	262^{2}	228	11	83	139	10.8	2.78	124	.238	.301	29	.305	10	25	20	1	3.4
1975	*Pit-N	13	11	.542	28	28	7	1	0	196^{2}	177	16	76	102	11.7	2.97	119	.238	.311	6	.095	-3	14	12	0	1.0
1976	Pit-N	15	8	.652	30	29	10	1	1	198^{2}	201	12	72	92	12.5	3.35	104	.263	.328	16	.216	3	3	3	-1	0.6
1977	Pit-N	14	9	.609	30	30	7	2	0	204^{1}	196	24	64	89	11.5	3.08	129	.253	.310	13	.186	0	19	20	-2	2.0
1978	Pit-N	9	11	.450	28	28	1	0	0	163^{1}	160	13	81	76	13.4	4.24	87	.259	.348	9	.161	0	-12	-10	1	-0.9
1979	*Pit-N	4	7	.364	19	17	1	0	0	103^{2}	106	11	39	44	12.6	4.60	84	.266	.331	4	.121	-1	-10	-8	-1	-1.0
1980	Pit-N	2	2	.500	4	4	0	0	0	18	16	0	12	8	14.0	3.50	104	.262	.384	1	.143	1	0	0	0	0.1
Total	13	103	109	.486	319	255	66	15	7	1810^{1}	1694	128	703	976	12.0	3.46	104	.249	.321	122	.201	22	34	30	-2	5.9
● **CHARLIE ROOT**	Root, Charles Henry "Chinski" b: 3/17/1899, Middletown, Ohio d: 11/5/70, Hollister, Cal. BR/TR, 5'10.5", 190 lbs. Deb: 4/18/23 C																									
1923	StL-A	0	4	.000	27	2	0	0	0	60	68	4	18	27	13.8	5.70	73	.302	.369	1	.077	-1	-11	-10	-1	-1.1
1926	Chi-N	18	17	.514	42	32	21	2	2	271^{1}	267	10	62	127	11.1	2.82	136	.264	.310	13	.143	-4	30	31	-1	2.6
1927	Chi-N	**26**	15	.634	**48**	36	21	4	2	**309**	296	16	117	145	12.3	3.76	103	.254	.326	27	.221	3	6	4	-4	0.2
1928	Chi-N	14	18	.438	40	30	13	1	2	237	214	15	73	122	11.2	3.57	108	.242	.305	13	.178	-0	11	7	-3	0.4
1929	*Chi-N	19	6	**.760**	43	31	19	4	5	272	286	12	83	124	12.3	3.47	133	.275	.330	15	.156	0	38	35	-4	2.8
1930	Chi-N	16	14	.533	37	30	15	**4**	3	220^{1}	247	17	63	124	12.9	4.33	113	.281	.334	21	.262	5	16	14	-3	1.4
1931	Chi-N	17	14	.548	39	31	19	3	2	251	240	7	71	131	11.4	3.48	111	.252	.309	20	.222	3	11	11	-3	1.1
1932	*Chi-N	15	10	.600	39	23	11	0	3	216^{1}	211	10	55	96	11.3	3.58	105	.253	.303	13	.171	-1	7	5	-3	0.0
1933	Chi-N	15	10	.600	35	30	20	2	0	242^{1}	232	14	61	86	11.3	2.60	126	.252	.306	8	.094	-4	20	18	-3	1.2
1934	Chi-N	4	7	.364	34	9	2	0	0	117^{2}	141	8	53	46	15.2	4.28	90	.298	.375	7	.175	1	-3	-5	-1	-0.4
1935	*Chi-N	15	8	.652	38	18	11	1	2	201^{1}	193	15	47	94	10.9	3.08	127	.252	.298	14	.203	2	21	19	-3	1.8
1936	Chi-N	3	6	.333	33	4	0	0	1	73^{2}	81	3	20	32	12.6	4.15	96	.280	.331	5	.333	1	-1	-1	-1	-0.1
1937	Chi-N	13	5	.722	43	15	5	0	5	178^{2}	173	18	32	74	10.5	3.38	118	.253	.290	12	.179	0	11	12	-1	1.1
1938	*Chi-N	8	7	.533	44	11	5	0	8	160^{2}	163	10	30	70	10.9	2.86	134	.258	.294	8	.167	-0	17	17	-2	1.5
1939	Chi-N	8	8	.500	35	16	8	0	4	167^{1}	189	11	34	65	12.1	4.03	98	.286	.323	10	.175	2	-2	-2	-3	-0.3
1940	Chi-N	2	4	.333	36	8	1	0	1	112	118	9	33	50	12.2	3.86	97	.265	.317	4	.129	-1	-0	-1	-0	-0.2
1941	Chi-N	8	7	.533	19	15	6	0	0	106^{2}	133	8	37	46	14.3	5.40	65	.306	.360	5	.152	2	-21	-22	-1	-2.1
Total	17	201	160	.557	632	341	177	21	40	3197^{1}	3252	187	889	1459	11.9	3.59	110	.264	.318	196	.180	8	148	129	-35	9.9
● **CHUCK ROSE**	Rose, Charles Alfred b: 9/1/1885, Macon, Mo. d: 8/4/61, Salina, Kan. BL/TL, 5'8.5", 158 lbs. Deb: 9/13/09																									
1909	StL-A	1	2	.333	3	3	3	0	0	25	32	1	7	6	15.1	5.40	45	.330	.393	0	.000	-1	-8	-8	-1	-0.9
● **DON ROSE**	Rose, Donald Gary b: 3/19/47, Covina, Cal. BR/TR, 6'3", 195 lbs. Deb: 9/15/71																									
1971	NY-N	0	0	—	1	0	0	0	0	2	2	0	0	1	9.0	0.00	—	.286	.286	0	—	0	1	1	-0	0.1
1972	Cal-A	1	4	.200	16	4	0	0	0	42^{2}	49	9	19	39	14.3	4.22	69	.283	.354	2	.200	1	-5	-6	-0	-0.6
1974	SF-N	0	0	—	2	0	0	0	0	1	4	0	1	0	45.0	9.00	42	.667	.714	0	—	0	-1	-1	0	-0.1
Total	3	1	4	.200	19	4	0	0	0	45^{2}	55	9	20	40	14.8	4.14	71	.296	.364	2	.200	1	-5	-6	-1	-0.6
● **ZEKE ROSEBRAUGH**	Rosebraugh, Eli Ethelbert b: 9/8/1870, Charleston, Ill. d: 7/16/30, Fresno, Cal. TL, Deb: 9/21/1898																									
1898	Pit-N	0	2	.000	4	2	2	0	0	21^{2}	23	0	9	6	14.5	3.32	107	.270	.360	3	.375	1	1	1	-0	0.1
1899	Pit-N	0	1	.000	2	2	0	0	0	6	14	0	3	2	27.0	9.00	42	.451	.513	0	.000	-0	-3	-3	-0	-0.3
Total	2	0	3	.000	6	4	2	0	0	27^{2}	37	0	12	8	17.2	4.55	79	.318	.401	3	.300	1	-3	-3	-0	-0.2
● **CHIEF ROSEMAN**	Roseman, James John b: 1856, New York, N.Y. d: 7/4/38, Brooklyn, N.Y. BR/TR, 5'7", 167 lbs. Deb: 5/01/1882 M♦																									
1885	NY-a	0	1	.000	1	1	0	0	0	1	3	0	2	0	45.0	27.00	11	.333	.455	114	.278	0	-3	-3	0	-0.2
1886	NY-a	0	0	—	1	0	0	0	0	7	6	0	0	0	7.7	5.14	66	.240	.240	127	.227	0	-1	-1	0	-0.1
1887	NY-a	0	0	—	2	0	0	0	0	8	11	0	5	1	20.3	7.88	54	.407	.529	55	.228	-0	-3	-3	-0	-0.3
Total	3	0	1	.000	4	1	0	0	0	16	20	0	7	1	16.3	7.88	48	.328	.414	726	.263	0	-7	-7	-0	-0.6
● **STEVE ROSENBERG**	Rosenberg, Steven Allen b: 10/31/64, Brooklyn, N.Y. BL/TL, 6', 186 lbs. Deb: 6/04/88																									
1988	Chi-A	0	1	.000	33	0	0	0	1	46	53	5	19	28	14.1	4.30	92	.298	.365	0	—	0	-2	-2	-0	-0.2
1989	Chi-A	4	13	.235	38	21	2	0	0	142	148	14	58	77	13.1	4.94	77	.273	.344	0	—	0	-17	-18	0	-1.8
1990	Chi-A	1	0	1.000	6	0	0	0	0	10	10	2	5	4	13.5	5.40	71	.256	.341	0	—	0	-2	-2	0	-0.2
1991	SD-N	1	1	.500	10	0	0	0	0	11^{2}	11	3	5	6	12.3	6.94	55	.250	.327	0	.000	-0	-4	-4	-0	-0.5

YEAR	TM/L	W	L	PCT	G	GS	CG	SH	SV	IP	H	HR	BB	SO	RAT	ERA	ERA+	OAV	OOB	BH	AVG	PB	PR	/A	PD	TPI
Total	4	6	15	.286	87	21	2	0	1	209^2	222	24	87	115	13.3	4.94	78	.276	.348	0	.000	-0	-24	-26	-0	-2.7
● **WAYNE ROSENTHAL**	Rosenthal, Wayne Scott b: 2/19/65, Brooklyn, N.Y. BR/TR, 6'5", 220 lbs. Deb: 6/26/91																									
1991	Tex-A	1	4	.200	36	0	0	0	1	70^1	72	9	36	61	13.9	5.25	77	.257	.344	0	—	0	-9	-10	-1	-1.0
1992	Tex-A	0	0	—	6	0	0	0	0	4^2	7	1	2	1	17.4	7.71	50	.333	.391	0	—	0	-2	-2	0	-0.2
Total	2	1	4	.200	42	0	0	0	1	75	79	10	38	62	14.2	5.40	74	.262	.347	0	—	0	-11	-12	-1	-1.2
● **STEVE ROSER**	Roser, Emerson Corey b: 1/25/18, Rome, N.Y. BR/TR, 6'4", 220 lbs. Deb: 5/05/44																									
1944	NY-A	4	3	.571	16	6	1	0	1	84	80	3	34	34	12.2	3.86	90	.256	.329	3	.100	-2	-4	-3	-1	-0.6
1945	NY-A	0	0	—	11	0	0	0	0	27	27	1	8	11	11.7	3.67	94	.262	.315	1	.125	-0	-1	-1	0	-0.1
1946	NY-A	1	1	.500	4	1	0	0	0	3^1	7	0	4	1	29.7	16.20	21	.438	.550	0	—	0	-5	-5	-0	-0.5
	Bos-N	1	1	.500	14	1	0	0	1	35	33	1	18	18	13.1	3.60	95	.250	.340	0	.000	-1	-1	-1	-0	-0.2
Total	3	6	5	.545	45	8	1	0	2	149^1	147	5	64	64	12.7	4.04	86	.261	.336	4	.093	-3	-10	-9	-1	-1.4
● **BUSTER ROSS**	Ross, Chester Franklin b: 3/11/03, Kuttawa, Ky. d: 4/24/82, Mayfield, Ky. BL/TL, 6'1", 195 lbs. Deb: 6/15/24																									
1924	Bos-A	4	3	.571	30	2	1	1	1	93^1	109	3	30	16	13.4	3.47	126	.307	.361	5	.200	-0	8	9	-1	0.8
1925	Bos-A	3	8	.273	33	8	0	0	0	94^1	119	9	40	15	15.6	6.20	73	.313	.386	3	.125	-1	-19	-17	-1	-1.8
1926	Bos-A	0	1	.000	1	0	0	0	0	2^2	5	0	4	0	30.4	16.88	24	.385	.529	0	.000	-0	-4	-4	0	-0.3
Total	3	7	12	.368	64	10	1	1	1	190^1	233	12	74	31	14.8	5.01	89	.311	.377	8	.160	-2	-15	-12	-2	-1.3
● **CLIFF ROSS**	Ross, Clifford Davis b: 8/3/28, Philadelphia, Pa. BL/TL, 6'4", 195 lbs. Deb: 9/11/54																									
1954	Cin-N	0	0	—	4	0	0	0	1	2^2	0	0	0	1	0.0	0.00	—	.000	.000	0	—	0	1	1	0	0.1
● **ERNIE ROSS**	Ross, Ernest Bertram "Curly" b: 3/31/1880, Toronto, Ont., Can. d: 3/28/50, Toronto, Ont., Can. BL/TL, 5'8", 150 lbs. Deb: 9/17/02																									
1902	Bal-A	1	1	.500	2	2	2	0	0	17	20	0	12	2	17.5	7.41	51	.293	.406	0	.000	-1	-7	-7	-1	-0.7
● **BOB ROSS**	Ross, Floyd Robert b: 11/2/28, Fullerton, Cal. BR/TL, 6', 165 lbs. Deb: 6/16/50																									
1950	Was-A	0	1	.000	6	2	0	0	0	12^2	15	1	15	2	21.3	8.53	53	.300	.462	0	.000	-0	-6	-6	0	-0.5
1951	Was-A	0	1	.000	11	1	0	0	0	31^2	36	3	21	23	16.2	6.54	63	.295	.399	1	.111	-0	-8	-9	-1	-0.9
1956	Phi-N	0	0	—	3	0	0	0	0	3^1	4	1	2	4	16.2	8.10	46	.333	.429	0	—	0	-2	-2	0	-0.1
Total	3	0	2	.000	20	3	0	0	0	47^2	55	5	38	29	17.6	7.17	58	.299	.419	1	.083	-1	-16	-16	-0	-1.5
● **GARY ROSS**	Ross, Gary Douglas b: 9/16/47, McKeesport, Pa. BR/TR, 6'1", 190 lbs. Deb: 6/28/68																									
1968	Chi-N	1	1	.500	13	5	1	0	0	41	44	1	25	31	15.1	4.17	76	.288	.388	1	.091	-1	-5	-5	0	-0.6
1969	Chi-N	0	0	—	2	1	0	0	0	2	1	0	2	2	13.5	13.50	30	.143	.333	0	—	0	-2	-2	-0	-0.2
	SD-N	3	12	.200	46	7	0	0	3	109^2	104	5	56	58	13.5	4.19	84	.252	.348	0	.000	-2	-7	-8	2	-0.9
	Yr	3	12	.200	48	8	0	0	3	111^2	105	5	58	60	13.5	4.35	81	.250	.348	0	.000	-2	-9	-10	2	-1.1
1970	SD-N	2	3	.400	33	2	0	0	1	62^1	72	8	36	39	16.0	5.20	76	.305	.404	4	.500	2	-8	-8	1	-0.6
1971	SD-N	1	3	.250	13	0	0	0	0	24^1	27	0	11	13	14.4	2.96	111	.300	.382	0	.000	-0	1	1	0	0.1
1972	SD-N	4	3	.571	60	0	0	0	3	91^2	87	2	49	46	13.7	2.45	134	.261	.363	2	.154	-0	10	8	1	1.0
1973	SD-N	4	4	.500	58	0	0	0	0	76^1	93	8	33	44	15.3	5.42	64	.304	.379	0	.000	-0	-15	-17	0	-1.7
1974	SD-N	0	0	—	9	0	0	0	0	18	23	1	6	11	14.5	4.50	79	.315	.367	0	.000	-0	-2	-2	0	-0.2
1975	Cal-A	0	1	.000	1	1	0	0	0	5	6	1	1	4	12.6	5.40	66	.273	.304	0	—	0	-1	-1	-0	0.0
1976	Cal-A	8	16	.333	34	31	7	2	0	225	224	12	58	100	11.5	3.00	111	.258	.308	0	—	0	13	8	5	1.4
1977	Cal-A	2	4	.333	14	12	0	0	0	58^1	83	10	11	30	14.8	5.55	70	.337	.371	0	—	0	-10	-11	1	-1.0
Total	10	25	47	.347	283	59	8	2	7	713^2	764	48	288	378	13.6	3.92	89	.278	.352	7	.115	-2	-26	-36	9	-2.7
● **GEORGE ROSS**	Ross, George Sidney b: 6/27/1892, San Rafael, Cal. d: 4/22/35, Amityville, N.Y. BL/TL, 5'10.5", 175 lbs. Deb: 6/27/18																									
1918	NY-N	0	0	—	1	0	0	0	1	2^1	2	0	3	2	19.3	0.00	—	.222	.417	0	.000	-0	1	1	0	0.1
● **BUCK ROSS**	Ross, Lee Ravon b: 2/2/15, Norwood, N.C. d: 11/23/78, Charlotte, N.C. BR/TR, 6'2", 170 lbs. Deb: 5/07/36																									
1936	Phi-A	9	14	.391	30	27	12	1	0	200^2	253	17	83	47	15.1	5.83	88	.304	.367	12	.169	-1	-18	-16	-2	-1.6
1937	Phi-A	5	10	.333	28	22	7	1	0	147^1	183	12	63	37	15.1	4.89	96	.306	.373	5	.102	-3	-4	-3	0	-0.5
1938	Phi-A	9	16	.360	29	28	10	0	0	184^1	218	23	80	54	14.5	5.32	91	.289	.357	12	.190	-0	-11	-10	-0	-0.9
1939	Phi-A	6	14	.300	29	28	6	1	0	174	216	17	95	43	16.1	6.00	78	.302	.384	12	.207	-1	-27	-25	-2	-2.4
1940	Phi-A	5	10	.333	24	19	10	0	1	156^1	160	15	60	43	12.7	4.38	102	.256	.322	7	.132	-2	0	1	-1	-0.2
1941	Phi-A	0	1	.000	1	1	0	0	0	4	10	2	2	0	27.0	18.00	23	.435	.480	0	.000	-0	-6	-6	0	-0.5
	Chi-A	3	8	.273	20	11	7	0	0	108^1	99	6	43	30	11.9	3.16	130	.239	.312	7	.219	1	12	11	-2	1.0
	Yr	3	9	.250	21	12	7	0	0	112^1	109	8	45	30	12.4	3.69	111	.249	.321	7	.212	1	6	5	-2	0.5
1942	Chi-A	5	7	.417	22	14	4	2	1	113^1	118	6	39	37	12.5	5.00	72	.264	.323	6	.158	0	-17	-18	-3	-2.0
1943	Chi-A	11	7	.611	21	21	7	1	0	149^1	140	6	56	41	11.9	3.19	105	.253	.324	4	.087	-1	2	2	-1	0.0
1944	Chi-A	2	7	.222	20	9	2	0	0	90^1	97	7	35	20	13.4	5.18	66	.280	.350	2	.077	-2	-18	-18	-2	-2.2
1945	Chi-A	1	1	.500	13	2	0	0	0	37^1	51	3	17	8	16.4	5.79	57	.327	.393	2	.182	-0	-10	-10	-1	-1.1
Total	10	56	95	.371	237	182	65	6	2	1365^1	1545	114	573	360	14.0	4.94	88	.283	.351	69	.154	-11	-97	-91	-13	-10.4
● **MARK ROSS**	Ross, Mark Joseph b: 8/8/57, Galveston, Tex. BR/TR, 6', 195 lbs. Deb: 9/12/82																									
1982	Hou-N	0	0	—	4	0	0	0	0	6	3	0	0	4	4.5	1.50	221	.143	.143	0	—	0	1	1	0	0.1
1984	Hou-N	1	0	1.000	2	0	0	0	0	2^1	1	0	0	1	3.9	0.00	—	.125	.125	0	—	0	1	1	-0	0.1
1985	Hou-N	0	2	.000	8	0	0	0	1	13	12	2	2	3	9.7	4.85	71	.240	.269	0	.000	-0	-2	-2	0	-0.2
1987	Pit-N	0	0	—	1	0	0	0	0	1	1	1	0	0	9.0	9.00	46	.250	.250	0	—	0	-1	-1	0	0.0
1988	Tor-A	0	0	—	3	0	0	0	0	7^1	5	0	4	4	11.0	4.91	80	.185	.290	0	—	0	-1	-1	-0	-0.1
1990	Pit-N	1	0	1.000	9	0	0	0	0	12^2	11	2	4	5	10.7	3.55	102	.244	.306	0	.000	-0	0	0	0	0.0
Total	6	2	2	.500	27	0	0	0	1	42^1	33	5	10	17	9.1	3.83	93	.213	.261	0	.000	-0	-0	-1	0	-0.1
● **FRANK ROSSO**	Rosso, Francis James b: 3/1/21, Agawam, Mass. d: 1/26/80, Ulrichsville, O. BR/TR, 5'11", 180 lbs. Deb: 9/15/44																									
1944	NY-N	0	0	—	2	0	0	0	0	4	11	0	3	1	31.5	9.00	41	.550	.609	0	—	0	-2	-2	0	-0.2
● **MARV ROTBLATT**	Rotblatt, Marvin "Rotty" b: 10/18/27, Chicago, Ill. BB/TL, 5'7", 160 lbs. Deb: 7/04/48																									
1948	Chi-A	0	1	.000	7	2	0	0	0	18^1	19	0	23	4	21.1	7.85	54	.271	.457	0	.000	-0	-7	-7	-1	-0.7
1950	Chi-A	0	0	—	2	0	0	0	0	8^2	11	2	5	6	16.6	6.23	72	.344	.432	0	.000	-0	-2	-2	0	-0.1
1951	Chi-A	4	2	.667	26	2	0	0	2	47^2	44	4	23	20	12.8	3.40	119	.244	.333	0	.000	-2	4	3	1	0.3
Total	3	4	3	.571	35	4	0	0	2	74^2	74	6	51	30	15.3	4.82	86	.262	.379	0	.000	-2	-5	-6	1	-0.5
● **JACK ROTHROCK**	Rothrock, John Houston b: 3/14/05, Long Beach, Cal. d: 2/2/80, San Bernardino, Cal BB/TR, 5'11.5", 165 lbs. Deb: 7/28/25 ♦																									
1928	Bos-A	0	0	—	1	0	0	0	0	1	0	0	0	0	0.0	0.00	—	.000	.000	92	.267	0	0	0	0	0.1
● **LARRY ROTHSCHILD**	Rothschild, Lawrence Lee b: 3/12/54, Chicago, Ill. BL/TR, 6'2", 180 lbs. Deb: 9/11/81 C																									
1981	Det-A	0	0	—	5	0	0	0	1	5^2	4	0	6	1	15.9	1.59	237	.200	.385	0	—	0	1	1	0	0.2
1982	Det-A	0	0	—	2	0	0	0	0	2^2	4	1	2	0	20.3	13.50	30	.333	.429	0	—	0	-3	-3	-0	-0.3
Total	2	0	0	—	7	0	0	0	1	8^1	8	1	8	1	17.3	5.40	72	.250	.400	0	—	0	-1	-1	0	-0.1
● **GENE ROUNSAVILLE**	Rounsaville, Virle Gene b: 9/27/44, Konawa, Okla. BR/TR, 6'3", 205 lbs. Deb: 4/07/70																									
1970	Chi-A	0	1	.000	8	0	0	0	0	6^1	10	1	2	3	17.1	9.95	39	.357	.400	0	—	0	-4	-4	-0	-0.4
● **JACK ROWAN**	Rowan, John Albert b: 6/16/1887, New Castle, Pa. d: 9/29/66, Dayton, Ohio BR/TR, 6'1", 210 lbs. Deb: 9/06/06																									
1906	Det-A	0	1	.000	1	1	1	0	0	9	15	0	6	0	21.0	11.00	25	.373	.455	1	.250	0	-8	-8	-0	-0.6

YEAR	TM/L	W	L	PCT	G	GS	CG	SH	SV	IP	H	HR	BB	SO	RAT	ERA	ERA+	OAV	OOB	BH	AVG	PB	PR	/A	PD	TPI
1908	Cin-N	3	3	.500	8	7	4	1	0	49^1	46	0	16	24	11.3	1.82	126	.253	.313	1	.071	-0	3	3	1	0.3
1909	Cin-N	11	12	.478	38	23	14	0	0	225^2	185	0	104	81	11.6	2.79	93	.233	.324	6	.092	-1	-5	-5	-5	-1.2
1910	Cin-N	14	13	.519	42	30	18	4	1	261	242	4	105	108	12.3	2.93	99	.254	.334	19	.229	3	3	-0	-4	-0.2
1911	Phi-N	2	4	.333	12	6	2	0	0	45^2	59	3	20	17	15.8	4.73	73	.316	.385	1	.077	-1	-7	-7	1	-0.7
	Chi-N	0	0	—	1	0	0	0	0	2	1	0	2	0	18.0	4.50	74	.143	.400	0	.000	-0	-0	-0	0	0.0
	Yr	2	4	.333	13	6	2	0	0	47^2	60	3	22	17	15.7	4.72	73	.308	.381	1	.071	-1	-7	-7	1	-0.7
1913	Cin-N	0	4	.000	5	5	5	0	0	39	37	0	9	21	10.8	3.00	108	.264	.313	2	.182	1	1	1	-0	0.2
1914	Cin-N	1	3	.250	12	2	0	0	2	39	38	1	10	16	11.1	3.46	85	.262	.310	0	.000	-1	-3	-2	-1	-0.4
Total	7	31	40	.437	119	74	44	5	3	670^2	623	8	272	267	12.2	3.07	92	.255	.333	30	.151	1	-16	-19	-9	-2.6

● DAVE ROWE

Rowe, David E. b: 2/1856, Jacksonville, Ill. BR/TR, 5′9″, 180 lbs. Deb: 5/30/1877 FM♦

YEAR	TM/L	W	L	PCT	G	GS	CG	SH	SV	IP	H	HR	BB	SO	RAT	ERA	ERA+	OAV	OOB	BH	AVG	PB	PR	/A	PD	TPI
1877	Chi-N	0	1	.000	1	1	0	0	0	1	3	0	2	0	45.0	18.00	17	.600	.714	2	.286	0	-2	-2	0	-0.1
1882	Cle-N	0	1	.000	1	1	1	0	0	9	29	3	7	0	36.0	12.00	23	.492	.545	25	.258	0	-9	-9	-0	-0.6
1883	Bal-a	0	0	—	1	0	0	0	0	4	12	1	2	1	31.5	20.25	17	.492	.530	80	.313	0	-8	-7	-0	-0.5
1884	StL-U	1	0	1.000	1	1	1	0	0	9	10	0	0	2	10.0	2.00	148	.263	.263	142	.293	0	1	1	0	0.1
Total	4	1	2	.333	4	3	2	0	0	23	54	4	11	3	25.4	9.78	31	.427	.473	383	.263	1	-17	-17	-0	-1.1

● DON ROWE

Rowe, Donald Howard b: 4/3/36, Brawley, Cal. BL/TL, 6′, 180 lbs. Deb: 4/09/63 C

YEAR	TM/L	W	L	PCT	G	GS	CG	SH	SV	IP	H	HR	BB	SO	RAT	ERA	ERA+	OAV	OOB	BH	AVG	PB	PR	/A	PD	TPI
1963	NY-N	0	0	—	26	1	0	0	0	54^2	59	6	21	27	13.3	4.28	81	.280	.348	3	.231	0	-6	-5	-1	-0.6

● KEN ROWE

Rowe, Kenneth Darrell b: 12/31/33, Ferndale, Mich. BR/TR, 6′2″, 185 lbs. Deb: 4/14/63 C

YEAR	TM/L	W	L	PCT	G	GS	CG	SH	SV	IP	H	HR	BB	SO	RAT	ERA	ERA+	OAV	OOB	BH	AVG	PB	PR	/A	PD	TPI
1963	LA-N	1	1	.500	14	0	0	0	1	27^2	28	2	11	12	13.0	2.93	103	.264	.339	0	.000	-0	1	0	-0	0.0
1964	Bal-A	1	0	1.000	6	0	0	0	0	4^1	10	1	1	4	22.8	8.31	43	.455	.478	0	—	0	-2	-2	0	-0.2
1965	Bal-A	0	0	—	6	0	0	0	0	13^1	17	0	2	3	12.8	3.38	103	.321	.345	1	1.000	0	0	0	-1	0.0
Total	3	2	1	.667	26	0	0	0	1	45^1	55	3	14	19	13.9	3.57	90	.304	.357	1	.167	0	-1	-2	-1	-0.2

● SCHOOLBOY ROWE

Rowe, Lynwood Thomas b: 1/11/10, Waco, Tex. d: 1/8/61, ElDorado, Ark. BR/TR, 6′4.5″, 210 lbs. Deb: 4/15/33 C♦

YEAR	TM/L	W	L	PCT	G	GS	CG	SH	SV	IP	H	HR	BB	SO	RAT	ERA	ERA+	OAV	OOB	BH	AVG	PB	PR	/A	PD	TPI
1933	Det-A	7	4	.636	19	15	8	1	0	123^1	129	7	31	75	11.7	3.58	121	.269	.315	11	.220	-0	10	10	2	1.1
1934	*Det-A	24	8	.750	45	30	20	3	1	266	259	12	81	149	11.5	3.45	127	.256	.312	33	.303	12	31	28	-0	3.7
1935	*Det-A☆	19	13	.594	42	34	21	**6**	3	275^2	272	11	68	140	11.2	3.69	113	.255	**.301**	34	.312	13	23	15	-2	2.5
1936	Det-A★	19	10	.655	41	35	19	4	3	245^1	266	15	64	115	12.2	4.51	110	.275	.321	23	.256	7	14	12	2	1.9
1937	Det-A	1	4	.200	10	2	1	0	0	31^1	49	7	9	6	16.9	8.62	54	.350	.393	2	.200	-0	-14	-14	0	-1.2
1938	Det-A	0	2	.000	4	3	0	0	0	21	20	1	11	4	13.3	3.00	167	.256	.348	1	.167	-0	4	5	1	0.5
1939	Det-A	10	12	.455	28	24	8	1	0	164	192	17	61	51	14.0	4.99	98	.291	.353	15	.246	2	-7	-2	0	0.0
1940	*Det-A	16	3	**.842**	27	23	11	1	0	169	170	15	43	61	11.4	3.46	137	.259	.305	18	.269	5	17	24	-0	2.9
1941	Det-A	8	6	.571	27	14	4	0	1	139	155	6	33	54	12.2	4.14	110	.278	.318	15	.273	5	0	6	1	1.2
1942	Det-A	1	0	1.000	2	1	0	0	0	10^1	9	0	2	7	9.6	0.00	—	.220	.256	0	.000	-1	4	5	0	0.5
	Bro-N	1	0	1.000	9	2	0	0	0	30^1	36	2	12	6	14.5	5.34	61	.288	.355	4	.211	0	-7	-7	0	-0.7
1943	Phi-N	14	8	.636	27	25	11	3	1	199	196	7	29	52	10.3	2.94	115	.249	.279	36	.300	16	10	10	0	3.0
1946	Phi-N	11	4	.733	17	16	9	2	0	136	112	3	21	51	9.2	2.12	162	.224	.263	11	.180	2	20	20	-2	2.3
1947	Phi-N★	14	10	.583	31	28	15	1	1	195^2	232	22	45	74	12.9	4.32	93	.292	.333	22	.278	10	-6	-7	-1	0.2
1948	Phi-N	10	10	.500	30	20	8	0	2	148	167	5	31	46	12.2	4.07	97	.281	.319	10	.192	1	-2	-2	1	0.0
1949	Phi-N	3	7	.300	23	6	2	0	0	65^1	68	2	17	22	12.0	4.82	82	.300	.354	4	.235	2	-6	-6	1	-0.4
Total	15	158	101	.610	382	278	137	22	12	2219^1	2332	132	558	913	11.8	3.87	110	.269	.315	239	.263	76	93	96	2	17.5

● MIKE ROWLAND

Rowland, Michael Evan b: 1/31/53, Chicago, Ill. BR/TR, 6′3″, 205 lbs. Deb: 7/25/80

YEAR	TM/L	W	L	PCT	G	GS	CG	SH	SV	IP	H	HR	BB	SO	RAT	ERA	ERA+	OAV	OOB	BH	AVG	PB	PR	/A	PD	TPI
1980	SF-N	1	1	.500	19	0	0	0	0	27	20	2	8	8	9.7	2.33	152	.206	.274	0	—	0	4	4	-0	0.4
1981	SF-N	0	1	.000	9	1	0	0	0	15^2	13	1	6	8	11.5	3.45	100	.232	.317	1	1.000	0	0	-0	-0	0.0
Total	2	1	2	.333	28	1	0	0	0	42^2	33	3	14	16	10.3	2.74	128	.216	.290	1	1.000	0	4	4	-0	0.4

● CHARLIE ROY

Roy, Charles Robert b: 6/22/1884, Beaulieu, Minn. d: 2/10/50, Blackfoot, Idaho BR/TR, 5′10″, 190 lbs. Deb: 6/27/06 F

YEAR	TM/L	W	L	PCT	G	GS	CG	SH	SV	IP	H	HR	BB	SO	RAT	ERA	ERA+	OAV	OOB	BH	AVG	PB	PR	/A	PD	TPI
1906	Phi-N	0	1	.000	7	1	0	0	0	18^1	24	0	5	6	14.7	4.91	53	.316	.366	0	.000	-1	-5	-5	-0	-0.6

● EMILE ROY

Roy, Emile Arthur b: 5/26/07, Brighton, Mass. BR/TR, 5′11″, 180 lbs. Deb: 9/30/33

YEAR	TM/L	W	L	PCT	G	GS	CG	SH	SV	IP	H	HR	BB	SO	RAT	ERA	ERA+	OAV	OOB	BH	AVG	PB	PR	/A	PD	TPI
1933	Phi-A	0	1	.000	1	1	0	0	0	2^1	4	0	4	3	30.9	27.00	16	.364	.533	0	—	0	-6	-6	-0	-0.4

● JEAN-PIERRE ROY

Roy, Jean-Pierre b: 6/26/20, Montreal, Que., Can. BB/TR, 5′10″, 160 lbs. Deb: 5/05/46

YEAR	TM/L	W	L	PCT	G	GS	CG	SH	SV	IP	H	HR	BB	SO	RAT	ERA	ERA+	OAV	OOB	BH	AVG	PB	PR	/A	PD	TPI
1946	Bro-N	0	0	—	3	1	0	0	0	6^1	5	2	5	6	14.2	9.95	34	.200	.333	0	.000	-0	-5	-5	-0	-0.5

● LUTHER ROY

Roy, Luther Franklin b: 7/29/02, Ooltewah, Tenn. d: 7/24/63, Grand Rapids, Mich. BR/TR, 5′10.5″, 161 lbs. Deb: 6/12/24 F

YEAR	TM/L	W	L	PCT	G	GS	CG	SH	SV	IP	H	HR	BB	SO	RAT	ERA	ERA+	OAV	OOB	BH	AVG	PB	PR	/A	PD	TPI
1924	Cle-A	0	5	.000	16	5	2	0	0	48^2	62	3	31	14	17.2	7.77	55	.318	.412	4	.267	-0	-19	-19	1	-1.7
1925	Cle-A	0	0	—	6	1	0	0	0	10	14	1	11	1	22.5	3.60	123	.368	.510	0	.000	-0	1	1	-0	0.0
1927	Chi-N	3	1	.750	11	0	0	0	0	19^2	14	0	11	5	11.9	2.29	169	.209	.329	1	.333	0	4	3	0	0.4
1929	Phi-N	3	6	.333	21	12	1	0	0	88^2	137	11	37	16	18.0	8.42	62	.350	.411	9	.281	2	-37	-32	1	-2.5
	Bro-N	0	0	—	2	0	0	0	0	3^2	4	0	2	0	14.7	4.91	94	.286	.375	0	.000	-0	-0	-0	0	0.0
	Yr	3	6	.333	23	12	1	0	0	92^1	141	11	39	16	17.5	8.29	62	.346	.403	9	.273	2	-37	-32	1	-2.5
Total	4	6	12	.333	56	18	3	0	0	170^2	231	15	92	36	17.2	7.17	66	.328	.408	14	.264	2	-51	-47	1	-3.8

● NORMIE ROY

Roy, Norman Brooks "Jumbo" b: 11/15/28, Newton, Mass. BR/TR, 6′, 200 lbs. Deb: 4/23/50

YEAR	TM/L	W	L	PCT	G	GS	CG	SH	SV	IP	H	HR	BB	SO	RAT	ERA	ERA+	OAV	OOB	BH	AVG	PB	PR	/A	PD	TPI
1950	Bos-N	4	3	.571	19	6	2	0	1	59^2	72	7	39	25	17.0	5.13	75	.305	.408	3	.167	0	-7	-8	0	-0.8

● DICK ROZEK

Rozek, Richard Louis b: 3/27/27, Cedar Rapids, Iowa BL/TL, 6′0.5″, 190 lbs. Deb: 4/29/50

YEAR	TM/L	W	L	PCT	G	GS	CG	SH	SV	IP	H	HR	BB	SO	RAT	ERA	ERA+	OAV	OOB	BH	AVG	PB	PR	/A	PD	TPI
1950	Cle-A	0	0	—	12	2	0	0	0	25^1	28	3	19	14	16.7	4.97	87	.283	.398	0	.000	-1	-1	-2	-1	-0.3
1951	Cle-A	0	0	—	7	1	0	0	0	15^1	18	1	11	5	17.6	2.93	129	.286	.400	1	.333	0	2	1	-1	0.1
1952	Cle-A	1	0	1.000	10	1	0	0	0	12^2	11	0	13	5	17.1	4.97	67	.224	.387	0	.000	-0	-2	-2	-0	-0.3
1953	Phi-A	0	0	—	2	0	0	0	0	10^2	8	3	9	2	14.3	5.06	85	.222	.378	0	.000	-0	-1	-1	-0	-0.1
1954	Phi-A	0	0	—	2	0	0	0	0	1^1	0	0	3	0	27.0	6.75	58	.000	.571	0	—	0	-0	-0	-0	0.0
Total	5	1	0	1.000	33	4	0	0	0	65^1	65	7	55	26	16.8	4.55	88	.260	.397	1	.083	-1	-3	-4	-2	-0.6

● DAVE ROZEMA

Rozema, David Scott b: 8/5/56, Grand Rapids, Mich. BR/TR, 6′4″, 200 lbs. Deb: 4/11/77

YEAR	TM/L	W	L	PCT	G	GS	CG	SH	SV	IP	H	HR	BB	SO	RAT	ERA	ERA+	OAV	OOB	BH	AVG	PB	PR	/A	PD	TPI
1977	Det-A	15	7	.682	28	28	16	1	0	218^1	222	25	34	92	10.8	3.09	139	.265	.299	0	—	0	23	29	0	3.1
1978	Det-A	9	12	.429	28	28	11	2	0	209^1	205	17	41	57	10.7	3.14	123	.260	.298	0	—	0	15	17	-1	1.7
1979	Det-A	4	4	.500	16	16	4	1	0	97^1	101	12	30	33	12.7	3.51	123	.270	.334	0	—	0	8	9	0	0.9
1980	Det-A	6	9	.400	42	13	2	1	4	144^2	152	11	49	49	12.8	3.92	105	.277	.342	0	—	0	2	3	1	0.3
1981	Det-A	5	5	.500	28	9	2	2	3	104	99	12	25	46	11.0	3.63	104	.256	.306	0	—	0	0	2	-1	0.1
1982	Det-A	3	0	1.000	8	2	0	0	1	27^2	17	2	7	15	8.1	1.63	250	.179	.243	0	—	0	8	7	1	0.9
1983	Det-A	8	3	.727	29	16	1	0	2	105	100	10	29	63	11.1	3.43	114	.248	.300	0	—	0	7	6	1	0.7
1984	Det-A	7	6	.538	29	16	0	0	0	101	110	13	18	48	11.6	3.74	105	.274	.309	0	—	0	3	2	1	0.3
1985	Tex-A	3	7	.300	34	4	0	0	7	88	100	10	22	42	12.7	4.19	101	.287	.333	0	—	0	-0	0	1	0.1
1986	Tex-A	0	0	—	6	0	0	0	0	10^2	19	1	3	3	18.6	5.91	73	.404	.440	0	—	0	-2	-2	0	-0.2
Total	10	60	53	.531	248	132	36	7	17	1106	1125	113	258	448	11.5	3.47	117	.266	.313	0	—	0	63	73	3	7.9

● JORGE RUBIO

Rubio, Jorge Jesus (Chavez) b: 4/23/45, Mexicali, Mexico BR/TR, 6′3″, 200 lbs. Deb: 4/21/66

YEAR	TM/L	W	L	PCT	G	GS	CG	SH	SV	IP	H	HR	BB	SO	RAT	ERA	ERA+	OAV	OOB	BH	AVG	PB	PR	/A	PD	TPI
1966	Cal-A	2	1	.667	7	4	1	1	0	27^1	22	2	16	27	12.8	2.96	113	.220	.333	0	.000	-1	1	1	-0	0.0
1967	Cal-A	0	2	.000	3	3	0	0	0	15	18	2	9	4	18.6	3.60	87	.316	.443	1	.333	1	-1	-1	0	0.0
Total	2	2	3	.400	10	7	1	1	0	42^1	40	4	25	31	14.9	3.19	103	.255	.374	1	.091	-0	1	0	-0	0.0

YEAR	TM/L	W	L	PCT	G	GS	CG	SH	SV	IP	H	HR	BB	SO	RAT	ERA	ERA+	OAV	OOB	BH	AVG	PB	PR	/A	PD	TPI
● DAVE RUCKER	Rucker, David Michael b: 9/1/57, San Bernardino, Cal BL/TL, 6'1", 190 lbs. Deb: 4/12/81																									
1981	Det-A	0	0	—	2	0	0	0	0	4	3	0	1	2	11.3	6.75	56	.188	.278	0	—	0	-1	-1	-0	-0.1
1982	Det-A	5	6	.455	27	4	1	0	0	64	62	4	23	31	12.2	3.38	120	.251	.320	0	—	0	5	5	0	0.5
1983	Det-A	1	2	.333	4	3	0	0	0	9	18	2	8	6	27.0	17.00	23	.419	.519	0	—	0	-13	-13	0	-1.1
	StL-N	5	3	.625	34	0	0	0	0	37	36	1	18	22	13.4	2.68	135	.263	.353	0	.000	-0	4	4	0	0.4
1984	StL-N	2	3	.400	50	0	0	0	0	73	62	0	34	38	12.0	2.10	166	.237	.327	1	.143	-0	12	11	-1	1.1
1985	Phi-N	3	2	.600	39	3	0	0	1	79^1	83	6	40	41	14.2	4.31	85	.279	.368	4	.333	2	-6	-6	0	-0.4
1986	Phi-N	0	2	.000	19	0	0	0	0	25	34	4	14	14	17.3	5.76	67	.340	.421	0	.000	-0	-6	-5	0	-0.5
1988	Pit-N	0	2	.000	31	0	0	0	0	28^1	39	2	9	16	15.2	4.76	71	.328	.375	0	.000	-0	-4	-4	-0	-0.5
Total	7	16	20	.444	206	10	1	0	1	319^2	337	19	147	170	13.9	3.97	93	.276	.357	5	.192	1	-9	-10	0	-0.6
● NAP RUCKER	Rucker, George Napoleon b: 9/30/1884, Crabapple, Ga. d: 12/19/70, Alpharetta, Ga. BR/TL, 5'11", 190 lbs. Deb: 4/15/07																									
1907	Bro-N	15	13	.536	37	30	26	4	0	275^1	242	3	80	131	10.8	2.06	114	.242	.303	15	.155	-1	13	9	-1	0.8
1908	Bro-N	17	19	.472	42	35	30	6	1	333^1	265	1	125	199	11.0	2.08	113	.231	.317	21	.179	-1	11	10	4	1.5
1909	Bro-N	13	19	.406	38	33	28	6	1	309^1	245	6	101	201	10.5	2.24	116	.228	.303	12	.119	-5	12	12	-2	0.6
1910	Bro-N	17	18	.486	41	39	**27**	**6**	0	**320^1**	293	5	84	147	10.8	2.58	117	.251	.306	23	.209	-1	16	16	-2	1.4
1911	Bro-N	22	18	.550	48	33	23	5	4	315^2	255	12	110	190	10.6	2.71	123	.226	.300	21	.202	2	24	22	2	2.6
1912	Bro-N	18	21	.462	45	34	23	**6**	4	297^2	272	6	72	151	10.5	2.21	152	.250	.298	25	.245	2	40	38	2	4.4
1913	Bro-N	14	15	.483	41	33	16	4	3	260	236	3	67	111	10.7	2.87	115	.249	.304	21	.241	2	10	12	-4	1.1
1914	Bro-N	7	6	.538	16	16	5	0	0	103^2	113	2	27	35	12.3	3.39	84	.275	.323	9	.265	2	-7	-6	0	-0.4
1915	Bro-N	9	4	.692	19	15	7	1	1	122^2	134	3	28	38	12.0	2.42	115	.279	.322	9	.214	1	4	5	1	0.8
1916	*Bro-N	2	1	.667	9	4	1	0	0	37^1	34	0	7	14	10.1	1.69	159	.241	.282	1	.091	-1	4	4	0	0.4
Total	10	134	134	.500	336	272	186	38	14	2375^1	2089	41	701	1217	10.8	2.42	119	.243	.306	157	.195	1	127	121	1	13.2
● ERNIE RUDOLPH	Rudolph, Ernest William b: 2/13/10, Black River Falls Wis. BL/TR, 5'8", 165 lbs. Deb: 6/16/45																									
1945	Bro-N	1	0	1.000	7	0	0	0	0	8^2	12	1	7	3	19.7	5.19	72	.333	.442	0	—	1	-1	-1	0	-0.1
● DON RUDOLPH	Rudolph, Frederick Donald b: 8/16/31, Baltimore, Md. d: 9/12/68, Granada Hills, Cal BL/TL, 5'11", 195 lbs. Deb: 9/21/57																									
1957	Chi-A	1	0	1.000	5	0	0	0	0	12	6	2	2	2	6.0	2.25	166	.146	.186	1	.500	1	2	2	-0	0.2
1958	Chi-A	1	0	1.000	7	0	0	0	1	7	4	0	5	2	11.6	2.57	141	.190	.346	0	—	0	1	1	0	0.1
1959	Chi-A	0	0	—	4	0	0	0	1	3	4	0	2	0	18.0	0.00	—	.333	.429	0	—	0	1	1	0	0.2
	Cin-N	0	0	—	5	0	0	0	0	7^1	13	1	3	8	19.6	4.91	83	.394	.444	0	.000	-0	-1	-1	0	-0.1
1962	Cle-A	0	0	—	1	0	0	0	0	0^1	1	0	0	0	27.0	0.00	—	1.000	1.000	0	—	0	0	0	0	0.0
	Was-A	8	10	.444	37	23	6	2	0	176^1	187	13	42	68	11.8	3.62	111	.274	.319	10	.175	1	7	8	-1	0.9
	Yr	8	10	.444	38	23	6	2	0	176^2	188	13	42	68	11.9	3.62	112	.275	.320	10	.175	1	7	8	-1	0.9
1963	Was-A	7	19	.269	37	26	4	0	1	174	189	28	36	70	11.9	4.55	82	.275	.317	8	.178	2	-18	-16	-1	-1.5
1964	Was-A	1	3	.250	28	8	0	0	0	70^1	81	10	12	32	11.9	4.09	90	.290	.320	1	.067	-1	-4	-3	-0	-0.4
Total	6	18	32	.360	124	57	10	2	3	450^1	485	54	102	182	11.9	4.00	96	.276	.319	20	.167	3	-11	-8	-1	-0.6
● DICK RUDOLPH	Rudolph, Richard "Baldy" b: 8/25/1887, New York, N.Y. d: 10/20/49, Bronx, N.Y. BR/TR, 5'9.5", 160 lbs. Deb: 9/30/10 C																									
1910	NY-N	0	1	.000	3	1	1	0	2	12	21	0	2	9	17.3	7.50	40	.350	.371	1	.250	0	-6	-6	-0	-0.6
1911	NY-N	0	0	—	1	0	0	0	0	2	2	0	0	0	9.0	9.00	37	.250	.250	1	1.000	0	-1	-1	-0	-0.1
1913	Bos-N	14	13	.519	33	22	17	2	0	249^1	258	4	59	109	11.5	2.92	112	.276	.320	21	.239	4	8	10	5	2.0
1914	*Bos-N	26	10	.722	42	36	31	6	0	336^1	288	9	61	138	**9.4**	2.35	117	.238	.276	15	.125	-1	16	15	2	1.7
1915	Bos-N	22	19	.537	44	43	30	3	1	341^1	304	4	64	147	9.9	2.37	109	.242	.282	23	.198	6	14	8	1	1.6
1916	Bos-N	19	12	.613	41	38	27	5	3	312	266	7	38	133	**8.9**	2.16	115	.235	**.261**	16	.158	1	16	11	6	2.1
1917	Bos-N	13	13	.500	31	30	22	5	0	242^2	252	1	54	96	11.5	3.41	75	.272	.314	20	.230	3	-19	-23	1	-2.2
1918	Bos-N	9	10	.474	21	20	15	3	0	154	144	2	30	48	10.2	2.57	104	.255	.292	10	.185	-1	3	2	1	0.2
1919	Bos-N	13	18	.419	37	32	24	2	2	273^2	282	2	54	76	11.1	2.17	132	.276	.314	17	.193	3	23	21	0	2.8
1920	Bos-N	4	8	.333	18	12	3	0	0	89	104	4	24	24	13.3	4.04	75	.294	.346	5	.185	-0	-9	-10	0	-1.0
1922	Bos-N	0	2	.000	3	3	1	0	0	16	22	2	5	3	15.2	5.06	79	.328	.375	2	.400	0	-2	-2	0	-0.1
1923	Bos-N	1	2	.333	4	4	1	1	0	19^1	27	0	10	3	17.7	3.72	107	.333	.413	0	.000	-1	1	1	0	0.0
1927	Bos-N	0	0	—	1	0	0	0	0	1^1	1	0	1	0	13.5	0.00	—	.200	.333	0	—	0	1	1	-0	0.1
Total	13	121	108	.528	279	241	172	27	8	2049	1971	35	402	786	10.5	2.66	104	.258	.298	131	.188	13	44	25	15	6.5
● DUTCH RUETHER	Ruether, Walter Henry b: 9/13/1893, Alameda, Cal. d: 5/16/70, Phoenix, Ariz. BL/TL, 6'1.5", 180 lbs. Deb: 4/13/17 ♦																									
1917	Chi-N	2	0	1.000	10	4	1	0	0	36^1	37	0	12	23	12.9	2.48	117	.285	.359	12	.273	2	1	2	1	0.6
	Cin-N	1	2	.333	7	4	1	1	0	35^2	43	0	14	12	14.9	3.53	74	.323	.396	5	.208	1	-3	-4	-0	-0.3
	Yr	3	2	.600	17	8	2	1	0	72	80	0	26	35	13.5	3.00	92	.301	.367	17	.250	3	-2	-2	0	0.3
1918	Cin-N	0	1	.000	2	2	1	0	0	10	10	0	3	10	12.6	2.70	99	.244	.311	0	.000	-0	0	-0	-0	-0.1
1919	*Cin-N	19	6	**.760**	33	29	20	3	0	242^2	195	1	83	78	10.6	1.82	153	.223	.295	24	.261	5	30	26	-3	3.3
1920	Cin-N	16	12	.571	37	33	23	5	3	265^2	235	2	96	99	11.5	2.47	123	.247	.321	20	.192	-1	20	17	0	1.7
1921	Bro-N	10	13	.435	36	27	12	1	2	211^1	247	7	67	78	13.7	4.26	91	.299	.356	34	.351	12	-11	-9	-1	0.3
1922	Bro-N	21	12	.636	35	35	26	2	0	267^1	290	11	92	89	13.1	3.53	115	.282	.345	26	.208	6	17	16	-0	2.0
1923	Bro-N	15	14	.517	34	34	20	0	0	275	308	11	86	87	13.1	4.22	92	.287	.343	32	.274	4	-7	-10	-2	-0.7
1924	Bro-N	8	13	.381	30	21	13	2	3	168	190	4	45	63	12.9	3.91	96	.282	.332	15	.242	2	-1	-3	1	0.0
1925	*Was-A	18	7	.720	30	29	16	1	0	223^1	241	5	105	68	14.3	3.87	109	.281	.365	36	.333	6	13	9	-3	1.6
1926	Was-A	12	6	.667	23	23	9	0	0	169^1	214	5	66	48	15.1	4.84	80	.311	.375	23	.250	4	-15	-18	-2	-1.5
	*NY-A	2	3	.400	5	5	1	0	0	36	32	0	18	8	12.8	3.50	110	.248	.345	2	.095	-2	2	1	-1	-0.1
	Yr	14	9	.609	28	28	10	0	0	205^1	246	5	84	56	14.5	4.60	84	.300	.366	25	.221	3	-13	-17	-3	-1.6
1927	NY-A	13	6	.684	27	26	12	3	0	184	202	9	52	45	12.8	3.38	114	.287	.343	21	.262	5	16	10	0	1.4
Total	11	137	95	.591	309	272	155	18	8	2124^2	2244	55	739	708	12.9	3.50	104	.277	.342	250	.258	45	60	36	-9	8.2
● BRUCE RUFFIN	Ruffin, Bruce Wayne b: 10/4/63, Lubbock, Tex BB/TL, 6'2", 205 lbs. Deb: 6/28/86																									
1986	Phi-N	9	4	.692	21	21	6	0	0	146^1	138	6	44	70	11.3	2.46	157	.251	.308	4	.073	-3	20	23	-1	2.0
1987	Phi-N	11	14	.440	35	35	3	1	0	204^2	236	17	73	93	13.7	4.35	97	.298	.359	4	.055	-5	-6	-3	-1	-0.8
1988	Phi-N	6	10	.375	55	15	3	0	3	144^1	151	7	80	82	14.6	4.43	80	.275	.370	4	.121	-0	-16	-14	1	-1.4
1989	Phi-N	6	10	.375	24	23	1	0	0	125^2	152	10	62	70	15.3	4.44	80	.301	.377	6	.176	2	-13	-13	2	-0.9
1990	Phi-N	6	13	.316	32	25	2	1	0	149	178	14	62	79	14.6	5.38	71	.297	.364	3	.068	-2	-26	-26	0	-2.7
1991	Phi-N	4	7	.364	31	15	1	1	0	119	125	6	38	85	12.4	3.78	97	.272	.329	0	.000	-1	-1	-2	-0	-0.3
1992	Mil-A	1	6	.143	25	6	1	0	0	58	66	7	41	45	16.6	6.67	57	.293	.402	0	—	0	-18	-18	-0	-1.8
Total	7	43	64	.402	223	140	17	3	3	947	1046	67	400	524	13.8	4.31	89	.284	.356	21	.080	-10	-60	-52	1	-5.9
● RED RUFFING	Ruffing, Charles Herbert b: 5/3/04, Granville, Ill. d: 2/17/86, Mayfield Hts., O. BR/TR, 6'1.5", 205 lbs. Deb: 5/31/24 CH♦																									
1924	Bos-A	0	0	—	8	2	0	0	0	23	29	0	9	10	16.0	6.65	66	.333	.414	1	.143	0	-6	-6	-1	-0.6
1925	Bos-A	9	18	.333	37	27	13	3	1	217^1	253	10	75	64	13.7	5.01	91	.299	.357	17	.215	-0	-15	-11	-1	-1.1
1926	Bos-A	6	15	.286	37	22	6	0	2	166	169	4	68	58	13.1	4.39	93	.274	.351	10	.196	0	-7	-6	-1	-0.7
1927	Bos-A	5	13	.278	26	18	10	0	2	158^1	160	7	87	77	14.3	4.66	91	.277	.375	14	.255	1	-9	-8	0	-0.6
1928	Bos-A	10	25	.286	42	34	**25**	1	2	289^1	303	8	96	118	12.7	3.89	106	.275	.339	38	.314	12	5	7	-3	1.6
1929	Bos-A	9	22	.290	35	30	18	1	1	244^1	280	17	118	109	14.7	4.86	88	.297	.376	35	.307	5	-17	-16	-1	-0.8
1930	Bos-A	0	3	.000	4	3	1	0	0	24	32	1	6	14	14.6	6.38	72	.323	.368	3	.273	1	-5	-5	-1	-0.4
	NY-A	15	5	.750	34	25	12	2	1	197^2	200	10	62	117	12.0	4.14	104	.260	.317	37	.374	16	11	3	-2	1.5
	Yr	15	8	.652	38	28	13	2	1	221^2	232	11	68	131	12.3	4.38	99	.267	.322	40	.364	17	7	-1	-3	1.1
1931	NY-A	16	14	.533	37	30	19	1	2	237	240	11	87	132	12.6	4.41	90	.256	.323	36	.330	10	-1	-12	-3	-0.2

YEAR	TM/L	W	L	PCT	G	GS	CG	SH	SV	IP	H	HR	BB	SO	RAT	ERA	ERA+	OAV	OOB	BH	AVG	PB	PR	/A	PD	TPI
1932	*NY-A	18	7	.720	35	29	22	3	2	259	219	16	115	**190**	11.7	3.09	132	**.226**	.311	38	.306	13	40	28	-2	3.8
1933	NY-A	9	14	.391	35	28	18	0	3	235	230	7	93	122	12.5	3.91	99	.258	.330	29	.252	8	10	-1	-0	0.6
1934	NY-A★	19	11	.633	36	31	19	5	0	256^1	232	18	104	149	11.8	3.93	103	.236	.310	28	.248	6	16	4	-3	0.6
1935	NY-A	16	11	.593	30	29	19	2	0	222	201	17	76	81	11.3	3.12	130	.239	.303	37	.339	13	33	23	-2	3.2
1936	*NY-A	20	12	.625	33	33	25	3	0	271	274	22	90	102	12.2	3.85	121	.263	.323	37	.291	15	36	24	2	3.7
1937	*NY-A	20	7	.741	31	31	22	4	0	256^1	242	17	68	131	10.9	2.98	149	.247	.296	26	.202	3	47	42	-4	3.9
1938	*NY-A☆	**21**	7	**.750**	31	31	22	3	0	247^1	246	16	82	127	11.9	3.31	137	.258	.317	24	.224	10	**41**	34	-2	3.9
1939	*NY-A★	21	7	.750	28	28	22	**5**	0	233^1	211	15	75	95	11.1	2.93	149	.240	.301	35	.307	8	44	37	-2	4.3
1940	NY-A★	15	12	.556	30	30	20	3	0	226	218	24	76	97	11.8	3.38	119	.252	.314	11	.124	-2	25	16	-3	1.0
1941	*NY-A☆	15	6	.714	23	23	13	2	0	185^2	177	13	54	60	11.2	3.54	111	.252	.306	27	.303	11	13	8	-3	1.6
1942	*NY-A☆	14	7	.667	24	24	16	4	0	193^2	183	10	41	80	10.5	3.21	107	.250	.292	20	.250	6	10	5	-2	1.0
1945	NY-A	7	3	.700	11	11	8	1	0	87^1	85	2	20	24	10.9	2.89	120	.251	.294	10	.217	1	5	6	-2	0.5
1946	NY-A	5	1	.833	8	8	4	2	0	61	37	2	23	19	8.9	1.77	195	.171	.251	3	.120	-1	12	11	-1	1.1
1947	Chi-A	3	5	.375	9	9	1	0	0	53	63	7	16	11	13.4	6.11	60	.290	.339	5	.208	-0	-14	-14	-0	-1.4
Total	22	273	225	.548	624	536	335	45	16	4344	4284	254	1541	1987	12.2	3.80	109	.258	.323	521	.269	135	272	174	-34	26.5

● VERN RUHLE Ruhle, Vernon Gerald b: 1/25/51, Coleman, Mich. BR/TR, 6'1", 187 lbs. Deb: 9/09/74

YEAR	TM/L	W	L	PCT	G	GS	CG	SH	SV	IP	H	HR	BB	SO	RAT	ERA	ERA+	OAV	OOB	BH	AVG	PB	PR	/A	PD	TPI
1974	Det-A	2	0	1.000	5	3	1	0	0	33	35	1	6	10	11.5	2.73	139	.273	.311	0	—	0	3	4	-1	0.1
1975	Det-A	11	12	.478	32	31	8	3	0	190	199	17	65	67	12.8	4.03	100	.266	.330	0	—	0	-5	-0	-2	-0.5
1976	Det-A	9	12	.429	32	32	5	1	0	199^2	227	19	59	88	13.1	3.92	95	.288	.340	0	—	0	-9	-5	-0	-0.8
1977	Det-A	3	5	.375	14	10	0	0	0	66^1	83	9	15	27	13.7	5.70	75	.305	.348	0	—	0	-12	-10	-1	-1.1
1978	Hou-N	3	3	.500	13	10	2	2	0	68	57	0	20	27	10.3	2.12	156	.224	.283	1	.056	-1	11	9	-1	0.8
1979	Hou-N	2	6	.250	13	10	2	2	0	66^1	64	9	8	33	10.0	4.07	86	.249	.277	1	.053	-1	-2	-4	-1	-0.6
1980	*Hou-N	12	4	.750	28	22	6	2	0	159^1	148	7	29	55	10.2	2.37	139	.251	.289	12	.245	4	22	16	-2	2.1
1981	*Hou-N	4	6	.400	20	15	1	0	1	102	97	6	20	39	10.4	2.91	113	.250	.289	6	.250	3	7	4	-2	0.6
1982	Hou-N	9	13	.409	31	21	3	2	1	149	169	12	24	56	11.9	3.93	84	.289	.321	4	.098	-0	-5	-10	-1	-1.2
1983	Hou-N	8	5	.615	41	9	0	0	3	114^2	107	13	36	43	11.5	3.69	92	.249	.312	2	.105	0	-1	-4	0	-0.3
1984	Hou-N	1	9	.100	40	6	0	0	2	90^1	112	5	29	60	14.3	4.58	72	.309	.365	1	.083	0	-10	-13	1	-1.2
1985	Cle-A	2	10	.167	42	16	1	0	3	125	139	16	30	54	12.3	4.32	96	.283	.326	0	—	0	-2	-3	-0	-0.3
1986	*Cal-A	1	3	.250	16	3	0	0	1	47^2	46	5	7	23	10.2	4.15	99	.247	.278	0	—	0	0	-0	1	0.0
Total	13	67	88	.432	327	188	29	12	11	1411^1	1483	119	348	582	11.9	3.73	97	.270	.318	27	.148	5	-5	-16	-8	-2.4

● ANDY RUSH Rush, Jesse Howard b: 12/26/1889, Longton, Kan. d: 3/16/69, Fresno, Cal. BR/TR, 6'3", 180 lbs. Deb: 4/16/25

YEAR	TM/L	W	L	PCT	G	GS	CG	SH	SV	IP	H	HR	BB	SO	RAT	ERA	ERA+	OAV	OOB	BH	AVG	PB	PR	/A	PD	TPI
1925	Bro-N	0	1	.000	4	2	0	0	0	9^2	16	3	5	4	19.6	9.31	45	.364	.429	0	.000	-0	-5	-6	0	-0.5

● BOB RUSH Rush, Robert Ransom b: 12/21/25, Battle Creek, Mich BR/TR, 6'4", 205 lbs. Deb: 4/22/48

YEAR	TM/L	W	L	PCT	G	GS	CG	SH	SV	IP	H	HR	BB	SO	RAT	ERA	ERA+	OAV	OOB	BH	AVG	PB	PR	/A	PD	TPI
1948	Chi-N	5	11	.313	36	16	4	0	0	133^1	153	8	37	72	12.9	3.92	100	.287	.335	5	.128	-2	1	-0	1	-0.1
1949	Chi-N	10	18	.357	35	27	9	1	4	201	197	10	79	80	12.4	4.07	99	.255	.324	2	.032	-7	-1	-1	1	-0.7
1950	Chi-N☆	13	20	.394	39	34	19	1	1	254^2	261	11	93	93	12.7	3.71	113	.265	.332	15	.167	-1	12	14	2	1.5
1951	Chi-N	11	12	.478	37	29	12	2	2	211^1	212	16	68	129	12.1	3.83	107	.254	.312	13	.191	-0	3	6	1	0.7
1952	Chi-N★	17	13	.567	34	32	17	4	0	250^1	205	14	81	157	10.5	2.70	143	.216	.282	28	.292	7	29	32	2	**4.7**
1953	Chi-N	9	14	.391	29	28	8	1	0	166^2	177	17	66	84	13.4	4.54	98	.270	.341	6	.111	-2	-5	-2	1	-0.3
1954	Chi-N	13	15	.464	33	32	11	0	0	236^1	213	12	103	124	12.2	3.77	111	.243	.326	23	.277	7	8	11	3	2.3
1955	Chi-N	13	11	.542	33	33	14	3	0	234	204	19	73	130	10.7	3.50	117	.234	.295	9	.110	-3	14	15	1	1.3
1956	Chi-N	13	10	.565	32	32	13	1	0	239^2	210	30	59	104	10.2	3.19	118	.233	.282	8	.098	-3	15	15	-2	1.1
1957	Chi-N	6	16	.273	31	29	5	0	0	205^1	211	16	66	103	12.2	4.38	88	.265	.323	14	.203	2	-12	-12	-2	-1.2
1958	*Mil-N	10	6	.625	28	20	5	2	0	147^1	142	13	31	84	10.6	3.42	103	.253	.293	9	.200	1	9	2	-2	0.1
1959	Mil-N	5	6	.455	31	9	1	1	0	101^1	102	5	23	64	11.2	2.40	148	.257	.299	6	.188	0	17	13	-1	1.3
1960	Mil-N	2	0	1.000	10	0	0	0	1	15	24	2	5	8	17.4	4.20	82	.369	.414	1	.333	1	-1	-1	-0	-0.1
	Chi-A	0	0	—	9	0	0	0	0	14^1	16	4	5	12	13.2	5.65	67	.302	.362	1	1.000	0	-3	-3	0	-0.2
Total	13	127	152	.455	417	321	118	16	8	2410^2	2327	177	789	1244	11.8	3.65	109	.251	.313	140	.173	0	88	90	7	10.4

● AMOS RUSIE Rusie, Amos Wilson "The Hoosier Thunderbolt" b: 5/30/1871, Mooresville, Ind. d: 12/6/42, Seattle, Wash. BR/TR, 6'1", 200 lbs. Deb: 5/09/1889 H

YEAR	TM/L	W	L	PCT	G	GS	CG	SH	SV	IP	H	HR	BB	SO	RAT	ERA	ERA+	OAV	OOB	BH	AVG	PB	PR	/A	PD	TPI
1889	Ind-N	12	10	.545	33	22	19	1	0	225	246	12	116	109	14.8	5.32	78	.270	.358	18	.175	-4	-33	-29	-2	-2.8
1890	NY-N	29	34	.460	67	63	56	4	1	548^2	436	3	289	**341**	12.3	2.56	137	**.212**	.316	79	.278	11	62	58	6	6.8
1891	NY-N	33	20	.623	61	57	52	**6**	1	500^1	391	7	262	**337**	12.1	2.55	125	**.207**	.310	54	.245	4	44	36	2	3.8
1892	NY-N	31	31	.500	64	61	58	2	0	532	405	7	267	288	11.6	2.88	112	.202	.300	53	.210	-0	24	20	5	2.4
1893	NY-N	33	21	.611	**56**	52	**50**	**4**	1	**482**	451	15	218	**208**	12.8	3.23	144	**.240**	.324	57	.269	3	**77**	**76**	3	**7.1**
1894	*NY-N	**36**	13	.735	54	50	45	**3**	1	444	426	10	200	**195**	**12.8**	**2.78**	**189**	**.250**	**.330**	52	.280	2	126	122	8	**11.0**
1895	NY-N	23	23	.500	49	47	42	**4**	0	393^1	384	9	159	**201**	12.6	3.73	124	.252	.325	44	.246	-5	46	40	3	3.1
1897	NY-N	28	10	.737	38	37	35	2	0	322^1	314	6	87	135	11.5	**2.54**	164	.253	.308	40	.278	2	64	58	2	5.7
1898	NY-N	20	11	.645	37	36	33	4	1	300	288	6	103	114	12.0	3.03	115	.251	.317	29	.210	-1	19	15	-0	1.3
1901	Cin-N	0	1	.000	3	2	2	0	0	22	43	1	3	6	18.8	8.59	37	.405	.422	1	.125	-1	-13	-13	0	-1.1
Total	10	245	174	.585	462	427	392	30	5	3769^2	3384	76	1704	1934	12.4	3.07	130	.234	.319	427	.247	12	416	381	27	37.3

● SCOTT RUSKIN Ruskin, Scott Drew b: 6/8/63, Jacksonville, Fla. BR/TL, 6'2", 185 lbs. Deb: 4/09/90

YEAR	TM/L	W	L	PCT	G	GS	CG	SH	SV	IP	H	HR	BB	SO	RAT	ERA	ERA+	OAV	OOB	BH	AVG	PB	PR	/A	PD	TPI
1990	Pit-N	2	2	.500	44	0	0	0	2	47^2	50	2	28	34	15.1	3.02	120	.269	.370	2	.333	1	4	3	0	0.5
	Mon-N	1	0	1.000	23	0	0	0	0	27^2	25	2	10	23	11.4	2.28	160	.243	.310	0	.000	-0	5	4	0	0.5
	Yr	3	2	.600	67	0	0	0	2	75^1	75	4	38	57	13.5	2.75	132	.256	.341	2	.250	1	9	7	0	1.0
1991	Mon-N	4	4	.500	64	0	0	0	6	63^2	57	4	30	46	12.7	4.24	85	.241	.333	0	.000	0	-4	-4	-0	-0.5
1992	Cin-N	4	3	.571	57	0	0	0	0	53^2	56	6	20	43	12.9	5.03	73	.275	.342	0	.000	-0	-9	-8	0	-0.9
Total	3	11	9	.550	188	0	0	0	8	192^2	188	14	88	146	13.2	3.88	94	.258	.342	2	.154	1	-4	-5	1	-0.4

● JOHN RUSS Russ, John b: Louisville, Ky. Deb: 7/04/1882 ♦

YEAR	TM/L	W	L	PCT	G	GS	CG	SH	SV	IP	H	HR	BB	SO	RAT	ERA	ERA+	OAV	OOB	BH	AVG	PB	PR	/A	PD	TPI
1882	Bal-a	0	1	.000	1	1	0	0	0	5	10	0	1	0	19.8	7.20	38	.391	.414	1	.333	0	-3	-2	-0	-0.2

● ALLAN RUSSELL Russell, Allan E. "Rubberarm" b: 7/31/1893, Baltimore, Md. d: 10/20/72, Baltimore, Md. BB/TR, 5'11", 165 lbs. Deb: 9/13/15 F

YEAR	TM/L	W	L	PCT	G	GS	CG	SH	SV	IP	H	HR	BB	SO	RAT	ERA	ERA+	OAV	OOB	BH	AVG	PB	PR	/A	PD	TPI
1915	NY-A	1	2	.333	5	3	1	0	0	27	21	1	21	21	14.3	2.67	110	.228	.377	2	.250	0	1	1	-0	0.1
1916	NY-A	6	10	.375	34	18	8	1	6	171^1	138	8	75	104	11.6	3.20	90	.232	.324	2	.044	-3	-7	-6	0	-1.0
1917	NY-A	7	8	.467	25	10	6	0	2	104^1	89	3	39	55	11.6	2.24	120	.236	.319	10	.323	4	5	5	-1	0.9
1918	NY-A	7	11	.389	27	18	7	2	4	141	139	6	73	54	13.9	3.26	87	.267	.363	7	.167	-1	-7	-7	-1	-1.0
1919	NY-A	5	5	.500	23	9	4	1	1	90^2	89	6	32	50	12.2	3.47	92	.251	.317	7	.233	0	-2	-3	0	-0.2
	Bos-A	10	4	.714	21	11	9	1	4	121^1	105	0	39	63	10.8	2.52	120	.246	.310	5	.122	-1	10	7	-1	0.5
	Yr	15	9	.625	44	20	13	2	**5**	212	194	6	71	113	11.3	2.93	106	.248	.311	12	.169	-1	7	4	-0	0.3
1920	Bos-A	5	6	.455	16	10	7	0	1	107^2	100	3	38	53	11.8	3.01	121	.251	.321	5	.122	-2	9	8	1	0.6
1921	Bos-A	7	11	.389	39	13	7	0	3	173	204	10	77	60	15.1	4.11	103	.303	.382	7	.123	-5	3	2	0	-0.2
1922	Bos-A	6	7	.462	34	11	1	0	2	125^2	152	6	57	34	15.3	5.01	82	.314	.392	3	.079	-3	-14	-13	2	-1.3
1923	Was-A	10	7	.588	52	5	4	0	**9**	181^1	177	9	77	67	12.7	3.03	124	.270	.348	10	.200	2	19	15	-3	1.3
1924	*Was-A	5	1	.833	37	0	0	0	8	82^1	83	1	45	17	14.1	4.37	92	.282	.379	5	.278	2	-1	-3	-0	-0.2
1925	Was-A	2	4	.333	32	2	0	0	2	68^2	85	6	37	25	16.1	5.77	73	.315	.399	2	.143	-1	-10	-12	2	-1.0
Total	11	71	76	.483	345	110	54	5	42	1394^1	1382	59	610	603	13.1	3.52	99	.269	.351	65	.157	-10	5	-4	-0	-1.5

● LEFTY RUSSELL Russell, Clarence Dickson b: 7/8/1890, Baltimore, Md. d: 1/22/62, Baltimore, Md. BL/TL, 6'1", 165 lbs. Deb: 10/01/10 F

YEAR	TM/L	W	L	PCT	G	GS	CG	SH	SV	IP	H	HR	BB	SO	RAT	ERA	ERA+	OAV	OOB	BH	AVG	PB	PR	/A	PD	TPI
1910	Phi-A	1	0	1.000	1	1	1	1	0	9	8	0	2	5	10.0	0.00	—	.258	.303	0	.000	-0	3	2	0	0.3
1911	Phi-A	0	3	.000	7	2	0	0	0	31^2	45	1	18	7	19.3	7.67	41	.357	.456	5	.385	1	-15	-16	1	-1.2

YEAR TM/L	W	L	PCT	G	GS	CG	SH	SV	IP	H	HR	BB	SO	RAT	ERA	ERA+	OAV	OOB	BH	AVG	PB	PR	/A	PD	TPI
1912 Phi-A	0	2	.000	5	2	1	0	0	17^{1}	18	1	14	9	18.2	7.27	42	.265	.412	0	.000	-0	-8	-8	0	-0.8
Total 3	1	5	.167	13	5	2	1	0	58	71	2	34	21	17.5	6.36	47	.316	.423	5	.250	0	-20	-22	1	-1.7

● REB RUSSELL Russell, Ewell Albert b: 4/12/1889, Jackson, Miss. d: 9/30/73, Indianapolis, Ind BL/TL, 5'11", 185 lbs. Deb: 4/18/13 ♦

YEAR TM/L	W	L	PCT	G	GS	CG	SH	SV	IP	H	HR	BB	SO	RAT	ERA	ERA+	OAV	OOB	BH	AVG	PB	PR	/A	PD	TPI
1913 Chi-A	22	16	.579	**52**	36	26	8	4	316^{2}	250	2	79	122	9.5	1.90	154	.219	.273	20	.189	3	36	36	-5	3.7
1914 Chi-A	8	12	.400	38	23	8	1	1	167^{1}	168	3	33	79	11.0	2.90	92	.268	.308	17	.266	4	-3	-4	0	-0.1
1915 Chi-A	11	10	.524	41	25	10	3	2	229^{1}	215	0	47	90	10.5	2.59	115	.249	.292	21	.244	4	9	10	-2	1.3
1916 Chi-A	18	11	.621	56	25	16	5	3	264^{1}	207	1	42	112	**8.5**	2.42	114	.220	**.254**	13	.143	-3	12	10	-2	0.5
1917 *Chi-A	15	5	**.750**	35	24	11	5	3	189^{1}	170	1	32	54	9.6	1.95	136	.245	.279	19	.279	5	15	15	-1	2.2
1918 Chi-A	7	5	.583	19	15	10	2	0	124^{2}	117	0	33	38	10.8	2.60	105	.252	.302	7	.140	-1	2	2	-1	-0.2
1919 Chi-A	0	0	—	1	0	0	0	0	0	1	0	1	0	—	—	—	1.000	1.000	0	—	0	0	0	0	0.0
Total 7	81	59	.579	242	148	81	24	13	1291^{2}	1128	7	267	495	9.8	2.33	120	.238	.281	262	.268	10	72	69	-11	7.4

● JACK RUSSELL Russell, Jack Erwin b: 10/24/05, Paris, Tex. d: 11/3/90, Clearwater, Fla. BR/TR, 6'1.5", 178 lbs. Deb: 5/05/26

YEAR TM/L	W	L	PCT	G	GS	CG	SH	SV	IP	H	HR	BB	SO	RAT	ERA	ERA+	OAV	OOB	BH	AVG	PB	PR	/A	PD	TPI
1926 Bos-A	0	5	.000	36	5	1	0	0	98	94	2	24	17	10.9	3.58	114	.268	.316	4	.190	-0	5	5	4	0.9
1927 Bos-A	4	9	.308	34	15	4	1	0	147	172	5	40	25	13.3	4.10	103	.298	.348	6	.125	-3	1	2	1	0.0
1928 Bos-A	11	14	.440	32	26	10	2	0	201^{1}	233	6	41	27	12.4	3.84	107	.294	.332	13	.210	-0	4	6	1	0.7
1929 Bos-A	6	18	.250	35	32	13	0	0	227^{1}	263	12	40	37	12.1	3.92	109	.290	.322	9	.129	-4	8	9	4	0.9
1930 Bos-A	9	20	.310	35	30	15	0	0	229^{2}	302	11	53	35	14.0	5.45	85	.321	.359	14	.177	-3	-20	-21	2	-1.9
1931 Bos-A	10	18	.357	36	31	13	0	0	232	298	7	65	45	14.2	5.16	83	.310	.355	16	.195	-0	-20	-22	3	-1.7
1932 Bos-A	1	7	.125	11	6	1	0	0	39^{2}	61	2	15	7	17.2	6.81	66	.343	.394	1	.091	-1	-10	-10	0	-1.0
Cle-A	5	7	.417	18	11	6	0	1	113	146	5	27	27	13.9	4.70	101	.310	.349	12	.300	2	-3	1	1	0.4
Yr	6	14	.300	29	17	7	0	1	152^{2}	207	7	42	34	14.7	5.25	89	.319	.361	13	.255	1	-13	-10	2	-0.6
1933 *Was-A	12	6	.667	50	3	2	0	**13**	124	119	3	32	28	11.0	2.69	156	.255	.305	5	.147	-1	**22**	**21**	4	2.3
1934 Was-A☆	5	10	.333	**54**	9	3	0	**7**	157^{2}	179	6	56	38	13.5	4.17	104	.287	.348	7	.159	3	6	3	3	0.7
1935 Was-A	4	9	.308	43	7	2	0	3	126	170	10	37	30	14.9	5.71	76	.324	.371	7	.200	1	-18	-20	3	-1.5
1936 Was-A	3	2	.600	18	5	1	0	3	49^{2}	66	3	25	6	16.5	6.34	75	.317	.391	0	.000	-2	-7	-9	1	-0.8
Bos-A	0	3	.000	23	2	0	0	0	40	57	2	16	9	16.4	5.62	94	.345	.403	2	.286	0	-3	-1	2	0.1
Yr	3	5	.375	41	7	1	0	3	89^{2}	123	5	41	15	16.5	6.02	83	.330	.396	2	.091	-1	-10	-10	3	-0.7
1937 Det-A	2	5	.286	25	0	0	0	4	40^{1}	63	4	20	10	18.7	7.59	62	.362	.431	0	.000	-1	-13	-13	1	-1.1
1938 *Chi-N	6	1	.857	42	0	0	0	3	102^{1}	100	1	30	29	11.5	3.34	115	.258	.313	7	.219	1	5	6	3	1.0
1939 Chi-N	4	3	.571	39	0	0	0	3	68^{2}	78	3	24	32	13.4	3.67	107	.282	.339	0	.000	-2	**2**	2	2	0.1
1940 StL-N	3	4	.429	26	0	0	0	1	54	53	1	26	16	13.2	2.50	160	.252	.335	0	.000	-2	8	9	1	0.8
Total 15	85	141	.376	557	182	71	3	38	2050^{2}	2454	83	571	418	13.4	4.46	97	.299	.346	103	.167	-11	-33	-33	36	-0.1

● JEFF RUSSELL Russell, Jeffrey Lee b: 9/2/61, Cincinnati, Ohio BR/TR, 6'3", 210 lbs. Deb: 8/13/83

YEAR TM/L	W	L	PCT	G	GS	CG	SH	SV	IP	H	HR	BB	SO	RAT	ERA	ERA+	OAV	OOB	BH	AVG	PB	PR	/A	PD	TPI
1983 Cin-N	4	5	.444	10	10	2	0	0	68^{1}	58	7	22	40	10.5	3.03	126	.233	.295	3	.143	1	5	6	-0	0.7
1984 Cin-N	6	18	.250	33	30	4	2	0	181^{2}	186	15	65	101	12.6	4.26	89	.263	.329	8	.140	-0	-14	-10	1	-0.9
1985 Tex-A	3	6	.333	13	13	0	0	0	62	85	10	27	44	16.5	7.55	56	.324	.392	0	—	0	-23	-23	1	-2.0
1986 Tex-A	5	2	.714	37	0	0	0	2	82	74	11	31	54	11.6	3.40	126	.244	.316	0	—	0	7	8	2	1.0
1987 Tex-A	5	4	.556	52	2	0	0	3	97^{1}	109	9	52	56	15.1	4.44	101	.285	.373	0	—	0	0	0	1	0.2
1988 Tex-A★	10	9	.526	34	24	5	0	0	188^{2}	183	15	66	88	12.2	3.82	107	.257	.326	0	.000	0	3	6	2	0.7
1989 Tex-A★	6	4	.600	71	0	0	0	**38**	72^{2}	45	4	24	77	8.9	1.98	200	.182	.263	0	—	0	15	16	2	1.8
1990 Tex-A	1	5	.167	27	0	0	0	10	25^{1}	23	1	16	16	13.9	4.26	92	.253	.364	0	—	0	-1	-1	0	-0.1
1991 Tex-A	6	4	.600	68	0	0	0	30	79^{1}	71	11	26	52	11.1	3.29	122	.235	.298	0	—	0	7	7	2	0.8
1992 Tex-A	2	3	.400	51	0	0	0	28	56^{2}	51	3	22	43	11.9	1.91	200	.238	.315	0	—	0	13	12	1	1.3
*Oak-A	2	0	1.000	8	0	0	0	2	9^{2}	4	0	3	5	6.5	0.00	—	.125	.200	0	—	0	4	4	-0	0.4
Yr	4	3	.571	59	0	0	0	30	66^{1}	55	3	25	48	10.9	1.63	234	.220	.291	0	—	0	17	16	0	1.7
Total 10	50	60	.455	404	79	11	2	113	923^{2}	889	86	354	576	12.3	3.79	107	.254	.326	11	.139	1	16	25	10	3.9

● JOHN RUSSELL Russell, John Albert b: 10/20/1894, San Mateo, Cal. d: 11/19/30, Ely, Nev. BL/TL, 6'2", 195 lbs. Deb: 7/04/17

YEAR TM/L	W	L	PCT	G	GS	CG	SH	SV	IP	H	HR	BB	SO	RAT	ERA	ERA+	OAV	OOB	BH	AVG	PB	PR	/A	PD	TPI
1917 Bro-N	0	1	.000	5	1	1	0	0	16	12	1	6	1	10.1	4.50	62	.222	.300	1	.250	0	-3	-3	-0	-0.3
1918 Bro-N	0	0	—	1	0	0	0	0	1	2	0	1	0	27.0	18.00	15	.500	.600	0	—	0	-2	-2	-0	-0.2
1921 Chi-A	2	5	.286	11	9	4	0	0	66^{1}	82	3	35	15	16.0	5.29	80	.314	.397	10	.400	3	-7	-8	-1	-0.5
1922 Chi-A	0	1	.000	4	1	0	0	1	6^{2}	7	0	4	3	14.9	6.75	60	.280	.379	0	.000	-0	-2	-2	0	-0.2
Total 4	2	7	.222	21	11	5	0	1	90	103	4	46	19	15.0	5.40	73	.299	.384	11	.367	3	-14	-14	-1	-1.2

● JOHN RUSSELL Russell, John William b: 1/5/61, Oklahoma City, Okla. BR/TR, 6', 200 lbs. Deb: 6/22/84 ♦

YEAR TM/L	W	L	PCT	G	GS	CG	SH	SV	IP	H	HR	BB	SO	RAT	ERA	ERA+	OAV	OOB	BH	AVG	PB	PR	/A	PD	TPI
1989 Atl-N	0	0	—	1	0	0	0	0	0^{1}	0	0	0	0	0.0	0.00	—	.000	.000	29	.182	0	0	0	0	0.0

● MARIUS RUSSO Russo, Marius Ugo "Lefty" b: 7/19/14, Brooklyn, N.Y. BR/TL, 6'1", 190 lbs. Deb: 6/06/39

YEAR TM/L	W	L	PCT	G	GS	CG	SH	SV	IP	H	HR	BB	SO	RAT	ERA	ERA+	OAV	OOB	BH	AVG	PB	PR	/A	PD	TPI
1939 NY-A	8	3	.727	21	11	9	2	2	116	86	6	41	55	9.9	2.41	181	.210	.283	10	.244	1	29	25	2	2.8
1940 NY-A	14	8	.636	30	24	15	0	1	189^{1}	181	17	55	87	11.3	3.28	123	.249	.303	12	.188	2	23	16	3	2.1
1941 *NY-A☆	14	10	.583	28	27	17	3	1	209^{2}	195	8	87	105	12.1	3.09	127	.247	.322	18	.231	2	25	20	2	2.4
1942 NY-A	4	1	.800	9	5	2	0	0	45^{1}	41	2	14	15	11.1	2.78	124	.244	.306	4	.235	1	4	3	0	0.5
1943 *NY-A	5	10	.333	24	14	5	1	1	101^{2}	89	7	45	42	12.0	3.72	87	.235	.319	6	.194	1	-5	-6	0	-0.5
1946 NY-A	0	2	.000	8	3	0	0	0	18^{2}	26	1	11	7	17.8	4.34	80	.333	.416	0	.000	-1	-2	-2	0	-0.2
Total 6	45	34	.570	120	84	48	6	5	680^{2}	618	41	253	311	11.6	3.13	124	.242	.312	50	.213	7	74	57	8	7.1

● DICK RUSTECK Rusteck, Richard Frank b: 7/12/41, Chicago, Ill. BR/TL, 6'1", 175 lbs. Deb: 6/10/66

YEAR TM/L	W	L	PCT	G	GS	CG	SH	SV	IP	H	HR	BB	SO	RAT	ERA	ERA+	OAV	OOB	BH	AVG	PB	PR	/A	PD	TPI
1966 NY-N	1	2	.333	8	3	1	1	0	24	24	1	8	9	12.0	3.00	121	.276	.337	0	.000	-1	2	2	-0	0.1

● BABE RUTH Ruth, George Herman "The Bambino" or "The Sultan Of Swat"
b: 2/6/1895, Baltimore, Md. d: 8/16/48, New York, N.Y. BL/TL, 6'2", 215 lbs. Deb: 7/11/14 CH♦

YEAR TM/L	W	L	PCT	G	GS	CG	SH	SV	IP	H	HR	BB	SO	RAT	ERA	ERA+	OAV	OOB	BH	AVG	PB	PR	/A	PD	TPI
1914 Bos-A	2	1	.667	4	3	1	0	0	23	21	1	7	3	11.0	3.91	69	.236	.292	2	.200	0	-3	-3	-0	-0.3
1915 *Bos-A	18	8	.692	32	28	16	1	0	217^{2}	166	3	85	112	10.6	2.44	114	.212	.294	29	.315	15	12	8	1	2.7
1916 *Bos-A	23	12	.657	44	41	23	**9**	1	323^{2}	230	0	118	170	9.9	**1.75**	**158**	**.201**	.280	37	.272	13	**39**	37	0	**6.0**
1917 Bos-A	24	13	.649	41	38	**35**	6	2	326^{1}	244	2	108	128	10.0	2.01	128	.211	.284	40	.325	17	24	21	2	4.6
1918 *Bos-A	13	7	.650	20	19	18	1	0	166^{1}	125	1	49	40	9.5	2.22	121	.214	.277	95	.300	12	10	9	4	2.8
1919 Bos-A	9	5	.643	17	15	12	0	1	133^{1}	148	2	58	30	14.0	2.97	102	.290	.365	139	.322	13	4	1	0	1.5
1920 NY-A	1	0	1.000	1	1	0	0	0	4	3	0	2	0	11.3	4.50	85	.200	.294	172	.376	1	-0	-0	-0	0.0
1921 *NY-A	2	0	1.000	2	1	0	0	0	9	14	1	9	2	23.0	9.00	47	.350	.469	204	.378	2	-5	-5	0	-0.3
1930 NY-A	1	0	1.000	1	1	1	0	0	9	11	0	2	3	13.0	3.00	143	.306	.342	186	.359	1	2	1	1	0.3
1933 NY-A★	1	0	1.000	1	1	1	0	0	9	12	0	3	0	15.0	5.00	78	.308	.357	138	.301	1	-1	-1	-0	0.0
Total 10	94	46	.671	163	148	107	17	4	1221^{1}	974	10	441	488	10.6	2.28	122	.221	.297	2873	.342	75	81	67	8	17.3

● JOHNNY RUTHERFORD Rutherford, John William "Doc" b: 5/5/25, Belleville, Ont., Canada BL/TR, 5'10.5", 170 lbs. Deb: 4/30/52

YEAR TM/L	W	L	PCT	G	GS	CG	SH	SV	IP	H	HR	BB	SO	RAT	ERA	ERA+	OAV	OOB	BH	AVG	PB	PR	/A	PD	TPI
1952 *Bro-N	7	7	.500	22	11	4	0	2	97^{1}	97	9	29	29	11.8	4.25	86	.262	.319	9	.290	2	-6	-7	1	-0.4

● DICK RUTHVEN Ruthven, Richard David b: 3/27/51, Sacramento, Cal. BR/TR, 6'3", 190 lbs. Deb: 4/17/73

YEAR TM/L	W	L	PCT	G	GS	CG	SH	SV	IP	H	HR	BB	SO	RAT	ERA	ERA+	OAV	OOB	BH	AVG	PB	PR	/A	PD	TPI
1973 Phi-N	6	9	.400	25	23	3	1	1	128^{1}	125	10	75	98	14.2	4.21	90	.257	.360	5	.132	-1	-8	-6	1	-0.6
1974 Phi-N	9	13	.409	35	35	6	0	0	212^{2}	182	11	116	153	12.7	4.02	94	.231	.332	13	.191	-1	-10	-6	-1	-0.8
1975 Phi-N	2	2	.500	11	7	0	0	0	40^{2}	37	2	22	26	13.3	4.20	89	.243	.343	2	.154	-0	-3	-2	-0	-0.3
1976 Atl-N☆	14	17	.452	36	36	8	4	0	240^{1}	255	14	90	142	13.2	4.19	90	.275	.345	13	.171	-0	-19	-11	2	-0.9
1977 Atl-N	7	13	.350	25	23	6	2	0	151	158	14	62	84	13.2	4.23	105	.267	.338	12	.267	3	-5	4	-2	0.5

YEAR	TM/L	W	L	PCT	G	GS	CG	SH	SV	IP	H	HR	BB	SO	RAT	ERA	ERA+	OAV	OOB	BH	AVG	PB	PR	/A	PD	TPI
1978	Atl-N	2	6	.250	13	13	2	1	0	81	78	8	28	45	11.8	4.11	98	.257	.319	2	.083	-2	-5	-1	-0	-0.3
	*Phi-N	13	5	.722	20	20	9	2	0	150^{2}	136	13	28	75	9.9	2.99	119	.248	.285	15	.283	4	10	10	-0	1.5
	Yr	15	11	.577	33	33	11	3	0	231^{2}	214	21	56	120	10.5	3.38	111	.250	.297	17	.221	3	5	9	-1	1.2
1979	Phi-N	7	5	.583	20	20	3	2	0	122^{1}	121	10	37	58	11.8	4.27	90	.256	.313	6	.146	-0	-7	-6	-2	-0.8
1980	*Phi-N	17	10	.630	33	33	6	1	0	223^{1}	241	9	74	86	12.8	3.55	107	.283	.342	16	.235	4	1	6	-0	1.0
1981	*Phi-N★	12	7	.632	23	22	5	0	0	146^{2}	162	10	54	80	13.4	5.15	70	.281	.346	7	.140	-0	-27	-25	-1	-2.6
1982	Phi-N	11	11	.500	33	31	8	2	0	204^{1}	189	18	59	115	11.2	3.79	97	.246	.305	7	.109	-2	-4	-3	-2	-0.8
1983	Phi-N	1	3	.250	7	7	0	0	0	33^{2}	46	5	10	26	15.0	5.61	64	.333	.378	1	.111	-0	-7	-8	0	-0.8
	Chi-N	12	9	.571	25	25	5	2	0	149^{1}	156	17	28	73	11.3	4.10	92	.269	.306	12	.226	2	-8	-5	2	-0.1
	Yr	13	12	.520	32	32	5	2	0	183	202	22	38	99	12.0	4.38	86	.279	.318	13	.210	2	-15	-13	2	-0.9
1984	Chi-N	6	10	.375	23	22	0	0	0	126^{2}	154	14	41	55	14.1	5.04	77	.302	.359	7	.159	0	-21	-16	-0	-1.6
1985	Chi-N	4	7	.364	20	15	0	0	0	87^{1}	103	6	37	26	14.4	4.53	88	.299	.367	5	.208	0	-9	-5	-1	-0.7
1986	Chi-N	0	0	—	6	0	0	0	0	10^{2}	12	4	6	3	15.2	5.06	80	.293	.383	0	.000	-0	-2	-1	-0	-0.2
Total	14	123	127	.492	355	332	61	17	1	2109	2155	165	767	1145	12.6	4.14	92	.267	.333	123	.183	6	-123	-75	-4	-7.5

● CYCLONE RYAN Ryan, Daniel R. b: 1866, Capperwhite, Ireland d: 1/30/17, Medfield, Mass. TR , 6′, Deb: 8/08/1887 ♦

YEAR	TM/L	W	L	PCT	G	GS	CG	SH	SV	IP	H	HR	BB	SO	RAT	ERA	ERA+	OAV	OOB	BH	AVG	PB	PR	/A	PD	TPI
1887	NY-a	0	1	.000	2	1	0	0	0	2^{1}	5	1	6	0	42.4	23.14	18	.455	.647	7	.219	-0	-5	-5	-0	-0.4
1891	Bos-N	0	0	—	1	0	0	0	0	3	2	0	1	0	9.0	0.00	—	.182	.251	0	.000	-0	1	1	0	0.1
Total	2	0	1	.000	3	1	0	0	0	5^{1}	7	1	7	0	23.6	10.13	39	.319	.483	7	.212	-0	-4	-4	0	-0.3

● JACK RYAN Ryan, Jack "Gulfport" b: 9/19/1884, Lawrenceville, Ill. d: 10/16/49, Hondsboro, Miss. BR/TR, 5′10″, 165 lbs. Deb: 7/02/08

YEAR	TM/L	W	L	PCT	G	GS	CG	SH	SV	IP	H	HR	BB	SO	RAT	ERA	ERA+	OAV	OOB	BH	AVG	PB	PR	/A	PD	TPI
1908	Cle-A	1	1	.500	8	1	1	0	1	35^{2}	27	3	2	7	7.6	2.27	105	.220	.238	1	.091	0	0	0	-0	0.1
1909	Bos-A	4	3	.571	13	8	2	0	0	61^{1}	65	0	20	24	13.1	3.23	77	.281	.349	4	.211	0	-5	-5	-1	-0.6
1911	Bro-N	0	1	.000	3	1	0	0	0	6	9	1	4	1	21.0	3.00	111	.375	.483	0	.000	-0	0	0	0	0.0
Total	3	5	5	.500	24	10	3	0	1	103	101	4	26	32	11.6	2.88	87	.267	.324	5	.161	1	-4	-4	-0	-0.5

● JIMMY RYAN Ryan, James Edward "Pony" b: 2/11/1863, Clinton, Mass. d: 10/26/23, Chicago, Ill. BR/TL, 5′9″, 162 lbs. Deb: 10/08/1885 ♦

YEAR	TM/L	W	L	PCT	G	GS	CG	SH	SV	IP	H	HR	BB	SO	RAT	ERA	ERA+	OAV	OOB	BH	AVG	PB	PR	/A	PD	TPI
1886	*Chi-N	0	0	—	5	0	0	0	1	23^{1}	19	2	13	15	12.3	4.63	79	.257	.368	100	.306	1	-3	-3	0	-0.1
1887	Chi-N	2	1	.667	8	3	2	0	0	45	53	3	17	14	15.2	4.20	107	.305	.386	145	.285	2	-1	1	2	0.4
1888	Chi-N	4	0	1.000	8	2	1	0	0	38^{1}	47	2	12	11	13.9	3.05	99	.297	.347	182	.332	5	-1	-0	0	0.2
1891	Chi-N	0	0	—	2	0	0	0	1	5^{2}	11	0	2	2	20.6	1.59	210	.394	.434	140	.277	1	1	1	-0	0.1
1893	Chi-N	0	0	—	1	0	0	0	0	4^{2}	3	0	0	1	5.8	0.00	—	.178	.178	102	.299	0	2	2	0	0.3
Total	5	6	1	.857	24	5	3	0	2	117	133	7	44	43	14.1	3.62	105	.295	.365	2502	.306	9	-1	2	2	0.9

● JOHNNY RYAN Ryan, John Joseph b: 10/1853, Philadelphia, Pa. d: 3/22/02, Philadelphia, Pa. 5′7.5″, 150 lbs. Deb: 8/19/1873 ♦

YEAR	TM/L	W	L	PCT	G	GS	CG	SH	SV	IP	H	HR	BB	SO	RAT	ERA	ERA+	OAV	OOB	BH	AVG	PB	PR	/A	PD	TPI
1874	Bal-n	0	0	—	1	0	0	0	0	1^{1}	9	0	0		60.8	*13.50*	23	.643	.643	33	.179	-0	-2	-2		-0.1
1875	NH-n	1	5	.167	10	6	4	0	0	59^{1}	69	1	9		11.8	*3.34*	69	.256	.280	23	.158	-1	-6	-7		-0.6
1876	Lou-N	0	0	—	1	0	0	0	0	8	22	0	0	1	24.8	5.63	48	.449	.449	61	.253	-0	-3	-3	-0	-0.2
Total	2 n	1	5	.167	11	6	4	0	0	60^{2}	78	1	9		12.9	*3.56*	65	.275	.297	58	.172	-1	-7	-8		-0.7

● JOHN RYAN Ryan, John M. b: Hamilton, Ohio Deb: 4/19/1884

YEAR	TM/L	W	L	PCT	G	GS	CG	SH	SV	IP	H	HR	BB	SO	RAT	ERA	ERA+	OAV	OOB	BH	AVG	PB	PR	/A	PD	TPI
1884	Bal-U	3	2	.600	6	6	5	0	0	51	61	1	16	33	13.6	3.35	99	.278	.327	2	.080	-3	-2	-0	-0	-0.3

● KEN RYAN Ryan, Kenneth Frederick b: 10/24/68, Pawtucket.R.I. BR/TR, 6′3″, 200 lbs. Deb: 8/31/92

YEAR	TM/L	W	L	PCT	G	GS	CG	SH	SV	IP	H	HR	BB	SO	RAT	ERA	ERA+	OAV	OOB	BH	AVG	PB	PR	/A	PD	TPI
1992	Bos-A	0	0	—	7	0	0	0	1	7	4	2	5	5	11.6	6.43	65	.174	.321	0	—	0	-2	-2	0	-0.2

● NOLAN RYAN Ryan, Lynn Nolan b: 1/31/47, Refugio, Tex. BR/TR, 6′2″, 195 lbs. Deb: 9/11/66

YEAR	TM/L	W	L	PCT	G	GS	CG	SH	SV	IP	H	HR	BB	SO	RAT	ERA	ERA+	OAV	OOB	BH	AVG	PB	PR	/A	PD	TPI
1966	NY-N	0	1	.000	2	1	0	0	0	3	5	1	3	6	24.0	15.00	24	.357	.471	0	—	0	-4	-4	0	-0.4
1968	NY-N	6	9	.400	21	18	3	0	0	134	93	12	75	133	11.6	3.09	98	.200	.317	5	.114	-1	-2	-1	-2	-0.5
1969	*NY-N	6	3	.667	25	10	2	0	1	89^{1}	60	3	53	92	11.5	3.53	104	.189	.307	3	.103	-1	1	1	-2	-0.2
1970	NY-N	7	11	.389	27	19	5	2	1	131^{2}	86	10	97	125	12.8	3.42	118	.188	.335	8	.178	-1	9	9	-1	0.7
1971	NY-N	10	14	.417	30	26	3	0	0	152	125	8	116	137	15.2	3.97	86	.219	.365	6	.128	-0	-8	-9	-1	-1.2
1972	Cal-A☆	19	16	.543	39	39	20	**9**	0	284	166	14	157	**329**	10.6	2.28	128	**.171**	.292	13	.135	0	25	20	-2	2.2
1973	Cal-A★	21	16	.568	41	39	26	4	1	326	238	18	162	**383**	11.2	2.87	123	.203	.304	0	—	0	34	24	-2	2.8
1974	Cal-A	22	16	.579	42	41	26	3	0	**332^{2}**	221	18	202	**367**	11.7	2.89	119	**.190**	.314	0	—	0	27	20	2	2.8
1975	Cal-A☆	14	12	.538	28	28	10	5	0	198	152	13	132	186	13.2	3.45	103	.213	.342	0	—	0	7	2	-2	0.5
1976	Cal-A	17	18	.486	39	39	21	**7**	0	284^{1}	193	13	183	**327**	12.1	3.36	99	**.195**	.323	0	—	0	5	-1	0	0.3
1977	Cal-A†	19	16	.543	37	37	**22**	4	0	299	198	12	204	**341**	12.4	2.77	141	**.193**	.331	0	—	0	**43**	**38**	0	4.0
1978	Cal-A	10	13	.435	31	31	14	3	0	234^{2}	183	12	148	**260**	12.8	3.72	97	.220	.340	0	—	0	1	-3	1	0.0
1979	*Cal-A★	16	14	.533	34	34	17	**5**	0	222^{2}	169	15	114	**223**	11.7	3.60	113	**.212**	.314	0	—	0	15	12	-0	1.3
1980	*Hou-N	11	10	.524	35	35	4	2	0	233^{2}	205	10	98	200	11.8	3.35	98	.236	.316	6	.086	-1	6	-2	-1	-0.5
1981	*Hou-N★	11	5	.688	21	21	5	3	0	149	99	2	68	140	10.1	**1.69**	**195**	**.188**	.281	11	.216	3	**30**	**27**	-1	**3.4**
1982	Hou-N	16	12	.571	35	35	10	3	0	250^{1}	196	20	109	245	11.3	3.16	105	**.213**	.302	10	.120	-1	12	4	-0	0.3
1983	Hou-N	14	9	.609	29	29	5	2	0	196^{1}	134	9	101	183	11.0	2.98	114	**.195**	.302	5	.072	-3	14	9	-0	0.6
1984	Hou-N	12	11	.522	30	30	5	2	0	183^{2}	143	12	69	197	10.6	3.04	109	.211	.288	6	.098	-1	11	6	-3	0.2
1985	Hou-N★	10	12	.455	35	35	4	0	0	232	205	12	95	209	12.0	3.80	91	.239	.322	7	.111	-1	-5	-9	-3	-1.3
1986	*Hou-N	12	8	.600	30	30	1	0	0	178	119	14	82	194	10.4	3.34	108	.188	.285	6	.102	-2	8	5	-1	0.1
1987	Hou-N	8	16	.333	34	34	0	0	0	211^{2}	154	14	87	**270**	10.4	**2.76**	**142**	**.199**	.284	4	.062	-3	**31**	**27**	-1	2.4
1988	Hou-N	12	11	.522	33	33	4	1	0	220	186	18	87	**228**	11.5	3.52	94	.227	.307	4	.057	-3	-2	-5	-3	-1.1
1989	Tex-A★	16	10	.615	32	32	6	2	0	239^{1}	162	17	98	**301**	10.1	3.20	124	**.187**	.276	0	—	0	18	20	-1	2.0
1990	Tex-A	13	9	.591	30	30	5	2	0	204	137	18	74	**232**	**9.6**	3.44	114	**.188**	**.269**	0	—	0	11	11	-2	0.9
1991	Tex-A	12	6	.667	27	27	2	2	0	173	102	12	72	203	**9.3**	2.91	138	**.172**	**.267**	0	—	0	23	21	-1	2.2
1992	Tex-A	5	9	.357	27	27	2	0	0	157^{1}	138	9	69	157	12.5	3.72	103	.238	.331	0	—	0	4	2	-1	0.1
Total	26	319	287	.526	794	760	222	61	3	5319^{2}	3869	316	2755	5668	11.5	3.17	112	.203	.309	94	.110	-16	313	224	-28	21.6

● ROSY RYAN Ryan, Wilfred Patrick Dolan b: 3/15/1898, Worcester, Mass. d: 12/10/80, Scottsdale, Ariz. BL/TR, 6′, 185 lbs. Deb: 9/07/19

YEAR	TM/L	W	L	PCT	G	GS	CG	SH	SV	IP	H	HR	BB	SO	RAT	ERA	ERA+	OAV	OOB	BH	AVG	PB	PR	/A	PD	TPI
1919	NY-N	1	2	.333	4	3	1	0	0	20^{1}	20	0	9	7	13.3	3.10	91	.260	.345	0	.000	-1	-0	-1	-1	-0.2
1920	NY-N	0	1	.000	3	1	1	0	0	15^{1}	14	1	4	5	10.6	1.76	170	.259	.310	0	.000	-1	2	2	0	0.2
1921	NY-N	7	10	.412	36	16	5	0	3	147^{1}	140	6	32	58	10.6	3.73	98	.255	.297	9	.200	1	1	-1	-1	-0.2
1922	*NY-N	17	12	.586	46	20	12	1	3	191^{2}	194	5	74	75	12.7	3.01	133	.269	.338	12	.194	1	23	21	-1	2.0
1923	*NY-N	16	5	.762	**45**	15	7	0	4	172^{2}	169	8	46	58	11.3	3.49	109	.257	.308	11	.208	0	10	6	0	0.6
1924	*NY-N	8	6	.571	37	9	2	0	5	124^{2}	137	1	37	36	12.7	4.26	86	.285	.339	5	.139	-1	-5	-8	-2	-1.1
1925	Bos-N	2	8	.200	37	7	1	0	2	122^{2}	152	7	52	48	15.0	6.31	64	.303	.368	11	.282	3	-28	-31	-1	-2.7
1926	Bos-N	0	2	.000	7	2	0	0	0	19	29	1	7	1	17.1	7.58	47	.392	.444	1	.200	-0	-8	-9	-0	-0.8
1928	NY-A	0	0	—	3	0	0	0	0	6	17	1	1	5	27.0	16.50	23	.486	.500	0	.000	-1	-8	-8	-0	-0.8
1933	Bro-N	1	1	.500	30	0	0	0	2	61^{1}	69	3	16	22	12.9	4.55	71	.276	.327	2	.154	0	-8	-9	-0	-1.0
Total	10	52	47	.525	248	73	29	1	19	881	941	33	278	315	12.6	4.14	91	.277	.333	51	.190	1	-22	-38	-5	-4.0

● MIKE RYBA Ryba, Dominic Joseph b: 6/9/03, DeLancey, Pa. d: 12/13/71, Brookline Station Mo. BR/TR, 5′11.5″, 180 lbs. Deb: 9/22/35 C

YEAR	TM/L	W	L	PCT	G	GS	CG	SH	SV	IP	H	HR	BB	SO	RAT	ERA	ERA+	OAV	OOB	BH	AVG	PB	PR	/A	PD	TPI
1935	StL-N	1	1	.500	2	1	1	0	0	16	15	0	1	6	9.0	3.38	121	.242	.254	2	.400	1	1	1	0	0.2
1936	StL-N	5	1	.833	14	0	0	0	0	45	55	3	16	25	14.6	5.40	73	.294	.356	3	.167	-0	-7	-7	-1	-0.8
1937	StL-N	9	6	.600	38	8	5	0	0	135	152	8	40	57	12.9	4.13	96	.284	.336	15	.313	4	-3	-2	0	0.2
1938	StL-N	1	1	.500	3	0	0	0	0	5	8	0	1	0	16.2	5.40	73	.348	.375	0	—	0	-1	-1	0	-0.1
1941	Bos-A	7	3	.700	40	3	0	0	6	121	143	14	42	54	13.8	4.46	93	.297	.353	8	.216	1	-4	-4	2	-0.1
1942	Bos-A	3	3	.500	18	0	0	0	3	44^{1}	49	5	13	16	12.8	3.86	97	.278	.332	5	.294	1	-1	-1	1	0.1

YEAR	TM/L	W	L	PCT	G	GS	CG	SH	SV	IP	H	HR	BB	SO	RAT	ERA	ERA+	OAV	OOB	BH	AVG	PB	PR	/A	PD	TPI
1943	Bos-A	7	5	.583	40	8	4	1	2	143^2	142	4	57	50	12.5	3.26	102	.262	.333	8	.186	0	1	1	-1	0.0
1944	Bos-A	12	7	.632	42	7	2	0	2	138	119	7	39	50	10.3	3.33	102	.233	.287	6	.146	-0	2	1	3	0.3
1945	Bos-A	7	6	.538	34	9	4	1	2	123	122	5	33	44	11.5	2.49	137	.259	.310	9	.250	2	12	13	-1	1.5
1946	*Bos-A	0	1	.000	9	0	0	0	1	12^2	12	1	5	5	12.1	3.55	103	.261	.333	2	1.000	1	-0	0	-0	0.1
Total	10	52	34	.605	240	36	16	2	16	783^2	817	47	247	307	12.3	3.66	100	.269	.326	58	.235	9	-1	1	3	1.4

● GARY RYERSON Ryerson, Gary Lawrence b: 6/7/48, Los Angeles, Cal. BR/TL, 6'1", 175 lbs. Deb: 6/28/72

YEAR	TM/L	W	L	PCT	G	GS	CG	SH	SV	IP	H	HR	BB	SO	RAT	ERA	ERA+	OAV	OOB	BH	AVG	PB	PR	/A	PD	TPI
1972	Mil-A	3	8	.273	20	14	4	1	0	102	119	9	21	45	12.4	3.62	84	.290	.324	1	.042	-1	-6	-7	-1	-1.0
1973	Mil-A	0	1	.000	9	4	0	0	0	23	32	0	7	10	15.3	7.83	48	.327	.371	0	—	0	-10	-10	0	-0.9
Total	2	3	9	.250	29	18	4	1	0	125	151	9	28	55	12.9	4.39	72	.297	.333	1	.042	-1	-17	-17	-1	-1.9

● BRET SABERHAGEN Saberhagen, Bret William b: 4/11/64, Chicago Heights, Ill. BR/TR, 6'1", 195 lbs. Deb: 4/04/84

YEAR	TM/L	W	L	PCT	G	GS	CG	SH	SV	IP	H	HR	BB	SO	RAT	ERA	ERA+	OAV	OOB	BH	AVG	PB	PR	/A	PD	TPI
1984	*KC-A	10	11	.476	38	18	2	1	1	157^2	138	13	36	73	10.0	3.48	116	.237	.283	0	—	0	9	10	0	1.0
1985	*KC-A	20	6	.769	32	32	10	1	0	235^1	211	19	38	158	**9.6**	2.87	145	.241	**.273**	0	—	0	33	34	2	3.8
1986	KC-A	7	12	.368	30	25	4	2	0	156	165	15	29	112	11.3	4.15	102	.268	.303	0	—	0	0	2	1	0.3
1987	KC-A★	18	10	.643	33	33	15	4	0	257	246	27	53	163	10.7	3.36	135	.252	.295	0	—	0	31	34	1	3.5
1988	KC-A	14	16	.467	35	35	9	0	0	260^2	271	18	59	171	11.5	3.80	105	.269	.312	0	—	0	5	5	0	0.6
1989	KC-A	**23**	6	**.793**	36	35	**12**	4	0	**262^1**	209	13	43	193	**8.7**	**2.16**	**178**	.217	**.252**	0	—	0	**50**	**49**	0	**5.5**
1990	KC-A★	5	9	.357	20	20	5	0	0	135	146	9	28	87	11.7	3.27	117	.279	.316	0	—	0	10	8	3	1.2
1991	KC-A	13	8	.619	28	28	7	2	0	196^1	165	12	45	136	10.0	3.07	134	.228	.281	0	—	0	22	23	1	2.5
1992	NY-N	3	5	.375	17	15	1	1	0	97^2	84	6	27	81	10.6	3.50	100	.233	.294	3	.107	-1	0	-0	3	0.2
Total	9	113	83	.577	269	241	65	15	1	1758	1635	132	358	1174	10.4	3.23	126	.247	.288	3	.107	-1	161	164	12	18.6

● RAY SADECKI Sadecki, Raymond Michael b: 12/26/40, Kansas City, Kan. BL/TL, 5'11", 180 lbs. Deb: 5/19/60

YEAR	TM/L	W	L	PCT	G	GS	CG	SH	SV	IP	H	HR	BB	SO	RAT	ERA	ERA+	OAV	OOB	BH	AVG	PB	PR	/A	PD	TPI
1960	StL-N	9	9	.500	26	26	7	1	0	157^1	148	15	86	95	13.4	3.78	109	.249	.345	12	.211	-0	-0	6	-2	0.4
1961	StL-N	14	10	.583	31	31	13	0	0	222^2	196	28	102	114	12.2	3.72	118	.238	.324	22	.253	2	8	17	-5	1.4
1962	StL-N	6	8	.429	22	17	4	1	1	102^1	121	13	43	50	14.7	5.54	77	.296	.367	3	.081	-2	-18	-14	-2	-1.7
1963	StL-N	10	10	.500	36	28	4	1	1	193^1	198	25	78	136	13.0	4.10	87	.266	.339	9	.141	-1	-17	-12	-3	-1.7
1964	*StL-N	20	11	.645	37	32	9	2	1	220	232	16	60	119	12.0	3.68	103	.273	.322	12	.160	2	-4	3	-3	0.2
1965	StL-N	6	15	.286	36	28	4	0	1	172^2	192	26	64	122	13.3	5.21	74	.284	.346	11	.200	2	-32	-26	-2	-2.7
1966	StL-N	2	1	.667	5	3	1	0	0	24^1	16	2	9	21	9.2	2.22	162	.188	.266	3	.429	2	4	4	0	0.6
	SF-N	3	7	.300	26	19	3	1	0	105	125	20	39	62	14.4	5.40	68	.293	.358	11	.324	6	-21	-20	-2	-1.7
	Yr	5	8	.385	31	22	4	1	0	129^1	141	22	48	83	13.4	4.80	76	.276	.343	14	.341	7	-17	-17	-2	-1.1
1967	SF-N	12	6	.667	35	24	10	2	0	188	165	8	58	145	10.9	2.78	118	.238	.301	18	.247	4	13	11	-1	1.6
1968	SF-N	12	18	.400	38	36	13	6	0	254	225	14	70	206	10.6	2.91	101	.237	.292	8	.094	-1	2	1	-2	-0.3
1969	SF-N	5	8	.385	29	17	4	3	0	138^1	137	18	53	104	12.5	4.23	83	.259	.329	5	.125	2	-10	-11	2	-0.8
1970	NY-N	8	4	.667	28	19	4	0	0	138^2	134	18	52	89	12.1	3.89	103	.255	.322	8	.205	1	2	2	-2	0.0
1971	NY-N	7	7	.500	34	20	5	2	0	163^1	139	10	44	120	10.3	2.92	117	.229	.285	10	.200	1	10	9	-2	0.9
1972	NY-N	2	1	.667	34	2	0	0	0	75^2	73	3	31	38	12.6	3.09	109	.257	.334	2	.154	-0	3	2	-1	0.1
1973	*NY-N	5	4	.556	31	11	1	0	1	116^2	109	11	41	87	11.6	3.39	107	.248	.314	7	.226	1	3	3	-3	0.2
1974	NY-N	8	8	.500	34	10	3	1	0	103	107	7	35	46	12.6	3.41	105	.274	.337	7	.259	1	2	2	-0	0.3
1975	StL-N	1	0	1.000	8	0	0	0	0	11	13	0	7	8	16.4	3.27	115	.289	.385	0	—	0	0	1	-0	0.0
	Atl-N	2	3	.400	25	5	0	0	1	66^1	73	3	21	24	13.3	4.21	90	.286	.350	3	.200	0	-4	-3	-1	-0.4
	Yr	3	3	.500	33	5	0	0	1	77^1	86	3	28	32	13.7	4.07	93	.285	.353	3	.200	0	-4	-3	-1	-0.4
	KC-A	1	0	1.000	5	0	0	0	0	3	5	0	3	0	24.0	3.00	128	.333	.444	0	—	0	0	0	-0	-0.1
1976	KC-A	0	0	—	3	0	0	0	0	4^2	7	0	3	1	19.3	0.00	—	.368	.455	0	—	0	2	2	-0	0.1
	Mil-A	2	0	1.000	36	0	0	0	1	37^1	38	2	20	27	14.7	4.34	81	.262	.363	0	—	0	-3	-4	-1	-0.3
	Yr	2	0	1.000	39	0	0	0	1	42	45	2	23	28	15.2	3.86	91	.274	.374	0	—	0	-2	-2	-1	-0.2
1977	NY-N	0	1	.000	4	0	0	0	0	3	3	1	3	0	18.0	6.00	62	.300	.462	0	—	0	-1	-1	-0	-0.1
Total	18	135	131	.508	563	328	85	20	7	2500^2	2456	240	922	1614	12.3	3.78	97	.258	.326	151	.191	19	-61	-32	-30	-4.0

● JIM SADOWSKI Sadowski, James Michael b: 8/7/51, Pittsburgh, Pa. BR/TR, 6'3", 195 lbs. Deb: 4/27/74

YEAR	TM/L	W	L	PCT	G	GS	CG	SH	SV	IP	H	HR	BB	SO	RAT	ERA	ERA+	OAV	OOB	BH	AVG	PB	PR	/A	PD	TPI
1974	Pit-N	0	1	.000	4	0	0	0	0	9	7	1	9	1	16.0	6.00	57	.233	.410	0	.000	0	-2	-3	1	-0.2

● BOB SADOWSKI Sadowski, Robert b: 2/19/38, Pittsburgh, Pa. BR/TR, 6'2", 195 lbs. Deb: 6/19/63 F

YEAR	TM/L	W	L	PCT	G	GS	CG	SH	SV	IP	H	HR	BB	SO	RAT	ERA	ERA+	OAV	OOB	BH	AVG	PB	PR	/A	PD	TPI
1963	Mil-N	5	7	.417	19	18	5	1	0	116^2	99	8	30	72	10.3	2.62	123	.231	.289	2	.057	-2	9	8	1	0.7
1964	Mil-N	9	10	.474	51	18	5	0	5	166^2	159	18	56	96	12.0	4.10	86	.251	.319	8	.154	0	-11	-11	3	-0.9
1965	Mil-N	5	9	.357	34	13	3	0	3	123	117	11	35	78	11.3	4.32	82	.250	.306	3	.086	-2	-11	-11	-1	-1.4
1966	Bos-A	1	1	.500	11	5	0	0	0	33^1	41	4	9	11	13.8	5.40	70	.311	.359	0	.000	-1	-7	-6	-0	-0.7
Total	4	20	27	.426	115	54	13	1	8	439^2	416	41	130	257	11.5	3.87	90	.250	.311	13	.101	-4	-20	-20	2	-2.3

● TED SADOWSKI Sadowski, Theodore b: 4/1/36, Pittsburgh, Pa. BR/TR, 6'1.5", 190 lbs. Deb: 9/02/60 F

YEAR	TM/L	W	L	PCT	G	GS	CG	SH	SV	IP	H	HR	BB	SO	RAT	ERA	ERA+	OAV	OOB	BH	AVG	PB	PR	/A	PD	TPI
1960	Was-A	1	0	1.000	9	1	0	0	1	17^1	17	4	9	12	14.0	5.19	75	.258	.355	0	.000	-0	-3	-3	-0	-0.3
1961	Min-A	0	2	.000	15	1	0	0	0	33	49	6	11	12	16.6	6.82	62	.348	.399	0	.000	-1	-10	-9	1	-0.9
1962	Min-A	1	1	.500	19	0	0	0	0	34	37	6	11	15	13.0	5.03	81	.301	.363	2	.500	1	-4	-4	0	-0.3
Total	3	2	3	.400	43	2	0	0	1	84^1	103	16	31	39	14.6	5.76	71	.312	.376	2	.154	-0	-17	-16	1	-1.5

● JOHNNY SAIN Sain, John Franklin b: 9/25/17, Havana, Ark. BR/TR, 6'2", 200 lbs. Deb: 4/24/42 C

YEAR	TM/L	W	L	PCT	G	GS	CG	SH	SV	IP	H	HR	BB	SO	RAT	ERA	ERA+	OAV	OOB	BH	AVG	PB	PR	/A	PD	TPI
1942	Bos-N	4	7	.364	40	3	0	0	6	97	79	8	63	68	13.6	3.90	86	.228	.354	2	.074	-2	-6	-6	1	-0.7
1946	Bos-N	20	14	.588	37	34	**24**	3	2	265	225	8	87	129	10.7	2.21	155	.230	.294	28	.298	5	35	36	3	**5.1**
1947	Bos-N★	21	12	.636	38	35	22	3	1	266	265	19	79	132	11.8	3.52	111	.255	.310	37	.346	12	16	11	1	2.4
1948	*Bos-N★	**24**	15	.615	42	39	**28**	4	1	**314^2**	297	19	83	137	11.0	2.60	147	.245	.296	25	.217	2	**47**	43	-2	4.6
1949	Bos-N	10	17	.370	37	36	16	1	0	243	285	15	75	73	13.5	4.81	78	.291	.344	20	.206	1	-21	-28	-2	-2.7
1950	Bos-N	20	13	.606	37	37	25	3	0	278^1	294	34	70	96	11.8	3.94	98	.269	.314	21	.206	4	6	-3	-2	-0.2
1951	Bos-N	5	13	.278	26	22	6	1	1	160^1	195	16	45	63	13.6	4.21	87	.299	.347	11	.212	3	-4	-10	0	-0.7
	*NY-A	2	1	.667	7	4	1	0	1	37	41	5	8	21	11.9	4.14	93	.281	.318	4	.286	1	-0	-1	1	0.0
1952	*NY-A	11	6	.647	35	16	8	0	7	148^1	149	15	38	57	11.5	3.46	96	.261	.310	19	.268	6	4	-2	-1	0.3
1953	*NY-A☆	14	7	.667	40	19	10	1	9	189	189	16	45	84	11.3	3.00	123	.262	.308	17	.250	4	21	15	-0	1.9
1954	NY-A	6	6	.500	45	0	0	0	**22**	77	66	11	15	33	9.5	3.16	109	.229	.267	6	.353	2	5	2	-0	0.5
1955	NY-A	0	0	—	3	0	0	0	0	5^1	6	4	1	5	11.8	6.75	55	.300	.333	0	.000	-0	-2	-2	0	-0.2
	KC-A	2	5	.286	25	0	0	0	1	44^2	54	10	10	12	12.9	5.44	77	.297	.333	0	.000	-1	-7	-6	-1	-0.8
	Yr	2	5	.286	28	0	0	0	1	50	60	14	11	17	12.8	5.58	74	.297	.333	0	.000	-1	-9	-8	-1	-1.0
Total	11	139	116	.545	412	245	140	16	51	2125^2	2145	180	619	910	11.8	3.49	106	.261	.315	190	.245	38	94	50	-2	9.5

● RANDY ST.CLAIRE St.Claire, Randy Anthony b: 8/23/60, Glens Falls, N.Y. BR/TR, 6'2", 190 lbs. Deb: 9/11/84 F

YEAR	TM/L	W	L	PCT	G	GS	CG	SH	SV	IP	H	HR	BB	SO	RAT	ERA	ERA+	OAV	OOB	BH	AVG	PB	PR	/A	PD	TPI
1984	Mon-N	0	0	—	4	0	0	0	0	8	11	0	2	4	15.8	4.50	76	.344	.400	0	—	0	-1	-1	-0	-0.1
1985	Mon-N	5	3	.625	42	0	0	0	0	68^2	69	3	26	25	12.6	3.93	86	.265	.334	1	.200	1	-3	-4	0	-0.3
1986	Mon-N	2	0	1.000	11	0	0	0	1	19	13	2	6	21	9.0	2.37	156	.186	.250	0	.000	-0	3	3	1	0.3
1987	Mon-N	3	3	.500	44	0	0	0	7	67	64	9	20	43	11.4	4.03	104	.249	.306	2	.333	1	0	1	-0	0.1
1988	Mon-N	0	0	—	6	0	0	0	0	7^1	11	2	5	6	19.6	6.14	59	.344	.432	0	—	0	-2	-2	0	-0.2
	Cin-N	1	0	1.000	10	0	0	0	0	13^2	13	3	5	8	11.9	2.63	136	.241	.305	0	.000	-0	1	1	-0	0.1
	Yr	1	0	1.000	16	0	0	0	0	21	24	5	10	14	14.6	3.86	93	.276	.351	0	.000	-0	-1	-1	0	-0.1
1989	Min-A	1	0	1.000	14	0	0	0	1	22^1	19	4	10	14	12.5	5.24	79	.226	.323	0	—	0	-3	-3	0	-0.3
1991	*Atl-N	0	0	—	19	0	0	0	0	28^2	31	4	9	30	12.6	4.08	95	.282	.336	1	.500	0	-1	-1	0	0.0
1992	Atl-N	0	0	—	10	0	0	0	0	15^1	17	1	8	7	14.7	5.87	64	.283	.368	0	—	0	-4	-4	0	-0.4

YEAR TM/L	W	L	PCT	G	GS	CG	SH	SV	IP	H	HR	BB	SO	RAT	ERA	ERA+	OAV	OOB	BH	AVG	PB	PR	/A	PD	TPI
Total 8	12	6	.667	160	0	0	0	9	250	248	28	91	158	12.4	4.10	92	.259	.326	4	.267	1	-10	-9	1	-0.8

● JIM ST.VRAIN St.Vrain, James Marcellin b: 6/6/1883, Ralls County, Mo. d: 6/12/37, Butte, Montana BR/TL, 5'9", 175 lbs. Deb: 4/20/02

YEAR TM/L	W	L	PCT	G	GS	CG	SH	SV	IP	H	HR	BB	SO	RAT	ERA	ERA+	OAV	OOB	BH	AVG	PB	PR	/A	PD	TPI
1902 Chi-N	4	6	.400	12	11	10	1	0	95	88	0	25	51	11.1	2.08	130	.246	.302	3	.097	-2	7	7	0	0.5

● LUIS SALAZAR Salazar, Luis Ernesto (Garcia) b: 5/19/56, Barcelona, Venez. BR/TR, 5'9", 180 lbs. Deb: 8/15/80 ♦

YEAR TM/L	W	L	PCT	G	GS	CG	SH	SV	IP	H	HR	BB	SO	RAT	ERA	ERA+	OAV	OOB	BH	AVG	PB	PR	/A	PD	TPI
1987 SD-N	0	0	—	2	0	0	0	0	2	2	0	1	0	13.5	4.50	88	.250	.333	48	.254	0	-0	-0	0	0.0

● FREDDY SALE Sale, Frederick Link b: 5/2/02, Chester, S.C. d: 5/27/56, Hermosa Beach, Cal BR/TR, 5'9", 160 lbs. Deb: 6/30/24

YEAR TM/L	W	L	PCT	G	GS	CG	SH	SV	IP	H	HR	BB	SO	RAT	ERA	ERA+	OAV	OOB	BH	AVG	PB	PR	/A	PD	TPI
1924 Pit-N	0	0	—	1	0	0	0	0	1	2	0	0	0	18.0	0.00	—	.500	.500	0	—	0	0	0	-0	0.0

● HARRY SALISBURY Salisbury, Henry H. b: 5/15/1855, Providence, R.I. d: 3/29/33, Chicago, Ill. BL , Deb: 8/28/1879

YEAR TM/L	W	L	PCT	G	GS	CG	SH	SV	IP	H	HR	BB	SO	RAT	ERA	ERA+	OAV	OOB	BH	AVG	PB	PR	/A	PD	TPI
1879 Tro-N	4	6	.400	10	10	9	0	0	89	103	0	11	31	11.5	2.22	112	.265	.285	2	.056	-4	3	3	2	0.1
1882 Pit-a	20	18	.526	38	38	38	1	0	335	315	1	37	135	9.5	2.63	99	.232	.253	22	.152	-6	2	-1	-2	-0.8
Total 2	24	24	.500	48	48	47	1	0	424	418	1	48	166	9.9	2.55	102	.239	.260	24	.133	-10	5	2	-1	-0.7

● BILL SALISBURY Salisbury, William Ansel "Solly" b: 11/12/1876, Algona, Iowa d: 1/17/52, Rowena, Ore. BR/TR, 6', 180 lbs. Deb: 4/19/02

YEAR TM/L	W	L	PCT	G	GS	CG	SH	SV	IP	H	HR	BB	SO	RAT	ERA	ERA+	OAV	OOB	BH	AVG	PB	PR	/A	PD	TPI
1902 Phi-N	0	0	—	2	1	0	0	0	6	15	1	2	0	25.5	13.50	21	.468	.499	0	.000	-0	-7	-7	-1	-0.7

● SLIM SALLEE Sallee, Harry Franklin "Scatter" b: 2/3/1885, Higginsport, Ohio d: 3/23/50, Higginsport, Ohio BL/TL, 6'3", 180 lbs. Deb: 4/16/08

YEAR TM/L	W	L	PCT	G	GS	CG	SH	SV	IP	H	HR	BB	SO	RAT	ERA	ERA+	OAV	OOB	BH	AVG	PB	PR	/A	PD	TPI
1908 StL-N	3	8	.273	25	12	7	1	0	128^2	144	1	36	39	12.8	3.15	75	.274	.324	2	.049	-3	-11	-11	-0	-1.6
1909 StL-N	10	11	.476	32	27	12	1	0	219	223	3	59	55	11.8	2.42	104	.264	.315	8	.113	-2	4	3	-0	0.1
1910 StL-N	7	8	.467	18	13	9	1	2	115	112	4	24	46	10.7	2.97	100	.251	.290	4	.108	-2	1	0	0	-0.2
1911 StL-N	15	9	.625	36	30	18	1	3	245	234	6	64	74	11.1	2.76	123	.257	.309	15	.169	-2	18	17	-3	1.2
1912 StL-N	16	17	.485	48	32	20	3	**6**	294	289	6	72	108	11.2	2.60	132	.266	.315	14	.136	-4	26	27	-2	2.1
1913 StL-N	19	15	.559	50	31	18	3	5	276	257	11	60	106	10.5	2.71	119	.255	.301	20	.211	2	15	16	1	2.0
1914 StL-N	18	17	.514	46	30	18	3	**6**	282^1	252	5	72	105	10.6	2.10	133	.246	.302	21	.231	2	22	22	-2	2.5
1915 StL-N	13	17	.433	46	33	17	2	3	275^1	245	6	57	91	10.0	2.84	98	.238	.280	11	.120	-4	-3	-2	-1	-0.7
1916 StL-N	5	5	.500	16	7	4	2	1	70	75	2	23	28	12.9	3.47	76	.290	.352	3	.167	-0	-7	-6	-1	-0.9
NY-N	9	4	.692	15	11	7	2	0	111^2	96	2	10	35	8.5	1.37	178	.234	.252	9	.257	2	15	13	-3	1.5
Yr	14	9	.609	31	18	11	4	1	181^2	171	4	33	63	10.1	2.18	115	.255	.290	12	.226	2	9	7	-4	0.6
1917 *NY-N	18	7	.720	34	24	18	1	**4**	215^2	199	4	34	54	9.8	2.17	118	.249	.280	17	.221	1	13	9	-4	0.7
1918 NY-N	8	8	.500	18	16	12	1	2	132	122	3	12	33	**9.1**	2.25	117	.241	**.259**	5	.122	-2	8	6	-2	0.2
1919 *Cin-N	21	7	.750	29	28	22	4	0	227^2	221	4	20	24	9.6	2.06	135	.258	.276	14	.189	2	22	18	-5	1.7
1920 Cin-N	5	6	.455	21	12	6	0	2	116	129	4	16	13	11.4	3.34	91	.293	.320	6	.171	-1	-3	-4	-3	-0.8
NY-N	1	0	1.000	5	1	1	0	0	17	16	0	0	2	8.5	1.59	189	.239	.239	1	.333	0	3	3	-0	0.3
Yr	6	6	.500	26	13	7	0	2	133	145	4	16	15	10.9	3.11	97	.284	.306	7	.184	-0	0	-1	-4	-0.5
1921 NY-N	6	4	.600	37	0	0	0	2	96^1	115	7	14	23	12.1	3.64	101	.307	.332	8	.364	2	1	0	-2	0.1
Total 14	174	143	.549	476	307	189	25	36	2821^2	2729	68	573	836	10.7	2.56	114	.258	.299	158	.171	-8	125	110	-26	8.2

● ROGER SALMON Salmon, Roger Elliott b: 5/11/1891, Newark, N.J. d: 6/17/74, Belfast, Me. BL/TL, 6'2", 170 lbs. Deb: 5/03/12

YEAR TM/L	W	L	PCT	G	GS	CG	SH	SV	IP	H	HR	BB	SO	RAT	ERA	ERA+	OAV	OOB	BH	AVG	PB	PR	/A	PD	TPI
1912 Phi-A	1	0	1.000	2	1	0	0	0	5	7	0	4	5	19.8	9.00	34	.318	.423	0	.000	-0	-3	-3	-0	-0.3

● GUS SALVE Salve, Augustus William b: 12/29/1885, Boston, Mass. d: 3/29/71, Providence, R.I. BL/TL, 6', 190 lbs. Deb: 9/14/08

YEAR TM/L	W	L	PCT	G	GS	CG	SH	SV	IP	H	HR	BB	SO	RAT	ERA	ERA+	OAV	OOB	BH	AVG	PB	PR	/A	PD	TPI
1908 Phi-A	0	1	.000	2	1	1	0	0	15^1	17	1	9	6	15.8	4.11	62	.266	.365	0	.000	-1	-3	-3	-1	-0.4

● JACK SALVESON Salveson, John Theodore b: 1/5/14, Fullerton, Cal. d: 12/28/74, Norwalk, Cal. BR/TR, 6'0.5", 180 lbs. Deb: 6/03/33

YEAR TM/L	W	L	PCT	G	GS	CG	SH	SV	IP	H	HR	BB	SO	RAT	ERA	ERA+	OAV	OOB	BH	AVG	PB	PR	/A	PD	TPI
1933 NY-N	0	2	.000	8	2	2	0	0	30^2	30	4	14	8	12.9	3.82	84	.252	.331	1	.111	-1	-2	-2	0	-0.2
1934 NY-N	3	1	.750	12	4	0	0	0	38^1	43	2	13	18	13.1	3.52	110	.281	.337	3	.300	0	2	1	1	0.2
1935 Pit-N	0	1	.000	5	0	0	0	0	7	11	1	5	2	21.9	9.00	46	.306	.405	0	.000	-0	-4	-4	1	-0.3
Chi-A	1	2	.333	20	2	2	0	1	66^2	79	6	23	22	13.8	4.86	95	.298	.354	6	.300	2	-3	-2	-0	0.0
1943 Cle-A	5	3	.625	23	11	4	3	3	86	87	5	26	24	11.9	3.35	93	.266	.322	6	.231	2	-0	-2	0	0.0
1945 Cle-A	0	0	—	19	0	0	0	0	44	52	3	6	11	12.1	3.68	88	.294	.321	4	.400	3	-2	-2	1	0.2
Total 5	9	9	.500	87	19	8	3	4	272^2	302	21	87	85	12.9	3.99	91	.280	.336	20	.260	6	-8	-11	2	-0.1

● MANNY SALVO Salvo, Manuel "Gyp" b: 6/30/13, Sacramento, Cal. BR/TR, 6'4", 210 lbs. Deb: 4/22/39

YEAR TM/L	W	L	PCT	G	GS	CG	SH	SV	IP	H	HR	BB	SO	RAT	ERA	ERA+	OAV	OOB	BH	AVG	PB	PR	/A	PD	TPI
1939 NY-N	4	10	.286	32	18	4	0	1	136	150	11	75	69	15.2	4.63	85	.285	.380	4	.098	-2	-11	-11	1	-1.1
1940 Bos-N	10	9	.526	21	20	14	**5**	0	160^2	151	9	43	60	11.0	3.08	121	.248	.300	6	.103	-2	14	11	-1	0.8
1941 Bos-N	7	16	.304	35	27	11	2	0	195	192	9	93	67	13.3	4.06	88	.255	.340	7	.113	-0	-9	-11	-0	-1.1
1942 Bos-N	7	8	.467	25	14	6	1	0	130^2	129	7	41	25	12.0	3.03	110	.260	.322	5	.122	-1	4	4	-1	0.2
1943 Bos-N	0	1	.000	1	1	0	0	0	5	5	0	6	1	19.8	7.20	47	.250	.423	2	1.000	2	-2	-2	-0	-0.1
Phi-N	0	0	—	1	0	0	0	0	0^1	2	0	1	0	81.0	27.00	12	.667	.750	0	—	0	-1	-1	0	-0.1
Bos-N	5	6	.455	20	13	5	1	0	93^2	94	6	25	25	11.5	3.27	105	.261	.311	6	.214	0	1	2	-1	0.2
Yr	5	7	.417	22	14	5	1	0	99	101	6	32	26	12.2	3.55	96	.264	.322	8	.267	2	-2	-1	-1	0.0
Total 5	33	50	.398	135	93	40	9	1	721^1	723	42	284	247	12.8	3.69	98	.261	.334	30	.129	-4	-4	-7	-3	-1.2

● JOE SAMBITO Sambito, Joseph Charles b: 6/28/52, Brooklyn, N.Y. BL/TL, 6'1", 190 lbs. Deb: 7/20/76

YEAR TM/L	W	L	PCT	G	GS	CG	SH	SV	IP	H	HR	BB	SO	RAT	ERA	ERA+	OAV	OOB	BH	AVG	PB	PR	/A	PD	TPI
1976 Hou-N	3	2	.600	20	4	1	1	1	53^1	45	4	14	26	10.0	3.54	90	.237	.289	2	.222	1	-0	-2	1	0.0
1977 Hou-N	5	5	.500	54	1	0	0	7	89	77	6	24	67	10.2	2.33	153	.235	.287	2	.154	-0	16	12	1	1.3
1978 Hou-N	4	9	.308	62	0	0	0	11	88	85	5	32	96	12.0	3.07	108	.260	.326	1	.167	0	5	2	1	0.4
1979 Hou-N★	8	7	.533	63	0	0	0	22	91^1	80	8	23	83	10.5	1.77	198	.235	.292	2	.286	2	**20**	18	1	2.2
1980 *Hou-N	8	4	.667	64	0	0	0	17	90^1	65	3	22	75	8.9	2.19	150	.200	.255	0	.000	-1	14	11	0	1.1
1981 *Hou-N	5	5	.500	49	0	0	0	10	63^2	43	4	22	41	9.5	1.84	179	.192	.270	0	.000	-1	12	10	1	1.1
1982 Hou-N	0	0	—	9	0	0	0	4	12^2	7	0	2	7	6.4	0.71	467	.159	.196	0	.000	-0	4	4	0	0.4
1984 Hou-N	0	0	—	32	0	0	0	0	47^2	39	5	16	26	10.4	3.02	110	.228	.294	0	.000	-0	3	2	-1	0.0
1985 NY-N	0	0	—	8	0	0	0	0	10^2	21	1	8	3	24.5	12.66	27	.420	.500	0	—	0	-11	-11	0	-1.0
1986 *Bos-A	2	0	1.000	53	0	0	0	12	44^2	54	4	16	30	14.5	4.84	86	.298	.362	0	—	0	-3	-3	0	-0.3
1987 Bos-A	2	6	.250	47	0	0	0	0	37^2	46	8	16	35	14.8	6.93	65	.301	.367	0	—	0	-10	-10	-0	-1.1
Total 11	37	38	.493	461	5	1	1	84	629	562	48	195	489	11.0	3.03	115	.241	.302	7	.135	2	49	32	4	4.1

● BILL SAMPEN Sampen, William Albert b: 1/18/63, Lincoln, Ill. BR/TR, 6'1", 185 lbs. Deb: 4/10/90

YEAR TM/L	W	L	PCT	G	GS	CG	SH	SV	IP	H	HR	BB	SO	RAT	ERA	ERA+	OAV	OOB	BH	AVG	PB	PR	/A	PD	TPI
1990 Mon-N	12	7	.632	59	4	0	0	2	90^1	94	7	33	69	12.9	2.99	122	.268	.334	0	.000	-1	8	7	-1	0.5
1991 Mon-N	9	5	.643	43	8	0	0	0	92^1	96	13	46	52	14.1	4.00	91	.273	.362	3	.231	0	-3	-4	-1	-0.5
1992 Mon-N	1	4	.200	44	1	0	0	0	63^1	62	4	29	23	13.1	3.13	112	.268	.352	0	.000	-1	3	3	1	0.3
KC-A	0	2	.000	8	1	0	0	0	19^2	21	0	3	14	12.4	3.66	109	.292	.346	0	—	0	1	1	0	0.1
Total 3	22	18	.550	154	14	0	0	2	265^2	273	24	111	158	13.3	3.42	106	.271	.349	3	.111	-1	8	6	-1	0.4

● JOE SAMUELS Samuels, Joseph Jonas "Skabotch" b: 3/21/05, Scranton, Pa. BR/TR, 6'1.5", 196 lbs. Deb: 4/23/30

YEAR TM/L	W	L	PCT	G	GS	CG	SH	SV	IP	H	HR	BB	SO	RAT	ERA	ERA+	OAV	OOB	BH	AVG	PB	PR	/A	PD	TPI
1930 Det-A	0	0	—	2	0	0	0	0	6	10	1	6	1	24.0	16.50	29	.417	.533	0	.000	-0	-8	-8	-0	-0.6

● ROGER SAMUELS Samuels, Roger Howard b: 1/3/61, San Jose, Cal. BL/TL, 6'5", 210 lbs. Deb: 7/20/88

YEAR TM/L	W	L	PCT	G	GS	CG	SH	SV	IP	H	HR	BB	SO	RAT	ERA	ERA+	OAV	OOB	BH	AVG	PB	PR	/A	PD	TPI
1988 SF-N	1	2	.333	15	0	0	0	0	23^1	17	4	7	22	9.6	3.47	94	.202	.272	0	.000	-0	-0	-1	0	-0.1
1989 Pit-N	0	0	—	5	0	0	0	0	3^2	9	1	4	2	31.9	9.82	34	.474	.565	0	—	0	-3	-3	-0	-0.3
Total 2	1	2	.333	20	0	0	0	0	27	26	5	11	24	12.7	4.33	76	.252	.330	0	.000	-0	-3	-3	0	-0.4

● ALEX SANCHEZ Sanchez, Alex Anthony b: 4/8/66, Concord, Cal. BR/TR, 6'2", 185 lbs. Deb: 5/23/89

YEAR TM/L	W	L	PCT	G	GS	CG	SH	SV	IP	H	HR	BB	SO	RAT	ERA	ERA+	OAV	OOB	BH	AVG	PB	PR	/A	PD	TPI
1989 Tor-A	0	1	.000	4	3	0	0	0	11^2	16	1	14	4	23.1	10.03	38	.356	.508	0	—	0	-8	-8	1	-0.7

● ISRAEL SANCHEZ Sanchez, Israel (Matos) b: 8/20/63, Falcon Lasvias, Cuba BL/TL, 5'9", 170 lbs. Deb: 7/07/88

YEAR TM/L	W	L	PCT	G	GS	CG	SH	SV	IP	H	HR	BB	SO	RAT	ERA	ERA+	OAV	OOB	BH	AVG	PB	PR	/A	PD	TPI
1988 KC-A	3	2	.600	19	1	0	0	1	35^2	36	0	18	14	13.6	4.54	88	.265	.351	0	—	0	-2	-2	0	-0.2
1990 KC-A	0	0	—	11	0	0	0	0	9^2	16	1	3	5	18.6	8.38	46	.381	.435	0	—	0	-5	-5	-0	-0.5
Total 2	3	2	.600	30	1	0	0	1	45^1	52	1	21	19	14.7	5.36	74	.292	.370	0	—	0	-7	-7	0	-0.7

● LUIS SANCHEZ Sanchez, Luis Mercedes (b: Luis Mercedes Escoba (Sanchez)) b: 8/24/53, Cariaco, Sucre, Ven. BR/TR, 6'2", 210 lbs. Deb: 4/10/81

YEAR TM/L	W	L	PCT	G	GS	CG	SH	SV	IP	H	HR	BB	SO	RAT	ERA	ERA+	OAV	OOB	BH	AVG	PB	PR	/A	PD	TPI
1981 Cal-A	0	2	.000	17	0	0	0	2	33^2	39	4	11	13	13.6	2.94	124	.287	.345	0	—	0	3	3	-0	0.3
1982 *Cal-A	7	4	.636	46	0	0	0	5	92^2	89	3	34	58	12.6	3.21	126	.259	.339	0	—	0	9	9	1	1.0
1983 Cal-A	10	8	.556	56	1	0	0	7	98^1	92	6	40	49	12.4	3.66	110	.254	.333	0	—	0	4	4	2	0.6
1984 Cal-A	9	7	.563	49	0	0	0	11	83^2	84	10	33	62	12.9	3.33	119	.268	.343	0	—	0	6	6	-0	0.6
1985 Cal-A	2	0	1.000	26	0	0	0	2	61^1	67	9	27	34	13.9	5.72	72	.283	.358	0	—	0	-11	-11	0	-1.0
Total 5	28	21	.571	194	1	0	0	27	369^2	371	32	145	216	12.9	3.75	107	.267	.342	0	—	0	11	10	2	1.5

● RAUL SANCHEZ Sanchez, Raul Guadalupe (Rodriguez) b: 12/12/30, Marianao, Cuba BR/TR, 6', 150 lbs. Deb: 4/17/52

YEAR TM/L	W	L	PCT	G	GS	CG	SH	SV	IP	H	HR	BB	SO	RAT	ERA	ERA+	OAV	OOB	BH	AVG	PB	PR	/A	PD	TPI
1952 Was-A	1	1	.500	3	2	1	1	0	12^2	13	0	7	6	14.2	3.55	100	.260	.351	0	.000	-1	0	0	0	-0.1
1957 Cin-N	3	2	.600	38	0	0	0	5	62^1	61	7	25	37	13.0	4.76	86	.262	.344	2	.286	1	-6	-5	1	-0.4
1960 Cin-N	1	0	1.000	8	0	0	0	0	14^2	12	1	11	5	16.0	4.91	78	.226	.388	1	.500	0	-2	-2	0	-0.1
Total 3	5	3	.625	49	2	1	1	5	89^2	86	8	43	48	13.7	4.62	86	.256	.352	3	.214	0	-8	-6	1	-0.6

● BEN SANDERS Sanders, Alexander Bennett b: 2/16/1865, Catharpen, Va. d: 8/29/30, Memphis, Tenn. BR/TR, 6', 210 lbs. Deb: 6/06/1888 ♦

YEAR TM/L	W	L	PCT	G	GS	CG	SH	SV	IP	H	HR	BB	SO	RAT	ERA	ERA+	OAV	OOB	BH	AVG	PB	PR	/A	PD	TPI
1888 Phi-N	19	10	.655	31	29	28	**8**	0	275^1	240	3	33	121	9.0	1.90	157	.228	.253	58	.246	5	29	33	4	4.4
1889 Phi-N	19	18	.514	44	39	34	1	1	349^2	406	9	96	123	13.0	3.55	122	.282	.328	47	.278	6	18	31	-2	3.2
1890 Phi-P	19	18	.514	43	40	37	2	1	346^2	412	13	69	107	12.7	3.76	114	.283	.320	59	.312	10	18	20	1	2.5
1891 Phi-a	11	5	.688	19	18	15	0	0	145	157	3	37	40	12.5	3.79	101	.267	.319	39	.250	2	-1	1	-1	0.2
1892 Lou-N	12	19	.387	31	31	30	3	0	268^1	281	6	62	77	11.6	3.22	95	.259	.300	54	.273	10	2	-5	-1	0.4
Total 5	80	70	.533	168	157	144	14	2	1385	1496	34	297	468	11.8	3.24	116	.266	.306	257	.271	33	66	79	1	10.7

● DEE SANDERS Sanders, Dee Wilma b: 4/8/21, Quitman, Tex. BR/TR, 6'3", 195 lbs. Deb: 8/12/45

YEAR TM/L	W	L	PCT	G	GS	CG	SH	SV	IP	H	HR	BB	SO	RAT	ERA	ERA+	OAV	OOB	BH	AVG	PB	PR	/A	PD	TPI
1945 StL-A	0	0	—	2	0	0	0	0	1^1	7	0	1	1	54.0	40.50	9	.700	.727	0	—	0	-6	-5	0	-0.5

● KEN SANDERS Sanders, Kenneth George "Daffy" b: 7/8/41, St.Louis, Mo. BR/TR, 5'11", 185 lbs. Deb: 8/06/64

YEAR TM/L	W	L	PCT	G	GS	CG	SH	SV	IP	H	HR	BB	SO	RAT	ERA	ERA+	OAV	OOB	BH	AVG	PB	PR	/A	PD	TPI
1964 KC-A	0	2	.000	21	0	0	0	1	27	23	2	17	18	13.7	3.67	104	.232	.350	0	—	0	-0	0	1	0.1
1966 Bos-A	3	6	.333	24	0	0	0	2	47^1	36	2	28	33	12.5	3.80	100	.214	.333	0	.000	-0	-2	0	-0	0.0
KC-A	3	4	.429	38	1	0	0	1	65^1	59	7	48	41	14.9	3.72	91	.250	.379	2	.250	0	-2	-2	1	-0.2
Yr	6	10	.375	62	1	0	0	3	112^2	95	9	76	74	13.7	3.75	95	.233	.355	2	.143	0	-4	-2	1	-0.2
1968 Oak-A	0	1	.000	7	0	0	0	0	10^2	8	1	8	6	13.5	3.38	84	.229	.372	0	—	0	-0	-1	0	-0.1
1970 Mil-A	5	2	.714	50	0	0	0	13	92^1	64	1	25	64	9.1	1.75	216	.201	.268	3	.231	1	20	21	1	2.5
1971 Mil-A	7	12	.368	**83**	0	0	0	**31**	136^1	111	9	34	80	9.8	1.91	181	.227	.282	0	.000	-1	**23**	**24**	2	2.7
1972 Mil-A	2	9	.182	62	0	0	0	17	92^1	88	10	31	51	11.8	3.12	97	.245	.309	1	.143	0	-1	-1	1	0.0
1973 Min-A	2	4	.333	27	0	0	0	8	44^1	53	4	21	19	15.4	6.09	65	.299	.380	0	—	0	-11	-11	0	-1.0
Cle-A	5	1	.833	15	0	0	0	5	27^1	18	2	9	14	8.9	1.65	238	.188	.257	0	—	0	7	7	0	0.7
Yr	7	5	.583	42	0	0	0	13	71^2	71	6	30	33	12.7	4.40	90	.255	.328	0	—	0	-5	-4	0	-0.3
1974 Cle-A	0	1	.000	9	0	0	0	1	11	21	5	5	4	21.3	9.82	37	.404	.456	0	—	0	-8	-8	0	-0.7
Cal-A	0	0	—	9	0	0	0	1	9^2	10	0	3	4	12.1	2.79	123	.278	.333	0	—	0	1	1	1	0.6
Yr	0	1	.000	18	0	0	0	2	20^2	31	5	8	8	17.0	6.53	54	.352	.406	0	—	0	-7	-7	1	-0.1
1975 NY-N	1	1	.500	29	0	0	0	5	43	31	2	14	8	9.4	2.30	150	.205	.273	0	.000	-0	6	5	-0	0.5
1976 NY-N	1	2	.333	31	0	0	0	1	47	39	4	12	16	10.0	2.87	115	.231	.286	0	.000	-0	3	2	1	0.3
KC-A	0	0	—	3	0	0	0	0	3	3	0	3	2	18.0	0.00	—	.273	.429	0	—	0	1	1	-0	0.1
Total 10	29	45	.392	408	1	0	0	86	656^2	564	49	258	360	11.5	2.97	118	.235	.314	6	.115	-0	38	39	7	5.5

● ROY SANDERS Sanders, Roy Garvin "Butch" or "Pepe" b: 8/1/1892, Stafford, Kan. d: 1/17/50, Kansas City, Mo. BR/TR, 6'0.5", 195 lbs. Deb: 4/16/17

YEAR TM/L	W	L	PCT	G	GS	CG	SH	SV	IP	H	HR	BB	SO	RAT	ERA	ERA+	OAV	OOB	BH	AVG	PB	PR	/A	PD	TPI
1917 Cin-N	0	1	.000	2	2	1	0	0	14	12	0	16	3	18.6	4.50	58	.273	.475	0	.000	-1	-3	-3	1	-0.3
1918 Pit-N	7	9	.438	28	14	6	1	1	156	135	1	52	55	10.9	2.60	111	.239	.305	8	.151	-1	3	5	2	0.6
Total 2	7	10	.412	30	16	7	1	1	170	147	1	68	58	11.5	2.75	104	.241	.321	8	.136	-2	0	2	2	0.3

● ROY SANDERS Sanders, Roy Lee "Simon" b: 6/10/1894, Missouri d: 7/8/63, Louisville, Ky. BR/TR, 6', 185 lbs. Deb: 8/06/18

YEAR TM/L	W	L	PCT	G	GS	CG	SH	SV	IP	H	HR	BB	SO	RAT	ERA	ERA+	OAV	OOB	BH	AVG	PB	PR	/A	PD	TPI
1918 NY-A	0	2	.000	6	2	0	0	0	25^2	28	0	16	8	16.1	4.21	67	.301	.414	0	.000	-1	-4	-4	-1	-0.6
1920 StL-A	1	1	.500	8	1	0	0	0	17^1	20	1	17	2	19.7	5.19	75	.313	.463	0	.000	-1	-3	-2	-1	-0.4
Total 2	1	3	.250	14	3	0	0	0	43	48	1	33	10	17.6	4.60	71	.306	.435	0	.000	-2	-7	-6	-1	-1.0

● WAR SANDERS Sanders, Warren Williams b: 8/2/1877, Maynardville, Tenn. d: 8/3/62, Chattanooga, Tenn. BR/TL, 5'10", 160 lbs. Deb: 4/18/03

YEAR TM/L	W	L	PCT	G	GS	CG	SH	SV	IP	H	HR	BB	SO	RAT	ERA	ERA+	OAV	OOB	BH	AVG	PB	PR	/A	PD	TPI
1903 StL-N	1	6	.143	8	6	3	0	0	40	48	0	21	9	16.0	6.07	54	.286	.372	1	.067	-2	-12	-12	-1	-1.3
1904 StL-N	1	2	.333	4	3	1	0	0	19	25	1	1	11	12.8	4.74	57	.298	.314	0	.000	-1	-4	-4	0	-0.5
Total 2	2	8	.200	12	9	4	0	0	59	73	1	22	20	14.9	5.64	55	.290	.354	1	.048	-2	-17	-17	-0	-1.8

● SCOTT SANDERSON Sanderson, Scott Douglas b: 7/22/56, Dearborn, Mich. BR/TR, 6'5", 200 lbs. Deb: 8/06/78

YEAR TM/L	W	L	PCT	G	GS	CG	SH	SV	IP	H	HR	BB	SO	RAT	ERA	ERA+	OAV	OOB	BH	AVG	PB	PR	/A	PD	TPI
1978 Mon-N	4	2	.667	10	9	1	1	0	61	52	3	21	50	10.9	2.51	140	.232	.301	2	.105	-1	7	7	-1	0.6
1979 Mon-N	9	8	.529	34	24	5	3	1	168	148	16	54	138	11.0	3.43	107	.236	.300	8	.160	-0	6	4	-2	0.2
1980 Mon-N	16	11	.593	33	33	7	3	0	211^1	206	18	56	125	11.3	3.11	115	.257	.308	5	.078	-3	12	11	-2	0.6
1981 *Mon-N	9	7	.563	22	22	4	1	0	137^1	122	10	31	77	10.1	2.95	118	.236	.281	4	.114	2	8	8	-2	0.9
1982 Mon-N	12	12	.500	32	32	7	0	0	224	212	24	58	158	11.0	3.46	105	.251	.301	8	.140	1	4	5	-3	0.2
1983 Mon-N	6	7	.462	18	16	0	0	1	81^1	98	12	20	55	13.1	4.65	77	.303	.344	4	.143	-0	-9	-10	-1	-1.1
1984 *Chi-N	8	5	.615	24	24	3	0	0	140^2	140	5	24	76	10.6	3.14	125	.264	.298	5	.119	-1	7	12	1	1.3
1985 Chi-N	5	6	.455	19	19	2	0	0	121	100	13	27	80	9.4	3.12	128	.228	.273	2	.065	-2	6	12	1	1.2
1986 Chi-N	9	11	.450	37	28	1	1	1	169^2	165	21	37	124	10.8	4.19	96	.255	.297	3	.059	-4	-9	-3	-1	-0.8
1987 Chi-N	8	9	.471	32	22	0	0	2	144^2	156	23	50	106	13.0	4.29	100	.274	.336	3	.075	-1	-3	-0	-1	-0.2
1988 Chi-N	1	2	.333	11	0	0	0	0	15^1	13	1	3	6	9.4	5.28	68	.232	.271	0	—	0	-3	-3	-0	-0.3
1989 *Chi-N	11	9	.550	37	23	2	0	0	146^1	155	16	31	86	11.6	3.94	95	.273	.313	2	.047	-2	-7	-3	-2	-0.7
1990 *Oak-A	17	11	.607	34	34	2	1	0	206^1	205	27	66	128	11.6	3.88	96	.255	.315	0	—	0	1	-4	-2	-0.5
1991 NY-A☆	16	10	.615	34	34	2	2	0	208	200	22	29	130	10.0	3.81	109	.252	.281	0	—	0	7	8	-3	0.5
1992 NY-A	12	11	.522	33	33	2	1	0	193^1	220	28	64	104	13.4	4.93	82	.286	.344	0	—	0	-21	-19	-2	-2.1
Total 15	143	121	.542	410	353	38	13	5	2228^1	2192	239	571	1443	11.3	3.72	103	.257	.307	46	.100	-11	4	25	-21	-0.2

● FRED SANFORD Sanford, John Frederick b: 8/9/19, Garfield, Utah BB/TR, 6'1", 200 lbs. Deb: 5/05/43

YEAR TM/L	W	L	PCT	G	GS	CG	SH	SV	IP	H	HR	BB	SO	RAT	ERA	ERA+	OAV	OOB	BH	AVG	PB	PR	/A	PD	TPI
1943 StL-A	0	0	—	3	0	0	0	0	9^1	7	0	4	2	10.6	1.93	172	.219	.306	0	—	0	1	1	0	0.2
1946 StL-A	2	1	.667	3	3	2	2	0	22	19	0	9	8	11.5	2.05	182	.235	.311	2	.286	1	4	4	-0	0.6
1947 StL-A	7	16	.304	34	23	9	0	4	186^2	186	17	76	62	12.6	3.71	104	.261	.332	11	.204	-0	-0	3	-1	0.1
1948 StL-A	12	21	.364	42	33	9	1	2	227	250	19	91	79	13.6	4.64	98	.279	.347	11	.151	-2	-9	-2	1	-0.3
1949 NY-A	7	3	.700	29	11	3	0	0	95^1	100	9	57	51	14.8	3.87	105	.270	.367	4	.118	-2	3	2	-0	-0.1
1950 NY-A	5	4	.556	26	12	2	0	0	112^2	103	9	79	54	14.6	4.55	94	.252	.374	8	.229	1	0	-3	3	0.0
1951 NY-A	0	3	.000	11	2	0	0	0	26^2	15	2	25	10	13.5	3.71	103	.169	.351	0	.000	-1	1	0	1	0.0
Was-A	2	3	.400	7	7	0	0	0	37	51	5	27	12	19.0	6.57	62	.329	.429	1	.071	-1	-10	-10	-1	-1.1

YEAR	TM/L	W	L	PCT	G	GS	CG	SH	SV	IP	H	HR	BB	SO	RAT	ERA	ERA+	OAV	OOB	BH	AVG	PB	PR	/A	PD	TPI
	StL-A	2	4	.333	9	7	1	0	0	27^1	37	6	23	7	19.8	10.21	43	.308	.420	2	.286	1	-18	-18	-0	-1.5
	Yr	4	10	.286	27	16	1	0	0	91	103	13	75	29	17.6	6.82	60	.283	.405	3	.115	-1	-27	-27	-0	-2.6
Total	7	37	55	.402	164	98	26	3	6	744	768	67	391	285	14.1	4.45	94	.268	.357	39	.170	-4	-28	-21	2	-2.1

● JACK SANFORD Sanford, John Stanley b: 5/18/29, Wellesley Hills, Mass. BR/TR, 6', 190 lbs. Deb: 9/16/56 C

YEAR	TM/L	W	L	PCT	G	GS	CG	SH	SV	IP	H	HR	BB	SO	RAT	ERA	ERA+	OAV	OOB	BH	AVG	PB	PR	/A	PD	TPI
1956	Phi-N	1	0	1.000	3	1	0	0	0	13	7	0	13	6	14.5	1.38	269	.184	.404	1	.333	0	3	3	0	0.4
1957	Phi-N★	19	8	.704	33	33	15	3	0	236^2	194	22	94	**188**	11.1	3.08	124	**.221**	.298	15	.169	-1	21	19	-1	1.8
1958	Phi-N	10	13	.435	38	27	7	2	0	186^1	197	15	81	106	13.6	4.44	89	.274	.350	10	.169	1	-10	-10	-2	-1.0
1959	SF-N	15	12	.556	36	31	10	0	1	222^1	198	22	70	132	11.1	3.16	121	.235	.300	8	.111	-1	20	16	-1	1.5
1960	SF-N	12	14	.462	37	34	11	**6**	0	219	199	11	99	125	12.3	3.82	91	.243	.326	13	.176	1	-1	-8	-1	-0.8
1961	SF-N	13	9	.591	38	33	6	0	0	217^1	203	22	87	112	12.2	4.22	90	.249	.325	16	.216	5	-5	-10	-1	-0.5
1962	*SF-N	24	7	.774	39	38	13	2	0	265^1	233	23	92	147	11.1	3.43	111	.234	.301	15	.153	0	15	11	2	1.3
1963	SF-N	16	13	.552	42	42	11	0	0	284^1	273	21	76	158	11.2	3.51	91	.251	.303	13	.138	3	-7	-10	3	-0.5
1964	SF-N	5	7	.417	18	17	3	1	1	106^1	91	7	37	64	11.2	3.30	108	.228	.300	4	.133	1	3	3	1	0.4
1965	SF-N	4	5	.444	23	16	0	0	2	91	92	11	30	43	12.8	3.96	91	.256	.325	3	.120	-0	-4	-4	-1	-0.5
	Cal-A	1	2	.333	9	5	0	0	1	29^1	35	2	10	13	13.8	4.60	74	.324	.381	1	.143	-0	-4	-4	1	-0.4
1966	Cal-A	13	7	.650	50	6	0	0	5	108	108	11	27	54	11.6	3.83	88	.271	.323	3	.136	1	-5	-6	1	-0.5
1967	Cal-A	3	2	.600	12	9	0	0	1	48^1	53	6	7	21	11.2	4.47	70	.288	.314	3	.200	1	-7	-7	1	-0.5
	KC-A	1	2	.333	10	1	0	0	0	22	24	1	14	13	16.4	6.55	49	.296	.412	0	.000	-0	-8	-8	1	-0.8
	Yr	4	4	.500	22	10	0	0	1	70^1	77	7	21	34	12.8	5.12	62	.288	.345	3	.167	1	-15	-15	2	-1.3
Total	12	137	101	.576	388	293	76	14	11	2049^1	1907	174	737	1182	11.8	3.69	98	.247	.316	105	.158	11	11	-14	3	-0.1

● MO SANFORD Sanford, Meredith Leroy b: 12/24/66, Americus, Ga. BR/TR, 6'6", 220 lbs. Deb: 8/09/91

YEAR	TM/L	W	L	PCT	G	GS	CG	SH	SV	IP	H	HR	BB	SO	RAT	ERA	ERA+	OAV	OOB	BH	AVG	PB	PR	/A	PD	TPI
1991	Cin-N	1	2	.333	5	5	0	0	0	28	19	3	15	31	11.3	3.86	99	.186	.297	0	.000	-1	-1	-0	-0	-0.1

● JOSE SANTIAGO Santiago, Jose Guillermo (Guzman) "Pants" b: 9/4/28, Coamo, P.R. BR/TR, 5'10", 175 lbs. Deb: 4/17/54

YEAR	TM/L	W	L	PCT	G	GS	CG	SH	SV	IP	H	HR	BB	SO	RAT	ERA	ERA+	OAV	OOB	BH	AVG	PB	PR	/A	PD	TPI
1954	Cle-A	0	0	—	1	0	0	0	0	1^2	0	0	2	1	10.8	0.00	—	.000	.286	0	—	0	1	1	-0	0.1
1955	Cle-A	2	0	1.000	17	0	0	0	0	32^2	31	1	14	19	13.8	2.48	161	.256	.357	2	.500	1	5	5	0	0.7
1956	KC-A	1	2	.333	9	5	0	0	0	21^2	36	8	17	9	24.1	8.31	52	.387	.504	2	.400	0	-10	-10	0	-0.8
Total	3	3	2	.600	27	5	0	0	0	56	67	9	33	29	17.7	4.66	88	.306	.420	4	.444	2	-4	-3	0	0.0

● JOSE SANTIAGO Santiago, Jose Rafael (Alfonso) b: 8/15/40, Juana Diaz, P.R. BR/TR, 6'2", 185 lbs. Deb: 9/09/63

YEAR	TM/L	W	L	PCT	G	GS	CG	SH	SV	IP	H	HR	BB	SO	RAT	ERA	ERA+	OAV	OOB	BH	AVG	PB	PR	/A	PD	TPI
1963	KC-A	1	0	1.000	4	0	0	0	0	7	8	4	2	6	12.9	9.00	43	.276	.323	0	—	0	-4	-4	0	-0.4
1964	KC-A	0	6	.000	34	8	0	0	0	83^2	84	9	35	64	13.2	4.73	81	.258	.337	0	.000	-2	-10	-9	-1	-1.1
1965	KC-A	0	0	—	4	0	0	0	0	5	8	1	4	8	21.6	9.00	39	.364	.462	0	—	0	-3	-3	0	-0.3
1966	Bos-A	12	13	.480	35	28	7	1	2	172	155	17	58	119	11.3	3.66	104	.238	.302	11	.196	0	-4	3	-1	0.2
1967	*Bos-A	12	4	.750	50	11	2	0	5	145^1	138	14	47	109	11.6	3.59	97	.251	.313	8	.190	2	-6	-2	0	0.1
1968	Bos-A†	9	4	.692	18	18	7	2	0	124	96	9	42	86	10.2	2.25	140	.215	.287	7	.163	1	10	13	-0	1.5
1969	Bos-A	0	0	—	10	0	0	0	0	7^2	11	2	4	4	17.6	3.52	108	.324	.395	0	—	0	0	0	-0	0.0
1970	Bos-A	0	2	.000	8	0	0	0	1	11^1	18	0	8	8	20.6	10.32	38	.353	.441	2	.667	1	-8	-8	-0	-0.7
Total	8	34	29	.540	163	65	16	3	8	556	518	56	200	404	11.8	3.74	96	.246	.314	28	.173	3	-26	-10	-2	-0.7

● AL SANTORINI Santorini, Alan Joel b: 5/19/48, Irvington, N.J. BR/TR, 6', 190 lbs. Deb: 9/10/68

YEAR	TM/L	W	L	PCT	G	GS	CG	SH	SV	IP	H	HR	BB	SO	RAT	ERA	ERA+	OAV	OOB	BH	AVG	PB	PR	/A	PD	TPI
1968	Atl-N	0	1	.000	1	1	0	0	0	3	4	1	0	0	12.0	0.00	—	.286	.286	0	—	0	1	1	-0	0.1
1969	SD-N	8	14	.364	32	30	2	1	0	184^2	194	11	73	111	13.4	3.95	90	.270	.343	7	.111	-1	-7	-8	1	-0.9
1970	SD-N	1	8	.111	21	12	0	0	1	75^2	91	11	43	41	16.3	6.07	66	.294	.385	0	.000	-2	-17	-18	-1	-1.9
1971	SD-N	0	2	.000	18	3	0	0	0	38^1	43	4	11	21	12.7	3.76	88	.285	.333	2	.400	1	-1	-2	-1	-0.2
	StL-N	0	2	.000	19	5	0	0	2	49^2	51	2	19	21	12.9	3.81	95	.270	.340	3	.300	1	-2	-1	-0	-0.1
	Yr	0	4	.000	37	8	0	0	2	88	94	6	30	42	12.8	3.78	92	.275	.335	5	.333	1	-3	-3	-1	-0.3
1972	StL-N	8	11	.421	30	19	3	3	0	133^2	136	6	46	72	12.3	4.11	83	.263	.324	3	.075	-2	-10	-10	-1	-1.4
1973	StL-N	0	0	—	6	0	0	0	0	8^1	14	1	2	2	18.4	5.40	67	.400	.447	0	.000	-0	-2	-2	-0	-0.2
Total	6	17	38	.309	127	70	5	4	3	493^1	533	36	194	268	13.5	4.29	83	.276	.346	15	.109	-4	-38	-40	-3	-4.6

● MANNY SARMIENTO Sarmiento, Manuel Eduardo (Aponte) b: 2/2/56, Cagua, Venez. BR/TR, 6', 170 lbs. Deb: 7/30/76

YEAR	TM/L	W	L	PCT	G	GS	CG	SH	SV	IP	H	HR	BB	SO	RAT	ERA	ERA+	OAV	OOB	BH	AVG	PB	PR	/A	PD	TPI
1976	*Cin-N	5	1	.833	22	0	0	0	0	43^2	36	1	12	20	10.1	2.06	170	.222	.280	0	.000	-1	7	7	-1	0.6
1977	Cin-N	0	0	—	24	0	0	0	1	40^1	28	6	11	23	8.7	2.45	160	.196	.253	0	.000	-0	7	7	-1	0.6
1978	Cin-N	9	7	.563	63	4	0	0	5	127^1	109	16	54	72	11.6	4.38	81	.234	.315	0	.000	-1	-11	-12	-1	-1.4
1979	Cin-N	0	4	.000	23	1	0	0	0	38^2	47	2	7	23	12.8	4.66	80	.311	.346	0	.000	-1	-4	-4	-0	-0.5
1980	Sea-A	0	1	.000	9	0	0	0	1	14^2	14	2	6	15	12.3	3.68	112	.255	.328	0	—	0	1	1	-0	0.0
1982	Pit-N	9	4	.692	35	17	4	0	1	164^2	153	7	46	81	10.9	3.39	109	.246	.298	9	.191	1	4	6	-2	0.5
1983	Pit-N	3	5	.375	52	0	0	0	4	84^1	74	8	36	49	11.7	2.99	124	.243	.324	0	.000	-1	6	7	-1	0.5
Total	7	26	22	.542	228	22	4	0	12	513^2	461	42	172	283	11.1	3.49	106	.242	.306	9	.103	-3	9	11	-6	0.3

● KEVIN SAUCIER Saucier, Kevin Andrew b: 8/9/56, Pensacola, Fla. BR/TL, 6'1", 196 lbs. Deb: 10/01/78

YEAR	TM/L	W	L	PCT	G	GS	CG	SH	SV	IP	H	HR	BB	SO	RAT	ERA	ERA+	OAV	OOB	BH	AVG	PB	PR	/A	PD	TPI
1978	Phi-N	0	1	.000	1	0	0	0	0	2	4	0	1	2	27.0	18.00	20	.400	.500	0	—	0	-3	-3	-0	-0.3
1979	Phi-N	1	4	.200	29	2	0	0	1	62^1	68	4	33	21	15.0	4.19	91	.291	.385	1	.100	-1	-3	-3	0	-0.3
1980	*Phi-N	7	3	.700	40	0	0	0	0	50	50	2	20	25	13.3	3.42	111	.281	.366	0	.000	-1	1	2	0	0.1
1981	Det-A	4	2	.667	38	0	0	0	13	49	26	1	21	23	9.6	1.65	228	.160	.277	0	—	0	11	12	0	1.2
1982	Det-A	3	1	.750	31	1	0	0	5	40^1	35	0	29	23	14.7	3.12	130	.254	.391	0	—	0	4	4	0	0.4
Total	5	15	11	.577	139	3	0	0	19	203^2	183	7	104	94	13.3	3.31	116	.253	.359	1	.056	-2	10	12	1	1.1

● DENNIS SAUNDERS Saunders, Dennis James b: 1/4/49, Alhambra, Cal. BB/TR, 6'3", 195 lbs. Deb: 5/21/70

YEAR	TM/L	W	L	PCT	G	GS	CG	SH	SV	IP	H	HR	BB	SO	RAT	ERA	ERA+	OAV	OOB	BH	AVG	PB	PR	/A	PD	TPI
1970	Det-A	1	1	.500	8	0	0	0	1	14	16	1	5	8	14.1	3.21	116	.286	.355	0	.000	-1	1	1	1	0.1

● RICH SAUVEUR Sauveur, Richard Daniel b: 11/23/63, Arlington, Va. BL/TL, 6'4", 163 lbs. Deb: 7/01/86

YEAR	TM/L	W	L	PCT	G	GS	CG	SH	SV	IP	H	HR	BB	SO	RAT	ERA	ERA+	OAV	OOB	BH	AVG	PB	PR	/A	PD	TPI
1986	Pit-N	0	0	—	3	3	0	0	0	12	17	3	6	6	18.8	6.00	64	.354	.446	1	.333	0	-3	-3	1	-0.2
1988	Mon-N	0	0	—	4	0	0	0	0	3	3	1	2	3	15.0	6.00	60	.250	.357	0	—	0	-1	-1	0	-0.1
1991	NY-N	0	0	—	6	0	0	0	0	3^1	7	1	2	4	24.3	10.80	34	.467	.529	0	—	0	-3	-3	0	-0.2
1992	KC-A	0	1	.000	8	0	0	0	0	14^1	15	1	8	7	15.7	4.40	91	.273	.385	0	—	0	-1	-1	-0	-0.1
Total	4	0	1	.000	21	3	0	0	0	32^2	42	6	18	20	17.6	5.79	67	.323	.421	1	.333	0	-7	-7	1	-0.6

● JACK SAVAGE Savage, John Joseph b: 4/22/64, Louisville, Ky. BR/TR, 6'3", 190 lbs. Deb: 9/14/87

YEAR	TM/L	W	L	PCT	G	GS	CG	SH	SV	IP	H	HR	BB	SO	RAT	ERA	ERA+	OAV	OOB	BH	AVG	PB	PR	/A	PD	TPI
1987	LA-N	0	0	—	3	0	0	0	0	3^1	4	0	0	0	10.8	2.70	147	.286	.286	0	—	0	1	0	-0	0.0
1990	Min-A	0	2	.000	17	0	0	0	1	26	37	3	11	12	16.6	8.31	50	.339	.400	0	—	0	-13	-12	-0	-1.2
Total	2	0	2	.000	20	0	0	0	1	29^1	41	3	11	12	16.0	7.67	54	.333	.388	0	—	0	-12	-12	-0	-1.2

● BOB SAVAGE Savage, John Robert b: 12/1/21, Manchester, N.H. BR/TR, 6'2", 180 lbs. Deb: 6/24/42

YEAR	TM/L	W	L	PCT	G	GS	CG	SH	SV	IP	H	HR	BB	SO	RAT	ERA	ERA+	OAV	OOB	BH	AVG	PB	PR	/A	PD	TPI
1942	Phi-A	0	1	.000	8	3	0	0	0	30^2	24	0	31	10	16.1	3.23	117	.220	.393	1	.111	0	1	2	-0	0.2
1946	Phi-A	3	15	.167	40	19	7	1	2	164	164	5	93	78	14.2	4.06	87	.259	.355	5	.122	1	-10	-9	-3	-1.2
1947	Phi-A	8	10	.444	44	8	2	1	2	146	135	8	55	56	11.7	3.76	101	.245	.314	2	.050	-4	-1	1	-2	-0.5
1948	Phi-A	5	1	.833	33	1	1	0	5	75^1	98	9	33	26	15.7	6.21	69	.318	.384	1	.077	-1	-16	-16	-1	-1.6
1949	StL-A	0	0	—	4	0	0	0	0	7	12	1	3	1	19.3	6.43	70	.400	.455	0	.000	-0	-2	-1	0	-0.1
Total	5	16	27	.372	129	31	10	2	9	423	433	23	215	171	13.8	4.32	88	.265	.352	9	.087	-4	-27	-24	-6	-3.2

● DON SAVIDGE Savidge, Donald Snyder b: 8/28/08, Berwick, Pa. d: 3/22/83, Santa Barbara, Cal BR/TR, 6'1", 180 lbs. Deb: 8/06/29 F

YEAR	TM/L	W	L	PCT	G	GS	CG	SH	SV	IP	H	HR	BB	SO	RAT	ERA	ERA+	OAV	OOB	BH	AVG	PB	PR	/A	PD	TPI
1929	Was-A	0	0	—	3	0	0	0	0	6	12	1	2	2	21.0	9.00	47	.414	.452	0	—	0	-3	-3	0	-0.3

YEAR	TM/L	W	L	PCT	G	GS	CG	SH	SV	IP	H	HR	BB	SO	RAT	ERA	ERA+	OAV	OOB	BH	AVG	PB	PR	/A	PD	TPI
● RALPH SAVIDGE	Savidge, Ralph Austin "The Human Whipcord" b: 2/3/1879, Jerseytown, Pa. d: 7/22/59, Berwick, Pa. BR/TR, 6'2", 210 lbs. Deb: 9/22/08 F																									
1908	Cin-N	0	1	.000	4	1	1	0	0	21	18	0	8	7	11.1	2.57	90	.247	.321	0	.000	-1	-0	-1	-1	-0.2
1909	Cin-N	0	0	—	1	0	0	0	0	4	10	1	3	2	31.5	22.50	12	.588	.667	0	.000	-0	-9	-9	0	-0.7
Total	2	0	1	.000	5	1	1	0	0	25	28	1	11	9	14.4	5.76	41	.311	.392	0	.000	-1	-9	-9	-1	-0.9
● MOE SAVRANSKY	Savransky, Morris b: 1/13/29, Cleveland, Ohio BL/TL, 5'11", 175 lbs. Deb: 4/23/54																									
1954	Cin-N	0	2	.000	16	0	0	0	0	24	23	6	8	7	12.4	4.88	86	.247	.320	1	.500	1	-2	-2	1	0.0
● RICK SAWYER	Sawyer, Richard Clyde b: 4/7/48, Bakersfield, Cal. BR/TR, 6'2", 205 lbs. Deb: 4/28/74																									
1974	NY-A	0	0	—	1	0	0	0	0	1^2	2	0	1	1	16.2	16.20	22	.500	.600	0	—	0	-2	-2	0	-0.1
1975	NY-A	0	0	—	4	0	0	0	0	6	7	0	2	3	13.5	3.00	121	.304	.360	0	—	0	1	0	-0	0.0
1976	SD-N	5	3	.625	13	11	4	2	0	81^2	84	2	38	33	13.6	2.53	129	.272	.353	5	.208	1	9	7	-0	0.8
1977	SD-N	7	6	.538	56	9	0	0	0	111	136	15	55	45	16.1	5.84	61	.316	.402	3	.150	1	-24	-28	1	-2.6
Total	4	12	9	.571	74	20	4	2	0	200^1	229	17	96	82	15.0	4.49	76	.299	.382	8	.182	2	-17	-24	1	-1.9
● WILL SAWYER	Sawyer, Willard Newton b: 7/29/1864, Brimfield, Ohio d: 1/5/36, Kent, Ohio BL/TL, Deb: 7/21/1883																									
1883	Cle-N	4	10	.286	17	15	15	0	0	141	119	1	47	76	10.6	2.36	133	**.217**	.279	1	.021	-7	12	12	-3	0.2
● BILL SAYLES	Sayles, William Nisbeth b: 7/27/17, Portland, Ore. BR/TR, 6'2", 175 lbs. Deb: 7/17/39																									
1939	Bos-A	0	0	—	5	0	0	0	0	14	14	1	13	9	17.4	7.07	67	.264	.409	1	.143	-0	-4	-4	0	-0.4
1943	NY-N	1	3	.250	18	3	1	0	0	53	60	1	23	38	14.1	4.75	72	.284	.355	4	.308	1	-8	-8	-0	-0.7
	Bro-N	0	0	—	5	0	0	0	0	11^2	13	0	10	5	17.7	7.71	44	.271	.397	1	.500	0	-6	-6	-0	-0.6
	Yr	1	3	.250	23	3	1	0	0	64^2	73	1	33	43	14.8	5.29	65	.282	.363	5	.333	1	-14	-13	-1	-1.3
Total	2	1	3	.250	28	3	1	0	0	78^2	87	2	46	52	15.2	5.61	65	.279	.372	6	.273	1	-17	-17	-0	-1.7
● PHIL SAYLOR	Saylor, Philip Andrew "Lefty" b: 1/2/1871, Van Wert Co., Ohio d: 7/23/37, W.Alexandria, O. TL, Deb: 7/11/1891																									
1891	Phi-N	0	0	—	1	0	0	0	0	3	2	1	0	0	6.0	6.00	57	.182	.182	0	.000	-0	-1	-1	-0	-0.1
● FRANK SCANLAN	Scanlan, Frank Aloysius b: 4/28/1890, Syracuse, N.Y. d: 4/9/69, Brooklyn, N.Y. BL/TL, 6'1.5", 175 lbs. Deb: 8/06/09 F																									
1909	Phi-N	0	0	—	6	0	0	0	1	11	8	0	5	5	10.6	1.64	159	.211	.302	0	.000	-1	1	1	-0	0.0
● BOB SCANLAN	Scanlan, Robert Guy b: 8/9/66, Los Angeles, Cal. BR/TR, 6'7", 215 lbs. Deb: 5/07/91																									
1991	Chi-N	7	8	.467	40	13	0	0	1	111	114	5	40	44	12.7	3.89	100	.268	.335	1	.042	-2	-3	-0	-0	-0.2
1992	Chi-N	3	6	.333	69	0	0	0	14	87^1	76	4	30	42	11.0	2.89	125	.235	.302	0	.000	-0	6	7	1	0.9
Total	2	10	14	.417	109	13	0	0	15	198^1	190	9	70	86	12.0	3.45	109	.254	.321	1	.036	-2	3	7	1	0.7
● DOC SCANLAN	Scanlan, William Dennis b: 3/7/1881, Syracuse, N.Y. d: 5/29/49, Brooklyn, N.Y. BL/TR, 5'8", 165 lbs. Deb: 9/24/03 F																									
1903	Pit-N	0	1	.000	1	1	1	0	0	9	5	0	6	0	11.0	4.00	81	.167	.306	0	.000	0	-1	-1	-0	-0.1
1904	Pit-N	1	3	.250	4	3	1	0	0	22	21	0	20	10	17.6	4.91	56	.236	.387	0	.000	-1	-5	-5	-0	-0.6
	Bro-N	6	6	.500	13	12	11	3	0	104	94	0	40	40	11.8	2.16	127	.242	.316	5	.143	-2	7	7	-2	0.4
	Yr	7	9	.438	17	15	12	3	0	126	115	0	60	50	12.6	2.64	104	.240	.327	5	.122	-2	1	1	-2	-0.2
1905	Bro-N	14	12	.538	33	28	22	2	0	249^2	220	4	104	135	12.0	2.92	99	.237	.319	16	.167	-2	2	-1	-2	-0.4
1906	Bro-N	18	13	.581	38	33	28	6	2	288	230	5	127	120	11.3	3.19	79	.214	.301	18	.186	3	-18	-21	-7	-2.7
1907	Bro-N	6	8	.429	17	15	10	2	0	107	90	1	61	59	13.0	3.20	73	.239	.349	9	.265	5	-9	-10	-2	-0.8
1909	Bro-N	8	7	.533	19	17	12	2	0	141^1	125	2	65	72	12.4	2.93	89	.252	.343	12	.273	5	-5	-5	-1	-0.1
1910	Bro-N	9	11	.450	34	25	14	0	2	217^1	175	1	116	103	12.3	2.61	116	.234	.341	14	.203	1	10	10	-2	1.0
1911	Bro-N	3	10	.231	22	15	3	0	1	113^2	101	2	69	45	13.9	3.64	92	.256	.374	4	.121	-2	-3	-4	-1	-0.7
Total	8	65	71	.478	181	149	102	15	5	1252	1061	15	608	584	12.3	3.00	93	.234	.330	78	.188	8	-21	-31	-17	-4.0
● PAT SCANTLEBURY	Scantlebury, Patrico Athelstan b: 11/11/17, Gatun, Canal Zone d: 5/24/91, Glen Ridge, N.J. BL/TL, 6'1", 180 lbs. Deb: 4/19/56																									
1956	Cin-N	0	1	.000	6	2	0	0	0	19	24	5	5	10	13.7	6.63	60	.293	.333	0	.000	-0	-6	-6	-0	-0.6
● RANDY SCARBERY	Scarbery, Randy James b: 6/22/52, Fresno, Cal. BB/TR, 6'1", 185 lbs. Deb: 4/16/79																									
1979	Chi-A	2	8	.200	45	5	0	0	4	101^1	102	9	34	45	12.3	4.62	92	.262	.326	0	—	0	-5	-4	0	-0.4
1980	Chi-A	1	2	.333	15	0	0	0	2	28^2	24	1	7	18	10.4	4.08	99	.238	.300	0	—	0	-0	-0	-0	0.0
Total	2	3	10	.231	60	5	0	0	6	130	126	10	41	63	11.9	4.50	93	.257	.320	0	—	0	-5	-4	-0	-0.4
● RAY SCARBOROUGH	Scarborough, Ray Wilson (b: Rae Wilson Scarborough) b: 7/23/17, Mt.Gilead, N.C. d: 7/1/82, Mount Olive, N.C. BR/TR, 6', 185 lbs. Deb: 6/26/42 C																									
1942	Was-A	2	1	.667	17	5	1	1	0	63^1	68	2	32	16	14.2	4.12	89	.272	.355	4	.190	0	-3	-3	1	-0.3
1943	Was-A	4	4	.500	24	6	2	0	3	86	93	2	46	43	14.5	2.83	113	.273	.359	8	.333	2	5	4	0	0.6
1946	Was-A	7	11	.389	32	20	6	1	1	155^2	176	8	74	46	14.5	4.05	83	.286	.364	7	.140	-2	-9	-12	2	-1.2
1947	Was-A	6	13	.316	33	18	8	2	0	161	165	5	67	63	13.0	3.41	109	.267	.339	6	.120	-3	5	6	-0	0.3
1948	Was-A	15	8	.652	31	26	9	0	1	185^1	166	10	72	76	11.7	2.82	154	.233	.307	14	.219	-0	30	31	1	3.4
1949	Was-A	13	11	.542	34	27	11	1	0	199^2	204	10	88	81	13.5	4.60	93	.265	.346	13	.194	-0	-9	-8	1	-0.6
1950	Was-A	3	5	.375	8	8	4	2	0	58^1	62	1	22	24	13.3	4.01	112	.276	.345	2	.100	-1	4	3	1	0.2
	Chi-A	10	13	.435	27	23	8	1	1	149^1	160	10	62	70	13.6	5.30	85	.274	.347	8	.174	-1	-12	-14	-1	-1.4
	Yr	13	18	.419	35	31	12	3	1	207^2	222	11	84	94	13.4	4.94	91	.273	.344	10	.152	-3	-8	-10	-0	-1.2
1951	Bos-A	12	9	.571	37	22	8	0	0	184	201	21	61	71	13.5	5.09	88	.275	.342	13	.191	-3	-20	-13	1	-1.5
1952	Bos-A	1	5	.167	28	8	1	1	4	76^2	79	8	35	29	13.9	4.81	82	.266	.351	4	.222	0	-10	-7	0	-0.7
	*NY-A	5	1	.833	9	4	1	0	0	34	27	4	15	13	11.4	2.91	114	.223	.314	5	.357	2	3	2	-0	0.3
	Yr	6	6	.500	37	12	2	1	4	110^2	106	12	50	42	12.8	4.23	89	.251	.332	9	.281	2	-7	-6	0	-0.4
1953	NY-A	2	2	.500	25	1	0	0	0	54^2	52	4	26	20	13.5	3.29	112	.250	.345	1	.083	-0	4	2	0	0.3
	Det-A	0	2	.000	13	0	0	0	2	20^2	34	3	11	12	20.9	8.27	49	.354	.436	0	.000	-0	-10	-10	-0	-1.0
	Yr	2	4	.333	38	1	0	0	2	75^1	86	7	37	32	15.1	4.66	81	.279	.362	1	.071	-0	-6	-7	-0	-0.7
Total	10	80	85	.485	318	168	59	9	12	1428^2	1487	88	611	564	13.5	4.13	97	.267	.344	85	.186	-6	-22	-19	4	-1.6
● MAC SCARCE	Scarce, Guerrant McCurdy b: 4/8/49, Danville, Va. BL/TL, 6'3", 200 lbs. Deb: 7/10/72																									
1972	Phi-N	1	2	.333	31	0	0	0	4	36^2	30	6	20	40	12.8	3.44	105	.222	.331	0	.000	-1	0	1	1	0.1
1973	Phi-N	1	8	.111	52	0	0	0	12	70^2	54	3	47	57	13.0	2.42	157	.220	.347	0	.000	-1	10	11	-1	1.0
1974	Phi-N	3	8	.273	58	0	0	0	5	70^1	72	6	35	50	13.9	4.99	76	.275	.365	0	.000	-1	-11	-9	-1	-1.2
1975	NY-N	0	0	—	1	0	0	0	0	0	1	0	0	0	—	—	—	1.000	1.000	0	—	0	0	0	0	0.0
1978	Min-A	1	1	.500	17	0	0	0	0	32	35	5	15	17	14.9	3.94	97	.292	.384	0	—	0	-1	-0	-1	-0.1
Total	5	6	19	.240	159	0	0	0	21	209^2	192	20	117	164	13.6	3.69	102	.251	.357	0	.000	-2	-2	2	-2	-0.2
● AL SCHACHT	Schacht, Alexander b: 11/11/1892, New York, N.Y. d: 7/14/84, Waterbury, Conn. BR/TR, 5'11", 142 lbs. Deb: 9/18/19 C																									
1919	Was-A	2	0	1.000	2	2	1	0	0	15	14	0	4	4	10.8	2.40	134	.233	.281	0	.000	0	1	1	-0	0.1
1920	Was-A	6	4	.600	22	11	5	1	1	99^1	130	2	30	19	14.6	4.44	84	.319	.367	5	.192	1	-7	-8	2	-0.5
1921	Was-A	6	6	.500	29	5	2	0	1	82^2	110	2	27	15	15.1	4.90	84	.332	.386	5	.227	1	-6	-7	-3	-0.9
Total	3	14	10	.583	53	18	8	1	2	197	254	4	61	38	14.5	4.48	86	.318	.368	10	.196	2	-11	-14	-2	-1.3
● SID SCHACHT	Schacht, Sidney b: 2/3/18, Bogota, N.J. BR/TR, 5'11", 170 lbs. Deb: 4/23/50																									
1950	StL-A	0	0	—	8	1	0	0	0	10^2	24	5	14	7	32.1	16.03	31	.429	.543	0	.000	-0	-14	-13	-0	-1.2
1951	StL-A	0	0	—	6	0	0	0	1	6	14	1	5	4	28.5	21.00	21	.452	.528	0	—	-0	-11	-11	-0	-1.0
	Bos-N	0	2	.000	5	0	0	0	0	4^2	6	0	2	1	15.4	1.93	191	.300	.364	0	—	0	1	1	-0	0.1
Total	2	0	2	.000	19	1	0	0	1	21^1	44	6	21	12	27.4	14.34	31	.411	.508	0	.000	-0	-24	-23	-1	-2.1

YEAR TM/L	W	L	PCT	G	GS	CG	SH	SV	IP	H	HR	BB	SO	RAT	ERA	ERA+	OAV	OOB	BH	AVG	PB	PR	/A	PD	TPI
● HAL SCHACKER Schacker, Harold b: 4/6/25, Brooklyn, N.Y. BR/TR, 6', 190 lbs. Deb: 5/09/45																								
1945 Bos-N	0	1	.000	6	0	0	0	0	15¹	14	2	9	6	13.5	5.28	73	.241	.343	0	.000	0	-3	-2	-0	-0.3
● GERMANY SCHAEFER Schaefer, Herman A. b: 2/4/1877, Chicago, Ill. d: 5/16/19, Saranac Lake, N.Y. BR/TR, 5'9", 175 lbs. Deb: 10/05/01 ♦																								
1912 Was-A	0	0	—	1	0	0	0	0	0²	1	0	0	0	13.5	0.00	—	.333	.333	41	.247	0	0	0	-0	0.0
1913 Was-A	0	0	—	1	0	0	0	0	0¹	2	1	0	0	54.0	54.00	5	.667	.667	32	.320	0	-2	-2	-0	-0.2
Total 2	0	0	—	2	0	0	0	0	1	3	1	0	0	27.0	18.00	18	.500	.500	972	.257	0	-2	-2	0	-0.2
● HARRY SCHAEFFER Schaeffer, Harry Edward "Lefty" b: 6/23/24, Reading, Pa. BL/TL, 6'2.5", 175 lbs. Deb: 7/28/52																								
1952 NY-A	0	1	.000	5	2	0	0	0	17	18	2	18	15	19.1	5.29	63	.265	.419	0	.000	-0	-3	-4	0	-0.4
● MARK SCHAEFFER Schaeffer, Mark Philip b: 6/5/48, Santa Monica, Cal. BL/TL, 6'5", 215 lbs. Deb: 4/18/72																								
1972 SD-N	2	0	1.000	41	0	0	0	1	41	52	3	28	25	18.0	4.61	71	.319	.425	0	.000	-0	-5	-6	1	-0.6
● JOE SCHAFFERNOTH Schaffernoth, Joseph Arthur b: 8/6/37, Trenton, N.J. BR/TR, 6'4.5", 195 lbs. Deb: 4/15/59																								
1959 Chi-N	1	0	1.000	5	1	0	0	0	7²	11	1	4	3	17.6	8.22	48	.355	.429	0	.000	-0	-4	-4	0	-0.4
1960 Chi-N	2	3	.400	33	0	0	0	3	55	46	2	17	33	10.5	2.78	136	.235	.299	2	.286	0	6	6	0	0.7
1961 Chi-N	0	4	.000	21	0	0	0	0	38¹	43	7	18	23	14.6	6.34	66	.293	.373	0	.000	-1	-10	-9	0	-1.0
Cle-A	0	1	.000	15	0	0	0	0	17	16	2	14	9	16.4	4.76	83	.242	.383	0	.000	-0	-1	-2	1	-0.1
Total 3	3	8	.273	74	1	0	0	3	118	116	12	53	68	13.1	4.58	86	.264	.347	2	.125	-1	-9	-8	1	-0.8
● ART SCHALLOCK Schallock, Arthur Lawrence b: 4/25/24, Mill Valley, Cal. BL/TL, 5'9", 160 lbs. Deb: 7/16/51																								
1951 NY-A	3	1	.750	11	6	1	0	0	46¹	50	3	20	19	13.8	3.88	99	.272	.346	5	.294	1	1	-0	0	0.1
1952 NY-A	0	0	—	2	0	0	0	0	2	3	0	2	1	22.5	9.00	37	.375	.500	0	—	0	-1	-1	-0	-0.1
1953 *NY-A	0	0	—	7	1	0	0	1	21¹	30	2	15	13	19.4	2.95	125	.345	.447	2	.333	0	2	2	-0	0.2
1954 NY-A	0	1	.000	6	1	1	0	0	17¹	20	3	11	9	16.6	4.15	83	.282	.386	0	.000	-0	-1	-1	-0	-0.2
1955 NY-A	0	0	—	2	0	0	0	0	3	4	1	1	2	15.0	6.00	62	.333	.385	0	—	0	-1	-1	-0	-0.1
Bal-A	3	5	.375	30	6	1	0	0	80¹	92	2	42	33	15.2	4.15	92	.294	.381	2	.105	-1	-2	-3	-1	-0.4
Yr	3	5	.375	32	6	1	0	0	83¹	96	3	43	35	15.2	4.21	90	.295	.381	2	.105	-1	-2	-4	-1	-0.5
Total 5	6	7	.462	58	14	3	0	1	170¹	199	11	91	77	15.6	4.02	94	.295	.383	9	.200	0	-1	-5	-1	-0.5
● CHARLEY SCHANZ Schanz, Charley Murrell b: 6/8/19, Anacortes, Wash. BR/TR, 6'3.5", 215 lbs. Deb: 4/20/44																								
1944 Phi-N	13	16	.448	40	30	13	1	3	241¹	231	6	103	84	12.7	3.32	109	.254	.334	12	.148	-1	8	8	-0	0.8
1945 Phi-N	4	15	.211	35	21	5	1	5	144²	165	5	87	56	16.2	4.35	88	.285	.387	6	.154	-0	-9	-8	1	-0.8
1946 Phi-N	6	6	.500	32	15	4	0	4	116¹	131	8	71	47	15.9	5.80	59	.286	.389	3	.083	-2	-31	-31	1	-3.2
1947 Phi-N	2	4	.333	34	6	1	0	2	101²	107	4	47	42	13.9	4.16	86	.295	.380	4	.148	-1	-1	-2	-0	-0.2
1950 Bos-A	3	2	.600	14	0	0	0	0	22²	25	3	24	14	19.9	8.34	59	.281	.439	1	.091	-1	-9	-9	-0	-0.9
Total 5	28	43	.394	155	72	23	2	14	626²	658	29	332	243	14.6	4.34	86	.275	.369	26	.134	-5	-43	-42	1	-4.3
● JOHN SCHAPPERT Schappert, John b: Brooklyn, N.Y. d: 7/29/16, Rockaway Beach, N.Y. BR/TR, 5'10", 170 lbs. Deb: 5/03/1882																								
1882 StL-a	8	7	.533	15	14	13	0	0	128	131	2	32	38	11.5	3.52	80	.248	.291	9	.180	0	-12	-10	-2	-1.1
● BILL SCHARDT Schardt, Wilburt "Big Bill" b: 1/20/1886, Cleveland, Ohio d: 7/20/64, Vermilion, Ohio BR/TR, 6'4", 210 lbs. Deb: 4/14/11																								
1911 Bro-N	5	15	.250	39	22	10	1	4	195¹	190	4	91	77	13.3	3.59	93	.266	.355	10	.169	0	-4	-6	0	-0.5
1912 Bro-N	0	1	.000	7	0	0	0	1	20²	25	1	6	7	14.4	4.35	77	.321	.384	-0	.000	-1	-2	-2	2	-0.1
Total 2	5	16	.238	46	22	10	1	5	216	215	5	97	84	13.4	3.67	91	.271	.358	10	.154	-1	-6	-8	2	-0.6
● JEFF SCHATTINGER Schattinger, Jeffrey Charles b: 10/25/55, Fresno, Cal. BL/TR, 6'5", 200 lbs. Deb: 9/21/81																								
1981 KC-A	0	0	—	1	0	0	0	0	3	2	0	1	1	15.0	0.00	—	.182	.357	0	—	0	1	1	-0	0.2
● DAN SCHATZEDER Schatzeder, Daniel Ernest b: 12/1/54, Elmhurst, Ill. BL/TL, 6', 195 lbs. Deb: 9/04/77																								
1977 Mon-N	2	1	.667	6	3	1	1	0	21²	16	0	13	14	12.0	2.49	153	.203	.315	2	.333	0	3	3	-0	0.4
1978 Mon-N	7	7	.500	29	18	2	0	0	143²	108	10	68	69	11.2	3.07	115	.213	.308	10	.222	3	8	7	-2	0.9
1979 Mon-N	10	5	.667	32	21	3	0	1	162	136	17	59	106	10.9	2.83	129	.225	.295	11	.216	4	16	15	-3	1.7
1980 Det-A	11	13	.458	32	26	9	2	0	192²	178	23	58	94	11.2	4.02	102	.246	.304	0	—	0	0	-2	-0	-0.1
1981 Det-A	6	8	.429	17	14	1	0	0	71¹	74	4	29	20	13.2	6.06	62	.265	.339	0	—	0	-19	-18	-0	-1.9
1982 SF-N	1	4	.200	13	3	0	0	0	33¹	47	3	12	18	15.9	7.29	49	.333	.386	1	.125	-0	-14	-14	0	-1.4
Mon-N	0	2	.000	26	1	0	0	0	36	37	1	12	15	12.8	3.50	104	.276	.345	2	.400	1	0	1	-0	0.1
Yr	1	6	.143	39	4	0	0	0	69¹	84	4	24	33	14.3	5.32	68	.304	.364	3	.231	1	-13	-13	0	-1.3
1983 Mon-N	5	2	.714	58	2	0	0	2	87	88	3	25	48	12.2	3.21	112	.265	.326	2	.200	0	4	4	-1	0.3
1984 Mon-N	7	7	.500	36	14	1	1	1	136	112	13	36	89	9.9	2.71	126	.224	.278	11	.314	5	13	11	-3	1.4
1985 Mon-N	3	5	.375	24	15	1	0	0	104¹	101	13	31	64	11.4	3.80	89	.259	.314	6	.194	3	-2	-5	-0	-0.2
1986 Mon-N	3	2	.600	30	1	0	0	1	59	53	6	19	33	11.0	3.20	115	.240	.300	9	.429	3	3	3	-1	0.9
Phi-N	3	3	.500	25	0	0	0	1	29¹	28	3	16	14	13.5	3.38	104	.252	.346	1	.200	1	2	2	-0	0.2
Yr	6	5	.545	55	1	0	0	2	88¹	81	9	35	47	11.8	3.26	115	.243	.314	10	.385	7	4	5	-1	1.1
1987 Phi-N	3	1	.750	26	0	0	0	0	37²	40	4	14	28	12.9	4.06	104	.278	.342	2	.167	0	0	1	-1	0.0
*Min-A	3	1	.750	30	1	0	0	0	43²	64	8	18	30	17.1	6.39	72	.342	.403	0	—	0	-9	-9	-0	-0.8
1988 Cle-A	0	2	.000	15	0	0	0	3	16	26	6	2	10	16.3	9.56	43	.351	.377	0	—	0	-10	-10	-0	-1.1
Min-A	0	1	.000	10	0	0	0	0	10¹	8	1	5	7	12.2	1.74	234	.216	.326	0	—	0	3	3	-0	0.1
Yr	0	3	.000	25	0	0	0	3	26¹	34	7	7	17	14.4	6.49	63	.304	.350	0	—	0	-7	-7	-0	-1.0
1989 Hou-N	4	1	.800	36	0	0	0	0	56²	64	2	28	46	15.1	4.45	76	.287	.374	0	.000	-1	-6	-7	-0	-0.8
1990 Hou-N	1	3	.250	45	2	0	0	6	64	61	2	23	37	11.8	2.39	155	.261	.327	1	.250	0	10	9	-0	1.0
NY-N	0	0	—	6	0	0	0	0	5²	5	0	0	2	7.9	0.00	—	.263	.263	0	—	0	2	2	-0	0.2
Yr	1	3	.250	51	2	0	0	6	69²	66	2	23	39	11.5	2.20	169	.256	.317	1	.250	0	12	12	-0	1.2
1991 KC-A	0	0	—	8	0	0	0	0	6²	11	0	7	4	24.3	9.45	44	.367	.486	0	—	0	-4	-4	-0	-0.4
Total 15	69	68	.504	504	121	18	4	10	1317	1257	128	475	748	12.0	3.74	99	.253	.321	58	.240	22	1	-4	-13	0.5
● RUBE SCHAUER Schauer, Alexander John (b: Dimitri Ivanovich Dimitrihoff) b: 3/19/1891, Odessa, Russia d: 4/15/57, Minneapolis, Minn. BR/TR, 6'2", 192 lbs. Deb: 8/27/13																								
1913 NY-N	0	1	.000	3	1	1	0	0	12	14	0	9	7	17.3	7.50	42	.292	.404	0	.000	-0	-6	-6	-0	-0.6
1914 NY-N	0	0	—	6	0	0	0	0	22¹	16	2	8	6	9.7	3.22	82	.205	.279	1	.143	-0	-1	-1	-1	-0.1
1915 NY-N	2	8	.200	32	7	4	0	0	105¹	101	4	35	65	11.8	3.50	73	.258	.322	2	.077	-2	-9	-11	-0	-1.4
1916 NY-N	1	4	.200	19	3	1	0	0	45²	44	0	16	24	12.2	2.96	82	.257	.328	2	.222	-0	-2	-3	-0	-0.3
1917 Phi-A	7	16	.304	33	21	10	0	1	215	209	6	69	62	11.8	3.14	88	.263	.324	11	.145	-3	-11	-9	-0	-1.4
Total 5	10	29	.256	93	32	16	0	1	400¹	384	12	137	164	11.9	3.35	80	.259	.324	16	.132	-4	-29	-30	-1	-3.7
● OWEN SCHEETZ Scheetz, Owen Franklin b: 12/24/13, New Bedford, Ohio BR/TR, 6', 190 lbs. Deb: 4/22/43																								
1943 Was-A	0	0	—	6	0	0	0	1	9	16	0	4	5	20.0	7.00	46	.381	.435	0	.000	-0	-4	-4	0	-0.4
● LEFTY SCHEGG Schegg, Gilbert Eugene (b: Gilbert Eugene Price) b: 8/28/1889, Leesville, Ohio d: 2/27/63, Niles, Ohio BL/TL, 5'11", 180 lbs. Deb: 8/20/12																								
1912 Was-A	0	0	—	2	1	0	0	0	5¹	7	0	4	3	18.6	3.38	99	.333	.440	0	—	0	-0	-0	-1	-0.1
● CARL SCHEIB Scheib, Carl Alvin b: 1/1/27, Gratz, Pa. BR/TR, 6'1", 192 lbs. Deb: 9/06/43																								
1943 Phi-A	0	1	.000	6	0	0	0	0	18²	24	4	3	3	13.5	4.34	78	.308	.341	0	.000	-0	-2	-2	-1	-0.3
1944 Phi-A	0	0	—	15	0	0	0	0	36¹	36	1	11	13	12.6	4.21	83	.257	.329	3	.300	1	-3	-3	1	-0.1
1945 Phi-A	0	0	—	4	0	0	0	0	8²	6	0	4	2	10.4	3.12	110	.207	.303	-0	.000	-0	0	0	0	0.0

YEAR TM/L	W	L	PCT	G	GS	CG	SH	SV	IP	H	HR	BB	SO	RAT	ERA	ERA+	OAV	OOB	BH	AVG	PB	PR	/A	PD	TPI
1947 Phi-A	4	6	.400	21	12	6	2	0	116	121	11	55	26	13.8	5.04	76	.274	.357	6	.133	-3	-17	-16	-2	-2.0
1948 Phi-A	14	8	.636	32	24	15	1	0	198^2	219	14	76	44	13.4	3.94	109	.286	.351	31	.298	7	8	8	1	1.9
1949 Phi-A	9	12	.429	38	23	11	2	0	182^2	191	16	118	43	15.3	5.12	80	.275	.382	17	.236	3	-19	-21	-3	-1.9
1950 Phi-A	3	10	.231	43	8	1	0	3	106	138	13	70	37	17.7	7.22	63	.317	.411	13	.250	2	-31	-31	-1	-2.7
1951 Phi-A	1	12	.077	46	11	3	0	10	143	132	7	71	49	13.3	4.47	96	.250	.347	21	.396	8	-6	-3	4	1.0
1952 Phi-A	11	7	.611	30	19	8	1	2	158	153	21	50	42	11.8	4.39	90	.253	.314	18	.220	-1	-12	-8	0	-0.8
1953 Phi-A	3	7	.300	28	8	3	0	2	96	99	9	29	25	12.7	4.88	88	.261	.325	8	.195	-1	-9	-6	-0	-0.7
1954 Phi-A	0	1	.000	1	1	0	0	0	2	5	0	1	1	31.5	22.50	17	.500	.583	0	—	0	-4	-4	-0	-0.4
StL-N	0	1	.000	3	1	0	0	0	4^2	6	3	5	5	21.2	11.57	36	.300	.440	0	.000	-0	-4	-4	0	-0.4
Total 11	45	65	.409	267	107	47	6	17	1070^2	1130	99	493	290	13.9	4.88	85	.274	.355	117	.250	16	-100	-89	0	-6.4

● FRANK SCHEIBECK Scheibeck, Frank S. b: 6/28/1865, Detroit, Mich. d: 10/22/56, Detroit, Mich. BR/TR, 5'7", 145 lbs. Deb: 5/09/1887 ♦

YEAR TM/L	W	L	PCT	G	GS	CG	SH	SV	IP	H	HR	BB	SO	RAT	ERA	ERA+	OAV	OOB	BH	AVG	PB	PR	/A	PD	TPI
1887 Cle-a	0	1	.000	1	1	1	0	0	9	17	1	4	3	22.0	12.00	36	.362	.423	2	.222	0	-8	-8	-0	-0.5

● JACK SCHEIBLE Scheible, John G. b: 2/16/1866, Youngstown, Ohio d: 8/9/1897, Youngstown, Ohio TL, Deb: 9/08/1893

YEAR TM/L	W	L	PCT	G	GS	CG	SH	SV	IP	H	HR	BB	SO	RAT	ERA	ERA+	OAV	OOB	BH	AVG	PB	PR	/A	PD	TPI
1893 Cle-N	1	1	.500	2	2	2	1	0	18	15	0	11	1	13.0	2.00	244	.220	.328	1	.143	-0	5	6	-0	0.5
1894 Phi-N	0	1	.000	1	1	0	0	0	0^1	6	0	2	0	243.0	189.00	3	.862	.904	0	—	0	-7	-7	-0	-0.4
Total 2	1	2	.333	3	3	2	1	0	18^1	21	0	13	1	17.2	5.40	91	.279	.392	1	.143	-0	-1	-1	-0	0.1

● RICH SCHEID Scheid, Richard Paul b: 2/3/65, Staten Island, N.Y. BL/TL, 6'3", 185 lbs. Deb: 9/11/92

YEAR TM/L	W	L	PCT	G	GS	CG	SH	SV	IP	H	HR	BB	SO	RAT	ERA	ERA+	OAV	OOB	BH	AVG	PB	PR	/A	PD	TPI
1992 Hou-N	0	1	.000	7	1	0	0	0	12	14	2	6	8	15.0	6.00	56	.280	.357	0	.000	-0	-3	-4	-0	-0.4

● JIM SCHELLE Schelle, Gerard Anthony b: 4/13/17, Baltimore, Md. BR/TR, 6'3", 204 lbs. Deb: 7/23/39

YEAR TM/L	W	L	PCT	G	GS	CG	SH	SV	IP	H	HR	BB	SO	RAT	ERA	ERA+	OAV	OOB	BH	AVG	PB	PR	/A	PD	TPI
1939 Phi-A	0	0	—	1	0	0	0	0	0	1	0	3	0	—	∞	—	1.000	1.000	0	—	0	-3	-3	0	-0.2

● FRED SCHEMANSKE Schemanske, Frederick George "Buck" b: 4/28/03, Detroit, Mich. d: 2/18/60, Detroit, Mich. BR/TR, 6'2", 190 lbs. Deb: 9/15/23 ♦

YEAR TM/L	W	L	PCT	G	GS	CG	SH	SV	IP	H	HR	BB	SO	RAT	ERA	ERA+	OAV	OOB	BH	AVG	PB	PR	/A	PD	TPI
1923 Was-A	0	0	—	1	0	0	0	0	1	3	0	0	0	27.0	27.00	14	.600	.600	2	1.000	1	-3	-3	-0	-0.1

● BILL SCHENCK Schenck, William G. b: Brooklyn, N.Y. 5'7", 171 lbs. Deb: 5/29/1882 ♦

YEAR TM/L	W	L	PCT	G	GS	CG	SH	SV	IP	H	HR	BB	SO	RAT	ERA	ERA+	OAV	OOB	BH	AVG	PB	PR	/A	PD	TPI
1882 Lou-a	1	0	1.000	2	1	1	0	0	10	6	0	1	4	6.3	0.90	275	.162	.184	60	.260	0	2	2	-0	0.1

● JOHN SCHENEBERG Scheneberg, John Bluford b: 11/20/1887, Guyandotte, W.Va. d: 9/26/50, Huntington, W.Va. BB/TR, 6'1", 180 lbs. Deb: 9/23/13

YEAR TM/L	W	L	PCT	G	GS	CG	SH	SV	IP	H	HR	BB	SO	RAT	ERA	ERA+	OAV	OOB	BH	AVG	PB	PR	/A	PD	TPI
1913 Pit-N	0	1	.000	1	1	0	0	0	6	10	0	2	1	18.0	6.00	50	.400	.444	1	.500	0	-2	-2	0	-0.1
1920 StL-A	0	0	—	1	0	0	0	0	2	7	0	1	0	36.0	27.00	15	.583	.615	0	—	0	-5	-5	-0	-0.4
Total 2	0	1	.000	2	1	0	0	0	8	17	0	3	1	22.5	11.25	29	.459	.500	1	.500	0	-7	-7	0	-0.5

● FRED SCHERMAN Scherman, Frederick John b: 7/25/44, Dayton, Ohio BL/TL, 6'1", 195 lbs. Deb: 4/26/69

YEAR TM/L	W	L	PCT	G	GS	CG	SH	SV	IP	H	HR	BB	SO	RAT	ERA	ERA+	OAV	OOB	BH	AVG	PB	PR	/A	PD	TPI
1969 Det-A	1	0	1.000	4	0	0	0	0	4	6	2	0	3	13.5	6.75	55	.333	.333	0	—	0	-1	-1	0	-0.1
1970 Det-A	4	4	.500	48	0	0	0	1	69^2	61	5	28	58	11.6	3.23	115	.237	.315	2	.167	-0	4	4	0	0.4
1971 Det-A	11	6	.647	69	1	1	0	20	113	91	11	49	46	11.5	2.71	133	.226	.318	5	.208	1	9	11	1	1.4
1972 *Det-A	7	3	.700	57	3	0	0	12	94	91	5	53	53	14.3	3.64	86	.269	.376	2	.091	-1	-6	-5	-1	-0.8
1973 Det-A	2	2	.500	34	0	0	0	1	61^2	59	6	30	28	13.4	4.23	97	.258	.351	0	—	0	-3	-1	-1	-0.2
1974 Hou-N	2	5	.286	53	0	0	0	4	61^1	67	5	26	35	14.7	4.11	84	.284	.372	0	.000	-0	-3	-4	-0	-0.5
1975 Hou-N	0	1	.000	16	0	0	0	0	16^1	21	4	4	13	14.3	4.96	68	.318	.366	0	.000	-0	-2	-3	0	-0.3
Mon-N	4	3	.571	34	7	0	0	0	76^1	84	3	41	43	15.3	3.54	108	.283	.379	1	.063	-1	1	2	1	0.3
Yr	4	4	.500	50	7	0	0	0	92^2	105	7	45	56	15.1	3.79	99	.288	.373	1	.059	-1	-2	-0	1	0.0
1976 Mon-N	2	2	.500	31	0	0	0	1	40	42	5	14	18	13.3	4.95	75	.261	.331	1	.250	0	-6	-5	-1	-0.6
Total 8	33	26	.559	346	11	1	0	39	536^1	522	46	245	297	13.4	3.66	99	.260	.350	11	.134	-1	-9	-3	-1	-0.4

● BILL SCHERRER Scherrer, William Joseph b: 1/20/58, Tonawanda, N.Y. BL/TL, 6'4", 180 lbs. Deb: 9/07/82

YEAR TM/L	W	L	PCT	G	GS	CG	SH	SV	IP	H	HR	BB	SO	RAT	ERA	ERA+	OAV	OOB	BH	AVG	PB	PR	/A	PD	TPI
1982 Cin-N	0	1	.000	5	2	0	0	0	17^1	17	0	0	7	8.8	2.60	142	.250	.250	1	.500	1	2	2	-0	0.3
1983 Cin-N	2	3	.400	73	0	0	0	10	92	73	6	33	57	10.4	2.74	139	.225	.296	1	.091	-0	9	11	1	1.2
1984 Cin-N	1	1	.500	36	0	0	0	1	52^1	64	6	15	35	13.6	4.99	76	.300	.346	0	.000	-0	-8	-7	0	-0.7
*Det-A	1	0	1.000	18	0	0	0	0	19	14	1	8	16	10.4	1.89	207	.206	.289	0	—	0	4	4	-0	0.4
1985 Det-A	3	2	.600	48	0	0	0	0	66	62	10	41	46	14.2	4.36	93	.248	.356	0	—	0	-2	-2	1	-0.1
1986 Det-A	0	1	.000	13	0	0	0	0	21	19	3	22	16	18.0	7.29	57	.244	.416	0	—	0	-7	-7	0	-0.7
1987 Cin-N	1	1	.500	23	0	0	0	0	33	43	3	16	24	16.1	4.36	97	.328	.401	0	.000	-0	-1	-0	-0	-0.1
1988 Bal-A	0	1	.000	4	0	0	0	0	4	8	2	3	3	24.8	13.50	29	.400	.478	0	—	0	-4	-4	-0	-0.3
Phi-N	0	0	—	8	0	0	0	0	6^2	7	0	2	3	12.2	5.40	66	.269	.321	0	—	0	-1	-1	0	-0.1
Total 7	8	10	.444	228	2	0	0	11	311^1	307	31	140	207	13.0	4.08	96	.260	.340	2	.118	-0	-8	-5	1	-0.1

● DUTCH SCHESLER Schesler, Charles b: 6/1/1900, Frankfurt, Germany d: 11/19/53, Harrisburg, Pa. BR/TR, 6'2", 185 lbs. Deb: 4/16/31

YEAR TM/L	W	L	PCT	G	GS	CG	SH	SV	IP	H	HR	BB	SO	RAT	ERA	ERA+	OAV	OOB	BH	AVG	PB	PR	/A	PD	TPI
1931 Phi-N	0	0	—	17	0	0	0	0	38^1	65	4	18	14	20.4	7.28	58	.385	.455	1	.111	-0	-15	-13	0	-1.2

● LOU SCHETTLER Schettler, Louis Martin b: 6/12/1886, Pittsburgh, Pa. d: 5/1/60, Youngstown, Ohio BR/TR, 5'11", 160 lbs. Deb: 4/25/10

YEAR TM/L	W	L	PCT	G	GS	CG	SH	SV	IP	H	HR	BB	SO	RAT	ERA	ERA+	OAV	OOB	BH	AVG	PB	PR	/A	PD	TPI
1910 Phi-N	2	6	.250	27	7	3	0	1	107	96	2	51	62	12.5	3.20	98	.247	.337	7	.171	-1	-2	-1	-1	-0.4

● CURT SCHILLING Schilling, Curtis Montague b: 11/14/66, Anchorage, Al. BR/TR, 6'5", 205 lbs. Deb: 9/07/88

YEAR TM/L	W	L	PCT	G	GS	CG	SH	SV	IP	H	HR	BB	SO	RAT	ERA	ERA+	OAV	OOB	BH	AVG	PB	PR	/A	PD	TPI
1988 Bal-A	0	3	.000	4	4	0	0	0	14^2	22	3	10	4	20.3	9.82	40	.355	.452	0	—	0	-10	-10	-1	-0.8
1989 Bal-A	0	1	.000	5	1	0	0	0	8^2	10	2	3	6	13.5	6.23	61	.286	.342	0	—	0	-2	-2	-0	-0.2
1990 Bal-A	1	2	.333	35	0	0	0	3	46	38	1	19	32	11.2	2.54	149	.229	.308	0	—	0	7	6	-1	0.6
1991 Hou-N	3	5	.375	56	0	0	0	8	75^2	79	2	39	71	14.0	3.81	92	.271	.358	1	.333	0	-1	-3	-1	-0.3
1992 Phi-N	14	11	.560	42	26	10	4	2	226^1	165	11	59	147	**8.9**	2.35	149	**.201**	**.256**	10	.156	-0	29	29	-3	3.0
Total 5	18	22	.450	142	31	10	4	13	371^1	314	19	130	260	10.8	3.05	117	.229	.296	11	.164	0	23	21	-5	2.3

● RED SCHILLINGS Schillings, Elbert Isaiah b: 3/29/1900, Deport, Tex. d: 1/7/54, Oklahoma City, Okla BR/TR, 5'10", 180 lbs. Deb: 9/11/22

YEAR TM/L	W	L	PCT	G	GS	CG	SH	SV	IP	H	HR	BB	SO	RAT	ERA	ERA+	OAV	OOB	BH	AVG	PB	PR	/A	PD	TPI
1922 Phi-A	0	0	—	4	0	0	0	0	8	10	1	11	4	23.6	6.75	63	.313	.488	0	.000	-0	-2	-2	-0	-0.3

● CALVIN SCHIRALDI Schiraldi, Calvin Drew b: 6/16/62, Houston, Tex. BR/TR, 6'4", 200 lbs. Deb: 9/01/84

YEAR TM/L	W	L	PCT	G	GS	CG	SH	SV	IP	H	HR	BB	SO	RAT	ERA	ERA+	OAV	OOB	BH	AVG	PB	PR	/A	PD	TPI
1984 NY-N	0	2	.000	5	3	0	0	0	17^1	20	3	10	16	15.6	5.71	62	.286	.375	0	.000	-0	-4	-4	0	-0.4
1985 NY-N	2	1	.667	10	4	0	0	0	26^1	43	4	11	21	19.5	8.89	39	.368	.435	1	.125	-0	-15	-16	0	-1.5
1986 *Bos-A	4	2	.667	25	0	0	0	9	51	36	5	15	55	9.2	1.41	295	.201	.267	0	—	0	16	16	-1	1.5
1987 Bos-A	8	5	.615	62	1	0	0	6	83^2	75	15	40	93	12.5	4.41	103	.240	.328	0	—	0	0	1	-0	0.1
1988 Chi-N	9	13	.409	29	27	2	1	1	166^1	166	13	63	140	12.5	4.38	82	.257	.325	6	.100	-2	-17	-14	-2	-1.9
1989 Chi-N	3	6	.333	54	0	0	0	4	78^2	60	7	50	54	12.7	3.78	100	.209	.328	0	.000	-1	-2	-0	-1	-0.2
SD-N	3	1	.750	5	4	0	0	0	21^1	12	1	13	17	10.5	2.53	138	.162	.287	1	.143	1	2	2	-0	0.3
Yr	6	7	.462	59	4	0	0	4	100	72	8	63	71	12.2	3.51	105	.198	.316	1	.063	0	-0	2	-2	0.1
1990 SD-N	3	8	.273	42	8	0	0	1	104	105	11	60	74	14.4	4.41	87	.264	.362	4	.190	2	-7	-7	-1	-0.6
1991 Tex-A	0	1	.000	3	0	0	0	0	4^2	5	3	5	1	19.3	11.57	35	.263	.417	0	—	0	-4	-4	0	-0.3
Total 8	32	39	.451	235	47	2	1	21	553^1	522	62	267	471	13.0	4.28	90	.248	.336	12	.111	-1	-32	-26	-5	-3.0

● BIFF SCHLITZER Schlitzer, Victor Joseph b: 12/4/1884, Rochester, N.Y. d: 1/4/48, Wellesley Hills, Mass. BR/TR, 5'11", 175 lbs. Deb: 4/17/08

YEAR TM/L	W	L	PCT	G	GS	CG	SH	SV	IP	H	HR	BB	SO	RAT	ERA	ERA+	OAV	OOB	BH	AVG	PB	PR	/A	PD	TPI
1908 Phi-A	6	8	.429	24	18	11	2	0	131	110	1	45	57	10.8	3.16	81	.234	.303	9	.196	-1	-11	-9	-2	-1.3
1909 Phi-A	0	3	.000	4	3	0	0	0	13^1	13	0	7	6	15.5	5.40	45	.245	.365	1	.250	0	-4	-4	1	-0.4
Bos-A	4	4	.500	13	8	5	0	1	69^2	68	0	17	23	11.1	3.49	72	.234	.279	4	.154	-0	-8	-8	1	-0.7
Yr	4	7	.364	17	11	5	0	1	83	81	0	24	29	11.5	3.80	65	.234	.286	5	.167	0	-12	-12	2	-1.1

YEAR TM/L	W	L	PCT	G	GS	CG	SH	SV	IP	H	HR	BB	SO	RAT	ERA	ERA+	OAV	OOB	BH	AVG	PB	PR	/A	PD	TPI
1914 Buf-F	0	0	—	3	0	0	0	0	3^1	7	3	2	1	24.3	16.20	20	.438	.500	1	1.000	0	-5	-5	0	-0.4
Total 3	10	15	.400	44	29	16	2	1	217^1	198	4	71	87	11.4	3.60	71	.239	.303	15	.195	-0	-28	-25	-0	-2.8

● GEORGE SCHMEES Schmees, George Edward "Rocky" b: 9/6/24, Cincinnati, Ohio BL/TL, 6', 190 lbs. Deb: 4/15/52 ♦

YEAR TM/L	W	L	PCT	G	GS	CG	SH	SV	IP	H	HR	BB	SO	RAT	ERA	ERA+	OAV	OOB	BH	AVG	PB	PR	/A	PD	TPI
1952 Bos-A	0	0	—	2	1	0	0	0	6	9	0	2	2	16.5	3.00	131	.346	.393	13	.203	0	0	1	1	0.1

● AL SCHMELZ Schmelz, Alan George b: 11/12/43, Whittier, Cal. BR/TR, 6'4", 210 lbs. Deb: 9/07/67

YEAR TM/L	W	L	PCT	G	GS	CG	SH	SV	IP	H	HR	BB	SO	RAT	ERA	ERA+	OAV	OOB	BH	AVG	PB	PR	/A	PD	TPI
1967 NY-N	0	0	—	2	0	0	0	0	3	4	1	1	2	15.0	3.00	113	.364	.417	0	—	0	0	0	0	0.0

● BUTCH SCHMIDT Schmidt, Charles John "Butcher Boy" b: 7/19/1886, Baltimore, Md. d: 9/4/52, Baltimore, Md. BL/TL, 6'1.5", 200 lbs. Deb: 5/11/09 ♦

YEAR TM/L	W	L	PCT	G	GS	CG	SH	SV	IP	H	HR	BB	SO	RAT	ERA	ERA+	OAV	OOB	BH	AVG	PB	PR	/A	PD	TPI
1909 NY-A	0	0	—	1	0	0	0	0	5	10	0	1	2	19.8	7.20	35	.435	.458	0	.000	-0	-3	-3	-0	-0.3

● DAVE SCHMIDT Schmidt, David Joseph b: 4/22/57, Niles, Mich. BR/TR, 6'1", 185 lbs. Deb: 5/01/81

YEAR TM/L	W	L	PCT	G	GS	CG	SH	SV	IP	H	HR	BB	SO	RAT	ERA	ERA+	OAV	OOB	BH	AVG	PB	PR	/A	PD	TPI
1981 Tex-A	0	1	.000	14	1	0	0	1	31^2	31	1	11	13	12.2	3.13	111	.258	.326	0	—	0	2	1	0	0.2
1982 Tex-A	4	6	.400	33	8	0	0	6	109^2	118	5	25	69	12.1	3.20	121	.279	.327	0	—	0	11	8	-0	1.1
1983 Tex-A	3	3	.500	31	0	0	0	2	46^1	42	3	14	29	11.1	3.88	103	.241	.302	0	—	0	1	1	0	0.2
1984 Tex-A	6	6	.500	43	0	0	0	12	70^1	69	3	20	46	11.4	2.56	162	.262	.314	0	—	0	11	12	1	1.4
1985 Tex-A	7	6	.538	51	4	1	1	5	85^2	81	6	22	46	10.8	3.15	134	.246	.293	0	—	0	9	10	1	1.1
1986 Chi-A	3	6	.333	49	1	0	0	8	92^1	94	10	27	67	12.3	3.31	130	.264	.325	0	—	0	9	10	-1	0.9
1987 Bal-A	10	5	.667	35	14	2	2	1	124	128	13	26	70	11.3	3.77	117	.263	.302	0	—	0	9	9	-1	0.7
1988 Bal-A	8	5	.615	41	9	0	0	2	129^2	129	14	38	67	11.8	3.40	115	.262	.319	0	—	0	8	7	2	1.1
1989 Bal-A	10	13	.435	38	26	2	0	0	156^2	196	24	36	46	13.4	5.69	67	.310	.349	0	—	0	-31	-33	1	-3.1
1990 Mon-N	3	3	.500	34	0	0	0	13	48	58	3	13	22	13.3	4.31	85	.297	.341	0	.000	-0	-3	-4	0	-0.4
1991 Mon-N	0	1	.000	4	0	0	0	0	4^1	9	2	2	3	22.8	10.38	35	.429	.478	0	—	0	-3	-3	0	-0.3
1992 Sea-A	0	0	—	3	0	0	0	0	3^1	7	1	3	1	27.0	18.90	21	.438	.526	0	—	0	-6	-6	-0	-0.5
Total 12	54	55	.495	376	63	5	3	50	902	962	85	237	479	12.1	3.88	103	.274	.323	0	.000	-0	17	13	3	2.4

● FREDDY SCHMIDT Schmidt, Frederick Albert b: 2/9/16, Hartford, Conn. BR/TR, 6'1", 185 lbs. Deb: 4/25/44

YEAR TM/L	W	L	PCT	G	GS	CG	SH	SV	IP	H	HR	BB	SO	RAT	ERA	ERA+	OAV	OOB	BH	AVG	PB	PR	/A	PD	TPI
1944 *StL-N	7	3	.700	37	9	3	2	5	114^1	94	5	58	58	12.0	3.15	112	.222	.317	7	.206	-0	6	5	-1	0.4
1946 StL-N	1	0	1.000	16	0	0	0	0	27^1	27	0	15	14	14.8	3.29	105	.276	.388	0	.000	-0	0	0	0	0.1
1947 StL-N	0	0	—	2	0	0	0	0	4	5	1	1	2	13.5	2.25	184	.333	.375	0	—	0	1	1	-0	0.1
Phi-N	5	8	.385	29	5	0	0	0	76^2	76	4	43	24	14.4	4.70	85	.285	.392	1	.050	-2	-5	-6	-1	-0.8
Chi-N	0	0	—	1	1	0	0	0	3	4	0	5	0	27.0	9.00	44	.333	.529	0	.000	-0	-2	-2	0	-0.2
Yr	5	8	.385	32	6	0	0	0	83^2	85	5	49	26	14.4	4.73	85	.285	.386	1	.045	-2	-6	-7	-1	-0.9
Total 3	13	11	.542	85	15	3	2	5	225^1	206	10	122	98	13.4	3.75	98	.252	.355	8	.140	-2	-0	-1	-1	-0.4

● PETE SCHMIDT Schmidt, Friedrich Christoph Herman b: 7/23/1890, Lowden, Iowa d: 3/11/73, Pembroke, Ont., Can BR/TR, 5'11", 175 lbs. Deb: 7/14/13

YEAR TM/L	W	L	PCT	G	GS	CG	SH	SV	IP	H	HR	BB	SO	RAT	ERA	ERA+	OAV	OOB	BH	AVG	PB	PR	/A	PD	TPI
1913 StL-A	0	0	—	1	0	0	0	1	2	3	0	2	0	22.5	4.50	65	.333	.455	0	—	0	-0	-0	-0	-0.1

● HENRY SCHMIDT Schmidt, Henry Martin b: 6/26/1873, Brownsville, Tex. d: 4/23/26, Nashville, Tenn. BR/TR, 5'11", 170 lbs. Deb: 4/17/03

YEAR TM/L	W	L	PCT	G	GS	CG	SH	SV	IP	H	HR	BB	SO	RAT	ERA	ERA+	OAV	OOB	BH	AVG	PB	PR	/A	PD	TPI
1903 Bro-N	22	13	.629	40	36	29	5	2	301	321	5	120	96	13.8	3.83	83	.280	.359	21	.196	3	-19	-21	6	-1.2

● WILLARD SCHMIDT Schmidt, Willard Raymond b: 5/29/28, Hays, Kan. BR/TR, 6'1", 187 lbs. Deb: 4/19/52

YEAR TM/L	W	L	PCT	G	GS	CG	SH	SV	IP	H	HR	BB	SO	RAT	ERA	ERA+	OAV	OOB	BH	AVG	PB	PR	/A	PD	TPI
1952 StL-N	2	3	.400	18	3	0	0	1	34^2	36	6	18	30	14.5	5.19	72	.267	.361	1	.125	-0	-6	-6	1	-0.5
1953 StL-N	0	2	.000	6	2	0	0	0	17^2	21	1	13	11	17.8	9.17	46	.288	.402	0	.000	-1	-10	-10	-0	-0.9
1955 StL-N	7	6	.538	20	15	8	1	0	129^2	89	7	57	86	10.3	2.78	146	.197	.291	5	.119	-3	18	19	1	1.7
1956 StL-N	6	8	.429	33	21	2	0	1	147^2	131	18	78	52	12.8	3.84	99	.246	.344	10	.233	1	-1	-1	2	0.2
1957 StL-N	10	3	.769	40	8	1	0	0	116^2	146	13	49	63	15.2	4.78	83	.312	.380	7	.212	0	-12	-11	1	-1.0
1958 Cin-N	3	5	.375	41	2	0	0	0	69^1	60	8	33	41	12.2	2.86	145	.235	.325	1	.091	-1	8	10	1	1.1
1959 Cin-N	3	2	.600	36	4	0	0	0	70^2	80	4	30	40	14.1	3.95	103	.296	.369	1	.083	0	-0	1	1	0.2
Total 7	31	29	.517	194	55	11	1	2	586^1	563	57	278	323	13.1	3.93	101	.258	.344	25	.163	-2	-1	2	6	0.8

● CRAZY SCHMIT Schmit, Frederick M. "Germany" b: 2/13/1866, Chicago, Ill. d: 10/5/40, Chicago, Ill. BL/TL, 5'10.5", 165 lbs. Deb: 4/21/1890

YEAR TM/L	W	L	PCT	G	GS	CG	SH	SV	IP	H	HR	BB	SO	RAT	ERA	ERA+	OAV	OOB	BH	AVG	PB	PR	/A	PD	TPI
1890 Pit-N	1	9	.100	11	10	9	1	0	83^1	108	3	42	35	17.1	5.83	57	.304	.390	2	.061	-3	-21	-23	-0	-2.1
1892 Bal-N	1	4	.200	6	6	6	0	0	47^1	37	0	26	17	12.0	3.23	106	.207	.307	2	.105	-1	0	1	1	0.1
1893 Bal-N	3	2	.600	9	6	4	0	0	49	67	1	22	10	16.7	6.61	72	.316	.386	5	.238	0	-11	-10	-1	-0.9
NY-N	0	2	.000	4	4	1	0	0	20^2	30	0	17	5	21.3	7.40	63	.329	.445	4	.444	1	-6	-6	0	-0.4
Yr	3	4	.429	13	10	5	0	0	69^2	97	1	39	15	17.8	6.85	69	.318	.399	9	.300	1	-17	-16	-1	-1.3
1899 Cle-N	2	17	.105	20	19	16	0	0	138^1	197	3	62	24	17.8	5.86	63	.334	.410	11	.157	-2	-31	-33	2	-2.8
1901 Bal-A	0	2	.000	4	3	1	0	0	22^2	25	0	16	2	16.3	1.99	195	.276	.385	2	.222	0	4	5	1	0.6
Total 5	7	36	.163	54	48	37	1	0	361^1	464	7	185	93	16.8	5.45	69	.306	.390	26	.161	-5	-64	-68	2	-5.5

● JOHNNY SCHMITZ Schmitz, John Albert "Bear Tracks" b: 11/27/20, Wausau, Wis. BR/TL, 6', 170 lbs. Deb: 9/06/41

YEAR TM/L	W	L	PCT	G	GS	CG	SH	SV	IP	H	HR	BB	SO	RAT	ERA	ERA+	OAV	OOB	BH	AVG	PB	PR	/A	PD	TPI
1941 Chi-N	2	0	1.000	5	3	1	0	0	20^2	12	0	9	11	9.6	1.31	269	.182	.289	4	.571	2	5	5	1	0.9
1942 Chi-N	3	7	.300	23	10	1	0	2	86^2	70	3	45	51	12.3	3.43	93	.230	.335	4	.154	-1	-1	-2	4	0.1
1946 Chi-N☆	11	11	.500	41	31	14	2	2	224^1	184	6	94	**135**	11.2	2.61	127	**.221**	.302	9	.129	-2	20	18	2	2.0
1947 Chi-N	13	18	.419	38	28	10	3	4	207	209	8	80	97	12.7	3.22	123	.262	.330	9	.132	-2	19	17	2	1.7
1948 Chi-N★	18	13	.581	34	30	18	2	1	242	186	11	97	100	10.6	2.64	148	**.215**	.295	11	.131	-2	35	34	5	4.0
1949 Chi-N	11	13	.458	36	31	9	3	3	207	227	11	92	75	14.0	4.35	93	.287	.363	10	.143	-1	-7	-7	5	-0.3
1950 Chi-N	10	16	.385	39	27	8	3	0	193	217	23	91	75	14.5	4.99	84	.284	.363	8	.119	-3	-18	-17	5	-1.4
1951 Chi-N	1	2	.333	8	3	0	0	0	18	22	1	15	6	18.5	8.00	51	.301	.420	1	.167	-0	-8	-8	1	-0.6
Bro-N	1	4	.200	16	7	0	0	0	55^2	55	4	28	20	13.7	5.34	74	.259	.351	4	.222	2	-9	-9	1	-0.6
Yr	2	6	.250	24	10	0	0	0	73^2	77	5	43	26	14.9	5.99	66	.270	.370	5	.208	1	-17	-17	2	-1.2
1952 Bro-N	1	1	.500	10	3	1	0	0	33^1	29	3	18	11	13.0	4.32	84	.238	.340	1	.125	-0	-2	-3	1	-0.2
NY-A	1	1	.500	5	2	1	0	1	15	15	0	9	3	15.0	3.60	92	.263	.373	3	.600	2	0	-0	0	0.2
Cin-N	1	0	1.000	3	0	0	0	0	5	3	0	3	3	10.8	0.00	—	.188	.316	0	—	0	2	2	0	0.2
1953 NY-A	0	0	—	3	0	0	0	2	4^1	2	1	3	0	10.4	2.08	178	.143	.294	0	—	0	1	1	0	0.1
Was-A	2	7	.222	24	13	5	0	4	107^2	118	9	37	39	13.3	3.68	106	.286	.351	2	.059	-4	4	3	1	-0.1
Yr	2	7	.222	27	13	5	0	6	112	120	10	40	39	13.2	3.62	108	.282	.349	2	.059	-4	5	3	1	0.0
1954 Was-A	11	8	.579	29	23	12	2	1	185^1	176	6	64	56	11.8	2.91	122	.255	.321	7	.117	-3	17	13	2	1.4
1955 Was-A	7	10	.412	32	21	6	1	1	165	187	8	54	49	13.5	3.71	103	.291	.352	10	.185	0	5	2	2	0.5
1956 Bos-A	0	0	—	2	0	0	0	0	4^1	5	0	4	0	18.7	0.00	—	.278	.409	0	.000	-0	2	2	0	0.2
Bal-A	0	3	.000	18	3	0	0	0	38^1	49	3	14	15	15.0	3.99	98	.318	.379	0	.000	-1	1	-0	1	-0.1
Yr	0	3	.000	20	3	0	0	0	42^2	54	3	18	15	15.4	3.59	111	.314	.382	0	.000	-1	3	2	1	0.1
Total 13	93	114	.449	366	235	86	16	21	1812^2	1766	97	757	746	12.7	3.55	107	.258	.335	83	.141	-14	66	50	35	8.0

● CHARLIE SCHMUTZ Schmutz, Charles Otto "King" b: 1/1/1890, San Diego, Cal. d: 6/27/62, Seattle, Wash. BR/TR, 6'1.5", 195 lbs. Deb: 5/13/14

YEAR TM/L	W	L	PCT	G	GS	CG	SH	SV	IP	H	HR	BB	SO	RAT	ERA	ERA+	OAV	OOB	BH	AVG	PB	PR	/A	PD	TPI
1914 Bro-N	1	3	.250	18	5	1	0	0	57^1	57	1	13	21	11.1	3.30	87	.265	.310	3	.188	1	-3	-3	0	-0.2
1915 Bro-N	0	0	—	1	0	0	0	0	4	7	0	1	1	18.0	6.75	41	.438	.471	0	.000	-0	-2	-2	0	-0.2
Total 2	1	3	.250	19	5	1	0	0	61^1	64	1	14	22	11.6	3.52	81	.277	.321	3	.176	0	-5	-5	1	-0.4

● FRANK SCHNEIBERG Schneiberg, Frank Frederick b: 3/12/1882, Milwaukee, Wis. d: 5/18/48, Milwaukee, Wis. TR, Deb: 6/08/10

YEAR TM/L	W	L	PCT	G	GS	CG	SH	SV	IP	H	HR	BB	SO	RAT	ERA	ERA+	OAV	OOB	BH	AVG	PB	PR	/A	PD	TPI
1910 Bro-N	0	0	—	1	0	0	0	0	1	5	0	4	0	81.0	63.00	5	.625	.750	0	—	0	-7	-7	-0	-0.5

● DAN SCHNEIDER Schneider, Daniel Louis b: 8/29/42, Evansville, Ind. BL/TL, 6'3", 170 lbs. Deb: 5/12/63

YEAR TM/L	W	L	PCT	G	GS	CG	SH	SV	IP	H	HR	BB	SO	RAT	ERA	ERA+	OAV	OOB	BH	AVG	PB	PR	/A	PD	TPI
1963 Mil-N	1	0	1.000	30	3	0	0	0	43^2	36	2	20	19	11.5	3.09	104	.225	.311	0	.000	-1	1	1	-1	-0.1

YEAR	TM/L	W	L	PCT	G	GS	CG	SH	SV	IP	H	HR	BB	SO	RAT	ERA	ERA+	OAV	OOB	BH	AVG	PB	PR	/A	PD	TPI
1964	Mil-N	1	2	.333	13	5	0	0	0	36^{1}	38	6	13	14	12.6	5.45	65	.270	.331	0	.000	-1	-8	-8	1	-0.8
1966	Atl-N	0	0	—	14	0	0	0	0	26^{1}	35	1	5	11	14.0	3.42	106	.324	.360	4	.500	1	1	1	-0	0.2
1967	Hou-N	0	2	.000	54	0	0	0	2	52^{2}	60	5	27	39	15.2	4.96	67	.296	.384	1	.200	0	-9	-10	1	-0.9
1969	Hou-N	0	1	.000	6	0	0	0	0	7^{1}	16	2	5	3	25.8	13.50	26	.485	.553	0	.000	-0	-8	-8	0	-0.8
Total	5	2	5	.286	117	8	0	0	2	166^{1}	185	16	70	86	14.0	4.71	72	.287	.359	5	.172	-0	-24	-24	1	-2.4
● **JEFF SCHNEIDER**	Schneider, Jeffrey Theodore b: 12/6/52, Bremerton, Wash. BB/TL, 6'3", 195 lbs. Deb: 8/12/81																									
1981	Bal-A	0	0	—	11	0	0	0	1	24	27	4	12	17	15.0	4.88	74	.290	.377	0	—	0	-3	-3	-0	-0.4
● **PETE SCHNEIDER**	Schneider, Peter Joseph b: 8/20/1895, Los Angeles, Cal. d: 6/1/57, Los Angeles, Cal. BR/TR, 6'1", 194 lbs. Deb: 6/20/14																									
1914	Cin-N	5	13	.278	29	20	11	1	1	144^{1}	143	1	56	62	12.8	2.81	104	.269	.347	8	.178	1	-0	2	-1	0.2
1915	Cin-N	14	19	.424	48	35	16	5	2	275^{2}	254	4	104	108	11.9	2.48	115	.251	.325	23	.245	5	8	12	-1	1.9
1916	Cin-N	10	19	.345	44	31	16	2	1	274^{1}	259	4	82	117	11.6	2.69	96	.255	.319	21	.236	2	-2	-3	-3	-0.4
1917	Cin-N	20	19	.513	46	42	24	0	0	333^{2}	311	4	117	138	11.8	2.10	124	.255	.326	19	.167	0	23	19	-5	1.6
1918	Cin-N	10	15	.400	33	30	17	2	0	217	213	2	117	51	14.1	3.53	76	.272	.374	24	.289	6	-18	-21	-3	-1.9
1919	NY-A	0	1	.000	7	4	0	0	0	29	19	1	22	11	13.7	3.41	94	.192	.355	1	.111	-1	-1	-1	-1	-0.2
Total	6	59	86	.407	207	162	84	10	4	1274	1199	16	498	487	12.4	2.66	102	.257	.336	96	.221	14	9	8	-13	1.2
● **KARL SCHNELL**	Schnell, Karl Otto b: 9/20/1899, Los Angeles, Cal. d: 5/31/92, Palo Alto, Cal. BR/TR, 6'1", 176 lbs. Deb: 4/24/22																									
1922	Cin-N	0	0	—	10	0	0	0	0	20	21	0	18	5	17.5	2.70	148	.300	.443	1	.250	0	3	3	0	0.3
1923	Cin-N	0	0	—	1	0	0	0	0	1	2	0	2	0	36.0	36.00	11	.667	.800	0	—	0	-4	-4	-0	-0.3
Total	2	0	0	—	11	0	0	0	0	21	23	0	20	5	18.4	4.29	93	.315	.462	1	.250	0	-0	-1	0	0.0
● **GERRY SCHOEN**	Schoen, Gerald Thomas b: 1/15/47, New Orleans, La. BR/TR, 6'3", 215 lbs. Deb: 9/14/68																									
1968	Was-A	0	1	.000	1	1	0	0	0	3^{2}	6	1	1	1	17.2	7.36	40	.400	.438	0	.000	-0	-2	-2	-0	-0.2
● **JUMBO SCHOENECK**	Schoeneck, Louis N. b: 3/3/1862, Chicago, Ill. d: 1/20/30, Chicago, Ill. BR/TR, 6'3", 223 lbs. Deb: 4/20/1884 ♦																									
1888	Ind-N	0	0	—	2	0	0	0	0	4^{1}	5	0	1	1	12.5	0.00	—	.227	.261	40	.237	0	1	1	-0	0.1
● **MIKE SCHOOLER**	Schooler, Michael Ralph b: 8/10/62, Anaheim, Cal. BR/TR, 6'3", 220 lbs. Deb: 6/10/88																									
1988	Sea-A	5	8	.385	40	0	0	0	15	48^{1}	45	4	24	54	13.0	3.54	118	.245	.335	0	—	0	2	3	-0	0.0
1989	Sea-A	1	7	.125	67	0	0	0	33	77	81	2	19	69	11.9	2.81	144	.266	.314	0	—	0	9	10	1	1.1
1990	Sea-A	1	4	.200	49	0	0	0	30	56	47	5	16	45	10.3	2.25	176	.227	.286	0	.000	0	10	11	0	1.1
1991	Sea-A	3	3	.500	34	0	0	0	7	34^{1}	25	2	10	31	9.2	3.67	112	.198	.257	0	—	0	2	2	-0	0.1
1992	Sea-A	2	7	.222	53	0	0	0	13	51^{2}	55	7	24	33	13.9	4.70	85	.275	.356	0	—	0	-4	-4	1	-0.4
Total	5	12	29	.293	243	0	0	0	98	267^{1}	253	20	93	232	11.8	3.30	122	.248	.314	0	.000	0	19	22	1	1.9
● **ED SCHORR**	Schorr, Edward Walter b: 2/14/1891, Bremen, Ohio d: 9/12/69, Atlantic City, N.J. BR/TR, 6'2.5", 180 lbs. Deb: 4/26/15																									
1915	Chi-N	0	0	—	2	0	0	0	0	6	9	0	5	3	21.0	7.50	37	.409	.519	1	.500	0	-3	-3	0	-0.3
● **GENE SCHOTT**	Schott, Eugene Arthur b: 7/14/13, Batavia, Ohio BR/TR, 6'2", 185 lbs. Deb: 4/16/35 ♦																									
1935	Cin-N	8	11	.421	33	19	9	1	0	159	153	5	64	49	12.3	3.91	102	.253	.326	12	.200	1	2	1	3	0.5
1936	Cin-N	11	11	.500	31	22	8	0	1	180	184	7	73	65	13.1	3.80	101	.262	.335	18	.300	7	4	0	1	0.8
1937	Cin-N	4	13	.235	37	17	7	2	1	154^{1}	150	2	48	56	11.6	2.97	125	.253	.310	7	.143	-1	16	13	1	1.3
1938	Cin-N	5	5	.500	31	4	0	0	2	83	89	8	32	21	13.2	4.45	82	.279	.347	3	.125	-1	-6	-7	1	-0.7
1939	Phi-N	0	1	.000	4	0	0	0	0	11	14	0	5	1	17.2	4.91	82	.326	.420	2	.333	1	-1	-1	-1	-0.1
Total	5	28	41	.406	136	62	24	3	4	587^{1}	590	22	222	192	12.6	3.72	103	.261	.329	42	.211	6	15	6	6	1.8
● **PETE SCHOUREK**	Schourek, Peter Alan b: 5/10/69, Austin, Tex. BL/TL, 6'5", 195 lbs. Deb: 4/09/91																									
1991	NY-N	5	4	.556	35	8	1	1	2	86^{1}	82	7	43	67	13.2	4.27	85	.248	.338	3	.136	0	-6	-6	1	-0.5
1992	NY-N	6	8	.429	22	21	0	0	0	136	137	9	44	60	12.1	3.64	96	.261	.321	2	.048	-3	-2	-2	-2	-0.8
Total	2	11	12	.478	57	29	1	1	2	222^{1}	219	16	87	127	12.5	3.89	91	.256	.328	5	.078	-3	-8	-8	-1	-1.3
● **BARNEY SCHREIBER**	Schreiber, David Henry b: 5/8/1882, Waverly, Ohio d: 10/6/64, Chillicothe, Ohio BL/TL, 6', 185 lbs. Deb: 5/15/11																									
1911	Cin-N	0	0	—	3	0	0	0	1	10	19	2	2	5	18.9	5.40	61	.413	.438	0	.000	-0	-2	-2	-0	-0.3
● **PAUL SCHREIBER**	Schreiber, Paul Frederick "Von" b: 10/8/02, Jacksonville, Fla. d: 1/28/82, Sarasota, Fla. BR/TR, 6'2", 180 lbs. Deb: 9/02/22 C																									
1922	Bro-N	0	0	—	1	0	0	0	0	1	2	0	0	0	18.0	0.00	—	.500	.500	0	—	0	0	0	0	0.1
1923	Bro-N	0	0	—	9	0	0	0	1	15	16	1	8	4	15.6	4.20	92	.276	.382	0	.000	-0	-0	-1	-0	-0.1
1945	NY-A	0	0	—	2	0	0	0	0	4^{1}	4	0	2	1	12.5	4.15	83	.267	.353	0	.000	-0	-0	-0	1	0.0
Total	3	0	0	—	12	0	0	0	1	20^{1}	22	1	10	5	15.0	3.98	96	.286	.382	0	.000	-0	-0	-0	1	0.0
● **AL SCHROLL**	Schroll, Albert Bringhurst "Bull" b: 3/22/32, New Orleans, La. BR/TR, 6'2", 210 lbs. Deb: 4/20/58																									
1958	Bos-A	0	0	—	5	0	0	0	0	10	6	1	4	7	9.0	4.50	89	.176	.263	1	1.000	0	-1	-1	0	0.0
1959	Phi-N	1	1	.500	3	0	0	0	0	9^{1}	12	1	6	4	17.4	8.68	47	.353	.450	1	.250	0	-5	-5	0	-0.4
	Bos-A	1	4	.200	14	5	1	0	0	46	47	3	22	26	13.7	4.70	86	.269	.354	1	.111	0	-4	-3	-1	-0.3
1960	Chi-N	0	0	—	2	0	0	0	0	2^{2}	3	1	5	2	27.0	10.13	37	.273	.500	1	1.000	0	-2	-2	-0	-0.2
1961	Min-A	4	4	.500	11	8	2	0	0	50	53	5	27	24	14.8	5.22	81	.266	.360	5	.278	2	-7	-5	-0	-0.3
Total	4	6	9	.400	35	13	3	0	0	118	121	11	64	63	14.3	5.34	77	.267	.362	9	.273	4	-19	-16	-1	-1.2
● **KEN SCHROM**	Schrom, Kenneth Marvin b: 11/23/54, Grangeville, Idaho BR/TR, 6'2", 195 lbs. Deb: 8/08/80																									
1980	Tor-A	1	0	1.000	17	0	0	0	1	31	32	2	19	13	14.8	5.23	82	.274	.375	0	—	0	-4	-3	0	-0.3
1982	Tor-A	1	0	1.000	6	0	0	0	0	15^{1}	13	3	15	8	16.4	5.87	76	.232	.394	0	—	0	-3	-2	-1	-0.7
1983	Min-A	15	8	.652	33	28	6	1	0	196^{1}	196	14	80	80	13.1	3.71	114	.266	.345	0	—	0	8	12	-3	0.9
1984	Min-A	5	11	.313	25	21	3	0	0	137	156	15	41	49	13.0	4.47	94	.285	.336	0	—	0	-7	-4	-2	-0.8
1985	Min-A	9	12	.429	29	26	6	0	0	160^{2}	164	28	59	74	12.5	4.99	88	.272	.337	0	—	0	-15	-10	1	-1.1
1986	Cle-A☆	14	7	.667	34	33	3	1	0	206	217	34	49	87	12.1	4.54	91	.271	.322	0	—	0	-8	-9	-3	-1.1
1987	Cle-A	6	13	.316	32	29	4	1	0	153^{2}	185	29	57	61	14.3	6.50	70	.298	.360	0	—	0	-35	-34	-2	-3.3
Total	7	51	51	.500	176	137	22	3	1	900	963	125	320	372	13.1	4.81	89	.276	.342	0	—	0	-65	-51	-10	-6.4
● **RON SCHUELER**	Schueler, Ronald Richard b: 4/18/48, Catherine, Kan. BR/TR, 6'4", 205 lbs. Deb: 4/16/72 C																									
1972	Atl-N	5	8	.385	37	18	3	0	2	144^{2}	122	16	60	96	11.4	3.67	103	.227	.307	8	.190	0	-3	2	-1	0.1
1973	Atl-N	8	7	.533	39	20	4	2	2	186	179	24	66	124	11.9	3.87	102	.255	.319	11	.177	-1	-4	1	-1	0.0
1974	Phi-N	11	16	.407	44	27	5	0	1	203^{1}	202	17	98	109	13.5	3.72	102	.264	.351	6	.118	-2	-2	1	-2	-0.4
1975	Phi-N	4	4	.500	46	6	1	0	0	92^{2}	88	6	40	69	12.5	5.24	71	.258	.338	2	.154	-0	-17	-16	1	-1.5
1976	Phi-N	1	0	1.000	35	0	0	0	3	49^{2}	44	4	16	43	11.2	2.90	122	.243	.312	0	.000	-0	3	4	-1	0.3
1977	Min-A	8	7	.533	52	7	0	0	3	134^{2}	131	16	61	77	13.2	4.41	90	.260	.347	0	—	0	-5	-6	2	-0.4
1978	Chi-A	3	5	.375	30	7	0	0	0	81^{2}	76	10	39	39	13.4	4.30	88	.251	.350	0	—	0	-5	-5	0	-0.4
1979	Chi-A	0	1	.000	8	1	0	0	0	19^{2}	19	3	13	6	15.6	7.32	58	.264	.391	0	—	0	-7	-7	-0	-0.6
Total	8	40	48	.455	291	86	13	2	11	912^{1}	861	96	393	563	12.6	4.08	94	.253	.334	27	.159	-3	-40	-25	-2	-2.9
● **DAVE SCHULER**	Schuler, David Paul b: 10/4/53, Framingham, Mass. BR/TL, 6'4", 210 lbs. Deb: 9/17/79																									
1979	Cal-A	0	0	—	1	0	0	0	0	1^{2}	2	1	0	0	10.8	10.80	38	.333	.333	0	—	0	-1	-1	-0	0.0
1980	Cal-A	0	1	.000	8	0	0	0	0	12^{2}	13	3	2	7	10.7	3.55	111	.271	.300	0	—	0	1	1	-0	0.0
1985	Atl-N	0	0	—	9	0	0	0	0	10^{2}	19	4	3	10	18.6	6.75	57	.404	.440	0	—	0	-4	-3	-0	-0.4
Total	3	0	1	.000	18	0	0	0	0	25	34	8	5	17	14.0	5.40	72	.337	.368	0	—	0	-4	-4	-1	-0.4

YEAR	TM/L	W	L	PCT	G	GS	CG	SH	SV	IP	H	HR	BB	SO	RAT	ERA	ERA+	OAV	OOB	BH	AVG	PB	PR	/A	PD	TPI
● **BUDDY SCHULTZ** Schultz, Charles Budd b: 9/19/50, Cleveland, Ohio BR/TL, 6', 175 lbs. Deb: 9/03/75																										
1975	Chi-N	2	0	1.000	6	0	0	0	0	5^2	11	0	5	4	25.4	6.35	60	.367	.457	0	—	0	-2	-2	-0	-0.2
1976	Chi-N	1	1	.500	29	0	0	0	2	23^2	37	3	9	15	17.5	6.08	63	.356	.407	0	.000	-0	-7	-6	1	-0.6
1977	StL-N	6	1	.857	40	3	0	0	1	85^1	76	5	24	66	10.5	2.32	166	.245	.299	2	.167	0	15	14	-1	1.5
1978	StL-N	2	4	.333	62	0	0	0	6	83	68	6	36	70	11.3	3.80	93	.226	.309	1	.200	1	-2	-3	-1	-0.3
1979	StL-N	4	3	.571	31	0	0	0	3	42^1	40	7	14	38	11.5	4.46	84	.256	.318	0	.000	-0	-3	-3	-0	-0.4
Total	5	15	9	.625	168	3	0	0	12	240	232	21	88	193	12.0	3.68	101	.257	.324	3	.120	0	1	1	-1	-0.0
● **BARNEY SCHULTZ** Schultz, George Warren b: 8/15/26, Beverly, N.J. BR/TR, 6'2", 200 lbs. Deb: 4/12/55 C																										
1955	StL-N	1	2	.333	19	0	0	0	4	29^2	28	5	15	19	14.3	7.89	52	.259	.370	0	.000	-1	-13	-13	1	-1.2
1959	Det-A	1	2	.333	13	0	0	0	0	18^1	17	1	14	17	15.7	4.42	92	.254	.390	2	1.000	1	-1	-1	-0	0.0
1961	Chi-N	7	6	.538	41	0	0	0	7	66^2	57	6	25	59	11.6	2.70	155	.228	.308	1	.100	-1	10	11	-0	1.0
1962	Chi-N	5	5	.500	51	0	0	0	5	77^2	66	7	23	58	10.8	3.82	108	.231	.297	0	.000	-0	1	3	0	0.3
1963	Chi-N	1	0	1.000	15	0	0	0	2	27^1	25	5	9	18	11.2	3.62	97	.263	.327	0	.000	-0	-1	-0	0	0.0
	StL-N	2	0	1.000	24	0	0	0	1	35^1	36	5	8	26	11.7	3.57	99	.263	.313	0	—	0	-1	-0	-0	0.0
	Yr	3	0	1.000	39	0	0	0	3	62^2	61	10	17	44	11.5	3.59	98	.263	.319	0	.000	-0	-2	-0	0	0.0
1964	*StL-N	1	3	.250	30	0	0	0	14	49^1	35	1	11	29	8.4	1.64	232	.201	.249	1	.167	-0	10	12	-1	1.2
1965	StL-N	2	2	.500	34	0	0	0	2	42^1	39	8	11	38	10.6	3.83	100	.242	.291	0	.000	-0	-1	0	0	0.0
Total	7	20	20	.500	227	0	0	0	35	346^2	303	38	116	264	11.3	3.63	109	.237	.308	4	.121	-1	4	12	-0	1.3
● **BOB SCHULTZ** Schultz, Robert Duffy b: 11/27/23, Louisville, Ky. d: 3/31/79, Nashville, Tenn. BR/TL, 6'3", 200 lbs. Deb: 4/20/51																										
1951	Chi-N	3	6	.333	17	10	2	0	0	77^1	75	9	51	27	14.9	5.24	78	.251	.364	4	.138	-1	-11	-10	-1	-1.2
1952	Chi-N	6	3	.667	29	5	1	0	0	74	63	3	51	31	14.1	4.01	96	.232	.357	4	.222	1	-2	-1	-2	-0.3
1953	Chi-N	0	2	.000	7	2	0	0	0	11^2	13	2	11	4	19.3	5.40	82	.289	.439	0	.000	-0	-1	-1	-1	-0.2
	Pit-N	0	2	.000	11	2	0	0	0	18^2	26	3	10	5	18.3	8.20	55	.321	.409	0	.000	0	-8	-8	-0	-0.7
	Yr	0	4	.000	18	4	0	0	0	30^1	39	5	21	9	18.4	7.12	63	.307	.413	0	.000	-0	-10	-9	-1	-0.9
1955	Det-A	0	0	—	1	0	0	0	0	1^1	2	0	2	0	27.0	20.25	19	.333	.500	0	—	0	-2	-2	-0	-0.2
Total	4	9	13	.409	65	19	3	0	0	183	179	17	125	67	15.3	5.16	79	.255	.372	8	.154	-1	-25	-23	-4	-2.6
● **WEBB SCHULTZ** Schultz, Webb Carl b: 1/31/1898, Wautoma, Wis. d: 7/26/86, Delavan, Wis. BR/TR, 5'11", 172 lbs. Deb: 8/03/24																										
1924	Chi-A	0	0	—	1	0	0	0	0	1	1	0	0	0	9.0	9.00	46	.250	.250	0	—	0	-1	-1	-0	-0.1
● **MIKE SCHULTZ** Schultz, William Michael b: 12/17/20, Syracuse, N.Y. BL/TL, 6'1", 175 lbs. Deb: 4/20/47																										
1947	Cin-N	0	0	—	1	0	0	0	0	2	4	0	2	0	27.0	4.50	91	.444	.545	0	—	0	-0	-0	-0	0.0
● **JOHN SCHULTZE** Schultze, John F. b: Burlington, N.J. 6'0.5", 165 lbs. Deb: 5/06/1891																										
1891	Phi-N	0	1	.000	6	1	0	0	0	15	18	1	11	4	17.4	6.60	52	.286	.393	1	.167	-0	-5	-5	-1	-0.5
● **AL SCHULZ** Schulz, Albert Christopher b: 5/12/1889, Toledo, Ohio d: 12/13/31, Gallipolis, Ohio BR/TL, 6', 182 lbs. Deb: 9/25/12																										
1912	NY-A	1	1	.500	3	1	1	0	0	16^1	11	0	11	8	12.1	2.20	163	.183	.310	0	.000	-0	2	3	1	0.3
1913	NY-A	7	13	.350	38	22	9	0	0	193	197	4	69	77	12.6	3.73	80	.266	.333	11	.175	0	-17	-16	-1	-1.7
1914	NY-A	1	3	.250	6	4	1	0	0	28^1	27	0	10	18	12.4	4.76	58	.237	.310	0	.000	-0	-6	-6	1	-0.6
	Buf-F	9	12	.429	27	23	10	0	2	171	160	3	77	87	12.6	3.37	98	.259	.343	10	.179	-0	-3	-1	2	0.0
1915	Buf-F	21	14	.600	42	38	25	5	0	309^2	264	8	149	160	12.2	3.08	101	.238	.332	18	.165	-2	-2	1	1	0.0
1916	Cin-N	8	19	.296	44	22	10	0	2	215	208	4	93	95	12.8	3.14	83	.268	.350	8	.125	-3	-12	-13	0	-1.8
Total	5	47	62	.431	160	110	56	5	4	933^1	867	19	409	445	12.5	3.32	90	.254	.337	47	.155	-7	-39	-33	3	-3.8
● **WALT SCHULZ** Schulz, Walter Frederick b: 4/16/1900, St.Louis, Mo. d: 2/27/28, Prescott, Ark. BR/TR, 6', 170 lbs. Deb: 9/24/20																										
1920	StL-N	0	0	—	2	0	0	0	0	6	10	0	2	0	18.0	6.00	50	.370	.414	0	.000	-0	-2	-2	0	-0.2
● **DON SCHULZE** Schulze, Donald Arthur b: 9/27/62, Roselle, Ill. BR/TR, 6'3", 225 lbs. Deb: 9/13/83																										
1983	Chi-N	0	1	.000	4	3	0	0	0	14	19	1	7	8	17.4	7.07	54	.322	.403	0	.000	0	-5	-5	0	-0.5
1984	Chi-N	0	0	—	1	1	0	0	0	3	8	0	1	2	27.0	12.00	33	.571	.600	0	—	0	-3	-3	0	-0.2
	Cle-A	3	6	.333	19	14	2	0	0	85^2	105	9	27	39	13.9	4.83	85	.302	.352	0	—	0	-8	-7	-0	-0.8
1985	Cle-A	4	10	.286	19	18	1	0	0	94^1	128	10	19	37	14.4	6.01	69	.322	.360	0	—	0	-20	-20	1	-1.8
1986	Cle-A	4	4	.500	19	13	1	0	0	84^2	88	9	34	33	13.5	5.00	83	.266	.343	0	—	0	-8	-8	-1	-0.8
1987	NY-N	1	2	.333	5	4	0	0	0	21^2	24	4	6	5	12.9	6.23	61	.296	.352	0	.000	0	-5	-6	1	-0.4
1989	NY-A	1	1	.500	2	2	0	0	0	11	12	1	5	5	14.7	4.09	95	.300	.391	0	—	0	-0	-0	-0	0.0
	SD-N	2	1	.667	7	4	0	0	0	24^1	38	6	6	15	16.3	5.55	63	.352	.386	0	.000	-0	-6	-6	1	-0.6
Total	6	15	25	.375	76	59	4	0	0	338^2	422	40	105	144	14.3	5.47	74	.306	.361	0	.000	0	-54	-54	1	-5.1
● **HAL SCHUMACHER** Schumacher, Harold Henry "Prince Hal" b: 11/23/10, Hinckley, N.Y. BR/TR, 6', 190 lbs. Deb: 4/15/31																										
1931	NY-N	1	1	.500	8	2	1	0	1	18^1	31	3	14	11	22.1	10.80	34	.387	.479	1	.143	-0	-14	-14	1	-1.3
1932	NY-N	5	6	.455	27	13	2	1	0	101^1	119	3	39	38	14.2	3.55	104	.288	.352	7	.226	1	4	2	2	0.5
1933	*NY-N☆	19	12	.613	35	33	21	7	1	258^2	199	9	84	96	9.9	2.16	149	**.214**	.280	21	.214	1	34	30	3	3.9
1934	NY-N	23	10	.697	41	36	18	2	0	297	299	16	89	112	11.8	3.18	122	.259	.313	28	.239	9	29	23	3	3.5
1935	NY-N★	19	9	.679	33	33	19	3	0	261^2	235	11	70	79	10.7	2.89	133	.238	.292	21	.196	2	33	28	7	3.8
1936	*NY-N	11	13	.458	35	30	9	3	1	215^1	234	15	69	75	12.7	3.47	112	.280	.336	16	.216	2	13	10	4	1.6
1937	*NY-N	13	12	.520	38	29	10	1	1	217^2	222	11	89	100	12.9	3.60	108	.264	.335	18	.222	3	8	7	1	1.1
1938	NY-N	13	8	.619	28	28	12	3	0	185	178	12	50	54	11.2	3.50	108	.248	.299	16	.239	4	6	5	2	1.2
1939	NY-N	13	10	.565	29	27	8	0	0	181^2	199	14	89	58	14.4	4.81	82	.276	.358	14	.203	1	-18	-18	-0	-1.7
1940	NY-N	13	13	.500	34	30	12	1	1	227	218	14	96	123	12.4	3.25	119	.251	.325	15	.192	2	15	16	4	2.4
1941	NY-N	12	10	.545	30	26	12	3	1	206	187	11	79	63	11.8	3.36	110	.243	.317	10	.152	-1	6	8	-1	0.6
1942	NY-N	12	13	.480	29	29	12	3	0	216	208	12	82	49	12.2	3.04	111	.251	.321	13	.173	1	7	8	2	1.1
1946	NY-N	4	4	.500	24	13	2	0	1	96^2	95	8	52	48	13.7	3.91	88	.255	.347	1	.038	-2	-5	-5	3	-0.5
Total	13	158	121	.566	391	329	138	27	7	2482^1	2424	139	902	906	12.1	3.36	111	.255	.321	181	.202	23	117	100	30	16.2
● **HACK SCHUMANN** Schumann, Carl J. b: 8/13/1884, Buffalo, N.Y. d: 3/25/46, Millgrove, N.Y. TR , 6'2", 230 lbs. Deb: 9/19/06																										
1906	Phi-A	0	2	.000	4	2	1	0	0	18	21	0	8	9	15.5	4.00	68	.294	.381	0	.000	-1	-3	-3	-0	-0.4
● **FERDIE SCHUPP** Schupp, Ferdinand Maurice b: 1/16/1891, Louisville, Ky. d: 12/16/71, Los Angeles, Cal. BR/TR, 5'10", 150 lbs. Deb: 4/19/13																										
1913	NY-N	0	0	—	5	1	0	0	0	12	10	0	3	2	9.8	0.75	416	.244	.295	1	.333	1	3	3	-0	0.4
1914	NY-N	0	0	—	8	0	0	0	1	17	19	0	9	9	15.9	5.82	46	.306	.411	0	.000	-0	-6	-6	-0	-0.7
1915	NY-N	1	0	1.000	23	1	0	0	0	54^2	57	1	29	28	14.7	5.10	50	.281	.379	2	.200	0	-14	-15	0	-1.6
1916	NY-N	9	3	.750	30	11	8	4	1	140^1	79	1	37	86	7.8	0.90	271	.167	.235	4	.098	-2	27	24	-3	2.2
1917	*NY-N	21	7	**.750**	36	32	25	6	0	272	202	7	70	147	9.1	1.95	131	**.209**	.265	15	.161	1	23	18	-3	1.8
1918	NY-N	0	1	.000	10	2	1	0	0	33^1	42	1	27	22	19.4	7.56	35	.328	.456	1	.111	-0	-18	-18	0	-1.9
1919	NY-N	1	3	.250	9	4	0	0	1	32	32	2	18	17	14.1	5.63	50	.269	.365	2	.333	0	-10	-10	-1	-1.1
	StL-N	4	4	.500	10	9	6	0	0	69^2	55	2	30	37	11.1	3.75	75	.221	.307	1	.050	-0	-6	-7	-1	-0.9
	Yr	5	7	.417	19	13	6	0	1	101^2	87	4	48	54	12.0	4.34	64	.236	.326	3	.115	-0	-16	-17	-2	-2.0
1920	StL-N	16	13	.552	38	37	17	0	0	250^2	246	5	127	119	13.7	3.52	85	.265	.358	22	.256	5	-11	-15	-2	-1.2
1921	StL-N	2	0	1.000	9	4	1	0	1	37^1	42	5	21	22	15.7	4.10	89	.276	.371	4	.286	0	-1	-2	-0	-0.2
	Bro-N	3	4	.429	20	7	1	0	2	61	75	2	27	26	15.3	4.57	85	.310	.384	1	.083	-1	-5	-5	0	-0.5
	Yr	5	4	.556	29	11	2	0	3	98^1	117	7	48	48	15.3	4.39	87	.295	.374	5	.192	-0	-7	-6	-0	-0.7
1922	Chi-A	4	4	.500	18	12	3	1	0	74	79	4	66	38	17.9	6.08	67	.284	.425	5	.217	1	-17	-17	-0	-1.6

YEAR	TM/L	W	L	PCT	G	GS	CG	SH	SV	IP	H	HR	BB	SO	RAT	ERA	ERA+	OAV	OOB	BH	AVG	PB	PR	/A	PD	TPI
Total	10	61	39	.610	216	120	62	11	6	1054	938	30	464	553	12.3	3.32	87	.244	.331	58	.182	5	-35	-51	-10	-5.3
● **WAYNE SCHURR**	Schurr, Wayne Allen b: 8/6/37, Garrett, Ind. BR/TR, 6'4", 185 lbs. Deb: 4/15/64																									
1964	Chi-N	0	0	—	26	0	0	0	0	48^1	57	3	11	29	12.7	3.72	100	.298	.337	0	.000	-0	-1	-0	-0	-0.1
● **MIKE SCHWABE**	Schwabe, Michael Scott b: 7/12/64, Ft.Dodge, Iowa BR/TR, 6'4", 200 lbs. Deb: 5/27/89																									
1989	Det-A	2	4	.333	13	4	0	0	0	44^2	58	6	16	13	15.1	6.04	63	.307	.364	0	—	0	-11	-11	1	-1.0
1990	Det-A	0	0	—	1	0	0	0	0	3^2	5	0	0	1	12.3	2.45	161	.357	.357	0	—	0	1	1	0	0.1
Total	2	2	4	.333	14	4	0	0	0	48^1	63	6	16	14	14.9	5.77	66	.310	.364	0	—	0	-10	-10	1	-0.9
● **DON SCHWALL**	Schwall, Donald Bernard b: 3/2/36, Wilkes-Barre, Pa. BR/TR, 6'6", 200 lbs. Deb: 5/21/61																									
1961	Bos-A★	15	7	.682	25	25	10	2	0	178^2	167	8	110	91	14.3	3.22	129	.255	.368	11	.180	-0	16	19	1	1.9
1962	Bos-A	9	15	.375	33	32	5	1	0	182^1	180	18	121	89	15.4	4.94	84	.260	.378	9	.136	-2	-20	-16	0	-1.8
1963	Pit-N	6	12	.333	33	24	3	2	0	167^2	158	13	74	86	12.8	3.33	99	.255	.340	8	.160	-0	-1	-1	2	0.1
1964	Pit-N	4	3	.571	15	9	0	0	0	49^2	53	1	15	36	12.3	4.35	81	.269	.321	5	.263	2	-4	-5	0	-0.3
1965	Pit-N	9	6	.600	43	1	0	0	4	77	77	5	30	55	12.7	2.92	120	.269	.343	0	.000	-2	5	5	2	0.5
1966	Pit-N	3	2	.600	11	4	0	0	0	41^2	31	3	21	24	11.4	2.16	165	.209	.312	1	.100	-0	7	7	0	0.7
	Atl-N	3	3	.500	11	8	0	0	0	45^1	44	2	19	27	12.9	4.37	83	.256	.337	0	.000	-2	-4	-4	-0	-0.6
	Yr	6	5	.545	22	12	0	0	0	87	75	5	40	51	12.1	3.31	109	.234	.322	1	.043	-2	3	3	-0	0.1
1967	Atl-N	0	0	—	1	0	0	0	0	0^2	0	0	1	0	13.5	0.00	—	.000	.500	0	—	0	0	0	-0	0.0
Total	7	49	48	.505	172	103	18	5	4	743	710	50	391	408	13.7	3.72	102	.257	.354	34	.145	-5	-1	5	4	0.5
● **BLACKIE SCHWAMB**	Schwamb, Ralph Richard b: 8/6/26, Lancaster, Cal. d: 12/21/89, Los Angeles, Cal. BR/TR, 6'5.5", 198 lbs. Deb: 7/25/48																									
1948	StL-A	1	1	.500	12	5	0	0	0	31^2	44	3	21	7	18.5	8.53	53	.331	.422	3	.300	1	-15	-14	0	-1.2
● **RUDY SCHWENCK**	Schwenck, Rudolph Christian b: 4/6/1884, Louisville, Ky. d: 11/27/41, Anchorage, Ky. BL/TL, 6', 174 lbs. Deb: 9/23/09																									
1909	Chi-N	1	1	.500	3	2	0	0	0	4	16	0	3	3	45.0	13.50	19	.308	.357	1	.250	0	-5	-5	1	-0.3
● **HAL SCHWENK**	Schwenk, Harold Edward b: 8/23/1890, Schuylkill Haven, Pa. d: 9/3/55, Kansas City, Mo. BL/TL, 6', 185 lbs. Deb: 9/04/13																									
1913	StL-A	1	0	1.000	1	1	1	0	0	11	12	0	4	3	13.1	3.27	90	.333	.400	1	.333	1	-0	-0	-0	0.0
● **JIM SCOGGINS**	Scoggins, Lynn J. "Lefty" b: 7/19/1891, Killeen, Tex. d: 8/16/23, Columbia, S.C. BL/TL, 5'11", 165 lbs. Deb: 8/26/13																									
1913	Chi-A	0	1	.000	1	1	0	0	0	0	0	0	1	0	—	—	—	.000	.500	0	—	0	0	0	0	0.0
● **HERB SCORE**	Score, Herbert Jude b: 6/7/33, Rosedale, N.Y. BL/TL, 6'2", 185 lbs. Deb: 4/15/55																									
1955	Cle-A☆	16	10	.615	33	32	11	2	0	227^1	158	18	154	**245**	12.4	2.85	140	.194	.323	10	.119	-4	28	29	-4	2.1
1956	Cle-A★	20	9	.690	35	33	16	**5**	0	249^1	162	18	129	**263**	**10.6**	2.53	**166**	**.186**	.292	16	.184	1	**45**	**46**	-4	4.6
1957	Cle-A	2	1	.667	5	5	3	1	0	36	18	0	26	39	11.3	2.00	186	.149	.304	1	.091	-0	7	7	0	0.7
1958	Cle-A	2	3	.400	12	5	2	1	3	41	29	1	34	48	13.8	3.95	92	.197	.348	1	.091	-0	-1	-1	-1	-0.3
1959	Cle-A	9	11	.450	30	25	9	1	0	160^2	123	28	115	147	13.4	4.71	78	**.210**	.341	5	.096	-3	-15	-18	-3	-2.3
1960	Chi-A	5	10	.333	23	22	5	1	0	113^2	91	10	87	78	14.3	3.72	102	.226	.366	3	.100	-0	2	1	-1	-0.1
1961	Chi-A	1	2	.333	8	5	1	0	0	24^1	22	3	24	14	17.0	6.66	59	.259	.422	0	.000	-1	-7	-7	0	-0.8
1962	Chi-A	0	0	—	4	0	0	0	0	6	6	1	4	3	15.0	4.50	87	.261	.370	0	—	0	-0	-0	0	0.0
Total	8	55	46	.545	150	127	47	11	3	858^1	609	79	573	837	12.5	3.36	117	.200	.328	36	.128	-7	59	55	-12	3.9
● **DICK SCOTT**	Scott, Amos Richard b: 2/5/1883, Bethel, Ohio d: 1/18/11, Chicago, Ill. BR/TR, 6', 180 lbs. Deb: 6/26/01																									
1901	Cin-N	0	2	.000	3	2	2	0	0	21	26	2	9	7	16.3	5.14	62	.302	.387	0	.000	-1	-4	-5	-1	-0.6
● **ED SCOTT**	Scott, Edward b: 8/12/1870, Walbridge, Ohio d: 11/1/33, Toledo, Ohio BR/TR, 6'3", Deb: 4/19/00																									
1900	Cin-N	17	20	.459	42	35	31	0	1	315	370	10	65	87	12.8	3.86	95	.292	.333	19	.154	-5	-6	-6	9	-0.2
1901	Cle-A	6	6	.500	17	16	11	0	1	124^2	149	2	38	23	13.9	4.40	81	.293	.349	10	.208	0	-10	-12	2	-0.8
Total	2	23	26	.469	59	51	42	0	2	439^2	519	12	103	110	13.1	4.01	91	.292	.338	29	.170	-5	-16	-18	11	-1.0
● **GEORGE SCOTT**	Scott, George William b: 11/17/1896, Trenton, Mo. BR/TR, 6'1", 175 lbs. Deb: 9/13/20																									
1920	StL-N	0	0	—	2	0	0	0	0	6	4	0	3	1	10.5	4.50	66	.200	.304	0	.000	-0	-1	-1	-0	-0.2
● **JIM SCOTT**	Scott, James "Death Valley Jim" b: 4/23/1888, Deadwood, S.Dak. d: 4/7/57, Palm Springs, Cal. BR/TR, 6'1", 235 lbs. Deb: 4/25/09																									
1909	Chi-A	12	12	.500	36	29	20	4	0	250^1	194	0	93	135	10.9	2.30	102	.223	.310	9	.106	-1	5	1	-1	-0.2
1910	Chi-A	8	18	.308	41	23	14	2	1	229^2	182	5	86	135	10.7	2.43	99	.226	.303	15	.203	1	2	-1	3	0.4
1911	Chi-A	14	11	.560	39	26	13	3	0	222	195	3	81	128	11.4	2.39	135	.240	.311	11	.155	-2	24	21	-4	1.5
1912	Chi-A	2	2	.500	6	4	2	1	0	37^2	36	0	15	23	12.4	2.15	149	.265	.342	0	.000	-2	5	4	-0	0.3
1913	Chi-A	20	20	.500	48	38	25	4	1	312^1	252	2	86	158	10.0	1.90	154	.221	.281	7	.072	-7	36	36	-0	3.2
1914	Chi-A	14	18	.438	43	33	12	2	1	253^1	228	5	75	138	10.9	2.84	94	.246	.306	14	.163	-0	-3	-4	3	-0.4
1915	Chi-A	24	11	.686	48	35	23	**7**	2	296^1	256	3	78	120	10.3	2.03	146	.238	.292	12	.126	-5	30	31	2	3.1
1916	Chi-A	7	14	.333	32	21	8	1	3	165^1	155	3	53	71	11.5	2.72	101	.258	.321	6	.115	-3	2	1	-1	-0.4
1917	Chi-A	6	7	.462	24	17	6	2	1	125	126	0	42	37	12.5	1.87	142	.272	.341	5	.119	-2	11	11	0	1.0
Total	9	107	113	.486	317	226	123	26	9	1892	1624	21	609	945	10.9	2.30	120	.238	.305	79	.129	-20	111	99	3	8.5
● **JACK SCOTT**	Scott, John William b: 4/18/1892, Ridgeway, N.C. d: 11/30/59, Durham, N.C. BL/TR, 6'2.5", 199 lbs. Deb: 9/06/16																									
1916	Pit-N	0	0	—	1	0	0	0	0	5	5	1	3	4	14.4	10.80	25	.278	.381	0	.000	0	-5	-5	0	-0.4
1917	Bos-N	1	2	.333	7	3	3	0	0	39^2	36	0	5	21	10.0	1.82	141	.255	.295	2	.125	-1	4	3	-1	0.2
1919	Bos-N	6	6	.500	19	12	7	0	1	103^2	109	3	39	44	12.9	3.13	91	.275	.341	7	.175	-1	-2	-3	-3	-0.7
1920	Bos-N	10	21	.323	44	32	22	3	1	291	308	6	85	94	12.6	3.53	87	.277	.336	21	.212	0	-13	-15	-4	-2.0
1921	Bos-N	15	13	.536	**47**	29	16	2	3	233^2	258	9	57	83	12.4	3.70	99	.283	.330	30	.341	10	2	-1	-1	0.7
1922	Cin-N	0	0	—	1	0	0	0	0	1	2	0	1	0	27.0	9.00	44	.500	.600	0	.000	-0	-1	-1	-0	-0.1
	*NY-N	8	2	.800	17	10	5	0	2	79^2	83	7	23	37	12.2	4.41	91	.265	.320	8	.267	1	-3	-4	-1	-0.4
	Yr	8	2	.800	18	10	5	0	2	80^2	85	7	24	37	12.4	4.46	90	.268	.324	8	.258	1	-3	-4	-1	-0.5
1923	*NY-N	16	7	.696	40	25	9	3	1	220	223	15	65	79	11.9	3.89	98	.267	.323	25	.316	7	3	-2	-2	0.3
1925	NY-N	14	15	.483	36	28	18	2	3	239^2	251	10	55	87	11.6	3.15	128	.269	.313	21	.241	5	30	24	2	3.0
1926	NY-N	13	15	.464	**50**	22	13	0	5	226	242	13	53	82	11.9	4.34	86	.276	.319	28	.337	9	-13	-15	-1	-0.6
1927	Phi-N	9	21	.300	**48**	25	17	1	1	233^1	304	15	69	69	14.5	5.09	81	.330	.379	33	.289	8	-30	-25	-0	-1.6
1928	NY-N	4	1	.800	16	3	3	0	1	50^1	59	3	11	17	12.9	3.58	109	.295	.338	4	.267	1	2	2	0	0.3
1929	NY-N	7	6	.538	30	6	2	0	1	91^2	89	12	27	40	11.4	3.53	130	.260	.314	8	.308	3	12	11	1	1.3
Total	12	103	109	.486	356	195	115	11	19	1814^2	1969	94	493	657	12.4	3.85	96	.281	.332	187	.275	43	-13	-30	-9	-0.0
● **LEFTY SCOTT**	Scott, Marshall b: 7/15/15, Roswell, N.Mex. d: 3/3/64, Houston, Tex. BR/TL, 6'0.5", 165 lbs. Deb: 6/15/45																									
1945	Phi-N	0	2	.000	8	2	0	0	0	22^1	29	1	12	5	16.5	4.43	86	.312	.390	0	.000	-0	-2	-1	-1	-0.2
● **MIKE SCOTT**	Scott, Michael Warren b: 4/26/55, Santa Monica, Cal. BR/TR, 6'3", 215 lbs. Deb: 4/18/79																									
1979	NY-N	1	3	.250	18	9	0	0	0	52^1	59	4	20	21	13.6	5.33	68	.289	.353	0	.000	-1	-9	-10	-0	-1.1
1980	NY-N	1	1	.500	6	6	1	1	0	29^1	40	1	8	13	14.7	4.30	83	.331	.372	1	.111	0	-2	-2	-0	-0.2
1981	NY-N	5	10	.333	23	23	1	0	0	136	130	11	34	54	10.9	3.90	89	.261	.309	3	.073	-2	-6	-6	3	-0.5
1982	NY-N	7	13	.350	37	22	1	0	3	147	185	13	60	63	15.1	5.14	71	.321	.387	7	.146	0	-25	-25	4	-2.1
1983	Hou-N	10	6	.625	24	24	2	2	0	145	143	8	46	73	12.0	3.72	91	.258	.320	8	.167	1	-2	-5	0	-0.4
1984	Hou-N	5	11	.313	31	29	0	0	0	154	179	7	43	83	13.1	4.68	71	.293	.343	6	.128	0	-19	-23	-0	-2.3
1985	Hou-N	18	8	.692	36	35	4	2	0	221^2	194	20	80	137	11.2	3.29	105	.235	.304	11	.153	2	7	4	-2	0.5

YEAR TM/L	W	L	PCT	G	GS	CG	SH	SV	IP	H	HR	BB	SO	RAT	ERA	ERA+	OAV	OOB	BH	AVG	PB	PR	/A	PD	TPI
1986 *Hou-N★	18	10	.643	37	37	7	**5**	0	**275**^{1}	182	17	72	**306**	**8.4**	**2.22**	**162**	**.186**	**.244**	12	.126	-2	**46**	**42**	2	**4.8**
1987 Hou-N★	16	13	.552	36	36	8	3	0	247^2	199	21	79	233	10.2	3.23	121	.217	**.282**	10	.125	-1	23	19	0	1.8
1988 Hou-N	14	8	.636	32	32	8	5	0	218^2	162	19	53	190	9.2	2.92	114	.204	.261	6	.085	-3	13	10	-1	0.7
1989 Hou-N†	**20**	10	.667	33	32	9	2	0	229	180	23	62	172	9.6	3.10	109	.212	.268	10	.133	-0	10	7	-2	0.5
1990 Hou-N	9	13	.409	32	32	4	2	0	205^2	194	27	66	121	11.4	3.81	98	.246	.305	7	.130	-0	-0	-2	-2	-0.4
1991 Hou-N	0	2	.000	2	2	0	0	0	7	11	2	4	3	20.6	12.86	27	.367	.457	0	.000	-0	-7	-7	-0	-0.6
Total 13	124	108	.534	347	319	45	22	3	2068^2	1858	173	627	1469	11.0	3.54	100	.240	.300	81	.124	-6	28	1	3	0.7

● **MILT SCOTT** Scott, Milton Parker "Mikado Milt" b: 1/17/1866, Chicago, Ill. d: 11/3/38, Baltimore, Md. 5'9", 160 lbs. Deb: 9/30/1882 ♦

YEAR TM/L	W	L	PCT	G	GS	CG	SH	SV	IP	H	HR	BB	SO	RAT	ERA	ERA+	OAV	OOB	BH	AVG	PB	PR	/A	PD	TPI
1886 Bal-a	0	0	—	1	0	0	0	0	3	2	0	2	0	15.0	3.00	114	.125	.263	92	.190	-0	0	0	-0	0.0

● **MICKEY SCOTT** Scott, Ralph Robert b: 7/25/47, Weimar, Germany BL/TL, 6'1", 165 lbs. Deb: 5/06/72

YEAR TM/L	W	L	PCT	G	GS	CG	SH	SV	IP	H	HR	BB	SO	RAT	ERA	ERA+	OAV	OOB	BH	AVG	PB	PR	/A	PD	TPI
1972 Bal-A	0	1	.000	15	0	0	0	0	23	23	2	5	11	11.3	2.74	112	.277	.326	0	.000	1	1	1	-0	0.1
1973 Bal-A	0	0	—	1	0	0	0	0	1^2	2	1	2	2	21.6	5.40	69	.286	.444	0	—	0	-0	-0	-0	0.0
Mon-N	1	2	.333	22	0	0	0	0	24	27	3	9	11	14.3	5.25	73	.287	.362	0	.000	-0	-4	-4	0	-0.4
1975 Cal-A	4	2	.667	50	0	0	0	1	68^1	59	8	18	31	10.3	3.29	108	.233	.287	0	—	0	4	2	-1	0.7
1976 Cal-A	3	0	1.000	33	0	0	0	3	39	47	3	12	10	13.6	3.23	103	.307	.358	0	—	0	1	0	-1	0.0
1977 Cal-A	0	2	.000	12	0	0	0	0	16	19	1	4	5	12.9	5.63	70	.302	.343	0	—	0	-3	-3	0	-0.2
Total 5	8	7	.533	133	0	0	0	4	172	177	18	50	70	12.1	3.72	94	.271	.327	0	.000	0	-2	-4	-1	0.2

● **DICK SCOTT** Scott, Richard Lewis b: 3/15/33, Portsmouth, N.H. BR/TL, 6'2", 185 lbs. Deb: 5/08/63

YEAR TM/L	W	L	PCT	G	GS	CG	SH	SV	IP	H	HR	BB	SO	RAT	ERA	ERA+	OAV	OOB	BH	AVG	PB	PR	/A	PD	TPI
1963 LA-N	0	0	—	9	0	0	0	2	12	17	6	3	6	15.0	6.75	45	.340	.377	0	—	0	-5	-5	0	-0.5
1964 Chi-N	0	0	—	3	0	0	0	0	4^1	10	2	1	1	22.8	12.46	30	.417	.440	0	—	0	-4	-4	0	-0.4
Total 2	0	0	—	12	0	0	0	2	16^1	27	8	4	7	17.1	8.27	39	.365	.397	0	—	0	-9	-9	0	-0.9

● **TIM SCOTT** Scott, Timothy Dale b: 11/16/66, Hanford, Cal. BR/TR, 6'2", 185 lbs. Deb: 6/25/91

YEAR TM/L	W	L	PCT	G	GS	CG	SH	SV	IP	H	HR	BB	SO	RAT	ERA	ERA+	OAV	OOB	BH	AVG	PB	PR	/A	PD	TPI
1991 SD-N	0	0	—	2	0	0	0	0	1	2	0	0	1	18.0	9.00	42	.400	.400	0	—	0	-1	-1	0	-0.1
1992 SD-N	4	1	.800	34	0	0	0	0	37^2	39	4	21	30	14.6	5.26	69	.267	.363	0	—	0	-7	-7	-1	-0.8
Total 2	4	1	.800	36	0	0	0	0	38^2	41	4	21	31	14.7	5.35	68	.272	.364	0	—	0	-8	-7	-1	-0.9

● **SCOTT SCUDDER** Scudder, William Scott b: 2/14/68, Paris, Tex. BR/TR, 6'2", 180 lbs. Deb: 6/06/89

YEAR TM/L	W	L	PCT	G	GS	CG	SH	SV	IP	H	HR	BB	SO	RAT	ERA	ERA+	OAV	OOB	BH	AVG	PB	PR	/A	PD	TPI
1989 Cin-N	4	9	.308	23	17	0	0	0	100^1	91	14	61	66	13.7	4.49	80	.239	.346	4	.167	1	-11	-10	-1	-1.1
1990 *Cin-N	5	5	.500	21	10	0	0	0	71^2	74	12	30	42	13.4	4.90	81	.265	.343	1	.056	-1	-9	-8	-1	-0.9
1991 Cin-N	6	9	.400	27	14	0	0	1	101^1	91	6	56	51	13.6	4.35	87	.246	.354	3	.103	-0	-8	-6	-1	-0.7
1992 Cle-A	6	10	.375	23	22	0	0	0	109	134	10	55	66	15.8	5.28	76	.303	.383	0	—	0	-16	-15	0	-1.5
Total 4	21	33	.389	94	63	0	0	1	382^1	390	42	202	225	14.2	4.76	81	.265	.358	8	.113	-0	-44	-39	-3	-4.2

● **ROD SCURRY** Scurry, Rodney Grant b: 3/17/56, Sacramento, Cal. d: 11/5/92 Reno, Nev. BL/TL, 6'2", 180 lbs. Deb: 4/17/80

YEAR TM/L	W	L	PCT	G	GS	CG	SH	SV	IP	H	HR	BB	SO	RAT	ERA	ERA+	OAV	OOB	BH	AVG	PB	PR	/A	PD	TPI
1980 Pit-N	0	2	.000	20	0	0	0	0	37^2	23	2	17	28	10.0	2.15	169	.176	.280	1	.250	0	6	6	-0	0.7
1981 Pit-N	4	5	.444	27	7	0	0	7	74	74	6	40	65	14.2	3.77	95	.261	.358	3	.158	0	-2	-1	-1	-0.2
1982 Pit-N	4	5	.444	76	0	0	0	14	103^2	79	3	64	94	12.8	1.74	213	.212	.334	5	.238	1	21	23	-1	2.5
1983 Pit-N	4	9	.308	61	0	0	0	7	68	63	6	53	67	15.9	5.56	67	.249	.387	0	.000	-1	-15	-14	-0	-1.5
1984 Pit-N	5	6	.455	43	0	0	0	4	46^1	28	1	22	48	9.7	2.53	143	.175	.275	0	.000	-0	5	6	0	0.6
1985 Pit-N	0	1	.000	30	0	0	0	2	47^2	42	4	28	43	13.2	3.21	111	.236	.340	0	.000	-0	2	2	0	0.2
NY-A	1	0	1.000	5	0	0	0	1	12^2	5	2	10	17	10.7	2.84	141	.125	.300	0	—	0	2	2	-0	0.2
1986 NY-A	1	2	.333	31	0	0	0	2	39^1	38	1	22	36	14.2	3.66	112	.252	.354	0	—	0	2	2	0	0.3
1988 Sea-A	0	2	.000	39	0	0	0	2	31^1	32	6	18	33	15.5	4.02	103	.258	.370	0	—	0	-0	0	0	-0.1
Total 8	19	32	.373	332	7	0	0	39	460^2	384	31	274	431	13.2	3.24	115	.227	.341	9	.164	0	22	25	-0	2.7

● **JOHNNIE SEALE** Seale, Johnny Ray "Durango Kid" b: 11/14/38, Edgewater, Colo. BL/TL, 5'10", 155 lbs. Deb: 9/20/64

YEAR TM/L	W	L	PCT	G	GS	CG	SH	SV	IP	H	HR	BB	SO	RAT	ERA	ERA+	OAV	OOB	BH	AVG	PB	PR	/A	PD	TPI
1964 Det-A	1	0	1.000	4	0	0	0	0	10	6	1	4	5	9.0	3.60	102	.171	.256	0	.000	-0	0	0	1	0.0
1965 Det-A	0	0	—	4	0	0	0	0	3	7	1	2	3	27.0	12.00	29	.500	.563	0	—	0	-3	-3	-0	-0.3
Total 2	1	0	1.000	8	0	0	0	0	13	13	2	6	8	13.2	5.54	65	.265	.345	0	.000	-0	-3	-3	0	-0.3

● **KIM SEAMAN** Seaman, Kim Michael b: 5/6/57, Pascagoula, Miss. BL/TL, 6'4", 205 lbs. Deb: 9/28/79

YEAR TM/L	W	L	PCT	G	GS	CG	SH	SV	IP	H	HR	BB	SO	RAT	ERA	ERA+	OAV	OOB	BH	AVG	PB	PR	/A	PD	TPI
1979 StL-N	0	0	—	1	0	0	0	0	2	0	0	2	3	9.0	0.00	—	.000	.250	0	—	0	1	1	0	0.1
1980 StL-N	3	2	.600	26	0	0	0	4	23^2	16	2	13	10	11.0	3.42	108	.188	.296	0	.000	-0	0	1	-0	0.0
Total 2	3	2	.600	27	0	0	0	4	25^2	16	2	15	13	10.9	3.16	117	.176	.292	0	.000	-0	1	2	-0	0.1

● **RUDY SEANEZ** Seanez, Rudy Caballero b: 10/20/68, Brawley, Cal. BR/TR, 5'10", 185 lbs. Deb: 9/07/89

YEAR TM/L	W	L	PCT	G	GS	CG	SH	SV	IP	H	HR	BB	SO	RAT	ERA	ERA+	OAV	OOB	BH	AVG	PB	PR	/A	PD	TPI
1989 Cle-A	0	0	—	5	0	0	0	0	5	1	0	4	7	9.0	3.60	110	.071	.278	0	—	0	0	0	-0	0.0
1990 Cle-A	2	1	.667	24	0	0	0	0	27^1	22	2	25	24	15.8	5.60	70	.220	.381	0	—	0	-5	-5	-1	-0.6
1991 Cle-A	0	0	—	5	0	0	0	0	5	10	2	7	7	30.6	16.20	26	.385	.515	0	—	0	-7	-7	-0	-0.6
Total 3	2	1	.667	34	0	0	0	0	37^1	33	4	36	38	16.9	6.75	59	.236	.395	0	—	0	-12	-12	-1	-1.2

● **RAY SEARAGE** Searage, Raymond Mark b: 5/1/55, Freeport, N.Y. BL/TL, 6'1", 180 lbs. Deb: 6/11/81

YEAR TM/L	W	L	PCT	G	GS	CG	SH	SV	IP	H	HR	BB	SO	RAT	ERA	ERA+	OAV	OOB	BH	AVG	PB	PR	/A	PD	TPI
1981 NY-N	1	0	1.000	26	0	0	0	1	36^2	34	2	17	16	12.5	3.68	95	.252	.336	1	1.000	0	-1	-1	-0	-0.1
1984 Mil-A	2	1	.667	21	0	0	0	6	38^1	20	0	16	29	8.7	0.70	546	.155	.253	0	—	0	14	13	-0	1.4
1985 Mil-A	1	4	.200	33	0	0	0	1	38	54	2	24	36	18.5	5.92	70	.338	.424	0	—	0	-7	-7	-1	-0.8
1986 Mil-A	0	1	.000	17	0	0	0	1	22	29	6	9	10	16.0	6.95	62	.315	.382	0	—	0	-7	-6	0	-0.7
Chi-A	1	0	1.000	29	0	0	0	0	29	15	1	19	26	10.6	0.62	694	.156	.296	0	—	0	11	12	0	1.1
Yr	1	1	.500	46	0	0	0	1	51	44	7	28	36	12.7	3.35	129	.233	.332	0	—	0	5	5	0	0.4
1987 Chi-A	2	3	.400	58	0	0	0	2	55^2	56	9	24	33	13.1	4.20	109	.264	.342	0	—	0	2	2	-0	0.1
1989 LA-N	3	4	.429	41	0	0	0	0	35^2	29	1	18	24	11.9	3.53	97	.225	.320	0	—	0	-0	-0	1	0.0
1990 LA-N	1	0	1.000	29	0	0	0	0	32^1	30	1	10	19	11.1	2.78	131	.250	.308	0	.000	-0	4	3	1	0.4
Total 7	11	13	.458	254	0	0	0	11	287^2	267	22	137	193	12.7	3.50	114	.249	.336	1	.333	0	15	15	0	1.4

● **STEVE SEARCY** Searcy, William Steven b: 6/4/64, Knoxville, Tenn. BL/TL, 6'1", 190 lbs. Deb: 8/29/88

YEAR TM/L	W	L	PCT	G	GS	CG	SH	SV	IP	H	HR	BB	SO	RAT	ERA	ERA+	OAV	OOB	BH	AVG	PB	PR	/A	PD	TPI
1988 Det-A	0	2	.000	2	2	0	0	0	8	8	3	4	5	13.5	5.63	68	.242	.324	0	—	0	-1	-2	-0	0.0
1989 Det-A	1	1	.500	8	2	0	0	0	22^1	27	3	12	11	15.7	6.04	63	.307	.390	0	—	0	-5	-6	-0	-0.6
1990 Det-A	2	7	.222	16	12	1	0	0	75^1	76	9	51	66	15.2	4.66	85	.270	.381	0	—	0	-6	-6	-0	-0.6
1991 Det-A	1	2	.333	16	5	0	0	0	40^2	52	8	30	32	18.1	8.41	49	.313	.418	0	—	0	-19	-19	-0	-1.8
Phi-N	2	1	.667	18	0	0	0	0	30^1	29	2	14	21	12.8	4.15	88	.252	.333	0	.000	-0	-2	-2	-0	-0.2
1992 Phi-N	0	0	—	10	0	0	0	0	10^1	13	0	8	5	18.3	6.10	57	.325	.438	0	—	0	-3	-3	0	-0.3
Total 5	6	13	.316	70	21	1	0	0	187	205	25	119	140	15.6	5.68	69	.283	.384	0	.000	-0	-37	-37	-1	-3.5

● **TOM SEATON** Seaton, Thomas Gordon b: 8/30/1887, Blair, Neb. d: 4/10/40, ElPaso, Tex. BB/TR, 6', 175 lbs. Deb: 4/13/12

YEAR TM/L	W	L	PCT	G	GS	CG	SH	SV	IP	H	HR	BB	SO	RAT	ERA	ERA+	OAV	OOB	BH	AVG	PB	PR	/A	PD	TPI
1912 Phi-N	16	12	.571	44	27	16	2	2	255	246	8	106	118	12.7	3.28	111	.261	.342	18	.217	-0	4	10	-2	0.8
1913 Phi-N	**27**	12	.692	52	35	21	5	1	**322**^{1}	262	6	136	**168**	11.4	2.60	128	.226	.313	12	.109	-5	22	26	2	2.4
1914 Bro-F	25	14	.641	44	38	26	7	2	302^2	299	6	102	172	12.3	3.03	105	.259	.326	22	.206	4	6	5	0	1.0
1915 Bro-F	12	11	.522	32	23	13	0	3	189^1	199	6	99	86	14.3	4.56	66	.273	.362	16	.242	4	-32	-32	1	-2.8
New-F	2	6	.250	12	10	7	0	1	75	61	1	21	28	10.1	2.28	125	.224	.285	4	.154	0	6	5	1	0.7
Yr	14	17	.452	44	33	20	0	4	264^1	260	7	120	114	13.0	3.92	76	.259	.339	20	.217	4	-26	-28	2	-2.1
1916 Chi-N	6	6	.500	31	14	4	0	1	121	108	3	43	45	11.5	3.27	89	.246	.319	7	.184	0	-9	-5	1	-0.5
1917 Chi-N	5	4	.556	16	9	3	1	1	74^2	60	0	23	27	10.1	2.53	114	.227	.292	5	.238	1	1	3	1	0.6
Total 6	93	65	.589	231	156	90	15	11	1340	1235	30	530	644	12.1	3.14	103	.249	.327	84	.186	3	-2	12	4	2.2

YEAR	TM/L	W	L	PCT	G	GS	CG	SH	SV	IP	H	HR	BB	SO	RAT	ERA	ERA+	OAV	OOB	BH	AVG	PB	PR	/A	PD	TPI
● TOM SEATS	Seats, Thomas Edward b: 9/24/10, Farmington, N.C. d: 5/10/92, San Ramon, Cal. BR/TL, 5'11", 190 lbs. Deb: 5/04/40																									
1940	Det-A	2	2	.500	26	2	0	0	1	55^2	67	4	21	25	14.2	4.69	101	.290	.349	1	.083	-1	-2	0	0	-0.1
1945	Bro-N	10	7	.588	31	18	6	2	0	121^2	127	8	37	44	12.5	4.36	86	.261	.320	9	.209	0	-8	-8	0	-0.8
Total	2	12	9	.571	57	20	6	2	1	177^1	194	12	58	69	13.0	4.47	91	.271	.329	10	.182	-1	-10	-8	0	-0.9
● TOM SEAVER	Seaver, George Thomas "Tom Terrific" b: 11/17/44, Fresno, Cal. BR/TR, 6'1", 206 lbs. Deb: 4/13/67 H																									
1967	NY-N★	16	13	.552	35	34	18	2	0	251	224	19	78	170	11.0	2.76	123	.241	.303	11	.143	2	17	18	0	2.3
1968	NY-N★	16	12	.571	36	35	14	5	1	277^2	224	15	48	205	9.1	2.20	137	.222	.262	15	.158	1	24	25	2	3.3
1969	*NY-N☆	**25**	7	**.781**	36	35	18	5	0	273^1	202	24	82	208	9.6	2.21	166	**.207**	.273	11	.121	-0	42	44	2	5.3
1970	NY-N★	18	12	.600	37	36	19	2	0	290^2	230	21	83	**283**	9.8	**2.82**	**143**	.214	.273	17	.179	4	**40**	**39**	2	**4.8**
1971	NY-N☆	20	10	.667	36	35	21	4	0	286^1	210	18	61	**289**	**8.6**	**1.76**	**194**	.206	**.253**	18	.196	4	**54**	**52**	1	**6.8**
1972	NY-N☆	21	12	.636	35	35	13	3	0	262	215	23	77	249	10.2	2.92	115	.224	.285	13	.146	4	16	13	2	2.1
1973	*NY-N★	19	10	.655	36	36	**18**	3	0	290	219	23	64	**251**	**8.9**	**2.08**	**174**	**.206**	**.254**	15	.161	2	**51**	**50**	-0	**6.0**
1974	NY-N	11	11	.500	32	32	12	5	0	236	199	19	75	201	10.6	3.20	111	.230	.293	7	.099	-2	11	9	2	1.0
1975	NY-N★	**22**	9	.710	36	36	15	5	0	280^1	217	11	88	**243**	9.9	2.38	145	.214	.280	17	.179	3	39	33	2	4.3
1976	NY-N★	14	11	.560	35	34	13	5	0	271	211	14	77	**235**	9.7	2.59	127	.213	.273	7	.085	-2	**27**	21	1	2.3
1977	NY-N	7	3	.700	13	13	5	3	0	96	79	7	28	72	10.0	3.00	125	.221	.277	5	.161	-0	10	8	1	0.9
	Cin-N	14	3	.824	20	20	14	4	0	165^1	120	12	38	124	8.6	2.34	168	.201	.249	12	.218	4	29	29	-1	3.6
	Yr	21	6	.778	33	33	19	**7**	0	261^1	199	19	66	196	**9.1**	2.58	149	**.208**	**.259**	17	.198	4	39	37	-0	4.5
1978	Cin-N☆	16	14	.533	36	36	8	1	0	259^2	218	26	89	226	10.6	2.88	123	.227	.292	9	.122	-0	20	19	-2	1.9
1979	*Cin-N	16	6	**.727**	32	32	9	**5**	0	215	187	16	61	131	10.4	3.14	119	.236	.291	12	.158	2	14	14	0	1.7
1980	Cin-N	10	8	.556	26	26	5	1	0	168	140	24	59	101	10.7	3.64	98	.225	.293	6	.130	1	-1	-1	1	0.1
1981	Cin-N★	**14**	2	**.875**	23	23	6	1	0	166^1	120	10	66	87	10.2	2.54	140	.205	.289	11	.200	4	17	19	-1	2.4
1982	Cin-N	5	13	.278	21	21	0	0	0	111^1	136	14	44	62	14.8	5.50	67	.302	.368	6	.176	1	-23	-22	-1	-2.3
1983	NY-N	9	14	.391	34	34	5	2	0	231	201	18	86	135	11.3	3.55	102	.235	.308	10	.156	2	2	2	-1	0.3
1984	Chi-A	15	11	.577	34	33	10	4	0	236^2	216	27	61	131	10.6	3.95	105	.240	.290	0	—	0	1	5	1	0.7
1985	Chi-A	16	11	.593	35	33	6	1	0	238^2	223	22	69	134	11.3	3.17	136	.248	.307	0	—	0	26	30	2	3.4
1986	Chi-A	2	6	.250	12	12	1	0	0	72	66	9	27	31	12.3	4.38	99	.242	.321	0	—	0	-2	-1	-1	-0.2
	Bos-A	5	7	.417	16	16	1	0	0	104^1	114	8	29	72	12.5	3.80	110	.278	.329	0	—	0	4	4	-0	0.4
	Yr	7	13	.350	28	28	2	0	0	176^1	180	17	56	103	12.1	4.03	105	.261	.318	0	—	0	3	4	-1	0.2
Total	20	311	205	.603	656	647	231	61	1	4782^2	3971	380	1390	3640	10.2	2.86	127	.226	.285	202	.154	28	419	411	13	51.1
● BOB SEBRA	Sebra, Robert Bush b: 12/11/61, Ridgewood, N.J. BR/TR, 6'2", 200 lbs. Deb: 6/26/85																									
1985	Tex-A	0	2	.000	7	4	0	0	0	20^1	26	4	14	13	18.1	7.52	56	.306	.410	0	—	0	-8	-7	-0	-0.7
1986	Mon-N	5	5	.500	17	13	3	1	0	91^1	82	9	25	66	10.8	3.55	104	.239	.296	6	.207	1	2	1	-1	0.2
1987	Mon-N	6	15	.286	36	27	4	1	0	177^1	184	15	67	156	12.9	4.42	95	.272	.340	8	.157	0	-7	-4	-1	-0.5
1988	Phi-N	1	2	.333	3	3	0	0	0	11^1	15	0	10	7	19.9	7.94	45	.333	.455	0	.000	-1	-6	-6	-0	-0.6
1989	Phi-N	2	3	.400	6	5	0	0	0	34^1	41	6	10	21	14.4	4.46	80	.295	.359	0	.000	-0	-4	-3	-0	-0.4
	Cin-N	0	0	—	15	0	0	0	1	21	24	2	18	14	19.3	6.43	56	.296	.441	0	.000	-0	-7	-7	-0	-0.7
	Yr	2	3	.400	21	5	0	0	1	55^1	65	8	28	35	15.6	5.20	68	.289	.375	0	.000	-1	-11	-10	-0	-1.1
1990	Mil-A	1	2	.333	10	0	0	0	0	11	20	1	5	4	21.3	8.18	47	.408	.473	0	—	0	-5	-5	1	-0.4
Total	6	15	29	.341	94	52	7	2	1	366^2	392	37	149	281	13.6	4.71	84	.276	.351	14	.146	-0	-34	-31	-2	-3.1
● DOC SECHRIST	Sechrist, Theodore O'Hara b: 2/10/1876, Williamstown, Ky. d: 4/2/50, Louisville, Ky. BR/TR, 5'9", 160 lbs. Deb: 4/28/1899																									
1899	NY-N	0	0	—	1	0	0	0	0	0	0	0	2	0	—	—	—	—	1.000	0	—	0	0	0	0	0.0
● DON SECRIST	Secrist, Donald Laverne b: 2/26/44, Seattle, Wash. BL/TL, 6'2", 195 lbs. Deb: 4/11/69																									
1969	Chi-A	0	1	.000	19	0	0	0	0	40	35	7	14	23	11.2	6.07	63	.227	.296	1	.143	0	-11	-10	0	-1.0
1970	Chi-A	0	0	—	9	0	0	0	0	14^2	19	2	12	9	19.0	5.52	71	.333	.449	0	—	0	-3	-3	-0	-0.3
Total	2	0	1	.000	28	0	0	0	0	54^2	54	9	26	32	13.3	5.93	65	.256	.340	1	.143	0	-14	-13	0	-1.3
● DUKE SEDGWICK	Sedgwick, Henry Kenneth b: 6/1/1898, Martins Ferry, O. d: 12/4/82, Clearwater, Fla. BR/TR, 6', 175 lbs. Deb: 7/12/21																									
1921	Phi-N	1	3	.250	16	5	1	0	0	71^1	81	3	32	21	14.8	4.92	86	.283	.363	5	.208	-1	-9	-5	-1	-0.7
1923	Was-A	0	1	.000	5	2	1	0	0	16	27	1	6	4	18.6	7.88	48	.415	.465	0	.000	-1	-7	-7	1	-0.7
Total	2	1	4	.200	21	7	2	0	0	87^1	108	4	38	25	15.5	5.46	76	.308	.382	5	.172	-2	-16	-13	-0	-1.4
● CHARLIE SEE	See, Charles Henry "Chad" b: 10/13/1896, Pleasantville, N.Y d: 7/19/48, Bridgeport, Conn. BL/TR, 5'10.5", 175 lbs. Deb: 8/06/19 ♦																									
1920	Cin-N	0	0	—	1	0	0	0	0	6	6	0	4	3	15.0	6.00	51	.286	.400	25	.305	0	-2	-2	-0	-0.2
● CHUCK SEELBACH	Seelbach, Charles Frederick b: 3/20/48, Lakewood, Ohio BR/TR, 6', 180 lbs. Deb: 6/29/71																									
1971	Det-A	0	0	—	5	0	0	0	0	4	6	2	7	1	31.5	13.50	27	.375	.583	0	—	0	-4	-4	-0	-0.5
1972	*Det-A	9	8	.529	61	3	0	0	14	112	96	6	39	76	11.1	2.89	109	.238	.310	3	.143	1	2	3	-1	0.4
1973	Det-A	1	0	1.000	5	0	0	0	0	7	7	1	2	2	11.6	3.86	106	.250	.300	0	—	0	-0	0	1	-0.4
1974	Det-A	0	0	—	4	0	0	0	0	7^2	9	2	3	0	15.3	4.70	81	.300	.382	0	—	0	-1	-1	-0	-0.3
Total	4	10	8	.556	75	3	0	0	14	130^2	118	11	51	79	12.0	3.38	96	.247	.326	3	.143	1	-3	-2	-0	-0.8
● EMMETT SEERY	Seery, John Emmett b: 2/13/1861, Princeville, Ill. BL/TR, Deb: 4/17/1884 ♦																									
1886	StL-N	0	0	—	2	0	0	0	0	7	8	1	3	2	14.1	7.71	42	.320	.393	108	.238	0	-3	-3	-0	-0.3
● HERMAN SEGELKE	Segelke, Herman Neils b: 4/24/58, San Mateo, Cal. BR/TR, 6'4", 200 lbs. Deb: 4/07/82																									
1982	Chi-N	0	0	—	3	0	0	0	0	4^1	6	1	6	4	24.9	8.31	45	.316	.480	0	—	0	-2	-2	0	-0.2
● DIEGO SEGUI	Segui, Diego Pablo (Gonzalez) b: 8/17/37, Holguin, Cuba BR/TR, 6', 190 lbs. Deb: 4/12/62 F																									
1962	KC-A	8	5	.615	37	13	2	0	6	116^2	89	16	46	71	10.5	3.86	108	.211	.291	8	.235	2	1	4	0	0.6
1963	KC-A	9	6	.600	38	23	4	1	0	167	173	17	73	116	13.4	3.77	102	.267	.343	12	.218	1	-3	1	1	0.3
1964	KC-A	8	17	.320	40	35	5	2	0	217	219	30	94	155	13.0	4.56	84	.260	.335	11	.155	0	-23	-18	2	-1.6
1965	KC-A	5	15	.250	40	25	5	1	0	163	166	18	67	119	13.0	4.64	75	.261	.334	9	.191	2	-21	-21	-1	-2.0
1966	Was-A	3	7	.300	21	13	1	1	0	72	82	8	24	54	13.3	5.00	69	.291	.346	2	.111	-1	-13	-12	-1	-1.4
1967	KC-A	3	4	.429	36	3	0	0	1	70	62	4	31	52	12.2	3.09	103	.238	.324	0	.000	-1	1	1	-0	-0.1
1968	Oak-A	6	5	.545	52	0	0	0	6	83	51	7	32	72	9.0	2.39	118	.173	.255	1	.111	0	5	4	-1	0.4
1969	Sea-A	12	6	.667	66	8	2	0	12	142^1	127	14	61	113	12.0	3.35	108	.238	.319	4	.148	-0	4	4	1	0.5
1970	Oak-A	10	10	.500	47	19	3	2	2	162	130	9	68	95	11.1	**2.56**	**138**	.222	.305	5	.116	-2	21	18	-1	1.5
1971	*Oak-A	10	8	.556	26	21	5	0	0	146^1	122	13	63	81	11.6	3.14	106	.229	.316	4	.085	-1	5	3	-1	0.1
1972	Oak-A	0	1	.000	7	3	0	0	0	22^2	25	2	7	11	12.7	3.57	80	.287	.340	1	.143	-0	-1	-2	-0	-0.3
	StL-N	3	1	.750	33	0	0	0	9	55^2	47	2	32	54	12.8	3.07	111	.229	.333	1	.143	0	2	2	1	0.3
1973	StL-N	7	6	.538	65	0	0	0	17	100^1	78	6	53	93	11.8	2.78	131	.211	.310	0	.000	-1	10	10	-1	0.8
1974	Bos-A	6	8	.429	58	0	0	0	10	108	106	9	49	76	13.0	4.00	96	.257	.337	0	—	0	-5	-2	-1	-0.8
1975	*Bos-A	2	5	.286	33	1	1	0	6	71	71	10	43	45	14.5	4.82	85	.270	.373	0	—	0	-8	-6	-1	-0.7
1977	Sea-A	0	7	.000	40	7	0	0	2	110^2	108	20	43	91	12.4	5.69	72	.251	.321	0	—	0	-20	-19	0	-1.9
Total	15	92	111	.453	639	171	28	7	71	1807^2	1656	185	786	1298	12.2	3.81	96	.243	.323	58	.151	-0	-43	-34	-3	-4.3
● JOSE SEGURA	Segura, Jose Altagracia (Mota) b: 1/26/63, Fundacion, D.R. BR/TR, 5'11", 180 lbs. Deb: 4/10/88																									
1988	Chi-A	0	0	—	4	0	0	0	0	8^2	19	1	8	2	28.0	13.50	29	.432	.519	0	—	0	-9	-9	0	-0.8
1989	Chi-A	0	1	.000	7	0	0	0	0	6	13	2	3	4	24.0	15.00	25	.464	.516	0	—	0	-7	-7	0	-0.7
1991	SF-N	0	1	.000	11	0	0	0	0	16^1	20	1	5	10	13.8	4.41	81	.303	.352	0	—	0	-1	-2	-0	-0.2

YEAR	TM/L	W	L	PCT	G	GS	CG	SH	SV	IP	H	HR	BB	SO	RAT	ERA	ERA+	OAV	OOB	BH	AVG	PB	PR	/A	PD	TPI
Total	3	0	2	.000	22	0	0	0	0	31	52	4	16	16	19.7	9.00	41	.377	.442	0	—	0	-18	-18	0	-1.7
● SOCKS SEIBOLD	Seibold, Harry b: 4/3/1896, Philadelphia, Pa. d: 9/21/65, Philadelphia, Pa. BR/TR, 5'8.5", 162 lbs. Deb: 9/18/15 ♦																									
1916	Phi-A	1	2	.333	3	2	1	1	0	21^{2}	22	0	9	5	12.9	4.15	69	.272	.344	2	.167	-0	-3	-3	1	-0.2
1917	Phi-A	4	16	.200	33	15	9	1	1	160	141	1	85	55	12.9	3.94	70	.243	.343	13	.220	2	-23	-21	-1	-2.2
1919	Phi-A	2	3	.400	14	4	1	0	0	45^{2}	58	2	26	19	17.3	5.32	64	.322	.419	2	.154	-1	-11	-10	0	-1.0
1929	Bos-N	12	17	.414	33	27	16	1	1	205^{2}	228	17	80	54	13.6	4.73	99	.285	.352	20	.286	4	-0	-1	-1	0.2
1930	Bos-N	15	16	.484	36	33	20	1	2	251	288	16	85	70	13.4	4.12	120	.290	.348	19	.211	0	24	23	-3	1.8
1931	Bos-N	10	18	.357	33	29	10	3	0	206^{1}	226	12	65	50	12.8	4.67	81	.279	.335	9	.129	-4	-18	-20	0	-2.3
1932	Bos-N	3	10	.231	28	20	6	1	0	136^{2}	173	12	41	33	14.2	4.68	80	.309	.358	7	.152	-1	-12	-14	2	-1.3
1933	Bos-N	1	4	.200	11	5	1	0	1	36^{2}	43	0	14	10	14.0	3.68	83	.295	.356	1	.111	0	-1	-3	0	-0.2
Total	8	48	86	.358	191	135	64	8	5	1063^{2}	1179	60	405	296	13.5	4.43	91	.284	.350	76	.192	-0	-45	-48	-1	-5.2
● EPP SELL	Sell, Lester Elwood b: 4/26/1897, Llewellyn, Pa. d: 2/19/61, Reading, Pa. BR/TR, 6', 175 lbs. Deb: 9/01/22																									
1922	StL-N	4	2	.667	7	5	0	0	0	33	47	2	6	5	15.0	6.82	57	.338	.374	4	.333	1	-10	-11	1	-0.8
1923	StL-N	0	1	.000	5	1	0	0	0	15	16	1	8	2	14.4	6.00	65	.291	.381	0	.000	-1	-3	-3	-0	-0.4
Total	2	4	3	.571	12	6	0	0	0	48	63	3	14	7	14.8	6.56	59	.325	.376	4	.211	0	-13	-14	0	-1.2
● JEFF SELLERS	Sellers, Jeffrey Doyle b: 5/11/64, Compton, Cal. BR/TR, 6'1", 175 lbs. Deb: 9/15/85																									
1985	Bos-A	2	0	1.000	4	4	1	0	0	22^{1}	24	1	7	6	12.5	3.63	118	.273	.326	0	—	0	1	2	-0	0.2
1986	Bos-A	3	7	.300	14	13	1	0	0	82	90	13	40	51	14.6	4.94	84	.282	.367	0	—	0	-7	-7	0	-0.7
1987	Bos-A	7	8	.467	25	22	4	2	0	139^{2}	161	10	61	99	14.5	5.28	86	.298	.373	0	—	0	-13	-12	1	-1.3
1988	Bos-A	1	7	.125	18	12	1	0	0	85^{2}	89	9	56	70	15.5	4.83	85	.268	.379	0	—	0	-8	-7	-0	-1.0
Total	4	13	22	.371	61	51	7	2	0	329^{2}	364	33	164	226	14.7	4.97	87	.285	.370	0	—	0	-27	-24	0	-2.8
● DAVE SELLS	Sells, David Wayne b: 9/18/46, Vacaville, Cal. BR/TR, 5'11", 175 lbs. Deb: 8/02/72																									
1972	Cal-A	2	0	1.000	10	0	0	0	0	16	11	0	5	2	9.0	2.81	103	.196	.262	0	—	0	0	0	0	0.1
1973	Cal-A	7	2	.778	51	0	0	0	10	68	72	2	35	25	14.8	3.71	96	.277	.373	0	—	0	1	-1	0	0.5
1974	Cal-A	2	3	.400	20	0	0	0	2	39	48	3	16	14	15.5	3.69	93	.312	.387	0	—	0	-0	-1	0	0.4
1975	Cal-A	0	0	—	4	0	0	0	0	8^{1}	9	3	8	7	18.4	8.64	41	.250	.386	0	—	0	-5	-5	0	-0.4
	LA-N	0	2	.000	5	0	0	0	0	7	6	2	3	1	11.6	3.86	88	.222	.300	1	1.000	0	-0	-0	0	0.0
Total	4	11	7	.611	90	0	0	0	12	138^{1}	146	10	67	49	14.4	3.90	88	.274	.363	1	1.000	0	-4	-7	1	0.6
● DICK SELMA	Selma, Richard Jay b: 11/4/43, Santa Ana, Cal. BR/TR, 5'11", 175 lbs. Deb: 9/02/65																									
1965	NY-N	2	1	.667	4	4	1	1	0	26^{2}	22	2	9	26	10.8	3.71	95	.229	.302	2	.222	0	-1	-1	1	0.0
1966	NY-N	4	6	.400	30	7	0	0	1	80^{2}	84	11	39	58	14.1	4.24	86	.274	.361	1	.071	0	-6	-5	2	-0.4
1967	NY-N	2	4	.333	38	4	0	0	2	81^{1}	71	3	36	52	12.1	2.77	122	.241	.328	2	.091	-1	6	6	1	0.6
1968	NY-N	9	10	.474	33	23	4	3	0	169^{2}	148	11	54	117	11.0	2.76	110	.233	.298	12	.207	2	4	5	2	1.0
1969	SD-N	2	2	.500	4	3	1	0	0	22	19	3	9	20	11.5	4.09	86	.229	.304	2	.286	0	-1	-1	0	-0.1
	Chi-N	10	8	.556	36	25	4	2	1	168^{2}	137	13	72	161	11.3	3.63	111	.222	.307	8	.154	-0	-1	7	-1	0.7
	Yr	12	10	.545	40	28	5	2	1	190^{2}	156	16	81	181	11.3	3.68	108	.223	.307	10	.169	-0	-2	6	-1	0.6
1970	Phi-N	8	9	.471	73	0	0	0	22	134^{1}	108	8	59	153	11.5	2.75	145	.226	.317	3	.150	0	**19**	**19**	2	2.1
1971	Phi-N	0	2	.000	17	0	0	0	1	24^{2}	21	2	8	15	11.3	3.28	107	.231	.307	1	1.000	0	0	1	0	0.1
1972	Phi-N	2	9	.182	46	10	1	0	3	98^{2}	91	13	73	58	15.4	5.56	65	.249	.381	4	.200	1	-23	-22	1	-2.1
1973	Phi-N	1	1	.500	6	0	0	0	0	8	6	1	5	4	12.4	5.63	67	.240	.367	0	—	0	-2	-2	1	-0.1
1974	Cal-A	2	2	.500	18	0	0	0	1	23	22	2	17	15	15.7	5.09	68	.272	.404	0	—	0	-4	-4	1	0.1
	Mil-A	0	0	—	2	0	0	0	0	2^{1}	5	0	0	2	23.1	19.29	19	.455	.500	0	—	0	-4	-4	-0	-0.3
	Yr	2	2	.500	20	0	0	0	1	25^{1}	27	2	17	17	16.0	6.39	54	.290	.405	0	—	0	-8	-8	1	-0.2
Total	10	42	54	.438	307	76	11	6	31	840	734	69	381	681	12.2	3.62	100	.238	.327	35	.172	2	-11	-2	8	1.6
● FRANK SELMAN	Selman, Frank C. (a.k.a. Frank C. Williams 1871-75) b: Baltimore, Md. Deb: 5/04/1871 ♦																									
1873	Mar-n	0	1	.000	1	1	1	0	0	9	21	0	0	0	21.0	8.00	40	.350	.350	1	.333	0	-5	-5		-0.3
● CARROLL SEMBERA	Sembera, Carroll William b: 7/26/41, Shiner, Tex. BR/TR, 6', 155 lbs. Deb: 9/28/65																									
1965	Hou-N	0	1	.000	2	1	0	0	0	7^{1}	5	0	3	4	9.8	3.68	91	.185	.267	0	.000	-0	-0	-0	0	0.0
1966	Hou-N	1	2	.333	24	0	0	0	1	33	36	3	16	21	14.2	3.00	114	.288	.369	0	.000	-0	2	2	0	0.2
1967	Hou-N	2	6	.250	45	0	0	0	3	59^{2}	66	7	19	48	13.0	4.83	69	.269	.325	1	.143	-0	-10	-10	1	-1.0
1969	Mon-N	0	2	.000	23	0	0	0	2	33	28	1	24	15	14.7	3.55	104	.246	.386	1	.250	0	0	0	-0	0.1
1970	Mon-N	0	0	—	5	0	0	0	0	6^{2}	14	2	11	6	35.1	18.90	22	.424	.578	0	—	0	-11	-11	0	-1.0
Total	5	3	11	.214	99	1	0	0	6	139^{2}	149	13	73	94	14.6	4.70	74	.274	.364	2	.133	-0	-18	-19	1	-1.7
● FRANK SEMINARA	Seminara, Frank Peter b: 5/16/67, Brooklyn, N.Y. BR/TR, 6'2", 205 lbs. Deb: 6/02/92																									
1992	SD-N	9	4	.692	19	18	0	0	0	100^{1}	98	5	46	61	13.2	3.68	99	.257	.342	4	.118	-1	-2	-1	2	0.0
● RAY SEMPROCH	Semproch, Roman Anthony "Baby" b: 1/7/31, Cleveland, Ohio BR/TR, 5'11", 180 lbs. Deb: 4/15/58																									
1958	Phi-N	13	11	.542	36	30	12	2	0	204^{1}	211	25	58	92	12.1	3.92	101	.264	.319	7	.095	-5	1	1	-1	-0.4
1959	Phi-N	3	10	.231	30	18	2	0	3	111^{2}	119	12	59	54	14.6	5.40	76	.277	.368	6	.176	-0	-18	-16	1	-1.5
1960	Det-A	3	0	1.000	17	0	0	0	0	27	29	2	16	9	15.0	4.00	99	.269	.363	0	.000	-0	-0	-0	1	0.1
1961	LA-A	0	0	—	2	0	0	0	0	1	1	0	3	1	36.0	9.00	50	.333	.667	0	—	0	-1	-0	0	0.0
Total	4	19	21	.475	85	48	14	2	3	344	360	39	136	156	13.2	4.42	91	.269	.340	13	.116	-5	-18	-16	1	-1.8
● STEVE SENTENEY	Senteney, Stephen Leonard b: 8/7/55, Indianapolis, Ind. d: 6/19/89, Colusa, Cal. BR/TR, 6'2", 205 lbs. Deb: 6/06/82																									
1982	Tor-A	0	0	—	11	0	0	0	0	22	23	5	6	20	11.9	4.91	91	.247	.293	0	—	0	-2	-1	-0	-0.2
● MANNY SEOANE	Seoane, Manuel Modesto b: 6/26/55, Tampa, Fla. BR/TR, 6'3", 187 lbs. Deb: 9/18/77																									
1977	Phi-N	0	0	—	2	1	0	0	0	6	11	0	3	4	21.0	6.00	67	.407	.467	1	.500	0	-1	-1	-0	-0.1
1978	Chi-N	1	0	1.000	7	1	0	0	0	8^{1}	11	0	6	5	18.4	5.40	75	.297	.395	0	—	0	-2	-1	-0	-0.2
Total	2	1	0	1.000	9	2	0	0	0	14^{1}	22	0	9	9	19.5	5.65	71	.344	.425	1	.500	0	-3	-3	-1	-0.3
● BILLY SERAD	Serad, William I. b: 1863, Philadelphia, Pa. d: 11/1/25, Chester, Pa. BR/TR, 5'7", 156 lbs. Deb: 5/05/1884																									
1884	Buf-N	16	20	.444	37	37	34	2	0	308	373	21	111	150	14.1	4.27	74	.281	.336	24	.175	-7	-44	-38	-3	-4.0
1885	Buf-N	7	21	.250	30	29	27	0	0	241^{1}	299	5	80	90	14.1	4.10	73	.293	.344	16	.154	-6	-34	-30	-3	-3.5
1887	Cin-a	10	11	.476	22	21	20	2	1	187^{1}	201	7	80	34	13.9	4.08	106	.266	.343	14	.177	-4	4	5	-1	0.1
1888	Cin-a	2	3	.400	6	5	5	0	0	50^{2}	62	1	19	4	15.5	3.55	89	.291	.365	3	.130	-1	-3	-2	-1	-0.4
Total	4	35	55	.389	95	92	86	4	1	787^{1}	935	34	290	278	14.2	4.13	82	.282	.342	57	.166	-18	-77	-64	-7	-7.8
● GARY SERUM	Serum, Gary Wayne b: 10/24/56, Fargo, N.D. BR/TR, 6'1", 180 lbs. Deb: 7/22/77																									
1977	Min-A	0	0	—	8	0	0	0	0	22^{2}	22	4	10	14	13.5	4.37	91	.268	.362	0	—	0	-1	-1	-0	-0.1
1978	Min-A	9	9	.500	34	23	6	1	1	184^{1}	188	14	44	80	11.5	4.10	93	.266	.311	0	—	0	-7	-6	0	-0.7
1979	Min-A	1	3	.250	20	5	0	0	0	64	93	10	20	31	15.9	6.61	66	.354	.399	0	—	0	-17	-16	0	-1.5
Total	3	10	12	.455	62	28	6	1	1	271	303	28	74	125	12.7	4.72	84	.288	.337	0	—	0	-25	-23	-0	-2.3
● SCOTT SERVICE	Service, Scott David b: 2/26/67, Cincinnati, Ohio BR/TR, 6'6", 230 lbs. Deb: 9/05/88																									
1988	Phi-N	0	0	—	5	0	0	0	0	5^{1}	7	0	1	6	15.2	1.69	211	.333	.391	0	—	0	1	1	-0	0.1
1992	Mon-N	0	0	—	5	0	0	0	0	7	15	1	5	11	25.7	14.14	25	.417	.488	0	.000	-0	-8	-8	-0	-0.8
Total	2	0	0	—	10	0	0	0	0	12^{1}	22	1	6	17	21.2	8.76	40	.386	.453	0	.000	-0	-7	-7	-0	-0.7

YEAR TM/L	W	L	PCT	G	GS	CG	SH	SV	IP	H	HR	BB	SO	RAT	ERA	ERA+	OAV	OOB	BH	AVG	PB	PR	/A	PD	TPI
● MERLE SETTLEMIRE	Settlemire, Edgar Merle "Lefty" b: 1/19/03, Santa Fe, Ohio d: 6/12/88, Russell's Point, Ohio BL/TL, 5'9", 156 lbs. Deb: 4/13/28																								
1928 Bos-A	0	6	.000	30	9	0	0	0	82^1	116	2	34	12	17.1	5.47	75	.345	.415	3	.176	-1	-13	-12	2	-1.0
● AL SEVERINSEN	Severinsen, Albert Henry b: 11/9/44, Brooklyn, N.Y. BR/TR, 6'3", 220 lbs. Deb: 7/01/69																								
1969 Bal-A	1	1	.500	12	0	0	0	0	19^2	14	2	10	13	11.0	2.29	156	.206	.308	1	.333	0	3	3	0	0.4
1971 SD-N	2	5	.286	59	0	0	0	8	70	77	4	30	31	14.0	3.47	95	.292	.368	0	.000	-0	-0	-1	1	0.0
1972 SD-N	0	1	.000	17	0	0	0	1	21^1	13	1	7	9	9.3	2.53	130	.173	.262	0	.000	-0	2	2	0	0.2
Total 3	3	7	.300	88	0	0	0	9	111	104	7	47	53	12.6	3.08	108	.256	.338	1	.200	0	5	3	2	0.6
● ED SEWARD	Seward, Edward William (b: Edward William Sourhardt) b: 6/29/1867, Cleveland, Ohio d: 7/30/47, Cleveland, Ohio TR , 5'7", 175 lbs. Deb: 9/30/1885 U♦																								
1885 Pro-N	0	0	—	1	0	0	0	0	6	2	0	0	1	3.0	0.00	—	.100	.100	0	.000	-0	2	2	1	0.2
1887 Phi-a	25	25	.500	55	52	52	3	0	470^2	445	7	140	155	11.6	4.13	104	.244	.306	50	.188	-5	9	8	-2	0.1
1888 Phi-a	35	19	.648	57	57	57	**6**	0	518^2	388	4	127	**272**	9.3	2.01	149	.200	.258	32	.142	-4	61	56	3	5.3
1889 Phi-a	21	15	.583	39	38	35	3	0	320	353	8	101	102	13.1	3.97	95	.271	.330	31	.217	6	-4	-6	-2	-0.1
1890 Phi-a	6	12	.333	21	19	15	1	0	154	165	4	72	55	14.3	4.73	81	.266	.349	10	.139	-1	-15	-15	-0	-1.4
1891 Cle-N	2	1	.667	3	3	0	0	0	16^1	16	0	1	4	9.4	3.86	90	.247	.258	4	.211	0	-1	-1	-1	-0.1
Total 6	89	72	.553	176	169	159	13	0	1485^2	1369	23	441	589	11.4	3.40	108	.237	.299	127	.174	-4	51	43	-2	4.0
● FRANK SEWARD	Seward, Frank Martin b: 4/7/21, Pennsauken, N.J. BR/TR, 6'3", 200 lbs. Deb: 9/28/43																								
1943 NY-N	0	1	.000	1	1	1	0	0	9	12	0	5	2	17.0	3.00	115	.324	.405	0	.000	-1	0	0	-0	-0.1
1944 NY-N	3	2	.600	25	7	2	0	0	78^1	98	8	32	16	15.2	5.40	68	.306	.373	2	.083	-2	-16	-15	-1	-1.8
Total 2	3	3	.500	26	8	3	0	0	87^1	110	8	37	18	15.4	5.15	71	.308	.376	2	.071	-2	-15	-15	-2	-1.9
● RIP SEWELL	Sewell, Truett Banks b: 5/11/07, Decatur, Ala. d: 9/3/89, Plant City, Fla. BL/TR, 6'1", 180 lbs. Deb: 6/14/32 C																								
1932 Det-A	0	0	—	5	0	0	0	0	10^2	19	2	8	2	22.8	12.66	37	.388	.474	1	.500	0	-10	-9	0	-0.8
1938 Pit-N	0	1	.000	17	0	0	0	1	38^1	41	3	21	17	15.0	4.23	90	.275	.372	1	.083	-1	-2	-2	1	-0.2
1939 Pit-N	10	9	.526	52	12	5	1	2	176^1	177	10	73	69	12.8	4.08	94	.265	.339	11	.200	1	-3	-5	3	-0.1
1940 Pit-N	16	5	.762	33	23	14	2	1	189^2	169	6	67	60	11.3	2.80	136	.238	.307	14	.192	2	22	21	2	2.7
1941 Pit-N	14	17	.452	39	32	18	2	2	249	225	18	84	76	11.3	3.72	97	.235	.299	16	.174	0	-2	-3	2	-0.1
1942 Pit-N	17	15	.531	40	33	18	5	2	248	259	13	72	69	12.1	3.41	99	.265	.317	13	.149	-2	-3	-1	-0	-0.3
1943 Pit-N★	**21**	9	.700	35	31	**25**	2	3	265^1	267	6	75	65	11.7	2.54	137	.260	.312	30	.286	6	25	28	1	**3.9**
1944 Pit-N★	21	12	.636	38	33	24	3	2	286	263	15	99	87	11.5	3.18	117	.240	.304	25	.223	3	14	17	-1	2.0
1945 Pit-N	11	9	.550	33	24	9	1	1	188	212	9	91	60	14.6	4.07	97	.279	.357	20	.313	6	-6	-3	-0	0.3
1946 Pit-N★	8	12	.400	25	20	11	2	0	149^1	140	6	53	33	11.7	3.68	96	.245	.310	9	.180	0	-4	-3	-1	-0.3
1947 Pit-N	6	4	.600	24	12	4	1	0	121	121	11	36	36	11.9	3.57	118	.263	.321	5	.125	-1	7	9	1	0.9
1948 Pit-N	13	3	.813	21	17	7	0	0	121^2	126	9	37	36	12.1	3.48	117	.262	.317	6	.143	1	6	8	-0	0.9
1949 Pit-N	6	1	.857	28	6	2	1	1	76	82	8	32	26	13.5	3.91	108	.280	.351	1	.063	-0	1	2	-1	0.2
Total 13	143	97	.596	390	243	137	20	15	2119^1	2101	116	748	636	12.2	3.48	107	.256	.320	152	.203	16	45	60	7	9.1
● ELMER SEXAUER	Sexauer, Elmer George b: 5/21/26, St.Louis Co., Mo. BR/TR, 6'4", 220 lbs. Deb: 9/06/48																								
1948 Bro-N	0	0	—	2	0	0	0	0	0^2	0	0	2	0	27.0	13.50	30	.000	.500	0	—	0	-1	-1	-0	-0.1
● FRANK SEXTON	Sexton, Frank Joseph b: 7/8/1872, Brockton, Mass. d: 1/4/38, Brighton, Mass. 160 lbs. Deb: 6/21/1895																								
1895 Bos-N	1	5	.167	7	5	4	0	0	49	59	2	22	14	15.2	5.69	90	.293	.369	5	.227	-1	-5	-3	-1	-0.4
● GORDON SEYFRIED	Seyfried, Gordon Clay b: 7/4/37, Long Beach, Cal. BR/TR, 6', 185 lbs. Deb: 9/13/63																								
1963 Cle-A	0	1	.000	3	1	0	0	0	7^1	9	0	3	1	14.7	1.23	295	.300	.364	0	.000	-0	2	2	0	0.2
1964 Cle-A	0	0	—	2	0	0	0	0	2^1	4	0	0	0	15.4	0.00	—	.444	.444	0	—	0	1	1	-0	0.1
Total 2	0	1	.000	5	1	0	0	0	9^2	13	0	3	1	14.9	0.93	388	.333	.381	0	.000	-0	3	3	0	0.3
● JAKE SEYMOUR	Seymour, Jacob (b: Jacob Semer) b: 1854, Pittsburgh, Pa. d: 8/1/1897, Allegheny, Pa. Deb: 9/23/1882																								
1882 Pit-a	0	1	.000	1	1	1	0	0	8	16	0	2	2	20.3	7.88	33	.391	.420	0	.000	-1	-5	-5	-0	-0.4
● CY SEYMOUR	Seymour, James Bentley b: 12/9/1872, Albany, N.Y. d: 9/20/19, New York, N.Y. BL/TL, 6', 200 lbs. Deb: 4/22/1896 ♦																								
1896 NY-N	2	4	.333	11	8	4	0	0	70^1	75	8	51	33	16.5	6.40	66	.271	.390	7	.219	-1	-16	-17	1	-1.4
1897 NY-N	18	14	.563	38	33	28	2	1	277^2	254	4	164	149	14.2	3.37	123	**.242**	.355	33	.241	1	29	24	8	2.9
1898 NY-N	25	19	.568	45	43	39	4	0	356^2	313	4	213	**239**	14.1	3.18	109	.234	.353	82	.276	7	17	12	8	2.5
1899 NY-N	14	18	.438	32	32	31	0	0	268^1	247	5	170	142	14.7	3.56	106	.245	.364	52	.327	7	9	6	5	1.9
1900 NY-N	2	1	.667	13	7	2	0	0	53	58	4	54	19	20.2	6.96	52	.278	.441	12	.300	1	-19	-20	1	-1.5
1902 Cin-N	0	0	—	1	0	0	0	0	3	4	0	3	2	21.0	9.00	33	.319	.451	83	.340	0	-2	-2	-0	-0.2
Total 6	61	56	.521	140	123	104	6	1	1029	951	25	655	584	14.8	3.76	101	.244	.364	1723	.303	15	18	3	23	4.2
● JOHN SHAFFER	Shaffer, John W. "Cannon Ball" b: 2/18/1864, Lock Haven, Pa. d: 11/21/26, Endicott, N.Y. Deb: 9/13/1886																								
1886 NY-a	5	3	.625	8	8	8	1	0	69	40	0	29	36	9.1	1.96	174	.164	.255	6	.240	1	11	11	-1	1.0
1887 NY-a	2	11	.154	13	13	13	0	0	112	148	3	53	22	17.0	6.19	69	.310	.391	8	.167	-3	-24	-24	2	-1.9
Total 2	7	14	.333	21	21	21	1	0	181	188	3	82	58	14.0	4.57	86	.260	.346	14	.192	-2	-12	-13	1	-0.9
● GUS SHALLIX	Shallix, August (b: August Schallick) b: 3/29/1858, Paderborn, Westphalia, Germany d: 10/28/37, Cincinnati, Ohio BR/TR, 5'11", 165 lbs. Deb: 6/22/1884																								
1884 Cin-a	11	10	.524	23	23	23	0	0	199^2	163	6	53	78	10.9	3.70	90	.212	.286	3	.036	-11	-10	-8	1	-1.6
1885 Cin-a	6	4	.600	13	12	7	0	0	91^1	95	1	33	15	13.9	3.25	100	.265	.349	5	.128	-2	-0	0	1	-0.1
Total 2	17	14	.548	36	35	30	0	0	291	258	7	86	93	11.8	3.56	93	.229	.306	8	.065	-13	-10	-8	2	-1.7
● GREG SHANAHAN	Shanahan, Paul Gregory b: 12/11/47, Eureka, Cal. BR/TR, 6'2", 190 lbs. Deb: 9/04/73																								
1973 LA-N	0	0	—	7	0	0	0	1	15^2	14	2	4	11	10.3	3.45	100	.230	.277	0	.000	0	0	-0	-0	0.0
1974 LA-N	0	0	—	4	0	0	0	0	7	7	1	5	2	15.4	3.86	88	.259	.375	0	—	0	-0	-0	0	0.0
Total 2	0	0	—	11	0	0	0	1	22^2	21	3	9	13	11.9	3.57	96	.239	.309	0	.000	0	-0	-0	0	0.0
● HARVEY SHANK	Shank, Harvey Tillman b: 7/29/46, Toronto, Ont., Can. BR/TR, 6'4", 220 lbs. Deb: 5/16/70																								
1970 Cal-A	0	0	—	1	0	0	0	0	3	2	0	2	1	12.0	0.00	—	.182	.308	0	—	0	1	1	-0	0.1
● BILL SHANNER	Shanner, Wilfred William b: 11/4/1894, Oakland City, Ind. d: 12/18/86, Evansville, Ind. BL/TR, Deb: 10/01/20																								
1920 Phi-A	0	0	—	1	0	0	0	0	4	6	2	1	1	15.8	6.75	60	.353	.389	0	.000	-0	-1	-1	0	-0.1
● BOBBY SHANTZ	Shantz, Robert Clayton b: 9/26/25, Pottstown, Pa. BR/TL, 5'6", 142 lbs. Deb: 5/01/49 F																								
1949 Phi-A	6	8	.429	33	7	4	1	2	127	100	9	74	58	12.5	3.40	121	.221	.334	7	.189	1	11	10	4	1.4
1950 Phi-A	8	14	.364	36	23	6	1	0	214^2	251	18	85	93	14.4	4.61	99	.294	.362	11	.167	-0	-1	-1	4	0.2
1951 Phi-A☆	18	10	.643	32	25	13	3	0	205^1	213	15	70	77	12.6	3.94	108	.270	.333	18	.250	2	4	8	3	1.3
1952 Phi-A★	**24**	7	**.774**	33	33	27	5	0	279^2	230	21	63	152	**9.6**	2.48	160	.225	**.272**	19	.198	2	37	**46**	2	**5.6**
1953 Phi-A	5	9	.357	16	16	6	0	0	105^2	107	10	26	58	11.3	4.09	105	.263	.307	9	.237	1	-1	2	2	0.6
1954 Phi-A	1	0	1.000	2	1	0	0	0	8	12	2	3	3	18.0	7.88	50	.364	.432	1	.333	0	-4	-4	0	-0.3
1955 KC-A	5	10	.333	23	17	4	1	0	125	124	8	66	58	13.8	4.54	92	.264	.356	6	.146	-2	-8	-5	1	-0.5
1956 KC-A	2	7	.222	45	2	1	0	9	101^1	95	12	37	67	12.0	4.35	99	.248	.319	2	.091	-1	-2	-0	1	0.0
1957 *NY-A☆	11	5	.688	30	21	9	1	5	173	157	15	40	72	10.6	**2.45**	**147**	.248	.299	10	.179	2	26	22	6	3.3
1958 NY-A	7	6	.538	33	13	3	0	0	126	127	8	35	80	11.7	3.36	105	.262	.315	8	.229	2	6	2	3	0.8

YEAR	TM/L	W	L	PCT	G	GS	CG	SH	SV	IP	H	HR	BB	SO	RAT	ERA	ERA+	OAV	OOB	BH	AVG	PB	PR	/A	PD	TPI
1959	NY-A	7	3	.700	33	4	2	2	3	94^2	64	4	33	66	9.2	2.38	153	.189	.261	5	.217	2	16	13	1	1.7
1960	*NY-A	5	4	.556	42	0	0	0	11	67^2	57	5	24	54	11.0	2.79	128	.235	.309	1	.100	-0	8	6	1	0.7
1961	Pit-N	6	3	.667	43	6	2	1	2	89^1	91	5	26	61	12.2	3.32	120	.271	.331	7	.438	3	7	7	2	1.2
1962	Hou-N	1	1	.500	3	3	1	0	0	20^2	15	1	5	14	8.7	1.31	286	.208	.260	0	.000	-1	6	6	2	0.8
	StL-N	5	3	.625	28	0	0	0	4	57^2	45	7	20	47	10.3	2.18	195	.211	.282	2	.154	-0	11	13	1	1.4
	Yr	6	4	.600	31	3	1	0	4	78^1	60	8	25	61	9.9	1.95	211	.210	.276	2	.095	-1	17	19	3	2.2
1963	StL-N	6	4	.600	55	0	0	0	11	79	55	6	17	70	8.4	2.62	135	.192	.243	1	.143	0	6	8	3	1.2
1964	StL-N	1	3	.250	16	0	0	0	0	17^1	14	2	7	12	10.9	3.12	122	.226	.304	0	—	0	1	1	1	0.3
	Chi-N	0	1	.000	20	0	0	0	1	11^1	15	2	6	12	16.7	5.56	67	.319	.396	0	—	0	-3	-2	0	-0.2
	Phi-N	1	1	.500	14	0	0	0	0	32	23	1	6	18	8.2	2.25	154	.204	.244	0	.000	-0	5	4	2	0.7
	Yr	2	5	.286	50	0	0	0	1	60^2	52	5	19	42	10.5	3.12	116	.233	.293	0	.000	0	3	3	4	0.8
Total	16	119	99	.546	537	171	78	15	48	1935^1	1795	151	643	1072	11.5	3.38	119	.248	.313	107	.195	11	125	137	39	20.2

● GEORGE SHARROTT Sharrott, George Oscar b: 11/2/1869, W.New Brighton, S.I., N.Y. d: 1/6/32, Jamaica, N.Y. BL/TL, 5'8", 164 lbs. Deb: 7/27/1893

YEAR	TM/L	W	L	PCT	G	GS	CG	SH	SV	IP	H	HR	BB	SO	RAT	ERA	ERA+	OAV	OOB	BH	AVG	PB	PR	/A	PD	TPI
1893	Bro-N	4	6	.400	13	10	10	0	1	95	114	3	58	24	17.1	5.87	75	.289	.390	9	.231	0	-13	-15	-1	-1.2
1894	Bro-N	0	1	.000	2	2	1	0	0	9	7	0	5	2	15.0	7.00	71	.213	.367	1	.333	0	-2	-2	-0	-0.2
Total	2	4	7	.364	15	12	11	0	1	104	121	3	63	26	16.9	5.97	75	.283	.388	10	.238	0	-14	-17	-1	-1.4

● JACK SHARROTT Sharrott, John Henry b: 8/13/1869, Bangor, Me. d: 12/31/27, Los Angeles, Cal. BR/TR, 5'9", 165 lbs. Deb: 4/22/1890 ♦

YEAR	TM/L	W	L	PCT	G	GS	CG	SH	SV	IP	H	HR	BB	SO	RAT	ERA	ERA+	OAV	OOB	BH	AVG	PB	PR	/A	PD	TPI
1890	NY-N	11	10	.524	25	20	18	0	0	184	162	3	88	84	12.7	2.89	121	.229	.322	22	.202	-2	14	13	3	1.1
1891	NY-N	5	5	.500	10	9	6	0	1	69^1	47	2	35	41	11.2	2.60	123	.185	.293	10	.333	4	6	5	1	0.8
1892	NY-N	0	0	—	1	0	0	0	0	2	2	0	1	1	13.5	4.50	72	.250	.333	1	.125	-0	-0	-0	-0	0.0
1893	Phi-N	4	2	.667	12	4	2	0	0	56	53	1	33	11	14.5	4.50	102	.242	.352	38	.250	1	1	0	0	0.1
Total	4	20	17	.541	48	33	26	0	1	311^1	264	6	157	137	12.7	3.12	116	.222	.322	71	.237	2	21	17	3	2.0

● JOE SHAUTE Shaute, Joseph Benjamin "Lefty" b: 8/1/1899, Peckville, Pa. d: 2/21/70, Scranton, Pa. BL/TL, 6', 190 lbs. Deb: 7/06/22

YEAR	TM/L	W	L	PCT	G	GS	CG	SH	SV	IP	H	HR	BB	SO	RAT	ERA	ERA+	OAV	OOB	BH	AVG	PB	PR	/A	PD	TPI
1922	Cle-A	0	0	—	2	0	0	0	0	3^2	7	2	3	3	24.5	19.64	20	.389	.476	0	.000	-0	-6	-6	-0	-0.6
1923	Cle-A	10	8	.556	33	16	7	0	0	172	176	4	53	61	12.0	3.51	113	.275	.332	11	.162	-4	9	9	-2	0.3
1924	Cle-A	20	17	.541	46	34	21	2	2	283	317	8	83	68	12.9	3.75	114	.287	.340	34	.318	9	15	16	-2	2.3
1925	Cle-A	4	12	.250	26	17	10	1	4	131	160	6	44	34	14.1	5.43	81	.304	.358	16	.302	3	-15	-15	-2	-1.2
1926	Cle-A	14	10	.583	34	25	15	1	1	206^2	215	9	65	47	12.3	3.53	115	.278	.337	20	.274	4	11	12	-5	1.1
1927	Cle-A	9	16	.360	45	28	14	0	2	230^1	255	9	75	63	13.0	4.22	100	.286	.343	27	.325	6	-2	-0	-2	0.3
1928	Cle-A	13	17	.433	36	31	21	1	2	253^2	295	9	68	81	13.1	4.04	102	.299	.348	21	.228	3	-0	3	1	0.7
1929	Cle-A	8	8	.500	26	24	8	0	0	162	211	6	52	43	14.7	4.28	104	.320	.370	17	.293	3	-1	3	-3	0.3
1930	Cle-A	0	0	—	4	0	0	0	0	4^2	8	0	4	2	23.1	15.43	31	.333	.429	0	—	0	-6	-5	0	-0.5
1931	Bro-N	11	8	.579	25	19	6	0	0	128^2	162	9	32	50	13.6	4.83	79	.305	.346	8	.178	-0	-14	-14	0	-1.4
1932	Bro-N	7	7	.500	34	9	1	0	4	117	147	8	21	32	13.1	4.54	84	.301	.333	9	.200	1	-9	-9	-2	-1.0
1933	Bro-N	3	4	.429	41	4	0	0	2	108^1	125	4	31	26	13.0	3.49	92	.287	.336	6	.222	1	-2	-3	1	-0.2
1934	Cin-N	0	2	.000	8	1	0	0	1	17^1	19	1	3	2	11.4	4.15	98	.268	.297	1	.250	0	-0	-0	-1	-0.1
Total	13	99	109	.476	360	208	103	5	18	1818^1	2097	75	534	512	13.1	4.15	99	.293	.345	170	.258	26	-18	-12	-14	0.0

● JEFF SHAVER Shaver, Jeffrey Thomas b: 7/30/63, Beaver, Pa. BR/TR, 6'3", 195 lbs. Deb: 7/06/88

YEAR	TM/L	W	L	PCT	G	GS	CG	SH	SV	IP	H	HR	BB	SO	RAT	ERA	ERA+	OAV	OOB	BH	AVG	PB	PR	/A	PD	TPI
1988	Oak-A	0	0	—	1	0	0	0	0	1	0	0	0	0	9.0	0.00	—	.000	.333	0	—	0	0	0	0	0.4

● DON SHAW Shaw, Donald Wellington b: 2/23/44, Pittsburgh, Pa. BL/TL, 6', 185 lbs. Deb: 4/11/67

YEAR	TM/L	W	L	PCT	G	GS	CG	SH	SV	IP	H	HR	BB	SO	RAT	ERA	ERA+	OAV	OOB	BH	AVG	PB	PR	/A	PD	TPI
1967	NY-N	4	5	.444	40	0	0	0	3	51^1	40	5	23	44	11.0	2.98	114	.219	.306	0	.000	0	2	2	-1	0.2
1968	NY-N	0	0	—	7	0	0	0	0	12^1	3	1	5	11	5.8	0.73	414	.086	.200	0	—	0	3	3	0	0.4
1969	Mon-N	2	5	.286	35	1	0	0	1	65^2	61	9	37	45	13.7	5.21	71	.254	.358	0	.000	-0	-12	-11	1	-1.1
1971	StL-N	7	2	.778	45	0	0	0	2	51	45	1	31	19	13.6	2.65	136	.237	.347	0	.000	-0	5	5	-0	0.5
1972	StL-N	0	1	.000	8	0	0	0	0	3	5	1	3	0	24.0	9.00	38	.417	.533	0	.000	-0	-2	-2	-0	-0.2
	Oak-A	0	1	.000	3	0	0	0	0	5^1	12	2	2	4	23.6	16.88	17	.500	.538	0	—	0	-8	-8	-0	-0.8
Total	5	13	14	.481	138	1	0	0	6	188^2	166	19	101	123	12.9	4.01	87	.243	.343	0	.000	-0	-12	-11	-0	-1.0

● DUPEE SHAW Shaw, Frederick Lander b: 5/31/1859, Charlestown, Mass. d: 6/11/38, Wakefield, Mass. BL/TL, 5'8", 165 lbs. Deb: 6/11/1883

YEAR	TM/L	W	L	PCT	G	GS	CG	SH	SV	IP	H	HR	BB	SO	RAT	ERA	ERA+	OAV	OOB	BH	AVG	PB	PR	/A	PD	TPI
1883	Det-N	10	15	.400	26	25	23	1	0	227	238	3	44	73	11.2	2.50	124	.256	.290	29	.206	-3	16	15	0	1.2
1884	Det-N	9	18	.333	28	28	25	0	0	227^2	219	8	72	142	11.5	3.04	95	.237	.292	26	.191	-1	-2	-4	2	-0.3
	Bos-U	21	15	.583	39	38	35	5	0	315^2	227	1	37	309	7.5	1.77	166	.188	.212	37	.242	1	**44**	41	-0	3.8
1885	Pro-N	23	26	.469	49	49	47	6	0	399^2	343	7	99	194	10.0	2.57	103	.209	.254	22	.133	-9	11	4	-2	-0.7
1886	Was-N	13	31	.295	45	44	43	1	0	385^2	384	12	91	177	11.1	3.34	98	.250	.291	13	.088	-10	-1	-2	-1	-1.2
1887	Was-N	7	13	.350	21	20	20	0	0	181^1	263	8	46	47	15.5	6.45	63	.328	.366	13	.186	-2	-48	-48	-2	-4.0
1888	Was-N	0	3	.000	3	3	3	0	0	25	36	2	7	8	15.5	6.48	43	.333	.374	0	.000	-1	-10	-10	-1	-1.0
Total	6	83	121	.407	211	207	196	13	0	1762	1710	41	396	950	10.8	3.10	99	.239	.279	140	.170	-25	11	-5	-5	-2.2

● JIM SHAW Shaw, James Aloysius "Grunting Jim" b: 8/19/1893, Pittsburgh, Pa. d: 1/27/62, Washington, D.C. BR/TR, 6', 180 lbs. Deb: 9/15/13

YEAR	TM/L	W	L	PCT	G	GS	CG	SH	SV	IP	H	HR	BB	SO	RAT	ERA	ERA+	OAV	OOB	BH	AVG	PB	PR	/A	PD	TPI
1913	Was-A	0	1	.000	2	1	0	0	0	13	8	0	7	14	11.1	2.08	142	.205	.340	0	.000	-0	1	1	1	0.2
1914	Was-A	15	17	.469	48	31	15	5	**4**	257	198	3	137	164	12.0	2.70	104	.216	.324	10	.118	-3	1	3	1	0.1
1915	Was-A	6	11	.353	25	18	7	1	1	133	102	2	76	78	12.2	2.50	119	.220	.333	10	.233	1	6	7	-1	0.7
1916	Was-A	3	8	.273	26	9	5	2	1	106^1	86	1	50	44	11.7	2.62	106	.227	.320	5	.156	-0	2	2	-3	-0.1
1917	Was-A	15	14	.517	47	31	15	2	1	266^1	233	1	123	118	12.1	3.21	82	.242	.328	14	.154	-2	-16	-17	-3	-2.4
1918	Was-A	16	12	.571	41	30	14	4	1	241^1	201	2	90	129	10.9	2.42	113	.228	.300	11	.133	-4	9	8	-5	-0.1
1919	Was-A	17	17	.500	**45**	37	23	3	**5**	**306^2**	274	5	101	128	11.2	2.73	118	.244	.309	17	.160	-1	17	16	-6	1.0
1920	Was-A	11	18	.379	38	32	17	0	1	236^1	285	12	87	88	14.3	4.27	87	.314	.376	14	.189	0	-12	-14	-4	-1.7
1921	Was-A	1	0	1.000	15	4	0	0	3	40^1	59	2	17	4	17.0	7.36	56	.345	.404	5	.417	2	-14	-15	0	-1.1
Total	9	84	98	.462	287	193	96	17	17	1600^1	1446	28	688	767	12.1	3.07	99	.247	.329	86	.163	-8	-4	-7	-19	-3.4

● JEFF SHAW Shaw, Jeffrey Lee b: 7/7/66, Washington Court House, Ohio BR/TR, 6'2", 185 lbs. Deb: 4/30/90

YEAR	TM/L	W	L	PCT	G	GS	CG	SH	SV	IP	H	HR	BB	SO	RAT	ERA	ERA+	OAV	OOB	BH	AVG	PB	PR	/A	PD	TPI
1990	Cle-A	3	4	.429	12	9	0	0	0	48^2	73	11	20	25	17.2	6.66	59	.356	.413	0	—	0	-15	-15	0	-1.4
1991	Cle-A	0	5	.000	29	1	0	0	1	72^1	72	6	27	31	12.8	3.36	124	.262	.337	0	—	0	6	6	0	0.6
1992	Cle-A	0	1	.000	2	1	0	0	0	7^2	7	2	4	3	12.9	8.22	49	.259	.355	0	—	0	-4	-4	0	-0.4
Total	3	3	10	.231	43	11	0	0	1	128^2	152	19	51	59	14.5	4.90	83	.300	.368	0	—	0	-13	-12	0	-1.2

● BOB SHAW Shaw, Robert John b: 6/29/33, Bronx, N.Y. BR/TR, 6'2", 195 lbs. Deb: 8/11/57 C

YEAR	TM/L	W	L	PCT	G	GS	CG	SH	SV	IP	H	HR	BB	SO	RAT	ERA	ERA+	OAV	OOB	BH	AVG	PB	PR	/A	PD	TPI
1957	Det-A	0	1	.000	7	0	0	0	0	9^2	11	2	7	4	16.8	7.45	52	.289	.400	0	.000	-0	-4	-4	-0	-0.4
1958	Det-A	1	2	.333	11	2	0	0	0	26^2	32	2	13	17	15.2	5.06	80	.302	.378	3	.375	1	-4	-3	1	-0.1
	Chi-A	4	2	.667	29	3	0	0	1	64	67	8	28	18	13.6	4.64	78	.271	.350	0	.000	-1	-6	-7	2	-0.7
	Yr	5	4	.556	40	5	0	0	1	90^2	99	10	41	35	14.1	4.76	79	.280	.358	3	.136	0	-10	-10	2	-0.8
1959	*Chi-A	18	6	**.750**	47	26	8	3	3	230^2	217	15	54	89	10.8	2.69	140	.249	.297	9	.123	-2	30	27	1	2.7
1960	Chi-A	13	13	.500	36	32	7	1	0	192^2	221	16	62	46	13.4	4.06	93	.292	.348	8	.138	-0	-4	-6	-1	-0.7
1961	Chi-A	3	4	.429	14	10	3	0	0	71^1	85	11	20	31	13.4	3.79	103	.302	.351	0	.000	-1	2	1	-0	0.0
	KC-A	9	10	.474	26	24	6	0	0	150^1	165	13	58	60	13.8	4.31	95	.281	.352	11	.200	-1	-5	-3	0	-0.4
	Yr	12	14	.462	40	34	9	0	0	221^2	250	24	78	91	13.6	4.14	98	.286	.349	11	.151	-2	-3	-2	-0	-0.4
1962	Mil-N★	15	9	.625	38	29	12	3	2	225	223	20	44	124	11.2	2.80	136	.260	.305	10	.137	1	29	25	-0	2.6
1963	Mil-N	7	11	.389	48	16	3	3	13	159	144	10	55	105	11.5	2.66	121	.243	.312	5	.122	0	11	10	-2	1.0
1964	SF-N	7	6	.538	61	1	0	0	11	93^1	105	5	31	57	13.6	3.76	95	.286	.350	0	.000	-1	-2	-2	-2	-0.5
1965	SF-N	16	9	.640	42	33	6	1	2	235	213	17	53	148	10.3	2.64	136	.236	.280	8	.101	-3	23	25	1	2.5

YEAR	TM/L	W	L	PCT	G	GS	CG	SH	SV	IP	H	HR	BB	SO	RAT	ERA	ERA+	OAV	OOB	BH	AVG	PB	PR	/A	PD	TPI
1966	SF-N	1	4	.200	13	6	0	0	0	31^2	45	9	7	21	14.8	6.25	59	.324	.356	0	.000	-1	-9	-9	-1	-1.0
	NY-N	11	10	.524	26	25	7	2	0	167^2	171	12	42	104	11.8	3.92	93	.261	.313	13	.260	3	-6	-5	1	-0.1
	Yr	12	14	.462	39	31	7	2	0	199^1	216	21	49	125	12.3	4.29	85	.272	.320	13	.232	2	-15	-14	0	-1.1
1967	NY-N	3	9	.250	23	13	3	1	0	98^2	105	9	28	49	12.3	4.29	79	.273	.326	1	.040	-2	-10	-10	-1	-1.3
	Chi-N	0	2	.000	9	3	0	0	0	22^1	33	0	9	7	18.5	6.04	59	.351	.430	1	.250	0	-7	-6	-1	-0.7
	Yr	3	11	.214	32	16	3	1	0	121	138	9	37	56	13.3	4.61	74	.286	.342	2	.069	-1	-17	-16	-2	-2.0
Total	11	108	98	.524	430	223	55	14	32	1778	1837	149	511	880	12.2	3.52	105	.267	.323	69	.133	-7	38	33	-2	2.9

● SAM SHAW

Shaw, Samuel E. b: 5/1864, Baltimore, Md. BR/TR, 5'5", 140 lbs. Deb: 5/03/1888

YEAR	TM/L	W	L	PCT	G	GS	CG	SH	SV	IP	H	HR	BB	SO	RAT	ERA	ERA+	OAV	OOB	BH	AVG	PB	PR	/A	PD	TPI
1888	Bal-a	2	4	.333	6	6	6	0	0	53	65	2	15	22	14.3	3.40	88	.291	.347	3	.150	-1	-2	-2	-1	-0.3
1893	Chi-N	1	0	1.000	2	2	1	0	0	16	12	2	13	1	19.1	5.63	82	.202	.418	2	.286	-0	-2	-2	-0	-0.2
Total	2	3	4	.429	8	8	7	0	0	69	77	4	28	23	15.4	3.91	86	.273	.365	5	.185	-1	-4	-4	-1	-0.5

● BOB SHAWKEY

Shawkey, James Robert b: 12/4/1890, Sigel, Pa. d: 12/31/80, Syracuse, N.Y. BR/TR, 5'11", 168 lbs. Deb: 7/16/13 MC

YEAR	TM/L	W	L	PCT	G	GS	CG	SH	SV	IP	H	HR	BB	SO	RAT	ERA	ERA+	OAV	OOB	BH	AVG	PB	PR	/A	PD	TPI
1913	Phi-A	6	5	.545	18	15	8	1	0	111^1	92	2	50	52	11.7	2.34	118	.207	.291	6	.136	-2	7	5	1	0.5
1914	*Phi-A	16	8	.667	38	31	18	5	2	237	223	4	75	89	11.4	2.73	96	.262	.323	17	.205	2	0	-3	-2	-0.4
1915	Phi-A	6	6	.500	17	13	7	1	0	100	103	3	38	56	12.8	4.05	72	.278	.346	4	.129	-1	-12	-12	0	-1.3
	NY-A	4	7	.364	16	9	5	1	0	85^2	78	2	35	31	12.1	3.26	90	.265	.347	7	.241	1	-3	-3	-1	-0.3
	Yr	10	13	.435	33	22	12	2	0	185^2	181	5	73	87	12.4	3.68	79	.272	.345	11	.183	1	-15	-16	-1	-1.6
1916	NY-A	24	14	.632	53	27	21	4	**8**	276^2	204	4	81	122	9.5	2.21	131	.209	.273	17	.183	-1	19	21	0	2.2
1917	NY-A	13	15	.464	32	26	16	2	0	236^1	207	2	72	97	10.9	2.44	110	.243	.306	16	.190	-0	6	7	3	1.1
1918	NY-A	1	1	.500	3	2	1	1	0	16	7	0	10	3	9.6	1.13	251	.143	.288	3	.750	2	3	3	0	0.6
1919	NY-A	20	11	.645	41	27	22	3	**5**	261^1	218	7	92	122	10.8	2.72	117	.231	.303	22	.234	-0	15	14	-1	1.3
1920	NY-A	20	13	.606	38	31	20	5	2	267^2	246	10	85	126	11.2	**2.45**	**156**	.248	.308	23	.230	-0	40	41	-3	3.8
1921	*NY-A	18	12	.600	38	31	18	3	2	245	245	15	86	126	12.4	4.08	104	.263	.329	27	.300	4	6	4	-4	0.3
1922	*NY-A	20	12	.625	39	34	22	3	1	299^2	286	16	98	130	11.5	2.91	138	.256	.316	21	.183	-3	38	36	-0	3.3
1923	*NY-A	16	11	.593	36	31	17	1	1	258^2	232	17	102	125	11.8	3.51	112	**.246**	.322	20	.202	-3	14	12	-1	0.8
1924	NY-A	16	11	.593	38	25	10	1	0	207^2	226	11	74	114	13.1	4.12	101	.286	.350	22	.319	7	3	1	-1	0.7
1925	NY-A	6	14	.300	33	20	9	1	0	186	209	12	67	81	13.6	4.11	104	.294	.359	10	.147	-4	6	3	-1	-0.2
1926	*NY-A	8	7	.533	29	10	3	1	3	104^1	102	8	37	63	12.2	3.62	106	.263	.330	9	.257	2	5	3	-0	0.4
1927	NY-A	2	3	.400	19	2	0	0	4	43^2	44	1	16	23	12.6	2.89	134	.262	.330	1	.091	-1	6	5	0	0.4
Total	15	196	150	.566	488	334	197	33	28	2937	2722	114	1018	1360	11.6	3.09	114	.251	.319	225	.214	4	151	136	-10	13.2

● SPEC SHEA

Shea, Francis Joseph "The Naugatuck Nuggett" (b: Francis Joseph O'Shea) b: 10/2/20, Naugatuck, Conn. BR/TR, 6', 195 lbs. Deb: 4/19/47

YEAR	TM/L	W	L	PCT	G	GS	CG	SH	SV	IP	H	HR	BB	SO	RAT	ERA	ERA+	OAV	OOB	BH	AVG	PB	PR	/A	PD	TPI
1947	*NY-A★	14	5	.737	27	23	13	3	1	178^2	127	10	89	89	11.1	3.07	115	**.200**	.303	11	.196	2	13	9	-3	0.9
1948	NY-A	9	10	.474	28	22	8	3	1	155^2	117	10	87	71	11.9	3.41	120	**.208**	.316	7	.149	1	15	12	-2	0.9
1949	NY-A	1	1	.500	20	3	0	0	1	52^1	48	5	43	22	15.6	5.33	76	.250	.387	3	.250	1	-7	-7	-0	-0.7
1951	NY-A	5	5	.500	25	11	2	2	0	95^2	112	11	50	38	15.6	4.33	88	.300	.389	6	.214	1	-2	-5	-0	-0.5
1952	Was-A	11	7	.611	22	21	12	2	0	169	144	6	92	65	12.7	2.93	121	.231	.331	15	.238	2	14	12	-1	1.4
1953	Was-A	12	7	.632	23	23	11	1	0	164^2	151	11	75	38	12.6	3.94	99	.244	.329	11	.177	-1	1	-1	-1	-0.2
1954	Was-A	2	9	.182	23	11	1	0	0	71^1	97	9	34	22	16.8	6.18	58	.340	.414	1	.050	-2	-19	-21	1	-2.1
1955	Was-A	2	2	.500	27	4	1	1	2	56^1	53	4	27	16	12.9	3.99	96	.251	.339	4	.400	2	-0	-1	-1	0.0
Total	8	56	46	.549	195	118	48	12	5	943^2	849	66	497	361	13.0	3.80	99	.243	.340	58	.195	6	14	-3	-8	-0.3

● JOHN SHEA

Shea, John Michael Joseph "Lefty" b: 12/27/04, Everett, Mass. d: 11/30/56, Malden, Mass. BL/TL, 5'10.5", 171 lbs. Deb: 6/30/28

YEAR	TM/L	W	L	PCT	G	GS	CG	SH	SV	IP	H	HR	BB	SO	RAT	ERA	ERA+	OAV	OOB	BH	AVG	PB	PR	/A	PD	TPI
1928	Bos-A	0	0	—	1	0	0	0	0	1	1	0	1	0	18.0	18.00	23	.250	.400	0	—	0	-2	-2	0	-0.1

● MIKE SHEA

Shea, Michael J. b: 3/10/1867, New Orleans, La. TR , 5'10", 170 lbs. Deb: 4/20/1887

YEAR	TM/L	W	L	PCT	G	GS	CG	SH	SV	IP	H	HR	BB	SO	RAT	ERA	ERA+	OAV	OOB	BH	AVG	PB	PR	/A	PD	TPI
1887	Cin-a	1	1	.500	2	2	2	0	0	16^2	26	0	10	0	19.4	7.02	62	.333	.409	2	.250	0	-5	-5	1	-0.3

● RED SHEA

Shea, Patrick Henry b: 11/29/1898, Ware, Mass. d: 11/17/81, Stafford Springs, Conn. BR/TR, 6', 165 lbs. Deb: 5/06/18

YEAR	TM/L	W	L	PCT	G	GS	CG	SH	SV	IP	H	HR	BB	SO	RAT	ERA	ERA+	OAV	OOB	BH	AVG	PB	PR	/A	PD	TPI
1918	Phi-A	0	0	—	3	0	0	0	0	9	14	0	2	2	16.0	4.00	73	.378	.410	0	.000	-0	-1	-1	-0	-0.2
1921	NY-N	5	2	.714	9	2	1	0	0	32	28	2	2	10	9.3	3.09	119	.239	.270	1	.111	-1	2	2	-1	0.1
1922	NY-N	0	3	.000	11	2	0	0	0	23	22	2	11	5	12.9	4.70	85	.256	.340	0	.000	-1	-2	-2	1	-0.2
Total	3	5	5	.500	23	4	1	0	0	64	64	4	15	17	11.5	3.80	97	.267	.318	1	.053	-2	-0	-1	-0	-0.3

● STEVE SHEA

Shea, Steven Francis b: 12/5/42, Worcester, Mass. BR/TR, 6'3", 215 lbs. Deb: 7/14/68

YEAR	TM/L	W	L	PCT	G	GS	CG	SH	SV	IP	H	HR	BB	SO	RAT	ERA	ERA+	OAV	OOB	BH	AVG	PB	PR	/A	PD	TPI
1968	Hou-N	4	4	.500	30	0	0	0	6	34^2	27	0	11	15	10.6	3.38	88	.229	.311	0	.000	-1	-2	-2	1	-0.2
1969	Mon-N	0	0	—	10	0	0	0	0	15^2	18	2	8	11	14.9	2.87	128	.300	.382	0	—	0	1	1	0	0.1
Total	2	4	4	.500	40	0	0	0	6	50^1	45	2	19	26	12.0	3.22	99	.253	.335	0	.000	-1	-0	-0	1	-0.1

● AL SHEALY

Shealy, Albert Berley b: 3/20/1900, Chapin, S.C. d: 3/7/67, Hagerstown, Md. BR/TR, 5'11", 175 lbs. Deb: 4/13/28

YEAR	TM/L	W	L	PCT	G	GS	CG	SH	SV	IP	H	HR	BB	SO	RAT	ERA	ERA+	OAV	OOB	BH	AVG	PB	PR	/A	PD	TPI
1928	NY-A	8	6	.571	23	12	3	0	2	96	124	4	42	39	15.7	5.06	74	.308	.375	9	.237	2	-11	-14	0	-1.1
1930	Chi-N	0	0	—	24	0	0	0	0	27	37	2	14	14	17.0	8.00	61	.327	.402	3	.600	1	-9	-9	-0	-0.7
Total	2	8	6	.571	47	12	3	0	2	123	161	6	56	53	16.0	5.71	70	.313	.381	12	.279	3	-20	-23	-0	-1.8

● JOHN SHEARON

Shearon, John M. b: 1870, Pittsburgh, Pa. d: 2/1/23, Bradford, Pa. Deb: 7/28/1891 ♦

YEAR	TM/L	W	L	PCT	G	GS	CG	SH	SV	IP	H	HR	BB	SO	RAT	ERA	ERA+	OAV	OOB	BH	AVG	PB	PR	/A	PD	TPI
1891	Cle-N	1	3	.250	6	5	4	0	0	46	57	2	24	19	16.0	3.52	98	.293	.373	30	.242	-0	-1	-0	-0	0.0

● GEORGE SHEARS

Shears, George Penfield b: 4/13/1890, Marshall, Mo. d: 11/12/78, Loveland, Colo. BR/TL, 6'3", 180 lbs. Deb: 4/24/12

YEAR	TM/L	W	L	PCT	G	GS	CG	SH	SV	IP	H	HR	BB	SO	RAT	ERA	ERA+	OAV	OOB	BH	AVG	PB	PR	/A	PD	TPI
1912	NY-A	0	0	—	4	0	0	0	0	15	24	1	11	9	21.0	5.40	67	.364	.455	1	.167	0	-3	-3	0	-0.3

● TOM SHEEHAN

Sheehan, Thomas Clancy b: 3/31/1894, Grand Ridge, Ill. d: 10/29/82, Chillicothe, Ohio BR/TR, 6'2.5", 190 lbs. Deb: 7/14/15 MC

YEAR	TM/L	W	L	PCT	G	GS	CG	SH	SV	IP	H	HR	BB	SO	RAT	ERA	ERA+	OAV	OOB	BH	AVG	PB	PR	/A	PD	TPI
1915	Phi-A	4	9	.308	15	13	8	1	0	102	131	1	38	22	15.0	4.15	71	.335	.395	4	.118	-3	-14	-14	-1	-1.7
1916	Phi-A	1	16	.059	38	17	8	0	0	188	197	2	94	54	14.0	3.69	78	.287	.374	7	.125	-2	-18	-17	3	-1.7
1921	NY-A	1	0	1.000	12	1	0	0	1	33	43	1	19	7	17.2	5.45	78	.326	.414	5	.625	2	-4	-4	2	-0.1
1924	Cin-N	9	11	.450	39	16	8	2	1	166^2	170	5	54	52	12.1	3.24	116	.269	.328	18	.310	4	12	10	-2	1.1
1925	Cin-N	1	0	1.000	10	3	1	0	1	29	37	3	12	5	15.2	8.07	51	.298	.360	1	.200	1	-12	-13	-1	-1.1
	Pit-N	1	1	.500	23	0	0	0	2	57^1	63	2	13	13	11.9	2.67	167	.286	.326	3	.150	-1	10	11	0	1.0
	Yr	2	1	.667	33	3	1	0	3	86^1	100	5	25	18	13.0	4.48	97	.291	.339	4	.160	-0	-2	-1	-1	-0.1
1926	Pit-N	0	2	.000	9	4	1	0	0	31	36	0	12	16	14.5	6.68	59	.298	.370	1	.111	-1	-10	-9	-0	-1.0
Total	6	17	39	.304	146	54	26	3	5	607	677	14	242	169	13.7	4.00	86	.294	.362	39	.205	0	-36	-36	1	-3.5

● ROLLIE SHELDON

Sheldon, Roland Frank b: 12/17/36, Putnam, Conn. BR/TR, 6'4", 190 lbs. Deb: 4/23/61

YEAR	TM/L	W	L	PCT	G	GS	CG	SH	SV	IP	H	HR	BB	SO	RAT	ERA	ERA+	OAV	OOB	BH	AVG	PB	PR	/A	PD	TPI
1961	NY-A	11	5	.688	35	21	6	2	0	162^2	149	17	55	84	11.4	3.60	103	.246	.311	7	.125	-2	8	2	1	0.1
1962	NY-A	7	8	.467	34	16	2	0	1	118	136	12	28	54	12.6	5.49	68	.289	.331	2	.077	0	-20	-23	-2	-2.4
1964	*NY-A	5	2	.714	19	12	3	0	1	102^1	92	18	18	57	9.8	3.61	100	.243	.279	3	.088	-2	0	0	1	-0.1
1965	NY-A	0	0	—	3	0	0	0	0	6^1	5	0	1	7	8.5	1.42	240	.238	.273	0	.000	-0	1	1	0	0.2
	KC-A	10	8	.556	32	29	4	1	0	186^2	180	22	56	105	11.7	3.95	88	.251	.312	4	.078	-3	-10	-10	-0	-1.3
	Yr	10	8	.556	35	29	4	1	0	193	185	22	57	112	11.6	3.87	90	.251	.310	4	.077	-3	-9	-8	0	-1.1
1966	KC-A	4	7	.364	14	13	1	1	0	69	73	3	26	26	13.0	3.13	109	.275	.342	2	.087	-1	2	2	0	0.1
	Bos-A	1	6	.143	23	10	1	0	0	79^2	106	15	23	38	14.8	4.97	77	.320	.368	2	.111	-1	-14	-10	0	-1.2
	Yr	5	13	.278	37	23	2	1	0	148^2	179	18	49	64	13.9	4.12	88	.297	.352	4	.098	-2	-11	-8	1	-1.1
Total	5	38	36	.514	160	101	17	4	2	724^2	741	87	207	371	11.9	4.09	89	.266	.320	20	.096	-9	-32	-36	0	-4.6

YEAR TM/L	W	L	PCT	G	GS	CG	SH	SV	IP	H	HR	BB	SO	RAT	ERA	ERA+	OAV	OOB	BH	AVG	PB	PR	/A	PD	TPI
● FRANK SHELLENBACK Shellenback, Frank Victor b: 12/16/1898, Joplin, Mo. d: 8/17/69, Newton, Mass. BR/TR, 6'2", 192 lbs. Deb: 5/08/18 C																									
1918 Chi-A	9	12	.429	28	21	10	2	2	182^{2}	180	1	74	47	12.7	2.66	103	.262	.338	7	.130	-1	2	2	-5	-0.5
1919 Chi-A	1	3	.250	8	4	2	0	0	35	40	1	16	10	14.4	5.14	62	.303	.378	1	.091	-0	-7	-8	-0	-0.8
Total 2	10	15	.400	36	25	12	2	2	217^{2}	220	2	90	57	13.0	3.06	92	.269	.344	8	.123	-1	-5	-6	-5	-1.3
● JIM SHELLENBACK Shellenback, James Philip b: 11/18/43, Riverside, Cal. BL/TL, 6'2", 200 lbs. Deb: 9/15/66 C																									
1966 Pit-N	0	0	—	2	0	0	0	0	3	3	2	3	0	18.0	9.00	40	.300	.462	0	—	0	-2	-2	0	-0.2
1967 Pit-N	1	1	.500	6	2	1	0	0	23^{1}	23	1	12	11	13.9	2.70	125	.250	.343	1	.167	-0	2	2	-0	0.2
1969 Pit-N	0	0	—	8	0	0	0	0	16^{2}	14	1	4	7	9.7	3.24	108	.233	.281	0	.000	-0	1	0	1	0.2
Was-A	4	7	.364	30	11	2	0	1	84^{2}	87	8	48	50	14.5	4.04	86	.268	.364	5	.185	-0	-4	-5	2	-0.4
1970 Was-A	6	7	.462	39	14	2	1	0	117^{1}	107	6	51	57	12.1	3.68	97	.246	.325	2	.067	-2	0	-2	-1	-0.4
1971 Was-A	3	11	.214	40	15	3	1	0	120	123	10	49	47	13.1	3.53	94	.267	.342	5	.167	0	-1	-3	1	-0.2
1972 Tex-A	2	4	.333	22	6	0	0	1	57	46	6	16	30	10.1	3.47	87	.221	.283	1	.100	-0	-3	-3	-1	-0.4
1973 Tex-A	0	0	—	2	0	0	0	0	1^{2}	0	0	0	3	0.0	0.00	—	.000	.000	0	—	0	1	1	0	0.2
1974 Tex-A	0	0	—	11	0	0	0	0	24^{2}	30	5	12	14	15.7	5.84	61	.306	.387	0	—	0	-6	-6	0	-0.6
1977 Min-A	0	0	—	5	0	0	0	0	5^{2}	10	1	5	3	23.8	7.94	50	.385	.484	0	—	0	-2	-2	0	-0.2
Total 9	16	30	.348	165	48	8	2	2	454	443	40	200	222	12.9	3.81	89	.258	.338	14	.135	-2	-14	-21	3	-1.8
● BERT SHEPARD Shepard, Robert Earl b: 6/28/20, Dana, Ind. BL/TL, 5'11", 185 lbs. Deb: 8/04/45																									
1945 Was-A	0	0	—	1	0	0	0	0	5^{1}	3	0	1	2	8.4	1.69	184	.167	.250	0	.000	-0	1	1	0	0.1
● KEITH SHEPHERD Shepherd, Keith Wayne b: 1/21/68, Wabash, Ind. BR/TR, 6'2", 205 lbs. Deb: 9/06/92																									
1992 Phi-N	1	1	.500	12	0	0	0	2	22	19	0	6	10	10.2	3.27	107	.244	.298	0	—	0	1	1	0	0.1
● BILL SHERDEL Sherdel, William Henry "Wee Willie" b: 8/15/1896, McSherrystown, Pa d: 11/14/68, McSherrystown, Pa BL/TL, 5'10", 160 lbs. Deb: 4/22/18																									
1918 StL-N	6	12	.333	35	17	9	1	0	182^{1}	174	3	49	40	11.2	2.71	100	.259	.313	15	.242	3	1	-0	-2	0.2
1919 StL-N	5	9	.357	36	10	7	0	1	137^{1}	137	3	42	52	11.9	3.47	80	.270	.328	13	.271	2	-9	-10	1	-0.8
1920 StL-N	11	10	.524	43	7	4	0	**6**	170	183	1	40	74	12.4	3.28	91	.297	.350	14	.222	2	-3	-6	1	-0.3
1921 StL-N	9	8	.529	38	8	5	1	1	144^{1}	137	7	38	57	11.1	3.18	115	.247	.299	5	.114	-2	10	8	1	0.6
1922 StL-N	17	13	.567	47	31	15	3	2	242	298	12	62	79	13.6	3.87	100	.303	.348	17	.193	1	6	-0	-3	-0.3
1923 StL-N	15	13	.536	39	26	14	0	2	225	270	15	59	78	13.4	4.32	90	.296	.343	28	.337	8	-8	-10	-3	-0.5
1924 StL-N	8	9	.471	35	10	6	0	1	168^{2}	188	9	38	57	12.3	3.42	111	.291	.335	15	.200	2	8	7	-2	0.7
1925 StL-N	15	6	**.714**	32	21	17	2	1	200	216	8	42	53	11.7	3.11	139	.277	.316	15	.205	2	26	27	-1	2.8
1926 *StL-N	16	12	.571	34	29	17	3	0	234^{2}	255	15	49	59	11.9	3.49	112	.278	.318	22	.244	2	9	11	-3	1.0
1927 StL-N	17	12	.586	39	28	18	0	**6**	232^{1}	241	17	48	59	11.3	3.53	112	.269	.308	14	.194	1	10	11	-4	0.8
1928 *StL-N	21	10	.677	38	27	20	0	**5**	248^{2}	251	17	56	72	11.2	2.86	140	.261	.303	19	.226	4	31	31	-5	3.1
1929 StL-N	10	15	.400	33	22	11	1	0	195^{2}	278	14	58	69	15.5	5.93	79	.337	.382	16	.229	2	-26	-28	-2	-2.5
1930 StL-N	3	2	.600	13	7	1	0	0	64	86	5	13	29	14.1	4.64	108	.325	.358	2	.105	-1	2	3	-1	0.1
Bos-N	6	5	.545	21	14	7	0	1	119^{1}	131	10	30	26	12.3	4.75	104	.283	.329	4	.095	-4	3	2	-1	-0.2
Yr	9	7	.563	34	21	8	0	1	183^{1}	217	15	43	55	12.9	4.71	105	.298	.339	6	.098	-5	5	5	-1	-0.1
1931 Bos-N	6	10	.375	27	16	8	0	0	137^{2}	163	13	35	34	13.0	4.25	89	.294	.337	14	.304	3	-6	-7	-2	-0.6
1932 Bos-N	0	0	—	1	0	0	0	0	1^{2}	3	0	1	0	21.6	0.00	—	.375	.444	0	—	0	1	1	-0	0.1
StL-N	0	0	—	3	0	0	0	0	5^{2}	7	0	1	1	12.7	4.76	83	.304	.333	1	1.000	1	-1	-1	0	0.0
Yr	0	0	—	4	0	0	0	0	7^{1}	10	0	2	1	14.7	3.68	106	.323	.364	1	1.000	1	0	0	0	0.1
Total 15	165	146	.531	514	273	159	11	26	2709^{1}	3018	149	661	839	12.4	3.72	103	.285	.330	214	.223	27	55	38	-25	4.2
● ROY SHERID Sherid, Royden Richard b: 1/25/07, Norristown, Pa. d: 2/28/82, Parker Ford, Pa. BR/TR, 6'2", 185 lbs. Deb: 5/11/29																									
1929 NY-A	6	6	.500	33	15	9	0	1	154^{2}	165	6	55	51	13.1	3.61	107	.277	.343	9	.180	-0	11	4	-1	0.3
1930 NY-A	12	13	.480	37	21	8	0	4	184	214	13	87	59	15.0	5.23	82	.289	.368	7	.101	-6	-12	-19	-1	-2.3
1931 NY-A	5	5	.500	17	8	3	0	2	74^{1}	94	4	24	39	14.7	5.69	70	.306	.362	10	.333	2	-11	-14	0	-1.1
Total 3	23	24	.489	87	44	20	0	7	413	473	23	166	149	14.2	4.71	87	.288	.358	26	.174	-4	-12	-29	-2	-3.1
● JOE SHERMAN Sherman, Joel Powers b: 11/4/1890, Yarmouth, Mass. d: 12/21/87, Cape Coral, Fla. BR/TR, 6', 165 lbs. Deb: 9/24/15																									
1915 Phi-A	1	0	1.000	2	1	1	0	0	15	15	0	1	5	10.8	2.40	122	.259	.295	2	.333	1	1	1	-0	0.1
● DAN SHERMAN Sherman, Lester Daniel "Babe" b: 5/9/1890, Hubbardsville, N.Y. d: 9/16/55, Highland Park, Mich. BR/TR, 5'6", 145 lbs. Deb: 6/04/14																									
1914 Chi-F	0	1	.000	1	1	0	0	0	0^{1}	0	0	2	0	54.0	0.00	—	.000	.667	0	—	0	0	0	0	0.0
● TIM SHERRILL Sherrill, Timothy Shawn b: 9/10/65, Harrison, Ark. BL/TL, 5'11", 170 lbs. Deb: 8/14/90																									
1990 StL-N	0	0	—	8	0	0	0	0	4^{1}	10	0	3	3	27.0	6.23	61	.476	.542	0	—	0	-1	-1	0	-0.1
1991 StL-N	0	0	—	10	0	0	0	0	14^{1}	20	2	3	4	15.7	8.16	46	.339	.391	0	—	0	-7	-7	0	-0.7
Total 2	0	0	—	18	0	0	0	0	18^{2}	30	2	6	7	18.3	7.71	48	.375	.432	0	—	0	-8	-8	0	-0.8
● FRED SHERRY Sherry, Fred Peter (b: Fred Peter Schuerholz) b: 1/13/1889, Honesdale, Pa. d: 7/27/75, Honesdale, Pa. BR/TR, 6', 170 lbs. Deb: 4/25/11																									
1911 Was-A	0	4	.000	10	3	2	0	0	52^{1}	63	1	19	20	14.1	4.30	76	.310	.369	3	.158	-0	-6	-6	0	-0.6
● LARRY SHERRY Sherry, Lawrence b: 7/25/35, Los Angeles, Cal. BR/TR, 6'2", 204 lbs. Deb: 4/17/58 FC																									
1958 LA-N	0	0	—	5	0	0	0	0	4^{1}	10	0	7	2	37.4	12.46	33	.476	.621	0	—	0	-4	-4	0	-0.4
1959 *LA-N	7	2	.778	23	9	1	1	3	94^{1}	75	9	43	72	11.4	2.19	193	.218	.308	7	.219	2	18	21	-1	2.4
1960 LA-N	14	10	.583	57	3	1	0	7	142^{1}	125	14	82	114	13.5	3.79	105	.238	.347	6	.162	1	-1	3	1	0.4
1961 LA-N	4	4	.500	53	1	0	0	15	94^{2}	90	10	39	79	12.6	3.90	111	.252	.333	2	.154	-0	1	5	-2	0.3
1962 LA-N	7	3	.700	58	0	0	0	11	90	81	8	44	71	13.1	3.20	113	.241	.339	2	.118	-0	7	4	-0	0.4
1963 LA-N	2	6	.250	36	3	0	0	3	79^{2}	82	8	24	47	12.4	3.73	81	.265	.325	1	.111	1	-4	-6	-0	-0.6
1964 Det-A	7	5	.583	38	0	0	0	11	66^{1}	52	7	37	58	12.5	3.66	100	.216	.327	0	.000	-2	-0	-0	-0	-0.2
1965 Det-A	3	6	.333	39	0	0	0	5	78^{1}	71	5	40	46	12.9	3.10	112	.254	.349	3	.300	2	3	3	0	0.6
1966 Det-A	8	5	.615	55	0	0	0	20	77^{2}	66	8	36	63	12.2	3.82	91	.232	.325	4	.400	2	-3	-3	-1	-0.2
1967 Det-A	0	1	.000	20	0	0	0	1	28	35	3	7	20	13.8	6.43	51	.289	.333	0	.000	-0	-10	-10	0	-1.0
Hou-N	1	2	.333	29	0	0	0	6	40^{2}	53	4	13	32	14.8	4.87	68	.327	.381	0	.000	-1	-7	-7	1	-0.7
1968 Cal-A	0	0	—	3	0	0	0	0	3	7	2	2	2	27.0	6.00	49	.467	.529	0	—	0	-1	-1	-0	-0.1
Total 11	53	44	.546	416	16	2	1	82	799^{1}	747	78	374	606	13.0	3.67	101	.249	.339	25	.169	5	0	5	-2	0.9
● BEN SHIELDS Shields, Benjamin Cowan "Big Ben" or "Lefty" b: 6/17/03, Huntersville, N.C d: 1/24/82, Woodruff, S.C. BR/TL, 6'1.5", 195 lbs. Deb: 4/17/24																									
1924 NY-A	0	0	—	2	0	0	0	0	2	6	0	2	3	36.0	27.00	15	.545	.615	0	—	0	-5	-5	-0	-0.4
1925 NY-A	3	0	1.000	4	2	2	0	0	24	24	2	12	5	14.3	4.88	87	.267	.365	1	.125	-1	-1	-2	-1	-0.3
1930 Bos-A	0	0	—	3	0	0	0	0	10	16	0	6	1	19.8	9.00	51	.400	.478	0	.000	-1	-5	-5	0	-0.4
1931 Phi-N	1	0	1.000	4	0	0	0	0	5^{1}	9	1	7	0	27.0	15.19	28	.391	.533	0	.000	-0	-7	-6	-0	-0.6
Total 4	4	0	1.000	13	2	2	0	0	41^{1}	55	3	27	9	18.3	8.27	53	.335	.435	1	.077	-2	-18	-18	-1	-1.7
● CHARLIE SHIELDS Shields, Charles S. b: 12/10/1879, Jackson, Tenn. d: 8/27/53, Memphis, Tenn. BL/TL, Deb: 4/23/02																									
1902 Bal-A	4	11	.267	23	15	10	1	1	142^{1}	201	7	32	28	14.9	4.24	89	.333	.368	8	.167	-1	-10	-7	-4	-1.2
StL-A	3	0	1.000	4	4	3	0	0	30	37	1	7	6	13.2	3.30	107	.303	.341	6	.462	2	1	1	-1	0.3
Yr	7	11	.389	27	19	13	1	1	172^{1}	238	8	39	34	14.5	4.07	92	.327	.361	14	.230	1	-10	-7	-5	-0.9
1907 StL-N	0	2	.000	3	2	0	0	0	6^{2}	12	0	7	1	28.4	9.45	26	.444	.583	0	.000	-0	-5	-5	0	-0.5
Total 2	7	13	.350	30	21	13	1	1	179	250	8	46	35	15.1	4.27	86	.332	.373	14	.222	1	-15	-12	-4	-1.4

● STEVE SHIELDS
Shields, Stephen Mack b: 11/30/58, Gasden, Ala. BR/TR, 6'5", 230 lbs. Deb: 6/01/85

YEAR	TM/L	W	L	PCT	G	GS	CG	SH	SV	IP	H	HR	BB	SO	RAT	ERA	ERA+	OAV	OOB	BH	AVG	PB	PR	/A	PD	TPI
1985	Atl-N	1	2	.333	23	6	0	0	0	68	86	9	32	29	15.8	5.16	75	.320	.394	2	.111	-1	-12	-10	-1	-1.2
1986	Atl-N	0	0	—	6	0	0	0	0	12^2	13	4	7	6	14.2	7.11	56	.271	.364	0	.000	-0	-5	-4	-0	-0.5
	KC-A	0	0	—	3	0	0	0	0	8^2	3	1	4	2	7.3	2.08	205	.111	.226	0	—	0	2	2	-0	0.1
1987	Sea-A	2	0	1.000	20	0	0	0	3	30	43	7	12	22	16.5	6.60	71	.333	.390	0	—	0	-7	-6	0	-0.9
1988	NY-A	5	5	.500	39	0	0	0	0	82^1	96	8	30	55	14.0	4.37	90	.298	.362	0	—	0	-4	-4	0	-0.4
1989	Min-A	0	1	.000	11	0	0	0	0	17^1	28	3	6	12	17.7	7.79	53	.354	.400	0	—	0	-8	-7	0	-0.8
Total	5	8	8	.500	102	6	0	0	3	219	269	32	91	126	14.9	5.26	77	.308	.375	2	.105	-1	-33	-29	-1	-3.7

● VINCE SHIELDS
Shields, Vincent William
b: 11/18/1900, Fredericton, N.B., Canada d: 10/17/52, Plaster Rock, N.B. Canada BL/TR, 5'11", 185 lbs. Deb: 9/20/24

YEAR	TM/L	W	L	PCT	G	GS	CG	SH	SV	IP	H	HR	BB	SO	RAT	ERA	ERA+	OAV	OOB	BH	AVG	PB	PR	/A	PD	TPI
1924	StL-N	1	1	.500	2	1	0	0	0	12	10	1	3	4	12.0	3.00	126	.227	.320	2	.400	0	1	1	-1	0.1

● GARLAND SHIFFLETT
Shifflett, Garland Jessie "Duck" b: 3/28/35, Elkton, Va. BR/TR, 5'10.5", 165 lbs. Deb: 4/22/57

YEAR	TM/L	W	L	PCT	G	GS	CG	SH	SV	IP	H	HR	BB	SO	RAT	ERA	ERA+	OAV	OOB	BH	AVG	PB	PR	/A	PD	TPI
1957	Was-A	0	0	—	6	1	0	0	0	8	6	0	10	2	18.0	10.13	38	.222	.432	0	—	0	-6	-6	-0	-0.6
1964	Min-A	0	2	.000	10	0	0	0	1	17^2	22	1	7	8	15.3	4.58	78	.297	.366	0	.000	-0	-2	-2	0	-0.2
Total	2	0	2	.000	16	1	0	0	1	25^2	28	1	17	10	16.1	6.31	58	.277	.387	0	.000	-0	-8	-8	0	-0.8

● STEVE SHIFFLETT
Shifflett, Stephen Earl b: 1/5/66, Kansas City, Mo. BR/TR, 6'1", 205 lbs. Deb: 7/03/92

YEAR	TM/L	W	L	PCT	G	GS	CG	SH	SV	IP	H	HR	BB	SO	RAT	ERA	ERA+	OAV	OOB	BH	AVG	PB	PR	/A	PD	TPI
1992	KC-A	1	4	.200	34	0	0	0	0	52	55	6	17	25	12.8	2.60	153	.279	.343	0	—	0	8	8	0	0.8

● RAY SHINES
Shines, Anthony Raymond b: 7/18/56, Durham, N.C. BB/TR, 6'1", 210 lbs. Deb: 9/09/83 ♦

YEAR	TM/L	W	L	PCT	G	GS	CG	SH	SV	IP	H	HR	BB	SO	RAT	ERA	ERA+	OAV	OOB	BH	AVG	PB	PR	/A	PD	TPI
1985	Mon-N	0	0	—	1	0	0	0	0	1	1	0	0	0	9.0	0.00	—	.250	.250	6	.120	-0	0	0	-0	0.0

● DAVE SHIPANOFF
Shipanoff, David Noel b: 11/13/59, Edmonton, Alb., Can. BR/TR, 6'2", 185 lbs. Deb: 8/09/85

YEAR	TM/L	W	L	PCT	G	GS	CG	SH	SV	IP	H	HR	BB	SO	RAT	ERA	ERA+	OAV	OOB	BH	AVG	PB	PR	/A	PD	TPI
1985	Phi-N	1	2	.333	26	0	0	0	3	36^1	33	3	16	26	12.4	3.22	114	.231	.313	0	.000	-0	1	2	-0	0.1

● JOE SHIPLEY
Shipley, Joseph Clark "Moses" b: 5/9/35, Morristown, Tenn. BR/TR, 6'4", 210 lbs. Deb: 7/14/58

YEAR	TM/L	W	L	PCT	G	GS	CG	SH	SV	IP	H	HR	BB	SO	RAT	ERA	ERA+	OAV	OOB	BH	AVG	PB	PR	/A	PD	TPI
1958	SF-N	0	0	—	1	0	0	0	0	1^1	3	0	3	0	54.0	33.75	11	.429	.667	0	—	0	-4	-4	-0	-0.4
1959	SF-N	0	0	—	10	1	0	0	0	18	16	2	17	11	17.0	4.50	85	.239	.400	0	.000	-0	-1	-1	-0	-0.2
1960	SF-N	0	0	—	15	0	0	0	0	20	20	2	9	9	14.4	5.40	64	.274	.376	0	—	0	-4	-4	1	-0.4
1963	Chi-A	0	1	.000	3	0	0	0	0	4^2	9	0	6	3	28.9	5.79	61	.409	.536	0	.000	-0	-1	-1	0	-0.1
Total	4	0	1	.000	29	1	0	0	0	44	48	4	35	23	18.2	5.93	61	.284	.424	0	.000	-1	-10	-11	0	-1.1

● DUKE SHIREY
Shirey, Clair Lee b: 6/20/1898, Jersey Shore, Pa. d: 9/1/62, Hagerstown, Pa. BR/TR, 6'1", 175 lbs. Deb: 9/28/20

YEAR	TM/L	W	L	PCT	G	GS	CG	SH	SV	IP	H	HR	BB	SO	RAT	ERA	ERA+	OAV	OOB	BH	AVG	PB	PR	/A	PD	TPI
1920	Was-A	0	1	.000	2	1	0	0	0	4	5	0	2	0	18.0	6.75	55	.313	.421	0	.000	-0	-1	-1	-0	-0.2

● TEX SHIRLEY
Shirley, Alvis Newman b: 4/25/18, Birthright, Tex. BB/TR, 6'1", 175 lbs. Deb: 9/06/41

YEAR	TM/L	W	L	PCT	G	GS	CG	SH	SV	IP	H	HR	BB	SO	RAT	ERA	ERA+	OAV	OOB	BH	AVG	PB	PR	/A	PD	TPI
1941	Phi-A	0	1	.000	5	0	0	0	1	7^1	8	1	6	1	17.2	2.45	171	.286	.412	0	.000	-0	1	1	0	0.2
1942	Phi-A	0	1	.000	15	1	0	0	1	35^2	37	0	22	10	15.4	5.30	71	.272	.381	0	.000	-1	-7	-6	-1	-0.8
1944	*StL-A	5	4	.556	23	11	2	1	0	80^1	59	4	64	35	13.9	4.15	87	.203	.348	4	.143	-2	-6	-5	-1	-0.8
1945	StL-A	8	12	.400	32	24	10	2	0	183^2	191	8	93	77	14.0	3.63	97	.274	.360	20	.286	2	-5	-2	-1	-0.1
1946	StL-A	6	12	.333	27	18	7	0	0	139^2	148	7	105	45	16.4	4.96	75	.273	.391	10	.196	-0	-23	-19	-1	-2.0
Total	5	19	30	.388	102	54	19	3	2	446^2	443	20	290	168	14.9	4.25	85	.261	.371	34	.214	-1	-39	-31	-3	-3.5

● BOB SHIRLEY
Shirley, Robert Charles b: 6/25/54, Cushing, Okla. BR/TL, 5'11", 185 lbs. Deb: 4/10/77

YEAR	TM/L	W	L	PCT	G	GS	CG	SH	SV	IP	H	HR	BB	SO	RAT	ERA	ERA+	OAV	OOB	BH	AVG	PB	PR	/A	PD	TPI
1977	SD-N	12	18	.400	39	35	1	0	0	214	215	22	100	146	13.4	3.70	96	.259	.341	9	.122	-2	5	-4	1	-0.5
1978	SD-N	8	11	.421	50	20	2	0	5	166	164	10	61	102	12.4	3.69	90	.262	.330	5	.125	0	-2	-7	2	-0.5
1979	SD-N	8	16	.333	49	25	4	1	0	205	196	15	59	117	11.5	3.38	104	.257	.316	5	.091	-2	8	3	0	0.2
1980	SD-N	11	12	.478	59	12	3	0	7	137	143	12	54	67	12.9	3.55	97	.276	.344	1	.033	-2	1	-2	2	-0.2
1981	StL-N	6	4	.600	28	11	1	0	1	79^1	78	6	34	36	12.8	4.08	87	.260	.337	3	.136	-1	-5	-5	-1	-0.7
1982	Cin-N	8	13	.381	41	20	1	0	0	152^2	138	17	73	89	12.6	3.60	103	.248	.338	6	.143	-1	0	2	1	0.2
1983	NY-A	5	8	.385	25	17	1	1	0	108	122	10	36	53	13.2	5.08	77	.293	.350	0	—	0	-12	-14	1	-1.2
1984	NY-A	3	3	.500	41	7	1	0	0	114^1	119	8	38	48	12.4	3.38	112	.274	.333	0	—	0	8	5	0	0.8
1985	NY-A	5	5	.500	48	8	2	0	2	109	103	5	26	55	10.7	2.64	151	.251	.295	0	—	0	18	16	-1	1.7
1986	NY-A	0	4	.000	39	6	0	0	3	105^1	108	13	40	64	12.9	5.04	81	.271	.342	0	—	0	-10	-11	1	-1.0
1987	NY-A	1	0	1.000	12	1	0	0	0	34	36	4	16	12	13.8	4.50	97	.277	.356	0	—	0	-0	-0	-1	0.0
	KC-A	0	0	—	3	0	0	0	0	7^1	10	5	6	1	19.6	14.73	31	.323	.432	0	—	0	-8	-8	-0	-0.8
	Yr	1	0	1.000	15	1	0	0	0	41^1	46	9	22	13	14.8	6.31	70	.275	.360	0	—	0	-9	-9	-1	-0.8
Total	11	67	94	.416	434	162	16	2	18	1432	1432	127	543	790	12.5	3.82	96	.264	.334	29	.110	-7	2	-24	5	-2.0

● STEVE SHIRLEY
Shirley, Steven Brian b: 10/12/56, San Francsico, Cal. BL/TL, 6', 185 lbs. Deb: 6/21/82

YEAR	TM/L	W	L	PCT	G	GS	CG	SH	SV	IP	H	HR	BB	SO	RAT	ERA	ERA+	OAV	OOB	BH	AVG	PB	PR	/A	PD	TPI
1982	LA-N	1	1	.500	11	0	0	0	0	12^2	15	0	7	8	15.6	4.26	81	.300	.386	1	1.000	0	-1	-1	0	0.0

● GEORGE SHOCH
Shoch, George Quintus b: 1/6/1859, Philadelphia, Pa. d: 9/30/37, Philadelphia, Pa. BR/TR, 5'6", 158 lbs. Deb: 9/10/1886 ♦

YEAR	TM/L	W	L	PCT	G	GS	CG	SH	SV	IP	H	HR	BB	SO	RAT	ERA	ERA+	OAV	OOB	BH	AVG	PB	PR	/A	PD	TPI
1888	Was-N	0	0	—	1	0	0	0	0	3	2	0	1	0	9.0	0.00	—	.167	.231	58	.183	0	1	1	-0	0.1

● URBAN SHOCKER
Shocker, Urban James (b: Urbain Jacques Shockcor)
b: 8/22/1890, Cleveland, Ohio d: 9/9/28, Denver, Colo. BR/TR, 5'10", 170 lbs. Deb: 4/24/16

YEAR	TM/L	W	L	PCT	G	GS	CG	SH	SV	IP	H	HR	BB	SO	RAT	ERA	ERA+	OAV	OOB	BH	AVG	PB	PR	/A	PD	TPI
1916	NY-A	4	3	.571	12	9	4	1	0	82^1	67	2	32	43	11.5	2.62	110	.230	.319	4	.190	1	2	2	-0	0.4
1917	NY-A	8	5	.615	26	13	7	0	1	145	124	4	46	68	10.6	2.61	103	.241	.303	8	.178	-1	1	1	2	0.2
1918	StL-A	6	5	.545	14	9	7	0	2	94^2	69	0	40	33	10.5	1.81	152	.209	.296	11	.324	4	10	10	1	1.7
1919	StL-A	13	11	.542	30	25	14	5	0	211	193	6	55	86	10.7	2.69	123	.244	.296	8	.138	-0	13	15	-1	1.4
1920	StL-A	20	10	.667	38	28	22	5	**5**	245^2	224	10	70	107	10.9	2.71	145	.248	.305	18	.225	3	30	33	-0	3.5
1921	StL-A	**27**	12	.692	47	38	30	4	4	326^2	345	21	86	132	12.0	3.55	126	.270	.319	27	.260	6	26	34	3	4.0
1922	StL-A	24	17	.585	48	38	29	2	3	348	365	22	57	**149**	11.0	2.97	139	.272	.304	22	.191	2	41	45	-3	4.5
1923	StL-A	20	12	.625	43	35	24	3	5	277^1	292	12	49	109	**11.2**	3.41	122	.272	**.306**	16	.200	2	18	24	-3	2.2
1924	StL-A	16	13	.552	40	33	17	4	1	246^1	270	11	52	88	11.9	4.20	107	.277	.315	16	.239	5	1	9	-2	1.1
1925	NY-A	12	12	.500	41	30	15	2	2	244^1	278	17	58	74	12.5	3.65	117	.294	.336	11	.172	5	20	17	-2	1.9
1926	*NY-A	19	11	.633	41	32	18	0	2	258^1	272	13	71	59	12.0	3.38	114	.269	.318	13	.171	1	18	14	-2	1.3
1927	NY-A	18	6	.750	31	27	13	2	0	200	207	8	41	35	11.2	2.84	136	.268	.306	13	.241	3	29	23	-2	2.3
1928	NY-A	0	0	—	1	0	0	0	0	2	3	0	0	0	13.5	0.00	—	.429	.429	0	—	0	1	1	-0	0.1
Total	13	187	117	.615	412	317	200	28	25	2681^2	2709	126	657	983	11.4	3.17	124	.265	.311	167	.209	29	210	226	-9	24.6

● MILT SHOFFNER
Shoffner, Milburn James b: 11/13/05, Sherman, Tex. d: 1/19/78, Madison, Ohio BL/TL, 6'1.5", 184 lbs. Deb: 7/20/29

YEAR	TM/L	W	L	PCT	G	GS	CG	SH	SV	IP	H	HR	BB	SO	RAT	ERA	ERA+	OAV	OOB	BH	AVG	PB	PR	/A	PD	TPI
1929	Cle-A	2	3	.400	11	3	1	0	0	44^2	46	4	22	15	14.3	5.04	88	.284	.380	0	.000	-3	-4	-3	0	-0.5
1930	Cle-A	3	4	.429	24	10	1	0	0	84^2	129	8	50	17	19.1	7.97	61	.362	.442	7	.212	1	-31	-30	-0	-2.4
1931	Cle-A	2	3	.400	12	4	1	0	0	41	55	4	26	12	18.2	7.24	64	.320	.415	1	.077	-1	-13	-12	-0	-1.2
1937	Bos-N	3	1	.750	6	5	3	1	1	42^2	38	1	9	13	10.1	2.53	142	.239	.284	2	.125	1	7	5	1	0.7
1938	Bos-N	8	7	.533	26	15	9	1	1	139^2	147	7	36	49	11.9	3.54	97	.270	.317	12	.211	3	4	-2	-2	-0.1
1939	Bos-N	4	6	.400	25	11	7	0	1	132^1	133	4	42	51	12.0	3.13	118	.265	.324	7	.159	-0	12	8	0	0.9
	Cin-N	2	2	.500	10	3	0	0	0	37^2	43	3	11	6	13.4	3.35	115	.289	.346	1	.091	-1	2	2	-0	0.1
	Yr	6	8	.429	35	14	7	0	1	170	176	7	53	57	12.2	3.18	117	.270	.327	8	.145	-1	14	10	0	1.0
1940	Cin-N	1	0	1.000	20	0	0	0	0	54^1	56	3	18	17	12.3	5.63	67	.268	.326	2	.125	-1	-11	-11	-1	-1.2
Total	7	25	26	.490	134	51	22	2	3	577	647	34	214	180	13.6	4.59	85	.287	.352	32	.156	-1	-35	-43	-2	-3.7

● **ERNIE SHORE** Shore, Ernest Grady b: 3/24/1891, East Bend, N.C. d: 9/24/80, Winston-Salem, N.C. BR/TR, 6'4", 220 lbs. Deb: 6/20/12

YEAR	TM/L	W	L	PCT	G	GS	CG	SH	SV	IP	H	HR	BB	SO	RAT	ERA	ERA+	OAV	OOB	BH	AVG	PB	PR	/A	PD	TPI
1912	NY-N	0	0	—	1	0	0	0	1	1	8	1	1	1	81.0	27.00	13	.667	.692	0	—	0	-3	-3	-0	-0.2
1914	Bos-A	10	5	.667	20	16	10	1	1	139^{2}	103	1	34	51	9.2	2.00	135	.204	.261	5	.102	-3	12	11	2	1.1
1915	*Bos-A	19	8	.704	38	32	17	4	0	247	207	3	66	102	10.1	1.64	170	.228	.283	8	.101	-3	36	31	4	3.6
1916	*Bos-A	16	10	.615	38	28	10	3	1	225^{2}	221	1	49	62	10.9	2.63	105	.259	.302	7	.091	-5	5	3	5	0.4
1917	Bos-A	13	10	.565	29	27	14	1	1	226^{2}	201	1	55	57	10.6	2.22	116	.240	.297	13	.167	-1	11	9	3	1.1
1919	NY-A	5	8	.385	20	13	3	0	0	95	105	4	44	24	14.2	4.17	77	.288	.366	4	.143	-1	-10	-10	0	-1.2
1920	NY-A	2	2	.500	14	5	2	0	1	44^{1}	61	1	21	12	16.8	4.87	78	.333	.405	2	.182	0	-5	-5	1	-0.4
Total	7	65	43	.602	160	121	56	9	5	979^{1}	906	12	270	309	11.1	2.47	113	.247	.304	39	.121	-13	45	36	14	4.4

● **RAY SHORE** Shore, Raymond Everett b: 6/9/21, Cincinnati, Ohio BR/TR, 6'3", 210 lbs. Deb: 9/21/46 C

YEAR	TM/L	W	L	PCT	G	GS	CG	SH	SV	IP	H	HR	BB	SO	RAT	ERA	ERA+	OAV	OOB	BH	AVG	PB	PR	/A	PD	TPI
1946	StL-A	0	0	—	1	0	0	0	0	1	3	0	1	1	36.0	18.00	21	.500	.571	0	—	0	-2	-2	0	-0.2
1948	StL-A	1	2	.333	17	4	0	0	0	38	40	2	35	12	18.7	6.39	71	.270	.422	0	.000	-2	-9	-8	0	-0.8
1949	StL-A	0	1	.000	13	0	0	0	0	23^{1}	27	3	31	13	23.1	10.80	42	.297	.484	0	.000	-1	-17	-16	1	-1.5
Total	3	1	3	.250	31	4	0	0	0	62^{1}	70	5	67	26	20.6	8.23	55	.286	.450	0	.000	-2	-28	-26	1	-2.5

● **BILL SHORES** Shores, William David b: 5/26/04, Abilene, Tex. d: 2/19/84, Purcell, Okla. BR/TR, 6', 185 lbs. Deb: 4/11/28

YEAR	TM/L	W	L	PCT	G	GS	CG	SH	SV	IP	H	HR	BB	SO	RAT	ERA	ERA+	OAV	OOB	BH	AVG	PB	PR	/A	PD	TPI
1928	Phi-A	1	1	.500	3	2	1	0	0	14	13	0	7	5	12.9	3.21	125	.250	.339	0	.000	-1	1	1	-0	0.0
1929	Phi-A	11	6	.647	39	13	5	1	7	152^{2}	150	9	59	49	12.5	3.60	118	.262	.334	5	.125	-2	11	11	-1	0.7
1930	*Phi-A	12	4	.750	31	19	7	1	0	159	169	11	70	48	13.7	4.19	112	.276	.353	11	.193	-2	8	9	0	0.6
1931	Phi-A	0	3	.000	6	2	0	0	0	16	26	3	10	2	20.3	5.06	89	.361	.439	1	.333	0	-1	-1	0	-0.1
1933	NY-N	2	1	.667	8	3	1	0	0	36^{2}	41	4	14	20	13.5	3.93	82	.291	.355	3	.273	1	-2	-3	1	-0.1
1936	Chi-A	0	0	—	9	0	0	0	0	17	26	1	8	5	18.0	9.53	55	.356	.420	1	.200	-0	-8	-8	0	-0.7
Total	6	26	15	.634	96	39	14	2	7	395^{1}	425	28	168	129	13.6	4.17	105	.279	.353	21	.174	-4	8	8	1	0.4

● **CHRIS SHORT** Short, Christopher Joseph b: 9/19/37, Milford, Del. d: 8/1/91, Wilmington, Del. BR/TL, 6'4", 205 lbs. Deb: 4/19/59

YEAR	TM/L	W	L	PCT	G	GS	CG	SH	SV	IP	H	HR	BB	SO	RAT	ERA	ERA+	OAV	OOB	BH	AVG	PB	PR	/A	PD	TPI
1959	Phi-N	0	0	—	3	2	0	0	0	14^{1}	19	3	10	8	18.8	8.16	50	.317	.423	0	.000	-1	-7	-6	-0	-0.6
1960	Phi-N	6	9	.400	42	10	2	0	3	107^{1}	101	8	52	54	13.1	3.94	99	.249	.339	0	.000	-3	-2	-1	0	-0.4
1961	Phi-N	6	12	.333	39	16	1	0	1	127^{1}	157	12	71	80	16.3	5.94	69	.304	.391	6	.162	-1	-27	-26	-1	-2.6
1962	Phi-N	11	9	.550	47	12	4	0	3	142	149	13	56	91	13.5	3.42	113	.272	.348	8	.222	1	8	7	0	0.8
1963	Phi-N	9	12	.429	38	27	6	3	0	198	185	12	69	160	11.7	2.95	109	.248	.315	7	.106	-2	7	6	4	0.9
1964	Phi-N★	17	9	.654	42	31	12	4	2	220^{2}	174	10	51	181	9.3	2.20	158	.217	.268	7	.108	-1	33	31	-1	3.2
1965	Phi-N	18	11	.621	47	40	15	5	2	297^{1}	260	18	89	237	10.7	2.82	123	.235	.295	13	.131	-2	24	21	-3	1.8
1966	Phi-N	20	10	.667	42	39	19	4	0	272	257	28	68	177	11.1	3.54	102	.250	.302	22	.208	1	2	2	0	0.3
1967	Phi-N★	9	11	.450	29	26	8	2	1	199^{1}	163	9	74	142	10.9	2.39	142	.225	.300	6	.091	-2	22	22	0	2.3
1968	Phi-N	19	13	.594	42	36	9	2	1	269^{2}	236	25	81	202	10.9	2.94	102	.236	.299	12	.152	0	1	2	-1	0.1
1969	Phi-N	0	0	—	2	2	0	0	0	10	11	2	4	5	14.4	7.20	49	.282	.364	0	.000	-0	-4	-4	0	-0.4
1970	Phi-N	9	16	.360	36	34	7	2	1	199	211	13	66	133	12.8	4.30	93	.272	.334	3	.049	-5	-6	-7	-2	-1.4
1971	Phi-N	7	14	.333	31	26	5	2	1	173	182	22	63	95	12.9	3.85	92	.274	.339	4	.083	-1	-7	-6	-1	-0.9
1972	Phi-N	1	1	.500	19	0	0	0	1	23	24	3	8	20	12.5	3.91	92	.267	.327	0	—	0	-1	-1	-0	-0.1
1973	Mil-A	3	5	.375	42	7	0	0	2	72	86	5	44	44	16.5	5.13	73	.299	.395	0	—	0	-10	-11	0	-1.1
Total	15	135	132	.506	501	308	88	24	18	2325	2215	183	806	1629	11.9	3.43	103	.252	.319	88	.126	-17	33	30	-4	1.9

● **BILL SHORT** Short, William Ross b: 11/27/37, Kingston, N.Y. BL/TL, 5'9", 170 lbs. Deb: 4/23/60

YEAR	TM/L	W	L	PCT	G	GS	CG	SH	SV	IP	H	HR	BB	SO	RAT	ERA	ERA+	OAV	OOB	BH	AVG	PB	PR	/A	PD	TPI
1960	NY-A	3	5	.375	10	10	2	0	0	47	49	5	30	14	15.3	4.79	75	.282	.390	3	.200	1	-5	-6	-1	-0.6
1962	Bal-A	0	0	—	5	0	0	0	0	4	8	0	6	3	33.8	15.75	24	.381	.536	0	.000	-0	-5	-5	0	-0.5
1966	Bal-A	2	3	.400	6	6	1	1	0	37^{2}	34	2	10	27	10.5	2.87	116	.239	.289	1	.091	-1	2	2	1	0.2
	Bos-A	0	0	—	8	0	0	0	0	8^{1}	10	1	2	2	13.0	4.32	88	.294	.333	0	.000	-0	-1	-0	0	0.0
	Yr	2	3	.400	14	6	1	1	0	46	44	3	12	29	11.0	3.13	109	.247	.295	1	.083	-1	2	1	1	0.2
1967	Pit-N	0	0	—	6	0	0	0	1	2^{1}	1	0	1	1	7.7	3.86	87	.143	.250	0	.000	-0	-0	-0	0	0.0
1968	NY-N	0	3	.000	34	0	0	0	1	30^{1}	24	0	14	24	11.6	4.75	64	.220	.315	0	.000	-0	-6	-6	1	-0.6
1969	Cin-N	0	0	—	4	0	0	0	0	2^{1}	4	0	1	0	19.3	15.43	24	.400	.455	0	.000	-0	-3	-3	-0	-0.3
Total	6	5	11	.313	73	16	3	1	2	132	130	8	64	71	13.4	4.70	73	.262	.349	4	.125	-1	-18	-19	2	-1.8

● **CLYDE SHOUN** Shoun, Clyde Mitchell "Hardrock" b: 3/20/12, Mountain City, Tenn. d: 3/20/68, Mountain Home, Tenn. BL/TL, 6'1", 188 lbs. Deb: 8/07/35

YEAR	TM/L	W	L	PCT	G	GS	CG	SH	SV	IP	H	HR	BB	SO	RAT	ERA	ERA+	OAV	OOB	BH	AVG	PB	PR	/A	PD	TPI
1935	Chi-N	1	0	1.000	5	1	0	0	0	12^{2}	14	2	5	5	13.5	2.84	138	.298	.365	0	.000	-0	2	2	-0	0.1
1936	Chi-N	0	0	—	4	0	0	0	0	4^{1}	3	0	6	1	18.7	12.46	32	.200	.429	0	—	0	-4	-4	0	-0.4
1937	Chi-N	7	7	.500	37	9	2	0	0	93	118	9	45	43	15.8	5.61	71	.309	.382	4	.138	-1	-18	-17	-1	-1.8
1938	StL-N	6	6	.500	40	12	3	0	1	117^{1}	130	8	43	37	13.3	4.14	96	.283	.345	8	.258	0	-5	-2	-1	-0.3
1939	StL-N	3	1	.750	**53**	2	0	0	**9**	103	98	4	42	50	12.4	3.76	109	.248	.323	3	.115	-1	2	**4**	-1	0.2
1940	StL-N	13	11	.542	**54**	19	13	1	5	197^{1}	193	13	46	82	11.0	3.92	102	.255	.299	12	.190	-1	-2	1	-0	0.0
1941	StL-N	3	5	.375	26	6	0	0	0	70	98	9	20	34	15.2	5.66	67	.337	.379	4	.182	0	-16	-15	1	-1.4
1942	StL-N	0	0	—	2	0	0	0	0	1^{2}	1	0	0	0	5.4	0.00	—	.167	.167	0	—	0	1	1	-0	0.1
	Cin-N	1	3	.250	34	0	0	0	0	72^{2}	55	2	24	32	9.8	2.23	147	.216	.283	4	.308	1	9	9	1	1.1
	Yr	1	3	.250	36	0	0	0	0	74^{1}	56	2	24	32	9.7	2.18	151	.215	.281	4	.308	1	9	9	1	1.2
1943	Cin-N	14	5	.737	45	5	2	0	7	147	131	5	46	61	10.8	3.06	108	.241	.300	13	.310	3	5	4	1	0.9
1944	Cin-N	13	10	.565	38	21	12	1	2	202^{2}	193	10	42	55	10.6	3.02	116	.248	.290	15	.224	1	13	11	-3	0.9
1946	Cin-N	1	6	.143	27	5	0	0	0	79	87	3	26	20	13.0	4.10	82	.292	.351	2	.095	-1	-6	-7	-2	-1.1
1947	Cin-N	0	0	—	10	0	0	0	0	14^{1}	16	2	5	7	13.8	5.02	82	.320	.393	0	—	0	-2	-1	0	-0.1
	Bos-N	5	3	.625	26	3	1	1	1	73^{2}	73	6	21	23	11.5	4.40	89	.254	.305	3	.158	-1	-3	-4	-1	-0.6
	Yr	5	3	.625	36	3	1	1	1	88	89	8	26	30	11.8	4.50	87	.263	.316	3	.158	-1	-4	-6	-1	-0.7
1948	Bos-N	5	1	.833	36	2	1	0	4	74	77	7	20	25	11.8	4.01	96	.267	.315	4	.190	0	-0	-1	-2	-0.3
1949	Bos-N	0	0	—	1	0	0	0	0	1	1	0	0	0	9.0	0.00	—	.250	.250	0	—	0	0	0	-0	0.0
	Chi-A	1	1	.500	16	0	0	0	0	23^{1}	37	1	13	8	19.3	5.79	72	.370	.442	1	.200	0	-4	-4	0	-0.4
Total	14	73	59	.553	454	85	34	3	29	1287	1325	81	404	483	12.2	3.91	96	.267	.324	73	.202	1	-27	-25	-9	-3.1

● **ERIC SHOW** Show, Eric Vaughn b: 5/19/56, Riverside, Cal. BR/TR, 6'1", 185 lbs. Deb: 9/02/81

YEAR	TM/L	W	L	PCT	G	GS	CG	SH	SV	IP	H	HR	BB	SO	RAT	ERA	ERA+	OAV	OOB	BH	AVG	PB	PR	/A	PD	TPI
1981	SD-N	1	3	.250	15	0	0	0	3	23	17	2	9	22	10.6	3.13	104	.213	.300	0	—	0	1	0	0	0.0
1982	SD-N	10	6	.625	47	14	2	2	3	150	117	10	48	88	10.2	2.64	130	.217	.287	6	.146	-1	16	13	2	1.5
1983	SD-N	15	12	.556	35	33	4	2	0	200^{2}	201	25	74	120	12.6	4.17	84	.263	.333	11	.172	1	-12	-15	-2	-1.6
1984	*SD-N	15	9	.625	32	32	3	1	0	206^{2}	175	18	88	104	11.6	3.40	105	.234	.317	17	.246	6	4	4	-1	1.0
1985	SD-N	12	11	.522	35	35	5	2	0	233	212	27	87	141	11.7	3.09	114	.243	.316	10	.127	-1	13	11	-3	0.8
1986	SD-N	9	5	.643	24	22	2	0	0	136^{1}	109	11	69	94	12.0	2.97	123	.225	.326	7	.163	1	11	10	-2	1.0
1987	SD-N	8	16	.333	34	34	5	3	0	206^{1}	188	26	85	117	12.3	3.84	103	.241	.323	5	.071	-4	6	3	-1	-0.2
1988	SD-N	16	11	.593	32	32	13	1	0	234^{2}	201	22	53	144	10.0	3.26	104	.231	.280	12	.148	-0	5	4	-4	-0.1
1989	SD-N	8	6	.571	16	16	1	0	0	106^{1}	113	9	39	66	13.0	4.23	83	.274	.340	8	.235	2	-9	-9	-1	-0.9
1990	SD-N	6	8	.429	39	12	0	0	1	106^{1}	131	16	41	55	14.9	5.76	66	.306	.372	5	.200	1	-23	-23	-1	-2.3
1991	Oak-A	1	2	.333	23	5	0	0	0	51^{2}	62	5	17	20	13.8	5.92	65	.298	.351	0	—	0	-10	-12	-1	-1.2
Total	11	101	89	.532	332	235	35	11	7	1655	1526	171	610	971	11.9	3.66	98	.247	.319	81	.160	3	1	-13	-13	-2.0

● **LEV SHREVE** Shreve, Leven Lawrence b: 1/14/1869, Louisville, Ky. d: 10/18/42, Detroit, Mich. BR/TR, 5'11", 150 lbs. Deb: 5/02/1887

YEAR	TM/L	W	L	PCT	G	GS	CG	SH	SV	IP	H	HR	BB	SO	RAT	ERA	ERA+	OAV	OOB	BH	AVG	PB	PR	/A	PD	TPI
1887	Bal-a	3	1	.750	5	5	4	1	0	38	33	0	19	13	12.6	3.79	108	.228	.321	4	.167	-1	2	1	0	0.1
	Ind-N	5	9	.357	14	14	14	1	0	122	141	5	65	22	15.5	4.72	88	.278	.365	13	.265	0	-9	-8	-2	-0.7
1888	Ind-N	11	24	.314	35	35	34	1	0	297^{2}	352	23	93	101	13.7	4.63	64	.288	.342	21	.183	-1	-59	-55	0	-5.1

YEAR TM/L	W	L	PCT	G	GS	CG	SH	SV	IP	H	HR	BB	SO	RAT	ERA	ERA+	OAV	OOB	BH	AVG	PB	PR	/A	PD	TPI
1889 Ind-N	0	3	.000	3	3	1	0	0	15^2	25	3	12	5	21.8	13.79	30	.350	.450	0	.000	-1	-17	-17	0	-1.2
Total 3	19	37	.339	57	57	53	3	0	473^1	551	31	189	141	14.3	4.89	70	.283	.351	38	.195	-2	-82	-78	-1	-6.9

● **HARRY SHRIVER** Shriver, Harry Graydon "Pop" b: 9/2/1896, Wadestown, W.Va. d: 1/21/70, Morgantown, W.Va. BR/TR, 6'2", 180 lbs. Deb: 4/14/22

YEAR TM/L	W	L	PCT	G	GS	CG	SH	SV	IP	H	HR	BB	SO	RAT	ERA	ERA+	OAV	OOB	BH	AVG	PB	PR	/A	PD	TPI
1922 Bro-N	4	6	.400	25	14	4	2	0	108^1	114	5	48	38	13.6	2.99	136	.287	.367	1	.037	-3	13	13	-2	0.7
1923 Bro-N	0	0	—	1	1	0	0	0	4	8	0	0	1	18.0	6.75	58	.444	.444	0	.000	-0	-1	-1	-0	-0.1
Total 2	4	6	.400	26	15	4	2	0	112^1	122	5	48	39	13.8	3.12	130	.294	.370	1	.036	-3	12	12	-3	0.6

● **TOOTS SHULTZ** Shultz, Wallace Luther b: 10/10/1888, Homestead, Pa. d: 1/30/59, McKeesport, Pa. BR/TR, 5'10", 175 lbs. Deb: 5/05/11

YEAR TM/L	W	L	PCT	G	GS	CG	SH	SV	IP	H	HR	BB	SO	RAT	ERA	ERA+	OAV	OOB	BH	AVG	PB	PR	/A	PD	TPI
1911 Phi-N	0	3	.000	5	3	2	0	0	25	30	5	15	9	17.6	9.36	37	.300	.412	2	.250	0	-17	-16	0	-1.4
1912 Phi-N	1	4	.200	22	4	1	0	1	59	75	2	35	20	17.2	4.58	79	.333	.430	5	.238	0	-8	-6	0	-0.6
Total 2	1	7	.125	27	7	3	0	1	84	105	7	50	29	17.4	6.00	60	.323	.424	7	.241	0	-24	-23	1	-2.0

● **HARRY SHUMAN** Shuman, Harry b: 3/5/16, Philadelphia, Pa. BR/TR, 6'2", 195 lbs. Deb: 9/14/42

YEAR TM/L	W	L	PCT	G	GS	CG	SH	SV	IP	H	HR	BB	SO	RAT	ERA	ERA+	OAV	OOB	BH	AVG	PB	PR	/A	PD	TPI
1942 Pit-N	0	0	—	1	0	0	0	0	2	0	0	1	1	4.5	0.00	—	.000	.167	0	—	0	1	1	-0	0.1
1943 Pit-N	0	0	—	11	0	0	0	0	22	30	0	8	5	16.4	5.32	65	.337	.404	0	.000	-0	-5	-4	0	-0.5
1944 Phi-N	0	0	—	18	0	0	0	0	26^2	26	1	11	4	12.5	4.05	89	.245	.316	0	.000	-0	-1	-1	0	-0.1
Total 3	0	0	—	30	0	0	0	0	50^2	56	1	20	10	13.9	4.44	80	.280	.351	0	.000	-0	-5	-5	0	-0.5

● **PAUL SIEBERT** Siebert, Paul Edward b: 6/5/53, Minneapolis, Minn. BL/TL, 6'2", 205 lbs. Deb: 9/07/74 F

YEAR TM/L	W	L	PCT	G	GS	CG	SH	SV	IP	H	HR	BB	SO	RAT	ERA	ERA+	OAV	OOB	BH	AVG	PB	PR	/A	PD	TPI
1974 Hou-N	1	1	.500	5	5	1	1	0	25^1	21	3	11	10	11.4	3.55	97	.236	.320	0	.000	-1	0	-0	1	0.0
1975 Hou-N	0	2	.000	7	2	0	0	2	18^1	20	0	6	6	13.3	2.95	114	.294	.360	0	.000	-0	1	1	0	0.1
1976 HouN	0	2	.000	19	0	0	0	0	25^2	29	0	18	10	16.8	3.16	101	.296	.410	0	.000	-0	1	0	-1	-0.1
1977 SD-N	0	0	—	4	0	0	0	0	3^2	3	1	4	1	17.2	2.45	144	.214	.389	0	—	0	1	0	-0	0.0
NY-N	2	1	.667	25	0	0	0	0	28	27	0	13	20	13.2	3.86	97	.257	.345	0	.000	-0	0	-0	-0	-0.1
Yr	2	1	.667	29	0	0	0	0	31^2	30	1	17	21	13.6	3.69	101	.250	.348	0	.000	-0	1	0	-0	-0.1
1978 NY-N	0	2	.000	27	0	0	0	1	28	30	2	21	12	16.7	5.14	68	.283	.406	0	.000	-0	-5	-5	0	-0.5
Total 5	3	8	.273	87	7	1	1	3	129	130	6	73	59	14.4	3.77	92	.271	.372	0	.000	-2	-2	-4	0	-0.6

● **SONNY SIEBERT** Siebert, Wilfred Charles b: 1/14/37, St.Mary's, Mo. BR/TR, 6'3", 198 lbs. Deb: 4/26/64

YEAR TM/L	W	L	PCT	G	GS	CG	SH	SV	IP	H	HR	BB	SO	RAT	ERA	ERA+	OAV	OOB	BH	AVG	PB	PR	/A	PD	TPI
1964 Cle-A	7	9	.438	41	14	3	1	3	156	142	15	57	144	11.6	3.23	111	.243	.313	13	.265	5	7	6	-2	1.1
1965 Cle-A	16	8	.667	39	27	4	1	1	188^2	139	14	46	191	9.1	2.43	143	.206	**.262**	7	.106	-2	22	22	1	2.4
1966 Cle-A★	16	8	**.667**	34	32	11	1	1	241	193	25	62	163	9.7	2.80	123	.221	.278	11	.129	-2	17	17	2	1.9
1967 Cle-A	10	12	.455	34	26	7	1	4	185^1	136	17	54	136	9.5	2.38	137	.202	.268	7	.135	1	18	18	-2	2.0
1968 Cle-A	12	10	.545	31	30	8	4	0	206	145	12	88	146	10.5	2.97	100	.198	.290	11	.157	1	0	-0	1	0.2
1969 Cle-A	0	1	.000	2	2	0	0	0	14	10	1	8	6	11.6	3.21	117	.196	.305	1	.250	0	1	1	-0	0.1
Bos-A	14	10	.583	43	22	2	0	5	163^1	151	21	68	127	12.3	3.80	100	.245	.324	8	.151	1	-3	0	2	0.3
Yr	14	11	.560	45	24	2	0	5	177^1	161	22	76	133	12.2	3.76	101	.241	.322	9	.158	1	-3	1	2	0.4
1970 Bos-A	15	8	.652	33	33	7	2	0	222^2	207	29	60	142	11.0	3.44	115	.248	.303	10	.130	-2	7	13	0	1.2
1971 Bos-A☆	16	10	.615	32	32	12	4	0	235^1	220	20	60	131	10.8	2.91	127	.245	.294	21	.266	10	15	21	1	3.6
1972 Bos-A	12	12	.500	32	30	7	3	0	196^1	204	17	59	123	12.4	3.80	84	.264	.322	17	.236	6	-16	-13	1	-0.6
1973 Bos-A	0	1	.000	2	0	0	0	0	2^1	5	1	1	5	23.1	7.71	52	.417	.462	0	—	0	-1	-1	0	-0.1
Tex-A	7	11	.389	25	20	1	1	2	119^2	120	11	37	76	12.0	3.99	93	.258	.317	0	—	0	-2	-4	2	-0.1
Yr	7	12	.368	27	20	1	1	2	122	125	12	38	81	12.2	4.06	92	.262	.320	0	—	0	-3	-4	2	-0.2
1974 StL-N	8	8	.500	28	20	5	3	0	133^2	150	8	51	68	13.7	3.84	93	.288	.355	5	.114	-2	-3	-4	-1	-0.7
1975 SD-N	3	2	.600	6	6	0	0	0	26^2	37	2	10	10	16.2	4.39	79	.330	.390	3	.375	2	-2	-3	0	-0.1
Oak-A	4	4	.500	17	13	0	0	0	61	60	4	31	44	13.4	3.69	98	.252	.338	0	.000	0	1	-0	-1	-0.1
Total 12	140	114	.551	399	307	67	21	16	2152	1919	197	692	1512	11.1	3.21	110	.238	.303	114	.173	19	57	73	5	11.1

● **DWIGHT SIEBLER** Siebler, Dwight Leroy b: 8/5/37, Columbus, Neb. BR/TR, 6'2", 184 lbs. Deb: 8/26/63

YEAR TM/L	W	L	PCT	G	GS	CG	SH	SV	IP	H	HR	BB	SO	RAT	ERA	ERA+	OAV	OOB	BH	AVG	PB	PR	/A	PD	TPI
1963 Min-A	2	1	.667	7	5	2	0	0	38^2	25	6	12	22	8.8	2.79	130	.182	.253	2	.133	-0	4	4	-1	0.3
1964 Min-A	0	0	—	9	0	0	0	0	11	10	1	6	10	13.1	4.91	73	.256	.356	0	—	0	-2	-2	-0	-0.2
1965 Min-A	0	0	—	7	1	0	0	0	15	11	2	11	15	13.2	4.20	85	.193	.324	0	.000	-0	-1	-1	0	-0.1
1966 Min-A	2	2	.500	23	2	0	0	1	49^2	47	6	14	24	11.2	3.44	104	.253	.308	0	.000	-1	-0	1	-1	-0.1
1967 Min-A	0	0	—	2	0	0	0	0	3	4	0	1	0	15.0	3.00	115	.364	.417	0	—	0	0	0	-0	0.0
Total 5	4	3	.571	48	8	2	0	1	117^1	97	15	44	71	11.0	3.45	104	.226	.300	2	.074	-1	1	2	-2	-0.1

● **CANDY SIERRA** Sierra, Ulises (Pizarro) b: 3/27/67, Rio Piedras, P.R. BR/TR, 6'2", 190 lbs. Deb: 4/06/88

YEAR TM/L	W	L	PCT	G	GS	CG	SH	SV	IP	H	HR	BB	SO	RAT	ERA	ERA+	OAV	OOB	BH	AVG	PB	PR	/A	PD	TPI
1988 SD-N	0	1	.000	15	0	0	0	0	23^2	36	2	11	20	17.9	5.70	60	.379	.443	0	.000	-0	-6	-6	-0	-0.7
Cin-N	0	0	—	1	0	0	0	0	4	5	0	1	4	13.5	4.50	80	.294	.333	0	.000	-0	-0	-0	0	0.0
Yr	0	1	.000	16	0	0	0	0	27^2	41	2	12	24	17.2	5.53	62	.363	.424	0	.000	-0	-6	-6	-0	-0.7

● **ED SIEVER** Siever, Edward T. b: 4/2/1877, Goddard, Kan. d: 2/4/20, Detroit, Mich. BL/TL, 5'11.5", 190 lbs. Deb: 4/26/01

YEAR TM/L	W	L	PCT	G	GS	CG	SH	SV	IP	H	HR	BB	SO	RAT	ERA	ERA+	OAV	OOB	BH	AVG	PB	PR	/A	PD	TPI
1901 Det-A	18	15	.545	38	33	30	2	0	288^2	334	9	65	85	12.7	3.24	119	.286	.328	18	.168	-5	14	19	-1	1.2
1902 Det-A	8	11	.421	25	23	17	4	1	188^1	166	0	32	36	9.6	**1.91**	**191**	.237	.273	10	.152	-4	35	36	-4	2.9
1903 StL-A	13	14	.481	31	27	24	1	0	254	245	6	39	90	10.2	2.48	117	.253	.285	13	.140	-4	14	12	2	1.1
1904 StL-A	10	15	.400	29	24	19	2	0	217	235	3	65	77	12.6	2.65	93	.277	.330	11	.155	-2	-1	-4	1	-0.6
1906 Det-A	14	11	.560	30	25	20	1	0	222^2	240	5	45	71	11.9	2.71	102	.278	.321	12	.156	-4	-0	1	-2	-0.5
1907 *Det-A	18	11	.621	39	33	22	3	1	274^2	256	1	52	88	10.4	2.16	121	.249	.291	15	.160	-3	12	14	-4	0.7
1908 Det-A	2	6	.250	11	9	4	1	0	61^2	74	0	13	23	12.7	3.50	69	.302	.337	3	.167	-1	-8	-7	-1	-1.0
Total 7	83	83	.500	203	174	136	14	2	1507	1550	24	311	470	11.3	2.60	116	.266	.308	82	.156	-22	65	70	-9	3.8

● **WALTER SIGNER** Signer, Walter Donald Aloysius b: 10/12/10, New York, N.Y. d: 7/23/74, Greenwich, Conn. BR/TR, 6', 185 lbs. Deb: 9/18/43

YEAR TM/L	W	L	PCT	G	GS	CG	SH	SV	IP	H	HR	BB	SO	RAT	ERA	ERA+	OAV	OOB	BH	AVG	PB	PR	/A	PD	TPI
1943 Chi-N	2	1	.667	4	2	1	0	0	25	24	3	4	5	10.1	2.88	116	.245	.275	2	.250	0	1	1	-0	0.2
1945 Chi-N	0	0	—	6	0	0	0	1	8	11	1	5	0	18.0	3.38	108	.256	.333	0	.000	-0	0	0	-0	0.0
Total 2	2	1	.667	10	2	1	0	1	33	35	4	9	5	12.0	3.00	114	.248	.293	2	.222	0	2	2	-0	0.2

● **SETH SIGSBY** Sigsby, Seth De Witt (b: Seth De Witt) b: 4/30/1874, Cobleskill, N.Y. d: 9/15/53, Schenectady, N.Y 6', 175 lbs. Deb: 6/27/1893

YEAR TM/L	W	L	PCT	G	GS	CG	SH	SV	IP	H	HR	BB	SO	RAT	ERA	ERA+	OAV	OOB	BH	AVG	PB	PR	/A	PD	TPI
1893 NY-N	0	0	—	1	0	0	0	0	3	1	0	4	2	18.0	9.00	52	.101	.403	0	.000	-0	-1	-1	-0	-0.1

● **AL SIMA** Sima, Albert b: 10/7/22, Mahwah, N.J. BR/TL, 6', 187 lbs. Deb: 6/28/50

YEAR TM/L	W	L	PCT	G	GS	CG	SH	SV	IP	H	HR	BB	SO	RAT	ERA	ERA+	OAV	OOB	BH	AVG	PB	PR	/A	PD	TPI
1950 Was-A	4	5	.444	17	9	1	0	0	77	89	9	26	23	13.6	4.79	94	.291	.348	3	.115	-2	-2	-3	-1	-0.6
1951 Was-A	3	7	.300	18	8	1	0	0	77	79	5	41	26	14.0	4.79	85	.261	.349	3	.176	1	-6	-6	-1	-0.5
1953 Was-A	2	3	.400	31	5	1	0	1	68^1	63	7	31	25	12.8	3.42	114	.249	.338	2	.118	-1	4	4	1	0.4
1954 Chi-A	0	1	.000	5	1	0	0	1	7	11	1	2	1	16.7	5.14	73	.393	.433	0	.000	-0	-1	-1	0	-0.1
Phi-A	2	5	.286	29	7	1	0	2	79^1	101	9	32	36	15.1	5.22	75	.309	.370	1	.050	-2	-13	-12	-1	-1.4
Yr	2	6	.250	34	8	1	0	3	86^1	112	10	34	37	15.2	5.21	75	.314	.373	1	.045	-2	-14	-13	-1	-1.5
Total 4	11	21	.344	100	30	4	0	4	308^2	343	31	132	111	14.0	4.61	89	.282	.354	9	.110	-5	-18	-17	-2	-2.2

● **CURT SIMMONS** Simmons, Curtis Thomas b: 5/19/29, Egypt, Pa. BL/TL, 6', 187 lbs. Deb: 9/28/47

YEAR TM/L	W	L	PCT	G	GS	CG	SH	SV	IP	H	HR	BB	SO	RAT	ERA	ERA+	OAV	OOB	BH	AVG	PB	PR	/A	PD	TPI
1947 Phi-N	1	0	1.000	1	1	1	0	0	9	5	0	6	9	11.0	1.00	401	.161	.297	1	.500	0	3	3	-0	0.4
1948 Phi-N	7	13	.350	31	22	7	0	0	170	169	8	108	86	14.8	4.87	81	.266	.374	7	.137	-1	-17	-17	1	-1.7
1949 Phi-N	4	10	.286	38	14	2	0	1	131^1	133	7	55	83	13.0	4.59	86	.275	.350	7	.171	-1	-8	-9	-0	-1.0
1950 Phi-N	17	8	.680	31	27	11	2	1	214^2	178	19	88	146	11.2	3.40	119	.223	.302	12	.156	-1	18	16	-0	1.4
1952 Phi-N★	14	8	.636	28	28	15	**6**	0	201^1	170	11	70	141	10.8	2.82	130	.227	.294	11	.164	2	20	19	-3	1.9
1953 Phi-N★	16	13	.552	32	30	19	4	0	238	211	17	82	138	11.2	3.21	131	.236	.302	13	.140	-3	28	26	-3	2.1

YEAR	TM/L	W	L	PCT	G	GS	CG	SH	SV	IP	H	HR	BB	SO	RAT	ERA	ERA+	OAV	OOB	BH	AVG	PB	PR	/A	PD	TPI
1954	Phi-N	14	15	.483	34	33	21	3	1	253	226	14	98	125	11.7	2.81	144	.239	.314	16	.176	-1	35	35	-3	3.1
1955	Phi-N	8	8	.500	25	22	3	0	0	130	148	15	50	58	13.9	4.92	81	.290	.356	8	.174	-1	-13	-14	-1	-1.5
1956	Phi-N	15	10	.600	33	27	14	0	0	198	186	17	65	88	11.5	3.36	111	.248	.311	17	.236	3	9	8	-1	1.1
1957	Phi-N★	12	11	.522	32	29	9	2	0	212	214	11	50	92	11.3	3.44	111	.264	.309	17	.239	4	10	9	-3	1.0
1958	Phi-N	7	14	.333	29	27	7	1	1	168^{1}	196	11	40	78	12.8	4.38	90	.293	.336	12	.203	0	-8	-8	-1	-0.9
1959	Phi-N	0	0	—	7	0	0	0	0	10	16	2	0	4	15.3	4.50	91	.400	.415	0	—	0	-1	-0	0	0.0
1960	Phi-N	0	0	—	4	2	0	0	0	4	13	3	6	4	42.8	18.00	22	.542	.633	0	—	0	-6	-6	1	-0.6
	StL-N	7	4	.636	23	17	3	1	0	152	149	11	31	63	10.7	2.66	154	.257	.295	10	.213	1	19	24	0	2.8
	Yr	7	4	.636	27	19	3	1	0	156	162	14	37	67	11.5	3.06	134	.269	.311	10	.213	1	12	18	1	2.2
1961	StL-N	9	10	.474	30	29	6	2	0	195^{2}	203	14	64	99	12.5	3.13	**141**	.269	.329	20	.303	6	20	**28**	-0	**3.5**
1962	StL-N	10	10	.500	31	22	9	4	0	154	167	18	32	74	11.8	3.51	122	.280	.320	8	.160	0	7	13	-1	1.3
1963	StL-N	15	9	.625	32	32	11	6	0	232^{2}	209	13	48	127	10.2	2.48	143	.239	.283	13	.160	0	21	28	-4	2.8
1964	*StL-N	18	9	.667	34	34	12	3	0	244	233	24	49	104	10.6	3.43	111	.249	.290	10	.106	-3	3	10	-1	0.6
1965	StL-N	9	15	.375	34	32	5	0	0	203	229	19	54	96	12.7	4.08	94	.283	.331	3	.047	-5	-12	-5	-2	-1.3
1966	StL-N	1	1	.500	10	5	1	0	0	33^{1}	35	3	14	14	13.2	4.59	78	.269	.340	1	.125	0	-4	-4	-1	-0.4
	Chi-N	4	7	.364	19	10	3	1	0	77^{1}	79	7	21	24	11.8	4.07	90	.268	.319	2	.111	-0	-4	-3	2	-0.3
	Yr	5	8	.385	29	15	4	1	0	110^{2}	114	10	35	38	12.2	4.23	86	.268	.325	3	.115	-0	-8	-7	1	-0.7
1967	Chi-N	3	7	.300	17	14	3	0	0	82	100	10	23	31	13.7	4.94	72	.300	.349	4	.143	-1	-14	-13	-0	-1.4
	Cal-A	2	1	.667	14	4	1	1	1	34^{2}	44	1	9	13	14.3	2.60	121	.321	.372	2	.222	1	2	2	-1	0.2
Total	20	193	183	.513	569	461	163	36	5	3348^{1}	3313	255	1063	1697	11.9	3.54	111	.259	.319	194	.171	2	109	142	-21	13.1
● **PAT SIMMONS**	Simmons, Patrick Clement (b: Patrick Clement Simoni) b: 11/29/08, Watervliet, N.Y. d: 7/3/68, Albany, N.Y. BR/TR, 5'11", 172 lbs. Deb: 4/18/28																									
1928	Bos-A	0	2	.000	31	3	0	0	1	69	69	4	38	16	14.1	4.04	102	.271	.367	2	.133	-1	0	**1**	-0	-0.1
1929	Bos-A	0	0	—	2	0	0	0	1	7	6	0	3	2	11.6	0.00	—	.231	.310	0	.000	-0	3	3	0	0.3
Total	2	0	2	.000	33	3	0	0	2	76	75	4	41	18	13.9	3.67	112	.267	.362	2	.125	-1	3	4	-0	0.2
● **DOUG SIMONS**	Simons, Douglas Eugene b: 9/15/66, Bakersfield, Cal. BL/TL, 6', 170 lbs. Deb: 4/09/91																									
1991	NY-N	2	3	.400	42	1	0	0	1	60^{2}	55	5	19	38	11.3	5.19	70	.246	.310	0	.000	-0	-10	-10	2	-0.9
1992	Mon-N	0	0	—	7	0	0	0	0	5^{1}	15	3	2	6	30.4	23.63	15	.500	.545	0	—	0	-12	-12	-0	-1.2
Total	2	2	3	.400	49	1	0	0	1	66	70	8	21	44	12.8	6.68	54	.276	.338	0	.000	-0	-22	-22	2	-2.1
● **JOE SIMPSON**	Simpson, Joe Allen b: 12/31/51, Purcell, Okla. BL/TL, 6'3", 175 lbs. Deb: 9/02/75 ♦																									
1983	KC-A	0	0	—	2	0	0	0	0	3	4	0	2	1	18.0	3.00	136	.308	.400	20	.168	1	0	0	-0	0.0
● **STEVE SIMPSON**	Simpson, Steven Edward b: 8/30/48, St.Joseph, Mo. d: 11/2/89, Omaha, Neb. BR/TR, 6'3", 200 lbs. Deb: 9/10/72																									
1972	SD-N	0	2	.000	9	0	0	0	2	11^{1}	10	0	8	9	14.3	4.76	69	.238	.360	0	—	0	-2	-2	-0	-0.2
● **DUKE SIMPSON**	Simpson, Thomas Leo b: 9/15/27, Columbus, Ohio BR/TR, 6'1.5", 190 lbs. Deb: 5/06/53																									
1953	Chi-N	1	2	.333	30	1	0	0	0	45	60	8	25	21	17.2	8.00	56	.314	.396	2	.250	0	-19	-18	-0	-1.7
● **WAYNE SIMPSON**	Simpson, Wayne Kirby b: 12/2/48, Los Angeles, Cal. BR/TR, 6'3", 220 lbs. Deb: 4/09/70																									
1970	Cin-N☆	14	3	.824	26	26	10	2	0	176	125	15	81	119	11.0	3.02	134	**.198**	.298	6	.094	-4	20	20	2	1.9
1971	Cin-N	4	7	.364	22	21	1	0	0	117^{1}	106	9	77	61	14.3	4.76	71	.244	.361	1	.031	-2	-17	-18	2	-1.9
1972	Cin-N	8	5	.615	24	22	1	0	0	130^{1}	124	17	49	70	12.1	4.14	78	.247	.316	3	.063	-3	-10	-13	-3	-1.9
1973	KC-A	3	4	.429	16	10	1	0	0	59^{2}	66	1	35	29	15.4	5.73	72	.284	.381	0	—	0	-13	-11	-0	-1.1
1975	Phi-N	1	0	1.000	7	5	0	0	0	30^{2}	31	1	11	19	12.6	3.23	116	.263	.331	2	.222	0	1	2	0	0.3
1977	Cal-A	6	12	.333	27	23	0	0	0	122	154	14	62	55	16.5	5.83	67	.308	.392	0	—	0	-24	-26	-1	-2.5
Total	6	36	31	.537	122	107	13	2	0	636	606	57	315	353	13.4	4.37	85	.251	.343	12	.078	-8	-42	-47	0	-5.2
● **PETE SIMS**	Sims, Clarence b: 5/24/1891, Crown City, Ohio d: 12/2/68, Dallas, Tex. BR/TR, 5'11.5", 165 lbs. Deb: 9/16/15																									
1915	StL-A	1	0	1.000	3	2	0	0	0	8^{1}	6	0	6	4	13.0	4.32	66	.214	.353	1	1.000	1	-1	-1	-0	-0.1
● **BERT SINCOCK**	Sincock, Herbert Sylvester b: 9/8/1887, Barkerville, B.C. Canada d: 8/1/46, Houghton, Mich. BL/TL, 5'10.5", 165 lbs. Deb: 6/25/08																									
1908	Cin-N	0	0	—	1	0	0	0	0	4^{2}	3	0	0	1	5.8	3.86	60	.176	.176	0	.000	-0	-1	-1	-0	-0.1
● **BILL SINGER**	Singer, William Robert "The Singer Throwing Machine" b: 4/24/44, Los Angeles, Cal. BR/TR, 6'4", 200 lbs. Deb: 9/24/64																									
1964	LA-N	0	1	.000	2	2	0	0	0	14	11	0	12	3	14.8	3.21	101	.216	.365	1	.167	0	1	0	-0	0.0
1965	LA-N	0	0	—	2	0	0	0	0	1	2	0	2	1	36.0	0.00	—	.400	.571	0	—	0	0	0	0	0.0
1966	LA-N	0	0	—	3	0	0	0	0	4	4	0	2	4	13.5	0.00	—	.286	.375	0	—	0	2	1	0	0.2
1967	LA-N	12	8	.600	32	29	7	3	0	204^{1}	185	5	61	169	11.2	2.64	117	.239	.301	6	.090	-3	17	10	1	0.9
1968	LA-N	13	17	.433	37	36	12	6	0	256^{1}	227	14	78	227	10.9	2.88	96	.237	.298	12	.148	3	3	-3	0	0.0
1969	LA-N★	20	12	.625	41	40	16	2	1	315^{2}	244	22	74	247	9.4	2.34	142	.210	.263	11	.102	-4	44	35	-2	3.2
1970	LA-N	8	5	.615	16	16	5	3	0	106^{1}	79	10	32	93	9.6	3.13	122	.203	.267	5	.132	-0	11	8	-1	0.8
1971	LA-N	10	17	.370	31	31	8	1	0	203^{1}	195	19	71	144	12.0	4.16	78	.252	.318	6	.103	-0	-16	-21	-1	-2.3
1972	LA-N	6	16	.273	26	25	4	3	0	169^{1}	148	8	60	101	11.3	3.67	91	.237	.309	4	.073	-3	-4	-6	1	-0.9
1973	Cal-A★	20	14	.588	40	40	19	2	0	315^{2}	280	15	130	241	11.9	3.22	110	.235	.314	0	—	0	21	11	-2	1.0
1974	Cal-A	7	4	.636	14	14	8	0	0	108^{2}	102	3	43	77	12.1	2.98	115	.250	.323	0	—	0	8	5	0	0.7
1975	Cal-A	7	15	.318	29	27	8	0	1	179	171	18	81	78	13.0	4.98	71	.257	.343	0	—	0	-24	-28	-1	-2.8
1976	Tex-A	4	1	.800	10	10	2	1	0	64^{2}	56	4	27	34	12.2	3.48	103	.239	.331	0	—	0	0	1	-1	0.0
	Min-A	9	9	.500	26	26	5	3	0	172	177	9	69	63	13.2	3.77	96	.274	.349	0	—	0	-5	-3	-2	-0.5
	Yr	13	10	.565	36	36	7	4	0	236^{2}	233	13	96	97	12.7	3.69	97	.262	.338	0	—	0	-4	-2	-2	-0.5
1977	Tor-A	2	8	.200	13	12	0	0	0	59^{2}	71	5	39	33	16.9	6.79	62	.296	.399	0	—	0	-18	-17	-0	-1.6
Total	14	118	127	.482	322	308	94	24	2	2174	1952	132	781	1515	11.6	3.39	99	.240	.311	45	.109	-6	39	-7	-7	-1.3
● **ELMER SINGLETON**	Singleton, Bert Elmer "Smoky" b: 6/26/18, Ogden, Utah BR/TR, 6'2", 174 lbs. Deb: 8/20/45																									
1945	Bos-N	1	4	.200	7	5	1	0	0	37^{1}	35	1	14	14	12.1	4.82	79	.248	.321	0	.000	-2	-4	-4	-0	-0.5
1946	Bos-N	0	1	.000	15	2	0	0	1	33^{2}	27	3	21	17	13.1	3.74	92	.221	.340	0	.000	-1	-1	-1	0	-0.2
1947	Pit-N	2	2	.500	36	3	0	0	1	67	70	9	39	24	14.9	6.31	67	.267	.366	4	.308	1	-17	-16	0	-1.4
1948	Pit-N	4	6	.400	38	5	1	0	2	92^{1}	90	11	40	53	12.8	4.97	82	.253	.330	2	.087	-2	-10	-9	1	-1.0
1950	Was-A	1	2	.333	21	1	0	0	0	36^{1}	39	4	17	19	13.9	5.20	86	.291	.371	3	.429	1	-3	-3	1	-0.1
1957	Chi-N	0	1	.000	5	2	0	0	0	13^{1}	20	3	2	6	14.9	6.75	57	.333	.355	0	.000	-0	-4	-4	0	-0.4
1958	Chi-N	1	0	1.000	2	0	0	0	0	4^{2}	1	0	1	2	3.9	0.00	—	.071	.133	0	.000	-0	2	2	-0	0.2
1959	Chi-N	2	1	.667	21	1	0	0	0	43	40	2	12	25	10.9	2.72	145	.252	.304	0	.000	-1	6	6	1	0.6
Total	8	11	17	.393	145	19	2	0	4	327^{2}	322	33	146	160	13.0	4.83	83	.258	.338	9	.132	-3	-32	-29	3	-2.8
● **JOHN SINGLETON**	Singleton, John Edward "Sheriff" b: 11/27/1896, Gallipolis, Ohio d: 10/23/37, Dayton, Ohio BR/TR, 5'11", 171 lbs. Deb: 6/08/22																									
1922	Phi-N	1	10	.091	22	9	3	1	0	93	127	6	38	27	16.5	5.90	79	.346	.415	5	.139	-3	-19	-13	-1	-1.5
● **DOUG SISK**	Sisk, Douglas Randall b: 9/26/57, Benton, Wash. BR/TR, 6'2", 210 lbs. Deb: 9/06/82																									
1982	NY-N	0	1	.000	8	0	0	0	1	8^{2}	5	1	4	4	10.4	1.04	349	.172	.294	0	—	0	2	2	0	0.3
1983	NY-N	5	4	.556	67	0	0	0	11	104^{1}	88	1	59	33	13.0	2.24	162	.235	.346	3	.500	1	16	16	-1	1.7
1984	NY-N	1	3	.250	50	0	0	0	15	77^{2}	57	1	54	32	13.2	2.09	169	.215	.354	1	.091	-0	13	12	0	1.3
1985	NY-N	4	5	.444	42	0	0	0	2	73	86	3	40	26	15.8	5.30	65	.291	.379	0	.000	-1	-14	-15	1	-1.6
1986	*NY-N	4	2	.667	41	0	0	0	1	70^{2}	77	0	31	31	14.4	3.06	116	.282	.366	0	.000	-0	5	4	-1	0.3
1987	NY-N	3	1	.750	55	0	0	0	3	78	83	5	22	37	12.5	3.46	109	.270	.325	0	.000	-0	5	3	1	0.4
1988	Bal-A	3	3	.500	52	0	0	0	0	94^{1}	109	3	45	26	14.9	3.72	105	.306	.387	0	—	0	3	2	1	0.2

YEAR TM/L	W	L	PCT	G	GS	CG	SH	SV	IP	H	HR	BB	SO	RAT	ERA	ERA+	OAV	OOB	BH	AVG	PB	PR	/A	PD	TPI
1990 Atl-N	0	0	—	3	0	0	0	0	2^{1}	1	0	4	1	19.3	3.86	105	.143	.455	0	—	0	-0	0	0	0.0
1991 Atl-N	2	1	.667	14	0	0	0	0	14^{1}	21	1	8	5	18.2	5.02	77	.333	.408	0	—	0	-2	-2	0	-0.2
Total 9	22	20	.524	332	0	0	0	33	523^{1}	527	15	267	195	14.0	3.27	112	.268	.361	4	.105	-1	29	23	2	2.4

● TOMMIE SISK Sisk, Tommie Wayne b: 4/12/42, Ardmore, Okla. BR/TR, 6'3", 195 lbs. Deb: 7/19/62

YEAR TM/L	W	L	PCT	G	GS	CG	SH	SV	IP	H	HR	BB	SO	RAT	ERA	ERA+	OAV	OOB	BH	AVG	PB	PR	/A	PD	TPI
1962 Pit-N	0	2	.000	5	3	1	0	0	17^{2}	18	1	8	6	13.8	4.08	97	.257	.342	1	.200	0	-0	-0	-0	-0.1
1963 Pit-N	1	3	.250	57	4	1	0	1	108	85	6	45	73	10.9	2.92	113	.222	.305	1	.063	-0	4	5	1	0.6
1964 Pit-N	1	4	.200	42	1	0	0	0	61^{1}	91	4	29	35	18.0	6.16	57	.364	.436	0	.000	-1	-18	-18	2	-1.8
1965 Pit-N	7	3	.700	38	12	1	1	0	111^{1}	103	6	50	66	12.4	3.40	103	.248	.330	2	.061	-2	2	1	-1	-0.2
1966 Pit-N	10	5	.667	34	23	4	1	1	150	146	14	52	60	12.1	4.14	86	.256	.323	5	.098	-1	-9	-9	0	-1.1
1967 Pit-N	13	13	.500	37	31	11	2	1	207^{2}	196	6	78	85	12.0	3.34	101	.253	.324	7	.101	-2	1	1	1	-0.1
1968 Pit-N	5	5	.500	33	11	0	0	1	96	101	3	35	41	13.0	3.28	89	.282	.351	2	.083	-1	-3	-4	0	-0.5
1969 SD-N	2	13	.133	53	13	1	0	6	143	160	11	48	59	13.2	4.78	74	.285	.342	3	.120	0	-19	-20	0	-2.0
1970 Chi-A	1	1	.500	17	1	0	0	0	33^{1}	37	6	13	16	13.5	5.40	72	.276	.340	1	.250	0	-6	-6	1	-0.5
Total 9	40	49	.449	316	99	19	4	10	928^{1}	937	57	358	441	12.7	3.92	88	.266	.337	22	.094	-7	-48	-50	3	-5.7

● DAVE SISLER Sisler, David Michael b: 10/16/31, St.Louis, Mo. BR/TR, 6'4", 200 lbs. Deb: 4/21/56 F

YEAR TM/L	W	L	PCT	G	GS	CG	SH	SV	IP	H	HR	BB	SO	RAT	ERA	ERA+	OAV	OOB	BH	AVG	PB	PR	/A	PD	TPI
1956 Bos-A	9	8	.529	39	14	3	0	3	142^{1}	120	13	72	93	12.6	4.62	100	.227	.328	5	.119	-3	-7	0	0	-0.2
1957 Bos-A	7	8	.467	22	19	5	0	1	122^{1}	135	15	61	55	14.6	4.71	85	.280	.363	7	.167	-0	-12	-10	1	-0.9
1958 Bos-A	8	9	.471	30	25	4	1	0	149^{1}	157	22	79	71	14.3	4.94	81	.276	.366	9	.196	0	-19	-16	-1	-1.6
1959 Bos-A	0	0	—	3	0	0	0	0	6^{2}	9	3	1	3	13.5	6.75	60	.310	.333	1	.500	0	-2	-2	-0	-0.2
Det-A	1	3	.250	32	0	0	0	7	51^{2}	46	4	36	29	14.5	4.01	101	.242	.366	1	.200	-0	-1	0	-1	0.0
Yr	1	3	.250	35	0	0	0	7	58^{1}	55	7	37	32	14.3	4.32	94	.251	.362	2	.286	0	-3	-2	-1	-0.2
1960 Det-A	7	5	.583	41	0	0	0	6	80	56	3	45	47	11.6	2.47	160	.199	.314	2	.125	-0	12	13	1	1.5
1961 Was-A	2	8	.200	45	1	0	0	11	60^{1}	55	6	48	30	15.8	4.18	96	.251	.393	0	.000	0	-1	-1	0	-0.1
1962 Cin-N	4	3	.571	35	0	0	0	1	43^{2}	44	4	26	27	14.4	3.92	103	.270	.370	0	—	0	0	1	-1	0.0
Total 7	38	44	.463	247	59	12	1	29	656^{1}	622	70	368	355	13.8	4.33	95	.253	.354	25	.157	-3	-31	-15	1	-1.5

● GEORGE SISLER Sisler, George Harold "Georgeous George" b: 3/24/1893, Manchester, Ohio d: 3/26/73, Richmond Heights, Mo. BL/TL, 5'11", 170 lbs. Deb: 6/28/15 FMCH♦

YEAR TM/L	W	L	PCT	G	GS	CG	SH	SV	IP	H	HR	BB	SO	RAT	ERA	ERA+	OAV	OOB	BH	AVG	PB	PR	/A	PD	TPI
1915 StL-A	4	4	.500	15	8	6	0	0	70	62	0	38	41	13.4	2.83	101	.247	.355	78	.285	3	1	0	0	0.2
1916 StL-A	1	2	.333	3	3	3	1	0	27	18	0	6	12	8.3	1.00	275	.198	.255	177	.305	1	5	5	1	0.9
1918 StL-A	0	0	—	2	1	0	0	1	8	10	0	4	4	16.9	4.50	61	.286	.375	154	.341	1	-2	-2	0	-0.1
1920 StL-A	0	0	—	1	0	0	0	1	1	0	0	0	2	0.0	0.00	—	.000	.000	257	.407	1	0	0	0	0.0
1925 StL-A	0	0	—	1	0	0	0	0	2	1	0	1	1	9.0	0.00	—	.167	.286	224	.345	0	1	1	0	0.1
1926 StL-A	0	0	—	1	0	0	0	1	2	0	0	2	3	9.0	0.00	—	.000	.286	178	.290	0	1	1	0	0.1
1928 Bos-N	0	0	—	1	0	0	0	0	1	0	0	1	0	9.0	0.00	—	.000	.333	167	.340	0	0	0	-0	0.0
Total 7	5	6	.455	24	12	9	1	3	111	91	0	52	63	12.1	2.35	123	.231	.330	2812	.340	7	8	7	1	1.2

● CARL SITTON Sitton, Carl Vetter b: 9/22/1882, Pendleton, S.C. d: 9/11/31, Valdosta, Ga. BR/TR, 5'10.5", 170 lbs. Deb: 4/24/09

YEAR TM/L	W	L	PCT	G	GS	CG	SH	SV	IP	H	HR	BB	SO	RAT	ERA	ERA+	OAV	OOB	BH	AVG	PB	PR	/A	PD	TPI
1909 Cle-A	3	2	.600	14	5	3	0	0	50	50	1	16	16	12.2	2.88	89	.263	.327	2	.154	0	-2	-2	-1	-0.2

● PETE SIVESS Sivess, Peter b: 9/23/13, South River, N.J. BR/TR, 6'3.5", 195 lbs. Deb: 6/13/36

YEAR TM/L	W	L	PCT	G	GS	CG	SH	SV	IP	H	HR	BB	SO	RAT	ERA	ERA+	OAV	OOB	BH	AVG	PB	PR	/A	PD	TPI
1936 Phi-N	3	4	.429	17	6	2	0	0	65	84	6	36	22	16.8	4.57	99	.310	.393	3	.120	-2	-4	-0	-2	-0.4
1937 Phi-N	1	1	.500	6	2	1	0	0	23	30	5	11	4	16.0	7.04	62	.330	.402	0	.000	-1	-8	-7	-1	-0.8
1938 Phi-N	3	6	.333	39	8	2	0	3	116	143	12	69	32	16.5	5.51	71	.306	.397	6	.188	-1	-22	-21	-1	-2.2
Total 3	7	11	.389	62	16	5	0	3	204	257	23	116	58	16.5	5.38	77	.310	.396	9	.143	-4	-34	-28	-3	-3.4

● JIM SIWY Siwy, James b: 9/20/58, Central Falls, R.I BR/TR, 6'4", 200 lbs. Deb: 8/20/82

YEAR TM/L	W	L	PCT	G	GS	CG	SH	SV	IP	H	HR	BB	SO	RAT	ERA	ERA+	OAV	OOB	BH	AVG	PB	PR	/A	PD	TPI
1982 Chi-A	0	0	—	2	1	0	0	0	7	10	1	5	3	19.3	10.29	39	.385	.484	0	—	0	-5	-5	-0	-0.5
1984 Chi-A	0	0	—	1	0	0	0	0	4^{1}	3	0	2	1	10.4	2.08	200	.231	.333	0	—	0	1	1	0	-0.1
Total 2	0	0	—	3	1	0	0	0	11^{1}	13	1	7	4	15.9	7.15	57	.333	.435	0	—	0	-4	-4	-0	-0.6

● JOE SKALSKI Skalski, Joseph Douglas b: 9/26/64, Burnham, Ill. BR/TR, 6'3", 190 lbs. Deb: 4/10/89

YEAR TM/L	W	L	PCT	G	GS	CG	SH	SV	IP	H	HR	BB	SO	RAT	ERA	ERA+	OAV	OOB	BH	AVG	PB	PR	/A	PD	TPI
1989 Cle-A	0	2	.000	2	1	0	0	0	6^{2}	7	0	4	3	17.6	6.75	59	.259	.394	0	—	0	-2	-2	-0	-0.2

● DAVE SKAUGSTAD Skaugstad, David Wendell b: 1/10/40, Algona, Iowa BL/TL, 6'1", 179 lbs. Deb: 9/25/57

YEAR TM/L	W	L	PCT	G	GS	CG	SH	SV	IP	H	HR	BB	SO	RAT	ERA	ERA+	OAV	OOB	BH	AVG	PB	PR	/A	PD	TPI
1957 Cin-N	0	0	—	2	0	0	0	0	5^{2}	4	0	6	4	15.9	1.59	259	.190	.370	0	.000	0	1	2	0	0.2

● DAVE SKEELS Skeels, David b: 12/29/1892, Washington State d: 12/2/26, Spokane, Wash. BL/TR, 6'1", 187 lbs. Deb: 9/14/10

YEAR TM/L	W	L	PCT	G	GS	CG	SH	SV	IP	H	HR	BB	SO	RAT	ERA	ERA+	OAV	OOB	BH	AVG	PB	PR	/A	PD	TPI
1910 Det-A	0	0	—	1	1	0	0	0	6	9	0	4	2	21.0	12.00	22	.333	.438	0	.000	-0	-6	-6	0	-0.5

● CRAIG SKOK Skok, Craig Richard b: 9/1/47, Dobbs Ferry, N.Y. BR/TL, 6', 190 lbs. Deb: 5/04/73

YEAR TM/L	W	L	PCT	G	GS	CG	SH	SV	IP	H	HR	BB	SO	RAT	ERA	ERA+	OAV	OOB	BH	AVG	PB	PR	/A	PD	TPI
1973 Bos-A	0	1	.000	11	0	0	0	1	28^{2}	35	2	11	22	14.4	6.28	64	.304	.365	0	—	0	-8	-7	-0	-0.8
1976 Tex-A	0	1	.000	9	0	0	0	0	5	13	2	3	5	28.8	12.60	28	.481	.533	0	—	0	-5	-5	0	-0.6
1978 Atl-N	3	2	.600	43	0	0	0	2	62	64	8	27	28	13.2	4.35	93	.266	.340	2	.250	0	-5	-2	-0	-0.2
1979 Atl-N	1	3	.250	44	0	0	0	2	54^{1}	58	7	17	30	12.9	3.98	102	.282	.345	0	.000	-0	-1	0	0	0.1
Total 4	4	7	.364	107	0	0	0	5	150	170	19	58	85	13.9	4.86	83	.289	.355	2	.182	0	-20	-14	-0	-1.5

● JOHN SKOPEC Skopec, John S. "Buckshot" b: 5/8/1880, Chicago, Ill. d: 10/20/12, Chicago.Ill. BR/TL, 5'10", 190 lbs. Deb: 4/25/01

YEAR TM/L	W	L	PCT	G	GS	CG	SH	SV	IP	H	HR	BB	SO	RAT	ERA	ERA+	OAV	OOB	BH	AVG	PB	PR	/A	PD	TPI
1901 Chi-A	6	3	.667	9	9	6	0	0	68^{1}	62	1	45	24	15.1	3.16	110	.239	.368	10	.333	3	4	2	3	0.8
1903 Det-A	2	2	.500	6	5	3	0	0	39^{1}	46	0	13	14	14.0	3.43	85	.291	.352	2	.154	-0	-2	-2	0	-0.3
Total 2	8	5	.615	15	14	9	0	0	107^{2}	108	1	58	38	14.7	3.26	101	.259	.363	12	.279	3	2	0	3	0.5

● JOHN SLAGLE Slagle, John A. b: Lawrence, Ind. BL/TR, Deb: 4/30/1891

YEAR TM/L	W	L	PCT	G	GS	CG	SH	SV	IP	H	HR	BB	SO	RAT	ERA	ERA+	OAV	OOB	BH	AVG	PB	PR	/A	PD	TPI
1891 Cin-a	0	0	—	1	0	0	0	1	1^{1}	3	0	1	1	27.0	0.00	—	.431	.502	0	.000	-0	1	1	0	0.0

● ROGER SLAGLE Slagle, Roger Lee b: 11/4/53, Wichita, Kan. BR/TR, 6'3", 190 lbs. Deb: 9/07/79

YEAR TM/L	W	L	PCT	G	GS	CG	SH	SV	IP	H	HR	BB	SO	RAT	ERA	ERA+	OAV	OOB	BH	AVG	PB	PR	/A	PD	TPI
1979 NY-A	0	0	—	1	0	0	0	0	2	0	0	0	2	0.0	0.00	—	.000	.000	0	—	0	1	1	0	0.1

● WALT SLAGLE Slagle, Walter Jennings b: 12/15/1878, Kenton, Ohio d: 6/17/74, San Gabriel, Cal. BB/TR, 6', 165 lbs. Deb: 5/04/10

YEAR TM/L	W	L	PCT	G	GS	CG	SH	SV	IP	H	HR	BB	SO	RAT	ERA	ERA+	OAV	OOB	BH	AVG	PB	PR	/A	PD	TPI
1910 Cin-N	0	0	—	1	0	0	0	0	1	0	0	3	0	36.0	9.00	32	.000	.571	0	—	0	-1	-1	-0	-0.1

● CY SLAPNICKA Slapnicka, Cyril Charles b: 3/23/1886, Cedar Rapids, Iowa d: 10/20/79, Cedar Rapids, Iowa BB/TR, 5'10", 165 lbs. Deb: 9/26/11

YEAR TM/L	W	L	PCT	G	GS	CG	SH	SV	IP	H	HR	BB	SO	RAT	ERA	ERA+	OAV	OOB	BH	AVG	PB	PR	/A	PD	TPI
1911 Chi-N	0	2	.000	3	2	1	0	0	24	21	0	7	10	11.6	3.38	98	.236	.313	2	.222	-0	0	-0	1	0.1
1918 Pit-N	1	4	.200	7	6	4	0	1	49^{1}	50	2	22	3	14.0	4.74	61	.269	.362	1	.071	-1	-11	-10	-0	-1.2
Total 2	1	6	.143	10	8	5	0	1	73^{1}	71	2	29	13	13.3	4.30	70	.258	.346	3	.130	-1	-11	-10	0	-1.1

● JOHN SLAPPEY Slappey, John Henry b: 8/8/1898, Albany, Ga. d: 6/10/57, Marietta, Ga. BL/TL, 6'4", 170 lbs. Deb: 8/23/20

YEAR TM/L	W	L	PCT	G	GS	CG	SH	SV	IP	H	HR	BB	SO	RAT	ERA	ERA+	OAV	OOB	BH	AVG	PB	PR	/A	PD	TPI
1920 Phi-A	0	1	.000	3	1	0	0	0	6^{1}	15	0	4	1	27.0	7.11	57	.441	.500	1	.500	1	-2	-2	-0	-0.2

● JIM SLATON Slaton, James Michael b: 6/19/50, Long Beach, Cal. BR/TR, 6', 185 lbs. Deb: 4/14/71

YEAR TM/L	W	L	PCT	G	GS	CG	SH	SV	IP	H	HR	BB	SO	RAT	ERA	ERA+	OAV	OOB	BH	AVG	PB	PR	/A	PD	TPI
1971 Mil-A	10	8	.556	26	23	5	4	0	147^{2}	140	16	71	63	12.9	3.78	92	.253	.339	5	.109	-1	-5	-5	-2	-0.9
1972 Mil-A	1	6	.143	9	8	0	0	0	44	50	3	21	17	14.7	5.52	55	.287	.367	1	.091	-1	-12	-12	1	-1.3
1973 Mil-A	13	15	.464	38	38	13	3	0	276^{1}	266	30	99	134	11.9	3.71	101	.251	.316	0	—	0	3	1	-3	-0.2
1974 Mil-A	13	16	.448	40	35	10	3	0	250	255	22	102	126	13.0	3.92	92	.268	.341	0	—	0	-9	-9	0	-0.8
1975 Mil-A	11	18	.379	37	33	10	3	0	217	238	28	90	119	13.7	4.52	85	.276	.346	0	—	0	-18	-17	1	-1.6

YEAR TM/L	W	L	PCT	G	GS	CG	SH	SV	IP	H	HR	BB	SO	RAT	ERA	ERA+	OAV	OOB	BH	AVG	PB	PR	/A	PD	TPI
1976 Mil-A	14	15	.483	38	38	12	2	0	292^2	287	14	94	138	11.9	3.44	101	.259	.320	0	—	0	2	2	-0	0.3
1977 Mil-A☆	10	14	.417	32	31	7	1	0	221	223	25	77	104	12.7	3.58	113	.266	.336	0	—	0	12	12	0	1.2
1978 Det-A	17	11	.607	35	34	11	2	0	233^2	235	27	85	92	12.6	4.12	94	.263	.332	0	—	0	-9	-7	-1	-0.8
1979 Mil-A	15	9	.625	32	31	12	3	0	213	229	15	54	80	12.0	3.63	115	.278	.323	0	—	0	14	13	1	1.3
1980 Mil-A	1	1	.500	3	3	0	0	0	16^1	17	3	5	4	12.1	4.41	88	.270	.324	0	—	0	-1	-1	0	-0.1
1981 *Mil-A	5	7	.417	24	21	0	0	0	117^1	120	10	50	47	13.2	4.37	78	.273	.350	0	—	0	-9	-12	-0	-1.0
1982 *Mil-A	10	6	.625	39	7	0	0	6	117^2	117	14	41	59	12.2	3.29	115	.264	.327	0	—	0	10	6	-0	0.6
1983 Mil-A	14	6	.700	46	0	0	0	5	112^1	112	12	56	38	13.7	4.33	86	.272	.363	0	—	0	-3	-7	-0	-0.7
1984 Cal-A	7	10	.412	32	22	5	1	0	163	192	22	56	67	13.8	4.97	80	.295	.353	0	—	0	-18	-18	0	-1.7
1985 Cal-A	6	10	.375	29	24	1	0	1	148^1	162	22	63	60	13.8	4.37	94	.284	.357	0	—	0	-4	-4	-0	-0.4
1986 Cal-A	4	6	.400	14	12	0	0	0	73^1	84	9	29	31	14.1	5.65	73	.295	.364	0	—	0	-12	-13	1	-1.1
Det-A	0	0	—	22	0	0	0	2	40	46	5	11	12	13.0	4.05	102	.287	.337	0	—	0	1	0	0	0.1
Yr	4	6	.400	36	12	0	0	2	113^1	130	14	40	43	13.6	5.08	81	.287	.346	0	—	0	-11	-12	1	-1.0
Total 16	151	158	.489	496	360	86	22	14	2683^2	2773	277	1004	1191	12.8	4.03	94	.270	.337	6	.105	-2	-58	-70	-4	-7.1
● **PHIL SLATTERY** Slattery, Philip Ryan b: 2/25/1893, Harper, Iowa d: 3/2/68, Long Beach, Cal. BR/TL, 5'11", 160 lbs. Deb: 9/16/15																									
1915 Pit-N	0	0	—	3	0	0	0	0	8	5	0	1	1	9.0	0.00	—	.185	.267	0	.000	-0	2	2	-1	0.2
● **BARNEY SLAUGHTER** Slaughter, Byron Atkins b: 10/6/1884, Smyrna, Del. d: 5/17/61, Philadelphia, Pa. BR/TR, 5'11.5", 165 lbs. Deb: 8/09/10																									
1910 Phi-N	0	1	.000	8	1	0	0	1	18	21	0	11	7	16.0	5.50	57	.318	.416	1	.200	0	-5	-5	0	-0.5
● **STERLING SLAUGHTER** Slaughter, Sterling Feore b: 11/18/41, Danville, Ill. BR/TR, 5'11", 165 lbs. Deb: 4/19/64																									
1964 Chi-N	2	4	.333	20	6	1	0	0	51^2	64	8	32	32	16.7	5.75	65	.305	.397	1	.083	-0	-13	-12	-1	-1.4
● **BILL SLAYBACK** Slayback, William Grover b: 2/21/48, Hollywood, Cal. BR/TR, 6'4", 200 lbs. Deb: 6/26/72																									
1972 Det-A	5	6	.455	23	13	3	1	0	81^2	74	4	25	65	11.0	3.20	98	.239	.298	4	.174	-0	-1	-0	1	0.0
1973 Det-A	0	0	—	3	0	0	0	0	2	5	0	0	1	27.0	4.50	91	.417	.462	0	—	0	-0	-0	-0	0.0
1974 Det-A	1	3	.250	16	4	0	0	0	54^2	57	1	26	23	14.2	4.77	80	.273	.361	0	—	0	-7	-6	-0	-0.7
Total 3	6	9	.400	42	17	3	1	0	138^1	136	5	51	89	12.5	3.84	89	.256	.327	4	.174	-0	-8	-7	0	-0.7
● **STEVE SLAYTON** Slayton, Foster Herbert b: 4/26/02, Barre, Vt. d: 12/20/84, Manchester, N.H. BR/TR, 6', 163 lbs. Deb: 7/21/28																									
1928 Bos-A	0	0	—	3	0	0	0	0	7	6	0	3	2	11.6	3.86	107	.240	.321	0	.000	-0	0	0	-0	0.0
● **LOU SLEATER** Sleater, Louis Mortimer b: 9/8/26, St.Louis, Mo. BL/TL, 5'10", 185 lbs. Deb: 4/25/50																									
1950 StL-A	0	0	—	1	0	0	0	0	1	0	0	0	1	0.0	0.00	—	.000	.000	0	—	0	1	1	0	0.0
1951 StL-A	1	9	.100	20	8	4	0	1	81	88	7	53	33	16.2	5.11	86	.271	.381	7	.226	0	-9	-6	-1	-0.7
1952 StL-A	0	1	.000	4	2	0	0	0	8^2	9	1	5	1	14.5	7.27	54	.265	.359	0	.000	-0	-3	-3	0	-0.3
Was-A	4	2	.667	14	9	3	1	0	57	56	4	30	22	13.9	3.63	98	.260	.356	1	.050	-2	0	-0	-1	-0.4
Yr	4	3	.571	18	11	3	1	0	65^2	65	5	35	23	14.0	4.11	88	.261	.357	1	.045	-2	-3	-4	-1	-0.7
1955 KC-A	1	1	.500	16	1	0	0	0	25^2	33	3	21	11	18.9	7.71	54	.324	.439	2	.154	-1	-11	-10	-0	-1.0
1956 Mil-N	2	2	.500	25	1	0	0	2	45^2	42	6	27	32	13.6	3.15	110	.240	.342	5	.500	2	3	2	1	0.5
1957 Det-A	3	3	.500	41	0	0	0	2	69^1	61	9	28	43	11.7	3.76	102	.237	.315	5	.250	3	0	1	-0	0.4
1958 Det-A	0	0	—	4	0	0	0	0	5^1	3	2	6	4	15.2	6.75	60	.158	.360	1	1.000	1	-2	-2	0	0.0
Bal-A	1	0	1.000	6	0	0	0	0	7	14	0	2	5	20.6	12.86	28	.438	.471	0	.000	-1	-7	-7	0	-0.8
Yr	1	0	1.000	10	0	0	0	0	12^1	17	2	8	9	18.2	10.22	37	.333	.424	1	.143	1	-9	-9	0	-0.8
Total 7	12	18	.400	131	21	7	1	5	300^2	306	32	172	152	14.5	4.70	83	.263	.362	21	.204	3	-28	-26	-2	-2.3
● **LEFTY SLOAT** Sloat, Dwain Clifford b: 12/1/18, Nokomis, Ill. BR/TL, 6', 168 lbs. Deb: 4/24/48																									
1948 Bro-N	0	1	.000	4	1	0	0	0	7^1	7	0	8	1	18.4	6.14	65	.280	.455	0	.000	-0	-2	-2	1	-0.1
1949 Chi-N	0	0	—	5	1	0	0	0	9	14	0	3	3	17.0	7.00	58	.400	.447	0	—	0	-3	-3	0	-0.3
Total 2	0	1	.000	9	2	0	0	0	16^1	21	0	11	4	17.6	6.61	61	.350	.451	0	.000	-0	-5	-5	1	-0.4
● **HEATHCLIFF SLOCUMB** Slocumb, Heathcliff b: 6/7/66, Jamaica, N.Y. BR/TR, 6'3", 210 lbs. Deb: 4/11/91																									
1991 Chi-N	2	1	.667	52	0	0	0	1	62^2	53	3	30	34	12.4	3.45	113	.231	.328	0	.000	-0	2	3	0	0.3
1992 Chi-N	0	3	.000	30	0	0	0	1	36	52	3	21	27	18.5	6.50	55	.351	.435	0	.000	-0	-12	-12	-0	-1.3
Total 2	2	4	.333	82	0	0	0	2	98^2	105	6	51	61	14.6	4.56	83	.279	.370	0	.000	-1	-10	-9	-0	-1.0
● **JOE SLUSARSKI** Slusarski, Joseph Andrew b: 12/19/66, Indianapolis, Ind. BR/TR, 6'4", 195 lbs. Deb: 4/11/91																									
1991 Oak-A	5	7	.417	20	19	1	0	0	109^1	121	14	52	60	14.6	5.27	73	.283	.366	0	—	0	-14	-17	-1	-1.6
1992 Oak-A	5	5	.500	15	14	0	0	0	76	85	15	27	38	14.0	5.45	69	.284	.355	0	—	0	-13	-14	-1	-1.5
Total 2	10	12	.455	35	33	1	0	0	185^1	206	29	79	98	14.3	5.34	71	.284	.362	0	—	0	-27	-32	-2	-3.1
● **WALT SMALLWOOD** Smallwood, Walter Clayton b: 4/24/1893, Dayton, Md. d: 4/29/67, Baltimore, Md. BR/TR, 6'2", 190 lbs. Deb: 9/19/17																									
1917 NY-A	0	0	—	2	0	0	0	0	2	1	0	1	1	9.0	0.00	—	.167	.286	0	—	0	1	1	0	0.1
1919 NY-A	0	0	—	6	0	0	0	0	21^2	20	1	9	6	12.9	4.98	64	.263	.356	0	.000	-1	-4	-4	-0	-0.5
Total 2	0	0	—	8	0	0	0	0	23^2	21	1	10	7	12.5	4.56	69	.256	.351	0	.000	-1	-4	-4	-0	-0.4
● **JOHN SMILEY** Smiley, John Patrick b: 3/17/65, Phoenixville, Pa. BL/TL, 6'4", 195 lbs. Deb: 9/01/86																									
1986 Pit-N	1	0	1.000	12	0	0	0	0	11^2	4	2	4	9	6.2	3.86	99	.105	.190	0	—	0	-0	-0	0	0.0
1987 Pit-N	5	5	.500	63	0	0	0	4	75	69	7	50	58	14.3	5.76	71	.244	.357	1	.143	0	-14	-14	0	-1.3
1988 Pit-N	13	11	.542	34	32	5	1	0	205	185	15	46	129	10.3	3.25	105	.241	.287	5	.079	-2	5	3	-1	0.1
1989 Pit-N	12	8	.600	28	28	8	1	0	205^1	174	22	49	123	9.9	2.81	120	.226	.276	9	.138	1	16	13	-2	1.2
1990 *Pit-N	9	10	.474	26	25	2	0	0	149^1	161	15	36	86	12.0	4.64	78	.275	.319	6	.122	-0	-14	-17	0	-1.7
1991 *Pit-N★	**20**	8	**.714**	33	32	2	1	0	207^2	194	17	44	129	10.4	3.08	116	.251	.294	7	.100	-2	14	11	-0	1.0
1992 Min-A	16	9	.640	34	34	5	2	0	241	205	17	65	163	10.3	3.21	125	.231	.288	0	—	0	19	22	0	2.3
Total 7	76	51	.598	230	151	22	5	4	1095	992	95	294	697	10.7	3.49	104	.242	.295	28	.110	-4	25	18	-2	1.6
● **SMITH** Smith Deb: 6/05/1884																									
1884 Bal-U	0	0	—	1	1	0	0	0	6	12	0	2	2	21.0	9.00	37	.391	.429	1	.200	-0	-4	-4	-0	-0.3
● **AL SMITH** Smith, Alfred John b: 10/12/07, Belleville, Ill. d: 4/28/77, Brownsville, Tex. BL/TL, 5'11", 180 lbs. Deb: 5/05/34 C																									
1934 NY-N	3	5	.375	30	5	0	0	5	66^2	70	2	21	27	12.3	4.32	90	.266	.320	4	.286	0	-2	-3	-0	-0.3
1935 NY-N	10	8	.556	40	10	4	1	5	124	125	6	32	44	11.9	3.41	113	.263	.319	4	.118	-0	8	6	-1	0.5
1936 *NY-N	14	13	.519	43	30	9	**4**	2	209^1	217	16	69	89	12.5	3.78	103	.274	.335	10	.137	-1	6	3	-1	0.0
1937 *NY-N	5	4	.556	33	9	2	0	0	85^2	91	8	30	41	12.9	4.20	93	.275	.339	3	.120	-2	-3	-3	-1	-0.5
1938 Phi-N	1	4	.200	37	1	0	0	1	86	115	7	40	46	16.2	6.28	62	.320	.388	0	.000	-2	-24	-23	0	-2.4
1939 Phi-N	0	0	—	5	0	0	0	0	9	11	1	5	2	18.0	4.00	100	.314	.429	0	.000	-0	-0	0	0	0.0
1940 Cle-A	15	7	.682	31	24	11	1	2	183	187	12	55	46	12.2	3.44	122	.270	.329	19	.306	7	19	16	2	2.4
1941 Cle-A	12	13	.480	29	27	13	2	0	206^2	204	12	75	76	12.2	3.83	103	.256	.321	11	.155	2	7	2	2	0.6
1942 Cle-A	10	15	.400	30	24	7	1	0	168^1	163	9	71	66	12.8	3.96	87	.251	.329	15	.250	3	-6	-9	-1	-0.7
1943 Cle-A☆	17	7	.708	29	27	14	3	1	208^1	186	7	72	72	11.1	2.55	122	.239	.303	14	.206	3	17	13	-0	1.8
1944 Cle-A	7	13	.350	28	26	7	1	0	181^2	197	6	69	44	13.3	3.42	96	.280	.347	10	.156	-1	0	-2	1	-0.2
1945 Cle-A	5	12	.294	21	19	8	3	1	133^2	141	8	48	34	12.9	3.84	85	.275	.340	12	.293	4	-7	-9	2	-0.3
Total 12	99	101	.495	356	202	75	16	17	1662^1	1707	94	587	587	12.6	3.72	99	.267	.332	102	.191	13	17	-10	4	0.9

YEAR	TM/L	W	L	PCT	G	GS	CG	SH	SV	IP	H	HR	BB	SO	RAT	ERA	ERA+	OAV	OOB	BH	AVG	PB	PR	/A	PD	TPI
● **AL SMITH** Smith, Alfred Kendricks b: 12/13/03, Norristown, Pa. BR/TR, 6', 170 lbs. Deb: 6/18/26																										
1926	NY-N	0	0	—	1	0	0	0	0	2	4	0	2	0	27.0	9.00	42	.444	.545	0	—	0	-1	-1	-0	-0.1
● **ART SMITH** Smith, Arthur Laird b: 6/21/06, Boston, Mass. BR/TR, 6', 175 lbs. Deb: 6/09/32																										
1932	Chi-A	0	1	.000	3	2	0	0	0	7	17	1	4	1	27.0	11.57	37	.500	.553	0	.000	-0	-6	-6	1	-0.4
● **BILLY SMITH** Smith, Billy Lavern b: 9/13/54, LaMarque, Tex. BR/TR, 6'7", 200 lbs. Deb: 6/09/81																										
1981	*Hou-N	1	1	.500	10	1	0	0	1	20^2	20	3	3	3	10.0	3.05	108	.263	.291	0	.000	-0	1	1	0	0.0
● **BRYN SMITH** Smith, Bryn Nelson b: 8/11/55, Marietta, Ga. BR/TR, 6'2", 205 lbs. Deb: 9/08/81																										
1981	Mon-N	1	0	1.000	7	0	0	0	0	13	14	1	3	9	11.8	2.77	126	.280	.321	0	.000	-0	1	1	-0	0.1
1982	Mon-N	2	4	.333	47	1	0	0	3	79^1	81	5	23	50	11.8	4.20	87	.264	.315	0	.000	-0	-5	-5	0	-0.5
1983	Mon-N	6	11	.353	49	12	5	3	3	155^1	142	13	43	101	11.0	2.49	144	.248	.306	5	.167	0	20	19	0	2.1
1984	Mon-N	12	13	.480	28	28	4	2	0	179	178	15	51	101	11.7	3.32	103	.259	.313	7	.132	1	5	2	2	0.5
1985	Mon-N	18	5	.783	32	32	4	2	0	222^1	193	12	41	127	9.5	2.91	116	.232	.269	14	.194	3	17	12	-1	1.5
1986	Mon-N	10	8	.556	30	30	1	0	0	187^1	182	15	63	105	12.1	3.94	94	.251	.316	8	.138	1	-5	-5	3	-0.1
1987	Mon-N	10	9	.526	26	26	2	0	0	150^1	164	16	31	94	11.8	4.37	96	.274	.312	6	.136	-0	-5	-3	-0	-0.3
1988	Mon-N	12	10	.545	32	32	1	0	0	198	179	15	32	122	10.0	3.00	120	.243	.284	6	.109	-1	10	13	-2	1.1
1989	Mon-N	10	11	.476	33	32	3	1	0	215^2	177	16	54	129	9.8	2.84	124	.223	.276	4	.065	-2	16	17	2	1.9
1990	StL-N	9	8	.529	26	25	0	0	0	141^1	160	11	30	78	12.4	4.27	89	.286	.327	10	.256	3	-7	-7	-1	-0.5
1991	StL-N	12	9	.571	31	31	3	0	0	198^2	188	16	45	94	10.9	3.85	97	.251	.300	16	.246	3	-4	-3	-1	-0.1
1992	StL-N	4	2	.667	13	1	0	0	0	21^1	20	3	5	9	11.8	4.64	74	.247	.315	0	.000	-0	-3	-3	0	-0.3
Total	12	106	90	.541	354	250	23	8	6	1761^2	1678	138	421	1019	11.0	3.44	106	.251	.300	76	.155	8	40	38	3	5.4
● **CHARLIE SMITH** Smith, Charles Edwin b: 4/20/1880, Cleveland, Ohio d: 1/3/29, Wickliffe, Ohio BR/TR, 6'1", 185 lbs. Deb: 8/06/02 F																										
1902	Cle-A	2	1	.667	3	3	2	1	0	20	23	0	5	5	12.6	4.05	85	.289	.331	1	.125	-0	-1	-1	0	-0.2
1906	Was-A	9	16	.360	33	22	17	2	0	235^1	250	2	75	105	12.7	2.91	91	.275	.335	16	.184	-1	-6	-7	-2	-1.1
1907	Was-A	10	20	.333	36	31	21	3	0	258^2	254	0	51	119	10.6	2.61	93	.259	.296	12	.143	-3	-2	-5	3	-0.6
1908	Was-A	9	13	.409	26	23	14	1	1	184	166	2	60	83	11.2	2.40	96	.247	.311	8	.123	-2	0	-2	-1	-0.6
1909	Was-A	3	12	.200	23	15	7	1	0	145^2	140	4	37	72	11.2	3.27	74	.250	.303	7	.156	-1	-13	-14	0	-1.5
	Bos-A	3	0	1.000	3	3	2	0	0	25	23	2	2	11	9.4	2.16	116	.237	.260	3	.300	1	1	1	0	0.2
	Yr	6	12	.333	26	18	9	1	0	170^2	163	6	39	83	10.7	3.11	78	.247	.290	10	.182	-0	-12	-13	1	-1.3
1910	Bos-A	11	6	.647	24	18	11	0	1	156^1	141	4	35	53	10.2	2.30	111	.248	.294	5	.114	-2	4	4	-2	-0.1
1911	Bos-A	0	0	—	1	1	0	0	0	2	2	1	1	0	13.5	9.00	36	.250	.333	0	—	0	-1	-1	0	-0.1
	Chi-N	3	2	.600	7	5	3	1	0	38	31	0	7	11	9.2	1.42	233	.228	.271	1	.077	-1	8	8	-1	0.6
1912	Chi-N	7	4	.636	20	5	1	0	1	94	92	2	31	47	12.1	4.21	79	.269	.335	9	.257	1	-8	-9	1	-0.7
1913	Chi-N	7	9	.438	20	17	8	1	0	137^2	138	2	34	47	11.5	2.55	125	.274	.325	4	.089	-3	10	10	0	0.7
1914	Chi-N	2	4	.333	16	5	1	0	0	53^2	49	3	15	17	10.9	3.86	72	.251	.308	1	.091	-1	-6	-6	-1	-0.9
Total	10	66	87	.431	212	148	87	10	3	1350^1	1309	22	353	570	11.3	2.81	94	.259	.311	67	.150	-13	-14	-24	-2	-4.3
● **POP SMITH** Smith, Charles Marvin b: 10/12/1856, Digby, N.S., Canada d: 4/18/27, Boston, Mass. BR/TR, 5'11", 170 lbs. Deb: 5/01/1880 ♦																										
1883	Col-a	0	0	—	3	0	0	0	0	5^2	10	0	0	0	15.9	6.35	48	.362	.362	106	.262	1	-2	-2	-0	-0.2
● **POP-BOY SMITH** Smith, Clarence Ossie b: 5/23/1892, Newport, Tenn. d: 2/16/24, Sweetwater, Tex. BR/TR, 6'1", 176 lbs. Deb: 4/19/13																										
1913	Chi-A	0	1	.000	15	2	0	0	0	32	31	0	11	13	12.7	3.38	87	.261	.338	0	.000	-1	-2	-2	1	-0.1
1916	Cle-A	1	2	.333	5	3	0	0	1	25^2	25	1	11	4	13.0	3.86	78	.253	.333	2	.286	0	-3	-2	-0	-0.3
1917	Cle-A	0	1	.000	6	0	0	0	0	8^2	14	0	4	3	19.7	8.31	34	.368	.442	0	.000	-0	-5	-5	1	-0.4
Total	3	1	4	.200	26	5	0	0	1	66^1	70	1	26	20	13.7	4.21	70	.273	.352	2	.154	-1	-10	-9	2	-0.8
● **CLAY SMITH** Smith, Clay Jamieson b: 9/11/14, Cambridge, Kan. BR/TR, 6'2", 190 lbs. Deb: 9/13/38																										
1938	Cle-A	0	0	—	4	0	0	0	0	11	18	1	2	3	16.4	6.55	71	.367	.392	0	.000	-0	-2	-2	0	-0.2
1940	*Det-A	1	1	.500	14	1	0	0	0	28^1	32	3	13	14	14.6	5.08	94	.283	.362	0	.000	-1	-2	-1	1	-0.1
Total	2	1	1	.500	18	1	0	0	0	39^1	50	4	15	17	15.1	5.49	86	.309	.371	0	.000	-1	-4	-3	1	-0.3
● **DAN SMITH** Smith, Daniel Scott b: 8/20/69, St.Paul, Minn. BL/TL, 6'5", 190 lbs. Deb: 9/12/92																										
1992	Tex-A	0	3	.000	4	2	0	0	0	14^1	18	1	8	5	16.3	5.02	76	.321	.406	0	—	0	-2	-2	-0	-0.2
● **DARYL SMITH** Smith, Daryl Clinton b: 7/29/60, Baltimore, Md. BR/TR, 6'4", 185 lbs. Deb: 9/18/90																										
1990	KC-A	0	1	.000	2	1	0	0	0	6^2	5	0	4	6	12.2	4.05	95	.238	.360	0	—	0	-0	-0	-0	0.0
● **DAVE SMITH** Smith, David Merwin b: 12/17/14, Sellers, S.C. BR/TR, 5'10", 170 lbs. Deb: 6/16/38																										
1938	Phi-A	2	1	.667	21	0	0	0	0	44^1	50	0	28	13	16.0	5.08	95	.284	.385	0	.000	-1	-1	-1	-0	-0.2
1939	Phi-A	0	0	—	1	0	0	0	0	0	1	0	2	0	—	—	—	1.000	1.000	0	—	0	0	0	0	0.0
Total	2	2	1	.667	22	0	0	0	0	44^1	51	0	30	13	16.6	5.08	95	.288	.394	0	.000	-1	-1	-1	-0	-0.2
● **DAVE SMITH** Smith, David Stanley b: 1/21/55, Richmond, Cal. BR/TR, 6'1", 195 lbs. Deb: 4/11/80																										
1980	*Hou-N	7	5	.583	57	0	0	0	10	102^2	90	1	32	85	11.0	1.93	170	.237	.304	0	.000	-1	19	15	-1	1.4
1981	*Hou-N	5	3	.625	42	0	0	0	8	75	54	2	23	52	9.5	2.76	119	.198	.265	2	.250	0	6	4	-0	0.5
1982	Hou-N	5	4	.556	49	1	0	0	11	63^1	69	4	31	28	14.2	3.84	86	.285	.366	0	.000	-0	-2	-4	-1	-0.5
1983	Hou-N	3	1	.750	42	0	0	0	6	72^2	72	2	36	41	13.4	3.10	110	.258	.343	0	.000	-1	4	2	-2	0.0
1984	Hou-N	5	4	.556	53	0	0	0	5	77^1	60	5	20	45	9.4	2.21	150	.214	.269	0	.000	-0	12	10	-1	1.0
1985	Hou-N	9	5	.643	64	0	0	0	27	79^1	69	3	17	40	9.9	2.27	153	.235	.280	0	.000	0	12	11	-1	1.0
1986	*Hou-N☆	4	7	.364	54	0	0	0	33	56	39	5	22	46	10.0	2.73	132	.200	.284	0	.000	-0	6	5	0	0.5
1987	Hou-N	2	3	.400	50	0	0	0	24	60	39	0	21	73	9.2	1.65	237	.182	.258	1	.500	1	16	15	-0	1.6
1988	Hou-N	4	5	.444	51	0	0	0	27	57^1	60	1	19	38	12.6	2.67	124	.268	.328	0	.000	-0	5	4	-0	0.4
1989	Hou-N	3	4	.429	52	0	0	0	25	58	49	1	19	31	10.7	2.64	128	.233	.300	0	.000	-0	6	5	1	0.6
1990	Hou-N★	6	6	.500	49	0	0	0	23	60^1	45	4	20	50	9.7	2.39	156	.210	.278	0	.000	0	9	9	-1	0.8
1991	Chi-N	0	6	.000	35	0	0	0	17	33	39	6	19	16	16.1	6.00	65	.302	.396	0	.000	-0	-8	-8	-0	-0.8
1992	Chi-N	0	0	—	11	0	0	0	0	14^1	15	0	4	3	11.9	2.51	144	.273	.322	0	—	0	2	2	-0	0.2
Total	13	53	53	.500	609	1	0	0	216	809^1	700	34	283	548	11.1	2.67	130	.234	.303	3	.068	-2	87	71	-7	6.7
● **DAVE SMITH** Smith, David Wayne b: 8/30/57, Tomball, Tex. BR/TR, 6'1", 190 lbs. Deb: 9/18/84																										
1984	Cal-A	0	0	—	1	0	0	0	0	1	4	1	0	0	36.0	18.00	22	.571	.571	0	—	0	-2	-2	0	-0.1
1985	Cal-A	0	0	—	4	0	0	0	0	5	5	1	1	3	10.8	7.20	57	.278	.316	0	—	0	-2	-2	0	-0.1
Total	2	0	0	—	5	0	0	0	0	6	9	2	1	3	15.0	9.00	45	.360	.385	0	—	0	-3	-3	0	-0.2
● **DOUG SMITH** Smith, Douglass Weldon b: 5/25/1892, Millers Falls, Mass. d: 9/18/73, Greenfield, Mass. BL/TL, 5'10", 168 lbs. Deb: 7/10/12																										
1912	Bos-A	0	0	—	1	0	0	0	0	3	4	0	0	1	12.0	3.00	113	.364	.364	0	—	0	0	0	-0	0.0
● **EDDIE SMITH** Smith, Edgar b: 12/14/13, Columbus, N.J. BB/TL, 5'10", 174 lbs. Deb: 9/20/36																										
1936	Phi-A	1	1	.500	2	2	2	0	0	19	22	3	8	7	14.2	1.89	269	.275	.341	1	.125	-1	7	7	0	0.6
1937	Phi-A	4	17	.190	38	23	14	1	5	196^2	178	18	90	79	12.4	3.94	120	.242	.327	17	.233	1	15	17	-2	1.6
1938	Phi-A	3	10	.231	43	7	0	0	4	130^2	151	13	76	78	15.9	5.92	82	.287	.381	12	.286	3	-16	-16	0	-1.1
1939	Phi-A	1	0	1.000	3	0	0	0	0	3^2	7	0	2	3	22.1	9.82	48	.412	.474	0	—	0	-2	-2	-0	-0.2
	Chi-A	9	11	.450	29	22	7	1	0	176^2	161	11	90	67	13.0	3.67	129	.247	.342	6	.115	-1	19	21	-2	1.7
	Yr	10	11	.476	32	22	7	1	0	180^1	168	11	92	70	13.2	3.79	125	.251	.346	6	.115	-1	17	19	-2	1.5

YEAR	TM/L	W	L	PCT	G	GS	CG	SH	SV	IP	H	HR	BB	SO	RAT	ERA	ERA+	OAV	OOB	BH	AVG	PB	PR	/A	PD	TPI
1940	Chi-A	14	9	.609	32	28	12	0	0	207^{1}	179	16	95	119	12.0	3.21	138	.228	.313	15	.217	2	27	28	-1	2.9
1941	Chi-A★	13	17	.433	34	33	21	1	1	263^{1}	243	13	114	111	12.4	3.18	129	.246	.328	19	.216	4	28	27	0	3.1
1942	Chi-A☆	7	20	.259	29	28	18	2	1	215	223	17	86	78	13.1	3.98	90	.269	.341	9	.123	-2	-8	-9	2	-0.9
1943	Chi-A	11	11	.500	25	25	14	2	0	187^{2}	197	2	76	66	13.3	3.69	90	.277	.351	11	.159	-1	-8	-7	1	-0.8
1946	Chi-A	8	11	.421	24	21	3	1	1	145^{1}	135	9	60	59	12.3	2.85	120	.246	.325	8	.178	0	11	9	-0	1.0
1947	Chi-A	1	3	.250	15	5	0	0	0	33^{1}	40	1	24	12	17.3	7.29	50	.299	.405	1	.167	-0	-13	-13	-1	-1.4
	Bos-A	1	3	.250	8	3	0	0	0	17	18	3	18	15	19.1	7.41	52	.269	.424	1	.167	0	-7	-7	-0	-0.7
	Yr	2	6	.250	23	8	0	0	0	50^{1}	58	4	42	27	17.9	7.33	51	.289	.412	2	.167	-0	-20	-20	-1	-2.1
Total	10	73	113	.392	282	197	91	8	12	1595^{2}	1554	106	739	694	13.1	3.82	108	.256	.340	100	.188	5	51	53	-3	5.8

● EDGAR SMITH Smith, Edgar Eugene b: 6/12/1862, Providence, R.I. d: 11/3/1892, Providence, R.I. BR/TR, 5'10", 160 lbs. Deb: 5/25/1883 ♦

YEAR	TM/L	W	L	PCT	G	GS	CG	SH	SV	IP	H	HR	BB	SO	RAT	ERA	ERA+	OAV	OOB	BH	AVG	PB	PR	/A	PD	TPI
1883	Phi-N	0	1	.000	1	1	0	0	0	7	18	0	3	2	27.0	15.43	20	.409	.447	3	.750	1	-10	-10	-0	-0.6
1884	Was-a	0	2	.000	3	2	2	0	0	22	27	0	5	4	13.5	4.91	62	.276	.317	5	.088	-1	-4	-5	-0	-0.4
1885	Pro-N	1	0	1.000	1	1	1	0	0	9	9	0	0	1	9.0	1.00	265	.273	.273	1	.250	0	2	2	0	0.2
1890	Cle-N	1	4	.200	6	6	5	0	0	44	42	1	10	11	10.8	4.30	83	.244	.289	7	.292	2	-4	-3	2	0.0
Total	4	2	7	.222	11	10	8	0	0	82	96	1	18	18	12.7	5.05	65	.276	.316	18	.184	2	-15	-16	1	-0.8

● ELMER SMITH Smith, Elmer Ellsworth b: 3/23/1868, Pittsburgh, Pa. d: 11/3/45, Pittsburgh, Pa. BL/TL, 5'11", 178 lbs. Deb: 5/31/1886 ♦

YEAR	TM/L	W	L	PCT	G	GS	CG	SH	SV	IP	H	HR	BB	SO	RAT	ERA	ERA+	OAV	OOB	BH	AVG	PB	PR	/A	PD	TPI
1886	Cin-a	4	5	.444	10	10	9	0	0	81^{2}	65	1	54	41	13.4	3.75	94	.213	.337	9	.281	4	-3	-2	-2	-0.1
1887	Cin-a	34	17	.667	52	52	49	3	0	447^{1}	400	5	126	176	**10.8**	**2.94**	**148**	**.230**	**.286**	47	.253	5	68	**70**	-5	5.9
1888	Cin-a	22	17	.564	40	40	37	5	0	348^{1}	309	1	89	154	10.8	2.74	116	.229	.286	29	.225	5	13	17	-5	1.5
1889	Cin-a	9	12	.429	29	22	16	0	0	203	253	11	101	104	16.0	4.88	80	.296	.375	23	.277	5	-23	-22	-4	-1.7
1892	Pit-N	6	7	.462	17	13	12	1	0	134	140	2	58	51	13.4	3.63	91	.258	.331	140	.274	6	-5	-5	-1	-0.1
1894	Pit-N	0	0	—	1	0	0	0	0	4	6	0	1	0	18.0	4.50	116	.342	.410	174	.356	0	0	0	-0	0.0
1898	Cin-N	0	0	—	1	0	0	0	0	1	2	0	3	0	45.0	18.00	21	.411	.635	166	.342	0	-2	-2	-0	-0.1
Total	7	75	58	.564	150	137	123	9	0	1219^{1}	1175	20	432	526	12.2	3.35	113	.244	.312	1455	.310	26	48	57	-19	5.4

● FRANK SMITH Smith, Frank Elmer "Nig" or "Piano Mover" (b: Frank Elmer Schmidt)
b: 10/28/1879, Pittsburgh, Pa. d: 11/3/52, Pittsburgh, Pa. BR/TR, 5'10.5", 194 lbs. Deb: 4/22/04

YEAR	TM/L	W	L	PCT	G	GS	CG	SH	SV	IP	H	HR	BB	SO	RAT	ERA	ERA+	OAV	OOB	BH	AVG	PB	PR	/A	PD	TPI
1904	Chi-A	16	9	.640	26	23	22	4	0	202^{1}	157	0	58	107	10.1	2.09	117	.215	.283	18	.250	4	11	8	-2	1.2
1905	Chi-A	19	13	.594	39	31	27	4	0	291^{2}	215	0	107	171	10.1	2.13	116	.207	.285	24	.226	6	17	11	-0	1.9
1906	Chi-A	5	5	.500	20	13	8	1	1	122	124	3	37	53	12.2	3.39	75	.267	.327	12	.293	5	-10	-12	1	-0.6
1907	Chi-A	23	10	.697	41	37	29	3	0	310	280	3	111	139	11.4	2.47	97	.243	.311	18	.196	4	3	-2	4	0.7
1908	Chi-A	16	17	.485	41	35	24	3	1	297^{2}	213	2	73	129	8.7	2.03	114	.203	.256	20	.189	2	12	10	3	1.7
1909	Chi-A	25	17	.595	**51**	40	**37**	7	1	**365**	278	1	70	**177**	8.7	1.80	130	.214	.257	22	.173	5	27	22	10	**4.4**
1910	Chi-A	4	9	.308	19	15	9	3	0	128^{2}	91	1	40	50	9.3	2.03	118	.204	.272	8	.186	2	7	5	4	1.2
	Bos-A	1	2	.333	4	3	2	0	0	28	22	0	11	8	10.9	4.82	53	.234	.321	1	.111	-0	-7	-7	-0	-0.7
	Yr	5	11	.313	23	18	11	3	0	156^{2}	113	1	51	58	9.5	2.53	96	.208	.277	9	.173	2	-0	-2	4	0.5
1911	Bos-A	0	0	—	1	1	0	0	0	2^{1}	6	0	3	1	34.7	15.43	21	.500	.600	0	—	0	-3	-3	0	-0.2
	Cin-N	10	14	.417	34	18	10	0	1	176^{1}	198	1	55	67	13.1	3.98	83	.289	.345	12	.214	3	-11	-13	4	-0.6
1912	Cin-N	1	1	.500	7	3	1	0	0	22^{2}	34	1	15	5	19.5	6.35	53	.370	.458	0	.000	-0	-7	-8	-0	-0.8
1914	Bal-F	10	8	.556	39	22	9	1	2	174^{2}	180	8	47	83	11.7	2.99	113	.259	.306	12	.203	1	4	7	2	1.1
1915	Bal-F	4	4	.500	17	9	2	0	0	88^{2}	108	5	31	37	14.1	4.67	68	.312	.369	5	.172	1	-16	-15	0	-1.4
	Bro-F	5	2	.714	15	5	4	1	0	63	69	2	18	24	12.4	3.14	96	.290	.340	4	.200	1	-1	-1	1	0.1
	Yr	9	6	.600	32	14	6	1	0	151^{2}	177	7	49	61	13.4	4.04	77	.303	.357	9	.184	2	-17	-15	1	-1.3
Total	11	139	111	.556	354	255	184	27	6	2273	1975	27	676	1051	10.6	2.59	100	.237	.297	156	.204	33	27	2	27	8.0

● FRANK SMITH Smith, Frank Thomas b: 4/4/28, Pierrepont Manor, N.Y. BR/TR, 6'3", 200 lbs. Deb: 4/18/50

YEAR	TM/L	W	L	PCT	G	GS	CG	SH	SV	IP	H	HR	BB	SO	RAT	ERA	ERA+	OAV	OOB	BH	AVG	PB	PR	/A	PD	TPI
1950	Cin-N	2	7	.222	38	4	0	0	3	90^{2}	73	12	39	55	11.9	3.87	109	.216	.312	2	.095	-2	3	4	-1	0.1
1951	Cin-N	5	5	.500	50	0	0	0	11	76	65	7	22	34	10.8	3.20	128	.230	.295	0	.000	-1	6	7	0	0.7
1952	Cin-N	12	11	.522	53	2	1	0	7	122^{1}	109	13	41	77	11.6	3.75	101	.242	.315	5	.172	0	-0	0	-2	-0.1
1953	Cin-N	8	1	.889	50	1	0	0	2	83^{2}	89	15	25	42	12.6	5.49	79	.272	.330	2	.154	-1	-11	-11	1	-1.0
1954	Cin-N	5	8	.385	50	0	0	0	20	81	60	15	29	51	10.2	2.67	157	.211	.291	1	.100	1	13	14	0	1.5
1955	StL-N	3	1	.750	28	0	0	0	1	39	27	3	23	17	12.7	3.23	126	.205	.344	0	.000	-1	3	4	-0	0.3
1956	Cin-N	0	0	—	2	0	0	0	0	3	3	2	2	1	15.0	12.00	33	.300	.417	0	—	0	-3	-3	-0	-0.3
Total	7	35	33	.515	271	7	1	0	44	495^{2}	426	67	181	277	11.6	3.81	107	.234	.313	10	.115	-3	11	16	-2	1.2

● FRED SMITH Smith, Frederick b: 11/24/1878, New Diggins, Wis. d: 2/4/64, Los Angeles, Cal. BL/TR, 6', 186 lbs. Deb: 6/14/07

YEAR	TM/L	W	L	PCT	G	GS	CG	SH	SV	IP	H	HR	BB	SO	RAT	ERA	ERA+	OAV	OOB	BH	AVG	PB	PR	/A	PD	TPI
1907	Cin-N	2	7	.222	18	9	5	0	1	85^{1}	90	3	24	19	12.4	2.85	91	.274	.331	3	.107	-2	-4	-2	0	-0.5

● FRED SMITH Smith, Frederick C. b: 3/25/1863, Greene, N.Y. d: 1/9/41, Syracuse, N.Y. BL/TR, 5'11", 156 lbs. Deb: 4/18/1890

YEAR	TM/L	W	L	PCT	G	GS	CG	SH	SV	IP	H	HR	BB	SO	RAT	ERA	ERA+	OAV	OOB	BH	AVG	PB	PR	/A	PD	TPI
1890	Tol-a	19	13	.594	35	34	31	2	0	286	273	13	90	116	11.8	3.27	121	.244	.307	21	.167	-2	19	22	3	2.0

● GEORGE SMITH Smith, George Allen "Columbia George" b: 5/31/1892, Byram, Conn. d: 1/7/65, Greenwich, Conn. BR/TR, 6'2", 163 lbs. Deb: 8/09/16

YEAR	TM/L	W	L	PCT	G	GS	CG	SH	SV	IP	H	HR	BB	SO	RAT	ERA	ERA+	OAV	OOB	BH	AVG	PB	PR	/A	PD	TPI
1916	NY-N	3	0	1.000	9	1	0	0	0	20^{2}	14	0	6	9	9.1	2.61	93	.197	.269	0	.000	-0	0	-0	0	0.0
1917	NY-N	0	3	.000	14	1	1	0	0	38	38	1	11	16	11.8	2.84	90	.270	.327	0	.000	-1	-1	-1	-0	-0.3
1918	Cin-N	2	3	.400	10	6	4	1	0	55^{1}	71	3	11	19	13.3	4.07	66	.329	.361	0	.000	-2	-8	-9	1	-1.1
	NY-N	2	3	.400	5	2	1	0	0	26^{2}	26	0	6	4	11.1	4.05	65	.255	.303	2	.250	0	-4	-4	-1	-0.6
	Bro-N	4	1	.800	8	5	4	0	0	50	43	0	5	18	9.0	2.34	119	.249	.278	3	.200	0	2	2	1	0.4
	Yr	8	7	.533	23	13	9	1	0	132	140	3	22	41	11.2	3.41	79	.285	.318	5	.125	-2	-9	-10	0	-1.3
1919	NY-N	0	2	.000	3	2	0	0	0	11	18	1	4	0	18.0	5.73	49	.383	.431	0	.000	-0	-3	-4	-0	-0.5
	Phi-N	5	11	.313	31	20	11	1	0	184^{2}	194	7	46	42	11.8	3.22	100	.278	.326	8	.133	-3	-6	0	-1	-0.4
	Yr	5	13	.278	34	22	11	1	0	195^{2}	212	8	50	42	12.2	3.36	95	.285	.332	8	.127	-4	-10	-3	-1	-0.9
1920	Phi-N	13	18	.419	43	28	10	1	2	250^{2}	265	10	51	51	11.6	3.45	99	.283	.324	7	.097	-6	-9	-1	-2	-0.9
1921	Phi-N	4	20	.167	39	28	12	1	1	221^{1}	303	12	52	45	14.6	4.76	89	.335	.373	4	.056	-9	-24	-13	-2	-2.2
1922	Phi-N	5	14	.263	42	18	6	1	0	194	250	16	35	44	13.5	4.78	98	.316	.350	5	.076	-8	-15	-2	-2	-1.1
1923	Bro-N	3	6	.333	25	7	3	0	1	91	99	4	28	15	12.9	3.66	106	.278	.336	5	.192	-1	3	2	-2	-0.1
Total	8	41	81	.336	229	118	52	5	4	1143^{1}	1321	54	255	263	12.6	3.89	94	.298	.340	34	.097	-31	-63	-31	-8	-6.8

● HEINIE SMITH Smith, George Henry b: 10/24/1871, Pittsburgh, Pa. d: 6/25/39, Buffalo, N.Y. BR/TR, 5'9.5", 160 lbs. Deb: 9/08/1897 M♦

YEAR	TM/L	W	L	PCT	G	GS	CG	SH	SV	IP	H	HR	BB	SO	RAT	ERA	ERA+	OAV	OOB	BH	AVG	PB	PR	/A	PD	TPI
1901	NY-N	0	1	.000	2	1	1	0	0	13^{1}	24	0	5	5	22.3	8.10	41	.386	.463	6	.207	0	-7	-7	-0	-0.6

● GERMANY SMITH Smith, George J. b: 4/21/1863, Pittsburgh, Pa. d: 12/1/27, Altoona, Pa. BR/TR, 6', 175 lbs. Deb: 4/17/1884 ♦

YEAR	TM/L	W	L	PCT	G	GS	CG	SH	SV	IP	H	HR	BB	SO	RAT	ERA	ERA+	OAV	OOB	BH	AVG	PB	PR	/A	PD	TPI
1884	Alt-U	0	0	—	1	0	0	0	0	1	3	0	0	1	27.0	9.00	36	.491	.491	34	.315	0	-1	-1	0	-0.1

● GEORGE SMITH Smith, George Shelby b: 10/27/01, Louisville, Ky. d: 5/26/81, Richmond, Va. BR/TR, 6'1", 175 lbs. Deb: 4/21/26

YEAR	TM/L	W	L	PCT	G	GS	CG	SH	SV	IP	H	HR	BB	SO	RAT	ERA	ERA+	OAV	OOB	BH	AVG	PB	PR	/A	PD	TPI
1926	Det-A	1	2	.333	23	1	0	0	0	44	55	3	33	15	18.4	6.95	58	.318	.433	0	.000	-0	-14	-14	-1	-1.5
1927	Det-A	4	1	.800	29	0	0	0	0	71^{1}	62	3	50	32	14.4	3.91	108	.240	.368	7	.368	3	2	2	-1	0.5
1928	Det-A	1	1	.500	39	2	0	0	3	106	103	3	50	54	13.0	4.42	93	.263	.346	3	.111	-2	-4	-4	-2	-0.7
1929	Det-A	3	2	.600	14	2	1	0	0	35^{2}	42	1	36	13	19.7	5.80	74	.307	.451	5	.417	2	-6	-6	1	-0.3
1930	Bos-A	1	2	.333	27	2	0	0	0	73^{2}	92	7	49	21	17.3	6.60	70	.317	.418	8	.333	2	-16	-16	0	-1.3
Total	5	10	8	.556	132	7	1	0	3	330^{2}	354	17	218	135	15.7	5.28	81	.283	.392	23	.264	4	-39	-38	-2	-3.3

● HAL SMITH Smith, Harold Laverne b: 6/30/02, Creston, Iowa BR/TR, 6'3", 195 lbs. Deb: 9/14/32

YEAR	TM/L	W	L	PCT	G	GS	CG	SH	SV	IP	H	HR	BB	SO	RAT	ERA	ERA+	OAV	OOB	BH	AVG	PB	PR	/A	PD	TPI
1932	Pit-N	1	0	1.000	2	1	1	1	0	12	9	0	2	4	8.3	0.75	508	.209	.244	0	.000	-0	4	4	0	0.4

YEAR TM/L	W	L	PCT	G	GS	CG	SH	SV	IP	H	HR	BB	SO	RAT	ERA	ERA+	OAV	OOB	BH	AVG	PB	PR	/A	PD	TPI
1933 Pit-N	8	7	.533	28	19	8	2	1	145	149	5	31	40	11.5	2.86	116	.261	.305	6	.128	-2	8	7	-2	0.4
1934 Pit-N	3	4	.429	20	5	1	0	0	50	72	3	18	15	16.9	7.20	57	.343	.405	1	.059	-2	-17	-17	-0	-1.8
1935 Pit-N	0	0	—	1	0	0	0	0	3	2	0	1	0	9.0	3.00	137	.200	.273	0	—	0	0	0	-0	0.0
Total 4	12	11	.522	51	25	10	3	1	210	232	8	52	59	12.6	3.77	94	.279	.328	7	.104	-4	-5	-5	-2	-1.0

● HARRY SMITH Smith, Harrison Morton b: 8/15/1889, Union, Neb. d: 7/26/64, Dunbar, Neb. BR/TR, 5'9", 160 lbs. Deb: 10/06/12

YEAR TM/L	W	L	PCT	G	GS	CG	SH	SV	IP	H	HR	BB	SO	RAT	ERA	ERA+	OAV	OOB	BH	AVG	PB	PR	/A	PD	TPI
1912 Chi-A	1	0	1.000	1	1	0	0	0	5	6	0	0	1	10.8	1.80	178	.333	.333	0	.000	-0	1	1	-0	0.1

● JACK SMITH Smith, Jack Hatfield b: 11/15/35, Pikeville, Ky. BR/TR, 6', 185 lbs. Deb: 9/10/62

YEAR TM/L	W	L	PCT	G	GS	CG	SH	SV	IP	H	HR	BB	SO	RAT	ERA	ERA+	OAV	OOB	BH	AVG	PB	PR	/A	PD	TPI
1962 LA-N	0	0	—	8	0	0	0	1	10	10	0	4	7	12.6	4.50	81	.263	.333	0	.000	-0	-1	-1	-0	-0.1
1963 LA-N	0	0	—	4	0	0	0	0	8^{1}	10	2	2	5	15.1	7.56	40	.303	.378	0	.000	-0	-4	-4	0	-0.4
1964 Mil-N	2	2	.500	22	0	0	0	0	31	28	3	11	19	11.3	3.77	93	.237	.302	1	.333	0	-1	-1	1	0.0
Total 3	2	2	.500	34	0	0	0	1	49^{1}	48	5	17	31	12.2	4.56	76	.254	.322	1	.167	-0	-5	-6	1	-0.5

● JAKE SMITH Smith, Jacob (b: Jacob Schmidt) b: 6/21/1887, Dravosburg, Pa d: 11/7/48, E.McKeesport, Pa. BB/TR, 6'5", 200 lbs. Deb: 10/03/11

YEAR TM/L	W	L	PCT	G	GS	CG	SH	SV	IP	H	HR	BB	SO	RAT	ERA	ERA+	OAV	OOB	BH	AVG	PB	PR	/A	PD	TPI
1911 Phi-N	0	0	—	2	0	0	0	0	5	3	0	2	1	9.0	0.00	—	.176	.263	0	.000	-0	2	2	0	0.2

● PHENOMENAL SMITH Smith, John Francis (b: John Francis Gammon) b: 12/12/1864, Philadelphia, Pa. d: 4/3/52, Manchester, N.H. BL/TL, 5'6.5", 161 lbs. Deb: 4/18/1884

YEAR TM/L	W	L	PCT	G	GS	CG	SH	SV	IP	H	HR	BB	SO	RAT	ERA	ERA+	OAV	OOB	BH	AVG	PB	PR	/A	PD	TPI
1884 Bal-U	3	4	.429	9	8	5	0	0	62	86	2	17	13	15.0	3.48	95	.308	.348	5	.147	-3	-3	-1	-1	-0.4
Phi-a	0	1	.000	1	1	1	0	0	9	14	0	1	3	15.0	4.00	85	.368	.385	1	.250	-0	-1	-1	0	0.0
Pit-a	0	1	.000	1	1	1	0	0	8	11	0	2	4	15.8	9.00	37	.306	.359	0	.000	-1	-5	-5	0	-0.4
Yr	0	2	.000	2	2	2	0	0	17	25	0	3	7	15.4	6.35	53	.338	.372	1	.125	-1	-6	-6	0	-0.4
1885 Bro-a	0	1	.000	1	1	1	0	0	8	12	0	6	2	21.4	12.38	27	.300	.404	1	.333	0	-8	-8	0	-0.5
Phi-a	0	1	.000	1	1	0	0	0	4	7	0	4	7	27.0	9.00	38	.368	.500	0	.000	-0	-3	-2	0	-0.2
Yr	0	2	.000	2	2	1	0	0	12	19	0	10	9	22.5	11.25	30	.317	.423	1	.200	-0	-11	-11	0	-0.7
1886 Det-N	1	1	.500	3	3	3	0	0	25	16	0	8	15	8.6	2.16	153	.174	.240	1	.111	-1	3	3	-1	0.2
1887 Bal-a	25	30	.455	58	55	54	1	0	491^{1}	526	7	176	206	13.1	3.79	108	.261	.325	48	.234	8	28	17	-1	2.0
1888 Bal-a	14	19	.424	35	32	31	0	0	292	249	5	137	152	12.6	3.61	83	.222	.320	27	.248	8	-18	-20	-4	-1.5
Phi-a	2	1	.667	3	3	3	0	0	22	21	0	10	19	12.7	2.86	104	.242	.321	3	.333	1	0	0	-0	0.1
Yr	16	20	.444	38	35	34	0	0	314	270	5	147	171	12.0	3.55	84	.219	.303	30	.254	9	-17	-20	-4	-1.4
1889 Phi-a	2	3	.400	5	5	5	0	0	43	53	2	25	12	17.0	4.40	86	.294	.389	3	.188	0	-3	-3	-1	-0.3
1890 Phi-N	8	12	.400	24	20	19	1	0	204	209	5	89	81	13.5	4.28	85	.257	.336	24	.279	4	-16	-14	-2	-1.1
Pit-N	1	3	.250	5	5	5	0	0	44	39	0	13	15	10.8	3.07	107	.230	.289	7	.412	2	2	1	-0	0.3
Yr	9	15	.375	29	25	24	1	0	248	248	5	102	96	12.7	4.06	88	.250	.321	31	.301	6	-14	-13	-3	-0.8
1891 Phi-N	1	1	.500	3	2	0	0	0	19	20	1	8	3	13.3	4.26	80	.260	.330	3	.375	1	-2	-2	-1	-0.1
Total 8	57	78	.422	149	137	128	2	0	1231^{1}	1263	22	496	532	13.2	3.87	94	.254	.329	123	.243	20	-24	-34	-10	-1.9

● CHICK SMITH Smith, John William (b: Jan Smadt) b: 12/2/1892, Dayton, Ky. d: 10/11/35, Dayton, Ohio BL/TL, 5'8", 165 lbs. Deb: 4/12/13

YEAR TM/L	W	L	PCT	G	GS	CG	SH	SV	IP	H	HR	BB	SO	RAT	ERA	ERA+	OAV	OOB	BH	AVG	PB	PR	/A	PD	TPI
1913 Cin-N	0	1	.000	5	1	0	0	0	17^{2}	15	1	11	11	13.2	3.57	91	.238	.351	0	.000	-1	-1	-1	0	-0.1

● LEE SMITH Smith, Lee Arthur b: 12/4/57, Shreveport, La. BR/TR, 6'6", 225 lbs. Deb: 9/01/80

YEAR TM/L	W	L	PCT	G	GS	CG	SH	SV	IP	H	HR	BB	SO	RAT	ERA	ERA+	OAV	OOB	BH	AVG	PB	PR	/A	PD	TPI
1980 Chi-N	2	0	1.000	18	0	0	0	0	21^{2}	21	0	14	17	14.5	2.91	135	.259	.368	0	—	0	2	2	-0	0.2
1981 Chi-N	3	6	.333	40	1	0	0	1	66^{2}	57	2	31	50	12.0	3.51	105	.239	.330	0	.000	-1	-0	1	-0	0.0
1982 Chi-N	2	5	.286	72	5	0	0	17	117	105	5	37	99	11.2	2.69	139	.245	.309	1	.063	-0	12	14	-1	1.3
1983 Chi-N★	4	10	.286	66	0	0	0	**29**	103^{1}	70	5	41	91	9.8	1.65	229	.194	.279	1	.111	-0	23	25	-1	2.5
1984 *Chi-N	9	7	.563	69	0	0	0	33	101	98	6	35	86	11.9	3.65	107	.255	.317	1	.077	-1	-1	3	0	0.2
1985 Chi-N	7	4	.636	65	0	0	0	33	97^{2}	87	9	32	112	11.1	3.04	131	.242	.305	0	.000	-0	6	10	-1	1.0
1986 Chi-N	9	9	.500	66	0	0	0	31	90^{1}	69	7	42	93	11.1	3.09	131	.215	.306	0	.000	-1	6	10	-0	0.9
1987 Chi-N★	4	10	.286	62	0	0	0	36	83^{2}	84	4	32	96	12.5	3.12	137	.259	.326	0	.000	-0	9	11	-1	1.0
1988 *Bos-A	4	5	.444	64	0	0	0	29	83^{2}	72	7	37	96	11.8	2.80	147	.225	.307	0	—	0	11	12	-1	1.2
1989 Bos-A	6	1	.857	64	0	0	0	25	70^{2}	53	6	33	96	11.0	3.57	115	.209	.301	0	—	0	2	4	-1	0.0
1990 Bos-A	2	1	.667	11	0	0	0	4	14^{1}	13	0	9	17	13.8	1.88	216	.236	.344	0	—	0	3	3	0	0.3
StL-N	3	4	.429	53	0	0	0	27	68^{2}	58	3	20	70	10.2	2.10	182	.227	.284	0	.000	-0	13	13	-2	1.2
1991 StL-N☆	6	3	.667	67	0	0	0	**47**	73	70	5	13	67	10.2	2.34	159	.249	.282	0	—	0	11	11	-1	1.1
1992 StL-N☆	4	9	.308	70	0	0	0	**43**	75	62	4	26	60	10.6	3.12	110	.221	.287	0	—	0	3	3	-1	0.2
Total 13	65	74	.468	787	6	0	0	355	1066^{2}	919	63	402	1050	11.2	2.86	136	.233	.305	3	.048	-4	100	122	-8	11.1

● ROY SMITH Smith, Le Roy Purdy b: 9/6/61, Mt.Vernon, N.Y. BR/TR, 6'3", 200 lbs. Deb: 6/23/84

YEAR TM/L	W	L	PCT	G	GS	CG	SH	SV	IP	H	HR	BB	SO	RAT	ERA	ERA+	OAV	OOB	BH	AVG	PB	PR	/A	PD	TPI
1984 Cle-A	5	5	.500	22	14	0	0	0	86^{1}	91	14	40	55	13.8	4.59	89	.270	.349	0	—	0	-6	-5	-2	-0.7
1985 Cle-A	1	4	.200	12	11	1	0	0	62^{1}	84	8	17	28	14.7	5.34	77	.321	.364	0	—	0	-8	-8	-1	-0.8
1986 Min-A	0	2	.000	5	0	0	0	0	10^{1}	13	1	5	8	16.5	6.97	62	.295	.380	0	—	0	-3	-3	-0	-0.4
1987 Min-A	1	0	1.000	7	1	0	0	0	16^{1}	20	3	6	8	15.4	4.96	93	.290	.364	0	—	0	-1	-1	-0	-0.1
1988 Min-A	3	0	1.000	9	4	0	0	0	37	29	3	12	17	10.2	2.68	152	.210	.278	0	—	0	5	6	-1	0.5
1989 Min-A	10	6	.625	32	26	2	0	1	172^{1}	180	22	51	92	12.3	3.92	106	.269	.326	0	—	0	-1	4	-3	-0.1
1990 Min-A	5	10	.333	32	23	1	1	0	153^{1}	191	20	47	87	14.0	4.81	86	.313	.362	0	—	0	-15	-11	-2	-1.5
1991 Bal-A	5	4	.556	17	14	0	0	0	80^{1}	99	9	24	25	13.9	5.60	71	.311	.362	0	—	0	-13	-15	-1	-1.3
Total 8	30	31	.492	136	93	4	1	1	618^{1}	707	80	202	320	13.4	4.60	90	.289	.346	0	—	0	-42	-33	-9	-4.4

● MARK SMITH Smith, Mark Christopher b: 11/23/55, Arlington, Va. BR/TR, 6'2", 215 lbs. Deb: 8/12/83

YEAR TM/L	W	L	PCT	G	GS	CG	SH	SV	IP	H	HR	BB	SO	RAT	ERA	ERA+	OAV	OOB	BH	AVG	PB	PR	/A	PD	TPI
1983 Oak-A	1	0	1.000	8	1	0	0	0	14^{2}	24	0	6	10	19.0	6.75	57	.387	.449	0	—	0	-4	-5	-0	-0.1

● MIKE SMITH Smith, Michael Anthony b: 2/23/61, Hinds, Miss. BR/TR, 6'1", 195 lbs. Deb: 4/06/84

YEAR TM/L	W	L	PCT	G	GS	CG	SH	SV	IP	H	HR	BB	SO	RAT	ERA	ERA+	OAV	OOB	BH	AVG	PB	PR	/A	PD	TPI
1984 Cin-N	1	0	1.000	8	0	0	0	0	10^{1}	12	1	5	7	14.8	5.23	72	.286	.362	0	—	0	-2	-2	-0	-0.2
1985 Cin-N	0	0	—	2	0	0	0	0	3^{1}	2	2	1	2	8.1	5.40	70	.167	.231	0	—	0	-1	-1	0	-0.1
1986 Cin-N	0	0	—	2	1	0	0	0	3^{1}	7	0	1	1	21.6	13.50	29	.412	.444	0	—	0	-4	-4	-0	-0.3
1988 Mon-N	0	0	—	5	0	0	0	1	8^{2}	6	0	5	4	11.4	3.12	115	.207	.324	0	.000	-0	0	0	-0	0.0
1989 Pit-N	0	1	.000	16	0	0	0	0	24	28	1	10	12	14.3	3.75	89	.301	.369	0	.000	-0	-1	-1	1	0.0
Total 5	1	1	.500	33	1	0	0	1	49^{2}	55	4	22	26	14.0	4.71	75	.285	.358	0	.000	-1	-7	-6	0	-0.6

● MIKE SMITH Smith, Michael Anthony b: 10/31/63, San Antonio, Tex. BR/TR, 6'3", 180 lbs. Deb: 6/30/89

YEAR TM/L	W	L	PCT	G	GS	CG	SH	SV	IP	H	HR	BB	SO	RAT	ERA	ERA+	OAV	OOB	BH	AVG	PB	PR	/A	PD	TPI
1989 Bal-A	2	0	1.000	13	1	0	0	0	20	25	3	14	12	17.5	7.65	50	.313	.415	0	—	0	-8	-9	0	-0.7
1990 Bal-A	0	0	—	2	0	0	0	0	3	4	2	1	2	15.0	12.00	32	.308	.357	0	—	0	-3	-3	0	-0.2
Total 2	2	0	1.000	15	1	0	0	0	23	29	5	15	14	17.2	8.22	46	.312	.407	0	—	0	-11	-11	0	-0.9

● PETE SMITH Smith, Peter John b: 2/27/66, Abington, Mass. BR/TR, 6'3", 200 lbs. Deb: 9/08/87

YEAR TM/L	W	L	PCT	G	GS	CG	SH	SV	IP	H	HR	BB	SO	RAT	ERA	ERA+	OAV	OOB	BH	AVG	PB	PR	/A	PD	TPI
1987 Atl-N	1	2	.333	6	6	0	0	0	31^{2}	39	3	14	11	15.1	4.83	90	.307	.376	1	.091	-1	-3	-2	-1	-0.3
1988 Atl-N	7	15	.318	32	32	5	3	0	195^{1}	183	15	88	124	12.5	3.69	100	.250	.331	6	.113	-2	-5	-0	-3	-0.5
1989 Atl-N	5	14	.263	28	27	1	0	0	142	144	13	57	115	12.7	4.75	77	.263	.333	4	.098	-0	-20	-17	-1	-1.9
1990 Atl-N	5	6	.455	13	13	3	0	0	77	77	11	24	56	11.8	4.79	84	.260	.316	2	.087	-1	-9	-6	-1	-0.8
1991 Atl-N	1	3	.250	14	10	0	0	0	48	48	5	22	29	13.1	5.06	77	.262	.341	2	.167	0	-7	-6	1	-0.5
1992 *Atl-N	7	0	1.000	12	11	2	1	0	79	63	3	28	43	10.4	2.05	183	.217	.286	1	.038	-2	13	15	-0	1.5
Total 6	26	40	.394	105	99	11	4	0	573	554	50	233	378	12.4	4.05	93	.255	.327	16	.096	-5	-31	-17	-5	-2.5

● PETE SMITH Smith, Peter Luke b: 3/19/40, Natick, Mass. BR/TR, 6'2", 190 lbs. Deb: 9/13/62

YEAR TM/L	W	L	PCT	G	GS	CG	SH	SV	IP	H	HR	BB	SO	RAT	ERA	ERA+	OAV	OOB	BH	AVG	PB	PR	/A	PD	TPI
1962 Bos-A	0	1	.000	1	1	0	0	0	3^{2}	7	3	2	1	22.1	19.64	21	.438	.500	0	.000	-0	-6	-6	0	-0.5

YEAR TM/L	W	L	PCT	G	GS	CG	SH	SV	IP	H	HR	BB	SO	RAT	ERA	ERA+	OAV	OOB	BH	AVG	PB	PR	/A	PD	TPI
1963 Bos-A	0	0	—	6	1	0	0	0	15	11	2	6	6	10.2	3.60	105	.212	.293	0	.000	-0	0	0	0	0.0
Total 2	0	1	.000	7	2	0	0	0	18^{2}	18	5	8	7	12.5	6.75	57	.265	.342	0	.000	-0	-6	-6	0	-0.5

● REGGIE SMITH Smith, Reginald b: Louisville, Ky. Deb: 7/11/1886

YEAR TM/L	W	L	PCT	G	GS	CG	SH	SV	IP	H	HR	BB	SO	RAT	ERA	ERA+	OAV	OOB	BH	AVG	PB	PR	/A	PD	TPI
1886 Phi-a	0	1	.000	1	1	1	0	0	9	15	0	5	4	20.0	7.00	50	.385	.455	0	.000	-1	-4	-3	-0	-0.3

● ED SMITH Smith, Rhesa Edward b: 2/21/1879, Mentone, Ind. d: 3/20/55, Tarpon Springs, Fla. BR/TR, 5'11", 170 lbs. Deb: 4/27/06

YEAR TM/L	W	L	PCT	G	GS	CG	SH	SV	IP	H	HR	BB	SO	RAT	ERA	ERA+	OAV	OOB	BH	AVG	PB	PR	/A	PD	TPI
1906 StL-A	8	11	.421	19	18	13	0	0	154^{2}	153	3	53	45	12.5	3.72	69	.261	.332	11	.204	2	-18	-20	1	-1.7

● BOB SMITH Smith, Robert Ashley (a.k.a. Robert M. Brown In 1914)
b: 7/20/1890, Woodbury, Vt. d: 12/27/65, West Los Angeles, Cal. BR/TR, 5'11", 160 lbs. Deb: 4/19/13

YEAR TM/L	W	L	PCT	G	GS	CG	SH	SV	IP	H	HR	BB	SO	RAT	ERA	ERA+	OAV	OOB	BH	AVG	PB	PR	/A	PD	TPI
1913 Chi-A	0	0	—	1	0	0	0	0	2	3	0	3	1	27.0	13.50	22	.273	.429	0	—	0	-2	-2	-0	-0.2
1914 Buf-F	0	0	—	15	1	0	0	3	36^{2}	39	3	16	13	14.0	3.44	96	.281	.363	2	.222	0	-1	-1	1	0.0
1915 Buf-F	0	0	—	1	0	0	0	0	1	1	0	2	0	36.0	18.00	17	.333	.667	0	—	0	-2	-2	0	-0.2
Total 3	0	0	—	17	1	0	0	3	39^{2}	43	3	21	14	15.2	4.31	76	.281	.379	2	.222	0	-5	-5	1	-0.4

● BOB SMITH Smith, Robert Eldridge b: 4/22/1895, Rogersville, Tenn. d: 7/19/87, Waycross, Ga. BR/TR, 5'10", 175 lbs. Deb: 4/19/23 ♦

YEAR TM/L	W	L	PCT	G	GS	CG	SH	SV	IP	H	HR	BB	SO	RAT	ERA	ERA+	OAV	OOB	BH	AVG	PB	PR	/A	PD	TPI
1925 Bos-N	5	3	.625	13	10	6	0	0	92^{2}	110	6	36	19	14.2	4.47	90	.304	.367	49	.282	2	-2	-5	-0	-0.2
1926 Bos-N	10	13	.435	33	23	14	4	1	201^{1}	199	10	75	44	12.2	3.75	94	.269	.336	25	.298	7	2	-5	2	0.4
1927 Bos-N	10	18	.357	41	32	16	1	3	260^{2}	297	9	75	81	12.9	3.76	99	.301	.351	27	.248	4	4	-1	2	0.5
1928 Bos-N	13	17	.433	38	25	14	0	2	244^{1}	274	11	74	59	12.9	3.87	101	.289	.342	23	.250	3	3	1	3	0.7
1929 Bos-N	11	17	.393	34	29	19	1	3	231	256	20	71	65	12.8	4.68	100	.285	.338	17	.172	-1	1	0	1	0.1
1930 Bos-N	10	14	.417	38	24	14	2	5	219^{2}	247	25	85	84	13.7	4.26	116	.290	.357	19	.235	-1	17	16	2	1.5
1931 Chi-N	15	12	.556	36	29	18	2	2	240^{1}	239	10	62	63	11.3	3.22	120	.256	.303	19	.218	2	17	17	1	2.0
1932 *Chi-N	4	3	.571	34	11	4	1	2	119	148	4	36	35	14.1	4.61	82	.303	.355	10	.238	2	-10	-11	1	-0.9
1933 Cin-N	4	4	.500	16	6	4	0	0	73^{2}	75	3	11	18	10.5	2.20	154	.260	.287	5	.200	0	9	10	-0	1.1
Bos-N	4	3	.571	14	4	3	1	1	58^{2}	68	3	7	16	11.5	3.22	95	.296	.316	4	.200	1	1	-1	1	0.1
Yr	8	7	.533	30	10	7	1	1	132^{1}	143	6	18	34	10.9	2.65	123	.276	.300	9	.200	1	10	9	1	1.2
1934 Bos-N	6	9	.400	39	5	3	0	5	121^{2}	133	9	36	26	12.5	4.66	82	.277	.328	9	.250	1	-8	-11	1	-0.9
1935 Bos-N	8	18	.308	46	20	8	2	5	203^{1}	232	13	61	58	13.1	3.94	96	.285	.337	17	.270	2	2	-3	-1	-0.2
1936 Bos-N	6	7	.462	35	11	5	2	8	136	142	3	35	36	11.8	3.77	102	.264	.311	10	.222	0	4	1	1	0.2
1937 Bos-N	0	1	.000	18	0	0	0	3	44	52	6	6	14	12.3	4.09	88	.295	.326	2	.200	0	-1	-2	-1	-0.3
Total 13	106	139	.433	435	229	128	16	40	2246^{1}	2472	132	670	618	12.7	3.94	100	.283	.335	409	.242	22	40	4	12	4.1

● BOB SMITH Smith, Robert Gilchrist b: 2/1/31, Woodsville, N.H. BR/TL, 6'1.5", 190 lbs. Deb: 4/29/55

YEAR TM/L	W	L	PCT	G	GS	CG	SH	SV	IP	H	HR	BB	SO	RAT	ERA	ERA+	OAV	OOB	BH	AVG	PB	PR	/A	PD	TPI
1955 Bos-A	0	0	—	1	0	0	0	0	1^{2}	1	0	1	1	10.8	0.00	—	.200	.333	0	—	0	1	1	-0	0.1
1957 StL-N	0	0	—	6	0	0	0	1	9^{2}	12	0	6	11	17.7	4.66	85	.267	.365	0	.000	-0	-1	-1	0	-0.1
Pit-N	2	4	.333	20	4	2	0	0	55	48	2	25	35	12.1	3.11	122	.229	.314	1	.077	-1	5	4	-1	0.2
Yr	2	4	.333	26	4	2	0	1	64^{2}	60	2	31	46	12.8	3.34	114	.234	.319	1	.067	-1	4	3	-1	0.1
1958 Pit-N	2	2	.500	35	4	0	0	1	61	61	6	31	24	13.9	4.43	87	.262	.353	1	.091	-1	-3	-4	1	-0.4
1959 Pit-N	0	0	—	20	0	0	0	0	28^{1}	32	1	17	12	15.6	3.49	111	.291	.386	0	.000	-0	1	1	-0	0.1
Det-A	0	3	.000	9	0	0	0	0	11	20	5	3	10	18.8	8.18	50	.417	.451	0	.000	-0	-5	-5	0	-0.5
Total 4	4	9	.308	91	8	2	0	2	166^{2}	174	14	83	93	14.1	4.05	95	.267	.354	2	.069	-2	-2	-3	-0	-0.6

● BOB SMITH Smith, Robert Walkay "Riverboat" b: 5/13/28, Clarence, Mo. BL/TL, 6', 185 lbs. Deb: 4/22/58

YEAR TM/L	W	L	PCT	G	GS	CG	SH	SV	IP	H	HR	BB	SO	RAT	ERA	ERA+	OAV	OOB	BH	AVG	PB	PR	/A	PD	TPI
1958 Bos-A	4	3	.571	17	7	1	0	0	66^{2}	61	4	45	43	14.3	3.78	106	.248	.364	2	.105	-1	-0	2	1	0.1
1959 Chi-N	0	0	—	1	0	0	0	0	0^{2}	5	0	2	0	94.5	81.00	5	.833	.875	0	—	0	-6	-6	0	-0.4
Cle-A	0	1	.000	12	3	0	0	0	29^{1}	31	2	12	17	13.2	5.22	71	.282	.352	0	.000	-1	-4	-5	0	-0.6
Total 2	4	4	.500	30	10	1	0	0	96^{2}	97	6	59	60	14.5	4.75	82	.268	.371	2	.080	-2	-10	-9	1	-0.9

● RUFUS SMITH Smith, Rufus Frazier "Shirt" b: 1/24/05, Guilford College, N.C. d: 8/21/84, Aiken, S.C. BR/TL, 5'8", 165 lbs. Deb: 10/02/27

YEAR TM/L	W	L	PCT	G	GS	CG	SH	SV	IP	H	HR	BB	SO	RAT	ERA	ERA+	OAV	OOB	BH	AVG	PB	PR	/A	PD	TPI
1927 Det-A	0	0	—	1	1	0	0	0	8	8	0	3	2	13.5	3.38	125	.242	.324	0	.000	-1	1	1	-0	0.0

● SHERRY SMITH Smith, Sherrod Malone b: 2/18/1891, Monticello, Ga. d: 9/12/49, Reidsville, Ga. BR/TL, 6'1", 170 lbs. Deb: 5/11/11

YEAR TM/L	W	L	PCT	G	GS	CG	SH	SV	IP	H	HR	BB	SO	RAT	ERA	ERA+	OAV	OOB	BH	AVG	PB	PR	/A	PD	TPI
1911 Pit-N	0	0	—	1	0	0	0	0	0^{2}	4	0	1	0	67.5	54.00	6	.667	.714	0	—	0	-4	-4	-0	-0.3
1912 Pit-N	0	0	—	3	0	0	0	1	4	6	0	1	3	15.8	6.75	48	.600	.636	0	—	0	-1	-2	-0	-0.2
1915 Bro-N	14	8	.636	29	20	11	2	2	173^{2}	169	3	42	52	11.2	2.59	107	.264	.315	14	.246	3	3	4	-0	0.6
1916 *Bro-N	14	10	.583	36	23	15	4	1	219	193	5	45	67	9.9	2.34	114	.239	.282	21	.273	6	7	8	0	1.6
1917 Bro-N	12	12	.500	38	23	15	0	3	211^{1}	210	5	51	58	11.2	3.32	84	.265	.311	15	.195	2	-14	-12	3	-0.7
1919 Bro-N	7	12	.368	30	19	13	2	1	173	181	3	29	40	11.1	2.24	133	.278	.313	8	.148	-2	13	14	3	1.7
1920 *Bro-N	11	9	.550	33	12	6	2	3	136^{1}	134	1	27	33	10.8	1.85	173	.264	.304	10	.233	2	19	21	5	3.1
1921 Bro-N	7	11	.389	35	17	9	0	4	175^{1}	232	4	34	36	13.7	3.90	100	.319	.350	13	.228	1	-2	-0	5	0.5
1922 Bro-N	4	8	.333	28	9	3	1	2	108^{2}	128	6	35	15	14.1	4.56	89	.309	.373	9	.257	2	-5	-6	1	-0.3
Cle-A	1	0	1.000	2	2	1	0	0	15^{2}	18	0	3	4	12.1	3.45	116	.295	.328	2	.333	1	1	1	0	0.2
1923 Cle-A	9	6	.600	30	16	10	1	1	124	129	4	37	23	12.2	3.27	121	.269	.324	11	.244	1	10	10	2	1.2
1924 Cle-A	12	14	.462	39	27	20	2	1	247^{2}	267	5	42	34	11.5	3.02	142	.277	.312	18	.202	-1	33	35	3	3.5
1925 Cle-A	11	14	.440	31	30	**22**	1	1	237	296	11	48	30	13.3	4.86	91	.306	.342	28	.304	7	-12	-12	-0	-0.4
1926 Cle-A	11	10	.524	27	24	16	1	0	188^{1}	214	8	31	25	11.9	3.73	109	.292	.324	14	.215	2	6	7	3	1.2
1927 Cle-A	1	4	.200	11	2	1	0	1	38	53	2	14	8	15.9	5.45	77	.342	.396	2	.167	-0	-6	-5	0	-0.5
Total 14	114	118	.491	373	224	142	16	21	2052^{2}	2234	57	440	428	11.9	3.32	108	.282	.324	165	.233	23	48	59	26	11.2

● TOM SMITH Smith, Thomas E. b: 12/5/1871, Boston, Mass. d: 3/2/29, Dorchester, Mass. BR/TR, 180 lbs. Deb: 6/06/1894

YEAR TM/L	W	L	PCT	G	GS	CG	SH	SV	IP	H	HR	BB	SO	RAT	ERA	ERA+	OAV	OOB	BH	AVG	PB	PR	/A	PD	TPI
1894 Bos-N	0	0	—	2	0	0	0	1	6	8	2	6	2	27.0	15.00	38	.316	.510	0	.000	-0	-6	-6	-0	-0.5
1895 Phi-N	2	3	.400	11	7	4	0	0	68	76	1	53	21	18.0	6.88	70	.278	.408	8	.242	-0	-16	-16	-1	-1.3
1896 Lou-N	2	3	.400	11	5	4	0	0	55	73	2	25	14	16.7	5.40	80	.316	.393	8	.205	-0	-6	-7	1	-0.5
1898 StL-N	0	1	.000	1	1	1	0	0	9	9	0	5	1	16.0	2.00	189	.258	.383	1	.500	1	2	2	0	0.3
Total 4	4	7	.364	25	13	9	0	1	138	166	5	89	38	17.7	6.33	72	.294	.406	17	.224	-0	-27	-27	-0	-2.0

● BILL SMITH Smith, William Garland b: 6/8/34, Washington, D.C. BL/TL, 6', 190 lbs. Deb: 9/13/58

YEAR TM/L	W	L	PCT	G	GS	CG	SH	SV	IP	H	HR	BB	SO	RAT	ERA	ERA+	OAV	OOB	BH	AVG	PB	PR	/A	PD	TPI
1958 StL-N	0	1	.000	2	1	0	0	0	9^{2}	12	0	4	4	14.9	6.52	63	.324	.390	0	.000	-0	-3	-3	0	-0.3
1959 StL-N	0	0	—	6	0	0	0	1	8^{1}	11	0	3	4	15.1	1.08	393	.333	.389	0	.000	-0	3	3	-0	0.3
1962 Phi-N	1	5	.167	24	5	0	0	0	50^{1}	59	8	10	26	12.5	4.29	90	.295	.332	2	.182	1	-2	-2	-0	-0.2
Total 3	1	6	.143	32	6	0	0	1	68^{1}	82	8	17	34	13.2	4.21	94	.304	.347	2	.143	0	-2	-2	-0	-0.2

● BILL SMITH Smith, William S. b: 1851, Guelph, Ont., Canada d: 10/27/1897, Guelph, Ont., Can. 6', 168 lbs. Deb: 7/06/1886

YEAR TM/L	W	L	PCT	G	GS	CG	SH	SV	IP	H	HR	BB	SO	RAT	ERA	ERA+	OAV	OOB	BH	AVG	PB	PR	/A	PD	TPI
1886 Det-N	5	4	.556	9	9	9	0	0	77	81	0	30	36	13.0	4.09	81	.259	.324	7	.184	-1	-7	-7	-1	-0.7

● WILLIE SMITH Smith, Willie b: 2/11/39, Anniston, Ala. BL/TL, 6', 190 lbs. Deb: 6/18/63 ♦

YEAR TM/L	W	L	PCT	G	GS	CG	SH	SV	IP	H	HR	BB	SO	RAT	ERA	ERA+	OAV	OOB	BH	AVG	PB	PR	/A	PD	TPI
1963 Det-A	1	0	1.000	11	2	0	0	2	21^{2}	24	2	13	16	15.4	4.57	82	.300	.398	1	.125	-0	-2	-2	0	-0.2
1964 LA-A	1	4	.200	15	1	0	0	0	31^{2}	34	5	10	20	12.8	2.84	116	.293	.354	108	.301	6	3	2	0	0.4
1968 Cle-A	0	0	—	2	0	0	0	0	5	2	0	1	1	5.4	0.00	—	.125	.176	6	.143	0	2	2	0	0.2
Chi-N	0	0	—	1	0	0	0	0	2^{2}	0	0	0	2	0.0	0.00	—	.000	.000	39	.275	0	1	1	0	0.2
Total 3	2	4	.333	29	3	0	0	2	61	60	7	24	39	12.5	3.10	110	.273	.347	410	.248	6	3	2	1	0.6

● ZANE SMITH Smith, Zane William b: 12/28/60, Madison, Wis. BL/TL, 6'2", 195 lbs. Deb: 9/10/84

YEAR TM/L	W	L	PCT	G	GS	CG	SH	SV	IP	H	HR	BB	SO	RAT	ERA	ERA+	OAV	OOB	BH	AVG	PB	PR	/A	PD	TPI
1984 Atl-N	1	0	1.000	3	3	0	0	0	20	16	1	13	16	13.0	2.25	171	.219	.337	5	.556	2	3	4	0	0.7

YEAR	TM/L	W	L	PCT	G	GS	CG	SH	SV	IP	H	HR	BB	SO	RAT	ERA	ERA+	OAV	OOB	BH	AVG	PB	PR	/A	PD	TPI
1985	Atl-N	9	10	.474	42	18	2	2	0	147	135	4	80	85	13.3	3.80	101	.254	.355	6	.162	-0	-3	1	2	0.3
1986	Atl-N	8	16	.333	38	32	3	1	1	204^2	209	8	105	139	14.0	4.05	98	.275	.367	5	.085	-3	-7	-2	3	-0.2
1987	Atl-N	15	10	.600	36	36	9	3	0	242	245	19	91	130	12.7	4.09	106	.266	.335	10	.132	-1	-0	7	1	0.8
1988	Atl-N	5	10	.333	23	22	3	0	0	140^1	159	8	44	59	13.2	4.30	86	.292	.348	7	.167	0	-13	-10	3	-0.7
1989	Atl-N	1	12	.077	17	17	0	0	0	99	102	5	33	58	12.5	4.45	82	.267	.329	5	.179	-0	-11	-9	2	-0.7
	Mon-N	0	1	.000	31	0	0	0	2	48	39	2	19	35	11.1	1.50	235	.220	.299	1	.250	0	11	11	1	1.3
	Yr	1	13	.071	48	17	0	0	2	147	141	7	52	93	11.9	3.49	103	.249	.313	6	.188	0	0	2	3	0.6
1990	Mon-N	6	7	.462	22	21	1	0	0	139^1	141	11	41	80	11.9	3.23	113	.266	.322	7	.175	1	9	6	1	0.9
	*Pit-N	6	2	.750	11	10	3	2	0	76	55	4	9	50	7.6	1.30	278	.203	.229	4	.143	0	21	20	-0	2.3
	Yr	12	9	.571	33	31	4	2	0	215^1	196	15	50	130	10.3	2.55	143	.243	.287	11	.162	1	30	26	1	3.2
1991	*Pit-N	16	10	.615	35	35	6	3	0	228	234	15	29	120	10.5	3.20	112	.268	.293	13	.183	2	12	9	1	1.4
1992	Pit-N	8	8	.500	23	22	4	3	0	141	138	8	19	56	10.1	3.06	111	.261	.289	6	.122	-0	7	5	1	0.7
Total	9	75	86	.466	281	216	31	14	3	1485^1	1473	85	483	828	12.0	3.53	107	.263	.325	69	.156	2	28	42	15	6.8

● **MIKE SMITHSON** Smithson, Billy Mike b: 1/21/55, Centerville, Tenn. BL/TR, 6′8″, 215 lbs. Deb: 8/27/82

YEAR	TM/L	W	L	PCT	G	GS	CG	SH	SV	IP	H	HR	BB	SO	RAT	ERA	ERA+	OAV	OOB	BH	AVG	PB	PR	/A	PD	TPI
1982	Tex-A	3	4	.429	8	8	3	0	0	46^2	51	5	13	24	12.9	5.01	77	.282	.340	0	—	0	-5	-6	-1	-0.6
1983	Tex-A	10	14	.417	33	33	10	0	0	223^1	233	14	71	135	12.6	3.91	102	.269	.330	0	—	0	4	2	1	0.4
1984	Min-A	15	13	.536	36	36	10	1	0	252	246	35	54	144	11.0	3.68	114	.252	.296	0	—	0	9	15	-1	1.4
1985	Min-A	15	14	.517	37	37	8	3	0	257	264	25	78	127	12.5	4.34	101	.270	.333	0	—	0	-6	2	-2	0.0
1986	Min-A	13	14	.481	34	33	8	1	0	198	234	26	57	114	13.9	4.77	90	.294	.352	0	—	0	-13	-10	1	-1.1
1987	Min-A	4	7	.364	21	20	0	0	0	109	126	17	38	53	14.3	5.94	78	.286	.355	0	—	0	-18	-16	-1	-1.6
1988	*Bos-A	9	6	.600	31	18	1	0	0	126^2	149	25	37	73	13.6	5.97	69	.292	.347	0	—	0	-28	-26	-1	-2.6
1989	Bos-A	7	14	.333	40	19	1	1	2	143^2	170	21	35	61	13.5	4.95	83	.297	.348	0	—	0	-17	-14	-1	-1.7
Total	8	76	86	.469	240	204	41	6	2	1356^1	1473	168	383	731	12.8	4.58	92	.277	.334	0	—	0	-74	-53	-4	-5.8

● **LEFTY SMOLL** Smoll, Clyde Hetrick b: 4/17/14, Quakertown, Pa. d: 8/31/85, Quakertown, Pa. BB/TL, 5′10″, 175 lbs. Deb: 4/26/40

YEAR	TM/L	W	L	PCT	G	GS	CG	SH	SV	IP	H	HR	BB	SO	RAT	ERA	ERA+	OAV	OOB	BH	AVG	PB	PR	/A	PD	TPI
1940	Phi-N	2	8	.200	33	9	0	0	0	109	145	6	36	31	15.3	5.37	73	.322	.378	5	.161	-1	-18	-18	-2	-2.0

● **JOHN SMOLTZ** Smoltz, John Andrew b: 5/15/67, Detroit, Mich. BR/TR, 6′3″, 210 lbs. Deb: 7/23/88

YEAR	TM/L	W	L	PCT	G	GS	CG	SH	SV	IP	H	HR	BB	SO	RAT	ERA	ERA+	OAV	OOB	BH	AVG	PB	PR	/A	PD	TPI
1988	Atl-N	2	7	.222	12	12	0	0	0	64	74	10	33	37	15.3	5.48	67	.285	.369	2	.118	-0	-14	-13	-1	-1.4
1989	Atl-N★	12	11	.522	29	29	5	0	0	208	160	15	72	168	10.1	2.94	124	.212	.282	7	.113	1	13	16	2	2.1
1990	Atl-N	14	11	.560	34	34	6	2	0	231^1	206	20	90	170	11.6	3.85	105	.240	.313	12	.162	1	-2	5	1	0.7
1991	*Atl-N	14	13	.519	36	36	5	0	0	229^2	206	16	77	148	11.2	3.80	102	.243	.308	7	.108	-1	-3	2	0	0.2
1992	*Atl-N★	15	12	.556	35	35	9	3	0	246^2	206	17	80	**215**	10.6	2.85	132	.224	.289	12	.160	2	18	25	-1	2.9
Total	5	57	54	.514	146	146	25	5	0	979^2	852	78	352	738	11.2	3.50	109	.234	.304	40	.137	3	12	35	1	4.5

● **HARRY SMYTHE** Smythe, William Henry b: 10/24/04, Augusta, Ga. d: 8/28/80, Augusta, Ga. BL/TL, 5′10.5″, 179 lbs. Deb: 7/21/29

YEAR	TM/L	W	L	PCT	G	GS	CG	SH	SV	IP	H	HR	BB	SO	RAT	ERA	ERA+	OAV	OOB	BH	AVG	PB	PR	/A	PD	TPI
1929	Phi-N	4	6	.400	19	7	2	0	1	68^2	94	3	15	12	14.4	5.24	99	.330	.365	5	.192	-1	-4	-0	2	0.1
1930	Phi-N	0	3	.000	25	3	0	0	2	49^2	84	3	31	9	21.4	7.79	70	.368	.450	4	.286	-0	-16	-13	-1	-1.2
1934	NY-A	0	2	.000	8	0	0	0	1	15	24	1	8	7	19.2	7.80	52	.381	.451	1	.200	-0	-6	-6	1	-0.5
	Bro-N	1	1	.500	8	0	0	0	0	21^1	30	3	8	5	16.5	5.91	66	.337	.398	3	.333	1	-4	-5	1	-0.3
Total	3	5	12	.294	60	10	2	0	4	154^2	232	10	62	33	17.4	6.40	78	.349	.408	13	.241	0	-29	-24	2	-1.9

● **NATE SNELL** Snell, Nathaniel b: 9/2/52, Orangeburg, S.C. BR/TR, 6′4″, 190 lbs. Deb: 9/20/84

YEAR	TM/L	W	L	PCT	G	GS	CG	SH	SV	IP	H	HR	BB	SO	RAT	ERA	ERA+	OAV	OOB	BH	AVG	PB	PR	/A	PD	TPI
1984	Bal-A	1	1	.500	5	0	0	0	0	7^2	8	1	1	7	10.6	2.35	165	.258	.281	0	—	0	1	1	-0	0.1
1985	Bal-A	3	2	.600	43	0	0	0	5	100^1	100	4	30	41	11.8	2.69	150	.260	.315	0	—	0	16	15	1	1.6
1986	Bal-A	2	1	.667	34	0	0	0	0	72^1	69	9	22	29	11.4	3.86	107	.257	.316	0	—	0	3	2	1	0.4
1987	Det-A	1	2	.333	22	2	0	0	0	38^2	39	5	19	19	13.5	3.96	107	.267	.352	0	—	0	2	1	-1	0.2
Total	4	7	6	.538	104	2	0	0	5	219	216	19	72	96	11.9	3.29	125	.260	.321	0	—	0	22	20	1	2.3

● **FRANK SNOOK** Snook, Frank Walter b: 3/28/49, Somerville, N.J. BR/TR, 6′2″, 180 lbs. , Deb: 7/13/73

YEAR	TM/L	W	L	PCT	G	GS	CG	SH	SV	IP	H	HR	BB	SO	RAT	ERA	ERA+	OAV	OOB	BH	AVG	PB	PR	/A	PD	TPI
1973	SD-N	0	2	.000	18	0	0	0	1	27^1	19	4	18	13	12.2	3.62	96	.200	.327	0	.000	-0	0	-0	1	0.0

● **COLONEL SNOVER** Snover, Colonel Lester "Bosco" b: 5/16/1895, Hallstead, Pa. d: 4/30/69, Rochester, N.Y. BL/TL, 6′0.5″, 200 lbs. Deb: 9/18/19

YEAR	TM/L	W	L	PCT	G	GS	CG	SH	SV	IP	H	HR	BB	SO	RAT	ERA	ERA+	OAV	OOB	BH	AVG	PB	PR	/A	PD	TPI
1919	NY-N	0	1	.000	2	1	0	0	0	9	7	0	3	4	11.0	1.00	281	.212	.297	0	.000	0	2	2	-0	0.2

● **BRIAN SNYDER** Snyder, Brian Robert b: 2/20/58, Flemington, N.J. BL/TL, 6′3″, 185 lbs. Deb: 5/25/85

YEAR	TM/L	W	L	PCT	G	GS	CG	SH	SV	IP	H	HR	BB	SO	RAT	ERA	ERA+	OAV	OOB	BH	AVG	PB	PR	/A	PD	TPI
1985	Sea-A	1	2	.333	15	6	0	0	1	35^1	44	2	19	23	16.3	6.37	66	.306	.390	0	—	0	-9	-8	1	-0.8
1989	Oak-A	0	0	—	2	0	0	0	0	0^2	2	1	2	1	54.0	27.00	14	.500	.667	0	—	0	-2	-2	0	0.0
Total	2	1	2	.333	17	6	0	0	1	36	46	3	21	24	17.0	6.75	62	.311	.400	0	—	0	-10	-10	1	-0.8

● **GENE SNYDER** Snyder, Gene Walter b: 3/31/31, York, Pa. BR/TL, 5′11″, 175 lbs. Deb: 4/26/59

YEAR	TM/L	W	L	PCT	G	GS	CG	SH	SV	IP	H	HR	BB	SO	RAT	ERA	ERA+	OAV	OOB	BH	AVG	PB	PR	/A	PD	TPI
1959	LA-N	1	1	.500	11	2	0	0	0	26^1	32	1	20	20	17.8	5.47	77	.299	.409	0	.000	-0	-4	-4	-0	-0.4

● **GEORGE SNYDER** Snyder, George T. b: 1849, Philadelphia, Pa. d: 8/2/05, Philadelphia, Pa. Deb: 9/30/1882

YEAR	TM/L	W	L	PCT	G	GS	CG	SH	SV	IP	H	HR	BB	SO	RAT	ERA	ERA+	OAV	OOB	BH	AVG	PB	PR	/A	PD	TPI
1882	Phi-a	1	0	1.000	1	1	1	0	0	9	4	0	2	0	6.0	0.00	—	.125	.177	1	.333	0	3	3	0	0.3

● **BILL SNYDER** Snyder, William Nicholas b: 1/28/1898, Mansfield, Ohio d: 10/8/34, Vicksburg, Mich. BR/TR, Deb: 9/04/19

YEAR	TM/L	W	L	PCT	G	GS	CG	SH	SV	IP	H	HR	BB	SO	RAT	ERA	ERA+	OAV	OOB	BH	AVG	PB	PR	/A	PD	TPI
1919	Was-A	0	1	.000	2	1	0	0	0	8	6	0	3	5	10.1	1.13	285	.200	.273	0	.000	-0	2	2	-0	0.1
1920	Was-A	2	1	.667	16	4	1	0	1	54	59	1	28	17	15.5	4.17	90	.280	.380	6	.316	1	-2	-3	-1	-0.3
Total	2	2	2	.500	18	5	1	0	1	62	65	1	31	22	14.8	3.77	97	.270	.367	6	.286	1	-0	-1	-1	-0.2

● **RAY SOFF** Soff, Raymond John b: 10/31/58, Adrian, Mich. BR/TR, 6′, 185 lbs. Deb: 7/17/86

YEAR	TM/L	W	L	PCT	G	GS	CG	SH	SV	IP	H	HR	BB	SO	RAT	ERA	ERA+	OAV	OOB	BH	AVG	PB	PR	/A	PD	TPI
1986	StL-N	4	2	.667	30	0	0	0	0	38^1	37	4	13	22	11.7	3.29	111	.255	.316	0	.000	-0	2	1	0	0.2
1987	StL-N	1	0	1.000	12	0	0	0	0	15^1	18	3	5	9	14.1	6.46	64	.295	.358	0	.000	-0	-4	-4	-0	-0.4
Total	2	5	2	.714	42	0	0	0	0	53^2	55	7	18	31	12.4	4.19	90	.267	.329	0	.000	-0	-2	-2	0	-0.2

● **JULIO SOLANO** Solano, Julio Cesar b: 1/8/60, Aqua Blanca, D.R. BR/TR, 6′1″, 160 lbs. Deb: 4/05/83

YEAR	TM/L	W	L	PCT	G	GS	CG	SH	SV	IP	H	HR	BB	SO	RAT	ERA	ERA+	OAV	OOB	BH	AVG	PB	PR	/A	PD	TPI
1983	Hou-N	0	2	.000	4	0	0	0	0	6	5	1	4	3	13.5	6.00	57	.217	.333	0	—	0	-2	-2	0	-0.2
1984	Hou-N	1	3	.250	31	0	0	0	0	50^2	31	3	18	33	8.7	1.95	170	.179	.257	1	.333	0	9	8	-1	0.8
1985	Hou-N	2	2	.500	20	0	0	0	0	33^2	34	5	13	17	12.6	3.48	100	.262	.329	0	.000	-0	0	-0	-1	-0.1
1986	Hou-N	3	1	.750	16	1	0	0	0	32	39	5	22	21	18.0	7.59	47	.310	.424	0	.000	-1	-14	-14	-0	-1.5
1987	Hou-N	0	0	—	11	0	0	0	0	20	25	5	9	12	15.3	7.65	51	.298	.366	0	.000	-0	-8	-8	0	-0.8
1988	Sea-A	0	0	—	17	0	0	0	3	22	22	3	12	10	13.9	4.09	102	.268	.362	0	—	0	-0	0	0	-0.2
1989	Sea-A	0	0	—	7	0	0	0	0	9^2	6	1	4	6	10.2	5.59	72	.176	.282	0	—	0	-2	-2	0	-0.3
Total	7	6	8	.429	106	1	0	0	3	174	162	23	82	102	12.8	4.55	79	.248	.336	1	.077	-1	-16	-18	-2	-2.3

● **MARCELINO SOLIS** Solis, Marcelino b: 7/19/30, San Luis Potosi, Mexico BL/TL, 6′1″, 185 lbs. Deb: 7/16/58

YEAR	TM/L	W	L	PCT	G	GS	CG	SH	SV	IP	H	HR	BB	SO	RAT	ERA	ERA+	OAV	OOB	BH	AVG	PB	PR	/A	PD	TPI
1958	Chi-N	3	3	.500	15	4	0	0	0	52	74	5	20	15	17.0	6.06	65	.339	.405	5	.250	1	-12	-12	-0	-1.1

● **EDDIE SOLOMON** Solomon, Eddie "Buddy" b: 2/9/51, Perry, Ga. d: 1/12/86, Macon, Ga. BR/TR, 6′3″, 190 lbs. Deb: 9/02/73

YEAR	TM/L	W	L	PCT	G	GS	CG	SH	SV	IP	H	HR	BB	SO	RAT	ERA	ERA+	OAV	OOB	BH	AVG	PB	PR	/A	PD	TPI
1973	LA-N	0	0	—	4	0	0	0	0	6^1	10	3	4	6	21.3	7.11	48	.357	.455	0	.000	-0	-2	-3	-0	-0.3
1974	*LA-N	0	0	—	4	0	0	0	1	6	5	1	2	2	10.5	1.50	227	.217	.280	0	—	0	1	1	0	0.2
1975	Chi-N	0	0	—	6	0	0	0	0	6^2	7	1	6	3	17.6	1.35	285	.269	.406	0	—	0	2	2	0	0.2
1976	StL-N	1	1	.500	26	2	0	0	0	37	45	2	16	19	15.1	4.86	73	.306	.378	2	.400	1	-6	-5	1	-0.4
1977	Atl-N	6	6	.500	18	16	0	0	0	88^2	110	10	34	54	14.8	4.57	97	.305	.368	4	.129	-1	-6	-1	-0	-0.3

YEAR	TM/L	W	L	PCT	G	GS	CG	SH	SV	IP	H	HR	BB	SO	RAT	ERA	ERA+	OAV	OOB	BH	AVG	PB	PR	/A	PD	TPI
1978	Atl-N	4	6	.400	37	8	0	0	2	106	98	12	50	64	12.7	4.08	99	.247	.335	4	.138	-1	-6	-0	-0	-0.2
1979	Atl-N	7	14	.333	31	30	4	0	0	186	184	19	51	96	11.7	4.21	96	.254	.308	13	.203	1	-10	-3	-1	-0.4
1980	Pit-N	7	3	.700	26	12	2	0	0	100^1	96	8	37	35	12.3	2.69	135	.253	.325	7	.219	1	10	11	-0	1.2
1981	Pit-N	8	6	.571	22	17	2	0	1	127	133	10	27	38	11.6	3.12	115	.278	.321	7	.163	-1	5	7	-1	0.5
1982	Pit-N	2	6	.250	11	10	0	0	0	46^2	69	9	18	18	17.0	6.75	55	.347	.404	2	.133	-1	-16	-16	-2	-1.7
	Chi-A	1	0	1.000	6	0	0	0	0	7^1	7	1	2	2	11.0	3.68	110	.241	.290	0	—	0	0	0	-0	0.0
Total	10	36	42	.462	191	95	8	0	4	718	764	76	247	337	12.9	4.00	97	.274	.337	39	.177	-1	-28	-8	-3	-1.2
● JOE SOMMER	Sommer, Joseph John b: 11/20/1858, Covington, Ky. d: 1/16/38, Cincinnati, Ohio BR/TR, Deb: 7/08/1880 ♦																									
1883	Cin-a	0	0	—	1	0	0	0	0	5	9	0	1	2	18.0	5.40	60	.367	.392	115	.278	0	-1	-1	-0	-0.1
1885	Bal-a	0	0	—	2	0	0	0	1	3	6	0	0	0	18.0	9.00	36	.429	.429	118	.251	0	-2	-2	-0	-0.2
1886	Bal-a	0	0	—	1	0	0	0	0	4	14	0	3	1	38.3	18.00	19	.519	.567	117	.209	-0	-6	-6	-0	-0.5
1887	Bal-a	0	0	—	1	0	0	0	0	1	2	0	1	0	27.0	9.00	46	.333	.429	123	.266	0	-1	-1	-0	0.0
1890	Cle-N	0	0	—	1	0	0	0	0	1	2	1	2	0	36.0	0.00	—	.403	.575	8	.229	-0	0	0	-0	0.0
Total	5	0	0	—	6	0	0	0	1	14	33	1	7	3	25.7	9.64	35	.431	.479	911	.248	1	-10	-10	-1	-0.8
● RUDY SOMMERS	Sommers, Rudolph b: 10/30/1888, Cincinnati, Ohio d: 3/18/49, Louisville, Ky. BB/TL, 5′11″, 165 lbs. Deb: 9/08/12																									
1912	Chi-N	0	1	.000	1	0	0	0	0	3	4	0	2	2	18.0	3.00	111	.333	.429	0	.000	0	0	0	-0	0.0
1914	Bro-F	2	7	.222	23	8	2	0	2	82	88	2	34	40	13.7	4.06	79	.282	.358	6	.250	2	-8	-8	-1	-0.6
1926	Bos-A	0	0	—	2	0	0	0	0	2	3	0	3	0	27.0	13.50	30	.333	.500	0	—	0	-2	-2	0	-0.2
1927	Bos-A	0	0	—	7	0	0	0	0	14	18	2	14	2	20.6	8.36	51	.353	.492	1	.500	0	-7	-6	1	-0.5
Total	4	2	8	.200	33	8	2	0	2	101	113	4	53	44	15.1	4.81	70	.294	.384	7	.259	2	-16	-16	-0	-1.3
● ANDY SOMMERVILLE	Sommerville, Andrew Henry (b: Henry Travers Summersgill) b: 2/6/1876, Brooklyn, N.Y. d: 6/16/31, Richmond Hill, N.Y. Deb: 8/08/1894																									
1894	Bro-N	0	1	.000	1	1	0	0	0	0^1	1	0	5	0	162.0	162.00	3	.510	.862	0	—	0	-6	-6	0	-0.4
● DON SONGER	Songer, Donald C. b: 1/31/1900, Walnut, Kan. d: 10/3/62, Kansas City, Mo. BL/TL, 6′, 165 lbs. Deb: 9/21/24																									
1924	Pit-N	0	0	—	4	1	0	0	1	9^1	14	1	3	3	16.4	6.75	57	.333	.378	0	.000	-0	-3	-3	0	-0.3
1925	Pit-N	0	1	.000	8	0	0	0	0	11^2	14	0	8	4	17.0	2.31	193	.298	.400	0	.000	-0	3	3	-0	0.2
1926	Pit-N	7	8	.467	35	14	5	1	2	126^1	118	4	52	27	12.9	3.13	126	.252	.340	4	.105	-2	10	11	1	0.9
1927	Pit-N	0	0	—	2	0	0	0	0	4^2	10	0	4	1	28.9	11.57	36	.526	.625	0	.000	-0	-4	-4	-0	-0.4
	NY-N	3	5	.375	22	1	0	0	1	50^1	48	4	31	9	14.3	2.86	135	.261	.370	3	.300	1	6	6	1	0.8
	Yr	3	5	.375	24	1	0	0	1	55	58	4	35	10	15.4	3.60	108	.284	.392	3	.273	1	2	2	1	0.4
Total	4	10	14	.417	71	16	5	1	4	202^1	204	9	98	44	14.0	3.38	117	.268	.361	7	.132	-2	11	13	2	1.2
● LARY SORENSEN	Sorensen, Lary Alan b: 10/4/55, Detroit, Mich. BR/TR, 6′2″, 210 lbs. Deb: 6/07/77																									
1977	Mil-A	7	10	.412	23	20	9	0	0	142^1	147	10	36	57	11.6	4.36	93	.270	.316	0	—	0	-5	-5	1	-0.4
1978	Mil-A★	18	12	.600	37	36	17	3	1	280^2	277	14	50	78	10.6	3.21	117	.259	.295	0	—	0	17	17	1	1.9
1979	Mil-A	15	14	.517	34	34	16	2	0	235^1	250	30	42	63	11.3	3.98	105	.275	.310	0	—	0	6	5	1	0.5
1980	Mil-A	12	10	.545	35	29	8	2	1	195^2	242	13	45	54	13.3	3.68	105	.311	.351	0	—	0	8	4	1	0.7
1981	StL-N	7	7	.500	23	23	3	1	0	140^1	149	3	26	52	11.3	3.27	109	.271	.305	3	.065	-3	3	4	0	0.2
1982	Cle-A	10	15	.400	32	30	6	1	0	189^1	251	19	55	62	14.7	5.61	73	.322	.369	0	—	0	-32	-32	-1	-3.1
1983	Cle-A	12	11	.522	36	34	8	1	0	222^2	238	21	65	76	12.3	4.24	100	.276	.328	0	—	0	-5	-0	2	0.1
1984	Oak-A	6	13	.316	46	21	2	0	1	183^1	240	21	44	63	14.2	4.91	76	.317	.359	0	—	0	-19	-24	-1	-2.4
1985	Chi-N	3	7	.300	45	3	0	0	0	82^1	86	8	24	34	12.5	4.26	94	.274	.333	0	.000	-0	-6	-3	-0	-0.3
1987	Mon-N	3	4	.429	23	5	0	0	1	47^2	56	7	12	21	13.4	4.72	89	.286	.336	0	.000	-1	-3	-3	-1	-0.4
1988	SF-N	0	0	—	12	0	0	0	2	16^2	24	1	3	9	14.6	4.86	67	.329	.355	0	.000	-0	-3	-3	-0	-0.4
Total	11	93	103	.474	346	235	69	10	6	1736^1	1960	147	402	569	12.4	4.15	95	.287	.329	3	.049	-4	-38	-38	1	-3.6
● VIC SORRELL	Sorrell, Victor Garland b: 4/9/01, Morrisville, N.C. d: 5/4/72, Raleigh, N.C. BR/TR, 5′10″, 180 lbs. Deb: 4/22/28																									
1928	Det-A	8	11	.421	29	23	8	0	0	171	182	9	83	67	14.2	4.79	86	.277	.363	6	.109	-5	-14	-13	-3	-1.9
1929	Det-A	14	15	.483	36	31	13	1	1	226	270	15	106	81	15.1	5.18	83	.302	.377	12	.145	-6	-23	-22	-1	-2.7
1930	Det-A	16	11	.593	35	30	14	2	1	233^1	245	13	106	97	13.5	3.86	124	.274	.351	15	.188	-3	21	24	-3	1.7
1931	Det-A	13	14	.481	35	32	19	1	1	245	267	8	114	99	14.0	4.15	110	.278	.355	14	.159	-4	6	12	1	0.8
1932	Det-A	14	14	.500	32	31	13	1	0	234^1	234	11	77	84	12.1	4.03	117	.259	.319	9	.118	-4	12	17	-2	1.1
1933	Det-A	11	15	.423	36	28	13	1	1	232^2	233	18	78	75	12.1	3.79	114	.260	.321	11	.149	-2	13	13	-0	1.0
1934	Det-A	6	9	.400	28	19	6	1	2	129^2	146	13	45	46	13.5	4.79	92	.283	.345	4	.108	-1	-4	-6	2	-0.5
1935	Det-A	4	3	.571	12	6	4	0	0	51^1	65	2	25	22	16.1	4.03	103	.319	.398	0	.000	-3	2	1	0	-0.2
1936	Det-A	6	7	.462	30	14	5	1	3	131^1	153	9	64	37	15.0	5.28	94	.294	.373	6	.154	1	-3	-5	2	-0.2
1937	Det-A	0	2	.000	7	2	0	0	1	17	25	3	8	11	17.5	9.00	52	.338	.402	0	.000	-0	-8	-8	0	-0.8
Total	10	92	101	.477	280	216	95	8	10	1671^2	1820	101	706	619	13.7	4.43	102	.279	.351	77	.139	-28	-0	14	-4	-1.7
● ELIAS SOSA	Sosa, Elias (Martinez) b: 6/10/50, LaVega, D.R. BR/TR, 6′2″, 190 lbs. Deb: 9/08/72																									
1972	SF-N	0	1	.000	8	0	0	0	3	15^2	10	0	12	10	12.6	2.30	152	.189	.338	0	.000	-0	2	2	-0	0.2
1973	SF-N	10	4	.714	71	1	0	0	18	107	95	7	41	70	11.8	3.28	116	.241	.318	1	.071	-0	5	6	-1	0.6
1974	SF-N	9	7	.563	68	0	0	0	6	101	94	8	45	48	12.5	3.48	109	.252	.334	1	.067	-1	2	4	-1	0.2
1975	StL-N	0	3	.000	14	1	0	0	0	27^1	22	3	14	15	12.2	3.95	95	.227	.330	1	.125	-0	-1	-1	-0	-0.1
	Atl-N	2	2	.500	43	0	0	0	2	62^1	70	3	29	31	14.7	4.48	84	.294	.378	1	.143	-0	-6	-5	-0	-0.5
	Yr	2	5	.286	57	1	0	0	2	89^2	92	6	43	46	13.9	4.32	87	.271	.358	2	.133	-1	-7	-5	-0	-0.6
1976	Atl-N	4	4	.500	21	0	0	0	3	35^1	41	3	13	32	14.0	5.35	71	.287	.350	1	.143	-0	-7	-6	-0	-0.7
	LA-N	2	4	.333	24	0	0	0	1	33^2	30	0	12	20	11.2	3.48	97	.242	.309	0	—	0	0	-0	0	0.0
	Yr	6	8	.429	45	0	0	0	4	69	71	3	25	52	12.5	4.43	81	.263	.325	1	.143	-0	-7	-6	-0	-0.7
1977	*LA-N	2	2	.500	44	0	0	0	1	63^2	42	7	12	47	7.8	1.98	193	.189	.234	1	.250	0	14	13	-0	1.3
1978	Oak-A	8	2	.800	68	0	0	0	14	109	106	5	44	61	12.5	2.64	138	.264	.338	0	—	0	14	12	0	1.3
1979	Mon-N	8	7	.533	62	0	0	0	18	96^2	77	2	37	59	10.8	1.96	187	.219	.297	2	.154	0	19	18	-1	1.7
1980	Mon-N	9	6	.600	67	0	0	0	9	93^2	104	5	19	58	11.9	3.07	116	.286	.323	1	.091	-1	5	5	-0	0.4
1981	*Mon-N	1	2	.333	32	0	0	0	3	39^1	46	3	8	18	12.6	3.66	95	.297	.335	2	1.000	1	-1	-1	0	0.1
1982	Det-A	3	3	.500	38	0	0	0	4	61	64	11	18	24	12.4	4.43	92	.270	.327	0	—	0	-2	-2	1	-0.2
1983	SD-N	1	4	.200	41	1	0	0	1	72^1	72	7	30	45	13.1	4.35	80	.268	.348	1	.143	-0	-6	-7	-1	-0.8
Total	12	59	51	.536	601	3	0	0	83	918	873	64	334	538	12.0	3.32	111	.255	.325	12	.130	-3	37	39	-3	3.5
● JOSE SOSA	Sosa, Jose Ynocencio (b: Jose Ynocencio (Sosa)) b: 12/28/52, Santo Domingo, D.R. BR/TR, 5′11″, 158 lbs. Deb: 7/22/75																									
1975	Hou-N	1	3	.250	25	2	0	0	1	47	51	5	23	31	14.4	4.02	84	.291	.377	3	.333	2	-2	-3	-1	-0.3
1976	Hou-N	0	0	—	9	0	0	0	0	11^2	16	0	6	5	19.3	6.94	46	.340	.446	0	—	0	-4	-5	1	-0.4
Total	2	1	3	.250	34	2	0	0	1	58^2	67	5	29	36	15.3	4.60	72	.302	.392	3	.333	2	-7	-8	-0	-0.7
● ALLEN SOTHORON	Sothoron, Allen Sutton b: 4/27/1893, Bradford, Ohio d: 6/17/39, St.Louis, Mo. BB/TR, 5′11″, 182 lbs. Deb: 9/17/14 MC																									
1914	StL-A	0	0	—	1	0	0	0	0	6	6	0	4	3	15.0	6.00	45	.261	.370	0	.000	-0	-2	-2	-0	-0.2
1915	StL-A	0	1	.000	3	1	0	0	0	3^2	8	0	5	2	31.9	7.36	39	.400	.520	0	.000	-0	-2	-2	0	-0.2
1917	StL-A	14	19	.424	48	32	17	3	4	276^2	259	2	96	85	11.8	2.83	92	.251	.320	20	.217	3	-5	-7	-1	-0.5
1918	StL-A	12	12	.500	29	24	14	2	0	209	152	3	67	71	9.6	1.94	141	**.205**	.274	10	.159	-2	20	19	-3	1.5
1919	StL-A	20	13	.606	40	30	21	3	3	270	256	4	87	106	11.8	2.20	151	.246	.311	17	.175	-3	31	34	-7	2.6
1920	StL-A	8	15	.348	36	26	12	1	2	218^1	263	6	89	81	14.8	4.70	83	.307	.376	16	.222	-1	-22	-19	-2	-2.1
1921	StL-A	1	2	.333	5	4	1	0	0	27^2	33	0	8	9	13.7	5.20	86	.314	.368	1	.111	-1	-3	-2	-0	-0.3
	Bos-A	0	2	.000	2	2	0	0	0	6	15	0	5	2	30.0	13.50	31	.455	.526	1	.500	1	-6	-6	0	-0.5

YEAR	TM/L	W	L	PCT	G	GS	CG	SH	SV	IP	H	HR	BB	SO	RAT	ERA	ERA+	OAV	OOB	BH	AVG	PB	PR	/A	PD	TPI
	Cle-A	12	4	.750	22	16	10	2	0	144^2	146	0	58	61	13.1	3.24	132	.279	.358	16	.276	2	17	17	-2	1.5
	Yr	13	8	.619	29	22	11	2	0	178^1	194	0	71	72	13.7	3.89	111	.293	.367	18	.261	2	8	8	-2	0.7
1922	Cle-A	1	3	.250	6	4	2	0	0	25^1	26	1	14	8	14.9	6.39	63	.274	.378	4	.444	1	-7	-7	-0	-0.5
1924	StL-N	10	16	.385	29	28	16	**4**	0	196^2	209	9	84	62	13.9	3.57	106	.275	.354	14	.194	-2	7	5	-3	0.0
1925	StL-N	10	10	.500	28	23	8	2	0	155^2	173	7	63	67	14.0	4.05	107	.280	.353	11	.196	-1	4	5	-4	-0.1
1926	StL-N	3	3	.500	15	4	1	0	0	42^2	37	2	16	19	11.2	4.22	93	.247	.319	3	.231	0	-2	-1	-1	-0.2
Total	11	91	100	.476	264	194	102	17	9	1582^1	1583	34	596	576	12.7	3.31	105	.264	.336	113	.207	-2	29	30	-24	1.0
● **MARIO SOTO**	Soto, Mario Melvin b: 7/12/56, Bani, D.R. BR/TR, 6′, 185 lbs. Deb: 7/21/77																									
1977	Cin-N	2	6	.250	12	10	2	1	0	60^2	60	12	26	44	13.2	5.34	74	.258	.340	1	.077	-0	-10	-10	0	-0.9
1978	Cin-N	1	0	1.000	5	1	0	0	0	18	13	1	13	13	13.0	2.50	142	.197	.329	0	.000	-0	2	2	-0	0.2
1979	*Cin-N	3	2	.600	25	0	0	0	0	37^1	33	2	30	32	15.4	5.30	70	.243	.383	4	.571	2	-7	-7	-1	-0.6
1980	Cin-N	10	8	.556	53	12	3	1	4	190^1	126	11	84	182	10.0	3.07	116	**.187**	.279	2	.043	-4	11	11	0	0.7
1981	Cin-N	12	9	.571	25	25	10	3	0	175	142	13	61	151	10.6	3.29	108	.220	.290	4	.068	-4	4	5	-1	0.0
1982	Cin-N★	14	13	.519	35	34	13	2	0	257^2	202	19	71	274	**9.7**	2.79	132	.215	**.273**	14	.167	1	23	26	-1	2.9
1983	Cin-N★	17	13	.567	34	34	**18**	3	0	273^2	207	28	95	242	10.1	2.70	141	.208	.280	11	.125	-2	28	**34**	-1	3.3
1984	Cin-N★	18	7	.720	33	33	**13**	0	0	237^1	181	26	87	185	10.4	3.53	107	.209	.286	18	.207	3	2	7	-3	0.8
1985	Cin-N	12	15	.444	36	36	9	1	0	256^2	196	30	104	214	10.6	3.58	106	.211	.292	11	.133	-2	0	6	-1	0.4
1986	Cin-N	5	10	.333	19	19	1	1	0	105	113	15	46	67	13.7	4.71	82	.280	.355	3	.111	-1	-12	-10	-1	-1.1
1987	Cin-N	3	2	.600	6	6	0	0	0	31^2	34	7	12	11	13.1	5.12	83	.279	.343	1	.083	-1	-4	-3	0	-0.4
1988	Cin-N	3	7	.300	14	14	3	1	0	87	88	8	28	34	12.2	4.66	77	.267	.328	1	.045	-1	-12	-10	-1	-1.2
Total	12	100	92	.521	297	224	72	13	4	1730^1	1395	172	657	1449	10.8	3.47	108	.220	.296	70	.132	-10	27	51	-8	4.1
● **MARK SOUZA**	Souza, Kenneth Mark b: 2/1/55, Redwood City, Cal. BL/TL, 6′, 180 lbs. Deb: 4/22/80																									
1980	Oak-A	0	0	—	5	0	0	0	0	7	9	1	5	2	18.0	7.71	49	.310	.412	0	—	0	-3	-3	-0	0.1
● **JOHN SOWDERS**	Sowders, John b: 12/10/1866, Louisville, Ky. d: 7/29/08, Indianapolis, Ind BR/TL, 6′, Deb: 6/28/1887 F♦																									
1887	Ind-N	0	0	—	1	0	0	0	0	3	11	0	5	0	48.0	21.00	20	.500	.593	0	.000	-0	-6	-6	-0	-0.4
1889	KC-a	6	16	.273	25	23	20	0	1	185	204	9	105	104	15.4	4.82	87	.271	.366	19	.218	-2	-20	-13	-2	-1.3
1890	Bro-P	19	16	.543	39	37	28	1	0	309	358	3	161	91	15.4	3.82	117	.278	.363	25	.189	-4	14	22	-2	1.2
Total	3	25	32	.439	65	60	48	1	1	497	573	12	271	195	15.6	4.29	102	.278	.366	44	.199	-7	-11	4	-4	-0.5
● **BILL SOWDERS**	Sowders, William Jefferson "Little Bill" b: 11/29/1864, Louisville, Ky. d: 2/2/51, Indianapolis, Ind. BR/TR, 6′, Deb: 4/24/1888 F																									
1888	Bos-N	19	15	.559	36	35	34	2	0	317	278	3	73	132	10.2	2.07	138	.226	.275	18	.148	-4	27	27	1	2.4
1889	Bos-N	1	2	.333	7	4	3	0	2	42	53	3	23	10	16.7	5.14	81	.299	.385	4	.235	0	-5	-5	1	-0.3
	Pit-N	6	5	.545	13	11	9	0	0	52^2	94	1	29	33	21.7	7.35	51	.376	.449	13	.271	2	-19	-21	2	-1.4
	Yr	7	7	.500	20	15	12	0	**2**	94^2	147	4	52	43	19.3	6.37	62	.342	.418	17	.262	2	-25	-26	3	-1.7
1890	Pit-N	3	8	.273	15	11	9	0	0	106	117	1	24	30	12.1	4.42	75	.271	.313	9	.180	-2	-10	-13	-2	-1.4
Total	3	29	30	.492	71	61	55	2	2	517^2	542	8	149	205	12.3	3.34	94	.260	.314	44	.186	-4	-7	-11	2	-0.7
● **BOB SPADE**	Spade, Robert b: 1/4/1877, Akron, Ohio d: 9/7/24, Cincinnati, Ohio BR/TR, 5′10″, 190 lbs. Deb: 9/22/07																									
1907	Cin-N	1	2	.333	3	3	3	1	0	27	21	0	9	7	10.3	1.00	260	.219	.292	2	.286	1	4	5	-1	0.7
1908	Cin-N	17	12	.586	35	28	22	2	1	249^1	230	2	85	74	11.6	2.74	84	.250	.317	17	.195	1	-11	-12	-4	-1.7
1909	Cin-N	5	5	.500	14	13	8	0	0	98	91	0	39	31	12.3	2.85	91	.236	.313	10	.294	4	-3	-3	-4	-0.4
1910	Cin-N	1	2	.333	3	3	1	0	0	17^1	35	1	9	1	23.4	6.75	43	.479	.542	0	.000	-1	-7	-7	-0	-0.7
	StL-A	1	3	.250	7	5	2	1	0	34^2	34	1	17	8	13.5	4.41	56	.270	.361	3	.273	2	-7	-7	-1	-0.7
Total	4	25	24	.510	62	52	36	4	1	426^1	411	4	159	121	12.3	2.96	82	.257	.329	32	.222	7	-23	-25	-9	-2.8
● **WARREN SPAHN**	Spahn, Warren Edward b: 4/23/21, Buffalo, N.Y. BL/TL, 6′, 175 lbs. Deb: 4/19/42 CH																									
1942	Bos-N	0	0	—	4	2	1	0	0	15^2	25	0	11	7	20.7	5.74	58	.368	.456	1	.167	-0	-4	-4	-0	-0.5
1946	Bos-N	8	5	.615	24	16	8	0	1	125^2	107	6	36	67	10.3	2.94	117	.228	.285	7	.163	-1	7	7	-2	0.4
1947	Bos-N★	21	10	.677	40	35	22	**7**	3	**289^2**	245	15	84	123	**10.3**	**2.33**	**167**	.226	**.283**	16	.163	1	**56**	**50**	-2	5.1
1948	*Bos-N	15	12	.556	36	35	16	3	1	257	237	19	77	114	11.0	3.71	103	.242	.298	15	.167	1	7	3	0	0.5
1949	Bos-N★	**21**	14	.600	38	38	**25**	4	0	**302^1**	283	27	86	**151**	11.1	3.07	123	.245	.299	18	.162	0	33	24	-2	2.2
1950	Bos-N☆	**21**	17	.553	41	39	25	1	1	293	248	22	111	**191**	11.1	3.16	122	.227	.299	23	.217	4	32	22	0	2.7
1951	Bos-N☆	22	14	.611	39	36	**26**	**7**	0	310^2	278	20	109	**164**	11.2	2.98	123	.238	.304	22	.190	5	34	24	-2	2.7
1952	Bos-N☆	14	19	.424	40	35	19	5	3	290	263	19	73	**183**	10.6	2.98	121	.240	.291	18	.161	2	24	20	1	2.6
1953	Mil-N★	**23**	7	.767	35	32	24	5	3	265^2	211	14	70	148	**9.6**	**2.10**	**187**	**.217**	**.270**	23	.219	4	**65**	54	2	**6.3**
1954	Mil-N★	21	12	.636	39	34	23	1	3	283^1	262	24	86	136	11.1	3.14	118	.245	.302	21	.208	6	29	18	1	2.6
1955	Mil-N	17	14	.548	39	32	16	1	1	245^2	249	25	65	110	11.6	3.26	115	.265	.314	17	.210	5	21	14	0	1.9
1956	Mil-N★	20	11	.645	39	35	20	3	3	281^1	249	25	52	128	9.7	2.78	124	.238	.276	22	.210	6	**31**	21	-1	2.8
1957	*Mil-N☆	**21**	11	.656	39	35	**18**	4	3	271	241	23	78	111	10.7	2.69	130	.237	.293	13	.138	1	**36**	24	0	2.7
1958	*Mil-N★	**22**	11	**.667**	38	36	**23**	2	1	**290**	257	29	76	150	**10.4**	3.07	115	.237	.288	36	.333	16	28	14	4	**3.6**
1959	Mil-N☆	**21**	15	.583	40	36	**21**	**4**	0	**292**	282	21	70	143	10.9	2.96	120	.253	.298	24	.231	7	32	19	-1	2.5
1960	Mil-N	**21**	10	.677	40	33	**18**	4	2	267^2	254	24	74	154	11.2	3.50	98	.250	.303	14	.147	3	8	-2	3	0.3
1961	Mil-N★	**21**	13	.618	38	34	**21**	**4**	0	262^2	236	24	64	115	**10.4**	**3.02**	124	.243	**.293**	21	.223	9	**30**	21	3	3.5
1962	Mil-N☆	18	14	.563	34	34	**22**	0	0	269^1	248	25	55	118	10.2	3.04	125	.246	.287	18	.184	4	27	23	1	2.9
1963	Mil-N☆	23	7	.767	33	33	**22**	7	0	259^2	241	23	49	102	10.1	2.60	124	.248	.284	16	.178	5	20	18	4	3.1
1964	Mil-N	6	13	.316	38	25	4	1	4	173^2	204	23	52	78	13.4	5.29	67	.297	.348	11	.186	2	-34	-34	-1	-3.3
1965	NY-N	4	12	.250	20	19	5	0	0	126	140	18	35	56	12.6	4.36	81	.281	.331	4	.114	1	-11	-12	0	-1.1
	SF-N	3	4	.429	16	11	3	0	0	71^2	70	8	21	34	11.6	3.39	106	.256	.312	3	.143	0	1	2	1	0.2
	Yr	7	16	.304	36	30	8	0	0	197^2	210	26	56	90	12.2	4.01	89	.271	.321	7	.125	2	-10	-10	1	-0.9
Total	21	363	245	.597	750	665	382	63	29	5243^2	4830	434	1434	2583	10.8	3.09	118	.244	.297	363	.194	82	470	330	9	43.7
● **AL SPALDING**	Spalding, Albert Goodwill b: 9/2/1850, Byron, Ill. d: 9/9/15, San Diego, Cal. BR/TR, 6′1″, 170 lbs. Deb: 5/05/1871 MH♦																									
1871	Bos-n	**19**	10	.655	31	31	22	**1**	0	257^1	333	2	38	23	13.0	3.36	124	.268	.290	39	.271	2	25	23		1.5
1872	Bos-n	**38**	8	**.826**	48	48	41	**3**	0	404^2	412	0	27	27	9.8	**1.98**	**188**	.240	.252	87	.357	19	**78**	**79**		**7.0**
1873	Bos-n	**41**	14	**.745**	**60**	55	48	1	**2**	**497^2**	643	5	28	31	12.1	2.46	135	.283	.292	106	.329	20	**44**	**47**		**4.4**
1874	Bos-n	**52**	16	**.765**	**71**	69	**65**	**4**	0	**616^1**	753	1	23		11.3	2.35	126	.273	.279	119	.331	22	44	42		**4.7**
1875	Bos-n	**55**	5	**.917**	**72**	63	52	**7**	**8**	575	571	1	14		9.2	**1.52**	156	.244	.249	107	.312	21	**60**	**54**		**6.2**
1876	Chi-N	**47**	12	**.797**	61	60	53	8	0	528^2	542	6	26	39	9.7	1.75	139	.247	.256	91	.312	10	33	41	4	4.7
1877	Chi-N	1	0	1.000	4	1	0	0	1	11	17	0	0	2	13.9	3.27	91	.321	.321	65	.256	0	-1	-0	1	0.0
Total	5 n	205	53	.795	282	266	228	16	10	2351	2712	9	130	81	10.9	2.22	142	.263	.272	458	.324	84	251	244		23.8
Total	2	48	12	.800	65	61	53	8	1	539^2	559	6	26	41	9.8	1.78	138	.249	.257	158	.287	84	32	40	5	4.7
● **BILL SPANSWICK**	Spanswick, William Henry b: 7/8/38, Springfield, Mass. BL/TL, 6′3″, 195 lbs. Deb: 4/18/64																									
1964	Bos-A	2	3	.400	29	7	0	0	0	65^1	75	9	44	55	16.8	6.89	56	.306	.418	4	.286	1	-24	-22	1	-2.0
● **TULLY SPARKS**	Sparks, Thomas Frank b: 12/12/1874, Aetna, Ga. d: 7/15/37, Anniston, Ala. BR/TR, Deb: 9/15/1897																									
1897	Phi-N	0	1	.000	1	1	1	0	0	8	12	0	4	0	18.0	10.13	41	.343	.411	0	.000	-1	-5	-5	0	-0.4
1899	Pit-N	8	6	.571	28	17	8	0	0	170	180	1	82	53	14.4	3.86	99	.271	.360	8	.129	-2	-0	-1	-1	-0.3
1901	Mil-A	7	16	.304	29	26	18	0	0	210	228	5	93	62	14.3	3.51	102	.273	.355	12	.169	-2	4	2	-0	0.1
1902	NY-N	4	10	.286	15	13	11	0	1	115	123	2	40	40	13.1	3.76	75	.273	.338	5	.135	-1	-12	-12	3	-1.0
	Bos-A	7	9	.438	17	15	15	1	0	142^2	151	4	40	37	12.6	3.47	103	.272	.330	8	.154	-1	2	2	0	0.0
1903	Phi-N	11	15	.423	28	28	27	0	0	248	248	3	56	88	11.3	2.72	120	.263	.310	10	.109	-5	15	15	-2	0.8

YEAR TM/L	W	L	PCT	G	GS	CG	SH	SV	IP	H	HR	BB	SO	RAT	ERA	ERA+	OAV	OOB	BH	AVG	PB	PR	/A	PD	TPI
1904 Phi-N	7	16	.304	26	25	19	3	0	200^2	208	1	43	67	11.5	2.65	101	.260	.302	8	.105	-5	2	1	-4	-0.8
1905 Phi-N	14	11	.560	34	26	20	3	1	259^2	217	2	73	98	10.4	2.18	134	.236	.298	12	.128	-2	24	21	-6	1.4
1906 Phi-N	19	16	.543	42	37	29	6	3	316^2	244	4	62	114	9.0	2.16	121	.211	.257	16	.154	0	17	16	-4	1.3
1907 Phi-N	22	8	.733	33	31	24	3	1	265	221	2	51	90	9.5	2.00	121	.228	.271	3	.034	-8	14	12	-5	-0.1
1908 Phi-N	16	15	.516	33	31	24	2	2	263^1	251	3	51	85	10.6	2.60	93	.257	.300	4	.052	-5	-7	-5	-2	-1.5
1909 Phi-N	6	11	.353	24	16	6	1	0	121^2	126	4	32	40	11.9	2.96	88	.280	.332	5	.139	-1	-5	-5	-1	-0.7
1910 Phi-N	0	2	.000	3	3	0	0	0	15	22	2	2	4	15.6	6.00	52	.324	.361	0	.000	-1	-5	-5	0	-0.5
Total 12	121	136	.471	313	269	202	19	8	2335^2	2231	33	629	778	11.4	2.79	105	.253	.309	91	.114	-33	42	37	-21	-1.7

● JOE SPARMA Sparma, Joseph Blase b: 2/4/42, Massillon, Ohio d: 5/14/86, Columbus, Ohio BR/TR, 6', 195 lbs. Deb: 5/20/64

YEAR TM/L	W	L	PCT	G	GS	CG	SH	SV	IP	H	HR	BB	SO	RAT	ERA	ERA+	OAV	OOB	BH	AVG	PB	PR	/A	PD	TPI
1964 Det-A	5	6	.455	21	11	3	2	0	84	62	4	45	71	11.8	3.00	122	.207	.316	4	.160	1	6	6	1	0.9
1965 Det-A	13	8	.619	30	28	6	0	0	167	142	13	75	127	11.9	3.18	109	.228	.314	7	.135	-0	5	6	-1	0.5
1966 Det-A	2	7	.222	29	13	0	0	0	91^2	103	14	52	61	15.5	5.30	66	.288	.383	5	.217	1	-19	-19	-2	-2.0
1967 Det-A	16	9	.640	37	37	11	5	0	217^2	186	20	85	153	11.5	3.76	87	.227	.306	4	.054	-5	-13	-12	-2	-2.1
1968 *Det-A	10	10	.500	34	31	7	1	0	182^1	169	14	77	110	12.5	3.70	81	.246	.328	8	.133	-1	-15	-14	-2	-1.9
1969 Det-A	6	8	.429	23	16	3	2	0	92^2	78	5	77	41	15.2	4.76	78	.231	.375	4	.138	-1	-12	-11	-1	-1.3
1970 Mon-N	0	4	.000	9	6	1	0	0	29^1	34	7	25	23	18.7	7.06	58	.296	.430	0	.000	-0	-10	-10	-0	-1.0
Total 7	52	52	.500	183	142	31	10	0	864^2	774	77	436	586	12.9	3.94	86	.239	.334	32	.119	-6	-57	-53	-7	-6.9

● TRIS SPEAKER Speaker, Tristram E "The Grey Eagle" b: 4/4/1888, Hubbard, Tex. d: 12/8/58, Lake Whitney, Tex. BL/TL, 5'11.5", 193 lbs. Deb: 9/14/07 MH♦

YEAR TM/L	W	L	PCT	G	GS	CG	SH	SV	IP	H	HR	BB	SO	RAT	ERA	ERA+	OAV	OOB	BH	AVG	PB	PR	/A	PD	TPI
1914 Bos-A	0	0	—	1	0	0	0	0	1	2	0	0	0	18.0	9.00	30	.500	.500	193	.338	1	-1	-1	0	0.0

● CLIFF SPECK Speck, Robert Clifford b: 8/8/56, Portland, Ore. BR/TR, 6'4", 195 lbs. Deb: 7/30/86

YEAR TM/L	W	L	PCT	G	GS	CG	SH	SV	IP	H	HR	BB	SO	RAT	ERA	ERA+	OAV	OOB	BH	AVG	PB	PR	/A	PD	TPI
1986 Atl-N	2	1	.667	13	1	0	0	0	28^1	25	2	15	21	13.0	4.13	96	.238	.339	0	.000	-0	-1	-0	0	0.0

● BY SPEECE Speece, Byron Franklin b: 1/6/1897, West Baden, Ind. d: 9/29/74, Elgin, Ore. BR/TR, 5'11", 170 lbs. Deb: 4/21/24

YEAR TM/L	W	L	PCT	G	GS	CG	SH	SV	IP	H	HR	BB	SO	RAT	ERA	ERA+	OAV	OOB	BH	AVG	PB	PR	/A	PD	TPI
1924 *Was-A	2	1	.667	21	1	0	0	0	54^1	60	0	27	15	14.7	2.65	152	.303	.392	3	.150	-1	**10**	**8**	1	0.9
1925 Cle-A	3	5	.375	28	3	3	0	1	90^1	106	0	28	26	13.6	4.28	103	.297	.353	5	.161	-2	1	1	0	0.0
1926 Cle-A	0	0	—	2	0	0	0	0	3	1	0	2	1	9.0	0.00	—	.125	.300	0	—	0	1	1	0	0.2
1930 Phi-N	0	0	—	11	0	0	0	0	19^2	41	1	4	9	20.6	13.27	41	.432	.455	1	.333	0	-18	-17	-0	-1.4
Total 4	5	6	.455	62	4	3	0	1	167^1	208	1	61	51	14.7	4.73	93	.316	.378	9	.167	-2	-6	-6	2	-0.3

● FLOYD SPEER Speer, Floyd Vernie b: 1/27/13, Booneville, Ark. d: 3/22/69, Little Rock, Ark. BR/TR, 6', 180 lbs. Deb: 4/25/43

YEAR TM/L	W	L	PCT	G	GS	CG	SH	SV	IP	H	HR	BB	SO	RAT	ERA	ERA+	OAV	OOB	BH	AVG	PB	PR	/A	PD	TPI
1943 Chi-A	0	0	—	1	0	0	0	0	1	1	0	2	1	27.0	9.00	37	.250	.500	0	—	0	-1	-1	0	0.0
1944 Chi-A	0	0	—	2	0	0	0	0	2	4	0	0	1	18.0	9.00	38	.500	.500	0	—	0	-1	-1	-0	-0.1
Total 2	0	0	—	3	0	0	0	0	3	5	0	2	2	21.0	9.00	38	.417	.500	0	—	0	-2	-2	0	-0.1

● KID SPEER Speer, George Nathan b: 6/16/1886, Corning, Mo. d: 1/13/46, Edmonton, Alberta, Canada BL/TL, 5'9", 152 lbs. Deb: 4/24/09

YEAR TM/L	W	L	PCT	G	GS	CG	SH	SV	IP	H	HR	BB	SO	RAT	ERA	ERA+	OAV	OOB	BH	AVG	PB	PR	/A	PD	TPI
1909 Det-A	4	4	.500	12	8	4	0	1	76^1	88	2	13	12	12.4	2.83	89	.293	.331	3	.120	-0	-3	-3	1	-0.3

● HACK SPENCER Spencer, Fred Calvin b: 4/25/1885, St.Cloud, Minn. d: 2/5/69, St.Anthony, Minn. BR/TR, 5'10.5", 172 lbs. Deb: 4/18/12

YEAR TM/L	W	L	PCT	G	GS	CG	SH	SV	IP	H	HR	BB	SO	RAT	ERA	ERA+	OAV	OOB	BH	AVG	PB	PR	/A	PD	TPI
1912 StL-A	0	0	—	1	0	0	0	0	1^2	2	0	0	0	10.8	0.00	—	.286	.286	0	—	0	1	1	0	0.1

● GEORGE SPENCER Spencer, George Elwell b: 7/7/26, Columbus, Ohio BR/TR, 6'1", 215 lbs. Deb: 8/17/50

YEAR TM/L	W	L	PCT	G	GS	CG	SH	SV	IP	H	HR	BB	SO	RAT	ERA	ERA+	OAV	OOB	BH	AVG	PB	PR	/A	PD	TPI
1950 NY-N	1	0	1.000	10	1	1	0	0	25^1	12	3	7	5	6.8	2.49	165	.141	.207	0	.000	-1	5	5	0	0.4
1951 *NY-N	10	4	.714	57	4	2	0	6	132	125	21	56	36	12.4	3.75	104	.254	.332	4	.125	-1	3	2	1	0.3
1952 NY-N	3	5	.375	35	4	0	0	3	60	57	13	21	27	12.2	5.55	67	.251	.323	2	.200	0	-12	-12	-0	-1.3
1953 NY-N	0	0	—	1	0	0	0	0	2^1	3	0	2	1	19.3	7.71	56	.300	.417	0	—	0	-1	-1	-0	-0.1
1954 NY-N	1	0	1.000	6	0	0	0	0	12^1	9	1	8	4	12.4	3.65	111	.209	.333	0	.000	-0	1	1	1	0.1
1955 NY-N	0	0	—	1	0	0	0	0	1^2	1	1	3	0	21.6	5.40	75	.167	.444	0	—	0	-0	-0	0	0.0
1958 Det-A	1	0	1.000	7	0	0	0	0	10	11	0	4	5	13.5	2.70	149	.289	.357	0	—	0	1	1	0	0.2
1960 Det-A	0	1	.000	5	0	0	0	0	7^2	10	1	5	4	17.6	3.52	112	.323	.417	0	.000	-0	0	0	-0	0.0
Total 8	16	10	.615	122	9	3	0	9	251^1	228	40	106	82	12.1	4.05	96	.245	.324	6	.120	-2	-3	-4	2	-0.4

● GLENN SPENCER Spencer, Glenn Edward b: 9/11/05, Corning, N.Y. d: 12/30/58, Binghamton, N.Y. BR/TR, 5'11", 155 lbs. Deb: 4/11/28

YEAR TM/L	W	L	PCT	G	GS	CG	SH	SV	IP	H	HR	BB	SO	RAT	ERA	ERA+	OAV	OOB	BH	AVG	PB	PR	/A	PD	TPI
1928 Pit-N	0	0	—	4	0	0	0	0	5^2	4	0	3	2	11.1	1.59	255	.200	.304	0	.000	-0	2	2	-0	0.1
1930 Pit-N	8	9	.471	41	10	5	0	4	156^2	185	16	63	60	14.4	5.40	92	.305	.372	6	.113	-4	-7	-7	-2	-1.2
1931 Pit-N	11	12	.478	38	18	11	1	3	186^2	180	8	65	51	12.1	3.42	112	.260	.328	5	.096	-3	9	9	-0	0.6
1932 Pit-N	4	8	.333	39	13	5	1	1	137^2	167	10	44	35	14.0	4.97	77	.288	.341	6	.162	-1	-17	-18	-1	-1.9
1933 NY-N	0	2	.000	17	3	1	0	0	47^1	52	3	26	14	15.0	5.13	63	.284	.376	2	.167	-0	-9	-10	-0	-1.0
Total 5	23	31	.426	139	44	22	2	8	534	588	37	201	162	13.5	4.53	91	.282	.349	19	.123	-9	-23	-25	-3	-3.4

● BOB SPICER Spicer, Robert Oberton b: 4/11/25, Richmond, Va. BL/TR, 5'10", 173 lbs. Deb: 4/17/55

YEAR TM/L	W	L	PCT	G	GS	CG	SH	SV	IP	H	HR	BB	SO	RAT	ERA	ERA+	OAV	OOB	BH	AVG	PB	PR	/A	PD	TPI
1955 KC-A	0	0	—	2	0	0	0	0	2^2	9	2	4	2	47.3	33.75	12	.529	.636	0	.000	-0	-9	-9	-0	-0.7
1956 KC-A	0	0	—	2	0	0	0	0	2^1	6	1	1	0	30.9	19.29	22	.545	.615	0	—	0	-4	-4	0	-0.3
Total 2	0	0	—	4	0	0	0	0	5	15	3	5	2	39.6	27.00	16	.536	.629	0	.000	-0	-13	-13	0	-1.0

● DAN SPILLNER Spillner, Daniel Ray b: 11/27/51, Casper, Wyo. BR/TR, 6'1", 190 lbs. Deb: 5/21/74

YEAR TM/L	W	L	PCT	G	GS	CG	SH	SV	IP	H	HR	BB	SO	RAT	ERA	ERA+	OAV	OOB	BH	AVG	PB	PR	/A	PD	TPI
1974 SD-N	9	11	.450	30	25	5	2	0	148	153	15	70	95	13.6	4.01	89	.267	.346	1	.023	-4	-7	-8	-1	-1.3
1975 SD-N	5	13	.278	37	25	3	0	1	166^2	194	14	63	104	14.0	4.27	81	.293	.356	6	.133	1	-12	-15	-0	-1.4
1976 SD-N	2	11	.154	32	14	0	0	0	106^2	120	11	55	57	14.8	5.06	65	.291	.374	1	.040	-1	-19	-21	1	-2.2
1977 SD-N	7	6	.538	76	0	0	0	6	123	130	12	60	74	14.0	3.73	95	.280	.363	2	.118	1	2	-3	-2	-0.4
1978 SD-N	1	0	1.000	17	0	0	0	0	25^2	32	2	7	16	13.7	4.56	73	.317	.361	0	—	0	-3	-4	-0	-0.4
Cle-A	3	1	.750	36	0	0	0	3	56^1	54	2	21	48	12.1	3.67	102	.254	.323	0	—	0	1	0	-1	0.0
1979 Cle-A	9	5	.643	49	13	3	0	1	157^2	153	16	64	97	12.6	4.62	92	.256	.331	0	—	0	-7	-6	-1	-0.7
1980 Cle-A	16	11	.593	34	30	7	1	0	194^1	225	23	74	100	14.0	5.28	77	.288	.352	0	—	0	-27	-26	-2	-2.7
1981 Cle-A	4	4	.500	32	5	1	0	7	97^1	86	3	39	59	11.6	3.14	115	.240	.314	0	—	0	6	5	0	0.6
1982 Cle-A	12	10	.545	65	0	0	0	21	133^2	117	9	45	90	10.9	2.49	164	.235	.299	0	—	0	**24**	**24**	-3	2.2
1983 Cle-A	2	9	.182	60	0	0	0	8	92^1	117	7	38	48	15.3	5.07	84	.315	.382	0	—	0	-10	-9	-1	-1.0
1984 Cle-A	0	5	.000	14	8	0	0	1	51	70	3	22	23	16.2	5.65	72	.332	.395	0	—	0	-9	-9	1	-0.8
Chi-A	1	0	1.000	22	0	0	0	1	48^1	51	7	14	26	12.3	4.10	101	.276	.330	0	—	0	-1	0	-0	0.0
Yr	1	5	.167	36	8	0	0	2	99^1	121	10	36	49	14.3	4.89	84	.301	.360	0	—	0	-10	-9	1	-0.8
1985 Chi-A	4	3	.571	52	3	0	0	1	91^2	83	10	33	41	11.4	3.44	126	.245	.312	0	—	0	7	9	-3	0.7
Total 12	75	89	.457	556	123	19	3	50	1492^2	1585	134	605	878	13.3	4.21	91	.275	.345	10	.077	-3	-55	-62	-12	-7.4

● SCIPIO SPINKS Spinks, Scipio Ronald b: 7/12/47, Chicago, Ill. BR/TR, 6'1", 185 lbs. Deb: 9/16/69

YEAR TM/L	W	L	PCT	G	GS	CG	SH	SV	IP	H	HR	BB	SO	RAT	ERA	ERA+	OAV	OOB	BH	AVG	PB	PR	/A	PD	TPI
1969 Hou-N	0	0	—	1	0	0	0	0	2	1	0	1	4	9.0	0.00	—	.143	.250	0	—	0	1	1	0	0.1
1970 Hou-N	0	1	.000	5	2	0	0	0	13^2	17	5	9	6	17.1	9.88	39	.293	.388	0	.000	-0	-9	-9	-1	-0.9
1971 Hou-N	1	0	1.000	5	3	1	0	0	29^1	22	2	13	26	11.0	3.68	91	.210	.303	2	.222	0	-1	-1	0	-0.1
1972 StL-N	5	5	.500	16	16	6	0	0	118	96	5	59	93	12.0	2.67	127	.221	.317	7	.167	-1	10	10	1	1.0
1973 StL-N	1	5	.167	8	8	0	0	0	38^2	39	4	25	25	14.9	4.89	75	.269	.376	2	.182	1	-5	-5	1	-0.4
Total 5	7	11	.389	35	29	7	0	0	201^2	175	16	107	154	12.7	3.70	94	.234	.332	11	.169	0	-4	-5	1	-0.3

● PAUL SPLITTORFF Splittorff, Paul William b: 10/8/46, Evansville, Ind. BL/TL, 6'3", 210 lbs. Deb: 9/23/70

YEAR TM/L	W	L	PCT	G	GS	CG	SH	SV	IP	H	HR	BB	SO	RAT	ERA	ERA+	OAV	OOB	BH	AVG	PB	PR	/A	PD	TPI
1970 KC-A	0	1	.000	2	1	0	0	0	8^2	16	1	5	10	21.8	7.27	51	.390	.457	1	.500	0	-3	-3	0	-0.3
1971 KC-A	8	9	.471	22	22	6	3	0	144^1	129	4	35	80	10.5	2.68	128	.243	.295	5	.104	-1	13	12	2	1.4

YEAR	TM/L	W	L	PCT	G	GS	CG	SH	SV	IP	H	HR	BB	SO	RAT	ERA	ERA+	OAV	OOB	BH	AVG	PB	PR	/A	PD	TPI
1972	KC-A	12	12	.500	35	33	12	2	0	216	189	11	67	140	10.8	3.13	97	.241	.304	16	.225	4	-2	-2	4	0.6
1973	KC-A	20	11	.645	38	38	12	3	0	262	279	19	78	110	12.4	3.98	103	.272	.327	0	—	0	-5	4	1	0.0
1974	KC-A	13	19	.406	36	36	8	1	0	226	252	23	75	90	13.1	4.10	93	.285	.342	0	—	0	-12	-7	0	-1.1
1975	KC-A	9	10	.474	35	23	6	3	1	159	156	10	56	76	12.1	3.17	121	.255	.319	0	—	0	11	12	2	1.4
1976	*KC-A	11	8	.579	26	23	5	1	0	158^{2}	169	11	59	59	13.1	3.97	88	.277	.343	0	—	0	-8	-8	1	-0.8
1977	*KC-A	16	6	**.727**	37	37	6	2	0	229	243	11	83	99	12.9	3.69	109	.278	.342	0	—	0	9	9	-0	0.8
1978	*KC-A	19	13	.594	39	38	13	2	0	262	244	22	60	76	10.5	3.40	112	.247	.293	0	—	0	11	12	1	1.4
1979	KC-A	15	17	.469	36	35	11	0	0	240	248	25	77	77	12.4	4.24	101	.268	.328	0	—	0	-1	1	-2	-0.2
1980	*KC-A	14	11	.560	34	33	4	0	0	204	236	17	43	53	12.4	4.15	98	.296	.333	0	—	0	-3	-2	-0	-0.3
1981	KC-A	5	5	.500	21	15	1	0	0	99	111	12	23	48	12.3	4.36	83	.294	.337	0	—	0	-8	-8	1	-0.7
1982	KC-A	10	10	.500	29	28	0	0	0	162	166	14	57	74	12.6	4.28	95	.266	.330	0	—	0	-4	-4	0	-0.3
1983	KC-A	13	8	.619	27	27	4	0	0	156	159	9	52	61	12.2	3.63	112	.262	.322	0	—	0	7	8	0	0.8
1984	KC-A	1	3	.250	12	3	0	0	0	28	47	3	10	4	18.3	7.71	52	.376	.422	0	—	0	-12	-11	1	-1.0
Total	15	166	143	.537	429	392	88	17	1	2554^{2}	2644	192	780	1057	12.2	3.81	101	.270	.326	22	.182	3	-6	10	10	1.7

● CARL SPONGBERG Spongberg, Carl Gustav b: 5/21/1884, Idaho Falls, Idaho d: 7/21/38, Los Angeles, Cal. BR/TR, 6'2", 208 lbs. Deb: 8/01/08

YEAR	TM/L	W	L	PCT	G	GS	CG	SH	SV	IP	H	HR	BB	SO	RAT	ERA	ERA+	OAV	OOB	BH	AVG	PB	PR	/A	PD	TPI
1908	Chi-N	0	0	—	1	0	0	0	0	7	9	1	6	4	21.9	9.00	26	.321	.472	2	.667	1	-5	-5	0	-0.4

● KARL SPOONER Spooner, Karl Benjamin b: 6/23/31, Oriskany Falls, N.Y. d: 4/10/84, Vero Beach, Fla. BR/TL, 6', 185 lbs. Deb: 9/22/54

YEAR	TM/L	W	L	PCT	G	GS	CG	SH	SV	IP	H	HR	BB	SO	RAT	ERA	ERA+	OAV	OOB	BH	AVG	PB	PR	/A	PD	TPI
1954	Bro-N	2	0	1.000	2	2	2	2	0	18	7	0	6	27	6.5	0.00	—	.113	.191	1	.167	0	8	8	-0	1.1
1955	*Bro-N	8	6	.571	29	14	2	1	2	98^{2}	79	8	41	78	11.4	3.65	111	.215	.302	8	.286	3	4	5	-0	0.7
Total	2	10	6	.625	31	16	4	3	2	116^{2}	86	8	47	105	10.6	3.09	132	.200	.286	9	.265	3	12	13	-1	1.8

● HOMER SPRAGINS Spragins, Homer Franklin b: 11/9/20, Grenada, Miss. BR/TR, 6'1", 190 lbs. Deb: 9/13/47

YEAR	TM/L	W	L	PCT	G	GS	CG	SH	SV	IP	H	HR	BB	SO	RAT	ERA	ERA+	OAV	OOB	BH	AVG	PB	PR	/A	PD	TPI
1947	Phi-N	0	0	—	4	0	0	0	0	5^{1}	3	0	3	3	10.1	6.75	59	.158	.273	0	—	0	-2	-2	0	-0.2

● CHARLIE SPRAGUE Sprague, Charles Wellington b: 10/10/1864, Cleveland, Ohio d: 12/31/12, Des Moines, Iowa BL/TL, 5'11", 150 lbs. Deb: 9/17/1887 ♦

YEAR	TM/L	W	L	PCT	G	GS	CG	SH	SV	IP	H	HR	BB	SO	RAT	ERA	ERA+	OAV	OOB	BH	AVG	PB	PR	/A	PD	TPI
1887	Chi-N	1	0	1.000	3	3	2	0	0	22	24	1	13	9	16.8	4.91	91	.276	.394	2	.154	-1	-2	-1	-1	-0.2
1889	Cle-N	0	2	.000	2	2	2	0	0	17	27	0	10	8	20.6	8.47	48	.349	.437	1	.143	-0	-8	-8	1	-0.6
1890	Tol-a	9	5	.643	19	12	9	0	0	122^{2}	111	0	78	59	15.2	3.89	102	.234	.363	47	.236	3	-0	1	-2	0.1
Total	3	10	7	.588	24	17	13	0	0	161^{2}	162	1	101	76	16.0	4.51	89	.254	.376	50	.228	1	-11	-9	-2	-0.7

● ED SPRAGUE Sprague, Edward Nelson Sr. b: 9/16/45, Boston, Mass. BR/TR, 6'4", 195 lbs. Deb: 4/10/68 F

YEAR	TM/L	W	L	PCT	G	GS	CG	SH	SV	IP	H	HR	BB	SO	RAT	ERA	ERA+	OAV	OOB	BH	AVG	PB	PR	/A	PD	TPI
1968	Oak-A	3	4	.429	47	1	0	0	4	68^{2}	51	5	34	34	11.4	3.28	86	.209	.311	0	.000	-1	-2	-3	1	-0.4
1969	Oak-A	1	1	.500	27	0	0	0	2	46^{1}	47	4	31	20	15.5	4.47	77	.267	.383	1	.200	0	-4	-5	2	-0.3
1971	Cin-N	1	0	1.000	7	0	0	0	0	11	8	0	1	7	7.4	0.00	—	.195	.214	0	.000	-0	4	4	-1	0.4
1972	Cin-N	3	3	.500	33	1	0	0	0	56^{2}	55	6	26	25	13.3	4.13	78	.261	.350	0	.000	-1	-4	-6	-1	-0.8
1973	Cin-N	1	3	.250	28	0	0	0	1	38^{2}	35	3	22	19	13.7	5.12	66	.246	.355	0	.000	-0	-6	-7	0	-0.7
	StL-N	0	0	—	8	0	0	0	0	8	8	1	4	2	13.5	2.25	162	.276	.364	0	—	0	1	1	0	0.1
	Yr	1	3	.250	36	0	0	0	1	46^{2}	43	4	26	21	13.3	4.63	74	.247	.345	0	.000	0	-5	-6	1	-0.6
	Mil-A	0	1	.000	7	0	0	0	1	9^{2}	13	0	14	3	27.0	9.31	40	.317	.509	0	—	0	-6	-6	-0	-0.5
1974	Mil-A	7	2	.778	20	10	3	0	0	94	94	3	31	57	12.4	2.39	151	.266	.332	0	—	0	13	13	-1	1.4
1975	Mil-A	1	7	.125	18	11	0	0	1	67^{1}	81	5	40	21	16.4	4.68	82	.297	.390	0	—	0	-7	-6	-1	-0.7
1976	Mil-A	0	2	.000	3	0	0	0	0	7^{2}	14	0	3	0	20.0	7.04	50	.438	.486	0	—	0	-3	-3	1	-0.2
Total	8	17	23	.425	198	23	3	0	9	408	406	27	206	188	13.9	3.84	89	.263	.356	1	.045	-1	-15	-19	2	-1.7

● JACK SPRING Spring, Jack Russell b: 3/11/33, Spokane, Wash. BR/TL, 6'1", 180 lbs. Deb: 4/16/55

YEAR	TM/L	W	L	PCT	G	GS	CG	SH	SV	IP	H	HR	BB	SO	RAT	ERA	ERA+	OAV	OOB	BH	AVG	PB	PR	/A	PD	TPI
1955	Phi-N	0	1	.000	2	0	0	0	0	2^{2}	2	2	1	2	10.1	6.75	59	.200	.273	0	.000	-0	-1	-1	-0	-0.1
1957	Bos-A	0	0	—	1	0	0	0	0	1	0	0	0	2	0.0	0.00	—	.000	.000	0	—	0	0	0	0	0.0
1958	Was-A	0	0	—	3	1	0	0	0	7	16	1	7	1	29.6	14.14	27	.457	.548	0	.000	-0	-8	-8	0	-0.7
1961	LA-A	3	0	1.000	18	4	0	0	0	38	35	4	15	27	12.6	4.26	106	.243	.327	0	.000	-1	-1	1	-0	0.0
1962	LA-A	4	2	.667	57	0	0	0	6	65	66	7	30	31	13.6	4.02	96	.270	.355	1	.091	-1	-0	-1	1	-0.1
1963	LA-A	3	0	1.000	45	0	0	0	2	38^{1}	40	3	9	13	11.5	3.05	112	.268	.310	1	.333	0	2	2	1	0.3
1964	LA-A	1	0	1.000	6	0	0	0	0	3^{1}	3	1	3	0	16.2	2.70	122	.273	.429	0	—	0	0	0	-0	0.0
	Chi-N	0	0	—	7	0	0	0	0	6	4	0	2	1	9.0	6.00	62	.200	.273	0	—	0	-2	-2	0	-0.1
	StL-N	0	0	—	2	0	0	0	0	3	8	1	1	0	27.0	3.00	127	.471	.500	0	—	0	0	0	0	0.0
	Yr	0	0	—	9	0	0	0	0	9	12	1	3	1	15.0	5.00	75	.316	.366	0	—	0	-1	-1	0	-0.1
1965	Cle-A	1	2	.333	14	0	0	0	0	21^{2}	21	2	10	9	12.9	3.74	93	.259	.341	1	.333	0	-1	-1	-1	-0.1
Total	8	12	5	.706	155	5	0	0	8	186	195	21	78	86	13.5	4.26	90	.273	.349	3	.107	-1	-9	-9	1	-0.8

● BRAD SPRINGER Springer, Bradford Louis b: 5/9/04, Detroit, Mich. d: 1/4/70, Birmingham, Mich. BL/TL, 6', 155 lbs. Deb: 5/01/25

YEAR	TM/L	W	L	PCT	G	GS	CG	SH	SV	IP	H	HR	BB	SO	RAT	ERA	ERA+	OAV	OOB	BH	AVG	PB	PR	/A	PD	TPI
1925	StL-A	0	0	—	2	0	0	0	0	3	1	0	7	0	24.0	3.00	156	.200	.667	0	—	0	0	1	0	0.1
1926	Cin-N	0	0	—	1	0	0	0	0	1^{1}	2	0	2	1	33.8	6.75	55	.286	.500	0	.000	-0	-0	-0	0	-0.1
Total	2	0	0	—	3	0	0	0	0	4^{1}	3	0	9	1	27.0	4.15	105	.250	.591	0	.000	-0	0	0	0	0.0

● ED SPRINGER Springer, Edward H. b: 2/9/1861, California d: 4/24/26, Los Angeles Co., Cal. 6'2", 187 lbs. Deb: 7/12/1889

YEAR	TM/L	W	L	PCT	G	GS	CG	SH	SV	IP	H	HR	BB	SO	RAT	ERA	ERA+	OAV	OOB	BH	AVG	PB	PR	/A	PD	TPI
1889	Lou-a	0	1	.000	1	1	1	0	0	5	8	0	2	1	21.6	9.00	43	.351	.447	0	.000	-0	-3	-3	-0	-0.3

● RUSS SPRINGER Springer, Russell Paul b: 11/7/68, Alexandria, La. BR/TR, 6'4", 195 lbs. Deb: 4/17/92

YEAR	TM/L	W	L	PCT	G	GS	CG	SH	SV	IP	H	HR	BB	SO	RAT	ERA	ERA+	OAV	OOB	BH	AVG	PB	PR	/A	PD	TPI
1992	NY-A	0	0	—	14	0	0	0	0	16	18	0	10	12	16.3	6.19	65	.281	.387	0	—	0	-4	-4	-0	-0.4

● CHARLIE SPROULL Sproull, Charles William b: 1/9/19, Taylorsville, Ga. d: 1/13/80, Rockford, Ill. BR/TR, 6'3", 185 lbs. Deb: 4/19/45

YEAR	TM/L	W	L	PCT	G	GS	CG	SH	SV	IP	H	HR	BB	SO	RAT	ERA	ERA+	OAV	OOB	BH	AVG	PB	PR	/A	PD	TPI
1945	Phi-N	4	10	.286	34	19	2	0	1	130^{1}	158	10	80	47	16.4	5.94	65	.298	.390	5	.143	-1	-31	-31	-1	-3.1

● BOB SPROUT Sprout, Robert Samiel b: 12/5/41, Florin, Pa. BL/TL, 6', 165 lbs. Deb: 9/27/61

YEAR	TM/L	W	L	PCT	G	GS	CG	SH	SV	IP	H	HR	BB	SO	RAT	ERA	ERA+	OAV	OOB	BH	AVG	PB	PR	/A	PD	TPI
1961	LA-A	0	0	—	1	1	0	0	0	4	4	0	3	2	15.8	4.50	100	.267	.389	0	—	0	-0	0	-0	0.0

● BOBBY SPROWL Sprowl, Robert John b: 4/14/56, Sandusky, Ohio BL/TL, 6'2", 190 lbs. Deb: 9/05/78

YEAR	TM/L	W	L	PCT	G	GS	CG	SH	SV	IP	H	HR	BB	SO	RAT	ERA	ERA+	OAV	OOB	BH	AVG	PB	PR	/A	PD	TPI
1978	Bos-A	0	2	.000	3	3	0	0	0	12^{2}	12	3	10	10	15.6	6.39	64	.245	.373	0	—	0	-4	-3	-0	-0.4
1979	Hou-N	0	0	—	3	0	0	0	0	4	1	0	2	3	6.8	0.00	—	.083	.214	0	—	0	2	2	-0	0.2
1980	Hou-N	0	0	—	1	0	0	0	0	1	1	0	1	3	18.0	0.00	—	.250	.400	0	—	0	0	0	0	0.0
1981	Hou-N	0	1	.000	15	1	0	0	0	28^{2}	40	1	14	18	17.0	5.97	55	.333	.403	1	.167	-0	-8	-9	-0	-0.9
Total	4	0	3	.000	22	4	0	0	0	46^{1}	54	4	27	34	15.7	5.44	65	.292	.382	1	.167	-0	-10	-10	-1	-1.1

● MIKE SQUIRES Squires, Michael Lynn b: 3/5/52, Kalamazoo, Mich. BL/TL, 5'11", 185 lbs. Deb: 9/01/75 C♦

YEAR	TM/L	W	L	PCT	G	GS	CG	SH	SV	IP	H	HR	BB	SO	RAT	ERA	ERA+	OAV	OOB	BH	AVG	PB	PR	/A	PD	TPI
1984	Chi-A	0	0	—	1	0	0	0	0	0^{1}	0	0	0	0	0.0	0.00	—	.000	.000	15	.183	0	0	0	0	0.0

● GEORGE STABLEIN Stablein, George Charles b: 10/29/57, Inglewood, Cal. BR/TR, 6'4", 185 lbs. Deb: 9/20/80

YEAR	TM/L	W	L	PCT	G	GS	CG	SH	SV	IP	H	HR	BB	SO	RAT	ERA	ERA+	OAV	OOB	BH	AVG	PB	PR	/A	PD	TPI
1980	SD-N	0	1	.000	4	2	0	0	0	11^{2}	16	0	3	4	14.7	3.09	111	.340	.380	0	.000	-0	1	0	-0	0.0

● EDDIE STACK Stack, William Edward b: 10/24/1887, Chicago, Ill. d: 8/28/58, Chicago, Ill. BR/TR, 6', 175 lbs. Deb: 6/07/10

YEAR	TM/L	W	L	PCT	G	GS	CG	SH	SV	IP	H	HR	BB	SO	RAT	ERA	ERA+	OAV	OOB	BH	AVG	PB	PR	/A	PD	TPI
1910	Phi-N	6	7	.462	20	16	8	1	0	117	115	7	34	48	11.8	4.00	78	.266	.326	3	.083	-3	-13	-11	-1	-1.6
1911	Phi-N	5	5	.500	13	10	5	0	0	77^{2}	67	3	41	36	13.2	3.59	96	.234	.342	2	.083	-2	-2	-1	0	-0.3
1912	Bro-N	7	5	.583	28	17	4	0	1	142	139	3	55	45	12.9	3.36	100	.264	.343	7	.135	-3	1	-0	-1	-0.4
1913	Bro-N	4	4	.500	23	9	4	1	0	87	79	0	32	34	11.6	2.38	138	.250	.321	4	.160	-1	8	9	-2	0.6
	Chi-N	4	2	.667	11	7	3	1	1	51	56	1	15	28	12.9	4.24	75	.280	.336	1	.063	-1	-6	-6	-1	-0.8

YEAR	TM/L	W	L	PCT	G	GS	CG	SH	SV	IP	H	HR	BB	SO	RAT	ERA	ERA+	OAV	OOB	BH	AVG	PB	PR	/A	PD	TPI
	Yr	8	6	.571	34	16	7	2	1	138	135	1	47	62	12.0	3.07	106	.261	.325	5	.122	-2	2	3	-3	-0.2
1914	Chi-N	0	1	.000	7	1	0	0	0	16^1	13	0	11	9	13.2	4.96	56	.220	.343	0	.000	-0	-4	-4	0	-0.4
Total	5	26	24	.520	102	60	24	3	2	491	469	14	188	200	12.4	3.52	93	.258	.334	17	.108	-10	-15	-14	-4	-2.9

● **GENERAL STAFFORD** Stafford, James Joseph "Jamsey" b: 7/9/1868, Webster, Mass. d: 9/18/23, Worcester, Mass. BR/TR, 5'8", 165 lbs. Deb: 8/27/1890 F♦

YEAR	TM/L	W	L	PCT	G	GS	CG	SH	SV	IP	H	HR	BB	SO	RAT	ERA	ERA+	OAV	OOB	BH	AVG	PB	PR	/A	PD	TPI
1890	Buf-P	3	9	.250	12	12	11	0	0	98	123	8	43	21	15.6	5.14	80	.294	.365	7	.143	-1	-10	-11	-1	-1.0

● **JOHN STAFFORD** Stafford, John Henry "Doc" b: 4/8/1870, Dudley, Mass. d: 7/3/40, Worcester, Mass. BR/TR, 5'10", 170 lbs. Deb: 6/15/1893 F

YEAR	TM/L	W	L	PCT	G	GS	CG	SH	SV	IP	H	HR	BB	SO	RAT	ERA	ERA+	OAV	OOB	BH	AVG	PB	PR	/A	PD	TPI
1893	Cle-N	0	1	.000	2	0	0	0	0	7	12	1	7	4	24.4	14.14	35	.367	.478	0	.000	-1	-7	-7	-0	-0.6

● **BILL STAFFORD** Stafford, William Charles b: 8/13/39, Catskill, N.Y. BR/TR, 6'2", 193 lbs. Deb: 4/17/60

YEAR	TM/L	W	L	PCT	G	GS	CG	SH	SV	IP	H	HR	BB	SO	RAT	ERA	ERA+	OAV	OOB	BH	AVG	PB	PR	/A	PD	TPI
1960	*NY-A	3	1	.750	11	8	2	1	0	60	50	3	18	36	10.4	2.25	159	.226	.287	1	.045	-2	11	9	1	0.8
1961	*NY-A	14	9	.609	36	25	8	3	2	195	168	13	59	101	10.7	2.68	139	.232	.294	12	.179	2	29	23	-1	2.4
1962	*NY-A	14	9	.609	35	33	7	2	0	213^1	188	23	77	109	11.3	3.67	102	.233	.303	17	.218	3	7	2	-1	0.3
1963	NY-A	4	8	.333	28	14	0	0	3	89^2	104	16	42	52	15.0	6.02	58	.287	.366	7	.292	3	-24	-25	-0	-2.3
1964	NY-A	5	0	1.000	31	1	0	0	4	60^2	50	4	22	39	11.0	2.67	136	.231	.308	1	.077	-1	6	6	0	0.6
1965	NY-A	3	8	.273	22	15	1	0	0	111^1	93	16	31	71	10.2	3.56	96	.229	.286	0	.000	-3	-1	-2	-0	-0.5
1966	KC-A	0	4	.000	9	8	0	0	0	39^2	42	2	12	31	12.7	4.99	68	.273	.333	0	.000	-1	-7	-7	-1	-0.9
1967	KC-A	0	1	.000	14	0	0	0	0	16	12	0	9	10	11.8	1.69	189	.214	.323	0	.000	-0	3	3	0	0.3
Total	8	43	40	.518	186	104	18	6	9	785^2	707	77	270	449	11.4	3.52	103	.240	.308	38	.155	0	24	9	-2	0.7

● **CHICK STAHL** Stahl, Charles Sylvester b: 1/10/1873, Avila, Ind. d: 3/28/07, W.Baden, Ind. BL/TL, 5'10", 160 lbs. Deb: 4/19/1897 M♦

YEAR	TM/L	W	L	PCT	G	GS	CG	SH	SV	IP	H	HR	BB	SO	RAT	ERA	ERA+	OAV	OOB	BH	AVG	PB	PR	/A	PD	TPI
1899	Bos-N	0	0	—	1	0	0	0	0	2	2	0	3	0	22.5	9.00	46	.260	.468	202	.351	0	-1	-1	0	-0.1

● **GERRY STALEY** Staley, Gerald Lee b: 8/21/20, Brush Prairie, Wash. BR/TR, 6', 195 lbs. Deb: 4/20/47

YEAR	TM/L	W	L	PCT	G	GS	CG	SH	SV	IP	H	HR	BB	SO	RAT	ERA	ERA+	OAV	OOB	BH	AVG	PB	PR	/A	PD	TPI
1947	StL-N	1	0	1.000	18	1	1	0	0	29^1	33	2	8	14	12.9	2.76	150	.287	.339	0	.000	-1	4	4	1	0.5
1948	StL-N	4	4	.500	31	3	0	0	0	52	61	5	21	23	14.2	6.92	59	.288	.352	2	.222	1	-17	-16	1	-1.4
1949	StL-N	10	10	.500	45	17	5	2	6	171^1	154	7	41	55	10.4	2.73	152	**.238**	.286	5	.122	-0	25	27	3	3.1
1950	StL-N	13	13	.500	42	22	7	1	3	169^2	201	14	61	62	14.3	4.99	86	.300	.365	8	.145	-1	-16	-13	3	-1.1
1951	StL-N	19	13	.594	42	30	10	4	3	227	244	14	74	67	12.9	3.81	104	.275	.337	13	.160	-1	4	4	2	0.5
1952	StL-N☆	17	14	.548	35	33	15	0	0	239^2	238	21	52	93	11.2	3.27	114	.256	.301	13	.153	-2	12	12	4	1.4
1953	StL-N☆	18	9	.667	40	32	10	1	4	230	243	31	54	88	12.3	3.99	107	.269	.322	8	.103	-4	8	7	2	0.4
1954	StL-N	7	13	.350	48	20	3	1	2	155^2	198	21	47	50	14.5	5.26	78	.308	.361	5	.139	-0	-21	-20	2	-1.7
1955	Cin-N	5	8	.385	30	18	2	0	0	119^2	146	22	28	40	13.3	4.66	91	.309	.351	2	.056	-4	-8	-6	1	-0.8
	NY-A	0	0	—	2	0	0	0	0	2	5	1	1	0	27.0	13.50	28	.417	.462	0	—	0	-2	-2	0	-0.2
1956	NY-A	0	0	—	1	0	0	0	0	0^1	4	0	0	1	108.0	108.00	4	.800	.800	0	.000	-0	-4	-4	0	-0.3
	Chi-A	8	3	.727	26	10	5	0	0	101^2	98	11	20	25	11.0	2.92	140	.251	.298	3	.094	-2	14	13	1	1.1
	Yr	8	3	.727	27	10	5	0	0	102	102	11	20	26	11.3	3.26	126	.258	.304	3	.091	-2	10	9	1	0.8
1957	Chi-A	5	1	.833	47	0	0	0	7	105	95	7	27	44	10.5	2.06	182	.244	.293	1	.045	-1	**20**	**20**	2	2.2
1958	Chi-A	4	5	.444	50	0	0	0	8	85^1	81	10	24	27	11.1	3.16	115	.259	.312	0	.000	-1	6	4	3	0.7
1959	*Chi-A	8	5	.615	**67**	0	0	0	14	116^1	111	5	25	54	10.5	2.24	167	.259	.300	2	.154	0	**21**	**20**	-0	2.0
1960	Chi-A★	13	8	.619	64	0	0	0	10	115^1	94	8	25	52	9.5	2.42	156	.227	.276	4	.235	1	**19**	**17**	3	2.2
1961	Chi-A	0	3	.000	16	0	0	0	0	18	17	3	5	8	11.0	5.00	78	.246	.297	0	—	0	-2	-2	0	-0.2
	KC-A	1	1	.500	23	0	0	0	2	30	32	4	10	16	13.2	3.60	114	.278	.346	0	.000	0	1	2	1	0.3
	Det-A	1	1	.500	13	0	0	0	2	13^1	15	1	6	8	14.2	3.38	121	.288	.362	0	.000	-0	1	1	0	0.1
	Yr	2	5	.286	52	0	0	0	4	61^1	64	8	21	32	12.5	3.96	102	.267	.326	0	.000	0	0	1	1	0.2
Total	15	134	111	.547	640	186	58	9	61	1981^2	2070	187	529	727	12.1	3.70	108	.270	.322	66	.126	-16	65	68	29	8.8

● **HARRY STALEY** Staley, Henry E. b: 11/3/1866, Jacksonville, Ill. d: 1/12/10, Battle Creek, Mich BR/TR, 5'10", 175 lbs. Deb: 6/23/1888

YEAR	TM/L	W	L	PCT	G	GS	CG	SH	SV	IP	H	HR	BB	SO	RAT	ERA	ERA+	OAV	OOB	BH	AVG	PB	PR	/A	PD	TPI
1888	Pit-N	12	12	.500	25	24	24	2	0	207^1	185	6	53	89	10.6	2.69	99	.235	.289	11	.129	-3	4	-1	-1	-0.4
1889	Pit-N	21	26	.447	49	47	46	1	1	420	433	11	116	159	11.9	3.51	107	.258	.309	30	.161	-6	23	11	2	0.7
1890	Pit-P	21	25	.457	46	46	44	3	0	387^2	392	5	74	145	**11.1**	3.23	121	.251	**.290**	34	.207	1	43	29	-2	2.3
1891	Pit-N	4	5	.444	9	7	6	0	0	71^2	77	4	11	25	11.3	2.89	114	.264	.296	7	.226	1	4	3	-0	0.4
	Bos-N	20	8	.714	31	30	26	1	0	252^1	236	11	69	114	11.0	2.50	146	.238	.291	17	.167	-2	24	33	-1	2.7
	Yr	24	13	.649	40	37	32	1	0	324	313	15	80	139	**11.0**	2.58	138	.244	**.290**	24	.180	-1	28	36	-1	3.1
1892	*Bos-N	22	10	.688	37	35	31	3	0	299^2	273	10	97	93	11.2	3.03	116	.233	.293	16	.131	-6	8	16	-2	0.7
1893	Bos-N	18	10	.643	36	31	23	0	0	263	344	22	81	61	14.7	5.13	96	.307	.356	30	.265	3	-14	-6	-1	-0.3
1894	Bos-N	12	10	.545	27	21	18	0	0	208^2	305	15	61	32	16.0	6.81	83	.337	.382	20	.235	0	-35	-26	-3	-2.2
1895	StL-N	6	13	.316	23	16	13	0	0	158^2	223	8	39	28	15.0	5.22	93	.326	.365	9	.134	-6	-8	-7	-2	-1.2
Total	8	136	119	.533	283	257	231	10	1	2269	2468	92	601	746	12.4	3.80	105	.269	.317	174	.182	-18	51	51	-9	2.7

● **TRACY STALLARD** Stallard, Evan Tracy b: 8/31/37, Coeburn, Va. BR/TR, 6'5", 205 lbs. Deb: 9/24/60

YEAR	TM/L	W	L	PCT	G	GS	CG	SH	SV	IP	H	HR	BB	SO	RAT	ERA	ERA+	OAV	OOB	BH	AVG	PB	PR	/A	PD	TPI
1960	Bos-A	0	0	—	4	0	0	0	0	4	0	0	2	6	4.5	0.00	—	.000	.133	0	—	0	2	2	0	0.2
1961	Bos-A	2	7	.222	43	14	1	0	2	132^2	110	15	96	109	14.0	4.88	85	.229	.359	3	.083	-3	-13	-11	-2	-1.4
1962	Bos-A	0	0	—	1	0	0	0	0	1	0	0	0	0	0.0	0.00	—	.000	.000	0	—	0	0	0	-0	0.0
1963	NY-N	6	17	.261	39	23	5	0	1	154^2	156	23	77	110	13.6	4.71	74	.262	.347	3	.063	-3	-24	-21	-1	-2.6
1964	NY-N	10	20	.333	36	34	11	2	0	225^2	213	20	73	118	11.6	3.79	94	.252	.316	15	.190	2	-6	-5	-2	-0.6
1965	StL-N	11	8	.579	40	26	4	1	0	194^1	172	25	70	99	11.5	3.38	114	.235	.307	6	.088	-4	3	10	-2	0.4
1966	StL-N	1	5	.167	20	7	0	0	1	52^1	65	9	25	35	15.8	5.68	63	.305	.383	0	.000	-2	-12	-12	0	-1.4
Total	7	30	57	.345	183	104	21	3	4	764^2	716	92	343	477	12.7	4.17	90	.248	.332	27	.110	-10	-50	-37	-7	-5.4

● **CHARLEY STANCEU** Stanceu, Charles b: 1/9/16, Canton, Ohio d: 4/3/69, Canton, Ohio BR/TR, 6'2", 190 lbs. Deb: 4/16/41

YEAR	TM/L	W	L	PCT	G	GS	CG	SH	SV	IP	H	HR	BB	SO	RAT	ERA	ERA+	OAV	OOB	BH	AVG	PB	PR	/A	PD	TPI
1941	NY-A	3	3	.500	22	2	0	0	0	48	58	3	35	21	17.6	5.63	70	.296	.405	0	.000	-2	-8	-9	-1	-1.1
1946	NY-A	0	0	—	3	0	0	0	0	4	6	0	5	3	24.8	9.00	38	.316	.458	0	—	0	-2	-2	0	-0.2
	Phi-N	2	4	.333	14	11	1	0	0	70^1	71	4	39	23	14.1	4.22	81	.270	.364	0	.000	-2	-6	-6	-1	-0.9
Total	2	5	7	.417	39	13	1	0	0	122^1	135	7	79	47	15.8	4.93	74	.282	.385	0	.000	-3	-17	-18	-2	-2.2

● **PETE STANDRIDGE** Standridge, Alfred Peter b: 4/25/1891, Black Diamond, Wash. d: 8/2/63, San Francisco, Cal. BR/TR, 5'10.5", 165 lbs. Deb: 9/19/11

YEAR	TM/L	W	L	PCT	G	GS	CG	SH	SV	IP	H	HR	BB	SO	RAT	ERA	ERA+	OAV	OOB	BH	AVG	PB	PR	/A	PD	TPI
1911	StL-N	0	0	—	2	0	0	0	0	4^2	10	0	4	3	28.9	9.64	35	.435	.536	0	.000	-0	-3	-3	0	-0.3
1915	Chi-N	4	1	.800	29	3	2	0	0	112^1	120	2	36	42	12.7	3.61	77	.274	.332	9	.225	3	-11	-10	0	-0.9
Total	2	4	1	.800	31	3	2	0	0	117	130	2	40	45	13.3	3.85	73	.282	.343	9	.220	3	-14	-14	0	-1.2

● **AL STANEK** Stanek, Albert Wilfred "Lefty" b: 12/24/43, Springfield, Mass. BL/TL, 5'11.5", 190 lbs. Deb: 4/26/63

YEAR	TM/L	W	L	PCT	G	GS	CG	SH	SV	IP	H	HR	BB	SO	RAT	ERA	ERA+	OAV	OOB	BH	AVG	PB	PR	/A	PD	TPI
1963	SF-N	0	0	—	11	0	0	0	0	13^1	10	1	12	5	14.9	4.73	68	.217	.379	0	.000	-0	-2	-2	1	-0.2

● **KEVIN STANFIELD** Stanfield, Kevin Bruce b: 12/19/55, Huron, S.Dak. BL/TL, 6', 190 lbs. Deb: 9/14/79

YEAR	TM/L	W	L	PCT	G	GS	CG	SH	SV	IP	H	HR	BB	SO	RAT	ERA	ERA+	OAV	OOB	BH	AVG	PB	PR	/A	PD	TPI
1979	Min-A	0	0	—	3	0	0	0	0	3	2	0	0	0	6.0	6.00	73	.200	.200	0	—	0	-1	-1	0	-0.1

● **LEE STANGE** Stange, Albert Lee b: 10/27/36, Chicago, Ill. BR/TR, 5'10", 170 lbs. Deb: 4/15/61 C

YEAR	TM/L	W	L	PCT	G	GS	CG	SH	SV	IP	H	HR	BB	SO	RAT	ERA	ERA+	OAV	OOB	BH	AVG	PB	PR	/A	PD	TPI
1961	Min-A	1	0	1.000	7	0	0	0	0	12^1	15	1	10	10	18.2	2.92	145	.294	.410	0	.000	-0	2	2	0	0.2
1962	Min-A	4	3	.571	44	6	1	0	3	95	98	14	39	70	13.1	4.45	92	.271	.343	1	.059	-1	-5	-4	-0	-0.5
1963	Min-A	12	5	.706	32	20	7	2	0	164^2	145	21	43	100	10.3	2.62	139	.233	.283	5	.096	-1	18	19	-0	1.8
1964	Min-A	3	6	.333	14	11	2	0	0	79^2	78	13	19	54	11.0	4.74	75	.255	.298	1	.040	-1	-10	-10	1	-1.1
	Cle-A	4	8	.333	23	14	0	0	0	91^2	98	14	31	78	12.8	4.12	87	.270	.329	2	.080	-1	-5	-5	-0	-0.7
	Yr	7	14	.333	37	25	2	0	0	171^1	176	27	50	132	11.9	4.41	81	.262	.314	3	.060	-2	-15	-16	0	-1.8
1965	Cle-A	8	4	.667	41	12	4	2	0	132	122	13	26	80	10.2	3.34	104	.247	.286	3	.107	1	2	2	-2	0.1

YEAR TM/L	W	L	PCT	G	GS	CG	SH	SV	IP	H	HR	BB	SO	RAT	ERA	ERA+	OAV	OOB	BH	AVG	PB	PR	/A	PD	TPI
1966 Cle-A	1	0	1.000	8	2	1	0	0	16	17	1	3	8	11.8	2.81	122	.279	.323	1	.250	0	1	1	-0	0.1
Bos-A	7	9	.438	28	19	8	2	0	153^1	140	17	43	77	10.8	3.35	114	.246	.300	3	.063	-4	2	8	-1	0.3
Yr	8	9	.471	36	21	9	2	0	169^1	157	18	46	85	10.8	3.30	114	.248	.300	4	.077	-3	3	9	-2	0.4
1967 *Bos-A	8	10	.444	35	24	6	2	1	181^2	171	14	32	101	10.2	2.77	126	.246	.282	3	.061	-3	9	14	-3	1.0
1968 Bos-A	5	5	.500	50	2	1	0	12	103	89	10	25	53	10.0	3.93	80	.237	.286	2	.133	0	-11	-9	-1	-1.1
1969 Bos-A	6	9	.400	41	15	2	0	3	137	137	14	56	59	13.1	3.68	103	.256	.333	3	.086	-2	-1	2	-2	-0.2
1970 Bos-A	2	2	.500	20	0	0	0	2	27^1	34	5	12	14	15.8	5.60	71	.301	.378	0	.000	-0	-6	-5	0	-0.5
Chi-A	1	0	1.000	16	0	0	0	0	22^1	28	5	5	14	13.3	5.24	74	.295	.330	0	.000	-0	-4	-3	-0	-0.4
Yr	3	2	.600	36	0	0	0	2	49^2	62	10	17	28	14.3	5.44	72	.291	.343	0	.000	-0	-10	-8	-0	-0.9
Total 10	62	61	.504	359	125	32	8	21	1216	1172	142	344	718	11.3	3.56	102	.252	.306	24	.079	-12	-8	12	-9	-1.0

● DON STANHOUSE Stanhouse, Donald Joseph b: 2/12/51, DuQuoin, Ill. BR/TR, 6'2", 195 lbs. Deb: 4/19/72

YEAR TM/L	W	L	PCT	G	GS	CG	SH	SV	IP	H	HR	BB	SO	RAT	ERA	ERA+	OAV	OOB	BH	AVG	PB	PR	/A	PD	TPI
1972 Tex-A	2	9	.182	24	16	1	0	0	104^2	83	8	73	78	13.5	3.78	80	.223	.351	4	.129	-0	-8	-9	2	-0.8
1973 Tex-A	1	7	.125	21	5	1	0	1	70	70	5	44	42	14.9	4.76	78	.262	.371	0	—	0	-7	-8	2	-0.6
1974 Tex-A	1	1	.500	18	0	0	0	0	31^1	38	4	17	26	16.4	4.88	73	.302	.393	0	—	0	-4	-5	1	-0.2
1975 Mon-N	0	0	—	4	3	0	0	0	13	19	1	11	5	20.8	8.31	46	.345	.455	1	.333	0	-7	-6	-0	-0.6
1976 Mon-N	9	12	.429	34	26	8	1	1	184	182	7	92	79	13.6	3.77	99	.263	.352	11	.212	2	-5	-1	3	0.4
1977 Mon-N	10	10	.500	47	16	1	1	10	158^1	147	12	84	89	13.4	3.41	112	.251	.349	9	.191	1	9	7	-1	0.7
1978 Bal-A	6	9	.400	56	0	0	0	24	74^2	60	0	52	42	13.5	2.89	121	.230	.358	0	—	0	7	5	0	0.6
1979 *Bal-A☆	7	3	.700	52	0	0	0	21	72^2	49	4	51	34	12.5	2.85	141	.202	.342	0	—	0	11	9	1	1.0
1980 LA-N	2	2	.500	21	0	0	0	7	25	30	4	16	5	16.6	5.04	69	.306	.404	0	.000	0	-4	-4	1	-0.4
1982 Bal-A	0	1	.000	17	0	0	0	0	26^2	29	3	15	8	15.5	5.40	75	.276	.377	0	—	0	-4	-4	0	-0.4
Total 10	38	54	.413	294	66	11	2	64	760^1	707	48	455	408	13.9	3.84	95	.252	.359	25	.185	4	-13	-16	8	-0.3

● JOE STANKA Stanka, Joe Donald b: 7/23/31, Hammon, Okla. BR/TR, 6'5", 201 lbs. Deb: 9/02/59

YEAR TM/L	W	L	PCT	G	GS	CG	SH	SV	IP	H	HR	BB	SO	RAT	ERA	ERA+	OAV	OOB	BH	AVG	PB	PR	/A	PD	TPI
1959 Chi-A	1	0	1.000	2	0	0	0	0	5^1	2	1	4	3	10.1	3.38	111	.111	.273	1	.333	0	0	0	-0	0.0

● BUCK STANLEY Stanley, John Leonard b: 11/13/1889, Washington, D.C. d: 8/13/40, Norfolk, Va. BL/TL, 5'10", 160 lbs. Deb: 9/12/11 F

YEAR TM/L	W	L	PCT	G	GS	CG	SH	SV	IP	H	HR	BB	SO	RAT	ERA	ERA+	OAV	OOB	BH	AVG	PB	PR	/A	PD	TPI
1911 Phi-N	0	0	—	4	0	0	0	0	11^1	14	0	9	5	18.3	6.35	54	.326	.442	0	.000	-1	-4	-4	-1	-0.5

● JOE STANLEY Stanley, Joseph Bernard b: 4/2/1881, Washington, D.C. d: 9/13/67, Detroit, Mich. BB/TR, 5'9.5", 150 lbs. Deb: 9/11/1897 F♦

YEAR TM/L	W	L	PCT	G	GS	CG	SH	SV	IP	H	HR	BB	SO	RAT	ERA	ERA+	OAV	OOB	BH	AVG	PB	PR	/A	PD	TPI
1897 Was-N	0	0	—	1	0	0	0	0	0^2	0	0	0	0	0.0	0.00	—	.000	.000	0	.000	-0	0	0	-0	0.0
1903 Bos-N	0	0	—	1	0	0	0	0	4	4	0	4	4	20.3	9.00	36	.286	.474	77	.250	0	-3	-3	-0	-0.2
1906 Was-A	0	0	—	1	0	0	0	0	3	3	1	1	0	15.0	12.00	22	.263	.373	36	.163	-0	-3	-3	-0	-0.3
Total 3	0	0	—	3	0	0	0	0	7^2	7	1	5	4	16.4	9.39	33	.256	.408	148	.213	-0	-5	-5	-1	-0.5

● BOB STANLEY Stanley, Robert William b: 11/10/54, Portland, Maine BR/TR, 6'4", 215 lbs. Deb: 4/16/77

YEAR TM/L	W	L	PCT	G	GS	CG	SH	SV	IP	H	HR	BB	SO	RAT	ERA	ERA+	OAV	OOB	BH	AVG	PB	PR	/A	PD	TPI
1977 Bos-A	8	7	.533	41	13	3	1	3	151	176	10	43	44	13.2	3.99	112	.294	.344	0	—	0	1	8	4	0.8
1978 Bos-A	15	2	.882	52	3	0	0	10	141^2	142	5	34	38	11.2	2.60	158	.266	.312	0	—	0	18	24	2	2.6
1979 Bos-A★	16	12	.571	40	30	9	4	1	216^2	250	14	44	56	12.4	3.99	111	.294	.332	0	—	0	5	10	2	1.1
1980 Bos-A	10	8	.556	52	17	5	1	14	175	186	11	52	71	12.6	3.39	124	.278	.337	0	—	0	12	16	3	1.9
1981 Bos-A	10	8	.556	35	1	0	0	0	98^2	110	3	38	28	14.0	3.83	101	.294	.368	0	—	0	-2	0	3	0.2
1982 Bos-A	12	7	.632	48	0	0	0	14	168^1	161	11	50	83	11.5	3.10	**139**	.255	.313	0	—	0	18	23	4	2.6
1983 Bos-A★	8	10	.444	64	0	0	0	33	145^1	145	7	38	65	11.5	2.85	153	.266	.317	0	—	0	20	24	-1	2.3
1984 Bos-A	9	10	.474	57	0	0	0	22	106^2	113	9	23	52	11.6	3.54	117	.267	.308	0	—	0	5	7	3	0.9
1985 Bos-A	6	6	.500	48	0	0	0	10	87^2	76	7	30	46	11.1	2.87	149	.237	.306	0	—	0	12	14	0	1.4
1986 *Bos-A	6	6	.500	66	1	0	0	16	82^1	109	9	22	54	14.3	4.37	95	.322	.364	0	—	0	-2	-2	1	-0.1
1987 Bos-A	4	15	.211	34	20	4	1	0	152^2	198	17	42	67	14.2	5.01	91	.321	.366	0	—	0	-9	-8	1	-0.8
1988 *Bos-A	6	4	.600	57	0	0	0	5	101^2	90	6	29	57	11.2	3.19	129	.242	.309	0	—	0	9	10	-0	0.9
1989 Bos-A	5	2	.714	43	0	0	0	4	79^1	102	4	26	32	14.6	4.88	84	.321	.374	0	—	0	-9	-7	1	-0.7
Total 13	115	97	.542	637	85	21	7	132	1707	1858	113	471	693	12.5	3.64	117	.282	.334	0	—	0	80	121	22	13.1

● MIKE STANTON Stanton, Michael Thomas b: 9/25/52, Phenix City, Ala. BB/TR, 6'2", 205 lbs. Deb: 7/09/75

YEAR TM/L	W	L	PCT	G	GS	CG	SH	SV	IP	H	HR	BB	SO	RAT	ERA	ERA+	OAV	OOB	BH	AVG	PB	PR	/A	PD	TPI
1975 Hou-N	0	2	.000	7	2	0	0	1	17^1	20	1	20	16	20.8	7.27	46	.290	.449	1	.250	0	-7	-8	0	-0.7
1980 Cle-A	1	3	.250	51	0	0	0	5	85^2	98	5	44	74	15.2	5.46	75	.297	.385	0	—	0	-14	-13	1	-1.2
1981 Cle-A	3	3	.500	24	0	0	0	2	43^1	43	4	18	34	12.7	4.36	83	.262	.335	0	—	0	-3	-4	-1	-0.4
1982 Sea-A	2	4	.333	56	1	0	0	7	71^1	70	5	21	49	11.5	4.16	102	.260	.314	0	—	0	-1	1	1	0.1
1983 Sea-A	2	3	.400	50	0	0	0	7	65	65	3	28	47	13.0	3.32	128	.273	.352	0	—	0	5	7	-0	0.6
1984 Sea-A	4	4	.500	54	0	0	0	8	61	55	3	22	55	11.7	3.54	113	.241	.313	0	—	0	3	3	-1	0.3
1985 Sea-A	1	2	.333	24	0	0	0	1	29	32	4	21	17	17.4	5.28	80	.278	.403	0	—	0	-4	-3	1	-0.3
Chi-A	0	1	.000	11	0	0	0	0	11^2	15	2	8	12	17.7	9.26	47	.294	.390	0	—	0	-7	-6	-0	-0.6
Yr	1	3	.250	35	0	0	0	1	40^2	47	6	29	29	16.8	6.42	66	.278	.384	0	—	0	-10	-10	1	-0.9
Total 7	13	22	.371	277	3	0	0	31	384^1	398	27	182	304	13.8	4.61	88	.272	.356	1	.250	0	-27	-24	1	-2.2

● MIKE STANTON Stanton, William Michael b: 6/2/67, Houston, Tex. BL/TL, 6'1", 190 lbs. Deb: 8/24/89

YEAR TM/L	W	L	PCT	G	GS	CG	SH	SV	IP	H	HR	BB	SO	RAT	ERA	ERA+	OAV	OOB	BH	AVG	PB	PR	/A	PD	TPI
1989 Atl-N	0	1	.000	20	0	0	0	7	24	17	0	8	27	9.4	1.50	243	.207	.278	0	—	0	5	6	-0	0.6
1990 Atl-N	0	3	.000	7	0	0	0	2	7	16	1	4	7	27.0	18.00	22	.444	.512	0	—	0	-11	-11	0	-1.0
1991 *Atl-N	5	5	.500	74	0	0	0	7	78	62	6	21	54	9.7	2.88	135	.217	.273	3	.500	2	7	9	1	1.2
1992 *Atl-N	5	4	.556	65	0	0	0	8	63^2	59	6	20	44	11.5	4.10	91	.247	.310	1	.500	0	-4	-3	0	-0.2
Total 4	10	13	.435	166	0	0	0	24	172^2	154	13	53	132	11.0	3.75	101	.240	.301	4	.500	2	-3	1	1	0.6

● DAVE STAPLETON Stapleton, David Earl b: 10/16/61, Miami, Arizona BL/TL, 6'1", 185 lbs. Deb: 9/14/87

YEAR TM/L	W	L	PCT	G	GS	CG	SH	SV	IP	H	HR	BB	SO	RAT	ERA	ERA+	OAV	OOB	BH	AVG	PB	PR	/A	PD	TPI
1987 Mil-A	2	0	1.000	4	0	0	0	0	14^2	13	0	3	14	9.8	1.84	248	.241	.281	0	—	0	4	4	-0	0.4
1988 Mil-A	0	0	—	6	0	0	0	0	13^2	20	1	9	6	19.8	5.93	67	.339	.435	0	—	0	-3	-3	-0	-0.3
Total 2	2	0	1.000	10	0	0	0	0	28^1	33	1	12	20	14.6	3.81	112	.292	.365	0	—	0	1	1	-0	0.1

● CON STARKEL Starkel, Conrad b: 11/16/1880, Germany d: 1/19/33, Tacoma, Wash. BR/TR, 6', 200 lbs. Deb: 4/19/06

YEAR TM/L	W	L	PCT	G	GS	CG	SH	SV	IP	H	HR	BB	SO	RAT	ERA	ERA+	OAV	OOB	BH	AVG	PB	PR	/A	PD	TPI
1906 Was-A	0	0	—	1	0	0	0	0	3	7	1	2	1	27.0	18.00	15	.455	.518	0	—	0	-5	-5	0	-0.4

● RAY STARR Starr, Raymond Francis "Iron Man" b: 4/23/06, Nowata, Okla. d: 2/9/63, Baylis, Ill. BR/TR, 6'1", 178 lbs. Deb: 9/11/32

YEAR TM/L	W	L	PCT	G	GS	CG	SH	SV	IP	H	HR	BB	SO	RAT	ERA	ERA+	OAV	OOB	BH	AVG	PB	PR	/A	PD	TPI
1932 StL-N	1	1	.500	3	2	1	1	0	20	19	2	10	6	13.5	2.70	146	.284	.385	1	.250	0	3	3	1	0.3
1933 NY-N	0	1	.000	6	2	0	0	0	13^1	19	0	10	2	20.3	5.40	59	.339	.448	0	.000	-0	-3	-3	-0	-0.4
Bos-N	0	1	.000	9	1	0	0	0	28	32	4	9	15	13.5	3.86	79	.296	.356	1	.143	0	-2	-2	0	-0.2
Yr	0	2	.000	15	3	0	0	0	41^1	51	4	19	17	15.5	4.35	71	.309	.384	1	.100	-0	-5	-6	0	-0.6
1941 Cin-N	3	2	.600	7	4	3	2	0	34	28	1	6	11	9.3	2.65	136	.219	.259	2	.182	-0	4	4	0	0.4
1942 Cin-N☆	15	13	.536	37	33	17	4	0	276^2	228	10	106	83	11.0	2.67	123	.226	.301	8	.091	-4	20	19	-2	1.4
1943 Cin-N	11	10	.524	36	33	9	2	1	217^1	201	9	91	42	12.3	3.64	91	.248	.328	9	.122	-4	-6	-8	-0	-1.3
1944 Pit-N	6	5	.545	27	12	5	0	3	89^2	116	6	36	25	15.4	5.02	74	.314	.377	3	.136	1	-14	-13	-1	-1.3
1945 Pit-N	0	2	.000	4	0	0	0	0	6^2	10	0	4	0	18.9	9.45	42	.370	.452	1	1.000	1	-4	-4	0	-0.3
Chi-N	1	0	1.000	9	1	0	0	0	13^1	17	1	7	5	16.2	7.43	49	.298	.375	1	.500	0	-5	-6	0	-0.5
Yr	1	2	.333	13	1	0	0	0	20	27	1	11	5	17.1	8.10	46	.321	.400	2	.667	1	-10	-10	0	-0.8
Total 7	37	35	.514	138	88	35	9	4	699	670	33	279	189	12.4	3.53	96	.255	.329	26	.123	-7	-8	-11	-1	-1.9

● DICK STARR Starr, Richard Eugene b: 3/2/21, Kittanning, Pa. BR/TR, 6'3", 190 lbs. Deb: 9/05/47

YEAR TM/L	W	L	PCT	G	GS	CG	SH	SV	IP	H	HR	BB	SO	RAT	ERA	ERA+	OAV	OOB	BH	AVG	PB	PR	/A	PD	TPI
1947 NY-A	1	0	1.000	4	1	1	0	0	12^1	12	1	8	1	14.6	1.46	242	.250	.357	1	.333	1	3	3	0	0.4

YEAR	TM/L	W	L	PCT	G	GS	CG	SH	SV	IP	H	HR	BB	SO	RAT	ERA	ERA+	OAV	OOB	BH	AVG	PB	PR	/A	PD	TPI
1948	NY-A	0	0	—	1	0	0	0	0	2	0	0	2	2	9.0	4.50	91	.000	.250	0	—	0	-0	-0	-0	0.0
1949	StL-A	1	7	.125	30	8	1	1	0	83^1	96	6	48	44	15.7	4.32	105	.292	.384	2	.087	-1	-1	2	-1	0.0
1950	StL-A	7	5	.583	32	16	4	1	2	123^2	140	11	74	30	16.1	5.02	99	.287	.389	5	.139	-3	-6	-1	-1	-0.4
1951	StL-A	2	5	.286	15	9	0	0	0	62	66	10	42	26	16.0	7.40	59	.273	.385	4	.222	0	-23	-21	-1	-1.9
	Was-A	1	7	.125	11	11	1	0	0	61^1	76	12	24	17	14.7	5.58	73	.304	.365	3	.176	1	-10	-10	-2	-1.1
	Yr	3	12	.200	26	20	1	0	0	123^1	142	22	66	43	15.2	6.49	65	.287	.371	7	.200	1	-33	-31	-2	-3.0
Total	5	12	24	.333	93	45	7	2	2	344^2	390	40	198	120	15.6	5.25	86	.286	.381	15	.155	-3	-37	-27	-4	-3.0
● **HERMAN STARRETTE** Starrette, Herman Paul b: 11/20/38, Statesville, N.C. BR/TR, 6', 175 lbs. Deb: 7/01/63 C																										
1963	Bal-A	0	1	.000	18	0	0	0	0	26	26	1	7	13	12.1	3.46	102	.271	.333	0	.000	0	0	0	1	0.1
1964	Bal-A	1	0	1.000	5	0	0	0	0	11	9	0	6	5	12.3	1.64	218	.250	.357	0	.000	-0	2	2	-0	0.2
1965	Bal-A	0	0	—	4	0	0	0	0	9	8	0	3	3	11.0	1.00	347	.258	.324	0	.000	-0	2	2	0	0.3
Total	3	1	1	.500	27	0	0	0	0	46	43	1	16	21	11.9	2.54	139	.264	.337	0	.000	-0	5	5	1	0.6
● **ED STAUFFER** Stauffer, Charles Edward b: 1/10/1898, Emsworth, Pa. d: 7/2/79, St.Petersburg, Fla BR/TR, 5'11", 185 lbs. Deb: 4/26/23																										
1923	Chi-N	0	0	—	1	0	0	0	0	2	5	0	1	0	27.0	13.50	30	.556	.600	0	—	0	-2	-2	0	-0.2
1925	StL-A	0	1	.000	20	1	0	0	0	30^1	34	1	21	13	16.3	5.34	87	.283	.390	1	.250	-0	-3	-2	-1	-0.3
Total	2	0	1	.000	21	1	0	0	0	32^1	39	1	22	13	17.0	5.85	79	.302	.404	1	.250	-0	-5	-4	-1	-0.5
● **BILL STEARNS** Stearns, William E. b: 3/20/1853, Washington, D.C. d: 12/30/1898, Washington, D.C. TR , Deb: 6/26/1871																										
1871	Oly-n	2	0	1.000	2	2	2	0	0	18	10	0	8	0	9.0	2.50	167	.149	.240	0	.000	-1	3	3		0.1
1872	Nat-n	0	11	.000	11	11	11	0	0	99	194	2	3	2	17.9	6.91	68	.339	.343	11	.234	-4	-35	-24		-1.8
1873	Was-n	7	25	.219	32	32	32	0	0	283	481	8	15	4	15.8	4.55	74	.330	.337	24	.180	-6	-41	-38		-2.9
1874	Har-n	2	14	.125	22	18	14	0	1	164	255	1	13		14.7	*4.50*	70	.311	.322	21	.159	-5	-27	-24		-2.1
1875	Was-n	1	14	.067	17	16	14	0	0	141	243	1	4		15.8	*5.36*	49	.332	.335	20	.260	0	-45	-43		-3.3
Total	5 n	12	64	.158	84	79	73	0	1	705	1183	12	43	6	15.7	*4.98*	53	.324	.332	76	.191	-17	-197	-185		-10.0
● **CHARLIE STECHER** Stecher, Charles b: Bordentown, N.J. Deb: 9/06/1890																										
1890	Phi-a	0	10	.000	10	10	9	0	0	68	111	1	60	18	24.5	10.32	37	.355	.479	7	.241	1	-49	-49	2	-3.5
● **ELMER STEELE** Steele, Elmer Rae b: 5/17/1886, Muitzeskill, N.Y. d: 3/9/66, Rhinebeck, N.Y. BB/TR, 5'11", 200 lbs. Deb: 9/12/07																										
1907	Bos-A	0	1	.000	4	1	0	0	0	11^1	11	0	1	10	9.5	1.59	163	.256	.273	0	.000	-1	1	1	0	0.1
1908	Bos-A	5	7	.417	16	13	9	1	0	118	85	1	13	37	7.7	1.83	135	.209	.239	2	.051	-4	7	8	-1	0.4
1909	Bos-A	4	4	.500	16	8	2	0	1	75^2	75	1	15	32	10.8	2.85	88	.255	.294	6	.250	1	-3	-3	0	-0.2
1910	Pit-N	0	3	.000	3	3	2	0	0	24	19	0	3	7	8.3	2.25	138	.221	.247	0	.000	-1	2	2	1	0.3
1911	Pit-N	9	9	.500	31	16	7	2	2	166	153	5	31	52	10.2	2.60	132	.256	.297	11	.180	-0	15	15	2	1.7
	Bro-N	0	0	—	5	2	0	0	0	23	24	0	5	9	11.3	3.13	107	.258	.296	0	.000	-1	1	1	0	0.0
	Yr	9	9	.500	36	18	7	2	2	189	177	5	36	61	10.1	2.67	128	.255	.292	11	.157	-1	15	16	2	1.7
Total	5	18	24	.429	75	43	20	3	3	418	367	7	68	147	9.5	2.41	122	.241	.278	19	.132	-5	23	25	3	2.3
● **BOB STEELE** Steele, Robert Wesley b: 1/5/1894, Cassburn, Ont., Can. d: 1/27/62, Ocala, Fla. BB/TL, 5'10.5", 175 lbs. Deb: 4/17/16																										
1916	StL-N	5	15	.250	29	22	7	1	0	148	156	6	42	67	12.2	3.41	78	.285	.340	10	.196	-1	-13	-13	-3	-1.8
1917	StL-N	1	3	.250	12	6	1	0	0	42	33	1	19	23	11.1	3.21	84	.223	.311	5	.385	2	-2	-2	-1	-0.2
	Pit-N	5	11	.313	27	19	13	1	1	179^2	158	0	53	82	10.8	2.76	103	.237	.298	17	.224	1	-1	2	-2	0.0
	Yr	6	14	.300	39	25	14	1	1	221^2	191	1	72	105	10.9	2.84	99	.235	.301	22	.247	2	-3	-1	-2	-0.2
1918	Pit-N	2	3	.400	10	4	2	1	1	49	44	2	17	21	11.6	3.31	87	.240	.312	2	.125	-0	-3	-2	-0	-0.3
	NY-N	3	5	.375	12	7	5	1	1	66	56	1	11	24	9.5	2.59	101	.226	.267	6	.286	2	1	0	-2	0.0
	Yr	5	8	.385	22	11	7	2	2	115	100	3	28	45	10.3	2.90	94	.231	.282	8	.216	2	-2	-2	-3	-0.3
1919	NY-N	0	1	.000	1	0	0	0	0	3	3	0	2	0	15.0	6.00	47	.250	.357	0	.000	-0	-1	-1	-0	-0.1
Total	4	16	38	.296	91	58	28	4	3	487^2	450	10	144	217	11.2	3.05	90	.249	.310	40	.225	3	-19	-16	-8	-2.4
● **BILL STEELE** Steele, William Mitchell "Big Bill" b: 10/5/1885, Milford, Pa. d: 10/19/49, Overland, Mo. BR/TR, 5'11", 200 lbs. Deb: 9/10/10																										
1910	StL-N	4	4	.500	9	8	8	0	1	71^2	71	1	24	25	12.7	3.27	91	.264	.338	8	.258	1	-2	-2	1	0.0
1911	StL-N	18	19	.486	43	34	23	1	3	287^1	287	8	113	115	12.8	3.73	91	.269	.345	21	.208	4	-10	-11	3	-0.4
1912	StL-N	9	13	.409	40	25	7	0	2	194	245	5	66	67	14.8	4.69	73	.322	.381	11	.180	1	-27	-27	4	-2.1
1913	StL-N	4	4	.500	12	9	2	0	0	54	58	3	18	10	13.2	5.00	65	.286	.353	1	.056	-1	-11	-11	-1	-1.2
1914	StL-N	1	2	.333	17	2	0	0	0	53^1	55	3	7	16	11.0	2.70	104	.274	.308	5	.294	2	1	1	1	0.3
	Bro-N	1	1	.500	8	1	0	0	1	16^1	17	1	7	3	13.2	5.51	52	.258	.329	1	.333	1	-5	-5	-0	-0.4
	Yr	2	3	.400	25	3	0	0	1	69^2	72	4	14	19	11.1	3.36	84	.267	.303	6	.300	3	-4	-4	1	-0.1
Total	5	37	43	.463	129	79	40	1	7	676^2	733	21	235	236	13.3	4.02	82	.286	.352	47	.203	8	-55	-55	8	-3.8
● **BILL STEEN** Steen, William John b: 11/11/1887, Pittsburgh, Pa. d: 3/13/79, Signal Hill, Cal. BR/TR, 6'0.5", 180 lbs. Deb: 4/15/12																										
1912	Cle-A	9	8	.529	26	16	6	1	0	143^1	163	3	45	61	13.1	3.77	90	.298	.352	13	.271	2	-7	-6	-1	-0.5
1913	Cle-A	4	5	.444	22	13	7	2	2	128^1	113	3	49	57	11.6	2.45	124	.237	.313	7	.171	-0	7	8	-0	0.8
1914	Cle-A	9	14	.391	30	22	13	1	0	200^2	201	0	68	97	12.2	2.60	111	.272	.337	14	.200	1	3	6	0	0.7
1915	Cle-A	1	4	.200	10	7	2	0	0	45^1	51	1	15	22	13.5	4.96	61	.290	.352	3	.188	-0	-10	-10	2	-0.8
	Det-A	5	1	.833	20	7	3	0	4	79^1	83	0	22	28	12.0	2.72	111	.269	.319	5	.179	-1	2	3	2	0.3
	Yr	6	5	.545	30	14	5	0	4	124^2	134	1	37	50	12.4	3.54	86	.275	.328	8	.182	-1	-8	-7	4	-0.5
Total	4	28	32	.467	108	65	31	4	6	597	611	7	199	265	12.4	3.05	101	.272	.334	42	.207	1	-6	2	2	0.5
● **MILT STEENGRAFE** Steengrafe, Milton Henry b: 5/26/1900, San Francisco, Cal d: 6/2/77, BR/TR, 6', 170 lbs. Deb: 5/05/24																										
1924	Chi-A	0	0	—	3	0	0	0	0	5^2	15	0	4	3	30.2	12.71	32	.484	.543	0	.000	-0	-5	-5	0	-0.5
1926	Chi-A	1	1	.500	13	1	0	0	0	38^1	43	1	19	10	15.0	3.99	97	.295	.383	0	.000	-2	0	-1	-1	-0.3
Total	2	1	1	.500	16	1	0	0	0	44	58	1	23	13	17.0	5.11	76	.328	.411	0	.000	-2	-5	-6	-1	-0.8
● **MORRIE STEEVENS** Steevens, Morris Dale b: 10/7/40, Salem, Ill. BL/TL, 6'2", 175 lbs. Deb: 4/13/62																										
1962	Chi-N	0	1	.000	12	1	0	0	0	15	10	0	11	5	13.2	2.40	173	.196	.349	0	.000	-0	3	3	0	0.3
1964	Phi-N	0	0	—	4	0	0	0	0	2^2	5	0	1	3	20.3	3.38	103	.385	.429	0	—	0	0	0	0	0.0
1965	Phi-N	0	1	.000	6	0	0	0	0	2^2	5	1	4	3	30.4	16.88	20	.417	.563	0	—	0	-4	-4	-0	-0.4
Total	3	0	2	.000	22	1	0	0	0	20^1	20	1	16	11	16.4	4.43	90	.263	.398	0	.000	-0	-1	-1	0	-0.1
● **ED STEIN** Stein, Edward F. b: 9/5/1869, Detroit, Mich. d: 5/10/28, Detroit, Mich. BR/TR, 5'11", 170 lbs. Deb: 7/24/1890																										
1890	Chi-N	12	6	.667	20	18	14	1	0	160^2	147	9	83	65	13.5	3.81	96	.236	.336	9	.153	-2	-4	-3	-1	-0.5
1891	Chi-N	7	6	.538	14	10	9	1	0	101	99	7	57	38	14.1	3.74	89	.247	.343	7	.163	-1	-4	-5	2	-0.4
1892	Bro-N	27	16	.628	48	42	38	6	1	377^1	310	6	150	190	11.3	2.84	111	.215	.296	31	.215	4	19	14	2	1.8
1893	Bro-N	19	15	.559	37	34	28	1	0	298^1	294	4	119	81	12.7	3.77	117	.250	.323	25	.212	-3	30	22	2	1.7
1894	Bro-N	26	14	.650	44	40	37	2	1	350	388	10	170	84	14.7	4.63	107	.278	.362	38	.259	4	27	12	-0	1.3
1895	Bro-N	15	13	.536	32	27	24	1	1	255^1	282	9	93	55	13.4	4.72	93	.276	.340	26	.250	1	2	-9	1	-0.5
1896	Bro-N	3	6	.333	17	10	6	0	0	90^1	130	6	51	16	18.2	4.88	84	.334	.414	10	.256	0	-5	-8	0	-0.6
1898	Bro-N	0	2	.000	3	2	2	0	0	23	39	0	9	6	18.8	5.48	65	.372	.421	4	.400	1	-5	-5	-0	-0.4
Total	8	109	78	.583	215	183	158	12	3	1656	1689	51	732	535	13.5	3.97	103	.258	.338	150	.226	4	59	22	5	2.4
● **IRV STEIN** Stein, Irvin Michael b: 5/21/11, Madisonville, La. d: 1/7/81, Covington, La. BR/TR, 6'2", 170 lbs. Deb: 7/07/32																										
1932	Phi-A	0	0	—	1	0	0	0	0	3	7	2	1	0	24.0	12.00	38	.500	.533	0	.000	-0	-3	-2	0	-0.2

YEAR	TM/L	W	L	PCT	G	GS	CG	SH	SV	IP	H	HR	BB	SO	RAT	ERA	ERA+	OAV	OOB	BH	AVG	PB	PR	/A	PD	TPI
● **RANDY STEIN** Stein, William Randolph b: 3/7/53, Pomona, Cal. BR/TR, 6'4", 210 lbs. Deb: 4/17/78																										
1978	Mil-A	3	2	.600	31	1	0	0	1	72^2	78	5	39	42	15.0	5.33	71	.280	.376	0	—	0	-13	-13	0	-1.3
1979	Sea-A	2	3	.400	23	1	0	0	0	41^1	48	7	27	39	16.5	5.88	74	.291	.394	0	—	0	-8	-7	-1	-0.8
1981	Sea-A	0	1	.000	5	0	0	0	0	9^1	18	1	8	6	25.1	10.61	36	.429	.520	0	—	0	-7	-7	0	-0.7
1982	Chi-N	0	0	—	6	0	0	0	0	10^1	7	2	7	6	12.2	3.48	107	.200	.333	0	—	0	0	0	-0	0.0
Total	4	5	6	.455	65	2	0	0	1	133^2	151	15	81	93	16.0	5.72	69	.290	.390	0	—	0	-27	-26	-1	-2.8
● **RAY STEINEDER** Steineder, Raymond J. b: 11/13/1895, Salem, N.J. d: 8/25/82, Vineland, N.J. BR/TR, 6'0.5", 160 lbs. Deb: 7/16/23																										
1923	Pit-N	2	0	1.000	15	2	1	0	0	55	58	3	18	23	12.8	4.75	85	.278	.341	7	.467	3	-5	-4	-1	-0.3
1924	Pit-N	0	1	.000	5	0	0	0	0	2^2	6	0	5	0	37.1	13.50	28	.400	.550	0	—	0	-3	-3	0	-0.3
	Phi-N	1	1	.500	9	0	0	0	0	28^2	29	1	16	11	14.1	4.40	101	.266	.360	3	.300	0	-2	0	0	0.1
	Yr	1	2	.333	14	0	0	0	0	31^1	35	1	21	11	16.1	5.17	85	.282	.386	3	.300	0	-5	-3	0	-0.2
Total	2	3	2	.600	29	2	1	0	0	86^1	93	4	39	34	14.0	4.90	85	.279	.358	10	.400	3	-9	-7	-1	-0.5
● **RICK STEIRER** Steirer, Ricky Francis b: 8/27/56, Baltimore, Md. BR/TR, 6'4", 200 lbs. Deb: 8/05/82																										
1982	Cal-A	1	0	1.000	10	1	0	0	0	26^1	25	2	11	14	12.6	3.76	108	.243	.322	0	—	0	1	1	0	0.1
1983	Cal-A	3	2	.600	19	5	0	0	0	61^2	77	3	18	25	14.3	4.82	83	.302	.355	0	—	0	-5	-6	1	-0.5
1984	Cal-A	0	1	.000	1	1	0	0	0	2^2	6	0	2	2	27.0	16.88	24	.500	.571	0	—	0	-4	-4	0	-0.3
Total	3	4	3	.571	30	7	0	0	0	90^2	108	5	31	41	14.2	4.86	83	.292	.353	0	—	0	-8	-8	1	-0.7
● **BILL STELLBERGER** Stellberger, William F. b: 4/22/1865, Detroit, Mich. d: 11/9/36, Detroit, Mich. BL/TL, Deb: 10/01/1885																										
1885	Pro-N	0	1	.000	1	1	1	0	0	8	14	0	4	0	20.3	7.88	34	.389	.450	0	.000	-1	-4	-5	0	-0.4
● **JEFF STEMBER** Stember, Jeffrey Alan b: 3/2/58, Elizabeth, N.J. BR/TR, 6'5", 220 lbs. Deb: 8/05/80																										
1980	SF-N	0	0	—	1	1	0	0	0	3	2	1	2	0	12.0	3.00	118	.167	.286	0	.000	-0	0	0	-0	0.0
● **BILL STEMMEYER** Stemmeyer, William "Cannon Ball" b: 5/6/1865, Cleveland, Ohio d: 5/3/45, Cleveland, Ohio BR/TR, 6'2", 190 lbs. Deb: 10/03/1885																										
1885	Bos-N	1	1	.500	2	2	2	1	0	11	7	0	11	8	14.7	0.00	—	.194	.383	3	.429	1	3	3	0	0.5
1886	Bos-N	22	18	.550	41	41	41	0	0	348^2	300	11	144	239	11.5	3.02	106	.218	.292	41	.277	9	11	7	-3	1.1
1887	Bos-N	6	8	.429	15	14	14	0	1	119^1	138	4	41	41	13.7	5.20	78	.274	.331	12	.255	2	-15	-15	-2	-1.2
1888	Cle-a	0	2	.000	2	2	2	0	0	16	37	0	9	7	26.4	9.00	34	.437	.496	4	.400	1	-11	-11	-0	-0.7
Total	4	29	29	.500	60	59	59	1	1	495	482	15	205	295	12.5	3.67	92	.241	.312	60	.283	13	-11	-16	-4	-0.3
● **DAVE STENHOUSE** Stenhouse, David Rotchford b: 9/12/33, Westerly, R.I. BR/TR, 6', 195 lbs. Deb: 4/18/62 F																										
1962	Was-A★	11	12	.478	34	26	9	2	0	197	169	24	90	123	11.9	3.65	110	.234	.320	3	.052	-5	7	8	2	0.5
1963	Was-A	3	9	.250	16	16	2	1	0	87	90	12	45	47	14.1	4.55	82	.260	.347	2	.080	-1	-9	-8	0	-0.9
1964	Was-A	2	7	.222	26	14	1	0	1	88	80	12	39	44	12.3	4.81	77	.239	.320	6	.300	2	-12	-11	-0	-0.9
Total	3	16	28	.364	76	56	12	3	1	372	339	48	174	214	12.5	4.14	94	.241	.327	11	.107	-4	-14	-11	1	-1.3
● **BUZZ STEPHEN** Stephen, Louis Roberts b: 7/13/44, Porterville, Cal. BR/TR, 6'4", 205 lbs. Deb: 9/20/68																										
1968	Min-A	1	1	.500	2	2	0	0	0	11^1	11	0	7	4	15.1	4.76	65	.275	.396	0	.000	-0	-2	-2	0	-0.3
● **BRYAN STEPHENS** Stephens, Bryan Maris b: 7/14/20, Fayetteville, Ark d: 11/21/91, Santa Ana, Cal. BR/TR, 6'4", 175 lbs. Deb: 5/15/47																										
1947	Cle-A	5	10	.333	31	5	1	0	1	92	79	6	39	34	11.7	4.01	87	.230	.312	3	.111	-2	-3	-5	-1	-0.9
1948	StL-A	3	6	.333	43	12	2	0	3	122^2	141	14	67	35	15.6	6.02	76	.289	.379	4	.125	-1	-24	-20	-1	-2.0
Total	2	8	16	.333	74	17	3	0	4	214^2	220	20	106	69	13.9	5.16	79	.264	.352	7	.119	-3	-27	-26	-2	-2.9
● **CLARENCE STEPHENS** Stephens, Clarence Wright b: 8/19/1863, Cincinnati, Ohio d: 2/28/45, Cincinnati, Ohio TR, Deb: 10/08/1886																										
1886	Cin-a	1	0	1.000	1	1	1	0	0	8	9	0	5	6	16.9	5.63	63	.273	.385	3	.600	1	-2	-2	0	0.0
1891	Cin-N	0	1	.000	1	1	1	0	0	8	9	1	3	3	13.5	7.88	43	.273	.334	0	.000	-0	-4	-4	-0	-0.4
1892	Cin-N	0	1	.000	1	1	0	0	0	7	12	0	4	1	20.6	1.29	254	.364	.432	0	.000	-0	2	2	0	0.2
Total	3	1	2	.333	3	3	2	0	0	23	30	1	12	10	16.8	5.09	67	.303	.384	3	.300	0	-4	-4	0	-0.2
● **BEN STEPHENS** Stephens, George Benjamin b: 9/28/1867, Romeo, Mich. d: 8/5/1896, Armada, Mich. 5'10.5", 170 lbs. Deb: 8/05/1892																										
1892	Bal-N	1	1	.500	5	2	2	0	1	29	37	2	9	7	14.6	2.79	123	.298	.351	0	.000	-2	2	2	-0	0.0
1893	Was-N	0	6	.000	9	6	6	0	0	63^2	83	1	31	14	16.7	5.80	80	.306	.385	3	.103	-3	-8	-8	1	-0.9
1894	Was-N	0	0	—	3	2	1	0	0	11	19	1	8	1	22.9	4.91	107	.375	.469	1	.250	-0	1	0	0	0.0
Total	3	1	7	.125	17	10	9	0	1	103^2	139	4	48	22	16.8	4.86	90	.312	.386	4	.087	-5	-6	-6	1	-0.9
● **EARL STEPHENSON** Stephenson, Chester Earl b: 7/31/47, Benson, N.C. BL/TL, 6'3", 175 lbs. Deb: 4/07/71																										
1971	Chi-N	1	0	1.000	16	0	0	0	1	20^1	24	1	11	11	15.5	4.43	89	.316	.402	0	.000	-0	-2	-1	0	-0.1
1972	Mil-A	3	5	.375	35	8	1	0	0	80^1	79	5	33	33	12.9	3.25	93	.262	.340	0	.000	-2	-2	-2	0	-0.4
1977	Bal-A	0	0	—	1	0	0	0	0	3	5	1	0	2	15.0	9.00	42	.357	.357	0	—	0	-2	-2	-0	0.3
1978	Bal-A	0	0	—	2	0	0	0	0	9^2	10	0	5	4	14.0	2.79	125	.294	.385	0	—	0	1	1	-0	0.4
Total	4	4	5	.444	54	8	1	0	1	113^1	118	7	49	50	13.5	3.57	91	.277	.356	0	.000	-2	-4	-4	-0	0.2
● **JERRY STEPHENSON** Stephenson, Jerry Joseph b: 10/6/43, Detroit, Mich. BL/TR, 6'2", 185 lbs. Deb: 4/14/63 F																										
1963	Bos-A	0	0	—	1	1	0	0	0	2^1	5	0	2	3	27.0	7.71	49	.556	.636	0	.000	-0	-1	-1	-0	-0.1
1965	Bos-A	1	5	.167	15	8	0	0	0	52	62	7	33	49	16.6	6.23	60	.287	.384	3	.231	1	-16	-14	0	-1.4
1966	Bos-A	2	5	.286	15	11	1	0	0	66^1	68	6	44	50	15.3	5.83	65	.264	.373	2	.118	-1	-18	-15	0	-1.6
1967	*Bos-A	3	1	.750	8	6	0	0	1	39^2	32	4	16	24	11.1	3.86	90	.227	.310	4	.250	0	-3	-2	0	-0.1
1968	Bos-A	2	8	.200	23	7	2	0	0	68^2	81	4	42	51	16.4	5.64	56	.295	.392	6	.353	2	-20	-19	1	-1.8
1969	Sea-A	0	0	—	2	0	0	0	0	2^2	6	0	3	1	33.8	10.13	36	.429	.556	0	—	0	-2	-2	0	-0.2
1970	LA-N	0	0	—	3	0	0	0	0	6^2	11	0	5	6	21.6	9.45	41	.379	.471	0	.000	-0	-4	-4	-0	-0.4
Total	7	8	19	.296	67	33	3	0	1	238^1	265	21	145	184	15.7	5.70	62	.281	.381	15	.231	2	-64	-57	1	-5.6
● **JOHN STERLING** Sterling, John A. b: Philadelphia, Pa. Deb: 10/12/1890																										
1890	Phi-a	0	1	.000	1	1	1	0	0	5	16	1	4	1	37.8	21.60	18	.519	.586	0	.000	-0	-10	-10	-0	-0.7
● **RANDY STERLING** Sterling, Randall Wayne b: 4/21/51, Key West, Fla. BB/TR, 6'2", 195 lbs. Deb: 9/16/74																										
1974	NY-N	1	1	.500	3	2	0	0	0	9^1	13	0	3	2	16.4	4.82	74	.351	.415	0	.000	0	-1	-1	0	-0.1
● **JIM STEVENS** Stevens, James Arthur "Steve" b: 8/25/1889, Williamsburg, Md. d: 9/25/66, Baltimore, Md. BR/TR, 5'11", 180 lbs. Deb: 8/24/14																										
1914	Was-A	0	0	—	2	0	0	0	0	3	4	0	2	0	21.0	9.00	31	.364	.500	0	.000	-0	-2	-2	-0	-0.2
● **DAVE STEWART** Stewart, David Keith b: 2/19/57, Oakland, Cal. BR/TR, 6'2", 200 lbs. Deb: 9/22/78																										
1978	LA-N	0	0	—	1	0	0	0	0	2	1	0	0	1	4.5	0.00	—	.167	.167	0	—	0	1	1	-0	0.1
1981	*LA-N	4	3	.571	32	0	0	0	6	43^1	40	3	14	29	11.2	2.49	133	.250	.310	2	.400	2	5	4	0	0.6
1982	LA-N	9	8	.529	45	14	0	0	1	146^1	137	14	49	80	11.6	3.81	91	.249	.313	7	.179	1	-3	-6	-1	-0.6
1983	LA-N	5	2	.714	46	1	0	0	8	76	67	4	33	54	12.1	2.96	121	.237	.321	1	.143	-0	6	5	-1	0.5
	Tex-A	5	2	.714	8	8	2	0	0	59	50	2	17	24	10.5	2.14	188	.233	.295	0	—	0	13	12	0	1.4
1984	Tex-A	7	14	.333	32	27	3	0	0	192^1	193	26	87	119	13.3	4.73	88	.258	.339	0	—	0	-16	-12	-1	-1.4
1985	Tex-A	0	6	.000	42	5	0	0	4	81^1	86	13	37	64	13.8	5.42	78	.273	.353	0	—	0	-12	-11	0	-1.1
	Phi-N	0	0	—	4	0	0	0	0	4^1	5	0	4	2	18.7	6.23	59	.278	.409	0	—	0	-1	-1	-0	-0.2
1986	Phi-N	0	0	—	8	0	0	0	0	12^1	15	1	4	9	13.9	6.57	59	.306	.358	0	—	0	-4	-4	-0	-0.4
	Oak-A	9	5	.643	29	17	4	1	0	149^1	137	15	65	102	12.4	3.74	103	.241	.322	0	—	0	7	2	-0	0.2

YEAR TM/L	W	L	PCT	G	GS	CG	SH	SV	IP	H	HR	BB	SO	RAT	ERA	ERA+	OAV	OOB	BH	AVG	PB	PR	/A	PD	TPI
1987 Oak-A	**20**	13	.606	37	37	8	1	0	261^1	224	24	105	205	11.5	3.68	112	.229	.307	0	—	0	22	13	-3	1.4
1988 *Oak-A	21	12	.636	37	37	**14**	2	0	**275^2**	240	14	110	192	11.5	3.23	117	.234	.310	0	—	0	22	17	-3	1.5
1989 *Oak-A★	21	9	.700	36	36	8	0	0	257^2	260	23	69	155	11.7	3.32	111	.263	.315	0	—	0	16	10	-1	1.2
1990 *Oak-A	22	11	.667	36	36	**11**	**4**	0	**267**	226	16	83	166	10.6	2.56	145	.231	.294	0	—	0	40	34	-2	3.7
1991 Oak-A	11	11	.500	35	35	2	1	0	226	245	24	105	144	14.3	5.18	74	.278	.361	0	—	0	-27	-34	-2	-3.4
1992 *Oak-A	12	10	.545	31	31	2	0	0	199^1	175	25	79	130	11.8	3.66	103	.237	.318	0	—	0	6	3	-3	0.1
Total 13	146	106	.579	459	284	54	9	19	2253^1	2101	204	861	1476	12.0	3.69	104	.247	.320	10	.196	2	75	34	-17	3.6
● **FRANK STEWART**	Stewart, Frank "Stewy" b: 9/8/06, Minneapolis, Minn. BR/TR, 6'1.5", 180 lbs. Deb: 10/02/27																								
1927 Chi-A	0	1	.000	1	1	0	0	0	4	5	0	4	0	20.3	9.00	45	.357	.500	0	.000	-0	-2	-2	1	-0.2
● **JOE STEWART**	Stewart, Joseph Lawrence "Ace" b: 3/11/1879, Monroe, N.C. d: 2/9/13, Youngstown, Ohio TR, 5'11", 175 lbs. Deb: 9/13/04																								
1904 Bos-N	0	0	—	2	0	0	0	0	9^1	12	0	4	1	16.4	9.64	29	.286	.362	1	.200	-0	-7	-7	-0	-0.7
● **SAMMY STEWART**	Stewart, Samuel Lee b: 10/28/54, Asheville, N.C. BR/TR, 6'3", 208 lbs. Deb: 9/01/78																								
1978 Bal-A	1	1	.500	2	2	0	0	0	11^1	10	0	3	11	10.3	3.18	110	.238	.289	0	—	0	1	0	0	0.4
1979 *Bal-A	8	5	.615	31	3	1	0	1	117^2	96	11	71	71	13.2	3.52	114	.232	.351	0	—	0	9	6	3	1.0
1980 Bal-A	7	7	.500	33	3	2	0	3	118^2	103	9	60	78	12.5	3.56	111	.235	.330	0	—	0	6	5	-0	0.5
1981 Bal-A	4	8	.333	29	3	0	0	4	112^1	89	8	57	57	11.9	2.32	156	.225	.327	0	—	0	17	16	-0	1.8
1982 Bal-A	10	9	.526	38	12	1	1	5	139	140	9	62	69	13.2	4.14	97	.263	.342	0	—	0	-1	-2	1	-0.1
1983 *Bal-A	9	4	.692	58	1	0	0	7	144^1	138	7	67	95	12.8	3.62	109	.253	.336	0	—	0	7	5	-1	0.5
1984 Bal-A	7	4	.636	60	0	0	0	13	93	81	7	47	56	12.5	3.29	118	.241	.336	0	—	0	7	6	0	0.6
1985 Bal-A	5	7	.417	56	1	0	0	9	129^2	117	15	66	77	12.8	3.61	112	.246	.339	0	—	0	8	6	-1	0.6
1986 Bos-A	4	1	.800	27	0	0	0	0	63^2	64	7	48	47	15.8	4.38	95	.266	.388	0	—	0	-1	-2	-0	-0.2
1987 Cle-A	4	2	.667	25	0	0	0	3	27	25	4	21	25	15.7	5.67	80	.234	.364	0	—	0	-4	-3	0	-0.3
Total 10	59	48	.551	359	25	4	1	45	956^2	863	77	502	586	13.0	3.59	110	.245	.341	0	—	0	49	39	1	4.8
● **BUNKY STEWART**	Stewart, Veston Goff b: 1/7/31, Jasper, N.C. BL/TL, 6', 155 lbs. Deb: 5/04/52																								
1952 Was-A	0	0	—	1	0	0	0	0	1	2	0	1	1	27.0	18.00	20	.500	.600	0	—	0	-2	-2	0	-0.1
1953 Was-A	0	2	.000	2	2	1	0	0	15^1	17	1	11	3	17.0	4.70	83	.283	.403	1	.200	-0	-1	-1	-0	-0.2
1954 Was-A	0	2	.000	29	2	0	0	1	50^2	67	3	27	27	17.4	7.64	47	.324	.412	0	.000	0	-22	-23	1	-2.1
1955 Was-A	0	0	—	7	1	0	0	0	15^1	18	0	6	10	14.1	4.11	93	.295	.358	0	.000	-0	-0	-0	0	-0.1
1956 Was-A	5	7	.417	33	9	1	0	2	105	111	15	82	36	17.0	5.57	78	.276	.405	7	.250	-0	-16	-15	1	-1.3
Total 5	5	11	.313	72	14	2	0	3	187^1	215	19	127	77	16.9	6.01	67	.293	.404	8	.211	-0	-42	-41	2	-3.8
● **LEFTY STEWART**	Stewart, Walter Cleveland b: 9/23/1900, Sparta, Tenn. d: 9/26/74, Knoxville, Tenn. BR/TL, 5'10", 160 lbs. Deb: 4/20/21																								
1921 Det-A	0	0	—	5	0	0	0	1	9	20	0	5	4	25.0	12.00	36	.455	.510	0	.000	-0	-8	-8	0	-0.7
1927 StL-A	8	11	.421	27	19	11	0	1	155^2	187	7	43	43	13.4	4.28	102	.310	.357	15	.306	3	-2	1	2	0.5
1928 StL-A	7	9	.438	29	17	7	1	3	142^2	173	5	32	25	13.1	4.67	90	.310	.350	14	.275	3	-10	-7	-0	-0.5
1929 StL-A	9	6	.600	23	18	8	1	0	149^2	137	11	49	47	11.4	3.25	136	.246	.312	6	.118	-4	17	20	-0	1.5
1930 StL-A	20	12	.625	35	33	23	1	0	271	281	21	70	79	11.7	3.45	141	.268	.315	22	.244	2	36	43	0	4.4
1931 StL-A	14	17	.452	36	33	20	1	0	258	287	17	85	89	13.1	4.40	105	.277	.334	22	.250	6	-0	7	1	1.4
1932 StL-A	15	19	.441	41	32	18	2	1	259^2	269	22	99	86	12.9	4.61	105	.270	.338	12	.146	-2	-4	7	-1	0.4
1933 *Was-A	15	6	.714	34	31	11	1	0	230^2	227	19	60	69	11.2	3.82	109	.256	.304	11	.143	1	12	9	1	1.0
1934 Was-A	7	11	.389	24	22	7	1	0	152	184	8	36	36	13.1	4.03	107	.303	.343	7	.156	-1	8	5	-0	0.3
1935 Was-A	0	1	.000	1	1	0	0	0	2^2	8	1	2	1	33.8	13.50	32	.533	.588	0	.000	-0	-3	-3	-0	-0.2
Cle-A	6	6	.500	24	10	2	0	2	91	122	6	17	24	13.8	5.44	83	.312	.342	6	.200	-1	-10	-9	-1	-1.1
Yr	6	7	.462	25	11	2	0	2	93^2	130	7	19	25	14.4	5.67	79	.320	.352	6	.194	-1	-13	-12	-1	-1.3
Total 10	101	98	.508	279	216	107	8	8	1722	1895	117	498	503	12.6	4.19	108	.281	.332	115	.204	7	35	64	0	7.0
● **MACK STEWART**	Stewart, William Macklin b: 9/23/14, Stevenson, Ala. d: 3/21/60, Macon, Ga. BR/TR, 6', 167 lbs. Deb: 7/07/44																								
1944 Chi-N	0	0	—	8	0	0	0	0	12^1	11	1	4	3	10.9	1.46	242	.239	.300	0	.000	-0	3	3	-0	0.3
1945 Chi-N	0	1	.000	16	1	0	0	0	28^1	37	0	14	9	16.2	4.76	77	.322	.395	1	.333	0	-3	-4	0	-0.3
Total 2	0	1	.000	24	1	0	0	0	40^2	48	1	18	12	14.6	3.76	96	.298	.369	1	.250	0	-0	-1	0	0.0
● **DAVE STIEB**	Stieb, David Andrew b: 7/22/57, Santa Ana, Cal. BR/TR, 6'1", 195 lbs. Deb: 6/29/79																								
1979 Tor-A	8	8	.500	18	18	7	1	0	129^1	139	11	48	52	13.3	4.31	101	.276	.344	0	—	0	-1	0	3	0.3
1980 Tor-A★	12	15	.444	34	32	14	4	0	242^2	232	12	83	108	11.9	3.71	116	.260	.327	0	.000	0	9	16	5	2.2
1981 Tor-A★	11	10	.524	25	25	11	2	0	183^2	148	10	61	89	10.8	3.19	124	.223	.299	0	—	0	10	15	2	1.9
1982 Tor-A	17	14	.548	38	38	**19**	**5**	0	**288^1**	271	27	75	141	11.0	3.25	138	.248	.299	0	—	0	27	**39**	4	**4.4**
1983 Tor-A★	17	12	.586	36	36	14	4	0	278	223	21	93	187	10.7	3.04	141	.219	.293	0	—	0	31	**39**	1	**4.2**
1984 Tor-A★	16	8	.667	35	35	11	2	0	**267**	215	19	88	198	10.6	2.83	**145**	**.221**	.293	0	—	0	34	**37**	1	**4.1**
1985 *Tor-A★	14	13	.519	36	36	8	2	0	265	206	22	96	167	10.6	**2.48**	**170**	**.213**	.290	0	—	0	**49**	**51**	5	**6.0**
1986 Tor-A	7	12	.368	37	34	1	1	1	205	239	29	87	127	15.0	4.74	89	.297	.376	0	—	0	-13	-12	1	-1.0
1987 Tor-A	13	9	.591	33	31	3	1	0	185	164	16	87	115	12.6	4.09	110	.239	.331	0	—	0	8	8	1	0.9
1988 Tor-A★	16	8	.667	32	31	8	4	0	207^1	157	15	79	147	10.8	3.04	129	.210	.296	0	—	0	21	21	1	2.2
1989 *Tor-A	17	8	.680	33	33	3	2	0	206^2	164	12	76	101	11.0	3.35	112	.219	.302	0	—	0	12	10	0	1.1
1990 Tor-A★	18	6	.750	33	33	2	2	0	208^2	179	11	64	125	10.9	2.93	134	.230	.297	0	—	0	23	23	3	2.8
1991 Tor-A	4	3	.571	9	9	1	0	0	59^2	52	4	23	29	11.6	3.17	133	.243	.322	0	—	0	6	7	1	0.8
1992 Tor-A	4	6	.400	21	14	1	0	0	96^1	98	9	43	45	13.5	5.04	81	.275	.359	0	—	0	-12	-10	2	-1.0
Total 14	174	132	.569	420	405	103	30	1	2822^2	2487	218	1003	1631	11.5	3.39	123	.238	.312	0	.000	0	204	245	30	28.9
● **FRED STIELY**	Stiely, Fred Warren "Lefty" b: 6/1/01, Pillow, Pa. d: 1/6/81, Valley View, Pa. BL/TL, 5'8", 170 lbs. Deb: 10/06/29																								
1929 StL-A	1	0	1.000	1	1	1	0	0	9	11	0	3	2	15.0	0.00	—	.297	.366	2	.667	1	4	4	0	0.8
1930 StL-A	0	1	.000	4	2	1	0	0	19	27	4	8	5	17.1	8.53	57	.346	.414	3	.429	2	-8	-8	-0	-0.5
1931 StL-A	0	0	—	4	0	0	0	0	6^2	7	0	3	2	14.9	6.75	69	.269	.367	0	—	0	-2	-2	-0	-0.2
Total 3	1	1	.500	9	3	2	0	0	34^2	45	4	14	9	16.1	5.97	79	.319	.392	5	.500	3	-6	-5	-1	0.1
● **DICK STIGMAN**	Stigman, Richard Lewis b: 1/24/36, Nimrod, Minn. BR/TL, 6'3", 200 lbs. Deb: 4/22/60																								
1960 Cle-A☆	5	11	.313	41	18	3	0	9	133^2	118	13	87	104	13.8	4.51	83	.238	.352	8	.222	2	-9	-11	-2	-1.1
1961 Cle-A	2	5	.286	22	6	0	0	0	64^1	65	9	25	48	12.6	4.62	85	.264	.332	2	.125	-1	-4	-5	0	-0.5
1962 Min-A	12	5	.706	40	15	6	0	3	142^2	122	19	64	116	11.9	3.66	112	.233	.319	2	.044	-4	5	7	-2	0.1
1963 Min-A	15	15	.500	33	33	15	3	0	241	210	32	81	193	10.9	3.25	112	.231	.294	9	.107	-2	10	11	-4	0.5
1964 Min-A	6	15	.286	32	29	5	1	0	190	160	31	70	159	11.1	4.03	89	.225	.299	7	.101	-3	-8	-9	-3	-1.5
1965 Min-A	4	2	.667	33	8	0	0	4	70	59	14	33	70	11.8	4.37	81	.227	.314	2	.133	-0	-7	-6	-1	-0.8
1966 Bos-A	2	1	.667	34	10	1	1	0	81	85	15	46	65	14.7	5.44	70	.268	.363	2	.118	-1	-18	-15	-1	-1.8
Total 7	46	54	.460	235	119	30	5	16	922^2	819	133	406	755	12.0	4.03	93	.237	.318	32	.113	-8	-32	-29	-13	-5.1
● **ROLLIE STILES**	Stiles, Rolland Mays "Lena" b: 11/17/06, Ratcliff, Ark. BR/TR, 6'1.5", 180 lbs. Deb: 6/19/30																								
1930 StL-A	3	6	.333	20	7	3	0	0	102	136	10	41	25	15.7	5.91	82	.337	.399	10	.270	0	-14	-12	-1	-1.1
1931 StL-A	3	1	.750	34	2	0	0	0	81	112	2	60	32	19.3	7.22	64	.352	.458	1	.045	-2	-26	-23	-0	-2.3
1933 StL-A	3	7	.300	31	9	6	1	1	115	154	4	47	29	15.9	5.01	93	.327	.390	2	.061	-3	-9	-5	-1	-0.8
Total 3	9	14	.391	85	18	9	1	1	298	402	16	148	86	16.8	5.92	80	.337	.412	13	.141	-5	-49	-40	-2	-4.2

● ARCHIE STIMMEL Stimmel, Archibald May "Lumbago" b: 5/30/1873, Woodsboro, Md. d: 8/18/58, Frederick, Md. BR/TR, 6', 175 lbs. Deb: 7/03/00

YEAR	TM/L	W	L	PCT	G	GS	CG	SH	SV	IP	H	HR	BB	SO	RAT	ERA	ERA+	OAV	OOB	BH	AVG	PB	PR	/A	PD	TPI
1900	Cin-N	1	1	.500	2	1	1	0	0	13	18	1	4	2	15.2	6.92	53	.327	.373	1	.200	-0	-5	-5	-0	-0.4
1901	Cin-N	4	14	.222	20	18	14	1	0	153^1	170	10	44	55	13.1	4.11	78	.279	.338	5	.081	-4	-13	-15	-3	-2.1
1902	Cin-N	0	4	.000	4	3	3	0	0	26	37	1	12	7	17.7	3.46	87	.334	.408	2	.200	-0	-2	-1	-0	-0.2
Total	3	5	19	.208	26	22	18	1	0	192^1	225	12	60	64	13.9	4.21	76	.290	.350	8	.104	-5	-20	-21	-3	-2.7

● CARL STIMSON Stimson, Carl Remus b: 7/18/1894, Hamburg, Iowa d: 11/9/36, Omaha, Neb. BB/TR, 6'5", 190 lbs. Deb: 6/06/23

YEAR	TM/L	W	L	PCT	G	GS	CG	SH	SV	IP	H	HR	BB	SO	RAT	ERA	ERA+	OAV	OOB	BH	AVG	PB	PR	/A	PD	TPI
1923	Bos-A	0	0	—	2	0	0	0	0	4	12	0	5	1	40.5	22.50	18	.750	.818	0	.000	-0	-8	-8	0	-0.7

● HARRY STINE Stine, Harry C. b: 2/20/1864, Shenandoah, Pa. d: 6/5/24, Niagara Falls, N.Y TL, 5'6", 150 lbs. Deb: 7/22/1890

YEAR	TM/L	W	L	PCT	G	GS	CG	SH	SV	IP	H	HR	BB	SO	RAT	ERA	ERA+	OAV	OOB	BH	AVG	PB	PR	/A	PD	TPI
1890	Phi-a	0	1	.000	1	1	1	0	0	8	17	0	4	1	23.6	9.00	43	.418	.470	0	.000	-0	-5	-5	-0	-0.4

● LEE STINE Stine, Lee Elbert b: 11/17/13, Stillwater, Okla. BR/TR, 5'11", 185 lbs. Deb: 4/17/34

YEAR	TM/L	W	L	PCT	G	GS	CG	SH	SV	IP	H	HR	BB	SO	RAT	ERA	ERA+	OAV	OOB	BH	AVG	PB	PR	/A	PD	TPI
1934	Chi-A	0	0	—	4	0	0	0	0	11	11	2	10	8	18.0	8.18	58	.268	.423	0	.000	0	-5	-4	-0	-0.4
1935	Chi-A	0	0	—	1	0	0	0	0	2	2	1	3	1	22.5	9.00	51	.286	.500	0	—	0	-1	-1	1	0.0
1936	Cin-N	3	8	.273	40	13	5	1	2	121^2	157	6	41	26	15.2	5.03	76	.318	.379	8	.296	3	-14	-16	2	-1.1
1938	NY-A	0	0	—	4	0	0	0	0	8^2	9	0	1	4	10.4	1.04	437	.333	.357	1	.500	0	4	3	-0	0.3
Total	4	3	8	.273	49	13	5	1	2	143^1	179	9	55	39	15.3	5.09	78	.315	.384	9	.300	3	-16	-18	2	-1.2

● JACK STIVETTS Stivetts, John Elmer "Happy Jack" b: 3/31/1868, Ashland, Pa. d: 4/18/30, Ashland, Pa. BR/TR, 6'2", 185 lbs. Deb: 6/26/1889 ♦

YEAR	TM/L	W	L	PCT	G	GS	CG	SH	SV	IP	H	HR	BB	SO	RAT	ERA	ERA+	OAV	OOB	BH	AVG	PB	PR	/A	PD	TPI
1889	StL-a	12	7	.632	26	20	18	2	1	191^2	153	4	68	143	**10.6**	**2.25**	**188**	**.212**	**.285**	18	.228	-1	34	42	0	3.7
1890	StL-a	27	21	.563	54	46	41	3	0	419^1	399	14	179	289	12.8	3.52	123	.243	.324	65	.288	16	16	37	3	5.0
1891	StL-a	33	22	.600	**64**	56	40	3	1	440	357	15	232	**259**	12.4	2.86	147	.214	.317	92	.305	11	42	**66**	3	**7.1**
1892	*Bos-N	35	16	.686	54	48	45	3	1	415^2	346	12	171	180	11.4	3.03	116	.217	.297	71	.296	16	12	22	1	3.7
1893	Bos-N	20	12	.625	38	34	29	1	1	283^2	315	17	115	61	14.0	4.41	112	.273	.344	51	.297	8	8	17	-2	1.8
1894	Bos-N	26	14	.650	45	39	30	0	0	338	429	27	127	76	15.2	4.90	116	.306	.369	80	.328	11	16	29	-3	3.0
1895	Bos-N	17	17	.500	38	34	30	0	0	291	341	15	89	111	13.7	4.64	110	.288	.344	30	.190	-7	5	15	-1	0.5
1896	Bos-N	22	14	.611	42	36	31	2	0	329	353	20	99	71	12.6	4.10	111	.272	.327	76	.344	12	9	16	-3	2.2
1897	*Bos-N	11	4	.733	18	15	10	0	0	129^1	147	5	43	27	13.6	3.41	131	.284	.344	73	.367	7	13	15	1	2.1
1898	Bos-N	0	1	.000	2	1	1	0	0	12	17	2	7	1	18.0	8.25	45	.331	.411	28	.252	0	-6	-6	0	-0.5
1899	Cle-N	0	4	.000	7	4	3	0	0	38	48	0	25	5	17.8	5.68	65	.308	.410	8	.205	1	-8	-8	2	-0.5
Total	11	203	132	.606	388	333	278	14	4	2887^2	2905	131	1155	1223	13.0	3.74	121	.255	.329	592	.297	72	141	247	0	28.1

● CHUCK STOBBS Stobbs, Charles Klein b: 7/2/29, Wheeling, W.Va. BL/TL, 6'1", 185 lbs. Deb: 9/15/47

YEAR	TM/L	W	L	PCT	G	GS	CG	SH	SV	IP	H	HR	BB	SO	RAT	ERA	ERA+	OAV	OOB	BH	AVG	PB	PR	/A	PD	TPI
1947	Bos-A	0	1	.000	4	1	0	0	0	9	10	0	10	5	20.0	6.00	65	.294	.455	0	.000	-0	-2	-2	-0	-0.2
1948	Bos-A	0	0	—	6	0	0	0	0	7	9	0	7	4	20.6	6.43	68	.321	.457	0	.000	-0	-2	-2	0	-0.1
1949	Bos-A	11	6	.647	26	19	10	0	0	152	145	10	75	70	13.1	4.03	108	.254	.343	11	.208	0	3	6	-1	0.5
1950	Bos-A	12	7	.632	32	21	6	0	1	169^1	158	17	88	78	13.3	5.10	96	.250	.346	14	.246	3	-10	-4	1	0.0
1951	Bos-A	10	9	.526	34	25	6	0	0	170	180	15	74	75	13.7	4.76	94	.271	.349	11	.180	-2	-12	-6	-2	-1.0
1952	Chi-A	7	12	.368	38	17	2	0	1	135	118	9	72	73	13.0	3.13	116	.237	.339	3	.079	-1	8	8	1	0.7
1953	Was-A	11	8	.579	27	20	8	0	0	153	146	11	44	67	11.2	3.29	118	.246	.299	10	.227	1	12	10	-0	1.1
1954	Was-A	11	11	.500	31	24	10	3	0	182	189	6	67	67	12.7	4.10	87	.270	.335	7	.137	0	-8	-11	1	-1.0
1955	Was-A	4	14	.222	41	16	2	0	3	140^1	169	13	57	60	14.6	5.00	77	.302	.368	6	.171	2	-16	-18	1	-1.5
1956	Was-A	15	15	.500	37	33	15	1	1	240	264	29	54	97	12.0	3.60	120	.279	.318	15	.179	-2	15	19	1	1.8
1957	Was-A	8	20	.286	42	31	5	2	1	211^2	235	28	80	114	13.6	5.36	73	.279	.345	16	.211	1	-37	-34	-3	-3.5
1958	Was-A	2	6	.250	19	8	0	0	0	56^2	87	7	16	23	16.7	6.04	63	.369	.413	0	.000	-2	-14	-14	0	-1.5
	StL-N	1	3	.250	17	0	0	0	1	39^2	40	4	14	25	12.3	3.63	114	.261	.323	1	.250	0	1	2	1	0.3
1959	Was-A	1	8	.111	41	7	0	0	7	90^2	82	13	24	50	10.7	2.98	131	.238	.291	2	.105	-1	9	9	-0	0.8
1960	Was-A	12	7	.632	40	13	1	1	2	119^1	115	13	38	72	11.8	3.32	117	.252	.313	3	.088	-2	7	8	-2	0.4
1961	Min-A	2	3	.400	24	3	0	0	2	44^2	56	8	15	17	14.7	7.46	57	.311	.371	3	.375	1	-17	-16	-1	-1.5
Total	15	107	130	.451	459	238	65	7	19	1920^1	2003	183	735	897	13.0	4.29	95	.269	.338	102	.176	-1	-63	-46	-3	-4.7

● WES STOCK Stock, Wesley Gay b: 4/10/34, Longview, Wash. BR/TR, 6'2", 188 lbs. Deb: 4/19/59 C

YEAR	TM/L	W	L	PCT	G	GS	CG	SH	SV	IP	H	HR	BB	SO	RAT	ERA	ERA+	OAV	OOB	BH	AVG	PB	PR	/A	PD	TPI
1959	Bal-A	0	0	—	7	0	0	0	1	12^2	16	1	2	8	12.8	3.55	107	.302	.327	0	.000	-0	0	0	-0	0.0
1960	Bal-A	2	2	.500	17	0	0	0	2	34^1	26	2	14	23	10.7	2.88	132	.218	.306	0	.000	-1	4	4	1	0.3
1961	Bal-A	5	0	1.000	35	1	0	0	3	71^2	58	3	27	47	10.9	3.01	130	.225	.303	0	.000	-1	8	7	2	0.8
1962	Bal-A	3	2	.600	53	0	0	0	3	65	50	7	36	34	12.0	4.43	85	.217	.326	0	.000	-0	-3	-5	3	-0.2
1963	Bal-A	7	0	1.000	47	0	0	0	1	75^1	69	11	31	55	11.9	3.94	89	.246	.321	0	.000	-1	-3	-3	1	-0.4
1964	Bal-A	2	0	1.000	14	0	0	0	0	20^2	17	5	8	14	10.9	3.92	91	.233	.309	0	.000	-0	-1	-1	0	-0.1
	KC-A	6	3	.667	50	0	0	0	5	93	69	10	34	101	10.4	1.94	197	.213	.296	3	.200	0	17	19	-1	2.0
	Yr	8	3	.727	64	0	0	0	5	113^2	86	15	42	115	10.5	2.30	164	.216	.297	3	.158	-0	17	19	-0	1.9
1965	KC-A	0	4	.000	62	2	0	0	4	99^2	96	18	40	52	12.6	5.24	67	.251	.328	0	.000	-1	-20	-19	2	-1.9
1966	KC-A	2	2	.500	35	0	0	0	3	44	30	3	21	31	11.0	2.66	128	.199	.309	0	.000	-0	4	4	-0	0.3
1967	KC-A	0	0	—	1	0	0	0	0	1	3	0	2	0	45.0	18.00	18	.500	.625	0	—	0	-2	-2	0	-0.2
Total	9	27	13	.675	321	3	0	0	22	517^1	434	60	215	365	11.6	3.60	102	.231	.315	3	.051	-4	6	4	7	0.6

● OTIS STOCKSDALE Stocksdale, Otis Hinkley "Old Gray Fox"
b: 8/7/1871, Near Arcadia, Md. d: 3/15/33, Pennsville, N.J. BL/TR, 5'10.5", 180 lbs. Deb: 7/24/1893

YEAR	TM/L	W	L	PCT	G	GS	CG	SH	SV	IP	H	HR	BB	SO	RAT	ERA	ERA+	OAV	OOB	BH	AVG	PB	PR	/A	PD	TPI
1893	Was-N	2	8	.200	11	11	7	0	0	69	111	4	32	12	19.3	8.22	56	.352	.420	12	.300	2	-27	-28	1	-1.9
1894	Was-N	5	9	.357	18	14	11	0	0	117^1	176	10	42	10	17.8	5.06	104	.342	.407	23	.324	1	3	3	1	0.3
1895	Was-N	6	11	.353	20	17	11	0	1	136	199	7	52	23	17.1	6.09	79	.335	.396	23	.311	3	-20	-19	-0	-1.3
	Bos-N	2	2	.500	4	4	1	0	0	23	31	2	8	2	15.3	5.87	87	.317	.369	4	.267	-0	-3	-2	-0	-0.2
	Yr	8	13	.381	24	21	12	0	1	159	230	9	60	25	16.4	6.06	80	.329	.382	27	.303	2	-23	-21	-1	-1.5
1896	Bal-N	0	1	.000	1	0	0	0	0	1^2	4	0	2	1	37.8	16.20	26	.455	.594	1	.333	1	-2	-2	-0	-0.1
Total	4	15	31	.326	54	46	30	0	1	347	521	23	136	48	17.8	6.20	80	.341	.405	63	.310	5	-49	-48	1	-3.2

● BOB STODDARD Stoddard, Robert Lyle b: 3/8/57, San Jose, Cal. BR/TR, 6'1", 200 lbs. Deb: 9/04/81

YEAR	TM/L	W	L	PCT	G	GS	CG	SH	SV	IP	H	HR	BB	SO	RAT	ERA	ERA+	OAV	OOB	BH	AVG	PB	PR	/A	PD	TPI
1981	Sea-A	2	1	.667	5	5	1	0	0	34^2	35	3	9	22	11.7	2.60	148	.269	.321	0	—	0	4	5	-0	0.5
1982	Sea-A	3	3	.500	9	9	2	1	0	67^1	48	7	18	24	9.2	2.41	176	.205	.271	0	—	0	12	14	0	1.5
1983	Sea-A	9	17	.346	35	23	2	1	0	175^2	182	29	58	87	12.5	4.41	97	.274	.336	0	—	0	-7	-3	3	0.0
1984	Sea-A	2	3	.400	27	6	0	0	0	79	86	10	37	39	14.2	5.13	78	.278	.359	0	—	0	-10	-10	1	-0.9
1985	Det-A	0	0	—	8	0	0	0	1	13^1	15	3	5	11	13.5	6.75	60	.268	.328	0	—	0	-4	-4	1	-0.3
1986	SD-N	1	0	1.000	18	0	0	0	1	23^1	20	1	11	17	12.3	2.31	158	.227	.320	0	.000	-0	4	3	-0	0.3
1987	KC-A	1	3	.250	17	2	0	0	1	40	51	3	22	23	17.1	4.27	107	.313	.404	0	—	0	1	1	1	0.2
Total	7	18	27	.400	119	45	5	2	3	433^1	437	56	160	223	12.7	4.03	103	.266	.336	0	.000	-0	0	6	5	1.3

● TIM STODDARD Stoddard, Timothy Paul b: 1/24/53, E.Chicago, Ind. BR/TR, 6'7", 250 lbs. Deb: 9/07/75

YEAR	TM/L	W	L	PCT	G	GS	CG	SH	SV	IP	H	HR	BB	SO	RAT	ERA	ERA+	OAV	OOB	BH	AVG	PB	PR	/A	PD	TPI
1975	Chi-A	0	0	—	1	0	0	0	0	1	2	1	0	0	18.0	9.00	43	.400	.400	0	—	0	-1	-1	0	-0.1
1978	Bal-A	0	1	.000	8	0	0	0	0	18	22	3	8	14	16.0	6.00	58	.301	.386	0	—	0	-4	-5	0	-0.2
1979	*Bal-A	3	1	.750	29	0	0	0	3	58	44	3	19	47	9.8	1.71	235	.212	.278	0	—	0	16	15	-0	1.6
1980	Bal-A	5	3	.625	64	0	0	0	26	86	72	2	38	64	11.6	2.51	157	.233	.319	0	—	0	15	14	-1	1.3
1981	Bal-A	4	2	.667	31	0	0	0	7	37^1	38	6	18	32	14.0	3.86	94	.268	.358	0	—	0	-1	-1	-0	-0.1
1982	Bal-A	3	4	.429	50	0	0	0	12	56	53	4	29	42	13.3	4.02	100	.249	.342	0	—	0	0	0	-0	0.0
1983	Bal-A	4	3	.571	47	0	0	0	9	57^2	65	10	29	50	14.8	6.09	65	.293	.377	0	—	0	-13	-14	0	-1.3
1984	*Chi-N	10	6	.625	58	0	0	0	7	92	77	9	57	87	13.2	3.82	102	.236	.352	1	.091	-1	-2	1	-1	-0.1

YEAR	TM/L	W	L	PCT	G	GS	CG	SH	SV	IP	H	HR	BB	SO	RAT	ERA	ERA+	OAV	OOB	BH	AVG	PB	PR	/A	PD	TPI
1985	SD-N	1	6	.143	44	0	0	0	1	60	63	3	37	42	15.0	4.65	76	.269	.369	0	.000	-1	-7	-7	-1	-0.9
1986	SD-N	1	3	.250	30	0	0	0	0	45^{1}	33	6	34	47	13.3	3.77	97	.200	.337	1	.250	1	-0	-1	0	0.1
	NY-A	4	1	.800	24	0	0	0	0	49^{1}	41	6	23	34	11.7	3.83	107	.232	.320	0	—	0	2	1	0	0.1
1987	NY-A	4	3	.571	57	0	0	0	8	92^{2}	83	13	30	78	11.0	3.50	125	.235	.295	0	—	0	10	9	-1	0.8
1988	NY-A	2	2	.500	28	0	0	0	3	55	62	5	27	33	14.9	6.38	62	.286	.370	0	—	0	-15	-15	0	-1.4
1989	Cle-A	0	0	—	14	0	0	0	0	21^{1}	25	1	7	12	13.5	2.95	134	.313	.368	0	—	0	2	2	0	0.2
Total	13	41	35	.539	485	0	0	0	76	729^{2}	680	72	356	582	12.9	3.95	100	.250	.339	2	.100	-0	2	-0	-3	0.0
● **ART STOKES**	Stokes, Arthur Milton b: 9/13/1896, Emmitsburg, Md. d: 6/3/62, Titusville, Pa. BR/TR, 5'10.5", 155 lbs. Deb: 5/05/25																									
1925	Phi-A	1	1	.500	12	0	0	0	0	24^{1}	24	0	10	7	13.3	4.07	114	.270	.356	0	.000	-0	1	2	-0	0.1
● **DICK STONE**	Stone, Charles Richard b: 12/5/11, Oklahoma City, Okla d: 2/18/1880, Oklahoma City, Okla. BL/TL, 5'9", 153 lbs. Deb: 8/26/45																									
1945	Was-A	0	0	—	3	0	0	0	0	5	6	0	2	0	14.4	0.00	—	.316	.381	0	—	0	2	2	0	0.2
● **DEAN STONE**	Stone, Darrah Dean b: 9/1/30, Moline, Ill. BL/TL, 6'4", 205 lbs. Deb: 9/13/53																									
1953	Was-A	0	1	.000	3	1	0	0	0	8^{2}	13	0	5	5	18.7	8.31	47	.361	.439	0	.000	-0	-4	-4	-0	-0.4
1954	Was-A★	12	10	.545	31	23	10	2	0	178^{2}	161	7	69	87	11.6	3.22	110	.240	.312	5	.096	-0	10	7	-3	0.4
1955	Was-A	6	13	.316	43	24	5	1	1	180	180	14	114	84	14.9	4.15	92	.267	.375	2	.043	-3	-4	-6	-2	-1.1
1956	Was-A	5	7	.417	41	21	2	0	3	132	148	10	93	86	16.9	6.27	69	.282	.397	3	.088	-1	-31	-29	-1	-2.8
1957	Was-A	0	0	—	3	0	0	0	0	3^{1}	5	0	2	3	18.9	8.10	48	.357	.438	0	—	0	-2	-2	-0	-0.2
	Bos-A	1	3	.250	17	8	0	0	1	51^{1}	56	5	35	32	16.0	5.08	78	.284	.392	0	.000	-1	-7	-6	1	-0.7
	Yr	1	3	.250	20	8	0	0	1	54^{2}	61	5	37	35	16.1	5.27	76	.288	.394	0	.000	-1	-9	-8	1	-0.9
1959	StL-N	0	1	.000	18	1	0	0	1	30	30	4	16	17	13.8	4.20	101	.273	.365	0	.000	-0	-1	0	-0	-0.1
1962	Hou-N	3	2	.600	15	7	2	2	0	52^{1}	61	4	20	31	14.1	4.47	84	.295	.360	4	.250	1	-3	-4	0	-0.3
	Chi-A	1	0	1.000	27	0	0	0	5	30^{1}	28	3	9	23	11.3	3.26	120	.255	.317	1	.500	1	2	2	-0	0.3
1963	Bal-A	1	2	.333	17	0	0	0	1	19^{1}	23	0	10	12	15.4	5.12	69	.307	.388	0	—	0	-3	-3	0	-0.3
Total	8	29	39	.426	215	85	19	5	12	686	705	47	373	380	14.3	4.47	86	.269	.363	15	.088	-6	-43	-46	-5	-5.2
● **DWIGHT STONE**	Stone, Dwight Ely b: 8/2/1886, Holt Co., Neb. d: 6/3/76, Glendale, Cal. BR/TR, 6'1.5", 170 lbs. Deb: 4/13/13																									
1913	StL-A	2	6	.250	18	7	4	1	0	91	94	0	46	37	14.5	3.56	82	.267	.363	9	.273	2	-6	-6	1	-0.4
1914	KC-F	8	14	.364	39	22	6	0	0	186^{2}	205	8	77	88	14.0	4.34	71	.281	.356	7	.121	-2	-23	-26	1	-2.8
Total	2	10	20	.333	57	29	10	1	0	277^{2}	299	8	123	125	14.2	4.08	74	.276	.358	16	.176	-1	-30	-32	2	-3.2
● **ARNIE STONE**	Stone, Edwin Arnold b: 10/9/1892, North Creek, N.Y. d: 7/29/48, Hudson Falls, N.Y BR/TL, 6', 180 lbs. Deb: 8/07/23																									
1923	Pit-N	0	1	.000	9	0	0	0	0	12^{1}	19	0	4	2	16.8	8.03	50	.352	.397	0	.000	-0	-6	-6	-1	-0.6
1924	Pit-N	4	2	.667	26	2	1	0	0	64	57	0	15	7	10.1	2.95	130	.259	.306	2	.133	-1	6	6	0	0.5
Total	2	4	3	.571	35	2	1	0	0	76^{1}	76	0	19	9	11.2	3.77	102	.277	.324	2	.125	-1	1	1	-0	-0.1
● **GEORGE STONE**	Stone, George Heard b: 7/9/46, Ruston, La. BL/TL, 6'3", 205 lbs. Deb: 9/15/67																									
1967	Atl-N	0	0	—	2	1	0	0	0	7^{1}	8	0	1	5	11.0	4.91	68	.267	.290	0	.000	-0	-1	-1	0	-0.2
1968	Atl-N	7	4	.636	17	10	2	0	0	75	63	9	19	52	9.8	2.76	108	.222	.271	9	.333	3	2	2	-1	0.4
1969	*Atl-N	13	10	.565	36	20	3	0	3	165^{1}	166	20	48	102	11.9	3.65	99	.260	.317	11	.186	1	-1	-1	-1	0.0
1970	Atl-N	11	11	.500	35	30	9	2	0	207^{1}	218	27	50	131	11.9	3.86	111	.267	.314	17	.236	4	4	10	3	1.7
1971	Atl-N	6	8	.429	27	24	4	2	0	172^{2}	186	19	35	110	11.8	3.60	103	.274	.315	11	.177	-0	-3	2	-0	0.2
1972	Atl-N	6	11	.353	31	16	2	1	1	111	143	18	44	63	15.5	5.51	69	.315	.380	5	.200	2	-25	-21	1	-1.9
1973	*NY-N	12	3	.800	27	20	2	0	1	148	157	16	31	77	11.4	2.80	129	.274	.311	13	.271	2	14	13	1	1.8
1974	NY-N	2	7	.222	15	13	1	0	0	77	103	10	21	29	14.5	5.03	71	.322	.364	3	.115	-1	-12	-13	0	-1.3
1975	NY-N	3	3	.500	13	11	1	0	0	57	75	3	21	21	15.2	5.05	68	.323	.379	3	.167	0	-9	-10	1	-0.9
Total	9	60	57	.513	203	145	24	5	5	1020^{2}	1119	122	270	590	12.4	3.89	96	.278	.326	72	.212	10	-31	-19	4	-0.2
● **ROCKY STONE**	Stone, John Vernon b: 8/23/18, Redding, Cal. d: 11/12/86, Fountain Valley, Cal. BR/TR, 6', 200 lbs. Deb: 5/02/43																									
1943	Cin-N	0	1	.000	13	0	0	0	0	24^{2}	23	0	8	11	11.3	4.38	76	.237	.295	1	.250	0	-3	-3	-1	-0.4
● **STEVE STONE**	Stone, Steven Michael b: 7/14/47, Euclid, Ohio BR/TR, 5'10", 175 lbs. Deb: 4/08/71																									
1971	SF-N	5	9	.357	24	19	2	2	0	110^{2}	110	9	55	63	13.7	4.15	82	.259	.349	0	.000	-2	-8	-9	2	-1.1
1972	SF-N	6	8	.429	27	16	4	1	0	123^{2}	97	11	49	85	10.8	2.98	117	.218	.298	4	.118	-1	6	7	0	0.7
1973	Chi-A	6	11	.353	36	22	3	0	1	176^{1}	163	11	82	138	12.9	4.24	93	.245	.335	0	—	0	-8	-5	0	-0.5
1974	Chi-N	8	6	.571	38	23	1	0	0	169^{2}	185	19	64	90	13.4	4.14	92	.278	.345	7	.121	-3	-10	-6	1	-0.8
1975	Chi-N	12	8	.600	33	32	6	1	0	214^{1}	198	24	80	139	11.9	3.95	97	.245	.317	8	.111	-2	-8	-3	0	-0.5
1976	Chi-N	3	6	.333	17	15	1	1	0	75	70	6	21	33	11.3	4.08	95	.250	.309	3	.143	-1	-5	-2	-1	-0.4
1977	Chi-A	15	12	.556	31	31	8	0	0	207^{1}	228	25	80	124	13.6	4.51	90	.281	.350	0	—	0	-10	-10	-0	-1.0
1978	Chi-A	12	12	.500	30	30	6	1	0	212	196	19	84	118	12.0	4.37	87	.247	.321	0	—	0	-14	-13	-1	-1.5
1979	*Bal-A	11	7	.611	32	32	3	0	0	186	173	31	73	96	12.0	3.77	106	.248	.320	0	—	0	9	5	1	0.7
1980	Bal-A★	**25**	7	**.781**	37	37	9	1	0	250^{2}	224	22	101	149	11.9	3.23	122	.240	.319	0	—	0	22	20	-2	1.8
1981	Bal-A	4	7	.364	15	12	0	0	0	62^{2}	63	7	27	30	13.1	4.60	79	.266	.343	0	—	0	-7	-7	-0	-0.7
Total	11	107	93	.535	320	269	43	7	1	1788^{1}	1707	184	716	1065	12.4	3.97	97	.253	.328	22	.100	-10	-32	-22	-0	-3.3
● **TIGE STONE**	Stone, William Arthur b: 9/18/01, Macon, Ga. d: 1/1/60, Jacksonville, Fla. BR/TR, 5'8", 145 lbs. Deb: 8/23/23 ♦																									
1923	StL-N	0	0	—	1	0	0	0	0	3	5	1	3	1	24.0	12.00	33	.455	.571	1	1.000	0	-3	-3	0	-0.2
● **BILL STONEMAN**	Stoneman, William Hambly b: 4/7/44, Oak Park, Ill. BR/TR, 5'10", 170 lbs. Deb: 7/16/67																									
1967	Chi-N	2	4	.333	28	2	0	0	4	63	51	7	22	52	10.4	3.29	108	.223	.291	0	.000	-1	1	2	-1	0.0
1968	Chi-N	0	1	.000	18	0	0	0	0	29^{1}	35	6	14	18	15.3	5.52	57	.310	.391	0	.000	-0	-8	-8	-0	-0.9
1969	Mon-N	11	19	.367	42	36	8	5	0	235^{2}	233	26	123	185	14.1	4.39	84	.261	.358	4	.055	-3	-21	-19	-1	-2.3
1970	Mon-N	7	15	.318	40	30	5	3	0	207^{2}	209	26	109	176	14.4	4.59	90	.263	.361	6	.100	-2	-13	-11	-1	-1.4
1971	Mon-N	17	16	.515	39	39	20	3	0	294^{2}	243	20	146	251	12.0	3.15	112	.225	.321	12	.129	-1	10	12	0	1.4
1972	Mon-N★	12	14	.462	36	35	13	4	0	250^{2}	213	15	102	171	11.4	2.98	119	.229	.308	6	.080	-4	13	16	0	1.3
1973	Mon-N	4	8	.333	29	17	0	0	1	96^{2}	120	12	55	48	16.9	6.80	56	.310	.404	1	.050	-1	-34	-32	0	-3.2
1974	Cal-A	1	8	.111	13	11	0	0	0	58^{2}	78	8	31	33	17.0	6.14	56	.322	.404	0	—	0	-16	-18	0	-1.7
Total	8	54	85	.388	245	170	46	15	5	1236^{1}	1182	120	602	934	13.3	4.08	90	.253	.344	29	.086	-13	-68	-57	-3	-6.8
● **LIL STONER**	Stoner, Ulysses Simpson Grant b: 2/28/1899, Bowie, Tex. d: 6/26/66, Enid, Okla. BR/TR, 5'9.5", 180 lbs. Deb: 4/15/22																									
1922	Det-A	4	4	.500	17	7	2	0	0	62^{2}	76	3	35	18	16.4	7.04	55	.315	.409	2	.100	-1	-21	-22	1	-2.0
1924	Det-A	11	11	.500	36	25	10	1	0	215^{2}	271	13	65	66	14.2	4.72	87	.316	.367	15	.195	1	-12	-14	-1	-1.3
1925	Det-A	10	9	.526	34	18	8	0	1	152	166	6	53	51	13.5	4.26	101	.283	.352	16	.291	4	2	1	-3	0.1
1926	Det-A	7	10	.412	32	22	7	0	0	159^{2}	179	11	63	57	13.8	5.47	74	.291	.359	9	.170	-2	-26	-25	-0	-2.5
1927	Det-A	10	13	.435	38	24	13	0	5	215	251	9	77	63	13.9	3.98	106	.301	.362	8	.108	-6	4	6	-2	-0.2
1928	Det-A	5	8	.385	36	11	4	0	4	126^{1}	151	16	42	29	14.0	4.35	95	.296	.353	7	.179	-1	-4	-3	-2	-0.6
1929	Det-A	3	3	.500	24	3	1	0	4	53	57	2	31	12	15.3	5.26	82	.288	.390	1	.067	-2	-6	-6	2	-0.6
1930	Pit-N	0	0	—	5	0	0	0	0	5^{2}	7	2	3	1	15.9	4.76	105	.318	.400	0	—	0	0	0	0	0.0
1931	Phi-N	0	0	—	7	1	0	0	0	13^{2}	22	0	5	2	17.8	6.59	64	.373	.422	0	.000	-1	-4	-4	-0	-0.4
Total	9	50	58	.463	229	111	45	1	14	1003^{2}	1180	62	374	299	14.2	4.76	87	.301	.366	58	.172	-7	-66	-67	-5	-7.5
● **MEL STOTTLEMYRE**	Stottlemyre, Melvin Leon Jr. b: 12/28/63, Prosser, Wash. BR/TR, 6', 190 lbs. Deb: 7/17/90 F																									
1990	KC-A	0	1	.000	13	2	0	0	0	31^{1}	35	3	12	14	13.5	4.88	78	.280	.343	0	—	0	-3	-4	0	-0.4

YEAR	TM/L	W	L	PCT	G	GS	CG	SH	SV	IP	H	HR	BB	SO	RAT	ERA	ERA+	OAV	OOB	BH	AVG	PB	PR	/A	PD	TPI
● **MEL STOTTLEMYRE**	Stottlemyre, Melvin Leon Sr. b: 11/13/41, Hazelton, Mo. BR/TR, 6'2", 190 lbs. Deb: 8/12/64 FC																									
1964	*NY-A	9	3	.750	13	12	5	2	0	96	77	3	35	49	10.7	2.06	176	.219	.294	9	.243	2	17	17	1	2.3
1965	NY-A☆	20	9	.690	37	37	**18**	4	0	**291**	250	18	88	155	10.7	2.63	129	.233	.295	13	.131	1	27	25	6	3.5
1966	NY-A★	12	20	.375	37	35	9	3	1	251	239	18	82	146	11.5	3.80	87	.253	.313	11	.138	1	-10	-13	4	-0.9
1967	NY-A	15	15	.500	36	36	10	4	0	255	235	20	88	151	11.5	2.96	105	.248	.313	8	.098	-3	8	5	6	0.8
1968	NY-A★	21	12	.636	36	36	19	6	0	278^{2}	243	21	65	140	10.0	2.45	118	.234	.281	13	.143	2	16	14	2	2.1
1969	NY-A★	20	14	.588	39	39	**24**	3	0	303	267	19	97	113	11.0	2.82	123	.239	.303	18	.178	5	27	22	8	3.8
1970	NY-A★	15	13	.536	37	37	14	0	0	271	262	23	84	126	11.7	3.09	114	.255	.315	16	.188	8	19	13	2	2.5
1971	NY-A	16	12	.571	35	35	19	7	0	269^{2}	234	16	69	132	10.2	2.87	113	.233	.285	16	.170	2	18	11	3	1.7
1972	NY-A	14	18	.438	36	36	9	7	0	260	250	13	85	110	11.7	3.22	92	.254	.316	16	.200	3	-5	-8	3	-0.2
1973	NY-A	16	16	.500	38	38	19	4	0	273	259	13	79	95	11.3	3.07	119	.253	.310	0	—	0	23	18	2	2.1
1974	NY-A	6	7	.462	16	15	6	0	0	113	119	7	37	40	12.7	3.58	97	.272	.335	0	—	0	0	-1	-1	-0.2
Total	11	164	139	.541	360	356	152	40	1	2661^{1}	2435	171	809	1257	11.1	2.97	112	.245	.304	120	.160	20	139	102	36	17.5
● **TODD STOTTLEMYRE**	Stottlemyre, Todd Vernon b: 5/20/65, Sunnyside, Wash. BL/TR, 6'3", 195 lbs. Deb: 4/06/88 F																									
1988	Tor-A	4	8	.333	28	16	0	0	0	98	109	15	46	67	14.6	5.69	69	.283	.366	0	—	0	-19	-19	-0	-1.9
1989	*Tor-A	7	7	.500	27	18	0	0	0	127^{2}	137	11	44	63	13.1	3.88	97	.282	.348	0	—	0	0	-2	-1	-0.3
1990	Tor-A	13	17	.433	33	33	4	0	0	203	214	18	69	115	12.9	4.34	91	.274	.339	0	—	0	-10	-9	1	-0.8
1991	*Tor-A	15	8	.652	34	34	1	0	0	219	194	21	75	116	11.5	3.78	111	.235	.308	0	—	0	8	10	-0	0.8
1992	*Tor-A	12	11	.522	28	27	6	2	0	174	175	20	63	98	12.8	4.50	91	.262	.334	0	—	0	-11	-8	-1	-1.0
Total	5	51	51	.500	150	128	11	2	0	821^{2}	829	85	297	459	12.8	4.32	93	.263	.334	0	—	0	-32	-28	-1	-3.2
● **ALLYN STOUT**	Stout, Allyn McClelland "Fish Hook" b: 10/31/04, Peoria, Ill. d: 12/22/74, Sikestown, Mo. BR/TR, 5'10", 167 lbs. Deb: 5/16/31																									
1931	StL-N	6	0	1.000	30	3	1	0	3	72^{2}	87	2	34	40	15.1	4.21	93	.305	.381	2	.105	-1	-3	-2	1	-0.3
1932	StL-N	4	5	.444	36	3	1	0	1	73^{2}	87	5	28	32	14.5	4.40	89	.305	.375	2	.100	-1	-4	-4	1	-0.5
1933	StL-N	0	0	—	1	0	0	0	0	2	1	0	1	1	9.0	0.00	—	.167	.286	0	—	0	1	1	0	0.1
	Cin-N	2	3	.400	23	5	2	0	0	71^{1}	85	3	26	29	14.0	3.79	90	.295	.354	4	.182	-0	-4	-3	-1	-0.4
	Yr	2	3	.400	24	5	2	0	0	73^{1}	86	3	27	30	13.9	3.68	92	.293	.352	4	.182	-0	-3	-2	-1	-0.3
1934	Cin-N	6	8	.429	41	16	4	0	1	140^{2}	170	10	47	51	14.1	4.86	84	.297	.354	8	.186	0	-13	-12	-0	-1.2
1935	NY-N	1	4	.200	40	2	0	0	5	88	99	7	37	29	14.3	4.91	79	.289	.365	2	.133	0	-9	-10	-1	-1.1
1943	Bos-N	1	0	1.000	9	0	0	0	1	9^{1}	17	1	4	3	20.3	6.75	51	.378	.429	0	.000	-0	-3	-3	-0	-0.4
Total	6	20	20	.500	180	29	8	0	11	457^{2}	546	28	177	185	14.5	4.54	85	.299	.365	18	.149	-3	-35	-34	-1	-3.8
● **JESSE STOVALL**	Stovall, Jesse Cramer "Scout" b: 7/24/1875, Independence, Mo. d: 7/12/55, San Diego, Cal. BL/TR, 6', 175 lbs. Deb: 8/31/03 F																									
1903	Cle-A	5	1	.833	6	6	6	2	0	57	44	0	21	12	10.7	2.05	139	.213	.295	1	.045	-2	6	5	-1	0.2
1904	Det-A	3	13	.188	22	17	13	1	0	146^{2}	170	3	45	41	14.2	4.42	58	.291	.359	11	.196	0	-30	-30	0	-3.1
Total	2	8	14	.364	28	23	19	3	0	203^{2}	214	3	66	53	13.3	3.76	70	.270	.342	12	.154	-2	-24	-25	-0	-2.9
● **HARRY STOVEY**	Stovey, Harry Duffield (b: Harry Duffield Stowe) b: 12/20/1856, Philadelphia, Pa. d: 9/20/37, New Bedford, Mass BR/TR, 5'11.5", 175 lbs. Deb: 5/01/1880 M♦																									
1880	Wor-N	0	0	—	2	0	0	0	0	6	8	0	3	3	16.5	4.50	58	.308	.379	94	.265	0	-1	-1	-0	-0.1
1883	Phi-a	0	0	—	1	0	0	0	0	3	5	0	0	4	15.0	9.00	39	.349	.349	127	.302	0	-2	-2	-0	-0.1
1886	Phi-a	0	0	—	1	0	0	0	0	0^{1}	2	0	0	0	54.0	27.00	13	.667	.667	144	.294	0	-1	-1	0	-0.1
Total	3	0	0	—	4	0	0	0	0	9^{1}	15	0	3	7	17.4	6.75	43	.346	.389	1769	.288	1	-4	-4	-0	-0.3
● **HAL STOWE**	Stowe, Harold Rudolph b: 8/29/37, Gastonia, N.C. BL/TL, 6', 170 lbs. Deb: 9/30/60																									
1960	NY-A	0	0	—	1	0	0	0	0	1	0	0	1	0	9.0	9.00	40	.000	.500	0	—	0	-1	-1	-0	-0.1
● **MIKE STRAHLER**	Strahler, Michael Wayne b: 3/14/47, Chicago, Ill. BR/TR, 6'4", 180 lbs. Deb: 9/12/70																									
1970	LA-N	1	1	.500	6	0	0	0	1	18^{2}	13	1	10	11	11.1	1.45	265	.194	.299	2	.250	0	5	5	0	0.5
1971	LA-N	0	0	—	6	0	0	0	0	12^{2}	10	1	8	7	12.8	2.84	114	.217	.333	0	.000	-0	1	1	-0	0.0
1972	LA-N	1	2	.333	19	2	1	0	0	47	42	5	22	25	12.4	3.26	102	.237	.325	2	.182	1	1	0	-0	0.1
1973	Det-A	4	5	.444	22	11	1	0	0	80^{1}	84	7	39	37	13.9	4.37	94	.273	.356	0	—	0	-5	-3	-1	-0.3
Total	4	6	8	.429	53	13	2	0	1	158^{2}	149	14	79	80	13.0	3.57	105	.249	.339	4	.200	1	2	3	-1	0.3
● **DICK STRAHS**	Strahs, Richard Bernard b: 12/4/24, Evanston, Ill. BL/TR, 6', 192 lbs. Deb: 7/24/54																									
1954	Chi-A	0	0	—	9	0	0	0	1	14^{1}	16	0	8	8	15.1	5.65	66	.271	.358	0	.000	-0	-3	-3	0	-0.3
● **LES STRAKER**	Straker, Lester Paul (Bolnalda) b: 10/10/59, Ciudad Bolivar, Ven BR/TR, 6'1", 193 lbs. Deb: 4/11/87																									
1987	*Min-A	8	10	.444	31	26	1	0	0	154^{1}	150	24	59	76	12.3	4.37	106	.257	.328	0	—	0	1	4	-2	0.3
1988	Min-A	2	5	.286	16	14	1	1	1	82^{2}	86	8	25	23	12.1	3.92	104	.276	.329	0	—	0	0	1	0	0.2
Total	2	10	15	.400	47	40	2	1	1	237	236	32	84	99	12.2	4.22	105	.264	.328	0	—	0	2	5	-1	0.5
● **BOB STRAMPE**	Strampe, Robert Edwin b: 6/13/50, Janesville, Wis. BB/TR, 6'1", 185 lbs. Deb: 5/10/72																									
1972	Det-A	0	0	—	7	0	0	0	0	4^{2}	6	0	7	4	25.1	11.57	27	.300	.481	0	—	0	-4	-4	-0	-0.5
● **PAUL STRAND**	Strand, Paul Edward b: 12/19/1893, Carbonado, Wash. d: 7/2/74, Salt Lake City, Utah BR/TL, 6'0.5", 190 lbs. Deb: 5/15/13 ♦																									
1913	Bos-N	0	0	—	7	0	0	0	0	17	22	1	12	6	18.0	2.12	155	.393	.500	1	.167	-0	2	2	0	0.2
1914	Bos-N	6	2	.750	16	3	1	0	1	55^{1}	47	1	23	33	11.5	2.44	113	.235	.317	8	.333	2	2	2	-0	0.4
1915	Bos-N	1	1	.500	6	2	2	0	1	22^{2}	26	0	3	13	11.5	2.38	109	.295	.319	2	.091	-0	1	1	-1	-0.1
Total	3	7	3	.700	29	5	3	0	2	95	95	2	38	52	12.7	2.37	119	.276	.350	49	.224	2	5	5	-1	0.5
● **SCOTT STRATTON**	Stratton, C. Scott b: 10/2/1869, Campbellsburg, Ky. d: 3/8/39, Louisville, Ky. BL/TR, 6', 180 lbs. Deb: 4/21/1888 ♦																									
1888	Lou-a	10	17	.370	33	28	28	2	0	269^{2}	287	7	53	97	11.8	3.64	85	.263	.306	64	.257	4	-17	-17	-1	-1.1
1889	Lou-a	3	13	.188	19	17	13	0	1	133^{2}	157	6	42	42	13.9	3.23	119	.284	.342	66	.288	4	9	9	2	1.4
1890	*Lou-a	34	14	**.708**	50	49	44	4	0	431	398	3	61	207	**9.9**	**2.36**	**163**	.238	**.270**	61	.323	15	**72**	**71**	6	**8.9**
1891	Pit-N	0	2	.000	2	2	2	0	0	18^{1}	16	0	5	5	10.3	2.45	134	.226	.277	1	.125	-1	2	2	1	0.2
	Lou-a	6	13	.316	20	20	20	1	0	172	204	10	34	52	12.8	4.08	90	.285	.324	27	.235	1	-7	-8	3	-0.3
1892	Lou-N	21	19	.525	42	40	39	2	0	351^{2}	342	1	70	93	10.8	2.92	105	.245	.285	56	.256	9	14	6	2	1.7
1893	Lou-N	12	23	.343	37	35	34	1	0	314^{2}	445	8	100	43	15.8	5.43	81	.323	.373	49	.226	3	-27	-36	5	-2.1
1894	Lou-N	1	5	.167	7	5	4	0	0	43	72	3	13	3	18.4	8.37	61	.368	.415	12	.324	2	-15	-16	0	-1.0
	Chi-N	8	5	.615	15	12	11	0	0	119^{1}	198	5	40	23	18.2	6.03	93	.366	.412	36	.375	7	-9	-6	0	0.2
	Yr	9	10	.474	22	17	15	0	0	162^{1}	270	8	53	26	18.1	6.65	82	.365	.409	48	.361	9	-24	-21	1	-0.8
1895	Chi-N	2	3	.400	5	5	3	0	0	30	51	1	14	4	20.7	9.60	53	.370	.442	7	.292	1	-16	-15	1	-1.0
Total	8	97	114	.460	230	213	198	10	1	1883^{1}	2170	44	432	569	12.8	3.87	99	.280	.324	379	.274	46	7	-10	20	6.9
● **MONTY STRATTON**	Stratton, Monty Franklin Pierce "Gander" b: 5/21/12, Celeste, Tex. d: 9/29/82, Greenville, Tex. BR/TR, 6'5", 180 lbs. Deb: 6/02/34 C																									
1934	Chi-A	0	0	—	1	0	0	0	0	3^{1}	4	0	1	0	13.5	5.40	88	.333	.385	0	.000	-0	-0	-0	-0	-0.1
1935	Chi-A	1	2	.333	5	5	2	0	0	38	40	0	9	8	12.1	4.03	115	.274	.325	2	.143	-1	2	3	0	0.2
1936	Chi-A	5	7	.417	16	14	3	0	0	95	117	8	46	37	15.5	5.21	100	.305	.381	8	.216	1	-2	-0	2	0.2
1937	Chi-A†	15	5	.750	22	21	14	5	0	164^{2}	142	6	37	69	**9.9**	2.40	**191**	.234	**.280**	12	.200	-0	41	40	1	4.1
1938	Chi-A	15	9	.625	26	22	17	0	2	186^{1}	186	18	56	82	12.0	4.01	122	.255	.315	21	.266	5	16	18	0	2.2
Total	5	36	23	.610	70	62	36	5	2	487^{1}	489	32	149	196	12.0	3.71	130	.261	.319	43	.224	5	56	61	3	6.6
● **ED STRATTON**	Stratton, William Edward b: Baltimore, Md. Deb: 5/14/1873																									
1873	Mar-n	0	3	.000	3	3	3	0	0	27	75	3	0	0	25.0	8.33	39	.410	.410	2	.125	-1	-15	-15		-1.0

YEAR TM/L	W	L	PCT	G	GS	CG	SH	SV	IP	H	HR	BB	SO	RAT	ERA	ERA+	OAV	OOB	BH	AVG	PB	PR	/A	PD	TPI

● JOE STRAUSS   Strauss, Joseph "Dutch" or "The Socker" (b: Joseph Strasser)
b: 11/16/1858, Cincinnati, Ohio   d: 6/24/06, Cincinnati, Ohio   BR/TR   Deb: 7/27/1884 ♦

| 1886 Lou-a | 0 | 0 | — | 2 | 0 | 0 | 0 | 1 | 4 | 6 | 0 | 3 | 0 | 20.3 | 4.50 | 81 | .231 | .310 | 64 | .215 | -0 | -0 | -0 | -0 | -0.1 |

● OSCAR STREIT   Streit, Oscar William   b: 7/7/1873, Florence, Ala.   d: 10/10/35, Birmingham, Ala.   BL/TL, 6'5", 190 lbs.   Deb: 4/21/1899

1899 Bos-N	1	0	1.000	2	1	1	0	0	14²	15	1	15	0	19.6	6.75	62	.264	.434	0	.000	-1	-5	-4	0	-0.4
1902 Cle-A	0	7	.000	8	7	4	0	0	51²	72	3	25	10	17.4	5.23	66	.330	.406	4	.211	1	-9	-10	-1	-0.9
Total 2	1	7	.125	10	8	5	0	0	66¹	87	4	40	10	17.9	5.56	65	.316	.412	4	.154	-0	-14	-14	-1	-1.3

● ED STRELECKI   Strelecki, Edward Harold   b: 4/10/05, Newark, N.J.   d: 1/9/68, Newark, N.J.   BR/TR, 5'11.5", 180 lbs.   Deb: 4/16/28

1928 StL-A	0	2	.000	22	2	1	0	1	50¹	49	4	17	8	12.0	4.29	98	.269	.335	2	.200	0	-1	-1	-0	0.0
1929 StL-A	1	1	.500	7	0	0	0	0	11	12	1	6	2	15.5	4.91	90	.279	.380	0	.000	-0	-1	-1	-0	-0.1
1931 Cin-N	0	0	—	13	0	0	0	0	24¹	37	2	9	3	18.1	9.25	40	.394	.462	1	.200	0	-15	-15	-0	-1.3
Total 3	1	3	.250	42	2	1	0	1	85²	98	7	32	13	14.2	5.78	71	.307	.379	3	.176	0	-17	-16	1	-1.4

● PHIL STREMMEL   Stremmel, Philip   b: 4/16/1880, Zanesville, Ohio   d: 12/26/47, Chicago, Ill.   BR/TR, 6', 175 lbs.   Deb: 9/16/09

1909 StL-A	0	2	.000	2	2	2	0	0	18	20	0	4	6	12.5	4.50	54	.308	.357	0	.000	-1	-4	-4	-0	-0.4
1910 StL-A	0	2	.000	5	2	2	0	0	29	31	0	16	7	14.6	3.72	66	.287	.379	1	.125	-0	-4	-4	2	-0.3
Total 2	0	4	.000	7	4	4	0	0	47	51	0	20	13	13.8	4.02	61	.295	.371	1	.071	-1	-8	-8	2	-0.7

● CUB STRICKER   Stricker, John A. (b: John A. Streaker)
b: 2/15/1860, Philadelphia, Pa.   d: 11/19/37, Philadelphia, Pa.   BR/TR, 5'3", 138 lbs.   Deb: 5/02/1882 M♦

1882 Phi-a	1	0	1.000	2	0	0	0	0	7	3	0	1	2	5.1	1.29	232	.121	.155	59	.217	-0	1	1	-0	0.1
1884 Phi-a	0	0	—	1	0	0	0	0	3	6	0	1	1	21.0	6.00	57	.333	.368	92	.231	0	-1	-1	-0	-0.1
1887 Cle-a	0	0	—	3	0	0	0	0	5²	5	0	7	2	19.1	3.18	137	.238	.429	141	.264	0	1	1	0	0.1
1888 Cle-a	1	0	1.000	2	0	0	0	1	12	16	0	2	5	14.3	4.50	69	.309	.347	115	.233	1	-2	-2	-0	-0.2
Total 4	2	0	1.000	8	0	0	0	1	27²	30	0	11	10	13.7	3.58	94	.260	.329	1107	.239	1	-1	-1	-0	-0.1

● JIM STRICKLAND   Strickland, James Michael   b: 6/12/46, Los Angeles, Cal.   BL/TL, 6', 175 lbs.   Deb: 5/19/71

1971 Min-A	1	0	1.000	24	0	0	0	1	31¹	20	2	18	21	11.5	1.44	247	.183	.310	0	.000	0	7	7	0	0.8
1972 Min-A	3	1	.750	25	0	0	0	3	36	28	7	19	30	11.8	2.50	128	.214	.313	1	.333	1	2	3	0	0.4
1973 Min-A	0	1	.000	7	0	0	0	0	5¹	11	0	5	6	27.0	11.81	34	.440	.533	0	—	0	-5	-5	-0	-0.5
1975 Cle-A	0	0	—	4	0	0	0	1	4²	4	0	2	3	13.5	1.93	196	.222	.333	0	—	0	1	1	-0	0.1
Total 4	4	2	.667	60	0	0	0	5	77¹	63	9	44	60	12.8	2.68	128	.223	.333	1	.250	1	6	7	0	0.8

● BILL STRICKLAND   Strickland, William Goss   b: 3/29/08, Nashville, Ga.   BR/TR, 6'2", 170 lbs.   Deb: 9/16/37

| 1937 StL-A | 0 | 0 | — | 9 | 0 | 0 | 0 | 0 | 21¹ | 28 | 2 | 15 | 6 | 19.0 | 5.91 | 82 | .341 | .455 | 1 | .167 | -0 | -3 | -3 | -0 | -0.3 |

● ELMER STRICKLETT   Stricklett, Elmer Griffin "Spitball"   b: 8/29/1876, Glasco, Kan.   d: 6/7/64, Santa Cruz, Cal.   BR/TR, 5'6", 140 lbs.   Deb: 4/22/04

1904 Chi-A	0	1	.000	1	1	0	0	0	7	12	0	2	3	18.0	10.29	24	.377	.414	0	.000	-0	-6	-6	0	-0.5
1905 Bro-N	9	18	.333	33	28	25	1	1	237¹	259	0	71	77	13.0	3.34	87	.282	.343	13	.148	-1	-9	-12	9	-0.4
1906 Bro-N	14	18	.438	41	35	28	5	5	291²	273	2	77	88	11.0	2.72	93	.253	.306	20	.206	5	-3	-6	9	0.8
1907 Bro-N	12	14	.462	29	26	25	4	0	229²	211	1	65	69	11.1	2.27	103	.255	.315	12	.148	1	5	2	7	1.1
Total 4	35	51	.407	104	90	78	10	6	765²	755	3	215	237	11.7	2.84	91	.264	.322	45	.167	4	-12	-22	25	1.0

● JOHN STRIKE   Strike, John   b: 1865, Pennsylvania   Deb: 9/24/1886

| 1886 Phi-N | 1 | 1 | .500 | 2 | 2 | 1 | 0 | 0 | 15 | 19 | 1 | 7 | 11 | 15.6 | 4.80 | 69 | .311 | .382 | 0 | .000 | -1 | -2 | -2 | -1 | -0.3 |

● JAKE STRIKER   Striker, Wilbur Scott   b: 10/23/33, New Washington, O.   BL/TL, 6'2", 200 lbs.   Deb: 9/25/59

1959 Cle-A	1	0	1.000	1	1	0	0	0	6²	8	0	4	5	16.2	2.70	136	.296	.387	1	.000	1	1	1	0	0.1
1960 Chi-A	0	0	—	2	0	0	0	0	3²	5	1	1	1	17.2	4.91	77	.357	.438	0	—	0	-0	-0	-0	-0.1
Total 2	1	0	1.000	3	1	0	0	0	10¹	13	1	5	6	16.5	3.48	107	.317	.404	1	.000	1	0	0	-0	0.0

● NICK STRINCEVICH   Strincevich, Nicholas Mihailovich "Jumbo"   b: 3/1/15, Gary, Ind.   BR/TR, 6'1", 180 lbs.   Deb: 4/23/40

1940 Bos-N	4	8	.333	32	14	5	0	1	128²	142	17	63	54	14.9	5.53	67	.278	.367	5	.116	-2	-24	-26	-2	-2.8
1941 Bos-N	0	0	—	3	0	0	0	0	3¹	7	0	6	1	37.8	10.80	33	.412	.583	0	—	-1	-3	-3	0	-0.2
Pit-N	1	2	.333	12	3	0	0	0	31	35	4	13	12	14.2	5.23	69	.280	.353	3	.429	1	-5	-5	0	-0.5
Yr	1	2	.333	15	3	0	0	0	34¹	42	4	19	13	16.3	5.77	63	.294	.380	3	.429	-0	-8	-8	0	-0.7
1942 Pit-N	0	0	—	7	1	0	0	0	22¹	19	2	9	10	11.7	2.82	120	.229	.312	0	.000	-1	1	1	-0	0.1
1944 Pit-N	14	7	.667	40	26	11	0	2	190	190	5	37	47	10.9	3.08	121	.257	.296	9	.158	-1	14	13	5	1.8
1945 Pit-N	16	10	.615	36	29	18	1	2	228¹	235	7	49	74	11.3	3.31	119	.260	.301	17	.202	0	12	16	-2	1.5
1946 Pit-N	10	15	.400	32	22	11	3	1	176	185	7	44	49	11.9	3.58	98	.268	.316	8	.154	1	-3	-1	-2	-0.2
1947 Pit-N	1	6	.143	32	7	1	0	0	89	111	9	37	22	15.2	5.26	80	.316	.385	1	.048	-2	-12	-10	-0	-1.2
1948 Pit-N	0	0	—	3	0	0	0	0	4²	8	0	2	1	20.8	8.31	49	.444	.500	0	—	0	-2	-2	-0	-0.2
Phi-N	0	1	.000	6	1	0	0	0	16²	26	1	10	4	19.4	9.18	43	.347	.424	0	.000	-1	-10	-10	-1	-1.0
Yr	0	1	.000	9	1	0	0	0	21	34	1	12	5	19.7	9.00	44	.366	.438	0	.000	-1	-12	-12	-1	-1.2
Total 8	46	49	.484	203	103	46	4	6	889²	958	52	270	274	12.7	4.05	93	.273	.329	43	.158	-4	-34	-26	-0	-2.7

● JOHN STROHMAYER   Strohmayer, John Emery   b: 10/13/46, Belle Fourche, S.D.   BR/TR, 6'1", 181 lbs.   Deb: 4/29/70

1970 Mon-N	3	1	.750	42	0	0	0	0	76	85	7	39	74	14.9	4.86	85	.279	.364	1	.167	-0	-7	-6	-0	-0.6
1971 Mon-N	7	5	.583	27	14	2	0	1	114	124	16	31	56	12.6	4.34	81	.281	.333	8	.229	1	-11	-10	-1	-1.1
1972 Mon-N	1	2	.333	48	0	0	0	3	76²	73	6	31	50	12.3	3.52	101	.256	.331	0	.000	-0	-1	0	1	0.1
1973 Mon-N	0	0	—	17	3	0	0	0	34²	34	4	22	15	14.8	5.19	73	.260	.370	1	.200	-0	-6	-5	-0	-0.5
NY-N	0	1	.000	7	0	0	0	0	10	13	2	4	5	15.3	8.10	45	.310	.370	0	—	0	-5	-5	-0	-0.5
Yr	0	1	.000	24	3	0	0	0	44²	47	6	26	20	14.7	5.84	65	.270	.365	1	.200	-0	-11	-10	-1	-1.0
1974 NY-N	0	0	—	1	0	0	0	0	1	0	0	1	0	9.0	0.00	—	.000	.250	0	—	0	0	0	0	0.0
Total 5	11	9	.550	142	17	2	0	4	312¹	329	35	128	200	13.4	4.47	83	.272	.346	10	.200	1	-29	-26	-0	-2.6

● BRENT STROM   Strom, Brent Terry   b: 10/14/48, San Diego, Cal.   BR/TL, 6'3", 190 lbs.   Deb: 7/31/72

1972 NY-N	0	3	.000	11	5	0	0	0	30¹	34	7	15	20	14.5	6.82	49	.296	.377	0	.000	-1	-11	-12	-1	-1.3
1973 Cle-A	2	10	.167	27	18	2	0	0	123	134	18	47	91	13.5	4.61	85	.278	.346	0	—	0	-11	-9	1	-0.9
1975 SD-N	8	8	.500	18	16	6	2	0	120¹	103	6	33	56	10.3	2.54	137	.233	.289	3	.100	-1	14	12	1	1.3
1976 SD-N	12	16	.429	36	33	8	1	0	210²	188	15	73	103	11.2	3.29	99	.239	.305	4	.063	-2	5	0	-0	-0.2
1977 SD-N	0	2	.000	8	3	0	0	0	16²	23	5	12	8	18.9	12.42	28	.329	.427	1	.333	0	-16	-16	-0	-1.5
Total 5	22	39	.361	100	75	16	3	0	501	482	51	180	278	12.0	3.95	88	.254	.321	8	.078	-3	-19	-26	0	-2.6

● FLOYD STROMME   Stromme, Floyd Marvin "Rock"   b: 8/1/16, Copperstown, N.Dak.   BR/TR, 5'11", 170 lbs.   Deb: 7/05/39

| 1939 Cle-A | 0 | 1 | .000 | 5 | 0 | 0 | 0 | 0 | 13 | 13 | 1 | 13 | 4 | 18.0 | 4.85 | 91 | .265 | .419 | 1 | .333 | 0 | -0 | -1 | -0 | -0.1 |

● SAILOR STROUD   Stroud, Ralph Vivian   b: 5/15/1885, Ironia, N.J.   d: 4/11/70, Stockton, Cal.   BR/TR, 6', 160 lbs.   Deb: 4/29/10

1910 Det-A	5	9	.357	28	15	7	3	1	130¹	123	9	41	63	11.8	3.25	81	.257	.325	1	.026	-4	-11	-9	-4	-1.8
1915 NY-N	12	9	.571	32	22	8	0	1	184	194	3	35	62	11.5	2.79	92	.281	.321	9	.161	-1	-1	-5	-0	-0.6
1916 NY-N	3	2	.600	10	4	0	0	1	46²	47	1	9	16	11.0	2.70	90	.266	.305	1	.071	-1	-0	-1	-0	-0.3
Total 3	20	20	.500	70	41	15	3	3	361	364	13	85	141	11.5	2.94	88	.271	.321	11	.101	-6	-12	-15	-4	-2.7

YEAR	TM/L	W	L	PCT	G	GS	CG	SH	SV	IP	H	HR	BB	SO	RAT	ERA	ERA+	OAV	OOB	BH	AVG	PB	PR	/A	PD	TPI

● **STEAMBOAT STRUSS** Struss, Clarence Herbert b: 2/24/09, Riverdale, Ill. d: 9/12/85, Grand Rapids, Mich. BR/TR, 5'11", 163 lbs. Deb: 9/30/34

| 1934 | Pit-N | 0 | 1 | .000 | 1 | 1 | 0 | 0 | 0 | 7 | 7 | 0 | 6 | 3 | 16.7 | 6.43 | 64 | .250 | .382 | 1 | .333 | 0 | -2 | -2 | 0 | -0.1 |

● **DUTCH STRYKER** Stryker, Sterling Alpa b: 7/29/1895, Atlantic Highlands, N.J. d: 11/5/64, Red Bank, N.J. BR/TR, 5'11.5", 180 lbs. Deb: 4/16/24

1924	Bos-N	3	8	.273	20	10	2	0	0	73¹	90	4	22	22	13.9	6.01	64	.314	.365	5	.217	-0	-17	-18	2	-1.5
1926	Bro-N	0	0	—	2	0	0	0	0	2	8	0	1	0	40.5	27.00	14	.571	.600	0	—	0	-5	-5	-0	-0.5
Total	2	3	8	.273	22	10	2	0	0	75¹	98	4	23	22	14.6	6.57	58	.326	.375	5	.217	-0	-23	-23	2	-2.0

● **JOHNNY STUART** Stuart, John Davis "Stud" b: 4/27/01, Clinton, Tenn. d: 5/13/70, Charleston, W.Va. BR/TR, 5'11", 170 lbs. Deb: 7/27/22

1922	StL-N	0	0	—	2	1	0	0	0	2	2	0	2	1	22.5	9.00	43	.222	.417	0	—	0	-1	-1	-0	-0.1
1923	StL-N	9	5	.643	37	10	7	1	3	149²	139	11	70	55	13.1	4.27	91	.252	.345	14	.246	1	-4	-6	-1	-0.7
1924	StL-N	9	11	.450	28	22	13	0	0	159	167	12	60	54	13.1	4.75	80	.273	.343	11	.204	-1	-16	-17	-3	-2.0
1925	StL-N	2	2	.500	15	1	1	0	0	47	52	6	24	14	14.9	6.13	71	.278	.366	4	.250	1	-10	-9	-0	-0.8
Total	4	20	18	.526	82	34	21	1	3	357²	360	29	156	124	13.4	4.76	82	.265	.348	29	.228	1	-31	-34	-5	-3.6

● **MARLIN STUART** Stuart, Marlin Henry b: 8/8/18, Paragould, Ark. BL/TR, 6'2", 185 lbs. Deb: 4/26/49

1949	Det-A	0	2	.000	14	2	0	0	0	29²	39	3	35	14	22.4	9.10	46	.348	.503	2	.333	1	-16	-16	0	-1.4
1950	Det-A	3	1	.750	19	1	0	0	0	43²	59	6	22	19	16.9	5.56	84	.330	.406	1	.083	-1	-5	-4	0	-0.5
1951	Det-A	4	6	.400	29	15	5	0	1	124	119	9	71	46	14.3	3.77	111	.258	.365	10	.233	1	5	6	0	0.7
1952	Det-A	3	2	.600	30	9	2	0	1	91¹	91	8	48	32	14.0	4.93	77	.265	.360	2	.087	-1	-13	-11	-0	-1.3
	StL-A	1	2	.333	12	2	0	0	1	26	26	3	9	13	12.1	4.15	94	.260	.321	0	.000	-1	-1	-1	-0	-0.2
	Yr	4	4	.500	42	11	2	0	2	117¹	117	11	57	45	13.3	4.76	81	.262	.346	2	.069	-2	-14	-12	-1	-1.5
1953	StL-A	8	2	.800	60	2	0	0	7	114¹	136	6	44	46	14.2	3.94	107	.300	.363	5	.192	-1	1	3	0	0.2
1954	Bal-A	1	2	.333	22	0	0	0	2	38¹	46	2	15	13	14.8	4.46	80	.300	.373	0	.000	-0	-4	-4	0	-0.4
	NY-A	3	0	1.000	10	0	0	0	1	18¹	28	0	12	2	19.6	5.40	64	.350	.435	2	.333	0	-3	-4	0	-0.3
	Yr	4	2	.667	32	0	0	0	3	56²	74	2	27	15	16.0	4.76	74	.315	.385	2	.222	0	-7	-8	1	-0.7
Total	6	23	17	.575	196	31	7	0	15	485²	544	37	256	185	15.1	4.65	87	.289	.378	22	.176	-1	-36	-31	-0	-3.2

● **GEORGE STUELAND** Stueland, George Anton b: 3/2/1899, Algona, Iowa d: 9/9/64, Onawa, Iowa BB/TR, 6'1.5", 174 lbs. Deb: 9/15/21

1921	Chi-N	0	1	.000	2	1	0	0	0	11	11	0	7	4	14.7	5.73	67	.282	.391	1	.333	0	-2	-2	0	-0.2
1922	Chi-N	9	4	.692	35	12	4	0	0	113	129	9	49	44	14.6	5.81	73	.297	.374	4	.129	-2	-22	-20	-1	-2.1
1923	Chi-N	0	1	.000	6	0	0	0	0	8	11	1	0	5	2	18.0	5.63	71	.478	.571	0	—	0	-1	-1	0	-0.1
1925	Chi-N	0	0	—	2	0	0	0	0	3	2	1	3	2	15.0	3.00	144	.182	.357	1	1.000	0	0	0	0	0.1
Total	4	9	6	.600	45	13	4	0	0	135	153	9	64	52	14.8	5.73	73	.301	.385	6	.171	-1	-25	-24	-1	-2.3

● **PAUL STUFFEL** Stuffel, Paul Harrington "Stu" b: 3/22/27, Canton, Ohio BR/TR, 6'2", 185 lbs. Deb: 9/16/50

1950	Phi-N	0	0	—	3	0	0	0	0	5	4	0	1	3	10.8	1.80	225	.211	.286	0	—	0	1	1	0	0.1
1952	Phi-N	1	0	1.000	2	1	0	0	0	6	5	0	7	3	18.0	3.00	122	.217	.400	0	.000	-0	0	0	0	0.1
1953	Phi-N	0	0	—	2	0	0	0	0	0	0	0	4	0	—	∞	—	—	1.000	0	—	0	-4	-4	0	-0.4
Total	3	1	0	1.000	7	1	0	0	0	11	9	0	12	6	18.0	5.73	67	.214	.400	0	.000	-0	-2	-2	0	-0.2

● **GEORGE STULTZ** Stultz, George Irvin b: 6/30/1873, Louisville, Ky. d: 3/19/55, Louisville, Ky. 5'10", 150 lbs. Deb: 9/22/1894

| 1894 | Bos-N | 1 | 0 | 1.000 | 1 | 1 | 1 | 0 | 0 | 9 | 4 | 0 | 5 | 1 | 9.0 | 0.00 | — | ¹34 | .258 | 1 | .333 | -0 | 5 | 6 | 1 | 0.6 |

● **JIM STUMP** Stump, James Gilbert b: 2/10/32, Lansing, Mich. BR/TR, 6', 188 lbs. Deb: 8/29/57

1957	Det-A	1	0	1.000	6	0	0	0	0	13¹	11	0	8	2	12.8	2.03	190	.220	.328	1	.500	1	3	3	0	0.3
1959	Det-A	0	0	—	5	0	0	0	0	11¹	12	1	4	6	12.7	2.38	170	.279	.340	1	1.000	1	2	2	0	0.3
Total	2	1	0	1.000	11	0	0	0	0	24²	23	1	12	8	12.8	2.19	180	.247	.333	2	.667	1	4	5	0	0.6

● **JOHN STUPER** Stuper, John Anton b: 5/9/57, Butler, Pa. BR/TR, 6'2", 200 lbs. Deb: 6/01/82

1982	*StL-N	9	7	.563	23	21	2	0	0	136²	137	8	55	53	12.6	3.36	108	.266	.337	5	.119	-1	4	4	-3	0.0
1983	StL-N	12	11	.522	40	30	6	1	1	198	202	15	71	81	12.5	3.68	98	.265	.329	8	.136	-1	-1	-1	-3	-0.3
1984	StL-N	3	5	.375	15	12	0	0	0	61¹	73	4	20	19	13.9	5.28	66	.297	.354	1	.063	-1	-12	-12	0	-1.3
1985	Cin-N	8	5	.615	33	13	1	0	0	99	116	8	37	38	13.9	4.55	83	.303	.364	1	.059	-0	-10	-8	0	-0.9
Total	4	32	28	.533	111	76	9	1	1	495	528	35	183	191	13.0	3.96	92	.277	.341	15	.112	-3	-20	-18	-4	-2.5

● **TOM STURDIVANT** Sturdivant, Thomas Virgil "Snake" b: 4/28/30, Gordon, Kan. BL/TR, 6'1", 186 lbs. Deb: 4/14/55

1955	*NY-A	1	3	.250	33	1	0	0	0	68¹	48	6	42	48	12.1	3.16	118	.203	.329	1	.083	-1	6	4	0	0.3
1956	*NY-A	16	8	.667	32	17	6	2	5	158¹	134	15	52	110	10.8	3.30	117	.224	**.291**	20	.313	4	15	10	-2	1.2
1957	*NY-A	16	6	**.727**	28	28	7	2	0	201²	170	14	80	118	11.3	2.54	141	.232	.311	13	.183	1	28	23	-2	2.4
1958	NY-A	3	6	.333	15	10	0	0	0	70²	77	6	38	41	15.0	4.20	84	.274	.366	4	.190	0	-3	-5	-2	-0.7
1959	NY-A	0	2	.000	7	3	0	0	0	25¹	20	4	9	16	10.3	4.97	73	.222	.293	0	.000	-1	-3	-4	0	-0.4
	KC-A	2	6	.250	36	3	0	0	5	71²	70	9	34	57	13.8	4.65	86	.258	.354	1	.059	-2	-6	-5	1	-0.6
	Yr	2	8	.200	43	6	0	0	5	97	90	13	43	73	12.9	4.73	83	.249	.338	1	.043	-3	-9	-9	2	-1.0
1960	Bos-A	3	3	.500	40	3	0	0	0	101¹	106	16	45	67	13.6	4.97	80	.279	.358	4	.182	-1	-12	-10	-0	-1.1
1961	Was-A	2	6	.250	15	10	1	1	0	80	67	6	40	39	12.4	4.61	87	.233	.332	2	.077	-1	-5	-5	1	-0.6
	Pit-N	5	2	.714	13	11	6	1	1	85²	81	6	17	45	10.4	2.84	141	.249	.289	8	.250	1	11	11	-1	1.1
1962	Pit-N	9	5	.643	49	12	1	1	2	125¹	120	12	39	76	11.6	3.73	105	.260	.321	6	.182	0	3	3	0	0.3
1963	Pit-N	0	0	—	3	0	0	0	0	8¹	8	1	4	6	13.0	6.48	51	.267	.353	0	.000	-0	-3	-3	0	-0.3
	Det-A	1	2	.333	28	0	0	0	0	55	43	7	24	36	11.1	3.76	99	.221	.309	0	.000	-1	-1	-0	1	-0.1
	KC-A	1	2	.333	17	0	0	0	0	53	47	3	17	26	11.0	3.74	103	.237	.301	0	.000	-1	-1	1	0	0.0
	Yr	2	4	.333	45	0	0	0	0	108	90	10	41	62	11.0	3.75	101	.226	.300	0	.000	-2	-1	1	1	-0.1
1964	KC-A	0	0	—	3	0	0	0	0	3²	4	0	1	1	17.2	9.82	39	.308	.438	1	1.000	0	-3	-2	0	-0.2
	NY-N	0	0	—	16	0	0	0	1	28²	34	2	7	18	13.5	5.97	60	.306	.358	0	.000	-0	-8	-8	-0	-0.8
Total	10	59	51	.536	335	101	22	7	17	1137	1029	107	449	704	12.0	3.74	102	.244	.322	60	.183	-2	18	10	-4	0.5

● **DICK SUCH** Such, Richard Stanley b: 10/15/44, Sanford, N.C. BL/TR, 6'4", 190 lbs. Deb: 4/06/70 C

| 1970 | Was-A | 1 | 5 | .167 | 21 | 5 | 0 | 0 | 0 | 50 | 48 | 9 | 45 | 41 | 17.3 | 7.56 | 47 | .258 | .410 | 3 | .231 | 1 | -21 | -22 | 0 | -2.1 |

● **CHARLEY SUCHE** Suche, Charles Morris b: 8/5/15, Cranes Mill, Tex. d: 2/11/84, San Antonio, Tex. BR/TL, 6'2", 190 lbs. Deb: 9/18/38

| 1938 | Cle-A | 0 | 0 | — | 1 | 0 | 0 | 0 | 0 | 1¹ | 4 | 0 | 3 | 1 | 47.3 | 27.00 | 17 | .571 | .700 | 1 | 1.000 | 1 | -3 | -3 | 0 | -0.2 |

● **JIM SUCHECKI** Suchecki, James Joseph b: 8/25/27, Chicago, Ill. BR/TR, 6', 185 lbs. Deb: 5/20/50

1950	Bos-A	0	0	—	4	0	0	0	0	4	3	2	8	3	15.8	4.50	109	.231	.412	0	—	0	0	-0	-0	0.0
1951	StL-A	0	6	.000	29	6	0	0	0	89²	113	6	42	47	15.7	5.42	81	.299	.371	2	.100	-2	-13	-10	-1	-1.2
1952	Pit-N	0	0	—	5	0	0	0	0	10	14	1	4	6	17.1	5.40	74	.326	.396	0	.000	-0	-2	-2	-0	-0.2
Total	3	0	6	.000	38	6	0	0	0	103²	130	9	50	56	15.8	5.38	81	.300	.374	2	.091	-2	-15	-12	-1	-1.4

● **WILLIE SUDHOFF** Sudhoff, John William "Wee Willie" b: 9/17/1874, St.Louis, Mo. d: 5/25/17, St.Louis, Mo. BR/TR, 5'7", 165 lbs. Deb: 8/20/1897

1897	StL-N	2	7	.222	11	9	8	0	0	92²	126	8	21	19	14.3	4.47	99	.321	.356	10	.238	-1	-2	-1	2	0.0
1898	StL-N	11	27	.289	41	38	35	0	1	315	355	11	102	65	13.8	4.34	87	.282	.349	19	.158	-7	-26	-19	8	-1.6
1899	Cle-N	3	8	.273	11	10	8	0	0	86¹	131	3	25	10	17.0	6.98	53	.348	.399	2	.065	-2	-30	-32	2	-2.3
	StL-N	13	10	.565	26	24	18	0	0	189¹	203	6	67	33	13.5	3.61	110	.274	.346	14	.206	0	5	8	4	1.1
	Yr	16	18	.471	37	34	26	0	0	275²	334	9	92	43	14.4	4.67	83	.297	.358	16	.162	-2	-25	-24	6	-1.4
1900	StL-N	6	8	.429	16	14	13	0	2	127	128	3	37	29	12.2	2.76	132	.261	.322	20	.189	-0	13	12	1	1.2

YEAR	TM/L	W	L	PCT	G	GS	CG	SH	SV	IP	H	HR	BB	SO	RAT	ERA	ERA+	OAV	OOB	BH	AVG	PB	PR	/A	PD	TPI
1901	StL-N	17	11	.607	38	26	25	1	2	276^{1}	281	4	92	78	12.7	3.52	90	.262	.330	19	.176	3	-6	-10	2	-0.5
1902	StL-A	12	12	.500	30	25	20	0	0	220	213	6	67	42	11.9	2.86	123	.255	.318	13	.169	-2	17	16	3	1.7
1903	StL-A	21	15	.583	38	35	30	5	0	293^{2}	262	4	56	104	10.0	2.27	128	.238	.281	20	.182	-1	23	21	3	2.5
1904	StL-A	8	15	.348	27	24	20	1	0	222^{1}	232	8	54	63	12.0	3.76	66	.269	.321	14	.165	-1	-29	-32	5	-2.8
1905	StL-A	10	20	.333	32	30	23	1	0	244	222	8	78	70	11.5	2.99	85	.244	.312	16	.186	2	-9	-12	4	-0.7
1906	Was-A	0	2	.000	9	5	0	0	0	19^{2}	30	1	9	7	18.8	9.15	29	.353	.427	3	.429	1	-14	-14	1	-1.3
Total	10	103	135	.433	279	240	201	10	3	2086^{1}	2183	62	608	520	12.6	3.56	92	.269	.329	150	.179	-8	-57	-65	34	-2.9

● **JOE SUGDEN** Sugden, Joseph b: 7/31/1870, Philadelphia, Pa. d: 6/28/59, Philadelphia, Pa. BB/TR, 5'10", 180 lbs. Deb: 7/20/1893 C♦

YEAR	TM/L	W	L	PCT	G	GS	CG	SH	SV	IP	H	HR	BB	SO	RAT	ERA	ERA+	OAV	OOB	BH	AVG	PB	PR	/A	PD	TPI
1902	StL-A	0	0	—	1	0	0	0	0	1	1	0	0	0	9.0	0.00	—	.261	.261	50	.250	0	0	0	0	0.1

● **GEORGE SUGGS** Suggs, George Franklin b: 7/7/1882, Kinston, N.C. d: 4/4/49, Kinston, N.C. BR/TR, 5'7.5", 168 lbs. Deb: 4/21/08

YEAR	TM/L	W	L	PCT	G	GS	CG	SH	SV	IP	H	HR	BB	SO	RAT	ERA	ERA+	OAV	OOB	BH	AVG	PB	PR	/A	PD	TPI
1908	Det-A	1	1	.500	6	1	1	0	1	27	32	0	2	8	11.3	1.67	145	.299	.312	2	.200	0	2	2	-1	0.2
1909	Det-A	1	3	.250	9	4	2	0	1	44^{1}	34	1	10	18	9.5	2.03	124	.228	.290	1	.067	-1	2	2	-0	0.1
1910	Cin-N	20	12	.625	35	30	23	2	3	266	248	6	48	91	10.5	2.40	121	.253	.297	14	.165	2	19	15	1	2.0
1911	Cin-N	15	13	.536	36	29	17	1	0	260^{2}	258	3	79	91	12.0	3.00	110	.268	.330	23	.256	6	12	9	3	1.9
1912	Cin-N	19	16	.543	42	36	25	5	3	303	320	6	56	104	11.5	2.94	114	.278	.318	17	.160	-1	16	14	1	1.4
1913	Cin-N	8	15	.348	36	22	9	2	2	199	220	6	35	73	11.8	4.03	81	.292	.329	17	.254	2	-18	-17	3	-1.2
1914	Bal-F	24	14	.632	46	38	26	6	4	319^{1}	322	6	57	132	11.0	2.90	116	.266	.304	21	.212	4	11	17	6	2.8
1915	Bal-F	11	17	.393	35	25	12	0	3	232^{2}	288	12	68	71	14.0	4.14	77	.318	.370	17	.221	2	-29	-25	2	-2.2
Total	8	99	91	.521	245	185	115	16	17	1652	1722	40	355	588	11.7	3.11	103	.277	.322	112	.204	14	14	18	14	5.0

● **ED SUKLA** Sukla, Edward Anthony (b: Edward Anthony Suckla) b: 3/3/43, Long Beach, Cal. BR/TR, 5'11", 170 lbs. Deb: 9/17/64

YEAR	TM/L	W	L	PCT	G	GS	CG	SH	SV	IP	H	HR	BB	SO	RAT	ERA	ERA+	OAV	OOB	BH	AVG	PB	PR	/A	PD	TPI
1964	LA-A	0	1	.000	2	0	0	0	0	2^{2}	2	1	1	3	10.1	6.75	49	.200	.273	0	—	0	-1	-1	0	-0.1
1965	Cal-A	2	3	.400	25	0	0	0	3	32	32	3	10	15	12.1	4.50	76	.264	.326	0	—	0	-4	-4	1	-0.3
1966	Cal-A	1	1	.500	12	0	0	0	1	16^{2}	18	4	6	8	13.0	6.48	52	.281	.343	0	.000	-0	-6	-6	-1	-0.7
Total	3	3	5	.375	39	0	0	0	4	51^{1}	52	8	17	26	12.3	5.26	64	.267	.329	0	.000	-0	-10	-11	0	-1.1

● **CHARLIE SULLIVAN** Sullivan, Charles Edward b: 5/23/03, Yadkin Valley, N.C d: 5/28/35, Maiden, N.C. BL/TR, 6'1", 185 lbs. Deb: 4/21/28

YEAR	TM/L	W	L	PCT	G	GS	CG	SH	SV	IP	H	HR	BB	SO	RAT	ERA	ERA+	OAV	OOB	BH	AVG	PB	PR	/A	PD	TPI
1928	Det-A	0	2	.000	3	2	0	0	0	12^{1}	18	1	6	2	17.5	6.57	63	.360	.429	0	.000	-1	-3	-3	0	-0.4
1930	Det-A	1	5	.167	40	3	2	0	5	93^{2}	112	9	53	38	16.0	6.53	73	.311	.401	7	.292	2	-20	-18	1	-1.4
1931	Det-A	3	2	.600	31	4	2	0	0	95	109	6	46	28	14.8	4.93	93	.288	.366	4	.167	-1	-6	-4	-0	-0.5
Total	3	4	9	.308	74	9	4	0	5	201	239	16	105	68	15.5	5.78	81	.303	.386	11	.212	-0	-29	-25	1	-2.3

● **FLEURY SULLIVAN** Sullivan, Florence P. b: 1862, E.St.Louis, Ill. d: 2/15/1897, E.St.Louis, Ill. Deb: 5/03/1884

YEAR	TM/L	W	L	PCT	G	GS	CG	SH	SV	IP	H	HR	BB	SO	RAT	ERA	ERA+	OAV	OOB	BH	AVG	PB	PR	/A	PD	TPI
1884	Pit-a	16	35	.314	51	51	51	2	0	441	496	15	96	189	12.5	4.20	80	.268	.311	29	.153	-9	-47	-41	1	-4.3

● **FRANK SULLIVAN** Sullivan, Franklin Leal b: 1/23/30, Hollywood, Cal. BR/TR, 6'6.5", 215 lbs. Deb: 7/31/53

YEAR	TM/L	W	L	PCT	G	GS	CG	SH	SV	IP	H	HR	BB	SO	RAT	ERA	ERA+	OAV	OOB	BH	AVG	PB	PR	/A	PD	TPI
1953	Bos-A	1	1	.500	14	0	0	0	0	25^{2}	24	3	11	17	12.6	5.61	75	.264	.350	1	.250	0	-5	-4	-0	-0.4
1954	Bos-A	15	12	.556	36	26	11	3	1	206^{1}	185	18	66	124	11.2	3.14	131	.240	.305	7	.103	-3	13	22	1	2.2
1955	Bos-A★	**18**	13	.581	35	35	16	3	0	**260**	235	23	100	129	11.8	2.91	147	.241	.316	10	.112	-5	30	40	1	3.8
1956	Bos-A☆	14	7	.667	34	33	12	1	0	242	253	22	82	116	12.8	3.42	135	.268	.332	12	.141	-6	20	32	0	2.7
1957	Bos-A	14	11	.560	31	30	14	3	0	240^{2}	206	16	48	127	**9.8**	2.73	146	.230	**.275**	13	.165	-2	28	34	2	**3.7**
1958	Bos-A	13	9	.591	32	29	10	2	3	199^{1}	216	12	49	103	12.1	3.57	112	.278	.324	11	.164	-1	4	10	-1	0.8
1959	Bos-A	9	11	.450	30	26	5	2	1	177^{2}	172	17	67	107	12.5	3.95	103	.258	.332	12	.200	-1	-2	2	-1	0.0
1960	Bos-A	6	16	.273	40	22	4	0	1	153^{2}	164	12	52	98	13.0	5.10	79	.269	.332	5	.125	-1	-21	-18	-1	-2.0
1961	Phi-N	3	16	.158	49	18	1	1	6	159^{1}	161	19	55	114	12.5	4.29	95	.262	.327	5	.152	0	-5	-4	1	-0.2
1962	Phi-N	0	2	.000	19	0	0	0	0	23	38	2	12	12	20.3	6.26	62	.396	.473	0	—	0	-6	-6	0	-0.6
	Min-A	4	1	.800	21	0	0	0	5	33^{1}	33	3	13	10	12.4	3.24	126	.258	.326	0	.000	-0	3	3	0	0.3
1963	Min-A	0	1	.000	10	0	0	0	1	11	15	1	4	2	15.5	5.73	64	.349	.404	0	—	0	-3	-3	0	-0.2
Total	11	97	100	.492	351	219	73	15	18	1732	1702	148	559	959	12.0	3.60	116	.257	.320	76	.144	-18	59	108	3	10.1

● **HARRY SULLIVAN** Sullivan, Harry Andrew b: 4/12/1888, Rockford, Ill. d: 9/22/19, Rockford, Ill. BL/TL, Deb: 8/11/09

YEAR	TM/L	W	L	PCT	G	GS	CG	SH	SV	IP	H	HR	BB	SO	RAT	ERA	ERA+	OAV	OOB	BH	AVG	PB	PR	/A	PD	TPI
1909	StL-N	0	0	—	2	1	0	0	0	1	4	1	2	1	54.0	36.00	7	.500	.600	0	.000	-0	-4	-4	-0	-0.4

● **JIM SULLIVAN** Sullivan, James E. b: 4/25/1869, Charlestown, Mass. d: 11/30/01, Roxbury, Mass. BR/TR, 5'10", 155 lbs. Deb: 4/22/1891

YEAR	TM/L	W	L	PCT	G	GS	CG	SH	SV	IP	H	HR	BB	SO	RAT	ERA	ERA+	OAV	OOB	BH	AVG	PB	PR	/A	PD	TPI
1891	Bos-N	0	0	—	1	0	0	0	0	0^{1}	2	0	5	0	189.0	81.00	5	.667	.875	0	—	0	-3	-3	-0	-0.2
	Col-a	0	1	.000	1	1	1	0	0	9	10	1	5	1	16.0	4.00	87	.272	.374	0	.000	-1	-0	-1	1	-0.1
1895	Bos-N	11	9	.550	21	19	16	0	0	179^{1}	236	10	58	46	15.6	4.82	106	.312	.374	15	.176	-6	-1	6	-2	-0.2
1896	Bos-N	11	12	.478	31	26	21	1	1	225^{1}	268	12	68	33	13.7	4.03	113	.293	.346	19	.216	-3	8	13	-3	0.6
1897	*Bos-N	4	5	.444	13	9	8	1	2	89	91	1	26	17	12.0	3.94	113	.263	.318	6	.182	-3	4	5	-1	0.1
Total	4	26	27	.491	67	55	46	2	3	503	607	24	162	97	14.2	4.35	108	.295	.354	40	.190	-12	8	20	-6	0.2

● **JIM SULLIVAN** Sullivan, James Richard b: 4/5/1894, Mine Run, Va. d: 2/12/72, Burtonsville, Md. BR/TR, 5'11", 165 lbs. Deb: 9/27/21

YEAR	TM/L	W	L	PCT	G	GS	CG	SH	SV	IP	H	HR	BB	SO	RAT	ERA	ERA+	OAV	OOB	BH	AVG	PB	PR	/A	PD	TPI
1921	Phi-A	0	2	.000	2	2	2	0	0	17	20	0	7	8	14.3	3.18	140	.294	.360	0	.000	-1	2	2	-0	0.1
1922	Phi-A	0	2	.000	20	2	1	0	0	51^{1}	76	3	25	15	17.9	5.44	78	.373	.443	1	.091	-1	-8	-7	-0	-0.7
1923	Cle-A	0	1	.000	3	0	0	0	0	5	10	0	5	4	28.8	14.40	28	.476	.593	0	.000	-0	-6	-6	0	-0.5
Total	3	0	5	.000	25	4	3	0	0	73^{1}	106	3	37	27	17.8	5.52	78	.362	.437	1	.056	-2	-12	-10	-1	-1.1

● **JOHN SULLIVAN** Sullivan, John Jeremiah "Lefty" b: 5/31/1894, Chicago, Ill. d: 7/7/58, Chicago, Ill. BL/TL, 5'11", 165 lbs. Deb: 7/18/19

YEAR	TM/L	W	L	PCT	G	GS	CG	SH	SV	IP	H	HR	BB	SO	RAT	ERA	ERA+	OAV	OOB	BH	AVG	PB	PR	/A	PD	TPI
1919	Chi-A	0	1	.000	4	2	1	0	0	15	24	0	8	9	19.8	4.20	76	.364	.440	0	.000	-0	-2	-2	-1	-0.2

● **JOE SULLIVAN** Sullivan, Joe b: 9/26/10, Mason City, Ill. d: 4/8/85, Sequim, Wash. BL/TL, 5'11", 175 lbs. Deb: 4/20/35

YEAR	TM/L	W	L	PCT	G	GS	CG	SH	SV	IP	H	HR	BB	SO	RAT	ERA	ERA+	OAV	OOB	BH	AVG	PB	PR	/A	PD	TPI
1935	Det-A	6	6	.500	25	12	5	0	0	125^{2}	119	4	71	53	13.8	3.51	119	.244	.344	7	.163	-1	13	9	-1	0.7
1936	Det-A	2	5	.286	26	4	1	0	1	79^{2}	111	4	40	32	17.3	6.78	73	.331	.406	5	.179	-1	-15	-16	-1	-1.5
1939	Bos-N	6	9	.400	31	11	7	0	2	113^{2}	114	3	50	46	13.1	3.64	101	.266	.346	12	.300	3	3	1	0	0.4
1940	Bos-N	10	14	.417	36	22	7	0	1	177^{1}	157	9	89	64	12.9	3.55	105	.240	.339	14	.197	-0	6	3	0	0.3
1941	Bos-N	2	2	.500	16	2	0	0	0	52^{1}	60	3	26	11	15.1	4.13	86	.290	.374	1	.067	-1	-3	-3	1	-0.4
	Pit-N	4	1	.800	16	4	0	0	1	39^{1}	40	2	22	10	14.2	2.97	121	.258	.350	4	.364	1	3	3	0	0.4
	Yr	6	3	.667	32	6	0	0	1	91^{2}	100	5	48	21	14.5	3.63	99	.275	.359	5	.192	-0	0	-0	1	0.0
Total	5	30	37	.448	150	55	20	0	5	588	601	25	298	216	14.0	4.01	99	.265	.355	43	.207	1	7	-3	0	-0.1

● **MARTY SULLIVAN** Sullivan, Martin C. b: 10/20/1862, Lowell, Mass. d: 1/6/1894, Lowell, Mass. BR/TR, Deb: 4/30/1887 ♦

YEAR	TM/L	W	L	PCT	G	GS	CG	SH	SV	IP	H	HR	BB	SO	RAT	ERA	ERA+	OAV	OOB	BH	AVG	PB	PR	/A	PD	TPI
1887	Chi-N	0	0	—	1	0	0	0	0	2^{1}	6	0	1	1	27.0	7.71	58	.500	.538	134	.284	0	-1	-1	-0	-0.1

● **MIKE SULLIVAN** Sullivan, Michael Joseph "Big Mike" b: 10/23/1866, Boston, Mass. d: 6/14/06, Boston, Mass. BL , 6'1", 210 lbs. Deb: 6/17/1889

YEAR	TM/L	W	L	PCT	G	GS	CG	SH	SV	IP	H	HR	BB	SO	RAT	ERA	ERA+	OAV	OOB	BH	AVG	PB	PR	/A	PD	TPI
1889	Was-N	0	3	.000	9	3	3	0	0	41	47	2	32	15	18.0	7.24	54	.279	.403	1	.053	-2	-15	-15	-0	-1.4
1890	Chi-N	5	6	.455	12	12	10	0	0	96	108	3	58	33	15.9	4.59	80	.275	.374	5	.125	-3	-11	-10	-0	-1.1
1891	Phi-a	0	2	.000	2	2	2	0	0	18	17	2	10	7	15.0	3.50	109	.241	.359	0	.000	-1	0	1	-0	-0.1
	NY-N	1	2	.333	3	3	3	0	0	24	24	0	8	11	12.4	3.38	95	.251	.315	2	.200	-0	-0	-0	0	-0.1
1892	Cin-N	12	4	.750	21	16	15	0	0	166^{1}	179	8	74	56	14.2	3.08	106	.264	.344	13	.176	-3	4	3	-2	-0.1
1893	Cin-N	8	11	.421	27	18	14	0	1	183^{2}	200	5	103	40	15.7	5.05	95	.269	.371	16	.203	-3	-8	-5	-0	-0.7
1894	Was-N	2	10	.167	20	12	11	0	1	117^{2}	166	10	74	21	19.0	6.58	80	.329	.423	9	.158	-4	-16	-17	-0	-1.6
	Cle-N	6	5	.545	13	11	9	0	0	90^{2}	128	4	47	19	17.7	6.35	86	.329	.405	13	.295	0	-10	-9	-1	-0.7
	Yr	8	15	.348	33	23	20	0	1	208^{1}	294	14	121	40	18.1	6.48	83	.326	.407	22	.218	-4	-27	-26	-1	-2.3
1895	Cle-N	1	2	.333	4	3	2	0	0	31	42	1	16	5	17.1	8.42	59	.318	.396	2	.133	-2	-13	-12	-1	-1.0

YEAR TM/L	W	L	PCT	G	GS	CG	SH	SV	IP	H	HR	BB	SO	RAT	ERA	ERA+	OAV	OOB	BH	AVG	PB	PR	/A	PD	TPI
1896 NY-N	10	13	.435	25	22	18	0	0	185^{1}	188	3	71	42	13.2	4.66	90	.261	.338	16	.208	-3	-6	-9	0	-1.1
1897 NY-N	8	7	.533	23	16	11	1	2	148^{2}	183	6	71	35	16.2	5.09	82	.300	.386	18	.273	0	-13	-15	1	-1.2
1898 Bos-N	0	1	.000	3	2	0	0	0	12	19	1	9	1	21.8	12.00	31	.356	.457	1	.333	0	-11	-11	-0	-0.9
1899 Bos-N	1	0	1.000	1	1	1	0	0	9	10	1	4	1	15.0	5.00	83	.281	.369	1	.333	0	-1	-1	-0	-0.1
Total 11	54	66	.450	163	121	99	1	4	1123^{1}	1311	46	577	286	15.8	5.11	84	.285	.375	97	.196	-21	-100	-102	-5	-10.1
● **PAT SULLIVAN** Sullivan, Patrick J. b: 12/22/1862, Milwaukee, Wis. TR , 5'11", 165 lbs. Deb: 8/30/1884 ♦																									
1884 KC-U	0	1	.000	1	1	0	0	0	7	15	1	5	1	25.7	11.57	24	.408	.479	22	.193	-0	-7	-7	-0	-0.5
● **LEFTY SULLIVAN** Sullivan, Paul Thomas b: 9/7/16, Nashville, Tenn. d: 11/1/88, Scottsdale, Ariz. BL/TL, 6'3", 204 lbs. Deb: 5/06/39																									
1939 Cle-A	0	1	.000	7	1	0	0	0	12^{2}	9	0	9	4	13.5	4.26	103	.214	.365	0	.000	-0	1	0	-1	-0.1
● **SUTER SULLIVAN** Sullivan, Suter G. b: 10/14/1872, Baltimore, Md. d: 4/19/25, Baltimore, Md. Deb: 7/24/1898 ♦																									
1898 StL-N	0	0	—	1	0	0	0	0	6	10	0	4	3	21.0	1.50	253	.367	.449	32	.222	-0	1	2	-0	0.1
● **TOM SULLIVAN** Sullivan, Thomas b: 3/1/1860, New York, N.Y. d: 4/12/47, Cincinnati, Ohio Deb: 9/27/1884																									
1884 Col-a	2	2	.500	4	4	4	0	0	31	42	2	3	12	13.1	4.06	75	.318	.333	1	.091	-1	-3	-4	-1	-0.4
1886 Lou-a	2	7	.222	9	9	8	0	0	75	94	6	33	27	15.5	3.96	92	.305	.376	3	.111	-2	-4	-3	0	-0.4
1888 KC-a	8	16	.333	24	24	24	0	0	214^{2}	227	2	68	84	13.4	3.40	101	.262	.332	10	.109	-6	-8	1	5	0.0
1889 KC-a	2	8	.200	10	10	10	0	0	87^{1}	111	2	48	24	17.1	5.67	74	.300	.391	5	.152	-1	-18	-14	-1	-1.3
Total 4	14	33	.298	47	47	46	0	0	408	474	12	152	147	14.5	4.04	89	.283	.354	19	.117	-10	-33	-20	4	-2.1
● **TOM SULLIVAN** Sullivan, Thomas Augustin b: 10/18/1895, Boston, Mass. d: 9/23/62, Boston, Mass. BL/TL, 5'11", 178 lbs. Deb: 5/15/22																									
1922 Phi-N	0	0	—	3	0	0	0	0	8	16	0	5	2	24.8	11.25	41	.410	.489	1	.250	1	-6	-6	0	-0.4
● **SLEEPER SULLIVAN** Sullivan, Thomas Jefferson "Old Iron Hands" b: St.Louis, Mo. d: 9/25/1899, Camden, N.J. BR/TR, 175 lbs. Deb: 5/03/1881 ♦																									
1884 StL-U	1	0	1.000	1	1	0	0	0	6	10	0	0	3	15.0	4.50	66	.349	.349	1	.111	-0	-1	-1	-0	-0.1
● **BILL SULLIVAN** Sullivan, William T. Deb: 4/19/1890																									
1890 Syr-a	1	4	.200	6	6	4	0	0	42	51	2	27	13	18.0	7.93	45	.291	.403	2	.091	-2	-19	-21	-0	-1.7
● **ED SUMMERS** Summers, Oron Edgar "Kickapoo Ed" or "Chief" b: 12/5/1884, Ladoga, Ind. d: 5/12/53, Indianapolis, Ind. BB/TR, 6'2", 180 lbs. Deb: 4/16/08																									
1908 *Det-A	24	12	.667	40	32	23	5	1	301	271	3	55	103	10.3	1.64	147	.242	.290	14	.124	-6	25	26	-1	2.1
1909 *Det-A	19	9	.679	35	32	24	3	1	281^{2}	243	4	52	107	9.7	2.24	113	.227	.269	10	.106	-4	8	9	1	0.6
1910 Det-A	13	12	.520	30	25	18	1	0	220^{1}	211	8	60	82	11.3	2.53	104	.254	.308	14	.184	-0	-0	2	1	0.3
1911 Det-A	11	11	.500	30	20	13	0	1	179^{1}	189	3	51	65	12.6	3.66	95	.274	.334	16	.254	1	-6	-4	-1	-0.4
1912 Det-A	1	1	.500	3	3	1	0	0	16^{2}	16	1	3	5	10.3	4.86	67	.250	.284	3	.500	1	-3	-3	0	-0.2
Total 5	68	45	.602	138	112	79	9	3	999	930	19	221	362	10.8	2.42	111	.246	.296	57	.162	-9	23	30	-0	2.4
● **BILLY SUNDAY** Sunday, William Ashley "Parson" or "The Evangelist" b: 11/19/1862, Ames, Iowa d: 11/6/35, Chicago, Ill. BL/TR, 5'10", 160 lbs. Deb: 5/22/1883 ♦																									
1890 Pit-N	0	0	—	1	0	0	0	0	0	2	0	0	0	—	∞	—	1.000	1.000	92	.257	0	-2	-2	0	-0.2
● **GORDIE SUNDIN** Sundin, Gordon Vincent b: 10/10/37, Minneapolis, Minn. BR/TR, 6'4", 215 lbs. Deb: 9/19/56																									
1956 Bal-A	0	0	—	1	0	0	0	0	0	0	0	2	0	—	∞	—	—	1.000	0	—	0	-1	-1	0	-0.1
● **STEVE SUNDRA** Sundra, Stephen Richard "Smokey" b: 3/27/10, Luxor, Pa. d: 3/23/52, Cleveland, Ohio BR/TR, 6'2", 190 lbs. Deb: 4/17/36																									
1936 NY-A	0	0	—	1	0	0	0	0	2	2	0	2	1	18.0	0.00	—	.286	.444	0	.000	-0	1	1	-0	0.1
1938 NY-A	6	4	.600	25	8	3	0	0	93^{2}	107	7	43	33	14.4	4.80	94	.291	.365	6	.182	1	-0	-3	1	-0.1
1939 *NY-A	11	1	.917	24	11	8	1	0	120^{2}	110	7	56	27	12.4	2.76	158	.240	.323	13	.265	3	25	21	1	2.5
1940 NY-A	4	6	.400	27	8	2	0	2	99^{1}	121	11	42	26	14.9	5.53	73	.299	.366	4	.138	-1	-13	-16	0	-1.5
1941 Was-A	9	13	.409	28	23	11	0	0	168^{1}	203	11	61	50	14.2	5.29	76	.294	.352	13	.217	2	-21	-23	-1	-2.0
1942 Was-A	1	3	.250	6	4	2	0	0	33^{2}	43	1	15	5	15.8	5.61	65	.305	.376	2	.167	-0	-7	-7	-0	-0.7
StL-A	8	3	.727	20	13	6	0	0	110^{2}	122	2	29	26	12.3	3.82	97	.275	.319	9	.225	3	-2	-1	-0	0.1
Yr	9	6	.600	26	17	8	0	0	144^{1}	165	3	44	31	13.0	4.24	87	.282	.332	11	.212	2	-9	-9	-0	-0.6
1943 StL-A	15	11	.577	32	29	13	3	0	208	212	10	66	44	12.0	3.25	103	.266	.322	16	.219	1	1	2	-0	0.3
1944 StL-A	2	0	1.000	3	3	2	0	0	19	15	1	4	1	9.0	1.42	253	.211	.253	0	.000	-0	4	5	-0	0.5
1946 StL-A	0	0	—	2	0	0	0	0	4	9	0	3	1	27.0	11.25	33	.409	.480	0	—	0	-3	-3	0	-0.3
Total 9	56	41	.577	168	99	47	4	2	859^{1}	944	50	321	214	13.3	4.17	94	.277	.340	63	.209	10	-16	-24	1	-1.1
● **TOM SUNKEL** Sunkel, Thomas Jacob "Lefty" b: 8/9/12, Paris, Ill. BL/TL, 6'1", 190 lbs. Deb: 8/26/37																									
1937 StL-N	0	0	—	9	1	0	0	1	29^{1}	24	0	11	9	10.7	2.76	144	.214	.285	1	.111	-1	4	4	-0	0.3
1939 StL-N	4	4	.500	20	11	2	1	0	85^{1}	79	4	56	54	14.3	4.22	98	.242	.354	9	.321	2	-3	-1	-1	0.0
1941 NY-N	1	1	.500	2	2	1	1	0	15^{1}	7	0	12	14	11.7	2.93	126	.140	.317	2	.333	0	1	1	-0	0.2
1942 NY-N	3	6	.333	19	11	3	0	0	63^{2}	65	5	41	29	15.0	4.81	70	.269	.375	2	.105	-1	-11	-10	-2	-1.4
1943 NY-N	0	1	.000	1	1	0	0	0	2^{2}	4	1	3	0	23.6	10.13	34	.308	.438	0	—	0	-2	-2	0	-0.2
1944 Bro-N	1	3	.250	12	3	0	0	1	24	39	1	10	6	18.4	7.50	47	.368	.422	0	.000	-1	-10	-11	-1	-1.2
Total 6	9	15	.375	63	29	6	2	2	220^{1}	218	11	133	112	14.4	4.53	83	.256	.358	14	.212	0	-21	-19	-4	-2.3
● **RICK SURHOFF** Surhoff, Richard Clifford b: 10/3/62, Bronx, N.Y. BR/TR, 6'3", 210 lbs. Deb: 9/08/85 F																									
1985 Phi-N	1	0	1.000	2	0	0	0	0	1	2	0	0	1	18.0	0.00	—	.500	.500	0	—	0	0	0	0	0.0
Tex-A	0	1	.000	7	0	0	0	2	8^{1}	12	2	3	8	16.2	7.56	56	.343	.395	0	—	0	-3	-3	-0	-0.4
Total 1	1	1	.500	9	0	0	0	2	9^{1}	14	2	3	9	16.4	6.75	62	.359	.405	0	—	0	-3	-3	-0	-0.4
● **MAX SURKONT** Surkont, Matthew Constantine b: 6/16/22, Central Falls, R.I. d: 10/8/86, Largo, Fla. BR/TR, 6', 205 lbs. Deb: 4/19/49																									
1949 Chi-A	3	5	.375	44	2	0	0	4	96	92	9	60	38	14.5	4.78	87	.255	.366	1	.045	-1	-6	-7	-1	-0.9
1950 Bos-N	5	2	.714	9	6	2	0	0	55^{2}	63	5	20	21	13.7	3.23	119	.285	.350	10	.435	5	6	4	-1	0.9
1951 Bos-N	12	16	.429	37	33	11	2	1	237	230	21	89	110	12.4	3.99	92	.252	.323	11	.151	0	-1	-8	-3	-1.0
1952 Bos-N	12	13	.480	31	29	12	3	0	215	201	19	76	125	11.7	3.77	96	.245	.311	7	.111	-1	-1	-4	-1	-0.5
1953 Mil-N	11	5	.688	28	24	11	2	0	170	168	22	64	83	12.3	4.18	94	.255	.321	16	.286	6	2	-5	1	0.2
1954 Pit-N	9	18	.333	33	29	11	0	0	208^{1}	216	25	78	78	12.9	4.41	95	.268	.335	10	.167	0	-8	-5	0	-0.4
1955 Pit-N	7	14	.333	35	22	5	0	2	166^{1}	194	23	78	84	14.9	5.57	74	.298	.376	7	.140	-1	-28	-27	-2	-2.8
1956 Pit-N	0	0	—	1	0	0	0	0	2	2	0	3	1	22.5	4.50	84	.333	.556	0	—	0	-0	-0	0	0.0
StL-N	0	0	—	5	0	0	0	0	5^{2}	10	3	2	5	19.1	9.53	40	.417	.462	0	.000	-0	-4	-4	-0	-0.4
NY-N	2	2	.500	8	4	1	0	1	32	24	5	9	18	9.3	4.78	79	.202	.258	1	.111	-0	-4	-4	-0	-0.4
Yr	2	2	.500	14	4	1	0	1	39^{2}	36	8	14	24	11.3	5.45	69	.240	.305	1	.100	-0	-7	-7	-1	-0.8
1957 NY-N	0	1	.000	5	0	0	0	0	6^{1}	9	2	2	8	15.6	9.95	40	.321	.367	0	—	0	-4	-4	0	-0.4
Total 9	61	76	.445	236	149	53	7	8	1194^{1}	1209	134	481	571	12.9	4.38	89	.262	.335	63	.176	8	-48	-63	-5	-5.7
● **GEORGE SUSCE** Susce, George Daniel b: 9/13/31, Pittsburgh, Pa. BR/TR, 6'1", 180 lbs. Deb: 4/15/55 F																									
1955 Bos-A	9	7	.563	29	15	6	1	1	144^{1}	123	12	49	60	11.2	3.06	140	.232	.306	7	.143	-2	15	20	-0	1.8
1956 Bos-A	2	4	.333	21	6	0	0	0	69^{2}	71	14	44	26	15.4	6.20	74	.262	.373	4	.222	1	-16	-12	-0	-1.1
1957 Bos-A	7	3	.700	29	5	0	0	1	88^{1}	93	6	41	40	14.0	4.28	93	.274	.358	3	.120	-1	-5	-3	-1	-0.5
1958 Bos-A	0	0	—	2	0	0	0	0	2	6	1	1	0	31.5	18.00	22	.600	.636	0	—	0	-3	-3	-0	-0.3
Det-A	4	3	.571	27	10	2	0	1	90^{2}	90	7	26	42	11.8	3.67	110	.259	.316	3	.125	-1	1	4	-2	0.1
Yr	4	3	.571	29	10	2	0	1	92^{2}	96	8	27	42	12.2	3.98	101	.268	.325	3	.125	-1	-2	1	-2	-0.2

YEAR	TM/L	W	L	PCT	G	GS	CG	SH	SV	IP	H	HR	BB	SO	RAT	ERA	ERA+	OAV	OOB	BH	AVG	PB	PR	/A	PD	TPI
1959	Det-A	0	0	—	9	0	0	0	0	14^{2}	24	4	9	9	21.5	12.89	32	.358	.449	0	.000	-0	-15	-14	-0	-1.4
Total	5	22	17	.564	117	36	8	1	3	409^{2}	407	44	170	177	13.1	4.42	95	.260	.340	17	.145	-2	-23	-9	-4	-1.4

● RICK SUTCLIFFE

Sutcliffe, Richard Lee b: 6/21/56, Independence, Mo. BL/TR, 6'7", 215 lbs. Deb: 9/29/76

YEAR	TM/L	W	L	PCT	G	GS	CG	SH	SV	IP	H	HR	BB	SO	RAT	ERA	ERA+	OAV	OOB	BH	AVG	PB	PR	/A	PD	TPI
1976	LA-N	0	0	—	1	1	0	0	0	5	2	0	1	3	5.4	0.00	—	.125	.176	0	.000	-0	2	2	-0	0.2
1978	LA-N	0	0	—	2	0	0	0	0	1^{2}	2	0	1	0	21.6	0.00	—	.286	.444	0	—	0	1	1	0	0.1
1979	LA-N	17	10	.630	39	30	5	1	0	242	217	16	97	117	11.8	3.46	105	.243	.319	21	.247	5	7	5	-2	0.8
1980	LA-N	3	9	.250	42	10	1	1	5	110	122	10	55	59	14.6	5.56	63	.285	.368	4	.148	-0	-24	-25	-1	-2.7
1981	LA-N	2	2	.500	14	6	0	0	0	47	41	5	20	16	12.1	4.02	83	.238	.325	2	.182	1	-3	-4	0	-0.3
1982	Cle-A	14	8	.636	34	27	6	1	1	216	174	16	98	142	11.5	**2.96**	138	**.226**	.317	0	—	0	**27**	27	1	2.9
1983	Cle-A☆	17	11	.607	36	35	10	2	0	243^{1}	251	23	102	160	13.3	4.29	99	.268	.344	0	—	0	-6	-1	2	-0.2
1984	Cle-A	4	5	.444	15	15	2	0	0	94^{1}	111	7	46	58	15.2	5.15	79	.298	.378	0	—	0	-12	-11	-0	-1.2
	*Chi-N	16	1	**.941**	20	20	7	3	0	150^{1}	123	9	39	155	9.8	2.69	145	.220	.272	14	.250	3	15	20	2	2.8
1985	Chi-N	8	8	.500	20	20	6	3	0	130	119	12	44	102	11.5	3.18	125	.240	.306	10	.233	2	6	12	1	1.7
1986	Chi-N	5	14	.263	28	27	4	1	0	176^{2}	166	18	96	122	13.4	4.64	87	.252	.348	11	.208	3	-18	-12	1	-0.8
1987	Chi-N★	**18**	10	.643	34	34	6	1	0	237^{1}	223	24	106	174	12.6	3.68	116	.252	.335	12	.148	2	11	16	4	2.3
1988	Chi-N	13	14	.481	32	32	12	2	0	226	232	18	70	144	12.1	3.86	93	.269	.325	12	.160	3	-10	-6	1	-0.2
1989	*Chi-N★	16	11	.593	35	34	5	1	0	229	202	18	69	153	10.7	3.66	103	.240	.299	10	.143	1	-4	3	1	0.6
1990	Chi-N	0	2	.000	5	5	0	0	0	21^{1}	25	2	12	7	15.6	5.91	69	.305	.394	0	.000	0	-5	-4	0	-0.4
1991	Chi-N	6	5	.545	19	18	0	0	0	96^{2}	96	4	45	52	13.1	4.10	95	.264	.345	3	.094	-1	-4	-2	0	-0.4
1992	Bal-A	16	15	.516	36	36	5	2	0	237^{1}	251	20	74	109	12.6	4.47	87	.273	.332	0	—	0	-14	-15	-2	-1.7
Total	16	155	125	.554	412	350	69	18	6	2464	2357	202	975	1573	12.3	3.90	100	.254	.328	99	.184	19	-33	4	7	3.5

● HARRY SUTER

Suter, Harry Richard "Handsome Harry" or "Rube" b: 9/15/1887, Independence, Mo. d: 7/24/71, Topeka, Kan. BL/TL, 5'10", 190 lbs. Deb: 4/16/09

YEAR	TM/L	W	L	PCT	G	GS	CG	SH	SV	IP	H	HR	BB	SO	RAT	ERA	ERA+	OAV	OOB	BH	AVG	PB	PR	/A	PD	TPI
1909	Chi-A	2	3	.400	18	7	3	1	1	87^{1}	72	2	28	53	10.7	2.47	95	.199	.264	3	.094	-1	0	-1	-1	-0.4

● DARRELL SUTHERLAND

Sutherland, Darrell Wayne b: 11/14/41, Glendale, Cal. BR/TR, 6'4", 169 lbs. Deb: 6/28/64 F

YEAR	TM/L	W	L	PCT	G	GS	CG	SH	SV	IP	H	HR	BB	SO	RAT	ERA	ERA+	OAV	OOB	BH	AVG	PB	PR	/A	PD	TPI
1964	NY-N	0	3	.000	10	4	0	0	0	26^{2}	32	1	12	9	15.5	7.76	46	.302	.383	1	.200	0	-13	-12	1	-1.1
1965	NY-N	3	1	.750	18	2	0	0	0	48	33	4	17	16	10.1	2.81	125	.199	.289	2	.154	0	4	4	2	0.6
1966	NY-N	2	0	1.000	31	0	0	0	1	44^{1}	60	6	25	23	17.7	4.87	75	.339	.426	2	.667	1	-6	-6	1	-0.4
1968	Cle-A	0	0	—	3	0	0	0	0	3^{1}	6	0	4	2	27.0	8.10	37	.375	.500	0	—	0	-2	-2	-0	-0.2
Total	4	5	4	.556	62	6	0	0	1	122^{1}	131	11	58	50	14.5	4.78	75	.282	.371	5	.238	1	-17	-17	3	-1.1

● SUDS SUTHERLAND

Sutherland, Harvey Scott b: 2/20/1894, Beaverton, Ore. d: 5/11/72, Portland, Ore. BR/TR, 6', 180 lbs. Deb: 4/14/21

YEAR	TM/L	W	L	PCT	G	GS	CG	SH	SV	IP	H	HR	BB	SO	RAT	ERA	ERA+	OAV	OOB	BH	AVG	PB	PR	/A	PD	TPI
1921	Det-A	6	2	.750	13	8	3	0	0	58	80	1	18	18	15.2	4.97	86	.328	.374	11	.407	2	-4	-4	2	0.0

● DIZZY SUTHERLAND

Sutherland, Howard Alvin b: 4/9/22, Washington, D.C. d: 8/26/79, Washington, D.C. BL/TL, 6', 200 lbs. Deb: 9/20/49

YEAR	TM/L	W	L	PCT	G	GS	CG	SH	SV	IP	H	HR	BB	SO	RAT	ERA	ERA+	OAV	OOB	BH	AVG	PB	PR	/A	PD	TPI
1949	Was-A	0	1	.000	1	1	0	0	0	1	2	0	6	0	72.0	45.00	9	.400	.727	0	—	0	-5	-5	0	-0.4

● BRUCE SUTTER

Sutter, Howard Bruce b: 1/8/53, Lancaster, Pa. BR/TR, 6'2", 190 lbs. Deb: 5/09/76

YEAR	TM/L	W	L	PCT	G	GS	CG	SH	SV	IP	H	HR	BB	SO	RAT	ERA	ERA+	OAV	OOB	BH	AVG	PB	PR	/A	PD	TPI
1976	Chi-N	6	3	.667	52	0	0	0	10	83^{1}	63	4	26	73	9.6	2.70	143	.209	.272	0	.000	-1	7	11	-0	1.1
1977	Chi-N†	7	3	.700	62	0	0	0	31	107^{1}	69	5	23	129	7.8	1.34	327	.183	.232	3	.150	-0	31	**36**	1	3.9
1978	Chi-N★	8	10	.444	64	0	0	0	27	99	82	10	34	106	10.6	3.18	127	.220	.287	1	.077	-0	4	9	0	1.0
1979	Chi-N★	6	6	.500	62	0	0	0	**37**	101^{1}	67	3	32	110	8.8	2.22	185	.186	.252	3	.250	1	17	**21**	1	2.4
1980	Chi-N★	5	8	.385	60	0	0	0	**28**	102^{1}	90	5	34	76	11.0	2.64	148	.242	.307	1	.111	-1	11	14	-0	1.5
1981	StL-N★	3	5	.375	48	0	0	0	**25**	82^{1}	64	5	24	57	9.7	2.62	136	.218	.279	0	.000	-1	8	9	-1	0.8
1982	*StL-N	9	8	.529	70	0	0	0	**36**	102^{1}	88	8	34	61	11.0	2.90	125	.235	.303	1	.125	-0	8	8	0	0.9
1983	StL-N	9	10	.474	60	0	0	0	21	89^{1}	90	8	30	64	12.2	4.23	86	.262	.324	0	.000	-1	-6	-6	2	-0.5
1984	StL-N☆	5	7	.417	71	0	0	0	**45**	122^{2}	109	9	23	77	9.8	1.54	225	.245	.284	0	.000	-1	**28**	**26**	1	2.8
1985	Atl-N	7	7	.500	58	0	0	0	23	88^{1}	91	13	29	52	12.5	4.48	86	.267	.330	0	.000	-0	-9	-6	-0	-0.7
1986	Atl-N	2	0	1.000	16	0	0	0	3	18^{2}	17	3	9	16	12.5	4.34	92	.243	.329	0	.000	-0	-1	-1	0	-0.1
1988	Atl-N	1	4	.200	38	0	0	0	14	45^{1}	49	4	11	40	12.1	4.76	77	.275	.321	0	.000	0	-7	-5	-0	-0.6
Total	12	68	71	.489	661	0	0	0	300	1042^{1}	879	77	309	861	10.4	2.83	135	.230	.289	9	.088	-5	91	116	4	12.5

● JACK SUTTHOFF

Sutthoff, John Gerhard "Sunny Jack" b: 6/29/1873, Cincinnati, Ohio d: 8/3/42, Cincinnati, Ohio BL/TR, 5'9", 175 lbs. Deb: 9/15/1898

YEAR	TM/L	W	L	PCT	G	GS	CG	SH	SV	IP	H	HR	BB	SO	RAT	ERA	ERA+	OAV	OOB	BH	AVG	PB	PR	/A	PD	TPI
1898	Was-N	0	0	—	2	1	0	0	0	8^{1}	16	1	8	3	25.9	12.96	28	.401	.501	1	.333	0	-9	-9	0	-0.6
1899	StL-N	0	2	.000	2	2	1	0	0	13	19	0	10	4	20.1	10.38	38	.339	.440	0	.000	-1	-9	-9	1	-0.7
1901	Cin-N	1	6	.143	10	4	4	0	0	70^{1}	82	2	39	12	15.9	5.50	58	.289	.381	3	.107	-2	-17	-18	-1	-1.9
1903	Cin-N	16	9	.640	30	27	21	3	0	224^{2}	207	2	79	76	12.1	2.80	127	.246	.323	12	.143	-3	12	19	-1	1.4
1904	Cin-N	5	6	.455	12	10	8	0	0	90	83	1	43	27	12.9	2.30	127	.255	.348	6	.182	-0	4	6	-2	0.4
	Phi-N	6	13	.316	19	18	17	0	0	163^{2}	172	2	71	46	13.9	3.68	73	.272	.354	10	.164	-0	-17	-18	-1	-2.0
	Yr	11	19	.367	31	28	25	0	0	253^{2}	255	3	114	73	13.4	3.19	87	.266	.349	16	.170	-1	-13	-12	-3	-1.6
1905	Phi-N	3	4	.429	13	6	4	1	0	77^{2}	82	2	36	26	14.1	3.82	76	.290	.378	2	.080	-1	-7	-8	0	-0.9
Total	6	31	40	.437	88	68	55	4	0	647^{2}	661	10	286	194	13.6	3.65	86	.269	.353	34	.142	-7	-43	-37	-5	-4.3

● DON SUTTON

Sutton, Donald Howard b: 4/2/45, Clio, Ala. BR/TR, 6'1", 185 lbs. Deb: 4/14/66

YEAR	TM/L	W	L	PCT	G	GS	CG	SH	SV	IP	H	HR	BB	SO	RAT	ERA	ERA+	OAV	OOB	BH	AVG	PB	PR	/A	PD	TPI
1966	LA-N	12	12	.500	37	35	6	2	0	225^{2}	192	19	52	209	9.9	2.99	110	.228	.276	15	.183	1	15	8	-0	0.9
1967	LA-N	11	15	.423	37	34	11	3	1	232^{2}	223	18	57	169	11.1	3.95	79	.250	.300	10	.133	-0	-15	-22	-2	-2.5
1968	LA-N	11	15	.423	35	27	7	2	1	207^{2}	179	6	59	162	10.4	2.60	106	.232	.288	11	.177	1	9	4	-1	0.4
1969	LA-N	17	18	.486	41	41	11	4	0	293^{1}	269	25	91	217	11.1	3.47	96	.242	.301	15	.153	-1	4	-5	0	-0.6
1970	LA-N	15	13	.536	38	38	10	4	0	260^{1}	251	38	78	201	11.7	4.08	94	.249	.310	13	.155	3	-1	-7	-1	-0.5
1971	LA-N	17	12	.586	38	37	12	4	1	265^{1}	231	10	55	194	9.9	2.54	127	.238	.282	19	.216	3	27	20	-1	2.5
1972	LA-N★	19	9	.679	33	33	18	**9**	0	272^{2}	186	13	63	207	**8.4**	2.08	160	**.189**	**.240**	13	.143	-1	42	38	-0	4.2
1973	LA-N★	18	10	.643	33	33	14	3	0	256^{1}	196	18	56	200	9.0	2.42	142	.209	.258	10	.119	-1	35	29	-1	2.9
1974	*LA-N	19	9	.679	40	40	10	5	0	276	241	23	80	179	10.7	3.23	105	.229	.288	18	.184	1	12	5	-1	0.5
1975	LA-N★	16	13	.552	35	35	11	4	0	254^{1}	202	17	62	175	9.4	2.87	119	.213	**.264**	11	.138	-1	21	15	-1	1.4
1976	LA-N	21	10	.677	35	34	15	4	0	267^{2}	231	22	82	161	10.6	3.06	111	.234	.295	7	.083	-3	13	10	-3	0.4
1977	*LA-N★	14	8	.636	33	33	9	3	0	240^{1}	207	23	69	150	10.4	3.18	120	.233	.291	11	.151	1	19	17	-1	1.7
1978	*LA-N	15	11	.577	34	34	12	2	0	238^{1}	228	29	54	154	10.8	3.55	99	.250	.295	6	.083	-3	1	-1	-2	-0.7
1979	LA-N	12	15	.444	33	32	6	1	1	226	201	21	61	146	10.5	3.82	95	.239	.291	11	.143	-2	-2	-5	-1	-0.8
1980	LA-N	13	5	.722	32	31	4	2	1	212^{1}	163	20	47	128	**9.0**	**2.20**	159	.211	**.258**	5	.078	-4	33	30	-0	2.9
1981	Hou-N	11	9	.550	23	23	6	3	0	158^{2}	132	6	29	104	**9.2**	2.61	126	.230	**.268**	7	.137	0	16	12	0	1.4
1982	Hou-N	13	8	.619	27	27	4	0	0	195	169	10	46	139	10.0	3.00	111	.232	.279	11	.162	-0	13	7	-1	0.6
	*Mil-A	4	1	.800	7	7	2	1	0	54^{2}	55	8	18	36	12.0	3.29	115	.263	.322	0	—	0	5	3	1	0.8
1983	Mil-A	8	13	.381	31	31	4	0	0	220^{1}	209	21	54	134	10.9	4.08	91	.246	.295	0	—	0	-1	-9	-1	-0.6
1984	Mil-A	14	12	.538	33	33	1	0	0	212^{2}	224	24	51	143	11.8	3.77	102	.266	.310	0	—	0	5	2	-2	0.2
1985	Oak-A	13	8	.619	29	29	1	1	0	194^{1}	194	19	51	91	11.3	3.89	99	.256	.302	0	—	0	6	-1	-0	0.3
	Cal-A	2	2	.500	5	5	0	0	0	31^{2}	27	6	8	16	9.9	3.69	111	.233	.282	0	—	0	2	1	-1	0.1
	Yr	15	10	.600	34	34	1	1	0	226	221	25	59	107	11.2	3.86	101	.251	.298	0	—	0	7	1	-1	0.4
1986	*Cal-A	15	11	.577	34	34	3	1	0	207	192	31	49	116	10.6	3.74	110	.242	.288	0	—	0	10	9	-3	0.7
1987	Cal-A	11	11	.500	35	34	1	0	0	191^{2}	199	38	41	99	11.6	4.70	92	.269	.313	0	—	0	-5	-8	-3	-0.8
1988	LA-N	3	6	.333	16	16	0	0	0	87^{1}	91	7	30	44	12.6	3.92	85	.270	.332	2	.087	-1	-5	-6	-1	-0.7
Total	23	324	256	.559	774	756	178	58	5	5282^{1}	4692	472	1343	3574	10.4	3.26	108	.236	.287	195	.144	-7	259	146	-26	14.7

YEAR TM/L	W	L	PCT	G	GS	CG	SH	SV	IP	H	HR	BB	SO	RAT	ERA	ERA+	OAV	OOB	BH	AVG	PB	PR	/A	PD	TPI
● EZRA SUTTON Sutton, Ezra Ballou b: 9/17/1850, Palmyra, N.Y. d: 6/20/07, Braintree, Mass. BR/TR, 5'8.5", 153 lbs. Deb: 5/04/1871 ♦																									
1875 Ath-n	0	0	—	2	0	0	0	0	6	14	0	0		21.0	*7.50*	35	.412	.412	116	.324	1	-3	-3		-0.2
● JOHN SUTTON Sutton, Johnny Ike b: 11/13/52, Dallas, Tex. BR/TR, 5'11", 185 lbs. Deb: 4/07/77																									
1977 StL-N	2	1	.667	14	0	0	0	0	24^1	28	1	9	9	13.7	2.59	149	.315	.378	0	.000	-0	4	3	0	0.4
1978 Min-A	0	0	—	17	0	0	0	0	44^1	46	3	15	18	12.6	3.45	111	.264	.326	0	—	0	2	2	-0	0.0
Total 2	2	1	.667	31	0	0	0	0	68^2	74	4	24	27	13.0	3.15	122	.281	.344	0	.000	-0	5	5	0	0.4
● BILL SWABACH Swabach, William Deb: 7/09/1887																									
1887 NY-N	0	2	.000	2	2	2	0	0	16	27	1	6	6	19.1	5.06	74	.346	.400	0	.000	-1	-2	-2	0	-0.3
● BILL SWAGGERTY Swaggerty, William David b: 12/5/56, Sanford, Fla. BR/TR, 6'2", 186 lbs. Deb: 8/13/83																									
1983 Bal-A	1	1	.500	7	2	0	0	0	21^2	23	1	6	7	12.0	2.91	136	.267	.315	0	—	0	3	3	1	0.5
1984 Bal-A	3	2	.600	23	6	0	0	0	57	68	7	21	18	14.1	5.21	74	.302	.362	0	—	0	-8	-8	-1	-0.9
1985 Bal-A	0	0	—	1	0	0	0	0	1^2	3	0	2	2	27.0	5.40	75	.375	.500	0	—	0	-0	-0	-0	0.1
1986 Bal-A	0	0	—	1	0	0	0	0	1	6	0	1	1	63.0	18.00	23	.750	.778	0	—	0	-2	-2	0	-0.1
Total 4	4	3	.571	32	8	0	0	0	81^1	100	8	30	28	14.4	4.76	82	.306	.364	0	—	0	-7	-8	0	-0.4
● CY SWAIM Swaim, John Hillary b: 3/11/1874, Cadwallader, Ohio 6'6", 180 lbs. Deb: 5/03/1897																									
1897 Was-N	10	11	.476	27	20	15	0	0	193	225	5	60	55	13.8	4.43	98	.289	.347	17	.227	-3	-2	-2	-3	-0.7
1898 Was-N	3	11	.214	16	13	9	0	1	101^1	119	4	28	30	13.4	4.26	86	.290	.342	5	.143	-3	-7	-7	-1	-1.0
Total 2	13	22	.371	43	33	24	0	1	294^1	344	9	88	85	13.6	4.37	94	.289	.346	22	.200	-6	-10	-9	-5	-1.7
● CRAIG SWAN Swan, Craig Steven b: 11/30/50, Van Nuys, Cal. BR/TR, 6'3", 215 lbs. Deb: 9/03/73																									
1973 NY-N	0	1	.000	3	1	0	0	0	8^1	16	2	2	4	19.4	8.64	42	.432	.462	0	.000	-0	-5	-5	-0	-0.5
1974 NY-N	1	3	.250	7	5	0	0	0	30^1	28	1	21	10	14.5	4.45	80	.255	.374	4	.364	1	-3	-3	0	-0.2
1975 NY-N	1	3	.250	6	6	0	0	0	31	38	4	13	19	15.1	6.39	54	.302	.371	0	.000	-1	-10	-10	-1	-1.1
1976 NY-N	6	9	.400	23	22	2	1	0	132^1	129	11	44	89	12.1	3.54	93	.254	.320	4	.103	-1	-1	-4	-1	-0.5
1977 NY-N	9	10	.474	26	24	2	1	0	146^2	153	10	56	71	12.9	4.23	88	.268	.334	9	.188	-0	-5	-8	-2	-1.1
1978 NY-N	9	6	.600	29	28	5	1	0	207^1	164	12	58	125	**9.7**	**2.43**	**143**	.219	.277	10	.154	-0	26	24	1	2.8
1979 NY-N	14	13	.519	35	35	10	3	0	251^1	241	20	57	145	10.7	3.29	110	.255	.299	10	.123	-1	12	10	-1	0.8
1980 NY-N	5	9	.357	21	21	4	1	0	128^1	117	20	30	79	10.3	3.58	99	.247	.292	7	.219	2	0	-0	-2	-0.1
1981 NY-N	0	2	.000	5	3	0	0	0	13^2	10	0	1	9	7.2	3.29	106	.204	.220	0	.000	-0	0	0	-0	0.0
1982 NY-N	11	7	.611	37	21	2	0	1	166^1	165	13	37	67	10.9	3.35	108	.256	.297	8	.182	3	5	5	-1	0.7
1983 NY-N	2	8	.200	27	18	0	0	1	96^1	112	14	42	43	14.4	5.51	66	.299	.369	2	.077	-2	-20	-20	-1	-2.3
1984 NY-N	1	0	1.000	10	0	0	0	0	18^2	18	5	7	10	12.1	8.20	43	.247	.313	0	—	0	-10	-10	-0	-1.0
Cal-A	0	1	.000	2	1	0	0	0	5	8	3	0	2	14.4	10.80	37	.348	.348	0	—	0	-4	-4	0	-0.3
Total 12	59	72	.450	231	185	25	7	2	1235^2	1199	115	368	673	11.5	3.74	95	.256	.312	54	.151	1	-13	-24	-10	-2.8
● DUCKY SWAN Swan, Harry Gordon b: 8/11/1887, Lancaster, Pa. d: 5/8/46, Pittsburgh, Pa. BR/TR, 5'10", 165 lbs. Deb: 4/28/14																									
1914 KC-F	0	0	—	1	0	0	0	0	1	0	0	1	1	9.0	0.00	—	.000	.250	0	—	0	0	0	-0	0.0
● RUSS SWAN Swan, Russell Howard b: 1/3/64, Fremont, Cal. BL/TL, 6'4", 210 lbs. Deb: 8/03/89																									
1989 SF-N	0	2	.000	2	2	0	0	0	6^2	11	4	4	2	20.3	10.80	31	.393	.469	0	.000	-0	-5	-6	0	-0.5
1990 SF-N	0	1	.000	2	1	0	0	0	2^1	6	0	4	1	38.6	3.86	94	.429	.556	0	.000	-0	-0	-0	0	0.0
Sea-A	2	3	.400	11	8	0	0	0	47	42	3	18	15	11.5	3.64	109	.244	.316	0	—	0	1	2	0	0.2
1991 Sea-A	6	2	.750	63	0	0	0	2	78^2	81	8	28	33	12.5	3.43	120	.269	.331	0	—	0	6	6	1	0.7
1992 Sea-A	3	10	.231	55	9	1	0	9	104^1	104	8	45	45	13.1	4.74	84	.262	.342	0	—	0	-9	-9	2	-0.7
Total 4	11	18	.379	133	20	1	0	11	239	244	23	99	96	13.0	4.26	94	.268	.341	0	.000	-0	-8	-7	2	-0.3
● RED SWANSON Swanson, Arthur Leonard b: 10/15/36, Baton Rouge, La. BR/TR, 6'1.5", 175 lbs. Deb: 9/10/55																									
1955 Pit-N	0	0	—	1	0	0	0	0	2	2	1	3	0	22.5	18.00	23	.286	.500	0	—	0	-3	-3	-0	-0.3
1956 Pit-N	0	0	—	9	0	0	0	0	11^2	21	1	8	5	22.4	10.03	38	.438	.518	0	—	0	-8	-8	1	-0.7
1957 Pit-N	3	3	.500	32	8	1	0	0	72^2	68	9	31	29	12.4	3.72	102	.248	.327	0	.000	-1	1	1	-1	-0.2
Total 3	3	3	.500	42	8	1	0	0	86^1	91	11	42	34	14.0	4.90	77	.277	.360	0	.000	-1	-10	-11	-0	-1.2
● ED SWARTWOOD Swartwood, Cyrus Edward b: 1/12/1859, Rockford, Ill. d: 5/15/24, Pittsburgh, Pa. BL/TR, 198 lbs. Deb: 8/11/1881 U♦																									
1884 Pit-a	0	0	—	1	0	0	0	0	2^1	6	0	1	0	27.0	11.57	29	.400	.438	115	.288	0	-2	-2	-0	-0.2
1890 Tol-a	0	0	—	1	0	0	0	0	3	2	0	0	1	6.0	3.00	132	.184	.184	151	.327	0	0	0	-0	0.0
Total 2	0	0	—	2	0	0	0	0	5^1	8	0	1	1	15.2	6.75	55	.309	.335	861	.299	1	-2	-2	-0	-0.2
● BUD SWARTZ Swartz, Sherwin Merle b: 6/13/29, Tulsa, Okla. BL/TL, 6'2.5", 180 lbs. Deb: 7/12/47																									
1947 StL-A	0	0	—	5	0	0	0	0	5^1	9	1	7	1	27.0	6.75	57	.360	.500	1	1.000	0	-2	-2	-0	-0.1
● MONTY SWARTZ Swartz, Vernon Monroe "Dazzy" b: 1/1/1897, Farmersville, Ohio d: 1/13/80, Germantown, Ohio BR/TR, 5'11", 182 lbs. Deb: 10/03/20																									
1920 Cin-N	0	1	.000	1	1	1	0	0	12	17	0	2	2	14.3	4.50	68	.333	.358	2	.500	1	-2	-2	0	-0.1
● PARK SWARTZEL Swartzel, Park B. b: 11/21/1865, Knightstown, Ind. d: 1/3/40, Los Angeles, Cal. BR/TR, Deb: 4/17/1889																									
1889 KC-a	19	27	.413	48	47	45	0	1	410^1	481	21	117	147	13.6	4.32	97	.283	.338	25	.144	-10	-22	-6	9	-0.5
● CHARLIE SWEENEY Sweeney, Charles J. b: 4/13/1863, San Francisco, Cal d: 4/4/02, San Francisco, Cal. BR/TR, 5'10.5", 181 lbs. Deb: 5/11/1882 ♦																									
1883 Pro-N	7	7	.500	20	18	14	0	0	146^2	142	3	28	48	10.4	3.13	99	.237	.272	19	.218	-1	0	-1	1	-0.1
1884 Pro-N	17	8	.680	27	24	22	4	1	221	153	4	29	145	**7.4**	1.55	182	**.187**	**.215**	50	.298	8	35	31	1	3.8
StL-U	24	7	.774	33	32	31	2	0	271	207	2	13	192	7.3	1.83	162	.197	.207	54	.316	11	36	34	5	4.6
1885 StL-N	11	21	.344	35	35	32	2	0	275	276	6	50	84	10.7	3.93	70	.250	.282	55	.206	0	-34	-36	0	-3.2
1886 StL-N	5	6	.455	11	11	11	0	0	93	108	9	39	28	14.2	4.16	78	.285	.352	16	.250	1	-9	-10	0	-0.7
1887 Cle-a	0	3	.000	3	3	3	0	0	24	42	0	13	8	20.6	8.25	53	.372	.437	30	.226	0	-11	-10	0	-0.7
Total 5	64	52	.552	129	123	113	8	1	1030^2	928	24	172	505	9.6	2.87	103	.228	.260	224	.251	19	18	8	8	3.7
● BILL SWEENEY Sweeney, William J. b: Philadelphia, Pa. d: 8/2/03, Philadelphia, Pa. TR , Deb: 6/27/1882																									
1882 Phi-a	9	10	.474	20	20	18	0	0	170	178	4	42	48	11.6	2.91	102	.252	.294	14	.159	-3	-4	1	-1	-0.2
1884 Bal-U	**40**	21	.656	**62**	60	**58**	4	0	**538**	522	13	74	374	10.0	2.59	128	.238	.263	71	.240	-5	25	**43**	1	3.5
Total 2	49	31	.613	82	80	76	4	0	708	700	17	116	422	10.4	2.67	121	.241	.270	85	.221	-8	21	44	1	3.3
● LES SWEETLAND Sweetland, Lester Leo (Born Leo Sweetland) b: 8/15/01, St.Ignace, Mich. d: 3/4/74, Melbourne, Fla. BR/TL, 5'11.5", 155 lbs. Deb: 7/04/27																									
1927 Phi-N	2	10	.167	21	13	6	0	0	103^2	147	3	53	21	17.6	6.16	67	.348	.425	12	.316	4	-26	-23	5	-1.4
1928 Phi-N	3	15	.167	37	18	5	0	2	135^1	163	15	97	23	18.3	6.58	65	.306	.426	9	.191	1	-39	-35	2	-2.9
1929 Phi-N	13	11	.542	43	25	10	2	2	204^1	255	23	87	47	15.5	5.11	102	.316	.389	26	.292	3	-9	2	4	0.8
1930 Phi-N	7	15	.318	34	25	8	1	0	167	271	24	60	36	18.1	7.71	71	.373	.425	16	.281	4	-51	-42	1	-3.1
1931 Chi-N	8	7	.533	26	14	9	0	0	130^1	156	3	61	32	15.3	5.04	77	.297	.375	15	.268	5	-17	-17	0	-1.2
Total 5	33	58	.363	161	95	38	3	4	740^2	992	68	358	159	16.9	6.10	77	.329	.407	78	.272	17	-142	-116	12	-7.8
● STEVE SWETONIC Swetonic, Stephen Albert b: 8/13/03, Mt.Pleasant, Pa. d: 4/22/74, Canonsburg, Pa. BR/TR, 5'11", 185 lbs. Deb: 4/17/29 ♦																									
1929 Pit-N	8	10	.444	41	12	3	0	5	143^2	172	6	50	35	14.2	4.82	99	.299	.360	13	.271	3	-2	-1	2	0.3
1930 Pit-N	6	6	.500	23	6	3	1	5	96^2	107	7	27	35	12.5	4.47	111	.276	.323	4	.111	-3	5	5	-1	0.2
1931 Pit-N	0	2	.000	14	0	0	0	1	27^2	28	0	16	8	14.3	3.90	99	.264	.361	1	.143	-0	-0	-0	-0	0.0

YEAR	TM/L	W	L	PCT	G	GS	CG	SH	SV	IP	H	HR	BB	SO	RAT	ERA	ERA+	OAV	OOB	BH	AVG	PB	PR	/A	PD	TPI
1932	Pit-N	11	6	.647	24	19	11	**4**	0	162^2	134	11	55	39	10.5	2.82	135	**.221**	.286	5	.093	-4	19	18	-1	1.3
1933	Pit-N	12	12	.500	31	21	8	3	0	164^2	166	10	64	37	12.7	3.50	95	.260	.330	11	.200	1	-3	-3	-1	-0.4
Total	5	37	36	.507	133	58	25	8	11	595^1	607	34	212	154	12.5	3.81	107	.262	.326	34	.170	-2	20	19	-2	1.4
● **BILL SWIFT**	Swift, William Charles b: 10/27/61, Portland, Maine BR/TR, 6', 180 lbs. Deb: 6/07/85																									
1985	Sea-A	6	10	.375	23	21	0	0	0	120^2	131	8	48	55	13.7	4.77	88	.279	.352	0	—	0	-8	-8	0	-0.7
1986	Sea-A	2	9	.182	29	17	1	0	0	115^1	148	5	55	55	16.4	5.46	78	.319	.399	0	—	0	-16	-16	1	-1.4
1988	Sea-A	8	12	.400	38	24	6	1	0	174^2	199	10	65	47	14.0	4.59	91	.294	.363	0	—	0	-12	-8	2	-0.9
1989	Sea-A	7	3	.700	37	16	0	0	1	130	140	7	38	45	12.5	4.43	91	.278	.331	0	—	0	-8	-6	5	-0.3
1990	Sea-A	6	4	.600	55	8	0	0	6	128	135	4	21	42	11.5	2.39	166	.272	.311	0	—	0	22	22	0	2.3
1991	Sea-A	1	2	.333	71	0	0	0	17	90^1	74	3	26	48	10.1	1.99	207	.224	.283	0	—	0	21	21	3	2.4
1992	SF-N	10	4	.714	30	22	3	2	1	164^2	144	6	43	77	10.4	**2.08**	161	.239	.293	8	.157	1	26	23	2	3.0
Total	7	40	44	.476	283	108	10	3	25	923^2	971	43	296	369	12.7	3.69	108	.274	.336	8	.157	1	24	29	14	4.4
● **BILL SWIFT**	Swift, William Vincent b: 1/10/08, Elmira, N.Y. d: 2/23/69, Bartow, Fla. BR/TR, 6'1.5", 192 lbs. Deb: 4/12/32																									
1932	Pit-N	14	10	.583	39	23	11	0	4	214^1	205	15	26	64	9.8	3.61	106	.248	.272	15	.192	-1	6	5	-4	0.0
1933	Pit-N	14	10	.583	37	29	13	2	0	218^1	214	11	36	64	10.5	3.13	106	.251	.285	20	.244	3	5	5	-2	0.6
1934	Pit-N	11	13	.458	37	24	13	1	0	212^2	244	15	46	81	12.6	3.98	103	.284	.326	18	.214	2	2	3	-1	0.3
1935	Pit-N	15	8	.652	39	21	11	3	1	203^2	193	6	37	74	10.2	2.70	152	.247	.282	19	.244	3	30	32	-4	3.1
1936	Pit-N	16	16	.500	45	31	17	0	2	262^1	275	18	63	92	11.8	4.01	101	.265	.310	31	.295	9	0	1	-5	0.5
1937	Pit-N	9	10	.474	36	17	9	0	3	164	160	14	34	84	10.8	3.95	98	.256	.297	9	.167	-1	-1	-2	-3	-0.5
1938	Pit-N	7	5	.583	36	9	2	0	4	150	155	9	40	77	11.9	3.24	117	.271	.323	10	.200	2	9	9	-1	1.0
1939	Pit-N	5	7	.417	36	8	2	1	4	129^2	150	6	28	56	12.6	3.89	99	.293	.333	10	.238	2	0	-1	-3	-0.2
1940	Bos-N	1	1	.500	4	0	0	0	1	9^1	12	0	7	7	18.3	2.89	129	.308	.413	0	.000	-0	1	1	0	0.1
1941	Bro-N	3	0	1.000	9	0	0	0	1	22	26	4	7	9	13.5	3.27	112	.289	.340	1	.200	-0	1	1	-0	0.0
1943	Chi-A	0	2	.000	18	1	0	0	0	51^1	48	5	27	28	14.2	4.21	79	.246	.355	1	.100	0	-5	-5	-2	-0.7
Total	11	95	82	.537	336	163	78	7	20	1637^2	1682	103	351	636	11.4	3.58	108	.263	.305	134	.227	18	49	49	-25	4.2
● **OAD SWIGART**	Swigart, Oadis Vaughn b: 2/13/15, Archie, Mo. BL/TR, 6', 175 lbs. Deb: 9/14/39																									
1939	Pit-N	1	1	.500	3	3	1	1	0	24^1	27	1	6	8	12.2	4.44	87	.293	.337	2	.250	0	-1	-2	-0	-0.2
1940	Pit-N	0	2	.000	7	2	0	0	0	22^1	27	1	10	9	14.9	4.43	86	.297	.366	1	.200	-0	-1	-2	0	-0.1
Total	2	1	3	.250	10	5	1	1	0	46^2	54	2	16	17	13.5	4.44	86	.295	.352	3	.231	0	-3	-3	0	-0.3
● **AD SWIGLER**	Swigler, Adam William "Doc" b: 9/21/1895, Philadelphia, Pa. d: 2/5/75, Philadelphia, Pa. BR/TR, 5'10", 180 lbs. Deb: 9/25/17																									
1917	NY-N	0	1	.000	1	1	0	0	0	6	7	0	8	4	22.5	6.00	43	.333	.517	0	.000	-0	-2	-2	0	-0.2
● **GREG SWINDELL**	Swindell, Forrest Gregory b: 1/2/65, Houston, Tex. BR/TL, 6'2", 225 lbs. Deb: 8/21/86																									
1986	Cle-A	5	2	.714	9	9	1	0	0	61^2	57	9	15	46	10.7	4.23	98	.243	.291	0	—	0	-0	-1	1	0.1
1987	Cle-A	3	8	.273	16	15	4	1	0	102^1	112	18	37	97	13.2	5.10	89	.283	.346	0	—	0	-7	-7	-0	-0.7
1988	Cle-A	18	14	.563	33	33	12	4	0	242	234	18	45	180	10.4	3.20	129	.252	.287	0	—	0	21	25	-1	2.3
1989	Cle-A★	13	6	.684	28	28	5	2	0	184^1	170	16	51	129	10.8	3.37	118	.246	.298	0	—	0	11	12	-0	1.1
1990	Cle-A	12	9	.571	34	34	3	0	0	214^2	245	27	47	135	12.3	4.40	89	.288	.326	0	—	0	-12	-12	-2	-1.4
1991	Cle-A	9	16	.360	33	33	7	0	0	238	241	21	31	169	10.4	3.48	119	.263	.289	0	—	0	16	18	-1	1.7
1992	Cin-N	12	8	.600	31	30	5	3	0	213^2	210	14	41	138	10.7	2.70	136	.260	.297	10	.125	-2	19	23	-1	2.3
Total	7	72	63	.533	184	182	37	10	0	1256^2	1269	123	267	894	11.1	3.60	112	.263	.303	10	.125	-2	47	59	-4	5.4
● **JOSH SWINDELL**	Swindell, Joshua Ernest b: 7/5/1883, Rose Hill, Kan. d: 3/19/69, Fruita, Colo. BR/TR, 6', 180 lbs. Deb: 9/16/11 ♦																									
1911	Cle-A	0	1	.000	4	1	1	0	0	17^1	19	0	4	6	12.5	2.08	164	.257	.304	1	.250	-0	2	3	-0	0.2
● **LEN SWORMSTEDT**	Swormstedt, Leonard Jordan b: 10/6/1878, Cincinnati, Ohio d: 7/19/64, Salem, Mass. BR/TR, 5'11.5", 165 lbs. Deb: 9/29/01																									
1901	Cin-N	2	1	.667	3	3	3	0	0	26	19	2	5	13	8.7	1.73	185	.203	.251	0	.000	-1	5	4	0	0.3
1902	Cin-N	0	2	.000	2	2	2	0	0	18	22	1	5	3	13.5	4.00	75	.301	.345	0	.000	-1	-2	-2	-0	-0.3
1906	Bos-A	1	1	.500	3	2	2	0	0	21	17	0	0	6	7.7	1.29	214	.224	.235	1	.125	-1	3	3	-1	0.3
Total	3	3	4	.429	8	7	7	0	0	65	58	3	10	22	9.7	2.22	136	.239	.275	1	.043	-3	5	6	-1	0.3
● **BOB SYKES**	Sykes, Robert Joseph b: 12/11/54, Neptune, N.J. BB/TL, 6'2", 200 lbs. Deb: 4/09/77																									
1977	Det-A	5	7	.417	32	20	3	0	0	132^2	141	15	50	58	13.1	4.41	97	.271	.337	0	—	0	-5	-2	-0	-0.6
1978	Det-A	6	6	.500	22	10	3	2	2	93^2	99	14	34	58	12.9	3.94	98	.275	.339	0	—	0	-2	-1	-2	-0.5
1979	StL-N	4	3	.571	13	11	0	0	0	67	86	11	34	35	16.3	6.18	61	.315	.393	2	.095	-0	-18	-18	-1	-1.8
1980	StL-N	6	10	.375	27	19	4	3	0	126	134	12	54	50	13.4	4.64	79	.277	.350	4	.103	-2	-15	-13	-2	-1.7
1981	StL-N	2	0	1.000	22	1	0	0	0	37^1	37	2	18	14	13.5	4.58	78	.266	.354	0	.000	0	-5	-4	1	-0.4
Total	5	23	26	.469	116	61	10	5	2	456^2	497	54	190	215	13.6	4.65	84	.280	.351	6	.097	-2	-44	-38	-4	-5.0
● **LOU SYLVESTER**	Sylvester, Louis J. b: 2/14/1855, Springfield, Ill. BR/TR, 5'3", 165 lbs. Deb: 4/18/1884 ♦																									
1884	Cin-U	0	1	.000	6	1	1	0	1	32^2	32	0	6	7	10.5	3.58	88	.239	.272	89	.267	1	-2	-2	-1	-0.2
● **LEFTY TABER**	Taber, Edward Timothy b: 1/11/1900, Rock Island, Ill. d: 11/5/83, Lincoln, Neb. BL/TL, 6', 180 lbs. Deb: 9/04/26																									
1926	Phi-N	0	0	—	6	0	0	0	0	8^1	8	0	5	0	16.2	7.56	55	.242	.375	0	.000	-0	-3	-3	-0	-0.3
1927	Phi-N	0	1	.000	3	1	0	0	0	3^1	8	0	5	0	37.8	18.90	22	.533	.667	0	.000	-0	-6	-5	0	-0.5
Total	2	0	1	.000	9	1	0	0	0	11^2	16	0	10	0	22.4	10.80	38	.333	.475	0	.000	-0	-9	-9	0	-0.8
● **JOHN TABER**	Taber, John Pardon b: 6/28/1868, Acushnet, Mass. d: 2/21/40, Boston, Mass. BR/TR, 5'8", Deb: 4/30/1890																									
1890	Bos-N	0	1	.000	2	1	1	0	1	13	11	0	8	3	13.2	4.15	90	.222	.330	0	.000	-1	-1	-1	0	-0.1
● **JOHN TAFF**	Taff, John Gallatin b: 6/3/1890, Austin, Tex. d: 5/15/61, Houston, Tex. BR/TR, 6', 170 lbs. Deb: 5/11/13																									
1913	Phi-A	0	1	.000	7	1	0	0	1	17^2	22	0	5	9	13.8	6.62	42	.293	.338	1	.200	-0	-7	-8	0	-0.8
● **DOUG TAITT**	Taitt, Douglas John "Poco" b: 8/3/02, Bay City, Mich. d: 12/12/70, Portland, Ore. BL/TR, 6', 176 lbs. Deb: 4/10/28 ♦																									
1928	Bos-A	0	0	—	1	0	0	0	0	1	2	0	2	1	36.0	27.00	15	.400	.571	144	.299	0	-3	-3	0	-0.2
● **FRED TALBOT**	Talbot, Frederick Lealand "Bubby" b: 6/28/41, Washington, D.C. BR/TR, 6'2", 195 lbs. Deb: 9/28/63																									
1963	Chi-A	0	0	—	1	0	0	0	0	3	2	0	4	2	18.0	3.00	117	.222	.462	0	.000	-0	0	0	0	0.0
1964	Chi-A	4	5	.444	17	12	3	2	0	75^1	83	7	20	34	12.8	3.70	93	.288	.343	5	.263	3	-1	-2	-1	0.0
1965	KC-A	10	12	.455	39	33	2	1	0	198	188	25	86	117	12.7	4.14	84	.251	.333	14	.200	3	-15	-14	-1	-1.2
1966	KC-A	4	4	.500	11	11	0	0	0	67^2	65	6	28	37	12.6	4.79	71	.248	.325	3	.150	0	-10	-10	-0	-1.0
	NY-A	7	7	.500	23	19	3	0	0	124^1	123	16	45	48	12.4	4.13	81	.262	.331	5	.143	1	-10	-11	-0	-1.1
	Yr	11	11	.500	34	30	3	0	0	192	188	22	73	85	12.4	4.36	77	.256	.326	8	.145	1	-20	-22	-0	-2.1
1967	NY-A	6	8	.429	29	22	2	0	0	138^2	132	20	54	61	12.5	4.22	74	.252	.329	6	.158	3	-15	-17	2	-1.2
1968	NY-A	1	9	.100	29	11	1	0	0	99	89	6	42	67	12.1	3.36	86	.241	.322	2	.118	1	-4	-5	1	-0.4
1969	NY-A	0	0	—	8	0	0	0	0	12^1	13	1	6	7	13.9	5.11	68	.283	.365	0	.000	-0	-2	-2	0	-0.2
	Sea-A	5	8	.385	25	16	1	1	0	114^2	125	12	41	67	13.3	4.16	87	.278	.343	6	.162	2	-7	-7	0	-0.5
	Oak-A	1	2	.333	12	2	0	0	1	19	22	2	7	9	13.7	5.21	66	.297	.358	1	.333	0	-3	-4	0	-0.4
	Yr	6	10	.375	45	18	1	1	1	146	160	15	54	83	13.2	4.38	82	.277	.339	7	.171	2	-12	-13	0	-1.1
1970	Oak-A	0	1	.000	1	0	0	0	0	1^2	2	1	1	0	16.2	10.80	33	.286	.375	0	—	0	-1	-1	0	-0.1
Total	8	38	56	.404	195	126	12	4	1	853^2	844	96	334	449	12.7	4.12	81	.260	.334	42	.174	13	-68	-74	2	-6.1

YEAR	TM/L	W	L	PCT	G	GS	CG	SH	SV	IP	H	HR	BB	SO	RAT	ERA	ERA+	OAV	OOB	BH	AVG	PB	PR	/A	PD	TPI
● ROY TALCOTT	Talcott, Le Roy Everett b: 1/16/20, Brookline, Mass. BR/TR, 6'1.5", 180 lbs. Deb: 6/24/43																									
1943	Bos-N	0	0	—	1	0	0	0	0	0^{2}	1	0	2	0	40.5	27.00	13	.333	.600	0	—	0	-2	-2	0	-0.2
● VITO TAMULIS	Tamulis, Vitautis Casimirus b: 7/11/11, Cambridge, Mass. d: 5/5/74, Nashville, Tenn. BL/TL, 5'9", 170 lbs. Deb: 9/25/34																									
1934	NY-A	1	0	1.000	1	1	1	1	0	9	7	0	1	5	8.0	0.00	—	.219	.242	1	.250	0	4	4	0	0.5
1935	NY-A	10	5	.667	30	19	9	3	1	160^{2}	178	7	55	57	13.2	4.09	99	.280	.339	14	.246	4	7	-1	-1	0.2
1938	StL-A	0	3	.000	3	2	0	0	0	15^{1}	26	2	10	11	21.1	7.63	65	.366	.444	2	.400	1	-5	-5	0	-0.3
	Bro-N	12	6	.667	38	18	9	0	2	159^{2}	181	11	40	70	12.6	3.83	102	.288	.333	7	.127	-3	-1	1	-2	-0.3
1939	Bro-N	9	8	.529	39	17	8	1	4	158^{2}	177	10	45	83	13.0	4.37	92	.287	.343	10	.182	-1	-8	-6	0	-0.6
1940	Bro-N	8	5	.615	41	12	4	1	2	154^{1}	147	5	34	55	10.7	3.09	129	.244	.288	6	.130	-1	13	16	-1	1.3
1941	Phi-N	0	1	.000	6	1	0	0	0	12	21	1	7	5	21.8	9.00	41	.382	.460	0	.000	-0	-7	-7	0	-0.7
	Bro-N	0	0	—	12	0	0	0	1	22	21	1	10	8	12.7	3.68	100	.244	.323	0	.000	-1	-0	-0	0	-0.1
	Yr	0	1	.000	18	1	0	0	1	34	42	2	17	13	15.6	5.56	66	.296	.371	0	.000	-1	-7	-7	0	-0.8
Total	6	40	28	.588	170	70	31	6	10	691^{2}	758	37	202	294	12.7	3.97	101	.278	.331	40	.175	-1	3	4	-2	-0.0
● FRANK TANANA	Tanana, Frank Daryl b: 7/3/53, Detroit, Mich. BL/TL, 6'3", 195 lbs. Deb: 9/09/73																									
1973	Cal-A	2	2	.500	4	4	2	1	0	26^{1}	20	2	8	22	9.6	3.08	115	.200	.259	0	—	0	2	1	0	0.2
1974	Cal-A	14	19	.424	39	35	12	4	0	268^{2}	262	27	77	180	11.6	3.12	110	.255	.312	0	—	0	15	10	0	1.5
1975	Cal-A	16	9	.640	34	33	16	5	0	257^{1}	211	21	73	**269**	10.2	2.62	135	.226	.288	0	—	0	33	26	3	3.6
1976	Cal-A★	19	10	.655	34	34	23	2	0	288^{1}	212	24	73	261	**9.2**	2.43	137	.203	**.261**	0	—	0	35	29	1	3.5
1977	Cal-A†	15	9	.625	31	31	20	**7**	0	241^{1}	201	19	61	205	10.2	**2.54**	**154**	.227	.286	0	—	0	41	37	1	**4.2**
1978	Cal-A☆	18	12	.600	33	33	10	4	0	239	239	26	60	137	11.6	3.65	99	.258	.309	0	—	0	3	-1	-2	-0.4
1979	*Cal-A	7	5	.583	18	17	2	1	0	90^{1}	93	9	25	46	12.0	3.89	105	.264	.317	0	—	0	3	2	-1	0.4
1980	Cal-A	11	12	.478	32	31	7	0	0	204	223	18	45	113	12.2	4.15	95	.277	.322	0	—	0	-3	-5	-1	-0.6
1981	Bos-A	4	10	.286	24	23	5	2	0	141^{1}	142	17	43	78	12.0	4.01	96	.265	.324	0	—	0	-6	-2	1	-0.2
1982	Tex-A	7	18	.280	30	30	7	0	0	194^{1}	199	16	55	87	12.1	4.21	92	.264	.320	0	—	0	-3	-7	-0	-0.6
1983	Tex-A	7	9	.438	29	22	3	0	0	159^{1}	144	14	49	108	11.3	3.16	127	.240	.304	0	—	0	16	15	3	2.0
1984	Tex-A	15	15	.500	35	35	9	1	0	246^{1}	234	30	81	141	11.7	3.25	127	.245	.308	0	—	0	20	24	1	2.4
1985	Tex-A	2	7	.222	13	13	0	0	0	77^{2}	89	15	23	52	13.1	5.91	72	.287	.338	0	—	0	-15	-15	0	-1.4
	Det-A	10	7	.588	20	20	4	0	0	137^{1}	131	13	34	107	10.9	3.34	122	.250	.298	0	—	0	12	11	1	1.2
	Yr	12	14	.462	33	33	4	0	0	215	220	28	57	159	11.7	4.27	97	.262	.311	0	—	0	-3	-3	1	-0.2
1986	Det-A	12	9	.571	32	31	3	1	0	188^{1}	196	23	65	119	12.6	4.16	99	.268	.330	0	—	0	0	-1	1	0.1
1987	*Det-A	15	10	.600	34	34	5	3	0	218^{2}	216	27	56	146	11.4	3.91	108	.256	.306	0	—	0	13	8	1	0.8
1988	Det-A	14	11	.560	32	32	2	0	0	203	213	25	64	127	12.5	4.21	91	.267	.324	0	—	0	-6	-9	1	-0.6
1989	Det-A	10	14	.417	33	33	6	1	0	223^{2}	227	21	74	147	12.4	3.58	107	.265	.329	0	—	0	7	6	2	1.0
1990	Det-A	9	8	.529	34	29	1	0	1	176^{1}	190	25	66	114	13.5	5.31	75	.280	.352	0	—	0	-27	-26	1	-2.5
1991	Det-A	13	12	.520	33	33	3	2	0	217^{1}	217	26	78	107	12.3	3.77	110	.265	.330	0	.000	0	8	9	1	1.0
1992	Det-A	13	11	.542	32	31	3	0	0	186^{2}	188	22	90	91	13.7	4.39	91	.267	.356	0	—	0	-9	-8	1	-0.8
Total	20	233	219	.515	606	584	143	34	1	3985^{2}	3847	420	1200	2657	11.7	3.63	106	.253	.313	0	.000	0	141	103	15	14.8
● JESSE TANNEHILL	Tannehill, Jesse Niles "Powder" b: 7/14/1874, Dayton, Ky. d: 9/22/56, Dayton, Ky. BB/TL, 5'8", 150 lbs. Deb: 6/17/1894 FC♦																									
1894	Cin-N	1	0	1.000	5	1	1	0	1	29	37	1	16	7	16.8	7.14	78	.307	.393	0	.000	-2	-6	-5	-1	-0.6
1897	Pit-N	9	9	.500	21	16	11	1	1	142	172	1	24	40	12.9	4.25	98	.297	.332	49	.266	3	1	-1	3	0.3
1898	Pit-N	25	13	.658	43	38	34	5	2	326^{2}	338	2	63	93	11.4	2.95	121	.265	.306	44	.289	7	24	22	3	3.3
1899	Pit-N	24	14	.632	40	35	32	3	1	313	354	4	51	61	12.0	2.73	140	.285	.320	34	.258	4	39	38	4	4.4
1900	Pit-N	20	6	.769	29	27	23	2	0	234	247	3	43	50	11.8	2.88	126	.270	.316	37	.336	8	21	19	1	2.7
1901	Pit-N	18	10	.643	32	30	25	4	1	252^{1}	240	1	36	118	10.2	**2.18**	150	.249	.283	33	.244	4	32	31	-3	3.2
1902	Pit-N	20	6	.769	26	24	23	2	0	231	203	0	25	100	9.3	1.95	140	.236	.266	43	.291	7	21	20	-0	3.1
1903	NY-A	15	15	.500	32	31	22	2	0	239^{2}	258	3	34	106	11.3	3.27	96	.274	.306	26	.234	5	-8	-4	2	0.4
1904	Bos-A	21	11	.656	33	31	30	4	0	281^{2}	256	5	33	116	9.6	2.04	131	.243	.275	24	.197	3	17	20	3	3.0
1905	Bos-A	22	9	.710	37	32	27	6	0	271^{2}	238	7	59	113	10.2	2.48	109	.237	.287	21	.226	6	5	7	2	1.6
1906	Bos-A	13	11	.542	27	26	18	2	0	196^{1}	207	9	39	82	11.7	3.16	87	.274	.318	22	.278	6	-10	-9	0	-0.3
1907	Bos-A	6	7	.462	18	16	10	2	1	131	131	3	20	29	10.7	2.47	104	.262	.297	10	.196	1	1	2	0	0.3
1908	Bos-A	0	0	—	1	1	0	0	0	5	4	0	3	2	12.6	3.60	68	.200	.304	1	.500	0	-1	-1	0	0.0
	Was-A	2	4	.333	10	9	5	0	0	71^{2}	77	0	23	14	13.3	3.77	61	.278	.346	11	.256	2	-11	-12	1	-0.9
	Yr	2	4	.333	11	10	5	0	0	76^{2}	81	0	26	16	13.3	3.76	61	.273	.343	12	.267	2	-12	-12	2	-0.9
1909	Was-A	1	1	.500	3	2	2	1	0	21	19	1	5	8	10.7	3.43	71	.268	.325	6	.167	0	-2	-2	1	-0.1
1911	Cin-N	0	0	—	1	0	0	0	0	4^{1}	6	0	3	1	18.7	6.23	53	.316	.409	0	.000	-0	-1	-1	0	-0.1
Total	15	197	116	.629	358	319	263	34	7	2750^{1}	2787	40	477	940	11.1	2.79	115	.263	.303	361	.256	53	123	125	16	20.3
● BRUCE TANNER	Tanner, Bruce Matthew b: 12/9/61, New Castle, Pa. BL/TR, 6'3", 220 lbs. Deb: 6/12/85 F																									
1985	Chi-A	1	2	.333	10	4	0	0	0	27	34	1	13	9	16.3	5.33	81	.309	.392	0	—	0	-4	-3	1	-0.4
● KEVIN TAPANI	Tapani, Kevin Ray b: 2/18/64, Des Moines, Iowa BR/TR, 6', 180 lbs. Deb: 7/04/89																									
1989	NY-N	0	0	—	3	0	0	0	0	7^{1}	5	1	4	2	11.0	3.68	89	.192	.300	0	.000	-0	-0	-0	0	-0.1
	Min-A	2	2	.500	5	5	0	0	0	32^{2}	34	2	8	21	11.6	3.86	107	.266	.309	0	—	0	0	1	-0	-0.2
1990	Min-A	12	8	.600	28	28	1	1	0	159^{1}	164	12	29	101	11.0	4.07	102	.264	.299	0	—	0	-3	2	0	0.0
1991	*Min-A	16	9	.640	34	34	4	1	0	244	225	23	40	135	9.8	2.99	143	.245	.278	0	—	0	30	35	-0	3.6
1992	Min-A	16	11	.593	34	34	4	1	0	220	226	17	48	138	11.4	3.97	101	.269	.313	0	—	0	-1	1	-0	0.1
Total	4	46	30	.605	104	101	9	3	0	663^{1}	654	55	129	397	10.7	3.62	114	.258	.297	0	.000	-0	26	38	-0	3.4
● AL TATE	Tate, Alvin Walter b: 7/1/18, Coleman, Okla. BR/TR, 6', 180 lbs. Deb: 9/27/46																									
1946	Pit-N	0	1	.000	2	1	1	0	0	9	8	0	7	2	15.0	5.00	70	.267	.405	1	.333	0	-2	-1	0	-0.1
● RANDY TATE	Tate, Randall Lee b: 10/23/52, Florence, Ala. BR/TR, 6'3", 190 lbs. Deb: 4/14/75																									
1975	NY-N	5	13	.278	26	23	2	0	0	137^{2}	121	8	86	99	13.9	4.45	78	.240	.356	0	.000	-4	-13	-15	0	-2.0
● STU TATE	Tate, Stuart Douglas b: 6/17/62, Huntsville, Ala. BR/TR, 6'3", 205 lbs. Deb: 9/20/89																									
1989	SF-N	0	0	—	2	0	0	0	0	2^{2}	3	0	0	4	10.1	3.38	100	.250	.250	0	—	0	0	-0	-0	0.0
● KEN TATUM	Tatum, Kenneth Ray b: 4/25/44, Alexandria, La. BR/TR, 6'2", 205 lbs. Deb: 5/28/69																									
1969	Cal-A	7	2	.778	45	0	0	0	22	86^{1}	51	1	39	65	9.8	1.36	257	.172	.277	6	.286	4	**22**	20	-0	2.6
1970	Cal-A	7	4	.636	62	0	0	0	17	88^{2}	68	12	26	50	10.0	2.94	123	.208	.277	2	.182	1	8	7	0	0.8
1971	Bos-A	2	4	.333	36	1	0	0	9	53^{2}	50	3	25	21	13.9	4.19	88	.255	.362	3	.300	2	-4	-3	0	-0.1
1972	Bos-A	0	2	.000	22	0	0	0	4	29^{1}	32	3	15	15	15.0	3.07	105	.283	.377	0	.000	0	-0	0	-0	0.0
1973	Bos-A	0	0	—	1	0	0	0	0	4	6	2	3	0	20.3	9.00	45	.462	.563	0	—	0	-2	-2	-0	-0.2
1974	Chi-A	0	0	—	10	1	0	0	0	20^{2}	23	3	9	5	13.9	4.79	78	.274	.344	0	.000	0	-3	-2	1	-0.2
Total	6	16	12	.571	176	2	0	0	52	282^{2}	230	24	117	156	11.7	2.93	122	.224	.314	11	.244	7	20	20	0	2.9
● WALT TAUSCHER	Tauscher, Walter Edward b: 11/22/01, LaSalle, Ill. BR/TR, 6'1", 186 lbs. Deb: 4/19/28																									
1928	Pit-N	0	0	—	17	0	0	0	1	29^{1}	28	0	12	7	13.2	4.91	83	.280	.374	1	.167	-0	-3	-3	-0	-0.3
1931	Was-A	1	0	1.000	6	0	0	0	0	12	24	2	4	5	21.0	7.50	57	.429	.467	0	—	0	-4	-4	2	-0.3
Total	2	1	0	1.000	23	0	0	0	1	41^{1}	52	2	16	12	15.5	5.66	73	.333	.406	1	.167	-0	-7	-7	1	-0.6

YEAR	TM/L	W	L	PCT	G	GS	CG	SH	SV	IP	H	HR	BB	SO	RAT	ERA	ERA+	OAV	OOB	BH	AVG	PB	PR	/A	PD	TPI
● **ARLAS TAYLOR**	Taylor, Arlas Walter "Lefty" or "Foxy" b: 3/16/1896, Warick County, Ind d: 9/10/58, Dade City, Fla. BR/TL, 5'11", Deb: 9/15/21																									
1921	Phi-A	0	1	.000	1	1	0	0	0	2	7	1	2	1	40.5	22.50	20	.636	.692	0	—	0	-4	-4	-0	-0.3
● **BEN TAYLOR**	Taylor, Benjamin Harrison b: 4/2/1889, Paoli, Ind. d: 11/3/46, Martin County, Ind. BR/TR, 5'11", 163 lbs. Deb: 6/28/12																									
1912	Cin-N	0	0	—	2	0	0	0	0	5^{2}	9	0	3	2	20.6	3.18	106	.360	.448	0	.000	0	0	0	-0	0.0
● **BRUCE TAYLOR**	Taylor, Bruce Bell b: 4/16/53, Holden, Mass. BR/TR, 6', 178 lbs. Deb: 8/05/77																									
1977	Det-A	1	0	1.000	19	0	0	0	2	29^{1}	23	2	10	19	10.4	3.38	127	.219	.293	0	—	0	2	3	0	0.2
1978	Det-A	0	0	—	1	0	0	0	0	1	0	0	0	0	0.0	0.00	—	.000	.000	0	—	0	0	0	0	0.0
1979	Det-A	1	2	.333	10	0	0	0	0	18^{2}	16	1	7	8	12.1	4.82	90	.242	.333	0	—	0	-1	-1	0	-0.3
Total	3	2	2	.500	30	0	0	0	2	49	39	3	17	27	10.8	3.86	111	.224	.304	0	—	0	1	2	0	-0.1
● **CHUCK TAYLOR**	Taylor, Charles Gilbert b: 4/18/42, Murfreesboro, Tenn. BR/TR, 6'2", 195 lbs. Deb: 5/27/69																									
1969	StL-N	7	5	.583	27	13	5	1	0	126^{2}	108	8	30	62	10.0	2.56	140	.235	.287	7	.179	1	15	14	-2	1.4
1970	StL-N	6	7	.462	56	7	1	1	8	124^{1}	116	5	31	64	10.8	3.11	132	.256	.306	3	.115	-1	13	14	1	1.4
1971	StL-N	3	1	.750	43	1	0	0	3	71^{1}	72	7	25	46	12.4	3.53	102	.267	.331	2	.167	0	-1	1	0	0.1
1972	NY-N	0	0	—	20	0	0	0	2	31	44	2	9	9	15.7	5.52	61	.341	.388	0	.000	-0	-7	-7	1	-0.7
	Mil-A	0	0	—	5	0	0	0	1	11^{2}	8	0	3	5	9.3	1.54	196	.200	.273	1	.500	0	2	2	0	0.3
1973	Mon-N	2	0	1.000	8	0	0	0	0	20^{1}	17	3	2	10	8.4	1.77	215	.230	.250	0	.000	-0	4	5	1	0.5
1974	Mon-N	6	2	.750	61	0	0	0	11	107^{2}	101	8	25	43	10.8	2.17	177	.256	.305	3	.300	1	17	20	-0	2.2
1975	Mon-N	2	2	.500	54	0	0	0	6	74	72	6	24	29	11.8	3.53	108	.264	.326	0	.000	-0	1	2	0	0.2
1976	Mon-N	2	3	.400	31	0	0	0	0	40	38	4	13	14	11.5	4.50	83	.273	.336	0	.000	-0	-4	-3	-0	-0.4
Total	8	28	20	.583	305	21	6	2	31	607	576	43	162	282	11.1	3.07	123	.258	.312	16	.158	0	40	47	1	5.0
● **DORN TAYLOR**	Taylor, Donald Clyde b: 8/11/58, Abington, Pa. BR/TR, 6'2", 180 lbs. Deb: 4/30/87																									
1987	Pit-N	2	3	.400	14	8	0	0	0	53^{1}	48	10	28	37	13.0	5.74	72	.247	.345	3	.167	-0	-10	-10	-1	-1.0
1989	Pit-N	1	1	.500	9	0	0	0	0	10^{2}	14	0	5	3	16.0	5.06	66	.333	.404	0	.000	-0	-2	-2	-0	-0.2
1990	Bal-A	0	1	.000	4	0	0	0	0	3^{2}	4	0	2	4	14.7	2.45	155	.250	.333	0	—	0	1	1	-0	0.2
Total	3	3	5	.375	27	8	0	0	0	67^{2}	66	10	35	44	13.6	5.45	73	.262	.354	3	.158	-0	-11	-11	-1	-1.0
● **ED TAYLOR**	Taylor, Edgar Ruben "Rube" b: 3/23/1877, Palestine, Tex. d: 1/31/12, Dallas, Tex. TL, Deb: 8/08/03																									
1903	StL-N	0	0	—	1	0	0	0	0	3	0	0	0	1	0.0	0.00	—	.000	.000	0	.000	-0	1	1	0	0.1
● **GARY TAYLOR**	Taylor, Gary William b: 10/19/45, Detroit, Mich. BR/TR, 6'2", 190 lbs. Deb: 9/02/69																									
1969	Det-A	0	1	.000	7	0	0	0	0	10^{1}	10	2	6	3	13.9	5.23	71	.244	.340	0	.000	-0	-2	-2	0	-0.2
● **HARRY TAYLOR**	Taylor, Harry Evans b: 12/2/35, San Angelo, Tex. BR/TR, 6', 185 lbs. Deb: 9/17/57																									
1957	KC-A	0	0	—	2	0	0	0	0	8^{2}	11	0	4	4	16.6	3.12	127	.314	.400	1	.250	0	1	1	-0	0.1
● **HARRY TAYLOR**	Taylor, James Harry b: 5/20/19, E.Glenn, Ind. BR/TR, 6'1", 175 lbs. Deb: 9/22/46																									
1946	Bro-N	0	0	—	4	0	0	0	1	4^{2}	5	0	1	6	11.6	3.86	88	.313	.353	0	—	0	-0	-0	0	0.0
1947	*Bro-N	10	5	.667	33	20	10	2	1	162	130	10	83	58	12.1	3.11	133	**.225**	.327	8	.129	-2	17	18	1	1.8
1948	Bro-N	2	7	.222	17	13	2	0	0	80^{2}	90	8	61	32	17.2	5.36	75	.288	.408	6	.273	1	-13	-12	2	-0.9
1950	Bos-A	2	0	1.000	3	2	2	1	0	19	13	0	8	8	9.9	1.42	345	.197	.284	2	.286	0	7	7	0	0.8
1951	Bos-A	4	9	.308	31	8	1	0	2	81^{1}	100	6	42	22	15.8	5.75	78	.307	.388	3	.103	-3	-15	-12	1	-1.3
1952	Bos-A	1	0	1.000	2	1	1	0	0	10	6	1	6	1	11.7	1.80	219	.176	.317	1	.250	0	2	2	0	0.3
Total	6	19	21	.475	90	44	16	3	4	357^{2}	344	25	201	127	14.0	4.10	102	.258	.359	20	.161	-3	-2	4	4	0.7
● **JACK TAYLOR**	Taylor, John Budd "Brewery Jack" b: 5/23/1873, W.New Brighton, N.Y. d: 2/7/1900, Staten Island, N.Y. BR/TR, 6'1", 190 lbs. Deb: 9/16/1891																									
1891	NY-N	0	1	.000	1	1	1	0	0	8	4	1	3	3	7.9	1.13	285	.143	.226	0	.000	0	2	2	-0	0.2
1892	Phi-N	1	0	1.000	3	3	2	0	0	26	28	2	10	7	13.2	1.38	234	.264	.328	2	.167	-0	5	5	-1	0.4
1893	Phi-N	10	9	.526	25	16	14	0	1	170	189	8	77	41	14.6	4.24	108	.273	.354	20	.215	-2	8	6	2	0.5
1894	Phi-N	23	13	.639	41	34	31	1	1	298	347	13	96	76	13.9	4.08	125	.288	.349	48	.333	8	41	34	2	3.5
1895	Phi-N	26	14	.650	41	37	33	1	1	335	403	7	83	93	13.5	4.49	107	.293	.340	45	.290	7	11	11	4	1.8
1896	Phi-N	20	21	.488	45	41	35	1	1	359	459	17	112	97	14.8	4.79	90	.308	.364	29	.185	-6	-17	-19	4	-1.8
1897	Phi-N	16	20	.444	40	37	35	2	2	317^{1}	376	5	76	88	13.6	4.23	99	.292	.345	35	.252	2	3	-1	3	0.3
1898	StL-N	15	29	.341	**50**	47	**42**	0	1	**397^{1}**	465	14	83	89	13.0	3.90	97	.290	.335	38	.242	3	-13	-5	8	0.7
1899	Cin-N	9	10	.474	24	18	15	2	2	168^{1}	197	7	41	34	13.3	4.12	95	.292	.341	17	.250	-0	-5	-4	-1	-0.5
Total	9	120	117	.506	270	234	208	7	9	2079	2468	74	581	528	13.7	4.23	103	.292	.346	234	.252	11	36	34	21	5.1
● **JACK TAYLOR**	Taylor, John W. b: 1/14/1874, New Straightsville, Ohio d: 3/4/38, Columbus, Ohio BR/TR, 5'10", 170 lbs. Deb: 9/25/1898																									
1898	Chi-N	5	0	1.000	5	5	5	0	0	41	32	0	10	11	9.4	2.20	163	.214	.268	3	.200	1	6	6	-0	0.7
1899	Chi-N	18	21	.462	41	39	39	1	0	354^{2}	380	6	84	67	12.3	3.76	100	.274	.325	37	.266	9	4	-0	1	0.9
1900	Chi-N	10	17	.370	28	26	25	2	1	222^{1}	226	4	58	57	11.8	2.55	141	.263	.316	19	.235	2	28	26	-3	2.5
1901	Chi-N	13	19	.406	33	31	30	0	0	275^{2}	341	5	44	68	12.9	3.36	96	.301	.334	23	.217	2	-1	-4	2	0.0
1902	Chi-N	23	11	.676	36	33	33	7	1	324^{2}	271	2	43	83	**9.0**	**1.33**	**203**	.227	**.259**	44	.237	3	**52**	**49**	4	**6.6**
1903	Chi-N	21	14	.600	37	33	33	1	1	312^{1}	277	2	57	83	9.8	2.45	128	.235	.273	28	.222	4	28	24	1	2.9
1904	StL-N	20	19	.513	41	39	**39**	2	1	352	297	5	82	103	10.0	2.22	121	.220	.271	28	.211	4	20	19	1	2.6
1905	StL-N	15	21	.417	37	34	34	3	1	309	302	10	85	102	11.6	3.44	87	.259	.315	23	.190	3	-15	-16	-2	-1.4
1906	StL-N	8	9	.471	17	17	17	1	0	155	133	3	47	27	10.9	2.15	122	.227	.292	11	.208	3	8	8	1	1.4
	Chi-N	12	3	.800	17	16	15	2	0	147^{1}	116	1	39	34	9.8	1.83	144	.223	.285	11	.208	2	13	13	-0	1.7
	Yr	20	12	.625	34	33	32	3	0	302^{1}	249	4	86	61	10.2	1.99	132	.224	.283	22	.208	5	21	21	0	3.1
1907	Chi-N	7	5	.583	18	13	8	0	0	123	127	3	33	22	11.8	3.29	76	.268	.318	9	.191	0	-11	-11	1	-1.1
Total	10	152	139	.522	310	286	278	19	5	2617	2502	41	582	657	10.9	2.66	115	.250	.298	236	.223	33	134	116	5	16.8
● **DUMMY TAYLOR**	Taylor, Luther Haden b: 2/21/1875, Oskaloosa, Kan. d: 8/22/58, Jacksonville, Ill. BR/TR, 6'1", 160 lbs. Deb: 8/27/00																									
1900	NY-N	4	3	.571	11	7	6	0	0	62^{1}	74	0	24	16	14.9	2.45	147	.294	.367	3	.136	-1	9	8	-2	0.5
1901	NY-N	18	27	.400	**45**	43	37	4	0	353^{1}	377	8	112	136	12.8	3.18	104	.271	.332	18	.132	-8	5	5	1	-0.2
1902	Cle-A	1	3	.250	4	4	4	1	0	34	37	0	8	8	12.4	1.59	217	.277	.328	1	.100	-1	8	7	1	0.8
	NY-N	7	15	.318	26	25	18	0	0	200^{2}	194	4	55	87	11.7	2.29	123	.254	.314	6	.092	-5	11	12	-1	0.6
1903	NY-N	13	13	.500	33	31	18	1	0	244^{2}	306	6	89	94	14.7	4.23	79	.314	.374	12	.146	-2	-26	-24	-1	-2.5
1904	NY-N	21	15	.583	37	36	29	5	0	296^{1}	231	6	75	138	9.6	2.34	117	.214	.270	16	.157	-1	13	13	3	1.5
1905	NY-N	16	9	.640	32	28	18	4	0	213^{1}	200	5	51	91	10.9	2.66	110	.247	.298	9	.130	-1	8	6	1	0.6
1906	NY-N	17	9	.654	31	27	13	2	0	213	186	4	57	91	10.5	2.20	119	.233	.289	14	.184	0	10	10	-1	1.0
1907	NY-N	11	7	.611	28	21	11	3	1	171	145	1	46	56	10.2	2.42	102	.232	.288	6	.125	-1	1	1	-1	-0.1
1908	NY-N	8	5	.615	27	15	6	1	2	127^{2}	127	5	34	50	11.6	2.33	104	.253	.306	8	.229	2	1	1	-0	0.3
Total	9	116	106	.523	274	237	160	21	3	1916^{1}	1877	39	551	767	11.7	2.75	107	.256	.314	93	.144	-18	40	39	0	2.5
● **WILEY TAYLOR**	Taylor, Philip Wiley b: 3/18/1888, Wamego, Kan. d: 7/8/54, Westmoreland, Kan. BR/TR, 6'1", 175 lbs. Deb: 9/06/11																									
1911	Det-A	0	2	.000	3	2	1	0	0	19	18	0	10	9	13.7	3.79	91	.247	.345	0	.000	-1	-1	-1	-1	-0.2
1912	Chi-A	0	1	.000	3	3	0	0	0	20	21	0	14	4	15.7	4.95	65	.309	.427	0	.000	-1	-4	-4	0	-0.4
1913	StL-A	0	2	.000	5	4	1	0	0	31^{2}	33	0	16	12	13.9	4.83	61	.280	.366	0	.000	-1	-7	-7	0	-0.7
1914	StL-A	2	5	.286	16	8	2	1	0	50	41	0	25	20	12.2	3.42	79	.209	.305	2	.167	-0	-4	-4	-0	-0.5
Total	4	2	10	.167	27	17	4	1	0	120^{2}	113	0	65	45	13.5	4.10	72	.248	.346	2	.061	-3	-15	-15	-0	-1.8

YEAR	TM/L	W	L	PCT	G	GS	CG	SH	SV	IP	H	HR	BB	SO	RAT	ERA	ERA+	OAV	OOB	BH	AVG	PB	PR	/A	PD	TPI
● SCOTT TAYLOR Taylor, Rodney Scott b: 8/2/67, Defiance, Ohio BL/TL, 6'1", 185 lbs. Deb: 9/17/92																										
1992	Bos-A	1	1	.500	4	1	0	0	0	14^2	13	4	4	7	10.4	4.91	84	.245	.298	0	—	0	-2	-1	0	-0.1
● RON TAYLOR Taylor, Ronald Wesley b: 12/13/37, Toronto, Ont., Can. BR/TR, 6'1", 195 lbs. Deb: 4/11/62																										
1962	Cle-A	2	2	.500	8	4	1	0	0	33^1	36	6	13	15	13.5	5.94	65	.281	.352	3	.273	0	-7	-8	-0	-0.7
1963	StL-N	9	7	.563	54	9	2	0	11	133^1	119	10	30	91	10.3	2.84	125	.243	.293	1	.031	-3	7	11	-3	0.6
1964	*StL-N	8	4	.667	63	2	0	0	7	101^1	109	15	33	69	12.7	4.62	82	.274	.331	2	.133	-0	-12	-9	2	-0.8
1965	StL-N	2	1	.667	25	0	0	0	1	43^2	43	6	15	26	12.2	4.53	85	.261	.326	2	.400	1	-5	-3	0	-0.3
	Hou-N	1	5	.167	32	1	0	0	4	57^2	68	5	16	37	13.9	6.40	52	.305	.365	0	.000	-1	-18	-19	-1	-2.2
	Yr	3	6	.333	57	1	0	0	5	101^1	111	11	31	63	13.1	5.60	64	.283	.343	2	.111	-0	-23	-23	-1	-2.5
1966	Hou-N	2	3	.400	36	1	0	0	0	64^2	89	5	10	29	14.5	5.71	60	.333	.369	2	.167	0	-15	-16	-1	-1.8
1967	NY-N	4	6	.400	50	0	0	0	8	73	60	1	23	46	10.4	2.34	145	.230	.295	0	.000	-1	8	8	0	0.9
1968	NY-N	1	5	.167	58	0	0	0	13	76^2	64	4	18	49	9.7	2.70	112	.228	.277	0	.000	-1	2	3	1	0.3
1969	*NY-N	9	4	.692	59	0	0	0	13	76	61	7	24	42	10.2	2.72	134	.228	.294	1	.250	0	7	8	0	0.9
1970	NY-N	5	4	.556	57	0	0	0	13	66^1	65	5	16	28	11.0	3.93	102	.265	.310	0	.000	-0	1	1	0	0.1
1971	NY-N	2	2	.500	45	0	0	0	2	69	71	7	11	32	10.8	3.65	93	.269	.301	1	.250	0	-1	-2	-0	-0.2
1972	SD-N	0	0	—	4	0	0	0	0	5	9	5	0	0	16.2	12.60	26	.375	.375	0	—	0	-5	-5	0	-0.5
Total	11	45	43	.511	491	17	3	0	72	800	794	76	209	464	11.5	3.93	91	.264	.316	12	.103	-5	-39	-32	-2	-3.7
● TERRY TAYLOR Taylor, Terry Derrell b: 7/28/64, Crestview, Fla. BR/TR, 6'1", 180 lbs. Deb: 8/19/88																										
1988	Sea-A	0	1	.000	5	5	0	0	0	23	26	2	11	9	14.5	6.26	66	.295	.374	0	—	0	-6	-5	-1	-0.8
● PETE TAYLOR Taylor, Vernon Charles b: 11/26/27, Severn, Md. BR/TR, 6'1", 170 lbs. Deb: 5/02/52																										
1952	StL-A	0	0	—	1	0	0	0	0	2	4	0	3	0	31.5	13.50	29	.500	.636	0	—	0	-2	-2	0	-0.2
● WADE TAYLOR Taylor, Wade Eric b: 10/19/65, Mobile, Ala. BR/TR, 6'1", 185 lbs. Deb: 6/02/91																										
1991	NY-A	7	12	.368	23	22	0	0	0	116^1	144	13	53	72	15.8	6.27	66	.314	.393	0	—	0	-28	-27	1	-2.5
● BILLY TAYLOR Taylor, William Henry "Bollicky Bill" b: 1855, Washington, D.C. d: 5/14/1900, Jacksonville, Fla. BR/TR, 5'11.5", 204 lbs. Deb: 5/21/1881 ♦																										
1881	Wor-N	0	1	.000	1	1	1	0	0	8	15	0	6	0	23.6	7.88	38	.366	.447	3	.107	-0	-5	-4	-0	-0.4
	Cle-N	0	0	—	1	0	0	0	0	3	0	0	1	2	3.0	0.00	—	.000	.100	25	.243	-0	1	1	-0	0.1
	Yr	0	1	.000	2	1	1	0	0	11	15	0	7	2	18.0	5.73	51	.300	.386	28	.214	-1	-4	-3	-0	-0.3
1882	Pit-a	0	1	.000	1	0	0	0	0	5	11	0	4	1	27.0	16.20	16	.414	.491	84	.281	0	-8	-8	-0	-0.5
1883	Pit-a	4	7	.364	19	9	8	0	0	127	166	4	34	41	14.2	5.39	60	.296	.337	96	.260	3	-29	-31	-2	-2.5
1884	StL-U	25	4	.862	33	29	29	2	**4**	263	222	2	40	154	9.0	1.68	177	.213	.243	68	.366	19	39	38	-1	**4.9**
	Phi-a	18	12	.600	30	30	30	1	0	260	232	3	44	130	10.0	2.53	134	.219	.258	28	.252	3	21	25	2	2.8
1885	Phi-a	1	5	.167	6	6	6	0	0	52^1	68	0	9	11	13.4	3.27	105	.343	.375	4	.190	-1	-0	1	-1	-0.1
1886	Bal-a	1	6	.143	8	8	8	0	0	72^1	87	1	20	37	13.6	5.72	60	.284	.332	12	.308	1	-18	-18	-0	-1.4
1887	Phi-a	1	0	1.000	1	1	1	0	0	9	10	1	7	0	17.0	3.00	143	.286	.405	1	.250	-0	1	1	-0	0.1
Total	7	50	36	.581	100	84	83	3	4	799^2	811	11	165	376	11.2	3.17	102	.248	.287	323	.277	25	2	5	-4	3.0
● BUD TEACHOUT Teachout, Arthur John b: 2/27/04, Los Angeles, Cal. d: 5/11/85, Laguna Beach, Cal BR/TL, 6'2", 183 lbs. Deb: 5/12/30																										
1930	Chi-N	11	4	.733	40	16	6	0	0	153	178	16	48	59	13.3	4.06	120	.296	.348	17	.270	3	16	14	-1	1.4
1931	Chi-N	1	2	.333	27	3	1	0	0	61^1	79	6	28	14	15.8	5.72	67	.305	.375	5	.238	0	-13	-13	1	-1.1
1932	StL-N	0	0	—	1	0	0	0	0	1	2	0	0	0	18.0	0.00	—	.400	.400	0	—	0	0	0	-0	0.0
Total	3	12	6	.667	68	19	7	0	0	215^1	259	22	76	73	14.0	4.51	102	.299	.356	22	.262	3	3	2	0	0.3
● GEORGE TEBEAU Tebeau, George E. "White Wings" b: 12/26/1861, St.Louis, Mo. d: 2/4/23, Denver, Colo. BR/TR, 5'9", 175 lbs. Deb: 4/16/1887 F♦																										
1887	Cin-a	0	1	.000	1	1	1	0	0	8	21	0	3	1	28.1	13.50	32	.488	.532	94	.296	0	-8	-8	0	-0.5
1890	Tol-a	0	0	—	1	0	0	0	0	5	9	0	5	0	25.2	9.00	44	.378	.486	102	.268	0	-3	-3	-0	-0.2
Total	2	0	1	.000	2	1	1	0	0	13	30	0	8	1	27.0	11.77	36	.449	.514	622	.269	1	-11	-11	0	-0.7
● PATSY TEBEAU Tebeau, Oliver Wendell b: 12/5/1864, St.Louis, Mo. d: 5/15/18, St.Louis, Mo. BR/TR, 5'8", 163 lbs. Deb: 9/20/1887 FM♦																										
1896	*Cle-N	0	0	—	1	0	0	0	0	0	1	0	0	0	—	—	—	1.000	1.000	146	.269	0	0	0	0	0.0
● AL TEDROW Tedrow, Allen Seymour b: 12/14/1891, Westerville, Ohio d: 1/23/58, Westerville, Ohio BR/TL, 6', 180 lbs. Deb: 9/15/14																										
1914	Cle-A	1	2	.333	4	3	1	0	0	22^1	19	0	14	4	14.5	1.21	239	.235	.367	1	.167	0	4	4	-0	0.5
● KENT TEKULVE Tekulve, Kenton Charles b: 3/5/47, Cincinnati, Ohio BR/TR, 6'4", 180 lbs. Deb: 5/20/74																										
1974	Pit-N	1	1	.500	8	0	0	0	0	9	12	1	5	6	18.0	6.00	57	.343	.439	0	—	0	-2	-3	1	-0.2
1975	*Pit-N	1	2	.333	34	0	0	0	5	56	43	2	23	28	10.8	2.25	157	.215	.299	1	.091	-0	9	8	2	1.0
1976	Pit-N	5	3	.625	64	0	0	0	9	102^2	91	3	25	68	10.2	2.45	142	.241	.288	0	.000	-1	12	12	2	1.3
1977	Pit-N	10	1	.909	72	0	0	0	7	103	89	5	33	59	10.7	3.06	130	.236	.299	3	.250	0	10	11	3	1.5
1978	Pit-N	8	7	.533	**91**	0	0	0	31	135	115	5	55	77	11.5	2.33	159	.228	.306	2	.095	-1	**19**	21	3	2.4
1979	*Pit-N	10	8	.556	**94**	0	0	0	31	134^1	109	5	49	75	10.7	2.75	141	.222	.296	2	.133	-0	15	17	2	1.9
1980	Pit-N☆	8	12	.400	78	0	0	0	21	93	96	6	40	47	13.3	3.39	107	.267	.342	0	.000	-1	2	3	1	0.3
1981	Pit-N	5	5	.500	45	0	0	0	3	65	61	1	17	34	10.9	2.49	144	.250	.302	0	.000	-0	7	8	1	1.0
1982	Pit-N	12	8	.600	**85**	0	0	0	20	128^2	113	7	46	66	11.3	2.87	129	.237	.309	1	.071	-1	10	12	2	1.3
1983	Pit-N	7	5	.583	76	0	0	0	18	99	78	1	36	52	10.4	1.64	226	.223	.296	0	.000	-1	22	23	1	2.4
1984	Pit-N	3	9	.250	72	0	0	0	13	88	86	4	33	36	12.3	2.66	135	.262	.331	0	.000	-1	9	9	3	1.2
1985	Pit-N	0	0	—	3	0	0	0	0	3^1	7	1	5	4	32.4	16.20	22	.467	.600	0	—	0	-5	-5	0	-0.4
	Phi-N	4	10	.286	58	0	0	0	14	72^1	67	4	25	36	11.7	2.99	123	.246	.314	0	.000	-0	5	6	0	0.6
	Yr	4	10	.286	61	0	0	0	14	75^2	74	5	30	40	12.6	3.57	103	.258	.332	0	.000	-0	0	1	0	0.2
1986	Phi-N	11	5	.688	73	0	0	0	4	110	99	2	25	57	10.1	2.54	152	.240	.283	0	.000	-0	14	16	0	1.7
1987	Phi-N	6	4	.600	**90**	0	0	0	3	105	96	8	29	60	10.7	3.09	137	.243	.295	0	.000	0	12	13	1	1.5
1988	Phi-N	3	7	.300	70	0	0	0	4	80	87	3	22	43	12.5	3.60	99	.276	.327	0	.000	-0	-1	-0	1	0.0
1989	Cin-N	0	3	.000	37	0	0	0	1	52	56	5	23	31	13.7	5.02	72	.272	.345	1	.500	0	-9	-8	0	-0.8
Total	16	94	90	.511	1050	0	0	0	184	1436^1	1305	63	491	779	11.4	2.85	131	.244	.309	10	.083	-6	128	141	22	16.7
● ANTHONY TELFORD Telford, Anthony Charles b: 3/6/66, San Jose, Cal. BR/TR, 6', 175 lbs. Deb: 8/19/90																										
1990	Bal-A	3	3	.500	8	8	0	0	0	36^1	43	4	19	20	15.6	4.95	77	.295	.380	0	—	0	-4	-5	0	-0.3
1991	Bal-A	0	0	—	9	1	0	0	0	26^2	27	3	6	24	11.1	4.05	98	.265	.306	0	—	0	0	-0	-0	0.0
Total	2	3	3	.500	17	9	0	0	0	63	70	7	25	44	13.7	4.57	84	.282	.350	0	—	0	-4	-5	-0	-0.3
● TOM TELLMANN Tellmann, Thomas John b: 3/29/54, Warren, Pa. BR/TR, 6'3", 195 lbs. Deb: 6/09/79																										
1979	SD-N	0	0	—	1	0	0	0	0	2^2	7	1	0	1	23.6	16.88	21	.467	.467	0	.000	-0	-4	-4	0	-0.3
1980	SD-N	3	0	1.000	6	2	2	0	1	22^1	23	0	8	9	12.5	1.61	213	.264	.326	1	.125	-0	5	5	0	0.5
1983	Mil-A	9	4	.692	44	0	0	0	8	99^2	95	7	35	48	11.9	2.80	133	.259	.327	0	—	0	14	10	3	1.8
1984	Mil-A	6	3	.667	50	0	0	0	4	81	82	6	31	28	12.7	2.78	138	.272	.342	0	—	0	11	10	1	1.0
1985	Oak-A	0	0	—	11	0	0	0	0	21^1	33	3	9	8	18.1	5.06	76	.347	.410	0	—	0	-2	-3	0	-0.2
Total	5	18	7	.720	112	2	2	0	13	227	240	17	83	94	13.0	3.05	123	.277	.343	1	.111	-0	24	18	4	2.8
● CHUCK TEMPLETON Templeton, Charles Sherman b: 6/1/32, Detroit, Mich. BR/TL, 6'3", 210 lbs. Deb: 9/09/55																										
1955	Bro-N	0	1	.000	4	0	0	0	0	4^2	5	2	5	3	21.2	11.57	35	.294	.478	0	—	0	-4	-4	0	-0.4
1956	Bro-N	0	1	.000	6	2	0	0	0	16^1	20	2	10	8	16.5	6.61	60	.294	.385	0	.000	-0	-5	-5	-0	-0.5

YEAR	TM/L	W	L	PCT	G	GS	CG	SH	SV	IP	H	HR	BB	SO	RAT	ERA	ERA+	OAV	OOB	BH	AVG	PB	PR	/A	PD	TPI
Total	2	0	2	.000	10	2	0	0	0	21	25	4	15	11	17.6	7.71	52	.294	.406	0	.000	-0	-9	-9	-0	-0.9
● **JOHN TENER** Tener, John Kinley b: 7/25/1863, County Tyrone, Ireland d: 5/19/46, Pittsburgh, Pa. BR/TR, 6'4", 180 lbs. Deb: 6/08/1885 ♦																										
1888	Chi-N	7	5	.583	12	12	11	1	0	102	90	6	25	39	10.9	2.74	111	.228	.288	9	.196	-1	1	3	1	0.4
1889	Chi-N	15	15	.500	35	30	28	1	0	287	302	16	105	105	13.0	3.64	114	.262	.328	41	.273	6	12	17	3	2.3
1890	Pit-P	3	11	.214	14	14	13	0	0	117	160	6	70	30	18.1	7.31	53	.312	.400	12	.190	1	-40	-44	4	-2.8
Total	3	25	31	.446	61	56	52	2	0	506	552	28	200	174	13.7	4.30	90	.268	.339	62	.236	6	-27	-23	8	-0.1
● **JIM TENNANT** Tennant, James McDonnell b: 3/3/07, Shepherdstown, W.Va d: 4/16/67, Trumbull, Conn. BR/TR, 6'1", 190 lbs. Deb: 9/28/29																										
1929	NY-N	0	0	—	1	0	0	0	0	1	1	0	0	1	9.0	0.00	—	.333	.333	0	—	0	1	1	0	0.0
● **FRED TENNEY** Tenney, Fred Clay b: 7/9/1859, Marlborough, N.H. d: 6/15/19, Fall River, Mass. Deb: 4/28/1884 ♦																										
1884	Bos-U	3	1	.750	4	4	4	0	0	35	31	0	5	18	9.3	2.31	127	.222	.248	2	.118	-2	3	2	-1	0.0
	Wil-U	0	1	.000	1	1	1	0	0	8	6	0	4	10	11.3	1.13	293	.194	.287	0	.000	-1	2	2	0	0.1
	Yr	3	2	.600	5	5	5	0	0	43	37	0	9	28	9.6	2.09	144	.217	.256	2	.100	-2	4	4	-1	0.1
● **FRED TENNEY** Tenney, Frederick b: 11/26/1871, Georgetown, Mass. d: 7/3/52, Boston, Mass. BL/TL, 5'9", 155 lbs. Deb: 6/16/1894 M♦																										
1905	Bos-N	0	0	—	1	0	0	0	0	2	5	0	1	0	27.0	4.50	69	.417	.462	158	.288	0	-0	-0	0	0.0
● **BOB TERLECKI** Terlecki, Robert Joseph b: 2/14/45, Trenton, N.J. BR/TR, 5'8", 185 lbs. Deb: 8/16/72																										
1972	Phi-N	0	0	—	9	0	0	0	0	13^{1}	16	2	10	5	17.6	4.73	76	.308	.419	0	—	0	-2	-2	0	-0.2
● **GREG TERLECKY** Terlecky, Gregory John b: 3/20/52, Culver City, Cal. BR/TR, 6'3", 200 lbs. Deb: 6/12/75																										
1975	StL-N	0	1	.000	20	0	0	0	0	30^{1}	38	4	12	13	14.8	4.45	84	.306	.368	1	.333	0	-3	-2	0	-0.2
● **JEFF TERPKO** Terpko, Jeffrey Michael b: 10/16/50, Sayre, Pa. BR/TR, 6', 180 lbs. Deb: 9/21/74																										
1974	Tex-A	0	0	—	3	0	0	0	0	7	6	0	4	3	12.9	1.29	277	.231	.333	0	—	0	2	2	-0	0.4
1976	Tex-A	3	3	.500	32	0	0	0	0	52^{2}	42	3	29	24	12.1	2.39	150	.223	.327	0	—	0	7	7	-0	0.6
1977	Mon-N	0	1	.000	13	0	0	0	0	20^{2}	28	2	15	14	18.7	5.66	67	.346	.448	0	.000	-0	-4	-4	-0	-0.5
Total	3	3	4	.429	48	0	0	0	0	80^{1}	76	5	48	41	13.9	3.14	116	.258	.362	0	.000	-0	4	5	-1	0.5
● **WALT TERRELL** Terrell, Charles Walter b: 5/11/58, Jeffersonville, Ind BL/TR, 6'2", 205 lbs. Deb: 9/08/82																										
1982	NY-N	0	3	.000	3	3	0	0	0	21	22	2	14	8	15.4	3.43	106	.268	.375	2	.400	1	0	0	-0	0.1
1983	NY-N	8	8	.500	21	20	4	2	0	133^{2}	123	7	55	59	12.1	3.57	102	.251	.329	8	.182	3	1	1	-0	0.4
1984	NY-N	11	12	.478	33	33	3	1	0	215	232	16	80	114	13.2	3.52	101	.282	.348	6	.080	-4	2	0	0	-0.3
1985	Det-A	15	10	.600	34	34	5	3	0	229	221	9	95	130	12.6	3.85	106	.255	.332	0	—	0	7	6	3	0.9
1986	Det-A	15	12	.556	34	33	9	2	0	217^{1}	199	30	98	93	12.4	4.56	90	.245	.329	0	—	0	-9	-10	2	-0.9
1987	*Det-A	17	10	.630	35	35	10	1	0	244^{2}	254	30	94	143	12.9	4.05	104	.268	.336	0	—	0	11	5	-1	0.7
1988	Det-A	7	16	.304	29	29	11	1	0	206^{1}	199	20	78	84	12.2	3.97	96	.258	.328	0	—	0	-0	-4	1	0.0
1989	SD-N	5	13	.278	19	19	4	1	0	123^{1}	134	14	26	63	11.7	4.01	87	.277	.314	4	.100	-0	-7	-7	3	-0.5
	NY-A	6	5	.545	13	13	1	1	0	83	102	9	24	30	13.9	5.20	74	.307	.358	0	—	0	-12	-12	-0	-1.2
1990	Pit-N	2	7	.222	16	16	0	0	0	82^{2}	98	13	33	34	14.7	5.88	62	.295	.366	3	.107	-1	-19	-21	1	-2.0
	Det-A	6	4	.600	13	12	0	0	0	75^{1}	86	7	24	30	14.1	4.54	87	.290	.359	0	—	0	-5	-5	-1	-0.6
1991	Det-A	12	14	.462	35	33	8	2	0	218^{2}	257	16	79	80	13.9	4.24	98	.301	.361	0	—	0	-4	-2	-1	-0.3
1992	Det-A	7	10	.412	36	14	1	0	0	136^{2}	163	14	48	61	14.1	5.20	77	.298	.358	0	—	0	-19	-18	1	-1.7
Total	11	111	124	.472	321	294	56	14	0	1986^{2}	2090	187	748	929	13.0	4.22	93	.274	.341	23	.120	-1	-54	-67	8	-5.4
● **JERRY TERRELL** Terrell, Jerry Wayne b: 7/13/46, Waseca, Minn. BR/TR, 6', 170 lbs. Deb: 4/14/73 ♦																										
1979	KC-A	0	0	—	1	0	0	0	0	1	0	0	0	0	0.0	0.00	—	.000	.000	12	.300	0	0	0	0	0.0
1980	KC-A	0	0	—	1	0	0	0	0	1	1	0	1	0	18.0	0.00	—	.250	.400	1	.063	0	0	0	0	0.1
Total	2	0	0	—	2	0	0	0	0	2	1	0	1	0	9.0	0.00	—	.143	.250	412	.253	1	1	1	0	0.1
● **JOHN TERRY** Terry, John Burchard b: 11/1/1879, Waterbury, Conn. d: 4/27/33, Kansas City, Mo. Deb: 9/17/02																										
1902	Det-A	0	1	.000	1	1	1	0	0	5	8	0	1	0	16.2	3.60	101	.361	.388	0	.000	-0	-0	0	-0	-0.1
1903	StL-A	1	1	.500	3	1	1	0	0	17^{2}	21	0	4	2	14.3	2.55	114	.294	.357	0	.000	-1	1	1	-0	-0.1
Total	2	1	2	.333	4	2	2	0	0	22^{2}	29	0	5	2	14.7	2.78	111	.310	.364	0	.000	-2	1	1	-1	-0.2
● **YANK TERRY** Terry, Lancelot Yank b: 2/11/11, Bedford, Ind. d: 11/4/79, Bloomington, Ind. BR/TR, 6'1", 180 lbs. Deb: 8/03/40																										
1940	Bos-A	1	0	1.000	4	1	0	0	0	19^{1}	24	2	11	9	16.3	8.84	51	.304	.389	2	.250	0	-10	-9	0	-0.8
1942	Bos-A	6	5	.545	20	11	3	0	1	85	82	5	43	37	13.4	3.92	95	.248	.339	3	.111	-1	-2	-2	-0	-0.3
1943	Bos-A	7	9	.438	30	22	7	0	1	163^{2}	147	8	63	63	11.6	3.52	94	.242	.314	3	.067	-3	-4	-4	0	-0.7
1944	Bos-A	6	10	.375	27	17	3	0	0	132^{2}	142	10	65	30	14.2	4.21	81	.276	.361	11	.234	1	-11	-12	0	-1.1
1945	Bos-A	0	4	.000	12	4	1	0	0	56^{2}	68	8	14	28	13.0	4.13	82	.296	.336	2	.111	-2	-5	-5	-1	-0.7
Total	5	20	28	.417	93	55	14	0	2	457^{1}	463	33	196	167	13.1	4.09	85	.263	.339	21	.145	-4	-32	-31	-1	-3.6
● **RALPH TERRY** Terry, Ralph Willard b: 1/9/36, Big Cabin, Okla. BR/TR, 6'3", 195 lbs. Deb: 8/06/56																										
1956	NY-A	1	2	.333	3	3	0	0	0	13^{1}	17	2	11	8	18.9	9.45	41	.347	.467	1	.167	-0	-8	-8	-0	-0.8
1957	NY-A	1	1	.500	7	2	1	1	0	20^{2}	18	1	8	7	11.3	3.05	118	.240	.313	1	.250	0	2	1	0	0.2
	KC-A	4	11	.267	21	19	3	1	0	130^{2}	119	15	47	80	11.7	3.38	117	.239	.310	6	.143	-2	6	8	0	0.7
	Yr	5	12	.294	28	21	4	2	0	151^{1}	137	16	55	87	11.7	3.33	117	.239	.310	7	.152	-2	8	10	0	0.9
1958	KC-A	11	13	.458	40	33	8	3	2	216^{2}	217	29	61	134	11.6	4.24	92	.262	.314	14	.197	-0	-11	-8	-2	-1.1
1959	KC-A	2	4	.333	9	7	2	0	0	46^{1}	56	9	19	35	14.8	5.24	76	.308	.376	3	.176	-1	-7	-6	1	-0.6
	NY-A	3	7	.300	24	16	5	1	0	127^{1}	130	7	30	55	11.5	3.39	107	.270	.316	4	.098	-3	7	4	-0	0.1
	Yr	5	11	.313	33	23	7	1	0	173^{2}	186	16	49	90	12.3	3.89	96	.280	.331	7	.121	-3	-0	-3	0	-0.5
1960	*NY-A	10	8	.556	35	23	7	3	1	166^{2}	149	15	52	92	11.1	3.40	105	.237	.300	6	.122	-2	9	3	0	0.2
1961	*NY-A	16	3	.842	31	27	9	2	0	188^{1}	162	19	42	86	9.8	3.15	118	.232	.277	15	.227	2	18	12	1	1.5
1962	*NY-A☆	**23**	12	.657	43	39	14	3	2	**298^{2}**	257	40	57	176	**9.6**	3.19	117	.231	.270	20	.189	1	26	18	-4	1.6
1963	*NY-A	17	15	.531	40	37	**18**	3	1	268	246	29	39	114	**9.7**	3.22	109	.242	.273	7	.080	-5	12	9	-1	0.2
1964	*NY-A	7	11	.389	27	14	2	1	4	115	130	20	31	77	12.7	4.54	80	.283	.329	7	.200	1	-12	-12	-0	-1.1
1965	Cle-A	11	6	.647	30	26	6	2	0	165^{2}	154	22	23	84	9.7	3.69	94	.242	.269	7	.143	2	-4	-4	-4	-0.6
1966	KC-A	1	5	.167	15	10	0	0	0	64	65	7	15	33	11.4	3.80	89	.263	.308	3	.214	1	-3	-3	-1	-0.3
	NY-N	0	1	.000	11	1	0	0	1	24^{2}	27	1	11	14	13.9	4.74	77	.293	.369	1	.167	-0	-3	-3	-0	-0.3
1967	NY-N	0	0	—	2	0	0	0	0	3^{1}	1	0	0	5	2.7	0.00	—	.091	.091	0	—	0	1	1	0	0.2
Total	12	107	99	.519	338	257	75	20	11	1849^{1}	1748	216	446	1000	10.8	3.62	102	.249	.296	95	.160	-6	32	13	-11	-0.1
● **SCOTT TERRY** Terry, Scott Ray b: 11/21/59, Hobbs, N.Mex. BR/TR, 5'11", 195 lbs. Deb: 4/09/86																										
1986	Cin-N	1	2	.333	28	3	0	0	0	55^{2}	66	8	32	32	15.8	6.14	63	.300	.389	1	.250	0	-15	-14	0	-1.4
1987	StL-N	0	0	—	11	0	0	0	0	13^{1}	13	0	8	9	14.2	3.38	123	.260	.362	0	.000	-0	1	1	0	0.1
1988	StL-N	9	6	.600	51	11	1	0	3	129^{1}	119	5	34	65	10.6	2.92	119	.247	.297	7	.250	2	8	8	0	1.1
1989	StL-N	8	10	.444	31	24	1	0	2	148^{2}	142	14	43	69	11.4	3.57	102	.253	.310	7	.156	2	-1	1	2	0.5
1990	StL-N	2	6	.250	50	2	0	0	2	72	75	7	27	35	13.3	4.75	80	.264	.337	5	.455	2	-8	-7	0	-0.5
1991	StL-N	4	4	.500	65	0	0	0	1	80^{1}	76	1	32	52	12.1	2.80	133	.249	.320	1	.143	-0	8	8	1	1.0
Total	6	24	28	.462	236	40	2	0	8	499^{1}	491	35	176	262	12.1	3.73	98	.258	.323	21	.216	6	-7	-3	4	0.8
● **ADONIS TERRY** Terry, William H b: 8/7/1864, Westfield, Mass. d: 2/24/15, Milwaukee, Wis. BR/TR, 5'11.5", 168 lbs. Deb: 5/01/1884 U♦																										
1884	Bro-a	19	35	.352	56	55	54	2	0	476	486	10	72	230	10.7	3.55	93	.248	.277	55	.233	3	-16	-12	-3	-1.1

YEAR	TM/L	W	L	PCT	G	GS	CG	SH	SV	IP	H	HR	BB	SO	RAT	ERA	ERA+	OAV	OOB	BH	AVG	PB	PR	/A	PD	TPI
1885	Bro-a	6	17	.261	25	23	23	0	1	209	213	9	42	96	11.2	4.26	77	.262	.301	45	.170	-3	-24	-22	1	-2.1
1886	Bro-a	18	16	.529	34	34	32	5	0	288^1	263	1	115	162	12.3	3.09	113	.231	.310	71	.237	2	12	13	4	1.7
1887	Bro-a	16	16	.500	40	35	35	1	**3**	318	331	10	99	138	12.4	4.02	107	.262	.320	103	.293	7	10	10	5	1.7
1888	Bro-a	13	8	.619	23	23	20	2	0	195	145	2	67	138	10.2	2.03	147	**.199**	.275	29	.252	3	22	21	1	2.3
1889	*Bro-a	22	15	.595	41	39	35	2	0	326	285	6	126	186	11.8	3.29	113	.228	.306	48	.300	12	20	16	6	2.9
1890	*Bro-N	26	16	.619	46	44	38	1	0	370	362	3	133	185	12.4	2.94	117	.248	.318	101	.278	14	26	20	1	3.1
1891	Bro-N	6	16	.273	25	22	18	1	1	194	207	5	80	65	13.6	4.22	78	.263	.336	19	.209	3	-19	-20	-1	-1.5
1892	Bal-N	0	1	.000	1	1	1	0	0	9	7	0	7	3	14.0	4.00	86	.206	.342	0	.000	-1	-1	-1	0	-0.1
	Pit-N	18	7	.720	30	26	24	2	1	240	185	3	106	95	11.2	2.51	131	.204	.293	16	.160	1	21	21	1	2.2
	Yr	18	8	.692	31	27	25	2	1	249	192	3	113	98	11.3	2.57	129	.205	.295	16	.154	1	20	20	1	2.1
1893	Pit-N	12	8	.600	26	19	14	0	0	170	177	5	99	52	15.2	4.45	102	.260	.363	18	.254	2	4	2	0	0.4
1894	Pit-N	0	1	.000	1	1	0	0	0	0^2	2	0	4	0	81.0	67.50	8	.510	.758	0	—	0	-5	-5	0	-0.3
	Chi-N	5	11	.313	23	21	16	0	0	163^1	232	12	123	39	20.4	5.84	96	.330	.441	33	.347	5	-9	-4	-1	0.0
	Yr	5	12	.294	24	22	16	0	0	164	234	12	127	39	20.7	6.09	92	.331	.444	33	.347	5	-14	-9	-1	-0.3
1895	Chi-N	21	14	.600	38	34	31	0	0	311^1	346	4	131	88	14.3	4.80	106	.277	.354	30	.219	-6	-1	10	2	0.5
1896	Chi-N	15	14	.517	30	28	25	1	0	235^1	268	6	88	74	14.0	4.28	106	.284	.351	26	.263	2	2	7	-2	0.6
1897	Chi-N	0	1	.000	1	1	1	0	0	8	11	0	6	1	21.4	10.13	44	.324	.453	0	.000	-1	-5	-5	0	-0.4
Total	14	197	196	.501	440	406	367	17	6	3514	3520	76	1298	1552	12.7	3.73	103	.252	.322	594	.249	45	38	47	15	9.9
● DICK TERWILLIGER Terwilliger, Richard Martin b: 6/27/06, Sand Lake, Mich. d: 1/21/69, Greenville, Mich. BR/TR, 5'11", 178 lbs. Deb: 8/18/32																										
1932	StL-N	0	0	—	1	0	0	0	0	3	1	0	2	2	12.0	0.00	—	.143	.400	0	.000	-0	1	1	0	0.2
● JEFF TESREAU Tesreau, Charles Monroe b: 3/5/1889, Silver Mine, Mo. d: 9/24/46, Hanover, N.H. BR/TR, 6'2", 218 lbs. Deb: 4/12/12																										
1912	*NY-N	17	7	.708	36	28	19	3	1	243	177	2	106	119	10.9	**1.96**	**172**	**.204**	.298	12	.146	-2	39	38	1	3.8
1913	*NY-N	22	13	.629	41	38	17	1	0	282	222	7	119	167	11.1	2.17	144	**.220**	.306	21	.221	2	32	30	1	3.5
1914	NY-N	26	10	.722	42	40	26	**8**	1	322^1	238	8	128	189	10.4	2.37	112	**.209**	.293	28	.239	5	15	10	-2	1.5
1915	NY-N	19	16	.543	43	38	24	8	3	306	235	4	75	176	9.3	2.29	112	.215	.269	24	.233	5	16	9	1	1.7
1916	NY-N	14	14	.500	40	33	23	5	2	268^1	249	9	65	113	10.7	2.92	83	.250	.300	18	.191	2	-9	-14	-0	-1.5
1917	*NY-N	13	8	.619	33	20	11	1	2	183^2	168	6	58	85	11.2	3.09	83	.249	.312	14	.230	2	-8	-11	2	-0.9
1918	NY-N	4	4	.500	12	9	3	1	0	73^2	61	1	21	31	10.0	2.32	113	.227	.283	7	.318	2	4	3	1	0.6
Total	7	115	72	.615	247	206	123	27	9	1679	1350	37	572	880	10.5	2.43	114	.223	.295	124	.216	16	89	63	3	8.7
● BOB TEWKSBURY Tewksbury, Robert Alan b: 11/30/60, Concord, N.H. BR/TR, 6'4", 200 lbs. Deb: 4/11/86																										
1986	NY-A	9	5	.643	23	20	2	0	0	130^1	144	8	31	49	12.4	3.31	123	.282	.329	0	—	0	12	11	2	1.4
1987	NY-A	1	4	.200	8	6	0	0	0	33^1	47	5	7	12	14.9	6.75	65	.338	.374	0	—	0	-9	-9	0	-0.7
	Chi-N	0	4	.000	7	3	0	0	0	18	32	1	13	10	22.5	6.50	66	.421	.506	0	.000	-1	-5	-4	-1	-0.5
1988	Chi-N	0	0	—	1	1	0	0	0	3^1	6	1	2	1	21.6	8.10	45	.400	.471	0	.000	-0	-2	-2	0	-0.2
1989	StL-N	1	0	1.000	7	4	1	1	0	30	25	2	10	17	11.1	3.30	110	.225	.301	1	.111	-0	1	1	-0	0.0
1990	StL-N	10	9	.526	28	20	3	2	1	145^1	151	7	15	50	10.5	3.47	110	.267	.290	7	.171	1	5	6	-1	0.6
1991	StL-N	11	12	.478	30	30	3	0	0	191	206	13	38	75	11.7	3.25	114	.281	.321	9	.155	1	9	10	0	1.2
1992	StL-N★	16	5	**.762**	33	32	5	0	0	233	217	15	20	91	9.3	2.16	159	.248	.267	6	.086	-2	35	33	0	3.6
Total	7	48	39	.552	137	116	14	3	1	784^1	828	52	136	305	11.3	3.22	116	.274	.309	23	.124	-1	47	46	1	5.4
● GRANT THATCHER Thatcher, Ulysses Grant b: 2/23/1877, Maytown, Pa. d: 3/17/36, Lancaster, Pa. TR , 5'10.5", 180 lbs. Deb: 9/09/03																										
1903	Bro-N	3	1	.750	4	4	4	0	0	28	33	1	7	9	12.9	2.89	110	.292	.333	2	.182	0	1	1	-0	0.1
1904	Bro-N	1	0	1.000	1	0	0	0	0	9	9	0	2	4	11.0	4.00	69	.281	.324	1	.250	0	-1	-1	-0	-0.1
Total	2	4	1	.800	5	4	4	0	0	37	42	1	9	13	12.4	3.16	98	.290	.331	3	.200	0	-0	-0	-0	0.0
● GREG THAYER Thayer, Gregory Allen b: 10/23/49, Cedar Rapids, Iowa BR/TR, 5'11", 182 lbs. Deb: 4/07/78																										
1978	Min-A	1	1	.500	20	0	0	0	0	45	40	5	30	30	14.6	3.80	100	.258	.388	0	—	0	-0	0	-0	0.0
● JACK THEIS Theis, John Louis b: 7/23/1891, Georgetown, Ohio d: 7/6/41, Georgetown, Ohio BR/TR, 6', 190 lbs. Deb: 7/05/20																										
1920	Cin-N	0	0	—	1	0	0	0	0	2	1	0	3	0	18.0	0.00	—	.143	.400	0	—	0	1	1	-0	0.1
● DUANE THEISS Theiss, Duane Charles b: 11/20/53, Zanesville, Ohio BR/TR, 6'3", 185 lbs. Deb: 8/05/77																										
1977	Atl-N	1	1	.500	17	0	0	0	0	20^2	26	1	16	7	18.7	6.53	68	.338	.457	0	.000	-0	-6	-5	0	-0.5
1978	Atl-N	0	0	—	3	0	0	0	0	6^1	3	0	3	3	9.9	1.42	285	.158	.304	0	.000	-0	2	2	0	0.2
Total	2	1	1	.500	20	0	0	0	0	27	29	1	19	10	16.7	5.33	82	.302	.427	0	.000	-0	-5	-3	0	-0.3
● JUG THESENGA Thesenga, Arnold Joseph b: 4/27/14, Jefferson, S.Dak. BR/TR, 6', 200 lbs. Deb: 9/01/44																										
1944	Was-A	0	0	—	5	1	0	0	0	12^1	18	0	12	2	21.9	5.11	64	.340	.462	0	.000	-0	-2	-3	0	-0.3
● BERT THIEL Thiel, Maynard Bert b: 5/4/26, Marion, Wis. BR/TR, 5'10", 185 lbs. Deb: 4/17/52																										
1952	Bos-N	1	1	.500	4	0	0	0	0	7	11	1	4	6	21.9	7.71	47	.344	.447	0	—	0	-3	-3	-0	-0.3
● HENRY THIELMAN Thielman, Henry Joseph b: 10/3/1880, St.Cloud, Minn. d: 9/2/42, New York, N.Y. BR/TR, 5'11", 175 lbs. Deb: 4/17/02 F♦																										
1902	NY-N	0	1	.000	2	2	0	0	0	6	8	0	6	5	21.0	1.50	187	.319	.451	1	.111	-0	1	1	0	0.1
	Cin-N	9	15	.375	25	23	22	0	1	211	201	2	78	49	12.7	3.24	92	.251	.332	12	.132	-4	-11	-6	-1	-1.1
	Yr	9	16	.360	27	25	22	0	1	217	209	2	84	54	12.9	3.19	94	.253	.336	13	.130	-4	-10	-5	-0	-1.0
1903	Bro-N	0	3	.000	4	3	3	0	0	29	31	3	14	10	14.6	4.66	69	.330	.427	5	.217	1	-4	-5	1	-0.3
Total	2	9	19	.321	31	28	25	0	1	246	240	5	98	64	13.1	3.37	90	.261	.346	18	.146	-3	-14	-9	0	-1.3
● JAKE THIELMAN Thielman, John Peter b: 5/20/1879, St.Cloud, Minn. d: 1/28/28, Minneapolis, Minn. BR/TR, 5'11", 175 lbs. Deb: 4/23/05 F																										
1905	StL-N	15	16	.484	32	29	26	0	0	242	265	4	62	87	12.6	3.50	85	.281	.333	21	.231	8	-13	-14	3	-0.3
1906	StL-N	0	1	.000	1	1	0	0	0	5	5	0	2	0	12.6	3.60	73	.263	.333	1	.500	0	-1	-1	-0	0.0
1907	Cle-A	11	8	.579	20	18	18	3	0	166	151	2	34	56	10.3	2.33	108	.244	.289	12	.203	1	4	3	-3	0.1
1908	Cle-A	4	3	.571	11	8	5	0	0	61^2	59	2	9	15	10.5	3.65	66	.260	.300	8	.348	4	-9	-9	2	-0.4
	Bos-A	0	0	—	1	0	0	0	0	0^2	3	1	0	0	40.5	40.50	6	.600	.600	0	—	0	-3	-3	-0	-0.3
	Yr	4	3	.571	12	8	5	0	0	62^1	62	3	9	15	10.3	4.04	59	.263	.290	8	.348	4	-11	-11	1	-0.7
Total	4	30	28	.517	65	56	49	3	0	475^1	483	9	107	158	11.6	3.16	86	.266	.315	42	.240	12	-21	-23	2	-0.9
● DAVE THIES Thies, David Robert b: 3/21/37, Minneapolis, Minn. BR/TR, 6'4", 205 lbs. Deb: 4/20/63																										
1963	KC-A	0	1	.000	9	2	0	0	0	25^1	26	2	12	9	14.2	4.62	83	.274	.367	2	.333	1	-3	-2	0	-0.1
● JAKE THIES Thies, Vernon Arthur b: 4/1/26, St.Louis, Mo. BR/TR, 5'11", 170 lbs. Deb: 4/24/54																										
1954	Pit-N	3	9	.250	33	18	3	1	0	130^1	120	13	49	57	11.9	3.87	108	.244	.317	1	.030	-2	3	5	0	0.3
1955	Pit-N	0	1	.000	1	1	0	0	0	3^2	5	0	3	0	22.1	4.91	84	.357	.500	0	—	0	-0	-0	-0	0.0
Total	2	3	10	.231	34	19	3	1	0	134	125	13	52	57	12.2	3.90	107	.248	.323	1	.030	-2	3	4	0	0.3
● BOBBY THIGPEN Thigpen, Robert Thomas b: 7/17/63, Tallahassee, Fla. BR/TR, 6'3", 195 lbs. Deb: 8/06/86																										
1986	Chi-A	2	0	1.000	20	0	0	0	7	35^2	26	1	12	20	9.8	1.77	244	.205	.279	0	—	0	10	10	-0	0.9
1987	Chi-A	7	5	.583	51	0	0	0	16	89	86	10	24	52	11.4	2.73	168	.256	.311	0	—	0	17	18	0	1.7
1988	Chi-A	5	8	.385	68	0	0	0	34	90	96	6	33	62	13.3	3.30	120	.273	.342	0	—	0	7	7	0	0.7
1989	Chi-A	2	6	.250	61	0	0	0	34	79	62	10	40	47	11.7	3.76	101	.218	.316	0	—	0	1	0	-1	0.1
1990	Chi-A★	4	6	.400	**77**	0	0	0	**57**	88^2	60	5	32	70	9.4	1.83	209	.195	.274	0	—	0	20	20	0	2.2
1991	Chi-A	7	5	.583	67	0	0	0	30	69^2	63	10	38	47	13.6	3.49	114	.245	.351	0	—	0	5	4	1	0.6

YEAR	TM/L	W	L	PCT	G	GS	CG	SH	SV	IP	H	HR	BB	SO	RAT	ERA	ERA+	OAV	OOB	BH	AVG	PB	PR	/A	PD	TPI
1992	Chi-A	1	3	.250	55	0	0	0	22	55	58	4	33	45	15.4	4.75	81	.275	.381	0	—	0	-5	-6	1	-0.3
Total	7	28	33	.459	399	0	0	0	200	507	451	46	212	343	12.1	3.09	130	.241	.323	0	—	0	55	53	1	5.9

● DICK THOENEN Thoenen, Richard Crispin b: 1/9/44, Mexico, Mo. BR/TR, 6'6", 215 lbs. Deb: 9/16/67

YEAR	TM/L	W	L	PCT	G	GS	CG	SH	SV	IP	H	HR	BB	SO	RAT	ERA	ERA+	OAV	OOB	BH	AVG	PB	PR	/A	PD	TPI
1967	Phi-N	0	0	—	1	0	0	0	0	1	2	0	0	0	18.0	9.00	38	.500	.500	0	—	0	-1	-1	0	0.0

● TOMMY THOMAS Thomas, Alphonse b: 12/23/1899, Baltimore, Md. d: 4/27/88, Dallastown, Pa. BR/TR, 5'10", 175 lbs. Deb: 4/17/26

YEAR	TM/L	W	L	PCT	G	GS	CG	SH	SV	IP	H	HR	BB	SO	RAT	ERA	ERA+	OAV	OOB	BH	AVG	PB	PR	/A	PD	TPI
1926	Chi-A	15	12	.556	44	32	13	2	2	249	225	7	110	127	12.1	3.80	102	**.244**	.325	16	.186	-1	6	2	-3	-0.2
1927	Chi-A	19	16	.543	40	36	24	3	1	$\mathbf{307}^2$	271	16	94	107	10.7	2.98	136	.244	.303	14	.147	-3	40	36	-4	2.8
1928	Chi-A	17	16	.515	36	32	24	3	2	283	277	14	76	129	11.4	3.08	131	.259	.310	21	.219	3	30	30	-3	3.0
1929	Chi-A	14	18	.438	36	31	**24**	2	1	259^2	270	17	60	62	11.4	3.19	134	.269	.310	25	.255	2	30	32	-3	3.0
1930	Chi-A	5	13	.278	34	27	7	0	0	169	229	13	44	58	14.6	5.22	89	.323	.364	7	.125	-4	-11	-11	0	-1.3
1931	Chi-A	10	14	.417	43	36	11	2	2	245^1	298	17	69	72	13.6	4.73	90	.292	.340	21	.241	1	-10	-13	-1	-1.1
1932	Chi-A	3	3	.500	12	3	1	0	0	43^2	55	6	15	11	14.6	6.18	70	.307	.364	1	.077	-1	-8	-9	-0	-0.9
	Was-A	8	7	.533	18	14	7	1	0	117	114	5	46	36	12.3	3.54	122	.255	.325	10	.238	1	12	10	-2	0.9
	Yr	11	10	.524	30	17	8	1	0	160^2	169	11	61	47	12.9	4.26	101	.270	.334	11	.200	0	4	1	-2	0.0
1933	*Was-A	7	7	.500	35	14	2	0	3	135	149	9	49	35	13.3	4.80	87	.273	.336	10	.238	1	-8	-9	-2	-0.9
1934	Was-A	8	9	.471	33	18	7	1	1	133^1	154	9	58	42	14.5	5.47	79	.294	.368	7	.184	-0	-14	-17	-2	-1.7
1935	Was-A	0	0	—	1	0	0	0	0	0^1	3	0	0	0	81.0	54.00	8	.750	.750	0	—	0	-2	-2	0	-0.2
	Phi-N	0	1	.000	4	1	0	0	0	12	15	2	5	3	15.0	5.25	86	.313	.377	0	.000	-0	-2	-1	-0	-0.2
1936	StL-A	11	9	.550	36	21	8	1	0	179^2	219	25	72	40	14.8	5.26	102	.297	.362	8	.138	-3	-4	2	-2	-0.3
1937	StL-A	0	1	.000	17	2	0	0	0	30^2	46	2	10	10	16.7	7.04	69	.348	.399	0	.000	-1	-8	-8	0	-0.7
	Bos-A	0	2	.000	9	0	0	0	0	11	16	2	4	4	17.2	4.09	116	.340	.404	1	.250	-0	1	1	-0	0.1
	Yr	0	3	.000	26	2	0	0	0	41^2	62	4	14	14	16.6	6.26	77	.344	.395	1	.125	-1	-8	-7	-0	-0.6
Total	12	117	128	.478	398	267	128	15	12	2176^1	2341	144	712	736	12.7	4.11	104	.275	.333	141	.195	-5	52	43	-22	2.3

● BLAINE THOMAS Thomas, Blaine M. "Baldy" b: 8/1888, Glendora, Cal. d: 8/21/15, Glendora, Cal. BR/TR, 5'10", 165 lbs. Deb: 8/25/11

YEAR	TM/L	W	L	PCT	G	GS	CG	SH	SV	IP	H	HR	BB	SO	RAT	ERA	ERA+	OAV	OOB	BH	AVG	PB	PR	/A	PD	TPI
1911	Bos-A	0	0	—	2	2	0	0	0	4^2	3	0	7	0	21.2	0.00	—	.273	.579	1	.500	0	2	2	0	0.2

● CARL THOMAS Thomas, Carl Leslie b: 5/28/32, Minneapolis, Minn. BR/TR, 6'5", 245 lbs. Deb: 4/19/60

YEAR	TM/L	W	L	PCT	G	GS	CG	SH	SV	IP	H	HR	BB	SO	RAT	ERA	ERA+	OAV	OOB	BH	AVG	PB	PR	/A	PD	TPI
1960	Cle-A	1	0	1.000	4	0	0	0	0	9^2	8	1	10	5	17.7	7.45	50	.229	.413	1	.333	1	-4	-4	0	-0.3

● LEFTY THOMAS Thomas, Clarence Fletcher b: 10/4/03, Glade Springs, Va. d: 3/21/52, Charlottesville, Va. BL/TL, 6', 183 lbs. Deb: 9/26/25

YEAR	TM/L	W	L	PCT	G	GS	CG	SH	SV	IP	H	HR	BB	SO	RAT	ERA	ERA+	OAV	OOB	BH	AVG	PB	PR	/A	PD	TPI
1925	Was-A	0	2	.000	2	2	1	0	0	13	14	0	7	10	14.5	2.08	204	.264	.350	0	.000	-1	3	3	0	0.2
1926	Was-A	0	0	—	6	0	0	0	0	8^2	8	0	10	3	18.7	5.19	74	.267	.450	0	.000	0	-1	-1	-1	-0.2
Total	2	0	2	.000	8	2	1	0	0	21^2	22	0	17	13	16.2	3.32	123	.265	.390	0	.000	-1	2	2	-1	0.0

● CLAUDE THOMAS Thomas, Claude Alfred "Lefty" b: 5/15/1890, Stanberry, Mo. d: 3/6/46, Sulphur, Okla. BL/TL, 6'1", 180 lbs. Deb: 9/14/16

YEAR	TM/L	W	L	PCT	G	GS	CG	SH	SV	IP	H	HR	BB	SO	RAT	ERA	ERA+	OAV	OOB	BH	AVG	PB	PR	/A	PD	TPI
1916	Was-A	1	2	.333	7	4	1	1	0	28^1	27	1	12	7	13.0	4.13	68	.265	.353	1	.100	-1	-4	-4	-0	-0.6

● FAY THOMAS Thomas, Fay Wesley "Scow" b: 10/10/04, Holyrood, Kan. d: 8/16/90, Chatsworth, Cal. BR/TR, 6'2", 195 lbs. Deb: 6/27/27

YEAR	TM/L	W	L	PCT	G	GS	CG	SH	SV	IP	H	HR	BB	SO	RAT	ERA	ERA+	OAV	OOB	BH	AVG	PB	PR	/A	PD	TPI
1927	NY-N	0	0	—	9	0	0	0	0	16^1	19	3	4	11	13.2	3.31	117	.302	.353	0	.000	-0	1	1	-0	0.0
1931	Cle-A	2	4	.333	16	2	1	0	0	48^2	63	2	32	25	17.8	5.18	89	.323	.421	2	.154	-1	-4	-3	-1	-0.4
1932	Bro-N	0	1	.000	7	2	0	0	0	17	22	0	8	9	15.9	7.41	51	.306	.375	0	.000	-0	-7	-7	0	-0.7
1935	StL-A	7	15	.318	49	19	4	0	1	147	165	11	89	67	15.7	4.78	100	.289	.388	4	.105	-3	-5	0	2	0.0
Total	4	9	20	.310	81	23	5	0	1	229	269	16	133	112	16.0	4.95	93	.299	.392	6	.107	-5	-15	-9	1	-1.1

● FROSTY THOMAS Thomas, Forrest b: 5/23/1881, Faucett, Mo. d: 3/18/70, St.Joseph, Mo. BR/TR, 6', 185 lbs. Deb: 5/01/05

YEAR	TM/L	W	L	PCT	G	GS	CG	SH	SV	IP	H	HR	BB	SO	RAT	ERA	ERA+	OAV	OOB	BH	AVG	PB	PR	/A	PD	TPI
1905	Det-A	0	1	.000	2	1	0	0	0	6	10	0	3	5	21.0	7.50	37	.371	.452	0	.000	-0	-3	-3	0	-0.3

● BUD THOMAS Thomas, Luther Baxter b: 9/9/10, Faber, Va. BR/TR, 6', 180 lbs. Deb: 9/13/32

YEAR	TM/L	W	L	PCT	G	GS	CG	SH	SV	IP	H	HR	BB	SO	RAT	ERA	ERA+	OAV	OOB	BH	AVG	PB	PR	/A	PD	TPI
1932	Was-A	0	0	—	2	0	0	0	0	3	1	0	2	1	9.0	0.00	—	.100	.250	0	—	0	1	1	-0	0.1
1933	Was-A	0	0	—	2	0	0	0	0	4	11	1	2	1	31.5	15.75	27	.550	.609	0	.000	-0	-5	-5	0	-0.4
1937	Phi-A	8	15	.348	35	26	6	1	0	169^2	208	15	52	54	13.8	4.99	95	.295	.344	6	.128	-1	-7	-5	-3	-0.8
1938	Phi-A	9	14	.391	42	29	7	1	0	212^1	259	23	62	48	13.7	4.92	98	.299	.347	9	.130	-3	-3	-2	-1	-0.5
1939	Phi-A	0	1	.000	2	2	0	0	0	4	8	2	1	0	20.3	15.75	30	.421	.450	0	.000	-0	-5	-5	0	-0.4
	Was-A	0	0	—	4	0	0	0	0	9	11	0	2	0	13.0	6.00	72	.306	.342	0	.000	-0	-1	-2	0	-0.2
	Det-A	7	0	1.000	27	0	0	0	1	47^1	45	7	20	14	12.4	4.18	117	.254	.330	1	.111	-1	2	4	0	0.3
	Yr	7	1	.875	33	2	0	0	1	60^1	64	9	23	14	13.0	5.22	92	.276	.341	1	.071	-2	-4	-3	0	-0.3
1940	Det-A	0	1	.000	3	0	0	0	0	4	8	1	3	0	24.8	9.00	53	.421	.500	0	—	0	-2	-2	1	-0.1
1941	Det-A	1	3	.250	26	1	0	0	2	72^2	74	4	22	17	11.9	4.21	108	.260	.313	2	.105	-1	-1	3	2	0.3
Total	7	25	34	.424	143	58	13	2	3	526	625	53	166	135	13.6	4.96	96	.292	.345	18	.120	-7	-20	-13	-1	-1.7

● MYLES THOMAS Thomas, Myles Lewis b: 10/22/1897, State College, Pa. d: 12/12/63, Toledo, Ohio BR/TR, 5'9.5", 170 lbs. Deb: 4/18/26

YEAR	TM/L	W	L	PCT	G	GS	CG	SH	SV	IP	H	HR	BB	SO	RAT	ERA	ERA+	OAV	OOB	BH	AVG	PB	PR	/A	PD	TPI
1926	*NY-A	6	6	.500	33	13	3	0	0	140^1	140	6	65	38	13.3	4.23	91	.271	.356	5	.116	-3	-3	-6	1	-0.8
1927	NY-A	7	4	.636	21	9	1	0	0	88^2	111	4	43	25	15.7	4.87	79	.322	.398	9	.333	2	-7	-10	0	-0.8
1928	NY-A	1	0	1.000	12	1	0	0	0	31^2	33	3	9	10	11.9	3.41	110	.277	.328	4	.400	1	2	1	-0	0.2
1929	NY-A	0	2	.000	5	1	0	0	0	15	27	1	9	3	21.6	10.80	36	.409	.480	1	.143	-0	-11	-12	1	-1.0
	Was-A	7	8	.467	22	14	7	0	2	125^1	139	3	48	33	13.4	3.52	121	.288	.352	14	.292	2	10	10	0	1.2
	Yr	7	10	.412	27	15	7	0	2	140^1	166	4	57	36	14.3	4.30	98	.302	.368	15	.273	1	-1	-2	1	0.2
1930	Was-A	2	2	.500	12	2	0	0	0	33^2	49	3	15	12	17.1	8.29	55	.358	.421	2	.182	-1	-14	-14	-1	-1.3
Total	5	23	22	.511	105	40	11	0	2	434^2	499	20	189	121	14.3	4.64	87	.299	.372	35	.240	1	-23	-30	1	-2.5

● ROY THOMAS Thomas, Roy Allen b: 3/24/1874, Norristown, Pa. d: 11/20/59, Norristown, Pa. BL/TL, 5'11", 150 lbs. Deb: 4/14/1899 FC♦

YEAR	TM/L	W	L	PCT	G	GS	CG	SH	SV	IP	H	HR	BB	SO	RAT	ERA	ERA+	OAV	OOB	BH	AVG	PB	PR	/A	PD	TPI
1900	Phi-N	0	0	—	1	0	0	0	0	2^2	4	0	0	0	13.5	3.38	107	.345	.345	168	.316	0	0	0	-0	0.0

● ROY THOMAS Thomas, Roy Justin b: 6/22/53, Quantico, Va. BR/TR, 6'6", 200 lbs. Deb: 9/21/77

YEAR	TM/L	W	L	PCT	G	GS	CG	SH	SV	IP	H	HR	BB	SO	RAT	ERA	ERA+	OAV	OOB	BH	AVG	PB	PR	/A	PD	TPI
1977	Hou-N	0	0	—	4	0	0	0	0	6^1	5	0	3	4	11.4	2.84	125	.208	.296	0	—	0	1	1	0	0.1
1978	StL-N	1	1	.500	16	1	0	0	3	28^1	21	0	16	16	11.8	3.81	92	.216	.327	1	.250	0	-1	-1	1	0.0
1979	StL-N	3	4	.429	26	6	0	0	1	77	66	9	24	44	10.5	2.92	129	.237	.298	1	.059	-1	7	7	1	0.7
1980	StL-N	2	3	.400	24	5	0	0	0	55	59	3	25	22	14.2	4.75	78	.274	.358	2	.154	-0	-7	-6	1	-0.6
1983	Sea-A	3	1	.750	43	0	0	0	1	88^2	95	3	32	77	13.1	3.45	123	.275	.340	0	—	0	6	8	-0	0.6
1984	Sea-A	3	2	.600	21	1	0	0	1	49^2	52	8	37	42	16.9	5.26	76	.280	.410	0	—	0	-7	-7	0	-0.6
1985	Sea-A	7	0	1.000	40	0	0	0	1	93^2	66	8	48	70	11.1	3.36	125	.202	.309	0	—	0	8	9	-1	0.8
1987	Sea-A	1	0	1.000	8	0	0	0	0	20^2	23	2	11	14	15.2	5.23	90	.299	.393	0	—	0	-2	-1	-1	-0.3
Total	8	20	11	.645	182	13	0	0	7	419^1	387	33	196	289	12.8	3.82	105	.250	.339	4	.118	-1	5	9	1	0.7

● STAN THOMAS Thomas, Stanley Brown b: 7/11/49, Rumford, Me. BR/TR, 6'2", 185 lbs. Deb: 7/05/74

YEAR	TM/L	W	L	PCT	G	GS	CG	SH	SV	IP	H	HR	BB	SO	RAT	ERA	ERA+	OAV	OOB	BH	AVG	PB	PR	/A	PD	TPI
1974	Tex-A	0	0	—	12	0	0	0	0	13^2	22	1	6	8	18.4	6.59	54	.379	.438	0	—	0	-5	-5	0	-0.4
1975	Tex-A	4	4	.500	46	1	0	0	3	81^1	72	2	34	46	12.1	3.10	121	.239	.322	0	—	0	6	6	0	0.7
1976	Cle-A	4	4	.500	37	7	2	0	6	105^2	88	5	41	54	11.3	2.30	152	.229	.310	0	—	0	14	14	3	1.9
1977	Sea-A	2	6	.250	13	9	1	0	0	58^1	74	8	25	14	15.7	6.02	68	.310	.382	0	—	0	-13	-12	-0	-1.2
	NY-A	1	0	1.000	3	0	0	0	0	6^1	7	0	4	1	15.6	7.11	55	.280	.379	0	—	0	-2	-2	-0	-0.2
	Yr	3	6	.333	16	9	1	0	0	64^2	81	8	29	15	15.3	6.12	67	.300	.368	0	—	0	-15	-15	-1	-1.4
Total	4	11	14	.440	111	17	3	0	9	265^1	263	16	110	123	13.0	3.70	101	.261	.340	0	—	0	1	1	3	0.8

YEAR TM/L	W	L	PCT	G	GS	CG	SH	SV	IP	H	HR	BB	SO	RAT	ERA	ERA+	OAV	OOB	BH	AVG	PB	PR	/A	PD	TPI

● **TOM THOMAS**   Thomas, Thomas R. "Savage Tom" b: 12/27/1873, Shawnee, Ohio   d: 9/23/42, Shawnee, Ohio   BR/TR, 6'4", 195 lbs.   Deb: 9/20/1894

1894 Cle-N	0	0	—	1	0	0	0	0	0¹	0	0	2	0	54.0	27.00	20	.000	.676	0	—	0	-1	-1	0	-0.1
1899 StL-N	1	1	.500	4	2	2	0	0	25	22	1	4	9	9.4	2.52	158	.236	.268	3	.250	0	4	4	0	0.4
1900 StL-N	2	2	.500	5	1	1	0	0	26¹	38	2	4	7	15.0	3.76	97	.336	.370	1	.091	-1	-0	-0	-1	-0.2
Total 3	3	3	.500	10	3	3	0	0	51²	60	3	10	15	12.5	3.31	115	.290	.329	4	.174	-0	3	3	-1	0.1

● **ERSKINE THOMASON**   Thomason, Melvin Erskine b: 8/13/48, Laurens, S.C.   BR/TR, 6'1", 190 lbs.   Deb: 9/18/74

| 1974 Phi-N | 0 | 0 | — | 1 | 0 | 0 | 0 | 0 | 1 | 0 | 0 | 0 | 1 | 0.0 | 0.00 | — | .000 | .000 | 0 | — | 0 | 0 | 0 | 0 | 0.0 |

● **ART THOMPSON**   Thompson, Arthur J.   Deb: 6/17/1884

| 1884 Was-U | 0 | 1 | .000 | 1 | 1 | 1 | 0 | 0 | 8 | 10 | 0 | 3 | 8 | 14.6 | 6.75 | 44 | .287 | .343 | 0 | .000 | -1 | -3 | -3 | 0 | -0.3 |

● **FORREST THOMPSON**   Thompson, David Forrest b: 3/3/18, Mooresville, N.C.   d: 2/26/79, Charlotte, N.C.   BL/TL, 5'11", 195 lbs.   Deb: 4/26/48

1948 Was-A	6	10	.375	46	7	0	0	4	131¹	134	9	54	40	13.0	3.84	113	.262	.334	10	.286	2	7	7	-0	1.0
1949 Was-A	1	3	.250	9	1	1	0	0	16¹	22	1	9	8	17.6	4.41	97	.328	.416	3	.600	2	-0	-0	0	0.2
Total 2	7	13	.350	55	8	1	0	4	147²	156	10	63	48	13.5	3.90	111	.270	.344	13	.325	4	6	7	-0	1.2

● **JUNIOR THOMPSON**   Thompson, Eugene Earl b: 6/7/17, Latham, Ill.   BR/TR, 6'1", 185 lbs.   Deb: 4/26/39

1939 *Cin-N	13	5	.722	42	11	5	3	2	152¹	130	6	55	87	11.1	2.54	151	.236	.309	11	.229	0	23	22	-1	2.1
1940 *Cin-N	16	9	.640	33	31	17	3	0	225³	197	10	96	103	11.8	3.32	114	.233	.313	18	.228	3	13	12	-1	1.4
1941 Cin-N	6	6	.500	27	15	4	0	1	109	117	6	57	46	14.6	4.87	74	.272	.361	7	.233	1	-15	-15	2	-1.2
1942 Cin-N	4	7	.364	29	10	1	0	0	101²	86	5	53	35	12.5	3.36	98	.226	.324	8	.267	2	-1	-1	4	0.5
1946 NY-N	4	6	.400	39	1	0	0	4	62²	36	5	40	31	10.9	1.29	266	.190	.332	1	.143	0	15	15	2	1.8
1947 NY-N	4	2	.667	15	0	0	0	0	35²	36	3	27	13	16.1	4.29	95	.279	.408	0	.000	-1	-1	-1	1	-0.1
Total 6	47	35	.573	185	68	27	6	7	686²	602	35	328	315	12.3	3.26	113	.239	.329	45	.225	6	35	32	6	4.5

● **FULLER THOMPSON**   Thompson, Fuller Weidner b: 5/1/1889, Los Angeles, Cal.   d: 2/19/72, Los Angeles, Cal.   BR/TR, 5'11.5", 164 lbs.   Deb: 8/19/11

| 1911 Bos-N | 0 | 0 | — | 3 | 0 | 0 | 0 | 0 | 4² | 5 | 0 | 2 | 0 | 13.5 | 3.86 | 99 | .294 | .368 | 0 | — | 0 | -0 | -0 | 0 | 0.0 |

● **HARRY THOMPSON**   Thompson, Harold b: 9/9/1889, Nanticoke, Pa.   d: 2/14/51, Reno, Nev.   BL/TL, 5'8", 150 lbs.   Deb: 4/24/19

1919 Was-A	0	3	.000	12	2	0	0	1	43¹	48	0	8	10	12.0	3.53	91	.293	.333	8	.250	1	-1	-2	0	0.0
Phi-A	0	1	.000	3	0	0	0	0	12	16	4	3	1	14.3	6.75	51	.327	.365	0	.000	-1	-5	-4	0	-0.5
Yr	0	4	.000	15	2	0	0	1	55¹	64	4	11	11	12.2	4.23	77	.298	.332	8	.211	0	-6	-6	1	-0.5

● **LEE THOMPSON**   Thompson, John Dudley "Lefty" b: 2/26/1898, Smithfield, Utah   d: 2/17/63, Santa Barbara, Cal   BL/TL, 6'1", 185 lbs.   Deb: 9/04/21

| 1921 Chi-A | 0 | 3 | .000 | 4 | 4 | 0 | 0 | 0 | 20² | 32 | 0 | 6 | 4 | 16.5 | 8.27 | 51 | .333 | .373 | 2 | .286 | 0 | -9 | -9 | -1 | -0.8 |

● **GUS THOMPSON**   Thompson, John Gustav b: 6/22/1877, Humboldt, Iowa   d: 3/28/58, Kalispell, Mont.   6'2", 185 lbs.   Deb: 8/31/03

1903 *Pit-N	2	2	.500	5	4	3	0	0	43	52	1	16	22	14.4	3.56	91	.295	.358	4	.250	0	-1	-2	-1	-0.2
1906 StL-N	2	11	.154	17	12	8	0	0	103	111	2	25	36	12.3	4.28	61	.285	.336	6	.176	-1	-19	-19	1	-1.9
Total 2	4	13	.235	22	16	11	0	0	146	163	3	41	58	12.9	4.07	69	.288	.343	10	.200	-1	-20	-20	0	-2.1

● **JOCKO THOMPSON**   Thompson, John Samuel b: 1/17/17, Beverly, Mass.   d: 2/3/88, Olney, Md.   BL/TL, 6', 185 lbs.   Deb: 9/21/48

1948 Phi-N	1	0	1.000	2	2	1	0	0	13	10	0	9	7	13.2	2.77	142	.233	.365	0	.000	0	2	2	-0	0.2
1949 Phi-N	1	3	.250	8	5	1	0	0	31¹	38	6	11	12	14.1	6.89	57	.314	.371	2	.182	-0	-10	-10	-0	-1.0
1950 Phi-N	0	0	—	2	0	0	0	0	4	1	0	4	2	11.3	0.00	—	.077	.294	0	—	0	2	2	0	0.2
1951 Phi-N	4	8	.333	29	14	3	2	1	119¹	102	12	59	60	12.3	3.85	100	.231	.325	4	.103	-1	2	0	-1	-0.2
Total 4	6	11	.353	41	21	5	2	1	167²	151	18	83	81	12.7	4.24	91	.244	.336	6	.113	-1	-5	-7	-1	-0.8

● **MIKE THOMPSON**   Thompson, Michael Wayne b: 9/6/49, Denver, Colo.   BR/TR, 6'3", 190 lbs.   Deb: 5/19/71

1971 Was-A	1	6	.143	16	12	0	0	0	66²	53	3	54	41	14.9	4.86	68	.222	.372	2	.118	0	-10	-12	0	-1.1
1973 StL-N	0	0	—	2	2	0	0	0	4	1	0	5	3	13.5	0.00	—	.077	.333	0	.000	-0	2	2	0	0.1
1974 StL-N	0	3	.000	19	4	0	0	0	38¹	37	1	35	25	17.4	5.63	63	.274	.430	0	.000	-1	-9	-9	-0	-1.0
Atl-N	0	0	—	1	1	0	0	0	4	7	0	2	2	20.3	4.50	84	.412	.474	1	1.000	0	-0	-0	0	0.0
Yr	0	3	.000	20	5	0	0	0	42¹	44	1	37	27	17.2	5.53	65	.286	.424	1	.111	-1	-9	-9	-0	-1.0
1975 Atl-N	0	6	.000	16	10	0	0	0	51²	60	2	32	42	16.0	4.70	80	.305	.402	1	.071	-1	-6	-5	1	-0.6
Total 4	1	15	.063	54	29	0	0	0	164²	158	6	128	113	15.9	4.86	73	.263	.396	4	.098	-1	-24	-24	1	-2.6

● **RICH THOMPSON**   Thompson, Richard Neil b: 11/1/58, New York, N.Y.   BR/TR, 6'3", 225 lbs.   Deb: 4/28/85

1985 Cle-A	3	8	.273	57	0	0	0	5	80	95	8	48	30	16.8	6.30	66	.303	.405	0	—	0	-19	-19	-2	-2.0
1989 Mon-N	0	2	.000	19	1	0	0	0	33	27	2	11	15	10.9	2.18	162	.241	.320	0	.000	0	5	5	-0	0.5
1990 Mon-N	0	0	—	1	0	0	0	0	1	1	0	0	0	9.0	0.00	—	.250	.250	0	—	0	0	0	0	0.0
Total 3	3	10	.231	77	1	0	0	5	114	123	10	59	45	15.0	5.05	78	.286	.382	0	.000	0	-14	-14	-2	-1.5

● **TOMMY THOMPSON**   Thompson, Thomas Carl b: 11/7/1889, Spring City, Tenn.   d: 1/16/63, LaJolla, Cal.   BR/TR, 5'9.5", 170 lbs.   Deb: 6/05/12   F

| 1912 NY-A | 0 | 2 | .000 | 7 | 2 | 1 | 0 | 0 | 32² | 43 | 0 | 13 | 15 | 16.3 | 6.06 | 59 | .341 | .415 | 3 | .300 | 1 | -10 | -9 | -1 | -0.8 |

● **WILL THOMPSON**   Thompson, Will McLain b: 8/30/1870, Pittsburgh, Pa.   d: 6/9/62, Pittsburgh, Pa.   BR/TR, 5'11.5", 190 lbs.   Deb: 7/09/1892

| 1892 Pit-N | 0 | 1 | .000 | 1 | 1 | 0 | 0 | 0 | 3 | 3 | 0 | 5 | 0 | 27.0 | 3.00 | 110 | .250 | .500 | 0 | — | 0 | 0 | 0 | 0 | 0.0 |

● **HANK THORMAHLEN**   Thormahlen, Herbert Ehler "Lefty" b: 7/5/1896, Jersey City, N.J.   d: 2/6/55, Los Angeles, Cal.   BL/TL, 6', 180 lbs.   Deb: 9/29/17

1917 NY-A	0	1	.000	1	1	0	0	0	8	9	0	4	5	15.8	2.25	119	.281	.378	0	.000	-0	0	0	-0	0.0
1918 NY-A	7	3	.700	16	12	5	2	0	112²	85	1	52	22	11.4	2.48	114	.217	.318	3	.077	-4	4	4	0	0.1
1919 NY-A	12	10	.545	30	25	13	2	1	188²	155	10	61	62	10.5	2.62	122	.228	.295	11	.186	-4	13	12	1	1.1
1920 NY-A	9	6	.600	29	15	6	0	0	143¹	178	5	43	35	14.0	4.14	92	.312	.362	10	.222	1	-6	-5	1	-0.3
1921 Bos-A	1	7	.125	23	9	3	0	0	96¹	101	3	34	17	13.2	4.48	94	.277	.349	4	.174	-1	-2	-3	-0	-0.3
1925 Bro-N	0	3	.000	5	2	0	0	0	16	22	0	9	7	18.6	3.94	106	.333	.429	1	.200	0	1	0	0	0.1
Total 6	29	30	.492	104	64	27	4	2	565	550	19	203	148	12.3	3.33	105	.261	.332	29	.168	-3	10	9	0	0.7

● **PAUL THORMODSGARD**   Thormodsgard, Paul Gayton b: 11/10/53, San Francisco, Cal.   BR/TR, 6'2", 190 lbs.   Deb: 4/10/77

1977 Min-A	11	15	.423	37	37	8	1	0	218	236	25	65	94	12.6	4.62	86	.280	.333	0	—	0	-14	-16	-1	-1.5
1978 Min-A	1	6	.143	12	12	1	0	0	66	81	7	17	23	13.5	5.05	76	.308	.352	0	—	0	-9	-9	-1	-1.1
1979 Min-A	0	0	—	1	0	0	0	0	1	3	1	0	1	27.0	9.00	49	.500	.500	0	—	0	-1	-1	0	-0.1
Total 3	12	21	.364	50	49	9	1	0	285	320	33	82	118	12.8	4.74	83	.288	.339	0	—	0	-24	-25	-2	-2.7

● **JOHN THORNTON**   Thornton, John b: 1870, Washington, D.C.   5'10.5", 175 lbs.   Deb: 8/14/1889 ◆

1889 Was-N	0	1	.000	1	1	1	0	0	9	8	0	7	3	15.0	5.00	79	.231	.360	0	.000	-1	-1	-1	-0	-0.1
1891 Phi-N	15	16	.484	37	32	23	1	2	269	268	3	115	52	13.1	3.68	93	.250	.328	17	.138	-7	-10	-8	2	-1.3
1892 Phi-N	0	2	.000	3	2	1	0	0	12	16	1	17	2	24.8	12.75	25	.308	.478	5	.385	1	-13	-13	-0	-0.9
Total 3	15	19	.441	41	35	25	1	2	290	292	4	139	57	13.7	4.10	83	.252	.337	22	.154	-7	-24	-22	2	-2.3

● **WALTER THORNTON**   Thornton, Walter Miller b: 2/18/1875, Lewiston, Maine   d: 7/14/60, Los Angeles, Cal.   TL, 6'1", 180 lbs.   Deb: 7/01/1895 ◆

1895 Chi-N	2	0	1.000	7	2	2	0	1	40	58	3	31	13	21.1	6.07	84	.333	.448	7	.318	2	-6	-4	-1	-0.3
1896 Chi-N	2	1	.667	5	5	2	0	0	23²	30	1	13	10	16.4	5.70	80	.306	.388	8	.364	2	-4	-3	-1	-0.2
1897 Chi-N	6	7	.462	16	16	15	0	0	130¹	164	4	51	55	15.3	4.70	95	.305	.371	85	.321	4	-6	-3	0	0.1
1898 Chi-N	13	10	.565	28	25	21	2	0	215¹	226	4	56	56	12.5	3.34	107	.268	.327	62	.295	6	6	6	-1	1.0

YEAR	TM/L	W	L	PCT	G	GS	CG	SH	SV	IP	H	HR	BB	SO	RAT	ERA	ERA+	OAV	OOB	BH	AVG	PB	PR	/A	PD	TPI
Total	4	23	18	.561	56	48	40	2	1	409^1	478	12	151	134	14.5	4.18	97	.289	.359	162	.312	13	-8	-6	-2	0.6

● BOB THORPE Thorpe, Robert Joseph b: 1/12/35, San Diego, Cal. d: 3/17/60, San Diego, Cal. BR/TR, 6'1", 170 lbs. Deb: 4/17/55

YEAR	TM/L	W	L	PCT	G	GS	CG	SH	SV	IP	H	HR	BB	SO	RAT	ERA	ERA+	OAV	OOB	BH	AVG	PB	PR	/A	PD	TPI
1955	Chi-N	0	0	—	2	0	0	0	0	3	4	0	0	0	12.0	3.00	136	.333	.333	0	—	0	0	0	0	0.1

● GEORGE THROOP Throop, George Lynford b: 11/24/50, Pasadena, Cal. BR/TR, 6'7", 205 lbs. Deb: 9/07/75

YEAR	TM/L	W	L	PCT	G	GS	CG	SH	SV	IP	H	HR	BB	SO	RAT	ERA	ERA+	OAV	OOB	BH	AVG	PB	PR	/A	PD	TPI
1975	KC-A	0	0	—	7	0	0	0	2	9	8	1	2	8	10.0	4.00	96	.250	.294	0	—	0	-0	-0	0	-0.1
1977	KC-A	0	0	—	4	0	0	0	1	5^1	1	1	4	1	8.4	3.38	120	.059	.238	0	—	0	0	0	0	0.0
1978	KC-A	1	0	1.000	1	0	0	0	0	3	2	0	3	2	15.0	0.00	—	.222	.417	0	—	0	1	1	0	0.0
1979	KC-A	0	0	—	4	0	0	0	0	2^2	7	0	5	1	40.5	13.50	32	.467	.600	0	—	0	-3	-3	-0	-0.4
	Hou-N	1	0	1.000	14	0	0	0	0	22^1	23	4	11	15	14.1	3.22	109	.271	.361	0	.000	-0	1	1	-0	0.0
Total	4	2	0	1.000	30	0	0	0	3	42^1	41	6	25	27	14.2	3.83	97	.259	.364	0	.000	-0	-0	-1	0	-0.5

● LOU THUMAN Thuman, Louis Charles Frank b: 12/13/16, Baltimore, Md. BR/TR, 6'2", 185 lbs. Deb: 9/08/39

YEAR	TM/L	W	L	PCT	G	GS	CG	SH	SV	IP	H	HR	BB	SO	RAT	ERA	ERA+	OAV	OOB	BH	AVG	PB	PR	/A	PD	TPI
1939	Was-A	0	0	—	3	0	0	0	0	4	5	0	2	1	15.8	9.00	48	.278	.350	0	—	0	-2	-2	0	-0.1
1940	Was-A	0	1	.000	2	0	0	0	0	5	10	0	7	0	30.6	14.40	29	.400	.531	0	.000	-0	-6	-6	0	-0.5
Total	2	0	1	.000	5	0	0	0	0	9	15	0	9	1	24.0	12.00	35	.349	.462	0	.000	-0	-8	-8	0	-0.6

● MARK THURMOND Thurmond, Mark Anthony b: 9/12/56, Houston, Tex. BL/TL, 6', 193 lbs. Deb: 5/14/83

YEAR	TM/L	W	L	PCT	G	GS	CG	SH	SV	IP	H	HR	BB	SO	RAT	ERA	ERA+	OAV	OOB	BH	AVG	PB	PR	/A	PD	TPI
1983	SD-N	7	3	.700	21	18	2	0	0	115^1	104	7	33	49	10.8	2.65	131	.248	.306	2	.054	-2	12	11	1	1.0
1984	*SD-N	14	8	.636	32	29	1	1	0	178^2	174	12	55	57	11.5	2.97	120	.256	.311	11	.190	1	12	12	2	1.6
1985	SD-N	7	11	.389	36	23	1	1	2	138^1	154	9	44	57	13.1	3.97	89	.291	.349	3	.088	-2	-6	-7	1	-0.8
1986	SD-N	3	7	.300	17	15	2	1	0	70^2	96	7	27	32	15.7	6.50	56	.325	.382	6	.250	1	-22	-22	0	-2.0
	Det-A	4	1	.800	25	4	0	0	3	51^2	44	7	17	17	10.6	1.92	215	.234	.298	0	—	0	13	13	-1	1.2
1987	*Det-A	0	1	.000	48	0	0	0	5	61^2	83	5	24	21	15.6	4.23	100	.331	.389	0	—	0	2	-0	-0	0.0
1988	Bal-A	1	8	.111	43	6	0	0	3	74^2	80	10	27	29	13.1	4.58	85	.277	.343	0	—	0	-5	-6	-1	-0.6
1989	Bal-A	2	4	.333	49	2	0	0	4	90	102	6	17	34	12.0	3.90	97	.288	.323	0	—	0	-0	-1	-1	-0.2
1990	SF-N	2	3	.400	43	0	0	0	4	56^2	53	6	18	24	11.3	3.34	109	.257	.317	0	.000	-0	3	2	1	0.3
Total	8	40	46	.465	314	97	6	3	21	837^2	890	69	262	320	12.5	3.69	100	.277	.333	22	.139	-1	9	1	2	0.5

● SLOPPY THURSTON Thurston, Hollis John b: 6/2/1899, Fremont, Neb. d: 9/14/73, Los Angeles, Cal. BR/TR, 5'11", 165 lbs. Deb: 4/19/23

YEAR	TM/L	W	L	PCT	G	GS	CG	SH	SV	IP	H	HR	BB	SO	RAT	ERA	ERA+	OAV	OOB	BH	AVG	PB	PR	/A	PD	TPI
1923	StL-A	0	0	—	2	1	0	0	0	4	8	0	2	0	22.5	6.75	62	.421	.476	0	—	0	-1	-1	-0	-0.1
	Chi-A	7	8	.467	44	12	8	0	4	191^2	223	11	36	55	12.2	3.05	130	.308	.341	25	.316	6	20	19	-0	2.4
	Yr	7	8	.467	46	13	8	0	4	195^2	231	11	38	55	12.4	3.13	127	.310	.345	25	.316	6	19	18	-1	2.3
1924	Chi-A	20	14	.588	38	36	**28**	1	1	291	330	17	60	37	12.2	3.80	108	.290	.329	31	.254	4	14	10	1	1.6
1925	Chi-A	10	14	.417	36	25	9	0	1	183	250	14	47	35	14.9	5.95	70	.335	.378	24	.286	6	-32	-37	2	-2.5
1926	Chi-A	6	8	.429	31	13	6	1	3	134^1	164	10	36	35	13.5	5.02	77	.311	.356	19	.311	5	-15	-17	-1	-1.3
1927	Was-A	13	13	.500	29	28	13	2	0	205^1	254	16	60	38	13.9	4.47	91	.308	.356	29	.315	9	-8	-9	-1	-0.1
1930	Bro-N	6	4	.600	24	11	5	2	1	106	110	4	17	26	10.8	3.40	145	.266	.295	10	.200	-0	19	18	2	1.8
1931	Bro-N	9	9	.500	24	17	11	0	0	143	175	3	39	23	13.5	3.97	96	.301	.346	13	.217	2	-2	-2	-1	-0.1
1932	Bro-N	12	8	.600	28	20	10	2	0	153	174	14	38	35	12.5	4.06	94	.287	.330	17	.304	5	-3	-4	1	0.2
1933	Bro-N	6	8	.429	32	15	5	0	3	131^1	171	4	34	22	14.5	4.52	71	.319	.366	7	.159	-1	-17	-19	2	-1.9
Total	9	89	86	.509	288	178	95	8	13	1542^2	1859	93	369	306	13.1	4.24	94	.304	.346	175	.270	37	-25	-42	3	0.0

● LUIS TIANT Tiant, Luis Clemente (Vega) b: 11/23/40, Marianao, Cuba BR/TR, 5'11", 190 lbs. Deb: 7/19/64

YEAR	TM/L	W	L	PCT	G	GS	CG	SH	SV	IP	H	HR	BB	SO	RAT	ERA	ERA+	OAV	OOB	BH	AVG	PB	PR	/A	PD	TPI
1964	Cle-A	10	4	.714	19	16	9	3	1	127	94	13	47	105	10.1	2.83	127	.207	.284	5	.111	-1	11	11	0	1.0
1965	Cle-A	11	11	.500	41	30	10	2	1	196^1	166	20	66	152	10.8	3.53	99	.228	.295	6	.088	-2	-2	-1	-0	-0.3
1966	Cle-A	12	11	.522	46	16	7	**5**	8	155	121	16	50	145	10.0	2.79	123	.213	.279	4	.111	-1	11	11	-1	1.0
1967	Cle-A	12	9	.571	33	29	9	1	2	213^2	177	24	67	219	10.3	2.74	119	.221	.282	18	.254	5	12	13	-2	1.7
1968	Cle-A★	21	9	.700	34	32	19	**9**	0	258^1	152	16	73	264	8.0	**1.60**	**185**	**.168**	**.233**	7	.080	-4	**40**	39	-3	4.0
1969	Cle-A	9	20	.310	38	37	9	1	0	249^2	229	37	129	156	13.2	3.71	101	.246	.343	19	.235	6	-3	1	-1	0.7
1970	*Min-A	7	3	.700	18	17	2	1	0	92^2	84	12	41	50	12.3	3.40	109	.246	.330	13	.406	5	3	3	-0	0.9
1971	Bos-A	1	7	.125	21	10	1	0	0	72^1	73	8	32	59	13.2	4.85	76	.259	.337	3	.158	-0	-11	-9	-0	-1.0
1972	Bos-A	15	6	.714	43	19	12	6	3	179	128	7	65	123	9.7	**1.91**	**168**	.202	.277	6	.107	-2	23	26	-1	2.7
1973	Bos-A	20	13	.606	35	35	23	0	0	272	217	32	78	206	**10.0**	3.34	120	.219	**.281**	0	—	0	14	20	-1	1.8
1974	Bos-A★	22	13	.629	38	38	25	**7**	0	311^1	281	21	82	176	10.6	2.92	132	.241	.293	0	—	0	24	32	-3	3.0
1975	*Bos-A	18	14	.563	35	35	18	2	0	260	262	25	72	142	11.7	4.02	101	.264	.316	0	.000	0	-7	2	-3	-0.2
1976	Bos-A★	21	12	.636	38	38	19	3	0	279	274	25	64	131	11.0	3.06	128	.260	.304	0	.000	0	14	26	-2	2.6
1977	Bos-A	12	8	.600	32	32	3	3	0	188^2	210	26	51	124	12.5	4.53	99	.279	.327	0	—	0	-10	-1	-2	-1.0
1978	Bos-A	13	8	.619	32	31	12	5	0	212^1	185	26	57	114	10.5	3.31	124	.234	.290	0	—	0	11	19	-2	1.0
1979	NY-A	13	8	.619	30	30	5	1	0	195^2	190	22	53	104	11.2	3.91	104	.251	.300	0	—	0	7	4	-0	0.5
1980	NY-A	8	9	.471	25	25	3	0	0	136^1	139	10	50	84	12.5	4.89	80	.265	.330	0	—	0	-13	-15	1	-1.3
1981	Pit-N	2	5	.286	9	9	1	0	0	57^1	54	3	19	32	11.5	3.92	92	.243	.303	3	.188	1	-3	-2	-1	-0.2
1982	Cal-A	2	2	.500	6	5	0	0	0	29^2	39	3	8	30	14.3	5.76	70	.310	.351	0	—	0	-6	-6	-1	-0.6
Total	19	229	172	.571	573	484	187	49	15	3486^1	3075	346	1104	2416	10.9	3.30	113	.236	.298	84	.164	6	116	173	-21	16.3

● JAY TIBBS Tibbs, Jay Lindsey b: 1/4/62, Birmingham, Ala. BR/TR, 6'3", 185 lbs. Deb: 7/15/84

YEAR	TM/L	W	L	PCT	G	GS	CG	SH	SV	IP	H	HR	BB	SO	RAT	ERA	ERA+	OAV	OOB	BH	AVG	PB	PR	/A	PD	TPI
1984	Cin-N	6	2	.750	14	14	3	1	0	100^2	87	4	33	40	10.7	2.86	132	.238	.302	5	.139	-1	8	10	-1	0.9
1985	Cin-N	10	16	.385	35	34	5	2	0	218	216	14	83	98	12.3	3.92	97	.262	.329	6	.092	-3	-8	-3	1	-0.6
1986	Mon-N	7	9	.438	35	31	3	2	0	190^1	181	12	70	117	12.0	3.97	93	.256	.326	7	.130	-0	-5	-6	-1	-0.7
1987	Mon-N	4	5	.444	19	12	0	0	0	83	95	10	34	54	14.0	4.99	84	.289	.355	3	.120	0	-8	-7	-1	-0.7
1988	Bal-A	4	15	.211	30	24	1	0	0	158^2	184	18	63	82	14.2	5.39	72	.293	.360	0	—	0	-25	-26	0	-2.5
1989	Bal-A	5	0	1.000	10	8	1	0	0	54^1	62	2	20	30	13.6	2.82	135	.287	.347	0	—	0	6	6	-0	0.6
1990	Bal-A	2	7	.222	10	10	0	0	0	50^2	55	8	14	23	12.3	5.68	67	.279	.327	0	—	0	-10	-11	0	-1.0
	Pit-N	1	0	1.000	5	0	0	0	0	7	7	0	2	4	11.6	2.57	141	.259	.310	0	—	0	1	1	0	0.1
Total	7	39	54	.419	158	133	13	5	0	862^2	887	68	319	448	12.6	4.20	91	.269	.335	21	.117	-4	-41	-36	-1	-3.9

● DICK TIDROW Tidrow, Richard William b: 5/14/47, San Francisco, Cal. BR/TR, 6'4", 213 lbs. Deb: 4/18/72

YEAR	TM/L	W	L	PCT	G	GS	CG	SH	SV	IP	H	HR	BB	SO	RAT	ERA	ERA+	OAV	OOB	BH	AVG	PB	PR	/A	PD	TPI
1972	Cle-A	14	15	.483	39	34	10	3	0	237^1	200	21	70	123	10.5	2.77	116	.230	.291	7	.100	-3	8	12	-4	0.6
1973	Cle-A	14	16	.467	42	40	13	2	0	274^2	289	31	95	138	12.8	4.42	89	.270	.334	0	—	0	-19	-15	-2	-1.8
1974	Cle-A	1	3	.250	4	4	0	0	0	19	21	4	13	8	17.1	7.11	51	.276	.396	0	—	0	-7	-7	0	-0.6
	NY-A	11	9	.550	33	25	5	0	1	190^2	205	14	53	100	12.4	3.87	90	.279	.331	0	—	0	-5	-8	-2	-0.9
	Yr	12	12	.500	37	29	5	0	1	209^2	226	18	66	108	12.7	4.16	84	.278	.335	0	—	0	-13	-15	-1	-1.5
1975	NY-A	6	3	.667	37	0	0	0	5	69^1	65	5	31	38	12.9	3.12	117	.256	.344	0	—	0	5	4	-1	0.3
1976	*NY-A	4	5	.444	47	2	0	0	10	92^1	80	5	24	65	10.2	2.63	130	.233	.285	0	—	0	9	8	-1	0.7
1977	*NY-A	11	4	.733	49	7	0	0	5	151	143	20	41	83	11.1	3.16	125	.250	.303	0	—	0	15	13	-1	1.3
1978	*NY-A	7	11	.389	31	25	4	0	0	185^1	191	13	53	73	12.1	3.84	94	.267	.322	0	—	0	-2	-4	-2	-0.5
1979	NY-A	2	1	.667	14	0	0	0	2	22^2	38	5	4	7	16.7	7.94	51	.409	.433	0	—	0	-9	-10	1	[illegible]
	Chi-N	11	5	.688	63	0	0	0	4	102^2	86	5	42	68	11.4	2.72	151	.231	.313	2	.200	0	12	16	[illegible]	[illegible]
1980	Chi-N	6	5	.545	**84**	0	0	0	6	116	97	10	53	97	12.0	2.79	140	.229	.322	0	.000	-1	10	[illegible]	[illegible]	[illegible]
1981	Chi-N	3	10	.231	51	0	0	0	9	74^2	73	6	30	39	12.5	5.06	73	.256	.329	0	.000	-1	[illegible]	[illegible]	[illegible]	[illegible]
1982	Chi-N	8	3	.727	65	0	0	0	6	103^2	106	6	29	62	12.0	3.39	110	.265	.319	0	.000	[illegible]	[illegible]	[illegible]	[illegible]	[illegible]
1983	*Chi-A	2	4	.333	50	1	0	0	7	91^2	86	13	34	66	11.9	4.22	99	.242	.310	0	[illegible]	[illegible]	[illegible]	[illegible]	[illegible]	[illegible]
1984	NY-N	0	0	—	11	0	0	0	0	15^2	25	5	7	8	18.4	9.19	38	.357	.416	0	[illegible]	[illegible]	[illegible]	[illegible]	[illegible]	[illegible]
Total	13	100	94	.515	620	138	32	5	55	1746^2	1705	163	579	975	12.0	3.68	101	.257	.321	[illegible]	[illegible]	[illegible]	[illegible]	[illegible]	[illegible]	[illegible]

YEAR	TM/L	W	L	PCT	G	GS	CG	SH	SV	IP	H	HR	BB	SO	RAT	ERA	ERA+	OAV	OOB	BH	AVG	PB	PR	/A	PD	TPI
● BOBBY TIEFENAUER	Tiefenauer, Bobby Gene b: 10/10/29, Desloge, Mo. BR/TR, 6'2", 185 lbs. Deb: 7/14/52 C																									
1952	StL-N	0	0	—	6	0	0	0	0	8	12	1	7	3	21.4	7.88	47	.343	.452	0	.000	-0	-4	-4	0	-0.4
1955	StL-N	1	4	.200	18	0	0	0	0	32^2	31	6	10	16	12.4	4.41	92	.261	.338	0	.000	-0	-1	-1	0	-0.1
1960	Cle-A	0	1	.000	6	0	0	0	0	9	8	0	3	2	11.0	2.00	187	.242	.306	0	.000	0	2	2	-0	0.2
1961	StL-N	0	0	—	3	0	0	0	0	4^1	9	0	4	3	27.0	6.23	71	.450	.542	0	—	0	-1	-1	-0	-0.1
1962	Hou-N	2	4	.333	43	0	0	0	1	85	91	6	21	60	12.1	4.34	86	.277	.324	1	.111	0	-4	-6	-2	-0.7
1963	Mil-N	1	1	.500	12	0	0	0	2	29^2	20	1	4	22	7.3	1.21	265	.194	.224	0	.000	-0	7	7	1	0.8
1964	Mil-N	4	6	.400	46	0	0	0	13	73	61	6	15	48	9.7	3.21	110	.225	.273	0	.000	-1	3	3	-1	0.1
1965	Mil-N	0	1	.000	6	0	0	0	0	7	8	1	3	7	15.4	7.71	46	.286	.375	0	—	0	-3	-3	0	-0.3
	NY-A	1	1	.500	10	0	0	0	2	20^1	19	3	5	15	11.1	3.54	96	.253	.309	0	.000	0	-0	-0	-0	0.0
	Cle-A	0	5	.000	15	0	0	0	4	22^1	24	3	10	13	14.1	4.84	72	.273	.354	0	.000	-0	-3	-3	-0	-0.4
	Yr	1	6	.143	25	0	0	0	6	42^2	43	6	15	28	12.4	4.22	82	.259	.324	0	.000	-0	-4	-4	-0	-0.4
1967	Cle-A	0	1	.000	5	0	0	0	0	11^1	9	0	3	6	9.5	0.79	411	.225	.279	0	—	0	3	3	-1	0.3
1968	Chi-N	0	1	.000	9	0	0	0	1	13^1	20	2	2	9	14.9	6.08	52	.351	.373	0	.000	-0	-5	-4	-0	-0.5
Total	10	9	25	.265	179	0	0	0	23	316	312	29	87	204	11.7	3.84	94	.260	.317	1	.026	-2	-7	-9	-2	-1.1
● VERLE TIEFENTHALER	Tiefenthaler, Verle Matthew b: 7/11/37, Breda, Iowa BL/TR, 6'1", 190 lbs. Deb: 4/19/62																									
1962	Chi-A	0	0	—	3	0	0	0	0	3^2	6	1	7	1	31.9	9.82	40	.353	.542	0	—	0	-2	-2	-0	-0.2
● EDDIE TIEMEYER	Tiemeyer, Edward Carl b: 5/9/1885, Cincinnati, Ohio d: 9/27/46, Cincinnati, Ohio BR/TR, 5'11.5", 185 lbs. Deb: 8/19/06 ♦																									
1906	Cin-N	0	0	—	1	0	0	0	0	1	1	0	1	1	18.0	0.00	—	.500	.667	2	.182	0	0	0	-0	0.0
● MIKE TIERNAN	Tiernan, Michael Joseph "Silent Mike" b: 1/21/1867, Trenton, N.J. d: 11/9/18, New York, N.Y. BL/TL, 5'11", 165 lbs. Deb: 4/30/1887 ♦																									
1887	NY-N	1	2	.333	5	0	0	0	1	19^2	33	2	7	3	18.8	8.69	43	.398	.451	117	.287	2	-10	-11	-0	-0.8
● LES TIETJE	Tietje, Leslie William "Toots" b: 9/11/11, Sumner, Iowa BR/TR, 6'0.5", 178 lbs. Deb: 9/18/33																									
1933	Chi-A	2	0	1.000	3	3	1	0	0	22^1	16	1	15	9	12.5	2.42	175	.203	.330	1	.125	0	5	5	0	0.5
1934	Chi-A	5	14	.263	34	22	6	1	0	176	174	20	96	81	13.9	4.81	98	.257	.351	1	.017	-8	-6	-1	2	-0.7
1935	Chi-A	9	15	.375	30	21	9	1	0	169^2	184	14	81	64	14.2	4.30	108	.277	.357	12	.197	-1	3	6	-2	0.3
1936	Chi-A	0	0	—	2	0	0	0	0	2^1	6	0	5	3	42.4	27.00	19	.462	.611	0	—	0	-6	-6	-0	-0.4
	StL-A	3	5	.375	14	7	2	0	0	50^1	65	2	30	16	17.3	6.62	81	.310	.401	1	.067	-2	-9	-7	1	-0.7
	Yr	3	5	.375	16	7	2	0	0	52^2	71	2	35	19	18.5	7.52	71	.318	.415	1	.067	-1	-15	-13	1	-1.1
1937	StL-A	1	2	.333	5	4	2	0	0	30	32	0	17	5	14.7	4.20	115	.283	.377	0	.000	-2	1	2	-1	0.0
1938	StL-A	2	5	.286	17	8	2	1	0	62	83	8	38	15	17.6	7.55	66	.327	.414	2	.111	-1	-19	-18	-0	-1.6
Total	6	22	41	.349	105	65	22	3	0	512^2	560	45	282	193	14.9	5.11	93	.279	.369	17	.099	-13	-31	-19	0	-2.6
● RAY TIFT	Tift, Raymond Frank b: 6/21/1884, Fitchburg, Mass. d: 3/29/45, Verona, N.J. TL , Deb: 8/07/07																									
1907	NY-A	0	0	—	4	1	0	0	0	19	33	0	4	6	17.5	4.74	59	.382	.409	0	.000	-1	-5	-4	-1	-0.5
● JOHNNY TILLMAN	Tillman, John Lawrence "Ducky" b: 10/6/1893, Bridgeport, Conn. d: 4/7/64, Harrisburg, Pa. BB/TR, 5'11", 170 lbs. Deb: 9/20/15																									
1915	StL-A	1	0	1.000	2	1	0	0	0	10	6	0	4	6	9.0	0.90	318	.176	.263	0	.000	-0	2	2	0	0.2
● THAD TILLOTSON	Tillotson, Thaddeus Asa b: 12/20/40, Merced, Cal. BR/TR, 6'2.5", 195 lbs. Deb: 4/14/67																									
1967	NY-A	3	9	.250	43	5	1	0	2	98^1	99	9	39	62	12.8	4.03	78	.261	.333	1	.063	-0	-9	-10	0	-1.1
1968	NY-A	1	0	1.000	7	0	0	0	0	10^1	11	0	7	1	15.7	4.35	67	.282	.391	0	.000	-0	-2	-2	0	-0.2
Total	2	4	9	.308	50	5	1	0	2	108^2	110	9	46	63	13.1	4.06	77	.263	.339	1	.059	-1	-10	-11	1	-1.3
● GARY TIMBERLAKE	Timberlake, Gary Dale b: 8/8/48, Laconia, Ind. BR/TL, 6'2", 205 lbs. Deb: 6/18/69																									
1969	Sea-A	0	0	—	2	2	0	0	0	6	7	0	9	4	24.0	7.50	48	.269	.457	0	.000	-0	-3	-3	-0	-0.3
● MIKE TIMLIN	Timlin, Michael August b: 3/10/66, Midland, Tex. BR/TR, 6'4", 205 lbs. Deb: 4/08/91																									
1991	*Tor-A	11	6	.647	63	3	0	0	3	108^1	94	6	50	85	12.0	3.16	133	.233	.319	0	—	0	11	13	1	1.3
1992	*Tor-A	0	2	.000	26	0	0	0	1	43^2	45	0	20	35	13.6	4.12	99	.271	.353	0	—	0	-1	-0	0	-0.1
Total	2	11	8	.579	89	3	0	0	4	152	139	6	70	120	12.5	3.43	121	.244	.329	0	—	0	10	12	1	1.2
● TOM TIMMERMANN	Timmermann, Thomas Henry b: 5/12/40, Breese, Ill. BR/TR, 6'4", 215 lbs. Deb: 6/18/69																									
1969	Det-A	4	3	.571	31	1	1	0	1	55^2	50	1	26	42	12.6	2.75	136	.238	.328	1	.111	-0	5	6	-1	0.5
1970	Det-A	6	7	.462	61	0	0	0	27	85^1	90	3	34	49	13.3	4.11	91	.273	.344	0	.000	-2	-4	-4	-0	-0.6
1971	Det-A	7	6	.538	52	2	0	0	4	84	82	6	37	51	13.1	3.86	93	.262	.346	1	.053	-1	-4	-2	0	-0.4
1972	Det-A	8	10	.444	34	25	3	2	0	149^2	121	12	41	88	10.0	2.89	109	.216	.276	6	.136	-0	3	4	-2	0.3
1973	Det-A	1	1	.500	17	1	0	0	1	39	39	4	11	21	11.5	3.69	111	.258	.309	0	—	0	1	2	-1	-0.2
	Cle-A	8	7	.533	29	15	4	0	2	124^1	117	15	54	62	12.6	4.92	80	.251	.332	0	—	0	-15	-14	-0	-1.5
	Yr	9	8	.529	46	16	4	0	3	163^1	156	19	65	83	12.3	4.63	86	.252	.327	0	—	0	-15	-12	-1	-1.7
1974	Cle-A	1	1	.500	4	0	0	0	0	10	9	1	5	2	12.6	5.40	67	.250	.341	0	—	0	-2	-2	1	-0.1
Total	6	35	35	.500	228	44	8	2	35	548	508	42	208	315	12.0	3.78	96	.246	.319	8	.091	-4	-16	-10	-3	-2.0
● BEN TINCUP	Tincup, Austin Ben b: 12/14/1890, Adair, Okla. d: 7/5/80, Claremore, Okla. BL/TR, 6'1", 180 lbs. Deb: 5/22/14 C♦																									
1914	Phi-N	8	10	.444	28	17	9	3	2	155	165	0	62	108	13.4	2.61	113	.286	.359	9	.170	-1	3	6	1	0.6
1915	Phi-N	0	0	—	10	0	0	0	0	31	26	1	9	10	10.2	2.03	135	.263	.324	0	.000	-1	2	2	0	0.2
1918	Phi-N	0	1	.000	8	1	0	0	0	16^2	24	0	6	6	16.2	7.56	40	.329	.380	1	.125	-0	-9	-8	1	-0.8
1928	Chi-N	0	0	—	2	0	0	0	0	9	14	0	1	3	15.0	7.00	55	.378	.395	0	.000	-0	-3	-3	0	-0.3
Total	4	8	11	.421	48	18	9	3	2	211^2	229	1	78	127	13.2	3.10	95	.291	.358	10	.135	-3	-6	-3	3	-0.3
● BUD TINNING	Tinning, Lyle Forrest b: 3/12/06, Pilger, Neb. d: 1/17/61, Evansville, Ind. BB/TR, 5'11", 198 lbs. Deb: 4/20/32																									
1932	*Chi-N	5	3	.625	24	7	2	0	0	93^1	93	3	24	30	11.5	2.80	135	.263	.313	2	.087	-1	11	10	0	0.9
1933	Chi-N	13	6	.684	32	21	10	3	1	175^1	169	3	60	59	12.0	3.18	103	.255	.320	14	.209	1	3	2	-2	0.0
1934	Chi-N	4	6	.400	39	7	1	1	3	129^1	134	9	46	44	12.6	3.34	116	.269	.332	7	.179	-1	10	8	-1	0.6
1935	StL-N	0	0	—	4	0	0	0	0	7^2	9	1	5	2	17.6	5.87	70	.300	.417	0	.000	-0	-2	-2	0	-0.2
Total	4	22	[illegible]	[illegible]95	99	35	13	4	4	405^2	405	16	135	135	12.2	3.19	113	.262	.325	23	.177	-1	23	18	-4	1.3
● DAN T[illegible]	[illegible]e, Daniel E. "Big Dan" or "Rusty" b: 2/13/1890, Rockford, Ill. d: 3/26/60, Omaha, Neb. BR/TR, 6', 176 lbs. Deb: 9/18/15																									
1915	[illegible]	[illegible]	[illegible]	[illegible]	3	2	2	0	0	19	14	1	11	14	11.8	0.95	309	.203	.313	0	.000	-1	4	4	-1	0.3
[illegible]	[illegible]ohnnie Joseph b: 10/9/03, High Point, Mo. d: 9/5/67, Leadville, Ohio BL/TR, 6'2", 180 lbs. Deb: 4/24/36																									
[illegible]	[illegible]	[illegible]	[illegible]	[illegible]	[illegible]	6	1	0	0	47	52	5	24	27	14.6	4.21	96	.272	.353	3	.273	0	-1	-1	-0	-0.1
[illegible]	Titcomb, Ledell b: 8/21/1866, W.Baldwin, Me. d: 6/8/50, Kingston, N.H. BL/TL, 5'6", 157 lbs. Deb: 5/05/1886																									
[illegible]	[illegible]	[illegible]	[illegible]	[illegible]	[illegible]	5	5	0	0	41	43	1	24	24	14.7	3.73	88	.244	.335	1	.063	-2	-2	-2	1	-0.3
[illegible]	[illegible]	[illegible]	[illegible]	[illegible]	[illegible]	[illegible]	3	0	0	24	31	1	19	16	18.8	6.75	64	.298	.407	0	.000	-1	-7	-7	-1	-0.6
[illegible]	[illegible]	[illegible]	[illegible]	[illegible]	[illegible]	[illegible]	9	0	0	72	68	3	37	34	13.3	3.88	97	.233	.321	2	.069	-4	2	-1	-1	-0.5
[illegible]	[illegible]	[illegible]	[illegible]	[illegible]	[illegible]	[illegible]	22	4	0	197	149	4	46	129	9.1	2.24	122	.201	.253	10	.122	-4	13	11	-4	0.2
[illegible]	[illegible]	[illegible]	[illegible]	[illegible]	[illegible]	[illegible]	3	0	0	26	27	1	16	7	15.6	6.58	60	.260	.369	1	.083	-1	-7	-8	-0	-0.7
[illegible]	[illegible]	[illegible]	[illegible]	[illegible]	[illegible]	[illegible]	[illegible]	1	0	168^2	168	6	97	73	14.9	3.74	95	.252	.358	8	.107	-5	3	-3	-3	-0.9
[illegible]	[illegible]	[illegible]	[illegible]	[illegible]	[illegible]	[illegible]	[illegible]	5	0	528^2	486	16	239	283	12.7	3.47	96	.233	.318	22	.098	-16	2	-9	-8	-2.8

● **DAVE TOBIK** Tobik, David Vance b: 3/2/53, Euclid, Ohio BR/TR, 6'1", 195 lbs. Deb: 8/26/78

YEAR	TM/L	W	L	PCT	G	GS	CG	SH	SV	IP	H	HR	BB	SO	RAT	ERA	ERA+	OAV	OOB	BH	AVG	PB	PR	/A	PD	TPI
1978	Det-A	0	0	—	5	0	0	0	0	12	12	1	3	11	11.3	3.75	103	.261	.306	0	—	0	0	0	-0	-0.2
1979	Det-A	3	5	.375	37	0	0	0	3	68^{2}	59	12	25	48	11.0	4.33	100	.231	.300	0	—	0	-1	-0	-1	-0.3
1980	Det-A	1	0	1.000	17	1	0	0	0	61	61	7	21	34	12.1	3.98	103	.266	.328	0	—	0	0	1	-0	0.0
1981	Det-A	2	2	.500	27	0	0	0	1	60^{1}	47	7	33	32	11.9	2.69	140	.215	.317	0	—	0	7	7	-1	0.5
1982	Det-A	4	9	.308	51	1	0	0	9	98^{2}	86	8	38	63	11.4	3.56	114	.241	.316	0	—	0	6	6	-1	0.4
1983	Tex-A	2	1	.667	27	0	0	0	9	44	36	2	13	30	10.0	3.68	109	.222	.280	0	—	0	2	2	0	0.3
1984	Tex-A	1	6	.143	24	0	0	0	5	42^{1}	44	5	17	30	13.2	3.61	115	.265	.337	0	—	0	2	2	1	0.0
1985	Sea-A	1	0	1.000	8	0	0	0	1	9	10	2	3	8	13.0	6.00	70	.286	.342	0	—	0	-2	-2	-0	-0.2
Total	8	14	23	.378	196	2	0	0	28	396	355	44	153	256	11.6	3.70	110	.242	.314	0	—	0	13	16	-3	0.5

● **JIM TOBIN** Tobin, James Anthony "Abba Dabba" b: 12/27/12, Oakland, Cal. d: 5/19/69, Oakland, Cal. BR/TR, 6', 185 lbs. Deb: 4/30/37 F♦

YEAR	TM/L	W	L	PCT	G	GS	CG	SH	SV	IP	H	HR	BB	SO	RAT	ERA	ERA+	OAV	OOB	BH	AVG	PB	PR	/A	PD	TPI
1937	Pit-N	6	3	.667	20	8	7	0	1	87	74	1	28	37	10.7	3.00	129	.226	.289	15	.441	7	9	8	-2	1.4
1938	Pit-N	14	12	.538	40	33	14	2	0	241^{1}	254	17	66	70	12.2	3.47	109	.270	.321	25	.243	7	9	9	-2	1.4
1939	Pit-N	9	9	.500	25	19	8	0	0	145^{1}	194	7	33	43	14.2	4.52	85	.319	.356	18	.243	5	-10	-11	-1	-0.7
1940	Bos-N	7	3	.700	15	11	9	0	0	96^{1}	102	8	24	29	11.8	3.83	97	.264	.307	12	.279	3	0	-1	-1	0.1
1941	Bos-N	12	12	.500	33	26	20	3	0	238	229	12	60	61	10.9	3.10	115	.253	.300	19	.184	3	14	12	4	2.1
1942	Bos-N	12	21	.364	37	33	**28**	1	0	**287^{2}**	283	20	96	71	12.0	3.97	84	.257	.320	28	.246	14	-21	-20	6	-0.1
1943	Bos-N	14	14	.500	33	30	24	1	0	250	241	12	69	52	11.2	2.66	128	.251	.303	30	.280	6	20	21	2	3.5
1944	Bos-N★	18	19	.486	43	36	**28**	5	3	299^{1}	271	18	97	83	11.2	3.01	127	.240	.302	22	.190	6	20	27	7	4.3
1945	Bos-N	9	14	.391	27	25	16	0	0	196^{2}	220	10	56	38	12.9	3.84	100	.282	.334	11	.143	5	-1	-0	2	0.7
	*Det-A	4	5	.444	14	6	2	0	1	58^{1}	61	2	28	14	14.3	3.55	99	.274	.365	3	.120	0	-1	-0	1	0.1
Total	9	105	112	.484	287	227	156	12	5	1900	1929	107	557	498	11.9	3.44	106	.262	.316	183	.230	54	39	45	16	12.8

● **PAT TOBIN** Tobin, Marion Brooks b: 1/28/16, Hermitage, Ark. d: 1/21/75, Shreveport, La. BR/TR, 6'1", 198 lbs. Deb: 8/21/41

YEAR	TM/L	W	L	PCT	G	GS	CG	SH	SV	IP	H	HR	BB	SO	RAT	ERA	ERA+	OAV	OOB	BH	AVG	PB	PR	/A	PD	TPI
1941	Phi-A	0	0	—	1	0	0	0	0	1	4	0	2	0	54.0	36.00	12	.571	.667	0	—	0	-4	-4	0	-0.3

● **FRANK TODD** Todd, George Franklin b: 10/18/1869, Aberdeen, Md. d: 8/11/19, Havre De Grace, Md. TL, Deb: 7/14/1898

YEAR	TM/L	W	L	PCT	G	GS	CG	SH	SV	IP	H	HR	BB	SO	RAT	ERA	ERA+	OAV	OOB	BH	AVG	PB	PR	/A	PD	TPI
1898	Lou-N	0	2	.000	4	2	0	0	0	11	23	0	8	5	27.0	13.91	26	.422	.511	1	.200	0	-13	-13	-1	-1.0

● **JACKSON TODD** Todd, Jackson A b: 11/20/51, Tulsa, Okla. BR/TR, 6'2", 180 lbs. Deb: 5/05/77

YEAR	TM/L	W	L	PCT	G	GS	CG	SH	SV	IP	H	HR	BB	SO	RAT	ERA	ERA+	OAV	OOB	BH	AVG	PB	PR	/A	PD	TPI
1977	NY-N	3	6	.333	19	10	0	0	0	71^{2}	78	8	20	39	12.6	4.77	78	.273	.325	1	.059	-1	-7	-8	0	-0.9
1979	Tor-A	0	1	.000	12	1	0	0	0	32^{1}	40	7	7	14	13.4	5.85	74	.299	.338	0	—	0	-6	-5	0	-0.6
1980	Tor-A	5	2	.714	12	12	4	0	0	85	90	14	30	44	12.9	4.02	107	.276	.341	0	—	0	0	3	1	0.2
1981	Tor-A	2	7	.222	21	13	3	0	0	97^{2}	94	10	31	41	11.9	3.96	99	.251	.315	0	—	0	-3	-0	1	-0.1
Total	4	10	16	.385	64	36	7	0	0	286^{2}	302	39	88	138	12.5	4.40	92	.270	.328	1	.059	-1	-16	-11	2	-1.4

● **JIM TODD** Todd, James Richard b: 9/21/47, Lancaster, Pa. BL/TR, 6'2", 190 lbs. Deb: 4/29/74

YEAR	TM/L	W	L	PCT	G	GS	CG	SH	SV	IP	H	HR	BB	SO	RAT	ERA	ERA+	OAV	OOB	BH	AVG	PB	PR	/A	PD	TPI
1974	Chi-N	4	2	.667	43	6	0	0	3	88	82	7	41	42	12.9	3.89	98	.252	.341	1	.063	-2	-3	-1	1	-0.2
1975	*Oak-A	8	3	.727	58	0	0	0	12	122	104	4	33	50	10.3	2.29	159	.234	.292	0	—	0	20	18	4	2.3
1976	Oak-A	7	8	.467	49	0	0	0	4	82^{2}	87	6	34	22	13.8	3.81	88	.276	.358	0	—	0	-3	-4	2	-0.3
1977	Chi-N	1	1	.500	20	0	0	0	0	30^{2}	47	1	19	17	20.0	9.10	48	.336	.422	0	.000	-0	-18	-16	0	-1.5
1978	Sea-A	3	4	.429	49	2	0	0	3	106^{2}	113	4	61	37	14.7	3.88	98	.280	.375	0	—	0	-1	-1	0	0.0
1979	Oak-A	2	5	.286	51	0	0	0	2	81	108	12	51	26	17.9	6.56	62	.329	.423	0	—	0	-21	-23	0	-1.7
Total	6	25	23	.521	270	8	0	0	24	511	541	34	239	194	14.0	4.23	89	.277	.360	1	.059	-2	-25	-26	7	-1.4

● **HAL TOENES** Toenes, William Harrel b: 10/8/17, Mobile, Ala. BR/TR, 5'11.5", 175 lbs. Deb: 9/17/47

YEAR	TM/L	W	L	PCT	G	GS	CG	SH	SV	IP	H	HR	BB	SO	RAT	ERA	ERA+	OAV	OOB	BH	AVG	PB	PR	/A	PD	TPI
1947	Was-A	0	1	.000	3	1	0	0	0	6^{2}	11	0	2	5	17.6	6.75	55	.379	.419	0	.000	0	-2	-2	-0	-0.2

● **FREDDIE TOLIVER** Toliver, Freddie Lee b: 2/3/61, Natchez, Miss. BR/TR, 6'1", 170 lbs. Deb: 9/15/84

YEAR	TM/L	W	L	PCT	G	GS	CG	SH	SV	IP	H	HR	BB	SO	RAT	ERA	ERA+	OAV	OOB	BH	AVG	PB	PR	/A	PD	TPI
1984	Cin-N	0	0	—	3	1	0	0	0	10	7	0	7	4	12.6	0.90	420	.206	.341	0	.000	-0	3	3	-0	0.3
1985	Phi-N	0	4	.000	11	3	0	0	1	25	27	2	17	23	15.8	4.68	79	.273	.379	2	.500	1	-3	-3	-0	-0.2
1986	Phi-N	0	2	.000	5	5	0	0	0	25^{2}	28	0	11	20	13.7	3.51	110	.286	.358	0	.000	-0	1	1	0	0.1
1987	Phi-N	1	1	.500	10	4	0	0	0	30^{1}	34	2	17	25	15.4	5.64	75	.291	.385	0	.000	-1	-5	-5	0	-0.5
1988	Min-A	7	6	.538	21	19	0	0	0	114^{2}	116	8	52	69	13.3	4.24	96	.270	.350	0	—	0	-3	-2	0	-0.2
1989	Min-A	1	3	.250	7	5	0	0	0	29	39	2	15	11	17.1	7.76	53	.317	.396	0	—	0	-12	-12	1	-1.0
	SD-N	0	0	—	9	0	0	0	0	14	17	5	9	14	17.4	7.07	49	.321	.429	0	—	0	-6	-6	-0	-0.6
Total	6	9	16	.360	66	37	0	0	1	248^{2}	268	19	128	166	14.5	4.81	83	.281	.368	2	.125	0	-26	-23	2	-2.1

● **DICK TOMANEK** Tomanek, Richard Carl "Bones" b: 1/6/31, Avon Lake, Ohio BL/TL, 6'1", 175 lbs. Deb: 9/25/53

YEAR	TM/L	W	L	PCT	G	GS	CG	SH	SV	IP	H	HR	BB	SO	RAT	ERA	ERA+	OAV	OOB	BH	AVG	PB	PR	/A	PD	TPI
1953	Cle-A	1	0	1.000	1	1	1	0	0	9	6	1	6	6	13.0	2.00	188	.176	.317	0	.000	-1	2	2	-0	0.1
1954	Cle-A	0	0	—	1	0	0	0	0	1^{2}	1	1	1	0	10.8	5.40	68	.167	.286	0	—	0	-0	-0	0	0.0
1957	Cle-A	2	1	.667	34	2	0	0	0	69^{2}	67	13	37	55	13.6	5.68	65	.248	.341	3	.231	0	-15	-15	0	-1.5
1958	Cle-A	2	3	.400	18	6	2	0	0	57^{2}	61	8	28	42	14.2	5.62	65	.276	.363	2	.118	0	-12	-13	0	-1.2
	KC-A	5	5	.500	36	2	1	0	5	72^{1}	69	5	28	50	12.1	3.61	108	.252	.321	3	.231	1	1	2	-0	0.3
	Yr	7	8	.467	54	8	3	0	5	130	130	13	56	92	12.9	4.50	84	.261	.336	5	.167	1	-11	-10	0	-0.9
1959	KC-A	0	1	.000	16	0	0	0	2	20^{2}	27	6	12	13	17.9	6.53	61	.310	.406	1	.500	0	-6	-6	0	-0.5
Total	5	10	10	.500	106	11	4	0	7	231	231	34	112	166	13.6	4.95	77	.259	.346	9	.180	1	-30	-30	1	-2.8

● **ANDY TOMASIC** Tomasic, Andrew John b: 12/10/19, Hokendauqua, Pa. BR/TR, 6', 175 lbs. Deb: 4/28/49

YEAR	TM/L	W	L	PCT	G	GS	CG	SH	SV	IP	H	HR	BB	SO	RAT	ERA	ERA+	OAV	OOB	BH	AVG	PB	PR	/A	PD	TPI
1949	NY-N	0	1	.000	2	0	0	0	0	5	9	2	5	2	25.2	18.00	22	.375	.483	0	.000	-0	-8	-8	-0	-0.7

● **DAVE TOMLIN** Tomlin, David Allen b: 6/22/49, Maysville, Ky. BL/TL, 6'3", 185 lbs. Deb: 9/02/72

YEAR	TM/L	W	L	PCT	G	GS	CG	SH	SV	IP	H	HR	BB	SO	RAT	ERA	ERA+	OAV	OOB	BH	AVG	PB	PR	/A	PD	TPI
1972	Cin-N	0	0	—	3	0	0	0	0	4	7	2	1	2	18.0	9.00	36	.412	.444	0	—	0	-2	-3	0	-0.3
1973	*Cin-N	1	2	.333	16	0	0	0	1	27^{2}	24	5	15	20	12.7	4.88	70	.238	.336	0	.000	-0	-4	-5	0	-0.5
1974	SD-N	2	0	1.000	47	0	0	0	2	58	59	4	30	29	14.1	4.34	82	.271	.364	0	.000	-0	-5	-5	1	-0.5
1975	SD-N	4	2	.667	67	0	0	0	1	83	87	5	31	48	13.0	3.25	107	.275	.344	1	.200	1	3	2	3	0.6
1976	SD-N	0	1	.000	49	1	0	0	0	73	62	4	20	43	10.2	2.84	115	.235	.291	0	.000	-1	5	4	2	0.6
1977	SD-N	4	4	.500	76	0	0	0	3	101^{2}	98	3	32	55	11.7	3.01	118	.259	.320	2	.286	0	10	6	1	0.8
1978	Cin-N	9	1	.900	57	0	0	0	4	62^{1}	88	3	30	32	17.5	5.78	61	.326	.399	1	.200	1	-15	-15	1	-1.6
1979	*Cin-N	2	2	.500	53	0	0	0	1	58^{1}	59	3	18	30	12.0	2.62	142	.269	.328	1	.500	1	7	7	0	0.8
1980	Cin-N	3	0	1.000	27	0	0	0	0	26	38	2	11	6	17.0	5.54	65	.355	.415	0	—	0	-6	-6	0	-0.5
1982	Mon-N	0	0	—	1	0	0	0	0	2	1	0	1	2	9.0	4.50	81	.167	.286	0	—	0	-0	-0	-0	0.0
1983	Pit-N	0	0	—	5	0	0	0	0	4	6	0	1	5	15.8	6.75	55	.316	.350	0	—	0	-1	-1	-0	-0.2
1985	Pit-N	0	0	—	1	0	0	0	0	1	1	0	1	0	18.0	0.00	—	.333	.500	0	—	0	0	0	-0	0.0
1986	Mon-N	0	0	—	7	0	0	0	0	10^{1}	13	1	7	6	18.3	5.23	71	.317	.429	0	—	0	-2	-2	0	-0.1
Total	13	25	12	.676	409	1	0	0	12	511^{1}	543	32	198	278	13.3	3.82	92	.277	.347	5	.147	1	-9	-17	9	-0.9

● **RANDY TOMLIN** Tomlin, Randy Leon b: 6/14/66, Bainbridge, Md. BL/TL, 5'11", 179 lbs. Deb: 8/06/90

YEAR	TM/L	W	L	PCT	G	GS	CG	SH	SV	IP	H	HR	BB	SO	RAT	ERA	ERA+	OAV	OOB	BH	AVG	PB	PR	/A	PD	TPI
1990	Pit-N	4	4	.500	12	12	2	0	0	77^{2}	62	5	12	42	8.7	2.55	142	.221	.256	1	.040	-1	11	9	1	1.0
1991	*Pit-N	8	7	.533	31	27	4	2	0	175	170	9	54	104	11.8	2.98	120	.254	.316	10	.192	1	14	11	2	1.6
1992	*Pit-N	14	9	.609	35	33	1	1	0	208^{2}	226	11	42	90	11.8	3.41	100	.282	.322	9	.138	-0	2	-0	3	0.3
Total	3	26	20	.565	78	72	7	3	0	461^{1}	458	25	108	236	11.3	3.10	113	.262	.309	20	.141	-0	27	21	6	2.9

YEAR	TM/L	W	L	PCT	G	GS	CG	SH	SV	IP	H	HR	BB	SO	RAT	ERA	ERA+	OAV	OOB	BH	AVG	PB	PR	/A	PD	TPI
● CHUCK TOMPKINS	Tompkins, Charles Herbert b: 9/1/1889, Prescott, Ark. d: 9/20/75, Prescott, Ark. BR/TR, 6', 185 lbs. Deb: 6/25/12																									
1912	Cin-N	0	0	—	1	0	0	0	0	3	5	0	0	1	15.0	0.00	—	.357	.357	1	1.000	0	1	1	-0	0.2
● RON TOMPKINS	Tompkins, Ronald Everett "Stretch" b: 11/27/44, San Diego, Cal. BR/TR, 6'4", 198 lbs. Deb: 9/09/65																									
1965	KC-A	0	0	—	5	1	0	0	0	10^1	9	0	3	4	11.3	3.48	100	.237	.310	0	.000	-0	-0	0	0	0.0
1971	Chi-N	0	2	.000	35	0	0	0	3	39^2	31	3	21	20	12.5	4.08	96	.214	.325	0	—	0	-3	-1	1	0.0
Total	2	0	2	.000	40	1	0	0	3	50	40	3	24	24	12.2	3.96	97	.219	.322	0	.000	-0	-3	-1	1	0.0
● TOMMY TOMS	Toms, Thomas Howard b: 10/15/51, Charlottesville, Va BR/TR, 6'4", 195 lbs. Deb: 5/04/75																									
1975	SF-N	0	1	.000	7	0	0	0	0	10^1	13	1	6	6	16.5	6.10	62	.317	.404	0	—	0	-3	-3	-0	-0.3
1976	SF-N	0	1	.000	7	0	0	0	1	8^2	13	1	1	4	14.5	6.23	58	.351	.368	0	—	0	-3	-3	0	-0.3
1977	SF-N	0	1	.000	4	0	0	0	0	4^1	7	0	2	2	18.7	2.08	188	.333	.391	0	—	0	1	1	-0	0.1
Total	3	0	3	.000	18	0	0	0	1	23^1	33	2	9	12	16.2	5.40	70	.333	.389	0	—	0	-5	-4	-0	-0.5
● FRED TONEY	Toney, Fred Alexandra b: 12/11/1888, Nashville, Tenn. d: 3/11/53, Nashville, Tenn. BR/TR, 6'1", 195 lbs. Deb: 4/15/11																									
1911	Chi-N	1	1	.500	18	4	1	0	0	67	55	2	35	27	12.8	2.42	137	.229	.339	2	.111	-1	7	7	1	0.6
1912	Chi-N	1	2	.333	9	2	0	0	0	24	21	0	11	9	12.4	5.25	63	.247	.340	0	.000	-0	-5	-5	-1	-0.6
1913	Chi-N	2	2	.500	7	5	2	0	0	39	52	1	22	12	17.3	6.00	53	.327	.412	3	.250	1	-12	-12	0	-1.1
1915	Cin-N	17	6	.739	36	23	18	6	2	222^2	160	1	73	108	9.5	1.58	181	.207	.278	7	.095	-5	29	32	1	3.3
1916	Cin-N	14	17	.452	41	38	21	3	1	300	247	7	78	146	10.0	2.28	114	.231	.288	12	.121	-4	11	11	-4	0.3
1917	Cin-N	24	16	.600	43	42	31	7	1	339^2	300	4	77	123	10.1	2.20	119	.238	.286	13	.112	-6	19	16	-5	0.6
1918	Cin-N	6	10	.375	21	19	9	1	2	136^2	148	2	31	32	11.8	2.90	92	.282	.322	9	.214	0	-2	-3	1	-0.3
	NY-N	6	2	.750	11	9	7	1	1	85^1	55	1	7	19	6.8	1.69	156	.192	.216	6	.188	-1	10	9	-1	0.9
	Yr	12	12	.500	32	28	16	2	**3**	222	203	3	38	51	9.9	2.43	109	.250	.285	15	.203	-0	8	5	0	0.6
1919	NY-N	13	6	.684	24	20	14	4	1	181	157	6	35	40	9.6	1.84	152	.235	.276	15	.227	1	22	19	-3	2.0
1920	NY-N	21	11	.656	42	37	17	4	1	278^1	266	8	57	81	10.6	2.65	113	.259	.302	23	.240	3	15	11	-2	1.2
1921	*NY-N	18	11	.621	42	32	16	1	3	249^1	274	14	65	63	12.4	3.61	102	.289	.338	18	.209	2	5	2	-1	0.2
1922	NY-N	5	6	.455	13	12	6	0	0	86^1	91	5	31	10	12.9	4.17	96	.277	.343	2	.067	-3	-1	-2	-2	-0.6
1923	StL-N	11	12	.478	29	28	16	1	0	196^2	211	8	61	48	12.7	3.84	102	.282	.341	8	.116	-5	3	1	3	0.0
Total	12	139	102	.577	336	271	158	28	12	2206	2037	59	583	718	10.9	2.69	113	.251	.305	118	.159	-17	102	85	-12	6.5
● DOC TONKIN	Tonkin, Harry Glenville b: 8/11/1881, Concord, N.H. d: 5/30/59, Miami, Fla. BL/TL, 5'9", 165 lbs. Deb: 8/19/07																									
1907	Was-A	0	0	—	1	0	0	0	0	2^2	6	0	5	0	37.1	6.75	36	.444	.594	2	1.000	1	-1	-1	0	0.0
● STEVE TOOLE	Toole, Stephen John b: 4/9/1859, New Orleans, La. d: 3/28/19, Pittsburgh, Pa. BR/TL, 6', 170 lbs. Deb: 4/20/1886 U																									
1886	Bro-a	6	6	.500	13	12	11	0	0	104	100	0	64	48	14.9	4.41	79	.246	.359	20	.351	4	-11	-11	2	-0.5
1887	Bro-a	14	10	.583	24	24	22	1	0	194	186	1	106	48	14.1	4.31	100	.254	.358	24	.233	-1	-0	-0	-1	-0.2
1888	KC-a	5	6	.455	12	10	10	0	0	91^2	124	4	50	35	17.6	6.68	51	.312	.396	10	.208	-0	-37	-33	0	-2.7
1890	Bro-a	2	4	.333	6	6	6	0	0	53^1	47	0	39	10	15.2	4.05	96	.229	.363	6	.300	1	-1	-1	0	0.1
Total	4	27	26	.509	55	52	49	1	0	443	457	5	259	141	15.1	4.79	81	.262	.367	60	.263	5	-49	-44	2	-3.3
● RUPE TOPPIN	Toppin, Ruperto b: 12/7/41, Panama City, Panama BR/TR, 6', 185 lbs. Deb: 7/28/62																									
1962	KC-A	0	0	—	2	0	0	0	0	2	1	0	5	1	27.0	13.50	31	.167	.545	1	1.000	0	-2	-2	-0	-0.2
● RED TORKELSON	Torkelson, Chester Leroy b: 3/19/1894, Chicago, Ill. d: 9/22/64, Chicago, Ill. BR/TR, 6', 175 lbs. Deb: 8/29/17																									
1917	Cle-A	2	1	.667	4	3	0	0	0	22^1	33	1	13	10	19.3	7.66	37	.333	.421	2	.222	-0	-12	-12	0	-1.1
● PABLO TORREALBA	Torrealba, Pablo Arnoldo (Torrealba) b: 4/28/48, Barquisimento, Ven. BL/TL, 5'9", 175 lbs. Deb: 4/09/75																									
1975	Atl-N	0	1	.000	6	0	0	0	0	6^2	7	0	3	5	13.5	1.35	279	.250	.323	1	1.000	0	2	2	1	0.3
1976	Atl-N	0	2	.000	36	0	0	0	2	53	67	0	22	33	15.6	3.57	106	.315	.387	0	.000	-0	-0	1	1	0.2
1977	Oak-A	4	6	.400	41	10	3	0	2	116^2	127	5	38	51	12.9	2.62	153	.279	.337	0	—	0	19	18	2	2.1
1978	Chi-A	2	4	.333	25	3	1	1	1	57^1	69	6	39	23	17.4	4.71	81	.301	.410	0	—	0	-6	-6	-1	-0.8
1979	Chi-A	0	0	—	3	0	0	0	0	5^2	5	1	2	1	11.1	1.59	268	.250	.318	0	—	0	2	2	0	0.2
Total	5	6	13	.316	111	13	4	1	5	239^1	275	12	104	113	14.6	3.27	120	.291	.366	1	.200	-0	16	17	2	2.0
● ANGEL TORRES	Torres, Angel Rafael (Ruiz) b: 10/24/52, Las Ciengas, Azua, D.R. BL/TL, 5'11", 168 lbs. Deb: 9/12/77																									
1977	Cin-N	0	0	—	5	0	0	0	0	8^1	7	2	8	8	16.2	2.16	182	.233	.395	0	—	0	2	2	0	0.2
● GIL TORRES	Torres, Don Gilberto (Nunez) b: 8/23/15, Regla, Cuba d: 1/10/83, Regla, Cuba BR/TR, 6', 155 lbs. Deb: 4/25/40 F♦																									
1940	Was-A	0	0	—	2	0	0	0	0	2^2	3	0	0	1	10.1	0.00	—	.273	.273	0	—	0	1	1	0	0.1
1946	Was-A	0	0	—	3	0	0	0	1	7	9	0	3	2	15.4	7.71	43	.310	.375	47	.254	1	-3	-3	-0	-0.3
Total	2	0	0	—	5	0	0	0	1	9^2	12	0	3	3	14.0	5.59	64	.300	.349	320	.252	1	-2	-2	-0	-0.2
● HECTOR TORRES	Torres, Hector Epitacio (Marroquin) b: 9/16/45, Monterrey, Mexico BR/TR, 6', 175 lbs. Deb: 4/10/68 C♦																									
1972	Mon-N	0	0	—	1	0	0	0	0	0^2	5	0	0	0	67.5	27.00	13	.714	.714	28	.155	0	-2	-2	0	-0.2
● MIKE TORREZ	Torrez, Michael Augustine b: 8/28/46, Topeka, Kan. BR/TR, 6'5", 220 lbs. Deb: 9/10/67																									
1967	StL-N	0	1	.000	3	1	0	0	0	5^2	5	0	1	5	11.1	3.18	103	.238	.304	0	.000	-0	0	0	-0	0.0
1968	StL-N	2	1	.667	5	2	0	0	0	19^1	20	1	12	6	15.4	2.79	104	.286	.398	2	.286	0	0	0	0	0.1
1969	StL-N	10	4	.714	24	15	3	0	0	107^2	96	7	62	61	13.5	3.59	99	.240	.346	3	.073	-2	-0	-0	0	-0.2
1970	StL-N	8	10	.444	30	28	5	1	0	179^1	168	12	103	100	13.8	4.22	98	.248	.350	17	.270	4	-3	-2	-0	0.2
1971	StL-N	1	2	.333	9	6	0	0	0	36	41	2	30	8	18.0	6.00	60	.304	.434	1	.143	1	-10	-10	0	-0.9
	Mon-N	0	0	—	1	0	0	0	0	3	4	0	1	2	15.0	0.00	—	.308	.357	0	—	0	1	1	0	0.2
	Yr	1	2	.333	10	6	0	0	0	39	45	2	31	10	17.5	5.54	65	.300	.420	1	.143	1	-9	-8	1	-0.7
1972	Mon-N	16	12	.571	34	33	13	0	0	243^1	215	15	103	112	12.0	3.33	107	.242	.325	15	.176	0	3	6	2	1.0
1973	Mon-N	9	12	.429	35	34	3	1	0	208	207	17	115	90	14.1	4.46	86	.262	.359	12	.174	-1	-18	-15	2	-1.4
1974	Mon-N	15	8	.652	32	30	6	1	0	186^1	184	10	84	92	13.1	3.57	107	.257	.337	8	.125	-3	1	5	5	0.8
1975	Bal-A	20	9	**.690**	36	36	16	2	0	270^2	238	15	133	119	12.5	3.06	115	.239	.332	0	—	0	22	14	1	1.5
1976	Oak-A	16	12	.571	39	39	13	4	0	266^1	231	15	87	115	10.9	2.50	134	.235	.301	0	—	0	30	25	-1	2.9
1977	Oak-A	3	1	.750	4	4	2	0	0	26^1	23	3	11	12	12.0	4.44	91	.242	.327	0	—	0	-1	-1	-0	-0.1
	*NY-A	14	12	.538	31	31	15	2	0	217	212	20	75	90	12.2	3.82	103	.259	.326	0	—	0	6	3	-2	0.1
	Yr	17	13	.567	35	35	17	2	0	243^1	235	23	86	102	12.1	3.88	102	.256	.324	0	—	0	5	2	-2	0.0
1978	Bos-A	16	13	.552	36	36	15	2	0	250	272	19	99	120	13.5	3.96	104	.281	.349	0	—	0	-6	4	-2	0.2
1979	Bos-A	16	13	.552	36	36	12	1	0	252^1	254	20	121	125	13.6	4.49	98	.264	.349	0	—	0	-8	-2	-0	-0.4
1980	Bos-A	9	16	.360	36	32	6	1	0	207^1	256	18	75	97	14.4	5.08	83	.313	.371	0	—	0	-24	-20	2	-1.8
1981	Bos-A	10	3	.769	22	22	2	0	0	127^1	130	10	51	54	12.8	3.68	105	.267	.337	0	—	0	-0	3	-1	0.1
1982	Bos-A	9	9	.500	31	31	1	0	0	175^2	196	20	74	84	14.1	5.23	82	.282	.356	0	—	0	-22	-18	-2	-2.0
1983	NY-N	10	17	.370	39	34	5	0	0	222^1	227	16	113	94	13.8	4.37	83	.271	.358	3	.046	-5	-18	-18	0	-2.3
1984	NY-N	1	5	.167	9	8	0	0	0	37^2	55	3	18	16	17.9	5.02	70	.369	.444	3	.300	1	-6	-6	0	-0.5
	Oak-A	0	0	—	2	0	0	0	0	2^1	9	0	3	2	46.3	27.00	14	.563	.632	0	—	0	-6	-6	-0	-0.3
Total	18	185	160	.536	494	458	117	15	0	3044	3043	223	1371	1404	13.2	3.96	97	.264	.345	64	.155	-4	-60	-38	3	-2.8
● LOU TOST	Tost, Louis Eugene b: 6/1/11, Cumberland, Wash. d: 2/22/67, Santa Clara, Cal. BL/TL, 6', 175 lbs. Deb: 4/20/42																									
1942	Bos-N	10	10	.500	35	22	5	1	0	147^2	146	12	52	43	12.3	3.53	94	.256	.322	9	.176	0	-4	-3	-1	-0.5
1943	Bos-N	0	1	.000	3	1	0	0	0	6^2	10	2	4	3	18.9	5.40	63	.357	.438	0	.000	-0	-1	-1	0	-0.2

YEAR	TM/L	W	L	PCT	G	GS	CG	SH	SV	IP	H	HR	BB	SO	RAT	ERA	ERA+	OAV	OOB	BH	AVG	PB	PR	/A	PD	TPI
1947	Pit-N	0	0	—	1	0	0	0	0	1	3	0	0	0	27.0	9.00	47	.600	.600	0	—	0	-1	-1	0	0.0
Total	3	10	11	.476	39	23	5	1	0	155^1	159	14	56	46	12.7	3.65	92	.263	.330	9	.173	-0	-6	-5	-1	-0.7
● PAUL TOTH Toth, Paul Louis b: 6/30/35, McRoberts, Ky. BR/TR, 6'1", 175 lbs. Deb: 4/22/62																										
1962	StL-N	1	0	1.000	6	1	1	0	0	16^2	18	1	4	5	11.9	5.40	79	.295	.338	2	.400	1	-3	-2	-0	-0.2
	Chi-N	3	1	.750	6	4	1	0	0	34	29	2	10	11	10.9	4.24	98	.240	.308	2	.182	0	-1	-0	-0	0.0
	Yr	4	1	.800	12	5	2	0	0	50^2	47	3	14	16	11.2	4.62	91	.257	.317	4	.250	1	-4	-2	-1	-0.2
1963	Chi-N	5	9	.357	27	14	3	2	0	130^2	115	9	35	66	10.5	3.10	113	.240	.294	1	.026	-3	3	6	-1	0.2
1964	Chi-N	0	2	.000	4	2	0	0	0	10^2	15	2	5	0	16.9	8.44	44	.341	.408	1	.333	0	-6	-6	1	-0.5
Total	3	9	12	.429	43	21	5	2	0	192	177	14	54	82	11.0	3.80	97	.251	.308	6	.103	-2	-7	-2	-1	-0.5
● CLAY TOUCHSTONE Touchstone, Clayland Maffitt b: 1/24/03, Moore, Pa. d: 4/28/49, Beaumont, Tex. BR/TR, 5'9", 175 lbs. Deb: 9/04/28																										
1928	Bos-N	0	0	—	5	0	0	0	0	8	15	0	2	1	20.3	4.50	87	.417	.462	0	.000	-0	-0	-1	0	-0.1
1929	Bos-N	0	0	—	1	0	0	0	0	2^2	6	1	0	1	20.3	16.88	28	.429	.429	1	1.000	0	-4	-4	-0	-0.3
1945	Chi-A	0	0	—	6	0	0	0	0	10	14	1	6	4	18.9	5.40	61	.311	.404	0	.000	-0	-2	-2	0	-0.3
Total	3	0	0	—	12	0	0	0	0	20^2	35	2	8	6	19.6	6.53	57	.368	.429	1	.250	0	-6	-6	0	-0.7
● CESAR TOVAR Tovar, Cesar Leonardo "Pepito" (b: Cesar Leonard Perez (Tovar)) b: 7/3/40, Caracas, Venez. BR/TR, 5'9", 155 lbs. Deb: 4/12/65 ♦																										
1968	Min-A	0	0	—	1	1	0	0	0	1	0	0	1	1	9.0	0.00	—	.000	.250	167	.272	0	0	0	0	0.0
● IRA TOWNSEND Townsend, Ira Dance "Pat" b: 1/9/1894, Weimar, Tex. d: 7/21/65, Schulenberg, Tex. BR/TR, 6'1", 180 lbs. Deb: 8/25/20																										
1920	Bos-N	0	0	—	4	1	0	0	0	6^2	10	0	2	1	17.6	1.35	226	.370	.433	0	.000	-0	1	1	-0	0.1
1921	Bos-N	0	0	—	4	0	0	0	0	7^1	11	1	4	0	20.9	6.14	59	.344	.447	0	.000	-0	-2	-2	0	-0.2
Total	2	0	0	—	8	1	0	0	0	14	21	1	6	1	19.3	3.86	87	.356	.441	0	.000	-1	-1	-1	0	-0.1
● HAPPY TOWNSEND Townsend, John b: 4/9/1879, Townsend, Del. d: 12/21/63, Wilmington, Del. BR/TR, 6', 190 lbs. Deb: 4/19/01																										
1901	Phi-N	9	6	.600	19	16	14	2	0	143^2	118	3	64	72	11.7	3.45	99	**.223**	.312	7	.109	-5	-2	-1	-2	-0.7
1902	Was-A	9	16	.360	27	26	22	0	0	220^1	233	12	89	71	13.7	4.45	83	.272	.349	23	.264	3	-21	-18	-1	-1.5
1903	Was-A	2	11	.154	20	13	10	0	0	126^2	145	3	48	54	14.3	4.76	66	.286	.358	2	.045	-4	-25	-23	0	-2.6
1904	Was-A	5	26	.161	36	34	31	2	0	291^1	319	3	100	143	13.3	3.58	74	.279	.342	20	.168	-2	-32	-30	-1	-3.5
1905	Was-A	7	16	.304	34	24	22	0	0	263	247	2	84	102	11.8	2.63	101	.250	.317	15	.181	1	1	1	-3	-0.1
1906	Cle-A	3	7	.300	17	12	8	1	0	92^2	92	1	31	31	12.5	2.91	90	.262	.332	4	.133	-1	-2	-3	-0	-0.5
Total	6	35	82	.299	153	125	107	5	0	1137^2	1154	24	416	473	12.9	3.59	84	.264	.335	71	.166	-9	-82	-75	-7	-8.9
● LEO TOWNSEND Townsend, Leo Alphonse "Lefty" b: 1/15/1891, Mobile, Ala. d: 12/3/76, Mobile, Ala. BL/TL, 5'10", 160 lbs. Deb: 9/08/20																										
1920	Bos-N	2	2	.500	7	1	1	0	0	24^1	18	1	2	0	7.4	1.48	206	.220	.238	1	.167	0	4	4	0	0.5
1921	Bos-N	0	1	.000	1	1	0	0	0	1^1	2	0	3	0	33.8	27.00	14	.400	.625	0	—	0	-3	-3	0	-0.3
Total	2	2	3	.400	8	2	1	0	0	25^2	20	1	5	0	8.8	2.81	110	.230	.272	1	.167	0	1	1	0	0.2
● BILL TOZER Tozer, William Louis b: 7/3/1882, St.Louis, Mo. d: 2/23/55, Belmont, Cal. BR/TR, 6', 200 lbs. Deb: 4/16/08																										
1908	Cin-N	0	0	—	4	0	0	0	0	10^2	11	0	4	5	13.5	1.69	137	.268	.348	0	.000	-0	1	1	0	0.1
● FRED TRAUTMAN Trautman, Frederick Orlando b: 3/24/1892, Bucyrus, Ohio d: 2/15/64, Bucyrus, Ohio BR/TR, 6'1", 175 lbs. Deb: 4/27/15																										
1915	New-F	0	0	—	1	0	0	0	0	3	4	0	1	2	18.0	6.00	47	.364	.462	0	.000	-0	-1	-1	-0	-0.1
● JOHN TRAUTWEIN Trautwein, John Howard b: 8/7/62, Lafayette Hills, Pa. BR/TR, 6'3", 205 lbs. Deb: 4/07/88																										
1988	Bos-A	0	1	.000	9	0	0	0	0	16	26	2	9	8	20.3	9.00	46	.382	.462	0	—	0	-9	-9	0	-1.1
● ALLAN TRAVERS Travers, Aloysius Joseph "Joe" b: 5/7/1892, Philadelphia, Pa. d: 4/19/68, Philadelphia, Pa. BR/TR, 6'1", 180 lbs. Deb: 5/18/12																										
1912	Det-A	0	1	.000	1	1	1	0	0	8	26	0	7	1	37.1	15.75	21	.605	.660	0	.000	-0	-11	-11	1	-0.7
● BILL TRAVERS Travers, William Edward b: 10/27/52, Norwood, Mass. BL/TL, 6'6", 200 lbs. Deb: 5/19/74																										
1974	Mil-A	2	3	.400	23	1	0	0	0	53	59	6	30	31	15.3	4.92	73	.296	.391	0	—	0	-8	-8	0	-0.7
1975	Mil-A	6	11	.353	28	23	5	0	1	136^1	130	15	60	57	13.3	4.29	89	.251	.342	0	—	0	-8	-7	-1	-0.8
1976	Mil-A☆	15	16	.484	34	34	15	3	0	240	211	21	95	120	11.8	2.81	124	.237	.316	0	—	0	19	18	-1	1.9
1977	Mil-A	4	12	.250	19	19	2	1	0	121^2	140	13	57	49	15.1	5.25	77	.291	.374	0	—	0	-16	-16	0	-1.5
1978	Mil-A	12	11	.522	28	28	8	3	0	175^2	184	20	58	66	12.7	4.41	85	.268	.331	0	—	0	-13	-13	1	-1.2
1979	Mil-A	14	8	.636	30	27	9	2	0	187^1	196	33	45	74	11.7	3.89	107	.270	.315	0	—	0	7	6	-2	0.4
1980	Mil-A	12	6	.667	29	25	7	1	0	154^1	147	20	47	62	11.7	3.91	99	.249	.311	0	—	0	2	-1	-1	0.1
1981	Cal-A	0	1	.000	4	4	0	0	0	9^2	14	2	4	5	16.8	8.38	44	.333	.391	0	—	0	-5	-5	-0	-0.5
1983	Cal-A	0	3	.000	10	7	0	0	0	42^2	58	4	19	24	16.7	5.91	68	.331	.403	0	—	0	-9	-9	0	-0.8
Total	9	65	71	.478	205	168	46	10	1	1120^2	1139	134	415	488	12.8	4.10	93	.264	.335	0	—	0	-30	-34	-3	-3.1
● HARRY TREKELL Trekell, Harry Roy b: 11/18/1892, Breda, Ill. d: 11/4/65, Spokane, Wash. BR/TR, 6'1.5", 170 lbs. Deb: 8/16/13																										
1913	StL-N	0	1	.000	7	1	1	0	0	30	25	2	8	15	10.5	4.50	72	.221	.285	1	.111	-0	-4	-4	-0	-0.5
● BILL TREMEL Tremel, William Leonard "Mumbles" b: 7/4/29, Lilly, Pa. BR/TR, 5'11", 180 lbs. Deb: 6/12/54																										
1954	Chi-N	1	2	.333	33	0	0	0	4	51^1	45	3	28	21	12.8	4.21	100	.243	.343	2	.250	0	-1	-0	-1	-0.1
1955	Chi-N	3	0	1.000	23	0	0	0	2	38^2	33	2	18	13	11.9	3.72	110	.239	.327	2	.286	0	1	2	-1	0.1
1956	Chi-N	0	0	—	1	0	0	0	0	1	3	0	0	0	27.0	9.00	42	.600	.600	0	—	0	-1	-1	-0	-0.1
Total	3	4	2	.667	57	0	0	0	6	91	81	5	46	34	12.6	4.05	102	.247	.340	4	.267	1	-0	1	-2	-0.1
● BOB TRICE Trice, Robert Lee b: 8/28/26, Newton, Ga. d: 9/16/88, Weirton, W.Va. BR/TR, 6'3", 190 lbs. Deb: 9/13/53																										
1953	Phi-A	2	1	.667	3	3	1	0	0	23	25	4	6	4	12.1	5.48	78	.275	.320	1	.143	0	-4	-3	1	-0.2
1954	Phi-A	7	8	.467	19	18	8	1	0	119	146	14	48	22	14.7	5.60	70	.305	.369	12	.286	5	-25	-22	0	-1.7
1955	KC-A	0	0	—	4	0	0	0	0	10	14	4	6	2	18.0	9.00	46	.326	.408	2	.667	1	-6	-5	1	-0.4
Total	3	9	9	.500	26	21	9	1	0	152	185	22	60	28	14.5	5.80	69	.302	.365	15	.288	5	-34	-31	2	-2.3
● JOE TRIMBLE Trimble, Joseph Gerard b: 10/12/30, Providence, R.I. BR/TR, 6'1", 190 lbs. Deb: 4/29/55																										
1955	Bos-A	0	0	—	2	0	0	0	0	2	0	0	3	1	13.5	0.00	—	.000	.375	0	—	0	1	1	0	0.1
1957	Pit-N	0	2	.000	5	4	0	0	0	19^2	23	7	13	9	16.9	8.24	46	.291	.398	1	.143	-0	-10	-10	0	-0.9
Total	2	0	2	.000	7	4	0	0	0	21^2	23	7	16	10	16.6	7.48	51	.274	.396	1	.143	-0	-9	-9	0	-0.8
● KEN TRINKLE Trinkle, Kenneth Wayne b: 12/15/19, Paoli, Ind. d: 5/10/76, Paoli, Ind. BR/TR, 6'1.5", 175 lbs. Deb: 4/25/43																										
1943	NY-N	1	5	.167	11	6	1	0	0	45^2	51	3	15	10	13.2	3.74	92	.276	.333	3	.250	1	-2	-2	1	0.1
1946	NY-N	7	14	.333	**48**	13	2	0	2	151	146	8	74	49	13.2	3.87	89	.253	.340	3	.079	-2	-8	-7	-0	-1.0
1947	NY-N	8	4	.667	**62**	0	0	0	10	93^2	100	3	48	37	14.3	3.75	109	.278	.364	3	.188	-0	3	3	2	0.5
1948	NY-N	4	5	.444	53	0	0	0	7	70^2	66	6	41	20	14.0	3.18	124	.244	.350	2	.250	0	6	6	1	0.7
1949	Phi-N	1	1	.500	42	0	0	0	2	74^1	79	3	30	14	13.6	4.00	99	.299	.377	0	.000	-0	0	-0	1	0.0
Total	5	21	29	.420	216	19	3	0	21	435^1	442	23	208	130	13.6	3.74	100	.267	.352	11	.138	-2	0	0	6	0.3
● RICKY TRLICEK Trlicek, Richard Alan b: 4/26/69, Houston, Tex. BR/TR, 6'3", 200 lbs. Deb: 4/08/92																										
1992	Tor-A	0	0	—	2	0	0	0	0	1^2	2	0	2	1	21.6	10.80	38	.286	.444	0	—	0	-1	-1	-0	-0.2
● RICH TROEDSON Troedson, Richard La Monte b: 5/1/50, Palo Alto, Cal. BL/TL, 6'1", 170 lbs. Deb: 4/09/73																										
1973	SD-N	7	9	.438	50	18	2	0	1	152^1	167	12	59	81	13.4	4.25	82	.284	.351	7	.175	0	-10	-13	2	-1.2
1974	SD-N	1	1	.500	15	1	0	0	1	18^2	24	6	8	11	15.9	8.68	41	.300	.371	0	.000	-0	-10	-11	0	-1.0

YEAR TM/L	W	L	PCT	G	GS	CG	SH	SV	IP	H	HR	BB	SO	RAT	ERA	ERA+	OAV	OOB	BH	AVG	PB	PR	/A	PD	TPI
Total 2	8	10	.444	65	19	2	0	2	171	191	18	67	92	13.7	4.74	73	.286	.353	7	.171	-0	-21	-24	2	-2.2
● MIKE TROMBLEY Trombley, Michael Scott b: 4/14/67, Springfield, Mass. BR/TR, 6'2", 200 lbs. Deb: 8/19/92																									
1992 Min-A	3	2	.600	10	7	0	0	0	46^1	43	5	17	38	11.8	3.30	122	.247	.318	0	—	0	3	4	0	0.3
● HAL TROSKY Trosky, Harold Arthur Jr. "Hoot" (b: Harold Arthur Troyavesky Jr.) b: 9/29/36, Cleveland, Ohio BR/TR, 6'3", 205 lbs. Deb: 9/25/58 F																									
1958 Chi-A	1	0	1.000	2	0	0	0	0	3	5	0	2	1	21.0	6.00	61	.385	.467	0	—	0	-1	-1	0	-0.1
● BILL TROTTER Trotter, William Felix b: 8/10/08, Cisne, Ill. d: 8/26/84, Arlington, Mass. BR/TR, 6'2", 195 lbs. Deb: 4/23/37																									
1937 StL-A	2	9	.182	34	12	3	0	1	122^1	150	14	50	37	15.2	5.81	83	.304	.376	1	.030	-3	-16	-13	-2	-1.6
1938 StL-A	0	1	.000	1	1	1	0	0	8	8	0	0	1	9.0	5.63	88	.242	.242	0	.000	-0	-1	-1	1	0.0
1939 StL-A	6	13	.316	41	13	4	0	0	156^2	205	16	54	61	15.2	5.34	91	.318	.376	4	.108	-1	-13	-8	1	-0.8
1940 StL-A	7	6	.538	36	4	1	0	2	98	117	5	31	29	13.7	3.77	122	.300	.353	1	.045	-2	7	**9**	1	0.7
1941 StL-A	4	2	.667	29	0	0	0	0	49^2	68	2	19	17	16.1	5.98	72	.332	.394	0	.000	-1	-10	-9	1	-0.9
1942 StL-A	0	1	.000	3	0	0	0	0	2	5	0	2	0	31.5	18.00	21	.385	.467	0	—	0	-3	-3	0	-0.3
Was-A	3	1	.750	17	0	0	0	0	40^2	52	4	14	13	14.6	5.75	63	.304	.357	0	.000	-0	-9	-9	0	-0.9
Yr	3	2	.600	20	0	0	0	0	42^2	57	4	16	13	15.4	6.33	58	.310	.365	0	.000	-0	-13	-13	1	-1.2
1944 StL-N	0	1	.000	2	1	0	0	0	6	14	5	4	0	27.0	13.50	26	.467	.529	0	.000	-0	-7	-7	0	-0.6
Total 7	22	34	.393	163	31	9	0	3	483^1	619	46	174	158	15.0	5.40	85	.313	.373	6	.055	-7	-52	-42	2	-4.4
● DIZZY TROUT Trout, Paul Howard b: 6/29/15, Sandcut, Ind. d: 2/28/72, Harvey, Ill. BR/TR, 6'2.5", 195 lbs. Deb: 4/25/39 F																									
1939 Det-A	9	10	.474	33	22	6	0	2	162	168	5	74	72	13.7	3.61	135	.270	.351	12	.211	-0	18	23	-1	2.0
1940 *Det-A	3	7	.300	33	10	1	0	2	100^2	125	4	54	64	16.3	4.47	106	.307	.392	4	.129	-2	-1	3	2	0.3
1941 Det-A	9	9	.500	37	18	6	1	2	151^2	144	7	84	88	13.6	3.74	122	.252	.350	9	.180	0	7	14	1	1.5
1942 Det-A	12	18	.400	35	29	13	1	0	223	214	15	89	91	12.4	3.43	115	.249	.322	16	.213	2	6	13	4	2.0
1943 Det-A	**20**	12	.625	44	30	18	**5**	6	246^2	204	6	101	111	11.1	2.48	142	.227	.305	20	.220	2	22	29	4	4.0
1944 Det-A☆	27	14	.659	49	40	**33**	**7**	0	**352^1**	314	9	83	144	10.2	**2.12**	**168**	.237	.284	36	.271	12	**51**	**57**	7	**8.8**
1945 *Det-A	18	15	.545	41	31	18	4	2	246^1	252	8	79	97	12.1	3.14	112	.267	.324	25	.245	4	6	10	3	1.9
1946 Det-A	17	13	.567	38	32	23	5	3	276^1	244	11	97	151	11.2	2.34	156	.238	.306	20	.194	3	36	40	4	5.3
1947 Det-A☆	10	11	.476	32	26	9	2	2	186^1	186	6	65	74	12.3	3.48	108	.261	.325	11	.162	3	5	6	3	1.3
1948 Det-A	10	14	.417	32	23	11	2	2	183^2	193	6	73	91	13.1	3.43	127	.269	.338	15	.217	2	18	19	2	2.2
1949 Det-A	3	6	.333	33	0	0	0	3	59^1	68	2	21	19	13.5	4.40	95	.292	.350	2	.143	0	-1	-2	2	0.0
1950 Det-A	13	5	.722	34	20	11	1	4	184^2	190	13	64	88	12.6	3.75	125	.267	.332	12	.190	1	17	19	3	2.3
1951 Det-A	9	14	.391	42	22	7	0	5	191^2	172	13	75	89	11.6	4.04	103	.240	.312	14	.269	5	2	3	4	1.2
1952 Det-A	1	5	.167	10	2	0	0	1	27	30	4	19	20	16.3	5.33	71	.286	.395	3	.333	1	-5	-5	1	-0.3
Bos-A	9	8	.529	26	17	2	0	1	133^2	133	3	68	57	13.7	3.64	108	.263	.354	6	.136	-1	1	5	1	0.4
Yr	10	13	.435	36	19	2	0	2	160^2	163	7	87	77	14.2	3.92	100	.267	.361	9	.170	-1	-4	-0	2	0.1
1957 Bal-A	0	0	—	2	0	0	0	0	0^1	4	0	0	0	108.0	81.00	4	.800	.800	0	—	0	-3	-3	0	-0.3
Total 15	170	161	.514	521	322	158	28	35	2725^2	2641	112	1046	1256	12.3	3.23	124	.255	.325	205	.213	32	177	232	38	32.6
● STEVE TROUT Trout, Steven Russell b: 7/30/57, Detroit, Mich. BL/TL, 6'4", 195 lbs. Deb: 7/01/78 F																									
1978 Chi-A	3	0	1.000	4	3	1	0	0	22^1	19	0	11	11	12.1	4.03	94	.229	.319	0	—	0	-1	-1	-0	-0.1
1979 Chi-A	11	8	.579	34	18	6	2	4	155	165	10	59	76	13.3	3.89	109	.273	.343	0	—	0	6	6	2	0.8
1980 Chi-A	9	16	.360	32	30	7	2	0	199^2	229	14	49	89	12.9	3.70	109	.290	.338	0	—	0	8	7	3	1.0
1981 Chi-A	8	7	.533	20	18	3	0	0	124^2	122	7	38	54	11.8	3.47	103	.261	.322	0	—	0	3	2	0	0.3
1982 Chi-A	6	9	.400	25	19	2	0	0	120^1	130	9	50	62	13.6	4.26	95	.273	.344	0	—	0	-3	-3	0	-0.3
1983 Chi-N	10	14	.417	34	32	1	0	0	180	217	13	59	80	13.9	4.65	82	.305	.360	12	.194	1	-20	-17	2	-1.5
1984 *Chi-N	13	7	.650	32	31	6	2	0	190	205	7	59	81	12.6	3.41	115	.285	.341	8	.131	-1	4	10	4	1.4
1985 Chi-N	9	7	.563	24	24	3	1	0	140^2	142	8	63	44	13.2	3.39	118	.270	.350	5	.109	-2	3	9	2	1.1
1986 Chi-N	5	7	.417	37	25	0	0	0	161	184	6	78	69	14.7	4.75	85	.298	.378	9	.209	1	-19	-13	1	-1.2
1987 Chi-N	6	3	.667	11	11	3	2	0	75	72	3	27	32	12.0	3.00	143	.260	.328	4	.154	-1	9	11	0	1.1
NY-A	0	4	.000	14	9	0	0	0	46^1	51	4	37	27	17.3	6.60	66	.274	.397	0	—	0	-11	-11	0	-0.9
1988 Sea-A	4	7	.364	15	13	0	0	0	56^1	86	6	31	14	19.5	7.83	53	.361	.445	0	—	0	-24	-23	0	-2.4
1989 Sea-A	4	3	.571	19	3	0	0	0	30	43	3	17	17	18.0	6.60	61	.333	.411	0	—	0	-9	-9	0	-1.0
Total 12	88	92	.489	301	236	32	9	4	1501^1	1665	90	578	656	13.6	4.18	96	.286	.354	38	.160	-2	-55	-30	14	-1.7
● BOB TROWBRIDGE Trowbridge, Robert b: 6/27/30, Hudson, N.Y. d: 4/3/80, Hudson, N.Y. BR/TR, 6'1", 190 lbs. Deb: 4/22/56																									
1956 Mil-N	3	2	.600	19	4	1	0	0	50^2	38	4	34	40	13.1	2.66	130	.210	.341	0	.000	-0	6	4	0	0.5
1957 *Mil-N	7	5	.583	32	16	3	1	1	126	118	9	52	75	12.2	3.64	96	.248	.323	4	.103	-1	3	-2	-1	-0.4
1958 Mil-N	1	3	.250	27	4	0	0	1	55	53	4	26	31	13.1	3.93	90	.252	.338	1	.111	-0	0	-2	-1	-0.4
1959 Mil-N	1	0	1.000	16	0	0	0	1	30^1	45	2	10	22	16.3	5.93	60	.344	.390	0	.000	-0	-7	-8	-0	-0.9
1960 KC-A	1	3	.250	22	1	0	0	2	68^1	70	6	34	33	13.8	4.61	86	.281	.370	1	.056	-1	-6	-5	0	-0.6
Total 5	13	13	.500	116	25	4	1	5	330^1	324	25	156	201	13.2	3.95	91	.260	.344	6	.078	-4	-3	-13	-1	-1.8
● BUN TROY Troy, Robert b: 8/22/1888, Germany d: 10/7/18, Meuse, France BR/TR, 6'4", 195 lbs. Deb: 9/15/12																									
1912 Det-A	0	1	.000	1	1	0	0	0	6^2	9	0	3	1	17.6	5.40	60	.346	.433	0	.000	-0	-2	-2	-0	-0.2
● VIRGIL TRUCKS Trucks, Virgil Oliver "Fire" b: 4/26/19, Birmingham, Ala. BR/TR, 5'11", 198 lbs. Deb: 9/27/41 C																									
1941 Det-A	0	0	—	1	0	0	0	0	2	4	0	0	3	18.0	9.00	50	.500	.500	0	—	0	-1	-1	0	-0.1
1942 Det-A	14	8	.636	28	20	8	2	0	167^2	147	3	74	91	12.0	2.74	144	.231	.314	8	.123	-4	17	23	-2	1.8
1943 Det-A	16	10	.615	33	25	10	2	2	202^2	170	11	52	118	9.9	2.84	124	.225	.276	13	.181	-2	10	15	-2	1.2
1945 *Det-A	0	0	—	1	1	0	0	0	5^1	3	0	2	3	8.4	1.69	208	.176	.263	0	.000	-0	1	1	0	0.1
1946 Det-A	14	9	.609	32	29	15	2	0	236^2	217	23	75	161	11.2	3.23	113	.241	.302	17	.179	-1	7	11	-1	0.9
1947 Det-A	10	12	.455	36	26	8	2	2	180^2	186	14	79	108	13.3	4.53	83	.263	.339	19	.271	2	-17	-15	-1	-1.4
1948 Det-A	14	13	.519	43	26	7	0	2	211^2	190	14	85	123	11.8	3.78	115	.240	.315	13	.165	-3	12	14	-1	0.9
1949 Det-A★	19	11	.633	41	32	17	**6**	4	275	209	16	124	**153**	11.0	2.81	148	.211	.301	12	.120	-6	42	41	-3	3.2
1950 Det-A	3	1	.750	7	7	2	1	0	48^1	45	6	21	25	12.5	3.54	133	.243	.324	3	.150	-1	6	6	1	0.6
1951 Det-A	13	8	.619	37	18	6	1	1	153^2	153	9	75	89	13.6	4.33	96	.262	.350	13	.236	-0	-4	-3	2	-0.1
1952 Det-A	5	19	.208	35	29	8	3	1	197	190	12	82	129	12.7	3.97	96	.251	.330	12	.188	-0	-7	-4	2	-0.2
1953 StL-A	5	4	.556	16	12	4	2	2	88	83	4	32	47	12.2	3.07	137	.249	.322	4	.160	-1	9	11	-1	1.0
Chi-A	15	6	.714	24	21	13	3	1	176^1	151	14	67	102	11.3	2.86	141	.232	.306	15	.238	2	22	23	1	2.7
Yr	20	10	.667	40	33	17	5	3	264^1	234	18	99	149	11.4	2.93	139	.237	.308	19	.216	1	31	34	0	3.7
1954 Chi-A★	19	12	.613	40	33	16	**5**	3	264^2	224	13	95	152	10.9	2.79	134	.228	.297	17	.183	-1	27	28	1	2.9
1955 Chi-A	13	8	.619	32	26	7	3	0	175	176	19	61	91	12.3	3.96	100	.260	.323	8	.125	-3	0	-0	0	-0.3
1956 Det-A	6	5	.545	22	16	3	1	1	120	104	15	63	43	13.0	3.83	108	.239	.343	11	.244	1	4	4	-1	0.3
1957 KC-A	9	7	.563	48	7	0	0	7	116	106	12	62	55	13.2	3.03	131	.248	.346	4	.143	-1	10	12	0	1.1
1958 KC-A	0	1	.000	16	0	0	0	3	22	18	2	15	15	13.5	2.05	191	.222	.344	0	.000	-0	4	5	0	0.5
NY-A	2	1	.667	25	0	0	0	1	39^2	40	1	24	26	15.0	4.54	78	.265	.373	2	.250	0	-3	-4	-0	-0.5
Yr	2	2	.500	41	0	0	0	4	61^2	58	3	39	41	14.4	3.65	100	.249	.361	2	.222	0	1	0	-0	0.0
Total 17	177	135	.567	517	328	124	33	30	2682^1	2416	188	1088	1534	11.9	3.39	117	.240	.317	171	.180	-20	141	167	-5	14.6
● MIKE TRUJILLO Trujillo, Michael Andrew b: 1/12/60, Denver, Colo. BR/TR, 6'1", 180 lbs. Deb: 4/14/85																									
1985 Bos-A	4	4	.500	27	7	1	0	1	84	112	7	23	19	14.8	4.82	89	.320	.367	0	—	0	-6	-5	2	-0.6
1986 Bos-A	0	0	—	3	0	0	0	0	5^2	7	0	6	4	20.6	9.53	44	.304	.448	0	—	0	-3	-3	1	-0.3
Sea-A	3	2	.600	11	4	1	1	1	41^1	32	5	15	19	10.2	2.40	177	.215	.287	0	—	0	8	8	-0	0.8

YEAR TM/L	W	L	PCT	G	GS	CG	SH	SV	IP	H	HR	BB	SO	RAT	ERA	ERA+	OAV	OOB	BH	AVG	PB	PR	/A	PD	TPI
Yr	3	2	.600	14	4	1	1	1	47	39	5	21	23	11.5	3.26	130	.227	.311	0	—	0	5	5	0	0.5
1987 Sea-A	4	4	.500	28	7	0	0	1	65^2	70	12	26	36	13.4	6.17	76	.277	.349	0	—	0	-12	-11	-1	-1.5
1988 Det-A	0	0	—	6	0	0	0	0	12^1	11	2	5	5	11.7	5.11	75	.234	.308	0	—	0	-2	-2	0	0.1
1989 Det-A	1	2	.333	8	4	1	0	0	25^2	35	3	13	13	16.8	5.96	64	.333	.407	0	—	0	-6	-6	0	-0.5
Total 5	12	12	.500	83	22	3	1	3	234^2	267	29	88	96	13.8	5.02	86	.288	.353	0	—	0	-21	-19	2	-2.0

● **ED TRUMBULL** Trumbull, Edward J. (b: Edward J. Trembly) b: 11/3/1860, Chicopee, Mass. d: 1/14/37, Kingston, Pa. Deb: 5/10/1884 ♦

YEAR TM/L	W	L	PCT	G	GS	CG	SH	SV	IP	H	HR	BB	SO	RAT	ERA	ERA+	OAV	OOB	BH	AVG	PB	PR	/A	PD	TPI
1884 Was-a	1	9	.100	10	10	10	0	0	84	108	4	31	43	15.0	4.71	64	.295	.352	10	.116	-2	-14	-16	-1	-1.5

● **JOHN TSITOURIS** Tsitouris, John Philip b: 5/4/36, Monroe, N.C. BR/TR, 6', 175 lbs. Deb: 6/13/57

YEAR TM/L	W	L	PCT	G	GS	CG	SH	SV	IP	H	HR	BB	SO	RAT	ERA	ERA+	OAV	OOB	BH	AVG	PB	PR	/A	PD	TPI
1957 Det-A	1	0	1.000	2	0	0	0	0	3^1	8	0	2	2	27.0	8.10	48	.500	.556	0	.000	-0	-2	-2	0	-0.2
1958 KC-A	0	0	—	1	1	0	0	0	3	2	0	2	1	12.0	3.00	130	.182	.308	0	.000	-0	0	0	0	0.0
1959 KC-A	4	3	.571	24	10	0	0	0	83^1	90	3	35	50	13.8	4.97	81	.271	.346	3	.150	-1	-10	-9	-1	-1.0
1960 KC-A	0	2	.000	14	2	0	0	0	33	38	3	21	12	18.3	6.55	61	.297	.427	0	.000	-1	-10	-9	0	-1.0
1962 Cin-N	1	0	1.000	4	2	1	1	0	21^1	13	0	7	7	9.7	0.84	477	.181	.280	0	.000	-1	7	8	-0	0.7
1963 Cin-N	12	8	.600	30	21	8	3	0	191	167	20	38	113	10.2	3.16	106	.232	.281	5	.081	-3	3	4	-3	-0.3
1964 Cin-N	9	13	.409	37	24	6	1	2	175^1	178	20	75	146	13.2	3.80	95	.263	.340	11	.190	2	-5	-4	-1	-0.3
1965 Cin-N	6	9	.400	31	20	3	0	1	131	134	18	65	91	14.3	4.95	76	.265	.359	3	.070	-2	-20	-17	-1	-2.1
1966 Cin-N	0	0	—	1	0	0	0	0	1	3	0	1	0	36.0	18.00	22	.750	.800	0	—	0	-2	-2	-0	-0.2
1967 Cin-N	1	0	1.000	2	1	0	0	0	8	4	1	6	4	11.3	3.38	111	.154	.313	0	—	0	0	0	0	0.1
1968 Cin-N	0	3	.000	3	3	0	0	0	12^2	16	6	8	6	17.8	7.11	44	.302	.403	0	.000	0	-6	-6	0	-0.6
Total 11	34	38	.472	149	84	18	5	3	663	653	71	260	432	12.9	4.13	88	.257	.335	22	.111	-6	-44	-36	-5	-4.9

● **TOMMY TUCKER** Tucker, Thomas Joseph "Foghorn" b: 10/28/1863, Holyoke, Mass. d: 10/22/35, Montague, Mass. BB/TR, 5'11", 165 lbs. Deb: 4/16/1887 ♦

YEAR TM/L	W	L	PCT	G	GS	CG	SH	SV	IP	H	HR	BB	SO	RAT	ERA	ERA+	OAV	OOB	BH	AVG	PB	PR	/A	PD	TPI
1888 Bal-a	0	0	—	1	0	0	0	0	2^1	4	0	0	2	15.4	3.86	77	.365	.365	149	.287	0	-0	-0	-0	0.0
1891 Bos-N	0	0	—	1	0	0	0	0	1	3	0	0	0	27.0	9.00	41	.501	.501	148	.270	0	-1	-1	-0	-0.1
Total 2	0	0	—	2	0	0	0	0	3^1	7	0	0	2	18.9	5.40	59	.413	.413	1882	.290	0	-1	-1	-0	-0.1

● **TOM TUCKEY** Tuckey, Thomas H. "Tabasco Tom" b: 10/7/1883, Connecticut d: 10/17/50, New York, N.Y. TL, 6'3", Deb: 8/11/08

YEAR TM/L	W	L	PCT	G	GS	CG	SH	SV	IP	H	HR	BB	SO	RAT	ERA	ERA+	OAV	OOB	BH	AVG	PB	PR	/A	PD	TPI
1908 Bos-N	3	3	.500	8	8	3	1	0	72	60	2	20	26	10.5	2.50	96	.265	.336	1	.050	-2	-1	-1	0	-0.3
1909 Bos-N	0	9	.000	17	10	4	0	0	90^2	104	1	22	16	12.8	4.27	66	.295	.342	4	.138	-2	-17	-15	1	-1.6
Total 2	3	12	.200	25	18	7	1	0	162^2	164	3	42	42	11.8	3.49	76	.284	.340	5	.102	-3	-18	-15	1	-1.9

● **JOHN TUDOR** Tudor, John Thomas b: 2/2/54, Schenectady, N.Y. BL/TL, 6', 185 lbs. Deb: 8/16/79

YEAR TM/L	W	L	PCT	G	GS	CG	SH	SV	IP	H	HR	BB	SO	RAT	ERA	ERA+	OAV	OOB	BH	AVG	PB	PR	/A	PD	TPI
1979 Bos-A	1	2	.333	6	6	1	0	0	28	39	2	9	11	15.4	6.43	69	.345	.393	0	—	0	-7	-6	1	-0.5
1980 Bos-A	8	5	.615	16	13	5	0	0	92^1	81	4	31	45	11.2	3.02	140	.238	.307	0	—	0	10	12	2	1.1
1981 Bos-A	4	3	.571	18	11	2	0	1	78^2	74	11	28	44	12.0	4.58	85	.252	.323	0	—	0	-8	-6	1	-0.9
1982 Bos-A	13	10	.565	32	30	6	1	0	195^2	215	20	59	146	13.0	3.63	119	.280	.338	0	—	0	10	15	2	1.4
1983 Bos-A	13	12	.520	34	34	7	2	0	242	236	32	81	136	11.9	4.09	106	.255	.317	0	—	0	-1	7	-1	0.3
1984 Pit-N	12	11	.522	32	32	6	1	0	212	200	19	56	117	10.9	3.27	110	.248	.297	16	.211	2	8	8	-1	1.0
1985 *StL-N	21	8	.724	36	36	14	**10**	0	275	209	14	49	169	**8.6**	1.93	183	.209	**.249**	13	.138	1	51	49	1	5.8
1986 StL-N	13	7	.650	30	30	3	0	0	219	197	22	53	107	10.3	2.92	125	.244	.291	11	.153	-0	19	18	1	1.9
1987 *StL-N	10	2	.833	16	16	0	0	0	96	100	11	32	54	12.5	3.84	108	.272	.333	7	.200	1	3	3	1	0.5
1988 StL-N	6	5	.545	21	21	4	1	0	145^1	131	5	31	55	10.1	2.29	152	.247	.290	5	.109	-1	19	19	1	2.2
*LA-N	4	3	.571	9	9	1	0	0	52^1	58	5	10	32	11.7	2.41	138	.284	.318	0	.000	-1	6	5	0	0.5
Yr	10	8	.556	30	30	5	1	0	197^2	189	10	41	87	10.5	2.32	148	.255	.294	5	.085	-2	25	24	1	2.7
1989 LA-N	0	0	—	6	3	0	0	0	14^1	17	1	6	9	14.4	3.14	109	.309	.377	0	.000	-0	1	0	0	0.0
1990 StL-N	12	4	.750	25	22	1	1	0	146^1	120	10	30	63	9.3	2.40	159	.225	.269	7	.152	0	23	23	2	2.8
Total 12	117	72	.619	281	263	50	16	1	1797	1677	156	475	988	10.9	3.12	123	.248	.301	59	.154	3	132	146	9	16.1

● **OSCAR TUERO** Tuero, Oscar (Monzon) (b: Oscar Tuero Monzon) b: 12/17/1898, Canada d: 10/21/60, Houston, Tex. BR/TR, 5'8.5", 158 lbs. Deb: 5/30/18

YEAR TM/L	W	L	PCT	G	GS	CG	SH	SV	IP	H	HR	BB	SO	RAT	ERA	ERA+	OAV	OOB	BH	AVG	PB	PR	/A	PD	TPI
1918 StL-N	1	2	.333	11	3	2	0	0	44^1	32	0	10	13	9.1	1.02	267	.208	.269	3	.250	0	9	8	-1	0.9
1919 StL-N	5	7	.417	**45**	17	4	0	**4**	154^2	137	4	42	45	11.0	3.20	87	.242	.306	8	.205	1	-5	-7	-0	-0.7
1920 StL-N	0	0	—	2	0	0	0	0	0^2	5	0	1	0	81.0	54.00	6	.833	.857	0	—	0	-4	-4	-0	-0.4
Total 3	6	9	.400	58	20	6	0	4	199^2	174	4	53	58	10.8	2.88	96	.240	.303	11	.216	1	-0	-2	-1	-0.2

● **BOB TUFTS** Tufts, Robert Malcolm b: 11/2/55, Medford, Mass. BL/TL, 6'5", 215 lbs. Deb: 8/10/81

YEAR TM/L	W	L	PCT	G	GS	CG	SH	SV	IP	H	HR	BB	SO	RAT	ERA	ERA+	OAV	OOB	BH	AVG	PB	PR	/A	PD	TPI
1981 SF-N	0	0	—	11	0	0	0	0	15^1	20	1	6	12	15.8	3.52	97	.308	.375	0	.000	-0	-0	-0	1	0.0
1982 KC-A	2	0	1.000	10	0	0	0	2	20	24	3	3	13	12.1	4.50	91	.293	.318	0	—	0	-1	-1	-1	-0.2
1983 KC-A	0	0	—	6	0	0	0	0	6^2	16	1	5	3	29.7	8.10	50	.444	.524	0	—	0	-3	-3	0	-0.3
Total 3	2	0	1.000	27	0	0	0	2	42	60	5	14	28	16.3	4.71	81	.328	.382	0	.000	-0	-4	-4	0	-0.5

● **LEE TUNNELL** Tunnell, Byron Lee b: 10/30/60, Tyler, Tex. BR/TR, 6'1", 180 lbs. Deb: 9/04/82

YEAR TM/L	W	L	PCT	G	GS	CG	SH	SV	IP	H	HR	BB	SO	RAT	ERA	ERA+	OAV	OOB	BH	AVG	PB	PR	/A	PD	TPI
1982 Pit-N	1	1	.500	5	3	0	0	0	18^1	17	1	5	4	11.8	3.93	94	.254	.324	0	.000	-0	-1	-0	0	-0.1
1983 Pit-N	11	6	.647	35	25	5	3	0	177^2	167	15	58	95	11.5	3.65	102	.252	.314	7	.121	-1	-0	1	2	0.2
1984 Pit-N	1	7	.125	26	6	0	0	1	68^1	81	6	40	51	15.9	5.27	68	.298	.388	1	.083	-1	-13	-13	1	-1.2
1985 Pit-N	4	10	.286	24	23	0	0	0	132^1	126	11	57	74	12.5	4.01	89	.251	.329	4	.085	-2	-6	-6	1	-0.8
1987 *StL-N	4	4	.500	32	9	0	0	0	74^1	90	5	34	49	15.1	4.84	86	.307	.381	4	.235	0	-6	-6	0	-0.5
1989 Min-A	1	0	1.000	10	0	0	0	0	12	18	1	6	7	18.0	6.00	69	.340	.407	0	—	0	-3	-2	-0	-0.7
Total 6	22	28	.440	132	66	5	3	1	483	499	39	200	280	13.1	4.23	88	.270	.343	16	.116	-4	-29	-27	4	-3.1

● **GEORGE TURBEVILLE** Turbeville, George Elkins b: 8/24/14, Turbeville, S.C. d: 10/5/83, Salisbury, N.C. BR/TR, 6'1", 175 lbs. Deb: 7/20/35

YEAR TM/L	W	L	PCT	G	GS	CG	SH	SV	IP	H	HR	BB	SO	RAT	ERA	ERA+	OAV	OOB	BH	AVG	PB	PR	/A	PD	TPI
1935 Phi-A	0	3	.000	19	6	2	0	0	63^2	74	2	69	20	20.2	7.63	60	.312	.467	2	.105	-2	-22	-22	-1	-2.2
1936 Phi-A	2	5	.286	12	6	2	0	0	43^2	42	6	32	10	16.5	6.39	80	.258	.398	2	.143	-1	-7	-6	-0	-0.6
1937 Phi-A	0	4	.000	31	3	0	0	0	77^1	80	2	56	17	15.8	4.77	99	.266	.381	6	.231	0	-1	-1	-1	-0.1
Total 3	2	12	.143	62	15	4	0	0	184^2	196	10	157	47	17.5	6.14	77	.280	.416	10	.169	-2	-30	-29	-2	-2.9

● **LUCAS TURK** Turk, Lucas Newton "Harlem" or "Chief" b: 5/2/1898, Homer, Ga. BR/TR, 6', 165 lbs. Deb: 6/07/22

YEAR TM/L	W	L	PCT	G	GS	CG	SH	SV	IP	H	HR	BB	SO	RAT	ERA	ERA+	OAV	OOB	BH	AVG	PB	PR	/A	PD	TPI
1922 Was-A	0	0	—	5	0	0	0	0	11^2	16	0	5	1	16.2	6.94	56	.340	.404	1	.250	0	-4	-4	-1	-0.4

● **BOB TURLEY** Turley, Robert Lee "Bullet Bob" b: 9/19/30, Troy, Ill. BR/TR, 6'2", 215 lbs. Deb: 9/29/51 C

YEAR TM/L	W	L	PCT	G	GS	CG	SH	SV	IP	H	HR	BB	SO	RAT	ERA	ERA+	OAV	OOB	BH	AVG	PB	PR	/A	PD	TPI
1951 StL-A	0	1	.000	1	1	0	0	0	7^1	11	0	3	5	17.2	7.36	60	.355	.412	0	.000	-0	-3	-2	0	-0.2
1953 StL-A	2	6	.250	10	7	3	1	0	60^1	39	4	44	61	12.7	3.28	128	.184	.329	5	.278	2	5	6	-1	0.8
1954 Bal-A☆	14	15	.483	35	35	14	0	0	247^1	178	7	181	**185**	13.3	3.46	104	**.203**	.343	11	.136	-2	7	3	-1	0.1
1955 *NY-A☆	17	13	.567	36	34	13	6	1	246^2	168	16	177	210	12.8	3.06	122	**.193**	.333	11	.134	-0	25	19	-2	1.7
1956 *NY-A	8	4	.667	27	21	5	1	1	132	138	13	103	91	16.7	5.05	77	.273	.400	8	.174	-0	-13	-17	-1	-1.8
1957 *NY-A	13	6	.684	32	23	9	4	3	176^1	120	17	85	152	10.9	2.71	133	**.194**	.300	5	.088	-1	21	17	-0	1.6
1958 *NY-A★	**21**	7	**.750**	33	31	**19**	6	1	245^1	178	24	128	168	11.5	2.97	119	**.206**	.313	12	.136	-1	22	15	-2	1.3
1959 NY-A	8	11	.421	33	22	7	3	0	154^1	141	15	83	111	13.2	4.32	84	.245	.343	4	.087	-2	-8	-11	-1	-1.4
1960 *NY-A	9	3	.750	34	24	4	1	5	173^1	138	14	87	87	11.9	3.27	110	.222	.322	4	.073	-3	12	6	-1	0.1
1961 NY-A	3	5	.375	15	12	1	0	0	72	74	11	51	48	16.1	5.75	65	.269	.391	2	.095	-1	-14	-16	-1	-1.7
1962 NY-A	3	3	.500	24	8	0	0	1	69	68	8	47	42	15.5	4.57	82	.263	.384	0	.000	-1	-5	-6	1	-0.7
1963 LA-A	2	7	.222	19	12	3	2	0	87^1	71	5	51	70	12.8	3.30	104	.222	.332	4	.160	1	3	1	-0	0.2
Bos-A	1	4	.200	11	7	0	0	0	41^1	42	6	28	35	15.5	6.10	62	.256	.368	3	.214	0	-11	-11	-0	-1.1
Yr	3	11	.214	30	19	3	2	0	128^2	113	11	79	105	13.5	4.20	84	.232	.340	7	.179	1	-8	-9	-1	-0.9

YEAR TM/L	W	L	PCT	G	GS	CG	SH	SV	IP	H	HR	BB	SO	RAT	ERA	ERA+	OAV	OOB	BH	AVG	PB	PR	/A	PD	TPI
Total 12	101	85	.543	310	237	78	24	12	1712^{2}	1366	140	1068	1265	13.1	3.64	101	.220	.340	69	.126	-11	41	4	-9	-1.1
● TUCK TURNER Turner, George A. b: 2/13/1873, W.New Brighton, N.Y. d: 7/16/45, Staten Island, N.Y. BB/TL, 5'6.5", 155 lbs. Deb: 8/18/1893 ♦																									
1894 Phi-N	0	0	—	1	0	0	0	0	6	9	1	2	3	18.0	7.50	68	.342	.410	141	.416	1	-1	-2	-0	-0.1
● JIM TURNER Turner, James Riley "Milkman Jim" b: 8/6/03, Antioch, Tenn. BL/TR, 6', 185 lbs. Deb: 4/30/37 C																									
1937 Bos-N	20	11	.645	33	30	**24**	**5**	1	256^{2}	228	13	52	69	**9.8**	**2.38**	**150**	.235	**.274**	24	.250	4	**44**	34	-0	**4.1**
1938 Bos-N☆	14	18	.438	35	34	22	3	0	268	267	21	54	71	10.9	3.46	99	.259	.299	22	.229	4	10	-1	4	0.7
1939 Bos-N	4	11	.267	25	22	9	0	0	157^{2}	181	10	51	50	13.5	4.28	86	.293	.351	13	.236	2	-6	-10	1	-0.7
1940 *Cin-N	14	7	.667	24	23	11	0	0	187	187	9	32	53	10.5	2.89	131	.264	.296	18	.240	3	20	19	-1	2.2
1941 Cin-N	6	4	.600	23	10	3	0	0	113	120	5	24	34	11.5	3.11	116	.277	.317	6	.146	-1	7	6	2	0.7
1942 Cin-N	0	0	—	3	0	0	0	0	3^{1}	5	1	3	0	21.6	10.80	30	.333	.444	0	.000	-0	-3	-3	0	-0.3
*NY-A	1	1	.500	5	0	0	0	1	7	4	0	1	2	6.4	1.29	268	.167	.200	0	.000	-0	2	2	0	0.2
1943 NY-A	3	0	1.000	18	0	0	0	1	43^{1}	44	1	13	15	11.8	3.53	91	.260	.313	1	.077	-1	-1	-2	-0	-0.3
1944 NY-A	4	4	.500	35	0	0	0	7	41^{2}	42	3	22	13	13.8	3.46	101	.264	.354	2	.200	0	-0	0	-1	0.0
1945 NY-A	3	4	.429	30	0	0	0	**10**	54^{1}	45	4	31	22	12.6	3.64	95	.225	.329	1	.091	-1	-2	-1	1	-0.2
Total 9	69	60	.535	231	119	69	8	20	1132	1123	67	283	329	11.3	3.22	111	.260	.307	87	.218	11	70	45	6	6.4
● KEN TURNER Turner, Kenneth Charles b: 8/17/43, Framingham, Mass. BR/TL, 6'2", 190 lbs. Deb: 6/11/67																									
1967 Cal-A	1	2	.333	13	1	0	0	0	17^{1}	16	4	4	6	10.9	4.15	76	.239	.292	0	.000	-0	-2	-2	0	-0.2
● TED TURNER Turner, Theodore Holhot b: 5/4/1892, Lawrenceburg, Ky. d: 2/4/58, Lexington, Ky. BR/TR, 6', 180 lbs. Deb: 4/20/20																									
1920 Chi-N	0	0	—	1	0	0	0	0	1^{1}	2	0	1	0	20.3	13.50	24	.400	.500	0	.000	-0	-2	-2	-0	-0.2
● TINK TURNER Turner, Thomas Lovatt b: 2/20/1890, Swarthmore, Pa. d: 2/25/62, Philadelphia, Pa. BR/TR, 6'1", 190 lbs. Deb: 9/24/15																									
1915 Phi-A	0	1	.000	1	1	0	0	0	2	5	1	3	0	36.0	22.50	13	.500	.615	0	—	0	-4	-4	0	-0.4
● ELMER TUTWILER Tutwiler, Elmer Strange b: 11/19/05, Carbon Hill, Ala. d: 5/3/76, Pensacola, Fla. BR/TR, 5'11", 158 lbs. Deb: 8/20/28																									
1928 Pit-N	0	0	—	2	0	0	0	0	3^{2}	4	0	0	1	9.8	4.91	83	.267	.267	0	.000	-0	-0	-0	-0	-0.1
● TWINK TWINING Twining, Howard Earle "Doc" b: 5/30/1894, Horsham, Pa. d: 6/14/73, Lansdale, Pa. BR/TR, 6', 168 lbs. Deb: 7/09/16																									
1916 Cin-N	0	0	—	1	0	0	0	0	2	4	1	1	0	27.0	13.50	19	.444	.545	0	—	0	-2	-2	0	-0.2
● LARRY TWITCHELL Twitchell, Lawrence Grant b: 2/18/1864, Cleveland, Ohio d: 8/23/30, Cleveland, Ohio BR/TR, 6', 185 lbs. Deb: 4/30/1886 ♦																									
1886 Det-N	0	2	.000	4	4	2	0	0	25	35	1	12	6	16.9	6.48	51	.347	.416	1	.063	-2	-9	-9	1	-0.8
1887 *Det-N	11	1	.917	15	12	11	0	**1**	112^{1}	120	3	36	24	13.3	4.33	94	.268	.336	88	.333	4	-3	-3	-1	-0.1
1888 Det-N	0	0	—	2	0	0	0	0	4	6	1	0	3	13.5	6.75	41	.375	.375	128	.244	0	-2	-2	0	-0.1
1889 Cle-N	0	0	—	1	0	0	0	0	1	0	0	1	0	9.0	0.00	—	.000	.252	151	.275	0	0	0	-0	0.0
1890 Buf-P	5	7	.417	13	12	12	0	0	104^{1}	112	3	72	29	17.2	4.57	90	.263	.388	38	.221	1	-4	-5	2	-0.2
1891 Col-a	1	1	.500	6	1	1	0	0	31	29	1	13	8	13.1	4.06	85	.239	.328	62	.277	2	-1	-2	-0	-0.1
1894 Lou-N	0	0	—	1	0	0	0	0	3	5	1	1	0	18.0	6.00	85	.367	.410	56	.267	0	-0	-0	0	0.0
Total 7	17	11	.607	42	29	26	0	2	280^{2}	307	10	135	70	15.1	4.62	85	.272	.364	676	.263	6	-19	-21	1	-1.3
● WAYNE TWITCHELL Twitchell, Wayne Lee b: 3/10/48, Portland, Ore. BR/TR, 6'6", 220 lbs. Deb: 9/07/70																									
1970 Mil-A	0	0	—	2	0	0	0	0	1^{2}	3	0	1	5	21.6	10.80	35	.333	.400	0	—	0	-1	-1	0	-0.1
1971 Phi-N	1	0	1.000	6	1	0	0	0	16	8	1	10	15	10.7	0.00	—	.145	.288	0	.000	-0	6	6	-0	0.7
1972 Phi-N	5	9	.357	49	15	1	1	1	139^{2}	138	6	56	112	12.6	4.06	88	.259	.332	2	.071	-2	-9	-7	-1	-1.1
1973 Phi-N★	13	9	.591	34	28	10	5	0	223^{1}	172	16	99	169	11.3	2.50	152	.219	.314	7	.097	-4	29	32	-3	2.7
1974 Phi-N	6	9	.400	25	18	2	0	0	112^{1}	122	11	65	72	15.5	5.21	73	.276	.377	6	.171	-1	-20	-18	-2	-2.0
1975 Phi-N	5	10	.333	36	20	0	0	0	134^{1}	132	10	78	101	14.1	4.42	84	.261	.361	3	.088	-2	-12	-10	-3	-1.5
1976 Phi-N	3	1	.750	26	2	0	0	1	61^{2}	55	3	18	67	11.1	1.75	203	.241	.305	1	.167	0	12	12	0	1.4
1977 Phi-N	0	5	.000	12	8	0	0	0	45^{2}	50	3	25	37	14.8	4.53	88	.287	.377	1	.091	-0	-3	-3	1	-0.3
Mon-N	6	5	.545	22	22	2	0	0	139	116	18	49	93	11.0	4.21	90	.230	.304	8	.205	2	-5	-6	-1	-0.5
Yr	6	10	.375	34	30	2	0	0	184^{2}	166	21	74	130	11.9	4.29	90	.244	.323	9	.180	2	-8	-9	-0	-0.8
1978 Mon-N	4	12	.250	33	15	0	0	0	112	121	16	71	69	15.8	5.38	65	.286	.395	2	.083	-1	-22	-23	-1	-2.5
1979 NY-N	5	3	.625	33	2	0	0	0	63^{2}	55	6	55	44	16.1	5.23	70	.243	.400	3	.375	1	-11	-11	-0	-1.1
Sea-A	0	2	.000	4	2	0	0	0	13^{2}	11	2	10	5	15.1	5.27	83	.220	.371	0	—	0	-2	-1	-0	-0.1
Total 10	48	65	.425	282	133	15	6	2	1063	983	92	537	789	13.2	3.98	94	.250	.346	33	.127	-7	-38	-31	-10	-4.4
● JEFF TWITTY Twitty, Jeffrey Dean b: 11/10/57, Lancaster, S.C. BL/TL, 6'2", 185 lbs. Deb: 7/05/80																									
1980 KC-A	2	1	.667	13	0	0	0	0	22^{1}	33	4	7	9	16.1	6.04	67	.351	.396	0	—	0	-5	-5	0	-0.5
● CY TWOMBLY Twombly, Edwin Parker b: 6/15/1897, Groveland, Mass. d: 12/3/74, Savannah, Ga. BL/TL, 5'10.5", 170 lbs. Deb: 6/25/21																									
1921 Chi-A	1	2	.333	7	4	0	0	0	27^{2}	26	1	25	7	17.2	5.86	72	.283	.445	0	.000	-2	-5	-5	1	-0.6
● LEFTY TYLER Tyler, George Albert b: 12/14/1889, Derry, N.H. d: 9/29/53, Lowell, Mass. BL/TL, 6', 175 lbs. Deb: 9/20/10 F																									
1910 Bos-N	0	0	—	2	0	0	0	0	11^{1}	11	1	6	6	13.5	2.38	140	.275	.370	2	.500	1	1	1	-0	0.2
1911 Bos-N	7	10	.412	28	20	10	1	0	165^{1}	150	11	109	90	14.6	5.06	76	.243	.365	10	.164	-1	-31	-23	3	-1.9
1912 Bos-N	12	22	.353	42	29	15	1	0	256^{1}	262	8	126	144	14.0	4.18	86	.276	.367	19	.198	-1	-22	-17	4	-1.4
1913 Bos-N	16	17	.485	39	34	**28**	4	2	290^{1}	245	2	108	143	11.3	2.79	118	.235	.313	21	.206	4	13	16	7	2.8
1914 *Bos-N	16	13	.552	38	34	21	5	2	271^{1}	247	7	101	140	12.0	2.69	103	.249	.327	19	.202	1	3	2	-2	0.1
1915 Bos-N	10	9	.526	32	24	15	1	0	204^{2}	182	6	84	89	11.9	2.86	91	.243	.324	23	.261	7	-2	-6	-1	0.0
1916 Bos-N	17	9	.654	34	28	21	6	1	249^{1}	200	6	58	117	9.4	2.02	123	.226	.276	19	.204	7	17	13	2	2.6
1917 Bos-N	14	12	.538	32	28	22	4	1	239	203	1	86	98	11.1	2.52	101	.240	.314	31	.231	4	5	1	3	1.0
1918 *Chi-N	19	8	.704	33	30	22	6	1	269^{1}	218	1	67	102	9.7	2.00	139	.226	.279	21	.210	1	23	23	3	3.2
1919 Chi-N	2	2	.500	6	5	3	0	0	30	20	0	13	9	9.9	2.10	137	.196	.287	1	.143	1	3	3	1	0.5
1920 Chi-N	11	12	.478	27	27	18	2	0	193	193	6	57	57	11.8	3.31	97	.268	.324	17	.262	5	-4	-2	3	0.6
1921 Chi-N	3	2	.600	10	6	4	0	0	50	59	2	14	8	13.1	3.24	118	.294	.340	6	.231	1	3	3	-1	0.3
Total 12	127	116	.523	323	265	179	30	7	2230	1990	51	829	1003	11.6	2.95	101	.245	.320	189	.217	29	9	11	21	8.0
● JIM TYNG Tyng, James Alexander b: 3/27/1856, Philadelphia, Pa. d: 10/30/31, New York, N.Y. 5'9", 155 lbs. Deb: 9/23/1879																									
1879 Bos-N	1	2	.333	3	3	3	0	0	27	35	0	6	7	13.7	5.00	50	.292	.325	5	.357	1	-8	-8	0	-0.5
1888 Phi-N	0	0	—	1	0	0	0	1	4	8	0	2	2	24.8	4.50	66	.381	.458	0	.000	-0	-1	-1	0	-0.1
Total 2	1	2	.333	4	3	3	0	1	31	43	0	8	9	15.1	4.94	51	.305	.347	5	.333	1	-8	-8	0	-0.6
● DAVE TYRIVER Tyriver, David Burton b: 10/31/37, Oshkosh, Wis. d: 10/28/88, Oshkosh, Wis. BR/TR, 6', 175 lbs. Deb: 8/21/62																									
1962 Cle-A	0	0	—	4	0	0	0	0	10^{2}	10	2	7	7	15.2	4.22	92	.250	.375	0	.000	-0	-0	-0	0	-0.1
● JIMMY UCHRINSCKO Uchrinscko, James Emerson b: 10/20/1900, W.Newton, Pa. BL/TR, 6', 180 lbs. Deb: 7/20/26																									
1926 Was-A	0	0	—	3	0	0	0	0	8	13	0	8	0	23.6	10.13	38	.433	.553	0	.000	-0	-5	-6	0	-0.5
● BOB UHL Uhl, Robert Ellwood "Lefty" b: 9/17/13, San Francisco, Cal. d: 8/21/90, Santa Rosa, Cal. BB/TL, 5'11", 175 lbs. Deb: 5/08/38																									
1938 Chi-A	0	0	—	1	0	0	0	0	2	1	0	0	0	4.5	0.00	—	.167	.167	0	—	0	1	1	-0	0.1
1940 Det-A	0	0	—	1	0	0	0	0	0	4	0	2	0	—	∞	—	1.000	1.000	0	—	0	-4	-4	0	-0.3
Total 2	0	0	—	2	0	0	0	0	2	5	0	2	0	31.5	18.00	27	.500	.583	0	—	0	-3	-3	-0	-0.2

YEAR	TM/L	W	L	PCT	G	GS	CG	SH	SV	IP	H	HR	BB	SO	RAT	ERA	ERA+	OAV	OOB	BH	AVG	PB	PR	/A	PD	TPI
● GEORGE UHLE	Uhle, George Ernest "The Bull" b: 9/18/1898, Cleveland, Ohio d: 2/26/85, Lakewood, Ohio BR/TR, 6', 190 lbs. Deb: 4/30/19 C♦																									
1919	Cle-A	10	5	.667	26	12	7	1	0	127	129	1	43	50	12.7	2.91	115	.261	.329	13	.302	3	5	6	0	1.0
1920	*Cle-A	4	5	.444	27	6	2	0	1	84^2	98	3	29	27	14.4	5.21	73	.296	.367	11	.344	2	-13	-13	0	-1.0
1921	Cle-A	16	13	.552	41	28	13	2	2	238	288	9	63	63	13.4	4.01	106	.306	.352	23	.245	3	7	7	-3	0.6
1922	Cle-A	22	16	.579	50	40	23	**5**	3	287^1	328	6	89	82	13.5	4.07	98	.290	.348	29	.266	9	-1	-2	-3	0.2
1923	Cle-A	**26**	16	.619	54	44	**29**	1	5	**357^2**	378	8	102	109	12.4	3.77	105	.271	.326	52	.361	16	8	8	0	2.4
1924	Cle-A	9	15	.375	28	25	15	0	1	196^1	238	6	75	57	14.9	4.77	90	.306	.376	33	.308	7	-12	-11	1	-0.3
1925	Cle-A	13	11	.542	29	26	17	1	0	210^2	218	5	78	68	13.0	4.10	108	.268	.339	29	.287	6	7	7	-3	1.0
1926	Cle-A	**27**	11	**.711**	39	36	**32**	3	1	**318^1**	300	7	118	159	12.2	2.83	143	.253	.328	30	.227	4	42	43	-0	**4.8**
1927	Cle-A	8	9	.471	25	22	10	1	1	153^1	187	3	59	69	15.0	4.34	97	.310	.379	21	.266	4	-3	-2	-1	0.0
1928	Cle-A	12	17	.414	31	28	18	2	1	214^1	252	8	48	74	12.9	4.07	102	.300	.344	28	.286	7	-1	2	3	1.1
1929	Det-A	15	11	.577	32	30	23	1	0	249	283	9	58	100	12.4	4.08	105	.287	.328	37	.343	8	4	6	-3	1.1
1930	Det-A	12	12	.500	33	29	18	1	3	239	239	18	75	117	12.0	3.65	131	.264	.323	36	.308	8	26	30	-3	3.4
1931	Det-A	11	12	.478	29	18	15	2	2	193	190	10	49	63	11.3	3.50	131	.255	.304	22	.244	5	19	23	-1	2.7
1932	Det-A	6	6	.500	33	15	6	1	5	146^2	152	15	42	51	12.1	4.48	105	.266	.320	10	.182	1	-0	4	-1	0.3
1933	Det-A	0	0	—	1	0	0	0	0	0^2	2	1	0	1	27.0	27.00	16	.500	.500	0	—	0	-2	-2	0	-0.2
	NY-N	1	1	.500	6	1	0	0	0	13^2	16	1	6	4	14.5	7.90	41	.302	.373	0	.000	-0	-7	-7	0	-0.7
	NY-A	6	1	.857	12	6	4	0	0	61	63	4	20	26	12.7	5.16	75	.257	.321	8	.400	4	-6	-9	-1	-0.5
1934	NY-A	2	4	.333	10	2	0	0	0	16^1	30	3	7	10	20.4	9.92	41	.400	.451	3	.600	2	-10	-11	-0	-0.8
1936	Cle-A	0	1	.000	7	0	0	0	0	12^2	26	2	5	5	22.0	8.53	59	.419	.463	8	.381	4	-5	-5	-1	-0.2
Total	17	200	166	.546	513	368	232	21	25	3119^2	3417	119	966	1135	13.0	3.99	105	.281	.340	393	.289	93	60	74	-15	14.9
● JERRY UJDUR	Ujdur, Gerald Raymond b: 3/5/57, Duluth, Minn. BR/TR, 6'1", 195 lbs. Deb: 8/17/80																									
1980	Det-A	1	0	1.000	9	2	0	0	0	21^1	36	5	10	8	19.8	7.59	54	.383	.448	0	—	0	-8	-8	-1	-1.0
1981	Det-A	0	0	—	4	4	0	0	0	14	19	2	5	5	15.4	6.43	59	.322	.375	0	—	0	-4	-4	0	-0.4
1982	Det-A	10	10	.500	25	25	7	0	0	178	150	29	69	86	11.2	3.69	110	.230	.306	0	—	0	8	7	-1	0.6
1983	Det-A	0	4	.000	11	6	0	0	0	34	41	6	20	13	16.4	7.15	55	.293	.385	0	—	0	-12	-12	-1	-1.1
1984	Cle-A	1	2	.333	4	3	0	0	0	14^1	22	1	6	6	18.8	6.91	59	.355	.429	0	—	0	-5	-4	-1	-0.6
Total	5	12	16	.429	53	40	7	0	0	261^2	268	43	110	118	13.2	4.78	84	.266	.342	0	—	0	-21	-22	-3	-2.5
● SANDY ULLRICH	Ullrich, Carlos Santiago (Castello) b: 7/25/21, Havana, Cuba BR/TR, 6'1", 180 lbs. Deb: 5/03/44																									
1944	Was-A	0	0	—	3	0	0	0	0	9^2	17	2	4	2	20.5	9.31	35	.386	.449	1	.333	0	-6	-7	0	-0.6
1945	Was-A	3	3	.500	28	6	0	0	1	81^1	91	3	34	26	13.8	4.54	68	.276	.343	6	.273	1	-11	-13	1	-1.1
Total	2	3	3	.500	31	6	0	0	1	91	108	5	38	28	14.5	5.04	62	.289	.356	7	.280	1	-17	-19	2	-1.7
● DUTCH ULRICH	Ulrich, Frank W. b: 11/18/1899, Baltimore, Md. d: 2/11/29, Baltimore, Md. BR/TR, 6'2", 195 lbs. Deb: 4/18/25																									
1925	Phi-N	3	3	.500	21	4	2	1	0	65	73	6	12	29	11.9	3.05	157	.285	.320	2	.125	-1	9	12	1	1.2
1926	Phi-N	8	13	.381	45	17	8	1	1	147^2	178	9	37	52	13.2	4.08	101	.304	.347	12	.245	2	-4	1	-0	0.2
1927	Phi-N	8	11	.421	32	18	14	1	1	193^1	201	6	40	42	11.2	3.17	131	.271	.308	9	.123	-6	16	21	-2	1.3
Total	3	19	27	.413	98	39	24	3	2	406	452	21	89	123	12.0	3.48	122	.286	.324	23	.167	-5	21	34	-2	2.7
● ARNOLD UMBACH	Umbach, Arnold William b: 12/6/42, Williamsburg, Va. BR/TR, 6'1", 180 lbs. Deb: 10/03/64																									
1964	Mil-N	1	0	1.000	1	1	0	0	0	8^1	11	0	4	7	16.2	3.24	109	.333	.405	0	.000	0	0	0	-0	0.0
1966	Atl-N	0	2	.000	22	3	0	0	0	40^2	40	1	18	23	13.3	3.10	117	.256	.341	1	.200	0	2	2	-0	0.3
Total	2	1	2	.333	23	4	0	0	0	49	51	1	22	30	13.8	3.12	116	.270	.352	1	.125	0	3	3	-0	0.3
● JIM UMBARGER	Umbarger, James Harold b: 2/17/53, Burbank, Cal. BL/TL, 6'6", 200 lbs. Deb: 4/08/75																									
1975	Tex-A	8	7	.533	56	12	3	2	2	131	134	11	59	50	13.4	4.12	91	.276	.357	0	—	0	-5	-5	1	-0.4
1976	Tex-A	10	12	.455	30	30	10	3	0	197^1	208	12	54	105	12.0	3.15	114	.274	.324	0	—	0	8	10	-0	1.0
1977	Oak-A	1	5	.167	12	8	1	0	0	44	62	3	28	24	19.2	6.55	61	.354	.454	0	—	0	-12	-12	0	-1.1
	Tex-A	1	1	.500	3	2	0	0	0	13	14	2	4	5	12.5	5.54	74	.275	.327	0	—	0	-2	-2	-0	-0.3
	Yr	2	6	.250	15	10	1	0	0	57	76	5	32	29	17.1	6.32	64	.326	.408	0	—	0	-14	-14	0	-1.4
1978	Tex-A	5	8	.385	32	9	1	0	1	97^2	116	9	36	60	14.2	4.88	77	.299	.362	0	—	0	-12	-12	1	-1.2
Total	4	25	33	.431	133	61	15	5	3	483	534	37	181	244	13.5	4.14	90	.287	.354	0	—	0	-23	-22	2	-2.0
● JIM UMBRICHT	Umbricht, James b: 9/17/30, Chicago, Ill. d: 4/8/64, Houston, Tex. BR/TR, 6'4", 215 lbs. Deb: 9/26/59																									
1959	Pit-N	0	0	—	1	1	0	0	0	7	7	3	4	3	14.1	6.43	60	.259	.355	0	.000	-0	-2	-2	0	-0.2
1960	Pit-N	1	2	.333	17	3	0	0	1	40^2	40	5	27	26	14.8	5.09	74	.270	.383	2	.333	0	-6	-6	-1	-0.6
1961	Pit-N	0	0	—	1	0	0	0	0	3^1	5	0	2	1	18.9	2.70	148	.333	.412	1	1.000	0	0	0	-0	0.1
1962	Hou-N	4	0	1.000	34	0	0	0	2	67	51	3	17	55	9.4	2.01	185	.213	.270	1	.111	-0	14	13	1	1.3
1963	Hou-N	4	3	.571	35	3	0	0	0	76	52	6	21	48	8.8	2.61	121	.195	.256	1	.111	-0	6	5	1	0.5
Total	5	9	5	.643	88	7	0	0	3	194	155	17	71	133	10.6	3.06	115	.222	.297	5	.179	-0	13	10	0	1.1
● WILLIE UNDERHILL	Underhill, Willie Vern b: 9/6/04, Yowell, Tex. d: 10/26/70, Bay City, Tex. BR/TR, 6'2", 185 lbs. Deb: 9/08/27																									
1927	Cle-A	0	2	.000	4	1	0	0	0	8^1	12	0	11	4	24.8	9.72	43	.375	.535	0	.000	-0	-5	-5	0	-0.5
1928	Cle-A	1	2	.333	11	3	1	0	0	28	33	0	20	16	17.4	4.50	92	.306	.419	4	.364	2	-1	-1	0	0.1
Total	2	1	4	.200	15	4	1	0	0	36^1	45	0	31	20	19.1	5.70	73	.321	.448	4	.333	1	-7	-6	0	-0.4
● FRED UNDERWOOD	Underwood, Frederick Theodore b: 10/14/1868, St.Louis Co., Mo. d: 1/26/06, Kansas City, Mo. Deb: 7/18/1894																									
1894	Bro-N	2	4	.333	7	6	5	0	0	47	80	1	30	10	21.4	7.85	63	.371	.453	7	.389	2	-13	-15	-0	-1.0
● PAT UNDERWOOD	Underwood, Patrick John b: 2/9/57, Kokomo, Ind. BL/TL, 6', 175 lbs. Deb: 5/31/79 F																									
1979	Det-A	6	4	.600	27	15	1	0	0	121^2	126	17	29	83	11.6	4.59	94	.269	.314	0	—	0	-5	-4	-1	-0.4
1980	Det-A	3	6	.333	49	7	0	0	5	112^2	121	12	35	60	12.6	3.59	114	.277	.333	0	—	0	6	6	-0	0.5
1982	Det-A	4	8	.333	33	12	2	0	3	99	108	17	22	43	11.8	4.73	86	.269	.307	0	—	0	-7	-7	1	-0.7
1983	Det-A	0	0	—	4	0	0	0	0	10^1	11	1	6	2	14.8	8.71	45	.289	.386	0	—	0	-5	-6	-0	-0.5
Total	4	13	18	.419	113	34	3	0	8	343^2	366	47	92	188	12.1	4.43	94	.272	.320	0	—	0	-12	-10	-1	-1.1
● TOM UNDERWOOD	Underwood, Thomas Gerald b: 12/22/53, Kokomo, Ind. BR/TL, 5'11", 170 lbs. Deb: 8/19/74 F																									
1974	Phi-N	1	0	1.000	7	0	0	0	0	13	15	1	5	8	13.8	4.85	78	.313	.377	0	.000	-0	-2	-2	-0	-0.2
1975	Phi-N	14	13	.519	35	35	7	2	0	219^1	221	12	84	123	12.8	4.14	90	.262	.333	9	.122	-2	-13	-10	-4	-1.6
1976	*Phi-N	10	5	.667	33	25	3	0	2	155^2	154	9	63	94	12.6	3.53	101	.260	.332	5	.109	-1	-0	0	-2	-0.3
1977	Phi-N	3	2	.600	14	0	0	0	1	33^1	44	2	18	20	16.7	5.13	78	.328	.408	0	.000	-0	-5	-4	-0	-0.5
	StL-N	6	9	.400	19	17	1	0	0	100	104	7	57	66	14.6	4.95	78	.278	.375	4	.133	-0	-12	-12	-1	-1.3
	Yr	9	11	.450	33	17	1	0	1	133^1	148	9	75	86	15.1	4.99	78	.290	.382	4	.121	-0	-16	-16	-2	-1.8
1978	Tor-A	6	14	.300	31	30	7	1	0	197^2	201	23	87	139	13.2	4.10	96	.263	.340	0	—	0	-7	-4	-3	-0.8
1979	Tor-A	9	16	.360	33	32	12	1	0	227	213	23	95	127	12.6	3.69	118	.253	.335	0	—	0	13	17	-0	1.6
1980	*NY-A	13	9	.591	38	27	2	2	2	187	163	15	66	116	11.2	3.66	107	.237	.307	0	—	0	8	5	-0	0.7
1981	NY-A	1	4	.200	9	6	0	0	0	32^2	32	2	13	29	12.4	4.41	81	.262	.333	0	—	0	-3	-3	-0	-0.3
	*Oak-A	3	2	.600	16	5	1	0	1	51	37	4	25	46	11.3	3.18	109	.202	.305	0	—	0	3	2	0	0.2
	Yr	4	6	.400	25	11	1	0	1	83^2	69	6	38	75	11.7	3.66	96	.226	.316	0	—	0	-0	-1	-0	-0.1
1982	Oak-A	10	6	.625	56	10	2	0	7	153	136	11	68	79	12.1	3.29	119	.241	.324	0	—	0	13	10	-2	0.9
1983	Oak-A	9	7	.563	51	15	0	0	4	144^2	156	13	50	62	12.9	4.04	95	.277	.338	0	—	0	0	-3	-3	-0.5
1984	Bal-A	1	0	1.000	37	1	0	0	1	71^2	78	8	31	39	13.7	3.52	110	.282	.354	0	—	0	4	3	1	0.5
Total	11	86	87	.497	379	203	35	6	18	1586	1554	130	662	948	12.7	3.89	100	.259	.336	18	.117	-4	0	-0	-15	-1.6

YEAR	TM/L	W	L	PCT	G	GS	CG	SH	SV	IP	H	HR	BB	SO	RAT	ERA	ERA+	OAV	OOB	BH	AVG	PB	PR	/A	PD	TPI
● **WOODY UPCHURCH** Upchurch, Jefferson Woodrow b: 4/13/11, Buies Creek, N.C. d: 10/23/71, Buies Creek, N.C. BR/TL, 6', 180 lbs. Deb: 9/14/35																										
1935	Phi-A	0	2	.000	3	3	1	0	0	21^{1}	23	3	12	2	14.8	5.06	90	.271	.361	2	.286	0	-1	-1	-0	-0.1
1936	Phi-A	0	2	.000	7	2	1	0	0	22^{1}	36	7	14	6	20.1	9.67	53	.353	.431	1	.143	-0	-12	-11	-1	-1.0
Total	2	0	4	.000	10	5	2	0	0	43^{2}	59	10	26	8	17.5	7.42	65	.316	.399	3	.214	-0	-13	-13	-1	-1.1
● **JOHN UPHAM** Upham, John Leslie b: 12/29/41, Windsor, Ont., Can. BL/TL, 6', 180 lbs. Deb: 4/16/67 ♦																										
1967	Chi-N	0	1	.000	5	0	0	0	0	1^{1}	4	1	2	2	40.5	33.75	11	.571	.667	2	.667	1	-5	-4	0	-0.4
1968	Chi-N	0	0	—	2	0	0	0	0	7	2	0	3	2	7.7	0.00	—	.087	.222	2	.200	0	2	2	0	0.4
Total	2	0	1	.000	7	0	0	0	0	8^{1}	6	1	5	4	13.0	5.40	60	.200	.333	4	.308	1	-2	-2	0	0.0
● **BILL UPHAM** Upham, William Lawrence b: 4/4/1888, Akron, Ohio d: 9/14/59, Newark, N.J. BB/TR, 6', 178 lbs. Deb: 4/10/15																										
1915	Bro-F	6	8	.429	33	11	4	2	5	121	129	0	40	46	12.6	3.05	99	.274	.331	4	.111	-2	-0	-0	2	0.0
1918	Bos-N	1	1	.500	3	2	2	0	0	20^{2}	28	2	1	8	12.6	5.23	51	.326	.333	2	.222	0	-6	-6	-0	-0.6
Total	2	7	9	.438	36	13	6	2	5	141^{2}	157	2	41	54	12.6	3.37	88	.282	.332	6	.133	-2	-6	-6	2	-0.6
● **JERRY UPP** Upp, George Henry b: 12/10/1883, Sandusky, Ohio d: 6/30/37, Sandusky, Ohio TL , Deb: 9/02/09																										
1909	Cle-A	2	1	.667	7	4	2	0	0	26^{2}	26	0	12	13	12.8	1.69	152	.260	.339	2	.222	0	2	3	1	0.4
● **CECIL UPSHAW** Upshaw, Cecil Lee b: 10/22/42, Spearsville, La. BR/TR, 6'6", 205 lbs. Deb: 10/01/66																										
1966	Atl-N	0	0	—	1	0	0	0	0	3	0	0	3	2	9.0	0.00	—	.000	.273	1	1.000	0	1	1	-0	0.2
1967	Atl-N	2	3	.400	30	0	0	0	8	45^{1}	42	4	8	31	10.7	2.58	129	.247	.297	1	.167	1	4	4	0	0.5
1968	Atl-N	8	7	.533	52	0	0	0	13	116^{2}	98	6	24	74	9.7	2.47	121	.229	.276	4	.174	0	7	7	-0	0.8
1969	*Atl-N	6	4	.600	62	0	0	0	27	105^{1}	102	7	29	57	11.3	2.91	124	.259	.311	5	.238	2	8	8	1	1.1
1971	Atl-N	11	6	.647	49	0	0	0	17	82	95	5	28	56	13.7	3.51	106	.292	.352	0	.000	-2	-0	2	-1	-0.1
1972	Atl-N	3	5	.375	42	0	0	0	13	53^{2}	50	5	19	23	11.7	3.69	103	.249	.317	1	.143	-0	-1	1	1	0.1
1973	Atl-N	0	1	.000	5	0	0	0	0	3^{2}	8	0	2	3	24.5	9.82	40	.444	.500	0	—	0	-3	-2	0	-0.2
	Hou-N	2	3	.400	35	0	0	0	1	38^{1}	38	3	15	21	12.7	4.46	81	.259	.331	0	.000	-0	-3	-4	1	-0.3
	Yr	2	4	.333	40	0	0	0	1	42	46	3	17	24	13.7	4.93	74	.277	.348	0	.000	-0	-6	-6	1	-0.5
1974	Cle-A	0	1	.000	7	0	0	0	0	8	10	1	4	7	15.8	3.38	107	.345	.424	0	—	0	0	0	-0	0.0
	NY-A	1	5	.167	36	0	0	0	6	59^{2}	53	1	24	27	12.1	3.02	116	.254	.339	0	—	0	4	3	1	0.4
	Yr	1	6	.143	43	0	0	0	6	67^{2}	63	2	28	34	12.5	3.06	115	.262	.347	0	—	0	4	3	1	0.4
1975	Chi-A	1	1	.500	29	0	0	0	1	47^{1}	49	5	21	22	14.1	3.23	120	.271	.359	0	—	0	3	3	-0	0.3
Total	9	34	36	.486	348	0	0	0	86	563	545	37	177	323	11.9	3.13	112	.258	.322	12	.160	1	19	23	2	2.8
● **BILL UPTON** Upton, William Ray b: 6/18/29, Esther, Mo. d: 1/2/87, San Diego, Cal. BR/TR, 6', 167 lbs. Deb: 4/13/54 F																										
1954	Phi-A	0	0	—	2	0	0	0	1	5	6	1	1	2	12.6	1.80	217	.300	.333	0	—	0	1	1	0	0.1
● **JACK URBAN** Urban, Jack Elmer b: 12/5/28, Omaha, Neb. BR/TR, 5'8", 155 lbs. Deb: 6/13/57																										
1957	KC-A	7	4	.636	31	13	3	0	0	129^{1}	111	7	45	55	10.9	3.34	118	.237	.305	11	.282	2	6	9	2	1.4
1958	KC-A	8	11	.421	30	24	5	1	1	132	150	17	51	54	13.8	5.93	66	.286	.351	7	.152	-2	-32	-30	-1	-3.2
1959	StL-N	0	0	—	8	0	0	0	0	10^{2}	18	1	7	4	21.1	9.28	46	.409	.490	0	.000	-0	-6	-6	-0	-0.6
Total	3	15	15	.500	69	37	8	1	1	272	279	25	103	113	12.7	4.83	82	.269	.337	18	.209	0	-32	-27	-0	-2.4
● **JOHN URREA** Urrea, John Godoy b: 2/9/55, Los Angeles, Cal. BR/TR, 6'3", 205 lbs. Deb: 4/10/77																										
1977	StL-N	7	6	.538	41	12	2	1	4	139^{2}	126	13	35	81	10.4	3.16	122	.244	.292	4	.138	2	12	11	1	1.3
1978	StL-N	4	9	.308	27	12	1	0	0	98^{2}	108	4	47	61	14.8	5.38	65	.284	.373	3	.125	-1	-20	-20	0	-2.1
1979	StL-N	0	0	—	3	2	0	0	0	11^{1}	13	0	9	5	17.5	3.97	95	.310	.431	1	.250	0	-0	-0	0	0.0
1980	StL-N	4	1	.800	30	1	0	0	3	64^{2}	57	2	41	36	13.9	3.48	106	.239	.356	3	.231	0	1	2	-1	0.1
1981	SD-N	2	2	.500	38	0	0	0	2	49	43	1	28	19	13.6	2.39	136	.239	.351	1	.250	0	6	5	-1	0.4
Total	5	17	18	.486	139	27	3	1	9	363^{1}	347	20	160	202	12.9	3.74	97	.256	.339	12	.162	2	-2	-4	-1	-0.3
● **BOB VAIL** Vail, Robert Garfield "Doc" b: 9/24/1881, Linneus, Maine d: 3/22/42, Philadelphia, Pa. BR/TR, 5'10", 165 lbs. Deb: 8/27/08																										
1908	Pit-N	1	2	.333	4	1	0	0	0	15	15	0	7	9	13.8	6.00	38	.268	.359	1	.333	1	-6	-6	-1	-0.7
● **EFRAIN VALDEZ** Valdez, Efrain Antonio b: 7/11/66, Nizao Bani, D.R. BL/TL, 5'11", 180 lbs. Deb: 8/13/90																										
1990	Cle-A	1	1	.500	13	0	0	0	0	23^{2}	20	2	14	13	12.9	3.04	129	.233	.340	0	—	0	2	2	-0	0.3
1991	Cle-A	0	0	—	7	0	0	0	0	6	5	0	3	1	13.5	1.50	277	.238	.360	0	—	0	2	2	0	0.2
Total	2	1	1	.500	20	0	0	0	0	29^{2}	25	2	17	14	13.0	2.73	145	.234	.344	0	—	0	4	4	-0	0.5
● **RAFAEL VALDEZ** Valdez, Rafael Emilio (Diaz) b: 12/17/67, Nizao Boni, D.R. BR/TR, 5'11", 165 lbs. Deb: 4/18/90																										
1990	SD-N	0	1	.000	3	0	0	0	0	5^{2}	11	4	2	3	20.6	11.12	34	.393	.433	0	.000	-0	-5	-5	-0	-0.5
● **RENE VALDEZ** Valdez, Rene Gutierrez (b: Rene Gutierrez (Valdez)) b: 6/2/29, Guanabacoa, Cuba BR/TR, 6'3", 175 lbs. Deb: 4/21/57																										
1957	Bro-N	1	1	.500	5	1	0	0	0	13	13	1	7	10	13.8	5.54	75	.265	.357	0	.000	0	-2	-2	-0	-0.2
● **SERGIO VALDEZ** Valdez, Sergio Sanchez (b: Sergio Sanchez (Valdez)) b: 9/7/64, Elias Pina, D.R. BR/TR, 6', 165 lbs. Deb: 9/10/86																										
1986	Mon-N	0	4	.000	5	5	0	0	0	25	39	2	11	20	18.4	6.84	54	.361	.425	1	.125	-0	-9	-9	-0	-0.9
1989	Atl-N	1	2	.333	19	1	0	0	0	32^{2}	31	5	17	26	13.2	6.06	60	.246	.336	1	1.000	0	-9	-9	-1	-0.9
1990	Atl-N	0	0	—	6	0	0	0	0	5^{1}	6	0	3	3	15.2	6.75	60	.273	.360	0	—	0	-2	-2	0	-0.1
	Cle-A	6	6	.500	24	13	0	0	0	102^{1}	109	17	35	63	12.8	4.75	82	.276	.336	0	—	0	-10	-9	-0	-0.9
1991	Cle-A	1	0	1.000	6	0	0	0	0	16^{1}	15	3	5	11	11.0	5.51	75	.238	.294	0	—	0	-3	-2	-1	-0.3
1992	Mon-N	0	2	.000	27	0	0	0	0	37^{1}	25	2	12	32	8.9	2.41	145	.185	.252	0	.000	-0	5	4	0	0.5
Total	5	8	14	.364	87	19	0	0	0	219	225	29	83	155	12.7	4.89	78	.265	.332	2	.167	-0	-27	-27	-1	-2.6
● **CORKY VALENTINE** Valentine, Harold Lewis b: 1/4/29, Troy, Ohio BR/TR, 6'1", 203 lbs. Deb: 4/17/54																										
1954	Cin-N	12	11	.522	36	28	7	3	1	194^{1}	211	24	60	73	12.7	4.45	94	.282	.339	9	.138	-2	-8	-5	-2	-0.9
1955	Cin-N	2	1	.667	10	5	0	0	0	26^{2}	29	5	16	14	15.5	7.43	57	.276	.377	0	.000	-1	-10	-9	1	-0.9
Total	2	14	12	.538	46	33	7	3	1	221	240	29	76	87	13.1	4.81	87	.282	.344	9	.125	-3	-18	-15	-1	-1.8
● **JOHN VALENTINE** Valentine, John Gill b: 11/21/1855, Brooklyn, N.Y. d: 10/10/03, Central Islip, N.Y Deb: 5/03/1883																										
1883	Col-a	2	10	.167	13	12	11	0	0	102	130	0	17	13	13.0	3.53	87	.291	.317	17	.283	3	-3	-5	1	-0.1
● **VITO VALENTINETTI** Valentinetti, Vito John b: 9/16/28, W.New York, N.J. BR/TR, 6', 195 lbs. Deb: 6/20/54																										
1954	Chi-A	0	0	—	1	0	0	0	0	1	4	1	2	1	54.0	54.00	7	.571	.667	0	—	0	-6	-6	0	-0.4
1956	Chi-N	6	4	.600	42	2	0	0	1	95^{1}	84	10	36	26	11.4	3.78	100	.243	.317	2	.100	-1	-0	-0	-1	-0.3
1957	Chi-N	0	0	—	9	0	0	0	0	12	12	1	7	8	14.3	2.25	172	.255	.352	0	.000	0	2	2	-0	0.2
	Cle-A	2	2	.500	11	2	1	0	0	23^{2}	26	3	13	9	15.2	4.94	75	.289	.385	1	.200	-0	-3	-3	0	-0.3
1958	Det-A	1	0	1.000	15	0	0	0	2	18^{2}	18	4	5	10	11.6	3.38	120	.257	.316	0	—	0	1	1	-0	0.1
	Was-A	4	6	.400	23	10	2	0	0	95^{2}	106	16	49	33	14.8	5.08	75	.286	.373	9	.321	2	-14	-13	2	-1.0
	Yr	5	6	.455	38	10	2	0	2	114^{1}	124	20	54	43	14.2	4.80	80	.281	.362	9	.321	2	-13	-12	1	-0.9
1959	Was-A	0	2	.000	7	1	0	0	0	10^{2}	16	0	10	7	22.8	10.13	39	.356	.482	0	—	0	-7	-7	0	-0.6
Total	5	13	14	.481	108	15	3	0	3	257	266	35	122	94	13.8	4.73	81	.273	.358	12	.218	1	-27	-26	0	-2.3
● **FERNANDO VALENZUELA** Valenzuela, Fernando (Anguamea) b: 11/1/60, Navoja, Mexico BL/TL, 5'11", 195 lbs. Deb: 9/15/80																										
1980	LA-N	2	0	1.000	10	0	0	0	1	17^{2}	8	0	5	16	6.6	0.00	—	.136	.203	0	.000	-0	7	7	0	0.8
1981	*LA-N★	13	7	.650	25	25	**11**	**8**	0	**192^{1}**	140	11	61	**180**	9.5	2.48	134	.205	.271	16	.250	3	22	18	2	2.6

YEAR TM/L	W	L	PCT	G	GS	CG	SH	SV	IP	H	HR	BB	SO	RAT	ERA	ERA+	OAV	OOB	BH	AVG	PB	PR	/A	PD	TPI
1982 LA-N★	19	13	.594	37	37	18	4	0	285	247	13	83	199	10.5	2.87	121	.236	.294	16	.168	1	23	19	5	2.7
1983 *LA-N☆	15	10	.600	35	35	9	4	0	257	245	16	99	189	12.2	3.75	96	.255	.327	17	.187	2	-3	-4	4	0.2
1984 LA-N★	12	17	.414	34	34	12	2	0	261	218	14	106	240	11.2	3.03	116	.229	.308	15	.190	4	16	14	4	2.4
1985 *LA-N★	17	10	.630	35	35	14	5	0	272^{1}	211	14	101	208	10.3	2.45	142	.214	.288	21	.216	4	35	31	2	4.0
1986 LA-N★	**21**	11	.656	34	34	**20**	3	0	269^{1}	226	18	85	242	10.4	3.14	110	.226	.288	24	.220	4	17	9	4	1.8
1987 LA-N	14	14	.500	34	34	**12**	1	0	251	254	25	124	190	13.7	3.98	100	.262	.349	13	.141	-1	3	-0	3	0.2
1988 LA-N	5	8	.385	23	22	3	0	1	142^{1}	142	11	76	64	13.8	4.24	79	.268	.360	8	.182	1	-12	-14	3	-1.1
1989 LA-N	10	13	.435	31	31	3	0	0	196^{2}	185	11	98	116	13.0	3.43	99	.251	.340	12	.182	1	1	-0	2	0.2
1990 LA-N	13	13	.500	33	33	5	2	0	204	223	19	77	115	13.2	4.59	80	.276	.339	21	.304	8	-18	-21	-0	-1.4
1991 Cal-A	0	2	.000	2	2	0	0	0	6^{2}	14	3	3	5	23.0	12.15	34	.452	.500	0	—	0	-6	-6	0	-0.5
Total 12	141	118	.544	333	322	107	29	2	2355^{1}	2113	155	918	1764	11.6	3.34	106	.241	.314	163	.202	28	84	52	27	11.9
● **JULIO VALERA** Valera, Julio Enrique (Torres) b: 10/13/68, Aguadilla, P.R. BR/TR, 6'2", 185 lbs. Deb: 9/01/90																									
1990 NY-N	1	1	.500	3	3	0	0	0	13	20	1	7	4	18.7	6.92	54	.351	.422	1	.200	0	-5	-5	-1	-0.5
1991 NY-N	0	0	—	2	0	0	0	0	2	1	0	4	3	22.5	0.00	—	.143	.455	0	—	0	1	1	0	0.1
1992 Cal-A	8	11	.421	30	28	4	2	0	188	188	15	64	113	12.2	3.73	105	.262	.324	0	—	0	4	4	-2	0.1
Total 3	9	12	.429	35	31	4	2	0	203	209	16	75	120	12.7	3.90	100	.267	.333	1	.200	0	1	-0	-3	-0.3
● **CLAY Van ALSTYNE** Van Alstyne, Clayton Emory "Spike" b: 5/24/1900, Stuyvesant, N.Y. d: 1/5/60, Hudson, N.Y. BR/TR, 5'11", 180 lbs. Deb: 8/20/27																									
1927 Was-A	0	0	—	2	0	0	0	0	3	3	0	0	0	9.0	3.00	136	.250	.250	0	—	0	0	0	-0	0.0
1928 Was-A	0	0	—	4	0	0	0	0	21^{1}	26	0	13	5	16.9	5.48	73	.329	.430	2	.250	1	-3	-3	1	-0.1
Total 2	0	0	—	6	0	0	0	0	24^{1}	29	0	13	5	15.9	5.18	78	.319	.410	2	.250	1	-3	-3	1	-0.1
● **RUSS Van ATTA** Van Atta, Russell "Sheriff" b: 6/21/06, Augusta, N.J. d: 10/10/86, Andover, N.J. BL/TL, 6', 184 lbs. Deb: 4/25/33																									
1933 NY-A	12	4	.750	26	22	10	2	1	157	160	8	63	76	12.8	4.18	93	.262	.332	17	.283	4	2	-5	0	-0.2
1934 NY-A	3	5	.375	28	9	0	0	0	88	107	3	46	39	15.9	6.34	64	.307	.390	6	.207	1	-18	-22	-1	-2.0
1935 NY-A	0	0	—	5	0	0	0	0	4^{2}	5	0	4	3	17.4	3.86	105	.263	.391	0	.000	-0	0	0	-0	0.0
StL-A	9	16	.360	53	17	1	0	3	170^{1}	201	10	87	87	15.4	5.34	90	.292	.374	9	.214	-1	-17	-10	-1	-1.1
Yr	9	16	.360	**58**	17	1	0	3	175	206	10	91	90	15.4	5.30	90	.291	.375	9	.209	-1	-16	-10	-2	-1.1
1936 StL-A	4	7	.364	**52**	9	2	0	2	122^{2}	164	9	68	59	17.2	6.60	81	.320	.401	5	.172	-1	-21	-17	1	-1.4
1937 StL-A	1	2	.333	16	6	1	0	0	58^{2}	74	2	32	34	16.3	5.52	87	.307	.388	6	.462	3	-6	-5	1	-0.1
1938 StL-A	4	7	.364	25	12	3	1	0	104	118	7	61	35	15.6	6.06	82	.289	.382	4	.133	-2	-15	-13	0	-1.2
1939 StL-A	0	0	—	2	1	0	0	0	7	9	0	7	6	21.9	11.57	42	.310	.459	0	.000	-0	-5	-5	-0	-0.5
Total 7	33	41	.446	207	76	17	3	6	712^{1}	838	39	368	339	15.4	5.60	82	.293	.376	47	.228	4	-80	-78	-1	-6.5
● **OZZIE Van BRABANT** Van Brabant, Camille Oscar b: 9/28/26, Kingsville, Ont., Canada BR/TR, 6'1", 165 lbs. Deb: 4/13/54																									
1954 Phi-A	0	2	.000	9	2	0	0	0	26^{2}	35	3	18	10	18.2	7.09	55	.347	.450	1	.200	1	-10	-9	1	-0.8
1955 KC-A	0	0	—	2	0	0	0	0	2	4	1	2	1	27.0	18.00	23	.400	.500	0	—	0	-3	-3	-0	-0.3
Total 2	0	2	.000	11	2	0	0	0	28^{2}	39	4	20	11	18.8	7.85	50	.351	.455	1	.200	1	-13	-13	1	-1.1
● **DAZZY VANCE** Vance, Clarence Arthur b: 3/4/1891, Orient, Iowa d: 2/16/61, Homosassa Springs Fla BR/TR, 6'2", 200 lbs. Deb: 4/16/15 H																									
1915 Pit-N	0	1	.000	1	1	0	0	0	2^{2}	3	0	5	0	30.4	10.13	27	.375	.643	0	.000	-0	-2	-2	0	-0.2
NY-A	0	3	.000	8	3	1	0	0	28	23	1	16	18	13.2	3.54	83	.232	.350	2	.667	2	-2	-2	-0	0.0
1918 NY-A	0	0	—	2	0	0	0	0	2^{1}	9	0	2	0	42.4	15.43	18	.692	.733	0	—	0	-3	-3	-0	-0.3
1922 Bro-N	18	12	.600	36	30	16	**5**	0	245^{2}	259	9	94	**134**	13.2	3.70	110	.276	.347	20	.225	1	11	10	0	1.2
1923 Bro-N	18	15	.545	37	35	21	3	0	280^{1}	263	10	100	**197**	12.0	3.50	111	.250	.322	7	.084	-3	16	12	0	0.9
1924 Bro-N	**28**	6	.824	35	34	**30**	3	0	308^{2}	238	11	77	**262**	**9.4**	**2.16**	**174**	**.213**	**.269**	16	.151	-2	**59**	**55**	1	**5.8**
1925 Bro-N	**22**	9	.710	31	31	26	**4**	0	265^{1}	247	8	66	**221**	11.0	3.53	118	.250	.304	14	.143	-0	22	19	1	2.0
1926 Bro-N	9	10	.474	24	22	12	0	1	169	172	7	58	**140**	12.3	3.89	98	.271	.333	10	.182	-1	-1	-1	2	-0.1
1927 Bro-N	16	15	.516	34	32	**25**	2	1	273^{1}	242	12	69	**184**	10.4	2.70	147	**.239**	.291	15	.167	-2	37	38	-2	3.7
1928 Bro-N	22	10	.688	38	32	24	**4**	2	280^{1}	226	11	72	**200**	**9.8**	**2.09**	**190**	**.221**	**.277**	17	.177	2	**59**	**59**	1	**6.6**
1929 Bro-N	14	13	.519	31	26	17	1	0	231^{1}	244	15	47	126	11.7	3.89	119	.274	.316	10	.135	-2	21	19	1	1.6
1930 Bro-N	17	15	.531	35	31	20	**4**	0	258^{2}	241	15	55	173	**10.5**	**2.61**	**188**	**.246**	**.289**	12	.135	-5	**68**	**66**	-1	**5.8**
1931 Bro-N	11	13	.458	30	29	12	2	0	218^{2}	221	12	53	150	11.3	3.38	113	.261	.304	9	.134	-2	12	11	1	0.9
1932 Bro-N	12	11	.522	27	24	9	1	1	175^{2}	171	10	57	103	11.7	4.20	91	.256	.315	5	.089	-4	-6	-7	-0	-1.1
1933 StL-N	6	2	.750	28	11	2	0	3	99	105	3	28	67	12.2	3.55	98	.267	.318	5	.179	-1	-2	-1	-1	-0.3
1934 Cin-N	0	2	.000	6	2	0	0	0	18	28	1	11	9	20.0	7.50	54	.350	.435	1	.250	0	-7	-7	0	-0.6
*StL-N	1	1	.500	19	4	1	0	1	59	62	4	14	33	11.9	3.66	115	.271	.318	2	.133	-0	3	4	-0	0.3
Yr	1	3	.250	25	6	1	0	1	77	90	5	25	42	13.7	4.56	92	.290	.347	3	.158	0	-4	-3	-0	-0.3
1935 Bro-N	3	2	.600	20	0	0	0	2	51	55	3	16	28	13.1	4.41	90	.268	.330	1	.059	-2	-2	-2	-0	-0.4
Total 16	197	140	.585	442	347	216	29	11	2967	2809	132	840	2045	11.3	3.24	125	.251	.308	146	.150	-17	281	266	3	25.8
● **SANDY VANCE** Vance, Gene Covington b: 1/5/47, Lamar, Colo. BR/TR, 6'2", 180 lbs. Deb: 4/26/70																									
1970 LA-N	7	7	.500	20	18	2	0	0	115	109	9	37	45	11.5	3.13	122	.248	.308	7	.189	1	12	9	-3	0.7
1971 LA-N	2	1	.667	10	3	0	0	0	26	38	1	9	11	16.3	6.92	47	.355	.405	0	.000	-0	-10	-11	-0	-1.1
Total 2	9	8	.529	30	21	2	0	0	141	147	10	46	56	12.4	3.83	97	.269	.327	7	.167	0	2	-2	-3	-0.4
● **JOE VANCE** Vance, Joseph Albert "Sandy" b: 9/16/05, Devine, Tex. d: 7/4/78, Devine, Tex. BR/TR, 6'1.5", 190 lbs. Deb: 4/18/35																									
1935 Chi-A	2	2	.500	10	0	0	0	0	31	36	1	21	12	16.5	6.68	69	.295	.399	2	.182	-1	-8	-7	1	-0.7
1937 NY-A	1	0	1.000	2	2	0	0	0	15	11	2	9	3	12.0	3.00	148	.204	.317	0	.000	-1	3	2	1	0.2
1938 NY-A	0	0	—	3	1	0	0	0	11^{1}	20	2	4	2	19.1	7.15	63	.408	.453	3	.750	2	-3	-3	0	-0.1
Total 3	3	2	.600	15	3	0	0	0	57^{1}	67	5	34	17	15.9	5.81	79	.298	.390	5	.250	1	-8	-8	1	-0.6
● **CHRIS Van CUYK** Van Cuyk, Christian Gerald b: 3/1/27, Kimberly, Wis. BL/TL, 6'6", 215 lbs. Deb: 7/16/50 F																									
1950 Bro-N	1	3	.250	12	4	1	0	0	33^{1}	33	3	12	21	12.4	4.86	84	.266	.336	1	.100	-1	-3	-3	-1	-0.4
1951 Bro-N	1	2	.333	9	6	0	0	0	29^{1}	33	4	11	16	14.7	5.52	71	.295	.378	2	.250	0	-5	-5	-0	-0.5
1952 Bro-N	5	6	.455	23	16	4	0	1	97^{2}	104	12	40	66	13.7	5.16	71	.271	.347	8	.242	2	-16	-17	-1	-1.6
Total 3	7	11	.389	44	26	5	0	1	160^{1}	170	19	63	103	13.6	5.16	73	.274	.351	11	.216	1	-23	-25	-2	-2.5
● **JOHNNY Van CUYK** Van Cuyk, John Henry b: 7/7/21, Little Chute, Wis. BL/TL, 6'1", 190 lbs. Deb: 9/18/47 F																									
1947 Bro-N	0	0	—	2	0	0	0	0	3^{1}	5	0	1	2	16.2	5.40	77	.357	.400	0	—	0	-0	-0	0	0.0
1948 Bro-N	0	0	—	3	0	0	0	0	5	4	1	1	1	9.0	3.60	111	.200	.238	0	—	0	0	0	0	0.0
1949 Bro-N	0	0	—	2	0	0	0	0	2	3	0	1	0	18.0	9.00	46	.429	.500	0	—	0	-1	-1	-0	-0.1
Total 3	0	0	—	7	0	0	0	0	10^{1}	12	1	3	3	13.1	5.23	78	.293	.341	0	—	0	-1	-1	0	-0.1
● **ED VANDE BERG** Vande Berg, Edward John b: 10/26/58, Redlands, Cal. BR/TL, 6'2", 180 lbs. Deb: 4/07/82																									
1982 Sea-A	9	4	.692	**78**	0	0	0	5	76	54	5	32	60	10.4	2.37	179	.207	.298	0	—	0	14	16	2	1.8
1983 Sea-A	2	4	.333	68	0	0	0	5	64^{1}	59	6	22	49	11.5	3.36	127	.246	.312	0	—	0	5	6	0	0.5
1984 Sea-A	8	12	.400	50	17	2	0	7	130^{1}	165	18	50	71	14.8	4.76	84	.313	.373	0	—	0	-11	-11	-0	-1.1
1985 Sea-A	2	1	.667	76	0	0	0	3	67^{2}	71	4	31	34	13.7	3.72	113	.274	.354	0	—	0	3	4	1	0.4
1986 LA-N	1	5	.167	60	0	0	0	0	71^{1}	83	8	33	42	14.8	3.41	101	.290	.366	0	.000	-0	2	0	1	0.1
1987 Cle-A	1	0	1.000	55	0	0	0	0	72^{1}	96	9	21	40	14.6	5.10	89	.325	.370	0	—	0	-5	-5	0	-0.4
1988 Tex-A	2	2	.500	26	0	0	0	2	37	44	2	11	18	13.4	4.14	99	.308	.357	0	—	0	-1	-0	-1	-0.2
Total 7	25	28	.472	413	17	2	0	22	519	572	52	200	314	13.5	3.92	104	.284	.351	0	.000	-0	8	10	3	1.1

● **HY VANDENBERG** Vandenberg, Harold Harris b: 3/17/06, Abilene, Kan. BR/TR, 6'2.5", 190 lbs. Deb: 6/08/35

YEAR	TM/L	W	L	PCT	G	GS	CG	SH	SV	IP	H	HR	BB	SO	RAT	ERA	ERA+	OAV	OOB	BH	AVG	PB	PR	/A	PD	TPI
1935	Bos-A	0	0	—	3	0	0	0	0	5^1	15	1	4	2	32.1	20.25	23	.500	.559	1	1.000	0	-9	-9	0	-0.7
1937	NY-N	0	1	.000	1	1	1	0	0	8	10	0	6	2	18.0	7.88	49	.313	.421	0	.000	-1	-4	-4	1	-0.3
1938	NY-N	0	1	.000	6	1	0	0	0	18	28	2	12	7	20.0	7.50	50	.368	.455	0	.000	-1	-7	-7	1	-0.7
1939	NY-N	0	0	—	2	1	0	0	0	6^1	10	0	6	3	22.7	5.68	69	.345	.457	0	.000	-0	-1	-1	0	-0.1
1940	NY-N	1	1	.500	13	3	1	0	1	32^1	27	2	16	17	12.2	3.90	100	.227	.324	1	.125	-0	-0	-0	-0	-0.1
1944	Chi-N	7	4	.636	35	9	2	0	2	126^1	123	8	51	54	12.5	3.63	97	.255	.327	9	.237	1	-0	-1	0	-0.1
1945	*Chi-N	7	3	.700	30	7	3	1	2	95^1	91	4	33	35	12.1	3.49	105	.259	.330	4	.125	-1	3	2	0	0.1
Total	7	15	10	.600	90	22	7	1	5	291^2	304	17	128	120	13.5	4.32	85	.271	.349	15	.169	-1	-19	-21	2	-1.9

● **JOHNNY VANDER MEER** Vander Meer, John Samuel "Double No-Hit" or "The Dutch Master"
b: 11/2/14, Prospect Park, N.J. BB/TL, 6'1", 190 lbs. Deb: 4/22/37

YEAR	TM/L	W	L	PCT	G	GS	CG	SH	SV	IP	H	HR	BB	SO	RAT	ERA	ERA+	OAV	OOB	BH	AVG	PB	PR	/A	PD	TPI
1937	Cin-N	3	5	.375	19	9	4	0	0	84^1	63	0	69	52	14.3	3.84	97	.209	.359	5	.217	1	1	-1	2	0.2
1938	Cin-N★	15	10	.600	32	29	16	3	0	225^1	177	12	103	125	11.3	3.12	117	**.213**	.302	15	.181	-2	17	13	-1	1.0
1939	Cin-N☆	5	9	.357	30	21	8	0	0	129	128	7	95	102	15.7	4.67	82	.264	.387	4	.111	-1	-11	-12	-1	-1.4
1940	*Cin-N	3	1	.750	10	7	2	0	1	48	38	3	41	41	15.0	3.75	101	.211	.360	6	.300	2	1	0	0	0.2
1941	Cin-N	16	13	.552	33	32	18	6	0	226^1	172	8	126	**202**	11.9	2.82	127	.214	.321	10	.132	-3	20	19	2	2.0
1942	Cin-N★	18	12	.600	33	33	21	4	0	244	188	6	102	**186**	10.7	2.43	135	.208	.290	11	.147	-1	24	23	1	2.6
1943	Cin-N★	15	16	.484	36	36	21	3	0	289	228	5	162	**174**	12.2	2.87	116	.224	.332	13	.137	-2	17	14	3	1.7
1946	Cin-N	10	12	.455	29	25	11	4	0	204^1	175	11	78	94	11.1	3.17	105	.233	.305	18	.247	2	5	4	-2	0.5
1947	Cin-N	9	14	.391	30	29	9	3	0	186	186	11	87	79	13.4	4.40	93	.261	.343	5	.088	-3	-7	-6	-1	-0.9
1948	Cin-N	17	14	.548	33	33	14	3	0	232	204	15	124	120	12.8	3.41	115	.239	.336	11	.141	0	14	13	-1	1.3
1949	Cin-N	5	10	.333	28	24	7	3	0	159^2	172	12	85	76	14.6	4.90	85	.281	.370	4	.077	-3	-15	-13	1	-1.4
1950	Chi-N	3	4	.429	32	6	0	0	1	73^2	60	10	59	41	14.8	3.79	111	.221	.363	2	.125	-0	3	3	-0	0.3
1951	Cle-A	0	1	.000	1	1	0	0	0	3	8	0	1	2	27.0	18.00	21	.500	.529	0	.000	-0	-5	-5	1	-0.4
Total	13	119	121	.496	346	285	131	29	2	2104^2	1799	100	1132	1294	12.6	3.44	107	.232	.332	104	.152	-9	63	53	3	5.7

● **BEN Van DYKE** Van Dyke, Benjamin Harrison b: 8/15/1888, Clintonville, Pa. d: 10/22/73, Sarasota, Fla. BR/TL, 6'1", 150 lbs. Deb: 5/11/09

YEAR	TM/L	W	L	PCT	G	GS	CG	SH	SV	IP	H	HR	BB	SO	RAT	ERA	ERA+	OAV	OOB	BH	AVG	PB	PR	/A	PD	TPI
1909	Phi-N	0	0	—	2	0	0	0	0	7^1	7	0	4	5	13.5	3.68	71	.269	.367	0	.000	-0	-1	-1	-0	-0.2
1912	Bos-A	0	0	—	3	1	0	0	0	14^1	13	0	7	8	13.2	3.14	108	.245	.344	1	.250	-0	0	0	-1	0.0
Total	2	0	0	—	5	1	0	0	0	21^2	20	0	11	13	13.3	3.32	94	.253	.352	1	.143	-0	-1	-0	-1	-0.2

● **ELAM VANGILDER** Vangilder, Elam Russell b: 4/23/1896, Cape Girardeau, Mo d: 4/30/77, Cape Girardeau, Mo BR/TR, 6'1", 192 lbs. Deb: 9/18/19

YEAR	TM/L	W	L	PCT	G	GS	CG	SH	SV	IP	H	HR	BB	SO	RAT	ERA	ERA+	OAV	OOB	BH	AVG	PB	PR	/A	PD	TPI
1919	StL-A	1	0	1.000	3	1	1	0	0	13	15	0	3	6	12.5	2.08	160	.306	.346	2	.667	1	2	2	1	0.4
1920	StL-A	3	8	.273	24	13	4	0	0	104^2	131	7	40	25	15.0	5.50	71	.310	.373	4	.133	-2	-20	-18	-0	-1.9
1921	StL-A	11	12	.478	31	21	10	1	0	180^1	196	10	67	48	13.2	3.94	114	.278	.342	13	.200	-2	7	11	-0	0.8
1922	StL-A	19	13	.594	43	30	19	3	4	245	248	13	48	63	11.1	3.42	121	.270	.310	32	.344	13	17	20	-3	3.1
1923	StL-A	16	17	.485	41	35	20	4	1	282^1	276	11	120	74	12.8	3.06	136	.266	.345	24	.218	-0	29	**35**	-4	3.1
1924	StL-A	5	10	.333	43	18	5	0	1	145^1	183	10	55	49	15.3	5.64	80	.317	.385	13	.295	4	-23	-18	2	-1.3
1925	StL-A	14	8	.636	52	16	4	1	6	193^1	225	11	92	61	15.0	4.70	99	.303	.385	13	.183	-3	-7	-1	-0	-0.4
1926	StL-A	9	11	.450	42	19	8	1	1	181	196	12	98	40	14.7	5.17	83	.285	.376	11	.190	1	-23	-18	-2	-1.8
1927	StL-A	10	12	.455	44	23	12	3	1	203	245	13	102	62	15.6	4.79	91	.310	.392	19	.279	3	-15	-10	-4	-1.0
1928	Det-A	11	10	.524	38	11	7	0	5	156^1	163	4	67	43	13.4	3.91	105	.272	.348	15	.259	2	2	3	0	0.5
1929	Det-A	0	1	.000	6	0	0	0	0	11^1	16	1	7	3	18.3	6.35	68	.348	.434	0	.000	-0	-3	-3	1	-0.2
Total	11	99	102	.493	367	187	90	13	19	1715^2	1894	92	699	474	13.8	4.28	100	.288	.360	146	.243	16	-33	3	-9	1.3

● **GEORGE Van HALTREN** Van Haltren, George Edward Martin "Rip"
b: 3/30/1866, St.Louis, Mo. d: 9/29/45, Oakland, Cal. BL/TL, 5'11", 170 lbs. Deb: 6/27/1887 M♦

YEAR	TM/L	W	L	PCT	G	GS	CG	SH	SV	IP	H	HR	BB	SO	RAT	ERA	ERA+	OAV	OOB	BH	AVG	PB	PR	/A	PD	TPI
1887	Chi-N	11	7	.611	20	18	18	1	**1**	161	177	7	66	76	14.5	3.86	116	.277	.359	35	.203	-2	4	11	-0	0.7
1888	Chi-N	13	13	.500	30	24	24	4	1	245^2	263	15	60	139	12.3	3.52	86	.267	.318	90	.283	11	-18	-13	2	-0.1
1890	Bro-P	15	10	.600	28	25	23	0	2	223	272	8	89	48	15.4	4.28	104	.288	.362	126	.335	10	-1	4	3	1.4
1891	Bal-a	0	1	.000	6	1	0	0	0	23	38	1	10	7	20.3	5.09	73	.357	.432	180	.318	3	-3	-3	-0	-0.2
1892	Bal-N	0	0	—	4	0	0	0	0	14^2	28	1	7	5	21.5	9.20	37	.389	.443	168	.302	2	-10	-9	0	-0.7
1895	NY-N	0	0	—	1	0	0	0	0	5	13	0	2	1	30.6	12.60	37	.473	.540	177	.340	0	-4	-4	-0	-0.3
1896	NY-N	1	0	1.000	2	0	0	0	0	8	5	1	1	3	6.8	2.25	187	.179	.207	197	.351	1	2	2	-0	0.2
1900	NY-N	0	0	—	1	0	0	0	0	3	1	0	3	0	12.0	0.00	—	.105	.319	180	.315	0	1	1	-0	0.1
1901	NY-N	0	0	—	1	0	0	0	0	6	12	0	6	2	28.5	3.00	110	.411	.525	182	.335	0	0	0	1	0.1
Total	9	40	31	.563	93	68	65	5	4	689^1	809	33	244	281	14.5	4.05	96	.285	.353	2532	.316	27	-30	-12	6	1.2

● **TODD Van POPPEL** Van Poppel, Todd Matthew b: 12/9/71, Hinsdale, Ill. BR/TR, 6'5", 210 lbs. Deb: 9/11/91

YEAR	TM/L	W	L	PCT	G	GS	CG	SH	SV	IP	H	HR	BB	SO	RAT	ERA	ERA+	OAV	OOB	BH	AVG	PB	PR	/A	PD	TPI
1991	Oak-A	0	0	—	1	1	0	0	0	4^2	7	1	2	6	17.4	9.64	40	.368	.429	0	—	0	-3	-3	0	0.0

● **IKE Van ZANDT** Van Zandt, Charles Isaac b: 1877, Brooklyn, N.Y. d: 9/14/08, Nashua, N.H. BL, Deb: 8/05/01 ♦

YEAR	TM/L	W	L	PCT	G	GS	CG	SH	SV	IP	H	HR	BB	SO	RAT	ERA	ERA+	OAV	OOB	BH	AVG	PB	PR	/A	PD	TPI
1901	NY-N	0	0	—	2	0	0	0	0	12^2	16	0	8	2	17.8	7.11	47	.306	.408	1	.167	-0	-5	-5	-1	-0.5
1905	StL-A	0	0	—	1	0	0	0	0	6^2	2	0	2	3	6.8	0.00	—	.096	.210	75	.233	0	2	2	0	0.3
Total	2	0	0	—	3	0	0	0	0	19^1	18	0	10	5	14.0	4.66	65	.246	.352	76	.224	-0	-3	-3	-1	-0.2

● **ANDY VARGA** Varga, Andrew William b: 12/11/30, Chicago, Ill. BR/TL, 6'4", 187 lbs. Deb: 9/09/50

YEAR	TM/L	W	L	PCT	G	GS	CG	SH	SV	IP	H	HR	BB	SO	RAT	ERA	ERA+	OAV	OOB	BH	AVG	PB	PR	/A	PD	TPI
1950	Chi-N	0	0	—	1	0	0	0	0	1	0	0	1	0	9.0	0.00	—	.000	.333	0	—	0	0	0	-0	0.0
1951	Chi-N	0	0	—	2	0	0	0	0	3	2	0	6	1	24.0	3.00	136	.200	.500	0	—	0	0	0	-0	0.0
Total	2	0	0	—	3	0	0	0	0	4	2	0	7	1	20.3	2.25	183	.167	.474	0	—	0	1	1	-0	0.0

● **ROBERTO VARGAS** Vargas, Roberto Enrique b: 5/29/29, Santurce, P.R. BL/TL, 5'11", 170 lbs. Deb: 4/17/55

YEAR	TM/L	W	L	PCT	G	GS	CG	SH	SV	IP	H	HR	BB	SO	RAT	ERA	ERA+	OAV	OOB	BH	AVG	PB	PR	/A	PD	TPI
1955	Mil-N	0	0	—	25	0	0	0	2	24^2	39	4	14	13	19.7	8.76	43	.355	.432	1	.500	0	-13	-14	1	-1.2

● **BILL VARGUS** Vargus, William Fay b: 11/11/1899, N.Scituate, Mass. d: 2/12/79, Hyannis, Mass. BL/TL, 6', 165 lbs. Deb: 6/23/25

YEAR	TM/L	W	L	PCT	G	GS	CG	SH	SV	IP	H	HR	BB	SO	RAT	ERA	ERA+	OAV	OOB	BH	AVG	PB	PR	/A	PD	TPI
1925	Bos-N	1	1	.500	11	2	1	0	0	36^1	45	1	13	5	14.9	3.96	101	.302	.366	3	.250	0	1	0	0	0.0
1926	Bos-N	0	0	—	4	0	0	0	0	3	4	0	1	0	15.0	3.00	118	.333	.385	0	—	0	0	0	0	0.0
Total	2	1	1	.500	15	2	1	0	0	39^1	49	1	14	5	14.9	3.89	102	.304	.367	3	.250	0	2	0	0	0.0

● **DIKE VARNEY** Varney, Lawrence Delano (b: Lawrence Delano De Varney)
b: 8/9/1880, Dover, N.H. d: 4/23/50, Long Island City, N.Y. BL/TL, 6', 165 lbs. Deb: 7/03/02

YEAR	TM/L	W	L	PCT	G	GS	CG	SH	SV	IP	H	HR	BB	SO	RAT	ERA	ERA+	OAV	OOB	BH	AVG	PB	PR	/A	PD	TPI
1902	Cle-A	1	1	.500	3	3	0	0	0	14^2	14	0	12	7	19.0	6.14	56	.252	.427	1	.167	-0	-4	-4	0	-0.4

● **CAL VASBINDER** Vasbinder, Moses Calhoun b: 7/19/1880, Scio, Ohio d: 12/22/50, Cadiz, Ohio BR/TR, 6'2", Deb: 4/27/02

YEAR	TM/L	W	L	PCT	G	GS	CG	SH	SV	IP	H	HR	BB	SO	RAT	ERA	ERA+	OAV	OOB	BH	AVG	PB	PR	/A	PD	TPI
1902	Cle-A	0	0	—	2	0	0	0	0	5	5	1	8	2	23.4	9.00	38	.261	.478	1	.500	0	-3	-3	0	-0.2

● **RAFAEL VASQUEZ** Vasquez, Rafael b: 6/28/58, LaRomana, D.R. BR/TR, 6', 160 lbs. Deb: 4/06/79

YEAR	TM/L	W	L	PCT	G	GS	CG	SH	SV	IP	H	HR	BB	SO	RAT	ERA	ERA+	OAV	OOB	BH	AVG	PB	PR	/A	PD	TPI
1979	Sea-A	1	0	1.000	9	0	0	0	0	16	23	4	6	9	16.9	5.06	86	.354	.417	0	—	0	-2	-1	-0	-0.2

● **PORTER VAUGHAN** Vaughan, Cecil Porter "Lefty" b: 5/11/19, Stevensville, Va. BR/TL, 6'1", 178 lbs. Deb: 6/16/40

YEAR	TM/L	W	L	PCT	G	GS	CG	SH	SV	IP	H	HR	BB	SO	RAT	ERA	ERA+	OAV	OOB	BH	AVG	PB	PR	/A	PD	TPI
1940	Phi-A	2	9	.182	18	15	5	0	2	99^1	104	9	61	46	15.2	5.35	83	.264	.367	8	.235	0	-11	-10	-1	-1.0
1941	Phi-A	0	2	.000	5	3	1	0	0	22^2	32	3	12	6	17.5	7.94	53	.327	.400	1	.143	-0	-10	-9	-0	-0.9
1946	Phi-A	0	0	—	1	0	0	0	0	0	1	0	1	0	—	—	—	1.000	1.000	0	—	0	0	0	0	0.0
Total	3	2	11	.154	24	18	6	0	2	122	137	12	74	52	15.8	5.83	75	.278	.375	9	.220	-0	-20	-19	-1	-1.9

YEAR TM/L	W	L	PCT	G	GS	CG	SH	SV	IP	H	HR	BB	SO	RAT	ERA	ERA+	OAV	OOB	BH	AVG	PB	PR	/A	PD	TPI

● CHARLIE VAUGHAN Vaughan, Charles Wayne b: 10/6/47, Mercedes, Tex. BR/TL, 6'1.5", 185 lbs. Deb: 9/03/66

1966 Atl-N	1	0	1.000	1	1	0	0	0	7	8	0	3	6	14.1	2.57	141	.296	.367	1	.250	0	1	1	0	0.1
1969 Atl-N	0	0	—	1	0	0	0	0	1	1	0	3	1	36.0	18.00	20	.250	.571	0	—	0	-2	-2	0	-0.1
Total 2	1	0	1.000	2	1	0	0	0	8	9	0	6	7	16.9	4.50	81	.290	.405	1	.250	0	-1	-1	0	0.0

● ROY VAUGHN Vaughn, Clarence Leroy b: 9/4/11, Sedalia, Mo. d: 3/1/37, Martinsville, Va. BB/TR, 6'0.5", 178 lbs. Deb: 7/01/34

| 1934 Phi-A | 0 | 0 | — | 2 | 0 | 0 | 0 | 0 | 4¹ | 3 | 1 | 3 | 1 | 12.5 | 2.08 | 211 | .176 | .300 | 0 | .000 | -0 | 1 | 1 | -0 | 0.1 |

● DE WAYNE VAUGHN Vaughn, De Wayne Mathew b: 7/22/59, Oklahoma City, Okla BR/TR, 5'11", 180 lbs. Deb: 4/17/88

| 1988 Tex-A | 0 | 0 | — | 8 | 0 | 0 | 0 | 0 | 15¹ | 24 | 4 | 4 | 8 | 16.4 | 7.63 | 53 | .348 | .384 | 0 | — | 0 | -6 | -6 | -1 | -0.7 |

● FARMER VAUGHN Vaughn, Harry Francis b: 3/1/1864, Rural Dale, Ohio d: 2/21/14, Cincinnati, Ohio BR/TR, 6'3", 177 lbs. Deb: 10/07/1886 ♦

| 1891 Cin-a | 0 | 0 | — | 1 | 0 | 0 | 0 | 0 | 7 | 12 | 0 | 1 | 0 | 18.0 | 3.86 | 107 | .366 | .402 | 45 | .257 | 0 | -0 | 0 | -0 | 0.0 |

● HIPPO VAUGHN Vaughan, James Leslie b: 4/9/1888, Weatherford, Tex. d: 5/29/66, Chicago, Ill. BB/TL, 6'4", 215 lbs. Deb: 6/19/08

1908 NY-A	0	0	—	2	0	0	0	0	2¹	1	0	4	2	19.3	3.86	64	.167	.500	-0	.000	-0	-0	-0	0	0.0
1910 NY-A	13	11	.542	30	25	18	5	1	221²	190	2	58	107	10.5	1.83	146	.237	.297	10	.133	-3	17	20	-0	2.0
1911 NY-A	8	10	.444	26	18	11	0	0	145²	158	2	54	74	13.5	4.39	82	.284	.354	7	.143	-1	-17	-13	1	-1.3
1912 NY-A	2	8	.200	15	10	5	1	0	63	66	1	37	46	14.9	5.14	70	.264	.361	2	.095	-2	-13	-11	1	-1.1
Was-A	4	3	.571	12	8	4	0	0	81	75	0	43	49	13.6	2.89	115	.253	.356	6	.200	-1	4	4	2	0.5
Yr	6	11	.353	27	18	9	1	0	144	141	1	80	95	14.1	3.88	89	.258	.357	8	.157	-3	-9	-7	3	-0.6
1913 Chi-N	5	1	.833	7	6	5	2	0	56	37	0	27	36	10.6	1.45	220	.182	.284	4	.190	-1	11	11	0	1.2
1914 Chi-N	21	13	.618	42	35	23	4	1	293²	236	1	109	165	10.8	2.05	135	.222	.299	14	.144	-0	24	24	-0	2.6
1915 Chi-N	20	12	.625	41	34	18	4	1	269²	240	4	77	148	10.9	2.87	97	.238	.299	14	.163	1	-4	-3	-1	-0.3
1916 Chi-N	17	15	.531	44	35	21	4	1	294	269	4	67	144	10.5	2.20	132	.250	.298	14	.135	-4	14	23	1	2.2
1917 Chi-N	23	13	.639	41	39	27	5	0	295²	255	3	91	195	10.8	2.01	144	.235	.300	16	.160	-1	23	29	3	3.7
1918 ∗Chi-N	**22**	10	.688	35	33	27	**8**	0	290¹	216	4	76	**148**	9.3	**1.74**	**160**	**.208**	.266	23	.240	4	**33**	**34**	-1	**4.4**
1919 Chi-N	21	14	.600	38	37	25	4	1	**306²**	264	3	62	**141**	9.7	1.79	161	.234	.278	17	.173	-1	**38**	**37**	-3	4.1
1920 Chi-N	19	16	.543	40	38	24	4	0	301	301	8	81	131	11.7	2.54	126	.264	.318	22	.216	4	20	22	-2	2.6
1921 Chi-N	3	11	.214	17	14	7	0	0	109¹	153	8	31	30	15.6	6.01	64	.341	.390	10	.244	2	-27	-27	-1	-2.4
Total 13	178	137	.565	390	332	215	41	5	2730	2461	39	817	1416	11.1	2.49	120	.244	.306	159	.173	-1	123	152	-1	18.2

● AL VEACH Veach, Alvis Lindel b: 8/6/09, Maylene, Ala. d: 9/6/90, Charlotte, N.C. BR/TR, 5'11", 178 lbs. Deb: 9/22/35

| 1935 Phi-A | 0 | 2 | .000 | 2 | 2 | 1 | 0 | 0 | 10 | 20 | 1 | 9 | 3 | 26.1 | 11.70 | 39 | .417 | .509 | 0 | .000 | -1 | -8 | -8 | 0 | -0.7 |

● BOBBY VEACH Veach, Robert Hayes b: 6/29/1888, Island, Ky. d: 8/7/45, Detroit, Mich. BL/TR, 5'11", 160 lbs. Deb: 8/06/12 ♦

| 1918 Det-A | 0 | 0 | — | 1 | 0 | 0 | 0 | 1 | 2 | 2 | 0 | 2 | 0 | 18.0 | 4.50 | 59 | .286 | .444 | 139 | .279 | 0 | -0 | -0 | -0 | -0.1 |

● PEEK-A-BOO VEACH Veach, William Walter b: 6/15/1862, Indianapolis, Ind d: 11/12/37, Indianapolis, Ind. Deb: 8/24/1884 ♦

1884 KC-U	3	9	.250	12	12	12	0	0	104	95	1	10	62	9.1	2.42	114	.227	.245	11	.134	-1	7	4	1	0.3
1887 Lou-a	0	1	.000	1	1	1	0	0	9	5	1	8	2	13.0	4.00	110	.172	.351	0	.000	-0	0	0	-0	0.0
Total 2	3	10	.231	13	13	13	0	0	113	100	2	18	64	9.4	2.55	113	.223	.253	76	.215	-1	7	4	1	0.3

● BOB VEALE Veale, Robert Andrew b: 10/28/35, Birmingham, Ala. BB/TL, 6'6", 212 lbs. Deb: 4/16/62

1962 Pit-N	2	2	.500	11	6	2	1	0	45²	39	2	25	42	12.6	3.74	105	.235	.335	4	.250	1	1	1	-0	0.1
1963 Pit-N	5	2	.714	34	7	3	2	3	77²	59	1	40	68	11.6	1.04	316	.215	.317	2	.087	-0	19	**19**	0	2.2
1964 Pit-N	18	12	.600	40	38	14	1	0	279²	222	8	124	**250**	11.2	2.74	128	.217	.303	15	.156	-0	25	24	-1	2.5
1965 Pit-N☆	17	12	.586	39	37	14	7	0	266	221	5	119	276	11.7	2.84	124	.225	.313	8	.086	-1	21	20	-2	1.5
1966 Pit-N☆	16	12	.571	38	37	12	3	0	268¹	228	18	102	229	11.2	3.02	118	.232	.307	13	.138	-2	18	17	-2	1.3
1967 Pit-N	16	8	.667	33	31	6	1	0	203	184	12	119	179	13.7	3.64	93	.245	.352	3	.043	-5	-6	-6	1	-1.1
1968 Pit-N	13	14	.481	36	33	13	4	0	245¹	187	13	94	171	10.4	2.05	142	.211	.288	9	.110	-2	25	24	-2	2.4
1969 Pit-N	13	14	.481	34	34	9	1	0	225²	232	8	91	213	13.0	3.23	108	.267	.338	4	.051	-5	9	6	-0	0.1
1970 Pit-N	10	15	.400	34	32	5	1	0	202	189	15	94	178	12.7	3.92	100	.246	.331	11	.164	1	3	-0	-2	-0.1
1971 ∗Pit-N	6	0	1.000	37	0	0	0	2	46¹	59	5	24	40	16.1	6.99	48	.314	.392	3	.333	1	-18	-19	-2	-2.0
1972 Pit-N	0	0	—	5	0	0	0	0	9	10	0	7	6	17.0	6.00	55	.313	.436	0	.000	-0	-3	-3	-0	-0.3
Bos-A	2	0	1.000	6	0	0	0	2	8	2	0	3	10	5.6	0.00	—	.083	.185	0	.000	-0	3	3	0	0.3
1973 Bos-A	2	3	.400	32	0	0	0	11	36¹	37	2	24	25	12.1	3.47	116	.268	.327	0	—	0	1	2	1	0.3
1974 Bos-A	0	1	.000	18	0	0	0	2	13	15	2	4	16	13.2	5.54	69	.283	.333	0	—	-0	-3	-2	-0	-0.3
Total 13	120	95	.558	397	255	78	20	21	1926	1684	91	858	1703	12.0	3.07	113	.236	.320	72	.114	-16	96	86	-9	6.9

● LOU VEDDER Vedder, Louis Edward b: 4/20/1897, Oakville, Mich. d: 3/9/90, Lake Placid, Fla. BR/TR, 5'10.5", 175 lbs. Deb: 9/18/20

| 1920 Det-A | 0 | 0 | — | 1 | 0 | 0 | 0 | 0 | 2 | 0 | 0 | 1 | 0 | 0.0 | 0.00 | — | .000 | .000 | 0 | — | 0 | 1 | 1 | 0 | 0.1 |

● AL VEIGEL Veigel, Allen Francis b: 1/30/17, Dover, Ohio BR/TR, 6'1", 180 lbs. Deb: 9/21/39

| 1939 Bos-N | 0 | 1 | .000 | 2 | 2 | 0 | 0 | 0 | 2² | 3 | 0 | 5 | 1 | 27.0 | 6.75 | 55 | .250 | .471 | 0 | .000 | -0 | -1 | -1 | -0 | -0.1 |

● BUCKY VEIL Veil, Frederick William b: 8/2/1881, Tyrone, Pa. d: 4/16/31, Altoona, Pa. BR/TR, 5'10", 165 lbs. Deb: 4/19/03

1903 ∗Pit-N	5	3	.625	12	6	4	0	0	70²	70	1	36	20	13.8	3.82	85	.269	.362	6	.207	-0	-4	-5	-0	-0.5
1904 Pit-N	0	0	—	1	1	0	0	0	4²	4	0	4	1	17.4	5.79	47	.250	.429	1	1.000	0	-2	-2	0	-0.1
Total 2	5	3	.625	13	7	4	0	0	75¹	74	1	40	21	14.0	3.94	81	.268	.367	7	.233	0	-6	-6	-0	-0.6

● CARLOS VELAZQUEZ Velazquez, Carlos (Quinones) b: 3/22/48, Loiza, P.R. BR/TR, 5'11", 180 lbs. Deb: 7/20/73

| 1973 Mil-A | 2 | 2 | .500 | 18 | 0 | 0 | 0 | 2 | 38¹ | 46 | 5 | 10 | 12 | 13.1 | 2.58 | 146 | .297 | .339 | 0 | — | 0 | 5 | 5 | 0 | 0.5 |

● JOE VERBANIC Verbanic, Joseph Michael b: 4/24/43, Washington, Pa. BR/TR, 6', 155 lbs. Deb: 7/22/66

1966 Phi-N	1	1	.500	17	0	0	0	0	14	12	2	10	7	14.1	5.14	70	.226	.349	0	—	0	-2	-2	-0	-0.3
1967 NY-A	4	3	.571	28	6	1	1	2	80¹	74	6	21	39	10.9	2.80	112	.249	.303	2	.111	-0	4	3	2	0.5
1968 NY-A	6	7	.462	40	11	2	1	4	97	104	6	41	40	14.0	3.15	92	.284	.366	2	.080	-1	-2	-3	1	-0.3
1970 NY-A	1	0	1.000	7	0	0	0	0	15²	20	1	12	8	19.0	4.60	76	.323	.440	1	.333	0	-2	-2	1	-0.1
Total 4	12	11	.522	92	17	3	2	6	207	210	15	84	94	13.2	3.26	95	.270	.348	5	.109	-1	-2	-4	4	-0.2

● AL VERDEL Verdel, Albert Alfred "Stumpy" b: 6/10/21, Punxsutawney, Pa. BR/TR, 5'9.5", 186 lbs. Deb: 4/20/44

| 1944 Phi-N | 0 | 0 | — | 1 | 0 | 0 | 0 | 0 | 2 | 1 | 0 | 1 | 0 | 9.0 | 0.00 | — | .000 | .000 | 0 | — | 0 | 0 | 0 | -0 | 0.0 |

● RANDY VERES Veres, Randolf Ruhland b: 11/25/65, Sacramento, Cal. BR/TR, 6'3", 190 lbs. Deb: 7/01/89

1989 Mil-A	0	1	.000	3	1	0	0	0	8¹	9	0	4	8	14.0	4.32	89	.290	.371	0	—	0	-0	-0	0	0.0
1990 Mil-A	0	3	.000	26	0	0	0	1	41²	38	5	16	16	11.9	3.67	105	.247	.322	0	—	0	1	1	1	0.2
Total 2	0	4	.000	29	1	0	0	1	50	47	5	20	24	12.2	3.78	102	.254	.330	0	—	0	1	0	1	0.2

● TOMMY VEREKER Vereker, John James b: 12/2/1893, Baltimore, Md. d: 4/2/74, Baltimore, Md. 5'10", 185 lbs. Deb: 6/17/15

| 1915 Bal-F | 0 | 0 | — | 2 | 0 | 0 | 0 | 0 | 3 | 3 | 1 | 2 | 1 | 18.0 | 15.00 | 21 | .273 | .429 | 0 | — | 0 | -4 | -4 | 0 | -0.4 |

● JOHN VERHOEVEN Verhoeven, John C b: 7/3/53, Long Beach, Cal. BR/TR, 6'5", 200 lbs. Deb: 7/06/76

1976 Cal-A	0	2	.000	21	0	0	0	4	37¹	35	2	14	23	11.8	3.38	99	.252	.320	0	—	0	1	-0	1	0.2
1977 Cal-A	0	2	.000	4	0	0	0	0	4²	4	0	4	3	17.4	3.86	101	.222	.391	0	—	0	0	0	0	0.0
Chi-A	0	0	—	6	0	0	0	0	10¹	9	0	2	6	9.6	2.61	156	.231	.268	0	—	0	2	2	1	0.2

YEAR TM/L	W	L	PCT	G	GS	CG	SH	SV	IP	H	HR	BB	SO	RAT	ERA	ERA+	OAV	OOB	BH	AVG	PB	PR	/A	PD	TPI
Yr	0	2	.000	9	0	0	0	0	15	13	0	6	9	11.4	3.00	134	.224	.297	0	—	0	2	2	1	0.4
1980 Min-A	3	4	.429	44	0	0	0	0	99^2	109	10	29	42	12.7	3.97	110	.289	.345	0	—	0	1	4	0	0.1
1981 Min-A	0	0	—	25	0	0	0	0	52	57	4	14	16	12.6	3.98	99	.288	.341	0	—	0	-2	-0	0	-0.2
Total 4	3	8	.273	99	0	0	0	4	204	214	16	63	90	12.5	3.79	106	.278	.337	0	—	0	1	5	2	0.5

● JOE VERNON Vernon, Joseph Henry b: 11/25/1889, Mansfield, Mass. d: 3/13/55, Philadelphia, Pa. BR/TR, 5'11", 160 lbs. Deb: 7/20/12

YEAR TM/L	W	L	PCT	G	GS	CG	SH	SV	IP	H	HR	BB	SO	RAT	ERA	ERA+	OAV	OOB	BH	AVG	PB	PR	/A	PD	TPI
1912 Chi-N	0	0	—	1	0	0	0	0	4	4	0	6	1	24.8	11.25	30	.286	.524	0	.000	-0	-3	-4	-0	-0.3
1914 Bro-F	0	0	—	1	1	0	0	0	3^1	4	0	5	0	24.3	10.80	30	.308	.500	0	.000	-0	-3	-3	0	-0.3
Total 2	0	0	—	2	1	0	0	0	7^1	8	0	11	1	24.5	11.05	30	.296	.513	0	.000	-0	-6	-6	-0	-0.6

● BOB VESELIC Veselic, Robert Michael b: 9/27/55, Pittsburgh, Pa. BR/TR, 6', 175 lbs. Deb: 9/18/80

YEAR TM/L	W	L	PCT	G	GS	CG	SH	SV	IP	H	HR	BB	SO	RAT	ERA	ERA+	OAV	OOB	BH	AVG	PB	PR	/A	PD	TPI
1980 Min-A	0	0	—	1	0	0	0	0	4	3	1	1	2	9.0	4.50	97	.214	.267	0	—	0	-0	-0	-0	-0.3
1981 Min-A	1	1	.500	5	0	0	0	0	22^2	22	1	12	13	13.5	3.18	124	.250	.340	0	—	0	1	2	-1	0.0
Total 2	1	1	.500	6	0	0	0	0	26^2	25	2	13	15	12.8	3.38	119	.245	.330	0	—	0	1	2	-1	-0.3

● LEE VIAU Viau, Leon A. b: 7/5/1866, Corinth, Vt. d: 12/17/47, Hopewell, N.J. BR/TR, 5'4", 160 lbs. Deb: 4/22/1888

YEAR TM/L	W	L	PCT	G	GS	CG	SH	SV	IP	H	HR	BB	SO	RAT	ERA	ERA+	OAV	OOB	BH	AVG	PB	PR	/A	PD	TPI
1888 Cin-a	27	14	.659	42	42	42	1	0	387^2	331	7	110	164	10.7	2.65	120	.222	.285	13	.087	-11	18	23	-2	0.8
1889 Cin-a	22	20	.524	47	42	38	1	1	373	379	8	136	152	12.7	3.79	103	.255	.322	21	.143	-9	3	5	-3	-0.5
1890 Cin-N	7	5	.583	13	10	7	1	0	90	97	8	39	41	13.7	4.50	79	.267	.339	5	.139	-2	-9	-9	1	-0.9
Cle-N	4	9	.308	13	13	13	1	0	107	101	4	42	30	12.4	3.36	106	.242	.318	7	.163	-2	2	3	-1	0.0
Yr	11	14	.440	26	23	20	2	0	197	198	12	81	71	13.0	3.88	92	.253	.327	12	.152	-4	-7	-7	0	-0.9
1891 Cle-N	18	17	.514	45	38	31	0	0	343^2	367	3	138	130	13.6	3.01	115	.263	.336	23	.160	-3	13	17	1	1.3
1892 Cle-N	0	1	.000	1	1	0	0	0	1	5	0	1	0	54.0	36.00	9	.625	.667	0	—	0	-4	-4	0	-0.3
Lou-N	4	11	.267	16	15	14	1	0	130^2	156	7	56	36	14.6	3.99	77	.285	.351	13	.197	1	-10	-13	2	-0.9
Bos-N	1	0	1.000	1	1	1	0	0	9	5	0	4	1	9.0	0.00	—	.156	.250	0	.000	-1	3	4	-0	0.3
Yr	5	12	.294	18	17	15	1	0	140^2	166	7	61	37	14.5	3.97	78	.282	.350	13	.188	0	-11	-14	2	-0.9
Total 5	83	77	.519	178	162	146	5	1	1442	1441	37	526	554	12.6	3.33	105	.251	.320	82	.139	-27	16	25	-1	-0.2

● RUBE VICKERS Vickers, Harry Porter b: 5/17/1878, St.Marys, Ont., Can d: 12/9/58, Belleville, Mich. BL/TR, 6'2", 225 lbs. Deb: 9/21/02

YEAR TM/L	W	L	PCT	G	GS	CG	SH	SV	IP	H	HR	BB	SO	RAT	ERA	ERA+	OAV	OOB	BH	AVG	PB	PR	/A	PD	TPI
1902 Cin-N	0	3	.000	3	3	3	0	0	21	31	0	8	6	17.1	6.00	50	.342	.401	4	.364	1	-8	-7	-1	-0.6
1903 Bro-N	0	1	.000	4	1	1	0	0	14	27	0	9	5	23.8	10.93	29	.415	.493	1	.100	-1	-12	-12	1	-1.0
1907 Phi-A	2	2	.500	10	4	3	1	0	50^1	44	1	12	21	10.2	3.40	77	.237	.287	3	.150	-1	-5	-4	0	-0.6
1908 Phi-A	18	19	.486	53	34	21	6	1	317	264	0	71	156	9.8	2.21	116	.231	.282	17	.160	-1	6	12	-3	0.9
1909 Phi-A	2	2	.500	18	3	1	0	1	55^2	60	0	19	25	13.1	3.40	71	.274	.338	1	.063	-1	-6	-6	-1	-1.0
Total 5	22	27	.449	88	45	29	7	2	458	426	1	119	213	11.0	2.93	89	.250	.305	26	.160	-3	-23	-17	-4	-2.3

● TOM VICKERY Vickery, Thomas Gill "Vinegar Tom" b: 5/5/1867, Milford, N.J. d: 3/21/21, Burlington, N.J. TR, 6', 170 lbs. Deb: 4/21/1890

YEAR TM/L	W	L	PCT	G	GS	CG	SH	SV	IP	H	HR	BB	SO	RAT	ERA	ERA+	OAV	OOB	BH	AVG	PB	PR	/A	PD	TPI
1890 Phi-N	24	22	.522	46	46	41	2	0	382	405	8	184	162	14.6	3.44	106	.264	.353	33	.208	-4	6	9	-2	0.2
1891 Chi-N	6	5	.545	14	12	7	0	0	79^2	72	4	44	39	13.7	4.07	82	.232	.337	7	.179	-1	-6	-7	1	-0.6
1892 Bal-N	8	10	.444	24	21	17	0	0	176	189	3	87	49	14.6	3.53	97	.264	.351	18	.243	2	-5	-2	-2	-0.1
1893 Phi-N	4	5	.444	13	11	7	0	0	80	100	1	37	15	16.1	5.40	85	.297	.377	11	.314	1	-7	-7	2	-0.3
Total 4	42	42	.500	97	90	72	2	0	717^2	766	16	352	265	14.6	3.75	98	.264	.354	69	.225	-3	-12	-6	-1	-0.8

● BOB VINES Vines, Robert Earl b: 2/25/1897, Waxahachie, Tex. d: 10/18/82, Orlando, Fla. BR/TR, 6'4", 184 lbs. Deb: 9/03/24

YEAR TM/L	W	L	PCT	G	GS	CG	SH	SV	IP	H	HR	BB	SO	RAT	ERA	ERA+	OAV	OOB	BH	AVG	PB	PR	/A	PD	TPI
1924 StL-N	0	0	—	2	0	0	0	0	10^2	23	1	0	0	19.4	9.28	41	.426	.426	0	.000	-1	-6	-7	-0	-0.6
1925 Phi-N	0	0	—	3	0	0	0	0	4	9	0	3	0	27.0	11.25	42	.450	.522	0	—	0	-3	-3	0	-0.3
Total 2	0	0	—	5	0	0	0	0	14^2	32	1	3	0	21.5	9.82	41	.432	.455	0	.000	-1	-10	-9	-0	-0.9

● DAVE VINEYARD Vineyard, David Kent b: 2/25/41, Clay, W.Va. BR/TR, 6'3", 195 lbs. Deb: 7/18/64

YEAR TM/L	W	L	PCT	G	GS	CG	SH	SV	IP	H	HR	BB	SO	RAT	ERA	ERA+	OAV	OOB	BH	AVG	PB	PR	/A	PD	TPI
1964 Bal-A	2	5	.286	19	6	1	0	0	54	57	5	27	50	14.0	4.17	86	.274	.357	2	.167	0	-3	-4	-1	-0.4

● BILL VINTON Vinton, William Miller b: 4/27/1865, Winthrop, Mass. d: 9/3/1893, Pawtucket, R.I. BR/TR, 6'1", 160 lbs. Deb: 7/03/1884

YEAR TM/L	W	L	PCT	G	GS	CG	SH	SV	IP	H	HR	BB	SO	RAT	ERA	ERA+	OAV	OOB	BH	AVG	PB	PR	/A	PD	TPI
1884 Phi-N	10	10	.500	21	21	20	0	0	182	166	6	35	105	9.9	2.23	134	.220	.255	9	.115	-6	15	15	3	1.2
1885 Phi-N	3	6	.333	9	9	8	0	0	77	90	0	23	21	13.2	3.04	92	.269	.317	2	.067	-3	-2	-2	0	-0.5
Phi-a	4	3	.571	7	7	6	2	0	55	46	1	15	34	10.6	2.45	140	.200	.261	4	.154	-0	5	6	-0	0.5
Total 2	17	19	.472	37	37	34	2	0	314	302	7	73	160	10.9	2.46	122	.229	.272	15	.112	-10	18	19	3	1.2

● FRANK VIOLA Viola, Frank John b: 4/19/60, Hempstead, N.Y. BL/TL, 6'4", 209 lbs. Deb: 6/06/82

YEAR TM/L	W	L	PCT	G	GS	CG	SH	SV	IP	H	HR	BB	SO	RAT	ERA	ERA+	OAV	OOB	BH	AVG	PB	PR	/A	PD	TPI
1982 Min-A	4	10	.286	22	22	3	1	0	126	152	22	38	84	13.6	5.21	81	.302	.351	0	—	0	-16	-14	-1	-1.4
1983 Min-A	7	15	.318	35	34	4	0	0	210	242	34	92	127	14.7	5.49	77	.287	.363	0	—	0	-33	-29	-1	-2.9
1984 Min-A	18	12	.600	35	35	10	4	0	257^2	225	28	73	149	10.5	3.21	131	.233	.290	0	—	0	22	28	-3	2.7
1985 Min-A	18	14	.563	36	36	9	0	0	250^2	262	26	68	135	11.9	4.09	108	.268	.316	0	—	0	1	9	-2	0.6
1986 Min-A	16	13	.552	37	37	7	1	0	245^2	257	37	83	191	12.6	4.51	96	.268	.329	0	—	0	-9	-5	-3	-0.8
1987 *Min-A	17	10	.630	36	36	7	1	0	251^2	230	29	66	197	10.8	2.90	159	.241	.294	0	—	0	44	48	-1	4.8
1988 Min-A★	**24**	7	**.774**	35	35	7	2	0	255^1	236	20	54	193	10.3	2.64	154	.245	.288	0	—	0	38	**40**	-1	4.2
1989 Min-A	8	12	.400	24	24	7	1	0	175^2	171	17	47	138	11.3	3.79	109	.256	.308	0	—	0	2	7	0	0.7
NY-N	5	5	.500	12	12	2	1	0	85^1	75	5	27	73	10.9	3.38	97	.236	.298	3	.130	-0	1	-1	-1	-0.2
1990 NY-N★	20	12	.625	35	35	7	3	0	**249^2**	227	15	60	182	10.4	2.67	140	.242	.289	13	.153	-1	**31**	30	-0	3.1
1991 NY-N★	13	15	.464	35	35	3	0	0	231^1	259	25	54	132	12.2	3.97	92	.286	.327	9	.127	-1	-7	-8	-1	-1.1
1992 Bos-A	13	12	.520	35	35	6	1	0	238	214	13	89	121	11.7	3.44	121	.242	.316	0	—	0	13	19	3	1.8
Total 11	163	137	.543	377	376	72	15	0	2577	2550	271	751	1722	11.7	3.70	112	.258	.313	25	.140	-2	87	122	-11	11.5

● JAKE VIRTUE Virtue, Jacob Kitchline "Guesses" b: 3/2/1865, Philadelphia, Pa. d: 2/3/43, Camden, N.J. BB/TR, 5'9.5", 165 lbs. Deb: 7/21/1890 ♦

YEAR TM/L	W	L	PCT	G	GS	CG	SH	SV	IP	H	HR	BB	SO	RAT	ERA	ERA+	OAV	OOB	BH	AVG	PB	PR	/A	PD	TPI
1893 Cle-N	0	0	—	1	0	0	0	0	5	3	0	3	2	10.8	1.80	271	.169	.289	100	.265	0	2	2	-0	0.1
1894 Cle-N	0	0	—	1	0	0	0	0	0	0	0	1	0	—	—	—	—	1.000	23	.258	0	0	0	0	0.0
Total 2	0	0	—	2	0	0	0	0	5	3	0	4	2	12.6	1.80	271	.169	.321	483	.274	0	2	2	-0	0.1

● JOE VITELLI Vitelli, Antonio Joseph b: 4/12/08, Mckee's Rocks, Pa. d: 2/7/67, Pittsburgh, Pa. BR/TR, 6'1", 195 lbs. Deb: 5/30/44 ♦

YEAR TM/L	W	L	PCT	G	GS	CG	SH	SV	IP	H	HR	BB	SO	RAT	ERA	ERA+	OAV	OOB	BH	AVG	PB	PR	/A	PD	TPI
1944 Pit-N	0	0	—	4	0	0	0	0	7	5	1	7	2	16.7	2.57	145	.185	.371	0	.000	-0	1	1	0	0.1

● JOE VITKO Vitko, Joseph John b: 2/7/70, Somerville, N.J. BR/TR, 6'8", 210 lbs. Deb: 9/18/92

YEAR TM/L	W	L	PCT	G	GS	CG	SH	SV	IP	H	HR	BB	SO	RAT	ERA	ERA+	OAV	OOB	BH	AVG	PB	PR	/A	PD	TPI
1992 NY-N	0	1	.000	3	1	0	0	0	4^2	12	1	1	6	25.1	13.50	26	.444	.464	0	—	0	-5	-5	-0	-0.5

● OLLIE VOIGT Voigt, Olen Edward "Ode" b: 1/29/1900, Wheaton, Ill. d: 4/7/70, Scottsdale, Ariz. BL/TR, 6'1", 170 lbs. Deb: 4/19/24

YEAR TM/L	W	L	PCT	G	GS	CG	SH	SV	IP	H	HR	BB	SO	RAT	ERA	ERA+	OAV	OOB	BH	AVG	PB	PR	/A	PD	TPI
1924 StL-A	1	0	1.000	8	1	0	0	0	16^1	21	1	13	4	18.7	5.51	82	.356	.472	1	.250	1	-2	-2	1	0.0

● BILL VOISELLE Voiselle, William Symmes "Big Bill" or "Ninety-Six" b: 1/29/19, Greenwood, S.C. BR/TR, 6'4", 200 lbs. Deb: 9/01/42

YEAR TM/L	W	L	PCT	G	GS	CG	SH	SV	IP	H	HR	BB	SO	RAT	ERA	ERA+	OAV	OOB	BH	AVG	PB	PR	/A	PD	TPI
1942 NY-N	0	1	.000	2	1	0	0	0	9	6	1	4	5	10.0	2.00	168	.176	.263	0	.000	0	1	1	0	0.2
1943 NY-N	1	2	.333	4	4	3	0	0	31	18	1	14	19	9.3	2.03	170	.154	.244	1	.111	-1	5	5	-1	0.4
1944 NY-N☆	21	16	.568	43	41	25	1	0	**312^2**	276	31	118	**161**	11.5	3.02	121	.232	.303	22	.210	3	20	22	-3	2.3
1945 NY-N†	14	14	.500	41	35	14	4	0	232^1	249	15	97	115	13.6	4.49	87	.273	.345	10	.127	-3	-18	-15	-0	-1.7
1946 NY-N	9	15	.375	36	25	10	2	0	178	171	14	85	89	12.9	3.74	92	.248	.330	9	.164	-1	-7	-6	-0	-0.8
1947 NY-N	1	4	.200	11	5	1	0	0	42^2	44	4	22	20	14.1	4.64	88	.284	.376	2	.133	-1	-3	-3	-0	-0.3
Bos-N	8	7	.533	22	20	7	0	0	131^1	146	10	51	59	13.6	4.32	90	.280	.345	9	.170	-1	-4	-6	1	-0.6
Yr	9	11	.450	33	25	8	0	0	174	190	14	73	79	13.7	4.40	90	.280	.351	11	.162	-1	-7	-9	1	-0.9
1948 *Bos-N	13	13	.500	37	30	9	2	2	215^2	226	18	90	89	13.3	3.63	106	.272	.345	7	.097	-4	8	5	-3	-0.1

YEAR	TM/L	W	L	PCT	G	GS	CG	SH	SV	IP	H	HR	BB	SO	RAT	ERA	ERA+	OAV	OOB	BH	AVG	PB	PR	/A	PD	TPI
1949	Bos-N	7	8	.467	30	22	5	4	1	169^{1}	170	14	78	63	13.2	4.04	94	.263	.343	7	.115	-2	0	-5	1	-0.6
1950	Chi-N	0	4	.000	19	7	0	0	0	51^{1}	64	7	29	25	16.5	5.79	73	.303	.390	1	.077	-1	-9	-9	-1	-1.0
Total	9	74	84	.468	245	190	74	13	3	1373^{1}	1370	115	588	645	12.9	3.83	98	.258	.334	68	.147	-10	-6	-10	-6	-2.2
● JAKE VOLZ	Volz, Jacob Phillip "Silent Jake" b: 4/4/1878, San Antonio, Tex. d: 8/11/62, San Antonio, Tex. BR/TR, 5'10", 175 lbs. Deb: 9/28/01																									
1901	Bos-A	1	0	1.000	1	1	1	0	0	7	6	2	9	5	19.3	9.00	39	.229	.426	0	.000	-1	-4	-4	-1	-0.4
1905	Bos-N	0	2	.000	3	2	0	0	0	8^{2}	12	0	8	1	21.8	10.38	30	.364	.500	0	.000	-0	-7	-7	-1	-0.7
1908	Cin-N	1	2	.333	7	4	1	0	0	22^{2}	16	1	12	6	11.9	3.57	65	.195	.313	1	.250	0	-3	-3	-1	-0.5
Total	3	2	4	.333	11	7	2	0	0	38^{1}	34	3	29	12	15.5	6.10	44	.241	.381	1	.100	-1	-14	-14	-2	-1.6
● TONY Von FRICKEN	Von Fricken, Anthony b: 5/30/1870, Brooklyn, N.Y. d: 3/22/47, Troy, N.Y. BB/TR, 5'11.5", 160 lbs. Deb: 5/09/1890																									
1890	Bos-N	0	1	.000	1	1	1	0	0	8	23	0	8	2	34.9	10.13	37	.493	.567	0	.000	-1	-6	-6	-0	-0.5
● BRUCE Von HOFF	Von Hoff, Bruce Frederick b: 11/17/43, Oakland, Cal. BR/TR, 6', 187 lbs. Deb: 9/28/65																									
1965	Hou-N	0	0	—	3	0	0	0	0	3	3	0	2	1	15.0	9.00	37	.250	.357	0	—	0	-2	-2	-0	-0.2
1967	Hou-N	0	3	.000	10	10	0	0	0	50^{1}	52	3	28	22	14.3	4.83	69	.268	.360	1	.067	-1	-8	-8	-1	-1.0
Total	2	0	3	.000	13	10	0	0	0	53^{1}	55	3	30	23	14.3	5.06	65	.267	.360	1	.067	-1	-10	-10	-1	-1.2
● DAVE Von OHLEN	Von Ohlen, David b: 10/25/58, Flushing, N.Y. BL/TL, 6'2", 200 lbs. Deb: 5/13/83																									
1983	StL-N	3	2	.600	46	0	0	0	2	68^{1}	71	3	25	21	13.0	3.29	110	.280	.351	1	.143	0	3	2	-0	0.2
1984	StL-N	1	0	1.000	27	0	0	0	1	34^{2}	39	0	8	19	12.2	3.12	111	.300	.341	1	1.000	0	2	1	1	0.3
1985	Cle-A	3	2	.600	26	0	0	0	0	43^{1}	47	3	20	12	13.9	2.91	142	.288	.366	0	—	0	6	6	1	0.6
1986	Oak-A	0	3	.000	24	0	0	0	1	15^{1}	18	0	7	4	14.7	3.52	110	.300	.373	0	—	0	1	1	0	0.2
1987	Oak-A	0	0	—	4	0	0	0	0	6	10	1	1	3	16.5	7.50	55	.400	.423	0	—	0	-2	-2	-0	-0.2
Total	5	7	7	.500	127	0	0	0	4	167^{2}	185	7	61	59	13.4	3.33	113	.293	.358	2	.250	1	9	8	1	1.1
● CY VORHEES	Vorhees, Henry Bert b: 9/30/1874, Lodi, Ohio d: 2/8/10, Perry, Ohio 6'3", 200 lbs. Deb: 4/17/02																									
1902	Phi-N	3	3	.500	10	4	3	1	0	53^{2}	63	1	20	24	14.1	3.86	73	.292	.355	7	.350	2	-6	-6	-1	-0.5
	Was-A	0	1	.000	1	1	1	0	0	8	10	0	2	1	13.5	4.50	82	.306	.346	2	.667	1	-1	-1	-0	0.0
Total	1	3	4	.429	11	5	4	1	0	61^{2}	73	1	22	25	14.0	3.94	74	.294	.354	9	.391	3	-7	-7	-1	-0.5
● ED VOSBERG	Vosberg, Edward John b: 9/28/61, Tucson, Ariz. BL/TL, 6'1", 190 lbs. Deb: 9/17/86																									
1986	SD-N	0	1	.000	5	3	0	0	0	13^{2}	17	1	9	8	17.1	6.59	55	.304	.400	0	.000	-0	-4	-4	-0	-0.5
1990	SF-N	1	1	.500	18	0	0	0	0	24^{1}	21	3	12	12	12.2	5.55	66	.233	.324	0	—	0	-5	-5	0	-0.5
Total	2	1	2	.333	23	3	0	0	0	38	38	4	21	20	14.0	5.92	62	.260	.353	0	.000	-0	-9	-10	-0	-1.0
● ALEX VOSS	Voss, Alexander b: 5/1855, Roswell, Ga. d: 8/31/06, Cincinnati, Ohio BR/TR, 6'1", 180 lbs. Deb: 4/17/1884 ♦																									
1884	Was-U	5	14	.263	27	20	18	0	0	186^{1}	206	2	32	112	11.5	3.57	83	.262	.291	47	.192	-3	-12	-13	3	-1.1
	KC-U	0	6	.000	7	6	6	0	0	53	74	2	7	17	13.8	4.25	65	.310	.329	4	.089	-2	-7	-9	1	-0.9
	Yr	5	20	.200	34	26	24	0	0	239^{1}	280	4	39	129	12.0	3.72	78	.273	.300	51	.176	-6	-19	-21	3	-2.0
● RIP VOWINKEL	Vowinkel, John Henry b: 11/18/1884, Oswego, N.Y. d: 7/13/66, Oswego, N.Y. BR/TR, 5'10", 195 lbs. Deb: 9/05/05																									
1905	Cin-N	3	3	.500	6	6	4	0	0	45^{1}	52	2	10	7	12.5	4.17	79	.302	.344	1	.071	-0	-6	-4	-2	-0.6
● PETE VUCKOVICH	Vuckovich, Peter Dennis b: 10/27/52, Johnstown, Pa. BR/TR, 6'4", 220 lbs. Deb: 8/03/75																									
1975	Chi-A	0	1	.000	4	2	0	0	0	10^{1}	17	0	7	5	20.9	13.06	30	.386	.471	0	—	0	-11	-11	0	-1.0
1976	Chi-A	7	4	.636	33	7	1	0	0	110^{1}	122	3	60	62	15.2	4.65	77	.287	.380	0	—	0	-14	-13	0	-1.4
1977	Tor-A	7	7	.500	53	8	3	1	8	148	143	13	59	123	12.6	3.47	121	.257	.333	0	—	0	10	12	1	1.2
1978	StL-N	12	12	.500	45	23	6	2	1	198^{1}	187	9	59	149	11.3	2.54	138	.253	.310	8	.138	-1	23	21	2	2.4
1979	StL-N	15	10	.600	34	32	9	0	0	233	229	22	64	145	11.4	3.59	105	.260	.312	12	.152	-2	4	4	-1	0.1
1980	StL-N	12	9	.571	32	30	7	3	1	222^{1}	203	18	68	132	11.1	3.40	109	.247	.306	13	.183	1	5	7	-1	0.9
1981	*Mil-A	**14**	4	**.778**	24	23	2	1	0	149^{2}	137	9	57	84	11.9	3.55	96	.249	.324	0	—	0	2	-2	1	0.0
1982	*Mil-A	18	6	**.750**	30	30	9	1	0	223^{2}	234	14	102	105	13.7	3.34	113	.275	.356	0	—	0	18	11	1	1.3
1983	Mil-A	0	2	.000	3	3	0	0	0	14^{2}	15	0	10	10	16.0	4.91	76	.259	.377	0	—	0	-1	-2	-0	-0.2
1985	Mil-A	6	10	.375	22	22	1	0	0	112^{2}	134	16	48	55	15.1	5.51	76	.298	.374	0	—	0	-17	-17	-1	-1.7
1986	Mil-A	2	4	.333	6	6	0	0	0	32^{1}	33	3	11	12	12.8	3.06	141	.273	.343	0	—	0	4	5	0	0.5
Total	11	93	69	.574	286	186	38	8	10	1455^{1}	1454	107	545	882	12.6	3.66	103	.264	.334	33	.159	-2	22	16	2	2.1
● PAUL WACHTEL	Wachtel, Paul Horine b: 4/30/1888, Myersville, Md. d: 12/15/64, San Antonio, Tex. BR/TR, 5'11", 175 lbs. Deb: 9/18/17																									
1917	Bro-N	0	0	—	2	0	0	0	0	6	9	0	4	3	19.5	10.50	27	.375	.464	1	.333	0	-5	-5	-0	-0.5
● CHARLIE WACKER	Wacker, Charles James b: 12/8/1883, Jeffersonville, Ind d: 8/7/48, Evansville, Ind. BL/TL, 5'9", Deb: 4/28/09																									
1909	Pit-N	0	0	—	1	0	0	0	0	2	2	0	1	0	13.5	0.00	—	.400	.500	0	—	0	1	1	0	0.1
● RUBE WADDELL	Waddell, George Edward b: 10/13/1876, Bradford, Pa. d: 4/1/14, San Antonio, Tex. BR/TL, 6'1.5", 196 lbs. Deb: 9/08/1897 H																									
1897	Lou-N	0	1	.000	2	1	1	0	0	14	17	0	6	5	15.4	3.21	133	.297	.374	0	.000	-1	2	2	0	0.1
1899	Lou-N	7	2	.778	10	9	9	1	1	79	69	4	14	44	10.4	3.08	125	.235	.288	8	.235	-0	7	7	-1	0.6
1900	*Pit-N	8	13	.381	29	22	16	2	0	208^{2}	176	3	55	130	10.5	**2.37**	**153**	**.229**	.290	14	.173	-2	31	29	1	2.7
1901	Pit-N	0	2	.000	2	2	0	0	0	7^{2}	10	0	9	4	23.5	9.39	35	.313	.476	0	.000	-0	-5	-5	0	-0.5
	Chi-N	14	14	.500	29	28	26	0	0	243^{2}	239	5	66	168	11.6	2.81	115	.255	.309	25	.255	6	14	12	3	2.2
	Yr	14	16	.467	31	30	26	0	0	251^{1}	249	5	75	172	11.9	3.01	108	.257	.315	25	.248	6	9	6	4	1.7
1902	Phi-A	24	7	.774	33	27	26	3	0	276^{1}	224	7	64	**210**	9.7	2.05	179	.222	.275	32	.286	7	47	50	-0	**5.9**
1903	Phi-A	21	16	.568	39	38	**34**	4	0	324	274	3	85	**302**	10.2	2.44	125	.229	.284	14	.122	-7	19	22	0	1.6
1904	Phi-A	25	19	.568	46	46	39	8	0	383	307	5	91	**349**	9.7	1.62	**165**	.221	.275	17	.122	-7	**42**	45	2	4.6
1905	Phi-A	**27**	10	**.730**	**46**	34	27	7	0	328^{2}	231	5	90	**287**	9.1	**1.48**	**180**	**.199**	.263	20	.172	-1	**43**	**43**	-0	4.8
1906	Phi-A	15	17	.469	43	34	22	8	0	272^{2}	221	1	92	**196**	10.7	2.21	123	.225	.298	14	.163	-0	15	16	-2	1.5
1907	Phi-A	19	13	.594	44	33	20	7	0	284^{2}	234	2	73	**232**	10.1	2.15	121	.226	.286	12	.119	-6	13	15	-2	0.7
1908	StL-A	19	14	.576	43	36	25	5	3	285^{2}	223	0	90	232	10.1	1.89	127	.213	.231	10	.110	-2	16	16	-1	1.6
1909	StL-A	11	14	.440	31	28	16	5	3	220^{1}	204	1	57	141	10.9	2.37	102	.267	.323	5	.067	-5	3	1	-1	-0.6
1910	StL-A	3	1	.750	10	2	0	0	1	33	31	1	11	16	11.7	3.55	70	.242	.307	1	.111	-0	-4	-4	-1	-0.6
Total	13	193	143	.574	407	340	261	50	5	2961^{1}	2460	37	803	2316	10.3	2.16	135	.228	.288	172	.161	-19	241	248	-1	24.6
● TOM WADDELL	Waddell, Thomas David b: 9/17/58, Dundee, Scotland BR/TR, 6'1", 185 lbs. Deb: 4/15/84																									
1984	Cle-A	7	4	.636	58	0	0	0	6	97	68	12	37	59	9.8	3.06	133	.202	.283	0	—	0	10	11	-1	1.0
1985	Cle-A	8	6	.571	49	9	1	0	9	112^{2}	104	20	39	53	11.5	4.87	85	.246	.312	0	—	0	-9	-9	0	-0.9
1987	Cle-A	0	1	.000	6	0	0	0	0	5^{2}	7	1	7	6	23.8	14.29	32	.292	.469	0	—	0	-6	-6	-0	-0.6
Total	3	15	11	.577	113	9	1	0	15	215^{1}	179	33	83	118	11.1	4.30	96	.229	.305	0	—	0	-5	-4	-1	-0.5
● BEN WADE	Wade, Benjamin Styron b: 11/26/22, Morehead City, N.C BR/TR, 6'3", 205 lbs. Deb: 4/30/48 F																									
1948	Chi-N	0	1	.000	2	0	0	0	0	5	4	0	4	1	14.4	7.20	54	.211	.348	0	.000	-0	-2	-2	0	-0.2
1952	Bro-N	11	9	.550	37	24	5	1	3	180	166	19	94	118	13.1	3.60	101	.246	.340	7	.117	1	3	1	-2	0.0
1953	*Bro-N	7	5	.583	32	0	0	0	3	90^{1}	79	15	33	65	11.6	3.79	113	.232	.308	4	.167	0	5	5	-2	0.3
1954	Bro-N	1	1	.500	23	0	0	0	3	45	62	9	21	25	16.6	8.20	50	.339	.407	0	.000	-1	-21	-21	-1	-2.1
	StL-N	0	0	—	13	0	0	0	0	23	27	3	15	19	17.2	5.48	75	.303	.415	0	.000	-0	-4	-3	0	-0.4
	Yr	1	1	.500	36	0	0	0	3	68	89	12	36	44	16.8	7.28	56	.319	.401	0	.000	-1	-24	-24	-1	-2.5
1955	Pit-N	0	1	.000	11	1	0	0	1	28	26	3	14	7	13.2	3.21	128	.252	.347	0	.000	-0	3	3	-0	0.2

YEAR	TM/L	W	L	PCT	G	GS	CG	SH	SV	IP	H	HR	BB	SO	RAT	ERA	ERA+	OAV	OOB	BH	AVG	PB	PR	/A	PD	TPI
Total	5	19	17	.528	118	25	5	1	10	371^1	364	49	181	235	13.4	4.34	90	.259	.347	11	.112	-0	-16	-18	-5	-2.2

● JAKE WADE Wade, Jacob Fields "Whistling Jake" b: 4/1/12, Morehead City, N.C. BL/TL, 6'2", 175 lbs. Deb: 4/22/36 F

YEAR	TM/L	W	L	PCT	G	GS	CG	SH	SV	IP	H	HR	BB	SO	RAT	ERA	ERA+	OAV	OOB	BH	AVG	PB	PR	/A	PD	TPI
1936	Det-A	4	5	.444	13	11	4	1	0	78^1	93	7	52	30	16.8	5.29	94	.296	.398	5	.172	-0	-2	-3	-1	-0.3
1937	Det-A	7	10	.412	33	25	7	1	0	165^1	160	13	107	69	14.7	5.39	87	.257	.368	11	.186	-1	-14	-13	1	-1.3
1938	Det-A	3	2	.600	27	2	0	0	0	70	73	9	48	23	15.6	6.56	76	.268	.378	1	.048	-2	-14	-12	0	-1.3
1939	Bos-A	1	4	.200	20	6	1	0	0	47^2	68	1	37	21	19.8	6.23	76	.358	.463	0	.000	-2	-9	-8	-0	-0.9
	StL-A	0	2	.000	4	2	1	0	0	16^1	26	1	19	9	24.8	11.02	44	.356	.489	0	.000	-1	-12	-11	0	-1.0
	Yr	1	6	.143	24	8	2	0	0	64	94	2	56	30	21.1	7.45	64	.357	.470	0	.000	-3	-20	-19	0	-1.9
1942	Chi-A	5	5	.500	15	10	3	0	0	85^2	84	2	56	32	14.7	4.10	88	.255	.363	7	.241	1	-4	-5	1	-0.3
1943	Chi-A	3	7	.300	21	9	3	1	0	83^2	66	3	54	41	13.3	3.01	111	.222	.349	4	.148	-0	3	3	-1	0.2
1944	Chi-A	2	4	.333	19	5	1	0	2	74^2	75	3	41	35	14.0	4.82	71	.261	.354	7	.292	1	-12	-12	-2	-1.3
1946	NY-A	2	1	.667	13	1	0	0	1	35^1	33	2	14	22	12.2	2.29	151	.250	.327	1	.111	-0	5	5	0	0.5
	Was-A	0	0	—	6	0	0	0	0	11^1	12	1	12	9	19.1	4.76	70	.279	.436	0	.000	-0	-2	-2	0	-0.2
	Yr	2	1	.667	19	1	0	0	1	46^2	45	3	26	31	13.7	2.89	118	.256	.351	1	.100	-0	3	3	1	0.3
Total	8	27	40	.403	171	71	20	3	3	668^1	690	42	440	291	15.3	5.00	84	.269	.378	36	.167	-5	-60	-58	-1	-5.9

● JACK WADSWORTH Wadsworth, John L. b: 12/17/1867, Wellington, Ohio d: 7/8/41, Elyria, Ohio BL/TR, 180 lbs. Deb: 5/01/1890

YEAR	TM/L	W	L	PCT	G	GS	CG	SH	SV	IP	H	HR	BB	SO	RAT	ERA	ERA+	OAV	OOB	BH	AVG	PB	PR	/A	PD	TPI
1890	Cle-N	2	16	.111	20	19	19	0	0	169^2	202	6	81	26	15.3	5.20	69	.287	.365	12	.176	-3	-31	-30	-1	-2.8
1893	Bal-N	0	3	.000	3	3	0	0	0	16	37	0	8	2	25.3	11.25	42	.439	.487	3	.429	1	-12	-12	-1	-0.8
1894	Lou-N	4	18	.182	22	22	20	0	0	173	261	10	103	57	19.1	7.60	67	.344	.425	19	.257	0	-44	-48	-0	-3.4
1895	Lou-N	0	1	.000	2	0	0	0	0	9	24	0	7	2	31.0	16.00	29	.479	.543	1	.250	-0	-11	-11	0	-0.8
Total	4	6	38	.136	47	44	39	0	0	367^2	524	16	199	87	17.9	6.85	64	.328	.406	35	.229	-2	-97	-101	-1	-7.8

● CHARLIE WAGNER Wagner, Charles Thomas "Broadway" b: 12/3/12, Reading, Pa. BR/TR, 5'11", 170 lbs. Deb: 4/19/38 C

YEAR	TM/L	W	L	PCT	G	GS	CG	SH	SV	IP	H	HR	BB	SO	RAT	ERA	ERA+	OAV	OOB	BH	AVG	PB	PR	/A	PD	TPI
1938	Bos-A	1	3	.250	13	6	1	0	0	36^2	47	5	24	14	17.7	8.35	59	.309	.407	2	.167	-1	-14	-14	-1	-1.3
1939	Bos-A	3	1	.750	9	5	0	0	0	38^1	49	3	14	13	14.8	4.23	112	.320	.377	1	.071	-2	2	2	-0	0.0
1940	Bos-A	1	0	1.000	12	1	0	0	0	29^1	45	5	8	13	16.3	5.52	81	.344	.381	1	.200	-0	-4	-3	-0	-0.3
1941	Bos-A	12	8	.600	29	25	12	3	0	187^1	175	14	85	51	12.5	3.07	136	.245	.326	10	.159	-1	22	23	-0	2.1
1942	Bos-A	14	11	.560	29	26	17	2	0	205^1	184	5	95	52	12.4	3.29	113	.247	.336	5	.077	-5	8	10	1	0.6
1946	Bos-A	1	0	1.000	8	4	0	0	0	30^2	32	6	19	14	15.0	5.87	62	.276	.378	1	.091	-1	-8	-8	-0	-0.9
Total	6	32	23	.582	100	67	30	5	0	527^2	532	38	245	157	13.4	3.91	104	.264	.346	20	.118	-9	6	10	-1	0.2

● GARY WAGNER Wagner, Gary Edward b: 6/28/40, Bridgeport, Ill. BR/TR, 6'4", 191 lbs. Deb: 4/18/65

YEAR	TM/L	W	L	PCT	G	GS	CG	SH	SV	IP	H	HR	BB	SO	RAT	ERA	ERA+	OAV	OOB	BH	AVG	PB	PR	/A	PD	TPI
1965	Phi-N	7	7	.500	59	0	0	0	7	105	87	6	49	91	11.8	3.00	115	.233	.325	1	.077	-0	6	5	1	0.6
1966	Phi-N	0	1	.000	5	1	0	0	0	6^1	8	1	5	2	18.5	8.53	42	.333	.448	0	—	0	-3	-3	-0	-0.4
1967	Phi-N	0	0	—	1	0	0	0	0	2	1	0	0	1	4.5	0.00	—	.167	.167	0	—	0	1	1	0	0.1
1968	Phi-N	4	4	.500	44	0	0	0	8	78	69	0	31	43	12.1	3.00	100	.243	.328	1	.083	-1	-0	0	1	0.0
1969	Phi-N	0	3	.000	9	2	0	0	0	19^1	31	3	7	8	17.7	7.91	45	.365	.413	0	.000	-0	-9	-9	-1	-1.0
	Bos-A	1	3	.250	6	1	0	0	0	16^1	18	1	15	9	18.2	6.06	63	.300	.440	0	.000	-0	-4	-4	0	-0.4
1970	Bos-A	3	1	.750	38	0	0	0	7	40^1	36	3	19	20	12.7	3.35	118	.232	.324	1	.167	-0	2	3	-1	0.2
Total	6	15	19	.441	162	4	0	0	22	267^1	250	14	126	174	13.0	3.70	93	.253	.343	3	.081	-2	-9	-8	1	-0.9

● HECTOR WAGNER Wagner, Hector Raul Guerrero (b: Hector Raul Guerrero (Wagner)) b: 11/26/68, San Juan, D.R. BR/TR, 6'3", 185 lbs. Deb: 9/10/90

YEAR	TM/L	W	L	PCT	G	GS	CG	SH	SV	IP	H	HR	BB	SO	RAT	ERA	ERA+	OAV	OOB	BH	AVG	PB	PR	/A	PD	TPI
1990	KC-A	0	2	.000	5	5	0	0	0	23^1	32	4	11	14	16.6	8.10	47	.323	.391	0	—	0	-11	-11	0	-0.9
1991	KC-A	1	1	.500	2	2	0	0	0	10	16	2	3	5	17.1	7.20	57	.348	.388	0	—	0	-3	-3	-0	-0.4
Total	2	1	3	.250	7	7	0	0	0	33^1	48	6	14	19	16.7	7.83	50	.331	.390	0	—	0	-14	-14	0	-1.3

● HONUS WAGNER Wagner, John Peter "The Flying Dutchman" b: 2/24/1874, Mansfield, Pa. d: 12/6/55, Carnegie, Pa. BR/TR, 5'11", 200 lbs. Deb: 7/19/1897 FMCH♦

YEAR	TM/L	W	L	PCT	G	GS	CG	SH	SV	IP	H	HR	BB	SO	RAT	ERA	ERA+	OAV	OOB	BH	AVG	PB	PR	/A	PD	TPI
1900	*Pit-N	0	0	—	1	0	0	0	0	3	3	0	4	1	21.0	0.00	—	.260	.450	201	.381	1	1	1	-0	0.1
1902	Pit-N	0	0	—	1	0	0	0	0	5^1	4	0	2	5	10.1	0.00	—	.209	.284	176	.330	0	2	2	-0	0.2
Total	2	0	0	—	2	0	0	0	0	8^1	7	0	6	6	14.0	0.00	—	.228	.354	3415	.327	1	3	3	-0	0.3

● MARK WAGNER Wagner, Mark Duane b: 3/4/54, Conneaut, Ohio BR/TR, 6'1", 175 lbs. Deb: 8/20/76 ♦

YEAR	TM/L	W	L	PCT	G	GS	CG	SH	SV	IP	H	HR	BB	SO	RAT	ERA	ERA+	OAV	OOB	BH	AVG	PB	PR	/A	PD	TPI
1984	Oak-A	0	0	—	1	0	0	0	0	1^2	2	0	1	1	16.2	0.00	—	.400	.500	20	.230	0	1	1	-0	0.1

● PAUL WAGNER Wagner, Paul Alan b: 11/14/67, Milwaukee, Wis. BR/TR, 6'3", 205 lbs. Deb: 7/26/92

YEAR	TM/L	W	L	PCT	G	GS	CG	SH	SV	IP	H	HR	BB	SO	RAT	ERA	ERA+	OAV	OOB	BH	AVG	PB	PR	/A	PD	TPI
1992	Pit-N	2	0	1.000	6	1	0	0	0	13	9	0	5	5	9.7	0.69	492	.191	.269	1	.333	0	4	4	0	0.5

● BULL WAGNER Wagner, William George b: 1/1/1888, Lilley, Mich. d: 10/2/67, Muskegon, Mich. BR/TR, 6'0.5", 225 lbs. Deb: 6/02/13

YEAR	TM/L	W	L	PCT	G	GS	CG	SH	SV	IP	H	HR	BB	SO	RAT	ERA	ERA+	OAV	OOB	BH	AVG	PB	PR	/A	PD	TPI
1913	Bro-N	4	2	.667	18	1	0	0	0	70^2	77	5	30	11	14.0	5.48	60	.285	.363	6	.231	1	-18	-17	-2	-1.8
1914	Bro-N	0	1	.000	6	0	0	0	0	12^1	14	0	12	4	19.7	6.57	44	.311	.466	0	.000	-0	-5	-5	-0	-0.5
Total	2	4	3	.571	24	1	0	0	0	83	91	5	42	15	14.9	5.64	57	.289	.380	6	.222	0	-23	-22	-2	-2.3

● DAVE WAINHOUSE Wainhouse, David Paul b: 11/7/67, Toronto, Ont., Can. BL/TR, 6'2", 190 lbs. Deb: 8/03/91

YEAR	TM/L	W	L	PCT	G	GS	CG	SH	SV	IP	H	HR	BB	SO	RAT	ERA	ERA+	OAV	OOB	BH	AVG	PB	PR	/A	PD	TPI
1991	Mon-N	0	1	.000	2	0	0	0	0	2^2	2	0	4	1	20.3	6.75	54	.222	.462	0	—	0	-1	-1	-0	-0.1

● RICK WAITS Waits, Michael Richard b: 5/15/52, Atlanta, Ga. BL/TL, 6'3", 195 lbs. Deb: 9/17/73

YEAR	TM/L	W	L	PCT	G	GS	CG	SH	SV	IP	H	HR	BB	SO	RAT	ERA	ERA+	OAV	OOB	BH	AVG	PB	PR	/A	PD	TPI
1973	Tex-A	0	0	—	1	0	0	0	1	1	1	0	1	0	18.0	9.00	41	.333	.500	0	—	0	-1	-1	0	0.0
1975	Cle-A	6	2	.750	16	7	3	0	1	70^1	57	3	25	34	10.6	2.94	128	.221	.292	0	—	0	7	7	0	0.7
1976	Cle-A	7	9	.438	26	22	4	2	0	123^2	143	7	54	65	14.3	4.00	87	.297	.368	0	—	0	-7	-7	1	-0.7
1977	Cle-A	9	7	.563	37	16	1	0	2	135^1	132	8	64	62	13.1	3.99	99	.262	.347	0	—	0	1	-1	-0	-0.1
1978	Cle-A	13	15	.464	34	33	15	2	0	230^1	206	16	86	97	11.5	3.20	117	.240	.310	0	—	0	14	14	3	1.8
1979	Cle-A	16	13	.552	34	34	8	3	0	231	230	26	91	91	12.7	4.44	96	.264	.336	0	—	0	-6	-5	2	-0.3
1980	Cle-A	13	14	.481	33	33	9	2	0	224^1	231	18	82	109	12.6	4.45	91	.270	.335	0	—	0	-10	-10	-1	-1.0
1981	Cle-A	8	10	.444	22	21	5	1	0	126^1	173	7	44	51	15.5	4.92	74	.330	.383	0	—	0	-18	-18	2	-1.6
1982	Cle-A	2	13	.133	25	21	2	0	0	115	128	13	57	44	14.6	5.40	76	.290	.372	0	—	0	-17	-17	1	-1.5
1983	Cle-A	0	1	.000	8	0	0	0	0	19^2	23	1	9	13	14.6	4.58	93	.307	.381	0	—	0	-1	-1	0	-0.1
	Mil-A	0	2	.000	10	2	0	0	0	30	39	1	11	20	15.0	5.10	73	.320	.376	0	—	0	-3	-5	-0	-0.5
	Yr	0	3	.000	18	2	0	0	0	49^2	62	2	20	33	14.9	4.89	80	.308	.371	0	—	0	-5	-5	-0	-0.6
1984	Mil-A	2	4	.333	47	1	0	0	3	73	84	7	24	49	13.3	3.58	108	.297	.352	0	—	0	3	2	0	0.3
1985	Mil-A	3	2	.600	24	0	0	0	1	47	67	3	20	24	16.7	6.51	64	.340	.401	0	.000	0	-12	-12	0	-1.2
Total	12	79	92	.462	317	190	47	10	8	1427	1514	110	568	659	13.2	4.25	92	.277	.346	0	.000	0	-50	-53	8	-4.2

● TIM WAKEFIELD Wakefield, Timothy Stephen b: 8/2/66, Melbourne, Fla. BR/TR, 6'2", 195 lbs. Deb: 7/31/92

YEAR	TM/L	W	L	PCT	G	GS	CG	SH	SV	IP	H	HR	BB	SO	RAT	ERA	ERA+	OAV	OOB	BH	AVG	PB	PR	/A	PD	TPI
1992	*Pit-N	8	1	.889	13	13	4	1	0	92	76	3	35	51	11.0	2.15	158	.232	.309	2	.071	-1	14	13	1	1.4

● BILL WAKEFIELD Wakefield, William Sumner b: 5/24/41, Kansas City, Mo. BR/TR, 6', 175 lbs. Deb: 4/18/64

YEAR	TM/L	W	L	PCT	G	GS	CG	SH	SV	IP	H	HR	BB	SO	RAT	ERA	ERA+	OAV	OOB	BH	AVG	PB	PR	/A	PD	TPI
1964	NY-N	3	5	.375	62	4	0	0	2	119^2	103	10	61	61	13.0	3.61	99	.235	.341	4	.167	-0	-1	-0	0	0.0

● RUBE WALBERG Walberg, George Elvin b: 7/27/1896, Pine City, Minn. d: 10/27/78, Tempe, Ariz. BL/TL, 6'1.5", 190 lbs. Deb: 4/29/23

YEAR	TM/L	W	L	PCT	G	GS	CG	SH	SV	IP	H	HR	BB	SO	RAT	ERA	ERA+	OAV	OOB	BH	AVG	PB	PR	/A	PD	TPI
1923	NY-N	0	0	—	2	0	0	0	0	5	4	0	1	1	9.0	1.80	212	.211	.250	0	.000	-0	1	1	-0	0.1
	Phi-A	4	8	.333	26	10	4	0	0	115	122	10	60	38	14.4	5.32	77	.280	.369	13	.317	3	-17	-16	1	-1.1
1924	Phi-A	0	0	—	6	2	0	0	0	7	10	0	10	3	25.7	12.86	33	.345	.513	1	.500	0	-7	-7	0	-0.6
1925	Phi-A	8	14	.364	53	20	7	0	7	191^2	197	11	77	82	13.0	3.99	117	.269	.340	10	.156	-4	9	14	1	1.0
1926	Phi-A	12	10	.545	40	19	5	2	2	151	168	4	60	72	13.9	2.80	149	.292	.365	7	.152	-2	20	23	-1	2.0

YEAR	TM/L	W	L	PCT	G	GS	CG	SH	SV	IP	H	HR	BB	SO	RAT	ERA	ERA+	OAV	OOB	BH	AVG	PB	PR	/A	PD	TPI
1927	Phi-A	16	12	.571	46	34	15	0	4	249^1	257	18	91	136	12.7	3.93	108	.271	.337	18	.207	3	6	9	-0	1.2
1928	Phi-A	17	12	.586	38	30	15	3	1	235^2	236	19	64	112	11.6	3.55	113	.265	.317	18	.209	1	13	12	1	1.3
1929	*Phi-A	18	11	.621	40	33	20	3	4	267^2	256	22	99	94	11.9	3.60	118	.254	.320	23	.223	-0	19	19	-2	1.6
1930	*Phi-A	13	12	.520	38	30	12	2	1	205^1	207	6	85	100	12.9	4.69	100	.262	.335	12	.164	-3	-1	-0	-1	-0.4
1931	*Phi-A	20	12	.625	44	35	19	1	3	**291**	298	16	109	106	12.6	3.74	120	.266	.331	13	.124	-6	21	24	-1	1.5
1932	Phi-A	17	10	.630	41	34	19	3	1	272	305	16	103	96	13.5	4.73	96	.282	.344	16	.170	-3	-8	-6	-0	-0.9
1933	Phi-A	9	13	.409	40	20	10	1	4	201	224	12	95	68	14.3	4.88	88	.278	.354	9	.132	-1	-13	-13	1	-1.4
1934	Bos-A	6	7	.462	30	10	2	0	1	104^2	118	5	41	38	13.8	4.04	119	.284	.350	6	.188	-1	5	9	1	0.8
1935	Bos-A	5	9	.357	44	10	4	0	3	142^2	152	10	54	44	13.1	3.91	121	.273	.340	6	.162	-2	9	13	-1	1.0
1936	Bos-A	5	4	.556	24	9	5	0	0	100^1	98	7	36	49	12.1	4.40	121	.257	.323	5	.156	-1	7	10	1	0.8
1937	Bos-A	5	7	.417	32	11	3	0	1	104^2	143	7	46	46	16.5	5.59	85	.332	.400	5	.147	-1	-11	-10	-0	-1.1
Total	15	155	141	.524	544	307	140	15	32	2644	2795	163	1031	1085	13.1	4.16	107	.273	.341	162	.179	-18	53	82	-2	5.8

● DOC WALDBAUER Waldbauer, Albert Charles b: 2/22/1892, Richmond, Va. d: 7/16/69, Yakima, Wash. BR/TR, 6', 172 lbs. Deb: 9/24/17

YEAR	TM/L	W	L	PCT	G	GS	CG	SH	SV	IP	H	HR	BB	SO	RAT	ERA	ERA+	OAV	OOB	BH	AVG	PB	PR	/A	PD	TPI
1917	Was-A	0	0	—	2	0	0	0	1	5	10	0	2	2	21.6	7.20	36	.476	.522	0	.000	-0	-3	-3	0	-0.2

● BOB WALK Walk, Robert Vernon b: 11/26/56, Van Nuys, Cal. BR/TR, 6'4", 208 lbs. Deb: 5/26/80

YEAR	TM/L	W	L	PCT	G	GS	CG	SH	SV	IP	H	HR	BB	SO	RAT	ERA	ERA+	OAV	OOB	BH	AVG	PB	PR	/A	PD	TPI
1980	*Phi-N	11	7	.611	27	27	2	0	0	151^2	163	8	71	94	14.0	4.57	83	.276	.356	7	.140	-0	-16	-13	-1	-1.4
1981	Atl-N	1	4	.200	12	8	0	0	0	43^1	41	6	23	16	13.3	4.57	78	.250	.342	1	.143	-0	-5	-5	-1	-0.6
1982	*Atl-N	11	9	.550	32	27	3	1	0	164^1	179	19	59	84	13.4	4.87	77	.280	.347	10	.196	2	-23	-21	-2	-2.2
1983	Atl-N	0	0	—	1	1	0	0	0	3^2	7	0	2	4	22.1	7.36	53	.412	.474	0	.000	-0	-2	-1	0	-0.1
1984	Pit-N	1	1	.500	2	2	0	0	0	10^1	8	1	4	10	10.5	2.61	138	.200	.273	0	.000	-0	1	1	-0	0.1
1985	Pit-N	2	3	.400	9	9	1	1	0	58^2	60	3	18	40	12.0	3.68	97	.265	.320	0	.000	-1	-1	-1	-1	-0.3
1986	Pit-N	7	8	.467	44	15	1	1	2	141^2	129	14	64	78	12.5	3.75	102	.251	.337	6	.154	0	-0	1	2	0.3
1987	Pit-N	8	2	.800	39	12	1	1	0	117	107	11	51	78	12.4	3.31	124	.245	.329	6	.231	1	10	10	1	1.2
1988	Pit-N★	12	10	.545	32	32	1	1	0	212^2	183	6	65	81	10.6	2.71	126	.230	.290	6	.087	-2	17	16	0	1.6
1989	Pit-N	13	10	.565	33	31	2	0	0	196	208	15	65	83	12.7	4.41	76	.271	.331	13	.186	2	-20	-23	1	-2.1
1990	*Pit-N	7	5	.583	26	24	1	1	1	129^2	136	17	36	73	12.2	3.75	97	.270	.324	6	.162	1	1	-2	-1	-0.3
1991	*Pit-N	9	2	.818	25	20	0	0	0	115	104	10	35	67	11.3	3.60	99	.240	.304	8	.205	2	1	-0	-0	0.2
1992	*Pit-N	10	6	.625	36	19	1	0	2	135	132	10	43	60	12.1	3.20	106	.258	.323	4	.093	-2	5	3	1	0.3
Total	13	92	67	.579	318	227	13	6	5	1479	1457	120	536	768	12.3	3.82	95	.258	.327	67	.148	3	-32	-34	-0	-3.3

● ED WALKER Walker, Edward Harrison b: 8/11/1874, Cambois, England d: 9/29/47, Akron, Ohio BL/TL, 6'5", 242 lbs. Deb: 9/26/02

YEAR	TM/L	W	L	PCT	G	GS	CG	SH	SV	IP	H	HR	BB	SO	RAT	ERA	ERA+	OAV	OOB	BH	AVG	PB	PR	/A	PD	TPI
1902	Cle-A	0	1	.000	1	1	1	0	0	8	11	0	3	1	15.8	3.38	102	.327	.382	1	.333	0	0	0	0	0.0
1903	Cle-A	0	0	—	3	3	0	0	0	12	13	0	10	4	17.3	5.25	54	.275	.402	0	.000	-0	-3	-3	-1	-0.4
Total	2	0	1	.000	4	4	1	0	0	20	24	0	13	5	16.6	4.50	69	.297	.394	1	.167	0	-3	-3	-1	-0.4

● DIXIE WALKER Walker, Ewart Gladstone b: 6/1/1887, Brownsville, Pa. d: 11/14/65, Leeds, Ala. BL/TR, 6', 192 lbs. Deb: 9/17/09 F

YEAR	TM/L	W	L	PCT	G	GS	CG	SH	SV	IP	H	HR	BB	SO	RAT	ERA	ERA+	OAV	OOB	BH	AVG	PB	PR	/A	PD	TPI
1909	Was-A	3	1	.750	4	4	4	1	0	36	31	0	6	25	9.3	2.50	97	.217	.248	2	.154	-0	-0	-0	-0	-0.1
1910	Was-A	11	11	.500	29	26	16	3	0	199^1	177	2	68	84	11.4	3.30	76	.245	.317	9	.130	-3	-17	-18	-1	-2.3
1911	Was-A	8	13	.381	32	24	15	2	0	185^2	205	2	50	65	12.7	3.39	97	.286	.339	20	.303	4	-1	-2	-1	0.0
1912	Was-A	3	6	.333	9	8	5	0	0	60	72	2	18	29	14.1	5.25	63	.300	.359	2	.125	1	-13	-13	-0	-1.1
Total	4	25	31	.446	74	62	40	5	0	481	485	6	142	203	12.1	3.52	82	.266	.326	33	.201	2	-31	-33	-3	-3.5

● MYSTERIOUS WALKER Walker, Frederick Mitchell b: 3/21/1884, Utica, Neb. d: 2/1/58, Oak Park, Ill. BR/TR, 5'10.5", 185 lbs. Deb: 6/28/10

YEAR	TM/L	W	L	PCT	G	GS	CG	SH	SV	IP	H	HR	BB	SO	RAT	ERA	ERA+	OAV	OOB	BH	AVG	PB	PR	/A	PD	TPI
1910	Cin-N	0	0	—	1	0	0	0	0	3	4	0	4	1	24.0	3.00	97	.333	.500	0	.000	-0	0	-0	0	0.0
1912	Cle-A	0	0	—	1	0	0	0	0	1	0	0	1	0	9.0	0.00	—	.000	.200	0	—	0	0	0	-0	0.0
1913	Bro-N	1	3	.250	11	8	3	0	0	58^1	44	3	35	35	13.0	3.55	93	.233	.367	3	.167	-0	-2	-2	2	0.0
1914	Pit-F	4	16	.200	35	21	12	0	0	169^1	197	3	74	79	14.6	4.31	74	.294	.367	6	.113	-2	-21	-21	3	-2.0
1915	Bro-F	2	4	.333	13	7	2	0	1	65^2	61	3	22	28	11.4	3.70	82	.242	.303	6	.222	1	-5	-5	1	-0.3
Total	5	7	23	.233	61	36	17	0	1	297^1	306	9	136	143	13.6	4.00	79	.272	.354	15	.152	-1	-27	-27	6	-2.3

● GEORGE WALKER Walker, George A. b: 1863, Hamilton, Ontario, Canada TR, 5'9", 184 lbs. Deb: 8/01/1888

YEAR	TM/L	W	L	PCT	G	GS	CG	SH	SV	IP	H	HR	BB	SO	RAT	ERA	ERA+	OAV	OOB	BH	AVG	PB	PR	/A	PD	TPI
1888	Bal-a	1	3	.250	4	4	4	1	0	35	36	2	14	18	12.9	5.91	50	.256	.324	1	.077	-1	-11	-11	-0	-1.1

● LUKE WALKER Walker, James Luke b: 9/2/43, DeKalb, Tex. BL/TL, 6'1.5", 192 lbs. Deb: 9/07/65

YEAR	TM/L	W	L	PCT	G	GS	CG	SH	SV	IP	H	HR	BB	SO	RAT	ERA	ERA+	OAV	OOB	BH	AVG	PB	PR	/A	PD	TPI
1965	Pit-N	0	0	—	2	0	0	0	0	5	2	0	1	5	5.4	0.00	—	.118	.167	0	—	0	2	2	0	0.2
1966	Pit-N	0	1	.000	10	1	0	0	0	10	8	0	15	7	21.6	4.50	79	.205	.436	0	.000	-0	-1	-1	-0	-0.1
1968	Pit-N	0	3	.000	39	2	0	0	3	61^2	42	1	39	66	12.0	2.04	143	.190	.314	0	.000	-1	6	6	1	0.7
1969	Pit-N	4	6	.400	31	15	3	1	0	118^2	98	5	57	96	11.9	3.64	96	.226	.319	0	.000	-3	-1	-2	1	-0.4
1970	*Pit-N	15	6	.714	42	19	5	3	3	163	129	6	89	124	12.1	3.04	128	.219	.323	6	.130	-1	18	16	-0	1.5
1971	*Pit-N	10	8	.556	28	24	4	2	0	159^2	157	9	53	86	11.9	3.55	95	.262	.324	1	.022	-3	-2	-3	-2	-0.8
1972	*Pit-N	4	6	.400	26	12	2	0	2	92^2	98	4	34	48	12.8	3.40	98	.278	.342	2	.083	-1	1	-1	-0	-0.3
1973	Pit-N	7	12	.368	37	18	2	1	1	122	129	9	66	74	14.5	4.65	76	.270	.360	2	.067	-2	-13	-15	-1	-1.9
1974	Det-A	5	5	.500	28	9	0	0	0	92	100	9	54	52	15.3	4.99	76	.278	.375	0	—	0	-14	-12	-0	-1.3
Total	9	45	47	.489	243	100	16	7	9	824^2	763	43	408	558	12.9	3.65	97	.247	.337	11	.059	-11	-3	-11	-2	-2.4

● ROY WALKER Walker, James Roy "Dixie" b: 4/13/1893, Lawrenceburg, Tenn d: 2/10/62, New Orleans, La. BR/TR, 6'1.5", 180 lbs. Deb: 9/16/12

YEAR	TM/L	W	L	PCT	G	GS	CG	SH	SV	IP	H	HR	BB	SO	RAT	ERA	ERA+	OAV	OOB	BH	AVG	PB	PR	/A	PD	TPI
1912	Cle-A	0	0	—	1	0	0	0	0	2	0	0	2	1	9.0	0.00	—	.000	.250	0	—	0	1	1	-0	0.1
1915	Cle-A	4	9	.308	25	15	4	0	1	131	122	1	65	57	13.3	3.98	77	.261	.360	5	.132	-2	-15	-14	-2	-1.9
1917	Chi-N	0	1	.000	2	1	0	0	0	7	8	0	5	4	16.7	3.86	75	.286	.394	0	.000	-0	-1	-1	-0	-0.1
1918	Chi-N	1	3	.250	13	7	2	0	1	43^1	50	1	15	20	13.7	2.70	103	.298	.359	0	.000	-1	0	0	0	-0.1
1921	StL-N	11	12	.478	38	24	11	0	3	170^2	194	10	53	52	13.1	4.22	87	.293	.347	11	.204	-0	-8	-10	-1	-1.2
1922	StL-N	1	2	.333	12	2	0	0	0	32	34	1	15	14	13.8	4.78	81	.293	.374	1	.143	-0	-2	-3	-1	-0.5
Total	6	17	27	.386	91	49	17	0	5	386	408	13	155	148	13.3	3.99	85	.282	.355	17	.153	-4	-26	-26	-5	-3.7

● JERRY WALKER Walker, Jerry Allen b: 2/12/39, Ada, Okla. BB/TR, 6'1", 195 lbs. Deb: 7/06/57 C

YEAR	TM/L	W	L	PCT	G	GS	CG	SH	SV	IP	H	HR	BB	SO	RAT	ERA	ERA+	OAV	OOB	BH	AVG	PB	PR	/A	PD	TPI
1957	Bal-A	1	0	1.000	13	3	1	1	1	27^2	24	1	14	13	12.4	2.93	123	.245	.339	0	.000	-1	3	2	-0	0.1
1958	Bal-A	0	0	—	6	0	0	0	0	10^1	16	2	5	6	18.3	6.97	52	.340	.404	0	.000	-0	-4	-4	-0	-0.4
1959	Bal-A★	11	10	.524	30	22	7	2	4	182	160	13	52	100	10.6	2.92	130	.240	.297	11	.169	-1	19	18	-0	1.8
1960	Bal-A	3	4	.429	29	18	1	0	5	118	107	15	56	48	12.7	3.74	102	.247	.337	14	.368	5	2	1	1	0.6
1961	KC-A	8	14	.364	36	24	4	0	2	168	161	23	96	56	14.3	4.82	85	.253	.359	16	.250	3	-15	-13	1	-0.9
1962	KC-A	8	9	.471	31	21	3	1	0	143^1	165	27	78	57	15.7	5.90	70	.288	.381	15	.263	5	-31	-28	1	-2.1
1963	Cle-A	6	6	.500	39	2	0	0	1	88	92	15	36	41	13.3	4.91	74	.265	.338	2	.105	-0	-13	-13	-0	-1.4
1964	Cle-A	0	1	.000	6	0	0	0	0	9^2	9	1	4	5	12.1	4.66	77	.257	.333	0	.000	-0	-1	-1	-0	-0.2
Total	8	37	44	.457	190	90	16	4	13	747	734	97	341	326	13.3	4.36	89	.259	.343	58	.230	10	-39	-38	1	-2.5

● MARTY WALKER Walker, Martin Van Buren "Buddy" b: 3/27/1899, Philadelphia, Pa. d: 4/24/78, Philadelphia, Pa. BL/TL, 6', 170 lbs. Deb: 9/30/28

YEAR	TM/L	W	L	PCT	G	GS	CG	SH	SV	IP	H	HR	BB	SO	RAT	ERA	ERA+	OAV	OOB	BH	AVG	PB	PR	/A	PD	TPI
1928	Phi-N	0	1	.000	1	1	0	0	0	0	2	0	3	0	—	∞	—	1.000	1.000	0	—	0	-2	-2	0	-0.2

● MIKE WALKER Walker, Michael Aaron b: 6/23/65, Houston, Tex. BR/TR, 6'3", 205 lbs. Deb: 6/16/92

YEAR	TM/L	W	L	PCT	G	GS	CG	SH	SV	IP	H	HR	BB	SO	RAT	ERA	ERA+	OAV	OOB	BH	AVG	PB	PR	/A	PD	TPI
1992	Sea-A	0	3	.000	5	3	0	0	0	14^2	21	4	9	5	18.4	7.36	54	.333	.417	0	—	0	-6	-5	0	-0.5

● MIKE WALKER Walker, Michael Charles b: 10/4/66, Chicago, Ill. BR/TR, 6'2", 195 lbs. Deb: 9/09/88

YEAR	TM/L	W	L	PCT	G	GS	CG	SH	SV	IP	H	HR	BB	SO	RAT	ERA	ERA+	OAV	OOB	BH	AVG	PB	PR	/A	PD	TPI
1988	Cle-A	0	1	.000	3	1	0	0	0	8^2	8	0	10	7	18.7	7.27	57	.258	.439	0	—	0	-3	-3	0	-0.4
1990	Cle-A	2	6	.250	18	11	0	0	0	75^2	82	6	42	34	15.5	4.88	80	.277	.378	0	—	0	-8	-8	-0	-0.8

YEAR TM/L	W	L	PCT	G	GS	CG	SH	SV	IP	H	HR	BB	SO	RAT	ERA	ERA+	OAV	OOB	BH	AVG	PB	PR	/A	PD	TPI
1991 Cle-A	0	1	.000	5	0	0	0	0	4^1	6	0	2	2	18.7	2.08	200	.316	.409	0	—	0	1	1	0	0.1
Total 3	2	8	.200	26	12	0	0	0	88^2	96	6	54	43	15.9	4.97	79	.277	.386	0	—	0	-10	-10	0	-1.1

● **TOM WALKER** Walker, Robert Thomas b: 11/7/48, Tampa, Fla. BR/TR, 6'1", 188 lbs. Deb: 4/23/72

YEAR TM/L	W	L	PCT	G	GS	CG	SH	SV	IP	H	HR	BB	SO	RAT	ERA	ERA+	OAV	OOB	BH	AVG	PB	PR	/A	PD	TPI
1972 Mon-N	2	2	.500	46	0	0	0	2	74^2	71	4	22	42	11.3	2.89	123	.248	.304	0	.000	-0	5	5	-0	0.5
1973 Mon-N	7	5	.583	54	0	0	0	4	91^2	95	7	42	68	13.7	3.63	105	.274	.357	0	.000	-1	0	2	-0	0.1
1974 Mon-N	4	5	.444	33	8	1	0	2	91^2	96	7	28	70	12.4	3.83	100	.266	.322	3	.188	0	-2	0	-1	0.0
1975 Det-A	3	8	.273	36	9	1	0	0	115^1	116	16	40	60	12.6	4.45	90	.261	.329	0	—	0	-9	-6	-2	-0.9
1976 StL-N	1	2	.333	10	0	0	0	3	19^2	22	2	3	11	11.4	4.12	86	.265	.291	2	.400	1	-1	-1	-1	-0.1
1977 Mon-N	1	1	.500	11	0	0	0	0	19	15	2	7	10	10.4	4.74	80	.221	.293	0	.000	-0	-2	-2	-0	-0.2
Cal-A	0	0	—	1	0	0	0	0	2	3	2	0	1	13.5	9.00	43	.375	.375	0	—	0	-1	-1	-0	-0.1
Total 6	18	23	.439	191	17	2	0	11	414	418	40	142	262	12.4	3.87	99	.262	.326	5	.152	-0	-10	-3	-3	-0.7

● **TOM WALKER** Walker, Thomas William b: 8/1/1881, Philadelphia, Pa. d: 7/10/44, Woodbury Heights N.J. BR/TR, 5'11", 170 lbs. Deb: 9/27/02

YEAR TM/L	W	L	PCT	G	GS	CG	SH	SV	IP	H	HR	BB	SO	RAT	ERA	ERA+	OAV	OOB	BH	AVG	PB	PR	/A	PD	TPI
1902 Phi-A	0	1	.000	1	1	1	0	0	8	10	0	0	2	12.4	5.63	65	.306	.327	1	.250	-0	-2	-2	1	-0.1
1904 Cin-N	15	8	.652	24	24	22	2	0	217	196	2	53	64	11.1	2.24	131	.238	.299	9	.117	-5	12	17	-2	1.1
1905 Cin-N	9	7	.563	23	19	12	1	0	144^2	171	3	44	28	13.7	3.24	102	.305	.362	7	.137	-1	-4	1	-0	-0.1
Total 3	24	16	.600	48	44	35	3	0	369^2	377	5	97	94	12.1	2.70	114	.266	.325	17	.129	-6	6	16	-1	0.9

● **BILL WALKER** Walker, William Henry b: 10/7/03, E.St.Louis, Ill. d: 6/14/66, E.St.Louis, Ill. BR/TL, 6', 175 lbs. Deb: 9/13/27

YEAR TM/L	W	L	PCT	G	GS	CG	SH	SV	IP	H	HR	BB	SO	RAT	ERA	ERA+	OAV	OOB	BH	AVG	PB	PR	/A	PD	TPI
1927 NY-N	0	0	—	3	0	0	0	0	4	6	0	5	4	24.8	9.00	43	.429	.579	0	—	0	-2	-2	-0	-0.2
1928 NY-N	3	6	.333	22	8	1	0	0	76^1	79	9	31	39	13.1	4.72	83	.275	.348	2	.091	-2	-6	-7	-0	-0.9
1929 NY-N	14	7	.667	29	23	13	1	0	177^2	188	11	57	65	12.6	**3.09**	148	.274	.334	7	.115	-3	32	29	-3	2.1
1930 NY-N	17	15	.531	39	34	13	2	1	245^1	258	19	88	105	12.9	3.93	121	.268	.334	16	.186	-1	29	22	-1	1.8
1931 NY-N	16	9	.640	37	28	19	**6**	3	239^1	212	6	64	121	10.5	**2.26**	**164**	.231	.283	5	.065	-6	**43**	**38**	-4	2.9
1932 NY-N	8	12	.400	31	22	9	0	2	163	177	23	55	74	13.0	4.14	90	.274	.334	7	.135	-2	-5	-8	2	-0.8
1933 StL-N	9	10	.474	29	20	6	2	0	158	168	8	67	41	13.4	3.42	102	.273	.346	7	.132	-2	-1	1	1	0.0
1934 *StL-N	12	4	.750	24	19	10	1	0	153	160	11	66	76	13.4	3.12	136	.270	.345	5	.093	-4	16	19	-1	1.3
1935 StL-N★	13	8	.619	37	25	8	2	1	193^1	222	7	78	79	14.2	3.82	107	.288	.357	6	.102	-4	4	6	-1	0.1
1936 StL-N	5	6	.455	21	13	4	1	1	79^2	106	5	27	22	15.3	5.87	67	.318	.373	7	.280	2	-16	-17	1	-1.4
Total 10	97	77	.557	272	192	83	15	8	1489^2	1576	99	538	626	12.9	3.59	114	.271	.335	62	.127	-23	93	83	-7	4.9

● **JIM WALKUP** Walkup, James Elton b: 12/14/09, Havana, Ark. BR/TR, 6'1", 170 lbs. Deb: 9/22/34

YEAR TM/L	W	L	PCT	G	GS	CG	SH	SV	IP	H	HR	BB	SO	RAT	ERA	ERA+	OAV	OOB	BH	AVG	PB	PR	/A	PD	TPI
1934 StL-A	0	0	—	3	0	0	0	0	8^1	6	0	5	6	11.9	2.16	231	.200	.314	1	.333	0	2	3	-0	0.2
1935 StL-A	6	9	.400	55	20	4	1	0	181^1	226	17	104	44	16.5	6.25	77	.305	.392	6	.128	-3	-36	-29	-1	-3.1
1936 StL-A	0	3	.000	5	2	0	0	0	15^2	20	0	6	5	14.9	8.04	67	.308	.366	0	.000	-1	-5	-5	1	-0.4
1937 StL-A	9	12	.429	27	18	6	0	0	150^1	218	16	83	46	18.0	7.36	66	.347	.423	14	.241	-1	-46	-42	2	-3.5
1938 StL-A	1	12	.077	18	13	1	0	0	94	127	13	53	28	17.5	6.80	73	.329	.414	4	.138	-2	-21	-19	0	-1.8
1939 StL-A	0	1	.000	1	0	0	0	0	0^2	2	0	1	0	40.5	0.00	—	.500	.600	0	—	0	0	0	0	0.0
Det-A	0	1	.000	7	0	0	0	0	12	15	3	8	5	17.3	7.50	65	.319	.418	1	.500	0	-4	-3	0	-0.3
Yr	0	2	.000	8	0	0	0	0	12^2	17	3	9	5	18.5	7.11	69	.333	.433	1	.500	0	-3	-3	0	-0.3
Total 6	16	38	.296	116	53	11	1	0	462^1	614	49	260	134	17.1	6.74	72	.323	.406	26	.182	-6	-110	-96	1	-8.9

● **JIM WALKUP** Walkup, James Huey b: 11/3/1895, Havana, Ark. d: 6/12/90, Duncan, Okla. BR/TL, 5'8", 150 lbs. Deb: 4/30/27

YEAR TM/L	W	L	PCT	G	GS	CG	SH	SV	IP	H	HR	BB	SO	RAT	ERA	ERA+	OAV	OOB	BH	AVG	PB	PR	/A	PD	TPI
1927 Det-A	0	0	—	2	0	0	0	0	1^2	3	0	0	0	16.2	5.40	78	.429	.429	0	.000	-0	-0	-0	0	0.0

● **MURRAY WALL** Wall, Murray Wesley b: 9/19/26, Dallas, Tex. d: 10/8/71, Lone Oak, Tex. BR/TR, 6'3", 185 lbs. Deb: 7/04/50

YEAR TM/L	W	L	PCT	G	GS	CG	SH	SV	IP	H	HR	BB	SO	RAT	ERA	ERA+	OAV	OOB	BH	AVG	PB	PR	/A	PD	TPI
1950 Bos-N	0	0	—	1	0	0	0	0	4	6	0	2	2	18.0	9.00	43	.333	.400	0	.000	-0	-2	-2	-0	-0.2
1957 Bos-A	3	0	1.000	11	0	0	0	1	24^1	21	3	2	13	8.5	3.33	120	.233	.250	2	.333	0	1	2	1	0.3
1958 Bos-A	8	9	.471	52	1	0	0	10	114^1	109	14	33	53	11.6	3.62	111	.255	.316	3	.107	-2	2	5	3	0.6
1959 Bos-A	1	4	.200	15	0	0	0	3	31^2	31	5	15	8	13.1	5.40	75	.267	.351	0	.000	-1	-5	-5	1	-0.5
Was-A	0	0	—	1	0	0	0	0	1^1	3	1	0	0	20.3	6.75	58	.600	.600	0	.000	-0	-0	-0	0	0.0
Bos-A	1	1	.500	11	0	0	0	0	17^1	26	2	11	6	19.7	5.71	71	.371	.463	0	.000	-0	-4	-3	-0	-0.4
Yr	2	5	.286	27	0	0	0	3	50^1	60	8	26	14	15.6	5.54	73	.313	.397	0	.000	-2	-9	-8	1	-0.9
Total 4	13	14	.481	91	1	0	0	14	193	196	25	63	82	12.4	4.20	96	.270	.333	5	.109	-3	-8	-4	5	-0.2

● **STAN WALL** Wall, Stanley Arthur b: 6/16/51, Butler, Mo. BL/TL, 6'1", 175 lbs. Deb: 7/19/75

YEAR TM/L	W	L	PCT	G	GS	CG	SH	SV	IP	H	HR	BB	SO	RAT	ERA	ERA+	OAV	OOB	BH	AVG	PB	PR	/A	PD	TPI
1975 LA-N	0	1	.000	10	0	0	0	0	16	12	0	7	6	11.3	1.69	201	.222	.323	0	—	0	3	3	0	0.3
1976 LA-N	2	2	.500	31	0	0	0	1	50	50	5	15	27	12.1	3.60	94	.269	.330	0	.000	-0	-1	-1	-1	-0.2
1977 LA-N	2	3	.400	25	0	0	0	0	32	36	3	13	22	14.1	5.34	72	.279	.350	0	.000	-0	-5	-5	-1	-0.6
Total 3	4	6	.400	66	0	0	0	1	98	98	8	35	55	12.6	3.86	91	.266	.336	0	.000	-1	-2	-4	-1	-0.5

● **DAVE WALLACE** Wallace, David William b: 9/7/47, Waterbury, Conn. BR/TR, 5'10", 185 lbs. Deb: 7/18/73

YEAR TM/L	W	L	PCT	G	GS	CG	SH	SV	IP	H	HR	BB	SO	RAT	ERA	ERA+	OAV	OOB	BH	AVG	PB	PR	/A	PD	TPI
1973 Phi-N	0	0	—	4	0	0	0	0	3^2	13	1	2	2	36.8	22.09	17	.591	.625	0	—	0	-8	-7	0	-0.7
1974 Phi-N	0	1	.000	3	0	0	0	0	3	4	2	3	3	21.0	9.00	42	.308	.438	0	—	0	-2	-2	0	-0.2
1978 Tor-A	0	0	—	6	0	0	0	0	14	12	1	11	7	14.8	3.86	102	.245	.383	0	—	0	-0	0	-0	0.0
Total 3	0	1	.000	13	0	0	0	0	20^2	29	4	16	12	19.6	7.84	49	.345	.450	0	—	0	-9	-9	0	-0.9

● **HUCK WALLACE** Wallace, Harry Clinton "Lefty" b: 7/27/1882, Richmond, Ind. d: 7/6/51, Cleveland, Ohio BL/TL, 5'6", 160 lbs. Deb: 6/05/12

YEAR TM/L	W	L	PCT	G	GS	CG	SH	SV	IP	H	HR	BB	SO	RAT	ERA	ERA+	OAV	OOB	BH	AVG	PB	PR	/A	PD	TPI
1912 Phi-N	0	0	—	4	0	0	0	0	4^2	7	0	4	4	21.2	0.00	—	.350	.458	0	—	0	2	2	0	0.2

● **LEFTY WALLACE** Wallace, James Harold b: 8/12/21, Evansville, Ind. d: 7/28/82, Evansville, Ind. BL/TL, 5'11", 160 lbs. Deb: 5/05/42

YEAR TM/L	W	L	PCT	G	GS	CG	SH	SV	IP	H	HR	BB	SO	RAT	ERA	ERA+	OAV	OOB	BH	AVG	PB	PR	/A	PD	TPI
1942 Bos-N	1	3	.250	19	3	1	0	0	49^1	39	3	24	20	11.9	3.83	87	.217	.316	2	.143	-0	-3	-3	-1	-0.4
1945 Bos-N	1	0	1.000	5	3	1	0	0	20	18	1	9	4	12.6	4.50	85	.240	.329	0	.000	-1	-2	-1	0	-0.2
1946 Bos-N	3	3	.500	27	8	2	0	0	75^1	76	5	31	27	12.9	4.18	82	.253	.325	1	.056	-1	-6	-6	2	-0.6
Total 3	5	6	.455	51	14	4	0	0	144^2	133	9	64	51	12.5	4.11	84	.240	.323	3	.079	-2	-11	-10	1	-1.2

● **MIKE WALLACE** Wallace, Michael Sherman b: 2/3/51, Gastonia, N.C. BL/TL, 6'2", 204 lbs. Deb: 6/27/73

YEAR TM/L	W	L	PCT	G	GS	CG	SH	SV	IP	H	HR	BB	SO	RAT	ERA	ERA+	OAV	OOB	BH	AVG	PB	PR	/A	PD	TPI
1973 Phi-N	1	1	.500	20	3	1	0	1	33^1	38	1	15	20	14.3	3.78	100	.304	.379	0	.000	-0	-0	0	-0	0.0
1974 Phi-N	1	0	1.000	8	0	0	0	0	8^1	12	0	2	1	15.1	5.40	70	.324	.359	0	—	0	-2	-2	-0	-0.2
NY-A	6	0	1.000	23	1	0	0	0	52^1	42	3	35	34	13.2	2.41	145	.222	.344	0	—	0	7	6	-1	0.6
1975 NY-A	0	0	—	3	0	0	0	0	4^1	11	1	1	2	24.9	14.54	25	.458	.480	0	—	0	-5	-5	0	-0.4
StL-N	0	0	—	9	0	0	0	0	8^2	9	0	5	6	14.5	2.08	181	.281	.378	0	—	0	1	2	0	0.2
1976 StL-N	3	2	.600	49	0	0	0	2	66^1	66	3	39	40	14.2	4.07	87	.264	.363	1	.333	0	-4	-4	0	-0.4
1977 Tex-A	0	0	—	5	0	0	0	0	8^1	10	1	10	2	21.6	7.56	54	.323	.488	0	—	0	-3	-3	0	-0.3
Total 5	11	3	.786	117	4	1	0	3	181^2	188	9	107	105	14.6	3.91	92	.273	.371	1	.143	0	-6	-6	-1	-0.5

● **BOBBY WALLACE** Wallace, Roderick John b: 11/4/1873, Pittsburgh, Pa. d: 11/3/60, Torrance, Cal. BR/TR, 5'8", 170 lbs. Deb: 9/15/1894 MUCH◆

YEAR TM/L	W	L	PCT	G	GS	CG	SH	SV	IP	H	HR	BB	SO	RAT	ERA	ERA+	OAV	OOB	BH	AVG	PB	PR	/A	PD	TPI
1894 Cle-N	2	1	.667	4	3	2	0	0	26	28	1	20	10	17.0	5.19	105	.272	.396	2	.154	-1	0	1	1	0.0
1895 Cle-N	12	14	.462	30	28	22	1	1	228^2	271	3	87	63	14.4	4.09	122	.290	.356	21	.214	-3	17	23	3	1.9
1896 *Cle-N	10	7	.588	22	16	13	2	0	145^1	167	2	49	46	13.6	3.34	136	.286	.345	35	.235	1	16	19	-0	1.7
1902 StL-A	0	0	—	1	1	0	0	0	2	3	0	0	1	13.5	0.00	—	.346	.346	141	.285	0	1	1	0	0.1
Total 4	24	22	.522	57	48	37	3	1	402	469	6	156	120	14.3	3.87	125	.288	.355	2309	.268	-3	35	44	4	3.7

● **TIM WALLACH** Wallach, Timothy Charles b: 9/14/57, Huntington Park, Cal. BR/TR, 6'3", 200 lbs. Deb: 9/06/80 ◆

YEAR TM/L	W	L	PCT	G	GS	CG	SH	SV	IP	H	HR	BB	SO	RAT	ERA	ERA+	OAV	OOB	BH	AVG	PB	PR	/A	PD	TPI
1987 Mon-N★	0	0	—	1	0	0	0	0	1	1	0	0	0	9.0	0.00	—	.333	.333	177	.298	1	0	0	-0	0.0

YEAR	TM/L	W	L	PCT	G	GS	CG	SH	SV	IP	H	HR	BB	SO	RAT	ERA	ERA+	OAV	OOB	BH	AVG	PB	PR	/A	PD	TPI
1989	Mon-N★	0	0	—	1	0	0	0	0	1	2	0	0	0	18.0	9.00	39	.500	.500	159	.277	0	-1	-1	0	-0.1
Total	2	0	0	—	2	0	0	0	0	2	3	0	0	0	13.5	4.50	86	.429	.429	1694	.259	1	-0	-0	-0	-0.1

● RED WALLER Waller, John Francis b: 6/16/1883, Washington, D.C. d: 2/9/15, Secaucus, N.J. Deb: 4/27/09

YEAR	TM/L	W	L	PCT	G	GS	CG	SH	SV	IP	H	HR	BB	SO	RAT	ERA	ERA+	OAV	OOB	BH	AVG	PB	PR	/A	PD	TPI
1909	NY-N	0	0	—	1	0	0	0	0	1	3	0	0	1	36.0	0.00	—	.429	.500	0	—	0	0	0	0	0.1

● AUGIE WALSH Walsh, August Sothley b: 8/17/04, Wilmington, Del. d: 11/12/85, San Rafael, Cal. BR/TR, 6', 175 lbs. Deb: 10/02/27

YEAR	TM/L	W	L	PCT	G	GS	CG	SH	SV	IP	H	HR	BB	SO	RAT	ERA	ERA+	OAV	OOB	BH	AVG	PB	PR	/A	PD	TPI
1927	Phi-N	0	1	.000	1	1	1	0	0	10	12	3	5	0	15.3	4.50	92	.333	.415	1	.250	-0	-1	-0	-0	-0.1
1928	Phi-N	4	9	.308	38	11	2	0	2	122^1	160	13	40	38	15.1	6.18	69	.321	.378	10	.256	2	-30	-26	-2	-2.4
Total	2	4	10	.286	39	12	3	0	2	132^1	172	16	45	38	15.1	6.05	70	.322	.380	11	.256	2	-30	-26	-2	-2.5

● CONNIE WALSH Walsh, Cornelius R. b: 4/23/1882, St.Louis, Mo. d: 4/5/53, St.Louis, Mo. Deb: 9/16/07

YEAR	TM/L	W	L	PCT	G	GS	CG	SH	SV	IP	H	HR	BB	SO	RAT	ERA	ERA+	OAV	OOB	BH	AVG	PB	PR	/A	PD	TPI
1907	Pit-N	0	0	—	1	0	0	0	0	1	1	0	1	0	18.0	9.00	27	.250	.400	0	—	0	-1	-1	-0	-0.1

● DAVE WALSH Walsh, David Peter b: 9/25/60, Arlington, Mass. BL/TL, 6'1", 185 lbs. Deb: 8/13/90

YEAR	TM/L	W	L	PCT	G	GS	CG	SH	SV	IP	H	HR	BB	SO	RAT	ERA	ERA+	OAV	OOB	BH	AVG	PB	PR	/A	PD	TPI
1990	LA-N	1	0	1.000	20	0	0	0	1	16^1	15	1	6	15	11.6	3.86	95	.242	.309	0	—	0	-0	-0	0	0.0

● ED WALSH Walsh, Edward Arthur b: 2/11/05, Meriden, Conn. d: 10/31/37, Meriden, Conn. BR/TR, 6'1", 180 lbs. Deb: 7/04/28 F

YEAR	TM/L	W	L	PCT	G	GS	CG	SH	SV	IP	H	HR	BB	SO	RAT	ERA	ERA+	OAV	OOB	BH	AVG	PB	PR	/A	PD	TPI
1928	Chi-A	4	7	.364	14	10	3	0	0	78	86	2	42	32	15.3	4.96	82	.290	.387	3	.111	-2	-8	-8	-1	-1.0
1929	Chi-A	6	11	.353	24	20	7	0	0	129	156	9	64	31	15.6	5.65	76	.312	.394	10	.233	2	-20	-20	1	-1.6
1930	Chi-A	1	4	.200	37	4	0	0	0	103^2	131	8	30	37	14.3	5.38	86	.316	.367	9	.265	1	-8	-9	1	-0.6
1932	Chi-A	0	2	.000	4	4	1	0	0	20^1	26	3	13	7	17.3	8.41	51	.299	.390	2	.286	0	-9	-9	-0	-0.8
Total	4	11	24	.314	79	38	11	0	0	331	399	22	149	107	15.3	5.57	78	.307	.384	24	.216	1	-45	-45	1	-4.0

● ED WALSH Walsh, Edward Augustine "Big Ed" b: 5/14/1881, Plains, Pa. d: 5/26/59, Pompano Beach, Fla BR/TR, 6'1", 193 lbs. Deb: 5/07/04 FMUCH

YEAR	TM/L	W	L	PCT	G	GS	CG	SH	SV	IP	H	HR	BB	SO	RAT	ERA	ERA+	OAV	OOB	BH	AVG	PB	PR	/A	PD	TPI
1904	Chi-A	6	3	.667	18	8	6	1	1	110^2	90	1	32	57	10.2	2.60	94	.223	.285	9	.220	3	-0	-2	1	0.1
1905	Chi-A	8	3	.727	22	13	9	1	0	136^2	121	0	29	71	10.1	2.17	114	.239	.285	9	.155	-0	7	5	0	0.5
1906	*Chi-A	17	13	.567	41	31	24	**10**	1	278^1	215	1	58	171	9.1	1.88	135	.216	.265	14	.141	-2	25	21	8	3.0
1907	Chi-A	24	18	.571	**56**	46	**37**	5	**4**	**422^1**	341	3	87	206	9.3	**1.60**	**150**	.223	.268	25	.162	-1	**45**	**38**	22	**6.8**
1908	Chi-A	**40**	15	**.727**	**66**	49	**42**	**11**	**6**	**464**	343	2	56	**269**	7.9	1.42	164	.203	.232	27	.172	2	**51**	**47**	14	**7.5**
1909	Chi-A	15	11	.577	31	28	20	**8**	2	230^1	166	0	50	127	**8.6**	1.41	166	.203	**.253**	18	.214	4	**27**	24	7	4.3
1910	Chi-A	18	20	.474	**45**	36	33	7	**5**	369^2	242	5	61	258	**7.5**	**1.27**	**189**	**.187**	**.226**	30	.217	4	**52**	46	10	**7.3**
1911	Chi-A	27	18	.600	**56**	37	33	5	**4**	**368^2**	327	4	72	**255**	9.9	2.22	145	.239	**.280**	34	.215	-2	46	41	15	5.6
1912	Chi-A	27	17	.614	**62**	41	32	6	**10**	**393**	332	6	94	254	9.8	2.15	149	.231	.279	33	.243	5	51	46	7	6.2
1913	Chi-A	8	3	.727	16	14	7	1	1	97^2	91	1	39	34	12.3	2.58	113	.243	.321	5	.156	-1	4	4	1	0.4
1914	Chi-A	2	3	.400	8	5	3	1	0	44^2	33	0	20	15	10.9	2.82	95	.212	.305	1	.063	-1	-0	-1	1	-0.1
1915	Chi-A	3	0	1.000	3	3	3	1	0	27	19	0	7	12	8.7	1.33	223	.202	.257	4	.364	1	5	5	-1	0.6
1916	Chi-A	0	1	.000	2	1	0	0	0	3^1	4	0	3	3	18.9	2.70	102	.286	.412	0	—	0	0	0	0	0.0
1917	Bos-N	0	1	.000	4	3	1	0	0	18	22	0	9	4	16.0	3.50	73	.314	.400	1	.250	1	-2	-2	0	-0.1
Total	14	195	126	.607	430	315	250	57	34	2964^1	2346	23	617	1736	9.2	1.82	145	.218	.264	210	.193	12	310	270	83	42.1

● JUNIOR WALSH Walsh, James Gerald b: 3/7/19, Newark, N.J. d: 11/12/90, Olyphant, Pa. BR/TR, 5'11", 185 lbs. Deb: 9/14/46

YEAR	TM/L	W	L	PCT	G	GS	CG	SH	SV	IP	H	HR	BB	SO	RAT	ERA	ERA+	OAV	OOB	BH	AVG	PB	PR	/A	PD	TPI
1946	Pit-N	0	1	.000	4	2	0	0	0	10^1	9	0	10	2	17.4	5.23	67	.237	.408	0	.000	-1	-2	-2	-0	-0.3
1948	Pit-N	1	0	1.000	2	0	0	0	0	4^1	4	1	5	0	18.7	10.38	39	.235	.409	0	.000	-0	-3	-3	0	-0.3
1949	Pit-N	1	4	.200	9	7	1	1	0	42^2	40	5	16	24	11.8	5.06	83	.244	.311	0	.000	-1	-5	-4	-1	-0.6
1950	Pit-N	1	1	.500	38	2	0	0	2	62^1	56	6	34	33	13.1	5.05	87	.246	.346	1	.167	1	-6	-5	0	-0.3
1951	Pit-N	1	4	.200	36	1	0	0	0	73^1	92	9	46	32	17.1	6.87	61	.304	.397	1	.143	0	-24	-22	0	-2.1
Total	5	4	10	.286	89	12	1	1	2	193	201	21	111	91	14.7	5.88	72	.268	.365	2	.065	-1	-40	-35	-0	-3.6

● JIM WALSH Walsh, James Thomas b: 7/10/1894, Roxbury, Mass. d: 5/13/67, Boston, Mass. BL/TL, 5'11", 175 lbs. Deb: 8/25/21

YEAR	TM/L	W	L	PCT	G	GS	CG	SH	SV	IP	H	HR	BB	SO	RAT	ERA	ERA+	OAV	OOB	BH	AVG	PB	PR	/A	PD	TPI
1921	Det-A	0	0	—	3	0	0	0	0	4	2	0	1	3	6.8	2.25	190	.125	.176	0	—	0	1	1	-0	0.1

● DEE WALSH Walsh, Leo Thomas b: 3/28/1890, St.Louis, Mo. d: 7/14/71, St.Louis, Mo. BB/TR, 5'9.5", 165 lbs. Deb: 4/10/13 ♦

YEAR	TM/L	W	L	PCT	G	GS	CG	SH	SV	IP	H	HR	BB	SO	RAT	ERA	ERA+	OAV	OOB	BH	AVG	PB	PR	/A	PD	TPI
1915	StL-A	0	0	—	1	0	0	0	0	2	2	0	2	0	18.0	13.50	21	.222	.364	33	.220	0	-2	-2	-0	-0.2

● JIMMY WALSH Walsh, Michael Timothy "Runt" b: 3/25/1886, Lima, Ohio d: 1/21/47, Baltimore, Md. BR/TR, 5'9", 174 lbs. Deb: 4/25/10 ♦

YEAR	TM/L	W	L	PCT	G	GS	CG	SH	SV	IP	H	HR	BB	SO	RAT	ERA	ERA+	OAV	OOB	BH	AVG	PB	PR	/A	PD	TPI
1911	Phi-N	0	1	.000	1	0	0	0	0	2^2	7	1	1	1	27.0	13.50	26	.500	.533	78	.270	0	-3	-3	-0	-0.3

● GENE WALTER Walter, Gene Winston b: 11/22/60, Chicago, Ill. BL/TL, 6'4", 200 lbs. Deb: 8/09/85

YEAR	TM/L	W	L	PCT	G	GS	CG	SH	SV	IP	H	HR	BB	SO	RAT	ERA	ERA+	OAV	OOB	BH	AVG	PB	PR	/A	PD	TPI
1985	SD-N	0	2	.000	15	0	0	0	3	22	12	0	8	18	8.2	2.05	173	.158	.238	0	.000	0	4	4	0	0.4
1986	SD-N	2	2	.500	57	0	0	0	1	98	89	7	49	84	13.0	3.86	95	.247	.343	2	.200	1	-2	-2	1	-0.1
1987	NY-N	1	2	.333	21	0	0	0	0	19^2	18	1	13	11	14.6	3.20	118	.243	.364	0	.000	0	2	1	-0	0.1
1988	NY-N	0	1	.000	19	0	0	0	0	16^2	21	0	11	14	17.3	3.78	85	.309	.405	0	—	0	-1	-1	-0	-0.1
	Sea-A	1	0	1.000	16	0	0	0	0	26^1	21	0	15	13	13.0	5.13	81	.216	.333	0	—	0	-3	-3	-0	-0.5
Total	4	4	7	.364	128	0	0	0	4	182^2	161	8	96	140	13.0	3.74	98	.238	.339	2	.167	1	0	-1	0	-0.2

● BERNIE WALTER Walter, James Bernard b: 8/15/08, Dover, Tenn. d: 10/30/88, Nashville, Tenn. BR/TR, 6'1", 175 lbs. Deb: 8/16/30

YEAR	TM/L	W	L	PCT	G	GS	CG	SH	SV	IP	H	HR	BB	SO	RAT	ERA	ERA+	OAV	OOB	BH	AVG	PB	PR	/A	PD	TPI
1930	Pit-N	0	0	—	1	0	0	0	0	1	0	0	0	1	0.0	0.00	—	.000	.000	0	—	0	1	1	0	0.1

● CHARLIE WALTERS Walters, Charles Leonard b: 2/21/47, Minneapolis, Minn. BR/TR, 6'4", 190 lbs. Deb: 4/11/69

YEAR	TM/L	W	L	PCT	G	GS	CG	SH	SV	IP	H	HR	BB	SO	RAT	ERA	ERA+	OAV	OOB	BH	AVG	PB	PR	/A	PD	TPI
1969	Min-A	0	0	—	6	0	0	0	0	6^2	6	1	3	2	13.5	5.40	68	.240	.345	0	—	0	-1	-1	-0	-0.1

● MIKE WALTERS Walters, Michael Charles b: 10/18/57, St.Louis, Mo. BR/TR, 6'5", 203 lbs. Deb: 7/08/83

YEAR	TM/L	W	L	PCT	G	GS	CG	SH	SV	IP	H	HR	BB	SO	RAT	ERA	ERA+	OAV	OOB	BH	AVG	PB	PR	/A	PD	TPI
1983	Min-A	1	1	.500	23	0	0	0	2	59	52	4	20	21	11.3	4.12	103	.243	.314	0	—	0	-0	1	0	0.0
1984	Min-A	0	3	.000	23	0	0	0	2	29	31	1	14	10	14.3	3.72	113	.287	.374	0	—	0	1	2	-0	-0.1
Total	2	1	4	.200	46	0	0	0	4	88	83	5	34	31	12.3	3.99	106	.258	.334	0	—	0	0	2	-0	-0.1

● BUCKY WALTERS Walters, William Henry b: 4/19/09, Philadelphia, Pa. d: 4/20/91, Abington, Pa. BR/TR, 6'1", 180 lbs. Deb: 9/18/31 MC♦

YEAR	TM/L	W	L	PCT	G	GS	CG	SH	SV	IP	H	HR	BB	SO	RAT	ERA	ERA+	OAV	OOB	BH	AVG	PB	PR	/A	PD	TPI
1934	Phi-N	0	0	—	2	1	0	0	0	7	8	1	2	7	14.1	1.29	367	.296	.367	78	.260	0	2	3	1	0.4
1935	Phi-N	9	9	.500	24	22	8	2	0	151	168	9	68	40	14.5	4.17	109	.289	.370	24	.250	2	-3	6	2	1.1
1936	Phi-N	11	21	.344	40	33	15	**4**	0	258	284	11	115	66	14.1	4.26	107	.277	.353	29	.240	3	-7	8	9	2.1
1937	Phi-N★	14	15	.483	37	34	15	3	0	246^1	292	14	86	87	13.9	4.75	91	.295	.353	38	.277	4	-23	-11	5	-0.1
1938	Phi-N	4	8	.333	12	12	9	1	0	82^2	91	8	42	28	14.8	5.23	74	.276	.363	10	.286	3	-13	-12	0	-0.8
	Cin-N	11	6	.647	27	22	11	2	1	168^1	168	5	66	65	12.6	3.69	99	.255	.324	9	.141	-0	2	-1	2	0.1
	Yr	15	14	.517	39	34	20	3	1	251	259	13	108	93	13.2	4.20	89	.261	.335	19	.192	3	-11	-13	3	-0.7
1939	*Cin-N☆	**27**	11	.711	39	36	**31**	2	0	**319**	250	15	109	**137**	10.3	**2.29**	**168**	**.220**	.291	39	.325	13	**58**	**55**	4	**8.0**
1940	*Cin-N★	**22**	10	.688	36	36	**29**	3	0	**305**	241	19	92	115	10.0	**2.48**	**153**	**.220**	.283	24	.205	2	**46**	**44**	-1	**5.0**
1941	Cin-N★	19	15	.559	37	35	**27**	5	2	**302**	292	10	88	129	11.4	2.83	127	.255	.309	20	.189	2	27	26	2	3.2
1942	Cin-N★	15	14	.517	34	32	21	2	0	253^2	223	8	73	109	10.7	2.66	123	.231	.289	24	.242	6	18	18	1	2.9
1943	Cin-N	15	15	.500	34	34	21	5	0	246^1	244	8	109	80	12.9	3.54	94	.264	.342	24	.267	8	-4	-6	1	0.2
1944	Cin-N★	**23**	8	.742	34	32	27	6	1	285	233	10	87	77	10.2	2.40	145	**.219**	.281	30	.280	8	**38**	**34**	1	**4.7**
1945	Cin-N	10	10	.500	22	22	12	3	0	168	166	6	51	45	11.7	2.68	140	.259	.316	14	.230	5	21	20	-0	2.7
1946	Cin-N	10	7	.588	22	22	10	2	0	151^1	146	9	64	60	12.6	2.56	131	.258	.336	7	.127	-1	14	13	2	1.6
1947	Cin-N	8	8	.500	20	20	5	2	0	122	137	15	49	43	13.9	5.75	71	.278	.347	12	.267	3	-23	-22	-1	-1.9
1948	Cin-N	0	3	.000	7	5	1	0	0	35	42	6	18	19	15.4	4.63	84	.316	.397	4	.267	0	-3	-3	1	-0.1
1950	Bos-N	0	0	—	1	0	0	0	0	4	5	0	2	0	15.8	4.50	86	.313	.389	0	.000	-0	-0	-0	-0	-0.1

YEAR TM/L	W	L	PCT	G	GS	CG	SH	SV	IP	H	HR	BB	SO	RAT	ERA	ERA+	OAV	OOB	BH	AVG	PB	PR	/A	PD	TPI
Total 16	198	160	.553	428	398	242	42	4	3104^{2}	2990	154	1121	1107	12.1	3.30	115	.253	.321	477	.243	58	152	168	27	29.0

● BRUCE WALTON
Walton, Bruce Kenneth b: 12/25/62, Bakersfield, Cal. BR/TR, 6'2", 195 lbs. Deb: 5/11/91

YEAR TM/L	W	L	PCT	G	GS	CG	SH	SV	IP	H	HR	BB	SO	RAT	ERA	ERA+	OAV	OOB	BH	AVG	PB	PR	/A	PD	TPI
1991 Oak-A	1	0	1.000	12	0	0	0	0	13	11	3	6	10	12.5	6.23	62	.229	.327	0	—	0	-3	-3	-0	-0.3
1992 Oak-A	0	0	—	7	0	0	0	0	10	17	1	3	7	18.0	9.90	38	.378	.417	0	—	0	-7	-7	-0	-0.7
Total 2	1	0	1.000	19	0	0	0	0	23	28	4	9	17	14.9	7.83	49	.301	.369	0	—	0	-10	-10	-0	-1.0

● DICK WANTZ
Wantz, Richard Carter b: 4/11/40, South Gate, Cal. d: 5/13/65, Inglewood, Cal. BR/TR, 6'5", 175 lbs. Deb: 4/13/65

YEAR TM/L	W	L	PCT	G	GS	CG	SH	SV	IP	H	HR	BB	SO	RAT	ERA	ERA+	OAV	OOB	BH	AVG	PB	PR	/A	PD	TPI
1965 Cal-A	0	0	—	1	0	0	0	0	1	3	0	0	2	27.0	18.00	19	.500	.500	0	—	0	-2	-2	0	-0.2

● STEVE WAPNICK
Wapnick, Steven Lee b: 9/25/65, Panorama City, Cal. BR/TR, 6'2", 200 lbs. Deb: 4/14/90

YEAR TM/L	W	L	PCT	G	GS	CG	SH	SV	IP	H	HR	BB	SO	RAT	ERA	ERA+	OAV	OOB	BH	AVG	PB	PR	/A	PD	TPI
1990 Det-A	0	0	—	4	0	0	0	0	7	8	0	10	6	23.1	6.43	62	.296	.486	0	—	0	-2	-2	-0	-0.2
1991 Chi-A	0	1	.000	6	0	0	0	0	5	2	0	4	1	10.8	1.80	221	.111	.273	0	—	0	1	1	-0	0.1
Total 2	0	1	.000	10	0	0	0	0	12	10	0	14	7	18.0	4.50	88	.222	.407	0	—	0	-1	-1	-0	-0.1

● COLIN WARD
Ward, Colin Norval b: 11/22/60, Los Angeles, Cal. BL/TL, 6'3", 190 lbs. Deb: 9/21/85

YEAR TM/L	W	L	PCT	G	GS	CG	SH	SV	IP	H	HR	BB	SO	RAT	ERA	ERA+	OAV	OOB	BH	AVG	PB	PR	/A	PD	TPI
1985 SF-N	0	0	—	6	2	0	0	0	12^{1}	10	0	7	8	12.4	4.38	78	.233	.340	0	.000	-0	-1	-1	0	-0.2

● JOHNNY WARD
Ward, John b: East St.Louis, Ill. Deb: 9/19/1885

YEAR TM/L	W	L	PCT	G	GS	CG	SH	SV	IP	H	HR	BB	SO	RAT	ERA	ERA+	OAV	OOB	BH	AVG	PB	PR	/A	PD	TPI
1885 Pro-N	0	1	.000	1	1	1	0	0	8	10	0	1	3	12.4	4.50	59	.286	.306	0	.000	-0	-1	-2	-0	-0.2

● JOHN WARD
Ward, John Montgomery b: 3/3/1860, Bellefonte, Pa. d: 3/4/25, Augusta, Ga. BL/TR, 5'9", 165 lbs. Deb: 7/15/1878 MH♦

YEAR TM/L	W	L	PCT	G	GS	CG	SH	SV	IP	H	HR	BB	SO	RAT	ERA	ERA+	OAV	OOB	BH	AVG	PB	PR	/A	PD	TPI
1878 Pro-N	22	13	.629	37	37	37	6	0	334	308	3	34	116	9.2	**1.51**	**146**	.231	.251	27	.196	2	**30**	26	2	**2.8**
1879 Pro-N	**47**	19	**.712**	70	60	58	2	**1**	587	571	5	36	**239**	9.3	2.15	110	.239	.250	104	.286	16	23	13	4	2.9
1880 Pro-N	39	24	.619	70	67	59	**8**	1	595	501	5	45	230	8.3	1.74	127	.217	.232	81	.228	1	**42**	31	5	3.5
1881 Pro-N	18	18	.500	39	35	32	3	0	330	326	2	53	119	10.3	2.13	125	.242	.271	87	.244	3	24	19	5	2.6
1882 Pro-N	19	12	.613	33	32	29	4	**1**	278	261	6	36	72	9.6	2.59	109	.232	.256	87	.245	1	10	7	4	1.0
1883 NY-N	16	13	.552	34	25	24	1	0	277	278	3	31	121	10.0	2.70	115	.246	.267	97	.255	6	14	12	4	1.9
1884 NY-N	3	3	.500	9	5	5	0	0	60^{2}	72	2	18	23	13.4	3.41	87	.280	.327	122	.253	1	-3	-3	1	-0.1
Total 7	164	102	.617	292	261	244	24	3	2461^{2}	2317	26	253	920	9.4	2.10	118	.235	.254	2105	.275	30	138	105	24	14.6

● DICK WARD
Ward, Richard Ole b: 5/21/09, Herrick, S.Dak. d: 5/30/66, Freeland, Wash. BR/TR, 6'1", 198 lbs. Deb: 5/03/34

YEAR TM/L	W	L	PCT	G	GS	CG	SH	SV	IP	H	HR	BB	SO	RAT	ERA	ERA+	OAV	OOB	BH	AVG	PB	PR	/A	PD	TPI
1934 Chi-N	0	0	—	3	0	0	0	0	6	9	0	2	1	16.5	3.00	129	.375	.423	0	.000	-0	1	1	-0	0.0
1935 StL-N	0	0	—	1	0	0	0	0	0	0	0	1	0	—	—	—	—	1.000	0	—	0	0	0	0	0.0
Total 2	0	0	—	4	0	0	0	0	6	9	0	3	1	18.0	3.00	129	.375	.444	0	.000	-0	1	1	-0	0.0

● COLBY WARD
Ward, Robert Colby b: 1/2/64, Lansing, Mich. BR/TR, 6'2", 185 lbs. Deb: 7/27/90

YEAR TM/L	W	L	PCT	G	GS	CG	SH	SV	IP	H	HR	BB	SO	RAT	ERA	ERA+	OAV	OOB	BH	AVG	PB	PR	/A	PD	TPI
1990 Cle-A	1	3	.250	22	0	0	0	1	36	31	3	21	23	13.3	4.25	92	.238	.349	0	—	0	-1	-1	-0	-0.1

● DUANE WARD
Ward, Roy Duane b: 5/28/64, Park View, N.Mex. BR/TR, 6'4", 215 lbs. Deb: 4/12/86

YEAR TM/L	W	L	PCT	G	GS	CG	SH	SV	IP	H	HR	BB	SO	RAT	ERA	ERA+	OAV	OOB	BH	AVG	PB	PR	/A	PD	TPI
1986 Atl-N	0	1	.000	10	0	0	0	0	16	22	2	8	8	16.9	7.31	54	.349	.423	0	.000	-0	-6	-6	1	-0.6
Tor-A	0	1	.000	2	1	0	0	0	2	3	0	4	1	36.0	13.50	31	.300	.533	0	—	0	-2	-2	0	-0.3
1987 Tor-A	1	0	1.000	12	1	0	0	0	11^{2}	14	0	12	10	20.1	6.94	65	.326	.473	0	—	0	-3	-3	0	-0.4
1988 Tor-A	9	3	.750	64	0	0	0	15	111^{2}	101	5	60	91	13.4	3.30	119	.245	.347	0	—	0	8	8	-0	0.7
1989 *Tor-A	4	10	.286	66	0	0	0	15	114^{2}	94	4	58	122	12.3	3.77	100	.230	.333	0	—	0	1	0	2	0.2
1990 Tor-A	2	8	.200	73	0	0	0	11	127^{2}	101	9	42	112	10.2	3.45	114	.221	.288	0	—	0	6	7	1	0.7
1991 *Tor-A	7	6	.538	**81**	0	0	0	23	107^{1}	80	3	33	132	9.6	2.77	152	.207	.273	0	—	0	16	17	0	1.8
1992 *Tor-A	7	4	.636	79	0	0	0	12	101^{1}	76	5	39	103	10.3	1.95	209	.207	.285	0	—	0	**22**	**24**	0	2.5
Total 7	30	33	.476	387	2	0	0	76	592^{1}	491	28	256	579	11.6	3.31	120	.229	.315	0	.000	-0	43	45	3	4.6

● JON WARDEN
Warden, Jonathan Edgar "Warbler" b: 10/1/46, Columbus, Ohio BB/TL, 6', 205 lbs. Deb: 4/11/68

YEAR TM/L	W	L	PCT	G	GS	CG	SH	SV	IP	H	HR	BB	SO	RAT	ERA	ERA+	OAV	OOB	BH	AVG	PB	PR	/A	PD	TPI
1968 Det-A	4	1	.800	28	0	0	0	3	37^{1}	30	5	15	25	10.8	3.62	83	.217	.294	0	.000	-0	-3	-3	-1	-0.4

● CURT WARDLE
Wardle, Curtis Ray b: 11/16/60, Downey, Cal. BL/TL, 6'5", 220 lbs. Deb: 8/30/84

YEAR TM/L	W	L	PCT	G	GS	CG	SH	SV	IP	H	HR	BB	SO	RAT	ERA	ERA+	OAV	OOB	BH	AVG	PB	PR	/A	PD	TPI
1984 Min-A	0	0	—	2	0	0	0	0	4	3	2	0	5	6.8	4.50	93	.200	.200	0	—	0	-0	-0	0	-0.3
1985 Min-A	1	3	.250	35	0	0	0	1	49	49	9	28	47	14.3	5.51	80	.266	.366	0	—	0	-7	-6	1	-0.9
Cle-A	7	6	.538	15	12	0	0	0	66	78	11	34	37	15.4	6.68	62	.297	.379	0	—	0	-19	-19	-1	-1.8
Yr	8	9	.471	50	12	0	0	1	115	127	20	62	84	14.9	6.18	69	.283	.371	0	—	0	-26	-25	-0	-2.7
Total 2	8	9	.471	52	12	0	0	1	119	130	22	62	89	14.7	6.13	69	.281	.369	0	—	0	-26	-25	0	-3.0

● JACK WARHOP
Warhop, John Milton "Chief" or "Crab" (b: John Milton Wauhop)
b: 7/4/1884, Hinton, W.Va. d: 10/4/60, Freeport, Ill. BR/TR, 5'9.5", 168 lbs. Deb: 9/19/08

YEAR TM/L	W	L	PCT	G	GS	CG	SH	SV	IP	H	HR	BB	SO	RAT	ERA	ERA+	OAV	OOB	BH	AVG	PB	PR	/A	PD	TPI
1908 NY-A	1	2	.333	5	4	3	0	0	36^{1}	40	0	8	11	12.9	4.46	56	.292	.349	1	.063	-1	-8	-8	0	-0.9
1909 NY-A	13	15	.464	36	23	21	3	2	243^{1}	197	2	81	95	11.2	2.40	105	.233	.319	11	.128	-2	2	3	1	0.2
1910 NY-A	14	14	.500	37	27	20	0	2	243	219	1	79	75	11.7	3.00	89	.246	.320	14	.177	-1	-13	-9	-4	-1.5
1911 NY-A	12	13	.480	31	25	17	1	0	209^{2}	239	6	44	71	12.8	4.16	86	.286	.333	12	.156	-4	-19	-13	-2	-1.8
1912 NY-A	10	19	.345	39	22	16	0	3	258	256	3	59	110	11.5	2.86	126	.266	.319	19	.207	-1	13	21	-3	1.8
1913 NY-A	4	6	.400	15	7	1	0	0	62^{1}	69	1	33	11	16.5	3.75	80	.292	.406	3	.130	-0	-6	-5	-2	-0.8
1914 NY-A	8	15	.348	37	23	15	0	0	216^{2}	182	8	44	56	9.8	2.37	117	.235	.286	10	.141	-1	9	9	-2	0.8
1915 NY-A	7	9	.438	21	19	12	0	0	143^{1}	164	7	52	34	14.3	3.96	74	.309	.384	7	.137	-2	-16	-16	-3	-2.0
Total 8	69	93	.426	221	150	105	4	7	1412^{2}	1366	28	400	463	12.0	3.12	96	.262	.328	77	.156	-12	-38	-19	-13	-4.2

● CY WARMOTH
Warmoth, Wallace Walter b: 2/2/1893, Bone Gap, Ill. d: 6/20/57, Mt.Carmel, Ill. BL/TL, 5'11", 158 lbs. Deb: 8/31/16

YEAR TM/L	W	L	PCT	G	GS	CG	SH	SV	IP	H	HR	BB	SO	RAT	ERA	ERA+	OAV	OOB	BH	AVG	PB	PR	/A	PD	TPI
1916 StL-N	0	0	—	3	0	0	0	0	5	12	0	4	1	30.6	14.40	18	.500	.586	0	.000	-0	-7	-7	-0	-0.7
1922 Was-A	1	0	1.000	5	1	1	0	0	19	15	0	9	8	11.4	1.42	272	.205	.293	1	.143	-0	6	5	-0	0.5
1923 Was-A	7	5	.583	21	13	4	0	0	105	103	4	76	45	15.4	4.29	88	.261	.381	8	.222	2	-4	-6	0	-0.4
Total 3	8	5	.615	29	14	5	0	0	129	130	4	89	54	15.4	4.26	88	.264	.379	9	.200	1	-5	-7	-0	-0.6

● LON WARNEKE
Warneke, Lonnie "The Arkansas Hummingbird" b: 3/28/09, Mt.Ida, Ark. d: 6/23/76, Hot Springs, Ark. BR/TR, 6'2", 185 lbs. Deb: 4/18/30 U

YEAR TM/L	W	L	PCT	G	GS	CG	SH	SV	IP	H	HR	BB	SO	RAT	ERA	ERA+	OAV	OOB	BH	AVG	PB	PR	/A	PD	TPI
1930 Chi-N	0	0	—	1	0	0	0	0	1^{1}	2	0	5	0	47.3	33.75	14	.400	.700	0	—	0	-4	-4	0	-0.3
1931 Chi-N	2	4	.333	20	7	3	0	0	64^{1}	67	1	37	27	15.0	3.22	120	.269	.370	5	.263	1	5	5	-1	0.4
1932 *Chi-N	**22**	6	**.786**	35	32	25	**4**	0	277	247	12	64	106	10.2	**2.37**	**159**	.237	.283	19	.192	-0	**46**	**43**	-0	4.5
1933 Chi-N★	18	13	.581	36	34	**26**	4	1	287^{1}	262	8	75	133	10.6	2.00	163	.244	.295	30	.300	10	43	40	3	6.3
1934 Chi-N★	22	10	.688	43	35	23	3	3	291^{1}	273	16	66	143	10.5	3.21	121	.244	.287	22	.195	-0	27	21	0	2.1
1935 *Chi-N	20	13	.606	42	30	20	1	4	261^{2}	257	19	50	120	10.7	3.06	128	.257	.294	20	.220	1	28	25	-1	2.5
1936 Chi-N★	16	13	.552	40	29	13	**4**	1	240^{1}	246	10	76	113	12.2	3.45	116	.264	.322	17	.202	0	15	14	-1	1.4
1937 StL-N	18	11	.621	36	33	18	2	0	238^{2}	280	32	69	87	13.2	4.53	88	.287	.335	21	.262	5	-16	-14	-3	-1.2
1938 StL-N	13	8	.619	31	26	12	4	0	197	199	14	64	89	12.1	3.97	100	.256	.314	23	.324	5	-4	-0	-2	0.3
1939 StL-N☆	13	7	.650	34	21	6	2	2	162	160	14	49	59	11.7	3.78	109	.259	.316	10	.192	1	3	6	-0	0.7
1940 StL-N	16	10	.615	33	31	17	1	0	232	235	17	47	85	11.1	3.14	127	.257	.296	18	.209	2	18	22	1	2.6
1941 StL-N☆	17	9	.654	37	30	12	4	0	246	227	19	82	83	11.4	3.15	120	.249	.313	9	.117	-2	13	17	-2	1.3
1942 StL-N	6	4	.600	12	12	5	0	0	82	76	8	15	31	10.0	3.29	104	.238	.272	10	.333	3	0	1	-1	0.4
Chi-N	5	7	.417	15	12	8	1	2	99	97	2	21	28	10.7	2.27	141	.259	.298	6	.188	-0	11	10	-0	1.1
Yr	11	11	.500	27	24	13	1	2	181	173	10	36	59	10.4	2.73	121	.249	.286	16	.258	3	12	11	-1	1.5
1943 Chi-N	4	5	.444	21	10	4	0	0	88^{1}	82	3	18	30	10.2	3.16	106	.246	.285	5	.192	1	2	2	1	0.4
1945 Chi-N	0	1	.000	9	1	0	0	0	14	16	0	1	6	10.9	3.86	95	.267	.279	0	.000	0	-0	-0	0	0.0

YEAR TM/L	W	L	PCT	G	GS	CG	SH	SV	IP	H	HR	BB	SO	RAT	ERA	ERA+	OAV	OOB	BH	AVG	PB	PR	/A	PD	TPI
Total 15	192	121	.613	445	343	192	30	13	2782^{1}	2726	175	739	1140	11.3	3.18	119	.255	.304	215	.223	28	188	188	-5	22.5
● **ED WARNER** Warner, Edward Emory b: 6/20/1889, Fitchburg, Mass. d: 2/5/54, New York, N.Y. BR/TL, 5'10.5", 165 lbs. Deb: 7/02/12																									
1912 Pit-N	1	1	.500	11	3	1	1	0	45	40	0	18	13	12.2	3.60	91	.242	.328	2	.133	-1	-1	-2	1	-0.2
● **JACK WARNER** Warner, Jack Dyer b: 7/12/40, Brandywine, W.Va. BR/TR, 5'11", 190 lbs. Deb: 4/10/62																									
1962 Chi-N	0	0	—	7	0	0	0	0	7	9	3	0	3	11.6	7.71	54	.321	.321	0	—	0	-3	-3	0	-0.2
1963 Chi-N	0	1	.000	8	0	0	0	0	22^{2}	21	1	8	7	11.5	2.78	126	.256	.322	1	.250	0	1	2	-0	0.2
1964 Chi-N	0	0	—	7	0	0	0	0	9^{1}	12	0	4	6	15.4	2.89	128	.333	.400	0	—	0	1	1	0	0.1
1965 Chi-N	0	1	.000	11	0	0	0	0	15^{2}	22	1	9	7	17.8	8.62	43	.355	.437	0	.000	-0	-9	-9	0	-0.9
Total 4	0	2	.000	33	0	0	0	0	54^{2}	64	5	21	23	14.0	5.10	72	.308	.371	1	.200	0	-10	-9	0	-0.8
● **MIKE WARREN** Warren, Michael Bruce b: 3/26/61, Inglewood, Cal. BR/TR, 6'1", 175 lbs. Deb: 6/12/83																									
1983 Oak-A	5	3	.625	12	9	3	1	0	65^{2}	51	4	18	30	9.6	4.11	94	.215	.273	0	—	0	-0	-2	-1	0.2
1984 Oak-A	3	6	.333	24	12	0	0	0	90	104	11	44	61	15.1	4.90	76	.291	.373	0	—	0	-9	-12	-2	-0.8
1985 Oak-A	1	4	.200	16	6	0	0	0	49	52	13	38	48	17.3	6.61	58	.261	.390	0	—	0	-13	-15	-1	-1.0
Total 3	9	13	.409	52	27	3	1	0	204^{2}	207	28	100	139	13.9	5.06	75	.261	.349	0	—	0	-23	-28	-4	-1.6
● **TOMMY WARREN** Warren, Thomas Gentry b: 7/5/17, Tulsa, Okla. d: 1/2/68, Tulsa, Okla. BB/TL, 6'1", 190 lbs. Deb: 4/18/44																									
1944 Bro-N	1	4	.200	22	4	2	0	0	68^{2}	74	4	40	18	14.9	4.98	71	.270	.363	11	.256	1	-10	-11	0	-0.9
● **DAN WARTHEN** Warthen, Daniel Dean b: 12/1/52, Omaha, Neb. BB/TL, 6', 200 lbs. Deb: 5/18/75 C																									
1975 Mon-N	8	6	.571	40	18	2	0	3	167^{2}	130	8	87	128	11.7	3.11	123	.217	.317	6	.118	-2	9	13	1	1.2
1976 Mon-N	2	10	.167	23	16	2	1	0	90	76	8	66	67	14.4	5.30	70	.232	.364	0	.000	-3	-18	-16	0	-1.9
1977 Mon-N	2	3	.400	12	6	1	0	0	35	33	7	38	26	18.3	7.97	48	.262	.433	1	.111	-0	-16	-16	1	-1.5
Phi-N	0	1	.000	3	0	0	0	0	3^{2}	4	0	5	1	22.1	0.00	—	.267	.450	0	—	0	2	2	-0	0.2
Yr	2	4	.333	15	6	1	0	0	38^{2}	37	7	43	27	18.6	7.22	53	.261	.432	1	.111	-0	-14	-15	0	-1.3
1978 Hou-N	0	1	.000	5	1	0	0	0	10^{2}	10	3	2	2	10.1	4.22	78	.250	.286	0	.000	-0	-1	-1	-0	-0.2
Total 4	12	21	.364	83	41	5	1	3	307	253	26	198	224	13.3	4.31	88	.228	.347	7	.079	-6	-23	-18	1	-2.2
● **GEORGE WASHBURN** Washburn, George Edward b: 10/6/14, Solon, Me. d: 1/5/79, Baton Rouge, La. BL/TR, 6'1", 175 lbs. Deb: 5/04/41																									
1941 NY-A	0	1	.000	1	1	0	0	0	2	2	0	5	1	31.5	13.50	29	.286	.583	0	.000	-0	-2	-2	0	-0.2
● **GREG WASHBURN** Washburn, Gregory James b: 12/3/46, Coal City, Ill. BR/TR, 6', 190 lbs. Deb: 6/07/69																									
1969 Cal-A	0	2	.000	8	2	0	0	0	11^{1}	21	0	5	4	21.4	7.94	44	.404	.466	0	—	0	-5	-6	0	-0.5
● **LIBE WASHBURN** Washburn, Libeus b: 6/16/1874, Lyme, N.H. d: 3/22/40, Malone, N.Y. BB/TL, 5'10", 180 lbs. Deb: 5/30/02 ♦																									
1903 Phi-N	0	4	.000	4	4	4	0	0	35	44	0	11	9	14.1	4.37	75	.326	.377	3	.167	-0	-4	-4	-1	-0.5
● **RAY WASHBURN** Washburn, Ray Clark b: 5/31/38, Pasco, Wash. BR/TR, 6'1", 205 lbs. Deb: 9/20/61																									
1961 StL-N	1	1	.500	3	2	1	0	0	20^{1}	10	1	7	12	8.0	1.77	248	.152	.243	1	.125	-1	5	6	0	0.6
1962 StL-N	12	9	.571	34	25	2	1	0	175^{2}	187	25	58	109	12.7	4.10	104	.273	.332	10	.179	1	-3	3	1	0.5
1963 StL-N	5	3	.625	11	11	4	2	0	64^{1}	50	5	14	47	9.1	3.08	115	.212	.259	1	.053	-1	2	3	1	0.3
1964 StL-N	3	4	.429	15	10	0	0	2	60	60	7	17	28	12.3	4.05	94	.264	.329	2	.133	-0	-3	-2	1	-0.1
1965 StL-N	9	11	.450	28	16	1	1	2	119^{1}	114	15	28	67	10.8	3.62	106	.254	.300	5	.152	0	-1	3	-1	0.3
1966 StL-N	11	9	.550	27	26	4	1	0	170	183	15	44	98	12.1	3.76	95	.280	.326	5	.093	-1	-3	-3	1	-0.4
1967 *StL-N	10	7	.588	27	27	3	1	0	186^{1}	190	14	42	98	11.4	3.53	93	.265	.309	6	.091	-2	-3	-5	2	-0.5
1968 *StL-N	14	8	.636	31	30	8	4	0	215	191	9	47	124	10.0	2.26	128	.239	.283	5	.083	0	17	15	-2	1.5
1969 StL-N	3	8	.273	28	16	2	0	1	132^{1}	133	9	49	80	12.4	3.06	117	.261	.327	3	.081	-2	8	8	1	0.6
1970 *Cin-N	4	4	.500	35	3	0	0	0	66^{1}	90	7	48	37	18.7	6.92	58	.324	.423	0	.000	-1	-21	-21	1	-2.1
Total 10	72	64	.529	239	166	25	10	5	1209^{2}	1208	107	354	700	11.8	3.53	101	.261	.316	38	.105	-7	-3	6	4	0.7
● **BUCK WASHER** Washer, William b: 10/11/1882, Akron, Ohio d: 12/8/55, Akron, Ohio BR/TR, 5'10", 175 lbs. Deb: 4/25/05																									
1905 Phi-N	0	0	—	1	0	0	0	0	3	4	0	5	0	27.0	6.00	49	—	1.800	0	.000	-0	-1	-1	0	-0.1
● **GARY WASLEWSKI** Waslewski, Gary Lee b: 7/21/41, Meriden, Conn. BR/TR, 6'4", 195 lbs. Deb: 6/11/67																									
1967 *Bos-A	2	2	.500	12	8	0	0	0	42	34	3	20	20	11.8	3.21	108	.225	.320	1	.091	-1	0	1	0	0.1
1968 Bos-A	4	7	.364	34	11	2	0	2	105^{1}	108	9	40	59	13.2	3.67	86	.269	.344	1	.038	-2	-8	-6	2	-0.7
1969 StL-N	0	2	.000	12	0	0	0	1	20^{2}	19	3	8	16	12.2	3.92	91	.244	.322	0	.000	-0	-1	-1	1	0.0
Mon-N	3	7	.300	30	14	3	1	1	109^{1}	102	5	63	63	14.2	3.29	112	.252	.364	1	.033	-2	4	5	1	0.3
Yr	3	9	.250	42	14	3	1	2	130	121	8	71	79	13.8	3.39	108	.250	.355	1	.032	-2	3	4	1	0.3
1970 Mon-N	0	2	.000	6	4	0	0	0	24^{2}	23	3	15	19	13.9	5.11	80	.247	.352	0	.000	-0	-3	-3	1	-0.3
NY-A	2	2	.500	26	5	0	0	0	55	42	4	27	27	11.9	3.11	113	.219	.327	1	.100	-1	4	2	1	0.3
1971 NY-A	0	1	.000	24	0	0	0	1	35^{2}	28	2	16	17	11.4	3.28	98	.214	.304	0	.000	-0	1	-0	-0	0.0
1972 Oak-A	0	3	.000	8	0	0	0	0	17^{2}	12	3	8	8	10.2	2.04	140	.190	.282	0	.000	-0	2	2	0	0.2
Total 6	11	26	.297	152	42	5	1	5	410^{1}	368	32	197	229	12.9	3.44	100	.243	.338	4	.045	-6	-2	1	4	-0.1
● **STEVE WATERBURY** Waterbury, Steven Craig b: 4/6/52, Carbondale, Ill. BR/TR, 6'5", 190 lbs. Deb: 9/14/76																									
1976 StL-N	0	0	—	5	0	0	0	0	6	7	0	3	4	15.0	6.00	59	.304	.385	0	—	0	-2	-2	-0	-0.2
● **FRED WATERS** Waters, Fred Warren b: 2/2/27, Benton, Miss. d: 8/28/89, Pensacola, Fla. BL/TL, 5'11", 185 lbs. Deb: 9/20/55																									
1955 Pit-N	0	0	—	2	0	0	0	0	5	7	1	2	0	16.2	3.60	114	.318	.375	0	.000	-0	0	0	0	0.0
1956 Pit-N	2	2	.500	23	5	1	0	0	51	48	3	30	14	13.9	2.82	134	.258	.364	1	.050	-1	5	5	-1	0.3
Total 2	2	2	.500	25	5	1	0	0	56	55	4	32	14	14.1	2.89	131	.264	.365	1	.048	-1	6	6	-1	0.3
● **BOB WATKINS** Watkins, Robert Cecil b: 3/12/48, San Francisco, Cal. BR/TR, 6'1", 170 lbs. Deb: 9/06/69																									
1969 Hou-N	0	0	—	5	0	0	0	0	15^{2}	13	1	13	11	14.9	5.17	68	.241	.388	0	.000	-0	-3	-3	-0	-0.3
● **DOC WATSON** Watson, Charles John b: 1/30/1886, Kensington, Ohio d: 12/30/49, San Diego, Cal. BR/TL, 6', 170 lbs. Deb: 9/03/13																									
1913 Chi-N	1	0	1.000	1	1	1	0	0	9	8	0	6	1	15.0	1.00	318	.242	.375	0	.000	0	2	2	-1	0.2
1914 Chi-F	9	8	.529	26	18	10	3	1	172	145	2	49	69	10.3	2.04	145	.236	.295	5	.093	-3	22	17	-1	1.3
StL-F	3	4	.429	9	7	4	2	0	56	41	1	24	18	11.1	1.93	175	.211	.311	2	.125	-1	8	9	-1	0.8
Yr	12	12	.500	35	25	14	5	1	228	186	3	73	87	10.4	2.01	152	.229	.296	7	.100	-4	30	26	-2	2.1
1915 StL-F	9	9	.500	33	20	6	0	0	135^{2}	132	1	58	45	12.9	3.98	80	.273	.355	5	.125	-3	-14	-12	-4	-1.9
Total 3	22	21	.512	69	46	21	5	1	372^{2}	326	4	137	133	11.5	2.70	115	.246	.322	12	.107	-7	18	17	-7	0.4
● **MULE WATSON** Watson, John Reeves b: 10/15/1896, Homer, La. d: 8/25/49, Shreveport, La. BR/TR, 6'1.5", 185 lbs. Deb: 7/04/18																									
1918 Phi-A	7	10	.412	21	19	11	3	0	141^{2}	139	0	44	30	11.8	3.37	87	.288	.350	6	.128	-3	-9	-7	-2	-1.3
1919 Phi-A	0	1	.000	4	2	0	0	0	14^{1}	17	2	7	6	15.1	6.91	50	.309	.387	0	.000	-1	-6	-6	1	-0.5
1920 Bos-N	0	0	—	1	0	0	0	0	3	0	0	0	0	0.0	0.00	—	.000	.000	0	.000	-0	1	1	0	0.1
Pit-N	0	0	—	5	0	0	0	0	11^{1}	15	2	7	1	17.5	8.74	37	.326	.415	0	.000	-0	-7	-7	0	-0.7
Bos-N	5	4	.556	12	10	4	2	0	71^{2}	79	0	17	16	12.2	3.77	81	.298	.343	3	.130	-1	-5	-6	-0	-0.7
Yr	5	4	.556	18	10	4	2	0	86	94	2	24	17	12.5	4.29	72	.294	.345	3	.111	-2	-11	-12	-0	-1.3
1921 Bos-N	14	13	.519	44	31	15	1	2	259^{1}	269	11	57	48	11.6	3.85	95	.270	.314	12	.138	-4	-2	-6	-1	-1.0
1922 Bos-N	8	14	.364	41	29	8	1	1	201	262	9	59	53	14.6	4.70	85	.317	.366	13	.197	-0	-13	-16	-0	-1.5
1923 Bos-N	1	2	.333	11	4	1	0	1	31^{1}	42	2	20	10	17.8	5.17	77	.339	.431	2	.250	-0	-4	-4	0	-0.4

YEAR	TM/L	W	L	PCT	G	GS	CG	SH	SV	IP	H	HR	BB	SO	RAT	ERA	ERA+	OAV	OOB	BH	AVG	PB	PR	/A	PD	TPI
	*NY-N	8	5	.615	17	15	8	0	0	108^1	117	11	21	26	11.5	3.41	112	.280	.316	8	.174	-1	7	5	-1	0.3
	Yr	9	7	.563	28	19	9	0	1	139^2	159	13	41	36	13.0	3.80	101	.293	.344	10	.185	-1	3	1	-1	-0.1
1924	*NY-N	7	4	.636	22	16	6	1	0	99^2	122	7	24	18	13.3	3.79	97	.303	.343	9	.257	4	1	-1	-1	0.1
Total	7	50	53	.485	178	126	53	8	4	941^2	1062	44	256	208	12.8	4.03	89	.293	.342	53	.165	-8	-38	-45	-3	-5.6

● MILT WATSON Watson, Milton Wilson "Mule" b: 1/10/1890, Flovilla, Ga. d: 4/10/62, Pine Bluff, Ark. BR/TR, 6'1", 180 lbs. Deb: 7/26/16

YEAR	TM/L	W	L	PCT	G	GS	CG	SH	SV	IP	H	HR	BB	SO	RAT	ERA	ERA+	OAV	OOB	BH	AVG	PB	PR	/A	PD	TPI
1916	StL-N	4	6	.400	18	13	5	2	0	103	109	3	33	27	12.8	3.06	86	.283	.346	7	.219	0	-5	-5	-1	-0.6
1917	StL-N	10	13	.435	41	20	5	3	0	161^1	149	3	51	45	11.7	3.51	77	.252	.321	5	.098	-4	-14	-15	1	-1.9
1918	Phi-N	5	7	.417	23	11	6	0	0	112^2	126	1	36	29	13.1	3.43	87	.293	.350	3	.075	-4	-8	-5	-1	-1.2
1919	Phi-N	2	4	.333	8	4	3	0	0	47	51	3	19	12	13.8	5.17	62	.282	.356	1	.063	-2	-12	-10	0	-1.2
Total	4	21	30	.412	90	48	19	5	0	424	435	10	139	113	12.5	3.57	79	.274	.339	16	.115	-9	-40	-35	-0	-4.9

● MOTHER WATSON Watson, Walter L. b: 1/27/1865, Middleport, Ohio d: 11/23/1898, Middleport, Ohio 5'9", 145 lbs. Deb: 5/19/1887

YEAR	TM/L	W	L	PCT	G	GS	CG	SH	SV	IP	H	HR	BB	SO	RAT	ERA	ERA+	OAV	OOB	BH	AVG	PB	PR	/A	PD	TPI
1887	Cin-a	0	1	.000	2	2	1	0	0	14	22	0	6	1	18.0	5.79	75	.328	.384	1	.125	-1	-2	-2	-1	-0.2

● EDDIE WATT Watt, Edward Dean b: 4/4/41, Lamoni, Iowa BR/TR, 5'10", 197 lbs. Deb: 4/12/66

YEAR	TM/L	W	L	PCT	G	GS	CG	SH	SV	IP	H	HR	BB	SO	RAT	ERA	ERA+	OAV	OOB	BH	AVG	PB	PR	/A	PD	TPI
1966	Bal-A	9	7	.563	43	13	1	0	4	145^2	123	11	44	102	10.6	3.83	87	.230	.295	14	.304	6	-6	-8	-2	-0.5
1967	Bal-A	3	5	.375	49	0	0	0	8	103^2	67	5	37	93	9.3	2.26	140	.183	.263	4	.182	2	11	10	0	1.3
1968	Bal-A	5	5	.500	59	0	0	0	11	83^1	63	1	35	72	10.8	2.27	129	.209	.295	0	.000	-0	7	6	0	0.7
1969	*Bal-A	5	2	.714	56	0	0	0	16	71	49	3	26	46	9.8	1.65	216	.194	.274	0	.000	-0	16	15	-0	1.6
1970	*Bal-A	7	7	.500	53	0	0	0	12	55^1	44	3	29	33	12.7	3.25	112	.239	.358	1	.125	-0	3	2	0	0.2
1971	*Bal-A	3	1	.750	35	0	0	0	11	39^2	39	1	8	26	10.7	1.82	185	.260	.297	0	.000	-0	7	7	-1	0.7
1972	Bal-A	2	3	.400	38	0	0	0	7	45^2	30	2	20	23	10.2	2.17	142	.191	.291	0	.000	-0	5	5	-0	0.5
1973	*Bal-A	3	4	.429	30	0	0	0	5	71	62	8	21	38	10.8	3.30	113	.235	.296	0	—	0	4	3	-1	0.2
1974	Phi-N	1	1	.500	42	0	0	0	6	38^1	39	3	26	23	15.7	3.99	95	.275	.394	0	.000	-0	-2	-1	0	-0.1
1975	Chi-N	0	1	.000	6	0	0	0	0	6	14	0	8	6	34.5	13.50	28	.452	.575	0	—	0	-7	-6	0	-0.6
Total	10	38	36	.514	411	13	1	0	80	659^2	530	37	254	462	11.0	2.91	116	.222	.304	19	.190	6	38	33	-3	4.0

● FRANK WATT Watt, Frank Marion "Kilo" b: 12/15/02, Washington, D.C. d: 8/31/56, Washington, D.C. BR/TR, 6'1", 205 lbs. Deb: 4/14/31 F

YEAR	TM/L	W	L	PCT	G	GS	CG	SH	SV	IP	H	HR	BB	SO	RAT	ERA	ERA+	OAV	OOB	BH	AVG	PB	PR	/A	PD	TPI
1931	Phi-N	5	5	.500	38	12	5	0	2	122^2	147	5	49	25	14.6	4.84	88	.296	.362	8	.205	0	-13	-8	-2	-0.9

● JIM WAUGH Waugh, James Elden b: 11/25/33, Lancaster, Ohio BR/TR, 6'3", 185 lbs. Deb: 4/19/52

YEAR	TM/L	W	L	PCT	G	GS	CG	SH	SV	IP	H	HR	BB	SO	RAT	ERA	ERA+	OAV	OOB	BH	AVG	PB	PR	/A	PD	TPI
1952	Pit-N	1	6	.143	17	7	1	0	0	52^1	61	4	32	18	16.3	6.36	63	.285	.383	1	.100	-0	-15	-14	-0	-1.4
1953	Pit-N	4	5	.444	29	11	1	0	0	90^1	108	21	56	23	16.3	6.48	69	.295	.389	5	.227	0	-22	-20	-1	-1.9
Total	2	5	11	.313	46	18	2	0	0	142^2	169	25	88	41	16.3	6.43	67	.291	.387	6	.188	0	-37	-34	-1	-3.3

● FRANK WAYENBERG Wayenberg, Frank b: 8/27/1898, Franklin, Kan. d: 4/16/75, Zanesville, Ohio BR/TR, 6'0.5", 172 lbs. Deb: 8/25/24

YEAR	TM/L	W	L	PCT	G	GS	CG	SH	SV	IP	H	HR	BB	SO	RAT	ERA	ERA+	OAV	OOB	BH	AVG	PB	PR	/A	PD	TPI
1924	Cle-A	0	0	—	2	1	0	0	0	6^2	7	0	5	3	17.6	5.40	79	.259	.394	1	.500	0	-1	-1	-0	-0.1

● GARY WAYNE Wayne, Gary Anthony b: 11/30/62, Dearborn, Mich. BL/TL, 6'3", 185 lbs. Deb: 4/07/89

YEAR	TM/L	W	L	PCT	G	GS	CG	SH	SV	IP	H	HR	BB	SO	RAT	ERA	ERA+	OAV	OOB	BH	AVG	PB	PR	/A	PD	TPI
1989	Min-A	3	4	.429	60	0	0	0	1	71	55	4	36	41	11.7	3.30	126	.212	.311	0	—	0	5	7	-0	0.3
1990	Min-A	1	1	.500	38	0	0	0	1	38^2	38	5	13	28	12.1	4.19	99	.255	.319	0	—	0	-1	-0	-0	-0.1
1991	Min-A	1	0	1.000	8	0	0	0	1	12^1	11	1	4	7	11.7	5.11	84	.244	.320	0	—	0	-1	-1	-0	-0.1
1992	Min-A	3	3	.500	41	0	0	0	0	48	46	2	19	29	12.8	2.63	153	.260	.342	0	—	0	7	7	1	0.9
Total	4	8	8	.500	147	0	0	0	3	170	150	12	72	105	12.1	3.44	120	.238	.322	0	—	0	9	13	1	1.0

● HAL WEAFER Weafer, Kenneth Albert "Al" b: 2/6/14, Woburn, Mass. BR/TR, 6'0.5", 183 lbs. Deb: 5/29/36

YEAR	TM/L	W	L	PCT	G	GS	CG	SH	SV	IP	H	HR	BB	SO	RAT	ERA	ERA+	OAV	OOB	BH	AVG	PB	PR	/A	PD	TPI
1936	Bos-N	0	0	—	1	0	0	0	0	3	6	1	3	0	27.0	12.00	32	.375	.474	0	.000	-0	-3	-3	-0	-0.3

● DAVE WEATHERS Weathers, John David b: 9/25/69, Lawrenceburg, Tenn. BR/TR, 6'3", 205 lbs. Deb: 8/02/91

YEAR	TM/L	W	L	PCT	G	GS	CG	SH	SV	IP	H	HR	BB	SO	RAT	ERA	ERA+	OAV	OOB	BH	AVG	PB	PR	/A	PD	TPI
1991	Tor-A	1	0	1.000	15	0	0	0	0	14^2	15	1	17	13	20.9	4.91	86	.263	.447	0	—	0	-1	-1	-0	-0.1
1992	Tor-A	0	0	—	2	0	0	0	0	3^1	5	1	2	3	18.9	8.10	50	.385	.467	0	—	0	-2	-1	-0	-0.2
Total	2	1	0	1.000	17	0	0	0	0	18	20	2	19	16	20.5	5.50	76	.286	.451	0	—	0	-3	-3	-0	-0.3

● FLOYD WEAVER Weaver, David Floyd b: 5/12/41, Ben Franklin, Tex. BR/TR, 6'4", 195 lbs. Deb: 9/30/62

YEAR	TM/L	W	L	PCT	G	GS	CG	SH	SV	IP	H	HR	BB	SO	RAT	ERA	ERA+	OAV	OOB	BH	AVG	PB	PR	/A	PD	TPI
1962	Cle-A	1	0	1.000	1	1	0	0	0	5	3	1	0	8	5.4	1.80	215	.167	.167	1	.500	0	1	1	-0	0.2
1965	Cle-A	2	2	.500	32	1	0	0	1	61^1	61	10	24	37	13.2	5.43	64	.265	.347	1	.091	0	-13	-13	-0	-1.4
1970	Chi-A	1	2	.333	31	3	0	0	0	61^2	52	7	31	51	12.4	4.38	89	.233	.332	0	.000	-1	-5	-3	-1	-0.5
1971	Mil-A	0	1	.000	21	0	0	0	0	27^1	33	3	18	12	17.1	7.24	48	.320	.426	0	—	0	-11	-11	0	-1.2
Total	4	4	5	.444	85	5	0	0	1	155^1	149	21	73	108	13.3	5.21	70	.260	.351	2	.100	-0	-28	-27	-1	-2.9

● HARRY WEAVER Weaver, Harry Abraham b: 2/26/1892, Clarendon, Pa. d: 5/30/83, Rochester, N.Y. BR/TR, 5'11", 160 lbs. Deb: 9/18/15

YEAR	TM/L	W	L	PCT	G	GS	CG	SH	SV	IP	H	HR	BB	SO	RAT	ERA	ERA+	OAV	OOB	BH	AVG	PB	PR	/A	PD	TPI
1915	Phi-A	0	2	.000	2	2	2	0	0	18	18	1	10	1	14.5	3.00	98	.290	.397	1	.167	0	-0	-0	1	0.1
1916	Phi-A	0	0	—	3	0	0	0	0	8	14	0	5	2	21.4	10.13	28	.424	.500	1	.500	0	-6	-6	0	-0.6
1917	Chi-N	1	1	.500	4	2	1	0	0	19^2	17	0	7	8	11.0	2.75	105	.230	.296	1	.200	-0	-0	0	1	0.1
1918	Chi-N	2	2	.500	8	3	1	1	1	32^2	27	1	7	9	9.4	2.20	126	.227	.270	2	.250	0	2	2	1	0.3
1919	Chi-N	0	1	.000	2	1	0	0	0	3^1	6	0	2	1	24.3	10.80	27	.375	.474	0	.000	-0	-3	-3	-0	-0.3
Total	5	3	6	.333	19	8	4	1	1	81^2	82	2	31	21	12.7	3.64	78	.270	.341	5	.227	0	-8	-7	2	-0.4

● JIM WEAVER Weaver, James Brian "Fluff" b: 2/19/39, Lancaster, Pa. BL/TL, 6', 178 lbs. Deb: 8/13/67

YEAR	TM/L	W	L	PCT	G	GS	CG	SH	SV	IP	H	HR	BB	SO	RAT	ERA	ERA+	OAV	OOB	BH	AVG	PB	PR	/A	PD	TPI
1967	Cal-A	3	0	1.000	13	2	0	0	1	30^1	26	2	9	20	10.7	2.67	118	.232	.295	0	.000	-1	2	2	2	0.3
1968	Cal-A	0	1	.000	14	0	0	0	0	22^2	22	4	10	8	12.7	2.38	122	.259	.337	0	.000	-0	2	1	-1	0.1
Total	2	3	1	.750	27	2	0	0	1	53	48	6	19	28	11.5	2.55	119	.244	.313	0	.000	-1	3	3	1	0.4

● JIM WEAVER Weaver, James Dement "Big Jim" b: 11/25/03, Obion County, Ky. d: 12/12/83, Lakeland, Fla. BR/TR, 6'6", 230 lbs. Deb: 8/27/28

YEAR	TM/L	W	L	PCT	G	GS	CG	SH	SV	IP	H	HR	BB	SO	RAT	ERA	ERA+	OAV	OOB	BH	AVG	PB	PR	/A	PD	TPI
1928	Was-A	0	0	—	3	0	0	0	0	6	2	0	6	2	13.5	1.50	267	.143	.429	0	.000	-0	2	2	0	0.1
1931	NY-A	2	1	.667	17	5	2	0	0	57^2	66	1	29	28	15.0	5.31	75	.280	.361	1	.050	-2	-6	-9	0	-1.0
1934	StL-A	2	0	1.000	5	5	2	0	0	19^2	17	3	20	11	16.9	6.41	78	.236	.402	1	.143	-0	-4	-3	1	-0.2
	Chi-N	11	9	.550	27	20	8	1	0	159	163	5	54	98	12.5	3.91	99	.263	.326	3	.058	-5	3	-1	-1	-0.6
1935	Pit-N	14	8	.636	33	22	11	**4**	0	176^1	177	9	58	87	12.1	3.42	120	.254	.313	4	.071	-4	12	13	1	1.0
1936	Pit-N	14	8	.636	38	31	11	1	0	225^2	239	12	74	108	12.5	4.31	94	.272	.329	8	.101	-5	-7	-6	-2	-1.3
1937	Pit-N	8	5	.615	32	9	2	1	0	109^2	106	2	31	44	11.2	3.20	121	.255	.307	4	.148	-0	9	8	-2	0.6
1938	StL-A	0	1	.000	1	1	0	0	0	7	9	0	9	4	23.1	9.00	55	.321	.486	0	.000	-0	-3	-3	-0	-0.3
	Cin-N	6	4	.600	30	15	2	0	3	129^1	109	6	54	64	11.4	3.13	117	.227	.306	9	.205	0	9	7	-1	0.7
1939	Cin-N	0	0	—	3	0	0	0	0	3	3	0	1	3	12.0	3.00	128	.250	.308	0	.000	-0	0	0	0	0.0
Total	8	57	36	.613	189	108	38	7	3	893^1	891	38	336	449	12.5	3.88	102	.258	.326	30	.104	-17	14	9	-4	-1.0

● MONTE WEAVER Weaver, Montie Morton "Prof" b: 6/15/06, Helton, N.C. BL/TR, 6', 170 lbs. Deb: 9/20/31

YEAR	TM/L	W	L	PCT	G	GS	CG	SH	SV	IP	H	HR	BB	SO	RAT	ERA	ERA+	OAV	OOB	BH	AVG	PB	PR	/A	PD	TPI
1931	Was-A	1	0	1.000	3	1	1	0	0	10	11	0	6	6	15.3	4.50	95	.268	.362	0	.000	-0	-0	-0	0	0.0
1932	Was-A	22	10	.688	43	30	13	1	2	234	236	9	112	83	13.4	4.08	106	.261	.342	27	.287	6	10	6	-2	0.9
1933	*Was-A	10	5	.667	23	21	12	1	0	152^1	147	3	53	45	11.9	3.25	129	.257	.322	7	.125	-3	17	16	-1	1.2
1934	Was-A	11	15	.423	31	31	11	0	0	204^2	255	16	63	51	14.0	4.79	90	.306	.355	13	.162	-2	-7	-11	-2	-1.3
1935	Was-A	1	1	.500	5	2	0	0	0	12	16	1	6	4	16.5	5.25	82	.320	.393	1	.333	0	-1	-1	0	-0.1
1936	Was-A	6	4	.600	26	5	3	0	1	91	92	3	38	15	12.9	4.35	110	.262	.334	5	.200	1	7	4	-0	0.4
1937	Was-A	12	9	.571	30	26	9	0	0	188^2	197	21	70	44	12.7	4.20	105	.266	.330	14	.206	1	9	5	1	0.6
1938	Was-A	7	6	.538	31	18	7	0	0	139	157	9	74	43	15.2	5.24	86	.282	.370	12	.267	4	-7	-11	-1	-0.7

YEAR	TM/L	W	L	PCT	G	GS	CG	SH	SV	IP	H	HR	BB	SO	RAT	ERA	ERA+	OAV	OOB	BH	AVG	PB	PR	/A	PD	TPI
1939	Bos-A	1	0	1.000	9	1	1	0	1	20^{1}	26	0	13	6	17.7	6.64	71	.321	.421	0	.000	-1	-5	-4	-1	-0.5
Total	9	71	50	.587	201	135	57	2	4	1052	1137	62	435	297	13.5	4.36	101	.276	.345	79	.209	5	24	3	-6	0.5

● ORLIE WEAVER Weaver, Orville Forest b: 6/4/1886, Newport, Ky. d: 11/28/70, New Orleans, La. BR/TR, 6', 180 lbs. Deb: 9/14/10

YEAR	TM/L	W	L	PCT	G	GS	CG	SH	SV	IP	H	HR	BB	SO	RAT	ERA	ERA+	OAV	OOB	BH	AVG	PB	PR	/A	PD	TPI
1910	Chi-N	1	1	.500	7	2	2	0	0	32	34	2	15	22	14.1	3.66	79	.270	.352	2	.154	-1	-2	-3	-1	-0.4
1911	Chi-N	2	2	.500	6	4	1	1	0	43^{2}	29	0	17	20	10.3	2.06	161	.196	.296	1	.059	-1	7	6	-0	0.4
	Bos-N	3	12	.200	27	17	4	0	0	121	140	9	84	50	17.2	6.47	59	.303	.418	5	.122	-2	-41	-36	-2	-3.7
	Yr	5	14	.263	33	21	5	1	0	164^{2}	169	9	101	70	15.1	5.30	70	.275	.384	6	.103	-4	-35	-29	-3	-3.3
Total	2	6	15	.286	40	23	7	1	0	196^{2}	203	11	116	92	15.1	5.03	71	.276	.383	8	.113	-4	-37	-32	-4	-3.7

● ROGER WEAVER Weaver, Roger Edward b: 10/6/54, Amsterdam, N.Y. BR/TR, 6'3", 190 lbs. Deb: 6/06/80

YEAR	TM/L	W	L	PCT	G	GS	CG	SH	SV	IP	H	HR	BB	SO	RAT	ERA	ERA+	OAV	OOB	BH	AVG	PB	PR	/A	PD	TPI
1980	Det-A	3	4	.429	19	6	0	0	0	63^{2}	56	5	34	42	12.9	4.10	100	.247	.347	0	—	0	-0	0	1	-0.1

● SAM WEAVER Weaver, Samuel H. b: 7/10/1855, Philadelphia, Pa. d: 2/1/14, Philadelphia, Pa. BR/TR, 5'10", 175 lbs. Deb: 10/25/1875

YEAR	TM/L	W	L	PCT	G	GS	CG	SH	SV	IP	H	HR	BB	SO	RAT	ERA	ERA+	OAV	OOB	BH	AVG	PB	PR	/A	PD	TPI
1875	Phi-n	1	0	1.000	1	1	1	0	0	6	6	0	2		12.0	*1.50*	168	.240	.296	1	.250	0	1	1		0.1
1878	Mil-N	12	31	.279	45	43	39	1	0	383	371	2	21	95	**9.2**	1.95	135	.237	**.247**	34	.200	-3	15	**29**	0	2.6
1882	Phi-a	26	15	.634	42	41	41	2	0	371	374	6	35	104	9.9	2.74	109	.245	.262	36	.232	1	-2	10	1	1.1
1883	Lou-a	26	22	.542	48	48	47	4	0	418^{2}	468	3	38	116	10.9	3.70	81	.265	.280	39	.192	0	-18	-33	0	-2.8
1884	Phi-U	5	10	.333	17	17	14	0	0	136	206	3	11	40	14.4	5.76	50	.327	.339	18	.214	-1	-41	-44	-1	-3.6
1886	Phi-a	0	2	.000	2	2	1	0	0	11	30	0	2	2	27.0	14.73	24	.423	.446	1	.143	-1	-14	-14	-0	-1.0
Total	5	69	80	.463	154	151	142	7	0	1319^{2}	1449	14	107	357	10.6	3.23	90	.260	.275	128	.207	-3	-61	-46	0	-3.7

● LEFTY WEBB Webb, Cleon Earl b: 3/1/1885, Mt.Gilead, Ohio d: 1/12/58, Circleville, Ohio BB/TL, 5'11", 165 lbs. Deb: 5/23/10

YEAR	TM/L	W	L	PCT	G	GS	CG	SH	SV	IP	H	HR	BB	SO	RAT	ERA	ERA+	OAV	OOB	BH	AVG	PB	PR	/A	PD	TPI
1910	Pit-N	2	1	.667	7	3	2	0	0	27	29	0	9	6	13.3	5.67	55	.266	.333	2	.200	-0	-8	-8	-0	-0.8

● HANK WEBB Webb, Henry Gaylon Matthew b: 5/21/50, Copiague, N.Y. BR/TR, 6'3", 175 lbs. Deb: 9/05/72

YEAR	TM/L	W	L	PCT	G	GS	CG	SH	SV	IP	H	HR	BB	SO	RAT	ERA	ERA+	OAV	OOB	BH	AVG	PB	PR	/A	PD	TPI
1972	NY-N	0	0	—	6	2	0	0	0	18^{1}	18	1	9	15	13.3	4.42	76	.261	.346	0	.000	-1	-2	-2	1	-0.2
1973	NY-N	0	0	—	2	0	0	0	0	1^{2}	2	1	2	1	21.6	10.80	33	.286	.444	0	—	0	-1	-1	-0	-0.1
1974	NY-N	0	2	.000	3	2	0	0	0	10	15	1	10	8	23.4	7.20	49	.341	.473	0	.000	-0	-4	-4	-0	-0.4
1975	NY-N	7	6	.538	29	15	3	1	0	115	102	12	62	38	12.9	4.07	85	.236	.333	8	.258	2	-6	-8	-1	-0.7
1976	NY-N	0	1	.000	8	0	0	0	0	16	17	2	7	7	14.6	4.50	73	.274	.366	0	.000	0	-2	-2	0	-0.2
1977	LA-N	0	0	—	5	0	0	0	0	8	5	1	1	2	7.9	2.25	170	.192	.250	0	—	0	1	1	-0	0.1
Total	6	7	9	.438	53	19	3	1	0	169	159	18	91	71	13.6	4.31	80	.248	.346	8	.200	1	-13	-16	-1	-1.5

● RED WEBB Webb, Samuel Henry b: 9/25/24, Washington, D.C. BL/TR, 6', 175 lbs. Deb: 9/15/48

YEAR	TM/L	W	L	PCT	G	GS	CG	SH	SV	IP	H	HR	BB	SO	RAT	ERA	ERA+	OAV	OOB	BH	AVG	PB	PR	/A	PD	TPI
1948	NY-N	2	1	.667	5	3	2	0	0	28	27	2	10	9	12.2	3.21	122	.248	.317	2	.222	0	2	2	0	0.3
1949	NY-N	1	1	.500	20	0	0	0	0	44^{2}	41	3	21	9	12.5	4.03	99	.248	.333	4	.400	2	0	-0	2	0.3
Total	2	3	2	.600	25	3	2	0	0	72^{2}	68	5	31	18	12.4	3.72	107	.248	.327	6	.316	2	2	2	2	0.6

● BILL WEBB Webb, William Frederick b: 12/12/13, Atlanta, Ga. BR/TR, 6'2", 180 lbs. Deb: 5/15/43

YEAR	TM/L	W	L	PCT	G	GS	CG	SH	SV	IP	H	HR	BB	SO	RAT	ERA	ERA+	OAV	OOB	BH	AVG	PB	PR	/A	PD	TPI
1943	Phi-N	0	0	—	1	0	0	0	0	1	1	1	1	0	18.0	9.00	37	.333	.500	0	—	0	-1	-1	-0	-0.1

● LES WEBBER Webber, Lester Elmer b: 5/6/15, Kelseyville, Cal. d: 11/13/86, Santa Maria, Cal. BR/TR, 6'0.5", 185 lbs. Deb: 5/17/42

YEAR	TM/L	W	L	PCT	G	GS	CG	SH	SV	IP	H	HR	BB	SO	RAT	ERA	ERA+	OAV	OOB	BH	AVG	PB	PR	/A	PD	TPI
1942	Bro-N	3	2	.600	19	3	1	0	1	51^{2}	46	2	22	23	11.8	2.96	110	.230	.306	1	.071	-1	2	2	1	0.2
1943	Bro-N	2	2	.500	54	0	0	0	**10**	115^{2}	112	6	69	24	14.5	3.81	88	.264	.373	3	.120	-1	-6	-6	2	-0.5
1944	Bro-N	7	8	.467	48	9	1	0	3	140^{1}	157	9	64	42	14.2	4.94	72	.282	.357	8	.205	1	-21	-22	4	-1.7
1945	Bro-N	7	3	.700	17	7	5	0	0	75^{1}	69	3	25	30	11.3	3.58	105	.237	.300	2	.091	-1	2	1	-1	-0.1
1946	Bro-N	3	3	.500	11	4	0	0	0	43	34	5	15	16	10.3	2.30	147	.225	.295	1	.100	-1	5	5	-1	0.4
	Cle-A	1	1	.500	4	2	0	0	0	5^{1}	13	0	5	5	30.4	23.63	14	.464	.545	0	.000	0	-12	-12	0	-1.0
1948	Cle-A	0	0	—	1	0	0	0	0	0^{2}	3	0	1	1	54.0	40.50	10	.750	.800	0	—	0	-3	-3	0	-0.2
Total	6	23	19	.548	154	25	7	0	14	432	434	25	201	141	13.4	4.19	83	.262	.345	15	.135	-2	-32	-34	5	-2.9

● CHARLIE WEBER Weber, Charles P. "Count" b: 10/22/1868, Cincinnati, Ohio d: 6/13/14, Beaumont, Tex. Deb: 7/30/1898

YEAR	TM/L	W	L	PCT	G	GS	CG	SH	SV	IP	H	HR	BB	SO	RAT	ERA	ERA+	OAV	OOB	BH	AVG	PB	PR	/A	PD	TPI
1898	Was-N	0	1	.000	1	1	0	0	0	4	9	0	1	0	27.0	15.75	23	.440	.511	0	.000	-0	-5	-5	-0	-0.4

● MIKE WEGENER Wegener, Michael Denis b: 10/8/46, Denver, Colo. BR/TR, 6'4", 215 lbs. Deb: 4/09/69

YEAR	TM/L	W	L	PCT	G	GS	CG	SH	SV	IP	H	HR	BB	SO	RAT	ERA	ERA+	OAV	OOB	BH	AVG	PB	PR	/A	PD	TPI
1969	Mon-N	5	14	.263	32	26	4	1	0	165^{2}	150	10	96	124	13.6	4.40	84	.243	.349	13	.241	2	-15	-13	1	-1.0
1970	Mon-N	3	6	.333	25	16	1	0	0	104^{1}	100	16	56	35	13.8	5.26	78	.252	.350	4	.118	-2	-14	-13	-1	-1.5
Total	2	8	20	.286	57	42	5	1	0	270	250	26	152	159	13.7	4.73	81	.247	.349	17	.193	0	-29	-27	1	-2.5

● BILL WEGMAN Wegman, William Edward b: 12/19/62, Cincinnati, Ohio BR/TR, 6'5", 200 lbs. Deb: 9/14/85

YEAR	TM/L	W	L	PCT	G	GS	CG	SH	SV	IP	H	HR	BB	SO	RAT	ERA	ERA+	OAV	OOB	BH	AVG	PB	PR	/A	PD	TPI
1985	Mil-A	2	0	1.000	3	3	0	0	0	17^{2}	17	3	3	6	10.2	3.57	117	.246	.278	0	—	0	1	1	-0	0.1
1986	Mil-A	5	12	.294	35	32	2	0	0	198^{1}	217	32	43	82	12.1	5.13	84	.279	.323	0	—	0	-21	-18	-1	-1.8
1987	Mil-A	12	11	.522	34	33	7	0	0	225	229	31	53	102	11.5	4.24	108	.265	.312	0	—	0	5	8	-0	0.8
1988	Mil-A	13	13	.500	32	31	4	1	0	199	207	24	50	84	11.8	4.12	97	.265	.313	0	—	0	-3	-3	-1	-0.4
1989	Mil-A	2	6	.250	11	8	0	0	0	51	69	6	21	27	15.9	6.71	57	.321	.381	0	—	0	-16	-16	1	-1.5
1990	Mil-A	2	2	.500	8	5	1	1	0	29^{2}	37	6	6	20	13.0	4.85	80	.298	.331	0	—	0	-3	-3	-1	-0.3
1991	Mil-A	15	7	.682	28	28	7	2	0	193^{1}	176	16	40	89	10.4	2.84	140	.242	.288	0	—	0	27	24	2	2.8
1992	Mil-A	13	14	.481	35	35	7	0	0	261^{2}	251	28	55	127	10.8	3.20	119	.250	.295	0	—	0	22	18	4	2.3
Total	8	64	65	.496	186	175	28	4	0	1175^{2}	1203	146	271	537	11.5	4.02	102	.264	.310	0	—	0	12	11	4	2.0

● BIGGS WEHDE Wehde, Wilbur b: 11/23/06, Holstein, Iowa d: 9/21/70, Sioux Falls, S.Dak. BR/TR, 5'10.5", 180 lbs. Deb: 9/15/30

YEAR	TM/L	W	L	PCT	G	GS	CG	SH	SV	IP	H	HR	BB	SO	RAT	ERA	ERA+	OAV	OOB	BH	AVG	PB	PR	/A	PD	TPI
1930	Chi-A	0	0	—	4	0	0	0	0	6^{1}	7	1	7	3	21.3	9.95	46	.304	.484	0	.000	-0	-4	-4	1	-0.3
1931	Chi-A	1	0	1.000	8	0	0	0	0	16	19	0	10	3	17.4	6.75	63	.333	.449	0	.000	-0	-4	-4	1	-0.4
Total	2	1	0	1.000	12	0	0	0	0	22^{1}	26	1	17	6	18.5	7.66	57	.325	.460	0	.000	-1	-8	-8	1	-0.7

● HERM WEHMEIER Wehmeier, Herman Ralph b: 2/18/27, Cincinnati, Ohio d: 5/21/73, Dallas, Tex. BR/TR, 6'2", 200 lbs. Deb: 9/07/45

YEAR	TM/L	W	L	PCT	G	GS	CG	SH	SV	IP	H	HR	BB	SO	RAT	ERA	ERA+	OAV	OOB	BH	AVG	PB	PR	/A	PD	TPI
1945	Cin-N	0	1	.000	2	2	0	0	0	5	10	0	4	0	25.2	12.60	30	.435	.519	0	.000	-0	-5	-5	0	-0.4
1947	Cin-N	0	0	—	1	0	0	0	0	1	0	0	0	0	0.0	0.00	—	.000	.000	0	—	0	0	0	-0	0.0
1948	Cin-N	11	8	.579	33	24	6	0	0	147^{1}	179	21	75	56	15.6	5.86	67	.299	.379	5	.091	-3	-31	-32	-0	-3.3
1949	Cin-N	11	12	.478	33	29	11	1	0	213^{1}	202	20	117	80	13.8	4.68	89	.253	.353	20	.256	2	-15	-12	-2	-1.1
1950	Cin-N	10	18	.357	41	32	12	0	4	230	255	27	135	121	15.4	5.67	75	.281	.376	14	.152	-3	-39	-37	-3	-4.0
1951	Cin-N	7	10	.412	39	22	10	2	2	184^{2}	167	15	89	93	12.7	3.70	110	.241	.330	17	.288	3	5	8	-2	1.0
1952	Cin-N	9	11	.450	33	26	6	1	0	190^{1}	197	23	103	83	14.5	5.15	73	.269	.365	12	.188	2	-30	-29	-4	-3.0
1953	Cin-N	1	6	.143	28	10	2	0	0	81^{2}	100	20	47	32	16.2	7.16	61	.299	.385	4	.200	-0	-26	-25	-1	-2.5
1954	Cin-N	0	3	.000	12	3	0	0	2	33^{2}	36	6	21	13	15.5	6.68	63	.271	.374	0	.000	-1	-10	-9	1	-0.9
	Phi-N	10	8	.556	25	17	10	2	0	138	117	10	51	49	11.0	3.85	105	.231	.302	6	.120	-2	3	3	-0	0.1
	Yr	10	11	.476	37	20	10	2	2	171^{2}	153	16	72	62	11.8	4.40	92	.238	.316	6	.102	-3	-6	-6	1	-0.8
1955	Phi-N	10	12	.455	31	29	10	1	0	193^{2}	176	21	67	85	11.4	4.41	90	.241	.307	20	.278	4	-8	-10	-1	-0.7
1956	Phi-N	0	2	.000	3	3	0	0	0	20	18	2	11	8	13.0	4.05	92	.240	.337	0	.000	-1	-1	-1	-1	-0.2
	StL-N	12	9	.571	34	19	7	2	1	170^{2}	150	16	71	68	11.7	3.69	102	.240	.319	13	.224	4	2	2	-1	0.5
	Yr	12	11	.522	37	22	7	2	1	190^{2}	168	18	82	76	11.8	3.73	101	.240	.320	13	.197	3	1	1	-2	0.3
1957	StL-N	10	7	.588	36	18	5	0	0	165	165	25	54	91	12.1	4.31	92	.253	.312	12	.203	0	-8	-6	-0	-0.6
1958	StL-N	0	1	.000	3	3	0	0	0	6	13	2	2	4	22.5	13.50	31	.448	.484	1	.500	1	-6	-6	0	-0.5
	Det-A	1	0	1.000	7	3	0	0	0	22^{2}	21	2	5	11	10.3	2.38	169	.241	.283	0	.000	-1	3	4	-0	0.4
Total	13	92	108	.460	361	240	79	9	9	1803	1806	210	852	794	13.4	4.80	84	.260	.344	124	.196	5	-165	-156	-14	-15.2

● DAVE WEHRMEISTER Wehrmeister, David Thomas b: 11/9/52, Berwyn, Ill. BR/TR, 6'4", 195 lbs. Deb: 4/16/76

YEAR	TM/L	W	L	PCT	G	GS	CG	SH	SV	IP	H	HR	BB	SO	RAT	ERA	ERA+	OAV	OOB	BH	AVG	PB	PR	/A	PD	TPI
1976	SD-N	0	4	.000	7	4	0	0	0	19^1	27	0	11	10	17.7	7.45	44	.333	.413	0	.000	-1	-8	-9	0	-0.9
1977	SD-N	1	3	.250	30	6	0	0	0	69^2	81	8	44	32	16.5	6.07	58	.293	.396	2	.167	0	-17	-20	-0	-1.9
1978	SD-N	1	0	1.000	4	0	0	0	0	7^1	8	1	5	2	16.0	6.14	54	.276	.382	0	—	0	-2	-2	-0	-0.3
1981	NY-A	0	0	—	5	0	0	0	0	7	6	0	7	7	16.7	5.14	69	.240	.406	0	—	0	-1	-1	0	-0.1
1984	Phi-N	0	0	—	7	0	0	0	0	15	18	1	7	13	15.6	7.20	50	.300	.382	0	.000	-0	-6	-6	0	-0.6
1985	Chi-A	2	2	.500	23	0	0	0	2	39^1	35	4	10	32	11.0	3.43	126	.241	.304	0	—	0	3	4	-0	0.4
Total	6	4	9	.308	76	10	0	0	2	157^2	175	14	84	96	15.2	5.65	65	.284	.376	2	.100	-1	-31	-34	0	-3.4

● STUMP WEIDMAN Weidman, George E. b: 2/17/1861, Rochester, N.Y. d: 3/2/05, New York, N.Y. BR/TR, Deb: 8/26/1880 U♦

YEAR	TM/L	W	L	PCT	G	GS	CG	SH	SV	IP	H	HR	BB	SO	RAT	ERA	ERA+	OAV	OOB	BH	AVG	PB	PR	/A	PD	TPI
1880	Buf-N	0	9	.000	17	13	9	0	0	113^2	141	1	9	25	11.9	3.40	72	.291	.304	8	.103	-6	-13	-12	-1	-1.6
1881	Det-N	8	5	.615	13	13	13	1	0	115	108	1	12	26	**9.4**	**1.80**	**162**	.238	**.258**	12	.255	0	12	14	-2	1.3
1882	Det-N	25	20	.556	46	45	43	4	0	411	391	10	39	161	9.4	2.63	112	.236	.253	42	.218	-5	12	14	-0	0.7
1883	Det-N	20	24	.455	52	47	41	3	**2**	402^1	435	8	72	183	11.3	3.53	88	.257	.288	58	.185	-8	-18	-19	0	-2.1
1884	Det-N	4	21	.160	26	26	24	0	0	212^2	257	9	57	96	13.3	3.72	78	.273	.314	49	.163	-4	-18	-20	-1	-2.0
1885	Det-N	14	24	.368	38	38	37	3	0	330	343	7	63	149	11.1	3.14	91	.252	.286	24	.157	-4	-12	-11	-3	-1.7
1886	KC-N	12	36	.250	51	51	48	1	0	427^2	549	11	112	168	13.9	4.50	84	.303	.344	30	.168	-11	-57	-35	4	-3.5
1887	Det-N	13	7	.650	21	21	20	0	0	183	221	9	60	56	14.3	5.36	76	.296	.356	17	.207	-3	-26	-27	-0	-2.4
	NY-a	4	8	.333	12	12	11	1	0	97	122	3	25	37	13.7	4.64	92	.292	.333	7	.152	-2	-4	-4	1	-0.4
	NY-N	0	1	.000	1	1	1	0	0	8	10	0	2	4	13.5	1.13	335	.286	.324	1	.333	0	3	2	-0	0.2
1888	NY-N	1	1	.500	2	2	2	0	0	18	17	2	8	5	13.5	3.50	78	.230	.321	0	.000	-0	-1	-2	-0	-0.2
Total	9	101	156	.393	279	269	249	13	2	2318^1	2594	61	459	910	11.9	3.60	89	.268	.302	248	.177	-42	-120	-98	-2	-11.7

● DICK WEIK Weik, Richard Henry "Legs" b: 11/17/27, Waterloo, Iowa d: 4/21/91, Harvey, Ill. BR/TR, 6'3.5", 184 lbs. Deb: 9/08/48 ♦

YEAR	TM/L	W	L	PCT	G	GS	CG	SH	SV	IP	H	HR	BB	SO	RAT	ERA	ERA+	OAV	OOB	BH	AVG	PB	PR	/A	PD	TPI
1948	Was-A	1	2	.333	3	3	0	0	0	12^2	14	1	22	8	25.6	5.68	76	.311	.537	3	.750	2	-2	-2	-0	0.0
1949	Was-A	3	12	.200	27	14	2	2	1	95^1	78	5	103	58	17.1	5.38	79	.230	.410	5	.179	-1	-13	-12	1	-1.1
1950	Was-A	1	3	.250	14	5	1	0	0	44	38	2	47	26	17.4	4.30	105	.236	.409	2	.154	-1	1	1	-1	0.0
	Cle-A	1	3	.250	11	2	0	0	0	26	18	1	26	16	15.6	3.81	114	.205	.391	1	.200	0	2	2	0	0.2
	Yr	2	6	.250	25	7	1	0	0	70	56	3	73	42	16.7	4.11	108	.225	.402	3	.167	-1	4	2	-1	0.2
1953	Det-A	0	1	.000	12	1	0	0	0	19^1	32	3	23	6	25.6	13.97	29	.386	.519	1	.500	1	-21	-21	0	-1.9
1954	Det-A	0	1	.000	9	1	0	0	0	16^1	23	3	16	9	22.0	7.16	52	.354	.488	0	.000	-0	-6	-6	-1	-0.7
Total	5	6	22	.214	76	26	3	2	1	213^2	203	15	237	123	18.6	5.90	72	.260	.433	12	.226	1	-39	-39	0	-3.5

● ED WEILAND Weiland, Edwin Nicholas b: 11/26/14, Evanston, Ill. d: 7/12/71, Chicago, Ill. BL/TR, 5'11", 180 lbs. Deb: 5/01/40 F

YEAR	TM/L	W	L	PCT	G	GS	CG	SH	SV	IP	H	HR	BB	SO	RAT	ERA	ERA+	OAV	OOB	BH	AVG	PB	PR	/A	PD	TPI
1940	Chi-A	0	0	—	5	0	0	0	0	14^1	15	5	7	3	13.8	8.79	50	.263	.344	1	.200	-0	-7	-7	-0	-0.7
1942	Chi-A	0	0	—	5	0	0	0	0	9^2	18	0	3	4	19.6	7.45	48	.383	.420	0	.000	-0	-4	-4	-0	-0.5
Total	2	0	0	—	10	0	0	0	0	24	33	5	10	7	16.1	8.25	50	.317	.377	1	.143	-0	-11	-11	-1	-1.2

● BOB WEILAND Weiland, Robert George "Lefty" b: 12/14/05, Chicago, Ill. d: 11/9/88, Chicago, Ill. BL/TL, 6'4", 215 lbs. Deb: 9/30/28 F

YEAR	TM/L	W	L	PCT	G	GS	CG	SH	SV	IP	H	HR	BB	SO	RAT	ERA	ERA+	OAV	OOB	BH	AVG	PB	PR	/A	PD	TPI
1928	Chi-A	1	0	1.000	1	1	1	1	0	9	7	0	5	9	13.0	0.00	—	.212	.333	1	.333	0	4	4	0	0.5
1929	Chi-A	2	4	.333	15	9	1	0	1	62	62	3	43	25	15.7	5.81	74	.268	.390	2	.111	-1	-11	-10	-1	-1.2
1930	Chi-A	0	4	.000	14	3	0	0	0	32^2	38	1	21	15	16.8	6.61	70	.297	.404	0	.000	-1	-7	-7	-0	-0.8
1931	Chi-A	2	7	.222	15	8	3	0	0	75	75	3	46	38	15.0	5.16	83	.259	.368	4	.182	1	-7	-8	1	-0.5
1932	Bos-A	6	16	.273	43	27	7	0	1	195^2	231	11	97	63	15.4	4.51	100	.295	.377	9	.148	-1	-1	-0	3	0.2
1933	Bos-A	8	14	.364	39	27	12	0	3	216^1	197	19	100	97	12.6	3.87	113	.244	.331	7	.108	-4	10	12	-2	0.6
1934	Bos-A	1	5	.167	11	7	2	0	0	55^2	63	4	27	29	14.6	5.50	87	.293	.372	2	.105	-1	-6	-4	0	-0.5
	Cle-A	1	5	.167	16	7	2	0	0	70	71	5	30	42	13.0	4.11	111	.262	.336	3	.125	-0	3	3	-1	0.2
	Yr	2	10	.167	27	14	4	0	0	125^2	134	9	57	71	13.7	4.73	99	.276	.352	5	.116	-2	-3	-1	-0	-0.3
1935	StL-A	0	2	.000	14	4	0	0	0	32	39	6	31	11	20.0	9.56	50	.298	.436	0	.000	-1	-18	-17	-1	-1.7
1937	StL-N	15	14	.517	41	34	21	2	0	264^1	283	14	94	105	13.0	3.54	112	.276	.339	15	.169	0	11	13	-2	1.2
1938	StL-N	16	11	.593	35	29	11	1	1	228^1	248	14	67	117	12.6	3.59	110	.272	.324	11	.138	-3	5	9	-1	0.5
1939	StL-N	10	12	.455	32	23	6	3	1	146^1	146	4	50	63	12.4	3.57	115	.264	.331	3	.065	-5	6	9	-1	0.3
1940	StL-N	0	0	—	1	0	0	0	0	1	3	1	0	0	27.0	27.00	15	.600	.600	0	—	0	-3	-3	-0	-0.2
Total	12	62	94	.397	277	179	66	7	7	1388^1	1463	85	611	614	13.7	4.24	100	.272	.350	57	.129	-17	-13	2	-4	-1.4

● CARL WEILMAN Weilman, Carl Woolworth "Zeke" (b: Carl Woolworth Weilenmann)
b: 11/29/1889, Hamilton, Ohio d: 5/25/24, Hamilton, Ohio BL/TL, 6'5.5", 187 lbs. Deb: 8/24/12

YEAR	TM/L	W	L	PCT	G	GS	CG	SH	SV	IP	H	HR	BB	SO	RAT	ERA	ERA+	OAV	OOB	BH	AVG	PB	PR	/A	PD	TPI
1912	StL-A	2	4	.333	8	6	5	2	1	48^1	42	0	3	24	8.4	2.79	119	.227	.239	2	.118	-1	3	3	0	0.3
1913	StL-A	10	20	.333	39	28	17	2	0	251^2	262	2	60	79	11.7	3.40	86	.281	.328	12	.146	-3	-13	-13	1	-1.5
1914	StL-A	18	13	.581	44	36	20	3	1	299	260	1	84	119	10.7	2.08	130	.237	.298	15	.149	-1	22	21	1	2.4
1915	StL-A	18	19	.486	47	31	19	3	4	295^2	240	6	83	125	9.9	2.34	122	.229	.287	23	.230	2	19	17	-1	2.0
1916	StL-A	17	18	.486	46	31	19	1	2	276	237	3	76	91	10.5	2.15	128	.242	.301	14	.154	-1	21	18	-3	1.6
1917	StL-A	1	2	.333	5	3	0	0	0	19	19	1	6	9	11.8	1.89	137	.268	.325	0	.000	-1	2	1	1	0.2
1919	StL-A	10	6	.625	20	20	12	3	0	148	133	3	45	44	11.0	2.07	160	.244	.305	9	.191	0	19	21	-0	2.3
1920	StL-A	9	13	.409	30	24	13	1	2	183^1	201	6	61	45	13.0	4.47	88	.291	.351	11	.175	-2	-14	-11	1	-1.2
Total	8	85	95	.472	239	179	105	15	10	1521	1394	22	418	536	10.9	2.67	112	.251	.307	86	.170	-7	59	56	1	6.1

● JAKE WEIMER Weimer, Jacob "Tornado Jake" b: 11/29/1873, Ottumwa, Iowa d: 6/19/28, Chicago, Ill. BR/TL, 5'11", 175 lbs. Deb: 4/17/03

YEAR	TM/L	W	L	PCT	G	GS	CG	SH	SV	IP	H	HR	BB	SO	RAT	ERA	ERA+	OAV	OOB	BH	AVG	PB	PR	/A	PD	TPI
1903	Chi-N	20	8	.714	35	33	27	3	0	282	241	4	104	128	11.4	2.30	136	**.225**	.301	21	.196	2	30	26	-1	2.7
1904	Chi-N	20	14	.588	37	37	31	5	0	307	229	1	97	177	9.8	1.91	140	.204	.272	21	.183	-2	28	26	3	2.9
1905	Chi-N	18	12	.600	33	30	26	2	1	250^1	212	1	80	107	10.9	2.26	132	.229	.299	19	.207	2	21	20	-1	2.2
1906	Cin-N	20	14	.588	41	39	31	6	1	304^2	263	0	99	141	11.1	2.22	124	.236	.306	29	.269	6	14	18	1	2.8
1907	Cin-N	11	14	.440	29	26	19	3	0	209	165	6	63	67	10.8	2.41	108	.226	.308	14	.194	2	1	4	2	1.0
1908	Cin-N	8	7	.533	15	15	9	2	0	116^2	110	2	50	36	12.8	2.39	96	.255	.341	11	.244	2	-0	-1	1	0.2
1909	NY-N	0	0	—	1	0	0	0	0	3	7	0	0	1	24.0	9.00	28	.467	.500	0	.000	-0	-2	-2	-0	-0.2
Total	7	97	69	.584	191	180	143	21	2	1472^2	1227	14	493	657	11.0	2.23	125	.227	.300	115	.213	11	93	93	5	11.6

● LEFTY WEINERT Weinert, Phillip Walter b: 4/21/02, Philadelphia, Pa. d: 4/17/73, Rockledge, Fla. BL/TL, 6'1", 195 lbs. Deb: 9/24/19

YEAR	TM/L	W	L	PCT	G	GS	CG	SH	SV	IP	H	HR	BB	SO	RAT	ERA	ERA+	OAV	OOB	BH	AVG	PB	PR	/A	PD	TPI
1919	Phi-N	0	0	—	1	0	0	0	0	4	11	0	2	0	29.3	18.00	18	.478	.520	2	1.000	1	-7	-7	0	-0.4
1920	Phi-N	1	1	.500	10	2	0	0	0	22	27	1	19	10	19.2	6.14	56	.333	.465	0	.000	-1	-7	-7	-0	-0.8
1921	Phi-N	1	0	1.000	8	0	0	0	0	12^1	8	1	5	2	10.2	1.46	290	.216	.326	1	1.000	0	3	4	-1	0.4
1922	Phi-N	8	11	.421	34	22	10	0	1	166^2	189	10	70	58	14.3	3.40	137	.289	.362	14	.241	0	13	23	-2	2.2
1923	Phi-N	4	17	.190	38	20	8	0	1	156	207	10	81	46	17.1	5.42	85	.327	.410	19	.322	3	-25	-14	-3	-1.4
1924	Phi-N	0	1	.000	8	1	0	0	0	14^2	10	0	11	7	12.9	2.45	182	.204	.350	0	.000	-1	2	3	0	0.3
1927	Chi-N	1	1	.500	5	3	1	0	0	19^2	21	2	6	5	12.4	4.58	84	.259	.310	1	.200	0	-1	-2	-0	-0.2
1928	Chi-N	1	0	1.000	10	1	0	0	0	17	24	0	9	8	18.0	5.29	73	.393	.479	0	.000	-0	-2	-3	-1	-0.4
1931	NY-A	2	2	.500	17	0	0	0	0	24^2	31	2	19	24	20.1	6.20	64	.316	.451	0	.000	-0	-5	-6	0	-0.6
Total	9	18	33	.353	131	49	19	0	2	437	528	26	222	160	15.9	4.59	97	.308	.393	37	.261	3	-29	-7	-6	-0.9

● ROY WEIR Weir, William Franklin "Bill" b: 2/25/11, Portland, Maine BL/TL, 5'8.5", 170 lbs. Deb: 6/25/36

YEAR	TM/L	W	L	PCT	G	GS	CG	SH	SV	IP	H	HR	BB	SO	RAT	ERA	ERA+	OAV	OOB	BH	AVG	PB	PR	/A	PD	TPI
1936	Bos-N	4	3	.571	12	7	3	2	0	57^1	53	0	24	29	12.1	2.83	136	.241	.316	5	.278	2	8	6	1	0.9
1937	Bos-N	1	1	.500	10	4	1	0	0	33	27	0	19	8	12.5	3.82	94	.227	.333	0	.000	-1	0	-1	1	-0.1
1938	Bos-N	1	0	1.000	5	0	0	0	0	13^1	14	4	6	3	13.5	6.75	51	.269	.345	1	.333	0	-4	-5	0	-0.4
1939	Bos-N	0	0	—	2	0	0	0	0	2^2	1	0	1	2	6.8	0.00	—	.125	.222	0	.000	-0	1	1	0	0.1

YEAR TM/L	W	L	PCT	G	GS	CG	SH	SV	IP	H	HR	BB	SO	RAT	ERA	ERA+	OAV	OOB	BH	AVG	PB	PR	/A	PD	TPI
Total 4	6	4	.600	29	11	4	2	0	106^{1}	95	4	50	42	12.3	3.55	104	.238	.323	6	.188	1	5	2	2	0.5
● **CURT WELCH** Welch, Curtis Benton b: 2/11/1862, E.Liverpool, Ohio d: 8/29/1896, E.Liverpool, Ohio BR/TR, 5'10", 175 lbs. Deb: 5/01/1884 ♦																									
1890 Phi-a	0	0	—	1	0	0	0	0	1	6	0	0	1	54.0	54.00	7	.670	.670	106	.268	0	-6	-6	0	-0.4
● **TED WELCH** Welch, Floyd John b: 10/17/1892, Coyville, Kan. d: 1/6/43, Great Bend, Kan. BL/TR, 5'9.5", 160 lbs. Deb: 5/15/14																									
1914 StL-F	0	0	—	3	0	0	0	0	6	6	0	3	2	18.0	6.00	56	.273	.429	0	.000	-0	-2	-2	-0	-0.2
● **JOHNNY WELCH** Welch, John Vernon b: 12/2/06, Washington, D.C. d: 9/2/40, St.Louis, Mo. BL/TR, 6'3", 184 lbs. Deb: 5/22/26																									
1926 Chi-N	0	0	—	3	0	0	0	0	4^{1}	5	0	1	0	12.5	2.08	185	.357	.400	1	1.000	0	1	1	-0	0.1
1927 Chi-N	0	0	—	1	0	0	0	0	1	0	0	3	1	27.0	9.00	43	.000	.500	0	—	0	-1	-1	0	-0.1
1928 Chi-N	0	0	—	3	0	0	0	0	4	13	0	0	2	29.3	15.75	24	.591	.591	0	—	0	-5	-5	0	-0.5
1931 Chi-N	2	1	.667	8	3	1	0	0	33^{2}	39	2	10	7	13.4	3.74	103	.291	.345	5	.417	2	0	0	0	0.2
1932 Bos-A	4	6	.400	20	8	3	1	0	72^{1}	93	3	38	26	16.7	5.23	86	.312	.395	9	.250	2	-6	-6	0	-0.4
1933 Bos-A	4	9	.308	47	7	1	0	3	129	142	6	67	68	14.7	4.60	95	.283	.370	6	.162	-1	-5	-3	1	-0.3
1934 Bos-A	13	15	.464	41	22	8	1	0	206^{1}	223	14	76	91	13.4	4.49	107	.274	.342	15	.203	-1	0	7	1	0.6
1935 Bos-A	10	9	.526	31	19	10	1	2	143	155	4	53	48	13.3	4.47	106	.273	.339	9	.180	-0	-0	4	-0	0.4
1936 Bos-A	2	1	.667	9	3	1	0	0	32^{2}	43	4	8	9	14.1	5.51	96	.305	.342	3	.273	1	-2	-1	0	0.0
Pit-N	0	0	—	9	1	0	0	1	22	22	3	6	5	11.5	4.50	90	.265	.315	2	.286	1	-1	-1	-1	-0.1
Total 9	35	41	.461	172	63	24	3	6	648^{1}	735	36	262	257	14.1	4.66	99	.285	.355	50	.219	3	-18	-4	1	-0.1
● **MICKEY WELCH** Welch, Michael Francis "Smiling Mickey" b: 7/4/1859, Brooklyn, N.Y. d: 7/30/41, Concord, N.H. BR/TR, 5'8", 160 lbs. Deb: 5/01/1880 H																									
1880 Tro-N	34	30	.531	65	64	64	4	0	574	575	7	80	123	10.3	2.54	99	.249	.274	72	.287	11	-11	-1	-7	0.3
1881 Tro-N	21	18	.538	40	40	40	4	0	368	371	7	78	104	11.0	2.67	111	.255	.293	30	.203	-4	4	12	-6	0.1
1882 Tro-N	14	16	.467	33	33	30	5	0	281	334	7	62	53	12.7	3.46	82	.280	.315	37	.245	1	-17	-20	-3	-1.9
1883 NY-N	25	23	.521	54	52	46	4	0	426	431	11	66	144	10.5	2.73	114	.244	.272	75	.234	3	20	18	-6	1.3
1884 NY-N	39	21	.650	65	65	62	4	0	557^{1}	528	12	146	345	10.9	2.50	119	.237	.284	60	.241	9	30	29	-5	3.0
1885 NY-N	44	11	**.800**	56	55	55	7	1	492	372	4	131	258	9.2	1.66	160	.203	.256	41	.206	5	63	55	-8	4.9
1886 NY-N	33	22	.600	59	59	56	1	0	500	514	13	163	272	12.2	2.99	108	.259	.315	46	.216	1	18	12	-2	0.8
1887 NY-N	22	15	.595	40	40	39	2	0	346	339	7	91	115	11.3	3.36	112	.253	.303	36	.243	4	28	16	-2	1.4
1888 *NY-N	26	19	.578	47	47	47	5	0	425^{1}	328	12	108	167	9.5	1.93	142	.207	.263	32	.189	1	44	38	-4	3.5
1889 *NY-N	27	12	.692	45	41	39	3	**2**	375	340	14	149	125	12.0	3.02	130	.234	.310	30	.192	-2	41	38	-3	3.0
1890 NY-N	17	14	.548	37	37	33	2	0	292^{1}	268	5	122	97	12.4	2.99	117	.236	.317	22	.179	-3	19	17	-3	0.9
1891 NY-N	5	9	.357	22	15	14	0	1	160	176	7	97	46	16.0	4.27	75	.269	.372	10	.141	-4	-16	-19	-3	-2.2
1892 NY-N	0	0	—	1	1	0	0	0	5	11	0	4	1	27.0	14.40	22	.423	.500	1	.333	0	-6	-6	-0	-0.4
Total 13	307	210	.594	564	549	525	41	4	4802	4587	106	1297	1850	11.1	2.71	114	.242	.292	492	.224	22	216	196	-52	14.7
● **BOB WELCH** Welch, Robert Lynn b: 11/3/56, Detroit, Mich. BR/TR, 6'3", 190 lbs. Deb: 6/20/78																									
1978 *LA-N	7	4	.636	23	13	4	3	3	111^{1}	92	6	26	66	9.6	2.02	174	.229	.277	5	.172	0	19	18	-1	1.9
1979 LA-N	5	6	.455	25	12	1	0	5	81^{1}	82	7	32	64	12.9	3.98	91	.265	.340	3	.158	-0	-2	-3	-1	-0.4
1980 LA-N★	14	9	.609	32	32	3	2	0	213^{2}	190	15	79	141	11.5	3.29	106	.242	.314	17	.243	3	7	5	-1	0.8
1981 *LA-N	9	5	.643	23	23	2	1	0	141^{1}	141	11	41	88	11.8	3.44	96	.259	.315	10	.222	2	1	-2	-1	-0.1
1982 LA-N	16	11	.593	36	36	9	3	0	235^{2}	199	19	81	176	10.9	3.36	103	.229	.299	12	.141	-1	6	3	-1	0.0
1983 *LA-N	15	12	.556	31	31	4	3	0	204	164	13	72	156	10.5	2.65	136	.222	.294	7	.096	-2	22	21	-0	2.0
1984 LA-N	13	13	.500	31	29	3	1	0	178^{2}	191	11	58	126	12.6	3.78	93	.273	.331	4	.078	-3	-4	-5	2	-0.6
1985 *LA-N	14	4	.778	23	23	8	3	0	167^{1}	141	16	35	96	9.8	2.31	150	.225	.273	9	.180	1	24	22	1	2.6
1986 LA-N	7	13	.350	33	33	7	3	0	235^{2}	227	14	55	183	11.0	3.28	105	.251	.299	8	.105	-0	11	4	-1	0.3
1987 LA-N	15	9	.625	35	35	6	**4**	0	251^{2}	204	21	86	196	10.5	3.22	123	.221	.291	13	.157	1	24	21	2	2.5
1988 *Oak-A	17	9	.654	36	36	4	2	0	244^{2}	237	22	81	158	12.1	3.64	104	.257	.323	0	—	0	9	4	0	0.6
1989 *Oak-A	17	8	.680	33	33	1	0	0	209^{2}	191	13	78	137	11.8	3.00	122	.241	.314	0	—	0	20	16	-1	1.7
1990 *Oak-A★	**27**	6	**.818**	35	35	2	2	0	238	214	26	77	127	11.2	2.95	126	.242	.306	0	—	0	25	20	0	2.4
1991 Oak-A	12	13	.480	35	35	7	1	0	220	220	25	91	101	13.2	4.58	84	.263	.343	0	—	0	-12	-18	-1	-1.8
1992 *Oak-A	11	7	.611	20	20	0	0	0	123^{2}	114	13	43	47	11.6	3.27	115	.247	.314	0	—	0	9	7	-1	0.8
Total 15	199	129	.607	451	426	61	28	8	2856^{2}	2607	232	935	1862	11.4	3.27	111	.244	.309	88	.151	2	161	113	-4	12.7
● **DON WELCHEL** Welchel, Donald Ray b: 2/3/57, Atlanta, Tex. BR/TR, 6'4", 205 lbs. Deb: 9/15/82																									
1982 Bal-A	1	0	1.000	2	0	0	0	0	4^{1}	6	0	2	3	16.6	8.31	49	.300	.364	0	—	0	-2	-2	-0	-0.2
1983 Bal-A	0	2	.000	11	0	0	0	0	26^{2}	33	1	10	16	14.5	5.40	73	.297	.355	0	—	0	-4	-4	-0	-0.4
Total 2	1	2	.333	13	0	0	0	0	31	39	1	12	19	14.8	5.81	68	.298	.357	0	—	0	-6	-6	-0	-0.6
● **DAVID WELLS** Wells, David Lee b: 5/20/63, Torrance, Cal. BL/TL, 6'3", 225 lbs. Deb: 6/30/87																									
1987 Tor-A	4	3	.571	18	2	0	0	1	29^{1}	37	0	12	32	15.0	3.99	113	.311	.374	0	—	0	2	2	0	0.2
1988 Tor-A	3	5	.375	41	0	0	0	4	64^{1}	65	12	31	56	13.7	4.62	85	.269	.356	0	—	0	-5	-5	-0	-0.5
1989 *Tor-A	7	4	.636	54	0	0	0	2	86^{1}	66	5	28	78	9.8	2.40	157	.207	.271	0	—	0	14	13	0	1.4
1990 Tor-A	11	6	.647	43	25	0	0	3	189	165	14	45	115	10.1	3.14	125	.235	.283	0	—	0	16	17	1	1.7
1991 *Tor-A	15	10	.600	40	28	2	0	1	198^{1}	188	24	49	106	10.8	3.72	113	.251	.299	0	—	0	8	11	1	1.1
1992 *Tor-A	7	9	.438	41	14	0	0	2	120	138	16	36	62	13.7	5.40	76	.289	.349	0	—	0	-19	-18	-0	-1.9
Total 6	47	37	.560	237	69	2	0	13	687^{1}	659	71	201	449	11.4	3.78	107	.253	.310	0	—	0	16	20	2	2.0
● **ED WELLS** Wells, Edwin Lee "Satchelfoot" b: 6/7/1900, Ashland, Ohio d: 5/1/86, Birmingham, Ala. BL/TL, 6'1.5", 183 lbs. Deb: 6/16/23																									
1923 Det-A	0	0	—	7	0	0	0	0	10	11	0	6	6	15.3	5.40	72	.306	.405	0	.000	-0	-2	-2	-0	-0.2
1924 Det-A	6	8	.429	29	15	5	0	4	102	117	2	42	33	14.1	4.06	101	.291	.360	7	.212	-1	2	1	1	0.1
1925 Det-A	6	9	.400	35	14	5	0	2	134^{1}	190	8	62	45	17.0	6.23	69	.345	.413	12	.279	2	-27	-29	1	-2.4
1926 Det-A	12	10	.545	36	26	9	**4**	0	178	201	7	76	58	14.1	4.15	98	.297	.370	15	.205	0	-2	-2	-3	-0.4
1927 Det-A	0	1	.000	8	1	0	0	1	20	28	3	5	5	14.8	6.75	62	.333	.371	2	.286	0	-6	-6	1	-0.5
1929 NY-A	13	9	.591	31	23	10	3	0	193^{1}	179	19	81	78	12.1	4.33	89	.248	.324	17	.230	2	-2	-10	-4	-1.2
1930 NY-A	12	3	.800	27	21	7	0	0	150^{2}	185	11	49	46	14.2	5.20	83	.302	.358	15	.259	0	-9	-15	-2	-1.5
1931 NY-A	9	5	.643	27	10	6	0	2	116^{2}	130	7	37	34	13.0	4.32	92	.286	.341	10	.222	1	1	-5	-2	-0.5
1932 NY-A	3	3	.500	22	0	0	0	2	31^{2}	38	1	12	13	14.2	4.26	96	.302	.362	0	.000	-1	1	-1	-0	-0.1
1933 StL-A	6	14	.300	36	22	10	0	1	203^{2}	230	13	63	58	13.0	4.20	111	.278	.330	14	.197	-1	2	10	-3	0.6
1934 StL-A	1	7	.125	33	8	2	0	1	92	108	7	35	27	14.0	4.79	104	.292	.353	1	.045	-2	-3	2	1	0.1
Total 11	68	69	.496	291	140	54	7	13	1232^{1}	1417	78	468	403	13.9	4.65	91	.291	.355	93	.215	1	-46	-55	-10	-6.0
● **JOHN WELLS** Wells, John Frederick b: 11/25/22, Junction City, Kan BR/TR, 5'11.5", 180 lbs. Deb: 9/14/44																									
1944 Bro-N	0	2	.000	4	2	0	0	0	15	18	1	11	7	17.4	5.40	66	.316	.426	1	.250	0	-3	-3	-0	-0.3
● **TERRY WELLS** Wells, Terry b: 9/10/63, Kankakee, Ill. BL/TL, 6'3", 205 lbs. Deb: 7/03/90																									
1990 LA-N	1	2	.333	5	5	0	0	0	20^{2}	25	4	14	18	17.0	7.84	47	.287	.386	0	.000	-1	-9	-10	-1	-1.0
● **CHRIS WELSH** Welsh, Christopher Charles b: 4/14/55, Wilmington, Del. BL/TL, 6'2", 185 lbs. Deb: 4/12/81																									
1981 SD-N	6	7	.462	22	19	4	2	0	123^{2}	122	9	41	51	11.9	3.78	86	.264	.325	6	.146	0	-4	-7	1	-0.6
1982 SD-N	8	8	.500	28	20	3	1	0	139^{1}	146	16	63	48	13.7	4.91	70	.268	.347	11	.262	4	-20	-23	1	-1.9
1983 SD-N	0	1	.000	7	1	0	0	0	14^{1}	13	2	2	5	9.4	2.51	139	.236	.263	0	.000	-0	2	2	-0	0.1
Mon-N	0	1	.000	16	5	0	0	0	44^{2}	46	5	18	17	13.7	5.04	71	.267	.351	4	.286	1	-7	-7	1	-0.5
Yr	0	2	.000	23	6	0	0	0	59	59	7	20	22	12.7	4.42	81	.260	.331	4	.222	1	-5	-6	1	-0.4

YEAR	TM/L	W	L	PCT	G	GS	CG	SH	SV	IP	H	HR	BB	SO	RAT	ERA	ERA+	OAV	OOB	BH	AVG	PB	PR	/A	PD	TPI
1985	Tex-A	2	5	.286	25	6	0	0	0	76^1	101	11	25	31	15.3	4.13	102	.316	.372	0	—	0	0	1	-1	0.0
1986	Cin-N	6	9	.400	24	24	1	0	0	139^1	163	9	40	40	13.3	4.78	81	.301	.353	5	.119	0	-16	-14	-1	-1.4
Total	5	22	31	.415	122	75	8	3	0	537^2	591	52	189	192	13.3	4.45	81	.282	.346	26	.182	5	-46	-49	2	-4.3
● DICK WELTEROTH Welteroth, Richard John b: 8/3/27, Williamsport, Pa. BR/TR, 5'11", 165 lbs. Deb: 5/16/48																										
1948	Was-A	2	1	.667	33	2	0	0	1	65^1	73	6	50	16	17.1	5.51	79	.286	.405	1	.100	-1	-9	-8	-0	-0.9
1949	Was-A	2	5	.286	52	2	0	0	2	95^1	107	6	89	37	18.6	7.36	58	.296	.437	1	.059	-1	-34	-33	0	-3.2
1950	Was-A	0	0	—	5	0	0	0	0	6	5	0	6	2	16.5	3.00	150	.217	.379	0	—	0	1	1	0	0.1
Total	3	4	6	.400	90	4	0	0	3	166^2	185	12	145	55	17.9	6.48	66	.290	.422	2	.074	-2	-41	-40	-0	-4.0
● TONY WELZER Welzer, Anton Frank b: 4/5/1899, Germany d: 3/18/71, Milwaukee, Wis. BR/TR, 5'11", 160 lbs. Deb: 4/13/26																										
1926	Bos-A	4	3	.571	39	6	1	1	0	139	167	5	53	29	14.4	4.86	84	.308	.373	8	.211	2	-13	-12	4	-0.6
1927	Bos-A	6	11	.353	37	19	8	0	1	171^2	214	10	71	56	15.2	4.72	89	.318	.386	4	.095	-2	-11	-9	1	-1.0
Total	2	10	14	.417	76	25	9	1	1	310^2	381	15	124	85	14.8	4.78	87	.313	.380	12	.150	-0	-24	-22	4	-1.6
● BUTCH WENSLOFF Wensloff, Charles William b: 12/3/15, Sausalito, Cal. BR/TR, 5'11", 185 lbs. Deb: 5/02/43																										
1943	NY-A	13	11	.542	29	27	18	1	1	223^1	179	7	70	105	10.1	2.54	127	.219	.282	14	.177	-0	19	17	-1	1.7
1947	*NY-A	3	1	.750	11	5	1	0	0	51^2	41	3	22	18	11.0	2.61	135	.217	.299	5	.263	1	6	5	-1	0.5
1948	Cle-A	0	1	.000	1	0	0	0	0	1^2	2	1	3	2	27.0	10.80	38	.286	.500	0	—	0	-1	-1	-0	-0.1
Total	3	16	13	.552	41	32	19	1	1	276^2	222	11	95	125	10.3	2.60	126	.219	.287	19	.194	0	24	21	-2	2.1
● FRED WENZ Wenz, Frederick Charles "Fireball" b: 8/26/41, Bound Brook, N.J. BR/TR, 6'3", 214 lbs. Deb: 6/04/68																										
1968	Bos-A	0	0	—	1	0	0	0	0	1	0	0	2	3	18.0	0.00	—	.000	.400	0	—	0	0	0	0	0.0
1969	Bos-A	1	0	1.000	8	0	0	0	0	11	9	7	10	11	15.5	5.73	66	.225	.380	0	—	0	-3	-2	0	-0.2
1970	Phi-N	2	0	1.000	22	0	0	0	1	30^1	27	2	13	24	12.2	4.45	90	.237	.320	0	.000	-1	-1	-2	-1	-0.3
Total	3	3	0	1.000	31	0	0	0	1	42^1	36	9	25	38	13.2	4.68	84	.229	.339	0	.000	-0	-4	-4	-1	-0.5
● PERRY WERDEN Werden, Percival Wheritt b: 7/21/1865, St.Louis, Mo. d: 1/9/34, Minneapolis, Minn. BR/TR, 6'2", 220 lbs. Deb: 4/24/1884 ♦																										
1884	StL-U	12	1	.923	16	16	12	1	0	141^1	113	1	22	51	8.6	1.97	150	.204	.235	18	.237	-0	16	15	1	1.4
● BILL WERLE Werle, William George "Bugs" b: 12/21/20, Oakland, Cal. BL/TL, 6'2.5", 182 lbs. Deb: 4/22/49																										
1949	Pit-N	12	13	.480	35	29	10	2	0	221	243	22	51	106	12.3	4.24	99	.278	.324	9	.117	-3	-5	-1	1	-0.3
1950	Pit-N	8	16	.333	48	22	6	0	8	215^1	249	25	65	78	13.4	4.60	95	.290	.344	13	.194	1	-11	-5	4	0.0
1951	Pit-N	8	6	.571	59	9	2	0	6	149^2	181	20	51	57	14.3	5.65	75	.304	.364	12	.300	4	-28	-24	3	-1.6
1952	Pit-N	0	0	—	5	0	0	0	0	4	9	1	1	1	22.5	9.00	44	.429	.455	0	—	0	-2	-2	0	-0.2
	StL-N	1	2	.333	19	0	0	0	1	39	40	6	15	23	12.9	4.85	77	.268	.339	1	.111	-0	-5	-5	1	-0.4
	Yr	1	2	.333	24	0	0	0	1	43	49	7	16	24	13.8	5.23	71	.288	.353	1	.111	-0	-7	-7	2	-0.6
1953	Bos-A	0	1	.000	5	0	0	0	0	11^2	7	1	1	4	6.2	1.54	273	.179	.200	0	.000	-0	3	3	1	0.4
1954	Bos-A	0	1	.000	14	0	0	0	0	24^2	41	5	10	14	19.3	4.38	94	.376	.438	0	.000	-0	-2	-1	-0	-0.1
Total	6	29	39	.426	185	60	18	2	15	665^1	770	80	194	283	13.4	4.69	90	.291	.345	35	.176	1	-50	-34	10	-2.2
● GEORGE WERLEY Werley, George William b: 9/8/38, St.Louis, Mo. BR/TR, 6'2", 196 lbs. Deb: 9/29/56																										
1956	Bal-A	0	0	—	1	0	0	0	0	1	1	0	2	0	27.0	9.00	44	.250	.500	0	—	0	-1	-1	0	0.0
● JOHNNY WERTS Werts, Henry Levi b: 4/20/1898, Pomaria, S.C. d: 9/24/90, Newberry, S.C. BR/TR, 5'10", 180 lbs. Deb: 4/14/26																										
1926	Bos-N	11	9	.550	32	23	7	1	0	189^1	212	6	47	65	12.8	3.28	108	.287	.338	17	.266	4	11	6	2	1.2
1927	Bos-N	4	10	.286	42	15	4	0	1	164^1	204	5	52	39	14.2	4.55	82	.315	.369	7	.163	-0	-11	-15	-1	-1.6
1928	Bos-N	0	2	.000	10	2	0	0	0	18^1	31	2	8	5	19.1	10.31	38	.369	.424	1	.333	0	-13	-13	0	-1.2
1929	Bos-N	0	0	—	4	0	0	0	1	6	13	1	4	2	25.5	10.50	45	.433	.500	1	1.000	0	-4	-4	-0	-0.3
Total	4	15	21	.417	88	40	11	1	2	378	460	14	111	111	13.9	4.29	85	.307	.360	26	.234	4	-17	-27	1	-1.9
● DAVID WEST West, David Lee b: 9/1/64, Memphis, Tenn. BL/TL, 6'6", 205 lbs. Deb: 9/24/88																										
1988	NY-N	1	0	1.000	2	1	0	0	0	6	6	0	3	3	13.5	3.00	107	.273	.360	2	1.000	1	0	0	-0	0.1
1989	NY-N	0	2	.000	11	2	0	0	0	24^1	25	4	14	19	14.8	7.40	44	.260	.360	1	.200	0	-11	-11	-1	-1.2
	Min-A	3	2	.600	10	5	0	0	0	39^1	48	5	19	31	15.8	6.41	65	.306	.388	0	—	0	-11	-10	-1	-1.2
1990	Min-A	7	9	.438	29	27	2	0	0	146^1	142	21	78	92	13.8	5.10	81	.256	.352	0	—	0	-19	-15	-1	-2.0
1991	*Min-A	4	4	.500	15	12	0	0	0	71^1	66	13	28	52	12.0	4.54	94	.244	.317	0	—	0	-4	-2	0	-0.2
1992	Min-A	1	3	.250	9	3	0	0	0	28^1	32	3	20	19	16.8	6.99	58	.276	.387	0	—	0	-10	-9	-0	-1.0
Total	5	16	20	.444	76	50	2	0	0	315^2	319	46	162	216	14.0	5.45	75	.262	.353	3	.429	1	-54	-48	-3	-5.5
● FRANK WEST West, Frank b: 1873, Wilmerding, Pa. Deb: 7/11/1894																										
1894	Bos-N	0	0	—	1	0	0	0	0	3	5	0	2	1	21.0	9.00	63	.367	.448	0	.000	-0	-1	-1	-0	-0.1
● HI WEST West, James Hiram b: 8/8/1884, Roseville, Ill. d: 5/25/63, Los Angeles, Cal. BR/TR, 6', 185 lbs. Deb: 9/08/05																										
1905	Cle-A	2	2	.500	6	4	4	1	0	33	43	0	10	15	15.3	4.09	64	.316	.375	1	.077	-1	-5	-5	-2	-0.8
1911	Cle-A	3	4	.429	13	8	3	0	1	64^2	84	1	18	17	14.6	3.76	91	.343	.395	3	.130	-2	-3	-2	-1	-0.5
Total	2	5	6	.455	19	12	7	1	1	97^2	127	1	28	32	14.8	3.87	81	.333	.388	4	.111	-3	-8	-8	-3	-1.3
● LEFTY WEST West, Weldon Edison b: 9/3/15, Gibsonville, N.C. d: 7/23/79, Hendersonville, N.C. BR/TL, 6', 165 lbs. Deb: 4/30/44																										
1944	StL-A	0	0	—	11	0	0	0	0	24^1	34	1	19	11	20.0	6.29	57	.366	.478	1	.143	-0	-8	-7	-0	-0.8
1945	StL-A	3	4	.429	24	8	1	0	0	74^1	71	2	31	38	12.3	3.63	97	.245	.318	2	.074	-3	-2	-1	-2	-0.6
Total	2	3	4	.429	35	8	1	0	0	98^2	105	3	50	49	14.2	4.29	83	.274	.359	3	.088	-3	-10	-8	-2	-1.4
● HUYLER WESTERVELT Westervelt, Huyler b: 10/1/1870, Piermont, N.Y. 5'9", 170 lbs. Deb: 4/21/1894																										
1894	NY-N	7	10	.412	23	18	11	1	0	141	170	4	76	35	16.0	5.04	104	.295	.382	8	.143	-5	4	3	0	-0.1
● MICKEY WESTON Weston, Michael Lee b: 3/26/61, Flint, Mich. BR/TR, 6'1", 180 lbs. Deb: 6/18/89																										
1989	Bal-A	1	0	1.000	7	0	0	0	1	13	18	1	2	7	14.5	5.54	68	.346	.382	0	—	0	-2	-3	-0	-0.2
1990	Bal-A	0	1	.000	9	2	0	0	0	21	28	6	6	9	14.6	7.71	49	.322	.366	0	—	0	-9	-9	-0	-0.8
1991	Tor-A	0	0	—	2	0	0	0	0	2	1	0	1	1	9.0	0.00	—	.143	.250	0	—	0	1	1	-0	0.1
1992	Phi-N	0	1	.000	1	1	0	0	0	3^2	7	1	1	0	22.1	12.27	28	.412	.474	0	.000	-0	-4	-4	-0	-0.3
Total	4	1	2	.333	19	3	0	0	1	39^2	54	8	10	17	15.0	7.03	54	.331	.377	0	.000	-0	-14	-14	-1	-1.2
● JOHN WETTELAND Wetteland, John Karl b: 8/21/66, San Mateo, Cal. BR/TR, 6'2", 195 lbs. Deb: 5/31/89																										
1989	LA-N	5	8	.385	31	12	0	0	1	102^2	81	8	34	96	10.1	3.77	91	.218	.284	3	.143	-0	-3	-4	-1	-0.6
1990	LA-N	2	4	.333	22	5	0	0	0	43	44	6	17	36	13.6	4.81	76	.263	.346	1	.143	1	-5	-6	-1	-0.6
1991	LA-N	1	0	1.000	6	0	0	0	0	9	5	0	3	9	9.0	0.00	—	.161	.257	0	—	0	4	4	0	0.4
1992	Mon-N	4	4	.500	67	0	0	0	37	83^1	64	6	36	99	11.2	2.92	120	.213	.305	1	.200	0	5	5	-1	0.5
Total	4	12	16	.429	126	17	0	0	38	238	194	20	90	240	11.1	3.52	99	.223	.302	5	.152	1	1	-1	-2	-0.3
● BUZZ WETZEL Wetzel, Charles Edward b: 8/25/1894, Jay, Okla. d: 3/7/41, Globe, Ariz. BR/TR, 6'1", 162 lbs. Deb: 7/25/27																										
1927	Phi-A	0	0	—	2	1	0	0	0	4^2	8	0	5	0	25.1	7.71	55	.400	.520	1	1.000	0	-2	-2	0	-0.1
● SHORTY WETZEL Wetzel, George William b: 1868, Philadelphia, Pa. d: 2/25/1899, Dayton, Ohio Deb: 8/26/1885																										
1885	Bal-a	0	2	.000	2	2	1	0	0	17	27	0	9	6	20.6	8.47	38	.333	.419	0	.000	-1	-10	-10	1	-0.7

YEAR TM/L	W	L	PCT	G	GS	CG	SH	SV	IP	H	HR	BB	SO	RAT	ERA	ERA+	OAV	OOB	BH	AVG	PB	PR	/A	PD	TPI

● STEFAN WEVER   Wever, Stefan Matthew b: 4/22/58, Marburg, W.Germ BR/TR, 6'8", 245 lbs. Deb: 9/17/82

| 1982 NY-A | 0 | 1 | .000 | 1 | 1 | 0 | 0 | 0 | 2² | 6 | 1 | 3 | 2 | 30.4 | 27.00 | 15 | .429 | .529 | 0 | — | 0 | -7 | -7 | -0 | -0.5 |

● GUS WEYHING   Weyhing, August "Cannonball" b: 9/29/1866, Louisville, Ky. d: 9/4/55, Louisville, Ky. BR/TR, 5'10", 145 lbs. Deb: 5/02/1887 F

1887 Phi-a	26	28	.481	55	55	53	2	0	466¹	465	12	167	193	12.9	4.27	101	.253	.328	42	.201	-8	2	1	-2	-0.7
1888 Phi-a	28	18	.609	47	47	45	3	0	404	314	4	111	204	10.4	2.25	133	.207	.279	40	.217	4	36	33	1	3.7
1889 Phi-a	30	21	.588	54	53	50	4	0	449	382	15	212	213	12.6	2.95	128	.223	.321	25	.131	-14	45	42	-3	2.1
1890 Bro-P	30	16	.652	49	46	38	3	0	390	419	10	179	177	14.2	3.60	124	.263	.343	27	.164	-6	27	37	-9	1.7
1891 Phi-a	31	20	.608	52	51	51	3	0	450	428	12	161	219	12.4	3.18	120	.242	.317	22	.150	-16	27	32	-5	1.0
1892 Phi-N	32	21	.604	59	49	46	6	3	469²	411	9	168	202	11.4	2.66	122	.226	.298	29	.136	-9	33	30	-9	1.0
1893 Phi-N	23	16	.590	42	40	33	2	0	345¹	399	10	145	101	14.7	4.74	96	.281	.356	22	.150	-9	-3	-6	-2	-1.4
1894 Phi-N	16	14	.533	38	34	25	2	1	266¹	365	12	116	81	16.8	5.81	88	.322	.393	20	.174	-8	-14	-21	-3	-2.4
1895 Phi-N	0	2	.000	2	2	0	0	0	9	23	0	13	5	36.0	20.00	24	.469	.580	0	.000	-1	-15	-15	0	-1.0
Pit-N	1	0	1.000	1	1	1	0	0	9	10	0	5	3	15.0	1.00	452	.277	.365	1	.250	0	4	4	1	0.4
Lou-N	7	19	.269	28	25	22	1	0	213	285	9	66	53	15.2	5.41	86	.316	.368	20	.225	0	-15	-18	0	-1.4
Yr	8	21	.276	31	28	23	1	0	231	318	9	84	61	16.0	5.81	80	.322	.380	21	.216	-1	-26	-30	1	-2.0
1896 Lou-N	2	3	.400	5	5	4	0	0	42	62	6	15	9	16.9	6.64	65	.340	.396	2	.133	-1	-11	-11	1	-0.8
1898 Was-N	15	26	.366	45	42	39	0	0	361	428	10	84	92	13.2	4.51	81	.292	.338	25	.177	-5	-36	-34	-2	-3.7
1899 Was-N	17	21	.447	43	38	34	2	0	334²	414	8	76	96	13.9	4.54	86	.303	.352	26	.206	-8	-26	-24	-6	-2.7
1900 StL-N	3	2	.600	7	5	3	0	0	46²	60	2	21	6	15.8	4.63	79	.311	.382	2	.095	-2	-5	-5	-1	-0.3
Bro-N	3	4	.429	8	8	3	0	0	48	66	1	20	8	16.5	4.31	89	.326	.392	4	.222	-0	-3	-3	-1	-1.0
Yr	6	6	.500	15	13	6	0	0	94²	126	3	41	14	16.1	4.47	84	.318	.384	6	.154	-3	-8	-8	-1	-1.0
1901 Cle-A	0	0	—	2	1	0	0	0	11¹	20	1	0	5	23.0	7.94	45	.379	.470	0	.000	-1	-5	-5	-0	-0.5
Cin-N	0	1	.000	1	1	0	0	0	6	11	0	2	3	15.0	3.00	107	.299	.368	0	.000	-0	0	0	-0	-0.1
Total 14	264	232	.532	538	503	448	28	4	4324¹	4562	120	1566	1665	13.3	3.89	102	.264	.335	307	.166	-80	41	38	-39	-5.8

● JOHN WEYHING   Weyhing, John b: 6/24/1869, Louisville, Ky. d: 6/20/1890, Louisville, Ky. BL/TL, 6'2", 185 lbs. Deb: 7/13/1888 F

1888 Cin-a	3	4	.429	8	8	7	0	0	65²	52	0	17	30	9.6	1.23	257	.210	.263	3	.130	-2	13	14	-1	1.2
1889 Col-a	0	0	—	1	0	0	0	0	1	1	0	4	0	45.0	27.00	13	.252	.628	0	—	0	-3	-3	-0	-0.2
Total 2	3	4	.429	9	8	7	0	0	66²	53	0	21	30	10.1	1.62	196	.210	.274	3	.130	-2	11	12	-1	1.0

● LEE WHEAT   Wheat, Leroy William b: 9/15/29, Edwardsville, Ill BR/TR, 6'4", 200 lbs. Deb: 4/21/54

1954 Phi-A	0	2	.000	8	1	0	0	0	28¹	38	1	9	7	15.2	5.72	68	.304	.356	1	.125	-0	-6	-6	-0	-0.6
1955 KC-A	0	0	—	3	0	0	0	0	2	8	1	3	1	49.5	22.50	19	.533	.611	0	—	0	-4	-4	-0	-0.4
Total 2	0	2	.000	11	1	0	0	0	30¹	46	2	12	8	17.5	6.82	57	.329	.386	1	.125	-0	-10	-10	-0	-1.0

● CHARLIE WHEATLEY   Wheatley, Charles b: 6/27/1893, Rosedale, Kan. d: 12/10/82, Tulsa, Okla. BR/TR, 5'11", 174 lbs. Deb: 9/06/12

| 1912 Det-A | 1 | 4 | .200 | 5 | 5 | 2 | 0 | 0 | 35 | 45 | 1 | 17 | 14 | 16.5 | 6.17 | 53 | .331 | .413 | 0 | .000 | -2 | -11 | -11 | 0 | -1.1 |

● WOODY WHEATON   Wheaton, Elwood Pierce b: 10/3/14, Philadelphia, Pa. BL/TL, 5'8.5", 160 lbs. Deb: 9/28/43 ♦

| 1944 Phi-A | 0 | 1 | .000 | 11 | 1 | 1 | 0 | 0 | 38 | 36 | 1 | 20 | 15 | 13.5 | 3.55 | 98 | .255 | .352 | 11 | .186 | 0 | -1 | -0 | -1 | -0.1 |

● RIP WHEELER   Wheeler, Floyd Clark b: 3/2/1898, Marion, Ky. d: 9/18/68, Marion, Ky. BR/TR, 6', 180 lbs. Deb: 9/30/21

1921 Pit-N	0	0	—	1	0	0	0	0	3	6	0	1	0	24.0	9.00	43	.500	.571	0	.000	-0	-2	-2	0	-0.2
1922 Pit-N	0	0	—	1	0	0	0	0	1	1	0	2	0	27.0	0.00	—	.333	.600	0	—	0	0	0	0	0.1
1923 Chi-N	1	2	.333	3	3	1	0	0	24	28	2	5	5	13.5	4.88	82	.298	.353	1	.111	-1	-2	-2	1	-0.2
1924 Chi-N	3	6	.333	29	4	0	0	0	101¹	103	8	21	16	11.0	3.91	100	.265	.303	7	.219	-1	-0	-0	0	-0.1
Total 4	4	8	.333	34	7	1	0	0	129¹	138	10	29	21	11.9	4.18	94	.278	.323	8	.190	-2	-4	-4	2	-0.4

● GEORGE WHEELER   Wheeler, George L. (b: George L. Heroux) b: 8/3/1869, Methuen, Mass. d: 3/23/46, Santa Ana, Cal. BB/TB, Deb: 9/18/1896

1896 Phi-N	1	1	.500	3	2	2	0	0	16¹	18	0	5	2	13.8	3.86	112	.277	.348	1	.111	-1	1	1	0	0.0
1897 Phi-N	11	10	.524	26	19	17	0	0	191	229	3	62	35	13.9	3.96	106	.295	.349	16	.203	-1	8	5	1	0.4
1898 Phi-N	6	8	.429	15	13	10	0	0	112¹	155	1	36	20	15.8	4.17	82	.325	.379	8	.186	-1	-7	-9	3	-0.7
1899 Phi-N	3	1	.750	6	5	3	0	0	39	44	1	13	3	13.8	6.00	61	.284	.351	4	.235	-1	-9	-10	0	-0.7
Total 4	21	20	.512	50	39	32	0	0	358²	446	5	116	60	14.5	4.24	92	.303	.359	29	.196	-2	-8	-13	4	-1.0

● HARRY WHEELER   Wheeler, Harry Eugene b: 3/3/1858, Versailles, Ind. d: 10/9/1900, Cincinnati, Ohio BR/TR, 5'11", 165 lbs. Deb: 6/19/1878 M♦

1878 Pro-N	6	1	.857	7	6	6	0	0	62	70	1	25	25	13.8	3.48	63	.275	.339	4	.148	-1	-8	-9	-2	-1.0
1879 Cin-N	0	1	.000	1	1	0	0	0	1	6	0	4	0	90.0	81.00	3	.667	.769	0	.000	-0	-9	-9	-0	-0.6
1882 Cin-a	1	2	.333	4	1	1	0	0	21²	21	0	12	10	13.7	5.40	49	.238	.329	86	.250	1	-7	-7	-0	-0.6
1883 Col-a	0	1	.000	1	1	0	0	0	5	13	0	2	0	27.0	7.20	47	.456	.492	84	.226	0	2	1	0	-0.2
1884 KC-U	0	1	.000	1	1	1	0	0	8	7	0	6	6	7.9	1.13	245	.220	.220	16	.258	-0	2	1	0	0.2
Total 5	7	6	.538	14	10	8	0	0	97²	117	1	43	41	14.7	4.70	51	.283	.351	256	.228	-0	-24	-25	-2	-2.2

● GARY WHEELOCK   Wheelock, Gary Richard b: 11/29/51, Bakersfield, Cal. BR/TR, 6'3", 205 lbs. Deb: 9/17/76

1976 Cal-A	0	0	—	2	0	0	0	0	2	6	0	1	2	36.0	27.00	12	.500	.571	0	—	0	-5	-5	-0	-0.5
1977 Sea-A	6	9	.400	17	17	2	0	0	88¹	94	16	26	47	12.4	4.89	84	.268	.322	0	—	0	-8	-8	-1	-0.8
1980 Sea-A	0	0	—	1	1	0	0	0	3	4	0	1	1	15.0	6.00	69	.333	.385	0	—	0	-1	-1	-0	-0.1
Total 3	6	9	.400	20	18	2	0	0	93¹	104	16	28	50	13.0	5.40	76	.277	.333	0	—	0	-14	-14	-1	-1.4

● JACK WHILLOCK   Whillock, Jack Franklin b: 11/4/42, Clinton, Ark. BR/TR, 6'3", 195 lbs. Deb: 8/29/71

| 1971 Det-A | 0 | 2 | .000 | 7 | 0 | 0 | 0 | 1 | 8 | 10 | 1 | 2 | 6 | 13.5 | 5.63 | 64 | .323 | .364 | 0 | .000 | -0 | -2 | -2 | 0 | -0.2 |

● PAT WHITAKER   Whitaker, William H. b: 11/1864, St.Louis, Mo. d: 7/15/02, St.Louis, Mo. TR, Deb: 10/11/1888

1888 Bal-a	1	1	.500	2	2	2	0	0	14	13	0	6	5	13.5	5.14	58	.237	.335	0	.000	-1	-3	-3	2	-0.2
1889 Bal-a	1	0	1.000	1	1	1	0	0	9	10	0	4	1	14.0	2.00	197	.273	.344	1	.250	-0	2	2	0	0.2
Total 2	2	1	.667	3	3	3	0	0	23	23	0	10	6	13.7	3.91	86	.251	.338	1	.100	-1	-1	-2	2	0.0

● BILL WHITBY   Whitby, William Edward b: 7/29/43, Crewe, Va. BR/TR, 6'1", 190 lbs. Deb: 6/17/64

| 1964 Min-A | 0 | 0 | — | 4 | 0 | 0 | 0 | 0 | 6¹ | 7 | 0 | 3 | 2 | 12.8 | 8.53 | 42 | .308 | .333 | 0 | .000 | -0 | -3 | -3 | -0 | -0.4 |

● BOB WHITCHER   Whitcher, Robert Arthur b: 4/29/17, Berlin, N.H. BL/TL, 5'8", 165 lbs. Deb: 8/20/45

| 1945 Bos-N | 0 | 2 | .000 | 6 | 3 | 0 | 0 | 0 | 15² | 12 | 1 | 12 | 6 | 13.8 | 2.87 | 133 | .235 | .381 | 1 | .333 | 0 | 2 | 2 | -0 | 0.2 |

● ABE WHITE   White, Adel b: 5/16/04, Winder, Ga. d: 10/1/78, Atlanta, Ga. BR/TL, 6', 185 lbs. Deb: 7/10/37

| 1937 StL-N | 0 | 1 | .000 | 5 | 0 | 0 | 0 | 0 | 9¹ | 14 | 1 | 3 | 2 | 16.4 | 6.75 | 59 | .341 | .386 | 1 | 1.000 | 0 | -3 | -3 | -0 | -0.2 |

● ERNIE WHITE   White, Ernest Daniel b: 9/5/16, Pacolet Mills, S.C d: 5/22/74, Augusta, Ga. BR/TL, 5'11.5", 175 lbs. Deb: 5/09/40 C

1940 StL-N	1	1	.500	8	1	0	0	0	21²	29	0	14	15	18.3	4.15	96	.315	.411	3	.429	1	-1	-0	1	0.1
1941 StL-N	17	7	.708	32	25	12	3	2	210	169	12	70	117	10.5	2.40	157	.217	.287	15	.190	0	29	32	-4	3.1
1942 *StL-N	7	5	.583	26	19	7	1	2	128¹	113	11	41	67	10.9	2.52	136	.232	.294	8	.195	0	11	13	-2	1.2
1943 *StL-N	5	5	.500	14	10	5	1	0	78²	74	4	33	28	12.8	3.78	89	.257	.332	6	.214	-0	-3	-4	-1	-0.5
1946 Bos-N	0	1	.000	12	1	0	0	0	23²	22	1	12	8	12.9	4.18	82	.256	.347	1	.250	-0	-2	-2	-1	-0.3
1947 Bos-N	0	0	—	1	1	0	0	0	4	1	0	1	4	4.5	0.00	—	.083	.154	1	1.000	0	2	2	-0	0.2
1948 Bos-N	0	2	.000	15	0	0	0	2	23	13	0	17	8	11.7	1.96	190	.167	.316	0	—	0	5	5	0	0.4
Total 7	30	21	.588	108	57	24	5	6	489¹	425	28	188	244	11.5	2.78	130	.231	.306	34	.209	2	41	45	-8	4.2

● DEKE WHITE White, George Frederick b: 9/8/1872, Albany, N.Y. d: 11/5/57, Ilion, N.Y. BB/TL, Deb: 9/14/1895

YEAR	TM/L	W	L	PCT	G	GS	CG	SH	SV	IP	H	HR	BB	SO	RAT	ERA	ERA+	OAV	OOB	BH	AVG	PB	PR	/A	PD	TPI
1895	Phi-N	1	0	1.000	3	1	1	0	1	17^{1}	17	1	13	6	16.6	9.87	49	.253	.389	1	.125	-1	-10	-10	-0	-0.8

● DOC WHITE White, Guy Harris b: 4/9/1879, Washington, D.C. d: 2/19/69, Silver Spring, Md. BL/TL, 6'1", 150 lbs. Deb: 4/22/01 ♦

YEAR	TM/L	W	L	PCT	G	GS	CG	SH	SV	IP	H	HR	BB	SO	RAT	ERA	ERA+	OAV	OOB	BH	AVG	PB	PR	/A	PD	TPI
1901	Phi-N	14	13	.519	31	27	22	0	0	236^{2}	241	2	56	132	11.8	3.19	106	.262	.314	27	.276	5	3	5	3	1.3
1902	Phi-N	16	20	.444	36	35	34	3	1	306	277	3	72	185	10.6	2.53	111	.242	.294	47	.263	5	9	10	2	1.9
1903	Chi-A	17	16	.515	37	36	29	3	0	300	258	4	69	114	10.2	2.13	132	.232	.285	20	.202	5	28	23	3	3.3
1904	Chi-A	16	12	.571	30	30	23	7	0	228	201	6	68	115	11.0	1.78	138	.238	.301	12	.158	0	21	17	1	2.1
1905	Chi-A	17	13	.567	36	33	25	4	0	260^{1}	204	2	58	120	9.4	1.76	140	.217	.269	15	.167	0	26	21	-0	2.3
1906	*Chi-A	18	6	.750	28	24	20	7	0	219^{1}	160	2	38	95	**8.3**	**1.52**	**167**	.207	**.249**	12	.185	3	29	25	2	3.6
1907	Chi-A	**27**	13	.675	46	35	24	6	1	291	270	3	38	141	9.6	2.26	106	.248	.276	20	.222	4	9	5	5	1.5
1908	Chi-A	18	13	.581	41	37	24	5	0	296	267	3	69	126	10.5	2.55	91	.244	.295	25	.229	4	-5	-8	7	0.4
1909	Chi-A	11	9	.550	24	21	14	3	0	177^{2}	149	1	31	77	9.5	1.72	136	.226	.269	45	.234	6	15	12	-1	2.0
1910	Chi-A	15	13	.536	33	29	20	2	1	236^{2}	219	2	50	111	10.7	2.66	90	.243	.291	25	.198	2	-4	-7	2	-0.2
1911	Chi-A	10	14	.417	34	29	16	4	2	214^{1}	219	2	35	72	11.0	2.98	108	.271	.309	20	.256	3	9	6	-1	0.8
1912	Chi-A	8	10	.444	32	19	9	1	0	172	172	1	47	57	11.9	3.24	99	.267	.325	7	.125	-1	1	-1	-1	-0.3
1913	Chi-A	2	4	.333	19	8	2	0	0	103	106	2	39	39	13.1	3.50	84	.278	.353	3	.120	-1	-6	-7	2	-0.5
Total	13	189	156	.548	427	363	262	45	5	3041	2743	33	670	1384	10.5	2.39	112	.242	.292	278	.217	36	134	100	24	18.2

● HAL WHITE White, Harold George b: 3/18/19, Utica, N.Y. BR/TR, 5'10", 170 lbs. Deb: 4/22/41

YEAR	TM/L	W	L	PCT	G	GS	CG	SH	SV	IP	H	HR	BB	SO	RAT	ERA	ERA+	OAV	OOB	BH	AVG	PB	PR	/A	PD	TPI
1941	Det-A	0	0	—	4	0	0	0	0	9	11	0	6	2	17.0	6.00	76	.306	.405	0	.000	-0	-2	-1	0	-0.2
1942	Det-A	12	12	.500	34	25	12	4	1	216^{2}	212	6	82	93	12.4	2.91	136	.252	.323	13	.169	-1	18	25	0	2.6
1943	Det-A	7	12	.368	32	24	7	2	2	177^{2}	150	6	71	58	11.2	3.39	104	.228	.304	8	.140	-1	-2	3	0	0.2
1946	Det-A	1	1	.500	11	1	1	0	0	27^{1}	34	5	15	12	16.1	5.60	65	.312	.395	0	.000	-1	-6	-6	1	-0.6
1947	Det-A	4	5	.444	35	5	0	0	2	84^{2}	91	5	47	33	14.9	3.61	104	.279	.373	3	.167	0	1	1	1	0.3
1948	Det-A	2	1	.667	27	0	0	0	1	42^{2}	46	2	26	17	15.4	6.12	71	.272	.372	2	.154	0	-9	-8	-1	-0.9
1949	Det-A	1	0	1.000	9	0	0	0	2	12	5	0	4	4	6.8	0.00	—	.125	.205	1	.333	0	6	6	1	0.6
1950	Det-A	9	6	.600	42	8	3	1	1	111	96	7	65	53	13.1	4.54	103	.239	.347	4	.121	-2	0	2	0	0.0
1951	Det-A	3	4	.429	38	4	0	0	4	76	74	7	49	23	14.8	4.74	88	.264	.378	4	.250	0	-5	-5	2	-0.3
1952	Det-A	1	8	.111	41	0	0	0	5	63^{1}	53	1	39	18	13.1	3.69	103	.237	.350	2	.182	-0	-0	1	1	0.2
1953	StL-A	0	0	—	10	0	0	0	0	10^{1}	8	1	3	2	10.5	2.61	161	.205	.279	0	.000	0	2	2	0	0.2
	StL-N	6	5	.545	49	0	0	0	7	84^{2}	84	5	39	32	13.1	2.98	143	.272	.353	0	.000	-2	12	12	1	1.0
1954	StL-N	0	0	—	4	0	0	0	0	5	11	2	4	2	28.8	19.80	21	.440	.533	0	.000	-0	-9	-9	-0	-0.8
Total	12	46	54	.460	336	67	23	7	25	920^{1}	875	47	450	349	13.1	3.78	106	.253	.342	37	.145	-7	6	23	6	2.3

● DEACON WHITE White, James Laurie b: 12/7/1847, Caton, N.Y. d: 7/7/39, Aurora, Ill. BL/TR, 5'11", 175 lbs. Deb: 5/04/1871 FM♦

YEAR	TM/L	W	L	PCT	G	GS	CG	SH	SV	IP	H	HR	BB	SO	RAT	ERA	ERA+	OAV	OOB	BH	AVG	PB	PR	/A	PD	TPI
1876	Chi-N	0	0	—	1	0	0	0	1	2	1	0	0	3	4.5	0.00	—	.143	.143	104	.343	0	1	1	0	0.1
1890	Buf-P	0	0	—	1	0	0	0	0	8	18	0	2	0	22.5	9.00	46	.427	.453	114	.260	0	-4	-4	-1	-0.3
Total	2	0	0	—	2	0	0	0	1	10	19	0	2	3	18.9	7.20	53	.387	.411	1619	.303	0	-4	-4	-0	-0.2

● LARRY WHITE White, Larry David b: 9/25/58, San Fernando, Cal. BR/TR, 6'5", 190 lbs. Deb: 9/20/83

YEAR	TM/L	W	L	PCT	G	GS	CG	SH	SV	IP	H	HR	BB	SO	RAT	ERA	ERA+	OAV	OOB	BH	AVG	PB	PR	/A	PD	TPI
1983	LA-N	0	0	—	4	0	0	0	0	7	4	0	3	5	9.0	1.29	279	.174	.269	0	—	0	2	2	0	0.2
1984	LA-N	0	1	.000	7	1	0	0	0	12	9	2	6	10	11.3	3.00	118	.209	.306	0	.000	-0	1	1	-0	0.0
Total	2	0	1	.000	11	1	0	0	0	19	13	2	9	15	10.4	2.37	150	.197	.293	0	.000	-0	3	3	-0	0.2

● KIRBY WHITE White, Oliver Kirby "Red" or "Buck" b: 1/3/1884, Hillsboro, Ohio d: 4/22/43, Hillsboro, Ohio BL/TR, 6', 190 lbs. Deb: 5/04/09

YEAR	TM/L	W	L	PCT	G	GS	CG	SH	SV	IP	H	HR	BB	SO	RAT	ERA	ERA+	OAV	OOB	BH	AVG	PB	PR	/A	PD	TPI
1909	Bos-N	6	13	.316	23	19	11	1	0	148^{1}	134	5	80	53	13.0	3.22	88	.245	.343	8	.160	-1	-10	-6	-1	-0.9
1910	Bos-N	1	2	.333	3	3	3	0	0	26	15	2	12	6	10.4	1.38	240	.188	.316	2	.333	1	5	6	0	0.8
	Pit-N	10	9	.526	30	21	7	3	2	153^{1}	142	2	75	42	13.0	3.46	90	.258	.352	12	.261	4	-7	-6	-3	-0.6
	Yr	11	11	.500	33	24	10	3	2	179^{1}	157	4	87	48	12.5	3.16	99	.248	.343	14	.269	4	-3	-1	-3	0.2
1911	Pit-N	0	1	.000	2	1	0	0	0	3	3	1	1	1	12.0	9.00	38	.250	.308	0	.000	-0	-2	-2	0	-0.2
Total	3	17	25	.405	58	44	21	4	2	330^{2}	294	10	168	102	12.8	3.24	93	.247	.345	22	.214	3	-15	-9	-4	-0.9

● STEVE WHITE White, Stephen Vincent b: 12/21/1884, Dorchester, Mass. d: 1/29/75, Braintree, Mass. BR/TR, 5'10", 160 lbs. Deb: 5/29/12

YEAR	TM/L	W	L	PCT	G	GS	CG	SH	SV	IP	H	HR	BB	SO	RAT	ERA	ERA+	OAV	OOB	BH	AVG	PB	PR	/A	PD	TPI
1912	Was-A	0	0	—	1	0	0	0	0	0^{2}	2	1	0	1	27.0	0.00	—	.667	.667	0	—	0	0	0	-0	0.0
	Bos-N	0	0	—	3	0	0	0	0	6	9	0	5	2	22.5	6.00	60	.429	.556	0	.000	-0	-2	-2	0	-0.2
Total	1	0	0	—	4	0	0	0	0	6^{2}	11	1	5	3	23.0	5.40	66	.458	.567	0	.000	-0	-1	-1	-0	-0.2

● BILL WHITE White, William Dighton b: 5/1/1860, Bridgeport, Ohio d: 12/29/24, Bellaire, Ohio TR, Deb: 5/03/1884 ♦

YEAR	TM/L	W	L	PCT	G	GS	CG	SH	SV	IP	H	HR	BB	SO	RAT	ERA	ERA+	OAV	OOB	BH	AVG	PB	PR	/A	PD	TPI
1886	Lou-a	0	0	—	1	0	0	0	0	1	2	0	2	1	36.0	9.00	40	.400	.571	143	.257	0	-1	-1	0	0.0

● WILL WHITE White, William Henry "Whoop-La" b: 10/11/1854, Caton, N.Y. d: 8/31/11, Port Carling, Ont. Canada BB/TR, 5'9.5", 175 lbs. Deb: 7/20/1877 FM

YEAR	TM/L	W	L	PCT	G	GS	CG	SH	SV	IP	H	HR	BB	SO	RAT	ERA	ERA+	OAV	OOB	BH	AVG	PB	PR	/A	PD	TPI
1877	Bos-N	2	1	.667	3	3	3	1	0	27	27	0	2	7	9.7	3.00	94	.243	.257	3	.200	-1	-1	-1	-1	-0.2
1878	Cin-N	30	21	.588	52	52	52	5	0	468	477	1	45	169	10.0	1.79	119	.252	.269	28	.142	-7	27	18	-2	0.8
1879	Cin-N	43	31	.581	**76**	75	**75**	4	0	**680**	676	10	68	232	9.8	1.99	117	.238	.256	40	.136	-15	**38**	26	-7	0.3
1880	Cin-N	18	42	.300	62	62	58	3	0	517^{1}	550	9	56	161	10.5	2.14	116	.255	.273	35	.169	-10	13	20	-7	0.4
1881	Det-N	0	2	.000	2	2	2	0	0	18	24	0	2	5	13.0	5.00	58	.296	.313	0	.000	-1	-4	-4	-1	-0.5
1882	Cin-a	**40**	12	**.769**	54	54	**52**	**8**	0	**480**	411	3	71	122	9.0	1.54	172	.216	.244	55	.266	6	**61**	**59**	13	**7.5**
1883	Cin-a	**43**	22	.662	65	64	64	**6**	0	577	473	16	104	141	9.0	**2.09**	155	.209	.244	54	.225	3	**78**	**74**	-3	6.5
1884	Cin-a	34	18	.654	52	52	52	**7**	0	456	479	16	74	118	11.6	3.32	101	.255	.296	35	.190	-2	-3	1	-6	-0.7
1885	Cin-a	18	15	.545	34	34	33	2	0	293^{1}	295	9	64	80	11.8	3.53	92	.255	.309	20	.169	-3	-9	-9	-3	-1.4
1886	Cin-a	1	2	.333	3	3	3	0	0	26	28	1	10	6	15.2	4.15	85	.280	.379	1	.111	-1	-2	-2	-0	-0.2
Total	10	229	166	.580	403	401	394	36	0	3542^{2}	3440	65	496	1041	10.2	2.28	120	.239	.268	271	.183	-31	198	179	-17	12.5

● JOHN WHITEHEAD Whitehead, John Henderson "Silent John" b: 4/27/09, Coleman, Tex. d: 10/20/64, Bonham, Tex. BR/TR, 6'2", 195 lbs. Deb: 4/19/35

YEAR	TM/L	W	L	PCT	G	GS	CG	SH	SV	IP	H	HR	BB	SO	RAT	ERA	ERA+	OAV	OOB	BH	AVG	PB	PR	/A	PD	TPI
1935	Chi-A	13	13	.500	28	27	18	1	0	222^{1}	209	17	101	72	12.6	3.72	124	.250	.332	12	.146	-5	18	22	3	1.9
1936	Chi-A	13	13	.500	34	32	15	1	1	230^{2}	254	9	98	70	13.9	4.64	112	.276	.349	21	.241	1	10	14	3	1.7
1937	Chi-A	11	8	.579	26	24	8	4	0	165^{2}	191	14	56	45	13.7	4.07	113	.294	.354	13	.224	1	10	10	-1	0.9
1938	Chi-A	10	11	.476	32	24	10	2	2	183^{1}	218	12	80	38	14.8	4.76	103	.299	.370	6	.100	-4	1	3	-1	-0.2
1939	Chi-A	0	3	.000	7	4	0	0	0	32	60	4	5	9	18.3	8.16	58	.408	.428	0	.000	-1	-13	-12	0	-1.2
	StL-A	1	3	.250	26	4	0	0	1	66	88	10	17	9	14.6	5.86	83	.321	.365	1	.059	-2	-9	-7	1	-0.7
	Yr	1	6	.143	33	8	0	0	1	98	148	14	22	18	15.8	6.61	73	.352	.387	1	.038	-3	-22	-20	1	-1.9
1940	StL-A	1	3	.250	15	4	1	1	0	40	46	3	14	11	13.5	5.40	85	.286	.343	2	.167	-1	-5	-4	-1	-0.4
1942	StL-A	0	0	—	4	0	0	0	0	4	8	0	1	0	22.5	6.75	55	.421	.476	0	—	0	-1	-1	-0	-0.1
Total	7	49	54	.476	172	119	52	9	4	944	1074	69	372	254	14.0	4.60	105	.287	.355	55	.169	-11	11	24	5	1.9

● MILT WHITEHEAD Whitehead, Milton P. b: 1862, Canada d: 8/15/01, Highland, Cal. Deb: 4/20/1884 ♦

YEAR	TM/L	W	L	PCT	G	GS	CG	SH	SV	IP	H	HR	BB	SO	RAT	ERA	ERA+	OAV	OOB	BH	AVG	PB	PR	/A	PD	TPI
1884	StL-U	0	1	.000	1	1	1	0	0	8	14	0	2	2	18.0	9.00	33	.360	.391	83	.211	-0	-5	-5	0	-0.4

● EARL WHITEHILL Whitehill, Earl Oliver b: 2/7/1900, Cedar Rapids, Iowa d: 10/22/54, Omaha, Neb. BL/TL, 5'9.5", 174 lbs. Deb: 9/15/23 C

YEAR	TM/L	W	L	PCT	G	GS	CG	SH	SV	IP	H	HR	BB	SO	RAT	ERA	ERA+	OAV	OOB	BH	AVG	PB	PR	/A	PD	TPI
1923	Det-A	2	0	1.000	8	3	1	0	0	33	22	2	15	19	10.9	2.73	142	.188	.296	4	.364	1	5	4	-0	0.5
1924	Det-A	17	9	.654	35	32	16	2	0	233	260	8	79	65	13.6	3.86	106	.288	.353	19	.213	1	10	6	-0	0.6
1925	Det-A	11	11	.500	35	33	15	1	2	239^{1}	267	13	88	83	13.7	4.66	92	.293	.361	19	.218	0	-7	-9	-1	-1.0
1926	Det-A	16	13	.552	36	34	13	0	0	252^{1}	271	7	79	109	12.8	3.99	102	.277	.336	23	.253	4	1	2	-1	0.5
1927	Det-A	16	14	.533	41	31	17	3	3	236	238	4	105	95	13.4	3.36	125	.267	.350	16	.205	-0	21	22	-3	1.9

YEAR	TM/L	W	L	PCT	G	GS	CG	SH	SV	IP	H	HR	BB	SO	RAT	ERA	ERA+	OAV	OOB	BH	AVG	PB	PR	/A	PD	TPI
1928	Det-A	11	16	.407	31	30	12	1	0	196^1	214	8	78	93	13.4	4.31	95	.277	.344	13	.194	-1	-6	-4	1	-0.5
1929	Det-A	14	15	.483	38	28	18	1	1	245^1	267	16	96	103	13.4	4.62	93	.280	.348	23	.256	5	-10	-9	-0	-0.4
1930	Det-A	17	13	.567	34	31	16	0	1	220^2	248	8	80	109	13.7	4.24	113	.285	.351	16	.193	-4	10	14	-2	0.7
1931	Det-A	13	16	.448	34	34	22	0	0	271^1	287	22	118	81	13.6	4.08	112	.274	.351	15	.155	-5	9	15	2	1.2
1932	Det-A	16	12	.571	33	31	17	3	0	244	255	17	93	81	13.0	4.54	104	.269	.337	22	.244	2	-2	5	-2	0.4
1933	*Was-A	22	8	.733	39	37	19	2	1	270	271	9	100	96	12.5	3.33	125	.262	.329	24	.222	2	28	25	-2	2.5
1934	Was-A	14	11	.560	32	31	15	0	0	235	269	10	94	96	14.0	4.52	96	.290	.357	17	.200	4	-1	-5	-0	-0.2
1935	Was-A	14	13	.519	34	34	19	1	0	279^1	318	16	104	102	13.8	4.29	101	.289	.354	19	.183	-1	5	1	1	0.1
1936	Was-A	14	11	.560	28	28	14	0	0	212^1	252	17	89	63	14.5	4.87	98	.294	.362	13	.169	-0	4	-2	-1	-0.3
1937	Cle-A	8	8	.500	33	22	6	1	2	147	189	9	80	53	16.8	6.49	71	.322	.409	11	.224	1	-31	-31	1	-2.5
1938	Cle-A	9	8	.529	26	23	4	0	0	160^1	187	18	83	60	15.7	5.56	83	.289	.378	7	.125	-2	-14	-16	-2	-1.7
1939	Chi-N	4	7	.364	24	11	2	1	1	89^1	102	8	50	42	15.8	5.14	77	.292	.389	3	.103	-2	-12	-12	-1	-1.4
Total	17	218	185	.541	541	473	226	16	11	3564^2	3917	192	1431	1350	13.8	4.36	100	.282	.353	264	.204	4	10	6	-9	0.4

● CHARLIE WHITEHOUSE Whitehouse, Charles Evis "Lefty" b: 1/25/1894, Charleston, Ill. d: 7/19/60, Indianapolis, Ind BB/TL, 6', 152 lbs. Deb: 8/29/14

1914	Ind-F	2	0	1.000	8	2	2	0	0	26	34	0	5	10	13.8	4.85	72	.324	.360	0	.000	-1	-5	-4	-0	-0.5
1915	New-F	2	2	.500	11	3	1	0	0	39^2	46	0	17	18	15.4	4.31	66	.299	.386	0	.000	-1	-6	-6	-1	-0.8
1919	Was-A	0	1	.000	6	1	0	0	0	12	13	1	6	5	14.3	4.50	71	.283	.365	0	.000	-0	-2	-2	-0	-0.2
Total	3	4	3	.571	25	6	3	0	0	77^2	93	1	28	33	14.7	4.52	69	.305	.375	0	.000	-2	-12	-12	-1	-1.5

● GIL WHITEHOUSE Whitehouse, Gilbert Arthur b: 10/15/1893, Somerville, Mass. d: 2/14/26, Brewer, Me. BB/TR, 5'10", 170 lbs. Deb: 6/20/12 ♦

1915	New-F	0	0	—	1	0	0	0	0	1	0	0	1	0	9.0	0.00	—	.000	.250	27	.225	0	0	0	-0	0.0

● LEN WHITEHOUSE Whitehouse, Leonard Joseph b: 9/10/57, Burlington, Vt. BL/TL, 5'11", 175 lbs. Deb: 9/01/81

1981	Tex-A	0	1	.000	2	1	0	0	0	3^1	8	1	2	2	27.0	16.20	21	.500	.556	0	—	0	-5	-5	-0	-0.3
1983	Min-A	7	1	.875	60	0	0	0	2	73^2	70	6	44	44	14.2	4.15	102	.261	.369	0	—	0	-1	1	-1	-0.3
1984	Min-A	2	2	.500	30	0	0	0	1	31^1	29	3	17	18	13.8	3.16	133	.254	.361	0	—	0	3	4	-0	0.1
1985	Min-A	0	0	—	5	0	0	0	1	7^1	12	4	2	4	17.2	11.05	40	.353	.389	0	—	0	-6	-5	-0	-0.9
Total	4	9	4	.692	97	1	0	0	4	115^2	119	14	65	68	14.6	4.67	90	.275	.375	0	—	0	-8	-6	-1	-1.4

● WALLY WHITEHURST Whitehurst, Walter Richard b: 4/11/64, Shreveport, La. BR/TR, 6'3", 180 lbs. Deb: 7/17/89

1989	NY-N	0	1	.000	9	1	0	0	0	14	17	2	5	9	14.1	4.50	73	.293	.349	0	.000	0	-2	-2	-0	-0.2
1990	NY-N	1	0	1.000	38	0	0	0	2	65^2	63	5	9	46	9.9	3.29	114	.251	.277	2	.250	0	4	3	0	0.4
1991	NY-N	7	12	.368	36	20	0	0	1	133^1	142	12	25	87	11.5	4.18	87	.274	.313	6	.182	1	-7	-8	1	-0.6
1992	NY-N	3	9	.250	44	11	0	0	0	97	99	4	33	70	12.6	3.62	97	.264	.330	4	.182	1	-1	-1	1	-0.1
Total	4	11	22	.333	127	32	0	0	3	310	321	23	72	212	11.6	3.83	94	.267	.313	12	.188	2	-7	-8	2	-0.5

● MATT WHITESIDE Whiteside, Matthew Christopher b: 8/8/67, Sikeston, Mo. BR/TR, 6', 185 lbs. Deb: 8/05/92

1992	Tex-A	1	1	.500	20	0	0	0	4	28	26	1	11	13	11.9	1.93	198	.245	.316	0	—	0	6	6	-0	0.8

● JESSE WHITING Whiting, Jesse W. b: 5/30/1879, Philadelphia, Pa. d: 10/28/37, Philadelphia, Pa. Deb: 9/27/02

1902	Phi-N	0	1	.000	1	1	1	0	0	9	13	0	6	0	19.0	5.00	56	.337	.426	1	.333	0	-2	-2	0	-0.2
1906	Bro-N	1	1	.500	3	2	2	1	0	24^2	26	0	6	7	12.0	2.92	86	.286	.337	3	.300	1	-1	-1	1	0.0
1907	Bro-N	0	0	—	1	0	0	0	0	3	3	0	3	2	18.0	12.00	20	.273	.429	0	.000	-0	-3	-3	0	-0.3
Total	3	1	2	.333	5	3	3	1	0	36^2	42	0	15	9	14.2	4.17	62	.299	.370	4	.267	0	-6	-6	1	-0.5

● ART WHITNEY Whitney, Arthur Wilson b: 1/16/1858, Brockton, Mass. d: 8/15/43, Lowell, Mass. BR/TR, 5'8", 155 lbs. Deb: 5/01/1880 F♦

1882	Det-N	0	1	.000	3	2	1	0	0	18	31	1	8	11	19.5	6.00	49	.373	.429	21	.183	-1	-6	-6	-1	-0.6
1886	Pit-a	0	0	—	1	0	0	0	0	6	7	0	3	2	15.0	3.00	113	.304	.385	122	.239	0	0	0	-0	0.0
1889	*NY-N	0	1	.000	1	0	0	0	0	6	7	0	3	3	15.0	3.00	131	.283	.360	103	.218	0	1	1	-0	0.0
Total	3	0	2	.000	5	2	1	0	0	30	45	1	14	16	17.7	4.80	67	.344	.408	820	.223	-1	-5	-5	-1	-0.6

● JIM WHITNEY Whitney, James Evans "Grasshopper Jim" b: 11/10/1857, Conklin, N.Y. d: 5/21/1891, Binghamton, N.Y. BL/TR, 6'2", 172 lbs. Deb: 5/02/1881 ♦

1881	Bos-N	**31**	33	.484	**66**	63	**57**	6	0	**552^1**	548	6	90	162	10.4	2.48	107	.248	.277	72	.255	11	18	11	-4	1.8
1882	Bos-N	24	21	.533	49	48	46	3	0	420	404	3	41	180	9.5	2.64	109	.237	.255	81	.323	23	12	11	1	3.2
1883	Bos-N	37	21	.638	62	56	54	1	**2**	514	492	7	35	**345**	9.2	2.24	138	.238	.251	115	.281	20	51	49	0	6.0
1884	Bos-N	23	14	.622	38	37	35	6	0	336	272	12	27	270	8.0	2.09	138	.207	.223	70	.259	9	33	30	4	4.0
1885	Bos-N	18	32	.360	51	50	50	2	0	441^1	503	14	37	200	11.0	2.98	90	.272	.286	68	.234	7	-8	-14	6	-0.2
1886	KC-N	12	32	.273	46	44	42	3	0	393	465	9	55	167	11.9	4.49	84	.284	.308	59	.239	7	-51	-31	6	-1.6
1887	Was-N	24	21	.533	47	47	46	3	0	404^2	430	16	42	146	10.9	3.22	126	.259	.284	53	.264	10	38	38	4	4.6
1888	Was-N	18	21	.462	39	39	37	2	0	325	317	7	54	79	10.5	3.05	92	.245	.280	24	.170	-1	-7	-9	-1	-1.0
1889	Ind-N	2	7	.222	9	8	7	0	0	70	106	4	19	16	16.3	6.81	61	.338	.380	12	.375	5	-22	-21	-1	-1.3
1890	Phi-a	2	2	.500	6	4	3	0	0	40	61	1	11	6	16.4	5.17	74	.340	.381	5	.238	0	-6	-6	-0	-0.5
Total	10	191	204	.484	413	396	377	26	2	3496^1	3598	79	411	1571	10.4	2.97	105	.253	.275	559	.261	89	60	55	15	15.0

● BILL WHITROCK Whitrock, William Franklin b: 3/4/1870, Cincinnati, Ohio d: 7/26/35, Derby, Conn. TR , 5'7.5", 170 lbs. Deb: 5/03/1890

1890	StL-a	5	6	.455	16	11	10	0	1	105	104	2	40	39	12.9	3.51	123	.251	.327	7	.146	-3	4	9	0	0.6
1893	Lou-N	2	5	.286	8	8	5	0	0	46^2	64	3	18	8	16.6	8.10	54	.317	.384	7	.280	1	-18	-19	0	-1.4
1894	Lou-N	0	1	.000	1	1	0	0	0	4	8	0	2	0	22.5	9.00	57	.410	.465	0	.000	-0	-2	-2	-0	-0.2
	Cin-N	2	6	.250	10	8	8	0	0	70^1	110	7	39	9	20.2	6.65	84	.352	.438	13	.217	-2	-10	-9	0	-0.8
	Yr	2	7	.222	11	9	8	0	0	74^1	118	7	41	9	20.3	6.78	82	.355	.440	13	.210	-3	-12	-10	0	-1.0
1896	Phi-N	0	1	.000	2	1	1	0	0	9	10	0	3	1	13.0	3.00	144	.279	.335	0	.000	-1	1	1	-0	0.1
Total	4	9	19	.321	37	29	24	0	1	235	296	12	102	57	16.0	5.44	87	.301	.378	27	.196	-5	-24	-18	0	-1.7

● ED WHITSON Whitson, Eddie Lee b: 5/19/55, Johnson City, Tenn. BR/TR, 6'3", 195 lbs. Deb: 9/04/77

1977	Pit-N	1	0	1.000	5	2	0	0	0	15^2	11	0	9	10	11.5	3.45	116	.204	.317	0	.000	-1	1	1	-0	0.0
1978	Pit-N	5	6	.455	43	0	0	0	4	74^1	66	5	37	64	12.7	3.27	113	.243	.338	2	.182	-0	3	4	-1	0.3
1979	Pit-N	2	3	.400	19	7	0	0	1	57^2	53	6	36	31	14.0	4.37	89	.238	.346	0	.000	-1	-4	-3	-1	-0.5
	SF-N	5	8	.385	18	17	2	0	0	100^1	98	5	39	62	12.6	3.95	89	.254	.329	5	.156	-0	-2	-5	-0	-0.6
	Yr	7	11	.389	37	24	2	0	1	158	151	11	75	93	13.1	4.10	89	.248	.334	5	.111	-2	-6	-8	-1	-1.1
1980	SF-N☆	11	13	.458	34	34	6	2	0	211^2	222	7	56	90	12.0	3.10	114	.271	.321	6	.091	-4	12	10	-2	0.4
1981	SF-N	6	9	.400	22	22	2	1	0	123	130	10	47	65	13.1	4.02	85	.273	.340	3	.091	-1	-7	-8	-2	-1.1
1982	Cle-A	4	2	.667	40	9	1	1	2	107^2	91	6	58	61	12.5	3.26	125	.231	.330	0	—	0	10	10	-2	0.9
1983	SD-N	5	7	.417	31	21	2	0	1	144^1	143	23	50	81	12.1	4.30	81	.256	.318	8	.182	1	-11	-13	-4	-1.6
1984	*SD-N	14	8	.636	31	31	1	0	0	189	181	16	42	103	10.8	3.24	110	.255	.299	3	.049	-5	7	7	1	0.4
1985	NY-A	10	8	.556	30	30	2	2	0	158^2	201	19	43	89	14.0	4.88	82	.309	.354	0	—	0	-13	-15	-2	-1.5
1986	NY-A	5	2	.714	14	4	0	0	0	37	54	5	23	27	18.7	7.54	54	.335	.418	0	—	0	-14	-14	-0	-1.3
	SD-N	1	7	.125	17	12	0	0	0	75^2	85	8	37	46	14.5	5.59	65	.287	.366	3	.167	-0	-16	-16	0	-1.6
1987	SD-N	10	13	.435	36	34	3	1	0	205^2	197	36	64	135	11.6	4.73	84	.251	.310	8	.123	-1	-15	-18	-2	-2.0
1988	SD-N	13	11	.542	34	33	3	1	0	205^1	202	17	45	118	10.9	3.77	90	.259	.301	11	.167	1	-7	-9	-1	-0.9
1989	SD-N	16	11	.593	33	33	5	1	0	227	198	22	48	117	10.0	2.66	132	.235	.281	10	.139	1	21	21	-2	2.2
1990	SD-N	14	9	.609	32	32	6	3	0	228^2	215	13	47	127	10.4	2.60	147	.251	.291	10	.149	1	30	**31**	3	**3.8**
1991	SD-N	4	6	.400	13	12	2	0	0	78^2	93	13	17	40	12.6	5.03	75	.299	.335	3	.125	-1	-12	-11	-1	-1.2
Total	15	126	123	.506	452	333	35	12	8	2240^1	2240	211	698	1266	11.9	3.79	97	.261	.319	72	.125	-10	-17	-28	-14	-4.3

● WALT WHITTAKER Whittaker, Walter Elton "Doc" b: 6/11/1894, Chelsea, Mass. d: 8/9/65, Pembroke, Mass. BL/TR, 5'9.5", 165 lbs. Deb: 7/06/16

YEAR TM/L	W	L	PCT	G	GS	CG	SH	SV	IP	H	HR	BB	SO	RAT	ERA	ERA+	OAV	OOB	BH	AVG	PB	PR	/A	PD	TPI
1916 Phi-A	0	0	—	1	0	0	0	0	2	3	0	2	0	22.5	4.50	63	.375	.500	0	—	0	-0	-0	0	0.0

● KEVIN WICKANDER Wickander, Kevin Dean b: 1/5/65, Fort Dodge, Iowa BL/TL, 6'2", 202 lbs. Deb: 8/10/89

YEAR TM/L	W	L	PCT	G	GS	CG	SH	SV	IP	H	HR	BB	SO	RAT	ERA	ERA+	OAV	OOB	BH	AVG	PB	PR	/A	PD	TPI
1989 Cle-A	0	0	—	2	0	0	0	0	2^{2}	6	0	2	0	27.0	3.38	117	.462	.533	0	—	0	0	0	-0	-0.1
1990 Cle-A	0	1	.000	10	0	0	0	0	12^{1}	14	0	4	10	13.9	3.65	107	.304	.373	0	—	0	0	0	-0	0.0
1992 Cle-A	2	0	1.000	44	0	0	0	1	41	39	1	28	38	15.6	3.07	131	.258	.388	0	—	0	4	4	0	0.4
Total 3	2	1	.667	56	0	0	0	1	56	59	1	34	48	15.8	3.21	124	.281	.394	0	—	0	4	5	-0	0.3

● KEMP WICKER Wicker, Kemp Caswell (b: Kemp Caswell Whicker) b: 8/13/06, Kernersville, N.C. d: 6/11/73, Kernersville, N.C BR/TL, 5'11", 182 lbs. Deb: 8/14/36

YEAR TM/L	W	L	PCT	G	GS	CG	SH	SV	IP	H	HR	BB	SO	RAT	ERA	ERA+	OAV	OOB	BH	AVG	PB	PR	/A	PD	TPI
1936 NY-A	1	2	.333	7	0	0	0	0	20	31	2	11	5	18.9	7.65	61	.356	.429	1	.143	-0	-6	-7	0	-0.6
1937 *NY-A	7	3	.700	16	10	6	1	0	88	107	8	26	14	13.6	4.40	101	.296	.343	4	.114	-3	2	0	-2	-0.4
1938 NY-A	1	0	1.000	1	0	0	0	0	1	0	0	1	0	9.0	0.00	—	.000	.250	0	—	0	1	1	-0	0.0
1941 Bro-N	1	2	.333	16	2	0	0	1	32	30	3	14	8	12.4	3.66	100	.252	.331	1	.250	0	-0	0	-0	0.0
Total 4	10	7	.588	40	12	6	1	1	141	168	13	52	27	14.0	4.66	92	.294	.353	6	.130	-2	-3	-5	-2	-1.0

● BOB WICKER Wicker, Robert Kitridge b: 5/24/1878, Bedford, Ind. d: 1/22/55, Evanston, Ill. BR/TR, 6'2", 180 lbs. Deb: 8/11/01

YEAR TM/L	W	L	PCT	G	GS	CG	SH	SV	IP	H	HR	BB	SO	RAT	ERA	ERA+	OAV	OOB	BH	AVG	PB	PR	/A	PD	TPI
1901 StL-N	0	0	—	1	0	0	0	0	3	4	0	1	2	15.0	0.00	—	.317	.368	1	.333	0	1	1	-0	0.1
1902 StL-N	5	12	.294	22	16	14	1	0	152^{1}	159	1	45	78	12.1	3.19	86	.269	.321	18	.234	1	-7	-8	3	-0.4
1903 StL-N	0	0	—	1	0	0	0	0	5	4	0	3	3	12.6	0.00	—	.174	.269	0	.000	-0	2	2	1	0.2
Chi-N	20	9	.690	32	27	24	1	1	247	236	3	74	110	11.4	3.02	104	.253	.311	24	.245	5	7	3	-5	0.3
Yr	20	9	.690	33	27	24	1	1	252	240	3	77	113	11.4	2.96	106	.252	.309	24	.240	4	9	5	-4	0.5
1904 Chi-N	17	9	.654	30	27	23	4	0	229	201	6	58	99	10.3	2.67	100	.232	.282	34	.219	1	2	-0	-5	-0.5
1905 Chi-N	13	6	.684	22	22	17	4	0	178	139	3	47	86	9.5	2.02	147	.221	.276	10	.139	-2	19	19	-3	1.5
1906 Chi-N	3	5	.375	10	8	5	0	0	72^{1}	70	0	19	25	11.1	2.99	88	.257	.306	2	.100	-1	-3	-3	-1	-0.6
Cin-N	6	11	.353	20	17	14	0	0	150	150	3	46	69	11.8	2.70	102	.263	.319	9	.180	2	-1	1	-4	-0.1
Yr	9	16	.360	30	25	19	0	0	222^{1}	220	3	65	94	11.6	2.79	97	.261	.315	11	.157	1	-4	-2	-5	-0.7
Total 6	64	52	.552	138	117	97	10	1	1036^{2}	963	16	293	472	11.0	2.73	105	.247	.301	98	.205	5	20	16	-15	0.5

● DAVE WICKERSHAM Wickersham, David Clifford b: 9/27/35, Erie, Pa. BR/TR, 6'3", 190 lbs. Deb: 9/18/60

YEAR TM/L	W	L	PCT	G	GS	CG	SH	SV	IP	H	HR	BB	SO	RAT	ERA	ERA+	OAV	OOB	BH	AVG	PB	PR	/A	PD	TPI
1960 KC-A	0	0	—	5	0	0	0	2	8^{1}	4	0	1	3	5.4	1.08	369	.148	.179	0	.000	-0	3	3	0	0.3
1961 KC-A	2	1	.667	17	0	0	0	2	21	25	0	5	10	13.7	5.14	80	.309	.364	2	.667	1	-3	-2	0	-0.1
1962 KC-A	11	4	.733	30	9	3	0	1	110	105	13	43	61	12.8	4.17	100	.257	.340	2	.057	-3	-2	-0	1	-0.2
1963 KC-A	12	15	.444	38	34	4	1	1	237^{2}	244	21	79	118	12.6	4.09	94	.268	.333	11	.138	-3	-12	-6	1	-0.9
1964 Det-A	19	12	.613	40	36	11	1	1	254	224	28	81	164	11.2	3.44	106	.232	.299	6	.073	-5	5	6	-0	0.0
1965 Det-A	9	14	.391	34	27	8	3	0	195^{1}	179	12	61	109	11.6	3.78	92	.241	.308	4	.069	-4	-7	-7	1	-1.0
1966 Det-A	8	3	.727	38	14	3	0	1	140^{2}	139	14	54	93	12.9	3.20	109	.261	.338	2	.044	-3	4	4	1	0.2
1967 Det-A	4	5	.444	36	4	0	0	4	85^{1}	72	6	33	44	11.5	2.74	119	.235	.318	0	.000	-2	5	5	1	0.5
1968 Pit-N	1	0	1.000	11	0	0	0	1	20^{2}	21	0	13	9	14.8	3.48	84	.276	.382	1	.333	0	-1	-1	-0	-0.1
1969 KC-A	2	3	.400	34	0	0	0	5	50	58	6	14	27	13.3	3.96	93	.294	.347	0	.000	0	-2	-2	0	-0.1
Total 10	68	57	.544	283	124	29	5	18	1123	1071	100	384	638	12.1	3.66	100	.252	.323	28	.086	-18	-11	-0	4	-1.4

● BOB WICKMAN Wickman, Robert Joe b: 2/6/69, Green Bay, Wis. BR/TR, 6'1", 207 lbs. Deb: 8/24/92

YEAR TM/L	W	L	PCT	G	GS	CG	SH	SV	IP	H	HR	BB	SO	RAT	ERA	ERA+	OAV	OOB	BH	AVG	PB	PR	/A	PD	TPI
1992 NY-A	6	1	.857	8	8	0	0	0	50^{1}	51	2	20	21	13.1	4.11	98	.273	.349	0	—	0	-1	-0	0	-0.2

● AL WIDMAR Widmar, Albert Joseph b: 3/20/25, Cleveland, Ohio BR/TR, 6'3", 185 lbs. Deb: 4/25/47 C

YEAR TM/L	W	L	PCT	G	GS	CG	SH	SV	IP	H	HR	BB	SO	RAT	ERA	ERA+	OAV	OOB	BH	AVG	PB	PR	/A	PD	TPI
1947 Bos-A	0	0	—	2	0	0	0	0	1^{1}	1	1	2	1	20.3	13.50	29	.200	.429	0	—	0	-1	-1	0	-0.1
1948 StL-A	2	6	.250	49	0	0	0	1	82^{2}	88	4	48	34	14.8	4.46	102	.275	.370	3	.300	1	-2	1	2	0.3
1950 StL-A	7	15	.318	36	26	8	1	4	194^{2}	211	16	74	78	13.3	4.76	104	.271	.337	10	.149	-4	-4	4	1	0.1
1951 StL-A	4	9	.308	26	16	4	0	0	107^{2}	157	19	52	28	17.6	6.52	67	.344	.414	5	.167	-1	-29	-25	1	-2.4
1952 Chi-A	0	0	—	1	0	0	0	0	2	4	1	0	2	18.0	4.50	81	.444	.444	0	—	0	-0	-0	-0	0.0
Total 5	13	30	.302	114	42	12	1	5	388^{1}	461	41	176	143	14.9	5.21	90	.294	.367	18	.168	-4	-36	-22	3	-2.1

● WILD BILL WIDNER Widner, William Waterfield b: 6/3/1867, Cincinnati, Ohio d: 12/10/08, Cincinnati, Ohio BR/TR, 6', 180 lbs. Deb: 6/08/1887

YEAR TM/L	W	L	PCT	G	GS	CG	SH	SV	IP	H	HR	BB	SO	RAT	ERA	ERA+	OAV	OOB	BH	AVG	PB	PR	/A	PD	TPI
1887 Cin-a	1	0	1.000	1	1	1	0	0	9	11	2	2	0	14.0	5.00	87	.275	.326	1	.250	-0	-1	-1	0	0.0
1888 Was-N	5	7	.417	13	13	13	0	0	115	111	7	22	33	10.9	2.82	100	.247	.291	12	.200	-1	0	-0	-0	-0.1
1889 Col-a	12	20	.375	41	34	25	2	1	294	368	11	85	63	14.4	5.20	70	.297	.351	28	.211	-1	-44	-52	0	-4.2
1890 Col-a	4	8	.333	13	10	8	1	0	96	103	3	24	14	12.2	3.28	109	.266	.314	8	.195	-1	6	3	2	0.4
1891 Cin-a	0	1	.000	1	1	1	0	0	8	13	0	4	0	21.4	7.88	52	.353	.444	1	.250	-0	-4	-3	-0	-0.3
Total 5	22	36	.379	69	59	48	3	1	522	606	23	137	110	13.3	4.36	79	.281	.333	50	.207	-3	-42	-52	2	-4.2

● TED WIEAND Wieand, Franklin Delano Roosevelt b: 4/4/33, Walnutport, Pa. BR/TR, 6'2", 195 lbs. Deb: 9/27/58

YEAR TM/L	W	L	PCT	G	GS	CG	SH	SV	IP	H	HR	BB	SO	RAT	ERA	ERA+	OAV	OOB	BH	AVG	PB	PR	/A	PD	TPI
1958 Cin-N	0	0	—	1	0	0	0	0	2	4	1	0	2	18.0	9.00	46	.400	.400	0	—	0	-1	-1	-0	-0.1
1960 Cin-N	0	1	.000	5	0	0	0	0	4^{1}	4	2	5	3	18.7	10.38	37	.250	.429	0	—	0	-3	-3	0	-0.3
Total 2	0	1	.000	6	0	0	0	0	6^{1}	8	3	5	5	18.5	9.95	39	.308	.419	0	—	0	-4	-4	0	-0.4

● CHARLIE WIEDEMEYER Wiedemeyer, Charles John "Chick" b: 1/31/14, Chicago, Ill. d: 10/27/79, Lake Geneva, Fla. BL/TL, 6'3", 180 lbs. Deb: 9/09/34

YEAR TM/L	W	L	PCT	G	GS	CG	SH	SV	IP	H	HR	BB	SO	RAT	ERA	ERA+	OAV	OOB	BH	AVG	PB	PR	/A	PD	TPI
1934 Chi-N	0	0	—	4	1	0	0	0	8^{1}	16	0	4	2	22.7	9.72	40	.432	.500	0	.000	-0	-5	-5	0	-0.5

● JACK WIENEKE Wieneke, John b: 3/10/1894, Saltzburg, Pa. d: 3/16/33, Pleasant Ridge, Mich. BR/TL, 6', 182 lbs. Deb: 7/04/21

YEAR TM/L	W	L	PCT	G	GS	CG	SH	SV	IP	H	HR	BB	SO	RAT	ERA	ERA+	OAV	OOB	BH	AVG	PB	PR	/A	PD	TPI
1921 Chi-A	0	1	.000	10	3	0	0	0	25^{1}	39	4	17	10	20.3	8.17	52	.351	.442	1	.111	-1	-11	-11	0	-1.0

● BOB WIESLER Wiesler, Robert George b: 8/13/30, St.Louis, Mo. BB/TL, 6'2", 195 lbs. Deb: 8/03/51

YEAR TM/L	W	L	PCT	G	GS	CG	SH	SV	IP	H	HR	BB	SO	RAT	ERA	ERA+	OAV	OOB	BH	AVG	PB	PR	/A	PD	TPI
1951 NY-A	0	2	.000	4	3	0	0	0	9^{1}	13	0	11	3	23.1	13.50	28	.361	.511	0	.000	-0	-10	-10	0	-0.9
1954 NY-A	3	2	.600	6	5	0	0	0	30^{1}	28	0	30	25	17.2	4.15	83	.259	.420	3	.273	1	-1	-2	-1	-0.2
1955 NY-A	0	2	.000	16	7	0	0	0	53	39	1	49	22	15.1	3.91	96	.212	.380	2	.143	-1	0	-1	1	-0.1
1956 Was-A	3	12	.200	37	21	3	0	0	123	141	11	112	49	18.7	6.44	67	.300	.438	3	.091	-3	-31	-29	1	-2.8
1957 Was-A	1	1	.500	3	2	1	0	0	16^{1}	15	2	11	9	14.9	4.41	88	.250	.375	1	.167	0	-1	-1	0	-0.1
1958 Was-A	0	0	—	4	0	0	0	0	9^{1}	14	2	5	5	19.3	6.75	56	.359	.444	0	.000	-0	-3	-3	1	-0.3
Total 6	7	19	.269	70	38	4	0	0	241^{1}	250	16	218	113	17.7	5.74	70	.279	.423	9	.130	-4	-46	-46	3	-4.4

● WHITEY WIETELMANN Wietelmann, William Frederick b: 3/15/19, Zanesville, Ohio BB/TR, 6', 170 lbs. Deb: 9/06/39 C♦

YEAR TM/L	W	L	PCT	G	GS	CG	SH	SV	IP	H	HR	BB	SO	RAT	ERA	ERA+	OAV	OOB	BH	AVG	PB	PR	/A	PD	TPI
1945 Bos-N	0	0	—	1	0	0	0	0	1	6	0	2	0	72.0	54.00	7	.667	.727	116	.271	0	-6	-6	-0	-0.4
1946 Bos-N	0	0	—	3	0	0	0	0	6^{2}	9	1	4	2	18.9	8.10	42	.310	.412	16	.205	0	-3	-3	-0	-0.4
Total 2	0	0	—	4	0	0	0	0	7^{2}	15	1	6	2	25.8	14.09	25	.395	.489	409	.232	1	-9	-9	-0	-0.8

● JIMMY WIGGS Wiggs, James Alvin "Big Jim" b: 9/1/1876, Trondheim, Norway d: 1/20/63, Xenia, Ohio BB/TR, 6'4", 200 lbs. Deb: 4/23/03

YEAR TM/L	W	L	PCT	G	GS	CG	SH	SV	IP	H	HR	BB	SO	RAT	ERA	ERA+	OAV	OOB	BH	AVG	PB	PR	/A	PD	TPI
1903 Cin-N	0	1	.000	2	1	0	0	0	5	12	0	2	2	27.0	5.40	66	.500	.556	0	.000	-0	-1	-1	-0	-0.1
1905 Det-A	3	3	.500	7	7	4	0	0	41^{1}	30	0	29	37	13.1	3.27	84	.204	.339	2	.133	-0	-3	-2	-0	-0.3
1906 Det-A	0	0	—	4	1	0	0	0	10^{1}	11	1	7	7	17.4	5.23	53	.276	.409	1	.333	0	-3	-3	0	-0.2
Total 3	3	4	.429	13	9	4	0	0	56^{2}	53	1	38	46	15.1	3.81	74	.252	.376	3	.158	-0	-7	-6	0	-0.6

● BILL WIGHT Wight, William Robert "Lefty" b: 4/12/22, Rio Vista, Cal. BL/TL, 6'1", 180 lbs. Deb: 4/17/46

YEAR TM/L	W	L	PCT	G	GS	CG	SH	SV	IP	H	HR	BB	SO	RAT	ERA	ERA+	OAV	OOB	BH	AVG	PB	PR	/A	PD	TPI
1946 NY-A	2	2	.500	14	4	1	0	0	40^{1}	44	1	30	11	16.7	4.46	77	.289	.410	0	.000	-1	-4	-5	0	-0.6
1947 NY-A	1	0	1.000	1	1	1	0	0	9	8	0	2	3	10.0	1.00	353	.242	.286	0	.000	0	3	3	0	0.4

YEAR	TM/L	W	L	PCT	G	GS	CG	SH	SV	IP	H	HR	BB	SO	RAT	ERA	ERA+	OAV	OOB	BH	AVG	PB	PR	/A	PD	TPI
1948	Chi-A	9	20	.310	34	32	7	1	1	223^1	238	9	135	68	15.1	4.80	89	.278	.377	6	.082	-7	-13	-13	1	-1.8
1949	Chi-A	15	13	.536	35	33	14	3	1	245	254	9	96	78	12.9	3.31	126	.275	.343	14	.165	-1	24	24	0	2.2
1950	Chi-A	10	16	.385	30	28	13	3	0	206	213	10	79	62	12.8	3.58	125	.270	.336	0	.000	-8	23	21	2	1.3
1951	Bos-A	7	7	.500	34	17	4	2	0	118^1	128	5	63	38	14.5	5.10	88	.282	.369	3	.073	-5	-13	-8	1	-1.2
1952	Bos-A	2	1	.667	10	2	0	0	0	24^1	14	3	14	5	10.7	2.96	133	.169	.296	1	.143	-0	2	3	0	0.3
	Det-A	5	9	.357	23	19	8	3	0	143^2	167	7	55	65	13.9	3.88	98	.291	.354	11	.220	1	-3	-1	2	0.2
	Yr	7	10	.412	33	21	8	3	0	168	181	10	69	70	13.4	3.75	102	.275	.344	12	.211	1	-1	1	2	0.5
1953	Det-A	0	3	.000	13	4	0	0	0	25^1	35	4	14	10	17.4	8.88	46	.333	.412	3	.429	1	-14	-14	-1	-1.3
	Cle-A	2	1	.667	20	0	0	0	1	26^2	29	1	16	14	15.2	3.71	101	.282	.378	0	.000	-1	-1	0	0	0.0
	Yr	2	4	.333	33	4	0	0	1	52	64	5	30	24	16.3	6.23	63	.308	.395	3	.250	0	-13	-13	-0	-1.3
1955	Cle-A	0	0	—	17	0	0	0	1	24	24	0	9	9	12.4	2.63	152	.261	.327	0	—	0	4	4	2	0.6
	Bal-A	6	8	.429	19	14	8	2	2	117^1	111	6	39	54	11.6	2.45	155	.252	.315	3	.083	-2	20	18	2	1.9
	Yr	6	8	.429	36	14	8	2	3	141^1	135	6	48	63	11.7	2.48	155	.254	.317	3	.083	-2	23	21	4	2.5
1956	Bal-A	9	12	.429	35	26	7	1	0	174^2	198	7	72	84	14.2	4.02	98	.289	.362	12	.200	-1	3	-2	-1	-0.3
1957	Bal-A	6	6	.500	27	17	2	0	0	121	122	4	54	50	13.4	3.64	99	.271	.354	1	.029	-3	2	-1	-1	-0.5
1958	Cin-N	0	1	.000	7	0	0	0	0	6^2	7	1	4	5	14.9	4.05	102	.292	.393	0	—	0	-0	0	0	0.0
	StL-N	3	0	1.000	28	1	1	0	2	57^1	64	7	32	18	15.1	5.02	82	.290	.379	1	.100	-0	-7	-6	1	-0.6
	Yr	3	1	.750	35	1	1	0	2	64	71	8	36	23	15.0	4.92	84	.290	.381	1	.100	-0	-7	-6	1	-0.6
Total	12	77	99	.438	347	198	66	15	8	1563	1656	74	714	574	13.7	3.95	103	.277	.355	55	.115	-28	27	22	9	0.6

● FRED WIGINGTON Wigington, Fred Thomas b: 12/16/1897, Rogers, Neb. d: 5/8/80, Mesa, Ariz. BR/TR, 5'10", 168 lbs. Deb: 4/20/23

YEAR	TM/L	W	L	PCT	G	GS	CG	SH	SV	IP	H	HR	BB	SO	RAT	ERA	ERA+	OAV	OOB	BH	AVG	PB	PR	/A	PD	TPI
1923	StL-N	0	0	—	4	0	0	0	0	8^1	11	0	5	2	17.3	3.24	121	.367	.457	0	.000	-0	1	1	0	0.1

● SANDY WIHTOL Wihtol, Alexander Ames b: 6/1/55, Palo Alto, Cal. BR/TR, 6'1", 195 lbs. Deb: 9/07/79

YEAR	TM/L	W	L	PCT	G	GS	CG	SH	SV	IP	H	HR	BB	SO	RAT	ERA	ERA+	OAV	OOB	BH	AVG	PB	PR	/A	PD	TPI
1979	Cle-A	0	0	—	5	0	0	0	0	10^2	10	0	3	6	11.0	3.38	126	.238	.289	0	—	0	1	1	0	0.1
1980	Cle-A	1	0	1.000	17	0	0	0	1	35^1	35	2	14	20	13.0	3.57	114	.257	.336	0	—	0	2	2	-1	0.1
1982	Cle-A	0	0	—	6	0	0	0	0	11^2	9	1	7	8	13.1	4.63	88	.220	.347	0	—	0	-1	-1	-0	-0.1
Total	3	1	0	1.000	28	0	0	0	1	57^2	54	3	24	34	12.6	3.75	110	.247	.329	0	—	0	2	2	-1	0.1

● MILT WILCOX Wilcox, Milton Edward b: 4/20/50, Honolulu, Hawaii BR/TR, 6'2", 185 lbs. Deb: 9/05/70

YEAR	TM/L	W	L	PCT	G	GS	CG	SH	SV	IP	H	HR	BB	SO	RAT	ERA	ERA+	OAV	OOB	BH	AVG	PB	PR	/A	PD	TPI
1970	*Cin-N	3	1	.750	5	2	1	1	1	22^1	19	2	7	13	10.9	2.42	167	.229	.297	1	.200	0	4	4	0	0.5
1971	Cin-N	2	2	.500	18	3	0	0	1	43^1	43	2	17	21	12.9	3.32	101	.269	.346	0	.000	-1	1	0	0	-0.1
1972	Cle-A	7	14	.333	32	27	4	2	0	156	145	18	72	90	12.8	3.40	94	.251	.339	9	.200	1	-6	-3	-3	-0.5
1973	Cle-A	8	10	.444	26	19	4	0	0	134^1	143	14	68	82	14.7	5.83	67	.275	.367	0	—	0	-30	-29	1	-2.7
1974	Cle-A	2	2	.500	41	2	1	0	4	71^1	74	10	24	33	13.0	4.67	77	.271	.341	0	—	0	-8	-8	1	-0.8
1975	Chi-N	0	1	.000	25	0	0	0	0	38^1	50	4	17	21	16.0	5.63	68	.323	.393	1	.333	0	-9	-8	0	-0.7
1977	Det-A	6	2	.750	20	13	1	0	0	106^1	96	13	37	82	11.3	3.64	118	.241	.307	0	—	0	5	8	-0	0.7
1978	Det-A	13	12	.520	29	27	16	2	0	215^1	208	22	68	132	11.9	3.76	103	.255	.318	0	—	0	0	2	1	0.3
1979	Det-A	12	10	.545	33	29	7	0	0	196^1	201	18	73	109	13.1	4.35	99	.267	.341	0	—	0	-3	-1	3	0.2
1980	Det-A	13	11	.542	32	31	13	1	0	198^2	201	24	68	97	12.5	4.48	92	.262	.327	0	—	0	-10	-8	1	-0.7
1981	Det-A	12	9	.571	24	24	8	1	0	166^1	152	10	52	79	11.4	3.03	124	.247	.312	0	—	0	12	14	1	1.5
1982	Det-A	12	10	.545	29	29	9	1	0	193^2	187	18	85	112	13.0	3.62	112	.257	.340	0	—	0	10	9	3	1.2
1983	Det-A	11	10	.524	26	26	9	2	0	186	164	19	74	101	11.7	3.97	98	.237	.314	0	—	0	2	-1	3	0.3
1984	*Det-A	17	8	.680	33	33	0	0	0	193^2	183	13	66	119	11.9	4.00	98	.252	.321	0	—	0	-0	-2	1	0.0
1985	Det-A	1	3	.250	8	8	0	0	0	39	51	6	14	20	15.0	4.85	84	.315	.369	0	—	0	-3	-3	-1	-0.2
1986	Sea-A	0	8	.000	13	10	0	0	0	55^2	74	11	28	26	16.7	5.50	77	.327	.404	0	—	0	-8	-8	0	-0.7
Total	16	119	113	.513	394	283	73	10	6	2016^2	1991	204	770	1137	12.7	4.07	96	.260	.334	11	.177	0	-44	-33	14	-1.7

● RANDY WILES Wiles, Randall E b: 9/10/51, Fort Belvoir, Va. BL/TL, 6'1", 185 lbs. Deb: 8/07/77

YEAR	TM/L	W	L	PCT	G	GS	CG	SH	SV	IP	H	HR	BB	SO	RAT	ERA	ERA+	OAV	OOB	BH	AVG	PB	PR	/A	PD	TPI
1977	Chi-A	1	1	.500	5	0	0	0	0	2^2	5	1	3	0	27.0	10.13	40	.417	.533	0	—	0	-2	-2	0	-0.2

● MARK WILEY Wiley, Mark Eugene b: 2/28/48, National City, Cal. BR/TR, 6'1", 200 lbs. Deb: 6/17/75 C

YEAR	TM/L	W	L	PCT	G	GS	CG	SH	SV	IP	H	HR	BB	SO	RAT	ERA	ERA+	OAV	OOB	BH	AVG	PB	PR	/A	PD	TPI
1975	Min-A	1	3	.250	15	3	1	0	2	38^2	50	4	13	15	14.9	6.05	64	.325	.381	0	—	0	-10	-9	-1	-1.0
1978	SD-N	1	0	1.000	4	1	0	0	0	7^2	11	1	1	1	14.1	5.87	57	.324	.343	0	.000	-0	-2	-2	-0	-0.3
	Tor-A	0	0	—	2	0	0	0	0	2^2	3	0	1	2	13.5	6.75	58	.273	.333	0	—	0	-1	-1	-0	-0.1
Total	2	2	3	.400	21	4	1	0	2	49	64	5	15	18	14.7	6.06	62	.322	.372	0	.000	-0	-13	-12	-1	-1.4

● HARRY WILHELM Wilhelm, Harry Lester b: 4/7/1874, Uniontown, Pa. d: 2/20/44, Republic, Pa. BR/TR, 5'7", 155 lbs. Deb: 8/12/1899

YEAR	TM/L	W	L	PCT	G	GS	CG	SH	SV	IP	H	HR	BB	SO	RAT	ERA	ERA+	OAV	OOB	BH	AVG	PB	PR	/A	PD	TPI
1899	Lou-N	1	1	.500	5	3	2	0	0	25	36	1	3	6	14.4	6.12	63	.336	.360	3	.250	2	-6	-6	0	-0.4

● KAISER WILHELM Wilhelm, Irvin Key b: 1/26/1874, Wooster, Ohio d: 5/21/36, Rochester, N.Y. BR/TR, 6', 162 lbs. Deb: 4/18/03 MUC

YEAR	TM/L	W	L	PCT	G	GS	CG	SH	SV	IP	H	HR	BB	SO	RAT	ERA	ERA+	OAV	OOB	BH	AVG	PB	PR	/A	PD	TPI
1903	Pit-N	5	3	.625	12	9	7	1	0	86	88	0	25	20	12.1	3.24	100	.264	.321	3	.088	-2	0	-0	2	-0.1
1904	Bos-N	14	20	.412	39	36	30	3	0	288	316	8	74	73	12.4	3.69	75	.285	.333	7	.070	-8	-30	-30	1	-3.7
1905	Bos-N	3	23	.115	34	27	23	0	0	242^1	287	7	75	76	13.6	4.53	68	.295	.349	16	.160	-3	-41	-39	2	-3.8
1908	Bro-N	16	22	.421	42	36	33	6	0	332	266	3	83	99	9.6	1.87	125	.217	.271	12	.108	-4	18	18	3	1.8
1909	Bro-N	3	13	.188	22	17	14	1	0	163	176	3	59	45	13.1	3.26	80	.289	.353	13	.228	2	-12	-12	1	-0.9
1910	Bro-N	3	7	.300	15	5	0	0	0	68^1	88	3	18	17	14.1	4.74	64	.314	.358	6	.316	2	-13	-13	1	-1.0
1914	Bal-F	12	17	.414	47	27	11	1	5	243^2	263	10	81	113	12.7	4.03	84	.291	.349	21	.250	2	-22	-18	3	-1.3
1915	Bal-F	0	0	—	1	0	0	0	0	1	0	0	0	0	0.0	0.00	—	.000	.000	0	—	0	0	0	-0	0.0
1921	Phi-N	0	0	—	4	0	0	0	0	8	11	0	3	1	15.8	3.38	125	.393	.452	0	.000	-0	0	1	-0	0.0
Total	9	56	105	.348	216	157	118	12	5	1432^1	1495	34	418	444	12.2	3.44	83	.274	.328	78	.154	-11	-99	-93	11	-9.0

● HOYT WILHELM Wilhelm, James Hoyt b: 7/26/23, Huntersville, N.C. BR/TR, 6', 195 lbs. Deb: 4/19/52 H

YEAR	TM/L	W	L	PCT	G	GS	CG	SH	SV	IP	H	HR	BB	SO	RAT	ERA	ERA+	OAV	OOB	BH	AVG	PB	PR	/A	PD	TPI
1952	NY-N	15	3	**.833**	**71**	0	0	0	11	159^1	127	12	57	108	10.7	**2.43**	**152**	.220	.296	6	.158	0	23	23	1	2.4
1953	NY-N☆	7	8	.467	**68**	0	0	0	15	145	127	13	77	71	12.9	3.04	141	.238	.339	5	.152	1	**20**	**20**	-1	2.0
1954	*NY-N	12	4	.750	57	0	0	0	7	111^1	77	5	52	64	10.8	2.10	192	.198	.300	1	.048	-2	**24**	**24**	1	2.3
1955	NY-N	4	1	.800	59	0	0	0	0	103	104	10	40	71	12.8	3.93	102	.266	.337	3	.158	-1	1	1	3	0.3
1956	NY-N	4	9	.308	64	0	0	0	8	89^1	97	7	43	71	14.3	3.83	99	.280	.362	2	.222	0	-1	-0	2	0.1
1957	StL-N	1	4	.200	40	0	0	0	11	55	52	7	21	29	12.4	4.25	93	.254	.332	0	.000	-1	-2	-2	-0	-0.3
	Cle-A	1	0	1.000	2	0	0	0	1	3^2	2	1	1	0	9.8	2.45	151	.154	.267	0	—	0	1	1	-0	0.0
1958	Cle-A	2	7	.222	30	6	1	0	5	90^1	70	4	35	57	10.6	2.49	146	.215	.294	2	.095	-1	13	12	1	1.2
	Bal-A	1	3	.250	9	4	3	1	0	40^2	25	2	10	35	8.0	1.99	180	.179	.238	1	.091	-1	8	7	-0	0.7
	Yr	3	10	.231	39	10	4	1	5	131	95	6	45	92	9.7	2.34	155	.203	.274	3	.094	-2	21	19	1	1.9
1959	Bal-A★	15	11	.577	32	27	13	3	0	226	178	13	77	139	10.6	**2.19**	**173**	.224	.301	4	.053	-6	**42**	**40**	-1	3.6
1960	Bal-A	11	8	.579	41	11	3	1	7	147	125	13	39	107	10.1	3.31	115	.228	.280	3	.071	-3	9	8	1	0.6
1961	Bal-A★	9	7	.563	51	1	0	0	18	109^2	89	5	41	87	11.0	2.30	170	.219	.296	1	.050	-1	21	20	1	2.0
1962	Bal-A†	7	10	.412	52	0	0	0	15	93	64	5	34	90	9.8	1.94	194	.197	.279	2	.125	-0	21	19	0	1.9
1963	Chi-A	5	8	.385	55	3	0	0	21	136^1	106	8	30	111	9.2	2.64	133	.215	.265	2	.069	-1	15	13	1	1.3
1964	Chi-A	12	9	.571	73	0	0	0	27	131^1	94	7	30	95	8.6	1.99	174	.202	.254	3	.143	-0	24	21	-1	2.2
1965	Chi-A	7	7	.500	66	0	0	0	20	144	88	11	32	106	7.6	1.81	176	.177	.229	0	.000	-2	**26**	**22**	-1	2.2
1966	Chi-A	5	2	.714	46	0	0	0	6	81^1	50	6	17	61	7.5	1.66	191	.178	.227	1	.125	0	16	14	-1	1.4
1967	Chi-A	8	3	.727	49	0	0	0	12	89	58	2	34	76	9.7	1.31	236	.183	.270	1	.077	-1	**19**	**18**	-1	1.8
1968	Chi-A	4	4	.500	72	0	0	0	12	93^2	69	4	24	72	9.1	1.73	175	.205	.262	0	.000	-0	13	13	-1	1.4
1969	Cal-A	5	7	.417	44	0	0	0	10	65^2	45	4	18	53	9.0	2.47	141	.194	.261	0	.000	-1	8	7	-0	0.7
	Atl-N	2	0	1.000	8	0	0	0	4	12^1	5	0	4	14	7.3	0.73	494	.119	.213	0	.000	-0	4	4	0	0.4

YEAR	TM/L	W	L	PCT	G	GS	CG	SH	SV	IP	H	HR	BB	SO	RAT	ERA	ERA+	OAV	OOB	BH	AVG	PB	PR	/A	PD	TPI
1970	Atl-N☆	6	4	.600	50	0	0	0	13	78^1	69	7	39	67	12.5	3.10	138	.234	.325	1	.091	-0	8	10	0	1.1
	Chi-N	0	1	.000	3	0	0	0	0	3^2	4	1	3	1	17.2	9.82	46	.286	.412	0	—	0	-2	-2	0	-0.2
	Yr	6	5	.545	53	0	0	0	13	82	73	8	42	68	12.6	3.40	126	.234	.325	1	.091	-0	6	8	1	0.9
1971	Atl-N	0	0	—	3	0	0	0	0	2^1	6	2	1	1	27.0	15.43	24	.500	.538	0	—	0	-3	-3	0	-0.3
	LA-N	0	1	.000	9	0	0	0	3	17^2	6	1	4	15	5.1	1.02	317	.111	.172	0	.000	-0	5	4	-0	0.4
	Yr	0	1	.000	12	0	0	0	3	20	12	3	5	16	7.6	2.70	122	.182	.239	0	.000	-0	2	1	0	0.1
1972	LA-N	0	1	.000	16	0	0	0	1	25^1	20	0	15	9	12.4	4.62	72	.217	.327	0	.000	-0	-3	-4	0	-0.4
Total	21	143	122	.540	1070	52	20	5	227	2254^1	1757	150	778	1610	10.4	2.52	146	.216	.290	38	.088	-20	310	289	5	28.8

● LEFTY WILKIE Wilkie, Aldon Jay b: 10/30/14, Zealandia, Sask., Canada BL/TL, 5'11.5", 175 lbs. Deb: 4/22/41

YEAR	TM/L	W	L	PCT	G	GS	CG	SH	SV	IP	H	HR	BB	SO	RAT	ERA	ERA+	OAV	OOB	BH	AVG	PB	PR	/A	PD	TPI
1941	Pit-N	2	4	.333	26	6	2	1	2	79	90	1	40	16	14.9	4.56	79	.289	.372	7	.292	1	-8	-8	1	-0.6
1942	Pit-N	6	7	.462	35	6	3	0	1	107^1	112	4	37	18	12.6	4.19	81	.269	.330	10	.263	2	-10	-10	2	-0.6
1946	Pit-N	0	0	—	7	0	0	0	0	7^2	13	0	3	3	18.8	10.57	33	.382	.432	0	—	0	-6	-6	-0	-0.6
Total	3	8	11	.421	68	12	5	1	3	194	215	5	80	37	13.8	4.59	76	.283	.352	17	.274	3	-25	-24	3	-1.8

● DEAN WILKINS Wilkins, Dean Allan b: 8/24/66, Blue Island, Ill. BR/TR, 6'1", 170 lbs. Deb: 8/21/89

YEAR	TM/L	W	L	PCT	G	GS	CG	SH	SV	IP	H	HR	BB	SO	RAT	ERA	ERA+	OAV	OOB	BH	AVG	PB	PR	/A	PD	TPI
1989	Chi-N	1	0	1.000	11	0	0	0	0	15^2	13	2	9	14	12.6	4.60	82	.228	.333	0	.000	-0	-2	-1	0	-0.1
1990	Chi-N	0	0	—	7	0	0	0	1	7^1	11	1	7	3	23.3	9.82	42	.333	.463	0	—	0	-5	-5	-0	-0.5
1991	Hou-N	2	1	.667	7	0	0	0	1	8	16	0	10	4	29.3	11.25	31	.410	.531	0	.000	-0	-7	-7	-0	-0.7
Total	3	3	1	.750	25	0	0	0	2	31	40	3	26	21	19.5	7.55	50	.310	.429	0	.000	-0	-14	-13	-0	-1.3

● ERIC WILKINS Wilkins, Eric Lamoine b: 12/9/56, St.Louis, Mo. BR/TR, 6'1", 190 lbs. Deb: 4/11/79

YEAR	TM/L	W	L	PCT	G	GS	CG	SH	SV	IP	H	HR	BB	SO	RAT	ERA	ERA+	OAV	OOB	BH	AVG	PB	PR	/A	PD	TPI
1979	Cle-A	2	4	.333	16	14	0	0	0	69^2	77	4	38	52	15.4	4.39	97	.289	.386	0	—	0	-1	-1	0	-0.1

● ROY WILKINSON Wilkinson, Roy Hamilton b: 5/8/1893, Canandaigua, N.Y. d: 7/2/56, Louisville, Ky. BR/TR, 6'1", 170 lbs. Deb: 4/29/18

YEAR	TM/L	W	L	PCT	G	GS	CG	SH	SV	IP	H	HR	BB	SO	RAT	ERA	ERA+	OAV	OOB	BH	AVG	PB	PR	/A	PD	TPI
1918	Cle-A	0	0	—	1	0	0	0	0	1	0	0	0	0	0.0	0.00	—	.000	.000	0	—	0	0	0	-0	0.0
1919	*Chi-A	1	1	.500	4	1	1	1	0	22	21	0	10	5	12.7	2.05	156	.266	.348	3	.375	2	3	3	1	0.6
1920	Chi-A	7	9	.438	34	11	8	0	2	145	162	6	48	30	13.2	4.03	93	.297	.356	7	.146	-3	-4	-4	-3	-0.9
1921	Chi-A	4	20	.167	36	23	11	0	3	198^1	259	4	78	50	15.5	5.13	83	.334	.397	8	.123	-4	-19	-20	5	-1.7
1922	Chi-A	0	1	.000	4	1	0	0	1	14^1	24	1	6	3	19.5	8.79	46	.393	.456	0	.000	-0	-8	-8	-0	-0.7
Total	5	12	31	.279	79	36	20	1	6	380^2	466	11	142	88	14.5	4.66	86	.318	.381	13	.145	-5	-27	-28	4	-2.7

● BILL WILKINSON Wilkinson, William Carl b: 8/10/64, Greybull, Wyoming BR/TL, 5'10", 160 lbs. Deb: 6/13/85 F

YEAR	TM/L	W	L	PCT	G	GS	CG	SH	SV	IP	H	HR	BB	SO	RAT	ERA	ERA+	OAV	OOB	BH	AVG	PB	PR	/A	PD	TPI
1985	Sea-A	0	2	.000	2	2	0	0	0	6	8	2	6	5	21.0	13.50	31	.333	.467	0	—	0	-6	-6	0	-0.5
1987	Sea-A	3	4	.429	56	0	0	0	10	76^1	61	8	21	73	9.7	3.66	129	.223	.278	0	—	0	7	9	-1	0.7
1988	Sea-A	2	2	.500	30	0	0	0	2	31	28	3	15	25	12.5	3.48	119	.233	.319	0	—	0	2	2	-1	0.0
Total	3	5	8	.385	88	2	0	0	12	113^1	97	13	42	103	11.0	4.13	110	.232	.302	0	—	0	2	5	-1	0.2

● TED WILKS Wilks, Theodore "Cork" b: 11/13/15, Fulton, N.Y. d: 8/21/89, Houston, Tex. BR/TR, 5'9.5", 178 lbs. Deb: 4/25/44 C

YEAR	TM/L	W	L	PCT	G	GS	CG	SH	SV	IP	H	HR	BB	SO	RAT	ERA	ERA+	OAV	OOB	BH	AVG	PB	PR	/A	PD	TPI
1944	*StL-N	17	4	**.810**	36	21	16	4	0	207^2	173	12	49	70	**9.7**	2.64	133	.227	**.275**	9	.141	-1	22	20	-4	1.6
1945	StL-N	4	7	.364	18	16	4	1	0	98^1	103	9	29	28	12.2	2.93	128	.270	.324	4	.133	-0	10	9	-2	0.7
1946	*StL-N	8	0	1.000	40	4	0	0	1	95	88	13	38	40	12.1	3.41	101	.248	.324	5	.208	0	0	0	-1	0.0
1947	StL-N	4	0	1.000	37	0	0	0	5	50^1	57	10	11	28	12.5	5.01	83	.279	.323	1	.167	0	-5	-5	-0	-0.5
1948	StL-N	6	6	.500	57	2	1	0	13	130^2	113	5	39	71	10.5	2.62	156	.235	.293	5	.167	0	**19**	**21**	-1	2.1
1949	StL-N	10	3	.769	**59**	0	0	0	**9**	118^1	105	7	38	71	10.9	3.73	112	.240	.301	1	.037	-3	4	6	-2	0.0
1950	StL-N	2	0	1.000	18	0	0	0	0	24^1	27	4	9	15	13.7	6.66	65	.287	.356	0	.000	-1	-7	-6	0	-0.7
1951	StL-N	0	0	—	17	0	0	0	1	18	19	1	5	5	12.0	3.00	132	.279	.329	0	.000	-0	2	2	-1	0.1
	Pit-N	3	5	.375	48	1	1	0	12	82^2	69	6	24	43	10.3	2.83	149	.231	.292	1	.083	-1	10	13	1	1.3
	Yr	3	5	.375	**65**	1	1	0	**13**	100^2	88	7	29	48	10.6	2.86	146	.240	.299	1	.077	-1	12	15	0	1.4
1952	Pit-N	5	5	.500	44	0	0	0	4	72^1	65	9	31	24	12.2	3.61	111	.245	.329	1	.125	-0	1	3	-1	0.2
	Cle-A	0	0	—	7	0	0	0	1	11^2	8	0	7	6	11.6	3.86	87	.186	.300	0	—	0	-0	-1	0	-0.1
1953	Cle-A	0	0	—	4	0	0	0	0	3^2	5	0	3	2	19.6	7.36	51	.278	.381	0	—	0	-1	-1	-0	-0.2
Total	10	59	30	.663	385	44	22	5	46	913	832	76	283	403	11.1	3.26	118	.244	.304	27	.131	-5	55	61	-11	4.5

● ED WILLETT Willett, Robert Edgar b: 3/7/1884, Norfolk, Va. d: 5/10/34, Wellington, Kan. BR/TR, 6', 183 lbs. Deb: 9/05/06

YEAR	TM/L	W	L	PCT	G	GS	CG	SH	SV	IP	H	HR	BB	SO	RAT	ERA	ERA+	OAV	OOB	BH	AVG	PB	PR	/A	PD	TPI
1906	Det-A	0	3	.000	3	3	3	0	0	25	24	0	8	16	12.2	3.96	70	.256	.327	0	.000	-1	-4	-3	1	-0.4
1907	Det-A	1	5	.167	10	6	1	0	0	48^2	47	0	20	27	12.8	3.70	71	.256	.335	1	.077	-1	-6	-6	1	-0.7
1908	Det-A	15	8	.652	30	23	18	2	1	197^1	186	2	60	77	11.9	2.28	106	.261	.331	11	.164	-2	3	3	4	0.6
1909	*Det-A	21	10	.677	41	34	25	3	1	292^2	239	5	76	89	10.1	2.34	108	.221	.281	22	.196	4	5	6	-1	0.9
1910	Det-A	16	11	.593	37	25	18	4	0	224^1	175	2	74	65	10.7	2.37	111	.217	.296	11	.133	-2	4	7	7	1.2
1911	Det-A	13	14	.481	38	27	15	2	1	231^1	261	5	80	86	13.8	3.66	95	.295	.363	22	.268	7	-8	-5	3	0.5
1912	Det-A	17	15	.531	37	31	28	1	0	284^1	281	3	84	89	12.1	3.29	99	.262	.326	19	.165	-2	1	-1	5	0.3
1913	Det-A	13	14	.481	34	30	19	0	0	242	237	0	89	59	12.5	3.09	95	.260	.333	26	.283	7	-4	-5	3	0.6
1914	StL-F	4	16	.200	27	21	14	0	0	175	208	5	56	73	14.1	4.22	80	.295	.355	15	.234	3	-20	-16	5	-0.9
1915	StL-F	2	3	.400	17	2	1	0	2	52^2	61	2	18	19	14.0	4.61	69	.295	.360	3	.200	0	-9	-8	0	-0.8
Total	10	102	99	.507	274	202	142	12	5	1773^1	1719	24	565	600	12.1	3.08	95	.258	.326	130	.199	12	-39	-29	28	1.3

● CARL WILLEY Willey, Carlton Francis b: 6/6/31, Cherryfield, Me. BR/TR, 6', 175 lbs. Deb: 4/30/58

YEAR	TM/L	W	L	PCT	G	GS	CG	SH	SV	IP	H	HR	BB	SO	RAT	ERA	ERA+	OAV	OOB	BH	AVG	PB	PR	/A	PD	TPI
1958	*Mil-N	9	7	.563	23	19	9	**4**	0	140	110	14	53	74	10.6	2.70	130	.215	.291	5	.104	-2	19	13	-2	0.9
1959	Mil-N	5	9	.357	26	15	5	2	0	117	126	12	31	51	12.2	4.15	85	.273	.322	4	.103	-1	-3	-8	-1	-1.0
1960	Mil-N	6	7	.462	28	21	2	1	0	144^2	136	19	65	109	12.9	4.35	79	.248	.335	7	.146	1	-10	-15	-1	-1.5
1961	Mil-N	6	12	.333	35	22	4	0	0	159^2	147	20	65	91	12.1	3.83	98	.247	.323	1	.019	-6	4	-2	3	-0.5
1962	Mil-N	2	5	.286	30	6	0	0	1	73^1	95	9	20	40	14.2	5.40	70	.319	.364	3	.273	1	-12	-13	-0	-1.2
1963	NY-N	9	14	.391	30	28	7	4	0	183	149	24	69	101	10.9	3.10	113	.220	.296	6	.111	-1	4	8	0	0.8
1964	NY-N	0	2	.000	14	3	0	0	0	30	37	5	8	14	13.8	3.60	99	.301	.348	0	.000	-0	-0	-0	-1	-0.2
1965	NY-N	1	2	.333	13	3	1	0	0	28	30	2	15	13	15.1	4.18	84	.270	.367	0	.000	-1	-2	-2	-0	-0.3
Total	8	38	58	.396	199	117	28	11	1	875^2	830	105	326	493	12.1	3.76	95	.250	.320	26	.099	-8	1	-17	-3	-3.0

● NICK WILLHITE Willhite, Jon Nicholas b: 1/27/41, Tulsa, Okla. BL/TL, 6'2", 195 lbs. Deb: 6/16/63

YEAR	TM/L	W	L	PCT	G	GS	CG	SH	SV	IP	H	HR	BB	SO	RAT	ERA	ERA+	OAV	OOB	BH	AVG	PB	PR	/A	PD	TPI
1963	LA-N	2	3	.400	8	8	1	1	0	38	44	5	10	28	12.8	3.79	80	.286	.329	3	.300	1	-2	-3	-1	-0.3
1964	LA-N	2	4	.333	10	7	2	0	0	43^2	43	4	13	24	11.5	3.71	87	.264	.318	0	.000	-0	-1	-2	1	-0.2
1965	Was-A	0	0	—	5	0	0	0	0	6^1	10	2	4	3	19.9	7.11	49	.345	.424	0	—	0	-3	-3	-0	-0.3
	LA-N	2	2	.500	15	6	0	0	1	42	47	7	22	28	15.2	5.36	61	.288	.380	4	.400	3	-8	-10	-0	-0.7
1966	LA-N	0	0	—	6	0	0	0	0	4^1	3	0	5	4	16.6	2.08	159	.214	.421	0	—	0	1	1	0	0.1
1967	Cal-A	0	2	.000	10	7	0	0	0	39^1	39	8	16	22	12.6	4.35	72	.258	.329	0	.000	-1	-5	-5	-0	-0.7
	NY-N	0	1	.000	4	1	0	0	0	8^1	9	1	5	9	15.1	8.64	39	.257	.350	0	.000	-0	-5	-5	0	-0.5
Total	5	6	12	.333	58	29	3	1	1	182	195	27	75	118	13.5	4.55	70	.275	.346	7	.163	2	-23	-27	0	-2.6

● ALBERT WILLIAMS Williams, Albert Hamilton (De Souza) b: 5/6/54, Pearl Lagoon, Nic. BR/TR, 6'4", 190 lbs. Deb: 5/07/80

YEAR	TM/L	W	L	PCT	G	GS	CG	SH	SV	IP	H	HR	BB	SO	RAT	ERA	ERA+	OAV	OOB	BH	AVG	PB	PR	/A	PD	TPI
1980	Min-A	6	2	.750	18	9	3	0	1	77	73	9	30	35	12.0	3.51	124	.253	.323	0	—	0	5	7	-1	0.3
1981	Min-A	6	10	.375	23	22	4	0	0	150	160	11	52	76	12.8	4.08	97	.276	.337	0	—	0	-7	-2	-2	-0.7
1982	Min-A	9	7	.563	26	26	3	0	0	153^2	166	18	55	61	12.9	4.22	101	.276	.337	0	—	0	-2	0	0	0.0
1983	Min-A	11	14	.440	36	29	4	1	1	193^1	196	21	68	68	12.5	4.14	103	.262	.327	0	—	0	-2	2	-2	0.0
1984	Min-A	3	5	.375	17	11	1	0	0	68^2	75	9	22	22	13.6	5.77	73	.284	.355	0	—	0	-14	-12	0	-1.3
Total	5	35	38	.479	120	97	15	1	2	642^2	670	68	227	262	12.7	4.24	99	.270	.334	0	—	0	-20	-4	-4	-1.7

YEAR	TM/L	W	L	PCT	G	GS	CG	SH	SV	IP	H	HR	BB	SO	RAT	ERA	ERA+	OAV	OOB	BH	AVG	PB	PR	/A	PD	TPI
● **AL WILLIAMS**	Williams, Almon Edward b: 5/11/14, Valhermosa Springs, Ala. d: 7/19/49, Groves, Tex. BR/TR, 6'3", 200 lbs. Deb: 4/19/37																									
1937	Phi-A	4	1	.800	16	8	2	0	1	75^{1}	88	0	49	27	16.5	5.38	88	.300	.402	2	.083	-2	-6	-6	0	-0.7
1938	Phi-A	0	7	.000	30	8	1	0	0	93^{1}	128	6	54	25	17.6	6.94	70	.324	.407	1	.040	-3	-22	-22	-0	-2.1
Total	2	4	8	.333	46	16	3	0	1	168^{2}	216	6	103	52	17.1	6.24	77	.314	.405	3	.061	-5	-29	-27	0	-2.8
● **GUS WILLIAMS**	Williams, Augustine H. b: 1870, New York, N.Y. d: 10/14/1890, New York, N.Y. 5'11", 170 lbs. Deb: 4/18/1890																									
1890	Bro-a	0	1	.000	2	2	1	0	0	12	13	0	12	2	18.8	7.50	52	.268	.413	2	.500	1	-5	-5	-1	-0.4
● **BRIAN WILLIAMS**	Williams, Brian O'Neal b: 2/15/69, Lancaster, S.C. BR/TR, 6'3", 205 lbs. Deb: 9/16/91																									
1991	Hou-N	0	1	.000	2	2	0	0	0	12	11	2	4	4	12.0	3.75	94	.250	.327	0	.000	-0	-0	-0	0	-0.1
1992	Hou-N	7	6	.538	16	16	0	0	0	96^{1}	92	10	42	54	12.5	3.92	85	.255	.333	4	.133	-0	-4	-6	0	-0.7
Total	2	7	7	.500	18	18	0	0	0	108^{1}	103	12	46	58	12.5	3.90	86	.254	.332	4	.121	-1	-5	-7	0	-0.8
● **CHARLIE WILLIAMS**	Williams, Charles Prosek b: 10/11/47, Flushing, N.Y. BR/TR, 6'2", 200 lbs. Deb: 4/23/71																									
1971	NY-N	5	6	.455	31	9	1	0	0	90^{1}	92	7	41	53	13.5	4.78	71	.267	.348	2	.087	-1	-13	-14	-1	-1.7
1972	SF-N	0	2	.000	3	2	0	0	0	9^{1}	14	3	3	3	16.4	8.68	40	.333	.378	0	.000	-0	-5	-5	-0	-0.6
1973	SF-N	3	0	1.000	12	2	0	0	0	23	32	2	7	11	15.3	6.65	57	.330	.375	1	.333	0	-8	-7	0	-0.7
1974	SF-N	1	3	.250	39	7	0	0	0	100^{1}	93	6	31	48	11.3	2.78	137	.250	.311	3	.136	-1	9	11	3	1.4
1975	SF-N	5	3	.625	55	2	0	0	3	98	94	2	66	45	15.1	3.49	109	.261	.381	2	.125	0	1	3	2	0.5
1976	SF-N	2	0	1.000	48	2	0	0	1	85	80	4	39	34	12.8	2.96	122	.256	.343	1	.125	-0	5	6	1	0.7
1977	SF-N	6	5	.545	55	8	1	0	0	119^{1}	116	9	60	41	13.5	4.00	98	.262	.354	4	.222	0	-1	-1	-0	-0.1
1978	SF-N	1	3	.250	25	1	0	0	0	48	60	5	28	22	16.7	5.44	63	.314	.405	0	.000	-1	-10	-11	0	-1.2
Total	8	23	22	.511	268	33	2	0	4	573^{1}	581	38	275	257	13.7	3.97	93	.269	.355	13	.134	-2	-22	-17	3	-1.7
● **LEFTY WILLIAMS**	Williams, Claude Preston b: 3/9/1893, Aurora, Mo. d: 11/4/59, Laguna Beach, Cal. BR/TL, 5'9", 160 lbs. Deb: 9/17/13																									
1913	Det-A	1	3	.250	5	4	3	0	1	29	34	0	4	9	12.1	4.97	59	.286	.315	1	.100	-0	-7	-7	-1	-0.8
1914	Det-A	0	1	.000	1	1	0	0	0	1	3	0	2	0	45.0	0.00	—	.429	.556	0	—	0	0	0	-0	0.0
1916	Chi-A	13	7	.650	43	26	10	2	1	224^{1}	220	5	65	138	11.8	2.89	96	.267	.327	10	.135	-0	-1	-3	-4	-0.9
1917	*Chi-A	17	8	.680	45	29	8	1	1	230	221	3	81	85	12.2	2.97	89	.252	.321	6	.090	-3	-8	-8	-5	-1.7
1918	Chi-A	6	4	.600	15	14	7	2	1	105^{2}	76	0	47	30	10.9	2.73	100	.209	.308	5	.132	-2	1	0	-2	-0.5
1919	*Chi-A	23	11	.676	41	40	27	5	1	297	265	8	58	125	10.1	2.64	121	.244	.289	17	.181	1	20	18	-5	1.4
1920	Chi-A	22	14	.611	39	38	25	0	0	299	302	15	90	128	12.2	3.91	96	.271	.332	22	.218	0	-4	-5	-3	-0.8
Total	7	82	48	.631	189	152	80	10	5	1186	1121	31	347	515	11.5	3.13	99	.255	.316	61	.159	-4	1	-4	-21	-3.3
● **MUTT WILLIAMS**	Williams, David Carter b: 7/31/1891, Ozark, Ark. d: 3/30/62, Fayetteville, Ark. BR/TR, 6'3.5", 195 lbs. Deb: 10/04/13																									
1913	Was-A	1	0	1.000	1	1	0	0	0	4	4	1	2	1	13.5	4.50	66	.286	.375	1	.500	0	-1	-1	0	0.0
1914	Was-A	0	0	—	5	0	0	0	1	7	5	0	4	3	11.6	5.14	55	.227	.346	0	—	0	-2	-2	-0	-0.2
Total	2	1	0	1.000	6	1	0	0	1	11	9	1	6	4	12.3	4.91	58	.250	.357	1	.500	0	-3	-2	-0	-0.2
● **DAVE WILLIAMS**	Williams, David Owen b: 2/7/1881, Scranton, Pa. d: 4/25/18, Hot Springs, Ark. BR/TL, 5'11.5", 167 lbs. Deb: 7/02/02																									
1902	Bos-A	0	0	—	3	0	0	0	0	18^{2}	22	0	11	7	16.4	5.30	67	.294	.391	3	.333	1	-4	-4	-1	-0.3
● **DON WILLIAMS**	Williams, Donald Fred b: 9/14/31, Floyd, Va. BR/TR, 6'2", 180 lbs. Deb: 9/12/58																									
1958	Pit-N	0	0	—	2	0	0	0	0	4	6	1	1	3	15.8	6.75	57	.375	.412	0	—	0	-1	-1	0	-0.1
1959	Pit-N	0	0	—	6	0	0	0	0	12	17	1	3	3	15.0	6.75	57	.362	.400	1	.333	1	-4	-4	-1	-0.3
1962	KC-A	0	0	—	3	0	0	0	0	4	6	0	0	1	15.8	9.00	46	.353	.389	0	.000	-0	-2	-2	-0	-0.2
Total	3	0	0	—	11	0	0	0	0	20	29	2	4	7	15.3	7.20	55	.363	.400	1	.250	1	-7	-7	-1	-0.6
● **DON WILLIAMS**	Williams, Donald Reid "Dino" b: 9/2/35, Los Angeles, Cal. d: 12/20/91, LaJolla, Cal. BR/TR, 6'5", 218 lbs. Deb: 8/04/63																									
1963	Min-A	0	0	—	3	0	0	0	0	4^{1}	8	1	6	2	29.1	10.38	35	.381	.519	0	—	0	-3	-3	0	-0.3
● **DALE WILLIAMS**	Williams, Elisha Alphonso b: 10/6/1855, Ludlow, Ky. d: 10/22/39, Covington, Ky. BR/TR, 5'9", 175 lbs. Deb: 8/12/1876																									
1876	Cin-N	1	8	.111	9	9	9	0	0	83	123	1	4	9	13.8	4.23	52	.339	.346	7	.200	-2	-18	-19	-0	-1.6
● **FRANK WILLIAMS**	Williams, Frank Lee b: 2/13/58, Seattle, Wash. BR/TR, 6'1", 190 lbs. Deb: 4/05/84																									
1984	SF-N	9	4	.692	61	1	1	1	3	106^{1}	88	2	51	91	12.0	3.55	99	.226	.321	4	.222	1	0	-1	4	0.5
1985	SF-N	2	4	.333	49	0	0	0	0	73	65	5	35	54	13.1	4.19	82	.242	.342	0	.000	-0	-5	-6	0	-0.7
1986	SF-N	3	1	.750	36	0	0	0	1	52^{1}	35	0	21	33	10.3	1.20	292	.212	.316	1	.500	0	15	13	1	1.5
1987	Cin-N	4	0	1.000	85	0	0	0	2	105^{2}	101	5	39	60	12.1	2.30	185	.254	.324	0	.000	-1	21	23	1	2.3
1988	Cin-N	3	2	.600	60	0	0	0	1	62^{2}	59	6	35	43	13.8	2.59	139	.252	.354	0	.000	-0	6	7	0	0.8
1989	Det-A	3	3	.500	42	0	0	0	1	71^{2}	70	5	46	33	14.9	3.64	105	.254	.366	0	—	0	2	1	-0	0.2
Total	6	24	14	.632	333	1	1	1	8	471^{2}	418	23	227	314	12.7	3.00	124	.242	.336	5	.172	1	39	38	5	4.6
● **JOHNNIE WILLIAMS**	Williams, John Brodie "Honolulu Johnnie" b: 7/16/1889, Honolulu, Hawaii d: 9/8/63, Long Beach, Cal. BR/TR, 6', 180 lbs. Deb: 4/21/14																									
1914	Det-A	0	2	.000	4	3	1	0	0	11^{1}	17	0	5	4	17.5	6.35	44	.378	.440	0	.000	-0	-5	-4	-0	-0.5
● **LEON WILLIAMS**	Williams, Leon Theo "Lefty" b: 12/2/05, Macon, Ga. d: 11/20/84, Atlanta, Ga. BL/TL, 5'10.5", 154 lbs. Deb: 6/02/26																									
1926	Bro-N	0	0	—	8	0	0	0	0	8^{1}	16	0	2	3	19.4	5.40	71	.421	.450	1	.200	0	-1	-1	1	-0.1
● **MARSH WILLIAMS**	Williams, Marshall McDiarmid "Cap" b: 2/21/1893, Faison, N.C. d: 2/22/35, Tucson, Ariz. BR/TR, 6', 180 lbs. Deb: 7/07/16																									
1916	Phi-A	0	6	.000	10	4	3	0	0	51^{1}	71	4	31	17	17.9	7.89	36	.350	.436	2	.105	-1	-29	-29	-1	-2.8
● **MATT WILLIAMS**	Williams, Matthew Evan b: 7/25/59, Houston, Tex. BR/TR, 6'1", 200 lbs. Deb: 8/02/83																									
1983	Tor-A	1	1	.500	4	3	0	0	0	8	13	5	7	5	23.6	14.63	29	.361	.477	0	—	0	-9	-9	0	-0.8
1985	Tex-A	2	1	.667	6	3	0	0	0	26	20	3	10	22	10.4	2.42	175	.211	.286	0	—	0	5	5	-1	0.4
Total	2	3	2	.600	10	6	0	0	0	34	33	8	17	27	13.5	5.29	80	.252	.342	0	—	0	-4	-4	-0	-0.4
● **MIKE WILLIAMS**	Williams, Michael Darren b: 7/29/69, Radford, Va. BR/TR, 6'2", 190 lbs. Deb: 6/30/92																									
1992	Phi-N	1	1	.500	5	5	1	0	0	28^{2}	29	3	7	5	11.3	5.34	66	.259	.303	4	.400	1	-6	-6	-0	-0.5
● **MITCH WILLIAMS**	Williams, Mitchell Steven b: 11/17/64, Santa Ana, Cal. BL/TL, 6'4", 205 lbs. Deb: 4/09/86																									
1986	Tex-A	8	6	.571	**80**	0	0	0	8	98	69	8	79	90	14.6	3.58	120	.202	.369	0	—	0	6	8	-1	0.7
1987	Tex-A	8	6	.571	85	1	0	0	6	108^{2}	63	9	94	129	13.6	3.23	138	.175	.355	0	—	0	15	15	1	1.5
1988	Tex-A	2	7	.222	67	0	0	0	18	68	48	4	47	61	13.4	4.63	88	.203	.349	0	—	0	-5	-4	0	-0.5
1989	*Chi-N★	4	4	.500	**76**	0	0	0	36	81^{2}	71	6	52	67	14.4	2.76	136	.238	.366	1	.200	1	7	9	-1	1.0
1990	Chi-N	1	8	.111	59	2	0	0	16	66^{1}	60	4	50	55	15.1	3.93	104	.239	.368	0	.000	-1	-1	1	-1	0.0
1991	Phi-N	12	5	.706	69	0	0	0	30	88^{1}	56	4	62	84	12.8	2.34	156	.182	.333	0	.000	0	13	13	-1	1.2
1992	Phi-N	5	8	.385	66	0	0	0	29	81	69	4	64	74	15.4	3.78	93	.240	.389	1	.250	0	-2	-3	-1	-0.3
Total	7	40	44	.476	502	3	0	0	143	592	436	39	448	560	14.2	3.41	118	.209	.361	2	.133	1	33	39	-4	3.6
● **STEAMBOAT WILLIAMS**	Williams, Rees Gephardt b: 1/31/1892, Cascade, Mont. d: 6/29/79, Deer River, Minn. BL/TR, 5'11", 170 lbs. Deb: 7/12/14																									
1914	StL-N	0	1	.000	5	1	0	0	0	11	13	1	6	2	15.5	6.55	43	.295	.380	0	.000	-0	-5	-5	-0	-0.5
1916	StL-N	6	7	.462	36	8	5	0	1	105	121	6	27	25	12.8	4.20	63	.291	.336	5	.208	1	-18	-18	-0	-1.9
Total	2	6	8	.429	41	9	5	0	1	116	134	7	33	27	13.0	4.42	60	.291	.340	5	.200	1	-23	-23	-0	-2.4
● **RICK WILLIAMS**	Williams, Richard Allen b: 11/9/52, Merced, Cal. BR/TR, 6'1", 180 lbs. Deb: 6/12/78																									
1978	Hou-N	1	2	.333	17	1	0	0	0	34^{2}	43	2	10	17	13.8	4.67	71	.301	.346	0	.000	-1	-4	-5	0	-0.6

YEAR TM/L	W	L	PCT	G	GS	CG	SH	SV	IP	H	HR	BB	SO	RAT	ERA	ERA+	OAV	OOB	BH	AVG	PB	PR	/A	PD	TPI
1979 Hou-N	4	7	.364	31	16	2	2	0	121^1	122	6	30	37	11.4	3.26	108	.261	.308	8	.258	3	6	3	0	0.7
Total 2	5	9	.357	48	17	2	2	0	156	165	8	40	54	11.9	3.58	97	.270	.317	8	.222	2	2	-2	1	0.1
● ACE WILLIAMS	Williams, Robert Fulton b: 3/18/17, Montclair, N.J. BR/TL, 6'2", 174 lbs. Deb: 7/15/40																								
1940 Bos-N	0	0	—	5	0	0	0	0	9	21	0	12	5	34.0	16.00	23	.375	.493	0	.000	-0	-12	-12	0	-1.1
1946 Bos-N	0	0	—	1	0	0	0	0	0	1	0	1	0	—	—	—	1.000	1.000	0	—	0	0	0	0	0.0
Total 2	0	0	—	6	0	0	0	0	9	22	0	13	5	36.0	16.00	23	.386	.507	0	.000	-0	-12	-12	0	-1.1
● STAN WILLIAMS	Williams, Stanley Wilson b: 9/14/36, Enfield, N.H. BR/TR, 6'5", 230 lbs. Deb: 5/17/58 C																								
1958 LA-N	9	7	.563	27	21	3	2	0	119	99	10	65	80	12.9	4.01	102	.228	.338	2	.050	-3	-1	1	0	-0.2
1959 *LA-N	5	5	.500	35	15	2	0	0	124^2	102	12	86	89	14.2	3.97	106	.228	.363	7	.194	1	-0	4	0	0.5
1960 LA-N★	14	10	.583	38	30	9	2	1	207^1	162	26	72	175	10.4	3.00	133	.210	.282	9	.141	0	18	22	1	2.5
1961 LA-N	15	12	.556	41	35	6	2	0	235^1	213	21	108	205	12.5	3.90	111	.242	.329	13	.167	-0	3	12	-1	1.0
1962 LA-N	14	12	.538	40	28	4	1	1	185^2	184	16	98	108	13.7	4.46	81	.253	.341	5	.076	-2	-11	-17	-1	-1.9
1963 *NY-A	9	8	.529	29	21	6	1	0	146	137	7	57	98	12.3	3.21	110	.249	.326	5	.102	-1	7	5	1	0.5
1964 NY-A	1	5	.167	21	10	1	0	0	82	76	7	38	54	12.5	3.84	94	.248	.330	3	.143	-0	-2	-2	1	-0.2
1965 Cle-A	0	0	—	3	0	0	0	0	4^1	6	1	3	1	18.7	6.23	56	.353	.450	0	—	0	-1	-1	0	-0.1
1967 Cle-A	6	4	.600	16	8	2	1	1	79	64	6	24	75	10.1	2.62	125	.218	.279	2	.091	-1	5	6	-2	0.3
1968 Cle-A	13	11	.542	44	24	6	2	9	194^1	163	14	51	147	10.4	2.50	118	.225	.285	9	.161	1	10	10	-1	1.2
1969 Cle-A	6	14	.300	61	15	3	0	12	178^1	155	25	67	139	11.8	3.94	96	.235	.317	4	.100	-1	-6	-3	-1	-0.5
1970 *Min-A	10	1	.909	68	0	0	0	15	113^1	85	8	32	76	9.7	1.99	187	.208	.274	0	.000	-2	22	22	-2	1.9
1971 Min-A	4	5	.444	46	1	0	0	4	78	63	7	44	47	13.3	4.15	86	.220	.340	0	.000	-1	-6	-5	-1	-0.7
StL-N	3	0	1.000	10	0	0	0	0	12^2	13	0	2	8	12.1	1.42	253	.265	.321	0	.000	-0	3	3	0	0.4
1972 Bos-A	0	0	—	3	0	0	0	0	4^1	5	0	1	3	12.5	6.23	52	.294	.333	0	—	0	-2	-1	0	-0.2
Total 14	109	94	.537	482	208	42	11	43	1764^1	1527	160	748	1305	12.0	3.48	108	.232	.317	59	.118	-10	39	53	-4	4.5
● TED WILLIAMS	Williams, Theodore Samuel "The Kid', "The Thumper" or "The Splendid Splinter" b: 8/30/18, San Diego, Cal. BL/TR, 6'3", 205 lbs. Deb: 4/20/39 MH♦																								
1940 Bos-A★	0	0	—	1	0	0	0	0	2	3	0	0	1	13.5	4.50	100	.333	.333	193	.344	1	-0	-0	0	0.0
● TOM WILLIAMS	Williams, Thomas C. b: 8/19/1870, Minersville, Ohio d: 7/27/40, Columbus, Ohio Deb: 5/01/1892																								
1892 Cle-N	1	0	1.000	2	1	1	0	0	9	9	1	1	3	10.0	3.00	113	.250	.270	1	.100	-1	0	0	-0	0.0
1893 Cle-N	1	1	.500	5	2	2	0	0	24	33	1	10	6	16.5	4.88	100	.317	.383	5	.278	1	-1	0	0	0.0
Total 2	2	1	.667	7	3	3	0	0	33	42	2	11	9	14.7	4.36	102	.300	.355	6	.214	-0	-0	0	-0	0.0
● POP WILLIAMS	Williams, Walter Merrill b: 5/19/1874, Bowdoinham, Me. d: 8/4/59, Topsham, Maine BL/TR, 5'11", 190 lbs. Deb: 9/14/1898																								
1898 Was-N	0	2	.000	2	2	2	0	0	17	32	0	7	3	20.6	8.47	43	.396	.444	3	.375	1	-9	-9	-1	-0.7
1902 Chi-N	11	16	.407	31	31	26	1	0	254^1	259	2	63	94	11.6	2.51	107	.264	.312	23	.198	2	8	5	3	1.1
1903 Chi-N	0	1	.000	1	1	1	0	0	5	9	0	0	2	16.2	5.40	58	.409	.409	0	.000	-0	-1	-1	-0	-0.1
Phi-N	1	1	.500	2	2	2	0	0	18	21	0	6	8	14.0	3.00	109	.304	.368	2	.286	0	1	1	0	0.2
Bos-N	4	5	.444	10	10	9	1	0	83	97	3	37	20	15.5	4.12	78	.295	.381	10	.238	-0	-8	-8	-1	-0.8
Yr	5	7	.417	13	13	12	1	0	106	127	3	43	30	15.2	3.99	81	.302	.378	12	.235	-0	-8	-9	0	-0.7
Total 3	16	25	.390	46	46	40	2	0	377^1	418	5	113	127	13.0	3.20	90	.282	.339	38	.217	2	-10	-13	2	-0.3
● WASH WILLIAMS	Williams, Washington J. b: Philadelphia, Pa. d: 1/1890, Philadelphia, Pa. 5'11", 180 lbs. Deb: 8/05/1884 ♦																								
1885 Chi-N	0	0	—	1	1	0	0	0	2	2	0	5	0	31.5	13.50	22	.400	.700	1	.250	-0	-2	-2	0	-0.2
● NED WILLIAMSON	Williamson, Edward Nagle b: 10/24/1857, Philadelphia, Pa. d: 3/3/1894, Willow Springs, Ark BR/TR, 5'11", 170 lbs. Deb: 5/01/1878 ♦																								
1881 Chi-N	1	1	.500	3	1	1	0	0	18	14	0	0	2	7.0	2.00	137	.209	.209	92	.268	1	2	1	-0	0.1
1882 Chi-N	0	0	—	1	0	0	0	0	3	9	1	1	0	30.0	6.00	48	.500	.526	98	.282	1	-1	-1	0	-0.1
1883 Chi-N	0	0	—	1	0	0	0	0	1	1	0	1	1	18.0	9.00	35	.167	.286	111	.276	0	-1	-1	0	-0.1
1884 Chi-N	0	0	—	2	0	0	0	0	2	8	0	2	0	45.0	18.00	17	.500	.556	116	.278	1	-3	-3	0	-0.3
1885 *Chi-N	0	0	—	2	0	0	0	**2**	6	2	0	0	3	3.0	0.00	—	.080	.080	97	.238	0	2	2	0	0.2
1886 *Chi-N	0	0	—	2	0	0	0	1	3	2	0	0	1	6.0	0.00	—	.143	.143	93	.216	0	1	1	-0	0.1
1887 Chi-N	0	0	—	1	0	0	0	0	2	2	0	1	0	13.5	9.00	50	.222	.300	117	.267	0	-1	-1	0	-0.1
Total 7	1	1	.500	12	1	1	0	3	35	38	1	5	7	11.1	3.34	90	.245	.269	1159	.255	3	-2	-1	0	-0.2
● MARK WILLIAMSON	Williamson, Mark Alan b: 7/21/59, Corpus Christi, Tex. BR/TR, 6', 171 lbs. Deb: 4/08/87																								
1987 Bal-A	8	9	.471	61	2	0	0	3	125	122	12	41	73	12.0	4.03	109	.261	.324	0	—	0	6	5	1	0.7
1988 Bal-A	5	8	.385	37	10	2	0	2	117^2	125	14	40	69	12.8	4.90	80	.272	.333	0	—	0	-12	-13	-0	-1.3
1989 Bal-A	10	5	.667	65	0	0	0	9	107^1	105	4	30	55	11.5	2.93	129	.261	.315	0	—	0	11	10	-1	1.1
1990 Bal-A	8	2	.800	49	0	0	0	1	85^1	65	8	28	60	9.8	2.21	171	.215	.282	0	—	0	16	15	1	1.7
1991 Bal-A	5	5	.500	65	0	0	0	4	80^1	87	9	35	53	13.7	4.48	88	.275	.348	0	—	0	-3	-5	-0	-0.5
1992 Bal-A	0	0	—	12	0	0	0	1	18^2	16	1	10	14	12.5	0.96	405	.239	.338	0	—	0	6	6	-1	0.6
Total 6	36	29	.554	289	12	2	0	20	534^1	520	48	184	324	12.0	3.67	109	.258	.322	0	—	0	24	19	0	2.3
● AL WILLIAMSON	Williamson, Silas Albert b: 2/20/1900, Bucksville, Ark. d: 11/29/78, Hot Springs, Ark. BR/TR, 5'11", 160 lbs. Deb: 4/27/28																								
1928 Chi-A	0	0	—	1	0	0	0	0	2	1	0	0	0	4.5	0.00	—	.167	.167	0	—	0	1	1	0	0.1
● CARL WILLIS	Willis, Carl Blake b: 12/28/60, Danville, Va. BL/TR, 6'4", 210 lbs. Deb: 6/09/84																								
1984 Det-A	0	2	.000	10	2	0	0	0	16	25	1	5	4	16.9	7.31	54	.362	.405	0	—	0	-6	-6	0	-0.6
Cin-N	0	1	.000	7	0	0	0	1	9^2	8	1	2	3	9.3	3.72	101	.222	.263	0	—	0	-0	0	0	0.0
1985 Cin-N	1	0	1.000	11	0	0	0	1	13^2	21	3	5	6	17.1	9.22	41	.344	.394	0	.000	0	-9	-8	-0	-0.9
1986 Cin-N	1	3	.250	29	0	0	0	0	52^1	54	4	32	24	15.0	4.47	87	.278	.383	1	.333	0	-4	-4	1	-0.3
1988 Chi-A	0	0	—	6	0	0	0	0	12	17	3	7	6	18.0	8.25	48	.362	.444	0	—	0	-6	-6	-0	-0.6
1991 *Min-A	8	3	.727	40	0	0	0	2	89	76	4	19	53	9.7	2.63	162	.232	.276	0	—	0	14	16	-1	1.5
1992 Min-A	7	3	.700	59	0	0	0	1	79^1	73	4	11	45	9.5	2.72	148	.246	.273	0	—	0	11	11	-1	1.1
Total 6	17	12	.586	162	2	0	0	5	272	274	20	81	141	11.8	3.90	104	.266	.320	1	.250	0	1	4	-2	0.2
● LEFTY WILLIS	Willis, Charles William b: 11/4/05, Leetown, W.Va. d: 5/10/62, Bethesda, Md. BL/TL, 6'1", 175 lbs. Deb: 10/03/25																								
1925 Phi-A	0	0	—	1	1	0	0	0	5	9	2	2	3	19.8	10.80	43	.409	.458	0	.000	-1	-4	-3	0	-0.3
1926 Phi-A	0	0	—	13	1	0	0	1	32^1	31	0	12	13	12.2	1.39	300	.270	.344	2	.222	-0	9	10	-0	0.9
1927 Phi-A	3	1	.750	15	2	1	0	0	27	32	2	11	7	14.3	5.67	75	.308	.374	0	.000	-1	-5	-4	1	-0.4
Total 3	3	1	.750	29	4	1	0	1	64^1	72	4	25	23	13.7	3.92	108	.299	.367	2	.111	-1	1	2	1	0.2
● DALE WILLIS	Willis, Dale Jerome b: 5/29/38, Calhoun, Ga. BR/TR, 5'11", 165 lbs. Deb: 4/14/63																								
1963 KC-A	0	2	.000	25	0	0	0	1	44^2	46	3	25	47	15.1	5.04	76	.266	.371	1	.167	-0	-7	-6	1	-0.6
● JIM WILLIS	Willis, James Gladden b: 3/20/27, Doyline, La. BL/TR, 6'3", 175 lbs. Deb: 4/22/53																								
1953 Chi-N	2	1	.667	13	3	2	0	0	43^1	37	1	17	15	11.8	3.12	143	.228	.313	0	.000	-1	6	6	1	0.6
1954 Chi-N	0	1	.000	14	1	0	0	0	23	22	1	18	5	16.8	3.91	107	.256	.402	0	.000	-1	0	1	1	0.1
Total 2	2	2	.500	27	4	2	0	0	66^1	59	2	35	20	13.6	3.39	129	.238	.346	0	.000	-2	6	7	2	0.7
● JOE WILLIS	Willis, Joseph Denk b: 4/9/1890, Coal Grove, Ohio d: 12/4/66, Ironton, Ohio BR/TL, 6'1", 185 lbs. Deb: 5/03/11																								
1911 StL-A	0	1	.000	1	1	0	0	0	7	8	0	3	0	14.1	5.14	66	.308	.379	0	.000	0	-1	-1	-1	-0.1
StL-N	0	1	.000	2	2	1	0	0	15	13	0	4	5	10.2	4.20	80	.232	.283	0	.000	-1	-1	-1	0	-0.2

YEAR TM/L	W	L	PCT	G	GS	CG	SH	SV	IP	H	HR	BB	SO	RAT	ERA	ERA+	OAV	OOB	BH	AVG	PB	PR	/A	PD	TPI
1912 StL-N	4	9	.308	31	17	4	0	2	129^{2}	143	3	62	55	14.6	4.44	77	.288	.372	6	.158	-2	-15	-15	-1	-1.6
1913 StL-N	0	0	—	7	0	0	0	1	9^{2}	9	0	11	6	18.6	7.45	43	.257	.435	0	.000	-0	-5	-5	-0	-0.5
Total 3	4	11	.267	41	20	5	0	3	161^{1}	173	3	80	66	14.4	4.63	74	.282	.369	6	.125	-2	-22	-22	-1	-2.4

● LES WILLIS Willis, Lester Evans "Wimpy" or "Lefty" b: 1/17/08, Nacogdoches, Tex. d: 1/22/82, Jasper, Tex. BL/TL, 5'9.5", 195 lbs. Deb: 4/28/47

YEAR TM/L	W	L	PCT	G	GS	CG	SH	SV	IP	H	HR	BB	SO	RAT	ERA	ERA+	OAV	OOB	BH	AVG	PB	PR	/A	PD	TPI
1947 Cle-A	0	2	.000	22	2	0	0	1	44	58	3	24	10	16.8	3.48	100	.324	.404	1	.091	-1	1	0	-1	-0.2

● MIKE WILLIS Willis, Michael Henry b: 12/26/50, Oklahoma City, Okla BL/TL, 6'2", 210 lbs. Deb: 4/13/77

YEAR TM/L	W	L	PCT	G	GS	CG	SH	SV	IP	H	HR	BB	SO	RAT	ERA	ERA+	OAV	OOB	BH	AVG	PB	PR	/A	PD	TPI
1977 Tor-A	2	6	.250	43	3	0	0	5	107^{1}	105	15	38	59	12.0	3.94	106	.260	.324	0	—	0	1	3	1	0.4
1978 Tor-A	3	7	.300	44	2	1	0	7	100^{2}	104	11	39	52	12.8	4.56	86	.271	.338	0	—	0	-9	-7	0	-0.7
1979 Tor-A	0	3	.000	17	1	0	0	0	26^{2}	35	1	16	8	17.6	8.44	51	.333	.426	0	—	0	-13	-12	0	-1.2
1980 Tor-A	2	1	.667	20	0	0	0	3	26^{1}	25	3	11	14	12.6	1.71	252	.248	.327	0	—	0	7	8	0	0.5
1981 Tor-A	0	4	.000	20	0	0	0	0	35	43	6	20	16	16.5	5.91	67	.301	.390	0	—	0	-9	-8	0	-0.8
Total 5	7	21	.250	144	6	1	0	15	296	312	36	124	149	13.3	4.59	89	.274	.347	0	—	0	-22	-16	1	-1.8

● RON WILLIS Willis, Ronald Earl b: 7/12/43, Willisville, Tenn. d: 11/21/77, Memphis, Tenn. BR/TR, 6'2", 195 lbs. Deb: 9/20/66

YEAR TM/L	W	L	PCT	G	GS	CG	SH	SV	IP	H	HR	BB	SO	RAT	ERA	ERA+	OAV	OOB	BH	AVG	PB	PR	/A	PD	TPI
1966 StL-N	0	0	—	4	0	0	0	1	3	1	0	1	2	6.0	0.00	—	.100	.182	0	—	0	1	1	-0	0.1
1967 *StL-N	6	5	.545	65	0	0	0	10	81	76	3	43	42	13.6	2.67	123	.257	.357	3	.375	1	6	6	2	1.0
1968 *StL-N	2	3	.400	48	0	0	0	4	63^{2}	50	4	28	39	11.2	3.39	85	.213	.299	0	.000	-1	-3	-4	1	-0.4
1969 StL-N	1	2	.333	26	0	0	0	0	32^{1}	26	4	19	23	12.8	4.18	86	.224	.338	1	1.000	0	-2	-2	1	-0.1
Hou-N	0	0	—	3	0	0	0	0	2^{1}	3	0	0	2	11.6	0.00	—	.300	.300	0	—	0	1	1	-0	0.1
Yr	1	2	.333	29	0	0	0	0	34^{2}	29	4	19	25	12.5	3.89	92	.223	.322	1	1.000	0	-1	-1	1	0.0
1970 SD-N	2	2	.500	42	0	0	0	4	56	53	4	28	20	13.7	4.02	99	.247	.344	0	.000	-1	0	-0	1	0.1
Total 5	11	12	.478	188	0	0	0	19	238^{1}	209	15	119	128	12.7	3.32	102	.237	.334	4	.160	0	4	2	5	0.8

● VIC WILLIS Willis, Victor Gazaway b: 4/12/1876, Cecil Co., Md. d: 8/3/47, Elkton, Md. BR/TR, 6'2", 185 lbs. Deb: 4/20/1898

YEAR TM/L	W	L	PCT	G	GS	CG	SH	SV	IP	H	HR	BB	SO	RAT	ERA	ERA+	OAV	OOB	BH	AVG	PB	PR	/A	PD	TPI
1898 Bos-N	25	13	.658	41	38	29	1	0	311	264	5	148	160	12.8	2.84	130	.228	.331	17	.145	-6	27	30	-0	2.2
1899 Bos-N	27	8	.771	41	38	35	**5**	2	342^{2}	277	6	117	120	11.1	**2.50**	**167**	**.221**	.303	29	.216	-4	52	**63**	0	5.8
1900 Bos-N	10	17	.370	32	29	22	2	0	236	258	11	106	53	14.3	4.19	98	.277	.359	12	.136	-7	-13	-2	-2	-0.9
1901 Bos-N	20	17	.541	38	35	33	**6**	0	305^{1}	262	6	78	133	10.3	2.36	**153**	.230	.286	20	.187	-1	33	**43**	-1	4.2
1902 Bos-N	27	20	.574	**51**	46	**45**	4	**3**	**410**	372	6	101	**225**	10.7	2.20	129	.242	.295	23	.153	-6	27	29	4	2.9
1903 Bos-N	12	18	.400	33	32	29	2	0	278	256	3	88	125	11.5	2.98	108	.251	.317	24	.188	-1	9	7	3	0.8
1904 Bos-N	18	25	.419	43	43	**39**	2	0	350	357	7	109	196	12.3	2.85	97	.266	.327	27	.182	1	-4	-4	7	0.5
1905 Bos-N	12	29	.293	41	41	36	4	0	342	340	7	107	149	12.1	3.21	97	.265	.328	20	.153	-3	-8	-4	6	-0.1
1906 Pit-N	23	13	.639	41	36	32	6	1	322	295	0	76	124	10.5	1.73	154	.250	.298	20	.174	-1	32	34	5	4.5
1907 Pit-N	21	11	.656	39	37	27	6	1	292^{2}	234	4	69	107	9.5	2.34	104	.219	.271	14	.136	-2	4	3	2	0.3
1908 Pit-N	23	11	.676	41	38	25	7	0	304^{2}	239	2	69	97	9.3	2.07	111	.213	.262	17	.165	-1	10	8	-1	0.7
1909 *Pit-N	22	11	.667	39	35	24	4	1	289^{2}	243	3	83	95	10.3	2.24	122	.231	.289	14	.136	-2	12	16	1	1.5
1910 StL-N	9	12	.429	33	23	12	1	3	212	224	6	61	67	12.1	3.35	89	.275	.326	11	.167	-2	-8	-9	2	-0.8
Total 13	249	205	.548	513	471	388	50	11	3996	3621	66	1212	1651	11.2	2.63	118	.243	.307	248	.166	-36	172	208	27	21.6

● CLAUDE WILLOUGHBY Willoughby, Claude William "Flunky" or "Weeping Willie" b: 11/14/1898, Fredonia, Kan. d: 8/14/73, McPherson, Kan. BR/TR, 5'9.5", 165 lbs. Deb: 9/18/25

YEAR TM/L	W	L	PCT	G	GS	CG	SH	SV	IP	H	HR	BB	SO	RAT	ERA	ERA+	OAV	OOB	BH	AVG	PB	PR	/A	PD	TPI
1925 Phi-N	2	1	.667	3	3	1	0	0	23	26	0	11	6	14.9	1.96	244	.295	.380	0	.000	-1	6	7	-1	0.5
1926 Phi-N	8	12	.400	47	18	6	0	1	168	218	7	71	37	15.8	5.95	70	.327	.396	11	.212	-1	-40	-34	3	-3.0
1927 Phi-N	3	7	.300	35	6	1	1	2	97^{2}	126	7	53	14	16.7	6.54	63	.321	.404	2	.077	-2	-28	-26	-1	-2.7
1928 Phi-N	6	5	.545	35	13	5	1	1	130^{2}	180	6	83	26	18.3	5.30	80	.340	.432	6	.150	-1	-19	-15	-1	-1.6
1929 Phi-N	15	14	.517	49	34	14	1	4	243^{1}	288	15	108	50	14.8	4.99	104	.296	.370	13	.143	-5	-7	5	4	0.4
1930 Phi-N	4	17	.190	41	24	5	1	1	153	241	17	68	38	18.3	7.59	72	.369	.430	5	.104	-4	-44	-36	2	-3.2
1931 Pit-N	0	2	.000	9	2	1	0	0	25^{2}	32	4	12	4	15.4	6.31	61	.305	.376	2	.286	0	-7	-7	0	-0.6
Total 7	38	58	.396	219	100	33	4	9	841^{1}	1111	56	406	175	16.4	5.84	81	.326	.401	39	.143	-15	-140	-106	8	-10.2

● JIM WILLOUGHBY Willoughby, James Arthur b: 1/31/49, Salinas, Cal. BR/TR, 6'2", 185 lbs. Deb: 9/05/71

YEAR TM/L	W	L	PCT	G	GS	CG	SH	SV	IP	H	HR	BB	SO	RAT	ERA	ERA+	OAV	OOB	BH	AVG	PB	PR	/A	PD	TPI
1971 SF-N	0	1	.000	2	1	0	0	0	4	8	0	1	3	20.3	9.00	38	.400	.429	0	.000	-0	-2	-2	0	-0.2
1972 SF-N	6	4	.600	11	11	7	0	0	87^{2}	72	8	14	40	9.0	2.36	148	.222	.259	5	.185	0	11	11	0	1.3
1973 SF-N	4	5	.444	39	12	1	1	1	123	138	21	37	60	13.0	4.68	82	.295	.350	4	.143	1	-14	-12	-1	-1.2
1974 SF-N	1	4	.200	18	4	0	0	0	40^{2}	51	7	9	12	13.3	4.65	82	.304	.339	1	.100	-0	-5	-4	1	-0.3
1975 *Bos-A	5	2	.714	24	0	0	0	8	48^{1}	46	6	16	29	11.9	3.54	115	.247	.314	0	—	0	1	3	0	0.1
1976 Bos-A	3	12	.200	54	0	0	0	10	99	94	4	31	37	12.1	2.82	139	.256	.328	0	.000	0	8	12	1	1.4
1977 Bos-A	6	2	.750	31	0	0	0	2	54^{2}	54	5	18	33	12.2	4.94	91	.258	.323	0	—	0	-5	-3	1	-0.2
1978 Chi-A	1	6	.143	59	0	0	0	13	93^{1}	95	6	19	36	11.4	3.86	99	.275	.320	0	—	0	-1	-1	2	0.1
Total 8	26	36	.419	238	28	8	1	34	550^{2}	558	57	145	250	11.8	3.79	102	.267	.321	10	.149	1	-8	4	5	1.0

● FRANK WILLS Wills, Frank Lee b: 10/26/58, New Orleans, La. BR/TR, 6'2", 202 lbs. Deb: 7/31/83

YEAR TM/L	W	L	PCT	G	GS	CG	SH	SV	IP	H	HR	BB	SO	RAT	ERA	ERA+	OAV	OOB	BH	AVG	PB	PR	/A	PD	TPI
1983 KC-A	2	1	.667	6	4	0	0	0	34^{2}	35	2	15	23	13.0	4.15	98	.259	.333	0	—	0	-0	-0	-0	-0.1
1984 KC-A	2	3	.400	10	5	0	0	0	37	39	3	13	21	12.6	5.11	79	.271	.331	0	—	0	-5	-4	-1	-0.5
1985 Sea-A	5	11	.313	24	18	1	0	1	123	122	18	68	67	14.1	6.00	70	.266	.365	0	—	0	-25	-24	0	-2.3
1986 Cle-A	4	4	.500	26	0	0	0	4	40^{1}	43	6	16	32	13.2	4.91	84	.272	.339	0	—	0	-3	-3	0	-0.3
1987 Cle-A	0	1	.000	6	0	0	0	1	5^{1}	3	0	7	4	16.9	5.06	89	.176	.417	0	—	0	-0	-0	0	0.0
1988 Tor-A	0	0	—	10	0	0	0	0	20^{2}	22	2	6	19	12.2	5.23	75	.272	.322	0	—	0	-3	-3	1	-0.2
1989 Tor-A	3	1	.750	24	4	0	0	0	71^{1}	65	4	30	41	12.1	3.66	103	.242	.320	0	—	0	2	1	-0	0.1
1990 Tor-A	6	4	.600	44	4	0	0	0	99	101	13	38	72	12.7	4.73	83	.266	.334	0	—	0	-9	-9	0	-0.9
1991 Tor-A	0	1	.000	4	0	0	0	0	4^{1}	8	2	5	2	29.1	16.62	25	.421	.560	0	—	0	-6	-6	0	-0.5
Total 9	22	26	.458	154	35	1	0	6	435^{2}	438	50	198	281	13.3	5.06	80	.264	.344	0	—	0	-50	-50	0	-4.7

● TED WILLS Wills, Theodore Carl b: 2/9/34, Fresno, Cal. BL/TL, 6'2", 200 lbs. Deb: 5/24/59

YEAR TM/L	W	L	PCT	G	GS	CG	SH	SV	IP	H	HR	BB	SO	RAT	ERA	ERA+	OAV	OOB	BH	AVG	PB	PR	/A	PD	TPI
1959 Bos-A	2	6	.250	9	8	2	0	0	56^{1}	68	9	24	24	14.9	5.27	77	.302	.372	4	.250	1	-9	-8	-0	-0.7
1960 Bos-A	1	1	.500	15	0	0	0	1	30^{1}	38	4	16	28	16.9	7.42	55	.317	.410	2	.250	1	-12	-11	1	-1.0
1961 Bos-A	3	2	.600	17	0	0	0	0	19^{2}	24	2	19	11	19.7	5.95	70	.304	.439	0	.000	-0	-4	-4	0	-0.4
1962 Bos-A	0	0	—	1	0	0	0	0	0	2	0	1	0	—	∞	—	1.000	1.000	0	—	0	-1	-1	0	-0.1
Cin-N	0	2	.000	26	5	0	0	3	61	61	12	23	58	13.1	5.31	76	.266	.346	5	.313	1	-9	-9	-0	-0.8
1965 Chi-A	2	0	1.000	15	0	0	0	1	19	17	2	14	12	15.2	2.84	112	.258	.395	0	.000	0	1	1	0	0.1
Total 5	8	11	.421	83	13	2	0	5	186^{1}	210	29	97	133	15.3	5.51	72	.291	.383	11	.250	3	-34	-32	1	-2.9

● PAUL WILMET Wilmet, Paul Richard b: 11/8/58, Green Bay, Wis. BR/TR, 5'11", 170 lbs. Deb: 7/25/89

YEAR TM/L	W	L	PCT	G	GS	CG	SH	SV	IP	H	HR	BB	SO	RAT	ERA	ERA+	OAV	OOB	BH	AVG	PB	PR	/A	PD	TPI
1989 Tex-A	0	0	—	3	0	0	0	0	2^{1}	5	0	2	1	27.0	15.43	26	.417	.500	0	—	0	-3	-3	0	-0.3

● WHITEY WILSHERE Wilshere, Vernon Sprague b: 8/3/12, Poplar Ridge, N.Y. d: 5/23/85, Cooperstown, N.Y. BL/TL, 6', 180 lbs. Deb: 6/24/34

YEAR TM/L	W	L	PCT	G	GS	CG	SH	SV	IP	H	HR	BB	SO	RAT	ERA	ERA+	OAV	OOB	BH	AVG	PB	PR	/A	PD	TPI
1934 Phi-A	0	1	.000	9	2	0	0	0	21^{2}	39	0	15	19	22.8	12.05	36	.394	.478	0	.000	-0	-18	-18	-1	-1.7
1935 Phi-A	9	9	.500	27	18	7	3	1	142^{1}	136	8	78	80	14.2	4.05	112	.253	.358	4	.093	-4	6	8	-0	0.4
1936 Phi-A	1	2	.333	5	3	0	0	0	18^{1}	21	1	19	4	19.6	6.87	74	.288	.435	0	.000	-0	-4	-4	-0	-0.3
Total 3	10	12	.455	41	23	7	3	1	182^{1}	196	9	112	103	15.7	5.28	87	.276	.383	4	.080	-4	-15	-14	-1	-1.6

● TERRY WILSHUSEN Wilshusen, Terry Wayne b: 3/22/49, Atascadero, Cal. BR/TR, 6'2", 210 lbs. Deb: 4/07/73

YEAR TM/L	W	L	PCT	G	GS	CG	SH	SV	IP	H	HR	BB	SO	RAT	ERA	ERA+	OAV	OOB	BH	AVG	PB	PR	/A	PD	TPI
1973 Cal-A	0	0	—	1	0	0	0	0	0^{1}	0	0	2	0	81.0	81.00	4	.000	.750	0	—	0	-3	-3	0	0.0

YEAR	TM/L	W	L	PCT	G	GS	CG	SH	SV	IP	H	HR	BB	SO	RAT	ERA	ERA+	OAV	OOB	BH	AVG	PB	PR	/A	PD	TPI
● DON WILSON Wilson, Donald Edward b: 2/12/45, Monroe, La. d: 1/5/75, Houston, Tex. BR/TR, 6'3", 205 lbs. Deb: 9/29/66																										
1966	Hou-N	1	0	1.000	1	0	0	0	0	6	5	1	1	7	9.0	3.00	114	.238	.273	1	.500	1	0	0	0	0.1
1967	Hou-N	10	9	.526	31	28	7	3	0	184	141	10	69	159	10.6	2.79	119	.209	.289	6	.091	-2	12	11	-2	0.7
1968	Hou-N	13	16	.448	33	30	9	3	0	208^2	187	9	70	175	11.3	3.28	90	.236	.302	15	.214	4	-7	-7	-2	-0.6
1969	Hou-N	16	12	.571	34	34	13	1	0	225	210	16	97	235	12.6	4.00	89	.245	.328	8	.099	-1	-10	-11	-0	-1.4
1970	Hou-N	11	6	.647	29	27	3	0	0	184^1	188	15	66	94	12.7	3.91	99	.259	.327	8	.116	-2	3	-1	-3	-0.6
1971	Hou-N★	16	10	.615	35	34	18	3	0	268	195	15	79	180	9.4	2.45	137	**.202**	.268	14	.154	-1	30	27	-3	2.6
1972	Hou-N	15	10	.600	33	33	13	3	0	228^1	196	16	66	172	10.4	2.68	125	.233	.290	8	.105	-2	20	17	1	1.7
1973	Hou-N	11	16	.407	37	32	10	3	2	239^1	187	21	92	149	10.8	3.20	114	.213	.293	14	.177	1	12	12	-2	1.1
1974	Hou-N	11	13	.458	33	27	5	4	0	204^2	170	16	100	112	12.0	3.08	112	.227	.321	13	.206	2	12	9	-3	0.9
Total	9	104	92	.531	266	245	78	20	2	1748^1	1479	119	640	1283	11.2	3.15	109	.228	.301	87	.146	-1	73	57	-14	4.5
● DUANE WILSON Wilson, Duane Lewis b: 6/29/34, Wichita, Kan. BL/TL, 6'1", 185 lbs. Deb: 7/03/58																										
1958	Bos-A	0	0	—	2	2	0	0	0	6^1	10	0	7	3	24.2	5.68	70	.400	.531	0	.000	-0	-1	-1	0	-0.1
● FIN WILSON Wilson, Finis Elbert b: 12/9/1889, East Fork, Ky. d: 3/9/59, Coral Gables, Fla. BL/TL, 6'1", 194 lbs. Deb: 9/26/14																										
1914	Bro-F	0	1	.000	2	1	1	0	0	7	7	0	11	4	23.1	7.71	41	.269	.486	1	.500	1	-4	-4	-0	-0.3
1915	Bro-F	1	8	.111	18	11	5	0	0	102^1	85	2	53	47	12.5	3.78	80	.249	.356	11	.314	3	-9	-9	0	-0.6
Total	2	1	9	.100	20	12	6	0	0	109^1	92	2	64	51	13.2	4.03	75	.250	.367	12	.324	3	-12	-12	-0	-0.9
● ZEKE WILSON Wilson, Frank Ealton b: 12/24/1869, Benton, Ala. d: 4/26/28, Montgomery, Ala. BR/TR, 5'10", 165 lbs. Deb: 4/23/1895																										
1895	Bos-N	2	4	.333	6	6	4	0	0	45	54	1	27	5	16.2	5.20	98	.293	.383	6	.316	1	-2	-0	1	0.1
	Cle-N	3	1	.750	8	7	3	0	0	44^2	63	3	20	16	17.1	4.23	118	.327	.396	2	.111	-2	3	4	-0	0.1
	Yr	5	5	.500	14	13	7	0	0	89^2	117	4	47	21	16.7	4.72	107	.310	.390	8	.216	-2	1	3	1	0.2
1896	Cle-N	17	9	.654	33	29	20	1	1	240	265	9	81	56	13.3	4.01	113	.278	.339	27	.270	2	9	14	6	1.9
1897	Cle-N	16	11	.593	34	30	26	1	0	263^2	323	9	83	69	14.2	4.16	108	.299	.354	26	.224	-3	4	10	1	0.6
1898	Cle-N	13	18	.419	33	31	28	1	0	254^2	307	4	51	45	12.9	3.60	100	.296	.333	21	.178	-4	0	0	4	0.1
1899	StL-N	1	1	.500	5	2	2	0	0	26	30	0	4	3	12.5	4.50	88	.289	.327	0	.000	-1	-2	-1	1	-0.2
Total	5	52	44	.542	119	105	83	3	1	874	1042	26	266	194	13.8	4.03	106	.293	.347	82	.215	-8	13	25	14	2.6
● GARY WILSON Wilson, Gary Steven b: 11/21/54, Camden, Ark. BR/TR, 6'2", 185 lbs. Deb: 4/13/79																										
1979	Hou-N	0	0	—	6	0	0	0	0	7^1	15	2	6	6	25.8	12.27	29	.441	.525	0	—	0	-7	-7	-0	-0.7
● GLENN WILSON Wilson, Glenn Dwight b: 12/22/58, Baytown, Tex. BR/TR, 6'1", 190 lbs. Deb: 4/15/82 ♦																										
1987	Phi-N	0	0	—	1	0	0	0	0	1	0	0	0	1	0.0	0.00	—	.000	.000	150	.264	0	0	0	0	0.1
● TEX WILSON Wilson, Gomer Russell b: 7/8/01, Trenton, Tex. d: 9/15/46, Sulphur Springs, Tex. BR/TL, 5'10", 170 lbs. Deb: 9/02/24																										
1924	Bro-N	0	0	—	2	0	0	0	0	3^2	7	0	1	1	19.6	14.73	25	.412	.444	0	.000	-0	-4	-4	0	-0.4
● HIGHBALL WILSON Wilson, Howard Paul b: 8/9/1878, Philadelphia, Pa. d: 10/16/34, Havre-De-Grace, Md TR , Deb: 9/13/1899																										
1899	Cle-N	0	1	.000	1	1	1	0	0	8	12	0	5	1	19.1	9.00	41	.345	.428	1	.333	0	-5	-5	-0	-0.3
1902	Phi-A	7	5	.583	13	10	8	0	0	96^1	103	1	19	18	12.0	2.43	151	.274	.319	6	.171	-1	12	13	-1	1.1
1903	Was-A	7	18	.280	30	28	25	1	0	242^1	269	7	43	56	11.9	3.31	95	.280	.317	17	.200	2	-9	-5	-4	-0.6
1904	Was-A	0	3	.000	3	3	3	0	0	25	33	0	4	11	14.0	4.68	57	.318	.355	2	.222	1	-6	-6	0	-0.5
Total	4	14	27	.341	47	42	37	1	0	371^2	417	8	71	86	12.2	3.29	99	.283	.323	26	.197	2	-7	-2	-5	-0.3
● JIM WILSON Wilson, James Alger b: 2/20/22, San Diego, Cal. d: 9/2/86, Newport Beach, Cal BR/TR, 6'1.5", 200 lbs. Deb: 4/18/45																										
1945	Bos-A	6	8	.429	23	21	8	2	0	144^1	121	7	88	50	13.1	3.30	103	.228	.339	13	.245	2	1	2	-2	0.1
1946	Bos-A	0	0	—	1	0	0	0	0	0^2	2	1	0	0	27.0	27.00	14	.500	.500	0	—	0	-2	-2	-0	-0.2
1948	StL-A	0	0	—	4	0	0	0	0	2^2	5	0	5	1	33.8	13.50	34	.417	.588	0	—	0	-3	-3	0	-0.2
1949	Phi-A	0	0	—	2	0	0	0	0	5	7	2	5	2	21.6	14.40	29	.350	.480	0	.000	-0	-6	-6	-0	-0.5
1951	Bos-N	7	7	.500	20	15	5	0	1	110	131	14	40	33	14.3	5.40	68	.294	.357	7	.179	0	-18	-21	-1	-2.1
1952	Bos-N	12	14	.462	33	33	14	0	0	234	234	19	90	104	12.6	4.23	85	.262	.333	14	.163	-0	-13	-16	-1	-1.8
1953	Mil-N	4	9	.308	20	18	5	0	0	114	107	16	43	71	12.1	4.34	90	.243	.315	6	.167	1	-1	-5	1	-0.3
1954	Mil-N☆	8	2	.800	27	19	6	4	0	127^2	129	12	36	52	12.0	3.52	106	.266	.323	7	.159	0	8	3	1	0.4
1955	Bal-A☆	12	18	.400	34	31	14	4	0	235^1	200	17	87	96	11.1	3.44	111	.228	.300	15	.169	-1	14	10	-0	0.8
1956	Bal-A	4	2	.667	7	7	1	0	0	48^1	49	5	16	31	12.5	5.03	78	.268	.333	4	.267	2	-5	-6	0	-0.3
	Chi-A	9	12	.429	28	21	6	3	0	159^2	149	15	70	82	12.5	4.06	101	.248	.329	19	.306	4	2	1	-0	0.5
	Yr	13	14	.481	35	28	7	3	0	208	198	20	86	113	12.4	4.28	95	.252	.327	23	.299	6	-3	-5	0	0.2
1957	Chi-A	15	8	.652	30	29	12	**5**	0	201^2	189	22	65	100	11.5	3.48	107	.249	.310	10	.147	-0	7	6	-2	0.4
1958	Chi-A	9	9	.500	28	23	4	1	1	155^2	156	21	63	70	12.7	4.10	89	.268	.341	4	.078	-3	-6	-8	-1	-1.2
Total	12	86	89	.491	257	217	75	19	2	1539	1479	151	608	692	12.4	4.01	93	.254	.327	99	.181	4	-21	-45	-5	-4.4
● JACK WILSON Wilson, John Francis "Black Jack" b: 4/12/12, Portland, Ore. BR/TR, 5'11", 210 lbs. Deb: 9/09/34																										
1934	Phi-A	0	1	.000	2	2	1	0	0	9	15	1	9	2	24.0	12.00	37	.405	.522	0	.000	-0	-8	-8	-0	-0.6
1935	Bos-A	3	4	.429	23	6	2	0	1	64	72	0	36	19	15.5	4.22	112	.290	.385	5	.313	2	2	4	1	0.7
1936	Bos-A	6	8	.429	43	9	2	0	3	136^1	152	4	86	74	15.8	4.42	120	.284	.384	11	.220	-0	9	13	0	1.2
1937	Bos-A	16	10	.615	51	21	14	1	7	221^1	209	13	119	137	13.5	3.70	128	.248	.343	14	.165	-3	23	26	1	2.2
1938	Bos-A	15	15	.500	37	27	11	3	1	194^2	200	16	91	96	13.5	4.30	115	.262	.342	15	.221	0	11	14	-1	1.2
1939	Bos-A	11	11	.500	36	22	6	0	2	177^1	198	10	75	80	13.9	4.67	101	.281	.351	10	.159	-4	-1	1	-0	-0.3
1940	Bos-A	12	6	.667	41	16	9	0	5	157^2	170	17	87	102	14.8	5.08	89	.270	.362	18	.273	4	-12	-10	-2	-0.7
1941	Bos-A	4	13	.235	27	12	4	1	1	116^1	140	7	70	55	16.6	5.03	83	.300	.397	7	.159	-1	-11	-11	2	-1.0
1942	Was-A	1	4	.200	12	6	1	0	0	42	57	2	23	18	17.4	6.64	55	.322	.403	2	.118	-1	-14	-14	-1	-1.5
	Det-A	0	0	—	9	0	0	0	0	13	20	3	5	7	17.3	4.85	81	.351	.403	0	.000	-0	-2	-1	0	-0.1
	Yr	1	4	.200	21	6	1	0	0	55	77	5	28	25	17.2	6.22	60	.328	.399	2	.111	-1	-16	-15	-0	-1.6
Total	9	68	72	.486	281	121	50	5	20	1131^2	1233	73	601	590	14.7	4.59	102	.276	.364	82	.199	-3	-4	13	1	1.1
● JOHN WILSON Wilson, John Nicodemus b: 6/15/1890, Boonsboro, Md. d: 9/23/54, Annapolis, Md. BR/TL, 6'1", 185 lbs. Deb: 6/11/13																										
1913	Was-A	0	0	—	3	0	0	0	0	4	4	0	3	1	15.8	4.50	66	.267	.389	0	—	0	-1	-1	0	0.0
● JOHN WILSON Wilson, John Samuel b: 4/25/03, Coal City, Ala. d: 8/27/80, Chattanooga, Tenn. BR/TR, 6'2", 164 lbs. Deb: 5/09/27																										
1927	Bos-A	0	2	.000	5	2	2	0	0	25^1	31	1	13	8	15.6	3.55	119	.326	.407	1	.111	-1	2	2	-0	0.1
1928	Bos-A	0	0	—	2	0	0	0	0	5	6	0	6	1	21.6	9.00	46	.333	.500	0	.000	-0	-3	-3	0	-0.2
Total	2	0	2	.000	7	2	2	0	0	30^1	37	1	19	9	16.6	4.45	94	.327	.424	1	.100	-1	-1	-1	-0	-0.1
● MAX WILSON Wilson, Max b: 6/3/16, Haw River, N.C. d: 1/2/77, Greensboro, N.C. BL/TL, 5'7", 160 lbs. Deb: 9/10/40																										
1940	Phi-N	0	0	—	3	0	0	0	0	7	16	1	2	3	23.1	12.86	30	.444	.474	0	.000	-0	-7	-7	0	-0.6
1946	Was-A	0	1	.000	9	0	0	0	0	12^2	16	1	9	8	17.8	7.11	47	.320	.424	0	.000	0	-5	-5	-0	-0.5
Total	2	0	1	.000	12	0	0	0	0	19^2	32	2	11	11	19.7	9.15	39	.372	.443	0	.000	-0	-12	-12	-0	-1.1
● PETE WILSON Wilson, Peter Alex b: 10/9/1885, Springfield, Mass. d: 6/5/57, St.Petersburg, Fla TL , Deb: 9/15/08																										
1908	NY-A	3	3	.500	6	6	4	1	0	39	27	0	33	28	14.1	3.46	72	.191	.349	1	.071	-1	-5	-4	-0	-0.6
1909	NY-A	6	5	.545	14	12	7	1	0	93^2	82	2	43	44	12.4	3.17	80	.230	.320	4	.118	-1	-7	-7	-1	-0.9
Total	2	9	8	.529	20	18	11	2	0	132^2	109	2	76	72	12.9	3.26	77	.219	.329	5	.104	-2	-12	-11	-1	-1.5

YEAR	TM/L	W	L	PCT	G	GS	CG	SH	SV	IP	H	HR	BB	SO	RAT	ERA	ERA+	OAV	OOB	BH	AVG	PB	PR	/A	PD	TPI
● EARL WILSON Wilson, Robert Earl (Name Changed From Wilson, Earl Lawrence) b: 10/2/34, Ponchatoula, La. BR/TR, 6'3", 216 lbs. Deb: 7/28/59																										
1959	Bos-A	1	1	.500	9	4	0	0	0	23^2	21	2	31	17	19.8	6.08	67	.241	.441	4	.500	2	-6	-5	0	-0.3
1960	Bos-A	3	2	.600	13	9	2	0	0	65	61	4	48	40	15.1	4.71	86	.247	.369	4	.174	-0	-6	-5	0	-0.5
1962	Bos-A	12	8	.600	31	28	4	1	0	191^1	163	21	111	137	13.2	3.90	106	.231	.340	12	.174	3	1	5	-1	0.7
1963	Bos-A	11	16	.407	37	34	6	3	0	210^2	184	18	105	123	12.4	3.76	101	.234	.325	15	.208	5	-3	1	1	0.7
1964	Bos-A	11	12	.478	33	31	5	0	0	202^1	213	37	73	166	12.8	4.49	86	.269	.332	15	.205	8	-20	-14	0	-0.6
1965	Bos-A	13	14	.481	36	36	8	1	0	230^2	221	27	77	164	11.8	3.98	94	.250	.313	14	.177	9	-13	-7	-1	0.1
1966	Bos-A	5	5	.500	15	14	5	1	0	100^2	88	14	36	67	11.3	3.84	99	.235	.306	8	.250	4	-5	-0	-0	0.3
	Det-A	13	6	.684	23	23	8	2	0	163^1	126	16	38	133	9.3	2.59	134	.213	.265	15	.234	9	15	16	2	3.1
	Yr	18	11	.621	38	37	13	3	0	264	214	30	74	200	10.0	3.07	117	.220	.278	23	.240	13	11	16	2	3.4
1967	Det-A	**22**	11	.667	39	38	12	0	0	264	216	34	92	184	10.6	3.27	100	.224	.294	20	.185	7	-1	-0	2	0.9
1968	*Det-A	13	12	.520	34	33	10	3	0	224^1	192	20	65	168	10.3	2.85	106	.231	.287	20	.227	10	3	4	1	1.8
1969	Det-A	12	10	.545	35	35	5	1	0	214^2	209	23	69	150	11.8	3.31	113	.256	.317	10	.132	-0	7	10	1	1.1
1970	Det-A	4	6	.400	18	16	4	1	0	96	87	15	32	74	11.3	4.41	85	.238	.303	6	.194	2	-7	-7	-0	-0.6
	SD-N	1	6	.143	15	9	0	0	0	65	82	5	19	29	14.3	4.85	82	.309	.360	1	.059	0	-6	-6	-1	-0.7
Total	11	121	109	.526	338	310	69	13	0	2051^2	1863	236	796	1452	11.8	3.69	99	.242	.315	144	.195	60	-39	-10	2	6.0
● ROY WILSON Wilson, Roy Edward "Lefty" b: 9/13/1896, Foster, Iowa d: 12/3/69, Clarion, Iowa BL/TL, 6', 175 lbs. Deb: 4/18/28																										
1928	Chi-A	0	0	—	1	0	0	0	0	3^1	2	0	3	2	13.5	0.00	—	.167	.333	0	.000	-0	1	2	0	0.2
● STEVE WILSON Wilson, Stephen Douglas b: 12/13/64, Victoria, B.C., Can. BL/TL, 6'4", 205 lbs. Deb: 9/16/88																										
1988	Tex-A	0	0	—	3	0	0	0	0	7^2	7	1	4	1	12.9	5.87	70	.259	.355	0	—	0	-2	-2	-0	-0.3
1989	*Chi-N	6	4	.600	53	8	0	0	2	85^2	83	6	31	65	12.1	4.20	89	.257	.324	1	.063	-1	-7	-4	0	-0.5
1990	Chi-N	4	9	.308	45	15	1	0	1	139	140	17	43	95	12.0	4.79	85	.259	.316	6	.162	1	-15	-11	-1	-1.2
1991	Chi-N	0	0	—	8	0	0	0	0	12^1	13	1	5	9	13.1	4.38	89	.277	.346	0	.000	-0	-1	-1	-0	-0.1
	LA-N	0	0	—	11	0	0	0	2	8^1	1	0	4	5	5.4	0.00	—	.042	.179	0	.000	-0	3	3	-0	0.3
	Yr	0	0	—	19	0	0	0	2	20^2	14	1	9	14	10.0	2.61	144	.194	.284	0	.000	-0	2	3	-1	0.2
1992	LA-N	2	5	.286	60	0	0	0	0	66^2	74	6	29	54	14.0	4.18	83	.282	.356	1	.333	0	-5	-5	-0	-0.6
Total	5	12	18	.400	180	23	1	0	5	319^2	318	31	116	229	12.3	4.39	87	.260	.326	8	.138	-0	-26	-20	-2	-2.4
● TREVOR WILSON Wilson, Trevor Kirk b: 6/7/66, Torrance, Cal. BL/TL, 6', 190 lbs. Deb: 9/05/88																										
1988	SF-N	0	2	.000	4	4	0	0	0	22	25	1	8	15	13.5	4.09	80	.298	.359	2	.286	0	-2	-2	-1	-0.2
1989	SF-N	2	3	.400	14	4	0	0	0	39^1	28	2	24	22	12.8	4.35	78	.207	.344	2	.250	1	-4	-4	-0	-0.3
1990	SF-N	8	7	.533	27	17	3	2	0	110^1	87	11	49	66	11.2	4.00	91	.218	.305	4	.138	0	-3	-4	2	-0.3
1991	SF-N	13	11	.542	44	29	2	1	0	202	173	13	77	139	11.4	3.56	100	.234	.310	12	.235	5	3	0	3	0.8
1992	SF-N	8	14	.364	26	26	1	1	0	154	152	18	64	88	13.0	4.21	80	.265	.345	3	.077	-1	-12	-15	1	-1.5
Total	5	31	37	.456	115	80	6	4	0	527^2	465	45	222	330	12.0	3.92	89	.241	.324	23	.172	5	-17	-25	5	-1.5
● WALTER WILSON Wilson, Walter Wood b: 11/24/13, Glenn, Ga. BL/TR, 6'4", 190 lbs. Deb: 4/17/45																										
1945	Det-A	1	3	.250	25	4	1	0	0	70^1	76	4	35	28	14.6	4.61	76	.284	.373	1	.053	-2	-10	-9	1	-1.0
● WILLY WILSON Wilson, William b: 1/7/1884, Columbus, Ohio d: 10/28/25, Seattle, Wash. BR/TR, Deb: 10/03/06																										
1906	Was-A	0	1	.000	1	1	1	0	0	7	3	0	2	1	7.7	2.57	102	.133	.235	0	.000	-0	0	0	0	0.0
● MUTT WILSON Wilson, William Clarence "Lank" b: 7/20/1896, Kiser, N.C. d: 8/31/62, Wildwood, Fla. BR/TR, 6'3", 167 lbs. Deb: 9/11/20																										
1920	Det-A	1	1	.500	3	2	1	0	0	13	12	0	5	4	11.8	3.46	108	.240	.309	1	.250	-0	0	0	-1	0.0
● BILL WILSON Wilson, William Donald b: 11/6/28, Central City, Neb. BR/TR, 6'2", 200 lbs. Deb: 9/24/50 ♦																										
1955	KC-A	0	0	—	1	0	0	0	0	1	1	0	1	1	18.0	0.00	—	.250	.400	61	.223	0	0	0	0	0.0
● BILL WILSON Wilson, William Harlan b: 9/21/42, Pomeroy, Ohio BR/TR, 6'2", 200 lbs. Deb: 4/08/69																										
1969	Phi-N	2	5	.286	37	0	0	0	6	62^1	53	6	36	48	13.0	3.32	107	.231	.338	0	.000	-0	2	2	-1	0.0
1970	Phi-N	1	0	1.000	37	0	0	0	0	58^1	57	5	33	41	13.9	4.78	83	.263	.360	1	.250	0	-5	-5	-0	-0.5
1971	Phi-N	4	6	.400	38	0	0	0	7	58^2	39	4	22	40	9.5	3.07	115	.188	.268	1	.100	-1	3	3	2	0.4
1972	Phi-N	1	1	.500	23	0	0	0	0	30	26	1	11	18	11.1	3.30	109	.234	.303	0	—	0	1	1	0	0.1
1973	Phi-N	1	3	.250	44	0	0	0	4	48^2	54	7	29	24	15.3	6.66	57	.293	.390	0	.000	-0	-16	-15	-0	-1.7
Total	5	9	15	.375	179	0	0	0	17	258	229	23	131	171	12.6	4.22	88	.241	.335	2	.083	-1	-16	-15	0	-1.7
● HOOKS WILTSE Wiltse, George Leroy b: 9/7/1880, Hamilton, N.Y. d: 1/21/59, Long Beach, N.Y. BR/TL, 6', 185 lbs. Deb: 4/21/04 FC																										
1904	NY-N	13	3	.813	24	16	14	2	3	164^2	150	8	61	105	11.8	2.84	96	.240	.313	15	.224	3	-2	-2	3	0.4
1905	NY-N	15	6	.714	32	19	18	1	4	197	158	5	61	120	10.2	2.47	119	.219	.284	20	.278	7	12	10	5	2.4
1906	NY-N	16	11	.593	38	26	21	4	6	249^1	227	3	58	125	10.4	2.27	115	.241	.288	18	.191	1	10	9	-1	1.1
1907	NY-N	13	12	.520	33	21	14	3	2	190^1	171	3	48	79	10.6	2.18	114	.241	.294	9	.134	-0	6	6	2	0.9
1908	NY-N	23	14	.622	44	38	30	7	2	330	266	4	73	118	9.5	2.24	108	.224	.274	26	.236	6	5	7	-0	1.4
1909	NY-N	20	11	.645	37	30	22	4	3	269^1	228	9	51	119	9.5	2.00	128	.233	.275	19	.200	2	18	17	-2	1.8
1910	NY-N	14	12	.538	36	30	18	2	2	235^1	232	4	52	88	10.9	2.72	109	.261	.303	13	.176	0	8	7	-3	0.3
1911	*NY-N	12	9	.571	30	24	11	4	0	187^1	177	7	39	92	10.5	3.27	103	.251	.292	13	.188	-1	3	2	0	0.1
1912	NY-N	9	6	.600	28	17	5	0	3	134	140	7	28	58	11.4	3.16	107	.273	.312	15	.326	4	4	3	2	0.8
1913	*NY-N	0	0	—	17	2	0	0	3	57^2	53	1	8	25	9.7	1.56	200	.237	.266	5	.208	0	11	10	0	1.1
1914	NY-N	1	1	.500	20	0	0	0	1	38	41	2	12	19	12.6	2.84	93	.289	.344	2	.667	1	-0	-1	0	0.1
1915	Bro-F	3	5	.375	18	3	1	0	5	59^1	49	1	7	17	8.8	2.28	133	.226	.257	1	.045	-2	5	5	-1	0.2
Total	12	139	90	.607	357	226	154	27	34	2112^1	1892	54	498	965	10.4	2.47	113	.241	.290	156	.210	21	79	74	5	10.6
● HAL WILTSE Wiltse, Harold James "Whitey" b: 8/6/03, Clay City, Ill. d: 11/2/83, Bunkie, La. BL/TL, 5'9", 168 lbs. Deb: 4/13/26																										
1926	Bos-A	8	15	.348	37	29	9	1	0	196^1	201	6	99	59	14.0	4.22	97	.273	.363	5	.085	-5	-4	-3	0	-0.7
1927	Bos-A	10	18	.357	36	29	13	1	1	219	276	5	76	47	14.6	5.10	83	.321	.379	16	.208	-2	-23	-21	1	-1.9
1928	Bos-A	0	2	.000	2	2	1	0	0	12	16	1	1	5	15.0	9.00	46	.314	.3[illegible]4	0	.000	-1	-7	-7	-0	-0.6
	StL-A	2	5	.286	26	5	0	0	0	72	93	4	35	23	16.4	5.25	80	.316	.395	5	.227	0	-10	-8	0	-0.8
	Yr	2	7	.222	28	7	1	0	0	84	109	5	36	28	15.9	5.79	72	.313	.382	5	.192	-1	-16	-15	-0	-1.4
1931	Phi-N	0	0	—	1	0	0	0	0	1	3	0	0	0	27.0	9.00	47	.600	.600	0	—	0	-1	-1	0	0.0
Total	4	20	40	.333	102	65	23	2	1	500^1	589	16	211	134	14.7	4.87	85	.303	.375	26	.160	-7	-44	-40	2	-4.0
● SNAKE WILTSE Wiltse, Lewis De Witt b: 12/5/1871, Bouckville, N.Y. d: 8/25/28, Harrisburg, Pa. BR/TL, Deb: 5/05/01 F																										
1901	Pit-N	1	4	.200	7	5	3	0	0	44^1	57	2	13	10	15.0	4.26	77	.310	.368	3	.158	-1	-5	-5	1	-0.5
	Phi-A	13	5	.722	19	19	18	2	0	166	185	1	35	40	12.3	3.58	105	.279	.321	25	.373	8	2	4	1	1.2
1902	Phi-A	8	8	.500	19	17	13	0	1	138	182	7	41	28	14.8	5.15	71	.318	.367	10	.175	-1	-24	-23	-1	-2.2
	Bal-A	7	11	.389	19	18	18	0	0	164	215	4	51	37	15.0	5.10	74	.316	.370	39	.295	6	-28	-24	-0	-1.7
	Yr	15	19	.441	38	35	31	0	1	302	397	11	92	65	14.8	5.13	73	.316	.366	49	.259	5	-52	-47	-1	-3.9
1903	NY-A	0	3	.000	4	3	2	0	1	25	35	1	6	6	15.1	5.40	58	.329	.371	2	.222	0	-7	-6	-0	-0.6
Total	3	29	31	.483	68	62	54	2	2	537^1	674	15	146	121	14.1	4.59	80	.305	.355	79	.278	12	-62	-55	0	-3.8
● FRED WINCHELL Winchell, Frederick Russell (b: Frederick Cook) b: 1/23/1882, Arlington, Mass. d: 8/8/58, Toronto, Ont., Can. TR, 5'8", Deb: 9/16/09																										
1909	Cle-A	0	3	.000	4	3	0	0	1	14^1	16	0	2	7	11.3	6.28	41	.296	.321	1	.200	0	-6	-6	-0	-0.6

YEAR	TM/L	W	L	PCT	G	GS	CG	SH	SV	IP	H	HR	BB	SO	RAT	ERA	ERA+	OAV	OOB	BH	AVG	PB	PR	/A	PD	TPI
● ED WINEAPPLE	Wineapple, Edward "Lefty" b: 8/10/05, Boston, Mass. BL/TL, 6', 210 lbs. Deb: 9/15/29																									
1929	Was-A	0	0	—	1	0	0	0	0	4	7	0	3	1	22.5	4.50	94	.467	.556	0	.000	-0	-0	-0	-0	-0.1
● RALPH WINEGARNER	Winegarner, Ralph Lee b: 10/29/09, Benton, Kan. d: 88, Benton, Kan. BR/TR, 6', 182 lbs. Deb: 9/20/30 C♦																									
1932	Cle-A	1	0	1.000	5	1	1	0	0	17^1	7	0	13	5	10.4	1.04	457	.123	.286	1	.143	-1	7	7	-0	0.6
1934	Cle-A	5	4	.556	22	6	4	0	0	78^1	91	1	39	32	15.2	5.51	82	.289	.371	10	.196	1	-9	-8	0	-0.7
1935	Cle-A	2	2	.500	25	4	2	0	0	67^1	89	10	29	41	15.9	5.75	78	.313	.379	26	.310	4	-10	-9	0	-0.4
1936	Cle-A	0	0	—	9	0	0	0	0	14^2	18	0	6	3	14.7	4.91	103	.295	.358	2	.125	-1	0	0	-0	-0.1
1949	StL-A	0	0	—	9	0	0	0	0	16^2	24	2	2	8	14.0	7.56	60	.329	.347	2	.400	2	-6	-6	-0	-0.4
Total	5	8	6	.571	70	11	7	0	0	194^1	229	13	89	89	14.9	5.33	86	.290	.364	51	.276	5	-18	-16	-1	-1.0
● JIM WINFORD	Winford, James Head "Cowboy" b: 10/9/09, Shelbyville, Tenn. d: 12/16/70, Miami, Okla. BR/TR, 6'1", 180 lbs. Deb: 9/10/32																									
1932	StL-N	1	1	.500	4	1	0	0	0	8^1	9	0	5	4	15.1	6.48	61	.273	.368	2	.667	1	-2	-2	0	-0.1
1934	StL-N	0	2	.000	5	1	0	0	0	12^2	17	0	6	3	17.8	7.82	54	.327	.417	0	.000	0	-5	-5	0	-0.4
1935	StL-N	0	0	—	2	1	0	0	0	11^1	13	1	5	7	14.3	3.97	103	.283	.353	0	.000	-0	0	0	-1	-0.1
1936	StL-N	11	10	.524	39	23	10	1	3	192	203	10	68	72	12.9	3.80	104	.269	.333	5	.085	-4	5	3	-4	-0.5
1937	StL-N	2	4	.333	16	4	0	0	0	46^1	56	2	27	17	16.1	5.83	68	.311	.401	1	.125	-1	-10	-10	-0	-1.0
1938	Bro-N	0	1	.000	2	1	0	0	0	5^2	9	1	4	4	20.6	11.12	35	.346	.433	0	.000	0	-5	-5	-0	-0.4
Total	6	14	18	.438	68	31	10	1	3	276^1	307	14	115	107	14.0	4.56	87	.281	.353	8	.108	-3	-17	-18	-5	-2.5
● ERNIE WINGARD	Wingard, Ernest James "Jim" b: 10/17/1900, Prattville, Ala. d: 1/17/77, Prattville, Ala. BL/TL, 6'2", 176 lbs. Deb: 5/01/24																									
1924	StL-A	13	12	.520	36	26	14	0	1	218	215	6	85	23	12.5	3.51	129	.262	.334	18	.234	2	17	24	-3	2.3
1925	StL-A	9	10	.474	32	18	8	0	0	145	183	10	77	20	16.3	5.52	85	.319	.403	15	.288	4	-18	-14	2	-0.7
1926	StL-A	5	8	.385	39	16	7	0	3	169	188	9	76	30	14.3	3.57	120	.290	.369	14	.230	1	8	14	3	1.8
1927	StL-A	2	13	.133	38	17	7	0	0	156^1	213	7	79	28	16.9	6.56	66	.340	.415	10	.179	2	-42	-38	2	-3.2
Total	4	29	43	.403	145	77	36	0	4	688^1	799	32	317	101	14.8	4.64	96	.299	.377	57	.232	8	-34	-14	4	0.2
● TED WINGFIELD	Wingfield, Frederick Davis b: 8/7/1899, Bedford, Va. d: 7/18/75, Johnson City, Tenn. BR/TR, 5'11", 168 lbs. Deb: 9/23/23																									
1923	Was-A	0	0	—	1	0	0	0	0	1	0	0	0	1	0.0	0.00	—	.000	.000	0	—	0	0	0	0	0.0
1924	Was-A	0	0	—	4	0	0	0	0	7	9	0	4	2	16.7	2.57	157	.300	.382	0	.000	-0	1	1	-0	0.1
	Bos-A	0	2	.000	4	3	2	0	0	25^2	23	0	8	4	10.9	2.45	178	.240	.298	3	.333	1	5	5	0	0.6
	Yr	0	2	.000	8	3	2	0	0	32^2	32	0	12	6	12.1	2.48	173	.254	.319	3	.273	0	6	7	-0	0.7
1925	Bos-A	12	19	.387	41	26	18	2	2	254^1	267	11	92	30	13.0	3.96	115	.278	.346	23	.245	1	12	16	7	2.3
1926	Bos-A	11	16	.407	43	20	9	1	3	190^2	220	11	50	30	12.8	4.44	92	.298	.344	15	.217	-0	-9	-8	2	-0.6
1927	Bos-A	1	7	.125	20	8	2	0	0	74^2	105	2	27	1	16.3	5.06	83	.357	.417	4	.222	0	-8	-7	2	-0.4
Total	5	24	44	.353	113	57	31	3	5	553^1	624	24	181	68	13.3	4.18	103	.294	.353	45	.234	1	3	9	11	2.0
● LAVE WINHAM	Winham, Lafayette Sharkey "Lefty" b: 10/23/1881, Brooklyn, N.Y. d: 9/12/51, Brooklyn, N.Y. BL/TL, 5'11", 200 lbs. Deb: 4/21/02																									
1902	Bro-N	0	0	—	1	0	0	0	0	3	4	0	2	1	18.0	0.00	—	.319	.413	0	.000	-0	1	1	0	0.1
1903	Pit-N	3	1	.750	5	4	3	1	0	36	33	0	21	22	13.5	2.25	144	.231	.329	1	.071	-1	4	4	-1	0.1
Total	2	3	1	.750	6	4	3	1	0	39	37	0	23	23	13.8	2.08	154	.238	.336	1	.063	-2	5	5	-1	0.2
● GEORGE WINKELMAN	Winkelman, George Edward b: 2/18/1865, Washington, D.C. d: 5/19/60, Washington, D.C. BL/TL, Deb: 8/04/1883 ♦																									
1886	Was-N	0	1	.000	1	1	0	0	0	6	12	0	5	4	25.5	10.50	31	.400	.486	1	.200	-0	-5	-5	-0	-0.4
● GEORGE WINN	Winn, George Benjamin "Breezy" or "Lefty" b: 10/26/1897, Perry, Ga. d: 11/1/69, Roberta, Ga. BL/TL, 5'11", 170 lbs. Deb: 4/29/19																									
1919	Bos-A	0	0	—	3	0	0	0	0	4^2	6	0	1	0	13.5	7.71	39	.353	.389	0	.000	-0	-2	-2	-0	-0.3
1922	Cle-A	1	2	.333	8	3	1	0	0	33^2	44	2	5	7	13.1	4.54	88	.317	.340	3	.333	1	-2	-2	0	-0.1
1923	Cle-A	0	0	—	1	0	0	0	0	2	0	0	1	0	4.5	0.00	—	.000	.143	0	—	0	1	1	-0	0.1
Total	3	1	2	.333	12	3	1	0	0	40^1	50	2	7	7	12.7	4.69	83	.309	.337	3	.300	1	-3	-4	-0	-0.3
● JIM WINN	Winn, James Francis b: 9/23/59, Stockton, Cal. BR/TR, 6'3", 210 lbs. Deb: 4/10/83																									
1983	Pit-N	0	0	—	7	0	0	0	0	11	12	2	6	3	14.7	7.36	50	.267	.353	0	—	0	-5	-4	0	-0.4
1984	Pit-N	1	0	1.000	9	0	0	0	1	18^2	19	2	9	11	13.5	3.86	93	.264	.346	0	.000	-0	-1	-1	0	-0.1
1985	Pit-N	3	6	.333	30	7	0	0	0	75^2	77	4	31	22	13.1	5.23	68	.266	.341	2	.111	-0	-14	-14	2	-1.3
1986	Pit-N	3	5	.375	50	3	0	0	3	88	85	9	38	70	12.8	3.58	107	.258	.338	1	.063	-1	1	2	1	0.3
1987	Chi-A	4	6	.400	56	0	0	0	6	94	95	10	62	44	15.6	4.79	96	.271	.390	0	—	0	-3	-2	3	-0.1
1988	Min-A	1	0	1.000	9	0	0	0	0	21	33	4	10	9	18.4	6.00	68	.355	.417	0	—	0	-5	-5	0	-0.6
Total	6	12	17	.414	161	10	0	0	10	308^1	321	31	156	159	14.2	4.67	85	.272	.362	3	.086	-1	-26	-23	6	-2.2
● TOM WINSETT	Winsett, John Thomas "Long Tom" b: 11/24/09, McKenzie, Tenn. BL/TR, 6'2", 190 lbs. Deb: 4/20/30 ♦																									
1937	Bro-N	0	0	—	1	0	0	0	0	1	3	0	2	0	45.0	18.00	22	.600	.714	83	.237	0	-2	-2	-0	-0.1
● HANK WINSTON	Winston, Henry Rudolph b: 6/15/04, Youngville, N.C. d: 2/4/74, Jacksonville, Fla. BL/TR, 6'3.5", 226 lbs. Deb: 9/30/33																									
1933	Phi-A	0	0	—	1	0	0	0	0	6^2	7	0	6	2	17.6	6.75	63	.280	.419	0	.000	-0	-2	-2	0	-0.2
1936	Bro-N	1	3	.250	14	0	0	0	0	32^1	40	2	16	8	15.9	6.12	67	.301	.380	1	.091	-1	-8	-7	-0	-0.8
Total	2	1	3	.250	15	0	0	0	0	39	47	2	22	10	16.2	6.23	67	.297	.387	1	.071	-1	-9	-9	0	-1.0
● GEORGE WINTER	Winter, George Lovington "Sassafras" b: 4/27/1878, New Providence, Pa d: 5/26/51, Franklin Lakes, N.J. TR , 5'8", 155 lbs. Deb: 6/15/01																									
1901	Bos-A	16	12	.571	28	28	26	1	0	241	234	4	66	63	11.4	2.80	126	.252	.304	19	.190	-4	23	20	-1	1.4
1902	Bos-A	11	9	.550	20	20	18	0	0	168^1	149	2	53	51	11.2	2.99	119	.238	.305	10	.164	-2	11	11	-0	0.8
1903	Bos-A	9	8	.529	24	19	14	0	0	178^1	182	4	37	64	11.4	3.08	99	.264	.308	7	.106	-4	-2	-1	-1	-0.6
1904	Bos-A	8	4	.667	20	16	12	1	0	135^2	126	4	27	31	10.5	2.32	115	.247	.293	5	.116	-2	4	5	-2	0.2
1905	Bos-A	16	17	.485	35	27	24	2	0	264^1	249	5	54	119	10.5	2.96	91	.250	.291	24	.261	3	-9	-8	0	-0.5
1906	Bos-A	6	18	.250	29	22	18	1	2	207^2	215	8	38	72	11.1	4.12	67	.270	.307	17	.246	2	-33	-32	-0	-3.1
1907	Bos-A	12	15	.444	35	27	21	4	1	256^2	198	2	61	88	9.2	2.07	125	.215	.267	21	.223	0	14	15	-2	1.6
1908	Bos-A	4	14	.222	22	17	8	0	0	147^2	150	3	34	55	11.5	3.05	81	.274	.321	9	.184	-1	-11	-10	-0	-1.2
	*Det-A	1	5	.167	7	6	5	0	1	56^1	49	0	7	25	9.4	1.60	152	.240	.276	2	.111	-1	5	5	1	0.6
	Yr	5	19	.208	29	23	13	0	1	204	199	3	41	80	10.7	2.65	93	.263	.304	11	.164	-2	-6	-4	1	-0.6
Total	8	83	102	.449	220	182	146	9	4	1656	1552	32	377	568	10.7	2.87	101	.250	.297	114	.193	-9	2	7	-4	-0.8
● CLARENCE WINTERS	Winters, Clarence John b: 9/7/1898, Detroit, Mich. d: 6/29/45, Detroit, Mich. Deb: 8/28/24																									
1924	Bos-A	0	1	.000	4	2	0	0	0	7	22	0	4	3	33.4	20.57	21	.512	.553	1	.333	0	-13	-13	-0	-1.1
● JESSE WINTERS	Winters, Jesse Franklin "Buck" or "T-Bone" b: 12/22/1893, Stephenville, Tex. d: 6/5/86, Abilene, Texas BR/TR, 6'1", 165 lbs. Deb: 5/03/19																									
1919	NY-N	1	2	.333	16	2	0	0	3	28	39	1	13	6	17.7	5.46	51	.339	.420	0	.000	-0	-8	-8	-0	-0.9
1920	NY-N	0	0	—	21	0	0	0	0	46^1	37	1	28	14	13.4	3.50	86	.233	.361	0	.000	-1	-2	-3	1	-0.3
1921	Phi-N	5	10	.333	18	14	10	0	0	114	142	4	28	22	13.7	3.63	116	.310	.355	5	.128	-3	2	8	2	0.6
1922	Phi-N	6	6	.500	34	9	4	0	2	138^1	176	8	56	29	15.4	5.33	87	.319	.386	11	.256	0	-19	-10	1	-0.9
1923	Phi-N	1	6	.143	21	6	1	0	1	78^1	116	7	39	23	18.3	7.35	63	.348	.423	4	.160	-1	-29	-24	-1	-2.3
Total	5	13	24	.351	110	31	15	0	6	405	510	21	164	94	15.4	5.04	83	.316	.385	20	.171	-5	-56	-39	2	-3.8
● ALAN WIRTH	Wirth, Alan Lee b: 12/8/56, Mesa, Ariz. BR/TR, 6'4", 190 lbs. Deb: 4/09/78																									
1978	Oak-A	5	6	.455	16	14	2	1	0	81^1	72	6	34	31	12.1	3.43	106	.252	.337	0	—	0	3	2	-1	0.2
1979	Oak-A	1	0	1.000	5	1	0	0	0	12	14	2	8	7	17.3	6.00	67	.298	.411	0	—	0	-2	-3	0	0.2
1980	Oak-A	0	0	—	2	0	0	0	0	2	3	0	0	1	13.5	4.50	84	.333	.333	0	—	0	-0	-0	-0	0.7

YEAR TM/L	W	L	PCT	G	GS	CG	SH	SV	IP	H	HR	BB	SO	RAT	ERA	ERA+	OAV	OOB	BH	AVG	PB	PR	/A	PD	TPI
Total 3	6	6	.500	23	15	2	1	0	95^{1}	89	8	42	39	12.7	3.78	98	.260	.348	0	—	0	1	-1	-1	1.1
● ARCHIE WISE Wise, Archibald Edwin b: 7/31/12, Waxahachie, Tex. d: 2/2/78, Dallas, Tex. BR/TR, 6', 165 lbs. Deb: 7/24/32																									
1932 Chi-A	0	0	—	2	0	0	0	0	7^{1}	8	1	5	2	17.2	4.91	88	.258	.378	0	.000	-1	-0	-0	0	-0.1
● RICK WISE Wise, Richard Charles b: 9/13/45, Jackson, Mich. BR/TR, 6'2", 195 lbs. Deb: 4/18/64																									
1964 Phi-N	5	3	.625	25	8	0	0	0	69	78	7	25	39	13.8	4.04	86	.277	.342	5	.294	2	-4	-4	-2	-0.4
1966 Phi-N	5	6	.455	22	13	3	0	0	99^{1}	100	5	24	58	11.5	3.71	97	.262	.311	0	.000	-3	-1	-1	-1	-0.6
1967 Phi-N	11	11	.500	36	25	6	3	0	181^{1}	177	8	45	111	11.2	3.28	104	.259	.308	11	.208	3	2	3	1	0.7
1968 Phi-N	9	15	.375	30	30	7	1	0	182	210	12	37	97	12.5	4.55	66	.292	.332	14	.241	7	-32	-31	1	-2.6
1969 Phi-N	15	13	.536	33	31	14	4	0	220	215	17	61	144	11.4	3.23	110	.257	.309	20	.270	7	9	8	1	1.7
1970 Phi-N	13	14	.481	35	34	5	1	0	220^{1}	253	15	65	113	13.1	4.17	96	.287	.338	15	.200	4	-3	-4	1	0.1
1971 Phi-N☆	17	14	.548	38	37	17	4	0	272^{1}	261	20	70	155	11.1	2.88	123	.254	.304	23	.237	10	18	20	0	3.4
1972 StL-N	16	16	.500	35	35	20	2	0	269	250	16	71	142	10.8	3.11	109	.251	.301	16	.172	1	10	9	2	1.3
1973 StL-N★	16	12	.571	35	34	14	5	0	259	259	18	59	144	11.2	3.37	108	.257	.300	17	.193	6	8	8	-1	1.4
1974 Bos-A	3	4	.429	9	9	1	0	0	49	47	2	16	25	11.8	3.86	100	.251	.314	0	—	0	-1	-0	-0	-0.1
1975 *Bos-A	19	12	.613	35	35	17	1	0	255^{1}	262	34	72	141	11.9	3.95	103	.263	.315	0	—	0	-5	4	-1	0.1
1976 Bos-A	14	11	.560	34	34	11	4	0	224^{1}	218	18	48	93	10.8	3.53	111	.255	.296	0	—	0	-0	9	2	1.2
1977 Bos-A	11	5	.688	26	20	4	2	0	128^{1}	151	19	28	85	12.8	4.77	94	.291	.332	0	—	0	-10	-4	1	-0.3
1978 Cle-A	9	19	.321	33	31	9	1	0	211^{2}	226	22	59	106	12.2	4.34	86	.275	.325	0	—	0	-14	-14	-0	-1.4
1979 Cle-A	15	10	.600	34	34	9	2	0	231^{2}	229	24	68	108	11.6	3.73	114	.256	.309	0	—	0	12	13	4	1.8
1980 SD-N	6	8	.429	27	27	1	0	0	154^{1}	172	14	37	59	12.2	3.67	93	.285	.326	8	.138	-1	-1	-4	-1	-0.6
1981 SD-N	4	8	.333	18	18	0	0	0	98	116	10	19	27	12.4	3.77	86	.296	.328	1	.040	-1	-3	-6	0	-0.7
1982 SD-N	0	0	—	1	0	0	0	0	2	3	0	0	0	13.5	9.00	38	.333	.333	0	—	0	-1	-1	0	-0.1
Total 18	188	181	.509	506	455	138	30	0	3127	3227	261	804	1647	11.7	3.69	100	.267	.315	130	.195	34	-15	2	9	4.9
● ROY WISE Wise, Roy Ogden b: 11/18/24, Springfield, Ill. BB/TR, 6'2", 170 lbs. Deb: 5/13/44																									
1944 Pit-N	0	0	—	2	0	0	0	0	3	4	0	3	1	21.0	9.00	41	.333	.467	0	—	0	-2	-2	-0	-0.2
● BILL WISE Wise, William E. b: 3/15/1861, Washington, D.C. d: 5/5/40, Washington, D.C. Deb: 5/02/1882																									
1882 Bal-a	1	2	.333	3	3	3	0	0	26	30	1	4	9	11.8	2.77	99	.271	.296	2	.100	-1	-0	-0	-0	-0.1
1884 Was-U	23	18	.561	50	41	34	4	0	364^{1}	383	5	60	268	10.9	3.04	98	.253	.281	79	.233	2	-1	-3	5	0.3
1886 Was-N	0	1	.000	1	1	0	0	0	3	6	0	2	0	24.0	9.00	37	.400	.471	0	.000	-0	-2	-2	-0	-0.2
Total 3	24	21	.533	54	45	37	4	0	393^{1}	419	6	66	277	11.1	3.07	96	.255	.284	81	.224	1	-3	-5	4	0.0
● JACK WISNER Wisner, John Henry b: 11/5/1899, Grand Rapids, Mich. d: 12/15/81, Jackson, Mich. BR/TR, 6'3", 195 lbs. Deb: 9/12/19																									
1919 Pit-N	1	0	1.000	4	1	1	0	0	18^{2}	12	0	7	4	9.6	0.96	313	.185	.274	0	.000	-1	4	4	-0	0.4
1920 Pit-N	1	3	.250	17	2	1	0	0	44^{2}	46	1	10	13	11.5	3.43	94	.274	.318	0	.000	-1	-1	-1	1	-0.1
1925 NY-N	0	0	—	25	0	0	0	0	40^{1}	33	4	14	13	10.9	3.79	106	.228	.304	0	.000	-1	2	1	0	0.0
1926 NY-N	2	2	.500	5	3	2	0	0	28	21	4	10	5	10.0	3.54	106	.208	.279	2	.200	-0	1	1	-0	0.0
Total 4	4	5	.444	51	6	4	0	0	131^{2}	112	9	41	35	10.7	3.21	111	.234	.300	2	.065	-3	6	5	1	0.3
● WHITEY WISTERT Wistert, Francis Michael b: 2/20/12, Chicago, Ill. d: 4/23/85, Painesville, Ohio BR/TR, 6'4", 210 lbs. Deb: 9/11/34																									
1934 Cin-N	0	1	.000	2	1	0	0	0	8	5	1	5	1	11.3	1.13	363	.185	.313	0	.000	-0	3	3	-0	0.2
● WITHEROW Witherow Deb: 7/01/1875																									
1875 Was-n	0	1	.000	1	1	0	0	0	1	5	0	0		45.0	*18.00*	15	.625	.625	0	.000	-0	-2	-2		-0.1
● ROY WITHERUP Witherup, Foster Leroy b: 7/26/1886, N.Washington, Pa. d: 12/23/41, New Bethlehem, Pa. BR/TR, 6', 185 lbs. Deb: 5/14/06																									
1906 Bos-N	0	3	.000	8	3	3	0	0	46	59	2	19	14	15.5	6.26	43	.322	.389	2	.133	-1	-19	-18	-1	-1.9
1908 Was-A	2	4	.333	6	6	4	0	0	48^{1}	51	0	8	31	11.2	2.98	77	.264	.297	3	.167	-1	-3	-4	0	-0.4
1909 Was-A	1	5	.167	12	8	5	0	0	68	79	1	20	26	13.1	4.24	57	.306	.356	1	.053	-2	-13	-14	-2	-1.8
Total 3	3	12	.200	26	17	12	0	0	162^{1}	189	3	47	71	13.2	4.44	55	.298	.348	6	.115	-3	-35	-36	-2	-4.1
● GEORGE WITT Witt, George Adrian "Red" b: 11/9/33, Long Beach, Cal. BR/TR, 6'3", 200 lbs. Deb: 9/21/57																									
1957 Pit-N	0	1	.000	1	1	0	0	0	1^{1}	4	1	5	1	60.8	40.50	9	.500	.692	0	—	0	-5	-5	0	-0.4
1958 Pit-N	9	2	.818	18	15	5	3	0	106	78	2	59	81	11.8	1.61	240	.209	.320	6	.154	-1	28	27	-0	2.7
1959 Pit-N	0	7	.000	15	11	0	0	0	50^{2}	58	7	32	30	16.2	6.93	56	.293	.394	0	.000	-1	-17	-17	-0	-1.8
1960 *Pit-N	1	2	.333	10	6	0	0	0	30	33	3	12	15	13.5	4.20	89	.300	.369	0	.000	-1	-1	-1	-0	-0.3
1961 Pit-N	0	1	.000	9	1	0	0	0	15^{2}	17	5	5	9	12.6	6.32	63	.274	.328	1	.500	1	-4	-4	-1	-0.4
1962 LA-A	1	1	.500	5	2	0	0	0	10	15	4	5	10	18.0	8.10	48	.349	.417	1	.333	0	-5	-5	-0	-0.4
Hou-N	0	2	.000	8	2	0	0	0	15^{1}	20	2	9	10	17.6	7.04	53	.339	.435	1	.250	0	-5	-6	0	-0.5
Total 6	11	16	.407	66	38	5	3	0	229	225	24	127	156	14.0	4.32	89	.263	.361	9	.130	-2	-10	-12	-2	-1.1
● MIKE WITT Witt, Michael Atwater b: 7/20/60, Fullerton, Cal. BR/TR, 6'7", 192 lbs. Deb: 4/11/81																									
1981 Cal-A	8	9	.471	22	21	7	1	0	129	123	9	47	75	12.6	3.28	111	.251	.330	0	—	0	5	5	-1	0.4
1982 *Cal-A	8	6	.571	33	26	5	1	0	179^{2}	177	8	47	85	11.6	3.51	116	.260	.314	0	—	0	11	11	-0	1.1
1983 Cal-A	7	14	.333	43	19	2	0	5	154	173	14	75	77	14.8	4.91	82	.293	.379	0	—	0	-14	-15	0	-1.4
1984 Cal-A	15	11	.577	34	34	9	2	0	246^{2}	227	17	84	196	11.5	3.47	114	.244	.310	0	—	0	14	14	-1	1.4
1985 Cal-A	15	9	.625	35	35	6	1	0	250	228	22	98	180	11.9	3.56	115	.243	.317	0	—	0	16	15	0	1.6
1986 *Cal-A☆	18	10	.643	34	34	14	3	0	269	218	22	73	208	9.8	2.84	144	.221	.277	0	—	0	40	38	2	4.3
1987 Cal-A☆	16	14	.533	36	36	10	0	0	247	252	34	84	192	12.4	4.01	107	.261	.323	0	—	0	12	8	-1	1.0
1988 Cal-A	13	16	.448	34	34	12	2	0	249^{2}	263	14	87	133	12.8	4.15	93	.272	.335	0	—	0	-5	-8	-0	-0.6
1989 Cal-A	9	15	.375	33	33	5	0	0	220	252	26	48	123	12.4	4.54	84	.292	.330	0	—	0	-16	-18	4	-1.4
1990 Cal-A	0	3	.000	10	0	0	0	1	20^{1}	19	1	13	14	14.6	1.77	216	.250	.367	0	—	0	5	5	1	0.6
NY-A	5	6	.455	16	16	2	1	0	96^{2}	87	8	34	60	11.6	4.47	89	.240	.312	0	—	0	-6	-5	0	-0.5
Yr	5	9	.357	26	16	2	1	1	117	106	9	47	74	12.1	4.00	99	.240	.319	0	—	0	-1	-1	1	0.1
1991 NY-A	0	1	.000	2	2	0	0	0	5^{1}	8	1	1	0	15.2	10.13	41	.320	.346	0	—	0	-4	-4	0	-0.3
Total 11	114	114	.500	332	290	72	11	6	2067^{1}	2027	176	691	1343	12.1	3.80	105	.257	.321	0	—	0	59	46	4	6.2
● BOBBY WITT Witt, Robert Andrew b: 5/11/64, Arlington, Mass. BR/TR, 6'2", 205 lbs. Deb: 4/10/86																									
1986 Tex-A	11	9	.550	31	31	0	0	0	157^{2}	130	18	143	174	15.8	5.48	78	.223	.379	0	—	0	-23	-21	0	-2.1
1987 Tex-A	8	10	.444	26	25	1	0	0	143	114	10	140	160	16.2	4.91	91	.219	.388	0	.000	0	-7	-7	0	-0.6
1988 Tex-A	8	10	.444	22	22	13	2	0	174^{1}	134	13	101	148	12.2	3.92	104	.216	.326	0	—	0	1	3	-1	0.1
1989 Tex-A	12	13	.480	31	31	5	1	0	194^{1}	182	14	114	166	13.8	5.14	77	.248	.351	0	—	0	-27	-25	-0	-2.5
1990 Tex-A	17	10	.630	33	32	7	1	0	222	197	12	110	221	12.6	3.36	116	.238	.330	0	—	0	13	14	-1	1.3
1991 Tex-A	3	7	.300	17	16	1	1	0	88^{2}	84	4	74	82	16.1	6.09	66	.254	.392	0	—	0	-20	-20	-1	-2.0
1992 Tex-A	9	13	.409	25	25	0	0	0	161^{1}	152	14	95	100	13.9	4.46	86	.254	.358	0	—	0	-9	-12	-0	-1.1
*Oak-A	1	1	.500	6	6	0	0	0	31^{2}	31	2	19	25	14.2	3.41	111	.265	.368	0	—	0	2	1	0	0.2
Yr	10	14	.417	31	31	0	0	0	193	183	16	114	125	13.8	4.29	89	.252	.354	0	—	0	-8	-10	-0	-0.9
Total 7	69	73	.486	191	188	27	5	0	1173	1024	87	796	1076	14.1	4.57	89	.236	.357	0	.000	0	-70	-67	-3	-6.7
● JOHNNIE WITTIG Wittig, John Carl "Hans" b: 6/16/14, Baltimore, Md. BR/TR, 6', 180 lbs. Deb: 8/04/38																									
1938 NY-N	2	3	.400	13	6	2	0	0	39^{1}	41	4	26	14	15.3	4.81	78	.263	.368	0	.000	-1	-4	-5	-1	-0.7
1939 NY-N	0	2	.000	5	2	1	0	0	16^{2}	18	0	14	4	17.8	7.56	52	.281	.418	0	.000	-1	-7	-7	0	-0.7
1941 NY-N	3	5	.375	25	9	0	0	0	85^{1}	111	5	45	47	16.6	5.59	66	.319	.398	5	.200	-0	-19	-18	-2	-1.9

YEAR TM/L	W	L	PCT	G	GS	CG	SH	SV	IP	H	HR	BB	SO	RAT	ERA	ERA+	OAV	OOB	BH	AVG	PB	PR	/A	PD	TPI
1943 NY-N	5	15	.250	40	22	4	1	4	164	172	14	76	56	13.6	4.23	82	.273	.352	5	.098	-3	-15	-14	-3	-2.1
1949 Bos-A	0	0	—	1	0	0	0	0	2	2	0	2	0	18.0	9.00	48	.286	.444	0	—	0	-1	-1	0	-0.1
Total 5	10	25	.286	84	39	7	1	4	307^1	344	23	163	121	14.9	4.89	73	.286	.372	10	.110	-6	-46	-44	-6	-5.5
● **MARK WOHLERS** Wohlers, Mark Edward b: 1/23/70, Holyoke, Mass. BR/TR, 6'4", 207 lbs. Deb: 8/17/91																									
1991 *Atl-N	3	1	.750	17	0	0	0	2	19^2	17	1	13	13	14.6	3.20	121	.239	.372	0	.000	-0	1	1	0	0.1
1992 *Atl-N	1	2	.333	32	0	0	0	4	35^1	28	0	14	17	11.0	2.55	147	.235	.321	0	.000	-0	4	5	0	0.5
Total 2	4	3	.571	49	0	0	0	6	55	45	1	27	30	12.3	2.78	136	.237	.341	0	.000	-0	5	6	0	0.6
● **PETE WOJEY** Wojey, Peter Paul b: 12/1/19, Stowe, Pa. BR/TR, 5'11", 185 lbs. Deb: 7/02/54																									
1954 Bro-N	1	1	.500	14	1	0	0	1	27^2	24	3	14	21	13.0	3.25	126	.242	.348	0	.000	-0	3	3	1	0.3
1956 Det-A	0	0	—	2	0	0	0	0	4	2	0	1	1	6.8	2.25	183	.167	.231	0	—	0	1	1	0	0.1
1957 Det-A	0	0	—	2	0	0	0	0	1^1	1	0	0	0	6.8	0.00	—	.200	.200	0	—	0	1	1	0	0.1
Total 3	1	1	.500	18	1	0	0	1	33	27	3	15	22	12.0	3.00	136	.233	.331	0	.000	-0	4	4	1	0.5
● **ED WOJNA** Wojna, Edward David b: 8/20/60, Bridgeport, Conn. BR/TR, 6'1", 185 lbs. Deb: 6/16/85																									
1985 SD-N	2	4	.333	15	7	0	0	0	42	53	6	19	18	16.1	5.79	61	.312	.391	2	.167	-0	-10	-11	0	-1.1
1986 SD-N	2	2	.500	7	7	1	0	0	39	42	2	16	19	13.6	3.23	113	.268	.339	2	.143	-0	2	2	-1	0.1
1987 SD-N	0	3	.000	5	3	0	0	0	18^1	25	2	6	13	15.7	5.89	67	.333	.390	0	.000	-1	-4	-4	1	-0.4
1989 Cle-A	0	1	.000	9	3	0	0	0	33	31	0	14	10	12.3	4.09	97	.254	.331	0	—	0	-1	-0	1	0.0
Total 4	4	10	.286	36	20	1	0	0	132^1	151	10	55	60	14.4	4.62	81	.288	.361	4	.129	-1	-13	-13	1	-1.4
● **ERNIE WOLF** Wolf, Ernest Adolph b: 2/2/1889, Newark, N.J. d: 5/23/64, Atlantic Highlands, N.J. BR/TR, 5'11", 174 lbs. Deb: 9/10/12																									
1912 Cle-A	0	0	—	1	0	0	0	0	5^2	8	0	4	1	19.1	6.35	54	.348	.444	0	.000	-0	-2	-2	-0	-0.2
● **WALLY WOLF** Wolf, Walter Beck b: 1/5/42, Los Angeles, Cal. BR/TR, 6'0.5", 191 lbs. Deb: 9/27/69																									
1969 Cal-A	0	0	—	2	0	0	0	0	2^1	3	1	3	2	23.1	11.57	30	.333	.500	0	—	0	-2	-2	-0	-0.2
1970 Cal-A	0	0	—	4	0	0	0	0	5^1	3	1	4	5	11.8	5.06	71	.176	.333	0	—	0	-1	-1	-0	-0.1
Total 2	0	0	—	6	0	0	0	0	7^2	6	2	7	7	15.3	7.04	51	.231	.394	0	—	0	-3	-3	-0	-0.3
● **LEFTY WOLF** Wolf, Walter Francis b: 6/10/1900, Hartford, Conn. d: 9/25/71, New Orleans, La. BR/TL, 5'10", 163 lbs. Deb: 7/04/21																									
1921 Phi-A	0	0	—	8	0	0	0	0	15	15	0	16	11	19.8	7.20	62	.273	.452	1	.250	-0	-5	-5	-0	-0.4
● **JIMMY WOLF** Wolf, William Van Winkle "Chicken" b: 5/12/1862, Louisville, Ky. d: 5/16/03, Louisville, Ky. BR/TR, 5'9", 190 lbs. Deb: 5/02/1882 M♦																									
1882 Lou-a	0	0	—	1	0	0	0	0	6	11	0	3	1	21.0	9.00	28	.371	.429	95	.299	0	-4	-4	-0	-0.4
1885 Lou-a	0	0	—	1	0	0	0	0	1	1	0	0	1	9.0	9.00	36	.200	.200	141	.292	0	-1	-1	0	0.0
1886 Lou-a	0	0	—	1	0	0	0	0	3	7	0	0	0	21.0	15.00	24	.350	.350	148	.272	0	-4	-4	0	-0.3
Total 3	0	0	—	3	0	0	0	0	10	19	0	3	2	19.8	10.80	27	.348	.382	1440	.290	1	-9	-9	-0	-0.7
● **CHUCK WOLFE** Wolfe, Charles Hunt b: 2/15/1897, Wolfsburg, Pa. d: 11/27/57, Schellsburg, Pa. BL/TR, 5'7", 175 lbs. Deb: 8/02/23																									
1923 Phi-A	0	0	—	3	0	0	0	0	9^2	6	1	8	1	13.0	3.72	110	.194	.359	1	.333	0	0	0	-0	0.0
● **ED WOLFE** Wolfe, Edward Anthony b: 1/2/29, Los Angeles, Cal. BR/TR, 6'3", 185 lbs. Deb: 4/19/52																									
1952 Pit-N	0	0	—	3	0	0	0	0	3^2	7	1	5	1	31.9	7.36	54	.467	.619	0	—	0	-1	-1	0	-0.1
● **BARNEY WOLFE** Wolfe, Wilbert Otto b: 1/9/1876, Independence, Pa. d: 2/27/53, N.Charleroi, Pa. BR/TR, 6'1", Deb: 4/24/03																									
1903 NY-A	6	9	.400	20	16	12	1	0	148^1	143	1	26	48	10.6	2.97	105	.253	.293	4	.075	-5	-0	2	-0	-0.3
1904 NY-A	0	3	.000	7	3	2	0	0	33^2	31	1	4	8	9.6	3.21	85	.246	.274	0	.000	-1	-2	-2	0	-0.3
Was-A	6	9	.400	17	16	13	2	0	126^2	131	0	22	44	11.6	3.27	81	.268	.313	5	.119	-2	-9	-9	-2	-1.3
Yr	6	12	.333	24	19	15	2	0	160^1	162	1	26	52	11.1	3.26	82	.263	.303	5	.096	-3	-12	-10	-2	-1.6
1905 Was-A	9	13	.409	28	23	17	1	1	182	162	1	37	52	10.2	2.57	103	.240	.287	8	.127	-2	2	2	-2	-0.2
1906 Was-A	0	3	.000	4	3	2	0	0	20	17	0	10	8	13.0	4.05	65	.233	.341	2	.286	0	-3	-3	0	-0.3
Total 4	21	37	.362	76	61	46	4	1	510^2	484	3	99	160	10.8	2.96	94	.251	.297	19	.109	-9	-13	-10	-4	-2.4
● **BILL WOLFE** Wolfe, William b: Jersey City, N.J. Deb: 9/10/02																									
1902 Phi-N	0	1	.000	1	1	1	0	0	9	11	0	4	3	16.0	4.00	70	.301	.385	1	.333	0	-1	-1	0	-0.1
● **ROGER WOLFF** Wolff, Roger Francis b: 4/10/11, Evansville, Ill. BR/TR, 6'0.5", 208 lbs. Deb: 9/20/41																									
1941 Phi-A	0	2	.000	2	2	2	0	0	17	15	0	4	2	10.1	3.18	132	.231	.275	1	.200	-0	2	2	-0	0.2
1942 Phi-A	12	15	.444	32	25	15	2	3	214^1	206	16	69	94	11.7	3.32	114	.249	.309	6	.088	-3	8	11	0	0.8
1943 Phi-A	10	15	.400	41	26	13	2	6	221	232	11	72	91	12.5	3.54	96	.274	.334	9	.122	-4	-6	-4	-3	-1.1
1944 Was-A	4	15	.211	33	21	5	0	2	155	186	9	60	73	14.6	4.99	65	.295	.362	12	.218	1	-27	-30	2	-2.7
1945 Was-A†	20	10	.667	33	29	21	4	2	250	200	7	53	108	**9.1**	2.12	146	.215	**.258**	9	.107	-4	35	27	-1	2.4
1946 Was-A	5	8	.385	21	17	6	0	0	122	115	8	30	50	11.1	2.58	130	.249	.302	4	.103	-1	12	10	-1	0.9
1947 Cle-A	0	0	—	7	2	0	0	0	16	15	1	10	5	15.2	3.94	88	.259	.386	0	.000	-0	-0	-1	1	0.0
Pit-N	1	4	.200	13	6	1	0	0	30	49	4	18	7	20.4	8.70	49	.368	.447	0	.000	-1	-15	-15	-1	-1.5
Total 7	52	69	.430	182	128	63	8	13	1025^1	1018	56	316	430	11.9	3.41	100	.258	.316	41	.122	-12	8	1	-3	-1.0
● **MELLIE WOLFGANG** Wolfgang, Meldon John "Red" b: 3/20/1890, Albany, N.Y. d: 6/30/47, Albany, N.Y. BR/TR, 5'9", 160 lbs. Deb: 4/18/14																									
1914 Chi-A	9	5	.643	24	11	9	2	0	119^1	96	0	32	50	9.7	1.89	142	.219	.272	7	.175	-0	11	11	4	1.7
1915 Chi-A	2	2	.500	17	2	0	0	0	53^2	39	0	12	21	8.7	1.84	161	.211	.263	2	.118	-1	7	7	-1	0.5
1916 Chi-A	4	6	.400	27	14	6	1	0	127	103	2	42	36	10.4	1.98	139	.228	.296	9	.225	0	12	11	1	1.4
1917 Chi-A	0	0	—	5	0	0	0	0	17^2	18	1	6	3	12.7	5.09	52	.305	.379	0	.000	-1	-5	-5	-0	-0.6
1918 Chi-A	0	1	.000	4	0	0	0	0	8^1	12	0	3	1	16.2	5.40	51	.333	.385	1	.500	0	-2	-2	0	-0.2
Total 5	15	14	.517	77	27	15	3	0	326	268	3	95	111	10.1	2.18	127	.229	.289	19	.184	-1	23	21	4	2.8
● **HARRY WOLTER** Wolter, Harry Meigs b: 7/11/1884, Monterey, Cal. d: 7/7/70, Palo Alto, Cal. BL/TL, 5'10", 175 lbs. Deb: 5/14/07 ♦																									
1907 Pit-N	0	0	—	1	0	0	0	0	2	3	0	2	0	22.5	4.50	54	.333	.455	0	.000	-0	-0	-0	-0	-0.1
StL-N	0	2	.000	3	3	1	0	0	23	27	1	18	8	18.4	4.30	58	.318	.448	16	.340	1	-5	-5	-1	-0.5
Yr	0	2	.000	4	3	1	0	0	25	30	1	20	8	18.7	4.32	58	.319	.448	16	.333	1	-5	-5	-1	-0.6
1909 Bos-A	4	4	.500	11	6	0	0	0	59	66	0	30	21	15.3	3.51	71	.303	.397	30	.246	2	-7	-7	-1	-0.6
Total 2	4	6	.400	15	9	1	0	0	84	96	1	50	29	16.3	3.75	67	.308	.413	515	.270	3	-12	-12	-2	-1.2
● **RYNIE WOLTERS** Wolters, Reinder Albertus b: 12/18/1842, U.S.A. d: 1/3/17, Newark, N.J. TR , 6', 165 lbs. Deb: 5/18/1871																									
1871 Mut-n	16	16	.500	**32**	32	**31**	**1**	0	**283**	345	7	39	22	12.2	3.43	110	**.263**	.285	51	.370	18	25	11		1.9
1872 Cle-n	3	6	.333	12	8	5	0	0	76^1	119	3	7	4	14.9	5.19	70	.302	.314	16	.232	-0	-12	-13		-0.9
1873 Res-n	0	1	.000	1	1	1	0	0	9	13	0	1	1	14.0	0.00	—	.220	.233	0	.000	-1	3	3		0.2
Total 3 n	19	23	.452	45	41	37	1	0	368^1	477	10	47	27	12.8	3.71	90	.271	.290	67	.318	17	-19	-15		1.2
● **DOOLEY WOMACK** Womack, Horace Guy b: 8/25/39, Columbia, S.C. BL/TR, 6', 170 lbs. Deb: 4/14/66																									
1966 NY-A	7	3	.700	42	1	0	0	4	75	52	6	23	50	9.4	2.64	126	.198	.270	1	.200	0	7	6	2	0.9
1967 NY-A	5	6	.455	65	0	0	0	18	97	80	6	35	57	10.9	2.41	130	.230	.306	4	.286	1	9	8	4	1.4
1968 NY-A	3	7	.300	45	0	0	0	2	61^2	53	6	29	27	12.1	3.21	90	.244	.336	1	.200	0	-2	-2	2	0.0
1969 Hou-N	2	1	.667	30	0	0	0	0	51^1	49	1	20	32	12.6	3.51	101	.259	.340	1	.167	-0	0	0	2	0.2
Sea-A	2	1	.667	9	0	0	0	0	14^1	15	0	3	8	11.3	2.51	145	.273	.310	0	.000	-0	2	2	0	0.2
1970 Oak-A	0	0	—	2	0	0	0	0	3	4	2	1	3	15.0	15.00	24	.308	.357	0	—	0	-4	-4	0	-0.3

YEAR TM/L	W	L	PCT	G	GS	CG	SH	SV	IP	H	HR	BB	SO	RAT	ERA	ERA+	OAV	OOB	BH	AVG	PB	PR	/A	PD	TPI
Total 5	19	18	.514	193	1	0	0	24	302^1	253	21	111	177	11.1	2.95	110	.233	.310	7	.226	1	12	9	11	2.4

● SPADES WOOD Wood, Charles Asher b: 1/13/09, Spartanburg, S.C. d: 5/18/86, Wichita, Kan. BL/TL, 5'10.5", 150 lbs. Deb: 8/16/30

YEAR TM/L	W	L	PCT	G	GS	CG	SH	SV	IP	H	HR	BB	SO	RAT	ERA	ERA+	OAV	OOB	BH	AVG	PB	PR	/A	PD	TPI
1930 Pit-N	4	3	.571	9	7	4	2	0	58	61	4	32	23	14.4	5.12	97	.270	.360	5	.250	1	-1	-1	-2	-0.2
1931 Pit-N	2	6	.250	15	10	2	0	0	64	69	2	46	33	16.3	6.05	64	.273	.387	5	.227	1	-16	-16	-0	-1.4
Total 2	6	9	.400	24	17	6	2	0	122	130	6	78	56	15.4	5.61	78	.271	.375	10	.238	1	-16	-17	-2	-1.6

● GEORGE WOOD Wood, George A. "Dandy" b: 11/9/1858, Boston, Mass. d: 4/4/24, Harrisburg, Pa. BL/TR, 5'10.5", 175 lbs. Deb: 5/01/1880 MU♦

YEAR TM/L	W	L	PCT	G	GS	CG	SH	SV	IP	H	HR	BB	SO	RAT	ERA	ERA+	OAV	OOB	BH	AVG	PB	PR	/A	PD	TPI
1883 Det-N	0	0	—	1	0	0	0	0	5	8	0	3	0	19.8	7.20	43	.348	.423	133	.302	0	-2	-2	0	-0.1
1885 Det-N	0	0	—	1	0	0	0	0	4	5	0	1	1	13.5	0.00	—	.333	.375	105	.290	0	1	1	-0	0.1
1888 Phi-N	0	0	—	2	0	0	0	**2**	2	3	0	1	0	18.0	4.50	66	.300	.364	99	.229	0	-0	-0	0	0.0
1889 Phi-N	0	0	—	1	0	0	0	0	1	2	0	0	2	18.0	18.00	24	.403	.403	106	.251	0	-2	-2	0	-0.1
Total 4	0	0	—	5	0	0	0	2	12	18	0	5	3	17.3	5.25	59	.340	.397	1467	.273	1	-3	-3	0	-0.1

● JOHN WOOD Wood, John B. b: 1871, 5'7", 142 lbs. Deb: 5/09/1896

YEAR TM/L	W	L	PCT	G	GS	CG	SH	SV	IP	H	HR	BB	SO	RAT	ERA	ERA+	OAV	OOB	BH	AVG	PB	PR	/A	PD	TPI
1896 StL-N	0	0	—	1	0	0	0	0	0	1	0	2	0	—	∞	—	1.000	1.000	0	—	0	-1	-1	0	-0.1

● JOE WOOD Wood, Joseph "Smokey Joe" (b: Howard Ellsworth Wood)
b: 10/25/1889, Kansas City, Mo. d: 7/27/85, West Haven, Conn BR/TR, 5'11", 180 lbs. Deb: 8/24/08 F♦

YEAR TM/L	W	L	PCT	G	GS	CG	SH	SV	IP	H	HR	BB	SO	RAT	ERA	ERA+	OAV	OOB	BH	AVG	PB	PR	/A	PD	TPI
1908 Bos-A	1	1	.500	6	2	1	1	0	22^2	14	0	16	11	12.3	2.38	103	.161	.298	0	.000	-1	0	0	-0	-0.1
1909 Bos-A	11	7	.611	24	19	13	4	0	160^2	121	1	43	88	9.5	2.18	114	.209	.270	9	.164	-0	5	6	-4	0.2
1910 Bos-A	12	13	.480	35	17	14	3	0	198^2	155	3	56	145	10.0	1.68	152	.220	.287	18	.261	5	19	19	2	3.1
1911 Bos-A	23	17	.575	44	33	25	5	3	275^2	226	2	76	231	10.2	2.02	162	.223	.284	23	.261	8	40	38	2	5.1
1912 *Bos-A	**34**	5	**.872**	43	38	**35**	**10**	1	344	267	2	82	258	9.4	1.91	178	.216	.272	36	.290	11	54	57	8	8.5
1913 Bos-A	11	5	.688	23	18	12	1	2	145^2	120	0	61	123	11.7	2.29	129	.229	.319	15	.268	4	10	11	4	2.1
1914 Bos-A	9	3	.750	18	14	11	1	1	113^1	94	1	34	67	10.2	2.62	103	.229	.288	6	.140	-0	2	1	1	0.2
1915 Bos-A	15	5	**.750**	25	16	10	3	2	157^1	120	1	44	63	9.4	**1.49**	187	.216	.275	14	.259	4	25	23	1	3.1
1917 Cle-A	0	1	.000	5	1	0	0	1	15^2	17	0	7	2	13.8	3.45	82	.309	.387	0	.000	-1	-1	-1	0	-0.2
1919 Cle-A	0	0	—	1	0	0	0	1	0^2	0	0	0	0	0.0	0.00	—	.000	.000	49	.255	0	0	0	0	0.0
1920 *Cle-A	0	0	—	1	0	0	0	0	2	4	0	2	1	27.0	22.50	17	.444	.545	37	.270	0	-4	-4	0	-0.3
Total 11	116	57	.671	225	158	121	28	11	1436^1	1138	10	421	989	10.1	2.03	146	.220	.285	553	.283	31	150	150	14	21.7

● JOE WOOD Wood, Joseph Frank b: 5/20/16, Shoshola, Pa. BR/TR, 6', 190 lbs. Deb: 5/01/44 F

YEAR TM/L	W	L	PCT	G	GS	CG	SH	SV	IP	H	HR	BB	SO	RAT	ERA	ERA+	OAV	OOB	BH	AVG	PB	PR	/A	PD	TPI
1944 Bos-A	0	1	.000	3	1	0	0	0	9^2	13	0	3	5	14.9	6.52	52	.317	.364	0	.000	-0	-3	-3	0	-0.3

● PETE WOOD Wood, Peter Burke b: 2/1/1857, Hamilton, Ont., Can. d: 3/15/23, Chicago, Ill. TR, 5'7", 185 lbs. Deb: 7/15/1885 F

YEAR TM/L	W	L	PCT	G	GS	CG	SH	SV	IP	H	HR	BB	SO	RAT	ERA	ERA+	OAV	OOB	BH	AVG	PB	PR	/A	PD	TPI
1885 Buf-N	8	15	.348	24	22	21	0	0	198^2	235	8	66	38	13.6	4.44	67	.280	.332	23	.221	-1	-36	-32	-1	-3.0
1889 Phi-N	1	1	.500	3	2	2	0	0	19	28	0	3	8	14.7	5.21	83	.332	.355	0	.000	-1	-3	-2	-0	-0.3
Total 2	9	16	.360	27	24	23	0	0	217^2	263	8	69	46	13.7	4.51	69	.285	.334	23	.205	-2	-38	-34	-1	-3.3

● WILBUR WOOD Wood, Wilbur Forrester b: 10/22/41, Cambridge, Mass. BR/TL, 6', 180 lbs. Deb: 6/30/61

YEAR TM/L	W	L	PCT	G	GS	CG	SH	SV	IP	H	HR	BB	SO	RAT	ERA	ERA+	OAV	OOB	BH	AVG	PB	PR	/A	PD	TPI
1961 Bos-A	0	0	—	6	1	0	0	0	13	14	2	7	7	14.5	5.54	75	.269	.356	0	.000	-0	-2	-2	-0	-0.3
1962 Bos-A	0	0	—	1	1	0	0	0	7^2	6	0	3	3	10.6	3.52	117	.214	.290	0	.000	-0	0	1	0	0.0
1963 Bos-A	0	5	.000	25	6	0	0	0	64^2	67	10	13	28	11.6	3.76	101	.270	.314	0	.000	-2	-1	0	-1	-0.2
1964 Bos-A	0	0	—	4	0	0	0	0	5^2	13	1	3	5	25.4	17.47	22	.433	.485	0	.000	-0	-9	-9	0	-0.8
Pit-N	0	2	.000	3	2	1	0	0	17^1	16	0	11	7	15.1	3.63	97	.246	.372	0	.000	-0	-0	-0	-1	-0.1
1965 Pit-N	1	1	.500	34	1	0	0	0	51^1	44	3	16	29	10.7	3.16	111	.237	.300	0	.000	-1	2	2	-1	0.1
1967 Chi-A	4	2	.667	51	8	0	0	4	95^1	95	2	28	47	11.7	2.45	126	.260	.315	1	.063	-0	8	7	-1	0.6
1968 Chi-A	13	12	.520	**88**	2	0	0	16	159	127	8	33	74	9.2	1.87	162	.222	.268	2	.091	-1	**20**	**20**	-0	2.3
1969 Chi-A	10	11	.476	**76**	0	0	0	15	119^2	113	13	40	73	11.7	3.01	128	.248	.313	0	.000	-2	8	11	1	1.1
1970 Chi-A	9	13	.409	**77**	0	0	0	21	121^2	118	7	36	85	11.5	2.81	139	.258	.315	2	.111	-1	12	15	2	1.7
1971 Chi-A☆	22	13	.629	44	42	22	7	1	334	272	21	62	210	9.2	1.91	**188**	.222	.264	5	.052	-5	**57**	**62**	2	**7.0**
1972 Chi-A★	**24**	17	.585	49	49	20	8	0	**376^2**	325	28	74	193	9.7	2.51	125	.235	.277	17	.136	-2	23	26	4	3.2
1973 Chi-A	**24**	20	.545	49	48	21	4	0	**359^1**	381	25	91	199	12.0	3.46	114	.270	.318	0	—	0	14	20	1	2.1
1974 Chi-A☆	20	19	.513	42	42	22	1	0	320^1	305	27	80	169	11.1	3.60	104	.254	.305	0	—	0	1	5	3	0.6
1975 Chi-A	16	20	.444	43	43	14	2	0	291^1	309	26	92	140	12.5	4.11	94	.272	.329	0	—	0	-11	-8	1	-0.7
1976 Chi-A	4	3	.571	7	7	5	1	0	56^1	51	3	11	31	9.9	2.24	159	.242	.279	0	—	0	8	8	1	1.0
1977 Chi-A	7	8	.467	24	18	5	1	0	122^2	139	10	50	42	14.6	4.99	82	.293	.373	0	—	0	-13	-12	2	-1.0
1978 Chi-A	10	10	.500	28	27	4	0	0	168	187	23	74	69	14.1	5.20	73	.285	.361	0	—	0	-27	-26	2	-2.4
Total 17	164	156	.512	651	297	114	24	57	2684	2582	209	724	1411	11.3	3.24	112	.254	.308	27	.084	-14	92	120	15	14.2

● GENE WOODBURN Woodburn, Eugene Stewart b: 8/20/1886, Bellaire, Ohio d: 1/18/61, Sandusky, Ohio BR/TR, 6', 175 lbs. Deb: 7/27/11

YEAR TM/L	W	L	PCT	G	GS	CG	SH	SV	IP	H	HR	BB	SO	RAT	ERA	ERA+	OAV	OOB	BH	AVG	PB	PR	/A	PD	TPI
1911 StL-N	1	5	.167	11	6	1	0	0	38^1	22	0	40	23	16.0	5.40	63	.167	.382	1	.167	1	-9	-9	1	-0.6
1912 StL-N	1	4	.200	20	5	1	0	0	48^1	60	0	42	25	19.7	5.59	61	.306	.438	0	.000	-2	-12	-12	-1	-1.3
Total 2	2	9	.182	31	11	2	0	0	86^2	82	0	82	48	18.1	5.50	62	.250	.414	1	.053	-0	-20	-20	0	-1.9

● FRED WOODCOCK Woodcock, Fred Wayland b: 5/17/1868, Winchendon, Mass. d: 8/11/43, Ashburnham, Mass. BL/TL, 6'2", 190 lbs. Deb: 5/17/1892

YEAR TM/L	W	L	PCT	G	GS	CG	SH	SV	IP	H	HR	BB	SO	RAT	ERA	ERA+	OAV	OOB	BH	AVG	PB	PR	/A	PD	TPI
1892 Pit-N	1	2	.333	5	4	3	0	0	33	42	1	17	8	16.6	3.55	93	.298	.381	3	.200	0	-1	-1	0	-0.1

● GEORGE WOODEND Woodend, George Anthony b: 12/9/17, Hartford, Conn. d: 2/6/80, Hartford, Conn. BR/TR, 6', 200 lbs. Deb: 4/22/44

YEAR TM/L	W	L	PCT	G	GS	CG	SH	SV	IP	H	HR	BB	SO	RAT	ERA	ERA+	OAV	OOB	BH	AVG	PB	PR	/A	PD	TPI
1944 Bos-N	0	0	—	3	0	0	0	0	2	5	0	5	0	45.0	13.50	28	.556	.714	0	—	0	-2	-2	0	-0.2

● HAL WOODESHICK Woodeshick, Harold Joseph b: 8/24/32, Wilkes-Barre, Pa. BR/TL, 6'3", 200 lbs. Deb: 9/14/56

YEAR TM/L	W	L	PCT	G	GS	CG	SH	SV	IP	H	HR	BB	SO	RAT	ERA	ERA+	OAV	OOB	BH	AVG	PB	PR	/A	PD	TPI
1956 Det-A	0	2	.000	2	2	0	0	0	5^1	12	1	3	1	25.3	13.50	30	.444	.500	0	—	0	-6	-6	0	-0.5
1958 Cle-A	6	6	.500	14	9	3	0	0	71^2	71	4	25	27	12.8	3.64	100	.265	.341	4	.167	-1	1	0	3	0.2
1959 Was-A	2	4	.333	31	3	0	0	0	61	58	2	36	30	14.0	3.69	106	.253	.357	0	.000	-1	1	2	1	0.1
1960 Was-A	4	5	.444	41	14	1	0	4	115	131	7	60	46	15.2	4.70	83	.289	.375	2	.069	-2	-11	-10	2	-1.0
1961 Was-A	3	2	.600	7	6	1	0	0	40^1	38	3	24	24	14.5	4.02	100	.257	.371	2	.125	-1	0	-0	1	0.0
Det-A	1	1	.500	12	2	0	0	0	18^1	25	3	17	13	20.6	7.85	52	.316	.438	0	.000	-0	-8	-8	1	-0.7
Yr	4	3	.571	19	8	1	0	0	58^2	63	6	41	37	16.0	5.22	77	.273	.382	2	.100	-1	-8	-8	2	-0.7
1962 Hou-N	5	16	.238	31	26	2	1	0	139^1	161	3	54	82	14.1	4.39	85	.290	.356	3	.081	-1	-7	-10	0	-1.1
1963 Hou-N★	11	9	.550	55	0	0	0	10	114	75	3	42	94	9.7	1.97	160	.186	.273	3	.130	-0	17	15	3	2.0
1964 Hou-N	2	9	.182	61	0	0	0	**23**	78^1	73	3	32	58	12.9	2.76	124	.249	.337	0	.000	-0	7	6	2	0.7
1965 Hou-N	3	4	.429	27	0	0	0	3	32^1	27	3	18	22	12.5	3.06	110	.227	.328	1	.167	-0	2	1	1	0.2
StL-N	3	2	.600	51	0	0	0	15	59^2	47	1	27	37	11.5	1.81	212	.221	.314	0	.000	-1	11	13	2	1.6
Yr	6	6	.500	78	0	0	0	18	92	74	4	45	59	11.8	2.25	163	.223	.319	1	.071	-1	13	15	2	1.8
1966 StL-N	2	1	.667	59	0	0	0	4	70^1	57	5	23	30	10.4	1.92	187	.224	.290	1	.200	0	13	13	3	1.8
1967 *StL-N	2	1	.667	36	0	0	0	2	41^2	41	2	28	20	15.6	5.18	63	.252	.371	0	.000	-0	-8	-9	1	-0.9
Total 11	44	62	.415	427	62	7	1	61	847^1	816	40	389	484	13.2	3.56	102	.254	.342	16	.092	-7	13	7	18	2.4

● DAN WOODMAN Woodman, Daniel Courtenay "Cocoa" b: 7/8/1893, Danvers, Mass. d: 12/14/62, Danvers, Mass. BR/TR, 5'8", 160 lbs. Deb: 7/10/14

YEAR TM/L	W	L	PCT	G	GS	CG	SH	SV	IP	H	HR	BB	SO	RAT	ERA	ERA+	OAV	OOB	BH	AVG	PB	PR	/A	PD	TPI
1914 Buf-F	0	0	—	13	0	0	0	1	33^2	30	0	11	13	11.2	2.41	137	.246	.313	1	.143	-0	3	3	-1	0.2
1915 Buf-F	0	0	—	5	1	0	0	0	15^1	14	0	9	1	13.5	4.11	76	.246	.348	1	.250	0	-2	-2	1	-0.1
Total 2	0	0	—	18	1	0	0	1	49	44	0	20	14	11.9	2.94	110	.246	.325	2	.182	-0	1	2	0	0.1

YEAR TM/L	W	L	PCT	G	GS	CG	SH	SV	IP	H	HR	BB	SO	RAT	ERA	ERA+	OAV	OOB	BH	AVG	PB	PR	/A	PD	TPI

● CLARENCE WOODS Woods, Clarence Cofield b: 6/11/1892, Woods Ridge, Ohio County, Ind. d: 7/2/69, Rising Sun, Ind. BR/TR, 6′5″, 230 lbs. Deb: 8/08/14

| 1914 Ind-F | 0 | 0 | — | 2 | 0 | 0 | 0 | 1 | 2 | 1 | 0 | 2 | 1 | 13.5 | 4.50 | 77 | .167 | .375 | 0 | — | 0 | -0 | -0 | 0 | 0.0 |

● PINKY WOODS Woods, George Rowland b: 5/22/15, Waterbury, Conn. d: 10/30/82, Los Angeles, Cal. BR/TR, 6′5″, 225 lbs. Deb: 6/20/43

1943 Bos-A	5	6	.455	23	12	2	0	1	100²	109	6	55	32	14.8	4.92	67	.284	.375	8	.222	-0	-18	-18	-0	-1.9
1944 Bos-A	4	8	.333	38	20	5	1	0	170²	171	4	88	56	14.0	3.27	104	.266	.360	7	.146	-1	3	2	2	0.3
1945 Bos-A	4	7	.364	24	12	3	0	2	107¹	108	3	63	36	14.4	4.19	81	.268	.368	9	.214	1	-10	-9	1	-0.8
Total 3	13	21	.382	85	44	10	1	3	378²	388	13	206	124	14.3	3.97	85	.272	.366	24	.190	-1	-25	-25	3	-2.4

● JOHN WOODS Woods, John Fulton "Abe" b: 1/18/1898, Princeton, W.Va. d: 10/4/46, Norfolk, Va. BR/TR, 6′, 175 lbs. Deb: 9/16/24

| 1924 Bos-A | 0 | 0 | — | 1 | 0 | 0 | 0 | 0 | 1 | 0 | 0 | 3 | 0 | 27.0 | 0.00 | — | .000 | .500 | 0 | — | 0 | 0 | 0 | 0 | 0.0 |

● WALT WOODS Woods, Walter Sydney b: 4/28/1875, Rye, N.H. d: 10/30/51, Portsmouth, N.H. BR/TR, 5′9.5″, 165 lbs. Deb: 4/20/1898

1898 Chi-N	9	13	.409	27	22	18	3	0	215	224	7	59	26	12.3	3.14	114	.266	.322	27	.175	-4	11	11	1	0.6
1899 Lou-N	9	13	.409	26	21	17	0	0	186¹	216	9	37	21	12.6	3.28	117	.290	.329	19	.151	-3	12	12	5	1.2
1900 Pit-N	0	0	—	1	0	0	0	0	3	9	0	1	1	30.0	21.00	17	.513	.539	0	.000	-0	-6	-6	-0	-0.4
Total 3	18	26	.409	54	43	35	3	0	404¹	449	16	97	48	12.5	3.34	111	.280	.328	46	.164	-7	17	17	5	1.4

● DICK WOODSON Woodson, Richard Lee b: 3/30/45, Oelwein, Iowa BR/TR, 6′5″, 207 lbs. Deb: 4/08/69

1969 *Min-A	7	5	.583	44	10	2	0	1	110¹	99	11	49	66	12.3	3.67	99	.237	.322	2	.074	-1	-1	-0	1	-0.1
1970 *Min-A	1	2	.333	21	0	0	0	0	30²	29	2	19	22	14.1	3.82	98	.244	.348	0	.000	-0	-0	-0	0	0.0
1972 Min-A	14	14	.500	36	36	9	3	0	251²	193	19	101	150	10.6	2.72	118	.211	.291	7	.080	-5	10	14	1	1.0
1973 Min-A	10	8	.556	23	23	4	2	0	141¹	137	12	68	53	13.2	3.95	100	.254	.339	0	—	0	-2	0	-2	-0.2
1974 Min-A	1	1	.500	5	4	0	0	0	27	30	5	4	12	11.7	4.33	87	.273	.304	0	—	0	-2	-2	1	-0.3
NY-A	1	2	.333	8	3	0	0	0	28	34	6	12	12	15.1	5.79	60	.301	.373	0	—	0	-7	-7	-1	-0.6
Yr	2	3	.400	13	7	0	0	0	55	64	11	16	24	13.3	5.07	71	.286	.336	0	—	0	-9	-9	-0	-0.9
Total 5	34	32	.515	137	76	15	5	2	589	522	55	253	315	12.0	3.47	102	.236	.317	9	.077	-7	-2	5	-0	-0.2

● KERRY WOODSON Woodson, Walter Browne b: 5/18/69, Jacksonville, Fla. BR/TR, 6′2″, 190 lbs. Deb: 7/19/92

| 1992 Sea-A | 0 | 1 | .000 | 8 | 1 | 0 | 0 | 0 | 13² | 12 | 0 | 11 | 6 | 16.5 | 3.29 | 121 | .245 | .403 | 0 | — | 0 | 1 | 1 | 0 | 0.1 |

● FRANK WOODWARD Woodward, Frank Russell b: 5/17/1894, New Haven, Conn. d: 6/11/61, New Haven, Conn. BR/TR, 5′10″, 175 lbs. Deb: 4/17/18

1918 Phi-N	0	0	—	2	0	0	0	0	6	6	0	4	4	15.0	6.00	50	.250	.357	1	.333	-2	-2	-2	-0	-0.2
1919 Phi-N	6	9	.400	17	12	6	0	0	100²	109	5	35	27	13.3	4.74	68	.291	.359	6	.207	1	-20	-17	-2	-1.9
StL-N	3	5	.375	17	7	2	0	1	72	65	1	28	18	11.8	2.63	106	.248	.323	1	.048	-2	2	1	-0	-0.1
Yr	9	14	.391	34	19	8	0	1	172²	174	6	63	45	12.4	3.86	79	.271	.337	7	.140	-1	-18	-16	-2	-2.0
1921 Was-A	0	0	—	3	1	0	0	0	10²	11	0	3	4	11.8	5.91	70	.282	.333	1	.333	-2	-2	-2	-0	-0.2
1922 Was-A	0	0	—	1	0	0	0	0	2¹	3	0	3	2	23.1	11.57	33	.375	.545	0	.000	-0	-2	-2	-0	-0.2
1923 Chi-A	0	1	.000	2	1	0	0	0	2	5	0	1	0	27.0	13.50	29	.500	.545	0	—	0	-2	-2	-0	-0.2
Total 5	9	15	.375	42	21	8	0	1	193²	199	6	74	55	13.0	4.23	74	.277	.350	9	.158	-1	-26	-24	-2	-2.8

● BOB WOODWARD Woodward, Robert John b: 9/28/62, Hanover, N.H. BR/TR, 6′3″, 185 lbs. Deb: 9/05/85

1985 Bos-A	1	0	1.000	5	2	0	0	0	26²	17	0	9	16	9.5	1.69	254	.168	.250	0	—	0	7	8	-1	0.4
1986 Bos-A	2	3	.400	9	6	0	0	0	35²	46	4	11	14	14.6	5.30	79	.313	.365	0	—	0	-4	-5	0	-0.4
1987 Bos-A	1	1	.500	9	6	0	0	0	37	53	6	15	15	16.8	7.05	64	.338	.399	0	—	0	-11	-10	-1	-1.0
1988 Bos-A	0	0	—	1	0	0	0	0	0²	2	0	1	0	40.5	13.50	30	.500	.600	0	—	0	-1	-1	-0	-0.1
Total 4	4	4	.500	24	14	0	0	0	100	118	10	36	45	14.2	5.04	86	.289	.352	0	—	0	-9	-8	-1	-1.1

● FLOYD WOOLDRIDGE Wooldridge, Floyd Lewis b: 8/25/28, Jerico Springs, Mo BR/TR, 6′1″, 185 lbs. Deb: 5/01/55

| 1955 StL-N | 2 | 4 | .333 | 18 | 8 | 2 | 0 | 0 | 57² | 64 | 9 | 27 | 14 | 14.4 | 4.84 | 84 | .281 | .359 | 4 | .222 | 0 | -5 | -5 | -1 | -0.6 |

● JUNIOR WOOTEN Wooten, Earl Hazwell b: 1/16/24, Pelzer, S.C. BR/TL, 5′11″, 160 lbs. Deb: 9/16/47 ♦

| 1948 Was-A | 0 | 0 | — | 1 | 0 | 0 | 0 | 0 | 2 | 2 | 0 | 2 | 1 | 18.0 | 9.00 | 48 | .250 | .400 | 66 | .256 | 0 | -1 | -1 | 0 | -0.1 |

● FRED WORDEN Worden, Fred B. b: 9/4/1894, St.Louis, Mo. d: 11/9/41, St.Louis, Mo. BR/TR, Deb: 9/28/14

| 1914 Phi-A | 0 | 0 | — | 1 | 0 | 0 | 0 | 0 | 2 | 8 | 0 | 0 | 1 | 36.0 | 18.00 | 15 | .615 | .615 | 0 | .000 | -0 | -3 | -3 | 0 | -0.3 |

● HOGE WORKMAN Workman, Harry Hall b: 9/25/1899, Huntington, W.Va. d: 5/20/72, Ft.Myers, Fla. BR/TR, 5′11″, 170 lbs. Deb: 6/27/24

| 1924 Bos-A | 0 | 0 | — | 11 | 0 | 0 | 0 | 0 | 18 | 25 | 2 | 11 | 7 | 19.0 | 8.50 | 51 | .325 | .422 | 0 | .000 | -0 | -9 | -8 | P0 | -0.8 |

● RALPH WORKS Works, Ralph Talmadge "Judge" b: 3/16/1888, Payson, Ill. d: 8/8/41, Pasadena, Cal. BL/TR, 6′2.5″, 185 lbs. Deb: 5/01/09

1909 *Det-A	4	1	.800	16	4	4	0	2	64	62	0	17	31	11.3	1.97	128	.261	.313	1	.059	-2	4	4	-1	0.2
1910 Det-A	3	6	.333	18	10	5	0	1	85²	73	1	39	36	12.2	3.57	74	.235	.328	8	.267	1	-10	-9	-1	-0.9
1911 Det-A	11	5	.688	30	15	9	3	0	167¹	173	6	67	68	13.2	3.87	89	.268	.342	9	.148	-3	-10	-8	-4	-1.5
1912 Det-A	5	10	.333	27	16	9	1	1	157	185	1	66	64	14.8	4.24	77	.308	.383	8	.143	-3	-16	-17	-1	-1.9
Cin-N	1	1	.500	3	1	1	0	0	9²	4	0	5	5	9.3	2.79	120	.133	.278	1	.200	-0	1	1	-0	0.0
1913 Cin-N	0	1	.000	5	2	0	0	0	15	15	0	8	4	15.6	7.80	42	.242	.356	1	.167	-0	-8	-8	-0	-0.7
Total 5	24	24	.500	99	48	28	4	4	498²	512	5	202	208	13.3	3.79	83	.271	.348	28	.160	-8	-39	-37	-6	-4.8

● TODD WORRELL Worrell, Todd Roland b: 9/28/59, Arcadia, Cal. BR/TR, 6′5″, 215 lbs. Deb: 8/28/85

1985 *StL-N	3	0	1.000	17	0	0	0	5	21²	17	2	7	17	10.0	2.91	122	.215	.279	0	.000	-0	2	2	-0	0.1
1986 StL-N	9	10	.474	74	0	0	0	36	103²	86	9	41	73	11.1	2.08	175	.229	.307	1	.143	0	19	18	-2	1.7
1987 *StL-N	8	6	.571	75	0	0	0	33	94²	86	8	34	92	11.4	2.66	156	.242	.308	1	.100	-0	15	16	0	1.6
1988 StL-N★	5	9	.357	68	0	0	0	32	90	69	7	34	78	10.4	3.00	116	.214	.291	0	.000	-0	4	5	-0	0.4
1989 StL-N	3	5	.375	47	0	0	0	20	51²	42	4	26	41	11.8	2.96	123	.222	.316	0	.000	-0	3	4	1	0.5
1992 StL-N	5	3	.625	67	0	0	0	3	64	45	4	25	64	10.0	2.11	163	.198	.281	0	—	0	10	9	-1	0.9
Total 6	33	33	.500	348	0	0	0	129	425²	345	34	167	365	10.9	2.56	144	.223	.300	2	.080	-1	53	53	-3	5.2

● RICH WORTHAM Wortham, Richard Cooper b: 10/22/53, Odessa, Tex. BR/TL, 6′, 185 lbs. Deb: 5/03/78

1978 Chi-A	3	2	.600	8	8	2	0	0	59	59	1	23	25	12.5	3.05	125	.267	.336	0	—	0	5	5	-0	0.5
1979 Chi-A	14	14	.500	34	33	5	0	0	204	195	21	100	119	13.1	4.90	87	.255	.343	0	—	0	-15	-15	-2	-1.5
1980 Chi-A	4	7	.364	41	10	0	0	1	92	102	4	58	45	15.9	5.97	67	.285	.389	0	—	0	-20	-20	1	-1.8
1983 Oak-A	0	0	—	1	0	0	0	0	0	3	0	1	0	—	∞	—	1.000	1.000	0	—	0	-1	-1	0	0.1
Total 4	21	23	.477	84	51	7	0	1	355	359	26	182	189	13.9	4.89	84	.266	.356	0	—	0	-32	-31	-1	-2.7

● AL WORTHINGTON Worthington, Allan Fulton "Red" b: 2/5/29, Birmingham, Ala. BR/TR, 6′2″, 205 lbs. Deb: 7/06/53 C

1953 NY-N	4	8	.333	20	17	5	2	0	102	103	6	54	52	14.0	3.44	125	.258	.349	2	.065	-2	10	10	0	0.8
1954 NY-N	0	2	.000	10	1	0	0	0	18	21	0	15	8	18.0	3.50	115	.333	.462	0	.000	-1	1	1	0	0.1
1956 NY-N	7	14	.333	28	24	4	0	0	165²	158	20	74	95	12.8	3.97	95	.254	.338	12	.235	2	-4	-3	2	0.0
1957 NY-N	8	11	.421	55	12	1	0	0	157²	140	19	56	90	11.5	4.22	93	.237	.309	4	.100	-2	-6	-5	-0	-0.7
1958 SF-N	11	7	.611	54	12	1	0	6	151¹	152	17	57	76	12.5	3.63	105	.255	.322	8	.182	-2	5	3	0	0.3
1959 SF-N	2	3	.400	42	3	0	0	0	73¹	68	8	37	45	13.5	3.68	103	.253	.354	1	.077	-1	1	1	0	0.1
1960 Bos-A	0	0	—	11	2	0	0	0	11²	17	2	9	7	21.6	7.71	52	.340	.459	0	.000	-0	-5	-5	0	-0.5
Chi-A	1	0	.500	10	0	0	0	0	5¹	3	0	4	1	11.8	3.38	112	.176	.333	2	1.000	1	0	0	0	0.0
Yr	1	2	.333	10	2	0	0	0	17	20	1	13	8	18.5	6.35	62	.299	.427	2	.667	1	-5	-5	0	-0.4
1963 Cin-N	4	4	.500	50	0	0	0	10	81¹	75	6	31	55	12.1	2.99	112	.248	.324	1	.083	-0	3	3	2	0.5

YEAR	TM/L	W	L	PCT	G	GS	CG	SH	SV	IP	H	HR	BB	SO	RAT	ERA	ERA+	OAV	OOB	BH	AVG	PB	PR	/A	PD	TPI
1964	Cin-N	1	0	1.000	6	0	0	0	0	7	14	0	2	6	21.9	10.29	35	.400	.447	0	—	0	-5	-5	-0	-0.5
	Min-A	5	6	.455	41	0	0	0	14	72^1	47	4	28	59	9.3	1.37	261	.183	.263	1	.063	-1	18	18	1	1.8
1965	*Min-A	10	7	.588	62	0	0	0	21	80^1	57	4	41	59	11.3	2.13	167	.207	.316	1	.100	0	12	13	2	1.6
1966	Min-A	6	3	.667	65	0	0	0	16	91^1	66	6	27	93	9.3	2.46	146	.199	.261	3	.273	1	10	11	1	1.5
1967	Min-A	8	9	.471	59	0	0	0	16	92	77	6	38	80	11.3	2.84	122	.229	.309	0	.000	-1	4	6	0	0.6
1968	Min-A	4	5	.444	54	0	0	0	**18**	76^1	67	1	32	57	11.7	2.71	114	.238	.315	0	.000	-1	2	3	0	0.3
1969	*Min-A	4	1	.800	46	0	0	0	3	61	65	7	20	51	12.5	4.57	80	.278	.335	0	.000	-1	-6	-6	-1	-0.8
Total	14	75	82	.478	602	69	11	3	110	1246^2	1130	105	527	834	12.2	3.39	110	.243	.323	35	.137	-5	41	46	7	5.2

● GENE WRIGHT Wright, Clarence Eugene "Big Gene" b: 12/11/1878, Cleveland, Ohio d: 10/29/30, Barberton, Ohio BR/TR, 6'2", 185 lbs. Deb: 10/05/01

YEAR	TM/L	W	L	PCT	G	GS	CG	SH	SV	IP	H	HR	BB	SO	RAT	ERA	ERA+	OAV	OOB	BH	AVG	PB	PR	/A	PD	TPI
1901	Bro-N	1	0	1.000	1	1	1	0	0	9	6	0	1	6	7.0	1.00	335	.189	.213	1	.333	0	2	2	-0	0.3
1902	Cle-A	7	11	.389	21	18	15	1	1	148	150	6	75	52	14.2	3.95	87	.263	.357	10	.143	-2	-6	-8	-2	-1.1
1903	Cle-A	3	9	.250	15	12	8	0	0	101^2	122	1	58	42	16.3	5.75	50	.296	.388	9	.209	2	-32	-33	2	-2.7
	StL-A	3	5	.375	8	8	7	1	0	61	73	2	16	37	13.7	3.69	79	.296	.348	3	.143	-1	-5	-5	1	-0.5
	Yr	6	14	.300	23	20	15	1	0	162^2	195	3	74	79	15.1	4.98	58	.294	.368	12	.188	1	-36	-38	3	-3.2
1904	StL-A	0	1	.000	1	1	0	0	0	4	10	0	2	3	27.0	13.50	18	.469	.515	0	.000	-0	-5	-5	1	-0.4
Total	4	14	26	.350	46	40	31	2	1	323^2	361	9	152	140	14.7	4.50	70	.282	.365	23	.167	-1	-45	-49	1	-4.4

● CLYDE WRIGHT Wright, Clyde b: 2/20/41, Jefferson City, Tenn. BR/TL, 6'1", 185 lbs. Deb: 6/15/66

YEAR	TM/L	W	L	PCT	G	GS	CG	SH	SV	IP	H	HR	BB	SO	RAT	ERA	ERA+	OAV	OOB	BH	AVG	PB	PR	/A	PD	TPI
1966	Cal-A	4	7	.364	20	13	3	1	0	91^1	92	11	25	37	11.6	3.74	90	.265	.316	3	.103	-1	-3	-4	0	-0.5
1967	Cal-A	5	5	.500	20	11	1	0	0	77^1	76	5	24	35	11.8	3.26	96	.260	.319	6	.273	2	-0	-1	0	0.1
1968	Cal-A	10	6	.625	41	13	2	1	3	125^2	123	13	44	71	12.1	3.94	74	.256	.321	8	.216	2	-13	-14	-1	-1.5
1969	Cal-A	1	8	.111	37	5	0	0	0	63^2	66	4	30	31	13.7	4.10	85	.278	.362	2	.182	0	-3	-4	0	-0.4
1970	Cal-A★	22	12	.647	39	39	7	2	0	260^2	226	24	88	110	11.1	2.83	128	.232	.300	18	.171	2	26	23	-2	2.5
1971	Cal-A	16	17	.485	37	37	10	2	0	276^2	225	17	82	135	10.1	2.99	108	.226	.287	14	.154	2	14	8	4	1.5
1972	Cal-A	18	11	.621	35	35	15	2	0	251	229	14	80	87	11.2	2.98	98	.246	.308	18	.217	7	2	-2	3	0.9
1973	Cal-A	11	19	.367	37	36	13	1	0	257	273	26	76	65	12.3	3.68	96	.273	.326	0	—	0	4	-4	4	0.2
1974	Mil-A	9	20	.310	38	32	15	0	0	232	264	22	54	64	12.3	4.42	82	.284	.323	0	—	0	-21	-21	2	-1.9
1975	Tex-A	4	6	.400	25	14	1	0	0	93^1	105	7	47	32	14.8	4.44	85	.294	.378	0	—	0	-7	-7	2	-0.5
Total	10	100	111	.474	329	235	67	9	3	1728^2	1679	143	550	667	11.7	3.50	96	.256	.316	69	.183	14	-1	-27	13	0.4

● DAVE WRIGHT Wright, David William b: 8/27/1875, Dennison, Ohio d: 1/18/46, Dennison, Ohio BR/TR, 6', 185 lbs. Deb: 7/22/1895

YEAR	TM/L	W	L	PCT	G	GS	CG	SH	SV	IP	H	HR	BB	SO	RAT	ERA	ERA+	OAV	OOB	BH	AVG	PB	PR	/A	PD	TPI
1895	Pit-N	0	0	—	1	0	0	0	0	2	6	0	1	0	31.5	27.00	17	.509	.547	0	.000	-0	-5	-5	0	-0.4
1897	Chi-N	1	0	1.000	1	1	1	0	0	7	17	1	2	4	27.0	15.43	29	.458	.511	1	.333	0	-9	-9	0	-0.5
Total	2	1	0	1.000	2	1	1	0	0	9	23	1	3	4	28.0	18.00	25	.470	.520	1	.250	0	-14	-14	0	-0.9

● GEORGE WRIGHT Wright, George b: 1/28/1847, Yonkers, N.Y. d: 8/21/37, Boston, Mass. BR/TR, 5'9.5", 150 lbs. Deb: 5/05/1871 FMH♦

YEAR	TM/L	W	L	PCT	G	GS	CG	SH	SV	IP	H	HR	BB	SO	RAT	ERA	ERA+	OAV	OOB	BH	AVG	PB	PR	/A	PD	TPI
1875	Bos-n	0	1	.000	2	0	0	0	0	4	5	0	0		11.3	2.25	105	.263	.263	135	.333	1	0	0		0.0
1876	Bos-N	0	0	—	1	0	0	0	0	1	1	0	0	1	9.0	0.00	—	.250	.250	100	.299	0	0	0	0	0.0

● ED WRIGHT Wright, Henderson Edward b: 5/15/19, Dyersburg, Tenn. BR/TR, 6'1", 180 lbs. Deb: 7/29/45

YEAR	TM/L	W	L	PCT	G	GS	CG	SH	SV	IP	H	HR	BB	SO	RAT	ERA	ERA+	OAV	OOB	BH	AVG	PB	PR	/A	PD	TPI
1945	Bos-N	8	3	.727	15	12	7	1	0	111^1	104	7	33	24	11.1	2.51	153	.254	.310	5	.128	-2	16	16	-1	1.4
1946	Bos-N	12	9	.571	36	21	8	2	0	176^1	164	8	71	44	12.1	3.52	97	.250	.325	18	.305	6	-2	-2	0	0.4
1947	Bos-N	3	3	.500	23	6	1	0	0	64^2	80	9	35	14	16.3	6.40	61	.305	.391	3	.130	-0	-17	-18	-0	-1.8
1948	Bos-N	0	0	—	3	0	0	0	0	4^2	9	0	2	2	21.2	1.93	199	.474	.524	0	—	0	1	1	0	0.1
1952	Phi-A	2	1	.667	24	0	0	0	1	41^1	55	6	20	9	17.0	6.53	61	.320	.400	1	.143	-0	-13	-12	-0	-1.2
Total	5	25	16	.610	101	39	16	3	1	398^1	412	30	161	93	13.1	4.00	92	.271	.344	27	.211	3	-15	-14	-2	-1.1

● JIM WRIGHT Wright, James "Jiggs" b: 9/19/1900, Hyde, England d: 4/10/63, Oakland, Cal. BR/TR, 6'2.5", 195 lbs. Deb: 9/14/27

YEAR	TM/L	W	L	PCT	G	GS	CG	SH	SV	IP	H	HR	BB	SO	RAT	ERA	ERA+	OAV	OOB	BH	AVG	PB	PR	/A	PD	TPI
1927	StL-A	1	0	1.000	2	1	1	0	0	12	8	0	4	4	9.0	4.50	97	.182	.250	0	.000	-0	-0	-0	-0	-0.1
1928	StL-A	0	0	—	2	0	0	0	0	2	3	0	2	2	22.5	13.50	31	.375	.500	0	—	0	-2	-2	0	-0.2
Total	2	1	0	1.000	4	1	1	0	0	14	11	0	6	6	10.9	5.79	75	.212	.293	0	.000	-0	-3	-2	0	-0.3

● JIM WRIGHT Wright, James Clifton b: 12/21/50, Reed City, Mich. BR/TR, 6'1", 165 lbs. Deb: 4/15/78

YEAR	TM/L	W	L	PCT	G	GS	CG	SH	SV	IP	H	HR	BB	SO	RAT	ERA	ERA+	OAV	OOB	BH	AVG	PB	PR	/A	PD	TPI
1978	Bos-A	8	4	.667	24	16	5	3	0	116	122	8	24	56	11.9	3.57	115	.276	.323	0	—	0	2	7	-2	0.5
1979	Bos-A	1	0	1.000	11	1	0	0	0	23	19	5	7	15	11.3	5.09	87	.226	.309	0	—	0	-2	-2	-0	-0.5
Total	2	9	4	.692	35	17	5	3	0	139	141	13	31	71	11.8	3.82	109	.268	.321	0	—	0	0	5	-2	0.0

● JIM WRIGHT Wright, James Leon b: 3/3/55, St.Joseph, Mo. BR/TR, 6'5", 205 lbs. Deb: 4/22/81

YEAR	TM/L	W	L	PCT	G	GS	CG	SH	SV	IP	H	HR	BB	SO	RAT	ERA	ERA+	OAV	OOB	BH	AVG	PB	PR	/A	PD	TPI
1981	KC-A	2	3	.400	17	4	0	0	0	52	57	5	21	27	13.8	3.46	104	.277	.349	0	—	0	1	1	-1	0.1
1982	KC-A	0	0	—	7	0	0	0	0	23^2	32	3	6	9	14.5	5.32	77	.320	.358	0	—	0	-3	-3	-1	-0.4
Total	2	2	3	.400	24	4	0	0	0	75^2	89	8	27	36	14.0	4.04	93	.291	.352	0	—	0	-2	-2	-1	-0.3

● RICKY WRIGHT Wright, James Richard b: 11/22/58, Paris, Tex. BL/TL, 6'3", 175 lbs. Deb: 7/28/82

YEAR	TM/L	W	L	PCT	G	GS	CG	SH	SV	IP	H	HR	BB	SO	RAT	ERA	ERA+	OAV	OOB	BH	AVG	PB	PR	/A	PD	TPI
1982	LA-N	2	1	.667	14	5	0	0	0	32^2	28	1	20	24	13.2	3.03	114	.233	.343	1	.125	0	2	2	0	0.2
1983	LA-N	0	0	—	6	0	0	0	0	6^1	5	0	2	5	9.9	2.84	126	.227	.292	0	—	0	1	1	-0	0.0
	Tex-A	0	0	—	1	0	0	0	0	2	0	0	1	2	4.5	0.00	—	.000	.167	0	—	0	1	1	-0	0.3
1984	Tex-A	0	2	.000	8	1	0	0	0	14^2	20	3	11	6	19.0	6.14	68	.357	.463	0	—	0	-3	-3	0	-0.4
1985	Tex-A	0	0	—	5	0	0	0	0	7^2	5	0	5	7	11.7	4.70	90	.185	.313	0	—	0	-0	-0	0	-0.1
1986	Tex-A	1	0	1.000	21	1	0	0	0	39^1	44	1	21	23	14.9	5.03	85	.284	.369	0	—	0	-4	-3	1	-0.3
Total	5	3	3	.500	55	7	0	0	0	102^2	102	5	60	67	14.2	4.30	92	.265	.364	1	.125	0	-4	-4	1	-0.3

● KEN WRIGHT Wright, Kenneth Warren b: 9/4/46, Pensacola, Fla. BR/TR, 6'2", 210 lbs. Deb: 4/10/70

YEAR	TM/L	W	L	PCT	G	GS	CG	SH	SV	IP	H	HR	BB	SO	RAT	ERA	ERA+	OAV	OOB	BH	AVG	PB	PR	/A	PD	TPI
1970	KC-A	1	2	.333	47	0	0	0	3	53^1	49	2	29	30	14.3	5.23	71	.261	.379	0	.000	-0	-9	-9	-0	-1.0
1971	KC-A	3	6	.333	21	12	1	1	1	78	66	6	47	56	13.4	3.69	93	.230	.344	2	.091	-1	-2	-2	1	-0.3
1972	KC-A	1	2	.333	17	0	0	0	4	18^1	15	0	15	18	15.2	4.91	62	.231	.383	0	.000	-0	-4	-4	0	-0.5
1973	KC-A	6	5	.545	25	12	1	0	0	80^2	60	6	82	75	15.8	4.91	84	.210	.386	0	—	0	-10	-7	-1	-1.0
1974	NY-A	0	0	—	3	0	0	0	0	5^2	5	0	7	2	19.1	3.18	110	.227	.414	0	—	0	0	0	0	0.2
Total	5	11	15	.423	113	24	2	1	8	236	195	14	180	181	14.7	4.54	81	.230	.372	2	.071	-2	-24	-22	-1	-2.6

● MEL WRIGHT Wright, Melvin James b: 5/11/28, Manila, Ark. d: 5/16/83, Montreal, Que. BR/TR, 6'3", 210 lbs. Deb: 4/17/54 C

YEAR	TM/L	W	L	PCT	G	GS	CG	SH	SV	IP	H	HR	BB	SO	RAT	ERA	ERA+	OAV	OOB	BH	AVG	PB	PR	/A	PD	TPI
1954	StL-N	0	0	—	9	0	0	0	0	10^1	16	2	11	4	25.3	10.45	39	.348	.492	0	.000	-0	-7	-7	0	-0.7
1955	StL-N	2	2	.500	29	0	0	0	1	36^1	44	4	9	18	13.4	6.19	66	.308	.353	0	.000	-1	-9	-9	0	-0.9
1960	Chi-N	0	1	.000	9	0	0	0	2	16^1	17	1	3	8	11.0	4.96	76	.279	.313	0	.000	-0	-2	-2	-1	-0.3
1961	Chi-N	0	1	.000	11	0	0	0	0	21	42	3	4	6	19.7	10.71	39	.416	.438	0	.000	-0	-16	-15	1	-1.4
Total	4	2	4	.333	58	0	0	0	3	84	119	10	27	36	16.0	7.61	53	.339	.391	0	.000	-2	-34	-33	1	-3.3

● BOB WRIGHT Wright, Robert Cassius b: 12/13/1891, Greensburg, Ind. BR/TR, 6'1.5", 175 lbs. Deb: 9/21/15

YEAR	TM/L	W	L	PCT	G	GS	CG	SH	SV	IP	H	HR	BB	SO	RAT	ERA	ERA+	OAV	OOB	BH	AVG	PB	PR	/A	PD	TPI
1915	Chi-N	0	0	—	2	0	0	0	0	4	6	0	0	3	13.5	2.25	123	.353	.353	0	—	0	0	0	0	0.0

● ROY WRIGHT Wright, Roy Earl b: 9/26/33, Buchtel, Ohio BR/TR, 6'2", 170 lbs. Deb: 9/30/56

YEAR	TM/L	W	L	PCT	G	GS	CG	SH	SV	IP	H	HR	BB	SO	RAT	ERA	ERA+	OAV	OOB	BH	AVG	PB	PR	/A	PD	TPI
1956	NY-N	0	1	.000	1	1	0	0	0	2^2	8	1	2	0	33.8	16.88	22	.533	.588	0	.000	-0	-4	-4	0	-0.3

● RASTY WRIGHT Wright, Wayne Bromley b: 11/5/1895, Ceredo, W.Va. d: 6/12/48, Columbus, Ohio BR/TR, 5'11", 160 lbs. Deb: 6/22/17

YEAR	TM/L	W	L	PCT	G	GS	CG	SH	SV	IP	H	HR	BB	SO	RAT	ERA	ERA+	OAV	OOB	BH	AVG	PB	PR	/A	PD	TPI
1917	StL-A	0	1	.000	16	1	0	0	0	39^2	48	0	10	5	13.4	5.45	48	.300	.345	2	.200	0	-12	-13	0	-1.3
1918	StL-A	8	2	.800	18	13	6	1	0	111^1	99	1	18	25	9.9	2.51	109	.244	.285	10	.294	3	3	3	-1	0.5

YEAR	TM/L	W	L	PCT	G	GS	CG	SH	SV	IP	H	HR	BB	SO	RAT	ERA	ERA+	OAV	OOB	BH	AVG	PB	PR	/A	PD	TPI
1919	StL-A	0	5	.000	24	5	2	0	0	63^1	79	1	20	14	14.2	5.54	60	.315	.368	1	.083	-1	-16	-16	0	-1.6
1922	StL-A	9	7	.563	31	16	5	0	5	154	148	7	50	44	12.0	2.92	142	.262	.331	7	.140	-2	19	21	1	2.0
1923	StL-A	7	4	.636	20	8	4	0	0	82^2	107	6	34	26	15.9	6.42	65	.317	.387	6	.222	0	-22	-21	0	-1.9
Total	5	24	19	.558	109	43	17	1	5	451	481	15	132	114	12.6	4.05	87	.280	.338	26	.195	1	-28	-26	0	-2.3

● HARRY WRIGHT

Wright, William Henry b: 1/10/1835, Sheffield, England d: 10/3/1895, Atlantic City, N.J. BR/TR, 5'9.5", 157 lbs. Deb: 5/05/1871 FMH♦

YEAR	TM/L	W	L	PCT	G	GS	CG	SH	SV	IP	H	HR	BB	SO	RAT	ERA	ERA+	OAV	OOB	BH	AVG	PB	PR	/A	PD	TPI
1871	Bos-n	1	0	1.000	9	0	0	0	**3**	18^2	34	0	4	0	18.3	6.27	66	.337	.362	44	.299	1	-4	-4		-0.3
1872	Bos-n	1	0	1.000	7	0	0	0	**1**	25^2	26	0	0	1	9.1	2.10	177	.241	.241	54	.260	0	**5**	**5**		0.3
1873	Bos-n	2	2	.500	12	5	0	0	1	38^1	65	0	7	0	16.9	4.23	78	.330	.353	67	.252	1	-4	-4		-0.3
1874	Bos-n	0	2	.000	6	2	0	0	**3**	16^2	24	0	4		15.1	*2.70*	110	.338	.373	56	.304	2	1	0		0.1
Total	4 n	4	4	.500	34	7	0	0	8	99^1	149	0	15	1	14.9	*3.81*	78	.312	.333	222	.274	5	-9	-9		-0.2

● LUCKY WRIGHT

Wright, William Simmons "William The Red" or "Deacon"
b: 2/21/1880, Tontogany, Ohio d: 7/6/41, Tontogany, Ohio BR/TR, 6', 178 lbs. Deb: 4/18/09

YEAR	TM/L	W	L	PCT	G	GS	CG	SH	SV	IP	H	HR	BB	SO	RAT	ERA	ERA+	OAV	OOB	BH	AVG	PB	PR	/A	PD	TPI
1909	Cle-A	0	4	.000	5	4	3	0	0	28	21	0	7	5	9.0	3.21	80	.223	.277	0	.000	-1	-2	-2	-0	-0.3

● FRANK WURM

Wurm, Frank James b: 4/27/24, Cambridge, N.Y. BB/TL, 6'1", 175 lbs. Deb: 9/04/44

YEAR	TM/L	W	L	PCT	G	GS	CG	SH	SV	IP	H	HR	BB	SO	RAT	ERA	ERA+	OAV	OOB	BH	AVG	PB	PR	/A	PD	TPI
1944	Bro-N	0	0	—	1	1	0	0	0	0^1	1	0	5	1	162.0	108.00	3	.500	.857	0	—	0	-4	-4	0	-0.3

● JOHN WYATT

Wyatt, John Thomas b: 4/19/35, Chicago, Ill. BR/TR, 5'11.5", 200 lbs. Deb: 9/08/61

YEAR	TM/L	W	L	PCT	G	GS	CG	SH	SV	IP	H	HR	BB	SO	RAT	ERA	ERA+	OAV	OOB	BH	AVG	PB	PR	/A	PD	TPI
1961	KC-A	0	0	—	5	0	0	0	1	7^1	8	0	4	6	16.0	2.45	168	.296	.406	0	—	0	1	1	0	0.1
1962	KC-A	10	7	.588	59	9	0	0	11	125	121	12	80	106	14.8	4.46	93	.253	.366	3	.103	-2	-7	-4	-1	-0.7
1963	KC-A	6	4	.600	63	0	0	0	21	92	83	12	43	81	12.3	3.13	123	.239	.323	0	.000	-1	5	7	-1	0.6
1964	KC-A★	9	8	.529	**81**	0	0	0	20	128	111	23	52	74	11.5	3.59	106	.236	.314	0	.000	-1	1	3	-1	0.1
1965	KC-A	2	6	.250	65	0	0	0	18	88^2	78	8	53	70	13.7	3.25	107	.241	.354	0	.000	-0	2	2	0	0.3
1966	KC-A	0	3	.000	19	0	0	0	2	23^2	19	3	16	25	14.1	5.32	64	.213	.346	0	—	0	-5	-5	1	-0.5
	Bos-A	3	4	.429	42	0	0	0	8	71^2	59	3	27	63	11.3	3.14	121	.229	.311	0	.000	-1	2	5	-1	0.3
	Yr	3	7	.300	61	0	0	0	10	95^1	78	6	43	88	11.8	3.68	101	.223	.316	0	.000	-1	-3	0	-1	-0.2
1967	*Bos-A	10	7	.588	60	0	0	0	20	93^1	71	6	39	68	10.8	2.60	134	.217	.304	1	.083	-0	7	9	1	1.1
1968	Bos-A	1	2	.333	8	0	0	0	0	10^2	9	2	6	11	13.5	4.22	75	.231	.348	0	—	0	-1	-1	0	-0.1
	NY-A	0	2	.000	7	0	0	0	0	8^1	7	1	9	6	17.3	2.16	134	.219	.390	0	.000	-0	1	1	-0	0.1
	Det-A	1	0	1.000	22	0	0	0	2	30^1	26	2	11	25	11.3	2.37	127	.236	.311	0	.000	-0	2	2	0	0.2
	Yr	2	4	.333	37	0	0	0	2	49^1	42	5	26	42	12.6	2.74	110	.230	.329	0	.000	-0	1	2	0	0.2
1969	Oak-A	0	1	.000	4	0	0	0	0	8^1	8	0	6	5	17.3	5.40	64	.250	.400	0	.000	-0	-2	-2	-0	-0.2
Total	9	42	44	.488	435	9	0	0	103	687^1	600	72	346	540	12.7	3.47	107	.237	.334	4	.048	-7	6	19	-2	1.3

● WHIT WYATT

Wyatt, John Whitlow b: 9/27/07, Kensington, Ga. BR/TR, 6'1", 185 lbs. Deb: 9/16/29 C

YEAR	TM/L	W	L	PCT	G	GS	CG	SH	SV	IP	H	HR	BB	SO	RAT	ERA	ERA+	OAV	OOB	BH	AVG	PB	PR	/A	PD	TPI
1929	Det-A	0	1	.000	4	4	1	0	0	25^1	30	1	18	14	17.4	6.75	64	.309	.422	1	.100	-1	-7	-7	1	-0.6
1930	Det-A	4	5	.444	21	7	2	0	2	85^2	76	6	35	68	12.0	3.57	134	.239	.320	12	.353	3	10	12	0	1.4
1931	Det-A	0	2	.000	4	1	1	0	0	20^1	30	2	12	8	19.0	8.85	52	.361	.448	2	.286	0	-10	-10	-1	-0.8
1932	Det-A	9	13	.409	43	22	10	0	1	205^2	228	12	102	82	14.6	5.03	93	.286	.369	15	.192	-0	-13	-8	-1	-0.8
1933	Det-A	0	1	.000	10	0	0	0	0	17	20	1	9	9	16.4	4.24	102	.299	.397	0	.000	-0	0	0	-0	0.0
	Chi-A	3	4	.429	26	7	2	0	1	87^2	91	7	45	31	14.2	4.62	92	.266	.355	6	.214	0	-3	-4	0	-0.3
	Yr	3	5	.375	36	7	2	0	1	104^2	111	8	54	40	14.4	4.56	93	.270	.358	6	.200	-0	-3	-4	-0	-0.3
1934	Chi-A	4	11	.267	23	6	2	0	2	67^2	83	10	37	36	16.1	7.18	66	.303	.388	6	.231	0	-20	-18	0	-1.6
1935	Chi-A	4	3	.571	30	1	0	0	5	52	65	6	25	22	15.9	6.75	68	.308	.387	3	.231	1	-13	-12	1	-0.9
1936	Chi-A	0	0	—	3	0	0	0	1	3	3	0	0	0	9.0	0.00	—	.273	.273	0	—	0	2	2	-0	0.1
1937	Cle-A	2	3	.400	29	4	2	0	0	73	67	3	40	52	13.2	4.44	104	.244	.340	7	.389	3	1	1	0	0.4
1939	Bro-N☆	8	3	.727	16	14	6	2	0	109	88	3	39	52	10.7	2.31	174	.224	.297	6	.167	-0	19	21	1	2.3
1940	Bro-N★	15	14	.517	37	34	16	**5**	0	239^1	233	19	62	124	11.3	3.46	116	.254	.304	14	.175	-0	10	14	-2	1.2
1941	*Bro-N★	**22**	10	.688	38	35	23	**7**	1	288^1	223	10	82	176	**9.6**	2.34	157	**.212**	**.270**	26	.239	7	**41**	**42**	-1	**5.3**
1942	Bro-N☆	19	7	.731	31	30	16	0	0	217^1	185	9	63	104	10.6	2.73	119	.225	.286	14	.182	1	14	13	-1	1.3
1943	Bro-N	14	5	.737	26	26	13	3	0	180^2	139	5	43	80	**9.1**	2.49	135	**.207**	**.255**	17	.283	4	18	17	-2	2.2
1944	Bro-N	2	6	.250	9	9	1	0	0	37^2	51	1	16	4	16.5	7.17	50	.311	.379	2	.154	-0	-15	-15	-0	-1.5
1945	Phi-N	0	7	.000	10	10	2	0	0	51^1	72	3	14	10	15.1	5.26	73	.330	.371	2	.125	0	-8	-8	1	-0.7
Total	16	106	95	.527	360	210	97	17	13	1761	1684	98	642	872	12.1	3.79	105	.251	.319	133	.219	18	27	39	-6	7.0

● WELDON WYCKOFF

Wyckoff, John Weldon b: 2/19/1892, Williamsport, Pa. d: 5/8/61, Sheboygan Falls, Wis. BR/TR, 6'1", 175 lbs. Deb: 4/19/13

YEAR	TM/L	W	L	PCT	G	GS	CG	SH	SV	IP	H	HR	BB	SO	RAT	ERA	ERA+	OAV	OOB	BH	AVG	PB	PR	/A	PD	TPI
1913	Phi-A	2	4	.333	17	7	4	0	0	61^2	56	1	46	31	15.3	4.38	63	.233	.363	4	.190	-0	-10	-11	0	-1.1
1914	*Phi-A	11	7	.611	32	20	11	0	2	185	153	2	103	86	12.6	3.02	87	.228	.334	11	.147	-0	-6	-8	-5	-1.4
1915	Phi-A	10	22	.313	43	34	20	1	0	276	238	1	165	157	13.3	3.52	83	.246	.359	12	.125	-3	-18	-18	2	-2.1
1916	Phi-A	0	1	.000	7	2	1	0	0	21^1	20	1	20	4	17.3	5.48	52	.247	.402	3	.375	1	-6	-6	0	-0.6
	Bos-A	0	0	—	8	0	0	0	1	22^2	19	0	18	18	14.7	4.76	58	.232	.370	1	.167	-0	-5	-5	-1	-0.6
	Yr	0	1	.000	15	2	1	0	1	44	39	1	38	22	15.8	5.11	55	.238	.381	4	.286	1	-11	-11	-1	-1.2
1917	Bos-A	0	0	—	1	0	0	0	0	5	4	0	4	1	16.2	1.80	143	.222	.391	0	.000	-0	0	0	0	0.1
1918	Bos-A	0	0	—	1	0	0	0	0	2	4	0	1	2	22.5	0.00	—	.400	.455	0	.000	-0	1	1	-0	0.0
Total	6	23	34	.404	109	63	36	1	3	573^2	494	5	357	299	13.6	3.55	79	.239	.355	31	.149	-3	-44	-48	-3	-5.7

● FRANK WYMAN

Wyman, Frank H. b: 5/10/1862, Haverhill, Mass. d: 2/4/16, Everett, Mass. Deb: 6/24/1884 ♦

YEAR	TM/L	W	L	PCT	G	GS	CG	SH	SV	IP	H	HR	BB	SO	RAT	ERA	ERA+	OAV	OOB	BH	AVG	PB	PR	/A	PD	TPI
1884	KC-U	0	1	.000	3	1	1	0	0	21	37	0	3	9	17.1	6.86	40	.362	.380	27	.218	-0	-9	-10	-1	-0.8

● EARLY WYNN

Wynn, Early "Gus" b: 1/6/20, Hartford, Ala. BB/TR, 6', 200 lbs. Deb: 9/13/39 CH♦

YEAR	TM/L	W	L	PCT	G	GS	CG	SH	SV	IP	H	HR	BB	SO	RAT	ERA	ERA+	OAV	OOB	BH	AVG	PB	PR	/A	PD	TPI
1939	Was-A	0	2	.000	3	3	1	0	0	20^1	26	0	10	1	15.9	5.75	76	.313	.387	1	.167	0	-3	-3	-1	-0.3
1941	Was-A	3	1	.750	5	5	4	0	0	40	35	1	10	15	10.1	1.57	257	.226	.273	2	.133	-0	11	11	0	1.2
1942	Was-A	10	16	.385	30	28	10	1	0	190	246	6	73	58	15.3	5.12	71	.314	.374	15	.217	2	-31	-31	-1	-2.9
1943	Was-A	18	12	.600	37	33	12	3	0	256^2	232	15	83	89	11.1	2.91	110	.240	.301	29	.296	7	11	8	-2	1.5
1944	Was-A	8	17	.320	33	25	19	2	2	207^2	221	3	67	65	12.6	3.38	96	.277	.334	19	.207	2	1	-3	-2	-0.3
1946	Was-A	8	5	.615	17	12	9	0	0	107	112	8	33	36	12.4	3.11	108	.267	.325	15	.319	6	5	3	-0	1.0
1947	Was-A	17	15	.531	33	31	22	2	0	247	251	13	90	73	12.6	3.64	102	.262	.329	33	.275	7	2	2	-1	0.9
1948	Was-A	8	19	.296	33	31	15	1	0	198	236	18	94	49	15.0	5.82	75	.295	.370	23	.217	3	-34	-32	-1	-2.8
1949	Cle-A	11	7	.611	26	23	6	0	0	164^2	186	8	57	62	13.3	4.15	96	.282	.340	10	.143	-1	1	-3	1	-0.4
1950	Cle-A	18	8	.692	32	28	14	2	0	213^2	166	20	101	143	**11.4**	**3.20**	135	**.212**	**.305**	18	.234	7	33	27	0	3.3
1951	Cle-A	20	13	.606	37	34	21	3	1	**274^1**	227	18	107	133	11.1	3.02	126	.225	.301	20	.185	2	**34**	23	-1	2.4
1952	Cle-A	23	12	.657	42	33	19	4	3	285^2	239	23	132	153	11.7	2.90	115	.231	.318	22	.222	5	25	14	-1	1.9
1953	Cle-A	17	12	.586	36	34	16	1	0	251^2	234	19	107	138	12.3	3.93	95	.245	.324	25	.275	8	2	-5	-1	0.2
1954	*Cle-A	**23**	11	.676	40	36	20	3	2	**270^2**	225	21	83	155	10.2	2.73	135	.225	.284	17	.183	1	30	29	-3	2.8
1955	Cle-A★	17	11	.607	32	31	16	6	0	230	207	19	80	122	11.3	2.82	142	.240	.307	15	.179	2	29	30	-3	3.0
1956	Cle-A★	20	9	.690	38	35	18	4	2	277^2	233	19	91	158	10.7	2.72	154	.228	.294	23	.228	3	44	46	1	**5.3**
1957	Cle-A★	14	17	.452	40	37	13	1	1	263	270	32	104	**184**	13.0	4.31	86	.265	.336	10	.116	-2	-15	-17	-1	-2.0
1958	Chi-A★	14	16	.467	40	34	11	4	2	239^2	214	27	104	**179**	12.2	4.13	88	.242	.325	15	.200	3	-10	-13	-2	-1.3
1959	*Chi-A★	**22**	10	.688	37	37	14	5	0	**255^2**	202	20	119	179	11.6	3.17	119	.216	.310	22	.244	9	20	17	-1	2.5
1960	Chi-A★	13	12	.520	36	35	13	**4**	1	237^1	220	20	112	158	12.7	3.49	108	.247	.334	15	.200	6	10	8	-2	1.2
1961	Chi-A	8	2	.800	17	16	5	0	0	110^1	88	11	47	64	11.1	3.51	112	.220	.304	6	.162	-0	6	5	-2	0.3
1962	Chi-A	7	15	.318	27	26	11	3	0	167^2	171	15	56	91	12.3	4.46	88	.264	.326	7	.130	0	-9	-10	-2	-1.2
1963	Cle-A	1	2	.333	20	5	1	0	1	55^1	50	2	15	29	10.6	2.28	159	.250	.302	3	.273	1	8	8	-0	1.0

YEAR	TM/L	W	L	PCT	G	GS	CG	SH	SV	IP	H	HR	BB	SO	RAT	ERA	ERA+	OAV	OOB	BH	AVG	PB	PR	/A	PD	TPI
Total	23	300	244	.551	691	612	290	49	15	4564	4291	338	1775	2334	12.1	3.54	106	.248	.321	365	.214	70	170	112	-25	17.3
● **BILLY WYNNE** Wynne, Billy Vernon b: 7/31/43, Williamston, N.C. BL/TR, 6'5", 206 lbs. Deb: 8/06/67																										
1967	NY-N	0	0	—	6	1	0	0	0	8^{2}	12	0	2	4	14.5	3.12	109	.324	.359	0	.000	-0	0	0	-0	0.0
1968	Chi-A	0	0	—	1	0	0	0	0	2	2	0	2	1	18.0	4.50	67	.250	.400	0	—	0	-0	-0	-0	0.0
1969	Chi-A	7	7	.500	20	20	6	1	0	128^{2}	143	14	50	67	13.7	4.06	95	.283	.351	5	.122	-1	-6	-3	0	-0.3
1970	Chi-A	1	4	.200	12	9	0	0	0	44	54	8	22	19	15.8	5.32	73	.298	.377	1	.077	-1	-8	-7	1	-0.7
1971	Cal-A	0	0	—	3	0	0	0	0	3^{2}	6	0	2	6	19.6	4.91	66	.375	.444	0	—	0	-1	-1	0	-0.1
Total	5	8	11	.421	42	30	6	1	0	187	217	22	78	97	14.4	4.33	88	.290	.361	6	.109	-2	-15	-11	1	-1.1
● **BILL WYNNE** Wynne, William Andrew b: 3/27/1869, Neuse, N.C. d: 8/7/51, Raleigh, N.C. BR/TR, 5'11.5", 161 lbs. Deb: 8/31/1894																										
1894	Was-N	0	1	.000	1	1	1	0	0	8	10	0	8	2	22.5	6.75	78	.303	.465	0	.000	-0	-1	-1	-0	-0.1
● **HANK WYSE** Wyse, Henry Washington "Hooks" b: 3/1/18, Lunsford, Ark. BR/TR, 5'11.5", 185 lbs. Deb: 9/07/42																										
1942	Chi-N	2	1	.667	4	4	1	1	0	28	33	1	6	8	12.5	1.93	166	.287	.322	1	.125	-0	4	4	-0	0.4
1943	Chi-N	9	7	.563	38	15	8	2	5	156	159	4	34	45	11.3	2.94	113	.264	.306	4	.080	-3	8	7	3	0.7
1944	Chi-N	16	15	.516	41	34	14	3	1	257^{1}	277	9	57	86	11.8	3.15	112	.278	.318	16	.178	-1	13	11	0	1.0
1945	*Chi-N	22	10	.688	38	34	23	2	0	278^{1}	272	17	55	77	10.7	2.68	136	.256	.296	17	.168	-2	**35**	30	2	3.1
1946	Chi-N	14	12	.538	40	27	12	2	1	201^{1}	206	7	52	52	11.7	2.68	124	.265	.313	18	.243	1	16	14	2	1.9
1947	Chi-N	6	9	.400	37	19	5	1	1	142	158	12	64	53	14.3	4.31	92	.286	.363	5	.111	-1	-4	-6	1	-0.6
1950	Phi-A	9	14	.391	41	23	4	0	0	170^{2}	192	16	87	33	15.1	5.85	78	.287	.376	9	.153	-3	-24	-25	0	-2.5
1951	Phi-A	1	2	.333	9	1	0	0	0	14^{2}	24	0	8	5	19.6	7.98	54	.381	.451	1	.250	-0	-6	-6	-0	-0.6
	Was-A	0	0	—	3	2	0	0	0	9^{1}	17	0	10	3	27.0	9.64	42	.378	.500	0	.000	-1	-6	-6	0	-0.6
	Yr	1	2	.333	12	3	0	0	0	24	41	0	18	8	22.5	8.63	49	.380	.472	1	.125	-1	-12	-12	0	-1.2
Total	8	79	70	.530	251	159	67	11	8	1257^{2}	1338	66	373	362	12.4	3.52	105	.274	.329	71	.163	-11	36	24	9	2.8
● **BIFF WYSONG** Wysong, Harlan b: 4/13/05, Clarksville, Ohio d: 8/8/51, Xenia, Ohio BL/TL, 6'3", 195 lbs. Deb: 8/10/30																										
1930	Cin-N	0	1	.000	1	1	0	0	0	2^{1}	6	0	3	1	34.7	19.29	25	.545	.643	0	—	0	-4	-4	-0	-0.3
1931	Cin-N	0	2	.000	12	2	0	0	0	21^{2}	25	2	23	5	19.9	7.89	47	.298	.449	1	.250	0	-10	-10	-1	-1.0
1932	Cin-N	1	0	1.000	7	0	0	0	0	12^{1}	13	0	8	5	15.3	3.65	106	.277	.382	0	.000	-0	0	0	0	0.0
Total	3	1	3	.250	20	3	0	0	0	36^{1}	44	2	34	11	19.3	7.18	54	.310	.443	1	.167	-0	-13	-13	-0	-1.3
● **RUSTY YARNALL** Yarnall, Waldo William b: 10/22/02, Chicago, Ill. d: 10/9/85, Lowell, Mass. BR/TR, 6', 175 lbs. Deb: 6/30/26																										
1926	Phi-N	0	1	.000	1	0	0	0	0	1	3	0	1	0	36.0	18.00	23	.500	.571	0	.000	-0	-2	-2	0	-0.1
● **RUBE YARRISON** Yarrison, Byron Wardsworth b: 3/9/1896, Montgomery, Pa. d: 4/22/77, Williamsport, Pa. BR/TR, 5'11", 165 lbs. Deb: 4/13/22																										
1922	Phi-A	1	2	.333	18	1	0	0	0	33^{2}	50	4	12	10	17.1	8.29	51	.362	.421	1	.167	-0	-16	-15	-0	-1.4
1924	Bro-N	0	2	.000	3	2	0	0	0	11	12	0	3	2	13.1	6.55	57	.267	.327	0	.000	-0	-3	-3	0	-0.3
Total	2	1	4	.200	21	3	0	0	0	44^{2}	62	4	15	12	16.1	7.86	53	.339	.398	1	.125	-0	-19	-19	0	-1.7
● **EMIL YDE** Yde, Emil Ogden b: 1/28/1900, Great Lakes, Ill. d: 12/4/68, Leesburg, Fla. BB/TL, 5'11", 165 lbs. Deb: 4/21/24																										
1924	Pit-N	16	3	**.842**	33	22	14	**4**	0	194	171	3	62	53	11.1	2.83	136	.244	.311	21	.239	2	22	22	1	2.5
1925	*Pit-N	17	9	.654	33	28	13	0	0	207	254	11	75	41	14.4	4.13	108	.309	.369	17	.191	-2	3	8	-0	0.5
1926	Pit-N	8	7	.533	37	22	12	1	0	187^{1}	181	3	81	34	12.7	3.65	108	.260	.339	17	.230	3	4	6	0	0.8
1927	*Pit-N	1	3	.250	9	2	0	0	0	29^{2}	45	1	15	9	18.8	9.71	42	.375	.453	3	.167	-0	-19	-18	1	-1.6
1929	Det-A	7	3	.700	29	6	4	1	0	86^{2}	100	8	63	23	16.9	5.30	81	.296	.406	16	.333	2	-10	-10	-1	-0.6
Total	5	49	25	.662	141	80	43	6	0	704^{2}	751	26	296	160	13.5	4.02	102	.281	.355	74	.233	5	-0	7	1	1.6
● **JOE YEAGER** Yeager, Joseph F. "Little Joe" b: 8/28/1875, Philadelphia, Pa. d: 7/2/37, Detroit, Mich. BR/TR, Deb: 4/22/1898 ♦																										
1898	Bro-N	12	22	.353	36	33	32	0	0	291^{1}	333	4	80	70	12.9	3.65	98	.285	.334	23	.172	-3	-1	-2	5	0.0
1899	Bro-N	2	2	.500	10	4	2	1	1	47^{2}	56	1	16	6	14.0	4.72	83	.292	.353	9	.191	-0	-5	-4	1	-0.3
1900	Bro-N	1	1	.500	2	2	2	0	0	17	21	1	5	2	13.8	6.88	56	.303	.349	3	.333	0	-6	-6	-0	-0.5
1901	Det-A	12	11	.522	26	25	22	2	1	199^{2}	209	4	46	38	11.9	2.61	147	.266	.313	37	.296	4	23	27	2	3.4
1902	Det-A	6	12	.333	19	15	14	0	0	140	171	5	41	28	13.9	4.82	76	.301	.354	39	.242	2	-19	-18	3	-1.2
1903	Det-A	0	1	.000	1	1	1	0	0	9	15	0	0	1	15.0	4.00	73	.369	.369	103	.256	0	-1	-1	0	-0.1
Total	6	33	49	.402	94	80	73	3	2	704^{2}	805	15	188	145	13.0	3.74	99	.285	.334	467	.252	4	-9	-4	11	1.3
● **AL YEARGIN** Yeargin, James Almond b: 10/16/01, Mauldin, S.C. d: 5/8/37, Greenville, S.C. BR/TR, 5'11", 170 lbs. Deb: 10/01/22																										
1922	Bos-N	0	1	.000	1	1	1	0	0	7	5	1	2	1	9.0	1.29	311	.192	.250	0	.000	-0	2	2	0	0.2
1924	Bos-N	1	11	.083	32	12	6	0	0	141^{1}	162	7	42	34	13.2	5.09	75	.293	.346	6	.143	-2	-19	-20	4	-1.8
Total	2	1	12	.077	33	13	7	0	0	148^{1}	167	8	44	35	13.0	4.91	78	.288	.342	6	.133	-2	-17	-18	4	-1.6
● **LARRY YELLEN** Yellen, Lawrence Alan b: 1/4/43, Brooklyn, N.Y. BR/TR, 5'11", 190 lbs. Deb: 9/26/63																										
1963	Hou-N	0	0	—	1	1	0	0	0	5	7	0	1	3	14.4	3.60	88	.280	.308	0	.000	-0	-0	-0	0	0.0
1964	Hou-N	0	0	—	13	1	0	0	0	21	27	4	10	9	15.9	6.86	50	.297	.366	0	.000	-0	-8	-8	-0	-0.9
Total	2	0	0	—	14	2	0	0	0	26	34	4	11	12	15.6	6.23	54	.293	.354	0	.000	-0	-8	-8	0	-0.9
● **CHIEF YELLOWHORSE** Yellowhorse, Moses J. b: 1/28/1898, Pawnee, Okla. d: 4/10/64, Pawnee, Okla. BR/TR, 5'10", 180 lbs. Deb: 4/15/21																										
1921	Pit-N	5	3	.625	10	4	1	0	1	48^{1}	45	1	13	19	10.8	2.98	129	.254	.305	0	.000	-2	4	5	-2	0.0
1922	Pit-N	3	1	.750	28	5	2	0	0	77^{2}	92	0	20	24	13.2	4.52	90	.305	.352	6	.316	1	-4	-4	-1	-0.3
Total	2	8	4	.667	38	9	3	0	1	126	137	1	33	43	12.3	3.93	101	.286	.335	6	.167	-2	1	1	-3	-0.3
● **CARROLL YERKES** Yerkes, Charles Carroll "Lefty" b: 6/13/03, McSherrystown, Pa. d: 12/20/50, Oakland, Cal. BR/TL, 5'11", 180 lbs. Deb: 5/31/27																										
1927	Phi-A	0	0	—	1	0	0	0	0	1	0	0	1	0	9.0	0.00	—	.000	.333	0	—	0	0	0	0	0.1
1928	Phi-A	0	1	.000	2	1	1	0	0	8^{2}	7	0	2	1	9.3	2.08	193	.233	.281	0	.000	-0	2	2	1	0.2
1929	Phi-A	1	0	1.000	19	2	0	0	1	37^{1}	47	0	13	11	14.7	4.58	92	.329	.389	0	.000	-2	-1	-1	2	-0.1
1932	Chi-N	0	0	—	2	0	0	0	0	9	5	2	3	4	8.0	3.00	126	.167	.242	1	.333	0	1	1	-0	0.1
1933	Chi-N	0	0	—	1	0	0	0	0	2	2	0	1	0	13.5	4.50	73	.286	.375	0	—	0	-0	-0	0	0.0
Total	5	1	1	.500	25	3	1	0	1	58	61	2	20	16	12.7	3.88	106	.288	.352	1	.063	-2	2	1	3	0.3
● **STAN YERKES** Yerkes, Stanley Lewis "Yank" b: 11/28/1874, Cheltenham, Pa. d: 7/28/40, Boston, Mass. BR/TR, 5'10", 165 lbs. Deb: 5/03/01																										
1901	Bal-A	0	1	.000	1	1	1	0	0	8	12	0	2	4	15.8	6.75	57	.342	.377	1	.333	0	-3	-3	0	-0.2
	StL-N	3	1	.750	4	4	4	0	0	34	35	2	6	15	10.9	3.18	100	.264	.296	1	.083	-1	1	0	-0	-0.1
1902	StL-N	12	21	.364	39	37	27	1	0	272^{2}	341	1	79	81	13.9	3.66	75	.306	.353	12	.132	-3	-27	-28	-2	-3.3
1903	StL-N	0	1	.000	1	1	0	0	0	5	8	0	0	3	14.4	1.80	181	.333	.333	0	.000	-0	1	1	-0	0.0
Total	3	15	24	.385	45	43	32	1	0	319^{2}	396	3	87	103	13.7	3.66	77	.303	.347	14	.130	-4	-28	-30	-3	-3.6
● **RICH YETT** Yett, Richard Martin b: 10/6/62, Pomona, Cal. BR/TR, 6'2", 187 lbs. Deb: 4/13/85																										
1985	Min-A	0	0	—	1	1	0	0	0	0^{1}	1	0	2	0	81.0	27.00	16	.333	.600	0	—	0	-1	-1	0	-0.3
1986	Cle-A	5	3	.625	39	3	1	1	1	78^{2}	84	10	37	50	14.0	5.15	80	.275	.355	0	—	0	-8	-9	-1	-0.9
1987	Cle-A	3	9	.250	37	11	2	0	1	97^{2}	96	21	49	59	13.6	5.25	86	.257	.347	0	—	0	-9	-8	-1	-0.8
1988	Cle-A	9	6	.600	23	22	0	0	0	134^{1}	146	11	55	71	13.5	4.62	89	.275	.344	0	—	0	-10	-8	-2	-0.9
1989	Cle-A	5	6	.455	32	12	1	0	0	99	111	10	47	47	14.5	5.00	79	.283	.363	0	—	0	-12	-11	-1	-1.4
1990	Min-A	0	0	—	4	0	0	0	0	4^{1}	6	1	1	2	14.5	2.08	200	.353	.389	0	—	0	1	1	0	-0.2
Total	6	22	24	.478	136	49	4	1	2	414^{1}	444	53	191	229	13.9	4.95	84	.274	.353	0	—	0	-39	-36	-5	-4.5

YEAR TM/L	W	L	PCT	G	GS	CG	SH	SV	IP	H	HR	BB	SO	RAT	ERA	ERA+	OAV	OOB	BH	AVG	PB	PR	/A	PD	TPI

● EARL YINGLING   Yingling, Earl Hershey "Chink" b: 10/29/1888, Chillicothe, Ohio d: 10/2/62, Columbus, Ohio BL/TL, 5'11.5", 180 lbs. Deb: 4/12/11

1911 Cle-A	1	0	1.000	4	3	1	0	0	22¹	30	1	9	6	16.1	4.43	77	.326	.392	3	.273	0	-3	-3	0	-0.2
1912 Bro-N	6	11	.353	25	16	12	0	0	163	186	1	56	51	13.4	3.59	93	.293	.351	16	.250	3	-3	-4	-1	-0.3
1913 Bro-N	8	8	.500	26	13	8	2	0	146²	158	2	10	40	10.4	2.58	128	.280	.295	23	.383	8	10	12	-1	2.1
1914 Cin-N	9	13	.409	34	27	8	3	0	198	207	6	54	80	12.1	3.45	85	.274	.328	23	.192	1	-15	-12	-2	-1.2
1918 Was-A	1	2	.333	5	2	2	0	0	38	30	0	12	15	9.9	2.13	128	.238	.304	7	.467	3	3	3	1	0.8
Total 5	25	34	.424	94	61	31	5	0	568	611	19	141	192	12.1	3.22	98	.281	.328	72	.267	16	-8	-4	-3	1.2

● JOE YINGLING   Yingling, Joseph Granville b: 7/23/1866, Westminster, Md. d: 10/24/46, Manchester, Md. BR/TL, 5'7.5", 145 lbs. Deb: 5/28/1886 ♦

| 1886 Was-N | 0 | 0 | — | 1 | 0 | 0 | 0 | 0 | 3 | 7 | 0 | 1 | 1 | 24.0 | 12.00 | 27 | .412 | .444 | 0 | .000 | -0 | -3 | -3 | 0 | -0.3 |

● LEN YOCHIM   Yochim, Leonard Joseph b: 10/16/28, New Orleans, La. BL/TL, 6'2", 200 lbs. Deb: 9/18/51 F

1951 Pit-N	1	1	.500	2	2	0	0	0	8²	10	0	11	5	22.8	8.31	51	.278	.458	0	.000	-0	-4	-4	0	-0.4
1954 Pit-N	0	1	.000	10	1	0	0	0	19²	30	2	8	7	17.4	7.32	57	.361	.418	1	.500	0	-7	-7	1	-0.6
Total 2	1	2	.333	12	3	0	0	0	28¹	40	2	19	12	19.1	7.62	55	.336	.432	1	.200	-0	-11	-11	1	-1.0

● RAY YOCHIM   Yochim, Raymond Austin Aloysius b: 7/19/22, New Orleans, La. BR/TR, 6'1", 170 lbs. Deb: 5/02/48 F

1948 StL-N	0	0	—	1	0	0	0	0	1	0	0	3	1	27.0	0.00	—	.000	.500	0	—	0	0	0	0	0.0
1949 StL-N	0	0	—	3	0	0	0	0	2¹	3	1	4	3	27.0	15.43	27	.273	.467	0	—	0	-3	-3	-0	-0.3
Total 2	0	0	—	4	0	0	0	0	3¹	3	1	7	4	27.0	10.80	38	.214	.476	0	—	0	-3	-2	-0	-0.3

● LEFTY YORK   York, James Edward b: 11/1/1892, West Fork, Ark. d: 4/9/61, York, Pa. BL/TL, 5'10", 185 lbs. Deb: 9/12/19

1919 Phi-A	0	2	.000	2	2	0	0	0	4¹	13	0	5	2	37.4	24.92	14	.500	.581	0	.000	-0	-10	-10	0	-0.9
1921 Chi-N	5	9	.357	40	10	4	1	1	139	170	5	63	57	15.4	4.73	81	.308	.384	5	.128	-2	-15	-14	-3	-1.9
Total 2	5	11	.313	42	12	4	1	1	143¹	183	5	68	59	16.1	5.34	71	.317	.393	5	.125	-2	-25	-24	-3	-2.8

● JIM YORK   York, James Harlan b: 8/27/47, Maywood, Cal. BR/TR, 6'3", 200 lbs. Deb: 9/21/70

1970 KC-A	1	1	.500	4	0	0	0	0	8	5	2	2	6	7.9	3.38	111	.179	.233	0	.000	-0	0	0	-0	0.0
1971 KC-A	5	5	.500	53	0	0	0	3	93¹	70	7	44	103	11.3	2.89	119	.203	.299	2	.118	1	6	6	-0	0.7
1972 Hou-N	0	1	.000	26	0	0	0	6	36	45	3	18	25	16.0	5.25	64	.321	.403	0	.000	-0	-7	-8	-0	-0.8
1973 Hou-N	3	4	.429	41	0	0	0	6	53	65	4	20	22	14.6	4.42	82	.305	.368	0	.000	-0	-4	-5	-2	-0.5
1974 Hou-N	2	2	.500	28	0	0	0	1	38¹	48	1	19	15	16.0	3.29	105	.298	.376	0	.000	-0	1	1	0	0.0
1975 Hou-N	4	4	.500	19	4	0	0	0	46²	43	1	25	17	14.1	3.86	87	.251	.363	1	.091	-1	-3	-3	-1	-0.4
1976 NY-A	1	0	1.000	3	0	0	0	0	9²	14	1	4	6	17.7	5.59	61	.333	.404	0	—	0	-2	-2	-0	-0.2
Total 7	16	17	.485	174	4	0	0	10	285	290	19	132	194	13.7	3.79	91	.264	.349	3	.075	-1	-7	-10	-1	-1.2

● MIKE YORK   York, Michael David b: 9/6/64, Oak Park, Ill. BR/TR, 6'1", 187 lbs. Deb: 8/17/90

1990 Pit-N	1	1	.500	4	1	0	0	0	12²	13	0	5	4	13.5	2.84	127	.277	.358	1	.333	0	1	1	0	0.2
1991 Cle-A	1	4	.200	14	4	0	0	0	34²	45	2	19	19	17.1	6.75	62	.333	.423	0	—	0	-10	-10	-0	-1.0
Total 2	2	5	.286	18	5	0	0	0	47¹	58	2	24	23	16.2	5.70	70	.319	.407	1	.333	0	-9	-9	-0	-0.8

● GUS YOST   Yost, August 6'5", Deb: 6/12/1893

| 1893 Chi-N | 0 | 1 | .000 | 1 | 1 | 0 | 0 | 0 | 2² | 3 | 0 | 8 | 1 | 37.1 | 13.50 | 34 | .275 | .582 | 0 | .000 | -0 | -3 | -3 | 0 | -0.2 |

● FLOYD YOUMANS   Youmans, Floyd Everett b: 5/11/64, Tampa, Fla. BR/TR, 6'1", 190 lbs. Deb: 7/01/85

1985 Mon-N	4	3	.571	14	12	0	0	0	77	57	3	49	54	12.5	2.45	138	.206	.327	1	.053	-0	10	8	-2	0.6
1986 Mon-N	13	12	.520	33	32	6	2	0	219	145	14	118	202	11.0	3.53	104	.188	.299	12	.160	2	4	4	-3	0.2
1987 Mon-N	9	8	.529	23	23	3	3	0	116¹	112	13	47	94	12.4	4.64	91	.251	.324	6	.150	1	-7	-6	-0	-0.5
1988 Mon-N	3	6	.333	14	13	1	1	0	84	64	8	41	54	11.5	3.21	112	.213	.311	4	.154	-0	2	4	-1	0.3
1989 Phi-N	1	5	.167	10	10	0	0	0	42²	50	7	25	20	16.2	5.70	62	.299	.397	1	.077	-1	-10	-10	-1	-1.1
Total 5	30	34	.469	94	90	10	6	0	539	428	45	280	424	12.0	3.74	100	.218	.319	24	.139	1	-1	-1	-6	-0.5

● ANTHONY YOUNG   Young, Anthony Wayne b: 1/19/66, Houston, Tex. BR/TR, 6'2", 200 lbs. Deb: 8/05/91

1991 NY-N	2	5	.286	10	8	0	0	0	49¹	48	4	12	20	11.1	3.10	117	.257	.305	2	.143	0	3	3	-1	0.2
1992 NY-N	2	14	.125	52	13	1	0	15	121	134	8	31	64	12.3	4.17	84	.285	.331	3	.111	-1	-9	-9	-0	-1.1
Total 2	4	19	.174	62	21	1	0	15	170¹	182	12	43	84	12.0	3.86	92	.277	.323	5	.122	-1	-6	-6	-1	-0.9

● PETE YOUNG   Young, Bryan Owen b: 3/19/68, Meadville, Miss. BR/TR, 6', 225 lbs. Deb: 6/05/92

| 1992 Mon-N | 0 | 0 | — | 13 | 0 | 0 | 0 | 0 | 20¹ | 18 | 0 | 9 | 11 | 12.4 | 3.98 | 88 | .247 | .337 | 0 | — | -0 | -1 | -1 | -0 | -0.1 |

● CHARLIE YOUNG   Young, Charles "Cy" b: 1/12/1893, Philadelphia, Pa. d: 5/12/52, Riverside, N.J. BB/TR, 5'10.5", 155 lbs. Deb: 9/05/15

| 1915 Bal-F | 2 | 3 | .400 | 9 | 5 | 1 | 0 | 0 | 35 | 39 | 0 | 21 | 13 | 16.5 | 5.91 | 54 | .289 | .400 | 2 | .222 | 0 | -11 | -11 | 2 | -0.9 |

● CLIFF YOUNG   Young, Clifford Raphael b: 8/2/64, Willis, Tex. BL/TL, 6'4", 200 lbs. Deb: 7/14/90

1990 Cal-A	1	1	.500	17	0	0	0	0	30²	40	2	7	19	14.1	3.52	108	.325	.366	0	—	0	1	1	-0	0.2
1991 Cal-A	1	0	1.000	11	0	0	0	0	12²	12	3	3	6	10.7	4.26	96	.261	.306	0	—	0	-0	-0	0	0.0
Total 2	2	1	.667	28	0	0	0	0	43¹	52	5	10	25	13.1	3.74	104	.308	.350	0	—	0	1	1	-0	0.2

● CURT YOUNG   Young, Curtis Allen b: 4/16/60, Saginaw, Mich. BR/TL, 6'1", 180 lbs. Deb: 6/24/83

1983 Oak-A	0	1	.000	8	2	0	0	0	9	17	1	5	5	23.0	16.00	24	.386	.460	0	—	0	-12	-12	-1	-1.0
1984 Oak-A	9	4	.692	20	17	2	1	0	108²	118	9	31	41	13.0	4.06	92	.274	.334	0	—	0	-1	-4	-1	-0.2
1985 Oak-A	0	4	.000	19	7	0	0	0	46	57	15	22	19	15.7	7.24	53	.300	.376	0	—	0	-16	-17	-1	-1.4
1986 Oak-A	13	9	.591	29	27	5	2	0	198	176	19	57	116	10.9	3.45	112	.236	.297	0	—	0	16	9	0	1.1
1987 Oak-A	13	7	.650	31	31	6	0	0	203	194	38	44	124	10.7	4.08	101	.252	.295	0	.000	0	8	1	0	0.1
1988 *Oak-A	11	8	.579	26	26	1	0	0	156¹	162	23	50	69	12.4	4.14	91	.275	.336	0	—	0	-3	-6	-1	-0.7
1989 Oak-A	5	9	.357	25	20	1	0	0	111	117	10	47	55	13.5	3.73	99	.264	.338	0	—	0	2	-1	-1	0.1
1990 Oak-A	9	6	.600	26	21	0	0	0	124¹	124	17	53	56	13.0	4.85	77	.266	.344	0	—	0	-13	-16	-1	-1.4
1991 Oak-A	4	2	.667	41	1	0	0	0	68¹	74	8	34	27	14.5	5.00	77	.278	.364	0	—	0	-7	-9	1	-0.8
1992 KC-A	1	2	.333	10	2	0	0	0	24¹	29	1	7	7	13.3	5.18	77	.293	.340	0	—	0	-3	-3	-0	-0.4
NY-A	3	0	1.000	13	5	0	0	0	43¹	51	1	10	13	13.1	3.32	122	.298	.344	0	—	0	3	3	0	0.4
Yr	4	2	.667	23	7	0	0	0	67²	80	2	17	20	13.2	3.99	101	.295	.341	0	—	0	-0	0	0	0.0
Total 10	68	52	.567	248	159	15	3	0	1092¹	1119	142	360	532	12.5	4.31	90	.265	.328	0	.000	0	-26	-54	-1	-4.2

● CY YOUNG   Young, Denton True b: 3/29/1867, Gilmore, Ohio d: 11/4/55, Newcomerstown, Ohio BR/TR, 6'2", 210 lbs. Deb: 8/06/1890 MH

1890 Cle-N	9	7	.563	17	16	16	0	0	147²	145	6	32	36	11.3	3.47	103	.249	.297	8	.123	-6	2	2	1	-0.2
1891 Cle-N	27	22	.551	55	46	43	0	2	423²	431	4	140	147	12.3	2.85	122	.254	.314	29	.167	-3	24	29	-1	2.2
1892 *Cle-N	36	12	.750	53	49	48	9	0	453	363	8	118	168	9.8	1.93	176	.211	.266	31	.158	-8	68	74	5	7.0
1893 Cle-N	34	16	.680	53	46	42	1	1	422²	442	10	103	102	11.8	3.36	145	.261	.307	44	.235	-8	61	71	4	5.3
1894 Cle-N	26	21	.553	52	47	44	2	1	408²	488	19	106	108	13.2	3.94	139	.293	.337	40	.215	-8	63	69	7	5.3
1895 *Cle-N	35	10	.778	47	40	36	4	0	369²	363	10	75	121	10.9	3.26	153	.253	.294	30	.214	-4	62	71	8	6.4
1896 *Cle-N	28	15	.651	51	46	42	5	3	414¹	477	7	62	140	11.9	3.24	140	.286	.316	52	.289	7	52	60	8	6.7
1897 Cle-N	21	19	.525	46	38	35	2	0	333²	391	7	49	88	12.1	3.80	118	.290	.319	34	.222	-5	19	26	3	2.0
1898 Cle-N	25	13	.658	46	41	40	1	1	377²	387	6	41	101	10.4	2.53	143	.263	.287	39	.253	4	45	46	7	5.8
1899 StL-N	26	16	.619	44	42	40	4	1	369¹	368	10	44	111	10.2	2.58	154	.259	.285	32	.216	-1	52	57	6	6.0
1900 StL-N	19	19	.500	41	35	32	4	0	321¹	337	7	36	115	10.5	3.00	121	.269	.291	22	.177	-3	25	23	0	1.9
1901 Bos-A	33	10	.767	43	41	38	5	0	371¹	324	6	37	158	8.9	1.62	217	.232	.256	32	.209	0	84	79	1	7.9

YEAR	TM/L	W	L	PCT	G	GS	CG	SH	SV	IP	H	HR	BB	SO	RAT	ERA	ERA+	OAV	OOB	BH	AVG	PB	PR	/A	PD	TPI
1902	Bos-A	**32**	11	.744	**45**	43	**41**	3	0	**384^{2}**	350	6	53	160	9.7	2.15	166	.243	.276	34	.230	2	**61**	**61**	-6	5.8
1903	*Bos-A	**28**	9	**.757**	40	35	**34**	**7**	**2**	**341^{2}**	294	6	37	176	9.0	2.08	146	.232	.259	44	.321	13	34	**36**	-3	**5.0**
1904	Bos-A	26	16	.619	43	41	40	**10**	1	380	327	6	29	200	**8.5**	1.97	136	.233	**.251**	33	.223	2	27	30	-5	3.1
1905	Bos-A	18	19	.486	38	33	31	4	0	320^{2}	248	3	30	210	**8.1**	1.82	148	.215	**.241**	18	.150	-2	30	31	-2	3.2
1906	Bos-A	13	21	.382	39	34	28	0	2	287^{2}	288	3	25	140	10.0	3.19	86	.264	.285	16	.154	-2	-16	-14	-1	-1.9
1907	Bos-A	21	15	.583	43	37	33	6	2	343^{1}	286	3	51	147	**9.0**	1.99	130	.228	**.263**	27	.216	-0	21	23	-6	1.9
1908	Bos-A	21	11	.656	36	33	30	3	2	299	230	1	37	150	8.1	1.26	195	.213	.240	26	.226	1	38	40	-6	4.2
1909	Cle-A	19	15	.559	35	34	30	3	0	295	267	4	59	109	10.2	2.26	113	.250	.294	21	.196	-0	7	10	-1	0.9
1910	Cle-A	7	10	.412	21	20	14	1	0	163^{1}	149	0	27	58	9.9	2.53	102	.252	.289	8	.145	-0	-0	1	1	0.2
1911	Cle-A	3	4	.429	7	7	4	0	0	46^{1}	54	2	13	20	13.2	3.88	88	.298	.349	1	.063	-2	-3	-2	-0	-0.4
	Bos-N	4	5	.444	11	11	8	2	0	80	83	4	15	35	11.4	3.71	103	.268	.308	2	.080	-3	-3	1	0	-0.2
Total	22	511	316	.618	906	815	749	76	17	7354^{2}	7092	138	1219	2800	10.4	2.63	138	.252	.287	623	.210	-23	753	819	19	78.8

● HARLEY YOUNG Young, Harlan Edward "Cy The Third" b: 9/28/1883, Portland, Ind. d: 3/26/75, Jacksonville, Fla. BR/TR, 6'2", Deb: 4/21/08

YEAR	TM/L	W	L	PCT	G	GS	CG	SH	SV	IP	H	HR	BB	SO	RAT	ERA	ERA+	OAV	OOB	BH	AVG	PB	PR	/A	PD	TPI
1908	Pit-N	0	2	.000	8	3	0	0	0	48^{1}	40	0	10	17	10.2	2.23	103	.234	.296	1	.083	-1	1	0	1	0.1
	Bos-N	0	1	.000	6	2	1	0	0	27^{1}	29	0	4	12	11.9	3.29	73	.269	.313	2	.200	0	-3	-3	-0	-0.3
	Yr	0	3	.000	14	5	1	0	0	75^{2}	69	0	14	29	10.2	2.62	89	.243	.286	3	.136	-0	-2	-2	1	-0.2

● IRV YOUNG Young, Irving Melrose "Young Cy" or "Cy The Second"
b: 7/21/1877, Columbia Falls, Maine d: 1/14/35, Brewer, Maine BL/TL, 5'10", 170 lbs. Deb: 4/14/05

YEAR	TM/L	W	L	PCT	G	GS	CG	SH	SV	IP	H	HR	BB	SO	RAT	ERA	ERA+	OAV	OOB	BH	AVG	PB	PR	/A	PD	TPI
1905	Bos-N	20	21	.488	43	42	**41**	7	0	**378**	337	6	71	156	9.9	2.90	107	.241	.282	14	.103	-8	4	8	4	0.4
1906	Bos-N	16	25	.390	43	41	**37**	4	0	**358^{1}**	349	7	83	151	11.0	2.91	92	.263	.309	12	.096	-7	-11	-9	3	-1.4
1907	Bos-N	10	23	.303	40	32	22	3	1	245^{1}	287	5	58	86	13.1	3.96	64	.306	.354	13	.162	-2	-41	-38	1	-4.1
1908	Bos-N	4	9	.308	16	11	7	1	0	85	94	2	19	32	12.2	2.86	84	.289	.332	5	.156	-1	-5	-4	-1	-0.7
	Pit-N	4	3	.571	16	7	3	1	1	89^{2}	73	1	21	31	9.9	2.01	115	.225	.283	6	.200	1	4	3	-1	0.4
	Yr	8	12	.400	32	18	10	2	1	174^{2}	167	3	40	63	10.9	2.42	97	.257	.305	11	.177	0	-1	-1	-2	-0.3
1910	Chi-A	4	8	.333	27	17	7	4	0	135^{2}	122	0	39	64	10.9	2.72	88	.247	.306	5	.114	-2	-3	-5	-0	-0.8
1911	Chi-A	5	6	.455	24	11	3	1	2	92^{2}	99	2	25	40	12.0	4.37	74	.229	.271	5	.179	-0	-11	-12	1	-1.1
Total	6	63	95	.399	209	161	120	21	4	1384^{2}	1361	23	316	560	11.1	3.11	88	.260	.307	60	.126	-19	-62	-57	6	-7.3

● J. B. YOUNG Young, J. B. b: Mt.Carmel, Pa. Deb: 6/10/1892

YEAR	TM/L	W	L	PCT	G	GS	CG	SH	SV	IP	H	HR	BB	SO	RAT	ERA	ERA+	OAV	OOB	BH	AVG	PB	PR	/A	PD	TPI
1892	StL-N	0	0	—	1	0	0	0	0	2	9	0	2	1	49.5	22.50	14	.600	.647	0	.000	-0	-4	-4	-0	-0.4

● KIP YOUNG Young, Kip Lane b: 10/29/54, Georgetown, Ohio BR/TR, 5'11", 175 lbs. Deb: 7/21/78

YEAR	TM/L	W	L	PCT	G	GS	CG	SH	SV	IP	H	HR	BB	SO	RAT	ERA	ERA+	OAV	OOB	BH	AVG	PB	PR	/A	PD	TPI
1978	Det-A	6	7	.462	14	13	7	0	0	105^{2}	94	9	30	49	10.7	2.81	137	.246	.304	0	—	0	11	12	-2	1.0
1979	Det-A	2	2	.500	13	7	0	0	0	43^{2}	60	11	11	22	14.8	6.39	68	.323	.364	0	—	0	-11	-10	1	-1.1
Total	2	8	9	.471	27	20	7	0	0	149^{1}	154	20	41	71	11.9	3.86	104	.271	.324	0	—	0	1	2	-1	-0.1

● MATT YOUNG Young, Matthew John b: 8/9/58, Pasadena, Cal. BL/TL, 6'3", 205 lbs. Deb: 4/06/83

YEAR	TM/L	W	L	PCT	G	GS	CG	SH	SV	IP	H	HR	BB	SO	RAT	ERA	ERA+	OAV	OOB	BH	AVG	PB	PR	/A	PD	TPI
1983	Sea-A★	11	15	.423	33	32	5	2	0	203^{2}	178	17	79	130	11.7	3.27	130	.236	.315	0	—	0	18	22	2	2.4
1984	Sea-A	6	8	.429	22	22	1	0	0	113^{1}	141	11	57	73	15.8	5.72	70	.307	.384	0	—	0	-22	-22	1	-2.0
1985	Sea-A	12	19	.387	37	35	5	2	1	218^{1}	242	23	76	136	13.4	4.91	86	.282	.345	0	—	0	-18	-17	-2	-1.8
1986	Sea-A	8	6	.571	65	5	1	0	13	103^{2}	108	9	46	82	14.1	3.82	111	.272	.359	0	—	0	4	5	-1	0.3
1987	LA-N	5	8	.385	47	0	0	0	11	54^{1}	62	3	17	42	13.1	4.47	89	.288	.341	0	.000	-0	-2	-3	-2	-0.5
1989	*Oak-A	1	4	.200	26	4	0	0	0	37^{1}	42	2	31	27	17.6	6.75	55	.286	.410	0	—	0	-12	-13	0	-1.0
1990	Sea-A	8	18	.308	34	33	7	1	0	225^{1}	198	15	107	176	12.4	3.51	113	.237	.328	0	—	0	10	11	-0	1.1
1991	Bos-A	3	7	.300	19	16	0	0	0	88^{2}	92	4	53	69	14.9	5.18	83	.266	.367	0	—	0	-11	-9	-0	-0.9
1992	Bos-A	0	4	.000	28	8	1	0	0	70^{2}	69	7	42	57	14.5	4.58	90	.257	.363	0	—	0	-5	-3	-1	-0.4
Total	9	54	89	.378	311	155	20	5	25	1115^{1}	1132	91	508	792	13.5	4.35	95	.264	.347	0	.000	-0	-38	-28	-3	-2.8

● CHIEF YOUNGBLOOD Youngblood, Albert Clyde b: 6/13/1900, Hillsboro, Tex. d: 7/6/68, Amarillo, Tex. BL/TR, 6'3", 202 lbs. Deb: 7/16/22

YEAR	TM/L	W	L	PCT	G	GS	CG	SH	SV	IP	H	HR	BB	SO	RAT	ERA	ERA+	OAV	OOB	BH	AVG	PB	PR	/A	PD	TPI
1922	Was-A	0	0	—	2	0	0	0	0	4^{1}	9	0	7	0	37.4	14.54	27	.429	.600	0	.000	-0	-5	-5	0	-0.5

● DUCKY YOUNT Yount, Herbert Macon "Hub" b: 12/7/1885, Iredell Co., N.C. d: 5/9/70, Winston-Salem, N.C. BR/TR, 6'2", 178 lbs. Deb: 5/28/14

YEAR	TM/L	W	L	PCT	G	GS	CG	SH	SV	IP	H	HR	BB	SO	RAT	ERA	ERA+	OAV	OOB	BH	AVG	PB	PR	/A	PD	TPI
1914	Bal-F	1	1	.500	13	1	1	0	0	41^{1}	44	2	19	19	14.2	4.14	81	.280	.365	1	.083	-1	-4	-4	1	-0.4

● LARRY YOUNT Yount, Lawrence King b: 2/15/50, Houston, Tex. BR/TR, 6'2", 185 lbs. Deb: 9/15/71 F

YEAR	TM/L	W	L	PCT	G	GS	CG	SH	SV	IP	H	HR	BB	SO	RAT	ERA	ERA+	OAV	OOB	BH	AVG	PB	PR	/A	PD	TPI
1971	Hou-N	0	0	—	1	0	0	0	0	0	0	0	0	0	—	—	—	—	—	0	—	0	0	0	0	0.0

● CARL YOWELL Yowell, Carl Columbus "Sundown" b: 12/20/02, Madison Va. d: 7/27/85, Jacksonville, Tex. BL/TL, 6'4", 180 lbs. Deb: 9/05/24

YEAR	TM/L	W	L	PCT	G	GS	CG	SH	SV	IP	H	HR	BB	SO	RAT	ERA	ERA+	OAV	OOB	BH	AVG	PB	PR	/A	PD	TPI
1924	Cle-A	1	1	.500	4	2	2	0	0	27	37	1	13	8	16.7	6.67	64	.343	.413	2	.182	-1	-7	-7	-0	-0.7
1925	Cle-A	2	3	.400	12	4	1	0	0	36^{1}	40	1	17	12	14.4	4.46	99	.310	.395	1	.125	-1	-0	-0	0	-0.1
Total	2	3	4	.429	16	6	3	0	0	63^{1}	77	2	30	20	15.3	5.40	81	.325	.403	3	.158	-1	-8	-7	0	-0.8

● EDDIE YUHAS Yuhas, John Edward b: 8/5/24, Youngstown, Ohio d: 7/6/86, Winston-Salem, N.C BR/TR, 6'1", 180 lbs. Deb: 4/17/52

YEAR	TM/L	W	L	PCT	G	GS	CG	SH	SV	IP	H	HR	BB	SO	RAT	ERA	ERA+	OAV	OOB	BH	AVG	PB	PR	/A	PD	TPI
1952	StL-N	12	2	.857	54	2	0	0	6	99^{1}	90	5	35	39	11.5	2.72	137	.243	.312	4	.190	1	11	11	-1	1.1
1953	StL-N	0	0	—	2	0	0	0	0	1	3	0	0	0	27.0	18.00	24	.500	.500	0	—	0	-2	-2	-0	-0.1
Total	2	12	2	.857	56	2	0	0	6	100^{1}	93	5	35	39	11.7	2.87	130	.247	.315	4	.190	1	10	9	-1	1.0

● ADRIAN ZABALA Zabala, Adrian (Rodriguez) b: 8/26/16, San Antonio De Los Banos, Cuba BL/TL, 5'11", 165 lbs. Deb: 8/11/45

YEAR	TM/L	W	L	PCT	G	GS	CG	SH	SV	IP	H	HR	BB	SO	RAT	ERA	ERA+	OAV	OOB	BH	AVG	PB	PR	/A	PD	TPI
1945	NY-N	2	4	.333	11	5	1	0	0	43^{1}	46	2	20	14	13.7	4.78	82	.284	.363	3	.231	1	-5	-4	0	-0.3
1949	NY-N	2	3	.400	15	4	2	1	1	41	44	5	10	13	12.1	5.27	76	.278	.325	1	.077	-1	-6	-6	-1	-0.8
Total	2	4	7	.364	26	9	3	1	1	84^{1}	90	7	30	27	12.9	5.02	79	.281	.345	4	.154	-0	-10	-10	-1	-1.1

● ZIP ZABEL Zabel, George Washington b: 2/18/1891, Wetmore, Kan. d: 5/31/70, Beloit, Wis. BR/TR, 6'1.5", 185 lbs. Deb: 10/05/13

YEAR	TM/L	W	L	PCT	G	GS	CG	SH	SV	IP	H	HR	BB	SO	RAT	ERA	ERA+	OAV	OOB	BH	AVG	PB	PR	/A	PD	TPI
1913	Chi-N	1	0	1.000	1	1	0	0	0	5	3	0	1	0	7.2	0.00	—	.167	.211	0	.000	0	2	2	0	0.2
1914	Chi-N	4	4	.500	29	7	2	0	3	128	104	5	45	50	10.6	2.18	128	.235	.309	7	.184	-1	9	9	-1	0.7
1915	Chi-N	7	10	.412	36	17	8	3	0	163	124	3	84	60	11.7	3.20	87	.218	.323	4	.074	-4	-8	-8	3	-0.8
Total	3	12	14	.462	66	25	10	3	3	296	231	8	130	110	11.2	2.71	103	.224	.315	11	.117	-4	2	3	2	0.1

● CHINK ZACHARY Zachary, Albert Myron (b: Albert Myron Zarski) b: 10/19/17, Brooklyn, N.Y. BR/TR, 5'11", 182 lbs. Deb: 4/23/44

YEAR	TM/L	W	L	PCT	G	GS	CG	SH	SV	IP	H	HR	BB	SO	RAT	ERA	ERA+	OAV	OOB	BH	AVG	PB	PR	/A	PD	TPI
1944	Bro-N	0	2	.000	4	2	0	0	0	10^{1}	10	2	7	3	15.7	9.58	37	.238	.360	0	.000	-0	-7	-7	-0	-0.7

● TOM ZACHARY Zachary, Jonathan Thompson Walton (a.k.a. Zach Walton In 1918)
b: 5/7/1896, Graham, N.C. d: 1/24/69, Burlington, N.C. BL/TL, 6'1", 187 lbs. Deb: 7/11/18

YEAR	TM/L	W	L	PCT	G	GS	CG	SH	SV	IP	H	HR	BB	SO	RAT	ERA	ERA+	OAV	OOB	BH	AVG	PB	PR	/A	PD	TPI
1918	Phi-A	2	0	1.000	2	2	0	0	0	8	9	0	7	1	18.0	5.63	52	.321	.457	2	.500	1	-3	-2	-0	-0.2
1919	Was-A	1	5	.167	17	7	0	0	0	61^{2}	68	0	20	9	13.0	2.92	110	.292	.350	5	.333	2	2	2	-1	0.3
1920	Was-A	15	16	.484	44	31	19	3	2	262^{2}	289	7	78	53	12.7	3.77	99	.285	.339	29	.261	6	1	-1	0	0.4
1921	Was-A	18	16	.529	39	31	17	2	1	250	314	10	59	53	13.6	3.96	104	.319	.361	23	.256	3	9	4	-0	0.7
1922	Was-A	15	10	.600	32	25	13	1	1	184^{2}	190	6	43	37	11.5	3.12	124	.275	.321	21	.296	5	19	15	0	2.0
1923	Was-A	10	16	.385	35	29	10	0	0	204^{1}	270	9	63	40	14.8	4.49	84	.321	.372	15	.192	-0	-12	-17	-1	-1.7
1924	*Was-A	15	9	.625	33	27	13	1	2	202^{2}	198	5	53	45	11.3	2.75	147	.264	.315	22	.306	4	33	29	2	3.4
1925	*Was-A	12	15	.444	38	33	11	1	2	217^{2}	247	10	74	58	13.4	3.85	110	.296	.355	12	.174	-2	13	9	-0	0.7
1926	StL-A	14	15	.483	34	31	18	3	0	247^{1}	264	14	97	53	13.4	3.60	119	.288	.359	23	.267	5	11	19	3	2.6
1927	StL-A	4	6	.400	13	12	6	0	0	78^{1}	110	4	27	13	15.7	4.37	100	.345	.396	3	.107	-2	-2	-0	-1	-0.3
	Was-A	4	7	.364	15	14	5	1	0	102^{2}	116	2	30	13	13.0	3.94	103	.290	.343	5	.139	-2	2	1	-3	-0.3

YEAR	TM/L	W	L	PCT	G	GS	CG	SH	SV	IP	H	HR	BB	SO	RAT	ERA	ERA+	OAV	OOB	BH	AVG	PB	PR	/A	PD	TPI
	Yr	8	13	.381	28	26	11	1	0	181	226	6	57	26	14.2	4.13	102	.314	.366	8	.125	-4	0	1	-3	-0.6
1928	Was-A	6	9	.400	20	14	5	1	0	102^2	130	5	40	19	15.0	5.44	74	.322	.384	10	.303	1	-16	-16	1	-1.3
	*NY-A	3	3	.500	7	6	3	0	1	45^2	54	1	15	7	13.6	3.94	95	.320	.375	2	.133	-0	1	-1	1	-0.1
	Yr	9	12	.429	27	20	8	1	1	148^1	184	6	55	26	14.5	4.98	79	.321	.380	12	.250	1	-15	-17	2	-1.4
1929	NY-A	12	0	1.000	26	11	7	2	2	119^2	131	5	30	35	12.3	2.48	155	.277	.323	10	.238	1	23	18	-3	1.6
1930	NY-A	1	1	.500	3	3	0	0	0	16^2	18	0	9	1	14.6	6.48	66	.269	.355	2	.250	1	-3	-4	1	-0.3
	Bos-N	11	5	.688	24	22	10	1	0	151^1	192	9	50	57	14.4	4.58	108	.317	.369	13	.241	2	7	6	-1	0.6
1931	Bos-N	11	15	.423	33	28	16	3	2	229	243	8	53	64	11.7	3.10	122	.272	.314	14	.167	-1	19	17	2	1.9
1932	Bos-N	12	11	.522	32	24	12	1	0	212	231	5	55	67	12.2	3.10	121	.280	.326	21	.273	5	18	16	-2	1.9
1933	Bos-N	7	9	.438	26	20	6	2	2	125	134	1	35	22	12.2	3.53	87	.276	.325	5	.119	-2	-3	-6	0	-0.8
1934	Bos-N	1	2	.333	5	4	2	1	0	24	27	1	8	4	13.1	3.38	113	.278	.333	0	.000	-1	2	1	-0	0.0
	Bro-N	5	6	.455	22	12	4	0	2	101^2	122	5	21	28	12.8	4.43	88	.301	.339	7	.184	1	-4	-6	-1	-0.5
	Yr	6	8	.429	27	16	6	1	2	125^2	149	6	29	32	12.9	4.23	92	.297	.338	7	.152	0	-2	-5	-1	-0.5
1935	Bro-N	7	12	.368	25	21	9	1	4	158	193	10	35	33	13.1	3.59	111	.297	.335	7	.135	-1	8	7	0	0.6
1936	Bro-N	0	0	—	1	0	0	0	0	0^1	2	0	1	0	81.0	54.00	8	1.000	1.000	0	—	0	-2	-2	0	-0.2
	Phi-N	0	3	.000	7	2	0	0	1	20^1	28	2	11	8	17.3	7.97	57	.329	.406	3	.333	1	-9	-8	0	-0.6
	Yr	0	3	.000	8	2	0	0	1	20^2	30	2	12	8	18.3	8.71	52	.345	.424	3	.333	1	-11	-10	0	-0.8
Total	19	186	191	.493	533	409	186	24	22	3126^1	3580	119	914	720	13.1	3.73	106	.294	.345	254	.226	25	116	82	-2	10.4
● **CHRIS ZACHARY**	Zachary, William Christopher b: 2/19/44, Knoxville, Tenn. BL/TR, 6'2", 200 lbs. Deb: 4/11/63																									
1963	Hou-N	2	2	.500	22	7	0	0	0	57	62	5	22	42	13.7	4.89	64	.272	.344	0	.000	-1	-10	-11	1	-1.2
1964	Hou-N	0	1	.000	1	1	0	0	0	4	6	1	1	2	15.8	9.00	38	.333	.368	0	.000	-0	-2	-2	0	-0.2
1965	Hou-N	0	2	.000	4	2	0	0	0	10^2	12	0	6	4	15.2	4.22	80	.273	.360	0	.000	-0	-1	-1	-0	-0.1
1966	Hou-N	3	5	.375	10	8	0	0	0	55	44	1	32	37	12.6	3.44	100	.221	.332	4	.222	1	1	-0	-1	0.0
1967	Hou-N	1	6	.143	9	7	0	0	0	36^1	42	5	12	18	13.9	5.70	58	.290	.352	1	.100	-0	-9	-10	-0	-1.0
1969	KC-A	0	1	.000	8	2	0	0	0	18^1	27	4	7	6	16.7	7.85	47	.346	.400	1	.500	0	-9	-8	-0	-0.8
1971	StL-N	3	10	.231	23	12	1	1	0	89^2	114	3	26	48	14.5	5.32	68	.316	.368	8	.242	1	-18	-17	0	-1.7
1972	*Det-A	1	1	.500	25	1	0	0	1	38^1	27	2	15	21	10.1	1.41	223	.201	.287	1	.500	1	7	7	-0	0.9
1973	Pit-N	0	1	.000	6	0	0	0	1	12	10	1	1	6	8.3	3.00	117	.222	.239	0	.000	-0	1	1	-0	0.0
Total	9	10	29	.256	108	40	1	1	2	321^1	344	22	122	184	13.4	4.57	74	.275	.344	15	.181	1	-41	-42	-1	-4.1
● **PAT ZACHRY**	Zachry, Patrick Paul b: 4/24/52, Richmond, Tex. BR/TR, 6'5", 180 lbs. Deb: 4/11/76																									
1976	*Cin-N	14	7	.667	38	28	6	1	0	204	170	8	83	143	11.3	2.74	128	.228	.307	7	.113	-2	17	17	-2	1.5
1977	Cin-N	3	7	.300	12	12	3	0	0	75	78	7	29	36	13.0	5.04	78	.273	.342	3	.136	-1	-9	-9	1	-0.8
	NY-N	7	6	.538	19	19	2	1	0	119^2	129	14	48	63	13.5	3.76	99	.278	.350	6	.143	-1	2	-0	-2	-0.3
	Yr	10	13	.435	31	31	5	1	0	194^2	207	21	77	99	13.3	4.25	90	.274	.344	9	.141	-2	-7	-10	-0	-1.1
1978	NY-N☆	10	6	.625	21	21	5	2	0	138	120	9	60	78	11.8	3.33	105	.236	.318	3	.070	-2	4	2	1	0.2
1979	NY-N	5	1	.833	7	7	1	0	0	42^2	44	3	21	17	14.1	3.59	101	.267	.356	2	.125	-1	1	0	0	0.0
1980	NY-N	6	10	.375	28	26	7	3	0	164^2	145	16	58	88	11.4	3.01	118	.240	.312	2	.043	-4	11	10	-2	0.5
1981	NY-N	7	14	.333	24	24	3	0	0	139	151	13	56	76	13.7	4.14	84	.282	.354	6	.158	0	-10	-10	1	-1.0
1982	NY-N	6	9	.400	36	16	2	0	1	137^2	149	10	57	69	13.5	4.05	90	.279	.349	3	.079	-2	-7	-6	-0	-0.9
1983	*LA-N	6	1	.857	40	1	0	0	0	61^1	63	4	21	36	12.5	2.49	144	.278	.341	2	.500	1	8	7	0	0.9
1984	LA-N	5	6	.455	58	0	0	0	2	82^2	84	3	51	55	14.9	3.81	93	.267	.372	2	.333	1	-2	-3	1	-0.1
1985	Phi-N	0	0	—	10	0	0	0	0	12^2	14	1	11	8	17.8	4.26	86	.280	.410	0	.000	-0	-1	-1	1	0.0
Total	10	69	67	.507	293	154	29	7	3	1177^1	1147	88	495	669	12.7	3.52	102	.259	.336	36	.113	-11	13	8	-1	-0.0
● **GEORGE ZACKERT**	Zackert, George Carl "Zeke" b: 12/24/1884, Buchanan Co., Mo. d: 2/18/77, Burlington, Iowa BL/TL, 6', 177 lbs. Deb: 9/22/11																									
1911	StL-N	0	2	.000	4	1	0	0	0	7^1	17	0	6	6	28.2	11.05	31	.486	.561	0	.000	-0	-6	-6	1	-0.6
1912	StL-N	0	0	—	1	0	0	0	0	1	2	0	1	0	36.0	18.00	19	.667	.800	0	—	0	-2	-2	0	-0.1
Total	2	0	2	.000	5	1	0	0	0	8^1	19	0	7	6	29.2	11.88	28	.500	.587	0	.000	-0	-8	-8	1	-0.7
● **GEOFF ZAHN**	Zahn, Geoffrey Clayton b: 12/19/45, Baltimore, Md. BL/TL, 6'1", 180 lbs. Deb: 9/02/73																									
1973	LA-N	1	0	1.000	6	1	0	0	0	13^1	5	2	2	9	4.7	1.35	255	.116	.156	0	.000	-0	3	3	0	0.3
1974	LA-N	3	5	.375	21	10	1	0	0	79^2	78	3	16	33	10.8	2.03	167	.254	.295	4	.174	-0	14	12	0	1.3
1975	LA-N	0	1	.000	2	0	0	0	0	3	2	0	5	1	21.0	9.00	38	.222	.500	0	—	0	-2	-2	-0	-0.2
	Chi-N	2	7	.222	16	10	0	0	1	62^2	67	2	26	21	13.4	4.45	86	.282	.352	2	.133	-1	-6	-4	1	-0.4
	Yr	2	8	.200	18	10	0	0	1	65^2	69	2	31	22	13.7	4.66	82	.279	.360	2	.133	-1	-8	-6	1	-0.6
1976	Chi-N	0	1	.000	3	2	0	0	0	8^1	16	0	2	4	20.5	10.80	36	.410	.452	0	.000	-0	-7	-6	0	-0.6
1977	Min-A	12	14	.462	34	32	7	1	0	198	234	20	66	88	13.9	4.68	85	.299	.358	0	—	0	-14	-15	2	-1.2
1978	Min-A	14	14	.500	35	35	12	1	0	252^1	260	18	81	106	12.3	3.03	126	.274	.334	0	—	0	20	22	-0	2.3
1979	Min-A	13	7	.650	26	24	4	0	0	169	181	13	41	58	11.8	3.57	123	.279	.322	0	—	0	12	15	2	1.4
1980	Min-A	14	18	.438	38	35	13	5	0	232^2	273	17	66	96	13.2	4.41	99	.302	.351	0	—	0	-10	-1	0	-0.7
1981	Cal-A	10	11	.476	25	25	9	0	0	161^1	181	18	43	52	12.5	4.41	83	.285	.330	0	—	0	-13	-14	0	-1.4
1982	*Cal-A	18	8	.692	34	34	12	4	0	229^1	225	18	65	81	11.5	3.73	109	.259	.314	0	—	0	9	8	-1	0.7
1983	Cal-A	9	11	.450	29	28	11	3	0	203	212	22	51	81	11.7	3.33	121	.269	.314	0	—	0	17	16	-2	1.5
1984	Cal-A	13	10	.565	28	27	9	**5**	0	199^1	200	11	48	61	11.2	3.12	127	.263	.308	0	—	0	19	19	1	2.1
1985	Cal-A	2	2	.500	7	7	1	1	0	37	44	5	14	14	14.1	4.38	94	.299	.360	0	—	0	-1	-1	1	0.0
Total	13	111	109	.505	304	270	79	20	1	1849	1978	149	526	705	12.3	3.74	107	.278	.329	6	.140	-2	43	51	4	5.1
● **PAUL ZAHNISER**	Zahniser, Paul Vernon b: 9/6/1896, Sac City, Iowa d: 9/26/64, Klamath Falls, Ore. BR/TR, 5'10.5", 170 lbs. Deb: 5/18/23																									
1923	Was-A	9	10	.474	33	21	10	1	0	177	201	7	76	52	14.2	3.86	97	.291	.364	5	.096	-1	2	-2	-2	-0.5
1924	Was-A	5	7	.417	24	14	5	1	0	92	98	2	49	28	14.8	4.40	92	.283	.378	4	.129	-2	-2	-4	-2	-0.7
1925	Bos-A	5	12	.294	37	21	7	1	1	176^2	232	6	89	30	16.4	5.15	88	.327	.403	8	.138	-4	-15	-12	-2	-1.6
1926	Bos-A	6	18	.250	30	24	7	1	0	172	213	5	69	35	14.9	4.97	82	.321	.387	8	.163	-1	-18	-17	3	-1.4
1929	Cin-N	0	0	—	1	0	0	0	0	1	2	1	1	0	27.0	27.00	17	.400	.500	0	—	0	-2	-2	-0	-0.2
Total	5	25	47	.347	125	80	29	4	1	618^2	746	21	284	145	15.1	4.66	88	.309	.384	25	.132	-8	-35	-37	-3	-4.4
● **CARL ZAMLOCH**	Zamloch, Carl Eugene b: 10/6/1889, Oakland, Cal. d: 8/19/63, Santa Barbara, Cal BR/TR, 6'1", 176 lbs. Deb: 5/07/13																									
1913	Det-A	1	6	.143	17	5	3	0	1	69^2	66	1	23	28	11.9	2.45	119	.257	.325	4	.182	-1	4	4	-1	0.2
● **OSCAR ZAMORA**	Zamora, Oscar Jose (Sosa) b: 9/23/44, Camaguey, Cuba BR/TR, 5'10", 178 lbs. Deb: 6/18/74																									
1974	Chi-N	3	9	.250	56	0	0	0	10	83^2	82	6	19	38	10.9	3.12	122	.264	.306	2	.182	-0	5	6	-0	0.6
1975	Chi-N	5	2	.714	52	0	0	0	10	71	84	17	15	28	12.5	5.07	76	.298	.333	1	.167	-0	-11	-10	-0	-1.1
1976	Chi-N	5	3	.625	40	2	0	0	3	55	70	8	17	27	14.4	5.24	74	.317	.368	0	.000	-1	-11	-8	-1	-1.1
1978	Hou-N	0	0	—	10	0	0	0	0	15	20	2	7	6	16.2	7.20	46	.328	.397	0	.000	-0	-6	-6	0	-0.7
Total	4	13	14	.481	158	2	0	0	23	224^2	256	33	58	99	12.6	4.53	84	.293	.337	3	.107	-2	-23	-18	-1	-2.3
● **DOM ZANNI**	Zanni, Dominick Thomas b: 3/1/32, Bronx, N.Y. BR/TR, 5'11", 180 lbs. Deb: 9/28/58																									
1958	SF-N	1	0	1.000	1	0	0	0	0	4	7	1	1	3	18.0	2.25	169	.412	.444	0	.000	-0	1	1	-0	0.0
1959	SF-N	0	0	—	9	0	0	0	0	11	12	2	8	11	17.2	6.55	58	.273	.396	0	—	0	-3	-3	1	-0.2
1961	SF-N	1	0	1.000	8	0	0	0	0	13^2	13	1	12	11	16.5	3.95	96	.277	.424	0	—	0	0	-0	0	0.0
1962	Chi-A	6	5	.545	44	2	0	0	5	86^1	67	12	31	66	10.3	3.75	104	.214	.287	5	.278	2	2	1	2	0.6
1963	Chi-A	0	0	—	5	0	0	0	0	4^1	5	1	4	2	18.7	8.31	42	.294	.429	0	—	0	-2	-2	0	-0.2
	Cin-N	1	1	.500	31	1	0	0	5	43	39	2	21	40	13.4	4.19	80	.247	.350	1	.333	0	-4	-4	1	-0.3
1965	Cin-N	0	0	—	8	0	0	0	0	13^1	7	1	5	10	8.1	1.35	278	.159	.245	0	.000	-0	3	4	0	0.4

YEAR TM/L	W	L	PCT	G	GS	CG	SH	SV	IP	H	HR	BB	SO	RAT	ERA	ERA+	OAV	OOB	BH	AVG	PB	PR	/A	PD	TPI
1966 Cin-N	0	0	—	5	0	0	0	0	7^1	5	0	3	5	11.0	0.00	—	.192	.300	1	1.000	0	3	3	-0	0.4
Total 7	9	6	.600	111	3	0	0	10	183	155	20	85	148	12.1	3.79	99	.233	.326	7	.280	2	-1	-1	4	0.7

● JEFF ZASKE Zaske, Lloyd Jeffrey b: 10/6/60, Seattle, Wash. BR/TR, 6'5", 180 lbs. Deb: 7/21/84

YEAR TM/L	W	L	PCT	G	GS	CG	SH	SV	IP	H	HR	BB	SO	RAT	ERA	ERA+	OAV	OOB	BH	AVG	PB	PR	/A	PD	TPI
1984 Pit-N	0	0	—	3	0	0	0	0	5	4	0	1	2	9.0	0.00	—	.211	.250	0	—	0	2	2	0	0.2

● CLINT ZAVARAS Zavaras, Clinton Wayne b: 1/4/67, Denver, Colo. BR/TR, 6'1", 175 lbs. Deb: 6/03/89

YEAR TM/L	W	L	PCT	G	GS	CG	SH	SV	IP	H	HR	BB	SO	RAT	ERA	ERA+	OAV	OOB	BH	AVG	PB	PR	/A	PD	TPI
1989 Sea-A	1	6	.143	10	10	0	0	0	52	49	4	30	31	14.0	5.19	78	.253	.358	0	—	0	-8	-7	-0	-0.9

● ZAY Zay Deb: 10/07/1886 ♦

YEAR TM/L	W	L	PCT	G	GS	CG	SH	SV	IP	H	HR	BB	SO	RAT	ERA	ERA+	OAV	OOB	BH	AVG	PB	PR	/A	PD	TPI
1886 Bal-a	0	1	.000	1	1	0	0	0	2	4	0	4	2	36.0	9.00	38	.333	.500	0	.000	-0	-1	-1	-0	-0.1

● MATT ZEISER Zeiser, Matthew J. b: 9/25/1888, Chicago, Ill. d: 6/10/42, Norwood Park, Ill BR/TR, 5'10", 170 lbs. Deb: 4/27/14

YEAR TM/L	W	L	PCT	G	GS	CG	SH	SV	IP	H	HR	BB	SO	RAT	ERA	ERA+	OAV	OOB	BH	AVG	PB	PR	/A	PD	TPI
1914 Bos-A	0	0	—	2	0	0	0	0	10	9	0	8	0	16.2	1.80	150	.281	.439	0	.000	-0	1	1	-1	0.0

● BILL ZEPP Zepp, William Clinton b: 7/22/46, Detroit, Mich. BR/TR, 6'2", 185 lbs. Deb: 8/12/69

YEAR TM/L	W	L	PCT	G	GS	CG	SH	SV	IP	H	HR	BB	SO	RAT	ERA	ERA+	OAV	OOB	BH	AVG	PB	PR	/A	PD	TPI
1969 Min-A	0	0	—	4	0	0	0	0	5^1	6	1	4	2	16.9	6.75	54	.286	.400	0	.000	-0	-2	-2	-0	-0.2
1970 *Min-A	9	4	.692	43	20	1	1	2	151	154	9	51	64	12.8	3.22	116	.266	.335	6	.136	-1	8	8	-2	0.6
1971 Det-A	1	1	.500	16	4	0	0	2	31^2	41	2	17	15	17.3	5.12	70	.328	.421	0	.000	-0	-6	-5	0	-0.6
Total 3	10	5	.667	63	24	1	1	4	188	201	12	72	81	13.6	3.64	102	.278	.353	6	.122	-2	1	1	-2	-0.2

● GEORGE ZETTLEIN Zettlein, George "Charmer" b: 7/18/1844, Brooklyn, N.Y. d: 5/23/05, Patchogue, N.Y. BR/TR, 5'9", 162 lbs. Deb: 5/08/1871

YEAR TM/L	W	L	PCT	G	GS	CG	SH	SV	IP	H	HR	BB	SO	RAT	ERA	ERA+	OAV	OOB	BH	AVG	PB	PR	/A	PD	TPI
1871 Chi-n	18	9	.667	28	28	25	0	0	240^2	298	6	25	22	**12.1**	**2.73**	**168**	.267	**.283**	32	.250	-8	**40**	**50**		**2.8**
1872 Tro-n	14	8	.636	25	22	17	2	0	187^2	209	2	8	17	10.4	2.54	146	.250	.257	29	.250	-0	25	24		1.7
Eck-n	1	8	.111	9	9	8	0	0	75^1	105	1	6	8	13.3	2.99	116	.298	.310	3	.088	-4	6	4		0.1
Yr	15	16	.484	34	31	25	2	0	263	314	3	14	25	11.2	2.67	136	.265	.273	32	.213	-4	31	28		1.8
1873 Phi-n	36	15	.706	51	51	49	0	0	460	593	3	41	28	12.4	2.70	122	.283	.297	50	.207	-8	28	31		1.6
1874 Chi-n	27	30	.474	57	57	57	3	0	515^2	653	3	46		12.2	*3.07*	99	.280	.294	47	.193	-11	-4	-1		-0.9
1875 Chi-n	17	14	.548	31	31	29	6	0	282	269	0	6		8.8	*1.82*	138	.232	.236	29	.223	-3	20	22		1.7
Phi-n	12	8	.600	21	21	20	1	0	180^1	208	0	10		10.9	*2.40*	105	.263	.272	15	.179	-4	1	2		-0.1
Yr	29	22	.569	52	52	49	**7**	0	462^1	477	0	16		9.6	*2.04*	123	.245	.251	44	.206	-7	21	24		1.6
1876 Phi-N	4	20	.167	28	25	23	1	2	234	358	2	6	10	14.0	3.88	62	.331	.334	27	.211	-5	-41	-38	-1	-3.5
Total 5 n	125	92	.576	222	219	205	12	0	1941^2	2335	15	142	75	11.5	*2.64*	123	.269	.281	205	.210	-38	116	130		6.9

● BOB ZICK Zick, Robert George b: 4/26/27, Chicago, Ill. BL/TR, 6', 168 lbs. Deb: 5/02/54

YEAR TM/L	W	L	PCT	G	GS	CG	SH	SV	IP	H	HR	BB	SO	RAT	ERA	ERA+	OAV	OOB	BH	AVG	PB	PR	/A	PD	TPI
1954 Chi-N	0	0	—	8	0	0	0	0	16^1	23	1	7	9	16.5	8.27	51	.343	.405	1	.250	0	-8	-7	-0	-0.7

● GEORGE ZIEGLER Ziegler, George J. b: 1872, Chicago, Ill. d: 7/22/16, Kankakee, Ill. Deb: 6/19/1890

YEAR TM/L	W	L	PCT	G	GS	CG	SH	SV	IP	H	HR	BB	SO	RAT	ERA	ERA+	OAV	OOB	BH	AVG	PB	PR	/A	PD	TPI
1890 Pit-N	0	1	.000	1	1	0	0	0	6	12	0	0	1	18.0	10.50	31	.403	.403	0	.000	-0	-5	-5	-0	-0.4

● STEVE ZIEM Ziem, Stephen Graeling b: 10/24/61, Milwaukee, Wis. BR/TR, 6'2", 210 lbs. Deb: 4/30/87

YEAR TM/L	W	L	PCT	G	GS	CG	SH	SV	IP	H	HR	BB	SO	RAT	ERA	ERA+	OAV	OOB	BH	AVG	PB	PR	/A	PD	TPI
1987 Atl-N	0	1	.000	2	0	0	0	0	2^1	4	0	1	0	19.3	7.71	56	.364	.417	0	—	0	-1	-1	-0	-0.1

● WALTER ZINK Zink, Walter Noble b: 11/21/1899, Pittsfield, Mass. d: 6/12/64, Quincy, Mass. BR/TR, 6', 165 lbs. Deb: 7/06/21

YEAR TM/L	W	L	PCT	G	GS	CG	SH	SV	IP	H	HR	BB	SO	RAT	ERA	ERA+	OAV	OOB	BH	AVG	PB	PR	/A	PD	TPI
1921 NY-N	0	0	—	2	0	0	0	0	4	4	0	3	1	15.8	2.25	163	.235	.350	0	.000	-0	1	1	-0	0.0

● JIMMY ZINN Zinn, James Edward b: 1/21/1895, Benton, Ark. d: 2/26/91, Memphis, Tenn. BL/TR, 6'0.5", 195 lbs. Deb: 9/04/19

YEAR TM/L	W	L	PCT	G	GS	CG	SH	SV	IP	H	HR	BB	SO	RAT	ERA	ERA+	OAV	OOB	BH	AVG	PB	PR	/A	PD	TPI
1919 Phi-A	1	3	.250	5	3	2	0	0	25^2	38	1	10	9	17.2	6.31	54	.365	.426	4	.308	2	-9	-8	-0	-0.6
1920 Pit-N	1	1	.500	6	3	2	0	0	31	32	2	5	18	11.0	3.48	92	.260	.295	3	.200	0	-1	-1	-0	-0.1
1921 Pit-N	7	6	.538	32	9	5	1	4	127^1	159	3	30	49	13.5	3.68	104	.318	.359	11	.224	0	2	2	-2	0.0
1922 Pit-N	0	0	—	5	0	0	0	1	9^2	11	1	2	3	12.1	1.86	219	.297	.333	0	.000	-0	2	2	-0	0.2
1929 Cle-A	4	6	.400	18	11	6	1	2	105^1	150	8	33	29	15.9	5.04	88	.340	.390	16	.381	7	-9	-7	-0	0.0
Total 5	13	16	.448	66	26	15	2	7	299	390	15	80	108	14.4	4.30	92	.324	.369	34	.283	9	-15	-12	-3	-0.5

● BILL ZINSER Zinser, William Francis b: 1/6/18, Astoria, N.Y. BR/TR, 6'1", 185 lbs. Deb: 8/19/44

YEAR TM/L	W	L	PCT	G	GS	CG	SH	SV	IP	H	HR	BB	SO	RAT	ERA	ERA+	OAV	OOB	BH	AVG	PB	PR	/A	PD	TPI
1944 Was-A	0	0	—	2	0	0	0	0	0^2	1	0	5	1	81.0	27.00	12	.333	.750	0	—	0	-2	-2	0	-0.2

● ED ZMICH Zmich, Edward Albert b: 10/1/1884, Cleveland, Ohio d: 8/20/50, Cleveland, Ohio BL/TL, 6', 180 lbs. Deb: 7/23/10

YEAR TM/L	W	L	PCT	G	GS	CG	SH	SV	IP	H	HR	BB	SO	RAT	ERA	ERA+	OAV	OOB	BH	AVG	PB	PR	/A	PD	TPI
1910 StL-N	0	5	.000	9	6	2	0	0	36	38	0	29	19	17.5	6.25	48	.304	.446	1	.077	-1	-13	-13	1	-1.3
1911 StL-N	1	0	1.000	4	0	0	0	0	12^2	8	0	8	4	12.1	2.13	158	.182	.321	0	.000	-1	2	2	-1	0.0
Total 2	1	5	.167	13	6	2	0	0	48^2	46	0	37	23	16.1	5.18	60	.272	.414	1	.059	-2	-11	-11	0	-1.3

● SAM ZOLDAK Zoldak, Samuel Walter "Sad Sam" b: 12/8/18, Brooklyn, N.Y. d: 8/25/66, New Hyde Park, N.Y BL/TL, 5'11.5", 185 lbs. Deb: 5/13/44

YEAR TM/L	W	L	PCT	G	GS	CG	SH	SV	IP	H	HR	BB	SO	RAT	ERA	ERA+	OAV	OOB	BH	AVG	PB	PR	/A	PD	TPI
1944 StL-A	0	0	—	18	0	0	0	0	38^2	49	1	19	15	15.8	3.72	97	.310	.384	2	.333	0	-1	-1	0	0.0
1945 StL-A	3	2	.600	26	1	1	0	0	69^2	74	3	18	19	11.9	3.36	105	.267	.312	1	.050	-3	0	1	-1	-0.3
1946 StL-A	9	11	.450	35	21	9	2	2	170^1	166	11	57	51	11.8	3.43	109	.256	.317	9	.173	-0	1	6	1	0.6
1947 StL-A	9	10	.474	35	19	6	1	1	171	162	7	76	36	12.5	3.47	112	.254	.334	10	.172	-1	4	8	3	1.0
1948 StL-A	2	4	.333	11	9	0	0	0	54	64	4	19	13	14.0	4.67	98	.296	.356	6	.273	0	-2	-1	0	0.0
Cle-A	9	6	.600	23	12	4	1	0	105^2	104	6	24	17	10.9	2.81	144	.261	.303	5	.139	-2	17	15	2	1.4
Yr	11	10	.524	34	21	4	1	0	159^2	168	10	43	30	11.9	3.44	123	.273	.321	11	.190	-1	15	14	2	1.4
1949 Cle-A	1	2	.333	27	0	0	0	0	53	60	4	18	11	13.2	4.25	94	.291	.348	3	.375	1	-0	-1	3	0.2
1950 Cle-A	4	2	.667	33	3	0	0	4	63^2	64	6	21	15	12.2	3.96	109	.259	.320	3	.188	0	4	3	-0	0.2
1951 Phi-A	6	10	.375	26	18	8	1	0	128	127	9	24	18	10.6	3.16	135	.257	.292	7	.156	-3	14	16	-2	1.1
1952 Phi-A	0	6	.000	16	10	2	0	1	75^1	86	3	25	12	13.3	4.06	97	.290	.345	4	.174	-1	-3	-1	2	0.0
Total 9	43	53	.448	250	93	30	5	8	929^1	956	54	301	207	12.2	3.54	112	.267	.325	50	.175	-8	34	45	7	4.2

● BILL ZUBER Zuber, William Henry "Goober" b: 3/26/13, Middle Amana, Iowa d: 11/2/82, Cedar Rapids, Iowa BR/TR, 6'2", 195 lbs. Deb: 9/16/36

YEAR TM/L	W	L	PCT	G	GS	CG	SH	SV	IP	H	HR	BB	SO	RAT	ERA	ERA+	OAV	OOB	BH	AVG	PB	PR	/A	PD	TPI
1936 Cle-A	1	1	.500	2	2	1	0	0	13^2	14	0	15	5	19.1	6.59	76	.269	.433	1	.200	-0	-2	-2	-0	-0.2
1938 Cle-A	0	3	.000	15	0	0	0	1	28^2	33	0	20	14	16.6	5.02	92	.295	.402	0	.000	-1	-1	-1	-0	-0.2
1939 Cle-A	2	0	1.000	16	1	0	0	0	31^2	41	2	19	16	17.3	5.97	74	.323	.415	1	.200	0	-5	-6	1	-0.4
1940 Cle-A	1	1	.500	17	0	0	0	0	24	25	3	14	12	14.6	5.63	75	.260	.355	1	.333	0	-3	-4	-0	-0.4
1941 Was-A	6	4	.600	36	7	1	0	2	96^1	110	5	61	51	16.2	5.42	75	.291	.392	0	.000	-3	-14	-15	-1	-1.8
1942 Was-A	9	9	.500	37	7	3	1	1	126^2	115	5	82	64	14.0	3.84	95	.243	.355	6	.154	0	-3	-3	-3	-0.5
1943 NY-A	8	4	.667	20	13	7	0	1	118	100	3	74	57	13.3	3.89	83	.234	.347	7	.184	2	-8	-9	-2	-0.9
1944 NY-A	5	7	.417	22	13	2	1	0	107	101	5	54	59	13.1	4.21	83	.255	.346	4	.129	-2	-9	-9	-1	-1.1
1945 NY-A	5	11	.313	21	14	7	0	1	127	121	2	56	50	12.5	3.19	109	.259	.338	7	.167	-1	2	4	-1	0.1
1946 NY-A	0	1	.000	3	0	0	0	0	5^2	10	2	3	3	20.6	12.71	27	.385	.448	0	.000	-0	-6	-6	-0	-0.6
*Bos-A	5	1	.833	15	7	2	1	0	56^2	37	4	39	29	12.1	2.54	144	.187	.321	2	.111	-1	6	7	0	0.7
Yr	5	2	.714	18	7	2	1	0	62^1	47	6	42	32	12.9	3.47	105	.210	.335	2	.100	-1	0	1	-0	0.1
1947 Bos-A	1	0	1.000	20	1	0	0	0	50^2	60	4	31	23	16.2	5.33	73	.311	.406	2	.154	-0	-9	-8	-0	-0.9
Total 11	43	42	.506	224	65	23	3	6	786	767	35	468	383	14.2	4.28	87	.260	.362	31	.135	-6	-51	-50	-8	-6.2

● GEORGE ZUVERINK Zuverink, George b: 8/20/24, Holland, Mich. BR/TR, 6'4", 200 lbs. Deb: 4/21/51

YEAR TM/L	W	L	PCT	G	GS	CG	SH	SV	IP	H	HR	BB	SO	RAT	ERA	ERA+	OAV	OOB	BH	AVG	PB	PR	/A	PD	TPI
1951 Cle-A	0	0	—	16	0	0	0	0	25^1	24	2	13	14	13.5	5.33	71	.253	.349	0	—	0	-3	-4	0	-0.4
1952 Cle-A	0	0	—	1	0	0	0	0	1^1	1	0	0	1	6.8	0.00	—	.200	.200	0	—	0	1	0	0	0.1
1954 Cin-N	0	0	—	2	0	0	0	0	6	10	1	1	2	16.5	9.00	47	.385	.407	1	.500	0	-3	-3	-0	-0.3

YEAR	TM/L	W	L	PCT	G	GS	CG	SH	SV	IP	H	HR	BB	SO	RAT	ERA	ERA+	OAV	OOB	BH	AVG	PB	PR	/A	PD	TPI
	Det-A	9	13	.409	35	25	9	2	4	203	201	22	62	70	12.0	3.59	103	.257	.318	8	.125	-3	3	2	3	0.2
1955	Det-A	0	5	.000	14	1	0	0	0	28¹	38	6	14	13	16.8	6.99	55	.309	.384	0	.000	-1	-10	-10	0	-1.0
	Bal-A	4	3	.571	28	5	0	0	4	86¹	80	5	17	31	10.5	2.19	174	.264	.312	5	.217	1	17	16	1	1.8
	Yr	4	8	.333	42	6	0	0	4	114²	118	11	31	44	12.0	3.38	113	.276	.331	5	.185	0	7	6	1	0.8
1956	Bal-A	7	6	.538	**62**	0	0	0	**16**	97¹	112	6	34	33	13.8	4.16	94	.294	.356	2	.118	-1	-0	-3	1	-0.3
1957	Bal-A	10	6	.625	**56**	0	0	0	9	112²	105	9	39	36	11.8	2.48	145	.257	.327	3	.130	-0	16	14	1	1.6
1958	Bal-A	2	2	.500	45	0	0	0	7	69	74	4	17	22	12.7	3.39	106	.286	.344	2	.222	1	3	2	1	0.4
1959	Bal-A	0	1	.000	6	0	0	0	0	13	15	1	6	1	14.5	4.15	91	.306	.382	0	—	1	-0	-1	0	0.0
Total	8	32	36	.471	265	31	9	2	40	642¹	660	56	203	223	12.5	3.54	105	.271	.334	21	.148	-2	23	13	7	2.1

YEAR	TM/L	WR	LR	GR	SV	IPR	ERAR	RR	/A	RNK	GS	IPS
■ Don Aase												
1977	Bos-A										13	92^1
1978	Cal-A										29	178^2
1979	Cal-A	1	1	9	2	20	6.30	-5	-5	-6	28	165^1
1980	Cal-A	3	0	19	2	52	2.08	11	11	6	21	123
1981	Cal-A	4	4	39	11	65^1	2.34	10	9	14		
1982	Cal-A	3	3	24	4	52	3.46	4	3	4		
1984	Cal-A	4	1	23	8	39	1.62	10	10	16		
1985	Bal-A	10	6	54	14	88	3.78	4	2	5		
1986	Bal-A	6	7	66	34	81^2	2.98	11	11	25		
1987	Bal-A	1	0	7	2	8	2.25	2	2	3		
1988	Bal-A	0	0	35	0	46^2	4.05	-0	-1	0		
1989	NY-N	1	5	49	2	59^1	3.94	-3	-4	-4		
1990	LA-N	3	1	32	3	38	4.97	-5	-6	-6		
Total	11	36	28	357	82	550	3.34	38	33	58	91	559^1
■ Ted Abernathy												
1955	Was-A	1	1	26	0	45	5.80	-9	-10	-4	14	74^1
1956	Was-A	0	0	1	0	0^1	0.00	0	0	0	4	30
1957	Was-A	1	0	10	0	11^2	6.94	-4	-4	-3	16	73^1
1960	Was-A	0	0	2	0	3	12.00	-3	-3	0		
1963	Cle-A	7	2	43	12	59^1	2.88	5	5	9		
1964	Cle-A	2	6	53	11	72^2	4.33	-6	-6	-8		
1965	Chi-N	4	6	84	31	136^1	2.57	15	17	20		
1966	Chi-N	1	3	20	4	27^2	6.18	-8	-8	-13		
	Atl-N	4	4	38	4	65^1	3.86	-2	-2	-2		
	Yr	5	7	58	8	93	4.55	-10	-9	-14		
1967	Cin-N	6	3	70	28	106^1	1.27	25	29	40		
1968	Cin-N	10	7	78	13	134^2	2.47	8	10	14		
1969	Chi-N	4	3	56	3	85^1	3.16	4	8	7		
1970	Chi-N	0	0	11	1	9	2.00	2	3	1		
	StL-N	1	0	11	1	18^1	2.95	2	2	1		
	Yr	1	0	22	2	27^1	2.63	4	5	2		
	KC-A	9	3	36	12	55^2	2.59	7	7	17		
1971	KC-A	4	6	63	23	81	2.56	8	8	14		
1972	KC-A	3	4	45	5	58^1	1.70	9	9	11		
Total	14	57	48	647	148	970	2.99	53	66	104	34	177^2
■ Jim Acker												
1983	Tor-A	2	1	33	1	72^2	3.34	6	8	3	5	25
1984	Tor-A	3	4	29	1	57^2	4.21	-1	-1	-1	3	14^1
1985	Tor-A	7	2	61	10	86^1	3.23	9	9	11		
1986	Tor-A	2	2	18	0	31^1	4.88	-2	-2	-3	5	28^2
	Atl-N	0	0	7	0	9	4.00	-0	-0	0	14	86
1987	Atl-N	4	9	68	14	114^2	4.16	-1	2	3		
1988	Atl-N	0	3	20	0	37	5.11	-7	-6	-4	1	5
1989	Atl-N	0	6	59	2	97^2	2.67	9	11	6		
	Tor-A	2	1	14	0	28^1	1.59	7	7	7		
1990	Tor-A	4	4	59	1	91^2	3.83	1	1	1		
1991	Tor-A	2	3	50	1	68	4.50	-3	-2	-2	4	20^1
1992	Sea-A	0	0	17	0	30^2	5.28	-5	-4	0		
Total	10	26	35	435	30	725	3.79	12	22	22	32	179^1
■ Ace Adams												
1941	NY-N	4	1	38	1	71	4.82	-9	-9	-6		
1942	NY-N	7	4	61	11	88	1.84	14	15	21		
1943	NY-N	9	7	67	9	121^1	2.67	10	10	14	3	19
1944	NY-N	6	9	61	13	114^1	3.94	-4	-3	-5	4	23^1
1945	NY-N	11	9	65	15	113	3.42	5	6	12		
1946	NY-N	0	1	3	0	2^2	16.88	-4	-4	-13		
Total	6	37	31	295	49	510^1	3.35	11	15	22	7	42^1
■ Juan Agosto												
1981	Chi-A	0	0	2	0	5^2	4.76	-1	-1	0		
1982	Chi-A	0	0	1	0	2	18.00	-3	-3	0		
1983	Chi-A	2	2	39	7	41^2	4.10	-0	0	0		
1984	Chi-A	2	1	49	7	55^1	3.09	6	7	5		
1985	Chi-A	4	3	54	1	60^1	3.58	4	5	5		
1986	Chi-A	0	2	9	0	4^2	7.71	-2	-2	-7		
	Min-A	1	1	16	1	19	7.58	-7	-7	-7	1	1^1
	Yr	1	3	25	1	23^2	7.61	-9	-9	-14	1	1^1
1987	Hou-N	1	1	27	2	27^1	2.63	4	4	3		
1988	Hou-N	10	2	75	4	91^2	2.26	12	11	14		
1989	Hou-N	4	5	71	1	83	2.93	5	4	4		
1990	Hou-N	9	8	82	4	92^1	4.29	-5	-6	-10		
1991	StL-N	5	3	72	2	86	4.81	-11	-10	-9		
1992	StL-N	2	4	22	0	31^2	6.25	-10	-10	-17		
	Sea-A	0	0	16	0	15^2	5.74	-3	-3	0	1	2^2
Total	12	40	32	535	29	616^1	3.93	-11	-11	-19	2	4
■ Rick Aguilera												
1985	NY-N	1	0	2	0	4	0.00	2	2	3	19	118^1
1986	NY-N	1	1	8	0	19^2	3.20	1	1	1	20	122
1987	NY-N	0	0	1	0	3^1	0.00	2	1	0	17	111^2
1988	NY-N	0	2	8	0	12^2	4.97	-2	-2	-4	3	12
1989	NY-N	6	6	36	7	69^1	2.34	9	7	13		
	Min-A										11	75^2
1990	Min-A	5	3	56	32	65^1	2.76	8	10	22		
1991	Min-A	4	5	63	42	69	2.35	13	15	37		
1992	Min-A	2	6	64	41	66^2	2.84	8	9	22		
Total	8	19	23	238	122	310	2.64	41	42	95	70	439^2
■ Jack Aker												
1964	KC-A	0	1	9	0	16^1	8.82	-9	-9	-5		
1965	KC-A	4	3	34	3	51^1	3.16	2	2	3		

YEAR	TM/L	WR	LR	GR	SV	IPR	ERAR	RR	/A	RNK	GS	IPS
1966	KC-A	8	4	66	32	113	1.99	18	18	28		
1967	KC-A	3	8	57	12	88	4.30	-10	-11	-16		
1968	Oak-A	4	4	54	11	74^2	4.10	-9	-11	-14		
1969	Sea-A	0	2	15	3	16^2	7.56	-7	-7	-11		
	NY-A	8	4	38	11	65^2	2.06	11	10	21		
	Yr	8	6	53	14	82^1	3.17	4	3	10		
1970	NY-A	4	2	41	16	70	2.06	13	11	15		
1971	NY-A	4	4	41	4	55^2	2.59	5	4	6		
1972	NY-A	0	0	4	0	6	3.00	0	-0	0		
	Chi-N	6	6	48	17	67	2.96	4	6	14		
1973	Chi-N	4	5	47	12	63^2	4.10	-3	-1	-2		
1974	Atl-N	0	1	17	0	16^2	3.78	-0	-0	-0		
	NY-N	2	1	24	2	41^1	3.48	1	0	0		
	Yr	2	2	41	2	58	3.57	0	0	0		
Total	11	47	45	495	123	746	3.28	14	13	39		
■ Neil Allen												
1979	NY-N	6	6	45	8	78^2	2.52	11	10	16	5	20^1
1980	NY-N	7	10	59	22	97^1	3.70	-1	-2	-3		
1981	NY-N	7	6	43	18	66^2	2.97	4	4	9		
1982	NY-N	3	7	50	19	64^2	3.06	4	4	8		
1983	NY-N	0	5	17	2	31^1	4.60	-3	-3	-5	4	22^2
	StL-N	3	0	7	0	14^1	1.88	3	3	5	18	107^1
	Yr	3	5	24	2	45^2	3.74	-1	-1	-0	22	130
1984	StL-N	9	5	56	3	117^1	3.61	-0	-2	-2	1	1^2
1985	StL-N	1	3	22	2	26^2	4.05	-1	-2	-2	1	2^1
	NY-A	1	0	17	1	29^1	2.76	5	4	2		
1986	Chi-A	0	0	5	0	7	11.57	-6	-6	0	17	106
1987	Chi-A	0	0	5	0	10^1	6.10	-2	-2	0	10	39^1
	NY-A	0	0	7	0	19^2	2.75	4	4	0	1	5
	Yr	0	0	12	0	30	3.90	2	2	0	11	44^1
1988	NY-A	5	1	39	0	107	3.70	3	3	1	2	10^1
1989	Cle-A	0	1	3	0	3	15.00	-4	-4	-11		
Total	11	42	44	375	75	673^1	3.53	15	12	17	59	315
■ Red Ames												
1903	NY-N										2	14
1904	NY-N	0	0	3	3	8	4.50	-2	-2	-1	13	107
1905	NY-N	1	0	3	0	11^2	1.54	2	2	1	31	251^1
1906	NY-N	1	0	6	1	21	2.57	0	0	0	25	182^1
1907	NY-N	0	3	13	1	33	0.82	6	6	5	26	200^1
1908	NY-N	1	0	3	1	11	0.00	3	3	3	15	103^1
1909	NY-N	1	0	8	1	20^1	3.98	-3	-3	-2	26	223^2
1910	NY-N	0	3	10	0	18^2	2.41	1	1	2	23	171^2
1911	NY-N	2	1	11	2	31^1	4.60	-4	-4	-4	23	173^2
1912	NY-N	1	0	11	2	35^1	2.29	4	4	2	22	143^2
1913	NY-N	0	0	3	1	5	1.80	1	1	0	5	36^2
	Cin-N	2	1	7	2	18^2	2.41	2	2	3	24	168^2
	Yr	2	1	10	3	23^2	2.28	2	2	3	29	205^1
1914	Cin-N	1	4	11	6	36^1	2.72	0	1	1	36	260^2
1915	Cin-N	0	0	10	1	18^2	6.27	-7	-7	-1	7	49^1
	StL-N	0	0	1	1	2	13.50	-2	-2	-3	14	111^1
	Yr	0	0	11	2	20^2	6.97	-10	-9	-4	21	160^2
1916	StL-N	4	5	23	8	65^2	2.88	-2	-2	-3	22	162^1
1917	StL-N	8	2	24	3	77	2.22	4	4	5	19	132
1918	StL-N	0	0	2	1	1^1	0.00	0	0	1	25	205^1
1919	StL-N	2	0	16	1	33^2	4.54	-6	-7	-4	7	36^1
	Phi-N	0	0	1	1	1	0.00	0	0	1	2	15
	Yr	2	0	17	2	34^2	4.41	-6	-6	-3	9	51^1
Total	16	24	19	166	36	449^2	2.88	-2	-2	7	367	2748^2
■ Larry Andersen												
1975	Cle-A	0	0	3	0	5^2	4.76	-1	-1	0		
1977	Cle-A	0	1	11	0	14^1	3.14	1	1	1		
1979	Cle-A	0	0	8	0	16^2	7.56	-6	-6	0		
1981	Sea-A	3	3	41	5	67^2	2.66	7	9	9		
1982	Sea-A	0	0	39	1	75	5.88	-15	-14	-0	1	4^2
1983	Phi-N	1	0	17	0	26^1	2.39	4	3	1		
1984	Phi-N	3	7	64	4	90^2	2.38	12	13	14		
1985	Phi-N	3	3	57	3	73	4.32	-6	-5	-4		
1986	Phi-N	0	0	10	0	12^2	4.26	-1	-1	0		
	Hou-N	2	1	38	1	64^2	2.78	7	6	3		
	Yr	2	1	48	1	77^1	3.03	6	5	3		
1987	Hou-N	9	5	67	5	101^2	3.45	7	5	7		
1988	Hou-N	2	4	53	5	82^2	2.94	5	3	3		
1989	Hou-N	4	4	60	3	87^2	1.54	19	18	16		
1990	Hou-N	5	2	50	6	73^2	1.95	15	14	15		
	Bos-A	0	0	15	1	22	1.23	7	7	1		
1991	SD-N	3	4	38	13	47	2.30	7	8	15		
1992	SD-N	1	1	34	2	35	3.34	1	1	1		
Total	15	36	35	605	49	896^1	3.09	63	63	80	1	4^2
■ Pete Appleton												
1927	Cin-N	0	0	4	0	11^2	1.54	3	3	0	2	18
1928	Cin-N	3	4	30	0	79^2	4.07	-1	-1	-1	1	3
1930	Cle-A	6	5	32	1	70^2	4.46	2	3	4	7	48
1931	Cle-A	1	3	25	0	48	5.06	-4	-2	-2	4	31^2
1932	Cle-A	0	0	4	0	5	16.20	-7	-6	0		
	Bos-A	0	0	8	0	28^2	4.08	1	1	0	3	17^1
	Yr	0	0	12	0	33^2	5.88	-5	-5	0	3	17^1
1933	NY-A	0	0	1	0	2	0.00	1	1	0		
1936	Was-A	4	1	18	3	55	2.62	15	13	12	20	146^2
1937	Was-A	3	4	17	2	53^1	2.53	12	11	14	18	114^2
1938	Was-A	3	4	33	5	102^2	4.21	7	3	2	10	61^2
1939	Was-A	4	7	36	6	76^2	3.76	7	5	7	4	26

YEAR	TM/L	WR	LR	GR	SV	IPR	ERAR	RR	/A	RNK	GS	IPS
1940	Chi-A	4	0	25	5	57^2	5.62	-8	-8	-6		
1941	Chi-A	0	3	13	1	27^1	5.27	-3	-4	-4		
1942	Chi-A	0	0	4	0	4^2	3.86	-0	-0	0		
	StL-A	1	1	14	2	27^1	2.96	2	2	2		
	Yr	1	1	18	2	32	3.09	2	2	2		
1945	StL-A	0	0	2	0	2^1	15.43	-3	-3	0		
	Was-A	0	0	4	1	7^1	3.68	-0	-0	-0	2	14
	Yr	0	0	6	1	9^2	6.52	-3	-4	-0	2	14
Total	14	29	32	270	26	660	4.13	24	18	30	71	481
■ Paul Assenmacher												
1986	Atl-N	7	3	61	7	68^1	2.50	9	11	17		
1987	Atl-N	1	1	52	2	54^2	5.10	-6	-5	-2		
1988	Atl-N	8	7	64	5	79^1	3.06	3	5	10		
1989	Atl-N	1	3	49	0	57^2	3.59	-1	0	0		
	Chi-N	2	1	14	0	19	5.21	-4	-3	-4		
	Yr	3	4	63	0	76^2	3.99	-4	-3	-4		
1990	Chi-N	7	2	73	10	102	2.47	15	18	18	1	1
1991	Chi-N	7	8	75	15	102^2	3.24	5	7	12		
1992	Chi-N	4	4	70	8	68	4.10	-5	-4	-5		
Total	7	37	29	458	47	551^2	3.38	18	31	47	1	1
■ Keith Atherton												
1983	Oak-A	2	5	29	4	68^1	2.77	10	8	9		
1984	Oak-A	7	6	57	2	104	4.33	-4	-7	-8		
1985	Oak-A	4	7	56	3	104^2	4.30	-2	-5	-5		
1986	Oak-A	1	2	13	0	15^1	5.87	-3	-3	-6		
	Min-A	5	8	47	10	81^2	3.75	4	5	9		
	Yr	6	10	60	10	97	4.08	1	2	3		
1987	Min-A	7	5	59	2	79^1	4.54	-1	1	1		
1988	Min-A	7	5	49	3	74	3.41	5	5	8		
1989	Cle-A	0	3	32	2	39	4.15	-1	-1	-1		
Total	7	33	41	342	26	566^1	3.99	8	3	7		
■ Doc Ayers												
1913	Was-A	0	0	2	1	2	4.50	-0	-0	-0	2	15^2
1914	Was-A	3	2	17	3	62^2	2.30	3	4	3	32	202^2
1915	Was-A	5	4	24	3	88^2	1.73	12	12	12	16	122^2
1916	Was-A	0	2	26	2	54^2	4.12	-8	-8	-3	17	102^1
1917	Was-A	5	4	25	1	80	3.15	-4	-5	-5	15	127^2
1918	Was-A	3	2	16	3	46^1	1.75	5	5	6	24	173^1
1919	Was-A	0	1	6	1	15^1	0.59	4	4	3	5	28^1
	Det-A	3	2	19	0	52	2.77	3	2	2	5	41^2
	Yr	3	3	25	1	67^1	2.27	7	7	5	10	70
1920	Det-A	0	2	23	1	47^1	4.37	-3	-3	-1	23	161^1
1921	Det-A	0	0	1	0	1	0.00	0	0	0	1	3
Total	9	19	19	159	15	450	2.72	12	12	16	140	978^2
■ Doug Bair												
1976	Pit-N	0	0	4	0	6^1	5.68	-2	-2	0		
1977	Oak-A	4	6	45	8	83^1	3.46	6	5	7		
1978	Cin-N	7	6	70	28	100^1	1.97	18	18	31		
1979	Cin-N	11	7	65	16	94^1	4.29	-6	-6	-12		
1980	Cin-N	3	6	61	6	85	4.24	-6	-6	-7		
1981	Cin-N	2	2	24	0	39	5.77	-10	-10	-9		
	StL-N	2	0	11	1	15^2	3.45	0	0	0		
	Yr	4	2	35	1	54^2	5.10	-10	-9	-9		
1982	StL-N	5	3	63	8	91^2	2.55	11	11	11		
1983	StL-N	1	1	26	1	29^2	3.03	2	2	1		
	Det-A	6	3	26	4	49^2	4.35	-2	-2	-4	1	6
1984	Det-A	5	2	46	4	91	3.26	7	7	5	1	2^2
1985	Det-A	1	0	18	0	37^2	5.50	-6	-6	-1	3	11^1
	StL-N	0	0	2	0	2	0.00	1	1	0		
1986	Oak-A	2	3	31	4	45	3.00	6	4	5		
1987	Phi-N	2	0	11	0	13^2	5.93	-3	-3	-3		
1988	Tor-A	0	0	10	0	13^1	4.05	-0	-0	0		
1989	Pit-N	2	3	44	1	67^1	2.27	9	8	6		
1990	Pit-N	0	0	22	0	24^1	4.81	-3	-3	0		
Total	15	53	42	579	81	889^1	3.54	23	18	29	5	20
■ Jack Baldschun												
1961	Phi-N	5	3	65	3	99^2	3.88	2	2	2		
1962	Phi-N	12	7	67	13	112^2	2.96	12	11	20		
1963	Phi-N	11	7	65	16	113^2	2.30	13	12	21		
1964	Phi-N	6	9	71	21	118^1	3.12	6	5	7		
1965	Phi-N	5	8	65	6	99	3.82	-3	-4	-5		
1966	Cin-N	1	5	42	0	57^1	5.49	-12	-10	-10		
1967	Cin-N	0	0	9	0	13	4.15	-1	-1	0		
1969	SD-N	7	2	61	1	77	4.79	-10	-11	-12		
1970	SD-N	1	0	12	0	13^1	10.13	-9	-9	-6		
Total	9	48	41	457	60	704	3.69	-3	-4	17		
■ Steve Bedrosian												
1981	Atl-N	1	1	14	0	19^1	4.19	-2	-1	-1	1	5
1982	Atl-N	7	5	61	11	122	2.29	18	20	21	3	15^2
1983	Atl-N	9	10	69	19	113	3.74	-1	2	3	1	7
1984	Atl-N	6	5	36	11	58	1.71	12	14	30	4	25^2
1985	Atl-N										37	206^2
1986	Phi-N	8	6	68	29	90^1	3.39	3	5	10		
1987	Phi-N	5	3	65	40	89	2.83	12	14	25		
1988	Phi-N	6	6	57	28	74^1	3.75	-3	-2	-4		
1989	Phi-N	2	3	28	6	33^2	3.21	1	1	2		
	SF-N	1	4	40	17	51	2.65	5	4	7		
	Yr	3	7	68	23	84^2	2.87	6	5	9		
1990	SF-N	9	9	68	17	79^1	4.20	-4	-5	-12		
1991	Min-A	5	3	56	6	77^1	4.42	-3	-1	-1		

YEAR	TM/L	WR	LR	GR	SV	IPR	ERAR	RR	/A	RNK	GS	IPS
Total	10	59	55	562	184	807^1	3.27	40	50	79	46	260
■ Joe Beggs												
1938	NY-A	0	0	5	0	8	5.63	-1	-1	0	9	50^1
1940	Cin-N	12	3	36	7	74	1.58	19	18	37	1	2^2
1941	Cin-N	4	3	37	5	57	3.79	-1	-1	-2		
1942	Cin-N	6	5	38	8	88^2	2.13	12	11	15		
1943	Cin-N	4	5	35	6	78^2	3.09	3	2	2	4	36^2
1944	Cin-N										1	9
1946	Cin-N	0	1	6	1	23	1.96	4	4	2	22	167
1947	Cin-N	0	0	7	0	12^1	5.11	-1	-1	0	4	20
	NY-N	3	3	32	2	66	4.23	-1	-1	-1		
	Yr	3	3	39	2	78^1	4.37	-3	-3	-1	4	20
1948	NY-N	0	0	1	0	0^1	0.00	0	0	0		
Total	8	29	20	197	29	408	2.93	32	30	53	41	285^2
■ Gary Bell												
1958	Cle-A	1	2	10	1	26^1	1.03	8	8	9	23	155^2
1959	Cle-A	3	1	16	5	39	3.92	-0	-1	-1	28	195
1960	Cle-A	0	0	5	1	8^1	6.48	-2	-3	-1	23	146^1
1961	Cle-A										34	228^1
1962	Cle-A	9	6	51	12	84^2	2.87	10	9	18	6	23
1963	Cle-A	7	1	51	5	81	1.89	16	16	16	7	38
1964	Cle-A	7	5	54	4	95^1	4.15	-6	-6	-7	2	10^2
1965	Cle-A	6	5	60	17	103^2	3.04	5	5	7		
1966	Cle-A	1	0	3	0	4	2.25	1	1	1	37	250^1
1967	Cle-A										9	60^2
	Bos-A	0	0	5	3	10^1	1.74	2	2	1	24	155
	Yr	1	0	5	3	71	0.38	2	3	2	33	215^2
1968	Bos-A	1	1	8	1	17^1	3.12	-0	0	0	27	182
1969	Sea-A	0	0	2	2	2^2	0.00	1	1	2	11	58^2
	Chi-A	0	0	21	0	30^2	5.58	-7	-6	0	2	8
	Yr	0	0	23	2	33^1	5.13	-6	-5	2	13	66^2
Total	10	35	21	286	51	503^1	3.16	27	26	45	233	1511^2
■ Chief Bender												
1903	Phi-A	1	1	3	0	8	6.75	-3	-3	-7	33	262
1904	Phi-A	2	0	9	0	46^2	2.70	-1	-0	-0	20	157
1905	Phi-A	7	1	12	0	49^1	1.82	5	5	7	23	179^2
1906	Phi-A	1	0	9	3	19	1.89	2	2	1	27	219^1
1907	Phi-A	0	2	9	3	19^1	1.40	2	3	3	24	200
1908	Phi-A	0	0	1	1	1	0.00	0	0	1	17	137^2
1909	Phi-A	0	0	5	1	4^2	0.00	1	1	1	29	245^1
1910	Phi-A	1	0	2	0	3	0.00	1	1	2	28	247
1911	Phi-A	2	1	7	3	16^2	3.78	-1	-1	-2	24	199^2
1912	Phi-A	2	3	8	2	22^1	1.21	5	5	10	19	148^2
1913	Phi-A	6	5	27	13	66^2	2.16	6	4	9	21	170
1914	Phi-A	1	1	5	2	13^2	5.93	-5	-5	-8	23	165^1
1915	Bal-F	0	1	3	1	7^2	8.22	-4	-4	-6	23	170^2
1916	Phi-N	2	1	14	3	27	3.33	-2	-2	-3	13	95^2
1917	Phi-N	0	0	10	2	29	2.17	2	2	0	10	84
1925	Chi-A	0	0	1	0	1	18.00	-2	-2	0		
Total	16	25	16	125	34	335	2.63	6	5	7	334	2682
■ Al Benton												
1934	Phi-A	1	1	11	1	27^2	4.23	1	0	0	21	127^1
1935	Phi-A	3	1	18	0	41^1	5.88	-7	-6	-5	9	37
1938	Det-A	0	0	9	0	18^2	3.38	3	3	0	10	76^2
1939	Det-A	1	3	21	5	41	4.83	-1	0	0	16	109
1940	Det-A	6	10	42	17	79^1	4.42	-0	3	7		
1941	Det-A	6	2	24	7	51	2.65	8	11	18	14	106^2
1942	Det-A	0	1	5	2	11^1	3.18	1	1	1	30	215^1
1945	Det-A	0	1	4	3	10^2	2.53	1	1	2	27	181
1946	Det-A	1	2	13	1	35^1	2.55	4	4	4	15	105^1
1947	Det-A	1	0	22	7	41^1	4.14	-2	-2	-1	14	91^2
1948	Det-A	2	2	30	3	44^1	5.68	-7	-6	-6		
1949	Cle-A	4	0	29	10	58	0.78	22	21	21	11	77^2
1950	Cle-A	4	2	36	4	63	3.57	7	5	5		
1952	Bos-A	4	3	24	6	37^2	2.39	5	6	13		
Total	14	33	28	288	66	560^2	3.64	35	42	59	167	1127^2
■ Juan Berenguer												
1978	NY-N	0	0	2	0	2	0.00	1	1	0	3	11
1979	NY-N										5	30^2
1980	NY-N	0	1	6	0	9^1	5.79	-2	-2	-2		
1981	KC-A	0	3	5	0	6^2	12.15	-6	-6	-26	3	13
	Tor-A	1	0	1	0	5	1.80	1	1	2	11	66
	Yr	1	3	6	0	11^2	7.71	-5	-5	-23	14	79
1982	Det-A	0	0	1	0	3^2	4.91	-0	-0	0	1	3
1983	Det-A	2	0	18	1	40^1	3.12	4	4	2	19	117^1
1984	Det-A	0	0	4	0	12^2	3.55	1	1	0	27	155^2
1985	Det-A	1	1	18	0	34^1	6.82	-10	-10	-5	13	60^2
1986	SF-N	2	2	42	4	56^1	2.08	10	9	7	4	17
1987	Min-A	6	1	41	4	75	4.44	0	1	1	6	37
1988	Min-A	8	4	56	2	96	3.84	1	2	3	1	4
1989	Min-A	9	3	56	3	106	3.48	5	8	8		
1990	Min-A	8	5	51	0	100^1	3.41	6	8	10		
1991	Atl-N	0	3	49	17	64^1	2.24	10	12	12		
1992	Atl-N	3	1	28	1	33^1	5.13	-6	-5	-6		
	KC-A	1	2	17	0	35^2	4.79	-3	-3	-2	2	9
Total	14	41	26	395	32	681	3.79	10	19	4	95	524^1
■ Doug Bird												
1973	KC-A	4	4	54	20	102^1	2.99	9	13	15		
1974	KC-A	7	5	54	10	84^1	2.77	8	10	15	1	8
1975	KC-A	9	5	47	11	84	3.21	5	6	11	4	21^1

YEAR	TM/L	WR	LR	GR	SV	IPR	ERAR	RR	/A	RNK	GS	IPS
1976	KC-A	3	0	12	2	27^2	2.60	3	3	3	27	170
1977	KC-A	11	3	48	14	96^2	2.79	14	13	22	5	21^2
1978	KC-A	5	3	34	1	66^2	4.59	-6	-6	-6	6	32
1979	Phi-N	1	0	31	0	55^2	5.34	-10	-9	-2	1	5^1
1980	NY-A	2	0	21	1	44^2	2.22	9	8	4	1	6
1981	NY-A	2	0	13	0	31	3.19	2	1	1	4	22^1
	Chi-N										12	75^1
1982	Chi-N	0	0	2	0	2	0.00	1	1	0	33	189
1983	Bos-A	0	1	16	1	37^2	6.45	-10	-9	-3	6	30
Total	11	44	21	332	60	632^2	3.47	24	31	59	100	581
■ Joe Boever												
1985	StL-N	0	0	13	0	16^1	4.41	-1	-2	0		
1986	StL-N	0	1	11	0	21^2	1.66	5	5	2		
1987	Atl-N	1	0	14	0	18^1	7.36	-7	-6	-3		
1988	Atl-N	0	2	16	1	20^1	1.77	4	4	4		
1989	Atl-N	4	11	66	21	82^1	3.94	-4	-3	-6		
1990	Atl-N	1	3	33	8	42^1	4.68	-4	-3	-4		
	Phi-N	2	3	34	6	46	2.15	8	9	11		
	Yr	3	6	67	14	88^1	3.36	4	6	7		
1991	Phi-N	3	5	68	0	98^1	3.84	-2	-2	-1		
1992	Hou-N	3	6	81	2	111^1	2.51	12	10	8		
Total	8	14	31	336	38	457	3.41	11	13	11		
■ Bobby Bolin												
1961	SF-N	2	2	36	5	44	2.45	8	7	7	1	4
1962	SF-N	3	2	36	5	55^1	2.93	6	5	5	5	36^2
1963	SF-N	7	2	35	7	62^1	3.75	-3	-4	-6	12	75
1964	SF-N	1	0	15	1	34^1	1.57	7	8	2	23	140^1
1965	SF-N	8	1	32	2	87^1	1.96	15	16	16	13	75^2
1966	SF-N	0	0	2	1	3^1	10.80	-3	-3	-2	34	221
1967	SF-N	4	0	22	0	45	3.20	1	0	0	15	75
1968	SF-N	2	0	15	0	39	1.38	7	7	3	19	137^2
1969	SF-N	0	1	8	0	18^2	3.38	0	0	0	22	127^2
1970	Mil-A	1	2	12	1	20^2	3.92	-0	-0	-0	20	111^1
	Bos-A	2	0	6	2	8	0.00	3	4	10		
	Yr	3	2	18	3	28^2	2.83	3	3	9	20	111^1
1971	Bos-A	5	3	52	6	69^2	4.26	-6	-4	-5		
1972	Bos-A	0	1	21	5	30^2	2.93	0	1	1		
1973	Bos-A	3	4	39	15	53^1	2.70	7	8	14		
Total	13	38	18	331	50	571^2	2.87	43	44	45	164	1004^1
■ Pedro Borbon												
1969	Cal-A	2	3	22	0	41	6.15	-12	-12	-13		
1970	Cin-N	0	1	11	0	13^1	7.43	-5	-5	-3	1	4
1971	Cin-N	0	0	3	0	4^1	4.15	-0	-0	0		
1972	Cin-N	8	2	60	11	119	2.87	8	4	4	2	3
1973	Cin-N	11	4	80	14	121	2.16	20	17	23		
1974	Cin-N	10	7	73	14	139	3.24	6	4	5		
1975	Cin-N	9	5	67	5	125	2.95	9	9	10		
1976	Cin-N	4	3	68	8	117^2	3.14	5	5	3	1	3^1
1977	Cin-N	10	5	73	18	127	3.19	10	10	14		
1978	Cin-N	8	2	62	4	99^1	4.98	-16	-16	-16		
1979	Cin-N	2	2	30	2	44^2	3.43	2	2	1		
	SF-N	4	3	30	3	46	4.89	-6	-7	-11		
	Yr	6	5	60	5	90^2	4.17	-4	-6	-9		
1980	StL-N	1	0	10	1	19	3.79	-0	-0	-0		
Total	12	69	37	589	80	1016^1	3.45	21	10	18	4	10^1
■ Garland Braxton												
1921	Bos-N	1	1	15	0	25^2	4.91	-3	-4	-3	2	11^2
1922	Bos-N	0	1	21	0	32^2	4.13	-0	-0	-0	4	34
1925	NY-A	0	0	1	0	4^1	2.08	1	1	0	2	15
1926	NY-A	5	1	36	2	64	2.25	13	11	10	1	3^1
1927	Was-A	10	7	56	13	146	2.40	28	27	34	2	9^1
1928	Was-A	1	3	14	6	31^1	1.72	8	8	13	24	187
1929	Was-A	4	1	17	4	48^1	4.47	-1	-1	-1	20	133^2
1930	Was-A	3	2	15	5	27^1	3.29	4	4	8		
	Chi-A	2	2	9	1	38^1	5.40	-3	-3	-3	10	52^1
	Yr	5	4	24	6	65^2	4.52	1	1	5	10	52^1
1931	Chi-A	0	1	14	1	33	5.73	-5	-5	-2	3	14^1
	StL-A	0	0	10	0	18	8.00	-7	-7	0	1	0
	Yr	0	1	24	1	51	6.53	-12	-12	-2	4	14^1
1933	StL-A	0	0	4	0	8	5.63	-1	-1	0	1	0^1
Total	10	26	19	212	32	477	3.58	33	30	56	70	461
■ Al Brazle												
1943	StL-N	1	0	4	0	8	2.25	1	1	1	9	80
1946	StL-N	4	2	22	0	51^2	3.66	-1	-1	-1	15	101^2
1947	StL-N	4	1	25	4	38^2	2.09	8	9	12	19	129^1
1948	StL-N	3	0	19	1	31^2	3.69	1	1	1	23	124^2
1949	StL-N	3	0	14	0	31^1	2.59	5	5	5	25	175
1950	StL-N	5	4	34	6	84^2	3.51	6	7	8	12	80
1951	StL-N	2	2	48	7	110^2	2.68	16	16	7	8	43^2
1952	StL-N	8	3	40	16	62	2.76	7	7	14	6	47^1
1953	StL-N	6	7	60	18	92	4.21	1	1	1		
1954	StL-N	5	4	58	8	84^1	4.16	-1	-0	-1		
Total	10	41	23	324	60	595	3.34	42	45	48	117	781^2
■ Jim Brewer												
1960	Chi-N	0	0	1	0	1	27.00	-3	-3	0	4	20^2
1961	Chi-N	0	1	25	0	35	4.89	-3	-3	-1	11	51^2
1962	Chi-N	0	1	5	0	4	6.75	-1	-1	-3	1	1^2
1963	Chi-N	3	1	28	0	45^2	4.34	-5	-4	-3	1	4
1964	LA-N	1	2	29	1	61^2	3.36	1	-1	-0	5	31^1
1965	LA-N	3	1	17	2	41^1	1.96	7	6	6	2	8

YEAR	TM/L	WR	LR	GR	SV	IPR	ERAR	RR	/A	RNK	GS	IPS
1966	LA-N	0	2	13	2	22	3.68	-0	-1	-1		
1967	LA-N	2	0	19	1	38^1	1.88	6	5	3	11	62^1
1968	LA-N	8	3	54	14	76^1	2.48	4	2	4		
1969	LA-N	7	6	59	20	88^1	2.55	10	8	14		
1970	LA-N	7	6	58	24	89	3.13	9	7	13		
1971	LA-N	6	5	55	22	81^1	1.88	14	12	22		
1972	LA-N	8	7	51	17	78^1	1.26	19	18	40		
1973	LA-N	6	8	56	20	71^2	3.01	5	3	8		
1974	LA-N	4	4	24	0	39^1	2.52	5	4	7		
1975	LA-N	3	1	21	2	33	5.18	-6	-7	-8		
	Cal-A	1	0	21	5	34^2	1.82	8	7	4		
1976	Cal-A	3	1	13	2	20	2.70	2	1	3		
Total	17	62	49	549	132	861	2.80	73	55	108	35	179^2
■ Jim Brosnan												
1954	Chi-N	1	0	18	0	33^1	9.45	-20	-19	-5		
1956	Chi-N	3	4	20	1	35	2.31	6	6	11	10	60
1957	Chi-N	4	4	36	0	72^1	3.11	6	6	6	5	26^1
1958	Chi-N										8	51^2
	StL-N	4	1	21	7	43	1.67	11	12	17	12	72
	Yr	8	5	21	7	94^2	3.14	17	18	23	20	123^2
1959	StL-N	1	3	19	2	32^2	3.86	0	1	2	1	0^1
	Cin-N	4	0	17	2	32^1	1.67	8	9	11	9	51
	Yr	5	3	36	4	65	2.77	9	10	12	10	51^1
1960	Cin-N	7	2	55	12	95	1.71	22	22	25	2	4
1961	Cin-N	10	4	53	16	80	3.04	9	9	18		
1962	Cin-N	4	4	48	13	64^2	3.34	4	5	8		
1963	Cin-N	0	1	6	0	4^2	7.71	-2	-2	-4		
	Chi-A	3	8	45	14	73	2.84	6	5	10		
Total	8	41	31	338	67	566	3.07	50	54	97	47	265^1
■ Clint Brown												
1928	Cle-A	0	0	1	0	2	0.00	1	1	0	1	9
1929	Cle-A	0	1	2	0	8^1	3.24	1	1	1	1	8
1930	Cle-A	0	0	4	1	8^1	12.96	-8	-8	-2	31	205^1
1931	Cle-A	0	0	6	0	13^2	5.27	-1	-1	0	33	219^2
1932	Cle-A	0	0	5	1	6^1	7.11	-2	-2	-1	32	256^1
1933	Cle-A	1	1	10	1	26^1	2.39	6	6	5	23	158^2
1934	Cle-A	4	2	15	1	44^1	4.87	-2	-2	-2	2	6
1935	Cle-A	3	0	18	2	28^2	4.71	-1	-1	-1	5	20^1
1936	Chi-A	6	1	36	5	75^2	4.16	7	9	9	2	7^1
1937	Chi-A	7	7	53	18	100	3.42	13	13	22		
1938	Chi-A	1	3	8	2	13^2	4.61	0	0	1		
1939	Chi-A	11	10	61	18	118^1	3.88	10	11	22		
1940	Chi-A	4	6	37	10	66	3.68	5	5	9		
1941	Cle-A	3	3	41	5	74^1	3.27	7	6	5		
1942	Cle-A	1	1	7	0	9	6.00	-2	-3	-5		
Total	15	41	35	304	64	595	4.01	35	37	63	130	890^2
■ Lloyd Brown												
1925	Bro-N	0	0	12	0	32^1	3.34	3	3	0	5	31
1928	Was-A	2	0	17	1	50^1	3.04	6	5	2	10	56^2
1929	Was-A	4	4	25	0	63	5.14	-6	-6	-7	15	105
1930	Was-A	6	2	16	0	42	4.07	3	2	4	22	155
1931	Was-A	1	2	10	0	21^2	4.98	-1	-2	-2	32	237
1932	Was-A	4	2	22	5	46	3.33	6	5	7	24	156^2
1933	StL-A	0	2	2	0	4^2	3.86	0	0	2	6	34^1
	Bos-A	0	3	12	1	14^2	6.75	-4	-4	-8	21	148^2
	Yr	0	5	14	1	19^1	6.05	-4	-3	-6	27	183
1934	Cle-A	3	1	23	6	48	2.06	13	13	14	15	69
1935	Cle-A	0	2	34	4	63^1	3.13	9	10	4	8	58^2
1936	Cle-A	1	1	8	1	20^2	1.74	8	8	7	16	119^2
1937	Cle-A	1	2	26	0	39^2	8.17	-16	-16	-11	5	37^1
1940	Phi-N	0	3	16	3	28	6.11	-7	-7	-8	2	9^2
Total	12	22	24	223	21	474^1	4.14	13	12	4	181	1218^2
■ Mace Brown												
1935	Pit-N	1	0	13	0	44	3.89	1	1	0	5	28^2
1936	Pit-N	6	4	37	3	105^1	3.84	2	2	2	10	59^2
1937	Pit-N	6	1	48	7	97^2	3.87	0	-0	-0	2	10
1938	Pit-N	15	8	49	5	124^1	3.62	2	2	4	2	8^1
1939	Pit-N	2	3	28	7	67^1	2.67	9	9	8	19	133
1940	Pit-N	5	2	31	7	54^2	2.30	9	9	13	17	118^1
1941	Pit-N	0	0	1	0	1^1	0.00	1	1	0		
	Bro-N	3	2	24	3	42^2	3.16	2	2	3		
	Yr	3	2	25	3	44	3.07	3	3	3		
1942	Bos-A	9	3	34	6	60^1	3.43	2	2	4		
1943	Bos-A	6	6	49	9	93^1	2.12	12	12	17		
1946	Bos-A	3	1	18	1	26^1	2.05	4	5	7		
Total	10	56	30	332	48	717^1	3.21	45	46	59	55	358
■ Mordecai Brown												
1903	StL-N	0	0	2	0	10	0.00	4	4	0	24	191
1904	Chi-N	2	0	3	1	17	1.06	3	3	4	23	195^1
1905	Chi-N	2	2	6	0	40	2.70	1	1	1	24	209
1906	Chi-N	1	0	4	3	9^1	0.00	3	3	5	32	268
1907	Chi-N	2	0	7	3	17^1	0.52	4	4	5	27	215^2
1908	Chi-N	4	1	13	5	42	2.36	0	-0	-0	31	270^1
1909	Chi-N	1	1	16	7	31^2	0.85	6	6	6	34	311
1910	Chi-N	2	3	15	7	35^2	1.77	5	4	8	31	259^2
1911	Chi-N	5	3	26	13	57^1	1.73	11	10	18	27	212^2
1912	Chi-N	2	3	7	0	26^2	2.36	3	3	5	8	62
1913	Cin-N	4	3	23	6	51	2.29	5	5	8	16	122^1
1914	StL-F	1	2	8	0	28^2	4.08	-3	-2	-2	18	146^1
	Bro-F	0	0	1	0	4	2.25	0	0	0	8	53^2

YEAR	TM/L	WR	LR	GR	SV	IPR	ERAR	RR	/A	RNK	GS	IPS
	Yr	1	2	9	0	32^2	3.86	-2	-2	-2	26	200
1915	Chi-F	3	2	10	4	34^1	2.36	3	2	3	25	202
1916	Chi-N	1	0	8	0	26^1	0.34	7	8	3	4	22
Total	14	30	20	149	49	431^1	1.90	52	51	63	332	2741
■ Warren Brusstar												
1977	Phi-N	7	2	46	3	71^1	2.65	10	11	13		
1978	Phi-N	6	3	58	0	88^2	2.33	12	12	11		
1979	Phi-N	1	0	13	1	14^1	6.91	-5	-5	-4		
1980	Phi-N	2	2	26	0	38^2	3.72	-1	0	0		
1981	Phi-N	0	1	14	0	12^1	4.38	-1	-1	-1		
1982	Phi-N	2	3	22	2	22^2	4.76	-3	-3	-6		
	Chi-A	2	0	10	0	18^1	3.44	1	1	1		
1983	Chi-N	3	1	59	1	80^1	2.35	11	13	6		
1984	Chi-N	1	1	41	3	63^2	3.11	3	6	2		
1985	Chi-N	4	3	51	4	74^1	6.05	-20	-17	-17		
Total	9	28	16	340	14	484^2	3.51	8	17	7		
■ Lew Burdette												
1950	NY-A	0	0	2	0	1^1	6.75	-0	-0	0		
1951	Bos-N	0	0	3	0	4^1	6.23	-1	-1	0		
1952	Bos-N	2	8	36	7	79	2.96	7	6	8	9	58
1953	Mil-N	8	0	33	8	78	3.23	9	6	7	13	97
1954	Mil-N	1	1	6	0	12	5.25	-2	-2	-3	32	226
1955	Mil-N	2	1	9	0	16	5.06	-2	-2	-4	33	214
1956	Mil-N	0	0	4	1	2^1	3.86	-0	-0	-0	35	254
1957	Mil-N	2	1	4	0	11^1	3.97	-0	-1	-1	33	245^1
1958	Mil-N	2	0	4	0	10^1	1.74	3	2	4	36	265
1959	Mil-N	0	0	2	1	1^2	0.00	1	1	1	39	288
1960	Mil-N	3	2	13	4	28^1	3.18	2	1	2	32	247^1
1961	Mil-N	2	0	4	0	11^2	0.77	4	4	6	36	260^2
1962	Mil-N	3	1	18	2	25	4.68	-2	-2	-4	19	118^2
1963	Mil-N	1	1	2	0	3	3.00	0	0	0	13	81
	StL-N	0	1	7	2	11^2	0.00	4	5	5	14	86^1
	Yr	1	2	9	2	14^2	0.61	4	5	6	27	167^1
1964	StL-N	1	0	8	0	10	1.80	2	2	2		
	Chi-N	1	1	11	0	20^1	7.97	-10	-10	-9	17	110^2
	Yr	2	1	19	0	30^1	5.93	-8	-7	-7	17	110^2
1965	Chi-N	0	0	4	0	6	4.50	-1	-1	0	3	14^1
	Phi-N	0	0	10	0	29^2	2.73	3	2	0	9	41
	Yr	0	0	14	0	35^2	3.03	2	2	0	12	55^1
1966	Cal-A	7	2	54	5	79^2	3.39	0	-0	-0		
1967	Cal-A	1	0	19	1	18^1	4.91	-3	-4	-2		
Total	18	36	19	253	31	460	3.50	14	5	11	373	2607^1
■ Tom Burgmeier												
1968	Cal-A	1	2	54	5	67^1	3.74	-6	-6	-4	2	5^1
1969	KC-A	3	1	31	0	54	4.17	-3	-3	-2		
1970	KC-A	6	6	41	1	68^1	3.16	4	4	7		
1971	KC-A	9	7	67	17	88^1	1.73	17	17	34		
1972	KC-A	6	2	51	9	55^1	4.23	-7	-7	-12		
1973	KC-A	0	0	6	1	10	5.40	-2	-1	-0		
1974	Min-A	5	3	50	4	91^2	4.52	-9	-8	-7		
1975	Min-A	5	8	46	11	75^2	3.09	6	6	12		
1976	Min-A	8	1	57	1	115^1	2.50	13	14	10		
1977	Min-A	6	4	61	7	97^1	5.09	-11	-12	-13		
1978	Bos-A	2	1	34	4	56^2	4.45	-4	-2	-1	1	4^2
1979	Bos-A	3	2	44	4	88^2	2.74	15	16	10		
1980	Bos-A	5	4	62	24	99	2.00	22	24	33		
1981	Bos-A	4	5	32	6	59^2	2.87	5	7	11		
1982	Bos-A	7	0	40	2	102^1	2.29	20	23	15		
1983	Oak-A	6	7	49	4	96	2.81	13	11	15		
1984	Oak-A	3	0	17	2	23	2.35	4	4	5		
Total	17	79	53	742	102	1248^2	3.19	78	87	113	3	10
■ Tim Burke												
1985	Mon-N	9	4	78	8	120^1	2.39	16	13	15		
1986	Mon-N	8	7	66	4	89^1	3.22	5	5	7	2	12
1987	Mon-N	7	0	55	18	91	1.19	29	30	35		
1988	Mon-N	3	5	61	18	82	3.40	0	2	2		
1989	Mon-N	9	3	68	28	84^2	2.55	9	9	19		
1990	Mon-N	3	3	58	20	75	2.52	11	9	12		
1991	Mon-N	3	4	37	5	46	4.11	-2	-3	-4		
	NY-N	3	3	35	1	55^2	2.75	6	6	6		
	Yr	6	7	72	6	101^2	3.36	4	3	2		
1992	NY-N	1	2	15	0	15^2	5.74	-4	-4	-7		
	NY-A	2	2	23	0	27^2	3.25	2	2	3		
Total	8	48	33	496	102	687^1	2.75	72	70	88	2	12
■ Guy Bush												
1923	Chi-N	0	0	1	0	1	0.00	0	0	0		
1924	Chi-N	0	1	8	0	18^1	7.85	-8	-8	-4	8	62^1
1925	Chi-N	4	2	27	4	71	3.93	3	3	3	15	111
1926	Chi-N	6	2	19	2	44^2	2.22	8	8	14	16	112^2
1927	Chi-N	3	0	14	2	26^2	1.69	7	6	8	22	166^2
1928	Chi-N	4	0	18	2	41	4.83	-4	-4	-4	24	163^1
1929	Chi-N	2	1	21	8	46	1.96	14	14	13	29	224^2
1930	Chi-N	3	2	21	3	64^2	6.82	-13	-14	-11	25	160^1
1931	Chi-N	4	0	15	2	21^1	4.64	-2	-2	-4	24	159
1932	Chi-N	4	2	10	0	11	7.36	-4	-4	-22	30	227^2
1933	Chi-N	1	1	9	2	13	4.15	-1	-1	-2	32	246
1934	Chi-N	3	1	13	2	21^1	5.48	-3	-4	-7	27	188
1935	Pit-N	5	1	16	2	45	2.80	6	7	8	25	159^1
1936	Pit-N	1	3	16	2	34^2	5.97	-8	-7	-9		
	Bos-N	1	0	4	0	27^1	1.32	8	8	3	11	63

YEAR	TM/L	WR	LR	GR	SV	IPR	ERAR	RR	/A	RNK	GS	IPS
	Yr	2	3	20	2	62	3.92	1	0	-6	11	63
1937	Bos-N	2	3	12	1	22^2	6.35	-6	-7	-15	20	158
1938	StL-N	0	1	6	1	6	4.50	-0	-0	-1		
1945	Cin-N	0	0	4	1	4^1	8.31	-2	-2	-1		
Total	17	43	20	234	34	520	4.28	-6	-9	-30	308	2202
■ Rick Camp												
1976	Atl-N	0	0	4	0	6	6.00	-2	-1	0	1	5^1
1977	Atl-N	6	3	54	10	78^2	4.00	-1	4	5		
1978	Atl-N	0	4	38	0	52^2	4.78	-7	-4	-3	4	21^2
1980	Atl-N	6	4	77	22	108^1	1.91	20	22	28		
1981	Atl-N	9	3	48	17	76	1.78	14	15	29		
1982	Atl-N	4	3	30	5	47^1	3.99	-2	-1	-2	21	130
1983	Atl-N	4	2	24	0	40^2	2.66	4	6	7	16	99^1
1984	Atl-N	1	0	10	0	20^1	3.54	0	1	0	21	128^1
1985	Atl-N	3	5	64	3	118^2	3.79	-3	1	0	2	9
Total	9	33	24	349	57	548^2	3.22	25	41	66	65	393^2
■ Bill Campbell												
1973	Min-A	3	2	26	7	47^1	2.09	9	10	13	2	4^1
1974	Min-A	8	7	63	19	120^1	2.62	13	15	22		
1975	Min-A	1	4	40	5	73^1	2.95	7	7	6	7	47^2
1976	Min-A	17	5	78	20	167^2	3.01	10	11	16		
1977	Bos-A	13	9	69	31	140	2.96	17	24	46		
1978	Bos-A	7	5	29	4	50^2	3.91	-1	1	3		
1979	Bos-A	3	4	41	9	54^2	4.28	-0	1	1		
1980	Bos-A	4	0	23	0	41^1	4.79	-3	-3	-2		
1981	Bos-A	1	1	30	7	48^1	3.17	3	4	3		
1982	Chi-N	3	6	62	8	100	3.69	-1	0	0		
1983	Chi-N	6	8	82	8	122^1	4.49	-12	-9	-11		
1984	Phi-N	6	5	57	1	81^1	3.43	1	2	2		
1985	StL-N	5	3	50	4	64^1	3.50	1	0	0		
1986	Det-A	3	6	34	3	55^2	3.88	2	1	2		
1987	Mon-N	0	0	7	0	10	8.10	-4	-4	0		
Total	15	80	65	691	126	1177^1	3.44	41	61	101	9	52
■ Clay Carroll												
1964	Mil-N	2	0	10	1	17^2	0.00	7	7	8	1	2^2
1965	Mil-N	0	1	18	1	29	4.97	-5	-5	-2	1	5^2
1966	Atl-N	8	6	70	11	137^1	2.10	23	24	26	3	7
1967	Atl-N	3	8	35	0	56	5.63	-14	-14	-25	7	37
1968	Atl-N	0	1	10	0	22^1	4.84	-5	-5	-2		
	Cin-N	7	7	57	17	112^2	2.48	6	9	12	1	9
	Yr	7	8	67	17	135	2.87	2	4	11	1	9
1969	Cin-N	11	6	67	7	125^1	3.23	5	7	10	4	25^1
1970	Cin-N	9	4	65	16	104^1	2.59	17	17	25		
1971	Cin-N	10	4	61	15	93^2	2.50	10	9	15		
1972	Cin-N	6	4	65	37	96	2.25	13	10	19		
1973	Cin-N	6	7	48	14	64^2	4.59	-7	-9	-20	5	28
1974	Cin-N	10	4	54	6	80^2	1.90	15	14	25	3	20
1975	Cin-N	7	5	54	7	87^1	2.37	12	12	17	2	9
1976	Chi-A	4	4	29	6	77^1	2.56	8	9	10		
1977	StL-N	4	2	50	4	85	2.54	13	12	9	1	5
	Chi-A	1	3	8	1	11^1	4.76	-1	-1	-3		
1978	Pit-N	0	0	2	0	4	2.25	1	1	0		
Total	15	88	66	703	143	1204^2	2.82	100	97	123	28	148^2
■ Hugh Casey												
1935	Chi-N	0	0	13	0	25^2	3.86	0	0	0		
1939	Bro-N	2	1	15	1	36^2	2.45	6	6	5	25	190^2
1940	Bro-N	6	5	34	2	88^1	2.55	13	14	17	10	65^2
1941	Bro-N	8	4	27	7	59	2.29	9	9	19	18	103
1942	Bro-N	6	1	48	13	103	2.18	13	12	11	2	9
1946	Bro-N	11	4	45	5	99^1	1.81	18	17	25	1	0^1
1947	Bro-N	10	4	46	18	76^2	3.99	1	1	3		
1948	Bro-N	3	0	22	4	36	8.00	-16	-16	-16		
1949	Pit-N	4	1	33	5	38^2	4.66	-3	-2	-3		
	NY-A	1	0	4	0	7^2	8.22	-3	-4	-4		
Total	9	51	20	287	55	571	3.14	37	39	57	56	368^2
■ George Caster												
1934	Phi-A	1	1	2	0	11	0.82	4	4	7	3	26
1935	Phi-A	1	3	24	1	59^1	5.46	-7	-6	-4	1	4
1937	Phi-A	0	0	1	0	2	4.50	0	0	0	33	229^2
1938	Phi-A	0	0	2	1	2^2	0.00	1	1	1	40	278^2
1939	Phi-A	2	0	11	0	18	5.50	-2	-2	-2	17	118
1940	Phi-A	1	1	12	2	21^1	5.48	-3	-2	-3	24	157
1941	StL-A	0	1	23	3	51^1	4.91	-4	-3	-1	9	53
1942	StL-A	8	2	39	5	80	2.81	8	8	10		
1943	StL-A	6	8	35	8	76^1	2.12	10	10	19		
1944	StL-A	6	6	42	12	81	2.44	9	10	17		
1945	StL-A	1	2	10	1	15^2	6.89	-6	-6	-11		
	Det-A	5	1	22	2	51^1	3.86	-3	-2	-2		
	Yr	6	3	32	3	67	4.57	-9	-8	-13		
1946	Det-A	2	1	26	4	41^1	5.66	-10	-9	-8		
Total	12	33	26	249	39	511^1	3.78	-2	4	25	127	866^1
■ Bill Caudill												
1979	Chi-N	1	0	17	0	28^2	4.08	-1	0	0	12	61^1
1980	Chi-N	4	6	70	1	115^2	2.10	19	23	19	2	12
1981	Chi-N	0	0	20	0	26^1	5.13	-5	-4	0	10	44^2
1982	Sea-A	12	9	70	26	95^2	2.35	18	20	52		
1983	Sea-A	2	8	63	26	72^2	4.71	-5	-4	-7		
1984	Oak-A	9	7	68	36	96^1	2.71	14	11	26		
1985	Tor-A	4	6	67	14	69^1	2.99	9	9	17		
1986	Tor-A	2	4	40	2	36^1	6.19	-8	-8	-13		

YEAR	TM/L	WR	LR	GR	SV	IPR	ERAR	RR	/A	RNK	GS	IPS
1987	Oak-A	0	0	6	1	8	9.00	-4	-4	-1		
Total	9	34	40	421	106	549	3.33	37	44	91	24	118
■ Mark Clear												
1979	Cal-A	11	5	52	14	109	3.63	7	5	9		
1980	Cal-A	11	11	58	9	106^1	3.30	9	7	15		
1981	Bos-A	8	3	34	9	76^2	4.11	-4	-2	-3		
1982	Bos-A	14	9	55	14	105	3.00	13	15	35		
1983	Bos-A	4	5	48	4	96	6.28	-24	-21	-19		
1984	Bos-A	8	3	47	8	67	4.03	-0	1	2		
1985	Bos-A	1	3	41	3	55^2	3.72	3	3	3		
1986	Mil-A	5	5	59	16	73^2	2.20	16	17	30		
1987	Mil-A	8	4	57	6	75	4.08	3	4	7	1	3^1
1988	Mil-A	1	0	25	0	29	2.79	4	4	1		
1990	Cal-A	0	0	4	0	7^2	5.87	-2	-2	0		
Total	11	71	48	480	83	801	3.81	24	33	78	1	3^1
■ Dick Coffman												
1927	Was-A	0	0	3	0	6	1.50	2	2	0	2	10
1928	StL-A	0	1	22	1	33^1	8.10	-15	-14	-5	7	52^1
1929	StL-A	0	1	24	1	35^2	7.32	-12	-11	-4	3	17
1930	StL-A	1	1	8	1	12^2	8.53	-5	-5	-8	30	183^1
1931	StL-A	2	4	15	1	36	5.50	-4	-3	-5	17	133^1
1932	StL-A	1	1	3	0	12	6.00	-2	-2	-2	6	49
	Was-A	0	0	13	0	24^1	2.59	5	5	0	9	52
	Yr	1	1	16	0	36^1	3.72	3	3	-2	15	101
1933	StL-A	0	1	8	1	17	5.29	-2	-1	-1	13	64
1934	StL-A	2	0	19	3	38	4.26	1	3	2	21	135
1935	StL-A	1	3	23	2	55^1	7.32	-18	-16	-11	18	88^1
1936	NY-N	7	3	40	7	90^2	4.07	-1	-2	-2	2	11
1937	NY-N	8	3	41	3	76	2.96	8	8	11	1	4
1938	NY-N	7	2	48	12	89^2	2.91	9	9	10	3	21^2
1939	NY-N	1	2	28	3	38	3.08	4	4	3		
1940	Bos-N	1	5	31	3	48^1	5.40	-8	-9	-11		
1945	Phi-N	2	1	14	0	26^1	5.13	-4	-4	-4		
Total	15	33	28	340	38	639^1	4.70	-43	-38	-28	132	821
■ Sarge Connally												
1921	Chi-A	0	0	3	0	9^1	6.75	-3	-3	0	2	13
1923	Chi-A	0	0	3	0	8^2	6.23	-2	-2	0		
1924	Chi-A	5	5	31	6	68^1	3.16	8	7	11	13	91^2
1925	Chi-A	5	6	38	8	96	4.50	-1	-4	-5	2	8^2
1926	Chi-A	2	4	23	3	46^2	3.28	4	3	4	8	61^2
1927	Chi-A	5	3	25	5	68	3.31	6	6	7	18	130^1
1928	Chi-A	1	4	23	2	51^1	4.56	-3	-3	-3	5	23
1929	Chi-A	0	0	11	1	11^1	4.76	-1	-1	-0		
1931	Cle-A	2	0	8	1	24^2	3.65	2	3	2	9	61
1932	Cle-A	4	4	28	3	63^2	4.52	-0	2	2	7	48^2
1933	Cle-A	4	2	38	1	87^2	4.83	-5	-4	-2	3	15^1
1934	Cle-A	0	0	5	1	5^1	5.06	-0	-0	-0		
Total	12	28	28	236	31	541	4.18	5	4	16	67	453^1
■ Doug Corbett												
1980	Min-A	8	6	73	23	136^1	1.98	31	36	47		
1981	Min-A	2	6	54	17	87^2	2.57	11	13	17		
1982	Min-A	0	2	10	3	22	5.32	-3	-3	-3		
	Cal-A	1	7	33	8	57	5.05	-6	-6	-10		
	Yr	1	9	43	11	79	5.13	-9	-9	-13		
1983	Cal-A	1	1	11	0	17^1	3.63	1	1	1		
1984	Cal-A	4	1	44	4	79^2	2.03	17	17	12	1	5^1
1985	Cal-A	3	3	30	0	46	4.89	-4	-4	-5		
1986	Cal-A	4	2	46	10	78^2	3.66	5	4	4		
1987	Bal-A	0	2	11	1	23	7.83	-9	-9	-8		
Total	8	23	30	312	66	547^2	3.32	43	49	55	1	5^1
■ Doc Crandall												
1908	NY-N	2	1	8	0	32	1.13	4	5	4	24	182^2
1909	NY-N	5	1	23	6	68	2.51	1	0	0	7	54
1910	NY-N	7	1	24	5	63	1.86	8	8	10	18	144^2
1911	NY-N	7	0	26	5	85^2	1.68	16	16	14	15	113
1912	NY-N	6	5	27	2	85	4.24	-8	-8	-10	10	77
1913	NY-N	2	4	24	0	55^1	3.09	1	0	0		
	NY-N	2	0	11	0	42^1	2.55	3	3	1		
	Yr	4	4	35	0	97^2	2.86	4	3	1		
1914	StL-F	1	0	6	0	13	4.15	-1	-1	-1	21	183
1915	StL-F	6	3	18	1	68^2	3.80	-6	-5	-6	33	244
1916	StL-A	0	0	2	0	1^1	27.00	-4	-4	0		
1918	Bos-N	0	0	2	0	7	0.00	2	2	0	3	27
Total	10	38	15	171	19	521^1	2.80	17	16	13	131	1025^1
■ Chuck Crim												
1987	Mil-A	5	4	48	12	104	3.29	13	15	15	5	26
1988	Mil-A	7	6	70	9	105	2.91	12	12	16		
1989	Mil-A	9	7	76	7	117^2	2.83	14	13	18		
1990	Mil-A	3	5	67	11	85^2	3.47	4	4	4		
1991	Mil-A	8	5	66	3	91^1	4.63	-5	-7	-9		
1992	Cal-A	7	6	57	1	87	5.17	-12	-12	-17		
Total	6	39	33	384	43	590^2	3.64	26	25	28	5	26
■ Danny Darwin												
1978	Tex-A	0	0	2	0	2^2	3.38	0	0	0	1	6
1979	Tex-A	1	3	14	0	38^2	3.26	4	4	4	6	39^1
1980	Tex-A	12	4	51	8	94^2	2.66	14	13	22	2	15
1981	Tex-A										22	146
1982	Tex-A	10	7	55	7	82^1	3.17	8	6	13	1	6^2
1983	Tex-A	0	0	2	0	6^2	0.00	3	3	0	26	176^1

YEAR	TM/L	WR	LR	GR	SV	IPR	ERAR	RR	/A	RNK	GS	IPS
1984	Tex-A	0	0	3	0	10^1	0.87	4	4	0	32	213^1
1985	Mil-A	1	2	10	2	13^2	3.29	1	1	3	29	204
1986	Mil-A	2	1	13	0	30	3.00	4	4	4	14	100^1
	Hou-N	1	0	4	0	5^2	1.59	1	1	2	8	48^2
1987	Hou-N	0	0	3	0	3^2	4.91	-0	-0	0	30	192
1988	Hou-N	4	3	24	3	58^2	2.15	8	8	9	20	133^1
1989	Hou-N	11	4	68	7	122	2.36	15	14	17		
1990	Hou-N	2	1	31	2	45	2.40	7	7	5	17	117^2
1991	Bos-A										12	68
1992	Bos-A	5	4	36	3	54^1	4.80	-5	-4	-6	15	107
Total	13	49	29	316	32	568^1	2.82	65	61	72	235	1573^2
■ Hooks Dauss												
1912	Det-A										2	17
1913	Det-A	0	1	4	1	7^2	5.87	-3	-3	-4	29	217^1
1914	Det-A	1	2	10	4	23	2.74	0	0	0	35	279
1915	Det-A	3	2	11	2	25^2	3.16	-1	-0	-1	35	284
1916	Det-A	4	0	10	4	26^2	4.05	-4	-4	-6	29	212
1917	Det-A	1	0	6	2	13^2	2.63	0	0	0	31	257
1918	Det-A	1	3	7	3	30	2.70	0	-0	-0	26	219^2
1919	Det-A	1	0	2	0	2^2	0.00	1	1	3	32	253^2
1920	Det-A	1	3	6	0	16^2	5.94	-4	-4	-9	32	253^2
1921	Det-A	1	1	4	1	13	6.23	-3	-3	-4	28	220
1922	Det-A	5	1	14	4	48	2.06	11	10	13	25	170^2
1923	Det-A	1	0	11	3	21^1	3.80	0	0	-1	39	294^2
1924	Det-A	8	5	30	6	58	4.19	0	-1	-1	10	73^1
1925	Det-A	2	1	5	1	7^1	2.45	2	2	6	30	220^2
1926	Det-A	11	4	30	9	95^1	3.59	5	5	8	5	29
Total	14	40	23	150	40	389	3.54	5	4	6	388	3001^2
■ Mark Davis												
1980	Phi-N	0	0	1	0	2	0.00	1	1	0	1	5
1981	Phi-N										9	43
1983	SF-N										20	111
1984	SF-N	3	4	19	0	35	3.60	-0	-0	-1	27	139^2
1985	SF-N	5	11	76	7	110^1	3.18	5	3	5	1	4
1986	SF-N	5	6	65	4	75^2	3.09	5	4	5	2	8^2
1987	SF-N	0	0	9	0	9^1	5.79	-2	-2	0	11	61^1
	SD-N	5	3	43	2	62^1	3.18	6	5	7		
	Yr	5	3	52	2	71^2	3.52	4	3	7	11	61^1
1988	SD-N	5	10	62	28	98^1	2.01	16	15	30		
1989	SD-N	4	3	70	44	92^2	1.85	17	17	30		
1990	KC-A	2	5	50	6	56^2	4.13	-1	-2	-3	3	12
1991	KC-A	3	2	24	1	34^1	6.29	-8	-8	-11	5	28^1
1992	KC-A	0	0	7	0	12^2	1.42	4	4	0	6	23^2
	Atl-N	1	0	14	0	16^2	7.02	-7	-6	-3		
Total	10	33	44	440	92	606	3.16	35	30	59	85	436^2
■ Ron Davis												
1978	NY-A	0	0	4	0	2^1	11.57	-2	-2	0		
1979	NY-A	14	2	44	9	85^1	2.85	13	12	22		
1980	NY-A	9	3	53	7	131	2.95	16	14	13		
1981	NY-A	4	5	43	6	73	2.71	8	7	9		
1982	Min-A	3	9	63	22	106	4.42	-4	-2	-3		
1983	Min-A	5	8	66	30	89	3.34	7	9	19		
1984	Min-A	7	11	64	29	83	4.55	-5	-3	-9		
1985	Min-A	2	6	57	25	64^2	3.48	5	7	13		
1986	Min-A	2	6	36	2	38^2	9.08	-21	-21	-41		
	Chi-N	0	2	17	0	20	7.65	-9	-8	-7		
1987	Chi-N	0	0	21	0	32^1	5.85	-6	-6	0		
	LA-N	0	0	4	0	4	6.75	-1	-1	0		
	Yr	0	0	25	0	36^1	5.94	-8	-7	0		
1988	SF-N	1	1	9	0	17^1	4.67	-2	-3	-3		
Total	11	47	53	481	130	746^2	4.05	-3	3	14		
■ Ken Dayley												
1982	Atl-N	2	0	9	0	14^2	3.68	-0	0	0	11	56^2
1983	Atl-N	1	2	8	0	12^1	3.65	-0	0	1	16	92^1
1984	Atl-N										4	18^2
	StL-N	0	0	1	0	2	13.50	-2	-2	0	2	3
	Yr	1	2	1	0	20^2	3.48	-2	-2	1	6	21^2
1985	StL-N	4	4	57	11	65^1	2.76	6	6	8		
1986	StL-N	0	3	31	5	38^2	3.26	2	2	2		
1987	StL-N	9	5	53	4	61	2.66	10	10	22		
1988	StL-N	2	7	54	5	55^1	2.77	4	4	7		
1989	StL-N	4	3	71	12	75^1	2.87	5	6	8		
1990	StL-N	4	4	58	2	73^1	3.56	2	2	2		
1991	Tor-A	0	0	8	0	4^1	6.23	-1	-1	0		
Total	9	26	28	350	39	402^1	3.11	26	27	50	33	170^2
■ Rob Dibble												
1988	Cin-N	1	1	37	0	59^1	1.82	11	12	4		
1989	Cin-N	10	5	74	2	99	2.09	15	17	23		
1990	Cin-N	8	3	68	11	98	1.74	22	24	30		
1991	Cin-N	3	5	67	31	82^1	3.17	5	6	10		
1992	Cin-N	3	5	63	25	70^1	3.07	3	5	8		
Total	5	25	19	309	69	409	2.35	57	63	76		
■ Murry Dickson												
1939	StL-N	0	0	1	0	3^2	0.00	2	2	0		
1940	StL-N										1	1^2
1942	StL-N	4	1	29	2	91^2	1.47	19	20	11	7	29
1943	StL-N	2	2	24	0	69^2	2.58	6	6	3	7	46
1946	StL-N	4	2	28	1	24^1	7.03	-10	-10	-22	19	160
1947	StL-N	3	2	22	3	57	3.16	6	6	6	25	174^2
1948	StL-N	2	4	13	1	35^1	3.31	3	3	5	29	217

YEAR	TM/L	WR	LR	GR	SV	IPR	ERAR	RR	/A	RNK	GS	IPS
1949	Pit-N	3	5	24	0	76	3.20	7	8	8	20	148^1
1950	Pit-N	5	3	29	3	74	3.41	6	8	9	22	151
1951	Pit-N	4	2	10	2	28^2	2.51	5	5	11	35	260
1952	Pit-N	2	0	9	2	16	0.00	7	7	10	34	261^2
1953	Pit-N	2	4	19	4	35^2	4.04	1	2	3	26	165
1954	Phi-N	1	1	9	3	15^2	3.45	1	1	2	31	210^2
1955	Phi-N	1	1	8	0	20^1	5.31	-3	-3	-3	28	195^2
1956	Phi-N										3	23
	StL-N	0	1	1	0	0		-12	-12	0	27	196^1
	Yr	1	2	1	0	23	5.48	-15	-15	-3	30	219^1
1957	StL-N	0	0	1	0	0^2	13.50	-1	-1	0	13	73^1
1958	KC-A	6	2	18	1	46^1	2.72	5	6	10	9	52^2
	NY-A	1	1	4	1	9	2.00	2	2	3	2	11^1
	Yr	7	3	22	2	55^1	2.60	7	8	13	11	64
1959	KC-A	2	1	38	0	71	4.94	-9	-7	-3		
Total	16	42	32	287	23	675	3.23	35	44	52	338	2377^1

■ Frank DiPino

YEAR	TM/L	WR	LR	GR	SV	IPR	ERAR	RR	/A	RNK	GS	IPS
1981	Mil-A	0	0	2	0	2^1	0.00	1	1	0		
1982	Hou-N										6	28^1
1983	Hou-N	3	4	53	20	71^1	2.65	8	6	9		
1984	Hou-N	4	9	57	14	75^1	3.35	2	-0	-0		
1985	Hou-N	3	7	54	6	76	4.03	-4	-5	-6		
1986	Hou-N	1	3	31	3	40^1	3.57	1	0	0		
	Chi-N	2	4	30	0	40	5.18	-6	-5	-7		
	Yr	3	7	61	3	80^1	4.37	-6	-5	-7		
1987	Chi-N	3	3	69	4	80	3.15	8	10	8		
1988	Chi-N	2	3	63	6	90^1	4.98	-15	-14	-9		
1989	StL-N	9	0	67	0	88^1	2.45	10	12	11		
1990	StL-N	5	2	62	3	81	4.56	-7	-7	-6		
1992	StL-N	0	0	9	0	11	1.64	2	2	0		
Total	10	32	35	497	56	656	3.66	-0	0	-1	6	28^1

■ Fritz Dorish

YEAR	TM/L	WR	LR	GR	SV	IPR	ERAR	RR	/A	RNK	GS	IPS
1947	Bos-A	4	3	32	2	79	4.10	-3	-2	-2	9	57
1948	Bos-A	0	1	9	0	14^1	5.65	-2	-2	-1		
1949	Bos-A	0	0	5	0	7^2	2.35	2	2	0		
1950	StL-A	1	2	16	0	32^1	6.12	-6	-4	-4	13	76^2
1951	Chi-A	3	5	28	0	72	3.38	6	5	5	4	24^2
1952	Chi-A	7	4	38	11	82	2.52	10	10	15	1	9
1953	Chi-A	7	4	49	18	102^2	3.51	6	6	8	6	43
1954	Chi-A	2	2	31	6	61^2	3.50	2	2	1	6	47^1
1955	Chi-A	2	0	13	1	17	1.59	4	4	5		
	Bal-A	3	2	34	6	63^2	2.69	9	8	7	1	2
	Yr	5	2	47	7	80^2	2.45	13	12	13	1	2
1956	Bal-A	0	0	13	0	19^2	4.12	0	-0	0		
	Bos-A	0	2	15	0	22^2	3.57	1	3	2		
	Yr	0	2	28	0	42^1	3.83	2	2	2		
Total	10	29	25	283	44	574^2	3.49	29	31	38	40	259^2

■ Moe Drabowsky

YEAR	TM/L	WR	LR	GR	SV	IPR	ERAR	RR	/A	RNK	GS	IPS
1956	Chi-N	0	0	2	0	2	0.00	1	1	0	7	49
1957	Chi-N	0	0	3	0	5	3.60	0	0	0	33	234^2
1958	Chi-N	1	1	2	0	2^2	3.38	0	0	1	20	123
1959	Chi-N	0	0	8	0	13^2	0.66	5	5	0	23	128
1960	Chi-N	2	0	25	1	30^2	4.70	-3	-3	-2	7	19^2
1961	Mil-N	0	2	16	2	25^1	4.62	-2	-2	-2		
1962	Cin-N	1	1	13	1	31	3.48	2	2	1	10	52
	KC-A	0	0	7	0	15^2	5.17	-2	-2	0	3	12^1
1963	KC-A	0	0	4	0	7^1	0.00	3	3	0	22	167
1964	KC-A	1	2	32	1	51^1	5.08	-8	-7	-4	21	117
1965	KC-A	1	2	9	0	14^1	2.51	2	2	3	5	24^1
1966	Bal-A	5	0	41	7	83	2.71	7	6	4	3	13
1967	Bal-A	7	5	43	12	95^1	1.60	17	16	23		
1968	Bal-A	4	4	45	7	61^1	1.91	7	7	10		
1969	KC-A	11	9	52	11	98	2.94	7	8	17		
1970	KC-A	1	2	24	2	35^2	3.28	2	2	2		
	Bal-A	4	2	21	1	33^1	3.78	-0	-0	-1		
	Yr	5	4	45	3	69	3.52	1	1	1		
1971	StL-N	6	1	51	8	60^1	3.43	0	1	2		
1972	StL-N	1	1	30	2	27^2	2.60	3	2	2		
	Chi-A	0	0	7	0	7^1	2.45	0	1	0		
Total	17	45	32	435	55	701	3.00	40	41	55	154	940

■ Dick Drago

YEAR	TM/L	WR	LR	GR	SV	IPR	ERAR	RR	/A	RNK	GS	IPS
1969	KC-A	0	1	15	1	23	4.30	-2	-2	-1	26	177^2
1970	KC-A	0	0	1	0	0^2	0.00	0	0	0	34	239^1
1971	KC-A	0	0	1	0	0^1	162.00	-6	-6	0	34	241
1972	KC-A	0	0	1	0	3	3.00	0	0	0	33	236^1
1973	KC-A	0	1	4	0	8^2	4.15	-0	-0	-0	33	204
1974	Bos-A	3	0	15	3	39^1	1.37	10	11	9	18	136^1
1975	Bos-A	2	2	38	15	64^1	2.94	6	8	9	2	8^1
1976	Cal-A	7	8	43	6	79^1	4.42	-8	-10	-18		
1977	Cal-A	0	1	13	2	21	3.00	2	2	1		
	Bal-A	6	3	36	3	39^2	3.63	2	1	2		
	Yr	6	4	49	5	60^2	3.41	4	3	3		
1978	Bos-A	3	4	36	7	71^1	2.78	8	11	12	1	6
1979	Bos-A	10	6	52	13	86	3.14	10	12	25	1	3
1980	Bos-A	4	5	36	3	91^1	4.53	-5	-3	-3	7	41^1
1981	Sea-A	4	6	39	5	53^2	5.53	-11	-10	-19		
Total	13	39	37	330	58	581^2	3.74	6	14	16	189	1293^1

■ Ryne Duren

YEAR	TM/L	WR	LR	GR	SV	IPR	ERAR	RR	/A	RNK	GS	IPS
1954	Bal-A	0	0	1	0	2	9.00	-1	-1	0		
1957	KC-A	0	0	8	1	10	9.00	-6	-6	-1	6	32^2
1958	NY-A	6	4	43	20	70^2	2.17	13	11	20	1	5
1959	NY-A	3	6	41	14	76^2	1.88	17	15	22		
1960	NY-A	3	4	41	9	45	5.20	-7	-8	-15	1	4
1961	NY-A	0	1	4	0	5	5.40	-1	-1	-2		
	LA-A	2	6	26	2	52^2	4.78	-4	-2	-2	14	46^1
	Yr	2	7	30	2	57^2	4.84	-5	-3	-4	14	46^1
1962	LA-A	2	8	39	8	63	4.57	-4	-5	-9	3	8^1
1963	Phi-N	3	1	26	2	45^1	2.98	2	1	1	7	42
1964	Phi-N	0	0	2	0	3	6.00	-1	-1	0		
	Cin-N	0	2	26	1	43^2	2.89	3	4	2		
	Yr	0	2	28	1	46^2	3.09	2	3	2		
1965	Phi-N	0	0	6	0	11	3.27	0	0	0		
	Was-A	1	1	16	0	23	6.65	-8	-8	-6		
Total	10	20	33	279	57	451	3.71	3	-1	10	32	138^1

■ Rawly Eastwick

YEAR	TM/L	WR	LR	GR	SV	IPR	ERAR	RR	/A	RNK	GS	IPS
1974	Cin-N	0	0	8	2	17^2	2.04	3	3	1		
1975	Cin-N	5	3	58	22	90	2.60	10	10	13		
1976	Cin-N	11	5	71	26	107^2	2.09	17	17	32		
1977	Cin-N	2	2	23	7	43^1	2.91	5	5	6		
	StL-N	3	6	40	4	51^1	4.56	-4	-4	-7	1	2^1
	Yr	5	8	63	11	94^2	3.80	1	1	-1	1	2^1
1978	NY-A	2	1	8	0	24^2	3.28	1	1	1		
	Phi-N	2	1	22	0	40^1	4.02	-2	-2	-1		
1979	Phi-N	3	6	51	6	82^2	4.90	-11	-10	-11		
1980	KC-A	0	1	14	0	22	5.32	-3	-3	-1		
1981	Chi-N	0	1	30	1	43^1	2.28	6	7	2		
Total	8	28	26	325	68	523	3.29	23	23	34	1	2^1

■ Dennis Eckersley

YEAR	TM/L	WR	LR	GR	SV	IPR	ERAR	RR	/A	RNK	GS	IPS
1975	Cle-A	1	0	10	2	12^1	0.00	5	5	6	24	174^1
1976	Cle-A	1	0	6	1	15	3.00	1	1	1	30	184^1
1977	Cle-A										33	247^1
1978	Bos-A										35	268^1
1979	Bos-A										33	246^2
1980	Bos-A										30	197^2
1981	Bos-A										23	154
1982	Bos-A										33	224^1
1983	Bos-A										28	176^1
1984	Bos-A										9	64^2
	Chi-N										24	160^1
1985	Chi-N										25	169^1
1986	Chi-N	0	0	1	0	1	0.00	0	0	0	32	200
1987	Oak-A	6	6	52	16	104	2.60	21	18	24	2	11^2
1988	Oak-A	4	2	60	45	72^2	2.35	13	12	25		
1989	Oak-A	4	0	51	33	57^2	1.56	15	14	26		
1990	Oak-A	4	2	63	48	73^1	0.61	27	25	56		
1991	Oak-A	5	4	67	43	76	2.96	10	7	17		
1992	Oak-A	7	1	69	51	80	1.91	18	17	39		
Total	9	32	15	379	239	492	2.03	110	98	193	361	2479^1

■ Mark Eichhorn

YEAR	TM/L	WR	LR	GR	SV	IPR	ERAR	RR	/A	RNK	GS	IPS
1982	Tor-A										7	38
1986	Tor-A	14	6	69	10	157	1.72	43	44	56		
1987	Tor-A	10	6	89	4	127^2	3.17	18	19	22		
1988	Tor-A	0	3	37	1	66^2	4.18	-2	-2	-1		
1989	Atl-N	5	5	45	0	68^1	4.35	-6	-5	-7		
1990	Cal-A	2	5	60	13	84^2	3.08	8	7	8		
1991	Cal-A	3	3	70	1	81^2	1.98	19	19	13		
1992	Cal-A	2	4	42	2	56^2	2.38	10	10	10		
	Tor-A	2	0	23	0	31	4.35	-1	-1	-1		
	Yr	4	4	65	2	87^2	3.08	8	9	9		
Total	7	38	32	435	31	673^2	2.89	88	90	101	7	38

■ Don Elston

YEAR	TM/L	WR	LR	GR	SV	IPR	ERAR	RR	/A	RNK	GS	IPS
1953	Chi-N	0	0	1	0	2	9.00	-1	-1	0	1	3
1957	Bro-N	0	0	1	0	1	0.00	0	0	0		
	Chi-N	3	1	25	8	48^2	2.96	5	5	5	14	95^1
	Yr	3	1	26	8	49^2	2.90	5	5	5	14	95^1
1958	Chi-N	9	8	69	10	97	2.88	12	11	20		
1959	Chi-N	10	8	65	13	97^2	3.32	7	7	13		
1960	Chi-N	8	9	60	11	127	3.40	5	5	7		
1961	Chi-N	6	7	58	8	93^1	5.59	-16	-15	-21		
1962	Chi-N	4	8	57	8	66^1	2.44	11	13	24		
1963	Chi-N	4	1	51	4	70	2.83	4	5	4		
1964	Chi-N	2	5	48	1	54^1	5.30	-11	-10	-12		
Total	9	46	47	435	63	657^1	3.60	16	21	42	15	98^1

■ Roy Face

YEAR	TM/L	WR	LR	GR	SV	IPR	ERAR	RR	/A	RNK	GS	IPS
1953	Pit-N	3	2	28	0	50	6.84	-14	-13	-12	13	69
1955	Pit-N	1	1	32	5	56	3.54	3	4	2	10	69^2
1956	Pit-N	11	12	65	6	119^1	3.32	6	6	11	3	16
1957	Pit-N	4	6	58	10	85^2	3.05	8	7	9	1	8
1958	Pit-N	5	2	57	20	84	2.89	10	9	12		
1959	Pit-N	18	1	57	10	93^1	2.70	13	12	25		
1960	Pit-N	10	8	68	24	114^2	2.90	11	11	20		
1961	Pit-N	6	12	62	17	92	3.82	2	2	4		
1962	Pit-N	8	7	63	28	91	1.88	21	21	45		
1963	Pit-N	3	9	56	16	69^2	3.23	0	1	1		
1964	Pit-N	3	3	55	4	79^2	5.20	-15	-15	-12		
1965	Pit-N	5	2	16	0	20^1	2.66	2	2	6		
1966	Pit-N	6	6	54	18	70	2.70	7	7	14		
1967	Pit-N	7	5	61	17	74^1	2.42	8	8	15		
1968	Pit-N	2	4	43	13	52	2.60	2	2	3		
	Det-A	0	0	2	0	1	0.00	0	0	0		

YEAR	TM/L	WR	LR	GR	SV	IPR	ERAR	RR	/A	RNK	GS	IPS
1969	Mon-N	4	2	44	5	59^1	3.94	-2	-2	-2		
Total	16	96	82	821	193	1212^1	3.28	63	61	143	27	162^2
■ Ed Farmer												
1971	Cle-A	5	2	39	4	62^1	3.75	-2	0	1	4	16^1
1972	Cle-A	2	4	45	7	60	3.75	-5	-4	-4	1	1^1
1973	Cle-A	0	2	16	1	17^1	4.67	-2	-1	-2		
	Det-A	3	0	24	2	45	5.00	-6	-5	-3		
	Yr	3	2	40	3	62^1	4.91	-8	-6	-5		
1974	Phi-N	1	0	11	0	18^1	9.33	-12	-11	-6	3	12^2
1977	Bal-A	0	0	1	0	0	0.00	0	0	0		
1978	Mil-A	1	0	3	1	11	0.82	4	4	4		
1979	Tex-A	1	0	9	0	21^1	3.38	2	2	1	2	11^2
	Chi-A	3	4	39	14	67^1	1.07	24	24	33	3	14
	Yr	4	4	48	14	88^2	1.62	26	26	34	5	25^2
1980	Chi-A	7	9	64	30	99^2	3.34	8	8	16		
1981	Chi-A	3	3	42	10	52^2	4.61	-6	-6	-9		
1982	Phi-N	1	5	43	6	56^1	5.59	-12	-12	-14	4	19^2
1983	Phi-N	0	4	9	0	16^2	7.56	-7	-7	-16	3	10
	Oak-A	0	0	4	0	6^1	2.84	1	1	0	1	4
Total	11	27	33	349	75	534^1	3.98	-14	-8	1	21	89^2
■ Steve Farr												
1984	Cle-A	1	2	15	1	31^1	2.59	5	5	5	16	84^2
1985	KC-A	1	0	13	1	24^1	2.59	4	4	2	3	13^1
1986	KC-A	8	4	56	8	109^1	3.13	13	14	16		
1987	KC-A	4	3	47	1	91	4.15	3	4	3		
1988	KC-A	4	4	61	20	76^2	2.70	11	11	17	1	6
1989	KC-A	1	5	49	18	51^1	4.73	-5	-5	-9	2	12
1990	KC-A	8	6	51	1	91^1	2.17	18	17	24	6	35^2
1991	NY-A	5	5	60	23	70	2.19	15	15	31		
1992	NY-A	2	2	50	30	52	1.56	14	14	29		
Total	9	34	31	402	103	597^1	2.92	77	80	116	28	151^2
■ Turk Farrell												
1956	Phi-N										1	4^1
1957	Phi-N	10	2	52	10	83^1	2.38	14	13	21		
1958	Phi-N	8	9	54	11	94	3.35	6	6	12		
1959	Phi-N	1	6	38	6	57	4.74	-5	-4	-5		
1960	Phi-N	10	6	59	11	103^1	2.70	12	14	22		
1961	Phi-N	2	1	5	0	9^2	6.52	-3	-3	-7		
	LA-N	6	6	50	10	89	5.06	-10	-7	-10		
	Yr	8	7	55	10	98^2	5.20	-13	-10	-18		
1962	Hou-N	2	4	14	4	34	1.59	9	8	15	29	207^2
1963	Hou-N	3	1	8	1	11^1	3.18	0	-0	-0	26	191
1964	Hou-N	0	1	5	0	6	7.50	-3	-3	-4	27	192^1
1965	Hou-N	1	0	4	1	5	5.40	-1	-1	-3	29	203^1
1966	Hou-N	2	0	11	2	26^1	4.10	-1	-2	-2	21	126^1
1967	Hou-N	1	0	7	0	11^2	4.63	-2	-2	-1		
	Phi-N	9	5	49	12	91^1	1.77	16	17	28	1	0^2
	Yr	10	5	56	12	103	2.10	15	15	26	1	0^2
1968	Phi-N	4	6	54	12	83	3.47	-4	-4	-6		
1969	Phi-N	3	4	46	3	74^1	4.00	-3	-4	-4		
Total	13	62	51	456	83	779^1	3.40	25	29	55	134	925^2
■ Tom Ferrick												
1941	Phi-A	3	0	32	7	92^1	3.02	12	12	6	4	27
1942	Cle-A	2	1	29	3	62	1.74	13	12	6	2	19^1
1946	Cle-A	0	0	9	1	18	5.00	-3	-3	-0		
	StL-A	4	1	24	5	30	1.80	6	6	12	1	2^1
	Yr	4	1	33	6	48	3.00	3	3	12	1	2^1
1947	Was-A	1	7	31	9	60	3.15	4	4	6		
1948	Was-A	2	5	37	10	73^2	4.15	1	2	2		
1949	StL-A	6	4	50	6	104^1	3.88	4	7	7		
1950	StL-A	1	3	16	2	24	4.13	1	2	4		
	NY-A	8	4	30	9	56^2	3.65	6	4	9		
	Yr	9	7	46	11	80^2	3.79	7	6	13		
1951	NY-A	1	1	9	1	12	7.50	-5	-5	-8		
	Was-A	2	0	22	2	41^2	2.38	8	8	4		
	Yr	3	1	31	3	53^2	3.52	4	3	-4		
1952	Was-A	4	3	27	1	50^2	3.02	4	3	4		
Total	9	34	29	316	56	625^1	3.32	50	52	52	7	48^2
■ Rollie Fingers												
1968	Oak-A	0	0	1	0	1^1	27.00	-4	-4	0		
1969	Oak-A	4	3	52	12	74^1	2.91	6	4	5	8	44^2
1970	Oak-A	3	1	26	2	48^2	2.77	5	4	3	19	99^1
1971	Oak-A	3	3	40	17	80	2.47	9	8	9	8	49^1
1972	Oak-A	11	9	65	21	111^1	2.51	7	4	9		
1973	Oak-A	7	6	60	22	119	1.97	24	21	29	2	7^2
1974	Oak-A	9	5	76	18	119	2.65	13	9	12		
1975	Oak-A	10	6	75	24	126^2	2.98	11	9	14		
1976	Oak-A	13	11	70	20	134^2	2.47	16	13	26		
1977	SD-N	8	9	78	35	132^1	2.99	13	8	14		
1978	SD-N	6	13	67	37	107^1	2.52	13	10	23		
1979	SD-N	9	9	54	13	83^2	4.52	-7	-9	-21		
1980	SD-N	11	9	66	23	103	2.80	9	7	16		
1981	Mil-A	6	3	47	28	78	1.04	23	21	38		
1982	Mil-A	5	6	50	29	79^2	2.60	13	11	22		
1984	Mil-A	1	2	33	23	46	1.96	10	10	17		
1985	Mil-A	1	6	47	17	55^1	5.04	-6	-5	-10		
Total	17	107	101	907	341	1500^1	2.74	156	120	206	37	201
■ Eddie Fisher												
1959	SF-N	0	4	12	1	16^2	9.72	-11	-11	-25	5	23^1
1960	SF-N	0	0	2	0	3^2	2.45	1	0	0	1	9

YEAR	TM/L	WR	LR	GR	SV	IPR	ERAR	RR	/A	RNK	GS	IPS
1961	SF-N	0	2	14	1	33^2	4.81	-3	-4	-2	1	0
1962	Chi-A	4	3	45	5	95	2.94	11	10	8	12	87^2
1963	Chi-A	2	3	18	0	37^1	4.34	-3	-3	-4	15	83^1
1964	Chi-A	6	3	57	9	116^1	2.79	11	9	8	2	8^2
1965	Chi-A	15	7	82	24	165^1	2.40	20	15	22		
1966	Chi-A	1	3	23	6	35^1	2.29	4	3	5		
	Bal-A	5	3	44	13	71^2	2.64	6	6	8		
	Yr	6	6	67	19	107	2.52	11	9	13		
1967	Bal-A	4	3	46	1	89^2	3.61	-4	-5	-3		
1968	Cle-A	4	2	54	4	94^2	2.85	1	1	1		
1969	Cal-A	2	2	51	2	88^2	3.76	-1	-3	-1	1	8
1970	Cal-A	4	4	65	8	117^2	3.14	8	6	5	2	12^2
1971	Cal-A	9	7	54	3	102^2	2.19	14	12	18	3	16^1
1972	Cal-A	4	4	42	4	74^1	3.75	-6	-7	-8	1	7
	Chi-A	0	0	2	0	1	0.00	0	0	0	4	21^1
	Yr	4	4	44	4	75^1	3.70	-5	-7	-8	5	28^1
1973	Chi-A	0	0	10	0	35^1	7.90	-16	-15	0	16	75^1
	StL-N	2	1	6	0	7	1.29	2	2	7		
Total	15	62	51	627	81	1186	3.25	35	17	37	63	352^2
■ Mike Fornieles												
1952	Was-A	1	1	2	0	9	1.00	3	3	5	2	17^1
1953	Chi-A	4	1	23	3	61^1	2.64	9	9	8	16	91^2
1954	Chi-A	1	1	9	1	15^1	5.28	-3	-3	-3	6	26^2
1955	Chi-A	3	1	17	2	47^1	3.23	4	4	3	9	39
1956	Chi-A	0	1	6	0	15^2	4.60	-1	-1	-0		
	Bal-A	3	1	19	1	50^1	3.22	5	4	3	11	60^2
	Yr	3	2	25	1	66	3.55	4	3	2	11	60^2
1957	Bal-A	1	3	11	0	29	4.97	-4	-4	-5	4	28
	Bos-A	2	0	7	2	8^1	2.16	2	2	5	18	117
	Yr	3	3	18	2	37^1	4.34	-2	-3	-1	22	145
1958	Bos-A	3	3	30	1	69	5.22	-11	-9	-8	7	41^2
1959	Bos-A	5	3	46	11	82	3.07	7	9	11		
1960	Bos-A	10	5	70	14	109	2.64	15	17	26		
1961	Bos-A	8	7	55	15	105^1	4.70	-8	-6	-10	2	14
1962	Bos-A	3	5	41	5	79^1	5.45	-13	-12	-12	1	3
1963	Bos-A	0	0	9	0	14	6.43	-4	-4	0		
	Min-A	1	1	11	0	22^2	4.76	-3	-3	-2		
	Yr	1	1	20	0	36^2	5.40	-7	-7	-2		
Total	12	45	33	356	55	717^2	3.94	-2	5	19	76	439
■ Ken Forsch												
1970	Hou-N										4	24
1971	Hou-N	0	0	10	0	20^1	1.33	5	5	0	23	168
1972	Hou-N	0	0	6	0	11	4.09	-1	-1	0	24	145^1
1973	Hou-N	1	3	20	4	33	4.91	-5	-5	-6	26	168^1
1974	Hou-N	8	7	70	10	103^1	2.79	10	8	12		
1975	Hou-N	2	3	25	2	48	2.25	7	6	6	9	61
1976	Hou-N	4	3	52	19	92	2.15	14	11	12		
1977	Hou-N	5	5	37	8	54^2	2.96	6	4	7	5	31^1
1978	Hou-N	6	4	46	7	85	3.07	5	2	3	6	48^1
1979	Hou-N	1	0	2	0	3	0.00	1	1	4	24	174^2
1980	Hou-N										32	222^1
1981	Cal-A										20	153
1982	Cal-A	1	0	2	0	3	3.00	0	0	1	35	225
1983	Cal-A										31	219^1
1984	Cal-A										2	16^1
1986	Cal-A	0	1	10	1	17	9.53	-10	-10	-7		
Total	11	28	26	280	51	470^1	3.02	32	21	32	241	1657
■ Terry Forster												
1971	Chi-A	2	2	42	1	37^2	4.30	-4	-3	-3	3	12
1972	Chi-A	6	5	62	29	100	2.25	9	10	16		
1973	Chi-A	3	4	39	16	90^2	2.18	16	18	20	12	82
1974	Chi-A	7	7	58	24	131	3.30	5	6	9	1	3^1
1975	Chi-A	3	3	16	4	36	2.00	7	7	13	1	1
1976	Chi-A	0	5	13	1	29^2	3.64	-0	-0	-0	16	81^2
1977	Pit-N	4	1	27	1	49^2	4.35	-2	-2	-2	6	37^2
1978	LA-N	5	4	47	22	65^1	1.93	12	11	23		
1979	LA-N	1	2	17	2	16^1	5.51	-3	-3	-7		
1980	LA-N	0	0	9	0	11^2	3.09	1	1	0		
1981	LA-N	0	1	21	0	30^2	4.11	-2	-3	-1		
1982	LA-N	5	6	56	3	83	3.04	5	4	5		
1983	Atl-N	3	2	56	13	79^1	2.16	13	15	14		
1984	Atl-N	2	0	25	5	26^2	2.70	3	3	4		
1985	Atl-N	2	3	46	1	59^1	2.28	9	10	8		
1986	Cal-A	4	1	41	5	41	3.51	3	3	4		
Total	16	47	46	575	127	888	2.89	71	78	102	39	217^2
■ John Franco												
1984	Cin-N	6	2	54	4	79^1	2.61	9	10	11		
1985	Cin-N	12	3	67	12	99	2.18	16	18	29		
1986	Cin-N	6	6	74	29	101	2.94	9	10	18		
1987	Cin-N	8	5	68	32	82	2.52	14	16	36		
1988	Cin-N	6	6	70	39	86	1.57	18	19	44		
1989	Cin-N	4	8	60	32	80^2	3.12	3	4	10		
1990	NY-N	5	3	55	33	67^2	2.53	10	9	20		
1991	NY-N	5	9	52	30	55^1	2.93	5	4	15		
1992	NY-N	6	2	31	15	33	1.64	7	7	22		
Total	9	58	44	531	226	684	2.49	89	98	204		
■ George Frazier												
1978	StL-N	0	3	14	0	22	4.09	-1	-1	-2		
1979	StL-N	2	4	25	0	32^1	4.45	-3	-2	-4		
1980	StL-N	1	4	22	3	23	2.74	2	2	5		

YEAR	TM/L	WR	LR	GR	SV	IPR	ERAR	RR	/A	RNK	GS	IPS
1981	NY-A	0	1	16	3	27^2	1.63	6	6	3		
1982	NY-A	4	4	63	1	111^2	3.47	8	6	4		
1983	NY-A	4	4	61	8	115^1	3.43	8	6	5		
1984	Cle-A	3	2	22	1	44^1	3.65	2	2	2		
	Chi-N	6	3	37	3	63^2	4.10	-4	-1	-2		
1985	Chi-N	7	8	51	2	76	6.39	-24	-20	-37		
1986	Chi-N	2	4	35	0	51^2	5.40	-10	-8	-8		
	Min-A	1	1	15	6	26^2	4.39	-1	-0	-0		
1987	Min-A	5	5	54	2	81^1	4.98	-5	-3	-4		
Total	10	35	43	415	29	675^2	4.20	-20	-14	-37		
■ **Danny Frisella**												
1967	NY-N	0	0	3	0	8	0.00	3	3	0	11	66
1968	NY-N	0	2	15	2	28^1	2.86	0	1	0	4	22^1
1969	NY-N	0	0	3	0	4^2	7.71	-2	-2	0		
1970	NY-N	7	3	29	1	58	3.10	6	6	9	1	7^2
1971	NY-N	8	5	53	12	90^2	1.99	15	14	23		
1972	NY-N	5	8	39	9	67^1	3.34	1	0	0		
1973	Atl-N	1	2	42	8	45	4.20	-3	-1	-1		
1974	Atl-N	3	4	35	6	37^2	4.78	-5	-4	-9	1	4
1975	SD-N	1	6	65	9	97^2	3.13	5	4	3		
1976	StL-N	0	0	18	1	22^2	3.97	-1	-1	-0		
	Mil-A	5	2	32	9	49^1	2.74	4	4	7		
Total	10	30	32	334	57	509^1	3.15	24	23	33	17	100
■ **Woodie Fryman**												
1966	Pit-N	1	0	8	1	10	1.80	2	2	2	28	171^2
1967	Pit-N	0	0	10	1	16^2	3.78	-1	-1	-0	18	96^2
1968	Phi-N	0	0	2	0	2^1	7.71	-1	-1	0	32	211^1
1969	Phi-N	0	0	1	0	5	0.00	2	2	0	35	223^1
1970	Phi-N	1	0	7	0	11^2	1.54	3	3	2	20	116
1971	Phi-N	3	2	20	2	42	2.36	5	5	6	17	107^1
1972	Phi-N	0	1	6	1	11^2	4.63	-2	-1	-1	17	108
	Det-A	0	0	2	0	6^1	0.00	2	2	0	14	107^1
1973	Det-A	0	0	5	0	11^1	5.56	-2	-2	0	29	158^1
1974	Det-A	0	0	5	0	21^1	1.27	6	6	0	22	120^1
1975	Mon-N	2	4	18	3	32	3.09	2	3	5	20	125
1976	Mon-N	0	0	2	2	4^1	0.00	2	2	2	32	212
1977	Cin-N	0	1	5	1	11^1	3.18	1	1	1	12	64
1978	Chi-N	1	0	4	0	9	6.00	-2	-2	-2	9	46^2
	Mon-N	0	0	2	1	1^1	0.00	1	1	1	17	93^1
	Yr	1	0	6	1	10^1	5.23	-2	-1	-1	26	140
1979	Mon-N	3	6	44	10	58	2.79	6	6	10		
1980	Mon-N	7	4	61	17	80	2.25	12	12	20		
1981	Mon-N	5	3	35	7	43	1.88	8	8	16		
1982	Mon-N	9	4	60	12	69^2	3.75	-1	-1	-2		
1983	Mon-N	0	3	6	0	3	21.00	-6	-6	-52		
Total	18	32	28	303	58	450	2.88	36	38	8	322	1961^1
■ **Gene Garber**												
1969	Pit-N	0	0	1	0	0^2	0.00	0	0	0	1	4^1
1970	Pit-N	0	3	14	0	22^1	5.24	-3	-3	-4		
1972	Pit-N	0	0	4	0	6^1	7.11	-3	-3	0		
1973	KC-A	7	4	40	11	99^2	4.33	-6	-2	-3	8	53
1974	KC-A	1	2	17	1	28	4.82	-4	-3	-3		
	Phi-N	4	0	34	4	48	2.06	8	9	9		
1975	Phi-N	10	12	71	14	110	3.60	0	2	3		
1976	Phi-N	9	3	59	11	92^2	2.82	7	8	11		
1977	Phi-N	8	6	64	19	103^1	2.35	18	19	31		
1978	Phi-N	2	1	22	3	38^2	1.40	9	9	8		
	Atl-N	4	4	43	22	78^1	2.53	9	13	21		
	Yr	6	5	65	25	117	2.15	18	23	29		
1979	Atl-N	6	16	68	25	106	4.33	-7	-3	-8		
1980	Atl-N	5	5	68	7	82^1	3.83	-2	-1	-1		
1981	Atl-N	4	6	35	2	58^2	2.61	6	6	10		
1982	Atl-N	8	10	69	30	119^1	2.34	17	18	35		
1983	Atl-N	4	5	43	9	60^2	4.60	-7	-5	-8		
1984	Atl-N	3	6	62	11	106	3.06	6	9	9		
1985	Atl-N	6	6	59	1	97^1	3.61	-0	3	3		
1986	Atl-N	5	5	61	24	78	2.54	10	12	23		
1987	Atl-N	8	10	49	10	69^1	4.41	-3	-1	-1		
	KC-A	0	0	13	8	14^1	2.51	3	3	4		
1988	KC-A	0	4	26	6	32^2	3.58	1	1	2		
Total	19	94	108	922	218	1452^2	3.30	62	93	141	9	57^1
■ **Dave Giusti**												
1962	Hou-N	2	0	17	0	47	4.98	-5	-6	-2	5	26^2
1964	Hou-N	0	0	8	0	25^2	3.16	1	1	0		
1965	Hou-N	4	3	25	3	55^1	3.42	1	-0	-0	13	76
1966	Hou-N	0	0	1	0	2	4.50	-0	-0	0	33	208
1967	Hou-N	0	1	4	1	11^2	3.09	0	0	0	33	210
1968	Hou-N	0	0	3	1	4^2	13.50	-5	-5	-3	34	246^1
1969	StL-N	0	0	10	0	20^2	3.05	1	1	0	12	79
1970	Pit-N	9	3	65	26	101	2.76	14	13	21	1	2
1971	Pit-N	5	6	58	30	86	2.93	5	4	8		
1972	Pit-N	7	4	54	22	74^2	1.93	13	12	23		
1973	Pit-N	9	2	67	20	98^2	2.37	14	13	18		
1974	Pit-N	6	5	62	12	91^2	3.63	-0	-2	-3	2	14
1975	Pit-N	5	4	61	17	91^2	2.95	7	6	8		
1976	Pit-N	5	4	40	6	58^1	4.32	-5	-5	-9		
1977	Oak-A	3	3	40	6	60^1	2.98	7	7	8		
	Chi-N	0	2	20	1	25^1	6.04	-6	-5	-4		
Total	15	55	37	535	145	854^2	3.24	41	32	66	133	862
■ **Fred Gladding**												
1961	Det-A	1	0	8	0	16^1	3.31	1	1	1		
1962	Det-A	0	0	6	0	5	0.00	2	2	0		
1963	Det-A	1	1	22	7	27^1	1.98	5	5	7		
1964	Det-A	7	4	42	7	67^1	3.07	4	4	7		
1965	Det-A	6	2	46	5	70	2.83	5	5	6		
1966	Det-A	5	0	51	2	74	3.28	1	2	1		
1967	Det-A	6	4	41	12	72	2.13	9	9	15	1	5
1968	Hou-N	0	0	7	2	4^1	14.54	-6	-6	-6		
1969	Hou-N	4	8	57	29	72^2	4.21	-5	-5	-13		
1970	Hou-N	7	4	63	18	71	4.06	-0	-1	-3		
1971	Hou-N	4	5	48	12	51^1	2.10	8	7	15		
1972	Hou-N	5	6	42	14	48^2	2.77	4	3	9		
1973	Hou-N	2	0	16	1	16	4.50	-1	-2	-2		
Total	13	48	34	449	109	596	3.16	27	26	37	1	5
■ **Rich Gossage**												
1972	Chi-A	7	0	35	2	77	3.39	-3	-2	-2	1	3
1973	Chi-A	0	0	16	0	31^1	7.76	-14	-13	0	4	18^1
1974	Chi-A	4	5	36	1	77^2	3.71	-1	0	0	3	11^2
1975	Chi-A	9	8	62	26	141^2	1.84	30	32	48		
1976	Chi-A	0	1	2	1	4^1	8.31	-2	-2	-6	29	219^2
1977	Pit-N	11	9	72	26	133	1.62	34	35	63		
1978	NY-A	10	11	63	27	134^1	2.01	26	24	45		
1979	NY-A	5	3	36	18	58^1	2.62	10	9	18		
1980	NY-A	6	2	64	33	99	2.27	19	18	27		
1981	NY-A	3	2	32	20	46^2	0.77	15	15	28		
1982	NY-A	4	5	56	30	93	2.23	19	18	29		
1983	NY-A	13	5	57	22	87^1	2.27	17	16	38		
1984	SD-N	10	6	62	25	102^1	2.90	8	8	15		
1985	SD-N	5	3	50	26	79	1.82	16	15	25		
1986	SD-N	5	7	45	21	64^2	4.45	-5	-6	-14		
1987	SD-N	5	4	40	11	52	3.12	6	5	10		
1988	Chi-N	4	4	46	13	43^2	4.33	-4	-4	-8		
1989	SF-N	2	1	31	4	43^2	2.68	4	3	3		
	NY-A	1	0	11	1	14^1	3.77	0	0	0		
1991	Tex-A	4	2	44	1	40^1	3.57	2	2	3		
1992	Oak-A	0	2	30	0	38	2.84	5	4	2		
Total	20	108	80	890	308	1461^2	2.67	182	177	322	37	252^2
■ **Jim Gott**												
1982	Tor-A	0	0	7	0	14^2	2.45	3	3	0	23	121^1
1983	Tor-A	0	1	4	0	5^1	5.06	-1	-0	-1	30	171^1
1984	Tor-A	2	1	23	2	33	3.27	3	3	3	12	76^2
1985	SF-N										26	148^1
1986	SF-N	0	0	7	1	7^2	2.35	1	1	0	2	5^1
1987	SF-N	1	0	27	0	41^1	3.70	2	1	0	3	14^2
	Pit-N	0	2	25	13	31	1.45	9	9	14		
	Yr	1	2	52	13	72^1	2.74	11	10	14	3	14^2
1988	Pit-N	6	6	67	34	77^1	3.49	-0	-1	-2		
1989	Pit-N	0	0	1	0	0^2	0.00	0	0	0		
1990	LA-N	3	5	50	3	62	2.90	6	5	7		
1991	LA-N	4	3	55	2	76	2.96	6	5	5		
1992	LA-N	3	3	68	6	88	2.45	10	10	8		
Total	10	19	21	334	61	437	2.92	39	36	34	96	537^2
■ **Wayne Granger**												
1968	StL-N	4	2	34	4	44	2.25	4	3	5		
1969	Cin-N	9	6	90	27	144^2	2.80	13	15	21		
1970	Cin-N	6	5	67	35	84^2	2.66	13	13	27		
1971	Cin-N	7	6	70	11	100	3.33	2	0	0		
1972	Min-A	4	6	63	19	89^2	3.01	0	2	3		
1973	StL-N	2	4	33	5	46^2	4.24	-3	-3	-4		
	NY-A	0	1	7	0	15^1	1.76	4	3	2		
1974	Chi-A	0	0	5	0	7^2	8.22	-4	-4	0		
1975	Hou-N	2	5	55	5	74	3.65	-0	-2	-2		
1976	Mon-N	1	0	27	2	32	3.66	-1	0	0		
Total	9	35	35	451	108	638^2	3.14	27	28	51		
■ **Jim Grant**												
1958	Cle-A	2	2	16	4	29^2	4.25	-2	-2	-3	28	174^1
1959	Cle-A	1	1	19	3	39	5.31	-6	-7	-4	19	126^1
1960	Cle-A	1	3	14	0	32^2	3.31	2	2	2	19	127
1961	Cle-A										35	244^2
1962	Cle-A	0	0	3	0	5^2	0.00	2	2	0	23	144
1963	Cle-A	1	0	6	1	10^1	3.48	0	0	0	32	219
1964	Cle-A	1	0	4	0	10^2	5.06	-2	-2	-1	9	51^1
	Min-A	0	0	3	1	4^1	2.08	1	1	0	23	161^2
	Yr	1	0	7	1	15	4.20	-1	-1	-1	32	213
1965	Min-A	0	1	2	0	2^2	13.50	-3	-3	-10	39	267^2
1966	Min-A										35	249
1967	Min-A	0	0	13	0	15^1	5.28	-3	-3	0	14	80
1968	LA-N	5	2	33	3	69^2	1.81	9	7	7	4	25
1969	Mon-N	0	0	1	0	1	0.00	0	0	0	10	49^2
	StL-N	6	3	27	7	50^1	3.22	2	2	4	3	13
	Yr	6	3	28	7	51^1	3.16	2	2	4	13	62^2
1970	Oak-A	6	2	72	24	123^1	1.82	26	24	24		
	Pit-N	2	1	8	0	12	2.25	2	2	5		
1971	Pit-N	5	3	42	7	75	3.60	-1	-2	-2		
	Oak-A	1	0	15	3	27^1	1.98	5	4	2		
Total	12	31	18	278	53	509	2.99	33	26	24	293	1932^2
■ **Marv Grissom**												
1946	NY-N	0	0	1	0	2	0.00	1	1	0	3	16^2
1949	Det-A	2	3	25	0	35^2	1.77	10	9	12	2	3^2

YEAR	TM/L	WR	LR	GR	SV	IPR	ERAR	RR	/A	RNK	GS	IPS
1952	Chi-A	0	1	4	0	4^2	5.79	-1	-1	-2	24	161^1
1953	Bos-A	0	0	2	0	1^2	43.20	-7	-7	0	11	57^2
	NY-N	0	1	14	0	39^1	3.43	4	4	1	7	45
1954	NY-N	9	7	53	19	101	2.41	19	18	34	3	21^1
1955	NY-N	5	4	55	8	89^1	2.92	11	11	12		
1956	NY-N	1	1	41	7	69	1.30	19	19	9	2	11^2
1957	NY-N	4	4	55	14	82^2	2.61	12	12	15		
1958	SF-N	7	5	51	10	65^1	3.99	-0	-1	-3		
1959	StL-N	0	0	3	0	2	22.50	-4	-4	0		
Total	10	28	26	304	58	492^2	2.87	62	61	78	52	317^1

■ Lefty Grove

YEAR	TM/L	WR	LR	GR	SV	IPR	ERAR	RR	/A	RNK	GS	IPS
1925	Phi-A	5	3	27	1	71^2	4.02	3	5	5	18	125^1
1926	Phi-A	1	1	12	6	28^1	2.86	4	4	5	33	229^2
1927	Phi-A	3	4	23	9	47	2.87	7	7	13	28	215^1
1928	Phi-A	1	0	8	4	9^1	5.79	-2	-2	-4	31	252^1
1929	Phi-A	0	0	5	4	6^2	0.00	3	3	4	37	268^2
1930	Phi-A	5	2	18	9	40	2.03	12	12	24	32	251
1931	Phi-A	4	1	11	5	28^1	2.86	5	5	10	30	260^1
1932	Phi-A	3	2	14	7	33^2	1.87	10	10	18	30	258
1933	Phi-A	6	2	17	6	44^1	0.81	17	17	33	28	231
1934	Bos-A	2	2	10	0	28	8.04	-11	-10	-13	12	81^1
1935	Bos-A	2	1	5	1	12	1.50	4	4	11	30	261
1936	Bos-A	0	2	5	2	16	1.69	6	6	9	30	237^1
1937	Bos-A										32	262
1938	Bos-A	0	0	3	1	6	0.00	3	3	1	21	157^2
1939	Bos-A										23	191
1940	Bos-A	0	0	1	0	2	0.00	1	1	0	21	151^1
1941	Bos-A										21	134
Total	14	32	20	159	55	373^1	2.92	61	67	117	457	3567^1

■ Cecilio Guante

YEAR	TM/L	WR	LR	GR	SV	IPR	ERAR	RR	/A	RNK	GS	IPS
1982	Pit-N	0	0	10	0	27	3.33	1	1	0		
1983	Pit-N	2	6	49	9	100^1	3.32	3	4	4		
1984	Pit-N	2	3	27	2	41^1	2.61	4	5	5		
1985	Pit-N	4	6	63	5	109	2.72	10	10	10		
1986	Pit-N	5	2	52	4	78	3.35	3	4	4		
1987	NY-A	3	2	23	1	44	5.73	-6	-7	-7		
1988	NY-A	5	6	56	11	75	2.88	9	9	15		
	Tex-A	0	0	7	1	4^2	1.93	1	1	1		
	Yr	5	6	63	12	79^2	2.82	10	10	15		
1989	Tex-A	6	6	50	2	69	3.91	-0	0	1		
1990	Cle-A	2	2	25	0	43^2	4.53	-3	-3	-2	1	3
Total	9	29	33	362	35	592	3.44	23	25	29	1	3

■ Lee Guetterman

YEAR	TM/L	WR	LR	GR	SV	IPR	ERAR	RR	/A	RNK	GS	IPS
1984	Sea-A	0	0	3	0	4^1	4.15	-0	-0	0		
1986	Sea-A	0	2	37	0	59^1	7.13	-19	-19	-6	4	16^2
1987	Sea-A	1	0	8	0	12^2	2.13	3	4	3	17	100^2
1988	NY-A	1	0	18	0	34	3.71	1	1	0	2	6^2
1989	NY-A	5	5	70	13	103	2.45	16	16	19		
1990	NY-A	11	7	64	2	93	3.39	5	6	11		
1991	NY-A	3	4	64	6	88	3.68	4	4	4		
1992	NY-A	1	1	15	0	22^2	9.53	-14	-14	-11		
	NY-N	3	4	43	2	43^1	5.82	-11	-11	-17		
Total	8	25	23	322	23	460^1	4.24	-15	-13	2	23	124

■ Harry Gumbert

YEAR	TM/L	WR	LR	GR	SV	IPR	ERAR	RR	/A	RNK	GS	IPS
1935	NY-N	0	0	3	0	3^1	18.90	-6	-6	0	3	20^1
1936	NY-N	4	0	24	0	48	2.81	6	6	4	15	92^2
1937	NY-N	0	0	10	1	20^1	4.43	-1	-1	-0	24	180
1938	NY-N	0	0	5	0	6^2	6.75	-2	-2	0	33	229
1939	NY-N	0	1	2	0	6	6.00	-1	-1	-2	34	237^2
1940	NY-N	2	0	5	2	15^2	2.87	2	2	3	30	221^1
1941	NY-N										5	32^1
	StL-N	4	0	16	1	35^2	2.27	5	6	6	17	108^2
	Yr	6	0	16	3	68	1.85	7	8	9	22	141
1942	StL-N	4	0	19	5	47^2	0.94	13	13	13	19	115^1
1943	StL-N	0	0	2	0	2^2	10.13	-2	-2	0	19	130^1
1944	StL-N	0	0	3	1	12^1	2.92	1	1	0	7	49
	Cin-N	1	2	5	2	18	0.50	6	6	10	19	137^1
	Yr	1	2	8	3	30^1	1.48	7	7	11	26	186^1
1946	Cin-N	4	0	26	4	34^1	3.67	-1	-1	-2	10	84^2
1947	Cin-N	10	10	46	10	90^1	3.89	2	2	5		
1948	Cin-N	10	8	61	17	106^1	3.47	6	5	10		
1949	Cin-N	4	3	29	2	40^2	5.53	-7	-6	-10		
	Pit-N	1	4	16	3	27^2	5.86	-6	-5	-10		
	Yr	5	7	45	5	68^1	5.66	-12	-11	-20		
1950	Pit-N	0	0	1	0	1^2	5.40	-0	-0	0		
Total	14	44	28	273	48	517^1	3.58	15	16	28	235	1638^2

■ Dick Hall

YEAR	TM/L	WR	LR	GR	SV	IPR	ERAR	RR	/A	RNK	GS	IPS
1955	Pit-N	0	0	2	1	1^2	0.00	1	1	1	13	92^2
1956	Pit-N	0	1	10	1	15	1.20	4	4	3	9	47^1
1957	Pit-N	0	0	8	0	10	10.80	-8	-8	0		
1959	Pit-N	0	0	1	0	0^2	40.50	-3	-3	0	1	8
1960	KC-A	0	1	1	0	2	13.50	-2	-2	-10	28	180^1
1961	Bal-A	2	1	16	4	42^1	1.06	14	13	11	13	80
1962	Bal-A	4	3	37	6	74^2	1.81	18	16	17	6	43^2
1963	Bal-A	5	2	44	12	93^1	2.12	16	15	14	3	18^1
1964	Bal-A	9	1	45	7	87^2	1.85	17	17	20		
1965	Bal-A	11	8	48	12	93^2	3.07	4	4	9		
1966	Bal-A	6	2	32	7	66	3.95	-4	-5	-6		
1967	Phi-N	9	8	47	8	77	2.34	9	9	20	1	9
1968	Phi-N	4	1	32	0	46	4.89	-10	-10	-9		
1969	Bal-A	5	2	39	6	65^2	1.92	12	12	14		
1970	Bal-A	10	5	32	3	61^1	3.08	4	4	9		
1971	Bal-A	6	6	27	1	43^1	4.98	-7	-8	-20		
Total	16	71	41	421	68	780^1	2.83	66	60	73	74	479^1

■ Steve Hamilton

YEAR	TM/L	WR	LR	GR	SV	IPR	ERAR	RR	/A	RNK	GS	IPS
1961	Cle-A	0	0	2	0	3	3.00	0	0	0		
1962	Was-A	2	4	31	2	47	2.49	8	8	10	10	60^1
1963	Was-A	0	1	3	0	2	13.50	-2	-2	-10		
	NY-A	5	1	34	5	62^1	2.60	7	6	7		
	Yr	5	2	37	5	64^1	2.94	5	4	-3		
1964	NY-A	5	2	27	3	39	3.46	1	1	1	3	21^1
1965	NY-A	3	1	45	5	52^1	1.38	12	12	11	1	6
1966	NY-A	7	2	41	3	74^1	3.03	3	2	3	3	15^2
1967	NY-A	2	4	44	4	62	3.48	-2	-2	-2		
1968	NY-A	2	2	40	11	50^2	2.13	5	4	5		
1969	NY-A	3	4	38	2	57	3.32	2	1	1		
1970	NY-A	4	3	35	3	45^1	2.78	5	4	6		
	Chi-A	0	0	3	0	3	6.00	-1	-1	0		
	Yr	4	3	38	3	48^1	2.98	4	3	6		
1971	SF-N	2	2	39	4	44^2	3.02	2	2	2		
1972	Chi-N	1	0	22	0	17	4.76	-2	-2	-1		
Total	12	36	26	404	42	559^2	2.89	38	33	32	17	103^1

■ Greg Harris

YEAR	TM/L	WR	LR	GR	SV	IPR	ERAR	RR	/A	RNK	GS	IPS
1981	NY-N	0	0	2	1	2	0.00	1	1	1	14	66^2
1982	Cin-N	0	1	24	1	40^2	3.54	0	1	0	10	50^2
1983	Cin-N	0	0	1	0	1	27.00	-3	-3	0		
1984	Mon-N	0	1	15	2	17^2	2.04	3	3	2		
	SD-N	1	1	18	1	31^2	3.13	2	2	1	1	5
	Yr	1	2	33	3	49^1	2.74	5	4	3	1	5
1985	Tex-A	5	4	58	11	113	2.47	21	22	21		
1986	Tex-A	10	8	73	20	111^1	2.83	17	18	34		
1987	Tex-A	1	4	23	0	36^1	4.95	-2	-2	-2	19	104^1
1988	Phi-N	4	5	65	1	102	2.29	13	14	12	1	5
1989	Phi-N	2	2	44	1	75^1	3.58	-1	-0	-0		
	Bos-A	2	2	15	0	28	2.57	4	5	6		
1990	Bos-A	1	0	4	0	5^2	4.76	-1	-0	-1	30	178^2
1991	Bos-A	4	2	32	2	52^1	2.24	11	12	13	21	120^2
1992	Bos-A	4	8	68	4	94^2	2.66	13	16	19	2	13
Total	12	34	38	442	44	711^2	2.88	79	88	106	98	544

■ Bryan Harvey

YEAR	TM/L	WR	LR	GR	SV	IPR	ERAR	RR	/A	RNK	GS	IPS
1987	Cal-A	0	0	3	0	5	0.00	2	2	0		
1988	Cal-A	7	5	50	17	76	2.13	15	15	28		
1989	Cal-A	3	3	51	25	55	3.44	3	2	5		
1990	Cal-A	4	4	54	25	64^1	3.22	5	4	9		
1991	Cal-A	2	4	67	46	78^2	1.60	22	22	44		
1992	Cal-A	0	4	25	13	28^2	2.83	4	3	8		
Total	6	16	20	250	126	307^2	2.49	51	49	93		

■ Joe Haynes

YEAR	TM/L	WR	LR	GR	SV	IPR	ERAR	RR	/A	RNK	GS	IPS
1939	Was-A	2	0	7	0	25^2	4.56	0	-1	-0	20	147^1
1940	Was-A	2	3	15	0	29	4.34	0	-1	-1	7	34^1
1941	Chi-A	0	0	8	0	28	3.86	1	1	0		
1942	Chi-A	8	4	39	6	95	2.56	12	11	14	1	8
1943	Chi-A	5	2	33	3	94^2	3.14	2	2	2	2	14^2
1944	Chi-A	2	0	21	2	48^1	2.79	3	3	2	12	106
1945	Chi-A	0	0	1	1	3	0.00	1	1	1	13	101
1946	Chi-A	0	0	9	2	17^1	2.08	3	3	1	23	160
1947	Chi-A	3	0	7	0	23^2	1.14	7	7	8	22	158^1
1948	Chi-A	1	0	5	0	9^1	1.93	2	2	2	22	140^1
1949	Was-A	0	5	27	2	44^2	5.64	-7	-7	-8	10	51^2
1950	Was-A	3	1	17	0	48^1	5.21	-3	-4	-3	10	53^1
1951	Was-A	1	3	23	2	59	4.12	0	-0	-0	3	14
1952	Was-A	0	1	20	3	58^2	3.22	3	2	1	2	7^1
Total	14	27	19	232	21	584^2	3.49	23	20	17	147	996^1

■ Dave Heaverlo

YEAR	TM/L	WR	LR	GR	SV	IPR	ERAR	RR	/A	RNK	GS	IPS
1975	SF-N	3	1	42	1	64	2.39	9	10	6		
1976	SF-N	4	4	61	1	75	4.44	-8	-7	-7		
1977	SF-N	5	1	56	1	98^2	2.55	15	15	8		
1978	Oak-A	3	6	69	10	130	3.25	7	6	4		
1979	Oak-A	4	11	62	9	85^2	4.20	0	-2	-3		
1980	Sea-A	6	3	60	4	78^2	3.89	1	2	2		
1981	Oak-A	1	0	6	0	5^2	1.59	1	1	2		
Total	7	26	26	356	26	537^2	3.41	26	25	14		

■ Tom Henke

YEAR	TM/L	WR	LR	GR	SV	IPR	ERAR	RR	/A	RNK	GS	IPS
1982	Tex-A	1	0	8	0	15^2	1.15	5	5	3		
1983	Tex-A	1	0	8	1	16	3.38	1	1	1		
1984	Tex-A	1	1	25	2	28^1	6.35	-7	-7	-6		
1985	Tor-A	3	3	28	13	40	2.03	9	10	20		
1986	Tor-A	9	5	63	27	91^1	3.35	8	9	18		
1987	Tor-A	0	6	72	34	94	2.49	21	21	29		
1988	Tor-A	4	4	52	25	68	2.91	8	8	15		
1989	Tor-A	8	3	64	20	89	1.92	19	18	30		
1990	Tor-A	2	4	61	32	74^2	2.17	14	15	25		
1991	Tor-A	0	2	49	32	50^1	2.32	10	11	19		
1992	Tor-A	3	2	57	34	55^2	2.26	10	11	25		
Total	11	32	30	487	220	623	2.64	99	101	177		

■ Mike Henneman

YEAR	TM/L	WR	LR	GR	SV	IPR	ERAR	RR	/A	RNK	GS	IPS
1987	Det-A	11	3	55	7	96^2	2.98	16	13	20		
1988	Det-A	9	6	65	22	91^1	1.87	21	20	40		
1989	Det-A	11	4	60	8	90	3.70	2	1	2		

YEAR	TM/L	WR	LR	GR	SV	IPR	ERAR	RR	/A	RNK	GS	IPS
1990	Det-A	8	6	69	22	94^1	3.05	9	9	18		
1991	Det-A	10	2	60	21	84^1	2.88	11	12	22		
1992	Det-A	2	6	60	24	77^1	3.96	-0	0	0		
Total	6	51	27	369	104	534	3.05	59	56	101		
■ **Bill Henry**												
1952	Bos-A	0	0	3	0	5^2	6.35	-2	-2	0	10	71
1953	Bos-A	1	0	9	1	12^2	2.84	2	2	2	12	73
1954	Bos-A	0	1	11	0	17^2	4.08	-1	0	0	13	78
1955	Bos-A	1	1	10	0	20	3.15	2	3	2	7	39^2
1958	Chi-N	5	4	44	6	81^1	2.88	10	9	11		
1959	Chi-N	9	8	65	12	134^1	2.68	19	19	25		
1960	Cin-N	1	5	51	17	67^2	3.19	4	5	6		
1961	Cin-N	2	1	47	16	53^1	2.19	11	11	13		
1962	Cin-N	4	2	40	11	37^1	4.58	-3	-2	-5		
1963	Cin-N	1	3	47	14	52	4.15	-5	-5	-6		
1964	Cin-N	2	2	37	6	52	0.87	15	16	15		
1965	Cin-N	2	0	3	0	5	0.00	2	2	7		
	SF-N	2	2	35	4	42	3.64	-0	-0	-0		
	Yr	4	2	38	4	47	3.26	1	2	7		
1966	SF-N	1	1	35	1	22	2.45	3	3	3		
1967	SF-N	2	0	27	2	19	2.37	2	2	2	1	2^2
1968	SF-N	0	1	6	0	4^2	3.86	-0	-0	-1	1	0^1
	Pit-N	0	0	10	0	16^2	8.10	-9	-10	0		
	Yr	0	1	16	0	21^1	7.17	-10	-10	-1	1	0^1
1969	Hou-N	0	0	3	0	5	0.00	2	2	0		
Total	16	33	31	483	90	648^1	3.04	51	55	75	44	264^2
■ **Ramon Hernandez**												
1967	Atl-N	0	2	46	5	51^2	4.18	-5	-5	-3		
1968	Chi-N	0	0	8	0	9	9.00	-6	-6	0		
1971	Pit-N	0	1	10	4	12^1	0.73	4	4	5		
1972	Pit-N	5	0	53	14	70	1.67	14	13	14		
1973	Pit-N	4	5	59	11	89^2	2.41	12	11	13		
1974	Pit-N	5	2	58	2	68^2	2.75	7	5	5		
1975	Pit-N	7	2	46	5	64	2.95	5	4	6		
1976	Pit-N	2	2	37	3	43	3.56	-0	-0	-0		
	Chi-N	0	0	2	0	1^2	0.00	1	1	0		
	Yr	2	2	39	3	44^2	3.43	0	0	-0		
1977	Chi-N	0	0	6	1	7^2	8.22	-4	-3	-1		
	Bos-A	0	1	12	1	12^2	5.68	-2	-2	-1		
Total	9	23	15	337	46	430^1	3.03	25	22	38		
■ **Willie Hernandez**												
1977	Chi-N	8	6	66	4	103	2.97	11	16	21	1	7
1978	Chi-N	8	2	54	3	59^2	3.77	-1	2	3		
1979	Chi-N	4	3	49	0	70^2	5.22	-12	-9	-8	2	8^1
1980	Chi-N	1	3	46	0	77^2	2.90	6	9	4	7	30^2
1981	Chi-N	0	0	12	2	13^2	3.95	-1	-0	-0		
1982	Chi-N	4	6	75	10	75	3.00	5	6	9		
1983	Chi-N	1	0	10	1	15^1	2.35	2	2	2	1	4^1
	Phi-N	8	4	63	7	95^2	3.29	4	3	4		
	Yr	9	4	73	8	111	3.16	6	5	6	1	4^1
1984	Det-A	9	3	80	32	140^1	1.92	32	31	40		
1985	Det-A	8	10	74	31	106^2	2.70	17	16	35		
1986	Det-A	8	7	64	24	88^2	3.55	6	6	12		
1987	Det-A	3	4	45	8	49	3.67	4	3	5		
1988	Det-A	6	5	63	10	67^2	3.06	7	6	10		
1989	Det-A	2	2	32	15	31^1	5.74	-6	-7	-15		
Total	13	70	55	733	147	994^1	3.21	74	84	122	11	50^1
■ **Joe Heving**												
1930	NY-N	7	5	39	6	80	5.06	-1	-3	-4	2	9^2
1931	NY-N	1	6	22	3	42^1	4.89	-5	-6	-9		
1933	Chi-A	5	1	34	6	80^1	1.68	23	23	19	6	37^2
1934	Chi-A	1	5	31	4	82	6.91	-22	-20	-15	2	6
1937	Cle-A	8	4	40	5	72^2	4.83	-2	-2	-3		
1938	Cle-A	1	1	3	0	6	9.00	-3	-3	-9		
	Bos-A	0	0	5	2	6^1	0.00	3	3	2	11	75^2
	Yr	1	1	8	2	12^1	4.38	1	1	-6	11	75^2
1939	Bos-A	11	2	41	7	91	3.07	16	17	24	5	16
1940	Bos-A	8	4	32	3	70^1	3.07	10	11	18	7	48^2
1941	Cle-A	3	2	24	5	48	2.44	9	8	9	3	22^2
1942	Cle-A	5	2	25	3	40	4.72	-5	-6	-10	2	6^1
1943	Cle-A	1	1	29	9	67^1	2.67	5	3	2	1	4^2
1944	Cle-A	8	2	62	10	113^2	1.74	21	20	19	1	6
1945	Bos-N	1	0	3	0	5^1	3.38	0	0	0		
Total	13	60	35	390	63	805^1	3.62	51	47	45	40	233^1
■ **John Hiller**												
1965	Det-A	0	0	5	1	6	0.00	2	2	1		
1966	Det-A	0	0	1	0	2	9.00	-1	-1	0		
1967	Det-A	1	1	17	3	22^2	3.18	0	0	0	6	42^1
1968	Det-A	4	3	27	2	50^1	2.32	4	4	5	12	77^2
1969	Det-A	3	1	32	4	53^1	3.54	0	1	1	8	46
1970	Det-A	5	3	42	3	71	2.79	7	7	8	5	33
1972	Det-A	0	0	21	3	28^1	2.22	3	3	1	3	16
1973	Det-A	10	5	65	38	125^1	1.44	33	37	65		
1974	Det-A	17	14	59	13	150	2.64	16	19	40		
1975	Det-A	2	3	36	14	70^2	2.17	13	15	16		
1976	Det-A	11	8	55	13	112	2.57	12	14	25	1	9
1977	Det-A	5	9	37	7	68^2	3.41	5	7	14	8	55^1
1978	Det-A	9	4	51	15	92^1	2.34	15	16	26		
1979	Det-A	4	7	43	9	79^1	5.22	-9	-8	-12		
1980	Det-A	1	0	11	0	30^2	4.40	-1	-1	-0		

YEAR	TM/L	WR	LR	GR	SV	IPR	ERAR	RR	/A	RNK	GS	IPS
Total	15	72	58	502	125	962^2	2.78	99	115	189	43	279^1
■ **Billy Hoeft**												
1952	Det-A	0	2	24	4	53^1	4.72	-6	-5	-3	10	71^2
1953	Det-A	0	0	2	2	2	0.00	1	1	2	27	195^2
1954	Det-A	1	1	9	1	18^2	3.86	-0	-0	-0	25	156^1
1955	Det-A	0	1	3	0	1^2	10.80	-1	-1	-7	29	218^1
1956	Det-A	2	0	4	0	7^2	4.70	-0	-0	-1	34	240^1
1957	Det-A	0	0	6	1	15^1	1.17	4	5	1	28	191^2
1958	Det-A	1	2	15	3	24	3.00	2	3	4	21	119
1959	Det-A										2	9
	Bos-A	0	0	2	0	6	3.00	1	1	0	3	11^2
	Bal-A	0	0	13	0	30^2	5.58	-6	-6	0	3	10^1
	Yr	1	2	15	3	45^2	5.72	-3	-3	4	8	31
1960	Bal-A	2	1	19	0	18^2	4.34	-1	-1	-2		
1961	Bal-A	2	1	23	3	51^2	1.74	13	12	8	12	86^1
1962	Bal-A	4	6	53	7	92^2	3.98	-0	-2	-3	4	21
1963	SF-N	2	0	23	4	24^1	4.44	-3	-3	-4		
1964	Mil-N	4	0	42	4	73^1	3.80	-2	-2	-1		
1965	Chi-N	1	1	27	1	38^1	2.35	5	6	3	2	13
1966	Chi-N	1	2	36	3	41	4.61	-5	-4	-3		
	SF-N	0	2	4	0	3^2	7.36	-2	-2	-7		
	Yr	1	4	40	3	44^2	4.84	-6	-6	-11		
Total	14	20	19	305	33	503	3.76	-0	-1	-14	200	1344^1
■ **Joe Hoerner**												
1963	Hou-N	0	0	1	0	3	0.00	1	1	0		
1964	Hou-N	0	0	7	0	11	4.91	-2	-2	0		
1966	StL-N	5	1	57	13	76	1.54	17	17	19		
1967	StL-N	4	4	57	15	66	2.59	6	5	8		
1968	StL-N	8	2	47	17	48^2	1.48	8	8	20		
1969	StL-N	2	3	45	15	53^1	2.87	4	4	6		
1970	Phi-N	9	5	44	9	57^2	2.65	9	9	22		
1971	Phi-N	4	5	49	9	73	1.97	12	13	17		
1972	Phi-N	0	2	15	3	21^2	2.08	3	4	4		
	Atl-N	1	3	25	2	23^1	6.56	-8	-7	-12		
	Yr	1	5	40	5	45	4.40	-5	-4	-8		
1973	Atl-N	2	2	20	2	12^2	6.39	-4	-3	-11		
	KC-A	2	0	22	4	19^1	5.12	-3	-2	-3		
1974	KC-A	2	3	30	2	35^1	3.82	-1	-0	-0		
1975	Phi-N	0	0	25	0	21	2.57	2	3	0		
1976	Tex-A	0	4	41	8	35	5.14	-6	-6	-9		
1977	Cin-N	0	0	8	0	5^2	12.71	-6	-6	0		
Total	14	39	34	493	99	562^2	2.99	35	37	61		
■ **Chief Hogsett**												
1929	Det-A										4	28^2
1930	Det-A	2	1	16	1	39^1	5.03	-2	-1	-1	17	106^2
1931	Det-A	0	2	10	2	27^2	4.88	-2	-1	-1	12	84^2
1932	Det-A	6	3	32	7	69	2.74	13	15	21	15	109
1933	Det-A	6	9	43	9	105	4.71	-5	-5	-7	2	11
1934	Det-A	3	2	26	3	50^1	4.29	1	1	1		
1935	Det-A	6	6	40	5	96^2	3.54	10	7	8		
1936	Det-A	0	1	3	0	4	9.00	-2	-2	-4		
	StL-A	1	1	10	1	24	8.25	-9	-8	-6	29	191^1
	Yr	1	2	13	1	28	8.36	-10	-9	-11	29	191^1
1937	StL-A	1	0	11	2	22	3.68	2	3	2	26	155^1
1938	Was-A	3	2	22	3	52^1	3.78	6	4	4	9	38^2
1944	Det-A	0	0	3	0	6^1	0.00	2	3	0		
Total	10	28	27	216	33	496^2	4.20	16	16	17	114	725^1
■ **Al Holland**												
1977	Pit-N	0	0	2	0	2^1	7.71	-1	-1	0		
1979	SF-N	0	0	3	0	7	0.00	3	3	0		
1980	SF-N	5	3	54	7	82^1	1.75	17	16	17		
1981	SF-N	6	-4	44	7	79	2.51	9	8	3	3	21^2
1982	SF-N	5	0	51	5	91^1	3.15	5	4	3	7	38^1
1983	Phi-N	8	4	68	25	91^2	2.26	14	13	24		
1984	Phi-N	5	10	68	29	98^1	3.39	2	3	5		
1985	Phi-N	0	1	3	1	4	4.50	-0	-0	-1		
	Pit-N	1	3	38	4	58^2	3.38	1	1	1		
	Yr	1	4	41	5	62^2	3.45	1	1	-0		
	Cal-A	0	1	15	0	24^1	1.48	7	7	3		
1986	NY-A	1	0	24	0	36	4.00	1	0	0	1	4^2
1987	NY-A	0	0	3	0	6^1	14.21	-7	-7	0		
Total	10	31	18	373	78	581^1	2.88	50	48	56	11	64^2
■ **Charlie Hough**												
1970	LA-N	0	0	8	2	17	5.29	-2	-3	-1		
1971	LA-N	0	0	4	0	4^1	4.15	-0	-0	0		
1972	LA-N	0	0	2	0	2^2	3.38	0	-0	0		
1973	LA-N	4	2	37	5	71^2	2.76	7	5	5		
1974	LA-N	9	4	49	1	96	3.75	-1	-4	-5		
1975	LA-N	3	7	38	4	61	2.95	5	3	5		
1976	LA-N	12	8	77	18	142^2	2.21	20	19	29		
1977	LA-N	5	12	69	22	122^1	3.46	6	5	8	1	5
1978	LA-N	5	5	55	7	93^1	3.28	3	2	3		
1979	LA-N	1	2	28	0	67^2	4.66	-7	-8	-3	14	83^2
1980	LA-N	1	2	18	1	28^1	4.76	-4	-4	-4	1	4
	Tex-A	1	1	14	0	43^1	4.98	-5	-5	-2	2	18
1981	Tex-A	0	0	16	1	42^2	4.01	-2	-3	-0	5	39^1
1982	Tex-A										34	228
1983	Tex-A	1	0	1	0	4	0.00	2	2	4	33	248
1984	Tex-A										36	266
1985	Tex-A										34	250^1

YEAR	TM/L	WR	LR	GR	SV	IPR	ERAR	RR	/A	RNK	GS	IPS
1986	Tex-A										33	230^1
1987	Tex-A										40	285^1
1988	Tex-A										34	252
1989	Tex-A										30	182
1990	Tex-A										32	218^2
1991	Cle-A										31	199^1
1992	Chi-A										27	176^1
Total	13	42	43	416	61	797	3.43	22	10	39	387	2686^1
■ **Steve Howe**												
1980	LA-N	7	9	59	17	84^2	2.66	9	8	17		
1981	LA-N	5	3	41	8	54	2.50	6	5	8		
1982	LA-N	7	5	66	13	99^1	2.08	17	15	21		
1983	LA-N	4	7	46	18	68^2	1.44	17	16	33		
1985	LA-N	1	1	19	3	22	4.91	-3	-4	-4		
	Min-A	2	3	13	0	19	6.16	-4	-4	-9		
1987	Tex-A	3	3	24	1	31^1	4.31	1	1	1		
1991	NY-A	3	1	37	3	48^1	1.68	13	13	12		
1992	NY-A	3	0	20	6	22	2.45	4	4	7		
Total	8	35	32	325	69	449^1	2.58	58	55	87		
■ **Jay Howell**												
1980	Cin-N	0	0	5	0	3^1	13.50	-4	-4	0		
1981	Chi-N	0	0	8	0	12	3.75	-0	-0	0	2	10^1
1982	NY-A										6	28
1983	NY-A	0	0	7	0	12	9.00	-7	-7	0	12	70
1984	NY-A	8	4	60	7	98^2	2.74	14	12	14	1	5
1985	Oak-A	9	8	63	29	98	2.85	14	11	24		
1986	Oak-A	3	6	38	16	53^1	3.38	5	3	6		
1987	Oak-A	3	4	36	16	44^1	5.89	-7	-9	-19		
1988	LA-N	5	3	50	21	65	2.08	10	9	17		
1989	LA-N	5	3	56	28	79^2	1.58	17	16	27		
1990	LA-N	5	5	45	16	66	2.18	12	11	21		
1991	LA-N	6	5	44	16	51	3.18	3	2	6		
1992	LA-N	1	3	41	4	46^2	1.54	10	10	10		
Total	12	45	41	453	153	630	2.90	67	55	107	21	113^1
■ **Waite Hoyt**												
1918	NY-N	0	0	1	0	1	0.00	0	0	0		
1919	Bos-A	0	0	2	0	5^2	1.59	1	1	0	11	99^2
1920	Bos-A	0	2	11	1	38^2	4.89	-5	-5	-3	11	82^2
1921	NY-A	3	2	11	3	44	2.25	10	10	11	32	238^1
1922	NY-A	3	1	6	0	29	2.79	4	4	5	31	236
1923	NY-A	3	0	9	1	22^2	3.57	1	1	1	28	216
1924	NY-A	3	2	14	4	33^2	1.87	9	9	14	32	213^1
1925	NY-A	0	1	16	6	23^1	3.47	2	2	2	30	219^2
1926	NY-A	4	1	12	4	33^1	1.35	10	9	15	28	184^1
1927	NY-A	0	1	4	1	9	2.00	2	2	2	32	247^1
1928	NY-A	2	1	11	8	22^1	1.61	6	5	11	31	250^2
1929	NY-A	0	0	5	1	10	5.40	-1	-2	-0	25	191^2
1930	NY-A	0	0	1	0	2	9.00	-1	-1	0	7	45^2
	Det-A	1	0	6	4	6^1	7.11	-2	-2	-5	20	129^1
	Yr	1	0	7	4	8^1	7.56	-3	-3	-5	27	175
1931	Det-A	0	0	4	0	12	8.25	-5	-5	0	12	80
	Phi-A	0	1	2	0	2	13.50	-2	-2	-9	14	109
	Yr	0	1	6	0	14	9.00	-7	-7	-9	26	189
1932	Bro-N	1	0	4	1	7^2	4.70	-1	-1	-1	4	19
	NY-N	1	1	6	0	22	3.27	1	1	1	12	75^1
	Yr	2	1	10	1	29^2	3.64	1	0	-0	16	94^1
1933	Pit-N	2	2	28	4	69^2	2.84	4	4	2	8	47^1
1934	Pit-N	7	1	33	5	76^1	1.89	18	19	21	15	114^1
1935	Pit-N	5	3	28	6	76^1	2.24	15	16	18	11	87^2
1936	Pit-N	2	2	13	1	35	4.11	-0	-0	-0	9	81^2
1937	Pit-N	1	2	11	2	28	4.50	-2	-2	-2		
	Bro-N	1	0	8	0	20^1	3.54	1	1	0	19	146^2
	Yr	2	2	19	2	48^1	4.10	-1	-1	-2	19	146^2
1938	Bro-N	0	2	5	0	9^1	4.82	-1	-1	-2	1	7
Total	21	39	25	251	52	639^2	3.05	66	63	81	423	3122^2
■ **Al Hrabosky**												
1970	StL-N	2	1	15	0	13^1	6.07	-3	-3	-6	1	5^2
1971	StL-N	0	0	1	0	2	0.00	1	1	0		
1972	StL-N	1	0	5	0	7	0.00	3	3	3		
1973	StL-N	2	4	44	5	56	2.09	10	10	11		
1974	StL-N	8	1	65	9	88^1	2.95	7	6	7		
1975	StL-N	13	3	65	22	97^1	1.66	21	23	45		
1976	StL-N	8	6	68	13	95^1	3.30	2	2	4		
1977	StL-N	6	5	65	10	86^1	4.38	-5	-5	-7		
1978	KC-A	8	7	58	20	75	2.88	7	8	19		
1979	KC-A	9	4	58	11	65	3.74	3	4	8		
1980	Atl-N	4	2	45	3	59^2	3.62	-0	1	1		
1981	Atl-N	1	1	24	1	33^2	1.07	9	9	6		
1982	Atl-N	2	1	31	3	37^1	5.54	-8	-8	-7		
Total	13	64	35	544	97	716^1	3.12	47	51	84	1	5^2
■ **Tom Hume**												
1977	Cin-N	1	1	9	0	21^1	6.75	-7	-7	-6	5	21^2
1978	Cin-N	2	0	19	1	33^1	2.43	4	4	3	23	140^2
1979	Cin-N	5	5	45	17	80^1	2.02	15	15	24	12	82^2
1980	Cin-N	9	10	78	25	137	2.56	16	15	26		
1981	Cin-N	9	4	51	13	67^2	3.46	0	1	2		
1982	Cin-N	2	6	46	17	63^2	3.11	3	4	7		
1983	Cin-N	3	5	48	9	66	4.77	-8	-7	-10		
1984	Cin-N	3	8	46	3	73^1	5.89	-19	-17	-25	8	40
1985	Cin-N	3	5	56	3	80	3.26	3	5	5		

YEAR	TM/L	WR	LR	GR	SV	IPR	ERAR	RR	/A	RNK	GS	IPS
1986	Phi-N	3	1	47	4	88^1	2.95	7	9	4	1	6
1987	Phi-N	0	1	32	0	38^2	5.82	-7	-7	-2	6	32
	Cin-N	1	0	11	0	13^1	4.05	0	0	0		
	Yr	1	1	43	0	52	5.37	-7	-7	-1	6	32
Total	11	41	46	488	92	763	3.56	8	16	29	55	323
■ **Bob Humphreys**												
1962	Det-A	0	1	4	1	5	7.20	-2	-2	-4		
1963	StL-N	0	1	9	0	10^2	5.06	-2	-2	-2		
1964	StL-N	2	0	28	2	42^2	2.53	5	6	3		
1965	Chi-N	2	0	41	0	65^2	3.15	3	4	1		
1966	Was-A	6	3	57	3	106^2	2.95	6	6	5	1	5
1967	Was-A	5	1	46	4	96^2	4.47	-13	-14	-9	2	9
1968	Was-A	5	7	56	2	92^2	3.69	-7	-8	-10		
1969	Was-A	3	3	47	5	79^2	3.05	5	4	3		
1970	Was-A	0	0	5	0	6^2	1.35	2	2	0		
	Mil-A	1	4	22	3	40^2	3.32	2	2	3	1	5
	Yr	1	4	27	3	47^1	3.04	4	4	3	1	5
Total	9	24	20	315	20	547	3.44	-3	-2	-9	4	19
■ **Grant Jackson**												
1965	Phi-N	1	1	4	0	3^2	14.73	-5	-5	-23	2	10
1966	Phi-N	0	0	2	0	1^2	5.40	-0	-0	0		
1967	Phi-N	2	1	39	1	66	1.36	15	15	7	4	18^1
1968	Phi-N	0	3	27	1	32^1	1.67	5	5	4	6	28^2
1969	Phi-N	0	0	3	1	1^1	0.00	1	1	1	35	251^2
1970	Phi-N	2	0	9	0	25	3.60	1	1	1	23	124^2
1971	Bal-A	0	0	20	0	28	2.89	2	1	0	9	49^2
1972	Bal-A	1	1	32	8	41	2.63	2	2	2		
1973	Bal-A	8	0	45	9	80^1	1.90	17	16	19		
1974	Bal-A	6	4	49	12	66^2	2.57	8	7	12		
1975	Bal-A	4	3	41	7	48^1	3.35	2	1	1		
1976	Bal-A	1	1	13	3	19^1	5.12	-3	-4	-5		
	NY-A	4	0	19	1	42^2	2.11	7	6	6	2	16
	Yr	5	1	32	4	62	3.05	3	2	0	2	16
1977	Pit-N	5	2	47	4	79^2	3.28	6	6	6	2	11^1
1978	Pit-N	7	5	60	5	77^1	3.26	3	4	6		
1979	Pit-N	8	5	72	14	82	2.96	7	8	15		
1980	Pit-N	8	4	61	9	71	2.92	5	6	10		
1981	Pit-N	1	2	35	4	32^1	2.51	4	4	4		
	Mon-N	1	0	10	0	10^2	7.59	-5	-5	-4		
	Yr	2	2	45	4	43	3.77	-1	-1	0		
1982	KC-A	3	1	20	0	38^1	5.17	-5	-5	-4		
	Pit-N	0	0	1	0	0^2	13.50	-1	-1	0		
Total	18	62	33	609	79	848^1	2.94	64	64	57	83	510^1
■ **Mike Jackson**												
1986	Phi-N	0	0	9	0	13^1	3.38	1	1	0		
1987	Phi-N	2	6	48	1	75^2	3.09	8	10	9	7	33^2
1988	Sea-A	6	5	62	4	99^1	2.63	15	17	18		
1989	Sea-A	4	6	65	7	99^1	3.17	8	9	10		
1990	Sea-A	5	7	63	3	77^1	4.54	-5	-5	-7		
1991	Sea-A	7	7	72	14	88^2	3.25	8	9	15		
1992	SF-N	6	6	67	2	82	3.73	-2	-3	-5		
Total	7	30	37	386	31	535^2	3.36	32	37	41	7	33^2
■ **Bob James**												
1978	Mon-N	0	0	3	0	3	0.00	1	1	0	1	1
1979	Mon-N	0	0	2	0	2	13.50	-2	-2	0		
1982	Mon-N	0	0	7	0	9	6.00	-2	-2	0		
	Det-A	0	2	11	0	17^1	4.67	-1	-1	-1	1	2^1
1983	Det-A	0	0	4	0	4	11.25	-3	-3	0		
	Mon-N	1	0	27	7	50	2.88	4	4	2		
1984	Mon-N	6	6	62	10	96	3.66	-1	-2	-3		
1985	Chi-A	8	7	69	32	110	2.13	25	27	50		
1986	Chi-A	5	4	49	14	58^1	5.25	-7	-6	-12		
1987	Chi-A	4	6	43	10	54	4.67	-1	-1	-1		
Total	8	24	25	277	73	403^2	3.70	12	14	35	2	3^1
■ **Jerry Johnson**												
1968	Phi-N	0	0	5	0	6^2	2.70	0	0	0	11	74
1969	Phi-N	0	1	12	1	18^1	4.91	-3	-3	-2	21	129
1970	StL-N	2	0	7	1	11^1	3.18	1	1	2		
	SF-N	3	3	32	3	61^1	3.82	2	1	1	1	4
	Yr	5	3	39	4	72^2	3.72	3	2	3	1	4
1971	SF-N	12	9	67	18	109	2.97	6	5	11		
1972	SF-N	8	6	48	8	73^1	4.42	-8	-8	-15		
1973	Cle-A	5	6	38	5	59	5.95	-14	-13	-25	1	0^2
1974	Hou-N	2	1	34	0	45	4.80	-6	-7	-4		
1975	SD-N	2	0	17	0	34	5.03	-5	-6	-3	4	20
1976	SD-N	1	2	23	0	37^1	4.82	-5	-6	-5	1	1^2
1977	Tor-A	2	4	43	5	86	4.60	-5	-4	-3		
Total	10	37	32	326	41	541^1	4.32	-38	-39	-42	39	229^1
■ **Si Johnson**												
1928	Cin-N	0	0	3	0	10^1	4.35	-0	-0	0		
1929	Cin-N	0	0	1	0	2	4.50	0	0	0		
1930	Cin-N	2	1	32	0	64^2	4.04	7	6	2	3	13^2
1931	Cin-N	0	2	9	0	12^1	8.03	-6	-6	-9	33	250
1932	Cin-N	1	0	15	2	37^2	3.11	3	3	1	27	207^1
1933	Cin-N	0	0	6	1	16^1	2.20	2	2	0	28	195
1934	Cin-N	0	2	15	3	30^2	6.46	-8	-8	-7	31	185
1935	Cin-N	0	0	10	0	24^1	8.51	-12	-12	0	20	105^2
1936	Cin-N	0	0	2	0	4	13.50	-4	-4	0		
	StL-N	1	1	3	0	5	1.80	1	1	4	9	56^2
	Yr	1	1	5	0	9	7.00	-3	-3	4	9	56^2

YEAR	TM/L	WR	LR	GR	SV	IPR	ERAR	RR	/A	RNK	GS	IPS
1937	StL-N	3	3	17	1	35^{1}	4.08	-1	-0	-1	21	157
1938	StL-N	0	0	3	0	4	2.25	1	1	0	3	11^{2}
1940	Phi-N	1	6	23	1	52^{2}	5.98	-12	-12	-15	14	85^{2}
1941	Phi-N	0	3	18	2	36	4.50	-3	-3	-3	21	127^{1}
1942	Phi-N	1	1	13	0	20^{2}	3.92	-1	-1	-1	26	174^{2}
1943	Phi-N	0	0	7	2	11	3.27	0	0	0	14	102
1946	Phi-N	0	0	1	0	3	3.00	0	0	0		
	Bos-N	0	0	16	1	38	3.55	-1	-1	-0	12	89
	Yr	0	0	17	1	41	3.51	-0	-0	-0	12	89
1947	Bos-N	2	2	26	2	43^{2}	3.09	5	4	4	10	69
Total	17	11	21	220	15	451^{2}	4.56	-30	-32	-23	272	1829^{2}

■ Syl Johnson

YEAR	TM/L	WR	LR	GR	SV	IPR	ERAR	RR	/A	RNK	GS	IPS
1922	Det-A	3	1	21	1	51	3.00	6	5	4	8	46
1923	Det-A	5	2	19	0	78^{1}	4.48	-4	-5	-4	18	98
1924	Det-A	2	2	20	3	52	4.67	-3	-3	-3	9	52
1925	Det-A	0	2	6	0	13	3.46	1	1	2		
1926	StL-N	0	0	13	1	14	5.79	-3	-3	-0	6	35
1927	StL-N	0	0	2	0	3	6.00	-1	-1	0		
1928	StL-N	4	2	28	3	78^{2}	3.78	2	2	1	6	41^{1}
1929	StL-N	3	2	23	3	42^{1}	3.19	7	7	8	19	140
1930	StL-N	2	1	8	2	24^{1}	2.96	5	6	7	24	163^{1}
1931	StL-N	1	0	8	2	11^{2}	4.63	-1	-1	-1	24	174^{1}
1932	StL-N	1	1	10	2	16^{1}	3.86	0	0	0	22	148^{1}
1933	StL-N	2	3	34	3	78	4.15	-7	-6	-4	1	6
1934	Cin-N	0	0	2	0	6^{2}	2.70	1	1	0		
	Phi-N	2	5	32	3	97	2.78	14	21	15	10	36^{2}
	Yr	2	5	34	3	103^{2}	2.78	15	22	15	10	36^{2}
1935	Phi-N	3	1	19	6	37^{2}	3.35	3	5	7	18	137
1936	Phi-N	1	4	31	7	67^{1}	4.28	-2	2	2	8	43^{2}
1937	Phi-N	1	2	17	3	33^{1}	5.94	-8	-6	-6	15	104^{2}
1938	Phi-N	1	3	16	0	53^{2}	4.02	-1	-1	-1	6	29^{1}
1939	Phi-N	2	0	8	2	13^{1}	4.05	-0	-0	-0	14	97^{2}
1940	Phi-N	0	2	15	2	22^{2}	5.96	-5	-5	-5	2	18
Total	19	33	33	332	43	794^{1}	3.95	4	19	22	210	1371^{1}

■ Walter Johnson

YEAR	TM/L	WR	LR	GR	SV	IPR	ERAR	RR	/A	RNK	GS	IPS
1907	Was-A	0	2	2	0	5^{1}	3.38	-0	-1	-2	12	105
1908	Was-A	0	1	7	1	17	4.24	-3	-4	-2	29	240^{1}
1909	Was-A	1	2	4	1	12^{2}	3.55	-2	-2	-4	36	284^{1}
1910	Was-A	1	1	3	1	8^{2}	2.08	0	0	1	42	365^{1}
1911	Was-A	1	1	3	1	6	0.00	2	2	7	37	317^{1}
1912	Was-A	5	2	13	2	51	0.35	17	17	22	37	317
1913	Was-A	7	0	12	2	35	0.26	10	10	20	36	311
1914	Was-A	4	3	11	1	27^{2}	4.55	-6	-5	-13	40	344
1915	Was-A	2	0	8	4	8^{2}	1.04	2	2	6	39	328
1916	Was-A	4	3	10	1	29^{2}	1.82	3	3	7	38	341^{1}
1917	Was-A	5	1	13	3	39^{2}	1.82	4	4	5	34	288^{1}
1918	Was-A	3	4	10	3	29^{1}	0.92	6	6	14	29	295^{2}
1919	Was-A	2	4	10	2	21^{1}	2.53	2	2	4	29	269
1920	Was-A	1	2	6	3	22	4.50	-2	-2	-3	15	121^{2}
1921	Was-A	1	1	3	1	6	4.50	-0	-0	-1	32	258
1922	Was-A	1	1	10	4	25	3.24	2	2	2	31	255
1923	Was-A	1	2	8	4	12	3.00	1	1	3	34	249^{1}
1924	Was-A										38	277^{2}
1925	Was-A	1	0	1	0	2	0.00	1	1	4	29	227
1926	Was-A										33	261^{2}
1927	Was-A	0	0	3	0	7	5.14	-1	-1	0	15	100^{2}
Total	19	40	30	137	34	366	2.19	37	36	72	665	5557^{2}

■ Barry Jones

YEAR	TM/L	WR	LR	GR	SV	IPR	ERAR	RR	/A	RNK	GS	IPS
1986	Pit-N	3	4	26	3	37^{1}	2.89	3	4	7		
1987	Pit-N	2	4	32	1	43^{1}	5.61	-7	-7	-9		
1988	Pit-N	1	1	42	2	56^{1}	3.04	3	2	1		
	Chi-A	2	2	17	1	26	2.42	4	4	7		
1989	Chi-A	3	2	22	1	30^{1}	2.37	5	5	8		
1990	Chi-A	11	4	65	1	74	2.31	13	12	23		
1991	Mon-N	4	9	77	13	88^{2}	3.35	3	3	4		
1992	Phi-N	5	6	44	0	54^{1}	4.64	-7	-7	-13		
	NY-N	2	0	17	1	15^{1}	9.39	-10	-10	-13		
	Yr	7	6	61	1	69^{2}	5.68	-17	-17	-26		
Total	7	33	32	342	23	425^{2}	3.57	8	6	14		

■ Doug Jones

YEAR	TM/L	WR	LR	GR	SV	IPR	ERAR	RR	/A	RNK	GS	IPS
1982	Mil-A	0	0	4	0	2^{2}	10.13	-2	-2	0		
1986	Cle-A	1	0	11	1	18	2.50	3	3	2		
1987	Cle-A	6	5	49	8	91^{1}	3.15	13	14	18		
1988	Cle-A	3	4	51	37	83^{1}	2.27	16	17	30		
1989	Cle-A	7	10	59	32	80^{2}	2.34	14	14	40		
1990	Cle-A	5	5	66	43	84^{1}	2.56	13	13	28		
1991	Cle-A	1	7	32	7	32^{1}	7.24	-11	-11	-30	4	31
1992	Hou-N	11	8	80	36	111^{2}	1.85	20	18	42		
Total	8	34	39	352	164	504^{1}	2.77	66	67	130	4	31

■ Jim Kaat

YEAR	TM/L	WR	LR	GR	SV	IPR	ERAR	RR	/A	RNK	GS	IPS
1959	Was-A	0	0	1	0	1	0.00	0	0	0	2	4
1960	Was-A	0	0	4	0	6^{2}	2.70	1	1	0	9	43^{1}
1961	Min-A	0	1	7	0	13^{1}	2.70	2	2	2	29	187^{1}
1962	Min-A	1	0	4	1	13^{2}	0.66	5	5	4	35	255^{1}
1963	Min-A	0	1	4	1	7^{2}	0.00	3	3	5	27	170^{2}
1964	Min-A	0	1	2	1	2	4.50	-0	-0	-1	34	241
1965	Min-A	0	0	3	2	2	0.00	1	1	2	42	262^{1}
1966	Min-A										41	304^{2}
1967	Min-A	0	0	4	0	3^{1}	13.50	-4	-4	0	38	260
1968	Min-A	0	0	1	0	3	0.00	1	1	0	29	205
1969	Min-A	3	1	8	1	28	2.25	4	4	6	32	214^{1}
1970	Min-A	1	0	11	0	17	2.65	2	2	1	34	213^{1}
1971	Min-A	0	0	1	0	0^{1}	54.00	-2	-2	0	38	260
1972	Min-A										15	113^{1}
1973	Min-A	1	0	1	0	6^{2}	2.70	1	1	1	28	175
	Chi-A										7	42^{2}
	Yr	2	0	1	0	49^{1}	0.73	2	2	3	35	217^{2}
1974	Chi-A	1	0	3	0	7^{1}	4.91	-1	-1	-1	39	270
1975	Chi-A	0	0	2	0	1	0.00	0	0	0	41	302^{2}
1976	Phi-N	0	1	3	0	4^{1}	2.08	1	1	1	35	223^{1}
1977	Phi-N	0	1	8	0	12^{2}	8.53	-6	-6	-5	27	147^{2}
1978	Phi-N	0	0	2	0	7	7.71	-3	-3	0	24	133^{1}
1979	Phi-N	1	0	2	0	6	1.50	1	2	2	1	2^{1}
	NY-A	2	3	39	2	54^{1}	4.14	0	-0	-0	1	4
1980	NY-A	0	1	4	0	5	7.20	-2	-2	-3		
	StL-N	3	2	35	4	40	3.15	2	2	3	14	89^{2}
1981	StL-N	6	5	40	4	49^{1}	2.92	3	3	8	1	3^{2}
1982	StL-N	4	3	60	2	66	4.36	-6	-5	-6	2	9
1983	StL-N	0	0	24	0	34^{2}	3.89	-1	-1	0		
Total	23	23	20	273	18	392^{1}	3.65	3	4	19	625	4138

■ Jim Kern

YEAR	TM/L	WR	LR	GR	SV	IPR	ERAR	RR	/A	RNK	GS	IPS
1974	Cle-A	0	0	1	0	2	13.50	-2	-2	0	3	13^{1}
1975	Cle-A	0	0	6	0	24^{2}	1.82	5	5	0	7	47
1976	Cle-A	9	6	48	15	105^{2}	2.21	15	15	24	2	12
1977	Cle-A	8	10	60	18	92	3.42	6	5	12		
1978	Cle-A	10	10	58	13	99^{1}	3.08	8	7	15		
1979	Tex-A	13	5	71	29	143	1.57	42	41	65		
1980	Tex-A	3	10	37	2	58^{2}	4.45	-3	-4	-7	1	4^{2}
1981	Tex-A	1	2	23	6	30	2.70	3	3	3		
1982	Cin-N	3	5	50	2	76	2.84	6	7	7		
	Chi-A	1	1	12	3	21^{2}	6.23	-5	-5	-6	1	6^{1}
1983	Chi-A	0	0	1	0	0^{2}	0.00	0	0	0		
1984	Phi-N	0	1	8	0	13^{1}	10.13	-10	-10	-6		
	Mil-A	1	0	6	0	4^{2}	0.00	2	2	4		
1985	Mil-A	0	1	5	0	11	6.55	-3	-3	-2		
1986	Cle-A	1	1	16	0	27^{1}	7.90	-11	-11	-8		
Total	13	50	52	402	88	710	3.19	55	51	100	14	83^{1}

■ Ellis Kinder

YEAR	TM/L	WR	LR	GR	SV	IPR	ERAR	RR	/A	RNK	GS	IPS
1946	StL-A	0	0	26	1	41^{1}	3.27	1	2	0	7	45^{1}
1947	StL-A	0	0	8	1	14^{2}	9.20	-9	-9	-1	26	179^{2}
1948	Bos-A	1	2	6	0	24^{1}	2.59	5	5	5	22	153^{2}
1949	Bos-A	2	1	13	4	23^{2}	2.28	5	5	8	30	228^{1}
1950	Bos-A	3	4	25	9	48^{2}	2.40	12	13	23	23	158^{1}
1951	Bos-A	10	1	61	14	113^{2}	2.14	25	29	34	2	13^{1}
1952	Bos-A	1	2	13	4	21^{1}	2.95	2	2	4	10	76^{1}
1953	Bos-A	10	6	69	27	107	1.85	26	28	54		
1954	Bos-A	7	8	46	15	93^{1}	3.57	2	6	10	2	13^{2}
1955	Bos-A	5	5	43	18	66^{2}	2.84	8	11	21		
1956	StL-N	2	0	22	6	25^{2}	3.51	1	1	1		
	Chi-A	3	1	29	3	29^{2}	2.73	5	5	7		
1957	Chi-A	0	0	1	0	1	0.00	0	0	0		
Total	12	44	30	362	102	611	2.78	82	99	166	122	868^{2}

■ Ron Kline

YEAR	TM/L	WR	LR	GR	SV	IPR	ERAR	RR	/A	RNK	GS	IPS
1952	Pit-N	0	1	16	0	29^{1}	2.45	4	5	2	11	49^{1}
1955	Pit-N	2	0	17	2	33^{2}	1.60	9	9	6	19	103
1956	Pit-N	0	0	5	2	8	3.38	0	0	0	39	256
1957	Pit-N	0	1	9	0	14^{2}	3.07	1	1	1	31	190^{1}
1958	Pit-N										32	237^{1}
1959	Pit-N	1	0	4	0	9	1.00	3	3	3	29	177
1960	StL-N	1	2	17	1	35	6.17	-9	-8	-7	17	82^{2}
1961	LA-A	1	3	14	1	30	3.90	0	2	3	12	74^{2}
	Det-A	0	0	2	0	2^{2}	6.75	-1	-1	0	8	53^{2}
	Yr	1	3	16	1	32^{2}	4.13	-0	1	3	20	128^{1}
1962	Det-A	3	3	32	2	54	4.33	-2	-2	-2	4	23^{1}
1963	Was-A	3	8	61	17	90^{2}	2.78	9	9	14	1	3
1964	Was-A	10	7	61	14	81^{1}	2.32	12	12	28		
1965	Was-A	7	6	74	29	99^{1}	2.63	9	9	17		
1966	Was-A	6	4	63	23	90^{1}	2.39	10	11	17		
1967	Min-A	7	1	54	5	71^{2}	3.77	-4	-2	-3		
1968	Pit-N	12	5	56	7	112^{2}	1.68	16	16	23		
1969	Pit-N	1	3	20	3	31	5.81	-8	-8	-11		
	SF-N	0	2	7	0	11	4.09	-1	-1	-1		
	Yr	1	5	27	3	42	5.36	-8	-9	-12		
	Bos-A	0	1	16	1	17	4.76	-2	-2	-1		
1970	Atl-N	0	0	5	1	6^{1}	7.11	-2	-2	-1		
Total	16	54	47	533	108	827^{2}	3.04	45	53	89	203	1250^{1}

■ Johnny Klippstein

YEAR	TM/L	WR	LR	GR	SV	IPR	ERAR	RR	/A	RNK	GS	IPS
1950	Chi-N	1	1	22	1	57	2.84	8	9	3	11	47^{2}
1951	Chi-N	4	0	24	2	53^{1}	4.39	-3	-2	-1	11	70^{1}
1952	Chi-N	4	0	16	3	51^{1}	3.16	3	4	3	25	151^{1}
1953	Chi-N	2	5	29	6	66^{1}	5.02	-5	-4	-5	19	101^{1}
1954	Chi-N	0	2	15	1	32^{2}	4.96	-3	-3	-2	21	115^{1}
1955	Cin-N	4	2	25	0	57	2.21	12	13	12	14	81
1956	Cin-N	2	0	8	1	15	2.40	2	3	4	29	196
1957	Cin-N	3	2	28	3	42^{2}	6.12	-11	-10	-12	18	103^{1}
1958	Cin-N	2	1	8	1	18^{1}	3.44	1	1	2	4	14^{2}
	LA-N	3	5	45	9	90	3.80	2	3	3		
	Yr	5	6	53	10	108^{1}	3.74	3	4	5	4	14^{2}
1959	LA-N	4	0	28	2	45^{2}	5.91	-10	-9	-8		
1960	Cle-A	5	5	49	14	74^{1}	2.91	8	7	11		
1961	Was-A	2	1	41	0	69^{1}	6.49	-19	-19	-7	1	2^{1}

YEAR	TM/L	WR	LR	GR	SV	IPR	ERAR	RR	/A	RNK	GS	IPS
1962	Cin-N	6	3	33	4	70	4.37	-3	-3	-3	7	38^2
1963	Phi-N	5	5	48	8	107	1.68	19	18	19	1	5
1964	Phi-N	2	1	11	1	22^1	4.03	-1	-1	-2		
	Min-A	0	4	33	2	45^2	1.97	8	8	7		
1965	Min-A	9	3	56	5	76^1	2.24	10	11	17		
1966	Min-A	1	1	26	3	39^2	3.40	0	1	1		
1967	Det-A	0	0	5	0	6^2	5.40	-2	-2	0		
Total	18	59	41	550	66	1040^2	3.68	17	26	43	161	927

■ **Darold Knowles**

YEAR	TM/L	WR	LR	GR	SV	IPR	ERAR	RR	/A	RNK	GS	IPS
1965	Bal-A	0	0	4	0	8^2	10.38	-7	-7	0	1	6
1966	Phi-N	6	5	69	13	100^1	3.05	6	6	8		
1967	Was-A	6	7	60	14	112	2.25	12	11	15	1	1^1
1968	Was-A	1	1	32	4	41^1	2.18	4	3	2		
1969	Was-A	9	2	53	13	84^1	2.24	13	11	17		
1970	Was-A	2	14	71	27	119^1	2.04	22	20	35		
1971	Was-A	2	2	12	2	15^1	3.52	-0	-0	-1		
	Oak-A	5	2	43	7	52^2	3.59	-1	-1	-2		
	Yr	7	4	55	9	68	3.57	-1	-2	-3		
1972	Oak-A	5	1	54	11	65^2	1.37	12	11	13		
1973	Oak-A	4	7	47	9	71^2	2.89	7	5	9	5	27^1
1974	Oak-A	2	3	44	3	48^1	4.47	-5	-6	-7	1	5
1975	Chi-N	6	9	58	15	88^1	5.81	-21	-19	-37		
1976	Chi-N	5	7	58	9	71^2	2.89	5	8	14		
1977	Tex-A	5	2	42	4	50^1	3.22	5	5	7		
1978	Mon-N	3	3	60	6	72	2.38	10	9	9		
1979	StL-N	2	5	48	6	48^2	4.07	-2	-2	-3		
1980	StL-N	0	1	2	0	1^2	10.80	-1	-1	-7		
Total	16	63	71	757	143	1052^1	3.04	59	53	72	8	39^2

■ **Ray Kolp**

YEAR	TM/L	WR	LR	GR	SV	IPR	ERAR	RR	/A	RNK	GS	IPS
1921	StL-A	1	2	19	0	45^2	5.91	-8	-7	-4	18	121
1922	StL-A	2	1	14	0	46	3.72	2	2	1	18	123^2
1923	StL-A	0	2	17	1	43^1	3.32	3	4	2	17	128
1924	StL-A	2	0	13	0	28	7.71	-11	-10	-6	12	68^2
1927	Cin-N	1	2	19	3	44^1	3.86	0	-0	-0	5	38
1928	Cin-N	3	1	20	3	48	3.00	5	5	5	24	161
1929	Cin-N	2	1	14	0	49^1	2.37	13	12	7	16	96
1930	Cin-N	1	2	18	3	47^2	3.40	8	8	5	19	120^2
1931	Cin-N	2	1	20	1	45^1	1.59	11	11	7	10	61^2
1932	Cin-N	0	0	13	1	24^2	4.38	-1	-1	-0	19	135
1933	Cin-N	3	2	16	3	52^2	2.56	5	5	5	14	97^2
1934	Cin-N	0	0	26	3	51^2	4.35	-2	-2	-0	2	10
Total	12	17	14	209	18	526^2	3.67	25	26	20	174	1161^1

■ **Jim Konstanty**

YEAR	TM/L	WR	LR	GR	SV	IPR	ERAR	RR	/A	RNK	GS	IPS
1944	Cin-N	2	1	8	0	38^2	4.19	-2	-3	-2	12	74
1946	Bos-N	0	0	9	0	12^1	6.57	-4	-4	0	1	3
1948	Phi-N	1	0	6	2	9^2	0.93	3	3	5		
1949	Phi-N	9	5	53	7	97	3.25	9	8	11		
1950	Phi-N	16	7	74	22	152	2.66	25	23	39		
1951	Phi-N	4	10	57	9	110^2	3.98	-0	-2	-2	1	5
1952	Phi-N	4	2	40	6	63	4.29	-4	-4	-5	2	17
1953	Phi-N	4	3	29	5	51	2.82	8	8	11	19	119^2
1954	Phi-N	2	3	32	3	46^1	3.69	2	2	2	1	4
	NY-A	1	1	9	2	18^1	0.98	6	5	6		
1955	NY-A	7	2	45	11	73^2	2.32	13	12	17		
1956	NY-A	0	0	8	2	11	4.91	-1	-1	-1		
	StL-N	1	1	27	5	39^1	4.58	-4	-3	-3		
Total	11	51	35	397	74	723	3.35	51	42	79	36	222^2

■ **Clem Labine**

YEAR	TM/L	WR	LR	GR	SV	IPR	ERAR	RR	/A	RNK	GS	IPS
1950	Bro-N	0	0	1	0	2	4.50	-0	-0	0		
1951	Bro-N	0	0	8	0	19	2.84	2	2	0	6	46^1
1952	Bro-N	6	1	16	0	40^2	3.54	1	0	1	9	36^1
1953	Bro-N	10	4	30	7	66^2	2.43	14	14	29	7	43^2
1954	Bro-N	6	5	45	5	96^2	4.00	1	1	1	2	11^2
1955	Bro-N	10	2	52	11	93^1	2.31	18	18	26	8	51
1956	Bro-N	9	6	59	19	97	3.34	5	7	12	3	18^2
1957	Bro-N	5	7	58	17	104^2	3.44	5	8	12		
1958	LA-N	5	5	50	14	90	4.30	-3	-2	-3	2	14
1959	LA-N	5	10	56	9	84^2	3.93	0	3	5		
1960	LA-N	0	1	13	1	17	5.82	-4	-4	-2		
	Det-A	0	3	14	2	19^1	5.12	-3	-2	-4		
	Pit-N	3	0	15	3	30^1	1.48	8	8	9		
1961	Pit-N	4	1	55	8	88^2	3.55	5	4	3	1	4
1962	NY-N	0	0	3	0	4	11.25	-3	-3	0		
Total	13	63	45	475	96	854	3.49	44	54	88	38	225^2

■ **Lerrin LaGrow**

YEAR	TM/L	WR	LR	GR	SV	IPR	ERAR	RR	/A	RNK	GS	IPS
1970	Det-A	0	1	10	0	12^1	7.30	-5	-5	-4		
1972	Det-A	0	1	16	2	27^1	1.32	5	6	3		
1973	Det-A	0	3	18	3	36^2	4.17	-1	-0	-0	3	17^1
1974	Det-A	0	0	3	0	6^1	9.95	-4	-4	0	34	210
1975	Det-A	0	0	6	0	19^1	3.72	0	1	0	26	145
1976	StL-N	0	0	6	0	9^1	0.96	3	3	0	2	15
1977	Chi-A	7	3	66	25	98^2	2.46	17	18	26		
1978	Chi-A	6	5	52	16	88	4.40	-6	-6	-9		
1979	Chi-A	0	2	9	1	8^1	11.88	-7	-7	-17	2	9^1
	LA-N	5	1	31	4	37	3.41	1	1	2		
1980	Phi-N	0	2	25	3	39	4.15	-2	-2	-1		
Total	10	18	18	242	54	382^1	3.77	0	3	-0	67	396^2

■ **Dennis Lamp**

YEAR	TM/L	WR	LR	GR	SV	IPR	ERAR	RR	/A	RNK	GS	IPS
1977	Chi-N	0	1	8	0	13^1	7.43	-5	-5	-3	3	16^2
1978	Chi-N	0	0	1	0	0^2	0.00	0	0	0	36	223
1979	Chi-N	0	0	6	0	12^1	0.73	4	5	0	32	188
1980	Chi-N	1	2	4	0	4	4.50	-0	-0	-2	37	198^2
1981	Chi-A	3	1	17	0	47^2	2.08	8	8	6	10	79^1
1982	Chi-A	1	1	17	5	27	3.00	3	3	3	27	162^2
1983	Chi-A	4	5	44	15	87^1	3.61	4	6	7	5	29
1984	Tor-A	5	7	52	9	64	4.50	-4	-3	-6	4	21
1985	Tor-A	11	0	52	2	100^2	3.31	9	10	10	1	5
1986	Tor-A	2	4	38	2	66^1	4.88	-5	-5	-4	2	6^2
1987	Oak-A	0	0	31	0	37	5.11	-3	-4	0	5	19^2
1988	Bos-A	7	6	46	0	82^2	3.48	4	6	8		
1989	Bos-A	4	2	42	2	112^1	2.32	19	22	12		
1990	Bos-A	3	5	46	0	100^2	4.74	-9	-7	-5	1	5
1991	Bos-A	6	3	51	0	92	4.70	-6	-4	-4		
1992	Pit-N	1	1	21	0	28	5.14	-5	-5	-3		
Total	16	48	38	476	35	876	3.83	16	26	20	163	954^2

■ **Bill Landrum**

YEAR	TM/L	WR	LR	GR	SV	IPR	ERAR	RR	/A	RNK	GS	IPS
1986	Cin-N	0	0	10	0	13^1	6.75	-4	-4	0		
1987	Cin-N	3	1	42	2	57^2	3.90	1	2	2	2	7^1
1988	Chi-N	1	0	7	0	12^1	5.84	-3	-3	-2		
1989	Pit-N	2	3	56	26	81	1.67	16	15	19		
1990	Pit-N	7	3	54	13	71^2	2.13	13	12	20		
1991	Pit-N	4	4	61	17	76^1	3.18	4	3	5		
1992	Mon-N	1	1	18	0	20	7.20	-8	-8	-7		
Total	7	18	12	248	58	332^1	3.20	19	17	36	2	7^1

■ **Dave LaRoche**

YEAR	TM/L	WR	LR	GR	SV	IPR	ERAR	RR	/A	RNK	GS	IPS
1970	Cal-A	4	1	38	4	49^2	3.44	1	1	1		
1971	Cal-A	5	1	56	9	72	2.50	8	6	6		
1972	Min-A	5	7	62	10	95^1	2.83	2	4	5		
1973	Chi-N	4	1	45	4	54^1	5.80	-13	-11	-11		
1974	Chi-N	4	5	45	5	74	4.86	-10	-9	-11	4	18
1975	Cle-A	5	3	61	17	82^1	2.19	15	15	20		
1976	Cle-A	1	4	61	21	96^1	2.24	14	13	13		
1977	Cle-A	2	2	13	4	18^2	5.30	-3	-3	-7		
	Cal-A	6	5	46	13	81^1	3.10	9	7	12		
	Yr	8	7	59	17	100	3.51	6	5	5		
1978	Cal-A	10	9	59	25	95^2	2.82	10	8	20		
1979	Cal-A	7	10	52	10	82^2	5.55	-12	-14	-29	1	3
1980	Cal-A	2	1	43	4	79^1	2.95	10	9	4	9	48^2
1981	NY-A	4	0	25	0	43^1	1.87	9	8	7	1	3^2
1982	NY-A	4	2	25	0	50	3.42	4	3	3		
1983	NY-A	0	0	1	0	1	18.00	-2	-2	0		
Total	14	63	51	632	126	976	3.36	41	37	33	15	73^1

■ **Gary Lavelle**

YEAR	TM/L	WR	LR	GR	SV	IPR	ERAR	RR	/A	RNK	GS	IPS
1974	SF-N	0	3	10	0	16^2	2.16	3	3	5		
1975	SF-N	6	3	65	8	82^1	2.95	6	8	9		
1976	SF-N	10	6	65	12	110^1	2.69	10	11	18		
1977	SF-N	7	7	73	20	118^1	2.05	24	24	35		
1978	SF-N	13	10	67	14	97^2	3.32	3	1	3		
1979	SF-N	7	9	70	20	96^2	2.51	13	11	21		
1980	SF-N	6	8	62	9	100	3.42	2	1	2		
1981	SF-N	2	4	31	4	58^1	2.78	5	4	5	3	7^1
1982	SF-N	10	7	68	8	104^2	2.67	11	11	18		
1983	SF-N	7	4	56	20	87	2.59	10	9	15		
1984	SF-N	5	4	77	12	101	2.76	9	8	9		
1985	Tor-A	5	7	69	8	72^2	3.10	8	9	16		
1987	Tor-A	2	3	23	1	27^2	5.53	-3	-3	-5		
	Oak-A	0	0	6	0	4^1	8.31	-2	-2	0		
	Yr	2	3	29	1	32	5.91	-5	-5	-5		
Total	13	80	75	742	136	1077^2	2.86	99	96	150	3	7^1

■ **Terry Leach**

YEAR	TM/L	WR	LR	GR	SV	IPR	ERAR	RR	/A	RNK	GS	IPS
1981	NY-N	1	1	20	0	30	3.00	2	2	1	1	5
1982	NY-N	1	1	20	3	35^1	5.35	-7	-7	-5	1	10
1985	NY-N	0	3	18	1	29	3.10	2	1	1	4	26^2
1986	NY-N	0	0	6	0	6^2	2.70	1	1	0		
1987	NY-N	4	0	32	0	57	2.84	8	6	4	12	74^1
1988	NY-N	7	2	52	3	92	2.54	9	7	7		
1989	NY-N	0	0	10	0	21^1	4.22	-2	-2	0		
	KC-A	4	4	27	0	59^2	3.32	4	4	4	3	14
1990	Min-A	2	5	55	2	81^2	3.20	6	9	7		
1991	Min-A	1	2	50	0	67^1	3.61	4	5	2		
1992	Chi-A	6	5	51	0	73^2	1.95	16	15	21		
Total	10	26	23	341	9	553^2	3.10	43	40	42	21	130

■ **Bob Lee**

YEAR	TM/L	WR	LR	GR	SV	IPR	ERAR	RR	/A	RNK	GS	IPS
1964	LA-A	5	4	59	19	110^1	1.31	28	24	27	5	26^2
1965	Cal-A	9	7	69	23	131^1	1.92	22	22	32		
1966	Cal-A	5	4	61	16	101^2	2.74	8	7	8		
1967	LA-N	0	0	4	0	6^2	5.40	-2	-2	0		
	Cin-N	2	3	26	2	45^2	4.34	-5	-3	-3	1	5
	Yr	2	3	30	2	52^1	4.47	-6	-5	-3	1	5
1968	Cin-N	2	4	43	3	62^2	5.03	-14	-13	-13	1	2^2
Total	5	23	22	262	63	458^1	2.67	38	35	52	7	34^1

■ **Craig Lefferts**

YEAR	TM/L	WR	LR	GR	SV	IPR	ERAR	RR	/A	RNK	GS	IPS
1983	Chi-N	2	3	51	1	60^1	3.13	3	4	3	5	28^2
1984	SD-N	3	4	62	10	105^2	2.13	17	17	14		
1985	SD-N	7	6	60	2	83^1	3.35	2	2	3		
1986	SD-N	9	8	83	4	107^2	3.09	7	7	10		
1987	SD-N	2	2	33	2	51^1	4.38	-2	-2	-2		
	SF-N	3	3	44	4	47^1	3.23	4	3	4		
	Yr	5	5	77	6	98^2	3.83	3	1	2		
1988	SF-N	3	8	64	11	92^1	2.92	5	3	5		

YEAR	TM/L	WR	LR	GR	SV	IPR	ERAR	RR	/A	RNK	GS	IPS
1989	SF-N	2	4	70	20	107	2.69	10	8	7		
1990	SD-N	7	5	56	23	78^2	2.52	11	11	23		
1991	SD-N	1	6	54	23	69	3.91	-2	-1	-1		
1992	SD-N										27	163^1
	Bal-A										5	33
Total	9	39	49	577	100	802^2	3.03	57	53	66	37	225

■ Dutch Leonard

YEAR	TM/L	WR	LR	GR	SV	IPR	ERAR	RR	/A	RNK	GS	IPS
1933	Bro-N	1	1	7	0	22	1.64	4	4	3	3	18
1934	Bro-N	5	3	24	5	43^1	3.74	2	1	2	20	140^1
1935	Bro-N	0	4	32	8	60	4.05	-0	-0	-0	11	77^2
1936	Bro-N	0	0	16	1	32	3.66	1	2	0		
1938	Was-A	1	0	2	0	1^2	0.00	1	1	5	31	221^2
1939	Was-A										34	269^1
1940	Was-A										35	289
1941	Was-A	0	0	1	0	1	0.00	0	0	0	33	255
1942	Was-A	0	0	1	0	2	4.50	-0	-0	0	5	33
1943	Was-A	0	0	1	1	0^1	0.00	0	0	1	30	219^1
1944	Was-A	0	1	1	0	4^2	11.57	-4	-4	-8	31	224^2
1945	Was-A	1	0	2	1	4^1	0.00	2	1	4	29	211^2
1946	Was-A	0	0	3	0	9^2	2.79	1	1	0	23	152
1947	Phi-N	1	1	3	0	5	3.60	0	0	1	29	230
1948	Phi-N	1	1	3	0	9	4.00	-0	-0	-0	31	216^2
1949	Chi-N	0	0	5	0	5^2	4.76	-0	-0	0	28	174^1
1950	Chi-N	4	1	34	6	65^1	3.58	4	4	4	1	8^2
1951	Chi-N	10	5	40	3	77	2.34	14	15	28	1	4^2
1952	Chi-N	2	2	45	11	66^2	2.16	12	13	11		
1953	Chi-N	2	3	45	8	62^2	4.60	-2	-1	-1		
Total	18	28	22	265	44	472^1	3.33	33	36	48	375	2746

■ Paul Lindblad

YEAR	TM/L	WR	LR	GR	SV	IPR	ERAR	RR	/A	RNK	GS	IPS
1965	KC-A	0	1	4	0	7^1	11.05	-6	-6	-8		
1966	KC-A	2	3	24	1	41	4.39	-4	-5	-5	14	80
1967	KC-A	3	3	36	6	63	2.57	5	4	5	10	52^2
1968	Oak-A	4	2	46	2	55	1.96	6	5	6	1	1^1
1969	Oak-A	9	6	60	9	78^1	4.14	-4	-6	-12		
1970	Oak-A	8	2	62	3	63^1	2.70	7	6	9		
1971	Oak-A	1	0	8	0	16	3.94	-1	-1	-1		
	Was-A	6	4	43	8	83^2	2.58	8	7	9		
	Yr	7	4	51	8	99^2	2.80	7	6	8		
1972	Tex-A	5	8	66	9	99^2	2.62	5	4	6		
1973	Oak-A	1	2	33	2	60^2	4.01	-1	-3	-2	3	17^1
1974	Oak-A	3	3	43	6	89^2	1.81	18	15	11	2	11
1975	Oak-A	9	1	68	7	122^1	2.72	14	12	11		
1976	Oak-A	6	5	65	5	114^2	3.06	6	4	4		
1977	Tex-A	4	4	41	4	93^2	3.94	1	1	1	1	5
1978	Tex-A	1	1	18	2	39^2	3.63	1	0	0		
	NY-A	0	0	6	0	15^1	4.11	-1	-1	0	1	3
	Yr	1	1	24	2	55	3.76	-0	-0	0	1	3
Total	14	62	45	623	64	1043^1	3.10	53	38	34	32	170^1

■ Frank Linzy

YEAR	TM/L	WR	LR	GR	SV	IPR	ERAR	RR	/A	RNK	GS	IPS
1963	SF-N	0	0	7	0	14^2	3.68	-1	-1	0	1	2
1965	SF-N	9	3	57	21	81^2	1.43	19	20	37		
1966	SF-N	7	11	51	16	100^1	2.96	7	8	16		
1967	SF-N	7	7	57	17	95^2	1.51	20	19	33		
1968	SF-N	9	8	57	12	94^2	2.09	9	9	17		
1969	SF-N	14	9	58	11	116^1	3.64	-1	-2	-3		
1970	SF-N	2	1	20	1	25^2	7.01	-8	-9	-10		
	StL-N	3	5	47	2	61^1	3.67	3	3	4		
	Yr	5	6	67	3	87	4.66	-6	-6	-6		
1971	StL-N	4	3	50	6	59^1	2.12	9	10	13		
1972	Mil-A	2	2	47	12	77^1	3.03	0	0	0		
1973	Mil-A	2	6	41	13	60	3.60	1	1	2	1	3
1974	Phi-N	3	2	22	0	24^2	3.28	1	1	2		
Total	11	62	57	514	111	811^2	2.83	60	59	110	2	5

■ Mark Littell

YEAR	TM/L	WR	LR	GR	SV	IPR	ERAR	RR	/A	RNK	GS	IPS
1973	KC-A	0	0	1	0	2^2	6.75	-1	-1	0	7	35^1
1975	KC-A	1	0	4	0	7	1.29	2	2	3	3	17^1
1976	KC-A	8	3	59	16	102	1.50	23	23	30	1	2
1977	KC-A	6	4	43	12	74^2	3.25	7	6	10	5	30
1978	StL-N	4	7	70	11	97^1	2.77	9	8	10	2	9
1979	StL-N	9	4	63	13	82^1	2.19	14	14	26		
1980	StL-N	0	2	14	2	10^2	9.28	-7	-7	-14		
1981	StL-N	1	2	27	2	36	4.25	-3	-3	-2	1	5
1982	StL-N	0	1	16	0	20^2	5.23	-4	-4	-2		
Total	9	29	23	297	56	433^1	2.85	40	40	61	19	98^2

■ Skip Lockwood

YEAR	TM/L	WR	LR	GR	SV	IPR	ERAR	RR	/A	RNK	GS	IPS
1969	Sea-A	0	0	3	0	3	9.00	-2	-2	0	3	20
1970	Mil-A	0	0	1	0	7	5.14	-1	-1	0	26	166^2
1971	Mil-A	0	0	1	0	1	0.00	0	0	0	32	207
1972	Mil-A	0	0	2	0	3	0.00	1	1	0	27	167
1973	Mil-A	3	3	22	0	70	2.96	7	6	5	15	84^2
1974	Cal-A	2	4	35	1	74^2	3.74	-1	-2	-2	2	6^2
1975	NY-N	1	3	24	2	48^1	1.49	11	11	9		
1976	NY-N	10	7	56	19	94^1	2.67	9	7	14		
1977	NY-N	4	8	63	20	104	3.38	6	4	6		
1978	NY-N	7	13	57	15	90^2	3.57	0	-1	-2		
1979	NY-N	2	5	27	9	42^1	1.49	11	10	20		
1980	Bos-A	3	1	23	2	42^2	5.48	-7	-6	-6	1	3
Total	12	32	44	314	68	581	3.18	34	27	44	106	655

■ Bob Locker

YEAR	TM/L	WR	LR	GR	SV	IPR	ERAR	RR	/A	RNK	GS	IPS
1965	Chi-A	5	2	51	2	91^1	3.15	3	0	0		
1966	Chi-A	9	8	56	12	95	2.46	10	7	14		
1967	Chi-A	7	5	77	20	124^2	2.09	16	14	17		
1968	Chi-A	5	4	70	10	90^1	2.29	7	7	8		
1969	Chi-A	2	3	17	4	22	6.55	-7	-7	-16		
	Sea-A	3	3	51	6	78^1	2.18	13	13	11		
	Yr	5	6	68	10	100^1	3.14	5	6	-5		
1970	Mil-A	0	1	28	3	31^2	3.41	1	1	1		
	Oak-A	3	3	38	4	56^1	2.88	5	4	5		
	Yr	3	4	66	7	88	3.07	6	5	5		
1971	Oak-A	7	2	47	6	72^1	2.86	5	4	5		
1972	Oak-A	6	1	56	10	78	2.65	4	2	2		
1973	Chi-N	10	6	63	18	106^1	2.54	13	17	29		
1975	Chi-N	0	1	22	0	32^2	4.96	-5	-4	-1		
Total	10	57	39	576	95	879	2.75	64	59	75		

■ Aurelio Lopez

YEAR	TM/L	WR	LR	GR	SV	IPR	ERAR	RR	/A	RNK	GS	IPS
1974	KC-A	0	0	7	0	12	5.25	-2	-2	0	1	4
1978	StL-N	2	1	21	0	38^2	3.96	-2	-2	-1	4	26^1
1979	Det-A	10	5	61	21	127	2.41	25	27	39		
1980	Det-A	13	5	66	21	119^2	3.46	8	9	15	1	4^1
1981	Det-A	3	1	26	3	66^1	3.39	2	3	2	3	15^1
1982	Det-A	3	1	19	3	41	5.27	-5	-5	-6		
1983	Det-A	9	8	57	18	115^1	2.81	16	14	24		
1984	Det-A	10	1	71	14	137^2	2.94	16	15	14		
1985	Det-A	3	7	51	5	86^1	4.80	-6	-7	-8		
1986	Hou-N	3	3	45	7	78	3.46	2	1	1		
1987	Hou-N	2	1	26	1	38	4.50	-2	-2	-2		
Total	11	58	33	450	93	860	3.44	52	50	77	9	50

■ Turk Lown

YEAR	TM/L	WR	LR	GR	SV	IPR	ERAR	RR	/A	RNK	GS	IPS
1951	Chi-N	1	2	13	0	22	6.14	-5	-5	-6	18	105
1952	Chi-N	1	2	14	0	42^1	4.25	-2	-2	-1	19	114^1
1953	Chi-N	7	3	37	3	93	4.65	-4	-2	-2	12	55^1
1954	Chi-N	0	2	15	0	22	6.14	-5	-5	-4		
1956	Chi-N	9	8	61	13	110^2	3.58	2	2	4		
1957	Chi-N	5	7	67	12	93	3.77	1	1	1		
1958	Chi-N	0	0	4	0	4	4.50	-0	-0	0		
	Cin-N	0	2	11	0	11^2	5.40	-2	-2	-3		
	Yr	0	2	15	0	15^2	5.17	-2	-2	-3		
	Chi-A	3	3	27	8	40^2	3.98	-1	-2	-3		
1959	Chi-A	9	2	60	15	93^1	2.89	10	9	13		
1960	Chi-A	2	3	45	5	67^1	3.88	-0	-1	-1		
1961	Chi-A	7	5	59	11	101	2.76	14	13	17		
1962	Chi-A	4	2	42	6	56^1	3.04	6	5	7		
Total	11	48	41	455	73	757^1	3.77	14	13	22	49	274^2

■ Gary Lucas

YEAR	TM/L	WR	LR	GR	SV	IPR	ERAR	RR	/A	RNK	GS	IPS
1980	SD-N	1	1	28	3	39^1	2.29	6	5	3	18	110^2
1981	SD-N	7	7	57	13	90	2.00	15	13	22		
1982	SD-N	1	10	65	16	97^1	3.24	4	2	3		
1983	SD-N	5	8	62	17	91	2.87	8	6	11		
1984	Mon-N	0	3	55	8	53	2.72	5	4	4		
1985	Mon-N	6	2	49	1	67^2	3.19	3	1	2		
1986	Cal-A	4	1	27	2	45^2	3.15	5	5	5		
1987	Cal-A	1	5	48	3	74^1	3.63	7	6	5		
Total	8	25	37	391	63	558^1	2.90	52	42	53	18	110^2

■ Sparky Lyle

YEAR	TM/L	WR	LR	GR	SV	IPR	ERAR	RR	/A	RNK	GS	IPS
1967	Bos-A	1	2	27	5	43^1	2.28	5	6	5		
1968	Bos-A	6	1	49	11	65^2	2.74	2	3	4		
1969	Bos-A	8	3	71	17	102^2	2.54	12	14	19		
1970	Bos-A	1	7	63	20	67^1	3.88	-1	1	1		
1971	Bos-A	6	4	50	16	52^1	2.75	4	5	13		
1972	NY-A	9	5	59	35	107^2	1.92	14	12	23		
1973	NY-A	5	9	51	27	82^1	2.51	12	11	24		
1974	NY-A	9	3	66	15	114	1.66	25	23	29		
1975	NY-A	5	7	49	6	89^1	3.12	6	5	7		
1976	NY-A	7	8	64	23	103^2	2.26	15	13	24		
1977	NY-A	13	5	72	26	137	2.17	29	27	43		
1978	NY-A	9	3	59	9	111^2	3.47	4	2	2		
1979	Tex-A	5	8	67	13	95	3.13	11	11	17		
1980	Tex-A	3	2	49	8	80^2	4.69	-6	-7	-6		
	Phi-N	0	0	10	2	14	1.93	3	3	1		
1981	Phi-N	9	6	48	2	75	4.44	-8	-7	-13		
1982	Phi-N	3	3	34	2	36^2	5.15	-6	-6	-10		
	Chi-A	0	0	11	1	12	3.00	1	1	0		
Total	16	99	76	899	238	1390^1	2.88	121	118	185		

■ Firpo Marberry

YEAR	TM/L	WR	LR	GR	SV	IPR	ERAR	RR	/A	RNK	GS	IPS
1923	Was-A	0	0	7	0	14	2.57	2	2	0	4	30^2
1924	Was-A	6	5	35	15	96	2.91	14	12	17	15	99^1
1925	Was-A	9	5	55	15	93^1	3.47	10	8	13		
1926	Was-A	9	5	59	22	103	2.97	12	10	17	5	35
1927	Was-A	8	2	46	9	85^2	3.68	4	4	5	10	69^2
1928	Was-A	7	9	37	3	87^1	3.71	3	3	5	11	74
1929	Was-A	3	4	23	11	41	3.95	1	1	3	26	209^1
1930	Was-A	0	3	11	1	26	4.85	-1	-1	-1	22	159
1931	Was-A	3	1	20	7	44	4.70	-2	-2	-2	25	175
1932	Was-A	1	1	39	13	81^2	3.42	10	8	5	15	116
1933	Det-A	2	0	5	2	8^1	0.00	4	4	11	32	230
1934	Det-A	6	0	19	3	38^2	1.86	11	11	17	19	117
1935	Det-A	0	0	3	0	3^2	9.82	-2	-2	0	2	15^1
1936	NY-N	0	0	1	0	0^1	0.00	0	0	0		
	Was-A	0	1	4	0	7	3.86	1	1	1	1	7
Total	14	54	36	364	101	730	3.42	69	59	90	187	1337^1

YEAR	TM/L	WR	LR	GR	SV	IPR	ERAR	RR	/A	RNK	GS	IPS
■ Mike Marshall												
1967	Det-A	1	3	37	10	59	1.98	8	8	8		
1969	Sea-A	0	1	6	0	9^1	3.86	-0	-0	-0	14	78^1
1970	Hou-N	0	1	4	0	5^1	8.44	-3	-3	-5		
	Mon-N	3	3	19	3	39	2.77	6	6	9	5	25^2
	Yr	3	4	23	3	44^1	3.45	3	3	5	5	25^2
1971	Mon-N	5	8	66	23	111^1	4.28	-10	-9	-14		
1972	Mon-N	14	8	65	18	116	1.78	22	23	47		
1973	Mon-N	14	11	92	31	179	2.66	20	23	38		
1974	LA-N	15	12	106	21	208^1	2.42	28	23	32		
1975	LA-N	9	14	57	13	109^1	3.29	4	1	3		
1976	LA-N	4	3	30	8	62^2	4.45	-7	-7	-10		
	Atl-N	2	1	24	6	36^2	3.19	1	2	3		
	Yr	6	4	54	14	99^1	3.99	-5	-5	-7		
1977	Atl-N	1	0	4	0	6	9.00	-3	-3	-5		
	Tex-A	0	2	8	1	14^1	3.77	0	0	1	4	21^1
1978	Min-A	10	12	54	21	99	2.45	14	15	37		
1979	Min-A	10	14	89	32	140^2	2.62	25	27	56	1	2
1980	Min-A	1	3	18	1	32^1	6.12	-8	-6	-8		
1981	NY-N	3	2	20	0	31	2.61	3	3	4		
Total	14	92	98	699	188	1259^1	2.96	100	103	197	24	127^1
■ Tippy Martinez												
1974	NY-A	0	0	10	0	12^2	4.26	-1	-1	0		
1975	NY-A	1	0	21	8	26^1	1.71	6	6	6	2	10^2
1976	NY-A	2	0	11	2	28	1.93	5	5	4		
	Bal-A	3	1	28	8	41^2	2.59	4	3	4		
	Yr	5	1	39	10	69^2	2.33	9	8	8		
1977	Bal-A	5	1	41	9	50	2.70	8	6	9		
1978	Bal-A	3	3	42	5	69	4.83	-8	-10	-10		
1979	Bal-A	10	3	39	3	78	2.88	12	10	15		
1980	Bal-A	4	4	53	10	80^2	3.01	9	8	10		
1981	Bal-A	3	3	37	11	59	2.90	5	5	6		
1982	Bal-A	8	8	76	16	95	3.41	7	7	12		
1983	Bal-A	9	3	65	21	103^1	2.35	20	18	28		
1984	Bal-A	4	9	55	17	89^2	3.91	1	-0	-1		
1985	Bal-A	3	3	49	4	70	5.40	-10	-11	-10		
1986	Bal-A	0	2	14	1	16	5.63	-3	-3	-3		
1988	Min-A	0	0	3	0	4	18.00	-6	-6	0		
Total	14	55	40	544	115	823^1	3.43	48	36	71	2	10^2
■ Jakie May												
1917	StL-N	0	0	14	0	21^1	4.64	-5	-5	0	1	8
1918	StL-N	2	0	13	0	41^1	3.92	-5	-6	-2	16	111^1
1919	StL-N	0	1	9	0	18^2	2.41	1	1	0	19	107
1920	StL-N	0	1	11	0	34	2.38	3	2	1	5	36^2
1921	StL-N										5	21
1924	Cin-N	2	2	34	6	77^1	2.91	8	7	5	4	21^2
1925	Cin-N	2	4	24	2	45	4.40	-1	-1	-2	12	92^1
1926	Cin-N	5	4	30	3	66^1	2.98	6	5	7	15	101^1
1927	Cin-N	2	0	16	1	30^1	5.93	-7	-7	-5	28	205^1
1928	Cin-N	2	2	10	1	18^2	3.38	1	1	2	11	60^2
1929	Cin-N	4	1	17	3	40^2	3.76	4	4	5	24	158^1
1930	Cin-N	0	1	8	0	8^1	14.04	-8	-9	-9	18	104
1931	Chi-N	3	4	27	2	54^1	3.81	0	0	0	4	24^2
1932	Chi-N	2	2	35	1	53^2	4.36	-3	-4	-3		
Total	13	24	22	248	19	510	3.85	-4	-10	-1	162	1052^1
■ Al McBean												
1961	Pit-N	3	1	25	0	59^1	3.79	2	1	1	2	15
1962	Pit-N	0	0	4	0	5^1	6.75	-2	-2	0	29	184^1
1963	Pit-N	11	2	48	11	89^1	2.12	12	12	19	7	33
1964	Pit-N	8	3	58	22	89^2	1.91	16	16	26		
1965	Pit-N	5	6	61	18	108	2.25	15	15	20	1	6
1966	Pit-N	4	3	47	3	86^2	3.22	4	3	3		
1967	Pit-N	3	2	43	4	66^1	2.85	4	4	3	8	64^2
1968	Pit-N	0	1	8	0	13^1	5.40	-4	-4	-2	28	185
1969	SD-N										1	7
	LA-N	2	6	31	4	48^1	3.91	-2	-3	-5		
	Yr	2	7	31	4	55^1	4.72	-5	-7	-8	1	7
1970	LA-N	0	0	1	0	1	0.00	0	0	0		
	Pit-N	0	0	7	1	10	8.10	-5	-5	-1		
	Yr	0	0	8	1	11	7.36	-4	-4	-1		
Total	9	36	24	333	63	577^1	2.90	42	39	62	76	495
■ Bob McClure												
1975	KC-A	1	0	12	1	15^1	0.00	6	7	5		
1976	KC-A	0	0	8	0	4	9.00	-2	-2	0		
1977	Mil-A	2	1	68	6	71^1	2.52	12	12	7		
1978	Mil-A	2	6	44	9	65	3.74	0	0	0		
1979	Mil-A	5	2	36	5	51	3.88	2	2	2		
1980	Mil-A	1	7	47	10	57	3.47	4	3	4	5	33^2
1981	Mil-A	0	0	4	0	7^2	3.52	0	-0	0		
1982	Mil-A	2	0	8	0	12	3.00	1	1	2	26	160^2
1983	Mil-A	0	0	1	0	0^2	0.00	0	0	0	23	141^1
1984	Mil-A	0	2	21	1	35	2.57	6	5	3	18	104^2
1985	Mil-A	4	1	37	3	80^2	4.24	-1	-1	-0	1	5
1986	Mil-A	2	1	13	0	16^1	3.86	1	1	1		
	Mon-N	2	5	52	6	62^2	3.02	5	5	6		
1987	Mon-N	6	1	52	5	52^1	3.44	4	4	6		
1988	Mon-N	1	3	19	2	19	6.16	-6	-5	-12		
	NY-N	1	0	14	1	11	4.09	-1	-1	-1		
	Yr	2	3	33	3	30	5.40	-7	-6	-13		
1989	Cal-A	6	1	48	3	52^1	1.55	14	13	18		
1990	Cal-A	2	0	11	0	7	6.43	-2	-2	-5		
1991	Cal-A	0	0	13	0	9^2	9.31	-6	-6	0		
	StL-N	1	1	32	0	23	3.13	1	1	1		
1992	StL-N	2	2	71	0	54	3.17	2	2	1		
Total	18	40	33	611	52	707	3.40	40	38	38	73	445^1
■ Billy McCool												
1964	Cin-N	5	2	37	7	66^2	2.30	9	10	12	3	22^2
1965	Cin-N	9	8	60	21	96^2	3.91	-4	-2	-4	2	8^2
1966	Cin-N	8	8	57	18	105^1	2.48	13	17	29		
1967	Cin-N	0	3	20	2	31^2	3.41	-0	1	1	11	65^2
1968	Cin-N	2	3	26	2	37^2	4.54	-7	-6	-8	4	13
1969	SD-N	3	5	54	7	58^2	4.30	-5	-5	-7		
1970	StL-N	0	3	18	1	21^2	6.23	-5	-5	-7		
Total	7	27	32	272	58	418^1	3.49	2	10	16	20	110
■ Lindy McDaniel												
1955	StL-N	0	0	2	0	4	4.50	-0	-0	0	2	15
1956	StL-N	5	2	32	0	80^1	2.58	11	11	8	7	36
1957	StL-N	3	0	4	0	11^1	3.18	1	1	2	26	179^2
1958	StL-N	0	2	9	0	20	5.40	-3	-3	-3	17	88^2
1959	StL-N	13	8	55	15	92^2	3.59	4	7	16	7	39^1
1960	StL-N	12	2	63	26	104^1	1.29	29	32	57	2	12
1961	StL-N	10	6	55	9	94^1	4.87	-9	-5	-9		
1962	StL-N	2	9	53	14	95	3.51	5	8	11	2	12
1963	Chi-N	13	7	57	22	88	2.86	4	6	16		
1964	Chi-N	1	7	63	15	95	3.88	-4	-2	-2		
1965	Chi-N	5	6	71	2	128^2	2.59	14	16	13		
1966	SF-N	10	5	64	6	121^2	2.66	13	14	17		
1967	SF-N	2	4	38	3	59^2	3.32	0	-0	-0	3	13
1968	SF-N	0	0	12	0	19^1	7.45	-10	-10	0		
	NY-A	4	1	24	10	51^1	1.75	7	7	9		
1969	NY-A	5	6	51	5	83^2	3.55	1	-1	-1		
1970	NY-A	9	5	62	29	111^2	2.01	21	19	32		
1971	NY-A	5	10	44	4	69^2	5.04	-12	-14	-29		
1972	NY-A	3	1	37	0	68	2.25	6	5	3		
1973	NY-A	12	4	44	10	138^1	2.60	19	16	20	3	22
1974	KC-A	0	2	33	1	79	3.42	2	4	1	5	27^2
1975	KC-A	5	1	40	1	78	4.15	-3	-3	-2		
Total	21	119	88	913	172	1694	3.14	94	108	160	74	445^1
■ Roger McDowell												
1985	NY-N	6	4	60	17	117	2.38	16	14	15	2	10^1
1986	NY-N	14	9	75	22	128	3.02	10	7	15		
1987	NY-N	7	5	56	25	88^2	4.16	-1	-4	-7		
1988	NY-N	5	5	62	16	89	2.63	8	6	8		
1989	NY-N	1	5	25	4	35^1	3.31	1	-0	-0		
	Phi-N	3	3	44	19	56^2	1.11	15	15	26		
	Yr	4	8	69	23	92	1.96	16	15	26		
1990	Phi-N	6	8	72	22	86^1	3.86	-1	-0	-1		
1991	Phi-N	3	6	38	3	59	3.20	3	3	5		
	LA-N	6	3	33	7	42^1	2.55	5	5	11		
	Yr	9	9	71	10	101^1	2.93	8	8	16		
1992	LA-N	6	10	65	14	83^2	4.09	-5	-6	-12		
Total	8	57	58	530	149	780	3.08	51	40	60	2	10^1
■ Andy McGaffigan												
1981	NY-A	0	0	2	0	7	2.57	1	1	0		
1982	SF-N	1	0	4	0	8	0.00	3	3	4		
1983	SF-N	1	0	27	2	50^1	2.68	5	5	1	16	84
1984	Mon-N	2	3	18	1	29^2	1.52	7	6	10	3	16^1
	Cin-N	0	0	6	0	9^1	2.89	1	1	0	3	13^2
	Yr	2	3	24	1	39	1.85	8	7	10	6	30
1985	Cin-N										15	94^1
1986	Mon-N	5	1	34	2	62^1	1.30	17	17	16	14	80^1
1987	Mon-N	5	2	69	12	120^1	2.39	23	24	18		
1988	Mon-N	6	0	63	4	91^1	2.76	7	8	6		
1989	Mon-N	3	5	57	2	75	4.68	-10	-10	-10		
1990	SF-N	0	0	4	0	4^2	17.36	-7	-7	0		
	KC-A	1	0	13	1	23^2	2.66	3	3	1	11	55
1991	KC-A	0	0	4	0	8	4.50	-0	-0	0		
Total	10	24	11	301	24	489^2	2.81	49	51	46	62	343^2
■ Tug McGraw												
1965	NY-N	0	1	28	1	41^2	3.02	2	2	1	9	56
1966	NY-N	0	0	3	0	2	0.00	1	1	0	12	60^1
1967	NY-N										4	17^1
1969	NY-N	8	2	38	12	79^2	1.58	18	18	27	4	20^2
1970	NY-N	4	6	57	10	90^2	3.28	8	8	9		
1971	NY-N	11	4	50	8	105	1.63	21	21	30	1	6
1972	NY-N	8	6	54	27	106	1.70	21	20	34		
1973	NY-N	5	6	58	25	107	3.70	-0	-1	-1	2	11^2
1974	NY-N	4	9	37	3	61^1	4.40	-5	-6	-12	4	27^1
1975	Phi-N	9	6	56	14	102^2	2.98	7	9	14		
1976	Phi-N	7	6	58	11	97^1	2.50	11	11	17		
1977	Phi-N	7	3	45	9	79	2.62	11	12	17		
1978	Phi-N	8	6	54	9	82^2	3.38	2	2	3	1	7
1979	Phi-N	4	3	64	16	79^2	4.97	-11	-10	-13	1	4
1980	Phi-N	5	4	57	20	92^1	1.46	22	24	33		
1981	Phi-N	2	4	34	10	44	2.66	4	5	8		
1982	Phi-N	3	3	34	5	39^2	4.31	-3	-3	-5		
1983	Phi-N	2	0	33	0	52^2	3.25	2	2	1	1	3
1984	Phi-N	2	0	25	0	38	3.79	-1	-1	-0		
Total	18	89	69	785	180	1301^1	2.87	110	113	163	39	213^1
■ Don McMahon												
1957	Mil-N	2	3	32	9	46^2	1.54	12	10	14		

YEAR	TM/L	WR	LR	GR	SV	IPR	ERAR	RR	/A	RNK	GS	IPS
1958	Mil-N	7	2	38	8	58^2	3.68	2	-1	-2		
1959	Mil-N	5	3	60	15	80^2	2.57	12	9	11		
1960	Mil-N	3	6	48	10	63^2	5.94	-15	-18	-29		
1961	Mil-N	6	4	53	8	92	2.84	12	9	11		
1962	Mil-N	0	1	2	0	3	6.00	-1	-1	-2		
	Hou-N	5	5	51	8	76^2	1.53	21	19	27		
	Yr	5	6	53	8	79^2	1.69	20	18	24		
1963	Hou-N	1	3	47	5	66^1	3.80	-4	-5	-3	2	13^2
1964	Cle-A	6	4	70	16	101	2.41	14	13	17		
1965	Cle-A	3	3	58	11	85	3.28	2	2	2		
1966	Cle-A	1	1	12	1	12^1	2.92	1	1	1		
	Bos-A	8	7	49	9	78	2.65	7	10	20		
	Yr	9	8	61	10	90^1	2.69	7	11	21		
1967	Bos-A	1	2	11	2	17^2	3.57	-1	-0	-0		
	Chi-A	5	0	52	3	91^2	1.67	16	15	8		
	Yr	6	2	63	5	109^1	1.98	15	14	8		
1968	Chi-A	2	1	25	0	46	1.96	5	5	3		
	Det-A	3	1	20	1	35^2	2.02	4	4	4		
	Yr	5	2	45	1	81^2	1.98	9	9	7		
1969	Det-A	3	5	34	11	37	3.89	-1	-1	-2		
	SF-N	3	1	13	2	23^2	3.04	1	1	2		
1970	SF-N	9	5	61	19	94^1	2.96	11	11	19		
1971	SF-N	10	6	61	4	82	4.06	-5	-6	-11		
1972	SF-N	3	3	44	5	63	3.71	-2	-2	-2		
1973	SF-N	4	0	22	6	30^1	1.48	7	8	13		
1974	SF-N	0	0	9	0	11^2	3.09	1	1	0		
Total	18	90	66	872	153	1297	2.94	99	85	101	2	13^2
■ Pete Mikkelsen												
1964	NY-A	7	4	50	12	86	3.56	1	1	1		
1965	NY-A	4	6	38	1	65^2	3.02	3	3	4	3	16^2
1966	Pit-N	9	8	71	14	126	3.07	7	7	10		
1967	Pit-N	1	2	32	2	56^1	4.31	-6	-6	-3		
	Chi-N	0	0	7	0	7	6.43	-2	-2	0		
	Yr	1	2	39	2	63^1	4.55	-8	-8	-3		
1968	Chi-N	0	0	3	0	4^2	7.71	-2	-2	0		
	StL-N	0	0	5	0	16	1.13	3	3	0		
	Yr	0	0	8	0	20^2	2.61	1	1	0		
1969	LA-N	7	5	48	4	81^1	2.77	7	5	7		
1970	LA-N	4	2	33	6	62	2.76	9	7	8		
1971	LA-N	8	5	41	5	74	3.65	-2	-3	-6		
1972	LA-N	5	5	33	5	57^2	4.06	-4	-5	-8		
Total	9	45	37	361	49	636^2	3.35	15	7	13	3	16^2
■ Bob Miller												
1957	StL-N	0	0	5	0	9	7.00	-3	-3	0		
1959	StL-N	0	0	1	0	2	0.00	1	1	0	10	68^2
1960	StL-N	1	0	8	0	15^2	1.72	4	4	2	7	37
1961	StL-N	1	1	29	3	56^2	3.18	5	8	3	5	17^2
1962	NY-N	0	1	12	0	25^2	4.21	-1	-0	-0	21	118
1963	LA-N	4	2	19	1	55^2	1.62	10	9	9	23	131^1
1964	LA-N	6	6	72	9	125^1	2.37	16	12	12	2	12^1
1965	LA-N	6	6	60	9	95	2.75	8	5	7	1	8
1966	LA-N	4	2	46	5	84^1	2.77	8	5	4		
1967	LA-N	2	6	48	0	65^2	3.84	-3	-5	-6	4	20
1968	Min-A	0	3	45	2	72^1	2.74	2	3	1		
1969	Min-A	0	4	37	3	49^1	2.74	5	5	4	11	70
1970	Cle-A	1	1	13	1	19	3.32	1	1	1	2	9
	Chi-A	1	0	3	0	5^1	18.56	-9	-9	-15	12	64^2
	Yr	2	1	16	1	24^1	6.66	-8	-7	-13	14	73^2
	Chi-N	0	0	6	2	7	3.86	0	1	0	1	2
1971	Chi-N	0	0	2	0	7	5.14	-1	-1	0		
	SD-N	7	3	38	7	63^2	1.41	15	13	22		
	Pit-N	1	2	16	3	28	1.29	7	7	8		
	Yr	8	5	56	10	98^2	1.64	20	19	30		
1972	Pit-N	5	2	36	3	54^1	2.65	5	4	5		
1973	SD-N	0	0	18	0	30^2	4.11	-2	-2	0		
	NY-N	0	0	1	0	1	0.00	0	0	0		
	Yr	0	0	19	0	31^2	3.98	-1	-2	0		
	Det-A	4	2	22	1	42	3.43	2	3	4		
1974	NY-N	2	2	58	2	78	3.58	0	-0	-0		
Total	17	45	43	595	51	992^2	2.91	70	61	64	99	558^2
■ Stu Miller												
1952	StL-N	1	0	1	0	0^2	0.00	0	0	4	11	87^1
1953	StL-N	0	1	22	4	31^1	7.18	-10	-10	-6	18	106^1
1954	StL-N	1	2	15	2	25^2	5.96	-5	-5	-6	4	21
1956	StL-N	0	1	3	1	7^1	4.91	-1	-1	-1		
	Phi-N	2	0	9	0	13^1	2.03	3	3	3	15	93^1
	Yr	2	1	12	1	20^2	3.05	2	2	2	15	93^1
1957	NY-N	6	3	25	1	48^1	3.17	4	4	7	13	75^2
1958	SF-N	0	2	21	0	44^1	0.81	15	15	6	20	137^2
1959	SF-N	7	4	50	8	110	2.54	17	16	17	9	57^2
1960	SF-N	5	5	44	2	81^1	4.09	-3	-6	-6	3	20^1
1961	SF-N	14	5	63	17	122	2.66	19	16	27		
1962	SF-N	5	8	59	19	107	4.12	-2	-4	-6		
1963	Bal-A	5	8	71	27	112^1	2.24	17	16	25		
1964	Bal-A	7	7	66	23	97	3.06	6	5	10		
1965	Bal-A	14	7	67	24	119^1	1.89	21	21	43		
1966	Bal-A	9	4	51	18	92	2.25	12	11	19		
1967	Bal-A	3	10	42	8	81^1	2.55	6	5	9		
1968	Atl-N	0	0	2	0	1^1	27.00	-4	-4	0		
Total	16	79	67	611	154	1094^2	2.95	96	83	144	93	599^1

YEAR	TM/L	WR	LR	GR	SV	IPR	ERAR	RR	/A	RNK	GS	IPS
■ Steve Mingori												
1970	Cle-A	1	0	21	1	20^1	2.66	2	3	2		
1971	Cle-A	1	2	54	4	56^2	1.43	13	15	10		
1972	Cle-A	0	6	41	10	57	3.95	-6	-5	-6		
1973	Cle-A	0	0	5	0	11^2	6.17	-3	-3	0		
	KC-A	3	2	18	1	49^1	2.92	5	7	6	1	7
	Yr	3	2	23	1	61	3.54	2	4	6	1	7
1974	KC-A	2	3	36	2	67^1	2.81	6	8	6		
1975	KC-A	0	3	36	2	50^1	2.50	7	8	5		
1976	KC-A	5	5	55	10	85^1	2.32	11	11	15		
1977	KC-A	2	4	43	4	64	3.09	7	7	7		
1978	KC-A	1	4	45	7	69	2.74	8	8	7		
1979	KC-A	3	2	29	1	40^2	5.75	-7	-7	-8	1	6
Total	10	18	31	383	42	571^2	2.99	44	52	42	2	13
■ Greg Minton												
1975	SF-N	0	0	2	0	3^1	8.10	-2	-2	0	2	13^2
1976	SF-N	0	2	8	0	14	4.50	-2	-1	-2	2	11^2
1977	SF-N										2	14
1978	SF-N	0	1	11	0	15^2	8.04	-8	-8	-5		
1979	SF-N	4	3	46	4	79^2	1.81	17	15	13		
1980	SF-N	4	6	68	19	91^1	2.46	12	11	16		
1981	SF-N	4	5	55	21	84^1	2.88	6	5	8		
1982	SF-N	10	4	78	30	123	1.83	24	24	38		
1983	SF-N	7	11	73	22	106^2	3.54	1	-0	-0		
1984	SF-N	4	9	73	19	120^1	3.74	-2	-3	-4	1	4
1985	SF-N	5	4	68	4	96^2	3.54	1	-1	-1		
1986	SF-N	4	4	48	5	68^2	3.93	-2	-3	-4		
1987	SF-N	1	0	15	1	23^1	3.47	2	1	0		
	Cal-A	5	4	41	10	76	3.08	12	10	14		
1988	Cal-A	4	5	44	7	79	2.85	10	9	11		
1989	Cal-A	4	3	62	8	90	2.20	17	16	15		
1990	Cal-A	1	1	11	0	15^1	2.35	3	3	3		
Total	15	57	62	703	150	1087^1	3.00	88	75	102	7	43^1
■ Randy Moffitt												
1972	SF-N	1	5	40	4	70^2	3.69	-2	-2	-1		
1973	SF-N	4	4	60	14	100^1	2.42	14	16	16		
1974	SF-N	5	7	60	15	95	4.55	-10	-8	-12	1	7
1975	SF-N	4	5	55	11	74	3.89	-2	-1	-1		
1976	SF-N	6	6	58	14	103	2.27	14	16	21		
1977	SF-N	4	9	64	11	87^2	3.59	3	3	5		
1978	SF-N	8	4	70	12	81^2	3.31	2	1	2		
1979	SF-N	2	5	28	2	35	7.71	-15	-16	-32		
1980	SF-N	1	1	13	0	16^2	4.86	-2	-2	-3		
1981	SF-N	0	0	10	0	11^1	7.94	-6	-6	0		
1982	Hou-N	2	4	30	3	41^2	3.02	3	1	2		
1983	Tor-A	6	2	45	10	57^1	3.77	2	3	6		
Total	12	43	52	533	96	774^1	3.65	1	5	3	1	7
■ Sid Monge												
1975	Cal-A	0	0	2	0	6^1	5.68	-1	-2	0	2	17^1
1976	Cal-A	2	2	19	0	40	2.70	4	3	3	13	77^2
1977	Cal-A	0	1	4	1	12^1	2.92	2	1	1		
	Cle-A	1	2	33	3	39	6.23	-9	-10	-9		
	Yr	1	3	37	4	51^1	5.44	-8	-9	-7		
1978	Cle-A	4	2	46	6	73	2.34	12	11	10	2	11^2
1979	Cle-A	12	10	76	19	131	2.40	26	27	49		
1980	Cle-A	3	5	67	14	94^1	3.53	5	6	6		
1981	Cle-A	3	5	31	4	58	4.34	-4	-5	-6		
1982	Phi-N	7	1	47	2	72	3.75	-1	-1	-1		
1983	Phi-N	3	0	14	0	11^2	6.94	-4	-4	-10		
	SD-N	7	3	47	7	68^2	3.15	4	3	4		
	Yr	10	3	61	7	80^1	3.70	-1	-2	-6		
1984	SD-N	2	1	13	0	15	4.80	-2	-2	-4		
	Det-A	1	0	19	0	36	4.25	-1	-1	-0		
Total	10	45	32	418	56	657^1	3.48	28	26	44	17	106^2
■ Jeff Montgomery												
1987	Cin-N	2	1	13	0	14^1	5.65	-3	-2	-4	1	5
1988	KC-A	7	2	45	1	62^2	3.45	4	4	5		
1989	KC-A	7	3	63	18	92	1.37	26	25	36		
1990	KC-A	6	5	73	24	94^1	2.39	16	15	25		
1991	KC-A	4	4	67	33	90	2.90	12	12	20		
1992	KC-A	1	6	65	39	82^2	2.18	16	17	30		
Total	6	27	21	326	115	436	2.50	71	71	111	1	5
■ Donnie Moore												
1975	Chi-N	0	0	3	0	3^1	2.70	0	0	0	1	5^1
1977	Chi-N	4	2	26	0	45	4.00	-0	2	2	1	3^2
1978	Chi-N	9	7	70	4	98^2	4.01	-5	0	0	1	4^1
1979	Chi-N	1	3	38	1	69	4.83	-8	-5	-3	1	4
1980	StL-N	1	1	11	0	21^2	6.23	-6	-6	-5		
1981	Mil-A	0	0	3	0	4	6.75	-1	-1	0		
1982	Atl-N	3	1	16	1	27^2	4.23	-2	-2	-2		
1983	Atl-N	2	3	43	6	68^2	3.67	-0	2	1		
1984	Atl-N	4	5	47	16	64^1	2.94	5	7	12		
1985	Cal-A	8	8	65	31	103	1.92	25	25	52		
1986	Cal-A	4	5	49	21	72^2	2.97	10	9	16		
1987	Cal-A	2	2	14	5	26^2	2.70	5	5	8		
1988	Cal-A	5	2	27	4	33	4.91	-3	-4	-8		
Total	13	43	39	412	89	637^2	3.58	18	31	74	4	17^1
■ Ray Moore												
1952	Bro-N	1	0	12	0	24	2.63	3	3	1	2	4^1
1953	Bro-N										1	8

YEAR	TM/L	WR	LR	GR	SV	IPR	ERAR	RR	/A	RNK	GS	IPS
1955	Bal-A	3	7	32	6	61^2	4.23	-2	-3	-5	14	90
1956	Bal-A	1	1	5	0	10^1	2.61	2	2	3	27	174^2
1957	Bal-A	0	1	2	0	5^1	3.38	0	0	0	32	222
1958	Chi-A	2	3	12	2	25^1	2.13	5	4	8	20	111^1
1959	Chi-A	2	1	21	0	41	4.17	-1	-2	-1	8	48^2
1960	Chi-A	1	1	14	0	20^2	5.66	-4	-4	-4		
	Was-A	3	2	37	13	65^2	2.88	7	7	8		
	Yr	4	3	51	13	86^1	3.54	3	3	5		
1961	Min-A	4	4	46	14	56^1	3.67	2	4	7		
1962	Min-A	8	3	49	9	64^2	4.73	-5	-5	-9		
1963	Min-A	1	2	30	2	38^2	6.28	-11	-11	-9	1	0
Total	10	26	25	260	46	413^2	4.00	-5	-6	-1	105	659

■ Wilcy Moore

YEAR	TM/L	WR	LR	GR	SV	IPR	ERAR	RR	/A	RNK	GS	IPS
1927	NY-A	13	3	38	13	120	1.95	29	25	37	12	93
1928	NY-A	3	3	33	2	53	3.91	1	-1	-1	2	7^1
1929	NY-A	6	4	41	8	61	4.13	1	-2	-3		
1931	Bos-A	7	2	38	10	84^1	3.31	10	9	11	15	101
1932	Bos-A	4	8	35	4	80^1	4.03	4	4	6	2	4
	NY-A	1	0	9	4	19	2.84	3	3	2	1	6
	Yr	5	8	44	8	99^1	3.81	7	7	8	3	10
1933	NY-A	5	6	35	8	62	5.52	-9	-11	-21		
Total	6	39	26	229	49	479^2	3.53	40	27	31	32	211^1

■ Tom Morgan

YEAR	TM/L	WR	LR	GR	SV	IPR	ERAR	RR	/A	RNK	GS	IPS
1951	NY-A	1	0	11	2	26^2	3.04	3	2	1	16	98
1952	NY-A	0	0	4	2	15	2.40	2	2	0	12	78^2
1954	NY-A	3	1	15	1	34^2	5.71	-8	-9	-10	17	108^1
1955	NY-A	7	3	39	10	69	2.87	8	7	11	1	3
1956	NY-A	6	7	41	11	71^1	4.16	-0	-2	-5		
1957	KC-A	6	2	33	7	63^2	4.66	-6	-5	-7	13	80
1958	Det-A	0	0	38	1	60^2	2.82	6	8	0	1	2
1959	Det-A	0	3	45	9	87^1	3.71	1	3	2	1	5^1
1960	Det-A	3	2	22	1	29	4.66	-3	-2	-4		
	Was-A	1	3	14	0	24	3.75	0	0	1		
	Yr	4	5	36	1	53	4.25	-2	-2	-3		
1961	LA-A	8	2	59	10	91^2	2.36	17	22	27		
1962	LA-A	5	2	48	9	58^2	2.91	7	6	9		
1963	LA-A	0	0	13	1	16^1	5.51	-3	-4	-1		
Total	12	40	25	382	64	648	3.56	26	28	25	61	375^1

■ Don Mossi

YEAR	TM/L	WR	LR	GR	SV	IPR	ERAR	RR	/A	RNK	GS	IPS
1954	Cle-A	4	0	35	7	59	2.14	10	10	9	5	34
1955	Cle-A	4	3	56	9	80^2	1.90	18	19	19	1	1
1956	Cle-A	0	4	45	11	78^1	2.76	12	13	10	3	9^1
1957	Cle-A	1	1	14	2	22^1	3.63	0	0	0	22	136^2
1958	Cle-A	7	4	38	3	75^2	3.81	-0	-1	-2	5	26
1959	Det-A	0	1	4	0	9	4.00	-0	0	0	30	219
1960	Det-A	1	0	1	0	4	0.00	2	2	4	22	154^1
1961	Det-A	0	0	1	1	0^2	0.00	0	0	1	34	239^2
1962	Det-A	0	2	8	1	8	3.38	1	1	2	27	172^1
1963	Det-A	2	0	8	2	25	0.72	8	8	8	16	97^2
1964	Chi-A	3	1	34	7	40	2.93	3	2	3		
1965	KC-A	5	8	51	7	55^1	3.74	-2	-2	-4		
Total	12	27	24	295	50	458	2.77	53	52	50	165	1090

■ Johnny Murphy

YEAR	TM/L	WR	LR	GR	SV	IPR	ERAR	RR	/A	RNK	GS	IPS
1932	NY-A	0	0	2	0	3^1	16.20	-4	-4	0		
1934	NY-A	3	3	20	4	48^2	2.03	13	11	14	20	159
1935	NY-A	6	4	32	5	71^1	3.91	4	1	2	8	45^2
1936	NY-A	5	2	22	5	53	2.21	17	14	20	5	35
1937	NY-A	12	4	35	10	89^2	3.61	10	8	15	4	20^1
1938	NY-A	8	1	30	11	77^1	4.07	6	4	5	2	14
1939	NY-A	3	6	38	19	61^1	4.40	1	-0	-1		
1940	NY-A	8	4	34	9	56^1	3.51	5	3	7	1	7
1941	NY-A	8	3	35	15	77^1	1.98	19	17	29		
1942	NY-A	4	10	31	11	58	3.41	2	0	0		
1943	NY-A	12	4	37	8	68	2.51	6	5	13		
1946	NY-A	4	2	27	7	45	3.40	1	0	0		
1947	Bos-A	0	0	32	3	54^2	2.80	6	7	1		
Total	13	73	43	375	107	764	3.25	85	66	107	40	281

■ Rob Murphy

YEAR	TM/L	WR	LR	GR	SV	IPR	ERAR	RR	/A	RNK	GS	IPS
1985	Cin-N	0	0	2	0	3	6.00	-1	-1	0		
1986	Cin-N	6	0	34	1	50^1	0.72	17	18	20		
1987	Cin-N	8	5	87	3	100^2	3.04	12	13	17		
1988	Cin-N	0	6	76	3	84^2	3.08	3	5	3		
1989	Bos-A	5	7	74	9	105	2.74	13	16	19		
1990	Bos-A	0	6	68	7	57	6.32	-15	-14	-17		
1991	Sea-A	0	1	57	4	48	3.00	6	6	2		
1992	Hou-N	3	1	59	0	55^2	4.04	-3	-4	-3		
Total	8	22	26	457	27	504^1	3.25	32	38	41		

■ Tom Murphy

YEAR	TM/L	WR	LR	GR	SV	IPR	ERAR	RR	/A	RNK	GS	IPS
1968	Cal-A										15	99^1
1969	Cal-A	0	0	1	0	1	0.00	0	0	0	35	214^2
1970	Cal-A	0	0	1	0	0		0	0	0	38	227
1971	Cal-A	0	0	1	0	1	0.00	0	0	0	36	242^1
1972	Cal-A	0	0	6	0	10	5.40	-3	-3	0		
	KC-A	1	0	9	1	16^1	0.55	5	4	3	9	54
	Yr	1	0	15	1	26^1	2.39	2	2	3	9	54
1973	StL-N	1	0	6	0	13^1	0.68	4	4	3	13	75^1
1974	Mil-A	10	10	70	20	123	1.90	23	23	43		
1975	Mil-A	1	9	52	20	72^1	4.60	-7	-6	-12		
1976	Mil-A	0	1	15	1	18^1	7.36	-8	-8	-5		
	Bos-A	4	5	37	8	81	3.44	1	4	5		
	Yr	4	6	52	9	99^1	4.17	-7	-4	0		
1977	Bos-A	0	1	16	0	30^2	6.75	-9	-8	-2		
	Tor-A	1	1	18	2	46	3.91	1	1	1	1	6
	Yr	1	2	34	2	76^2	5.05	-8	-6	-2	1	6
1978	Tor-A	6	9	50	7	94	3.93	-2	-0	-0		
1979	Tor-A	1	2	10	0	18^1	5.40	-2	-2	-3		
Total	11	25	38	292	59	525^1	3.65	4	12	33	147	918^2

■ Dale Murray

YEAR	TM/L	WR	LR	GR	SV	IPR	ERAR	RR	/A	RNK	GS	IPS
1974	Mon-N	1	1	32	10	69^2	1.03	20	22	13		
1975	Mon-N	15	8	63	9	111^1	3.96	-4	-2	-3		
1976	Mon-N	4	9	81	13	113^1	3.26	3	6	8		
1977	Cin-N	7	2	60	4	101	4.46	-6	-6	-5	1	1
1978	Cin-N	1	1	15	2	32^2	4.13	-2	-2	-1		
	NY-N	8	5	53	5	86^1	3.65	-1	-2	-2		
	Yr	9	6	68	7	119	3.78	-3	-4	-4		
1979	NY-N	4	8	58	4	97	4.82	-12	-13	-15		
	Mon-N	1	2	9	1	13^1	2.70	2	1	3		
	Yr	5	10	67	5	110^1	4.57	-10	-11	-12		
1980	Mon-N	0	1	16	0	29^1	6.14	-8	-8	-3		
1981	Tor-A	1	0	11	0	15^1	1.17	4	5	3		
1982	Tor-A	8	7	56	11	111	3.16	11	16	23		
1983	NY-A	2	4	40	1	94^1	4.48	-4	-6	-4		
1984	NY-A	1	2	19	0	23^2	4.94	-3	-3	-3		
1985	NY-A	0	0	3	0	2	13.50	-2	-2	0		
	Tex-A	0	0	1	0	1	18.00	-2	-2	0		
	Yr	0	0	4	0	3	15.00	-4	-4	0		
Total	12	53	50	517	60	901^1	3.79	-4	5	12	1	1

■ Randy Myers

YEAR	TM/L	WR	LR	GR	SV	IPR	ERAR	RR	/A	RNK	GS	IPS
1985	NY-N	0	0	1	0	2	0.00	1	1	0		
1986	NY-N	0	0	10	0	10^2	4.22	-1	-1	0		
1987	NY-N	3	6	54	6	75	3.96	1	-2	-2		
1988	NY-N	7	3	55	26	68	1.72	13	11	25		
1989	NY-N	7	4	65	24	84^1	2.35	11	9	16		
1990	Cin-N	4	6	66	31	86^2	2.08	17	18	33		
1991	Cin-N	4	7	46	6	61^2	3.65	0	1	2	12	70^1
1992	SD-N	3	6	66	38	79^2	4.29	-7	-6	-12		
Total	8	28	32	363	131	468	3.00	35	32	61	12	70^1

■ Ray Narleski

YEAR	TM/L	WR	LR	GR	SV	IPR	ERAR	RR	/A	RNK	GS	IPS
1954	Cle-A	3	2	40	13	78^1	1.95	15	15	14	2	10^2
1955	Cle-A	8	1	59	19	102^2	3.94	0	0	1	1	9
1956	Cle-A	3	2	32	4	59^1	1.52	17	18	16		
1957	Cle-A	5	0	31	16	48	2.63	6	6	10	15	106^1
1958	Cle-A	2	1	20	1	31	2.90	3	3	2	24	152^1
1959	Det-A	2	7	32	5	53	5.94	-12	-11	-19	10	51^1
Total	6	23	13	214	58	372^1	3.17	30	30	24	52	329^2

■ Gene Nelson

YEAR	TM/L	WR	LR	GR	SV	IPR	ERAR	RR	/A	RNK	GS	IPS
1981	NY-A	0	0	1	0	3^1	2.70	0	0	0	7	36
1982	Sea-A	0	1	3	0	5^2	7.94	-2	-2	-4	19	117
1983	Sea-A	0	0	5	0	11^2	4.63	-1	-0	0	5	20^1
1984	Chi-A	2	0	11	1	21^1	2.95	2	3	3	9	53^1
1985	Chi-A	4	3	28	2	47^2	3.02	6	7	10	18	98
1986	Chi-A	6	5	53	6	108	3.75	5	7	7	1	6^2
1987	Oak-A	5	2	48	3	95	3.51	10	7	5	6	28^2
1988	Oak-A	9	5	53	3	108	2.83	14	11	14	1	3^2
1989	Oak-A	3	5	50	3	80	3.26	6	4	4		
1990	Oak-A	3	3	51	5	74^2	1.57	19	18	16		
1991	Oak-A	1	5	44	0	48^2	6.84	-15	-16	-18		
1992	Oak-A	2	1	26	0	43	7.12	-15	-16	-10	2	8^2
Total	12	35	30	373	23	647	3.67	29	21	26	68	372^1

■ Tom Niedenfuer

YEAR	TM/L	WR	LR	GR	SV	IPR	ERAR	RR	/A	RNK	GS	IPS
1981	LA-N	3	1	17	2	26	3.81	-1	-1	-2		
1982	LA-N	3	4	55	9	69^2	2.71	7	6	7		
1983	LA-N	8	3	66	11	94^2	1.90	18	18	23		
1984	LA-N	2	5	33	11	47^1	2.47	6	6	10		
1985	LA-N	7	9	64	19	106^1	2.71	10	9	16		
1986	LA-N	6	6	60	11	80	3.71	0	-2	-4		
1987	LA-N	1	0	15	1	16^1	2.76	2	2	2		
	Bal-A	3	5	45	13	52^1	4.99	-3	-3	-7		
1988	Bal-A	3	4	52	18	59	3.51	3	3	5		
1989	Sea-A	0	3	25	0	36^1	6.69	-11	-11	-8		
1990	StL-N	0	6	52	2	65	3.46	2	3	2		
Total	10	36	46	484	97	653	3.29	34	28	44		

■ Edwin Nunez

YEAR	TM/L	WR	LR	GR	SV	IPR	ERAR	RR	/A	RNK	GS	IPS
1982	Sea-A	0	0	3	0	10^2	1.69	3	3	0	5	24^2
1983	Sea-A	0	0	9	0	16^2	1.08	6	6	0	5	20^1
1984	Sea-A	2	2	37	7	67^2	3.19	6	6	5		
1985	Sea-A	7	3	70	16	90^1	3.09	11	11	16		
1986	Sea-A	0	2	13	0	16^2	7.56	-6	-6	-7	1	5
1987	Sea-A	3	4	48	12	47^1	3.80	3	5	9		
1988	Sea-A	1	1	11	0	16^2	8.64	-9	-8	-9	3	12^2
	NY-N	1	0	10	0	14	4.50	-2	-2	-1		
1989	Det-A	3	4	27	1	54	4.17	-2	-2	-3		
1990	Det-A	3	1	42	6	80^1	2.24	15	15	9		
1991	Mil-A	2	1	23	8	25^1	6.04	-5	-6	-10		
1992	Mil-A	1	1	10	0	13^2	2.63	2	2	2		
	Tex-A	0	2	39	3	45^2	5.52	-8	-9	-5		
	Yr	1	3	49	3	59^1	4.85	-6	-7	-2		
Total	11	23	21	342	53	499	3.79	13	15	7	14	62^2

■ Billy O'Dell

YEAR	TM/L	WR	LR	GR	SV	IPR	ERAR	RR	/A	RNK	GS	IPS
1954	Bal-A	0	0	5	0	7	1.29	2	2	0	2	9^{1}
1956	Bal-A	0	0	3	0	4	0.00	2	2	0	1	4
1957	Bal-A	0	1	20	4	44^{2}	2.22	8	7	3	15	95^{2}
1958	Bal-A	2	1	16	8	47^{2}	1.89	10	9	9	25	173^{2}
1959	Bal-A	2	4	14	1	30^{2}	1.76	7	7	13	24	168^{2}
1960	SF-N	1	3	19	2	35^{1}	2.55	5	4	4	24	167^{1}
1961	SF-N	3	2	32	2	54^{1}	2.82	7	6	5	14	76
1962	SF-N	1	0	4	0	1^{1}	13.50	-1	-1	-10	39	279^{1}
1963	SF-N	0	1	3	1	3^{2}	7.36	-2	-2	-5	33	218^{2}
1964	SF-N	8	3	28	2	51^{1}	3.33	1	1	3	8	33^{2}
1965	Mil-N	10	5	61	18	107^{1}	2.01	18	18	29	1	4
1966	Atl-N	2	3	24	6	41^{1}	2.40	6	6	8		
	Pit-N	2	2	35	4	61^{2}	2.92	5	4	3	2	9^{2}
	Yr	4	5	59	10	103	2.71	10	10	11	2	9^{2}
1967	Pit-N	1	1	16	0	27	5.00	-5	-5	-3	11	59^{2}
Total	13	32	26	280	48	517^{1}	2.59	62	57	59	199	1299^{2}

■ Gregg Olson

YEAR	TM/L	WR	LR	GR	SV	IPR	ERAR	RR	/A	RNK	GS	IPS
1988	Bal-A	1	1	10	0	11	3.27	1	1	1		
1989	Bal-A	5	2	64	27	85	1.69	21	20	29		
1990	Bal-A	6	5	64	37	74^{1}	2.42	12	11	28		
1991	Bal-A	4	6	72	31	73^{2}	3.18	8	6	14		
1992	Bal-A	1	5	60	36	61^{1}	2.05	13	13	28		
Total	5	17	19	270	131	305^{1}	2.36	54	51	99		

■ Jesse Orosco

YEAR	TM/L	WR	LR	GR	SV	IPR	ERAR	RR	/A	RNK	GS	IPS
1979	NY-N	1	2	16	0	26^{1}	5.13	-4	-4	-4	2	8^{2}
1981	NY-N	0	1	8	1	17^{1}	1.56	4	4	2		
1982	NY-N	4	8	52	4	99^{2}	2.17	16	16	19	2	9^{2}
1983	NY-N	13	7	62	17	110	1.47	26	26	52		
1984	NY-N	10	6	60	31	87	2.59	10	9	23		
1985	NY-N	8	6	54	17	79	2.73	8	6	13		
1986	NY-N	8	6	58	21	81	2.33	12	11	23		
1987	NY-N	3	9	58	16	77	4.44	-3	-6	-11		
1988	LA-N	3	2	55	9	53	2.72	4	4	4		
1989	Cle-A	3	4	69	3	78	2.08	16	16	15		
1990	Cle-A	5	4	55	2	64^{2}	3.90	0	0	0		
1991	Cle-A	2	0	47	0	45^{2}	3.74	2	2	1		
1992	Cle-A	3	1	59	1	39	3.23	3	3	3		
Total	13	63	56	653	122	857^{2}	2.76	93	88	141	4	18^{1}

■ Dan Osinski

YEAR	TM/L	WR	LR	GR	SV	IPR	ERAR	RR	/A	RNK	GS	IPS
1962	KC-A	0	0	4	0	4^{2}	17.36	-7	-7	0		
	LA-A	6	4	33	4	54^{1}	2.82	7	6	11		
	Yr	6	4	37	4	59	3.97	0	-1	11		
1963	LA-A	4	2	31	0	62	2.90	5	4	3	16	97^{1}
1964	LA-A	2	2	43	2	72^{1}	3.98	-3	-6	-3	4	20^{2}
1965	Mil-N	0	3	61	6	83	2.82	7	6	3		
1966	Bos-A	3	3	43	2	61^{2}	3.79	-2	0	0	1	5^{2}
1967	Bos-A	3	1	34	2	63^{2}	2.54	5	7	4		
1969	Chi-A	5	5	51	2	60^{2}	3.56	0	2	3		
1970	Hou-N	0	1	3	0	3^{2}	9.82	-2	-2	-6		
Total	8	23	21	303	18	466	3.40	9	10	16	21	123^{2}

■ Joe Page

YEAR	TM/L	WR	LR	GR	SV	IPR	ERAR	RR	/A	RNK	GS	IPS
1944	NY-A	0	0	3	0	6	4.50	-1	-1	0	16	96^{2}
1945	NY-A	2	0	11	0	37	2.19	5	5	3	9	65
1946	NY-A	2	4	14	3	31	4.06	-2	-2	-4	17	105
1947	NY-A	14	7	54	17	134	2.15	23	21	35	2	7^{1}
1948	NY-A	7	8	54	16	102	4.06	3	0	0	1	5^{2}
1949	NY-A	13	8	60	27	135^{1}	2.59	24	22	40		
1950	NY-A	3	7	37	13	55^{1}	5.04	-3	-5	-10		
1954	Pit-N	0	0	7	0	9^{2}	11.17	-8	-8	0		
Total	8	41	34	240	76	510^{1}	3.28	42	33	64	45	279^{2}

■ Jeff Parrett

YEAR	TM/L	WR	LR	GR	SV	IPR	ERAR	RR	/A	RNK	GS	IPS
1986	Mon-N	0	1	12	0	20^{1}	4.87	-3	-3	-1		
1987	Mon-N	7	6	45	6	62	4.21	-1	-0	-0		
1988	Mon-N	12	4	61	6	91^{2}	2.65	8	10	17		
1989	Phi-N	12	6	72	6	105^{2}	2.98	6	7	11		
1990	Phi-N	3	6	42	1	55^{1}	5.53	-11	-10	-16	5	26^{1}
	Atl-N	1	1	20	1	27	3.00	2	3	2		
	Yr	4	7	62	2	82^{1}	4.70	-8	-7	-13	5	26^{1}
1991	Atl-N	1	2	18	1	21^{1}	6.33	-6	-6	-8		
1992	Oak-A	9	1	66	0	98^{1}	3.02	10	8	8		
Total	7	45	27	336	21	481^{2}	3.61	6	9	12	5	26^{1}

■ Marty Pattin

YEAR	TM/L	WR	LR	GR	SV	IPR	ERAR	RR	/A	RNK	GS	IPS
1968	Cal-A	3	3	48	3	62^{1}	2.60	3	2	2	4	21^{2}
1969	Sea-A	0	0	7	0	9^{2}	12.10	-9	-9	0	27	149
1970	Mil-A	2	1	8	0	19^{2}	5.49	-4	-4	-5	29	213^{2}
1971	Mil-A										36	264^{2}
1972	Bos-A	0	1	3	0	2^{2}	10.13	-2	-2	-7	35	250^{1}
1973	Bos-A	1	0	4	1	12^{2}	1.42	3	4	3	30	206^{2}
1974	KC-A	2	2	14	0	56^{1}	2.24	9	10	6	11	61
1975	KC-A	4	4	29	5	73^{2}	2.69	9	10	11	15	103^{1}
1976	KC-A	1	8	29	5	36^{2}	4.42	-4	-4	-9	15	104^{1}
1977	KC-A	5	1	21	0	54^{1}	4.47	-2	-3	-3	10	74
1978	KC-A	2	1	27	4	48	3.19	3	3	3	5	30^{2}
1979	KC-A	2	1	24	3	51	4.76	-3	-3	-2	7	43^{1}
1980	KC-A	4	0	37	4	89	3.64	4	4	2		
Total	12	26	22	251	25	516	3.65	6	9	1	224	1522^{2}

■ Alejandro Pena

YEAR	TM/L	WR	LR	GR	SV	IPR	ERAR	RR	/A	RNK	GS	IPS
1981	LA-N	1	1	14	2	25^{1}	2.84	2	1	1		
1982	LA-N	0	2	29	0	35^{2}	4.79	-5	-5	-3		
1983	LA-N	3	1	8	1	12^{1}	1.46	3	3	9	26	164^{2}
1984	LA-N										28	199^{1}
1985	LA-N	0	1	1	0	2	18.00	-3	-3	-15	1	2^{1}
1986	LA-N	0	1	14	1	23^{1}	5.01	-3	-4	-2	10	46^{2}
1987	LA-N	2	2	30	11	51^{2}	2.26	10	10	11	7	35^{2}
1988	LA-N	6	7	60	12	94^{1}	1.91	16	15	23		
1989	LA-N	4	3	53	5	76	2.13	12	11	11		
1990	NY-N	3	3	52	5	76	3.20	5	5	4		
1991	NY-N	6	1	44	4	63	2.71	7	6	7		
	Atl-N	2	0	15	11	19^{1}	1.40	5	5	12		
	Yr	8	1	59	15	82^{1}	2.40	12	12	19		
1992	Atl-N	1	6	41	15	42	4.07	-3	-2	-4		
Total	11	28	28	361	67	521	2.85	46	42	56	72	448^{2}

■ Orlando Pena

YEAR	TM/L	WR	LR	GR	SV	IPR	ERAR	RR	/A	RNK	GS	IPS
1958	Cin-N	1	0	9	3	15	0.60	6	6	6		
1959	Cin-N	2	4	38	5	87^{2}	4.21	-3	-2	-1	8	48^{1}
1960	Cin-N	0	1	4	0	9^{1}	2.89	1	1	1		
1962	KC-A	0	0	1	0	1	0.00	0	0	0	12	88^{2}
1963	KC-A	1	0	2	0	6	1.50	1	2	2	33	211
1964	KC-A	0	0	8	0	14^{2}	7.36	-6	-6	0	32	204^{2}
1965	KC-A	0	1	7	0	10^{1}	12.19	-10	-10	-9	5	25
	Det-A	4	6	30	4	57^{1}	2.51	6	6	11		
	Yr	4	7	37	4	67^{2}	3.99	-4	-4	2	5	25
1966	Det-A	4	2	54	7	108	3.08	4	5	3		
1967	Det-A	0	1	2	0	2	13.50	-2	-2	-10		
	Cle-A	0	2	47	8	83^{1}	3.46	-2	-2	-1	1	5
	Yr	0	3	49	8	85^{1}	3.69	-4	-4	-11	1	5
1970	Pit-N	2	1	23	2	37^{2}	4.78	-3	-4	-3		
1971	Bal-A	0	1	5	0	14^{2}	3.07	1	0	0		
1973	Bal-A	1	0	9	1	31^{1}	3.73	0	-0	-0	2	13^{1}
	StL-N	4	4	42	6	62	2.18	10	10	14		
1974	StL-N	5	2	42	1	45	2.60	5	5	7		
	Cal-A	0	0	4	3	8	0.00	3	3	3		
1975	Cal-A	0	2	7	0	12^{2}	2.13	2	2	3		
Total	14	24	27	334	40	606	3.40	14	15	26	93	596

■ Ron Perranoski

YEAR	TM/L	WR	LR	GR	SV	IPR	ERAR	RR	/A	RNK	GS	IPS
1961	LA-N	7	5	52	6	87^{2}	2.46	15	18	25	1	4
1962	LA-N	6	6	70	20	107^{1}	2.85	13	9	13		
1963	LA-N	16	3	69	21	129	1.67	23	19	33		
1964	LA-N	5	7	72	14	125^{1}	3.09	6	2	2		
1965	LA-N	6	6	59	17	104^{2}	2.24	15	12	17		
1966	LA-N	6	7	55	7	82	3.18	4	1	2		
1967	LA-N	6	7	70	16	110	2.45	11	8	11		
1968	Min-A	8	7	66	6	87	3.10	-1	-0	-0		
1969	Min-A	9	10	75	31	119^{2}	2.11	20	21	41		
1970	Min-A	7	8	67	34	111	2.43	16	16	30		
1971	Min-A	1	4	36	5	42^{2}	6.75	-16	-15	-20		
	Det-A	0	1	11	2	18	2.50	2	2	2		
	Yr	1	5	47	7	60^{2}	5.49	-14	-13	-18		
1972	Det-A	0	1	17	0	18^{2}	7.71	-10	-9	-5		
	LA-N	2	0	9	0	16^{2}	2.70	1	1	1		
1973	Cal-A	0	2	8	0	11	4.09	-0	-1	-1		
Total	13	79	74	736	179	1170^{2}	2.78	100	84	152	1	4

■ Horacio Pina

YEAR	TM/L	WR	LR	GR	SV	IPR	ERAR	RR	/A	RNK	GS	IPS
1968	Cle-A	0	0	9	2	10^{2}	1.69	2	2	1	3	20^{2}
1969	Cle-A	3	1	27	1	30^{2}	4.99	-5	-4	-5	4	16
1970	Was-A	5	3	61	6	71	2.79	7	6	7		
1971	Was-A	1	1	56	2	57^{2}	3.59	-1	-2	-1		
1972	Tex-A	2	7	60	15	76	3.20	-1	-2	-2		
1973	Oak-A	6	3	47	8	88	2.76	10	8	9		
1974	Chi-N	3	4	34	4	47^{1}	3.99	-2	-1	-1		
	Cal-A	1	2	11	0	11^{2}	2.31	2	1	3		
1978	Phi-N	0	0	2	0	2^{1}	0.00	1	1	0		
Total	8	21	21	307	38	395^{1}	3.23	13	9	10	7	36^{2}

■ Dan Plesac

YEAR	TM/L	WR	LR	GR	SV	IPR	ERAR	RR	/A	RNK	GS	IPS
1986	Mil-A	10	7	51	14	91	2.97	12	14	28		
1987	Mil-A	5	6	57	23	79^{1}	2.61	16	17	33		
1988	Mil-A	1	2	50	30	52^{1}	2.41	9	9	16		
1989	Mil-A	3	4	52	33	61^{1}	2.35	10	10	23		
1990	Mil-A	3	7	66	24	69	4.43	-4	-4	-9		
1991	Mil-A	0	4	35	8	44^{1}	3.86	1	1	1	10	48
1992	Mil-A	4	3	40	1	58	2.17	11	11	12	4	21
Total	7	26	33	351	133	455^{1}	2.96	57	57	103	14	69

■ Ted Power

YEAR	TM/L	WR	LR	GR	SV	IPR	ERAR	RR	/A	RNK	GS	IPS
1981	LA-N	1	1	3	0	6	1.50	1	1	4	2	8^{1}
1982	LA-N	0	0	8	0	15^{1}	7.04	-6	-6	0	4	18^{1}
1983	Cin-N	4	3	43	2	73^{1}	4.42	-6	-5	-5	6	37^{2}
1984	Cin-N	9	7	78	11	108^{2}	2.82	9	12	18		
1985	Cin-N	8	6	64	27	80	2.70	8	10	23		
1986	Cin-N	4	5	46	1	63	4.86	-8	-7	-9	10	66
1987	Cin-N										34	204
1988	KC-A	2	2	10	0	20^{2}	5.66	-4	-4	-7	12	59^{2}
	Det-A	1	0	2	0	10^{2}	3.38	1	1	0	2	8
	Yr	3	2	12	0	31^{1}	4.88	-3	-3	-6	14	67^{2}
1989	StL-N	2	0	8	0	13	1.38	3	3	4	15	84
1990	Pit-N	1	3	40	7	51^{2}	3.66	1	-0	-0		
1991	Cin-N	5	3	68	3	87	3.62	1	2	2		
1992	Cle-A	3	3	64	6	99^{1}	2.54	15	16	11		
Total	11	40	33	434	57	628^{2}	3.49	15	22	41	85	486

YEAR	TM/L	WR	LR	GR	SV	IPR	ERAR	RR	/A	RNK	GS	IPS
■ Jack Quinn												
1909	NY-A	3	0	12	1	34^2	1.82	3	3	2	11	84
1910	NY-A	3	0	4	0	15	1.20	2	2	4	31	220^2
1911	NY-A	2	2	24	2	65^1	4.68	-10	-8	-5	16	109^1
1912	NY-A	2	0	7	0	30^1	3.86	-2	-1	-1	11	72^1
1913	Bos-N	0	0	1	0	4	0.00	1	1	0	7	52^1
1914	Bal-F	2	1	4	1	18^1	0.98	5	5	8	42	324^1
1915	Bal-F	2	2	13	1	37	3.16	-1	0	0	31	236^2
1918	Chi-A	1	0	1	0	6	0.00	2	2	3	5	45
1919	NY-A	3	1	7	0	10^1	2.61	1	1	2	31	255^2
1920	NY-A	1	0	9	3	14	1.29	4	4	4	32	239^1
1921	NY-A	3	2	20	0	52^1	3.44	5	5	4	13	66^2
1922	Bos-A	1	3	8	0	18	3.00	2	2	4	32	238
1923	Bos-A	2	2	14	7	31^1	2.87	4	4	7	28	211^2
1924	Bos-A	3	0	19	7	42^2	2.95	6	7	7	25	186
1925	Bos-A	1	2	4	0	12^1	5.84	-2	-2	-4	15	92^2
	Phi-A	0	0	4	0	8^1	3.24	1	1	0	14	91^1
	Yr	1	2	8	0	20^2	4.79	-1	-0	-4	29	184
1926	Phi-A	1	2	10	1	26	2.77	4	4	5	21	137^2
1927	Phi-A	1	2	9	1	22	3.27	2	2	3	25	179^1
1928	Phi-A	0	0	3	1	2^1	11.57	-2	-2	-2	28	209
1929	Phi-A	4	2	17	2	55^2	3.40	5	5	5	18	105^1
1930	Phi-A	8	3	28	6	67^2	3.33	10	10	17	7	22
1931	Bro-N	5	3	38	15	58^1	2.01	12	12	21	1	6
1932	Bro-N	3	7	42	8	87^1	3.30	6	5	6		
1933	Cin-N	0	1	14	1	15^2	4.02	-1	-1	-1		
Total	23	51	35	312	57	735	3.11	57	62	92	444	3185^1
■ Dan Quisenberry												
1979	KC-A	3	2	32	5	40	3.15	5	5	7		
1980	KC-A	12	7	75	33	128^1	3.09	14	14	26		
1981	KC-A	1	4	40	18	62^1	1.73	13	13	18		
1982	KC-A	9	7	72	35	136^2	2.57	23	23	37		
1983	KC-A	5	3	69	45	139	1.94	33	33	41		
1984	KC-A	6	3	72	44	129^1	2.64	19	20	28		
1985	KC-A	8	9	84	37	129	2.37	25	26	47		
1986	KC-A	3	7	62	12	81^1	2.77	13	13	19		
1987	KC-A	4	1	47	8	49	2.76	9	10	13		
1988	KC-A	0	1	20	1	25^1	3.55	1	1	1		
	StL-N	2	0	33	0	38	6.16	-11	-11	-5		
1989	StL-N	3	1	63	6	78^1	2.64	7	9	5		
1990	SF-N	0	1	5	0	6^2	13.50	-7	-7	-10		
Total	12	56	46	674	244	1043^1	2.76	144	147	227		
■ Dick Radatz												
1962	Bos-A	9	6	62	24	124^2	2.24	24	26	40		
1963	Bos-A	15	6	66	25	132^1	1.97	24	27	49		
1964	Bos-A	16	9	79	29	157	2.29	23	27	50		
1965	Bos-A	9	11	63	22	124^1	3.91	-6	-3	-5		
1966	Bos-A	0	2	16	4	19	4.74	-3	-2	-3		
	Cle-A	0	3	39	10	56^2	4.61	-7	-7	-6		
	Yr	0	5	55	14	75^2	4.64	-10	-9	-9		
1967	Cle-A	0	0	3	0	3	6.00	-1	-1	0		
	Chi-N	1	0	20	5	23^1	6.56	-8	-8	-7		
1969	Det-A	2	2	11	0	18^2	3.38	1	1	1		
	Mon-N	0	4	22	3	34^2	5.71	-8	-8	-10		
Total	7	52	43	381	122	693^2	3.13	38	52	111		
■ Pedro Ramos												
1955	Was-A	3	4	36	5	70^1	3.58	3	2	2	9	59^2
1956	Was-A	6	2	19	0	47	5.36	-6	-5	-8	18	105
1957	Was-A	4	2	13	0	35^1	3.82	-0	0	0	30	195^2
1958	Was-A	1	0	6	3	12^2	0.00	5	5	7	37	246^2
1959	Was-A	1	1	2	0	1^2	10.80	-1	-1	-14	35	232
1960	Was-A	1	0	7	2	14	1.29	4	4	4	36	260
1961	Min-A	1	2	8	2	27	2.00	6	7	8	34	237^1
1962	Cle-A	0	1	10	1	16^2	7.02	-6	-6	-4	27	184^2
1963	Cle-A	2	1	14	0	29^2	2.12	5	5	4	22	155
1964	Cle-A	3	1	17	0	31^2	4.55	-3	-3	-4	19	101^1
	NY-A	1	0	13	8	21^2	1.25	6	6	7		
	Yr	4	1	30	8	53^1	3.21	2	2	3	19	101^1
1965	NY-A	5	5	65	19	92^1	2.92	5	5	7		
1966	NY-A	3	8	51	13	85^2	3.36	1	-0	-1	1	4
1967	Phi-N	0	0	6	0	8	9.00	-5	-5	0		
1969	Pit-N	0	1	5	0	6	6.00	-2	-2	-3		
	Cin-N	4	3	38	2	66^1	5.16	-12	-10	-10		
	Yr	4	4	43	2	72^1	5.23	-13	-12	-13		
1970	Was-A	0	0	4	0	8^1	7.56	-4	-4	0		
Total	15	35	31	314	55	574^1	3.75	-3	-3	-4	268	1781^1
■ Claude Raymond												
1959	Chi-A	0	0	3	0	4	9.00	-2	-2	0		
1961	Mil-N	1	0	13	2	20^1	3.98	0	-1	-0		
1962	Mil-N	5	5	26	10	42^2	2.74	6	5	13		
1963	Mil-N	4	6	45	5	53^1	5.40	-13	-13	-25		
1964	Hou-N	5	5	38	0	79^2	2.82	6	5	6		
1965	Hou-N	3	2	26	5	46^1	3.30	1	0	0	7	50
1966	Hou-N	7	5	62	16	92	3.13	5	3	5		
1967	Hou-N	0	4	21	5	31	3.19	1	0	1		
	Atl-N	4	1	28	5	34^1	2.62	3	3	4		
	Yr	4	5	49	10	65^1	2.89	4	3	5		
1968	Atl-N	3	5	36	10	60^1	2.83	1	1	2		
1969	Atl-N	2	2	33	1	48	5.25	-9	-9	-7		
	Mon-N	1	2	15	1	22	4.09	-1	-1	-1		
	Yr	3	4	48	2	70	4.89	-10	-10	-8		
1970	Mon-N	6	7	59	23	83^1	4.43	-4	-3	-6		
1971	Mon-N	1	7	37	0	53^2	4.70	-7	-7	-9		
Total	12	42	51	442	83	671	3.74	-13	-18	-18	7	50
■ Jeff Reardon												
1979	NY-N	1	2	18	2	20^2	1.74	5	4	7		
1980	NY-N	8	7	61	6	110^1	2.61	12	12	15		
1981	NY-N	1	0	18	2	28^2	3.45	0	0	0		
	Mon-N	2	0	25	6	41^2	1.30	10	10	8		
	Yr	3	0	43	8	70^1	2.18	10	10	8		
1982	Mon-N	7	4	75	26	109	2.06	19	19	28		
1983	Mon-N	7	9	66	21	92	3.03	6	6	12		
1984	Mon-N	7	7	68	23	87	2.90	7	5	10		
1985	Mon-N	2	8	63	41	87^2	3.18	4	2	4		
1986	Mon-N	7	9	62	35	89	3.94	-2	-3	-6		
1987	Min-A	8	8	63	31	80^1	4.48	-0	1	3		
1988	Min-A	2	4	63	42	73	2.47	12	13	26		
1989	Min-A	5	4	65	31	73	4.07	-2	1	1		
1990	Bos-A	5	3	47	21	51^1	3.16	4	5	12		
1991	Bos-A	1	4	57	40	59^1	3.03	7	8	19		
1992	Bos-A	2	2	46	27	42^1	4.25	-1	-0	-1		
	Atl-N	3	0	14	3	15^2	1.15	4	5	10		
Total	14	68	71	811	357	1061	3.05	84	88	148		
■ Ron Reed												
1966	Atl-N										2	8^1
1967	Atl-N										3	21^1
1968	Atl-N	0	0	7	0	19^2	2.29	2	2	0	28	182
1969	Atl-N	0	0	3	0	2	0.00	1	1	0	33	239^1
1970	Atl-N	1	1	3	0	9	5.00	-1	-1	-1	18	125^2
1971	Atl-N										32	222^1
1972	Atl-N	0	0	1	0	4	0.00	2	2	0	30	209
1973	Atl-N	0	0	1	1	3^1	2.70	0	0	0	19	113
1974	Atl-N										28	186
1975	Atl-N										10	74^2
	StL-N										24	175^2
	Yr										34	250^1
1976	Phi-N	6	7	55	14	107	2.27	15	15	21	4	21
1977	Phi-N	7	5	57	15	111	2.51	17	18	23	3	13^1
1978	Phi-N	3	4	66	17	108^2	2.24	16	16	15		
1979	Phi-N	13	8	61	5	102	4.15	-5	-4	-7		
1980	Phi-N	7	5	55	9	91^1	4.04	-4	-3	-4		
1981	Phi-N	5	3	39	8	61^1	3.08	3	4	5		
1982	Phi-N	4	4	55	14	86^1	2.29	13	13	16	2	11^2
1983	Phi-N	9	1	61	8	95^2	3.48	2	1	1		
1984	Chi-A	0	6	51	12	73	3.08	7	9	10		
Total	14	55	44	515	103	874^1	2.97	66	74	79	236	1603^1
■ Phil Regan												
1960	Det-A	0	0	10	1	26^2	3.71	0	1	0	7	41^1
1961	Det-A	2	2	16	2	18^2	6.27	-5	-4	-10	16	101^1
1962	Det-A	1	2	12	0	16^2	4.32	-1	-0	-1	23	154^2
1963	Det-A	2	1	11	1	17^2	4.08	-1	-1	-1	27	171^1
1964	Det-A	1	0	11	1	27	4.00	-1	-1	-0	21	119^2
1965	Det-A	0	0	9	0	13	4.85	-2	-2	0	7	38^2
1966	LA-N	14	1	65	21	116^2	1.62	26	22	34		
1967	LA-N	5	7	52	6	79	2.96	4	1	2	3	17^1
1968	LA-N	2	0	5	0	7^2	3.52	-0	-1	-2		
	Chi-N	10	5	68	25	127	2.20	11	14	20		
	Yr	12	5	73	25	134^2	2.27	11	13	19		
1969	Chi-N	12	6	71	17	112	3.70	-1	4	7		
1970	Chi-N	5	9	54	12	75^2	4.76	-6	-2	-4		
1971	Chi-N	4	5	47	6	65^1	4.13	-5	-1	-2	1	8
1972	Chi-N	0	1	5	0	4	2.25	1	1	2		
	Chi-A	0	1	10	0	13^1	4.05	-1	-1	-1		
Total	13	58	40	446	92	720^1	3.29	18	28	44	105	652^1
■ Allie Reynolds												
1942	Cle-A	0	0	2	0	5	0.00	2	2	0		
1943	Cle-A	1	6	13	3	45	3.80	-3	-3	-5	21	153^2
1944	Cle-A	0	3	7	1	20^1	1.77	4	3	5	21	137^2
1945	Cle-A	2	1	14	4	25^2	4.21	-2	-3	-4	30	221^2
1946	Cle-A	0	0	3	0	1^1	0.00	1	0	0	28	182
1947	NY-A	1	1	4	2	9	3.00	1	1	1	30	232^2
1948	NY-A	0	0	8	3	15^1	0.59	6	6	3	31	221
1949	NY-A	2	0	4	1	15^1	0.00	7	7	9	31	198^1
1950	NY-A	1	3	6	2	14^2	7.36	-5	-5	-14	29	226
1951	NY-A	1	2	14	7	23^2	5.32	-3	-4	-7	26	197^1
1952	NY-A	0	0	6	6	9^1	0.00	4	3	5	29	235
1953	NY-A	7	1	26	13	51^2	2.79	7	5	10	15	93^1
1954	NY-A	3	2	18	7	39^2	2.50	5	4	6	18	117^2
Total	13	18	19	125	49	276	3.00	24	17	9	309	2216^1
■ Pete Richert												
1962	LA-N	1	1	7	0	18^1	4.42	-1	-2	-2	12	63
1963	LA-N	1	1	8	0	14^2	6.75	-6	-6	-7	12	63^1
1964	LA-N	0	0	2	0	3	9.00	-2	-2	0	6	31^2
1965	Was-A	1	0	5	0	6^1	1.42	1	1	2	29	187^2
1966	Was-A	0	0	2	0	9^1	3.86	-0	-0	0	34	236^1
1967	Was-A	0	0	1	0	0		-4	-4	0	10	54^1
	Bal-A	2	0	7	2	13	0.00	5	5	8	19	119^1
	Yr	2	0	8	2	13	1.38	1	1	8	29	173^2
1968	Bal-A	6	3	36	6	62^1	3.47	-3	-4	-6		
1969	Bal-A	7	4	44	12	57^1	2.20	9	9	19		
1970	Bal-A	7	2	50	13	54^2	1.98	11	10	20		

YEAR	TM/L	WR	LR	GR	SV	IPR	ERAR	RR	/A	RNK	GS	IPS
1971	Bal-A	3	5	35	4	36^1	3.47	-0	-0	-1		
1972	LA-N	2	3	37	6	52	2.25	7	6	7		
1973	LA-N	3	3	39	7	51	3.18	3	1	2		
1974	StL-N	0	0	13	1	11^1	2.38	2	2	0		
	Phi-N	2	1	21	0	20^1	2.21	3	4	5		
	Yr	2	1	34	1	31^2	2.27	5	5	5		
Total	13	35	23	307	51	410	2.92	24	19	48	122	755^2
■ **Steve Ridzik**												
1950	Phi-N	0	0	1	0	3	6.00	-1	-1	0		
1952	Phi-N	2	0	15	0	29^2	3.64	0	0	0	9	63
1953	Phi-N	7	1	30	0	62^1	3.03	9	8	9	12	61^2
1954	Phi-N	4	1	29	0	53^2	3.86	1	1	1	6	27
1955	Phi-N	0	0	2	0	4^1	0.00	2	2	0	1	6^2
	Cin-N	0	1	11	0	28^2	2.83	4	4	1	2	1^1
	Yr	0	1	13	0	33	2.45	6	6	1	3	8
1956	NY-N	3	1	36	0	64^1	4.20	-3	-3	-2	5	28
1957	NY-N	0	2	15	0	26^2	4.72	-3	-2	-2		
1958	Cle-A	0	2	6	0	8^2	2.08	2	2	3		
1963	Was-A	2	2	10	1	32^1	2.78	3	3	4	10	57^1
1964	Was-A	5	3	46	2	97	2.60	11	12	9	3	15
1965	Was-A	6	4	63	8	109^2	4.02	-7	-7	-7		
1966	Phi-N	0	0	2	0	2^1	7.71	-1	-1	0		
Total	12	29	17	266	11	522^2	3.48	18	19	18	48	260
■ **Dave Righetti**												
1979	NY-A										3	17^1
1981	NY-A										15	105^1
1982	NY-A	0	0	6	1	13^1	2.03	3	3	0	27	169^2
1983	NY-A										31	217
1984	NY-A	5	6	64	31	96^1	2.34	18	16	27		
1985	NY-A	12	7	74	29	107	2.78	16	15	32		
1986	NY-A	8	8	74	46	106^2	2.45	20	19	45		
1987	NY-A	8	6	60	31	95	3.51	10	9	19		
1988	NY-A	5	4	60	25	87	3.52	4	4	6		
1989	NY-A	2	6	55	25	69	3.00	7	7	12		
1990	NY-A	1	1	53	36	53	3.57	2	2	4		
1991	SF-N	2	7	61	24	71^2	3.39	2	2	3		
1992	SF-N	2	5	50	3	59^2	3.92	-3	-4	-4	4	18^2
Total	10	45	50	557	251	758^2	3.06	80	73	146	80	528
■ **Don Robinson**												
1978	Pit-N	0	0	3	1	12^1	2.92	1	1	0	32	216
1979	Pit-N	0	1	4	0	7^2	3.52	0	0	0	25	153
1980	Pit-N	0	0	5	1	10	3.60	0	0	0	24	150^1
1981	Pit-N	0	2	14	2	29	5.28	-6	-5	-4	2	9^1
1982	Pit-N	2	0	8	0	28	1.29	7	8	5	30	199
1983	Pit-N	1	0	3	0	10	0.90	3	3	3	6	26^1
1984	Pit-N	5	5	50	10	115	2.90	9	9	9	1	7
1985	Pit-N	4	7	38	3	62	3.77	-1	-1	-2	6	33^1
1986	Pit-N	3	4	50	14	69^1	3.38	3	4	5		
1987	Pit-N	6	6	42	12	65^1	3.86	2	2	4		
	SF-N	5	1	25	7	42^2	2.74	6	5	9		
	Yr	11	7	67	19	108	3.42	8	7	12		
1988	SF-N	2	1	32	6	45^1	2.78	3	2	2	19	131^1
1989	SF-N	0	1	2	0	4	2.25	1	0	1	32	193
1990	SF-N	0	0	1	0	1	27.00	-3	-3	0	25	156^2
1991	SF-N	0	1	18	1	36^2	2.45	5	5	1	16	84^2
1992	Cal-A										3	16^1
Total	14	28	29	295	57	538^1	3.19	30	30	32	221	1376^1
■ **Dob Robinson**												
1992	Phi-N										8	43^2
■ **Jeff Robinson**												
1984	SF-N	0	1	1	0	2	13.50	-2	-2	-10	33	169^2
1985	SF-N	0	0	8	0	12^1	5.11	-2	-2	0		
1986	SF-N	6	3	63	8	100^1	3.05	7	5	5	1	4
1987	SF-N	6	8	63	10	96^2	2.79	14	11	17		
	Pit-N	2	1	18	4	26^2	3.04	3	3	4		
	Yr	8	9	81	14	123^1	2.85	17	14	22		
1988	Pit-N	11	5	75	9	124^2	3.03	6	5	7		
1989	Pit-N	2	6	31	4	39^1	7.32	-17	-17	-36	19	102
1990	NY-A	1	5	50	0	62^1	3.61	2	2	2	4	26^1
1991	Cal-A	0	3	39	3	57	5.37	-8	-8	-5		
1992	Chi-N	3	2	44	1	56^2	2.54	6	7	6	5	21^1
Total	9	31	34	392	39	578	3.61	9	4	-9	70	367
■ **Ed Roebuck**												
1955	Bro-N	5	6	47	12	84	4.71	-6	-6	-9		
1956	Bro-N	5	4	43	1	89^1	3.93	-2	0	0		
1957	Bro-N	8	1	43	8	91^1	2.66	12	15	17	1	5
1958	LA-N	0	1	32	5	44	3.48	2	3	1		
1960	LA-N	8	3	58	8	116^2	2.78	13	15	15		
1961	LA-N	2	0	5	0	9	5.00	-1	-1	-1		
1962	LA-N	10	2	64	9	119^1	3.09	11	7	8		
1963	LA-N	2	4	29	0	40^1	4.24	-4	-5	-7		
	Was-A	2	1	26	4	57^1	3.30	2	3	2		
1964	Was-A	0	0	2	0	1	9.00	-1	-1	0		
	Phi-N	5	3	60	12	77^1	2.21	11	11	14		
1965	Phi-N	5	3	44	3	50^1	3.40	1	0	1		
1966	Phi-N	0	2	6	0	6	6.00	-2	-2	-5		
Total	11	52	30	459	62	786	3.34	38	41	35	1	5
■ **Eddie Rommel**												
1920	Phi-A	3	1	21	1	75^1	3.11	6	8	4	12	98^1

YEAR	TM/L	WR	LR	GR	SV	IPR	ERAR	RR	/A	RNK	GS	IPS
1921	Phi-A	4	7	14	3	47	1.72	13	14	32	32	238^1
1922	Phi-A	8	1	18	2	45	2.60	7	8	16	33	249
1923	Phi-A	3	4	25	5	62	3.05	6	7	9	31	235^2
1924	Phi-A	1	1	9	1	15^2	7.47	-6	-6	-7	34	262^1
1925	Phi-A	7	2	24	3	55	2.45	12	13	21	28	206
1926	Phi-A	2	1	11	0	26	4.15	-0	0	0	26	193
1927	Phi-A	0	1	13	1	29	9.93	-19	-18	-7	17	117^2
1928	Phi-A	8	1	32	4	97^1	2.68	15	14	13	11	76^1
1929	Phi-A	8	2	26	4	73^2	3.05	10	10	13	6	40
1930	Phi-A	5	3	26	3	84	4.71	-1	-0	-0	9	46^1
1931	Phi-A	1	0	15	0	43^2	3.71	3	4	1	10	74^1
1932	Phi-A	1	2	17	2	65^1	5.51	-7	-7	-3		
Total	13	51	26	251	29	719	3.72	40	48	91	249	1837^1
■ **Enrique Romo**												
1977	Sea-A	8	9	55	16	98^2	3.01	11	12	23	3	15^2
1978	Sea-A	11	7	56	10	107^1	3.69	1	1	2		
1979	Pit-N	10	5	84	5	129^1	2.99	11	13	14		
1980	Pit-N	5	5	74	11	123^2	3.27	4	5	5		
1981	Pit-N	1	3	33	9	41^2	4.54	-5	-4	-6		
1982	Pit-N	9	3	45	1	86^2	4.36	-7	-6	-8		
Total	6	44	32	347	52	587^1	3.49	15	21	31	3	15^2
■ **Vicente Romo**												
1968	LA-N	0	0	1	0	1	0.00	0	0	0		
	Cle-A	5	2	39	12	77^1	1.51	13	12	14	1	6
1969	Cle-A	1	1	3	0	8	2.25	1	1	3		
	Bos-A	2	7	41	11	62^1	3.90	-2	-1	-1	11	65
	Yr	3	8	44	11	70^1	3.71	-1	1	2	11	65
1970	Bos-A	6	0	38	6	59^1	2.43	8	10	11	10	48^2
1971	Chi-A	1	5	43	5	67^2	2.39	8	9	9	2	4^1
1972	Chi-A	3	0	28	1	51^2	3.31	-1	-1	-1		
1973	SD-N	2	2	48	7	82^1	3.72	-1	-2	-1	1	5^1
1974	SD-N	5	5	53	9	70^1	4.61	-8	-8	-13	1	0^2
1982	LA-N	0	1	9	1	14	1.29	4	3	3	6	21^2
Total	8	25	23	303	52	494	3.04	23	24	24	32	151^2
■ **Charlie Root**												
1923	StL-A	0	2	25	0	55^2	5.17	-7	-6	-2	2	4^1
1926	Chi-N	2	3	10	2	17	6.35	-5	-5	-14	32	254^1
1927	Chi-N	5	2	12	2	26^2	4.39	-1	-2	-4	36	282^1
1928	Chi-N	1	2	10	2	28^1	4.76	-2	-3	-3	30	208^2
1929	Chi-N	2	0	12	5	31^1	2.87	6	6	6	31	240^2
1930	Chi-N	0	1	7	3	7	6.43	-1	-1	-3	30	213^1
1931	Chi-N	2	1	8	2	19^2	3.66	0	0	1	31	231^1
1932	Chi-N	3	2	16	3	47	2.49	7	7	7	23	169^1
1933	Chi-N	1	1	5	0	8^2	5.19	-2	-2	-4	30	233^2
1934	Chi-N	3	2	25	0	77	3.16	8	6	4	9	40^2
1935	Chi-N	5	3	20	2	64	2.25	13	12	14	18	137^1
1936	Chi-N	2	5	29	1	51^1	3.33	4	4	5	4	22^1
1937	Chi-N	8	0	28	5	74	2.68	10	11	12	15	104^2
1938	Chi-N	4	1	33	8	88^1	2.45	13	14	10	11	72^1
1939	Chi-N	1	1	19	4	46^2	5.01	-6	-6	-3	16	120^2
1940	Chi-N	2	0	28	1	61^2	2.63	8	8	3	8	50^1
1941	Chi-N	1	0	4	0	13^2	1.98	3	2	2	15	93
Total	17	42	26	291	40	718	3.36	48	45	29	341	2479^1
■ **Allan Russell**												
1915	NY-A	0	0	2	0	5	0.00	2	2	0	3	22
1916	NY-A	2	0	16	6	46^1	1.55	7	7	5	18	125
1917	NY-A	4	2	15	2	39^1	0.92	8	8	12	10	65
1918	NY-A	1	3	9	4	28^1	2.86	-0	-0	-0	18	112^2
1919	NY-A	2	1	14	1	27^1	4.28	-3	-3	-4	9	63^1
	Bos-A	3	0	10	4	29	0.93	7	7	8	11	92^1
	Yr	5	1	24	5	56^1	2.56	4	3	5	20	155^2
1920	Bos-A	1	1	6	1	32^1	1.11	10	9	6	10	75^1
1921	Bos-A	4	2	26	3	52	5.71	-8	-9	-10	13	121
1922	Bos-A	3	2	23	2	70	4.50	-4	-3	-2	11	55^2
1923	Was-A	9	7	47	9	144^2	2.55	23	20	22	5	36^2
1924	Was-A	5	1	37	8	82^1	4.37	-1	-3	-3		
1925	Was-A	2	2	30	2	53^2	4.86	-3	-4	-3	2	15
Total	11	36	21	235	42	610^1	3.23	37	30	31	110	784
■ **Jack Russell**												
1926	Bos-A	0	2	31	0	67	2.82	9	9	3	5	31
1927	Bos-A	1	1	19	0	52^2	2.91	7	8	3	15	94^1
1928	Bos-A	1	0	6	0	16	3.38	1	1	1	26	185^1
1929	Bos-A	0	0	3	0	3	3.00	0	0	0	32	224^1
1930	Bos-A	0	0	5	0	13	9.00	-6	-6	0	30	216^2
1931	Bos-A	0	1	5	0	12^1	6.57	-3	-3	-2	31	219^2
1932	Bos-A	0	2	5	0	6	13.50	-6	-6	-18	6	33^2
	Cle-A	0	1	7	1	26	3.46	3	4	2	11	87
	Yr	0	3	12	1	32	5.34	-3	-2	-16	17	120^2
1933	Was-A	11	4	47	13	102	2.56	20	18	30	3	22
1934	Was-A	2	7	45	7	94^2	4.18	3	1	1	9	63
1935	Was-A	4	5	36	3	80^1	5.04	-5	-6	-7	7	45^2
1936	Was-A	1	2	13	3	21^2	5.82	-2	-3	-4	5	28
	Bos-A	0	2	21	0	33^1	4.86	1	2	1	2	6^2
	Yr	1	4	34	3	55	5.24	-1	-1	-3	7	34^2
1937	Det-A	2	5	25	4	40^1	7.59	-13	-13	-23		
1938	Chi-N	6	1	42	3	102^1	3.34	5	6	4		
1939	Chi-N	4	3	39	3	68^2	3.67	2	2	2		
1940	StL-N	3	4	26	1	54	2.50	8	9	11		
Total	15	35	40	375	38	793^1	3.98	24	23	2	182	1257^1

YEAR	TM/L	WR	LR	GR	SV	IPR	ERAR	RR	/A	RNK	GS	IPS
■ Jeff Russell												
1983	Cin-N										10	68^1
1984	Cin-N	0	0	3	0	8^1	0.00	3	3	0	30	173^1
1985	Tex-A										13	62
1986	Tex-A	5	2	37	2	82	3.40	7	8	7		
1987	Tex-A	5	3	50	3	88	4.30	2	2	2	2	9^1
1988	Tex-A	1	0	10	0	14^2	3.07	1	2	1	24	174
1989	Tex-A	6	4	71	38	72^2	1.98	15	16	39		
1990	Tex-A	1	5	27	10	25^1	4.26	-1	-1	-3		
1991	Tex-A	6	4	68	30	79^1	3.29	7	7	13		
1992	Tex-A	2	3	51	28	56^2	1.91	13	12	23		
	Oak-A	2	0	8	2	9^2	0.00	4	4	9		
	Yr	4	3	59	30	66^1	1.63	17	16	32		
Total	8	28	21	325	113	436^2	3.03	52	53	90	79	487
■ Mike Ryba												
1935	StL-N	1	0	1	0	7	1.29	2	2	3	1	9
1936	StL-N	5	1	14	0	45	5.40	-7	-7	-9		
1937	StL-N	6	3	30	0	75^2	3.45	4	4	5	8	59^1
1938	StL-N	1	1	3	0	5	5.40	-1	-1	-3		
1941	Bos-A	6	2	37	6	105^2	4.00	2	2	2	3	15^1
1942	Bos-A	3	3	18	3	44^1	3.86	-1	-1	-1		
1943	Bos-A	4	4	32	2	83	3.04	2	3	2	8	60^2
1944	Bos-A	9	5	35	2	90	3.10	3	3	4	7	48
1945	Bos-A	4	2	25	2	62	1.74	11	11	11	9	61
1946	Bos-A	0	1	9	1	12^2	3.55	-0	0	0		
Total	10	39	22	204	16	530^1	3.43	16	17	14	36	253^1
■ Johnny Sain												
1942	Bos-N	3	6	37	6	77^1	4.19	-8	-7	-9	3	19^2
1946	Bos-N	1	0	3	2	21^1	0.84	6	6	4	34	243^2
1947	Bos-N	0	0	3	1	9	2.00	2	2	0	35	257
1948	Bos-N	1	0	3	1	10^2	4.22	-0	-0	-0	39	304
1949	Bos-N	0	0	1	0	1^2	5.40	-0	-0	0	36	241^1
1950	Bos-N										37	278^1
1951	Bos-N	0	0	4	1	6^2	10.80	-5	-5	-2	22	153^2
	NY-A	0	0	3	1	14^1	1.88	4	3	0	4	22^2
1952	NY-A	3	1	19	7	44^1	1.22	12	10	12	16	104
1953	NY-A	4	1	21	9	50^2	1.24	15	14	18	19	138^1
1954	NY-A	6	6	45	22	77	3.16	5	2	5		
1955	NY-A	0	0	3	0	5^1	6.75	-2	-2	0		
	KC-A	2	5	25	1	44^2	5.44	-7	-6	-9		
	Yr	2	5	28	1	50	5.58	-9	-8	-9		
Total	10	20	19	167	51	363	3.17	22	16	19	245	1762^2
■ Slim Sallee												
1908	StL-N	1	0	13	0	45	4.40	-10	-10	-2	12	83^2
1909	StL-N	0	2	5	0	12	4.50	-3	-3	-4	27	207
1910	StL-N	1	2	5	2	12^1	2.92	0	0	0	13	102^2
1911	StL-N	1	1	6	3	11^2	3.09	0	0	1	30	233^1
1912	StL-N	4	3	16	6	48^2	2.22	6	7	10	32	245^1
1913	StL-N	2	1	19	5	45^1	2.18	5	5	4	31	230^2
1914	StL-N	2	5	16	6	41^1	2.40	2	2	3	30	241
1915	StL-N	0	2	13	3	25^2	4.56	-5	-5	-5	33	249^2
1916	StL-N	2	1	9	1	15^2	4.60	-3	-3	-6	7	54^1
	NY-N	2	0	4	0	14^2	0.61	3	3	4	11	97
	Yr	4	1	13	1	30^1	2.67	-0	-0	-3	18	151^1
1917	NY-N	2	3	10	4	29	3.72	-3	-4	-7	24	186^2
1918	NY-N	0	0	2	2	2	4.50	-0	-0	-1	16	130
1919	Cin-N	1	0	1	0	3	6.00	-1	-1	-3	28	224^2
1920	Cin-N	0	1	9	2	28^1	2.22	3	3	1	12	87^2
	NY-N	0	0	4	0	8	2.25	1	1	0	1	9
	Yr	0	1	13	2	36^1	2.23	4	3	1	13	96^2
1921	NY-N	6	4	37	2	96^1	3.64	1	0	0		
Total	14	24	25	169	36	439	3.18	-4	-6	-4	307	2382^2
■ Joe Sambito												
1976	Hou-N	1	0	16	1	27^1	3.95	-1	-2	-1	4	26
1977	Hou-N	5	4	53	7	85^2	2.31	15	12	13	1	3^1
1978	Hou-N	4	9	62	11	88	3.07	5	2	4		
1979	Hou-N	8	7	63	22	91^1	1.77	20	18	36		
1980	Hou-N	8	4	64	17	90^1	2.19	14	11	18		
1981	Hou-N	5	5	49	10	63^2	1.84	12	10	18		
1982	Hou-N	0	0	9	4	12^2	0.71	4	4	3		
1984	Hou-N	0	0	32	0	47^2	3.02	3	2	0		
1985	NY-N	0	0	8	0	10^2	12.66	-11	-11	0		
1986	Bos-A	2	0	53	12	44^2	4.84	-3	-3	-3		
1987	Bos-A	2	6	47	0	37^2	6.93	-10	-10	-19		
Total	11	35	35	456	84	599^2	3.03	47	32	68	5	29^1
■ Ken Sanders												
1964	KC-A	0	2	21	1	27	3.67	-0	0	0		
1966	Bos-A	3	6	24	2	47^1	3.80	-2	0	0		
	KC-A	3	4	37	1	61^1	3.82	-3	-3	-3	1	4
	Yr	6	10	61	3	108^2	3.81	-5	-3	-3	1	4
1968	Oak-A	0	1	7	0	10^2	3.38	-0	-1	-1		
1970	Mil-A	5	2	50	13	92^1	1.75	20	21	21		
1971	Mil-A	7	12	83	31	136^1	1.91	23	24	42		
1972	Mil-A	2	9	62	17	92^1	3.12	-1	-1	-1		
1973	Min-A	2	4	27	8	44^1	6.09	-11	-11	-17		
	Cle-A	5	1	15	5	27^1	1.65	7	7	16		
	Yr	7	5	42	13	71^2	4.40	-5	-4	-1		
1974	Cle-A	0	1	9	1	11	9.82	-8	-8	-8		
	Cal-A	0	0	9	1	9^2	2.79	1	1	0		
	Yr	0	1	18	2	20^2	6.53	-7	-7	-8		

YEAR	TM/L	WR	LR	GR	SV	IPR	ERAR	RR	/A	RNK	GS	IPS
1975	NY-N	1	1	29	5	43	2.30	6	5	4		
1976	NY-N	1	2	31	1	47	2.87	3	2	1		
	KC-A	0	0	3	0	3	0.00	1	1	0		
Total	10	29	45	407	86	652^2	2.98	37	39	55	1	4
■ Dan Schatzeder												
1977	Mon-N	0	0	3	0	4^1	8.31	-2	-2	0	3	17^1
1978	Mon-N	2	0	11	0	30^2	2.64	3	3	2	18	113
1979	Mon-N	1	1	11	1	26^2	1.69	6	6	4	21	135^1
1980	Det-A	2	0	6	0	14	1.29	4	4	6	26	178^2
1981	Det-A	2	0	3	0	12^1	1.46	3	3	5	14	59
1982	SF-N	1	1	10	0	21^1	6.33	-6	-6	-5	3	12
	Mon-N	0	1	25	0	30	2.40	4	4	1	1	6
	Yr	1	2	35	0	51^1	4.03	-2	-2	-4	4	18
1983	Mon-N	4	1	56	2	76^2	2.93	6	6	4	2	10^1
1984	Mon-N	1	2	22	1	40^2	2.43	5	4	3	14	95^1
1985	Mon-N	0	0	9	0	17	6.88	-6	-7	0	15	87^1
1986	Mon-N	3	2	29	1	55^2	2.91	5	5	4	1	3^1
	Phi-N	3	3	25	1	29^1	3.38	1	2	3		
	Yr	6	5	54	2	85	3.07	6	6	7	1	3^1
1987	Phi-N	3	1	26	0	37^2	4.06	0	1	1		
	Min-A	3	1	29	0	40^2	6.20	-8	-7	-6	1	3
1988	Cle-A	0	2	15	3	16	9.56	-10	-10	-15		
	Min-A	0	1	10	0	10^1	1.74	3	3	2		
	Yr	0	3	25	3	26^1	6.49	-7	-7	-13		
1989	Hou-N	4	1	36	1	56^2	4.45	-6	-7	-6		
1990	Hou-N	1	1	43	0	58	1.86	12	12	4	2	6
	NY-N	0	0	6	0	5^2	0.00	2	2	0		
	Yr	1	1	49	0	63^2	1.70	15	14	4	2	6
1991	KC-A	0	0	8	0	6^2	9.45	-4	-4	0		
Total	15	30	18	383	10	590^1	3.57	13	12	6	121	726^2
■ Fred Scherman												
1969	Det-A	1	0	4	0	4	6.75	-1	-1	-3		
1970	Det-A	4	4	48	1	69^2	3.23	4	4	4		
1971	Det-A	10	6	68	20	104	2.68	9	10	19	1	9
1972	Det-A	7	1	54	12	85^2	2.94	1	2	2	3	8^1
1973	Det-A	2	2	34	1	61^2	4.23	-3	-1	-1		
1974	Hou-N	2	5	53	4	61^1	4.11	-3	-4	-5		
1975	Hou-N	0	1	16	0	16^1	4.96	-2	-3	-2		
	Mon-N	4	0	27	0	37^2	3.35	1	2	2	7	38^2
	Yr	4	1	43	0	54	3.83	-1	-1	0	7	38^2
1976	Mon-N	2	2	31	1	40	4.95	-6	-5	-5		
Total	8	32	21	335	39	480^1	3.54	-1	3	12	11	56
■ Dave Schmidt												
1981	Tex-A	0	0	13	1	25	2.88	2	2	0	1	6^2
1982	Tex-A	3	1	25	6	63^1	1.99	15	13	10	8	46^1
1983	Tex-A	3	3	31	2	46^1	3.88	1	1	1		
1984	Tex-A	6	6	43	12	70^1	2.56	11	12	24		
1985	Tex-A	5	4	47	5	62^2	2.87	9	9	14	4	23
1986	Chi-A	3	5	48	8	87^2	3.08	11	12	12	1	4^2
1987	Bal-A	6	1	21	1	45^1	3.38	5	5	7	14	78^2
1988	Bal-A	3	3	32	2	75	3.96	0	-0	-0	9	54^2
1989	Bal-A	1	0	12	0	20	4.50	-1	-2	-1	26	136^2
1990	Mon-N	3	3	34	13	48	4.31	-3	-4	-6		
1991	Mon-N	0	1	4	0	4^1	10.38	-3	-3	-7		
1992	Sea-A	0	0	3	0	3^1	18.90	-6	-6	0		
Total	12	33	27	313	50	551^1	3.38	41	40	55	63	350^2
■ Mike Schooler												
1988	Sea-A	5	8	40	15	48^1	3.54	2	3	10		
1989	Sea-A	1	7	67	33	77	2.81	9	10	20		
1990	Sea-A	1	4	49	30	56	2.25	10	11	21		
1991	Sea-A	3	3	34	7	34^1	3.67	2	2	3		
1992	Sea-A	2	7	53	13	51^2	4.70	-4	-4	-9		
Total	5	12	29	243	98	267^1	3.30	19	22	46		
■ Rod Scurry												
1980	Pit-N	0	2	20	0	37^2	2.15	6	6	3		
1981	Pit-N	2	2	20	7	30^1	2.67	3	3	5	7	43^2
1982	Pit-N	4	5	76	14	103^2	1.74	21	23	25		
1983	Pit-N	4	9	61	7	68	5.56	-15	-14	-27		
1984	Pit-N	5	6	43	4	46^1	2.53	5	6	13		
1985	Pit-N	0	1	30	2	47^2	3.21	2	2	1		
	NY-A	1	0	5	1	12^2	2.84	2	2	1		
1986	NY-A	1	2	31	2	39^1	3.66	2	2	1		
1988	Sea-A	0	2	39	2	31^1	4.02	-0	0	0		
Total	8	17	29	325	39	417	3.11	27	29	22	7	43^2
■ Diego Segui												
1962	KC-A	3	2	24	6	30^1	3.56	1	2	4	13	86^1
1963	KC-A	1	0	15	0	23^2	5.32	-4	-4	-1	23	143^1
1964	KC-A	0	0	5	0	7^1	3.68	-0	0	0	35	209^2
1965	KC-A	0	2	15	0	35^2	3.28	1	1	0	25	127^1
1966	Was-A	1	0	8	0	14	5.79	-4	-4	-2	13	58
1967	KC-A	3	1	33	1	58^1	2.93	2	2	1	3	11^2
1968	Oak-A	6	5	52	6	83	2.39	5	4	5		
1969	Sea-A	8	4	58	12	93^2	3.17	5	5	7	8	48^2
1970	Oak-A	2	4	28	2	46^1	3.11	3	2	3	19	115^2
1971	Oak-A	1	0	5	0	14^2	2.45	2	1	1	21	131^2
1972	Oak-A	0	0	4	0	12	0.00	4	4	0	3	10^2
	StL-N	3	1	33	9	55^2	3.07	2	2	2		
1973	StL-N	7	6	65	17	100^1	2.78	10	10	15		
1974	Bos-A	6	8	58	10	108	4.00	-5	-2	-3		
1975	Bos-A	2	4	32	6	62	4.94	-8	-6	-6	1	9

YEAR	TM/L	WR	LR	GR	SV	IPR	ERAR	RR	/A	RNK	GS	IPS
1977	Sea-A	0	3	33	2	84	5.04	-9	-9	-3	7	26^2
Total	15	43	40	468	71	829	3.52	5	8	22	171	978^2
■ **Bobby Shantz**												
1949	Phi-A	3	4	26	2	83^1	2.59	15	14	11	7	43^2
1950	Phi-A	2	0	13	0	51^2	4.53	0	0	0	23	163
1951	Phi-A	2	1	7	0	25^2	4.91	-2	-2	-2	25	179^2
1952	Phi-A										33	279^2
1953	Phi-A										16	105^2
1954	Phi-A	0	0	1	0	3	15.00	-4	-4	0	1	5
1955	KC-A	2	0	6	0	17	2.12	3	4	4	17	108
1956	KC-A	1	6	43	9	88^2	4.47	-3	-1	-1	2	12^2
1957	NY-A	1	0	9	5	15	2.40	2	2	3	21	158
1958	NY-A	5	5	20	0	28^1	3.18	2	1	4	13	97^2
1959	NY-A	5	1	29	3	65^1	2.48	10	8	8	4	29^1
1960	NY-A	5	4	42	11	67^2	2.79	8	6	9		
1961	Pit-N	3	1	37	2	55	3.27	5	4	3	6	34^1
1962	Hou-N										3	20^2
	StL-N	5	3	28	4	57^2	2.18	11	13	19		
	Yr	8	4	28	6	78^1	3.91	16	18	22	3	20^2
1963	StL-N	6	4	55	11	79	2.62	6	8	12		
1964	StL-N	1	3	16	0	17^1	3.12	1	1	3		
	Chi-N	0	1	20	1	11^1	5.56	-3	-2	-2		
	Phi-N	1	1	14	0	32	2.25	5	4	2		
	Yr	2	5	50	1	60^2	3.12	3	3	3		
Total	13	42	34	366	48	698	3.20	57	58	72	171	1237^1
■ **Bill Sherdel**												
1918	StL-N	1	4	18	0	60^1	2.39	3	2	2	17	122
1919	StL-N	3	1	26	1	68^2	3.80	-7	-8	-4	10	68^2
1920	StL-N	8	8	36	6	132^1	2.92	3	1	1	7	37^2
1921	StL-N	4	6	30	1	91	3.26	5	4	4	8	53^1
1922	StL-N	2	1	16	2	26	3.46	2	1	1	31	216
1923	StL-N	3	2	13	2	22^1	5.24	-3	-3	-7	26	202^2
1924	StL-N	6	3	25	1	95^2	3.29	6	5	5	10	73
1925	StL-N	0	0	11	1	22	2.05	5	6	1	21	178
1926	StL-N	1	2	5	0	15^2	2.30	3	3	5	29	219
1927	StL-N	3	0	11	6	17	2.12	3	3	8	28	215^1
1928	StL-N	3	2	11	5	25	1.80	6	6	14	27	223^2
1929	StL-N	3	2	11	0	34	5.56	-3	-3	-4	22	161^2
1930	StL-N	1	0	6	0	15^2	1.15	7	7	4	7	48^1
	Bos-N	0	0	7	1	19^2	5.03	-0	-0	-0	14	99^2
	Yr	1	0	13	1	35^1	3.31	7	7	4	21	148
1931	Bos-N	1	1	11	0	23	3.91	-0	-0	-0	16	114^2
1932	Bos-N	0	0	1	0	1^2	0.00	1	1	0		
	StL-N	0	0	3	0	5^2	4.76	-1	-1	0		
	Yr	0	0	4	0	7^1	3.68	0	0	0		
Total	15	39	32	241	26	675^2	3.25	30	23	28	273	2033^2
■ **Larry Sherry**												
1958	LA-N	0	0	5	0	4^1	12.46	-4	-4	0		
1959	LA-N	2	0	14	3	36^1	0.74	13	14	10	9	58
1960	LA-N	13	8	54	7	119^2	3.46	4	7	12	3	22^2
1961	LA-N	4	3	52	15	92^2	3.40	7	10	10	1	2
1962	LA-N	7	3	58	11	90	3.20	7	4	5		
1963	LA-N	2	4	33	3	65	3.46	-1	-3	-3	3	14^2
1964	Det-A	7	5	38	11	66^1	3.66	-0	-0	-0		
1965	Det-A	3	6	39	5	78^1	3.10	3	3	4		
1966	Det-A	8	5	55	20	77^2	3.82	-3	-3	-6		
1967	Det-A	0	1	20	1	28	6.43	-10	-10	-4		
	Hou-N	1	2	29	6	40^2	4.87	-7	-7	-7		
1968	Cal-A	0	0	3	0	3	6.00	-1	-1	0		
Total	11	47	37	400	82	702	3.56	7	10	20	16	97^1
■ **Clyde Shoun**												
1935	Chi-N	0	0	4	0	5^2	4.76	-0	-1	0	1	7
1936	Chi-N	0	0	4	0	4^1	12.46	-4	-4	0		
1937	Chi-N	3	3	28	0	52	4.33	-2	-2	-2	9	41
1938	StL-N	2	2	28	1	42	3.43	2	2	2	12	75^1
1939	StL-N	3	1	51	9	94	3.45	5	7	4	2	9
1940	StL-N	3	4	35	5	56^2	4.76	-6	-5	-6	19	140^2
1941	StL-N	3	1	20	0	41	4.17	-2	-2	-2	6	29
1942	StL-N	0	0	2	0	1^2	0.00	1	1	0		
	Cin-N	1	3	34	0	72^2	2.23	9	9	4		
	Yr	1	3	36	0	74^1	2.18	9	9	4		
1943	Cin-N	13	3	40	7	117^2	2.75	8	7	10	5	29^1
1944	Cin-N	3	2	17	2	37^1	1.93	7	6	9	21	165^1
1946	Cin-N	1	3	22	0	50^1	3.40	0	-0	-0	5	28^2
1947	Cin-N	0	0	10	0	14^1	5.02	-2	-1	0		
	Bos-N	4	1	23	1	69	3.39	5	4	3	3	4^2
	Yr	4	1	33	1	83^1	3.67	4	2	3	3	4^2
1948	Bos-N	4	1	34	4	62^1	3.90	0	-0	-0	2	11^2
1949	Bos-N	0	0	1	0	1	0.00	0	0	0		
	Chi-A	1	1	16	0	23^1	5.79	-4	-4	-3		
Total	14	41	25	369	29	745^1	3.53	16	17	18	85	541^2
■ **Doug Sisk**												
1982	NY-N	0	1	8	1	8^2	1.04	2	2	3		
1983	NY-N	5	4	67	11	104^1	2.24	16	16	16		
1984	NY-N	1	3	50	15	77^2	2.09	13	12	11		
1985	NY-N	4	5	42	2	73	5.30	-14	-15	-18		
1986	NY-N	4	2	41	1	70^2	3.06	5	4	3		
1987	NY-N	3	1	55	3	78	3.46	5	3	2		
1988	Bal-A	3	3	52	0	94^1	3.72	3	2	1		
1990	Atl-N	0	0	3	0	2^1	3.86	-0	0	0		

YEAR	TM/L	WR	LR	GR	SV	IPR	ERAR	RR	/A	RNK	GS	IPS
1991	Atl-N	2	1	14	0	14^1	5.02	-2	-2	-3		
Total	9	22	20	332	33	523^1	3.27	29	23	15		
■ **Bob Smith**												
1925	Bos-N	0	1	3	0	9^2	9.31	-5	-6	-5	10	83
1926	Bos-N	2	0	10	1	29	2.79	3	2	2	23	172^1
1927	Bos-N	2	2	9	3	25^2	3.16	2	2	3	32	235
1928	Bos-N	2	2	13	2	46^1	4.08	-0	-1	-1	25	198
1929	Bos-N	0	1	5	3	6^2	2.70	1	1	3	29	224^1
1930	Bos-N	2	0	14	5	34	2.65	9	9	7	24	185^2
1931	Chi-N	0	0	7	2	15^1	2.93	2	2	0	29	225
1932	Chi-N	0	1	23	2	44^2	4.63	-4	-4	-1	11	74^1
1933	Cin-N	1	1	10	0	26	1.73	5	5	3	6	47^2
	Bos-N	2	1	10	1	32^2	2.76	2	1	1	4	26
	Yr	3	2	20	1	58^2	2.30	7	6	4	10	73^2
1934	Bos-N	4	6	34	5	83^2	4.73	-6	-8	-10	5	38
1935	Bos-N	3	3	26	5	77^2	2.32	15	13	11	20	125^2
1936	Bos-N	2	1	24	8	65^2	2.74	9	8	5	11	70^1
1937	Bos-N	0	1	18	3	44	4.09	-1	-2	-1		
Total	13	20	20	206	40	541	3.46	31	20	18	229	1705^1
■ **Dave Smith**												
1980	Hou-N	7	5	57	10	102^2	1.93	19	15	20		
1981	Hou-N	5	3	42	8	75	2.76	6	4	5		
1982	Hou-N	5	4	48	11	61^1	3.52	1	-1	-2	1	2
1983	Hou-N	3	1	42	6	72^2	3.10	4	2	2		
1984	Hou-N	5	4	53	5	77^1	2.21	12	10	11		
1985	Hou-N	9	5	64	27	79^1	2.27	12	11	25		
1986	Hou-N	4	7	54	33	56	2.73	6	5	17		
1987	Hou-N	2	3	50	24	60	1.65	16	15	25		
1988	Hou-N	4	5	51	27	57^1	2.67	5	4	10		
1989	Hou-N	3	4	52	25	58	2.64	6	5	10		
1990	Hou-N	6	6	49	23	60^1	2.39	9	9	24		
1991	Chi-N	0	6	35	17	33	6.00	-8	-8	-22		
1992	Chi-N	0	0	11	0	14^1	2.51	2	2	0		
Total	13	53	53	608	216	807^1	2.64	89	73	124	1	2
■ **Lee Smith**												
1980	Chi-N	2	0	18	0	21^2	2.91	2	2	2		
1981	Chi-N	3	5	39	1	60^2	3.56	-0	1	1	1	6
1982	Chi-N	2	1	67	17	86	1.88	16	18	13	5	31
1983	Chi-N	4	10	66	29	103^1	1.65	23	25	45		
1984	Chi-N	9	7	69	33	101	3.65	-1	3	6		
1985	Chi-N	7	4	65	33	97^2	3.04	6	10	18		
1986	Chi-N	9	9	66	31	90^1	3.09	6	10	25		
1987	Chi-N	4	10	62	36	83^2	3.12	9	11	27		
1988	Bos-A	4	5	64	29	83^2	2.80	11	12	21		
1989	Bos-A	6	1	64	25	70^2	3.57	2	4	7		
1990	Bos-A	2	1	11	4	14^1	1.88	3	3	9		
	StL-N	3	4	53	27	68^2	2.10	13	13	24		
1991	StL-N	6	3	67	47	73	2.34	11	11	29		
1992	StL-N	4	9	70	43	75	3.12	3	3	8		
Total	13	65	69	781	355	1029^2	2.80	104	126	234	6	37
■ **Elias Sosa**												
1972	SF-N	0	1	8	3	15^2	2.30	2	2	2		
1973	SF-N	10	3	70	18	103^1	2.87	9	11	17	1	3^2
1974	SF-N	9	7	68	6	101	3.48	2	4	6		
1975	StL-N	0	2	13	0	23	2.74	2	3	2	1	4^1
	Atl-N	2	2	43	2	62^1	4.48	-6	-5	-3		
	Yr	2	4	56	2	85^1	4.01	-4	-2	-1	1	4^1
1976	Atl-N	4	4	21	3	35^1	5.35	-7	-6	-14		
	LA-N	2	4	24	1	33^2	3.48	0	-0	-1		
	Yr	6	8	45	4	69	4.43	-7	-6	-14		
1977	LA-N	2	2	44	1	63^2	1.98	14	13	8		
1978	Oak-A	8	2	68	14	109	2.64	14	12	13		
1979	Mon-N	8	7	62	18	96^2	1.96	19	18	33		
1980	Mon-N	9	6	67	9	93^2	3.07	5	5	8		
1981	Mon-N	1	2	32	3	39^1	3.66	-1	-1	-1		
1982	Det-A	3	3	38	4	61	4.43	-2	-2	-3		
1983	SD-N	1	4	40	1	67^1	4.28	-5	-6	-4	1	5
Total	12	59	49	598	83	905	3.23	46	47	65	3	13
■ **Dan Spillner**												
1974	SD-N	0	0	5	0	4^2	3.86	-0	-0	0	25	143^1
1975	SD-N	0	0	12	1	25^2	2.81	2	2	0	25	141
1976	SD-N	1	1	18	0	31	5.52	-7	-8	-4	14	75^2
1977	SD-N	7	6	76	6	123	3.73	2	-3	-3		
1978	SD-N	1	0	17	0	25^2	4.56	-3	-4	-1		
	Cle-A	3	1	36	3	56^1	3.67	1	0	0		
1979	Cle-A	4	2	36	1	75^2	4.28	-1	-0	-0	13	82
1980	Cle-A	1	0	4	0	12	3.00	1	1	1	30	182^1
1981	Cle-A	3	1	27	7	62^1	2.17	10	10	8	5	35
1982	Cle-A	12	10	65	21	133^2	2.49	24	24	43		
1983	Cle-A	2	9	60	8	92^1	5.07	-10	-9	-11		
1984	Cle-A	0	0	6	1	15	4.20	-0	-0	-0	8	36
	Chi-A	1	0	22	1	48^1	4.10	-1	0	0		
	Yr	1	0	28	2	63^1	4.12	-1	0	0	8	36
1985	Chi-A	4	3	49	1	79^2	3.39	7	8	7	3	12
Total	12	39	33	433	50	785^1	3.66	26	23	40	123	707^1
■ **Gerry Staley**												
1947	StL-N	0	0	17	0	20^1	3.54	1	1	0	1	9
1948	StL-N	4	3	28	0	46^1	5.44	-8	-7	-9	3	5^2
1949	StL-N	4	2	28	6	57^2	1.25	18	19	22	17	113^2
1950	StL-N	6	1	20	3	41	5.71	-7	-6	-11	22	128^2

YEAR	TM/L	WR	LR	GR	SV	IPR	ERAR	RR	/A	RNK	GS	IPS
1951	StL-N	6	1	12	3	26^1	2.05	6	6	15	30	200^2
1952	StL-N	0	2	2	0	1	18.00	-2	-2	-29	33	238^2
1953	StL-N	0	0	8	4	8^1	4.32	-0	-0	-0	32	221^2
1954	StL-N	3	6	28	2	43	3.77	1	2	3	20	112^2
1955	Cin-N	0	1	12	0	16	5.06	-2	-1	-1	18	103^2
	NY-A	0	0	2	0	2	13.50	-2	-2	0		
1956	NY-A	0	0	1	0	0^1	0.00	0	0	0		
	Chi-A	1	1	16	0	30^1	5.93	-6	-6	-4	10	71^1
	Yr	1	1	17	0	30^2	5.87	-6	-6	-4	10	71^1
1957	Chi-A	5	1	47	7	105	2.06	20	20	13		
1958	Chi-A	4	5	50	8	85^1	3.16	6	4	5		
1959	Chi-A	8	5	67	14	116^1	2.24	21	20	25		
1960	Chi-A	13	8	64	10	115^1	2.42	19	17	32		
1961	Chi-A	0	3	16	0	18	5.00	-2	-2	-3		
	KC-A	1	1	23	2	30	3.60	1	2	1		
	Det-A	1	1	13	2	13^1	3.38	1	1	2		
	Yr	2	5	52	4	61^1	3.96	0	1	-0		
Total	15	56	41	454	61	776	3.17	66	64	61	186	1205^2

■ **Don Stanhouse**

YEAR	TM/L	WR	LR	GR	SV	IPR	ERAR	RR	/A	RNK	GS	IPS
1972	Tex-A	0	0	8	0	13	3.46	-1	-1	0	16	91^2
1973	Tex-A	0	4	16	1	22	8.59	-12	-12	-21	5	48
1974	Tex-A	1	1	18	0	31^1	4.88	-4	-5	-3		
1975	Mon-N	0	0	1	0	1^1	20.25	-2	-2	0	3	11^2
1976	Mon-N	2	0	8	1	18	1.50	4	4	5	26	166
1977	Mon-N	6	2	31	10	71^1	1.39	20	19	25	16	87
1978	Bal-A	6	9	56	24	74^2	2.89	7	5	13		
1979	Bal-A	7	3	52	21	72^2	2.85	11	9	18		
1980	LA-N	2	2	21	7	25	5.04	-4	-4	-9		
1982	Bal-A	0	1	17	0	26^2	5.40	-4	-4	-1		
Total	10	24	22	228	64	356	3.46	15	10	27	66	404^1

■ **Bob Stanley**

YEAR	TM/L	WR	LR	GR	SV	IPR	ERAR	RR	/A	RNK	GS	IPS
1977	Bos-A	3	2	28	3	69^1	3.12	7	11	8	13	81^2
1978	Bos-A	13	2	49	10	120^2	2.76	13	18	24	3	21
1979	Bos-A	3	1	10	1	20	3.60	1	2	3	30	196^2
1980	Bos-A	4	2	35	14	65^1	1.52	18	20	26	17	109^2
1981	Bos-A	10	7	34	0	91^1	3.84	-2	0	0	1	7^1
1982	Bos-A	12	7	48	14	168^1	3.10	18	23	27		
1983	Bos-A	8	10	64	33	145^1	2.85	20	24	39		
1984	Bos-A	9	10	57	22	106^2	3.54	5	7	15		
1985	Bos-A	6	6	48	10	87^2	2.87	12	14	20		
1986	Bos-A	6	5	65	16	76^1	4.24	-1	-1	-1	1	6
1987	Bos-A	0	3	14	0	25	4.68	-1	-0	-0	20	127^2
1988	Bos-A	6	4	57	5	101^2	3.19	9	10	10		
1989	Bos-A	5	2	43	4	79^1	4.88	-9	-7	-6		
Total	13	85	61	552	132	1157	3.27	93	121	166	85	550

■ **Sammy Stewart**

YEAR	TM/L	WR	LR	GR	SV	IPR	ERAR	RR	/A	RNK	GS	IPS
1978	Bal-A										2	11^1
1979	Bal-A	5	5	28	1	93^2	3.94	3	1	1	3	24
1980	Bal-A	6	5	30	3	95	3.51	6	5	5	3	23^2
1981	Bal-A	4	5	26	4	96^2	1.58	22	22	20	3	15^2
1982	Bal-A	7	4	26	5	75^2	3.09	8	8	12	12	63^1
1983	Bal-A	9	3	57	7	140^1	3.46	9	8	7	1	4
1984	Bal-A	7	4	60	13	93	3.29	7	6	8		
1985	Bal-A	5	6	55	9	127^1	3.32	12	10	9	1	2^1
1986	Bos-A	4	1	27	0	63^2	4.38	-1	-2	-1		
1987	Cle-A	4	2	25	3	27	5.67	-4	-3	-8		
Total	9	51	35	334	45	812^1	3.37	62	54	53	25	144^1

■ **Wes Stock**

YEAR	TM/L	WR	LR	GR	SV	IPR	ERAR	RR	/A	RNK	GS	IPS
1959	Bal-A	0	0	7	1	12^2	3.55	0	0	0		
1960	Bal-A	2	2	17	2	34^1	2.88	4	4	4		
1961	Bal-A	5	0	34	3	66^2	3.24	6	5	4	1	5
1962	Bal-A	3	2	53	3	65	4.43	-3	-5	-4		
1963	Bal-A	7	0	47	1	75^1	3.94	-3	-3	-3		
1964	Bal-A	2	0	14	0	20^2	3.92	-1	-1	-1		
	KC-A	6	3	50	5	93	1.94	17	19	19		
	Yr	8	3	64	5	113^2	2.30	17	19	19		
1965	KC-A	0	3	60	4	90^1	4.98	-15	-15	-6	2	9^1
1966	KC-A	2	2	35	3	44	2.66	4	4	4		
1967	KC-A	0	0	1	0	1	18.00	-2	-2	0		
Total	9	27	12	318	22	503	3.56	8	6	17	3	14^1

■ **Tim Stoddard**

YEAR	TM/L	WR	LR	GR	SV	IPR	ERAR	RR	/A	RNK	GS	IPS
1975	Chi-A	0	0	1	0	1	9.00	-1	-1	0		
1978	Bal-A	0	1	8	0	18	6.00	-4	-5	-3		
1979	Bal-A	3	1	29	3	58	1.71	16	15	11		
1980	Bal-A	5	3	64	26	86	2.51	15	14	21		
1981	Bal-A	4	2	31	7	37^1	3.86	-1	-1	-2		
1982	Bal-A	3	4	50	12	56	4.02	0	0	0		
1983	Bal-A	4	3	47	9	57^2	6.09	-13	-14	-20		
1984	Chi-N	10	6	58	7	92	3.82	-2	1	2		
1985	SD-N	1	6	44	1	60	4.65	-7	-7	-8		
1986	SD-N	1	3	30	0	45^1	3.77	-0	-1	-0		
	NY-A	4	1	24	0	49^1	3.83	2	1	1		
1987	NY-A	4	3	57	8	92^2	3.50	10	9	8		
1988	NY-A	2	2	28	3	55	6.38	-15	-15	-12		
1989	Cle-A	0	0	14	0	21^1	2.95	2	2	0		
Total	13	41	35	485	76	729^2	3.95	2	-1	-1		

■ **Bruce Sutter**

YEAR	TM/L	WR	LR	GR	SV	IPR	ERAR	RR	/A	RNK	GS	IPS
1976	Chi-N	6	3	52	10	83^1	2.70	7	11	13		
1977	Chi-N	7	3	62	31	107^1	1.34	31	36	54		
1978	Chi-N	8	10	64	27	99	3.18	4	9	21		
1979	Chi-N	6	6	62	37	101^1	2.22	17	21	40		
1980	Chi-N	5	8	60	28	102^1	2.64	11	14	25		
1981	StL-N	3	5	48	25	82^1	2.62	8	9	13		
1982	StL-N	9	8	70	36	102^1	2.90	8	8	19		
1983	StL-N	9	10	60	21	89^1	4.23	-6	-6	-15		
1984	StL-N	5	7	71	45	122^2	1.54	28	26	45		
1985	Atl-N	7	7	58	23	88^1	4.48	-9	-6	-13		
1986	Atl-N	2	0	16	3	18^2	4.34	-1	-1	-1		
1988	Atl-N	1	4	38	14	45^1	4.76	-7	-5	-9		
Total	12	68	71	661	300	1042^1	2.83	91	117	193		

■ **Ron Taylor**

YEAR	TM/L	WR	LR	GR	SV	IPR	ERAR	RR	/A	RNK	GS	IPS
1962	Cle-A	1	0	4	0	7	6.43	-2	-2	-3	4	26^1
1963	StL-N	7	3	45	11	78^1	2.30	9	11	16	9	55
1964	StL-N	8	2	61	7	90^2	4.47	-9	-7	-8	2	10^2
1965	StL-N	2	1	25	1	43^2	4.53	-5	-3	-2		
	Hou-N	1	5	31	4	52^1	5.85	-13	-14	-17	1	5^1
	Yr	3	6	56	5	96	5.25	-18	-18	-20	1	5^1
1966	Hou-N	2	3	35	0	59^2	6.03	-16	-17	-13	1	5
1967	NY-N	4	6	50	8	73	2.34	8	8	13		
1968	NY-N	1	5	58	13	76^2	2.70	2	3	3		
1969	NY-N	9	4	59	13	76	2.72	7	8	15		
1970	NY-N	5	4	57	13	66^1	3.93	1	1	1		
1971	NY-N	2	2	45	2	69	3.65	-1	-2	-1		
1972	SD-N	0	0	4	0	5	12.60	-5	-5	0		
Total	11	42	35	474	72	697^2	3.81	-25	-20	4	17	102^1

■ **Kent Tekulve**

YEAR	TM/L	WR	LR	GR	SV	IPR	ERAR	RR	/A	RNK	GS	IPS
1974	Pit-N	1	1	8	0	9	6.00	-2	-3	-5		
1975	Pit-N	1	2	34	5	56	2.25	9	8	5		
1976	Pit-N	5	3	64	9	102^2	2.45	12	12	11		
1977	Pit-N	10	1	72	7	103	3.06	10	11	12		
1978	Pit-N	8	7	91	31	135	2.33	19	21	31		
1979	Pit-N	10	8	94	31	134^1	2.75	15	17	29		
1980	Pit-N	8	12	78	21	93	3.39	2	3	6		
1981	Pit-N	5	5	45	3	65	2.49	7	8	12		
1982	Pit-N	12	8	85	20	128^2	2.87	10	12	21		
1983	Pit-N	7	5	76	18	99	1.64	22	23	34		
1984	Pit-N	3	9	72	13	88	2.66	9	9	14		
1985	Pit-N	0	0	3	0	3^1	16.20	-5	-5	0		
	Phi-N	4	10	58	14	72^1	2.99	5	6	12		
	Yr	4	10	61	14	75^2	3.57	0	1	12		
1986	Phi-N	11	5	73	4	110	2.54	14	16	22		
1987	Phi-N	6	4	90	3	105	3.09	12	13	12		
1988	Phi-N	3	7	70	4	80	3.60	-1	-0	-0		
1989	Cin-N	0	3	37	1	52	5.02	-9	-8	-5		
Total	16	94	90	1050	184	1436^1	2.85	128	142	212		

■ **Bobby Thigpen**

YEAR	TM/L	WR	LR	GR	SV	IPR	ERAR	RR	/A	RNK	GS	IPS
1986	Chi-A	2	0	20	7	35^2	1.77	10	10	10		
1987	Chi-A	7	5	51	16	89	2.73	17	18	30		
1988	Chi-A	5	8	68	34	90	3.30	7	7	14		
1989	Chi-A	2	6	61	34	79	3.76	1	0	1		
1990	Chi-A	4	6	77	57	88^2	1.83	20	20	48		
1991	Chi-A	7	5	67	30	69^2	3.49	5	4	9		
1992	Chi-A	1	3	55	22	55	4.75	-5	-6	-9		
Total	7	28	33	399	200	507	3.09	55	53	103		

■ **Dick Tidrow**

YEAR	TM/L	WR	LR	GR	SV	IPR	ERAR	RR	/A	RNK	GS	IPS
1972	Cle-A	1	0	5	0	14^2	0.61	4	4	3	34	222^2
1973	Cle-A	0	0	2	0	5	1.80	1	1	0	40	269^2
1974	Cle-A										4	19
	NY-A	2	0	8	1	33	1.64	7	7	4	25	157^2
	Yr	2	0	8	1	52	1.21	8	8	4	29	176^2
1975	NY-A	6	3	37	5	69^1	3.12	5	4	5		
1976	NY-A	3	5	45	10	76^2	2.70	7	6	8	2	15^2
1977	NY-A	6	4	42	5	104^1	3.54	6	5	5	7	46^2
1978	NY-A	0	1	6	0	30^2	3.52	1	0	0	25	154^2
1979	NY-A	2	1	14	2	22^2	7.94	-9	-10	-14		
	Chi-N	11	5	63	4	102^2	2.72	12	16	24		
1980	Chi-N	6	5	84	6	116	2.79	10	14	14		
1981	Chi-N	3	10	51	9	74^2	5.06	-13	-11	-21		
1982	Chi-N	8	3	65	6	103^2	3.39	2	4	4		
1983	Chi-A	2	4	49	7	88^2	4.26	-2	-1	-1	1	3
1984	NY-N	0	0	11	0	15^2	9.19	-10	-10	0		
Total	12	50	41	482	55	857^2	3.50	22	30	31	138	889

■ **Dave Tomlin**

YEAR	TM/L	WR	LR	GR	SV	IPR	ERAR	RR	/A	RNK	GS	IPS
1972	Cin-N	0	0	3	0	4	9.00	-2	-3	0		
1973	Cin-N	1	2	16	1	27^2	4.88	-4	-5	-5		
1974	SD-N	2	0	47	2	58	4.34	-5	-5	-2		
1975	SD-N	4	2	67	1	83	3.25	3	2	1		
1976	SD-N	0	0	48	0	71	2.28	10	8	0	1	2
1977	SD-N	4	4	76	3	101^2	3.01	10	6	5		
1978	Cin-N	9	1	57	4	62^1	5.78	-15	-15	-25		
1979	Cin-N	2	2	53	1	58^1	2.62	7	7	5		
1980	Cin-N	3	0	27	0	26	5.54	-6	-6	-6		
1982	Mon-N	0	0	1	0	2	4.50	-0	-0	0		
1983	Pit-N	0	0	5	0	4	6.75	-1	-1	0		
1985	Pit-N	0	0	1	0	1	0.00	0	0	0		
1986	Mon-N	0	0	7	0	10^1	5.23	-2	-2	0		
Total	13	25	11	408	12	509^1	3.75	-4	-13	-26	1	2

■ **Cecil Upshaw**

YEAR	TM/L	WR	LR	GR	SV	IPR	ERAR	RR	/A	RNK	GS	IPS
1966	Atl-N	0	0	1	0	3	0.00	1	1	0		
1967	Atl-N	2	3	30	8	45^1	2.58	4	4	5		

YEAR	TM/L	WR	LR	GR	SV	IPR	ERAR	RR	/A	RNK	GS	IPS
1968	Atl-N	8	7	52	13	116^2	2.47	7	7	10		
1969	Atl-N	6	4	62	27	105^1	2.91	8	8	12		
1971	Atl-N	11	6	49	17	82	3.51	-0	2	4		
1972	Atl-N	3	5	42	13	53^2	3.69	-1	1	1		
1973	Atl-N	0	1	5	0	3^2	9.82	-3	-2	-6		
	Hou-N	2	3	35	1	38^1	4.46	-3	-4	-4		
	Yr	2	4	40	1	42	4.93	-6	-6	-10		
1974	Cle-A	0	1	7	0	8	3.38	0	0	0		
	NY-A	1	5	36	6	59^2	3.02	4	3	4		
	Yr	1	6	43	6	67^2	3.06	4	3	4		
1975	Chi-A	1	1	29	1	47^1	3.23	3	3	1		
Total	9	34	36	348	86	563	3.13	19	23	27		

■ Ed Vande Berg

YEAR	TM/L	WR	LR	GR	SV	IPR	ERAR	RR	/A	RNK	GS	IPS
1982	Sea-A	9	4	78	5	76	2.37	14	16	27		
1983	Sea-A	2	4	68	5	64^1	3.36	5	6	7		
1984	Sea-A	3	1	33	7	35^1	2.29	7	7	10	17	95
1985	Sea-A	2	1	76	3	67^2	3.72	3	4	2		
1986	LA-N	1	5	60	0	71^1	3.41	2	0	0		
1987	Cle-A	1	0	55	0	72^1	5.10	-5	-5	-1		
1988	Tex-A	2	2	26	2	37	4.14	-1	-0	-0		
Total	7	20	17	396	22	424	3.52	26	28	44	17	95

■ Rube Walberg

YEAR	TM/L	WR	LR	GR	SV	IPR	ERAR	RR	/A	RNK	GS	IPS
1923	NY-N	0	0	2	0	5	1.80	1	1	0		
	Phi-A	3	1	16	0	53	3.74	1	2	1	10	62
1924	Phi-A	0	0	4	0	4^1	10.38	-3	-3	0	2	2^2
1925	Phi-A	3	4	33	7	70	2.19	17	19	22	20	121^2
1926	Phi-A	3	1	21	2	41^2	2.16	9	9	9	19	109^1
1927	Phi-A	2	2	12	4	31^1	2.30	6	7	10	34	218
1928	Phi-A	3	1	8	1	26^2	3.04	3	3	4	30	209
1929	Phi-A	1	1	7	4	19^1	3.26	2	2	3	33	248^1
1930	Phi-A	4	1	8	1	22^1	3.63	3	3	5	30	183
1931	Phi-A	1	0	9	3	13^1	0.68	5	6	7	35	277^2
1932	Phi-A	0	0	7	1	19	3.32	2	3	0	34	253
1933	Phi-A	3	3	20	4	45^2	7.69	-17	-17	-24	20	155^1
1934	Bos-A	4	2	20	1	50^1	2.50	11	13	14	10	54^1
1935	Bos-A	4	3	34	3	75	3.24	10	13	12	10	67^2
1936	Bos-A	1	2	15	0	33	5.73	-3	-2	-1	9	67^1
1937	Bos-A	2	2	21	1	33^1	7.29	-10	-9	-11	11	71^1
Total	15	34	23	237	32	543^1	3.71	39	49	52	307	2100^2

■ Ed Walsh

YEAR	TM/L	WR	LR	GR	SV	IPR	ERAR	RR	/A	RNK	GS	IPS
1904	Chi-A	2	0	10	1	43^2	2.47	1	-0	-0	8	67
1905	Chi-A	1	0	9	0	42	1.71	4	4	1	13	94^2
1906	Chi-A	1	1	10	1	37^1	3.13	-2	-2	-1	31	241
1907	Chi-A	0	1	10	4	42^2	0.84	8	7	3	46	379^2
1908	Chi-A	5	1	17	6	38^2	0.93	6	6	10	49	425^1
1909	Chi-A	0	1	3	2	3^2	2.45	0	-0	-0	28	226^2
1910	Chi-A	2	2	9	5	25^2	1.05	4	4	7	36	344
1911	Chi-A	7	5	19	4	41	2.63	3	3	8	37	327^2
1912	Chi-A	4	2	21	10	56	1.13	14	13	18	41	337
1913	Chi-A	0	0	2	1	5	1.80	1	1	0	14	92^2
1914	Chi-A	0	0	3	0	7^2	5.87	-3	-3	0	5	37
1915	Chi-A										3	27
1916	Chi-A	0	0	1	0	1	0.00	0	0	0	1	2^1
1917	Bos-N	0	0	1	0	2	4.50	-0	-0	0	3	16
Total	13	22	13	115	34	346^1	1.85	37	31	45	315	2618

■ Duane Ward

YEAR	TM/L	WR	LR	GR	SV	IPR	ERAR	RR	/A	RNK	GS	IPS
1986	Atl-N	0	1	10	0	16	7.31	-6	-6	-3		
	Tor-A	0	0	1	0	1	0.00	0	0	0	1	1
1987	Tor-A	1	0	11	0	10^2	3.38	1	1	1	1	1
1988	Tor-A	9	3	64	15	111^2	3.30	8	8	10		
1989	Tor-A	4	10	66	15	114^2	3.77	1	0	0		
1990	Tor-A	2	8	73	11	127^2	3.45	6	7	6		
1991	Tor-A	7	6	81	23	107^1	2.77	16	17	27		
1992	Tor-A	7	4	79	12	101^1	1.95	22	24	30		
Total	7	30	32	385	76	590^1	3.20	50	52	71	2	2

■ Eddie Watt

YEAR	TM/L	WR	LR	GR	SV	IPR	ERAR	RR	/A	RNK	GS	IPS
1966	Bal-A	7	2	30	4	82^1	3.50	-1	-2	-2	13	63^1
1967	Bal-A	3	5	49	8	103^2	2.26	11	10	9		
1968	Bal-A	5	5	59	11	83^1	2.27	7	6	8		
1969	Bal-A	5	2	56	16	71	1.65	16	15	21		
1970	Bal-A	7	7	53	12	55^1	3.25	3	2	7		
1971	Bal-A	3	1	35	11	39^2	1.82	7	7	10		
1972	Bal-A	2	3	38	7	45^2	2.17	5	5	6		
1973	Bal-A	3	4	30	5	71	3.30	4	3	4		
1974	Phi-N	1	1	42	6	38^1	3.99	-2	-1	-1		
1975	Chi-N	0	1	6	0	6	13.50	-7	-6	-10		
Total	10	36	31	398	80	596^1	2.76	43	40	53	13	63^1

■ Hal White

YEAR	TM/L	WR	LR	GR	SV	IPR	ERAR	RR	/A	RNK	GS	IPS
1941	Det-A	0	0	4	0	9	6.00	-2	-1	0		
1942	Det-A	1	3	9	1	25^1	2.13	4	5	8	25	191^1
1943	Det-A	0	2	8	2	21	4.29	-2	-2	-2	24	156^2
1946	Det-A	0	1	10	0	18^1	7.36	-8	-8	-4	1	9
1947	Det-A	4	2	30	2	56^2	3.02	4	5	5	5	28
1948	Det-A	2	1	27	1	42^2	6.12	-9	-8	-6		
1949	Det-A	1	0	9	2	12	0.00	6	6	6		
1950	Det-A	6	3	34	1	66^2	3.92	5	6	7	8	44^1
1951	Det-A	2	1	34	4	57	4.58	-3	-3	-2	4	19
1952	Det-A	1	8	41	5	63^1	3.69	-0	1	1		
1953	StL-A	0	0	10	0	10^1	2.61	2	2	0		
	StL-N	6	5	49	7	84^2	2.98	12	12	16		
1954	StL-N	0	0	4	0	5	19.80	-9	-9	0		
Total	12	23	26	269	25	472	4.02	1	5	31	67	448^1

■ Hoyt Wilhelm

YEAR	TM/L	WR	LR	GR	SV	IPR	ERAR	RR	/A	RNK	GS	IPS
1952	NY-N	15	3	71	11	159^1	2.43	23	23	26		
1953	NY-N	7	8	68	15	145	3.04	20	20	23		
1954	NY-N	12	4	57	7	111^1	2.10	24	24	34		
1955	NY-N	4	1	59	0	103	3.93	1	1	0		
1956	NY-N	4	9	64	8	89^1	3.83	-1	-0	-1		
1957	StL-N	1	4	40	11	55	4.25	-2	-2	-2		
	Cle-A	1	0	2	1	3^2	2.45	1	1	2		
1958	Cle-A	2	4	24	5	49^1	1.64	12	11	15	6	41
	Bal-A	0	1	5	0	6^2	2.70	1	1	1	4	34
	Yr	2	5	29	5	56	1.77	12	12	15	10	75
1959	Bal-A	0	2	5	0	15^1	2.35	3	2	3	27	210^2
1960	Bal-A	8	4	30	7	75^1	2.51	11	11	18	11	71^2
1961	Bal-A	9	7	50	18	106^2	2.11	23	21	37	1	3
1962	Bal-A	7	10	52	15	93	1.94	21	19	38		
1963	Chi-A	5	7	52	21	113^1	2.86	10	8	11	3	23
1964	Chi-A	12	9	73	27	131^1	1.99	24	21	41		
1965	Chi-A	7	7	66	20	144	1.81	26	22	26		
1966	Chi-A	5	2	46	6	81^1	1.66	16	14	13		
1967	Chi-A	8	3	49	12	89	1.31	19	18	25		
1968	Chi-A	4	4	72	12	93^2	1.73	13	13	14		
1969	Cal-A	5	7	44	10	65^2	2.47	8	7	15		
	Atl-N	2	0	8	4	12^1	0.73	4	4	9		
1970	Atl-N	6	4	50	13	78^1	3.10	8	10	16		
	Chi-N	0	1	3	0	3^2	9.82	-2	-2	-5		
	Yr	6	5	53	13	82	3.40	6	8	10		
1971	Atl-N	0	0	3	0	2^1	15.43	-3	-3	0		
	LA-N	0	1	9	3	17^2	1.02	5	4	4		
	Yr	0	1	12	3	20	2.70	2	1	4		
1972	LA-N	0	1	16	1	25^1	4.62	-3	-4	-2		
Total	21	124	103	1018	227	1871	2.49	261	245	360	52	383^1

■ Ted Wilks

YEAR	TM/L	WR	LR	GR	SV	IPR	ERAR	RR	/A	RNK	GS	IPS
1944	StL-N	2	1	15	0	31^1	2.30	5	4	4	21	176^1
1945	StL-N	0	0	2	0	5	0.00	2	2	0	16	93^1
1946	StL-N	6	0	36	1	77	2.45	8	9	6	4	18
1947	StL-N	4	0	37	5	50^1	5.01	-5	-5	-5		
1948	StL-N	5	6	55	13	117	2.38	20	22	24	2	13^2
1949	StL-N	10	3	59	9	118^1	3.73	4	6	7		
1950	StL-N	2	0	18	0	24^1	6.66	-7	-6	-5		
1951	StL-N	0	0	17	1	18	3.00	2	2	0		
	Pit-N	2	5	47	12	75^2	2.85	9	12	14	1	7
	Yr	2	5	64	13	93^2	2.88	11	13	14	1	7
1952	Pit-N	5	5	44	4	72^1	3.61	1	3	4		
	Cle-A	0	0	7	1	11^2	3.86	-0	-1	-0		
1953	Cle-A	0	0	4	0	3^2	7.36	-1	-1	0		
Total	10	36	20	341	46	604^2	3.30	38	46	50	44	308^1

■ Frank Williams

YEAR	TM/L	WR	LR	GR	SV	IPR	ERAR	RR	/A	RNK	GS	IPS
1984	SF-N	8	4	60	3	101^1	3.73	-2	-2	-3	1	5
1985	SF-N	2	4	49	0	73	4.19	-5	-6	-5		
1986	SF-N	3	1	36	1	52^1	1.20	15	13	10		
1987	Cin-N	4	0	85	2	105^2	2.30	21	23	9		
1988	Cin-N	3	2	60	1	62^2	2.59	6	7	5		
1989	Det-A	3	3	42	1	71^2	3.64	2	1	1		
Total	6	23	14	332	8	466^2	3.03	37	36	18	1	5

■ Mitch Williams

YEAR	TM/L	WR	LR	GR	SV	IPR	ERAR	RR	/A	RNK	GS	IPS
1986	Tex-A	8	6	80	8	98	3.58	6	8	12		
1987	Tex-A	8	5	84	6	104^2	3.10	16	16	20	1	4
1988	Tex-A	2	7	67	18	68	4.63	-5	-4	-7		
1989	Chi-N	4	4	76	36	81^2	2.76	7	9	17		
1990	Chi-N	1	7	57	16	60	3.30	3	5	9	2	6^1
1991	Phi-N	12	5	69	30	88^1	2.34	13	13	32		
1992	Phi-N	5	8	66	29	81	3.78	-2	-3	-6		
Total	7	40	42	499	143	581^2	3.31	38	44	77	3	10^1

■ Stan Williams

YEAR	TM/L	WR	LR	GR	SV	IPR	ERAR	RR	/A	RNK	GS	IPS
1958	LA-N	1	1	6	0	12	8.25	-6	-6	-8	21	107
1959	LA-N	2	2	20	0	43^2	2.27	8	10	8	15	81
1960	LA-N	0	0	8	1	14^1	5.65	-3	-3	-0	30	193
1961	LA-N	1	0	6	0	11^1	2.38	2	2	2	35	224
1962	LA-N	1	1	12	1	25	7.20	-9	-10	-8	28	160^2
1963	NY-A	2	2	8	0	15^1	1.76	3	3	7	21	130^2
1964	NY-A	1	1	11	0	27^1	2.63	3	3	2	10	54^2
1965	Cle-A	0	0	3	0	4^1	6.23	-1	-1	0		
1967	Cle-A	3	0	8	1	22	2.05	3	3	4	8	57
1968	Cle-A	2	0	20	9	29	2.48	2	2	2	24	165^1
1969	Cle-A	2	9	46	12	82^1	3.72	-1	0	1	15	96
1970	Min-A	10	1	68	15	113^1	1.99	22	22	26		
1971	Min-A	4	5	45	4	74	4.01	-5	-4	-5	1	4
	StL-N	3	0	10	0	12^2	1.42	3	3	7		
1972	Bos-A	0	0	3	0	4	6.75	-2	-2	0		
Total	14	32	22	274	43	490^2	3.26	19	23	36	208	1273^1

■ Hooks Wiltse

YEAR	TM/L	WR	LR	GR	SV	IPR	ERAR	RR	/A	RNK	GS	IPS
1904	NY-N	0	0	8	3	32^2	3.31	-2	-2	-0	16	132
1905	NY-N	2	0	13	4	34	3.71	-3	-3	-2	19	163
1906	NY-N	4	0	12	6	37^1	1.45	5	5	6	26	212
1907	NY-N	2	2	12	2	29	3.10	-2	-2	-3	21	161^1
1908	NY-N	0	2	6	2	10^1	4.35	-2	-2	-5	38	319^2
1909	NY-N	1	2	7	3	22^2	1.59	3	2	4	30	246^2
1910	NY-N	2	1	6	2	19	1.42	3	3	5	30	216^1

YEAR	TM/L	WR	LR	GR	SV	IPR	ERAR	RR	/A	RNK	GS	IPS
1911	NY-N	2	2	6	0	18²	3.38	0	-0	-0	24	168²
1912	NY-N	2	1	11	3	31¹	3.16	1	1	1	17	102²
1913	NY-N	0	0	15	3	48	1.31	10	10	1	2	9²
1914	NY-N	1	1	20	1	38	2.84	-0	-1	-0		
1915	Bro-F	3	2	15	5	32²	2.48	2	2	3	3	26²
Total	12	19	13	131	34	353²	2.54	15	13	10	226	1758²

■ Wilbur Wood

YEAR	TM/L	WR	LR	GR	SV	IPR	ERAR	RR	/A	RNK	GS	IPS
1961	Bos-A	0	0	5	0	10	4.50	-1	-0	0	1	3
1962	Bos-A										1	7²
1963	Bos-A	0	1	19	0	38	2.37	5	6	1	6	26²
1964	Bos-A	0	0	4	0	5²	17.47	-9	-9	0		
	Pit-N	0	0	1	0	3¹	0.00	1	1	0	2	14
1965	Pit-N	1	0	33	0	47¹	2.85	4	3	1	1	4
1967	Chi-A	0	0	43	4	53¹	1.86	8	7	1	8	42
1968	Chi-A	12	11	86	16	145	1.92	17	18	30	2	14
1969	Chi-A	10	11	76	15	119²	3.01	8	11	21		
1970	Chi-A	9	13	77	21	121²	2.81	12	15	30		
1971	Chi-A	0	0	2	1	2	0.00	1	1	1	42	332
1972	Chi-A										49	376²
1973	Chi-A	1	0	1	0	5	0.00	2	2	4	48	354¹
1974	Chi-A										42	320¹
1975	Chi-A										43	291¹
1976	Chi-A										7	56¹
1977	Chi-A	0	0	6	0	13	6.23	-3	-3	0	18	109²
1978	Chi-A	0	1	1	0	2	0.00	1	1	0	27	166
Total	12	33	36	354	57	566	2.70	47	54	89	297	2118

■ Hal Woodeshick

YEAR	TM/L	WR	LR	GR	SV	IPR	ERAR	RR	/A	RNK	GS	IPS
1956	Det-A										2	5¹
1958	Cle-A	3	0	5	0	7²	0.00	3	3	11	9	64
1959	Was-A	2	1	28	0	53	3.06	5	5	3	3	8
1960	Was-A	2	1	27	4	41²	5.18	-6	-6	-5	14	73¹
1961	Was-A	0	0	1	0	5²	1.59	2	2	0	6	34²
	Det-A	1	0	10	0	13²	6.59	-4	-4	-2	2	4²
	Yr	1	0	11	0	19¹	5.12	-2	-2	-2	8	39¹
1962	Hou-N	0	1	5	0	7²	4.70	-1	-1	-1	26	131²
1963	Hou-N	11	9	55	10	114	1.97	17	15	27		
1964	Hou-N	2	9	61	23	78¹	2.76	7	6	11		
1965	Hou-N	3	4	27	3	32¹	3.06	2	1	2		
	StL-N	3	2	51	15	59²	1.81	11	13	18		
	Yr	6	6	78	18	92	2.25	13	15	20		
1966	StL-N	2	1	59	4	70¹	1.92	13	13	7		
1967	StL-N	2	1	36	2	41²	5.18	-8	-9	-7		
Total	10	31	29	365	61	525²	2.88	40	39	63	62	321²

■ Todd Worrell

YEAR	TM/L	WR	LR	GR	SV	IPR	ERAR	RR	/A	RNK	GS	IPS
1985	StL-N	3	0	17	5	21²	2.91	2	2	3		
1986	StL-N	9	10	74	36	103²	2.08	19	19	44		
1987	StL-N	8	6	75	33	94²	2.66	15	16	33		
1988	StL-N	5	9	68	32	90	3.00	4	5	10		
1989	StL-N	3	5	47	20	51²	2.96	3	4	9		
1992	StL-N	5	3	67	3	64	2.11	10	9	12		
Total	6	33	33	348	129	425²	2.56	53	53	110		

■ Al Worthington

YEAR	TM/L	WR	LR	GR	SV	IPR	ERAR	RR	/A	RNK	GS	IPS
1953	NY-N	0	1	3	0	5	5.40	-1	-1	-1	17	97
1954	NY-N	0	0	9	0	14	2.57	2	2	0	1	4
1956	NY-N	0	1	4	0	7	7.71	-3	-3	-4	24	158²
1957	NY-N	7	5	43	4	94¹	3.15	8	8	10	12	63¹
1958	SF-N	3	4	42	6	82¹	3.61	3	2	2	12	69
1959	SF-N	1	2	39	2	56²	3.97	-0	-1	-1	3	16²
1960	Bos-A	0	1	6	0	11²	7.71	-5	-5	-4		
	Chi-A	1	1	4	0	5¹	3.38	0	0	1		
	Yr	1	2	10	0	17	6.35	-5	-5	-3		
1963	Cin-N	4	4	50	10	81¹	2.99	3	3	4		
1964	Cin-N	1	0	6	0	7	10.29	-5	-5	-7		
	Min-A	5	6	41	14	72¹	1.37	18	18	32		
1965	Min-A	10	7	62	21	80¹	2.13	12	13	32		
1966	Min-A	6	3	65	16	91¹	2.46	10	11	15		
1967	Min-A	8	9	59	16	92	2.84	4	6	13		
1968	Min-A	4	5	54	18	76¹	2.71	2	3	5		
1969	Min-A	4	1	46	3	61	4.57	-6	-6	-5		
Total	14	54	50	533	110	838	3.10	42	47	92	69	408²

■ John Wyatt

YEAR	TM/L	WR	LR	GR	SV	IPR	ERAR	RR	/A	RNK	GS	IPS
1961	KC-A	0	0	5	1	7¹	2.45	1	1	0		
1962	KC-A	7	4	50	11	81	3.89	1	2	4	9	44
1963	KC-A	6	4	63	21	92	3.13	5	7	11		
1964	KC-A	9	8	81	20	128	3.59	1	3	5		
1965	KC-A	2	6	65	18	88²	3.25	2	2	3		
1966	KC-A	0	3	19	2	23²	5.32	-5	-5	-7		
	Bos-A	3	4	42	8	71²	3.14	2	5	6		
	Yr	3	7	61	10	95¹	3.68	-3	0	-1		
1967	Bos-A	10	7	60	20	93¹	2.60	7	9	19		
1968	Bos-A	1	2	8	0	10²	4.22	-1	-1	-3		
	NY-A	0	2	7	0	8¹	2.16	1	1	1		
	Det-A	1	0	22	2	30¹	2.37	2	2	1		
	Yr	2	4	37	2	49¹	2.74	1	2	-1		
1969	Oak-A	0	1	4	0	8¹	5.40	-2	-2	-2		
Total	9	39	41	426	103	643¹	3.33	13	26	39	9	44

The Annual Record

T his section contains the season-by-season stand- ings and records for all teams since 1871, plus 28 statistical categories for each team's batting and baserunning, and 26 categories for its pitch- ing and fielding. In those years in which major league play consisted of more than one league, the statis- tics are presented in the order of the leagues' founding: that is, the National Association comes first; the National League record precedes those of all its rivals; the Ameri- can Association precedes the Union Association and Players League; and the American League follows the National League but precedes the Federal League.

The figure for the leading team in a given category is displayed in boldface. Where data are unavailable, the statistical column is blank. In the case of the National Association, much of the data that had been missing from the records for the five years of its existence, 1871–1875, are at last available. A research project of the Society for American Baseball Research to reconstruct all data from this period, based on original box scores and play-by-plays collected over decades by Michael Stagno of New York, is still in progress, though. It is hoped that additional, au- thoritative records can be developed for the next edition of *Total Baseball*.

Also presented here are the top three to five players/ pitchers in up to 48 categories per season. When fewer than 48 categories are shown, it means that official records are lacking; that data is not reconstructible at present, which is the case for records of stolen bases before 1886 (with the single exception, to date, being 1871); or that available data is not meaningful, such as for Relief Runs or Relief Ranking in the early years of this century. When fewer than five individuals appear in a given category, credible standouts are lacking, as in the case of Stolen Base Wins in most years. The criterion used for identifying pitching leaders is a minimum of one in- ning pitched per scheduled game; for batters the criterion employed is the one officially in place at the time or, in the absence of any known practice, 3.1 plate appearances per scheduled game.

Ties in counting stats are common, and occasionally they are so numerous that space does not permit listing all the players by name; ties for fifth place are not shown. Highly uncommon are ties in stats based on a large array of data, as with batting averages, on base percentages, earned run averages, and sabermetric stats such as Runs Created, Total Average, or the various Linear Weights measures. Where rounding off has created the appear- ance of a tie, the true leader—as extra decimal places for a complete calculation would have revealed—is listed first. An example is the AL batting race of 1949, in which

George Kell and Ted Williams are both shown as hitting .343; Kell in fact hit .3429 and Williams .3428. Both men are credited with batting averages of .343, but Kell, the actual leader, is listed first. (This procedure does not hold for calculated stats based on pitchers' won-lost percent- ages, where the narrow array of data frequently produces actual ties.)

For additional useful information about a team in a given year, we refer the reader to the preceding registers, the various rosters, and the Appendixes. Team abbrevia- tions used in the Annual Record are to be found on the last page of this book.

The abbreviations employed in the team statistical re- views of the Annual Record, plus brief descriptions of what the less common statistics measure, follow. For fuller explanations, see the general introduction to Part Two, and for more technical information about formulas and computation, see the Glossary. Also included below are descriptions of statistics computed for league-leading players shown in the Annual Record.

Batting and Baserunning

G	Games played
W	Wins
L	Losses
PCT	Percentage of games won
GB	Games Behind the league or division leader
R	Runs scored
OR	Opponents' Runs scored
AB	At-Bats
H	Hits
2B	Doubles
3B	Triples
HR	Home Runs
BB	Bases on Balls
SO	Strikeouts
AVG	Batting Average
OBP	On Base Percentage
SLG	Slugging Average
PRO	Production (On Base Percentage plus Slug- ging Average)

PRO⁺   Normalized and park-adjusted Production. A figure of 100 is a league-average performance.

BR   Batting Runs (Linear Weights measure of runs contributed *beyond* what a league-average batter or team might have contributed, defined as zero.)

/A   Adjusted (Signifies that the stat to the immediate left, in this instance Batting Runs, is here normalized to league average and adjusted for home-park factor. A mark of 100 is a league-average performance. Pitcher batting is removed from all league batting statistics before normalization for a variety of reasons expanded upon in the Glossary.)

PF   Park Factor (Calculated separately for batters and pitchers: above 100 signifies a park favorable to hitters, below 100 signifies a park favorable to pitchers; see Glossary for further data and technical information.)

CHI   Clutch Hitting Index (Calculated for individuals, actual RBIs over expected RBIs, adjusted for league average and position in batting order; calculated for teams, actual runs scored divided by Batting Runs. Marks above the median of 100 are superior. See Glossary for precise formula.)

RC   Runs Created (Bill James's formulation for run contribution from a variety of batting and baserunning events; many different formulas are applied, depending on data available; see Glossary.)

SB   Stolen Bases (1886 to the present.)

CS   Caught Stealing (Available 1915, 1916 for players with more than 20 steals, 1920–1925, 1951–1990 NL; 1914–1915, 1916 for players with more than 20 steals, 1920–1990 AL.)

SBA   Stolen Base Average (Stolen bases divided by attempts; availability dependent upon CS, as shown above.)

SBR   Stolen Base Runs (Linear Weights measure of runs contributed *beyond* what a league-average base stealer or team might have gained, defined as zero; individual SBRs are calculated on the basis of a 66.7 percent success rate, the rate necessary to produce benefit, while team SBRs are normalized to the success rate for the league in that season; availability dependent upon CS.)

Pitching and Fielding

CG   Complete Games

SH   Shutouts (Individual and combined when calculated for teams; individual only for top five leaders.)

SV   Saves (Employing definition in force at the time, and 1969 definition for years prior to 1969.)

IP   Innings Pitched (Fractional innings given for teams; rounded-off whole innings for individuals.)

H   Hits allowed

H/G   Hits allowed per Game (Game defined as nine innings.)

HR   Home Runs allowed

BB   Bases on Balls allowed

SO   Strikeouts

RAT   Hits allowed plus walks allowed per nine innings.

ERA   Earned Run Average

ERA⁺   Normalized and park-adjusted ERA. A mark of 100 is a league-average performance, while marks over 100 are superior to league average and those below 100 indicate poor pitching performance.

OAV   Opponents' Batting Average

OOB   Opponents' On Base Percentage

PR   Pitching Runs (Linear Weights measure of runs saved *beyond* what a league-average pitcher or team might have saved, defined as zero.)

/A   Adjusted (Signifies that the stat to the immediate left, in this instance Pitching Runs, is here normalized to league average and adjusted for home-park factor.)

PF   Park Factor (Calculated separately for batters and pitchers; above 100 signifies a park favorable to hitters, below 100 signifies a park favorable to pitchers; see Glossary for further data and technical information.)

CPI   Clutch Pitching Index (Expected runs over actual runs, with 100 being a league-average performance and marks above 100 indicating better than expected results. See Glossary.)

FA   Fielding Average

E   Errors

DP   Double Plays

FW   Fielding Wins (Fielding Runs divided by the number of runs required to create an additional win beyond average; average is defined as a team record of .500 because a league won-lost average must be .500. For more technical data about Runs Per Win and Fielding Run formulas, see Glossary.)

PW   Pitching Wins (Adjusted Pitching Runs divided by the number of runs required to create an additional win beyond average; average is defined as a team record of .500 because a league won-lost average must be .500. For more technical data about Runs Per Win and Pitching Run formulas, see Glossary.)

BW   Batting Wins (Adjusted Batting Runs divided by the number of runs required to create an additional win beyond average; average is defined as a team record of .500 because a league won-lost average must be .500. For more technical data about Runs Per Win and Batting Run formulas, see Glossary.)

SBW   Stolen Base Wins (Stolen Base Runs divided by the number of runs required to create an additional win beyond average; average is defined as a team record of .500 because a league won-lost average must be .500. For more technical data about Runs Per Win and Stolen Base Run formulas, see Glossary.)

DIF   Differential (Difference between the team's actual won-lost record and that predicted by the total of its Pitching Wins, Batting Wins, Fielding Wins, and Stolen Base Wins; indicates the extent to which a team outperformed or underperformed its talent.)

Other stats carried only on an individual basis in the Annual Record portion of *Total Baseball* are as follows:

Total Average   Tom Boswell's formulation for offensive contribution from a variety of batting and baserunning events; calculated to make use of the maximum available data.

Fielding Runs   The Linear Weights measure of runs saved *beyond* what a league-average player at that position might have saved, defined as zero; calculated to take into account the particular demands of the different positions. See Glossary for formulas.

Total Player Rating   The sum of a player's Adjusted Batting Runs, Fielding Runs, and Base Stealing Runs, minus his positional adjustment, all divided by the Runs Per Win factor for that year (generally around 10, historically in the 9–11 range).

Bases on Balls Per Game   Game defined as nine innings; league leaders calculated on the basis of fewest walks per nine innings.

Strikeouts Per Game   Game defined as nine innings; league leaders calculated on the basis of most strikeouts per nine innings.

Starter Runs   Identical to Pitching Runs but confined to starting pitchers, defined as pitchers who average more than three innings per appearance.

Relief Runs   Identical to Pitching Runs but confined to relief pitchers.

Relief Ranking   Adjusted Relief Runs, weighted for the greater value of a bullpen "closer" who limits his opponents' scoring in the late innings; see Glossary for formula. Relief Runs will tend to benefit long and middle relievers, who are effective over many innings, while Relief Ranking will tend to benefit relievers with perhaps fewer innings but more saves and decisions.

Total Pitcher Index   The sum of a pitcher's Pitching Runs, Batting Runs (in the AL since 1973, zero), and Fielding Runs, all divided by the Runs Per Win factor for that year (generally around 10, historically in the 9–11 range).

Total Baseball Ranking   The "MVP" of statistics, this ranks pitchers and position players by the total runs contributed in all their endeavors, revealing the most valuable performers in a given year. For rare individuals like Babe Ruth in his Red Sox years, or Bob Caruthers, both of whom played a position in the field when they were not pitching, the TPR will sum up their records in both endeavors.

How to Read a Team Line

TEAM	G	W	L	PCT	GB	R	OR	AB	H	2B	3B	HR	BB	SO	AVG	OBP	SLG	PRO	PRO+	BR	/A	PF	CHI	RC	SB	CS	SBA	SBR
EAST																												
NY	160	100	60	.625		703	532	5408	1387	251	24	152	544	842	.256	.328	.396	.724	120	95	126	95	97	717	140	51	73	11
PIT	160	85	75	.531	15	651	616	5379	1327	240	45	110	553	947	.247	.321	.369	.690	105	33	42	99	99	648	119	60	66	0
MON	163	81	81	.500	20	628	592	5573	1400	260	48	107	454	1053	.251	.311	.373	.684	98	12	-17	99	97	636	189	89	68	3
CHI	163	77	85	.475	24	660	694	5675	1481	262	46	113	403	910	.261	.312	.383	.695	100	31	2	105	99	673	120	46	72	8
STL	162	76	86	.469	25	578	633	5518	1373	207	33	71	484	827	.249	.312	.337	.649	92	-47	-53	101	98	601	234	64	79	32
PHI	162	65	96	.404	35.5	597	734	5403	1294	246	31	106	489	981	.239	.308	.355	.663	94	-22	-35	102	100	599	112	49	70	4
WEST																												
LA	162	94	67	.584		628	544	5431	1346	217	25	99	437	947	.248	.308	.352	.660	99	-32	-13	97	107	590	131	46	74	12
CIN	161	87	74	.540	7	641	596	5426	1334	246	25	122	479	922	.246	.311	.368	.679	97	6	-19	104	102	639	207	56	79	29
SD	161	83	78	.516	11	594	583	5366	1325	205	35	94	494	892	.247	.313	.351	.664	99	-19	-8	98	99	594	123	50	71	7
SF	162	83	79	.512	11.5	670	626	5450	1353	227	44	113	550	1023	.248	.321	.368	.689	109	32	59	96	101	650	121	78	61	-11
HOU	162	82	80	.506	12.5	617	631	5494	1338	239	31	96	474	840	.244	.308	.351	.659	99	-32	-7	96	103	604	198	71	74	17
ATL	160	54	106	.338	39.5	555	741	5440	1319	228	28	96	432	848	.242	.301	.348	.649	88	-56	-87	105	99	549	95	69	58	-13
TOT	969					7522		65563	16277	2828	415	1279	5793	11032	.248	.313	.363	.675							1789	729	71	99

TEAM	CG	SH	SV	IP	H	H/G	HR	BB	SO	RAT	ERA	ERA+	OAV	OOB	PR	/A	PF	CPI	FA	E	DP	FW	PW	BW	SBW	DIF
EAST																										
NY	31	22	46	1439	1253	7.8	78	404	1100	10.6	2.91	111	.235	.293	86	50	93	97	.981	115	127	.9	5.4	13.6	.3	-.2
PIT	12	11	46	1440²	1349	8.4	108	469	790	11.6	3.47	98	.250	.314	-3	-10	99	101	.980	125	128	.3	-1.1	4.5	-.9	2.1
MON	18	12	43	1482²	1310	8.0	122	476	923	11.1	3.08	117	.238	.303	60	84	104	105	.978	142	145	-.5	9.1	-1.8	-.6	-6.2
CHI	30	10	29	1464¹	1494	9.2	115	490	897	12.4	3.84	94	.265	.327	-64	-38	105	102	.980	125	128	.5	-4.1	.2	-.0	-.5
STL	17	14	42	1470²	1387	8.5	91	486	881	11.6	3.47	100	.252	.314	-4	1	101	99	.981	121	131	.6	.1	-5.7	2.6	-2.6
PHI	16	6	36	1433	1447	9.1	118	628	859	13.3	4.14	86	.265	.344	-110	-92	103	102	.976	145	139	-.7	-9.9	-3.8	-.5	-.6
WEST																										
LA	32	24	49	1463¹	1291	7.9	84	473	1029	11.0	2.96	112	.237	.301	78	59	97	102	.977	142	126	-.5	6.4	-1.4	.4	8.7
CIN	24	13	43	1455	1271	7.9	121	504	934	11.1	3.35	107	.237	.306	16	38	104	98	.980	125	131	.4	4.1	-2.0	2.2	1.9
SD	30	9	39	1449	1332	8.3	112	439	885	11.1	3.28	104	.247	.306	27	19	99	102	.981	120	147	.6	2.0	-.9	-.1	.8
SF	25	13	42	1462¹	1323	8.1	99	422	875	10.9	3.39	96	.242	.300	10	-20	95	93	.980	129	145	.2	-2.2	6.4	-2.1	-.3
HOU	21	15	40	1474²	1339	8.2	123	478	1049	11.3	3.41	97	.242	.307	7	-14	96	99	.978	138	124	-.3	-1.5	-.8	.9	2.6
ATL	14	4	25	1446	1481	9.2	108	524	810	12.7	4.09	90	.268	.336	-103	-67	107	100	.976	151	138	-1.1	-7.2	-9.4	-2.3	-6.0
TOT	270	153	480	17480²		8.4				11.6	3.45		.248	.313					.979	1578	1609					

The Los Angeles Dodgers had a miracle season in 1988, winning the National League pennant and the World Series against seemingly far superior opponents, the New York Mets and the Oakland Athletics, respectively. But their first miracle was to win the National League's Western Division title after finishing 73-89 in each of the previous two seasons. How did they win the West? With mirrors, mostly, for they had below-average fielding and hitting that should have negated their outstanding pitching.

Let's just track the Dodgers' performance in some of the key categories to show how illuminating a close examination of team data in the Annual Record can be. The Dodgers' on base percentage (OBP) and slugging average (SLG) reveal them to have been a weak hitting club, though their Adjusted Production (PRO+) is a bit better, for they scored more runs in their park than might have been expected from the total run-scoring picture at Chavez Ravine (Park Factor 97). However, their Clutch Hitting Index (CHI) was the best in their division, testifying to their character, their good fortune, or both. Their Stolen Base Average was above average, but still only accounted for 12 extra runs over the course of the season, so this wasn't the secret of their success.

The pitching numbers are superlative—fewest runs allowed in the West and lowest ERA—despite the fact that Cincinnati held opponents to the same batting average (OAV) and San Francisco to a lower on base percentage (OOB). Their Clutch Pitching Index (CPI) suggests that Dodger hurlers pulled their belts a notch tighter when men were on base, and their Home Runs allowed (HR) gives another tip that they knew how to stay away from the big inning. And maybe all those Shutouts (SH) are indicative of the many games they won while scoring few runs themselves.

Look at their batting (which cost them 1.4 wins in the BW, or Batting Wins, column) and baserunning and fielding (which are a virtual wash at +0.4 and −0.5, respectively, in the SBW and FW columns), and notice that their pitching, good as it was, only supplied 6.4 wins beyond average (.500). On balance, then, their offense and defense combined to produce only 5 wins beyond average. They should have finished with a record of 86–76, or five games beyond the 81–81 league average. Instead they finished 94–67, eight wins beyond their expectations, as indicated in the Differential (DIF) column. Maybe it was manager Tommy Lasorda's doing after all.

TEAM	G	W	L	PCT	GB	R	OR	AB	H	2B	3B	HR	BB	SO	AVG	OBP	SLG	PRO	PRO+	BR	/A	PF	CHI	RC	SB	CS	SBA	SBR
ATH	28	21	7	.750		376	266	1281	410	66	27	9	46	23	.320	.344	.435	.779	125	38	41	99	107	216	56			
BOS	31	20	10	.667	2	401	303	1372	426	70	37	3	60	19	.310	.339	.422	.761	115	33	22	103	108	227	73			
CHI	28	19	9	.679	2	302	241	1196	323	52	21	10	60	22	.270	.305	.374	.679	86	-7	-39	111	104	161	69			
MUT	33	16	17	.485	7.5	302	313	1404	403	43	21	1	33	15	.287	.303	.350	.653	97	-20	10	91	94	167	46			
OLY	32	15	15	.500	7	310	303	1353	375	54	26	6	48	13	.277	.302	.369	.671	98	-12	5	95	97	169	48			
TRO	29	13	15	.464	8	351	362	1248	384	51	34	6	49	19	.308	.334	.417	.751	114	25	21	101	106	199	62			
CLE	29	10	19	.345	11.5	249	341	1186	328	35	40	7	26	25	.277	.292	.391	.683	102	-7	9	95	89	144	18			
KEK	19	7	12	.368	9.5	137	243	746	178	19	8	2	33	9	.239	.271	.294	.565	63	-34	-38	102	91	65	16			
ROK	25	4	21	.160	15.5	231	287	1036	274	44	25	3	38	30	.264	.291	.364	.655	92	-16	-5	96	97	128	53			
TOT	127					2659		10822	3101	434	239	47	393	175	.287	.312	.384	.695						441				

TEAM	CG	SH	SV	IP	H	H/G	HR	BB	SO	RAT	ERA	ERA+	OAV	OOB	PR	/A	PF	CPI	FA	E	DP	FW	PW	BW	SBW	DIF
ATH	27	0	0	249	329	11.9	3	53	16	13.8	4.95	81	.284	.315	-20	-26	95	85	.845	**194**	13	1.1	-1.7	**2.7**		4.9
BOS	22	1	3	276	367	12.0	2	42	23	13.3	3.55	117	.273	.296	20	18	99	101	.834	243	24	-.3	1.2	1.4		2.7
CHI	25	0	1	251	**308**	11.0	6	28	22	12.0	2.76	166	.264	.281	41	51	109	121	.829	229	16	-.8	3.3	-2.5		5.0
MUT	32	1	0	293	373	11.5	7	42	22	12.7	3.72	102	.271	.292	16	2	90	98	.840	235	14	1.0	.1	.7		-2.3
OLY	32	0	0	282	371	11.8	4	45	13	13.3	4.37	95	.281	.305	-5	-6	99	90	**.850**	218	20	1.5	-.4	.3		-1.4
TRO	28	0	0	250	431	15.5	4	75	12	18.2	5.51	76	.342	.378	-36	-36	100	118	.845	198	22	1.3	-2.3	1.4		-1.3
CLE	23	0	0	254	346	12.3	13	53	**34**	14.1	4.11	100	.283	.312	3	0	98	107	.818	234	15	-.6	.0	.6		-4.5
KEK	19	1	0	169	261	13.9	5	21	17	15.0	5.17	88	.305	.322	-18	-11	108	93	.803	163	8	-.9	-.7	-2.5		1.6
ROK	23	1	0	226	315	12.5	3	34	16	13.9	4.30	95	.282	.303	-2	-5	97	91	.821	220	14	-1.5	-.3	-.3		-6.3
TOT	231	4	4	2250		12.4				14.0	4.22		.287	.312					.833	1934	146					

Runs
Barnes-Bos	66
Birdsall-Bos	51
Radcliff-Ath	47
Cuthbert-Ath	47
Waterman-Oly	46

Hits
McVey-Bos	66
Meyerle-Ath	64
Barnes-Bos	63
Start-Mut	58
King-Tro	57

Doubles
Anson-Rok	11

Triples
Bass-Cle	10
Wolters-Mut	9
Barnes-Bos	9
Pratt-Cle	8

Home Runs
Treacey-Chi	4
Pike-Tro	4
Meyerle-Ath	4

Total Bases
Meyerle-Ath	91
Barnes-Bos	91
Pike-Tro	85
McVey-Bos	85
King-Tro	79

Runs Batted In
Wolters-Mut	44
McVey-Bos	43
Meyerle-Ath	40
Pike-Tro	39

Runs Produced
Barnes-Bos	100
McVey-Bos	86
Meyerle-Ath	81
King-Tro	79
Pike-Tro	78

Bases On Balls
Pinkham-Chi	18
W.Wright-Bos	13
Barnes-Bos	13
Wood-Chi	11

Batting Average
Meyerle-Ath	.492
McVey-Bos	.431
G.Wright-Bos	.412
Barnes-Bos	.401
King-Tro	.396

On Base Percentage
Meyerle-Ath	.500
G.Wright-Bos	.453
Barnes-Bos	.447
McVey-Bos	.435
Wood-Chi	.425

Slugging Average
Meyerle-Ath	.700
Pike-Tro	.654
Bass-Cle	.640
G.Wright-Bos	.625
Barnes-Bos	.580

Production
Meyerle-Ath	1.200
G.Wright-Bos	1.078
Pike-Tro	1.054
Barnes-Bos	1.027
McVey-Bos	.991

Adjusted Production
Meyerle-Ath	243
G.Wright-Bos	199
Pike-Tro	194
Wolters-Mut	188
Barnes-Bos	186

Batter Runs
Meyerle-Ath	22.6
Barnes-Bos	18.9
Pike-Tro	15.5
McVey-Bos	15.5
Wolters-Mut	14.8

Adjusted Batter Runs
Meyerle-Ath	22.9
Wolters-Mut	17.9
Barnes-Bos	17.6
Pike-Tro	15.1
McVey-Bos	14.3

Clutch Hitting Index
McMullin-Tro	173
Barrows-Bos	162
Brainard-Oly	155
Wolters-Mut	147
Ferguson-Mut	141

Runs Created
Meyerle-Ath	49
Barnes-Bos	47
Wood-Chi	41
McVey-Bos	41
Pike-Tro	36

Total Average
Meyerle-Ath	1.470
G.Wright-Bos	1.383
Wood-Chi	1.250
Barnes-Bos	1.223
Pike-Tro	1.148

Stolen Bases
McGeary-Tro	20
Wood-Chi	18
Cuthbert-Ath	16
Leonard-Oly	14
Eggler-Mut	14

Stolen Base Average

Stolen Base Runs

Fielding Runs

Total Player Rating
Meyerle-Ath	1.3
Barnes-Bos	1.0
Pike-Tro	1.0
McVey-Bos	.9
King-Tro	.8

Wins
Spalding-Bos	19
Zettlein-Chi	18
McBride-Ath	18
Wolters-Mut	16

Win Percentage
McBride-Ath	.783
Zettlein-Chi	.667
Spalding-Bos	.655
Wolters-Mut	.500

Games
Wolters-Mut	32
Spalding-Bos	31
Brainard-Oly	30
McMullin-Tro	29

Complete Games
Wolters-Mut	31
Brainard-Oly	30
McMullin-Tro	28
Zettlein-Chi	25
McBride-Ath	25

Shutouts
Wolters-Mut	1
Spalding-Bos	1
Mathews-Kek	1
Fisher-Rok	1

Saves
W.Wright-Bos	3
Pinkham-Chi	1

Innings Pitched
Wolters-Mut	283.0
Brainard-Oly	264.0
Spalding-Bos	257.1
McMullin-Tro	249.0
Zettlein-Chi	240.2

Fewest Hits/Game
Wolters-Mut	10.97
Zettlein-Chi	11.14
McBride-Ath	11.55
Spalding-Bos	11.65
Pratt-Cle	11.86

Fewest BB/Game
Zettlein-Chi	.93
Mathews-Kek	1.12
Wolters-Mut	1.24
Brainard-Oly	1.26
Fisher-Rok	1.31

Strikeouts
Pratt-Cle	34
Spalding-Bos	23
Zettlein-Chi	22
Wolters-Mut	22
Mathews-Kek	17

Strikeouts/Game
Pratt-Cle	1.36
Mathews-Kek	.91
Zettlein-Chi	.82
Spalding-Bos	.80
Wolters-Mut	.70

Ratio
Zettlein-Chi	12.08
Wolters-Mut	12.21
Spalding-Bos	12.98
McBride-Ath	13.18
Brainard-Oly	13.57

Earned Run Average
Zettlein-Chi	2.73
Spalding-Bos	3.36
Wolters-Mut	3.43
Pratt-Cle	3.77
Fisher-Rok	4.35

Adjusted ERA
Zettlein-Chi	168
Spalding-Bos	124
Wolters-Mut	110
Pratt-Cle	110
Fisher-Rok	94

Opponents' Batting Avg.
Wolters-Mut	.263
Zettlein-Chi	.267
Spalding-Bos	.268
Pratt-Cle	.277
McBride-Ath	.280

Opponents' On Base Pct.
Zettlein-Chi	.283
Wolters-Mut	.285
Spalding-Bos	.290
Fisher-Rok	.302
McBride-Ath	.307

Starter Runs
Zettlein-Chi	39.8
Wolters-Mut	24.7
Spalding-Bos	24.7
Pratt-Cle	11.3
Stearns-Oly	3.4

Adjusted Starter Runs
Zettlein-Chi	49.7
Spalding-Bos	22.9
Wolters-Mut	11.2
Pratt-Cle	9.0
Stearns-Oly	3.3

Clutch Pitching Index
Zettlein-Chi	124
McMullin-Tro	118
Pratt-Cle	110
Spalding-Bos	101
Wolters-Mut	99

Relief Runs
Pinkham-Chi	.8

Adjusted Relief Runs
Pinkham-Chi	1.3

Relief Ranking
Pinkham-Chi	1.4

Total Pitcher Index
Zettlein-Chi	2.8
Wolters-Mut	1.9
Spalding-Bos	1.5
Pratt-Cle	.8
Stearns-Oly	.1

Total Baseball Ranking
Zettlein-Chi	3.1
Wolters-Mut	1.9
Spalding-Bos	1.9
Meyerle-Ath	1.3
Pratt-Cle	1.1

TEAM	G	W	L	PCT	GB	R	OR	AB	H	2B	3B	HR	BB	SO	AVG	OBP	SLG	PRO	PRO+	BR	/A	PF	CHI	RC	SB	CS	SBA	SBR
BOS	48	39	8	.830		521	236	2137	677	114	31	7	28	26	.317	.326	.409	.735	122	65	41	105	99	301	47	14	77	6
BAL	58	35	19	.648	7.5	617	434	2576	747	94	35	14	27	28	.290	.297	.370	.667	102	19	-6	105	108	295	35	15	70	2
MUT	56	34	20	.630	8.5	523	362	2423	668	86	13	4	55	52	.276	.292	.327	.619	99	-19	15	94	103	246	56	21	73	4
ATH	47	30	14	.682	7.5	539	349	2140	678	77	23	4	69	47	.317	.338	.380	.718	124	59	57	100	102	289	58	32	64	-2
TRO	25	15	10	.600	13	273	191	1124	329	56	11	5	7	14	.293	.297	.375	.672	107	10	7	101	109	129	9	7	56	-2
ATL	37	9	28	.243	25	237	473	1466	370	46	10	0	19	24	.252	.262	.297	.559	63	-42	-96	117	87	117	17	14	55	-3
CLE	22	6	16	.273	20.5	174	254	935	272	37	6	0	17	13	.291	.304	.343	.647	107	2	13	95	85	103	12	3	80	2
MAN	24	5	19	.208	22.5	220	348	1014	305	31	8	1	5	12	.301	.304	.350	.654	109	4	17	94	100	111	5	3	63	0
ECK	29	3	26	.103	27	152	413	1075	235	26	6	0	14	29	.219	.229	.254	.483	59	-59	-24	85	88	65	8	4	67	0
OLY	9	2	7	.222	18	54	140	363	93	12	3	0	4	4	.256	.264	.306	.570	81	-9	-5	95	78	29	0	3	0	-2
NAT	11	0	11	.000	21	80	190	460	105	3	2	0	1	3	.228	.230	.243	.473	41	-27	-43	117	113	26				
TOT	183					3390		15713	4479	582	148	35	246	252	.285	.296	.348	.644							247	116	68	5

TEAM	CG	SH	SV	IP	H	H/G	HR	BB	SO	RAT	ERA	ERA+	OAV	OOB	PR	/A	PF	CPI	FA	E	DP	FW	PW	BW	SBW	DIF
BOS	41	3	1	430¹	438	9.2	0	27		9.7	1.99	188	.240	.251	83	83	100	118				5.8	2.9	.4		6.5
BAL	48	1	1	515²	566	9.9	3	63		11.0	3.02	124	.243	.263	40	42	101	84				2.9	-.4	.1		5.4
MUT	54	3	0	512	618	10.9	2	32		11.4	2.55	135	.269	.279	66	51	93	125				3.6	1.0	.2		2.2
ATH	47	1	0	419	513	11.0	3	26		11.6	3.01	121	.268	.278	33	29	98	104				2.0	4.0	-.2		2.2
TRO	17	2	0	225	282	11.3	2	10		11.7	3.08	120	.272	.279	16	16	100	105				1.1	.5	-.2		1.1
ATL	37	0	0	336	561	15.0	6	19		15.5	5.06	91	.323	.331	-50	-17	124	100				-1.2	-6.7	-.2		-1.4
CLE	15	0	0	199	289	13.1	6	24		14.2	4.57	80	.291	.307	-19	-21	98	91				-1.5	.9	.1		-4.6
MAN	22	0	0	211	368	15.7	5	13		16.3	5.97	61	.320	.328	-53	-54	99	84				-3.8	1.2	-.0		-4.4
ECK	28	0	0	259¹	503	17.5	6	24		18.3	5.73	61	.355	.365	-58	-65	93	112				-4.5	-1.7	-.0		-5.3
OLY	9	0	0	79	147	16.7	0	5		17.3	6.38	58	.332	.339	-23	-24	99	84				-1.7	-.3	-.2		-.3
NAT	11	0	0	99	194	17.6	2	3		17.9	6.91	68	.339	.343	-35	-24	127	83				-1.7	-3.0	-.0		-.8
TOT	329	10	2	3285¹		12.3				12.9	3.72		.285	.296												

Runs
Eggler-Mut	95
G.Wright-Bos	87
Cuthbert-Ath	82
Barnes-Bos	81
Hatfield-Mut	75

Hits
Eggler-Mut	97
Barnes-Bos	97
Force-Tro-Bal	93
Hatfield-Mut	91
Cuthbert-Ath	90

Doubles
Barnes-Bos	28
Eggler-Mut	20
G.Wright-Bos	16
Hall-Bal	14
Fisler-Ath	14

Triples
Hall-Bal	8
Gould-Bal	8
Anson-Ath	7
Meyerle-Ath	6

Home Runs
Pike-Bal	6
Gedney-Tro-Eck	3

Total Bases
Barnes-Bos	132
Pike-Bal	120
G.Wright-Bos	119
Eggler-Mut	117
Hall-Bal	115

Runs Batted In
Pike-Bal	62
Anson-Ath	50
Start-Mut	49
Spalding-Bos	48
Fisler-Ath	48

Runs Produced
Cuthbert-Ath	128
Pike-Bal	124
Barnes-Bos	124
Hatfield-Mut	119
G.Wright-Bos	118

Bases On Balls
Mack-Ath	23
Anson-Ath	16
McMullin-Mut	11

Batting Average
Barnes-Bos	.422
Anson-Ath	.414
Force-Tro-Bal	.406
Hastings-Cle-Bal	.360
McGeary-Ath	.358

On Base Percentage
Anson-Ath	.455
Barnes-Bos	.444
Force-Tro-Bal	.411
Hastings-Cle-Bal	.374
White-Cle	.366

Slugging Average
Barnes-Bos	.574
Anson-Ath	.521
Meyerle-Ath	.479
Force-Tro-Bal	.476
G.Wright-Bos	.467

Production
Barnes-Bos	1.017
Anson-Ath	.975
Force-Tro-Bal	.887
G.Wright-Bos	.816
Spalding-Bos	.815

Adjusted Production
Barnes-Bos	200
Anson-Ath	199
Force-Tro-Bal	168
Hastings-Cle-Bal	147
White-Cle	146

Batter Runs
Barnes-Bos	29.2
Anson-Ath	25.5
Force-Tro-Bal	18.6
G.Wright-Bos	13.9
Spalding-Bos	13.5

Adjusted Batter Runs
Barnes-Bos	26.5
Anson-Ath	25.3
Force-Tro-Bal	17.3
Eggler-Mut	15.4
Hatfield-Mut	11.3

Clutch Hitting Index
Tipper-Man	170
Start-Mut	157
Boyd-Mut	156
Malone-Ath	155
Fisher-Bal	153

Runs Created
Barnes-Bos	64
Anson-Ath	52
Force-Tro-Bal	47
Eggler-Mut	47
G.Wright-Bos	45

Total Average
Barnes-Bos	1.119
Anson-Ath	.970
Force-Tro-Bal	.826
G.Wright-Bos	.767
Wood-Tro-Eck	.765

Stolen Bases
Eggler-Mut	17
G.Wright-Bos	14
Cuthbert-Ath	14
McGeary-Ath	13
Barnes-Bos	12

Stolen Base Average
Eggler-Mut	77.3

Stolen Base Runs
Barnes-Bos	2.4
Eggler-Mut	2.1
Bechtel-Mut	2.1

Fielding Runs

Total Player Rating
Barnes-Bos	1.7
Anson-Ath	1.4
Eggler-Mut	1.4
Force-Tro-Bal	1.0
Cuthbert-Ath	.9

Wins
Spalding-Bos	38
Cummings-Mut	33
McBride-Ath	30
Mathews-Bal	25
Zettlein-Tro-Eck	15

Win Percentage
Spalding-Bos	.826
McBride-Ath	.682
Cummings-Mut	.623
Mathews-Bal	.581
Zettlein-Tro-Eck	.484

Games
Cummings-Mut	55
Mathews-Bal	49
Spalding-Bos	48
McBride-Ath	47
Britt-Atl	37

Complete Games
Cummings-Mut	53
McBride-Ath	47
Spalding-Bos	41
Mathews-Bal	39
Britt-Atl	37

Shutouts
Spalding-Bos	3
Cummings-Mut	3
Zettlein-Tro-Eck	2
McBride-Ath	1
Fisher-Bal	1

Saves
W.Wright-Bos	1
Fisher-Bal	1

Innings Pitched
Cummings-Mut	497.0
McBride-Ath	419.0
Mathews-Bal	405.1
Spalding-Bos	404.2
Britt-Atl	336.0

Fewest Hits/Game
Fisher-Bal	7.26
Spalding-Bos	9.16
Mathews-Bal	10.59
Zettlein-Tro-Eck	10.75
Cummings-Mut	10.87

Fewest BB/Game
Buttery-Man	.18
Stearns-Mut	.18
A.Martin-Tro-Eck	.44
Zettlein-Tro-Eck	.48
Britt-Atl	.51

Strikeouts
Mathews-Bal	55
McBride-Ath	44
Cummings-Mut	43
Spalding-Bos	27
Zettlein-Tro-Eck	25

Strikeouts/Game
Fisher-Bal	1.63
Mathews-Bal	1.22
McBride-Ath	.95
Zettlein-Tro-Eck	.86
Cummings-Mut	.78

Ratio
Fisher-Bal	8.16
Spalding-Bos	9.76
Zettlein-Tro-Eck	11.22
Cummings-Mut	11.41
McBride-Ath	11.58

Earned Run Average
Spalding-Bos	1.98
Cummings-Mut	2.52
Fisher-Bal	2.53
Zettlein-Tro-Eck	2.67
McBride-Ath	3.01

Adjusted ERA
Spalding-Bos	188
Fisher-Bal	148
Cummings-Mut	137
Zettlein-Tro-Eck	136
McBride-Ath	121

Opponents' Batting Avg.
Fisher-Bal	.189
Spalding-Bos	.240
Mathews-Bal	.256
Zettlein-Tro-Eck	.265
McBride-Ath	.268

Opponents' On Base Pct.
Fisher-Bal	.207
Spalding-Bos	.252
Zettlein-Tro-Eck	.273
Mathews-Bal	.277
McBride-Ath	.278

Starter Runs
Spalding-Bos	78.1
Cummings-Mut	66.3
McBride-Ath	33.1
Zettlein-Tro-Eck	30.6
Mathews-Bal	25.4

Adjusted Starter Runs
Spalding-Bos	78.6
Cummings-Mut	51.1
McBride-Ath	28.7
Zettlein-Tro-Eck	28.4
Mathews-Bal	26.8

Clutch Pitching Index
Cummings-Mut	127
Spalding-Bos	119
Zettlein-Tro-Eck	114
A.Martin-Tro-Eck	109
McBride-Ath	104

Relief Runs
W.Wright-Bos	4.6

Adjusted Relief Runs
W.Wright-Bos	4.6

Relief Ranking
W.Wright-Bos	2.0

Total Pitcher Index
Spalding-Bos	7.0
Cummings-Mut	3.3
McBride-Ath	2.2
Zettlein-Tro-Eck	1.7
Mathews-Bal	1.3

Total Baseball Ranking
Spalding-Bos	7.6
Cummings-Mut	3.9
McBride-Ath	2.2
Zettlein-Tro-Eck	2.1
Mathews-Bal	1.7

1873 National Association

TEAM	G	W	L	PCT	GB	R	OR	AB	H	2B	3B	HR	BB	SO	AVG	OBP	SLG	PRO	PRO+	BR	/A	PF	CHI	RC	SB	CS	SBA	SBR
BOS	60	43	16	.729		739	460	2755	930	137	46	13	62	24	.338	.352	.435	.787	126	117	69	108	106	434	39	27	59	-5
PHI	53	36	17	.679	4	526	396	2325	645	83	20	8	62	39	.277	.296	.341	.637	89	-21	-39	104	111	249	44	14	76	5
BAL	57	34	22	.607	7.5	644	451	2563	810	119	39	12	40	25	.316	.327	.407	.734	121	59	62	100	108	352	21	10	68	0
MUT	53	29	24	.547	11	424	385	2214	622	67	41	5	42	22	.281	.294	.355	.649	96	-13	-10	99	93	240	15	5	75	2
ATH	52	28	23	.549	11	474	403	2266	683	76	22	4	35	32	.301	.312	.360	.672	95	6	-30	108	98	261	29	24	55	-6
ATL	55	17	37	.315	23.5	366	549	2210	588	60	27	6	53	43	.266	.283	.326	.609	93	-42	8	89	86	211	18	9	67	0
WAS	39	8	31	.205	25	283	485	1563	408	45	25	3	19	33	.261	.270	.328	.598	83	-38	-28	97	98	141	5	5	50	-2
RES	23	2	21	.087	23	98	299	868	204	21	8	0	8	22	.235	.242	.278	.520	62	-44	-30	92	71	60	2	1	67	0
MAR	6	0	6	.000	16.5	26	152	211	33	5	0	0	0	0	.156	.156	.180	.336	1	-24	-14	77	132	6				
TOT	199					3580		16975	4923	613	228	51	321	240	.290	.303	.362	.665							173	95	65	-5

TEAM	CG	SH	SV	IP	H	H/G	HR	BB	SO	RAT	ERA	ERA+	OAV	OOB	PR	/A	PF	CPI	FA	E	DP	FW	PW	BW	SBW	DIF
BOS	48	1	3	536	708	11.9	5	35	31	12.5	2.59	128	.287	.297	40	44	102	118	.838	465	45	.4	3.1	4.9	-.3	5.4
PHI	50	0	0	481	627	11.7	3	44	28	12.6	2.77	119	.284	.298	26	28	101	109	.848	379	43	2.0	2.0	-2.8	.4	7.9
BAL	55	1	0	508²	680	12.0	4	42	34	12.8	3.01	108	.285	.297	14	14	100	100	.859	353	33	5.0	1.0	4.4	.0	-4.4
MUT	48	2	0	477	539	10.2	5	69	76	11.5	2.62	121	.254	.278	33	29	97	87	.820	424	28	-.3	2.1	-.7	.2	1.3
ATH	44	3	1	475	553	10.5	4	58	41	11.6	3.03	113	.257	.276	12	20	105	75	.842	383	30	1.4	1.4	-2.1	-.4	2.2
ATL	52	1	0	500	737	13.3	8	42	15	14.0	3.98	76	.303	.315	-40	-52	93	93	.830	471	30	-1.9	-3.7	.6	.0	-5.0
WAS	39	0	0	346	593	15.4	11	22	7	16.0	4.71	71	.335	.343	-56	-52	103	104	.817	337	27	-1.5	-3.7	-2.0	-.1	-4.2
RES	22	0	0	207	342	14.9	7	9	8	15.3	3.22	104	.310	.316	1	3	103	124	.790	243	9	-3.2	.2	-2.1	.0	-4.4
MAR	6	0	0	54	144	24.0	4	0	0	24.0	8.00	40	.392	.392	-28	-29	100	102	.781	66	2	-1.0	-2.1	-1.0	.0	1.0
TOT	364	8	4	3584²		12.4				13.2	3.25		.290	.303					.833	3121	247					

Runs		Hits		Doubles		Triples		Home Runs		Total Bases	
Barnes-Bos	125	Barnes-Bos	137	Barnes-Bos	28	Barnes-Bos	10	Pike-Bal	4	Barnes-Bos	194
Wright-Bos	99	Wright-Bos	126	O'Rourke-Bos	22	White-Bos	8	Wright-Bos	3	Wright-Bos	162
Spalding-Bos	83	White-Bos	121	White-Bos	20	Pike-Bal	8	Meyerle-Phi	3	White-Bos	157
Eggler-Mut	82	Spalding-Bos	106	Pike-Bal	18	Holdsworth-Mut	8	McVey-Bal	3	Pike-Bal	136
Leonard-Bos	81	Anson-Ath	101	Carey-Bal	18			Barnes-Bos	3	O'Rourke-Bos	129

Runs Batted In		Runs Produced		Bases On Balls		Batting Average		On Base Percentage		Slugging Average	
White-Bos	64	Barnes-Bos	183	Barnes-Bos	18	Barnes-Bos	.425	Barnes-Bos	.456	Barnes-Bos	.602
Barnes-Bos	61	Wright-Bos	144	Mack-Phi	15	Anson-Ath	.398	Anson-Ath	.409	McVey-Bal	.521
Spalding-Bos	59	White-Bos	143	O'Rourke-Bos	14	White-Bos	.390	Wright-Bos	.402	White-Bos	.506
Leonard-Bos	58	Spalding-Bos	141	Malone-Phi	14	Wright-Bos	.388	Force-Bal	.391	Wright-Bos	.498
Mills-Bal	57	Leonard-Bos	139			McVey-Bal	.380	White-Bos	.390	Meyerle-Phi	.479

Production		Adjusted Production		Batter Runs		Adjusted Batter Runs		Clutch Hitting Index		Runs Created	
Barnes-Bos	1.058	Barnes-Bos	193	Barnes-Bos	43.2	Barnes-Bos	37.3	Cummings-Bal	192	Barnes-Bos	94
McVey-Bal	.911	McVey-Bal	166	Wright-Bos	25.0	Wright-Bos	19.3	Addy-Phi-Bos	156	Wright-Bos	66
Wright-Bos	.901	Pabor-Atl	151	White-Bos	22.6	White-Bos	17.3	Leonard-Bos	147	White-Bos	64
White-Bos	.897	Wright-Bos	151	Anson-Ath	16.3	McVey-Bal	15.2	Mills-Bal	144	O'Rourke-Bos	51
Anson-Ath	.858	White-Bos	149	O'Rourke-Bos	16.3	Pabor-Atl	15.1	Bechtel-Phi	138	Pike-Bal	48

Total Average		Stolen Bases		Stolen Base Average		Stolen Base Runs		Fielding Runs		Total Player Rating	
Barnes-Bos	1.169	Cuthbert-Phi	13			Cuthbert-Phi	2.7			Barnes-Bos	2.4
McVey-Bal	.874	Barnes-Bos	13			McMullin-Ath	2.1			White-Bos	1.3
White-Bos	.843	McMullin-Ath	9							Pabor-Atl	1.2
Wright-Bos	.824	Wood-Phi	8							Wright-Bos	1.1
O'Rourke-Bos	.788									McVey-Bal	1.1

Wins		Win Percentage		Games		Complete Games		Shutouts		Saves	
Spalding-Bos	41	Spalding-Bos	.745	Spalding-Bos	60	Britt-Atl	51	McBride-Ath	3	Spalding-Bos	2
Zettlein-Phi	36	Zettlein-Phi	.706	Britt-Atl	54	Zettlein-Phi	49	Mathews-Mut	2	Wright-Bos	1
Mathews-Mut	29	Cummings-Bal	.667	Mathews-Mut	52	Spalding-Bos	48	Spalding-Bos	1	Fisher-Ath	1
Cummings-Bal	28	McBride-Ath	.558	Zettlein-Phi	51	Mathews-Mut	47	Cummings-Bal	1		
McBride-Ath	24	Mathews-Mut	.558	McBride-Ath	46	Cummings-Bal	42	Britt-Atl	1		

Innings Pitched		Fewest Hits/Game		Fewest BB/Game		Strikeouts		Strikeouts/Game		Ratio	
Spalding-Bos	497.2	Fisher-Ath	9.60	Campbell-Res	.38	Mathews-Mut	75	Mathews-Mut	1.52	Fisher-Ath	10.67
Britt-Atl	480.2	Mathews-Mut	9.93	Stearns-Was	.48	Spalding-Bos	31	Fisher-Ath	1.49	Mathews-Mut	11.19
Zettlein-Phi	460.0	McBride-Ath	10.65	Spalding-Bos	.51	Cummings-Bal	31	Cummings-Bal	.73	McBride-Ath	11.76
Mathews-Mut	443.0	Cummings-Bal	11.19	Brainard-Bal	.75	Zettlein-Phi	28	McBride-Ath	.59	Cummings-Bal	11.97
McBride-Ath	382.2	Zettlein-Phi	11.60	Britt-Atl	.75	McBride-Ath	25	Spalding-Bos	.56	Spalding-Bos	12.13

Earned Run Average		Adjusted ERA		Opponents' Batting Avg.		Opponents' On Base Pct.		Starter Runs		Adjusted Starter Runs	
Fisher-Ath	1.81	Fisher-Ath	188	Fisher-Ath	.227	Fisher-Ath	.246	Spalding-Bos	43.8	Spalding-Bos	47.4
Spalding-Bos	2.46	Spalding-Bos	135	Mathews-Mut	.251	Mathews-Mut	.274	Mathews-Mut	34.0	Zettlein-Phi	30.5
Mathews-Mut	2.56	Mathews-Mut	124	McBride-Ath	.263	McBride-Ath	.282	Zettlein-Phi	28.2	Mathews-Mut	29.7
Cummings-Bal	2.66	Cummings-Bal	122	Cummings-Bal	.274	Cummings-Bal	.287	Cummings-Bal	25.0	Cummings-Bal	25.0
Zettlein-Phi	2.70	Zettlein-Phi	122	Zettlein-Phi	.283	Spalding-Bos	.292	Fisher-Ath	13.5	Fisher-Ath	15.0

Clutch Pitching Index		Relief Runs		Adjusted Relief Runs		Relief Ranking		Total Pitcher Index		Total Baseball Ranking	
Campbell-Res	124							Spalding-Bos	4.4	Spalding-Bos	5.2
Spalding-Bos	118							Cummings-Bal	2.0	Mathews-Mut	2.5
Zettlein-Phi	110							Mathews-Mut	1.9	Barnes-Bos	2.4
Greyson-Was	108							Zettlein-Phi	1.6	Zettlein-Phi	2.2
Brainard-Bal	103							Fisher-Ath	1.1	Cummings-Bal	2.0

TEAM	G	W	L	PCT	GB	R	OR	AB	H	2B	3B	HR	BB	SO	AVG	OBP	SLG	PRO	PRO+	BR	/A	PF	CHI	RC	SB	CS	SBA	SBR
BOS	71	52	18	.743		735	415	3122	981	130	57	18	32		.314	.321	.410	.731	128	114	82	106	108	421				
MUT	65	42	23	.646	7.5	500	377	2719	709	100	31	8	38		.261	.271	.329	.600	90	-19	-34	103	105	249				
ATH	55	33	22	.600	11.5	441	344	2260	646	87	17	6	24		.286	.293	.347	.640	98	15	-20	109	104	236				
PHI	58	29	29	.500	17	476	428	2432	690	74	51	3	28		.284	.292	.360	.640	106	25	10	104	102	262				
CHI	59	28	31	.475	18.5	418	480	2457	690	89	3	3	34		.281	.291	.323	.614	98	-4	-8	101	94	237				
ATL	56	22	33	.400	22.5	301	449	2165	497	50	11	1	32		.230	.241	.264	.505	71	-83	-37	88	97	141				
HAR	53	16	37	.302	27.5	371	471	2140	587	92	19	2	26		.274	.283	.338	.621	95	0	-19	105	95	210				
BAL	47	9	38	.191	31.5	227	505	1781	435	53	8	1	24		.244	.254	.285	.539	75	-48	-46	99	82	132				
TOT	232					3469		19076	5235	675	197	42	238		.274	.283	.337	.620										

TEAM	CG	SH	SV	IP	H	H/G	HR	BB	SO	RAT	ERA	ERA+	OAV	OOB	PR	/A	PF	CPI	FA	E	DP	FW	PW	BW	SBW	DIF
BOS	65	4	3	633	777	11.0	1	27		11.4	2.36	126	.274	.281	45	42	99	123					3.3	6.4		7.4
MUT	62	4	0	586	658	10.1	3	40		10.7	2.30	133	.259	.271	45	50	103	111					3.9	-2.6		8.3
ATH	55	0	0	487	514	9.5	5	29		10.0	2.55	124	.241	.251	24	33	106	80					2.6	-1.6		4.5
PHI	56	3	0	524	666	11.4	4	21		11.8	2.95	103	.275	.281	3	5	101	100					.4	.8		-1.2
CHI	58	3	0	533²	696	11.7	7	48		12.5	3.25	94	.285	.299	-15	-12	102	106					-.9	-.6		.0
ATL	56	1	0	506	621	11.0	16	13		11.3	3.20	88	.268	.272	-11	-22	94	90					-1.7	-2.9		-.9
HAR	45	0	1	481	660	12.3	2	23		12.8	3.54	89	.288	.295	-29	-20	105	94					-1.6	-1.5		-7.5
BAL	43	0	0	420	643	13.8	4	37		14.6	4.31	71	.306	.319	-61	-59	102	96					-4.6	-3.6		-6.4
TOT	440	15	4	4170²		11.3				11.8	3.00		.274	.283												

Runs	Hits	Doubles	Triples	Home Runs	Total Bases
McVey-Bos 91	McVey-Bos 124	Pike-Har 24	G.Wright-Bos 15	O'Rourke-Bos 5	McVey-Bos 166
O'Rourke-Bos 82	Spalding-Bos 119	McVey-Bos 22	Craver-Phi 11	McVey-Bos 4	G.Wright-Bos 153
Spalding-Bos 80	Leonard-Bos 109	Meyerle-Chi 20	Holdsworth-Phi 9	White-Bos 3	O'Rourke-Bos 144
G.Wright-Bos 76	G.Wright-Bos 106	Leonard-Bos 18	York-Phi 8	Clapp-Ath 3	Spalding-Bos 136
White-Bos 75	White-Bos 106	Burdock-Mut 16			Leonard-Bos 135

Runs Batted In	Runs Produced	Bases On Balls	Batting Average	On Base Percentage	Slugging Average
	McVey-Bos 87	Nelson-Mut 9	Meyerle-Chi 403	Meyerle-Chi 410	Pike-Har 496
	Spalding-Bos 80	Stearns-Har 8	McVey-Bos 364	McVey-Bos 364	Meyerle-Chi 494
	O'Rourke-Bos 77	Hatfield-Mut 8	Craver-Phi 352	Barnes-Bos 363	G.Wright-Bos 489
	G.Wright-Bos 74	Barnes-Bos 8	Barnes-Bos 344	Craver-Phi 362	McVey-Bos 487
			Pike-Har 340	McMullin-Ath 357	Craver-Phi 483

Production	Adjusted Production	Batter Runs	Adjusted Batter Runs	Clutch Hitting Index	Runs Created
Meyerle-Chi 904	Meyerle-Chi 185	McVey-Bos 24.7	Meyerle-Chi 23.1		McVey-Bos 62
McVey-Bos 850	Craver-Phi 161	Meyerle-Chi 23.6	McVey-Bos 21.2		G.Wright-Bos 55
Craver-Phi 845	McVey-Bos 159	G.Wright-Bos 22.1	G.Wright-Bos 18.9		Meyerle-Chi 53
G.Wright-Bos 842	G.Wright-Bos 156	Spalding-Bos 20.8	Craver-Phi 17.4		Craver-Phi 48
Pike-Har 836	Pike-Har 155	Craver-Phi 19.1	Spalding-Bos 17.1		O'Rourke-Bos 47

Total Average	Stolen Bases	Stolen Base Average	Stolen Base Runs	Fielding Runs	Total Player Rating
Meyerle-Chi 848					McVey-Bos 1.7
G.Wright-Bos 773					Meyerle-Chi 1.7
Craver-Phi 769					G.Wright-Bos 1.3
McVey-Bos 765					Craver-Phi 1.2
Pike-Har 752					Pike-Har 1.0

Wins	Win Percentage	Games	Complete Games	Shutouts	Saves
Spalding-Bos 52	Spalding-Bos 765	Spalding-Bos 71	Spalding-Bos 65	Spalding-Bos 4	W.Wright-Bos 3
Mathews-Mut 42	Mathews-Mut 656	Mathews-Mut 65	Mathews-Mut 62	Mathews-Mut 4	Stearns-Har 1
McBride-Ath 33	McBride-Ath 600	Zettlein-Chi 57	Zettlein-Chi 57	Zettlein-Chi 3	
Cummings-Phi 28	Cummings-Phi 519	McBride-Ath 55	McBride-Ath 55	Cummings-Phi 3	
Zettlein-Chi 27	Zettlein-Chi 474	Bond-Atl 55	Bond-Atl 55	Bond-Atl 1	

Innings Pitched	Fewest Hits/Game	Fewest BB/Game	Strikeouts	Strikeouts/Game	Ratio
Spalding-Bos 616.1	McBride-Ath 9.50	Bond-Atl 18			McBride-Ath 10.03
Mathews-Mut ... 578.0	Mathews-Mut ... 10.07	Fisher-Har 28			Mathews-Mut ... 10.68
Zettlein-Chi ... 515.2	Spalding-Bos 11.00	Spalding-Bos 34			Bond-Atl 11.21
Bond-Atl 497.0	Bond-Atl 11.03	Cummings-Phi 39			Spalding-Bos 11.33
McBride-Ath 487.0	Cummings-Phi ... 11.24	McBride-Ath 54			Cummings-Phi ... 11.63

Earned Run Average	Adjusted ERA	Opponents' Batting Avg.	Opponents' On Base Pct.	Starter Runs	Adjusted Starter Runs
Mathews-Mut 2.30	Mathews-Mut 133	McBride-Ath 241	McBride-Ath 251	Mathews-Mut 44.5	Mathews-Mut 49.5
Spalding-Bos 2.35	Spalding-Bos 126	Mathews-Mut 258	Mathews-Mut 270	Spalding-Bos 44.3	Spalding-Bos 42.0
McBride-Ath 2.55	McBride-Ath 124	Bond-Atl 268	Bond-Atl 271	McBride-Ath 24.2	McBride-Ath 33.3
Cummings-Phi.... 2.88	Cummings-Phi.... 106	Cummings-Phi.....271	Cummings-Phi.....278	Cummings-Phi 6.5	Cummings-Phi 8.6
Fisher-Har 3.04	Fisher-Har 104	Spalding-Bos 273	Spalding-Bos 279		Fisher-Har 4.2

Clutch Pitching Index	Relief Runs	Adjusted Relief Runs	Relief Ranking	Total Pitcher Index	Total Baseball Ranking
Spalding-Bos 120				Spalding-Bos 4.7	Spalding-Bos 4.7
Mathews-Mut 110				Mathews-Mut 3.6	Mathews-Mut 3.6
Zettlein-Chi 105				McBride-Ath 1.8	McBride-Ath 1.8
Cummings-Phi..... 99				Cummings-Phi......5	McVey-Bos 1.7
Brainard-Bal 99				W.Wright-Bos 0	Meyerle-Chi 1.7

TEAM	G	W	L	PCT	GB	R	OR	AB	H	2B	3B	HR	BB	SO	AVG	OBP	SLG	PRO	PRO+	BR	/A	PF	CHI	RC	SB	CS	SBA	SBR
BOS	82	71	8	.899		831	343	3516	1124	157	54	14	31		.320	.326	.407	.733	151	184	164	104	112	478				
HAR	86	54	28	.659	18.5	557	343	3342	873	98	34	2	40		.261	.270	.313	.583	99	12	-14	105	103	289				
ATH	77	53	20	.726	15	699	402	3245	940	126	61	10	40		.290	.298	.375	.673	122	107	50	111	112	372				
STL	70	39	29	.574	26.5	386	369	2679	641	84	27	0	33		.239	.249	.291	.540	98	-29	10	91	97	198				
PHI	70	37	31	.544	28.5	470	376	2717	681	65	28	5	22		.251	.257	.301	.558	91	-13	-30	104	113	215				
MUT	71	30	38	.441	35.5	328	425	2683	626	84	24	7	21		.233	.239	.290	.529	81	-38	-61	105	85	191				
CHI	69	30	37	.448	35	379	416	2658	697	85	13	0	24		.262	.269	.304	.573	100	1	-3	101	90	223				
NH	47	7	40	.149	48	170	397	1708	374	42	12	2	13		.219	.225	.261	.486	80	-48	-14	87	77	103				
WAS	28	5	23	.179	40.5	107	338	997	194	12	11	0	5		.195	.199	.229	.428	52	-48	-42	96	98	46				
RS	19	4	15	.211	37	60	161	688	138	20	1	0	14		.201	.217	.233	.450	64	-27	-16	90	72	36				
CEN	14	2	12	.143	36.5	70	138	529	126	19	3	0	8		.238	.250	.285	.535	95	-6	1	92	90	39				
ATL	44	2	42	.45	51.5	132	438	1547	304	32	9	2	10		.197	.202	.233	.435	60	-70	-39	87	76	74				
WES	13	1	12	.77	37	45	88	449	81	9	6	0	1		.180	.182	.227	.409	41	-24	-28	105	97	19				
TOT	345					4234		26758	6799	833	283	42	262		.254	.261	.311	.572										

TEAM	CG	SH	SV	IP	H	H/G	HR	BB	SO	RAT	ERA	ERA+	OAV	OOB	PR	/A	PF	CPI	FA	E	DP	FW	PW	BW	SBW	DIF
BOS	60	10	17	732	751	9.2	2	29		9.6	1.70	140	.249	.256	62	55	96	135					4.7	14.0		12.8
HAR	83	13	0	771	706	8.2	4	16		8.4	1.61	161	.228	.231	73	84	105	106					7.2	-1.2		7.0
ATH	75	6	0	687	775	10.2	4	40		10.7	2.11	125	.268	.278	27	41	107	137					3.5	4.3		8.7
STL	67	5	1	630	634	9.1	3	20		9.3	2.11	105	.240	.245	24	8	90	96					.7	.9		3.5
PHI	64	5	0	627	650	9.3	6	30		9.8	2.15	117	.244	.252	21	25	102	103					2.1	-2.6		3.4
MUT	70	2	0	637²	716	10.1	3	24		10.4	2.40	107	.258	.264	4	13	105	106					1.1	-5.2		.1
CHI	65	7	0	625	652	9.4	0	28		9.8	2.40	104	.244	.252	4	7	102	89					.6	-.3		-3.8
NH	40	0	0	426	500	10.6	5	22		11.0	3.34	69	.255	.263	-42	-49	93	76					-4.2	-1.2		-11.1
WAS	23	0	0	250²	397	14.3	6	11		14.6	4.85	54	.312	.318	-66	-62	107	93					-5.3	-3.6		-.1
RS	16	2	0	171	207	10.9	0	3		11.1	3.37	72	.264	.267	-17	-18	98	78					-1.5	-1.4		-2.6
CEN	14	0	0	126	170	12.1	0	3		12.4	3.93	61	.277	.281	-21	-21	98	78					-1.8	.0		-3.3
ATL	31	0	0	396	531	12.1	9	22		12.6	3.95	58	.285	.293	-66	-73	94	90					-6.2	-3.3		-10.4
WES	13	0	0	112	110	8.8	0	14		10.0	2.81	96	.225	.247	-4	-1	110	65					-.0	-2.4		-3.0
TOT	621	50	18	6191¹		9.9				10.3	2.46		.254	.261												

Runs	Hits	Doubles	Triples	Home Runs	Total Bases
Barnes-Bos 114	Barnes-Bos 142	McVey-Bos 33	Craver-Cen-Ath 13	O'Rourke-Bos 6	McVey-Bos 197
G.Wright-Bos 105	McVey-Bos 137	Barnes-Bos 22	Hall-Ath 13	Hall-Ath 5	Barnes-Bos 179
O'Rourke-Bos 98	White-Bos 136	Pike-StL 21	Pike-StL 10	Start-Mut 4	G.Wright-Bos 170
McVey-Bos 88	G.Wright-Bos 135	Force-Ath 21	Meyerle-Phi 9	Hallinan-Wes-Mut .. 3	White-Bos 167
Leonard-Bos 87	Leonard-Bos 127	White-Bos 20	McVey-Bos 9	McVey-Bos 3	Hall-Ath 160

Runs Batted In	Runs Produced	Bases On Balls	Batting Average	On Base Percentage	Slugging Average
	Barnes-Bos 113	Harbidge-Har...... 12	White-Bos 366	Barnes-Bos 373	McVey-Bos 506
	G.Wright-Bos 104	Dehlman-StL 11	Barnes-Bos 361	White-Bos 369	Pike-StL 474
	O'Rourke-Bos 92	O'Rourke-Bos 10	McVey-Bos 352	McVey-Bos 354	Craver-Cen-Ath ...458
	Leonard-Bos 86	Nelson-Mut 10	Pike-StL 343	Pike-StL 349	Barnes-Bos 455
	McVey-Bos 85	Hastings-Chi 9	G.Wright-Bos 333	Anson-Ath 336	White-Bos 449

Production	Adjusted Production	Batter Runs	Adjusted Batter Runs	Clutch Hitting Index	Runs Created
McVey-Bos 860	Pike-StL 200	McVey-Bos 35.0	McVey-Bos 32.8		McVey-Bos 71
Barnes-Bos 828	McVey-Bos 187	Barnes-Bos 32.3	Barnes-Bos 30.0		Barnes-Bos 68
Pike-StL 824	Barnes-Bos 178	White-Bos 28.9	Pike-StL 29.1		White-Bos 63
White-Bos 818	White-Bos 175	Pike-StL 24.7	White-Bos 26.8		G.Wright-Bos 59
Craver-Cen-Ath 778	Luff-NH.......... 158	G.Wright-Bos ... 23.0	G.Wright-Bos 20.7		Pike-StL 53

Total Average	Stolen Bases	Stolen Base Average	Stolen Base Runs	Fielding Runs	Total Player Rating
McVey-Bos 786					McVey-Bos 2.8
Barnes-Bos 741					White-Bos 2.5
Pike-StL 737					Pike-StL 2.5
White-Bos 716					Barnes-Bos 2.4
Craver-Cen-Ath 683					G.Wright-Bos 1.5

Wins	Win Percentage	Games	Complete Games	Shutouts	Saves
Spalding-Bos...... 55	Spalding-Bos......917	Spalding-Bos 72	Mathews-Mut 69	Zettlein-Chi-Phi 7	Spalding-Bos 8
McBride-Ath 44	Manning-Bos......882	Mathews-Mut 70	McBride-Ath 59	Spalding-Bos 7	Manning-Bos 7
Cummings-Har 35	McBride-Ath 759	McBride-Ath 60	Bradley-StL 57	Cummings-Har 7	McVey-Bos 1
Bradley-StL 33	Cummings-Har 745	Bradley-StL 60	Spalding-Bos 52	McBride-Ath 6	Heifer-Bos 1
	Zettlein-Chi-Phi 569	Zettlein-Chi-Phi 52	Zettlein-Chi-Phi 49	Bond-Har 6	Galvin-StL 1

Innings Pitched	Fewest Hits/Game	Fewest BB/Game	Strikeouts	Strikeouts/Game	Ratio
Mathews-Mut ... 626.2	Borden-Phi 6.41	Cummings-Har 13			Borden-Phi 7.36
Spalding-Bos ... 575.0	Galvin-StL 7.69	Blong-RS 14			Galvin-StL 7.84
McBride-Ath ... 538.0	Bond-Har 7.70	Galvin-StL 15			Bond-Har 7.95
Bradley-StL 535.2	Cummings-Har ... 8.55	Spalding-Bos 22			Cummings-Har 8.68
Zettlein-Chi-Phi .. 462.1	Fisher-Phi 8.71	Fisher-Phi 23			Fisher-Phi 8.93

Earned Run Average	Adjusted ERA	Opponents' Batting Avg.	Opponents' On Base Pct.	Starter Runs	Adjusted Starter Runs
Spalding-Bos 1.52	Bond-Har 166	Borden-Phi 181	Borden-Phi 203	Spalding-Bos 60.2	Spalding-Bos 54.4
Bond-Har........ 1.56	Cummings-Har ... 162	Galvin-StL 209	Galvin-StL 213	Cummings-Har ... 40.0	Cummings-Har ... 46.1
Cummings-Har ... 1.60	Spalding-Bos 156	Bond-Har 215	Bond-Har 220	Bond-Har 35.3	Bond-Har 40.4
Borden-Phi 1.64	Borden-Phi 154	Fisher-Phi 232	Fisher-Phi 237	McBride-Ath ... 29.1	McBride-Ath 40.0
Fisher-Phi 1.92	McBride-Ath 134	Cummings-Har 235	Cummings-Har ... 237	Bradley-StL 24.5	Zettlein-Chi-Phi ... 24.0

Clutch Pitching Index	Relief Runs	Adjusted Relief Runs	Relief Ranking	Total Pitcher Index	Total Baseball Ranking
McBride-Ath 142				Spalding-Bos...... 6.2	Spalding-Bos 6.9
Spalding-Bos 140				Bond-Har 3.9	Bond-Har 4.3
Manning-Bos 124				McBride-Ath 3.8	Cummings-Har 4.0
Cummings-Har ... 114				Cummings-Har ... 3.6	McBride-Ath 3.8
Knight-Ath 113				Fisher-Phi 1.9	McVey-Bos 2.7

TEAM	G	W	L	PCT	GB	R	OR	AB	H	2B	3B	HR	BB	SO	AVG	OBP	SLG	PRO	PRO+	BR	/A	PF	CHI	RC	SB	CS	SBA	SBR
CHI	66	52	14	.788		624	257	2748	926	131	32	8	70	45	.337	.353	.417	.770	140	160	110	112	107	415				
STL	64	45	19	.703	6	386	229	2478	642	73	27	2	59	63	.259	.276	.313	.589	102	-6	14	95	103	219				
HAR	69	47	21	.691	6	429	261	2664	711	96	22	2	39	78	.267	.277	.322	.599	92	1	-33	108	106	244				
BOS	70	39	31	.557	15	471	450	2722	723	96	24	9	58	98	.266	.281	.328	.609	102	11	4	102	110	257				
LOU	69	30	36	.455	22	280	344	2570	641	68	14	6	24	98	.249	.256	.294	.550	71	-42	-112	118	81	198				
NY	57	21	35	.375	26	260	412	2180	494	39	15	2	18	35	.227	.233	.261	.494	75	-76	-33	87	103	136				
PHI	60	14	45	.237	34.5	378	534	2387	646	79	35	7	27	36	.271	.279	.342	.621	108	16	19	99	100	233				
CIN	65	9	56	.138	42.5	238	579	2372	555	51	12	4	41	136	.234	.247	.271	.518	86	-63	-11	86	80	163				
TOT	260					3066		20121	5338	633	181	40	336	589	.265	.277	.321	.598										

TEAM	CG	SH	SV	IP	H	H/G	HR	BB	SO	RAT	ERA	ERA+	OAV	OOB	PR	/A	PF	CPI	FA	E	DP	FW	PW	BW	SBW	DIF
CHI	59	9	4	592¹	608	9.2	6	29	51	9.7	1.76	139	.247	.256	36	45	106	100	.899	282	33	6.0	4.0	9.7		-.6
STL	63	16	0	577	472	7.4	3	39	103	8.0	1.22	175	.210	.224	70	59	93	74	.902	268	33	6.1	5.2	1.2		.5
HAR	69	11	0	624	570	8.2	2	27	114	8.6	1.67	142	.227	.235	44	49	103	72	.888	337	27	4.0	4.3	-2.9		7.6
BOS	49	3	7	632	732	10.4	7	104	77	11.9	2.51	90	.268	.295	-14	-18	98	106	.860	442	42	-1.1	-1.6	.4		6.3
LOU	67	5	0	643	605	8.5	3	38	125	9.0	1.69	160	.229	.240	44	73	118	75	.875	397	44	.9	6.4	-9.8		-.5
NY	56	2	0	530	718	12.2	8	24	37	12.6	2.94	73	.302	.309	-37	-47	93	114	.825	473	18	-6.8	-4.1	-2.9		6.8
PHI	53	1	2	550	783	12.8	2	41	22	13.5	3.22	75	.310	.321	-56	-49	105	112	.839	456	32	-5.0	-4.3	1.7		-7.9
CIN	57	0	0	591	850	12.9	9	34	60	13.5	3.62	61	.313	.322	-86	-94	95	103	.841	469	45	-4.1	-8.3	-1.0		-10.2
TOT	473	47	13	4739¹		10.1				10.8	2.31		.265	.277					.866	3124	274					

Runs
Barnes-Chi 126
G.Wright-Bos 72
Peters-Chi 70
White-Chi 66
Burdock-Har 66

Hits
Barnes-Chi 138
Peters-Chi 111
Anson-Chi 110
McVey-Chi 107
White-Chi 104

Doubles
Hines-Chi 21
Higham-Har 21
Barnes-Chi 21
Pike-StL 19

Triples
Barnes-Chi 14
Hall-Phi 13
Pike-StL 10
Meyerle-Phi 8

Home Runs
Hall-Phi 5
Jones-Cin 4

Total Bases
Barnes-Chi 190
Hall-Phi 146
Anson-Chi 139
Hines-Chi 134

Runs Batted In
White-Chi 60
Hines-Chi 59
Barnes-Chi 59
Anson-Chi 59
McVey-Chi 53

Runs Produced
Barnes-Chi 184
White-Chi 125
Anson-Chi 120
Hines-Chi 119
Peters-Chi 116

Bases On Balls
Barnes-Chi 20
O'Rourke-Bos 15
Burdock-Har 13
Glenn-Chi 12
Anson-Chi 12

Batting Average
Barnes-Chi 429
Hall-Phi 366
Anson-Chi 356
Peters-Chi 351
McVey-Chi 347

On Base Percentage
Barnes-Chi 462
Hall-Phi 384
Anson-Chi 380
White-Chi 358
O'Rourke-Bos 358

Slugging Average
Barnes-Chi 590
Hall-Phi 545
Pike-StL 472
Anson-Chi 450
Meyerle-Phi 449

Production
Barnes-Chi . . . 1.052
Hall-Phi 929
Anson-Chi 830
Pike-StL 813
Meyerle-Phi 797

Adjusted Production
Barnes-Chi 222
Hall-Phi 208
Pike-StL 178
Meyerle-Phi 165
Jones-Cin 162

Batter Runs
Barnes-Chi 50.0
Hall-Phi 29.1
Anson-Chi 24.2
Pike-StL 19.7
O'Rourke-Bos 19.1

Adjusted Batter Runs
Barnes-Chi 44.0
Hall-Phi 29.4
Pike-StL 22.0
Anson-Chi 18.5
O'Rourke-Bos 18.4

Clutch Hitting Index
White-Chi 165
Hines-Chi 151
Schafer-Bos 145
Battin-StL 144
Spalding-Chi 139

Runs Created
Barnes-Chi 90
Hall-Phi 57
Anson-Chi 54
Peters-Chi 48
O'Rourke-Bos 48

Total Average
Barnes-Chi 1.141
Hall-Phi 906
Anson-Chi 759
Pike-StL 738
Meyerle-Phi 698

Stolen Bases

Stolen Base Average

Stolen Base Runs

Fielding Runs
Somerville-Lou . . . 29.7
Force-Phi-NY 21.1
Battin-StL 13.6
G.Wright-Bos 13.3
Anson-Chi 12.8

Total Player Rating
Barnes-Chi 4.2
Anson-Chi 2.9
Hall-Phi 2.4
Battin-StL 2.2
G.Wright-Bos 2.1

Wins
Spalding-Chi 47
Bradley-StL 45
Bond-Har 31
Devlin-Lou 30
Mathews-NY 21

Win Percentage
Spalding-Chi 797
Manning-Bos 783
Bond-Har 705
Bradley-StL 703
Cummings-Har 667

Games
Devlin-Lou 68
Bradley-StL 64
Spalding-Chi 61
Mathews-NY 56
Bond-Har 45

Complete Games
Devlin-Lou 66
Bradley-StL 63
Mathews-NY 55
Spalding-Chi 53
Bond-Har 45

Shutouts
Bradley-StL 16
Spalding-Chi 8
Bond-Har 6
Devlin-Lou 5
Cummings-Har 5

Saves
Manning-Bos 5
Zettlein-Phi 2
McVey-Chi 2

Innings Pitched
Devlin-Lou 622.0
Bradley-StL 573.0
Spalding-Chi 528.2
Mathews-NY 516.0
Bond-Har 408.0

Fewest Hits/Game
Bradley-StL 7.38
Bond-Har 7.83
Devlin-Lou 8.19
Cummings-Har 8.96
Spalding-Chi 9.23

Fewest BB/Game
Zettlein-Phi 23
Fisher-Cin 24
Bond-Har 29
Mathews-NY 42
Williams-Cin 43

Strikeouts
Devlin-Lou 122
Bradley-StL 103
Bond-Har 88
Spalding-Chi 39
Mathews-NY 37

Strikeouts/Game
Bond-Har 1.94
Devlin-Lou 1.77
Bradley-StL 1.62
Borden-Bos 1.40
Fisher-Cin 1.14

Ratio
Bradley-StL 7.98
Bond-Har 8.12
Devlin-Lou 8.73
Cummings-Har 9.54
Spalding-Chi 9.67

Earned Run Average
Bradley-StL 1.23
Devlin-Lou 1.56
Cummings-Har . . . 1.67
Bond-Har 1.68
Spalding-Chi 1.75

Adjusted ERA
Bradley-StL 174
Devlin-Lou 174
Cummings-Har 142
Bond-Har 141
Spalding-Chi 139

Opponents' Batting Avg.
Bradley-StL 211
Bond-Har 220
Devlin-Lou 224
Cummings-Har 239
Spalding-Chi 247

Opponents' On Base Pct.
Bradley-StL 224
Bond-Har 227
Devlin-Lou 235
Cummings-Har 251
Spalding-Chi 256

Starter Runs
Bradley-StL 68.9
Devlin-Lou 51.5
Spalding-Chi 32.5
Bond-Har 28.6
Cummings-Har 15.4

Adjusted Starter Runs
Devlin-Lou 79.8
Bradley-StL 57.9
Spalding-Chi 40.5
Bond-Har 31.5
Cummings-Har 16.9

Clutch Pitching Index
Knight-Phi 126
Mathews-NY 116
Borden-Bos 108
Dean-Cin 108
Zettlein-Phi 107

Relief Runs

Adjusted Relief Runs

Relief Ranking

Total Pitcher Index
Devlin-Lou 7.9
Bradley-StL 5.7
Spalding-Chi 4.7
Bond-Har 3.3
McVey-Chi 7

Total Baseball Ranking
Devlin-Lou 7.9
Bradley-StL 5.7
Spalding-Chi 4.5
Barnes-Chi 3.9
Bond-Har 3.3

1877 National League

TEAM	G	W	L	PCT	GB	R	OR	AB	H	2B	3B	HR	BB	SO	AVG	OBP	SLG	PRO	PRO+	BR	/A	PF	CHI	RC	SB	CS	SBA	SBR
BOS	61	42	18	.700		419	263	2368	700	91	37	4	65	121	.296	.314	.370	.684	114	47	34	104	104	283				
LOU	61	35	25	.583	7	339	288	2355	659	75	36	9	58	140	.280	.297	.354	.651	92	19	-44	118	92	254				
HAR	60	31	27	.534	10	341	311	2358	637	63	31	4	30	97	.270	.279	.328	.607	105	-17	20	89	103	222				
STL	60	28	32	.467	14	284	318	2178	531	51	36	1	57	147	.244	.263	.302	.565	84	-46	-29	95	102	177				
CHI	60	26	33	.441	15.5	366	375	2273	633	79	30	0	57	111	.278	.296	.340	.636	92	8	-32	112	105	234				
CIN	58	15	42	.263	25.5	291	485	2135	545	72	34	6	78	110	.255	.282	.329	.611	107	-11	25	89	94	203				
TOT	180					2040		13667	3705	431	204	24	345	726	.271	.289	.338	.627										

TEAM	CG	SH	SV	IP	H	H/G	HR	BB	SO	RAT	ERA	ERA+	OAV	OOB	PR	/A	PF	CPI	FA	E	DP	FW	PW	BW	SBW	DIF
BOS	61	7	0	548	557	9.1	5	38	177	9.8	2.15	130	.249	.261	40	40	100	98	.889	290	36	1.2	3.6	3.0		4.2
LOU	61	4	0	559	617	9.9	4	41	141	10.6	2.25	147	.270	.283	34	65	118	119	.904	267	37	2.4	5.8	-3.9		.8
HAR	59	4	0	544	572	9.5	2	56	99	10.4	2.32	105	.253	.271	30	7	87	97	.885	313	32	-.2	.6	1.8		-.2
STL	52	1	0	541	582	9.7	2	92	132	11.2	2.66	98	.262	.291	9	-4	93	102	.892	281	29	1.4	-.4	-2.6		-.5
CHI	45	3	3	534	630	10.6	7	58	92	11.6	3.37	88	.274	.292	-33	-24	106	87	.883	313	43	-.2	-2.1	-2.9		1.7
CIN	48	1	1	515	747	13.1	4	61	85	14.1	4.19	63	.318	.335	-79	-89	94	102	.851	394	33	-4.7	-7.9	2.2		-3.1
TOT	326	20	4	3241		10.3				11.2	2.81		.271	.289					.884	1858	210					

Runs
O'Rourke-Bos 68
G.Wright-Bos 58
McVey-Chi 58
Start-Har 55

Hits
J.White-Bos 103
McVey-Chi 98
O'Rourke-Bos 96
Cassidy-Har....... 95
Start-Har 90

Doubles
Anson-Chi 19
York-Har 16
Manning-Cin 16
G.Wright-Bos 15
Hall-Lou 15

Triples
J.White-Bos 11
Jones-Cin-Chi-Cin . 10
Hall-Lou 8
Brown-Bos 8

Home Runs
Pike-Cin 4
Shaffer-Lou 3
Jones-Cin-Chi-Cin .. 2
J.White-Bos 2
Snyder-Lou 2

Total Bases
J.White-Bos 145
McVey-Chi 121
O'Rourke-Bos 118
Hall-Lou 118
Cassidy-Har 115

Runs Batted In
J.White-Bos 49
Peters-Chi 41
Sutton-Bos 39
Jones-Cin-Chi-Cin . 38
York-Har 37

Runs Produced
J.White-Bos 98
McVey-Chi 94
G.Wright-Bos 93
O'Rourke-Bos 91
Jones-Cin-Chi-Cin . 89

Bases On Balls
O'Rourke-Bos 20
Jones-Cin-Chi-Cin . 15
Hall-Lou 12
Booth-Cin......... 12
Force-StL 11

Batting Average
J.White-Bos 387
Cassidy-Har 378
McVey-Chi 368
O'Rourke-Bos 362
Anson-Chi 337

On Base Percentage
O'Rourke-Bos 407
J.White-Bos 405
McVey-Chi 387
Cassidy-Har 386
Anson-Chi 360

Slugging Average
J.White-Bos 545
Jones-Cin-Chi-Cin .471
Cassidy-Har......458
McVey-Chi 455
O'Rourke-Bos 445

Production
J.White-Bos 950
O'Rourke-Bos 852
Cassidy-Har......844
McVey-Chi 842
Jones-Cin-Chi-Cin .824

Adjusted Production
J.White-Bos 190
Cassidy-Har 184
Jones-Cin-Chi-Cin 175
O'Rourke-Bos 162
Manning-Cin 157

Batter Runs
J.White-Bos 28.2
O'Rourke-Bos ... 21.2
McVey-Chi 18.9
Cassidy-Har...... 17.6
Jones-Cin-Chi-Cin 15.6

Adjusted Batter Runs
J.White-Bos 26.8
Cassidy-Har...... 21.6
O'Rourke-Bos ... 19.7
Jones-Cin-Chi-Cin 19.4
Manning-Cin 15.0

Clutch Hitting Index
Ferguson-Har 165
Croft-StL 162
Bond-Bos 150
Spalding-Chi 150
Sutton-Bos 146

Runs Created
J.White-Bos 60
O'Rourke-Bos ... 49
McVey-Chi 48
Cassidy-Har 45
Hall-Lou 43

Total Average
J.White-Bos 939
O'Rourke-Bos 817
Jones-Cin-Chi-Cin .776
McVey-Chi 768
Cassidy-Har......756

Stolen Bases

Stolen Base Average

Stolen Base Runs

Fielding Runs
Gerhardt-Lou..... 19.8
Peters-Chi 19.1
Ferguson-Har 17.2
Brown-Bos 15.4
Snyder-Lou 15.2

Total Player Rating
Jones-Cin-Chi-Cin . 2.6
J.White-Bos 2.4
Peters-Chi 1.8
Gerhardt-Lou..... 1.8
Anson-Chi 1.6

Wins
Bond-Bos......... 40
Devlin-Lou 35
Larkin-Har 29
Nichols-StL 18
Bradley-Chi 18

Win Percentage
Bond-Bos.........702
Devlin-Lou 583
Larkin-Har 537
Nichols-StL 439
Bradley-Chi 439

Games
Devlin-Lou 61
Bond-Bos......... 58
Larkin-Har 56
Bradley-Chi 50
Nichols-StL 42

Complete Games
Devlin-Lou 61
Bond-Bos......... 58
Larkin-Har 55
Nichols-StL 35
Bradley-Chi 35

Shutouts
Bond-Bos......... 6
Larkin-Har 4
Devlin-Lou 4
Bradley-Chi 2

Saves
McVey-Chi 2
Spalding-Chi 1
Manning-Cin 1

Innings Pitched
Devlin-Lou 559.0
Bond-Bos 521.0
Larkin-Har 501.0
Bradley-Chi 394.0
Nichols-StL 350.0

Fewest Hits/Game
Bond-Bos........ 9.16
Larkin-Har 9.16
Nichols-StL 9.67
Blong-StL 9.75
Devlin-Lou 9.93

Fewest BB/Game
Bond-Bos.........62
Devlin-Lou 66
Cummings-Cin ...75
Bradley-Chi 89
Larkin-Har 95

Strikeouts
Bond-Bos....... 170
Devlin-Lou 141
Larkin-Har 96
Nichols-StL 80
Bradley-Chi 59

Strikeouts/Game
Mitchell-Cin 3.69
Bond-Bos 2.94
Blong-StL 2.45
Devlin-Lou 2.27
Nichols-StL 2.06

Ratio
Bond-Bos........ 9.78
Larkin-Har 10.11
Devlin-Lou 10.59
Nichols-StL 11.03
Bradley-Chi 11.22

Earned Run Average
Bond-Bos........ 2.11
Larkin-Har 2.14
Devlin-Lou 2.25
Nichols-StL 2.60
Blong-StL........ 2.74

Adjusted ERA
Devlin-Lou 147
Bond-Bos........ 133
Larkin-Har 114
Nichols-StL 100
Blong-StL......... 95

Opponents' Batting Avg.
Larkin-Har 245
Bond-Bos.........249
Blong-StL.........262
Nichols-StL 263
Bradley-Chi 269

Opponents' On Base Pct.
Bond-Bos.........261
Larkin-Har 264
Devlin-Lou 283
Bradley-Chi 286
Nichols-StL 289

Starter Runs
Bond-Bos........ 40.5
Larkin-Har 37.3
Devlin-Lou 34.4
Reis-Chi 8.2
Nichols-StL 8.2

Adjusted Starter Runs
Devlin-Lou 65.4
Bond-Bos........ 40.5
Larkin-Har 16.3
Reis-Chi 8.9

Clutch Pitching Index
Mathews-Cin 123
Devlin-Lou 119
Booth-Cin....... 104
Nichols-StL 104
Blong-StL........ 101

Relief Runs

Adjusted Relief Runs

Relief Ranking

Total Pitcher Index
Devlin-Lou 6.3
Bond-Bos........ 3.6
Larkin-Har 1.8
Reis-Chi 6
Spalding-Chi 0

Total Baseball Ranking
Devlin-Lou 6.3
Bond-Bos........ 3.5
Jones-Cin-Chi-Cin . 2.6
J.White-Bos 2.4
Peters-Chi 1.8

TEAM	G	W	L	PCT	GB	R	OR	AB	H	2B	3B	HR	BB	SO	AVG	OBP	SLG	PRO	PRO+	BR	/A	PF	CHI	RC	SB	CS	SBA	SBR
BOS	60	41	19	.683		298	241	2220	535	75	25	2	35	154	.241	.253	.300	.553	79	-35	-59	108	110	173				
CIN	61	37	23	.617	4	333	281	2281	629	67	22	5	58	141	.276	.294	.331	.625	120	21	51	91	98	227				
PRO	62	33	27	.550	8	353	337	2298	604	107	30	8	50	218	.263	.279	.346	.625	109	19	20	100	104	227				
CHI	61	30	30	.500	11	371	331	2333	677	91	20	3	88	157	.290	.316	.350	.666	115	56	35	107	96	265				
IND	63	24	36	.400	17	293	328	2300	542	76	15	3	64	197	.236	.256	.286	.542	95	-43	0	87	105	173				
MIL	61	15	45	.250	26	256	386	2212	552	65	20	2	69	214	.250	.272	.300	.572	86	-18	-39	107	88	185				
TOT	184					1904		13644	3539	481	132	23	364	1081	.259	.279	.319	.598										

TEAM	CG	SH	SV	IP	H	H/G	HR	BB	SO	RAT	ERA	ERA+	OAV	OOB	PR	/A	PF	CPI	FA	E	DP	FW	PW	BW	SBW	DIF
BOS	58	9	0	544	595	9.8	6	38	184	10.5	2.32	102	.272	.284	-1	2	102	111	.914	228	48	3.5	.2	-5.5		12.8
CIN	61	6	0	548	546	9.0	2	63	220	10.0	1.84	116	.248	.269	28	17	92	108	.900	269	37	1.5	1.6	4.8		-.9
PRO	59	6	0	556	609	9.9	5	86	173	11.3	2.38	93	.265	.291	-5	-11	96	108	.892	311	42	-.5	-1.0	1.9		2.7
CHI	61	1	0	551	577	9.4	4	35	175	10.0	2.37	102	.253	.265	-4	3	105	85	.891	304	37	-.4	.3	3.3		-3.1
IND	59	2	1	578	621	9.7	3	87	182	11.0	2.32	87	.262	.288	-1	-19	88	106	.898	290	37	.9	-1.8	.0		-5.1
MIL	54	1	0	547	589	9.7	3	55	147	10.6	2.60	101	.255	.272	-18	1	114	82	.866	376	32	-4.4	.0	-3.6		-7.0
TOT	352	25	1	3324		9.6				10.6	2.30		.259	.279					.893	1778	233					

Runs
Higham-Pro	60
Start-Chi	58
York-Pro	56
Anson-Chi	55
Dalrymple-Mil	52

Hits
Start-Chi	100
Dalrymple-Mil	96
Hines-Pro	92
Ferguson-Chi	91

Doubles
Higham-Pro	22
Brown-Pro	21
York-Pro	19
Shaffer-Ind	19
O'Rourke-Bos	17

Triples
York-Pro	10
O'Rourke-Bos	7
Jones-Cin	7

Home Runs
Hines-Pro	4
Jones-Cin	3
McVey-Cin	2
McKelvy-Ind	2

Total Bases
York-Pro	125
Start-Chi	125
Hines-Pro	125
Shaffer-Ind	121
Higham-Pro	117

Runs Batted In
Hines-Pro	50
Brown-Pro	43
Anson-Chi	40
Jones-Cin	39
Ferguson-Chi	39

Runs Produced
Anson-Chi	95
Hines-Pro	88
Higham-Pro	88
Jones-Cin	86
Brown-Pro	86

Bases On Balls
Remsen-Chi	17
Larkin-Chi	17
Shaffer-Ind	13
Clapp-Ind	13
Anson-Chi	13

Batting Average
Hines-Pro	.358
Dalrymple-Mil	.354
Ferguson-Chi	.351
Start-Chi	.351
Anson-Chi	.341

On Base Percentage
Ferguson-Chi	.375
Anson-Chi	.372
Shaffer-Ind	.369
Dalrymple-Mil	.368
Hines-Pro	.363

Slugging Average
Hines-Pro	.486
York-Pro	.465
Shaffer-Ind	.455
Brown-Pro	.453
Jones-Cin	.441

Production
Hines-Pro	.849
Shaffer-Ind	.824
Start-Chi	.794
York-Pro	.793
Dalrymple-Mil	.789

Adjusted Production
Shaffer-Ind	196
Hines-Pro	177
Jones-Cin	163
York-Pro	159
Brown-Pro	153

Batter Runs
Hines-Pro	20.0
Shaffer-Ind	19.6
Start-Chi	17.2
Dalrymple-Mil	16.4
York-Pro	16.1

Adjusted Batter Runs
Shaffer-Ind	24.7
Hines-Pro	20.2
York-Pro	16.2
Jones-Cin	16.1
Start-Chi	14.6

Clutch Hitting Index
McClellan-Chi	193
Hague-Pro	166
McKelvy-Ind	164
Redmon-Pro	148
Harbidge-Chi	145

Runs Created
Hines-Pro	47
Shaffer-Ind	46
Start-Chi	46
Dalrymple-Mil	43
York-Pro	42

Total Average
Hines-Pro	.770
Shaffer-Ind	.761
York-Pro	.715
Brown-Pro	.692
Start-Chi	.686

Stolen Bases

Stolen Base Average

Stolen Base Runs

Fielding Runs
Burdock-Bos	21.3
Hague-Pro	18.7
Ferguson-Chi	15.9
Kelly-Cin	11.1
Wright-Bos	10.5

Total Player Rating
Ferguson-Chi	2.9
Shaffer-Ind	2.7
Burdock-Bos	2.2
Hines-Pro	1.8
Jones-Cin	1.7

Wins
Bond-Bos	40
W.White-Cin	30
Larkin-Chi	29
Ward-Pro	22
Nolan-Ind	13

Win Percentage
Bond-Bos	.678
Ward-Pro	.629
W.White-Cin	.588
Larkin-Chi	.527

Games
Bond-Bos	59
Larkin-Chi	56
W.White-Cin	52
Weaver-Mil	45
Nolan-Ind	38

Complete Games
Bond-Bos	57
Larkin-Chi	56
W.White-Cin	52
Weaver-Mil	39

Shutouts
Bond-Bos	9
Ward-Pro	6
W.White-Cin	5

Saves
Healey-Pro-Ind	1

Innings Pitched
Bond-Bos	532.2
Larkin-Chi	506.0
W.White-Cin	468.0
Weaver-Mil	383.0
Nolan-Ind	347.0

Fewest Hits/Game
Mitchell-Cin	7.76
Ward-Pro	8.30
Weaver-Mil	8.72
Larkin-Chi	9.09
W.White-Cin	9.17

Fewest BB/Game
Weaver-Mil	.49
Larkin-Chi	.55
Bond-Bos	.56
Nichols-Pro	.73
W.White-Cin	.87

Strikeouts
Bond-Bos	182
W.White-Cin	169
Larkin-Chi	163
Nolan-Ind	125
Ward-Pro	116

Strikeouts/Game
Mitchell-Cin	5.74
Wheeler-Pro	3.63
W.White-Cin	3.25
Nolan-Ind	3.24
Ward-Pro	3.13

Ratio
Weaver-Mil	9.21
Ward-Pro	9.22
Larkin-Chi	9.64
Mitchell-Cin	9.79
W.White-Cin	10.04

Earned Run Average
Ward-Pro	1.51
McCormick-Ind	1.69
W.White-Cin	1.79
Weaver-Mil	1.95
Bond-Bos	2.06

Adjusted ERA
Ward-Pro	146
Weaver-Mil	134
McCormick-Ind	120
W.White-Cin	119
Bond-Bos	114

Opponents' Batting Avg.
Mitchell-Cin	.223
Ward-Pro	.231
Weaver-Mil	.237
Larkin-Chi	.246
W.White-Cin	.252

Opponents' On Base Pct.
Weaver-Mil	.247
Ward-Pro	.251
Larkin-Chi	.257
Mitchell-Cin	.265
W.White-Cin	.269

Starter Runs
Ward-Pro	29.5
W.White-Cin	26.8
Weaver-Mil	15.1
Bond-Bos	14.4
McCormick-Ind	8.0

Adjusted Starter Runs
Weaver-Mil	28.6
Ward-Pro	25.7
Bond-Bos	17.6
W.White-Cin	17.6
Larkin-Chi	10.2

Clutch Pitching Index
McCormick-Ind	152
Healey-Pro-Ind	122
Bond-Bos	119
W.White-Cin	114
Nichols-Pro	112

Relief Runs

Adjusted Relief Runs

Relief Ranking

Total Pitcher Index
Ward-Pro	2.8
Weaver-Mil	2.6
Larkin-Chi	1.9
Bond-Bos	1.3
W.White-Cin	.8

Total Baseball Ranking
Ferguson-Chi	2.9
Ward-Pro	2.8
Shaffer-Ind	2.7
Weaver-Mil	2.4
Burdock-Bos	2.2

TEAM	G	W	L	PCT	GB	R	OR	AB	H	2B	3B	HR	BB	SO	AVG	OBP	SLG	PRO	PRO+	BR	/A	PF	CHI	RC	SB	CS	SBA	SBR
PRO	85	59	25	.702		612	355	3392	1003	142	55	12	91	172	.296	.314	.381	.695	134	110	118	98	103	416				
BOS	84	54	30	.643	5	562	348	3217	883	138	51	20	90	222	.274	.294	.368	.662	118	68	58	102	107	357				
BUF	79	46	32	.590	10	394	365	2906	733	105	54	2	78	314	.252	.272	.328	.600	98	1	-9	102	95	265				
CHI	83	46	33	.582	10.5	437	411	3116	808	167	32	5	73	294	.259	.276	.336	.612	98	14	-12	106	96	297				
CIN	81	43	37	.538	14	485	464	3085	813	127	53	8	66	207	.264	.279	.347	.626	-115	27	49	95	105	306				
CLE	82	27	55	.329	31	322	461	2987	666	116	29	4	37	214	.223	.232	.285	.517	73	-83	-79	99	96	203				
SYR	71	22	48	.314	30	276	462	2611	592	61	19	5	28	238	.227	.235	.270	.505	78	-82	-41	89	98	170				
TRO	77	19	56	.253	35.5	321	543	2841	673	102	24	4	45	182	.237	.249	.294	.543	87	-54	-27	93	93	213				
TOT	321					3409		24155	6171	958	317	58	508	1843	.255	.271	.329	.599										

TEAM	CG	SH	SV	IP	H	H/G	HR	BB	SO	RAT	ERA	ERA+	OAV	OOB	PR	/A	PF	CPI	FA	E	DP	FW	PW	BW	SBW	DIF
PRO	73	3	2	776	765	8.9	9	62	329	9.6	2.18	108	.243	.258	27	15	94	99	.902	382	41	1.8	1.4	10.9		2.9
BOS	80	13	0	753	757	9.0	9	46	230	9.6	2.19	114	.251	.262	26	25	100	107	.913	319	58	4.9	2.3	5.3		-.5
BUF	78	8	0	713	698	8.8	3	47	198	9.4	2.34	112	.242	.254	13	22	105	87	.906	331	62	2.9	2.0	-.8		2.9
CHI	82	6	0	744	762	9.2	5	57	211	9.9	2.46	105	.244	.258	3	9	103	86	.900	381	52	1.3	.8	-1.1		5.4
CIN	79	4	0	726	756	9.4	11	81	246	10.4	2.29	102	.248	.267	16	4	93	104	.877	454	48	-3.1	.4	4.5		1.2
CLE	79	3	0	741	818	9.9	4	116	287	11.3	2.65	95	.265	.292	-12	-12	100	111	.889	406	42	-.3	-1.1	-7.3		-5.4
SYR	64	5	0	649	775	10.7	4	52	132	11.5	3.19	74	.277	.290	-50	-59	95	96	.873	398	37	-2.7	-5.4	-3.8		-1.1
TRO	75	3	0	695	840	10.9	13	47	210	11.5	2.80	89	.275	.286	-23	-22	100	110	.875	460	44	-4.4	-2.0	-2.5		-9.6
TOT	610	45	2	5797		9.6				10.4	2.50		.255	.271					.892	3131	384					

Runs
Jones-Bos	85
Hines-Pro	81
Wright-Pro	79
Kelly-Cin	78
Dickerson-Cin	73

Hits
Hines-Pro	146
O'Rourke-Pro	126
Kelly-Cin	120
Jones-Bos	112
J.White-Cin	110

Doubles
Eden-Cle	31
York-Pro	25
Hines-Pro	25
Dalrymple-Chi	25
Houck-Bos	24

Triples
Dickerson-Cin	14
Williamson-Chi	13
Kelly-Cin	12
O'Rourke-Bos	11

Home Runs
Jones-Bos	9
O'Rourke-Bos	6
Brouthers-Tro	4
Eden-Cle	3

Total Bases
Hines-Pro	197
Jones-Bos	181
Kelly-Cin	170
O'Rourke-Pro	166
O'Rourke-Bos	165

Runs Batted In
O'Rourke-Bos	62
Jones-Bos	62
Dickerson-Cin	57
McVey-Cin	55

Runs Produced
Jones-Bos	138
Hines-Pro	131
Dickerson-Cin	128
O'Rourke-Bos	125
Kelly-Cin	123

Bases On Balls
Jones-Bos	29
Williamson-Chi	24
York-Pro	19
Richardson-Buf	16
Barnes-Cin	16

Batting Average
Hines-Pro	.357
O'Rourke-Pro	.348
Kelly-Cin	.348
O'Rourke-Bos	.341
J.White-Cin	.330

On Base Percentage
O'Rourke-Pro	.371
Hines-Pro	.369
Jones-Bos	.367
Kelly-Cin	.363
O'Rourke-Bos	.357

Slugging Average
O'Rourke-Bos	.521
Jones-Bos	.510
Kelly-Cin	.493
Hines-Pro	.482
O'Rourke-Pro	.459

Production
O'Rourke-Bos	.877
Jones-Bos	.877
Kelly-Cin	.855
Hines-Pro	.851
O'Rourke-Pro	.829

Adjusted Production
Kelly-Cin	188
Jones-Bos	182
O'Rourke-Bos	181
Hines-Pro	181
O'Rourke-Pro	174

Batter Runs
Jones-Bos	33.1
Hines-Pro	32.9
Kelly-Cin	28.1
O'Rourke-Bos	28.0
O'Rourke-Pro	27.2

Adjusted Batter Runs
Hines-Pro	33.8
Jones-Bos	31.9
Kelly-Cin	30.6
O'Rourke-Pro	28.0
O'Rourke-Bos	27.0

Clutch Hitting Index
Gerhardt-Cin	162
Brown-Pro-Chi	148
Morrill-Bos	145
McVey-Cin	137
J.White-Cin	134

Runs Created
Hines-Pro	75
Jones-Bos	68
Kelly-Cin	63
O'Rourke-Pro	63
O'Rourke-Bos	60

Total Average
Jones-Bos	.864
O'Rourke-Bos	.828
Kelly-Cin	.791
Hines-Pro	.779
O'Rourke-Pro	.758

Stolen Bases

Stolen Base Average

Stolen Base Runs

Fielding Runs
Snyder-Cin	23.9
Wright-Pro	20.5
Shaffer-Chi	20.3
Evans-Tro	17.7
Fulmer-Buf	17.4

Total Player Rating
Kelly-Cin	3.8
Jones-Bos	3.6
Hines-Pro	3.3
Williamson-Chi	3.3
Wright-Pro	3.2

Wins
Ward-Pro	47
W.White-Cin	43
Bond-Bos	43
Galvin-Buf	37
Larkin-Chi	31

Win Percentage
Ward-Pro	.712
Bond-Bos	.694
Hankinson-Chi	.600
W.White-Cin	.581
Galvin-Buf	.578

Games
W.White-Cin	76
Ward-Pro	70
Galvin-Buf	66
Bond-Bos	64
McCormick-Cle	62

Complete Games
W.White-Cin	75
Galvin-Buf	65
McCormick-Cle	59
Bond-Bos	59
Ward-Pro	58

Shutouts
Bond-Bos	11
Galvin-Buf	6
McCormick-Syr	5
W.White-Cin	4
Larkin-Chi	4

Saves
Ward-Pro	1
Mathews-Pro	1

Innings Pitched
W.White-Cin	680.0
Galvin-Buf	593.0
Ward-Pro	587.0
Bond-Bos	555.1
McCormick-Cle	546.1

Fewest Hits/Game
McGunnigle-Buf	8.48
Ward-Pro	8.75
Bond-Bos	8.80
Galvin-Buf	8.88
W.White-Cin	8.95

Fewest BB/Game
Bond-Bos	.39
Galvin-Buf	.47
Bradley-Tro	.48
Larkin-Chi	.53
Ward-Pro	.55

Strikeouts
Ward-Pro	239
W.White-Cin	232
McCormick-Cle	197
Bond-Bos	155
Larkin-Chi	142

Strikeouts/Game
McGunnigle-Buf	4.65
Mathews-Pro	4.29
Mitchell-Cle	4.16
Ward-Pro	3.66
McCormick-Cle	3.25

Ratio
Bond-Bos	9.19
Ward-Pro	9.31
Galvin-Buf	9.35
Larkin-Chi	9.54
McGunnigle-Buf	9.68

Earned Run Average
Bond-Bos	1.96
W.White-Cin	1.99
Ward-Pro	2.15
Salisbury-Tro	2.22
Galvin-Buf	2.28

Adjusted ERA
Bond-Bos	127
W.White-Cin	117
Galvin-Buf	115
Salisbury-Tro	112
Ward-Pro	110

Opponents' Batting Avg.
McGunnigle-Buf	.235
W.White-Cin	.238
Ward-Pro	.239
Larkin-Chi	.240
Galvin-Buf	.243

Opponents' On Base Pct.
Larkin-Chi	.250
Ward-Pro	.250
Galvin-Buf	.253
W.White-Cin	.256
Bond-Bos	.259

Starter Runs
W.White-Cin	38.6
Bond-Bos	33.0
Ward-Pro	22.8
Galvin-Buf	14.5
Goldsmith-Tro	6.5

Adjusted Starter Runs
Bond-Bos	32.3
W.White-Cin	26.2
Galvin-Buf	22.2
Ward-Pro	13.7
Larkin-Chi	7.4

Clutch Pitching Index
Salisbury-Tro	125
Mathews-Pro	122
Bond-Bos	117
McCormick-Cle	111
Mitchell-Cle	109

Relief Runs

Adjusted Relief Runs

Relief Ranking

Total Pitcher Index
Bond-Bos	3.8
Galvin-Buf	2.9
Ward-Pro	2.9
McCormick-Cle	.7
Goldsmith-Tro	.7

Total Baseball Ranking
Kelly-Cin	3.8
Bond-Bos	3.6
Jones-Bos	3.6
Hines-Pro	3.3
Williamson-Chi	3.3

TEAM	G	W	L	PCT	GB	R	OR	AB	H	2B	3B	HR	BB	SO	AVG	OBP	SLG	PRO	PRO+	BR	/A	PF	CHI	RC	SB	CS	SBA	SBR
CHI	86	67	17	.798		538	317	3135	876	164	39	4	104	217	.279	.303	.360	.663	119	81	56	106	109	350				
PRO	87	52	32	.619	15	419	299	3196	793	114	34	8	89	186	.248	.268	.313	.581	101	-6	7	97	102	275				
CLE	85	47	37	.560	20	387	337	3002	726	130	52	7	76	237	.242	.261	.327	.588	102	15	-6	105	95	275				
TRO	83	41	42	.494	25.5	392	438	3007	755	114	37	5	120	260	.251	.280	.319	.599	100	-1	7	98	99	260				
WOR	85	40	43	.482	26.5	412	370	3024	699	129	54	8	81	278	.231	.251	.316	.567	86	-21	-55	109	110	246				
BOS	86	40	44	.476	27	416	456	3080	779	134	41	20	105	221	.253	.278	.343	.621	115	34	47	97	95	300				
BUF	85	24	58	.293	42	331	502	2962	669	104	37	3	90	327	.226	.249	.289	.538	82	-48	-55	102	97	218				
CIN	83	21	59	.263	44	296	472	2895	649	91	36	7	75	267	.224	.244	.288	.532	82	-54	-49	99	91	208				
TOT	340					3191		24301	5946	980	328	62	740	1993	.245	.267	.320	.587										

TEAM	CG	SH	SV	IP	H	H/G	HR	BB	SO	RAT	ERA	ERA+	OAV	OOB	PR	/A	PF	CPI	FA	E	DP	FW	PW	BW	SBW	DIF
CHI	80	8	3	775	622	7.2	8	129	367	8.7	1.93	126	.209	.242	38	43	102	83	.913	329	41	2.3	4.2	5.4		13.1
PRO	75	13	2	799	663	7.5	7	51	286	8.0	1.64	134	.215	.228	65	49	93	87	.910	357	53	1.1	4.8	.7		3.5
CLE	83	7	1	759²	685	8.1	4	98	289	9.3	1.90	124	.228	.253	40	39	99	101	.910	330	52	2.0	3.8	.7		-1.5
TRO	81	4	0	738	763	9.3	8	113	173	10.7	2.74	92	.256	.283	-30	-18	106	101	.900	366	58	-.3	-1.7	-.6		2.2
WOR	68	7	5	762²	709	8.4	13	97	297	9.5	2.27	115	.233	.257	9	28	109	94	.906	355	49	.7	2.7	-5.3		.4
BOS	70	4	0	744²	840	10.2	2	86	187	11.2	3.08	74	.276	.296	-59	-67	96	102	.901	367	54	.3	-6.5	4.6		-.4
BUF	72	6	1	739	879	10.7	10	78	186	11.7	3.09	79	.279	.297	-59	-52	104	108	.891	408	55	-2.1	-5.1	-5.3		-4.5
CIN	79	3	0	713¹	785	9.9	10	88	208	11.0	2.44	102	.259	.280	-5	5	105	116	.877	437	49	-4.1	.5	-4.8		-10.7
TOT	608	52	12	6031¹		8.9				10.0	2.37		.245	.267					.901	2949	411					

Runs
Dalrymple-Chi 91
Stovey-Wor 76
Kelly-Chi 72
J.O'Rourke-Bos ... 71
Gore-Chi 70

Hits
Dalrymple-Chi 126
Anson-Chi 120
Gore-Chi 116
Hines-Pro 115
Connor-Tro 113

Doubles
Dunlap-Cle 27
Dalrymple-Chi 25
Anson-Chi 24
Gore-Chi 23
J.O'Rourke-Bos ... 22

Triples
Stovey-Wor 14
Dalrymple-Chi 12
J.O'Rourke-Bos ... 11
Hornung-Buf 11
Phillips-Cle 10

Home Runs
Stovey-Wor 6
J.O'Rourke-Bos ... 6
Jones-Bos 5
Dunlap-Cle 4

Total Bases
Dalrymple-Chi 175
Stovey-Wor 161
J.O'Rourke-Bos .. 160
Dunlap-Cle 160
Connor-Tro 156

Runs Batted In
Anson-Chi 74
Kelly-Chi 60
Gore-Chi 47
Connor-Tro 47
J.O'Rourke-Bos ... 45

Runs Produced
Kelly-Chi 131
Dalrymple-Chi 127
Anson-Chi 127
Gore-Chi 115
J.O'Rourke-Bos .. 110

Bases On Balls
Ferguson-Tro 24
J.O'Rourke-Bos ... 21
Gore-Chi 21
Clapp-Cin 21
Crowley-Buf 19

Batting Average
Gore-Chi .... .360
Anson-Chi .... .337
Connor-Tro ...... .332
Dalrymple-Chi .... .330
Burns-Chi .... .309

On Base Percentage
Gore-Chi .... .399
Anson-Chi .... .362
Connor-Tro ...... .357
Dalrymple-Chi .... .335
Burns-Chi .... .333

Slugging Average
Gore-Chi .... .463
Connor-Tro ...... .459
Dalrymple-Chi .... .458
Stovey-Wor ...... .454
J.O'Rourke-Bos .. .441

Production
Gore-Chi .... .862
Connor-Tro ...... .816
Dalrymple-Chi .... .793
Anson-Chi .... .781
J.O'Rourke-Bos ...756

Adjusted Production
Gore-Chi 180
Connor-Tro 166
Jones-Bos 159
J.O'Rourke-Bos .. 158
Dalrymple-Chi ... 156

Batter Runs
Gore-Chi 30.4
Connor-Tro 25.4
Dalrymple-Chi .. 24.5
Anson-Chi 22.9
J.O'Rourke-Bos .. 19.9

Adjusted Batter Runs
Gore-Chi 27.8
Connor-Tro 23.1
Dalrymple-Chi .. 21.6
J.O'Rourke-Bos .. 21.5
Anson-Chi 20.1

Clutch Hitting Index
Anson-Chi 171
Kelly-Chi 165
Richmond-Wor ... 153
Hanlon-Cle 146
Whitney-Wor 145

Runs Created
Gore-Chi 61
Dalrymple-Chi 60
Connor-Tro 57
Anson-Chi 55
J.O'Rourke-Bos ... 52

Total Average
Gore-Chi .... .825
Connor-Tro ...... .744
Dalrymple-Chi .... .695
Anson-Chi .... .691
J.O'Rourke-Bos .. .688

Stolen Bases

Stolen Base Average

Stolen Base Runs

Fielding Runs
Irwin-Wor 31.2
Force-Buf 30.9
Bradley-Pro 19.2
Shaffer-Cle 17.2
Clapp-Cin 17.2

Total Player Rating
Irwin-Wor 3.4
Gore-Chi 3.0
Clapp-Cin 2.9
Dunlap-Cle 2.7
Hines-Pro 2.4

Wins
McCormick-Cle ... 45
Corcoran-Chi 43
Ward-Pro 39
Welch-Tro 34
Richmond-Wor 32

Win Percentage
Goldsmith-Chi 875
Corcoran-Chi 754
Ward-Pro 619
McCormick-Cle 616
Welch-Tro 531

Games
Richmond-Wor 74
McCormick-Cle 74
Ward-Pro 70
Welch-Tro 65

Complete Games
McCormick-Cle ... 72
Welch-Tro 64
Ward-Pro 59
W.White-Cin 58

Shutouts
Ward-Pro 8
McCormick-Cle 7
Richmond-Wor 5
Galvin-Buf 5

Saves
Richmond-Wor 3
Corey-Wor 2
Corcoran-Chi 2

Innings Pitched
McCormick-Cle .. 657.2
Ward-Pro 595.0
Richmond-Wor .. 590.2
Welch-Tro 574.0
Corcoran-Chi 536.1

Fewest Hits/Game
Keefe-Tro 6.09
Corcoran-Chi 6.78
Bradley-Pro 7.26
Ward-Pro 7.58
Corey-Wor 7.95

Fewest BB/Game
Bradley-Pro 28
Galvin-Buf 63
Ward-Pro 68
Weidman-Buf 71
Goldsmith-Chi 77

Strikeouts
Corcoran-Chi 268
McCormick-Cle ... 260
Richmond-Wor ... 243
Ward-Pro 230
W.White-Cin 161

Strikeouts/Game
Corcoran-Chi 4.50
Goldsmith-Chi 3.85
Richmond-Wor ... 3.70
Keefe-Tro 3.69
McCormick-Cle ... 3.56

Ratio
Bradley-Pro 7.53
Keefe-Tro 7.54
Ward-Pro 8.26
Corcoran-Chi 8.44
Goldsmith-Chi 8.86

Earned Run Average
Keefe-Tro .... .86
Bradley-Pro 1.38
Ward-Pro 1.74
Goldsmith-Chi 1.75
McCormick-Cle ... 1.85

Adjusted ERA
Keefe-Tro 294
Bradley-Pro 160
Goldsmith-Chi 138
McCormick-Cle ... 127
Ward-Pro 127

Opponents' Batting Avg.
Keefe-Tro 187
Corcoran-Chi 199
Bradley-Pro 210
Ward-Pro 217
Corey-Wor 219

Opponents' On Base Pct.
Bradley-Pro 217
Keefe-Tro 222
Ward-Pro 232
Corcoran-Chi 236
Corey-Wor 239

Starter Runs
Ward-Pro 42.0
McCormick-Cle ... 38.5
Corcoran-Chi 25.5
Bradley-Pro 21.7
Keefe-Tro 17.7

Adjusted Starter Runs
McCormick-Cle ... 36.8
Ward-Pro 30.8
Richmond-Wor ... 29.5
Corcoran-Chi 28.3
W.White-Cin 19.6

Clutch Pitching Index
W.White-Cin 124
Keefe-Tro 120
Bond-Bos 114
Poorman-Buf-Chi . 112
Galvin-Buf 111

Relief Runs

Adjusted Relief Runs

Relief Ranking

Total Pitcher Index
McCormick-Cle 4.0
Ward-Pro 3.5
Corcoran-Chi 3.2
Keefe-Tro 2.2
Richmond-Wor 2.0

Total Baseball Ranking
Ward-Pro 4.3
McCormick-Cle 3.7
Irwin-Wor 3.4
Bradley-Pro 3.4
Gore-Chi 3.0

1881 National League

TEAM	G	W	L	PCT	GB	R	OR	AB	H	2B	3B	HR	BB	SO	AVG	OBP	SLG	PRO	PRO+	BR	/A	PF	CHI	RC	SB	CS	SBA	SBR
CHI	84	56	28	.667		550	379	3114	918	157	36	12	140	224	.295	.325	.380	.705	119	85	64	105	105	394				
PRO	85	47	37	.560	9	447	426	3077	780	144	37	11	146	214	.253	.287	.335	.622	100	-4	3	98	104	304				
BUF	83	45	38	.542	10.5	440	447	3019	797	157	50	12	108	270	.264	.289	.361	.650	109	22	28	99	99	323				
DET	84	41	43	.488	15	439	429	2995	780	131	53	17	136	250	.260	.293	.357	.650	103	22	5	104	99	320				
TRO	85	39	45	.464	17	399	429	3046	754	124	31	5	140	240	.248	.281	.314	.595	86	-32	-54	105	100	275				
BOS	83	38	45	.458	17.5	349	410	2916	733	121	27	5	110	193	.251	.279	.317	.596	94	-31	-12	95	93	264				
CLE	85	36	48	.429	20	392	414	3117	796	120	39	7	132	224	.255	.286	.326	.612	100	-16	7	95	93	297				
WOR	83	32	50	.390	23	410	492	3093	781	114	31	7	121	169	.253	.281	.316	.597	86	-31	-56	106	102	281				
TOT	336					3426		24377	6339	1068	304	76	1033	1784	.260	.289	.338	.627										

TEAM	CG	SH	SV	IP	H	H/G	HR	BB	SO	RAT	ERA	ERA+	OAV	OOB	PR	/A	PF	CPI	FA	E	DP	FW	PW	BW	SBW	DIF
CHI	81	9	0	744²	722	8.7	14	122	228	10.2	2.43	113	.243	.273	29	26	99	97	.916	309	54	2.1	2.4	6.0		3.5
PRO	76	7	0	757²	756	9.0	5	138	264	10.6	2.40	111	.243	.275	32	22	96	94	.896	390	66	-2.0	2.1	.3		4.7
BUF	72	5	0	742¹	881	10.7	9	89	185	11.8	2.84	98	.281	.301	-5	-5	100	114	.892	408	48	-3.4	-.5	2.6		4.8
DET	83	10	0	744²	785	9.5	8	137	265	11.1	2.65	110	.257	.289	11	22	105	102	.906	338	80	.5	2.1	.5		-4.0
TRO	85	8	0	770	813	9.5	11	159	207	11.4	2.97	99	.265	.301	-17	-2	106	102	.917	311	70	2.2	-.2	-5.0		.0
BOS	72	6	3	730²	763	9.4	9	143	199	11.2	2.71	98	.258	.292	5	-4	96	103	.909	325	54	1.0	-.4	-1.1		-3.0
CLE	82	2	0	760	737	8.7	9	126	240	10.2	2.68	98	.244	.274	8	-5	94	87	.904	348	68	.2	-.5	.7		-6.4
WOR	80	5	0	737¹	882	10.8	11	120	196	12.2	3.54	85	.288	.315	-63	-43	109	101	.903	353	50	-.5	-4.0	-5.2		.8
TOT	631	52	3	5987¹		9.5				11.1	2.77		.260	.289					.905	2782	490					

Runs		Hits		Doubles		Triples		Home Runs		Total Bases	
Gore-Chi	86	Anson-Chi	137	Kelly-Chi	27	Rowe-Buf	11	Brouthers-Buf	8	Anson-Chi	175
Kelly-Chi	84	Dalrymple-Chi	117	Hines-Pro	27	Phillips-Cle	10	Bennett-Det	7	Dunlap-Cle	156
Dalrymple-Chi	72	Dickerson-Wor	116	Stovey-Wor	25			Farrell-Pro	5	Kelly-Chi	153
O'Rourke-Buf	71			Dunlap-Cle	25			Burns-Chi	4	Dalrymple-Chi	150
Farrell-Pro	69			White-Buf	24					Dickerson-Wor	149

Runs Batted In		Runs Produced		Bases On Balls		Batting Average		On Base Percentage		Slugging Average	
Anson-Chi	82	Anson-Chi	148	Clapp-Cle	35	Anson-Chi	.399	Anson-Chi	.442	Brouthers-Buf	.541
Bennett-Det	64	Kelly-Chi	137	York-Pro	29	Start-Pro	.328	York-Pro	.362	Anson-Chi	.510
Kelly-Chi	55	Gore-Chi	129	Ferguson-Tro	29	Dunlap-Cle	.325	Brouthers-Buf	.361	Bennett-Det	.478
		Knight-Det	118	Farrell-Pro	29	Dalrymple-Chi	.323	Dunlap-Cle	.358	Dunlap-Cle	.444
		Richardson-Buf	113			Kelly-Chi	.323	Gore-Chi	.354	Kelly-Chi	.433

Production		Adjusted Production		Batter Runs		Adjusted Batter Runs		Clutch Hitting Index		Runs Created	
Anson-Chi	.952	Anson-Chi	189	Anson-Chi	38.9	Anson-Chi	36.5	Anson-Chi	169	Anson-Chi	79
Brouthers-Buf	.902	Brouthers-Buf	182	Brouthers-Buf	24.1	Brouthers-Buf	24.6	Ward-Pro	167	Dunlap-Cle	57
Bennett-Det	.819	Dunlap-Cle	159	Dunlap-Cle	20.0	Dunlap-Cle	22.6	White-Buf	149	Kelly-Chi	55
Dunlap-Cle	.802	York-Pro	150	Bennett-Det	18.3	York-Pro	18.6	Richmond-Wor	147	Brouthers-Buf	54
York-Pro	.790	Bennett-Det	149	Kelly-Chi	18.0	Bennett-Det	16.5	Radbourn-Pro	146	Dalrymple-Chi	54

Total Average		Stolen Bases		Stolen Base Average		Stolen Base Runs		Fielding Runs		Total Player Rating	
Anson-Chi	.976							Ewing-Tro	25.3	Bennett-Det	3.4
Brouthers-Buf	.891							Richardson-Buf	24.6	Anson-Chi	3.3
Bennett-Det	.770							Force-Buf	24.3	Richardson-Buf	3.1
York-Pro	.745							Williamson-Chi	22.2	Dunlap-Cle	2.9
Dunlap-Cle	.734							Bennett-Det	18.3	Williamson-Chi	2.2

Wins		Win Percentage		Games		Complete Games		Shutouts		Saves	
Whitney-Bos	31	Radbourn-Pro	.694	Whitney-Bos	66	Whitney-Bos	57	Derby-Det	9	Mathews-Pro-Bos	2
Corcoran-Chi	31	Corcoran-Chi	.689	McCormick-Cle	59	McCormick-Cle	57	Whitney-Bos	6	Morrill-Bos	1
Derby-Det	29	Goldsmith-Chi	.649	Galvin-Buf	57	Derby-Det	55	Goldsmith-Chi	5		
Galvin-Buf	28	Welch-Tro	.538	Derby-Det	56	Richmond-Wor	50	Galvin-Buf	5		
McCormick-Cle	26	Galvin-Buf	.538	Richmond-Wor	53	Galvin-Buf	48				

Innings Pitched		Fewest Hits/Game		Fewest BB/Game		Strikeouts		Strikeouts/Game		Ratio	
Whitney-Bos	552.1	McCormick-Cle	8.28	Galvin-Buf	.87	Derby-Det	212	Derby-Det	3.86	Weidman-Det	9.39
McCormick-Cle	526.0	Weidman-Det	8.45	Weidman-Det	.94	McCormick-Cle	178	Corcoran-Chi	3.40	McCormick-Cle	9.72
Derby-Det	494.2	Radbourn-Pro	8.55	Goldsmith-Chi	1.20	Whitney-Bos	162	Ward-Pro	3.25	Goldsmith-Chi	10.15
Galvin-Buf	474.0	Corcoran-Chi	8.62	Richmond-Wor	1.32	Richmond-Wor	156	Radbourn-Pro	3.24	Radbourn-Pro	10.32
Richmond-Wor	462.1	Ward-Pro	8.89	McCormick-Cle	1.44	Corcoran-Chi	150	McCormick-Cle	3.05	Ward-Pro	10.34

Earned Run Average		Adjusted ERA		Opponents' Batting Avg.		Opponents' On Base Pct.		Starter Runs		Adjusted Starter Runs	
Weidman-Det	1.80	Weidman-Det	162	Radbourn-Pro	.235	Weidman-Det	.258	Derby-Det	31.5	Derby-Det	39.3
Ward-Pro	2.13	Derby-Det	132	McCormick-Cle	.235	McCormick-Cle	.265	Ward-Pro	23.7	Galvin-Buf	21.3
Derby-Det	2.20	Ward-Pro	125	Weidman-Det	.238	Radbourn-Pro	.270	Galvin-Buf	21.1	Ward-Pro	19.4
Corcoran-Chi	2.31	Corcoran-Chi	118	Corcoran-Chi	.242	Goldsmith-Chi	.271	Corcoran-Chi	20.3	Corcoran-Chi	18.7
Galvin-Buf	2.37	Galvin-Buf	117	Ward-Pro	.242	Ward-Pro	.271	McCormick-Cle	19.2	Weidman-Det	14.3

Clutch Pitching Index		Relief Runs		Adjusted Relief Runs		Relief Ranking		Total Pitcher Index		Total Baseball Ranking	
Galvin-Buf	123							Derby-Det	3.0	Bennett-Det	3.4
Derby-Det	112							Galvin-Buf	2.6	Anson-Chi	3.3
Weidman-Det	109							Ward-Pro	2.6	Richardson-Buf	3.1
Fox-Bos	108							Whitney-Bos	1.8	Dunlap-Cle	2.9
Lynch-Buf	106							Corcoran-Chi	1.4	Derby-Det	2.8

TEAM	G	W	L	PCT	GB	R	OR	AB	H	2B	3B	HR	BB	SO	AVG	OBP	SLG	PRO	PRO+	BR	/A	PF	CHI	RC	SB	CS	SBA	SBR
CHI	84	55	29	.655		604	353	3225	892	209	54	15	142	262	.277	.307	.389	.696	119	82	60	105	108	395				
PRO	84	52	32	.619	3	463	356	3104	776	121	53	11	102	255	.250	.274	.334	.608	96	-16	-15	100	105	291				
BUF	84	45	39	.536	10	500	461	3128	858	146	47	18	116	228	.274	.300	.368	.668	113	50	42	102	98	355				
BOS	85	45	39	.536	10	472	414	3118	823	114	50	15	134	244	.264	.294	.347	.641	107	23	22	100	97	326				
CLE	84	42	40	.512	12	402	411	3009	716	139	40	20	122	261	.238	.268	.331	.599	96	-24	-9	97	95	273				
DET	86	42	41	.506	12.5	407	488	3144	724	117	44	19	122	308	.230	.259	.314	.573	84	-53	-52	100	99	262				
TRO	85	35	48	.422	19.5	430	522	3057	747	116	59	12	109	298	.244	.270	.333	.603	99	-20	2	95	100	282				
WOR	84	18	66	.214	37	379	652	2984	689	109	57	16	113	303	.231	.259	.322	.581	85	-43	-54	102	95	255				
TOT	338					3657		24769	6225	1071	404	126	960	2159	.251	.279	.342	.622										

TEAM	CG	SH	SV	IP	H	H/G	HR	BB	SO	RAT	ERA	ERA+	OAV	OOB	PR	/A	PF	CPI	FA	E	DP	FW	PW	BW	SBW	DIF
CHI	83	7	0	763²	667	7.9	13	102	279	9.1	2.22	129	.221	.246	57	51	99	87	.898	376	54	.1	4.6	5.5		2.8
PRO	80	10	1	752	690	8.3	12	87	273	9.3	2.27	123	.228	.250	51	47	97	94	.901	371	67	.4	4.3	-1.4		6.7
BUF	79	3	0	737	778	9.5	16	114	287	10.9	3.25	90	.254	.280	-30	-30	101	89	.910	315	42	3.3	-2.7	3.8		-1.4
BOS	81	4	0	749	738	8.9	10	77	352	9.8	2.80	102	.239	.258	7	4	99	83	.910	314	37	3.6	.4	2.0		-2.9
CLE	81	4	0	751²	743	8.9	22	132	232	10.5	2.75	101	.249	.280	11	1	97	106	.905	358	71	1.1	.0	-.8		.7
DET	82	7	0	793	808	9.2	19	129	354	10.6	2.98	98	.248	.277	-9	-8	101	94	.893	396	44	-.4	-.7	-4.7		6.4
TRO	81	6	0	757	837	10.0	13	168	189	11.9	3.08	91	.268	.305	-16	-24	98	113	.887	432	70	-2.5	-2.2	.2		-2.0
WOR	75	0	0	738¹	964	11.8	21	151	195	13.6	3.75	83	.294	.325	-71	-54	107	115	.878	468	66	-4.6	-4.9	-4.9		-9.6
TOT	642	41	1	6041²		9.3				10.7	2.89		.251	.279					.897	3030	451					

Runs		Hits		Doubles		Triples		Home Runs		Total Bases	
Gore-Chi	99	Brouthers-Buf	129	Kelly-Chi	37	Connor-Tro	18	Wood-Det	7	Brouthers-Buf	192
Dalrymple-Chi	96	Anson-Chi	126	Anson-Chi	29	Wood-Det	12	Muldoon-Cle	6	Connor-Tro	185
Stovey-Wor	90			Hines-Pro	28	Corey-Wor	12	Brouthers-Buf	6	Hines-Pro	177
Kelly-Chi	81			Williamson-Chi	27					Anson-Chi	174
Purcell-Buf	79			Glasscock-Cle	27					Dalrymple-Chi	167

Runs Batted In		Runs Produced		Bases On Balls		Batting Average		On Base Percentage		Slugging Average	
Anson-Chi	83	Anson-Chi	151	Gore-Chi	29	Brouthers-Buf	.368	Brouthers-Buf	.403	Brouthers-Buf	.547
Brouthers-Buf	63	Gore-Chi	147	Williamson-Chi	27	Anson-Chi	.362	Anson-Chi	.397	Connor-Tro	.530
Williamson-Chi	60	Kelly-Chi	135	Shaffer-Cle	27	Connor-Tro	.330	Whitney-Bos	.382	Whitney-Bos	.510
Richardson-Buf	57	Dalrymple-Chi	131	Hanlon-Det	26	Start-Pro	.329	Gore-Chi	.369	Anson-Chi	.500
Kelly-Chi	55	Brouthers-Buf	128			Whitney-Bos	.323	Connor-Tro	.354	Hines-Pro	.467

Production		Adjusted Production		Batter Runs		Adjusted Batter Runs		Clutch Hitting Index		Runs Created	
Brouthers-Buf	.950	Brouthers-Buf	198	Brouthers-Buf	39.1	Brouthers-Buf	38.2	Anson-Chi	167	Brouthers-Buf	79
Anson-Chi	.897	Connor-Tro	188	Anson-Chi	32.7	Connor-Tro	32.1	Pfeffer-Tro	159	Anson-Chi	71
Whitney-Bos	.892	Whitney-Bos	183	Connor-Tro	29.7	Anson-Chi	30.3	Holbert-Tro	152	Connor-Tro	67
Connor-Tro	.884	Anson-Chi	177	Whitney-Bos	23.7	Whitney-Bos	23.6	Rowen-Bos	150	Hines-Pro	59
Hines-Pro	.793	Hines-Pro	151	Gore-Chi	22.2	Hines-Pro	20.7	Williamson-Chi	142	Gore-Chi	59

Total Average		Stolen Bases	Stolen Base Average	Stolen Base Runs	Fielding Runs		Total Player Rating	
Brouthers-Buf	.959				Glasscock-Cle	24.0	Glasscock-Cle	4.1
Whitney-Bos	.894				A.Irwin-Wor	20.5	Connor-Tro	2.7
Anson-Chi	.874				Evans-Wor	19.8	Williamson-Chi	2.7
Connor-Tro	.846				Dunlap-Cle	17.6	Brouthers-Buf	2.7
Gore-Chi	.736				Williamson-Chi	16.2	Dunlap-Cle	2.5

Wins		Win Percentage		Games		Complete Games		Shutouts		Saves	
McCormick-Cle	36	Corcoran-Chi	.692	McCormick-Cle	68	McCormick-Cle	65	Radbourn-Pro	6	Ward-Pro	1
Radbourn-Pro	33	Radbourn-Pro	.623	Radbourn-Pro	55	Radbourn-Pro	51	Welch-Tro	5		
Goldsmith-Chi	28	Goldsmith-Chi	.622	Galvin-Buf	52	Galvin-Buf	48				
Galvin-Buf	28	Ward-Pro	.613	Whitney-Bos	49	Whitney-Bos	46				
Corcoran-Chi	27	Mathews-Bos	.559	Richmond-Wor	48	Goldsmith-Chi	45				

Innings Pitched		Fewest Hits/Game		Fewest BB/Game		Strikeouts		Strikeouts/Game		Ratio	
McCormick-Cle	595.2	Corcoran-Chi	7.11	Mathews-Bos	.69	Radbourn-Pro	201	Mathews-Bos	4.83	Corcoran-Chi	8.70
Radbourn-Pro	474.0	Radbourn-Pro	8.15	Galvin-Buf	.81	McCormick-Cle	200	Derby-Det	4.52	Radbourn-Pro	9.11
Galvin-Buf	445.1	McCormick-Cle	8.31	Goldsmith-Chi	.84	Derby-Det	182	Corcoran-Chi	4.30	Goldsmith-Chi	9.22
Whitney-Bos	420.0	Goldsmith-Chi	8.38	Weidman-Det	.85	Whitney-Bos	180	Daily-Buf	4.08	Weidman-Det	9.42
		Ward-Pro	8.45	Whitney-Bos	.88	Corcoran-Chi	170	Whitney-Bos	3.86	Mathews-Bos	9.47

Earned Run Average		Adjusted ERA		Opponents' Batting Avg.		Opponents' On Base Pct.		Starter Runs		Adjusted Starter Runs	
Corcoran-Chi	1.95	Corcoran-Chi	147	Corcoran-Chi	.200	Corcoran-Chi	.234	Radbourn-Pro	42.0	Radbourn-Pro	37.6
Radbourn-Pro	2.09	Radbourn-Pro	134	Radbourn-Pro	.226	Mathews-Bos	.246	Corcoran-Chi	37.0	Corcoran-Chi	35.9
McCormick-Cle	2.37	Goldsmith-Chi	118	Mathews-Bos	.232	Radbourn-Pro	.246	McCormick-Cle	34.0	McCormick-Cle	27.5
Goldsmith-Chi	2.42	McCormick-Cle	118	Ward-Pro	.232	Weidman-Det	.253	Goldsmith-Chi	20.8	Goldsmith-Chi	19.5
Keefe-Tro	2.50	Keefe-Tro	113	Daily-Buf	.234	Goldsmith-Chi	.254	Keefe-Tro	16.2	Weidman-Det	13.5

Clutch Pitching Index		Relief Runs	Adjusted Relief Runs	Relief Ranking	Total Pitcher Index		Total Baseball Ranking	
Egan-Tro	120				Radbourn-Pro	3.4	Glasscock-Cle	4.1
Richmond-Wor	116				Corcoran-Chi	3.2	Radbourn-Pro	3.2
F.Mountain-Wor-Wor	115				Whitney-Bos	3.2	Corcoran-Chi	3.2
Welch-Tro	113				Keefe-Tro	2.2	Whitney-Bos	3.1
Corey-Wor	112				McCormick-Cle	2.0	Connor-Tro	2.7

TEAM	G	W	L	PCT	GB	R	OR	AB	H	2B	3B	HR	BB	SO	AVG	OBP	SLG	PRO	PRO+	BR	/A	PF	CHI	RC	SB	CS	SBA	SBR
CIN	80	55	25	.688		489	268	3007	795	95	47	5	102	204	.264	.289	.332	.621	107	38	14	106	104	295				
PHI	75	41	34	.547	11.5	406	389	2707	660	89	21	5	125	164	.244	.277	.298	.575	88	-4	-50	112	104	229				
LOU	80	42	38	.525	13	443	352	2806	728	110	28	9	128	193	.259	.292	.328	.620	120	37	59	95	95	275				
PIT	79	39	39	.500	15	428	418	2904	730	110	59	18	90	183	.251	.274	.348	.622	118	35	54	95	95	284				
STL	80	37	43	.463	18	399	496	2865	663	87	41	11	112	226	.231	.260	.302	.562	90	-19	-35	104	101	231				
BAL	74	19	54	.260	32.5	273	515	2583	535	60	24	4	72	215	.207	.229	.254	.483	72	-87	-59	92	97	153				
TOT	234					2438		16872	4111	551	220	52	629	1185	.244	.271	.312	.582										

TEAM	CG	SH	SV	IP	H	H/G	HR	BB	SO	RAT	ERA	ERA+	OAV	OOB	PR	/A	PF	CPI	FA	E	DP	FW	PW	BW	SBW	DIF
CIN	77	11	0	721¹	609	7.6	7	125	165	9.2	1.65	160	.214	.247	83	79	98	119	.907	332	41	3.7	7.3	1.3		2.8
PHI	72	2	0	663	682	9.3	13	99	190	10.6	2.97	100	.249	.275	-21	0	111	97	.895	361	36	1.2	.0	-4.6		6.9
LOU	73	6	0	693¹	637	8.3	6	112	240	9.7	2.03	122	.229	.259	51	34	92	113	.893	385	57	1.3	3.1	5.4		-7.8
PIT	77	2	0	696²	694	9.0	4	82	252	10.0	2.79	93	.243	.264	-8	-14	97	90	.889	397	40	.5	-1.3	5.0		-4.1
STL	75	3	1	688¹	729	9.5	7	103	225	10.9	2.92	96	.254	.280	-18	-9	105	101	.875	446	41	-1.6	-.8	-3.2		2.6
BAL	64	1	0	646¹	760	10.6	15	108	113	12.1	3.88	71	.275	.302	-86	-82	102	94	.859	490	41	-5.0	-7.5	-5.4		.5
TOT	438	25	1	4109		9.0				10.4	2.68		.244	.271					.886	2411	256					

Runs		Hits		Doubles		Triples		Home Runs		Total Bases	
Swartwood-Pit	86	Carpenter-Cin	120	Swartwood-Pit	18	Mansell-Pit	16	Walker-StL	7	Swartwood-Pit	159
Sommer-Cin	82	Browning-Lou	109	Mansell-Pit	18	Taylor-Pit	13	Browning-Lou	5	Mansell-Pit	152
Carpenter-Cin	78	Swartwood-Pit	107	Browning-Lou	17	Wheeler-Cin	11	Swartwood-Pit	4	Carpenter-Cin	148
Browning-Lou	67	Sommer-Cin	102	Taylor-Pit	16	Swartwood-Pit	11			Browning-Lou	147
Birchall-Phi	65	W.Gleason-StL	100	Cuthbert-StL	16	Wolf-Lou	8			Taylor-Pit	135

Runs Batted In		Runs Produced		Bases On Balls		Batting Average		On Base Percentage		Slugging Average	
		Swartwood-Pit	82	J.Gleason-StL	27	Browning-Lou	.378	Browning-Lou	.430	Browning-Lou	.510
		Sommer-Cin	81	Browning-Lou	26	Carpenter-Cin	.342	Swartwood-Pit	.370	Swartwood-Pit	.489
		Carpenter-Cin	77	Sommer-Cin	24	Swartwood-Pit	.329	Carpenter-Cin	.360	Taylor-Pit	.452
		Birchall-Phi	65	J.Reccius-Lou	23	O'Brien-Phi	.303	O'Brien-Phi	.339	Mansell-Pit	.438
				Swartwood-Pit	21	Wolf-Lou	.299	Sommer-Cin	.333	Carpenter-Cin	.422

Production		Adjusted Production		Batter Runs		Adjusted Batter Runs		Clutch Hitting Index		Runs Created	
Browning-Lou	.940	Browning-Lou	228	Browning-Lou	35.3	Browning-Lou	37.7			Browning-Lou	65
Swartwood-Pit	.859	Swartwood-Pit	197	Swartwood-Pit	29.3	Swartwood-Pit	31.5			Swartwood-Pit	60
Carpenter-Cin	.782	Taylor-Pit	157	Carpenter-Cin	22.0	Carpenter-Cin	19.2			Carpenter-Cin	55
O'Brien-Phi	.758	Carpenter-Cin	154	Taylor-Pit	14.5	Mansell-Pit	16.7			Mansell-Pit	45
Taylor-Pit	.749	Mansell-Pit	150	Mansell-Pit	14.5	Taylor-Pit	16.4			Sommer-Cin	44

Total Average		Stolen Bases		Stolen Base Average		Stolen Base Runs		Fielding Runs		Total Player Rating	
Browning-Lou	.966							Stricker-Phi	22.5	Browning-Lou	4.6
Swartwood-Pit	.826							Snyder-Cin	19.1	Snyder-Cin	2.3
Carpenter-Cin	.684							White-Cin	12.1	Swartwood-Pit	2.0
O'Brien-Phi	.679							Browning-Lou	11.8	O'Brien-Phi	2.0
Taylor-Pit	.660							O'Brien-Phi	11.2	Carpenter-Cin	1.8

Wins		Win Percentage		Games		Complete Games		Shutouts		Saves	
White-Cin	40	White-Cin	.769	Mullane-Lou	55	White-Cin	52	White-Cin	8	Fusselback-StL	1
Mullane-Lou	30	Weaver-Phi	.634	White-Cin	54	Mullane-Lou	51	Mullane-Lou	5		
Weaver-Phi	26	McGinnis-StL	.581	McGinnis-StL	45	McGinnis-StL	43	McGinnis-StL	3		
McGinnis-StL	25	Mullane-Lou	.556	Landis-Phi-Bal	44	Weaver-Phi	41	McCormick-Cin	3		
Salisbury-Pit	20	Salisbury-Pit	.526	Weaver-Phi	42	Salisbury-Pit	38	Weaver-Phi	2		

Innings Pitched		Fewest Hits/Game		Fewest BB/Game		Strikeouts		Strikeouts/Game		Ratio	
White-Cin	480.0	Hecker-Lou	6.49	Hecker-Lou	.43	Mullane-Lou	170	Salisbury-Pit	3.63	Hecker-Lou	6.92
Mullane-Lou	460.1	McCormick-Cin	7.25	Driscoll-Pit	.54	Salisbury-Pit	135	Arundel-Pit	3.53	Driscoll-Pit	7.79
McGinnis-StL	388.1	Driscoll-Pit	7.25	Weaver-Phi	.85	McGinnis-StL	134	Mullane-Lou	3.32	McCormick-Cin	8.97
Weaver-Phi	371.0	White-Cin	7.71	Salisbury-Pit	.99	White-Cin	122	McGinnis-StL	3.11	White-Cin	9.04
Landis-Phi-Bal	358.0	Geis-Bal	7.90	Landis-Phi-Bal	1.18	Weaver-Phi	104	J.Reccius-Lou	2.94	Salisbury-Pit	9.46

Earned Run Average		Adjusted ERA		Opponents' Batting Avg.		Opponents' On Base Pct.		Starter Runs		Adjusted Starter Runs	
Driscoll-Pit	1.21	Driscoll-Pit	216	Hecker-Lou	.188	Hecker-Lou	.199	White-Cin	61.1	White-Cin	58.7
Hecker-Lou	1.30	Hecker-Lou	191	McCormick-Cin	.206	Driscoll-Pit	.218	Mullane-Lou	41.2	Driscoll-Pit	31.2
McCormick-Cin	1.52	McCormick-Cin	174	Driscoll-Pit	.206	McCormick-Cin	.243	Driscoll-Pit	32.9	Mullane-Lou	30.7
White-Cin	1.54	White-Cin	172	White-Cin	.216	White-Cin	.244	McCormick-Cin	28.5	McCormick-Cin	27.4
Mullane-Lou	1.88	Mullane-Lou	132	Geis-Bal	.220	Salisbury-Pit	.253	Hecker-Lou	16.0	Hecker-Lou	13.6

Clutch Pitching Index		Relief Runs		Adjusted Relief Runs		Relief Ranking		Total Pitcher Index		Total Baseball Ranking	
White-Cin	124							White-Cin	7.5	White-Cin	7.4
McCormick-Cin	124							Mullane-Lou	4.9	Mullane-Lou	4.8
Mullane-Lou	120							Driscoll-Pit	2.5	Browning-Lou	4.6
J.Reccius-Lou	119							McCormick-Cin	2.0	Driscoll-Pit	2.5
Driscoll-Pit	113							Hecker-Lou	2.0	Snyder-Cin	2.3

TEAM	G	W	L	PCT	GB	R	OR	AB	H	2B	3B	HR	BB	SO	AVG	OBP	SLG	PRO	PRO+	BR	/A	PF	CHI	RC	SB	CS	SBA	SBR
BOS	98	63	35	.643		669	456	3657	1010	209	86	34	123	423	.276	.300	.408	.708	114	68	54	102	104	459				
CHI	98	59	39	.602	4	679	540	3658	1000	277	61	13	129	399	.273	.298	.393	.691	106	49	16	106	109	439				
PRO	98	58	40	.592	5	636	436	3685	1001	189	59	21	149	309	.272	.300	.372	.672	106	29	13	103	104	422				
CLE	100	55	42	.567	7.5	476	443	3457	852	184	38	8	139	374	.246	.276	.329	.605	88	-53	-46	99	97	321				
BUF	98	52	45	.536	10.5	614	576	3729	1058	184	59	8	147	342	.284	.311	.371	.682	108	44	31	102	97	441				
NY	98	46	50	.479	16	530	577	3524	900	139	69	24	127	297	.255	.281	.354	.635	96	-18	-12	99	99	360				
DET	101	40	58	.408	23	524	650	3726	931	164	48	13	166	378	.250	.282	.330	.612	93	-46	-19	95	96	355				
PHI	99	17	81	.173	46	437	887	3576	859	181	48	3	141	355	.240	.269	.320	.589	90	-74	-24	91	89	316				
TOT	395					4565		29012	7611	1527	468	124	1121	2877	.262	.290	.360	.650										

TEAM	CG	SH	SV	IP	H	H/G	HR	BB	SO	RAT	ERA	ERA+	OAV	OOB	PR	/A	PF	CPI	FA	E	DP	FW	PW	BW	SBW	DIF
BOS	89	6	3	860	853	8.9	11	90	538	9.9	2.55	121	.245	.264	56	52	99	96	.901	409	58	3.1	4.5	4.7		1.6
CHI	91	5	1	862	942	9.8	21	123	299	11.1	2.78	115	.260	.284	34	37	102	109	.879	543	76	-3.5	3.2	1.4		8.8
PRO	88	4	1	871	827	8.5	12	111	376	9.7	2.37	130	.238	.262	75	68	98	99	.903	419	75	2.7	5.9	1.1		-.7
CLE	92	5	2	879	818	8.4	7	217	402	10.6	2.22	142	.237	.282	89	92	100	118	.909	389	69	4.6	8.0	-4.0		-2.1
BUF	90	5	2	859[1]	971	10.2	12	101	362	11.2	3.32	96	.268	.288	-17	-8	101	97	.896	445	52	1.4	-.7	2.7		.1
NY	87	5	0	866	907	9.4	19	170	323	11.2	2.94	105	.253	.287	19	11	99	101	.889	468	52	.2	1.0	-1.0		-2.1
DET	89	5	2	894[1]	1026	10.3	22	184	324	12.2	3.58	87	.270	.303	-44	-49	99	98	.893	470	77	.9	-4.3	-1.7		-3.9
PHI	91	3	0	864[2]	1267	13.2	20	125	253	14.5	5.34	58	.318	.338	-212	-216	98	92	.858	639	62	-8.0	-18.9	-2.1		-3.1
TOT	717	38	11	6956[1]		9.8				11.3	3.14		.262	.290					.891	3782	521					

Runs
Hornung-Bos 107
Gore-Chi 105
O'Rourke-Buf 102
Sutton-Bos 101
Hines-Pro 94

Hits
Brouthers-Buf 159
Connor-NY 146
O'Rourke-Buf 143
Sutton-Bos 134
Wood-Det 133

Doubles
Williamson-Chi 49
Brouthers-Buf 41
Burns-Chi 37
Anson-Chi 36

Triples
Brouthers-Buf 17
Morrill-Bos 16
Sutton-Bos 15
Connor-NY 15

Home Runs
Ewing-NY 10
Hornung-Bos 8
Denny-Pro 8
Ward-NY 7
Morrill-Bos 6

Total Bases
Brouthers-Buf 243
Morrill-Bos 212
Connor-NY 207
Sutton-Bos 201
Hornung-Bos 199

Runs Batted In
Brouthers-Buf 97
Burdock-Bos 88
Sutton-Bos 73
Morrill-Bos 68
Anson-Chi 68

Runs Produced
Brouthers-Buf 179
Sutton-Bos 171
Hornung-Bos 165
Burdock-Bos 163
Gore-Chi 155

Bases On Balls
York-Cle 37
Hanlon-Det 34
Powell-Det 28
Shaffer-Buf 27
Gore-Chi 27

Batting Average
Brouthers-Buf 374
Connor-NY 357
Gore-Chi 334
Burdock-Bos 330
O'Rourke-Buf 328

On Base Percentage
Brouthers-Buf 397
Connor-NY 394
Gore-Chi 377
Dunlap-Cle 361
Burdock-Bos 353

Slugging Average
Brouthers-Buf 572
Morrill-Bos 525
Connor-NY 506
Sutton-Bos 486
Ewing-NY 481

Production
Brouthers-Buf 969
Connor-NY 900
Morrill-Bos 868
Gore-Chi 849
Sutton-Bos 836

Adjusted Production
Brouthers-Buf 186
Connor-NY 173
Morrill-Bos 155
Bennett-Det 155
Gore-Chi 148

Batter Runs
Brouthers-Buf ... 44.4
Connor-NY 34.6
Morrill-Bos 27.6
Gore-Chi 26.5
Sutton-Bos 24.4

Adjusted Batter Runs
Brouthers-Buf ... 42.9
Connor-NY 35.3
Morrill-Bos 26.0
Bennett-Det 23.9
Sutton-Bos 22.9

Clutch Hitting Index
Burdock-Bos 157
Anson-Chi 144
Brouthers-Buf 141
Burns-Chi 134
Start-Pro 134

Runs Created
Brouthers-Buf 99
Connor-NY 84
Morrill-Bos 75
Sutton-Bos 72
Gore-Chi 72

Total Average
Brouthers-Buf ...974
Connor-NY 882
Morrill-Bos 825
Gore-Chi 812
Bennett-Det 783

Fielding Runs
Farrell-Pro 24.9
Shaffer-Buf 20.0
Ward-NY 19.3
Richardson-Buf ... 18.7
Williamson-Chi ... 17.8

Total Player Rating
Farrell-Pro 3.3
Richardson-Buf ... 3.1
Brouthers-Buf 3.0
Gore-Chi 2.8
Dunlap-Cle 2.7

Wins
Radbourn-Pro 48
Galvin-Buf 46
Whitney-Bos 37
Corcoran-Chi 34
McCormick-Cle ... 28

Win Percentage
McCormick-Cle ...700
Radbourn-Pro 658
Buffinton-Bos 641
Whitney-Bos 638
Corcoran-Chi 630

Games
Radbourn-Pro 76
Galvin-Buf 76
Coleman-Phi 65
Whitney-Bos 62
Corcoran-Chi 56

Complete Games
Galvin-Buf 72
Radbourn-Pro 66
Coleman-Phi 59
Whitney-Bos 54
Corcoran-Chi 51

Shutouts
Galvin-Buf 5
Welch-NY 4
Radbourn-Pro 4
Daily-Cle........... 4
Buffinton-Bos 4

Saves
Whitney-Bos 2
Weidman-Det 2

Innings Pitched
Galvin-Buf 656.1
Radbourn-Pro ... 632.1
Coleman-Phi ... 538.1
Whitney-Bos 514.0
Corcoran-Chi ... 473.2

Fewest Hits/Game
Sawyer-Cle 7.60
Radbourn-Pro ... 8.01
McCormick-Cle .. 8.32
Daily-Cle 8.56
Whitney-Bos 8.61

Fewest BB/Game
Whitney-Bos 61
Galvin-Buf 69
Radbourn-Pro 80
Coleman-Phi 80
Goldsmith-Chi 92

Strikeouts
Whitney-Bos 345
Radbourn-Pro ... 315
Galvin-Buf 279
Corcoran-Chi 216
Buffinton-Bos 188

Strikeouts/Game
Whitney-Bos 6.04
Buffinton-Bos ... 5.08
Sawyer-Cle 4.85
Radbourn-Pro ... 4.48
Corcoran-Chi 4.10

Ratio
Radbourn-Pro 8.81
Whitney-Bos 9.23
Galvin-Buf 9.96
McCormick-Cle .. 10.03
Ward-NY........ 10.04

Earned Run Average
McCormick-Cle ... 1.84
Radbourn-Pro 2.05
Whitney-Bos 2.24
Sawyer-Cle 2.36
Daily-Cle......... 2.42

Adjusted ERA
McCormick-Cle ... 171
Radbourn-Pro 150
Whitney-Bos 138
Sawyer-Cle 133
Daily-Cle 130

Opponents' Batting Avg.
Sawyer-Cle 217
Radbourn-Pro 227
McCormick-Cle ...233
Sweeney-Pro 237
Whitney-Bos 238

Opponents' On Base Pct.
Radbourn-Pro 244
Whitney-Bos 251
Galvin-Buf 265
Ward-NY.........267
McCormick-Cle ...268

Starter Runs
Radbourn-Pro 76.4
Whitney-Bos 51.2
McCormick-Cle .. 49.2
Corcoran-Chi 34.1
Galvin-Buf 30.8

Adjusted Starter Runs
Radbourn-Pro 72.7
McCormick-Cle .. 49.7
Whitney-Bos 49.0
Corcoran-Chi 36.8
Galvin-Buf 33.5

Clutch Pitching Index
McCormick-Cle ... 125
Shaw-Det 121
Daily-Cle......... 119
O'Neill-NY 118
Goldsmith-Chi 113

Total Pitcher Index
Radbourn-Pro 8.1
Whitney-Bos 6.0
McCormick-Cle ... 5.2
Corcoran-Chi 3.2
Galvin-Buf 2.5

Total Baseball Ranking
Radbourn-Pro 7.8
Whitney-Bos 6.0
McCormick-Cle ... 5.0
Farrell-Pro 3.3
Ward-NY.......... 3.2

1883 American Association

TEAM	G	W	L	PCT	GB	R	OR	AB	H	2B	3B	HR	BB	SO	AVG	OBP	SLG	PRO	PRO+	BR	/A	PF	CHI	RC	SB	CS	SBA	SBR
PHI	98	66	32	.673		720	547	3714	972	149	50	20	194	268	.262	.298	.345	.643	101	42	-8	109	115	392				
STL	98	65	33	.663	1	549	409	3495	892	118	46	7	125	240	.255	.281	.321	.602	92	-12	-42	106	104	323				
CIN	98	61	37	.622	5	662	413	3669	961	122	74	34	139	261	.262	.289	.363	.652	106	47	16	106	107	395				
NY	97	54	42	.563	11	498	405	3534	883	111	58	6	142	259	.250	.279	.319	.598	92	-17	-38	104	93	322				
LOU	98	52	45	.536	13.5	564	562	3553	891	114	64	14	140	305	.251	.279	.331	.610	107	-4	37	93	103	336				
COL	97	32	65	.330	33.5	476	659	3553	854	101	79	15	134	410	.240	.268	.326	.594	102	-24	-22	92	90	318				
PIT	98	31	67	.316	35	525	728	3609	892	120	58	13	162	345	.247	.280	.323	.603	102	-11	15	95	95	334				
BAL	96	28	68	.292	37	471	742	3534	870	125	49	5	162	331	.246	.279	.314	.593	91	-21	-38	103	89	317				
TOT	390					4465		28661	7215	960	478	114	1198	2419	.252	.282	.331	.612										

TEAM	CG	SH	SV	IP	H	H/G	HR	BB	SO	RAT	ERA	ERA+	OAV	OOB	PR	/A	PF	CPI	FA	E	DP	FW	PW	BW	SBW	DIF
PHI	92	1	0	873	921	9.5	22	95	347	10.5	2.88	121	.254	.273	41	59	106	113	.865	584	40	-4.1	5.2	-.7		16.6
STL	93	9	1	879¹	729	7.5	7	150	325	9.0	2.23	156	.211	.244	104	122	106	97	.909	388	62	4.5	10.7	-3.7		4.5
CIN	96	8	0	866²	766	8.0	17	168	215	9.7	2.26	143	.222	.258	100	94	98	115	.905	383	57	4.7	8.3	1.4		-2.4
NY	97	6	0	874	749	7.7	12	123	480	9.0	2.90	114	.217	.244	38	40	101	78	.905	391	45	4.1	3.5	-3.3		1.7
LOU	96	7	0	873²	987	10.2	7	110	269	11.3	3.50	85	.267	.288	-20	-50	91	101	.886	478	67	.6	-4.4	3.3		4.1
COL	90	4	0	840¹	980	10.5	16	211	222	12.8	3.96	78	.273	.314	-62	-83	93	105	.874	535	69	-2.1	-7.3	1.8		-8.8
PIT	82	1	1	867²	1140	11.8	21	151	271	13.4	4.62	69	.298	.325	-127	-137	97	102	.884	504	55	-.6	-12.1	1.3		-6.7
BAL	86	1	0	844²	943	10.0	12	190	290	12.1	4.08	85	.265	.303	-74	-58	105	93	.855	624	44	-6.3	-5.1	-3.3		-5.3
TOT	732	37	2	6919¹		9.4				10.9	3.30		.252	.282					.885	3887	439					

Runs
Stovey-Phi 110
Reilly-Cin 103
Carpenter-Cin 99
Knight-Phi 98

Hits
Swartwood-Pit ... 147
Reilly-Cin 136
Carpenter-Cin ... 129
Stovey-Phi 127
Nelson-NY 127

Doubles
Stovey-Phi 31
Swartwood-Pit 24
Knight-Phi 23
Hayes-Pit 23

Triples
Smith-Col 17
Reilly-Cin 14
Kuehne-Col 14
Mansell-Pit 13
Mann-Col 13

Home Runs
Stovey-Phi 14
Jones-Cin......... 10
Reilly-Cin 9
Fulmer-Cin 5
Brown-Col 5

Total Bases
Stovey-Phi 212
Reilly-Cin 212
Swartwood-Pit ... 196
Jones-Cin 184
W.Gleason-StL ... 167

Runs Batted In

Runs Produced
Knight-Phi 97
Stovey-Phi 96
Carpenter-Cin 96
Reilly-Cin 94
Birchall-Phi 94

Bases On Balls
Stearns-Bal 34
Nelson-NY 31
Moynahan-Phi 30
J.Gleason-StL-Lou . 29
Clinton-Bal 27

Batting Average
Swartwood-Pit ...356
Browning-Lou 338
Clinton-Bal 313
Reilly-Cin 311
Moynahan-Phi ...308

On Base Percentage
Swartwood-Pit 391
Browning-Lou 378
Clinton-Bal 357
Moynahan-Phi 356
Nelson-NY 353

Slugging Average
Stovey-Phi 504
Reilly-Cin 485
Swartwood-Pit 475
Jones-Cin.........471
Browning-Lou 464

Production
Swartwood-Pit 866
Stovey-Phi 846
Browning-Lou 842
Reilly-Cin 810
Jones-Cin.........799

Adjusted Production
Swartwood-Pit ... 186
Browning-Lou 183
Stovey-Phi 156
Reilly-Cin 149
Jones-Cin........ 146

Batter Runs
Swartwood-Pit ...35.0
Stovey-Phi ...31.5
Browning-Lou 27.4
Reilly-Cin 26.1
Jones-Cin.........22.8

Adjusted Batter Runs
Swartwood-Pit ...38.0
Browning-Lou 31.7
Stovey-Phi 25.8
Reilly-Cin 22.5
Jones-Cin.........19.4

Clutch Hitting Index

Runs Created
Swartwood-Pit 79
Stovey-Phi 74
Reilly-Cin 71
Browning-Lou 64
Jones-Cin 62

Total Average
Swartwood-Pit 827
Stovey-Phi 810
Browning-Lou 797
Jones-Cin.........739
Reilly-Cin 734

Stolen Bases

Stolen Base Average

Stolen Base Runs

Fielding Runs
Holbert-NY 35.3
Battin-Pit 29.0
Richmond-Col 25.5
Latham-StL 21.9
Gerhardt-Lou 20.4

Total Player Rating
Richmond-Col 3.4
Smith-Col 3.1
Swartwood-Pit 2.9
Gerhardt-Lou 2.4
Holbert-NY 2.3

Wins
White-Cin 43
Keefe-NY 41
Mullane-StL 35
Mathews-Phi 30
McGinnis-StL...... 28

Win Percentage
Mullane-StL 700
Mathews-Phi 698
Bradley-Phi 696
White-Cin 662
McGinnis-StL.....636

Games
Keefe-NY 68
White-Cin 65
Mountain-Col 59
Mullane-StL 53
Hecker-Lou 51

Complete Games
Keefe-NY 68
White-Cin 64
Mountain-Col 57
Mullane-StL 49
Hecker-Lou 49

Shutouts
White-Cin 6
McGinnis-StL...... 6
Keefe-NY 5
Weaver-Lou 4
Mountain-Col 4

Saves
Mullane-StL 1
Barr-Pit 1

Innings Pitched
Keefe-NY 619.0
White-Cin 577.0
Mountain-Col ... 503.0
Mullane-StL 460.2
Hecker-Lou 451.0

Fewest Hits/Game
Keefe-NY 7.07
Mullane-StL 7.27
White-Cin 7.38
McGinnis-StL..... 7.64
Deagle-Cin 8.27

Fewest BB/Game
Mathews-Phi 73
Weaver-Lou 82
Lynch-NY 88
Bradley-Phi 92
Driscoll-Pit 1.04

Strikeouts
Keefe-NY 361
Mathews-Phi 203
Mullane-StL 191
Mountain-Col 159
Hecker-Lou 153

Strikeouts/Game
Keefe-NY 5.25
Mathews-Phi 4.80
Lynch-NY 4.20
Mullane-StL 3.73
Henderson-Bal ... 3.64

Ratio
Keefe-NY 8.49
Mullane-StL 8.71
White-Cin 9.00
McGinnis-StL..... 9.27
Bradley-Phi 9.95

Earned Run Average
White-Cin 2.09
Mullane-StL 2.19
Deagle-Cin 2.31
McGinnis-StL..... 2.33
Keefe-NY 2.41

Adjusted ERA
Mullane-StL 159
White-Cin 155
McGinnis-StL..... 149
Mathews-Phi 142
Deagle-Cin 140

Opponents' Batting Avg.
Keefe-NY .... .202
Mullane-StL ..... .207
White-Cin .... .209
McGinnis-StL..... .215
Deagle-Cin ...... .229

Opponents' On Base Pct.
Keefe-NY .... .233
Mullane-StL ..... .238
White-Cin .... .244
McGinnis-StL..... .249
Bradley-Phi ...... .263

Starter Runs
White-Cin 77.4
Keefe-NY 60.8
Mullane-StL 56.8
McGinnis-StL..... 41.2
Mathews-Phi 35.6

Adjusted Starter Runs
White-Cin 73.8
Mullane-StL 66.1
Keefe-NY 62.4
McGinnis-StL..... 48.9
Mathews-Phi 43.7

Clutch Pitching Index
Mathews-Phi 127
Corey-Phi 124
McCormick-Cin ... 123
Valentine-Col 122
Deagle-Cin 117

Relief Runs

Adjusted Relief Runs

Relief Ranking

Total Pitcher Index
Keefe-NY 6.6
White-Cin 6.5
Mullane-StL 6.3
McGinnis-StL...... 4.0
Mathews-Phi 3.2

Total Baseball Ranking
Keefe-NY 6.6
White-Cin 6.5
Mullane-StL 6.1
McGinnis-StL..... 3.8
Richmond-Col 3.4

TEAM	G	W	L	PCT	GB	R	OR	AB	H	2B	3B	HR	BB	SO	AVG	OBP	SLG	PRO	PRO+	BR	/A	PF	CHI	RC	SB	CS	SBA	SBR
PRO	114	84	28	.750		665	388	4093	987	153	43	21	300	469	.241	.293	.315	.608	97	-18	-2	98	107	387				
BOS	116	73	38	.658	10.5	684	468	4189	1063	179	60	36	207	660	.254	.289	.351	.640	105	17	20	100	104	435				
BUF	115	64	47	.577	19.5	700	626	4197	1099	163	69	39	215	458	.262	.298	.361	.659	106	46	24	103	102	463				
NY	116	62	50	.554	22	693	623	4124	1053	149	67	23	249	492	.255	.298	.341	.639	102	20	5	102	105	429				
CHI	113	62	50	.554	22	834	647	4182	1176	162	50	142	264	469	.281	.324	.446	.770	133	201	148	108	98	619				
PHI	113	39	73	.348	45	549	824	3998	934	149	39	14	209	512	.234	.272	.301	.573	88	-72	-43	95	101	335				
CLE	113	35	77	.313	49	458	716	3934	934	147	49	16	170	576	.237	.269	.312	.581	83	-63	-83	103	86	338				
DET	114	28	84	.250	56	445	736	3970	825	114	47	31	207	699	.208	.247	.284	.531	74	-132	-95	94	93	285				
TOT	457					5028		32687	8071	1216	424	322	1821	4335	.247	.287	.340	.626										

TEAM	CG	SH	SV	IP	H	H/G	HR	BB	SO	RAT	ERA	ERA+	OAV	OOB	PR	/A	PF	CPI	FA	E	DP	FW	PW	BW	SBW	DIF
PRO	107	16	2	1036[1]	825	7.2	26	172	639	8.7	1.61	176	.209	.242	158	141	95	110	.918	398	50	5.1	12.6	-.2		10.4
BOS	109	14	2	1037	932	8.1	30	135	742	9.3	2.47	117	.226	.250	58	49	97	84	.922	384	46	6.3	4.4	1.8		5.0
BUF	108	14	1	1001	1041	9.4	46	189	534	11.1	2.95	107	.254	.286	3	21	106	105	.905	462	71	1.9	1.9	2.1		2.5
NY	111	4	0	1014	1011	9.0	28	326	567	11.9	3.12	95	.245	.300	-16	-19	100	98	.895	514	69	-.6	-1.7	.4		7.9
CHI	106	9	0	997[1]	1028	9.3	83	231	472	11.4	3.03	103	.250	.290	-6	11	105	112	.886	595	107	-5.6	1.0	13.2		-2.6
PHI	106	3	1	981	1090	10.0	38	254	411	12.3	3.93	76	.261	.304	-103	-106	100	87	.888	536	67	-2.5	-9.5	-3.8		-1.2
CLE	107	7	0	994[2]	1046	9.5	35	269	482	11.9	3.43	92	.256	.302	-50	-32	106	97	.897	512	75	-1.2	-2.9	-7.4		-9.5
DET	109	3	0	984[2]	1097	10.0	36	245	488	12.3	3.38	86	.262	.302	-44	-54	97	100	.886	550	62	-3.0	-4.8	-8.5		-11.7
TOT	863	70	6	8046		9.0				11.1	2.98		.247	.287					.899	3951	547					

Runs
Kelly-Chi 120
O'Rourke-Buf 119
Hornung-Bos 119
Dalrymple-Chi 111
Anson-Chi 108

Hits
Sutton-Bos 162
O'Rourke-Buf 162
Dalrymple-Chi 161
Kelly-Chi 160
Anson-Chi 159

Doubles
Hines-Pro 36
O'Rourke-Buf 33
Anson-Chi 30
Manning-Phi 29

Triples
Ewing-NY 20
Brouthers-Buf 15
Rowe-Buf 14
Phillips-Cle 12
McKinnon-NY 12

Home Runs
Williamson-Chi 27
Pfeffer-Chi 25
Dalrymple-Chi 22
Anson-Chi 21
Brouthers-Buf 14

Total Bases
Dalrymple-Chi 263
Anson-Chi 258
Pfeffer-Chi 240
Kelly-Chi 237
Williamson-Chi . . . 231

Runs Batted In
Anson-Chi 102
Pfeffer-Chi 101
Kelly-Chi 95
Williamson-Chi . . . 84
Connor-NY 82

Runs Produced
Kelly-Chi 202
Anson-Chi 189
Pfeffer-Chi 181
O'Rourke-Buf 177
Connor-NY 176

Bases On Balls
Gore-Chi 61
Kelly-Chi 46
Hines-Pro 44
Williamson-Chi . . . 42

Batting Average
Kelly-Chi 354
O'Rourke-Buf 347
Sutton-Bos 346
Anson-Chi 335
Brouthers-Buf 327

On Base Percentage
Kelly-Chi 414
Gore-Chi 404
O'Rourke-Buf 392
Sutton-Bos 384
Brouthers-Buf 378

Slugging Average
Brouthers-Buf 563
Williamson-Chi 554
Anson-Chi 543
Kelly-Chi 524
Pfeffer-Chi 514

Production
Brouthers-Buf 941
Kelly-Chi 938
Anson-Chi 916
Williamson-Chi 898
O'Rourke-Buf 872

Adjusted Production
Brouthers-Buf 186
Kelly-Chi 178
Anson-Chi 170
O'Rourke-Buf 167
Williamson-Chi . . . 164

Batter Runs
Kelly-Chi 48.8
Anson-Chi 44.6
Brouthers-Buf 41.2
O'Rourke-Buf 38.8
Williamson-Chi . . . 36.7

Adjusted Batter Runs
Kelly-Chi 42.9
Brouthers-Buf 39.1
Anson-Chi 38.6
O'Rourke-Buf 36.3
Sutton-Bos 33.7

Clutch Hitting Index
Dorgan-NY 144
Caskin-NY 142
McKinnon-NY 137
Morrill-Bos 137
Lillie-Buf 135

Runs Created
Kelly-Chi 100
Anson-Chi 99
O'Rourke-Buf 90
Dalrymple-Chi 88
Brouthers-Buf 87

Total Average
Kelly-Chi 969
Brouthers-Buf 959
Anson-Chi 908
Williamson-Chi 907
O'Rourke-Buf 849

Stolen Bases

Stolen Base Average

Stolen Base Runs

Fielding Runs
Pfeffer-Chi 45.5
Williamson-Chi . . . 23.8
Gilligan-Pro 17.2
Lillie-Buf 16.0
Hanlon-Det 13.4

Total Player Rating
Pfeffer-Chi 6.3
Williamson-Chi 4.9
Kelly-Chi 3.5
Sutton-Bos 2.7
Brouthers-Buf 2.6

Wins
Radbourn-Pro 59
Buffinton-Bos 48
Galvin-Buf 46
Welch-NY 39
L.Corcoran-Chi 35

Win Percentage
Radbourn-Pro 831
Buffinton-Bos 750
Sweeney-Pro 680
Galvin-Buf 676
Welch-NY 650

Games
Radbourn-Pro 75
Galvin-Buf 72
Buffinton-Bos 67
Welch-NY 65
L.Corcoran-Chi 60

Complete Games
Radbourn-Pro 73
Galvin-Buf 71
Buffinton-Bos 63
Welch-NY 62
L.Corcoran-Chi 57

Shutouts
Galvin-Buf 12
Radbourn-Pro 11
Buffinton-Bos 8
L.Corcoran-Chi 7
Whitney-Bos 6

Saves
Morrill-Bos 2
Sweeney-Pro 1
Radbourn-Pro 1
O'Rourke-Buf 1
Ferguson-Phi 1

Innings Pitched
Radbourn-Pro . . . 678.2
Galvin-Buf 636.1
Buffinton-Bos . . . 587.0
Welch-NY 557.1
L.Corcoran-Chi . . 516.2

Fewest Hits/Game
Sweeney-Pro 6.23
Radbourn-Pro 7.00
Clarkson-Chi 7.17
Getzien-Det 7.21
Whitney-Bos 7.29

Fewest BB/Game
Whitney-Bos 72
Galvin-Buf 89
Buffinton-Bos 1.17
Sweeney-Pro 1.18
Coleman-Phi 1.28

Strikeouts
Radbourn-Pro 441
Buffinton-Bos . . . 417
Galvin-Buf 369
Welch-NY 345
L.Corcoran-Chi . . . 272

Strikeouts/Game
Clarkson-Chi 7.78
Whitney-Bos 7.23
Getzien-Det 6.54
Buffinton-Bos 6.39
Sweeney-Pro 5.90

Ratio
Sweeney-Pro 7.41
Whitney-Bos 8.01
Radbourn-Pro 8.30
Getzien-Det 8.74
Galvin-Buf 8.90

Earned Run Average
Radbourn-Pro 1.38
Sweeney-Pro 1.55
Getzien-Det 1.95
Galvin-Buf 1.99
Whitney-Bos 2.09

Adjusted ERA
Radbourn-Pro 204
Sweeney-Pro 182
Galvin-Buf 158
Getzien-Det 148
Clarkson-Chi 147

Opponents' Batting Avg.
Sweeney-Pro 187
Getzien-Det 204
Radbourn-Pro 205
Whitney-Bos 207
Clarkson-Chi 208

Opponents' On Base Pct.
Sweeney-Pro 215
Whitney-Bos 223
Radbourn-Pro 234
Getzien-Det 237
Buffinton-Bos 244

Starter Runs
Radbourn-Pro . . . 120.5
Galvin-Buf 69.5
Buffinton-Bos 54.2
Sweeney-Pro 35.1
Whitney-Bos 33.2

Adjusted Starter Runs
Radbourn-Pro . . . 108.6
Galvin-Buf 81.5
Buffinton-Bos 48.2
L.Corcoran-Chi . . . 41.7
Sweeney-Pro 31.2

Clutch Pitching Index
Radbourn-Pro 117
Meinke-Det 116
L.Corcoran-Chi . . . 113
Moffett-Cle 110
Welch-NY 107

Relief Runs

Adjusted Relief Runs

Relief Ranking

Total Pitcher Index
Radbourn-Pro 10.4
Galvin-Buf 7.1
Buffinton-Bos 5.8
L.Corcoran-Chi . . . 4.6
Whitney-Bos 4.0

Total Baseball Ranking
Radbourn-Pro 10.1
Galvin-Buf 7.0
Pfeffer-Chi 6.3
Buffinton-Bos 5.3
Williamson-Chi . . . 4.7

TEAM	G	W	L	PCT	GB	R	OR	AB	H	2B	3B	HR	BB	SO	AVG	OBP	SLG	PRO	PRO+	BR	/A	PF	CHI	RC	SB	CS	SBA	SBR
NY	112	75	32	.701		734	423	4012	1052	155	64	22	203	315	.262	.304	.349	.653	122	82	99	97	107	436				
COL	110	69	39	.639	6.5	585	459	3759	901	107	96	40	196	404	.240	.288	.351	.639	124	59	104	92	93	390				
LOU	110	68	40	.630	7.5	573	425	3957	1004	152	69	17	146	408	.254	.286	.340	.626	115	41	67	96	91	395				
STL	110	67	40	.626	8	658	539	3952	986	151	60	11	174	339	.249	.288	.326	.614	102	28	7	104	107	381				
CIN	112	68	41	.624	8	754	512	4090	1037	109	96	36	154	404	.254	.289	.354	.643	110	65	36	105	112	429				
BAL	108	63	43	.594	11.5	636	515	3845	896	133	84	19	211	545	.233	.284	.336	.620	104	38	15	104	102	377				
PHI	108	61	46	.570	14	700	546	3959	1057	167	100	26	153	425	.267	.301	.379	.680	120	112	72	107	100	463				
TOL	110	46	58	.442	27.5	463	571	3712	859	153	48	8	157	541	.231	.268	.305	.573	90	-27	-46	104	88	310				
BRO	109	40	64	.385	33.5	476	644	3763	845	112	47	16	179	417	.225	.263	.292	.555	86	-49	-53	101	93	296				
RIC	46	12	30	.286	30.5	194	285	1469	325	40	33	7	53	284	.221	.260	.308	.568	92	-14	-11	99	95	120				
PIT	110	30	78	.278	45.5	406	725	3689	777	105	50	2	143	411	.211	.248	.268	.516	73	-97	-106	102	90	251				
IND	110	29	78	.271	46	462	755	3813	890	129	62	20	125	560	.233	.262	.315	.577	95	-26	-11	97	86	323				
WAS	63	12	51	.190	41	248	481	2166	434	61	24	6	102	377	.200	.242	.259	.501	78	-68	-30	88	97	139				
TOT	659					6889		46186	11063	1574	833	243	1996	5430	.240	.271	.325	.597										

TEAM	CG	SH	SV	IP	H	H/G	HR	BB	SO	RAT	ERA	ERA+	OAV	OOB	PR	/A	PF	CPI	FA	E	DP	FW	PW	BW	SBW	DIF
NY	111	9	0	984²	800	7.3	15	119	611	8.6	2.46	126	.209	.237	86	71	96	90	.907	441	42	2.3	6.5	9.0		3.6
COL	102	8	1	962¹	815	7.6	22	172	526	9.5	2.68	113	.217	.256	60	36	93	98	.908	433	74	2.3	3.3	9.5		-.0
LOU	101	6	0	989²	836	7.6	9	97	470	8.8	2.17	142	.216	.241	118	100	95	106	.912	426	84	2.6	9.1	6.1		-3.9
STL	99	8	0	987	881	8.0	16	172	477	10.0	2.67	122	.226	.266	63	63	100	106	.900	490	65	-.2	5.8	.6		7.3
CIN	111	11	0	983²	956	8.7	27	181	308	11.1	3.33	100	.243	.290	-10	-1	103	106	.909	430	82	2.8	-.0	3.3		7.5
BAL	105	8	1	955²	869	8.2	16	219	635	10.5	2.71	128	.224	.271	56	79	107	107	.899	461	61	.7	7.2	1.4		.7
PHI	105	5	0	948²	920	8.7	16	127	530	10.3	3.42	99	.237	.269	-18	-3	105	89	.901	457	63	.9	-.3	6.6		.3
TOL	103	9	1	946	885	8.4	12	169	501	10.5	3.06	111	.233	.275	19	35	105	99	.900	469	67	.7	3.2	-4.2		-5.7
BRO	105	6	0	948²	996	9.4	20	163	378	11.2	3.79	87	.254	.288	-58	-51	102	94	.889	520	68	-1.6	-4.7	-4.8		-.8
RIC	45	1	0	370¹	402	9.8	14	52	167	11.4	4.52	73	.257	.288	-53	-50	102	83	.874	239	27	-1.5	-4.6	-1.0		-1.9
PIT	108	4	0	943¹	1059	10.1	25	216	338	12.7	4.35	77	.265	.312	-116	-104	104	96	.889	523	71	-1.6	-9.5	-9.7		-3.2
IND	107	2	0	937²	1001	9.6	30	199	479	11.8	4.20	78	.255	.295	-100	-97	101	90	.889	515	45	-1.2	-8.9	-1.0		-13.4
WAS	62	3	0	543²	643	10.6	21	110	235	12.8	4.01	76	.273	.311	-46	-59	93	109	.858	400	40	-5.3	-5.4	-2.7		-6.1
TOT	1264	80	3	115501¹		8.7				10.6	3.24		.240	.271					.897	5804	789					

Runs
Stovey-Phi 124
Jones-Cin 117
Latham-StL 115
Reilly-Cin 114
Nelson-NY 114

Hits
Orr-NY 162
Reilly-Cin 152
Esterbrook-NY ... 150
Browning-Lou 150
Jones-Cin........ 148

Doubles
Barkley-Tol 39
Browning-Lou 33
Orr-NY 32
Esterbrook-NY ... 29
Lewis-StL 25

Triples
Stovey-Phi 23
Reilly-Cin 19
Mann-Col 18
Peltz-Ind 17
Jones-Cin 17

Home Runs
Reilly-Cin 11
Stovey-Phi 10
Orr-NY 9
Mann-Col 7
Jones-Cin......... 7

Total Bases
Reilly-Cin 247
Orr-NY 247
Stovey-Phi 244
Jones-Cin........ 222
Browning-Lou 211

Runs Batted In
(none listed)

Runs Produced
Stovey-Phi 114
Latham-StL 114
Nelson-NY 113
Jones-Cin....... 110
Esterbrook-NY ... 109

Bases On Balls
Nelson-NY 74
Geer-Bro 38
Jones-Cin 37
Macullar-Bal 36
Richmond-Col 35

Batting Average
Orr-NY .... .354
Reilly-Cin .... .339
Browning-Lou .... .336
Stovey-Phi ...... .326
Lewis-StL .... .323

On Base Percentage
Jones-Cin .... .376
Nelson-NY ...... .375
Stovey-Phi ...... .368
Fennelly-Was-Cin ..367
Reilly-Cin .... .366

Slugging Average
Reilly-Cin .... .551
Stovey-Phi ...... .545
Orr-NY .... .539
Fennelly-Was-Cin ..480
Browning-Lou .... .472

Production
Reilly-Cin .... .918
Stovey-Phi ...... .913
Orr-NY .... .901
Fennelly-Was-Cin ..847
Jones-Cin........ .846

Adjusted Production
Orr-NY 199
Fennelly-Was-Cin . 190
Reilly-Cin 190
Stovey-Phi 185
Browning-Lou 180

Batter Runs
Stovey-Phi 46.2
Reilly-Cin 45.9
Orr-NY 43.4
Jones-Cin........ 40.4
Browning-Lou 32.9

Adjusted Batter Runs
Orr-NY 45.3
Reilly-Cin 42.7
Stovey-Phi 41.6
Jones-Cin........ 36.9
Browning-Lou 35.9

Clutch Hitting Index
(none listed)

Runs Created
Reilly-Cin 93
Stovey-Phi 92
Orr-NY 92
Jones-Cin........ 85
Browning-Lou 77

Total Average
Stovey-Phi ...... .907
Reilly-Cin .... .899
Orr-NY .... .855
Jones-Cin........ .830
Fennelly-Was-Cin ..824

Stolen Bases
(none listed)

Stolen Base Average
(none listed)

Stolen Base Runs
(none listed)

Fielding Runs
Latham-StL 39.5
Smith-Col 29.1
Snyder-Cin....... 27.4
Gerhardt-Lou..... 27.3
Barkley-Tol 24.6

Total Player Rating
Barkley-Tol 4.6
Latham-StL 4.5
Smith-Col 4.0
Fennelly-Was-Cin . 3.9
Esterbrook-NY ... 3.5

Wins
Hecker-Lou 52
Lynch-NY 37
Keefe-NY 37
Mullane-Tol 36

Win Percentage
Morris-Col .... .723
Hecker-Lou ...... .722
Foutz-StL .... .714
Lynch-NY .... .712
Keefe-NY .... .685

Games
Hecker-Lou 75
Mullane-Tol 67
McKeon-Ind 61
Keefe-NY 57
Terry-Bro 56

Complete Games
Hecker-Lou 72
Mullane-Tol 64
McKeon-Ind 59
Keefe-NY 56

Shutouts
White-Cin 7
Mullane-Tol 7
Hecker-Lou 6

Saves
O'Day-Tol 1
Mountain-Col...... 1
T.Burns-Bal 1

Innings Pitched
Hecker-Lou 670.2
Mullane-Tol 567.0
McKeon-Ind 512.0
Lynch-NY 496.0
Keefe-NY 482.2

Fewest Hits/Game
Morris-Col 7.02
Keefe-NY 7.05
Hecker-Lou 7.06
Mountain-Col 7.21
Foutz-StL 7.27

Fewest BB/Game
Driscoll-Lou 62
Hecker-Lou 75
Lynch-NY 76
E.Dugan-Ric 81
McGinnis-StL 89

Strikeouts
Hecker-Lou 385
Henderson-Bal ... 346
Mullane-Tol 325
Keefe-NY 317
McKeon-Ind 308

Strikeouts/Game
Henderson-Bal ... 7.09
Davis-StL 6.49
Morris-Col 6.33
Mathews-Phi 5.98
Keefe-NY 5.91

Ratio
Hecker-Lou 8.02
Morris-Col 8.36
Lynch-NY 8.56
Keefe-NY 8.73
Foutz-StL 9.23

Earned Run Average
Hecker-Lou 1.80
Foutz-StL 2.18
Morris-Col 2.18
Keefe-NY 2.26
Mountain-Col 2.45

Adjusted ERA
Hecker-Lou 171
Foutz-StL 149
Morris-Col 139
Keefe-NY 138
Mullane-Tol 135

Opponents' Batting Avg.
Keefe-NY .... .203
Hecker-Lou ...... .204
Morris-Col ...... .204
Mountain-Col .... .209
Foutz-StL .... .212

Opponents' On Base Pct.
Hecker-Lou ...... .226
Morris-Col ...... .234
Lynch-NY .... .236
Keefe-NY .... .240
Foutz-StL .... .255

Starter Runs
Hecker-Lou 107.6
Keefe-NY 52.9
Morris-Col 50.8
Mullane-Tol 45.3
Mountain-Col 32.0

Adjusted Starter Runs
Hecker-Lou 95.6
Mullane-Tol 55.7
Keefe-NY 45.6
Henderson-Bal ... 40.9
Morris-Col 40.3

Clutch Pitching Index
Comiskey-StL 127
Foutz-StL 122
Davis-StL 120
O'Neill-StL 118
White-Cin 116

Relief Runs
(none listed)

Adjusted Relief Runs
(none listed)

Relief Ranking
(none listed)

Total Pitcher Index
Hecker-Lou 12.9
Mullane-Tol 7.9
Keefe-NY 5.4
Henderson-Bal ... 4.3
Morris-Col 4.2

Total Baseball Ranking
Hecker-Lou 12.8
Mullane-Tol 7.9
Keefe-NY 5.6
Barkley-Tol 4.6
Latham-StL 4.5

TEAM	G	W	L	PCT	GB	R	OR	AB	H	2B	3B	HR	BB	SO	AVG	OBP	SLG	PRO	PRO+	BR	/A	PF	CHI	RC	SB	CS	SBA	SBR
STL	114	94	19	.832		887	429	4285	1251	259	41	32	181	542	.292	.321	.394	.715	138	182	158	104	103	555				
MIL	12	8	4	.667	35.5	53	34	395	88	25	0	0	20	70	.223	.260	.286	.546	159	-5	24	54	91	30				
CIN	105	69	36	.657	21	703	466	3786	1027	118	63	26	147	482	.271	.298	.356	.654	113	85	38	108	102	413				
BAL	106	58	47	.552	32	662	627	3883	952	150	26	17	144	652	.245	.272	.310	.582	89	-7	-71	110	109	336				
BOS	111	58	51	.532	34	636	558	3940	928	168	32	19	128	787	.236	.260	.309	.569	95	-28	-18	98	107	324				
CP	93	41	50	.451	42	438	482	3212	742	127	26	10	119	505	.231	.258	.296	.554	89	-36	-33	99	93	252				
WAS	114	47	65	.420	46.5	572	679	3926	931	120	26	4	118	558	.237	.259	.284	.543	88	-59	-39	97	102	296				
PHI	67	21	46	.313	50	414	545	2518	618	108	35	7	103	405	.245	.275	.324	.599	112	10	40	93	101	230				
STP	9	2	6	.250	39.5	24	57	272	49	13	1	0	7	47	.180	.201	.235	.436	89	-14	6	54	84	13				
ALT	25	6	19	.240	44	90	216	899	223	30	6	2	22	130	.248	.266	.301	.567	92	-7	-9	101	67	74				
KC	82	16	63	.203	61	311	618	2802	557	104	15	6	123	529	.199	.232	.253	.485	75	-95	-37	87	88	169				
WIL	18	2	16	.111	44.5	35	114	521	91	8	8	2	22	123	.175	.208	.232	.440	49	-26	-28	103	61	26				
TOT	428					4825		30439	7457	1230	279	125	1134	4830	.245	.272	.316	.588										

TEAM	CG	SH	SV	IP	H	H/G	HR	BB	SO	RAT	ERA	ERA+	OAV	OOB	PR	/A	PF	CPI	FA	E	DP	FW	PW	BW	SBW	DIF
STL	104	8	6	993	838	7.6	9	110	550	8.6	1.96	151	.214	.235	116	110	98	104	.888	554	79	3.8	9.6	13.8		10.3
MIL	12	3	0	104	49	4.2	1	13	139	5.4	2.25	73	.132	.161	9	-7	54	11	.892	53	4	.6	-.6	2.1		-.1
CIN	95	11	1	914¹	831	8.2	17	90	503	9.1	2.38	133	.226	.245	64	79	105	100	.882	532	45	2.6	6.9	3.3		3.7
BAL	92	4	0	946²	1002	9.5	24	177	628	11.2	3.20	103	.254	.286	-20	11	110	107	.872	616	53	-.8	1.0	-6.2		11.6
BOS	100	5	1	953¹	885	8.4	17	110	753	9.4	2.70	109	.231	.252	33	24	98	94	.868	633	39	-.3	2.1	-1.6		3.3
CP	86	6	0	803²	743	8.3	12	137	679	9.9	2.18	138	.230	.261	74	74	100	121	.882	459	38	2.8	6.5	-2.9		-10.9
WAS	94	5	0	953²	992	9.4	16	168	684	10.9	3.44	86	.251	.282	-45	-51	98	94	.869	625	55	.7	-4.5	-3.4		-1.9
PHI	64	1	0	593¹	726	11.0	7	105	310	12.6	4.63	62	.283	.311	-106	-116	95	89	.841	501	36	-5.3	-10.2	3.5		-.6
STP	7	1	0	71	72	9.1	1	27	44	12.5	3.17	52	.248	.312	-1	-12	54	116	.872	47	6	.2	-1.1	.5		-1.6
ALT	20	0	0	219²	292	12.0	3	52	93	14.1	4.67	70	.300	.335	-40	-34	109	103	.862	156	4	-.6	-3.0	-.8		-2.1
KC	70	0	0	702²	862	11.0	14	127	334	12.7	4.07	68	.283	.312	-83	-103	92	103	.861	520	51	-2.5	-9.0	-3.2		-8.8
WIL	15	0	0	142	165	10.5	4	18	113	11.6	3.04	108	.273	.294	0	4	109	125	.860	104	10	-.1	.4	-2.5		-4.8
TOT	759	44	8	7397¹		9.1				10.5	3.01		.245	.272					.872	4800	420					

Runs		Hits		Doubles		Triples		Home Runs		Total Bases	
Dunlap-StL	160	Dunlap-StL	185	Shaffer-StL	40	Burns-Cin	12	Dunlap-StL	13	Dunlap-StL	279
Shaffer-StL	130	Shaffer-StL	168	Dunlap-StL	39	Rowe-StL	11	Crane-Bos	12	Shaffer-StL	234
Seery-Bal-KC	115	Moore-Was	155	Rowe-StL	32	Shaffer-StL	10	Levis-Bal-Was	6	Rowe-StL	208
Robinson-Bal	101	Seery-Bal-KC	146	O'Brien-Bos	31					Crane-Bos	193
Rowe-StL	95	Rowe-StL	142	Gleason-StL	30					Seery-Bal-KC	192

Runs Batted In		Runs Produced		Bases On Balls		Batting Average		On Base Percentage		Slugging Average	
		Dunlap-StL	147	Robinson-Bal	37	Dunlap-StL	.412	Dunlap-StL	.448	Dunlap-StL	.621
		Shaffer-StL	128	Shaffer-StL	30	Hoover-Phi	.364	Shaffer-StL	.398	Shaffer-StL	.501
		Seery-Bal-KC	113	Dunlap-StL	29	Shaffer-StL	.360	Hoover-Phi	.390	Hoover-Phi	.495
		Robinson-Bal	99	Harbidge-Cin	25	Moore-Was	.336	Moore-Was	.363	Burns-Cin	.457
		Rowe-StL	91	Gleason-StL	23	Gleason-StL	.324	Gleason-StL	.361	Crane-Bos	.451

Production		Adjusted Production		Batter Runs		Adjusted Batter Runs		Clutch Hitting Index		Runs Created	
Dunlap-StL	1.069	Dunlap-StL	249	Dunlap-StL	72.5	Dunlap-StL	69.9			Dunlap-StL	128
Shaffer-StL	.899	Hoover-Phi	213	Shaffer-StL	49.1	Shaffer-StL	46.5			Shaffer-StL	96
Hoover-Phi	.885	Shaffer-StL	195	Moore-Was	28.9	Moore-Was	31.3			Moore-Was	71
Gleason-StL	.802	Moore-Was	168	Gleason-StL	28.3	Hoover-Phi	30.3			Seery-Bal-KC	67
Moore-Was	.777	Gleason-StL	164	Hoover-Phi	27.0	Gleason-StL	26.1			Rowe-StL	65

Total Average		Stolen Bases		Stolen Base Average		Stolen Base Runs		Fielding Runs		Total Player Rating	
Dunlap-StL	1.167							Dunlap-StL	30.5	Dunlap-StL	8.6
Shaffer-StL	.883							Fusselback-Bal	18.1	Shaffer-StL	3.6
Hoover-Phi	.846							Krieg-CP	17.4	Hoover-Phi	2.4
Gleason-StL	.738							Baker-StL	16.1	Robinson-Bal	2.4
Moore-Was	.686							Robinson-Bal	15.8	Fusselback-Bal	2.1

Wins		Win Percentage		Games		Complete Games		Shutouts		Saves	
W.Sweeney-Bal	40	McCormick-Cin	.875	W.Sweeney-Bal	62	W.Sweeney-Bal	58	McCormick-Cin	7	Taylor-StL	4
Daily-CP-Was	28	Taylor-StL	.862	Daily-CP-Was	58	Daily-CP-Was	56	Daily-CP-Was	5	Sylvester-Cin	1
Taylor-StL	25	Boyle-StL	.833	Wise-Was	50	Bakely-Phi-Wil-KC	43	Shaw-Bos	5	Dunlap-StL	1
Bradley-Cin	25	Sweeney-StL	.774	Bakely-Phi-Wil-KC	46	Bradley-Cin	36	Wise-Was	4	Brown-Bos	1
Sweeney-StL	24	W.Sweeney-Bal	.656	Bradley-Cin	41	Shaw-Bos	35	W.Sweeney-Bal	4	Boyle-StL	1

Innings Pitched		Fewest Hits/Game		Fewest BB/Game		Strikeouts		Strikeouts/Game		Ratio	
W.Sweeney-Bal	538.0	McCormick-Cin	6.47	Sweeney-StL	.43	Daily-CP-Was	483	Shaw-Bos	8.81	McCormick-Cin	7.07
Daily-CP-Was	500.2	Shaw-Bos	6.47	McCormick-Cin	.60	W.Sweeney-Bal	374	Daily-CP-Was	8.68	Sweeney-StL	7.31
Bakely-Phi-Wil-KC	394.2	Sweeney-StL	6.87	Boyle-StL	.60	Gagus-Was	309	Gagus-Was	7.92	Shaw-Bos	7.53
Wise-Was	364.1	Boyle-StL	7.08	Bradley-Cin	.61	Wise-Was	268	Robinson-Bal	7.32	Boyle-StL	7.68
Bradley-Cin	342.0	Werden-StL	7.20	Murphy-Wil-Alt	.62	Burke-Bos	255	Burke-Bos	7.13	Werden-StL	8.60

Earned Run Average		Adjusted ERA		Opponents' Batting Avg.		Opponents' On Base Pct.		Starter Runs		Adjusted Starter Runs	
McCormick-Cin	1.54	McCormick-Cin	205	McCormick-Cin	.188	McCormick-Cin	.202	Shaw-Bos	43.7	W.Sweeney-Bal	42.7
Taylor-StL	1.68	Taylor-StL	176	Shaw-Bos	.188	Sweeney-StL	.207	Taylor-StL	39.0	Shaw-Bos	41.0
Boyle-StL	1.74	Boyle-StL	170	Sweeney-StL	.197	Shaw-Bos	.212	Sweeney-StL	35.7	McCormick-Cin	37.7
Shaw-Bos	1.77	Shaw-Bos	166	Boyle-StL	.202	Boyle-StL	.215	McCormick-Cin	34.3	Taylor-StL	37.4
Sweeney-StL	1.83	Sweeney-StL	162	Werden-StL	.205	Werden-StL	.235	Daily-CP-Was	32.6	Sweeney-StL	34.0

Clutch Pitching Index		Relief Runs		Adjusted Relief Runs		Relief Ranking		Total Pitcher Index		Total Baseball Ranking	
Hodnett-StL	139							Taylor-StL	4.9	Dunlap-StL	8.6
Robinson-Bal	131							Sweeney-StL	4.6	Taylor-StL	5.5
Taylor-StL	127							Shaw-Bos	3.8	Sweeney-StL	4.7
W.Sweeney-Bal	109							McCormick-Cin	3.5	Shaw-Bos	3.7
Murphy-Wil-Alt	109							W.Sweeney-Bal	3.5	W.Sweeney-Bal	3.6

TEAM	G	W	L	PCT	GB	R	OR	AB	H	2B	3B	HR	BB	SO	AVG	OBP	SLG	PRO	PRO+	BR	/A	PF	CHI	RC	SB	CS	SBA	SBR
CHI	113	87	25	.777		**834**	470	4093	1079	**184**	75	54	340	429	.264	**.320**	**.385**	**.705**	115	143	55	115	**113**	517				
NY	112	85	27	.759	2	691	370	4029	**1085**	150	**82**	16	221	312	**.269**	.307	.359	.666	**122**	82	**90**	99	106	456				
PHI	111	56	54	.509	30	513	511	3893	891	156	35	20	220	401	.229	.270	.302	.572	91	-45	-34	98	102	326				
PRO	110	53	57	.482	33	442	531	3727	820	114	30	6	265	430	.220	.272	.272	.544	83	-74	-53	96	96	282				
BOS	113	46	66	.411	41	528	589	3950	915	144	53	22	190	522	.232	.267	.312	.579	94	-41	-21	96	103	337				
DET	108	41	67	.380	44	514	582	3773	917	149	66	25	216	451	.243	.284	.337	.621	105	17	16	100	93	371				
BUF	112	38	74	.339	49	495	761	3900	980	149	50	23	179	380	.251	.284	.333	.617	100	11	-8	103	89	378				
STL	111	36	72	.333	49	390	593	3758	829	121	21	8	214	412	.221	.263	.270	.533	81	-92	-58	94	89	273				
TOT	445					4407		31123	7516	1167	412	174	1845	3337	.241	.284	.322	.606										

TEAM	CG	SH	SV	IP	H	H/G	HR	BB	SO	RAT	ERA	ERA+	OAV	OOB	PR	/A	PF	CPI	FA	E	DP	FW	PW	BW	SBW	DIF
CHI	108	14	4	1015²	868	7.7	37	202	458	9.5	2.23	136	.221	.259	66	89	108	102	.903	496	80	-2.4	8.4	5.2		19.9
NY	109	**16**	1	994	758	6.9	11	265	**516**	9.3	**1.72**	**155**	**.205**	.258	121	106	95	114	**.929**	331	85	**6.0**	**10.0**	**8.5**		4.5
PHI	108	10	0	976	860	7.9	18	218	378	9.9	2.39	117	.224	.266	46	41	99	96	.905	447	66	-.3	3.9	-3.2		.6
PRO	108	8	0	960²	912	8.5	18	235	371	10.7	2.71	98	.235	.278	12	-7	94	96	.903	459	70	-1.1	-.7	-5.0		4.7
BOS	**111**	10	0	981	1045	9.6	26	**188**	480	11.3	3.03	89	.261	.294	-23	-38	95	107	.901	478	79	-1.5	-3.6	-2.0		-3.0
DET	105	6	1	954¹	966	9.1	18	224	475	11.2	2.88	99	.249	.290	-6	-2	101	104	.901	463	61	-1.7	-.2	1.5		-12.6
BUF	107	4	1	956	1175	11.1	31	234	320	13.3	4.29	69	.289	.328	-157	-140	106	99	.901	464	65	-.9	-13.2	-.8		-3.1
STL	107	4	0	965¹	935	8.7	15	278	337	11.3	3.37	82	.245	.296	-59	-68	97	89	.916	398	67	2.3	-6.4	-5.5		-8.4
TOT	863	72	7	7803		8.7				10.8	2.82		.241	.284					.908	3536	573					

Runs
Kelly-Chi 124
O'Rourke-NY 119
Gore-Chi 115
Dalrymple-Chi 109
Connor-NY 102

Hits
Connor-NY 169
Brouthers-Buf ... 146
Anson-Chi 144
Sutton-Bos 143
O'Rourke-NY 143

Doubles
Anson-Chi 35
Brouthers-Buf 32
Rowe-Buf 28
Dalrymple-Chi 27
Mulvey-Phi 25

Triples
O'Rourke-NY 16
Connor-NY 15
Gore-Chi 13
Bennett-Det 13

Home Runs
Dalrymple-Chi 11
Kelly-Chi 9

Total Bases
Connor-NY 225
Brouthers-Buf 221
Dalrymple-Chi 219
Anson-Chi 214
O'Rourke-NY 211

Runs Batted In
Anson-Chi 108
Kelly-Chi 75
Pfeffer-Chi 73
Burns-Chi 71

Runs Produced
Anson-Chi 201
Kelly-Chi 190
Gore-Chi 167
Connor-NY 166
Dalrymple-Chi 159

Bases On Balls
Williamson-Chi 75
Gore-Chi 68
Morrill-Bos 64
Connor-NY 51

Batting Average
Connor-NY 371
Brouthers-Buf 359
Dorgan-NY 326
Richardson-Buf ...319
Gore-Chi 313

On Base Percentage
Connor-NY 435
Brouthers-Buf 408
Gore-Chi 405
Hanlon-Det 372
Anson-Chi 357

Slugging Average
Brouthers-Buf 543
Connor-NY 495
Ewing-NY 471
Anson-Chi 461
Richardson-Buf ..458

Production
Brouthers-Buf 951
Connor-NY 929
Gore-Chi 858
Anson-Chi 819
Bennett-Det 812

Adjusted Production
Connor-NY 203
Brouthers-Buf ... 199
Bennett-Det 161
Ewing-NY 159
O'Rourke-NY 158

Batter Runs
Connor-NY 51.7
Brouthers-Buf 46.8
Gore-Chi 40.6
Anson-Chi 31.7
O'Rourke-NY 29.5

Adjusted Batter Runs
Connor-NY 52.6
Brouthers-Buf 44.8
O'Rourke-NY 30.5
Gore-Chi 30.5
Richardson-Buf ... 24.6

Clutch Hitting Index
Williamson-Chi 170
Anson-Chi 169
Pfeffer-Chi 159
Gerhardt-NY 150
White-Buf 140

Runs Created
Connor-NY 100
Brouthers-Buf 92
Gore-Chi 83
Anson-Chi 78
O'Rourke-NY 77

Total Average
Brouthers-Buf 977
Connor-NY 965
Gore-Chi 884
Bennett-Det 808
Anson-Chi 775

Stolen Bases

Stolen Base Average

Stolen Base Runs

Fielding Runs
Dunlap-StL 25.8
Pfeffer-Chi 25.4
Fogarty-Phi 24.8
Glasscock-StL 19.4
Richardson-Buf ... 13.0

Total Player Rating
Connor-NY 4.0
Dunlap-StL 3.9
Richardson-Buf 3.5
Ewing-NY 3.2
Glasscock-StL 3.1

Wins
Clarkson-Chi 53
Welch-NY 44
Keefe-NY 32
Radbourn-Pro 28

Win Percentage
Welch-NY 800
Clarkson-Chi 768
McCormick-Pro-Chi ..750
Keefe-NY 711
Radbourn-Pro 571

Games
Clarkson-Chi 70
Welch-NY 56
Whitney-Bos 51
Buffinton-Bos 51
Daily-Phi 50

Complete Games
Clarkson-Chi 68
Welch-NY 55
Whitney-Bos 50

Shutouts
Clarkson-Chi 10
Welch-NY 7
Keefe-NY 7
Shaw-Pro 6
Buffinton-Bos 6

Saves
Williamson-Chi 2
Pfeffer-Chi 2
Welch-NY 1
Galvin-Buf 1
Baldwin-Det 1

Innings Pitched
Clarkson-Chi 623.0
Welch-NY 492.0
Radbourn-Pro ... 445.2
Whitney-Bos 441.1
Daily-Phi 440.0

Fewest Hits/Game
Keefe-NY 6.75
Welch-NY 6.80
Baldwin-Det 6.88
Clarkson-Chi 7.18
Daily-Phi 7.57

Fewest BB/Game
Whitney-Bos ...... .75
Galvin-Buf 1.17
Clarkson-Chi 1.40
Baldwin-Det 1.41
C.Sweeney-StL ... 1.64

Strikeouts
Clarkson-Chi 308
Welch-NY 258
Buffinton-Bos 242
Keefe-NY 227
Whitney-Bos 200

Strikeouts/Game
Baldwin-Det 6.78
Keefe-NY 5.11
Buffinton-Bos 5.01
Welch-NY 4.72
Clarkson-Chi 4.45

Ratio
Baldwin-Det 8.28
Clarkson-Chi 8.58
Keefe-NY 9.05
Welch-NY 9.20
Daily-Phi 9.41

Earned Run Average
Keefe-NY 1.58
Welch-NY 1.66
Clarkson-Chi 1.85
Baldwin-Det 1.86
Radbourn-Pro 2.20

Adjusted ERA
Keefe-NY 169
Clarkson-Chi 164
Welch-NY 160
Baldwin-Det 153
Daily-Phi 126

Opponents' Batting Avg.
Baldwin-Det 197
Welch-NY 203
Keefe-NY 203
Clarkson-Chi 208
Shaw-Pro 209

Opponents' On Base Pct.
Baldwin-Det 228
Clarkson-Chi 239
Shaw-Pro 254
Keefe-NY 255
Daily-Phi 256

Starter Runs
Clarkson-Chi 67.0
Welch-NY 63.0
Keefe-NY 55.2
Radbourn-Pro ... 30.5
Daily-Phi 29.7

Adjusted Starter Runs
Clarkson-Chi 82.0
Welch-NY 54.7
Keefe-NY 48.4
Daily-Phi 28.2
Ferguson-Phi 25.4

Clutch Pitching Index
Keefe-NY 121
Getzien-Det 118
Radbourn-Pro ... 116
Welch-NY 112
Whitney-Bos 111

Relief Runs

Adjusted Relief Runs

Relief Ranking

Total Pitcher Index
Clarkson-Chi 8.9
Welch-NY 4.9
Keefe-NY 4.7
Ferguson-Phi 4.2
Radbourn-Pro 3.5

Total Baseball Ranking
Clarkson-Chi 8.8
Welch-NY 4.9
Keefe-NY 4.6
Ferguson-Phi 4.4
Connor-NY 4.0

TEAM	G	W	L	PCT	GB	R	OR	AB	H	2B	3B	HR	BB	SO	AVG	OBP	SLG	PRO	PRO+	BR	/A	PF	CHI	RC	SB	CS	SBA	SBR
STL	112	79	33	.705		677	461	3972	979	132	57	17	234	282	.246	.297	.321	.618	98	14	-14	105	107	388				
CIN	112	63	49	.563	16	642	575	4050	1046	108	77	26	153	420	.258	.294	.342	.636	106	31	19	102	99	417				
PIT	111	56	55	.505	22.5	547	539	3975	955	123	79	5	189	537	.240	.282	.315	.597	96	-19	-10	99	92	362				
PHI	113	55	57	.491	24	764	691	4142	1099	169	76	30	223	410	.265	.310	.365	.675	113	90	52	106	105	480				
LOU	112	53	59	.473	26	564	598	3969	986	126	83	19	152	448	.248	.281	.336	.617	101	2	3	100	93	384				
BRO	112	53	59	.473	26	624	650	3943	966	121	65	14	238	324	.245	.295	.319	.614	100	9	5	101	100	381				
NY	108	44	64	.407	33	526	688	3731	921	123	57	21	217	428	.247	.295	.327	.622	112	16	62	92	88	369				
BAL	110	41	68	.376	36.5	541	683	3820	837	124	59	17	279	529	.219	.280	.296	.576	90	-40	-31	99	96	324				
TOT	445					4885		31602	7789	1026	553	149	1685	3378	.246	.285	.328	.613										

TEAM	CG	SH	SV	IP	H	H/G	HR	BB	SO	RAT	ERA	ERA+	OAV	OOB	PR	/A	PF	CPI	FA	E	DP	FW	PW	BW	SBW	DIF
STL	111	11	0	1002	879	7.9	12	168	378	9.8	2.44	134	.228	.268	89	91	101	106	.920	381	64	3.0	8.2	-1.3		13.1
CIN	102	7	1	999¹	998	9.0	24	250	330	11.9	3.26	100	.253	.309	-2	-1	100	112	.911	423	86	.8	-.0	1.7		4.6
PIT	104	8	0	1011	918	8.2	14	201	454	10.3	2.92	110	.232	.275	36	32	99	95	.912	422	77	.6	2.9	-.9		-2.1
PHI	105	5	0	1003¹	1038	9.3	11	212	506	11.6	3.23	106	.254	.298	2	23	106	104	.901	483	79	-2.2	2.1	4.7		-5.6
LOU	109	3	1	1002	927	8.3	13	217	462	10.6	2.68	120	.232	.278	63	60	99	104	.905	460	75	-1.2	5.4	.3		-7.5
BRO	110	3	1	991²	955	8.7	27	211	436	10.8	3.46	95	.240	.283	-24	-19	102	89	.910	434	56	.2	-1.7	.5		-2.0
NY	103	2	0	937	1015	9.7	36	204	408	11.9	4.15	71	.262	.303	-94	-125	91	91	.901	452	62	-1.6	-11.3	5.6		-2.8
BAL	103	2	4	971	1059	9.8	12	222	395	12.3	3.90	83	.269	.316	-71	-71	100	100	.910	418	71	.6	-6.4	-2.8		-5.0
TOT	847	41	7	7917¹		8.9				11.1	3.24		.246	.285					.909	3473	570					

Runs		Hits		Doubles		Triples		Home Runs		Total Bases	
Stovey-Phi	130	Browning-Lou	174	Larkin-Phi	37	Orr-NY	21	Stovey-Phi	13	Browning-Lou	255
Larkin-Phi	114	Jones-Cin	157	Browning-Lou	34	Kuehne-Pit	19	Fennelly-Cin	10	Orr-NY	241
Jones-Cin	108	Stovey-Phi	153	Orr-NY	29	Wolf-Lou	17	Browning-Lou	9	Larkin-Phi	238
Nelson-NY	98	Orr-NY	152	Stovey-Phi	27	Jones-Cin	17	Larkin-Phi	8	Stovey-Phi	237
Browning-Lou	98	Larkin-Phi	149			Fennelly-Cin	17	Orr-NY	6	Jones-Cin	225

Runs Batted In	Runs Produced		Bases On Balls		Batting Average		On Base Percentage		Slugging Average	
	Stovey-Phi	117	Nelson-NY	61	Browning-Lou	.362	Browning-Lou	.393	Orr-NY	.543
	Larkin-Phi	106	Macullar-Bal	49	Orr-NY	.342	Larkin-Phi	.372	Browning-Lou	.530
	Jones-Cin	103	Hotaling-Bro	49	Larkin-Phi	.329	Stovey-Phi	.371	Larkin-Phi	.525
	Nelson-NY	97	Stovey-Phi	39	Jones-Cin	.322	Brown-Pit	.366	Stovey-Phi	.488
	Browning-Lou	89			Stovey-Phi	.315	Phillips-Bro	.364	Jones-Cin	.462

Production		Adjusted Production		Batter Runs		Adjusted Batter Runs		Clutch Hitting Index	Runs Created	
Browning-Lou	.923	Orr-NY	201	Browning-Lou	48.4	Browning-Lou	48.6		Browning-Lou	103
Orr-NY	.901	Browning-Lou	193	Larkin-Phi	41.7	Orr-NY	44.7		Larkin-Phi	91
Larkin-Phi	.897	Larkin-Phi	174	Orr-NY	39.5	Larkin-Phi	37.5		Stovey-Phi	90
Stovey-Phi	.858	Stovey-Phi	163	Stovey-Phi	39.5	Stovey-Phi	34.9		Orr-NY	88
Jones-Cin	.824	Jones-Cin	159	Jones-Cin	33.0	Jones-Cin	31.6		Jones-Cin	83

Total Average		Stolen Bases	Stolen Base Average	Stolen Base Runs	Fielding Runs		Total Player Rating	
Browning-Lou	.912				G.Smith-Bro	39.9	Browning-Lou	4.5
Larkin-Phi	.885				Smith-Pit	33.2	Larkin-Phi	4.1
Orr-NY	.863				Houck-Phi	21.8	G.Smith-Bro	3.9
Stovey-Phi	.841				Hankinson-NY	18.0	Jones-Cin	3.6
Jones-Cin	.773				Corkhill-Cin	17.1	Smith-Pit	3.4

Wins		Win Percentage		Games		Complete Games		Shutouts		Saves	
Caruthers-StL	40	Caruthers-StL	.755	Morris-Pit	63	Morris-Pit	63	Morris-Pit	7	Burns-Bal	3
Morris-Pit	39	Foutz-StL	.702	Henderson-Bal	61	Henderson-Bal	59	Caruthers-StL	6	Terry-Bro	1
Porter-Bro	33	Mathews-Phi	.638	Porter-Bro	54	Porter-Bro	53	McGinnis-StL	3	Sommer-Bal	1
Foutz-StL	33	Morris-Pit	.619	Hecker-Lou	53	Caruthers-StL	53			Reccius-Lou	1
		Porter-Bro	.611	Caruthers-StL	53	Hecker-Lou	51			Corkhill-Cin	1

Innings Pitched		Fewest Hits/Game		Fewest BB/Game		Strikeouts		Strikeouts/Game		Ratio	
Morris-Pit	581.0	Morris-Pit	7.11	Lynch-NY	1.00	Morris-Pit	298	Mathews-Phi	6.09	Morris-Pit	8.89
Henderson-Bal	539.1	Mays-Lou	7.74	Hecker-Lou	1.01	Mathews-Phi	286	Cushman-Phi-NY	5.50	Caruthers-StL	9.44
Caruthers-StL	482.1	Foutz-StL	7.75	Caruthers-StL	1.06	Henderson-Bal	263	Morris-Pit	4.62	Hecker-Lou	9.86
Porter-Bro	481.2	McGinnis-StL	7.87	Mathews-Phi	1.21	Hecker-Lou	209	Henderson-Bal	4.39	McGinnis-StL	9.88
Hecker-Lou	480.0	Porter-Bro	7.98	McGinnis-StL	1.53	Porter-Bro	197	Harkins-Bro	4.33	Mathews-Phi	10.04

Earned Run Average		Adjusted ERA		Opponents' Batting Avg.		Opponents' On Base Pct.		Starter Runs		Adjusted Starter Runs	
Caruthers-StL	2.07	Caruthers-StL	158	Morris-Pit	.208	Morris-Pit	.247	Caruthers-StL	62.9	Caruthers-StL	64.1
Hecker-Lou	2.17	Hecker-Lou	148	Mays-Lou	.219	Caruthers-StL	.260	Morris-Pit	57.4	Hecker-Lou	55.8
Morris-Pit	2.35	Mathews-Phi	141	Porter-Bro	.223	Hecker-Lou	.265	Hecker-Lou	57.0	Morris-Pit	55.6
Mathews-Phi	2.43	Morris-Pit	137	McGinnis-StL	.225	Cushman-Phi-NY	.266	Mathews-Phi	38.2	Mathews-Phi	47.2
Foutz-StL	2.63	Foutz-StL	124	Foutz-StL	.227	Mathews-Phi	.267	Foutz-StL	28.0	Foutz-StL	29.0

Clutch Pitching Index		Relief Runs	Adjusted Relief Runs	Relief Ranking	Total Pitcher Index		Total Baseball Ranking	
Knight-Phi	283				Hecker-Lou	6.7	Caruthers-StL	6.6
Hecker-Lou	121				Caruthers-StL	6.7	Hecker-Lou	6.4
Caruthers-StL	118				Morris-Pit	4.7	Morris-Pit	4.7
Mountjoy-Cin-Bal	111				Mathews-Phi	3.8	Browning-Lou	4.5
Foutz-StL	107				Foutz-StL	3.7	Larkin-Phi	4.1

1886 National League

TEAM	G	W	L	PCT	GB	R	OR	AB	H	2B	3B	HR	BB	SO	AVG	OBP	SLG	PRO	PRO+	BR	/A	PF	CHI	RC	SB	CS	SBA	SBR
CHI	126	90	34	.726		900	555	4378	1223	198	87	53	460	513	.279	.348	.401	.749	115	176	71	115	104	701	213			
DET	126	87	36	.707	2.5	829	538	4501	1260	176	81	53	374	426	.280	.335	.390	.725	122	137	117	103	100	670	194			
NY	124	75	44	.630	12.5	692	558	4298	1156	175	68	21	237	410	.269	.307	.356	.663	106	29	23	101	102	531	155			
PHI	119	71	43	.623	14	621	498	4072	976	145	66	26	282	516	.240	.289	.327	.616	91	-37	-43	101	106	461	226			
BOS	118	56	61	.479	30.5	657	661	4180	1085	151	59	24	250	537	.260	.301	.341	.642	104	0	23	96	104	489	156			
STL	126	43	79	.352	46	547	712	4250	1001	183	46	30	235	656	.236	.276	.321	.597	92	-71	-30	94	96	430	156			
KC	126	30	91	.248	58.5	494	872	4236	967	177	48	19	269	608	.228	.274	.306	.580	76	-92	-133	106	90	392	96			
WAS	125	28	92	.233	60	445	791	4082	856	135	51	23	265	582	.210	.258	.285	.543	73	-143	-107	94	93	345	143			
TOT	495					5185		33997	8524	1340	506	249	2372	4248	.251	.300	.342	.641							1339			

TEAM	CG	SH	SV	IP	H	H/G	HR	BB	SO	RAT	ERA	ERA+	OAV	OOB	PR	/A	PF	CPI	FA	E	DP	FW	PW	BW	SBW	DIF
CHI	116	8	3	1097²	988	8.1	49	262	647	10.2	2.54	142	.232	.277	91	131	110	111	.912	475	82	-1.8	11.9	6.4		11.4
DET	122	8	0	1103²	995	8.1	20	270	592	10.3	2.85	115	.231	.276	53	52	100	90	.928	373	82	3.8	4.7	10.6		6.4
NY	119	3	1	1062	1029	8.7	23	280	588	11.1	2.86	111	.247	.294	50	26	97	104	.927	359	70	4.2	2.4	2.1		6.9
PHI	110	10	2	1045²	923	7.9	29	264	540	10.2	2.45	134	.224	.271	97	94	100	101	.921	393	46	1.4	8.5	-3.9		8.0
BOS	116	3	0	1029	1049	9.2	33	298	511	11.8	3.24	98	.252	.302	5	-7	97	104	.905	465	63	-2.7	-.6	2.1		-1.2
STL	118	6	0	1077¹	1050	8.8	34	392	501	12.0	3.24	99	.246	.309	5	-7	97	105	.914	452	92	-.5	-.6	-2.7		-14.1
KC	117	4	0	1066²	1345	11.3	27	246	442	13.4	4.84	77	.295	.331	-184	-132	114	90	.910	482	79	-2.1	-12.0	-12.1		-4.3
WAS	116	4	0	1041	1147	9.9	34	379	500	13.2	4.30	76	.271	.331	-117	-124	99	95	.910	458	69	-1.0	-11.2	-9.7		-10.0
TOT	934	46	6	8523		9.0				11.5	3.29		.251	.300					.916	3457	583					

Runs
Kelly-Chi 155
Gore-Chi 150
Brouthers-Det ... 139
Richardson-Det ... 125
Anson-Chi 117

Hits
Richardson-Det ... 189
Anson-Chi 187
Brouthers-Det ... 181
Kelly-Chi 175
Connor-NY 172

Doubles
Brouthers-Det 40
Anson-Chi 35
Kelly-Chi 32
Hines-Was 30

Triples
Connor-NY 20
Wood-Phi 15
Brouthers-Det 15
Thompson-Det 13

Home Runs
Richardson-Det 11
Brouthers-Det 11
Anson-Chi 10
Hines-Was 9
Denny-StL 9

Total Bases
Brouthers-Det ... 284
Anson-Chi 274
Richardson-Det ... 271
Connor-NY 262
Kelly-Chi 241

Runs Batted In
Anson-Chi 147
Pfeffer-Chi 95
Thompson-Det ... 89
Rowe-Det 87
Ward-NY 81

Runs Produced
Anson-Chi 254
Kelly-Chi 230
Gore-Chi 207
Brouthers-Det ... 200
Thompson-Det ... 182

Bases On Balls
Gore-Chi 102
Kelly-Chi 83
Williamson-Chi ... 80
Brouthers-Det 66
Radford-KC 58

Batting Average
Kelly-Chi .... .388
Anson-Chi .... .371
Brouthers-Det ... .370
Connor-NY .... .355
Richardson-Det ... .351

On Base Percentage
Kelly-Chi .... .483
Brouthers-Det .... .445
Gore-Chi .... .434
Anson-Chi .... .433
Connor-NY .... .405

Slugging Average
Brouthers-Det .... .581
Anson-Chi .... .544
Connor-NY .... .540
Kelly-Chi .... .534
Richardson-Det ... .504

Production
Brouthers-Det ... 1.026
Kelly-Chi 1.018
Anson-Chi .... .977
Connor-NY .... .945
Richardson-Det ... .906

Adjusted Production
Brouthers-Det 204
Connor-NY 183
Kelly-Chi 182
Anson-Chi 170
Richardson-Det ... 169

Batter Runs
Brouthers-Det ... 65.9
Kelly-Chi 64.3
Anson-Chi 58.3
Connor-NY 48.7
Richardson-Det ... 47.4

Adjusted Batter Runs
Brouthers-Det ... 63.6
Kelly-Chi 52.7
Connor-NY 48.0
Anson-Chi 46.1
Richardson-Det ... 45.0

Clutch Hitting Index
Pfeffer-Chi 164
Dorgan-NY 162
Anson-Chi 151
White-Det 148
Ward-NY 147

Runs Created
Kelly-Chi 146
Brouthers-Det ... 139
Anson-Chi 134
Richardson-Det ... 129
Connor-NY 116

Total Average
Kelly-Chi 1.366
Brouthers-Det ... 1.205
Anson-Chi 1.129
Gore-Chi 1.042
Richardson-Det ... 1.029

Stolen Bases
Andrews-Phi 56
Kelly-Chi 53
Hanlon-Det 50
Richardson-Det ... 42
Radford-KC 39

Stolen Base Average

Stolen Base Runs

Fielding Runs
Knowles-Was 27.7
Denny-StL 22.7
Dunlap-StL-Det ... 19.4
Johnston-Bos 16.7
Glasscock-StL 13.8

Total Player Rating
Kelly-Chi 5.3
Richardson-Det ... 4.9
Glasscock-StL 4.1
Connor-NY 3.9
Brouthers-Det 3.7

Wins
Keefe-NY 42
Baldwin-Det 42
Clarkson-Chi 36
Welch-NY 33
McCormick-Chi ... 31

Win Percentage
Flynn-Chi 793
Ferguson-Phi 769
Baldwin-Det 764
McCormick-Chi ...738
Getzien-Det 732

Games
Keefe-NY 64
Welch-NY 59
Radbourn-Bos 58
Baldwin-Det 56
Clarkson-Chi 55

Complete Games
Keefe-NY 62
Radbourn-Bos 57
Welch-NY 56
Baldwin-Det 55
Clarkson-Chi 50

Shutouts
Baldwin-Det 7
Ferguson-Phi 4
Casey-Phi 4

Saves
Ferguson-Phi 2
Williamson-Chi 1
Ryan-Chi 1
Flynn-Chi 1
Devlin-NY 1

Innings Pitched
Keefe-NY 535.0
Radbourn-Bos ... 509.1
Welch-NY 500.0
Baldwin-Det 487.0
Clarkson-Chi ... 466.2

Fewest Hits/Game
Baldwin-Det 6.86
Ferguson-Phi 7.21
Flynn-Chi 7.25
Stemmeyer-Bos ... 7.74
Boyle-StL 7.84

Fewest BB/Game
Whitney-KC 1.26
Ferguson-Phi 1.57
Clarkson-Chi 1.66
Keefe-NY 1.72
Baldwin-Det 1.85

Strikeouts
Baldwin-Det 323
Clarkson-Chi 313
Keefe-NY 297
Welch-NY 272
Stemmeyer-Bos ... 239

Strikeouts/Game
Stemmeyer-Bos ... 6.17
Clarkson-Chi 6.04
Baldwin-Det 5.97
Healy-StL 5.42
Flynn-Chi 5.11

Ratio
Baldwin-Det 8.70
Ferguson-Phi 8.78
Flynn-Chi 9.46
Clarkson-Chi 9.74
Keefe-NY 9.77

Earned Run Average
Boyle-StL 1.76
Ferguson-Phi 1.98
Baldwin-Det 2.24
Flynn-Chi 2.24
Clarkson-Chi 2.41

Adjusted ERA
Boyle-StL 182
Ferguson-Phi 166
Flynn-Chi 161
Clarkson-Chi 150
Baldwin-Det 147

Opponents' Batting Avg.
Baldwin-Det ..... .202
Ferguson-Phi .... .210
Flynn-Chi .... .210
Stemmeyer-Bos ... .218
Boyle-StL .... .220

Opponents' On Base Pct.
Baldwin-Det ..... .243
Ferguson-Phi .... .244
Flynn-Chi .... .257
Boyle-StL .... .261
Clarkson-Chi .... .264

Starter Runs
Ferguson-Phi 57.5
Baldwin-Det 56.9
Clarkson-Chi 45.4
Keefe-NY 43.4
Casey-Phi 35.8

Adjusted Starter Runs
Clarkson-Chi 62.7
Ferguson-Phi 57.1
Baldwin-Det 57.1
Flynn-Chi 39.3
Keefe-NY 37.5

Clutch Pitching Index
Boyle-StL 127
McCormick-Chi ... 126
Welch-NY 121
Kirby-StL 112
Radbourn-Bos 108

Relief Runs

Adjusted Relief Runs

Relief Ranking

Total Pitcher Index
Ferguson-Phi 7.1
Clarkson-Chi 6.4
Baldwin-Det 6.0
Flynn-Chi 4.1
Boyle-StL 3.8

Total Baseball Ranking
Ferguson-Phi 7.0
Clarkson-Chi 6.2
Baldwin-Det 5.9
Kelly-Chi 5.3
Richardson-Det 4.8

TEAM	G	W	L	PCT	GB	R	OR	AB	H	2B	3B	HR	BB	SO	AVG	OBP	SLG	PRO	PRO+	BR	/A	PF	CHI	RC	SB	CS	SBA	SBR
STL	139	93	46	.669		944	592	5009	1365	206	85	20	400	425	.273	.333	.360	.693	117	126	88	105	100	729	336			
PIT	140	80	57	.584	12	810	647	4854	1171	186	96	16	478	713	.241	.314	.329	.643	108	43	47	100	96	598	260			
BRO	141	76	61	.555	16	832	832	5053	1261	196	80	16	433	523	.250	.311	.330	.641	105	35	28	101	97	610	248			
LOU	138	66	70	.485	25.5	833	805	4921	1294	182	88	20	410	558	.263	.323	.348	.671	109	86	40	106	94	634	202			
CIN	141	65	73	.471	27.5	883	865	4915	1225	145	95	45	374	633	.249	.311	.345	.656	107	57	31	103	103	599	185			
PHI	139	63	72	.467	28	772	942	4856	1142	192	82	21	330	697	.235	.296	.321	.617	97	-10	-18	101	99	560	284			
NY	137	53	82	.393	38	628	766	4683	1047	108	72	18	330	578	.224	.279	.289	.568	86	-90	-57	96	95	422	120			
BAL	139	48	83	.366	41	625	878	4639	945	124	51	8	379	603	.204	.269	.258	.527	72	-151	-132	98	104	404	269			
TOT	557					6327		38930	9450	1339	649	164	3182	4730	.243	.300	.323	.623							1904			

TEAM	CG	SH	SV	IP	H	H/G	HR	BB	SO	RAT	ERA	ERA+	OAV	OOB	PR	/A	PF	CPI	FA	E	DP	FW	PW	BW	SBW	DIF
STL	134	14	2	1229¹	1087	8.0	13	329	583	10.6	2.49	138	.227	.281	130	128	100	113	.915	494	96	3.3	11.2	7.7		1.2
PIT	137	15	1	1226	1226	8.3	10	299	515	10.7	2.83	120	.235	.285	84	74	98	104	.917	487	90	3.9	6.5	4.1		-3.0
BRO	138	6	0	1234²	1202	8.8	17	464	540	12.4	3.42	102	.243	.312	3	9	101	104	.900	610	87	-2.2	.8	2.5		6.5
LOU	131	5	2	1209²	1109	8.3	16	432	720	11.7	3.07	118	.230	.297	51	75	106	101	.901	593	89	-2.0	6.6	3.5		-10.1
CIN	129	3	0	1247²	1267	9.1	25	481	495	13.0	4.18	84	.255	.327	-103	-94	102	95	.905	582	122	-.8	-8.3	2.7		2.3
PHI	134	4	0	1218²	1308	9.7	35	388	513	13.0	3.97	88	.259	.319	-72	-66	102	100	.894	637	99	-4.0	-5.8	-1.6		6.9
NY	134	5	0	1186¹	1148	8.7	23	386	559	11.8	3.50	97	.243	.304	-8	-14	99	98	.907	544	81	.3	-1.2	-5.0		-8.6
BAL	134	5	0	1206²	1197	8.9	25	403	805	12.3	4.08	84	.244	.308	-85	-90	99	87	.910	523	59	1.8	-7.9	-11.6		.2
TOT	1071	57	5	9759		8.7				11.9	3.44		.243	.300					.906	4470	723					

Runs
Latham-StL 152
McPhee-Cin 139
Larkin-Phi 133
McClellan-Bro 131
Pinkney-Bro 119

Hits
Orr-NY 193
O'Neill-StL 190
Larkin-Phi 180
Latham-StL 174
Phillips-Bro 160

Doubles
Larkin-Phi 36
McClellan-Bro 33
Welch-StL 31
Barkley-Pit 31
Browning-Lou 29

Triples
Orr-NY 31
Coleman-Phi-Pit ... 17
Kuehne-Pit 17
Fennelly-Cin 17
Larkin-Phi 16

Home Runs
McPhee-Cin 8
Stovey-Phi 7
Orr-NY 7

Total Bases
Orr-NY 301
O'Neill-StL 255
Larkin-Phi 254
Welch-StL 221
McPhee-Cin 221

Runs Batted In

Runs Produced
Latham-StL 151
McPhee-Cin 131
Larkin-Phi 131
McClellan-Bro 130
Pinkney-Bro 119

Bases On Balls
Swartwood-Bro 70
Pinkney-Bro 70
Mack-Lou 68
Kerins-Lou 66

Batting Average
Browning-Lou .... .340
Orr-NY .... .338
O'Neill-StL ...... .328
Larkin-Phi .... .319
Latham-StL ...... .301

On Base Percentage
Larkin-Phi .... .390
Browning-Lou .... .389
O'Neill-StL ...... .385
Stovey-Phi .... .377
Swartwood-Bro ... .377

Slugging Average
Orr-NY .... .527
Larkin-Phi .... .450
Browning-Lou .... .441
O'Neill-StL ...... .440
Stovey-Phi .... .440

Production
Orr-NY .... .890
Larkin-Phi .... .839
Browning-Lou .... .830
O'Neill-StL ...... .826
Stovey-Phi .... .817

Adjusted Production
Orr-NY 188
Larkin-Phi 163
Stovey-Phi 156
O'Neill-StL 153
Browning-Lou 153

Batter Runs
Orr-NY 47.2
Larkin-Phi 42.6
Caruthers-StL 42.1
O'Neill-StL 39.9
Stovey-Phi 33.3

Adjusted Batter Runs
Orr-NY 51.1
Larkin-Phi 41.7
Caruthers-StL 39.4
O'Neill-StL 35.5
Stovey-Phi 32.5

Clutch Hitting Index

Runs Created
Orr-NY 118
Larkin-Phi 114
Stovey-Phi 109
O'Neill-StL 104
Latham-StL 104

Total Average
Stovey-Phi 1.009
Larkin-Phi .... .914
Robinson-StL ..... .903
Orr-NY .... .897
Browning-Lou .... .873

Stolen Bases
Stovey-Phi 68
Latham-StL 60
Welch-StL 59
Robinson-StL 51
McClellan-Bro 43

Stolen Base Average

Stolen Base Runs

Fielding Runs
Kerins-Lou 39.1
McPhee-Cin 30.5
Hankinson-NY ... 25.4
Smith-Pit 21.0
Peoples-Bro 18.5

Total Player Rating
Kerins-Lou 4.8
McPhee-Cin 4.7
Larkin-Phi 3.8
Carroll-Pit 3.7
O'Neill-StL 3.5

Wins
Morris-Pit 41
Foutz-StL 41
Ramsey-Lou 38
Mullane-Cin 33
Caruthers-StL 30

Win Percentage
Foutz-StL .... .719
Caruthers-StL .... .682
Morris-Pit .... .672
Hudson-StL ...... .615
Atkinson-Phi ..... .595

Games
Kilroy-Bal 68
Ramsey-Lou 67
Morris-Pit 64
Mullane-Cin 63
Foutz-StL 59

Complete Games
Ramsey-Lou 66
Kilroy-Bal 66
Morris-Pit 63
Mullane-Cin 55
Foutz-StL 55

Shutouts
Morris-Pit 12
Foutz-StL 11
Terry-Bro 5
Kilroy-Bal 5
Ramsey-Lou 3

Saves
Morris-Pit 1
Hudson-StL 1
Foutz-StL 1
Ely-Lou 1

Innings Pitched
Ramsey-Lou 588.2
Kilroy-Bal 583.0
Morris-Pit 555.1
Mullane-Cin 529.2
Foutz-StL 504.0

Fewest Hits/Game
Ramsey-Lou 6.83
Kilroy-Bal 7.35
Morris-Pit 7.37
Foutz-StL 7.46
Caruthers-StL 7.51

Fewest BB/Game
Galvin-Pit 1.55
Morris-Pit 1.91
Caruthers-StL 2.00
McGinnis-StL-Bal . 2.27
Atkinson-Phi 2.29

Strikeouts
Kilroy-Bal 513
Ramsey-Lou 499
Morris-Pit 326
Foutz-StL 283
Mullane-Cin 250

Strikeouts/Game
Kilroy-Bal 7.92
Ramsey-Lou 7.63
Morris-Pit 5.28
Miller-Phi 5.25
Terry-Bro 5.06

Ratio
Morris-Pit 9.40
Caruthers-StL 9.67
Ramsey-Lou 10.18
Foutz-StL 10.21
Cushman-NY 10.45

Earned Run Average
Foutz-StL 2.11
Caruthers-StL 2.32
Ramsey-Lou 2.45
Morris-Pit 2.45
Galvin-Pit 2.67

Adjusted ERA
Foutz-StL 163
Ramsey-Lou 148
Caruthers-StL 148
Morris-Pit 138
Hecker-Lou 127

Opponents' Batting Avg.
Ramsey-Lou ..... .198
Kilroy-Bal .... .210
Morris-Pit .... .214
Foutz-StL .... .216
Caruthers-StL .... .217

Opponents' On Base Pct.
Morris-Pit .... .258
Caruthers-StL .... .263
Ramsey-Lou ..... .269
Foutz-StL .... .274
Kilroy-Bal .... .274

Starter Runs
Foutz-StL 74.8
Ramsey-Lou 65.2
Morris-Pit 61.4
Caruthers-StL 48.2
Galvin-Pit 37.3

Adjusted Starter Runs
Ramsey-Lou 77.6
Foutz-StL 74.2
Morris-Pit 57.6
Caruthers-StL 47.7
Hecker-Lou 35.8

Clutch Pitching Index
Galvin-Pit 130
McGinnis-StL-Bal . 127
Foutz-StL 122
Miller-Phi 119
Mays-NY 107

Relief Runs

Adjusted Relief Runs

Relief Ranking

Total Pitcher Index
Foutz-StL 8.0
Caruthers-StL 6.8
Ramsey-Lou 6.6
Hecker-Lou 5.2
Morris-Pit 4.5

Total Baseball Ranking
Foutz-StL 8.0
Caruthers-StL 8.0
Ramsey-Lou 6.6
Hecker-Lou 5.3
Kerins-Lou 4.8

1887 National League

TEAM	G	W	L	PCT	GB	R	OR	AB	H	2B	3B	HR	BB	SO	AVG	OBP	SLG	PRO	PRO+	BR	/A	PF	CHI	RC	SB	CS	SBA	SBR
DET	127	79	45	.637		969	714	4689	1404	213	126	55	352	258	.299	.353	.434	.787	120	146	120	103	102	833	267			
PHI	128	75	48	.610	3.5	901	702	4630	1269	213	89	47	385	346	.274	.337	.389	.726	101	48	2	106	106	744	355			
CHI	127	71	50	.587	6.5	813	716	4350	1177	178	98	80	407	400	.271	.336	.412	.748	100	74	-25	113	98	748	382			
NY	129	68	55	.553	10.5	816	723	4516	1259	167	93	48	361	326	.279	.339	.389	.728	113	49	86	95	98	753	415			
BOS	127	61	60	.504	16.5	831	792	4531	1255	185	94	53	340	392	.277	.333	.394	.727	107	44	43	100	101	736	373			
PIT	125	55	69	.444	24	621	750	4414	1141	183	78	20	319	381	.258	.314	.349	.663	96	-56	-10	94	88	567	221			
WAS	126	46	76	.377	32	601	818	4314	1039	149	63	47	269	339	.241	.292	.337	.629	84	-114	-76	95	97	535	334			
IND	127	37	89	.294	43	628	965	4368	1080	162	70	33	300	379	.247	.302	.339	.641	86	-92	-65	96	96	562	334			
TOT	508					6180		35812	9624	1450	711	383	2733	2821	.269	.321	.381	.702						2681				

TEAM	CG	SH	SV	IP	H	H/G	HR	BB	SO	RAT	ERA	ERA+	OAV	OOB	PR	/A	PF	CPI	FA	E	DP	FW	PW	BW	SBW	DIF
DET	122	3	1	1116¹	1172	9.4	52	344	337	12.5	3.95	102	.264	.322	12	-3	99	97	.925	394	92	3.3	-.3	10.2		3.8
PHI	119	7	1	1132²	1173	9.3	48	305	435	12.0	3.47	121	.259	.311	72	89	104	104	.912	471	76	-.4	7.5	.2		6.2
CHI	117	4	3	1126	1156	9.2	55	338	510	12.4	3.46	129	.257	.317	73	120	110	108	.914	472	99	-.6	10.2	-2.1		3.1
NY	123	5	1	1113²	1096	8.9	27	373	415	12.2	3.57	105	.250	.314	59	18	93	96	.920	431	83	1.8	1.5	7.3		-4.1
BOS	123	4	1	1100²	1226	10.0	55	396	254	13.6	4.41	91	.273	.338	-44	-46	100	99	.905	522	94	-3.1	-3.9	3.6		3.9
PIT	123	3	0	1108²	1287	10.4	39	246	248	12.7	4.12	94	.281	.322	-9	-32	95	99	.921	425	70	1.4	-2.7	-.8		-4.8
WAS	124	4	0	1090¹	1216	10.0	47	299	396	12.9	4.19	96	.272	.323	-18	-21	100	96	.909	483	77	-1.4	-1.8	-6.4		-5.4
IND	118	4	1	1088	1289	10.7	60	431	245	14.6	5.24	79	.284	.352	-145	-139	102	92	.912	479	105	-1.0	-11.8	-5.5		-7.7
TOT	969	34	8	8876¹		9.7				12.8	4.05		.269	.321					.915	3677	696					

Runs
Brouthers-Det 153
Rowe-Det 135
Richardson-Det ... 131
Kelly-Bos 120

Hits
Thompson-Det ... 203
Ward-NY 184
Richardson-Det... 178
Rowe-Det 171
Brouthers-Det ... 169

Doubles
Brouthers-Det 36
Kelly-Bos 34
Denny-Ind 34
Anson-Chi 33

Triples
Thompson-Det 23
Connor-NY 22
Johnston-Bos 20
Brouthers-Det 20
Wood-Phi 19

Home Runs
W.O'Brien-Was 19
Connor-NY 17
Pfeffer-Chi 16
Wood-Phi 14

Total Bases
Thompson-Det 311
Brouthers-Det ... 281
Richardson-Det ... 263
Denny-Ind 256
Connor-NY 255

Runs Batted In
Thompson-Det ... 166
Connor-NY 104
Anson-Chi 102
Brouthers-Det ... 101
Denny-Ind 97

Runs Produced
Thompson-Det ... 273
Brouthers-Det ... 242
Rowe-Det........ 225
Richardson-Det ... 217
Anson-Chi 202

Bases On Balls
Fogarty-Phi 82
Connor-NY 75
Williamson-Chi 73
Seery-Ind 71
Brouthers-Det 71

Batting Average
Thompson-Det 372
Anson-Chi 347
Brouthers-Det 338
Ward-NY..........338
Wise-Bos 334

On Base Percentage
Brouthers-Det 426
Anson-Chi 422
Thompson-Det ...416
Schomberg-Ind ...397
Kelly-Bos 393

Slugging Average
Thompson-Det 571
Brouthers-Det 562
Connor-NY.......541
Wise-Bos 522
Anson-Chi 517

Production
Brouthers-Det 988
Thompson-Det ...987
Anson-Chi 939
Connor-NY 933
Wise-Bos 913

Adjusted Production
Brouthers-Det 169
Thompson-Det 168
Connor-NY 166
Carroll-Pit....... 155
Wise-Bos 153

Batter Runs
Thompson-Det ... 52.5
Brouthers-Det ... 51.8
Anson-Chi 40.6
Connor-NY 38.4
Wise-Bos 32.9

Adjusted Batter Runs
Thompson-Det ... 49.5
Brouthers-Det ... 48.9
Connor-NY 42.6
Wise-Bos 32.8
Kelly-Bos 30.0

Clutch Hitting Index
O'Rourke-NY 167
Thompson-Det ... 143
Mulvey-Phi 140
McGeachey-Ind ... 132
Donnelly-Was 129

Runs Created
Thompson-Det ... 142
Brouthers-Det ... 138
Kelly-Bos 129
Ward-NY 125
Connor-NY 120

Total Average
Brouthers-Det ... 1.184
Kelly-Bos 1.146
Connor-NY 1.131
Thompson-Det ...1.094
Fogarty-Phi 1.085

Stolen Bases
Ward-NY 111
Fogarty-Phi 102
Kelly-Bos 84
Hanlon-Det....... 69
Glasscock-Ind 62

Stolen Base Average

Stolen Base Runs

Fielding Runs
Glasscock-Ind 35.0
Fogarty-Phi 31.7
Ward-NY 29.6
Johnston-Bos ... 25.3
Pfeffer-Chi 24.6

Total Player Rating
Thompson-Det 4.5
Denny-Ind 4.0
Ward-NY 3.9
Glasscock-Ind 3.6
Fogarty-Phi 3.4

Wins
Clarkson-Chi 38
Keefe-NY 35
Getzien-Det 29
Galvin-Pit 28
Casey-Phi 28

Win Percentage
Getzien-Det 690
Ferguson-Phi 688
Casey-Phi 683
Keefe-NY 648
Clarkson-Chi 644

Games
Clarkson-Chi 60
Keefe-NY 56
Radbourn-Bos..... 50
Galvin-Pit 49
Whitney-Was 47

Complete Games
Clarkson-Chi 56
Keefe-NY 54
Radbourn-Bos..... 48
Galvin-Pit 47
Whitney-Was 46

Shutouts
Casey-Phi 4
Whitney-Was 3
Madden-Bos 3
Healy-Ind 3

Saves
VanHaltren-Chi 1
Twitchell-Det 1
Tiernan-NY 1
Stemmeyer-Bos 1
Pettit-Chi 1
Ferguson-Phi 1
Fast-Ind 1
Baldwin-Chi 1

Innings Pitched
Clarkson-Chi 523.0
Keefe-NY 476.2
Galvin-Pit 440.2
Radbourn-Bos ... 425.0
Whitney-Was 404.2

Fewest Hits/Game
Keefe-NY 8.08
Conway-Det 8.14
Casey-Phi 8.69
Welch-NY 8.82
Clarkson-Chi 8.83

Fewest BB/Game
Whitney-Was 93
Galvin-Pit 1.37
Ferguson-Phi 1.42
Clarkson-Chi 1.58
Boyle-Ind 1.89

Strikeouts
Clarkson-Chi 237
Keefe-NY 189
Baldwin-Chi 164
Buffinton-Phi 160
Whitney-Was 146

Strikeouts/Game
Baldwin-Chi 4.42
Gilmore-Was 4.37
Buffinton-Phi 4.33
VanHaltren-Chi ... 4.25
Clarkson-Chi 4.08

Ratio
Keefe-NY 10.33
Clarkson-Chi 10.55
Ferguson-Phi 10.75
Whitney-Was 10.85
Welch-NY 11.32

Earned Run Average
Casey-Phi 2.86
Conway-Det 2.90
Ferguson-Phi 3.00
Clarkson-Chi 3.08
Keefe-NY 3.12

Adjusted ERA
Casey-Phi 147
Clarkson-Chi 145
Ferguson-Phi 140
Conway-Det 139
Baldwin-Chi 131

Opponents' Batting Avg.
Keefe-NY .... .230
Conway-Det ...... .235
Casey-Phi .... .246
Clarkson-Chi ..... .246
Baldwin-Chi ...... .248

Opponents' On Base Pct.
Keefe-NY .... .276
Clarkson-Chi ..... .281
Whitney-Was ..... .284
Ferguson-Phi ..... .289
Galvin-Pit .... .299

Starter Runs
Clarkson-Chi 56.1
Casey-Phi 51.5
Keefe-NY 49.3
Galvin-Pit 37.1
Whitney-Was 36.9

Adjusted Starter Runs
Clarkson-Chi 80.1
Casey-Phi 58.3
Ferguson-Phi 39.9
Baldwin-Chi 39.5
Whitney-Was 36.4

Clutch Pitching Index
VanHaltren-Chi ... 123
Casey-Phi 117
Baldwin-Chi 114
Ferguson-Phi 108
Madden-Bos 105

Relief Runs

Adjusted Relief Runs

Relief Ranking

Total Pitcher Index
Clarkson-Chi 8.3
Ferguson-Phi 4.9
Whitney-Was 4.6
Casey-Phi 4.0
Keefe-NY 3.8

Total Baseball Ranking
Clarkson-Chi 8.1
Ferguson-Phi 5.0
Thompson-Det 4.5
Whitney-Was 4.4
Denny-Ind 4.0

TEAM	G	W	L	PCT	GB	R	OR	AB	H	2B	3B	HR	BB	SO	AVG	OBP	SLG	PRO	PRO+	BR	/A	PF	CHI	RC	SB	CS	SBA	SBR
STL	138	95	40	.704		1131	761	5048	1550	261	78	39	442	340	.307	.371	.413	.784	113	168	68	111	102	1012	581			
CIN	136	81	54	.600	14	892	745	4797	1285	179	102	37	382	366	.268	.329	.371	.700	99	5	-15	102	100	778	527			
BAL	141	77	58	.570	18	975	861	4825	1337	202	100	31	469	334	.277	.349	.380	.729	116	67	120	94	100	852	545			
LOU	139	76	60	.559	19.5	956	854	4916	1420	194	98	27	436	356	.289	.352	.385	.737	110	77	59	102	96	850	466			
PHI	137	64	69	.481	30	893	890	4954	1370	231	84	29	321	388	.277	.327	.375	.702	101	4	3	100	98	782	476			
BRO	138	60	74	.448	34.5	904	918	4913	1281	200	82	25	456	365	.261	.330	.350	.680	94	-23	-34	101	101	720	409			
NY	138	44	89	.331	50	754	1093	4820	1197	193	66	21	439	463	.248	.318	.329	.647	90	-81	-41	96	92	615	305			
CLE	133	39	92	.298	54	729	1112	4649	1170	178	77	14	375	463	.252	.314	.332	.646	89	-83	-58	97	94	611	355			
TOT	550					7234		38922	10610	1638	687	223	3320	3075	.273	.330	.367	.697							3664			

TEAM	CG	SH	SV	IP	H	H/G	HR	BB	SO	RAT	ERA	ERA+	OAV	OOB	PR	/A	PF	CPI	FA	E	DP	FW	PW	BW	SBW	DIF
STL	132	7	2	1199¹	1254	9.4	19	323	334	12.2	3.77	120	.258	.311	69	100	106	94	.916	481	86	3.6	8.1	5.5		10.3
CIN	129	11	1	1182²	1202	9.1	28	396	330	12.6	3.58	121	.257	.322	93	99	101	107	.916	484	106	3.0	8.0	-1.2		3.7
BAL	132	8	0	1220	1288	9.5	16	418	470	13.0	3.87	106	.262	.326	58	30	95	100	.907	549	66	.8	2.4	9.7		-3.4
LOU	133	3	1	1205²	1274	9.5	31	357	544	12.5	3.82	115	.260	.316	63	75	102	98	.903	574	83	-.9	6.1	4.8		-2.0
PHI	131	5	1	1186¹	1227	9.3	29	433	417	13.1	4.59	93	.260	.331	-39	-41	100	88	.907	528	95	1.0	-3.3	.2		-.4
BRO	132	3	3	1185¹	1348	10.2	27	454	332	14.0	4.47	96	.281	.348	-24	-24	100	103	.905	562	88	-.5	-1.9	-2.8		-1.8
NY	132	1	0	1180¹	1545	11.8	39	406	316	15.3	5.28	80	.308	.365	-130	-138	99	102	.894	632	102	-4.0	-11.2	-3.3		-4.0
CLE	127	2	1	1136	1472	11.7	34	533	332	16.4	4.99	87	.308	.384	-88	-84	101	115	.898	576	97	-2.2	-6.8	-4.7		-12.8
TOT	1048	40	9	9495²		10.1				13.6	4.29		.273	.330					.906	4386	723					

Runs
O'Neill-StL 167
Latham-StL 163
Griffin-Bal 142
Poorman-Phi 140
Comiskey-StL 139

Hits
O'Neill-StL 225
Browning-Lou 220
Lyons-Phi 209
Latham-StL 198
Burns-Bal 188

Doubles
O'Neill-StL 52
Lyons-Phi 43
Reilly-Cin 35
Latham-StL 35
Browning-Lou 35

Triples
Poorman-Phi 19
O'Neill-StL 19
McPhee-Cin 19
Kerins-Lou 19
Davis-Bal 19
Burns-Bal 19

Home Runs
O'Neill-StL 14
Reilly-Cin 10
Burns-Bal 9

Total Bases
O'Neill-StL 357
Browning-Lou 299
Lyons-Phi 298
Burns-Bal 286
Reilly-Cin 263

Runs Batted In / Runs Produced
Latham-StL 161
O'Neill-StL 153
Griffin-Bal 139
Poorman-Phi 136

Bases On Balls
Radford-NY 106
Robinson-StL 92
Nicol-Cin 86
Mack-Lou 83
Fennelly-Cin 82

Batting Average
O'Neill-StL 435
Browning-Lou 402
Lyons-Phi 367
Caruthers-StL 357
Foutz-StL 357

On Base Percentage
O'Neill-StL 490
Browning-Lou 464
Caruthers-StL 463
Robinson-StL 445
Lyons-Phi 421

Slugging Average
O'Neill-StL 691
Caruthers-StL 547
Browning-Lou 547
Lyons-Phi 523
Burns-Bal 519

Production
O'Neill-StL ...1.180
Browning-Lou ...1.011
Caruthers-StL ...1.010
Lyons-Phi 943
Burns-Bal 933

Adjusted Production
O'Neill-StL 208
Browning-Lou 180
Burns-Bal 172
Caruthers-StL 166
Lyons-Phi 165

Batter Runs
O'Neill-StL 87.9
Browning-Lou 62.5
Lyons-Phi 48.5
Burns-Bal 45.5
Caruthers-StL 44.0

Adjusted Batter Runs
O'Neill-StL 77.6
Browning-Lou 60.4
Burns-Bal 51.6
Lyons-Phi 48.4
Caruthers-StL 36.2

Clutch Hitting Index

Runs Created
O'Neill-StL 194
Browning-Lou 191
Lyons-Phi 160
Burns-Bal 146
Latham-StL 146

Total Average
O'Neill-StL ...1.514
Browning-Lou ...1.422
Caruthers-StL ...1.368
Robinson-StL ...1.197
Lyons-Phi 1.175

Stolen Bases
Nicol-Cin 138
Latham-StL 129
Comiskey-StL 117
Browning-Lou 103
McPhee-Cin 95

Stolen Base Average

Stolen Base Runs

Fielding Runs
Smith-Bro 32.0
McPhee-Cin 26.2
Kerins-Lou 24.8
White-Lou 21.5
Welch-StL 19.4

Total Player Rating
O'Neill-StL 5.5
Browning-Lou 4.4
Lyons-Phi 3.6
McPhee-Cin 3.2
Smith-Bro 2.9

Wins
Kilroy-Bal 46
Ramsey-Lou 37
Smith-Cin 34
King-StL 32
Mullane-Cin 31

Win Percentage
Caruthers-StL 763
King-StL 727
Kilroy-Bal 708
Foutz-StL 676
Smith-Cin 667

Games
Kilroy-Bal 69
Ramsey-Lou 65
Smith-Bal 58
Weyhing-Phi 55
Seward-Phi 55

Complete Games
Kilroy-Bal 66
Ramsey-Lou 61
Smith-Bal 54
Weyhing-Phi 53
Seward-Phi 52

Shutouts
Mullane-Cin 6
Kilroy-Bal 6
Smith-Cin 3
Seward-Phi 3

Saves
Terry-Bro 3

Innings Pitched
Kilroy-Bal 589.1
Ramsey-Lou 561.0
Smith-Bal 491.1
Seward-Phi 470.2
Weyhing-Phi 466.1

Fewest Hits/Game
Smith-Cin 8.05
Seward-Phi 8.51
Toole-Bro 8.63
Ramsey-Lou 8.73
Caruthers-StL 8.89

Fewest BB/Game
Hecker-Lou 1.58
Caruthers-StL 1.61
Lynch-NY 1.73
Foutz-StL 2.39
Kilroy-Bal 2.40

Strikeouts
Ramsey-Lou 355
Kilroy-Bal 217
Smith-Bal 206
Weyhing-Phi 193
Smith-Cin 176

Strikeouts/Game
Ramsey-Lou 5.70
Morrison-Cle 4.49
Terry-Bro 3.91
Smith-Bal 3.77
Weyhing-Phi 3.72

Ratio
Smith-Cin 10.76
Caruthers-StL 10.93
Kilroy-Bal 11.64
Seward-Phi 11.65
Ramsey-Lou 11.66

Earned Run Average
Smith-Cin 2.94
Kilroy-Bal 3.07
Mullane-Cin 3.24
Caruthers-StL ... 3.30
Ramsey-Lou 3.43

Adjusted ERA
Smith-Cin 148
Caruthers-StL 137
Mullane-Cin 134
Kilroy-Bal 133
Ramsey-Lou 128

Opponents' Batting Avg.
Smith-Cin 230
Ramsey-Lou 242
Seward-Phi 244
Caruthers-StL 247
Kilroy-Bal 253

Opponents' On Base Pct.
Smith-Cin 286
Caruthers-StL 287
Ramsey-Lou 299
Kilroy-Bal 306
Foutz-StL 306

Starter Runs
Kilroy-Bal 80.0
Smith-Cin 67.3
Ramsey-Lou 53.5
Mullane-Cin 48.5
Caruthers-StL 37.6

Adjusted Starter Runs
Smith-Cin 69.6
Kilroy-Bal 67.0
Ramsey-Lou 59.3
Mullane-Cin 50.7
Caruthers-StL 46.7

Clutch Pitching Index
Daily-Cle......... 140
Crowell-Cle 122
Morrison-Cle 121
Mullane-Cin 119
Chamberlain-Lou . 117

Relief Runs

Adjusted Relief Runs

Relief Ranking

Total Pitcher Index
Kilroy-Bal 7.3
Caruthers-StL 6.4
Smith-Cin 5.9
Mullane-Cin 4.4
Ramsey-Lou 3.4

Total Baseball Ranking
Caruthers-StL 8.2
Kilroy-Bal 7.2
Smith-Cin 5.8
O'Neill-StL 5.5
Browning-Lou 4.4

TEAM	G	W	L	PCT	GB	R	OR	AB	H	2B	3B	HR	BB	SO	AVG	OBP	SLG	PRO	PRO+	BR	/A	PF	CHI	RC	SB	CS	SBA	SBR
NY	138	84	47	.641		659	479	4747	1149	130	76	55	270	456	.242	.287	.336	.623	107	33	40	99	100	562	314			
CHI	136	77	58	.570	9	734	659	4616	1201	147	95	77	290	563	.260	.308	.383	.691	119	139	95	107	98	649	287			
PHI	132	69	61	.531	14.5	535	509	4528	1021	151	46	16	268	485	.225	.276	.290	.566	84	-50	-81	105	97	441	246			
BOS	137	70	64	.522	15.5	669	619	4834	1183	167	89	56	282	524	.245	.291	.351	.642	110	63	52	102	96	593	293			
DET	134	68	63	.519	16	721	629	4849	1275	177	72	51	307	396	.263	.313	.361	.674	123	122	123	100	94	623	193			
PIT	139	66	68	.493	19.5	534	580	4713	1070	150	49	14	194	583	.227	.264	.289	.553	91	-80	-33	92	100	446	287			
IND	136	50	85	.370	36	603	731	4623	1100	180	33	34	236	492	.238	.281	.313	.594	95	-11	-23	102	101	518	350			
WAS	136	48	86	.358	37.5	482	731	4546	944	98	49	30	246	499	.208	.255	.271	.526	79	-117	-83	94	100	408	331			
TOT	544					4937		37456	8943	1200	509	333	2093	3998	.239	.279	.325	.604							2301			

TEAM	CG	SH	SV	IP	H	H/G	HR	BB	SO	RAT	ERA	ERA+	OAV	OOB	PR	/A	PF	CPI	FA	E	DP	FW	PW	BW	SBW	DIF
NY	133	20	1	1208	907	6.8	27	307	726	9.3	1.96	139	.199	.255	117	103	96	95	.924	432	76	1.2	10.1	3.9		3.2
CHI	123	13	1	1186¹	1139	8.6	63	308	588	11.4	2.96	102	.246	.301	-17	6	106	112	.927	417	112	1.7	.6	9.3		-2.1
PHI	125	16	3	1167	1072	8.3	26	196	519	10.0	2.38	124	.236	.271	58	69	104	103	.923	424	70	.6	6.8	-8.0		4.6
BOS	134	7	0	1225¹	1104	8.1	36	269	484	10.4	2.61	109	.232	.280	30	27	100	100	.917	494	91	-2.2	2.7	5.1		-2.5
DET	130	10	1	1199	1115	8.4	44	183	522	10.0	2.74	100	.234	.266	12	-2	97	90	.919	463	83	-1.1	-.2	12.1		-8.3
PIT	135	13	0	1203¹	1190	8.9	23	223	367	10.8	2.67	99	.249	.287	22	-4	94	107	.927	416	88	2.3	-.4	-3.2		.4
IND	132	6	0	1187²	1260	9.5	64	308	388	12.2	3.81	77	.263	.313	-129	-117	104	98	.921	449	84	-.0	-11.5	-2.3		-3.7
WAS	133	6	0	1179¹	1157	8.8	50	298	406	11.5	3.54	79	.248	.300	-93	-104	98	91	.912	494	69	-2.4	-10.2	-8.2		1.8
TOT	1045	91	6	9556		8.4				10.7	2.83		.239	.279					.921	3589	673					

Runs
Brouthers-Det 118
Ryan-Chi 115
Johnston-Bos 102
Anson-Chi 101
Connor-NY 98

Hits
Ryan-Chi 182
Anson-Chi 177
Johnston-Bos 173
Brouthers-Det 160
White-Det 157

Doubles
Ryan-Chi 33
Brouthers-Det 33
Johnston-Bos 31
Denny-Ind 27
Hines-Ind 26

Triples
Johnston-Bos 18
Connor-NY 17
Nash-Bos 15
Ewing-NY 15

Home Runs
Ryan-Chi 16
Connor-NY 14
Johnston-Bos 12
Denny-Ind 12
Anson-Chi 12

Total Bases
Ryan-Chi 283
Johnston-Bos 276
Anson-Chi 257
Brouthers-Det 242
Connor-NY 231

Runs Batted In
Anson-Chi 84
Nash-Bos 75
Rowe-Det 74
Williamson-Chi 73

Runs Produced
Brouthers-Det 175
Anson-Chi 173
Ryan-Chi 163
Johnston-Bos 158
Connor-NY 155

Bases On Balls
Connor-NY 73
Hoy-Was 69
Brouthers-Det 68
Williamson-Chi 65
Seery-Ind 64

Batting Average
Anson-Chi .... .344
Ryan-Chi .... .332
Kelly-Bos .... .318
Brouthers-Det .... .307
Ewing-NY .... .306

On Base Percentage
Anson-Chi .... .400
Brouthers-Det .... .399
Connor-NY .... .389
Ryan-Chi .... .377
Hoy-Was .... .374

Slugging Average
Ryan-Chi .... .515
Anson-Chi .... .499
Connor-NY .... .480
Kelly-Bos .... .480
Johnston-Bos .... .472

Production
Anson-Chi .... .899
Ryan-Chi .... .892
Connor-NY .... .869
Brouthers-Det .... .862
Kelly-Bos .... .848

Adjusted Production
Connor-NY 181
Brouthers-Det 177
Anson-Chi 175
Ryan-Chi 172
Kelly-Bos 168

Batter Runs
Ryan-Chi 50.7
Anson-Chi 50.5
Brouthers-Det 48.0
Connor-NY 44.9
Kelly-Bos 34.5

Adjusted Batter Runs
Brouthers-Det 48.0
Connor-NY 45.7
Anson-Chi 45.5
Ryan-Chi 45.5
Kelly-Bos 33.5

Clutch Hitting Index
Burns-Chi 162
Rowe-Det 147
Bassett-Ind 147
Williamson-Chi ... 139
Smith-Pit 138

Runs Created
Ryan-Chi 133
Anson-Chi 117
Brouthers-Det 113
Connor-NY 103
Kelly-Bos 101

Total Average
Ryan-Chi 1.044
Kelly-Bos 1.007
Anson-Chi .... .985
Brouthers-Det .... .983
Connor-NY .... .982

Stolen Bases
Hoy-Was 82
Seery-Ind 80
Sunday-Pit 71
Pfeffer-Chi 64
Ryan-Chi 60

Stolen Base Average

Stolen Base Runs

Fielding Runs
Pfeffer-Chi 38.3
Nash-Bos 25.6
Denny-Ind 24.5
Burns-Chi 17.1
Sunday-Pit 16.6

Total Player Rating
Nash-Bos 5.0
Pfeffer-Chi 4.6
Ryan-Chi 4.3
Anson-Chi 4.2
Ewing-NY 3.9

Wins
Keefe-NY 35
Clarkson-Bos 33
Conway-Det 30
Morris-Pit 29
Buffinton-Phi 28

Win Percentage
Keefe-NY .... .745
Conway-Det .... .682
Sanders-Phi ...... .655
Krock-Chi .... .641
Clarkson-Bos ..... .623

Games
Morris-Pit 55
Clarkson-Bos 54
Keefe-NY 51
Galvin-Pit 50
Welch-NY 47

Complete Games
Morris-Pit 54
Clarkson-Bos 53
Galvin-Pit 49
Keefe-NY 48
Welch-NY 47

Shutouts
Sanders-Phi 8
Keefe-NY 8
Galvin-Pit 6
Buffinton-Phi 6

Saves
Wood-Phi 2
VanHaltren-Chi ... 1
Tyng-Phi 1
Twitchell-Det 1
Crane-NY 1

Innings Pitched
Clarkson-Bos 483.1
Morris-Pit 480.0
Galvin-Pit 437.1
Keefe-NY 434.1
Welch-NY 425.1

Fewest Hits/Game
Keefe-NY 6.57
Titcomb-NY 6.81
Welch-NY 6.94
Conway-Det 7.25
Buffinton-Phi 7.28

Fewest BB/Game
Sanders-Phi 1.08
Galvin-Pit 1.09
Krock-Chi 1.19
Getzien-Det 1.20
Madden-Bos 1.31

Strikeouts
Keefe-NY 335
Clarkson-Bos 223
Getzien-Det 202
Buffinton-Phi 199
O'Day-Was 186

Strikeouts/Game
Keefe-NY 6.94
Titcomb-NY 5.89
Baldwin-Chi 5.63
VanHaltren-Chi ... 5.09
Getzien-Det 4.50

Ratio
Keefe-NY 8.68
Buffinton-Phi 8.70
Conway-Det 8.86
Sanders-Phi 9.02
Gruber-Det 9.04

Earned Run Average
Keefe-NY 1.74
Sanders-Phi 1.90
Buffinton-Phi 1.91
Welch-NY 1.93
Sowders-Bos 2.07

Adjusted ERA
Keefe-NY 156
Sanders-Phi 156
Buffinton-Phi 154
Welch-NY 141
Sowders-Bos 137

Opponents' Batting Avg.
Keefe-NY .... .196
Titcomb-NY .... .201
Welch-NY .... .207
Conway-Det .... .208
Buffinton-Phi .... .213

Opponents' On Base Pct.
Conway-Det .... .243
Keefe-NY .... .243
Buffinton-Phi .... .244
Gruber-Det .... .249
Titcomb-NY .... .253

Starter Runs
Keefe-NY 52.6
Welch-NY 42.8
Buffinton-Phi 40.9
Sanders-Phi 28.6
Morris-Pit 28.0

Adjusted Starter Runs
Keefe-NY 47.3
Buffinton-Phi 46.2
Welch-NY 37.6
Sanders-Phi 32.2
Sowders-Bos 26.7

Clutch Pitching Index
Baldwin-Chi 137
Gleason-Phi 125
Burdick-Ind 116
Sowders-Bos 113
Morris-Pit 112

Relief Runs

Adjusted Relief Runs

Relief Ranking

Total Pitcher Index
Buffinton-Phi 5.8
Sanders-Phi 4.4
Keefe-NY 4.4
Conway-Det 3.9
Welch-NY 3.5

Total Baseball Ranking
Buffinton-Phi 5.7
Nash-Bos 5.0
Pfeffer-Chi 4.6
Ryan-Chi 4.5
Keefe-NY 4.3

TEAM	G	W	L	PCT	GB	R	OR	AB	H	2B	3B	HR	BB	SO	AVG	OBP	SLG	PRO	PRO+	BR	/A	PF	CHI	RC	SB	CS	SBA	SBR
STL	137	92	43	.681		789	501	4755	1189	149	47	36	410	521	.250	.316	.324	.640	102	74	-5	111	99	651	468			
BRO	143	88	52	.629	6.5	758	584	4871	1177	172	70	25	353	439	.242	.300	.321	.621	106	37	39	100	99	584	334			
PHI	136	81	52	.609	10	827	594	4828	1209	183	89	31	303	473	.250	.305	.344	.649	116	79	84	99	103	656	434			
CIN	137	80	54	.597	11.5	745	628	4801	1161	132	82	32	345	555	.242	.301	.323	.624	102	41	3	105	98	623	469			
BAL	137	57	80	.416	36	653	779	4656	1068	162	70	19	298	479	.229	.284	.306	.590	99	-17	2	97	97	511	326			
CLE	135	50	82	.379	40.5	651	839	4603	1076	128	59	12	315	559	.234	.294	.295	.589	99	-13	7	97	96	516	353			
LOU	139	48	87	.356	44	689	870	4881	1177	183	67	14	322	604	.241	.297	.315	.612	105	21	36	98	92	565	318			
KC	132	43	89	.326	47.5	579	896	4588	1000	142	61	19	288	604	.218	.273	.288	.561	81	-65	-108	106	94	441	257			
TOT	548					5691		37983	9057	1251	545	188	2634	4234	.238	.288	.315	.603						2959				

TEAM	CG	SH	SV	IP	H	H/G	HR	BB	SO	RAT	ERA	ERA+	OAV	OOB	PR	/A	PF	CPI	FA	E	DP	FW	PW	BW	SBW	DIF
STL	132	12	0	1212²	939	7.0	19	225	517	9.1	2.09	156	.206	.254	130	156	107	96	.924	430	73	3.4	14.4	-.5		7.1
BRO	138	9	0	1286¹	1059	7.4	15	285	577	9.7	2.33	128	.217	.266	104	92	97	97	.918	502	88	.6	8.5	3.6		5.3
PHI	133	13	0	1208²	988	7.4	14	324	596	10.4	2.41	124	.216	.279	87	76	98	102	.919	475	73	.7	7.0	7.8		-1.0
CIN	132	10	2	1237²	1103	8.0	19	310	539	10.8	2.73	116	.230	.288	46	60	104	102	.923	456	100	2.0	5.5	.3		5.2
BAL	130	3	0	1200¹	1162	8.7	23	419	525	12.5	3.78	79	.245	.318	-96	-108	97	93	.920	461	88	1.7	-10.0	.2		-3.4
CLE	131	6	1	1171	1235	9.5	38	389	500	12.9	3.72	83	.261	.324	-86	-82	101	105	.915	488	87	-.2	-7.6	.6		-8.8
LOU	133	6	0	1231¹	1264	9.2	28	281	599	11.7	3.25	95	.256	.304	-26	-24	100	105	.900	609	75	-6.2	-2.2	3.3		-14.4
KC	128	4	0	1157²	1306	10.2	32	401	381	13.8	4.29	80	.275	.340	-159	-112	112	101	.914	507	95	-1.9	-10.3	-10.0		-.8
TOT	1057	63	3	9705²		8.4				11.3	3.06		.238	.288					.917	3928	679					

Runs		Hits		Doubles		Triples		Home Runs		Total Bases	
Pinkney-Bro	134	O'Neill-StL	177	Collins-Lou-Bro	31	Stovey-Phi	20	Reilly-Cin	13	Reilly-Cin	264
Collins-Lou-Bro	133	Reilly-Cin	169	Wolf-Lou	28	Burns-Bal-Bro	15	Stovey-Phi	9	Stovey-Phi	244
Stovey-Phi	127	McKean-Cle	164	Reilly-Cin	28	McKean-Cle	15	Larkin-Phi	7	O'Neill-StL	236
Welch-Phi	125	Collins-Lou-Bro	162	Larkin-Phi	28	Reilly-Cin	14			McKean-Cle	233
Latham-StL	119	Corkhill-Cin-Bro	160			Foutz-Bro	13			Burns-Bal-Bro	230

Runs Batted In		Runs Produced		Bases On Balls		Batting Average		On Base Percentage		Slugging Average	
Reilly-Cin	103	Reilly-Cin	202	Robinson-StL	116	O'Neill-StL	.335	Robinson-StL	.400	Reilly-Cin	.501
Larkin-Phi	101	O'Neill-StL	189	Fennelly-Cin-Phi	72	Reilly-Cin	.321	O'Neill-StL	.390	Stovey-Phi	.460
Foutz-Bro	99	Foutz-Bro	187	Nicol-Cin	67	Browning-Lou	.313	Browning-Lou	.380	O'Neill-StL	.446
O'Neill-StL	98	Larkin-Phi	186	McTamany-KC	67	Collins-Lou-Bro	.307	Collins-Lou-Bro	.373	Browning-Lou	.436
Corkhill-Cin-Bro	93	Welch-Phi	185	Pinkney-Bro	66	McKean-Cle	.299	Stovey-Phi	.365	Burns-Bal-Bro	.435

Production		Adjusted Production		Batter Runs		Adjusted Batter Runs		Clutch Hitting Index		Runs Created	
Reilly-Cin	.864	Reilly-Cin	170	Reilly-Cin	43.8	Stovey-Phi	40.5	Gleason-Phi	154	Reilly-Cin	129
O'Neill-StL	.836	Stovey-Phi	169	O'Neill-StL	41.7	Reilly-Cin	39.7	Smith-Bro	151	Stovey-Phi	124
Stovey-Phi	.825	Browning-Lou	168	Stovey-Phi	39.9	Collins-Lou-Bro	36.2	Fennelly-Cin-Phi	149	Collins-Lou-Bro	112
Browning-Lou	.816	Collins-Lou-Bro	162	Collins-Lou-Bro	34.7	O'Neill-StL	33.0	Gilks-Cle	144	Welch-Phi	106
Collins-Lou-Bro	.796	Burns-Bal-Bro	155	Burns-Bal-Bro	29.8	Burns-Bal-Bro	31.1	Lyons-StL	142	O'Neill-StL	105

Total Average		Stolen Bases		Stolen Base Average	Stolen Base Runs	Fielding Runs		Total Player Rating	
Reilly-Cin	1.064	Latham-StL	109			Shindle-Bal	36.8	Collins-Lou-Bro	4.1
Stovey-Phi	1.048	Nicol-Cin	103			McPhee-Cin	31.3	Stovey-Phi	3.6
Collins-Lou-Bro	.956	Welch-Phi	95			Davis-KC	29.8	McPhee-Cin	3.5
Robinson-StL	.934	McCarthy-StL	93			McCarthy-StL	29.8	Davis-KC	3.2
Browning-Lou	.928	Stovey-Phi	87			Easterday-KC	26.4	McKean-Cle	3.1

Wins		Win Percentage		Games		Complete Games		Shutouts		Saves	
King-StL	45	Hudson-StL	.714	King-StL	66	King-StL	64	Seward-Phi	6	Mullane-Cin	1
Seward-Phi	35	Chamberlain-Lou-StL	.694	Bakely-Cle	61	Bakely-Cle	60	King-StL	6	Gilks-Cle	1
Caruthers-Bro	29	King-StL	.682	Seward-Phi	57	Seward-Phi	57	Smith-Cin	5		
Weyhing-Phi	28	Caruthers-Bro	.659	Porter-KC	55	Porter-KC	53	Hudson-StL	5		
Viau-Cin	27	Viau-Cin	.659	Cunningham-Bal	51	Cunningham-Bal	50				

Innings Pitched		Fewest Hits/Game		Fewest BB/Game		Strikeouts		Strikeouts/Game		Ratio	
King-StL	585.2	Terry-Bro	6.69	King-StL	1.17	Seward-Phi	272	Terry-Bro	6.37	King-StL	8.34
Bakely-Cle	532.2	King-StL	6.72	Caruthers-Bro	1.22	King-StL	258	Ramsey-Lou	5.99	Caruthers-Bro	9.19
Seward-Phi	518.2	Seward-Phi	6.73	Hudson-StL	1.59	Ramsey-Lou	228	Chamberlain-Lou-StL	5.14	Seward-Phi	9.32
Porter-KC	474.0	Chamberlain-Lou-StL	6.95	Ewing-Lou	1.60	Bakely-Cle	212	Smith-Bal-Phi	4.90	Foutz-Bro	9.51
Cunningham-Bal	453.1	Hughes-Bro	6.97	Hecker-Lou	1.73	Weyhing-Phi	204	Seward-Phi	4.72	Hughes-Bro	9.55

Earned Run Average		Adjusted ERA		Opponents' Batting Avg.		Opponents' On Base Pct.		Starter Runs		Adjusted Starter Runs	
King-StL	1.64	King-StL	198	Terry-Bro	.200	King-StL	.237	King-StL	92.0	King-StL	104.9
Seward-Phi	2.01	Seward-Phi	148	King-StL	.200	Caruthers-Bro	.255	Seward-Phi	60.2	Seward-Phi	56.0
Terry-Bro	2.03	Terry-Bro	147	Seward-Phi	.201	Seward-Phi	.258	Hughes-Bro	37.3	Hughes-Bro	34.1
Hughes-Bro	2.13	Chamberlain-Lou-StL	143	Chamberlain-Lou-StL	.206	Foutz-Bro	.262	Weyhing-Phi	36.3	Weyhing-Phi	33.0
Chamberlain-Lou-StL	2.19	Hughes-Bro	140	Hughes-Bro	.206	Hughes-Bro	.262	Chamberlain-Lou-StL	29.7	Chamberlain-Lou-StL	32.4

Clutch Pitching Index		Relief Runs	Adjusted Relief Runs	Relief Ranking	Total Pitcher Index		Total Baseball Ranking	
Sullivan-KC	115				King-StL	11.4	King-StL	11.4
Hecker-Lou	112				Seward-Phi	5.3	Seward-Phi	5.3
Terry-Bro	110				Weyhing-Phi	3.7	Collins-Lou-Bro	4.1
Ramsey-Lou	106				Caruthers-Bro	3.5	Caruthers-Bro	3.7
Bakely-Cle	106				Chamberlain-Lou-StL	2.9	Stovey-hi	3.6

TEAM	G	W	L	PCT	GB	R	OR	AB	H	2B	3B	HR	BB	SO	AVG	OBP	SLG	PRO	PRO+	BR	/A	PF	CHI	RC	SB	CS	SBA	SBR
NY	131	83	43	.659		935	708	4671	1319	208	77	52	538	386	.282	.360	.393	.753	119	120	118	100	103	785	292			
BOS	133	83	45	.648	1	826	626	4628	1251	196	54	42	471	450	.270	.343	.363	.706	99	38	-8	106	102	707	331			
CHI	136	67	65	.508	19	867	814	4849	1274	184	66	79	518	516	.263	.338	.377	.715	103	48	8	105	101	716	243			
PHI	130	63	64	.496	20.5	742	748	4695	1248	215	52	44	393	353	.266	.327	.362	.689	92	-1	-68	109	97	660	269			
PIT	134	61	71	.462	25	726	801	4748	1202	209	65	42	420	467	.253	.320	.351	.671	105	-32	43	90	97	622	231			
CLE	136	61	72	.459	25.5	656	720	4673	1167	131	59	25	429	417	.250	.318	.319	.637	87	-81	-66	98	95	563	237			
IND	135	59	75	.440	28	819	894	4879	1356	228	35	62	377	447	.278	.335	.377	.712	105	39	24	102	98	719	252			
WAS	127	41	83	.331	41	632	892	4395	1105	151	57	25	466	456	.251	.329	.329	.658	98	-38	7	94	91	566	232			
TOT	531					6203		37538	9922	1522	465	371	3612	3492	.264	.329	.359	.688						2087				

TEAM	CG	SH	SV	IP	H	H/G	HR	BB	SO	RAT	ERA	ERA+	OAV	OOB	PR	/A	PF	CPI	FA	E	DP	FW	PW	BW	SBW	DIF
NY	118	6	3	1151	1073	8.4	38	523	558	12.9	3.47	114	.241	.327	71	56	98	102	.919	437	90	-.3	4.9	10.2		5.3
BOS	121	10	4	1166	1152	8.9	41	413	497	12.4	3.36	124	.250	.317	86	106	104	105	.926	413	105	1.2	9.2	-.7		9.3
CHI	123	6	2	1237	1313	9.6	71	408	434	12.8	3.73	112	.262	.323	41	64	104	106	.923	463	91	-.8	5.5	.7		-4.4
PHI	106	4	2	1153¹	1288	10.1	33	428	443	13.6	4.00	109	.275	.339	3	42	108	103	.915	466	92	-2.0	3.6	-5.9		3.7
PIT	125	5	1	1130²	1296	10.3	42	374	345	13.5	4.51	83	.272	.329	-60	-78	93	92	.931	385	94	2.8	-6.8	3.7		-4.8
CLE	132	6	1	1191¹	1182	8.9	36	519	435	13.2	3.66	110	.251	.332	48	47	100	102	.936	365	108	4.2	4.1	-5.7		-8.0
IND	109	3	2	1174¹	1365	10.5	73	420	408	14.0	4.85	86	.282	.344	-108	-88	104	95	.926	420	102	1.2	-7.6	2.1		-3.6
WAS	113	1	0	1103	1261	10.3	37	527	388	14.9	4.68	85	.279	.359	-80	-90	98	99	.904	519	91	-5.2	-7.8	.6		-8.6
TOT	947	41	15	9307		9.6				13.4	4.02		.264	.329					.923	3468	773					

Runs		Hits		Doubles		Triples		Home Runs		Total Bases	
Tiernan-NY	147	Glasscock-Ind	205	Kelly-Bos	41	Wilmot-Was	19	Thompson-Phi	20	Ryan-Chi	287
Duffy-Chi	144	Brouthers-Bos	181	Glasscock-Ind	40	Fogarty-Phi	17	Denny-Ind	18	Glasscock-Ind	272
Ryan-Chi	140	Ryan-Chi	177	Thompson-Phi	36	Connor-NY	17	Ryan-Chi	17	Thompson-Phi	262
Gore-NY	132	Duffy-Chi	172	O'Rourke-NY	36	Tiernan-NY	14	Connor-NY	13	Connor-NY	262
Glasscock-Ind	128	VanHaltren-Chi	168	Richardson-Bos	33	Ryan-Chi	14	Duffy-Chi	12	Tiernan-NY	248

Runs Batted In		Runs Produced		Bases On Balls		Batting Average		On Base Percentage		Slugging Average	
Connor-NY	130	Connor-NY	234	Tiernan-NY	96	Brouthers-Bos	.373	Carroll-Pit	.486	Connor-NY	.528
Brouthers-Bos	118	Duffy-Chi	221	Connor-NY	93	Glasscock-Ind	.352	Brouthers-Bos	.462	Brouthers-Bos	.507
Anson-Chi	117	Brouthers-Bos	216	Radford-Cle	91	Tiernan-NY	.335	Tiernan-NY	.447	Ryan-Chi	.498
Denny-Ind	112	Tiernan-NY	210	Anson-Chi	86	Carroll-Pit	.330	Connor-NY	.426	Tiernan-NY	.497
Thompson-Phi	111	Anson-Chi	210	Carroll-Pit	85	Ewing-NY	.327	Gore-NY	.416	Thompson-Phi	.492

Production		Adjusted Production		Batter Runs		Adjusted Batter Runs		Clutch Hitting Index		Runs Created	
Carroll-Pit	.970	Carroll-Pit	192	Brouthers-Bos	50.7	Tiernan-NY	48.1	Quinn-NY	144	Ryan-Chi	132
Brouthers-Bos	.969	Connor-NY	168	Tiernan-NY	48.3	Connor-NY	47.1	Dunlap-Pit	144	Glasscock-Ind	132
Connor-NY	.955	Tiernan-NY	165	Connor-NY	47.3	Brouthers-Bos	45.6	Richardson-NY	144	Tiernan-NY	129
Tiernan-NY	.944	Brouthers-Bos	163	Carroll-Pit	38.7	Carroll-Pit	44.6	Whitney-NY	144	Brouthers-Bos	127
Ryan-Chi	.886	Wilmot-Was	147	Ryan-Chi	36.7	Ryan-Chi	31.8	Nash-Bos	138	Connor-NY	124

Total Average		Stolen Bases		Stolen Base Average	Stolen Base Runs	Fielding Runs		Total Player Rating	
Carroll-Pit	1.263	Fogarty-Phi	99			Glasscock-Ind	35.7	Glasscock-Ind	6.0
Tiernan-NY	1.151	Kelly-Bos	68			Pfeffer-Chi	19.5	Ewing-NY	4.0
Brouthers-Bos	1.145	Brown-Bos	63			Fogarty-Phi	19.4	Tiernan-NY	3.6
Connor-NY	1.115	Ward-NY	62			Ewing-NY	17.3	Brouthers-Bos	3.3
Ryan-Chi	1.023	Glasscock-Ind	57			Wilmot-Was	14.5	Wilmot-Was	3.2

Wins		Win Percentage		Games		Complete Games		Shutouts		Saves	
Clarkson-Bos	49	Clarkson-Bos	.721	Clarkson-Bos	73	Clarkson-Bos	68	Clarkson-Bos	8	Sowders-Bos-Pit	2
Keefe-NY	28	Welch-NY	.692	Staley-Pit	49	Staley-Pit	46	Galvin-Pit	4	Welch-NY	2
Buffinton-Phi	28	Keefe-NY	.683	Keefe-NY	47	Welch-NY	39			Bishop-Chi	2
Welch-NY	27	Radbourn-Bos	.645	Buffinton-Phi	47	O'Brien-Cle	39				
Galvin-Pit	23	Buffinton-Phi	.636	Boyle-Ind	46	Keefe-NY	39				

Innings Pitched		Fewest Hits/Game		Fewest BB/Game		Strikeouts		Strikeouts/Game		Ratio	
Clarkson-Bos	620.0	Keefe-NY	7.89	Galvin-Pit	2.06	Clarkson-Bos	284	Keefe-NY	5.56	Clarkson-Bos	11.74
Staley-Pit	420.0	Welch-NY	8.16	Boyle-Ind	2.26	Keefe-NY	225	Crane-NY	5.09	Radbourn-Bos	11.76
Buffinton-Phi	380.0	Clarkson-Bos	8.55	Radbourn-Bos	2.34	Staley-Pit	159	Rusie-Ind	4.36	Staley-Pit	11.94
Boyle-Ind	378.2	Crane-NY	8.65	Dwyer-Chi	2.35	Buffinton-Phi	153	Healy-Was-Chi	4.35	Welch-NY	11.98
Welch-NY	375.0	Hutchinson-Chi	8.66	Sanders-Phi	2.47	Getzien-Ind	139	Clarkson-Bos	4.12	Keefe-NY	12.07

Earned Run Average		Adjusted ERA		Opponents' Batting Avg.		Opponents' On Base Pct.		Starter Runs		Adjusted Starter Runs	
Clarkson-Bos	2.73	Clarkson-Bos	153	Keefe-NY	.228	Clarkson-Bos	.305	Clarkson-Bos	89.2	Clarkson-Bos	99.4
Bakely-Cle	2.96	Bakely-Cle	136	Welch-NY	.234	Radbourn-Bos	.306	Welch-NY	41.7	Buffinton-Phi	47.0
Welch-NY	3.02	Buffinton-Phi	134	Clarkson-Bos	.243	Staley-Pit	.309	Bakely-Cle	36.1	Welch-NY	38.5
Buffinton-Phi	3.24	Welch-NY	131	Crane-NY	.245	Welch-NY	.310	Buffinton-Phi	32.9	Bakely-Cle	36.5
Keefe-NY	3.31	Sanders-Phi	123	Hutchinson-Chi	.245	Keefe-NY	.311	Keefe-NY	28.7	Sanders-Phi	31.3

Clutch Pitching Index		Relief Runs	Adjusted Relief Runs	Relief Ranking	Total Pitcher Index		Total Baseball Ranking	
Casey-Phi	118				Clarkson-Bos	10.2	Clarkson-Bos	10.2
Clarkson-Bos	116				Buffinton-Phi	4.1	Glasscock-Ind	6.0
Bakely-Cle	113				Bakely-Cle	3.4	Buffinton-Phi	4.1
Sanders-Phi	113				Sanders-Phi	3.2	Ewing-NY	4.0
Crane-NY	112				Welch-NY	3.0	Tiernan-NY	3.6

TEAM	G	W	L	PCT	GB	R	OR	AB	H	2B	3B	HR	BB	SO	AVG	OBP	SLG	PRO	PRO+	BR	/A	PF	CHI	RC	SB	CS	SBA	SBR
BRO	140	93	44	.679	—	995	706	4815	1265	188	79	47	550	401	.263	.344	.364	.708	108	60	57	100	109	756	389			
STL	141	90	45	.667	2	957	680	4939	1312	211	64	58	493	477	.266	.339	.370	.709	96	56	-56	113	104	751	336			
PHI	138	75	58	.564	16	880	787	4868	1339	239	65	43	534	496	.275	.354	.377	.731	117	103	114	99	91	758	252			
CIN	141	76	63	.547	18	897	769	4844	1307	197	96	52	452	511	.270	.340	.382	.722	109	74	49	103	98	806	462			
BAL	139	70	65	.519	22	791	795	4756	1209	155	68	20	418	536	.254	.325	.328	.653	90	-38	-52	102	100	624	311			
COL	140	60	78	.435	33.5	779	924	4816	1247	171	95	36	507	609	.259	.335	.356	.691	88	26	68	95	90	693	304			
KC	139	55	82	.401	38	852	1031	4947	1256	162	76	18	430	626	.254	.322	.328	.650	86	-48	-98	106	105	692	472			
LOU	140	27	111	.196	66.5	632	1091	4955	1249	170	75	22	320	521	.252	.303	.330	.633	88	-91	-75	98	85	571	203			
TOT	559					6783		38940	10184	1493	618	296	3704	4177	.262	.326	.354	.680						2729				

TEAM	CG	SH	SV	IP	H	H/G	HR	BB	SO	RAT	ERA	ERA+	OAV	OOB	PR	/A	PF	CPI	FA	E	DP	FW	PW	BW	SBW	DIF
BRO	120	10	1	1212²	1205	8.9	33	400	471	12.2	3.61	103	.251	.315	31	14	97	93	.928	421	92	4.6	1.2	4.8		13.9
STL	121	7	3	1237²	1166	8.5	39	413	617	11.9	3.00	141	.242	.309	116	167	110	106	.925	438	100	3.8	14.1	-4.7		9.3
PHI	130	9	1	1199¹	1200	9.0	35	509	479	13.4	3.53	107	.253	.335	42	33	98	107	.920	465	120	1.7	2.8	9.6		-5.6
CIN	114	3	8	1243	1270	9.2	35	475	562	13.0	3.50	111	.257	.328	47	54	102	105	.926	440	121	3.7	4.6	4.1		-5.9
BAL	128	10	1	1192	1168	8.8	27	424	540	12.6	3.56	111	.249	.322	38	49	103	97	.907	536	104	-2.1	4.1	-4.4		4.8
COL	114	9	4	1199	1274	9.6	33	551	610	14.1	4.39	82	.264	.346	-73	-103	94	93	.915	497	92	.3	-8.7	5.8		-6.4
KC	128	0	2	1204¹	1373	10.3	51	457	447	14.1	4.36	96	.278	.347	-69	-25	109	101	.899	611	109	-6.3	-2.1	-8.3		3.2
LOU	127	2	1	1226¹	1529	11.2	43	475	451	15.1	4.81	80	.297	.362	-132	-133	100	101	.906	584	117	-4.5	-11.3	-6.3		-19.9
TOT	982	50	21	9714¹		9.4				13.3	3.84		.262	.326					.916	3992	855					

Runs		Hits		Doubles		Triples		Home Runs		Total Bases	
Stovey-Phi	152	Tucker-Bal	196	Welch-Phi	39	Marr-Col	15	Stovey-Phi	19	Stovey-Phi	292
Griffin-Bal	150	Orr-Col	183	Stovey-Phi	38	Griffin-Bal	14	Holliday-Cin	19	Holliday-Cin	280
O'Brien-Bro	146	Holliday-Cin	181	Lyons-Phi	36	Beard-Cin	14	Duffee-StL	15	Tucker-Bal	255
Hamilton-KC	144	O'Neill-StL	179	O'Neill-StL	33			Milligan-StL	12	O'Neill-StL	255
Collins-Bro	139	Shindle-Bal	178	Long-KC	32					Orr-Col	250

Runs Batted In		Runs Produced		Bases On Balls		Batting Average		On Base Percentage		Slugging Average	
Stovey-Phi	119	Stovey-Phi	252	Robinson-StL	118	Tucker-Bal	.372	Tucker-Bal	.450	Stovey-Phi	.525
Foutz-Bro	113	Foutz-Bro	225	McTamany-Col	116	O'Neill-StL	.335	Larkin-Phi	.428	Holliday-Cin	.497
O'Neill-StL	110	O'Neill-StL	224	Griffin-Bal	91	Lyons-Phi	.329	Lyons-Phi	.426	Tucker-Bal	.484
Bierbauer-Phi	105	O'Brien-Bro	221	Marr-Col	87	Orr-Col	.327	O'Neill-StL	.419	O'Neill-StL	.478
Holliday-Cin	104	Hamilton-KC	218	Hamilton-KC	87	Holliday-Cin	.321	Hamilton-KC	.413	Lyons-Phi	.469

Production		Adjusted Production		Batter Runs		Adjusted Batter Runs		Clutch Hitting Index		Runs Created	
Tucker-Bal	.934	Tucker-Bal	166	Tucker-Bal	49.8	Tucker-Bal	48.2	Hornung-Bal	149	Tucker-Bal	147
Stovey-Phi	.918	Stovey-Phi	165	Stovey-Phi	44.6	Stovey-Phi	45.9	Robinson-StL	144	Stovey-Phi	143
O'Neill-StL	.897	Lyons-Phi	159	O'Neill-StL	41.7	Lyons-Phi	42.2	Mack-Bal	141	Hamilton-KC	136
Lyons-Phi	.895	Larkin-Phi	148	Lyons-Phi	41.0	Larkin-Phi	37.2	Foutz-Bro	139	O'Brien-Bro	129
Holliday-Cin	.869	Holliday-Cin	144	Larkin-Phi	36.0	Marr-Col	34.7	Manning-KC	136	Holliday-Cin	124

Total Average		Stolen Bases		Stolen Base Average		Stolen Base Runs		Fielding Runs		Total Player Rating	
Tucker-Bal	1.187	Hamilton-KC	111					McPhee-Cin	41.1	Stovey-Phi	5.0
Hamilton-KC	1.134	O'Brien-Bro	91					Bierbauer-Phi	36.6	Bierbauer-Phi	4.6
Stovey-Phi	1.125	Long-KC	89					Long-KC	32.2	Lyons-Phi	4.6
O'Brien-Bro	1.020	Nicol-Cin	80					Tomney-Lou	26.7	McPhee-Cin	4.2
O'Neill-StL	1.014	Latham-StL	69					Shindle-Bal	20.3	Marr-Col	4.1

Wins		Win Percentage		Games		Complete Games		Shutouts		Saves	
Caruthers-Bro	40	Caruthers-Bro	.784	Baldwin-Col	63	Kilroy-Bal	55	Caruthers-Bro	7	Mullane-Cin	5
King-StL	35	King-StL	.686	King-StL	59	Baldwin-Col	54	Baldwin-Col	6		
Duryea-Cin	32	Chamberlain-StL	.681	King-StL	56	Weyhing-Phi	50	Kilroy-Bal	5		
Chamberlain-StL	32	Lovett-Bro	.630	Caruthers-Bro	56	King-StL	47	Foreman-Bal	5		
Weyhing-Phi	30	Duryea-Cin	.627	Weyhing-Phi	54	Caruthers-Bro	46	Weyhing-Phi	4		

Innings Pitched		Fewest Hits/Game		Fewest BB/Game		Strikeouts		Strikeouts/Game		Ratio	
Baldwin-Col	513.2	Stivetts-StL	7.18	Caruthers-Bro	2.10	Baldwin-Col	368	Stivetts-StL	6.71	Stivetts-StL	10.61
Kilroy-Bal	480.2	Weyhing-Phi	7.66	Conway-KC	2.42	Kilroy-Bal	217	Baldwin-Col	6.45	Caruthers-Bro	11.35
King-StL	458.0	Terry-Bro	7.87	King-StL	2.46	Weyhing-Phi	213	Terry-Bro	5.13	Duryea-Cin	11.56
Weyhing-Phi	449.0	Foreman-Bal	7.91	Lovett-Bro	2.55	Chamberlain-StL	202	Sowders-KC	5.06	Foreman-Bal	11.76
Caruthers-Bro	445.0	Baldwin-Col	8.02	Swartzel-KC	2.57	King-StL	188	Gastright-Col	4.65	Conway-KC	11.77

Earned Run Average		Adjusted ERA		Opponents' Batting Avg.		Opponents' On Base Pct.		Starter Runs		Adjusted Starter Runs	
Stivetts-StL	2.25	Stivetts-StL	187	Stivetts-StL	.212	Stivetts-StL	.285	Duryea-Cin	57.3	Duryea-Cin	59.8
Duryea-Cin	2.56	Duryea-Cin	152	Weyhing-Phi	.223	Caruthers-Bro	.299	Kilroy-Bal	53.3	Chamberlain-StL	58.7
Kilroy-Bal	2.85	Chamberlain-StL	142	Terry-Bro	.228	Duryea-Cin	.303	Weyhing-Phi	44.8	Kilroy-Bal	58.4
Weyhing-Phi	2.95	Kilroy-Bal	138	Foreman-Bal	.229	Foreman-Bal	.306	Chamberlain-StL	41.1	King-StL	54.8
Chamberlain-StL	2.97	King-StL	134	Baldwin-Col	.231	Conway-KC	.306	King-StL	35.6	Stivetts-StL	41.9

Clutch Pitching Index		Relief Runs		Adjusted Relief Runs		Relief Ranking		Total Pitcher Index		Total Baseball Ranking	
Mullane-Cin	119							Kilroy-Bal	7.0	Kilroy-Bal	6.9
Duryea-Cin	116							Duryea-Cin	5.9	Duryea-Cin	5.9
Kilroy-Bal	114							Chamberlain-StL	4.8	Stovey-Phi	5.0
Hughes-Bro	110							King-StL	4.6	Chamberlain-StL	4.7
Weyhing-Phi	109							Caruthers-Bro	4.2	Bierbauer-Phi	4.6

TEAM	G	W	L	PCT	GB	R	OR	AB	H	2B	3B	HR	BB	SO	AVG	OBP	SLG	PRO	PRO+	BR	/A	PF	CHI	RC	SB	CS	SBA	SBR
BRO	129	86	43	.667		884	620	4419	1166	184	75	43	517	361	.264	.346	.369	.715	115	90	87	100	110	702	349			
CHI	139	84	53	.613	6	847	692	4891	1271	147	59	67	516	514	.260	.336	.355	.691	104	54	23	104	101	712	329			
PHI	133	78	54	.591	9.5	823	707	4707	1267	220	78	23	522	403	.269	.350	.364	.714	112	96	77	103	96	735	335			
CIN	134	77	55	.583	10.5	753	633	4644	1204	150	120	27	433	377	.259	.329	.361	.690	109	42	46	100	97	670	312			
BOS	134	76	57	.571	12	763	633	4722	1220	175	62	31	530	515	.258	.342	.341	.683	98	46	-15	108	94	665	285			
NY	135	63	68	.481	24	713	698	4832	1250	208	89	25	350	479	.259	.315	.354	.669	101	1	-1	100	95	647	289			
CLE	136	44	88	.333	43.5	630	832	4633	1073	132	59	21	497	474	.232	.312	.299	.611	86	-80	-66	98	95	491	152			
PIT	138	23	113	.169	66.5	597	1235	4739	1088	160	43	20	408	458	.230	.300	.294	.594	89	-117	-30	88	94	492	208			
TOT	539					6010		37587	9539	1376	585	257	3773	3581	.254	.322	.342	.664							2259			

TEAM	CG	SH	SV	IP	H	H/G	HR	BB	SO	RAT	ERA	ERA+	OAV	OOB	PR	/A	PF	CPI	FA	E	DP	FW	PW	BW	SBW	DIF
BRO	115	6	2	1145	1102	8.7	27	401	403	12.2	3.06	112	.246	.315	64	47	96	104	.940	320	92	4.5	4.2	7.7		5.1
CHI	126	6	3	1237¹	1103	8.0	41	481	504	11.9	3.24	113	.234	.311	44	50	103	93	.940	344	89	4.9	4.4	2.0		4.2
PHI	122	9	2	1194²	1210	9.1	22	486	507	13.2	3.32	110	.255	.331	32	43	102	107	.929	398	122	.4	3.8	6.8		.9
CIN	124	9	1	1190²	1097	8.3	41	407	488	11.8	2.79	127	.238	.307	102	100	100	109	.932	382	106	1.6	8.9	4.1		-3.6
BOS	132	13	1	1187	1132	8.6	27	354	506	11.5	2.93	128	.245	.303	83	104	105	101	.935	359	77	3.0	9.2	-1.3		-1.4
NY	115	6	1	1177	1029	7.9	14	607	612	13.0	3.06	114	.230	.331	66	52	98	104	.921	449	104	-2.3	4.6	-.0		-4.7
CLE	129	2	0	1184¹	1322	10.0	33	464	303	14.0	4.13	86	.273	.343	-75	-70	100	99	.930	405	108	.6	-6.2	-5.9		-10.5
PIT	119	3	0	1176¹	1520	11.6	52	573	381	16.6	5.97	55	.304	.384	-315	-350	92	91	.897	607	94	-11.5	-31.1	-2.7		.2
TOT	982	54	10	9492¹		9.0				13.0	3.56		.254	.322					.928	3264	792					

Runs		Hits		Doubles		Triples		Home Runs		Total Bases	
Collins-Bro	148	Thompson-Phi	172	Thompson-Phi	41	Reilly-Cin	26	Wilmot-Chi	13	Tiernan-NY	274
Carroll-Chi	134	Glasscock-NY	172	Glasscock-NY	32	McPhee-Cin	22	Tiernan-NY	13	Reilly-Cin	261
Hamilton-Phi	133	Tiernan-NY	168	Collins-Bro	32	Tiernan-NY	21	Burns-Bro	13	Thompson-Phi	243
Tiernan-NY	132	Reilly-Cin	166	Myers-Phi	29	Beard-Cin	15	Long-Bos	8	Wilmot-Chi	237
McPhee-Cin	125	Carroll-Chi	166	O'Brien-Bro	28					Glasscock-NY	225

Runs Batted In		Runs Produced		Bases On Balls		Batting Average		On Base Percentage		Slugging Average	
Burns-Bro	128	Burns-Bro	217	Anson-Chi	113	Glasscock-NY	.336	Anson-Chi	.443	Tiernan-NY	.495
Anson-Chi	107	Thompson-Phi	214	McKean-Cle	87	Hamilton-Phi	.325	Hamilton-Phi	.430	Clements-Phi	.472
Thompson-Phi	102	Collins-Bro	214	Allen-Phi	87	Clements-Phi	.315	Pinkney-Bro	.411	Reilly-Cin	.472
Wilmot-Chi	99	Wilmot-Chi	200	Collins-Bro	85	Thompson-Phi	.313	McKean-Cle	.401	Burns-Bro	.464
Foutz-Bro	98	Foutz-Bro	199	Hamilton-Phi	83	Knight-Cin	.312	Glasscock-NY	.395	Burkett-NY	.461

Production		Adjusted Production		Batter Runs		Adjusted Batter Runs		Clutch Hitting Index		Runs Created	
Tiernan-NY	.880	Tiernan-NY	158	Tiernan-NY	39.8	Tiernan-NY	39.6	Burns-Bro	144	Hamilton-Phi	132
Clements-Phi	.864	Clements-Phi	150	Anson-Chi	39.3	Anson-Chi	35.7	Mayer-Phi	142	Tiernan-NY	130
Anson-Chi	.844	Pinkney-Bro	148	Hamilton-Phi	33.3	McKean-Cle	32.5	Anson-Chi	139	Wilmot-Chi	113
Pinkney-Bro	.842	Glasscock-NY	145	Pinkney-Bro	32.5	Pinkney-Bro	32.1	Hornung-NY	139	Glasscock-NY	113
Glasscock-NY	.834	McKean-Cle	144	McKean-Cle	30.8	Hamilton-Phi	31.2	Clarke-NY	134	Collins-Bro	111

Total Average		Stolen Bases		Stolen Base Average	Stolen Base Runs	Fielding Runs		Total Player Rating	
Hamilton-Phi	1.170	Hamilton-Phi	102			Allen-Phi	38.6	Glasscock-NY	5.1
Tiernan-NY	1.047	Collins-Bro	85			McPhee-Cin	30.0	McPhee-Cin	4.7
Pinkney-Bro	1.015	Sunday-Pit-Phi	84			Glasscock-NY	22.1	Allen-Phi	4.2
Anson-Chi	1.009	Wilmot-Chi	76			Smalley-Cle	16.5	Clements-Phi	3.0
Collins-Bro	1.005	Tiernan-NY	56			Carroll-Chi	14.5	Collins-Bro	2.9

Wins		Win Percentage		Games		Complete Games		Shutouts		Saves	
W.Hutchinson-Chi	42	Lovett-Bro	.732	W.Hutchinson-Chi	71	W.Hutchinson-Chi	65	Nichols-Bos	7	W.Hutchinson-Chi	2
Gleason-Phi	38	Gleason-Phi	.691	Rusie-NY	67	Rusie-NY	56	Rhines-Cin	6	Gleason-Phi	2
Lovett-Bro	30	Luby-Chi	.690	Gleason-Phi	60	Gleason-Phi	54	Gleason-Phi	6	Foutz-Bro	2
Rusie-NY	29	Caruthers-Bro	.676	Beatin-Cle	54	Beatin-Cle	53	W.Hutchinson-Chi	5		
Rhines-Cin	28	W.Hutchinson-Chi	.627	Nichols-Bos	48	Nichols-Bos	47				

Innings Pitched		Fewest Hits/Game		Fewest BB/Game		Strikeouts		Strikeouts/Game		Ratio	
W.Hutchinson-Chi	603.0	Rusie-NY	7.15	Young-Cle	1.95	Rusie-NY	341	Rusie-NY	5.59	Rhines-Cin	10.43
Rusie-NY	548.2	Mullane-Cin	7.54	Duryea-Cin	1.97	W.Hutchinson-Chi	289	Nichols-Bos	4.71	Nichols-Bos	10.55
Gleason-Phi	506.0	W.Hutchinson-Chi	7.54	Getzien-Bos	2.11	Nichols-Bos	222	Terry-Bro	4.50	W.Hutchinson-Chi	10.70
Beatin-Cle	474.1	Rhines-Cin	7.56	Nichols-Bos	2.38	Gleason-Phi	222	W.Hutchinson-Chi	4.31	Getzien-Bos	10.98
Nichols-Bos	424.0	Luby-Chi	7.60	Rhines-Cin	2.53	Terry-Bro	185	Sharrott-NY	4.11	Duryea-Cin	11.10

Earned Run Average		Adjusted ERA		Opponents' Batting Avg.		Opponents' On Base Pct.		Starter Runs		Adjusted Starter Runs	
Rhines-Cin	1.95	Rhines-Cin	182	Rusie-NY	.212	Rhines-Cin	.282	Rhines-Cin	71.8	Nichols-Bos	71.3
Nichols-Bos	2.23	Nichols-Bos	168	Mullane-Cin	.221	Nichols-Bos	.284	Nichols-Bos	62.8	Rhines-Cin	71.3
Mullane-Cin	2.24	Mullane-Cin	159	W.Hutchinson-Chi	.221	W.Hutchinson-Chi	.287	Rusie-NY	61.1	W.Hutchinson-Chi	63.6
Rusie-NY	2.56	Gleason-Phi	139	Rhines-Cin	.221	Getzien-Bos	.292	W.Hutchinson-Chi	57.6	Gleason-Phi	57.0
Gleason-Phi	2.63	Rusie-NY	137	Luby-Chi	.222	Duryea-Cin	.295	Gleason-Phi	52.2	Rusie-NY	57.0

Clutch Pitching Index		Relief Runs	Adjusted Relief Runs	Relief Ranking	Total Pitcher Index		Total Baseball Ranking	
Mullane-Cin	131				Nichols-Bos	6.9	Nichols-Bos	6.8
Vickery-Phi	120				Rusie-NY	6.8	Rusie-NY	6.5
Rhines-Cin	118				Rhines-Cin	6.4	Rhines-Cin	6.4
Gleason-Phi	112				W.Hutchinson-Chi	5.9	W.Hutchinson-Chi	5.9
Nichols-Bos	110				Gleason-Phi	4.7	Glasscock-NY	5.1

TEAM	G	W	L	PCT	GB	R	OR	AB	H	2B	3B	HR	BB	SO	AVG	OBP	SLG	PRO	PRO+	BR	/A	PF	CHI	RC	SB	CS	SBA	SBR
LOU	136	88	44	.667		819	588	4687	1310	156	65	15	410	460	.279	.344	.350	.694	116	73	90	98	99	699	341			
COL	140	79	55	.590	10	831	617	4741	1225	159	77	16	545	557	.258	.341	.335	.676	115	49	103	93	100	677	353			
STL	139	78	58	.574	12	870	736	4800	1308	178	73	48	474	490	.273	.350	.370	.720	105	120	9	114	96	746	307			
TOL	134	68	64	.515	20	739	689	4575	1152	152	108	24	486	558	.252	.333	.348	.681	105	50	29	103	92	687	421			
ROC	133	63	63	.500	22	709	711	4553	1088	131	64	31	446	538	.239	.315	.316	.631	101	-33	23	93	100	564	310			
BAL	38	15	19	.441	24	182	192	1213	278	34	16	2	125	152	.229	.316	.289	.605	81	-18	-27	105	100	146	101			
SYR	128	55	72	.433	30.5	698	831	4469	1158	151	59	14	457	482	.259	.333	.329	.662	115	19	95	90	94	600	292			
PHI	132	54	78	.409	34	702	945	4490	1057	181	51	24	475	540	.235	.320	.314	.634	96	-21	-4	98	98	564	305			
BRO	100	26	73	.263	45.5	492	733	3475	769	116	47	13	328	456	.221	.294	.293	.587	83	-83	-64	97	103	362	182			
TOT	540					6042		37003	9345	1258	560	187	3746	4233	.253	.321	.332	.653							2612			

TEAM	CG	SH	SV	IP	H	H/G	HR	BB	SO	RAT	ERA	ERA+	OAV	OOB	PR	/A	PF	CPI	FA	E	DP	FW	PW	BW	SBW	DIF
LOU	114	13	7	1206	1120	8.4	18	293	587	10.9	2.57	149	.239	.291	173	169	100	117	.934	380	79	2.8	14.9	7.9		-3.6
COL	120	14	3	1214²	976	7.2	20	471	624	11.2	2.99	120	.214	.297	118	80	93	95	.932	396	101	2.6	7.0	9.1		-6.7
STL	118	4	1	1195¹	1127	8.5	38	447	733	12.3	3.67	117	.242	.316	25	82	112	98	.916	478	93	-1.8	7.2	.8		3.8
TOL	122	4	2	1159¹	1122	8.7	23	429	533	12.6	3.56	111	.247	.321	39	49	102	102	.925	419	75	.4	4.3	2.6		-5.3
ROC	122	5	2	1161²	1115	8.6	19	530	477	13.2	3.56	100	.246	.331	39	-2	92	106	.926	416	95	.4	-.2	-.0		-2.3
BAL	36	1	0	315¹	307	8.8	3	123	134	13.0	4.00	101	.248	.328	-5	2	105	92	.928	109	21	.6	-2.4			-.4
SYR	115	5	0	1089²	1158	9.6	28	518	454	14.4	4.98	71	.265	.351	-135	-176	91	89	.925	391	90	.9	-15.5	8.4		-2.3
PHI	119	3	2	1132	1405	11.2	17	514	461	15.8	5.22	73	.296	.373	-171	-176	99	99	.918	452	93	-1.6	-15.5	-.4		5.4
BRO	96	0	0	879	1011	10.4	21	421	230	15.2	4.71	83	.281	.365	-83	-81	101	104	.909	404	92	-4.4	-7.1	-5.6		-6.3
TOT	962	49	17	9353		9.0				13.1	3.86		.253	.321					.923	3445	739					

Runs
McTamany-Col ... 140
McCarthy-StL 137
Fuller-StL 118
Sneed-Tol-Col ... 117
Welch-Phi-Bal ... 116

Hits
Wolf-Lou 197
McCarthy-StL 192
Johnson-Col 186
Childs-Syr 170
Taylor-Lou 169

Doubles
Childs-Syr 33
Wolf-Lou 29
Lyons-Phi 29

Triples
Werden-Tol 20
Johnson-Col 18
Alvord-Tol 16
Sneed-Tol-Col 15

Home Runs
Campau-StL 9
Cartwright-StL 8
Stivetts-StL 7
Lyons-Phi 7

Total Bases
Wolf-Lou 260
McCarthy-StL 256
Johnson-Col 248
Childs-Syr 237
Werden-Tol 227

Runs Batted In

Runs Produced
McTamany-Col ... 139
McCarthy-StL 131
Fuller-StL 117
Sneed-Tol-Col ... 115
Taylor-Lou 115

Bases On Balls
McTamany-Col ... 112
Crooks-Col 96
Swartwood-Tol 80
Werden-Tol 78
Scheffler-Roc 78

Batting Average
Wolf-Lou .... .363
Lyons-Phi .... .354
McCarthy-StL ..... .350
Johnson-Col ...... .346
Childs-Syr .... .345

On Base Percentage
Lyons-Phi .... .461
Swartwood-Tol .... .444
Childs-Syr .... .434
McCarthy-StL ..... .430
Wright-Syr .... .428

Slugging Average
Lyons-Phi .... .531
Childs-Syr .... .481
Wolf-Lou .... .479
McCarthy-StL ..... .467
Johnson-Col ...... .461

Production
Lyons-Phi .... .992
Childs-Syr .... .915
Wolf-Lou .... .900
McCarthy-StL ..... .898
Swartwood-Tol .... .887

Adjusted Production
Lyons-Phi 200
Childs-Syr 193
Wolf-Lou 172
Johnson-Col 171
Swartwood-Tol ... 160

Batter Runs
McCarthy-StL 47.6
Childs-Syr 46.5
Wolf-Lou 45.3
Lyons-Phi 42.7
Swartwood-Tol ... 42.4

Adjusted Batter Runs
Childs-Syr 55.2
Wolf-Lou 47.3
Johnson-Col 45.3
Lyons-Phi 44.0
Swartwood-Tol ... 40.1

Clutch Hitting Index

Runs Created
McCarthy-StL 150
Wolf-Lou 132
Childs-Syr 130
Johnson-Col 122
Werden-Tol 118

Total Average
Lyons-Phi 1.224
McCarthy-StL 1.169
Childs-Syr 1.149
Swartwood-Tol .. 1.141
Werden-Tol 1.074

Stolen Bases
McCarthy-StL 83
Scheffler-Roc 77
VanDyke-Tol 73
Welch-Phi-Bal 72

Stolen Base Average

Stolen Base Runs

Fielding Runs
Gerhardt-Bro-StL . 41.5
Reilly-Col 28.2
Ely-Syr 19.3
Tomney-Lou 17.6
Welch-Phi-Bal 15.7

Total Player Rating
Childs-Syr 6.4
Lyons-Phi 4.9
Swartwood-Tol ... 3.8
O'Connor-Col 3.7
Wolf-Lou 3.6

Wins
McMahon-Phi-Bal .. 36
Stratton-Lou 34
Gastright-Col 30
Barr-Roc 28
Stivetts-StL 27

Win Percentage
Stratton-Lou ..... .708
Chamberlain-StL-Col .682
Gastright-Col .... .682
Ehret-Lou .... .641
McMahon-Phi-Bal . .632

Games
McMahon-Phi-Bal .. 60
Barr-Roc 57
Stivetts-StL 54
Stratton-Lou 50
Gastright-Col 48

Complete Games
McMahon-Phi-Bal .. 55
Barr-Roc 52
Stratton-Lou 44
Healy-Tol 44

Shutouts
Chamberlain-StL-Col ... 6
Stratton-Lou 4
Gastright-Col 4
Ehret-Lou 4

Saves
Goodall-Lou 4
Knauss-Col 2
Ehret-Lou 2

Innings Pitched
McMahon-Phi-Bal 509.0
Barr-Roc 493.1
Stratton-Lou ... 431.0
Stivetts-StL ... 419.1
Gastright-Col .. 401.1

Fewest Hits/Game
Knauss-Col 6.73
Gastright-Col ... 7.00
Easton-Col 7.50
Chamberlain-StL-Col . 7.50
Healy-Tol 7.54

Fewest BB/Game
Stratton-Lou ... 1.27
Ehret-Lou 1.98
Ramsey-StL 2.63
Smith-Tol 2.83
McMahon-Phi-Bal . 2.94

Strikeouts
McMahon-Phi-Bal . 291
Stivetts-StL 289
Ramsey-StL 257
Healy-Tol 225
Barr-Roc 209

Strikeouts/Game
Ramsey-StL 6.63
Stivetts-StL 6.20
Meakim-Lou 5.77
Chamberlain-StL-Col . 5.49
Healy-Tol 5.21

Ratio
Stratton-Lou 9.86
Gastright-Col ... 10.43
Knauss-Col 10.87
Healy-Tol 11.04
Ehret-Lou 11.21

Earned Run Average
Stratton-Lou 2.36
Ehret-Lou 2.53
Knauss-Col 2.81
Chamberlain-StL-Col . 2.83
Healy-Tol 2.89

Adjusted ERA
Stratton-Lou 163
Ehret-Lou 152
Healy-Tol 136
Meakim-Lou 132
Chamberlain-StL-Col . 131

Opponents' Batting Avg.
Knauss-Col .... .202
Gastright-Col .... .208
Easton-Col .... .220
Chamberlain-StL-Col . .220
Healy-Tol .... .221

Opponents' On Base Pct.
Stratton-Lou ..... .270
Gastright-Col .... .282
Knauss-Col .... .290
Healy-Tol .... .293
Ehret-Lou .... .296

Starter Runs
Stratton-Lou 72.0
Ehret-Lou 53.1
Healy-Tol 42.0
Gastright-Col 41.3
Barr-Roc 33.8

Adjusted Starter Runs
Stratton-Lou 71.1
Ehret-Lou 52.3
Healy-Tol 45.5
Stivetts-StL 36.7
McMahon-Phi-Bal .. 33.8

Clutch Pitching Index
Ehret-Lou 126
Titcomb-Roc 121
Daily-Bro-Lou 113
Stratton-Lou 110
Chamberlain-StL-Col . 110

Relief Runs

Adjusted Relief Runs

Relief Ranking

Total Pitcher Index
Stratton-Lou 8.9
Stivetts-StL 5.0
Healy-Tol 4.8
Ehret-Lou 4.4
McMahon-Phi-Bal .. 4.1

Total Baseball Ranking
Stratton-Lou 9.0
Childs-Syr 6.4
Stivetts-StL 5.2
Lyons-Phi 4.9
Healy-Tol 4.7

TEAM	G	W	L	PCT	GB	R	OR	AB	H	2B	3B	HR	BB	SO	AVG	OBP	SLG	PRO	PRO+	BR	/A	PF	CHI	RC	SB	CS	SBA	SBR
BOS	130	81	48	.628		992	767	4626	1306	223	76	54	652	435	.282	.376	.398	.774	107	105	45	107	99	869	412			
BRO	133	76	56	.576	6.5	964	893	4887	1354	186	93	34	502	369	.277	.349	.374	.723	94	4	-52	106	104	752	272			
NY	132	74	57	.565	8	1018	875	4913	1393	204	97	66	486	364	.284	.352	.405	.757	100	56	-25	109	104	800	231			
CHI	138	75	62	.547	10	886	770	4968	1311	200	95	31	492	410	.264	.335	.361	.696	89	-49	-87	104	100	712	276			
PHI	132	68	63	.519	14	941	855	4855	1348	187	113	49	431	321	.278	.343	.393	.736	101	-5		102	102	742	203			
PIT	128	60	68	.469	20.5	835	892	4577	1192	168	113	35	569	375	.260	.349	.369	.718	108	0	72	92	95	694	249			
CLE	131	55	75	.423	26.5	849	1027	4804	1373	213	94	27	509	345	.286	.360	.386	.746	115	47	121	92	89	751	180			
BUF	134	36	96	.273	46.5	793	1199	4795	1249	180	64	20	541	367	.260	.347	.337	.684	98	-53	23	92	92	632	160			
TOT	529					7278		38425	10526	1561	745	316	4182	2986	.274	.345	.378	.723							1983			

TEAM	CG	SH	SV	IP	H	H/G	HR	BB	SO	RAT	ERA	ERA+	OAV	OOB	PR	/A	PF	CPI	FA	E	DP	FW	PW	BW	SBW	DIF
BOS	105	6	2	1137.1	1291	10.2	49	467	345	14.3	3.79	116	.274	.346	55	76	104	111	.918	460	109	1.7	6.1	3.6		5.1
BRO	111	4	7	1184	1334	10.1	26	570	377	14.9	3.95	113	.273	.356	37	65	105	106	.909	531	114	-1.8	5.2	-4.1		10.7
NY	111	3	6	1172.1	1224	9.4	37	569	449	14.1	4.17	109	.257	.343	8	47	107	92	.921	450	94	2.8	3.8	-2.0		4.0
CHI	124	5	2	1219.1	1238	9.1	27	503	460	13.2	3.39	128	.252	.327	114	128	103	100	.918	492	107	1.6	10.2	-6.9		1.6
PHI	118	4	2	1154.1	1292	10.1	33	495	361	14.4	4.05	105	.271	.347	22	27	101	100	.910	510	118	-.7	2.2	-.4		1.5
PIT	121	7	0	1116.2	1267	10.2	32	334	318	13.2	4.22	93	.274	.328	2	-39	92	89	.907	512	80	-1.7	-3.1	5.7		-4.9
CLE	115	1	0	1143.2	1386	10.9	45	571	325	15.8	4.23	94	.287	.369	0	-33	94	114	.907	533	103	-2.3	-2.6	9.7		-14.7
BUF	125	2	0	1141	1499	11.8	67	673	351	17.5	6.11	67	.304	.393	-239	-257	97	93	.914	491	116	.8	-20.5	1.8		-12.1
TOT	930	32	19	9268.2		10.2				14.7	4.23		.274	.345					.913	3979	841					

Runs
Duffy-Chi 161
Brown-Bos 146
Stovey-Bos 142
Ward-Bro 134
Connor-NY 133

Hits
Duffy-Chi 191
Ward-Bro 189
Shindle-Phi 188
Browning-Cle 184
Richardson-Bos 181

Doubles
Browning-Cle 40
Beckley-Pit 38
O'Rourke-NY 37
Duffy-Chi 36
Brouthers-Bos..... 36

Triples
Visner-Pit 22
Beckley-Pit 22
Shindle-Phi 21
Fields-Pit 20
Joyce-Bro 18

Home Runs
Connor-NY........ 14
Richardson-Bos .. 13
Stovey-Bos 12
Shindle-Phi 10
Gore-NY 10

Total Bases
Shindle-Phi 281
Duffy-Chi 280
Beckley-Pit........ 276
Richardson-Bos .. 274
Connor-NY........ 265

Runs Batted In
Richardson-Bos .. 146
Orr-Bro 124
Beckley-Pit 120
O'Rourke-NY 115
Larkin-Cle 112

Runs Produced
Richardson-Bos .. 259
Duffy-Chi 236
Connor-NY....... 222
Bierbauer-Bro 220
Beckley-Pit....... 220

Bases On Balls
Joyce-Bro 123
Robinson-Pit 101
Brouthers-Bos.... 99
Hoy-Buf 94

Batting Average
Browning-Cle 373
Orr-Bro 373
O'Rourke-NY 360
Connor-NY.......349
Ryan-Chi 340

On Base Percentage
Brouthers-Bos.....466
Browning-Cle 459
Connor-NY.......450
Robinson-Pit 434
Gore-NY 432

Slugging Average
Connor-NY.......548
Orr-Bro 537
Beckley-Pit.......535
Browning-Cle 517
O'Rourke-NY 515

Production
Connor-NY.......998
Browning-Cle 976
Orr-Bro 952
Gore-NY 931
O'Rourke-NY 925

Adjusted Production
Browning-Cle 177
Beckley-Pit....... 158
Larkin-Cle 156
Connor-NY....... 154
Orr-Bro........... 147

Batter Runs
Connor-NY....... 49.1
Browning-Cle 46.7
Brouthers-Bos.... 39.6
Orr-Bro........... 34.4
Larkin-Cle 32.6

Adjusted Batter Runs
Browning-Cle 54.6
Larkin-Cle 40.7
Connor-NY....... 40.6
Beckley-Pit....... 37.8
Brouthers-Bos.... 33.1

Clutch Hitting Index
Nash-Bos......... 130
McGeachey-Bro .. 129
Rowe-Buf 127
Farrell-Chi 125
Fogarty-Phi 124

Runs Created
Duffy-Chi 141
Browning-Cle 136
Stovey-Bos 134
Connor-NY 132
Shindle-Phi 126

Total Average
Stovey-Bos 1.210
Connor-NY 1.194
Browning-Cle ...1.191
Brouthers-Bos...1.149
Gore-NY 1.129

Stolen Bases
Stovey-Bos 97
Brown-Bos 79
Duffy-Chi 78
Hanlon-Pit 65
Ward-Bro 63

Stolen Base Average

Stolen Base Runs

Fielding Runs
Farrell-Chi 26.5
Richardson-Bos .. 25.3
Bierbauer-Bro 24.8
Pfeffer-Chi 24.1
Ward-Bro 21.3

Total Player Rating
Browning-Cle 4.3
Connor-NY........ 3.6
W.Ewing-NY 3.2
Ward-Bro 3.1
Shindle-Phi 2.7

Wins
Baldwin-Chi 34
Weyhing-Bro 30
King-Chi 30
Radbourn-Bos 27
Gumbert-Bos 23

Win Percentage
Daley-Bos 720
Radbourn-Bos 692
Knell-Phi 667
Gumbert-Bos.....657
Weyhing-Bro 652

Games
Baldwin-Chi 59
King-Chi 56
Weyhing-Bro 49
Gruber-Cle 48
Staley-Pit 46

Complete Games
Baldwin-Chi 54
King-Chi 48
Staley-Pit 44
Gruber-Cle 39
Weyhing-Bro 38

Shutouts
King-Chi 4
Weyhing-Bro 3
Staley-Pit 3

Saves
Hemming-Cle-Bro ... 3
O'Day-NY.......... 3

Innings Pitched
Baldwin-Chi 501.0
King-Chi 461.0
Weyhing-Bro 390.0
Staley-Pit 387.2
Gruber-Cle 383.1

Fewest Hits/Game
King-Chi 8.20
Crane-NY 8.80
Hemming-Cle-Bro . 8.88
Baldwin-Chi 8.95
Keefe-NY 8.96

Fewest BB/Game
Staley-Pit 1.72
Sanders-Phi 1.79
Galvin-Pit 2.03
Morris-Pit 2.18
Radbourn-Bos 2.62

Strikeouts
Baldwin-Chi 211
King-Chi 185
Weyhing-Bro 177
Staley-Pit 145
J.Ewing-NY 145

Strikeouts/Game
J.Ewing-NY 4.88
Daley-Bos 4.21
Weyhing-Bro 4.08
McGill-Cle 4.02
Haddock-Buf 3.81

Ratio
Staley-Pit 11.07
King-Chi 11.67
Radbourn-Bos... 12.15
Keefe-NY 12.62
Sanders-Phi..... 12.75

Earned Run Average
King-Chi 2.69
Staley-Pit 3.23
Baldwin-Chi 3.31
Radbourn-Bos.... 3.31
Keefe-NY 3.38

Adjusted ERA
King-Chi 161
Keefe-NY 134
Radbourn-Bos.... 133
Baldwin-Chi 131
Weyhing-Bro 124

Opponents' Batting Avg.
King-Chi 232
Crane-NY 245
Hemming-Cle-Bro .247
Baldwin-Chi 248
Keefe-NY 249

Opponents' On Base Pct.
Staley-Pit 290
King-Chi 301
Radbourn-Bos....310
Keefe-NY 318
Sanders-Phi......320

Starter Runs
King-Chi 78.6
Baldwin-Chi 51.4
Staley-Pit 43.2
Radbourn-Bos.... 35.2
Weyhing-Bro 27.2

Adjusted Starter Runs
King-Chi 84.2
Baldwin-Chi 57.5
Radbourn-Bos.... 41.4
Weyhing-Bro 37.0
Keefe-NY 29.5

Clutch Pitching Index
O'Brien-Cle 126
Daley-Bos 124
McGill-Cle 117
Kilroy-Bos 114
Gruber-Cle 114

Relief Runs

Adjusted Relief Runs

Relief Ranking

Total Pitcher Index
King-Chi 7.0
Baldwin-Chi 5.0
Radbourn-Bos..... 3.6
Sanders-Phi...... 2.5
Staley-Pit 2.3

Total Baseball Ranking
King-Chi 7.0
Baldwin-Chi 5.0
Browning-Cle 4.3
Connor-NY....... 3.6
Radbourn-Bos..... 3.4

TEAM	G	W	L	PCT	GB	R	OR	AB	H	2B	3B	HR	BB	SO	AVG	OBP	SLG	PRO	PRO+	BR	/A	PF	CHI	RC	SB	CS	SBA	SBR
BOS	140	87	51	.630		847	658	4956	1264	181	80	54	532	538	.255	.337	.357	.694	98	68	-25	112	99	711	289			
CHI	137	82	53	.607	3.5	832	730	4873	1233	159	88	60	526	457	.253	.332	.359	.691	109	58	59	100	100	676	238			
NY	136	71	61	.538	13	754	711	4833	1271	189	72	46	438	394	.263	.329	.360	.689	113	49	80	96	94	663	224			
PHI	138	68	69	.496	18.5	756	773	4929	1244	180	51	21	482	412	.252	.326	.322	.648	94	-12	-31	103	99	609	232			
CLE	141	65	74	.468	22.5	835	888	5074	1294	183	88	22	519	464	.255	.330	.339	.669	99	22	-11	104	102	663	242			
BRO	137	61	76	.445	25.5	765	820	4748	1233	200	69	23	464	435	.260	.330	.345	.675	105	30	35	99	99	669	337			
CIN	138	56	81	.409	30.5	646	790	4791	1158	148	90	40	414	439	.242	.308	.335	.643	94	-33	-38	101	91	584	244			
PIT	137	55	80	.407	30.5	679	744	4794	1148	148	71	29	427	503	.239	.308	.318	.626	92	-57	-38	98	99	547	205			
TOT	552					6114		38998	9845	1388	609	295	3802	3642	.252	.319	.342	.661							2011			

TEAM	CG	SH	SV	IP	H	H/G	HR	BB	SO	RAT	ERA	ERA+	OAV	OOB	PR	/A	PF	CPI	FA	E	DP	FW	PW	BW	SBW	DIF
BOS	126	9	6	1241²	1223	8.9	51	364	525	11.8	2.76	132	.248	.305	80	122	109	109	.938	358	96	4.7	10.9	-2.2		4.7
CHI	114	6	3	1220²	1207	8.9	53	475	477	12.7	3.47	96	.249	.322	-17	-21	100	96	.932	397	119	1.5	-1.9	5.3		9.6
NY	117	11	3	1204	1098	8.2	27	593	651	13.1	2.99	107	.234	.327	47	28	96	104	.933	384	104	2.2	2.5	7.1		-6.8
PHI	105	3	5	1229¹	1280	9.4	29	505	343	13.4	3.73	91	.259	.333	-53	-46	102	94	.925	443	108	-1.3	-4.1	-2.8		7.7
CLE	118	1	3	1244	1371	9.9	24	466	400	13.6	3.50	99	.270	.336	-22	-7	103	105	.920	485	86	-3.5	-.6	-1.0		.6
BRO	121	8	3	1204²	1272	9.5	40	459	407	13.4	3.86	86	.261	.332	-68	-75	99	93	.924	432	73	-.8	-6.7	3.1		-3.1
CIN	125	6	1	1218²	1234	9.1	40	465	393	13.0	3.55	95	.253	.326	-28	-25	101	96	.931	409	101	.9	-2.2	-3.4		-7.8
PIT	122	7	2	1197²	1160	8.7	31	465	446	12.7	2.89	114	.245	.320	61	51	98	109	.917	475	76	-3.6	4.6	-3.4		-10.0
TOT	948	51	26	9760²		9.1				12.9	3.34		.252	.319					.928	3383	763					

Runs		Hits		Doubles		Triples		Home Runs		Total Bases	
Hamilton-Phi	141	Hamilton-Phi	179	Griffin-Bro	36	Stovey-Bos	20	Tiernan-NY	16	Stovey-Bos	271
Long-Bos	129	McKean-Cle	170	Davis-Cle	35	Beckley-Pit	19	Stovey-Bos	16	Tiernan-NY	268
Childs-Cle	120	Tiernan-NY	166	Stovey-Bos	31	McPhee-Cin	16	Wilmot-Chi	11	Long-Bos	236
Latham-Cin	119	Davis-Cle	165	Tiernan-NY	30	Ryan-Chi	15	Long-Bos	10	Davis-Cle	233
Stovey-Bos	118	O'Rourke-NY	164			Virtue-Cle	14			Beckley-Pit	232

Runs Batted In		Runs Produced		Bases On Balls		Batting Average		On Base Percentage		Slugging Average	
Anson-Chi	120	Davis-Cle	201	Hamilton-Phi	102	Hamilton-Phi	.340	Hamilton-Phi	.453	Stovey-Bos	.498
Stovey-Bos	95	Childs-Cle	201	Childs-Cle	97	Holliday-Cin	.319	Connor-NY	.399	Tiernan-NY	.494
O'Rourke-NY	95	Hamilton-Phi	199	Connor-NY	83	Browning-Pit-Cin	.317	Childs-Cle	.395	Holliday-Cin	.473
Nash-Bos	95	Connor-NY	199	Long-Bos	80	Clements-Phi	.310	Browning-Pit-Cin	.395	Connor-NY	.449
Connor-NY	94	Stovey-Bos	197	Pfeffer-Chi	79	Tiernan-NY	.306	Tiernan-NY	.388	Ryan-Chi	.434

Production		Adjusted Production		Batter Runs		Adjusted Batter Runs		Clutch Hitting Index		Runs Created	
Tiernan-NY	.882	Tiernan-NY	165	Hamilton-Phi	45.7	Hamilton-Phi	43.4	Anson-Chi	151	Hamilton-Phi	155
Hamilton-Phi	.874	Connor-NY	156	Tiernan-NY	39.5	Tiernan-NY	43.0	Brodie-Bos	139	Tiernan-NY	128
Stovey-Bos	.870	Hamilton-Phi	154	Stovey-Bos	36.7	Connor-NY	35.5	Nash-Bos	133	Stovey-Bos	125
Holliday-Cin	.848	Holliday-Cin	148	Connor-NY	32.2	Stovey-Bos	26.3	Myers-Phi	132	Long-Bos	115
Connor-NY	.848	Browning-Pit-Cin	142	Holliday-Cin	25.7	Holliday-Cin	25.2	Zimmer-Cle	129	Latham-Cin	112

Total Average		Stolen Bases		Stolen Base Average		Stolen Base Runs		Fielding Runs		Total Player Rating	
Hamilton-Phi	1.270	Hamilton-Phi	111					Richardson-NY	49.1	Richardson-NY	4.6
Tiernan-NY	1.045	Latham-Cin	87					Griffin-Bro	25.7	Hamilton-Phi	3.9
Stovey-Bos	1.041	Griffin-Bro	65					Pfeffer-Chi	25.0	Latham-Cin	3.9
Latham-Cin	.974	Long-Bos	60					McPhee-Cin	23.3	Pfeffer-Chi	3.3
Connor-NY	.968							Latham-Cin	20.4	McPhee-Cin	3.3

Wins		Win Percentage		Games		Complete Games		Shutouts		Saves	
Hutchinson-Chi	44	J.Ewing-NY	.724	Hutchinson-Chi	66	Hutchinson-Chi	56	Rusie-NY	6	Nichols-Bos	3
Rusie-NY	33	Hutchinson-Chi	.698	Rusie-NY	61	Rusie-NY	52	Nichols-Bos	5	Clarkson-Bos	3
Clarkson-Bos	33	Staley-Pit-Bos	.649	Young-Cle	55	Baldwin-Pit	48	J.Ewing-NY	5	Young-Cle	2
Nichols-Bos	30	Nichols-Bos	.638	Clarkson-Bos	55	Clarkson-Bos	47	Hutchinson-Chi	4	Thornton-Phi	2
Young-Cle	27	Clarkson-Bos	.635			Nichols-Bos	45				

Innings Pitched		Fewest Hits/Game		Fewest BB/Game		Strikeouts		Strikeouts/Game		Ratio	
Hutchinson-Chi	561.0	Rusie-NY	7.03	Nichols-Bos	2.18	Rusie-NY	337	Rusie-NY	6.06	Staley-Pit-Bos	11.08
Rusie-NY	500.1	Baldwin-Pit	7.92	Staley-Pit-Bos	2.22	Hutchinson-Chi	261	Nichols-Bos	5.08	Hutchinson-Chi	11.12
Clarkson-Bos	460.2	J.Ewing-NY	7.92	Galvin-Pit	2.26	Nichols-Bos	240	J.Ewing-NY	4.61	Nichols-Bos	11.28
Baldwin-Pit	437.2	Hutchinson-Chi	8.15	Radbourn-Cin	2.56	Baldwin-Pit	197	Hutchinson-Chi	4.19	J.Ewing-NY	11.80
Mullane-Cin	426.1	Mullane-Cin	8.23	Hutchinson-Chi	2.86	King-Pit	160	Baldwin-Pit	4.05	Clarkson-Bos	11.80

Earned Run Average		Adjusted ERA		Opponents' Batting Avg.		Opponents' On Base Pct.		Starter Runs		Adjusted Starter Runs	
J.Ewing-NY	2.27	Nichols-Bos	153	Rusie-NY	.207	Staley-Pit-Bos	.292	Nichols-Bos	45.1	Nichols-Bos	59.6
Nichols-Bos	2.39	J.Ewing-NY	141	Baldwin-Pit	.228	Hutchinson-Chi	.293	Rusie-NY	43.9	Clarkson-Bos	43.9
Rusie-NY	2.55	Staley-Pit-Bos	138	J.Ewing-NY	.228	Nichols-Bos	.296	Hutchinson-Chi	33.5	Rusie-NY	35.7
Staley-Pit-Bos	2.58	Clarkson-Bos	131	Hutchinson-Chi	.233	J.Ewing-NY	.305	J.Ewing-NY	32.1	Staley-Pit-Bos	35.5
Baldwin-Pit	2.76	Rusie-NY	125	Mullane-Cin	.234	Clarkson-Bos	.305	Baldwin-Pit	28.6	Hutchinson-Chi	32.4

Clutch Pitching Index		Relief Runs		Adjusted Relief Runs		Relief Ranking		Total Pitcher Index		Total Baseball Ranking	
Viau-Cle	117							Nichols-Bos	5.8	Nichols-Bos	5.8
Nichols-Bos	116							Clarkson-Bos	4.8	Clarkson-Bos	4.7
Caruthers-Bro	116							Rusie-NY	3.8	Richardson-NY	4.6
Galvin-Pit	112							Staley-Pit-Bos	3.1	Hamilton-Phi	3.9
J.Ewing-NY	111							Hutchinson-Chi	2.7	Latham-Cin	3.9

1891 American Association

TEAM	G	W	L	PCT	GB	R	OR	AB	H	2B	3B	HR	BB	SO	AVG	OBP	SLG	PRO	PRO+	BR	/A	PF	CHI	RC	SB	CS	SBA	SBR
BOS	139	93	42	.689		1028	675	4889	1341	163	100	52	651	499	.274	.367	.380	.747	124	149	162	99	104	868	447			
STL	141	86	52	.623	8.5	976	753	5005	1330	169	51	58	625	440	.266	.357	.355	.712	97	88	-41	115	103	753	283			
MIL	36	21	15	.583	22.5	227	156	1271	332	58	15	13	107	114	.261	.333	.361	.694	88	9	-34	120	103	173	47			
BAL	139	71	64	.526	22	850	798	4771	1217	142	99	30	551	553	.255	.346	.345	.691	105	45	36	101	99	705	342			
PHI	143	73	66	.525	22	817	794	5039	1301	182	123	55	447	548	.258	.328	.376	.704	106	46	21	103	93	686	149			
COL	138	61	76	.445	33	702	777	4697	1113	154	61	20	529	530	.237	.319	.308	.627	92	-70	-25	94	97	565	280			
CIN	102	43	57	.430	32.5	549	643	3574	838	105	58	28	428	385	.234	.322	.320	.642	84	-34	-87	109	96	432	164			
LOU	141	55	84	.396	40	713	890	4833	1247	130	69	17	468	473	.258	.329	.324	.653	95	-30	-20	99	92	606	230			
WAS	139	44	91	.326	49	691	1067	4715	1183	147	84	19	468	485	.251	.328	.330	.658	101	-21	15	96	90	597	219			
TOT	559					6553		38794	9902	1250	660	292	4249	4027	.255	.329	.344	.673						2161				

TEAM	CG	SH	SV	IP	H	H/G	HR	BB	SO	RAT	ERA	ERA+	OAV	OOB	PR	/A	PF	CPI	FA	E	DP	FW	PW	BW	SBW	DIF
BOS	108	9	7	1219²	1158	8.5	42	497	524	12.6	3.03	115	.242	.321	94	62	94	109	.934	392	115	4.0	5.3	14.0		2.2
STL	103	8	5	1222²	1106	8.1	50	576	621	12.9	3.27	129	.234	.325	61	126	113	102	.920	468	91	-.2	10.9	-3.5		9.8
MIL	35	3	0	309²	291	8.5	6	120	137	12.2	2.50	176	.241	.314	42	65	118	122	.922	116	20	.2	5.6	-2.9		.2
BAL	118	6	2	1217	1238	9.2	33	472	408	13.1	3.43	109	.255	.329	39	40	100	103	.915	503	103	-2.6	3.4	3.1		-.4
PHI	135	3	0	1233²	1274	9.3	35	520	533	13.6	4.01	95	.258	.338	-40	-27	103	93	.933	389	109	4.9	-2.3	1.8		-.9
COL	118	6	0	1213¹	1141	8.5	29	588	502	13.5	3.75	92	.241	.336	-4	-39	93	93	.935	379	126	4.5	-3.4	-2.2		-6.5
CIN	86	2	1	902	921	9.2	20	446	331	14.2	3.43	120	.256	.347	29	68	111	112	.913	389	68	-3.1	5.9	-7.5		-2.3
LOU	128	9	1	1226	1353	9.9	33	464	485	13.8	4.27	85	.271	.341	-75	-85	98	92	.922	458	113	.4	-7.3	-1.7		-5.9
WAS	123	2	2	1181	1420	10.8	44	566	486	15.9	4.83	77	.288	.374	-146	-144	101	101	.900	589	95	-7.7	-12.4	1.3		-4.7
TOT	954	48	18	9725		9.2				13.6	3.72		.255	.329					.922	3683	840					

Runs
Brown-Bos 177
VanHaltren-Bal .. 136
Hoy-StL 136
Duffy-Bos 134
McCarthy-StL ... 127

Hits
Brown-Bos 189
VanHaltren-Bal .. 180
Duffy-Bos 180
McCarthy-StL ... 179
Brouthers-Bos ... 170

Doubles
Milligan-Phi 35
Brown-Bos 30
O'Neill-StL 28
Duffee-Col 28
Larkin-Phi 27

Triples
Brown-Bos 21
Brouthers-Bos 19
Canavan-Cin-Mil .. 18
Werden-Bal 18

Home Runs
Farrell-Bos 12
Milligan-Phi 11
Lyons-StL 11

Total Bases
Brown-Bos 276
VanHaltren-Bal ... 251
Brouthers-Bos ... 249
Duffy-Bos 243
McCarthy-StL 236

Runs Batted In
Farrell-Bos 110
Duffy-Bos 110
Brouthers-Bos ... 109
Milligan-Phi 106
Werden-Bal 104

Runs Produced
Brown-Bos 243
Duffy-Bos 235
Brouthers-Bos ... 221
McCarthy-StL ... 214
VanHaltren-Bal ... 210

Bases On Balls
Hoy-StL 119
Crooks-Col 103
McTamany-Col-Phi 101
Radford-Bos 96
Johnson-Bal 89

Batting Average
Brouthers-Bos .... .350
Duffy-Bos .... .336
Brown-Bos .... .321
O'Neill-StL .... .321
VanHaltren-Bal ... .318

On Base Percentage
Brouthers-Bos .... .471
Lyons-StL .... .445
Hoy-StL .... .424
Seery-Cin .... .423
Duffy-Bos .... .408

Slugging Average
Brouthers-Bos .... .512
Milligan-Phi ...... .505
Farrell-Bos .... .474
Brown-Bos .... .469
Cross-Phi .... .458

Production
Brouthers-Bos .... .983
Milligan-Phi ...... .903
Lyons-StL .... .900
Brown-Bos .... .865
Duffy-Bos .... .861

Adjusted Production
Brouthers-Bos 188
Milligan-Phi 157
Brown-Bos 153
Duffy-Bos 152
Farrell-Bos 151

Batter Runs
Brouthers-Bos 59.1
Lyons-StL 41.2
Brown-Bos 37.9
Milligan-Phi 35.5
Duffy-Bos 34.5

Adjusted Batter Runs
Brouthers-Bos 60.5
Brown-Bos 39.4
Duffy-Bos 35.9
Milligan-Phi 33.1
VanHaltren-Bal ... 31.5

Clutch Hitting Index
Sneed-Col 154
Comiskey-StL 150
Wolf-Lou 143
Radford-Bos 138
Johnson-Bal 132

Runs Created
Brown-Bos 155
Duffy-Bos 137
Brouthers-Bos ... 135
VanHaltren-Bal ... 133
Hoy-StL 114

Total Average
Brouthers-Bos ... 1.237
Brown-Bos 1.140
Duffy-Bos 1.104
VanHaltren-Bal .. 1.039
Lyons-StL 1.036

Stolen Bases
Brown-Bos 106
Duffy-Bos 85
VanHaltren-Bal ... 75
Hoy-StL 59
Radford-Bos 55

Stolen Base Average

Stolen Base Runs

Fielding Runs
Stricker-Bos 24.2
Radford-Bos 19.9
Crooks-Col 19.6
Eagan-StL 19.5
Farrell-Bos 19.0

Total Player Rating
Farrell-Bos 4.6
Brouthers-Bos 4.0
Crooks-Col 3.5
Milligan-Phi 3.4
Radford-Bos 3.1

Wins
McMahon-Bal 35
Haddock-Bos 34
Stivetts-StL 33
Weyhing-Phi 31
Buffinton-Bos 29

Win Percentage
Buffinton-Bos .... .763
Haddock-Bos .... .756
Weyhing-Phi ..... .608
Stivetts-StL ...... .600
McMahon-Bal .... .593

Games
Stivetts-StL 64
McMahon-Bal 61
Knell-Col 58
Carsey-Was 54
Weyhing-Phi 52

Complete Games
McMahon-Bal 53
Weyhing-Phi 51
Knell-Col 47
Carsey-Was 46
Chamberlain-Phi .. 44

Shutouts
McMahon-Bal 5
Knell-Col 5
Haddock-Bos 5

Saves
O'Brien-Bos 2
Daley-Bos 2

Innings Pitched
McMahon-Bal .. 503.0
Knell-Col 462.0
Weyhing-Phi 450.0
Stivetts-StL 440.0
Carsey-Was 415.0

Fewest Hits/Game
Knell-Col 7.07
Stivetts-StL 7.30
Buffinton-Bos 7.50
Crane-Cin 7.78
Haddock-Bos 7.82

Fewest BB/Game
Stratton-Lou 1.78
Sanders-Phi 2.30
McMahon-Bal 2.67
Ehret-Lou 2.85
Griffith-StL-Bos ... 2.90

Strikeouts
Stivetts-StL 259
Knell-Col 228
Weyhing-Phi 219
McMahon-Bal 219
Chamberlain-Phi .. 204

Strikeouts/Game
Meekin-Lou 5.68
Stivetts-StL 5.30
McGill-Cin-StL 4.96
Daley-Bos 4.83
Chamberlain-Phi .. 4.53

Ratio
Buffinton-Bos ... 10.64
Haddock-Bos ... 11.40
McMahon-Bal ... 11.79
Weyhing-Phi 12.40
Stivetts-StL 12.42

Earned Run Average
Crane-Cin 2.45
Haddock-Bos 2.49
Buffinton-Bos 2.55
McMahon-Bal 2.81
Stivetts-StL 2.86

Adjusted ERA
Crane-Cin 168
Stivetts-StL 147
Haddock-Bos 140
Buffinton-Bos 137
Mains-Cin-Mil 134

Opponents' Batting Avg.
Knell-Col .... .209
Stivetts-StL ...... .215
Buffinton-Bos .... .219
Crane-Cin .... .225
Haddock-Bos .... .226

Opponents' On Base Pct.
Buffinton-Bos .... .285
Haddock-Bos .... .299
McMahon-Bal .... .306
Weyhing-Phi ..... .317
Stivetts-StL ...... .317

Starter Runs
Haddock-Bos 51.9
McMahon-Bal 50.9
Buffinton-Bos 47.3
Stivetts-StL 41.8
Knell-Col 40.9

Adjusted Starter Runs
Stivetts-StL 65.5
McMahon-Bal 51.7
Crane-Cin 46.3
Haddock-Bos 42.0
Buffinton-Bos 37.8

Clutch Pitching Index
Daley-Bos 134
Crane-Cin 128
O'Brien-Bos 123
Mains-Cin-Mil 122
Foreman-Was 113

Relief Runs

Adjusted Relief Runs

Relief Ranking

Total Pitcher Index
Stivetts-StL 7.1
Haddock-Bos 5.0
McMahon-Bal 4.8
Buffinton-Bos 3.9
Crane-Cin 3.5

Total Baseball Ranking
Stivetts-StL 7.0
Haddock-Bos 4.8
McMahon-Bal 4.7
Farrell-Bos 4.6
Brouthers-Bos 4.0

TEAM	G	W	L	PCT	GB	R	OR	AB	H	2B	3B	HR	BB	SO	AVG	OBP	SLG	PRO	PRO+	BR	/A	PF	CHI	RC	SB	CS	SBA	SBR
BOS	152	102	48	.680		862	649	5301	1324	203	51	34	526	488	.250	.325	.327	.652	95	32	-39	109	106	689	338			
CLE	153	93	56	.624	8.5	855	613	5412	1375	196	96	26	552	536	.254	.328	.340	.668	105	62	30	104	99	694	225			
BRO	158	95	59	.617	9	935	733	5485	1439	183	105	30	629	506	.262	.344	.350	.694	121	124	154	96	99	822	409			
PHI	155	87	66	.569	16.5	860	690	5413	1420	225	95	50	528	515	.262	.334	.367	.701	119	-9	2	99	99	753	216			
CIN	155	82	68	.547	20	766	731	5349	1288	155	75	44	503	474	.241	.311	.322	.633	99			99	99	635	270			
PIT	155	80	73	.523	23.5	802	796	5469	1288	143	108	38	435	453	.236	.297	.322	.619	94	-44	-47	100	107	604	222			
CHI	147	70	76	.479	30	635	735	5063	1188	149	92	26	427	482	.235	.299	.316	.615	92	-46	-54	101	92	561	233			
NY	153	71	80	.470	31.5	811	826	5291	1326	173	85	39	510	469	.251	.320	.338	.658	108	39	51	98	100	686	301			
LOU	154	63	89	.414	40	649	804	5334	1208	133	61	18	433	508	.226	.290	.284	.574	87	-120	-58	92	99	533	275			
WAS	153	58	93	.384	44.5	731	869	5204	1245	149	78	37	529	553	.239	.314	.319	.633	101	-4	18	97	96	624	276			
STL	155	56	94	.373	46	703	922	5259	1187	160	53	45	607	491	.226	.312	.298	.610	96	-40	-1	95	94	568	209			
BAL	152	46	101	.313	54.5	779	1020	5296	1342	160	111	30	499	480	.253	.325	.343	.668	106	58	37	103	93	680	227			
TOT	921					9388		63876	15630	2007	1010	417	6178	5955	.245	.311	.327	.639							3201			

TEAM	CG	SH	SV	IP	H	H/G	HR	BB	SO	RAT	ERA	ERA+	OAV	OOB	PR	/A	PF	CPI	FA	E	DP	FW	PW	BW	SBW	DIF
BOS	142	15	1	1336	1156	7.8	41	460	509	11.1	2.86	123	.224	.292	64	96	107	93	.929	454	127	.5	8.9	-3.6		21.3
CLE	140	11	2	1336	1178	7.9	28	413	472	10.9	2.41	140	.228	.289	130	143	103	107	.935	407	95	3.4	13.2	2.8		-.9
BRO	132	12	5	1405²	1285	8.2	26	600	597	12.4	3.25	97	.234	.315	6	-14	96	95	.940	398	98	4.8	-1.3	14.3		.2
PHI	131	10	5	1379	1297	8.5	24	492	502	12.0	2.93	111	.239	.309	54	47	99	103	.939	393	128	4.5	4.4	11.4		-9.8
CIN	130	8	2	1377¹	1327	8.7	39	535	437	12.5	3.17	103	.243	.317	18	15	99	104	.939	402	140	4.0	1.4	.2		1.4
PIT	130	3	1	1347¹	1300	8.7	28	537	455	12.7	3.10	106	.244	.320	28	27	100	106	.927	483	113	-.7	2.5	-4.4		6.0
CHI	133	6	1	1298	1269	8.8	35	424	518	12.0	3.16	105	.246	.308	18	22	101	100	.932	424	85	1.3	2.0	-5.0		-1.4
NY	139	5	1	1322²	1165	7.9	32	635	641	12.6	3.29	98	.227	.318	-1	-11	98	94	.912	565	97	-5.8	-1.0	4.7		-2.4
LOU	147	9	0	1346	1358	9.1	26	441	430	12.3	3.34	97	.252	.313	-8	-41	93	97	.928	451	133	-.2	-3.8	-5.4		-3.7
WAS	129	5	3	1315¹	1293	8.8	40	556	479	13.1	3.46	94	.247	.327	-26	-32	99	102	.926	547	122	-4.8	-3.0	1.7		-11.4
STL	139	4	1	1344²	1466	9.8	47	543	478	13.8	4.20	76	.267	.339	-137	-151	97	96	.929	452	100	1.1	-14.0	-.0		-6.0
BAL	131	2	2	1298²	1537	10.7	51	536	437	14.7	4.28	80	.284	.353	-144	-124	104	106	.910	584	100	-7.1	-11.5	3.4		-12.3
TOT	1623	90	24	16106²		8.7				12.5	3.28		.245	.311					.928	5580	1338					

Split Season: First-half Winner BOS (52-22); Second-half Winner CLE (53-23)

Runs		Hits		Doubles		Triples		Home Runs		Total Bases	
Childs-Cle	136	Brouthers-Bro	197	Connor-Phi	37	Delahanty-Phi	21	Holliday-Cin	13	Brouthers-Bro	282
Hamilton-Phi	132	Thompson-Phi	186	Long-Bos	33	Virtue-Cle	20	Connor-Phi	12	Holliday-Cin	270
Duffy-Bos	125	Duffy-Bos	184	Delahanty-Phi	30	Brouthers-Bro	20	Ryan-Chi	10	Thompson-Phi	263
Connor-Phi	123	Hamilton-Phi	183	Brouthers-Bro	30	Dahlen-Chi	19	Beckley-Pit	10	Connor-Phi	261
Brouthers-Bro	121	Long-Bos	181	Zimmer-Cle	29	Beckley-Pit	19	Thompson-Phi	9	Duffy-Bos	251

Runs Batted In		Runs Produced		Bases On Balls		Batting Average		On Base Percentage		Slugging Average	
Brouthers-Bro	124	Brouthers-Bro	240	Crooks-StL	136	Brouthers-Bro	.335	Childs-Cle	.443	Delahanty-Phi	.495
Thompson-Phi	104	Thompson-Phi	204	Childs-Cle	117	Hamilton-Phi	.330	Brouthers-Bro	.432	Brouthers-Bro	.480
Larkin-Was	96	Duffy-Bos	201	Connor-Phi	116	Childs-Cle	.317	Hamilton-Phi	.423	Connor-Phi	.463
Burns-Bro	96	Holliday-Cin	192	McCarthy-Bos	93	Burns-Bro	.315	Connor-Phi	.420	Burns-Bro	.454
Beckley-Pit	96					Delahanty-Phi	.306	Crooks-StL	.400	Holliday-Cin	.449

Production		Adjusted Production		Batter Runs		Adjusted Batter Runs		Clutch Hitting Index		Runs Created	
Brouthers-Bro	.911	Brouthers-Bro	185	Brouthers-Bro	58.4	Brouthers-Bro	61.8	McKean-Cle	159	Brouthers-Bro	138
Connor-Phi	.883	Connor-Phi	170	Connor-Phi	52.1	Connor-Phi	52.4	Nash-Bos	158	Hamilton-Phi	123
Delahanty-Phi	.855	Burns-Bro	165	Childs-Cle	47.0	Childs-Cle	43.4	Larkin-Was	152	Connor-Phi	122
Burns-Bro	.849	Delahanty-Phi	160	Hamilton-Phi	40.4	Burns-Bro	41.8	Corcoran-Bro	138	VanHaltren-Bal-Pit	117
Childs-Cle	.841	Hamilton-Phi	155	Burns-Bro	38.8	Hamilton-Phi	40.6	Comiskey-Cin	137	Holliday-Cin	114

Total Average		Stolen Bases		Stolen Base Average	Stolen Base Runs	Fielding Runs		Total Player Rating	
Brouthers-Bro	1.056	Ward-Bro	88			D.Richardson-Was	57.6	Brouthers-Bro	6.1
Connor-Phi	1.018	Brown-Lou	78			Shindle-Bal	35.5	Dahlen-Chi	4.7
Hamilton-Phi	1.005	Latham-Cin	66			Bierbauer-Pit	31.7	McPhee-Cin	4.6
Childs-Cle	.982	Hoy-Was	60			McPhee-Cin	25.3	Hamilton-Phi	4.4
Burns-Bro	.943	Dahlen-Chi	60			Dahlen-Chi	25.2	D.Richardson-Was	4.2

Wins		Win Percentage		Games		Complete Games		Shutouts		Saves	
Hutchinson-Chi	37	Young-Cle	.750	Hutchinson-Chi	75	Hutchinson-Chi	67	Young-Cle	9	Weyhing-Phi	3
Young-Cle	36	Terry-Bal-Pit	.692	Rusie-NY	64	Rusie-NY	58	Weyhing-Phi	6	Duryea-Cin-Was	2
Stivetts-Bos	35	Haddock-Bro	.690	Killen-Was	60	Nichols-Bos	49	Stein-Bro	6		
Nichols-Bos	35	Staley-Bos	.688	Weyhing-Phi	59	Young-Cle	48				
Weyhing-Phi	32			Baldwin-Pit	56						

Innings Pitched		Fewest Hits/Game		Fewest BB/Game		Strikeouts		Strikeouts/Game		Ratio	
Hutchinson-Chi	627.0	Mullane-Cin	6.77	Stratton-Lou	1.79	Hutchinson-Chi	316	Kennedy-Bro	5.09	Young-Cle	9.77
Rusie-NY	532.0	Rusie-NY	6.85	Dwyer-StL-Cin	2.03	Rusie-NY	288	Rusie-NY	4.87	Nichols-Bos	10.63
Weyhing-Phi	469.2	Terry-Bal-Pit	6.94	Sanders-Lou	2.08	Weyhing-Phi	202	Hutchinson-Chi	4.54	Stratton-Lou	10.77
Killen-Was	459.2	Young-Cle	7.21	Young-Cle	2.34	Stein-Bro	190	Stein-Bro	4.53	Keefe-Phi	10.83
		Duryea-Cin-Was	7.25	Ehret-Pit	2.36	Nichols-Bos	187	Crane-NY	4.30	Mullane-Cin	11.01

Earned Run Average		Adjusted ERA		Opponents' Batting Avg.		Opponents' On Base Pct.		Starter Runs		Adjusted Starter Runs	
Young-Cle	1.93	Young-Cle	176	Mullane-Cin	.201	Young-Cle	.266	Young-Cle	68.3	Young-Cle	73.4
Keefe-Phi	2.36	J.Clarkson-Bos-Cle	139	Rusie-NY	.203	Nichols-Bos	.283	Hutchinson-Chi	37.8	J.Clarkson-Bos-Cle	41.3
J.Clarkson-Bos-Cle	2.48	Keefe-Phi	138	Terry-Bal-Pit	.205	Stratton-Lou	.286	J.Clarkson-Bos-Cle	35.0	Hutchinson-Chi	40.3
Cuppy-Cle	2.51	Cuppy-Cle	135	Young-Cle	.211	Keefe-Phi	.287	Weyhing-Phi	32.4	Cuppy-Cle	36.5
Terry-Bal-Pit	2.57	Davies-Cle	131	Duryea-Cin-Was	.212	Mullane-Cin	.290	Keefe-Phi	32.3	Nichols-Bos	33.6

Clutch Pitching Index		Relief Runs	Adjusted Relief Runs	Relief Ranking	Total Pitcher Index		Total Baseball Ranking	
Sullivan-Cin	136				Young-Cle	7.0	Young-Cle	7.0
Galvin-Pit-StL	122				Hutchinson-Chi	4.6	Brouthers-Bro	6.1
Luby-Chi	117				Cuppy-Cle	3.9	Dahlen-Chi	4.7
Vickery-Bal	116				Stivetts-Bos	3.7	McPhee-Cin	4.6
McMahon-Bal	115				J.Clarkson-Bos-Cle	3.5	Hutchinson-Chi	4.5

TEAM	G	W	L	PCT	GB	R	OR	AB	H	2B	3B	HR	BB	SO	AVG	OBP	SLG	PRO	PRO+	BR	/A	PF	CHI	RC	SB	CS	SBA	SBR
BOS	131	86	43	.667		1008	795	4678	1358	178	50	65	**561**	292	.290	.372	.391	.763	101	70	2	108	**109**	790	243			
PIT	131	81	48	.628	5	970	**766**	4834	1447	176	**127**	37	537	273	.299	.377	.411	.788	118	113	**130**	98	98	848	210			
CLE	129	73	55	.570	12.5	976	839	4747	1425	222	98	32	532	**229**	.300	.374	.408	.782	108	100	48	106	102	841	252			
PHI	133	72	57	.558	14	**1011**	841	5151	**1553**	**246**	90	**80**	468	335	.301	.368	**.431**	**.799**	119	**125**	128	100	97	**912**	202			
NY	136	68	64	.515	19.5	941	845	4858	1424	182	101	61	04	279	.293	.366	.410	.776	113	85	82	100	98	860	**299**			
CIN	131	65	63	.508	20.5	759	814	4617	1195	161	65	29	532	256	.259	.342	.341	.683	86	-72	-92	102	99	634	238			
BRO	130	65	63	.508	20.5	775	845	4511	1200	173	83	45	473	296	.266	.341	.371	.712	100	-30	7	95	99	659	213			
BAL	130	60	70	.462	26.5	820	893	4651	1281	164	86	27	537	323	.275	.359	.365	.724	97	3	-11	102	96	711	233			
CHI	128	56	71	.441	29	829	874	4664	1299	186	93	32	465	262	.279	.348	.379	.727	101	-4	9	99	100	722	255			
STL	135	57	75	.432	30.5	745	829	4879	1288	152	98	10	524	251	.264	.343	.341	.684	88	-72	-74	100	92	674	250			
LOU	126	50	75	.400	34	759	942	4566	1185	177	73	19	485	306	.260	.338	.343	.681	94	-77	-12	92	101	612	203			
WAS	130	40	89	.310	46	722	1032	4742	1260	180	83	23	524	237	.266	.347	.353	.700	95	-44	-21	97	88	650	154			
TOT	785					10315		56898	15915	2197	1047	460	6142	3339	.280	.350	.379	.729						2752				

TEAM	CG	SH	SV	IP	H	H/G	HR	BB	SO	RAT	ERA	ERA+	OAV	OOB	PR	/A	PF	CPI	FA	E	DP	FW	PW	BW	SBW	DIF
BOS	**114**	2	2	1163²	1314	10.2	66	402	253	**13.6**	4.43	111	.277	**.339**	30	64	106	100	.936	353	118	1.8	5.2	.2		14.3
PIT	104	**8**	2	1167	**1232**	9.5	29	504	280	13.8	4.08	112	.263	.342	75	60	98	101	.938	347	112	2.1	4.9	**10.7**		-1.2
CLE	110	2	2	1140¹	1361	10.7	35	**356**	242	13.8	4.20	116	.288	.342	59	86	105	**106**	.929	395	92	-.9	7.1	3.9		-1.1
PHI	107	4	2	1189	1359	10.3	30	521	283	14.8	4.68	98	.279	.358	-2	-14	98	99	**.944**	318	121	**4.1**	-1.1	10.5		-5.9
NY	111	6	4	1211¹	1271	**9.4**	36	581	**395**	14.2	4.29	108	**.262**	.347	49	48	100	99	.927	432	95	-1.8	3.9	6.7		-6.8
CIN	97	4	**5**	1172	1305	10.0	38	549	258	14.8	4.55	105	.243	.357	15	30	103	101	.943	321	**138**	3.6	2.5	-7.5		2.5
BRO	109	3	3	1154	1262	9.8	41	547	297	14.4	4.55	97	.270	.352	15	-16	95	98	.930	385	88	-.2	-1.3	.6		1.9
BAL	104	1	2	1123²	1325	10.6	29	534	275	15.2	4.97	95	.285	.364	-39	-30	102	97	.929	384	95	-.1	-2.5	-.9		-1.5
CHI	101	4	5	1117¹	1278	10.4	26	553	273	15.3	4.81	96	.271	.365	-18	-24	99	99	.922	421	92	-2.5	-2.0	.7		-3.7
STL	**114**	4	4	1207	1292	9.6	38	542	301	14.1	4.06	116	.266	.346	80	88	101	105	.930	398	110	-.0	**7.2**	-6.1		-10.1
LOU	113	4	1	1080	1431	11.9	38	479	190	16.3	5.90	74	.310	.380	-149	-181	94	94	.937	330	111	2.2	-14.8	-1.0		1.1
WAS	110	2	0	1139	1485	11.7	54	574	292	16.7	5.56	83	.306	.387	-114	-120	99	103	.912	497	96	-6.5	-9.8	-1.7		-6.5
TOT	1294	43	32	13864¹		10.3				14.7	4.66		.280	.350					.931	4581	1268					

Runs		Hits		Doubles		Triples		Home Runs		Total Bases	
Long-Bos	149	Thompson-Phi	222	Thompson-Phi	37	Werden-StL	29	Delahanty-Phi	19	Delahanty-Phi	347
Duffy-Bos	147	Delahanty-Phi	219	Delahanty-Phi	35	Davis-NY	27	Clements-Phi	17	Thompson-Phi	318
Delahanty-Phi	145	Duffy-Bos	203	Tebeau-Cle	32	McKean-Cle	24	Tiernan-NY	14	Davis-NY	304
Childs-Cle	145	Davis-NY	195	Beckley-Pit	32	Smith-Pit	23	Lowe-Bos	14	Smith-Pit	272
Burkett-Cle	145	Ward-NY	193			Beckley-Pit	19				

Runs Batted In		Runs Produced		Bases On Balls		Batting Average		On Base Percentage		Slugging Average	
Delahanty-Phi	146	Delahanty-Phi	272	Crooks-StL	121	Hamilton-Phi	.380	Hamilton-Phi	.490	Delahanty-Phi	.583
McKean-Cle	133	Duffy-Bos	259	Childs-Cle	120	Thompson-Phi	.370	Childs-Cle	.463	Davis-NY	.554
Thompson-Phi	126	Thompson-Phi	245	Radford-Was	105	Delahanty-Phi	.368	Burkett-Cle	.459	Thompson-Phi	.530
Nash-Bos	123	Ewing-Cle	233	McGraw-Bal	101	Duffy-Bos	.363	McGraw-Bal	.454	Smith-Pit	.525
Ewing-Cle	122	McKean-Cle	232	Burkett-Cle	98	Davis-NY	.355	Smith-Pit	.435	Hamilton-Phi	.524

Production		Adjusted Production		Batter Runs		Adjusted Batter Runs		Clutch Hitting Index		Runs Created	
Hamilton-Phi	1.014	Hamilton-Phi	172	Delahanty-Phi	54.6	Delahanty-Phi	54.9	Anson-Chi	172	Delahanty-Phi	167
Delahanty-Phi	1.007	Delahanty-Phi	169	Burkett-Cle	45.3	Thompson-Phi	45.6	Vaughn-Cin	172	Thompson-Phi	146
Davis-NY	.964	Smith-Pit	160	Thompson-Phi	45.3	Smith-Pit	45.0	Nash-Bos	149	Davis-NY	143
Smith-Pit	.960	Davis-NY	157	Smith-Pit	43.1	Davis-NY	41.5	McCarthy-Bos	140	Burkett-Cle	137
Thompson-Phi	.954	Thompson-Phi	155	Davis-NY	41.8	Hamilton-Phi	41.2	Lyons-Pit	139	Smith-Pit	133

Total Average		Stolen Bases		Stolen Base Average		Stolen Base Runs		Fielding Runs		Total Player Rating	
Hamilton-Phi	1.386	T.Brown-Lou	66					McPhee-Cin	34.0	Delahanty-Phi	6.4
Burkett-Cle	1.186	Dowd-StL	59					Delahanty-Phi	30.8	McPhee-Cin	3.7
Delahanty-Phi	1.173	Latham-Cin	57					T.Brown-Lou	27.1	Davis-NY	3.6
Smith-Pit	1.121	Burke-NY	54					G.Smith-Cin	19.5	Childs-Cle	3.4
Davis-NY	1.107	Brodie-StL-Bal	49					Allen-Phi	18.4	Smith-Pit	3.4

Wins		Win Percentage		Games		Complete Games		Shutouts		Saves	
Killen-Pit	36	Gastright-Pit-Bos	.750	Rusie-NY	56	Rusie-NY	50	Rusie-NY	4	Mullane-Cin-Bal	2
Young-Cle	34	Killen-Pit	.720	Killen-Pit	55	Nichols-Bos	43	Ehret-Pit	4	Baldwin-Pit-NY	2
Nichols-Bos	34	Nichols-Bos	.708	Young-Cle	53	Young-Cle	42			Dwyer-Cin	2
Rusie-NY	33	Young-Cle	.680	Nichols-Bos	52	Kennedy-Bro	40			Donnelly-Chi	2
Kennedy-Bro	25	Staley-Bos	.643	Mullane-Cin-Bal	49					Colcolough-Pit	2

Innings Pitched		Fewest Hits/Game		Fewest BB/Game		Strikeouts		Strikeouts/Game		Ratio	
Rusie-NY	482.0	Rusie-NY	8.42	Young-Cle	2.19	Rusie-NY	208	Rusie-NY	3.88	Young-Cle	11.82
Nichols-Bos	425.0	Breitenstein-StL	8.44	Nichols-Bos	2.50	Kennedy-Bro	107	Meekin-Was	3.34	Nichols-Bos	11.84
Young-Cle	422.2	Killen-Pit	8.70	Cuppy-Cle	2.77	Young-Cle	102	Hawley-StL	2.89	Killen-Pit	12.06
Killen-Pit	415.0	Kennedy-Bro	8.84	Staley-Bos	2.77	Breitenstein-StL	102	Terry-Pit	2.75	Breitenstein-StL	12.30
		Stein-Bro	8.87	Stratton-Lou	2.86	Weyhing-Phi	101	Hawke-StL-Bal	2.74	Stein-Bro	12.70

Earned Run Average		Adjusted ERA		Opponents' Batting Avg.		Opponents' On Base Pct.		Starter Runs		Adjusted Starter Runs	
Breitenstein-StL	3.18	Breitenstein-StL	149	Rusie-NY	.240	Young-Cle	.308	Rusie-NY	76.6	Rusie-NY	76.1
Rusie-NY	3.23	Young-Cle	145	Breitenstein-StL	.241	Nichols-Bos	.308	Breitenstein-StL	63.2	Young-Cle	71.2
Young-Cle	3.36	Rusie-NY	144	Killen-Pit	.246	Killen-Pit	.312	Young-Cle	60.9	Nichols-Bos	66.9
Ehret-Pit	3.44	Nichols-Bos	140	Kennedy-Bro	.249	Breitenstein-StL	.316	Nichols-Bos	54.1	Breitenstein-StL	65.9
Clarkson-StL	3.48	Clarkson-StL	136	Stein-Bro	.250	Stein-Bro	.323	Killen-Pit	46.9	Killen-Pit	41.8

Clutch Pitching Index		Relief Runs		Adjusted Relief Runs		Relief Ranking		Total Pitcher Index		Total Baseball Ranking	
Esper-Was	120							Rusie-NY	7.1	Rusie-NY	7.1
Clarkson-StL	117							Young-Cle	6.0	Delahanty-Phi	6.4
McNabb-Bal	113							Breitenstein-StL	5.5	Young-Cle	6.0
Cuppy-Cle	111							Nichols-Bos	5.4	Breitenstein-StL	5.4
Rusie-NY	111							Killen-Pit	4.9	Nichols-Bos	5.3

TEAM	G	W	L	PCT	GB	R	OR	AB	H	2B	3B	HR	BB	SO	AVG	OBP	SLG	PRO	PRO+	BR	/A	PF	CHI	RC	SB	CS	SBA	SBR
BAL	129	89	39	.695		1171	819	4799	1647	271	150	33	516	200	.343	.418	.483	.901	118	188	144	104	98	1146	324			
NY	137	88	44	.667	3	940	789	4806	1446	197	96	43	476	217	.301	.368	.409	.777	94	-52	-44	99	102	869	319			
BOS	133	83	49	.629	8	1220	1002	5011	1658	272	94	103	535	261	.331	.401	.484	.885	110	151	70	108	104	1102	241			
PHI	129	71	57	.555	18	1143	966	4967	1732	252	131	40	496	245	.349	.414	.476	.890	123	172	198	97	96	1132	273			
BRO	134	70	61	.534	20.5	1021	1007	4816	1507	228	130	42	466	294	.313	.378	.440	.818	111	20	89	93	102	941	282			
CLE	130	68	61	.527	21.5	932	896	4764	1442	241	90	37	471	301	.303	.368	.414	.782	91	-41	-78	104	101	837	220			
PIT	132	65	65	.500	25	955	972	4676	1458	222	124	48	434	208	.312	.379	.443	.822	105	26	36	99	96	921	256			
CHI	135	57	75	.432	34	1041	1066	4960	1555	265	86	65	496	298	.314	.380	.441	.821	98	28	-26	105	101	987	327			
STL	133	56	76	.424	35	771	953	4610	1320	171	113	54	442	289	.286	.354	.408	.762	89	-85	-85	100	90	763	190			
CIN	132	55	75	.423	35	910	1085	4671	1374	224	67	61	508	252	.294	.368	.410	.778	90	-46	-82	104	100	812	215			
WAS	132	45	87	.341	46	882	1122	4581	1317	218	118	59	467	375	.287	.381	.425	.806	103	9	40	97	91	864	249			
LOU	130	36	94	.277	54	692	1001	4482	1206	173	88	42	350	364	.269	.330	.375	.705	80	-184	-123	93	97	859	217			
TOT	793					11678		57143	17662	2734	1287	627	5807	3304	.309	.373	.435	.808							3113			

TEAM	CG	SH	SV	IP	H	H/G	HR	BB	SO	RAT	ERA	ERA+	OAV	OOB	PR	/A	PF	CPI	FA	E	DP	FW	PW	BW	SBW	DIF
BAL	97	1	11	1116[1]	1371	11.1	31	472	275	15.2	5.00	109	.299	.371	39	55	103	98	.944	293	105	5.6	4.2	11.0		4.1
NY	111	5	5	1212	1292	9.6	37	539	395	13.8	3.83	137	.271	.349	200	187	99	101	.924	443	101	-1.6	14.3	-3.4		12.6
BOS	108	3	1	1166	1529	11.8	89	411	262	15.3	5.41	105	.314	.372	-12	33	107	101	.925	415	120	-.7	2.5	5.4		9.8
PHI	102	3	4	1125[2]	1482	11.8	62	469	262	16.1	5.63	90	.314	.384	-39	-68	96	99	.935	338	111	3.0	-5.2	15.2		-6.0
BRO	105	3	5	1162[1]	1447	11.2	41	555	285	16.0	5.51	90	.302	.382	-25	-75	93	95	.928	390	85	.9	-5.8	6.8		2.5
CLE	106	6	1	1124[1]	1390	11.1	54	435	254	14.9	4.97	110	.301	.366	43	59	103	100	.935	344	107	2.9	4.5	-6.0		2.1
PIT	106	2	0	1164[2]	1552	12.0	39	457	304	14.8	5.60	97	.317	.380	-37	-50	98	96	.936	354	106	2.6	-3.8	2.8		-1.6
CHI	117	0	0	1148	1561	12.2	43	557	281	17.1	5.68	99	.322	.398	-47	-11	106	103	.918	452	113	-2.4	-.8	-2.0		-3.7
STL	114	2	0	1161	1418	11.0	48	500	319	15.2	5.29	102	.299	.371	4	14	102	94	.923	426	109	-1.3	1.1	-6.5		-3.3
CIN	110	4	3	1147[1]	1585	12.4	85	491	219	16.7	5.99	93	.325	.393	-85	-56	104	101	.925	423	119	-1.3	-4.3	-6.3		1.9
WAS	101	0	4	1107	1573	12.8	59	446	190	16.9	5.51	95	.331	.396	-24	-32	99	110	.908	499	81	-5.6	-2.5	3.1		-16.0
LOU	113	2	1	1096[2]	1462	12.0	39	475	258	16.3	5.45	93	.317	.386	-16	-44	96	101	.920	428	130	-1.9	-3.4	-9.4		-14.0
TOT	1290	31	35	13731[1]		11.6				15.8	5.32		.309	.373					.927	4805	1287					

Runs
Hamilton-Phi	192
Kelley-Bal	165
Keeler-Bal	165
Duffy-Bos	160
Lowe-Bos	158

Hits
Duffy-Bos	237
Hamilton-Phi	220
Keeler-Bal	219
Lowe-Bos	212
Brodie-Bal	210

Doubles
Duffy-Bos	51
Kelley-Bal	48
Wilmot-Chi	45

Triples
Reitz-Bal	31
Thompson-Phi	27
Treadway-Bro	26
Connor-NY-StL	25
Brouthers-Bal	23

Home Runs
Duffy-Bos	18
Lowe-Bos	17
Joyce-Was	17
Dahlen-Chi	15

Total Bases
Duffy-Bos	374
Lowe-Bos	319
Kelley-Bal	305
Keeler-Bal	305
Stenzel-Pit	303

Runs Batted In
Duffy-Bos	145
Thompson-Phi	141
E.Delahanty-Phi	131
Wilmot-Chi	130

Runs Produced
Duffy-Bos	287
Hamilton-Phi	275
E.Delahanty-Phi	274
Kelley-Bal	270
Wilmot-Chi	259

Bases On Balls
Hamilton-Phi	126
Kelley-Bal	107
Childs-Cle	107
Nash-Bos	91
McGraw-Bal	91

Batting Average
Duffy-Bos	.440
Thompson-Phi	.407
E.Delahanty-Phi	.407
Hamilton-Phi	.404
Kelley-Bal	.393

On Base Percentage
Hamilton-Phi	.523
Kelley-Bal	.502
Duffy-Bos	.502
Joyce-Was	.496
E.Delahanty-Phi	.478

Slugging Average
Duffy-Bos	.694
Thompson-Phi	.686
Joyce-Was	.648
Kelley-Bal	.602
E.Delahanty-Phi	.585

Production
Duffy-Bos	1.196
Thompson-Phi	1.145
Joyce-Was	1.143
Kelley-Bal	1.104
E.Delahanty-Phi	1.063

Adjusted Production
Joyce-Was	182
Thompson-Phi	179
Duffy-Bos	174
E.Delahanty-Phi	161
Kelley-Bal	160

Batter Runs
Duffy-Bos	77.2
Kelley-Bal	61.7
Hamilton-Phi	61.5
Thompson-Phi	50.6
Joyce-Was	48.3

Adjusted Batter Runs
Duffy-Bos	68.4
Hamilton-Phi	64.7
Kelley-Bal	56.7
Thompson-Phi	52.9
Joyce-Was	50.9

Clutch Hitting Index
Robinson-Bal	152
Bierbauer-Pit	141
Shindle-Bro	137
Decker-Chi	136
Ward-NY	136

Runs Created
Duffy-Bos	217
Hamilton-Phi	207
Kelley-Bal	182
Stenzel-Pit	165
Thompson-Phi	152

Total Average
Duffy-Bos	1.619
Hamilton-Phi	1.605
Joyce-Was	1.528
Kelley-Bal	1.503
Thompson-Phi	1.409

Stolen Bases
Hamilton-Phi	98
McGraw-Bal	78
Wilmot-Chi	74
T.Brown-Lou	66
Lange-Chi	65

Stolen Base Average

Stolen Base Runs

Fielding Runs
Jennings-Bal	33.1
Dahlen-Chi	31.6
McPhee-Cin	31.2
Farrell-NY	29.4
Reitz-Bal	26.4

Total Player Rating
Dahlen-Chi	5.0
Duffy-Bos	4.9
E.Delahanty-Phi	4.6
Hamilton-Phi	4.6
Kelley-Bal	3.8

Wins
Rusie-NY	36
Meekin-NY	33
Nichols-Bos	32
Breitenstein-StL	27

Win Percentage
Meekin-NY	.786
McMahon-Bal	.758
Rusie-NY	.735
Nichols-Bos	.711

Games
Breitenstein-StL	56
Rusie-NY	54
Hawley-StL	53
Young-Cle	52
Meekin-NY	52

Complete Games
Breitenstein-StL	46
Rusie-NY	45
Young-Cle	44
Nichols-Bos	40
Meekin-NY	40

Shutouts
Rusie-NY	3
Nichols-Bos	3
Cuppy-Cle	3

Saves
Mullane-Bal-Cle	4
Mercer-Was	3
Hawke-Bal	3

Innings Pitched
Breitenstein-StL	447.1
Rusie-NY	444.0
Meekin-NY	409.0
Young-Cle	408.2
Nichols-Bos	407.0

Fewest Hits/Game
Rusie-NY	8.64
Meekin-NY	8.89
Stein-Bro	9.98
Breitenstein-StL	10.00
Clarkson-Cle	10.33

Fewest BB/Game
Young-Cle	2.33
Menefee-Lou-Pit	2.48
Gleason-StL-Bal	2.54
Staley-Bos	2.63
Nichols-Bos	2.68

Strikeouts
Rusie-NY	195
Breitenstein-StL	140
Meekin-NY	133
Hawley-StL	120
Nichols-Bos	113

Strikeouts/Game
Rusie-NY	3.95
Hawke-Bal	2.97
Wadsworth-Lou	2.97
Meekin-NY	2.93
Chamberlain-Cin	2.89

Ratio
Rusie-NY	12.79
Meekin-NY	12.89
Clarkson-Cle	13.08
Young-Cle	13.19
Nichols-Bos	13.67

Earned Run Average
Rusie-NY	2.78
Meekin-NY	3.70
Mercer-Was	3.85
Young-Cle	3.94
Taylor-Phi	4.08

Adjusted ERA
Rusie-NY	189
Meekin-NY	142
Young-Cle	138
Mercer-Was	136
McMahon-Bal	129

Opponents' Batting Avg.
Rusie-NY	.250
Meekin-NY	.256
Stein-Bro	.278
Breitenstein-StL	.279
Clarkson-Cle	.285

Opponents' On Base Pct.
Rusie-NY	.331
Meekin-NY	.333
Clarkson-Cle	.336
Young-Cle	.338
Nichols-Bos	.346

Starter Runs
Rusie-NY	125.3
Meekin-NY	73.6
Young-Cle	62.4
Mercer-Was	54.7
Taylor-Phi	41.0

Adjusted Starter Runs
Rusie-NY	121.3
Meekin-NY	70.0
Young-Cle	68.7
Mercer-Was	52.5
Nichols-Bos	41.5

Clutch Pitching Index
Mercer-Was	134
Rusie-NY	125
Terry-Pit-Chi	121
Hemming-Lou-Bal	112
Killen-Pit	111

Relief Runs

Adjusted Relief Runs

Relief Ranking

Total Pitcher Index
Rusie-NY	11.0
Meekin-NY	5.9
Young-Cle	5.3
Mercer-Was	4.6
Nichols-Bos	3.5

Total Baseball Ranking
Rusie-NY	11.0
Meekin-NY	5.9
Young-Cle	5.3
Dahlen-Chi	5.0
Duffy-Bos	4.9

TEAM	G	W	L	PCT	GB	R	OR	AB	H	2B	3B	HR	BB	SO	AVG	OBP	SLG	PRO	PRO+	BR	/A	PF	CHI	RC	SB	CS	SBA	SBR
BAL	132	87	43	.669		1009	646	4725	1530	235	89	25	355	243	.324	.384	.427	.811	112	109	84	103	102	930	310			
CLE	131	84	46	.646	3	917	720	4658	1423	194	67	29	472	361	.305	.375	.395	.770	99	43	-8	106	100	790	187			
PHI	133	78	53	.595	9.5	1068	957	5037	1664	272	73	61	463	262	.330	.394	.450	.844	124	178	174	100	95	1040	276			
CHI	133	72	58	.554	15	866	854	4708	1401	171	85	55	422	344	.298	.361	.405	.766	97	23	-32	106	97	810	260			
BRO	133	71	60	.542	16.5	867	834	4717	1330	189	77	39	397	318	.282	.346	.379	.725	100	-49	21	92	106	707	183			
BOS	132	71	60	.542	16.5	907	826	4715	1369	197	57	54	500	236	.290	.365	.391	.756	94	13	-57	108	100	778	199			
PIT	134	71	61	.538	17	811	787	4645	1349	190	89	26	376	299	.290	.352	.386	.738	101	-24	22	95	97	753	257			
CIN	132	66	64	.508	21	903	854	4684	1395	235	105	36	414	249	.298	.359	.416	.775	101	35	0	104	101	844	326			
NY	132	66	65	.504	21.5	852	834	4605	1324	191	90	32	454	292	.288	.355	.389	.744	99	-12	8	98	102	763	292			
WAS	132	43	85	.336	43	837	1048	4577	1314	207	101	55	518	396	.287	.366	.412	.778	107	48	59	99	92	805	237			
STL	135	39	92	.298	48.5	747	1032	4781	1344	155	88	38	384	279	.281	.338	.374	.712	90	-76	-65	99	94	699	205			
LOU	133	35	96	.267	52.5	698	1090	4724	1320	171	73	34	346	323	.279	.339	.368	.707	94	-82	-28	94	90	665	156			
TOT	796					10482		56576	16763	2407	994	484	5101	3602	.296	.354	.400	.754						2888				

TEAM	CG	SH	SV	IP	H	H/G	HR	BB	SO	RAT	ERA	ERA+	OAV	OOB	PR	/A	PF	CPI	FA	E	DP	FW	PW	BW	SBW	DIF
BAL	104	10	4	1134¹	1216	9.6	31	430	244	13.4	3.80	125	.271	.340	123	118	100	105	.946	288	108	5.4	9.6	6.8		.3
CLE	108	6	3	1143²	1272	10.0	33	346	326	13.0	3.91	127	.278	.333	110	135	104	101	.936	348	77	1.8	10.9	-.6		6.9
PHI	106	2	7	1161	1467	11.4	36	485	330	15.6	5.47	88	.304	.375	-89	-88	100	94	.933	369	93	1.0	-7.1	14.1		4.5
CHI	119	3	1	1150²	1422	11.1	38	432	297	15.0	4.67	109	.300	.366	14	52	106	105	.928	401	113	-.8	4.2	-2.6		6.2
BRO	103	5	6	1150²	1360	10.6	41	395	216	14.1	4.94	89	.290	.351	-21	-71	92	91	.941	325	96	3.5	-5.8	1.7		6.1
BOS	116	4	4	1175¹	1364	10.4	56	363	370	13.6	4.27	119	.286	.343	66	107	107	103	.934	364	104	1.1	8.7	-4.6		.3
PIT	106	4	6	1171²	1263	9.7	17	500	382	14.2	4.05	112	.272	.353	95	60	95	102	.930	392	95	-.1	4.9	1.8		-1.5
CIN	97	2	6	1147¹	1451	11.4	39	362	245	14.7	4.81	103	.304	.361	-4	19	104	101	.931	377	112	.4	1.5	.0		-.9
NY	115	6	1	1147¹	1359	10.7	34	415	409	14.3	4.51	103	.291	.354	34	16	97	100	.922	438	106	-3.0	1.3	.6		1.6
WAS	99	0	5	1101²	1507	12.3	55	465	258	16.7	5.28	91	.321	.391	-61	-60	100	110	.917	447	96	-3.5	-4.9	4.8		-17.4
STL	105	1	1	1152¹	1562	12.2	64	439	280	16.0	5.76	84	.319	.381	-126	-120	101	98	.930	380	94	.7	-9.7	-5.3		-12.2
LOU	104	3	1	1117¹	1520	12.2	40	470	245	16.5	5.90	78	.320	.389	-139	-158	97	96	.913	477	104	-5.1	-12.8	-2.3		-10.4
TOT	1282	46	45	13753¹		11.0				14.7	4.78		.296	.354					.930	4606	1198					

Runs
Hamilton-Phi 166
Keeler-Bal 162
Jennings-Bal 159
Burkett-Cle 153
Delahanty-Phi 149

Hits
Burkett-Cle 225
Keeler-Bal 213
Thompson-Phi 211
Jennings-Bal 204
Hamilton-Phi 201

Doubles
Delahanty-Phi 49
Thompson-Phi 45
Jennings-Bal 41
Stenzel-Pit 38
Griffin-Bro 38

Triples
Selbach-Was 22
Tiernan-NY 21
Thompson-Phi 21
Cooley-StL 20

Home Runs
Thompson-Phi 18
Joyce-Was 17
Clements-Phi 13
Delahanty-Phi 11

Total Bases
Thompson-Phi 352
Delahanty-Phi ... 296
Burkett-Cle 288
McKean-Cle 283
Kelley-Bal 283

Runs Batted In
Thompson-Phi 165
Kelley-Bal 134
Brodie-Bal 134
Jennings-Bal 125
McKean-Cle 119

Runs Produced
Jennings-Bal 280
Thompson-Phi 278
Kelley-Bal 272
Delahanty-Phi 244
McKean-Cle 242

Bases On Balls
Joyce-Was 96
Hamilton-Phi 96
Griffin-Bro 93
Delahanty-Phi 86
Kelley-Bal 77

Batting Average
Burkett-Cle ...... .409
Delahanty-Phi .... .404
Thompson-Phi ..... .392
Lange-Chi .... .389
Hamilton-Phi ..... .389

On Base Percentage
Delahanty-Phi .... .500
Hamilton-Phi ..... .490
Burkett-Cle ...... .486
McGraw-Bal .... .459
Lange-Chi .... .456

Slugging Average
Thompson-Phi ..... .654
Delahanty-Phi .... .617
Lange-Chi .... .575
Kelley-Bal .... .546
Stenzel-Pit ...... .539

Production
Delahanty-Phi ... 1.117
Thompson-Phi ... 1.085

Lange-Chi 1.032
Burkett-Cle 1.009
Kelley-Bal 1.003

Adjusted Production
Delahanty-Phi 189
Thompson-Phi 179

Stenzel-Pit 165
Lange-Chi 157
Hamilton-Phi 157

Batter Runs
Delahanty-Phi 67.9
Thompson-Phi 58.7

Burkett-Cle 56.0
Hamilton-Phi 51.3
Kelley-Bal 49.0

Adjusted Batter Runs
Delahanty-Phi 67.6
Thompson-Phi 58.3

Hamilton-Phi 50.9
Burkett-Cle 49.8
Stenzel-Pit 49.1

Clutch Hitting Index
Brodie-Bal 163
Cross-Phi 149
Hassamaer-Was-Lou ..
.... 139
Childs-Cle 136
McCarthy-Bos 135

Runs Created
Hamilton-Phi 178
Delahanty-Phi 176

Thompson-Phi 167
Burkett-Cle 165
Lange-Chi 160

Total Average
Delahanty-Phi ... 1.517
Hamilton-Phi 1.443
Lange-Chi 1.373
Kelley-Bal 1.289
Thompson-Phi 1.269

Stolen Bases
Hamilton-Phi 97
Lange-Chi 67
McGraw-Bal 61
Kelley-Bal 54

Stolen Base Average

Stolen Base Runs

Fielding Runs
Jennings-Bal 35.7
Dahlen-Chi 35.2
Fuller-NY 34.2
Cross-Phi 33.4
Collins-Bos-Lou .. 19.0

Total Player Rating
Jennings-Bal 6.2
Delahanty-Phi 4.9
Thompson-Phi 4.9
Kelley-Bal 3.8
Griffin-Bro 3.5

Wins
Young-Cle 35
Hoffer-Bal 31
Hawley-Pit 31

Win Percentage
Hoffer-Bal .... .838
Young-Cle .... .778
Rhines-Cin .... .655

Games
Hawley-Pit 56
Breitenstein-StL ... 54
Rusie-NY 49

Complete Games
Breitenstein-StL ... 46
Hawley-Pit 44
Rusie-NY 42
Nichols-Bos 42
Griffith-Chi 39

Shutouts
Young-Cle 4
Rusie-NY 4
McMahon-Bal 4
Hoffer-Bal 4
Hawley-Pit 4

Saves
Parrott-Cin 3
Nichols-Bos 3
Beam-Phi 3

Innings Pitched
Hawley-Pit 444.1
Breitenstein-StL . 429.2
Rusie-NY 393.1
Nichols-Bos 379.2
Young-Cle 369.2

Fewest Hits/Game
Foreman-Pit 8.44
Hoffer-Bal 8.48
Rusie-NY 8.79
Young-Cle 8.84
Maul-Was 9.02

Fewest BB/Game
Young-Cle 1.83
Clarke-NY 1.92
Nichols-Bos 2.04
Staley-StL 2.21
Taylor-Phi 2.23

Strikeouts
Rusie-NY 201
Hawley-Pit 142
Nichols-Bos 140
Breitenstein-StL . 127
Young-Cle 121

Strikeouts/Game
Rusie-NY 4.60
McGill-Phi 4.32
Foreman-Pit 3.48
Stivetts-Bos 3.43
Nichols-Bos 3.32

Ratio
Young-Cle 10.86
Maul-Was 11.68
Nichols-Bos 12.04
Hawley-Pit 12.23
Cuppy-Cle 12.42

Earned Run Average
Maul-Was 2.45
Hawley-Pit 3.18
Hoffer-Bal 3.21
Foreman-Pit 3.22
Young-Cle 3.26

Adjusted ERA
Maul-Was 195
Young-Cle 153
Nichols-Bos 149
Hoffer-Bal 148
Hawley-Pit 142

Opponents' Batting Avg.
Foreman-Pit ...... .245
Hoffer-Bal .... .246
Rusie-NY .... .252
Young-Cle .... .253
Maul-Was .... .257

Opponents' On Base Pct.
Young-Cle .... .294
Maul-Was .... .309
Nichols-Bos ...... .316
Hawley-Pit .... .320
Cuppy-Cle .... .323

Starter Runs
Hawley-Pit 78.8
Young-Cle 62.2
Nichols-Bos 57.5
Hoffer-Bal 54.6
Cuppy-Cle 48.3

Adjusted Starter Runs
Nichols-Bos 71.0
Young-Cle 70.6
Hawley-Pit 65.8
Cuppy-Cle 56.4
Hoffer-Bal 53.8

Clutch Pitching Index
Maul-Was 137
Mercer-Was 126
Clarke-NY 119
Foreman-Cin 116
Griffith-Chi 115

Relief Runs

Adjusted Relief Runs

Relief Ranking

Total Pitcher Index
Hawley-Pit 6.9
Young-Cle 6.4
Cuppy-Cle 5.8
Nichols-Bos 5.7
Griffith-Chi 4.5

Total Baseball Ranking
Hawley-Pit 6.9
Young-Cle 6.4
Jennings-Bal 6.2
Cuppy-Cle 5.8
Nichols-Bos 5.6

TEAM	G	W	L	PCT	GB	R	OR	AB	H	2B	3B	HR	BB	SO	AVG	OBP	SLG	PRO	PRO+	BR	/A	PF	CHI	RC	SB	CS	SBA	SBR
BAL	132	90	39	.698		995	662	4719	1548	207	100	23	386	201	.328	.393	.429	.822	122	167	156	101	101	1003	441			
CLE	135	80	48	.625	9.5	840	650	4856	1463	207	72	28	436	316	.301	.363	.391	.754	99	43	-5	106	96	785	175			
CIN	128	77	50	.606	12	783	620	4360	1283	204	73	20	382	226	.294	.357	.388	.745	97	22	-28	107	101	761	350			
BOS	132	74	57	.565	17	860	761	4717	1416	175	74	36	414	274	.300	.363	.392	.755	100	43	-5	106	100	791	241			
CHI	132	71	57	.555	18.5	815	799	4582	1311	182	97	34	409	290	.286	.349	.390	.739	97	10	-21	104	102	769	332			
PIT	131	66	63	.512	24	787	741	4701	1371	169	94	27	387	286	.292	.353	.385	.738	105	9	41	96	96	746	217			
NY	133	64	67	.489	27	829	821	4661	1383	159	87	40	439	271	.297	.364	.394	.758	110	49	71	97	97	795	274			
PHI	130	62	68	.477	28.5	890	891	4680	1382	234	84	49	438	297	.295	.363	.413	.776	112	74	84	99	101	801	191			
WAS	133	58	73	.443	33	818	920	4639	1328	179	79	45	516	365	.286	.365	.388	.753	105	46	47	100	95	783	258			
BRO	133	58	73	.443	33	692	764	4548	1292	174	87	28	344	269	.284	.340	.379	.719	102	-28	16	94	93	680	198			
STL	131	40	90	.308	50.5	593	929	4520	1162	134	78	37	332	300	.257	.313	.346	.659	82	-132	-101	96	94	572	185			
LOU	134	38	93	.290	53	653	997	4588	1197	142	80	37	371	427	.261	.322	.351	.673	86	-106	-76	96	97	603	195			
TOT	792					9555		55571	16136	2166	1005	404	4854	3522	.290	.347	.387	.735						3057				

TEAM	CG	SH	SV	IP	H	H/G	HR	BB	SO	RAT	ERA	ERA+	OAV	OOB	PR	/A	PF	CPI	FA	E	DP	FW	PW	BW	SBW	DIF
BAL	115	9	1	1168¹	1281	9.9	22	339	302	12.7	3.67	116	.277	.331	89	77	98	100	.945	296	114	2.6	6.5	13.2		3.1
CLE	113	9	5	1195²	1363	10.3	27	280	336	12.6	3.46	131	.285	.329	119	141	104	109	.949	288	117	3.6	12.0	-.4		.9
CIN	105	12	4	1108	1240	10.1	27	310	219	13.0	3.67	125	.281	.335	84	114	106	105	.951	252	107	4.7	9.7	-2.4		1.5
BOS	110	6	3	1155²	1254	9.8	57	397	277	13.1	3.78	120	.275	.337	74	97	104	106	.934	368	94	-1.7	8.2	-.4		2.4
CHI	118	2	1	1161	1302	10.1	30	467	353	14.3	4.41	103	.282	.358	-7	-15	104	97	.934	366	115	-1.6	1.3	-1.8		9.1
PIT	108	8	1	1159¹	1286	10.0	18	439	362	13.9	4.30	98	.280	.351	7	-15	96	94	.941	317	103	1.2	-1.3	3.5		-1.9
NY	104	1	2	1136²	1303	10.3	33	403	312	14.0	4.54	92	.286	.352	-24	-45	96	94	.933	365	90	-1.3	-3.8	6.0		-2.4
PHI	107	3	2	1117	1473	11.9	39	387	243	15.4	5.20	83	.316	.375	-104	-112	99	99	.941	313	112	1.3	-9.5	7.1		-1.9
WAS	106	2	3	1156²	1435	11.4	24	435	292	15.2	4.61	95	.306	.372	-32	-28	101	105	.927	398	99	-3.3	-2.4	4.0		-5.8
BRO	97	3	1	1144	1353	10.6	39	400	259	14.1	4.25	97	.292	.354	14	-17	95	104	.945	297	104	2.7	-1.4	1.4		-10.2
STL	115	1	1	1130²	1448	11.5	40	456	279	15.5	5.33	82	.309	.376	-122	-124	100	95	.936	345	73	-.5	-10.5	-8.6		-5.5
LOU	108	1	4	1148²	1398	11.0	48	541	288	15.9	5.12	84	.298	.381	-98	-103	99	99	.916	475	110	-7.8	-8.7	-6.4		-4.5
TOT	1306	57	28	13761²		10.6				14.1	4.36		.290	.347					.938	4080	1238					

Runs
Burkett-Cle 160
Keeler-Bal 153
Hamilton-Bos ... 152
Kelley-Bal 148
Dahlen-Chi 137

Hits
Burkett-Cle 240
Keeler-Bal 210
Jennings-Bal 209
Delahanty-Phi ... 198
VanHaltren-NY ... 197

Doubles
Delahanty-Phi 44
Miller-Cin 38
Kelley-Bal 31
Dahlen-Chi 30

Triples
VanHaltren-NY 21
McCreery-Lou 21
Kelley-Bal 19
Dahlen-Chi 19
Clarke-Lou 18

Home Runs
Joyce-Was-NY 13
Delahanty-Phi 13
Thompson-Phi 12
Connor-StL 11

Total Bases
Burkett-Cle 317
Delahanty-Phi ... 315
Kelley-Bal 282
VanHaltren-NY ... 272
Keeler-Bal 270

Runs Batted In
Delahanty-Phi ... 126
Jennings-Bal 121
Duffy-Bos 113
McKean-Cle 112

Runs Produced
Jennings-Bal 246
Delahanty-Phi ... 244
Kelley-Bal 240
Keeler-Bal 231
Burkett-Cle 226

Bases On Balls
Hamilton-Bos 110
Joyce-Was-NY ... 101
Childs-Cle 100
Kelley-Bal 91
Tiernan-NY 77

Batting Average
Burkett-Cle ...... .410
Jennings-Bal ..... .401
Delahanty-Phi ... .397
Keeler-Bal .... .386
Tiernan-NY ...... .369

On Base Percentage
Hamilton-Bos .... .477
Jennings-Bal ..... .472
Delahanty-Phi ... .472
Joyce-Was-NY ... .470
Kelley-Bal .... .469

Slugging Average
Delahanty-Phi ... .631
Dahlen-Chi .... .553
McCreery-Lou ... .546
Kelley-Bal .... .543
Burkett-Cle ...... .541

Production
Delahanty-Phi ... 1.103
Kelley-Bal 1.013
Burkett-Cle 1.002
Dahlen-Chi ...... .990
Joyce-Was-NY ... .988

Adjusted Production
Delahanty-Phi ... 194
Kelley-Bal 167
Joyce-Was-NY ... 165
Tiernan-NY 162
E.Smith-Pit 160

Batter Runs
Delahanty-Phi ... 66.3
Kelley-Bal 56.4
Burkett-Cle 56.3
Joyce-Was-NY ... 50.1
Hamilton-Bos ... 46.5

Adjusted Batter Runs
Delahanty-Phi ... 67.4
Kelley-Bal 55.0
Joyce-Was-NY ... 51.1
Burkett-Cle 50.6
Tiernan-NY 48.3

Clutch Hitting Index
Reitz-Bal 176
Anson-Chi 165
McPhee-Cin 156
Cross-Phi 150
Tebeau-Cle 150

Runs Created
Kelley-Bal 178
Delahanty-Phi ... 170
Burkett-Cle 166
Hamilton-Bos ... 160
Jennings-Bal 158

Total Average
Kelley-Bal 1.430
Delahanty-Phi ... 1.405
Hamilton-Bos ... 1.316
Joyce-Was-NY ... 1.306
Jennings-Bal 1.263

Stolen Bases
Kelley-Bal 87
Lange-Chi 84
Hamilton-Bos 83
Miller-Cin 76
Doyle-Bal 73

Stolen Base Average

Stolen Base Runs

Fielding Runs
Childs-Cle 42.2
Jennings-Bal 34.4
Dahlen-Chi 24.6
Corcoran-Bro 23.6
Clingman-Lou ... 23.6

Total Player Rating
Jennings-Bal 6.9
Childs-Cle 6.9
Delahanty-Phi 6.1
Dahlen-Chi 5.7
Joyce-Was-NY 4.1

Wins
Nichols-Bos 30
Killen-Pit 30
Young-Cle 28
Meekin-NY 26

Win Percentage
Hoffer-Bal .... .781
Hemming-Bal ..... .714
Dwyer-Cin .... .686
Nichols-Bos ...... .682
Griffith-Chi ...... .676

Games
Killen-Pit 52
Young-Cle 51
Nichols-Bos 49
Hawley-Pit 49
Clarke-NY 48

Complete Games
Killen-Pit 44
Young-Cle 42
Mercer-Was 38

Shutouts
Young-Cle 5
Killen-Pit 5

Saves
Young-Cle 3
Hill-Lou 2
Fisher-Cin 2

Innings Pitched
Killen-Pit 432.1
Young-Cle 414.1
Hawley-Pit 378.0
Nichols-Bos 372.1
Mercer-Was 366.1

Fewest Hits/Game
Rhines-Cin 8.06
Hawley-Pit 9.10
Sullivan-NY 9.13
Friend-Chi 9.23
Hoffer-Bal 9.23

Fewest BB/Game
Young-Cle 1.35
Clarke-NY 1.54
Dwyer-Cin 1.87
Cuppy-Cle 1.89
Griffith-Chi 1.98

Strikeouts
Young-Cle 140
Hawley-Pit 137
Killen-Pit 134
Breitenstein-StL .. 114
Meekin-NY 110

Strikeouts/Game
Briggs-Chi 3.90
Pond-Bal 3.36
McJames-Was 3.31
Hawley-Pit 3.26
Young-Cle 3.04

Ratio
Rhines-Cin 11.64
Cuppy-Cle 11.82
Nichols-Bos 11.95
Nichols-Bos 11.97
Esper-Bal 12.08

Earned Run Average
Rhines-Cin 2.45
Nichols-Bos 2.83
Cuppy-Cle 3.12
Dwyer-Cin 3.15
Young-Cle 3.24

Adjusted ERA
Rhines-Cin 188
Nichols-Bos 160
Dwyer-Cin 146
Cuppy-Cle 145
Young-Cle 140

Opponents' Batting Avg.
Rhines-Cin ...... .238
Hawley-Pit ...... .261
Sullivan-NY ..... .261
Friend-Chi ...... .264
Hoffer-Bal ...... .264

Opponents' On Base Pct.
Rhines-Cin ...... .311
Cuppy-Cle .... .314
Young-Cle .... .317
Nichols-Bos ..... .317
Esper-Bal .... .319

Starter Runs
Nichols-Bos 63.2
Young-Cle 51.5
Cuppy-Cle 49.3
Killen-Pit 45.3
Dwyer-Cin 38.7

Adjusted Starter Runs
Nichols-Bos 70.6
Young-Cle 59.6
Cuppy-Cle 56.2
Dwyer-Cin 46.7
Killen-Pit 37.5

Clutch Pitching Index
Nichols-Bos 122
Wallace-Cle 120
Payne-Bro 116
Dwyer-Cin 115
Rhines-Cin 114

Relief Runs

Adjusted Relief Runs

Relief Ranking

Total Pitcher Index
Young-Cle 6.7
Nichols-Bos 6.2
Cuppy-Cle 6.0
Dwyer-Cin 4.3
Killen-Pit 4.2

Total Baseball Ranking
Jennings-Bal 6.9
Childs-Cle 6.9
Young-Cle 6.7
Delahanty-Phi 6.1
Nichols-Bos 6.1

TEAM	G	W	L	PCT	GB	R	OR	AB	H	2B	3B	HR	BB	SO	AVG	OBP	SLG	PRO	PRO+	BR	/A	PF	CHI	RC	SB	CS	SBA	SBR
BOS	135	93	39	.705		1025	665	4937	1574	230	83	45	423	262	.319	.378	.426	.804	110	117	65	106	108	919	233			
BAL	136	90	40	.692	2	964	674	4872	1584	243	66	19	437	256	.325	.394	.414	.808	118	138	138	100	100	984	401			
NY	137	83	48	.634	9.5	895	695	4844	1449	188	84	31	404	327	.299	.361	.392	.753	106	24	47	97	108	829	328			
CIN	134	76	56	.576	17	763	705	4524	1311	219	69	22	380	218	.290	.353	.383	.736	93	-7	-58	107	100	714	194			
CLE	132	69	62	.527	23.5	773	680	4604	1374	192	88	16	435	344	.298	.364	.389	.753	98	26	-16	105	96	747	181			
WAS	135	61	71	.462	32	781	793	4636	1376	194	77	36	374	348	.297	.357	.395	.752	104	18	22	100	98	755	208			
BRO	136	61	71	.462	32	802	845	4810	1343	202	72	24	351	255	.279	.335	.366	.701	94	-75	-31	95	110	684	187			
PIT	135	60	71	.458	32.5	676	835	4590	1266	140	108	25	359	334	.276	.337	.370	.707	95	-61	-32	96	95	657	170			
CHI	138	59	73	.447	34	832	894	4803	1356	189	97	38	430	317	.282	.347	.386	.733	94	-16	-47	104	105	766	264			
PHI	134	55	77	.417	38	752	792	4756	1392	213	83	40	399	299	.293	.353	.398	.751	106	13	34	97	93	754	163			
LOU	134	52	78	.400	40	669	859	4520	1197	160	70	40	370	453	.265	.329	.358	.687	89	-94	-68	97	100	624	195			
STL	132	29	102	.221	63.5	588	1083	4642	1277	149	67	31	354	314	.275	.336	.356	.692	89	-84	-68	98	85	639	172			
TOT	809					9520		56538	16499	2319	964	367	4716	3727	.292	.354	.386	.741							2696			

TEAM	CG	SH	SV	IP	H	H/G	HR	BB	SO	RAT	ERA	ERA+	OAV	OOB	PR	/A	PF	CPI	FA	E	DP	FW	PW	BW	SBW	DIF
BOS	115	8	7	1194¹	1273	9.6	39	393	329	12.9	3.65	122	.271	.333	87	107	104	102	.951	272	80	3.9	9.2	5.6		8.3
BAL	118	3	0	1197²	1296	9.7	18	382	361	13.2	3.55	117	.274	.338	100	81	97	104	.951	277	110	3.8	6.9	11.8		2.4
NY	118	8	3	1187¹	1214	9.2	26	486	456	13.4	3.47	120	.263	.342	110	89	96	107	.930	397	109	-3.3	7.6	4.0		9.2
CIN	100	4	2	1156²	1375	10.7	18	329	270	13.7	4.09	111	.294	.347	29	58	106	101	.948	273	100	3.7	5.0	-5.0		6.3
CLE	111	6	0	1119¹	1297	10.4	32	289	277	13.1	3.95	114	.288	.337	45	67	104	100	.950	261	74	4.2	5.7	-1.4		-5.0
WAS	102	7	6	1148	1383	10.8	27	400	348	14.6	4.01	108	.296	.362	37	40	101	112	.933	369	103	-1.9	3.4	1.9		-8.4
BRO	114	4	2	1194²	1417	10.7	34	410	256	14.2	4.60	89	.293	.355	-39	-68	95	94	.936	364	99	-1.5	-5.8	-2.7		4.9
PIT	112	2	2	1153¹	1397	10.9	22	318	342	13.9	4.67	89	.297	.350	-47	-66	97	91	.936	346	70	-.5	-5.7	-2.7		3.4
CHI	131	2	1	1197	1485	11.2	30	433	361	14.9	4.53	98	.303	.361	-30	-12	104	103	.932	393	111	-2.9	-1.0	-4.0		1.0
PHI	115	4	2	1155¹	1415	11.0	28	364	253	14.3	4.60	91	.300	.356	-38	-53	97	96	.944	296	72	2.3	-4.5	2.9		-11.7
LOU	114	2	0	1138	1363	10.8	39	459	267	15.1	4.42	96	.295	.369	-14	-22	99	106	.929	395	84	-3.6	-1.9	-5.8		-1.7
STL	109	1	1	1127¹	1584	12.6	54	453	207	16.8	6.21	71	.329	.395	-239	-228	102	93	.933	375	84	-2.7	-19.5	-5.8		-8.4
TOT	1359	51	26	13969		10.6				14.1	4.31		.292	.354					.939	4018	1096					

Runs		Hits		Doubles		Triples		Home Runs		Total Bases	
Hamilton-Bos	152	Keeler-Bal	239	Stenzel-Bal	43	Davis-Pit	28	Duffy-Bos	11	Lajoie-Phi	310
Keeler-Bal	145	F.Clarke-Lou	202	Lajoie-Phi	40	Lajoie-Phi	23	Davis-NY	10	Keeler-Bal	304
Griffin-Bro	136	Delahanty-Phi	200	Delahanty-Phi	40	Wallace-Cle	21	Lajoie-Phi	9	Delahanty-Phi	285
Jones-Bro	134	Burkett-Cle	198	Wallace-Cle	33	Keeler-Bal	19	Beckley-NY-Cin	8	F.Clarke-Lou	276
Jennings-Bal	133	Lajoie-Phi	197	Ryan-Chi	33					Duffy-Bos	265

Runs Batted In		Runs Produced		Bases On Balls		Batting Average		On Base Percentage		Slugging Average	
Davis-NY	136	Duffy-Bos	248	Hamilton-Bos	105	Keeler-Bal	.424	McGraw-Bal	.471	Lajoie-Phi	.569
Collins-Bos	132	Davis-NY	238	McGraw-Bal	99	F.Clarke-Lou	.390	Burkett-Cle	.468	Keeler-Bal	.539
Duffy-Bos	129	Collins-Bos	229	Griffin-Bro	81	Burkett-Cle	.383	Keeler-Bal	.464	Delahanty-Phi	.538
Lajoie-Phi	127	Kelley-Bal	226	Selbach-Was	80	Delahanty-Phi	.377	Jennings-Bal	.463	F.Clarke-Lou	.533
Kelley-Bal	118			Joyce-NY	78	Kelley-Bal	.362	F.Clarke-Lou	.462	Davis-NY	.509

Production		Adjusted Production		Batter Runs		Adjusted Batter Runs		Clutch Hitting Index		Runs Created	
Keeler-Bal	1.003	F.Clarke-Lou	168	Keeler-Bal	52.2	Keeler-Bal	52.2	Gleason-NY	163	Keeler-Bal	176
F.Clarke-Lou	.994	Keeler-Bal	164	F.Clarke-Lou	48.5	F.Clarke-Lou	51.5	Lowe-Bos	147	F.Clarke-Lou	158
Delahanty-Phi	.981	Delahanty-Phi	162	Delahanty-Phi	45.1	Delahanty-Phi	47.5	Collins-Bos	144	Delahanty-Phi	142
Lajoie-Phi	.960	Lajoie-Phi	156	Burkett-Cle	42.1	Lajoie-Phi	38.3	Anson-Chi	143	Davis-NY	137
Burkett-Cle	.944	Kelley-Bal	147	Kelley-Bal	37.2	Kelley-Bal	37.2	Davis-NY	143	Stenzel-Bal	136

Total Average		Stolen Bases		Stolen Base Average		Stolen Base Runs		Fielding Runs		Total Player Rating	
F.Clarke-Lou	1.272	Lange-Chi	73					Clingman-Lou	29.2	Jennings-Bal	5.4
Keeler-Bal	1.262	Stenzel-Bal	69					Cross-StL	28.1	Davis-NY	4.8
Jennings-Bal	1.251	Hamilton-Bos	66					Jennings-Bal	27.2	F.Clarke-Lou	4.1
Hamilton-Bos	1.162	Davis-NY	65					Davis-NY	22.0	Delahanty-Phi	3.9
Kelley-Bal	1.143	Keeler-Bal	64					Reitz-Bal	21.4	Collins-Bos	3.6

Wins		Win Percentage		Games		Complete Games		Shutouts		Saves	
Nichols-Bos	31	Klobedanz-Bos	.788	Young-Cle	46	Killen-Pit	38	Mercer-Was	3	Nichols-Bos	3
Rusie-NY	28	Nops-Bal	.769	Nichols-Bos	46	Griffith-Chi	38	McJames-Was	3	Mercer-Was	3
Klobedanz-Bos	26	Corbett-Bal	.750	Mercer-Was	46	Donahue-StL	38				
Corbett-Bal	24	Nichols-Bos	.738	Donahue-StL	46	Nichols-Bos	37				
Breitenstein-Cin	23	Rusie-NY	.737			Kennedy-Bro	36				

Innings Pitched		Fewest Hits/Game		Fewest BB/Game		Strikeouts		Strikeouts/Game		Ratio	
Nichols-Bos	368.0	Seymour-NY	8.23	Young-Cle	1.32	McJames-Was	156	Seymour-NY	4.83	Nichols-Bos	10.59
Donahue-StL	348.0	Rusie-NY	8.77	Tannehill-Pit	1.52	Seymour-NY	149	McJames-Was	4.34	Rusie-NY	11.50
Griffith-Chi	343.2	Nichols-Bos	8.85	Nichols-Bos	1.66	Corbett-Bal	149	Corbett-Bal	4.28	Cuppy-Cle	11.69
Kennedy-Bro	343.1	Hill-Lou	9.45	Cuppy-Cle	1.68	Rusie-NY	135	Rusie-NY	3.77	Nops-Bal	12.07
Killen-Pit	337.1	Corbett-Bal	9.49	Killen-Pit	2.03	Nichols-Bos	127	Nichols-Bos	3.11	Young-Cle	12.11

Earned Run Average		Adjusted ERA		Opponents' Batting Avg.		Opponents' On Base Pct.		Starter Runs		Adjusted Starter Runs	
Rusie-NY	2.54	Nichols-Bos	169	Seymour-NY	.242	Nichols-Bos	.291	Nichols-Bos	68.1	Nichols-Bos	74.6
Nichols-Bos	2.64	Rusie-NY	163	Rusie-NY	.254	Rusie-NY	.308	Rusie-NY	63.3	Rusie-NY	57.7
Nops-Bal	2.81	Nichols-Bos	148	Nichols-Bos	.256	Cuppy-Cle	.312	Corbett-Bal	41.8	Mercer-Was	40.5
Corbett-Bal	3.11	Powell-Cle	142	Hill-Lou	.268	Nops-Bal	.319	Mercer-Was	39.4	Corbett-Bal	36.8
Powell-Cle	3.16	Cuppy-Cle	142	Corbett-Bal	.269	Young-Cle	.319	Nops-Bal	36.6	Powell-Cle	33.2

Clutch Pitching Index		Relief Runs		Adjusted Relief Runs		Relief Ranking		Total Pitcher Index		Total Baseball Ranking	
Mercer-Was	132							Nichols-Bos	7.0	Nichols-Bos	7.0
Nops-Bal	120							Rusie-NY	5.7	Rusie-NY	5.7
Corbett-Bal	117							Mercer-Was	4.3	Jennings-Bal	5.4
Rusie-NY	117							Corbett-Bal	3.4	Davis-NY	4.8
McJames-Was	117							Breitenstein-Cin	3.2	Mercer-Was	4.3

TEAM	G	W	L	PCT	GB	R	OR	AB	H	2B	3B	HR	BB	SO	AVG	OBP	SLG	PRO	PRO+	BR	/A	PF	CHI	RC	SB	CS	SBA	SBR
BOS	152	102	47	.685		872	614	5276	1531	190	55	53	405	303	.290	.344	.377	.721	106	72	32	105	104	780	172			
BAL	154	96	53	.644	6	933	623	5242	1584	154	77	12	519	316	.302	.382	.368	.750	119	158	144	102	99	864	250			
CIN	157	92	60	.605	11.5	831	740	5334	1448	207	101	19	455	300	.271	.334	.359	.693	97	21	-33	107	104	729	165			
CHI	152	85	65	.567	17.5	828	679	5219	1431	175	84	18	476	394	.274	.343	.350	.693	104	29	31	100	104	735	220			
CLE	156	81	68	.544	21	730	683	5246	1379	162	56	18	545	306	.263	.337	.325	.662	96	-23	-13	99	97	640	93			
PHI	150	78	71	.523	24	823	784	5118	1431	238	81	33	472	382	.280	.348	.377	.725	118	84	116	96	98	769	182			
NY	157	77	73	.513	25.5	837	800	5349	1422	190	86	34	428	372	.266	.328	.353	.681	103	-5	20	97	109	714	214			
PIT	152	72	76	.486	29.5	634	694	5087	1313	140	88	14	336	343	.258	.313	.328	.641	90	-78	-63	98	96	589	107			
LOU	154	70	81	.464	33	728	833	5193	1389	150	71	32	375	429	.267	.324	.342	.666	98	-31	-18	98	101	686	235			
BRO	149	54	91	.372	46	638	811	5126	1314	156	66	17	328	314	.256	.309	.322	.631	85	-97	-94	100	100	577	130			
WAS	155	51	101	.336	52.5	704	939	5257	1423	177	80	16	370	386	.271	.327	.355	.682	100	-4	-2	100	94	703	197			
STL	154	39	111	.260	63.5	571	929	5214	1290	149	55	13	383	402	.247	.309	.305	.614	79	-126	-143	102	91	552	104			
TOT	921					9129		62661	16955	2088	900	299	5092	4247	.271	.334	.347	.681							2069			

TEAM	CG	SH	SV	IP	H	H/G	HR	BB	SO	RAT	ERA	ERA+	OAV	OOB	PR	/A	PF	CPI	FA	E	DP	FW	PW	BW	SBW	DIF
BOS	127	9	8	1340	1186	8.0	37	470	432	11.6	2.98	124	.236	.310	93	105	102	97	.950	310	102	3.1	9.8	3.0		11.6
BAL	138	12	0	1323	1236	8.4	17	400	422	11.5	2.90	123	.246	.310	104	98	99	99	.947	326	105	2.5	9.2	13.5		-3.6
CIN	131	10	2	1385¹	1484	9.6	16	449	294	13.0	3.50	110	.272	.336	17	51	106	103	.950	325	128	2.9	4.8	-3.1		11.4
CHI	137	13	0	1342²	1357	9.1	17	364	323	12.1	2.83	126	.261	.319	115	111	99	113	.936	412	149	-2.9	10.4	2.9		-.4
CLE	142	9	0	1334	1429	9.6	26	309	339	12.1	3.20	113	.272	.320	59	60	100	105	.952	301	95	4.2	5.6	-1.2		-2.1
PHI	129	10	0	1288¹	1440	10.1	23	399	325	13.4	3.72	92	.281	.342	-17	-42	95	104	.937	379	102	-1.2	-3.9	10.8		-2.2
NY	141	9	1	1353²	1359	9.0	21	587	558	13.5	3.44	101	.260	.344	25	4	96	106	.932	447	113	-4.2	.4	1.9		4.0
PIT	131	10	3	1323²	1400	9.5	14	346	330	12.3	3.41	104	.270	.323	29	21	99	98	.946	340	105	1.4	2.0	-5.9		.6
LOU	137	4	0	1323	1457	9.8	33	470	271	13.6	4.24	84	.276	.346	-95	-101	99	99	.939	382	114	-.8	-9.4	-1.7		6.4
BRO	134	1	0	1298²	1446	10.0	34	476	294	13.7	4.01	89	.280	.348	-59	-63	99	100	.947	334	125	1.3	-5.9	-8.8		-5.1
WAS	129	0	1	1307	1577	10.9	29	450	371	14.5	4.52	81	.297	.360	-134	-127	102	98	.929	443	119	-4.2	-11.9	-.2		-8.7
STL	133	0	2	1324¹	1584	10.8	32	372	288	13.9	4.53	83	.295	.350	-137	-111	105	93	.939	388	97	-1.2	-10.4	-13.4		-11.1
TOT	1609	87	17	15954²		9.6				12.9	3.60		.271	.334					.942	4387	1354					

Runs
McGraw-Bal	143
Jennings-Bal	135
VanHaltren-NY	129
Keeler-Bal	126
Cooley-Phi	123

Hits
Keeler-Bal	216
Burkett-Cle	213
VanHaltren-NY	204
Lajoie-Phi	197

Doubles
Lajoie-Phi	43
Delahanty-Phi	36
Dahlen-Chi	35
Collins-Bos	35
Anderson-Bro-Was-Bro	33

Triples
Anderson-Bro-Was-Bro	22
VanHaltren-NY	16
Hoy-Lou	16

Home Runs
Collins-Bos	15
Wagner-Lou	10
Joyce-NY	10
Anderson-Bro-Was-Bro	9
McKean-Cle	9

Total Bases
Collins-Bos	286
Lajoie-Phi	280
VanHaltren-NY	270
Anderson-Bro-Was-Bro	257
Cooley-Phi	256

Runs Batted In
Lajoie-Phi	127
Collins-Bos	111
Kelley-Bal	110
Duffy-Bos	108
McGann-Bal	106

Runs Produced
Lajoie-Phi	234
Jennings-Bal	221
Delahanty-Phi	203
Collins-Bos	203
McGann-Bal	200

Bases On Balls
McGraw-Bal	112
Joyce-NY	88
Hamilton-Bos	87
Flick-Phi	86
Jennings-Bal	78

Batting Average
Keeler-Bal	.385
Hamilton-Bos	.369
McGraw-Bal	.342
Smith-Cin	.342
Burkett-Cle	.341

On Base Percentage
Hamilton-Bos	.480
McGraw-Bal	.475
Jennings-Bal	.454
Flick-Phi	.430
Delahanty-Phi	.426

Slugging Average
Anderson-Bro-Was-Bro	.494
Collins-Bos	.479
Lajoie-Phi	.461
Delahanty-Phi	.454
Hamilton-Bos	.453

Production
Hamilton-Bos	.933
Delahanty-Phi	.880
Flick-Phi	.878
Jennings-Bal	.876
McGraw-Bal	.871

Adjusted Production
Hamilton-Bos	159
Delahanty-Phi	159
Flick-Phi	158
Jennings-Bal	149
McGraw-Bal	148

Batter Runs
McGraw-Bal	45.2
Jennings-Bal	44.3
Hamilton-Bos	43.5
Delahanty-Phi	40.3
Flick-Phi	35.2

Adjusted Batter Runs
Delahanty-Phi	43.9
McGraw-Bal	43.7
Jennings-Bal	42.7
Hamilton-Bos	40.0
Flick-Phi	38.4

Clutch Hitting Index
Kelley-Bal	169
Hartman-NY	158
McGann-Bal	151
Duffy-Bos	147
Connor-Chi	147

Runs Created
Delahanty-Phi	135
McGraw-Bal	121
Hamilton-Bos	120
Jennings-Bal	119
Ryan-Chi	119

Total Average
Hamilton-Bos	1.262
McGraw-Bal	1.115
Delahanty-Phi	1.082
Jennings-Bal	1.050
Flick-Phi	1.035

Stolen Bases
Delahanty-Phi	58
Hamilton-Bos	54
DeMontreville-Bal	49
Dexter-Lou	44
McGraw-Bal	43

Stolen Base Average

Stolen Base Runs

Fielding Runs
Davis-NY	35.8
Dahlen-Chi	25.3
Selbach-Was	20.3
Gleason-NY	19.4
Cross-StL	18.4

Total Player Rating
Dahlen-Chi	4.6
Jennings-Bal	4.6
Davis-NY	4.5
Collins-Bos	4.0
Delahanty-Phi	3.6

Wins
Nichols-Bos	31
Cunningham-Lou	28
McJames-Bal	27
Hawley-Cin	27
Lewis-Bos	26

Win Percentage
Lewis-Bos	.765
Maul-Bal	.741
Nichols-Bos	.721
Hawley-Cin	.711
Griffith-Chi	.706

Games
Taylor-StL	50
Nichols-Bos	50
Young-Cle	46

Complete Games
Taylor-StL	42
Cunningham-Lou	41
Young-Cle	40
Nichols-Bos	40
McJames-Bal	40

Shutouts
Powell-Cle	6
Piatt-Phi	6
Tannehill-Pit	5
Nichols-Bos	5
Hughes-Bal	5

Saves
Nichols-Bos	4
Tannehill-Pit	2
Lewis-Bos	2
Hickman-Bos	2
Dammann-Cin	2

Innings Pitched
Taylor-StL	397.1
Nichols-Bos	388.0
Young-Cle	377.2
McJames-Bal	374.0
Cunningham-Lou	362.0

Fewest Hits/Game
Nichols-Bos	7.33
Willis-Bos	7.64
Lewis-Bos	7.67
Maul-Bal	7.77
McJames-Bal	7.87

Fewest BB/Game
Young-Cle	.98
Dwyer-Cin	1.58
Cunningham-Lou	1.62
Tannehill-Pit	1.74
Griffith-Chi	1.77

Strikeouts
Seymour-NY	239
McJames-Bal	178
Willis-Bos	160
Nichols-Bos	138
Piatt-Phi	121

Strikeouts/Game
Seymour-NY	6.03
Willis-Bos	4.63
McJames-Bal	4.28
Doheny-NY	4.06
Piatt-Phi	3.56

Ratio
Nichols-Bos	9.63
Maul-Bal	9.76
Young-Cle	10.41
Griffith-Chi	10.75
McJames-Bal	10.88

Earned Run Average
Griffith-Chi	1.88
Maul-Bal	2.10
Nichols-Bos	2.13
McJames-Bal	2.36
Callahan-Chi	2.46

Adjusted ERA
Griffith-Chi	190
Nichols-Bos	173
Maul-Bal	170
McJames-Bal	152
Callahan-Chi	145

Opponents' Batting Avg.
Nichols-Bos	.221
Willis-Bos	.229
Lewis-Bos	.229
Maul-Bal	.232
McJames-Bal	.234

Opponents' On Base Pct.
Nichols-Bos	.272
Maul-Bal	.275
Young-Cle	.288
Griffith-Chi	.294
McJames-Bal	.297

Starter Runs
Nichols-Bos	63.3
Griffith-Chi	62.4
McJames-Bal	51.7
Young-Cle	45.2
Maul-Bal	39.9

Adjusted Starter Runs
Nichols-Bos	67.1
Griffith-Chi	61.5
McJames-Bal	50.5
Young-Cle	45.6
Maul-Bal	39.2

Clutch Pitching Index
Griffith-Chi	136
Orth-Phi	120
Dammann-Cin	119
Doheny-NY	117
Callahan-Chi	116

Relief Runs

Adjusted Relief Runs

Relief Ranking

Total Pitcher Index
Nichols-Bos	6.8
Griffith-Chi	6.2
Young-Cle	5.8
McJames-Bal	4.2
Callahan-Chi	4.0

Total Baseball Ranking
Nichols-Bos	6.7
Griffith-Chi	6.2
Young-Cle	5.8
Dahlen-Chi	4.6
Jennings-Bal	4.6

TEAM	G	W	L	PCT	GB	R	OR	AB	H	2B	3B	HR	BB	SO	AVG	OBP	SLG	PRO	PRO+	BR	/A	PF	CHI	RC	SB	CS	SBA	SBR
BRO	150	101	47	.682		892	658	4937	1436	178	97	27	477	263	.291	.368	.383	.751	110	87	70	102	103	824	271			
BOS	153	95	57	.625	8	858	645	5290	1517	178	90	39	431	269	.287	.345	.377	.722	94	22	-56	110	103	787	185			
PHI	154	94	58	.618	9	916	743	5353	1613	241	83	31	441	341	.301	.363	.395	.758	118	96	125	97	99	879	212			
BAL	152	86	62	.581	15	827	691	5073	1509	204	71	17	448	383	.297	.365	.376	.741	104	69	28	105	96	861	364			
STL	155	84	67	.556	18.5	819	739	5304	1514	172	88	47	468	262	.285	.347	.378	.725	102	29	10	102	97	801	210			
CIN	156	83	67	.553	19	856	770	5225	1439	194	105	13	485	295	.275	.344	.360	.704	97	-6	-21	102	106	760	228			
PIT	154	76	73	.510	25.5	834	765	5450	1574	196	121	27	384	345	.289	.342	.384	.726	104	26	29	100	97	815	179			
CHI	152	75	73	.507	26	812	763	5148	1428	173	82	27	406	342	.277	.338	.359	.697	100	-25	-3	97	105	743	247			
LOU	155	75	77	.493	28	827	775	5307	1484	192	68	40	436	375	.280	.343	.364	.707	99	-4	-3	100	101	780	233			
NY	152	60	90	.400	42	734	863	5092	1431	161	65	23	387	360	.281	.337	.352	.689	97	-39	-12	97	100	707	234			
WAS	155	54	98	.355	49	743	983	5256	1429	162	87	47	350	341	.272	.327	.363	.690	95	-46	-37	99	99	710	176			
CLE	154	20	134	.130	84	529	1252	5279	1333	142	50	12	289	280	.253	.299	.305	.604	76	-208	-151	93	92	541	127			
TOT	921					9647		62714	17707	2193	1007	350	4972	3856	.282	.343	.366	.709						2666				

TEAM	CG	SH	SV	IP	H	H/G	HR	BB	SO	RAT	ERA	ERA+	OAV	OOB	PR	/A	PF	CPI	FA	E	DP	FW	PW	BW	SBW	DIF
BRO	121	9	9	1269¹	1320	9.4	32	463	331	13.0	3.25	120	.268	.337	85	92	102	111	.948	314	125	2.9	8.3	6.3		9.4
BOS	138	13	4	1348	1273	8.5	44	432	385	11.8	3.26	127	.250	.317	88	133	108	95	.952	303	124	4.0	12.1	-5.1		8.1
PHI	129	15	2	1333¹	1398	9.4	17	370	281	12.5	3.47	106	.270	.328	56	30	96	97	.940	379	110	-.4	2.7	11.3		4.3
BAL	132	10	4	1304¹	1403	9.7	13	349	294	12.6	3.31	119	.275	.330	78	93	103	103	.949	308	96	3.5	8.4	2.5		-2.5
STL	134	7	1	1340²	1476	9.9	41	321	331	12.4	3.36	118	.280	.327	73	91	103	107	.939	397	117	-1.3	8.2	.9		.6
CIN	130	8	5	1361	1484	9.8	26	370	360	12.8	3.70	106	.278	.333	23	32	102	97	.947	339	111	2.3	2.9	-1.9		4.7
PIT	117	9	4	1364	1464	9.7	27	437	334	13.0	3.60	106	.274	.337	38	32	99	101	.945	361	98	.7	2.9	2.6		-4.7
CHI	147	8	1	1331¹	1433	9.7	20	330	313	12.5	3.37	111	.275	.328	71	55	97	102	.935	428	145	-3.5	5.0	-.3		-.2
LOU	134	5	2	1351²	1509	10.0	33	323	287	12.6	3.45	112	.282	.331	60	60	100	106	.939	394	101	-1.1	5.4	-.3		-5.1
NY	138	4	0	1278¹	1454	10.2	19	628	397	15.3	4.29	87	.286	.375	-63	-78	97	104	.932	433	140	-3.8	-7.1	-1.1		-3.1
WAS	131	3	0	1300¹	1649	11.4	35	422	328	14.9	4.93	79	.309	.368	-157	-149	102	95	.935	403	99	-1.6	-13.5	-3.4		-3.5
CLE	138	0	0	1264	1844	13.1	43	527	215	17.7	6.37	58	.340	.409	-353	-378	96	94	.937	388	121	-.9	-34.3	-13.7		-8.2
TOT	1589	91	32	15846¹		10.1				13.4	3.85		.282	.343					.942	4447	1387					

Runs
McGraw-Bal...... 140
Keeler-Bro....... 140
Thomas-Phi....... 137
Delahanty-Phi.... 135
Williams-Pit..... 126

Hits
Delahanty-Phi.... 238
Burkett-StL...... 221
Williams-Pit..... 219
Keeler-Bro....... 216
Tenney-Bos....... 209

Doubles
Delahanty-Phi.... 55
Wagner-Lou....... 43
Holmes-Bal....... 31
Long-Bos......... 30
Duffy-Bos........ 29

Triples
Williams-Pit..... 27
Freeman-Was...... 25
Stahl-Bos........ 19
Tenney-Bos....... 17
McCarthy-Pit..... 17

Home Runs
Freeman-Was...... 25
Wallace-StL...... 12
Williams-Pit..... 9
Mertes-Chi....... 9
Delahanty-Phi.... 9

Total Bases
Delahanty-Phi.... 338
Freeman-Was...... 331
Williams-Pit..... 328
Stahl-Bos........ 284
Wagner-Lou....... 282

Runs Batted In
Delahanty-Phi.... 137
Freeman-Was...... 122
Williams-Pit..... 116
Wagner-Lou....... 113
Wallace-StL...... 108

Runs Produced
Delahanty-Phi.... 263
Williams-Pit..... 233
Wagner-Lou....... 204
Freeman-Was...... 204

Bases On Balls
McGraw-Bal....... 124
Thomas-Phi....... 115
VanHaltren-NY.... 74
Childs-StL....... 74

Batting Average
Delahanty-Phi.....410
Burkett-StL.......396
McGraw-Bal.......391
Keeler-Bro........379
Williams-Pit......355

On Base Percentage
McGraw-Bal........547
Delahanty-Phi.....464
Burkett-StL.......463
Thomas-Phi........457
Stahl-Bos.........426

Slugging Average
Delahanty-Phi.....582
Freeman-Was.......563
Williams-Pit......532
Burkett-StL.......500
Wagner-Lou........494

Production
Delahanty-Phi...1.046
McGraw-Bal.......994
Burkett-StL......963
Williams-Pit.....948
Freeman-Was......924

Adjusted Production
Delahanty-Phi....193
McGraw-Bal.......165
Burkett-StL......160
Williams-Pit.....160
Freeman-Was......154

Batter Runs
Delahanty-Phi....67.9
McGraw-Bal.......56.9
Burkett-StL......51.6
Williams-Pit.....48.7
Stahl-Bos........42.3

Adjusted Batter Runs
Delahanty-Phi....71.0
McGraw-Bal.......53.0
Burkett-StL......49.6
Williams-Pit.....49.1
Freeman-Was......36.9

Clutch Hitting Index
Corcoran-Cin.....150
Flick-Phi........143
Duffy-Bos........140
Magoon-Bal-Chi...139
Lauder-Phi.......139

Runs Created
Delahanty-Phi....175
Williams-Pit.....152
Burkett-StL......145
McGraw-Bal.......141
Stahl-Bos........139

Total Average
McGraw-Bal.......1.601
Delahanty-Phi....1.245
Burkett-StL......1.107
Williams-Pit.....1.053
Stahl-Bos........1.051

Stolen Bases
Sheckard-Bal..... 77
McGraw-Bal....... 73
Heidrick-StL..... 55
Holmes-Bal....... 50
Clarke-Lou....... 49

Stolen Base Average

Stolen Base Runs

Fielding Runs
G.Davis-NY....... 46.3
Wallace-StL...... 38.3
Cross-Cle-StL.... 32.9
Gleason-NY....... 25.7
Collins-Bos...... 21.0

Total Player Rating
G.Davis-NY....... 6.2
Delahanty-Phi.... 5.4
Wallace-StL...... 5.3
Williams-Pit..... 5.1
McGraw-Bal....... 5.0

Wins
McGinnity-Bal.... 28
Hughes-Bro....... 28
Willis-Bos....... 27
Young-StL........ 26
Tannehill-Pit.... 24

Win Percentage
Hughes-Bro.......824
Willis-Bos........771
Hahn-Cin.........742
Donahue-Phi......724
Kennedy-Bro......710

Games
Leever-Pit....... 51
Powell-StL....... 48
McGinnity-Bal.... 48
Young-StL........ 44
Carrick-NY....... 44

Complete Games
Young-StL........ 40
Powell-StL....... 40
Carrick-NY....... 40
Taylor-Chi....... 39
McGinnity-Bal.... 38

Shutouts
Willis-Bos......... 5

Saves
Leever-Pit......... 3

Innings Pitched
Leever-Pit......379.0
Powell-StL......373.0
Young-StL.......369.1
McGinnity-Bal...366.1
Carrick-NY......361.2

Fewest Hits/Game
Willis-Bos........7.28
Hughes-Bro.......7.71
Hahn-Cin.........8.16
Seymour-NY.......8.28
Leever-Pit.......8.38

Fewest BB/Game
Young-StL........1.07
Cuppy-StL........1.36
Tannehill-Pit....1.47
Kitson-Bal.......1.79
Woods-Lou........1.79

Strikeouts
Hahn-Cin......... 145
Seymour-NY...... 142
Leever-Pit....... 121
Willis-Bos....... 120
Doheny-NY........ 115

Strikeouts/Game
Seymour-NY...... 4.76
Hahn-Cin......... 4.22
Doheny-NY........ 3.90
McJames-Bro..... 3.43
Willis-Bos....... 3.15

Ratio
Young-StL........10.19
Hahn-Cin.........10.43
Nichols-Bos......10.85
Willis-Bos.......11.14
Kitson-Bal.......11.15

Earned Run Average
Willis-Bos........ 2.50
Young-StL........ 2.58
McGinnity-Bal.... 2.68
Hahn-Cin......... 2.68
Hughes-Bro....... 2.68

Adjusted ERA
Willis-Bos....... 166
Young-StL........ 154
McGinnity-Bal.... 148
Hahn-Cin......... 146
Hughes-Bro....... 146

Opponents' Batting Avg.
Willis-Bos.......222
Hughes-Bro.......232
Hahn-Cin.........242
Seymour-NY.......245
Leever-Pit.......247

Opponents' On Base Pct.
Young-StL........285
Hahn-Cin.........290
Nichols-Bos......298
Willis-Bos.......303
Kitson-Bal.......304

Starter Runs
Young-StL........ 52.0
Willis-Bos....... 51.6
McGinnity-Bal.... 47.7
Hahn-Cin......... 40.2
Kitson-Bal....... 39.2

Adjusted Starter Runs
Willis-Bos....... 63.1
Young-StL........ 57.2
McGinnity-Bal.... 52.1
Nichols-Bos...... 44.5
Kitson-Bal....... 43.1

Clutch Pitching Index
Kennedy-Bro...... 130
Tannehill-Pit.... 124
Dowling-Lou...... 122
Callahan-Chi..... 121
Woods-Lou........ 118

Relief Runs

Adjusted Relief Runs

Relief Ranking

Total Pitcher Index
Young-StL........ 6.0
Willis-Bos....... 5.8
McGinnity-Bal.... 4.5
Hughes-Bro....... 4.5
Griffith-Chi..... 4.4

Total Baseball Ranking
G.Davis-NY....... 6.2
Young-StL........ 6.0
Willis-Bos....... 5.8
Delahanty-Phi.... 5.4
Wallace-StL...... 5.3

TEAM	G	W	L	PCT	GB	R	OR	AB	H	2B	3B	HR	BB	SO	AVG	OBP	SLG	PRO	PRO+	BR	/A	PF	CHI	RC	SB	CS	SBA	SBR
BRO	142	82	54	.603		816	722	4860	1423	199	81	26	421	272	.293	.359	.383	.742	105	72	27	106	100	795	274			
PIT	140	79	60	.568	4.5	733	612	4817	1312	185	100	26	327	321	.272	.327	.368	.695	96	-24	-29	101	104	666	174			
PHI	141	75	63	.543	8	810	792	4969	1439	187	82	29	440	374	.290	.356	.378	.734	109	59	65	99	99	774	205			
BOS	142	66	72	.478	17	778	739	4952	1403	163	68	48	395	278	.283	.342	.373	.715	92	16	-76	112	102	724	182			
STL	142	65	75	.464	19	744	748	4877	1420	141	81	36	406	318	.291	.355	.375	.730	108	52	58	99	94	765	243			
CHI	146	65	75	.464	19	635	751	4907	1276	202	51	33	343	383	.260	.317	.342	.659	90	-87	-60	96	97	622	189			
CIN	144	62	77	.446	21.5	703	745	5026	1335	178	83	33	333	408	.266	.317	.354	.671	92	-72	-53	98	103	650	183			
NY	141	60	78	.435	23	713	823	4724	1317	177	61	23	369	343	.279	.338	.357	.695	102	-17	16	95	102	675	236			
TOT	569					5932		39132	10925	1432	607	254	3034	2697	.279	.339	.366	.705							1686			

TEAM	CG	SH	SV	IP	H	H/G	HR	BB	SO	RAT	ERA	ERA+	OAV	OOB	PR	/A	PF	CPI	FA	E	DP	FW	PW	BW	SBW	DIF
BRO	104	8	4	1225[2]	1370	10.1	30	405	300	13.5	3.89	99	.282	.346	-27	-8	104	99	.948	303	102	2.6	-.7	2.5		9.7
PIT	114	11	1	1229	1232	9.0	24	295	415	11.6	3.06	119	.261	.313	87	77	98	97	.945	322	106	1.1	7.0	-2.7		4.0
PHI	116	7	3	1248[2]	1506	10.9	29	402	284	14.2	4.12	88	.298	.357	-59	-71	98	103	.945	330	125	.8	-6.5	5.9		5.8
BOS	116	8	2	1240[1]	1263	9.2	59	463	340	12.9	3.72	111	.264	.335	-4	55	112	97	.953	273	86	4.4	5.0	-6.9		-5.5
STL	117	12	0	1217[1]	1373	10.2	37	299	325	12.7	3.75	97	.284	.331	-7	-16	98	97	.943	331	73	.8	-1.5	5.3		-9.7
CHI	137	9	1	1271	1375	9.7	21	324	357	12.6	3.23	112	.276	.330	66	52	98	106	.933	418	98	-3.9	4.8	-5.5		-.3
CIN	118	9	1	1274[2]	1383	9.8	28	404	399	13.0	3.83	96	.276	.337	-20	-24	99	94	.945	341	120	.5	-2.2	-4.8		-1.0
NY	113	4	0	1207[1]	1423	10.6	26	442	277	14.6	3.96	91	.293	.363	-35	-47	98	108	.928	439	124	-6.0	-4.3	1.5		-.2
TOT	935	68	12	9914		9.9				13.1	3.69		.279	.339					.942	2757	834					

Runs
Thomas-Phi 132
Slagle-Phi 115
VanHaltren-NY 114
Barrett-Cin 114
Wagner-Pit 107

Hits
Keeler-Bro 204
Burkett-StL 203
Wagner-Pit 201
Flick-Phi 200
Beckley-Cin 190

Doubles
Wagner-Pit 45
Lajoie-Phi 33
Flick-Phi 32
Delahanty-Phi 32
VanHaltren-NY 30

Triples
Wagner-Pit 22
Kelley-Bro 17
Hickman-NY 17
Stahl-Bos 16
Flick-Phi 16

Home Runs
Long-Bos 12
Flick-Phi 11
Donlin-StL 10
Hickman-NY 9
Sullivan-Bos 8

Total Bases
Wagner-Pit 302
Flick-Phi 297
Burkett-StL 265
Keeler-Bro 253
Beckley-Cin 242

Runs Batted In
Flick-Phi 110
Delahanty-Phi . . . 109
Wagner-Pit 100
Collins-Bos 95
Beckley-Cin 94

Runs Produced
Flick-Phi 205
Wagner-Pit 203
Collins-Bos 193
Beckley-Cin 190
Delahanty-Phi . . . 189

Bases On Balls
Thomas-Phi 115
Hamilton-Bos 107
McGraw-StL 85
Dahlen-Bro 73

Batting Average
Wagner-Pit 381
Flick-Phi 367
Burkett-StL 363
Keeler-Bro 362
McGraw-StL 344

On Base Percentage
McGraw-StL 503
Thomas-Phi 451
Hamilton-Bos 449
Flick-Phi 441
Wagner-Pit 434

Slugging Average
Wagner-Pit 573
Flick-Phi 545
Lajoie-Phi 510
Kelley-Bro 485
Hickman-NY 482

Production
Wagner-Pit 1.007
Flick-Phi 986
McGraw-StL 920
Burkett-StL 904
Selbach-NY 885

Adjusted Production
Wagner-Pit 175
Flick-Phi 173
McGraw-StL 156
Selbach-NY 151
Burkett-StL 150

Batter Runs
Flick-Phi 53.6
Wagner-Pit 53.3
Burkett-StL 39.0
McGraw-StL 35.8
Selbach-NY 34.3

Adjusted Batter Runs
Flick-Phi 54.3
Wagner-Pit 52.7
Burkett-StL 39.7
Selbach-NY 38.2
McGraw-StL 36.2

Clutch Hitting Index
Cross-Phi 153
Delahanty-Phi . . . 138
Dahlen-Bro 135
Jennings-Bro 133
Lowe-Bos 132

Runs Created
Wagner-Pit 152
Flick-Phi 151
Burkett-StL 133
Keeler-Bro 123
Selbach-NY 121

Total Average
McGraw-StL 1.256
Wagner-Pit 1.193
Flick-Phi 1.171
Selbach-NY 1.029
Burkett-StL 1.017

Stolen Bases
VanHaltren-NY 45
Donovan-StL 45
Barrett-Cin 44
Keeler-Bro 41

Stolen Base Average

Stolen Base Runs

Fielding Runs
Steinfeldt-Cin . . . 35.9
Lajoie-Phi 29.5
Davis-NY 29.1
Dahlen-Bro 19.3
Bradley-Chi 16.8

Total Player Rating
Lajoie-Phi 5.0
Davis-NY 4.5
Flick-Phi 4.3
Selbach-NY 3.4
Wagner-Pit 3.4

Wins
McGinnity-Bro 28
Tannehill-Pit 20
Phillippe-Pit 20
Kennedy-Bro 20
Dinneen-Bos 20

Win Percentage
McGinnity-Bro 778
Tannehill-Pit 769
Fraser-Phi 625
Phillippe-Pit 606
Kennedy-Bro 606

Games
Carrick-NY 45
McGinnity-Bro . . . 44
Scott-Cin 42
Kennedy-Bro 42

Complete Games
Hawley-NY 34
Dinneen-Bos 33

Shutouts
Young-StL 4
Nichols-Bos 4
Hahn-Cin 4
Griffith-Chi 4

Saves
Kitson-Bro 4
Bernhard-Phi 2

Innings Pitched
McGinnity-Bro . . . 343.0
Carrick-NY 341.2
Hawley-NY 329.1
Young-StL 321.1
Dinneen-Bos 320.2

Fewest Hits/Game
Waddell-Pit 7.59
Garvin-Chi 8.22
Nichols-Bos 8.36
Dinneen-Bos 8.53
Phillippe-Pit 8.84

Fewest BB/Game
Young-StL 1.01
Phillippe-Pit 1.35
Tannehill-Pit 1.65
Griffith-Chi 1.85
Leever-Pit 1.86

Strikeouts
Hahn-Cin 132
Waddell-Pit 130
Young-StL 115
Garvin-Chi 107
Dinneen-Bos 107

Strikeouts/Game
Waddell-Pit 5.61
Garvin-Chi 3.91
Hahn-Cin 3.82
Newton-Cin 3.38
Leever-Pit 3.25

Ratio
Phillippe-Pit 10.45
Waddell-Pit 10.48
Young-StL 10.53
Garvin-Chi 11.14
Griffith-Chi 11.29

Earned Run Average
Waddell-Pit 2.37
Garvin-Chi 2.41
Taylor-Chi 2.55
Leever-Pit 2.71
Phillippe-Pit 2.84

Adjusted ERA
Waddell-Pit 153
Garvin-Chi 149
Taylor-Chi 141
Nichols-Bos 134
Leever-Pit 134

Opponents' Batting Avg.
Waddell-Pit 229
Garvin-Chi 243
Nichols-Bos 246
Dinneen-Bos 250
Phillippe-Pit 257

Opponents' On Base Pct.
Phillippe-Pit 290
Waddell-Pit 290
Young-StL 291
Garvin-Chi 303
Griffith-Chi 306

Starter Runs
Garvin-Chi 35.1
Waddell-Pit 30.7
McGinnity-Bro . . . 28.8
Taylor-Chi 28.3
Phillippe-Pit 26.5

Adjusted Starter Runs
Dinneen-Bos 35.9
McGinnity-Bro . . . 34.2
Garvin-Chi 32.6
Waddell-Pit 29.1
Nichols-Bos 27.0

Clutch Pitching Index
Fraser-Phi 131
Taylor-Chi 120
McGinnity-Bro . . . 118
Carrick-NY 115
Donahue-Phi 114

Relief Runs

Adjusted Relief Runs

Relief Ranking

Total Pitcher Index
Dinneen-Bos 3.8
Garvin-Chi 3.1
Waddell-Pit 2.7
Tannehill-Pit 2.7
McGinnity-Bro . . . 2.5

Total Baseball Ranking
Lajoie-Phi 5.0
Davis-NY 4.5
Flick-Phi 4.3
Dinneen-Bos 3.8
Wagner-Pit 3.5

TEAM	G	W	L	PCT	GB	R	OR	AB	H	2B	3B	HR	BB	SO	AVG	OBP	SLG	PRO	PRO+	BR	/A	PF	CHI	RC	SB	CS	SBA	SBR
PIT	140	90	49	.647		776	**534**	4913	1407	182	92	29	386	493	.286	**.344**	.379	**.723**	113	**99**	79	103	102	**742**	203			
PHI	140	83	57	.593	7.5	668	543	4793	1275	194	58	24	**430**	549	.266	.334	.346	.680	102	30	17	102	97	652	199			
BRO	137	79	57	.581	9.5	744	600	4879	1399	**206**	93	32	312	449	**.287**	.334	**.387**	.721	112	84	67	103	102	715	178			
STL	142	76	64	.543	14.5	**792**	689	5039	**1430**	187	**94**	**39**	314	540	.284	.336	.381	.717	**120**	86	**120**	95	**104**	**742**	190			
BOS	140	69	69	.500	20.5	531	556	4746	1180	135	36	28	303	519	.249	.298	.310	.608	75	-103	-161	109	100	514	158			
CHI	140	53	86	.381	37	578	699	4844	1250	153	61	18	314	532	.258	.310	.326	.636	94	-56	-32	96	99	575	**204**			
NY	141	52	85	.380	37	544	755	4839	1225	167	46	19	303	575	.253	.302	.318	.620	89	-84	-60	96	98	528	133			
CIN	142	52	87	.374	38	561	818	4914	1232	173	70	38	323	584	.251	.302	.338	.640	97	-56	-13	93	94	569	137			
TOT	561					5194		38967	10398	1397	550	227	2685	4241	.267	.320	.348	.669						1402				

TEAM	CG	SH	SV	IP	H	H/G	HR	BB	SO	RAT	ERA	ERA+	OAV	OOB	PR	/A	PF	CPI	FA	E	DP	FW	PW	BW	SBW	DIF
PIT	119	**15**	4	1244²	1198	8.7	20	**244**	505	10.8	2.58	126	.252	**.296**	102	94	98	105	.950	287	97	1.2	9.2	7.7		2.3
PHI	125	**15**	2	1246²	1221	8.8	19	259	480	11.0	2.87	119	.255	.300	63	73	102	97	**.954**	**262**	65	**2.7**	7.2	1.7		1.5
BRO	111	7	5	1213²	1244	9.2	**18**	435	583	12.8	3.14	107	.264	.333	24	27	101	**109**	.950	281	99	1.2	2.6	6.6		.6
STL	118	5	5	1269²	1333	9.4	39	332	445	12.1	3.68	86	.268	.320	-51	-71	96	92	.949	305	108	.4	-7.0	11.8		.8
BOS	128	11	0	1263	1196	**8.5**	29	349	558	11.3	2.90	125	**.249**	.304	59	**99**	109	98	.952	282	89	1.5	**9.7**	-15.8		4.6
CHI	**131**	2	0	1241²	1348	9.8	27	324	**586**	12.5	3.33	97	.275	.326	-2	-14	97	105	.943	336	87	-1.8	-1.4	-3.1		-10.2
NY	118	11	1	1232	1389	10.1	24	377	542	13.3	3.87	85	.283	.340	-75	-78	100	99	.941	348	81	-2.3	-7.6	-5.9		-.6
CIN	126	4	0	1265²	1469	10.4	51	365	542	13.5	4.17	77	.289	.344	-120	-138	96	99	.940	355	102	-2.6	-13.5	-1.3		-.0
TOT	976	70	17	9977		9.4				12.2	3.32		.267	.320					.947	2456	728					

Runs
Burkett-StL 142
Keeler-Bro 123
Beaumont-Pit 120
Clarke-Pit 118
Sheckard-Bro 116

Hits
Burkett-StL 226
Keeler-Bro 202
Sheckard-Bro 196
Wagner-Pit 194
Delahanty-Phi 192

Doubles
Delahanty-Phi 38
Daly-Bro 38
Wagner-Pit 37
Beckley-Cin 36
Wallace-StL 34

Triples
Sheckard-Bro 19
Flick-Phi 17

Home Runs
Crawford-Cin 16
Sheckard-Bro 11
Burkett-StL 10

Total Bases
Burkett-StL 306
Sheckard-Bro 296
Delahanty-Phi 286
Wagner-Pit 271

Runs Batted In
Wagner-Pit 126
Delahanty-Phi 108
Sheckard-Bro 104
Crawford-Cin 104

Runs Produced
Wagner-Pit 221
Sheckard-Bro 209
Burkett-StL 207
Delahanty-Phi ... 206
Flick-Phi 192

Bases On Balls
Thomas-Phi 100
Hartsel-Phi......... 74
Davis-Bro-Chi 66
Delahanty-Phi 65
Hamilton-Bos 64

Batting Average
Burkett-StL 376
Delahanty-Phi ... .354
Sheckard-Bro .... .354
Wagner-Pit .... .353
Keeler-Bro .... .339

On Base Percentage
Burkett-StL 440
Thomas-Phi ...... .437
Delahanty-Phi ... .427
Wagner-Pit .... .416
Hartsel-Chi........414

Slugging Average
Sheckard-Bro .... .534
Delahanty-Phi ... .528
Crawford-Cin .... .524
Burkett-StL .... .509
Flick-Phi .... .500

Production
Delahanty-Phi .... .955
Burkett-StL ...... .949
Sheckard-Bro .... .944
Wagner-Pit .... .910
Crawford-Cin .... .903

Adjusted Production
Burkett-StL 184
Delahanty-Phi ... 173
Crawford-Cin 172
Sheckard-Bro 168
Hartsel-Chi....... 164

Batter Runs
Burkett-StL 58.9
Delahanty-Phi ... 53.5
Sheckard-Bro 49.9
Wagner-Pit 44.8
Hartsel-Chi....... 42.8

Adjusted Batter Runs
Burkett-StL 62.9
Delahanty-Phi ... 51.9
Sheckard-Bro 47.9
Hartsel-Chi....... 45.7
Wagner-Pit 42.5

Clutch Hitting Index
Ganzel-NY 163
Dexter-Chi 158
Long-Bos 155
Long-Bos 155
Dahlen-Bro 149

Runs Created
Burkett-StL 151
Sheckard-Bro 139
Delahanty-Phi ... 139
Wagner-Pit 137
Hartsel-Chi....... 130

Total Average
Delahanty-Phi 1.097
Burkett-StL 1.072
Sheckard-Bro 1.070
Wagner-Pit 1.068
Hartsel-Chi...... 1.027

Stolen Bases
Wagner-Pit 49
Hartsel-Chi 41
Strang-NY 40
Harley-Cin 37
Beaumont-Pit 36

Stolen Base Average

Stolen Base Runs

Fielding Runs
Wallace-StL 29.6
Davis-NY 23.1
Flick-Phi 14.9
Dahlen-Bro 13.5
Kittridge-Bos 12.1

Total Player Rating
Wallace-StL 6.1
Wagner-Pit 5.2
Burkett-StL 5.0
Davis-NY 4.9
Sheckard-Bro 4.4

Wins
Donovan-Bro 25
Harper-StL 23
Phillippe-Pit 22
Hahn-Cin 22

Win Percentage
Chesbro-Pit ...... .677
Phillippe-Pit ...... .647
Tannehill-Pit ..... .643
Harper-StL ...... .639
Kitson-Bro .... .633

Games
Taylor-NY 45
Powell-StL 45
Donovan-Bro 45
Hahn-Cin 42
Mathewson-NY 40

Complete Games
Hahn-Cin 41
Taylor-NY 37
Mathewson-NY ... 36
Donovan-Bro 36
Donahue-Phi 34

Shutouts
Willis-Bos.......... 6
Orth-Phi 6
Chesbro-Pit 6

Saves
Powell-StL 3
Donovan-Bro 3
Sudhoff-StL 2
Phillippe-Pit 2
Kitson-Bro 2

Innings Pitched
Hahn-Cin 375.1
Taylor-NY 353.1
Donovan-Bro ... 351.0
Powell-StL 338.1
Mathewson-NY .. 336.0

Fewest Hits/Game
Townsend-Phi 7.39
Mathewson-NY .. 7.71
Willis-Bos 7.72
Orth-Phi 7.99
Chesbro-Pit 8.17

Fewest BB/Game
Orth-Phi 1.02
Phillippe-Pit 1.16
Tannehill-Pit 1.28
Duggleby-Phi 1.31
Powell-StL 1.33

Strikeouts
Hahn-Cin 239
Donovan-Bro 226
Hughes-Chi 225
Mathewson-NY ... 221
Waddell-Pit-Chi ... 172

Strikeouts/Game
Hughes-Chi 6.57
Waddell-Pit-Chi .. 6.16
Mathewson-NY ... 5.92
Donovan-Bro 5.79
Hahn-Cin 5.73

Ratio
Orth-Phi 9.27
Phillippe-Pit 9.79
Tannehill-Pit 10.17
Chesbro-Pit 10.17
Willis-Bos 10.35

Earned Run Average
Tannehill-Pit 2.18
Phillippe-Pit 2.22
Orth-Phi 2.27
Willis-Bos 2.36
Chesbro-Pit 2.38

Adjusted ERA
Willis-Bos 153
Tannehill-Pit 150
Orth-Phi 150
Phillippe-Pit 147
Chesbro-Pit 137

Opponents' Batting Avg.
Townsend-Phi .... .223
Mathewson-NY ... .230
Willis-Bos .... .231
Orth-Phi .... .237
Chesbro-Pit ..... .241

Opponents' On Base Pct.
Orth-Phi .... .264
Phillippe-Pit ..... .275
Tannehill-Pit ..... .283
Chesbro-Pit ..... .283
Willis-Bos .... .286

Starter Runs
Phillippe-Pit 36.2
Mathewson-NY ... 34.0
Orth-Phi 32.9
Willis-Bos 32.7
Tannehill-Pit 32.1

Adjusted Starter Runs
Willis-Bos 42.6
Orth-Phi 35.3
Phillippe-Pit 34.4
Mathewson-NY ... 33.3
Tannehill-Pit 30.5

Clutch Pitching Index
Kitson-Bro 122
Taylor-Chi........ 117
Hughes-Bro 114
Taylor-NY 112
Duggleby-Phi..... 109

Relief Runs

Adjusted Relief Runs

Relief Ranking

Total Pitcher Index
Orth-Phi 4.6
Phillippe-Pit 4.3
Willis-Bos 4.2
Mathewson-NY ... 4.2
Tannehill-Pit 3.2

Total Baseball Ranking
Wallace-StL 6.1
Wagner-Pit 5.2
Burkett-StL 5.0
Davis-NY 4.9
Orth-Phi 4.5

TEAM	G	W	L	PCT	GB	R	OR	AB	H	2B	3B	HR	BB	SO	AVG	OBP	SLG	PRO	PRO+	BR	/A	PF	CHI	RC	SB	CS	SBA	SBR
CHI	137	83	53	.610		**819**	631	4725	1303	173	89	32	**475**	337	.276	.350	.370	.720	**108**	41	**61**	97	103	744	**280**			
BOS	138	79	57	.581	4	759	**608**	4866	1353	183	104	**37**	331	**282**	.278	.330	.381	.711	104	9	22	98	101	693	157			
DET	136	74	61	.548	8.5	741	694	4676	1303	180	80	29	380	346	.279	.340	.370	.710	98	16	-17	105	99	690	204			
PHI	137	74	62	.544	9	805	761	4882	**1409**	239	87	35	301	344	.289	.336	.395	.731	102	42	9	104	103	733	173			
BAL	135	68	65	.511	13.5	760	750	4589	1348	179	**111**	24	369	377	**.294**	**.353**	**.397**	**.750**	**108**	**80**	49	104	96	**745**	207			
WAS	138	61	72	.459	20.5	682	771	4772	1282	191	83	33	356	340	.269	.326	.364	.690	97	-24	-13	99	96	633	127			
CLE	138	54	82	.397	29	667	831	4833	1311	197	68	12	243	326	.271	.313	.348	.661	92	-81	-51	96	**104**	588	125			
MIL	139	48	89	.350	35.5	641	828	4795	1250	192	66	26	325	384	.261	.313	.345	.658	91	-82	-46	95	98	601	176			
TOT	549					5874		38138	10559	1534	688	228	2780	2736	.277	.333	.371	.704						1449				

TEAM	CG	SH	SV	IP	H	H/G	HR	BB	SO	RAT	ERA	ERA+	OAV	OOB	PR	/A	PF	CPI	FA	E	DP	FW	PW	BW	SBW	DIF
CHI	110	**11**	2	1218[1]	1250	9.2	27	312	394	11.9	**2.98**	117	.263	.314	**93**	68	95	106	.941	345	100	.9	6.1	**5.5**		2.5
BOS	123	7	1	1217	**1178**	8.7	33	294	**396**	11.2	3.04	116	**.251**	**.301**	84	66	96	94	**.943**	337	104	1.6	6.0	2.0		1.5
DET	118	8	2	1188[2]	1328	10.1	22	313	307	12.8	3.30	116	.280	.330	48	**71**	105	**109**	.930	410	**127**	-3.3	**6.4**	-1.5		4.9
PHI	**124**	6	1	1200[2]	1346	10.1	**20**	374	350	13.3	4.00	94	.280	.339	-45	-32	103	94	.942	337	93	1.4	-2.9	.8		6.7
BAL	115	4	3	1158	1313	10.2	21	344	271	13.3	3.73	104	.282	.338	-9	17	106	102	.926	401	76	-2.9	1.5	4.4		-1.5
WAS	118	8	2	1183	1396	10.6	51	**284**	308	13.2	4.09	89	.291	.338	-57	-58	100	100	**.943**	**323**	97	**2.4**	-5.2	-1.2		-1.5
CLE	122	7	**4**	1182[1]	1365	10.4	22	464	334	14.4	4.12	86	.286	.357	-60	-75	97	102	.942	329	99	2.1	-6.8	-4.6		-4.7
MIL	107	3	**4**	1218	1383	10.2	32	395	376	13.6	4.06	89	.283	.344	-53	-63	98	98	.934	393	106	-1.8	-5.7	-4.2		-8.9
TOT	937	54	19	9566		9.9				12.9	3.66		.277	.333					.938	2875	802					

Runs		Hits		Doubles		Triples		Home Runs		Total Bases	
Lajoie-Phi	145	Lajoie-Phi	232	Lajoie-Phi	48	Williams-Bal	21	Lajoie-Phi	14	Lajoie-Phi	350
Jones-Chi	120	Anderson-Mil	190	Anderson-Mil	46	Keister-Bal	21	Freeman-Bos	12	Collins-Bos	279
Williams-Bal	113	Collins-Bos	187	Collins-Bos	42	Mertes-Chi	17	Grady-Was	9	Anderson-Mil	274
Hoy-Chi	112	Waldron-Mil-Was	186	Farrell-Was	32	Stahl-Bos	16			Freeman-Bos	255
Barrett-Det	110	Dungan-Was	179			Collins-Bos	16			Williams-Bal	248

Runs Batted In		Runs Produced		Bases On Balls		Batting Average		On Base Percentage		Slugging Average	
Lajoie-Phi	125	Lajoie-Phi	256	Hoy-Chi	86	Lajoie-Phi	.426	Lajoie-Phi	.463	Lajoie-Phi	.643
Freeman-Bos	114	Williams-Bal	202	Jones-Chi	84	Donlin-Bal	.340	Jones-Chi	.412	Freeman-Bos	.520
Anderson-Mil	99	Collins-Bos	196	Barrett-Det	76	Freeman-Bos	.339	Donlin-Bal	.409	Seybold-Phi	.503
Mertes-Chi	98	Freeman-Bos	190	McFarland-Chi	75	Seybold-Phi	.334	Hoy-Chi	.407	Williams-Bal	.495
Williams-Bal	96	Mertes-Chi	187	McGraw-Bal	61	Collins-Bos	.332	Freeman-Bos	.400	Collins-Bos	.495

Production		Adjusted Production		Batter Runs		Adjusted Batter Runs		Clutch Hitting Index		Runs Created	
Lajoie-Phi	1.106	Lajoie-Phi	196	Lajoie-Phi	74.1	Lajoie-Phi	70.6	Burke-Mil-Chi	151	Lajoie-Phi	179
Freeman-Bos	.920	Freeman-Bos	157	Freeman-Bos	35.0	Freeman-Bos	36.3	Keister-Bal	142	Collins-Bos	116
Seybold-Phi	.901	Seybold-Phi	142	McGraw-Bal	31.1	Collins-Bos	29.8	Hartman-Chi	140	Anderson-Mil	114
Donlin-Bal	.883	Collins-Bos	142	Donlin-Bal	29.5	McGraw-Bal	29.2	Freeman-Bos	131	Freeman-Bos	112
Williams-Bal	.883	Donlin-Bal	138	Williams-Bal	29.4	Donlin-Bal	26.2	Elberfeld-Det	131	Donlin-Bal	109

Total Average		Stolen Bases		Stolen Base Average		Stolen Base Runs		Fielding Runs		Total Player Rating	
Lajoie-Phi	1.327	Isbell-Chi	52					Lajoie-Phi	28.7	Lajoie-Phi	9.2
Donlin-Bal	1.000	Mertes-Chi	46					Elberfeld-Det	22.6	Elberfeld-Det	4.3
Freeman-Bos	.994	Seymour-Bal	38					Conroy-Mil	19.8	Collins-Bos	4.0
Seybold-Phi	.963	Jones-Chi	38					Clingman-Was	17.8	Freeman-Bos	2.7
Williams-Bal	.956							Farrell-Was	16.6	Williams-Bal	2.6

Wins		Win Percentage		Games		Complete Games		Shutouts		Saves	
Young-Bos	33	Griffith-Chi	.774	McGinnity-Bal	48	McGinnity-Bal	39	Young-Bos	5	Hoffer-Cle	3
McGinnity-Bal	26	Young-Bos	.767	Dowling-Mil-Cle	43	Young-Bos	38	Griffith-Chi	5	Garvin-Mil	2
Griffith-Chi	24	Callahan-Chi	.652	Young-Bos	43	Miller-Det	35	Patterson-Chi	4		
Miller-Det	23	Patten-Was	.643	Carrick-Was	42	Fraser-Phi	35	Patten-Was	4		
Fraser-Phi	22	Miller-Det	.639	Patterson-Chi	41	Carrick-Was	34	Moore-Cle	4		

Innings Pitched		Fewest Hits/Game		Fewest BB/Game		Strikeouts		Strikeouts/Game		Ratio	
McGinnity-Bal	382.0	Young-Bos	7.85	Young-Bos	.90	Young-Bos	158	Garvin-Mil	4.27	Young-Bos	8.94
Young-Bos	371.1	Callahan-Chi	8.15	Gear-Was	1.21	Patterson-Chi	127	Patten-Was	3.86	Callahan-Chi	10.57
Miller-Det	332.0	Moore-Cle	8.38	Lee-Was	1.55	Dowling-Mil-Cle	124	Young-Bos	3.83	Griffith-Chi	11.10
Fraser-Phi	331.0	Lewis-Bos	8.51	Griffith-Chi	1.69	Garvin-Mil	122	Patterson-Chi	3.66	Lewis-Bos	11.32
Carrick-Was	324.0	Winter-Bos	8.74	Cronin-Det	1.72	Fraser-Phi	110	Dowling-Mil-Cle	3.65	Winter-Bos	11.35

Earned Run Average		Adjusted ERA		Opponents' Batting Avg.		Opponents' On Base Pct.		Starter Runs		Adjusted Starter Runs	
Young-Bos	1.62	Young-Bos	217	Young-Bos	.232	Young-Bos	.256	Young-Bos	84.1	Young-Bos	78.5
Callahan-Chi	2.42	Yeager-Det	147	Callahan-Chi	.239	Callahan-Chi	.290	Callahan-Chi	29.6	Miller-Det	32.8
Yeager-Det	2.61	Callahan-Chi	143	Moore-Cle	.244	Griffith-Chi	.300	Griffith-Chi	29.5	Yeager-Det	27.3
Griffith-Chi	2.67	Griffith-Chi	130	Lewis-Bos	.247	Lewis-Bos	.304	Miller-Det	26.1	Callahan-Chi	25.2
Winter-Bos	2.80	Miller-Det	130	Winter-Bos	.252	Winter-Bos	.304	Yeager-Det	23.2	Griffith-Chi	24.1

Clutch Pitching Index		Relief Runs		Adjusted Relief Runs		Relief Ranking		Total Pitcher Index		Total Baseball Ranking	
Katoll-Chi	125							Young-Bos	7.9	Lajoie-Phi	9.2
Yeager-Det	121							Callahan-Chi	4.0	Young-Bos	7.9
Siever-Det	116							Miller-Det	3.6	Elberfeld-Det	4.3
Sparks-Mil	115							Griffith-Chi	3.5	Collins-Bos	4.0
Young-Bos	114							Yeager-Det	3.4	Callahan-Chi	4.0

1902 National League

TEAM	G	W	L	PCT	GB	R	OR	AB	H	2B	3B	HR	BB	SO	AVG	OBP	SLG	PRO	PRO+	BR	/A	PF	CHI	RC	SB	CS	SBA	SBR
PIT	142	103	36	.741		775	440	4926	1410	189	95	18	372	446	.286	.345	.374	.719	124	153	133	104	105	744	222			
BRO	141	75	63	.543	27.5	564	519	4845	1242	147	49	19	319	489	.256	.310	.319	.629	98	-6	-10	101	100	551	145			
BOS	142	73	64	.533	29	572	516	4728	1178	142	39	14	398	481	.249	.313	.305	.618	95	-16	-22	101	104	541	189			
CIN	141	70	70	.500	33.5	633	566	4908	1383	188	77	18	297	465	.282	.328	.362	.690	108	96	42	110	95	655	131			
CHI	141	68	69	.496	34	530	501	4802	1200	131	40	6	353	565	.250	.307	.298	.605	95	-42	-26	97	101	539	222			
STL	140	56	78	.418	44.5	517	695	4751	1226	116	37	10	273	438	.258	.306	.304	.610	97	-37	-15	96	101	516	158			
PHI	138	56	81	.409	46	484	649	4615	1139	110	43	5	356	481	.247	.306	.293	.599	90	-49	-50	100	98	473	108			
NY	139	48	88	.353	53.5	401	590	4571	1088	147	34	8	252	530	.238	.283	.290	.573	83	-100	-96	99	94	451	187			
TOT	562					4476		38146	9866	1170	414	98	2620	3895	.259	.313	.319	.631						1362				

TEAM	CG	SH	SV	IP	H	H/G	HR	BB	SO	RAT	ERA	ERA+	OAV	OOB	PR	/A	PF	CPI	FA	E	DP	FW	PW	BW	SBW	DIF
PIT	131	21	3	1264²	1142	8.1	4	250	564	10.3	2.30	119	.241	.287	67	61	98	93	.958	247	87	3.4	6.4	14.0		9.6
BRO	132	14	3	1256	1113	8.0	10	363	536	10.8	2.69	102	.238	.298	12	9	99	86	.952	275	79	1.5	.9	-1.1		4.6
BOS	124	14	4	1259²	1233	8.8	16	372	523	11.6	2.61	108	.257	.316	24	29	102	109	.959	240	90	3.8	3.1	-2.3		-.0
CIN	130	9	1	1239	1228	8.9	15	352	430	11.9	2.67	112	.259	.317	14	43	108	108	.945	322	108	1.4	4.5	4.4		-7.6
CHI	132	17	2	1275¹	1235	8.7	9	279	437	11.0	2.21	122	.254	.300	81	69	97	113	.945	327	111	-1.7	7.3	-2.7		-3.4
STL	112	7	4	1227²	1399	10.3	16	338	400	13.0	3.47	79	.287	.337	-95	-101	99	102	.944	336	107	-2.4	-10.7	-1.6		3.6
PHI	118	8	3	1211	1323	9.8	12	334	504	12.7	3.50	80	.278	.333	-97	-93	101	95	.946	305	81	-.7	-9.8	-5.3		3.3
NY	118	11	1	1226¹	1193	8.8	16	332	501	11.6	2.82	99	.255	.312	-5	-3	101	98	.943	330	104	-2.1	-.3	-10.1		-7.4
TOT	997	101	21	9959²		8.9				11.6	2.78		.259	.313					.949	2382	777					

Runs
Wagner-Pit 105
Clarke-Pit 103
Beaumont-Pit 100
Leach-Pit 97
Crawford-Cin 92

Hits
Beaumont-Pit 193
Keeler-Bro 186
Crawford-Cin 185
Wagner-Pit 176
Beckley-Cin 175

Doubles
Wagner-Pit 30
Clarke-Pit 27
Cooley-Bos 26
Dahlen-Bro 25
Beckley-Cin 23

Triples
Leach-Pit 22
Crawford-Cin 22
Wagner-Pit 16
Clarke-Pit 14
Gremminger-Bos .. 12

Home Runs
Leach-Pit 6
Beckley-Cin 5
Sheckard-Bro 4
McCreery-Bro 4

Total Bases
Crawford-Cin 256
Wagner-Pit 247
Beckley-Cin 227
Beaumont-Pit 226
Leach-Pit 219

Runs Batted In
Wagner-Pit 91
Leach-Pit 85
Crawford-Cin 78
Dahlen-Bro 74

Runs Produced
Wagner-Pit 193
Leach-Pit 176
Crawford-Cin 167
Beaumont-Pit 167
Clarke-Pit 154

Bases On Balls
R.Thomas-Phi 107
Lush-Bos 76
Tenney-Bos 73
Sheckard-Bro 57

Batting Average
Beaumont-Pit ... .357
Crawford-Cin .... .333
Keeler-Bro ...... .333
Wagner-Pit ...... .330
Beckley-Cin ..... .330

On Base Percentage
R.Thomas-Phi .... .415
Tenney-Bos ...... .410
Clarke-Pit ...... .408
Beaumont-Pit .... .403
Wagner-Pit ...... .391

Slugging Average
Wagner-Pit ...... .463
Crawford-Cin .... .461
Clarke-Pit ...... .449
Beckley-Cin ..... .427
Leach-Pit .... .426

Production
Clarke-Pit .... .856
Wagner-Pit .... .854
Crawford-Cin ..... .848
Beaumont-Pit ..... .821
Beckley-Cin ...... .803

Adjusted Production
Clarke-Pit 159
Wagner-Pit 158
Beaumont-Pit 148
Crawford-Cin 147
Tenney-Bos 141

Batter Runs
Wagner-Pit 39.0
Crawford-Cin ... 38.6
Clarke-Pit 36.7
Beaumont-Pit ... 33.8
Tenney-Bos 29.0

Adjusted Batter Runs
Wagner-Pit 36.8
Clarke-Pit 34.7
Crawford-Cin ... 32.4
Beaumont-Pit ... 31.6
Tenney-Bos 28.4

Clutch Hitting Index
Hartman-StL 173
Bransfield-Pit ... 155
Ritchey-Pit 145
McCreery-Bro ... 144
Dahlen-Bro 141

Runs Created
Wagner-Pit 117
Beaumont-Pit ... 109
Crawford-Cin 108
Clarke-Pit 99
Beckley-Cin 94

Total Average
Clarke-Pit .... .975
Wagner-Pit .... .958
Beaumont-Pit ..... .865
Crawford-Cin ..... .865
Tenney-Bos ...... .848

Stolen Bases
Wagner-Pit 42
Slagle-Chi 40
Donovan-StL 34
Beaumont-Pit 33
Smith-NY 32

Stolen Base Average

Stolen Base Runs

Fielding Runs
Farrell-StL 33.3
Lowe-Chi 26.0
H.Long-Bos 22.5
Steinfeldt-Cin 21.2
Leach-Pit 12.7

Total Player Rating
Wagner-Pit 4.4
Tenney-Bos 4.0
Farrell-StL 3.3
Leach-Pit 3.3
Crawford-Cin 2.8

Wins
Chesbro-Pit 28
Willis-Bos 27
Pittinger-Bos 27
Taylor-Chi 23
Hahn-Cin 23

Win Percentage
Chesbro-Pit ...... .824
Doheny-Pit .... .800
Tannehill-Pit ..... .769
Phillippe-Pit ..... .690
Leever-Pit .... .682

Games
Willis-Bos 51
Pittinger-Bos 46
Yerkes-StL 39

Complete Games
Willis-Bos 45
Pittinger-Bos 36
Hahn-Cin 35
White-Phi 34
Taylor-Chi 33

Shutouts
Mathewson-NY 8
Chesbro-Pit 8
Taylor-Chi 7
Pittinger-Bos 7
Hahn-Cin 6

Saves
Willis-Bos 3
M.O'Neill-StL 2
Newton-Bro 2
Leever-Pit 2

Innings Pitched
Willis-Bos 410.0
Pittinger-Bos ... 389.1
Taylor-Chi 324.2
Hahn-Cin 321.0
White-Phi 306.0

Fewest Hits/Game
Newton-Bro 7.08
McGinnity-NY ... 7.18
Taylor-Chi 7.51
Donovan-Bro ... 7.56
Chesbro-Pit 7.61

Fewest BB/Game
Phillippe-Pit .... .86
Tannehill-Pit ...... .97
Menefee-Chi 1.19
Taylor-Chi 1.19
Leever-Pit 1.26

Strikeouts
Willis-Bos 225
White-Phi 185
Pittinger-Bos ... 174
Donovan-Bro 170
Mathewson-NY ... 159

Strikeouts/Game
White-Phi 5.44
Mathewson-NY ... 5.17
Donovan-Bro 5.14
Willis-Bos 4.94
Wicker-StL 4.61

Ratio
Taylor-Chi 8.95
Tannehill-Pit 9.27
McGinnity-NY 9.53
Hahn-Cin 9.70
Phillippe-Pit 9.73

Earned Run Average
Taylor-Chi 1.33
Hahn-Cin 1.77
Tannehill-Pit 1.95
Lundgren-Chi 1.97
Phillippe-Pit 2.05

Adjusted ERA
Taylor-Chi 203
Hahn-Cin 169
Poole-Pit-Cin 142
Tannehill-Pit 140
Lundgren-Chi 137

Opponents' Batting Avg.
Newton-Bro ...... .217
McGinnity-NY .... .219
Taylor-Chi .... .227
Donovan-Bro ..... .228
Chesbro-Pit ...... .229

Opponents' On Base Pct.
Taylor-Chi .... .259
Tannehill-Pit .... .266
McGinnity-NY .... .272
Hahn-Cin .... .275
Phillippe-Pit ..... .276

Starter Runs
Taylor-Chi 52.2
Hahn-Cin 36.1
Willis-Bos 26.5
Phillippe-Pit 22.0
Tannehill-Pit 21.3

Adjusted Starter Runs
Taylor-Chi 49.3
Hahn-Cin 43.7
Willis-Bos 28.4
Mathewson-NY ... 21.2
Phillippe-Pit 20.6

Clutch Pitching Index
Lundgren-Chi 144
Eason-Chi-Bos ... 140
Poole-Pit-Cin ... 140
Taylor-NY 124
Taylor-Chi 121

Relief Runs

Adjusted Relief Runs

Relief Ranking

Total Pitcher Index
Taylor-Chi 6.6
Hahn-Cin 4.7
Tannehill-Pit 3.1
Phillips-Cin 3.1
Mathewson-NY ... 3.0

Total Baseball Ranking
Taylor-Chi 6.3
Wagner-Pit 4.7
Hahn-Cin 4.6
Tenney-Bos 4.0
Farrell-StL 3.3

TEAM	G	W	L	PCT	GB	R	OR	AB	H	2B	3B	HR	BB	SO	AVG	OBP	SLG	PRO	PRO+	BR	/A	PF	CHI	RC	SB	CS	SBA	SBR
PHI	137	83	53	.610		775	636	4762	1369	235	67	38	343	293	.287	.340	.389	.729	104	49	21	104	107	729	201			
STL	140	78	58	.574	5	619	607	4736	1254	208	61	29	373	327	.265	.324	.353	.677	95	-39	-30	99	97	613	137			
BOS	138	77	60	.562	6.5	664	600	4875	1356	195	95	42	275	375	.278	.322	.383	.705	98	0	-19	103	98	672	132			
CHI	138	74	60	.552	8	675	602	4654	1248	170	50	14	411	381	.268	.333	.335	.668	95	-42	-12	96	95	712	265			
CLE	137	69	67	.507	14	686	667	4840	1401	248	68	33	308	356	.289	.336	.389	.725	111	40	67	96	95	712	140			
WAS	138	61	75	.449	22	707	790	4734	1338	262	66	47	329	296	.283	.336	.396	.732	108	51	46	101	98	697	121			
DET	137	52	93	.385	30.5	566	657	4644	1167	141	55	22	359	287	.251	.312	.320	.632	79	-110	-123	102	103	527	130			
BAL	141	50	88	.362	34	715	848	4760	1318	202	107	33	417	429	.277	.342	.385	.727	103	51	21	104	97	723	189			
TOT	553					5407		38005	10451	1661	569	258	2815	2744	.275	.331	.369	.700									1315	

TEAM	CG	SH	SV	IP	H	H/G	HR	BB	SO	RAT	ERA	ERA+	OAV	OOB	PR	/A	PF	CPI	FA	E	DP	FW	PW	BW	SBW	DIF
PHI	114	5	2	1216¹	1292	9.6	33	368	455	12.7	3.29	111	.273	.333	39	51	103	109	.953	270	75	1.4	4.8	2.0		6.8
STL	120	7	2	1244	1273	9.2	36	343	348	12.0	3.34	106	.266	.320	32	26	99	99	.953	274	122	1.5	2.5	-2.8		8.8
BOS	123	6	1	1238	1217	8.8	27	326	431	11.5	3.02	118	.258	.311	75	75	100	99	.955	263	101	2.0	7.1	-1.8		1.2
CHI	116	11	0	1221²	1269	9.3	30	331	346	12.1	3.41	99	.269	.323	22	-5	95	98	.955	257	125	2.3	-.5	-1.1		6.3
CLE	116	16	3	1204¹	1199	9.0	26	411	361	12.4	3.28	105	.260	.327	39	21	96	100	.950	287	96	.3	2.0	6.4		-7.7
WAS	130	2	1	1207²	1403	10.5	56	312	300	13.2	4.36	85	.291	.341	-106	-88	104	94	.945	316	70	-1.3	-8.3	4.4		-1.7
DET	116	9	3	1190²	1267	9.6	20	370	245	12.7	3.56	102	.274	.333	1	10	102	99	.943	332	111	-2.5	.9	-11.7		-2.3
BAL	119	3	1	1210¹	1531	11.4	30	354	258	14.3	4.33	87	.309	.360	-102	-77	106	104	.938	357	109	-3.5	-7.3	2.0		-10.2
TOT	954	59	13	9733		9.7				12.6	3.57		.275	.331					.949	2356	809					

Runs
Hartsel-Phi 109
Fultz-Phi 109
Strang-Chi 108
Bradley-Cle 104
Delahanty-Was ... 103

Hits
Hickman-Bos-Cle . 193
L.Cross-Phi 191
Bradley-Cle 187
Delahanty-Was ... 178
Freeman-Bos 174

Doubles
Delahanty-Was ... 43
Davis-Phi 43
L.Cross-Phi 39
Bradley-Cle 39
Freeman-Bos 38

Triples
Williams-Bal 21
Freeman-Bos 19
Ferris-Bos 14
Delahanty-Was ... 14
Hickman-Bos-Cle .. 13

Home Runs
Seybold-Phi 16
Hickman-Bos-Cle .. 11
Freeman-Bos 11
Bradley-Cle 11
Delahanty-Was ... 10

Total Bases
Hickman-Bos-Cle . 288
Freeman-Bos 283
Bradley-Cle 283
Delahanty-Was ... 279
Seybold-Phi 264

Runs Batted In
Freeman-Bos 121
Hickman-Bos-Cle . 110
L.Cross-Phi 108
Seybold-Phi 97

Runs Produced
L.Cross-Phi 198
Delahanty-Was ... 186
Freeman-Bos 185
Davis-Phi 175
Hickman-Bos-Cle . 173

Bases On Balls
Hartsel-Phi 87
Strang-Chi 76
Barrett-Det 74
Burkett-StL 71
Davis-Chi 65

Batting Average
Delahanty-Was ... .376
Hickman-Bos-Cle .. .361
Dougherty-Bos .... .342
L.Cross-Phi ...... .342
Bradley-Cle ...... .340

On Base Percentage
Delahanty-Was ... .454
Dougherty-Bos .... .411
Barrett-Det .... .397
Jones-Chi .... .394
Selbach-Bal ...... .394

Slugging Average
Delahanty-Was ... .590
Hickman-Bos-Cle .. .539
Bradley-Cle ...... .515
Seybold-Phi ...... .506
Freeman-Bos ..... .502

Production
Delahanty-Was .. 1.044
Hickman-Bos-Cle .. .926
Bradley-Cle ...... .890
Seybold-Phi ...... .881
Williams-Bal ...... .864

Adjusted Production
Delahanty-Was ... 186
Hickman-Bos-Cle .. 159
Bradley-Cle 151
Seybold-Phi 137
Williams-Bal 132

Batter Runs
Delahanty-Was ... 57.2
Hickman-Bos-Cle . 36.2
Lajoie-Phi-Cle ... 32.4
Bradley-Cle 30.6
Seybold-Phi 28.4

Adjusted Batter Runs
Delahanty-Was ... 56.6
Hickman-Bos-Cle . 38.0
Lajoie-Phi-Cle ... 34.3
Bradley-Cle 33.7
Seybold-Phi 25.2

Clutch Hitting Index
Davis-Chi 159
L.Cross-Phi 153
Mertes-Chi 151
Daly-Chi 126
Anderson-StL 126

Runs Created
Delahanty-Was .. 137
Hickman-Bos-Cle . 118
Bradley-Cle 114
Freeman-Bos 109
L.Cross-Phi 105

Total Average
Delahanty-Was .. 1.227
Hickman-Bos-Cle .. .935
Bradley-Cle ...... .895
Hartsel-Phi .... .895
Seybold-Phi ...... .894

Stolen Bases
Hartsel-Phi 47
Mertes-Chi 46
Fultz-Phi 44

Stolen Base Average

Stolen Base Runs

Fielding Runs
Ferris-Bos 26.6
Schreck-Cle-Phi-Cle . 21.2
Padden-StL 17.9
Jones-Chi 12.5
Coughlin-Was 11.8

Total Player Rating
Lajoie-Phi-Cle 6.1
Delahanty-Was 4.8
Bradley-Cle 4.3
Schreck-Cle-Phi-Cle .. 2.7
Hickman-Bos-Cle .. 2.7

Wins
Young-Bos 32
Waddell-Phi 24
Powell-StL 22
F.Donahue-StL 22
Dinneen-Bos 21

Win Percentage
Bernhard-Phi-Cle .783
Waddell-Phi ...... .774
Young-Bos .... .744
F.Donahue-StL .... .667
Griffith-Chi .... .625

Games
Young-Bos 45
Powell-StL 42
Dinneen-Bos 42
Wiltse-Phi-Bal 38
Orth-Was 38

Complete Games
Young-Bos 41
Dinneen-Bos 39
Powell-StL 36
Orth-Was 36

Shutouts
Joss-Cle 5
Siever-Det 4
Moore-Cle 4
Mercer-Det 4

Saves
Powell-StL 2

Innings Pitched
Young-Bos 384.2
Dinneen-Bos 371.1
Powell-StL 328.1
Orth-Was 324.0
F.Donahue-StL ... 316.1

Fewest Hits/Game
Bernhard-Phi-Cle . 7.01
Waddell-Phi 7.30
Joss-Cle 7.52
Siever-Det 7.93
Winter-Bos 7.97

Fewest BB/Game
Orth-Was 1.11
Young-Bos 1.24
Bernhard-Phi-Cle . 1.47
Siever-Det 1.53
Plank-Phi 1.83

Strikeouts
Waddell-Phi 210
Young-Bos 160
Powell-StL 137
Dinneen-Bos 136
Plank-Phi 107

Strikeouts/Game
Waddell-Phi 6.84
Powell-StL 3.76
Young-Bos 3.74
Joss-Cle 3.54
Piatt-Chi 3.51

Ratio
Bernhard-Phi-Cle . 8.68
Siever-Det 9.56
Waddell-Phi 9.67
Young-Bos 9.71
Joss-Cle 10.43

Earned Run Average
Siever-Det 1.91
Waddell-Phi 2.05
Bernhard-Phi-Cle . 2.15
Young-Bos 2.15
Garvin-Chi 2.21

Adjusted ERA
Siever-Det 191
Waddell-Phi 179
Young-Bos 166
Bernhard-Phi-Cle . 160
Garvin-Chi 153

Opponents' Batting Avg.
Bernhard-Phi-Cle .216
Waddell-Phi ...... .223
Joss-Cle .... .228
Siever-Det .... .237
Winter-Bos .... .238

Opponents' On Base Pct.
Bernhard-Phi-Cle .254
Siever-Det .... .273
Waddell-Phi ...... .275
Young-Bos .... .276
Joss-Cle .... .290

Starter Runs
Young-Bos 60.6
Waddell-Phi 46.6
Bernhard-Phi-Cle . 35.7
Siever-Det 34.7
F.Donahue-StL ... 28.5

Adjusted Starter Runs
Young-Bos 60.6
Waddell-Phi 49.5
Siever-Det 36.2
Bernhard-Phi-Cle . 32.6
F.Donahue-StL ... 26.9

Clutch Pitching Index
Garvin-Chi 128
Shields-Bal-StL ... 123
Husting-Bos-Phi .. 120
Moore-Cle 119
Sudhoff-StL 109

Relief Runs

Adjusted Relief Runs

Relief Ranking

Total Pitcher Index
Waddell-Phi 5.9
Young-Bos 5.8
Bernhard-Phi-Cle . 3.2
Siever-Det 2.9
F.Donahue-StL 2.4

Total Baseball Ranking
Lajoie-Phi-Cle 6.1
Waddell-Phi 5.9
Young-Bos 5.8
Delahanty-Was ... 4.8
Bradley-Cle 4.3

TEAM	G	W	L	PCT	GB	R	OR	AB	H	2B	3B	HR	BB	SO	AVG	OBP	SLG	PRO	PRO+	BR	/A	PF	CHI	RC	SB	CS	SBA	SBR
PIT	141	91	49	.650		793	613	4988	1429	208	110	34	364		.286	.341	.393	.734	113	90	68	103	101	756	172			
NY	142	84	55	.604	6.5	729	567	4741	1290	181	49	20	379		.272	.334	.344	.678	96	2	-24	104	107	670	264			
CHI	139	82	56	.594	8	695	599	4733	1300	191	62	9	422		.275	.340	.347	.687	106	22	41	97	100	678	259			
CIN	141	74	65	.532	16.5	765	656	4857	1399	228	92	28	403		.288	.346	.390	.736	105	98	23	111	98	735	144			
BRO	139	70	66	.515	19	667	682	4534	1201	177	56	15	522		.265	.345	.339	.684	105	23	42	97	98	656	273			
BOS	140	58	80	.420	32	578	699	4682	1145	176	47	25	398		.245	.312	.318	.630	90	-80	-54	96	100	540	159			
PHI	139	49	86	.363	39.5	617	738	4781	1283	186	62	12	338		.268	.321	.341	.662	98	-31	-9	97	97	596	120			
STL	139	43	94	.314	46.5	505	795	4689	1176	138	65	8	277		.251	.296	.313	.609	83	-124	-103	97	98	510	171			
TOT	560					5349		38005	10223	1485	543	151	3103	3767	.269	.330	.349	.678						1562				

TEAM	CG	SH	SV	IP	H	H/G	HR	BB	SO	RAT	ERA	ERA+	OAV	OOB	PR	/A	PF	CPI	FA	E	DP	FW	PW	BW	SBW	DIF
PIT	117	16	5	1251¹	1215	8.7	9	384	454	11.8	2.91	111	.255	.316	48	44	99	96	.951	295	100	1.6	4.2	6.5		8.7
NY	115	8	8	1262²	1257	9.0	20	371	628	11.9	2.95	113	.258	.316	43	56	102	99	.951	287	87	2.3	5.4	-2.3		9.1
CHI	117	6	6	1240¹	1182	8.6	14	354	451	11.4	2.77	113	.250	.307	67	46	96	94	.946	312	78	-1.6	4.4	3.9		6.3
CIN	126	11	1	1230	1277	9.3	14	378	480	12.6	3.07	116	.268	.331	26	65	109	105	.946	312	84	.4	6.2	2.2		-4.4
BRO	118	11	4	1221¹	1276	9.4	18	377	438	12.7	3.44	92	.275	.339	-25	-38	98	101	.951	284	98	2.0	-3.6	4.0		-.4
BOS	125	8	1	1228²	1310	9.6	30	460	516	13.4	3.44	96	.274	.348	-11	-21	98	112	.939	361	89	-3.0	-2.0	-5.2		-.8
PHI	126	5	3	1212¹	1347	10.0	21	425	381	13.6	3.96	82	.285	.352	-95	-97	100	97	.947	300	76	1.0	-9.3	-.9		-9.3
STL	111	4	2	1212¹	1353	10.0	25	430	419	13.6	3.67	89	.284	.350	-55	-56	100	105	.940	354	111	-2.7	-5.4	-9.9		-7.5
TOT	955	69	30	9859		9.3				12.6	3.26		.269	.330					.946	2531	723					

Runs
Beaumont-Pit 137
Donlin-Cin 110
Browne-NY 105
Slagle-Chi 104
Strang-Bro 101

Hits
Beaumont-Pit 209
Seymour-Cin 191
Browne-NY 185
Wagner-Pit 182
Donlin-Cin 174

Doubles
Steinfeldt-Cin 32
Mertes-NY 32
Clarke-Pit 32

Triples
Wagner-Pit 19
Donlin-Cin 18
Leach-Pit 17

Home Runs
Sheckard-Bro 9

Total Bases
Beaumont-Pit 272
Seymour-Cin 267
Wagner-Pit 265
Donlin-Cin 256
Sheckard-Bro 245

Runs Batted In
Mertes-NY 104
Wagner-Pit 101
Doyle-Bro 91
Leach-Pit 87
Steinfeldt-Cin 83

Runs Produced
Beaumont-Pit 198
Mertes-NY 197
Wagner-Pit 193
Leach-Pit 177
Doyle-Bro 175

Bases On Balls
Thomas-Phi 107
Dahlen-Bro 82
Slagle-Chi 81
Chance-Chi 78

Batting Average
Wagner-Pit 355
Clarke-Pit 351
Donlin-Cin 351
Bresnahan-NY 350
Seymour-Cin 342

On Base Percentage
Thomas-Phi 453
Chance-Chi 439
Bresnahan-NY 438
Sheckard-Bro 422
Donlin-Cin 420

Slugging Average
Clarke-Pit 532
Wagner-Pit 518
Donlin-Cin 516
Bresnahan-NY 493
Steinfeldt-Cin 481

Production
Clarke-Pit 945
Donlin-Cin 936
Wagner-Pit 931
Bresnahan-NY 931
Sheckard-Bro 898

Adjusted Production
Clarke-Pit 164
Sheckard-Bro 161
Wagner-Pit 160
Bresnahan-NY 159
Chance-Chi 155

Batter Runs
Donlin-Cin 42.8
Wagner-Pit 42.4
Sheckard-Bro 39.8
Clarke-Pit 37.2
Bresnahan-NY 36.8

Adjusted Batter Runs
Sheckard-Bro 42.1
Wagner-Pit 40.1
Chance-Chi 36.1
Clarke-Pit 35.3
Donlin-Cin 35.0

Clutch Hitting Index
Doyle-Bro 153
Corcoran-Cin 153
Mertes-NY 143
Chance-Chi 138
Dobbs-Chi-Bro . . . 138

Runs Created
Sheckard-Bro 137
Wagner-Pit 133
Donlin-Cin 122
Beaumont-Pit 119
Chance-Chi 118

Total Average
Chance-Chi 1.175
Sheckard-Bro . . 1.140
Bresnahan-NY . . 1.129
Wagner-Pit 1.097
Donlin-Cin 1.059

Stolen Bases
Sheckard-Bro 67
Chance-Chi 67
Wagner-Pit 46
Strang-Bro 46
Mertes-NY 45

Stolen Base Average

Stolen Base Runs

Fielding Runs
Farrell-StL 28.1
Wagner-Pit 24.6
Sheckard-Bro 23.4
Moran-Bos 19.3
Ritchey-Pit 19.0

Total Player Rating
Wagner-Pit 6.4
Sheckard-Bro 5.3
Thomas-Phi 3.7
Moran-Bos 3.5
Farrell-StL 3.0

Wins
McGinnity-NY 31
Mathewson-NY . . . 30
Phillippe-Pit 25
Leever-Pit 25

Win Percentage
Leever-Pit 781
Phillippe-Pit 735
Weimer-Chi 714
Mathewson-NY 698
Wicker-StL-Chi 690

Games
McGinnity-NY 55
Mathewson-NY 45
Pittinger-Bos 44
Schmidt-Bro 40

Complete Games
McGinnity-NY 44
Mathewson-NY 37
Pittinger-Bos 35
Hahn-Cin 34
Taylor-Chi 33

Shutouts
Leever-Pit 7
Schmidt-Bro 5
Hahn-Cin 5
Phillippe-Pit 4
Jones-Bro 4

Saves
Miller-NY 3
Lundgren-Chi 3

Innings Pitched
McGinnity-NY . . . 434.0
Mathewson-NY . . 366.1
Pittinger-Bos 351.2
Jones-Bro 324.1
Taylor-Chi 312.1

Fewest Hits/Game
Weimer-Chi 7.69
Mathewson-NY . . . 7.89
Taylor-Chi 7.98
Leever-Pit 8.07
McGinnity-NY 8.11

Fewest BB/Game
Phillippe-Pit 90
Hahn-Cin 1.43
Taylor-Chi 1.64
McFarland-StL 1.89
Leever-Pit 1.90

Strikeouts
Mathewson-NY . . . 267
McGinnity-NY 171
Garvin-Bro 154
Pittinger-Bos 140
Weimer-Chi 128

Strikeouts/Game
Mathewson-NY . . . 6.56
Piatt-Bos 4.97
Garvin-Bro 4.65
Weimer-Chi 4.09
Willis-Bos 4.05

Ratio
Phillippe-Pit 9.39
Taylor-Chi 9.77
Leever-Pit 10.13
Mathewson-NY . . . 10.59
Hahn-Cin 10.70

Earned Run Average
Leever-Pit 2.06
Mathewson-NY . . . 2.26
Weimer-Chi 2.30
Phillippe-Pit 2.43
McGinnity-NY 2.43

Adjusted ERA
Leever-Pit 157
Mathewson-NY . . . 148
Hahn-Cin 141
McGinnity-NY 138
Weimer-Chi 136

Opponents' Batting Avg.
Weimer-Chi 225
Mathewson-NY 231
Taylor-Chi 235
McGinnity-NY 236
Leever-Pit 238

Opponents' On Base Pct.
Phillippe-Pit 263
Taylor-Chi 273
Leever-Pit 282
Mathewson-NY 287
McGinnity-NY 291

Starter Runs
Mathewson-NY . . . 40.7
McGinnity-NY 40.2
Leever-Pit 38.0
Weimer-Chi 30.2
Taylor-Chi 28.2

Adjusted Starter Runs
McGinnity-NY 44.0
Mathewson-NY . . . 43.9
Leever-Pit 37.0
Hahn-Cin 33.8
Weimer-Chi 26.0

Clutch Pitching Index
Brown-StL 153
Pittinger-Bos 127
Malarkey-Bos 116
Piatt-Bos 115
Poole-Cin 114

Relief Runs

Adjusted Relief Runs

Relief Ranking

Total Pitcher Index
Mathewson-NY 4.9
McGinnity-NY 3.7
Leever-Pit 3.3
Hahn-Cin 3.1
Ewing-Cin 3.0

Total Baseball Ranking
Wagner-Pit 6.4
Sheckard-Bro 5.3
Mathewson-NY 4.9
Thomas-Phi 3.7
McGinnity-NY 3.7

TEAM	G	W	L	PCT	GB	R	OR	AB	H	2B	3B	HR	BB	SO	AVG	OBP	SLG	PRO	PRO+	BR	/A	PF	CHI	RC	SB	CS	SBA	SBR
BOS	141	91	47	.659		708	504	4919	1336	222	113	48	262	561	.272	.313	.392	.705	111	91	60	105	103	680	141			
PHI	137	75	60	.556	14.5	597	519	4673	1236	227	68	32	268	513	.264	.309	.363	.672	102	37	11	105	100	598	157			
CLE	140	77	63	.550	15	639	579	4773	1265	231	95	31	259	595	.265	.308	.373	.681	112	51	61	98	102	634	175			
NY	136	72	62	.537	17	579	573	4565	1136	193	62	19	332	465	.249	.307	.330	.637	91	-10	-45	106	105	540	160			
DET	137	65	71	.478	25	567	539	4582	1229	162	91	12	292	526	.268	.318	.351	.669	110	39	55	97	94	589	128			
STL	139	65	74	.468	26.5	500	525	4639	1133	166	68	12	271	539	.244	.290	.317	.607	90	-66	-51	97	102	480	101			
CHI	138	60	77	.438	30.5	516	613	4670	1152	176	49	14	325	537	.247	.301	.314	.615	95	-46	-21	96	98	526	180			
WAS	140	43	94	.314	47.5	437	691	4613	1066	172	72	17	257	463	.231	.277	.311	.588	80	-98	-109	102	96	454	131			
TOT	554					4543		37434	9553	1549	618	184	2266	4199	.255	.303	.344	.647						1173				

TEAM	CG	SH	SV	IP	H	H/G	HR	BB	SO	RAT	ERA	ERA+	OAV	OOB	PR	/A	PF	CPI	FA	E	DP	FW	PW	BW	SBW	DIF
BOS	123	20	4	1255	1142	8.2	23	269	579	10.4	2.57	118	.242	.288	55	64	102	100	.959	239	86	2.3	6.6	6.2		6.9
PHI	112	10	1	1207	1124	8.4	20	315	728	11.3	2.98	103	.246	.305	-2	10	103	97	.960	217	66	3.2	1.0	1.1		2.2
CLE	125	20	1	1243²	1161	8.4	16	271	521	10.6	2.73	105	.247	.293	32	17	96	98	.946	322	99	-3.2	1.8	6.3		2.1
NY	111	7	2	1201¹	1171	8.8	19	245	463	10.9	3.08	101	.255	.299	-16	5	105	93	.953	264	87	.0	.5	-4.7		9.1
DET	123	15	2	1196	1169	8.8	19	336	554	11.5	2.75	106	.256	.310	28	20	98	111	.950	281	82	.2	2.1	5.7		-9.9
STL	124	12	3	1222¹	1220	9.0	26	237	511	11.0	2.77	105	.260	.300	26	19	98	108	.953	268	94	.2	2.0	-5.3		-1.3
CHI	114	9	4	1235	1233	9.0	23	287	391	11.5	3.02	93	.260	.309	-8	-29	95	103	.949	297	85	-1.8	-3.0	-2.2		-1.5
WAS	122	6	3	1223²	1333	9.8	38	306	452	12.3	3.82	82	.277	.325	-116	-94	106	97	.954	260	86	.8	-9.8	-11.3		-5.2
TOT	954	99	20	9784		8.8				11.2	2.96		.255	.303					.953	2148	685					

Runs
Dougherty-Bos 107
Bradley-Cle 101
Keeler-NY 95
Barrett-Det 95
Bay-Cle 94

Hits
Dougherty-Bos ... 195
Crawford-Det ... 184
Parent-Bos 170
Bay-Cle 169
Bradley-Cle 168

Doubles
Seybold-Phi 45
Lajoie-Cle 41
Freeman-Bos 39
Bradley-Cle 36
Anderson-StL 34

Triples
Crawford-Det 25
Bradley-Cle 22
Freeman-Bos 20
Parent-Bos 17
Collins-Cle 17

Home Runs
Freeman-Bos 13
Hickman-Cle 12
Ferris-Bos 9
Seybold-Phi 8

Total Bases
Freeman-Bos 281
Crawford-Det 269
Bradley-Cle 266
Lajoie-Cle 251
Dougherty-Bos ... 250

Runs Batted In
Freeman-Bos 104
Hickman-Cle 97
Lajoie-Cle 93
L.Cross-Phi 90
Crawford-Det 89

Runs Produced
Lajoie-Cle 176
Crawford-Det 173
Freeman-Bos 165
Bradley-Cle 163
Dougherty-Bos ... 162

Bases On Balls
Barrett-Det 74
Lush-Det 70
Pickering-Phi 53
Burkett-StL 52
Flick-Cle 51

Batting Average
Lajoie-Cle .... .344
Crawford-Det .... .335
Dougherty-Bos .... .331
Barrett-Det .... .315
Bradley-Cle .... .313

On Base Percentage
Barrett-Det .... .407
Hartsel-Phi .... .391
Lajoie-Cle .... .379
Lush-Det .... .379
Green-Chi .... .375

Slugging Average
Lajoie-Cle .... .518
Bradley-Cle .... .496
Freeman-Bos .... .496
Crawford-Det .... .489
Hartsel-Phi .... .477

Production
Lajoie-Cle .... .896
Hartsel-Phi .... .868
Crawford-Det .... .855
Bradley-Cle .... .844
Freeman-Bos .... .823

Adjusted Production
Lajoie-Cle 170
Crawford-Det 159
Bradley-Cle 154
Hartsel-Phi 152
Green-Chi 146

Batter Runs
Lajoie-Cle 37.6
Crawford-Det 34.6
Bradley-Cle 30.9
Barrett-Det 29.7
Freeman-Bos 28.1

Adjusted Batter Runs
Lajoie-Cle 38.7
Crawford-Det 36.5
Bradley-Cle 32.1
Barrett-Det 31.7
Green-Chi 27.9

Clutch Hitting Index
Gochnauer-Cle ... 168
L.Cross-Phi 168
Williams-NY 152
Ganzel-NY 143
Carr-Det 143

Runs Created
Dougherty-Bos ... 111
Crawford-Det 110
Lajoie-Cle 107
Bradley-Cle 104
Barrett-Det 98

Total Average
Lajoie-Cle .... .940
Hartsel-Phi ...... .934
Barrett-Det ...... .873
Crawford-Det ..... .858
Bradley-Cle ...... .856

Stolen Bases
Bay-Cle 45
Pickering-Phi 40
Holmes-Was-Chi ... 35
Dougherty-Bos 35
Conroy-NY 33

Fielding Runs
Lajoie-Cle 40.1
Criger-Bos 22.8
Schreckengost-Phi 18.2
Wallace-StL 18.1
Williams-NY 15.6

Total Player Rating
Lajoie-Cle 8.3
Bradley-Cle 4.6
Crawford-Det 3.2
Elberfeld-Det-NY . 3.2
Barrett-Det 3.1

Wins
Young-Bos 28
Plank-Phi 23

Win Percentage
Young-Bos .... .757
Hughes-Bos ...... .741
Moore-Cle .... .679
Dinneen-Bos ..... .618
Plank-Phi .... .590

Games
Plank-Phi 43
Mullin-Det 41
Young-Bos 40
Flaherty-Chi 40
Chesbro-NY 40

Complete Games
Young-Bos 34
Waddell-Phi 34
Donovan-Det 34

Shutouts
Young-Bos 7
Mullin-Det 6
Dinneen-Bos 6
Sudhoff-StL 5
Hughes-Bos 5

Saves
Young-Bos 2
Powell-StL 2
Orth-Was 2
Mullin-Det 2
Dinneen-Bos 2

Innings Pitched
Young-Bos 341.2
Plank-Phi 336.0
Chesbro-NY 324.2
Waddell-Phi 324.0
Mullin-Det 320.2

Fewest Hits/Game
Moore-Cle 7.12
Donovan-Det 7.24
Joss-Cle 7.36
Waddell-Phi 7.61
Dinneen-Bos 7.68

Fewest BB/Game
Young-Bos .... .97
Bernhard-Cle 1.14
Donahue-StL-Cle .. 1.14
Joss-Cle 1.17
Tannehill-NY 1.28

Strikeouts
Waddell-Phi 302
Donovan-Det 187
Young-Bos 176
Plank-Phi 176
Mullin-Det 170

Strikeouts/Game
Waddell-Phi 8.39
Donovan-Det 5.48
Moore-Cle 5.38
Powell-StL 4.97
Mullin-Det 4.77

Ratio
Joss-Cle 8.85
Young-Bos 8.96
Bernhard-Cle 9.34
Moore-Cle 9.56
Dinneen-Bos 9.78

Earned Run Average
Moore-Cle 1.74
Young-Bos 2.08
Bernhard-Cle 2.12
White-Chi 2.13
Joss-Cle 2.19

Adjusted ERA
Moore-Cle 164
Young-Bos 146
Bernhard-Cle 135
Dinneen-Bos 134
White-Chi 132

Opponents' Batting Avg.
Moore-Cle .... .217
Donovan-Det ..... .220
Joss-Cle .... .223
Waddell-Phi ..... .229
Dinneen-Bos ..... .230

Opponents' On Base Pct.
Joss-Cle .... .257
Young-Bos .... .259
Bernhard-Cle .... .267
Moore-Cle .... .271
Dinneen-Bos ..... .276

Starter Runs
Moore-Cle 33.5
Young-Bos 33.4
White-Chi 27.7
Mullin-Det 25.5
Joss-Cle 24.4

Adjusted Starter Runs
Young-Bos 36.1
Moore-Cle 30.5
Dinneen-Bos 25.8
Plank-Phi 24.9
Mullin-Det 23.6

Clutch Pitching Index
Kitson-Det 128
Mullin-Det 121
Donahue-StL-Cle .. 119
Plank-Phi 116
White-Chi 111

Total Pitcher Index
Young-Bos 5.0
Mullin-Det 4.2
White-Chi 3.3
Joss-Cle 2.7
Dinneen-Bos 2.5

Total Baseball Ranking
Lajoie-Cle 8.3
Young-Bos 5.0
Bradley-Cle 4.6
Mullin-Det 4.1
White-Chi 3.3

1904 National League

TEAM	G	W	L	PCT	GB	R	OR	AB	H	2B	3B	HR	BB	SO	AVG	OBP	SLG	PRO	PRO+	BR	/A	PF	CHI	RC	SB	CS	SBA	SBR
NY	158	106	47	.693		744	476	5150	1347	202	65	31	434		.262	.324	.344	.668	108	80	53	104	106	703	283			
CHI	156	93	60	.608	13	599	517	5210	1294	157	62	22	298		.248	.295	.315	.610	95	-35	-36	100	104	581	227			
CIN	157	88	65	.575	18	695	547	5231	1332	189	92	21	399		.255	.311	.338	.649	98	39	-16	109	105	636	179			
PIT	156	87	66	.569	19	675	592	5160	1333	164	102	15	391		.258	.316	.338	.654	106	51	36	103	101	638	178			
STL	155	75	79	.487	31.5	602	595	5104	1292	175	66	24	343		.253	.306	.327	.633	107	9	36	96	98	601	199			
BRO	154	56	97	.366	50	497	614	4917	1142	159	53	15	411		.232	.294	.295	.589	90	-60	-45	98	94	516	205			
BOS	155	55	98	.359	51	491	749	5135	1217	153	50	24	316		.237	.286	.300	.586	90	-75	-53	96	93	507	143			
PHI	155	52	100	.342	53.5	571	784	5103	1268	170	54	23	377		.248	.305	.316	.621	102	-9	13	96	96	569	159			
TOT	623					4874		41010	10225	1369	544	175	2969	4277	.249	.305	.322	.627						1573				

TEAM	CG	SH	SV	IP	H	H/G	HR	BB	SO	RAT	ERA	ERA+	OAV	OOB	PR	/A	PF	CPI	FA	E	DP	FW	PW	BW	SBW	DIF
NY	127	21	15	1396²	1151	7.4	36	349	707	9.9	2.17	125	.222	.276	86	83	100	94	.956	294	93	2.3	8.8	5.6		12.8
CHI	139	18	6	1383²	1150	7.5	16	402	618	10.3	2.30	115	.224	.285	65	53	97	92	.954	298	89	1.8	5.6	-3.8		12.9
CIN	142	12	2	1392²	1256	8.1	13	343	502	10.7	2.34	125	.241	.295	60	88	107	103	.954	301	81	1.7	9.3	-1.7		2.2
PIT	133	15	1	1348¹	1273	8.5	13	379	455	11.4	2.89	95	.248	.306	-24	-24	100	93	.955	291	93	2.2	-2.5	3.6		7.2
STL	146	7	2	1368	1286	8.5	23	319	529	10.8	2.64	102	.239	.286	13	5	99	86	.952	307	83	1.1	.5	3.8		-7.4
BRO	135	12	2	1337¹	1281	8.6	27	414	453	11.8	2.70	101	.255	.319	4	4	100	113	.945	343	87	-1.4	.4	-4.8		-14.8
BOS	136	13	0	1348¹	1405	9.4	25	500	544	13.1	3.43	80	.272	.343	-105	-105	101	106	.945	353	91	-1.9	-11.1	-5.6		-2.9
PHI	131	10	2	1339¹	1418	9.5	22	425	469	12.9	3.39	79	.270	.332	-99	-110	98	101	.936	403	93	-5.1	-11.6	1.4		-8.7
TOT	1089	108	30	10914¹		8.4				11.3	2.73		.249	.305					.950	2590	710					

Runs
Browne-NY 99
Wagner-Pit 97
Beaumont-Pit 97
Huggins-Cin 96

Hits
Beaumont-Pit 185
Beckley-StL 179
Wagner-Pit 171
Browne-NY 169
Seymour-Cin 166

Doubles
Wagner-Pit 44
Mertes-NY 28
Delahanty-Bos 27
Seymour-Cin 26
Dahlen-NY 26

Triples
Lumley-Bro 18
Wagner-Pit 14
Tinker-Chi 13
Seymour-Cin 13
Kelley-Cin 13

Home Runs
Lumley-Bro 9
Brain-StL 7

Total Bases
Wagner-Pit 255
Lumley-Bro 247
Seymour-Cin 233
Beaumont-Pit 230
Beckley-StL 222

Runs Batted In
Dahlen-NY 80
Mertes-NY 78
Lumley-Bro 78
Wagner-Pit 75
Corcoran-Cin 74

Runs Produced
Wagner-Pit 168
Mertes-NY 157
Lumley-Bro 148
Dahlen-NY 148
Beaumont-Pit 148

Bases On Balls
Thomas-Phi 102
Huggins-Cin 88
Devlin-NY 62
Wagner-Pit 59
Ritchey-Pit 59

Batting Average
Wagner-Pit 349
Beckley-StL 325
Seymour-Cin 313
Chance-Chi 310
Beaumont-Pit 301

On Base Percentage
Wagner-Pit 423
Thomas-Phi 415
Chance-Chi 382
Huggins-Cin 376
Beckley-StL 374

Slugging Average
Wagner-Pit 520
Seymour-Cin 439
Chance-Chi 430
Lumley-Bro 428
Brain-StL 408

Production
Wagner-Pit 944
Chance-Chi 812
Seymour-Cin 787
Beckley-StL 777
Thomas-Phi 760

Adjusted Production
Wagner-Pit 186
Chance-Chi 151
Beckley-StL 147
Thomas-Phi 141
Lumley-Bro 137

Batter Runs
Wagner-Pit 53.0
Thomas-Phi 28.4
Chance-Chi 27.6
Beckley-StL 25.7
Donlin-Cin-NY ... 24.6

Adjusted Batter Runs
Wagner-Pit 51.4
Thomas-Phi 30.8
Beckley-StL 28.7
Chance-Chi 27.5
Grady-StL 24.8

Clutch Hitting Index
Dahlen-NY 170
Corcoran-Cin 159
Bransfield-Pit..... 154
Cooley-Bos 144
Kelley-Cin 141

Runs Created
Wagner-Pit 134
Lumley-Bro 94
Chance-Chi 93
Beckley-StL 93
Mertes-NY 93

Total Average
Wagner-Pit 1.163
Chance-Chi 926
Thomas-Phi 866
Mertes-NY 810
McGann-NY 789

Stolen Bases
Wagner-Pit 53
Mertes-NY 47
Dahlen-NY 47
McGann-NY 42
Chance-Chi 42

Stolen Base Average

Stolen Base Runs

Fielding Runs
Leach-Pit 35.8
Evers-Chi 31.3
Dahlen-NY 27.6
Tinker-Chi 19.3
Farrell-StL 16.3

Total Player Rating
Wagner-Pit 5.0
Leach-Pit 4.1
Thomas-Phi 3.9
Chance-Chi 3.8
Dahlen-NY 3.4

Wins
McGinnity-NY 35
Mathewson-NY 33
Harper-Cin 23
Taylor-NY 21
Nichols-StL 21

Win Percentage
McGinnity-NY 814
Mathewson-NY ...733
Harper-Cin 719
Flaherty-Pit 679

Games
McGinnity-NY 51
Mathewson-NY ... 48
Jones-Bro 46
Willis-Bos 43
Fraser-Phi 42

Complete Games
Willis-Bos 39
Taylor-StL 39
McGinnity-NY 38
Jones-Bro 38

Shutouts
McGinnity-NY 9
Harper-Cin 6

Saves
McGinnity-NY 5
Wiltse-NY 3
Briggs-Chi 3
Ames-NY 3

Innings Pitched
McGinnity-NY ... 408.0
Jones-Bro 377.0
Mathewson-NY ... 367.2
Taylor-StL 352.0
Willis-Bos 350.0

Fewest Hits/Game
Brown-Chi 6.57
Weimer-Chi 6.71
McGinnity-NY 6.77
Garvin-Bro 6.99
Taylor-NY 7.02

Fewest BB/Game
Hahn-Cin 1.06
Phillippe-Pit 1.40
Nichols-StL 1.42
Kellum-Cin 1.84
McFarland-StL.... 1.87

Strikeouts
Mathewson-NY ... 212
Willis-Bos 196
Weimer-Chi 177
Pittinger-Bos 146
McGinnity-NY 144

Strikeouts/Game
Wiltse-NY 5.74
Mathewson-NY ... 5.19
Weimer-Chi 5.19
Willis-Bos 5.04
Phillippe-Pit 4.43

Ratio
Brown-Chi 8.94
McGinnity-NY 8.96
Hahn-Cin 9.07
Nichols-StL 9.17
Mathewson-NY ... 9.50

Earned Run Average
McGinnity-NY 1.61
Garvin-Bro 1.68
Brown-Chi 1.86
Weimer-Chi 1.91
Nichols-StL 2.02

Adjusted ERA
McGinnity-NY 169
Garvin-Bro 162
Brown-Chi 142
Hahn-Cin 142
Weimer-Chi 139

Opponents' Batting Avg.
Brown-Chi 199
Weimer-Chi 204
McGinnity-NY 206
Taylor-NY 214
Garvin-Bro 218

Opponents' On Base Pct.
Brown-Chi 253
Nichols-StL 256
McGinnity-NY 256
Hahn-Cin 262
Mathewson-NY ...270

Starter Runs
McGinnity-NY 50.6
Mathewson-NY ... 28.4
Weimer-Chi 28.0
Nichols-StL 25.0
Hahn-Cin 22.2

Adjusted Starter Runs
McGinnity-NY 50.1
Hahn-Cin 28.5
Mathewson-NY ... 28.0
Weimer-Chi 25.6
Nichols-StL 23.6

Clutch Pitching Index
Garvin-Bro 154
O'Neill-StL 132
Briggs-Chi 129
Jones-Bro 118
Mitchell-Phi-Bro .. 117

Relief Runs

Adjusted Relief Runs

Relief Ranking

Total Pitcher Index
McGinnity-NY 5.7
Mathewson-NY 4.4
Flaherty-Pit 3.3
Hahn-Cin 3.2
Weimer-Chi 2.9

Total Baseball Ranking
McGinnity-NY 5.7
Wagner-Pit 5.0
Mathewson-NY ... 4.4
Leach-Pit 4.1
Thomas-Phi 3.9

TEAM	G	W	L	PCT	GB	R	OR	AB	H	2B	3B	HR	BB	SO	AVG	OBP	SLG	PRO	PRO+	BR	/A	PF	CHI	RC	SB	CS	SBA	SBR
BOS	157	95	59	.617		608	466	5231	1294	194	105	26	347	570	.247	.301	.340	.641	102	43	12	106	101	597	101			
NY	155	92	59	.609	1.5	598	526	5220	1354	195	91	27	312	548	.259	.307	.347	.654	107	66	40	105	96	636	163			
CHI	156	89	65	.578	6	600	482	5027	1217	193	68	14	373	586	.242	.300	.316	.616	104	5	27	96	109	578	216			
CLE	154	86	65	.570	7.5	647	482	5152	1340	225	90	27	307	714	.260	.308	.354	.662	116	79	83	99	103	650	178			
PHI	155	81	70	.536	12.5	557	503	5088	1266	197	77	31	313	605	.249	.297	.336	.633	100	28	1	105	98	579	137			
STL	156	65	87	.428	29	481	604	5291	1266	153	53	10	332	609	.239	.291	.294	.585	96	-53	-18	94	94	526	150			
DET	162	62	90	.408	32	505	627	5321	1231	154	69	11	344	635	.231	.282	.292	.574	90	-74	-56	97	102	501	112			
WAS	157	38	113	.252	55.5	437	743	5149	1170	171	57	10	283	759	.227	.275	.288	.563	84	-94	-85	98	97	475	150			
TOT	626					4433		41479	10138	1482	610	156	2611	5026	.244	.295	.321	.616							1207			

TEAM	CG	SH	SV	IP	H	H/G	HR	BB	SO	RAT	ERA	ERA+	OAV	OOB	PR	/A	PF	CPI	FA	E	DP	FW	PW	BW	SBW	DIF
BOS	148	21	1	1406	1208	7.7	31	233	612	9.4	2.12	126	.233	.270	75	86	103	102	.962	242	83	1.6	9.6	1.3		5.5
NY	123	15	1	1380²	1180	7.7	29	311	684	10.0	2.57	106	.232	.282	4	22	104	90	.958	275	90	-.8	2.5	4.5		10.4
CHI	134	26	3	1380	1161	7.6	13	303	550	9.8	2.30	107	.229	.279	45	23	95	93	.964	238	95	1.7	2.6	3.0		4.7
CLE	141	20	0	1356²	1273	8.4	10	285	627	10.5	2.22	114	.249	.293	56	47	98	116	.959	255	86	.4	5.3	9.3		-4.4
PHI	136	26	0	1361¹	1149	7.6	13	366	887	10.4	2.35	114	.230	.291	38	49	103	100	.959	250	67	.8	5.5	.1		-.9
STL	135	13	1	1410	1335	8.5	25	333	577	11.0	2.83	88	.251	.303	-36	-55	96	100	.960	267	78	-.2	-6.1	-2.0		-2.7
DET	143	15	2	1430	1345	8.5	16	433	556	11.6	2.77	92	.250	.313	-27	-35	98	106	.959	273	92	.0	-3.9	-6.3		-3.9
WAS	137	7	4	1359²	1487	9.8	19	347	533	12.5	3.62	73	.279	.330	-155	-145	102	99	.951	314	97	-3.1	-16.2	-9.5		-8.6
TOT	1097143		12	11084¹		8.2				10.7	2.60		.244	.295					.959	2114	688					

Runs
Dougherty-Bos-NY 113
Flick-Cle 97
Bradley-Cle 94
Lajoie-Cle 92

Hits
Lajoie-Cle 208
Keeler-NY 186
Bradley-Cle 183
Dougherty-Bos-NY 181
Flick-Cle 177

Doubles
Lajoie-Cle 49
Collins-Bos 33
Bradley-Cle 32

Triples
Stahl-Bos 19
Freeman-Bos. 19
Cassidy-Was 19
Murphy-Phi 17
Flick-Cle 17

Home Runs
Davis-Phi 10
Murphy-Phi 7
Freeman-Bos. 7

Total Bases
Lajoie-Cle 305
Flick-Cle 260
Freeman-Bos. 246
Bradley-Cle 246

Runs Batted In
Lajoie-Cle 102
Freeman-Bos 84
Bradley-Cle 83
Anderson-NY 82

Runs Produced
Lajoie-Cle 188
Bradley-Cle 172
Parent-Bos 156
Collins-Bos 149
Murphy-Phi 148

Bases On Balls
Barrett-Det 79
Burkett-StL 78
Hartsel-Phi 75
Selbach-Was-Bos . . 72
Lush-Cle 72

Batting Average
Lajoie-Cle 376
Keeler-NY 343
Flick-Cle 306
Bradley-Cle 300
Seybold-Phi 292

On Base Percentage
Lajoie-Cle 413
Keeler-NY 388
Flick-Cle 371
Stahl-Bos 366
Burkett-StL 362

Slugging Average
Lajoie-Cle 552
Flick-Cle 449
Murphy-Phi 440
Hickman-Cle-Det . . .437
Stahl-Bos 416

Production
Lajoie-Cle 965
Flick-Cle 820
Keeler-NY 796
Stahl-Bos 782
Murphy-Phi 760

Adjusted Production
Lajoie-Cle 205
Flick-Cle 160
Keeler-NY 145
Stahl-Bos 139
Hickman-Cle-Det . . 138

Batter Runs
Lajoie-Cle 62.5
Flick-Cle 38.8
Stahl-Bos 32.8
Keeler-NY 32.2
Davis-Phi 27.5

Adjusted Batter Runs
Lajoie-Cle 63.0
Flick-Cle 39.3
Keeler-NY 29.4
Stahl-Bos 29.1
Davis-Phi 25.5

Clutch Hitting Index
Anderson-NY 145
Williams-NY 143
Carr-Det-Cle 143
Tannehill-Chi 140
Crawford-Det 138

Runs Created
Lajoie-Cle 142
Flick-Cle 115
Keeler-NY 100
Stahl-Bos 99
Bradley-Cle 95

Total Average
Lajoie-Cle 1.070
Flick-Cle 891
Keeler-NY 793
Stahl-Bos 782
Murphy-Phi 741

Stolen Bases
Flick-Cle 38
Bay-Cle 38
Heidrick-StL 35
Davis-Chi 32
Conroy-NY 30

Stolen Base Average

Stolen Base Runs

Fielding Runs
Tannehill-Chi 27.8
Davis-Chi 16.8
Williams-NY 16.8
Carr-Det-Cle 15.9
Elberfeld-NY 15.3

Total Player Rating
Lajoie-Cle 7.2
Flick-Cle 4.5
Murphy-Phi 4.0
Bradley-Cle 3.8
Davis-Chi 3.4

Wins
Chesbro-NY 41
Young-Bos 26
Plank-Phi 26
Waddell-Phi 25

Win Percentage
Chesbro-NY 774
Tannehill-Bos 656
Smith-Chi 640
Bernhard-Cle 639
Dinneen-Bos 622

Games
Chesbro-NY 55
Powell-NY 47
Waddell-Phi 46
Patten-Was 45
Mullin-Det 45

Complete Games
Chesbro-NY 48
Mullin-Det 42
Young-Bos 40
Waddell-Phi 39
Powell-NY 38

Shutouts
Young-Bos 10
Waddell-Phi 8
White-Chi 7
Plank-Phi 7
Mullin-Det 7

Saves
Patten-Was 3

Innings Pitched
Chesbro-NY 454.2
Powell-NY 390.1
Waddell-Phi 383.0
Mullin-Det 382.1
Young-Bos 380.0

Fewest Hits/Game
Chesbro-NY 6.69
Owen-Chi 6.94
Smith-Chi 6.98
Gibson-Bos 7.12
Waddell-Phi 7.21

Fewest BB/Game
Young-Bos 69
Tannehill-Bos 1.05
Patterson-Chi 1.31
Joss-Cle 1.40
Altrock-Chi 1.41

Strikeouts
Waddell-Phi 349
Chesbro-NY 239
Powell-NY 202
Plank-Phi 201
Young-Bos 200

Strikeouts/Game
Waddell-Phi 8.20
Bender-Phi 6.58
Moore-Cle 5.49
Plank-Phi 5.06
Glade-StL 4.86

Ratio
Young-Bos 8.53
Chesbro-NY 8.57
Owen-Chi 8.97
Joss-Cle 9.17
Dinneen-Bos 9.33

Earned Run Average
Joss-Cle 1.59
Waddell-Phi 1.62
White-Chi 1.78
Chesbro-NY 1.82
Owen-Chi 1.94

Adjusted ERA
Waddell-Phi 165
Joss-Cle 159
Chesbro-NY 149
White-Chi 138
Young-Bos 136

Opponents' Batting Avg.
Chesbro-NY 208
Owen-Chi 214
Smith-Chi 215
Gibson-Bos 219
Waddell-Phi 221

Opponents' On Base Pct.
Young-Bos 251
Chesbro-NY 252
Owen-Chi 261
Joss-Cle 265
Dinneen-Bos 268

Starter Runs
Waddell-Phi 41.5
Chesbro-NY 39.2
Young-Bos 26.6
Owen-Chi 22.9
Joss-Cle 21.5

Adjusted Starter Runs
Chesbro-NY 45.0
Waddell-Phi 44.8
Young-Bos 29.8
Joss-Cle 20.2
Plank-Phi 20.2

Clutch Pitching Index
White-Chi 153
Siever-StL 134
Bernhard-Cle 130
Waddell-Phi 126
Donahue-Cle 118

Relief Runs

Adjusted Relief Runs

Relief Ranking

Total Pitcher Index
Chesbro-NY 6.7
Waddell-Phi 4.6
Owen-Chi 3.4
Mullin-Det 3.2
Young-Bos 3.1

Total Baseball Ranking
Lajoie-Cle 7.2
Chesbro-NY 6.7
Waddell-Phi 4.6
Flick-Cle 4.5
Murphy-Phi 4.0

1905 National League

TEAM	G	W	L	PCT	GB	R	OR	AB	H	2B	3B	HR	BB	SO	AVG	OBP	SLG	PRO	PRO+	BR	/A	PF	CHI	RC	SB	CS	SBA	SBR
NY	155	105	48	.686		780	505	5094	1392	191	88	39	517		.273	.350	.368	.718	119	143	129	102	99	794	291			
PIT	155	96	57	.627	9	692	570	5213	1385	190	91	22	382		.266	.320	.350	.670	104	39	23	103	102	682	202			
CHI	155	92	61	.601	13	667	442	5108	1249	157	82	12	448		.245	.313	.314	.627	90	-28	-53	104	108	624	267			
PHI	155	83	69	.546	21.5	708	602	5243	1362	187	82	16	406		.260	.318	.336	.654	106	14	38	96	107	654	180			
CIN	155	79	74	.516	26	735	698	5205	1401	160	101	27	434		.269	.329	.354	.683	100	69	-1	111	103	704	181			
STL	154	58	96	.377	47.5	535	734	5066	1254	140	85	20	391		.248	.306	.321	.627	97	-35	-16	97	91	574	162			
BOS	156	51	103	.331	54.5	468	733	5190	1217	148	52	17	302		.234	.283	.293	.576	80	-134	-120	98	96	490	132			
BRO	155	48	104	.316	56.5	506	807	5100	1255	154	60	29	327		.246	.295	.317	.612	96	-68	-22	93	92	562	186			
TOT	620					5091		41219	10515	1327	641	182	3207	4462	.255	.314	.332	.646						1601				

TEAM	CG	SH	SV	IP	H	H/G	HR	BB	SO	RAT	ERA	ERA+	OAV	OOB	PR	/A	PF	CPI	FA	E	DP	FW	PW	BW	SBW	DIF
NY	117	18	15	1370	1160	7.6	25	364	760	10.2	2.39	122	.229	.284	91	80	98	93	.960	258	93	2.3	8.3	13.4		4.5
PIT	113	12	6	1382²	1270	8.3	12	389	512	11.2	2.86	104	.248	.308	20	16	100	95	.961	255	112	2.5	1.7	2.4		13.0
CHI	133	23	2	1407¹	1135	7.3	14	385	627	10.0	2.04	146	.224	.286	149	144	99	105	.962	248	99	2.9	15.0	-5.5		3.1
PHI	119	12	5	1398²	1303	8.4	21	411	516	11.5	2.81	104	.253	.316	28	12	97	106	.957	275	99	1.2	1.2	4.0		.6
CIN	119	10	2	1365²	1409	9.3	22	439	547	12.5	3.01	109	.272	.335	-3	41	110	116	.953	310	122	-1.0	4.3	-.1		-.7
STL	135	10	2	1347²	1431	9.6	28	367	411	12.3	3.59	83	.276	.329	-89	-93	99	98	.957	274	83	1.2	-9.7	-1.7		-8.8
BOS	139	14	0	1383	1390	9.0	36	433	533	12.1	3.52	88	.265	.326	-81	-68	103	95	.951	325	89	-1.8	-7.1	-12.5		-4.6
BRO	125	7	3	1347	1416	9.5	24	476	556	13.1	3.76	77	.274	.343	-114	-132	96	98	.937	408	101	-7.2	-13.7	-2.3		-4.8
TOT	1000106		35	11002		8.6				11.6	2.99		.255	.314					.954	2353	798					

Runs		Hits		Doubles		Triples		Home Runs		Total Bases	
Donlin-NY	124	Seymour-Cin	219	Seymour-Cin	40	Seymour-Cin	21	Odwell-Cin	9	Seymour-Cin	325
Thomas-Phi	118	Donlin-NY	216	Titus-Phi	36	Mertes-NY	17	Seymour-Cin	8	Donlin-NY	300
Huggins-Cin	117	Wagner-Pit	199	Wagner-Pit	32	Magee-Phi	17	Lumley-Bro	7	Wagner-Pit	277
Wagner-Pit	114	Barry-Chi-Cin	182	Donlin-NY	31	Smoot-StL	16	Donlin-NY	7	Magee-Phi	253
		Magee-Phi	180	Ritchey-Pit	29	Donlin-NY	16	Dahlen-NY	7	Titus-Phi	239

Runs Batted In		Runs Produced		Bases On Balls		Batting Average		On Base Percentage		Slugging Average	
Seymour-Cin	121	Wagner-Pit	209	Huggins-Cin	103	Seymour-Cin	.377	Chance-Chi	.449	Seymour-Cin	.559
Mertes-NY	108	Seymour-Cin	208	Slagle-Chi	97	Wagner-Pit	.363	Seymour-Cin	.428	Wagner-Pit	.505
Wagner-Pit	101	Donlin-NY	197	Thomas-Phi	93	Donlin-NY	.356	Wagner-Pit	.424	Donlin-NY	.495
Magee-Phi	98	Magee-Phi	193	Chance-Chi	78	Thomas-Phi	.317	Thomas-Phi	.417	Titus-Phi	.436
Titus-Phi	89	Titus-Phi	186	Titus-Phi	69	Chance-Chi	.316	Donlin-NY	.413	McGann-NY	.434

Production		Adjusted Production		Batter Runs		Adjusted Batter Runs		Clutch Hitting Index		Runs Created	
Seymour-Cin	.988	Seymour-Cin	175	Seymour-Cin	64.7	Seymour-Cin	57.0	Mertes-NY	162	Seymour-Cin	153
Wagner-Pit	.930	Wagner-Pit	173	Wagner-Pit	51.6	Donlin-NY	50.0	Corcoran-Cin	153	Wagner-Pit	146
Donlin-NY	.908	Donlin-NY	167	Donlin-NY	51.6	Wagner-Pit	49.9	Dahlen-NY	147	Donlin-NY	142
Chance-Chi	.882	Chance-Chi	157	Chance-Chi	37.1	Titus-Phi	36.9	Chance-Chi	146	Magee-Phi	110
Titus-Phi	.832	Titus-Phi	154	Titus-Phi	34.3	Chance-Chi	34.9	Magee-Phi	135	Mertes-NY	103

Total Average		Stolen Bases		Stolen Base Average	Stolen Base Runs	Fielding Runs		Total Player Rating	
Chance-Chi	1.127	Maloney-Chi	59			Huggins-Cin	36.2	Wagner-Pit	7.4
Wagner-Pit	1.123	Devlin-NY	59			Gilbert-NY	26.4	Seymour-Cin	6.3
Seymour-Cin	1.099	Wagner-Pit	57			Tenney-Bos	22.2	Huggins-Cin	4.7
Donlin-NY	1.003	Mertes-NY	52			Wagner-Pit	20.3	Thomas-Phi	4.4
McGann-NY	.898	Magee-Phi	48			Dahlen-NY	19.8	Titus-Phi	3.9

Wins		Win Percentage		Games		Complete Games		Shutouts		Saves	
Mathewson-NY	31	Leever-Pit	.800	Pittinger-Phi	46	Young-Bos	41	Mathewson-NY	8	Elliott-NY	6
Pittinger-Phi	23	Mathewson-NY	.775	McGinnity-NY	46	Willis-Bos	36	Young-Bos	7	Wiltse-NY	4
Ames-NY	22	Ames-NY	.733	Young-Bos	43	Fraser-Bos	35	Reulbach-Chi	5	McGinnity-NY	3
McGinnity-NY	21	Wiltse-NY	.714	Mathewson-NY	43	Taylor-StL	34	Phillippe-Pit	5		
		Lynch-Pit	.680	Overall-Cin	42			Briggs-Chi	5		

Innings Pitched		Fewest Hits/Game		Fewest BB/Game		Strikeouts		Strikeouts/Game		Ratio	
Young-Bos	378.0	Reulbach-Chi	6.42	Phillippe-Pit	1.55	Mathewson-NY	206	Ames-NY	6.78	Mathewson-NY	8.42
Willis-Bos	342.0	Mathewson-NY	6.70	Brown-Chi	1.59	Ames-NY	198	Wiltse-NY	5.48	Reulbach-Chi	9.23
Mathewson-NY	338.2	Lundgren-Chi	7.02	Young-Bos	1.69	Overall-Cin	173	Mathewson-NY	5.47	Phillippe-Pit	9.45
Pittinger-Phi	337.1	Wicker-Chi	7.03	Mathewson-NY	1.70	Ewing-Cin	164	Overall-Cin	4.90	Wicker-Chi	9.46
Fraser-Bos	334.1	Wiltse-NY	7.22	McGinnity-NY	1.99	Young-Bos	156	Scanlan-Bro	4.87	Brown-Chi	9.54

Earned Run Average		Adjusted ERA		Opponents' Batting Avg.		Opponents' On Base Pct.		Starter Runs		Adjusted Starter Runs	
Mathewson-NY	1.28	Mathewson-NY	229	Reulbach-Chi	.201	Mathewson-NY	.245	Mathewson-NY	64.6	Mathewson-NY	61.9
Reulbach-Chi	1.42	Reulbach-Chi	209	Mathewson-NY	.205	Reulbach-Chi	.266	Reulbach-Chi	50.9	Reulbach-Chi	50.3
Wicker-Chi	2.02	Wicker-Chi	147	Wiltse-NY	.219	Brown-Chi	.271	Phillippe-Pit	24.7	Ewing-Cin	27.1
Briggs-Chi	2.14	Briggs-Chi	139	Lundgren-Chi	.220	Phillippe-Pit	.274	Sparks-Phi	23.3	Phillippe-Pit	24.7
Brown-Chi	2.17	Brown-Chi	137	Wicker-Chi	.221	Wicker-Chi	.276	Brown-Chi	22.8	Brown-Chi	22.2

Clutch Pitching Index		Relief Runs	Adjusted Relief Runs	Relief Ranking	Total Pitcher Index		Total Baseball Ranking	
Chech-Cin	133				Mathewson-NY	9.0	Mathewson-NY	9.0
Duggleby-Phi	127				Reulbach-Chi	4.8	Wagner-Pit	7.4
Briggs-Chi	120				Ewing-Cin	3.1	Seymour-Cin	6.3
Overall-Cin	120				Wiltse-NY	2.4	Reulbach-Chi	4.8
Case-Pit	116				Brown-Chi	2.2	Huggins-Cin	4.7

TEAM	G	W	L	PCT	GB	R	OR	AB	H	2B	3B	HR	BB	SO	AVG	OBP	SLG	PRO	PRO+	BR	/A	PF	CHI	RC	SB	CS	SBA	SBR
PHI	152	92	56	.622		623	492	5146	1310	256	51	24	376		.255	.309	.338	.647	109	59	50	102	98	631	190			
CHI	158	92	60	.605	2	612	451	5114	1213	200	55	11	439		.237	.305	.304	.609	103	2	26	96	104	577	194			
DET	154	79	74	.516	15.5	512	602	4971	1209	190	54	13	375		.243	.301	.311	.612	99	2	-2	101	91	540	129			
BOS	153	78	74	.513	16	579	564	5049	1179	165	69	29	486		.234	.305	.311	.616	100	15	9	101	98	550	131			
CLE	155	76	78	.494	19	567	587	5166	1318	211	72	18	286		.255	.301	.334	.635	106	34	26	101	94	608	188			
NY	152	71	78	.477	21.5	586	622	4957	1228	163	61	23	360		.248	.305	.319	.624	93	21	-42	111	102	576	200			
WAS	154	64	87	.424	29.5	559	623	5015	1121	193	68	22	298		.224	.274	.302	.576	92	-69	-47	96	115	492	169			
STL	156	54	99	.353	40.5	511	608	5204	1205	153	49	16	362		.232	.288	.289	.577	94	-64	-33	95	99	501	130			
TOT	617					4549		40622	9783	1531	479	156	2982	5107	.241	.299	.314	.612						1331				

TEAM	CG	SH	SV	IP	H	H/G	HR	BB	SO	RAT	ERA	ERA+	OAV	OOB	PR	/A	PF	CPI	FA	E	DP	FW	PW	BW	SBW	DIF
PHI	117	19	0	1383¹	1137	7.4	21	409	895	10.4	2.19	121	.227	.293	70	68	100	110	.957	265	64	.2	7.5	5.5		4.8
CHI	131	15	0	1427	1163	7.3	11	329	613	9.6	1.99	124	.226	.277	105	72	93	106	.968	217	95	4.1	7.9	2.9		1.1
DET	124	17	1	1348	1226	8.2	11	474	578	11.7	2.83	96	.246	.318	-27	-19	103	104	.957	265	80	.5	-2.1	-.2		4.3
BOS	124	14	1	1356¹	1198	7.9	33	292	652	10.2	2.84	95	.241	.289	-29	-26	102	90	.953	294	75	-1.6	-2.9	1.0		5.4
CLE	140	16	0	1363¹	1251	8.3	23	334	555	10.8	2.85	92	.246	.299	-30	-34	99	96	.963	229	84	3.0	-3.7	2.9		-3.1
NY	88	16	4	1353²	1235	8.2	26	396	642	11.1	2.93	100	.246	.306	-42	-2	111	98	.952	293	88	-1.6	-.2	-4.6		3.0
WAS	118	12	1	1362¹	1250	8.3	12	385	539	11.2	2.87	92	.247	.307	-33	-35	100	98	.951	318	76	-3.1	-3.8	-5.2		.6
STL	134	10	2	1384²	1245	8.1	19	389	633	10.9	2.74	93	.243	.302	-14	-33	96	99	.955	295	78	-1.3	-3.6	-3.6		-14.0
TOT	976	119	9	10978²		8.0				10.7	2.65		.241	.299					.957	2176	640					

Runs		Hits		Doubles		Triples		Home Runs		Total Bases	
Davis-Phi	93	Stone-StL	187	Davis-Phi	47	Flick-Cle	18	Davis-Phi	8	Stone-StL	259
Jones-Chi	91	Davis-Phi	173	Crawford-Det	38	Ferris-Bos	16	Stone-StL	7	Davis-Phi	256
Bay-Cle	90	Crawford-Det	171	Hickman-Det-Was	37	Turner-Cle	14			Crawford-Det	247
Hartsel-Phi	88	Keeler-NY	169	Seybold-Phi	37	Stone-StL	13			Hickman-Det-Was	232
Keeler-NY	81	Bay-Cle	166			Burkett-Bos	13			Flick-Cle	231

Runs Batted In		Runs Produced		Bases On Balls		Batting Average		On Base Percentage		Slugging Average	
Davis-Phi	83	Davis-Phi	168	Hartsel-Phi	121	Flick-Cle	.308	Hartsel-Phi	.408	Flick-Cle	.462
L.Cross-Phi	77	Donahue-Chi	146	Jones-Chi	73	Keeler-NY	.302	Flick-Cle	.382	Crawford-Det	.430
Donahue-Chi	76	L.Cross-Phi	146	Selbach-Bos	67	Bay-Cle	.301	Crawford-Det	.357	Davis-Phi	.422
Crawford-Det	75	Crawford-Det	142	Burkett-Bos	67	Crawford-Det	.297	Keeler-NY	.356	Stone-StL	.410
Turner-Cle	72	Murphy-Phi	136	Davis-Chi	60	Stone-StL	.296	Selbach-Bos	.355	Hickman-Det-Was	.405

Production		Adjusted Production		Batter Runs		Adjusted Batter Runs		Clutch Hitting Index		Runs Created	
Flick-Cle	.844	Flick-Cle	165	Flick-Cle	38.4	Flick-Cle	37.6	Donahue-Chi	152	Flick-Cle	105
Crawford-Det	.786	Crawford-Det	148	Hartsel-Phi	32.7	Hartsel-Phi	31.6	L.Cross-Phi	150	Stone-StL	102
Stone-StL	.756	Stone-StL	148	Crawford-Det	31.1	Stone-StL	30.7	Gleason-StL	145	Davis-Phi	101
Davis-Phi	.756	Hartsel-Phi	138	Stone-StL	27.1	Crawford-Det	30.6	Williams-NY	131	Crawford-Det	99
Hartsel-Phi	.754	Davis-Phi	137	Davis-Phi	25.1	Davis-Phi	24.0	Fultz-NY	131	Hartsel-Phi	96

Total Average		Stolen Bases		Stolen Base Average	Stolen Base Runs	Fielding Runs		Total Player Rating	
Flick-Cle	.942	Hoffman-Phi	46			Cassidy-Was	33.1	Davis-Chi	4.0
Hartsel-Phi	.882	Fultz-NY	44			Tannehill-Chi	27.8	Crawford-Det	3.9
Crawford-Det	.797	Stahl-Was	41			Wallace-StL	19.0	Wallace-StL	3.7
Davis-Phi	.776	Hartsel-Phi	37			McIntyre-Det	16.4	Flick-Cle	3.4
Stone-StL	.751					Jones-Was	16.1	Bradley-Cle	2.8

Wins		Win Percentage		Games		Complete Games		Shutouts		Saves	
Waddell-Phi	27	Waddell-Phi	.730	Waddell-Phi	46	Plank-Phi	35	Killian-Det	8	Buchanan-StL	2
Plank-Phi	24	Tannehill-Bos	.710	Mullin-Det	44	Mullin-Det	35	Waddell-Phi	7		
Killian-Det	23	Coakley-Phi	.692	Patten-Was	42	Howell-StL	35	Tannehill-Bos	6		
Altrock-Chi	23	Plank-Phi	.667	Owen-Chi	42	Killian-Det	33	Orth-NY	6		
Tannehill-Bos	22	Altrock-Chi	.657			Owen-Chi	32	Hughes-Was	6		

Innings Pitched		Fewest Hits/Game		Fewest BB/Game		Strikeouts		Strikeouts/Game		Ratio	
Mullin-Det	347.2	Waddell-Phi	6.33	Young-Bos	.84	Waddell-Phi	287	Waddell-Phi	7.86	Young-Bos	8.08
Plank-Phi	346.2	Smith-Chi	6.63	Joss-Cle	1.45	Young-Bos	210	Young-Bos	5.89	Waddell-Phi	9.06
Owen-Chi	334.0	Young-Bos	6.96	Owen-Chi	1.51	Plank-Phi	210	Bender-Phi	5.58	Owen-Chi	9.16
Waddell-Phi	328.2	Howell-StL	7.02	Bernhard-Cle	1.76	Howell-StL	198	Howell-StL	5.52	White-Chi	9.37
Howell-StL	323.0	White-Chi	7.05	Altrock-Chi	1.80	Smith-Chi	171	Hogg-NY	5.49	Joss-Cle	9.57

Earned Run Average		Adjusted ERA		Opponents' Batting Avg.		Opponents' On Base Pct.		Starter Runs		Adjusted Starter Runs	
Waddell-Phi	1.48	Waddell-Phi	179	Waddell-Phi	.200	Young-Bos	.242	Waddell-Phi	42.7	Waddell-Phi	42.7
White-Chi	1.76	Young-Bos	147	Smith-Chi	.208	Waddell-Phi	.264	Young-Bos	29.3	Young-Bos	30.9
Young-Bos	1.82	Coakley-Phi	144	Young-Bos	.216	Owen-Chi	.266	Altrock-Chi	26.9	Chesbro-NY	24.6
Coakley-Phi	1.84	White-Chi	140	Howell-StL	.217	White-Chi	.270	White-Chi	25.6	Coakley-Phi	23.0
Altrock-Chi	1.88	Chesbro-NY	133	White-Chi	.218	Joss-Cle	.275	Howell-StL	24.0	Altrock-Chi	20.3

Clutch Pitching Index		Relief Runs	Adjusted Relief Runs	Relief Ranking	Total Pitcher Index		Total Baseball Ranking	
Coakley-Phi	142				Howell-StL	4.8	Waddell-Phi	4.8
Altrock-Chi	118				Waddell-Phi	4.8	Howell-StL	4.7
Waddell-Phi	116				Young-Bos	3.2	Davis-Chi	4.0
Townsend-Was	115				Chesbro-NY	3.0	Crawford-Det	3.9
Mullin-Det	114				Altrock-Chi	2.9	Wallace-StL	3.7

1906 National League

TEAM	G	W	L	PCT	GB	R	OR	AB	H	2B	3B	HR	BB	SO	AVG	OBP	SLG	PRO	PRO+	BR	/A	PF	CHI	RC	SB	CS	SBA	SBR
CHI	155	116	36	.763		705	381	5018	1316	181	71	20	448		.262	.328	.339	.667	110	86	53	106	108	694	283			
NY	153	96	56	.632	20	625	510	4768	1217	162	53	15	563		.255	.340	.321	.661	112	89	77	102	99	655	288			
PIT	154	93	60	.608	23.5	623	470	5030	1313	164	67	12	424		.261	.323	.327	.650	105	56	31	104	101	623	162			
PHI	154	71	82	.464	45.5	528	564	4911	1183	197	47	12	432		.241	.306	.307	.613	98	-8	-9	100	99	549	180			
BRO	153	66	86	.434	50	496	625	4897	1156	141	68	25	388		.236	.295	.308	.603	103	-32	10	92	98	529	175			
CIN	155	64	87	.424	51.5	533	582	5025	1198	140	71	16	395		.238	.298	.304	.602	91	-32	-56	104	102	540	170			
STL	154	52	98	.347	63	470	607	5075	1195	137	69	10	361		.235	.290	.296	.586	93	-65	-42	96	97	496	110			
BOS	152	49	102	.325	66.5	408	649	4925	1115	136	43	16	356		.226	.285	.281	.566	85	-94	-80	97	92	447	93			
TOT	615					4388		39649	9693	1258	489	126	3367	4537	.244	.308	.310	.619						1461				

TEAM	CG	SH	SV	IP	H	H/G	HR	BB	SO	RAT	ERA	ERA+	OAV	OOB	PR	/A	PF	CPI	FA	E	DP	FW	PW	BW	SBW	DIF
CHI	125	30	10	1388[1]	1018	6.6	12	446	702	9.8	1.75	150	.207	.280	135	135	100	101	.969	194	100	4.5	15.0	5.9		14.6
NY	105	19	18	1334[1]	1207	8.1	13	394	639	11.0	2.49	105	.241	.300	20	15	99	97	.963	233	84	1.8	1.7	8.6		8.0
PIT	116	27	2	1358	1234	8.2	13	309	532	10.5	2.21	120	.245	.294	62	70	102	108	.964	228	109	2.2	7.8	3.4		3.1
PHI	108	21	5	1354[1]	1201	8.0	18	436	500	11.3	2.58	101	.235	.304	7	0	99	94	.956	271	83	-.6	.0	-1.0		-3.9
BRO	119	22	11	1348[2]	1255	8.4	15	453	476	11.7	3.13	80	.249	.316	-76	-93	96	89	.955	283	73	-1.5	-10.3	1.1		.7
CIN	126	12	5	1369[2]	1248	8.2	14	470	567	11.6	2.69	102	.250	.320	-10	6	105	106	.959	262	97	.0	.7	-6.2		-6.0
STL	118	4	2	1354	1246	8.3	17	479	559	11.9	3.04	86	.246	.318	-63	-65	100	92	.957	272	92	-.7	-7.2	-4.7		-10.4
BOS	137	10	0	1334[1]	1291	8.7	24	436	562	12.0	3.14	85	.261	.328	-76	-70	102	100	.947	337	102	-5.2	-7.8	-8.9		-4.7
TOT	954	145	53	10841[2]		8.1				11.2	2.62		.244	.308					.959	2080	740					

Runs		Hits		Doubles		Triples		Home Runs		Total Bases	
Wagner-Pit	103	Steinfeldt-Chi	176	Wagner-Pit	38	Schulte-Chi	13	Jordan-Bro	12	Wagner-Pit	237
Chance-Chi	103	Wagner-Pit	175	Magee-Phi	36	Clarke-Pit	13	Lumley-Bro	12	Steinfeldt-Chi	232
Sheckard-Chi	90	Seymour-Cin-NY	165	Bransfield-Phi	28	Nealon-Pit	12	Seymour-Cin-NY	8	Lumley-Bro	231
Nealon-Pit	82	Magee-Phi	159	Steinfeldt-Chi	27	Lumley-Bro	12	Schulte-Chi	7	Magee-Phi	229
		Huggins-Cin	159	Sheckard-Chi	27					Schulte-Chi	223

Runs Batted In		Runs Produced		Bases On Balls		Batting Average		On Base Percentage		Slugging Average	
Steinfeldt-Chi	83	Wagner-Pit	172	Thomas-Phi	107	Wagner-Pit	.339	Chance-Chi	.418	Lumley-Bro	.477
Nealon-Pit	83	Chance-Chi	171	Bresnahan-NY	81	Steinfeldt-Chi	.327	Bresnahan-NY	.414	Wagner-Pit	.459
Seymour-Cin-NY	80	Nealon-Pit	162	Titus-Phi	78	Lumley-Bro	.324	Wagner-Pit	.411	Steinfeldt-Chi	.430
Jordan-Bro	78	Steinfeldt-Chi	161	Dahlen-NY	76	Chance-Chi	.319	Steinfeldt-Chi	.395	Chance-Chi	.430
		Seymour-Cin-NY	142	Devlin-NY	74	Clarke-Pit	.309	Devlin-NY	.394	Jordan-Bro	.422

Production		Adjusted Production		Batter Runs		Adjusted Batter Runs		Clutch Hitting Index		Runs Created	
Wagner-Pit	.870	Lumley-Bro	184	Wagner-Pit	43.4	Lumley-Bro	41.8	Tinker-Chi	161	Wagner-Pit	123
Lumley-Bro	.864	Wagner-Pit	165	Chance-Chi	39.0	Wagner-Pit	40.9	Nealon-Pit	156	Chance-Chi	114
Chance-Chi	.848	Chance-Chi	156	Lumley-Bro	37.5	Chance-Chi	35.8	Ritchey-Pit	138	Steinfeldt-Chi	109
Steinfeldt-Chi	.825	Jordan-Bro	153	Steinfeldt-Chi	36.4	Steinfeldt-Chi	32.8	Mertes-NY-StL	135	Lumley-Bro	107
Devlin-NY	.784	Steinfeldt-Chi	149	Devlin-NY	28.8	Devlin-NY	27.5	Jordan-Bro	133	Magee-Phi	102

Total Average		Stolen Bases		Stolen Base Average		Stolen Base Runs		Fielding Runs		Total Player Rating	
Chance-Chi	1.059	Chance-Chi	57					Devlin-NY	28.0	Wagner-Pit	7.4
Wagner-Pit	1.035	Magee-Phi	55					Brain-Bos	25.7	Devlin-NY	6.5
Lumley-Bro	.963	Devlin-NY	54					Wagner-Pit	23.8	Huggins-Cin	4.0
Devlin-NY	.934	Wagner-Pit	53					Gilbert-NY	22.6	Lumley-Bro	4.0
Bresnahan-NY	.897	Evers-Chi	49					Huggins-Cin	21.5	Bresnahan-NY	3.8

Wins		Win Percentage		Games		Complete Games		Shutouts		Saves	
McGinnity-NY	27	Reulbach-Chi	.826	McGinnity-NY	45	Young-Bos	37	Brown-Chi	9	Ferguson-NY	7
Brown-Chi	26	Brown-Chi	.813	Young-Bos	43	Pfeffer-Bos	33	Leifield-Pit	8	Wiltse-NY	6
Willis-Pit	23	Leever-Pit	.759	Sparks-Phi	42					Stricklett-Bro	5
C.Mathewson-NY	22	Lundgren-Chi	.739	Duggleby-Phi	42						
Leever-Pit	22	Pfiester-Chi	.714								

Innings Pitched		Fewest Hits/Game		Fewest BB/Game		Strikeouts		Strikeouts/Game		Ratio	
Young-Bos	358.1	Reulbach-Chi	5.33	Phillippe-Pit	1.07	Beebe-Chi-StL	171	Ames-NY	6.90	Brown-Chi	8.53
McGinnity-NY	339.2	Pfiester-Chi	6.21	Leever-Pit	1.66	Pfeffer-Bos	158	Beebe-Chi-StL	6.67	Pfiester-Chi	8.94
Willis-Pit	322.0	Brown-Chi	6.43	Sparks-Phi	1.76	Ames-NY	156	Pfiester-Chi	5.49	Sparks-Phi	8.98
Sparks-Phi	316.2	Beebe-Chi-StL	6.67	Ewing-Cin	1.88	Pfiester-Chi	153	Overall-Cin-Chi	5.05	Reulbach-Chi	9.66
Lindaman-Bos	307.1	Lundgren-Chi	6.93	McGinnity-NY	1.88			Lush-Phi	4.84	Ewing-Cin	9.70

Earned Run Average		Adjusted ERA		Opponents' Batting Avg.		Opponents' On Base Pct.		Starter Runs		Adjusted Starter Runs	
Brown-Chi	1.04	Brown-Chi	253	Reulbach-Chi	.175	Brown-Chi	.252	Brown-Chi	48.9	Brown-Chi	49.0
Pfiester-Chi	1.51	Pfiester-Chi	174	Pfiester-Chi	.194	Sparks-Phi	.257	Willis-Pit	31.9	Willis-Pit	33.3
Reulbach-Chi	1.65	Reulbach-Chi	159	Brown-Chi	.202	Pfiester-Chi	.258	Pfiester-Chi	31.1	Pfiester-Chi	31.3
Willis-Pit	1.73	Willis-Pit	154	Beebe-Chi-StL	.209	Phillippe-Pit	.276	Reulbach-Chi	23.6	Reulbach-Chi	23.7
Leifield-Pit	1.87	Leifield-Pit	143	Sparks-Phi	.211	Reulbach-Chi	.278	Leifield-Pit	21.6	Leifield-Pit	22.7

Clutch Pitching Index		Relief Runs		Adjusted Relief Runs		Relief Ranking		Total Pitcher Index		Total Baseball Ranking	
Willis-Pit	140	Ferguson-NY	.3	Ferguson-NY	.1	Ferguson-NY	.0	Brown-Chi	6.4	Wagner-Pit	7.4
Lindaman-Bos	127							Willis-Pit	4.5	Devlin-NY	6.5
Brown-Chi	124							Taylor-StL-Chi	3.1	Brown-Chi	6.4
Leifield-Pit	121							Weimer-Cin	2.8	Willis-Pit	4.5
Lush-Phi	115							Reulbach-Chi	2.8	Huggins-Cin	4.0

TEAM	G	W	L	PCT	GB	R	OR	AB	H	2B	3B	HR	BB	SO	AVG	OBP	SLG	PRO	PRO+	BR	/A	PF	CHI	RC	SB	CS	SBA	SBR
CHI	154	93	58	.616		570	460	4925	1133	152	52	7	453		.230	.301	.286	.587	91	-44	-29	97	109	531	214			
NY	155	90	61	.596	3	644	543	5095	1354	166	77	17	331		.266	.313	.339	.652	100	53	-5	110	104	638	192			
CLE	157	89	64	.582	5	663	482	5426	1516	240	73	12	330		.279	.326	.357	.683	122	114	122	99	93	737	203			
PHI	149	78	67	.538	12	561	543	4883	1206	213	49	32	385		.247	.306	.330	.636	102	28	12	103	98	578	165			
STL	154	76	73	.510	16	558	498	5030	1244	145	60	20	366		.247	.304	.312	.616	103	-5	19	96	100	579	221			
DET	151	71	78	.477	21	518	599	4930	1195	154	64	10	333		.242	.294	.306	.600	91	-35	-50	103	101	538	206			
WAS	151	55	95	.367	37.5	518	664	4956	1180	144	65	26	306		.238	.286	.309	.595	97	-47	-21	95	104	535	233			
BOS	155	49	105	.318	45.5	463	706	5168	1223	160	75	13	298		.237	.283	.304	.587	89	-65	-64	100	93	502	99			
TOT	613					4495		40413	10051	1374	515	137	2802	4561	.249	.302	.318	.620						1533				

TEAM	CG	SH	SV	IP	H	H/G	HR	BB	SO	RAT	ERA	ERA+	OAV	OOB	PR	/A	PF	CPI	FA	E	DP	FW	PW	BW	SBW	DIF
CHI	117	32	3	1375[1]	1212	7.9	11	255	543	9.8	2.13	119	.239	.280	85	63	94	104	.963	243	80	1.8	6.9	-3.2		11.9
NY	99	18	5	1357[2]	1236	8.2	21	351	605	10.8	2.78	107	.246	.301	-13	28	110	96	.957	272	69	.1	3.1	-.5		11.9
CLE	133	27	4	1412[2]	1197	7.6	16	365	530	10.2	2.60	125	.232	.289	94	84	97	111	.957	216	111	3.9	9.2	13.4		-14.0
PHI	107	19	4	1322	1135	7.7	9	425	749	11.0	2.60	105	.236	.305	13	16	101	98	.957	267	86	-.2	1.8	1.3		2.7
STL	133	17	5	1357[2]	1132	7.5	14	314	558	10.0	2.23	116	.230	.284	70	54	96	98	.954	290	80	-1.1	5.9	2.1		-5.4
DET	128	7	4	1334[1]	1398	9.4	14	389	469	12.4	3.06	90	.272	.330	-55	-43	103	111	.959	260	86	.4	-4.7	-5.5		6.3
WAS	115	13	1	1322[2]	1331	9.1	15	451	558	12.4	3.25	81	.264	.330	-83	-90	98	102	.955	279	78	-.8	-9.9	-2.3		-7.0
BOS	124	6	6	1382	1360	8.9	37	285	549	11.0	3.41	81	.262	.306	-111	-106	102	87	.949	335	84	-3.9	-11.7	-7.0		-5.4
TOT	956	139	32	10864[1]		8.3				10.9	2.69		.249	.302					.958	2162	674					

Runs
Flick-Cle 98
Keeler-NY 96
Hartsel-Phi 96
Davis-Phi 94
Stone-StL 91

Hits
Lajoie-Cle 214
Stone-StL 208
Flick-Cle 194
Chase-NY 193
Keeler-NY 180

Doubles
Lajoie-Cle 48
Davis-Phi 42
Flick-Cle 34
Murphy-Phi 28
Turner-Cle 27

Triples
Flick-Cle 22
Stone-StL 20
Crawford-Det 16
Ferris-Bos 13

Home Runs
Davis-Phi 12
Hickman-Was 9
Stone-StL 6
Seybold-Phi 5

Total Bases
Stone-StL 291
Lajoie-Cle 280
Flick-Cle 275
Davis-Phi 253
Chase-NY 236

Runs Batted In
Davis-Phi 96
Lajoie-Cle 91
Davis-Chi 80
Williams-NY 77
Chase-NY 76

Runs Produced
Lajoie-Cle 179
Davis-Phi 178
Chase-NY 160
Flick-Cle 159
Stone-StL 156

Bases On Balls
Hartsel-Phi 88
Jones-Chi 83
W.Hahn-NY-Chi ... 72
Wallace-StL 58
McIntyre-Det 56

Batting Average
Stone-StL .... .358
Lajoie-Cle .... .355
Chase-NY .... .323
Flick-Cle .... .311
Keeler-NY .... .304

On Base Percentage
Stone-StL .... .416
Lajoie-Cle .... .392
Flick-Cle .... .372
Hartsel-Phi ...... .362
Davis-Phi .... .355

Slugging Average
Stone-StL .... .501
Lajoie-Cle .... .465
Davis-Phi .... .459
Flick-Cle .... .441
Hickman-Was ..... .421

Production
Stone-StL .... .917
Lajoie-Cle .... .857
Davis-Phi .... .815
Flick-Cle .... .813
Crawford-Det ..... .747

Adjusted Production
Stone-StL 195
Lajoie-Cle 170
Flick-Cle 157
Davis-Phi 150
Hickman-Was 134

Batter Runs
Stone-StL 57.8
Lajoie-Cle 45.1
Flick-Cle 38.7
Davis-Phi 33.4
Seybold-Phi 21.0

Adjusted Batter Runs
Stone-StL 60.6
Lajoie-Cle 46.0
Flick-Cle 39.6
Davis-Phi 31.6
Seybold-Phi 19.6

Clutch Hitting Index
Davis-Chi 180
Wallace-StL 152
Williams-NY 152
Coughlin-Det 145
Stahl-Was 144

Runs Created
Stone-StL 141
Lajoie-Cle 122
Flick-Cle 121
Davis-Phi 101
Chase-NY 94

Total Average
Stone-StL 1.029
Flick-Cle .... .872
Lajoie-Cle .... .866
Davis-Phi .... .846
Hartsel-Phi ...... .751

Stolen Bases
Flick-Cle 39
Anderson-Was 39
Isbell-Chi 37
Altizer-Was 37
Donahue-Chi 36

Stolen Base Average

Stolen Base Runs

Fielding Runs
Tannehill-Chi 39.6
Lajoie-Cle 31.9
Turner-Cle 23.6
Schlafly-Was 14.0
McIntyre-Det 11.9

Total Player Rating
Lajoie-Cle 8.5
Stone-StL 5.6
Turner-Cle 4.7
Davis-Phi 2.9
Davis-Chi 2.8

Wins
Orth-NY 27
Chesbro-NY 23
Rhoads-Cle 22
Owen-Chi 22

Win Percentage
Plank-Phi .... .760
White-Chi .... .750
Joss-Cle .... .700
Rhoads-Cle ...... .688
Owen-Chi .... .629

Games
Chesbro-NY 49
Orth-NY 45
Waddell-Phi 43
Hess-Cle 43
Owen-Chi 42

Complete Games
Orth-NY 36
Mullin-Det 35
Hess-Cle 33
Rhoads-Cle 31

Shutouts
Walsh-Chi 10
Joss-Cle 9
Waddell-Phi 8

Saves
Hess-Cle 3
Bender-Phi 3

Innings Pitched
Orth-NY 338.2
Hess-Cle 333.2
Mullin-Det 330.0
Chesbro-NY 325.0
Rhoads-Cle 315.0

Fewest Hits/Game
Pelty-StL 6.53
White-Chi 6.57
Walsh-Chi 6.95
Joss-Cle 7.02
Powell-StL 7.23

Fewest BB/Game
Young-Bos .... .78
Altrock-Chi 1.31
Joss-Cle 1.37
White-Chi 1.56
Jacobson-StL 1.57

Strikeouts
Waddell-Phi 196
Falkenberg-Was .. 178
Walsh-Chi 171
Hess-Cle 167
Bender-Phi 159

Strikeouts/Game
Waddell-Phi 6.47
Bender-Phi 6.00
Walsh-Chi 5.53
Falkenberg-Was .. 5.36
Powell-StL 4.87

Ratio
White-Chi 8.33
Joss-Cle 8.49
Walsh-Chi 9.05
Pelty-StL 9.22
Powell-StL 9.48

Earned Run Average
White-Chi 1.52
Pelty-StL 1.59
Joss-Cle 1.72
Powell-StL 1.77
Rhoads-Cle 1.80

Adjusted ERA
White-Chi 167
Pelty-StL 163
Joss-Cle 152
Powell-StL 146
Rhoads-Cle 146

Opponents' Batting Avg.
Pelty-StL .... .206
White-Chi .... .207
Walsh-Chi .... .217
Joss-Cle .... .218
Powell-StL ...... .223

Opponents' On Base Pct.
White-Chi .... .249
Joss-Cle .... .252
Walsh-Chi .... .265
Pelty-StL .... .268
Powell-StL ...... .274

Starter Runs
Pelty-StL 31.9
Hess-Cle 31.7
Rhoads-Cle 31.1
Joss-Cle 30.3
White-Chi 28.6

Adjusted Starter Runs
Hess-Cle 29.1
Pelty-StL 28.8
Rhoads-Cle 28.7
Joss-Cle 28.1
White-Chi 24.9

Clutch Pitching Index
Rhoads-Cle 126
Siever-Det 126
Hess-Cle 123
Donahue-Det 121
Smith-Was 121

Relief Runs

Adjusted Relief Runs

Relief Ranking

Total Pitcher Index
Joss-Cle 3.8
Pelty-StL 3.7
White-Chi 3.6
Orth-NY 3.3
Hess-Cle 3.2

Total Baseball Ranking
Lajoie-Cle 8.5
Stone-StL 5.6
Turner-Cle 4.7
Joss-Cle 3.9
Pelty-StL 3.7

TEAM	G	W	L	PCT	GB	R	OR	AB	H	2B	3B	HR	BB	SO	AVG	OBP	SLG	PRO	PRO+	BR	/A	PF	CHI	RC	SB	CS	SBA	SBR
CHI	155	107	45	.704		574	390	4892	1224	162	48	13	435		.250	.318	.311	.629	98	27	-6	106	104	596	235			
PIT	157	91	63	.591	17	634	510	4957	1261	133	78	19	469		.254	.324	.324	.648	109	62	55	101	106	644	264			
PHI	149	83	64	.565	21.5	512	476	4725	1113	162	65	12	424		.236	.304	.305	.609	99	-10	-2	99	104	513	154			
NY	155	82	71	.536	25.5	574	510	4874	1222	160	48	23	516		.251	.329	.317	.646	107	66	49	103	96	614	205			
BRO	153	65	83	.439	40	446	522	4895	1135	142	63	18	336		.232	.285	.298	.583	97	-65	-24	92	99	485	121			
CIN	156	66	87	.431	41.5	526	519	4966	1226	126	90	15	372		.247	.303	.318	.621	98	4	-18	104	99	563	158			
BOS	152	58	90	.392	47	502	652	5020	1222	142	61	22	413		.243	.308	.309	.617	100	4	6	100	94	545	118			
STL	155	52	101	.340	55.5	419	608	5008	1163	121	51	19	312		.232	.282	.288	.570	88	-87	-70	97	97	473	125			
TOT	616					4187		39337	9566	1148	504	141	3277	4217	.243	.307	.309	.616						1380				

TEAM	CG	SH	SV	IP	H	H/G	HR	BB	SO	RAT	ERA	ERA+	OAV	OOB	PR	/A	PF	CPI	FA	E	DP	FW	PW	BW	SBW	DIF
CHI	114	32	8	1373¹	1054	6.9	11	402	586	9.8	1.73	144	.216	.281	112	115	101	102	.967	211	110	3.1	13.1	-.7		15.5
PIT	111	24	5	1363	1207	8.0	12	368	497	10.7	2.30	106	.241	.299	25	19	99	99	.959	256	75	.2	2.2	6.3		5.4
PHI	110	21	4	1299¹	1095	7.6	13	422	499	10.9	2.43	99	.233	.304	5	-3	98	94	.957	256	104	-.7	-.3	-.2		10.8
NY	109	22	13	1371	1219	8.0	25	369	655	10.7	2.45	101	.238	.294	2	1	100	91	.963	232	75	1.6	.1	5.6		-1.8
BRO	125	20	1	1356¹	1218	8.1	16	463	479	11.4	2.38	98	.249	.319	12	-9	95	113	.959	262	94	-.7	-1.0	-2.7		-4.6
CIN	118	10	2	1351¹	1223	8.1	16	444	481	11.5	2.41	107	.251	.322	8	25	105	115	.963	227	118	2.1	2.8	-2.0		-13.4
BOS	121	9	2	1338²	1324	8.9	28	458	426	12.4	3.33	76	.268	.339	-129	-119	103	99	.961	249	128	.1	-13.5	.7		-3.3
STL	127	19	2	1365²	1212	8.0	20	500	594	11.6	2.70	93	.243	.318	-35	-32	101	98	.948	340	105	-5.8	-3.6	-8.0		-7.1
TOT	935	157	37	10818²		7.9				11.1	2.46		.243	.307					.960	2033	809					

Runs	Hits	Doubles	Triples	Home Runs	Total Bases
Shannon-NY 104	Beaumont-Bos ... 187	Wagner-Pit 38	Ganzel-Cin 16	Brain-Bos 10	Wagner-Pit 264
Leach-Pit 102	Wagner-Pit 180	Magee-Phi 28	Alperman-Bro ... 16	Lumley-Bro 9	Beaumont-Bos ... 246
Wagner-Pit 98	Leach-Pit 166	Steinfeldt-Chi ... 25	Wagner-Pit 14	Murray-StL 7	Magee-Phi 229
Clarke-Pit 97	Magee-Phi 165	Seymour-NY 25	Beaumont-Bos 14	Wagner-Pit 6	Leach-Pit 221
Tenney-Bos 83	Mitchell-Cin 163	Brain-Bos 24	Clarke-Pit 13	Browne-NY 5	Brain-Bos 214

Runs Batted In	Runs Produced	Bases On Balls	Batting Average	On Base Percentage	Slugging Average
Magee-Phi 85	Wagner-Pit 174	Thomas-Phi 83	Wagner-Pit .... .350	Wagner-Pit .... .407	Wagner-Pit .... .513
Wagner-Pit 82	Magee-Phi 156	Huggins-Cin 83	Magee-Phi .... .328	Magee-Phi .... .396	Magee-Phi .... .455
Abbaticchio-Pit ... 82	Clarke-Pit 154	Tenney-Bos 82	Beaumont-Bos ... .322	Clarke-Pit .... .382	Lumley-Bro .... .425
Seymour-NY 75	Abbaticchio-Pit ... 143	Shannon-NY 82	Leach-Pit .... .303	Thomas-Phi .... .375	Beaumont-Bos ... .424
Steinfeldt-Chi 70	Leach-Pit 141	Anderson-Pit 80	Seymour-NY ..... .294		Brain-Bos .... .420

Production	Adjusted Production	Batter Runs	Adjusted Batter Runs	Clutch Hitting Index	Runs Created
Wagner-Pit .... .920	Wagner-Pit 186	Wagner-Pit 50.4	Wagner-Pit 49.6	Abbaticchio-Pit ... 194	Wagner-Pit 137
Magee-Phi .... .852	Magee-Phi 170	Magee-Phi 38.6	Magee-Phi 39.4	Seymour-NY 152	Magee-Phi 113
Beaumont-Bos ... .790	Beaumont-Bos ... 148	Beaumont-Bos ... 29.7	Beaumont-Bos ... 29.9	Steinfeldt-Chi ... 152	Beaumont-Bos ... 103
Clarke-Pit .... .771	Lumley-Bro 144	Clarke-Pit 26.4	Clarke-Pit 25.6	Magee-Phi 142	Leach-Pit 98
Leach-Pit .... .756	Jordan-Bro 142	Leach-Pit 21.6	Jordan-Bro 23.8	Ganzel-Cin 129	Clarke-Pit 93

Total Average	Stolen Bases	Stolen Base Average	Stolen Base Runs	Fielding Runs	Total Player Rating
Wagner-Pit 1.119	Wagner-Pit 61			Evers-Chi 29.2	Wagner-Pit 6.3
Magee-Phi .... .982	Magee-Phi 46			Brain-Bos 24.8	Brain-Bos 5.0
Clarke-Pit .... .862	Evers-Chi 46			Byrne-StL 22.4	Magee-Phi 4.6
Leach-Pit .... .801	Leach-Pit 43			Mitchell-Cin 22.2	Beaumont-Bos ... 3.3
Beaumont-Bos ... .791	Devlin-NY 38			Tinker-Chi 15.7	Mitchell-Cin 3.2

Wins	Win Percentage	Games	Complete Games	Shutouts	Saves
C.Mathewson-NY .. 24	Reulbach-Chi ..... .810	McGinnity-NY 47	McGlynn-StL 33	Overall-Chi 8	McGinnity-NY 4
Overall-Chi 23	Brown-Chi .... .769	McGlynn-StL 45	Ewing-Cin 32	C.Mathewson-NY ... 8	Overall-Chi 3
Sparks-Phi 22	Overall-Chi .... .767	C.Mathewson-NY .. 41	C.Mathewson-NY .. 31	Lundgren-Chi 7	Brown-Chi 3
Willis-Pit 21	Sparks-Phi .... .733	Ewing-Cin 41	Karger-StL 29		
	Lundgren-Chi ..... .720		Willis-Pit 27		

Innings Pitched	Fewest Hits/Game	Fewest BB/Game	Strikeouts	Strikeouts/Game	Ratio
McGlynn-StL 352.1	Lundgren-Chi 5.65	Phillippe-Pit 1.51	C.Mathewson-NY . 178	Ames-NY 5.63	C.Mathewson-NY . 8.71
Ewing-Cin 332.2	Pfiester-Chi 6.60	C.Mathewson-NY .. 1.51	Ewing-Cin 147	Beebe-StL 5.32	Brown-Chi 8.73
C.Mathewson-NY 315.0	Overall-Chi 6.74	Brown-Chi 1.55	Ames-NY 146	C.Mathewson-NY . 5.09	Pfiester-Chi 9.05
Karger-StL 314.0	Camnitz-Pit 6.75	McGinnity-NY 1.68	Overall-Chi 141	Overall-Chi 4.73	Overall-Chi 9.42
McGinnity-NY 310.1	Reulbach-Chi 6.89	Sparks-Phi 1.73	Beebe-StL 141	Reulbach-Chi 4.50	Sparks-Phi 9.48

Earned Run Average	Adjusted ERA	Opponents' Batting Avg.	Opponents' On Base Pct.	Starter Runs	Adjusted Starter Runs
Pfiester-Chi 1.15	Pfiester-Chi 215	Lundgren-Chi ..... .185	C.Mathewson-NY .. .247	Lundgren-Chi 29.7	Ewing-Cin 31.6
Lundgren-Chi 1.17	Lundgren-Chi 212	Pfiester-Chi ...... .207	Brown-Chi .... .262	Pfiester-Chi 28.4	Lundgren-Chi 30.2
Brown-Chi 1.39	Brown-Chi 179	Overall-Chi .... .208	Pfiester-Chi ...... .263	Brown-Chi 27.8	Pfiester-Chi 28.9
Leever-Pit 1.66	Ewing-Cin 149	Camnitz-Pit .... .211	Overall-Chi .... .268	Ewing-Cin 27.1	Brown-Chi 28.4
Overall-Chi 1.68	Overall-Chi 148	C.Mathewson-NY .. .212	Karger-StL .... .270	Overall-Chi 23.5	Overall-Chi 24.1

Clutch Pitching Index	Relief Runs	Adjusted Relief Runs	Relief Ranking	Total Pitcher Index	Total Baseball Ranking
Coakley-Cin 133				Brown-Chi 3.8	Wagner-Pit 6.3
Pastorius-Bro 129				Overall-Chi 3.5	Brain-Bos 5.0
Brown-StL-Phi ... 126				Lundgren-Chi 3.2	Magee-Phi 4.6
McIntire-Bro 126				Ewing-Cin 3.0	Brown-Chi 3.8
Leifield-Pit 123				Pfiester-Chi 2.8	Overall-Chi 3.5

TEAM	G	W	L	PCT	GB	R	OR	AB	H	2B	3B	HR	BB	SO	AVG	OBP	SLG	PRO	PRO+	BR	/A	PF	CHI	RC	SB	CS	SBA	SBR
DET	153	92	58	.613		694	532	5204	1383	179	75	11	315		.266	.313	.335	.648	108	63	43	104	110	640	192			
PHI	150	88	57	.607	1.5	582	511	5008	1274	223	43	22	384		.254	.310	.329	.639	106	51	38	102	96	590	137			
CHI	157	87	64	.576	5.5	588	474	5070	1205	149	33	5	421		.238	.302	.283	.585	95	-35	-16	97	110	522	175			
CLE	158	85	67	.559	8	530	525	5068	1221	182	68	11	335		.241	.295	.310	.605	97	-10	-14	101	96	555	193			
NY	152	70	78	.473	21	605	665	5044	1258	150	67	15	304		.249	.297	.315	.612	93	-2	-46	108	111	562	206			
STL	155	69	83	.454	24	542	555	5224	1324	154	63	10	370		.253	.308	.313	.621	103	19	21	100	91	580	144			
BOS	155	59	90	.396	32.5	464	558	5235	1224	154	48	18	305		.234	.280	.292	.572	88	-74	-69	99	94	493	125			
WAS	154	49	102	.325	43.5	506	691	5112	1243	134	58	12	390		.243	.302	.299	.601	105	-12	32	92	92	560	223			
TOT	617					4511		40965	10132	1325	455	104	2824	4479	.247	.301	.310	.610							1395			

TEAM	CG	SH	SV	IP	H	H/G	HR	BB	SO	RAT	ERA	ERA+	OAV	OOB	PR	/A	PF	CPI	FA	E	DP	FW	PW	BW	SBW	DIF
DET	120	15	7	1370²	1281	8.4	8	380	512	11.3	2.33	112	.251	.309	32	40	102	115	.959	260	79	1.0	4.4	4.7		6.9
PHI	106	27	6	1354²	1106	7.3	13	378	789	10.3	2.35	111	.226	.289	29	38	102	91	.958	263	67	.4	4.2	4.2		6.7
CHI	112	17	9	1406¹	1279	8.2	13	305	604	10.3	2.22	108	.245	.289	50	26	94	105	.966	233	101	3.4	2.9	-1.8		7.0
CLE	127	20	5	1392²	1253	8.1	8	362	513	10.8	2.26	111	.244	.300	43	36	99	109	.960	264	137	1.3	4.0	-1.5		5.2
NY	93	10	5	1333²	1327	9.0	13	428	511	12.2	3.03	92	.264	.328	-73	-40	110	103	.947	334	79	-4.4	-4.4	-5.1		9.9
STL	129	15	9	1381¹	1254	8.2	17	352	463	10.8	2.61	96	.245	.301	-10	-16	99	97	.959	266	97	.8	-1.8	2.3		-8.4
BOS	100	17	7	1414	1222	7.8	22	337	517	10.2	2.45	105	.238	.290	14	15	101	94	.959	274	100	.2	1.7	-7.6		-9.8
WAS	106	12	5	1351¹	1383	9.2	10	344	570	11.8	3.11	78	.268	.319	-86	-106	95	98	.951	311	69	-2.5	-11.7	3.5		-15.8
TOT	893	133	53	11004²		8.3				10.9	2.54		.247	.301					.957	2205	729					

Runs		Hits		Doubles		Triples		Home Runs		Total Bases	
Crawford-Det	102	Cobb-Det	212	Davis-Phi	37	Flick-Cle	18	Davis-Phi	8	Cobb-Det	283
D.Jones-Det	101	Stone-StL	191	Crawford-Det	34	Crawford-Det	17	Seybold-Phi	5	Crawford-Det	268
Cobb-Det	97	Crawford-Det	188	J.Collins-Bos-Phi	30	Cobb-Det	14	Hoffman-NY	5	Stone-StL	238
Hartsel-Phi	93	Ganley-Was	167	Lajoie-Cle	30	Unglaub-Bos	13	Cobb-Det	5	Davis-Phi	232
Hahn-Chi	87	Flick-Cle	166	Seybold-Phi	29					Flick-Cle	226

Runs Batted In		Runs Produced		Bases On Balls		Batting Average		On Base Percentage		Slugging Average	
Cobb-Det	119	Cobb-Det	211	Hartsel-Phi	106	Cobb-Det	.350	Hartsel-Phi	.405	Cobb-Det	.468
Seybold-Phi	92	Crawford-Det	179	Hahn-Chi	84	Crawford-Det	.323	Stone-StL	.387	Crawford-Det	.460
Davis-Phi	87	Davis-Phi	163	Jones-Chi	67	Stone-StL	.320	Flick-Cle	.386	Flick-Cle	.412
Crawford-Det	81	Seybold-Phi	145	Flick-Cle	64	Flick-Cle	.302	Cobb-Det	.380	Stone-StL	.399
Wallace-StL	70	Donahue-Chi	143	D.Jones-Det	60	Nicholls-Phi	.302	Crawford-Det	.366	Davis-Phi	.399

Production		Adjusted Production		Batter Runs		Adjusted Batter Runs		Clutch Hitting Index		Runs Created	
Cobb-Det	.848	Cobb-Det	164	Cobb-Det	44.4	Cobb-Det	42.1	Wallace-StL	155	Cobb-Det	130
Crawford-Det	.826	Crawford-Det	158	Crawford-Det	38.8	Crawford-Det	36.5	Davis-Phi	144	Crawford-Det	108
Flick-Cle	.798	Flick-Cle	153	Flick-Cle	35.8	Stone-StL	35.8	Seybold-Phi	144	Flick-Cle	107
Stone-StL	.787	Stone-StL	152	Stone-StL	35.6	Flick-Cle	35.3	Rohe-Chi	141	Stone-StL	105
Hartsel-Phi	.771	Hartsel-Phi	143	Hartsel-Phi	33.2	Hartsel-Phi	31.7	Cobb-Det	138	Hartsel-Phi	87

Total Average		Stolen Bases		Stolen Base Average		Stolen Base Runs		Fielding Runs		Total Player Rating	
Cobb-Det	.919	Cobb-Det	49					Lajoie-Cle	45.0	Lajoie-Cle	6.7
Flick-Cle	.893	Flick-Cle	41					Donahue-Chi	20.7	Cobb-Det	5.2
Hartsel-Phi	.855	Conroy-NY	41					Ferris-Bos	14.6	Crawford-Det	4.2
Crawford-Det	.825	Ganley-Was	40					D.Jones-Det	13.0	Flick-Cle	3.3
Stone-StL	.805	Altizer-Was	38					Murphy-Phi	12.7	Stone-StL	2.9

Wins		Win Percentage		Games		Complete Games		Shutouts		Saves	
White-Chi	27	Donovan-Det	.862	Walsh-Chi	56	Walsh-Chi	37	Plank-Phi	8	Dinneen-Bos-StL	4
Joss-Cle	27	Dygert-Phi	.724	White-Chi	46	Mullin-Det	35	Waddell-Phi	7	Walsh-Chi	4
Killian-Det	25	Joss-Cle	.711	Mullin-Det	46	Joss-Cle	34	Young-Bos	6	Hughes-Was	4
Donovan-Det	25	Smith-Chi	.697	Waddell-Phi	44	Young-Bos	33	White-Chi	6		
		White-Chi	.675			Plank-Phi	33	Joss-Cle	6		

Innings Pitched		Fewest Hits/Game		Fewest BB/Game		Strikeouts		Strikeouts/Game		Ratio	
Walsh-Chi	422.1	Dygert-Phi	6.88	White-Chi	1.18	Waddell-Phi	232	Waddell-Phi	7.33	Young-Bos	9.02
Mullin-Det	357.1	Winter-Bos	6.94	Altrock-Chi	1.31	Walsh-Chi	206	Dygert-Phi	5.19	Joss-Cle	9.04
Plank-Phi	343.2	Walsh-Chi	7.27	Young-Bos	1.34	Plank-Phi	183	Plank-Phi	4.79	Bender-Phi	9.15
Young-Bos	343.1	Howell-StL	7.34	Bender-Phi	1.40	Dygert-Phi	151	Bender-Phi	4.60	Winter-Bos	9.22
Joss-Cle	338.2	Donovan-Det	7.37	Joss-Cle	1.44	Young-Bos	147	Walsh-Chi	4.39	Walsh-Chi	9.27

Earned Run Average		Adjusted ERA		Opponents' Batting Avg.		Opponents' On Base Pct.		Starter Runs		Adjusted Starter Runs	
Walsh-Chi	1.60	Walsh-Chi	150	Dygert-Phi	.214	Young-Bos	.263	Walsh-Chi	44.2	Walsh-Chi	37.3
Killian-Det	1.78	Killian-Det	146	Winter-Bos	.216	Joss-Cle	.264	Killian-Det	26.6	Killian-Det	28.8
Joss-Cle	1.83	Joss-Cle	136	Walsh-Chi	.224	Bender-Phi	.266	Joss-Cle	26.6	Joss-Cle	25.2
Howell-StL	1.93	Howell-StL	130	Howell-StL	.225	Winter-Bos	.268	Howell-StL	21.3	Young-Bos	22.2
Young-Bos	1.99	Young-Bos	129	Donovan-Det	.226	Walsh-Chi	.269	Young-Bos	20.9	Howell-StL	20.2

Clutch Pitching Index		Relief Runs		Adjusted Relief Runs		Relief Ranking		Total Pitcher Index		Total Baseball Ranking	
Killian-Det	147							Walsh-Chi	6.8	Walsh-Chi	6.8
Hogg-NY	126							Killian-Det	4.3	Lajoie-Cle	6.7
Liebhardt-Cle	125							Howell-StL	4.0	Cobb-Det	5.2
Rhoads-Cle	120							Joss-Cle	3.3	Killian-Det	4.5
Walsh-Chi	112							Young-Bos	1.9	Crawford-Det	4.2

TEAM	G	W	L	PCT	GB	R	OR	AB	H	2B	3B	HR	BB	SO	AVG	OBP	SLG	PRO	PRO+	BR	/A	PF	CHI	RC	SB	CS	SBA	SBR
CHI	158	99	55	.643		624	461	5085	1267	196	56	19	418		.249	.311	.321	.632	105	49	27	104	107	584	212			
PIT	155	98	56	.636	1	585	469	5109	1263	162	98	25	420		.247	.309	.332	.641	112	64	64	100	99	582	186			
NY	157	98	56	.636	1	652	456	5006	1339	182	43	20	494		.267	.342	.333	.675	117	136	110	105	97	645	181			
PHI	155	83	71	.539	16	504	445	5012	1223	194	68	11	334		.244	.298	.316	.614	100	12	-5	103	96	535	200			
CIN	155	73	81	.474	26	489	544	4879	1108	129	77	14	372		.227	.288	.294	.582	95	-41	-27	97	105	473	196			
BOS	156	63	91	.409	36	537	622	5131	1228	137	43	17	414		.239	.303	.293	.596	99	-12	-4	98	104	501	134			
BRO	154	53	101	.344	46	377	516	4897	1044	110	60	28	323		.213	.265	.277	.542	82	-113	-94	96	98	390	113			
STL	154	49	105	.318	50	371	626	4959	1105	134	57	17	282		.223	.271	.283	.554	87	-95	-71	95	92	420	150			
TOT	622					4139		40078	9577	1244	502	151	3057	4180	.239	.299	.306	.605						1372				

TEAM	CG	SH	SV	IP	H	H/G	HR	BB	SO	RAT	ERA	ERA+	OAV	OOB	PR	/A	PF	CPI	FA	E	DP	FW	PW	BW	SBW	DIF
CHI	108	29	12	1433²	1137	7.1	20	437	668	10.1	2.14	109	.221	.287	33	30	100	93	.969	205	76	3.7	3.5	3.1		11.7
PIT	100	24	9	1402¹	1142	7.3	16	406	468	10.3	2.12	108	.223	.287	34	24	97	92	.964	226	74	1.9	2.8	7.4		8.9
NY	95	25	18	1411	1214	7.7	26	288	656	9.8	2.14	112	.233	.277	32	39	102	92	.962	250	79	.4	4.5	12.8		3.3
PHI	116	22	6	1393	1167	7.5	8	379	476	10.3	2.10	115	.234	.294	38	46	103	103	.963	238	75	1.0	5.3	-.6		.2
CIN	110	17	8	1384	1218	7.9	19	415	433	10.9	2.37	96	.243	.307	-4	-19	98	104	.959	255	72	-.2	-2.2	-3.1		1.5
BOS	92	14	1	1404²	1262	8.1	29	423	416	11.2	2.79	86	.245	.310	-70	-68	102	93	.962	253	90	.0	-7.9	-.5		-5.7
BRO	118	20	4	1369	1165	7.7	17	444	535	11.0	2.47	94	.235	.306	-18	-24	99	97	.961	247	66	.3	-2.8	-10.9		-10.6
STL	97	13	4	1368	1217	8.0	16	430	528	11.1	2.64	89	.232	.296	-44	-51	100	82	.946	348	68	-6.8	-5.9	-8.2		-7.0
TOT	836	164	62	11165²		7.7				10.6	2.35		.239	.299					.961	2022	600					

Runs		Hits		Doubles		Triples		Home Runs		Total Bases	
Tenney-NY	101	Wagner-Pit	201	Wagner-Pit	39	Wagner-Pit	19	Jordan-Bro	12	Wagner-Pit	308
Wagner-Pit	100	Donlin-NY	198	Magee-Phi	30	Lobert-Cin	18	Wagner-Pit	10	Donlin-NY	268
Leach-Pit	93	Murray-StL	167	Chance-Chi	27	Magee-Phi	16	Murray-StL	7	Murray-StL	237
Evers-Chi	83	Lobert-Cin	167	Knabe-Phi	26	Leach-Pit	16	Tinker-Chi	6	Lobert-Cin	232
Clarke-Pit	83	Bransfield-Phi	160	Donlin-NY	26			Donlin-NY	6	Leach-Pit	222

Runs Batted In		Runs Produced		Bases On Balls		Batting Average		On Base Percentage		Slugging Average	
Wagner-Pit	109	Wagner-Pit	199	Bresnahan-NY	83	Wagner-Pit	.354	Wagner-Pit	.415	Wagner-Pit	.542
Donlin-NY	106	Donlin-NY	171	Tenney-NY	72	Donlin-NY	.334	Evers-Chi	.402	Donlin-NY	.452
Seymour-NY	92	Tenney-NY	148	Evers-Chi	66	Bransfield-Phi	.304	Bresnahan-NY	.400	Magee-Phi	.417
Bransfield-Phi	71	Seymour-NY	147	Clarke-Pit	65	Evers-Chi	.300	Donlin-NY	.364	Lobert-Cin	.407
Tinker-Chi	68					Lobert-Cin	.293	Titus-Phi	.364	Murray-StL	.400

Production		Adjusted Production		Batter Runs		Adjusted Batter Runs		Clutch Hitting Index		Runs Created	
Wagner-Pit	.957	Wagner-Pit	205	Wagner-Pit	65.3	Wagner-Pit	65.3	Seymour-NY	175	Wagner-Pit	148
Donlin-NY	.816	Donlin-NY	153	Donlin-NY	36.7	Donlin-NY	33.8	McGann-Bos	155	Donlin-NY	108
Evers-Chi	.777	Lobert-Cin	145	Magee-Phi	27.4	Lobert-Cin	26.7	Abbaticchio-Pit	154	Lobert-Cin	97
Magee-Phi	.776	Magee-Phi	143	Bresnahan-NY	26.8	Magee-Phi	25.6	Donlin-NY	151	Murray-StL	92
Bresnahan-NY	.759	Evers-Chi	143	Evers-Chi	26.5	Evers-Chi	24.5	Steinfeldt-Chi	150	Magee-Phi	90

Total Average		Stolen Bases		Stolen Base Average		Stolen Base Runs		Fielding Runs		Total Player Rating	
Wagner-Pit	1.144	Wagner-Pit	53					Dahlen-Bos	37.5	Wagner-Pit	7.0
Evers-Chi	.904	Murray-StL	48					Tinker-Chi	30.4	Tinker-Chi	4.9
Magee-Phi	.857	Lobert-Cin	47					Ritchey-Bos	15.6	Dahlen-Bos	4.2
Donlin-NY	.825	Magee-Phi	40					Devlin-NY	12.8	Donlin-NY	3.2
Bresnahan-NY	.817	Evers-Chi	36					Burch-Bro	12.6	Ritchey-Bos	3.1

Wins		Win Percentage		Games		Complete Games		Shutouts		Saves	
Mathewson-NY	37	Reulbach-Chi	.774	Mathewson-NY	56	Mathewson-NY	34	Mathewson-NY	11	McGinnity-NY	5
Brown-Chi	29	Mathewson-NY	.771	Raymond-StL	48	Wilhelm-Bro	33	Brown-Chi	9	Mathewson-NY	5
Reulbach-Chi	24	Brown-Chi	.763	McQuillan-Phi	48	McQuillan-Phi	32			Brown-Chi	5
		Maddox-Pit	.742	Reulbach-Chi	46	Wiltse-NY	30			Overall-Chi	4
		Leever-Pit	.682			Rucker-Bro	30			Ewing-Cin	3

Innings Pitched		Fewest Hits/Game		Fewest BB/Game		Strikeouts		Strikeouts/Game		Ratio	
Mathewson-NY	390.2	Brown-Chi	6.17	Mathewson-NY	.97	Mathewson-NY	259	Overall-Chi	6.68	Mathewson-NY	7.60
McQuillan-Phi	359.2	Raymond-StL	6.55	Brown-Chi	1.41	Rucker-Bro	199	Mathewson-NY	5.97	Brown-Chi	7.72
Rucker-Bro	333.1	Mathewson-NY	6.57	Sparks-Phi	1.74	Overall-Chi	167	Rucker-Bro	5.37	McQuillan-Phi	9.01
Wilhelm-Bro	332.0	McQuillan-Phi	6.58	Ewing-Cin	1.75	Raymond-StL	145	Camnitz-Pit	4.49	Willis-Pit	9.28
Wiltse-NY	330.0	Overall-Chi	6.60	Campbell-Cin	1.79	Reulbach-Chi	133	Ferguson-Bos	4.24	Ewing-Cin	9.47

Earned Run Average		Adjusted ERA		Opponents' Batting Avg.		Opponents' On Base Pct.		Starter Runs		Adjusted Starter Runs	
Mathewson-NY	1.43	Mathewson-NY	168	Beebe-StL	.193	Mathewson-NY	.225	Mathewson-NY	39.8	Mathewson-NY	42.1
Brown-Chi	1.47	Brown-Chi	159	Brown-Chi	.195	Brown-Chi	.232	McQuillan-Phi	32.7	McQuillan-Phi	35.2
McQuillan-Phi	1.53	McQuillan-Phi	158	Mathewson-NY	.200	Willis-Pit	.262	Brown-Chi	30.4	Brown-Chi	30.1
Camnitz-Pit	1.56	Camnitz-Pit	147	McQuillan-Phi	.207	McQuillan-Phi	.263	Camnitz-Pit	20.7	Camnitz-Pit	19.1
Coakley-Cin-Chi	1.78	Richie-Phi	132	Raymond-StL	.207	Beebe-StL	.267	Wilhelm-Bro	17.5	Wilhelm-Bro	16.8

Clutch Pitching Index		Relief Runs		Adjusted Relief Runs		Relief Ranking		Total Pitcher Index		Total Baseball Ranking	
Coakley-Cin-Chi	134							Mathewson-NY	6.6	Wagner-Pit	7.0
McGinnity-NY	134							McQuillan-Phi	3.9	Mathewson-NY	6.6
Richie-Phi	127							Brown-Chi	3.6	Tinker-Chi	4.9
Fraser-Chi	126							Raymond-StL	2.0	Dahlen-Bos	4.2
Rucker-Bro	119							Wilhelm-Bro	1.8	McQuillan-Phi	3.9

TEAM	G	W	L	PCT	GB	R	OR	AB	H	2B	3B	HR	BB	SO	AVG	OBP	SLG	PRO	PRO+	BR	/A	PF	CHI	RC	SB	CS	SBA	SBR
DET	154	90	63	.588		647	547	5115	1347	199	86	19	320		.263	.312	.347	.659	115	102	80	104	102	604	165			
CLE	157	90	64	.584	0.5	568	457	5108	1221	188	58	18	364		.239	.297	.309	.606	103	15	13	100	101	528	177			
CHI	156	88	64	.579	1.5	537	470	5027	1127	145	41	3	463		.224	.298	.271	.569	92	-37	-28	98	105	479	209			
STL	155	83	69	.546	6.5	544	483	5151	1261	173	52	20	343		.245	.296	.310	.606	102	14	11	101	98	514	126			
BOS	155	75	79	.487	15.5	564	513	5048	1239	117	88	14	289		.245	.295	.312	.607	100	13	-2	103	104	513	167			
PHI	157	68	85	.444	22	486	562	5065	1131	183	50	21	368		.223	.281	.292	.573	86	-46	-82	107	100	449	116			
WAS	155	67	85	.441	22.5	479	539	5041	1186	132	74	8	368		.235	.293	.296	.589	106	-14	30	92	92	489	170			
NY	155	51	103	.331	39.5	459	713	5046	1190	142	50	13	288		.236	.282	.292	.574	91	-47	-53	101	97	475	231			
TOT	622					4284		40601	9702	1279	499	116	2803	4930	.239	.294	.304	.598						1361				

TEAM	CG	SH	SV	IP	H	H/G	HR	BB	SO	RAT	ERA	ERA+	OAV	OOB	PR	/A	PF	CPI	FA	E	DP	FW	PW	BW	SBW	DIF
DET	119	15	5	1374[1]	1313	8.6	12	318	553	11.1	2.40	100	.255	.306	-3	2	101	114	.953	305	95	-2.1	.2	9.1		6.2
CLE	108	18	5	1424[1]	1172	7.4	16	328	548	9.7	2.02	118	.229	.280	59	56	100	102	.962	257	95	1.6	6.4	1.5		3.5
CHI	107	15	10	1414	1170	7.4	11	284	623	9.4	2.22	104	.226	.270	26	13	97	83	.966	232	82	3.2	1.5	-3.2		10.5
STL	107	15	5	1397	1151	7.4	7	387	607	10.3	2.15	111	.230	.294	37	36	100	97	.964	237	71	2.7	4.1	1.3		-1.1
BOS	102	12	7	1380[1]	1200	7.8	18	364	624	10.5	2.28	108	.238	.295	17	27	103	105	.955	297	71	-1.4	3.1	-.2		-3.4
PHI	102	23	4	1400[1]	1194	7.7	10	410	741	10.6	2.56	100	.235	.298	-27	-4	107	92	.957	272	68	.6	-.5	-9.4		.8
WAS	106	15	7	1392[2]	1236	8.0	16	348	649	10.5	2.34	97	.241	.294	7	-14	96	102	.958	275	89	.1	-1.6	3.4		-10.9
NY	90	11	3	1366	1288	8.5	26	458	585	12.0	3.16	78	.251	.322	-117	-106	104	96	.947	337	78	-4.1	-12.1	-6.0		-3.7
TOT	841	132	46	11149		7.8				10.5	2.39		.239	.294					.958	2212	675					

Runs		Hits		Doubles		Triples		Home Runs		Total Bases	
McIntyre-Det	105	Cobb-Det	188	Cobb-Det	36	Cobb-Det	20	Crawford-Det	7	Cobb-Det	276
Crawford-Det	102	Crawford-Det	184	Rossman-Det	33	Stahl-NY-Bos	16	Hinchman-Cle	6	Crawford-Det	270
Schaefer-Det	96	McIntyre-Det	168	Crawford-Det	33	Crawford-Det	16	Niles-NY-Bos	5	Rossman-Det	219
Jones-Chi	92	Lajoie-Cle	168	Lajoie-Cle	32	Gessler-Bos	14	Stone-StL	5	McIntyre-Det	218
Stone-StL	89	Stone-StL	165	Stovall-Cle	29			Davis-Phi	5	Lajoie-Cle	218

Runs Batted In		Runs Produced		Bases On Balls		Batting Average		On Base Percentage		Slugging Average	
Cobb-Det	108	Cobb-Det	192	Hartsel-Phi	93	Cobb-Det	.324	Gessler-Bos	.394	Cobb-Det	.475
Crawford-Det	80	Crawford-Det	175	Jones-Chi	86	Crawford-Det	.311	McIntyre-Det	.392	Crawford-Det	.457
Lajoie-Cle	74	Lajoie-Cle	149	McIntyre-Det	83	Gessler-Bos	.308	Hemphill-NY	.373	Gessler-Bos	.423
Ferris-StL	74	Schaefer-Det	145	J.Clarke-Cle	76	Hemphill-NY	.297	Hartsel-Phi	.371	Rossman-Det	.418
Rossman-Det	71	Jones-Chi	141	Davis-Phi	61	McIntyre-Det	.295	Dougherty-Chi	.367	McIntyre-Det	.383

Production		Adjusted Production		Batter Runs		Adjusted Batter Runs		Clutch Hitting Index		Runs Created	
Cobb-Det	.842	Cobb-Det	166	Cobb-Det	43.9	Cobb-Det	41.4	Wallace-StL	148	Cobb-Det	114
Gessler-Bos	.817	Gessler-Bos	161	Crawford-Det	38.1	Crawford-Det	35.5	Ferris-StL	146	Crawford-Det	100
Crawford-Det	.811	Crawford-Det	157	McIntyre-Det	36.5	McIntyre-Det	33.9	Cobb-Det	135	McIntyre-Det	93
McIntyre-Det	.775	McIntyre-Det	146	Gessler-Bos	33.3	Gessler-Bos	31.9	Gessler-Bos	130	Lajoie-Cle	83
Rossman-Det	.748	Rossman-Det	137	Lajoie-Cle	23.4	Lajoie-Cle	23.2	Murphy-Phi	128	Hemphill-NY	82

Total Average		Stolen Bases		Stolen Base Average		Stolen Base Runs		Fielding Runs		Total Player Rating	
Cobb-Det	.903	Dougherty-Chi	47					Lajoie-Cle	49.3	Lajoie-Cle	7.8
Gessler-Bos	.880	Hemphill-NY	42					McBride-Was	32.8	McIntyre-Det	4.8
McIntyre-Det	.818	Schaefer-Det	40					Wagner-Bos	31.7	Cobb-Det	4.4
Hemphill-NY	.797	Cobb-Det	39					Tannehill-Chi	18.0	McBride-Was	3.6
Crawford-Det	.796	J.Clarke-Cle	37					Wallace-StL	18.0	Wallace-StL	3.1

Wins		Win Percentage		Games		Complete Games		Shutouts		Saves	
Walsh-Chi	40	Walsh-Chi	.727	Walsh-Chi	66	Walsh-Chi	42	Walsh-Chi	11	Walsh-Chi	6
Summers-Det	24	Donovan-Det	.720	Vickers-Phi	53	Young-Bos	30	Joss-Cle	9	Hughes-Was	4
Joss-Cle	24	Joss-Cle	.686	Chesbro-NY	45	Joss-Cle	29	Vickers-Phi	6	Waddell-StL	3
Young-Bos	21	Summers-Det	.667	Waddell-StL	43	Howell-StL	27	Johnson-Was	6		
Waddell-StL	19	Young-Bos	.656	Hughes-Was	43	Mullin-Det	26	Donovan-Det	6		

Innings Pitched		Fewest Hits/Game		Fewest BB/Game		Strikeouts		Strikeouts/Game		Ratio	
Walsh-Chi	464.0	Joss-Cle	6.42	Joss-Cle	.83	Walsh-Chi	269	Waddell-StL	7.31	Joss-Cle	7.31
Joss-Cle	325.0	Smith-Chi	6.44	Burns-Was	.98	Waddell-StL	232	Dygert-Phi	6.18	Walsh-Chi	7.91
Howell-StL	324.1	Walsh-Chi	6.65	Walsh-Chi	1.09	Hughes-Was	165	Johnson-Was	5.60	Young-Bos	8.07
Vickers-Phi	317.0	Johnson-Was	6.78	Young-Bos	1.11	Dygert-Phi	164	Hughes-Was	5.37	Burns-Was	8.56
Summers-Det	301.0	Berger-Cle	6.86	Summers-Det	1.64	Johnson-Was	160	Donovan-Det	5.23	Smith-Chi	8.71

Earned Run Average		Adjusted ERA		Opponents' Batting Avg.		Opponents' On Base Pct.		Starter Runs		Adjusted Starter Runs	
Joss-Cle	1.16	Joss-Cle	205	Joss-Cle	.197	Joss-Cle	.218	Walsh-Chi	50.0	Walsh-Chi	46.0
Young-Bos	1.26	Young-Bos	194	Smith-Chi	.203	Walsh-Chi	.232	Joss-Cle	44.2	Joss-Cle	44.0
Walsh-Chi	1.42	Walsh-Chi	163	Walsh-Chi	.203	Young-Bos	.240	Young-Bos	37.3	Young-Bos	39.5
Johnson-Was	1.64	Summers-Det	147	Johnson-Was	.211	Smith-Chi	.256	Summers-Det	24.8	Summers-Det	25.6
Summers-Det	1.64	Johnson-Was	139	Young-Bos	.213	Burns-Was	.257	Johnson-Was	21.2	Rhoads-Cle	18.4

Clutch Pitching Index		Relief Runs		Adjusted Relief Runs		Relief Ranking		Total Pitcher Index		Total Baseball Ranking	
Summers-Det	142							Walsh-Chi	7.5	Lajoie-Cle	7.8
Willett-Det	140							Joss-Cle	6.1	Walsh-Chi	7.5
Rhoads-Cle	137							Young-Bos	4.2	Joss-Cle	6.1
Howell-StL	123							Rhoads-Cle	2.9	McIntyre-Det	4.8
Cicotte-Bos	123							Howell-StL	2.3	Cobb-Det	4.4

TEAM	G	W	L	PCT	GB	R	OR	AB	H	2B	3B	HR	BB	SO	AVG	OBP	SLG	PRO	PRO+	BR	/A	PF	CHI	RC	SB	CS	SBA	SBR
PIT	153	110	42	.724		699	447	5129	1332	218	92	25	479		.260	.327	.353	.680	109	100	52	108	103	656	185			
CHI	155	104	49	.680	6.5	635	390	4999	1227	203	60	20	420		.245	.308	.322	.630	100	7	-6	102	112	562	187			
NY	158	92	61	.601	18.5	623	546	5218	1327	173	68	26	530		.254	.329	.328	.657	109	70	61	102	95	640	234			
CIN	156	77	76	.503	33.5	606	599	5088	1273	159	72	22	478		.250	.319	.323	.642	107	35	40	99	100	618	280			
PHI	154	74	79	.484	36.5	516	518	5034	1228	185	53	12	369		.244	.303	.309	.612	95	-26	-30	101	96	534	185			
BRO	155	55	98	.359	55.5	444	627	5056	1157	176	59	16	330		.229	.279	.296	.575	87	-98	-78	96	98	456	141			
STL	154	54	98	.355	56	583	731	5108	1242	148	56	15	568		.243	.326	.303	.629	109	25	61	94	97	556	161			
BOS	155	45	108	.294	65.5	435	683	5017	1121	124	43	15	400		.223	.285	.274	.559	76	-116	-142	105	99	435	135			
TOT	620					4541		40649	9907	1386	503	151	3574	4437	.244	.310	.314	.624							1508			

TEAM	CG	SH	SV	IP	H	H/G	HR	BB	SO	RAT	ERA	ERA+	OAV	QOB	PR	/A	PF	CPI	FA	E	DP	FW	PW	BW	SBW	DIF
PIT	93	21	11	1401²	1174	7.5	12	320	490	9.9	2.07	131	.232	.284	81	100	105	97	.964	228	100	3.4	11.1	5.8		13.7
CHI	111	32	11	1399¹	1094	7.0	6	364	680	9.6	1.75	145	.215	.272	131	124	98	94	.962	244	95	2.6	13.8	-.7		11.8
NY	105	17	15	1440²	1248	7.8	29	397	735	10.5	2.27	112	.238	.295	51	42	98	103	.954	307	99	-1.1	4.7	6.8		5.2
CIN	91	10	8	1407	1233	7.9	5	510	477	11.4	2.52	103	.240	.314	11	9	100	100	.952	309	120	-1.5	1.0	4.4		-3.5
PHI	89	17	6	1391	1190	7.7	23	472	612	11.0	2.44	106	.235	.304	23	20	100	99	.962	241	97	2.7	2.2	-3.3		-4.1
BRO	126	18	3	1384¹	1277	8.3	31	528	594	12.1	3.10	83	.256	.333	-79	-84	100	101	.955	282	86	.2	-9.3	-8.7		-3.7
STL	84	5	4	1379²	1368	8.9	22	483	435	12.4	3.41	74	.263	.331	-126	-139	97	92	.950	322	90	-2.5	-15.4	6.8		-10.8
BOS	98	13	6	1370²	1329	8.7	23	543	414	12.6	3.20	88	.263	.339	-93	-60	109	103	.948	342	101	-3.7	-6.7	-15.8		-5.4
TOT	797	133	64	11174¹		8.0				11.2	2.59		.244	.310					.956	2275	788					

Runs		Hits		Doubles		Triples		Home Runs		Total Bases	
Leach-NY	126	Doyle-NY	172	Wagner-Pit	39	Mitchell-Cin	17	Murray-NY	7	Wagner-Pit	242
Clarke-Pit	97	Grant-Phi	170	Magee-Phi	33	Magee-Phi	14	Leach-Pit	6	Doyle-NY	239
Byrne-StL-Pit	92	Wagner-Pit	168	J.Miller-Pit	31	Konetchy-StL	14	Doyle-NY	6	Konetchy-StL	228
Wagner-Pit	92	Konetchy-StL	165	Sheckard-Chi	29	J.Miller-Pit	13	Becker-Bos	6	Mitchell-Cin	225
		Burch-Bro	163	Leach-Pit	29			Wagner-Pit	5	J.Miller-Pit	222

Runs Batted In		Runs Produced		Bases On Balls		Batting Average		On Base Percentage		Slugging Average	
Wagner-Pit	100	Wagner-Pit	187	Clarke-Pit	80	Wagner-Pit	.339	Wagner-Pit	.420	Wagner-Pit	.489
Murray-NY	91	Mitchell-Cin	165	Byrne-StL-Pit	78	Mitchell-Cin	.310	Bridwell-NY	.386	Mitchell-Cin	.430
J.Miller-Pit	87	Konetchy-StL	164	Evers-Chi	73	Hoblitzel-Cin	.308	Clarke-Pit	.384	Doyle-NY	.419
Mitchell-Cin	86	Leach-Pit	163	Sheckard-Chi	72	Doyle-NY	.302	Mitchell-Cin	.378	Hoblitzel-Cin	.418
Konetchy-StL	80	Clarke-Pit	162	Bridwell-NY	67	Bridwell-NY	.294	Evers-Chi	.369	Magee-Phi	.398

Production		Adjusted Production		Batter Runs		Adjusted Batter Runs		Clutch Hitting Index		Runs Created	
Wagner-Pit	.909	Wagner-Pit	168	Wagner-Pit	48.1	Wagner-Pit	43.3	Murray-NY	152	Wagner-Pit	117
Mitchell-Cin	.808	Mitchell-Cin	152	Mitchell-Cin	30.3	Mitchell-Cin	30.8	Abstein-Pit	151	Mitchell-Cin	98
Hoblitzel-Cin	.782	Konetchy-StL	145	Doyle-NY	26.2	Konetchy-StL	28.9	Wagner-Pit	150	Doyle-NY	96
Doyle-NY	.779	Hoblitzel-Cin	144	Clarke-Pit	25.4	Doyle-NY	25.3	Lobert-Cin	146	Clarke-Pit	92
Konetchy-StL	.762	Doyle-NY	140	Konetchy-StL	24.9	Hoblitzel-Cin	24.8	J.Miller-Pit	145	Konetchy-StL	92

Total Average		Stolen Bases		Stolen Base Average	Stolen Base Runs	Fielding Runs		Total Player Rating	
Wagner-Pit	1.058	Bescher-Cin	54			Doolan-Phi	24.4	Wagner-Pit	5.6
Mitchell-Cin	.884	Murray-NY	48			Egan-Cin	24.0	Konetchy-StL	3.5
Clarke-Pit	.821	Egan-Cin	39			Bergen-Bro	22.0	Devlin-NY	3.5
Doyle-NY	.809	Magee-Phi	38			Byrne-StL-Pit	20.6	Mitchell-Cin	3.4
Konetchy-StL	.791	Burch-Bro	38			Devlin-NY	15.8	Egan-Cin	2.7

Wins		Win Percentage		Games		Complete Games		Shutouts		Saves	
M.Brown-Chi	27	Mathewson-NY	.806	M.Brown-Chi	50	M.Brown-Chi	32	Overall-Chi	9	M.Brown-Chi	7
Mathewson-NY	25	S.Camnitz-Pit	.806	Mattern-Bos	47	Bell-Bro	29	Mathewson-NY	8	Crandall-NY	6
S.Camnitz-Pit	25	M.Brown-Chi	.750	Gaspar-Cin	44	Rucker-Bro	28	M.Brown-Chi	8		
Willis-Pit	22	Pfiester-Chi	.739	Beebe-StL	44	Mathewson-NY	26				
		Leifield-Pit	.704								

Innings Pitched		Fewest Hits/Game		Fewest BB/Game		Strikeouts		Strikeouts/Game		Ratio	
M.Brown-Chi	342.2	Mathewson-NY	6.28	Mathewson-NY	1.18	Overall-Chi	205	Overall-Chi	6.47	Mathewson-NY	7.45
Mattern-Bos	316.1	Fromme-Cin	6.28	M.Brown-Chi	1.39	Rucker-Bro	201	Rucker-Bro	5.85	M.Brown-Chi	8.04
Rucker-Bro	309.1	Overall-Chi	6.44	Wiltse-NY	1.70	Moore-Phi	173	Ames-NY	5.75	S.Camnitz-Pit	8.97
Moore-Phi	299.2	M.Brown-Chi	6.46	Maddox-Pit	1.73	M.Brown-Chi	172	Marquard-NY	5.67	Overall-Chi	9.22
Willis-Pit	289.2	S.Camnitz-Pit	6.58	McQuillan-Phi	1.96	Ames-NY	156	Moore-Phi	5.20	McQuillan-Phi	9.34

Earned Run Average		Adjusted ERA		Opponents' Batting Avg.		Opponents' On Base Pct.		Starter Runs		Adjusted Starter Runs	
Mathewson-NY	1.14	Mathewson-NY	223	Overall-Chi	.198	Mathewson-NY	.228	M.Brown-Chi	48.6	M.Brown-Chi	46.5
M.Brown-Chi	1.31	M.Brown-Chi	193	Mathewson-NY	.200	M.Brown-Chi	.239	Mathewson-NY	44.2	Mathewson-NY	43.0
Overall-Chi	1.42	Overall-Chi	178	Fromme-Cin	.201	Overall-Chi	.262	Overall-Chi	37.0	Overall-Chi	35.2
S.Camnitz-Pit	1.62	S.Camnitz-Pit	167	M.Brown-Chi	.202	S.Camnitz-Pit	.267	S.Camnitz-Pit	30.4	S.Camnitz-Pit	34.3
Reulbach-Chi	1.78	Reulbach-Chi	142	Moore-Phi	.210	McQuillan-Phi	.271	Reulbach-Chi	23.6	Adams-Pit	23.2

Clutch Pitching Index		Relief Runs	Adjusted Relief Runs	Relief Ranking	Total Pitcher Index		Total Baseball Ranking	
Richie-Phi-Bos	126				Mathewson-NY	6.9	Mathewson-NY	6.9
Corridon-Phi	123				M.Brown-Chi	5.4	Wagner-Pit	5.6
Sallee-StL	119				Overall-Chi	5.2	M.Brown-Chi	5.4
Wilhelm-Bro	117				S.Camnitz-Pit	3.6	Overall-Chi	5.2
Marquard-NY	117				Fromme-Cin	3.0	S.Camnitz-Pit	3.6

TEAM	G	W	L	PCT	GB	R	OR	AB	H	2B	3B	HR	BB	SO	AVG	OBP	SLG	PRO	PRO+	BR	/A	PF	CHI	RC	SB	CS	SBA	SBR
DET	158	98	54	.645		666	493	5095	1360	209	58	19	397		.267	.325	.342	.667	113	98	74	104	103	660	280			
PHI	153	95	58	.621	3.5	605	408	4905	1257	186	88	21	403		.256	.321	.343	.664	115	91	80	102	97	613	205			
BOS	152	88	63	.583	9.5	597	550	4979	1307	151	69	20	348		.263	.321	.333	.654	112	73	61	102	99	599	215			
CHI	159	78	74	.513	20	492	463	5017	1110	145	56	4	441		.221	.292	.275	.567	90	-5	-13	99	104	474	211			
NY	153	74	77	.490	23.5	590	587	4981	1234	143	61	16	407		.248	.313	.311	.624	103	25	21	101	105	547	187			
CLE	155	71	82	.464	27.5	493	532	5048	1216	173	81	10	283		.241	.288	.313	.601	93	-28	-50	104	99	501	174			
STL	154	61	89	.407	36	441	575	4964	1151	116	45	10	331		.232	.287	.279	.566	91	-79	-42	93	100	436	136			
WAS	156	42	110	.276	56	380	656	4983	1112	149	41	9	321		.223	.276	.275	.551	84	-109	-84	95	91	419	136			
TOT	620					4264		39972	9747	1272	499	109	2931	4918	.244	.303	.309	.611						1544				

TEAM	CG	SH	SV	IP	H	H/G	HR	BB	SO	RAT	ERA	ERA+	OAV	OOB	PR	/A	PF	CPI	FA	E	DP	FW	PW	BW	SBW	DIF
DET	117	17	12	1420¹	1254	7.9	16	359	528	10.6	2.26	111	.238	.293	33	40	102	100	.959	276	87	.4	4.5	8.4		8.7
PHI	110	27	3	1378	1069	7.0	9	386	728	9.9	1.93	124	.217	.282	82	72	97	96	.961	245	92	1.8	8.2	9.1		-.6
BOS	75	11	15	1360¹	1214	8.0	18	384	555	10.9	2.59	96	.243	.303	-19	-16	101	96	.955	292	95	-1.3	-1.8	6.9		8.7
CHI	115	26	4	1430¹	1182	7.4	8	340	669	9.9	2.05	114	.229	.283	67	44	95	96	.964	246	101	2.4	5.0	-5.6		.2
NY	94	18	7	1350¹	1223	8.2	21	422	597	11.4	2.65	95	.248	.316	-26	-22	102	104	.948	329	94	-3.6	-2.5	2.4		2.2
CLE	110	15	3	1361	1212	8.0	9	348	568	10.6	2.40	106	.250	.307	11	21	103	107	.957	278	110	-.0	2.4	-5.7		-2.1
STL	105	21	4	1354²	1287	8.6	16	383	620	11.4	2.88	84	.261	.319	-61	-72	98	101	.958	267	107	.5	-8.2	-4.8		-1.5
WAS	99	11	2	1375¹	1288	8.4	12	424	653	11.6	3.04	80	.248	.312	-86	-96	98	87	.957	280	100	-.1	-10.9	-9.6		-13.4
TOT	825	146	50	11030¹		7.9				10.8	2.47		.244	.303					.957	2213	786					

Runs
Cobb-Det 116
Bush-Det 114
Collins-Phi 104
Lord-Bos 86
Crawford-Det 83

Hits
Cobb-Det 216
Collins-Phi 198
Crawford-Det 185
Speaker-Bos 168
Lord-Bos 166

Doubles
Crawford-Det 35
Lajoie-Cle 33
Cobb-Det 33
Collins-Phi 30
Murphy-Phi 28

Triples
Baker-Phi 19
Murphy-Phi 14
Crawford-Det 14

Home Runs
Cobb-Det 9
Speaker-Bos 7
Stahl-Bos 6
Crawford-Det 6
Murphy-Phi 5

Total Bases
Cobb-Det 296
Crawford-Det 266
Collins-Phi 257
Baker-Phi 242
Speaker-Bos 241

Runs Batted In
Cobb-Det 107
Crawford-Det 97
Baker-Phi 85
Speaker-Bos 77
Davis-Phi 75

Runs Produced
Cobb-Det 214
Crawford-Det 174
Collins-Phi 157
Baker-Phi 154
Bush-Det 147

Bases On Balls
Bush-Det 88
Collins-Phi 62
Demmitt-NY 55
McIntyre-Det 54

Batting Average
Cobb-Det .... .377
Collins-Phi ...... .346
Lajoie-Cle .... .324
Crawford-Det ..... .314
Lord-Bos .... .311

On Base Percentage
Cobb-Det .... .431
Collins-Phi ...... .416
Bush-Det .... .380
Lajoie-Cle .... .378
Stahl-Bos .... .377

Slugging Average
Cobb-Det .... .517
Crawford-Det ..... .452
Collins-Phi ...... .449
Baker-Phi .... .447
Speaker-Bos ..... .443

Production
Cobb-Det .... .947
Collins-Phi ...... .865
Crawford-Det ..... .817
Stahl-Bos .... .812
Lajoie-Cle .... .809

Adjusted Production
Cobb-Det 190
Collins-Phi 170
Stahl-Bos 153
Crawford-Det 151
Speaker-Bos 151

Batter Runs
Cobb-Det 63.3
Collins-Phi 48.9
Crawford-Det 36.7
Speaker-Bos 31.5
Lajoie-Cle 28.8

Adjusted Batter Runs
Cobb-Det 60.6
Collins-Phi 47.6
Crawford-Det 33.9
Speaker-Bos 30.3
Stahl-Bos 27.4

Clutch Hitting Index
Engle-NY 153
Davis-Phi 143
Gessler-Bos-Was . 137
Ferris-StL 135
Baker-Phi 134

Runs Created
Cobb-Det 159
Collins-Phi 134
Crawford-Det 108
Speaker-Bos 99
Baker-Phi 90

Total Average
Cobb-Det 1.193
Collins-Phi 1.048
Stahl-Bos .... .857
Speaker-Bos ..... .854
Crawford-Det .... .851

Stolen Bases
Cobb-Det 76
Collins-Phi 67
Bush-Det 53
Lord-Bos 36
Dougherty-Chi 36

Fielding Runs
Speaker-Bos 22.7
Lajoie-Cle 18.6
Parent-Chi 16.5
McConnell-Bos .. 14.4
Wagner-Bos 14.0

Total Player Rating
Cobb-Det 6.4
Collins-Phi 5.8
Speaker-Bos 5.3
Lajoie-Cle 4.8
Baker-Phi 2.6

Wins
Mullin-Det 29
Smith-Chi 25
Willett-Det 21

Win Percentage
Mullin-Det ..... .784
Krause-Phi ..... .692
Bender-Phi ..... .692
Summers-Det .... .679
Willett-Det .... .677

Games
Smith-Chi 51
Arellanes-Bos 45
Groom-Was 44
Willett-Det 41

Complete Games
Smith-Chi 37
Young-Cle 30
Mullin-Det 29
Johnson-Was 27
Morgan-Bos-Phi ... 26

Shutouts
Walsh-Chi 8
Smith-Chi 7
Krause-Phi 7
Coombs-Phi 6

Saves
Arellanes-Bos 8
Powell-StL 3

Innings Pitched
Smith-Chi 365.0
Mullin-Det 303.2
Johnson-Was 297.0
Young-Cle 295.0
Morgan-Bos-Phi . 293.1

Fewest Hits/Game
Morgan-Bos-Phi . 6.26
Krause-Phi 6.38
Walsh-Chi 6.49
Cicotte-Bos 6.59
Wood-Bos 6.78

Fewest BB/Game
Joss-Cle 1.15
White-Chi 1.57
Powell-StL 1.58
Bender-Phi 1.62
Summers-Det 1.66

Strikeouts
Smith-Chi 177
Johnson-Was 164
Berger-Cle 162
Bender-Phi 161
Waddell-StL 141

Strikeouts/Game
Berger-Cle 5.90
Krause-Phi 5.87
Bender-Phi 5.80
Waddell-StL 5.76
Bailey-StL 5.16

Ratio
Walsh-Chi 8.60
Joss-Cle 8.64
Smith-Chi 8.73
Bender-Phi 8.86
Krause-Phi 9.00

Earned Run Average
Krause-Phi 1.39
Walsh-Chi 1.41
Bender-Phi 1.66
Joss-Cle 1.71
Killian-Det 1.71

Adjusted ERA
Krause-Phi 172
Walsh-Chi 166
Joss-Cle 149
Killian-Det 146
Bender-Phi 145

Opponents' Batting Avg.
Morgan-Bos-Phi . .202
Walsh-Chi ...... .203
Krause-Phi ..... .204
Wood-Bos .... .209
Cicotte-Bos .... .210

Opponents' On Base Pct.
Walsh-Chi ...... .253
Bender-Phi ..... .254
Joss-Cle .... .255
Smith-Chi ...... .257
Krause-Phi ..... .266

Starter Runs
Walsh-Chi 27.2
Smith-Chi 27.2
Krause-Phi 25.5
Bender-Phi 22.6
Morgan-Bos-Phi . 21.5

Adjusted Starter Runs
Krause-Phi 23.8
Walsh-Chi 23.8
Joss-Cle 22.7
Smith-Chi 21.7
Bender-Phi 20.6

Clutch Pitching Index
Burns-Was-Chi ... 142
Killian-Det 132
Brockett-NY 132
Waddell-StL 125
Bailey-StL 117

Total Pitcher Index
Smith-Chi 4.4
Walsh-Chi 4.3
Bender-Phi 3.1
Plank-Phi 2.7
Lake-NY 2.6

Total Baseball Ranking
Cobb-Det 6.4
Collins-Phi 5.8
Speaker-Bos 5.3
Lajoie-Cle 4.8
Smith-Chi 4.4

TEAM	G	W	L	PCT	GB	R	OR	AB	H	2B	3B	HR	BB	SO	AVG	OBP	SLG	PRO	PRO+	BR	/A	PF	CHI	RC	SB	CS	SBA	SBR
CHI	154	104	50	.675		712	499	4977	1333	219	84	34	542	501	.268	.344	.366	.710	114	81	86	99	101	696	173			
NY	155	91	63	.591	13	715	567	5061	1391	204	83	31	562	489	.275	.354	.366	.720	116	106	105	100	97	759	282			
PIT	154	86	67	.562	17.5	655	576	5125	1364	214	83	33	437	524	.266	.328	.360	.688	100	30	-6	106	100	655	148			
PHI	157	78	75	.510	25.5	674	639	5171	1319	223	71	22	506	559	.255	.327	.338	.665	97	-4	-25	103	106	641	199			
CIN	156	75	79	.487	29	620	684	5121	1326	150	79	23	529	515	.259	.332	.333	.665	105	0	28	96	98	669	310			
BRO	156	64	90	.416	40	497	623	5125	1174	166	73	25	434	706	.229	.294	.305	.599	82	-132	-113	97	101	506	151			
STL	153	63	90	.412	40.5	639	718	4912	1217	167	70	15	655	581	.248	.345	.319	.664	103	19	42	96	99	609	179			
BOS	157	53	100	.346	50.5	495	701	5123	1260	173	49	31	359	540	.246	.301	.317	.618	81	-99	-127	105	96	536	152			
TOT	621					5007		40615	10384	1516	592	214	4024	4415	.256	.328	.338	.666						1594				

TEAM	CG	SH	SV	IP	H	H/G	HR	BB	SO	RAT	ERA	ERA+	OAV	OOB	PR	/A	PF	CPI	FA	E	DP	FW	PW	BW	SBW	DIF
CHI	100	25	13	1378²	1171	7.6	18	474	609	11.0	2.51	115	.235	.307	79	54	95	95	.963	230	110	2.1	5.7	9.1		10.2
NY	96	9	10	1391²	1290	8.3	30	397	717	11.2	2.68	110	.250	.308	54	44	98	99	.955	291	117	-1.7	4.6	11.1		.0
PIT	73	13	12	1376	1254	8.2	20	392	479	11.1	2.83	109	.250	.311	29	38	102	93	.961	245	102	1.1	4.0	-.6		5.0
PHI	84	17	9	1411¹	1297	8.3	36	547	657	12.1	3.05	102	.253	.330	-5	9	103	101	.960	258	132	.6	.9	-2.6		2.6
CIN	86	16	11	1386²	1334	8.7	27	528	497	12.5	3.08	94	.261	.338	-9	-29	96	105	.955	291	103	-1.6	-3.1	2.9		-.3
BRO	103	15	5	1420¹	1331	8.4	17	545	555	12.1	3.07	99	.259	.335	-7	-9	100	101	.964	235	125	2.0	-.9	-11.9		-2.1
STL	81	4	14	1337¹	1396	9.4	30	541	466	13.3	3.78	79	.275	.350	-112	-120	98	96	.959	261	109	.0	-12.6	4.4		-5.3
BOS	72	12	9	1390¹	1328	8.6	36	599	531	12.8	3.22	103	.265	.349	-30	14	110	110	.954	305	137	-2.4	1.5	-13.4		-9.2
TOT	695	111	83	11092¹		8.4				12.0	3.02		.256	.328					.959	2116	935					

Runs
Magee-Phi 110
Huggins-StL 101
Byrne-Pit 101
Doyle-NY 97
Bescher-Cin....... 95

Hits
Wagner-Pit 178
Byrne-Pit 178
Wheat-Bro 172
Magee-Phi 172
Hoblitzel-Cin 170

Doubles
Byrne-Pit 43
Magee-Phi 39
Wheat-Bro 36
Merkle-NY 35
Wagner-Pit 34

Triples
Mitchell-Cin 18
Magee-Phi 17
Konetchy-StL 16
Hofman-Chi 16

Home Runs
Schulte-Chi 10
Beck-Bos 10
Doyle-NY 8
Daubert-Bro....... 8

Total Bases
Magee-Phi 263
Schulte-Chi 257
Byrne-Pit 251
Wheat-Bro 244
Wagner-Pit 240

Runs Batted In
Magee-Phi 123
Mitchell-Cin 88
Murray-NY 87
Hofman-Chi 86
Wagner-Pit 81

Runs Produced
Magee-Phi 227
Wagner-Pit 167
Hofman-Chi 166
Mitchell-Cin 162
Konetchy-StL..... 162

Bases On Balls
Huggins-StL 116
Evers-Chi 108
Magee-Phi 94
Titus-Phi 93
Sheckard-Chi...... 83

Batting Average
Magee-Phi 331
Mitchell-Cin .... .325
Snodgrass-NY....321
Wagner-Pit 320
Bates-Phi 305

On Base Percentage
Magee-Phi 445
Snodgrass-NY..... .440
Evers-Chi 413
Hofman-Chi 406
Huggins-StL 399

Slugging Average
Magee-Phi 507
Hofman-Chi 461
Schulte-Chi 460
Merkle-NY 441
Snodgrass-NY.......432

Production
Magee-Phi 952
Snodgrass-NY.....871
Hofman-Chi 867
Konetchy-StL......822
Wagner-Pit 822

Adjusted Production
Magee-Phi 172
Snodgrass-NY..... 154
Hofman-Chi 154
Konetchy-StL..... 145
Schulte-Chi 137

Batter Runs
Magee-Phi 54.9
Hofman-Chi 32.4
Snodgrass-NY.... 31.9
Konetchy-StL..... 28.0
Wagner-Pit 27.9

Adjusted Batter Runs
Magee-Phi 52.6
Hofman-Chi 32.9
Snodgrass-NY..... 31.9
Konetchy-StL..... 30.5
Wagner-Pit 23.9

Clutch Hitting Index
Magee-Phi 162
Evans-StL 158
Murray-NY 146
Steinfeldt-Chi..... 145
Devlin-NY 143

Runs Created
Magee-Phi 139
Byrne-Pit 104
Wagner-Pit 103
Hofman-Chi 102
Doyle-NY 101

Total Average
Magee-Phi 1.205
Snodgrass-NY... 1.071
Hofman-Chi 975
Konetchy-StL.....884
Paskert-Cin 884

Stolen Bases
Bescher-Cin....... 70
Murray-NY 57
Paskert-Cin 51
Magee-Phi 49
Devore-NY 43

Stolen Base Average

Stolen Base Runs

Fielding Runs
Shean-Bos 42.5
Doolan-Phi 20.7
Tinker-Chi 15.5
Paskert-Cin 14.1
Knabe-Phi 13.9

Total Player Rating
Konetchy-StL..... 4.0
Wagner-Pit 3.4
Hofman-Chi 3.4
Magee-Phi 3.3
Mowrey-StL 3.1

Wins
Mathewson-NY 27
Brown-Chi 25
Moore-Phi 22
Suggs-Cin 20
Cole-Chi 20

Win Percentage
Cole-Chi 833
Crandall-NY ...810
Mathewson-NY ...750
Adams-Pit 667
Brown-Chi 641

Games
Mattern-Bos 51
Gaspar-Cin 48

Complete Games
Rucker-Bro 27
Mathewson-NY 27
Brown-Chi 27
Bell-Bro 25
Barger-Bro........ 25

Shutouts
Rucker-Bro 6
Moore-Phi 6
Mattern-Bos 6
Brown-Chi 6

Saves
Gaspar-Cin 7
Brown-Chi 7
Crandall-NY 5
Richie-Bos-Chi 4
Phillippe-Pit 4

Innings Pitched
Rucker-Bro 320.1
Mathewson-NY ... 318.1
Bell-Bro 310.0
Mattern-Bos 305.0
Brown-Chi 295.1

Fewest Hits/Game
Cole-Chi 6.53
Scanlan-Bro...... 7.25
Moore-Phi 7.25
Drucke-NY 7.27
Ames-NY 7.61

Fewest BB/Game
Suggs-Cin 1.62
Mathewson-NY ... 1.70
Crandall-NY 1.86
Brown-Chi 1.95
Wiltse-NY 1.99

Strikeouts
Moore-Phi 185
Mathewson-NY ... 184
Frock-Pit-Bos ... 171
Drucke-NY 151
Rucker-Bro 147

Strikeouts/Game
Drucke-NY 6.31
Frock-Pit-Bos ... 5.98
Moore-Phi 5.88
Mathewson-NY ... 5.20
Ames-NY 4.44

Ratio
Brown-Chi 9.87
Mathewson-NY ... 10.04
Bell-Bro 10.25
Adams-Pit 10.40
Crandall-NY 10.44

Earned Run Average
Cole-Chi 1.80
Brown-Chi 1.86
Mathewson-NY ... 1.89
Ames-NY 2.22
Adams-Pit 2.24

Adjusted ERA
Cole-Chi 159
Mathewson-NY ... 156
Brown-Chi 155
Adams-Pit 138
Ames-NY 133

Opponents' Batting Avg.
Cole-Chi 211
Drucke-NY 228
Moore-Phi 228
Brown-Chi 232
Scanlan-Bro......234

Opponents' On Base Pct.
Brown-Chi 277
Mathewson-NY ...286
Crandall-NY 289
Adams-Pit 291
Bell-Bro 296

Starter Runs
Mathewson-NY ... 40.0
Brown-Chi 38.2
Cole-Chi 32.5
McQuillan-Phi ... 24.2
Adams-Pit 21.3

Adjusted Starter Runs
Mathewson-NY ... 37.6
Brown-Chi 33.3
Cole-Chi 28.5
McQuillan-Phi ... 25.8
Adams-Pit 23.1

Clutch Pitching Index
Cole-Chi 136
Brown-Bos 122
Barger-Bro 122
Mathewson-NY ... 117
Curtis-Bos 116

Relief Runs

Adjusted Relief Runs

Relief Ranking

Total Pitcher Index
Mathewson-NY 5.9
Brown-Chi 3.9
Cole-Chi 3.3
McQuillan-Phi ... 2.7
Brown-Bos 2.3

Total Baseball Ranking
Mathewson-NY 5.9
Konetchy-StL..... 3.9
Brown-Chi 3.9
Wagner-Pit........ 3.4
Hofman-Chi 3.4

TEAM	G	W	L	PCT	GB	R	OR	AB	H	2B	3B	HR	BB	SO	AVG	OBP	SLG	PRO	PRO+	BR	/A	PF	CHI	RC	SB	CS	SBA	SBR
PHI	155	102	48	.680		673	441	5156	1373	191	105	19	409		.266	.326	.355	.681	120	104	110	99	99	665	207			
NY	156	88	63	.583	14.5	626	557	5051	1254	164	75	20	464		.248	.320	.322	.642	101	44	11	106	102	614	288			
DET	155	86	68	.558	18	679	582	5039	1317	190	72	28	459		.261	.329	.344	.673	110	96	58	107	102	655	249			
BOS	158	81	72	.529	22.5	638	564	5204	1350	175	87	43	430		.259	.323	.351	.674	114	94	80	102	94	656	194			
CLE	161	71	81	.467	32	548	657	5385	1316	188	64	9	366		.244	.297	.308	.605	94	-37	-45	101	99	549	189			
CHI	156	68	85	.444	35.5	457	479	5024	1058	115	58	7	403		.211	.275	.261	.536	76	-150	-126	96	112	415	183			
WAS	157	66	85	.437	36.5	501	550	4989	1175	145	46	9	449		.236	.309	.288	.597	97	-32	-6	95	94	508	192			
STL	158	47	107	.305	57	451	743	5077	1105	131	60	12	415		.218	.281	.274	.555	84	-117	-82	94	102	438	169			
TOT	628					4573		40925	9948	1299	567	147	3395	5278	.243	.308	.313	.621							1671			

TEAM	CG	SH	SV	IP	H	H/G	HR	BB	SO	RAT	ERA	ERA+	OAV	OOB	PR	/A	PF	CPI	FA	E	DP	FW	PW	BW	SBW	DIF
PHI	123	24	5	1421²	1103	7.0	8	450	789	10.2	1.79	133	.221	.292	115	91	94	111	.965	230	117	3.8	10.1	12.2		.8
NY	110	14	8	1399	1238	8.0	16	364	654	10.7	2.61	102	.243	.300	-15	4	106	90	.956	285	95	.2	.4	1.2		10.6
DET	108	17	5	1380¹	1257	8.2	34	460	532	11.6	2.82	93	.248	.319	-47	-28	104	101	.956	288	79	-.0	-3.1	6.4		5.8
BOS	100	12	6	1430	1236	7.8	30	414	670	10.7	2.45	104	.235	.297	10	14	101	94	.954	309	80	-1.1	1.6	8.9		-4.8
CLE	92	13	5	1467	1394	8.6	10	488	617	11.9	2.88	90	.261	.330	-60	-51	103	105	.964	247	112	3.4	-5.7	-5.0		2.2
CHI	103	23	7	1421	1130	7.2	16	381	785	9.8	2.03	118	.222	.281	77	56	95	91	.954	314	100	-1.7	6.2	-14.0		1.0
WAS	119	19	3	1377¹	1222	8.0	19	375	674	10.8	2.46	101	.246	.305	9	4	99	102	.959	264	99	1.8	.4	-.7		-11.1
STL	101	9	3	1391	1356	8.8	14	532	557	12.6	3.09	80	.265	.341	-89	-95	98	106	.943	385	113	-6.3	-10.6	-9.1		-4.0
TOT	856	131	42	11287¹		7.9				11.0	2.52		.243	.308					.956	2322	795					

Runs
Cobb-Det	106
Lajoie-Cle	94
Speaker-Bos	92
Bush-Det	90
Milan-Was	89

Hits
Lajoie-Cle	227
Cobb-Det	194
Collins-Phi	188
Speaker-Bos	183
Crawford-Det	170

Doubles
Lajoie-Cle	51
Cobb-Det	35
Lewis-Bos	29
Murphy-Phi	28
Oldring-Phi	27

Triples
Crawford-Det	19
Lord-Cle-Phi	18
Murphy-Phi	18
Stahl-Bos	16
Cree-NY	16

Home Runs
Stahl-Bos	10
Lewis-Bos	8
Cobb-Det	8
Speaker-Bos	7
Crawford-Det	5

Total Bases
Lajoie-Cle	304
Cobb-Det	279
Speaker-Bos	252
Crawford-Det	249
Murphy-Phi	244

Runs Batted In
Crawford-Det	120
Cobb-Det	91
Collins-Phi	81
Stahl-Bos	77
Lajoie-Cle	76

Runs Produced
Crawford-Det	198
Cobb-Det	189
Lajoie-Cle	166
Collins-Phi	159
Baker-Phi	155

Bases On Balls
Bush-Det	78
Milan-Was	71
Wolter-NY	66
Cobb-Det	64

Batting Average
Lajoie-Cle	.384
Cobb-Det	.383
Speaker-Bos	.340
Collins-Phi	.322
Oldring-Phi	.308

On Base Percentage
Cobb-Det	.456
Lajoie-Cle	.445
Speaker-Bos	.404
Collins-Phi	.381
Milan-Was	.379

Slugging Average
Cobb-Det	.551
Lajoie-Cle	.514
Speaker-Bos	.468
Murphy-Phi	.436
Oldring-Phi	.430

Production
Cobb-Det	1.008
Lajoie-Cle	.960
Speaker-Bos	.873
Collins-Phi	.798
Cree-NY	.775

Adjusted Production
Cobb-Det	202
Lajoie-Cle	198
Speaker-Bos	169
Collins-Phi	151
Murphy-Phi	143

Batter Runs
Lajoie-Cle	68.2
Cobb-Det	67.9
Speaker-Bos	44.9
Collins-Phi	33.0
Murphy-Phi	23.6

Adjusted Batter Runs
Lajoie-Cle	67.4
Cobb-Det	64.0
Speaker-Bos	43.5
Collins-Phi	33.6
Murphy-Phi	24.2

Clutch Hitting Index
Crawford-Det	178
LaPorte-NY	166
McBride-Was	143
Purtell-Chi-Bos	138
Moriarty-Det	137

Runs Created
Cobb-Det	156
Lajoie-Cle	147
Collins-Phi	122
Speaker-Bos	115
Crawford-Det	89

Total Average
Cobb-Det	1.321
Lajoie-Cle	1.085
Speaker-Bos	.972
Collins-Phi	.959
Cree-NY	.820

Stolen Bases
Collins-Phi	81
Cobb-Det	65
Zeider-Chi	49
Bush-Det	49
Milan-Was	44

Stolen Base Average

Stolen Base Runs

Fielding Runs
Collins-Phi	35.5
McBride-Was	26.6
Wallace-StL	22.0
Lajoie-Cle	16.9
Speaker-Bos	15.0

Total Player Rating
Lajoie-Cle	8.7
Cobb-Det	7.2
Collins-Phi	7.1
Speaker-Bos	5.6
Wallace-StL	3.6

Wins
Coombs-Phi	31
Ford-NY	26
Johnson-Was	25
Bender-Phi	23
Mullin-Det	21

Win Percentage
Bender-Phi	.821
Ford-NY	.813
Coombs-Phi	.775
Donovan-Det	.708
Mullin-Det	.636

Games
Walsh-Chi	45
Johnson-Was	45
Coombs-Phi	45
Scott-Chi	41

Complete Games
Johnson-Was	38
Coombs-Phi	35
Walsh-Chi	33
Ford-NY	29
Mullin-Det	27

Shutouts
Coombs-Phi	13
Johnson-Was	8
Ford-NY	8
Walsh-Chi	7

Saves
Walsh-Chi	5
Browning-Det	3

Innings Pitched
Johnson-Was	374.0
Walsh-Chi	369.2
Coombs-Phi	353.0
Ford-NY	299.2
Morgan-Phi	290.2

Fewest Hits/Game
Ford-NY	5.83
Walsh-Chi	5.89
Coombs-Phi	6.32
Johnson-Was	6.47
Bender-Phi	6.55

Fewest BB/Game
Walsh-Chi	1.49
Young-NY	1.49
Collins-Bos	1.51
Bender-Phi	1.69
Johnson-Was	1.83

Strikeouts
Johnson-Was	313
Walsh-Chi	258
Coombs-Phi	224
Ford-NY	209
Bender-Phi	155

Strikeouts/Game
Johnson-Was	7.53
Wood-Bos	6.57
Walsh-Chi	6.28
Ford-NY	6.28
Coombs-Phi	5.71

Ratio
Walsh-Chi	7.47
Ford-NY	8.17
Bender-Phi	8.60
Johnson-Was	8.61
Collins-Bos	9.09

Earned Run Average
Walsh-Chi	1.27
Coombs-Phi	1.30
Johnson-Was	1.35
Morgan-Phi	1.55
Bender-Phi	1.58

Adjusted ERA
Walsh-Chi	189
Johnson-Was	185
Coombs-Phi	182
Ford-NY	161
Collins-Bos	157

Opponents' Batting Avg.
Walsh-Chi	.187
Ford-NY	.188
Coombs-Phi	.201
Hall-Bos	.207
Bender-Phi	.207

Opponents' On Base Pct.
Walsh-Chi	.226
Ford-NY	.245
Bender-Phi	.255
Johnson-Was	.262
Collins-Bos	.264

Starter Runs
Walsh-Chi	51.3
Johnson-Was	48.5
Coombs-Phi	47.7
Morgan-Phi	31.2
Ford-NY	28.8

Adjusted Starter Runs
Johnson-Was	47.4
Walsh-Chi	46.3
Coombs-Phi	41.9
Ford-NY	33.4
Morgan-Phi	26.5

Clutch Pitching Index
Morgan-Phi	142
Olmstead-Chi	142
Vaughn-NY	121
Wood-Bos	117
Coombs-Phi	114

Relief Runs

Adjusted Relief Runs

Relief Ranking

Total Pitcher Index
Walsh-Chi	7.3
Johnson-Was	5.7
Coombs-Phi	4.7
Ford-NY	4.2
Bender-Phi	3.7

Total Baseball Ranking
Lajoie-Cle	8.7
Walsh-Chi	7.3
Cobb-Det	7.2
Collins-Phi	7.1
Johnson-Was	5.7

TEAM	G	W	L	PCT	GB	R	OR	AB	H	2B	3B	HR	BB	SO	AVG	OBP	SLG	PRO	PRO+	BR	/A	PF	CHI	RC	SB	CS	SBA	SBR
NY	154	99	54	.647		756	542	5006	1399	225	103	41	530	506	.279	.358	.390	.748	113	109	88	103	96	820	347			
CHI	157	92	62	.597	7.5	757	607	5130	1335	218	101	54	585	617	.260	.341	.374	.715	107	44	43	100	102	729	214			
PIT	155	85	69	.552	14.5	744	557	5137	1345	206	106	49	525	583	.262	.336	.372	.708	101	28	2	104	104	698	160			
PHI	153	79	73	.520	19.5	658	669	5044	1307	214	56	60	490	588	.259	.328	.359	.687	98	-11	-19	101	100	647	153			
STL	158	75	74	.503	22	671	745	5132	1295	199	86	26	592	650	.252	.337	.340	.677	99	-18	1	97	99	651	175			
CIN	159	70	83	.458	29	682	706	5291	1379	180	105	21	578	594	.261	.337	.346	.683	102	-10	16	96	97	716	289			
BRO	154	64	86	.427	33.5	539	659	5059	1198	151	71	28	425	683	.237	.301	.311	.612	80	-152	-124	96	106	528	184			
BOS	156	44	107	.291	54	699	1021	5308	1417	249	54	37	554	577	.267	.340	.355	.695	93	10	-47	108	98	696	169			
TOT	623					5506		41107	10675	1642	682	316	4279	4798	.260	.335	.356	.691							1691			

TEAM	CG	SH	SV	IP	H	H/G	HR	BB	SO	RAT	ERA	ERA+	OAV	OOB	PR	/A	PF	CPI	FA	E	DP	FW	PW	BW	SBW	DIF
NY	95	19	13	1368	1267	8.3	33	369	771	11.0	2.69	125	.246	.300	106	100	99	97	.959	256	86	.5	10.0	8.8		3.1
CHI	85	12	16	1411	1270	8.1	26	525	582	11.7	2.90	114	.245	.320	78	62	97	100	.960	260	114	.6	6.2	4.3		3.9
PIT	91	13	11	1380[1]	1249	8.1	36	375	605	10.8	2.84	121	.248	.306	85	87	101	97	.963	232	131	2.1	8.7	.2		-3.0
PHI	90	20	10	1373[1]	1285	8.4	43	598	697	12.7	3.30	104	.255	.340	14	19	101	104	.963	231	113	1.9	1.9	-1.9		1.1
STL	88	6	10	1402[1]	1296	8.3	39	701	561	13.2	3.68	91	.254	.350	-46	-52	99	97	.960	261	106	.6	-5.2	.1		5.0
CIN	77	4	12	1425	1410	8.9	36	476	557	12.3	3.26	101	.265	.332	21	5	97	103	.955	295	108	-1.4	.5	1.6		-7.2
BRO	81	13	10	1371[2]	1310	8.6	27	566	533	12.6	3.39	98	.263	.344	0	-12	98	103	.962	241	112	1.4	-1.2	-12.5		1.2
BOS	73	5	7	1374	1570	10.3	76	672	486	15.1	5.08	75	.296	.381	-258	-195	113	96	.947	347	110	-5.0	-19.6	-4.7		-2.2
TOT	680	92	89	11105[2]		8.6				12.4	3.39		.260	.335					.958	2123	880					

Runs
Sheckard-Chi..... 121
Huggins-StL 106
Bescher-Cin...... 106
Schulte-Chi 105
Doyle-NY 102

Hits
Miller-Bos 192
Hoblitzel-Cin 180
Daubert-Bro 176
Schulte-Chi 173
Luderus-Phi 166

Doubles
Konetchy-StL..... 38
Miller-Bos 36
Wilson-Pit........ 34
Herzog-Bos-NY ... 33
Sweeney-Bos 33

Triples
Doyle-NY 25
Mitchell-Cin 22
Schulte-Chi 21
Zimmerman-Chi ... 17
Byrne-Pit 17

Home Runs
Schulte-Chi 21
Luderus-Phi 16
Magee-Phi 15
Doyle-NY 13

Total Bases
Schulte-Chi 308
Doyle-NY 277
Luderus-Phi 260
Hoblitzel-Cin 258
Wilson-Pit........ 257

Runs Batted In
Wilson-Pit........ 107
Schulte-Chi 107
Luderus-Phi 99
Magee-Phi 94

Runs Produced
Schulte-Chi 191
Konetchy-StL 172
Wilson-Pit 167
Wagner-Pit 167
Sheckard-Chi..... 167

Bases On Balls
Sheckard-Chi..... 147
Bates-Cin 103
Bescher-Cin...... 102
Huggins-StL 96
Knabe-Phi 94

Batting Average
Wagner-Pit 334
Miller-Bos 333
Sweeney-Bos 314
Doyle-NY 310
Daubert-Bro......307

On Base Percentage
Sheckard-Chi.....434
Wagner-Pit 423
Bates-Cin 415
Sweeney-Bos 404
Doyle-NY 397

Slugging Average
Schulte-Chi 534
Doyle-NY 527
Wagner-Pit 507
Magee-Phi 483
Wilson-Pit........472

Production
Wagner-Pit 930
Doyle-NY 924
Schulte-Chi 918
Magee-Phi 849
Wilson-Pit........826

Adjusted Production
Schulte-Chi 155
Wagner-Pit 154
Doyle-NY 153
Magee-Phi 135
Konetchy-StL..... 132

Batter Runs
Schulte-Chi..... 40.6
Doyle-NY 39.3
Wagner-Pit 38.8
Sheckard-Chi.... 31.7
Clarke-Pit 27.0

Adjusted Batter Runs
Schulte-Chi 40.4
Doyle-NY 37.0
Wagner-Pit 36.4
Sheckard-Chi..... 31.6
Bates-Cin 26.6

Clutch Hitting Index
Hofman-Chi 155
Miller-Pit 138
Grant-Cin 136
Mitchell-Cin 130
Magee-Phi 130

Runs Created
Schulte-Chi 127
Doyle-NY 124
Bescher-Cin 114
Wagner-Pit 109
Miller-Bos 107

Total Average
Doyle-NY 1.077
Wagner-Pit 1.057
Schulte-Chi 1.015
Sheckard-Chi 1.003
Bates-Cin 943

Stolen Bases
Bescher-Cin....... 80
Devore-NY 61
Snodgrass-NY..... 51
Merkle-NY 49

Stolen Base Average

Stolen Base Runs

Fielding Runs
Tinker-Chi 23.4
Doolan-Phi 20.3
Ingerton-Bos 18.2
Herzog-Bos-NY ... 17.8
Merkle-NY 15.3

Total Player Rating
Wagner-Pit 4.6
Sheckard-Chi..... 3.8
Herzog-Bos-NY... 3.2
Tinker-Chi 3.1
Schulte-Chi 2.7

Wins
Alexander-Phi 28
Mathewson-NY ... 26
Marquard-NY 24
Harmon-StL 23

Win Percentage
Marquard-NY......774
Crandall-NY 750
Cole-Chi 720
Alexander-Phi 683
Mathewson-NY 667

Games
Brown-Chi 53
Harmon-StL 51
Rucker-Bro 48
Alexander-Phi 48

Complete Games
Alexander-Phi 31
Mathewson-NY ... 29
Harmon-StL 28
Leifield-Pit 26
Adams-Pit 24

Shutouts
Alexander-Phi 7
Adams-Pit 6

Saves
Brown-Chi 13
Crandall-NY 5

Innings Pitched
Alexander-Phi ... 367.0
Harmon-StL 348.0
Leifield-Pit 318.0
Rucker-Bro 315.2
Moore-Phi 308.1

Fewest Hits/Game
Alexander-Phi 6.99
Marquard-NY 7.16
Rucker-Bro 7.27
Ames-NY 7.46
Harmon-StL 7.50

Fewest BB/Game
Mathewson-NY ... 1.11
Adams-Pit 1.29
Steele-Pit-Bro 1.71
Brown-Chi 1.83
Wiltse-NY 1.87

Strikeouts
Marquard-NY..... 237
Alexander-Phi 227
Rucker-Bro 190
Moore-Phi 174
Harmon-StL 144

Strikeouts/Game
Marquard-NY..... 7.68
Alexander-Phi 5.57
Rucker-Bro 5.42
Ames-NY 5.18
Moore-Phi 5.08

Ratio
Adams-Pit 9.30
Ames-NY 10.01
Mathewson-NY .. 10.03
Steele-Pit-Bro ... 10.33
Alexander-Phi ... 10.35

Earned Run Average
Mathewson-NY ... 1.99
Richie-Chi 2.31
Adams-Pit 2.33
Marquard-NY..... 2.50
Alexander-Phi 2.57

Adjusted ERA
Mathewson-NY ... 168
Adams-Pit 147
Richie-Chi 143
Marquard-NY 134
Alexander-Phi ... 133

Opponents' Batting Avg.
Alexander-Phi 219
Marquard-NY......219
Ames-NY 223
Rucker-Bro 226
Keefe-Cin 229

Opponents' On Base Pct.
Adams-Pit 271
Ames-NY 277
Mathewson-NY 283
Wiltse-NY 292
Alexander-Phi 293

Starter Runs
Mathewson-NY ... 47.7
Adams-Pit 34.5
Alexander-Phi 33.3
Richie-Chi 30.3
Marquard-NY..... 27.6

Adjusted Starter Runs
Mathewson-NY ... 46.4
Adams-Pit 35.5
Alexander-Phi 34.9
Leifield-Pit 27.9
Richie-Chi 27.8

Clutch Pitching Index
Moore-Phi 130
Mathewson-NY ... 122
Richie-Chi 119
Leifield-Pit 117
Gaspar-Cin 115

Relief Runs
Richter-Chi........ 1.6

Adjusted Relief Runs
Richter-Chi........ 1.1

Relief Ranking
Richter-Chi..........8

Total Pitcher Index
Mathewson-NY 5.8
Alexander-Phi 3.5
Leifield-Pit 3.5
Adams-Pit 3.4
Richie-Chi 2.6

Total Baseball Ranking
Mathewson-NY ... 5.8
Wagner-Pit........ 4.6
Sheckard-Chi..... 3.8
Alexander-Phi 3.5
Leifield-Pit 3.4

TEAM	G	W	L	PCT	GB	R	OR	AB	H	2B	3B	HR	BB	SO	AVG	OBP	SLG	PRO	PRO+	BR	/A	PF	CHI	RC	SB	CS	SBA	SBR
PHI	152	101	50	.669		861	601	5199	1540	237	93	35	424		.296	.357	.398	.755	119	108	122	98	104	821	226			
DET	154	89	65	.578	13.5	831	776	5294	1544	230	96	30	471		.292	.355	.388	.743	108	91	55	105	102	825	276			
CLE	156	80	73	.523	22	691	712	5321	1501	238	81	20	354		.282	.333	.369	.702	101	1	-8	101	97	716	209			
CHI	154	77	74	.510	24	719	624	5213	1401	179	92	20	385		.269	.325	.320	.645	97	-46	-23	97	108	659	201			
BOS	153	78	75	.510	24	680	643	5014	1379	203	66	35	506		.275	.350	.363	.713	106	39	45	99	91	710	190			
NY	153	76	76	.500	25.5	684	724	5052	1374	190	96	25	493		.272	.344	.362	.706	97	24	-22	107	94	724	269			
WAS	154	64	90	.416	38.5	625	766	5065	1308	159	54	16	466		.258	.330	.320	.650	89	-75	-62	98	100	607	215			
STL	152	45	107	.296	56.5	567	812	4996	1192	187	63	17	460		.239	.307	.311	.618	81	-142	-115	96	105	515	125			
TOT	614					5658		41154	11239	1623	641	198	3559	5093	.273	.338	.358	.696							1711			

TEAM	CG	SH	SV	IP	H	H/G	HR	BB	SO	RAT	ERA	ERA+	OAV	OOB	PR	/A	PF	CPI	FA	E	DP	FW	PW	BW	SBW	DIF
PHI	97	13	13	1375²	1343	8.8	17	487	739	12.5	3.01	105	.264	.338	50	20	94	106	.964	225	100	4.9	2.0	12.0		6.7
DET	108	8	3	1387²	1514	9.8	28	460	538	13.3	3.73	93	.283	.348	-60	-45	104	97	.951	318	78	-1.0	-4.4	5.4		12.0
CLE	93	6	6	1390²	1382	8.9	17	552	675	12.9	3.36	101	.267	.345	-3	7	102	100	.954	302	108	.3	.7	-.8		3.3
CHI	85	17	11	1386¹	1349	8.8	22	384	752	11.5	2.97	108	.255	.310	57	38	96	88	.961	252	98	3.4	3.7	-2.3		-3.3
BOS	87	10	8	1351²	1309	8.7	21	473	711	12.2	2.74	119	.262	.332	89	78	98	113	.949	323	93	-1.4	7.7	4.4		-9.2
NY	91	5	3	1360²	1404	9.3	26	406	667	12.8	3.54	101	.270	.329	-30	9	108	89	.949	328	99	-1.7	.9	-2.2		3.0
WAS	106	13	3	1354¹	1471	9.8	39	410	628	12.8	3.52	93	.277	.334	-27	-38	98	96	.953	305	90	-.1	-3.7	-6.1		-3.1
STL	92	8	1	1332¹	1465	9.9	28	463	383	13.4	3.86	87	.278	.342	-77	-73	101	90	.945	358	104	-3.8	-7.2	-11.3		-8.7
TOT	759	80	48	10939¹		9.2				12.6	3.34		.273	.338					.953	2411	770					

Runs		Hits		Doubles		Triples		Home Runs		Total Bases	
Cobb-Det	147	Cobb-Det	248	Cobb-Det	47	Cree-NY	24	Baker-Phi	11	Cobb-Det	367
Jackson-Cle	126	Jackson-Cle	233	Jackson-Cle	45	Jackson-Cle	22	Speaker-Bos	8	Jackson-Cle	337
Bush-Det	126	Crawford-Det	217	Baker-Phi	42	Jackson-Cle	19	Cobb-Det	8	Crawford-Det	302
Milan-Was	109	Baker-Phi	198	Lord-Phi	37	Lord-Chi	18			Baker-Phi	301
Crawford-Det	109	Milan-Was	194	LaPorte-StL	37	Wolter-NY	15			Cree-NY	267

Runs Batted In		Runs Produced		Bases On Balls		Batting Average		On Base Percentage		Slugging Average	
Cobb-Det	127	Cobb-Det	266	Bush-Det	98	Cobb-Det	.420	Jackson-Cle	.468	Cobb-Det	.621
Crawford-Det	115	Crawford-Det	217	Milan-Was	74	Jackson-Cle	.408	Cobb-Det	.467	Jackson-Cle	.590
Baker-Phi	115	Jackson-Cle	202	Gessler-Was	74	Crawford-Det	.378	Collins-Phi	.451	Crawford-Det	.526
Bodie-Chi	97	Baker-Phi	200	Hooper-Bos	73	Collins-Phi	.365	Crawford-Det	.438	Cree-NY	.513
Delahanty-Det	94			Austin-StL	69	Cree-NY	.348	Speaker-Bos	.418	Baker-Phi	.508

Production		Adjusted Production		Batter Runs		Adjusted Batter Runs		Clutch Hitting Index		Runs Created	
Cobb-Det	1.088	Cobb-Det	193	Cobb-Det	78.4	Cobb-Det	74.4	Stovall-Cle	176	Cobb-Det	207
Jackson-Cle	1.058	Jackson-Cle	192	Jackson-Cle	71.8	Jackson-Cle	70.8	Hartzell-NY	153	Jackson-Cle	175
Crawford-Det	.964	Collins-Phi	163	Crawford-Det	52.4	Crawford-Det	48.4	Bodie-Chi	147	Crawford-Det	147
Collins-Phi	.932	Crawford-Det	160	Collins-Phi	43.0	Collins-Phi	44.3	McBride-Was	141	Cree-NY	129
Cree-NY	.928	Speaker-Bos	158	Cree-NY	39.9	Speaker-Bos	39.0	Gessler-Was	141	Baker-Phi	127

Total Average		Stolen Bases		Stolen Base Average		Stolen Base Runs		Fielding Runs		Total Player Rating	
Cobb-Det	1.464	Cobb-Det	83					Tannehill-Chi	42.5	Cobb-Det	7.4
Jackson-Cle	1.308	Milan-Was	58					Gardner-Bos	23.6	Jackson-Cle	6.8
Collins-Phi	1.125	Cree-NY	48					McBride-Was	23.5	Collins-Phi	4.3
Crawford-Det	1.120	Callahan-Chi	45					Bush-Det	16.7	Speaker-Bos	3.7
Cree-NY	1.103	Lord-Chi	43					Austin-StL	16.3	Baker-Phi	3.5

Wins		Win Percentage		Games		Complete Games		Shutouts		Saves	
Coombs-Phi	28	Bender-Phi	.773	Walsh-Chi	56	Johnson-Was	36	Plank-Phi	6	Walsh-Chi	4
Walsh-Chi	27	Gregg-Cle	.767	Coombs-Phi	47	Walsh-Chi	33	Johnson-Was	6	Plank-Phi	4
Johnson-Was	25	Plank-Phi	.742	Wood-Bos	44	Ford-NY	26	Wood-Bos	5	Hall-Bos	4
		Coombs-Phi	.700	Caldwell-NY	41	Coombs-Phi	26	Walsh-Chi	5	Wood-Bos	3
		Morgan-Phi	.682					Gregg-Cle	5	Bender-Phi	3

Innings Pitched		Fewest Hits/Game		Fewest BB/Game		Strikeouts		Strikeouts/Game		Ratio	
Walsh-Chi	368.2	Gregg-Cle	6.33	White-Chi	1.47	Walsh-Chi	255	Wood-Bos	7.54	Gregg-Cle	9.86
Coombs-Phi	336.2	Wood-Bos	7.38	Lake-StL	1.67	Wood-Bos	231	Walsh-Chi	6.23	Walsh-Chi	9.91
Johnson-Was	323.1	Krapp-Cle	7.62	Walsh-Chi	1.76	Johnson-Was	207	Lange-Chi	5.79	Wood-Bos	10.22
Ford-NY	281.1	Morgan-Phi	7.82	Warhop-NY	1.89	Coombs-Phi	185	Johnson-Was	5.76	Johnson-Was	10.30
Wood-Bos	275.2	Scott-Chi	7.91	Powell-StL	1.91	Ford-NY	158	Kahler-Cle	5.66	Ford-NY	10.59

Earned Run Average		Adjusted ERA		Opponents' Batting Avg.		Opponents' On Base Pct.		Starter Runs		Adjusted Starter Runs	
Gregg-Cle	1.80	Gregg-Cle	189	Gregg-Cle	.205	Walsh-Chi	.280	Johnson-Was	51.9	Johnson-Was	49.8
Johnson-Was	1.89	Johnson-Was	173	Wood-Bos	.223	Johnson-Was	.283	Walsh-Chi	45.8	Gregg-Cle	43.7
Wood-Bos	2.02	Wood-Bos	162	Krapp-Cle	.232	Wood-Bos	.284	Gregg-Cle	41.8	Ford-NY	41.2
Plank-Phi	2.10	Ford-NY	158	Ford-NY	.237	Gregg-Cle	.286	Wood-Bos	40.3	Walsh-Chi	40.8
Bender-Phi	2.16	Plank-Phi	149	Johnson-Was	.238	Ford-NY	.291	Plank-Phi	35.2	Wood-Bos	38.2

Clutch Pitching Index		Relief Runs		Adjusted Relief Runs		Relief Ranking		Total Pitcher Index		Total Baseball Ranking	
Plank-Phi	133							Johnson-Was	6.0	Cobb-Det	7.4
Pape-Bos	130							Walsh-Chi	5.6	Jackson-Cle	6.8
Cicotte-Bos	122							Wood-Bos	5.1	Johnson-Was	6.0
Bender-Phi	117							Gregg-Cle	4.2	Walsh-Chi	5.6
Willett-Det	111							Ford-NY	4.0	Wood-Bos	5.1

TEAM	G	W	L	PCT	GB	R	OR	AB	H	2B	3B	HR	BB	SO	AVG	OBP	SLG	PRO	PRO+	BR	/A	PF	CHI	RC	SB	CS	SBA	SBR
NY	154	103	48	.682		823	571	5067	1451	231	89	47	514	497	.286	.360	.395	.755	110	89	68	103	104	830	319			
PIT	152	93	58	.616	10	751	565	5252	1493	222	129	39	420	514	.284	.340	.398	.738	110	44	55	98	99	767	177			
CHI	152	91	59	.607	11.5	756	668	5048	1398	245	90	43	560	615	.277	.354	.387	.741	109	62	64	100	98	750	164			
CIN	155	75	78	.490	29	656	722	5115	1310	183	89	21	479	492	.256	.323	.339	.662	90	-90	-69	97	107	639	248			
PHI	152	73	79	.480	30.5	670	688	5077	1354	244	68	43	464	615	.267	.332	.367	.699	91	-23	-69	107	99	671	159			
STL	153	63	90	.412	41	659	830	5092	1366	190	77	27	508	620	.268	.340	.352	.692	97	-27	-10	98	97	675	193			
BRO	153	58	95	.379	46	651	754	5141	1377	220	73	32	490	584	.268	.336	.358	.694	100	-28	0	96	96	677	179			
BOS	155	52	101	.340	52	693	861	5361	1465	227	68	35	454	690	.273	.335	.361	.696	94	-28	-40	102	99	693	137			
TOT	613					5659		41153	11214	1762	683	287	3889	4627	.272	.340	.369	.710							1576			

TEAM	CG	SH	SV	IP	H	H/G	HR	BB	SO	RAT	ERA	ERA+	OAV	OOB	PR	/A	PF	CPI	FA	E	DP	FW	PW	BW	SBW	DIF
NY	93	8	15	1369²	1352	8.9	36	338	652	11.3	2.58	130	.259	.307	124	118	99	103	.956	280	123	-2.1	11.6	6.7		11.3
PIT	94	18	7	1385	1268	8.2	28	497	664	11.8	2.85	114	.251	.324	84	60	96	99	.972	169	125	6.0	5.9	5.4		.2
CHI	80	15	9	1358²	1307	8.7	33	493	554	12.2	3.42	97	.259	.331	-4	-19	98	89	.960	249	125	-.0	-1.9	6.3		11.6
CIN	86	13	10	1377²	1455	9.5	28	452	561	12.9	3.42	98	.279	.344	-4	-14	99	102	.960	249	102	.4	-1.4	-6.8		6.3
PHI	81	10	9	1355	1381	9.2	43	515	616	12.9	3.25	111	.272	.344	23	54	106	107	.963	231	98	1.3	5.3	-6.8		-2.9
STL	61	6	12	1353	1466	9.8	31	560	487	13.7	3.85	89	.286	.361	-68	-63	101	102	.957	274	113	-1.8	-6.2	-1.0		-4.6
BRO	71	10	8	1357	1399	9.3	45	510	553	12.9	3.64	92	.273	.343	-37	-49	98	96	.959	255	96	-.3	-4.8	.0		-13.3
BOS	88	5	5	1390²	1544	10.0	43	521	542	13.6	4.17	86	.291	.359	-119	-98	105	95	.954	297	129	-3.2	-9.6	-3.9		-7.7
TOT	654	85	75	10946²		9.2				12.7	3.40		.272	.340					.960	2004	911					

Runs		Hits		Doubles		Triples		Home Runs		Total Bases	
Bescher-Cin	120	Zimmerman-Chi	207	Zimmerman-Chi	41	Wilson-Pit	36	Zimmerman-Chi	14	Zimmerman-Chi	318
Carey-Pit	114	Sweeney-Bos	204	Paskert-Phi	37	Wagner-Pit	20	Schulte-Chi	12	Wilson-Pit	299
Paskert-Phi	102	Campbell-Bos	185	Wagner-Pit	35	Murray-NY	20	Wilson-Pit	11	Wagner-Pit	277
Campbell-Bos	102	Doyle-NY	184	Miller-Pit	33	Daubert-Bro	16	Merkle-NY	11	Sweeney-Bos	264
		Wagner-Pit	181	Doyle-NY	33			Cravath-Phi	11	Doyle-NY	263

Runs Batted In		Runs Produced		Bases On Balls		Batting Average		On Base Percentage		Slugging Average	
Wagner-Pit	102	Wagner-Pit	186	Sheckard-Chi	122	Zimmerman-Chi	.372	Evers-Chi	.431	Zimmerman-Chi	.571
Sweeney-Bos	100	Sweeney-Bos	183	Paskert-Phi	91	Sweeney-Bos	.344	Huggins-StL	.422	Wilson-Pit	.513
Zimmerman-Chi	99	Zimmerman-Chi	180	Huggins-StL	87	Evers-Chi	.341	Paskert-Phi	.420	Wagner-Pit	.496
Wilson-Pit	95	Doyle-NY	178	Bescher-Cin	83	Doyle-NY	.330	Zimmerman-Chi	.418	Doyle-NY	.471
Murray-NY	92	Carey-Pit	175	Titus-Phi-Bos	82	Wagner-Pit	.324	Sweeney-Bos	.416	Cravath-Phi	.470

Production		Adjusted Production		Batter Runs		Adjusted Batter Runs		Clutch Hitting Index		Runs Created	
Zimmerman-Chi	.989	Zimmerman-Chi	169	Zimmerman-Chi	49.8	Zimmerman-Chi	50.0	Murray-NY	139	Zimmerman-Chi	141
Wagner-Pit	.891	Wagner-Pit	145	Wagner-Pit	32.1	Wagner-Pit	33.3	Miller-Phi	131	Sweeney-Bos	123
Evers-Chi	.873	Evers-Chi	139	Sweeney-Bos	30.9	Sweeney-Bos	29.5	Mitchell-Cin	127	Wagner-Pit	118
Doyle-NY	.864	Wilson-Pit	134	Evers-Chi	29.1	Evers-Chi	29.3	Tinker-Chi	126	Doyle-NY	116
Titus-Phi-Bos	.862	Konetchy-StL	134	Meyers-NY	28.2	Meyers-NY	26.7	Mowrey-StL	123	Paskert-Phi	108

Total Average		Stolen Bases		Stolen Base Average	Stolen Base Runs	Fielding Runs		Total Player Rating	
Zimmerman-Chi	1.100	Bescher-Cin	67			Sweeney-Bos	26.9	Wagner-Pit	6.6
Wagner-Pit	.976	Carey-Pit	45			Tinker-Chi	24.7	Sweeney-Bos	5.1
Paskert-Phi	.965	Snodgrass-NY	43			Wagner-Pit	22.9	Zimmerman-Chi	5.1
Evers-Chi	.962	Murray-NY	38			Herzog-NY	19.2	Evers-Chi	3.1
Doyle-NY	.955					Fletcher-NY	15.8	Meyers-NY	2.7

Wins		Win Percentage		Games		Complete Games		Shutouts		Saves	
Marquard-NY	26	Hendrix-Pit	.727	Benton-Cin	50	Cheney-Chi	28	Rucker-Bro	6	Sallee-StL	6
Cheney-Chi	26	Cheney-Chi	.722	Sallee-StL	48	Mathewson-NY	27	Suggs-Cin	5	Rucker-Bro	4
Hendrix-Pit	24	Tesreau-NY	.708	Alexander-Phi	46	Suggs-Cin	25	O'Toole-Pit	5	Reulbach-Chi	4
Mathewson-NY	23	Marquard-NY	.703	Rucker-Bro	45	Hendrix-Pit	25			Mathewson-NY	4
Camnitz-Pit	22	Richie-Chi	.667	Seaton-Phi	44	Alexander-Phi	25				

Innings Pitched		Fewest Hits/Game		Fewest BB/Game		Strikeouts		Strikeouts/Game		Ratio	
Alexander-Phi	310.1	Tesreau-NY	6.56	Mathewson-NY	0.99	Alexander-Phi	195	Alexander-Phi	5.66	Robinson-Pit	9.57
Mathewson-NY	310.0	Robinson-Pit	7.51	Robinson-Pit	1.54	Hendrix-Pit	176	Hendrix-Pit	5.49	Mathewson-NY	10.07
Cheney-Chi	303.1	O'Toole-Pit	7.75	Suggs-Cin	1.66	Marquard-NY	175	Marquard-NY	5.35	Rucker-Bro	10.49
Suggs-Cin	303.0	Cheney-Chi	7.77	Ames-NY	1.76	Benton-Cin	162	Tyler-Bos	5.06	Tesreau-NY	10.85
Benton-Cin	302.0	Brown-Bos	7.81	Adams-Pit	1.85	Rucker-Bro	151	O'Toole-Pit	4.90	Adams-Pit	10.94

Earned Run Average		Adjusted ERA		Opponents' Batting Avg.		Opponents' On Base Pct.		Starter Runs		Adjusted Starter Runs	
Tesreau-NY	1.96	Tesreau-NY	172	Tesreau-NY	.204	Mathewson-NY	.281	Mathewson-NY	44.1	Mathewson-NY	43.0
Mathewson-NY	2.12	Mathewson-NY	159	Cheney-Chi	.234	Robinson-Pit	.284	Rucker-Bro	39.4	Tesreau-NY	37.9
Rucker-Bro	2.21	Rucker-Bro	151	Robinson-Pit	.237	Rucker-Bro	.298	Tesreau-NY	38.8	Rucker-Bro	37.4
Robinson-Pit	2.26	Rixey-Phi	145	Brown-Bos	.239	Tesreau-NY	.298	Marquard-NY	27.3	Alexander-Phi	27.7
Ames-NY	2.46	Robinson-Pit	144	O'Toole-Pit	.241	Adams-Pit	.303	Sallee-StL	26.0	Sallee-StL	26.6

Clutch Pitching Index		Relief Runs	Adjusted Relief Runs	Relief Ranking	Total Pitcher Index		Total Baseball Ranking	
Ames-NY	125				Mathewson-NY	5.0	Wagner-Pit	6.6
Geyer-StL	125				Rucker-Bro	4.4	Sweeney-Bos	5.1
Benton-Cin	116				Hendrix-Pit	4.2	Zimmerman-Chi	5.1
Dickson-Bos	116				Tesreau-NY	3.8	Mathewson-NY	5.0
Yingling-Bro	114				Alexander-Phi	2.9	Rucker-Bro	4.4

TEAM	G	W	L	PCT	GB	R	OR	AB	H	2B	3B	HR	BB	SO	AVG	OBP	SLG	PRO	PRO+	BR	/A	PF	CHI	RC	SB	CS	SBA	SBR
BOS	154	105	47	.691		799	544	5071	1404	269	84	29	565		.277	.355	.380	.735	110	104	69	105	100	752	185			
WAS	154	91	61	.599	14	699	581	5075	1298	202	86	20	472		.256	.324	.341	.665	94	-32	-37	101	108	645	274			
PHI	153	90	62	.592	15	779	658	5111	1442	204	108	22	485		.282	.349	.377	.726	117	83	109	96	101	763	258			
CHI	158	78	76	.506	28	639	648	5182	1321	174	80	17	423		.255	.317	.329	.646	93	-68	-46	97	102	610	205			
CLE	155	75	78	.490	30.5	677	681	5133	1403	219	77	12	407		.273	.333	.353	.686	98	5	-17	103	98	671	194			
DET	154	69	84	.451	36.5	720	777	5143	1376	189	86	19	530		.268	.343	.349	.692	106	26	48	97	100	705	270			
STL	157	53	101	.344	53	552	764	5080	1262	166	71	19	449		.248	.315	.320	.635	90	-86	-62	96	94	565	176			
NY	153	50	102	.329	55	630	842	5092	1320	168	79	18	463		.259	.329	.334	.663	90	-31	-72	106	97	638	247			
TOT	619					5495		40887	10826	1591	671	156	3794	5157	.265	.333	.348	.681							1809			

TEAM	CG	SH	SV	IP	H	H/G	HR	BB	SO	RAT	ERA	ERA+	OAV	OOB	PR	/A	PF	CPI	FA	E	DP	FW	PW	BW	SBW	DIF
BOS	108	18	6	1362	1243	8.2	18	385	712	11.0	2.76	124	.248	.306	88	104	103	98	.957	267	88	2.4	10.4	6.9		9.3
WAS	98	11	7	1375²	1219	8.0	24	525	828	11.8	2.70	124	.242	.320	98	105	100	108	.954	297	92	.7	10.5	-3.7		7.6
PHI	95	11	9	1357	1273	8.4	12	518	601	12.3	3.32	93	.258	.336	2	-31	93	99	.959	263	115	2.5	-3.1	10.9		3.7
CHI	85	14	16	1413	1398	8.9	26	426	698	11.8	3.06	105	.264	.322	44	26	96	104	.956	291	102	1.5	2.6	-4.6		1.5
CLE	94	7	7	1352²	1367	9.1	15	523	622	12.9	3.30	104	.272	.346	6	21	103	110	.954	287	124	1.4	2.1	-1.7		-3.3
DET	107	7	5	1367¹	1438	9.5	16	521	512	13.3	3.77	87	.277	.350	-66	-71	98	100	.950	338	91	-1.7	-7.1	4.8		-3.5
STL	85	8	5	1369²	1433	9.4	17	442	547	12.7	3.71	90	.277	.341	-56	-55	100	97	.947	341	127	-1.6	-5.5	-6.2		-10.8
NY	105	5	3	1335	1448	9.8	28	436	637	13.0	4.13	88	.282	.344	-117	-71	108	92	.940	382	77	-4.4	-7.1	-7.2		-7.3
TOT	777	81	58	10932¹		8.9				12.3	3.34		.265	.333					.952	2466	816					

Runs
Collins-Phi 137
Speaker-Bos 136
Jackson-Cle 121
Cobb-Det 120
Baker-Phi 116

Hits
Jackson-Cle 226
Cobb-Det 226
Speaker-Bos 222
Baker-Phi 200

Doubles
Speaker-Bos 53
Jackson-Cle 44
Baker-Phi 40
Lewis-Bos 36

Triples
Jackson-Cle 26
Cobb-Det 23
Crawford-Det 21
Baker-Phi 21
Gardner-Bos 18

Home Runs
Baker-Phi 10
Cobb-Det 7

Total Bases
Jackson-Cle 331
Speaker-Bos 329
Cobb-Det 323
Baker-Phi 312
Crawford-Det 273

Runs Batted In
Baker-Phi 130
Lewis-Bos 109
Crawford-Det 109
McInnis-Phi 101

Runs Produced
Baker-Phi 236
Speaker-Bos 216
Jackson-Cle 208
Collins-Phi 201
Cobb-Det 196

Bases On Balls
Bush-Det 117
Collins-Phi 101
Rath-Chi 95
Shotton-StL 86
Speaker-Bos 82

Batting Average
Cobb-Det 409
Jackson-Cle 395
Speaker-Bos 383
Lajoie-Cle 368
Collins-Phi 348

On Base Percentage
Speaker-Bos 464
Jackson-Cle 458
Cobb-Det 456
Collins-Phi 450
Lajoie-Cle 414

Slugging Average
Cobb-Det 584
Jackson-Cle 579
Speaker-Bos 567
Baker-Phi 541
Crawford-Det 470

Production
Cobb-Det 1.040
Jackson-Cle 1.036
Speaker-Bos . . . 1.031
Baker-Phi 945
Collins-Phi 885

Adjusted Production
Cobb-Det 203
Jackson-Cle 190
Speaker-Bos 185
Baker-Phi 176
Collins-Phi 159

Batter Runs
Speaker-Bos 72.8
Jackson-Cle 70.3
Cobb-Det 67.1
Baker-Phi 49.2
Collins-Phi 43.7

Adjusted Batter Runs
Cobb-Det 69.4
Speaker-Bos 68.8
Jackson-Cle 67.8
Baker-Phi 52.0
Collins-Phi 46.7

Clutch Hitting Index
Lewis-Bos 151
Gandil-Was 145
McInnis-Phi 140
Lajoie-Cle 140
Crawford-Det 135

Runs Created
Speaker-Bos 175
Cobb-Det 173
Jackson-Cle 166
Baker-Phi 140
Collins-Phi 136

Total Average
Cobb-Det 1.321
Speaker-Bos . . . 1.310
Jackson-Cle 1.249
Collins-Phi 1.130
Baker-Phi 1.082

Stolen Bases
Milan-Was 88
Collins-Phi 63
Cobb-Det 61
Speaker-Bos 52
Zeider-Chi 47

Stolen Base Average

Stolen Base Runs

Fielding Runs
McBride-Was 31.1
Bush-Det 29.4
Louden-Det 22.8
Speaker-Bos 21.6
Rath-Chi 18.3

Total Player Rating
Speaker-Bos 8.0
Jackson-Cle 7.1
Cobb-Det 6.2
Baker-Phi 6.1
Collins-Phi 5.7

Wins
Wood-Bos 34
Johnson-Was 33
Walsh-Chi 27
Plank-Phi 26
Groom-Was 24

Win Percentage
Wood-Bos 872
Plank-Phi 813
Johnson-Was 733
Bedient-Bos 690
Coombs-Phi 677

Games
Walsh-Chi 62
Johnson-Was 50
Wood-Bos 43
Groom-Was 43
Benz-Chi 42

Complete Games
Wood-Bos 35
Johnson-Was 34
Walsh-Chi 32
Ford-NY 30

Shutouts
Wood-Bos 10
Johnson-Was 7
Walsh-Chi 6
Plank-Phi 5
Collins-Bos 4

Saves
Walsh-Chi 10
Warhop-NY 3
Mogridge-Chi 3
Lange-Chi 3
Dubuc-Det 3

Innings Pitched
Walsh-Chi 393.0
Johnson-Was . . . 368.0
Wood-Bos 344.0
Groom-Was 316.0
Ford-NY 291.2

Fewest Hits/Game
Johnson-Was 6.33
Wood-Bos 6.99
Houck-Phi 7.37
Walsh-Chi 7.60
O'Brien-Bos 7.74

Fewest BB/Game
Bender-Phi 1.74
Johnson-Was 1.86
Collins-Bos 1.90
Powell-StL 1.99
Warhop-NY 2.06

Strikeouts
Johnson-Was . . . 303
Wood-Bos 258
Walsh-Chi 254
Gregg-Cle 184
Groom-Was 179

Strikeouts/Game
Johnson-Was 7.41
Wood-Bos 6.75
Gregg-Cle 6.10
Walsh-Chi 5.82
Lange-Chi 5.23

Ratio
Johnson-Was 8.58
Wood-Bos 9.44
Walsh-Chi 9.78
Bedient-Bos 10.29
Collins-Bos 10.66

Earned Run Average
Johnson-Was 1.39
Wood-Bos 1.91
Walsh-Chi 2.15
Plank-Phi 2.22
Collins-Bos 2.53

Adjusted ERA
Johnson-Was 240
Wood-Bos 179
Walsh-Chi 149
Plank-Phi 140
Collins-Bos 135

Opponents' Batting Avg.
Johnson-Was 196
Wood-Bos 216
Walsh-Chi 231
Houck-Phi 234
Dubuc-Det 235

Opponents' On Base Pct.
Johnson-Was 248
Wood-Bos 272
Walsh-Chi 279
Bedient-Bos 288
Collins-Bos 297

Starter Runs
Johnson-Was 79.5
Wood-Bos 54.6
Walsh-Chi 51.8
Plank-Phi 32.3
Groom-Was 25.2

Adjusted Starter Runs
Johnson-Was 80.0
Wood-Bos 57.8
Walsh-Chi 46.5
O'Brien-Bos 25.8
Groom-Was 25.7

Clutch Pitching Index
Hughes-Was 129
McConnell-NY 121
Cashion-Was 120
Kahler-Cle 120
Plank-Phi 119

Relief Runs

Adjusted Relief Runs

Relief Ranking

Total Pitcher Index
Johnson-Was 10.0
Wood-Bos 8.5
Walsh-Chi 6.2
McConnell-NY 2.9
Plank-Phi 2.9

Total Baseball Ranking
Johnson-Was 10.0
Wood-Bos 8.5
Speaker-Bos 8.0
Jackson-Cle 7.1
Walsh-Chi 6.2

TEAM	G	W	L	PCT	GB	R	OR	AB	H	2B	3B	HR	BB	SO	AVG	OBP	SLG	PRO	PRO+	BR	/A	PF	CHI	RC	SB	CS	SBA	SBR
NY	156	101	51	.664		684	515	5218	1427	226	71	30	444	501	.273	.338	.361	.699	105	43	38	101	99	708	296			
PHI	159	88	63	.583	12.5	693	636	5400	1433	257	78	73	383	578	.265	.318	.382	.700	102	29	2	104	100	695	156			
CHI	155	88	65	.575	13.5	720	630	5022	1289	195	96	59	554	634	.257	.335	.369	.704	107	52	51	100	104	683	181			
PIT	155	78	71	.523	21.5	673	585	5252	1383	210	86	35	391	545	.263	.319	.356	.675	104	-13	15	96	106	641	181			
BOS	154	69	82	.457	31.5	641	640	5145	1318	191	60	32	488	640	.256	.326	.335	.661	93	-26	-39	102	103	619	177			
BRO	152	65	84	.436	34.5	595	613	5165	1394	193	86	39	361	555	.270	.321	.363	.684	98	4	-13	103	94	646	188			
CIN	156	64	89	.418	37.5	607	717	5132	1339	170	96	27	458	579	.261	.325	.347	.672	98	-10	-7	100	96	639	226			
STL	153	51	99	.340	49	528	755	4967	1229	152	72	15	451	573	.247	.316	.316	.632	88	-78	-69	99	97	550	171			
TOT	620					5141		41301	10812	1594	645	310	3530	4605	.262	.325	.354	.679							1576			

TEAM	CG	SH	SV	IP	H	H/G	HR	BB	SO	RAT	ERA	ERA+	OAV	OOB	PR	/A	PF	CPI	FA	E	DP	FW	PW	BW	SBW	DIF
NY	82	12	17	1422	1276	8.1	38	315	651	10.2	2.42	128	.243	.289	122	107	97	99	.961	254	107	-.6	11.1	4.0		10.5
PHI	77	20	11	1455¹	1407	8.7	40	512	667	12.1	3.15	106	.261	.330	7	27	104	103	.968	214	112	2.2	2.8	.2		7.3
CHI	89	12	15	1372¹	1330	8.7	39	478	556	12.1	3.13	101	.260	.328	9	6	99	103	.959	260	106	-1.1	.6	5.3		6.7
PIT	74	9	7	1400	1344	8.6	26	434	590	11.6	2.90	104	.260	.320	46	16	94	104	.964	226	94	1.1	1.7	1.6		-.8
BOS	105	13	3	1373¹	1343	8.8	37	419	597	11.8	3.19	103	.263	.324	1	12	103	100	.957	273	82	-2.0	1.2	-4.1		-1.6
BRO	71	9	7	1373	1287	8.4	33	439	548	11.6	3.13	105	.255	.321	11	23	103	97	.961	243	125	-.3	2.4	-1.4		-10.2
CIN	71	10	10	1380	1398	9.1	40	456	522	12.4	3.46	94	.273	.338	-40	-36	101	102	.961	251	104	-.4	-3.7	-.7		-7.6
STL	74	6	11	1351²	1426	9.5	57	477	465	13.0	4.23	76	.280	.348	-156	-152	101	92	.965	219	113	1.3	-15.8	-7.2		-2.3
TOT	643	91	81	11127²		8.7				11.9	3.20		.262	.325					.962	1940	843					

Runs
Leach-Chi 99
Carey-Pit 99
Lobert-Phi 98
Saier-Chi 94
Magee-Phi 92

Hits
Cravath-Phi 179
Burns-NY 178
Lobert-Phi 172
Carey-Pit 172

Doubles
Smith-Bro 40
Burns-NY 37
Magee-Phi 36
Cravath-Phi 34

Triples
Saier-Chi 21
Miller-Pit 20
Konetchy-StL 17
Wilson-Pit 14
Cravath-Phi 14

Home Runs
Cravath-Phi 19
Luderus-Phi 18
Saier-Chi 14
Magee-Phi 11
Wilson-Pit 10

Total Bases
Cravath-Phi 298
Luderus-Phi 254
Saier-Chi 249
Miller-Pit 243
Lobert-Phi 243

Runs Batted In
Cravath-Phi 128
Zimmerman-Chi ... 95
Saier-Chi 92
Miller-Pit 90
Luderus-Phi 86

Runs Produced
Cravath-Phi 187
Saier-Chi 172
Miller-Pit 158
Zimmerman-Chi ... 155
Magee-Phi 151

Bases On Balls
Bescher-Cin 94
Huggins-StL 92
Leach-Chi 77
Bridwell-Chi 74

Batting Average
Daubert-Bro ...... .350
Cravath-Phi ...... .341
Viox-Pit .... .317
Zimmerman-Chi .. .313
Magee-Phi .... .306

On Base Percentage
Huggins-StL ...... .432
Cravath-Phi ...... .407
Daubert-Bro ...... .405
Viox-Pit .... .399
Leach-Chi .... .391

Slugging Average
Cravath-Phi ...... .568
Zimmerman-Chi .. .490
Saier-Chi .... .480
Magee-Phi .... .479
Smith-Bro .... .441

Production
Cravath-Phi ..... .974
Zimmerman-Chi .. .868
Saier-Chi .... .850
Magee-Phi .... .848
Daubert-Bro ...... .829

Adjusted Production
Cravath-Phi 169
Zimmerman-Chi .. 147
Viox-Pit 142
Saier-Chi 141
Magee-Phi 136

Batter Runs
Cravath-Phi 50.5
Saier-Chi 27.5
Zimmerman-Chi .. 26.3
Daubert-Bro 25.2
Viox-Pit 24.8

Adjusted Batter Runs
Cravath-Phi 47.8
Viox-Pit 27.7
Saier-Chi 27.4
Zimmerman-Chi .. 26.2
Daubert-Bro 23.5

Clutch Hitting Index
Zimmerman-Chi .. 143
Doyle-NY 139
Cravath-Phi 134
Miller-Pit 131
Murray-NY 123

Runs Created
Cravath-Phi 124
Saier-Chi 100
Lobert-Phi 94
Daubert-Bro 94
Smith-Bro 91

Total Average
Cravath-Phi 1.058
Saier-Chi .... .927
Zimmerman-Chi .. .925
Magee-Phi .... .905
Leach-Chi .... .895

Stolen Bases
Carey-Pit 61
Myers-Bos 57
Lobert-Phi 41
Burns-NY 40
Cutshaw-Bro 39

Stolen Base Average

Stolen Base Runs

Fielding Runs
Evers-Chi 29.9
Whitted-StL 22.8
Killefer-Phi 17.9
Paskert-Phi 17.7
Cutshaw-Bro 17.5

Total Player Rating
Tinker-Cin 3.9
Cravath-Phi 3.9
Evers-Chi 3.5
Meyers-NY 3.4
Zimmerman-Chi .. 3.2

Wins
Seaton-Phi 27
Mathewson-NY ... 25
Marquard-NY 23
Tesreau-NY 22
Alexander-Phi 22

Win Percentage
Humphries-Chi ... .800
Seaton-Phi .... .733
Marquard-NY ..... .697
Mathewson-NY ... .694
Seaton-Phi .... .692

Games
Cheney-Chi 54
Seaton-Phi 52
Sallee-StL 50
Alexander-Phi 47
Camnitz-Pit-Phi ... 45

Complete Games
Tyler-Bos 28
Mathewson-NY ... 25
Cheney-Chi 25
Adams-Pit 24
Alexander-Phi 23

Shutouts
Alexander-Phi 9
Seaton-Phi 5

Saves
Cheney-Chi 11
Crandall-NY-StL-NY 6
Brown-Cin 6
Sallee-StL 5

Innings Pitched
Seaton-Phi 322.1
Adams-Pit 313.2
Alexander-Phi .. 306.1
Mathewson-NY . 306.0
Cheney-Chi 305.0

Fewest Hits/Game
Tesreau-NY 7.09
Seaton-Phi 7.32
Allen-Bro 7.42
Pearce-Chi 7.55
Tyler-Bos 7.59

Fewest BB/Game
Mathewson-NY ... 0.62
Humphries-Chi ... 1.19
Adams-Pit 1.41
Marquard-NY 1.53
Suggs-Cin 1.58

Strikeouts
Seaton-Phi 168
Tesreau-NY 167
Alexander-Phi 159
Marquard-NY 151
Adams-Pit 144

Strikeouts/Game
Tesreau-NY 5.33
Hendrix-Pit 5.15
Marquard-NY 4.72
Seaton-Phi 4.69
Alexander-Phi ... 4.67

Ratio
Mathewson-NY ... 9.18
Adams-Pit 9.18
Marquard-NY 9.38
Humphries-Chi ... 9.70
Demaree-NY 9.87

Earned Run Average
Mathewson-NY ... 2.06
Adams-Pit 2.15
Tesreau-NY 2.17
Demaree-NY 2.21
Pearce-Chi 2.31

Adjusted ERA
Mathewson-NY ... 151
Tesreau-NY 143
Demaree-NY 141
Adams-Pit 140
Brennan-Phi 139

Opponents' Batting Avg.
Tesreau-NY ...... .220
Seaton-Phi ...... .226
Allen-Bro .... .231
Pearce-Chi ...... .234
Tyler-Bos .... .235

Opponents' On Base Pct.
Mathewson-NY ... .266
Adams-Pit .... .267
Marquard-NY .... .273
Humphries-Chi ... .277
Demaree-NY ..... .286

Starter Runs
Mathewson-NY ... 38.7
Adams-Pit 36.4
Tesreau-NY 32.2
Marquard-NY 22.3
Demaree-NY 21.9

Adjusted Starter Runs
Mathewson-NY ... 35.9
Adams-Pit 29.8
Tesreau-NY 29.5
Seaton-Phi 26.2
Brennan-Phi 21.5

Clutch Pitching Index
Brennan-Phi 128
Packard-Cin 127
Brown-Cin 119
Ames-NY-Cin 119
Pearce-Chi 112

Relief Runs
Crandall-NY-StL-NY 3.7

Adjusted Relief Runs
Crandall-NY-StL-NY 2.8

Relief Ranking
Crandall-NY-StL-NY 2.4

Total Pitcher Index
Mathewson-NY 4.3
Adams-Pit 4.0
Tesreau-NY 3.5
Tyler-Bos 2.8
Seaton-Phi 2.4

Total Baseball Ranking
Mathewson-NY 4.3
Adams-Pit 4.0
Tinker-Cin 3.9
Cravath-Phi 3.9
Evers-Chi 3.5

TEAM	G	W	L	PCT	GB	R	OR	AB	H	2B	3B	HR	BB	SO	AVG	OBP	SLG	PRO	PRO+	BR	/A	PF	CHI	RC	SB	CS	SBA	SBR
PHI	153	96	57	.627		794	592	5044	1412	223	80	33	534	547	.280	.356	.375	.731	124	135	149	98	105	747	221			
WAS	155	90	64	.584	6.5	596	561	5074	1281	156	81	19	440	595	.252	.317	.326	.643	92	-35	-48	102	105	593	287			
CLE	155	86	66	.566	9.5	633	536	5031	1349	206	74	16	420	557	.268	.331	.348	.679	102	29	11	103	99	636	191			
BOS	151	79	71	.527	15.5	631	610	4965	1334	220	101	17	466	534	.269	.336	.364	.700	109	66	51	103	95	664	189			
CHI	153	78	74	.513	17.5	488	498	4822	1139	157	66	24	398	550	.236	.299	.311	.610	85	-94	-88	99	100	496	156			
DET	153	66	87	.431	30	624	716	5064	1344	180	101	24	496	501	.265	.336	.355	.691	111	56	65	99	93	669	218			
NY	153	57	94	.377	38	529	668	4880	1157	155	45	19	534	617	.237	.320	.292	.612	85	-75	-77	100	101	525	203			
STL	155	57	96	.373	39	528	642	5031	1193	179	73	18	455	769	.237	.306	.312	.618	90	-80	-63	97	101	538	209			
TOT	614					4823		39911	10209	1476	621	159	3743	4670	.256	.325	.336	.661							1674			

TEAM	CG	SH	SV	IP	H	H/G	HR	BB	SO	RAT	ERA	ERA+	OAV	OOB	PR	/A	PF	CPI	FA	E	DP	FW	PW	BW	SBW	DIF
PHI	69	17	22	1351[1]	1200	8.0	24	532	630	11.8	3.19	86	.229	.304	-39	-66	94	70	.966	212	108	3.2	-7.0	15.9		7.4
WAS	78	23	20	1396	1177	7.6	35	465	758	11.0	2.73	108	.225	.297	30	34	101	80	.960	261	122	.3	3.6	-5.1		14.2
CLE	93	18	5	1386[2]	1278	8.3	19	502	689	11.8	2.54	119	.249	.321	59	74	104	108	.962	242	124	1.5	7.9	1.2		-.6
BOS	83	12	10	1358[1]	1323	8.8	6	442	710	11.9	2.94	100	.260	.323	-2	-3	100	96	.961	237	84	1.4	-.3	5.4		-2.5
CHI	84	17	8	1360[1]	1190	7.9	10	438	602	11.0	2.33	125	.237	.302	91	89	100	97	.960	255	104	.5	9.5	-9.4		1.4
DET	90	4	7	1360	1359	9.0	13	504	468	12.6	3.38	86	.265	.336	-68	-71	100	94	.954	300	105	-2.4	-7.6	6.9		-7.5
NY	75	8	7	1344	1318	8.8	31	455	530	12.2	3.27	91	.260	.327	-51	-42	102	94	.954	293	94	-1.9	-4.5	-8.2		-3.9
STL	104	14	5	1382[1]	1369	8.9	21	454	476	12.2	3.06	96	.266	.332	-20	-22	100	103	.954	301	125	-2.2	-2.3	-6.7		-8.2
TOT	676	113	84	10939		8.4				11.8	2.93		.256	.325					.959	2101	866					

Runs
Collins-Cle	125
Baker-Phi	116
Jackson-Cle	109
Shotton-StL	105
J.Murphy-Phi	105

Hits
Jackson-Cle	197
Crawford-Det	193
Baker-Phi	190
Speaker-Bos	189
Collins-Phi	184

Doubles
Jackson-Cle	39
Speaker-Bos	35
Baker-Phi	34
Crawford-Det	32

Triples
Crawford-Det	23
Speaker-Bos	22
Jackson-Cle	17
Williams-StL	16
Cobb-Det	16

Home Runs
Baker-Phi	12
Crawford-Det	9
Bodie-Chi	8
Jackson-Cle	7

Total Bases
Crawford-Det	298
Jackson-Cle	291
Baker-Phi	278
Speaker-Bos	277
Collins-Phi	242

Runs Batted In
Baker-Phi	117
McInnis-Phi	90
Lewis-Bos	90
Pratt-StL	87
Barry-Phi	85

Runs Produced
Baker-Phi	221
Collins-Phi	195
Jackson-Cle	173
Oldring-Phi	167
McInnis-Phi	165

Bases On Balls
Shotton-StL	99
Collins-Phi	85
Wolter-NY	80
Jackson-Cle	80
Bush-Det	80

Batting Average
Cobb-Det	.390
Jackson-Cle	.373
Speaker-Bos	.363
Collins-Phi	.345
Baker-Phi	.337

On Base Percentage
Cobb-Det	.467
Jackson-Cle	.460
Collins-Phi	.441
Speaker-Bos	.441
Baker-Phi	.413

Slugging Average
Jackson-Cle	.551
Cobb-Det	.535
Speaker-Bos	.533
Baker-Phi	.493
Crawford-Det	.489

Production
Jackson-Cle	1.011
Cobb-Det	1.002
Speaker-Bos	.974
Baker-Phi	.906
Collins-Phi	.894

Adjusted Production
Cobb-Det	196
Jackson-Cle	190
Speaker-Bos	180
Baker-Phi	169
Collins-Phi	165

Batter Runs
Jackson-Cle	65.5
Speaker-Bos	55.9
Cobb-Det	51.8
Baker-Phi	45.9
Collins-Phi	45.7

Adjusted Batter Runs
Jackson-Cle	63.5
Speaker-Bos	54.3
Cobb-Det	52.6
Baker-Phi	47.5
Collins-Phi	47.3

Clutch Hitting Index
Barry-Phi	176
Lewis-Bos	155
McInnis-Phi	142
Turner-Cle	142
Baker-Phi	140

Runs Created
Jackson-Cle	144
Speaker-Bos	135
Collins-Phi	125
Baker-Phi	125
Cobb-Det	121

Total Average
Cobb-Det	1.310
Jackson-Cle	1.215
Speaker-Bos	1.193
Collins-Phi	1.111
Baker-Phi	1.029

Stolen Bases
Milan-Was	75
Moeller-Was	62
Collins-Phi	55
Cobb-Det	51
Speaker-Bos	46

Stolen Base Average

Stolen Base Runs

Fielding Runs
Weaver-Chi	33.5
Speaker-Bos	23.9
Turner-Cle	16.3
Collins-Phi	15.6
Shotton-StL	12.8

Total Player Rating
Speaker-Bos	7.4
Collins-Phi	6.3
Jackson-Cle	6.2
Baker-Phi	6.0
Cobb-Det	5.3

Wins
Johnson-Was	36
Falkenberg-Cle	23
Russell-Chi	22
Bender-Phi	21

Win Percentage
Johnson-Was	.837
Bush-Phi	.714
Boehling-Was	.708
Collins-Bos	.704
Falkenberg-Cle	.697

Games
Russell-Chi	52
Scott-Chi	48
Johnson-Was	48
Bender-Phi	48
S.Gregg-Cle	44

Complete Games
Johnson-Was	29
Russell-Chi	26
Scott-Chi	25

Shutouts
Johnson-Was	11
Russell-Chi	8
Plank-Phi	7
Falkenberg-Cle	6

Saves
Bender-Phi	13
Hughes-Was	6
Bedient-Bos	5

Innings Pitched
Johnson-Was	346.0
Russell-Chi	316.2
Scott-Chi	312.1
S.Gregg-Cle	285.2
Falkenberg-Cle	276.0

Fewest Hits/Game
Johnson-Was	6.03
Mitchell-Cle	6.35
Engel-Was	6.78
Leverenz-StL	7.06
Russell-Chi	7.11

Fewest BB/Game
Johnson-Was	0.99
Collins-Bos	1.35
Mitchell-StL	1.72
Plank-Phi	2.11
Weilman-StL	2.15

Strikeouts
Johnson-Was	243
S.Gregg-Cle	166
Falkenberg-Cle	166
Scott-Chi	158
Groom-Was	156

Strikeouts/Game
Johnson-Was	6.32
Mitchell-Cle	5.85
Plank-Phi	5.60
Falkenberg-Cle	5.41
Groom-Was	5.31

Ratio
Johnson-Was	7.26
Russell-Chi	9.55
Scott-Chi	10.00
Cicotte-Chi	10.07
Plank-Phi	10.13

Earned Run Average
Johnson-Was	1.14
Cicotte-Chi	1.58
Scott-Chi	1.90
Russell-Chi	1.90
Mitchell-Cle	1.91

Adjusted ERA
Johnson-Was	258
Cicotte-Chi	185
Mitchell-Cle	159
Scott-Chi	154
Russell-Chi	153

Opponents' Batting Avg.
Johnson-Was	.187
Mitchell-Cle	.199
Engel-Was	.207
Houck-Phi	.214
Russell-Chi	.219

Opponents' On Base Pct.
Johnson-Was	.217
Russell-Chi	.273
Bender-Phi	.277
Cicotte-Chi	.281
Scott-Chi	.281

Starter Runs
Johnson-Was	68.6
Cicotte-Chi	40.2
Russell-Chi	36.1
Scott-Chi	35.7
Mitchell-Cle	24.6

Adjusted Starter Runs
Johnson-Was	69.4
Cicotte-Chi	40.0
Russell-Chi	35.8
Scott-Chi	35.4
Mitchell-Cle	27.2

Clutch Pitching Index
Blanding-Cle	141
S.Gregg-Cle	130
Ford-NY	123
Baumgardner-StL	118
Cicotte-Chi	114

Relief Runs

Adjusted Relief Runs

Relief Ranking

Total Pitcher Index
Johnson-Was	9.7
Cicotte-Chi	5.1
Russell-Chi	3.7
Scott-Chi	3.2
Boehling-Was	2.7

Total Baseball Ranking
Johnson-Was	9.6
Speaker-Bos	7.4
Collins-Phi	6.3
Jackson-Cle	6.2
Baker-Phi	6.0

TEAM	G	W	L	PCT	GB	R	OR	AB	H	2B	3B	HR	BB	SO	AVG	OBP	SLG	PRO	PRO+	BR	/A	PF	CHI	RC	SB	CS	SBA	SBR
BOS	158	94	59	.614		657	548	5206	1307	213	60	35	502	617	.251	.323	.335	.658	103	17	21	99	103	618	139			
NY	156	84	70	.545	10.5	672	576	5146	1363	222	59	30	447	479	.265	.330	.348	.678	112	53	73	97	103	655	239			
STL	157	81	72	.529	13	558	540	5046	1249	203	65	33	445	618	.248	.314	.333	.647	100	-9	-2	99	95	585	204			
CHI	156	78	76	.506	16.5	605	638	5050	1229	199	74	42	501	577	.243	.317	.337	.654	101	7	9	100	100	595	164			
BRO	154	75	79	.487	19.5	622	618	5152	1386	172	90	31	376	559	.269	.323	.355	.678	106	43	30	102	97	636	173			
PHI	154	74	80	.481	20.5	651	687	5110	1345	211	52	62	472	570	.263	.329	.361	.690	105	69	30	107	97	654	145			
PIT	158	69	85	.448	25.5	503	540	5145	1197	148	79	18	416	608	.233	.295	.303	.598	88	-101	-75	96	101	503	147			
CIN	157	60	94	.390	34.5	530	651	4991	1178	142	64	16	441	627	.236	.305	.300	.605	83	-79	-97	103	105	517	224			
TOT	625					4798		40846	10254	1510	543	267	3600	4655	.251	.317	.334	.651						1435				

TEAM	CG	SH	SV	IP	H	H/G	HR	BB	SO	RAT	ERA	ERA+	OAV	OOB	PR	/A	PF	CPI	FA	E	DP	FW	PW	BW	SBW	DIF
BOS	104	19	6	1421	1272	8.1	38	477	606	11.4	2.74	100	.249	.319	7	1	99	102	.963	246	143	1.8	.1	2.3		13.3
NY	88	20	9	1390²	1298	8.4	47	367	563	11.0	2.94	90	.253	.306	-25	-46	95	92	.961	254	119	1.1	-5.0	7.9		3.0
STL	84	16	12	1424²	1279	8.1	26	422	531	11.1	2.38	117	.250	.313	64	64	100	112	.964	239	109	2.2	6.9	-.2		-4.4
CHI	70	14	11	1389¹	1169	7.6	37	528	651	11.2	2.71	103	.233	.311	12	9	100	92	.951	310	87	-2.7	1.0	1.0		1.8
BRO	80	11	11	1368¹	1282	8.4	36	466	605	11.8	2.82	101	.255	.323	-5	7	103	105	.961	248	112	1.2	.8	3.2		-7.2
PHI	85	14	7	1379¹	1403	9.2	26	452	650	12.4	3.06	96	.270	.335	-42	-21	105	106	.950	324	81	-3.9	-2.3	3.2		-.0
PIT	86	10	11	1405	1272	8.1	27	392	488	10.9	2.70	98	.249	.308	13	-9	95	95	.966	223	96	3.4	-1.0	-8.1		-2.3
CIN	74	15	15	1387¹	1259	8.2	30	489	607	11.7	2.94	100	.248	.320	-24	-3	105	95	.952	314	113	-2.9	-.3	-10.5		-3.4
TOT	671	119	82	11165²		8.2				11.4	2.78		.251	.317					.958	2158	860					

Runs
Burns-NY 100
Magee-Phi 96
Daubert-Bro 89
Saier-Chi 87
Doyle-NY 87

Hits
Magee-Phi 171
Wheat-Bro 170
Burns-NY 170
Zimmerman-Chi . . . 167
Becker-Phi 167

Doubles
Magee-Phi 39
Zimmerman-Chi . . . 36
Burns-NY 35
Connolly-Bos 28

Triples
Carey-Pit 17
Zimmerman-Chi . . . 12
Wilson-StL 12
Cutshaw-Bro 12

Home Runs
Cravath-Phi 19
Saier-Chi 18
Magee-Phi 15
Luderus-Phi 12

Total Bases
Magee-Phi 277
Cravath-Phi 249
Wheat-Bro 241
Zimmerman-Chi . . 239
Burns-NY 234

Runs Batted In
Magee-Phi 103
Cravath-Phi 100
Wheat-Bro 89
J.Miller-StL 88
Zimmerman-Chi . . . 87

Runs Produced
Magee-Phi 184
Zimmerman-Chi . . 158
Cravath-Phi 157
Burns-NY 157
J.Miller-StL 151

Bases On Balls
Huggins-StL 105
Saier-Chi 94
Burns-NY 89
Evers-Bos 87
Cravath-Phi 83

Batting Average
Daubert-Bro 329
Becker-Phi 325
Dalton-Bro 319
Wheat-Bro 319
Stengel-Bro 316

On Base Percentage
Stengel-Bro 404
Burns-NY 403
Cravath-Phi 402
Huggins-StL 396
Dalton-Bro 396

Slugging Average
Magee-Phi 509
Cravath-Phi 499
Wheat-Bro 452
Becker-Phi 446
Daubert-Bro 432

Production
Cravath-Phi 901
Magee-Phi 890
Wheat-Bro 830
Stengel-Bro 829
Burns-NY 820

Adjusted Production
Cravath-Phi 157
Magee-Phi 154
Burns-NY 149
Stengel-Bro 143
Wheat-Bro 143

Batter Runs
Cravath-Phi 42.7
Magee-Phi 40.7
Burns-NY 34.0
Connolly-Bos . . . 31.0
Wheat-Bro 29.3

Adjusted Batter Runs
Cravath-Phi 38.7
Magee-Phi 36.5
Burns-NY 36.3
Connolly-Bos 31.3
Wheat-Bro 27.9

Clutch Hitting Index
Fletcher-NY 151
Maranville-Bos . . 148
Cutshaw-Bro 144
J.Miller-StL 143
Schmidt-Bos 141

Runs Created
Burns-NY 113
Magee-Phi 111
Cravath-Phi 108
Wheat-Bro 96
Saier-Chi 89

Total Average
Burns-NY 997
Cravath-Phi 997
Magee-Phi 965
Stengel-Bro 904
Wheat-Bro 857

Stolen Bases
Burns-NY 62
Herzog-Cin 46
Dolan-StL 42
Carey-Pit 38

Stolen Base Average

Stolen Base Runs

Fielding Runs
Maranville-Bos . . . 51.8
Herzog-Cin 30.6
Cutshaw-Bro 27.5
Smith-Bro-Bos . . . 22.6
Wheat-Bro 18.2

Total Player Rating
Maranville-Bos . . . 5.9
Magee-Phi 4.8
Herzog-Cin 4.8
Smith-Bro-Bos . . . 4.3
Wheat-Bro 4.2

Wins
Alexander-Phi 27
Tesreau-NY 26
Rudolph-Bos 26
James-Bos 26
Mathewson-NY . . . 24

Win Percentage
James-Bos 788
Doak-StL 760
Tesreau-NY 722
Rudolph-Bos 722
Pfeffer-Bro 657

Games
Cheney-Chi 50
Mayer-Phi 48
Ames-Cin 47

Complete Games
Alexander-Phi 32
Rudolph-Bos 31
James-Bos 30
Mathewson-NY . . . 29
Pfeffer-Bro 27

Shutouts
Tesreau-NY 8
Doak-StL 7
Rudolph-Bos 6
Cheney-Chi 6
Alexander-Phi 6

Saves
Sallee-StL 6
Ames-Cin 6
Cheney-Chi 5
Pfeffer-Bro 4
McQuillan-Pit 4

Innings Pitched
Alexander-Phi . . . 355.0
Rudolph-Bos 336.1
James-Bos 332.1
Tesreau-NY 322.1
Mayer-Phi 321.0

Fewest Hits/Game
Tesreau-NY 6.65
Doak-StL 6.79
Cheney-Chi 6.91
Douglas-Cin 6.99
James-Bos 7.07

Fewest BB/Game
Mathewson-NY . . . 0.66
Adams-Pit 1.24
Marquard-NY 1.58
Rudolph-Bos 1.63
Alexander-Phi 1.93

Strikeouts
Alexander-Phi 214
Tesreau-NY 189
Vaughn-Chi 165
Cheney-Chi 157
James-Bos 156

Strikeouts/Game
Alexander-Phi 5.43
Tesreau-NY 5.28
Vaughn-Chi 5.06
G.Tyler-Bos 4.64
Ragan-Bro 4.58

Ratio
Rudolph-Bos 9.45
Adams-Pit 9.51
Mathewson-NY 9.78
Doak-StL 10.09
Pfeffer-Bro 10.34

Earned Run Average
Doak-StL 1.72
James-Bos 1.90
Pfeffer-Bro 1.97
Vaughn-Chi 2.05
Sallee-StL 2.10

Adjusted ERA
Doak-StL 162
James-Bos 145
Pfeffer-Bro 145
Vaughn-Chi 135
Sallee-StL 133

Opponents' Batting Avg.
Tesreau-NY 209
Cheney-Chi 215
Doak-StL 216
Vaughn-Chi 222
Douglas-Cin 223

Opponents' On Base Pct.
Adams-Pit 276
Rudolph-Bos 276
Mathewson-NY 278
Alexander-Phi 290
Doak-StL 290

Starter Runs
James-Bos 32.8
Doak-StL 30.2
Pfeffer-Bro 28.5
Vaughn-Chi 23.9
Sallee-StL 21.4

Adjusted Starter Runs
James-Bos 31.6
Pfeffer-Bro 30.9
Doak-StL 30.4
Vaughn-Chi 23.6
Alexander-Phi 21.8

Clutch Pitching Index
Cooper-Pit 126
James-Bos 121
Crutcher-Bos 120
Perritt-StL 116
Sallee-StL 116

Relief Runs

Adjusted Relief Runs

Relief Ranking

Total Pitcher Index
James-Bos 4.0
Doak-StL 3.7
Alexander-Phi 3.2
Pfeffer-Bro 3.0
Vaughn-Chi 2.6

Total Baseball Ranking
Maranville-Bos . . . 5.9
Magee-Phi 4.8
Herzog-Cin 4.8
Smith-Bro-Bos . . . 4.3
Wheat-Bro 4.2

TEAM	G	W	L	PCT	GB	R	OR	AB	H	2B	3B	HR	BB	SO	AVG	OBP	SLG	PRO	PRO+	BR	/A	PF	CHI	RC	SB	CS	SBA	SBR
PHI	158	99	53	.651		749	529	5126	1392	165	80	29	545	517	.272	.348	.352	.700	123	112	136	96	107	662	231	188	55	-44
BOS	159	91	62	.595	8.5	589	510	5117	1278	226	85	18	490	549	.250	.320	.338	.658	105	26	26	100	98	567	177	176	50	-53
WAS	158	81	73	.526	19	572	519	5108	1245	176	81	18	470	640	.244	.313	.320	.633	93	-17	-39	104	102	544	220	163	57	-32
DET	157	80	73	.523	19.5	615	618	5102	1318	195	84	25	557	537	.258	.336	.344	.680	109	76	58	103	93	630	211	154	58	-29
STL	159	71	82	.464	28.5	523	615	5101	1241	185	75	17	423	863	.243	.306	.319	.625	99	-38	-16	96	99	516	233	189	55	-44
NY	157	70	84	.455	30	537	550	4992	1144	149	52	12	577	711	.229	.315	.287	.602	88	-60	-58	100	105	484	251	191	57	-39
CHI	157	70	84	.455	30	487	560	5040	1205	161	71	19	408	609	.239	.302	.311	.613	92	-59	-51	99	96	497	167	152	52	-41
CLE	157	51	102	.333	48.5	538	709	5157	1262	178	70	10	450	685	.245	.310	.312	.622	90	-39	-61	104	100	517	167	157	52	-44
TOT	631					4610		40743	10085	1435	598	148	3920	5111	.248	.319	.323	.642							1657	1370	55	-325

TEAM	CG	SH	SV	IP	H	H/G	HR	BB	SO	RAT	ERA	ERA+	OAV	OOB	PR	/A	PF	CPI	FA	E	DP	FW	PW	BW	SBW	DIF
PHI	89	24	17	1404	1264	8.1	18	521	720	11.6	2.78	94	.249	.322	-6	-27	95	100	.966	213	116	3.5	-3.0	15.0	-.4	7.8
BOS	88	24	8	1427¹	1207	7.6	18	393	602	10.3	2.36	114	.236	.295	59	50	98	94	.963	242	99	1.8	5.5	2.9	-1.4	5.6
WAS	75	25	20	1420²	1170	7.4	20	520	784	11.0	2.54	111	.233	.311	31	41	103	97	.961	254	116	1.0	4.5	-4.3	1.0	1.8
DET	81	14	12	1412	1285	8.2	17	498	567	11.8	2.86	98	.249	.322	-19	-10	103	97	.958	286	101	-1.1	-1.1	6.4	1.3	-2.0
STL	81	15	11	1410²	1309	8.4	20	540	553	12.1	2.85	95	.251	.327	-17	-22	99	103	.952	317	114	-2.7	-2.4	-1.8	.4	1.8
NY	98	9	5	1397¹	1277	8.2	30	390	563	10.9	2.81	98	.250	.308	-12	-10	101	94	.963	238	93	1.9	-1.1	-6.4	.2	-1.5
CHI	74	17	11	1398²	1207	7.8	15	401	660	10.5	2.48	108	.239	.298	40	30	98	92	.955	299	90	-1.9	3.3	-5.6	-.0	-2.8
CLE	69	9	3	1391²	1365	8.8	10	666	688	13.4	3.21	90	.267	.357	-74	-55	105	110	.953	300	119	-1.9	-6.1	-6.7	-.4	-10.4
TOT	655	137	87	11262¹		8.1				11.5	2.73		.248	.319					.959	2149	848					

Runs
Collins-Phi	122
Speaker-Bos	101
Murphy-Phi	101
Bush-Det	97

Hits
Speaker-Bos	193
Crawford-Det	183
Baker-Phi	182
McInnis-Phi	181
Collins-Phi	181

Doubles
Speaker-Bos	46
Lewis-Bos	37
Pratt-StL	34
Collins-Chi	34
Leary-StL	28

Triples
Crawford-Det	26
Gardner-Bos	19
Speaker-Bos	18
C.Walker-StL	16
Hooper-Bos	15

Home Runs
Baker-Phi	9
Crawford-Det	8
C.Walker-StL	6
Fournier-Chi	6

Total Bases
Speaker-Bos	287
Crawford-Det	281
Baker-Phi	252
Pratt-StL	240
Collins-Phi	238

Runs Batted In
Crawford-Det	104
McInnis-Phi	95
Speaker-Bos	90
Baker-Phi	89
Collins-Phi	85

Runs Produced
Collins-Phi	205
Speaker-Bos	187
Crawford-Det	170
McInnis-Phi	168
Baker-Phi	164

Bases On Balls
Bush-Det	112
Collins-Phi	97
Murphy-Phi	87
Speaker-Bos	77
Maisel-NY	76

Batting Average
Collins-Phi	.344
Speaker-Bos	.338
Jackson-Cle	.338
Baker-Phi	.319
Crawford-Det	.314

On Base Percentage
Collins-Phi	.452
Speaker-Bos	.423
Jackson-Cle	.399
Crawford-Det	.388
Baker-Phi	.380

Slugging Average
Speaker-Bos	.503
Crawford-Det	.483
Jackson-Cle	.464
Collins-Phi	.452
Baker-Phi	.442

Production
Speaker-Bos	.926
Collins-Phi	.904
Crawford-Det	.871
Jackson-Cle	.862
Baker-Phi	.822

Adjusted Production
Collins-Phi	179
Speaker-Bos	178
Crawford-Det	157
Baker-Phi	153
Jackson-Cle	153

Batter Runs
Speaker-Bos	54.9
Collins-Phi	51.6
Cobb-Det	42.3
Crawford-Det	42.1
Jackson-Cle	31.6

Adjusted Batter Runs
Speaker-Bos	54.9
Collins-Phi	54.3
Cobb-Det	41.0
Crawford-Det	40.0
Baker-Phi	33.7

Clutch Hitting Index
McInnis-Phi	171
Lewis-Bos	146
Veach-Det	135
Shanks-Was	134
Gandil-Was	133

Runs Created
Speaker-Bos	124
Collins-Phi	120
Crawford-Det	113
Baker-Phi	95
C.Walker-StL	87

Total Average
Collins-Phi	.984
Speaker-Bos	.943
Crawford-Det	.867
Jackson-Cle	.835
C.Walker-StL	.776

Stolen Bases
Maisel-NY	74
Collins-Phi	58
Speaker-Bos	42
Shotton-StL	40

Stolen Base Average
Maisel-NY	81.3
Sweeney-NY	76.0
Chapman-Cle	72.7
Moriarty-Det	69.4
Peckinpaugh-NY	69.1

Stolen Base Runs
Maisel-NY	12.0
Sweeney-NY	2.1
Kopf-Phi	1.8
Chapman-Cle	1.8

Fielding Runs
Bush-Det	33.6
Speaker-Bos	27.6
Gandil-Was	23.7
Boone-NY	22.7
Turner-Cle	21.3

Total Player Rating
Speaker-Bos	7.6
Collins-Phi	5.7
Bush-Det	5.0
Baker-Phi	4.6
C.Walker-StL	3.8

Wins
Johnson-Was	28
Coveleski-Det	22
Collins-Bos	20
Leonard-Bos	19

Win Percentage
Bender-Phi	.850
Leonard-Bos	.792
Plank-Phi	.682
Shawkey-Phi	.667
Caldwell-NY	.654

Games
Johnson-Was	51
Ayers-Was	49
Shaw-Was	48
Benz-Chi	48

Complete Games
Johnson-Was	33
Coveleski-Det	23
Dauss-Det	22
Caldwell-NY	22

Shutouts
Johnson-Was	9
Leonard-Bos	7
Bender-Phi	7
Collins-Bos	6

Saves
Shaw-Was	4
Mitchell-StL	4
Faber-Chi	4
Dauss-Det	4
Bentley-Was	4

Innings Pitched
Johnson-Was	371.2
Coveleski-Det	303.1
Hamilton-StL	302.1
Dauss-Det	302.0
Weilman-StL	299.0

Fewest Hits/Game
Leonard-Bos	5.57
Caldwell-NY	6.46
Shaw-Was	6.93
Johnson-Was	6.95
Foster-Bos	6.97

Fewest BB/Game
McHale-NY	1.55
Russell-Chi	1.77
Johnson-Was	1.79
Warhop-NY	1.83
Ayers-Was	1.83

Strikeouts
Johnson-Was	225
Mitchell-Cle	179
Leonard-Bos	176
Shaw-Was	164
Dauss-Det	150

Strikeouts/Game
Leonard-Bos	7.05
Mitchell-Cle	6.27
Shaw-Was	5.74
Johnson-Was	5.45
Bender-Phi	5.38

Ratio
Leonard-Bos	8.29
Caldwell-NY	8.79
Johnson-Was	9.01
Foster-Bos	9.48
Ayers-Was	9.60

Earned Run Average
Leonard-Bos	.96
Foster-Bos	1.70
Johnson-Was	1.72
Caldwell-NY	1.94
Cicotte-Chi	2.04

Adjusted ERA
Leonard-Bos	279
Johnson-Was	163
Foster-Bos	158
Caldwell-NY	142
Cicotte-Chi	131

Opponents' Batting Avg.
Leonard-Bos	.180
Caldwell-NY	.205
Shaw-Was	.216
Johnson-Was	.217
Foster-Bos	.218

Opponents' On Base Pct.
Leonard-Bos	.246
Caldwell-NY	.260
Johnson-Was	.265
Foster-Bos	.274
Benz-Chi	.282

Starter Runs
Leonard-Bos	44.3
Johnson-Was	41.9
Foster-Bos	24.3
Weilman-StL	21.8
Cicotte-Chi	20.8

Adjusted Starter Runs
Johnson-Was	45.0
Leonard-Bos	43.0
Foster-Bos	23.2
Weilman-StL	20.7
Caldwell-NY	19.2

Clutch Pitching Index
Hagerman-Cle	126
Steen-Cle	123
Shawkey-Phi	109
James-StL	106
Bender-Phi	106

Relief Runs

Adjusted Relief Runs

Relief Ranking

Total Pitcher Index
Johnson-Was	6.6
Leonard-Bos	4.7
Cicotte-Chi	2.9
Foster-Bos	2.7
Weilman-StL	2.4

Total Baseball Ranking
Speaker-Bos	7.5
Johnson-Was	6.6
Collins-Phi	5.7
Bush-Det	5.0
Leonard-Bos	4.7

TEAM	G	W	L	PCT	GB	R	OR	AB	H	2B	3B	HR	BB	SO	AVG	OBP	SLG	PRO	PRO+	BR	/A	PF	CHI	RC	SB	CS	SBA	SBR
IND	157	88	65	.575		762	622	5176	1474	230	90	33	470	668	.285	.349	.383	.732	103	94	23	111	102	763	273			
CHI	157	87	67	.565	1.5	621	517	5098	1314	227	50	52	520	645	.258	.331	.352	.683	106	7	45	94	95	653	171			
BAL	160	84	70	.545	4.5	645	628	5120	1374	222	67	32	487	589	.268	.337	.357	.694	100	27	7	103	96	670	152			
BUF	155	80	71	.530	7	620	602	5064	1264	177	74	38	430	761	.250	.311	.336	.647	88	-67	-80	102	111	585	228			
BRO	157	77	77	.500	11.5	662	677	5221	1402	225	85	42	404	665	.269	.326	.368	.694	104	17	22	99	100	680	220			
KC	154	67	84	.444	20	644	683	5127	1369	226	77	39	399	621	.267	.324	.364	.688	105	5	31	96	101	650	171			
PIT	154	64	86	.427	22.5	605	698	5114	1339	180	90	34	410	575	.262	.321	.352	.673	98	-20	-14	99	98	624	153			
STL	154	62	89	.411	25	565	697	5078	1254	193	65	26	503	662	.247	.319	.326	.645	85	-64	-97	105	98	577	113			
TOT	624					5124		40998	10790	1680	598	296	3623	5186	.263	.328	.355	.683						1481				

TEAM	CG	SH	SV	IP	H	H/G	HR	BB	SO	RAT	ERA	ERA+	OAV	OOB	PR	/A	PF	CPI	FA	E	DP	FW	PW	BW	SBW	DIF
IND	104	15	9	1397²	1352	8.7	29	476	664	12.1	3.06	113	.258	.325	23	63	108	100	.956	289	113	-1.2	6.6	2.4		3.8
CHI	93	17	8	1420¹	1204	7.6	43	393	650	10.3	2.44	121	.233	.291	121	80	92	94	.962	249	114	1.1	8.3	4.7		-4.1
BAL	88	15	13	1392	1389	9.0	34	392	732	11.7	3.13	108	.268	.323	12	36	105	101	.960	263	105	.6	3.7	.7		1.9
BUF	89	15	16	1387	1249	8.1	45	505	662	11.7	3.16	104	.245	.318	7	19	103	91	.962	242	109	1.3	2.0	-8.3		9.5
BRO	91	11	9	1385¹	1375	8.9	31	559	636	12.9	3.33	96	.264	.341	-20	-22	100	102	.956	283	120	-.9	-2.3	2.3		.9
KC	82	10	12	1361	1387	9.2	37	445	600	12.4	3.41	91	.268	.331	-30	-49	96	98	.957	279	135	-.9	-5.1	3.2		-5.7
PIT	97	9	6	1370	1416	9.3	39	444	510	12.4	3.56	89	.273	.333	-54	-59	99	96	.960	253	92	.6	-6.1	-1.5		-4.0
STL	97	9	6	1367²	1418	9.3	38	409	661	12.3	3.59	94	.267	.324	-58	-32	105	89	.957	273	94	-.6	-3.3	-10.1		.5
TOT	741	101	79	11081		8.8				12.0	3.20		.263	.328					.959	2131	882					

Runs
Kauff-Ind 120
McKechnie-Ind ... 107
Duncan-Bal 99
Kenworthy-KC 93
Evans-Bro 93

Hits
Kauff-Ind 211
Zwilling-Chi 185
Evans-Bro 179
Oakes-Pit 178
Hanford-Buf 174

Doubles
Kauff-Ind 44
Evans-Bro 41
Kenworthy-KC.... 40
Zwilling-Chi 38

Triples
Evans-Bro 15
Esmond-Ind 15
Kenworthy-KC..... 14

Home Runs
Zwilling-Chi 16
Kenworthy-KC 15
Hanford-Buf 13
Evans-Bro 12

Total Bases
Kauff-Ind 305
Zwilling-Chi 287
Kenworthy-KC.... 286
Evans-Bro 286
Hanford-Buf...... 267

Runs Batted In
LaPorte-Ind 107
Evans-Bro 96
Zwilling-Chi 95
Kauff-Ind 95
Kenworthy-KC.... 91

Runs Produced
Kauff-Ind 207
LaPorte-Ind 189
Evans-Bro 177
Zwilling-Chi 170
Kenworthy-KC.... 169

Bases On Balls
Wickland-Chi 81
Agler-Buf 77
Kauff-Ind 72

Batting Average
Kauff-Ind 370
Evans-Bro 348
Campbell-Ind 318
Kenworthy-KC.....317
Louden-Buf 313

On Base Percentage
Kauff-Ind 447
Evans-Bro 416
Lennox-Pit 414
Meyer-Bal 395
Wilson-Chi 394

Slugging Average
Evans-Bro 556
Kauff-Ind 534
Kenworthy-KC.....525
Lennox-Pit 493
Zwilling-Chi 485

Production
Kauff-Ind 981
Evans-Bro 973
Lennox-Pit 907
Kenworthy-KC.....896
Wilson-Chi 860

Adjusted Production
Evans-Bro 177
Kauff-Ind 161
Kenworthy-KC.... 160
Lennox-Pit 159
Wilson-Chi 153

Batter Runs
Kauff-Ind 60.4
Evans-Bro 49.6
Kenworthy-KC.... 35.1
Lennox-Pit 34.1
Zwilling-Chi 28.3

Adjusted Batter Runs
Kauff-Ind 52.4
Evans-Bro 50.1
Kenworthy-KC.... 37.8
Lennox-Pit 34.7
Zwilling-Chi 32.5

Clutch Hitting Index
LaPorte-Ind 176
Swacina-Bal 160
Carr-Ind 148
Wisterzil-Bro 139
Stovall-KC 138

Runs Created
Kauff-Ind 156
Evans-Bro 124
Kenworthy-KC ... 113
Zwilling-Chi 108
Lennox-Pit 96

Total Average
Kauff-Ind 1.278
Evans-Bro 1.087
Lennox-Pit 1.034
Kenworthy-KC....995
Wilson-Chi 939

Stolen Bases
Kauff-Ind 75
McKechnie-Ind ... 47
Myers-Bro 43
Chadbourne-KC .. 42

Stolen Base Average

Stolen Base Runs

Fielding Runs
Doolan-Bal 29.3
McKechnie-Ind ... 23.0
Kenworthy-KC.... 20.8
Rariden-Ind 20.1
Tinker-Chi 19.1

Total Player Rating
Kauff-Ind 6.2
Kenworthy-KC 5.9
Wilson-Chi 5.6
Evans-Bro 4.1
McKechnie-Ind ... 3.1

Wins
Hendrix-Chi 29
Quinn-Bal 26
Seaton-Bro 25
Falkenberg-Ind 25
Suggs-Bal 24

Win Percentage
Ford-Buf 778
Hendrix-Chi 744
Quinn-Bal.........650
Seaton-Bro 641
Suggs-Bal.........632

Games
Hendrix-Chi 49
Falkenberg-Ind 49
Wilhelm-Bal 47
Suggs-Bal 46
Quinn-Bal......... 46

Complete Games
Hendrix-Chi 34
Falkenberg-Ind ... 33
Moseley-Ind....... 29
Quinn-Bal 27

Shutouts
Falkenberg-Ind 9
Seaton-Bro 7
Suggs-Bal 6
Hendrix-Chi 6

Saves
Ford-Buf 6
Wilhelm-Bal 5
Packard-KC 5
Hendrix-Chi 5

Innings Pitched
Falkenberg-Ind .. 377.1
Hendrix-Chi 362.0
Quinn-Bal....... 342.2
Suggs-Bal 319.1
Moseley-Ind 316.2

Fewest Hits/Game
Hendrix-Chi 6.51
Ford-Buf 6.91
Krapp-Buf 7.05
Fiske-Chi 7.32
Watson-Chi-StL ... 7.34

Fewest BB/Game
Ford-Buf 1.49
Suggs-Bal 1.61
Quinn-Bal 1.71
Hendrix-Chi 1.91
Keupper-StL 2.07

Strikeouts
Falkenberg-Ind ... 236
Moseley-Ind 205
Hendrix-Chi 189
Seaton-Bro 172
Groom-StL 167

Strikeouts/Game
Davenport-StL ... 5.93
Moseley-Ind 5.83
Groom-StL 5.36
Falkenberg-Ind ... 5.63
Seaton-Bro 5.11

Ratio
Hendrix-Chi 8.55
Ford-Buf 8.66
Falkenberg-Ind .. 10.16
Fiske-Chi 10.32
Lange-Chi 10.42

Earned Run Average
Hendrix-Chi 1.69
Ford-Buf 1.82
Watson-Chi-StL ... 2.01
Falkenberg-Ind ... 2.22
Lange-Chi 2.23

Adjusted ERA
Ford-Buf 181
Hendrix-Chi 174
Falkenberg-Ind ... 156
Watson-Chi-StL ... 152
Lange-Chi 132

Opponents' Batting Avg.
Hendrix-Chi 203
Krapp-Buf 210
Ford-Buf 214
Lange-Chi 224
Watson-Chi-StL....230

Opponents' On Base Pct.
Hendrix-Chi 251
Ford-Buf 254
Lange-Chi 282
Falkenberg-Ind ...284
Anderson-Buf 297

Starter Runs
Hendrix-Chi 60.9
Falkenberg-Ind .. 41.4
Ford-Buf 38.1
Watson-Chi-StL .. 30.2
Cullop-KC 28.3

Adjusted Starter Runs
Falkenberg-Ind ... 52.3
Hendrix-Chi 50.6
Ford-Buf 40.4
Quinn-Bal........ 29.2
Watson-Chi-StL .. 26.4

Clutch Pitching Index
Mullin-Ind 128
Lafitte-Bro 122
Watson-Chi-StL ... 114
Kaiserling-Ind 109
Quinn-Bal 106

Relief Runs

Adjusted Relief Runs

Relief Ranking

Total Pitcher Index
Hendrix-Chi 7.0
Falkenberg-Ind ... 5.8
Quinn-Bal 4.2
Ford-Buf.......... 4.2
Krapp-Buf 2.9

Total Baseball Ranking
Hendrix-Chi 7.0
Kauff-Ind 6.2
Kenworthy-KC 5.9
Falkenberg-Ind 5.8
Wilson-Chi 5.6

TEAM	G	W	L	PCT	GB	R	OR	AB	H	2B	3B	HR	BB	SO	AVG	OBP	SLG	PRO	PRO+	BR	/A	PF	CHI	RC	SB	CS	SBA	SBR
PHI	153	90	62	.592		589	463	4916	1216	202	39	58	460	600	.247	.316	.340	.656	104	31	25	101	101	550	121	113	52	-32
BOS	157	83	69	.546	7	582	545	5070	1219	231	57	17	549	620	.240	.321	.319	.640	105	15	41	96	98	554	121	98	55	-23
BRO	154	80	72	.526	10	536	560	5120	1268	165	75	14	313	496	.248	.295	.317	.612	89	-56	-66	102	107	496	131	126	51	-36
CHI	156	73	80	.477	17.5	570	620	5114	1246	212	66	53	469	639	.244	.303	.334	.645	102	4	3	100	100	555	166	124	57	-25
PIT	156	73	81	.474	18	557	520	5113	1259	197	91	24	419	656	.246	.309	.334	.643	102	8	16	99	97	563	182	111	62	-12
STL	157	72	81	.471	18.5	590	601	5106	1297	159	92	20	457	658	.254	.320	.333	.653	104	30	29	100	98	568	162	144	53	-38
CIN	160	71	83	.461	20	516	585	5231	1323	194	84	15	360	512	.253	.308	.331	.639	98	-5	-15	102	91	553	156	142	52	-38
NY	155	69	83	.454	21	582	628	5218	1312	195	68	24	315	547	.251	.300	.329	.629	103	-27	6	94	109	526	155	137	53	-36
TOT	624					4522		40888	10140	1555	572	225	3266	4728	.248	.309	.331	.640							1194	995	55	-239

TEAM	CG	SH	SV	IP	H	H/G	HR	BB	SO	RAT	ERA	ERA+	OAV	OOB	PR	/A	PF	CPI	FA	E	DP	FW	PW	BW	SBW	DIF
PHI	98	20	8	1374[1]	1161	7.6	26	342	652	10.0	2.17	126	.234	.288	87	85	100	103	.966	216	99	.8	9.4	2.8	-.2	1.2
BOS	95	17	13	1405[2]	1257	8.0	23	366	630	10.7	2.57	100	.246	.302	27	1	94	100	.966	213	115	1.4	.1	4.6	.8	.2
BRO	87	16	8	1389[2]	1252	8.1	29	473	499	11.6	2.66	104	.245	.318	14	17	101	108	.963	238	96	-.5	1.9	-7.3	-.7	10.7
CHI	71	18	8	1399	1272	8.2	28	480	657	11.6	3.11	89	.247	.316	-57	-54	101	91	.958	268	94	-2.3	-6.0	.3	.5	4.0
PIT	91	18	11	1380	1229	8.0	21	384	544	10.8	2.60	105	.246	.304	23	19	99	100	.966	214	100	1.2	2.1	1.8	2.0	-11.1
STL	79	13	9	1400[2]	1320	8.5	30	402	538	11.3	2.89	96	.256	.314	-22	-17	101	101	.964	235	109	-.0	-1.9	3.2	-.9	-4.9
CIN	80	19	12	1432[1]	1304	8.2	28	497	572	11.6	2.84	101	.250	.321	-15	2	104	104	.966	222	148	1.1	.2	-1.7	-.9	-4.8
NY	78	15	9	1385	1350	8.8	40	325	637	11.2	3.11	82	.260	.308	-57	-86	93	94	.960	256	119	-1.6	-9.6	.7	-.7	4.2
TOT	679	136	78	11166[2]		8.2				11.1	2.75		.248	.309					.964	1862	880					

Runs
Cravath-Phi 89
Doyle-NY 86
Bancroft-Phi 85
Burns-NY 83
O'Mara-Bro 77

Hits
Doyle-NY 189
Griffith-Cin 179
Hinchman-Pit 177
Groh-Cin 170
Burns-NY 169

Doubles
Doyle-NY 40
Luderus-Phi 36
Saier-Chi 35
Smith-Bos 34
Magee-Bos 34

Triples
Long-Stl 25
J.Wagner-Pit 17
Griffith-Cin 16
Hinchman-Pit 14
Burns-NY 14

Home Runs
Cravath-Phi 24
Williams-Chi 13
Schulte-Chi 12
Saier-Chi 11
Becker-Phi 11

Total Bases
Cravath-Phi 266
Doyle-NY 261
Griffith-Cin 254
Hinchman-Pit 253
J.Wagner-Pit 239

Runs Batted In
Cravath-Phi 115
Magee-Bos 87
Griffith-Cin 85
J.Wagner-Pit 78
Hinchman-Pit 77

Runs Produced
Cravath-Phi 180
Magee-Bos 157
Doyle-NY 152
Hinchman-Pit 144
Miller-Stl 143

Bases On Balls
Cravath-Phi 86
Bancroft-Phi 77
Viox-Pit 75
Huggins-Stl 74
Smith-Bos 67

Batting Average
Doyle-NY .... .320
Luderus-Phi .... .315
Griffith-Cin .... .307
Hinchman-Pit .... .307
Daubert-Bro .... .301

On Base Percentage
Cravath-Phi .... .393
Luderus-Phi .... .376
Daubert-Bro .... .369
Hinchman-Pit .... .368
Doyle-NY .... .358

Slugging Average
Cravath-Phi .... .510
Luderus-Phi .... .457
Long-Stl .... .446
Saier-Chi .... .445
Doyle-NY .... .442

Production
Cravath-Phi .... .902
Luderus-Phi .... .833
Hinchman-Pit .... .807
Doyle-NY .... .799
Saier-Chi .... .795

Adjusted Production
Cravath-Phi 170
Doyle-NY 150
Luderus-Phi 150
Hinchman-Pit 146
Saier-Chi 140

Batter Runs
Cravath-Phi 46.8
Luderus-Phi 30.3
Hinchman-Pit 29.7
Doyle-NY 27.1
Griffith-Cin 25.4

Adjusted Batter Runs
Cravath-Phi 46.1
Doyle-NY 30.8
Hinchman-Pit 30.6
Luderus-Phi 29.7
Griffith-Cin 24.2

Clutch Hitting Index
Fletcher-NY 156
Magee-Bos 153
Miller-Stl 149
Schmidt-Bos 145
Cutshaw-Bro 143

Runs Created
Cravath-Phi 105
Doyle-NY 94
Hinchman-Pit 94
Luderus-Phi 87
Griffith-Cin 85

Total Average
Cravath-Phi .... .942
Saier-Chi .... .819
Luderus-Phi .... .799
Hinchman-Pit .... .741
Doyle-NY .... .714

Stolen Bases
Carey-Pit 36
Herzog-Cin 35
Saier-Chi 29
Baird-Pit 29
Cutshaw-Bro 28

Stolen Base Average
Bresnahan-Chi 86.4
Saier-Chi 76.3
Baird-Pit 70.7
Robertson-NY 68.8
Herzog-Cin 68.6

Stolen Base Runs
Bresnahan-Chi 3.9
Saier-Chi 3.3
Costello-Pit 1.5
Baird-Pit 1.5
Gerber-Pit 1.2

Fielding Runs
Fletcher-NY 34.1
Herzog-Cin 30.9
Maranville-Bos 20.9
Cutshaw-Bro 16.8
Magee-Bos 15.4

Total Player Rating
Cravath-Phi 5.0
Herzog-Cin 4.2
Luderus-Phi 3.8
Fletcher-NY 3.2
Snyder-Stl 3.1

Wins
Alexander-Phi 31
Rudolph-Bos 22
Mayer-Phi 21
Mamaux-Pit 21
Vaughn-Chi 20

Win Percentage
Alexander-Phi .... .756
Toney-Cin .... .739
Mamaux-Pit .... .724
Vaughn-Chi .... .625
Coombs-Bro .... .600

Games
Hughes-Bos 50
Dale-Cin 49
Alexander-Phi 49
Schneider-Cin 48
Sallee-Stl 46

Complete Games
Alexander-Phi 36
Rudolph-Bos 30
Pfeffer-Bro 26
Harmon-Pit 25
Tesreau-NY 24

Shutouts
Alexander-Phi 12
Tesreau-NY 8
Mamaux-Pit 8
Toney-Cin 6
Pfeffer-Bro 6

Saves
Hughes-Bos 9
Benton-Cin-NY 5
Lavender-Chi 4
Cooper-Pit 4

Innings Pitched
Alexander-Phi 376.1
Rudolph-Bos 341.1
Tesreau-NY 306.0
Dale-Cin 296.2
Pfeffer-Bro 291.2

Fewest Hits/Game
Alexander-Phi 6.05
Toney-Cin 6.47
Mamaux-Pit 6.51
Hughes-Bos 6.68
Zabel-Chi 6.85

Fewest BB/Game
Mathewson-NY .... .97
Humphries-Chi 1.21
Adams-Pit 1.25
Alexander-Phi 1.53
Rudolph-Bos 1.69

Strikeouts
Alexander-Phi 241
Tesreau-NY 176
Hughes-Bos 171
Mamaux-Pit 152
Vaughn-Chi 148

Strikeouts/Game
Alexander-Phi 5.76
Hughes-Bos 5.49
Mamaux-Pit 5.44
Douglas-Cin-Bro-Chi 5.26
Tesreau-NY 5.18

Ratio
Alexander-Phi 7.82
Hughes-Bos 8.89
Tesreau-NY 9.26
Toney-Cin 9.54
Adams-Pit 9.73

Earned Run Average
Alexander-Phi 1.22
Toney-Cin 1.58
Mamaux-Pit 2.04
Pfeffer-Bro 2.10
Hughes-Bos 2.12

Adjusted ERA
Alexander-Phi 224
Toney-Cin 181
Mamaux-Pit 134
Pfeffer-Bro 132
Hughes-Bos 122

Opponents' Batting Avg.
Alexander-Phi .... .191
Toney-Cin .... .207
Mamaux-Pit .... .208
Hughes-Bos .... .213
Tesreau-NY .... .215

Opponents' On Base Pct.
Alexander-Phi .... .234
Hughes-Bos .... .265
Tesreau-NY .... .269
Toney-Cin .... .278
Adams-Pit .... .280

Starter Runs
Alexander-Phi 63.8
Toney-Cin 28.9
Pfeffer-Bro 21.0
Mamaux-Pit 19.8
Hughes-Bos 19.5

Adjusted Starter Runs
Alexander-Phi 63.4
Toney-Cin 31.6
Pfeffer-Bro 21.9
Mamaux-Pit 19.2
Hughes-Bos 14.5

Clutch Pitching Index
Humphries-Chi 139
Perritt-NY 122
Schneider-Cin 121
Rixey-Phi 120
Stroud-NY 118

Relief Runs

Adjusted Relief Runs

Relief Ranking

Total Pitcher Index
Alexander-Phi 8.6
Toney-Cin 3.3
Pfeffer-Bro 2.5
Mayer-Phi 2.0
Schneider-Cin 1.9

Total Baseball Ranking
Alexander-Phi 8.6
Cravath-Phi 5.0
Herzog-Cin 4.2
Luderus-Phi 3.8
Toney-Cin 3.3

TEAM	G	W	L	PCT	GB	R	OR	AB	H	2B	3B	HR	BB	SO	AVG	OBP	SLG	PRO	PRO+	BR	/A	PF	CHI	RC	SB	CS	SBA	SBR
BOS	155	101	50	.669		669	499	5024	1308	202	76	14	527	476	.260	.336	.339	.675	110	46	65	97	100	611	118	117	50	-35
DET	156	100	54	.649	2.5	778	597	5128	1372	207	94	23	681	527	.268	.357	.358	.715	114	131	99	105	101	711	241	146	62	-15
CHI	155	93	61	.604	9.5	717	509	4914	1269	163	102	25	583	575	.258	.345	.348	.693	110	83	64	103	102	637	233	183	56	-40
WAS	155	85	68	.556	17	569	491	5029	1225	152	79	12	458	541	.244	.312	.312	.624	90	-52	-64	102	103	535	186	106	64	-8
NY	154	69	83	.454	32.5	584	588	4982	1162	167	50	31	570	669	.233	.317	.305	.622	91	-46	-45	100	103	523	198	133	60	-20
STL	159	63	91	.409	39.5	521	680	5112	1255	166	65	19	472	765	.246	.315	.315	.630	98	-44	-21	96	91	535	202	160	56	-35
CLE	154	57	95	.375	44.5	539	670	5034	1210	169	79	20	490	681	.240	.312	.317	.629	91	-43	-55	102	95	526	138	117	54	-29
PHI	154	43	109	.283	58.5	545	888	5081	1204	183	72	16	436	634	.237	.304	.311	.615	92	-74	-53	97	103	507	127	89	59	-15
TOT	621					4922		40304	10005	1409	617	160	4217	4868	.248	.325	.326	.651							1443	1051	58	-198

TEAM	CG	SH	SV	IP	H	H/G	HR	BB	SO	RAT	ERA	ERA+	OAV	OOB	PR	/A	PF	CPI	FA	E	DP	FW	PW	BW	SBW	DIF
BOS	81	19	15	1397	1164	7.5	18	446	634	10.7	2.39	116	.231	.300	84	59	95	97	.964	226	95	2.5	6.3	6.9	-1.1	11.0
DET	86	10	19	1413¹	1259	8.0	14	492	550	11.5	2.86	106	.243	.316	11	25	103	94	.961	258	107	.5	2.7	10.5	1.0	8.3
CHI	91	16	9	1401	1242	8.0	14	350	635	10.4	2.43	122	.241	.294	78	84	101	95	.965	222	95	2.7	8.9	6.8	-1.6	-.8
WAS	87	21	13	1393²	1161	7.5	12	455	715	10.7	2.31	129	.232	.302	97	102	101	102	.964	230	101	2.2	10.8	-6.8	1.8	.5
NY	101	12	2	1382²	1272	8.3	41	517	559	12.0	3.06	96	.254	.329	-20	-21	100	104	.966	217	118	2.9	-2.2	-4.8	.5	-3.4
STL	76	6	7	1403	1256	8.1	21	612	566	12.4	3.04	94	.249	.338	-17	-31	98	103	.949	336	144	-4.3	-3.3	-2.2	-1.1	-3.1
CLE	62	11	10	1372	1287	8.4	18	518	610	12.0	3.13	97	.256	.329	-30	-13	104	98	.957	280	82	-1.2	-1.4	-5.8	-.5	-10.1
PHI	78	6	2	1348¹	1358	9.1	22	827	588	15.0	4.29	68	.278	.388	-204	-206	100	102	.947	338	118	-5.0	-21.9	-5.6	1.0	-1.5
TOT	662	101	77	11111		8.1				11.8	2.93		.248	.325					.959	2107	860					

Runs
Cobb-Det 144
E.Collins-Chi 118
Vitt-Det 116
Speaker-Bos 108
Chapman-Cle ... 101

Hits
Cobb-Det 208
Crawford-Det... 183
Veach-Det 178
Speaker-Bos 176
Pratt-StL 175

Doubles
Veach-Det 40
Pratt-StL 31
Lewis-Bos 31
Crawford-Det..... 31
Cobb-Det 31

Triples
Crawford-Det...... 19
Fournier-Chi...... 18
Roth-Chi-Cle 17
J.Collins-Chi 17
Chapman-Cle 17

Home Runs
Roth-Chi-Cle 7
Oldring-Phi......... 6

Total Bases
Cobb-Det 274
Crawford-Det.... 264
Veach-Det 247
Pratt-StL 237
E.Collins-Chi 227

Runs Batted In
Veach-Chi 112
Crawford-Det ... 112
Cobb-Det 99
J.Collins-Chi 85
J.Jackson-Cle-Chi . 81

Runs Produced
Cobb-Det 240
E.Collins-Chi 191
Veach-Det 190
Crawford-Det... 189
Speaker-Bos 177

Bases On Balls
E.Collins-Chi 119
Shotton-StL 118
Cobb-Det 118
Bush-Det 118
Hooper-Bos 89

Batting Average
Cobb-Det .... .369
E.Collins-Chi .... .332
Fournier-Chi..... .322
Speaker-Bos .... .322
McInnis-Phi ..... .314

On Base Percentage
Cobb-Det .... .486
E.Collins-Chi .... .460
Fournier-Chi..... .429
Speaker-Bos .... .416
Shotton-StL ..... .409

Slugging Average
Fournier-Chi...... .491
Cobb-Det .... .487
J.Jackson-Cle-Chi .445
E.Collins-Chi ..... .436
Veach-Det .... .434

Production
Cobb-Det .... .973
Fournier-Chi..... .920
E.Collins-Chi .... .896
J.Jackson-Cle-Chi .830
Speaker-Bos .... .827

Adjusted Production
Cobb-Det 182
Fournier-Chi..... 170
E.Collins-Chi 163
Speaker-Bos 152
J.Jackson-Cle-Chi 145

Batter Runs
Cobb-Det 71.6
E.Collins-Chi 51.9
Fournier-Chi...... 40.9
Speaker-Bos 35.0
Veach-Det 32.3

Adjusted Batter Runs
Cobb-Det 67.9
E.Collins-Chi 49.7
Fournier-Chi..... 39.3
Speaker-Bos 37.2
Shotton-StL 30.1

Clutch Hitting Index
Veach-Det 158
J.Collins-Chi 140
Gardner-Bos 133
Schalk-Chi 133
Crawford-Det.... 133

Runs Created
Cobb-Det 155
E.Collins-Chi 116
Crawford-Det.... 101
Speaker-Bos 97
Veach-Det 97

Total Average
Cobb-Det 1.170
E.Collins-Chi .... .971
Fournier-Chi.....964
Speaker-Bos .... .801
Veach-Det 771

Stolen Bases
Cobb-Det 96
Maisel-NY 51
E.Collins-Chi 46
Shotton-StL 43
J.Milan-Was 40

Stolen Base Average
Schang-Phi 85.7
Maisel-NY 81.0
Foster-Was 76.9
Moeller-Was 76.2
Roth-Chi-Cle 72.2

Stolen Base Runs
Maisel-NY 8.1
Cobb-Det 6.0
Schang-Phi 3.6
Moeller-Was 3.6
Williams-StL 2.7

Fielding Runs
Boone-NY 20.8
C.Walker-StL 14.8
Vitt-Det 14.4
Lajoie-Phi 14.1
Speaker-Bos 13.4

Total Player Rating
Cobb-Det 6.6
E.Collins-Chi 6.3
Speaker-Bos 3.9
Fournier-Chi...... 3.6
Chapman-Cle 3.5

Wins
Johnson-Was 27
Scott-Chi 24
Faber-Chi 24
Dauss-Det 24
Coveleski-Det 22

Win Percentage
Wood-Bos .... .750
Shore-Bos .... .704
Foster-Bos .... .704
Ruth-Bos .... .692
Scott-Chi .... .686

Games
Faber-Chi 50
Coveleski-Det 50
Scott-Chi 48
Jones-Cle........ 48

Complete Games
Johnson-Was 35
Caldwell-NY 31
Dauss-Det 27
Scott-Chi 23
Dubuc-Det 22

Shutouts
Scott-Chi 7
Johnson-Was 7
Morton-Cle 6
Foster-Bos 5
Dubuc-Det 5

Saves
Mays-Bos 7

Innings Pitched
Johnson-Was ...336.2
Coveleski-Det ...312.2
Dauss-Det 309.2
Caldwell-NY 305.0
Faber-Chi 299.2

Fewest Hits/Game
Leonard-Bos 6.38
Ruth-Bos 6.86
Wood-Bos 6.86
Johnson-Was 6.90
Morton-Cle 7.09

Fewest BB/Game
Johnson-Was 1.50
Ayers-Was 1.62
Benz-Chi 1.62
Russell-Chi 1.84
Cicotte-Chi 1.93

Strikeouts
Johnson-Was ... 203
Faber-Chi 182
Wyckoff-Phi 157
Coveleski-Det ... 150
Mitchell-Cle 149

Strikeouts/Game
Leonard-Bos 5.69
Mitchell-Cle 5.68
Faber-Chi 5.47
Johnson-Was 5.43
Lowdermilk-StL-De 5.32

Ratio
Johnson-Was 8.90
Morton-Cle 9.41
Wood-Bos 9.44
Ayers-Was 9.50
Benz-Chi 9.63

Earned Run Average
Wood-Bos 1.49
Johnson-Was 1.55
Shore-Bos 1.64
Scott-Chi 2.03
Fisher-NY 2.11

Adjusted ERA
Johnson-Was 191
Wood-Bos 187
Shore-Bos 169
Scott-Chi 146
Morton-Cle 142

Opponents' Batting Avg.
Leonard-Bos 208
Ruth-Bos 212
Johnson-Was 214
Morton-Cle 216
Wood-Bos 216

Opponents' On Base Pct.
Johnson-Was 260
Morton-Cle 268
Wood-Bos 275
Benz-Chi 276
Ayers-Was 276

Starter Runs
Johnson-Was 51.7
Shore-Bos 35.5
Scott-Chi 29.5
Wood-Bos 25.2
Foster-Bos 23.2

Adjusted Starter Runs
Johnson-Was 52.9
Shore-Bos 31.2
Scott-Chi 30.9
Morton-Cle 24.1
Benz-Chi 22.7

Clutch Pitching Index
Hamilton-StL 125
Shore-Bos 122
Foster-Bos 121
Fisher-NY 119
Wood-Bos 118

Relief Runs

Adjusted Relief Runs

Relief Ranking

Total Pitcher Index
Johnson-Was 7.1
Shore-Bos 3.6
Scott-Chi 3.1
Wood-Bos 3.1
Dauss-Det 3.1

Total Baseball Ranking
Johnson-Was 6.9
Cobb-Det 6.6
E.Collins-Chi 6.3
Speaker-Bos 3.9
Fournier-Chi.......3.6

TEAM	G	W	L	PCT	GB	R	OR	AB	H	2B	3B	HR	BB	SO	AVG	OBP	SLG	PRO	PRO+	BR	/A	PF	CHI	RC	SB	CS	SBA	SBR
CHI	155	86	66	.566		640	538	5133	1320	185	77	50	444	590	.257	.320	.352	.672	109	17	52	94	104	650	161			
STL	159	87	67	.565		634	527	5145	1344	199	81	23	576	502	.261	.340	.345	.685	102	56	24	105	93	698	195			
PIT	156	86	67	.562	0.5	592	524	5040	1318	180	80	20	448	561	.262	.326	.341	.667	103	14	19	99	97	655	224			
KC	153	81	72	.529	5.5	547	551	4937	1206	200	66	28	368	503	.244	.303	.329	.632	95	-58	-34	96	105	559	144			
NEW	155	80	72	.526	6	585	562	5097	1283	210	80	17	438	550	.252	.315	.334	.649	102	-22	13	94	101	618	184			
BUF	153	74	78	.487	12	574	634	5065	1261	193	68	40	420	587	.249	.309	.338	.647	94	-32	-44	102	104	594	184			
BRO	153	70	82	.461	16	647	673	5035	1348	205	75	36	473	654	.268	.336	.360	.696	112	66	71	99	98	704	249			
BAL	154	47	107	.305	40	550	760	5060	1235	196	53	36	470	641	.244	.313	.325	.638	90	-40	-59	103	99	578	128			
TOT	619					4769		40512	10315	1568	580	250	3637	4588	.255	.320	.340	.661						1469				

TEAM	CG	SH	SV	IP	H	H/G	HR	BB	SO	RAT	ERA	ERA+	OAV	OOB	PR	/A	PF	CPI	FA	E	DP	FW	PW	BW	SBW	DIF
CHI	97	21	10	1397²	1232	7.9	33	402	576	10.7	2.64	106	.240	.299	61	23	92	95	.964	233	102	.4	2.5	5.6		1.5
STL	94	24	9	1426	1267	8.0	22	396	698	10.7	2.73	117	.243	.300	47	73	105	92	.967	212	111	2.0	7.9	2.6		-2.5
PIT	88	16	12	1382¹	1273	8.3	37	441	517	11.4	2.79	108	.253	.317	37	33	99	107	.971	182	98	3.5	3.6	2.0		.4
KC	95	16	11	1359	1210	8.0	29	390	526	10.8	2.82	103	.242	.301	32	14	96	91	.962	246	96	-.5	1.5	-3.7		7.2
NEW	100	16	7	1406²	1308	8.4	15	453	581	11.6	2.60	109	.253	.319	67	37	94	111	.963	239	124	.0	4.0	1.4		-1.4
BUF	79	14	11	1360	1271	8.4	35	553	594	12.3	3.38	92	.254	.331	-53	-41	103	95	.964	232	112	.3	-4.4	-4.7		6.9
BRO	78	10	16	1355²	1299	8.6	27	536	467	12.3	3.37	90	.258	.332	-50	-53	100	97	.955	290	103	-3.1	-5.7	7.6		-4.8
BAL	85	5	7	1360¹	1455	9.6	52	466	570	13.0	3.96	81	.284	.349	-140	-117	105	100	.957	273	140	-2.0	-12.6	-6.3		-9.0
TOT	716	122	83	11047²		8.4				11.6	3.03		.255	.320					.963	1907	886					

Runs
Borton-StL 97
Berghammer-Pit ... 96
Evans-Bro-Bal 94
Tobin-StL 92
Kauff-Bro 92

Hits
Tobin-StL 184
Konetchy-Pit 181
Evans-Bro-Bal 171
Kauff-Bro 165
Chase-Buf 165

Doubles
Evans-Bro-Bal 34
Zwilling-Chi 32
Konetchy-Pit 31
Chase-Buf 31

Triples
Mann-Chi 19
Konetchy-Pit 18
Kelly-Pit 17
Gilmore-KC 15

Home Runs
Chase-Buf 17
Zwilling-Chi 13
Kauff-Bro 12
Konetchy-Pit 10
Walsh-Bal-StL 9

Total Bases
Konetchy-Pit 278
Chase-Buf 267
Tobin-StL 254
Kauff-Bro 246
Zwilling-Chi 242

Runs Batted In
Zwilling-Chi 94
Konetchy-Pit 93
Chase-Buf 89
Kauff-Bro 83
Borton-StL 83

Runs Produced
Borton-StL 177
Kauff-Bro 163
Konetchy-Pit 162
Evans-Bro-Bal 157
Chase-Buf 157

Bases On Balls
Borton-StL 92
Kauff-Bro 85
Berghammer-Pit ... 83
W.Miller-StL 79

Batting Average
Kauff-Bro .... .342
Magee-Bro .... .323
Konetchy-Pit ..... .314
Flack-Chi .... .314
Campbell-New ..... .310

On Base Percentage
Kauff-Bro .... .446
W.Miller-StL ..... .400
Borton-StL .... .395
Evans-Bro-Bal .... .392
Cooper-Bro ...... .388

Slugging Average
Kauff-Bro .... .509
Konetchy-Pit ..... .483
Chase-Buf .... .471
Zwilling-Chi ..... .442
Mann-Chi .... .438

Production
Kauff-Bro .... .955
Konetchy-Pit ..... .846
Evans-Bro-Bal .... .818
Zwilling-Chi ..... .808
Mann-Chi .... .795

Adjusted Production
Kauff-Bro 182
Konetchy-Pit 149
Zwilling-Chi 146
Mann-Chi 142
Flack-Chi 139

Batter Runs
Kauff-Bro 52.5
Konetchy-Pit 31.4
Evans-Bro-Bal 29.8
Borton-StL 25.5
Zwilling-Chi 25.1

Adjusted Batter Runs
Kauff-Bro 53.0
Konetchy-Pit 32.0
Zwilling-Chi 29.0
Evans-Bro-Bal ... 28.8
Wilson-Chi 26.2

Clutch Hitting Index
Oakes-Pit 146
Borton-StL 142
Engle-Buf 140
F.Smith-Buf-Bro ... 134
Zwilling-Chi 128

Runs Created
Kauff-Bro 132
Konetchy-Pit 111
Tobin-StL 106
Zwilling-Chi 99
Evans-Bro-Bal 99

Total Average
Kauff-Bro 1.233
Konetchy-Pit ..... .884
Cooper-Bro ...... .868
W.Miller-StL ..... .863
Zwilling-Chi ..... .857

Stolen Bases
Kauff-Bro 55
Mowrey-Pit 40
Kelly-Pit 38
Flack-Chi 37
Magee-Bro 34

Stolen Base Average

Stolen Base Runs

Fielding Runs
Doolan-Bal-Chi ... 32.1
Rariden-New 23.0
Cooper-Bro 18.3
Johnson-StL 17.7
Perring-KC 14.8

Total Player Rating
Kauff-Bro 6.4
Rariden-New 5.0
Cooper-Bro 3.8
Zwilling-Chi 3.2
Louden-Buf 3.0

Wins
McConnell-Chi 25
Allen-Pit 23
Davenport-StL 22
Cullop-KC 22

Win Percentage
McConnell-Chi .... .714
Brown-Chi .... .680
Reulbach-New ..... .677
Cullop-KC .... .667
Plank-StL .... .656

Games
Davenport-StL 55
Bedient-Buf 53
Crandall-StL 51
Johnson-KC 46

Complete Games
Davenport-StL 30
Hendrix-Chi 26
Schulz-Buf 25
Allen-Pit 24

Shutouts
Davenport-StL 10
Plank-StL 6
Allen-Pit 6

Saves
Bedient-Buf 10
Barger-Pit 6
Wiltse-Bro 5
Upham-Bro 5

Innings Pitched
Davenport-StL ... 392.2
Crandall-StL 312.2
Schulz-Buf 309.2
McConnell-Chi ... 303.0
Cullop-KC 302.1

Fewest Hits/Game
Davenport-StL 6.88
Main-KC 7.08
Plank-StL 7.11
Brown-Chi 7.20
Anderson-Buf 7.20

Fewest BB/Game
Plank-StL 1.81
Bender-Bal 1.87
Hearn-Pit 1.90
Cullop-KC 1.99
Quinn-Bal 2.07

Strikeouts
Davenport-StL 229
Schulz-Buf 160
McConnell-Chi ... 151
Plank-StL 147

Strikeouts/Game
Anderson-Buf 5.33
Davenport-StL 5.25
Plank-StL 4.93
Bailey-Bal-Chi 4.91
Groom-StL 4.78

Ratio
Plank-StL 9.02
Davenport-StL 9.19
Brown-Chi 9.90
Anderson-Buf 10.01
Reulbach-New ... 10.17

Earned Run Average
Moseley-New 1.91
Plank-StL 2.08
Brown-Chi 2.09
McConnell-Chi ... 2.20
Davenport-StL 2.20

Adjusted ERA
Plank-StL 154
Moseley-New 149
Davenport-StL 145
Brown-Chi 133
Reulbach-New 127

Opponents' Batting Avg.
Davenport-StL ..... .215
Plank-StL .... .218
Brown-Chi .... .220
Main-KC .... .222
Anderson-Buf .... .222

Opponents' On Base Pct.
Plank-StL .... .262
Davenport-StL .... .268
Brown-Chi .... .279
Anderson-Buf ..... .285
Reulbach-New ... .287

Starter Runs
Davenport-StL 36.3
Moseley-New 33.3
Plank-StL 28.4
McConnell-Chi ... 28.1
Brown-Chi 24.6

Adjusted Starter Runs
Davenport-StL 43.4
Plank-StL 33.3
Moseley-New 27.7
Crandall-StL 21.0
McConnell-Chi 19.9

Clutch Pitching Index
Moran-New 129
Kaiserling-New ... 127
Rogge-Pit 127
Moseley-New 122
Suggs-Bal 117

Relief Runs

Adjusted Relief Runs

Relief Ranking

Total Pitcher Index
Crandall-StL 4.1
Plank-StL 4.0
McConnell-Chi 3.2
Brown-Chi 3.0
Davenport-StL 2.9

Total Baseball Ranking
Kauff-Bro 6.4
Rariden-New 5.0
Crandall-StL 4.1
Plank-StL 4.0
Cooper-Bro 3.8

TEAM	G	W	L	PCT	GB	R	OR	AB	H	2B	3B	HR	BB	SO	AVG	OBP	SLG	PRO	PRO+	BR	/A	PF	CHI	RC	SB	CS	SBA	SBR
BRO	156	94	60	.610		585	471	5234	1366	195	80	28	355	550	.261	.313	.345	.658	105	46	31	103	99	645	187			
PHI	154	91	62	.595	2.5	581	489	4985	1244	223	53	42	399	571	.250	.310	.341	.651	102	34	15	104	104	593	149			
BOS	158	89	63	.586	4	542	453	5075	1181	166	73	22	437	646	.233	.299	.307	.606	96	-38	-15	96	108	535	141			
NY	155	86	66	.566	7	597	504	5152	1305	188	74	42	356	558	.253	.307	.343	.650	112	31	59	95	106	617	206			
CHI	156	67	86	.438	26.5	520	541	5179	1237	194	56	46	399	662	.239	.298	.325	.623	88	-18	-76	111	99	559	133			
PIT	157	65	89	.422	29	484	586	5181	1246	147	91	20	372	618	.240	.298	.316	.614	94	-32	-37	101	95	556	173			
STL	153	60	93	.392	33.5	476	629	5030	1223	155	74	25	335	651	.243	.295	.318	.613	95	-35	-32	99	99	535	182			
CIN	155	60	93	.392	33.5	505	617	5254	1336	187	88	14	362	573	.254	.307	.331	.638	105	13	26	98	91	596	157			
TOT	622					4290		41090	10138	1455	589	239	3015	4829	.247	.303	.328	.632						1328				

TEAM	CG	SH	SV	IP	H	H/G	HR	BB	SO	RAT	ERA	ERA+	OAV	OOB	PR	/A	PF	CPI	FA	E	DP	FW	PW	BW	SBW	DIF
BRO	96	22	9	1427[1]	1201	7.6	24	372	634	10.2	2.12	126	.232	.289	78	86	102	103	.965	224	90	1.2	9.8	3.5		2.4
PHI	97	25	9	1382[1]	1238	8.1	28	295	601	10.3	2.36	112	.244	.292	39	44	101	101	.963	234	119	.4	5.0	1.7		7.3
BOS	97	23	11	1415[2]	1206	7.7	24	325	644	9.9	2.19	113	.235	.285	66	45	95	99	.967	212	124	2.1	5.1	-1.7		7.4
NY	88	22	12	1397[1]	1267	8.2	41	310	638	10.4	2.60	93	.245	.293	2	-28	93	95	.966	217	108	1.5	-3.2	6.7		4.9
CHI	72	17	13	1416[2]	1265	8.0	32	365	616	10.6	2.65	110	.244	.298	-6	39	111	94	.957	286	104	-2.6	4.5	-8.7		-2.7
PIT	88	11	7	1419[2]	1277	8.1	24	443	596	11.1	2.76	97	.247	.311	-24	-14	103	97	.959	260	97	-.9	-1.6	-4.2		-5.3
STL	58	13	15	1355	1331	8.8	31	445	529	12.1	3.14	84	.265	.330	-80	-77	101	104	.957	278	124	-2.4	-8.8	-3.7		-1.7
CIN	86	7	6	1408	1356	8.7	35	461	569	11.9	3.10	84	.261	.326	-76	-82	99	102	.965	228	126	.9	-9.4	3.0		-11.0
TOT	682	140	82	11222		8.1				10.8	2.61		.247	.303					.963	1939	892					

Runs
Burns-NY 105
Carey-Pit 90
Robertson-NY 88
Groh-Cin 85
Paskert-Phi 82

Hits
Chase-Cin 184
Robertson-NY 180
Z.Wheat-Bro 177
Hinchman-Pit 175
Burns-NY 174

Doubles
Niehoff-Phi 42
Z.Wheat-Bro 32
Paskert-Phi 30

Triples
Hinchman-Pit 16
Roush-NY-Cin 15
Kauff-NY 15
Hornsby-StL 15

Home Runs
Williams-Chi 12
Robertson-NY 12
Cravath-Phi 11
Z.Wheat-Bro 9
Kauff-NY 9

Total Bases
Z.Wheat-Bro 262
Robertson-NY 250
Chase-Cin 249
Hinchman-Pit 237
Burns-NY 229

Runs Batted In
Zimmerman-Chi-NY 83
Chase-Cin 82
Hinchman-Pit 76
Kauff-NY 74
Z.Wheat-Bro 73

Runs Produced
Zimmerman-Chi-NY 153
Robertson-NY 145
Chase-Cin 144
Konetchy-Bos 143
Burns-NY 141

Bases On Balls
Groh-Cin 84
Saier-Chi 79
Bancroft-Phi 74
Kauff-NY 68
Cravath-Phi 64

Batting Average
Chase-Cin .... .339
Daubert-Bro ...... .316
Hinchman-Pit .... .315
Hornsby-StL ...... .313
Z.Wheat-Bro ...... .312

On Base Percentage
Cravath-Phi ...... .379
Hinchman-Pit .... .378
Williams-Chi ..... .372
Daubert-Bro ...... .371
Groh-Cin .... .370

Slugging Average
Z.Wheat-Bro ..... .461
Chase-Cin .... .459
Williams-Chi ..... .459
Hornsby-StL ...... .444
Cravath-Phi ...... .440

Production
Williams-Chi ...... .831
Z.Wheat-Bro ...... .828
Chase-Cin .... .822
Cravath-Phi ...... .819
Hornsby-StL ...... .814

Adjusted Production
Chase-Cin 155
Hornsby-StL 150
Z.Wheat-Bro 149
Cravath-Phi 146
Hinchman-Pit 146

Batter Runs
Z.Wheat-Bro 34.5
Hinchman-Pit 31.1
Chase-Cin 30.2
Cravath-Phi 28.7
Hornsby-StL 28.2

Adjusted Batter Runs
Z.Wheat-Bro 32.9
Chase-Cin 31.5
Hinchman-Pit 30.6
Hornsby-StL 28.5
Cravath-Phi 26.9

Clutch Hitting Index
Mowrey-Bro 157
Magee-Bos 156
Zimmerman-Chi-NY 145
Fletcher-NY 139
Cutshaw-Bro 138

Runs Created
Z.Wheat-Bro 103
Hinchman-Pit 96
Chase-Cin 93
Hornsby-StL 88
Carey-Pit 87

Total Average
Williams-Chi ...... .863
Cravath-Phi ...... .857
Z.Wheat-Bro ...... .844
Hornsby-StL ...... .826
Hinchman-Pit ..... .797

Stolen Bases
Carey-Pit 63
Kauff-NY 40
Bescher-StL 39
Burns-NY 37
Herzog-Cin-NY ... 34

Stolen Base Average
Carey-Pit 76.8
Bescher-StL 76.5
Daubert-Bro 75.0
Maranville-Bos ... 68.1
Chase-Cin 66.7

Stolen Base Runs
Carey-Pit 7.5
Bescher-StL 4.5
Daubert-Bro 2.1
Maranville-Bos 0.6

Fielding Runs
Carey-Pit 29.9
Betzel-StL 28.4
Bancroft-Phi 24.5
Maranville-Bos ... 21.5
Doyle-NY-Chi..... 20.0

Total Player Rating
Groh-Cin 5.3
Carey-Pit 4.7
Fletcher-NY 4.2
Doyle-NY-Chi..... 4.2
Z.Wheat-Bro 3.9

Wins
Alexander-Phi 33
Pfeffer-Bro 25
Rixey-Phi 22
Mamaux-Pit 21

Win Percentage
Hughes-Bos ...... .842
Alexander-Phi .... .733
Pfeffer-Bro .... .694
Rixey-Phi .... .688
Benton-NY ...... .667

Games
Meadows-StL 51
Alexander-Phi 48
Mamaux-Pit 45
Ames-StL 45

Complete Games
Alexander-Phi 38
Pfeffer-Bro 30
Rudolph-Bos 27
Mamaux-Pit 26
Demaree-Phi 25

Shutouts
Alexander-Phi 16
Tyler-Bos 6
Pfeffer-Bro 6

Saves
Ames-StL 8
Packard-Chi 5
Marquard-Bro 5
Hughes-Bos 5

Innings Pitched
Alexander-Phi ... 388.2
Pfeffer-Bro 328.2
Rudolph-Bos 312.0
Mamaux-Pit 310.0
Toney-Cin 300.0

Fewest Hits/Game
Cheney-Bro 6.33
Hughes-Bos 6.76
Cooper-Pit 6.91
Miller-Pit 7.02
Ragan-Bos........ 7.07

Fewest BB/Game
Rudolph-Bos 1.10
Alexander-Phi 1.16
Demaree-Phi 1.52
Sallee-StL-NY 1.63
Marquard-Bro ... 1.67

Strikeouts
Alexander-Phi 167
Cheney-Bro 166
Mamaux-Pit 163
Toney-Cin 146
Vaughn-Chi 144

Strikeouts/Game
Cheney-Bro 5.91
Hughes-Bos 5.42
Hendrix-Chi 4.83
Mamaux-Pit 4.73
Marquard-Bro ... 4.70

Ratio
Rudolph-Bos 8.86
Alexander-Phi 8.87
Marquard-Bro ... 9.09
McConnell-Chi.... 9.30
Ragan-Bos....... 9.40

Earned Run Average
Alexander-Phi 1.55
Marquard-Bro ... 1.58
Rixey-Phi 1.85
Cooper-Pit 1.87
Pfeffer-Bro 1.92

Adjusted ERA
Alexander-Phi 171
Marquard-Bro ... 169
Cooper-Pit 144
Rixey-Phi 143
Pfeffer-Bro 140

Opponents' Batting Avg.
Cheney-Bro ...... .198
Cooper-Pit .... .215
Hughes-Bos ...... .215
Ragan-Bos........ .218
McConnell-Chi.... .223

Opponents' On Base Pct.
Rudolph-Bos ..... .261
Alexander-Phi .... .262
Marquard-Bro ... .267
Ragan-Bos........ .270
McConnell-Chi.... .271

Starter Runs
Alexander-Phi 45.8
Schupp-NY 26.7
Pfeffer-Bro 25.4
Rixey-Phi 24.3
Marquard-Bro ... 23.5

Adjusted Starter Runs
Alexander-Phi 47.3
Pfeffer-Bro 27.7
Rixey-Phi 25.4
Marquard-Bro ... 24.9
Schupp-NY 23.8

Clutch Pitching Index
Dell-Bro 124
Sallee-StL-NY 117
Meadows-StL 116
Schulz-Cin 114
Alexander-Phi 114

Relief Runs

Adjusted Relief Runs

Relief Ranking

Total Pitcher Index
Alexander-Phi 7.0
Pfeffer-Bro 3.7
Rixey-Phi 3.2
Cooper-Pit 2.6
Tyler-Bos 2.6

Total Baseball Ranking
Alexander-Phi 7.0
Groh-Cin 5.3
Carey-Pit 4.7
Fletcher-NY 4.2
Doyle-NY-Chi...... 4.2

TEAM	G	W	L	PCT	GB	R	OR	AB	H	2B	3B	HR	BB	SO	AVG	OBP	SLG	PRO	PRO+	BR	/A	PF	CHI	RC	SB	CS	SBA	SBR
BOS	156	91	63	.591		550	**480**	5018	1246	197	56	14	464	**482**	.248	.317	.318	.635	97	-20	-22	100	101	580	129			
CHI	155	89	65	.578	2	601	497	5081	1277	194	**100**	17	447	591	.251	.319	.339	.658	103	18	12	101	102	638	197			
DET	155	87	67	.565	4	**670**	595	5193	**1371**	202	96	17	545	529	**.264**	**.337**	**.350**	**.687**	**109**	**78**	**57**	104	101	**700**	190			
NY	156	80	74	.519	11	577	561	5198	1277	194	59	**35**	516	632	.246	.318	.326	.644	98	-4	-16	102	100	613	179			
STL	158	79	75	.513	12	588	545	5159	1262	181	50	14	**627**	640	.245	.331	.307	.638	103	2	30	95	99	620	**234**			
CLE	157	77	77	.500	14	630	602	5064	1264	**233**	66	16	522	605	.250	.324	.331	.655	97	17	-17	106	**106**	625	160			
WAS	159	76	77	.497	14.5	536	543	5114	1238	170	60	12	535	597	.242	.320	.306	.626	95	-30	-24	99	98	579	185			
PHI	154	36	117	.235	54.5	447	776	5010	1212	169	65	19	406	631	.242	.303	.313	.616	96	-61	-35	95	91	538	151			
TOT	625					4599		40837	10147	1540	552	144	4062	4707	.248	.321	.324	.645							1425			

TEAM	CG	SH	SV	IP	H	H/G	HR	BB	SO	RAT	ERA	ERA+	OAV	OOB	PR	/A	PF	CPI	FA	E	DP	FW	PW	BW	SBW	DIF
BOS	76	**24**	16	1410^{2}	1221	7.8	**10**	463	584	11.0	2.48	112	.239	.307	55	44	98	99	**.972**	**183**	108	**3.0**	4.9	-2.4		8.5
CHI	73	20	15	1412^{1}	**1189**	**7.6**	14	**405**	644	**10.3**	**2.36**	**117**	**.236**	**.296**	**72**	**61**	98	96	.968	205	**134**	1.5	**6.8**	1.3		2.4
DET	81	8	13	1410	1254	8.0	12	578	531	12.1	2.97	96	.248	.333	-23	-18	101	100	.968	211	110	1.1	-2.0	**6.3**		4.5
NY	84	12	**17**	1428	1249	7.9	37	476	616	11.2	2.77	104	.244	.314	8	17	102	100	.967	219	119	.7	1.9	-1.8		2.2
STL	74	9	13	1443^{2}	1292	8.1	15	478	505	11.3	2.58	106	.248	.316	39	26	97	105	.963	248	120	-.9	2.9	3.3		-3.3
CLE	65	9	16	1410	1383	8.8	16	467	537	12.0	2.90	103	.264	.328	-13	16	106	**107**	.965	232	130	.0	1.8	-1.9		.1
WAS	85	11	7	1432	1271	8.0	14	490	**706**	11.3	2.66	105	.244	.314	25	17	99	99	.964	232	119	.2	1.9	-2.7		.0
PHI	**94**	11	3	1343^{2}	1311	8.8	26	715	575	13.8	3.92	73	.267	.364	-163	-161	101	97	.951	314	126	-5.5	-17.8	-3.9		-13.3
TOT	632	104	100	11290^{1}		8.1				11.6	2.82		.248	.321					.965	1844	966					

Runs
Cobb-Det 113
Graney-Cle 106
Speaker-Cle 102
Shotton-StL 97
Veach-Det 92

Hits
Speaker-Cle 211
Jackson-Chi 202
Cobb-Det 201
Sisler-StL 177
Shotton-StL 174

Doubles
Speaker-Cle 41
Graney-Cle 41
Jackson-Chi 40
Pratt-StL 35
Veach-Det 33

Triples
Jackson-Chi 21
E.Collins-Chi 17
Witt-Phi 15
Veach-Det 15

Home Runs
Pipp-NY 12
Baker-NY 10
Schang-Phi 7
Felsch-Chi 7

Total Bases
Jackson-Chi 293
Speaker-Cle 274
Cobb-Det 267
Veach-Det 245

Runs Batted In
Pratt-StL 103
Pipp-NY 93
Veach-Det 91
Speaker-Cle 79
Jackson-Chi 78

Runs Produced
Veach-Det 180
Speaker-Cle 179
Cobb-Det 176
Jackson-Chi 166
Pratt-StL 162

Bases On Balls
Shotton-StL 111
Graney-Cle 102
E.Collins-Chi 86
Speaker-Cle 82
Hooper-Bos 80

Batting Average
Speaker-Cle .386
Cobb-Det .371
Jackson-Chi .341
Strunk-Phi .316
Gardner-Bos .308

On Base Percentage
Speaker-Cle .470
Cobb-Det .452
E.Collins-Chi .405
Jackson-Chi .393
Strunk-Phi .393

Slugging Average
Speaker-Cle .502
Jackson-Chi .495
Cobb-Det .493
Veach-Det .433
Felsch-Chi .427

Production
Speaker-Cle .972
Cobb-Det .944
Jackson-Chi .888
Strunk-Phi .814
E.Collins-Chi .802

Adjusted Production
Speaker-Cle 181
Cobb-Det 177
Jackson-Chi 165
Strunk-Phi 152
E.Collins-Chi 139

Batter Runs
Speaker-Cle 64.6
Cobb-Det 57.5
Jackson-Chi 44.9
E.Collins-Chi 30.5
Strunk-Phi 30.2

Adjusted Batter Runs
Speaker-Cle 60.8
Cobb-Det 55.3
Jackson-Chi 44.2
Strunk-Phi 33.2
E.Collins-Chi 29.8

Clutch Hitting Index
Pratt-StL 158
Gandil-Cle 151
Marsans-StL 143
Heilmann-Det 138
Burns-Det 137

Runs Created
Cobb-Det 136
Speaker-Cle 132
Jackson-Chi 119
E.Collins-Chi 99
Veach-Det 94

Total Average
Cobb-Det 1.071
Speaker-Cle 1.017
Jackson-Chi .876
E.Collins-Chi .814
Graney-Cle .761

Stolen Bases
Cobb-Det 68
Marsans-StL 46
Shotton-StL 41
E.Collins-Chi 40
Speaker-Cle 35

Stolen Base Average
Cobb-Det 73.9
Hooper-Bos 71.1
Schalk-Chi 69.8
Roth-Cle 67.4
Shanks-Was 65.7

Stolen Base Runs
Cobb-Det 6.0
Hooper-Bos 1.5
Schalk-Chi 1.2
Roth-Cle .3

Fielding Runs
Lavan-StL 34.2
Lajoie-Phi 30.4
Vitt-Det 27.6
Pratt-StL 22.4
Milan-Was 16.5

Total Player Rating
Speaker-Cle 6.1
Cobb-Det 5.7
Pratt-StL 4.2
Jackson-Chi 3.7
Lavan-StL 3.4

Wins
Johnson-Was 25
Shawkey-NY 24
Ruth-Bos 23
Coveleski-Det 21
Dauss-Det 19

Win Percentage
Cicotte-Chi .682
Ruth-Bos .657
Coveleski-Det .656
Faber-Chi .654
Shawkey-NY .632

Games
Davenport-StL 59
Russell-Chi 56
Shawkey-NY 53
Gallia-Was 49

Complete Games
Johnson-Was 36
Myers-Phi 31
Bush-Phi 25
Ruth-Bos 23
Coveleski-Det 22

Shutouts
Ruth-Bos 9
Bush-Phi 8
Leonard-Bos 6
Russell-Chi 5

Saves
Shawkey-NY 8
Russell-NY 6
Leonard-Bos 6
Cicotte-Chi 5
Bagby-Cle 5

Innings Pitched
Johnson-Was 371.0
Coveleski-Det 324.1
Ruth-Bos 323.2
Myers-Phi 315.0
Davenport-StL 290.2

Fewest Hits/Game
Ruth-Bos 6.40
Shawkey-NY 6.64
Cicotte-Chi 6.64
Bush-Phi 6.97
Johnson-Was 7.04

Fewest BB/Game
Russell-Chi 1.43
Cullop-NY 1.72
Coveleski-Det 1.75
Shore-Bos 1.95
Johnson-Was 1.99

Strikeouts
Johnson-Was 228
Myers-Phi 182
Ruth-Bos 170
Bush-Phi 157
Harper-Was 149

Strikeouts/Game
Williams-Chi 5.54
Johnson-Was 5.53
Russell-NY 5.46
Harper-Was 5.37
Myers-Phi 5.20

Ratio
Russell-Chi 8.51
Johnson-Was 9.24
Shawkey-NY 9.47
Coveleski-Det 9.77
Ruth-Bos 9.90

Earned Run Average
Ruth-Bos 1.75
Cicotte-Chi 1.78
Johnson-Was 1.89
Coveleski-Det 1.97
Faber-Chi 2.02

Adjusted ERA
Ruth-Bos 158
Cicotte-Chi 155
Johnson-Was 147
Coveleski-Det 145
Cullop-NY 141

Opponents' Batting Avg.
Ruth-Bos .201
Shawkey-NY .209
Cicotte-Chi .218
Bush-Phi .219
Johnson-Was .220

Opponents' On Base Pct.
Russell-Chi .254
Johnson-Was .270
Shawkey-NY .273
Ruth-Bos .280
Coveleski-Det .282

Starter Runs
Ruth-Bos 38.5
Johnson-Was 38.4
Coveleski-Det 30.7
Cicotte-Chi 21.7
Weilman-StL 20.6

Adjusted Starter Runs
Johnson-Was 36.9
Ruth-Bos 36.4
Coveleski-Det 32.1
Shawkey-NY 20.7
Cicotte-Chi 20.3

Clutch Pitching Index
Cicotte-Chi 117
Gallia-Was 117
Mogridge-NY 113
Fisher-NY 113
Weilman-StL 113

Relief Runs

Adjusted Relief Runs

Relief Ranking

Total Pitcher Index
Ruth-Bos 6.0
Johnson-Was 4.7
Coveleski-Det 4.3
Mays-Bos 3.0
Cicotte-Chi 2.6

Total Baseball Ranking
Speaker-Cle 6.1
Ruth-Bos 6.0
Cobb-Det 5.7
Johnson-Was 4.7
Coveleski-Det 4.3

1917 National League

TEAM	G	W	L	PCT	GB	R	OR	AB	H	2B	3B	HR	BB	SO	AVG	OBP	SLG	PRO	PRO+	BR	/A	PF	CHI	RC	SB	CS	SBA	SBR
NY	158	98	56	.636		635	457	5211	1360	170	71	39	373	533	.261	.317	.343	.660	113	50	68	97	105	610	162			
PHI	154	87	65	.572	10	578	500	5084	1262	225	60	38	435	533	.248	.310	.339	.649	101	29	6	104	100	573	109			
STL	154	82	70	.539	15	531	567	5083	1271	159	93	26	359	652	.250	.303	.333	.636	104	2	17	97	98	552	159			
CIN	157	78	76	.506	20	601	611	5251	1385	196	100	26	312	477	.264	.309	.354	.663	114	48	71	96	101	607	153			
CHI	157	74	80	.481	24	552	567	5135	1229	194	67	17	415	599	.239	.299	.313	.612	86	-35	-79	108	107	524	127			
BOS	157	72	81	.471	25.5	536	552	5201	1280	169	75	22	427	587	.246	.309	.320	.629	105	-2	30	94	96	563	155			
BRO	156	70	81	.464	26.5	511	559	5251	1299	159	78	25	334	527	.247	.296	.322	.618	93	-32	-47	103	98	534	130			
PIT	157	51	103	.331	47	464	595	5169	1230	160	61	9	399	580	.238	.298	.298	.596	86	-61	-80	103	94	506	150			
TOT	625					4408		41385	10316	1432	605	202	3054	4488	.249	.305	.328	.633						1145				

TEAM	CG	SH	SV	IP	H	H/G	HR	BB	SO	RAT	ERA	ERA+	OAV	OOB	PR	/A	PF	CPI	FA	E	DP	FW	PW	BW	SBW	DIF
NY	92	18	14	1426²	1221	7.7	29	327	551	9.9	2.27	112	.234	.283	69	43	94	97	.968	208	122	1.8	4.9	7.7		6.6
PHI	102	22	5	1389	1258	8.2	25	325	616	10.5	2.46	114	.246	.295	38	53	104	102	.967	212	112	1.2	6.0	.7		3.1
STL	66	16	10	1392²	1257	8.1	29	421	502	11.1	3.03	89	.248	.311	-51	-55	99	92	.967	221	112	.6	-6.2	1.9		9.7
CIN	94	12	6	1397¹	1358	8.7	20	402	488	11.5	2.70	97	.260	.317	1	-15	97	110	.962	247	120	-.7	-1.7	8.0		-4.6
CHI	79	15	9	1404	1303	8.4	34	400	654	10.9	2.62	110	.253	.307	14	40	107	108	.959	267	121	-1.9	4.5	-8.9		3.3
BOS	105	22	3	1424²	1309	8.3	19	371	593	10.8	2.77	92	.251	.304	-10	-38	94	96	.966	224	122	.7	-4.3	3.4		-4.3
BRO	99	8	9	1421¹	1288	8.2	32	405	582	11.0	2.78	100	.247	.307	-12	0	103	98	.962	245	102	-.7	.0	-5.3		.5
PIT	84	17	6	1417²	1318	8.4	14	432	509	11.3	3.01	94	.253	.314	-48	-29	105	94	.961	251	119	-.9	-3.3	-9.0		-12.7
TOT	721	130	62	11273¹		8.2				10.9	2.70		.249	.305					.964	1875	971					

Runs
Burns-NY	103
Groh-Cin	91
Kauff-NY	89
Hornsby-StL	86

Hits
Groh-Cin	182
Burns-NY	180
Roush-Cin	178
Zimmerman-NY	174
Carey-Pit	174

Doubles
Groh-Cin	39
Merkle-Bro-Chi	31
Smith-Bos	31
Cravath-Phi	29
Chase-Cin	28

Triples
Hornsby-StL	17
Cravath-Phi	16
Chase-Cin	15
Roush-Cin	14
Long-StL	14

Home Runs
Robertson-NY	12
Cravath-Phi	12
Hornsby-StL	8

Total Bases
Hornsby-StL	253
Groh-Cin	246
Burns-NY	246
Cravath-Phi	238

Runs Batted In
Zimmerman-NY	102
Chase-Cin	86
Cravath-Phi	83
Stengel-Bro	73
Luderus-Phi	72

Runs Produced
Zimmerman-NY	158
Chase-Cin	153
Kauff-NY	152
Roush-Cin	145
Hornsby-StL	144

Bases On Balls
Burns-NY	75
Groh-Cin	71
Cravath-Phi	70
Luderus-Phi	65
Paskert-Phi	62

Batting Average
Roush-Cin	.341
Hornsby-StL	.327
Kauff-NY	.308
Groh-Cin	.304
Burns-NY	.302

On Base Percentage
Groh-Cin	.385
Hornsby-StL	.385
Burns-NY	.380
Roush-Cin	.379
Kauff-NY	.379

Slugging Average
Hornsby-StL	.484
Cravath-Phi	.473
Roush-Cin	.454
Burns-NY	.412
Groh-Cin	.411

Production
Hornsby-StL	.868
Cravath-Phi	.842
Roush-Cin	.833
Groh-Cin	.796
Burns-NY	.792

Adjusted Production
Hornsby-StL	170
Roush-Cin	162
Cravath-Phi	151
Groh-Cin	150
Burns-NY	148

Batter Runs
Hornsby-StL	39.6
Cravath-Phi	34.7
Groh-Cin	33.5
Roush-Cin	32.3
Burns-NY	32.2

Adjusted Batter Runs
Hornsby-StL	41.2
Groh-Cin	36.2
Roush-Cin	34.6
Burns-NY	34.3
Cravath-Phi	32.3

Clutch Hitting Index
Zimmerman-NY	171
Ward-Pit	143
Luderus-Phi	143
Deal-Chi	141
Chase-Cin	141

Runs Created
Burns-NY	105
Groh-Cin	102
Hornsby-StL	102
Carey-Pit	94
Roush-Cin	93

Total Average
Hornsby-StL	.906
Cravath-Phi	.870
Burns-NY	.868
Roush-Cin	.843
Groh-Cin	.815

Stolen Bases
Carey-Pit	46
Burns-NY	40
Kauff-NY	30
Maranville-Bos	27
Baird-Pit-StL	26

Stolen Base Average

Stolen Base Runs

Fielding Runs
Bancroft-NY	27.9
Fletcher-NY	27.4
Carey-Pit	24.5
Hornsby-StL	21.3
Miller-StL	18.6

Total Player Rating
Hornsby-StL	7.6
Groh-Cin	5.2
Fletcher-NY	4.1
Carey-Pit	4.0
Burns-NY	3.4

Wins
Alexander-Phi	30
Toney-Cin	24
Vaughn-Chi	23
Schupp-NY	21
Schneider-Cin	20

Win Percentage
Schupp-NY	.750
Sallee-NY	.720
Perritt-NY	.708
Alexander-Phi	.698
Nehf-Bos	.680

Games
Douglas-Chi	51
Barnes-Bos	50
Schneider-Cin	46
Alexander-Phi	45
Doak-StL	44

Complete Games
Alexander-Phi	34
Toney-Cin	31
Vaughn-Chi	27
Barnes-Bos	27
Schupp-NY	25

Shutouts
Alexander-Phi	8
Toney-Cin	7
Cooper-Pit	7
Schupp-NY	6

Saves
Sallee-NY	4

Innings Pitched
Alexander-Phi	387.2
Toney-Cin	339.2
Schneider-Cin	333.2
Cooper-Pit	297.2
Vaughn-Chi	295.2

Fewest Hits/Game
Schupp-NY	6.68
Anderson-NY	6.78
Nehf-Bos	7.60
Pfeffer-Bro	7.61
Tyler-Bos	7.64

Fewest BB/Game
Alexander-Phi	1.30
Sallee-NY	1.42
Nehf-Bos	1.50
Barnes-Bos	1.53
Douglas-Chi	1.53

Strikeouts
Alexander-Phi	200
Vaughn-Chi	195
Douglas-Chi	151
Schupp-NY	147
Schneider-Cin	138

Strikeouts/Game
Vaughn-Chi	5.94
Schupp-NY	4.86
Alexander-Phi	4.64
Douglas-Chi	4.63
Marquard-Bro	4.53

Ratio
Anderson-NY	8.78
Schupp-NY	9.13
Alexander-Phi	9.24
Nehf-Bos	9.26
Barnes-Bos	9.58

Earned Run Average
Anderson-NY	1.44
Alexander-Phi	1.83
Perritt-NY	1.88
Schupp-NY	1.95
Vaughn-Chi	2.01

Adjusted ERA
Anderson-NY	176
Alexander-Phi	153
Vaughn-Chi	144
Perritt-NY	135
Schupp-NY	130

Opponents' Batting Avg.
Schupp-NY	.209
Anderson-NY	.209
Nehf-Bos	.231
Marquard-Bro	.232
Pfeffer-Bro	.234

Opponents' On Base Pct.
Anderson-NY	.255
Schupp-NY	.265
Alexander-Phi	.266
Nehf-Bos	.268
Barnes-Bos	.277

Starter Runs
Alexander-Phi	37.4
Vaughn-Chi	22.8
Schupp-NY	22.7
Anderson-NY	22.7
Schneider-Cin	22.2

Adjusted Starter Runs
Alexander-Phi	41.6
Vaughn-Chi	28.8
Anderson-NY	19.8
Schneider-Cin	18.7
Schupp-NY	17.9

Clutch Pitching Index
Schneider-Cin	145
Vaughn-Chi	120
Perritt-NY	118
Hendrix-Chi	117
Mayer-Phi	114

Relief Runs

Adjusted Relief Runs

Relief Ranking

Total Pitcher Index
Alexander-Phi	5.9
Vaughn-Chi	3.7
Rixey-Phi	2.2
Anderson-NY	1.9
Schupp-NY	1.8

Total Baseball Ranking
Hornsby-StL	7.6
Alexander-Phi	5.9
Groh-Cin	5.2
Fletcher-NY	4.1
Carey-Pit	4.0

TEAM	G	W	L	PCT	GB	R	OR	AB	H	2B	3B	HR	BB	SO	AVG	OBP	SLG	PRO	PRO+	BR	/A	PF	CHI	RC	SB
CHI	156	100	54	.649		**656**	464	5057	1281	152	**81**	18	522	479	.253	**.329**	.326	.655	103	36	24	102	**108**	615	**219**
BOS	157	90	62	.592	9	555	**454**	5048	1243	198	64	14	466	596	.246	.314	.319	.633	100	-10	-4	99	99	558	210
CLE	156	88	66	.571	12	584	543	4994	1224	218	64	13	**549**	596	.245	.324	.322	.646	96	21	-21	107	99	595	163
DET	154	78	75	.510	21.5	639	577	5093	**1317**	204	77	25	483	476	**.259**	.328	**.344**	**.672**	111	61	63	100	102	**630**	166
WAS	157	74	79	.484	25.5	543	566	5142	1238	173	70	4	500	574	.241	.313	.304	.617	95	-34	-27	99	101	548	136
NY	155	71	82	.464	28.5	524	558	5136	1226	172	52	27	496	535	.239	.310	.308	.618	93	-34	-39	101	98	544	157
STL	155	57	97	.370	43	510	687	5091	1250	183	63	15	405	540	.246	.305	.315	.620	98	-39	-18	96	99	535	112
PHI	154	55	98	.359	44.5	529	691	5109	1296	177	62	17	435	519	.254	.316	.323	.639	101	-1	7	99	94	566	105
TOT	622					4540		40670	10075	1477	533	133	3856	4192	.248	.318	.320	.638							1268

TEAM	CG	SH	SV	IP	H	H/G	HR	BB	SO	RAT	ERA	ERA+	OAV	OOB	PR	/A	PF	CPI	FA	E	DP	FW	PW	BW	SBW	DIF
CHI	78	**22**	21	1424¹	1236	7.8	10	413	517	10.6	**2.16**	123	.238	.298	79	76	100	102	.967	204	117	2.3	**8.5**	2.7		9.6
BOS	115	15	7	1421¹	**1197**	7.6	12	413	509	10.5	2.20	117	**.231**	.295	73	60	97	95	**.972**	183	116	3.9	6.7	-.4		3.9
CLE	73	20	22	1412²	1270	8.1	17	438	451	11.1	2.52	112	.247	.310	22	48	106	101	.964	242	136	-.5	5.3	-2.3		8.5
DET	78	20	15	1396¹	1209	7.8	12	504	516	11.4	2.56	103	.240	.316	16	13	99	99	.964	234	95	-.1	1.4	**7.0**		-6.8
WAS	84	14	11	1411¹	1217	7.7	12	537	**637**	11.4	2.75	95	.239	.316	-14	-20	99	91	.961	251	127	-1.0	-2.2	-3.0		3.8
NY	87	10	6	1411¹	1280	8.2	28	427	571	11.1	2.66	101	.252	.314	0	3	101	**102**	.965	225	129	.6	.3	-4.3		-2.1
STL	66	12	12	1385¹	1320	8.6	19	537	429	12.3	3.20	81	.257	.332	-84	-96	98	94	.957	281	**139**	-3.4	-10.7	-2.0		-3.9
PHI	80	8	8	1365²	1310	8.6	23	562	516	12.5	3.27	84	.261	.338	-92	-79	103	97	.961	251	106	-1.4	-8.8	.8		-12.1
TOT	661	128	101	11232		8.0				11.4	2.66		.248	.318					.964	1871	965					

Runs
Bush-Det ... 112
Cobb-Det ... 107
Chapman-Cle ... 98
Jackson-Chi ... 91
E.Collins-Chi ... 91

Hits
Cobb-Det ... 225
Sisler-StL ... 190
Speaker-Cle ... 184
Veach-Det ... 182

Doubles
Cobb-Det ... 44
Speaker-Cle ... 42
Veach-Det ... 31
Sisler-StL ... 30
Roth-Cle ... 30

Triples
Cobb-Det ... 24
Jackson-Chi ... 17
Judge-Was ... 15
Chapman-Cle ... 13

Home Runs
Pipp-NY ... 9
Veach-Det ... 8
Bodie-Phi ... 7

Total Bases
Cobb-Det ... 335
Veach-Det ... 261
Speaker-Cle ... 254
Sisler-StL ... 244
Bodie-Phi ... 233

Runs Batted In
Veach-Det ... 103
Felsch-Chi ... 102
Cobb-Det ... 102
Heilmann-Det ... 86
Jackson-Chi ... 75

Runs Produced
Cobb-Det ... 203
Veach-Det ... 174
Felsch-Chi ... 171
Jackson-Chi ... 161
E.Collins-Chi ... 158

Bases On Balls
Graney-Cle ... 94
E.Collins-Chi ... 89
Hooper-Bos ... 80
Bush-Det ... 80
Leibold-Chi ... 74

Batting Average
Cobb-Det ... .383
Sisler-StL ... .353
Speaker-Cle ... .352
Veach-Det ... .319
Felsch-Chi ... .308

On Base Percentage
Cobb-Det ... .444
Speaker-Cle ... .432
Veach-Det ... .393
Sisler-StL ... .390
E.Collins-Chi ... .389

Slugging Average
Cobb-Det ... .570
Speaker-Cle ... .486
Veach-Det ... .457
Sisler-StL ... .453
Jackson-Chi ... .429

Production
Cobb-Det ... 1.014
Speaker-Cle ... .918
Veach-Det ... .850
Sisler-StL ... .843
Jackson-Chi ... .805

Adjusted Production
Cobb-Det ... 210
Speaker-Cle ... 168
Sisler-StL ... 163
Veach-Det ... 160
Jackson-Chi ... 142

Batter Runs
Cobb-Det ... 74.4
Speaker-Cle ... 51.2
Veach-Det ... 40.1
Sisler-StL ... 34.0
Jackson-Chi ... 28.8

Adjusted Batter Runs
Cobb-Det ... 74.7
Speaker-Cle ... 46.8
Veach-Det ... 40.3
Sisler-StL ... 36.1
Jackson-Chi ... 27.5

Clutch Hitting Index
Bates-Phi ... 156
Felsch-Chi ... 155
Heilmann-Det ... 142
Schalk-Chi ... 141
Roth-Cle ... 135

Runs Created
Cobb-Det ... 162
Speaker-Cle ... 120
Veach-Det ... 110
Sisler-StL ... 102
Chapman-Cle ... 98

Total Average
Cobb-Det ... 1.253
Speaker-Cle ... 1.056
Veach-Det ... .905
Sisler-StL ... .900
E.Collins-Chi ... .873

Stolen Bases
Cobb-Det ... 55
E.Collins-Chi ... 53
Chapman-Cle ... 52
Roth-Cle ... 51
Sisler-StL ... 37

Stolen Base Average

Stolen Base Runs

Fielding Runs
Chapman-Cle ... 24.4
Felsch-Chi ... 19.1
Wambsganss-Cle ... 15.3
Pratt-StL ... 14.8
Ainsmith-Was ... 14.6

Total Player Rating
Cobb-Det ... 8.5
Chapman-Cle ... 5.6
Speaker-Cle ... 5.1
Veach-Det ... 3.9
Sisler-StL ... 3.8

Wins
Cicotte-Chi ... 28
Ruth-Bos ... 24
Johnson-Was ... 23
Bagby-Cle ... 23
Mays-Bos ... 22

Win Percentage
Russell-Chi ... .750
Mays-Bos ... .710
Cicotte-Chi ... .700
Williams-Chi ... .680
Ruth-Bos ... .649

Games
Danforth-Chi ... 50
Cicotte-Chi ... 49
Bagby-Cle ... 49
Sothoron-StL ... 48

Complete Games
Ruth-Bos ... 35
Johnson-Was ... 30
Cicotte-Chi ... 29
Mays-Bos ... 27

Shutouts
Coveleski-Cle ... 9
Johnson-Was ... 8
Bagby-Cle ... 8
Cicotte-Chi ... 7

Saves
Danforth-Chi ... 9
Bagby-Cle ... 7
Boland-Det ... 6
Coumbe-Cle ... 5

Innings Pitched
Cicotte-Chi ... 346.2
Johnson-Was ... 328.0
Ruth-Bos ... 326.1
Bagby-Cle ... 320.2
Coveleski-Cle ... 298.1

Fewest Hits/Game
Coveleski-Cle ... 6.09
Cicotte-Chi ... 6.39
Ruth-Bos ... 6.73
Johnson-Was ... 6.80
Mays-Bos ... 7.16

Fewest BB/Game
Russell-Chi ... 1.52
Mogridge-NY ... 1.79
Cicotte-Chi ... 1.82
Johnson-Was ... 1.87
Bagby-Cle ... 2.05

Strikeouts
Johnson-Was ... 188
Cicotte-Chi ... 150
Leonard-Bos ... 144
Coveleski-Cle ... 133
Ruth-Bos ... 128

Strikeouts/Game
Johnson-Was ... 5.16
Harper-Was ... 4.97
Bush-Phi ... 4.67
Leonard-Bos ... 4.40
Danforth-Chi ... 4.11

Ratio
Cicotte-Chi ... 8.28
Coveleski-Cle ... 8.96
Johnson-Was ... 9.05
Russell-Chi ... 9.65
Mays-Bos ... 9.90

Earned Run Average
Cicotte-Chi ... 1.53
Mays-Bos ... 1.74
Coveleski-Cle ... 1.81
Faber-Chi ... 1.92
Russell-Chi ... 1.95

Adjusted ERA
Cicotte-Chi ... 173
Coveleski-Cle ... 156
Mays-Bos ... 148
Bagby-Cle ... 144
Faber-Chi ... 138

Opponents' Batting Avg.
Coveleski-Cle ... .194
Cicotte-Chi ... .203
Ruth-Bos ... .211
Johnson-Was ... .211
Mays-Bos ... .221

Opponents' On Base Pct.
Cicotte-Chi ... .248
Coveleski-Cle ... .261
Johnson-Was ... .263
Russell-Chi ... .279
Mays-Bos ... .282

Starter Runs
Cicotte-Chi ... 43.5
Mays-Bos ... 29.4
Coveleski-Cle ... 28.2
Bagby-Cle ... 24.8
Ruth-Bos ... 23.5

Adjusted Starter Runs
Cicotte-Chi ... 43.3
Coveleski-Cle ... 33.8
Bagby-Cle ... 30.9
Mays-Bos ... 26.8
Ruth-Bos ... 20.5

Clutch Pitching Index
Faber-Chi ... 136
Ayers-Was ... 128
James-Det ... 127
Morton-Cle ... 117
Mitchell-Det ... 116

Relief Runs

Adjusted Relief Runs

Relief Ranking

Total Pitcher Index
Cicotte-Chi ... 5.0
Mays-Bos ... 4.9
Ruth-Bos ... 4.6
Bagby-Cle ... 3.6
Coveleski-Cle ... 3.0

Total Baseball Ranking
Cobb-Det ... 8.5
Chapman-Cle ... 5.6
Speaker-Cle ... 5.1
Cicotte-Chi ... 5.0
Mays-Bos ... 4.9

TEAM	G	W	L	PCT	GB	R	OR	AB	H	2B	3B	HR	BB	SO	AVG	OBP	SLG	PRO	PRO+	BR	/A	PF	CHI	RC	SB	CS	SBA	SBR
CHI	131	84	45	.651		538	393	4325	1147	164	53	21	358	343	.265	.325	.342	.667	106	48	37	102	102	528	159			
NY	124	71	53	.573	10.5	480	415	4164	1081	150	53	13	271	365	.260	.310	.330	.640	103	1	10	98	107	459	130			
CIN	129	68	60	.531	15.5	530	496	4265	1185	165	84	15	304	303	.278	.330	.366	.696	120	86	94	98	96	551	128			
PIT	126	65	60	.520	17	466	412	4091	1016	107	72	15	371	285	.248	.315	.321	.636	96	1	-15	104	102	467	200			
BRO	126	57	69	.452	25.5	360	463	4212	1052	121	62	10	212	326	.250	.291	.315	.606	90	-53	-51	100	91	411	113			
PHI	125	55	68	.447	26	430	454	4192	1022	158	28	25	346	400	.244	.305	.313	.618	88	-29	-60	107	101	432	97			
BOS	124	53	71	.427	28.5	424	469	4162	1014	107	59	13	350	438	.244	.307	.307	.614	97	-32	-13	96	100	426	83			
STL	131	51	78	.395	33	454	527	4369	1066	147	64	27	329	461	.244	.301	.325	.626	99	-21	-4	97	100	461	119			
TOT	508					3682		33780	8583	1119	475	139	2541	2921	.254	.311	.328	.638						1029				

TEAM	CG	SH	SV	IP	H	H/G	HR	BB	SO	RAT	ERA	ERA+	OAV	OOB	PR	/A	PF	CPI	FA	E	DP	FW	PW	BW	SBW	DIF
CHI	92	23	8	1197	1050	7.9	13	296	472	10.3	2.18	128	.239	.291	77	80	101	104	.966	188	91	.5	8.9	4.1		5.9
NY	74	18	11	1111²	1002	8.1	20	228	330	10.1	2.64	100	.243	.287	15	-1	95	87	.971	152	78	2.1	-.1	1.1		5.9
CIN	84	14	6	1142¹	1136	9.0	19	381	321	12.1	3.00	89	.268	.332	-30	-42	97	109	.964	192	127	.0	-4.7	10.5		-1.9
PIT	85	10	7	1140¹	1005	7.9	13	299	367	10.5	2.48	116	.243	.300	36	51	104	95	.966	179	108	.6	5.7	-1.7		-2.1
BRO	85	17	2	1131¹	1024	8.1	22	320	395	10.9	2.81	99	.248	.307	-6	-4	101	95	.963	193	74	-.3	-.4	-5.7		.4
PHI	78	10	6	1139²	1086	8.6	22	369	312	11.7	3.15	95	.258	.323	-49	-20	109	96	.961	211	91	-1.5	-2.2	-6.7		4.0
BOS	96	13	0	1117¹	1111	8.9	14	277	340	11.4	2.90	93	.266	.316	-17	-27	97	102	.965	184	89	.0	-3.0	-1.5		-4.6
STL	72	3	5	1193	1148	8.7	16	352	361	11.6	2.96	91	.261	.321	-27	-34	98	101	.962	220	116	-1.5	-3.8	-.4		-7.7
TOT	666	108	45	9172²		8.4				11.1	2.76		.254	.311					.965	1519	774					

Runs
Groh-Cin 86
Burns-NY 80
Flack-Chi 74
Hollocher-Chi 72

Hits
Hollocher-Chi 161
Groh-Cin 158
Roush-Cin 145
Youngs-NY 143
Merkle-Chi 143

Doubles
Groh-Cin 28
Mann-Chi 27
Cravath-Phi 27
Meusel-Phi 25
Merkle-Chi 25

Triples
Daubert-Bro 15
Wickland-Bos 13
S.Magee-Cin 13
L.Magee-Cin 13

Home Runs
Cravath-Phi 8
Williams-Phi 6
Cruise-StL 6

Total Bases
Hollocher-Chi 202
Roush-Cin 198
Groh-Cin 195
Mann-Chi 188
Merkle-Chi 187

Runs Batted In
S.Magee-Cin 76
Cutshaw-Pit 68
Luderus-Phi 67
J.Smith-Bos 65
Merkle-Chi 65

Runs Produced
Burns-NY 127
Paskert-Chi 125
Mann-Chi 122
Groh-Cin 122
S.Magee-Cin 120

Bases On Balls
Carey-Pit 62
Flack-Chi 56
Groh-Cin 54
Cravath-Phi 54
Bancroft-Phi 54

Batting Average
Z.Wheat-Bro ..... .335
Roush-Cin .... .333
Groh-Cin .... .320
Hollocher-Chi ... .316
Daubert-Bro ..... .308

On Base Percentage
Groh-Cin .... .395
Hollocher-Chi ... .379
J.Smith-Bos ..... .373
S.Magee-Cin .... .370
Z.Wheat-Bro .... .369

Slugging Average
Roush-Cin .... .455
Daubert-Bro ...... .429
Hornsby-StL ..... .416
S.Magee-Cin ..... .415
Wickland-Bos .... .398

Production
Roush-Cin .... .823
Groh-Cin .... .791
Daubert-Bro ..... .789
S.Magee-Cin .... .785
Hollocher-Chi ... .775

Adjusted Production
Roush-Cin 153
Groh-Cin 144
S.Magee-Cin 142
Daubert-Bro 141
Wickland-Bos ... 139

Batter Runs
Groh-Cin 26.4
Roush-Cin 24.3
Hollocher-Chi ... 23.0
S.Magee-Cin 19.2
Daubert-Bro 18.2

Adjusted Batter Runs
Groh-Cin 27.4
Roush-Cin 25.2
Hollocher-Chi ... 21.6
S.Magee-Cin 20.0
Daubert-Bro 18.4

Clutch Hitting Index
S.Magee-Cin 170
Konetchy-Bos ... 160
J.Smith-Bos 157
Paulette-StL 142
Luderus-Phi 140

Runs Created
Hollocher-Chi 84
Groh-Cin 83
Roush-Cin 77
Carey-Pit 74
Burns-NY 73

Total Average
Roush-Cin .... .848
Carey-Pit .... .844
Wickland-Bos .... .812
Burns-NY .... .809
S.Magee-Cin .... .804

Stolen Bases
Carey-Pit 58
Burns-NY 40
Hollocher-Chi 26
Cutshaw-Pit 25
Baird-StL 25

Stolen Base Average

Stolen Base Runs

Fielding Runs
Fletcher-NY 22.3
Carey-Pit 18.6
Bancroft-Phi 17.9
Schmidt-Pit 15.8
Myers-Bro 13.0

Total Player Rating
Groh-Cin 3.5
Hornsby-StL 3.5
Fisher-StL 3.5
L.Magee-Cin 3.0
Roush-Cin 3.0

Wins
Vaughn-Chi 22
Hendrix-Chi 20
Tyler-Chi 19
Grimes-Bro 19
Cooper-Pit 19

Win Percentage
Hendrix-Chi ...... .741
Tyler-Chi .... .704
Mayer-Phi-Pit .... .696
Vaughn-Chi ...... .688
Grimes-Bro ...... .679

Games
Grimes-Bro 40
Cooper-Pit 38
Eller-Cin 37

Complete Games
Nehf-Bos 28
Vaughn-Chi 27
Cooper-Pit 26
Tyler-Chi 22
Hendrix-Chi 21

Shutouts
Vaughn-Chi 8
Grimes-Bro 7
Tyler-Chi 6
Perritt-NY 6

Saves
Toney-Cin-NY 3
Oeschger-Phi 3
Cooper-Pit 3
Anderson-NY 3

Innings Pitched
Vaughn-Chi 290.1
Nehf-Bos 284.1
Cooper-Pit 273.1
Grimes-Bro 269.2
Tyler-Chi 269.1

Fewest Hits/Game
Vaughn-Chi 6.70
Grimes-Bro 7.01
Cooper-Pit 7.21
Tyler-Chi 7.28
Jacobs-Pit-Phi ... 7.50

Fewest BB/Game
Sallee-NY .... .82
Perritt-NY 1.47
G.Smith-Cin-NY-Bro 1.50
Toney-Cin-NY 1.54
Demaree-NY 1.58

Strikeouts
Vaughn-Chi 148
Cooper-Pit 117
Grimes-Bro 113
Tyler-Chi 102
Nehf-Bos 96

Strikeouts/Game
Vaughn-Chi 4.59
Cooper-Pit 3.85
Grimes-Bro 3.77
Cheney-Bro 3.72
May-StL 3.60

Ratio
Sallee-NY 9.14
Vaughn-Chi 9.27
Grimes-Bro 9.68
Cooper-Pit 9.68
Tyler-Chi 9.69

Earned Run Average
Vaughn-Chi 1.74
Tyler-Chi 2.00
Cooper-Pit 2.11
Douglas-Chi 2.13
Grimes-Bro 2.14

Adjusted ERA
Vaughn-Chi 160
Tyler-Chi 139
Cooper-Pit 136
Douglas-Chi 131
Grimes-Bro 130

Opponents' Batting Avg.
Vaughn-Chi ...... .208
Grimes-Bro ...... .216
Cooper-Pit .... .223
Tyler-Chi .... .226
Jacobs-Pit-Phi ... .233

Opponents' On Base Pct.
Sallee-NY .... .259
Vaughn-Chi ...... .266
Grimes-Bro ...... .276
Perritt-NY .... .278
Cooper-Pit .... .279

Starter Runs
Vaughn-Chi 33.1
Tyler-Chi 22.7
Cooper-Pit 19.9
Grimes-Bro 18.8
Hamilton-Pit 11.6

Adjusted Starter Runs
Vaughn-Chi 33.8
Cooper-Pit 23.3
Tyler-Chi 23.3
Grimes-Bro 19.4
Hamilton-Pit 12.2

Clutch Pitching Index
Bressler-Cin 123
Mayer-Phi-Pit 117
Schneider-Cin ... 113
Eller-Cin 112
Demaree-NY 112

Relief Runs

Adjusted Relief Runs

Relief Ranking

Total Pitcher Index
Vaughn-Chi 4.4
Tyler-Chi 3.2
Cooper-Pit 2.8
Grimes-Bro 2.7
Hogg-Phi 2.0

Total Baseball Ranking
Vaughn-Chi 4.4
Groh-Cin 3.5
Hornsby-StL 3.5
Fisher-StL 3.5
Tyler-Chi 3.2

TEAM	G	W	L	PCT	GB	R	OR	AB	H	2B	3B	HR	BB	SO	AVG	OBP	SLG	PRO	PRO+	BR	/A	PF	CHI	RC	SB	CS	SBA	SBR
BOS	126	75	51	.595		474	380	3982	990	159	54	15	406	324	.249	.322	.327	.649	103	5	13	98	105	465	110			
CLE	129	73	54	.575	2.5	504	447	4166	1084	176	67	9	491	386	.260	.344	.341	.685	102	68	23	110	93	552	165			
WAS	130	72	56	.563	4	461	412	4472	1144	156	49	4	376	361	.256	.318	.315	.633	98	-21	-12	98	99	492	137			
NY	126	60	63	.488	13.5	493	475	4224	1085	160	45	20	367	370	.257	.320	.330	.650	99	2	-8	102	106	482	88			
STL	123	58	64	.475	15	426	448	4019	1040	152	40	5	397	340	.259	.331	.320	.651	105	11	25	97	93	476	138			
CHI	124	57	67	.460	17	457	446	4132	1057	136	55	8	375	358	.256	.322	.321	.643	98	-5	-10	101	102	469	116			
DET	128	55	71	.437	20	476	557	4262	1063	141	56	13	452	380	.249	.325	.318	.643	103	-2	17	96	101	488	123			
PHI	130	52	76	.406	24	412	538	4278	1039	124	44	22	343	485	.243	.303	.308	.611	88	-59	-64	101	102	431	83			
TOT	508					3703		33535	8502	1204	410	96	3207	3004	.254	.323	.322	.646							960			

TEAM	CG	SH	SV	IP	H	H/G	HR	BB	SO	RAT	ERA	ERA+	OAV	OOB	PR	/A	PF	CPI	FA	E	DP	FW	PW	BW	SBW	DIF
BOS	105	26	2	1120	931	7.5	9	380	392	10.8	2.31	116	.231	.302	58	47	97	95	.971	152	89	2.5	5.2	1.5		2.8
CLE	78	5	13	1161	1126	8.7	9	343	364	11.5	2.64	114	.262	.319	18	46	108	105	.962	207	82	-.7	5.1	2.6		2.5
WAS	75	19	8	1227	1021	7.5	10	395	505	10.6	2.14	127	.231	.298	86	80	98	99	.960	226	95	-1.8	8.9	-1.3		2.2
NY	59	8	13	1157[1]	1103	8.6	25	463	370	12.5	3.00	94	.261	.340	-29	-23	102	107	.970	161	137	1.9	-2.6	-.9		.0
STL	67	8	8	1111[1]	993	8.0	11	402	346	11.5	2.75	99	.246	.319	2	-2	99	95	.963	190	86	-.2	-.2	2.8		-5.4
CHI	76	9	8	1126	1092	8.7	9	300	349	11.3	2.73	100	.261	.314	5	-3	99	97	.967	169	98	1.2	-.3	-1.1		-4.8
DET	74	8	7	1160[2]	1130	8.8	10	437	374	12.4	3.40	78	.263	.335	-81	-99	96	89	.960	212	77	-1.1	-11.0	1.9		2.2
PHI	80	13	9	1155	1106	8.6	13	486	277	12.7	3.23	91	.266	.348	-58	-39	106	103	.959	228	136	-1.9	-4.4	-7.1		1.4
TOT	614	96	68	9218[1]		8.3				11.7	2.77		.254	.323					.964	1545	800					

Runs
Chapman-Cle 84
T.Cobb-Det 83
Hooper-Bos 81
Bush-Det 74
Speaker-Cle 73

Hits
Burns-Phi 178
T.Cobb-Det 161
Sisler-StL 154
Baker-NY 154
Speaker-Cle 150

Doubles
Speaker-Cle 33
Ruth-Bos 26
Hooper-Bos 26
Baker-NY 24

Triples
T.Cobb-Det 14
Veach-Det 13
Hooper-Bos 13
Roth-Cle 12

Home Runs
Walker-Phi 11
Ruth-Bos 11
Burns-Phi 6
Baker-NY 6

Total Bases
Burns-Phi 236
T.Cobb-Det 217
Baker-NY 206
Speaker-Cle 205
Sisler-StL 199

Runs Batted In
Veach-Det 78
Burns-Phi 70
Wood-Cle 66
Ruth-Bos 66
T.Cobb-Det 64

Runs Produced
T.Cobb-Det 144
Veach-Det 134
Speaker-Cle 134
Burns-Phi 125
Hooper-Bos 124

Bases On Balls
Chapman-Cle 84
Bush-Det 79
Hooper-Bos 75
E.Collins-Chi 73
Shotton-Was 67

Batting Average
T.Cobb-Det 382
Burns-Phi 352
Sisler-StL 341
Speaker-Cle 318
Baker-NY 306

On Base Percentage
T.Cobb-Det 440
E.Collins-Chi 407
Speaker-Cle 403
Sisler-StL 400
Hooper-Bos 391

Slugging Average
T.Cobb-Det 515
Burns-Phi 467
Sisler-StL 440
Speaker-Cle 435
Walker-Phi 423

Production
T.Cobb-Det 955
Burns-Phi 857
Sisler-StL 841
Speaker-Cle 839
Hooper-Bos 796

Adjusted Production
T.Cobb-Det 196
Sisler-StL 159
Burns-Phi 157
Hooper-Bos 142
Speaker-Cle 140

Batter Runs
T.Cobb-Det 44.0
Ruth-Bos 34.8
Burns-Phi 32.8
Speaker-Cle 31.3
Sisler-StL 28.8

Adjusted Batter Runs
T.Cobb-Det 45.9
Ruth-Bos 35.4
Burns-Phi 32.3
Sisler-StL 30.3
Speaker-Cle 26.2

Clutch Hitting Index
McInnis-Bos 159
Demmitt-StL 148
Gandil-Chi 147
Roth-Cle 145
Shanks-Was 144

Runs Created
T.Cobb-Det 104
Burns-Phi 93
Speaker-Cle 92
Sisler-StL 90
Hooper-Bos 85

Total Average
T.Cobb-Det 1.131
Sisler-StL 970
Speaker-Cle 931
Roth-Cle 929
Hooper-Bos 875

Stolen Bases
Sisler-StL 45
Roth-Cle 35
T.Cobb-Det 34
Chapman-Cle 30
Speaker-Cle 27

Stolen Base Average

Stolen Base Runs

Fielding Runs
Peckinpaugh-NY .. 25.0
Scott-Bos 17.5
Dugan-Phi 17.0
Gedeon-StL 15.8
J.Collins-Chi 14.1

Total Player Rating
T.Cobb-Det 4.6
Sisler-StL 3.7
Burns-Phi 3.6
Speaker-Cle 3.3
Baker-NY 3.2

Wins
Johnson-Was 23
Coveleski-Cle 22
Mays-Bos 21
Perry-Phi 20
Bagby-Cle 17

Win Percentage
Jones-Bos 762
Johnson-Was 639
Coveleski-Cle 629
Mays-Bos 618
Shaw-Was 571

Games
Mogridge-NY 45
Bagby-Cle 45
Perry-Phi 44
Shaw-Was 41
Ayers-Was 40

Complete Games
Perry-Phi 30
Mays-Bos 30
Johnson-Was 29
Bush-Bos 26
Coveleski-Cle 25

Shutouts
Mays-Bos 8
Johnson-Was 8
Bush-Bos 7
Jones-Bos 5

Saves
Mogridge-NY 7
Bagby-Cle 6
Russell-NY 4
Geary-Phi 4

Innings Pitched
Perry-Phi 332.1
Johnson-Was .. 325.0
Coveleski-Cle .. 311.0
Mays-Bos 293.1
Bush-Bos 272.2

Fewest Hits/Game
Sothoron-StL 6.55
Johnson-Was 6.67
Harper-Was 6.71
Ruth-Bos 6.76
Mays-Bos 7.06

Fewest BB/Game
Cicotte-Chi 1.35
Mogridge-NY 1.62
Benz-Chi 1.64
Enzmann-Cle 1.91
Johnson-Was 1.94

Strikeouts
Johnson-Was 162
Shaw-Was 129
Bush-Bos 125
Morton-Cle 123
Mays-Bos 114

Strikeouts/Game
Morton-Cle 5.16
Shaw-Was 4.81
Johnson-Was 4.49
Bush-Bos 4.13
Love-NY 3.74

Ratio
Johnson-Was 8.83
Ruth-Bos 9.52
Sothoron-StL 9.56
Coveleski-Cle ... 9.87
Mays-Bos 9.88

Earned Run Average
Johnson-Was 1.27
Coveleski-Cle ... 1.82
Sothoron-StL 1.94
Perry-Phi 1.98
Bush-Bos 2.11

Adjusted ERA
Johnson-Was 214
Coveleski-Cle ... 164
Perry-Phi 148
Sothoron-StL 141
Mogridge-NY 129

Opponents' Batting Avg.
Sothoron-StL 205
Johnson-Was 210
Harper-Was 212
Ruth-Bos 214
Mays-Bos 221

Opponents' On Base Pct.
Johnson-Was 260
Sothoron-StL 274
Ruth-Bos 277
Coveleski-Cle 279
Mays-Bos 284

Starter Runs
Johnson-Was 54.1
Coveleski-Cle ... 32.8
Perry-Phi 29.4
Bush-Bos 20.0
Sothoron-StL 19.4

Adjusted Starter Runs
Johnson-Was 52.3
Coveleski-Cle ... 40.6
Perry-Phi 35.1
Sothoron-StL 18.5
Bush-Bos 17.1

Clutch Pitching Index
Perry-Phi 125
Mogridge-NY 123
Coumbe-Cle 119
Russell-NY 119
Shellenback-Chi .. 116

Relief Runs
Houck-StL 3.1

Adjusted Relief Runs
Houck-StL 2.8

Relief Ranking
Houck-StL 2.3

Total Pitcher Index
Johnson-Was 7.4
Coveleski-Cle 4.5
Mays-Bos 4.0
Perry-Phi 3.6
Bush-Bos 3.1

Total Baseball Ranking
Johnson-Was 7.4
Ruth-Bos 5.4
T.Cobb-Det 4.5
Coveleski-Cle 4.5
Mays-Bos 4.0

TEAM	G	W	L	PCT	GB	R	OR	AB	H	2B	3B	HR	BB	SO	AVG	OBP	SLG	PRO	PRO+	BR	/A	PF	CHI	RC	SB	CS	SBA	SBR
CIN	140	96	44	.686		577	401	4577	1204	135	83	20	405	368	.263	.327	.342	.669	110	43	56	97	104	560	143			
NY	140	87	53	.621	9	605	470	4664	1254	204	64	40	328	407	.269	.322	.366	.688	113	64	70	99	106	587	157			
CHI	140	75	65	.536	21	454	407	4581	1174	166	58	21	298	359	.256	.308	.332	.640	98	-14	-17	101	93	505	150			
PIT	139	71	68	.511	24.5	472	466	4538	1132	130	82	17	344	381	.249	.306	.325	.631	91	-25	-45	104	100	498	196			
BRO	141	69	71	.493	27	525	513	4844	1272	167	66	25	258	405	.263	.304	.340	.644	97	-13	-24	102	104	525	112			
BOS	140	57	82	.410	38.5	465	563	4746	1201	142	62	24	355	481	.253	.311	.324	.635	100	-17	4	96	92	520	145			
STL	138	54	83	.394	40.5	463	552	4588	1175	163	52	18	304	418	.256	.305	.326	.631	101	-28	2	94	99	491	148			
PHI	138	47	90	.343	47.5	510	699	4746	1191	208	50	42	323	469	.251	.303	.342	.645	92	-9	-45	107	101	521	114			
TOT	558					4071		37284	9603	1315	517	207	2615	3288	.258	.311	.337	.648							1165			

TEAM	CG	SH	SV	IP	H	H/G	HR	BB	SO	RAT	ERA	ERA+	OAV	OOB	PR	/A	PF	CPI	FA	E	DP	FW	PW	BW	SBW	DIF
CIN	89	23	9	1274	1104	7.8	21	298	407	10.0	2.23	124	.239	.288	96	75	95	104	.974	151	98	2.7	8.3	6.2		8.7
NY	72	11	13	1256	1153	8.3	34	305	340	10.6	2.70	104	.247	.296	29	14	96	96	.964	216	96	-1.0	1.6	7.8		8.7
CHI	80	21	5	1265	1127	8.0	14	294	495	10.3	2.21	130	.242	.291	98	93	99	106	.969	185	87	.7	10.3	-1.9		-4.2
PIT	91	17	4	1249	1113	8.0	23	263	391	10.2	2.88	105	.244	.290	4	19	104	84	.970	165	89	1.8	2.1	-5.0		2.6
BRO	98	12	1	1281	1256	8.8	21	292	476	11.1	2.73	109	.262	.309	25	33	102	106	.963	219	84	-1.1	3.7	-2.7		-.9
BOS	79	5	9	1270[1]	1313	9.3	29	337	374	11.8	3.17	90	.276	.327	-36	-45	98	107	.966	204	111	-.4	-5.0	.4		-7.6
STL	55	6	8	1217[1]	1146	8.5	25	415	414	11.9	3.23	86	.256	.326	-44	-60	96	97	.963	214	112	-1.1	-6.7	.2		-7.0
PHI	93	6	2	1252	1391	10.0	40	408	397	13.3	4.14	78	.294	.356	-171	-129	111	100	.963	218	112	-1.3	-14.3	-5.0		-.8
TOT	657	101	51	10064[2]		8.6				11.2	2.91		.258	.311					.967	1572	789					

Runs		Hits		Doubles		Triples		Home Runs		Total Bases	
Burns-NY	86	Olson-Bro	164	Youngs-NY	31	Southworth-Pit	14	Cravath-Phi	12	Myers-Bro	223
Groh-Cin	79	Hornsby-StL	163	Luderus-Phi	30	Myers-Bro	14	Kauff-NY	10	Hornsby-StL	220
Daubert-Cin	79	Roush-Cin	162	Burns-NY	30			Williams-Phi	9	Z.Wheat-Bro	219
Rath-Cin	77	Burns-NY	162	Kauff-NY	27			Hornsby-StL	8	Roush-Cin	217
				Meusel-Phi	26			Doyle-NY	7	Burns-NY	216

Runs Batted In		Runs Produced		Bases On Balls		Batting Average		On Base Percentage		Slugging Average	
Myers-Bro	73	Roush-Cin	140	Burns-NY	82	Roush-Cin	.321	Burns-NY	.396	Myers-Bro	.436
Roush-Cin	71	Groh-Cin	137	Rath-Cin	64	Hornsby-StL	.318	Groh-Cin	.392	Groh-Cin	.431
Hornsby-StL	71	Hornsby-StL	131	Groh-Cin	56	Youngs-NY	.311	Hornsby-StL	.384	Roush-Cin	.431
Kauff-NY	67			Luderus-Phi	54	Groh-Cin	.310	Youngs-NY	.384	Hornsby-StL	.430
Groh-Cin	63			Boeckel-Pit-Bos	53	Stock-StL	.307	Roush-Cin	.380	Kauff-NY	.422

Production		Adjusted Production		Batter Runs		Adjusted Batter Runs		Clutch Hitting Index		Runs Created	
Groh-Cin	.823	Hornsby-StL	154	Cravath-Phi	32.2	Hornsby-StL	32.0	Kopf-Cin	146	Burns-NY	98
Hornsby-StL	.814	Groh-Cin	151	Burns-NY	30.0	Burns-NY	30.7	Zimmerman-NY	141	Hornsby-StL	90
Roush-Cin	.811	Roush-Cin	147	Hornsby-StL	28.5	Cravath-Phi	30.4	Merkle-Chi	140	Roush-Cin	88
Burns-NY	.801	Burns-NY	142	Groh-Cin	27.4	Groh-Cin	28.7	Neale-Cin	138	Youngs-NY	85
Youngs-NY	.799	Youngs-NY	142	Roush-Cin	26.9	Roush-Cin	28.4	Deal-Chi	127	Groh-Cin	83

Total Average		Stolen Bases		Stolen Base Average	Stolen Base Runs	Fielding Runs		Total Player Rating	
Burns-NY	.909	Burns-NY	40			Maranville-Bos	28.7	Maranville-Bos	4.7
Groh-Cin	.887	Cutshaw-Pit	36			Fletcher-NY	24.0	Hornsby-StL	4.3
Youngs-NY	.846	Bigbee-Pit	31			Bigbee-Pit	17.9	Stock-StL	4.3
Hornsby-StL	.837	Smith-StL	30			Killefer-Chi	17.4	Groh-Cin	3.4
Roush-Cin	.833					Stock-StL	16.8	Roush-Cin	3.2

Wins		Win Percentage		Games		Complete Games		Shutouts		Saves	
J.Barnes-NY	25	Ruether-Cin	.760	Tuero-StL	45	Cooper-Pit	27	Alexander-Chi	9	Tuero-StL	4
Vaughn-Chi	21	Sallee-Cin	.750	Meadows-StL-Phi	40	Pfeffer-Bro	26	Eller-Cin	7		
Sallee-Cin	21	J.Barnes-NY	.735	Vaughn-Chi	38	Vaughn-Chi	25	Adams-Pit	6		
		Eller-Cin	.679	Eller-Cin	38	Rudolph-Bos	24	Fisher-Cin	5		
		Adams-Pit	.630	J.Barnes-NY	38						

Innings Pitched		Fewest Hits/Game		Fewest BB/Game		Strikeouts		Strikeouts/Game		Ratio	
Vaughn-Chi	306.2	Alexander-Chi	6.89	Adams-Pit	.79	Vaughn-Chi	141	Eller-Cin	4.97	Adams-Pit	8.17
J.Barnes-NY	295.2	Cooper-Pit	7.19	Sallee-Cin	.79	Eller-Cin	137	Alexander-Chi	4.63	Alexander-Chi	8.35
Cooper-Pit	286.2	Ruether-Cin	7.23	J.Barnes-NY	1.07	Alexander-Chi	121	Meadows-StL-Phi	4.17	J.Barnes-NY	9.13
Rudolph-Bos	273.2	Carlson-Pit	7.28	Cadore-Bro	1.40	Meadows-StL-Phi	116	Vaughn-Chi	4.14	Fisher-Cin	9.29
Nehf-Bos-NY	270.2	Fisher-Cin	7.28	Alexander-Chi	1.46	Cooper-Pit	106	Grimes-Bro	4.07	Miller-Pit	9.33

Earned Run Average		Adjusted ERA		Opponents' Batting Avg.		Opponents' On Base Pct.		Starter Runs		Adjusted Starter Runs	
Alexander-Chi	1.72	Alexander-Chi	167	Alexander-Chi	.211	Adams-Pit	.241	Vaughn-Chi	38.1	Vaughn-Chi	37.0
Vaughn-Chi	1.79	Vaughn-Chi	161	Adams-Pit	.220	Alexander-Chi	.245	Alexander-Chi	31.0	Adams-Pit	30.3
Ruether-Cin	1.82	Ruether-Cin	152	Ruether-Cin	.223	J.Barnes-NY	.260	Ruether-Cin	29.4	Alexander-Chi	30.1
Toney-NY	1.84	Toney-NY	152	Cooper-Pit	.225	Fisher-Cin	.271	Adams-Pit	27.1	Ruether-Cin	25.7
Adams-Pit	1.98	Adams-Pit	152	Nehf-Bos-NY	.225	Miller-Pit	.272	Rudolph-Bos	22.5	Rudolph-Bos	20.8

Clutch Pitching Index		Relief Runs	Adjusted Relief Runs	Relief Ranking	Total Pitcher Index		Total Baseball Ranking	
Rudolph-Bos	141				Alexander-Chi	4.3	Maranville-Bos	4.7
Smith-Bro	141				Vaughn-Chi	4.1	Hornsby-StL	4.3
Martin-Chi	122				Ruether-Cin	3.3	Alexander-Chi	4.3
Jacobs-Phi-StL	122				Adams-Pit	3.0	Stock-StL	4.3
Toney-NY	120				Rudolph-Bos	2.8	Vaughn-Chi	4.1

TEAM	G	W	L	PCT	GB	R	OR	AB	H	2B	3B	HR	BB	SO	AVG	OBP	SLG	PRO	PRO+	BR	/A	PF	CHI	RC	SB	CS	SBA	SBR
CHI	140	88	52	.629		667	534	4675	1343	218	70	25	427	358	.287	.351	.380	.731	111	69	67	100	103	674	150			
CLE	139	84	55	.604	3.5	636	537	4565	1268	254	71	25	498	367	.278	.354	.381	.735	106	78	43	106	98	667	113			
NY	141	80	59	.576	7.5	578	506	4775	1275	193	49	45	386	479	.267	.326	.356	.682	96	-20	-24	101	104	590	101			
DET	140	80	60	.571	8	618	578	4665	1319	222	84	23	429	427	.283	.346	.355	.681	95	60	73	98	97	659	121			
STL	140	67	72	.482	20.5	533	567	4672	1234	187	73	31	391	443	.264	.336	.344	.680	103	-22	-36	103	97	575	74			
BOS	138	66	71	.482	20.5	564	552	4548	1188	181	49	33	471	411	.261	.336	.344	.680	103	-11	22	94	102	577	108			
WAS	142	56	84	.400	32	533	570	4757	1238	177	63	24	416	511	.260	.325	.339	.664	93	-47	-42	99	100	571	142			
PHI	140	36	104	.257	52	457	742	4730	1156	175	71	35	349	565	.244	.300	.334	.634	82	-108	-115	101	100	505	103			
TOT	560					4586		37387	10021	1607	530	241	3367	3561	.268	.333	.359	.692							912			

TEAM	CG	SH	SV	IP	H	H/G	HR	BB	SO	RAT	ERA	ERA+	OAV	OOB	PR	/A	PF	CPI	FA	E	DP	FW	PW	BW	SBW	DIF
CHI	88	14	3	1265²	1245	8.9	25	342	468	11.5	3.04	105	.262	.315	26	19	99	93	.969	176	116	1.6	2.0	7.0		7.3
CLE	80	10	10	1245	1242	9.0	19	362	432	11.8	2.94	114	.264	.321	39	53	104	98	.965	201	102	-.0	5.5	4.5		4.5
NY	85	14	7	1287	1143	8.0	47	433	500	11.3	2.82	113	.240	.309	-11	-14	99	98	.964	205	81	-.2	-1.5	7.6		4.0
DET	85	10	4	1256	1254	9.0	35	436	428	12.4	3.30	97	.266	.333	13	24	103	99	.968	193	108	.7	5.5	-2.5		6.8
STL	78	14	4	1256	1255	9.0	35	421	415	12.3	3.13	106	.263	.328	-12	-41	94	101	.975	140	118	3.8	-4.3	2.3		-4.3
BOS	89	15	8	1224¹	1251	9.2	16	421	381	12.5	3.31	91	.275	.341	-12	28	99	99	.960	227	86	-1.4	2.9	-4.4		-11.1
WAS	68	13	10	1274¹	1237	8.7	20	451	536	12.2	3.01	106	.259	.328	30	28	99	99	.956	257	96	-3.5	-12.4	-12.0		-6.1
PHI	72	1	3	1239¹	1371	10.0	44	503	417	13.8	4.26	80	.292	.364	-143	-118	106	96	.963	215	98	-.8	2.5	-3.8		-.4
TOT	645	91	49	10047²		9.0				12.2	3.22		.268	.333					.965	1614	805					

Runs
Ruth-Bos 103
Sisler-StL 96
Cobb-Det 92
Weaver-Chi 89
Peckinpaugh-NY ... 89

Hits
Veach-Det 191
Cobb-Det 191
Jackson-Chi 181
Sisler-StL 180
Rice-Was 179

Doubles
Veach-Det 45
Speaker-Cle 38
Cobb-Det 36
O'Neill-Cle 35

Triples
Veach-Det 17
Sisler-StL 15
Heilmann-Det 15
Jackson-Chi 14
Cobb-Det 13

Home Runs
Ruth-Bos 29
C.Walker-Phi 10
Sisler-StL 10
Baker-NY 10
Smith-Cle 9

Total Bases
Ruth-Bos 284
Veach-Det 279
Sisler-StL 271
Jackson-Chi 261

Runs Batted In
Ruth-Bos 114
Veach-Det 101
Jackson-Chi 96
Heilmann-Det 93
Lewis-NY 89

Runs Produced
Ruth-Bos 188
Veach-Det 185
Sisler-StL 169
Jackson-Chi 168
E.Collins-Chi ... 163

Bases On Balls
Graney-Cle 105
Ruth-Bos 101
Judge-Was 81
Hooper-Bos 79
Bush-Det 75

Batting Average
Cobb-Det .... .384
Veach-Det .... .355
Sisler-StL .... .352
Jackson-Chi ..... .351
Tobin-StL .... .327

On Base Percentage
Ruth-Bos .... .456
Cobb-Det .... .429
Jackson-Chi ..... .422
Leibold-Chi ..... .404
E.Collins-Chi ... .400

Slugging Average
Ruth-Bos .... .657
Sisler-StL .... .530
Veach-Det .... .519
Cobb-Det .... .515
Jackson-Chi ..... .506

Production
Ruth-Bos 1.114
Cobb-Det .... .944
Jackson-Chi .... .928
Sisler-StL ..... .921
Veach-Det ...... .916

Adjusted Production
Ruth-Bos 224
Cobb-Det 168
Veach-Det 160
Jackson-Chi 159
Sisler-StL 153

Batter Runs
Ruth-Bos 66.5
Jackson-Chi 41.7
Cobb-Det 41.6
Veach-Det 37.7
Sisler-StL 35.8

Adjusted Batter Runs
Ruth-Bos 69.9
Cobb-Det 43.0
Jackson-Chi 41.5
Veach-Det 39.2
Sisler-StL 34.3

Clutch Hitting Index
Lewis-NY 152
Gardner-Cle 143
Jones-Det 141
Felsch-Chi 140
Veach-Det 135

Runs Created
Ruth-Bos 138
Cobb-Det 115
Jackson-Chi 115
Veach-Det 114
Sisler-StL 110

Total Average
Ruth-Bos 1.358
Cobb-Det 1.056
Sisler-StL 1.000
Jackson-Chi .... .997
Veach-Det ...... .968

Stolen Bases
E.Collins-Chi 33
Sisler-StL 28
Cobb-Det 28
Rice-Was 26

Stolen Base Average

Stolen Base Runs

Fielding Runs
Pratt-NY 28.0
Peckinpaugh-NY . 27.7
Felsch-Chi 21.4
Speaker-Cle 19.1
Young-Det 17.3

Total Player Rating
Ruth-Bos 6.0
Peckinpaugh-NY ... 5.1
Sisler-StL 4.4
Veach-Det 4.2
Pratt-NY 3.8

Wins
Cicotte-Chi 29
Coveleski-Cle 24
Williams-Chi 23
Dauss-Det 21

Win Percentage
Cicotte-Chi ..... .806
Dauss-Det .... .700
Williams-Chi .... .676
Pennock-Bos ..... .667
Coveleski-Cle ... .667

Games
Shaw-Was 45
Russell-NY-Bos ... 44
Kinney-Phi 43
Coveleski-Cle 43

Complete Games
Cicotte-Chi 30
Williams-Chi 27
Johnson-Was 27
Mays-Bos-NY 26
Coveleski-Cle 24

Shutouts
Johnson-Was 7

Saves
Russell-NY-Bos 5
Shawkey-NY 5
Shaw-Was 5
Coveleski-Cle 4

Innings Pitched
Shaw-Was 306.2
Cicotte-Chi ... 306.2
Williams-Chi .. 297.0
Johnson-Was ... 290.1
Coveleski-Cle . 286.0

Fewest Hits/Game
Johnson-Was 7.28
Thormahlen-NY .. 7.39
Shawkey-NY 7.51
Cicotte-Chi 7.51
Mays-Bos-NY 7.68

Fewest BB/Game
Cicotte-Chi 1.44
Johnson-Was 1.58
Bagby-Cle 1.64
Williams-Chi ... 1.76
Coveleski-Cle .. 1.89

Strikeouts
Johnson-Was 147
Shaw-Was 128
Williams-Chi ... 125
Shawkey-NY 122
Coveleski-Cle .. 118

Strikeouts/Game
Erickson-Det-Was 5.52
Russell-NY-Bos . 4.80
Johnson-Was 4.56
Kinney-Phi 4.31
Leonard-Det 4.22

Ratio
Cicotte-Chi 9.01
Johnson-Was 9.08
Williams-Chi .. 10.12
Thormahlen-NY . 10.49
Quinn-NY 10.59

Earned Run Average
Johnson-Was 1.49
Cicotte-Chi 1.82
Weilman-StL 2.07
Mays-Bos-NY 2.10
Sothoron-StL ... 2.20

Adjusted ERA
Johnson-Was 215
Cicotte-Chi 175
Weilman-StL 160
Sothoron-StL ... 151
Mays-Bos-NY 147

Opponents' Batting Avg.
Johnson-Was .... .219
Cicotte-Chi .... .228
Thormahlen-NY .. .228
Shawkey-NY ..... .231
Mays-Bos-NY .... .233

Opponents' On Base Pct.
Johnson-Was .... .259
Cicotte-Chi .... .261
Williams-Chi ... .289
Morton-Cle ..... .293
Quinn-NY .... .295

Starter Runs
Johnson-Was 56.0
Cicotte-Chi 47.8
Mays-Bos-NY 33.3
Sothoron-StL ... 30.7
Coveleski-Cle .. 19.4

Adjusted Starter Runs
Johnson-Was 55.3
Cicotte-Chi 46.3
Sothoron-StL ... 33.4
Mays-Bos-NY 29.4
Coveleski-Cle .. 23.2

Clutch Pitching Index
Weilman-StL 119
Sothoron-StL ... 114
Ehmke-Det 113
Harper-Was 107
Pennock-Bos 107

Relief Runs
Phillips-Cle 1.7

Adjusted Relief Runs
Phillips-Cle 2.4

Relief Ranking
Phillips-Cle 2.0

Total Pitcher Index
Johnson-Was 6.7
Cicotte-Chi 4.8
Mays-Bos-NY 3.9
Coveleski-Cle ... 3.2
Sothoron-StL 2.6

Total Baseball Ranking
Ruth-Bos 7.4
Johnson-Was 6.6
Peckinpaugh-NY .. 5.1
Cicotte-Chi 4.8
Sisler-StL 4.4

1964   1920 National League

TEAM	G	W	L	PCT	GB	R	OR	AB	H	2B	3B	HR	BB	SO	AVG	OBP	SLG	PRO	PRO+	BR	/A	PF	CHI	RC	SB	CS	SBA	SBR
BRO	155	93	61	.604		660	528	5399	1493	205	99	28	359	391	.277	.324	.367	.691	100	19	-1	103	103	637	70	80	47	-27
NY	155	86	68	.558	7	682	543	5309	1427	210	76	46	432	545	.269	.327	.363	.690	104	23	30	99	107	628	131	113	54	-29
CIN	154	82	71	.536	10.5	639	569	5176	1432	169	76	18	382	367	.277	.332	.349	.681	102	11	19	99	104	602	158	128	55	-29
PIT	155	79	75	.513	14	530	552	5219	1342	162	90	16	374	405	.257	.310	.332	.642	86	-67	-86	103	99	544	181	117	61	-16
STL	155	75	79	.487	18	675	682	5495	1589	238	96	32	373	484	.289	.337	.385	.722	117	83	106	96	94	704	126	114	53	-31
CHI	154	75	79	.487	18	619	635	5117	1350	223	67	34	428	421	.264	.326	.354	.680	98	7	-5	102	101	589	115	129	47	-43
BOS	153	62	90	.408	30	523	670	5218	1358	168	86	23	385	488	.260	.315	.339	.654	97	-45	-19	96	93	557	88	98	47	-32
PHI	153	62	91	.405	30.5	565	714	5264	1385	229	54	64	283	531	.263	.305	.364	.669	93	-30	-58	105	99	577	100	83	55	-20
TOT	617					4893		42197	11376	1604	644	261	3016	3632	.270	.322	.357	.679							969	862	53	-227

TEAM	CG	SH	SV	IP	H	H/G	HR	BB	SO	RAT	ERA	ERA+	OAV	OOB	PR	/A	PF	CPI	FA	E	DP	FW	PW	BW	SBW	DIF
BRO	89	17	10	1427^1	1381	8.7	25	327	553	10.9	2.62	122	.259	.304	81	91	102	102	.966	226	118	-.2	9.7	-.1	.1	6.4
NY	86	18	9	1408^2	1379	8.8	44	297	380	10.8	2.80	107	.261	.303	51	30	96	99	.969	210	137	-.2	3.2	3.2	-.0	1.9
CIN	90	12	9	1391^2	1327	8.6	26	393	435	11.3	2.90	105	.256	.313	36	22	97	97	.968	200	125	.8	2.4	2.0	-.0	-.1
PIT	92	17	10	1415^1	1389	8.8	25	280	444	10.8	2.89	111	.261	.301	39	51	103	91	.971	186	119	1.3	5.5	-.6	.1	2.2
STL	72	9	12	1426^2	1488	9.4	30	479	529	12.8	3.43	87	.277	.343	-47	-72	95	103	.961	256	136	2.2	5.5	-9.2	1.3	2.2
CHI	95	13	9	1388^2	1459	9.5	37	382	508	12.1	3.27	98	.276	.328	-21	-10	102	101	.965	239	125	-2.0	-7.7	11.4	-.3	-3.4
BOS	93	14	6	1386^1	1480	9.6	39	415	368	12.4	3.54	86	.280	.337	-62	-75	97	100	.964	225	112	-.2	-1.1	-.5	-1.6	1.4
PHI	77	8	11	1380^2	1480	9.6	35	444	419	12.8	3.63	94	.284	.345	-76	-35	109	102	.964	232	135	-1.1	-8.0	-2.0	-.4	-2.4
TOT	694	108	76	11225^1		9.1				11.7	3.13		.270	.322					.966	1774	1007	-.7	-3.7	-6.2	.9	-4.7

Runs
Burns-NY 115
Bancroft-Phi-NY .. 102
Daubert-Cin 97
Hornsby-StL 96
Youngs-NY 92

Hits
Hornsby-StL 218
Youngs-NY 204
Stock-StL 204
Roush-Cin 196
Williams-Phi 192

Doubles
Hornsby-StL 44
Bancroft-Phi-NY .. 36
Williams-Phi 36
Myers-Bro 36
Burns-NY 35

Triples
Myers-Bro 22
Hornsby-StL 20
Roush-Cin 16
Maranville-Bos ... 15
Bigbee-Pit 15

Home Runs
Williams-Phi 15
Meusel-Phi 14
Kelly-NY 11
Robertson-Chi 10
McHenry-StL 10

Total Bases
Hornsby-StL 329
Williams-Phi 293
Youngs-NY 277
Wheat-Bro 270
Myers-Bro 269

Runs Batted In
Kelly-NY 94
Hornsby-StL 94
Roush-Cin 90
Duncan-Cin 83
Myers-Bro 80

Runs Produced
Hornsby-StL 181
Roush-Cin 167
Youngs-NY 164
Stock-StL 161
Myers-Bro 159

Bases On Balls
Burns-NY 76
Youngs-NY 75
Paskert-Chi 64
Hornsby-StL 60
Groh-Cin 60

Batting Average
Hornsby-StL ..... .370
Youngs-NY .... .351
Roush-Cin .... .339
Wheat-Bro .... .328
Williams-Phi .... .325

On Base Percentage
Hornsby-StL ..... .431
Youngs-NY .... .427
Roush-Cin .... .386
Wheat-Bro .... .385
Groh-Cin .... .375

Slugging Average
Hornsby-StL ..... .559
Williams-Phi .... .497
Youngs-NY .... .477
Meusel-Phi ...... .473
Wheat-Bro .... .463

Production
Hornsby-StL ..... .990
Youngs-NY .... .904
Williams-Phi .... .861
Wheat-Bro .... .848
Roush-Cin .... .839

Adjusted Production
Hornsby-StL 190
Youngs-NY 161
Roush-Cin 142
Williams-Phi 139
Wheat-Bro 138

Batter Runs
Hornsby-StL 62.6
Youngs-NY 47.1
Williams-Phi 32.1
Wheat-Bro 31.9
Roush-Cin 29.7

Adjusted Batter Runs
Hornsby-StL 65.2
Youngs-NY 47.9
Roush-Cin 30.7
Wheat-Bro 29.8
Williams-Phi 29.0

Clutch Hitting Index
Whitted-Pit 176
Kopf-Cin 172
Duncan-Cin 153
Kelly-NY 142
Paskert-Chi 138

Runs Created
Hornsby-StL 138
Youngs-NY 118
Williams-Phi 103
Wheat-Bro 102
Roush-Cin 98

Total Average
Hornsby-StL 1.008
Youngs-NY .... .896
Williams-Phi .... .817
Wheat-Bro .... .801
Roush-Cin .... .784

Stolen Bases
Carey-Pit 52
Roush-Cin 36
Frisch-NY 34
Bigbee-Pit 31
Neale-Cin 29

Stolen Base Average
Carey-Pit 83.9
Frisch-NY 75.6
Neale-Cin 70.7
Bigbee-Pit 67.4
Meusel-Phi 60.7

Stolen Base Runs
Carey-Pit 9.6
Frisch-NY 3.6
Neale-Cin 1.5
Tragesser-Phi 1.2
Gowdy-Bos 1.2

Fielding Runs
Bancroft-Phi-NY .. 39.0
Lavan-StL 16.2
Roush-Cin 15.7
Maranville-Bos .. 14.3
Neale-Cin 14.3

Total Player Rating
Hornsby-StL 7.9
Bancroft-Phi-NY .. 5.7
Youngs-NY 3.5
Roush-Cin 3.4
Williams-Phi 2.8

Wins
Alexander-Chi 27
Cooper-Pit 24
Grimes-Bro 23
Toney-NY 21
Nehf-NY 21

Win Percentage
Grimes-Bro ...... .676
Alexander-Chi ... .659
Toney-NY .... .656
Pfeffer-Bro ..... .640
Nehf-NY .... .636

Games
Haines-StL 47
Douglas-NY 46
Alexander-Chi 46
Scott-Bos 44
Cooper-Pit 44

Complete Games
Alexander-Chi 33
Cooper-Pit 28
Rixey-Phi 25
Grimes-Bro 25
Vaughn-Chi 24

Shutouts
Adams-Pit 8
Alexander-Chi 7

Saves
Sherdel-StL 6
McQuillan-Bos 5
Alexander-Chi 5
Hubbell-NY-Phi 4
Mamaux-Bro 4

Innings Pitched
Alexander-Chi ... 363.1
Cooper-Pit 327.0
Grimes-Bro 303.2
Haines-StL 301.2
Vaughn-Chi 301.0

Fewest Hits/Game
Luque-Cin 7.28
Ruether-Cin 7.96
Grimes-Bro 8.03
Mamaux-Bro 8.12
Adams-Pit 8.21

Fewest BB/Game
Adams-Pit .... .62
Cooper-Pit 1.43
Nehf-NY 1.44
Benton-NY 1.44
Marquard-Bro 1.66

Strikeouts
Alexander-Chi ... 173
Vaughn-Chi 131
Grimes-Bro 131
Haines-StL 120
Schupp-StL 119

Strikeouts/Game
Mamaux-Bro 4.77
Alexander-Chi ... 4.29
Schupp-StL 4.27
Marquard-Bro 4.22
Sherdel-StL 3.92

Ratio
Adams-Pit 8.86
Alexander-Chi .. 10.03
Luque-Cin 10.05
J.Barnes-NY 10.12
Grimes-Bro 10.14

Earned Run Average
Alexander-Chi ... 1.91
Adams-Pit 2.16
Grimes-Bro 2.22
Cooper-Pit 2.39
Ruether-Cin 2.47

Adjusted ERA
Alexander-Chi ... 168
Adams-Pit 149
Grimes-Bro 144
Cooper-Pit 134
Vaughn-Chi 126

Opponents' Batting Avg.
Luque-Cin .... .225
Grimes-Bro ...... .238
Adams-Pit .... .244
Ponder-Pit ...... .246
Ruether-Cin ..... .247

Opponents' On Base Pct.
Adams-Pit .... .259
Grimes-Bro ...... .282
Alexander-Chi ... .285
Luque-Cin .... .286
Ponder-Pit ...... .286

Starter Runs
Alexander-Chi ... 49.5
Grimes-Bro 30.7
Adams-Pit 28.5
Cooper-Pit 26.8
Vaughn-Chi 19.8

Adjusted Starter Runs
Alexander-Chi ... 52.4
Grimes-Bro 33.0
Adams-Pit 30.9
Cooper-Pit 29.8
Vaughn-Chi 22.2

Clutch Pitching Index
Meadows-Phi 121
Alexander-Chi ... 120
Vaughn-Chi 119
Fillingim-Bos ... 118
Benton-NY 115

Relief Runs

Adjusted Relief Runs

Relief Ranking

Total Pitcher Index
Alexander-Chi 6.8
Grimes-Bro 5.3
Smith-Bro 3.1
Cooper-Pit 2.9
Adams-Pit 2.7

Total Baseball Ranking
Hornsby-StL 7.9
Alexander-Chi 6.8
Bancroft-Phi-NY .. 5.7
Grimes-Bro 5.3
Youngs-NY 3.5

TEAM	G	W	L	PCT	GB	R	OR	AB	H	2B	3B	HR	BB	SO	AVG	OBP	SLG	PRO	PRO+	BR	/A	PF	CHI	RC	SB	CS	SBA	SBR
CLE	154	98	56	.636		857	642	5196	1574	300	95	35	576	379	.303	.376	.417	.793	113	125	102	103	98	827	73	92	44	-33
CHI	154	96	58	.623	2	794	665	5328	1574	263	98	37	471	353	.295	.357	.402	.759	107	49	49	100	100	769	112	96	54	-24
NY	154	95	59	.617	3	838	629	5176	1448	268	71	115	539	626	.280	.350	.426	.776	107	71	46	104	105	773	64	82	44	-30
STL	154	76	77	.497	21.5	797	766	5358	1651	279	83	50	427	339	.308	.363	.419	.782	110	93	71	103	95	822	118	79	60	-12
BOS	154	72	81	.471	25.5	650	698	5199	1397	216	71	22	533	429	.269	.342	.350	.692	93	-70	-38	96	97	637	98	111	47	-37
WAS	153	68	84	.447	29	723	802	5251	1526	233	81	36	433	543	.291	.351	.386	.737	104	7	27	97	98	718	161	114	59	-20
DET	155	61	93	.396	37	652	833	5215	1408	228	72	30	479	391	.270	.334	.359	.693	91	-80	-62	98	100	640	76	66	54	-17
PHI	156	48	106	.312	50	558	834	5256	1324	220	49	44	353	593	.252	.305	.338	.643	74	-188	-195	101	106	543	50	67	43	-25
TOT	617					5869		41979	11902	2007	620	369	3811	3653	.284	.347	.387	.734							752	707	52	-199

TEAM	CG	SH	SV	IP	H	H/G	HR	BB	SO	RAT	ERA	ERA+	OAV	OOB	PR	/A	PF	CPI	FA	E	DP	FW	PW	BW	SBW	DIF
CLE	94	11	7	1377	1448	9.5	31	401	466	12.3	3.41	111	.276	.331	57	58	100	98	.971	184	124	2.1	5.6	9.9	-.8	4.1
CHI	109	9	10	1386²	1467	9.5	45	405	438	12.3	3.59	105	.280	.335	31	24	99	98	.968	198	142	1.2	2.3	4.8	.0	10.7
NY	88	15	11	1368	1414	9.3	48	420	480	12.3	3.32	115	.270	.328	72	75	101	99	.969	194	129	1.4	7.3	4.5	-.5	5.3
STL	84	9	14	1378²	1481	9.7	53	578	444	13.7	4.03	97	.283	.359	-38	-23	103	99	.972	183	131	2.2	-2.9	-3.7	-1.2	1.1
BOS	92	11	6	1395¹	1481	9.6	39	461	481	12.7	3.82	95	.279	.339	-5	-30	96	93	.963	233	119	-1.3	-6.8	2.6	.5	-3.0
WAS	81	10	10	1367	1521	10.0	51	520	418	13.7	4.17	89	.288	.357	-58	-70	98	97	.964	230	95	-.9	-4.9	-6.0	.8	-4.9
DET	74	9	7	1385	1487	9.7	46	561	483	13.7	4.04	92	.284	.359	-38	-51	98	99	.963	232	95	-1.2	-2.2	6.9	1.2	-5.2
PHI	79	6	2	1380¹	1612	10.5	56	461	423	13.8	3.93	102	.302	.362	-21	12	106	110	.959	266	125	-3.3	1.2	-18.9	-.0	-7.9
TOT	701	80	67	11038		9.7				13.1	3.79		.284	.347					.966	1720	960					

Runs
Ruth-NY 158
Speaker-Cle 137
Sisler-StL 137
E.Collins-Chi 117

Hits
Sisler-StL 257
E.Collins-Chi 224
Jackson-Chi 218
Jacobson-StL 216
Speaker-Cle 214

Doubles
Speaker-Cle 50
Sisler-StL 49
Jackson-Chi 42

Triples
Jackson-Chi 20
Sisler-StL 18
Hooper-Bos 17

Home Runs
Ruth-NY 54
Sisler-StL 19
C.Walker-Phi 17
Felsch-Chi 14

Total Bases
Sisler-StL 399
Ruth-NY 388
Jackson-Chi 336
Speaker-Cle 310
Jacobson-StL 305

Runs Batted In
Ruth-NY 137
Sisler-StL 122
Jacobson-StL 122
Jackson-Chi 121
Gardner-Cle 118

Runs Produced
Ruth-NY 241
Sisler-StL 240
Speaker-Cle 236
Jackson-Chi 214
Jacobson-StL 210

Bases On Balls
Ruth-NY 148
Speaker-Cle 97
Hooper-Bos 88
Young-Det 85
Roth-Was 75

Batting Average
Sisler-StL 407
Speaker-Cle 388
Jackson-Chi 382
Ruth-NY 376
E.Collins-Chi 372

On Base Percentage
Ruth-NY 530
Speaker-Cle 483
Sisler-StL 449
Jackson-Chi 444
E.Collins-Chi 438

Slugging Average
Ruth-NY 847
Sisler-StL 632
Jackson-Chi 589
Speaker-Cle 562
Felsch-Chi 540

Production
Ruth-NY 1.378
Sisler-StL 1.082
Speaker-Cle 1.045
Jackson-Chi 1.033
E.Collins-Chi 932

Adjusted Production
Ruth-NY 252
Sisler-StL 179
Jackson-Chi 172
Speaker-Cle 171
E.Collins-Chi 146

Batter Runs
Ruth-NY 113.2
Sisler-StL 73.2
Speaker-Cle 65.7
Jackson-Chi 58.4
E.Collins-Chi 42.3

Adjusted Batter Runs
Ruth-NY 110.5
Sisler-StL 70.7
Speaker-Cle 63.2
Jackson-Chi 58.4
E.Collins-Chi 42.3

Clutch Hitting Index
Gardner-Cle 168
Roth-Was 141
Pratt-NY 138
Jacobson-StL 134
Smith-Cle 133

Runs Created
Ruth-NY 211
Sisler-StL 176
Speaker-Cle 152
Jackson-Chi 145
E.Collins-Chi 133

Total Average
Ruth-NY 1.797
Sisler-StL 1.207
Speaker-Cle 1.165
Jackson-Chi 1.088
E.Collins-Chi .... .982

Stolen Bases
Rice-Was 63
Sisler-StL 42
Roth-Was 24
Menosky-Bos 23
Tobin-StL 21

Stolen Base Average
Sisler-StL 71.2
E.Collins-Chi 70.4
Williams-StL 69.2
Rice-Was 67.7
Roth-Was 66.7

Stolen Base Runs
Sisler-StL 2.4
Burns-Phi-Cle 1.5
Smith-Cle 9
Rice-Was 9
E.Collins-Chi 9

Fielding Runs
Perkins-Phi 23.2
Ward-NY 21.8
Rice-Was 21.4
Pinelli-Det 19.9
Felsch-Chi 17.7

Total Player Rating
Ruth-NY 8.9
Sisler-StL 8.0
E.Collins-Chi 5.6
Speaker-Cle 5.4
Jackson-Chi 4.0

Wins
Bagby-Cle 31
Mays-NY 26
Coveleski-Cle 24
Faber-Chi 23
Williams-Chi 22

Win Percentage
Bagby-Cle 721
Mays-NY 703
Kerr-Chi 700
Cicotte-Chi 677

Games
Bagby-Cle 48
Ayers-Det 46
Mays-NY 45
Kerr-Chi 45
Zachary-Was 44

Complete Games
Bagby-Cle 30
Faber-Chi 28
Cicotte-Chi 28
Mays-NY 26
Coveleski-Cle 26

Shutouts
Mays-NY 6
Shocker-StL 5
Shawkey-NY 5

Saves
Shocker-StL 5
Kerr-Chi 5
Burwell-StL 4

Innings Pitched
Bagby-Cle 339.2
Faber-Chi 319.0
Coveleski-Cle ... 315.0
Mays-NY 312.0
Cicotte-Chi 303.1

Fewest Hits/Game
Coveleski-Cle ... 8.11
Shocker-StL 8.21
Collins-NY 8.22
Shawkey-NY 8.27
Davis-StL 8.35

Fewest BB/Game
Quinn-NY 1.71
Coveleski-Cle ... 1.86
Bagby-Cle 2.09
Cicotte-Chi 2.20
Perry-Phi 2.22

Strikeouts
Coveleski-Cle 133
Williams-Chi 128
Shawkey-NY 126
Faber-Chi 108
Shocker-StL 107

Strikeouts/Game
Ayers-Det 4.44
Shawkey-NY 4.24
Harper-Bos 3.93
Shocker-StL 3.92
Williams-Chi 3.85

Ratio
Coveleski-Cle ... 10.09
Shocker-StL 10.92
Rommel-Phi 10.99
Shawkey-NY ... 11.16
Bagby-Cle 11.18

Earned Run Average
Shawkey-NY 2.45
Coveleski-Cle ... 2.49
Shocker-StL 2.71
Rommel-Phi 2.85
Bagby-Cle 2.89

Adjusted ERA
Shawkey-NY 155
Coveleski-Cle ... 153
Shocker-StL 144
Rommel-Phi 141
Bagby-Cle 131

Opponents' Batting Avg.
Coveleski-Cle 243
Collins-NY 247
Shawkey-NY 248
Shocker-StL 248
Ehmke-Det 253

Opponents' On Base Pct.
Coveleski-Cle 285
Shocker-StL 305
Shawkey-NY 308
Quinn-NY 308
Rommel-Phi 309

Starter Runs
Coveleski-Cle 45.6
Shawkey-NY 39.6
Bagby-Cle 33.9
Shocker-StL 29.4
Faber-Chi 28.2

Adjusted Starter Runs
Coveleski-Cle 45.7
Shawkey-NY 40.3
Bagby-Cle 34.1
Shocker-StL 32.7
Faber-Chi 27.2

Clutch Pitching Index
Naylor-Phi 130
Harper-Bos 128
Davis-StL 117
Oldham-Det 116
Perry-Phi 113

Relief Runs

Adjusted Relief Runs

Relief Ranking

Total Pitcher Index
Coveleski-Cle 5.4
Shawkey-NY 3.8
Shocker-StL 3.5
Mays-NY 3.4
Bagby-Cle 3.3

Total Baseball Ranking
Ruth-NY 8.9
Sisler-StL 8.0
E.Collins-Chi 5.6
Speaker-Cle 5.4
Coveleski-Cle 5.4

1921 National League

TEAM	G	W	L	PCT	GB	R	OR	AB	H	2B	3B	HR	BB	SO	AVG	OBP	SLG	PRO	PRO+	BR	/A	PF	CHI	RC	SB	CS	SBA	SBR
NY	153	94	59	.614		840	637	5278	1575	237	93	75	469	390	.298	.359	.421	.780	112	94	93	100	104	795	137	114	55	-27
PIT	154	90	63	.588	4	692	595	5379	1533	231	104	37	341	371	.285	.330	.387	.717	93	-37	-56	103	102	684	134	93	59	-16
STL	154	87	66	.569	7	809	681	5309	1635	260	88	83	382	452	.308	.358	.437	.795	118	114	129	98	98	816	94	94	50	-28
BOS	153	79	74	.516	15	721	697	5385	1561	209	100	61	377	470	.290	.339	.400	.739	107	6	45	95	100	718	94	100	48	-32
BRO	152	77	75	.507	16.5	667	681	5263	1476	209	85	59	325	400	.280	.325	.386	.711	90	-52	-77	104	104	655	91	73	55	-17
CIN	153	70	83	.458	24	618	649	5112	1421	221	94	20	375	308	.278	.333	.370	.703	96	-56	-24	95	98	623	117	120	49	-37
CHI	153	64	89	.418	30	668	773	5321	1553	234	56	37	343	374	.292	.339	.378	.717	95	-31	-32	100	99	671	70	97	42	-37
PHI	154	51	103	.331	43.5	617	919	5329	1512	238	50	88	294	615	.284	.324	.397	.721	89	-37	-92	108	94	668	66	80	45	-28
TOT	613					5632		42376	12266	1839	670	460	2906	3380	.289	.338	.397	.736							803	771	51	-222

TEAM	CG	SH	SV	IP	H	H/G	HR	BB	SO	RAT	ERA	ERA+	OAV	OOB	PR	/A	PF	CPI	FA	E	DP	FW	PW	BW	SBW	DIF
NY	71	9	18	1372¹	1497	9.8	79	295	357	11.9	3.55	103	.286	.326	34	16	97	102	.971	187	155	1.3	1.6	9.2	.0	5.4
PIT	88	10	10	1415²	1448	9.2	37	322	500	11.5	3.17	121	.271	.316	96	104	101	96	.973	172	129	2.3	10.3	-5.5	1.2	5.3
STL	70	10	16	1371²	1486	9.8	61	399	464	12.6	3.62	101	.282	.337	24	5	97	100	.965	219	130	-.6	.5	12.7	-.0	-2.1
BOS	74	11	12	1385	1488	9.7	54	420	382	12.6	3.90	94	.280	.337	-18	-38	97	93	.969	199	122	.5	-3.8	4.4	-.4	1.7
BRO	82	8	12	1363¹	1556	10.3	46	361	471	12.9	3.70	100	.293	.342	13	28	103	103	.964	232	142	-1.5	2.8	-7.6	1.1	6.3
CIN	83	7	9	1363	1500	9.9	37	305	408	12.0	3.46	103	.287	.328	48	17	95	100	.969	193	139	.9	1.7	-2.4	-.9	-5.8
CHI	73	7	7	1363	1605	10.6	67	409	441	13.6	4.39	87	.303	.357	-93	-88	101	99	.974	166	129	2.5	-8.7	-3.2	-.9	-2.3
PHI	82	5	8	1348²	1665	11.1	79	371	333	13.8	4.48	94	.308	.356	-105	-39	112	99	.955	295	127	-5.2	-3.9	-9.1	-.0	-7.8
TOT	623	67	92	10982²		10.0				12.6	3.78		.289	.338					.967	1663	1073					

Runs
Hornsby-StL 131
Frisch-NY 121
Bancroft-NY 121
Powell-Bos 114
Burns-NY 111

Hits
Hornsby-StL 235
Frisch-NY 211
C.Bigbee-Pit 204
Johnston-Bro . . . 203

Doubles
Hornsby-StL 44
Kelly-NY 42
Johnston-Bro 41
Grimes-Chi 38
McHenry-StL 37

Triples
Powell-Bos 18
Hornsby-StL 18
Grimm-Pit 17
Frisch-NY 17
C.Bigbee-Pit 17

Home Runs
Kelly-NY 23
Hornsby-StL 21
Williams-Phi 18
McHenry-StL 17
Fournier-StL 16

Total Bases
Hornsby-StL 378
Kelly-NY 310
McHenry-StL 305
Meusel-Phi-NY . . 302
Frisch-NY 300

Runs Batted In
Hornsby-StL 126
Kelly-NY 122
Youngs-NY 102
McHenry-StL 102
Frisch-NY 100

Runs Produced
Hornsby-StL 236
Frisch-NY 213
Kelly-NY 194
Youngs-NY 189
Bancroft-NY 182

Bases On Balls
Burns-NY 80
Youngs-NY 71
Grimes-Chi 70
Carey-Pit 70
Bancroft-NY 66

Batting Average
Hornsby-StL 397
McHenry-StL 350
Fournier-StL 343
Meusel-Phi-NY . . .343
Frisch-NY 341

On Base Percentage
Hornsby-StL 458
Youngs-NY 411
Fournier-StL 409
Grimes-Chi 406
Carey-Pit 395

Slugging Average
Hornsby-StL 639
McHenry-StL 531
Kelly-NY 528
Meusel-Phi-NY . . .515
Fournier-StL 505

Production
Hornsby-StL 1.097
McHenry-StL 924
Fournier-StL 914
Meusel-Phi-NY . . .895
Kelly-NY 884

Adjusted Production
Hornsby-StL 191
McHenry-StL 145
Fournier-StL 144
Kelly-NY 131
Youngs-NY 129

Batter Runs
Hornsby-StL 74.4
Fournier-StL 34.5
McHenry-StL 33.5
Meusel-Phi-NY . . 27.6
Frisch-NY 24.8

Adjusted Batter Runs
Hornsby-StL 76.1
Fournier-StL 36.1
McHenry-StL 35.0
Cruise-Bos 27.1
Roush-Cin 25.6

Clutch Hitting Index
Youngs-NY 166
Lavan-StL 152
Barnhart-Pit 133
Myers-Bro 130
Kelly-NY 125

Runs Created
Hornsby-StL 169
Frisch-NY 118
Fournier-StL 114
McHenry-StL 111
Meusel-Phi-NY . . 110

Total Average
Hornsby-StL 1.203
Frisch-NY 902
Fournier-StL 882
Carey-Pit 868
Youngs-NY 860

Stolen Bases
Frisch-NY 49
Carey-Pit 37
Johnston-Bro . . . 28
Bohne-Cin 26
Maranville-Pit 25

Stolen Base Average
Frisch-NY 79.0
Carey-Pit 75.5
Maisel-Chi 70.8
Maranville-Pit . . . 67.6
Johnston-Bro 63.6

Stolen Base Runs
Frisch-NY 6.9
Carey-Pit 3.9
Stock-StL 1.5
Cutshaw-Pit 1.2

Fielding Runs
Lavan-StL 18.5
Bancroft-NY 17.4
Williams-Phi 16.3
C.Bigbee-Pit 16.2
Carey-Pit 16.1

Total Player Rating
Hornsby-StL 7.0
Bancroft-NY 4.8
Frisch-NY 4.3
Johnston-Bro . . . 3.0
Kelly-NY 2.5

Wins
Grimes-Bro 22
Cooper-Pit 22
Oeschger-Bos 20
Nehf-NY 20
Rixey-Cin 19

Win Percentage
Doak-StL 714
Nehf-NY 667
Grimes-Bro 629
Barnes-NY 625
Toney-NY 621

Games
Scott-Bos 47
Oeschger-Bos 46
McQuillan-Bos . . . 45
Watson-Bos 44
Fillingim-Bos 44

Complete Games
Grimes-Bro 30
Cooper-Pit 29
Luque-Cin 25

Shutouts
Oeschger-Bos 3
J.Morrison-Pit . . . 3
Mitchell-Bro 3
Luque-Cin 3
Haines-StL 3
Fillingim-Bos 3
Douglas-NY 3
Alexander-Chi 3

Saves
North-StL 7
Barnes-NY 6
McQuillan-Bos 5

Innings Pitched
Cooper-Pit 327.0
Luque-Cin 304.0
Grimes-Bro 302.1
Rixey-Cin 301.0
Oeschger-Bos . . . 299.0

Fewest Hits/Game
Glazner-Pit 8.23
Adams-Pit 8.72
Oeschger-Bos . . . 9.12
Pertica-StL 9.16
Nehf-NY 9.18

Fewest BB/Game
Adams-Pit 1.01
Alexander-Chi 1.18
Barnes-NY 1.53
Hubbell-Phi 1.55
Doak-StL 1.60

Strikeouts
Grimes-Bro 136
Cooper-Pit 134
Luque-Cin 102
McQuillan-Bos 94

Strikeouts/Game
Grimes-Bro 4.05
Cooper-Pit 3.69
Doak-StL 3.58
Martin-Chi 3.56
Glazner-Pit 3.38

Ratio
Adams-Pit 9.73
Glazner-Pit 10.92
Nehf-NY 11.15
Luque-Cin 11.34
Alexander-Chi . . . 11.43

Earned Run Average
Doak-StL 2.59
Adams-Pit 2.64
Glazner-Pit 2.77
Rixey-Cin 2.78
Grimes-Bro 2.83

Adjusted ERA
Adams-Pit 145
Doak-StL 142
Glazner-Pit 138
Grimes-Bro 137
Mitchell-Bro 134

Opponents' Batting Avg.
Glazner-Pit 250
Adams-Pit 251
Pertica-StL 267
Watson-Bos 270
Nehf-NY 271

Opponents' On Base Pct.
Adams-Pit 272
Glazner-Pit 306
Nehf-NY 311
Luque-Cin 312
Doak-StL 313

Starter Runs
Rixey-Cin 33.4
Grimes-Bro 32.0
Doak-StL 27.6
Glazner-Pit 26.3
Adams-Pit 20.2

Adjusted Starter Runs
Grimes-Bro 35.5
Glazner-Pit 27.6
Rixey-Cin 26.6
Doak-StL 24.9
Cooper-Pit 21.2

Clutch Pitching Index
Barnes-NY 124
Mitchell-Bro 118
Doak-StL 116
Rixey-Cin 113
Grimes-Bro 112

Relief Runs
North-StL 2.3
Sallee-NY 1.5

Adjusted Relief Runs
North-StL 1.1
Sallee-NY 2

Relief Ranking
North-StL 1.1
Sallee-NY 2

Total Pitcher Index
Grimes-Bro 4.4
Mitchell-Bro 2.8
Rixey-Cin 2.5
Doak-StL 2.4
Adams-Pit 2.4

Total Baseball Ranking
Hornsby-StL 7.0
Bancroft-NY 4.8
Grimes-Bro 4.4
Frisch-NY 4.3
Johnston-Bro 3.0

TEAM	G	W	L	PCT	GB	R	OR	AB	H	2B	3B	HR	BB	SO	AVG	OBP	SLG	PRO	PRO+	BR	/A	PF	CHI	RC	SB	CS	SBA	SBR
NY	153	98	55	.641		948	708	5249	1576	285	87	134	588	569	.300	.375	.464	.839	116	142	125	102	102	929	89	64	58	-12
CLE	154	94	60	.610	4.5	925	712	5383	1656	355	90	42	623	376	.308	.383	.430	.813	111	112	100	102	100	916	50	42	54	-10
STL	154	81	73	.526	17.5	835	845	5442	1655	246	106	67	413	407	.304	.357	.425	.782	98	28	-19	106	102	827	111	66	63	-6
WAS	154	80	73	.523	18	704	738	5294	1468	240	96	42	462	472	.277	.342	.383	.725	95	-80	-43	95	101	712	83	65	56	-14
BOS	154	75	79	.487	23.5	668	696	5206	1440	248	69	17	428	344	.277	.335	.361	.696	84	-133	-113	97	107	642	95	89	52	-25
DET	154	71	82	.464	27	883	852	5461	1724	268	100	58	582	376	.316	.385	.433	.818	115	120	128	99	94	921	97	93	51	-27
CHI	154	62	92	.403	36.5	683	858	5329	1509	242	82	35	445	474	.283	.343	.379	.722	90	-86	-76	99	99	696	68	55	55	-13
PHI	155	53	100	.346	45	657	894	5465	1497	256	64	82	424	565	.274	.331	.389	.720	88	-102	-106	101	96	710	92	71	56	-15
TOT	616					6303		42829	12525	2140	694	477	3965	3583	.292	.356	.408	.765							685	545	56	-122

TEAM	CG	SH	SV	IP	H	H/G	HR	BB	SO	RAT	ERA	ERA+	OAV	OOB	PR	/A	PF	CPI	FA	E	DP	FW	PW	BW	SBW	DIF
NY	92	8	15	1364	1461	9.6	51	470	481	13.1	3.82	111	.277	.342	70	62	99	99	.965	222	138	-.3	5.8	11.7	.3	4.0
CLE	81	11	14	1377	1534	10.0	43	431	475	13.0	3.90	109	.288	.344	58	55	100	100	.967	204	124	.8	5.1	9.3	.5	1.2
STL	77	9	9	1379	1541	10.1	71	556	477	13.9	4.61	97	.288	.360	-51	-22	105	94	.964	224	127	-.3	-2.1	-1.8	.0	8.1
WAS	80	10	10	1383²	1568	10.2	51	442	452	13.3	3.97	104	.291	.349	47	22	96	102	.963	235	153	-.9	2.1	-4.0	.9	5.5
BOS	88	9	5	1364¹	1521	10.0	53	452	446	13.3	3.98	106	.291	.352	45	37	99	104	.975	157	151	3.5	3.5	-10.6	.1	1.5
DET	73	4	16	1386¹	1634	10.6	71	495	452	14.2	4.40	97	.297	.361	-18	-20	100	102	.963	232	107	-.8	-1.9	12.0	-.9	-13.9
CHI	84	7	9	1365¹	1603	10.6	52	549	392	14.4	4.94	86	.303	.372	-99	-107	99	94	.969	200	155	1.0	-10.0	-7.1	-1.1	2.2
PHI	75	2	7	1400¹	1645	10.6	85	548	431	14.3	4.61	97	.300	.367	-52	-25	104	102	.958	274	144	-3.1	-2.3	-9.9	.2	-8.4
TOT	650	60	85	11020		10.2				13.7	4.28		.292	.356					.965	1748	1099					

Runs
Ruth-NY 177
Tobin-StL 132
Peckinpaugh-NY .. 128
Sisler-StL 125
Cobb-Det 124

Hits
Heilmann-Det 237
Tobin-StL 236
Sisler-StL 216
Jacobson-StL 211
Veach-Det 207

Doubles
Speaker-Cle 52
Ruth-NY 44
Veach-Det 43
Heilmann-Det 43
Meusel-NY 40

Triples
Tobin-StL 18
Sisler-StL 18
Shanks-Was 18

Home Runs
Ruth-NY 59
Williams-StL 24
Meusel-NY 24
C.Walker-Phi 23
Heilmann-Det 19

Total Bases
Ruth-NY 457
Heilmann-Det 365
Meusel-NY 334
Tobin-StL 327
Sisler-StL 326

Runs Batted In
Ruth-NY 171
Heilmann-Det 139
Meusel-NY 135
Veach-Det 128
Gardner-Cle 120

Runs Produced
Ruth-NY 289
Heilmann-Det 234
Veach-Det 222
Gardner-Cle 218
Sisler-StL 217

Bases On Balls
Ruth-NY 144
Blue-Det 103
Peckinpaugh-NY ... 84
J.Sewell-Cle 80
Schang-NY 78

Batting Average
Heilmann-Det ..... .394
Cobb-Det .... .389
Ruth-NY .... .378
Sisler-StL .... .371
Speaker-Cle ...... .362

On Base Percentage
Ruth-NY .... .512
Cobb-Det .... .452
Heilmann-Det ..... .444
Speaker-Cle ...... .439
Williams-StL ..... .429

Slugging Average
Ruth-NY .... .846
Heilmann-Det ..... .606
Cobb-Det .... .596
Williams-StL ..... .561
Sisler-StL .... .560

Production
Ruth-NY 1.358
Heilmann-Det 1.051
Cobb-Det 1.048
Williams-StL ..... .990
Speaker-Cle ...... .977

Adjusted Production
Ruth-NY 236
Heilmann-Det 167
Cobb-Det 167
Speaker-Cle 146
Williams-StL 142

Batter Runs
Ruth-NY 119.2
Heilmann-Det 58.4
Cobb-Det 50.3
Williams-StL 42.5
Speaker-Cle 38.2

Adjusted Batter Runs
Ruth-NY 117.3
Heilmann-Det 59.3
Cobb-Det 51.0
Williams-StL 37.5
Speaker-Cle 37.1

Clutch Hitting Index
Gardner-Cle 164
Pratt-Bos 145
Severeid-StL 132
Pipp-NY 128
J.Sewell-Cle 127

Runs Created
Ruth-NY 238
Heilmann-Det 159
Cobb-Det 134
Sisler-StL 133
Williams-StL 130

Total Average
Ruth-NY 1.745
Cobb-Det 1.132
Heilmann-Det 1.121
Speaker-Cle 1.040
Williams-StL 1.037

Stolen Bases
Sisler-StL 35
Harris-Was 29
Rice-Was 25
Johnson-Chi 22
Cobb-Det 22

Stolen Base Average
Judge-Was 77.8
Harris-Was 76.3
Sisler-StL 76.1
Meusel-NY 73.9
Rice-Was 67.6

Stolen Base Runs
Sisler-StL 3.9
Harris-Was 3.3
Judge-Was 2.7
Welch-Phi 1.8

Fielding Runs
Scott-Bos 38.1
Collins-Chi 27.1
Dykes-Phi 25.0
Ward-NY 18.8
Johnson-Chi 18.0

Total Player Rating
Ruth-NY 9.6
Cobb-Det 4.8
Collins-Chi 3.9
Sisler-StL 3.8
Speaker-Cle 3.3

Wins
Shocker-StL 27
Mays-NY 27
Faber-Chi 25
Jones-Bos 23
Coveleski-Cle 23

Win Percentage
Mays-NY .... .750
Shocker-StL ...... .692
Bush-Bos .... .640
Coveleski-Cle .... .639
Faber-Chi .... .625

Games
Mays-NY 49
Shocker-StL 47
Bayne-StL 47
Rommel-Phi 46

Complete Games
Faber-Chi 32
Shocker-StL 30
Mays-NY 30
Coveleski-Cle 28

Shutouts
Jones-Bos 5
Shocker-StL 4
Mogridge-Was 4
Faber-Chi 4

Saves
Middleton-Det 7
Mays-NY 7

Innings Pitched
Mays-NY 336.2
Faber-Chi 330.2
Shocker-StL 326.2
Coveleski-Cle ... 315.0
Kerr-Chi 308.2

Fewest Hits/Game
Faber-Chi 7.97
Bush-Bos 8.63
Mays-NY 8.88
Shawkey-NY 9.00
Johnson-Was 9.03

Fewest BB/Game
Hasty-Phi 2.01
Mays-NY 2.03
Mogridge-Was 2.06
Bagby-Cle 2.07
Zachary-Was 2.12

Strikeouts
Johnson-Was 143
Shocker-StL 132
Shawkey-NY 126
Faber-Chi 124
Leonard-Det 120

Strikeouts/Game
Johnson-Was 4.88
Shawkey-NY 4.63
Bayne-StL 4.50
Leonard-Det 4.41
Mails-Cle 4.03

Ratio
Faber-Chi 10.53
Mays-NY 11.15
Mogridge-Was ... 11.69
Shocker-StL 12.04
Jones-Bos 12.11

Earned Run Average
Faber-Chi 2.48
Mogridge-Was 3.00
Mays-NY 3.05
Hoyt-NY 3.09
Jones-Bos 3.22

Adjusted ERA
Faber-Chi 171
Mays-NY 139
Mogridge-Was 137
Hoyt-NY 137
Jones-Bos 131

Opponents' Batting Avg.
Faber-Chi .... .242
Mays-NY .... .257
Bush-Bos .... .260
Shawkey-NY ...... .263
Johnson-Was ..... .263

Opponents' On Base Pct.
Faber-Chi .... .297
Mays-NY .... .303
Mogridge-Was .... .313
Shocker-StL ..... .319
Johnson-Was ..... .326

Starter Runs
Faber-Chi 66.3
Mays-NY 46.2
Mogridge-Was 41.0
Hoyt-NY 37.3
Jones-Bos 35.1

Adjusted Starter Runs
Faber-Chi 64.6
Mays-NY 44.4
Hoyt-NY 35.8
Mogridge-Was 35.7
Shocker-StL 33.6

Clutch Pitching Index
Russell-Bos 122
Zachary-Was 118
Keefe-Phi 114
Uhle-Cle 108
Sothoron-StL-Bos-Cle 108

Relief Runs

Adjusted Relief Runs

Relief Ranking

Total Pitcher Index
Faber-Chi 6.3
Mays-NY 5.8
Shocker-StL 4.0
Jones-Bos 3.4
Hoyt-NY 3.2

Total Baseball Ranking
Ruth-NY 9.3
Faber-Chi 6.3
Mays-NY 5.8
Cobb-Det 4.8
Shocker-StL 4.0

TEAM	G	W	L	PCT	GB	R	OR	AB	H	2B	3B	HR	BB	SO	AVG	OBP	SLG	PRO	PRO+	BR	/A	PF	CHI	RC	SB	CS	SBA	SBR
NY	156	93	61	.604		852	658	5454	1661	253	90	80	448	421	.305	.363	.428	.791	109	77	71	101	99	848	116	83	58	-15
CIN	156	86	68	.558	7	766	677	5282	1561	226	99	45	436	381	.296	.353	.401	.754	102	8	23	98	99	737	130	136	49	-43
STL	154	85	69	.552	8	863	819	5425	1634	280	88	107	447	425	.301	.357	.444	.801	118	91	128	95	99	860	73	63	54	-16
PIT	155	85	69	.552	8	865	736	5521	1698	239	110	52	423	326	.308	.360	.419	.779	106	56	47	101	102	848	145	59	71	8
CHI	156	80	74	.519	13	771	808	5335	1564	248	71	42	525	447	.293	.359	.390	.749	97	7	-8	102	98	752	97	108	47	-36
BRO	155	76	78	.494	17	743	744	5413	1569	235	76	56	339	318	.290	.335	.392	.727	94	-58	-51	99	105	709	79	60	57	-12
PHI	154	57	96	.373	35.5	738	920	5459	1537	268	55	116	450	611	.282	.341	.415	.756	92	-3	-77	110	95	771	48	60	44	-22
BOS	154	53	100	.346	39.5	596	822	5161	1355	162	73	32	387	451	.263	.317	.341	.658	78	-179	-146	96	106	566	67	65	51	-19
TOT	620					6194		43050	12579	1911	662	530	3455	3380	.292	.348	.404	.753							755	634	54	-154

TEAM	CG	SH	SV	IP	H	H/G	HR	BB	SO	RAT	ERA	ERA+	OAV	OOB	PR	/A	PF	CPI	FA	E	DP	FW	PW	BW	SBW	DIF
NY	76	7	15	1396[1]	1454	9.4	71	393	388	12.0	3.45	116	.272	.324	100	83	98	99	.970	194	145	1.1	7.8	6.7	.4	-.0
CIN	88	8	3	1385[2]	1481	9.6	49	326	357	11.9	3.53	113	.322	.322	87	69	97	95	.968	205	147	.4	6.5	2.2	-2.2	2.2
STL	60	8	12	1362[2]	1609	10.6	61	447	465	13.9	4.44	87	.299	.358	-52	-87	94	98	.961	239	122	-2.0	-8.2	12.1	.3	5.8
PIT	88	15	7	1387[1]	1613	10.5	52	358	490	13.0	3.98	102	.296	.343	18	13	99	99	.970	187	126	1.5	1.2	4.4	2.6	-1.7
CHI	74	8	12	1397[2]	1579	10.2	77	475	402	13.6	4.34	97	.292	.356	-38	-24	102	99	.968	204	154	.5	-2.3	-.8	-1.6	7.1
BRO	82	12	8	1385[2]	1574	10.2	74	490	499	13.6	4.05	100	.293	.356	8	2	99	106	.967	208	139	.1	.2	-4.8	.7	2.8
PHI	73	6	5	1372	1692	11.1	89	460	394	14.4	4.64	101	.307	.365	-82	7	114	102	.965	225	152	-1.1	.7	-7.3	-.3	-11.5
BOS	63	7	6	1348	1565	10.4	57	489	360	13.9	4.37	91	.298	.361	-41	-57	98	100	.965	215	121	-.4	-5.4	-13.8	.0	-3.9
TOT	604	71	68	11035[1]		10.2				13.3	4.10		.292	.348					.967	1677	1106					

Runs
Hornsby-StL	141
Carey-Pit	140
Smith-StL	117
Bancroft-NY	117
Maranville-Pit	115

Hits
Hornsby-StL	250
Bigbee-Pit	215
Bancroft-NY	209
Carey-Pit	207
Daubert-Cin	205

Doubles
Hornsby-StL	46
Grimes-Chi	45
Duncan-Cin	44
Bancroft-NY	41
Hollocher-Chi	37

Triples
Daubert-Cin	22
Meusel-NY	17
Maranville-Pit	15
Bigbee-Pit	15

Home Runs
Hornsby-StL	42
Williams-Phi	26
Lee-Phi	17
Kelly-NY	17

Total Bases
Hornsby-StL	450
Meusel-NY	314
Wheat-Bro	302
Williams-Phi	300
Daubert-Cin	300

Runs Batted In
Hornsby-StL	152
Meusel-NY	132
Wheat-Bro	112
Kelly-NY	107

Runs Produced
Hornsby-StL	251
Meusel-NY	216
Bigbee-Pit	207
Carey-Pit	200
Wheat-Bro	188

Bases On Balls
Carey-Pit	80
O'Farrell-Chi	79
Bancroft-NY	79
Burns-Cin	78
Grimes-Chi	75

Batting Average
Hornsby-StL	.401
Grimes-Chi	.354
Miller-Chi	.352
Bigbee-Pit	.350
Tierney-Pit	.345

On Base Percentage
Hornsby-StL	.459
Grimes-Chi	.442
O'Farrell-Chi	.439
Carey-Pit	.408
Bigbee-Pit	.405

Slugging Average
Hornsby-StL	.722
Grimes-Chi	.572
Tierney-Pit	.515
Williams-Phi	.514
Miller-Chi	.511

Production
Hornsby-StL	1.181
Grimes-Chi	1.014
Williams-Phi	.905
Miller-Chi	.899
Walker-Phi	.899

Adjusted Production
Hornsby-StL	210
Grimes-Chi	157
Daubert-Cin	130
Wheat-Bro	129
Miller-Chi	128

Batter Runs
Hornsby-StL	90.0
Grimes-Chi	47.1
Williams-Phi	27.5
Walker-Phi	26.3
Daubert-Cin	24.7

Adjusted Batter Runs
Hornsby-StL	94.2
Grimes-Chi	45.6
Daubert-Cin	26.4
Wheat-Bro	25.0
Russell-Pit	23.7

Clutch Hitting Index
Terry-Chi	146
Meusel-NY	135
Traynor-Pit	133
Pinelli-Cin	125
Tierney-Pit	124

Runs Created
Hornsby-StL	200
Carey-Pit	131
Grimes-Chi	130
Walker-Phi	118
Bigbee-Pit	116

Total Average
Hornsby-StL	1.353
Grimes-Chi	1.107
Carey-Pit	.995
O'Farrell-Chi	.951
Walker-Phi	.918

Stolen Bases
Carey-Pit	51
Frisch-NY	31
Burns-Cin	30
Maranville-Pit	24
Bigbee-Pit	24

Stolen Base Average
Carey-Pit	96.2
Traynor-Pit	85.0
Smith-StL	72.0
Johnston-Bro	66.7
Youngs-NY	65.4

Stolen Base Runs
Carey-Pit	14.1
Traynor-Pit	3.3
Kelly-NY	1.8
T.Griffith-Bro	1.5
Smith-StL	1.2

Fielding Runs
Parkinson-Pit	31.0
Bancroft-NY	21.9
Pinelli-Cin	21.1
Carey-Pit	19.5
Bigbee-Pit	17.4

Total Player Rating
Hornsby-StL	8.1
Bancroft-NY	4.5
Carey-Pit	4.2
O'Farrell-Chi	3.8
Grimes-Chi	3.4

Wins
Rixey-Cin	25
Cooper-Pit	23
Ruether-Bro	21
Pfeffer-StL	19
Nehf-NY	19

Win Percentage
Donohue-Cin	.667
Rixey-Cin	.658
Couch-Cin	.640
Ruether-Bro	.636
Cooper-Pit	.622

Games
North-StL	53
Sherdel-StL	47
Ryan-NY	46
Oeschger-Bos	46
Morrison-Pit	45

Complete Games
Cooper-Pit	27
Ruether-Bro	26
Rixey-Cin	26

Shutouts
Vance-Bro	5
Morrison-Pit	5
Cooper-Pit	4
Adams-Pit	4
Sherdel-StL	3

Saves
Jonnard-NY	5
North-StL	4

Innings Pitched
Rixey-Cin	313.1
Cooper-Pit	294.2
Morrison-Pit	286.1
Nehf-NY	268.1
Ruether-Bro	267.1

Fewest Hits/Game
Douglas-NY	8.79
Osborne-Chi	8.95
Ryan-NY	9.11
Luque-Cin	9.17
Vance-Bro	9.49

Fewest BB/Game
Adams-Pit	.79
Alexander-Chi	1.25
Rixey-Cin	1.29
Donohue-Cin	1.60
J.Barnes-NY	1.61

Strikeouts
Vance-Bro	134
Cooper-Pit	129
Ring-Phi	116
Morrison-Pit	104
Grimes-Bro	99

Strikeouts/Game
Vance-Bro	4.91
Ring-Phi	4.19
Osborne-Chi	3.96
Cooper-Pit	3.94
Doak-StL	3.64

Ratio
Douglas-NY	11.02
Adams-Pit	11.03
Rixey-Cin	11.09
Donohue-Cin	11.34
Luque-Cin	11.69

Earned Run Average
Douglas-NY	2.63
Ryan-NY	3.01
Donohue-Cin	3.12
Cooper-Pit	3.18
Nehf-NY	3.29

Adjusted ERA
Douglas-NY	152
Weinert-Phi	137
Ryan-NY	133
Cooper-Pit	128
Donohue-Cin	128

Opponents' Batting Avg.
Douglas-NY	.257
Luque-Cin	.268
Ryan-NY	.269
Osborne-Chi	.271
Rixey-Cin	.275

Opponents' On Base Pct.
Douglas-NY	.302
Rixey-Cin	.303
Adams-Pit	.307
J.Barnes-NY	.311
Donohue-Cin	.312

Starter Runs
Cooper-Pit	30.2
Donohue-Cin	26.2
Douglas-NY	25.8
Nehf-NY	24.2
Ryan-NY	23.3

Adjusted Starter Runs
Cooper-Pit	29.4
Douglas-NY	24.1
Weinert-Phi	23.4
Donohue-Cin	23.2
Nehf-NY	21.3

Clutch Pitching Index
Weinert-Phi	129
Ryan-NY	116
Cooper-Pit	113
Morrison-Pit	111
McQuillan-Bos-NY	110

Relief Runs
McNamara-Bos	13.2
Causey-NY	7.2
Braxton-Bos	5.4
Mamaux-Bro	3.9
V.Barnes-NY	3.5

Adjusted Relief Runs
McNamara-Bos	12.4
Causey-NY	6.4
Braxton-Bos	4.6
Mamaux-Bro	3.6
V.Barnes-NY	3.0

Relief Ranking
McNamara-Bos	11.0
Causey-NY	5.9
Mamaux-Bro	2.1
Braxton-Bos	1.9
Jonnard-NY	1.3

Total Pitcher Index
Cooper-Pit	3.7
Douglas-NY	2.5
Meadows-Phi	2.4
Nehf-NY	2.3
Aldridge-Chi	2.3

Total Baseball Ranking
Hornsby-StL	8.1
Bancroft-NY	4.5
Carey-Pit	4.2
O'Farrell-Chi	3.8
Cooper-Pit	3.7

TEAM	G	W	L	PCT	GB	R	OR	AB	H	2B	3B	HR	BB	SO	AVG	OBP	SLG	PRO	PRO+	BR	/A	PF	CHI	RC	SB	CS	SBA	SBR
NY	154	94	60	.610		758	618	5245	1504	220	75	95	497	532	.287	.353	.412	.765	103	36	20	102	99	774	62	59	51	-17
STL	154	93	61	.604	1	867	643	5416	1693	291	94	98	473	381	.313	.372	.455	.827	117	157	131	104	96	924	132	73	64	-4
DET	155	79	75	.513	15	828	791	5360	1641	250	87	54	530	378	.306	.372	.415	.787	115	94	118	97	98	848	78	61	56	-13
CLE	155	78	76	.506	16	768	817	5293	1544	320	73	32	554	331	.292	.364	.398	.762	104	43	38	101	97	792	89	58	61	-8
CHI	155	77	77	.500	17	691	691	5267	1463	243	62	45	482	463	.278	.343	.373	.716	92	-52	-48	95	103	690	106	84	50	-19
WAS	154	69	85	.448	25	650	706	5201	1395	229	76	45	458	442	.268	.334	.367	.701	93	-84	-48	100	101	659	94	54	64	-4
PHI	155	65	89	.422	29	705	830	5211	1409	229	63	111	437	591	.270	.331	.402	.733	94	-36	-55	103	104	697	60	63	49	-20
BOS	154	61	93	.396	33	598	769	5288	1392	250	55	45	366	455	.263	.316	.357	.673	82	-149	-143	99	105	600	60	63	49	-20
TOT	618					5865		42281	12041	2032	585	525	3797	3573	.285	.348	.398	.746							681	515	57	-105

TEAM	CG	SH	SV	IP	H	H/G	HR	BB	SO	RAT	ERA	ERA+	OAV	OOB	PR	/A	PF	CPI	FA	E	DP	FW	PW	BW	SBW	DIF
NY	100	7	14	1393²	1402	9.1	73	423	458	11.9	3.39	118	.268	.325	99	91	99	101	.975	157	124	2.0	8.8	1.9	-.4	4.6
STL	79	8	22	1392	1412	9.1	71	419	534	12.1	3.38	122	.268	.327	101	115	103	103	.968	201	158	-.5	11.2	12.7	.9	-8.3
DET	67	7	15	1391	1554	10.1	62	473	461	13.7	4.27	91	.288	.354	-37	-64	96	97	.970	191	133	.2	-6.2	11.5	.0	-3.4
CLE	76	14	7	1383²	1605	10.4	58	464	489	13.7	4.59	87	.296	.356	-85	-92	99	93	.975	155	143	-.5	-8.9	3.7	.5	6.2
CHI	86	13	8	1403²	1472	9.4	57	529	484	13.0	3.94	103	.278	.346	15	15	101	98	.968	202	147	2.2	1.5	-4.7	-.6	1.5
WAS	84	13	10	1362¹	1485	9.8	49	500	422	13.4	3.81	101	.286	.354	33	5	96	107	.969	196	168	-.2	.5	-4.7	.9	-4.5
PHI	73	4	6	1362¹	1573	10.4	107	469	373	13.7	4.59	92	.297	.357	-85	-55	105	99	.966	215	118	-1.2	-5.3	-5.3	-.7	.6
BOS	71	10	6	1373¹	1508	9.9	48	503	359	13.5	4.30	95	.287	.354	-41	-32	102	94	.965	224	145	-1.8	-3.1	-13.9	-.7	3.5
TOT	636	76	88	11062		9.8				13.1	4.03		.285	.348					.969	1541	1136					

Runs
Sisler-StL 134
Blue-Det 131
Williams-StL 128
Tobin-StL 122

Hits
Sisler-StL 246
Cobb-Det 211
Tobin-StL 207
Veach-Det 202

Doubles
Speaker-Cle 48
Pratt-Bos 44
Sisler-StL 42
Cobb-Det 42

Triples
Sisler-StL 18
Jacobson-StL 16
Cobb-Det 16
Judge-Was 15
Mostil-Chi 14

Home Runs
Williams-StL 39
Walker-Phi 37
Ruth-NY 35
Miller-Phi 21
Heilmann-Det 21

Total Bases
Williams-StL 367
Sisler-StL 348
Walker-Phi 310
Cobb-Det 297
Tobin-StL 296

Runs Batted In
Williams-StL 155
Veach-Det 126
McManus-StL 109
Sisler-StL 105
Jacobson-StL 102

Runs Produced
Williams-StL 244
Sisler-StL 231
Veach-Det 213
Cobb-Det 194
McManus-StL ... 186

Bases On Balls
Witt-NY 89
Ruth-NY 84
Blue-Det 82
Speaker-Cle 77
Williams-StL 74

Batting Average
Sisler-StL .... .420
Cobb-Det .... .401
Speaker-Cle ..... .378
Heilmann-Det .... .356
Miller-Phi .... .335

On Base Percentage
Speaker-Cle .... .474
Sisler-StL .... .467
Cobb-Det ...... .462
Ruth-NY .... .434
Heilmann-Det ... .432

Slugging Average
Ruth-NY .... .672
Williams-StL ..... .627
Speaker-Cle ..... .606
Heilmann-Det ... .598
Sisler-StL .... .594

Production
Ruth-NY 1.106
Speaker-Cle 1.080
Sisler-StL 1.061
Williams-StL 1.040
Heilmann-Det ... 1.030

Adjusted Production
Ruth-NY 181
Speaker-Cle 178
Cobb-Det 172
Heilmann-Det ... 172
Sisler-StL 169

Batter Runs
Sisler-StL 64.4
Williams-StL 56.1
Speaker-Cle 52.8
Cobb-Det 52.4
Ruth-NY 50.5

Adjusted Batter Runs
Sisler-StL 61.6
Cobb-Det 54.8
Williams-StL 53.2
Speaker-Cle 52.3
Ruth-NY 49.2

Clutch Hitting Index
J.Sewell-Cle 142
O'Neill-Cle 138
Veach-Det 137
Jacobson-StL ... 136
Wood-Cle 136

Runs Created
Sisler-StL 162
Williams-StL 150
Cobb-Det 133
Speaker-Cle 127
Ruth-NY 120

Total Average
Speaker-Cle 1.272
Ruth-NY 1.246
Sisler-StL 1.203
Williams-StL 1.137
Heilmann-Det ... 1.135

Stolen Bases
Sisler-StL 51
Williams-StL 37
Harris-Was 25
Johnson-Chi 21

Stolen Base Average
Jacobson-StL 76.0
Sisler-StL 72.9
Harris-Was 69.4
Rice-Was 69.0
Rigney-Det 68.0

Stolen Base Runs
Sisler-StL 3.9
Veach-Det 2.1
Jacobson-StL ... 2.1
Evans-Cle 2.1
Shanks-Was 1.8

Fielding Runs
Harris-Was 26.4
Peckinpaugh-Was .. 22.2
Schalk-Chi 20.2
Scott-NY 19.1
J.Sewell-Cle 14.7

Total Player Rating
Sisler-StL 6.8
Speaker-Cle 5.1
Williams-StL 4.6
Cobb-Det 4.2
Ruth-NY 3.7

Wins
Rommel-Phi 27
Bush-NY 26
Shocker-StL 24
Uhle-Cle 22
Faber-Chi 21

Win Percentage
Bush-NY .... .788
Rommel-Phi ..... .675
Shawkey-NY ..... .625
Pillette-Det ...... .613
Hoyt-NY .... .613

Games
Rommel-Phi 51
Uhle-Cle 50
Shocker-StL 48
Harriss-Phi 47

Complete Games
Faber-Chi 31
Shocker-StL 29
Uhle-Cle 23
Johnson-Was 23

Shutouts
Uhle-Cle 5

Saves
Jones-NY 8
Pruett-StL 7
Wright-StL 5

Innings Pitched
Faber-Chi 352.0
Shocker-StL 348.0
Shawkey-NY 299.2
Rommel-Phi 294.0
Uhle-Cle 287.1

Fewest Hits/Game
Davis-StL 8.36
Bush-NY 8.46
Faber-Chi 8.54
Shawkey-NY 8.59
Wright-StL 8.65

Fewest BB/Game
Shocker-StL 1.47
Vangilder-StL 1.76
Mays-NY 1.88
Kolp-StL 1.91
Hasty-Phi 1.92

Strikeouts
Shocker-StL 149
Faber-Chi 148
Shawkey-NY 130
Ehmke-Det 108
Johnson-Was ... 105

Strikeouts/Game
Morton-Cle 4.53
Harriss-Phi 4.00
Shawkey-NY 3.90
Shocker-StL 3.85
Faber-Chi 3.78

Ratio
Faber-Chi 10.82
Shocker-StL 11.02
Rommel-Phi 11.08
Vangilder-StL ... 11.09
Quinn-Bos 11.43

Earned Run Average
Faber-Chi 2.81
Pillette-Det 2.85
Shawkey-NY 2.91
Wright-StL 2.92
Shocker-StL 2.97

Adjusted ERA
Faber-Chi 144
Wright-StL 141
Shocker-StL 139
Shawkey-NY 137
Pillette-Det 136

Opponents' Batting Avg.
Davis-StL .... .250
Bush-NY .... .252
Faber-Chi .... .252
Shawkey-NY ..... .256
Pillette-Det ...... .258

Opponents' On Base Pct.
Faber-Chi .... .299
Shocker-StL ..... .304
Rommel-Phi ..... .309
Vangilder-StL .... .310
Quinn-Bos .... .311

Starter Runs
Faber-Chi 47.7
Shocker-StL 40.9
Shawkey-NY 37.2
Pillette-Det 36.0
Johnson-Was ... 32.4

Adjusted Starter Runs
Faber-Chi 48.8
Shocker-StL 44.8
Shawkey-NY 36.0
Rommel-Phi 31.5
Pillette-Det 31.1

Clutch Pitching Index
Mogridge-Was 124
Wright-StL 118
Johnson-Was 114
Pillette-Det 110
Shawkey-NY 109

Relief Runs
Murray-NY 4

Adjusted Relief Runs
Murray-NY 2

Relief Ranking
Murray-NY 1

Total Pitcher Index
Faber-Chi 4.8
Shocker-StL 4.5
Shawkey-NY 3.3
Rommel-Phi 3.2
Pillette-Det 3.1

Total Baseball Ranking
Sisler-StL 6.8
Speaker-Cle 5.1
Faber-Chi 4.8
Williams-StL 4.6
Shocker-StL 4.5

1923 National League

TEAM	G	W	L	PCT	GB	R	OR	AB	H	2B	3B	HR	BB	SO	AVG	OBP	SLG	PRO	PRO+	BR	/A	PF	CHI	RC	SB	CS	SBA	SBR
NY	153	95	58	.621		854	679	5452	1610	248	76	85	487	406	.295	.356	.415	.771	110	72	82	99	103	816	106	70	60	-10
CIN	154	91	63	.591	4.5	708	629	5278	1506	237	95	45	439	367	.285	.344	.392	.736	102	-1	14	98	96	707	96	105	48	-34
PIT	154	87	67	.565	8.5	786	696	5405	1592	224	111	49	407	362	.295	.347	.404	.751	102	26	10	102	103	766	154	75	67	1
CHI	154	83	71	.539	12.5	756	704	5259	1516	243	52	90	455	485	.288	.348	.406	.754	104	33	32	100	99	735	181	143	56	-32
STL	154	79	74	.516	16	746	732	5526	1582	274	76	63	438	446	.286	.343	.398	.741	103	5	21	98	97	761	89	61	59	-10
BRO	155	76	78	.494	19.5	753	741	5476	1559	214	81	62	425	382	.285	.340	.387	.727	100	-20	1	97	102	730	71	50	59	-9
BOS	155	54	100	.351	41.5	636	798	5329	1455	213	58	32	429	404	.273	.331	.353	.684	90	-99	-69	96	99	625	57	80	42	-31
PHI	155	50	104	.325	45.5	748	1008	5491	1528	259	39	112	414	556	.278	.333	.401	.734	89	-15	-102	112	101	729	70	73	49	-23
TOT	617					5987		43216	12348	1912	588	538	3494	3408	.286	.343	.395	.737							824	657	56	-147

TEAM	CG	SH	SV	IP	H	H/G	HR	BB	SO	RAT	ERA	ERA+	OAV	OOB	PR	/A	PF	CPI	FA	E	DP	FW	PW	BW	SBW	DIF
NY	62	10	18	1378	1440	9.4	82	424	453	12.3	3.90	98	.271	.328	15	-13	96	93	.972	176	141	2.4	-1.3	7.9	.8	8.7
CIN	88	11	9	1391¹	1465	9.5	28	359	450	12.0	3.21	120	.273	.322	121	99	97	101	.969	202	144	.9	9.5	1.3	-1.5	3.7
PIT	92	5	9	1376¹	1513	9.9	53	402	414	12.7	3.87	103	.284	.337	19	19	100	98	.971	179	157	2.3	1.8	1.0	1.9	3.1
CHI	80	8	11	1366²	1419	9.3	86	435	408	12.4	3.82	105	.269	.329	27	25	100	96	.967	208	144	.5	2.4	3.1	-1.3	1.3
STL	77	9	7	1398¹	1539	9.9	70	456	398	13.1	3.87	101	.284	.344	20	5	98	104	.963	232	141	-.9	.5	2.0	.8	.0
BRO	94	8	5	1396²	1503	9.7	55	476	548	13.0	3.74	103	.277	.340	39	20	97	100	.955	293	137	-4.4	1.9	.0	.9	.5
BOS	54	13	7	1392²	1662	10.7	64	394	351	13.5	4.21	94	.302	.352	-34	-41	100	102	.964	230	157	-.7	-3.9	-6.6	-1.2	-10.5
PHI	68	3	8	1376¹	1801	11.8	100	549	384	15.6	5.34	86	.322	.386	-205	-115	115	102	.966	217	172	.0	-11.1	-9.8	-.4	-5.8
TOT	615	67	74	11076¹		10.0				13.1	3.99		.286	.343					.966	1737	1193					

Runs
Youngs-NY 121
Carey-Pit 120
Frisch-NY 116
Johnston-Bro 111
Statz-Chi 110

Hits
Frisch-NY 223
Statz-Chi 209
Traynor-Pit 208
Johnston-Bro 203
Youngs-NY 200

Doubles
Roush-Cin 41
Tierney-Pit-Phi .. 36
Grantham-Chi 36
Bottomley-StL 34

Triples
Traynor-Pit 19
Carey-Pit 19
Roush-Cin 18
Southworth-Bos ... 16

Home Runs
Williams-Phi 41
Fournier-Bro 22
Miller-Chi 20
Meusel-NY 19
Hornsby-StL 17

Total Bases
Frisch-NY 311
Williams-Phi 308
Fournier-Bro 303
Traynor-Pit 301
Statz-Chi 288

Runs Batted In
Meusel-NY 125
Williams-Phi 114
Frisch-NY 111
Kelly-NY 103
Fournier-Bro 102

Runs Produced
Frisch-NY 215
Meusel-NY 208
Youngs-NY 205
Traynor-Pit 197
Carey-Pit 177

Bases On Balls
Burns-Cin 101
Sand-Phi 82
Youngs-NY 73
Carey-Pit 73
Grantham-Chi 71

Batting Average
Hornsby-StL ..... .384
Bottomley-StL .... .371
Fournier-Bro ..... .351
Roush-Cin .... .351
Frisch-NY .... .348

On Base Percentage
Hornsby-StL ..... .459
Bottomley-StL .... .425
Youngs-NY .... .412
Fournier-Bro ..... .411
O'Farrell-Chi ..... .408

Slugging Average
Hornsby-StL ...... .627
Fournier-Bro ..... .588
Williams-Phi ..... .576
Bottomley-StL .... .535
Roush-Cin .... .531

Production
Hornsby-StL 1.086
Fournier-Bro 999
Bottomley-StL 960
Williams-Phi 947
Roush-Cin 938

Adjusted Production
Hornsby-StL 188
Fournier-Bro 165
Bottomley-StL 155
Roush-Cin 149
Frisch-NY 133

Batter Runs
Hornsby-StL 52.1
Fournier-Bro 43.7
Bottomley-StL 39.2
Roush-Cin 34.0
Williams-Phi 33.2

Adjusted Batter Runs
Hornsby-StL 53.3
Fournier-Bro 45.7
Bottomley-StL 40.7
Roush-Cin 35.5
Frisch-NY 29.5

Clutch Hitting Index
Stock-StL 159
McInnis-Bos 145
Meusel-NY 137
Kelly-NY 123
Grimm-Pit 122

Runs Created
Fournier-Bro 125
Frisch-NY 123
Hornsby-StL 120
Bottomley-StL 117
Carey-Pit 117

Total Average
Hornsby-StL 1.194
Fournier-Bro 1.071
Bottomley-StL 976
Williams-Phi 966
Carey-Pit 928

Stolen Bases
Carey-Pit 51
Grantham-Chi 43
Smith-StL 32
Heathcote-Chi 32

Stolen Base Average
Carey-Pit 86.4
Smith-StL 74.4
Frisch-NY 70.7
Traynor-Pit 68.3
Heathcote-Chi ... 65.3

Stolen Base Runs
Carey-Pit 10.5
Smith-StL 3.0
Rawlings-Pit 2.7

Fielding Runs
Bancroft-NY 21.3
Carey-Pit 19.7
Johnston-Bro 19.4
Statz-Chi 17.7
Tierney-Pit-Phi.... 14.4

Total Player Rating
Fournier-Bro 4.1
Traynor-Pit 4.1
Carey-Pit 3.6
Bancroft-NY 3.6
Johnston-Bro 3.5

Wins
Luque-Cin 27
Morrison-Pit....... 25
Alexander-Chi 22
Grimes-Bro 21
Donohue-Cin 21

Win Percentage
Luque-Cin 771
Ryan-NY 762
Scott-NY 696
Morrison-Pit.......658
Alexander-Chi ...647

Games
Ryan-NY 45
Jonnard-NY 45
Oeschger-Bos 44
J.Barnes-NY-Bos .. 43
Genewich-Bos..... 43

Complete Games
Grimes-Bro 33
Luque-Cin 28
Morrison-Pit....... 27
Cooper-Pit 26
Alexander-Chi 26

Shutouts
Luque-Cin 6
J.Barnes-NY-Bos .. 5
McQuillan-NY 5

Saves
Jonnard-NY 5
Ryan-NY.......... 4

Innings Pitched
Grimes-Bro 327.0
Luque-Cin 322.0
Rixey-Cin 309.0
Alexander-Chi ... 305.0
Ring-Phi 304.1

Fewest Hits/Game
Luque-Cin 7.80
Vance-Bro 8.44
Morrison-Pit..... 8.56
Keen-Chi 8.59
Aldridge-Chi..... 8.67

Fewest BB/Game
Alexander-Chi 89
C.Adams-Pit 1.42
Genewich-Bos.... 1.82
Rixey-Cin 1.89
Meadows-Phi-Pit.. 2.15

Strikeouts
Vance-Bro 197
Luque-Cin 151
Grimes-Bro 119
Morrison-Pit..... 114
Ring-Phi 112

Strikeouts/Game
Vance-Bro 6.32
Luque-Cin 4.22
Bentley-NY....... 3.93
Osborne-Chi 3.46
Morrison-Pit...... 3.40

Ratio
Alexander-Chi ... 9.97
Luque-Cin 10.40
Ryan-NY........ 11.31
Aldridge-Chi..... 11.49
McQuillan-NY ... 11.56

Earned Run Average
Luque-Cin 1.93
Rixey-Cin 2.80
Keen-Chi 3.00
Kaufmann-Chi ... 3.10
Haines-StL 3.11

Adjusted ERA
Luque-Cin 200
Rixey-Cin 138
Keen-Chi 133
Kaufmann-Chi 129
Alexander-Chi ... 125

Opponents' Batting Avg.
Luque-Cin ...... .235
Vance-Bro ...... .250
Aldridge-Chi..... .251
Morrison-Pit..... .253
Osborne-Chi ..... .255

Opponents' On Base Pct.
Alexander-Chi ... .277
Luque-Cin ...... .291
Aldridge-Chi..... .307
Ryan-NY........ .308
McQuillan-NY ... .315

Starter Runs
Luque-Cin 73.9
Rixey-Cin 41.1
Alexander-Chi ... 27.4
Haines-StL 26.1
Kaufmann-Chi ... 20.6

Adjusted Starter Runs
Luque-Cin 69.1
Rixey-Cin 36.5
Alexander-Chi ... 27.4
Ring-Phi 24.3
Haines-StL 23.2

Clutch Pitching Index
Kaufmann-Chi 118
Rixey-Cin 116
Genewich-Bos.... 116
Doak-StL 116
Luque-Cin 115

Relief Runs
Decatur-Bro 15.3
Jonnard-NY 7.6
Keck-Cin 2.6
V.Barnes-NY 5

Adjusted Relief Runs
Decatur-Bro 14.0
Jonnard-NY 4.4
Keck-Cin 1.3

Relief Ranking
Decatur-Bro 8.7
Jonnard-NY 4.4
Keck-Cin 1.3

Total Pitcher Index
Luque-Cin 7.5
Rixey-Cin 3.3
Alexander-Chi ... 3.2
Kaufmann-Chi ... 2.3
Haines-StL 2.1

Total Baseball Ranking
Luque-Cin 7.5
Fournier-Bro 4.1
Traynor-Pit 4.1
Carey-Pit 3.6
Bancroft-NY 3.6

TEAM	G	W	L	PCT	GB	R	OR	AB	H	2B	3B	HR	BB	SO	AVG	OBP	SLG	PRO	PRO+	BR	/A	PF	CHI	RC	SB	CS	SBA	SBR
NY	152	98	54	.645		823	622	5347	1554	231	79	105	521	516	.291	.357	.422	.779	108	73	60	102	101	811	69	74	48	-24
DET	155	83	71	.539	16	831	741	5266	1579	270	69	41	596	385	.300	.377	.401	.778	113	91	106	98	98	827	87	62	58	-11
CLE	153	82	71	.536	16.5	888	746	5290	1594	301	75	59	633	384	.301	.381	.420	.801	117	135	137	100	100	869	79	77	51	-23
WAS	155	75	78	.490	23.5	720	747	5244	1436	224	93	26	532	448	.274	.346	.367	.713	98	-46	-8	95	104	693	102	67	60	-10
STL	154	74	78	.487	24	688	720	5298	1489	248	62	82	442	423	.281	.339	.398	.737	94	-15	-56	106	96	724	64	54	54	-13
PHI	153	69	83	.454	29	661	761	5196	1407	229	64	53	445	517	.271	.333	.370	.703	89	-26	-16	99	97	706	191	119	62	-14
CHI	156	69	85	.448	30	692	741	5246	1463	254	57	42	532	458	.279	.350	.373	.723	97	-74	-83	101	103	653	72	62	54	-16
BOS	154	61	91	.401	37	584	809	5181	1354	253	54	34	391	480	.261	.318	.351	.669	81	-143	-147	101	104	578	77	91	46	-32
TOT	616					5887		42068	11876	2010	553	442	4092	3611	.282	.351	.388	.739							741	606	55	-141

TEAM	CG	SH	SV	IP	H	H/G	HR	BB	SO	RAT	ERA	ERA+	OAV	OOB	PR	/A	PF	CPI	FA	E	DP	FW	PW	BW	SBW	DIF
NY	101	9	10	1380.2	1365	8.9	68	491	506	12.3	3.62	109	.263	.330	55	49	99	96	.977	144	131	3.3	4.7	5.8	-.6	8.8
DET	61	9	12	1373.2	1502	9.8	58	449	447	13.1	4.09	94	.283	.345	-16	-34	97	96	.968	200	103	.0	-3.3	10.3	.6	-1.7
CLE	77	10	11	1376	1517	9.9	36	465	407	13.2	3.91	101	.285	.346	11	4	100	97	.964	226	143	-1.7	.4	13.2	-.5	-5.9
WAS	71	8	16	1374.2	1527	10.0	56	563	474	14.0	3.98	95	.291	.364	0	-30	95	109	.966	216	182	-.9	-2.9	-.8	.7	2.3
STL	83	10	10	1373.1	1430	9.4	59	528	488	13.2	3.93	106	.275	.348	9	37	105	98	.971	177	145	1.4	3.6	-5.4	.5	-2.0
PHI	65	7	12	1364.2	1465	9.7	68	550	400	13.5	4.08	101	.280	.352	-15	1	103	99	.965	221	127	-1.4	.0	-8.0	.2	2.1
CHI	74	5	11	1397	1512	9.7	49	534	467	13.4	4.05	98	.283	.353	-10	-13	99	99	.971	184	138	1.1	-1.3	-1.5	.4	-6.7
BOS	77	3	11	1372	1534	10.1	48	520	412	13.9	4.20	98	.294	.366	-33	-15	103	104	.963	232	126	-2.0	-1.5	-14.2	-1.4	4.0
TOT	609	61	93	11012		9.7				13.3	3.98		.282	.351					.968	1600	1095					

Runs
Ruth-NY 151
Speaker-Cle 133
Jamieson-Cle 130
Heilmann-Det 121
Rice-Was 117

Hits
Jamieson-Cle ... 222
Speaker-Cle 218
Heilmann-Det 211
Ruth-NY 205
Tobin-StL 202

Doubles
Speaker-Cle 59
Burns-Bos 47
Ruth-NY 45
Heilmann-Det 44
J.Sewell-Cle 41

Triples
Rice-Was 18
Goslin-Was 18
Tobin-StL 15
Mostil-Chi 15

Home Runs
Ruth-NY 41
Williams-StL 29
Heilmann-Det 18
Speaker-Cle 17
Hauser-Phi 17

Total Bases
Ruth-NY 399
Speaker-Cle 350
Williams-StL 346
Heilmann-Det 331
Tobin-StL 303

Runs Batted In
Ruth-NY 131
Speaker-Cle 130
Heilmann-Det 115
J.Sewell-Cle 109
Pipp-NY 108

Runs Produced
Speaker-Cle 246
Ruth-NY 241
Heilmann-Det 218
J.Sewell-Cle 204
Rice-Was 189

Bases On Balls
Ruth-NY 170
J.Sewell-Cle 98
Blue-Det 96
Speaker-Cle 93
Collins-Chi 84

Batting Average
Heilmann-Det 403
Ruth-NY 393
Speaker-Cle 380
Collins-Chi 360
Williams-StL 357

On Base Percentage
Ruth-NY 545
Heilmann-Det 481
Speaker-Cle 469
J.Sewell-Cle 456
Collins-Chi 455

Slugging Average
Ruth-NY 764
Heilmann-Det 632
Williams-StL 623
Speaker-Cle 610
Harris-Bos 520

Production
Ruth-NY 1.309
Heilmann-Det ..1.113
Speaker-Cle 1.079
Williams-StL 1.062
J.Sewell-Cle 935

Adjusted Production
Ruth-NY 238
Heilmann-Det 195
Speaker-Cle 183
Williams-StL 168
J.Sewell-Cle 147

Batter Runs
Ruth-NY 119.1
Speaker-Cle 70.9
Heilmann-Det 70.7
Williams-StL 61.2
J.Sewell-Cle 42.8

Adjusted Batter Runs
Ruth-NY 117.7
Heilmann-Det 72.2
Speaker-Cle 71.1
Williams-StL 56.8
J.Sewell-Cle 42.9

Clutch Hitting Index
Pipp-NY 160
J.Sewell-Cle 144
Sheely-Chi 142
Rigney-Det 134
Judge-Was....... 130

Runs Created
Ruth-NY 223
Speaker-Cle 166
Heilmann-Det 159
Williams-StL 148
J.Sewell-Cle 128

Total Average
Ruth-NY 1.683
Heilmann-Det ..1.284
Speaker-Cle 1.227
Williams-StL 1.144
J.Sewell-Cle 1.025

Stolen Bases
Collins-Chi 49
Mostil-Chi 41
Harris-Was 23
Rice-Was 20
Jamieson-Cle 19

Stolen Base Average
Rice-Was 71.4
Mostil-Chi 70.7
Collins-Chi 62.8
Jamieson-Cle ... 61.3
Harris-Was 59.0

Stolen Base Runs
Mostil-Chi 2.1
Barrett-Chi 1.8
Veach-Det 1.2
Rice-Was 1.2

Fielding Runs
Peckinpaugh-Was . 22.8
Mostil-Chi 22.0
Lutzke-Cle 20.4
Harris-Was 19.7
Flagstead-Det-Bos 18.7

Total Player Rating
Ruth-NY 10.8
Speaker-Cle...... 6.5
Heilmann-Det 6.0
J.Sewell-Cle 5.9
Williams-StL 5.0

Wins
Uhle-Cle 26
Jones-NY 21
Dauss-Det 21
Shocker-StL 20
Ehmke-Bos 20

Win Percentage
Pennock-NY 760
Jones-NY 724
Hoyt-NY 654
Shocker-StL 625
Uhle-Cle 619

Games
Rommel-Phi 56
Uhle-Cle 54
Russell-Was 52
Cole-Det 52
Dauss-Det 50

Complete Games
Uhle-Cle 29
Ehmke-Bos 28
Shocker-StL 24
Dauss-Det 22
Bush-NY 22

Shutouts
Coveleski-Cle 5
Vangilder-StL 4
Dauss-Det 4

Saves
Russell-Was........ 9
Quinn-Bos 7
Harriss-Phi......... 6

Innings Pitched
Uhle-Cle 357.2
Ehmke-Bos 316.2
Dauss-Det 316.0
Rommel-Phi 297.2
Vangilder-StL ... 282.1

Fewest Hits/Game
Shawkey-NY 8.07
Hoyt-NY 8.56
Bush-NY 8.59
Russell-Was...... 8.78
Danforth-StL 8.79

Fewest BB/Game
Shocker-StL 1.59
Coveleski-Cle 1.66
Thurston-StL-Chi . 1.75
Quinn-Bos 1.96
Dauss-Det 2.22

Strikeouts
Johnson-Was 130
Shawkey-NY 125
Bush-NY 125
Ehmke-Bos 121

Strikeouts/Game
Johnson-Det 4.75
Johnson-Was 4.48
Shawkey-NY 4.35
Bush-NY 4.08
Harriss-Phi....... 3.83

Ratio
Shocker-StL 11.16
Hoyt-NY 11.20
Pennock-NY 11.52
Jones-NY 11.63
Coveleski-Cle ... 11.64

Earned Run Average
Coveleski-Cle 2.76
Hoyt-NY 3.02
Russell-Was...... 3.03
Vangilder-StL 3.06
Mogridge-Was ... 3.11

Adjusted ERA
Coveleski-Cle 143
Vangilder-StL 136
Hoyt-NY 131
Thurston-StL-Chi . 127
Rommel-Phi 126

Opponents' Batting Avg.
Shawkey-NY 246
Hoyt-NY 253
Jones-NY 257
Faber-Chi 259
Bush-NY 260

Opponents' On Base Pct.
Shocker-StL 306
Hoyt-NY 307
Faber-Chi 311
Jones-NY 312
Pennock-NY 314

Starter Runs
Coveleski-Cle 30.9
Vangilder-StL 28.9
Hoyt-NY 25.6
Rommel-Phi 23.7
Pennock-NY 22.4

Adjusted Starter Runs
Vangilder-StL 34.8
Coveleski-Cle 30.4
Rommel-Phi 27.8
Hoyt-NY 24.4
Shocker-StL 23.5

Clutch Pitching Index
Thurston-StL-Chi . 139
Russell-Was 128
Mogridge-Was.... 122
Vangilder-StL 121
Coveleski-Cle 121

Relief Runs

Adjusted Relief Runs

Relief Ranking

Total Pitcher Index
Rommel-Phi....... 3.5
Vangilder-StL 3.1
Coveleski-Cle 2.6
Bush-NY 2.4
Uhle-Cle 2.4

Total Baseball Ranking
Ruth-NY 10.8
Speaker-Cle 6.5
Heilmann-Det 6.0
J.Sewell-Cle 5.9
Williams-StL 5.0

TEAM	G	W	L	PCT	GB	R	OR	AB	H	2B	3B	HR	BB	SO	AVG	OBP	SLG	PRO	PRO+	BR	/A	PF	CHI	RC	SB	CS	SBA	SBR
NY	154	93	60	.608		857	641	5445	1634	269	81	95	467	479	.300	.358	.432	.790	120	124	144	97	102	849	82	53	61	-7
BRO	154	92	62	.597	1.5	717	675	5339	1534	227	54	72	447	357	.287	.345	.391	.736	105	19	42	97	99	725	34	46	43	-17
PIT	153	90	63	.588	3	724	588	5288	1517	222	122	44	366	396	.287	.336	.400	.736	100	11	0	102	103	715	181	92	66	-1
CIN	153	83	70	.542	10	649	629	5301	1539	236	111	36	349	334	.290	.337	.397	.734	103	8	18	99	93	698	103	98	51	-28
CHI	154	81	72	.529	12	698	699	5134	1419	207	59	66	469	521	.276	.340	.378	.718	96	-10	-16	101	103	652	137	149	48	-48
STL	154	65	89	.422	28.5	740	750	5349	1552	270	87	67	382	418	.290	.341	.411	.752	108	42	55	98	100	740	86	86	50	-26
PHI	152	55	96	.364	37	676	849	5306	1459	256	56	94	382	452	.275	.328	.397	.725	88	-13	-98	112	99	687	57	67	46	-23
BOS	154	53	100	.346	40	520	800	5283	1355	194	52	25	354	451	.256	.306	.327	.633	77	-181	-152	96	103	532	74	68	52	-19
TOT	614					5581		42445	12009	1881	622	499	3216	3408	.283	.337	.392	.729							754	659	53	-169

TEAM	CG	SH	SV	IP	H	H/G	HR	BB	SO	RAT	ERA	ERA+	OAV	OOB	PR	/A	PF	CPI	FA	E	DP	FW	PW	BW	SBW	DIF
NY	71	4	21	1378²	1464	9.6	77	392	406	12.2	3.62	101	.274	.326	38	7	95	100	.971	186	160	.4	.7	14.3	1.4	-.3
BRO	97	10	5	1376¹	1432	9.4	58	403	638	12.2	3.64	103	.270	.326	35	16	97	96	.968	196	121	-.2	1.6	4.2	.4	9.0
PIT	85	15	5	1382	1387	9.0	42	323	364	11.3	3.27	117	.267	.313	92	88	99	97	.971	183	161	.5	8.7	.0	2.0	2.3
CIN	77	14	9	1378	1408	9.2	30	293	451	11.3	3.12	121	.267	.309	115	99	97	97	.966	217	142	-1.4	9.8	1.8	-.7	-3.0
CHI	85	4	6	1380²	1459	9.5	89	438	416	12.5	3.83	102	.275	.333	6	11	101	101	.966	218	153	-1.4	1.1	-1.6	-2.7	9.1
STL	79	7	6	1364²	1528	10.1	70	486	393	13.5	4.15	91	.290	.354	-43	-57	98	104	.969	188	162	.3	-5.7	5.5	-.5	-11.6
PHI	59	7	10	1354¹	1689	11.2	84	469	349	14.5	4.87	92	.313	.372	-151	-60	115	103	.972	175	168	.8	-6.0	-9.7	-.2	-5.5
BOS	66	10	4	1379¹	1607	10.5	49	402	364	13.3	4.46	86	.301	.353	-92	-100	99	96	.973	168	154	1.4	-9.9	-15.1	.2	-.0
TOT	619	71	66	10994		9.8				12.6	3.87		.283	.337					.970	1531	1221					

Runs
Hornsby-StL 121
Frisch-NY 121
Carey-Pit 113
Youngs-NY 112
Williams-Phi 101

Hits
Hornsby-StL 227
Wheat-Bro 212
Frisch-NY 198
High-Bro 191
Fournier-Bro 188

Doubles
Hornsby-StL 43
Wheat-Bro 41
Kelly-NY 37

Triples
Roush-Cin 21
Maranville-Pit 20
Wright-Pit 18
Cuyler-Pit 16
Frisch-NY 15

Home Runs
Fournier-Bro 27
Hornsby-StL 25
Williams-Phi 24
Kelly-NY 21

Total Bases
Hornsby-StL 373
Wheat-Bro 311
Williams-Phi 308
Kelly-NY 303
Fournier-Bro 302

Runs Batted In
Kelly-NY 136
Fournier-Bro 116
Wright-Pit 111
Bottomley-StL 111
Meusel-NY 102

Runs Produced
Kelly-NY 206
Hornsby-StL 190
Wright-Pit 184
Bottomley-StL 184
Frisch-NY 183

Bases On Balls
Hornsby-StL 89
Fournier-Bro 83
Youngs-NY 77
Williams-Phi 67
Friberg-Chi 66

Batting Average
Hornsby-StL 424
Wheat-Bro 375
Youngs-NY 356
Cuyler-Pit 354
Roush-Cin 348

On Base Percentage
Hornsby-StL 507
Youngs-NY 441
Fournier-Bro 428
Wheat-Bro 428
Williams-Phi 403

Slugging Average
Hornsby-StL 696
Williams-Phi 552
Wheat-Bro 549
Cuyler-Pit 539
Fournier-Bro 536

Production
Hornsby-StL 1.203
Wheat-Bro 978
Fournier-Bro 965
Youngs-NY 962
Williams-Phi 955

Adjusted Production
Hornsby-StL 223
Wheat-Bro 165
Fournier-Bro 162
Youngs-NY 161
Cuyler-Pit 147

Batter Runs
Hornsby-StL 94.1
Wheat-Bro 48.2
Fournier-Bro 48.1
Youngs-NY 45.3
Williams-Phi 42.0

Adjusted Batter Runs
Hornsby-StL 95.5
Fournier-Bro 50.6
Wheat-Bro 50.6
Youngs-NY 47.3
Williams-Phi 32.8

Clutch Hitting Index
Friberg-Chi 164
Meusel-NY 158
Wright-Pit 152
Griffith-Bro 146
Brown-Bro 145

Runs Created
Hornsby-StL 186
Fournier-Bro 133
Wheat-Bro 132
Youngs-NY 123
Williams-Phi 121

Total Average
Hornsby-StL 1.424
Fournier-Bro 1.045
Youngs-NY 1.023
Wheat-Bro 1.014
Cuyler-Pit 990

Stolen Bases
Carey-Pit 49
Cuyler-Pit 32
Heathcote-Chi 26
Traynor-Pit 24
Smith-StL 24

Stolen Base Average
Carey-Pit 79.0
Cuyler-Pit 74.4
Frisch-NY 71.0
Critz-Cin 63.3
Smith-StL 60.0

Stolen Base Runs
Carey-Pit 6.9
Cuyler-Pit 3.0
Hartnett-Chi 1.8

Fielding Runs
Pinelli-Cin 26.7
Frisch-NY 24.9
Statz-Chi 14.5
Ford-Phi 11.9
Wright-Pit 10.7

Total Player Rating
Hornsby-StL 8.4
Frisch-NY 5.3
Fournier-Bro 4.6
Wheat-Bro 4.3
Youngs-NY 3.4

Wins
Vance-Bro 28
Grimes-Bro 22
Mays-Cin 20
Cooper-Pit 20
Kremer-Pit 18

Win Percentage
Yde-Pit 842
Vance-Bro 824
Bentley-NY 762
Mays-Cin 690
Kremer-Pit 643

Games
Morrison-Pit 41
Kremer-Pit 41
Keen-Chi 40
Sheehan-Cin 39

Complete Games
Vance-Bro 30
Grimes-Bro 30
Cooper-Pit 25
Barnes-Bos 21
Aldridge-Chi 20

Shutouts
Yde-Pit 4
Sothoron-StL 4
Rixey-Cin 4
Kremer-Pit 4
Cooper-Pit 4
Barnes-Bos 4

Saves
May-Cin 6
Ryan-NY 5
Jonnard-NY 5

Innings Pitched
Grimes-Bro 310.2
Vance-Bro 308.2
Cooper-Pit 268.2
Barnes-Bos 267.2
Kremer-Pit 259.1

Fewest Hits/Game
Vance-Bro 6.94
Yde-Pit 7.93
Morrison-Pit 8.07
Doak-StL-Bro . . . 8.14
Rixey-Cin 8.27

Fewest BB/Game
Benton-Cin 1.33
Alexander-Chi . . . 1.33
Cooper-Pit 1.34
Mays-Cin 1.43
Donohue-Cin 1.46

Strikeouts
Vance-Bro 262
Grimes-Bro 135
Luque-Cin 86
Morrison-Pit 85
Kaufmann-Chi 79

Strikeouts/Game
Vance-Bro 7.64
Grimes-Bro 3.91
Nehf-NY 3.77
Luque-Cin 3.53
Kaufmann-Chi 3.41

Ratio
Vance-Bro 9.45
Rixey-Cin 10.12
Benton-Cin 10.73
Doak-StL-Bro . . . 10.87
McQuillan-NY . . . 10.96

Earned Run Average
Vance-Bro 2.16
McQuillan-NY . . . 2.69
Rixey-Cin 2.76
Benton-Cin 2.77
Yde-Pit 2.83

Adjusted ERA
Vance-Bro 174
Rixey-Cin 137
McQuillan-NY . . . 136
Benton-Cin 136
Yde-Pit 136

Opponents' Batting Avg.
Vance-Bro 213
Yde-Pit 244
Morrison-Pit 245
Rixey-Cin 246
Doak-StL-Bro 249

Opponents' On Base Pct.
Vance-Bro 269
Rixey-Cin 285
Benton-Cin 297
Alexander-Chi 299
Nehf-NY 301

Starter Runs
Vance-Bro 58.6
Rixey-Cin 29.4
McQuillan-NY . . . 24.0
Yde-Pit 22.3
Barnes-NY 20.5

Adjusted Starter Runs
Vance-Bro 54.5
Rixey-Cin 26.7
Yde-Pit 21.7
McQuillan-NY . . . 19.9
Kremer-Pit 18.6

Clutch Pitching Index
Sherdel-StL 117
Sothoron-StL 115
Ring-Phi 113
McQuillan-NY . . . 113
Aldridge-Chi 110

Relief Runs
Jonnard-NY 14.5
May-Cin 9.5
Stone-Pit 6.5

Adjusted Relief Runs
Jonnard-NY 12.5
May-Cin 8.4
Stone-Pit 6.3

Relief Ranking
Jonnard-NY 12.9
May-Cin 5.7
Stone-Pit 5.3

Total Pitcher Index
Vance-Bro 5.8
Mays-Cin 3.2
Rixey-Cin 2.8
Yde-Pit 2.5
Cooper-Pit 2.2

Total Baseball Ranking
Hornsby-StL 8.4
Vance-Bro 5.8
Frisch-NY 5.3
Fournier-Bro 4.6
Wheat-Bro 4.3

TEAM	G	W	L	PCT	GB	R	OR	AB	H	2B	3B	HR	BB	SO	AVG	OBP	SLG	PRO	PRO+	BR	/A	PF	CHI	RC	SB	CS	SBA	SBR
WAS	156	92	62	.597		755	613	5304	1558	255	**88**	22	513	392	.294	.361	.387	.748	101	-8	16	97	98	761	115	87	57	-18
NY	153	89	63	.586	2	798	667	5240	1516	248	86	**98**	478	420	.289	.352	**.426**	.778	106	29	31	100	102	790	100	76	57	-16
DET	156	86	68	.558	6	849	796	5389	**1604**	315	76	35	**607**	400	.298	.356	.404	.764	**108**	53	**66**	98	100	**837**	85	50	50	-26
STL	153	74	78	.487	17	769	809	5236	1543	266	62	67	465	349	.295	.356	.408	.764	96	9	-38	106	101	762	79	66	54	-16
PHI	152	71	81	.467	20	685	778	5184	1459	251	59	63	374	482	.281	.334	.389	.723	90	-77	-84	101	105	675	84	56	60	**-8**
CLE	153	67	86	.438	24.5	755	814	5332	1580	306	59	41	492	371	.296	.361	.399	.760	100	8	-2	101	97	784	79	61	56	-13
BOS	157	67	87	.435	25	737	806	5340	1481	302	63	30	603	417	.277	.356	.374	.730	94	-42	-43	100	99	741	69	61	56	-13
CHI	154	66	87	.431	25.5	793	858	5255	1512	254	58	41	604	418	.288	.365	.382	.747	101	-6	18	97	103	763	**138**	86	**62**	-10
TOT	617					6141		42280	12253	2197	551	397	4136	3249	.290	.358	.397	.755							749	581	56	-124

TEAM	CG	SH	SV	IP	H	H/G	HR	BB	SO	RAT	ERA	ERA+	OAV	OOB	PR	/A	PF	CPI	FA	E	DP	FW	PW	BW	SBW	DIF
WAS	74	13	25	1383	**1329**	8.6	34	505	469	12.2	3.34	121	.259	.330	136	106	95	99	.972	171	149	1.3	**10.0**	1.5	-.2	2.4
NY	76	13	13	1359¹	1483	9.8	59	522	**487**	13.4	3.86	108	.284	.353	56	44	98	107	**.974**	156	131	**2.0**	4.2	2.9	-.2	4.1
DET	60	5	20	1394²	1586	10.2	55	**467**	441	13.5	4.19	98	.293	.354	5	-12	97	101	.971	187	142	.4	-1.1	**6.2**	-.0	3.6
STL	65	11	7	1353¹	1511	10.0	68	517	386	13.8	4.57	99	.289	.358	-51	-9	107	95	.969	184	142	.3	-.8	-3.6	-1.0	3.1
PHI	68	8	10	1345	1527	10.2	43	597	371	14.4	4.39	98	.292	.368	-24	-15	101	101	.971	180	**157**	-1.0	-1.4	-7.9	-.0	3.9
CLE	**87**	7	7	1349	1603	10.7	43	503	315	14.3	4.40	97	.300	.365	-25	-20	101	101	.967	205	130	-1.0	-1.9	-.2	.7	-7.1
BOS	73	8	16	1391¹	1563	10.1	43	523	414	13.9	4.35	100	.290	.359	-19	2	103	97	.967	210	126	-1.0	.2	-4.1	.2	-5.4
CHI	76	1	11	1370²	1635	10.7	52	512	360	14.3	4.74	87	.305	.368	-78	-95	97	98	.963	229	136	-2.4	-9.0	1.7	.5	-1.4
TOT	579	66	109	10946¹		10.1				13.7	4.23		.290	.358					.969	1522	1113					

Runs
Ruth-NY	143
Cobb-Det	115
Collins-Chi	108
Hooper-Chi	107
Heilmann-Det	107

Hits
Rice-Was	216
Jamieson-Cle	213
Cobb-Det	211
Ruth-NY	200
Goslin-Was	199

Doubles
J.Sewell-Cle	45
Heilmann-Det	45
Wambsganss-Bos	41
Jacobson-StL	41
Meusel-NY	40

Triples
Pipp-NY	19
Goslin-Was	17
Heilmann-Det	16
Rice-Was	14
Jacobson-StL	12

Home Runs
Ruth-NY	46
Hauser-Phi	27
Jacobson-StL	19
Williams-StL	18
Boone-Bos	13

Total Bases
Ruth-NY	391
Jacobson-StL	306
Heilmann-Det	304
Goslin-Was	299
Hauser-Phi	290

Runs Batted In
Goslin-Was	129
Ruth-NY	121
Meusel-NY	120
Hauser-Phi	115
Heilmann-Det	114

Runs Produced
Ruth-NY	218
Goslin-Was	217
Heilmann-Det	211
J.Sewell-Cle	201
Meusel-NY	201

Bases On Balls
Ruth-NY	142
Rigney-Det	102
Sheely-Chi	95
Collins-Chi	89
Cobb-Det	85

Batting Average
Ruth-NY	.378
Jamieson-Cle	.359
Falk-Chi	.352
Collins-Chi	.349
Heilmann-Det	.346

On Base Percentage
Ruth-NY	.513
Collins-Chi	.441
Speaker-Cle	.432
Heilmann-Det	.428
Sheely-Chi	.426

Slugging Average
Ruth-NY	.739
Heilmann-Det	.533
Williams-StL	.533
Jacobson-StL	.528
Goslin-Was	.516

Production
Ruth-NY	1.252
Heilmann-Det	.961
Williams-StL	.958
Speaker-Cle	.943
Goslin-Was	.937

Adjusted Production
Ruth-NY	221
Heilmann-Det	149
Goslin-Was	145
Speaker-Cle	141
Williams-StL	137

Batter Runs
Ruth-NY	100.8
Heilmann-Det	40.4
Goslin-Was	35.6
Speaker-Cle	32.4
Collins-Chi	30.5

Adjusted Batter Runs
Ruth-NY	100.9
Heilmann-Det	41.8
Goslin-Was	38.2
Collins-Chi	33.1
Speaker-Cle	31.5

Clutch Hitting Index
Kamm-Chi	150
Pratt-Det	149
Rigney-Det	148
Sheely-Chi	143
Veach-Bos	142

Runs Created
Ruth-NY	205
Heilmann-Det	134
Goslin-Was	126
Cobb-Det	121
Collins-Chi	119

Total Average
Ruth-NY	1.558
Heilmann-Det	1.042
Williams-StL	1.039
Speaker-Cle	.988
Collins-Chi	.976

Stolen Bases
Collins-Chi	42
Meusel-NY	26
Rice-Was	24
Cobb-Det	23
Jamieson-Cle	21

Stolen Base Average
Collins-Chi	71.2
Jamieson-Cle	65.6
Harris-Was	65.5
Meusel-NY	65.0
Rice-Was	64.9

Stolen Base Runs
Collins-Chi	2.4

Fielding Runs
J.Sewell-Cle	21.4
Lutzke-Cle	19.4
Dykes-Phi	15.9
Jacobson-StL	15.8
Wambsganss-Bos	14.4

Total Player Rating
Ruth-NY	8.5
J.Sewell-Cle	4.4
Heilmann-Det	3.9
Rigney-Det	3.4
Goslin-Was	2.8

Wins
Johnson-Was	23
Pennock-NY	21
Thurston-Chi	20
Shaute-Cle	20
Ehmke-Bos	19

Win Percentage
Johnson-Was	.767
Pennock-NY	.700
Whitehill-Det	.654
Zachary-Was	.625

Games
Marberry-Was	50
Holloway-Det	49
Shaute-Cle	46
Hoyt-NY	46
Ehmke-Bos	45

Complete Games
Thurston-Chi	28
Ehmke-Bos	26
Pennock-NY	25
Shaute-Cle	21
Rommel-Phi	21

Shutouts
Johnson-Was	6
Davis-StL	5
Shocker-StL	4
Pennock-NY	4
Ehmke-Bos	4

Saves
Marberry-Was	15
Russell-Was	8
Quinn-Bos	7
Dauss-Det	6
Connally-Chi	6

Innings Pitched
Ehmke-Bos	315.0
Thurston-Chi	291.0
Pennock-NY	286.1
Shaute-Cle	283.0
Rommel-Phi	278.0

Fewest Hits/Game
Johnson-Was	7.55
Collins-Det	8.29
Marberry-Was	8.75
Zachary-Was	8.79
Wingard-StL	8.88

Fewest BB/Game
Smith-Cle	1.53
Thurston-Chi	1.86
Shocker-StL	1.90
Pennock-NY	2.01
Quinn-Bos	2.05

Strikeouts
Johnson-Was	158
Ehmke-Bos	119
Shawkey-NY	114
Pennock-NY	101
Shocker-StL	88

Strikeouts/Game
Johnson-Was	5.12
Shawkey-NY	4.94
Ehmke-Bos	3.40
Shocker-StL	3.22
Pennock-NY	3.17

Ratio
Johnson-Was	10.37
Collins-Det	11.08
Zachary-Was	11.28
Smith-Cle	11.48
Pennock-NY	11.54

Earned Run Average
Johnson-Was	2.72
Zachary-Was	2.75
Pennock-NY	2.83
Baumgartner-Phi	2.88
Smith-Cle	3.02

Adjusted ERA
Baumgartner-Phi	149
Johnson-Was	148
Pennock-NY	147
Zachary-Was	147
Smith-Cle	142

Opponents' Batting Avg.
Johnson-Was	.224
Collins-Det	.249
Marberry-Was	.262
Wingard-StL	.262
Davis-StL	.263

Opponents' On Base Pct.
Johnson-Was	.284
Collins-Det	.307
Smith-Cle	.312
Pennock-NY	.314
Zachary-Was	.315

Starter Runs
Johnson-Was	46.5
Pennock-NY	44.6
Smith-Cle	33.4
Zachary-Was	33.2
Baumgartner-Phi	27.1

Adjusted Starter Runs
Pennock-NY	42.3
Johnson-Was	40.5
Smith-Cle	34.5
Ehmke-Bos	31.9
Zachary-Was	28.9

Clutch Pitching Index
Baumgartner-Phi	132
Pennock-NY	117
Zachary-Was	113
Ferguson-Bos	113
Hoyt-NY	112

Relief Runs
Speece-Was	9.5

Adjusted Relief Runs
Speece-Was	8.4

Relief Ranking
Speece-Was	4.2

Total Pitcher Index
Johnson-Was	4.6
Pennock-NY	3.9
Smith-Cle	3.5
Zachary-Was	3.4
Ehmke-Bos	3.1

Total Baseball Ranking
Ruth-NY	8.5
Johnson-Was	4.6
J.Sewell-Cle	4.4
Pennock-NY	3.9
Heilmann-Det	3.9

1925 National League

TEAM	G	W	L	PCT	GB	R	OR	AB	H	2B	3B	HR	BB	SO	AVG	OBP	SLG	PRO	PRO+	BR	/A	PF	CHI	RC	SB	CS	SBA	SBR
PIT	153	95	58	.621		912	715	5372	1651	316	105	78	499	363	.307	.369	.449	.818	108	116	63	107	101	909	159	63	72	10
NY	152	86	66	.566	8.5	736	702	5327	1507	239	61	114	411	494	.283	.337	.415	.752	101	-26	4	96	100	742	79	65	55	-15
CIN	153	80	73	.523	15	690	643	5233	1490	221	90	44	409	327	.285	.339	.387	.726	93	-66	-48	98	100	680	108	107	50	-32
STL	153	77	76	.503	18	828	764	5329	1592	292	80	109	446	414	.299	.356	.445	.801	108	72	54	102	98	846	70	51	58	-10
BOS	153	70	83	.458	25	708	802	5365	1567	260	70	41	405	380	.292	.345	.390	.735	102	-48	20	91	98	722	77	72	52	-20
PHI	153	68	85	.444	27	812	930	5412	1598	288	58	100	456	542	.295	.354	.425	.779	96	35	-34	109	99	814	48	59	45	-21
BRO	153	68	85	.444	27	786	866	5468	1617	250	80	64	437	383	.296	.351	.406	.757	102	-6	15	97	101	787	37	30	55	-7
CHI	154	68	86	.442	27.5	723	773	5353	1473	254	70	86	397	470	.275	.329	.397	.726	89	-77	-89	102	104	700	94	70	57	-14
TOT	612					6195		42859	12495	2120	614	636	3460	3373	.292	.348	.414	.762							672	517	57	-109

TEAM	CG	SH	SV	IP	H	H/G	HR	BB	SO	RAT	ERA	ERA+	OAV	OOB	PR	/A	PF	CPI	FA	E	DP	FW	PW	BW	SBW	DIF
PIT	77	2	13	1354²	1526	10.1	81	387	386	12.9	3.87	115	.287	.339	59	88	105	105	.964	224	171	-.9	8.2	5.9	2.2	3.1
NY	80	6	8	1354¹	1532	10.2	73	408	446	13.0	3.94	102	.289	.342	49	17	95	104	.968	199	129	.5	1.6	.4	-.1	7.7
CIN	92	11	12	1375¹	1447	9.5	35	324	437	11.8	3.38	121	.272	.317	135	110	96	95	.968	203	161	.3	10.3	-4.5	-1.7	-.9
STL	82	8	7	1335²	1480	10.0	86	470	428	13.4	4.36	99	.283	.347	-14	-7	101	96	.966	204	156	.3	-.7	5.1	.3	-4.5
BOS	77	5	4	1366²	1567	10.3	67	458	351	13.4	4.39	91	.291	.348	-19	-58	94	96	.964	221	145	-.7	-5.4	1.9	-.6	-1.6
PHI	69	8	9	1350²	1753	11.7	117	444	371	14.8	5.02	95	.315	.368	-114	-39	112	103	.966	211	147	-.1	-3.7	-3.2	-.7	-.8
BRO	82	4	4	1350²	1608	10.7	75	477	518	14.1	4.77	88	.301	.362	-76	-90	98	97	.966	210	130	-.0	-8.4	1.4	.6	-2.0
CHI	75	5	10	1370	1575	10.3	102	485	435	13.7	4.41	98	.292	.353	-21	-14	101	102	.969	198	161	.7	-1.3	-8.3	-.0	-.0
TOT	634	49	67	10857²		10.4				13.4	4.27		.292	.348					.966	1670	1200					

Runs
Cuyler-Pit 144
Hornsby-StL 133
Wheat-Bro 125
Traynor-Pit 114
Blades-StL 112

Hits
Bottomley-StL 227
Wheat-Bro 221
Cuyler-Pit 220
Hornsby-StL 203
Stock-Bro 202

Doubles
Bottomley-StL 44
Cuyler-Pit 43
Wheat-Bro 42
Hornsby-StL 41
Burrus-Bos 41

Triples
Cuyler-Pit 26
Walker-Cin 16
Roush-Cin 16
Fournier-Bro 16

Home Runs
Hornsby-StL 39
Hartnett-Chi 24
Fournier-Bro 22
Meusel-NY 21
Bottomley-StL . . . 21

Total Bases
Hornsby-StL 381
Cuyler-Pit 369
Bottomley-StL 358
Wheat-Bro 333
Fournier-Bro 310

Runs Batted In
Hornsby-StL 143
Fournier-Bro 130
Bottomley-StL . . . 128
Wright-Pit 121
Barnhart-Pit 114

Runs Produced
Hornsby-StL 237
Cuyler-Pit 228
Wheat-Bro 214
Traynor-Pit 214
Fournier-Bro 207

Bases On Balls
Fournier-Bro 86
Hornsby-StL 83
Moore-Pit 73
Youngs-NY 66
Carey-Pit 66

Batting Average
Hornsby-StL 403
Bottomley-StL 367
Wheat-Bro 359
Cuyler-Pit 357
Fournier-Bro 350

On Base Percentage
Hornsby-StL 489
Fournier-Bro 446
Blades-StL 423
Cuyler-Pit 423
Carey-Pit 418

Slugging Average
Hornsby-StL 756
Cuyler-Pit 598
Bottomley-StL 578
Fournier-Bro 569
Harper-Phi 558

Production
Hornsby-StL 1.245
Cuyler-Pit 1.021
Fournier-Bro 1.015
Bottomley-StL 992
Blades-StL 958

Adjusted Production
Hornsby-StL 208
Fournier-Bro 162
Cuyler-Pit 148
Bottomley-StL . . . 147
Wheat-Bro 143

Batter Runs
Hornsby-StL 87.1
Cuyler-Pit 53.1
Fournier-Bro 50.1
Bottomley-StL . . . 45.5
Wheat-Bro 35.0

Adjusted Batter Runs
Hornsby-StL 85.3
Fournier-Bro 52.4
Cuyler-Pit 46.9
Bottomley-StL . . . 43.5
Wheat-Bro 37.3

Clutch Hitting Index
Barnhart-Pit 170
Traynor-Pit 137
E.Brown-Bro 133
Wright-Pit 131
Fournier-Bro 130

Runs Created
Hornsby-StL 187
Cuyler-Pit 158
Bottomley-StL . . . 145
Fournier-Bro 141
Wheat-Bro 134

Total Average
Hornsby-StL 1.539
Cuyler-Pit 1.141
Fournier-Bro 1.117
Bottomley-StL . . . 1.025
Carey-Pit 1.011

Stolen Bases
Carey-Pit 46
Cuyler-Pit 41
Adams-Chi 26
Roush-Cin 22
Frisch-NY 21

Stolen Base Average
Smith-StL 90.9
Carey-Pit 80.7
Cuyler-Pit 75.9
Moore-Pit 73.1
Adams-Chi 68.4

Stolen Base Runs
Carey-Pit 7.2
Smith-StL 4.8
Cuyler-Pit 4.5
Stock-Bro 1.8
Grantham-Pit 1.8

Fielding Runs
Adams-Chi 28.1
Traynor-Pit 22.9
Critz-Cin 21.6
Pinelli-Cin 20.8
Kelly-NY 17.8

Total Player Rating
Hornsby-StL 6.2
Cuyler-Pit 4.4
Fournier-Bro 4.1
Bancroft-Bos 3.7
Traynor-Pit 3.6

Wins
Vance-Bro 22
Rixey-Cin 21
Donohue-Cin 21
Meadows-Pit 19

Win Percentage
Sherdel-StL 714
Vance-Bro 710
Aldridge-Pit 682
Kremer-Pit 680
Rixey-Cin 656

Games
Morrison-Pit 44
Donohue-Cin 42
Bush-Chi 42
Osborne-Bro 41
Kremer-Pit 40

Complete Games
Donohue-Cin 27
Vance-Bro 26
Rixey-Cin 22
Luque-Cin 22
Ring-Phi 21

Shutouts
Vance-Bro 4
Luque-Cin 4
Carlson-Phi 4
Donohue-Cin 3

Saves
Morrison-Pit 4
Bush-Chi 4

Innings Pitched
Donohue-Cin 301.0
Luque-Cin 291.0
Rixey-Cin 287.1
Ring-Phi 270.0
Vance-Bro 265.1

Fewest Hits/Game
Alexander-Chi 8.13
Benton-Bos 8.35
Vance-Bro 8.38
Aldridge-Pit 9.20
Donohue-Cin 9.27

Fewest BB/Game
Alexander-Chi 1.11
Donohue-Cin 1.47
Rixey-Cin 1.47
Cooney-Bos 1.83
Sherdel-StL 1.89

Strikeouts
Vance-Bro 221
Luque-Cin 140
Ring-Phi 93
Blake-Chi 93
Aldridge-Pit 88

Strikeouts/Game
Vance-Bro 7.50
Luque-Cin 4.33
Sothoron-StL 3.87
Bush-Chi 3.76
Aldridge-Pit 3.71

Ratio
Luque-Cin 10.61
Donohue-Cin . . . 10.79
Vance-Bro 10.96
Rixey-Cin 11.15
Alexander-Chi . . . 11.52

Earned Run Average
Luque-Cin 2.63
Rixey-Cin 2.88
Donohue-Cin 3.08
Benton-Bos 3.09
Sherdel-StL 3.11

Adjusted ERA
Luque-Cin 156
Rixey-Cin 143
Sherdel-StL 139
Donohue-Cin 133
Benton-Bos 130

Opponents' Batting Avg.
Luque-Cin 239
Benton-Bos 249
Vance-Bro 250
Donohue-Cin 268
Scott-NY 269

Opponents' On Base Pct.
Luque-Cin 291
Donohue-Cin 299
Vance-Bro 304
Rixey-Cin 307
Cooney-Bos 312

Starter Runs
Luque-Cin 53.0
Rixey-Cin 44.2
Donohue-Cin 39.7
Scott-NY 29.6
Sherdel-StL 25.8

Adjusted Starter Runs
Luque-Cin 47.9
Rixey-Cin 39.2
Donohue-Cin 34.4
Sherdel-StL 27.0
Alexander-Chi . . . 24.4

Clutch Pitching Index
Nehf-NY 122
Yde-Pit 117
Sherdel-StL 109
Rixey-Cin 108
Morrison-Pit 107

Relief Runs
Huntzinger-NY 5.5

Adjusted Relief Runs
Huntzinger-NY 3.9

Relief Ranking
Huntzinger-NY 3.2

Total Pitcher Index
Luque-Cin 5.8
Donohue-Cin 3.8
Rixey-Cin 3.6
Scott-NY 3.0
Sherdel-StL 2.8

Total Baseball Ranking
Hornsby-StL 6.2
Luque-Cin 5.8
Cuyler-Pit 4.4
Fournier-Bro 4.1
Donohue-Cin 3.8

TEAM	G	W	L	PCT	GB	R	OR	AB	H	2B	3B	HR	BB	SO	AVG	OBP	SLG	PRO	PRO+	BR	/A	PF	CHI	RC	SB	CS	SBA	SBR
WAS	152	96	55	.636		829	670	5206	1577	251	71	56	533	427	.303	.373	.411	.784	106	39	55	98	100	816	134	88	60	-13
PHI	153	88	64	.579	8.5	831	713	5399	1659	298	79	76	453	432	.307	.364	.434	.798	101	54	1	107	97	857	67	59	53	-15
STL	154	82	71	.536	15	900	906	5440	1620	304	68	110	498	375	.298	.360	.439	.799	103	52	11	105	105	859	85	78	52	-21
DET	156	81	73	.526	16.5	903	829	5371	1621	277	84	50	640	386	.302	.379	.413	.792	109	63	75	99	102	872	97	63	61	-9
CHI	154	79	75	.513	18.5	811	770	5224	1482	299	59	38	662	405	.284	.370	.385	.755	102	-7	36	95	101	781	129	88	59	-14
CLE	155	70	84	.455	27.5	782	817	5436	1613	285	58	52	520	379	.297	.361	.399	.760	97	-12	-18	101	98	795	90	77	54	-19
NY	156	69	85	.448	28.5	706	774	5353	1471	247	74	110	470	482	.275	.336	.364	.700	96	-61	-47	98	97	738	67	73	48	-24
BOS	152	47	105	.309	49.5	639	922	5166	1375	257	64	41	513	422	.266	.336	.364	.700	83	-131	-130	100	100	647	42	56	43	-21
TOT	616					6401		42595	12418	2218	557	533	4289	3308	.292	.360	.408	.768							711	582	55	-136

TEAM	CG	SH	SV	IP	H	H/G	HR	BB	SO	RAT	ERA	ERA+	OAV	OOB	PR	/A	PF	CPI	FA	E	DP	FW	PW	BW	SBW	DIF
WAS	69	10	21	1358¹	1428	9.5	49	543	463	13.3	3.70	114	.277	.349	105	79	96	106	.972	170	166	1.8	7.3	5.1	.4	5.9
PHI	61	8	18	1381²	1468	9.6	60	544	495	13.3	3.87	120	.276	.347	81	119	106	101	.966	211	148	-.6	11.0	.0	.2	1.3
STL	67	7	10	1379²	1588	10.4	99	675	419	15.0	4.92	95	.298	.380	-80	-39	106	102	.964	226	164	-1.4	-3.6	1.0	-.4	9.9
DET	66	2	15	1383²	1582	10.3	70	556	419	14.2	4.61	94	.296	.366	-32	-46	98	99	.972	173	143	1.9	-4.3	6.9	.7	-1.3
CHI	71	12	13	1385²	1579	10.3	69	489	374	13.6	4.29	97	.296	.356	17	-21	95	102	.967	210	146	.2	-1.9	3.3	.3	.2
CLE	93	6	9	1372¹	1604	10.5	41	493	345	14.0	4.49	98	.296	.359	-15	-9	101	95	.974	160	150	2.7	-1.0	-4.4	-.6	-4.7
NY	80	8	13	1387²	1560	10.1	78	505	492	13.6	4.33	98	.289	.353	10	-11	97	99	.968	200	162	-.4	-.8	-1.7	-.2	-4.0
BOS	68	6	6	1326²	1615	11.0	67	510	310	14.7	4.97	92	.308	.374	-84	-62	103	98	.957	271	150	-4.2	-5.7	-12.0	-.4	-6.6
TOT	575	59	108	10975²		10.2				13.9	4.39		.292	.360					.968	1621	1229					

Runs
Mostil-Chi 135
Simmons-Phi 122
Combs-NY 117
Goslin-Was 116
Rice-Was 111

Hits
Simmons-Phi 253
Rice-Was 227
Heilmann-Det 225
Sisler-StL 224
J.Sewell-Cle 204

Doubles
McManus-StL 44
Simmons-Phi 43
Sheely-Chi 43
Burns-Cle 41

Triples
Goslin-Was 20
Mostil-Chi 16
Sisler-StL 15

Home Runs
Meusel-NY 33
Williams-StL 25
Ruth-NY 25
Simmons-Phi 24
Gehrig-NY 20

Total Bases
Simmons-Phi 392
Meusel-NY 338
Goslin-Was 329
Heilmann-Det 326
Sisler-StL 311

Runs Batted In
Meusel-NY 138
Heilmann-Det 134
Simmons-Phi 129
Goslin-Was 113
Sheely-Chi 111

Runs Produced
Simmons-Phi 227
Heilmann-Det 218
Goslin-Was 211
Meusel-NY 206
Rice-Was 197

Bases On Balls
Mostil-Chi 90
Kamm-Chi 90
Collins-Chi 87
Bishop-Phi 87
Blue-Det 83

Batting Average
Heilmann-Det 393
Speaker-Cle 389
Simmons-Phi 387
Cobb-Det 378
Wingo-Det 370

On Base Percentage
Speaker-Cle 479
Cobb-Det 468
Collins-Chi 461
Heilmann-Det 457
Wingo-Det 456

Slugging Average
Simmons-Phi 599
Cobb-Det 598
Speaker-Cle 578
Heilmann-Det 569
Goslin-Was 547

Production
Cobb-Det 1.066
Speaker-Cle 1.057
Heilmann-Det 1.026
Simmons-Phi 1.018
Wingo-Det 983

Adjusted Production
Cobb-Det 171
Speaker-Cle 166
Heilmann-Det 161
Wingo-Det 151
Simmons-Phi 146

Batter Runs
Heilmann-Det 52.5
Simmons-Phi 51.4
Speaker-Cle 47.0
Cobb-Det 45.3
Wingo-Det 35.3

Adjusted Batter Runs
Heilmann-Det 53.8
Speaker-Cle 46.4
Cobb-Det 46.3
Simmons-Phi 45.3
Wingo-Det 36.3

Clutch Hitting Index
Galloway-Phi 155
Blue-Det 147
Collins-Chi 144
Falk-Chi 136
J.Sewell-Cle 133

Runs Created
Simmons-Phi 155
Heilmann-Det 149
Goslin-Was 131
Speaker-Cle 123
Cobb-Det 118

Total Average
Speaker-Cle 1.231
Cobb-Det 1.206
Heilmann-Det 1.113
Wingo-Det 1.041
Collins-Chi 1.028

Stolen Bases
Mostil-Chi 43
Rice-Was 26
Goslin-Was 26

Stolen Base Average
Blue-Det 79.2
Goslin-Was 76.5
Collins-Chi 76.0
Rice-Was 70.3
Mostil-Chi 67.2

Stolen Base Runs
Goslin-Was 3.0
Haney-Det 2.7
Blue-Det 2.7
Collins-Chi 2.1
Peckinpaugh-Was . . 1.5

Fielding Runs
Flagstead-Bos 20.0
J.Sewell-Cle 16.3
O'Rourke-Det 14.6
Goslin-Was 13.6
Ruel-Was 11.5

Total Player Rating
Speaker-Cle 4.5
J.Sewell-Cle 3.8
Heilmann-Det 3.6
Goslin-Was 3.6
Cobb-Det 3.3

Wins
Rommel-Phi 21
Lyons-Chi 21
Johnson-Was 20
Coveleski-Was 20
Harriss-Phi 19

Win Percentage
Coveleski-Was 800
Johnson-Was 741
Ruether-Was 720
Blankenship-Chi . . .680
Rommel-Phi 677

Games
Marberry-Was 55
Walberg-Phi 53
Vangilder-StL 52
Rommel-Phi 52
Pennock-NY 47

Complete Games
Smith-Cle 22
Ehmke-Bos 22
Pennock-NY 21
Lyons-Chi 19
Wingfield-Bos 18

Shutouts
Lyons-Chi 5
Gray-Phi 4
Giard-StL 4

Saves
Marberry-Was 15
Doyle-Det 8
Connally-Chi 8
Walberg-Phi 7

Innings Pitched
Pennock-NY 277.0
Lyons-Chi 262.2
Rommel-Phi 261.0
Ehmke-Bos 260.2
Wingfield-Bos 254.1

Fewest Hits/Game
Johnson-Was 8.29
Blankenship-Chi . . 8.46
Coveleski-Was . . . 8.59
Pennock-NY 8.68
Gray-Phi 8.79

Fewest BB/Game
Smith-Cle 1.82
Quinn-Bos-Phi . . . 1.85
Shocker-NY 2.14
Faber-Chi 2.23
Pennock-NY 2.31

Strikeouts
Grove-Phi 116
Johnson-Was 108
Harriss-Phi 95
Ehmke-Bos 95
Jones-NY 92

Strikeouts/Game
Grove-Phi 5.30
Johnson-Was 4.24
Shawkey-NY 3.92
Walberg-Phi 3.85
Gray-Phi 3.54

Ratio
Pennock-NY 11.05
Blankenship-Chi . . 11.13
Coveleski-Was . . . 11.39
Johnson-Was 11.63
Gray-Phi 11.71

Earned Run Average
Coveleski-Was . . . 2.84
Pennock-NY 2.96
Blankenship-Chi . . 3.03
Johnson-Was 3.07
Dauss-Det 3.16

Adjusted ERA
Coveleski-Was . . . 149
Pennock-NY 144
Gray-Phi 142
Johnson-Was 138
Blankenship-Chi . . 137

Opponents' Batting Avg.
Johnson-Was 243
Blankenship-Chi . . .253
Pennock-NY 254
Coveleski-Was 255
Gray-Phi 260

Opponents' On Base Pct.
Pennock-NY 303
Blankenship-Chi . . .308
Johnson-Was 311
Coveleski-Was 312
Gray-Phi 319

Starter Runs
Pennock-NY 44.2
Coveleski-Was . . . 41.7
Blankenship-Chi . . 35.3
Johnson-Was 33.8
Lyons-Chi 33.3

Adjusted Starter Runs
Pennock-NY 40.2
Coveleski-Was . . . 37.2
Harriss-Phi 32.5
Gray-Phi 31.2
Johnson-Was 29.6

Clutch Pitching Index
Dauss-Det 119
Shocker-NY 114
Zachary-Was 113
Lyons-Chi 111
Shawkey-NY 110

Relief Runs
Marberry-Was 9.6
Gregg-Was 2.3

Adjusted Relief Runs
Marberry-Was 7.8
Gregg-Was 9

Relief Ranking
Marberry-Was 13.4
Gregg-Was 5

Total Pitcher Index
Johnson-Was 4.1
Pennock-NY 3.3
Harriss-Phi 3.2
Rommel-Phi 3.0
Coveleski-Was . . . 2.8

Total Baseball Ranking
Speaker-Cle 4.5
Johnson-Was 4.1
J.Sewell-Cle 3.8
Heilmann-Det 3.6
Goslin-Was 3.6

TEAM	G	W	L	PCT	GB	R	OR	AB	H	2B	3B	HR	BB	SO	AVG	OBP	SLG	PRO	PRO+	BR	/A	PF	CHI	RC	SB	CS	SBA	SBR
STL	156	89	65	.578		817	678	5381	1541	259	82	90	478	518	.286	.348	.415	.763	107	76	48	104	102	770	83			
CIN	157	87	67	.565	2	747	651	5320	1541	242	120	35	454	333	.290	.349	.400	.749	110	52	71	97	97	738	51			
PIT	157	84	69	.549	4.5	769	689	5312	1514	243	106	44	434	350	.285	.343	.396	.739	99	28	-10	105	104	713	91			
CHI	155	82	72	.532	7	682	602	5229	1453	291	49	66	445	447	.278	.338	.390	.728	100			105	104	685	85			
NY	151	74	77	.490	13.5	663	668	5167	1435	214	55	73	339	420	.278	.325	.384	.709	97	-36	-28	99	104	631	94			
BRO	155	71	82	.464	17.5	623	705	5130	1348	246	62	40	475	464	.263	.328	.358	.686	91	-65	-55	99	100	607	76			
BOS	153	66	86	.434	22	624	686	5216	1444	209	62	16	460	348	.277	.335	.350	.685	99	-66	-3	91	99	612	81			
PHI	152	58	93	.384	29.5	687	900	5254	1479	244	50	75	422	479	.281	.337	.390	.727	96	5	-30	105	98	683	47			
TOT	618					5612		42009	11755	1948	589	439	3473	3359	.280	.338	.386	.724						608				

TEAM	CG	SH	SV	IP	H	H/G	HR	BB	SO	RAT	ERA	ERA+	OAV	OOB	PR	/A	PF	CPI	FA	E	DP	FW	PW	BW	SBW	DIF
STL	90	10	6	1398²	1423	9.2	76	397	365	11.8	3.67	106	.269	.322	24	36	102	96	.969	198	141	.3	3.6	4.7		3.4
CIN	88	14	8	1408²	1449	9.3	40	324	424	11.5	3.42	108	.271	.316	64	42	97	95	.972	183	160	1.3	4.2	7.0		-2.5
PIT	83	12	18	1379¹	1422	9.3	50	455	387	12.5	3.67	107	.272	.334	24	42	103	99	.965	220	161	-.9	4.2	-1.0		5.2
CHI	77	13	14	1378¹	1407	9.2	39	486	508	12.6	3.26	118	.273	.340	87	89	101	113	.974	162	174	2.4	8.8	-.0		-6.1
NY	61	4	15	1341²	1370	9.2	70	427	419	12.2	3.77	100	.269	.328	8	-3	98	96	.970	186	150	.7	-.3	-2.8		.9
BRO	83	5	9	1361²	1440	9.5	50	472	517	12.8	3.82	100	.276	.339	1	0	100	98	.963	229	95	-1.5	.0	-5.4		1.5
BOS	60	9	9	1365¹	1536	10.1	46	455	408	13.4	4.01	88	.294	.354	-28	-71	93	105	.967	208	150	-.5	-7.0	-.3		-2.2
PHI	68	5	5	1334¹	1699	11.5	68	454	331	14.7	5.03	82	.315	.371	-179	-133	108	98	.964	224	153	-1.5	-13.1	-3.0		.0
TOT	610	72	84	10968		9.6				12.7	3.82		.280	.338					.968	1610	1184					

Runs
Cuyler-Pit 113
Waner-Pit 101
Southworth-NY-StL 99
Sand-Phi 99

Hits
Brown-Bos 201
Cuyler-Pit 197
Adams-Chi 193
L.Bell-StL 189

Doubles
Bottomley-StL 40
Roush-Cin 37
Wilson-Chi 36

Triples
Waner-Pit 22
Walker-Cin 20
Traynor-Pit 17

Home Runs
Wilson-Chi 21
Bottomley-StL 19
Williams-Phi 18
L.Bell-StL 17
Southworth-NY-StL 16

Total Bases
Bottomley-StL 305
L.Bell-StL 301
Wilson-Chi 285
Waner-Pit 283
Cuyler-Pit 282

Runs Batted In
Bottomley-StL 120
Wilson-Chi 109
L.Bell-StL 100
Southworth-NY-StL 99
Pipp-Cin 99

Runs Produced
Bottomley-StL 199
Cuyler-Pit 197
Wilson-Chi 185
Southworth-NY-StL 182
Hornsby-StL 178

Bases On Balls
Wilson-Chi 69
Waner-Pit 66
Sand-Phi 66
Bancroft-Bos 64
Blades-StL 62

Batting Average
Waner-Pit 336
Leach-Phi 329
Brown-Bos 328
L.Bell-StL 325
Roush-Cin 323

On Base Percentage
Waner-Pit 413
Blades-StL 409
Wilson-Chi 406
Grantham-Pit 400
Bancroft-Bos 399

Slugging Average
Wilson-Chi 539
Waner-Pit 528
L.Bell-StL 518
Bottomley-StL 506
Herman-Bro.......500

Production
Wilson-Chi 944
Waner-Pit 941
L.Bell-StL 901
Grantham-Pit 890
Herman-Bro 875

Adjusted Production
Wilson-Chi 150
Waner-Pit 144
Herman-Bro 136
L.Bell-StL 135
Grantham-Pit 131

Batter Runs
Waner-Pit 39.5
Wilson-Chi 39.2
L.Bell-StL 31.6
Williams-Phi 29.8
Bottomley-StL 25.2

Adjusted Batter Runs
Wilson-Chi 38.3
Waner-Pit 35.6
L.Bell-StL 28.5
Williams-Phi 27.4
Herman-Bro 23.3

Clutch Hitting Index
Pipp-Cin 142
Butler-Bro 135
Traynor-Pit 130
Burrus-Bos 125
Critz-Cin 124

Runs Created
Waner-Pit 115
Wilson-Chi 115
L.Bell-StL 112
Bottomley-StL 109
Cuyler-Pit 105

Total Average
Wilson-Chi 1.031
Waner-Pit 1.022
Grantham-Pit 938
Blades-StL 938
L.Bell-StL 929

Stolen Bases
Cuyler-Pit 35
Adams-Chi 27
Frisch-NY 23
Douthit-StL 23
Youngs-NY 21

Stolen Base Average

Stolen Base Runs

Fielding Runs
Critz-Cin 24.0
Friberg-Phi 22.4
Cooney-Chi 19.4
Thevenow-StL 18.4
Douthit-StL 17.8

Total Player Rating
Waner-Pit 3.3
Wilson-Chi 3.0
O'Farrell-StL 2.7
Bancroft-Bos 2.6
Jackson-NY 2.5

Wins
Rhem-StL 20
Meadows-Pit 20
Kremer-Pit 20
Donohue-Cin 20
Mays-Cin 19

Win Percentage
Kremer-Pit 769
Rhem-StL 741
Meadows-Pit 690
Mays-Cin 613
Donohue-Cin 588

Games
Scott-NY 50
Willoughby-Phi ... 47
Donohue-Cin 47
Ulrich-Phi 45
May-Cin 45

Complete Games
Mays-Cin 24
Petty-Bro 23
Root-Chi 21
Rhem-StL 20
Carlson-Phi 20

Shutouts
Donohue-Cin 5
R.Smith-Bos 4
Blake-Chi 4

Saves
Davies-NY 6
Scott-NY 5
Kremer-Pit 5
Ehrhardt-Bro 4

Innings Pitched
Donohue-Cin 285.2
Mays-Cin 281.0
Petty-Bro 275.2
Root-Chi 271.1
Carlson-Phi 267.1

Fewest Hits/Game
Petty-Bro 8.03
Greenfield-NY 8.33
Rhem-StL 8.41
Jones-Chi 8.48
Bush-Chi 8.52

Fewest BB/Game
Donohue-Cin ... 1.23
Alexander-Chi-StL 1.39
Carlson-Phi 1.58
Mays-Cin 1.70
Lucas-Cin 1.75

Strikeouts
Vance-Bro 140
Root-Chi 127
May-Cin 103
Benton-Bos 103
Petty-Bro 101

Strikeouts/Game
Vance-Bro 7.46
May-Cin 5.53
Jones-Chi 4.49
Blake-Chi 4.33
Root-Chi 4.21

Ratio
Alexander-Chi-StL 10.06
Petty-Bro 10.71
Kremer-Pit 10.74
Donohue-Cin 10.90
Mays-Cin 10.99

Earned Run Average
Kremer-Pit 2.61
Root-Chi 2.82
Petty-Bro 2.84
Bush-Chi 2.86
Barnes-NY 2.87

Adjusted ERA
Kremer-Pit 151
Root-Chi 136
Petty-Bro 134
Bush-Chi 134
Barnes-NY 131

Opponents' Batting Avg.
Petty-Bro 240
Alexander-Chi-StL .250
Rhem-StL 250
Greenfield-NY 251
Kremer-Pit 252

Opponents' On Base Pct.
Alexander-Chi-StL .281
Petty-Bro 296
Kremer-Pit 296
Donohue-Cin 298
Rhem-StL 305

Starter Runs
Kremer-Pit 31.3
Root-Chi 30.3
Petty-Bro 30.1
Fitzsimmons-NY ... 23.0
Mays-Cin 21.4

Adjusted Starter Runs
Kremer-Pit 34.1
Root-Chi 30.9
Petty-Bro 30.0
Carlson-Phi 27.0
Fitzsimmons-NY ... 21.3

Clutch Pitching Index
Jones-Chi 122
Blake-Chi 119
Fitzsimmons-NY .. 118
Werts-Bos 117
Root-Chi 111

Relief Runs
Hallahan-StL 1.1

Adjusted Relief Runs
Hallahan-StL 1.6

Relief Ranking
Hallahan-StL 1.3

Total Pitcher Index
Kremer-Pit 3.5
Mays-Cin 3.0
Carlson-Phi 2.7
Root-Chi 2.6
Petty-Bro 2.4

Total Baseball Ranking
Kremer-Pit 3.5
Waner-Pit 3.3
Mays-Cin 3.0
Wilson-Chi 3.0
O'Farrell-StL 2.7

TEAM	G	W	L	PCT	GB	R	OR	AB	H	2B	3B	HR	BB	SO	AVG	OBP	SLG	PRO	PRO+	BR	/A	PF	CHI	RC	SB	CS	SBA	SBR
NY	155	91	63	.591		847	713	5221	1508	262	75	121	642	580	.289	.369	.437	.806	119	123	135	98	98	866	79	60	57	-12
CLE	154	88	66	.571	3	738	612	5293	1529	333	49	27	455	332	.289	.349	.386	.735	97	-17	-24	101	103	735	88	43	67	1
PHI	150	83	67	.553	6	677	570	5046	1359	259	65	61	523	452	.269	.341	.383	.724	90	-39	-79	106	101	681	56	46	55	-11
WAS	152	81	69	.540	8	802	761	5223	1525	244	97	43	555	369	.292	.364	.401	.765	109	48	66	98	103	780	122	89	58	-17
CHI	155	81	72	.529	9.5	730	665	5220	1508	314	60	32	556	381	.289	.361	.390	.751	106	24	50	96	96	761	121	77	61	-10
DET	157	79	75	.513	12	793	830	5315	1547	281	90	36	599	423	.291	.367	.398	.765	105	52	42	101	99	800	88	72	55	-17
STL	155	62	92	.403	29	682	845	5259	1449	253	78	72	437	465	.276	.321	.394	.729	92	-38	-72	105	100	698	62	71	47	-24
BOS	154	46	107	.301	44.5	562	835	5185	1325	249	54	32	465	450	.256	.321	.343	.664	82	-156	-133	97	101	586	48	51	48	-16
TOT	616					5831		41762	11750	2195	568	424	4232	3452	.281	.351	.392	.743							664	509	57	-106

TEAM	CG	SH	SV	IP	H	H/G	HR	BB	SO	RAT	ERA	ERA+	OAV	OOB	PR	/A	PF	CPI	FA	E	DP	FW	PW	BW	SBW	DIF
NY	63	4	20	1372¹	1442	9.5	56	478	486	12.8	3.86	100	.274	.337	24	-1	96	96	.966	210	117	-1.1	-.0	13.1	.1	2.0
CLE	96	11	4	1374	1412	9.2	49	450	381	12.5	3.40	119	.271	.334	94	101	101	105	.972	173	153	1.1	9.8	-2.3	1.4	1.1
PHI	62	10	16	1346	1362	9.1	38	451	571	12.3	3.00	139	.268	.331	153	174	104	114	.972	171	131	.9	16.9	-7.7	.2	-2.3
WAS	65	5	26	1349¹	1489	9.9	45	566	418	14.0	4.34	89	.287	.361	-48	-71	96	98	.969	184	129	.2	-6.9	6.4	-.4	6.6
CHI	85	11	12	1380	1426	9.3	47	506	458	12.7	3.74	103	.271	.336	43	16	96	96	.973	165	122	1.6	1.6	4.8	.3	-3.8
DET	57	10	18	1394²	1570	10.1	58	565	469	14.0	4.41	92	.292	.363	-61	-54	101	99	.969	193	151	.0	-5.2	4.1	-.4	3.5
STL	64	5	9	1368	1549	10.2	86	654	337	14.7	4.66	92	.297	.379	-99	-59	107	105	.963	235	167	-2.6	-5.7	-7.0	-1.0	1.3
BOS	53	6	5	1362	1520	10.0	45	546	336	13.9	4.72	86	.294	.365	-107	-101	101	92	.970	193	143	-.2	-9.8	-12.9	-.3	-7.4
TOT	545	62	110	10946¹		9.7				13.3	4.02		.281	.351					.969	1524	1113					

Runs
Ruth-NY 139
Gehrig-NY 135
Mostil-Chi 120
Combs-NY 113
Goslin-Was 105

Hits
Rice-Was 216
Burns-Cle 216
Goslin-Was 201
Simmons-Phi 199
Mostil-Chi 197

Doubles
Burns-Cle 64
Simmons-Phi 53
Speaker-Cle 52
Jacobson-StL-Bos . 51
Gehrig-NY 47

Triples
Gehrig-NY 20
Gehringer-Det 17
Mostil-Chi 15
Goslin-Was 15

Home Runs
Ruth-NY 47
Simmons-Phi 19
Lazzeri-NY 18
Williams-StL 17
Goslin-Was 17

Total Bases
Ruth-NY 365
Simmons-Phi 329
Gehrig-NY 314
Goslin-Was 308
Burns-Cle 298

Runs Batted In
Ruth-NY 146
Lazzeri-NY 114
Burns-Cle 114
Gehrig-NY 112
Simmons-Phi 109

Runs Produced
Ruth-NY 238
Gehrig-NY 231
Burns-Cle 207
Goslin-Was 196
Falk-Chi 186

Bases On Balls
Ruth-NY 144
Bishop-Phi 116
Rigney-Bos 108
Gehrig-NY 105
Speaker-Cle 94

Batting Average
Manush-Det ...... .378
Ruth-NY .... .372
Heilmann-Det .... .367
Burns-Cle .... .358
Goslin-Was ...... .354

On Base Percentage
Ruth-NY .... .516
Heilmann-Det .... .445
Bishop-Phi ...... .431
Goslin-Was ...... .425
Manush-Det ...... .421

Slugging Average
Ruth-NY .... .737
Simmons-Phi ..... .564
Manush-Det ...... .564
Gehrig-NY .... .549
Goslin-Was ...... .542

Production
Ruth-NY 1.253
Manush-Det ..... .985
Heilmann-Det ... .979
Gehrig-NY ...... .969
Goslin-Was ..... .967

Adjusted Production
Ruth-NY 228
Goslin-Was 155
Gehrig-NY 154
Manush-Det 153
Heilmann-Det 152

Batter Runs
Ruth-NY 97.4
Gehrig-NY 44.2
Goslin-Was 42.3
Heilmann-Det ... 41.7
Manush-Det 38.2

Adjusted Batter Runs
Ruth-NY 98.7
Gehrig-NY 45.5
Goslin-Was 44.3
Heilmann-Det ... 40.8
Manush-Det 37.3

Clutch Hitting Index
Judge-Was 144
Haney-Bos 138
Dugan-NY 136
Sheely-Chi 135
Burns-Cle 133

Runs Created
Ruth-NY 196
Gehrig-NY 137
Goslin-Was 131
Simmons-Phi 129
Mostil-Chi 122

Total Average
Ruth-NY 1.606
Gehrig-NY 1.058
Heilmann-Det .. 1.040
Manush-Det 1.029
Goslin-Was 1.008

Stolen Bases
Mostil-Chi 35
Rice-Was 25
Hunnefield-Chi ... 24
McNeely-Was 18
J.Sewell-Cle 17

Stolen Base Average
McNeely-Was 75.0
Hunnefield-Chi . 72.7
Mostil-Chi 71.4
J.Sewell-Cle ... 70.8
Lazzeri-NY 69.6

Stolen Base Runs
Mostil-Chi 2.1
McNeely-Was 1.8
Kamm-Chi 1.8
Hunnefield-Chi .. 1.8

Fielding Runs
Dykes-Phi 26.4
Rigney-Bos 19.6
Goslin-Was 18.5
Regan-Bos 17.4
Mostil-Chi 17.1

Total Player Rating
Ruth-NY 8.2
Goslin-Was 4.8
Rigney-Bos 3.9
Mostil-Chi 3.9
J.Sewell-Cle 3.4

Wins
Uhle-Cle 27
Pennock-NY 23
Shocker-NY 19
Lyons-Chi 18

Win Percentage
Uhle-Cle .... .711
Pennock-NY ...... .676
Shocker-NY ...... .633
Faber-Chi .... .625
Hoyt-NY .... .571

Games
Marberry-Was 64
Pate-Phi 47
Grove-Phi 45
Thomas-Chi 44

Complete Games
Uhle-Cle 32
Lyons-Chi 24
Johnson-Was 22
Grove-Phi 20
Pennock-NY 19

Shutouts
Wells-Det 4

Saves
Marberry-Was 22
Dauss-Det 9
Pate-Phi 6
Grove-Phi 6
Jones-NY 5

Innings Pitched
Uhle-Cle 318.1
Lyons-Chi 283.2
Pennock-NY 266.1
Johnson-Was 261.2
Shocker-NY 258.1

Fewest Hits/Game
Grove-Phi 7.92
Thomas-Chi 8.13
Uhle-Cle 8.48
Lyons-Chi 8.50
Buckeye-Cle 8.69

Fewest BB/Game
Pennock-NY 1.45
Smith-Cle 1.48
Quinn-Phi 1.98
Rommel-Phi 2.22
Wingfield-Bos ... 2.36

Strikeouts
Grove-Phi 194
Uhle-Cle 159
Thomas-Chi 127
Johnson-Was 125
Whitehill-Det ... 109

Strikeouts/Game
Grove-Phi 6.77
Thomas-Chi 4.59
Uhle-Cle 4.50
Johnson-Was 4.30
Whitehill-Det ... 3.89

Ratio
Pennock-NY 11.52
Rommel-Phi 11.55
Johnson-Was ... 11.59
Grove-Phi 11.65
Lyons-Chi 11.90

Earned Run Average
Grove-Phi 2.51
Uhle-Cle 2.83
Lyons-Chi 3.01
Rommel-Phi 3.08
Buckeye-Cle 3.10

Adjusted ERA
Grove-Phi 166
Uhle-Cle 143
Rommel-Phi 135
Buckeye-Cle 131
Lyons-Chi 128

Opponents' Batting Avg.
Thomas-Chi ...... .244
Grove-Phi .... .244
Lyons-Chi .... .252
Uhle-Cle .... .253
Levsen-Cle ...... .261

Opponents' On Base Pct.
Pennock-NY ...... .313
Rommel-Phi ...... .314
Hoyt-NY .... .316
Johnson-Was ..... .317
Shocker-NY ...... .318

Starter Runs
Grove-Phi 43.1
Uhle-Cle 42.1
Lyons-Chi 31.6
Coveleski-Was ... 24.5
Rommel-Phi 22.7

Adjusted Starter Runs
Grove-Phi 47.4
Uhle-Cle 43.3
Lyons-Chi 26.7
Rommel-Phi 26.3
Walberg-Phi 22.9

Clutch Pitching Index
Wingard-StL 128
Zachary-StL 122
Grove-Phi 119
Coveleski-Was ... 117
Buckeye-Cle 114

Relief Runs
Pate-Phi 16.4
Marberry-Was 15.6
Braxton-NY 10.0
Russell-Bos 4.7

Adjusted Relief Runs
Pate-Phi 18.3
Marberry-Was 13.2
Braxton-NY 8.8
Russell-Bos 5.3

Relief Ranking
Marberry-Was 21.2
Pate-Phi 15.3
Braxton-NY 7.7
Russell-Bos 2.4

Total Pitcher Index
Uhle-Cle 4.8
Grove-Phi 4.2
Lyons-Chi 3.0
Zachary-StL 2.6
Rommel-Phi 2.5

Total Baseball Ranking
Ruth-NY 8.2
Uhle-Cle 4.8
Goslin-Was 4.8
Grove-Phi 4.2
Rigney-Bos 3.9

TEAM	G	W	L	PCT	GB	R	OR	AB	H	2B	3B	HR	BB	SO	AVG	OBP	SLG	PRO	PRO+	BR	/A	PF	CHI	RC	SB	CS	SBA	SBR
PIT	156	94	60	.610		817	659	5397	1648	258	54	54	437	355	.305	.361	.412	.773	106	99	48	107	99	791	65			
STL	153	92	61	.601	1.5	754	665	5207	1450	264	79	84	484	511	.278	.343	.408	.751	104	47	25	103	101	723	110			
NY	155	92	62	.597	2	817	720	5372	1594	251	62	109	461	462	.297	.356	.427	.783	116	113	114	100	98	805	73			
CHI	153	85	68	.556	8.5	750	661	5303	1505	266	63	74	481	492	.284	.346	.400	.746	106	43	42	100	99	730	65			
CIN	153	75	78	.490	18.5	643	653	5185	1439	222	77	29	402	332	.278	.332	.367	.699	96	-47	-26	97	100	628	62			
BRO	154	65	88	.425	28.5	541	619	5193	1314	195	74	39	368	494	.253	.306	.342	.648	79	-152	-154	100	102	539	106			
BOS	155	60	94	.390	34	651	771	5370	1498	216	61	37	346	363	.279	.326	.363	.689	98	-73	-18	92	103	626	100			
PHI	155	51	103	.331	43	678	903	5317	1487	216	46	57	434	482	.280	.337	.370	.707	94	-30	-39	101	100	660	68			
TOT	617					5651		42344	11935	1888	540	483	3413	3491	.282	.339	.386	.725						649				

TEAM	CG	SH	SV	IP	H	H/G	HR	BB	SO	RAT	ERA	ERA+	OAV	OOB	PR	/A	PF	CPI	FA	E	DP	FW	PW	BW	SBW	DIF
PIT	90	10	10	1385	1400	9.1	58	418	435	12.0	3.66	112	.267	.324	39	68	105	95	.969	187	130	.6	6.7	4.7		4.9
STL	89	14	11	1367¹	1416	9.3	72	363	394	11.8	3.57	110	.271	.320	52	57	101	99	.966	213	170	-1.0	5.6	2.5		8.4
NY	65	7	16	1381²	1520	9.9	77	453	442	13.0	3.97	97	.283	.341	-8	-17	98	102	.969	195	160	.1	-1.7	11.3		5.3
CHI	75	11	5	1385	1439	9.4	50	514	465	12.9	3.65	106	.273	.342	40	31	99	104	.971	181	152	.8	3.1	4.1		.5
CIN	87	12	12	1368	1472	9.7	36	316	407	11.9	3.54	107	.281	.325	57	36	97	100	.973	165	160	1.6	3.6	-2.6		-4.1
BRO	74	7	10	1375¹	1382	9.0	63	418	574	11.9	3.36	118	.265	.323	85	90	101	103	.963	229	117	-1.8	8.9	-15.2		-3.4
BOS	52	3	11	1390	1602	10.4	43	468	402	13.6	4.22	88	.296	.356	-48	-79	95	102	.963	231	130	-1.8	-7.8	-1.8		-5.6
PHI	81	5	6	1355¹	1710	11.4	84	462	377	14.7	5.36	77	.317	.374	-218	-187	106	96	.972	169	152	1.5	-18.5	-3.8		-5.2
TOT	613	69	81	11007²		9.8				12.7	3.91		.282	.339					.969	1570	1171					

Runs
L.Waner-Pit 133
Hornsby-NY 133
Wilson-Chi 119
P.Waner-Pit 114
Frisch-StL 112

Hits
P.Waner-Pit 237
L.Waner-Pit 223
Frisch-StL 208
Hornsby-NY 205
Stephenson-Chi 199

Doubles
Stephenson-Chi ... 46
P.Waner-Pit 42
Lindstrom-NY 36
Dressen-Cin 36
Brown-Bos 35

Triples
P.Waner-Pit 18
Bottomley-StL 15
Thompson-Phi 14
Terry-NY 13
Wilson-Chi 12

Home Runs
Wilson-Chi 30
Williams-Phi 30
Hornsby-NY 26
Terry-NY 20
Bottomley-StL 19

Total Bases
P.Waner-Pit 342
Hornsby-NY 333
Wilson-Chi 319
Terry-NY 307
Bottomley-StL 292

Runs Batted In
P.Waner-Pit 131
Wilson-Chi 129
Hornsby-NY 125
Bottomley-StL 124
Terry-NY 121

Runs Produced
P.Waner-Pit 236
Hornsby-NY 232
Wilson-Chi 218
Terry-NY 202
Bottomley-StL 200

Bases On Balls
Hornsby-NY 86
Harper-NY 84
Grantham-Pit 74
Bottomley-StL 74

Batting Average
P.Waner-Pit 380
Hornsby-NY 361
L.Waner-Pit 355
Stephenson-Chi ...344
Traynor-Pit 342

On Base Percentage
Hornsby-NY 448
P.Waner-Pit 437
Harper-NY 435
Stephenson-Chi ...415
Harris-Pit 402

Slugging Average
Hornsby-NY 586
Wilson-Chi 579
P.Waner-Pit 549
Terry-NY 529
Bottomley-StL 509

Production
Hornsby-NY 1.035
P.Waner-Pit 986
Wilson-Chi 980
Harper-NY 930
Terry-NY 907

Adjusted Production
Hornsby-NY 175
Wilson-Chi 159
P.Waner-Pit 152
Harper-NY 149
Stephenson-Chi ... 141

Batter Runs
Hornsby-NY 62.5
P.Waner-Pit 55.6
Wilson-Chi 45.7
Harper-NY 37.1
Stephenson-Chi .. 35.7

Adjusted Batter Runs
Hornsby-NY 62.7
P.Waner-Pit 49.7
Wilson-Chi 45.6
Harper-NY 37.2
Stephenson-Chi .. 35.6

Clutch Hitting Index
Wright-Pit 157
Bressler-Cin 155
Traynor-Pit 142
Farrell-NY-Bos 141
Felix-Bro 131

Runs Created
Hornsby-NY 148
P.Waner-Pit 145
Wilson-Chi 126
Stephenson-Chi ... 117
Bottomley-StL 112

Total Average
Hornsby-NY 1.190
Wilson-Chi 1.088
P.Waner-Pit 1.062
Harper-NY 1.037
Stephenson-Chi ...955

Stolen Bases
Frisch-StL 48
Carey-Bro 32
Hendrick-Bro 29
Adams-Chi 26
Richbourg-Bos 24

Stolen Base Average

Stolen Base Runs

Fielding Runs
Frisch-StL 48.6
Jackson-NY 27.9
Friberg-Phi 25.3
Beck-Chi 22.0
Statz-Bro 15.2

Total Player Rating
Frisch-StL 7.3
Hornsby-NY 6.9
Jackson-NY 5.4
P.Waner-Pit 4.6
Wilson-Chi 3.5

Wins
Root-Chi.......... 26
Haines-StL 24
Hill-Pit.......... 22
Alexander-StL 21

Win Percentage
Benton-Bos-NY 708
Haines-StL 706
Kremer-Pit 704
Grimes-NY 704
Alexander-StL 677

Games
Scott-Phi 48
Root-Chi 48
Ehrhardt-Bro 46
Henry-NY 45
May-Cin 44

Complete Games
Vance-Bro 25
Meadows-Pit 25
Haines-StL 25
Hill-Pit.......... 22
Alexander-StL 22

Shutouts
Haines-StL 6
Root-Chi 4
Lucas-Cin 4
Kremer-Pit 3

Saves
Sherdel-StL 6
Nehf-Cin-Chi 5
Mogridge-Bos 5
Henry-NY 4

Innings Pitched
Root-Chi........ 309.0
Haines-StL 300.2
Meadows-Pit 299.1
Hill-Pit........ 277.2
Vance-Bro 273.1

Fewest Hits/Game
Vance-Bro 7.97
Kremer-Pit 8.16
Haines-StL 8.17
Bush-Chi 8.24
Hill-Pit......... 8.43

Fewest BB/Game
Alexander-StL 1.28
Lucas-Cin 1.46
Donohue-Cin 1.51
Carlson-Phi-Chi .. 1.63
Henry-NY 1.70

Strikeouts
Vance-Bro 184
Root-Chi 145
May-Cin 121
Grimes-NY 102
Petty-Bro 101

Strikeouts/Game
Vance-Bro 6.06
Elliott-Bro 4.73
May-Cin 4.62
Pruett-Phi 4.35
Root-Chi 4.22

Ratio
Alexander-StL 10.07
Lucas-Cin....... 10.14
Kremer-Pit 10.27
Vance-Bro 10.44
Petty-Bro 10.60

Earned Run Average
Kremer-Pit 2.47
Alexander-StL 2.52
Vance-Bro 2.70
Haines-StL 2.72
Petty-Bro 2.98

Adjusted ERA
Kremer-Pit 166
Alexander-StL 157
Vance-Bro 147
Haines-StL 145
Petty-Bro 133

Opponents' Batting Avg.
Vance-Bro 239
Kremer-Pit 244
Haines-StL 245
Hill-Pit..........249
Bush-Chi 250

Opponents' On Base Pct.
Alexander-StL 286
Lucas-Cin.........287
Kremer-Pit 289
Vance-Bro 291
Petty-Bro 293

Starter Runs
Alexander-StL 41.5
Haines-StL 39.8
Vance-Bro 36.9
Kremer-Pit 36.3
Petty-Bro 28.1

Adjusted Starter Runs
Alexander-StL 42.5
Kremer-Pit 41.1
Haines-StL 40.8
Vance-Bro 38.2
Petty-Bro 29.4

Clutch Pitching Index
Blake-Chi 117
McWeeny-Bro 116
R.Smith-Bos 114
Donohue-Cin 111
Alexander-StL 109

Relief Runs
Clark-Bro 13.0
Ehrhardt-Bro 3.6
Cvengros-Pit 3.3
Songer-Pit-NY 1.9

Adjusted Relief Runs
Clark-Bro 13.4
Cvengros-Pit 4.5
Ehrhardt-Bro 4.1
Songer-Pit-NY 1.7

Relief Ranking
Clark-Bro 15.5
Ehrhardt-Bro 4.0
Cvengros-Pit 2.4
Songer-Pit-NY 2.3

Total Pitcher Index
Alexander-StL 4.9
Haines-StL 4.2
Kremer-Pit 3.8
Vance-Bro 3.7
Hill-Pit.......... 2.9

Total Baseball Ranking
Frisch-StL 7.3
Hornsby-NY 6.9
Jackson-NY 5.4
Alexander-StL 4.9
P.Waner-Pit 4.6

TEAM	G	W	L	PCT	GB	R	OR	AB	H	2B	3B	HR	BB	SO	AVG	OBP	SLG	PRO	PRO+	BR	/A	PF	CHI	RC	SB	CS	SBA	SBR
NY	155	110	44	.714		975	599	5347	1644	291	103	158	635	605	.307	.383	.489	.872	135	235	259	97	95	1016	90	64	58	-11
PHI	155	91	63	.591	19	841	726	5296	1606	281	70	56	551	326	.303	.372	.414	.786	103	79	36	106	99	839	98	63	61	-8
WAS	157	85	69	.552	25	782	730	5389	1549	268	87	29	498	359	.287	.351	.386	.737	97	-25	-16	99	104	758	133	52	72	9
DET	156	82	71	.536	27.5	845	805	5299	1533	282	100	51	587	420	.289	.363	.409	.772	105	47	36	101	103	814	141	73	66	-2
CHI	153	70	83	.458	39.5	662	708	5157	1433	285	61	36	493	389	.278	.344	.378	.722	94	-54	-35	98	95	685	90	75	55	-18
CLE	153	66	87	.431	43.5	668	766	5202	1471	321	52	26	381	366	.283	.337	.379	.716	90	-70	-75	101	100	668	63	72	47	-24
STL	155	59	94	.386	50.5	724	904	5220	1440	262	59	55	443	420	.276	.338	.380	.718	88	-68	-93	103	106	683	91	66	58	-12
BOS	154	51	103	.331	59	597	856	5207	1348	271	78	28	430	456	.259	.320	.357	.677	82	-149	-133	98	100	614	82	46	64	-3
TOT	619					6094		42117	12024	2261	610	439	4018	3341	.285	.352	.399	.751							788	511	61	-70

TEAM	CG	SH	SV	IP	H	H/G	HR	BB	SO	RAT	ERA	ERA+	OAV	OOB	PR	/A	PF	CPI	FA	E	DP	FW	PW	BW	SBW	DIF
NY	82	11	20	1389²	1403	9.1	42	409	431	11.9	3.20	120	.267	.323	145	100	93	104	.969	195	123	.7	9.5	24.6	-.2	-1.6
PHI	66	8	25	1384	1467	9.5	65	442	553	12.6	3.97	107	.278	.338	26	45	103	97	.970	190	124	1.0	4.3	3.4	.0	5.2
WAS	62	10	23	1402	1434	9.2	53	491	497	12.6	3.97	102	.269	.335	26	14	98	91	.969	195	125	.8	1.3	-1.5	1.7	5.7
DET	75	5	17	1387²	1542	10.0	52	577	421	14.0	4.14	102	.290	.364	0	9	102	106	.968	206	173	.1	.9	3.4	.6	.5
CHI	85	10	8	1367	1467	9.7	55	440	365	12.7	3.91	103	.283	.342	34	19	98	101	.971	178	131	1.6	1.8	-3.3	-.9	-5.7
CLE	72	5	8	1353¹	1542	10.0	37	508	366	13.9	4.27	98	.295	.361	-20	-11	102	102	.968	201	146	.2	-1.0	-7.1	-1.4	-1.0
STL	80	4	8	1353¹	1592	10.6	79	604	385	14.7	4.95	88	.304	.378	-122	-91	105	101	.960	248	166	-2.5	-8.6	-8.8	-.3	2.8
BOS	63	6	7	1366¹	1603	10.6	56	558	381	14.5	4.72	89	.305	.376	-88	-77	102	102	.964	228	167	-1.4	-7.3	-12.6	.5	-5.2
TOT	585	59	116	11003¹		9.9				13.4	4.14		.285	.352					.967	1641	1155					

Runs		Hits		Doubles		Triples		Home Runs		Total Bases	
Ruth-NY	158	Combs-NY	231	Gehrig-NY	52	Combs-NY	23	Ruth-NY	60	Gehrig-NY	447
Gehrig-NY	149	Gehrig-NY	218	Burns-Cle	51	Manush-Det	18	Gehrig-NY	47	Ruth-NY	417
Combs-NY	137	Sisler-StL	201	Heilmann-Det	50	Gehrig-NY	18	Lazzeri-NY	18	Combs-NY	331
Gehringer-Det	110	Heilmann-Det	201	J.Sewell-Cle	48	Goslin-Was	15	Williams-StL	17	Heilmann-Det	311
Heilmann-Det	106	Goslin-Was	194	Meusel-NY	47	Rice-Was	14	Simmons-Phi	15	Goslin-Was	300

Runs Batted In		Runs Produced		Bases On Balls		Batting Average		On Base Percentage		Slugging Average	
Gehrig-NY	175	Gehrig-NY	277	Ruth-NY	138	Heilmann-Det	.398	Ruth-NY	.487	Ruth-NY	.772
Ruth-NY	164	Ruth-NY	262	Gehrig-NY	109	Gehrig-NY	.373	Heilmann-Det	.475	Gehrig-NY	.765
Heilmann-Det	120	Heilmann-Det	212	Bishop-Phi	105	Fothergill-Det	.359	Gehrig-NY	.474	Heilmann-Det	.616
Goslin-Was	120	Goslin-Was	203	Heilmann-Det	72	Cobb-Phi	.357	Bishop-Phi	.442	Williams-StL	.525
Fothergill-Det	114	Fothergill-Det	198	Blue-Det	71	Combs-NY	.356	Cobb-Phi	.440	Goslin-Was	.516

Production		Adjusted Production		Batter Runs		Adjusted Batter Runs		Clutch Hitting Index		Runs Created	
Ruth-NY	1.259	Ruth-NY	229	Gehrig-NY	100.8	Gehrig-NY	103.5	J.Sewell-Cle	133	Gehrig-NY	212
Gehrig-NY	1.240	Gehrig-NY	224	Ruth-NY	100.7	Ruth-NY	103.3	Cobb-Phi	130	Ruth-NY	208
Heilmann-Det	1.091	Heilmann-Det	179	Heilmann-Det	62.3	Heilmann-Det	61.3	Fothergill-Det	129	Heilmann-Det	150
Fothergill-Det	.929	Combs-NY	143	Simmons-Phi	44.1	Simmons-Phi	40.9	Hale-Phi	126	Combs-NY	138
Williams-StL	.928	Fothergill-Det	138	Combs-NY	37.1	Combs-NY	39.8	Barrett-Chi	124	Goslin-Was	119

Total Average		Stolen Bases		Stolen Base Average		Stolen Base Runs		Fielding Runs		Total Player Rating	
Ruth-NY	1.571	Sisler-StL	27	Harris-Was	85.7	Sisler-StL	3.9	Gehringer-Det	19.8	Ruth-NY	8.9
Gehrig-NY	1.500	Meusel-NY	24	Sisler-StL	79.4	Harris-Was	3.6	Falk-Chi	18.2	Gehrig-NY	7.8
Heilmann-Det	1.265	Neun-Det	22	Goslin-Was	77.8	Goslin-Was	2.7	Metzler-Chi	15.7	Heilmann-Det	4.2
Williams-StL	.959	Lazzeri-NY	22	Rice-Was	76.0			Bluege-Was	15.0	Simmons-Phi	3.6
Combs-NY	.955	Cobb-Phi	22	Neun-Det	75.9			Koenig-NY	13.8	Gehringer-Det	3.1

Wins		Win Percentage		Games		Complete Games		Shutouts		Saves	
Lyons-Chi	22	Hoyt-NY	.759	Braxton-Was	58	Lyons-Chi	30	Lisenbee-Was	4	Moore-NY	13
Hoyt-NY	22	Shocker-NY	.750	Marberry-Was	56	Thomas-Chi	24			Braxton-Was	13
Grove-Phi	20	Moore-NY	.731	Grove-Phi	51	Hoyt-NY	23			Marberry-Was	9
		Pennock-NY	.704	Moore-NY	50	Gaston-StL	21			Grove-Phi	9
		Lisenbee-Was	.667	Walberg-Phi	46						

Innings Pitched		Fewest Hits/Game		Fewest BB/Game		Strikeouts		Strikeouts/Game		Ratio	
Thomas-Chi	307.2	Moore-NY	7.82	Quinn-Phi	1.65	Grove-Phi	174	Grove-Phi	5.97	Moore-NY	10.35
Lyons-Chi	307.2	Thomas-Chi	7.93	Shocker-NY	1.85	Walberg-Phi	136	Braxton-Was	5.56	Braxton-Was	10.37
Hudlin-Cle	264.2	Pipgras-NY	8.01	Hoyt-NY	1.90	Thomas-Chi	107	Walberg-Phi	4.91	Lyons-Chi	10.47
Grove-Phi	262.1	Hadley-Was	8.02	Braxton-Was	1.91	Lisenbee-Was	105	Pipgras-NY	4.38	Hoyt-NY	10.53
Hoyt-NY	256.1	Lisenbee-Was	8.22	Lyons-Chi	1.96	Braxton-Was	96	Ruffing-Bos	4.38	Thomas-Chi	10.71

Earned Run Average		Adjusted ERA		Opponents' Batting Avg.		Opponents' On Base Pct.		Starter Runs		Adjusted Starter Runs	
Moore-NY	2.28	Moore-NY	169	Moore-NY	.234	Moore-NY	.289	Lyons-Chi	44.4	Lyons-Chi	41.3
Hoyt-NY	2.63	Hoyt-NY	146	Thomas-Chi	.244	Braxton-Was	.289	Moore-NY	43.9	Moore-NY	37.1
Shocker-NY	2.84	Lyons-Chi	143	Hadley-Was	.244	Lyons-Chi	.292	Hoyt-NY	42.8	Thomas-Chi	36.3
Lyons-Chi	2.84	Hadley-Was	142	Lisenbee-Was	.245	Hoyt-NY	.294	Thomas-Chi	39.4	Hoyt-NY	34.7
Hadley-Was	2.85	Braxton-Was	137	Braxton-Was	.246	Thomas-Chi	.303	Shocker-NY	28.9	Grove-Phi	31.2

Clutch Pitching Index		Relief Runs		Adjusted Relief Runs		Relief Ranking		Total Pitcher Index		Total Baseball Ranking	
Ruether-NY	121	Braxton-Was	20.4	Braxton-Was	19.1	Braxton-Was	24.6	Lyons-Chi	4.8	Ruth-NY	8.9
Gibson-Det	119	Burke-Was	1.9	G.Smith-Det	2.3	G.Smith-Det	1.5	Moore-NY	3.9	Gehrig-NY	7.8
Pennock-NY	118	G.Smith-Det	1.8	Burke-Was	1.1	Burke-Was	.5	Hoyt-NY	3.4	Lyons-Chi	4.8
Zachary-StL-Was	115							Hadley-Was	2.9	Heilmann-Det	4.2
Stoner-Det	114							Thomas-Chi	2.8	Moore-NY	3.9

TEAM	G	W	L	PCT	GB	R	OR	AB	H	2B	3B	HR	BB	SO	AVG	OBP	SLG	PRO	PRO+	BR	/A	PF	CHI	RC	SB	CS	SBA	SBR
STL	154	95	59	.617		807	636	5357	1505	292	70	113	568	438	.281	.353	.425	.778	108	73	60	102	99	802	82			
NY	155	93	61	.604	2	807	653	5459	1600	276	59	118	444	376	.293	.349	.430	.779	110	68	65	100	100	805	62			
CHI	154	91	63	.591	4	714	615	5260	1460	251	64	92	508	517	.278	.345	.402	.747	103	11	21	99	97	728	83			
PIT	152	85	67	.559	9	837	704	5371	1659	246	100	52	435	352	.309	.364	.421	.785	108	89	60	104	103	809	64			
CIN	153	78	74	.513	16	648	686	5184	1449	229	67	32	386	330	.280	.333	.368	.701	91	-76	-65	98	104	630	83			
BRO	155	77	76	.503	17.5	665	640	5243	1393	229	70	66	557	510	.266	.340	.374	.714	94	-46	-36	99	98	673	81			
BOS	153	50	103	.327	44.5	631	878	5228	1439	241	41	52	447	377	.275	.335	.367	.702	95	-70	-33	95	99	643	60			
PHI	152	43	109	.283	51	660	957	5234	1396	257	47	85	503	510	.267	.333	.382	.715	90	-49	-73	103	99	667	53			
TOT	614					5769		42336	11901	2021	518	610	3848	3410	.281	.344	.397	.741						568				

TEAM	CG	SH	SV	IP	H	H/G	HR	BB	SO	RAT	ERA	ERA+	OAV	OOB	PR	/A	PF	CPI	FA	E	DP	FW	PW	BW	SBW	DIF
STL	83	4	21	1415[1]	1470	9.3	86	399	422	12.1	3.38	118	.270	.323	95	97	100	104	.974	160	134	1.3	9.5	5.9		1.3
NY	79	7	16	1394	1454	9.4	77	405	399	12.1	3.67	106	.273	.327	49	36	98	98	.972	178	175	.3	3.5	6.4		5.8
CHI	75	12	14	1380[2]	1383	9.0	56	508	531	12.5	3.40	113	.267	.336	90	68	96	105	.975	156	176	1.6	6.6	2.1		3.7
PIT	82	8	11	1354	1422	9.5	66	446	385	12.6	3.95	103	.274	.335	5	15	102	93	.967	201	123	-1.3	1.5	5.9		2.9
CIN	68	11	11	1371[2]	1516	9.9	58	410	355	12.7	3.94	100	.289	.342	7	1	99	100	.974	162	194	1.1	.0	-6.4		7.1
BRO	75	16	15	1378	1378	8.9	59	468	551	12.1	3.25	122	.261	.324	114	111	100	101	.965	217	113	-2.0	10.9	-3.5		-4.8
BOS	54	1	6	1360	1596	10.6	100	524	343	14.2	4.83	81	.298	.363	-128	-141	98	97	.969	193	141	-.7	-13.8	-3.2		-8.8
PHI	42	4	11	1352[2]	1654	11.0	108	671	403	15.7	5.52	77	.315	.397	-231	-193	107	100	.971	181	171	-.0	-18.9	-7.1		-6.9
TOT	558	63	105	11024[1]		9.7				13.0	3.98		.281	.344					.971	1448	1227					

Runs		Hits		Doubles		Triples		Home Runs		Total Bases	
P.Waner-Pit	142	Lindstrom-NY	231	P.Waner-Pit	50	Bottomley-StL	20	Wilson-Chi	31	Bottomley-StL	362
Bottomley-StL	123	P.Waner-Pit	223	Hafey-StL	46	P.Waner-Pit	19	Bottomley-StL	31	Lindstrom-NY	330
L.Waner-Pit	121	L.Waner-Pit	221	Hornsby-Bos	42	L.Waner-Pit	14	Hafey-StL	27	P.Waner-Pit	329
Douthit-StL	111	Richbourg-Bos	206	Bottomley-StL	42	Bressler-Bro	13	Bissonette-Bro	25	Bissonette-Bro	319
Frisch-StL	107	Traynor-Pit	192	Lindstrom-NY	39	Bissonette-Bro	13	Hornsby-Bos	21	Hafey-StL	314

Runs Batted In		Runs Produced		Bases On Balls		Batting Average		On Base Percentage		Slugging Average	
Bottomley-StL	136	Bottomley-StL	228	Hornsby-Bos	107	Hornsby-Bos	.387	Hornsby-Bos	.498	Hornsby-Bos	.632
Traynor-Pit	124	P.Waner-Pit	222	Douthit-StL	84	P.Waner-Pit	.370	P.Waner-Pit	.446	Bottomley-StL	.628
Wilson-Chi	120	Traynor-Pit	212	Bressler-Bro	80	Lindstrom-NY	.358	Grantham-Pit	.408	Hafey-StL	.604
Hafey-StL	111	Lindstrom-NY	192	Wilson-Chi	77	Sisler-Bos	.340	Stephenson-Chi	.407	Wilson-Chi	.588
Lindstrom-NY	107	Hafey-StL	185	P.Waner-Pit	77	Herman-Bro	.340	Wilson-Chi	.404	P.Waner-Pit	.547

Production		Adjusted Production		Batter Runs		Adjusted Batter Runs		Clutch Hitting Index		Runs Created	
Hornsby-Bos	1.130	Hornsby-Bos	204	Hornsby-Bos	72.5	Hornsby-Bos	76.3	Traynor-Pit	172	Hornsby-Bos	154
Bottomley-StL	1.030	Bottomley-StL	163	P.Waner-Pit	53.4	Bottomley-StL	51.0	Walker-Cin	137	P.Waner-Pit	145
Wilson-Chi	.992	Wilson-Chi	159	Bottomley-StL	52.5	P.Waner-Pit	50.0	Whitney-Phi	134	Bottomley-StL	142
P.Waner-Pit	.992	Hafey-StL	152	Wilson-Chi	42.1	Wilson-Chi	43.1	Ford-Cin	133	Bissonette-Bro	125
Hafey-StL	.990	P.Waner-Pit	152	Hafey-StL	38.5	Bissonette-Bro	37.5	Wilson-Phi-StL	131	Wilson-Chi	122

Total Average		Stolen Bases		Stolen Base Average		Stolen Base Runs		Fielding Runs		Total Player Rating	
Hornsby-Bos	1.409	Cuyler-Chi	37					Maguire-Chi	50.5	Hornsby-Bos	5.4
Bottomley-StL	1.147	Frisch-StL	29					Jackson-NY	28.3	Lindstrom-NY	4.8
P.Waner-Pit	1.100	Walker-Cin	19					Douthit-StL	24.3	Jackson-NY	4.3
Wilson-Chi	1.090	Thompson-Phi	19					Lindstrom-NY	15.1	P.Waner-Pit	4.2
Hafey-StL	1.055							Ford-Cin	11.9	Hartnett-Chi	4.2

Wins		Win Percentage		Games		Complete Games		Shutouts		Saves	
Grimes-Pit	25	Benton-NY	.735	Grimes-Pit	48	Grimes-Pit	28	Vance-Bro	4	Sherdel-StL	5
Benton-NY	25	Haines-StL	.714	Kolp-Cin	44	Benton-NY	28	McWeeny-Bro	4	Haid-StL	5
Vance-Bro	22	Bush-Chi	.714	Rixey-Cin	43	Vance-Bro	24	Lucas-Cin	4	Carlson-Chi	4
Sherdel-StL	21	Fitzsimmons-NY	.690			Sherdel-StL	20	Grimes-Pit	4	Benton-NY	4
		Vance-Bro	.688			Haines-StL	20	Blake-Chi	4		

Innings Pitched		Fewest Hits/Game		Fewest BB/Game		Strikeouts		Strikeouts/Game		Ratio	
Grimes-Pit	330.2	Vance-Bro	7.26	Alexander-StL	1.37	Vance-Bro	200	Vance-Bro	6.42	Vance-Bro	9.79
Benton-NY	310.1	Blake-Chi	7.82	Sherdel-StL	2.03	Malone-Chi	155	Malone-Chi	5.57	Benton-NY	10.73
Rixey-Cin	291.1	Malone-Chi	7.83	Benton-NY	2.06	Root-Chi	122	Root-Chi	4.63	Grimes-Pit	10.81
Vance-Bro	280.1	McWeeny-Bro	8.04	Rixey-Cin	2.07	Grimes-Pit	97	Clark-Bro	3.93	Lucas-Cin	11.08
Fitzsimmons-NY	261.1	Root-Chi	8.13	Grimes-Pit	2.10	Benton-NY	90	Ring-Phi	3.75	Alexander-StL	11.12

Earned Run Average		Adjusted ERA		Opponents' Batting Avg.		Opponents' On Base Pct.		Starter Runs		Adjusted Starter Runs	
Vance-Bro	2.09	Vance-Bro	190	Vance-Bro	.221	Vance-Bro	.277	Vance-Bro	59.0	Vance-Bro	58.5
Blake-Chi	2.47	Blake-Chi	156	McWeeny-Bro	.235	Grimes-Pit	.297	Benton-NY	43.3	Benton-NY	40.6
Nehf-Chi	2.65	Clark-Bro	148	Malone-Chi	.236	Benton-NY	.300	Blake-Chi	40.5	Grimes-Pit	38.8
Clark-Bro	2.68	Nehf-Chi	145	Blake-Chi	.240	Sherdel-StL	.303	Grimes-Pit	36.3	Blake-Chi	36.7
Benton-NY	2.73	Benton-NY	143	Root-Chi	.242	Lucas-Cin	.304	Malone-Chi	31.9	Sherdel-StL	31.2

Clutch Pitching Index		Relief Runs		Adjusted Relief Runs		Relief Ranking		Total Pitcher Index		Total Baseball Ranking	
Nehf-Chi	133							Vance-Bro	6.6	Vance-Bro	6.6
Bush-Chi	117							Grimes-Pit	5.7	Grimes-Pit	5.7
Blake-Chi	115							Benton-NY	3.8	Hornsby-Bos	5.4
Kolp-Cin	114							Blake-Chi	3.6	Lindstrom-NY	4.8
Rhem-StL	114							Sherdel-StL	3.1	Jackson-NY	4.3

TEAM	G	W	L	PCT	GB	R	OR	AB	H	2B	3B	HR	BB	SO	AVG	OBP	SLG	PRO	PRO+	BR	/A	PF	CHI	RC	SB	CS	SBA	SBR
NY	154	101	53	.656		894	685	5337	1578	269	79	133	562	544	.296	.365	.450	.815	124	146	170	97	100	888	51	51	50	-15
PHI	153	98	55	.641	2.5	829	615	5226	1540	323	75	89	533	442	.295	.363	.436	.799	112	115	95	103	97	843	59	48	55	-11
STL	154	82	72	.532	19	772	742	5217	1431	276	76	63	548	479	.274	.346	.393	.739	97	2	-21	103	104	736	76	43	64	-3
WAS	155	75	79	.487	26	718	705	5320	1510	277	93	40	481	390	.284	.346	.393	.739	101	1	6	99	97	743	110	59	65	-2
CHI	155	72	82	.468	29	656	725	5207	1405	231	77	24	469	488	.270	.334	.358	.692	88	-88	-78	99	102	641	139	82	63	-8
DET	154	68	86	.442	33	744	804	5292	1476	265	97	62	469	438	.279	.340	.401	.741	99	-2	-13	102	102	730	113	77	59	-12
CLE	155	62	92	.403	39	674	830	5386	1535	299	61	34	377	426	.285	.335	.382	.717	93	-49	-56	101	98	693	50	52	49	-16
BOS	154	57	96	.373	43.5	589	770	5132	1356	260	62	38	389	512	.264	.319	.361	.680	86	-119	-106	98	100	602	99	64	61	-9
TOT	617					5876		42117	11831	2200	620	483	3828	3719	.281	.344	.397	.741							697	476	59	-77

TEAM	CG	SH	SV	IP	H	H/G	HR	BB	SO	RAT	ERA	ERA+	OAV	OOB	PR	/A	PF	CPI	FA	E	DP	FW	PW	BW	SBW	DIF
NY	82	13	21	1375¹	1466	9.6	59	452	487	12.7	3.74	101	.276	.335	46	3	93	102	.968	194	136	-.0	.3	16.4	-.5	7.9
PHI	81	15	16	1367²	1349	8.9	66	424	607	11.8	3.36	119	.259	.318	103	97	99	99	.970	181	124	.6	9.4	9.2	-.1	2.4
STL	80	6	15	1374¹	1487	9.7	93	454	456	12.8	4.17	101	.282	.340	-20	3	104	100	.969	189	146	.2	.3	-2.0	.6	5.9
WAS	77	15	10	1384	1420	9.2	40	466	462	12.5	3.88	103	.272	.335	25	19	99	94	.972	178	146	1.0	1.8	.6	.7	-6.1
CHI	88	6	11	1378	1518	9.9	66	501	418	13.4	3.98	102	.287	.352	8	8	100	108	.970	186	149	.5	.8	-7.5	.2	1.1
DET	65	5	16	1372	1481	9.7	58	567	451	13.7	4.32	95	.281	.355	-42	-34	102	97	.965	218	140	-1.5	-3.3	-1.3	-.2	-2.7
CLE	71	4	15	1378	1615	10.5	52	511	416	14.2	4.47	93	.303	.369	-66	-52	103	105	.965	221	187	-1.6	-5.0	-5.4	-.6	-2.4
BOS	70	5	9	1352	1492	9.9	49	452	407	13.2	4.39	93	.288	.349	-53	-44	102	94	.971	178	139	.9	-4.3	-10.2	.0	-6.0
TOT	614	69	113	10981¹		9.7				13.0	4.04		.281	.344					.969	1545	1167					

Runs
Ruth-NY 163
Gehrig-NY 139
Combs-NY 118
Blue-StL 116
Gehringer-Det 108

Hits
Manush-StL 241
Gehrig-NY 210
Rice-Was 202
Combs-NY 194
Gehringer-Det 193

Doubles
Manush-StL 47
Gehrig-NY 47
Meusel-NY 45
Schulte-StL 44
Lind-Cle 42

Triples
Combs-NY 21
Manush-StL 20
Gehringer-Det 16

Home Runs
Ruth-NY 54
Gehrig-NY 27
Goslin-Was 17
Hauser-Phi 16
Simmons-Phi 15

Total Bases
Ruth-NY 380
Manush-StL 367
Gehrig-NY 364
Combs-NY 290
Heilmann-Det 283

Runs Batted In
Ruth-NY 142
Gehrig-NY 142
Meusel-NY 113
Manush-StL 108

Runs Produced
Gehrig-NY 254
Ruth-NY 251
Manush-StL 199
Blue-StL 182
Meusel-NY 179

Bases On Balls
Ruth-NY 135
Blue-StL 105
Bishop-Phi 97
Gehrig-NY 95
Judge-Was 80

Batting Average
Goslin-Was .379
Manush-StL .378
Gehrig-NY .374
Simmons-Phi .351
Miller-Phi .329

On Base Percentage
Gehrig-NY .467
Ruth-NY .461
Goslin-Was .442
Bishop-Phi .435
Manush-StL .414

Slugging Average
Ruth-NY .709
Gehrig-NY .648
Goslin-Was .614
Manush-StL .575
Simmons-Phi .558

Production
Ruth-NY 1.170
Gehrig-NY 1.115
Goslin-Was 1.056
Manush-StL .989
Simmons-Phi .954

Adjusted Production
Ruth-NY 210
Gehrig-NY 196
Goslin-Was 176
Manush-StL 153
Simmons-Phi 144

Batter Runs
Ruth-NY 83.9
Gehrig-NY 76.0
Manush-StL 50.3
Goslin-Was 49.0
Foxx-Phi 30.5

Adjusted Batter Runs
Ruth-NY 86.6
Gehrig-NY 78.6
Goslin-Was 49.4
Manush-StL 47.7
Foxx-Phi 28.9

Clutch Hitting Index
Meusel-NY 149
Judge-Was 144
Cissell-Chi 141
Kress-StL 135
Kamm-Phi 133

Runs Created
Ruth-NY 182
Gehrig-NY 169
Manush-StL 150
Goslin-Was 125
Combs-NY 114

Total Average
Ruth-NY 1.405
Gehrig-NY 1.256
Goslin-Was 1.203
Manush-StL 1.040
Simmons-Phi .951

Stolen Bases
Myer-Bos 30
Mostil-Chi 23
Rice-Det 20
Cissell-Chi 18
Bluege-Was 18

Stolen Base Average
Rice-Was 84.2
Goslin-Was 84.2
Judge-Was 80.0
Manush-StL 77.3

Stolen Base Runs
Rice-Was 3.0
Goslin-Was 3.0
Reynolds-Chi 2.7
Judge-Was 2.4
Manush-StL 2.1

Fielding Runs
Gerber-StL-Bos 32.0
J.Sewell-Cle 27.0
Jamieson-Cle 19.9
Mostil-Chi 17.8
Schulte-StL 17.3

Total Player Rating
Ruth-NY 6.8
J.Sewell-Cle 5.5
Gehrig-NY 4.9
Goslin-Was 4.5
Manush-StL 3.9

Wins
Pipgras-NY 24
Grove-Phi 24
Hoyt-NY 23
Crowder-StL 21
Gray-StL 20

Win Percentage
Crowder-StL .808
Hoyt-NY .767
Grove-Phi .750
Pennock-NY .739
Quinn-Phi .720

Games
Marberry-Was 48
Morris-Bos 47
Pipgras-NY 46
Rommel-Phi 43

Complete Games
Ruffing-Bos 25
Thomas-Chi 24
Grove-Phi 24
Pipgras-NY 22

Shutouts
Pennock-NY 5
Quinn-Phi 4
Pipgras-NY 4
Jones-Was 4
Grove-Phi 4

Saves
Hoyt-NY 8
Hudlin-Cle 7
Lyons-Chi 6
Braxton-Was 6

Innings Pitched
Pipgras-NY 300.2
Ruffing-Bos 289.1
Thomas-Chi 283.0
Hoyt-NY 273.0
Gray-StL 262.2

Fewest Hits/Game
Braxton-Was 7.30
Grove-Phi 7.84
Earnshaw-Phi 8.13
Jones-Was 8.37
Johnson-NY 8.50

Fewest BB/Game
Rommel-Phi 1.35
Quinn-Phi 1.45
Pennock-NY 1.71
Braxton-Was 1.81
Russell-Bos 1.83

Strikeouts
Grove-Phi 183
Pipgras-NY 139
Thomas-Chi 129
Ruffing-Bos 118
Earnshaw-Phi 117

Strikeouts/Game
Earnshaw-Phi 6.65
Grove-Phi 6.29
Johnson-NY 4.97
Walberg-Phi 4.28
Whitehill-Det 4.26

Ratio
Braxton-Was 9.32
Grove-Phi 10.08
Rommel-Phi 10.62
Pennock-NY 10.88
Hoyt-NY 11.21

Earned Run Average
Braxton-Was 2.51
Pennock-NY 2.56
Grove-Phi 2.58
Jones-Was 2.84
Quinn-Phi 2.90

Adjusted ERA
Braxton-Was 159
Grove-Phi 155
Pennock-NY 147
Jones-Was 141
Quinn-Phi 138

Opponents' Batting Avg.
Braxton-Was .222
Grove-Phi .229
Earnshaw-Phi .240
Johnson-NY .250
Jones-Was .252

Opponents' On Base Pct.
Braxton-Was .267
Grove-Phi .277
Rommel-Phi .295
Pennock-NY .302
Thomas-Chi .310

Starter Runs
Grove-Phi 42.4
Braxton-Was 37.0
Pennock-NY 34.7
Thomas-Chi 30.0
Jones-Was 29.8

Adjusted Starter Runs
Grove-Phi 41.5
Braxton-Was 36.2
Thomas-Chi 30.2
Gray-StL 29.4
Jones-Was 29.0

Clutch Pitching Index
Miller-Cle 119
Quinn-Phi 119
Blankenship-Chi 114
Pennock-NY 113
Adkins-Chi 113

Relief Runs

Adjusted Relief Runs
Simmons-Bos .5

Relief Ranking
Simmons-Bos 1

Total Pitcher Index
Grove-Phi 4.0
Jones-Was 3.6
Braxton-Was 3.3
Gray-StL 3.1
Thomas-Chi 3.0

Total Baseball Ranking
Ruth-NY 6.8
J.Sewell-Cle 5.5
Gehrig-NY 4.9
Goslin-Was 4.5
Grove-Phi 4.0

TEAM	G	W	L	PCT	GB	R	OR	AB	H	2B	3B	HR	BB	SO	AVG	OBP	SLG	PRO	PRO+	BR	/A	PF	CHI	RC	SB	CS	SBA	SBR
CHI	156	98	54	.645		982	758	5471	1655	310	46	139	589	567	.303	.373	.452	.825	111	92	90	100	104	916	103			
PIT	154	88	65	.575	10.5	904	780	5490	1663	285	116	60	503	335	.303	.364	.430	.794	101	28	8	102	104	850	94			
NY	152	84	67	.556	13.5	897	709	5388	1594	251	47	136	482	405	.296	.358	.436	.794	103	18	20	100	106	827	85			
STL	154	78	74	.513	20	831	806	5364	1569	310	84	100	490	455	.293	.354	.438	.792	101	12	4	101	100	819	72			
PHI	154	71	82	.464	27.5	897	1032	5484	1693	305	51	153	573	470	.309	.377	.467	.844	108	125	70	107	92	951	59			
BRO	153	70	83	.458	28.5	755	888	5273	1535	282	69	99	504	454	.291	.355	.427	.782	102	-1	15	98	93	792	80			
CIN	155	66	88	.429	33	686	760	5269	1478	258	79	34	412	347	.281	.336	.379	.715	87	-133	-95	95	103	664	134			
BOS	154	56	98	.364	43	657	876	5291	1481	252	77	33	408	432	.280	.335	.375	.710	85	-142	-110	96	99	659	65			
TOT	616					6609		43030	12668	2253	569	754	3961	3465	.294	.357	.426	.783						692				

TEAM	CG	SH	SV	IP	H	H/G	HR	BB	SO	RAT	ERA	ERA+	OAV	OOB	PR	/A	PF	CPI	FA	E	DP	FW	PW	BW	SBW	DIF
CHI	79	14	21	1398²	1542	9.9	77	537	548	13.5	4.16	111	.284	.350	86	70	98	104	.975	154	169	1.4	6.4	8.2		6.0
PIT	79	5	13	1379	1530	10.0	96	439	409	13.0	4.36	109	.284	.340	54	62	101	98	.970	181	136	-.2	5.6	.7		5.4
NY	68	9	13	1372	1536	10.1	102	431	431	13.0	3.97	115	.287	.337	113	93	97	109	.975	158	163	.9	8.5	1.8		-2.7
STL	83	6	8	1359²	1604	10.6	101	474	453	13.9	4.66	100	.297	.357	8	-1	99	102	.971	174	149	.2	-.0	.4		1.6
PHI	45	5	24	1348	1743	11.6	122	616	369	16.0	6.13	85	.319	.391	-212	-142	110	96	.969	191	153	-.8	-12.9	6.4		1.8
BRO	59	8	16	1358	1553	10.3	92	549	549	14.2	4.92	94	.290	.360	-32	-48	98	95	.968	192	113	-.9	-4.4	1.4		-2.6
CIN	75	5	8	1369¹	1558	10.2	61	413	347	13.1	4.41	103	.292	.345	46	22	97	97	.974	162	148	.9	2.0	-8.6		-5.3
BOS	78	4	12	1352²	1604	10.7	103	530	366	14.4	5.12	91	.302	.367	-62	-68	99	99	.967	204	146	-1.5	-6.2	-10.0		-3.3
TOT	566	56	115	10937¹		10.4				13.8	4.71		.294	.357					.971	1416	1177					

Runs
Hornsby-Chi 156
O'Doul-Phi 152
Ott-NY 138
Wilson-Chi 135
L.Waner-Pit 134

Hits
O'Doul-Phi 254
L.Waner-Pit 234
Hornsby-Chi 229
Terry-NY 226
Klein-Phi 219

Doubles
Frederick-Bro ... 52
Hornsby-Chi 47
Hafey-StL 47
Klein-Phi 45
Kelly-Cin 45

Triples
L.Waner-Pit 20
P.Waner-Pit 15
Walker-Cin 15
Whitney-Phi 14

Home Runs
Klein-Phi 43
Ott-NY 42
Wilson-Chi 39
Hornsby-Chi 39
O'Doul-Phi 32

Total Bases
Hornsby-Chi 409
Klein-Phi 405
O'Doul-Phi 397
Wilson-Chi 355
Herman-Bro 348

Runs Batted In
Wilson-Chi 159
Ott-NY 151
Hornsby-Chi 149
Klein-Phi 145
Bottomley-StL ... 137

Runs Produced
Hornsby-Chi 266
Wilson-Chi 255
Ott-NY 247
O'Doul-Phi 242
Klein-Phi 228

Bases On Balls
Ott-NY 113
Grantham-Pit 93
P.Waner-Pit 89
Hornsby-Chi 87
Walker-Cin 85

Batting Average
O'Doul-Phi .... .398
Herman-Bro .... .381
Hornsby-Chi ...... .380
Terry-NY .... .372
Stephenson-Chi ... .362

On Base Percentage
O'Doul-Phi .... .465
Hornsby-Chi ...... .459
Ott-NY .... .449
Stephenson-Chi ... .445
Cuyler-Chi .... .438

Slugging Average
Hornsby-Chi ...... .679
Klein-Phi .... .657
Ott-NY .... .635
Hafey-StL .... .632
O'Doul-Phi .... .622

Production
Hornsby-Chi 1.139
O'Doul-Phi 1.087
Ott-NY 1.084
Klein-Phi 1.065
Herman-Bro 1.047

Adjusted Production
Hornsby-Chi 178
Ott-NY 166
Herman-Bro 160
O'Doul-Phi 157
Wilson-Chi 155

Batter Runs
Hornsby-Chi 74.1
O'Doul-Phi 68.5
Ott-NY 58.4
Klein-Phi 53.3
Herman-Bro 49.6

Adjusted Batter Runs
Hornsby-Chi 73.9
O'Doul-Phi 62.0
Ott-NY 58.7
Herman-Bro 51.4
Wilson-Chi 48.8

Clutch Hitting Index
Sheely-Pit 148
Comorosky-Pit 144
Kelly-Cin 143
Grimm-Chi 137
Traynor-Pit 133

Runs Created
Hornsby-Chi 183
O'Doul-Phi 180
Klein-Phi 158
Ott-NY 157
Wilson-Chi 148

Total Average
Hornsby-Chi 1.338
Ott-NY 1.287
O'Doul-Phi 1.247
Herman-Bro 1.205
Cuyler-Chi 1.181

Stolen Bases
Cuyler-Chi 43
Swanson-Cin 33
Frisch-StL 24
Herman-Bro 21
Allen-Cin 21

Stolen Base Average

Stolen Base Runs

Fielding Runs
Whitney-Phi 21.3
Maranville-Bos ... 19.5
Jackson-NY 19.2
L.Waner-Pit 15.7
English-Chi 15.4

Total Player Rating
Hornsby-Chi 7.2
Ott-NY 5.2
O'Doul-Phi 5.0
Jackson-NY 4.1
Wilson-Chi 3.3

Wins
Malone-Chi 22
Root-Chi 19
Lucas-Cin 19

Win Percentage
Root-Chi .... .760
Bush-Chi .... .720
Grimes-Pit .... .708
Malone-Chi .... .688
Kremer-Pit .... .643

Games
Bush-Chi 50
Willoughby-Phi ... 49
Sweetland-Phi 43
Root-Chi 43
Collins-Phi 43

Complete Games
Lucas-Cin 28

Shutouts
Malone-Chi 5
Root-Chi 4
Fitzsimmons-NY ... 4

Saves
Morrison-Bro 8
Bush-Chi 8
Koupal-Bro-Phi 6

Innings Pitched
Clark-Bro 279.0
Root-Chi 272.0
Bush-Chi 270.2
Lucas-Cin 270.0
Hubbell-NY 268.0

Fewest Hits/Game
Lucas-Cin 8.90
Hubbell-NY 9.17
Kremer-Pit 9.18
Johnson-StL 9.18
Bush-Chi 9.21

Fewest BB/Game
Vance-Bro 1.83
Lucas-Cin 1.93
Petty-Pit 2.05
Hubbell-NY 2.25
Clark-Bro 2.29

Strikeouts
Malone-Chi 166
Clark-Bro 140
Vance-Bro 126
Root-Chi 124
Hubbell-NY 106

Strikeouts/Game
Malone-Chi 5.60
Vance-Bro 4.90
Clark-Bro 4.52
May-Cin 4.16
Root-Chi 4.10

Ratio
Lucas-Cin 10.87
Hubbell-NY 11.62
Kremer-Pit 11.65
Petty-Pit 11.67
Vance-Bro 11.67

Earned Run Average
Walker-NY 3.09
Grimes-Pit 3.13
Root-Chi 3.47
Malone-Chi 3.57
Lucas-Cin 3.60

Adjusted ERA
Grimes-Pit 152
Walker-NY 148
Root-Chi 133
Johnson-StL 129
Malone-Chi 129

Opponents' Batting Avg.
Lucas-Cin .... .257
Johnson-StL ...... .265
Hubbell-NY .... .265
Bush-Chi .... .265
Grimes-Pit .... .269

Opponents' On Base Pct.
Lucas-Cin .... .297
Hubbell-NY .... .313
Clark-Bro .... .316
Vance-Bro .... .316
Petty-Pit .... .317

Starter Runs
Grimes-Pit 40.8
Root-Chi 37.4
Malone-Chi 33.8
Lucas-Cin 33.3
Walker-NY 32.0

Adjusted Starter Runs
Grimes-Pit 42.2
Root-Chi 34.4
Malone-Chi 30.8
Walker-NY 29.4
Lucas-Cin 28.8

Clutch Pitching Index
Mitchell-StL 129
Walker-NY 129
Sweetland-Phi ... 116
Grimes-Pit 116
Malone-Chi 115

Relief Runs
Hill-Pit-StL 2.9
Cvengros-Chi 5

Adjusted Relief Runs
Hill-Pit-StL 3.3

Relief Ranking
Hill-Pit-StL 2.0

Total Pitcher Index
Grimes-Pit 5.0
Lucas-Cin 3.9
Root-Chi 2.8
Malone-Chi 2.7
Hubbell-NY 2.3

Total Baseball Ranking
Hornsby-Chi 7.2
Ott-NY 5.2
O'Doul-Phi 5.0
Grimes-Pit 5.0
Jackson-NY 4.1

TEAM	G	W	L	PCT	GB	R	OR	AB	H	2B	3B	HR	BB	SO	AVG	OBP	SLG	PRO	PRO+	BR	/A	PF	CHI	RC	SB	CS	SBA	SBR
PHI	151	104	46	.693		901	615	5204	1539	288	76	122	543	440	.296	.365	.451	.816	111	113	85	104	102	875	61	38	62	-5
NY	154	88	66	.571	18	899	775	5379	1587	262	74	142	554	518	.295	.364	.450	.814	123	111	163	93	101	892	51	44	54	-11
CLE	152	81	71	.533	24	717	736	5187	1525	294	79	62	453	363	.294	.354	.417	.771	100	26	-1	104	92	763	75	85	47	-29
STL	154	79	73	.520	26	733	713	5174	1426	277	64	46	589	431	.276	.352	.381	.733	91	-33	-62	104	100	723	72	46	61	-6
WAS	153	71	81	.467	34	730	776	5237	1445	244	66	48	556	400	.276	.347	.375	.722	90	-56	-61	101	102	706	86	61	59	-11
DET	155	70	84	.455	36	926	928	5592	1671	339	97	110	521	496	.299	.360	.453	.813	114	110	107	100	101	914	95	72	57	-15
CHI	152	59	93	.388	46	627	792	5248	1406	240	74	37	425	436	.268	.325	.363	.688	83	-134	-125	99	102	633	109	65	63	-6
BOS	155	58	96	.377	48	605	803	5160	1377	285	69	28	413	494	.267	.325	.365	.690	85	-130	-112	98	99	616	85	80	52	-23
TOT	613					6138		42181	11976	2229	599	595	4054	3578	.284	.349	.407	.756							634	491	56	-104

TEAM	CG	SH	SV	IP	H	H/G	HR	BB	SO	RAT	ERA	ERA+	OAV	OOB	PR	/A	PF	CPI	FA	E	DP	FW	PW	BW	SBW	DIF
PHI	70	9	24	1357	1371	9.1	73	487	573	12.4	3.44	123	.264	.329	121	119	100	105	.975	146	117	2.6	11.2	8.0	.8	6.4
NY	64	12	18	1366²	1475	9.7	83	485	484	13.1	4.19	92	.278	.341	7	-52	91	96	.971	178	153	.8	-4.9	15.4	.2	-.5
CLE	80	8	10	1352	1570	10.5	56	488	389	13.9	4.05	109	.295	.357	28	57	105	109	.968	198	162	-.6	5.4	-.0	-1.5	1.8
STL	83	15	10	1371	1469	9.6	100	462	415	12.8	4.08	108	.279	.340	25	51	104	102	.975	156	148	2.2	4.8	-5.8	.7	1.2
WAS	62	3	17	1354²	1429	9.5	48	496	494	12.9	4.34	98	.276	.342	-15	-16	100	89	.968	195	156	-.3	-1.5	-5.8	.2	2.4
DET	82	5	9	1390¹	1641	10.6	73	646	467	15.0	4.96	86	.301	.377	-111	-105	101	100	.961	242	149	-3.0	-9.9	10.1	-.2	-4.0
CHI	78	5	7	1357²	1481	9.8	84	505	328	13.4	4.41	97	.284	.351	-26	-22	101	98	.970	188	153	.0	-2.1	-11.8	.7	-3.9
BOS	84	9	5	1366²	1537	10.1	78	496	416	13.6	4.43	96	.291	.355	-28	-25	101	100	.965	218	159	-1.6	-2.4	-10.6	-.9	-3.6
TOT	603	66	100	10916		9.9				13.4	4.24		.284	.349					.969	1521	1197					

Runs		Hits		Doubles		Triples		Home Runs		Total Bases	
Gehringer-Det	131	Gehringer-Det	215	Manush-StL	45	Gehringer-Det	19	Ruth-NY	46	Simmons-Phi	373
Johnson-Det	128	Alexander-Det	215	Johnson-Det	45	Scarritt-Bos	17	Gehrig-NY	35	Alexander-Det	363
Gehrig-NY	127	Simmons-Phi	212	Gehringer-Det	45	E.Miller-Phi	16	Simmons-Phi	34	Ruth-NY	348
Foxx-Phi	123	Fonseca-Cle	209	Fonseca-Cle	44			Foxx-Phi	33	Gehringer-Det	337
Ruth-NY	121	Manush-StL	204					Alexander-Det	25		

Runs Batted In		Runs Produced		Bases On Balls		Batting Average		On Base Percentage		Slugging Average	
Simmons-Phi	157	Simmons-Phi	237	Bishop-Phi	128	Fonseca-Cle	.369	Foxx-Phi	.463	Ruth-NY	.697
Ruth-NY	154	Ruth-NY	229	Blue-StL	126	Simmons-Phi	.365	Gehrig-NY	.431	Simmons-Phi	.642
Alexander-Det	137	Gehringer-Det	224	Gehrig-NY	122	Manush-StL	.355	Ruth-NY	.430	Foxx-Phi	.625
Gehrig-NY	126	Alexander-Det	222	Foxx-Phi	103	Lazzeri-NY	.354	Lazzeri-NY	.429	Gehrig-NY	.584
Heilmann-Det	120	Gehrig-NY	218	Cronin-Was	85	Foxx-Phi	.354	Fonseca-Cle	.427	Alexander-Det	.580

Production		Adjusted Production		Batter Runs		Adjusted Batter Runs		Clutch Hitting Index		Runs Created	
Ruth-NY	1.128	Ruth-NY	199	Foxx-Phi	63.1	Ruth-NY	66.9	Kress-StL	144	Foxx-Phi	154
Foxx-Phi	1.088	Foxx-Phi	171	Ruth-NY	61.9	Foxx-Phi	60.2	West-Was	141	Ruth-NY	150
Simmons-Phi	1.040	Gehrig-NY	170	Gehrig-NY	51.6	Gehrig-NY	57.4	Heilmann-Det	139	Gehrig-NY	146
Gehrig-NY	1.015	Lazzeri-NY	164	Simmons-Phi	50.3	Lazzeri-NY	49.3	Schulte-StL	136	Simmons-Phi	145
Lazzeri-NY	.991	Simmons-Phi	158	Lazzeri-NY	43.9	Simmons-Phi	47.4	Cochrane-Phi	130	Alexander-Det	140

Total Average		Stolen Bases		Stolen Base Average		Stolen Base Runs		Fielding Runs		Total Player Rating	
Ruth-NY	1.288	Gehringer-Det	27	Gehringer-Det	75.0	Gehringer-Det	2.7	Durocher-NY	26.2	Simmons-Phi	5.1
Foxx-Phi	1.261	Cissell-Chi	25	E.Miller-Phi	72.7	E.Miller-Phi	1.8	Kerr-Chi	24.0	Ruth-NY	4.5
Gehrig-NY	1.151	E.Miller-Phi	24	Myer-Was	72.0	Myer-Was	1.2	Melillo-StL	22.5	Lazzeri-NY	4.5
Simmons-Phi	1.097	Rothrock-Bos	23	Reynolds-Chi	67.9	Goslin-Was	1.2	Simmons-Phi	17.3	Gehringer-Det	3.9
Lazzeri-NY	1.041	Johnson-Det	20	Rice-Was	66.7	Berg-Chi	.9	West-Was	15.0	Foxx-Phi	3.8

Wins		Win Percentage		Games		Complete Games		Shutouts		Saves	
Earnshaw-Phi	24	Grove-Phi	.769	Marberry-Was	49	Thomas-Chi	24	MacFayden-Bos	4	Marberry-Was	11
Ferrell-Cle	21	Earnshaw-Phi	.750	Earnshaw-Phi	44	Uhle-Det	23	Gray-StL	4	Moore-NY	8
Grove-Phi	20	Ferrell-Cle	.677	Gray-StL	43	Gray-StL	23	Crowder-StL	4	Shores-Phi	7
Marberry-Was	19	Walberg-Phi	.621	Ferrell-Cle	43	Hudlin-Cle	22	Blaeholder-StL	4	Ferrell-Cle	5
		Marberry-Was	.613			Lyons-Chi	21				

Innings Pitched		Fewest Hits/Game		Fewest BB/Game		Strikeouts		Strikeouts/Game		Ratio	
Gray-StL	305.0	Earnshaw-Phi	8.23	Russell-Bos	1.58	Grove-Phi	170	Grove-Phi	5.56	Marberry-Was	11.07
Hudlin-Cle	280.1	Wells-NY	8.33	Pennock-NY	1.60	Earnshaw-Phi	149	Earnshaw-Phi	5.27	Thomas-Chi	11.44
Grove-Phi	275.1	Marberry-Was	8.38	Thomas-Chi	2.08	Pipgras-NY	125	Pipgras-NY	4.99	Grove-Phi	11.83
Walberg-Phi	267.2	Walberg-Phi	8.61	Uhle-Det	2.10	Marberry-Was	121	Hadley-Was	4.52	Walberg-Phi	11.94
Crowder-StL	266.2	McKain-Chi	9.00	Quinn-Phi	2.18			Marberry-Was	4.35	Faber-Chi	11.96

Earned Run Average		Adjusted ERA		Opponents' Batting Avg.		Opponents' On Base Pct.		Starter Runs		Adjusted Starter Runs	
Grove-Phi	2.81	Grove-Phi	150	Earnshaw-Phi	.241	Marberry-Was	.308	Grove-Phi	43.7	Grove-Phi	43.3
Marberry-Was	3.06	Marberry-Was	139	Wells-NY	.248	Thomas-Chi	.310	Marberry-Was	32.9	Hudlin-Cle	34.3
Thomas-Chi	3.19	Thomas-Chi	134	Marberry-Was	.252	Grove-Phi	.316	Thomas-Chi	30.3	Marberry-Was	32.8
Earnshaw-Phi	3.29	Hudlin-Cle	133	Walberg-Phi	.254	Hudlin-Cle	.318	Hudlin-Cle	28.1	Thomas-Chi	31.4
Hudlin-Cle	3.34	Earnshaw-Phi	129	Grove-Phi	.262	Walberg-Phi	.320	Earnshaw-Phi	27.0	Earnshaw-Phi	26.6

Clutch Pitching Index		Relief Runs		Adjusted Relief Runs	Relief Ranking	Total Pitcher Index		Total Baseball Ranking	
McKain-Chi	130	Moore-NY	.7			Grove-Phi	4.0	Simmons-Phi	5.1
N.Gaston-Bos	116					Hudlin-Cle	3.8	Ruth-NY	4.5
Shaute-Cle	116					Marberry-Was	3.1	Lazzeri-NY	4.5
Ferrell-Cle	116					Thomas-Chi	3.0	Grove-Phi	4.0
Collins-StL	113					Ferrell-Cle	2.9	Gehringer-Det	3.9

TEAM	G	W	L	PCT	GB	R	OR	AB	H	2B	3B	HR	BB	SO	AVG	OBP	SLG	PRO	PRO+	BR	/A	PF	CHI	RC	SB	CS	SBA	SBR
STL	154	92	62	.597		1004	784	5512	1732	373	89	104	479	496	.314	.372	.471	.843	105	72	43	103	104	944	72			
CHI	156	90	64	.584	2	998	870	5581	1722	305	72	171	588	635	.309	.378	.481	.859	111	110	104	101	98	1001	70			
NY	154	87	67	.565	5	959	814	5553	1769	264	83	143	422	382	.319	.369	.473	.842	110	67	86	98	101	941	59			
BRO	154	86	68	.558	6	871	814	5433	1654	303	73	122	446	541	.304	.364	.454	.818	103	21	31	99	97	881	53			
PIT	154	80	74	.519	12	891	928	5346	1622	285	119	86	494	449	.303	.365	.449	.814	101	15	12	100	101	862	76			
BOS	154	70	84	.455	22	693	835	5356	1503	246	78	66	332	397	.281	.326	.393	.719	81	-186	-157	97	105	669	48			
CIN	154	59	95	.383	33	665	857	5245	1475	265	67	74	445	489	.281	.339	.400	.739	87	-135	-93	95	94	703	48			
PHI	156	52	102	.338	40	944	1199	5667	1783	345	44	126	450	459	.315	.367	.458	.825	97	37	-28	107	100	929	34			
TOT	618					7025		43693	13260	2386	625	892	3691	3848	.303	.360	.448	.808							481			

TEAM	CG	SH	SV	IP	H	H/G	HR	BB	SO	RAT	ERA	ERA+	OAV	OOB	PR	/A	PF	CPI	FA	E	DP	FW	PW	BW	SBW	DIF
STL	63	5	21	1380²	1596	10.4	87	476	639	13.7	4.39	114	.294	.353	89	95	101	104	.970	183	176	.2	8.4	3.8		2.7
CHI	67	6	12	1403²	1642	10.5	111	528	601	14.1	4.80	102	.294	.357	26	14	98	99	.973	170	167	1.0	1.2	9.2		1.5
NY	64	6	19	1363¹	1546	10.2	117	439	522	13.3	4.61	103	.290	.348	54	18	95	99	.974	164	144	1.3	1.6	7.6		-.4
BRO	74	13	15	1372	1480	9.7	115	394	526	12.4	4.03	122	.278	.330	144	135	99	102	.972	174	167	.7	11.9	2.7		-6.3
PIT	80	7	13	1361¹	1730	11.4	128	438	393	14.5	5.24	95	.313	.367	-41	-40	100	101	.965	216	164	-1.8	-3.5	1.1		7.2
BOS	71	6	11	1361	1624	10.7	117	475	424	14.0	4.91	100	.302	.360	9	3	99	102	.971	178	167	.4	.3	-13.9		6.2
CIN	61	6	11	1335	1650	11.1	75	394	361	13.9	5.08	95	.310	.361	-15	-37	97	96	.973	161	164	1.4	-3.3	-8.2		-8.0
PHI	54	3	7	1372²	1993	13.1	142	543	384	16.8	6.71	81	.346	.405	-266	-189	110	99	.962	239	169	-3.0	-16.7	-2.5		-2.9
TOT	534	52	109	10949²		10.9				14.1	4.97		.303	.360					.970	1485	1318					

Runs
Klein-Phi 158
Cuyler-Chi 155
English-Chi 152
Wilson-Chi 146
Herman-Bro 143

Hits
Terry-NY 254
Klein-Phi 250
Herman-Bro 241
Lindstrom-NY 231
Cuyler-Chi 228

Doubles
Klein-Phi 59
Cuyler-Chi 50
Herman-Bro 48
Comorosky-Pit 47
Frisch-StL 46

Triples
Comorosky-Pit . . . 23
P.Waner-Pit 18
English-Chi 17
Cuyler-Chi 17
Terry-NY 15

Home Runs
Wilson-Chi 56
Klein-Phi 40
Berger-Bos 38
Hartnett-Chi 37
Herman-Bro 35

Total Bases
Klein-Phi 445
Wilson-Chi 423
Herman-Bro 416
Terry-NY 392
Cuyler-Chi 351

Runs Batted In
Wilson-Chi 190
Klein-Phi 170
Cuyler-Chi 134
Herman-Bro 130
Terry-NY 129

Runs Produced
Klein-Phi 288
Wilson-Chi 280
Cuyler-Chi 276
Terry-NY 245
Herman-Bro 238

Bases On Balls
Wilson-Chi 105
Ott-NY 103
English-Chi 100
Grantham-Pit 81
Suhr-Pit 80

Batting Average
Terry-NY 401
Herman-Bro 393
Klein-Phi 386
O'Doul-Phi 383
Lindstrom-NY 379

On Base Percentage
Ott-NY 458
Herman-Bro 455
Wilson-Chi 454
O'Doul-Phi 453
Terry-NY 452

Slugging Average
Wilson-Chi 723
Klein-Phi 687
Herman-Bro 678
Hafey-StL 652
Hartnett-Chi 630

Production
Wilson-Chi 1.177
Herman-Bro 1.132
Klein-Phi 1.123
Terry-NY 1.071
Hafey-StL 1.059

Adjusted Production
Wilson-Chi 177
Herman-Bro 171
Terry-NY 159
Klein-Phi 155
Ott-NY 152

Batter Runs
Wilson-Chi 75.4
Herman-Bro 68.7
Klein-Phi 67.3
Terry-NY 57.6
O'Doul-Phi 46.9

Adjusted Batter Runs
Wilson-Chi 74.7
Herman-Bro 69.9
Klein-Phi 59.8
Terry-NY 59.8
Ott-NY 47.3

Clutch Hitting Index
Traynor-Pit 155
Thevenow-Phi 144
Whitney-Phi 140
Wright-Bro 130
Grimm-Chi 121

Runs Created
Wilson-Chi 189
Klein-Phi 186
Herman-Bro 183
Terry-NY 170
Cuyler-Chi 148

Total Average
Wilson-Chi 1.411
Herman-Bro 1.351
Klein-Phi 1.274
Ott-NY 1.224
Terry-NY 1.208

Stolen Bases
Cuyler-Chi 37
P.Waner-Pit 18
Herman-Bro 18

Stolen Base Average

Stolen Base Runs

Fielding Runs
Frisch-StL 27.5
Klein-Phi 23.0
Whitney-Phi 20.3
Terry-NY 12.6
Cuyler-Chi 12.2

Total Player Rating
Klein-Phi 6.2
Terry-NY 4.9
Wilson-Chi 4.9
Lindstrom-NY 4.8
Frisch-StL 4.5

Wins
Malone-Chi 20
Kremer-Pit 20
Fitzsimmons-NY . . . 19

Win Percentage
Fitzsimmons-NY . . .731
Malone-Chi 690
Brame-Pit 680
Kremer-Pit 625
Hallahan-StL 625

Games
Elliott-Phi 48
Collins-NY 47
Bush-Chi 46
Pruett-NY 45
Malone-Chi 45

Complete Games
Malone-Chi 22
Brame-Pit 22
French-Pit 21
Vance-Bro 20
Seibold-Bos 20

Shutouts
Vance-Bro 4
Root-Chi 4
Hubbell-NY 3
French-Pit 3

Saves
Bell-StL 8
Heving-NY 6
Clark-Bro 6

Innings Pitched
Kremer-Pit 276.0
French-Pit 274.2
Malone-Chi 271.2
Vance-Bro 258.2
Seibold-Bos 251.0

Fewest Hits/Game
Vance-Bro 8.39
Hallahan-StL 8.84
Fitzsimmons-NY . . 9.23
Elliott-Bro 9.26
Clark-Bro 9.41

Fewest BB/Game
Clark-Bro 1.71
Kolp-Cin 1.82
Johnson-StL 1.82
Lucas-Cin 1.88
Vance-Bro 1.91

Strikeouts
Hallahan-StL 177
Vance-Bro 173
Malone-Chi 142
Root-Chi 124
Hubbell-NY 117

Strikeouts/Game
Hallahan-StL 6.71
Vance-Bro 6.02
Root-Chi 5.07
Malone-Chi 4.70
Johnson-StL 4.41

Ratio
Vance-Bro 10.47
Clark-Bro 11.11
Kolp-Cin 11.44
Fitzsimmons-NY . 11.63
Johnson-StL 12.33

Earned Run Average
Vance-Bro 2.61
Hubbell-NY 3.87
Walker-NY 3.93
Malone-Chi 3.94
Elliott-Bro 3.95

Adjusted ERA
Vance-Bro 188
Elliott-Bro 124
Malone-Chi 124
Grimes-Bos-StL . . . 123
Hubbell-NY 122

Opponents' Batting Avg.
Vance-Bro 246
Hallahan-StL 260
Fitzsimmons-NY . . .266
Walker-NY 268
Malone-Chi 271

Opponents' On Base Pct.
Vance-Bro 289
Clark-Bro 306
Fitzsimmons-NY . . .314
Kolp-Cin 314
Hubbell-NY 327

Starter Runs
Vance-Bro 67.9
Malone-Chi 31.1
Hubbell-NY 29.5
Walker-NY 28.5
Seibold-Bos 23.7

Adjusted Starter Runs
Vance-Bro 66.2
Malone-Chi 28.5
Hubbell-NY 23.1
Seibold-Bos 22.7
Walker-NY 22.0

Clutch Pitching Index
Grimes-Bos-StL . . 119
Smith-Bos 117
Haines-StL 109
Vance-Bro 108
Seibold-Bos 107

Relief Runs
Bell-StL 13.7
Lindsey-StL 6.4
Johnson-Cin 3

Adjusted Relief Runs
Bell-StL 14.3
Lindsey-StL 6.9

Relief Ranking
Bell-StL 10.0
Lindsey-StL 7.8

Total Pitcher Index
Vance-Bro 5.8
Malone-Chi 2.8
Grimes-Bos-StL . . . 2.2
Fitzsimmons-NY . . . 2.1
Seibold-Bos 1.8

Total Baseball Ranking
Klein-Phi 6.2
Vance-Bro 5.8
Terry-NY 4.9
Wilson-Chi 4.9
Lindstrom-NY 4.8

TEAM	G	W	L	PCT	GB	R	OR	AB	H	2B	3B	HR	BB	SO	AVG	OBP	SLG	PRO	PRO+	BR	/A	PF	CHI	RC	SB	CS	SBA	SBR
PHI	154	102	52	.662		951	751	5345	1573	319	74	125	599	531	.294	.369	.452	.821	108	102	65	104	100	913	48	33	59	-5
WAS	154	94	60	.610	8	892	689	5370	1620	300	98	57	537	438	.302	.369	.426	.795	106	59	56	100	99	860	101	67	60	-10
NY	154	86	68	.558	16	1062	898	5448	1683	298	110	152	644	569	.309	.384	.488	.872	131	206	245	96	99	1035	91	60	60	-9
CLE	154	81	73	.526	21	890	915	5439	1654	358	59	72	490	461	.304	.364	.431	.795	102	54	22	104	99	863	51	47	52	-13
DET	154	75	79	.487	27	783	833	5297	1504	298	90	82	461	508	.284	.344	.421	.765	96	-18	-34	102	98	771	98	70	58	-13
STL	154	64	90	.416	38	751	886	5278	1415	289	67	75	497	550	.268	.333	.391	.724	85	-96	-124	103	104	696	93	71	57	-15
CHI	154	62	92	.403	40	729	884	5419	1496	256	90	63	389	479	.276	.328	.391	.719	89	-111	-83	97	102	706	74	40	65	-2
BOS	154	52	102	.338	50	612	814	5286	1393	257	68	47	358	552	.264	.313	.365	.678	79	-192	-161	96	100	608	42	35	55	-8
TOT	616					6670		42882	12338	2375	656	673	3975	4088	.288	.351	.421	.772							598	423	59	-74

TEAM	CG	SH	SV	IP	H	H/G	HR	BB	SO	RAT	ERA	ERA+	OAV	OOB	PR	/A	PF	CPI	FA	E	DP	FW	PW	BW	SBW	DIF
PHI	72	8	21	1371	1457	9.6	84	488	672	12.9	4.28	109	.274	.337	56	58	101	98	.975	145	121	3.0	5.2	5.9	.4	10.5
WAS	78	6	14	1369	1367	9.0	52	504	524	12.5	3.96	116	.264	.332	104	96	99	97	.974	157	99	2.3	8.7	5.1	-.0	1.1
NY	65	7	15	1367²	1566	10.3	93	542	572	13.9	4.88	88	.287	.352	-36	-90	93	96	.965	207	132	-.7	-8.1	22.2	.0	-4.3
CLE	68	5	14	1360	1663	11.0	85	528	441	14.6	4.88	99	.305	.368	-36	-9	104	107	.962	237	156	-2.5	-.8	2.0	-.3	5.7
DET	68	4	17	1351²	1507	10.0	86	570	574	14.0	4.70	102	.286	.359	-8	13	103	102	.967	192	156	.2	1.2	-3.1	-.3	.0
STL	68	5	10	1371²	1639	10.8	124	449	470	13.9	5.07	96	.300	.356	-65	-31	105	101	.970	188	152	.4	-2.8	-11.2	-.5	1.1
CHI	63	2	10	1361	1629	10.8	74	407	471	13.6	4.71	98	.300	.352	-10	-15	99	101	.962	235	136	-2.4	-1.4	-7.5	.7	-4.4
BOS	78	4	5	1360¹	1515	10.0	75	488	356	13.4	4.68	98	.286	.348	-6	-12	99	97	.968	196	161	-.0	-1.1	-14.6	.1	-9.4
TOT	560	41	106	10912¹		10.2				13.6	4.65		.288	.351					.968	1557	1164					

Runs
Simmons-Phi.....152
Ruth-NY.....150
Gehringer-Det....144
Gehrig-NY.......143
Combs-NY.......129

Hits
Hodapp-Cle.......225
Gehrig-NY.......220
Simmons-Phi.....211
Rice-Was.......207
Morgan-Cle......204

Doubles
Hodapp-Cle.......51
Manush-StL-Was...49
Morgan-Cle.......47
Gehringer-Det.....47

Triples
Combs-NY.......22
Reynolds-Chi.......18
Gehrig-NY.......17
Simmons-Phi.......16

Home Runs
Ruth-NY.........49
Gehrig-NY........41
Goslin-Was-StL....37
Foxx-Phi.......37
Simmons-Phi.....36

Total Bases
Gehrig-NY.......419
Simmons-Phi.....392
Ruth-NY.........379
Foxx-Phi.........358

Runs Batted In
Gehrig-NY.......174
Simmons-Phi.....165
Foxx-Phi........156
Ruth-NY.........153
Goslin-Was-StL...138

Runs Produced
Simmons-Phi.....281
Gehrig-NY.......276
Ruth-NY.......254
Foxx-Phi.......246
Cronin-Was.......240

Bases On Balls
Ruth-NY.......136
Bishop-Phi.......128
Gehrig-NY.......101
Foxx-Phi.........93
Blue-StL.........81

Batting Average
Simmons-Phi.....381
Gehrig-NY.......379
Ruth-NY.......359
Reynolds-Chi.......359
Cochrane-Phi.......357

On Base Percentage
Ruth-NY.......493
Gehrig-NY.......473
Foxx-Phi.........429
Bishop-Phi.......426
Combs-NY.......424

Slugging Average
Ruth-NY.......732
Gehrig-NY.......721
Simmons-Phi.....708
Foxx-Phi.......637

Production
Ruth-NY.......1.225
Gehrig-NY.......1.194
Simmons-Phi....1.130
Foxx-Phi........1.066
Morgan-Cle.....1.014

Adjusted Production
Ruth-NY.......216
Gehrig-NY.......207
Simmons-Phi.....173
Foxx-Phi.......159
Morgan-Cle......148

Batter Runs
Ruth-NY.......89.5
Gehrig-NY.......88.4
Simmons-Phi.....64.2
Foxx-Phi.......57.0
Morgan-Cle......46.3

Adjusted Batter Runs
Ruth-NY.......93.7
Gehrig-NY.......92.8
Simmons-Phi.....60.5
Foxx-Phi........52.9
Morgan-Cle......42.8

Clutch Hitting Index
Lazzeri-NY.....146
Rice-Det-NY.....142
Cronin-Was.....130
Alexander-Det....130
Hodapp-Cle.....123

Runs Created
Gehrig-NY.......195
Ruth-NY.......191
Simmons-Phi.....163
Foxx-Phi.......154
Morgan-Cle......144

Total Average
Ruth-NY.......1.509
Gehrig-NY.....1.389
Simmons-Phi....1.272
Foxx-Phi.......1.184
Morgan-Cle.....1.089

Stolen Bases
McManus-Det.....23
Gehringer-Det.....19
Goslin-Was-StL....17
Johnson-Det.......17
Cronin-Was.......17

Stolen Base Average
Reynolds-Chi.....80.0
McManus-Det.....74.2
Cissell-Chi.....64.0
Johnson-Det.......63.0
Cronin-Was.......63.0

Stolen Base Runs
Lary-NY.......3.0
Reynolds-Chi.....2.4
McManus-Det.....2.1

Fielding Runs
Melillo-StL......26.8
Cronin-Was.....26.2
Goldman-Cle....20.7
Oliver-Bos.......15.2
Kamm-Chi.......14.9

Total Player Rating
Ruth-NY.........7.0
Cronin-Was.......6.7
Gehrig-NY.......6.5
Simmons-Phi.....5.1
Cochrane-Phi.....4.1

Wins
Grove-Phi.........28
Ferrell-Cle.....25
Lyons-Chi.......22
Earnshaw-Phi.....22
Stewart-StL.......20

Win Percentage
Grove-Phi.......848
Marberry-Was....750
Jones-Was.......682
Ferrell-Cle.....658
Ruffing-Bos-NY...652

Games
Grove-Phi.......50
Earnshaw-Phi.....49
Pipgras-NY.......44
Johnson-NY.......44
Ferrell-Cle.......43

Complete Games
Lyons-Chi.......29
Crowder-StL-Was..25
Ferrell-Cle.......25
Stewart-StL.......23
Grove-Phi.........22

Shutouts
Pipgras-NY........3
Earnshaw-Phi.......3
Brown-Cle.........3

Saves
Grove-Phi.........9
Braxton-Was-Chi....6
Quinn-Phi.........6
Sullivan-Det.......5
McKain-Chi.......5

Innings Pitched
Lyons-Chi.....297.2
Ferrell-Cle.....296.2
Earnshaw-Phi.....296.0
Grove-Phi.......291.0
Crowder-StL-Was 279.2

Fewest Hits/Game
Hadley-Was.....8.37
Grove-Phi.......8.44
Collins-StL.....8.81
Crowder-StL-Was .8.88
Gaston-Bos.....8.97

Fewest BB/Game
Pennock-NY.....1.15
Lyons-Chi.......1.72
Grove-Phi.......1.86
Russell-Bos.....2.08
Brown-Cle.......2.15

Strikeouts
Grove-Phi.......209
Earnshaw-Phi.....193
Hadley-Was.....162
Ferrell-Cle.....143
Ruffing-Bos-NY...131

Strikeouts/Game
Grove-Phi.......6.46
Johnson-NY.....5.90
Earnshaw-Phi.....5.87
Hadley-Was.....5.60
Ruffing-Bos-NY...5.32

Ratio
Grove-Phi.......10.45
Stewart-StL.....11.69
Lyons-Chi......11.79
Marberry-Was...11.82
Caraway-Chi.....11.82

Earned Run Average
Grove-Phi.........2.54
Ferrell-Cle.....3.31
Stewart-StL.....3.45
Uhle-Det.........3.65
Hadley-Was.....3.73

Adjusted ERA
Grove-Phi.........184
Ferrell-Cle.....146
Stewart-StL.....141
Uhle-Det.........131
Sorrell-Det.......124

Opponents' Batting Avg.
Grove-Phi.........247
Hadley-Was.....247
Crowder-StL-Was ..259
Collins-StL.....259
Gaston-Bos.......259

Opponents' On Base Pct.
Grove-Phi.........288
Stewart-StL.....315
Lyons-Chi.......319
Marberry-Was....321
Crowder-StL-Was .321

Starter Runs
Grove-Phi.......68.3
Ferrell-Cle.....44.2
Stewart-StL.....35.9
Lyons-Chi.......28.7
Hadley-Was.....26.4

Adjusted Starter Runs
Grove-Phi.........69.0
Ferrell-Cle.....50.0
Stewart-StL.....42.7
Uhle-Det.........30.4
Lyons-Chi.......27.8

Clutch Pitching Index
Henry-Chi........122
Harder-Cle.......115
Sorrell-Det.......115
Hoyt-NY-Det.....113
Ferrell-Cle.......113

Relief Runs
Quinn-Phi.........2.3

Adjusted Relief Runs
Quinn-Phi.........2.5

Relief Ranking
Quinn-Phi.........4.5

Total Pitcher Index
Grove-Phi.........6.6
Ferrell-Cle.....5.4
Stewart-StL.......4.4
Lyons-Chi........3.7
Uhle-Det.........3.4

Total Baseball Ranking
Ruth-NY..........7.3
Cronin-Was.......6.7
Grove-Phi.........6.6
Gehrig-NY.......6.5
Ferrell-Cle.......5.4

TEAM	G	W	L	PCT	GB	R	OR	AB	H	2B	3B	HR	BB	SO	AVG	OBP	SLG	PRO	PRO+	BR	/A	PF	CHI	RC	SB	CS	SBA	SBR
STL	154	101	53	.656		815	614	5435	1554	353	74	60	432	475	.286	.342	.411	.753	105	61	34	104	107	787	114			
NY	153	87	65	.572	13	768	599	5372	1554	251	64	101	383	395	.289	.340	.416	.756	112	61	78	98	103	776	83			
CHI	156	84	70	.545	17	828	710	5451	1578	340	66	84	577	641	.289	.360	.422	.782	115	131	119	102	97	865	49			
BRO	153	79	73	.520	21	681	673	5309	1464	240	77	71	409	512	.276	.331	.390	.721	101	-3	2	99	101	705	45			
PIT	155	75	79	.487	26	636	691	5360	1425	243	70	41	493	454	.266	.330	.360	.690	93	-54	-47	99	98	667	59			
PHI	155	66	88	.429	35	684	828	5375	1502	299	52	81	437	492	.279	.336	.400	.736	96	27	-28	108	95	745	42			
BOS	156	64	90	.416	37	533	680	5296	1367	221	59	34	368	430	.258	.309	.341	.650	84	-137	-113	96	98	580	46			
CIN	154	58	96	.377	43	592	742	5343	1439	241	70	21	403	463	.269	.323	.352	.675	94	-85	-44	94	99	631	24			
TOT	618					5537		42941	11883	2188	532	493	3502	3862	.277	.334	.387	.721						462				

TEAM	CG	SH	SV	IP	H	H/G	HR	BB	SO	RAT	ERA	ERA+	OAV	OOB	PR	/A	PF	CPI	FA	E	DP	FW	PW	BW	SBW	DIF
STL	80	17	20	1384²	1470	9.6	65	449	626	12.6	3.45	114	.273	.332	63	74	102	110	.974	160	169	1.0	7.4	3.4		12.3
NY	90	17	12	1360²	1341	8.9	71	422	570	11.8	3.30	112	.255	.313	85	58	96	100	.974	159	126	1.0	5.8	7.8		-3.5
CHI	80	8	8	1385²	1448	9.4	54	524	541	13.0	3.97	97	.268	.337	-17	-19	100	94	.973	169	141	.6	-1.9	11.8		-3.5
BRO	64	9	18	1356	1520	10.1	56	351	546	12.5	3.84	99	.283	.329	3	-5	99	100	.969	187	154	-.7	-.5	.2		4.0
PIT	89	9	5	1390	1489	9.6	55	442	345	12.6	3.66	105	.274	.331	32	28	100	102	.968	194	167	-.9	2.8	-4.7		.8
PHI	60	6	16	1603¹	1603	10.6	75	511	499	14.2	4.58	93	.293	.358	-108	-51	110	100	.966	210	149	-1.9	-5.1	-2.8		-1.3
BOS	78	12	9	1380¹	1465	10.6	66	406	419	12.3	3.90	97	.272	.325	-5	-18	98	94	.973	170	141	.5	-1.8	-11.2		-.5
CIN	70	7	6	1345	1545	10.3	51	399	317	13.1	4.22	89	.294	.346	-53	-72	97	101	.973	165	194	.7	-7.2	-4.4		-8.1
TOT	611	85	94	10962²		9.8				12.8	3.86		.277	.334					.971	1414	1241					

Runs
Terry-NY 121
Klein-Phi 121
English-Chi 117
Ott-NY 104
Cuyler-Chi 100

Hits
L.Waner-Pit 214
Terry-NY 213
English-Chi 202
Cuyler-Chi 202
Klein-Phi 200

Doubles
Adams-StL 46
Berger-Bos 44
Terry-NY 43
Herman-Bro 43
Bartell-Phi 43

Triples
Terry-NY 20
Herman-Bro 16
Traynor-Pit 15
Bissonette-Bro 14

Home Runs
Klein-Phi 31
Ott-NY 29
Berger-Bos 19
Herman-Bro 18
Arlett-Phi 18

Total Bases
Klein-Phi 347
Terry-NY 323
Herman-Bro 320
Berger-Bos 316
Cuyler-Chi 290

Runs Batted In
Klein-Phi 121
Ott-NY 115
Terry-NY 112
Traynor-Pit 103
Herman-Bro 97

Runs Produced
Terry-NY 224
Klein-Phi 211
Ott-NY 190
Traynor-Pit 182
Cuyler-Chi 179

Bases On Balls
Ott-NY 80
P.Waner-Pit 73
Cuyler-Chi 72
Grantham-Pit 71
English-Chi 68

Batting Average
Hafey-StL .... .349
Terry-NY .... .349
Klein-Phi .... .337
O'Doul-Bro .... .336
Grimm-Chi .... .331

On Base Percentage
Hafey-StL .... .404
Cuyler-Chi .... .404
P.Waner-Pit ...... .404
Grantham-Pit ...... .400
Klein-Phi .... .398

Slugging Average
Klein-Phi .... .584
Hafey-StL .... .569
Ott-NY .... .545
Terry-NY .... .529
Herman-Bro .... .525

Production
Klein-Phi .... .982
Hafey-StL .... .973
Ott-NY .... .937
Terry-NY .... .926
Berger-Bos .... .892

Adjusted Production
Ott-NY 153
Hafey-StL 153
Terry-NY 150
Klein-Phi 149
Berger-Bos 143

Batter Runs
Klein-Phi 48.9
Terry-NY 39.0
Hafey-StL 36.2
Ott-NY 35.0
Hornsby-Chi 33.5

Adjusted Batter Runs
Klein-Phi 42.8
Terry-NY 41.0
Ott-NY 36.7
Berger-Bos 34.4
Hafey-StL 34.0

Clutch Hitting Index
Sheely-Bos 163
Traynor-Pit 148
Frisch-StL 143
Cuccinello-Cin ... 138
Gelbert-StL 127

Runs Created
Klein-Phi 140
Terry-NY 130
Cuyler-Chi 122
Berger-Bos 122
Herman-Bro 118

Total Average
Hafey-StL 1.055
Klein-Phi 1.051
Ott-NY 1.031
Terry-NY .... .955
Cuyler-Chi .... .925

Stolen Bases
Frisch-StL 28
Herman-Bro 17
Martin-StL 16
Adams-StL 16
Watkins-StL 15

Stolen Base Average

Stolen Base Runs

Fielding Runs
L.Waner-Pit 18.3
Frisch-StL 16.3
P.Waner-Pit 14.6
Gelbert-StL 12.9
Hurst-Phi 11.4

Total Player Rating
Ott-NY 3.5
Terry-NY 3.5
Berger-Bos 3.4
Cuccinello-Cin 3.2
English-Chi 3.1

Wins
Meine-Pit 19
Hallahan-StL 19
J.Elliott-Phi 19

Win Percentage
Derringer-StL ..... .692
Hallahan-StL ..... .679
Bush-Chi .... .667
Grimes-StL .... .654

Games
J.Elliott-Phi 52
Johnson-Cin 42
Collins-Phi 42

Complete Games
Lucas-Cin 24
Brandt-Bos 23
Meine-Pit 22
Hubbell-NY 21
French-Pit 20

Shutouts
Walker-NY 6
Hubbell-NY 4
Fitzsimmons-NY ... 4
Derringer-StL 4

Saves
Quinn-Bro 15
Hallahan-StL 7
J.Elliott-Phi 5
Hallahan-StL 4
Collins-Phi 4

Innings Pitched
Meine-Pit 284.0
French-Pit 275.2
Johnson-Cin 262.1
Fitzsimmons-NY . 253.2
Root-Chi 251.0

Fewest Hits/Game
Hubbell-NY 7.66
Walker-NY 7.97
Brandt-Bos 8.21
Fitzsimmons-NY .. 8.59
Root-Chi 8.61

Fewest BB/Game
Johnson-StL 1.40
Lucas-Cin 1.47
Cantwell-Bos 1.96
Clark-Bro 2.01
Zachary-Bos 2.08

Strikeouts
Hallahan-StL 159
Hubbell-NY 155
Vance-Bro 150
Derringer-StL 134
Root-Chi 131

Strikeouts/Game
Vance-Bro 6.17
Hallahan-StL 5.75
Derringer-StL 5.70
Hubbell-NY 5.63
Root-Chi 4.70

Ratio
Hubbell-NY 10.23
Walker-NY 10.49
Johnson-StL 10.50
Fitzsimmons-NY .10.79
Brandt-Bos 11.12

Earned Run Average
Walker-NY 2.26
Hubbell-NY 2.65
Brandt-Bos 2.92
Meine-Pit 2.98
Johnson-StL 3.00

Adjusted ERA
Walker-NY 164
Hubbell-NY 139
Benge-Phi 134
Johnson-StL 131
Brandt-Bos 130

Opponents' Batting Avg.
Hubbell-NY ...... .227
Walker-NY .... .231
Brandt-Bos ...... .244
Fitzsimmons-NY .. .251
Root-Chi .... .252

Opponents' On Base Pct.
Hubbell-NY ...... .282
Walker-NY .... .283
Johnson-StL ..... .286
Fitzsimmons-NY .. .296
Cantwell-Bos ..... .301

Starter Runs
Walker-NY 42.7
Hubbell-NY 33.5
Meine-Pit 27.9
Brandt-Bos 26.3
Fitzsimmons-NY .. 22.9

Adjusted Starter Runs
Walker-NY 38.1
Benge-Phi 29.4
Hubbell-NY 28.7
Meine-Pit 27.3
Brandt-Bos 24.2

Clutch Pitching Index
Benton-Cin 125
Dudley-Phi 120
Grimes-StL 114
Hallahan-StL 113
Derringer-StL 112

Relief Runs
Lindsey-StL 9.1
Quinn-Bro 8.6
Moore-Bro 5

Adjusted Relief Runs
Lindsey-StL 9.6
Quinn-Bro 8.2
Moore-Bro 1

Relief Ranking
Quinn-Bro 14.7
Lindsey-StL 13.6
Moore-Bro 0

Total Pitcher Index
Fitzsimmons-NY ... 3.6
Brandt-Bos 3.4
Hubbell-NY 3.2
Walker-NY 2.9
Benge-Phi 2.7

Total Baseball Ranking
Fitzsimmons-NY ...3.6
Ott-NY 3.5
Terry-NY 3.5
Berger-Bos 3.4
Brandt-Bos 3.4

TEAM	G	W	L	PCT	GB	R	OR	AB	H	2B	3B	HR	BB	SO	AVG	OBP	SLG	PRO	PRO+	BR	/A	PF	CHI	RC	SB	CS	SBA	SBR
PHI	153	107	45	.704		858	626	5377	1544	311	64	118	528	543	.287	.355	.435	.790	107	93	45	106	98	843	25	23	52	-6
NY	155	94	59	.614	13.5	1067	760	5608	1667	277	78	155	748	554	.297	.383	.457	.840	135	220	267	94	100	1016	138	68	67	1
WAS	156	92	62	.597	16	843	691	5576	1588	308	93	49	481	459	.285	.345	.400	.745	100	91	46	106	100	840	63	60	51	-17
CLE	155	78	76	.506	30	885	833	5445	1612	321	69	71	555	433	.296	.363	.419	.782	105	-40	-67	104	98	696	73	80	48	-26
STL	154	63	91	.409	45	722	870	5374	1455	287	62	76	488	580	.271	.333	.390	.723	92	-154	-112	95	102	596	42	43	49	-13
BOS	153	62	90	.408	45	625	800	5379	1409	289	34	37	405	565	.262	.315	.349	.664	85	-79	-106	103	93	675	117	75	61	-10
DET	154	61	93	.396	47	651	836	5430	1456	292	69	43	480	468	.268	.330	.371	.701	87	-79	-106	103	93	675	117	75	61	-10
CHI	156	56	97	.366	51.5	704	939	5481	1423	238	69	27	483	445	.260	.323	.343	.666	86	-146	-99	94	108	632	94	39	71	5
TOT	618					6355		43670	12154	2323	538	576	4168	4047	.278	.344	.396	.740							624	452	58	-84

TEAM	CG	SH	SV	IP	H	H/G	HR	BB	SO	RAT	ERA	ERA+	OAV	OOB	PR	/A	PF	CPI	FA	E	DP	FW	PW	BW	SBW	DIF
PHI	97	12	16	1365[1]	1342	8.8	73	457	574	11.9	3.47	130	.256	.316	138	155	103	105	.976	141	151	3.2	14.4	4.2	.4	8.8
NY	78	4	17	1410[1]	1461	9.3	67	543	686	12.9	4.20	94	.263	.332	28	-37	91	94	.976	169	131	1.7	-3.4	24.9	1.1	-6.7
WAS	60	7	24	1394[1]	1434	9.3	73	498	582	12.6	3.76	114	.264	.327	95	82	98	104	.976	142	148	3.3	7.6	.4	-.6	4.3
CLE	76	6	9	1354[2]	1577	10.5	64	561	470	14.4	4.63	100	.286	.355	-38	-2	106	100	.963	232	143	-2.0	-.2	4.3	-.6	-.5
STL	65	4	10	1362	1623	10.7	84	444	436	13.8	4.76	97	.293	.348	-57	-18	106	99	.963	232	160	-2.1	-1.7	-6.2	-1.4	-2.5
BOS	61	5	10	1366[2]	1559	10.3	54	473	365	13.5	4.60	94	.285	.344	-33	-44	98	95	.970	188	127	.4	-4.1	-10.4	-.2	.4
DET	86	5	6	1384[1]	1549	10.1	79	597	511	14.1	4.59	100	.282	.355	-32	-1	105	102	.964	220	139	-1.4	-.0	-9.9	.0	-4.7
CHI	54	6	10	1390[1]	1613	10.4	82	588	421	14.5	5.04	85	.287	.358	-101	-122	97	96	.961	245	131	-2.7	-11.4	-9.2	1.4	1.4
TOT	577	49	102	11028		9.9				13.5	4.38		.278	.344					.968	1569	1130					

Runs
Gehrig-NY 163
Ruth-NY 149
Averill-Cle 140
Combs-NY 120
Chapman-NY 120

Hits
Gehrig-NY 211
Averill-Cle 209
Simmons-Phi 200
Ruth-NY 199
Webb-Bos 196

Doubles
Webb-Bos 67
Alexander-Det 47
Kress-StL 46
Cronin-Was 44

Triples
Johnson-Det 19
Gehrig-NY 15
Blue-Chi 15
Vosmik-Cle 14
Reynolds-Chi 14

Home Runs
Ruth-NY 46
Gehrig-NY 46
Averill-Cle 32
Foxx-Phi 30
Goslin-StL 24

Total Bases
Gehrig-NY 410
Ruth-NY 374
Averill-Cle 361
Simmons-Phi 329
Goslin-StL 328

Runs Batted In
Gehrig-NY 184
Ruth-NY 163
Averill-Cle 143
Simmons-Phi 128
Cronin-Was 126

Runs Produced
Gehrig-NY 301
Ruth-NY 266
Averill-Cle 251
Chapman-NY 225
Cronin-Was 217

Bases On Balls
Ruth-NY 128
Blue-Chi 127
Gehrig-NY 117
Bishop-Phi 112
Lary-NY 88

Batting Average
Simmons-Phi 390
Ruth-NY 373
Morgan-Cle 351
Cochrane-Phi 349
Gehrig-NY 341

On Base Percentage
Ruth-NY 495
Morgan-Cle 451
Gehrig-NY 446
Simmons-Phi 444
Blue-Chi 430

Slugging Average
Ruth-NY 700
Gehrig-NY 662
Simmons-Phi 641
Averill-Cle 576
Foxx-Phi 567

Production
Ruth-NY 1.195
Gehrig-NY 1.108
Simmons-Phi 1.085
Averill-Cle .... .979
Cochrane-Phi .... .976

Adjusted Production
Ruth-NY 223
Gehrig-NY 199
Simmons-Phi 172
Webb-Bos 151
Goslin-StL 147

Batter Runs
Ruth-NY 91.5
Gehrig-NY 79.9
Simmons-Phi 59.6
Averill-Cle 48.2
Goslin-StL 44.7

Adjusted Batter Runs
Ruth-NY 96.4
Gehrig-NY 85.3
Simmons-Phi 55.1
Averill-Cle 43.1
Goslin-StL 41.6

Clutch Hitting Index
Kamm-Chi-Cle 145
Vosmik-Cle 139
Bluege-Was 136
Cronin-Was 134
Lary-NY 132

Runs Created
Ruth-NY 192
Gehrig-NY 185
Simmons-Phi 145
Averill-Cle 144
Goslin-StL 137

Total Average
Ruth-NY 1.487
Gehrig-NY 1.267
Simmons-Phi 1.199
Morgan-Cle 1.046
Cochrane-Phi ... 1.033

Stolen Bases
Chapman-NY 61
Johnson-Det 33
Burns-StL 19
Lazzeri-NY 18
Cissell-Chi 18

Stolen Base Average
Cissell-Chi 75.0
Reynolds-Chi 73.9
Chapman-NY 72.6
Lazzeri-NY 66.7
Bluege-Was 61.5

Stolen Base Runs
Chapman-NY 4.5
H.Walker-Det 2.4
Blue-Chi 2.1
Cissell-Chi 1.8

Fielding Runs
Melillo-StL 33.1
McManus-Det-Bos 21.1
West-Was 21.0
Burns-StL 18.4
Rhyne-Bos 16.9

Total Player Rating
Ruth-NY 6.8
Gehrig-NY 5.3
Simmons-Phi 4.9
Cronin-Was 4.6
Cochrane-Phi 4.5

Wins
Grove-Phi 31
Ferrell-Cle 22
Gomez-NY 21
Earnshaw-Phi 21
Walberg-Phi 20

Win Percentage
Grove-Phi .... .886
Marberry-Was .... .800
Mahaffey-Phi ..... .789
Earnshaw-Phi .... .750
Gomez-NY .... .700

Games
Hadley-Was 55
Moore-Bos 53
Caraway-Chi 51
Frasier-Chi 46
Fischer-Was 46

Complete Games
Grove-Phi 27
Ferrell-Cle 27
Earnshaw-Phi 23
Whitehill-Det 22
Stewart-StL 20

Shutouts
Grove-Phi 4
Earnshaw-Phi 3

Saves
Moore-Bos 10
Hadley-Was 8
Marberry-Was 7
Kimsey-StL 7
Earnshaw-Phi 6

Innings Pitched
Walberg-Phi 291.0
Grove-Phi 288.2
Earnshaw-Phi 281.2
Ferrell-Cle 276.1
Whitehill-Det 271.1

Fewest Hits/Game
Hadley-Was 7.26
Gomez-NY 7.63
Grove-Phi 7.76
Johnson-NY 8.07
Earnshaw-Phi 8.15

Fewest BB/Game
Pennock-NY 1.43
Gray-StL 1.88
Grove-Phi 1.93
Brown-Cle 2.12
Blaeholder-StL ... 2.23

Strikeouts
Grove-Phi 175
Earnshaw-Phi 152
Gomez-NY 150
Ruffing-NY 132
Hadley-Was 124

Strikeouts/Game
Hadley-Was 6.21
Gomez-NY 5.56
Bridges-Det 5.46
Grove-Phi 5.46
Ruffing-NY 5.01

Ratio
Grove-Phi 9.73
Earnshaw-Phi 10.64
Gomez-NY 10.93
Coffman-StL 11.27
Uhle-Det 11.33

Earned Run Average
Grove-Phi 2.06
Gomez-NY 2.67
Hadley-Was 3.06
Brown-Was 3.20
Marberry-Was 3.45

Adjusted ERA
Grove-Phi 218
Gomez-NY 149
Hadley-Was 140
Brown-Was 134
Uhle-Det 131

Opponents' Batting Avg.
Hadley-Was ...... .218
Gomez-NY .... .226
Grove-Phi .... .229
Johnson-NY ...... .234
Earnshaw-Phi .... .236

Opponents' On Base Pct.
Grove-Phi .... .271
Earnshaw-Phi .... .288
Gomez-NY .... .295
Coffman-StL ...... .298
Uhle-Det .... .304

Starter Runs
Grove-Phi 74.5
Gomez-NY 46.2
Brown-Was 33.9
Hadley-Was 26.4
Marberry-Was 22.6

Adjusted Starter Runs
Grove-Phi 78.1
Gomez-NY 35.1
Brown-Was 31.3
Ferrell-Cle 26.9
Earnshaw-Phi 25.6

Clutch Pitching Index
Grove-Phi 118
Faber-Chi 116
Whitehill-Det 115
Pennock-NY 110
Brown-Was 110

Relief Runs
Kimsey-StL 2.6

Adjusted Relief Runs
Kimsey-StL 2.9

Relief Ranking
Kimsey-StL 2.9

Total Pitcher Index
Grove-Phi 7.5
Ferrell-Cle 4.9
Brown-Was 3.4
Earnshaw-Phi 3.1
Gomez-NY 3.0

Total Baseball Ranking
Grove-Phi 7.5
Ruth-NY 6.8
Gehrig-NY 5.3
Ferrell-Cle 4.9
Simmons-Phi 4.9

1932 National League

TEAM	G	W	L	PCT	GB	R	OR	AB	H	2B	3B	HR	BB	SO	AVG	OBP	SLG	PRO	PRO+	BR	/A	PF	CHI	RC	SB	CS	SBA	SBR
CHI	154	90	64	.584		720	633	5462	1519	296	60	69	398	514	.278	.330	.392	.722	101	0	7	99	101	728	48			
PIT	154	86	68	.558	4	701	711	5421	1543	274	90	48	358	385	.285	.333	.395	.728	103	9	22	98	99	729	71			
BRO	154	81	73	.526	9	752	747	5433	1538	296	59	110	388	574	.283	.334	.420	.754	110	55	**70**	98	99	778	61			
PHI	154	78	76	.506	12	**844**	796	5510	**1608**	330	67	122	446	547	**.292**	**.348**	**.442**	**.790**	105	132		98	99	**870**	71			
BOS	155	77	77	.500	13	649	655	5506	1460	262	53	63	347	496	.265	.311	.366	.677	90	-94	-67	96	105	643	36			
STL	156	72	82	.468	18	684	717	5458	1467	307	51	76	420	514	.269	.324	.385	.709	93	-27	-48	103	100	702	**92**			
NY	154	72	82	.468	18	755	706	5530	1527	263	54	116	348	391	.276	.322	.406	.728	103	1	16	98	**107**	735	31			
CIN	155	60	94	.390	30	575	715	5443	1429	265	68	47	436	436	.263	.320	.362	.682	92	-77	-54	97	91	654	35			
TOT	618					5680		43763	12091	2293	502	651	3141	3857	.276	.328	.396	.724							445			

TEAM	CG	SH	SV	IP	H	H/G	HR	BB	SO	RAT	ERA	ERA+	OAV	OOB	PR	/A	PF	CPI	FA	E	DP	FW	PW	BW	SBW	DIF
CHI	79	9	7	1401	**1444**	9.3	68	409	527	12.1	3.44	109	.264	.319	68	50	97	102	.973	173	146	.4	**4.9**	.7		7.0
PIT	71	12	12	1377	1472	9.6	86	338	377	11.9	3.75	102	.270	.314	20	10	98	96	.969	185	124	-.4	1.0	2.2		6.2
BRO	61	7	16	1379²	1538	10.0	72	403	497	12.8	4.27	89	.282	.334	-60	-68	98	94	.971	183	**169**	-.3	-6.7	**6.9**		4.1
PHI	59	4	**17**	1384	1589	10.3	107	450	459	13.5	4.47	99	.287	.344	-91	-9	114	100	.968	194	133	-.9	-.9	4.6		-1.7
BOS	72	8	8	1414	1483	9.4	**61**	420	440	12.3	3.53	107	.272	.328	55	36	97	105	**.976**	152	145	1.7	3.6	-6.6		1.3
STL	70	**13**	9	1396	1533	9.9	76	455	**681**	13.0	3.97	99	.282	.340	-14	-6	101	104	.971	175	155	.4	-.6	-4.7		-.0
NY	57	3	16	1375¹	1533	10.0	112	387	506	12.7	3.83	97	.280	.330	8	-18	96	**108**	.969	191	143	-.7	-1.8	1.6		-4.1
CIN	**83**	6	6	1394²	1505	9.7	69	**276**	359	**11.6**	3.79	102	.274	**.311**	14	10	99	92	.971	178	129	.1	1.0	-5.3		-12.8
TOT	552	62	91	11121²		9.8				12.5	3.88		.276	.328					.971	1431	1144					

Runs
Klein-Phi 152
Terry-NY 124
O'Doul-Bro . . . 120
Ott-NY 119
Bartell-Phi 118

Hits
Klein-Phi 226
Terry-NY 225
O'Doul-Bro 219
P.Waner-Pit 215
Herman-Chi 206

Doubles
P.Waner-Pit 62
Klein-Phi 50
Stephenson-Chi 49
Bartell-Phi 48

Triples
Herman-Cin 19
Suhr-Pit 16
Klein-Phi 15

Home Runs
Ott-NY 38
Klein-Phi 38
Terry-NY 28
Hurst-Phi 24
Wilson-Bro 23

Total Bases
Klein-Phi 420
Terry-NY 373
Ott-NY 340
O'Doul-Bro 330
P.Waner-Pit 321

Runs Batted In
Hurst-Phi 143
Klein-Phi 137
Whitney-Phi 124
Wilson-Bro 123
Ott-NY 123

Runs Produced
Klein-Phi 251
Hurst-Phi 228
Terry-NY 213
Whitney-Phi 204
Ott-NY 204

Bases On Balls
Ott-NY 100
Hurst-Phi 65
Bartell-Phi 64
Suhr-Pit 63

Batting Average
O'Doul-Bro 368
Terry-NY 350
Klein-Phi 348
P.Waner-Pit 341
Hurst-Phi 339

On Base Percentage
Ott-NY 424
O'Doul-Bro 423
Hurst-Phi 412
Klein-Phi 404
P.Waner-Pit 397

Slugging Average
Klein-Phi 646
Ott-NY 601
Terry-NY 580
O'Doul-Bro 555
Hurst-Phi 547

Production
Klein-Phi 1.050
Ott-NY 1.025
O'Doul-Bro 978
Terry-NY 962
Hurst-Phi 959

Adjusted Production
Ott-NY 175
O'Doul-Bro 164
Klein-Phi 158
Terry-NY 158
Herman-Cin 152

Batter Runs
Klein-Phi 68.2
Ott-NY 59.8
O'Doul-Bro . . . 51.2
Terry-NY 46.4
Hurst-Phi 46.2

Adjusted Batter Runs
Ott-NY 61.5
Klein-Phi 58.1
O'Doul-Bro 52.8
Terry-NY 48.1
Herman-Cin 40.5

Clutch Hitting Index
Whitney-Phi 153
Hurst-Phi 145
Wilson-Bro 142
Hogan-NY 134
Piet-Pit 132

Runs Created
Klein-Phi 171
Ott-NY 151
O'Doul-Bro 142
Terry-NY 142
Hurst-Phi 134

Total Average
Klein-Phi 1.182
Ott-NY 1.166
O'Doul-Bro 1.059
Hurst-Phi 1.042
Terry-NY 981

Stolen Bases
Klein-Phi 20
Piet-Pit 19
Watkins-StL 18
Frisch-StL 18
G.Davis-Phi 16

Stolen Base Average

Stolen Base Runs

Fielding Runs
Jurges-Chi 31.7
Cuccinello-Bro 19.0
Herman-Chi 16.8
Frisch-StL 16.4
Stripp-Bro 15.9

Total Player Rating
Klein-Phi 5.6
Ott-NY 5.2
Terry-NY 4.8
Herman-Cin 4.6
O'Doul-Bro 3.8

Wins
Warneke-Chi 22
Clark-Bro 20
Bush-Chi 19

Win Percentage
Warneke-Chi 786
Bush-Chi 633
Rhem-StL-Phi 625
Clark-Bro 625
Hubbell-NY 621

Games
French-Pit 47
Dean-StL 46
Carleton-StL 44
Collins-Phi 43

Complete Games
Lucas-Cin 28
Warneke-Chi 25
Hubbell-NY 22

Shutouts
Warneke-Chi 4
Swetonic-Pit 4
Dean-StL 4

Saves
Quinn-Bro 8
Benge-Phi 6
Luque-NY 5
Cantwell-Bos 5

Innings Pitched
Dean-StL 286.0
Hubbell-NY 284.0
Warneke-Chi . . . 277.0
French-Pit 274.1
Clark-Bro 273.0

Fewest Hits/Game
Swetonic-Pit 7.41
Brown-Bos 7.90
Warneke-Chi 8.03
Hubbell-NY 8.24
Malone-Chi 8.43

Fewest BB/Game
Swift-Pit 1.09
Lucas-Cin 1.17
Hubbell-NY 1.27
Benton-Cin 1.35
Betts-Bos 1.42

Strikeouts
Dean-StL 191
Hubbell-NY 137
Malone-Chi 120
Carleton-StL 113
Brown-Bos 110

Strikeouts/Game
Dean-StL 6.01
Hallahan-StL 5.51
Vance-Bro 5.28
Carleton-StL 5.18
Brown-Bos 4.65

Ratio
Hubbell-NY 9.63
Swift-Pit 9.78
Lucas-Cin 9.92
Warneke-Chi 10.17
Swetonic-Pit 10.46

Earned Run Average
Warneke-Chi 2.37
Hubbell-NY 2.50
Betts-Bos 2.80
Swetonic-Pit 2.82
Lucas-Cin 2.94

Adjusted ERA
Warneke-Chi 159
Hubbell-NY 148
Swetonic-Pit 135
Betts-Bos 134
Lucas-Cin 131

Opponents' Batting Avg.
Swetonic-Pit 221
Warneke-Chi 237
Hubbell-NY 238
Brown-Bos 238
Malone-Chi 244

Opponents' On Base Pct.
Hubbell-NY 268
Swift-Pit 272
Lucas-Cin 274
Warneke-Chi 283
Swetonic-Pit 286

Starter Runs
Warneke-Chi 46.4
Hubbell-NY 43.4
Lucas-Cin 28.1
Betts-Bos 26.5
French-Pit 26.2

Adjusied Starter Runs
Warneke-Chi 42.9
Hubbell-NY 38.1
Lucas-Cin 27.4
French-Pit 24.2
Betts-Bos 23.6

Clutch Pitching Index
Bush-Chi 123
French-Pit 123
Zachary-Bos 117
Hallahan-StL 113
Derringer-StL 113

Relief Runs
Quinn-Bro 5.6
Frankhouse-Bos . . . 3.8

Adjusted Relief Runs
Quinn-Bro 5.0
Frankhouse-Bos . . . 2.4

Relief Ranking
Quinn-Bro 6.2
Frankhouse-Bos . . . 2.0

Total Pitcher Index
Hubbell-NY 5.1
Warneke-Chi 4.5
Lucas-Cin 4.4
Betts-Bos 2.4
Dean-StL 2.4

Total Baseball Ranking
Klein-Phi 5.6
Ott-NY 5.2
Hubbell-NY 5.1
Terry-NY 4.8
Herman-Cin 4.6

TEAM	G	W	L	PCT	GB	R	OR	AB	H	2B	3B	HR	BB	SO	AVG	OBP	SLG	PRO	PRO+	BR	/A	PF	CHI	RC	SB	CS	SBA	SBR
NY	156	107	47	.695		1002	724	5477	1564	279	82	160	766	527	.286	.376	.454	.830	128	172	216	95	99	961	77	66	54	-17
PHI	154	94	60	.610	13	981	752	5537	1606	303	52	172	647	630	.290	.366	.457	.823	115	148	118	104	100	951	38	23	62	-2
WAS	154	93	61	.604	14	840	716	5515	1565	303	100	61	505	442	.284	.347	.408	.755	102	8	19	99	103	793	52	54	49	-17
CLE	153	87	65	.572	19	845	747	5412	1544	310	74	78	566	454	.285	.357	.413	.770	99	44	-9	107	99	811	103	49	68	2
DET	153	76	75	.503	29.5	799	787	5409	1479	291	80	80	486	523	.273	.335	.401	.736	92	-35	-67	104	106	741	69	62	53	-17
STL	154	63	91	.409	44	736	898	5449	1502	274	69	67	507	528	.276	.339	.388	.727	89	-45	-91	106	97	726	69	62	53	-17
CHI	152	49	102	.325	56.5	667	897	5336	1426	274	56	36	459	386	.267	.327	.360	.687	90	-122	-71	94	101	642	89	58	61	-8
BOS	154	43	111	.279	64	566	915	5295	1331	253	57	53	469	539	.251	.314	.351	.665	80	-171	-149	97	94	593	46	46	50	-14
TOT	615					6436		43430	12017	2287	570	707	4405	4029	.277	.346	.404	.750							544	405	57	-80

TEAM	CG	SH	SV	IP	H	H/G	HR	BB	SO	RAT	ERA	ERA+	OAV	OOB	PR	/A	PF	CPI	FA	E	DP	FW	PW	BW	SBW	DIF
NY	96	11	15	1408	1425	9.1	93	561	780	12.8	3.98	102	.260	.331	78	15	91	101	.969	188	124	.2	1.4	20.0	-.6	9.1
PHI	95	10	10	1386	1477	9.6	112	511	595	13.0	4.45	102	.271	.336	4	11	101	98	.979	124	142	3.8	1.0	10.9	.7	.5
WAS	66	11	22	1383¹	1463	9.5	73	526	437	13.0	4.16	104	.271	.337	49	24	96	100	.979	125	157	3.8	2.2	1.8	.3	8.0
CLE	94	6	8	1377¹	1506	9.8	70	446	439	12.8	4.12	115	.273	.329	55	96	106	98	.969	191	129	-.2	8.9	-.8	-.6	3.8
DET	67	9	17	1362²	1421	9.4	89	592	521	13.5	4.30	109	.269	.346	27	61	105	102	.969	187	154	.0	5.6	-6.2	1.1	-.0
STL	63	7	11	1376²	1592	10.4	103	574	496	14.3	5.01	97	.290	.359	-81	-24	108	100	.969	188	156	.0	-2.2	-8.4	-.6	-2.8
CHI	50	2	12	1348²	1551	10.4	88	580	379	14.4	4.82	90	.287	.359	-52	-75	97	101	.958	264	170	-4.6	-6.9	-6.6	.2	-8.6
BOS	42	3	7	1362	1574	10.4	79	612	365	14.6	5.02	90	.289	.364	-81	-79	100	99	.963	233	165	-2.6	-7.3	-13.8	-.4	-9.9
TOT	573	59	102	11004²		9.8				13.6	4.48		.277	.346					.969	1500	1197					

Runs
Foxx-Phi 151
Simmons-Phi 144
Combs-NY 143
Gehrig-NY 138
Manush-Was 121

Hits
Simmons-Phi 216
Manush-Was 214
Foxx-Phi 213
Gehrig-NY 208
Averill-Cle 198

Doubles
McNair-Phi 47
Gehringer-Det 44
Cronin-Was 43

Triples
Cronin-Was 18
Myer-Was 16
Lazzeri-NY 16
Chapman-NY 15

Home Runs
Foxx-Phi 58
Ruth-NY 41
Simmons-Phi 35
Gehrig-NY 34
Averill-Cle 32

Total Bases
Foxx-Phi 438
Gehrig-NY 370
Simmons-Phi 367
Averill-Cle 359
Manush-Was 325

Runs Batted In
Foxx-Phi 169
Simmons-Phi 151
Gehrig-NY 151
Ruth-NY 137
Averill-Cle 124

Runs Produced
Foxx-Phi 262
Simmons-Phi 260
Gehrig-NY 255
Manush-Was 223
Ruth-NY 216

Bases On Balls
Ruth-NY 130
Foxx-Phi 116
Bishop-Phi 110
Gehrig-NY 108
Cochrane-Phi 100

Batting Average
Foxx-Phi .... .364
Gehrig-NY .... .349
Manush-Was ..... .342
Ruth-NY .... .341
Walker-Det .... .323

On Base Percentage
Ruth-NY .... .489
Foxx-Phi .... .469
Gehrig-NY .... .451
Bishop-Phi .... .412
Cochrane-Phi ..... .412

Slugging Average
Foxx-Phi .... .749
Ruth-NY .... .661
Gehrig-NY .... .621
Averill-Cle .... .569
Simmons-Phi ..... .548

Production
Foxx-Phi 1.218
Ruth-NY 1.150
Gehrig-NY 1.072
Averill-Cle .... .961
Cochrane-Phi .... .921

Adjusted Production
Ruth-NY 206
Foxx-Phi 203
Gehrig-NY 184
Lazzeri-NY 140
Averill-Cle 137

Batter Runs
Foxx-Phi 96.7
Ruth-NY 71.2
Gehrig-NY 68.6
Averill-Cle 41.1
Alexander-Det-Bos 31.8

Adjusted Batter Runs
Foxx-Phi 93.4
Ruth-NY 75.3
Gehrig-NY 73.5
Averill-Cle 35.0
Alexander-Det-Bos 32.8

Clutch Hitting Index
Cronin-Was 141
Dykes-Phi 134
Kamm-Cle 129
Lazzeri-NY 127
Cissell-Chi-Cle 126

Runs Created
Foxx-Phi 207
Gehrig-NY 168
Ruth-NY 157
Averill-Cle 140
Simmons-Phi 134

Total Average
Foxx-Phi 1.451
Ruth-NY 1.432
Gehrig-NY 1.188
Cochrane-Phi ... 1.000
Averill-Cle .... .991

Stolen Bases
Chapman-NY 38
Walker-Det 30
Johnson-Det-Bos . 20
Cissell-Chi-Cle 18

Stolen Base Average
Walker-Det 83.3
Johnson-Det-Bos . 76.9
Blue-Chi 73.9
Chapman-NY 67.9
Burns-StL 60.7

Stolen Base Runs
Walker-Det 5.4
Johnson-Det-Bos . 2.4
Blue-Chi 1.5

Fielding Runs
Warstler-Bos 27.9
Vosmik-Cle 23.8
West-Was 19.3
Appling-Chi 18.1
Kress-StL-Chi 12.8

Total Player Rating
Foxx-Phi 6.8
Ruth-NY 5.4
Gehrig-NY 4.5
Cochrane-Phi 4.2
Cronin-Was 3.8

Wins
Crowder-Was 26
Grove-Phi 25
Gomez-NY 24
Ferrell-Cle 23
Weaver-Was 22

Win Percentage
Allen-NY .... .810
Gomez-NY .... .774
Ruffing-NY .... .720
Grove-Phi .... .714
Weaver-Was ...... .688

Games
Marberry-Was 54
Gray-StL 52
Crowder-Was 50

Complete Games
Grove-Phi 27
Ferrell-Cle 26
Ruffing-NY 22

Shutouts
Grove-Phi 4
Bridges-Det 4

Saves
Marberry-Was 13
Moore-Bos-NY ... 8
Hogsett-Det 7
Grove-Phi 7
Faber-Chi 6

Innings Pitched
Crowder-Was ... 327.0
Grove-Phi 291.2
Ferrell-Cle 287.2
Walberg-Phi 272.0
Gomez-NY 265.1

Fewest Hits/Game
Allen-NY 7.59
Ruffing-NY 7.61
Bridges-Det 7.79
Grove-Phi 8.30
Crowder-Was 8.78

Fewest BB/Game
Brown-Cle 1.71
Crowder-Was 2.12
Gray-StL 2.31
Harder-Cle 2.40
Grove-Phi 2.44

Strikeouts
Ruffing-NY 190
Grove-Phi 188
Gomez-NY 176
Hadley-Chi-StL ... 145
Pipgras-NY 111

Strikeouts/Game
Ruffing-NY 6.60
Gomez-NY 5.97
Grove-Phi 5.80
Hadley-Chi-StL ... 5.26
Allen-NY 5.11

Ratio
Grove-Phi 10.77
Crowder-Was 10.90
Allen-NY 11.39
Ruffing-NY 11.71
Sorrell-Det 12.06

Earned Run Average
Grove-Phi 2.84
Ruffing-NY 3.09
Lyons-Chi 3.28
Crowder-Was 3.33
Bridges-Det 3.36

Adjusted ERA
Grove-Phi 159
Bridges-Det 140
Hogsett-Det 133
Lyons-Chi 132
Ruffing-NY 132

Opponents' Batting Avg.
Ruffing-NY .... .226
Allen-NY .... .228
Bridges-Det ...... .233
Grove-Phi .... .241
Crowder-Was .... .252

Opponents' On Base Pct.
Grove-Phi .... .292
Crowder-Was .... .295
Allen-NY .... .306
Ruffing-NY .... .311
Brown-Cle .... .314

Starter Runs
Grove-Phi 53.2
Crowder-Was 41.7
Ruffing-NY 39.9
Lyons-Chi 30.8
Ferrell-Cle 26.2

Adjusted Starter Runs
Grove-Phi 54.6
Crowder-Was 35.7
Ferrell-Cle 34.6
Bridges-Det 30.0
Ruffing-NY 28.3

Clutch Pitching Index
Hogsett-Det 129
Lyons-Chi 120
Weiland-Bos 117
Bridges-Det 116
Gaston-Chi 115

Relief Runs
Faber-Chi 8.8
Kimsey-StL-Chi ... 6.5

Adjusted Relief Runs
Kimsey-StL-Chi .. 9.5
Faber-Chi 7.0

Relief Ranking
Kimsey-StL-Chi ... 8.9
Faber-Chi 8.6

Total Pitcher Index
Grove-Phi 5.1
Ferrell-Cle 3.9
Ruffing-NY 3.8
Crowder-Was 3.2
Lyons-Chi 3.0

Total Baseball Ranking
Foxx-Phi 6.8
Ruth-NY 5.4
Grove-Phi 5.1
Gehrig-NY 4.5
Cochrane-Phi 4.2

TEAM	G	W	L	PCT	GB	R	OR	AB	H	2B	3B	HR	BB	SO	AVG	OBP	SLG	PRO	PRO+	BR	/A	PF	CHI	RC	SB	CS	SBA	SBR
NY	156	91	61	.599		636	515	5461	1437	204	41	82	377	477	.263	.312	.361	.673	100	-14	-4	98	104	667	31			
PIT	154	87	67	.565	5	667	619	5429	1548	249	84	39	366	334	.285	.333	.383	.716	111	71	72	100	96	750	34			
CHI	154	86	68	.558	6	646	536	5255	1422	256	51	72	392	475	.271	.325	.380	.705	107	47	49	100	99	705	52			
BOS	156	83	71	.539	9	552	531	5243	1486	217	56	54	326	428	.252	.299	.345	.644	98	-70	-21	92	104	588	25			
STL	154	82	71	.536	9.5	687	609	5387	1486	256	61	57	391	528	.276	.329	.378	.707	103	53	21	105	102	726	99			
BRO	157	65	88	.425	26.5	617	695	5367	1413	224	51	62	397	453	.263	.316	.359	.675	103	-8	19	96	101	662	82			
PHI	152	60	92	.395	31	607	760	5261	1439	240	41	60	381	479	.274	.326	.369	.695	93	32	-45	113	95	689	55			
CIN	153	58	94	.382	33	496	643	5156	1267	208	37	34	349	354	.246	.298	.320	.618	83	-111	-102	99	103	540	30			
TOT	618					4908		42559	11332	1854	422	460	2979	3528	.266	.317	.362	.679						408				

TEAM	CG	SH	SV	IP	H	H/G	HR	BB	SO	RAT	ERA	ERA+	OAV	OOB	PR	/A	PF	CPI	FA	E	DP	FW	PW	BW	SBW	DIF
NY	75	23	15	1408²	1280	8.2	61	400	555	10.9	2.71	118	.242	.299	98	78	96	102	.973	178	156	-.5	8.3	-.4		7.6
PIT	70	16	12	1373¹	1417	9.3	54	313	401	11.5	3.27	101	.264	.308	10	7	99	95	.972	166	133	.2	.7	7.6		1.5
CHI	95	16	9	1362	1316	8.7	61	413	488	11.6	2.93	112	.254	.312	62	52	98	105	.973	168	163	.0	5.5	5.2		-1.7
BOS	85	15	16	1403	1391	8.9	54	355	383	11.3	2.96	103	.261	.309	58	14	92	105	.978	138	148	2.1	1.5	-2.2		4.6
STL	73	11	16	1382²	1391	9.1	55	452	635	12.1	3.37	103	.261	.321	-5	16	104	98	.973	162	119	.4	1.7	2.2		1.2
BRO	71	9	10	1386¹	1502	9.8	51	374	415	12.4	3.73	86	.275	.326	-60	-79	96	95	.971	177	120	-.3	-8.4	2.0		-4.8
PHI	52	10	13	1336²	1563	10.5	87	410	341	13.6	4.34	88	.293	.348	-150	-79	114	101	.970	183	156	-1.1	-8.4	-4.8		-1.8
CIN	74	13	8	1352	1470	9.8	47	257	310	11.6	3.42	99	.279	.314	-13	-5	102	99	.971	177	139	-.6	-.5	-10.8		-6.1
TOT	595	113	99	11004²		9.3				11.9	3.34		.266	.317					.973	1349	1134					

Runs
Martin-StL 122
P.Waner-Pit 101
Klein-Phi 101
Ott-NY 98
Medwick-StL 92

Hits
Klein-Phi 223
Fullis-Phi 200
P.Waner-Pit 191
Traynor-Pit 190
Martin-StL 189

Doubles
Klein-Phi 44
Medwick-StL 40
Lindstrom-Pit 39
P.Waner-Pit 38
Berger-Bos 37

Triples
Vaughan-Pit 19
P.Waner-Pit 16
Martin-StL 12
F.Herman-Chi 12

Home Runs
Klein-Phi 28
Berger-Bos 27
Ott-NY 23
Medwick-StL 18

Total Bases
Klein-Phi 365
Berger-Bos 299
Medwick-StL 296
P.Waner-Pit 282
Vaughan-Pit 274

Runs Batted In
Klein-Phi 120
Berger-Bos 106
Ott-NY 103
Medwick-StL 98
Vaughan-Pit 97

Runs Produced
Klein-Phi 193
Ott-NY 178
Vaughan-Pit 173
Medwick-StL 172
Martin-StL 171

Bases On Balls
Ott-NY 75
Suhr-Pit 72
Martin-StL 67
Vaughan-Pit 64
P.Waner-Pit 60

Batting Average
Klein-Phi 368
Davis-Phi 349
Terry-NY 322
Schulmerich-Bos-Phi . .318
Martin-StL 316

On Base Percentage
Klein-Phi 422
Davis-Phi 395
Vaughan-Pit 388
Martin-StL 387
Terry-NY 375

Slugging Average
Klein-Phi 602
Berger-Bos 566
F.Herman-Chi 502
Medwick-StL 497
Vaughan-Pit 478

Production
Klein-Phi 1.025
Berger-Bos 932
Davis-Phi 867
Vaughan-Pit 866
F.Herman-Chi 855

Adjusted Production
Berger-Bos 177
Klein-Phi 168
Vaughan-Pit 146
F.Herman-Chi 142
Ott-NY 139

Batter Runs
Klein-Phi 69.1
Berger-Bos 40.5
Vaughan-Pit 35.2
Martin-StL 32.3
Davis-Phi 29.8

Adjusted Batter Runs
Klein-Phi 60.2
Berger-Bos 45.4
Vaughan-Pit 35.4
Ott-NY 29.5
P.Waner-Pit 28.8

Clutch Hitting Index
Traynor-Pit 139
Hartnett-Chi 130
Bottomley-Cin 129
Vaughan-Pit 128
Hurst-Phi 127

Runs Created
Klein-Phi 162
Berger-Bos 113
Vaughan-Pit 112
Martin-StL 111
P.Waner-Pit 109

Total Average
Klein-Phi 1.132
Berger-Bos 935
Martin-StL 881
Vaughan-Pit 861
F.Herman-Chi 827

Stolen Bases
Martin-StL 26
Fullis-Phi 18
Frisch-StL 18
Klein-Phi 15
Orsatti-StL 14

Stolen Base Average

Stolen Base Runs

Fielding Runs
Critz-NY 46.5
W.Herman-Chi 29.1
Jurges-Chi 20.1
Lopez-Bro 18.4
Ryan-NY 17.4

Total Player Rating
Klein-Phi 6.2
Berger-Bos 4.3
Vaughan-Pit 3.8
Martin-StL 3.7
W.Herman-Chi 3.5

Wins
Hubbell-NY 23
Dean-StL 20
Cantwell-Bos 20
Bush-Chi 20
Schumacher-NY . . . 19

Win Percentage
Cantwell-Bos 667
Hubbell-NY 657
Meine-Pit 652
Bush-Chi 625
Schumacher-NY 613

Games
Dean-StL 48
French-Pit 47
Liska-Phi 45
Hubbell-NY 45
Carleton-StL 44

Complete Games
Warneke-Chi 26
Dean-StL 26
Brandt-Bos 23
Hubbell-NY 22

Shutouts
Hubbell-NY 10
Schumacher-NY . . . 7
French-Pit 5

Saves
Collins-Phi 6
Hubbell-NY 5
Harris-Pit 5
Bell-NY 5

Innings Pitched
Hubbell-NY 308.2
Dean-StL 293.0
French-Pit 291.1
Brandt-Bos 287.2
Warneke-Chi 287.1

Fewest Hits/Game
Schumacher-NY . . 6.92
Hubbell-NY 7.46
Parmelee-NY 7.87
Brandt-Bos 8.01
Mungo-Bro 8.09

Fewest BB/Game
Lucas-Cin 74
Hubbell-NY 1.37
Swift-Pit 1.48
Hansen-Phi 1.60
French-Pit 1.70

Strikeouts
Dean-StL 199
Hubbell-NY 156
Carleton-StL 147
Warneke-Chi 133
Parmelee-NY 132

Strikeouts/Game
Dean-StL 6.11
Parmelee-NY 5.44
Carleton-StL 4.78
Hubbell-NY 4.55
Warneke-Chi 4.17

Ratio
Hubbell-NY 8.92
Schumacher-NY . . 9.88
Betts-Bos 10.41
Swift-Pit 10.47
Brandt-Bos 10.51

Earned Run Average
Hubbell-NY 1.66
Warneke-Chi 2.00
Schumacher-NY . . 2.16
Brandt-Bos 2.60
Root-Chi 2.60

Adjusted ERA
Hubbell-NY 193
Warneke-Chi 163
Schumacher-NY . . 149
Root-Chi 126
French-Pit 122

Opponents' Batting Avg.
Schumacher-NY . . .214
Hubbell-NY 227
Parmelee-NY 232
Mungo-Bro 236
Warneke-Chi 244

Opponents' On Base Pct.
Hubbell-NY 260
Schumacher-NY . . .280
Swift-Pit 285
Betts-Bos 290
Cantwell-Bos 291

Starter Runs
Hubbell-NY 57.4
Warneke-Chi 42.5
Schumacher-NY . . 33.9
Brandt-Bos 23.6
Cantwell-Bos 20.4

Adjusted Starter Runs
Hubbell-NY 53.1
Warneke-Chi 40.4
Schumacher-NY . . 30.2
French-Pit 19.3
Root-Chi 18.0

Clutch Pitching Index
Warneke-Chi 131
Root-Chi 120
Walker-StL 117
Holley-Phi 115
Hubbell-NY 112

Relief Runs
Bell-NY 15.0
Luque-NY 5.8
Harris-Pit 7

Adjusted Relief Runs
Bell-NY 13.6
Luque-NY 4.6
Harris-Pit 6

Relief Ranking
Bell-NY 14.2
Luque-NY 5.7
Harris-Pit 9

Total Pitcher Index
Hubbell-NY 7.1
Warneke-Chi 6.3
Schumacher-NY . . 3.9
Brandt-Bos 2.6
Bush-Chi 1.9

Total Baseball Ranking
Hubbell-NY 7.1
Warneke-Chi 6.3
Klein-Phi 6.2
Berger-Bos 4.3
Schumacher-NY . . 3.9

TEAM	G	W	L	PCT	GB	R	OR	AB	H	2B	3B	HR	BB	SO	AVG	OBP	SLG	PRO	PRO+	BR	/A	PF	CHI	RC	SB	CS	SBA	SBR
WAS	153	99	53	.651		850	665	5524	**1586**	281	**86**	60	539	395	**.287**	.353	.402	.755	107	47	56	99	102	798	65	50	57	-11
NY	152	91	59	.607	7	**927**	768	5274	1495	241	75	**144**	**700**	506	.283	**.369**	**.440**	**.809**	129	155	201	94	100	**880**	76	59	56	-13
PHI	152	79	72	.523	19.5	875	853	5330	1519	298	56	139	625	618	.285	.362	**.440**	**.802**	118	135	127	101	97	867	36	34	50	-10
CLE	151	75	76	.497	23.5	654	669	5240	1366	218	77	50	448	426	.261	.321	.360	.681	82	-103	-136	105	**103**	616	36	40	47	-13
DET	155	75	79	.487	25	722	733	5502	1479	283	78	57	475	523	.269	.329	.380	.709	92	-54	-69	102	101	698	68	50	58	-10
CHI	151	67	83	.447	31	683	814	5318	1448	231	53	43	538	416	.272	.342	.360	.702	96	-50	-18	96	96	674	43	46	48	-15
BOS	149	63	86	.423	34.5	700	758	5201	1407	294	56	50	525	464	.271	.339	.377	.716	97	-28	-21	99	98	687	58	37	**61**	**-5**
STL	153	55	96	.364	43.5	669	820	5285	1337	244	64	64	520	556	.253	.322	.360	.682	81	-102	-149	106	**103**	625	72	60	55	-14
TOT	608					6080		42674	11637	2090	545	607	4370	3904	.273	.342	.390	.732							452	376	55	-90

TEAM	CG	SH	SV	IP	H	H/G	HR	BB	SO	RAT	ERA	ERA+	OAV	OOB	PR	/A	PF	CPI	FA	E	DP	FW	PW	BW	SBW	DIF
WAS	68	5	**26**	1389²	1415	9.2	64	**452**	447	12.2	3.82	109	.263	**.322**	71	56	98	98	**.979**	131	149	**2.6**	5.3	5.3	.0	9.8
NY	70	8	13	1354²	1426	9.5	66	612	**711**	13.6	4.36	89	.267	.344	-13	-72	91	96	.972	165	122	.4	-6.8	**19.0**	-.2	3.6
PHI	69	6	14	1343²	1523	10.2	77	644	423	14.6	4.81	89	.283	.361	-79	-78	100	99	.966	203	121	-1.9	-7.4	12.0	.1	.7
CLE	**74**	**12**	7	1350	**1382**	9.2	60	465	437	12.4	**3.71**	**120**	.264	.325	**86**	**111**	104	102	.974	156	127	.9	**10.5**	-12.9	-.2	1.1
DET	69	6	17	1398	1415	**9.1**	84	561	575	12.9	3.95	109	**.263**	.335	52	57	101	103	.971	178	**167**	-.2	5.4	-6.5	.1	-.8
CHI	53	8	13	1371¹	1505	9.9	85	519	423	13.5	4.45	95	.277	.343	-26	-32	99	99	.970	186	143	-1.0	-3.0	-1.7	-.4	-1.9
BOS	60	4	14	1327²	1396	9.5	75	591	467	13.6	4.35	101	.271	.348	-10	4	102	100	.966	204	133	-2.2	.4	-2.0	**.6**	-8.3
STL	55	7	10	1360²	1574	10.4	96	531	426	14.0	4.82	97	.289	.354	-82	-25	109	100	.976	149	162	1.5	-2.4	-14.1	-.3	-5.2
TOT	518	56	123	10895²		9.6				13.3	4.28		.273	.342					.972	1372	1124					

Runs
Gehrig-NY 138
Foxx-Phi 125
Manush-Was 115
Chapman-NY 112
Cramer-NY 109

Hits
Manush-Was 221
Gehringer-Det 204
Foxx-Phi 204
Simmons-Chi 200
Gehrig-NY 198

Doubles
Cronin-Was 45
Johnson-Phi 44
Burns-StL 43
Rogell-Det 42
Gehringer-Det 42

Triples
Manush-Was 17
Combs-NY 16
Averill-Cle 16
Myer-Was 15
Reynolds-StL 14

Home Runs
Foxx-Phi 48
Ruth-NY 34
Gehrig-NY 32
Johnson-Phi 21
Lazzeri-NY 18

Total Bases
Foxx-Phi 403
Gehrig-NY 359
Manush-Was 302
Gehringer-Det 294
Simmons-Chi 291

Runs Batted In
Foxx-Phi 163
Gehrig-NY 139
Simmons-Chi 119
Cronin-Was 118
Kuhel-Was 107

Runs Produced
Gehrig-NY 245
Foxx-Phi 240
Manush-Was 205
Cronin-Was 202
Chapman-NY 201

Bases On Balls
Ruth-NY 114
Cochrane-Phi 106
Bishop-Phi 106
Foxx-Phi 96
Swanson-Chi 93

Batting Average
Foxx-Phi 356
Manush-Was 336
Gehrig-NY 334
Simmons-Chi 331
Gehringer-Det 325

On Base Percentage
Cochrane-Phi 459
Foxx-Phi 449
Bishop-Phi 446
Ruth-NY 442
Gehrig-NY 424

Slugging Average
Foxx-Phi 703
Gehrig-NY 605
Ruth-NY 582
Cochrane-Phi 515
Johnson-Phi 505

Production
Foxx-Phi 1.153
Gehrig-NY 1.030
Ruth-NY 1.023
Cochrane-Phi 974
Johnson-Phi 892

Adjusted Production
Foxx-Phi 199
Gehrig-NY 181
Ruth-NY 180
Cochrane-Phi 156
Dickey-NY 138

Batter Runs
Foxx-Phi 82.7
Gehrig-NY 59.5
Ruth-NY 49.5
Cochrane-Phi 41.6
Johnson-Phi 26.8

Adjusted Batter Runs
Foxx-Phi 81.9
Gehrig-NY 64.7
Ruth-NY 53.9
Cochrane-Phi 40.9
Lazzeri-NY 26.3

Clutch Hitting Index
Cronin-Was 147
Melillo-StL 136
Ferrell-StL-Bos . . . 134
Bluege-Was 133
R.Johnson-Bos . . . 127

Runs Created
Foxx-Phi 184
Gehrig-NY 151
Ruth-NY 124
Gehringer-Det 117
Manush-Was 111

Total Average
Foxx-Phi 1.348
Ruth-NY 1.172
Cochrane-Phi . . . 1.118
Gehrig-NY 1.098
Johnson-Phi 940

Stolen Bases
Chapman-NY 27
Walker-Det 26
Swanson-Chi 19
Kuhel-Was 17

Stolen Base Average
Walker-Det 74.3
Kuhel-Was 68.0
Swanson-Chi 63.3
Chapman-NY 60.0

Stolen Base Runs
Walker-Det 2.4
Werber-NY-Bos 1.5
Stumpf-Bos 1.2

Fielding Runs
Melillo-StL 23.3
Rogell-Det 19.5
Schulte-Was 15.8
Simmons-Chi 14.3
Scharein-StL 14.0

Total Player Rating
Foxx-Phi 6.7
Cronin-Was 4.0
Gehrig-NY 3.9
Cochrane-Phi 3.8
Gehringer-Det 3.6

Wins
Grove-Phi 24
Crowder-Was 24
Whitehill-Was 22

Win Percentage
Grove-Phi 750
Whitehill-Was 733
Stewart-Was 714
Allen-NY 682

Games
Crowder-Was 52
Russell-Was 50
Welch-Bos 47
Kline-Bos 46

Complete Games
Grove-Phi 21
Whitehill-Was 19
Hadley-StL 19
Ruffing-NY 18

Shutouts
Hildebrand-Cle 6
Gomez-NY 4
Blaeholder-StL 3

Saves
Russell-Was 13
Hogsett-Det 9
Moore-NY 8
Heving-Chi 6
Grove-Phi 6

Innings Pitched
Hadley-StL 316.2
Crowder-Was . . . 299.1
Grove-Phi 275.1
Whitehill-Was . . . 270.0
Blaeholder-StL . . 255.2

Fewest Hits/Game
Bridges-Det 7.42
Weiland-Bos 8.20
Allen-NY 8.33
Gomez-NY 8.36
Hildebrand-Cle . . . 8.37

Fewest BB/Game
Brown-Cle 1.65
Marberry-Det 2.30
Stewart-Was 2.34
Harder-Cle 2.38
Blaeholder-StL . . . 2.43

Strikeouts
Gomez-NY 163
Hadley-StL 149
Ruffing-NY 122
Bridges-Det 120
Allen-NY 119

Strikeouts/Game
Gomez-NY 6.25
Allen-NY 5.80
Ruffing-NY 4.67
Bridges-Det 4.64
Fischer-Det 4.58

Ratio
Marberry-Det 11.10
Stewart-Was 11.24
Harder-Cle 11.53
Brown-Cle 11.58
Weaver-Was 11.88

Earned Run Average
Harder-Cle 2.95
Bridges-Det 3.09
Gomez-NY 3.18
Grove-Phi 3.20
Weaver-Was 3.25

Adjusted ERA
Harder-Cle 151
Bridges-Det 140
Grove-Phi 134
Marberry-Det 131
Brown-Cle 130

Opponents' Batting Avg.
Bridges-Det 226
Gomez-NY 240
Allen-NY 242
Weiland-Bos 244
Hildebrand-Cle . . .245

Opponents' On Base Pct.
Marberry-Det 302
Stewart-Was 304
Harder-Cle 309
Brown-Cle 310
Grove-Phi 316

Starter Runs
Harder-Cle 37.4
Grove-Phi 33.0
Bridges-Det 30.8
Pearson-Cle 29.4
Gomez-NY 28.6

Adjusted Starter Runs
Harder-Cle 41.9
Grove-Phi 33.1
Pearson-Cle 31.8
Bridges-Det 31.6
Marberry-Det 27.2

Clutch Pitching Index
Cain-Phi 125
Jones-Chi 124
Harder-Cle 115
Whitehill-Was 112
Grove-Phi 111

Relief Runs
Russell-Was 22.0
Heving-Chi 21.1
Faber-Chi 8.1
Burke-Was 7.4
Herring-Det 3.0

Adjusted Relief Runs
Russell-Was 20.6
Heving-Chi 20.6
Faber-Chi 7.7
Gray-StL 6.9
Burke-Was 6.7

Relief Ranking
Russell-Was 31.8
Heving-Chi 21.2
Gray-StL 6.7
Burke-Was 6.6
Faber-Chi 6.6

Total Pitcher Index
Harder-Cle 4.9
Bridges-Det 3.4
Pearson-Cle 3.3
Grove-Phi 2.6
Whitehill-Was 2.5

Total Baseball Ranking
Foxx-Phi 6.7
Harder-Cle 4.9
Cronin-Was 4.0
Gehrig-NY 3.9
Cochrane-Phi 3.8

1934 National League

TEAM	G	W	L	PCT	GB	R	OR	AB	H	2B	3B	HR	BB	SO	AVG	OBP	SLG	PRO	PRO+	BR	/A	PF	CHI	RC	SB	CS	SBA	SBR
STL	154	95	58	.621		799	656	5502	1582	294	75	104	392	535	.288	.337	.425	.762	102	63	16	107	101	796	69			
NY	153	93	60	.608	2	760	583	5396	1485	240	41	126	406	526	.275	.329	.405	.734	105	8	25	98	105	736	19			
CHI	152	86	65	.570	8	705	639	5347	1494	263	44	101	375	630	.279	.330	.402	.732	103	5	19	98	99	719	59			
BOS	152	78	73	.517	16	683	714	5370	1460	233	44	83	375	440	.272	.323	.378	.701	101	-52	-4	98	104	660	30			
PIT	151	74	76	.493	19.5	735	713	5361	1541	281	77	52	440	398	.287	.344	.398	.742	102	34	18	102	99	742	44			
BRO	153	71	81	.467	23.5	748	795	5427	1526	284	52	79	548	555	.281	.350	.396	.746	112	51	88	95	95	782	55			
PHI	149	56	93	.376	37	675	754	5218	1480	286	35	56	398	534	.284	.338	.384	.722	87	-3	-95	113	98	685	52			
CIN	152	52	99	.344	42	590	801	5361	1428	227	65	55	313	532	.266	.311	.364	.675	88	-105	-88	98	99	603	34			
TOT	608					5695		42982	11996	2108	433	656	3247	4150	.279	.333	.394	.727						362				

TEAM	CG	SH	SV	IP	H	H/G	HR	BB	SO	RAT	ERA	ERA+	OAV	OOB	PR	/A	PF	CPI	FA	E	DP	FW	PW	BW	SBW	DIF
STL	78	15	16	1386²	1463	9.5	77	411	689	12.4	3.69	115	.268	.323	58	83	104	101	.972	166	141	.3	8.1	1.6		8.5
NY	68	13	30	1370	1384	9.1	75	351	499	11.5	3.19	121	.260	.308	132	102	95	105	.972	179	141	-.5	9.9	2.4		4.6
CHI	73	11	9	1361¹	1432	9.5	80	417	633	12.3	3.76	103	.269	.325	46	18	95	101	.977	137	135	1.9	1.8	1.9		5.0
BOS	62	12	20	1359²	1512	10.0	78	405	462	12.8	4.11	93	.279	.331	-7	-44	94	97	.972	169	120	.0	-4.3	.0		6.7
PIT	63	8	8	1329²	1523	10.3	78	354	487	12.9	4.20	98	.284	.332	-20	-13	101	98	.975	145	118	1.4	-1.3	1.8		-2.8
BRO	66	6	12	1354¹	1540	10.2	81	475	520	13.6	4.48	87	.285	.346	-63	-87	96	97	.970	180	141	-.6	-8.5	8.6		-4.5
PHI	52	8	15	1297	1501	10.4	126	437	416	13.6	4.76	99	.288	.347	-101	-4	116	99	.966	197	140	-1.8	-.4	-9.3		-7.0
CIN	51	3	19	1347²	1645	11.0	61	389	438	13.8	4.37	93	.299	.348	-46	-43	101	102	.970	181	136	-.7	-4.2	-8.6		-10.0
TOT	513	76	129	10806¹		10.0				12.9	4.06		.279	.333					.972	1354	1072					

Runs
P.Waner-Pit 122
Ott-NY 119
Collins-StL 116
Vaughan-Pit 115
Medwick-StL 110

Hits
P.Waner-Pit 217
Terry-NY 213
Collins-StL 200
Medwick-StL 198

Doubles
Cuyler-Chi 42
Allen-Phi 42
Vaughan-Pit 41
Medwick-StL 40
Collins-StL 40

Triples
Medwick-StL 18
P.Waner-Pit 16
Suhr-Pit 13
Collins-StL 12

Home Runs
Ott-NY 35
Collins-StL 35
Berger-Bos 34
Hartnett-Chi 22
Klein-Chi 20

Total Bases
Collins-StL 369
Ott-NY 344
Berger-Bos 336
Medwick-StL 328
P.Waner-Pit 323

Runs Batted In
Ott-NY 135
Collins-StL 128
Berger-Bos 121
Medwick-StL 106
Suhr-Pit 103

Runs Produced
Ott-NY 219
Collins-StL 209
P.Waner-Pit 198
Medwick-StL 198
Vaughan-Pit 197

Bases On Balls
Vaughan-Pit 94
Ott-NY 85
Koenecke-Bro 70
Leslie-Bro 69
P.Waner-Pit 68

Batting Average
P.Waner-Pit 362
Terry-NY 354
Cuyler-Chi 338
Vaughan-Pit 333
Collins-StL 333

On Base Percentage
Vaughan-Pit 431
P.Waner-Pit 429
Ott-NY 415
Terry-NY 414
Koenecke-Bro 411

Slugging Average
Collins-StL 615
Ott-NY 591
Berger-Bos 546
P.Waner-Pit 539
Medwick-StL 529

Production
Collins-StL 1.008
Ott-NY 1.006
P.Waner-Pit 968
Vaughan-Pit 942
Koenecke-Bro 919

Adjusted Production
Ott-NY 170
Collins-StL 155
P.Waner-Pit 154
Koenecke-Bro 152
Berger-Bos 148

Batter Runs
Ott-NY 55.2
Collins-StL 53.3
P.Waner-Pit 50.2
Vaughan-Pit 44.3
Terry-NY 31.5

Adjusted Batter Runs
Ott-NY 57.1
P.Waner-Pit 48.3
Collins-StL 48.1
Vaughan-Pit 42.5
Berger-Bos 35.3

Clutch Hitting Index
Thevenow-Pit 138
Durocher-StL 137
Leslie-Bro 136
Jackson-NY 135
Cuccinello-Bro 134

Runs Created
Ott-NY 150
Collins-StL 148
P.Waner-Pit 142
Vaughan-Pit 135
Terry-NY 122

Total Average
Ott-NY 1.075
Collins-StL 1.046
Vaughan-Pit 1.043
P.Waner-Pit 1.010
Koenecke-Bro 981

Stolen Bases
Martin-StL 23
Cuyler-Chi 15
Bartell-Phi 13
Taylor-Bro 12

Stolen Base Average

Stolen Base Runs

Fielding Runs
Critz-NY 25.0
G.Davis-StL-Phi . . 17.8
W.Herman-Chi . . . 15.6
Bartell-Phi 13.5
Hartnett-Chi 13.5

Total Player Rating
Vaughan-Pit 5.2
P.Waner-Pit 4.7
Collins-StL 4.1
Ott-NY 4.0
Hartnett-Chi 3.5

Wins
J.Dean-StL 30
Schumacher-NY . . . 23
Warneke-Chi 22
Hubbell-NY 21

Win Percentage
J.Dean-StL 811
Hoyt-Pit 714
Schumacher-NY . . .697
Warneke-Chi 688
Frankhouse-Bos . . .654

Games
C.Davis-Phi 51
Hansen-Phi 50
J.Dean-StL 50
Hubbell-NY 49
French-Pit 49

Complete Games
Hubbell-NY 25
J.Dean-StL 24
Warneke-Chi 23
Mungo-Bro 22
Brandt-Bos 20

Shutouts
J.Dean-StL 7
Hubbell-NY 5
P.Dean-StL 5
Lee-Chi 4

Saves
Hubbell-NY 8
Luque-NY 7
J.Dean-StL 7
Bell-NY 6

Innings Pitched
Mungo-Bro 315.1
Hubbell-NY 313.0
J.Dean-StL 311.2
Schumacher-NY . 297.0
Warneke-Chi . . . 291.1

Fewest Hits/Game
Parmelee-NY 7.90
Hubbell-NY 8.22
J.Dean-StL 8.32
Warneke-Chi 8.43
Mungo-Bro 8.56

Fewest BB/Game
Hubbell-NY 1.06
Freitas-Cin 1.47
Frey-Cin 1.54
Leonard-Bro 1.62
Fitzsimmons-NY . 1.74

Strikeouts
J.Dean-StL 195
Mungo-Bro 184
P.Dean-StL 150
Warneke-Chi 143
Derringer-Cin 122

Strikeouts/Game
P.Dean-StL 5.79
J.Dean-StL 5.63
Weaver-Chi 5.55
Mungo-Bro 5.25
Malone-Chi 5.23

Ratio
Hubbell-NY 9.35
Warneke-Chi . . . 10.53
J.Dean-StL 10.66
Hoyt-Pit 10.81
Fitzsimmons-NY . 10.87

Earned Run Average
Hubbell-NY 2.30
J.Dean-StL 2.66
Hoyt-Pit 2.93
C.Davis-Phi 2.95
Fitzsimmons-NY . 3.04

Adjusted ERA
Hubbell-NY 168
C.Davis-Phi 160
J.Dean-StL 159
Hoyt-Pit 141
Walker-StL 135

Opponents' Batting Avg.
Parmelee-NY 238
Hubbell-NY 239
J.Dean-StL 241
Warneke-Chi 244
P.Dean-StL 248

Opponents' On Base Pct.
Hubbell-NY 263
Warneke-Chi 287
J.Dean-StL 289
P.Dean-StL 292
Hoyt-Pit 296

Starter Runs
Hubbell-NY 61.3
J.Dean-StL 48.7
C.Davis-Phi 33.8
Fitzsimmons-NY . 29.8
Schumacher-NY . 29.0

Adjusted Starter Runs
Hubbell-NY 54.5
J.Dean-StL 54.3
C.Davis-Phi 54.0
Hoyt-Pit 25.2
Fitzsimmons-NY . 24.1

Clutch Pitching Index
Walker-StL 137
Leonard-Bro 121
C.Davis-Phi 120
Freitas-Cin 111
Frankhouse-Bos . . 110

Relief Runs
Haines-StL 5.6
Bell-NY 2.4
Brennan-Cin 2.2

Adjusted Relief Runs
Haines-StL 7.2
Brennan-Cin 2.4
Bell-NY 1.2

Relief Ranking
Haines-StL 6.0
Brennan-Cin 2.1
Bell-NY 1.7

Total Pitcher Index
C.Davis-Phi 6.4
Hubbell-NY 6.0
J.Dean-StL 5.7
Schumacher-NY . . 3.5
Fitzsimmons-NY . . 3.4

Total Baseball Ranking
C.Davis-Phi 6.4
Hubbell-NY 6.0
J.Dean-StL 5.7
Vaughan-Pit 5.2
P.Waner-Pit 4.7

TEAM	G	W	L	PCT	GB	R	OR	AB	H	2B	3B	HR	BB	SO	AVG	OBP	SLG	PRO	PRO+	BR	/A	PF	CHI	RC	SB	CS	SBA	SBR
DET	154	101	53	.656		**958**	708	5475	**1644**	349	53	74	639	528	**.300**	.376	.424	**.800**	113	**112**	110	100	104	**905**	**125**	55	69	5
NY	154	94	60	.610	7	842	**669**	5368	1494	226	61	135	**700**	597	.278	.364	.419	.783	**117**	70	**125**	93	96	848	71	46	61	-6
CLE	154	85	69	.552	16	814	763	5396	1550	340	46	100	526	433	.287	.350	.423	.776	105	44	32	102	98	820	52	32	62	-4
BOS	153	76	76	.500	24	820	775	5339	1465	287	**70**	51	610	535	.274	.350	.383	.733	90	-28	-84	107	**108**	748	**116**	47	**71**	7
PHI	153	68	82	.453	31	764	838	5317	1491	236	50	**144**	491	584	.280	.343	**.425**	.768	108	20	48	96	97	785	57	35	62	-4
STL	154	67	85	.441	33	674	800	5288	1417	252	59	62	514	**631**	.268	.335	.373	.708	82	-84	-149	108	98	680	43	31	58	-6
WAS	155	66	86	.434	34	729	806	5448	1512	278	**70**	51	570	447	.278	.348	.382	.730	99	-35	-5	96	95	747	47	42	53	-11
CHI	153	53	99	.349	47	704	946	5301	1395	237	40	71	565	524	.263	.336	.363	.699	84	-97	-120	103	103	672	36	27	57	-5
TOT	615					6305		42932	11968	2205	449	688	4615	4279	.279	.351	.399	.750							547	315	63	-25

TEAM	CG	SH	SV	IP	H	H/G	HR	BB	SO	RAT	ERA	ERA+	OAV	OOB	PR	/A	PF	CPI	FA	E	DP	FW	PW	BW	SBW	DIF
DET	74	**13**	14	1370²	1467	9.6	86	488	640	12.9	4.06	108	.273	.335	67	50	98	102	**.974**	159	150	1.2	4.6	10.2	.8	7.2
NY	83	**13**	10	1382²	1349	8.8	71	542	**656**	12.4	3.76	108	**.254**	.324	114	48	90	97	.973	**157**	151	**1.3**	4.5	**11.6**	-.3	-.0
CLE	72	8	19	1367	1476	9.7	**70**	582	554	13.7	4.28	106	.275	.349	33	40	101	101	.972	172	164	.4	3.7	3.0	-.0	1.0
BOS	68	9	9	1361	1527	10.1	**70**	543	538	13.8	4.32	**111**	.283	.351	27	73	107	103	.969	188	141	-.5	6.8	-7.8	**.9**	.6
PHI	68	8	8	1337	1429	9.6	84	693	480	14.4	5.01	87	.275	.363	-77	-94	97	94	.967	196	166	-1.0	-8.7	4.5	-.0	-1.7
STL	50	6	**20**	1350	1499	10.0	94	632	499	14.3	4.49	**111**	.283	.361	1	75	111	**107**	.969	187	160	-.4	**7.0**	-13.9	-.3	-1.4
WAS	61	4	12	1381¹	1622	10.6	74	503	412	13.9	4.68	92	.295	.355	-28	-55	96	101	**.974**	162	167	1.0	-5.1	-.5	-.7	-4.7
CHI	72	5	8	1355	1599	10.6	139	628	506	14.9	5.41	88	.292	.367	-137	-101	105	97	.966	207	126	-1.6	-9.4	-11.2	-.2	-.7
TOT	548	66	100	10904²		9.9				13.8	4.50		.279	.351					.970	1428	1225					

Runs		Hits		Doubles		Triples		Home Runs		Total Bases	
Gehringer-Det	134	Gehringer-Det	214	Greenberg-Det	63	Chapman-NY	13	Gehrig-NY	49	Gehrig-NY	409
Werber-Bos	129	Gehrig-NY	210	Gehringer-Det	50	Manush-Was	11	Foxx-Phi	44	Trosky-Cle	374
Gehrig-NY	128	Trosky-Cle	206	Averill-Cle	48			Trosky-Cle	35	Greenberg-Det	356
Averill-Cle	128	Cramer-Phi	202	Trosky-Cle	45			Johnson-Phi	34	Foxx-Phi	352
Foxx-Phi	120	Greenberg-Det	201	Hale-Cle	44			Averill-Cle	31	Averill-Cle	340

Runs Batted In		Runs Produced		Bases On Balls		Batting Average		On Base Percentage		Slugging Average	
Gehrig-NY	165	Gehringer-Det	250	Foxx-Phi	111	Gehrig-NY	.363	Gehrig-NY	.465	Gehrig-NY	.706
Trosky-Cle	142	Gehrig-NY	244	Gehrig-NY	109	Gehringer-Det	.356	Gehringer-Det	.450	Foxx-Phi	.653
Greenberg-Det	139	Greenberg-Det	231	Ruth-NY	103	Manush-Was	.349	Foxx-Phi	.449	Greenberg-Det	.600
Foxx-Phi	130	Trosky-Cle	224	Myer-Was	102	Simmons-Chi	.344	Cochrane-Det	.428	Trosky-Cle	.598
Gehringer-Det	127	Rogell-Det	211			Greenberg-Det	.339	Myer-Was	.419	Averill-Cle	.569

Production		Adjusted Production		Batter Runs		Adjusted Batter Runs		Clutch Hitting Index		Runs Created	
Gehrig-NY	1.172	Gehrig-NY	213	Gehrig-NY	85.6	Gehrig-NY	91.7	Cronin-Was	153	Gehrig-NY	195
Foxx-Phi	1.102	Foxx-Phi	188	Foxx-Phi	66.4	Foxx-Phi	69.5	Dykes-Chi	148	Foxx-Phi	165
Greenberg-Det	1.005	Greenberg-Det	156	Gehringer-Det	47.8	Gehringer-Det	47.6	Rogell-Det	147	Averill-Cle	145
Trosky-Cle	.987	Trosky-Cle	149	Greenberg-Det	46.7	Greenberg-Det	46.5	R.Johnson-Bos	147	Trosky-Cle	145
Averill-Cle	.982	Averill-Cle	149	Averill-Cle	45.6	Averill-Cle	44.3	Morgan-Bos	143	Gehringer-Det	144

Total Average		Stolen Bases		Stolen Base Average		Stolen Base Runs		Fielding Runs		Total Player Rating	
Gehrig-NY	1.401	Werber-Bos	40	White-Det	82.4	White-Det	4.8	Hale-Cle	25.7	Gehrig-NY	7.2
Foxx-Phi	1.310	White-Det	28	Werber-Bos	72.7	Werber-Bos	3.0	Hemsley-StL	23.3	Foxx-Phi	5.8
Averill-Cle	1.075	Chapman-NY	26	Fox-Det	71.4	Lazzeri-NY	2.7	Werber-Bos	20.3	Gehringer-Det	5.7
Greenberg-Det	1.071	Fox-Det	25	Walker-Det	69.0	Cronin-Was	2.4	Cronin-Was	18.4	Averill-Cle	4.2
Gehringer-Det	1.053	Walker-Det	20	Chapman-NY	61.9			Melillo-StL	18.1	Werber-Bos	4.2

Wins		Win Percentage		Games		Complete Games		Shutouts		Saves	
Gomez-NY	26	Gomez-NY	.839	Russell-Was	54	Gomez-NY	25	Harder-Cle	6	Russell-Was	7
Rowe-Det	24	Rowe-Det	.750	Newsom-StL	47	Bridges-Det	23	Gomez-NY	6	L.Brown-Cle	6
Bridges-Det	22	Marberry-Det	.750	Rowe-Det	45	Lyons-Chi	21	Ruffing-NY	5	Newsom-StL	5
Harder-Cle	20	Auker-Det	.682	Knott-StL	45	Rowe-Det	20	Dietrich-Phi	4		
Ruffing-NY	19	Bridges-Det	.667								

Innings Pitched		Fewest Hits/Game		Fewest BB/Game		Strikeouts		Strikeouts/Game		Ratio	
Gomez-NY	281.2	Gomez-NY	7.13	W.Ferrell-Bos	2.44	Gomez-NY	158	Ruffing-NY	5.23	Gomez-NY	10.19
Bridges-Det	275.0	Ruffing-NY	8.15	Auker-Det	2.46	Bridges-Det	151	Gomez-NY	5.05	Rowe-Det	11.54
Rowe-Det	266.0	Bridges-Det	8.15	Blaeholder-StL	2.61	Ruffing-NY	149	Rowe-Det	5.04	Bridges-Det	11.65
Newsom-StL	262.1	Burke-Was	8.30	Rowe-Det	2.74	Rowe-Det	149	Pearson-Cle	4.95	Murphy-NY	11.66
Ruffing-NY	256.1	Murphy-NY	8.36	Weaver-Was	2.77	Pearson-Cle	140	Bridges-Det	4.94	Harder-Cle	11.77

Earned Run Average		Adjusted ERA		Opponents' Batting Avg.		Opponents' On Base Pct.		Starter Runs		Adjusted Starter Runs	
Gomez-NY	2.33	Harder-Cle	174	Gomez-NY	.215	Gomez-NY	.282	Gomez-NY	67.7	Harder-Cle	55.0
Harder-Cle	2.61	Gomez-NY	174	Ruffing-NY	.236	Ruffing-NY	.310	Harder-Cle	53.6	Gomez-NY	54.2
Murphy-NY	3.12	Ostermueller-Bos	138	Bridges-Det	.241	Rowe-Det	.312	Murphy-NY	31.8	Ostermueller-Bos	29.0
Burke-Was	3.21	Burke-Was	134	Burke-Was	.245	Bridges-Det	.312	Rowe-Det	30.9	Newsom-StL	28.6
Auker-Det	3.42	W.Ferrell-Bos	132	Benton-Phi	.249	Harder-Cle	.316	Bridges-Det	25.4	Rowe-Det	27.7

Clutch Pitching Index		Relief Runs		Adjusted Relief Runs		Relief Ranking		Total Pitcher Index		Total Baseball Ranking	
Harder-Cle	127	Pennock-Bos	10.0	Pennock-Bos	12.1	Bean-Cle	4.1	Harder-Cle	5.5	Gehrig-NY	7.2
Auker-Det	123	McColl-Was	8.0	McColl-Was	5.7	Pennock-Bos	3.9	Gomez-NY	4.9	Foxx-Phi	5.8
Ostermueller-Bos	116	Russell-Was	5.8	Bean-Cle	3.9	McColl-Was	3.3	Rowe-Det	3.7	Gehringer-Det	5.7
Murphy-NY	113	Bean-Cle	3.7	Russell-Was	2.6	Russell-Was	2.5	W.Ferrell-Bos	3.0	Harder-Cle	5.5
Coffman-StL	109			Wells-StL	2.1	Wells-StL	1.7	Ostermueller-Bos	2.9	Gomez-NY	4.9

1935 National League

TEAM	G	W	L	PCT	GB	R	OR	AB	H	2B	3B	HR	BB	SO	AVG	OBP	SLG	PRO	PRO+	BR	/A	PF	CHI	RC	SB	CS	SBA	SBR
CHI	154	100	54	.649		847	597	5486	1581	303	62	88	464	471	.288	.347	.414	.761	110	81	77	101	102	812	66			
STL	154	96	58	.623	4	829	625	5457	1548	286	59	86	404	521	.284	.335	.405	.740	101	33	4	104	109	759	71			
NY	156	91	62	.595	8.5	770	675	5623	1608	248	56	123	392	479	.286	.336	.416	.752	110	54	68	98	96	797	32			
PIT	153	86	67	.562	13.5	743	647	5415	1543	255	90	66	457	437	.285	.343	.402	.745	103	49	26	103	96	751	30			
BRO	154	70	83	.458	29.5	711	767	5410	1496	235	62	59	430	520	.277	.333	.376	.709	99	-21	-5	98	101	691	60			
CIN	154	68	85	.444	31.5	646	772	5296	1403	244	68	73	392	547	.265	.319	.378	.697	96	-51	-29	97	99	658	72			
PHI	156	64	89	.418	35.5	685	871	5442	1466	249	32	92	392	661	.269	.322	.378	.700	85	-47	-120	110	101	681	52			
BOS	153	38	115	.248	61.5	575	852	5309	1396	233	33	75	353	436	.263	.311	.362	.673	93	-98	-42	92	95	596	20			
TOT	617					5806		43438	12041	2053	462	662	3284	4072	.277	.331	.391	.722						403				

TEAM	CG	SH	SV	IP	H	H/G	HR	BB	SO	RAT	ERA	ERA+	OAV	OOB	PR	/A	PF	CPI	FA	E	DP	FW	PW	BW	SBW	DIF
CHI	81	12	14	1394[1]	1417	9.1	85	400	589	11.9	3.26	121	.263	.317	118	103	98	111	.970	186	163	.3	10.0	7.5		5.2
STL	73	10	18	1384[2]	1445	9.4	68	377	602	12.0	3.52	116	.267	.318	76	89	102	101	.972	164	133	1.6	8.6	.4		8.4
NY	76	10	11	1403[2]	1433	9.2	106	411	524	12.0	3.78	102	.262	.318	37	11	96	98	.972	174	129	1.1	1.1	6.6		5.7
PIT	76	15	11	1365[2]	1428	9.4	63	312	549	11.6	3.42	120	.265	.307	91	103	102	98	.968	190	94	.0	10.0	2.5		-3.0
BRO	62	11	20	1358	1519	10.1	88	436	480	13.1	4.22	94	.281	.337	-31	-37	99	100	.969	188	146	.2	-3.6	-.5		-2.6
CIN	59	9	13	1356	1490	9.9	65	438	500	13.0	4.30	93	.278	.336	-43	-49	99	99	.966	204	139	-.7	-4.8	-2.8		-.2
PHI	53	8	15	1374[2]	1652	10.8	106	505	475	14.4	4.76	95	.295	.358	-113	-35	113	102	.963	228	145	-2.0	-3.4	-11.7		4.5
BOS	54	6	5	1330	1645	11.1	81	404	355	14.0	4.93	77	.303	.354	-135	-169	94	96	.967	197	101	-.4	-16.4	-4.1		-17.6
TOT	534	81	107	10967		9.9				12.7	4.02		.277	.331					.968	1531	1050					

Runs		Hits		Doubles		Triples		Home Runs		Total Bases	
Galan-Chi	133	Herman-Chi	227	Herman-Chi	57	Goodman-Cin	18	Berger-Bos	34	Medwick-StL	365
Medwick-StL	132	Medwick-StL	224	Medwick-StL	46	L.Waner-Pit	14	Ott-NY	31	Ott-NY	329
Martin-StL	121			Allen-Phi	46	Medwick-StL	13	Camilli-Phi	25	Berger-Bos	323
Ott-NY	113			Martin-StL	41			Medwick-StL	23	Herman-Chi	317
Herman-Chi	113			Galan-Chi	41			J.Collins-StL	23	Leiber-NY	314

Runs Batted In		Runs Produced		Bases On Balls		Batting Average		On Base Percentage		Slugging Average	
Berger-Bos	130	Medwick-StL	235	Vaughan-Pit	97	Vaughan-Pit	.385	Vaughan-Pit	.491	Vaughan-Pit	.607
Medwick-StL	126	J.Collins-StL	208	Galan-Chi	87	Medwick-StL	.353	Ott-NY	.407	Medwick-StL	.576
J.Collins-StL	122	Galan-Chi	200	Ott-NY	82	Herman-Chi	.341	Hack-Chi	.406	Ott-NY	.555
Ott-NY	114	Ott-NY	196	Suhr-Pit	70	Terry-NY	.341	Galan-Chi	.399	Berger-Bos	.548
Leiber-NY	107	Leiber-NY	195	Frey-Bro	66	Leiber-NY	.331	P.Waner-Pit	.392	J.Collins-StL	.529

Production		Adjusted Production		Batter Runs		Adjusted Batter Runs		Clutch Hitting Index		Runs Created	
Vaughan-Pit	1.098	Vaughan-Pit	187	Vaughan-Pit	71.9	Vaughan-Pit	69.5	Leslie-Bro	146	Vaughan-Pit	163
Medwick-StL	.962	Ott-NY	159	Ott-NY	47.6	Ott-NY	49.1	Young-Pit	138	Ott-NY	144
Ott-NY	.962	Berger-Bos	151	Medwick-StL	46.0	Medwick-StL	42.7	Jurges-Chi	131	Medwick-StL	139
J.Collins-StL	.915	Medwick-StL	149	J.Collins-StL	35.0	Berger-Bos	36.1	Durocher-StL	130	Galan-Chi	133
Berger-Bos	.903	Leiber-NY	143	Leiber-NY	34.3	Leiber-NY	35.8	J.Collins-StL	124	J.Collins-StL	125

Total Average		Stolen Bases		Stolen Base Average	Stolen Base Runs	Fielding Runs		Total Player Rating	
Vaughan-Pit	1.317	Galan-Chi	22			Jurges-Chi	30.2	Vaughan-Pit	6.3
Ott-NY	1.037	Martin-StL	20			Herman-Chi	18.9	Herman-Chi	5.4
Medwick-StL	.948	Bordagaray-Bro	18			Allen-Phi	16.5	Ott-NY	4.8
Galan-Chi	.937	Hack-Chi	14			Hartnett-Chi	14.5	Hartnett-Chi	4.8
J.Collins-StL	.930	Goodman-Cin	14			T.Moore-StL	13.8	Berger-Bos	3.8

Wins		Win Percentage		Games		Complete Games		Shutouts		Saves	
J.Dean-StL	28	Lee-Chi	.769	Jorgens-Phi	53	J.Dean-StL	29	Weaver-Bro	4	Leonard-Bro	8
Hubbell-NY	23	Castleman-NY	.714	J.Dean-StL	50	Hubbell-NY	24	Mungo-Bro	4	Johnson-Phi	6
Derringer-Cin	22	J.Dean-StL	.700	Bivin-Phi	47	Blanton-Pit	23	French-Chi	4	Hoyt-Pit	6
Warneke-Chi	20	Schumacher-NY	.679	Smith-Bos	46	Warneke-Chi	20	Fitzsimmons-NY	4		
Lee-Chi	20	Hubbell-NY	.657	P.Dean-StL	46	Derringer-Cin	20	Blanton-Pit	4		

Innings Pitched		Fewest Hits/Game		Fewest BB/Game		Strikeouts		Strikeouts/Game		Ratio	
J.Dean-StL	325.1	Blanton-Pit	7.79	Clark-Bro	1.22	J.Dean-StL	190	Mungo-Bro	6.00	Blanton-Pit	9.80
Hubbell-NY	302.2	Schumacher-NY	8.08	Hubbell-NY	1.46	Hubbell-NY	150	J.Dean-StL	5.26	Swift-Pit	10.21
Derringer-Cin	276.2	Parmelee-NY	8.52	Hoyt-Pit	1.48	Mungo-Bro	143	Blanton-Pit	5.02	Clark-Bro	10.61
P.Dean-StL	269.2	Swift-Pit	8.53	Derringer-Cin	1.59	P.Dean-StL	143	P.Dean-StL	4.77	Warneke-Chi	10.66
		Hollingsworth-Cin	8.57	Johnson-Phi	1.60	Blanton-Pit	142	Hollingsworth-Cin	4.62	Schumacher-NY	10.66

Earned Run Average		Adjusted ERA		Opponents' Batting Avg.		Opponents' On Base Pct.		Starter Runs		Adjusted Starter Runs	
Blanton-Pit	2.58	Blanton-Pit	159	Blanton-Pit	.229	Blanton-Pit	.272	Blanton-Pit	40.6	Blanton-Pit	43.0
Swift-Pit	2.70	Swift-Pit	152	Schumacher-NY	.238	Swift-Pit	.282	J.Dean-StL	35.3	J.Dean-StL	38.2
Schumacher-NY	2.89	J.Dean-StL	135	Hollingsworth-Cin	.243	Clark-Bro	.289	Schumacher-NY	32.8	Swift-Pit	31.9
French-Chi	2.96	Schumacher-NY	133	Swift-Pit	.247	Schumacher-NY	.292	Swift-Pit	29.9	Schumacher-NY	28.0
Lee-Chi	2.96	French-Chi	133	P.Dean-StL	.249	P.Dean-StL	.292	Lee-Chi	29.5	Lee-Chi	27.0

Clutch Pitching Index		Relief Runs	Adjusted Relief Runs	Relief Ranking	Total Pitcher Index		Total Baseball Ranking	
French-Chi	126				Blanton-Pit	4.2	Vaughan-Pit	6.3
Zachary-Bro	121				Schumacher-NY	3.8	Herman-Chi	5.4
Walker-StL	116				J.Dean-StL	3.7	Ott-NY	4.8
Lee-Chi	111				Swift-Pit	3.1	Hartnett-Chi	4.8
Hallahan-StL	111				Lee-Chi	2.9	Blanton-Pit	4.2

TEAM	G	W	L	PCT	GB	R	OR	AB	H	2B	3B	HR	BB	SO	AVG	OBP	SLG	PRO	PRO+	BR	/A	PF	CHI	RC	SB	CS	SBA	SBR
DET	152	93	58	.616		919	665	5423	1573	301	83	106	627	456	.290	.366	.435	.801	116	95	123	97	104	885	70	45	61	-6
NY	149	89	60	.597	3	818	632	5214	1462	255	70	104	604	469	.280	.358	.416	.774	111	42	84	94	102	799	68	46	60	-7
CLE	156	82	71	.536	12	776	739	5534	1573	324	77	93	460	567	.284	.341	.421	.762	100	3	-11	102	99	796	63	54	54	-14
BOS	154	78	75	.510	16	718	732	5288	1458	281	63	69	609	470	.276	.353	.392	.745	92	-11	-63	107	94	757	91	59	61	-8
CHI	153	74	78	.487	19.5	738	750	5314	1460	262	42	74	580	405	.275	.348	.382	.730	92	-41	-60	103	101	733	46	28	62	-3
WAS	154	67	86	.438	27	823	903	5592	1591	255	95	32	596	406	.285	.357	.381	.738	90	-18	9	97	104	788	54	37	59	-6
STL	155	65	87	.428	28.5	718	930	5365	1446	291	51	73	593	561	.270	.344	.384	.728	90	-49	-85	105	98	735	45	25	64	-2
PHI	149	58	91	.389	34	710	869	5269	1470	243	44	112	475	602	.279	.341	.406	.747	99	-23	-17	99	98	738	43	35	55	-8
TOT	611					6220		42999	12033	2212	525	663	4544	3936	.280	.351	.402	.753							480	329	59	-53

TEAM	CG	SH	SV	IP	H	H/G	HR	BB	SO	RAT	ERA	ERA+	OAV	OOB	PR	/A	PF	CPI	FA	E	DP	FW	PW	BW	SBW	DIF
DET	87	16	11	1364	1440	9.5	78	522	584	13.1	3.82	109	.271	.339	96	53	94	107	.978	128	154	2.3	5.0	11.5	.0	-1.3
NY	76	12	13	1331	1276	8.6	91	516	594	12.2	3.60	112	.251	.321	126	66	91	101	.974	151	114	.8	6.2	7.9	-.0	-.3
CLE	67	12	21	1396	1527	9.8	68	457	498	12.9	4.15	108	.278	.335	47	55	101	97	.972	177	147	-.3	5.2	-1.0	-.7	2.3
BOS	82	6	11	1376	1520	9.9	67	520	470	13.5	4.05	117	.280	.346	62	106	107	105	.969	194	136	-1.4	9.9	-5.9	-.1	-1.0
CHI	80	8	8	1360²	1443	9.5	105	574	436	13.5	4.38	106	.272	.346	12	36	104	100	.976	146	133	1.3	3.4	-5.6	.3	-1.4
WAS	67	5	12	1378²	1672	10.9	89	613	456	15.1	5.25	82	.302	.374	-122	-142	97	99	.972	171	186	-.0	-13.3	.8	.0	2.9
STL	42	4	15	1380¹	1667	10.9	92	641	435	15.2	5.26	91	.297	.371	-124	-72	108	97	.970	187	138	-.9	-6.7	-8.0	.4	4.2
PHI	58	7	10	1326¹	1486	10.1	73	704	469	15.0	5.12	89	.285	.372	-97	-84	102	96	.968	190	150	-1.4	-7.9	-1.6	-.1	-5.5
TOT	559	70	101	10913		9.9				13.8	4.46		.280	.351					.972	1344	1158					

Runs
Gehrig-NY 125
Gehringer-Det 123
Greenberg-Det ... 121
Foxx-Phi 118
Chapman-NY 118

Hits
Vosmik-Cle....... 216
Myer-Was........ 215
Cramer-Phi 214
Greenberg-Det ... 203

Doubles
Vosmik-Cle........ 47
Greenberg-Det 46
Solters-Bos-StL ... 45
Fox-Det 38
Chapman-NY 38

Triples
Vosmik-Cle 20
Stone-Was 18
Greenberg-Det 16
Cronin-Bos 14
Averill-Cle 13

Home Runs
Greenberg-Det ... 36
Foxx-Phi 36
Gehrig-NY 30
Johnson-Phi 28
Trosky-Cle 26

Total Bases
Greenberg-Det ... 389
Foxx-Phi 340
Vosmik-Cle 333
Solters-Bos-StL ... 314
Gehrig-NY 312

Runs Batted In
Greenberg-Det ... 170
Gehrig-NY 119
Foxx-Phi 115
Trosky-Cle 113
Solters-Bos-StL .. 112

Runs Produced
Greenberg-Det ... 255
Gehrig-NY 214
Gehringer-Det ... 212
Myer-Was 210
Foxx-Phi 197

Bases On Balls
Gehrig-NY 132
Appling-Chi 122
Foxx-Phi 114
Myer-Was 96
Cochrane-Det 96

Batting Average
Myer-Was.........349
Vosmik-Cle........348
Foxx-Phi..........346
Cramer-Phi 332
Gehringer-Det 330

On Base Percentage
Gehrig-NY 466
Foxx-Phi..........461
Cochrane-Det 452
Myer-Was 440
Appling-Chi 437

Slugging Average
Foxx-Phi..........636
Greenberg-Det ...628
Gehrig-NY 583
Vosmik-Cle........537
Fox-Det 513

Production
Foxx-Phi......... 1.096
Gehrig-NY 1.049
Greenberg-Det .. 1.039
Vosmik-Cle.......946
Gehringer-Det 911

Adjusted Production
Foxx-Phi......... 182
Gehrig-NY 180
Greenberg-Det ... 171
Vosmik-Cle 140
Myer-Was 139

Batter Runs
Foxx-Phi 67.2
Gehrig-NY 61.6
Greenberg-Det ... 57.5
Vosmik-Cle 38.3
Myer-Was 36.5

Adjusted Batter Runs
Foxx-Phi 67.9
Gehrig-NY 66.4
Greenberg-Det ... 60.7
Myer-Was 39.6
Vosmik-Cle 36.7

Clutch Hitting Index
Goslin-Det 144
Owen-Det........ 139
Powell-Was 134
Dykes-Chi 126
Stone-Was 125

Runs Created
Foxx-Phi 163
Greenberg-Det ... 161
Gehrig-NY 154
Vosmik-Cle 137
Myer-Was........ 132

Total Average
Foxx-Phi......... 1.288
Gehrig-NY 1.230
Greenberg-Det .. 1.138
Cochrane-Det ... 1.000
Vosmik-Cle.......980

Stolen Bases
Werber-Bos 29
Lary-Was-StL 28
Almada-Bos 20
White-Det 19
Chapman-NY 17

Stolen Base Average
Lary-Was-StL 87.5
Werber-Bos 80.6
Almada-Bos 69.0
White-Det 65.5
Chapman-NY 63.0

Stolen Base Runs
Lary-Was-StL 6.0
Werber-Bos 4.5
Solters-Bos-StL ... 2.1
Hughes-Cle 2.1

Fielding Runs
Appling-Chi 21.3
Travis-Was 21.3
Solters-Bos-StL .. 18.6
Melillo-StL-Bos .. 18.6
Werber-Bos 17.2

Total Player Rating
Foxx-Phi 5.7
Myer-Was......... 5.3
Gehringer-Det ... 4.6
Greenberg-Det ... 4.5
Gehrig-NY 4.5

Wins
W.Ferrell-Bos 25
Harder-Cle 22
Bridges-Det 21
Grove-Bos 20
Rowe-Det......... 19

Win Percentage
Auker-Det.........720
Broaca-NY 682
Bridges-Det 677
Harder-Cle 667
Lyons-Chi 652

Games
VanAtta-NY-StL 58
Walkup-StL 55
Andrews-StL 50
Thomas-StL 49
Knott-StL 48

Complete Games
W.Ferrell-Bos 31
Grove-Bos 23
Bridges-Det 23
Rowe-Det 21

Shutouts
Rowe-Det......... 6
Harder-Cle 4
Bridges-Det 4

Saves
Knott-StL 7

Innings Pitched
W.Ferrell-Bos ... 322.1
Harder-Cle 287.1
Whitehill-Was 279.1
Rowe-Det....... 275.2
Bridges-Det 274.1

Fewest Hits/Game
Allen-NY 8.03
Ruffing-NY 8.15
Gomez-NY 8.16
Whitehead-Chi ... 8.46
Grove-Bos 8.87

Fewest BB/Game
Harder-Cle 1.66
Grove-Bos 2.14
Rowe-Det 2.22
Andrews-StL 2.24
Hudlin-Cle 2.37

Strikeouts
Bridges-Det 163
Rowe-Det 140
Gomez-NY 138
Grove-Bos 121
Allen-NY 113

Strikeouts/Game
Allen-NY 6.09
Bridges-Det 5.35
Gomez-NY 5.05
VanAtta-NY-StL .. 4.63
Rowe-Det 4.57

Ratio
Grove-Bos 11.11
Rowe-Det 11.17
Ruffing-NY 11.27
Allen-NY 11.37
Gomez-NY 11.38

Earned Run Average
Grove-Bos 2.70
Lyons-Chi 3.02
Ruffing-NY 3.12
Gomez-NY 3.18
Harder-Cle 3.29

Adjusted ERA
Grove-Bos 176
Lyons-Chi 153
Harder-Cle 137
Andrews-StL 135
W.Ferrell-Bos 135

Opponents' Batting Avg.
Allen-NY 238
Ruffing-NY 239
Gomez-NY 242
Whitehead-Chi 250
Broaca-NY 254

Opponents' On Base Pct.
Rowe-Det 301
Grove-Bos 302
Ruffing-NY 303
Allen-NY 307
Harder-Cle 307

Starter Runs
Grove-Bos 53.1
Harder-Cle 37.2
Gomez-NY 34.8
W.Ferrell-Bos 33.6
Ruffing-NY 32.9

Adjusted Starter Runs
Grove-Bos 61.9
W.Ferrell-Bos 43.9
Harder-Cle 38.8
Lyons-Chi 33.9
Andrews-StL 29.6

Clutch Pitching Index
Lyons-Chi 124
Bridges-Det 113
Auker-Det....... 112
Grove-Bos 112
Tietje-Chi 110

Relief Runs
L.Brown-Cle 11.4
Hogsett-Det 9.9
DeShong-NY 9.2
Murphy-NY 4.9
Wilson-Bos 1.7

Adjusted Relief Runs
L.Brown-Cle 12.1
Hogsett-Det 6.8
DeShong-NY 6.0
Wilson-Bos 3.7

Relief Ranking
L.Brown-Cle 14.2
Hogsett-Det 8.4
DeShong-NY 4.5
Wilson-Bos 3.8

Total Pitcher Index
W.Ferrell-Bos 6.9
Grove-Bos 5.9
Harder-Cle 4.2
Lyons-Chi 3.3
Ruffing-NY 3.2

Total Baseball Ranking
W.Ferrell-Bos 6.9
Grove-Bos 5.9
Foxx-Phi 5.7
Myer-Was 5.3
Gehringer-Det 4.6

TEAM	G	W	L	PCT	GB	R	OR	AB	H	2B	3B	HR	BB	SO	AVG	OBP	SLG	PRO	PRO+	BR	/A	PF	CHI	RC	SB	CS	SBA	SBR
NY	154	92	62	.597		742	621	5449	1529	237	48	97	431	452	.281	.337	.395	.732	104	19	27	99	99	744	31			
STL	155	87	67	.565	5	795	794	5537	1554	332	60	88	442	577	.281	.336	.410	.746	106	40	43	100	103	772	69			
CHI	154	87	67	.565	5	755	603	5409	1545	275	36	76	491	462	.286	.349	.392	.741	104	44	28	102	97	757	68			
PIT	156	84	70	.545	8	804	718	5586	1596	283	80	60	517	502	.286	.349	.392	.746	105	56	39	102	100	798	37			
CIN	154	74	80	.481	18	722	760	5393	1476	224	73	82	410	584	.274	.329	.388	.717	106	-14	31	94	104	699	68			
BOS	157	71	83	.461	21	631	715	5478	1450	207	45	67	433	582	.265	.322	.356	.678	94	-86	-39	94	98	635	23			
BRO	156	67	87	.435	25	662	752	5574	1518	263	43	33	390	458	.272	.323	.353	.676	87	-92	-99	101	104	649	55			
PHI	154	54	100	.351	38	726	874	5465	1538	250	46	103	451	586	.281	.339	.401	.740	95	32	-41	110	96	757	50			
TOT	620					5837		43891	12206	2071	431	606	3565	4203	.278	.335	.386	.722						401				

TEAM	CG	SH	SV	IP	H	H/G	HR	BB	SO	RAT	ERA	ERA+	OAV	OOB	PR	/A	PF	CPI	FA	E	DP	FW	PW	BW	SBW	DIF
NY	60	12	22	1385[2]	1458	9.5	75	401	500	12.2	3.46	113	.273	.327	86	67	97	110	.974	168	164	1.1	6.5	2.6		4.7
STL	65	5	24	1398	1610	10.4	89	434	559	13.4	4.47	88	.289	.344	-71	-84	98	98	.974	156	134	1.9	-8.2	4.2		12.1
CHI	77	18	10	1382[1]	1413	9.2	77	434	597	12.2	3.54	113	.265	.324	74	68	99	104	.976	146	156	2.4	6.6	2.7		-1.7
PIT	67	5	12	1395[1]	1475	9.5	74	379	559	12.1	3.89	104	.269	.319	20	25	101	92	.967	199	113	-.5	2.4	3.8		1.3
CIN	50	6	23	1367[1]	1576	10.4	51	418	459	13.3	4.22	91	.287	.341	-31	-61	95	97	.969	191	150	-.2	-6.0	3.0		.1
BOS	61	7	13	1413[1]	1566	10.0	69	451	421	13.0	3.94	97	.281	.337	12	-18	95	103	.971	189	175	.1	-1.8	-3.8		-.6
BRO	59	7	18	1403	1466	9.4	84	528	651	13.0	3.98	104	.266	.333	5	22	103	97	.966	208	107	-1.0	2.1	-9.7		-1.5
PHI	51	7	14	1365[1]	1630	10.7	87	515	454	14.4	4.64	98	.292	.356	-95	-17	113	100	.959	252	144	-3.7	-1.7	-4.0		-13.7
TOT	490	67	136	11110[1]		9.9				12.9	4.02		.278	.335					.969	1509	1143					

Runs
Vaughan-Pit 122
J.Martin-StL 121
Ott-NY 120
Medwick-StL 115
Suhr-Pit 111

Hits
Medwick-StL 223
P.Waner-Pit 218
Demaree-Chi 212
Herman-Chi 211
Moore-NY 205

Doubles
Medwick-StL 64
Herman-Chi 57
P.Waner-Pit 53
Moore-StL 39
Moore-Bos 38

Triples
Goodman-Cin 14
Medwick-StL 13
Camilli-Phi 13

Home Runs
Ott-NY 33
Camilli-Phi 28
Klein-Chi-Phi 25
Berger-Bos 25
Mize-StL 19

Total Bases
Medwick-StL 367
Ott-NY 314
Klein-Chi-Phi 308
Camilli-Phi 306
P.Waner-Pit 304

Runs Batted In
Medwick-StL 138
Ott-NY 135
Suhr-Pit 118
Klein-Chi-Phi 104

Runs Produced
Medwick-StL 235
Ott-NY 222
Suhr-Pit 218
P.Waner-Pit 196
Vaughan-Pit 191

Bases On Balls
Vaughan-Pit 118
Camilli-Phi 116
Ott-NY 111
Suhr-Pit 95
Hack-Chi 89

Batting Average
P.Waner-Pit 373
Medwick-StL 351
Demaree-Chi 350
Vaughan-Pit 335
Herman-Chi 334

On Base Percentage
Vaughan-Pit 453
Ott-NY 448
P.Waner-Pit 446
Camilli-Phi 441
Suhr-Pit 410

Slugging Average
Ott-NY 588
Camilli-Phi 577
Medwick-StL 577
P.Waner-Pit 520
Klein-Chi-Phi 512

Production
Ott-NY 1.036
Camilli-Phi 1.018
P.Waner-Pit 965
Medwick-StL 964
Vaughan-Pit 927

Adjusted Production
Ott-NY 179
Medwick-StL 157
Camilli-Phi 156
P.Waner-Pit 156
Vaughan-Pit 146

Batter Runs
Ott-NY 61.9
Camilli-Phi 58.0
P.Waner-Pit 51.4
Vaughan-Pit 47.3
Medwick-StL 46.9

Adjusted Batter Runs
Ott-NY 62.8
Camilli-Phi 50.1
P.Waner-Pit 49.5
Medwick-StL 47.2
Vaughan-Pit 45.3

Clutch Hitting Index
Brubaker-Pit 160
Suhr-Pit 145
Young-Pit 141
Cuccinello-Bos . . . 130
Galan-Chi 130

Runs Created
Ott-NY 153
Camilli-Phi 148
Medwick-StL 141
P.Waner-Pit 140
Vaughan-Pit 137

Total Average
Ott-NY 1.188
Camilli-Phi 1.162
Vaughan-Pit 1.034
P.Waner-Pit 1.016
Medwick-StL 956

Stolen Bases
J.Martin-StL 23
S.Martin-StL 17
Hack-Chi 17
Chiozza-Phi 17

Stolen Base Average

Stolen Base Runs

Fielding Runs
Bartell-NY 44.8
Whitehead-NY 29.2
Kampouris-Cin 28.0
Berres-Bro 23.0

Total Player Rating
Bartell-NY 5.7
Medwick-StL 5.3
Ott-NY 5.1
P.Waner-Pit 5.0
Herman-Chi 5.0

Wins
Hubbell-NY 26
J.Dean-StL 24
Derringer-Cin 19

Win Percentage
Hubbell-NY 813
Lucas-Pit 789
French-Chi 667
J.Dean-StL 649
Lee-Chi 621

Games
Derringer-Cin 51
J.Dean-StL 51
Passeau-Phi 49
M.Brown-Pit 47

Complete Games
J.Dean-StL 28
Hubbell-NY 25
Mungo-Bro 22
MacFayden-Bos . . 21
Lee-Chi 20

Shutouts
Warneke-Chi 4
Walters-Phi 4
Smith-NY 4
Lee-Chi 4
French-Chi 4
Carleton-Chi 4
Blanton-Pit 4

Saves
J.Dean-StL 11
Brennan-Cin 9
Smith-Bos 8
Johnson-Phi 7
Coffman-NY 7

Innings Pitched
J.Dean-StL 315.0
Mungo-Bro 311.2
Hubbell-NY 304.0
Derringer-Cin 282.1
MacFayden-Bos . 266.2

Fewest Hits/Game
Hubbell-NY 7.85
Mungo-Bro 7.94
Lee-Chi 8.28
J.Dean-StL 8.86
Blanton-Pit 8.97

Fewest BB/Game
Lucas-Pit 1.33
Derringer-Cin 1.34
J.Dean-StL 1.51
Hubbell-NY 1.69
Gabler-NY 1.89

Strikeouts
Mungo-Bro 238
J.Dean-StL 195
Blanton-Pit 127
Hubbell-NY 123
Derringer-Cin 121

Strikeouts/Game
Mungo-Bro 6.87
J.Dean-StL 5.57
Blanton-Pit 4.85
Weaver-Pit 4.31
Warneke-Chi 4.23

Ratio
Hubbell-NY 9.68
J.Dean-StL 10.46
Lucas-Pit 10.61
Blanton-Pit 11.19
Davis-Phi-Chi 11.35

Earned Run Average
Hubbell-NY 2.31
MacFayden-Bos . . 2.87
Gabler-NY 3.12
J.Dean-StL 3.17
Lucas-Pit 3.18

Adjusted ERA
Hubbell-NY 169
MacFayden-Bos . . 134
Passeau-Phi 130
Lucas-Pit 128
Gabler-NY 125

Opponents' Batting Avg.
Mungo-Bro 234
Hubbell-NY 236
Lee-Chi 246
J.Dean-StL 253
Blanton-Pit 257

Opponents' On Base Pct.
Hubbell-NY 276
J.Dean-StL 285
Lucas-Pit 287
Blanton-Pit 301
Mungo-Bro 305

Starter Runs
Hubbell-NY 57.7
MacFayden-Bos . . 34.0
J.Dean-StL 29.6
Mungo-Bro 23.1
Lee-Chi 20.4

Adjusted Starter Runs
Hubbell-NY 53.5
MacFayden-Bos . . 28.5
Mungo-Bro 27.0
J.Dean-StL 26.9
Passeau-Phi 25.4

Clutch Pitching Index
Schumacher-NY . . 120
Gabler-NY 119
Chaplin-Bos 111
Smith-NY 110
Carleton-Chi 109

Relief Runs
Bryant-Chi 4.6
Coffman-NY 1.4

Adjusted Relief Runs
Bryant-Chi 4.4
Johnson-Phi 2.9

Relief Ranking
Johnson-Phi 3.2
Bryant-Chi 2.1

Total Pitcher Index
Hubbell-NY 5.7
Passeau-Phi 3.1
MacFayden-Bos . . 2.8
Mungo-Bro 2.5
J.Dean-StL 2.5

Total Baseball Ranking
Hubbell-NY 5.7
Bartell-NY 5.7
Medwick-StL 5.3
Ott-NY 5.1
P.Waner-Pit 5.0

TEAM	G	W	L	PCT	GB	R	OR	AB	H	2B	3B	HR	BB	SO	AVG	OBP	SLG	PRO	PRO+	BR	/A	PF	CHI	RC	SB	CS	SBA	SBR
NY	155	102	51	.667		**1065**	**731**	5591	1676	315	83	**182**	**700**	594	.300	**.381**	**.483**	**.864**	124	162	194	97	100	**1056**	77	40	66	-1
DET	154	83	71	.539	19.5	921	871	5464	1638	326	55	94	640	462	.300	.377	.431	.808	106	57	54	100	98	912	73	49	60	-8
CHI	153	81	70	.536	20	920	873	5466	1597	282	56	60	684	417	.292	.374	.397	.771	94	-9	-41	104	**104**	851	66	29	69	2
WAS	153	82	71	.536	20	889	799	5433	1601	293	**84**	62	576	**398**	.295	.365	.414	.779	105	-7	41	94	**104**	847	**104**	42	71	6
CLE	157	80	74	.519	22.5	921	862	5646	**1715**	**357**	82	123	514	470	**.304**	.364	.461	.825	109	70	63	101	96	948	66	53	55	-12
BOS	155	74	80	.481	28.5	775	764	5383	1485	288	62	86	584	465	.276	.349	.400	.749	86	-72	-121	106	98	773	55	44	56	-10
STL	155	57	95	.375	44.5	804	1064	5391	1502	299	66	79	625	627	.279	.356	.403	.759	91	-51	-75	103	99	804	62	20	**76**	7
PHI	154	53	100	.346	49	714	1045	5373	1443	240	60	72	524	590	.269	.336	.376	.712	84	-151	-134	98	102	694	59	43	58	-8
TOT	618					7009		43747	12657	2400	548	758	4847	4023	.289	.363	.421	.784							562	320	64	-23

TEAM	CG	SH	SV	IP	H	H/G	HR	BB	SO	RAT	ERA	ERA+	OAV	OOB	PR	/A	PF	CPI	FA	E	DP	FW	PW	BW	SBW	DIF
NY	77	6	**21**	1400[1]	1474	9.5	84	663	**624**	13.8	**4.17**	112	**.271**	.351	135	75	92	**108**	.973	163	148	.8	6.6	**17.1**	.2	.8
DET	76	**13**	13	1360	1568	10.4	100	562	526	14.2	5.00	99	.289	.358	6	-7	98	100	.973	153	159	**1.3**	-.6	4.8	-.4	1.0
CHI	**80**	5	8	1365	1603	10.6	104	578	414	14.5	5.06	103	.293	.363	-4	21	103	102	.973	168	**174**	.4	1.9	-3.6	.4	6.5
WAS	78	8	14	1345[2]	1484	9.9	**73**	588	462	14.0	4.58	104	.279	.353	68	29	95	101	.970	182	163	-.4	2.6	3.6	.8	-1.1
CLE	74	6	12	1389[1]	1604	10.4	**73**	607	619	14.5	4.83	104	.289	.362	32	32	100	102	.971	178	154	.0	2.8	5.6	-.8	-4.7
BOS	78	11	9	1372[1]	1501	9.8	78	**552**	584	**13.6**	4.39	**121**	.277	**.346**	99	**142**	106	102	.972	165	139	.7	**12.5**	-10.7	-.6	-4.9
STL	54	3	13	1348[1]	1776	11.9	115	609	399	16.2	6.24	86	.314	.385	-180	-130	107	95	.969	188	143	-.6	-11.5	-6.6	.9	-1.2
PHI	68	3	12	1352[1]	1645	10.9	131	696	405	15.7	6.08	84	.300	.381	-156	-146	101	94	.965	209	152	-1.9	-12.9	-11.8	-.4	3.5
TOT	585	55	102	10933[1]		10.4				14.6	5.04		.289	.363					.971	1406	1232					

Runs
Gehrig-NY 167
Clift-StL 145
Gehringer-Det 144
Crosetti-NY 137
Averill-Cle 136

Hits
Averill-Cle 232
Gehringer-Det 227
Trosky-Cle 216
Bell-StL 212
Radcliff-Chi 207

Doubles
Gehringer-Det 60
Walker-Det 55
Chapman-NY-Was .. 50
Hale-Cle 50

Triples
Rolfe-NY 15
DiMaggio-NY 15
Averill-Cle 15
R.Johnson-Phi 14

Home Runs
Gehrig-NY 49
Trosky-Cle 42
Foxx-Bos 41
DiMaggio-NY 29
Averill-Cle 28

Total Bases
Trosky-Cle 405
Gehrig-NY 403
Averill-Cle 385
Foxx-Bos 369
DiMaggio-NY 367

Runs Batted In
Trosky-Cle 162
Gehrig-NY 152
Foxx-Bos 143
Bonura-Chi 138
Solters-StL 134

Runs Produced
Gehrig-NY 270
Bonura-Chi 246
Gehringer-Det 245
Trosky-Cle 244
Averill-Cle 234

Bases On Balls
Gehrig-NY 130
Lary-StL 117
Clift-StL 115
Foxx-Bos 105
Lazzeri-NY 97

Batting Average
Appling-Chi .... .388
Averill-Cle .... .378
Gehringer-Det ..... .354
Gehrig-NY .... .354
Walker-Det .... .353

On Base Percentage
Gehrig-NY .... .478
Appling-Chi .... .474
Foxx-Bos .... .440
Averill-Cle .... .438
Gehringer-Det ..... .431

Slugging Average
Gehrig-NY .... .696
Trosky-Cle .... .644
Foxx-Bos .... .631
Averill-Cle .... .627
DiMaggio-NY ...... .576

Production
Gehrig-NY 1.174
Foxx-Bos 1.071
Averill-Cle 1.065
Trosky-Cle 1.026
Gehringer-Det ..... .987

Adjusted Production
Gehrig-NY 193
Averill-Cle 159
Foxx-Bos 153
Trosky-Cle 148
Stone-Was 145

Batter Runs
Gehrig-NY 82.2
Foxx-Bos 56.8
Averill-Cle 56.4
Gehringer-Det 43.0
Trosky-Cle 41.9

Adjusted Batter Runs
Gehrig-NY 85.8
Averill-Cle 55.6
Foxx-Bos 51.2
Gehringer-Det 42.7
Trosky-Cle 41.1

Clutch Hitting Index
Appling-Chi 154
Bonura-Chi 148
Sewell-Chi 137
Owen-Det 137
Vosmik-Cle 135

Runs Created
Gehrig-NY 199
Averill-Cle 168
Foxx-Bos 168
Gehringer-Det 157
Trosky-Cle 150

Total Average
Gehrig-NY 1.426
Foxx-Bos 1.238
Averill-Cle 1.171
Appling-Chi 1.088
Gehringer-Det ... 1.075

Stolen Bases
Lary-StL 37
Powell-Was-NY ... 26
Werber-Bos 23
Chapman-NY-Was . 20
Hughes-Cle 20

Stolen Base Average
Lary-StL 80.4
Crosetti-NY 72.0
Powell-Was-NY ... 70.3
Chapman-NY-Was 69.0
Hughes-Cle 69.0

Stolen Base Runs
Lary-StL 5.7
Hill-Was 3.3
Stone-Was 2.4
Sewell-Chi 2.1

Fielding Runs
Hayes-Chi 17.1
Hale-Cle 16.5
Cramer-Bos 16.3
Gehringer-Det 15.7
Appling-Chi 15.2

Total Player Rating
Gehrig-NY 6.1
Gehringer-Det 6.1
Appling-Chi 5.3
Averill-Cle 3.9
Dickey-NY 3.7

Wins
Bridges-NY 23
Kennedy-Chi 21
Ruffing-NY 20
W.Ferrell-Bos 20
Allen-Cle 20

Win Percentage
Pearson-NY ...... .731
Kennedy-Chi ..... .700
Bridges-Det ...... .676
Allen-Cle .... .667
Rowe-Det .... .655

Games
VanAtta-StL 52
Knott-StL 47

Complete Games
W.Ferrell-Bos 28
Bridges-Det 26
Ruffing-NY 25
Newsom-Was 24
Grove-Bos 22

Shutouts
Grove-Bos 6
Bridges-Det 5
Rowe-Det 4
Newsom-Was 4
Allen-Cle 4

Saves
Malone-NY 9
Knott-StL 6
Murphy-NY 5
Brown-Chi 5
Hildebrand-Cle 4

Innings Pitched
W.Ferrell-Bos 301.0
Bridges-Det 294.2
Newsom-Was ... 285.2
Kennedy-Chi 274.1
Ruffing-NY 271.0

Fewest Hits/Game
Pearson-NY 7.71
Grove-Bos 8.42
Allen-Cle 8.67
Gomez-NY 8.78
Bridges-Det 8.83

Fewest BB/Game
Lyons-Chi 2.23
Grove-Bos 2.31
Rowe-Det 2.35
Andrews-StL 2.35
Marcum-Bos 2.69

Strikeouts
Bridges-Det 175
Allen-Cle 165
Newsom-Was 156
Grove-Bos 130
Pearson-NY 118

Strikeouts/Game
Allen-Cle 6.11
Bridges-Det 5.35
Gomez-NY 5.01
Newsom-Was 4.91
Pearson-NY 4.76

Ratio
Grove-Bos 10.87
Rowe-Det 12.18
Ruffing-NY 12.19
Allen-Cle 12.30
Appleton-Was ... 12.45

Earned Run Average
Grove-Bos 2.81
Allen-Cle 3.44
Appleton-Was 3.53
Bridges-Det 3.60
Pearson-NY 3.71

Adjusted ERA
Grove-Bos 189
Allen-Cle 146
Bridges-Det 137
Appleton-Was ... 135
Kelley-Phi 132

Opponents' Batting Avg.
Pearson-NY ...... .233
Grove-Bos .... .246
Gomez-NY .... .254
Appleton-Was .... .254
Bridges-Det ..... .255

Opponents' On Base Pct.
Grove-Bos .... .297
Rowe-Det .... .321
Ruffing-NY .... .323
Appleton-Was .... .324
Bridges-Det ..... .326

Starter Runs
Grove-Bos 62.8
Bridges-Det 46.9
Allen-Cle 43.0
Ruffing-NY 35.7
Appleton-Was ... 33.9

Adjusted Starter Runs
Grove-Bos 70.6
Bridges-Det 44.1
Allen-Cle 43.0
W.Ferrell-Bos 37.8
Kelley-Phi 32.4

Clutch Pitching Index
Hadley-NY 116
Kelley-Phi 115
Grove-Bos 115
Bridges-Det 109
Thomas-StL 107

Relief Runs
Lee-Cle 2.1
Gumpert-Phi 1.9
Kimsey-Det 1.1
Brown-Chi 5

Adjusted Relief Runs
Gumpert-Phi 2.3
Lee-Cle 2.1
Brown-Chi 1.9
Kimsey-Det 6

Relief Ranking
Brown-Chi 2.0
Lee-Cle 1.3
Gumpert-Phi 1.2
Kimsey-Det 6

Total Pitcher Index
Grove-Bos 6.6
W.Ferrell-Bos 4.4
Bridges-Det 4.3
Allen-Cle 3.9
Ruffing-NY 3.7

Total Baseball Ranking
Grove-Bos 6.6
Gehrig-NY 6.1
Gehringer-Det 6.1
Appling-Chi 5.3
W.Ferrell-Bos 4.4

TEAM	G	W	L	PCT	GB	R	OR	AB	H	2B	3B	HR	BB	SO	AVG	OBP	SLG	PRO	PRO+	BR	/A	PF	CHI	RC	SB	CS	SBA	SBR
NY	152	95	57	.625		732	602	5329	1484	251	41	111	412	492	.278	.334	.403	.737	105	40	32	101	100	734	45			
CHI	154	93	61	.604	3	811	682	5349	1537	253	74	96	538	496	.287	.355	.416	.771	111	117	88	104	98	816	71			
PIT	154	86	68	.558	10	704	646	5433	1550	223	86	47	463	480	.285	.343	.384	.727	104	30	30	100	96	734	32			
STL	157	81	73	.526	15	789	733	5476	1543	264	67	94	385	569	.282	.331	.406	.737	104	36	22	102	107	744	78			
BOS	152	79	73	.520	16	579	556	5124	1265	200	41	63	485	707	.247	.314	.339	.653	91	-109	-48	91	102	565	45			
BRO	155	62	91	.405	33.5	616	772	5295	1401	258	53	37	469	583	.265	.327	.354	.681	90	-57	-68	102	97	629	69			
PHI	155	61	92	.399	34.5	724	869	5424	1482	258	37	103	478	640	.273	.334	.391	.725	95	21	-36	108	100	730	66			
CIN	155	56	98	.364	40	612	707	5230	1329	215	59	73	437	586	.254	.315	.360	.675	94	-78	-45	95	102	599	53			
TOT	617					5567		42660	11591	1922	458	624	3667	4553	.272	.332	.382	.714							459			

TEAM	CG	SH	SV	IP	H	H/G	HR	BB	SO	RAT	ERA	ERA+	OAV	OOB	PR	/A	PF	CPI	FA	E	DP	FW	PW	BW	SBW	DIF
NY	67	11	17	1361	1341	8.9	85	404	653	11.7	3.43	113	.258	.314	73	69	99	102	.974	159	143	.9	6.8	3.2		8.1
CHI	73	11	13	1381¹	1434	9.3	91	502	596	12.8	3.97	100	.267	.332	-10	0	102	99	.975	151	141	1.5	.0	8.7		5.8
PIT	67	12	17	1366¹	1398	9.2	71	428	643	12.2	3.56	108	.264	.321	53	45	99	101	.970	181	135	-.2	4.5	3.0		1.8
STL	81	10	4	1392	1546	10.0	95	448	571	13.0	3.98	100	.281	.337	-10	-1	102	105	.973	164	127	1.0	-.0	2.2		1.0
BOS	85	16	10	1359¹	1344	8.9	60	372	387	11.4	3.22	111	.259	.310	105	55	92	103	.975	157	128	1.0	5.5	-4.8		1.3
BRO	63	5	8	1362²	1470	9.7	68	476	592	13.0	4.13	98	.274	.336	-33	-14	103	96	.964	217	127	-2.2	-1.4	-6.7		-4.2
PHI	59	6	15	1373²	1629	10.7	116	501	529	14.2	5.05	86	.297	.359	-174	-114	111	97	.970	184	157	-.3	-11.3	-3.6		-.3
CIN	64	10	18	1358¹	1428	9.5	38	533	581	13.1	3.94	95	.270	.339	-4	-32	95	97	.966	208	139	-1.6	-3.2	-4.5		-11.7
TOT	559	81	102	10954²		9.5				12.7	3.91		.272	.332					.971	1421	1097					

Runs
Medwick-StL 111
Herman-Chi 106
Hack-Chi 106
Galan-Chi 104
Demaree-Chi 104

Hits
Medwick-StL 237
P.Waner-Pit 219
Mize-StL 204
Demaree-Chi 199
Herman-Chi 189

Doubles
Medwick-StL 56
Mize-StL 40
Bartell-NY 38
Phelps-Bro 37
Moore-NY 37

Triples
Vaughan-Pit 17
Suhr-Pit 14
Handley-Pit 12
Goodman-Cin 12
Herman-Chi 11

Home Runs
Ott-NY 31
Medwick-StL 31
Camilli-Phi 27
Mize-StL 25
Galan-Chi 18

Total Bases
Medwick-StL 406
Mize-StL 333
Demaree-Chi 298
Ott-NY 285
Camilli-Phi 279

Runs Batted In
Medwick-StL 154
Demaree-Chi 115
Mize-StL 113
Suhr-Pit 97
Ott-NY 95

Runs Produced
Medwick-StL 234
Demaree-Chi 202
Mize-StL 191
Hack-Chi 167
P.Waner-Pit 166

Bases On Balls
Ott-NY 102
Camilli-Phi 90
Suhr-Pit 83
Hack-Chi 83
Galan-Chi 79

Batting Average
Medwick-StL ..... .374
Mize-StL ..... .364
P.Waner-Pit ..... .354
Whitney-Phi ..... .341
Camilli-Phi ..... .339

On Base Percentage
Camilli-Phi ..... .446
Mize-StL ..... .427
Medwick-StL ..... .414
P.Waner-Pit ..... .413
Ott-NY ..... .408

Slugging Average
Medwick-StL ..... .641
Mize-StL ..... .595
Camilli-Phi ..... .587
Ott-NY ..... .523
Demaree-Chi ..... .485

Production
Medwick-StL 1.056
Camilli-Phi 1.034
Mize-StL 1.021
Ott-NY ..... .931
Herman-Chi ..... .875

Adjusted Production
Medwick-StL 179
Mize-StL 171
Camilli-Phi 165
Ott-NY 149
P.Waner-Pit 132

Batter Runs
Medwick-StL 68.8
Mize-StL 57.4
Camilli-Phi 54.9
Ott-NY 41.2
Hartnett-Chi 31.1

Adjusted Batter Runs
Medwick-StL 67.2
Mize-StL 56.0
Camilli-Phi 49.5
Ott-NY 40.3
P.Waner-Pit 29.8

Clutch Hitting Index
Suhr-Pit 151
Durocher-StL 144
Scharein-Phi 142
Jurges-Chi 134
Todd-Pit 130

Runs Created
Medwick-StL 170
Mize-StL 150
Camilli-Phi 137
Ott-NY 128
P.Waner-Pit 118

Total Average
Camilli-Phi 1.189
Medwick-StL 1.113
Mize-StL 1.097
Ott-NY 1.021
Vaughan-Pit ..... .864

Stolen Bases
Galan-Chi 23
Hack-Chi 16

Stolen Base Average

Stolen Base Runs

Fielding Runs
Bartell-NY 37.5
Whitehead-NY 26.1
Riggs-Cin 19.5
Herman-Chi 18.6
Young-Pit 18.1

Total Player Rating
Medwick-StL 6.3
Bartell-NY 6.1
Herman-Chi 5.3
Ott-NY 3.8
Camilli-Phi 3.8

Wins
Hubbell-NY 22
Turner-Bos 20
Melton-NY 20
Fette-Bos 20
Warneke-StL 18

Win Percentage
Hubbell-NY ..... .733
Melton-NY ..... .690
Fette-Bos ..... .667
Carleton-Chi ..... .667
Turner-Bos ..... .645

Games
Mulcahy-Phi 56
Jorgens-Phi 52

Complete Games
Turner-Bos 24
Fette-Bos 23
Weiland-StL 21

Shutouts
Turner-Bos 5
Grissom-Cin 5
Fette-Bos 5

Saves
Melton-NY 7
Brown-Pit 7
Grissom-Cin 6
Root-Chi 5
Hollingsworth-Cin ... 5

Innings Pitched
Passeau-Phi 292.1
Lee-Chi 272.1
Weiland-StL 264.1
Hubbell-NY 261.2
Fette-Bos 259.0

Fewest Hits/Game
Mungo-Bro 7.60
Grissom-Cin 7.77
Melton-NY 7.84
Carleton-Chi 7.91
Turner-Bos 7.99

Fewest BB/Game
J.Dean-StL 1.51
Root-Chi 1.61
Hoyt-Pit-Bro 1.66
Turner-Bos 1.82
Castleman-NY 1.85

Strikeouts
Hubbell-NY 159
Grissom-Cin 149
Blanton-Pit 143
Melton-NY 142

Strikeouts/Game
Mungo-Bro 6.82
Grissom-Cin 6.00
Bauers-Pit 5.66
Henshaw-Bro 5.64
LaMaster-Phi 5.51

Ratio
Turner-Bos 9.82
Melton-NY 10.05
Castleman-NY 10.16
Root-Chi 10.53
J.Dean-StL 10.72

Earned Run Average
Turner-Bos 2.38
Melton-NY 2.61
J.Dean-StL 2.69
Bauers-Pit 2.88
Fette-Bos 2.88

Adjusted ERA
Turner-Bos 150
Melton-NY 149
J.Dean-StL 148
Mungo-Bro 139
Bauers-Pit 134

Opponents' Batting Avg.
Mungo-Bro ..... .229
Grissom-Cin ..... .232
Melton-NY ..... .233
Turner-Bos ..... .235
Carleton-Chi ..... .236

Opponents' On Base Pct.
Turner-Bos ..... .274
Melton-NY ..... .280
Castleman-NY ..... .287
Root-Chi ..... .290
J.Dean-StL ..... .291

Starter Runs
Turner-Bos 43.5
Melton-NY 35.8
Fette-Bos 29.5
MacFayden-Bos 26.9
J.Dean-StL 26.7

Adjusted Starter Runs
Melton-NY 35.0
Turner-Bos 34.2
J.Dean-StL 28.2
Bauers-Pit 20.5
Mungo-Bro 20.1

Clutch Pitching Index
Johnson-StL 128
Brandt-Pit 124
Weiland-StL 115
Frankhouse-Bro .. 113
MacFayden-Bos .. 112

Relief Runs
Coffman-NY 7.8
Hutchinson-Bos ... 1.8

Adjusted Relief Runs
Coffman-NY 7.5

Relief Ranking
Coffman-NY 9.9

Total Pitcher Index
Turner-Bos 4.1
Melton-NY 3.5
J.Dean-StL 2.8
Mungo-Bro 2.7
Bauers-Pit 2.5

Total Baseball Ranking
Medwick-StL 6.3
Bartell-NY 6.1
Herman-Chi 5.3
Turner-Bos 4.1
Ott-NY 3.8

TEAM	G	W	L	PCT	GB	R	OR	AB	H	2B	3B	HR	BB	SO	AVG	OBP	SLG	PRO	PRO+	BR	/A	PF	CHI	RC	SB	CS	SBA	SBR
NY	157	102	52	.662		**979**	671	5487	1554	282	73	**174**	**709**	607	.283	.369	**.456**	**.825**	113	**112**	**107**	101	**103**	952	60	36	63	-4
DET	155	89	65	.578	13	935	841	5516	**1611**	309	62	150	656	711	**.292**	**.370**	.452	.822	111	106	88	102	100	947	89	45	66	0
CHI	154	86	68	.558	16	780	730	5277	1478	280	76	67	549	**447**	.280	.350	.400	.750	95	-38	-37	100	103	763	70	34	**67**	1
CLE	156	83	71	.539	19	817	768	5353	1499	304	76	103	570	551	.280	.352	.423	.775	100	4	-1	101	101	813	78	51	60	-7
BOS	154	80	72	.526	21	821	775	5354	1506	269	64	100	601	557	.281	.357	.411	.768	96	-1	-32	104	102	804	79	61	56	-13
WAS	158	73	80	.477	28.5	757	841	5578	1559	245	**84**	47	591	503	.279	.351	.379	.730	94	-74	-37	96	100	767	61	35	64	-3
PHI	154	54	97	.358	46.5	699	854	5228	1398	278	60	94	583	557	.267	.348	.397	.738	93	-63	-50	98	97	732	**95**	48	66	0
STL	156	46	108	.299	56	715	1023	5510	1573	**327**	44	71	514	510	.285	.348	.399	.747	93	-47	-52	101	93	780	30	27	53	-7
TOT	622					6503		43303	12178	2294	539	806	4773	4443	.281	.355	.415	.770							562	337	63	-34

TEAM	CG	SH	SV	IP	H	H/G	HR	BB	SO	RAT	ERA	ERA+	OAV	OOB	PR	/A	PF	CPI	FA	E	DP	FW	PW	BW	SBW	DIF
NY	**82**	15	21	1396	**1417**	9.1	92	**506**	652	12.5	3.65	122	**.261**	**.325**	151	124	96	103	.972	170	134	.2	11.4	9.8	.0	3.6
DET	70	6	11	1378	1521	9.9	102	635	485	14.2	4.87	96	.279	.357	-38	-30	101	95	**.976**	147	149	1.4	-2.8	8.1	.4	4.9
CHI	70	15	21	1351[1]	1435	9.6	115	532	533	13.2	4.17	110	.273	.341	68	65	100	104	.971	174	173	-.2	6.0	-3.4	.5	6.2
CLE	64	4	15	1364[2]	1529	10.1	**61**	566	630	14.0	4.39	105	.285	.356	35	33	100	102	.974	159	153	.8	3.0	-.0	-.3	2.5
BOS	74	6	14	1366	1518	10.0	92	597	**682**	14.0	4.48	106	.279	.352	21	41	103	100	.970	177	139	-.4	3.8	-2.9	-.8	4.4
WAS	75	5	14	1398[2]	1498	9.6	96	671	524	14.1	4.58	97	.275	.357	7	-23	96	99	.972	170	**181**	.3	-2.1	-3.4	.1	1.6
PHI	65	6	9	1335	1490	10.0	105	613	469	14.3	4.85	97	.281	.358	-35	-21	102	97	.967	198	150	-1.7	-1.9	-4.6	.4	-13.7
STL	55	2	8	1363	1768	11.7	143	653	468	16.2	6.00	80	.315	.390	-209	-178	105	100	.972	173	166	-.0	-16.3	-4.8	-.3	-9.6
TOT	555	59	113	10952[2]		10.0				14.1	4.62		.281	.355					.972	1368	1245					

Runs		Hits		Doubles		Triples		Home Runs		Total Bases	
DiMaggio-NY	151	Bell-StL	218	Bell-StL	51	Walker-Chi	16	DiMaggio-NY	46	DiMaggio-NY	418
Rolfe-NY	143	DiMaggio-NY	215	Greenberg-Det	49	Kreevich-Chi	16	Greenberg-Det	40	Greenberg-Det	397
Gehrig-NY	138	Walker-Det	213	Moses-Phi	48	Stone-Was	15	Gehrig-NY	37	Gehrig-NY	366
Greenberg-Det	137	Lewis-Was	210	Vosmik-StL	47	DiMaggio-NY	15	Foxx-Bos	36	Moses-Phi	357
Gehringer-Det	133	Gehringer-Det	209	Lary-Cle	46	Greenberg-Det	14	York-Det	35	Trosky-Cle	329

Runs Batted In		Runs Produced		Bases On Balls		Batting Average		On Base Percentage		Slugging Average	
Greenberg-Det	183	Greenberg-Det	280	Gehrig-NY	127	Gehringer-Det	.371	Gehrig-NY	.473	DiMaggio-NY	.673
DiMaggio-NY	167	DiMaggio-NY	272	Greenberg-Det	102	Gehrig-NY	.351	Gehringer-Det	.458	Greenberg-Det	.668
Gehrig-NY	159	Gehrig-NY	260	Foxx-Bos	99	DiMaggio-NY	.346	Greenberg-Det	.436	Gehrig-NY	.643
Dickey-NY	133	Gehringer-Det	215	Johnson-Phi	98	Bonura-Chi	.345	Johnson-Phi	.425	Bonura-Chi	.573
Trosky-Cle	128	Foxx-Bos	202	Clift-StL	98	Travis-Was	.344	Dickey-NY	.417	Dickey-NY	.570

Production		Adjusted Production		Batter Runs		Adjusted Batter Runs		Clutch Hitting Index		Runs Created	
Gehrig-NY	1.116	Gehrig-NY	177	Gehrig-NY	73.3	Gehrig-NY	72.7	Hayes-Cle	146	Gehrig-NY	181
Greenberg-Det	1.105	Greenberg-Det	171	Greenberg-Det	67.2	Greenberg-Det	65.2	Higgins-Bos	138	Greenberg-Det	178
DiMaggio-NY	1.085	DiMaggio-NY	168	DiMaggio-NY	61.3	DiMaggio-NY	60.7	Myer-Was	135	DiMaggio-NY	173
Dickey-NY	.987	Johnson-Phi	147	Gehringer-Det	44.0	Gehringer-Det	42.1	Greenberg-Det	128	Gehringer-Det	140
Bonura-Chi	.984	Bonura-Chi	146	Dickey-NY	37.5	Dickey-NY	37.0	Hale-Cle	127	Clift-StL	134

Total Average		Stolen Bases		Stolen Base Average		Stolen Base Runs		Fielding Runs		Total Player Rating	
Gehrig-NY	1.339	Chapman-Was-Bos	35	Hill-Was-Phi	81.8	Chapman-Was-Bos	3.3	Clift-StL	41.0	Clift-StL	7.2
Greenberg-Det	1.277	Werber-Phi	35	Walker-Det	76.7	Hill-Was-Phi	3.0	Hale-Cle	25.9	DiMaggio-NY	6.1
DiMaggio-NY	1.207	Walker-Det	23	Pytlak-Cle	76.2	Werber-Phi	2.7	Hayes-Chi	20.5	Gehringer-Det	5.3
Gehringer-Det	1.089			Chapman-Was-Bos	74.5	Walker-Det	2.7	Appling-Chi	13.8	Dickey-NY	5.1
Johnson-Phi	1.083			Werber-Phi	72.9	Kreevich-Chi	2.4	Dickey-NY	12.3	Greenberg-Det	4.8

Wins		Win Percentage		Games		Complete Games		Shutouts		Saves	
Gomez-NY	21	Allen-Cle	.938	Brown-Chi	53	W.Ferrell-Bos-Was	26	Gomez-NY	6	Brown-Chi	18
Ruffing-NY	20	Stratton-Chi	.750	Wilson-Bos	51	Gomez-NY	25	Stratton-Chi	5	Murphy-NY	10
Lawson-Det	18	Ruffing-NY	.741	Newsom-Was-Bos	41	Ruffing-NY	22	Whitehead-Chi	4	Wilson-Bos	7
Grove-Bos	17	Lawson-Det	.720	Kelley-Phi	41	Grove-Bos	21	Ruffing-NY	4	Malone-NY	6
Auker-Det	17	Gomez-NY	.656	Heving-Cle	40	DeShong-Was	20	Appleton-Was	4		

Innings Pitched		Fewest Hits/Game		Fewest BB/Game		Strikeouts		Strikeouts/Game		Ratio	
W.Ferrell-Bos-Was	281.0	Gomez-NY	7.53	Stratton-Chi	2.02	Gomez-NY	194	Gomez-NY	6.27	Stratton-Chi	9.89
Gomez-NY	278.1	Stratton-Chi	7.76	Hudlin-Cle	2.20	Newsom-Was-Bos	166	Wilson-Bos	5.57	Gomez-NY	10.57
Newsom-Was-Bos	275.1	Smith-Phi	8.15	Marcum-Bos	2.30	Grove-Bos	153	Newsom-Was-Bos	5.43	Ruffing-NY	10.92
DeShong-Was	264.1	Allen-Cle	8.17	Ruffing-NY	2.39	Feller-Cle	150	Grove-Bos	5.26	Allen-Cle	11.55
Grove-Bos	262.0	Ruffing-NY	8.50	Lyons-Chi	2.39	Bridges-Det	138	Bridges-Det	5.06	Lee-Chi	11.87

Earned Run Average		Adjusted ERA		Opponents' Batting Avg.		Opponents' On Base Pct.		Starter Runs		Adjusted Starter Runs	
Gomez-NY	2.33	Stratton-Chi	191	Gomez-NY	.223	Stratton-Chi	.280	Gomez-NY	70.9	Gomez-NY	65.5
Stratton-Chi	2.40	Gomez-NY	191	Stratton-Chi	.234	Gomez-NY	.287	Ruffing-NY	46.6	Grove-Bos	50.2
Allen-Cle	2.55	Allen-Cle	181	Smith-Phi	.242	Ruffing-NY	.296	Grove-Bos	46.5	Ruffing-NY	41.6
Ruffing-NY	2.98	Grove-Bos	157	Allen-Cle	.244	Lee-Chi	.312	Stratton-Chi	40.6	Stratton-Chi	40.2
Grove-Bos	3.02	Ruffing-NY	149	Ruffing-NY	.247	Allen-Cle	.313	Allen-Cle	39.8	Allen-Cle	39.6

Clutch Pitching Index		Relief Runs		Adjusted Relief Runs		Relief Ranking		Total Pitcher Index		Total Baseball Ranking	
Allen-Cle	120	Brown-Chi	13.3	Brown-Chi	13.1	Brown-Chi	21.9	Gomez-NY	6.2	Clift-StL	7.2
Whitehead-Chi	119	Cohen-Was	9.2	Cohen-Was	8.1	Cohen-Was	9.2	Grove-Bos	4.6	Gomez-NY	6.2
Knott-StL	112	Murphy-NY	5.5	Fink-Phi	5.9	Murphy-NY	5.3	Stratton-Chi	4.1	DiMaggio-NY	6.1
Grove-Bos	111	Fink-Phi	5.1	Murphy-NY	3.3	Fink-Phi	2.2	Ruffing-NY	3.9	Gehringer-Det	5.3
Galehouse-Cle	110	Wyatt-Cle	1.5	Wyatt-Cle	1.4	Wyatt-Cle	.8	Allen-Cle	3.4	Dickey-NY	5.1

TEAM	G	W	L	PCT	GB	R	OR	AB	H	2B	3B	HR	BB	SO	AVG	OBP	SLG	PRO	PRO+	BR	/A	PF	CHI	RC	SB	CS	SBA	SBR
CHI	154	89	63	.586		713	598	5333	1435	242	70	65	522	476	.269	.338	.377	.715	100	25	7	103	101	689	49			
PIT	152	86	64	.573	2	707	630	5422	1511	265	66	65	485	409	.279	.340	.388	.728	106	48	43	101	96	727	47			
NY	152	83	67	.553	5	705	637	5255	1424	210	36	125	465	528	.271	.334	.396	.730	106	45	40	101	99	715	31			
CIN	151	82	68	.547	6	723	644	5391	1495	251	57	110	366	518	.277	.327	.406	.733	110	43	61	97	101	720	19			
BOS	153	77	75	.507	12	561	618	5250	1311	199	39	54	424	548	.250	.309	.333	.642	91	-119	-53	90	104	549	49			
STL	156	71	80	.470	17.5	725	721	5528	1542	288	74	91	412	492	.279	.331	.407	.738	103	56	17	106	97	752	55			
BRO	151	69	80	.463	18.5	704	710	5142	1322	225	79	61	611	615	.257	.338	.367	.705	98	13	-2	102	103	671	66			
PHI	151	45	105	.300	43	550	840	5192	1318	233	29	40	423	507	.254	.312	.333	.645	85	-111	-93	97	101	549	38			
TOT	610					5388		42513	11358	1913	450	611	3708	4093	.267	.329	.376	.705							354			

TEAM	CG	SH	SV	IP	H	H/G	HR	BB	SO	RAT	ERA	ERA+	OAV	OOB	PR	/A	PF	CPI	FA	E	DP	FW	PW	BW	SBW	DIF
CHI	67	16	18	1396²	1414	9.1	71	454	583	12.1	3.37	113	.262	.322	64	66	101	105	.978	135	151	2.3	6.6	.7		3.4
PIT	57	8	15	1379²	1406	9.2	71	432	557	12.2	3.46	109	.266	.324	49	50	100	106	.974	163	168	.5	5.0	4.3		1.2
NY	59	8	18	1349	1370	9.1	87	389	497	11.9	3.62	104	.261	.314	24	20	99	97	.973	168	147	.2	2.0	4.0		1.8
CIN	72	11	16	1362	1329	8.8	75	463	542	11.9	3.62	101	.254	.316	25	3	96	94	.971	172	133	-.1	.3	6.1		.7
BOS	83	15	12	1380	1375	9.0	66	465	413	12.2	3.40	101	.258	.322	58	3	91	103	.972	173	136	-.0	.3	-5.3		6.1
STL	58	10	16	1384²	1482	9.6	77	474	534	12.8	3.84	103	.272	.333	-9	17	104	102	.967	199	145	-1.4	1.7	1.7		-6.5
BRO	56	12	14	1332	1464	9.9	88	446	469	13.1	4.07	96	.278	.338	-42	-26	103	102	.973	157	148	.8	-2.6	-.2		-3.4
PHI	68	3	6	1329¹	1516	10.3	76	582	492	14.4	4.93	79	.285	.358	-169	-155	103	92	.966	201	135	-1.8	-15.6	-9.4		-3.2
TOT	520	83	115	10913¹		9.4				12.6	3.78		.267	.329					.972	1368	1163					

Runs
Ott-NY 116
Hack-Chi 109
Camilli-Bro 106
Goodman-Cin 103
Medwick-StL 100

Hits
McCormick-Cin ... 209
Hack-Chi 195
L.Waner-Pit 194
Medwick-StL 190
Mize-StL 179

Doubles
Medwick-StL 47
McCormick-Cin ... 40
Young-Pit 36
Martin-Phi 36

Triples
Mize-StL 16
Gutteridge-StL 15
Suhr-Pit 14
Riggs-Cin 13
Koy-Bro 13

Home Runs
Ott-NY 36
Goodman-Cin 30
Mize-StL 27
Camilli-Bro 24
Rizzo-Pit 23

Total Bases
Mize-StL 326
Medwick-StL 316
Ott-NY 307
Goodman-Cin 303
Rizzo-Pit 285

Runs Batted In
Medwick-StL 122
Ott-NY 116
Rizzo-Pit 111
McCormick-Cin ... 106
Mize-StL 102

Runs Produced
Medwick-StL 201
Ott-NY 196
McCormick-Cin ... 190
Rizzo-Pit 185
Camilli-Bro 182

Bases On Balls
Camilli-Bro 119
Ott-NY 118
Vaughan-Pit 104
Hack-Chi 94
Suhr-Pit 87

Batting Average
Lombardi-Cin..... .342
Mize-StL .... .337
McCormick-Cin ... .327
Medwick-StL ..... .322
Vaughan-Pit ...... .322

On Base Percentage
Ott-NY .... .442
Vaughan-Pit ...... .433
Mize-StL .... .422
Hack-Chi .... .411
Suhr-Pit .... .394

Slugging Average
Mize-StL .... .614
Ott-NY .... .583
Medwick-StL ..... .536
Goodman-Cin .... .533
Lombardi-Cin..... .524

Production
Mize-StL 1.036
Ott-NY 1.024
Lombardi-Cin..... .915
Medwick-StL ..... .905
Goodman-Cin .... .901

Adjusted Production
Ott-NY 178
Mize-StL 172
Lombardi-Cin..... 154
Goodman-Cin ... 149
Vaughan-Pit 140

Batter Runs
Ott-NY 61.9
Mize-StL 59.2
Vaughan-Pit 36.4
Medwick-StL 34.4
Goodman-Cin ... 33.5

Adjusted Batter Runs
Ott-NY 61.3
Mize-StL 55.3
Vaughan-Pit 35.9
Goodman-Cin ... 35.5
Lombardi-Cin..... 33.5

Clutch Hitting Index
Durocher-Bro 146
Arnovich-Phi 139
Lavagetto-Bro ... 135
Todd-Pit 132
Young-Pit 129

Runs Created
Ott-NY 149
Mize-StL 141
Hack-Chi 119
Goodman-Cin ... 116
Vaughan-Pit 115

Total Average
Ott-NY 1.164
Mize-StL 1.104
Camilli-Bro ...... .964
Vaughan-Pit ...... .960
Goodman-Cin ... .908

Stolen Bases
Hack-Chi 16
Lavagetto-Bro 15
Koy-Bro 15
Vaughan-Pit 14
Gutteridge-StL..... 14

Stolen Base Average

Stolen Base Runs

Fielding Runs
Young-Pit 31.8
Herman-Chi 24.8
Bartell-NY 22.4
Vaughan-Pit 18.3
Arnovich-Phi 16.7

Total Player Rating
Vaughan-Pit 6.5
Ott-NY 6.2
Lombardi-Cin..... 3.7
Hack-Chi 3.7
Mize-StL 3.7

Wins
Lee-Chi........... 22
Derringer-Cin..... 21
Bryant-Chi 19
Weiland-StL 16

Win Percentage
Lee-Chi........... .710
Bryant-Chi .... .633
Brown-Pit .... .625
VanderMeer-Cin ... .600
Derringer-Cin...... .600

Games
Coffman-NY 51
Brown-Pit 51
McGee-StL 47
Mulcahy-Phi....... 46

Complete Games
Derringer-Cin 26
Turner-Bos 22
Walters-Phi-Cin ... 20
MacFayden-Bos ... 19
Lee-Chi........... 19

Shutouts
Lee-Chi........... 9
MacFayden-Bos ... 5
Warneke-StL 4
Derringer-Cin...... 4

Saves
Coffman-NY 12
Root-Chi.......... 8
Hamlin-Bro 6
Errickson-Bos 6

Innings Pitched
Derringer-Cin 307.0
Lee-Chi......... 291.0
Bryant-Chi 270.1
Turner-Bos 268.0
Mulcahy-Phi..... 267.1

Fewest Hits/Game
VanderMeer-Cin .. 7.07
Bauers-Pit 7.67
Bryant-Chi 7.82
MacFayden-Bos .. 8.52
Klinger-Pit 8.59

Fewest BB/Game
Davis-StL 1.40
Derringer-Cin 1.44
Hubbell-NY 1.66
Root-Chi......... 1.68
Turner-Bos 1.81

Strikeouts
Bryant-Chi 135
Derringer-Cin 132
VanderMeer-Cin ... 125
Lee-Chi.......... 121

Strikeouts/Game
Hubbell-NY 5.23
VanderMeer-Cin .. 4.99
Weiland-StL 4.61
Bryant-Chi 4.49

Ratio
Hubbell-NY 10.36
Derringer-Cin.... 10.67
Root-Chi........ 10.92
Turner-Bos 10.95
Lee-Chi.......... 11.04

Earned Run Average
Lee-Chi........... 2.66
Root-Chi......... 2.86
Derringer-Cin..... 2.93
MacFayden-Bos .. 2.95
Klinger-Pit 2.99

Adjusted ERA
Lee-Chi.......... 144
Root-Chi......... 134
Fitzsimmons-Bro . 129
Klinger-Pit 127
Derringer-Cin..... 124

Opponents' Batting Avg.
VanderMeer-Cin .. .213
Bauers-Pit .... .233
Bryant-Chi .... .235
MacFayden-Bos .. .247
Schumacher-NY ...248

Opponents' On Base Pct.
Hubbell-NY ...... .285
Derringer-Cin ..... .291
Root-Chi......... .294
Lohrman-NY ..... .294
Schumacher-NY ...299

Starter Runs
Lee-Chi.......... 36.3
Derringer-Cin..... 29.1
Bryant-Chi 20.6
MacFayden-Bos .. 20.3
Bauers-Pit 19.2

Adjusted Starter Runs
Lee-Chi.......... 37.6
Derringer-Cin.... 24.3
Bryant-Chi 21.8
Fitzsimmons-Bro . 19.8
Bauers-Pit 19.4

Clutch Pitching Index
Lee-Chi........... 119
Pressnell-Bro 111
Blanton-Pit 111
Tamulis-Bro 110
Fette-Bos 110

Relief Runs
Brown-NY 19.8
Russell-Chi 5.0
Coffman-NY 3.8

Adjusted Relief Runs
Brown-NY 19.6
Russell-Chi 5.5
Coffman-NY 3.5

Relief Ranking
Brown-NY 18.1
Coffman-NY 4.3
Russell-Chi 3.7

Total Pitcher Index
Lee-Chi........... 4.1
Fitzsimmons-Bro . 2.6
Bryant-Chi 2.4
Derringer-Cin..... 2.3
Bauers-Pit 2.0

Total Baseball Ranking
Vaughan-Pit 6.5
Ott-NY 6.2
Lee-Chi.......... 4.1
Lombardi-Cin..... 3.7
Hack-Chi 3.7

TEAM	G	W	L	PCT	GB	R	OR	AB	H	2B	3B	HR	BB	SO	AVG	OBP	SLG	PRO	PRO+	BR	/A	PF	CHI	RC	SB	CS	SBA	SBR
NY	157	99	53	.651		966	710	5410	1480	283	63	174	749	616	.274	.366	.446	.812	111	77	81	100	104	926	91	28	76	11
BOS	150	88	61	.591	9.5	902	751	5229	1566	298	56	98	650	463	.299	.378	.434	.812	105	87	49	105	100	881	55	51	52	-14
CLE	153	86	66	.566	13	847	782	5356	1506	300	89	113	550	605	.281	.350	.434	.784	104	9	25	98	102	832	83	36	70	3
DET	155	84	70	.545	16	862	795	5270	1434	219	52	137	693	581	.272	.359	.411	.770	94	0	-47	106	104	812	76	41	65	-2
WAS	152	75	76	.497	23.5	814	873	5474	1602	278	72	85	573	379	.293	.362	.416	.778	108	12	70	93	96	845	65	37	64	-3
CHI	149	65	83	.439	32	709	752	5199	1439	239	55	67	514	489	.277	.343	.383	.726	86	-91	-109	102	101	700	56	39	59	-7
STL	156	55	97	.362	44	755	962	5333	1498	273	36	92	590	528	.281	.355	.397	.752	95	-38	-36	100	96	774	51	40	56	-9
PHI	154	53	99	.349	46	726	956	5229	1410	243	62	98	605	590	.270	.348	.396	.744	95	-57	-36	97	97	741	65	53	55	-12
TOT	613					6581		42500	11935	2133	485	864	4924	4251	.281	.358	.415	.773							542	325	63	-32

TEAM	CG	SH	SV	IP	H	H/G	HR	BB	SO	RAT	ERA	ERA+	OAV	OOB	PR	/A	PF	CPI	FA	E	DP	FW	PW	BW	SBW	DIF
NY	91	11	13	1382	1436	9.4	85	566	567	13.1	3.91	116	.268	.339	134	95	95	106	.973	169	177	.5	8.6	7.3	1.4	5.3
BOS	67	10	15	1316[1]	1472	10.1	102	528	484	13.8	4.46	111	.281	.349	48	70	103	103	.968	190	172	-1.1	6.3	4.4	-.9	4.8
CLE	68	5	17	1353	1416	9.4	100	681	717	14.1	4.60	101	.268	.355	29	7	97	99	.974	151	145	1.2	.6	2.3	.6	5.2
DET	75	3	11	1348[1]	1532	10.2	110	608	435	14.4	4.79	104	.287	.361	1	32	104	103	.976	147	172	1.6	2.9	-4.2	.2	6.6
WAS	59	6	11	1360[1]	1472	9.7	92	655	515	14.3	4.94	91	.276	.358	-22	-64	94	94	.970	180	179	-.5	-5.8	6.3	.0	-1.7
CHI	83	5	9	1316[1]	1449	9.9	101	550	432	13.8	4.36	112	.279	.350	62	78	102	106	.967	196	155	-1.6	7.0	-9.8	-.3	-4.4
STL	71	3	7	1344[2]	1584	10.6	132	737	632	15.7	5.80	86	.295	.382	-151	-124	104	96	.975	145	163	1.8	-11.2	-3.3	-.4	-7.9
PHI	56	4	12	1324	1573	10.7	142	599	473	14.9	5.48	88	.292	.365	-101	-95	101	96	.965	206	119	-1.8	-8.6	-3.3	-.7	-8.6
TOT	570	47	95	10745		10.0				14.3	4.79		.281	.358					.971	1384	1282					

Runs
Greenberg-Det ... 144
Foxx-Bos ... 139
Gehringer-Det 133
Rolfe-NY ... 132
DiMaggio-NY 129

Hits
Vosmik-Bos 201
Cramer-Bos 198
Almada-Was-StL .. 197
Foxx-Bos 197
Rolfe-NY 196

Doubles
Cronin-Bos 51
McQuinn-StL 42
Trosky-Cle 40
Chapman-Bos 40
Vosmik-Bos 37

Triples
Heath-Cle 18
Averill-Cle 15
DiMaggio-NY 13

Home Runs
Greenberg-Det ... 58
Foxx-Bos 50
Clift-StL 34
York-Det 33
DiMaggio-NY 32

Total Bases
Foxx-Bos 398
Greenberg-Det ... 380
DiMaggio-NY 348
Johnson-Phi 311
Heath-Cle 302

Runs Batted In
Foxx-Bos 175
Greenberg-Det ... 146
DiMaggio-NY 140
York-Det 127
Clift-StL 118

Runs Produced
Foxx-Bos 264
DiMaggio-NY 237
Greenberg-Det ... 232
Gehringer-Det 220
Clift-StL 203

Bases On Balls
Greenberg-Det ... 119
Foxx-Bos 119
Clift-StL 118
Gehringer-Det ... 113
Gehrig-NY 107

Batting Average
Foxx-Bos 349
Heath-Cle 343
Chapman-Bos 340
Myer-Was 336
Travis-Was 335

On Base Percentage
Foxx-Bos 462
Myer-Was 454
Greenberg-Det 438
Averill-Cle 429
Cronin-Bos 428

Slugging Average
Foxx-Bos 704
Greenberg-Det ...683
Heath-Cle 602
DiMaggio-NY 581
York-Det 579

Production
Foxx-Bos 1.166
Greenberg-Det ..1.122
York-Det 995
Heath-Cle 985
Dickey-NY 981

Adjusted Production
Foxx-Bos 180
Greenberg-Det ... 167
Heath-Cle 146
Dickey-NY 144
Clift-StL 143

Batter Runs
Foxx-Bos 78.2
Greenberg-Det ... 66.0
Clift-StL 37.7
Cronin-Bos 34.8
York-Det 33.9

Adjusted Batter Runs
Foxx-Bos 73.9
Greenberg-Det ... 60.7
Clift-StL 37.9
Johnson-Phi 35.0
Averill-Cle 33.3

Clutch Hitting Index
Higgins-Bos 164
Heffner-StL 149
Doerr-Bos 125
Radcliff-Chi 123
R.Ferrell-Was 121

Runs Created
Foxx-Bos 189
Greenberg-Det ... 172
DiMaggio-NY 136
Clift-StL 133
Gehrig-NY 131

Total Average
Foxx-Bos 1.392
Greenberg-Det ..1.306
Clift-StL 1.104
York-Det 1.104
Dickey-NY 1.083

Stolen Bases
Crosetti-NY 27
Lary-Cle 23
Werber-Phi 19
Lewis-Was 17
Fox-Det 16

Stolen Base Average
Lary-Cle 79.3
Fox-Det 69.6
Crosetti-NY 69.2
Lewis-Was 65.4
Werber-Phi 55.9

Stolen Base Runs
Gehringer-Det 3.6
Rolfe-NY 3.3
Lary-Cle 3.3
Hale-Cle 1.8

Fielding Runs
Gordon-NY 23.7
Crosetti-NY 17.6
Clift-StL 14.0
Johnson-Phi 10.3
Cramer-Bos 8.7

Total Player Rating
Foxx-Bos 5.5
Clift-StL 4.8
Greenberg-Det ... 4.3
Cronin-Bos 4.3
Dickey-NY 3.7

Wins
Ruffing-NY 21
Newsom-StL 20
Gomez-NY 18
Harder-Cle 17
Feller-Cle 17

Win Percentage
Ruffing-NY 750
Pearson-NY 696
Harder-Cle 630
Stratton-Chi 625
Feller-Cle 607

Games
Humphries-Cle 45
Newsom-StL 44
E.Smith-Phi 43
Bagby-Bos 43
Appleton-Was 43

Complete Games
Newsom-StL 31
Ruffing-NY 22
Gomez-NY 20
Feller-Cle 20
Caster-Phi 20

Shutouts
Gomez-NY 4
Wilson-Bos 3
Ruffing-NY 3
Leonard-Was 3

Saves
Murphy-NY 11
McKain-Bos 6
Humphries-Cle 6
Potter-Phi 5
Appleton-Was 5

Innings Pitched
Newsom-StL 329.2
Caster-Phi 281.1
Feller-Cle 277.2
Ruffing-NY 247.1
Lee-Chi......... 245.1

Fewest Hits/Game
Feller-Cle 7.29
Allen-Cle 8.51
Pearson-NY 8.82
Rigney-Chi 8.84
Hadley-NY 8.87

Fewest BB/Game
Leonard-Was 2.14
Harder-Cle 2.33
Lyons-Chi 2.40
Chandler-NY 2.46
Thomas-Phi 2.63

Strikeouts
Feller-Cle 240
Newsom-StL 226
H.Mills-StL 134
Gomez-NY 129
Ruffing-NY 127

Strikeouts/Game
Feller-Cle 7.78
Newsom-StL 6.17
H.Mills-StL 5.73
Grove-Bos 5.44
Allen-Cle 5.04

Ratio
Leonard-Was 11.32
Ruffing-NY 11.94
Stratton-Chi 12.03
Chandler-NY 12.14
Harder-Cle 12.15

Earned Run Average
Grove-Bos 3.08
Ruffing-NY 3.31
Gomez-NY 3.35
Leonard-Was 3.43
Lee-Chi......... 3.49

Adjusted ERA
Grove-Bos 160
Lee-Chi......... 140
Rigney-Chi 138
Ruffing-NY 137
Gomez-NY 135

Opponents' Batting Avg.
Feller-Cle 220
Allen-Cle 246
Hadley-NY 254
Stratton-Chi 255
Rigney-Chi 256

Opponents' On Base Pct.
Leonard-Was 305
Stratton-Chi 315
Ruffing-NY 317
Harder-Cle 319
Grove-Bos 319

Starter Runs
Ruffing-NY 40.6
Gomez-NY 38.2
Lee-Chi.......... 35.6
Leonard-Was 33.8
Grove-Bos 31.1

Adjusted Starter Runs
Lee-Chi.......... 38.4
Grove-Bos 33.7
Ruffing-NY 33.6
Gomez-NY 31.4
Leonard-Was 27.0

Clutch Pitching Index
Lyons-Chi 125
Gill-Det 119
Grove-Bos 118
Rigney-Chi 117
Ruffing-NY 110

Relief Runs
Murphy-NY 5.6
McKain-Bos 3.0

Adjusted Relief Runs
McKain-Bos 4.6
Murphy-NY 3.0

Relief Ranking
McKain-Bos 4.4
Murphy-NY 3.8

Total Pitcher Index
Lee-Chi........... 4.1
Ruffing-NY 3.9
Grove-Bos 3.1
Gomez-NY 2.9
Leonard-Was 2.9

Total Baseball Ranking
Foxx-Bos 5.5
Clift-StL 4.8
Greenberg-Det ... 4.3
Cronin-Bos 4.3
Lee-Chi........... 4.1

1939 National League

TEAM	G	W	L	PCT	GB	R	OR	AB	H	2B	3B	HR	BB	SO	AVG	OBP	SLG	PRO	PRO+	BR	/A	PF	CHI	RC	SB	CS	SBA	SBR
CIN	156	97	57	.630		767	595	5378	1493	269	60	98	500	538	.278	.343	.405	.748	106	51	47	101	102	759	46			
STL	155	92	61	.601	4.5	779	633	5447	1601	332	62	98	475	566	.294	.354	.432	.786	110	122	79	106	94	834	44			
BRO	157	84	69	.549	12.5	708	645	5350	1420	265	57	78	564	639	.265	.338	.380	.718	96	0	-25	104	102	697	59			
CHI	156	84	70	.545	13	724	678	5293	1407	263	62	91	523	553	.266	.336	.391	.727	99	10	-2	102	103	702	61			
NY	151	77	74	.510	18.5	703	685	5129	1395	211	38	116	498	499	.272	.340	.396	.736	103	28	23	101	101	683	26			
PIT	153	68	85	.444	28.5	666	721	5269	1453	261	60	63	477	420	.276	.338	.384	.722	102	4	15	98	97	687	44			
BOS	152	63	88	.417	32.5	572	659	5286	1395	199	39	56	366	494	.264	.314	.348	.662	91	-117	-69	93	104	575	41			
PHI	152	45	106	.298	50.5	553	856	5133	1341	232	40	49	421	486	.261	.318	.351	.669	89	-98	-79	97	99	570	47			
TOT	616					5472		42285	11505	2032	418	649	3824	4195	.272	.335	.386	.721						368				

TEAM	CG	SH	SV	IP	H	H/G	HR	BB	SO	RAT	ERA	ERA+	OAV	OOB	PR	/A	PF	CPI	FA	E	DP	FW	PW	BW	SBW	DIF
CIN	86	13	9	1403²	1340	8.6	81	499	637	12.0	3.27	117	.255	.322	101	87	98	107	.974	162	170	.6	8.7	4.7		6.0
STL	45	18	32	1384²	1377	9.0	76	498	603	12.3	3.59	115	.260	.326	50	80	105	100	.971	177	140	-.2	8.0	7.9		-.2
BRO	69	9	13	1410¹	1431	9.1	93	399	528	11.9	3.64	110	.263	.317	43	60	103	97	.972	176	157	-.0	6.0	-2.5		4.0
CHI	72	8	13	1392¹	1504	9.7	74	430	584	12.6	3.80	104	.276	.331	18	21	101	101	.970	186	126	-.6	2.1	-.2		5.7
NY	55	6	20	1319	1412	9.6	86	477	505	13.1	4.07	96	.275	.340	-22	-20	100	100	.975	153	151	.8	-2.0	2.3		.4
PIT	53	10	15	1354	1537	10.2	70	423	464	13.2	4.15	92	.287	.342	-36	-49	98	100	.972	168	153	.1	-4.9	1.5		-5.2
BOS	68	11	15	1358¹	1400	9.3	63	513	430	12.8	3.71	100	.271	.339	31	-3	94	104	.971	181	178	-.6	-.3	-6.9		-4.7
PHI	67	3	12	1326²	1502	10.2	106	579	447	14.4	5.17	77	.289	.365	-185	-171	102	93	.970	171	136	-.0	-17.1	-7.9		-5.4
TOT	515	78	129	10949		9.5				12.8	3.92		.272	.335					.972	1374	1211					

Runs		Hits		Doubles		Triples		Home Runs		Total Bases	
Werber-Cin	115	McCormick-Cin	209	Slaughter-StL	52	Herman-Chi	18	Mize-StL	28	Mize-StL	353
Hack-Chi	112	Medwick-StL	201	Medwick-StL	48	Goodman-Cin	16	Ott-NY	27	McCormick-Cin	312
Herman-Chi	111	Mize-StL	197	Mize-StL	44	Mize-StL	14	Camilli-Bro	26	Medwick-StL	307
Camilli-Bro	105	Slaughter-StL	193	McCormick-Cin	41	Camilli-Bro	12	Leiber-Chi	24	Camilli-Bro	296
		Brown-StL	192					Lombardi-Cin	20	Slaughter-StL	291

Runs Batted In		Runs Produced		Bases On Balls		Batting Average		On Base Percentage		Slugging Average	
McCormick-Cin	128	McCormick-Cin	209	Camilli-Bro	110	Mize-StL	.349	Ott-NY	.449	Mize-StL	.626
Medwick-StL	117	Medwick-StL	201	Ott-NY	100	McCormick-Cin	.332	Mize-StL	.444	Ott-NY	.581
Mize-StL	108	Mize-StL	184	Mize-StL	92	Medwick-StL	.332	Camilli-Bro	.409	Camilli-Bro	.524
Camilli-Bro	104	Camilli-Bro	183	Werber-Cin	91	P.Waner-Pit	.328	Goodman-Cin	.401	Goodman-Cin	.515
Leiber-Chi	88	Herman-Chi	174	Lavagetto-Bro	78	Arnovich-Phi	.324	Arnovich-Phi	.397	Medwick-StL	.507

Production		Adjusted Production		Batter Runs		Adjusted Batter Runs		Clutch Hitting Index		Runs Created	
Mize-StL	1.070	Mize-StL	174	Mize-StL	68.7	Mize-StL	64.0	McCormick-Cin	136	Mize-StL	162
Ott-NY	1.030	Ott-NY	173	Ott-NY	45.9	Ott-NY	45.5	Bonura-NY	132	Camilli-Bro	128
Camilli-Bro	.933	Camilli-Bro	144	Camilli-Bro	41.8	Camilli-Bro	39.0	May-Phi	130	Medwick-StL	114
Goodman-Cin	.916	Goodman-Cin	144	Leiber-Chi	30.5	Leiber-Chi	29.6	Medwick-StL	130	Ott-NY	112
Medwick-StL	.886	West-Bos	139	Goodman-Cin	29.8	Goodman-Cin	29.5	G.Russell-Chi	125	McCormick-Cin	110

Total Average		Stolen Bases		Stolen Base Average	Stolen Base Runs	Fielding Runs		Total Player Rating	
Mize-StL	1.194	Handley-Pit	17			Slaughter-StL	15.8	Mize-StL	4.3
Ott-NY	1.194	Hack-Chi	17			Frey-Cin	15.1	Frey-Cin	4.0
Camilli-Bro	.995	Werber-Cin	15			Arnovich-Phi	14.9	Vaughan-Pit	3.9
Goodman-Cin	.941	Lavagetto-Bro	14			Jurges-NY	14.9	Ott-NY	3.6
Frey-Cin	.860	Hassett-Bos	13			Werber-Cin	12.6	Camilli-Bro	3.2

Wins		Win Percentage		Games		Complete Games		Shutouts		Saves	
Walters-Cin	27	Derringer-Cin	.781	Shoun-StL	53	Walters-Cin	31	Fette-Bos	6	Shoun-StL	9
Derringer-Cin	25	Walters-Cin	.711	Sewell-Pit	51	Derringer-Cin	28	Posedel-Bos	5	Bowman-StL	9
Davis-StL	22	French-Chi	.652	Bowman-StL	51	Lee-Chi	20	Derringer-Cin	5	Davis-StL	7
Hamlin-Bro	20	Gumbert-NY	.621	Davis-StL	49	Hamlin-Bro	19	McGee-StL	4	Brown-NY	7
Lee-Chi	19	Hamlin-Bro	.606	Brown-Pit	47	Posedel-Bos	18			Brown-Pit	7

Innings Pitched		Fewest Hits/Game		Fewest BB/Game		Strikeouts		Strikeouts/Game		Ratio	
Walters-Cin	319.0	Walters-Cin	7.05	Derringer-Cin	1.05	Passeau-Phi-Chi	137	Cooper-StL	5.55	Hubbell-NY	10.29
Derringer-Cin	301.0	Bowman-StL	7.49	Hubbell-NY	1.40	Walters-Cin	137	Tamulis-Bro	4.71	Walters-Cin	10.30
Lee-Chi	282.1	Moore-Cin	8.49	Davis-StL	1.74	Cooper-StL	130	French-Chi	4.55	Hamlin-Bro	10.31
Passeau-Phi-Chi	274.1	Hamlin-Bro	8.51	Hamlin-Bro	1.80	Derringer-Cin	128	Passeau-Phi-Chi	4.49	Derringer-Cin	10.73
Hamlin-Bro	269.2	Hubbell-NY	8.77	Root-Chi	1.83	Lee-Chi	105	Bowman-StL	4.15	Bowman-StL	10.74

Earned Run Average		Adjusted ERA		Opponents' Batting Avg.		Opponents' On Base Pct.		Starter Runs		Adjusted Starter Runs	
Walters-Cin	2.29	Walters-Cin	168	Walters-Cin	.220	Hubbell-NY	.280	Walters-Cin	57.8	Walters-Cin	54.7
Bowman-StL	2.60	Bowman-StL	158	Bowman-StL	.232	Hamlin-Bro	.285	Derringer-Cin	33.0	Derringer-Cin	30.1
Hubbell-NY	2.75	Hubbell-NY	143	Hamlin-Bro	.248	Walters-Cin	.291	Casey-Bro	24.9	Bowman-StL	28.4
Casey-Bro	2.93	Casey-Bro	137	Hubbell-NY	.249	Derringer-Cin	.295	Bowman-StL	24.7	Casey-Bro	27.7
Derringer-Cin	2.93	Derringer-Cin	131	Moore-Cin	.254	Bowman-StL	.302	Thompson-Cin	23.3	Thompson-Cin	21.8

Clutch Pitching Index		Relief Runs		Adjusted Relief Runs		Relief Ranking		Total Pitcher Index		Total Baseball Ranking	
Brown-Pit	120	J.Russell-Chi	1.9	Shoun-StL	4.1	Shoun-StL	2.2	Walters-Cin	8.0	Walters-Cin	8.0
Shoffner-Bos-Cin	115	Shoun-StL	1.8	J.Russell-Chi	2.0	J.Russell-Chi	2.1	Casey-Bro	3.1	Mize-StL	4.3
Casey-Bro	113							Derringer-Cin	2.8	Frey-Cin	4.0
Cooper-StL	113							Davis-StL	2.8	Vaughan-Pit	3.9
Moore-Cin	113							Bowman-StL	2.5	Ott-NY	3.6

TEAM	G	W	L	PCT	GB	R	OR	AB	H	2B	3B	HR	BB	SO	AVG	OBP	SLG	PRO	PRO+	BR	/A	PF	CHI	RC	SB	CS	SBA	SBR
NY	152	106	45	.702		967	556	5300	1521	259	55	166	701	543	.287	.374	.451	.825	119	134	147	98	102	923	72	37	66	-1
BOS	152	89	62	.589	17	890	795	5308	1543	287	57	124	591	505	.291	.363	.436	.799	106	78	48	104	101	831	42	44	49	-14
CLE	154	87	67	.565	20.5	797	700	5316	1490	291	79	85	557	574	.280	.350	.413	.763	105	4	32	97	100	775	72	46	61	-6
CHI	155	85	69	.552	22.5	755	737	5279	1451	220	56	64	579	502	.275	.349	.374	.723	89	-62	-83	103	103	708	113	61	65	-3
DET	155	81	73	.526	26.5	849	762	5326	1487	277	67	124	620	592	.279	.356	.426	.782	99	43	-18	108	100	821	88	38	70	4
WAS	153	65	87	.428	41.5	702	797	5334	1483	249	79	44	547	460	.278	.346	.379	.725	98	-62	-3	93	96	718	94	47	67	0
PHI	153	55	97	.362	51.5	711	1022	5309	1438	282	55	98	503	532	.271	.336	.400	.736	96	-55	-38	98	97	713	60	34	64	-2
STL	156	43	111	.279	64.5	733	1035	5422	1453	242	50	91	559	606	.268	.339	.381	.720	88	-79	-96	102	100	706	48	38	56	-8
TOT	615					6404		42594	11866	2107	498	796	4657	4314	.279	.352	.407	.759							589	345	63	-30

TEAM	CG	SH	SV	IP	H	H/G	HR	BB	SO	RAT	ERA	ERA+	OAV	OOB	PR	/A	PF	CPI	FA	E	DP	FW	PW	BW	SBW	DIF
NY	87	15	26	1348²	1208	8.1	85	567	565	11.9	3.31	132	.241	.319	196	157	94	107	.978	126	159	2.9	14.5	13.5	.3	-.7
BOS	52	4	20	1350²	1533	10.2	77	543	539	14.0	4.56	104	.287	.355	9	25	102	102	.970	180	147	.0	2.3	4.4	-.9	7.6
CLE	69	10	13	1364²	1394	9.2	75	602	614	13.3	4.08	108	.267	.344	81	49	95	103	.970	180	148	.2	4.5	2.9	-.2	2.5
CHI	62	5	21	1377	1470	9.6	99	454	535	12.7	4.31	110	.275	.333	48	65	102	98	.972	167	140	1.0	6.0	-7.6	.0	8.6
DET	64	8	16	1367¹	1430	9.4	104	574	633	13.3	4.29	114	.268	.341	50	91	106	100	.967	198	147	-.6	8.4	-1.7	.7	-2.8
WAS	72	4	10	1354²	1420	9.4	75	602	521	13.6	4.60	94	.271	.348	2	-39	99	94	.966	205	167	-1.1	-3.6	-.3	.3	-6.3
PHI	50	6	12	1342²	1687	11.3	148	579	397	15.3	5.79	81	.307	.375	-175	-162	102	99	.964	210	131	-1.4	-14.9	-3.5	.2	-1.3
STL	56	3	3	1371¹	1724	11.3	133	739	516	16.4	6.01	81	.310	.393	-212	-175	105	100	.968	199	144	-.6	-16.1	-8.8	-.4	-8.0
TOT	512	55	121	10877		9.8				13.8	4.62		.279	.352					.969	1465	1183					

Runs
Rolfe-NY 139
Williams-Bos 131
Foxx-Bos 130
McCosky-Det. 120
Johnson-Phi 115

Hits
Rolfe-NY 213
McQuinn-StL 195
Keltner-Cle 191
McCosky-Det. 190
Williams-Bos 185

Doubles
Rolfe-NY 46
Williams-Bos 44
Greenberg-Det . . . 42
McQuinn-StL 37
Keltner-Cle 35

Triples
Lewis-Was 16
McCosky-Det 14
McQuinn-StL 13
Campbell-Cle 13

Home Runs
Foxx-Bos 35
Greenberg-Det . . . 33
Williams-Bos 31
DiMaggio-NY 30
Gordon-NY 28

Total Bases
Williams-Bos 344
Foxx-Bos 324
Rolfe-NY 321
McQuinn-StL 318
Greenberg-Det . . . 311

Runs Batted In
Williams-Bos 145
DiMaggio-NY 126
Johnson-Phi 114
Greenberg-Det . . . 112

Runs Produced
Williams-Bos 245
Johnson-Phi 206
Rolfe-NY 205
DiMaggio-NY 204
Foxx-Bos 200

Bases On Balls
Clift-StL 111
Williams-Bos 107
Appling-Chi 105
Selkirk-NY 103
Johnson-Phi 99

Batting Average
DiMaggio-NY 381
Foxx-Bos 360
Johnson-Phi 338
Trosky-Cle 335
Keller-NY 334

On Base Percentage
Foxx-Bos 464
Selkirk-NY 452
DiMaggio-NY 448
Keller-NY 447
Johnson-Phi 440

Slugging Average
Foxx-Bos 694
DiMaggio-NY 671
Greenberg-Det 622
Williams-Bos 609
Trosky-Cle 589

Production
Foxx-Bos 1.158
DiMaggio-NY 1.119
Williams-Bos 1.045
Greenberg-Det . . 1.042
Trosky-Cle 994

Adjusted Production
DiMaggio-NY 185
Foxx-Bos 185
Williams-Bos 158
Trosky-Cle 157
Johnson-Phi 156

Batter Runs
Foxx-Bos 66.1
Williams-Bos 56.3
DiMaggio-NY 56.0
Greenberg-Det . . . 47.3
Johnson-Phi 45.7

Adjusted Batter Runs
Foxx-Bos 63.2
DiMaggio-NY 57.1
Williams-Bos 52.9
Johnson-Phi 47.5
Greenberg-Det . . . 41.3

Clutch Hitting Index
Wright-Was 140
Walker-Cle 131
Keller-NY 128
Vosmik-Bos 127
McNair-Chi 126

Runs Created
Williams-Bos 157
Foxx-Bos 150
DiMaggio-NY 139
Johnson-Phi 138
Greenberg-Det . . . 136

Total Average
Foxx-Bos 1.304
DiMaggio-NY 1.242
Williams-Bos 1.161
Greenberg-Det . . 1.152
Selkirk-NY 1.121

Stolen Bases
Case-Was 51
Kreevich-Chi 23
Fox-Det 23
McCosky-Det 20

Stolen Base Average
McCosky-Det. 83.3
Kuhel-Chi 78.3
Chapman-Cle 75.0
Case-Was 75.0
Walker-Chi 73.9

Stolen Base Runs
Case-Was 5.1
McCosky-Det 3.6
Welaj-Was 2.7
Kuhel-Chi 2.4
Henrich-NY 2.1

Fielding Runs
Doerr-Bos 27.3
Kreevich-Chi 16.1
Tebbetts-Det 14.5
Lewis-Was 13.6
Clift-StL 12.0

Total Player Rating
DiMaggio-NY 5.6
Foxx-Bos 5.1
Johnson-Phi 4.6
Williams-Bos 4.5
Dickey-NY 3.8

Wins
Feller-Cle 24
Ruffing-NY 21
Newsom-StL-Det. . . 20
Leonard-Was 20
Bridges-Det 17

Win Percentage
Grove-Bos 789
Dean-Phi 750
Feller-Cle 727
Leonard-Was 714
Bridges-Det 708

Games
Brown-Chi 61
Dean-Phi 54
Dickman-Bos 48
Heving-Bos 46

Complete Games
Newsom-StL-Det. . . 24
Feller-Cle 24
Ruffing-NY 22
Leonard-Was 21
Grove-Bos 17

Shutouts
Ruffing-NY 5
Feller-Cle 4
Newsom-StL-Det. . . . 3

Saves
Murphy-NY 19
Brown-Chi 18
Heving-Bos 7
Dean-Phi 7
Appleton-Was 6

Innings Pitched
Feller-Cle 296.2
Newsom-StL-Det. . 291.2
Leonard-Was 269.1
Lee-Chi. 235.0
Ruffing-NY 233.1

Fewest Hits/Game
Feller-Cle 6.89
Hadley-NY 7.71
Gomez-NY 7.86
Ruffing-NY 8.14
Chase-Was 8.34

Fewest BB/Game
Lyons-Chi 1.36
Leonard-Was 1.97
Beckmann-Phi 2.38
Lee-Chi. 2.68
Grove-Bos 2.73

Strikeouts
Feller-Cle 246
Newsom-StL-Det. . 192
Bridges-Det 129
Rigney-Chi 119
Chase-Was 118

Strikeouts/Game
Feller-Cle 7.46
Newsom-StL-Det. . 5.92
Bridges-Det 5.86
Rigney-Chi 4.90
Gomez-NY 4.64

Ratio
Lyons-Chi 9.85
Ruffing-NY 11.11
Leonard-Was 11.26
Grove-Bos 11.26
Feller-Cle 11.29

Earned Run Average
Grove-Bos 2.54
Lyons-Chi 2.76
Feller-Cle 2.85
Ruffing-NY 2.93
Hadley-NY 2.98

Adjusted ERA
Grove-Bos 186
Lyons-Chi 171
Feller-Cle 154
Ruffing-NY 149
Hadley-NY 146

Opponents' Batting Avg.
Feller-Cle 210
Gomez-NY 235
Hadley-NY 237
Ruffing-NY 240
Bridges-Det 243

Opponents' On Base Pct.
Lyons-Chi 276
Ruffing-NY 301
Feller-Cle 303
Bridges-Det 304
Leonard-Was 305

Starter Runs
Feller-Cle 58.3
Grove-Bos 44.0
Ruffing-NY 43.8
Lyons-Chi 35.6
Newsom-StL-Det. . 33.7

Adjusted Starter Runs
Feller-Cle 51.1
Grove-Bos 46.3
Newsom-StL-Det. . 42.3
Lyons-Chi 37.8
Ruffing-NY 36.9

Clutch Pitching Index
Hadley-NY 132
Grove-Bos 126
Trout-Det 116
Harder-Cle 116
Milnar-Cle 110

Relief Runs
Heving-Bos 10.9
Brown-Chi 9.7
Dickman-Bos 2.3
Murphy-NY 1.5
Appleton-Was 7

Adjusted Relief Runs
Heving-Bos 12.2
Brown-Chi 11.2
Dickman-Bos. 3.7

Relief Ranking
Brown-Chi 21.7
Heving-Bos 16.1
Dickman-Bos. 3.6

Total Pitcher Index
Feller-Cle 5.6
Ruffing-NY 4.3
Grove-Bos 4.2
Lyons-Chi 4.1
Newsom-StL-Det. . 3.6

Total Baseball Ranking
DiMaggio-NY 5.6
Feller-Cle 5.6
Foxx-Bos 5.2
Johnson-Phi 4.6
Williams-Bos 4.5

TEAM	G	W	L	PCT	GB	R	OR	AB	H	2B	3B	HR	BB	SO	AVG	OBP	SLG	PRO	PRO+	BR	/A	PF	CHI	RC	SB	CS	SBA	SBR
CIN	155	100	53	.654		707	528	5372	1427	264	38	89	453	503	.266	.327	.379	.706	100	6	-1	101	103	672	72			
BRO	156	88	65	.575	12	697	621	5470	1421	256	70	93	522	570	.260	.327	.383	.710	96	15	-27	106	98	692	56			
STL	156	84	69	.549	16	747	699	5499	1514	266	61	119	479	610	.275	.336	.411	.747	106	83	44	106	96	764	97			
PIT	156	78	76	.506	22.5	809	783	5466	1511	276	68	76	553	494	.276	.346	.394	.740	112	84	90	99	104	757	69			
CHI	154	75	79	.487	25.5	681	636	5389	1441	272	48	86	482	566	.267	.331	.384	.715	106	25	39	98	97	691	63			
NY	152	72	80	.474	27.5	663	659	5324	1423	201	46	91	453	478	.267	.329	.374	.703	99	3	-2	101	98	653	45			
BOS	152	65	87	.428	34.5	623	745	5329	1366	219	50	59	402	581	.256	.311	.349	.660	93	-83	-47	95	108	581	48			
PHI	153	50	103	.327	50	494	750	5137	1225	180	35	75	435	527	.238	.300	.331	.631	83	-133	-108	96	96	512	25			
TOT	617					5421		42986	11328	1934	416	688	3779	4329	.264	.326	.376	.702							475			

TEAM	CG	SH	SV	IP	H	H/G	HR	BB	SO	RAT	ERA	ERA+	OAV	OOB	PR	/A	PF	CPI	FA	E	DP	FW	PW	BW	SBW	DIF
CIN	91	10	11	1407²	1263	8.1	73	445	557	11.0	3.05	124	.240	.302	125	115	98	102	.981	117	158	2.9	11.6	-.1		9.1
BRO	65	17	14	1433	1366	8.6	101	393	639	11.2	3.50	114	.248	.302	56	79	104	95	.970	183	110	-.3	8.0	-2.7		6.6
STL	71	10	14	1396	1457	9.4	83	488	550	12.7	3.83	104	.266	.329	3	24	104	102	.971	174	134	.1	2.4	4.5		.5
PIT	49	8	24	1388²	1569	10.2	72	492	491	13.6	4.36	87	.283	.345	-79	-85	99	99	.966	217	161	-2.0	-8.6	9.1		2.5
CHI	69	12	14	1392	1418	9.2	74	430	564	12.1	3.54	106	.262	.319	47	32	97	103	.968	199	143	-1.2	3.2	3.9		-8.0
NY	57	11	18	1360¹	1383	9.1	110	473	606	12.4	3.79	102	.262	.325	9	14	101	104	.977	139	132	1.6	1.4	-.2		-6.8
BOS	76	9	12	1359	1444	9.6	83	573	435	13.6	4.36	85	.274	.349	-77	-97	97	100	.970	184	169	-.6	-9.8	-4.8		4.2
PHI	66	5	8	1357	1429	9.5	92	475	485	12.8	4.40	89	.270	.333	-83	-75	101	93	.970	181	136	-.4	-7.6	-10.9		-7.6
TOT	544	82	115	11093²		9.2				12.4	3.85		.264	.326					.972	1394	1143					

Runs		Hits		Doubles		Triples		Home Runs		Total Bases	
Vaughan-Pit	113	F.McCormick-Cin	191	F.McCormick-Cin	44	Vaughan-Pit	15	Mize-StL	43	Mize-StL	368
Mize-StL	111	Hack-Chi	191	Vaughan-Pit	40	Ross-Bos	14	Nicholson-Chi	25	F.McCormick-Cin	298
Werber-Cin	105	Mize-StL	182	Gleeson-Chi	39	Slaughter-StL	13	Rizzo-Pit-Cin-Phi	24	Medwick-StL-Bro	280
Frey-Cin	102	Vaughan-Pit	178	Hack-Chi	38	Mize-StL	13	Camilli-Bro	23	Camilli-Bro	271
Hack-Chi	101	Medwick-StL-Bro	175	Walker-Bro	37	Camilli-Bro	13			Vaughan-Pit	269

Runs Batted In		Runs Produced		Bases On Balls		Batting Average		On Base Percentage		Slugging Average	
Mize-StL	137	Mize-StL	205	Fletcher-Pit	119	Hack-Chi	.317	Fletcher-Pit	.418	Mize-StL	.636
F.McCormick-Cin	127	Vaughan-Pit	201	Ott-NY	100	Mize-StL	.314	Ott-NY	.407	Nicholson-Chi	.534
VanRobays-Pit	116	F.McCormick-Cin	201	Camilli-Bro	89	Gleeson-Chi	.313	Mize-StL	.404	Camilli-Bro	.529
Fletcher-Pit	104	VanRobays-Pit	187	Vaughan-Pit	88	F.McCormick-Cin	.309	Camilli-Bro	.397	Slaughter-StL	.504
Young-NY	101	Fletcher-Pit	182	Mize-StL	82	Walker-Bro	.308	Hack-Chi	.395	F.McCormick-Cin	.482

Production		Adjusted Production		Batter Runs		Adjusted Batter Runs		Clutch Hitting Index		Runs Created	
Mize-StL	1.039	Mize-StL	173	Mize-StL	63.9	Mize-StL	59.6	VanRobays-Pit	167	Mize-StL	152
Camilli-Bro	.926	Nicholson-Chi	148	Camilli-Bro	38.7	Camilli-Bro	34.5	Fletcher-Pit	151	Camilli-Bro	114
Nicholson-Chi	.899	Camilli-Bro	144	Fletcher-Pit	31.8	Fletcher-Pit	32.4	F.McCormick-Cin	141	Vaughan-Pit	113
Slaughter-StL	.874	Gleeson-Chi	139	Ott-NY	31.7	Ott-NY	31.1	Young-NY	134	Hack-Chi	112
Ott-NY	.864	Fletcher-Pit	137	Vaughan-Pit	28.8	Nicholson-Chi	29.9	West-Bos	131	Ott-NY	107

Total Average		Stolen Bases		Stolen Base Average	Stolen Base Runs	Fielding Runs		Total Player Rating	
Mize-StL	1.135	Frey-Cin	22			Witek-NY	19.0	Vaughan-Pit	5.0
Camilli-Bro	1.005	Hack-Chi	21			Herman-Chi	18.9	Hack-Chi	4.4
Fletcher-Pit	.930	Moore-StL	18			Frey-Cin	18.2	Mize-StL	3.8
Ott-NY	.915	Werber-Cin	16			Moore-StL	16.8	Miller-Bos	3.4
Nicholson-Chi	.901	Reese-Bro	15			Miller-Bos	14.7	Frey-Cin	3.1

Wins		Win Percentage		Games		Complete Games		Shutouts		Saves	
Walters-Cin	22	Fitzsimmons-Bro	.889	Shoun-StL	54	Walters-Cin	29	Wyatt-Bro	5	Brown-NY	7
Passeau-Chi	20	Sewell-Pit	.762	Brown-Pit	48	Derringer-Cin	26	Salvo-Bos	5	Brown-Pit	7
Derringer-Cin	20	Walters-Cin	.688	Passeau-Chi	46	Mulcahy-Phi	21			Beggs-Cin	7
		Thompson-Cin	.640	Casey-Bro	44	Passeau-Chi	20			Shoun-StL	5
		Derringer-Cin	.625	Raffensberger-Chi	43	Higbe-Phi	20			Passeau-Chi	5

Innings Pitched		Fewest Hits/Game		Fewest BB/Game		Strikeouts		Strikeouts/Game		Ratio	
Walters-Cin	305.0	Walters-Cin	7.11	Derringer-Cin	1.46	Higbe-Phi	137	Melton-NY	4.91	Derringer-Cin	9.95
Derringer-Cin	296.2	Higbe-Phi	7.70	Turner-Cin	1.54	Wyatt-Bro	124	Schumacher-NY	4.88	Walters-Cin	9.97
Higbe-Phi	283.0	Thompson-Cin	7.87	Hamlin-Bro	1.68	Passeau-Chi	124	Wyatt-Bro	4.66	Passeau-Chi	10.33
Passeau-Chi	280.2	Casey-Bro	7.95	Davis-StL-Bro	1.79	Schumacher-NY	123	Hamlin-Bro	4.49	Turner-Cin	10.54
Mulcahy-Phi	280.0	Sullivan-Bos	7.97	Warneke-StL	1.82			Higbe-Phi	4.36	Tamulis-Bro	10.73

Earned Run Average		Adjusted ERA		Opponents' Batting Avg.		Opponents' On Base Pct.		Starter Runs		Adjusted Starter Runs	
Walters-Cin	2.48	Walters-Cin	153	Walters-Cin	.220	Derringer-Cin	.276	Walters-Cin	46.4	Walters-Cin	44.3
Passeau-Chi	2.50	Passeau-Chi	150	Higbe-Phi	.232	Passeau-Chi	.278	Passeau-Chi	42.0	Passeau-Chi	38.9
Sewell-Pit	2.80	Sewell-Pit	136	Thompson-Cin	.233	Walters-Cin	.283	Derringer-Cin	25.8	Derringer-Cin	23.8
Turner-Cin	2.89	Turner-Cin	131	Passeau-Chi	.237	Tamulis-Bro	.288	Sewell-Pit	22.1	Warneke-StL	21.8
Olsen-Chi	2.97	Hamlin-Bro	131	Casey-Bro	.237	Hamlin-Bro	.292	Turner-Cin	20.0	Sewell-Pit	21.3

Clutch Pitching Index		Relief Runs		Adjusted Relief Runs		Relief Ranking		Total Pitcher Index		Total Baseball Ranking	
Errickson-Bos	124	Beggs-Cin	15.8	Beggs-Cin	15.3	Beggs-Cin	30.0	Walters-Cin	5.0	Vaughan-Pit	5.0
Olsen-Chi	119	Russell-StL	8.1	Russell-StL	8.9	Russell-StL	10.8	Passeau-Chi	4.9	Walters-Cin	5.0
Schumacher-NY	113	Raffensberger-Chi	6.0	Raffensberger-Chi	4.8	Raffensberger-Chi	6.2	Sewell-Pit	2.7	Passeau-Chi	4.9
Turner-Cin	113	MacFayden-Pit	3.0	Brown-NY	2.9	Brown-NY	3.6	Warneke-StL	2.6	Hack-Chi	4.4
Hamlin-Bro	111	Joiner-NY	2.7	Joiner-NY	2.9	Pressnell-Bro	3.6	Schumacher-NY	2.4	Mize-StL	3.8

TEAM	G	W	L	PCT	GB	R	OR	AB	H	2B	3B	HR	BB	SO	AVG	OBP	SLG	PRO	PRO+	BR	/A	PF	CHI	RC	SB	CS	SBA	SBR
DET	155	90	64	.584		888	717	5418	1549	312	65	134	664	556	.286	.366	.442	.808	105	124	49	110	97	913	66	39	63	-4
CLE	155	89	65	.578	1	710	637	5361	1422	287	61	101	519	597	.265	.332	.398	.730	98	-43	-21	97	99	724	53	36	60	-6
NY	155	88	66	.571	2	817	671	5286	1371	243	66	155	648	606	.259	.344	.418	.762	107	25	56	96	103	789	59	36	62	-4
CHI	155	82	72	.532	8	735	672	5386	1499	238	63	73	496	569	.278	.340	.387	.727	93	-41	-50	101	102	713	52	60	46	-20
BOS	154	82	72	.532	8	872	825	5481	1566	301	80	145	590	597	.286	.356	.449	.805	110	109	78	104	97	889	55	49	53	-13
STL	156	67	87	.435	23	757	882	5416	1423	278	58	118	556	642	.263	.333	.401	.734	94	-35	-51	102	103	744	51	40	56	-9
WAS	154	64	90	.416	26	665	811	5365	1453	266	67	52	468	504	.271	.331	.374	.705	95	-85	-36	94	100	690	94	40	70	4
PHI	154	54	100	.351	36	703	932	5304	1391	242	53	105	556	656	.262	.334	.387	.721	95	-53	-37	98	100	704	48	33	59	-5
TOT	619					6147		43017	11674	2167	513	883	4497	4727	.271	.342	.407	.750							478	333	59	-56

TEAM	CG	SH	SV	IP	H	H/G	HR	BB	SO	RAT	ERA	ERA+	OAV	OOB	PR	/A	PF	CPI	FA	E	DP	FW	PW	BW	SBW	DIF
DET	59	10	23	1375[1]	1425	9.3	102	570	752	13.2	4.01	119	.266	.338	57	114	109	105	.968	194	116	-.7	10.8	4.6	.3	-2.0
CLE	72	13	22	1375	1328	8.7	86	512	686	12.2	3.63	116	.254	.324	115	89	96	102	.975	149	164	1.7	8.4	-2.0	.0	3.8
NY	76	10	14	1373	1389	9.1	119	511	559	12.6	3.89	104	.261	.328	76	22	92	104	.975	152	158	1.6	2.1	5.3	.3	1.8
CHI	83	10	18	1386[2]	1335	8.7	111	480	574	11.9	3.74	118	.250	.313	99	105	101	96	.969	185	125	-.2	9.9	-4.7	-1.2	1.2
BOS	51	4	16	1379[2]	1568	10.2	124	625	613	14.5	4.89	92	.284	.359	-77	-60	103	101	.972	173	156	.4	-5.7	7.4	-.6	3.5
STL	64	4	9	1373[1]	1592	10.4	113	646	439	14.8	5.12	89	.290	.367	-113	-82	105	100	.974	158	179	1.3	-7.7	-4.8	-.2	1.4
WAS	74	6	7	1350	1494	10.0	93	618	618	14.2	4.59	91	.281	.359	-31	-64	95	103	.968	194	166	-.7	-6.0	-3.4	1.0	-3.9
PHI	72	4	12	1345	1543	10.3	135	534	488	14.0	5.22	85	.283	.348	-125	-116	101	91	.960	238	131	-3.1	-11.0	-3.5	.2	-5.7
TOT	551	61	121	10958		9.6				13.4	4.38		.271	.342					.970	1443	1195					

Runs
Williams-Bos 134
Greenberg-Det ... 129
McCosky-Det 123
Gordon-NY 112
Kuhel-Chi 111

Hits
Radcliff-StL 200
McCosky-Det 200
Cramer-Bos 200
Appling-Chi 197
Wright-Chi 196

Doubles
Greenberg-Det 50
York-Det 46
Boudreau-Cle 46
Williams-Bos 43
Moses-Phi 41

Triples
McCosky-Det 19
Keller-NY 15
Finney-Bos 15
Williams-Bos 14
Appling-Chi 13

Home Runs
Greenberg-Det 41
Foxx-Bos 36
York-Det 33
Johnson-Phi 31
DiMaggio-NY 31

Total Bases
Greenberg-Det ... 384
York-Det 343
Williams-Bos 333
DiMaggio-NY 318
Gordon-NY 315

Runs Batted In
Greenberg-Det ... 150
York-Det 134
DiMaggio-NY 133
Foxx-Bos 119
Williams-Bos 113

Runs Produced
Greenberg-Det ... 238
Williams-Bos 224
York-Det 206
DiMaggio-NY 195
Cronin-Bos 191

Bases On Balls
Keller-NY 106
Clift-StL 104
Gehringer-Det 101
Foxx-Bos 101
Williams-Bos 96

Batting Average
DiMaggio-NY ..... .352
Appling-Chi ...... .348
Williams-Bos ..... .344
Radcliff-StL ...... .342
Greenberg-Det ... .340

On Base Percentage
Williams-Bos ..... .442
Greenberg-Det ... .433
Gehringer-Det .... .428
DiMaggio-NY ..... .425
Appling-Chi ...... .420

Slugging Average
Greenberg-Det ... .670
DiMaggio-NY ..... .626
Williams-Bos ..... .594
York-Det .... .583
Foxx-Bos .... .581

Production
Greenberg-Det .. 1.103
DiMaggio-NY 1.051
Williams-Bos 1.036
York-Det .... .993
Foxx-Bos .... .993

Adjusted Production
DiMaggio-NY 176
Greenberg-Det ... 166
Williams-Bos 159
Foxx-Bos 148
Keller-NY 142

Batter Runs
Greenberg-Det .. 68.8
Williams-Bos 57.2
DiMaggio-NY 50.8
York-Det 47.3
Foxx-Bos 42.6

Adjusted Batter Runs
Greenberg-Det .. 60.7
Williams-Bos 53.8
DiMaggio-NY 53.7
Foxx-Bos 39.5
York-Det 39.1

Clutch Hitting Index
Tresh-Chi 142
Heffner-StL 127
Bloodworth-Was .. 125
DiMaggio-NY 124
Bell-Cle 123

Runs Created
Greenberg-Det ... 171
Williams-Bos 154
York-Det 147
DiMaggio-NY 135
Foxx-Bos 124

Total Average
Greenberg-Det .. 1.215
Williams-Bos 1.122
DiMaggio-NY 1.098
York-Det 1.050
Foxx-Bos 1.026

Stolen Bases
Case-Was 35
Walker-Was 21
Gordon-NY 18
Lewis-Was 15
Kreevich-Chi 15

Stolen Base Average
Walker-Was 84.0
Case-Was 77.8
Gordon-NY 69.2

Stolen Base Runs
Case-Was 4.5
Walker-Was 3.9
Gehringer-Det 3.0
Bartell-Det 2.4
Rosar-NY 1.5

Fielding Runs
Heffner-StL 19.1
Doerr-Bos 18.3
Tebbetts-Det 18.2
Travis-Was 15.7
Gordon-NY 14.0

Total Player Rating
Greenberg-Det 5.0
DiMaggio-NY 4.4
Williams-Bos 4.2
Gordon-NY 3.8
Doerr-Bos 3.6

Wins
Feller-Cle 27
Newsom-Det 21
Milnar-Cle 18
Hudson-Was 17

Win Percentage
Rowe-Det .... .842
Newsom-Det ..... .808
Feller-Cle .... .711
Smith-Cle .... .682
Milnar-Cle ...... .643

Games
Feller-Cle 43
Benton-Det 42
Wilson-Bos 41
Heusser-Phi 41
Dobson-Cle 40

Complete Games
Feller-Cle 31
Lee-Chi 24
Leonard-Was 23

Shutouts
Milnar-Cle 4
Lyons-Chi 4
Feller-Cle 4

Saves
Benton-Det 17
Brown-Chi 10
Murphy-NY 9

Innings Pitched
Feller-Cle 320.1
Leonard-Was 289.0
Rigney-Chi 280.2
Newsom-Det 264.0
Auker-StL 263.2

Fewest Hits/Game
Feller-Cle 6.88
Rigney-Chi 7.70
Smith-Chi 7.77
Bridges-Det 7.79
Newsom-Det 8.01

Fewest BB/Game
Lyons-Chi 1.79
Lee-Chi 2.21
Rowe-Det 2.29
Leonard-Was 2.43
Russo-NY 2.61

Strikeouts
Feller-Cle 261
Newsom-Det 164
Rigney-Chi 141
Bridges-Det 133
Chase-Was 129

Strikeouts/Game
Feller-Cle 7.33
Bridges-Det 6.06
Wilson-Bos 5.82
Newsom-Det 5.59
Smith-Chi 5.17

Ratio
Feller-Cle 10.34
Rigney-Chi 10.65
Lyons-Chi 10.87
Lee-Chi 11.09
Russo-NY 11.27

Earned Run Average
Feller-Cle 2.61
Newsom-Det 2.83
Rigney-Chi 3.11
Smith-Chi 3.21
Chase-Was 3.23

Adjusted ERA
Newsom-Det 168
Feller-Cle 161
Rigney-Chi 142
Bridges-Det 141
Smith-Chi 138

Opponents' Batting Avg.
Feller-Cle .... .210
Smith-Chi .... .228
Bridges-Det ..... .229
Rigney-Chi ...... .230
Newsom-Det ..... .238

Opponents' On Base Pct.
Feller-Cle .... .285
Lyons-Chi .... .287
Rigney-Chi ...... .292
Lee-Chi .... .300
Russo-NY .... .303

Starter Runs
Feller-Cle 63.0
Newsom-Det 45.6
Rigney-Chi 39.7
Chase-Was 33.4
Milnar-Cle 30.0

Adjusted Starter Runs
Feller-Cle 57.1
Newsom-Det 56.5
Rigney-Chi 40.9
Bridges-Det 30.5
Smith-Chi 27.9

Clutch Pitching Index
Chase-Was 134
Leonard-Was 122
Newsom-Det 119
Smith-Cle 117
Milnar-Cle 115

Relief Runs
Eisenstat-Cle 9.9
Trotter-StL 6.7
Brown-Chi 5.1
Murphy-NY 4.8

Adjusted Relief Runs
Trotter-StL 8.9
Eisenstat-Cle 8.6
Brown-Chi 5.4
Benton-Det 2.9
Murphy-NY 2.4

Relief Ranking
Trotter-StL 11.1
Brown-Chi 9.3
Benton-Det 6.7
Eisenstat-Cle 6.5
Murphy-NY 4.8

Total Pitcher Index
Feller-Cle 5.5
Newsom-Det 5.3
Rigney-Chi 4.0
Rowe-Det 2.9
Smith-Chi 2.9

Total Baseball Ranking
Feller-Cle 5.5
Newsom-Det 5.3
Greenberg-Det ... 5.0
DiMaggio-NY 4.4
Williams-Bos 4.3

TEAM	G	W	L	PCT	GB	R	OR	AB	H	2B	3B	HR	BB	SO	AVG	OBP	SLG	PRO	PRO+	BR	/A	PF	CHI	RC	SB	CS	SBA	SBR
BRO	157	100	54	.649		800	581	5485	1494	286	69	101	600	535	.272	.347	.405	.752	113	128	99	104	98	792	36			
STL	155	97	56	.634	2.5	734	589	5457	1482	254	56	70	540	543	.272	.340	.377	.717	102	62	17	107	99	719	47			
CIN	154	88	66	.571	12	616	564	5218	1288	213	33	64	477	428	.247	.313	.337	.650	89	-72	-74	100	108	556	68			
PIT	156	81	73	.526	19	690	643	5297	1417	233	65	56	547	516	.268	.338	.368	.706	105	39	42	100	99	670	59			
NY	156	74	79	.484	25.5	667	667	5395	1401	248	35	95	504	518	.260	.326	.371	.697	101	15	2	102	98	659	36			
CHI	155	70	84	.455	30	666	670	5230	1323	239	25	99	559	670	.253	.327	.365	.692	105	9	32	96	101	642	39			
BOS	156	62	92	.403	38	592	720	5414	1357	231	38	48	471	608	.251	.312	.334	.646	92	-82	-54	96	103	568	61			
PHI	155	43	111	.279	57	501	793	5233	1277	188	38	64	451	596	.244	.307	.331	.638	89	-97	-73	96	93	528	65			
TOT	622					5266		42729	11039	1892	359	597	4149	4414	.258	.326	.361	.688						411				

TEAM	CG	SH	SV	IP	H	H/G	HR	BB	SO	RAT	ERA	ERA+	OAV	OOB	PR	/A	PF	CPI	FA	E	DP	FW	PW	BW	SBW	DIF
BRO	66	17	22	1421	1236	7.8	81	495	603	11.1	3.14	117	.233	.300	78	83	101	93	.974	162	125	.9	8.5	10.2		3.4
STL	64	15	20	1416¹	1289	8.2	85	502	659	11.5	3.19	118	.242	.310	70	90	104	101	.973	172	146	.2	9.2	1.7		9.3
CIN	89	19	10	1386²	1300	8.4	61	510	627	11.9	3.17	114	.250	.319	72	66	99	106	.975	152	147	1.3	6.8	-7.6		10.6
PIT	71	8	12	1374¹	1392	9.1	66	492	410	12.4	3.48	104	.260	.323	23	19	99	102	.968	196	130	-1.1	2.0	4.3		-1.1
NY	55	12	18	1391²	1455	9.4	90	539	566	13.0	3.94	94	.269	.337	-48	-39	102	102	.974	160	144	.9	-4.0	.2		.4
CHI	74	8	9	1364²	1431	9.4	60	449	548	12.5	3.72	94	.267	.327	-13	-32	97	98	.970	180	139	-.3	-3.3	3.3		-6.7
BOS	62	10	9	1385²	1440	9.4	75	554	446	13.2	3.95	90	.269	.341	-49	-58	98	102	.969	191	174	-.9	-6.0	-5.5		-2.6
PHI	35	4	9	1372¹	1499	9.8	79	606	552	14.0	4.50	82	.279	.355	-132	-121	102	98	.969	187	147	-.7	-12.4	-7.5		-13.4
TOT	516	93	109	11112²		8.9				12.4	3.63		.258	.326					.972	1400	1152					

Runs
Reiser-Bro 117
Hack-Chi 114
Medwick-Bro 100
Rucker-NY 95
Fletcher-Pit 95

Hits
Hack-Chi 186
Reiser-Bro 184
Litwhiler-Phi 180
Rucker-NY 179
Medwick-Bro 171

Doubles
Reiser-Bro 39
Mize-StL 39
Rucker-NY 38
Dallessandro-Chi .. 36

Triples
Reiser-Bro 17
Fletcher-Pit 13
Hopp-StL 11
Medwick-Bro 10
Elliott-Pit 10

Home Runs
Camilli-Bro 34
Ott-NY 27
Nicholson-Chi 26
Young-NY 25
Dahlgren-Bos-Chi .. 23

Total Bases
Reiser-Bro 299
Camilli-Bro 294
Medwick-Bro 278
Litwhiler-Phi 275
Young-NY 265

Runs Batted In
Camilli-Bro 120
Young-NY 104
Mize-StL 100
DiMaggio-Pit 100
Nicholson-Chi 98

Runs Produced
Reiser-Bro 179
Camilli-Bro 178
Medwick-Bro 170
Young-NY 169
Fletcher-Pit 158

Bases On Balls
Fletcher-Pit 118
Camilli-Bro 104
Ott-NY 100
Hack-Chi 99

Batting Average
Reiser-Bro .... .343
Medwick-Bro ..... .318
Hack-Chi .... .317
Mize-StL .... .317
Etten-Phi .... .311

On Base Percentage
Fletcher-Pit ...... .421
Hack-Chi .... .417
Camilli-Bro .... .407
Reiser-Bro .... .406
Mize-StL .... .406

Slugging Average
Reiser-Bro .... .558
Camilli-Bro .... .556
Mize-StL .... .535
Medwick-Bro ..... .517
Slaughter-StL ..... .496

Production
Reiser-Bro .... .964
Camilli-Bro .... .962
Mize-StL .... .941
Ott-NY .... .898
Slaughter-StL ..... .886

Adjusted Production
Reiser-Bro 163
Camilli-Bro 162
Mize-StL 153
Ott-NY 149
Fletcher-Pit 148

Batter Runs
Camilli-Bro 50.2
Reiser-Bro 48.0
Mize-StL 40.2
Ott-NY 38.7
Fletcher-Pit 38.2

Adjusted Batter Runs
Camilli-Bro 47.1
Reiser-Bro 45.1
Fletcher-Pit 38.5
Ott-NY 37.3
Hack-Chi 36.7

Clutch Hitting Index
Lavagetto-Bro 173
VanRobays-Pit 154
Dallessandro-Chi . 150
Elliott-Pit 141
Bragan-Phi 134

Runs Created
Camilli-Bro 128
Reiser-Bro 124
Ott-NY 115
Hack-Chi 114
Fletcher-Pit 111

Total Average
Camilli-Bro 1.057
Reiser-Bro 1.006
Mize-StL .... .991
Ott-NY .... .976
Fletcher-Pit ...... .965

Stolen Bases
Murtaugh-Phi 18
Benjamin-Phi 17
Handley-Pit 16
Frey-Cin 16
Hopp-StL 15

Stolen Base Average

Stolen Base Runs

Fielding Runs
May-Phi 25.2
Stringer-Chi 20.1
Litwhiler-Phi 17.1
Werber-Cin 12.5
Miller-Bos 12.2

Total Player Rating
Reiser-Bro 4.9
Camilli-Bro 3.9
Fletcher-Pit 3.7
Ott-NY 3.4
Litwhiler-Phi 3.1

Wins
Wyatt-Bro 22
Higbe-Bro 22
Walters-Cin 19
E.Riddle-Cin 19

Win Percentage
E.Riddle-Cin ..... .826
Higbe-Bro .... .710
White-StL .... .708
Wyatt-Bro .... .688
Warneke-StL ..... .654

Games
Higbe-Bro 48
Pearson-Phi 46
Casey-Bro 45
Hutchings-Cin-Bos . 44
Johnson-Bos 43

Complete Games
Walters-Cin 27
Wyatt-Bro 23
Tobin-Bos 20
Passeau-Chi 20

Shutouts
Wyatt-Bro 7
VanderMeer-Cin ... 6
Walters-Cin 5
Davis-Bro 5

Saves
Brown-NY 8
Crouch-Phi-StL 7
Casey-Bro 7
Pearson-Phi 6

Innings Pitched
Walters-Cin 302.0
Higbe-Bro 298.0
Wyatt-Bro 288.1
Sewell-Pit 249.0
Warneke-StL 246.0

Fewest Hits/Game
VanderMeer-Cin .. 6.84
Wyatt-Bro 6.96
White-StL 7.24
Higbe-Bro 7.37
E.Riddle-Cin 7.48

Fewest BB/Game
Passeau-Chi 2.03
Derringer-Cin ... 2.13
Lohrman-NY 2.26
Tobin-Bos 2.27
Lee-Chi 2.31

Strikeouts
VanderMeer-Cin .. 202
Wyatt-Bro 176
Walters-Cin 129
Higbe-Bro 121
M.Cooper-StL 118

Strikeouts/Game
VanderMeer-Cin .. 8.03
M.Cooper-StL 5.69
Wyatt-Bro 5.49
White-StL 5.01
Melton-NY 4.63

Ratio
Wyatt-Bro 9.58
E.Riddle-Cin 10.14
White-StL 10.50
Tobin-Bos 10.93
Sewell-Pit 11.28

Earned Run Average
E.Riddle-Cin 2.24
Wyatt-Bro 2.34
White-StL 2.40
VanderMeer-Cin .. 2.82
Walters-Cin 2.83

Adjusted ERA
E.Riddle-Cin 160
White-StL 157
Wyatt-Bro 157
VanderMeer-Cin .. 127
Walters-Cin 127

Opponents' Batting Avg.
Wyatt-Bro .... .212
VanderMeer-Cin .. .214
White-StL .... .217
Higbe-Bro .... .220
E.Riddle-Cin ..... .224

Opponents' On Base Pct.
Wyatt-Bro .... .270
E.Riddle-Cin ..... .282
White-StL .... .287
Sewell-Pit .... .299
Tobin-Bos .... .300

Starter Runs
Wyatt-Bro 41.4
E.Riddle-Cin 33.5
White-StL 28.8
Walters-Cin 26.9
VanderMeer-Cin .. 20.4

Adjusted Starter Runs
Wyatt-Bro 42.4
E.Riddle-Cin 32.6
White-StL 31.8
Walters-Cin 25.7
VanderMeer-Cin .. 19.5

Clutch Pitching Index
V.Olsen-Chi 120
Heintzelman-Pit ... 117
Butcher-Pit 112
Johnson-Bos 111
Walters-Cin 111

Relief Runs
Pressnell-Chi 4.3
Brown-NY 2.0
Pearson-Phi 9
Sullivan-Bos-Pit 0

Adjusted Relief Runs
Pressnell-Chi 3.3
Brown-NY 2.4
Pearson-Phi 1.9

Relief Ranking
Pressnell-Chi 3.5
Brown-NY 3.0
Pearson-Phi 2.5

Total Pitcher Index
Wyatt-Bro 5.3
E.Riddle-Cin 3.8
Walters-Cin 3.2
White-StL 3.1
Gumbert-NY-StL ... 2.5

Total Baseball Ranking
Wyatt-Bro 5.3
Reiser-Bro 4.9
Camilli-Bro 3.9
E.Riddle-Cin 3.8
Fletcher-Pit 3.7

TEAM	G	W	L	PCT	GB	R	OR	AB	H	2B	3B	HR	BB	SO	AVG	OBP	SLG	PRO	PRO+	BR	/A	PF	CHI	RC	SB	CS	SBA	SBR
NY	156	101	53	.656		830	631	5444	1464	243	60	151	616	565	.269	.346	.419	.765	111	64	74	99	103	822	51	33	61	-5
BOS	155	84	70	.545	17	865	750	5359	1517	304	55	124	683	567	.283	.366	.430	.796	115	136	118	102	98	872	67	51	57	-11
CHI	156	77	77	.500	24	638	649	5404	1376	245	47	47	510	476	.255	.322	.343	.665	84	-128	-119	99	106	612	43	28	61	-4
DET	155	75	79	.487	26	686	743	5370	1412	247	55	81	602	584	.263	.340	.375	.715	87	-27	-101	110	97	713	43	28	61	-4
CLE	155	75	79	.487	26	677	668	5283	1350	249	84	103	512	605	.256	.323	.393	.716	101	-40	-5	95	100	691	63	47	57	-9
WAS	156	70	84	.455	31	728	798	5521	1502	257	80	52	470	488	.272	.331	.376	.707	99	-53	-18	95	107	702	79	36	69	2
STL	157	70	84	.455	31	765	823	5408	1440	281	58	91	775	552	.266	.360	.390	.750	103	56	31	103	93	804	50	39	56	-8
PHI	154	64	90	.416	37	713	840	5336	1431	240	69	85	574	588	.268	.340	.387	.727	102	-7	11	98	99	711	27	36	43	-14
TOT	622					5902		43125	11492	2066	508	734	4742	4425	.266	.341	.389	.730							471	323	59	-53

TEAM	CG	SH	SV	IP	H	H/G	HR	BB	SO	RAT	ERA	ERA+	OAV	OOB	PR	/A	PF	CPI	FA	E	DP	FW	PW	BW	SBW	DIF
NY	75	13	26	1396[1]	1309	8.4	81	598	589	12.4	3.53	112	.248	.325	96	63	95	102	.973	165	196	.5	6.1	7.2	.2	10.1
BOS	70	8	11	1372	1453	9.5	88	611	574	13.7	4.19	100	.270	.347	-6	-3	101	102	.972	172	148	.0	-.3	11.4	-.4	-3.8
CHI	106	14	4	1416	1362	8.7	89	521	564	12.1	3.52	116	.252	.320	99	91	99	102	.971	180	145	-.3	8.8	-11.5	.2	2.9
DET	52	8	16	1381[2]	1399	9.1	80	645	697	13.4	4.18	109	.260	.341	-4	57	110	96	.969	186	129	-.7	5.5	-9.8	.2	2.7
CLE	68	10	19	1377	1366	8.9	71	660	617	13.4	3.90	101	.259	.344	39	7	95	103	.976	142	158	1.7	.7	-.5	-.2	-3.7
WAS	69	8	7	1389[1]	1524	9.9	69	603	544	13.9	4.35	93	.279	.353	-32	-48	98	101	.969	187	169	-.7	-4.7	-1.7	.8	-.7
STL	65	7	10	1389	1563	10.1	120	549	454	13.8	4.72	91	.283	.350	-88	-64	104	99	.975	151	156	1.3	-6.2	3.0	-.1	-5.0
PHI	64	3	18	1365[1]	1516	10.0	136	557	386	13.8	4.83	87	.279	.348	-104	-98	101	97	.967	200	150	-1.6	-9.5	1.1	-.7	-2.3
TOT	569	71	111	11086[2]		9.3				13.3	4.15		.266	.341					.972	1383	1242					

Runs
Williams-Bos 135
DiMaggio-NY 122
DiMaggio-Bos 117
Clift-StL 108

Hits
Travis-Was 218
Heath-Cle 199
DiMaggio-NY 193
Appling-Chi 186
Williams-Bos 185

Doubles
Boudreau-Cle 45
DiMaggio-NY 43
Judnich-StL 40
Travis-Was 39
Kuhel-Chi 39

Triples
Heath-Cle 20
Travis-Was 19
Keltner-Cle 13

Home Runs
Williams-Bos 37
Keller-NY 33
Henrich-NY 31
DiMaggio-NY 30
York-Det 27

Total Bases
DiMaggio-NY 348
Heath-Cle 343
Williams-Bos 335
Travis-Was 316
S.Chapman-Phi ... 300

Runs Batted In
DiMaggio-NY 125
Heath-Cle 123
Keller-NY 122
Williams-Bos 120
York-Det 111

Runs Produced
Williams-Bos 218
DiMaggio-NY 217
Travis-Was 200
Keller-NY 191
Heath-Cle 188

Bases On Balls
Williams-Bos 145
Cullenbine-StL ... 121
Clift-StL 113
Keller-NY 102

Batting Average
Williams-Bos ..... .406
Travis-Was .... .359
DiMaggio-NY ..... .357
Heath-Cle .... .340
Siebert-Phi .... .334

On Base Percentage
Williams-Bos ..... .551
Cullenbine-StL .... .452
DiMaggio-NY ..... .440
Keller-NY .... .416
Foxx-Bos .... .412

Slugging Average
Williams-Bos ..... .735
DiMaggio-NY ..... .643
Heath-Cle .... .586
Keller-NY .... .580
S.Chapman-Phi ... .543

Production
Williams-Bos 1.286
DiMaggio-NY 1.083
Keller-NY .... .996
Heath-Cle .... .982
Travis-Was .... .930

Adjusted Production
Williams-Bos 232
DiMaggio-NY 186
Heath-Cle 165
Keller-NY 163
Travis-Was 152

Batter Runs
Williams-Bos 102.0
DiMaggio-NY 64.3
Keller-NY 45.7
Heath-Cle 44.8
Cullenbine-StL 38.3

Adjusted Batter Runs
Williams-Bos 100.3
DiMaggio-NY 65.4
Heath-Cle 48.6
Keller-NY 46.7
Travis-Was 41.8

Clutch Hitting Index
Berardino-StL 165
Cullenbine-StL ... 136
Tabor-Bos 135
Wright-Chi 135
Vernon-Was 133

Runs Created
Williams-Bos 202
DiMaggio-NY 162
Heath-Cle 138
Keller-NY 134
Travis-Was 131

Total Average
Williams-Bos 1.688
DiMaggio-NY 1.208
Keller-NY 1.099
Cullenbine-StL ... 1.023
Heath-Cle 1.000

Stolen Bases
Case-Was 33
Kuhel-Chi 20
Heath-Cle 18
Tabor-Bos 17
Kreevich-Chi 17

Stolen Base Average
Kuhel-Chi 80.0
Case-Was 78.6
Kreevich-Chi 77.3
Tabor-Bos 65.4
Heath-Cle 60.0

Stolen Base Runs
Case-Was 4.5
Kuhel-Chi 3.0
Kreevich-Chi 2.1
Fox-Bos 1.5

Fielding Runs
Bloodworth-Was .. 34.7
Keltner-Cle 22.5
Rizzuto-NY 15.6
Case-Was 15.2
S.Chapman-Phi ... 14.4

Total Player Rating
Williams-Bos 8.1
DiMaggio-NY 6.3
Travis-Was 5.1
Keller-NY 4.0
Keltner-Cle 3.5

Wins
Feller-NY 25
Lee-Chi 22
H.Newsome-Bos ... 19
Leonard-Was 18

Win Percentage
Gomez-NY .... .750
Ruffing-NY ...... .714
Benton-Det ..... .714
Lee-Chi .... .667
Feller-Cle .... .658

Games
Feller-Cle 44
Newsom-Det 43
Brown-Cle 41
Ryba-Bos 40
Benton-Det 38

Complete Games
Lee-Chi 30
Feller-Cle 28
Smith-Chi 21
Lyons-Chi 19
Leonard-Was 19

Shutouts
Feller-Cle 6
Leonard-Was 4
Humphries-Chi ... 4
Chandler-NY 4

Saves
Murphy-NY 15
Ferrick-Phi 7
Benton-Det 7
Ryba-Bos 6

Innings Pitched
Feller-Cle 343.0
Lee-Chi 300.1
Smith-Chi 263.1
Leonard-Was 256.0
Newsom-Det 250.1

Fewest Hits/Game
Benton-Det 7.42
Feller-Cle 7.45
Lee-Chi 7.73
Donald-NY 7.98
Chandler-NY 8.03

Fewest BB/Game
Lyons-Chi 1.78
Leonard-Was 1.90
Muncrief-StL 2.23
Ruffing-NY 2.62
Lee-Chi 2.76

Strikeouts
Feller-Cle 260
Newsom-Det 175
Lee-Chi 130
Rigney-Chi 119

Strikeouts/Game
Feller-Cle 6.82
Newsom-Det 6.29
Newhouser-Det .. 5.51
Harris-Bos 5.15
Rigney-Chi 4.52

Ratio
Lee-Chi 10.61
Ruffing-NY 11.25
Benton-Det 11.30
Chandler-NY 11.33
Lyons-Chi 11.53

Earned Run Average
Lee-Chi 2.37
Benton-Det 2.97
Wagner-Bos 3.07
Russo-NY 3.09
Feller-Cle 3.15

Adjusted ERA
Lee-Chi 173
Benton-Det 153
Wagner-Bos 136
Smith-Chi 129
Harris-Bos 128

Opponents' Batting Avg.
Benton-Det ..... .221
Feller-Cle ...... .226
Lee-Chi .... .232
Donald-NY ...... .237
Chandler-NY .... .239

Opponents' On Base Pct.
Lee-Chi .... .293
Benton-Det ..... .302
Ruffing-NY ...... .306
Chandler-NY .... .307
Lyons-Chi ...... .308

Starter Runs
Lee-Chi 59.4
Feller-Cle 38.1
Smith-Chi 28.4
Russo-NY 24.6
Wagner-Bos 22.3

Adjusted Starter Runs
Lee-Chi 57.7
Feller-Cle 30.2
Benton-Det 27.6
Smith-Chi 26.9
Wagner-Bos 22.8

Clutch Pitching Index
Lee-Chi 122
Wagner-Bos 120
Gomez-NY 115
Marchildon-Phi ... 115
Smith-Chi 112

Relief Runs
Murphy-NY 18.6
Heving-Cle 14.6
Carrasquel-Was ... 7.5
Brown-Cle 7.3

Adjusted Relief Runs
Murphy-NY 16.8
Heving-Cle 12.9
Carrasquel-Was ... 6.4
Brown-Cle 5.5
Thomas-Det 2.7

Relief Ranking
Murphy-NY 28.8
Heving-Cle 13.6
Carrasquel-Was ... 5.1
Brown-Cle 4.9
Thomas-Det 1.5

Total Pitcher Index
Lee-Chi 6.6
Feller-Cle 3.1
Smith-Chi 3.1
Russo-NY 2.4
Benton-Det 2.2

Total Baseball Ranking
Williams-Bos 8.1
Lee-Chi 6.6
DiMaggio-NY 6.3
Travis-Was 5.1
Keller-NY 4.0

TEAM	G	W	L	PCT	GB	R	OR	AB	H	2B	3B	HR	BB	SO	AVG	OBP	SLG	PRO	PRO+	BR	/A	PF	CHI	RC	SB	CS	SBA	SBR
STL	156	106	48	.688		755	482	5421	1454	282	69	60	551	507	.268	.338	.379	.717	109	109	62	108	103	718	71			
BRO	155	104	50	.675	2	742	510	5285	1398	263	34	62	572	484	.265	.338	.362	.700	110	80	70	102	107	671	81			
NY	154	85	67	.559	20	675	600	5210	1323	162	35	109	558	511	.254	.330	.361	.691	108	59	56	101	102	627	39			
CIN	154	76	76	.500	29	527	545	5260	1216	198	39	66	483	549	.231	.299	.321	.620	88	-81	-80	100	102	519	42			
PIT	151	66	81	.449	36.5	585	631	5104	1250	173	49	54	537	536	.245	.320	.330	.650	95	-15	-30	103	102	556	41			
CHI	155	68	86	.442	38	591	665	5352	1360	224	41	75	509	607	.254	.321	.353	.674	108	23	46	96	93	619	63			
BOS	150	59	89	.399	44	515	645	5077	1216	210	19	68	474	507	.240	.307	.329	.636	94	-48	-36	98	97	520	49			
PHI	151	42	109	.278	62.5	394	706	5060	1174	168	37	44	392	488	.232	.289	.306	.595	84	-125	-97	95	89	451	37			
TOT	613					4784		41769	10391	1680	323	538	4076	4189	.249	.318	.343	.661							423			

TEAM	CG	SH	SV	IP	H	H/G	HR	BB	SO	RAT	ERA	ERA+	OAV	OOB	PR	/A	PF	CPI	FA	E	DP	FW	PW	BW	SBW	DIF
STL	70	18	15	1410¹	1192	7.6	49	473	651	10.7	2.55	134	.228	.294	120	137	103	102	.972	169	137	-.1	14.7	6.7		7.8
BRO	67	16	24	1398²	1205	7.8	73	493	612	11.1	2.84	115	.231	.302	73	64	98	101	.977	138	150	1.7	6.9	7.5		10.9
NY	70	12	13	1370	1299	8.5	94	493	497	11.9	3.31	101	.250	.316	0	7	101	104	.977	138	128	1.6	.8	6.0		.6
CIN	80	12	8	1411²	1213	7.7	47	526	616	11.2	2.82	117	.230	.302	78	73	99	97	.971	177	158	-.7	7.8	-8.6		1.5
PIT	64	13	11	1351¹	1376	9.2	62	435	426	12.1	3.58	94	.262	.320	-41	-30	102	97	.969	184	128	-1.3	-3.2	-3.2		.3
CHI	71	10	14	1400²	1447	9.3	70	525	507	12.8	3.60	89	.267	.334	-44	-62	97	105	.973	170	136	-.2	-6.7	4.9		-7.1
BOS	68	9	8	1334	1326	8.9	82	518	414	12.6	3.76	89	.260	.331	-66	-62	101	100	.976	142	138	1.1	-6.7	-3.9		-5.6
PHI	51	2	6	1341	1328	8.9	61	605	472	13.1	4.12	80	.260	.342	-120	-122	100	93	.968	194	147	-1.9	-13.1	-10.4		-8.1
TOT	541	92	99	11017²		8.5				11.9	3.31		.249	.318					.973	1312	1122					

Runs
Ott-NY 118
Slaughter-StL 100
Mize-NY 97
Hack-Chi 91

Hits
Slaughter-StL 188
Nicholson-Chi . . . 173
Medwick-Bro 166
Hack-Chi 166
Elliott-Pit 166

Doubles
Marion-StL 38
Medwick-Bro 37
Hack-Chi 36
Herman-Bro 34
Reiser-Bro 33

Triples
Slaughter-StL 17
Nicholson-Chi . . . 11
Musial-StL 10
Litwhiler-Phi 9

Home Runs
Ott-NY 30
Mize-NY 26
Camilli-Bro 26
Nicholson-Chi . . . 21
West-Bos 16

Total Bases
Slaughter-StL 292
Mize-NY 282
Nicholson-Chi . . . 280
Ott-NY 273
Camilli-Bro 247

Runs Batted In
Mize-NY 110
Camilli-Bro 109
Slaughter-StL 98
Medwick-Bro 96
Ott-NY 93

Runs Produced
Slaughter-StL 185
Ott-NY 181
Mize-NY 181
Camilli-Bro 172
Medwick-Bro 161

Bases On Balls
Ott-NY 109
Fletcher-Pit 105
Camilli-Bro 97
Hack-Chi 94
Slaughter-StL 88

Batting Average
Slaughter-StL 318
Musial-StL 315
Reiser-Bro 310
Mize-NY 305
Novikoff-Chi 300

On Base Percentage
Fletcher-Pit 417
Ott-NY 415
Slaughter-StL 412
Hack-Chi 402
Musial-StL 397

Slugging Average
Mize-NY 521
Ott-NY 497
Slaughter-StL 494
Musial-StL 490
Nicholson-Chi 476

Production
Ott-NY 912
Slaughter-StL 906
Mize-NY 901
Musial-StL 888
Nicholson-Chi 859

Adjusted Production
Ott-NY 165
Mize-NY 161
Nicholson-Chi . . . 156
Slaughter-StL 153
Musial-StL 148

Batter Runs
Slaughter-StL 49.8
Ott-NY 49.3
Mize-NY 40.8
Nicholson-Chi . . . 37.6
Musial-StL 35.0

Adjusted Batter Runs
Ott-NY 49.0
Slaughter-StL 44.6
Mize-NY 40.4
Nicholson-Chi . . . 40.2
Hack-Chi 32.4

Clutch Hitting Index
Medwick-Bro 154
F.McCormick-Cin . . 134
Elliott-Pit 134
Camilli-Bro 127
Herman-Bro 125

Runs Created
Slaughter-StL 128
Ott-NY 122
Nicholson-Chi . . . 112
Mize-NY 110
Hack-Chi 100

Total Average
Ott-NY 990
Slaughter-StL 966
Musial-StL 926
Mize-NY 911
Camilli-Bro 888

Stolen Bases
Reiser-Bro 20
Reese-Bro 15
Fernandez-Bos . . . 15
Merullo-Chi 14
Hopp-StL 14

Stolen Base Average

Stolen Base Runs

Fielding Runs
DiMaggio-Pit . . . 19.8
Reese-Bro 17.4
May-Phi 17.2
Holmes-Bos 14.8
Fletcher-Pit 11.5

Total Player Rating
Nicholson-Chi 4.6
Slaughter-StL 4.3
Ott-NY 4.2
Fletcher-Pit 3.3
Mize-NY 3.1

Wins
M.Cooper-StL 22
Beazley-StL 21
Wyatt-Bro 19
Passeau-Chi 19
VanderMeer-Cin . . 18

Win Percentage
French-Bro 789
Beazley-StL 778
M.Cooper-StL 759
Wyatt-Bro 731
Davis-Bro 714

Games
Adams-NY 61
Casey-Bro 50
Podgajny-Phi 43
Beazley-StL 43

Complete Games
Tobin-Bos 28
Passeau-Chi 24
M.Cooper-StL 22
Walters-Cin 21
VanderMeer-Cin . . 21

Shutouts
M.Cooper-StL 10
Sewell-Pit 5
Javery-Bos 5
Davis-Bro 5

Saves
Casey-Bro 13
Adams-NY 11
Beggs-Cin 8
Sain-Bos 6
Gumbert-StL 5

Innings Pitched
Tobin-Bos 287.2
M.Cooper-StL . . . 278.2
Passeau-Chi 278.1
Starr-Cin 276.2
Javery-Bos 261.0

Fewest Hits/Game
M.Cooper-StL . . . 6.69
VanderMeer-Cin . 6.93
Higbe-Bro 7.31
Starr-Cin 7.42
Beazley-StL 7.57

Fewest BB/Game
Warneke-StL 1.79
Lohrman-StL-NY . . 1.85
Hubbell-NY 1.94
Derringer-Cin 2.11
M.Cooper-StL . . . 2.20

Strikeouts
VanderMeer-Cin . . 186
M.Cooper-StL . . . 152
Higbe-Bro 115
Walters-Cin 109
Melton-Phi 107

Strikeouts/Game
VanderMeer-Cin . 6.86
Lanier-StL 5.20
M.Cooper-StL . . . 4.91
Higbe-Bro 4.67
Melton-Phi 4.60

Ratio
M.Cooper-StL . . . 9.04
Lohrman-StL-NY . 10.07
Davis-Bro 10.35
Warneke-StL-Chi . 10.39
Wyatt-Bro 10.56

Earned Run Average
M.Cooper-StL 1.78
Beazley-StL 2.13
Davis-Bro 2.36
VanderMeer-Cin . . 2.43
Lohrman-StL-NY . . 2.48

Adjusted ERA
M.Cooper-StL 193
Beazley-StL 161
Davis-Bro 138
Lohrman-StL-NY . . 136
VanderMeer-Cin . . 135

Opponents' Batting Avg.
M.Cooper-StL 204
VanderMeer-Cin . .208
Higbe-Bro 223
Wyatt-Bro 225
Starr-Cin 226

Opponents' On Base Pct.
M.Cooper-StL 258
Lohrman-StL-NY . .281
Wyatt-Bro 286
Warneke-StL-Chi . .286
Davis-Bro 287

Starter Runs
M.Cooper-StL . . . 47.6
Beazley-StL 28.3
French-Bro 24.4
VanderMeer-Cin . 23.8
Davis-Bro 21.8

Adjusted Starter Runs
M.Cooper-StL . . . 51.0
Beazley-StL 30.9
French-Bro 23.5
VanderMeer-Cin . 23.0
Davis-Bro 20.6

Clutch Pitching Index
Bithorn-Chi 130
Passeau-Chi 121
Beazley-StL 114
Schumacher-NY . . 113
Carpenter-NY 112

Relief Runs
Adams-NY 14.4
Casey-Bro 13.2
Beggs-Cin 11.6
Shoun-StL-Cin . . . 9.4
Webber-Bro 2.0

Adjusted Relief Runs
Adams-NY 14.8
Casey-Bro 12.6
Beggs-Cin 11.3
Shoun-StL-Cin . . . 9.1
Webber-Bro 1.7

Relief Ranking
Adams-NY 20.9
Beggs-Cin 15.0
Casey-Bro 12.4
Shoun-StL-Cin . . . 4.4
Webber-Bro 1.6

Total Pitcher Index
M.Cooper-StL 5.4
Beazley-StL 3.4
French-Bro 3.0
Walters-Cin 2.9
Davis-Bro 2.6

Total Baseball Ranking
M.Cooper-StL 5.4
Nicholson-Chi 4.6
Slaughter-StL 4.3
Ott-NY 4.2
Beazley-StL 3.4

TEAM	G	W	L	PCT	GB	R	OR	AB	H	2B	3B	HR	BB	SO	AVG	OBP	SLG	PRO	PRO+	BR	/A	PF	CHI	RC	SB	CS	SBA	SBR
NY	154	103	51	.669		801	507	5305	1429	223	57	108	591	556	.269	.346	.394	.740	118	104	118	98	104	759	69	33	68	1
BOS	152	93	59	.612	9	761	594	5248	1451	244	55	103	591	508	.276	.352	.403	.755	116	132	110	103	96	774	68	61	53	-16
STL	151	82	69	.543	19.5	730	637	5229	1354	239	62	98	609	607	.259	.338	.385	.723	109	68	58	102	101	703	37	38	49	-12
CLE	156	75	79	.487	28	590	659	5317	1344	223	58	50	500	544	.253	.320	.345	.665	100	-43	-4	94	96	596	69	74	48	-24
DET	156	73	81	.474	30	589	587	5327	1313	217	37	76	509	476	.246	.314	.344	.658	85	-57	-110	108	98	582	39	40	49	-12
CHI	148	66	82	.446	34	538	609	4949	1215	214	36	25	497	427	.246	.316	.318	.634	87	-87	-73	98	102	520	114	70	62	-8
WAS	151	62	89	.411	39.5	653	817	5295	1364	224	49	40	581	536	.258	.333	.341	.674	98	-14	-7	99	101	641	98	29	77	12
PHI	154	55	99	.357	48	549	801	5285	1315	213	46	33	440	490	.249	.309	.325	.634	86	-101	-97	99	101	536	44	45	49	-14
TOT	611					5211		41955	10785	1797	400	533	4318	4144	.257	.329	.357	.686		538	390	58	-73					

TEAM	CG	SH	SV	IP	H	H/G	HR	BB	SO	RAT	ERA	ERA+	OAV	OOB	PR	/A	PF	CPI	FA	E	DP	FW	PW	BW	SBW	DIF
NY	88	18	17	1375	1259	8.2	71	431	558	11.2	2.91	118	.244	.304	115	82	94	108	.976	142	190	2.0	8.4	12.1	1.0	2.5
BOS	84	11	17	1358²	1260	8.3	65	553	500	12.1	3.44	108	.247	.322	32	43	102	99	.974	157	156	1.0	4.4	11.3	-.7	1.0
STL	68	12	13	1363	1387	9.2	63	505	488	12.7	3.59	103	.262	.330	10	17	101	103	.972	167	143	.4	1.7	5.9	-.3	-1.3
CLE	61	12	11	1402²	1353	8.7	61	560	448	12.4	3.59	96	.254	.327	10	-23	94	99	.974	163	175	1.0	-2.4	-.4	-1.5	1.3
DET	65	12	14	1399¹	1321	8.5	60	598	671	12.5	3.13	126	.248	.326	82	127	108	111	.969	194	142	-.8	13.0	-11.3	-.3	-4.7
CHI	86	8	8	1314¹	1304	8.9	74	473	432	12.3	3.58	100	.258	.325	11	3	98	102	.970	173	144	-.1	.3	-7.5	.1	-.8
WAS	68	12	11	1346²	1496	10.0	50	558	496	13.8	4.58	80	.279	.349	-139	-139	100	91	.962	222	133	-2.7	-14.2	-.7	2.2	1.9
PHI	67	5	9	1374²	1404	9.2	89	639	546	13.5	4.45	85	.263	.344	-120	-102	103	93	.969	188	124	-.6	-10.4	-9.9	-.5	-.6
TOT	587	90	100	10934¹		8.9				12.6	3.66		.257	.329					.971	1406	1207					

Runs
Williams-Bos 141
DiMaggio-NY 123
DiMaggio-Bos 110
Clift-StL 108
Keller-NY 106

Hits
Pesky-Bos 205
Spence-Was 203
Williams-Bos 186
DiMaggio-NY 186
Keltner-Cle 179

Doubles
Kolloway-Chi 40
Clift-StL 39
Heath-Cle 37
DiMaggio-Bos 36

Triples
Spence-Was 15
Heath-Cle 13
DiMaggio-NY 13
McQuillen-StL 12

Home Runs
Williams-Bos 36
Laabs-StL 27
Keller-NY 26
York-Det 21
DiMaggio-NY 21

Total Bases
Williams-Bos 338
DiMaggio-NY 304
Keller-NY 279
Spence-Was 272
DiMaggio-Bos 272

Runs Batted In
Williams-Bos 137
DiMaggio-NY 114
Keller-NY 108
Gordon-NY 103
Doerr-Bos 102

Runs Produced
Williams-Bos 242
DiMaggio-NY 216
Keller-NY 188
Gordon-NY 173
Spence-Was 169

Bases On Balls
Williams-Bos 145
Keller-NY 114
Fleming-Cle 106
Clift-StL 106
Cullenbine-StL-Was-NY . 92

Batting Average
Williams-Bos ..... .356
Pesky-Bos .... .331
Spence-Was ...... .323
Gordon-NY .... .322
Case-Was .... .320

On Base Percentage
Williams-Bos ..... .499
Keller-NY .... .417
Judnich-StL ...... .413
Fleming-Cle ...... .412
Gordon-NY .... .409

Slugging Average
Williams-Bos ..... .648
Keller-NY .... .513
Judnich-StL ...... .499
DiMaggio-NY ..... .498
Laabs-StL .... .498

Production
Williams-Bos 1.147
Keller-NY .... .930
Judnich-StL ...... .912
Gordon-NY .... .900
Laabs-StL .... .878

Adjusted Production
Williams-Bos 214
Keller-NY 164
Gordon-NY 156
Judnich-StL 153
DiMaggio-NY 148

Batter Runs
Williams-Bos 92.6
Keller-NY 46.9
Gordon-NY 38.6
Judnich-StL 35.4
DiMaggio-NY 34.5

Adjusted Batter Runs
Williams-Bos 90.1
Keller-NY 48.4
Gordon-NY 40.0
Fleming-Cle 36.3
DiMaggio-NY 36.0

Clutch Hitting Index
Lupien-Bos 135
Siebert-Phi 132
Kuhel-Chi 130
Doerr-Bos 130
Cullenbine-StL-Was-NY 126

Runs Created
Williams-Bos 185
Keller-NY 131
DiMaggio-NY 120
Spence-Was 111
Gordon-NY 108

Total Average
Williams-Bos 1.394
Keller-NY 1.038
Judnich-StL ...... .950
Gordon-NY .... .891
Laabs-StL .... .878

Stolen Bases
Case-Was 44
Vernon-Was 25
Rizzuto-NY 22
Kuhel-Chi 22

Stolen Base Average
Case-Was 88.0
Vernon-Was 80.6
Rizzuto-NY 78.6
Appling-Chi 77.3
Kuhel-Chi 71.0

Stolen Base Runs
Case-Was 9.6
Vernon-Was 3.9
Rizzuto-NY 3.0
Keller-NY 3.0
Appling-Chi 2.1

Fielding Runs
Rizzuto-NY 25.0
Pesky-Bos 17.7
DiMaggio-Bos 16.9
Keltner-Cle 15.6
York-Det 15.4

Total Player Rating
Williams-Bos 8.4
Gordon-NY 5.3
Keller-NY 4.3
Pesky-Bos 4.1
Rizzuto-NY 4.0

Wins
Hughson-Bos 22
Bonham-NY 21
Marchildon-Phi .. 17
Bagby-Cle 17
Chandler-NY 16

Win Percentage
Bonham-NY .... .808
Borowy-NY .... .789
Hughson-Bos ..... .786
Chandler-NY ..... .762
Bagby-Cle .... .654

Games
Haynes-Chi 40
Caster-StL 39

Complete Games
Hughson-Bos 22
Bonham-NY 22
Lyons-Chi 20
Hudson-Was 19

Shutouts
Bonham-NY 6

Saves
Murphy-NY 11
Haynes-Chi 6
Brown-Bos 6
Newhouser-Det ... 5
Caster-StL 5

Innings Pitched
Hughson-Bos 281.0
Bagby-Cle 270.2
Auker-StL 249.0
Marchildon-Phi . 244.0
Hudson-Was 239.1

Fewest Hits/Game
Newhouser-Det ... 6.71
Niggeling-StL ... 7.55
Dobson-Bos 7.64
Trucks-Det 7.89
Chandler-NY 7.89

Fewest BB/Game
Bonham-NY .... .96
Lyons-Chi 1.30
Ruffing-NY 1.91
Breuer-NY 2.03
Bagby-Cle 2.13

Strikeouts
Newsom-Was 113
Hughson-Bos 113
Marchildon-Phi . 110
Benton-Det 110
Niggeling-StL .. 107

Strikeouts/Game
Newhouser-Det ... 5.05
Bridges-Det 5.02
Trucks-Det 4.88
Newsom-Was 4.76
Niggeling-StL ... 4.67

Ratio
Bonham-NY 8.92
Lyons-Chi 9.73
Ruffing-NY 10.55
Breuer-NY 10.68
Hughson-Bos ... 10.70

Earned Run Average
Lyons-Chi 2.10
Bonham-NY 2.27
Chandler-NY ... 2.38
Newhouser-Det . 2.45
Borowy-NY 2.52

Adjusted ERA
Lyons-Chi 172
Newhouser-Det .. 161
Bonham-NY 152
Chandler-NY ... 145
Trucks-Det 144

Opponents' Batting Avg.
Newhouser-Det ... .207
Niggeling-StL .... .226
Dobson-Bos ...... .231
Trucks-Det ...... .231
Borowy-NY .... .233

Opponents' On Base Pct.
Bonham-NY ...... .259
Lyons-Chi ...... .275
Ruffing-NY ..... .292
Breuer-NY ...... .295
Hughson-Bos .... .296

Starter Runs
Bonham-NY 34.8
Hughson-Bos 33.2
Lyons-Chi 31.3
Chandler-NY 28.5
Humphries-Chi .. 24.8

Adjusted Starter Runs
Hughson-Bos 35.5
Newhouser-Det .. 30.6
Lyons-Chi 30.1
Bonham-NY 29.4
Benton-Det 26.5

Clutch Pitching Index
Chandler-NY 136
Lyons-Chi 131
Hollingsworth-StL 123
Humphries-Chi .. 121
Niggeling-StL .. 119

Relief Runs
Ferrick-Cle 15.0
Haynes-Chi 11.9
Caster-StL 7.5
Murphy-NY 1.6
Brown-Bos 1.5

Adjusted Relief Runs
Ferrick-Cle 13.2
Haynes-Chi 11.2
Caster-StL 7.9
Brown-Bos 2.0
Murphy-NY 2

Relief Ranking
Haynes-Chi 14.2
Caster-StL 10.0
Ferrick-Cle 8.4
Brown-Bos 4.0
Murphy-NY 5

Total Pitcher Index
Hughson-Bos 4.1
Lyons-Chi 4.0
Newhouser-Det ... 3.5
Chandler-NY 3.3
Humphries-Chi ... 2.9

Total Baseball Ranking
Williams-Bos 8.4
Gordon-NY 5.3
Keller-NY 4.3
Pesky-Bos 4.1
Hughson-Bos 4.1

TEAM	G	W	L	PCT	GB	R	OR	AB	H	2B	3B	HR	BB	SO	AVG	OBP	SLG	PRO	PRO+	BR	/A	PF	CHI	RC	SB	CS	SBA	SBR
STL	157	105	49	.682		679	475	5438	1515	259	72	70	428	438	.279	.333	.391	.724	110	92	65	104	95	720	40			
CIN	155	87	67	.565	18	608	543	5329	1362	229	47	43	445	476	.256	.315	.340	.655	96	-35	-26	99	106	581	49			
BRO	153	81	72	.529	23.5	716	674	5309	1444	263	35	39	580	422	.272	.346	.357	.703	110	70	69	100	104	675	58			
PIT	157	80	74	.519	25	669	605	5353	1401	240	73	42	573	566	.262	.335	.357	.692	103	45	24	103	100	657	64			
CHI	154	74	79	.484	30.5	632	600	5279	1380	207	56	52	574	522	.261	.336	.351	.687	107	38	47	99	97	641	53			
BOS	153	68	85	.444	36.5	465	612	5196	1213	202	36	39	469	609	.233	.299	.309	.608	82	-121	-112	99	98	491	56			
PHI	157	64	90	.416	41	571	676	5297	1321	186	36	66	499	556	.249	.316	.335	.651	98	-38	-14	96	100	565	29			
NY	156	55	98	.359	49.5	558	713	5290	1309	153	33	81	480	470	.247	.313	.335	.648	92	-48	-52	101	100	552	35			
TOT	621					4898		42491	10945	1739	388	432	4048	4059	.258	.324	.347	.672							384			

TEAM	CG	SH	SV	IP	H	H/G	HR	BB	SO	RAT	ERA	ERA+	OAV	OOB	PR	/A	PF	CPI	FA	E	DP	FW	PW	BW	SBW	DIF
STL	94	21	15	1427	1246	7.9	33	477	639	11.0	2.57	131	.237	.303	129	126	99	105	.976	151	183	.9	13.5	6.9		6.7
CIN	78	18	17	1404	1299	8.3	38	579	498	12.1	3.13	106	.251	.328	39	28	98	105	.980	125	193	2.2	3.0	-2.8		7.6
BRO	50	13	22	1369²	1326	8.7	59	637	588	13.1	3.88	86	.254	.338	-76	-80	99	93	.972	168	137	-.3	-8.5	7.4		6.0
PIT	74	11	12	1404	1424	9.1	44	422	396	11.9	3.08	113	.264	.319	47	60	103	107	.973	170	159	-.2	6.4	2.6		-5.8
CHI	67	13	14	1386	1379	9.0	53	394	513	11.6	3.31	101	.258	.311	11	3	99	95	.973	168	138	-.3	.3	5.0		-7.6
BOS	87	13	4	1397²	1361	8.8	66	441	409	11.8	3.25	105	.255	.314	20	25	101	100	.972	176	139	-.8	2.7	-12.0		1.6
PHI	66	10	14	1392²	1436	9.3	59	451	431	12.3	3.79	89	.267	.326	-62	-64	100	93	.969	189	143	-1.3	-6.8	-1.5		-3.4
NY	35	6	19	1394²	1474	9.5	80	626	588	13.7	4.08	84	.272	.350	-108	-99	102	101	.973	166	140	-.0	-10.6	-5.6		-5.3
TOT	551	105	117	11175²		8.8				12.2	3.38		.258	.324					.974	1313	1232					

Runs		Hits		Doubles		Triples		Home Runs		Total Bases	
Vaughan-Bro	112	Musial-StL	220	Musial-StL	48	Musial-StL	20	Nicholson-Chi	29	Musial-StL	347
Musial-StL	108	Witek-NY	195	Herman-Bro	41	Klein-StL	14	Ott-NY	18	Nicholson-Chi	323
Nicholson-Chi	95	Herman-Bro	193	DiMaggio-Pit	41	Lowrey-Chi	12	Northey-Phi	16	Elliott-Pit	258
Cavarretta-Chi	93	Nicholson-Chi	188	Vaughan-Bro	39	Elliott-Pit	12	Triplett-StL-Phi	15	Klein-StL	257
Stanky-Chi	92	Vaughan-Bro	186	Holmes-Bos	33			DiMaggio-Pit	15		

Runs Batted In		Runs Produced		Bases On Balls		Batting Average		On Base Percentage		Slugging Average	
Nicholson-Chi	128	Nicholson-Chi	194	Galan-Bro	103	Musial-StL	.357	Musial-StL	.425	Musial-StL	.562
Elliott-Pit	101	Musial-StL	176	Ott-NY	95	Herman-Bro	.330	Galan-Bro	.412	Nicholson-Chi	.531
Herman-Bro	100	Elliott-Pit	176	Fletcher-Pit	95	Elliott-Pit	.315	Herman-Bro	.398	Elliott-Pit	.444
DiMaggio-Pit	88	Herman-Bro	174	Stanky-Chi	92	Witek-NY	.314	Fletcher-Pit	.395	Kurowski-StL	.439
		Vaughan-Bro	173	Tipton-Cin	85	Nicholson-Chi	.309	Tipton-Cin	.395	Northey-Phi	.430

Production		Adjusted Production		Batter Runs		Adjusted Batter Runs		Clutch Hitting Index		Runs Created	
Musial-StL	.988	Musial-StL	176	Musial-StL	65.5	Musial-StL	62.3	Herman-Bro	153	Musial-StL	147
Nicholson-Chi	.917	Nicholson-Chi	166	Nicholson-Chi	47.7	Nicholson-Chi	48.8	Miller-Cin	149	Nicholson-Chi	129
Elliott-Pit	.820	Tipton-Cin	138	Galan-Bro	28.5	Galan-Bro	28.3	Elliott-Pit	133	Herman-Bro	97
Tipton-Cin	.819	Galan-Bro	136	Herman-Bro	28.0	Herman-Bro	27.9	Wasdell-Pit-Phi	130	Vaughan-Bro	96
Galan-Bro	.818	Herman-Bro	135	Elliott-Pit	26.5	Tipton-Cin	26.7	Stanky-Chi	127	Elliott-Pit	96

Total Average		Stolen Bases		Stolen Base Average		Stolen Base Runs		Fielding Runs		Total Player Rating	
Musial-StL	1.039	Vaughan-Bro	20					Miller-Cin	26.6	Musial-StL	6.7
Nicholson-Chi	.944	Lowrey-Chi	13					Marion-StL	25.3	Nicholson-Chi	4.9
Ott-NY	.895	Workman-Bos	12					Mueller-Cin	20.2	Galan-Bro	3.9
Galan-Bro	.876	Russell-Pit	12					Wietelmann-Bos	20.0	Mueller-Cin	3.8
Tipton-Cin	.825	Gustine-Pit	12					Galan-Bro	16.1	Witek-NY	3.3

Wins		Win Percentage		Games		Complete Games		Shutouts		Saves	
Sewell-Pit	21	M.Cooper-StL	.724	Adams-NY	70	Sewell-Pit	25	Bithorn-Chi	7	Webber-Bro	10
Riddle-Cin	21	Sewell-Pit	.700	Webber-Bro	54	Tobin-Bos	24	M.Cooper-StL	6	Adams-NY	9
M.Cooper-StL	21	Lanier-StL	.682	Head-Bro	47	M.Cooper-StL	24			Shoun-Cin	7
Bithorn-Chi	18	Riddle-Cin	.656	Shoun-Cin	45	Andrews-Bos	23			Head-Bro	6
Javery-Bos	17	Bithorn-Chi	.600	Mungo-NY	45					Beggs-Cin	6

Innings Pitched		Fewest Hits/Game		Fewest BB/Game		Strikeouts		Strikeouts/Game		Ratio	
Javery-Bos	303.0	Wyatt-Bro	6.92	Rowe-Phi	1.31	VanderMeer-Cin	174	VanderMeer-Cin	5.42	Wyatt-Bro	9.07
VanderMeer-Cin	289.0	VanderMeer-Cin	7.10	Wyse-Chi	1.96	M.Cooper-StL	141	Higbe-Bro	5.25	M.Cooper-StL	10.25
Andrews-Bos	283.2	M.Cooper-StL	7.49	Derringer-Chi	2.02	Javery-Bos	134	Lanier-StL	5.19	Rowe-Phi	10.31
M.Cooper-StL	274.0	Krist-StL	7.72	Davis-Bro	2.14	Lanier-StL	123	M.Cooper-StL	4.63	Andrews-Bos	10.60
Sewell-Pit	265.1	Barrett-Chi-Phi	7.94	Wyatt-Bro	2.14	Higbe-Bro	108	Head-Bro	4.40	Bithorn-Chi	10.60

Earned Run Average		Adjusted ERA		Opponents' Batting Avg.		Opponents' On Base Pct.		Starter Runs		Adjusted Starter Runs	
Lanier-StL	1.90	Lanier-StL	177	Wyatt-Bro	.207	Wyatt-Bro	.255	Lanier-StL	35.2	Lanier-StL	34.7
M.Cooper-StL	2.30	M.Cooper-StL	146	VanderMeer-Cin	.224	Rowe-Phi	.279	M.Cooper-StL	33.0	M.Cooper-StL	32.4
Wyatt-Bro	2.49	Sewell-Pit	137	M.Cooper-StL	.226	M.Cooper-StL	.286	Andrews-Bos	25.6	Sewell-Pit	27.5
Sewell-Pit	2.54	Wyatt-Bro	135	Krist-StL	.233	Andrews-Bos	.291	Sewell-Pit	24.7	Andrews-Bos	26.6
Andrews-Bos	2.57	Butcher-Pit	134	Barrett-Chi-Phi	.237	Bithorn-Chi	.294	Riddle-Cin	21.9	Pollet-StL	21.2

Clutch Pitching Index		Relief Runs		Adjusted Relief Runs		Relief Ranking		Total Pitcher Index		Total Baseball Ranking	
Lanier-StL	151	Beggs-Cin	13.4	Beggs-Cin	12.5	Beggs-Cin	14.1	Sewell-Pit	3.9	Musial-StL	6.7
Butcher-Pit	122	Adams-NY	8.8	Adams-NY	9.7	Adams-NY	12.6	Lanier-StL	3.7	Nicholson-Chi	4.9
Sewell-Pit	121	Prim-Chi	5.6	Prim-Chi	5.2	Prim-Chi	5.7	Tobin-Bos	3.5	Galan-Bro	3.9
Riddle-Cin	118	Brandt-Pit	1.6	Brandt-Pit	2.2	Brandt-Pit	1.7	M.Cooper-StL	3.2	Sewell-Pit	3.9
Tobin-Bos	113							Andrews-Bos	3.2	Mueller-Cin	3.8

TEAM	G	W	L	PCT	GB	R	OR	AB	H	2B	3B	HR	BB	SO	AVG	OBP	SLG	PRO	PRO+	BR	/A	PF	CHI	RC	SB	CS	SBA	SBR
NY	155	98	56	.636		669	542	5282	1350	218	59	100	624	562	.256	.337	.376	.713	114	97	93	101	95	683	46	60	43	-22
WAS	153	84	69	.549	13.5	666	595	5233	1328	245	50	47	605	579	.254	.336	.347	.683	110	45	67	96	103	656	142	55	72	10
CLE	153	82	71	.536	15.5	600	577	5269	1344	246	45	55	567	521	.255	.329	.350	.679	112	32	69	94	95	626	47	58	45	-21
CHI	155	82	72	.532	16	573	594	5254	1297	193	46	33	561	581	.247	.322	.320	.642	94	-33	-32	100	102	570	173	87	67	0
DET	155	78	76	.506	20	632	560	5364	1401	200	47	77	483	553	.261	.324	.359	.683	98	32	-14	108	99	620	40	43	48	-14
STL	153	72	80	.474	25	596	604	5175	1269	229	36	78	569	646	.245	.308	.349	.671	100	14	2	102	98	603	37	43	46	-15
BOS	155	68	84	.447	29	563	607	5392	1314	223	42	57	486	591	.244	.308	.332	.640	92	-48	-58	102	101	570	86	61	59	-11
PHI	155	49	105	.318	49	497	717	5244	1219	174	44	26	430	465	.232	.294	.297	.591	78	-137	-134	100	111	466	55	42	57	-9
TOT	617					4796		42213	10522	1728	369	473	4325	4498	.249	.322	.341	.663							626	449	58	-82

TEAM	CG	SH	SV	IP	H	H/G	HR	BB	SO	RAT	ERA	ERA+	OAV	OOB	PR	/A	PF	CPI	FA	E	DP	FW	PW	BW	SBW	DIF
NY	83	14	13	1415¹	1229	7.8	60	489	653	11.0	2.93	110	.234	.301	58	46	98	95	.974	160	166	.2	5.0	10.1	-1.3	7.0
WAS	61	16	21	1388	1293	8.4	48	540	495	12.0	3.18	101	.246	.318	17	3	97	99	.971	179	145	-1.0	.3	7.2	2.2	-1.3
CLE	64	14	20	1406¹	1234	7.9	52	606	585	11.9	3.15	99	.239	.322	23	-6	94	100	.975	157	183	.3	-.6	7.5	-1.2	-.4
CHI	70	12	19	1400¹	1352	8.7	54	501	476	12.1	3.20	104	.255	.324	15	21	101	105	.973	166	167	-.0	2.3	-3.5	1.1	5.2
DET	67	18	20	1411²	1226	7.8	51	549	706	11.4	3.00	117	.234	.308	46	81	107	95	.971	177	130	-.7	8.8	-1.5	-.4	-5.1
STL	64	10	14	1385	1397	9.1	74	488	572	12.4	3.41	97	.263	.327	-18	-13	101	106	.975	152	127	.6	-1.4	.2	-.5	-2.9
BOS	62	13	16	1426¹	1369	8.6	61	615	513	12.6	3.45	96	.257	.335	-25	-22	101	105	.976	153	179	.6	-2.4	-6.3	-.0	.0
PHI	73	5	13	1394	1421	9.2	73	536	503	12.9	4.05	84	.265	.336	-117	-101	103	94	.973	162	148	.1	-10.9	-14.5	.1	-2.8
TOT	544	102	136	11227		8.4				12.0	3.30		.249	.322					.973	1306	1245					

Runs
Case-Was 102
Keller-NY 97
Wakefield-Det 91
York-Det 90
Vernon-Was 89

Hits
Wakefield-Det 200
Appling-Chi 192
Cramer-Det 182
Case-Was 180

Doubles
Wakefield-Det 38
Case-Was 36
Gutteridge-StL ... 35
Etten-NY 35

Triples
Moses-Chi 12
Lindell-NY 12
York-Det 11
Keller-NY 11
Spence-Was 10

Home Runs
York-Det 34
Keller-NY 31
Stephens-StL 22
Heath-Cle 18

Total Bases
York-Det 301
Wakefield-Det 275
Keller-NY 269
Doerr-Bos 249
Stephens-StL 247

Runs Batted In
York-Det 118
Etten-NY 107
Johnson-NY 94
Stephens-StL 91
Spence-Was 88

Runs Produced
York-Det 174
Etten-NY 171
Wakefield-Det 163
Johnson-NY 159
Case-Was 153

Bases On Balls
Keller-NY 106
Gordon-NY 98
Cullenbine-Cle ... 96
Boudreau-Cle 90
Appling-Chi 90

Batting Average
Appling-Chi ...... .328
Wakefield-Det .... .316
Cramer-Det .... .300
Case-Was .... .294
Curtright-Chi .... .291

On Base Percentage
Appling-Chi ...... .419
Cullenbine-Cle ... .407
Keller-NY .... .396
Boudreau-Cle ..... .388
Curtright-Chi .... .382

Slugging Average
York-Det .... .527
Keller-NY .... .525
Stephens-StL ..... .482
Heath-Cle .... .481
Wakefield-Det .... .434

Production
Keller-NY .... .922
York-Det .... .893
Heath-Cle .... .850
Stephens-StL ..... .839
Appling-Chi ...... .825

Adjusted Production
Keller-NY 167
Heath-Cle 157
York-Det 148
Cullenbine-Cle ... 146
Appling-Chi 142

Batter Runs
Keller-NY 45.8
York-Det 41.0
Appling-Chi 35.0
Wakefield-Det 28.8
Cullenbine-Cle ... 27.4

Adjusted Batter Runs
Keller-NY 45.3
York-Det 35.9
Appling-Chi 35.1
Cullenbine-Cle ... 31.1
Heath-Cle 28.1

Clutch Hitting Index
Sullivan-Was 175
Johnson-NY 157
Siebert-Phi 150
Etten-NY 144
Higgins-Det 143

Runs Created
Keller-NY 116
Appling-Chi 109
York-Det 108
Wakefield-Det 101
Spence-Was 93

Total Average
Keller-NY .... .979
York-Det .... .871
Appling-Chi ...... .841
Heath-Cle .... .828
Cullenbine-Cle ... .816

Stolen Bases
Case-Was 61
Moses-Chi 56
Tucker-Chi 29
Appling-Chi 27
Vernon-Was 24

Stolen Base Average
Case-Was 81.3
Moses-Chi 80.0
Appling-Chi 77.1
Vernon-Was 75.0
Fox-Bos 73.3

Stolen Base Runs
Case-Was 9.9
Moses-Chi 8.4
Culberson-Bos 4.2
Appling-Chi 3.3
Vernon-Was 2.4

Fielding Runs
Boudreau-Cle 28.4
Gordon-NY 25.7
Clift-StL-Was 18.3
York-Det 17.6
Bloodworth-Det ... 17.2

Total Player Rating
Boudreau-Cle 6.5
Appling-Chi 6.0
Gordon-NY 5.5
York-Det 4.6
Keller-NY 4.3

Wins
Trout-Det 20
Chandler-NY 20
Wynn-Was 18
Smith-Cle 17
Bagby-Cle 17

Win Percentage
Chandler-NY ...... .833
Smith-Cle .... .708
Bonham-NY .... .652
Trout-Det .... .625
Grove-Chi .... .625

Games
Brown-Bos 49
Trout-Det 44
Wolff-Phi 41
Ryba-Bos 40
Carrasquel-Was ... 39

Complete Games
Hughson-Bos 20
Chandler-NY 20
Wensloff-NY 18
Trout-Det 18
Grove-Chi 18

Shutouts
Trout-Det 5
Chandler-NY 5
Hughson-Bos 4
Bonham-NY 4

Saves
Maltzberger-Chi ... 14
Heving-Cle 9
Brown-Bos 9
Murphy-NY 8
Caster-StL 8

Innings Pitched
Bagby-Cle 273.0
Hughson-Bos 266.0
Wynn-Was 256.2
Chandler-NY 253.0
Trout-Det 246.2

Fewest Hits/Game
Reynolds-Cle 6.34
Niggeling-StL-Was 6.66
Haefner-Was 6.86
Chandler-NY 7.01
Wensloff-NY 7.21

Fewest BB/Game
Leonard-Was 1.88
Chandler-NY 1.92
Bonham-NY 2.07
Muncrief-StL 2.11
Trucks-Det 2.31

Strikeouts
Reynolds-Cle 151
Newhouser-Det ... 144
Chandler-NY 134
Bridges-Det 124
Trucks-Det 118

Strikeouts/Game
Reynolds-Cle 6.84
Newhouser-Det ... 6.62
Bridges-Det 5.82
Trucks-Det 5.24
Chandler-NY 4.77

Ratio
Chandler-NY 9.07
Trucks-Det 9.90
Bonham-NY 9.97
Wensloff-NY 10.07
Niggeling-StL-Was 10.24

Earned Run Average
Chandler-NY 1.64
Bonham-NY 2.27
Haefner-Was 2.29
Bridges-Det 2.39
Trout-Det 2.48

Adjusted ERA
Chandler-NY 197
Bridges-Det 147
Trout-Det 142
Bonham-NY 141
Haefner-Was 140

Opponents' Batting Avg.
Reynolds-Cle ..... .202
Niggeling-StL-Was .204
Haefner-Was ...... .208
Chandler-NY ...... .215
Wensloff-NY ...... .219

Opponents' On Base Pct.
Chandler-NY ...... .261
Trucks-Det .... .276
Wensloff-NY ...... .282
Bonham-NY .... .282
Niggeling-StL-Was .282

Starter Runs
Chandler-NY 46.6
Bonham-NY 25.6
Trout-Det 22.3
Hughson-Bos 19.4
Bridges-Det 19.2

Adjusted Starter Runs
Chandler-NY 44.4
Trout-Det 28.5
Bridges-Det 24.0
Bonham-NY 23.6
Hughson-Bos 19.9

Clutch Pitching Index
Hughson-Bos 124
Muncrief-StL 120
Bonham-NY 116
Galehouse-StL 115
Candini-Was 115

Relief Runs
Brown-Bos 12.2
Caster-StL 10.0
Maltzberger-Chi .. 9.1
Naymick-Cle 6.9
Murphy-NY 5.9

Adjusted Relief Runs
Brown-Bos 12.3
Caster-StL 10.2
Maltzberger-Chi .. 9.6
Naymick-Cle 5.6
Murphy-NY 5.3

Relief Ranking
Caster-StL 19.2
Brown-Bos 17.0
Maltzberger-Chi .. 12.7
Murphy-NY 12.6
Naymick-Cle 6.9

Total Pitcher Index
Chandler-NY 6.6
Trout-Det 4.0
Bridges-Det 2.9
Bonham-NY 2.2
Hughson-Bos 1.9

Total Baseball Ranking
Chandler-NY 6.6
Boudreau-Cle 6.5
Appling-Chi 6.0
Gordon-NY 5.5
York-Det 4.6

TEAM	G	W	L	PCT	GB	R	OR	AB	H	2B	3B	HR	BB	SO	AVG	OBP	SLG	PRO	PRO+	BR	/A	PF	CHI	RC	SB	CS	SBA	SBR
STL	157	105	49	.682		772	490	5475	1507	274	59	100	544	473	.275	.344	.402	.746	114	110	98	102	98	775	37			
PIT	158	90	63	.588	14.5	744	662	5428	1441	248	80	70	573	616	.265	.338	.379	.717	104	58	30	104	102	707	87			
CIN	155	89	65	.578	16	573	537	5271	1340	229	31	51	423	391	.254	.313	.338	.651	92	-74	-50	96	101	558	51			
CHI	157	75	79	.487	30	702	669	5462	1425	236	46	71	520	521	.261	.328	.360	.688	101	-2	2	99	104	658	53			
NY	155	67	87	.435	38	682	773	5306	1398	191	47	93	512	480	.263	.331	.370	.701	103	22	24	100	100	656	39			
BOS	155	65	89	.422	40	593	674	5282	1299	250	39	79	456	509	.246	.308	.353	.661	88	-61	-88	104	101	586	37			
BRO	155	63	91	.409	42	690	832	5393	1450	255	51	56	486	451	.269	.331	.366	.697	104	16	28	98	101	664	45			
PHI	154	61	92	.399	43.5	539	658	5301	1331	199	42	55	470	500	.251	.316	.336	.652	92	-70	-48	97	92	571	32			
TOT	623					5295		42918	11191	1882	395	575	3984	3941	.261	.326	.363	.689							381			

TEAM	CG	SH	SV	IP	H	H/G	HR	BB	SO	RAT	ERA	ERA+	OAV	OOB	PR	/A	PF	CPI	FA	E	DP	FW	PW	BW	SBW	DIF
STL	89	26	12	1427	1228	7.7	55	468	637	10.8	2.67	132	.233	.298	148	134	98	103	.982	112	162	3.7	13.8	10.1		.5
PIT	77	10	19	1414[1]	1466	9.3	65	435	452	12.2	3.44	108	.265	.321	27	45	103	103	.970	191	122	-1.1	4.6	3.1		6.9
CIN	93	17	12	1398[1]	1292	8.3	60	390	369	10.9	2.97	117	.246	.300	99	80	97	99	.978	137	153	2.0	8.2	-5.1		6.9
CHI	70	11	13	1400[2]	1484	9.5	75	458	545	12.5	3.59	98	.274	.331	4	-8	98	108	.970	186	151	-.8	-.8	.2		-.5
NY	47	4	21	1363[2]	1413	9.3	116	587	499	13.4	4.29	85	.265	.342	-103	-94	102	98	.971	179	128	-.5	-9.6	2.5		-2.3
BOS	70	13	12	1388[1]	1430	9.3	80	527	454	12.8	3.67	104	.267	.335	-9	23	106	106	.971	182	160	-.7	2.4	-9.0		-4.6
BRO	50	4	13	1367[2]	1471	9.7	75	660	487	14.3	4.68	76	.274	.357	-162	-172	98	93	.966	197	112	-1.7	-17.7	2.9		2.4
PHI	66	11	6	1395[1]	1407	9.1	49	459	496	12.2	3.64	99	.261	.321	-4	-5	100	93	.972	177	138	-.5	-.5	-4.9		-9.6
TOT	562	96	108	11155[1]		9.0				12.4	3.61		.261	.326					.972	1361	1126					

Runs
Nicholson-Chi 116
Musial-StL 112
Russell-Pit 109
Hopp-StL 106
Cavarretta-Chi 106

Hits
Musial-StL 197
Cavarretta-Chi ... 197
Holmes-Bos 195
Walker-Bro 191
Russell-Pit 181

Doubles
Musial-StL 51
Galan-Bro 43
Holmes-Bos 42

Triples
Barrett-Pit 19
Elliott-Pit.......... 16
Cavarretta-Chi 15
Russell-Pit 14
Musial-StL 14

Home Runs
Nicholson-Chi 33
Ott-NY 26
Northey-Phi 22
McCormick-Cin ... 20
Kurowski-StL...... 20

Total Bases
Nicholson-Chi 317
Musial-StL 312
Holmes-Bos 288
Walker-Bro 283
Northey-Phi 283

Runs Batted In
Nicholson-Chi ... 122
Elliott-Pit......... 108
Northey-Phi 104
Sanders-StL 102
McCormick-Cin ... 102

Runs Produced
Nicholson-Chi 205
Musial-StL 194
Elliott-Pit........ 183
Cavarretta-Chi ... 183

Bases On Balls
Galan-Bro 101
Nicholson-Chi 93
Ott-NY 90
Musial-StL 90
Barrett-Pit 86

Batting Average
Walker-Bro........357
Musial-StL........347
Medwick-NY 337
Hopp-StL.........336
Cavarretta-Chi.....321

On Base Percentage
Musial-StL......440
Walker-Bro......434
Galan-Bro 426
Ott-NY 423
Hopp-StL......404

Slugging Average
Musial-StL........549
Nicholson-Chi....545
Ott-NY 544
Walker-Bro.......529
Hopp-StL........499

Production
Musial-StL.......990
Ott-NY 967
Walker-Bro......963
Nicholson-Chi....935
Galan-Bro 922

Adjusted Production
Musial-StL 174
Walker-Bro....... 173
Ott-NY 171
Nicholson-Chi 162
Galan-Bro 162

Batter Runs
Musial-StL 60.9
Walker-Bro....... 51.2
Nicholson-Chi ... 47.4
Galan-Bro 46.5
Ott-NY 40.4

Adjusted Batter Runs
Musial-StL 59.6
Walker-Bro....... 52.4
Nicholson-Chi ... 47.9
Galan-Bro 47.8
Ott-NY 40.6

Clutch Hitting Index
Elliott-Pit......... 146
Olmo-Bro 143
Medwick-NY 136
Dahlgren-Pit..... 129
Sanders-StL 129

Runs Created
Musial-StL 145
Nicholson-Chi ... 132
Walker-Bro 128
Galan-Bro 123
Russell-Pit 112

Total Average
Musial-StL 1.095
Ott-NY 1.087
Walker-Bro 1.034
Nicholson-Chi ... 1.002
Galan-Bro .... .992

Stolen Bases
Barrett-Pit 28
Lupien-Phi 18
Hughes-Chi 16
Hopp-StL 15
Kerr-NY 14

Stolen Base Average

Stolen Base Runs

Fielding Runs
Kerr-NY 16.8
Luby-NY 16.4
Williams-Cin 15.0
Pafko-Chi 14.7
Russell-Pit 13.3

Total Player Rating
Musial-StL 5.5
Walker-Bro 4.3
Nicholson-Chi 4.2
Galan-Bro 3.9
Russell-Pit 3.6

Wins
Walters-Cin 23
M.Cooper-StL 22
Voiselle-NY 21
Sewell-Pit 21
Tobin-Bos......... 18

Win Percentage
Wilks-StL.........810
Brecheen-StL.....762
M.Cooper-StL.....759
Walters-Cin 742
Sewell-Pit 636

Games
Adams-NY 65
Webber-Bro 48
Rescigno-Pit 48
Voiselle-NY 43
Tobin-Bos 43

Complete Games
Tobin-Bos......... 28
Walters-Cin 27
Voiselle-NY 25
Sewell-Pit 24
M.Cooper-StL 22

Shutouts
M.Cooper-StL 7
Walters-Cin 6
Tobin-Bos.......... 5
Lanier-StL 5
Butcher-Pit........ 5

Saves
Adams-NY 13
Schmidt-StL....... 5
Rescigno-Pit 5
Davis-Bro 4
Cuccurullo-Pit 4

Innings Pitched
Voiselle-NY ... 312.2
Tobin-Bos...... 299.1
Sewell-Pit 286.0
Walters-Cin 285.0
Raffensberger-Phi 258.2

Fewest Hits/Game
Walters-Cin 7.36
Wilks-StL........ 7.50
Lanier-StL 7.70
Heusser-Cin...... 7.71
Voiselle-NY 7.94

Fewest BB/Game
Raffensberger-Phi. 1.57
Strincevich-Pit ... 1.75
Davis-Bro 1.81
Shoun-Cin 1.87
Derringer-Chi 1.95

Strikeouts
Voiselle-NY 161
Lanier-StL 141
Javery-Bos 137
Raffensberger-Phi. 136

Strikeouts/Game
Lanier-StL 5.66
Javery-Bos 4.85
Raffensberger-Phi. 4.73
Voiselle-NY 4.63
Melton-Bro....... 4.37

Ratio
Wilks-StL 9.66
Heusser-Cin...... 9.72
De LaCruz-Cin... 10.16
Walters-Cin 10.23
M.Cooper-StL ... 10.41

Earned Run Average
Heusser-Cin 2.38
Walters-Cin 2.40
M.Cooper-StL 2.46
Wilks-StL 2.64
Lanier-StL 2.65

Adjusted ERA
Heusser-Cin 146
Walters-Cin 145
M.Cooper-StL 143
Wilks-StL 133
Lanier-StL 133

Opponents' Batting Avg.
Walters-Cin 219
Wilks-StL........227
Heusser-Cin......231
Voiselle-NY 232
Lanier-StL 234

Opponents' On Base Pct.
Wilks-StL.........275
Heusser-Cin......275
Walters-Cin 281
De LaCruz-Cin....284
Raffensberger-Phi..285

Starter Runs
Walters-Cin 38.3
M.Cooper-StL 32.2
Munger-StL 30.5
Heusser-Cin...... 26.3
Lanier-StL 24.0

Adjusted Starter Runs
Walters-Cin 34.4
M.Cooper-StL 29.8
Munger-StL 29.4
Tobin-Bos........ 27.0
Ostermueller-Bro-Pit . 23.9

Clutch Pitching Index
Fleming-Chi 121
Ostermueller-Bro-Pit . 120
Chipman-Bro-Chi . 119
Wyse-Chi 113
Javery-Bos 111

Relief Runs
Karl-Phi 12.7
Donnelly-StL 12.6

Adjusted Relief Runs
Karl-Phi 12.7
Donnelly-StL 11.9

Relief Ranking
Karl-Phi 7.1
Donnelly-StL 4.9

Total Pitcher Index
Walters-Cin 4.7
Tobin-Bos......... 4.3
Munger-StL 3.3
M.Cooper-StL 2.9
Ostermueller-Bro-Pit .. 2.6

Total Baseball Ranking
Musial-StL 5.5
Walters-Cin 4.7
Tobin-Bos......... 4.3
Walker-Bro........ 4.3
Nicholson-Chi 4.2

TEAM	G	W	L	PCT	GB	R	OR	AB	H	2B	3B	HR	BB	SO	AVG	OBP	SLG	PRO	PRO+	BR	/A	PF	CHI	RC	SB	CS	SBA	SBR
STL	154	89	65	.578		684	587	5269	1328	223	45	72	531	604	.252	.323	.352	.675	94	-4	-40	106	110	629	44	33	57	-7
DET	156	88	66	.571	1	658	581	5344	1405	220	44	60	532	500	.263	.332	.354	.686	97	21	-14	106	100	641	61	55	53	-15
NY	154	83	71	.539	6	674	617	5331	1410	216	74	96	522	627	.264	.333	.387	.720	108	73	81	99	103	707	91	31	75	9
BOS	156	77	77	.500	12	739	676	5400	1456	277	56	69	522	505	.270	.336	.380	.716	112	73	81	99	103	710	60	40	60	-6
PHI	155	72	82	.468	17	525	594	5312	1364	169	47	36	422	490	.257	.314	.327	.641	90	-73	-64	99	96	547	42	32	57	-7
CLE	155	72	82	.468	17	643	677	5481	1458	270	50	70	512	593	.266	.331	.372	.703	111	46	71	96	93	684	66	47	58	-8
CHI	154	71	83	.461	18	543	662	5292	1307	210	55	23	439	448	.247	.320	.320	.627	86	-97	-89	99	104	533	48	42	53	-11
WAS	154	64	90	.416	25	592	664	5319	1386	186	42	33	470	477	.261	.324	.330	.654	97	-41	-13	96	101	594	127	59	68	3
TOT	619					5058		42748	11114	1771	413	459	3951	4244	.260	.325	.353	.678							539	339	61	-42

TEAM	CG	SH	SV	IP	H	H/G	HR	BB	SO	RAT	ERA	ERA+	OAV	OOB	PR	/A	PF	CPI	FA	E	DP	FW	PW	BW	SBW	DIF
STL	71	16	17	1397.1	1392	9.0	58	469	581	12.1	3.17	114	.259	.320	41	66	105	105	.972	171	142	.5	6.9	-4.2	-.2	9.0
DET	87	20	8	1400	1373	8.8	39	452	568	11.9	3.09	116	.257	.318	54	75	104	103	.970	190	184	-.5	7.9	-1.5	-1.0	6.1
NY	78	9	13	1390.1	1351	8.7	82	532	529	12.3	3.39	103	.257	.326	7	15	102	105	.974	156	170	1.3	1.6	5.7	1.5	-4.1
BOS	58	7	17	1394.1	1404	9.1	66	592	524	13.0	3.82	89	.263	.339	-60	-65	99	98	.972	171	154	.6	-6.8	8.5	-.0	-2.2
PHI	72	10	14	1397.1	1345	8.7	58	390	534	11.4	3.26	107	.252	.307	-35	-56	96	102	.971	176	127	.2	-6.7	-.2		-2.0
CLE	48	7	18	1419.1	1428	9.1	40	621	524	13.2	3.65	90	.265	.344	-23	-23	100	93	.974	165	192	.9	-5.9	7.5	-.6	-6.8
CHI	64	5	17	1390.2	1411	9.1	68	420	481	12.0	3.58	96	.264	.320	-23	-23	100	97	.970	183	154	-.2	-2.4	-9.4	-.3	6.3
WAS	83	13	11	1381	1410	9.2	48	475	503	12.4	3.49	93	.264	.327	-10	-36	95	99	.964	218	156	-2.3	-3.8	-1.4	.9	-6.4
TOT	561	87	115	11170.1		9.0				12.3	3.43		.260	.325					.971	1430	1279					

Runs
Stirnweiss-NY 125
R.Johnson-Bos ... 106
Cullenbine-Cle 98
Doerr-Bos 95
Metkovich-Bos 94

Hits
Stirnweiss-NY 205
Boudreau-Cle 191
Spence-Was 187
Lindell-NY 178
Rocco-Cle 174

Doubles
Boudreau-Cle 45
Keltner-Cle........ 41
R.Johnson-Bos 40
Fox-Det 37
Stirnweiss-NY 35

Triples
Stirnweiss-NY 16
Lindell-NY 16
Gutteridge-StL 11
Doerr-Bos 10

Home Runs
Etten-NY 22
Stephens-StL 20
York-Det 18
Spence-Was 18
Lindell-NY 18

Total Bases
Lindell-NY 297
Stirnweiss-NY 296
Spence-Was 288
R.Johnson-Bos ... 277

Runs Batted In
Stephens-StL 109
R.Johnson-Bos ... 106
Lindell-NY 103
Spence-Was 100
York-Det 98

Runs Produced
R.Johnson-Bos ... 195
Stephens-StL 180
Lindell-NY 176
Spence-Was 165
Cullenbine-Cle 162

Bases On Balls
Etten-NY 97
R.Johnson-Bos ... 95
Cullenbine-Cle 87
McQuinn-StL 85
Higgins-Det 81

Batting Average
Boudreau-Cle 327
Doerr-Bos 325
R.Johnson-Bos ...324
Stirnweiss-NY 319
Spence-Was 316

On Base Percentage
R.Johnson-Bos 431
Boudreau-Cle 406
Doerr-Bos 399
Etten-NY 399
Byrnes-StL........396

Slugging Average
Doerr-Bos 528
R.Johnson-Bos ...528
Lindell-NY 500
Spence-Was 486

Production
R.Johnson-Bos 959
Doerr-Bos 927
Spence-Was 877
Etten-NY 865
Lindell-NY 851

Adjusted Production
R.Johnson-Bos ... 175
Doerr-Bos 166
Spence-Was 157
Boudreau-Cle 146
Etten-NY 142

Batter Runs
R.Johnson-Bos 52.9
Spence-Was 38.1
Doerr-Bos 38.0
Etten-NY 37.3
Wakefield-Det 36.7

Adjusted Batter Runs
R.Johnson-Bos ... 53.7
Spence-Was 41.3
Stephens-StL 38.7
Boudreau-Cle 35.9
Etten-NY 34.9

Clutch Hitting Index
Christman-StL 145
Carnett-Chi 133
Stephens-StL 131
Torres-Was 124
Trosky-Chi 124

Runs Created
Stirnweiss-NY 128
R.Johnson-Bos ... 124
Spence-Was 118
Etten-NY 114
Boudreau-Cle 112

Total Average
R.Johnson-Bos 987
Doerr-Bos 945
Stirnweiss-NY 910
Etten-NY 879
Spence-Was 856

Stolen Bases
Stirnweiss-NY 55
Case-Was 49
Myatt-Was 26
Moses-Chi 21
Gutteridge-StL..... 20

Stolen Base Average
Stirnweiss-NY 83.3
Moses-Chi 75.0
Case-Was 73.1
Myatt-Was 72.2
Gutteridge-StL.... 71.4

Stolen Base Runs
Stirnweiss-NY 9.9
Case-Was 3.9
Moses-Chi 2.1
Myatt-Was 1.8
Grimes-NY 1.8

Fielding Runs
Mayo-Det 29.4
Boudreau-Cle 25.8
Stirnweiss-NY ... 18.9
Spence-Was 18.6
Tucker-Chi 17.7

Total Player Rating
Boudreau-Cle 7.7
Stirnweiss-NY ... 7.2
Doerr-Bos 5.1
Spence-Was 5.0
R.Johnson-Bos ... 4.8

Wins
Newhouser-Det 29
Trout-Det 27
Potter-StL 19
Hughson-Bos 18

Win Percentage
Hughson-Bos 783
Newhouser-Det ...763
Potter-StL 731
Trout-Det 659
Borowy-NY 586

Games
Heving-Cle 63
Berry-Phi 53
Trout-Det 49
Newhouser-Det ... 47
Klieman-Cle 47

Complete Games
Trout-Det 33
Newhouser-Det 25

Shutouts
Trout-Det 7
Newhouser-Det 6
Jakucki-StL 4

Saves
Maltzberger-Chi ... 12
Caster-StL 12
Berry-Phi 12
Heving-Cle 10
Barrett-Bos 8

Innings Pitched
Trout-Det 352.1
Newhouser-Det .. 312.1
Newsom-Phi 265.0
Kramer-StL 257.0
Borowy-NY 252.2

Fewest Hits/Game
Gromek-Cle 7.07
Niggeling-Was ... 7.17
Newhouser-Det ... 7.61
Hughson-Bos 7.61
Borowy-NY 7.98

Fewest BB/Game
Harris-Phi 1.34
Leonard-Was 1.45
Bonham-NY 1.73
Gorsica-Det 1.78
Hamlin-Phi 1.80

Strikeouts
Newhouser-Det ... 187
Trout-Det 144
Newsom-Phi 142
Kramer-StL 124
Niggeling-Was ... 121

Strikeouts/Game
Newhouser-Det ...5.39
Niggeling-Was ... 5.29
Gromek-Cle 5.08
Hughson-Bos 4.96
Newsom-Phi 4.82

Ratio
Hughson-Bos 9.52
Trout-Det 10.24
Leonard-Was 10.28
Gromek-Cle 10.30
Newhouser-Det .. 10.58

Earned Run Average
Trout-Det 2.12
Newhouser-Det ... 2.22
Hughson-Bos 2.26
Niggeling-Was ... 2.32
Kramer-StL 2.49

Adjusted ERA
Trout-Det 168
Newhouser-Det ... 161
Hughson-Bos 151
Kramer-StL 145
Niggeling-Was ... 141

Opponents' Batting Avg.
Gromek-Cle 219
Niggeling-Was 221
Hughson-Bos 225
Newhouser-Det ...230
Borowy-NY 236

Opponents' On Base Pct.
Hughson-Bos 267
Leonard-Was 284
Trout-Det 284
Gromek-Cle 290
Newhouser-Det ...293

Starter Runs
Trout-Det 51.3
Newhouser-Det .. 42.1
Kramer-StL 27.0
Hughson-Bos 26.5
Niggeling-Was ... 25.5

Adjusted Starter Runs
Trout-Det 56.7
Newhouser-Det .. 46.8
Kramer-StL 31.8
Hughson-Bos 25.8
Borowy-NY 23.9

Clutch Pitching Index
Donald-NY 129
Woods-Bos 122
Smith-Cle 116
Haynes-Chi 116
Bonham-NY 115

Relief Runs
Heving-Cle 19.6
Berry-Phi 18.4
Caster-StL 8.9
Maltzberger-Chi ... 4.8

Adjusted Relief Runs
Berry-Phi 19.1
Heving-Cle 17.9
Caster-StL 10.4
Maltzberger-Chi ... 4.8

Relief Ranking
Berry-Phi 32.4
Heving-Cle 18.2
Caster-StL 17.3
Maltzberger-Chi ... 8.5

Total Pitcher Index
Trout-Det 8.8
Newhouser-Det ... 5.9
Kramer-StL 4.1
Hughson-Bos 2.8
Borowy-NY 2.3

Total Baseball Ranking
Trout-Det 8.8
Boudreau-Cle 7.7
Stirnweiss-NY ... 7.2
Newhouser-Det ... 5.9
Doerr-Bos 5.1

TEAM	G	W	L	PCT	GB	R	OR	AB	H	2B	3B	HR	BB	SO	AVG	OBP	SLG	PRO	PRO+	BR	/A	PF	CHI	RC	SB	CS	SBA	SBR
CHI	155	98	56	.636		735	532	5298	1465	229	52	57	554	462	.277	.349	.372	.721	109	53	68	98	99	714	69			
STL	155	95	59	.617	3	756	583	5487	1498	256	44	64	515	488	.273	.338	.371	.709	102	25	8	102	103	716	55			
BRO	155	87	67	.565	11	795	724	5418	1468	257	71	57	629	434	.271	.349	.376	.725	109	66	72	99	102	746	75			
PIT	155	82	72	.532	16	753	686	5343	1425	259	56	57	590	480	.267	.342	.377	.719	102	45	18	104	102	701	81			
NY	154	78	74	.513	19	668	700	5350	1439	175	35	114	501	457	.269	.336	.379	.715	103	33	23	102	93	692	38			
BOS	154	67	85	.441	30	721	728	5441	1453	229	25	101	520	510	.267	.334	.374	.708	102	20	17	101	100	692	82			
CIN	154	61	93	.396	37	536	694	5283	1317	221	26	56	392	532	.249	.304	.333	.637	85	-122	-107	98	99	537	71			
PHI	154	46	108	.299	52	548	865	5203	1278	197	27	56	449	501	.246	.307	.326	.633	84	-122	-104	97	102	527	54			
TOT	618					5512		42823	11343	1823	336	577	4150	3864	.265	.333	.364	.696							525			

TEAM	CG	SH	SV	IP	H	H/G	HR	BB	SO	RAT	ERA	ERA+	OAV	OOB	PR	/A	PF	CPI	FA	E	DP	FW	PW	BW	SBW	DIF
CHI	86	15	14	1366¹	1301	8.6	57	385	541	11.3	2.98	123	.249	.304	125	102	96	102	.980	121	124	3.4	10.2	6.8		.6
STL	77	18	9	1408²	1351	8.6	70	497	510	12.0	3.24	116	.253	.320	88	79	99	106	.977	137	150	2.4	7.9	.8		6.9
BRO	61	7	18	1392¹	1357	8.8	74	586	557	12.8	3.70	101	.253	.331	15	7	99	98	.962	230	144	-3.2	.7	7.2		5.3
PIT	73	8	16	1387¹	1477	9.6	61	455	518	12.7	3.76	105	.272	.331	6	27	104	100	.971	178	141	-.0	2.7	1.8		.6
NY	53	13	21	1374²	1401	9.2	85	528	530	12.8	4.06	96	.263	.332	-40	-23	103	95	.973	166	112	.6	-2.3	2.3		1.4
BOS	57	7	13	1391²	1474	9.5	99	557	404	13.3	4.04	95	.272	.342	-37	-32	101	104	.969	193	160	-1.1	-3.2	1.7		-6.4
CIN	77	11	6	1365²	1438	9.5	70	534	372	13.2	4.00	94	.271	.340	-31	-36	99	100	.976	146	138	1.8	-3.6	-10.7		-3.5
PHI	31	4	26	1352²	1544	10.3	61	608	432	14.5	4.64	83	.285	.360	-126	-123	101	97	.962	234	150	-3.5	-12.3	-10.4		-4.7
TOT	515	83	123	11039¹		9.2				12.8	3.80		.265	.333					.971	1405	1119					

Runs
Stanky-Bro 128
Rosen-Bro 126
Holmes-Bos 125
Galan-Bro 114
Hack-Chi 110

Hits
Holmes-Bos 224
Rosen-Bro 197
Hack-Chi 193
Clay-Cin 184

Doubles
Holmes-Bos 47
Walker-Bro 42
Galan-Bro 36
Elliott-Pit 36
Cavarretta-Chi 34

Triples
Olmo-Bro 13
Pafko-Chi 12
Rucker-NY 11
Rosen-Bro 11
Cavarretta-Chi 10

Home Runs
Holmes-Bos 28
Workman-Bos 25
Adams-Phi-StL ... 22
Ott-NY 21
Kurowski-StL 21

Total Bases
Holmes-Bos 367
Adams-Phi-StL ... 279
Rosen-Bro 279
Walker-Bro 266
Kurowski-StL 261

Runs Batted In
Walker-Bro 124
Holmes-Bos 117
Pafko-Chi 110
Olmo-Bro 110
Adams-Phi-StL ... 109

Runs Produced
Walker-Bro 218
Holmes-Bos 214
Galan-Bro 197
Adams-Phi-StL ... 191
Rosen-Bro 189

Bases On Balls
Stanky-Bro 148
Galan-Bro 114
Hack-Chi 99
Nicholson-Chi 92
Sanders-StL 83

Batting Average
Cavarretta-Chi 355
Holmes-Bos 352
Rosen-Bro 325
Hack-Chi 323
Kurowski-StL......323

On Base Percentage
Cavarretta-Chi 449
Galan-Bro 423
Hack-Chi 420
Holmes-Bos 420
Stanky-Bro........417

Slugging Average
Holmes-Bos 577
Kurowski-StL.....511
Cavarretta-Chi 500
Ott-NY 499
Olmo-Bro 462

Production
Holmes-Bos 997
Cavarretta-Chi 949
Ott-NY 910
Kurowski-StL.....894
Galan-Bro 864

Adjusted Production
Holmes-Bos 175
Cavarretta-Chi 167
Ott-NY 150
Kurowski-StL..... 144
Galan-Bro 142

Batter Runs
Holmes-Bos 62.9
Cavarretta-Chi 46.4
Galan-Bro 36.8
Ott-NY 33.4
Kurowski-StL..... 30.7

Adjusted Batter Runs
Holmes-Bos 62.5
Cavarretta-Chi 47.8
Galan-Bro 37.4
Ott-NY 32.5
Hack-Chi 31.0

Clutch Hitting Index
Walker-Bro 157
Elliott-Pit 157
Pafko-Chi 145
Lowrey-Chi 139
Olmo-Bro 136

Runs Created
Holmes-Bos 156
Cavarretta-Chi 119
Galan-Bro 116
Hack-Chi 111
Rosen-Bro 110

Total Average
Holmes-Bos ... 1.078
Cavarretta-Chi ... 1.037
Ott-NY 959
Galan-Bro 936
Kurowski-StL......876

Stolen Bases
Schoendienst-StL .. 26
Barrett-Pit 25
Clay-Cin 19

Stolen Base Average

Stolen Base Runs

Fielding Runs
Kerr-NY 28.3
Gillenwater-Bos .. 23.8
Coscarart-Pit 21.1
Hack-Chi 18.0
Walker-Bro 12.4

Total Player Rating
Holmes-Bos 5.4
Hack-Chi 5.2
Cavarretta-Chi 3.7
Stanky-Bro........ 3.6
Kurowski-StL...... 3.4

Wins
Barrett-Bos-StL.... 23
Wyse-Chi 22
Gregg-Bro 18
Burkhart-StL 18
Passeau-Chi 17

Win Percentage
Brecheen-StL 789
Burkhart-StL 692
Wyse-Chi 688
Barrett-Bos-StL....657
Passeau-Chi 654

Games
Karl-Phi 67
Adams-NY 65
Hutchings-Bos 57
Barrett-Bos-StL ... 45
Fox-Cin 45

Complete Games
Barrett-Bos-StL ... 24
Wyse-Chi 23
Passeau-Chi 19
Strincevich-Pit 18
Heusser-Cin....... 18

Shutouts
Passeau-Chi 5
Voiselle-NY 4
Heusser-Cin 4
Donnelly-StL 4
Burkhart-StL 4

Saves
Karl-Phi 15
Adams-NY 15
Rescigno-Pit 9

Innings Pitched
Barrett-Bos-StL .. 284.2
Wyse-Chi 278.1
Gregg-Bro 254.1
Roe-Pit 235.0
Voiselle-NY 232.1

Fewest Hits/Game
Prim-Chi 7.73
Brecheen-StL 7.78
Gregg-Bro 7.82
Mungo-NY 7.92
Passeau-Chi 8.13

Fewest BB/Game
Prim-Chi 1.25
Barrett-Bos-StL... 1.71
Roe-Pit 1.76
Wyse-Chi 1.78
Strincevich-Pit 1.93

Strikeouts
Roe-Pit 148
Gregg-Bro 139
Voiselle-NY 115
Mungo-NY 101
Hutchings-Bos 99

Strikeouts/Game
Roe-Pit 5.67
Mungo-NY 4.97
Gregg-Bro 4.92
Hutchings-Bos 4.82
Prim-Chi 4.79

Ratio
Prim-Chi 9.04
Roe-Pit 10.53
Passeau-Chi 10.55
Brecheen-StL 10.58
Wyse-Chi 10.74

Earned Run Average
Prim-Chi 2.40
Passeau-Chi 2.46
Brecheen-StL 2.52
Walters-Cin 2.68
Wyse-Chi 2.68

Adjusted ERA
Prim-Chi 152
Brecheen-StL 149
Passeau-Chi 149
Walters-Cin 140
Roe-Pit 137

Opponents' Batting Avg.
Prim-Chi .... .228
Gregg-Bro .... .232
Brecheen-StL .... .238
Mungo-NY .... .238
Passeau-Chi 238

Opponents' On Base Pct.
Prim-Chi .... .256
Passeau-Chi ...... .289
Barrett-Bos-StL... .295
Wyse-Chi .... .296
Roe-Pit .... .296

Starter Runs
Wyse-Chi 34.5
Passeau-Chi 33.8
Prim-Chi 25.8
Barrett-Bos-StL... 25.2
Roe-Pit 24.2

Adjusted Starter Runs
Passeau-Chi 30.1
Wyse-Chi 29.9
Roe-Pit 28.0
Barrett-Bos-StL... 23.7
Prim-Chi 23.1

Clutch Pitching Index
Butcher-Pit 124
Logan-Bos 124
Walters-Cin 124
Lee-Phi-Bos 123
Wyse-Chi 117

Relief Runs
Karl-Phi 16.3
Buker-Bro 4.9
Adams-NY 4.7
Chipman-Chi 2.4

Adjusted Relief Runs
Karl-Phi 16.9
Adams-NY 6.1
Buker-Bro 4.4
Chipman-Chi 1.2

Relief Ranking
Karl-Phi 16.6
Adams-NY 11.5
Buker-Bro 4.7
Chipman-Chi 1.4

Total Pitcher Index
Passeau-Chi 3.6
Wyse-Chi 3.1
Walters-Cin 2.7
Roe-Pit 2.6
Prim-Chi 2.6

Total Baseball Ranking
Holmes-Bos 5.4
Hack-Chi 5.2
Cavarretta-Chi 3.7
Passeau-Chi 3.6
Stanky-Bro........ 3.6

TEAM	G	W	L	PCT	GB	R	OR	AB	H	2B	3B	HR	BB	SO	AVG	OBP	SLG	PRO	PRO+	BR	/A	PF	CHI	RC	SB	CS	SBA	SBR
DET	155	88	65	.575		633	565	5257	1345	**227**	47	77	517	533	.256	.324	.361	.685	98	20	-18	106	102	627	60	54	53	-14
WAS	156	87	67	.565	1.5	622	562	5326	1375	197	**63**	27	545	489	.258	.330	.334	.664	107	-8	44	92	103	612	**110**	65	**63**	**-6**
STL	154	81	70	.536	6	597	**548**	5227	1302	215	37	63	500	555	.249	.316	.341	.657	91	-29	-59	105	105	584	25	31	45	-11
NY	152	81	71	.533	6.5	**676**	606	5176	1343	189	61	43	**618**	567	.259	**.343**	**.373**	**.716**	108	**90**	**62**	105	97	**698**	64	43	60	-7
CLE	147	73	72	.503	11	557	**548**	4898	1249	216	48	65	505	578	.255	.326	.359	.685	**109**	23	47	96	95	588	19	31	38	-13
CHI	150	71	78	.477	15	596	633	5077	1330	204	55	22	470	467	**.262**	.326	.337	.663	101	-13	3	97	**105**	571	78	54	59	-9
BOS	157	71	83	.461	17.5	599	674	5367	**1393**	225	44	50	541	534	.260	.330	.346	.676	100	12	-2	102	96	634	72	50	59	-8
PHI	153	52	98	.347	34.5	494	638	5296	1297	201	37	33	449	**463**	.245	.306	.316	.622	86	-96	-94	100	98	523	25	45	36	-20
TOT	612					4774		41624	10634	1674	392	430	4145	4186	.255	.325	.346	.671							453	373	55	-88

TEAM	CG	SH	SV	IP	H	H/G	HR	BB	SO	RAT	ERA	ERA+	OAV	OOB	PR	/A	PF	CPI	FA	E	DP	FW	PW	BW	SBW	DIF
DET	78	**19**	16	1393²	1305	8.4	48	538	**588**	12.1	2.99	118	.250	.322	58	81	105	**108**	.975	158	173	.4	**8.7**	-1.9	-.3	4.7
WAS	82	**19**	11	1412¹	1307	**8.3**	42	**440**	550	11.2	**2.92**	106	**.242**	**.301**	69	28	92	93	.970	143	124	1.2	6.2	-6.3	.0	4.4
STL	**91**	10	8	1382²	1307	8.5	59	506	570	11.8	3.14	112	.249	.316	34	58	105	101	.976	143	123	1.2	6.2	-6.3	.0	4.4
NY	78	9	14	1355	1277	8.5	66	485	474	11.8	3.45	100	.250	.316	-13	1	103	93	.971	175	170	-.7	.1	6.6	.4	-1.4
CLE	76	14	12	1302¹	**1269**	8.8	**39**	501	497	12.4	3.31	98	.257	.328	8	-9	97	102	**.977**	126	149	**1.7**	-1.0	5.0	-.2	-5.1
CHI	84	13	13	1330²	1400	9.5	63	448	486	12.7	3.69	90	.270	.332	-49	-55	99	100	.970	180	139	-1.1	-5.9	.3	.2	3.0
BOS	71	15	13	1390²	1389	9.0	58	656	490	13.4	3.80	90	.264	.348	-67	-61	101	102	.973	169	**198**	-.1	-6.5	-.2	.3	.5
PHI	65	11	8	1381	1380	9.0	55	571	531	12.9	3.62	95	.262	.337	-40	-29	102	101	.973	168	160	-.3	-3.1	-10.1	-1.0	-8.6
TOT	625	110	95	10948¹		8.7				12.3	3.36		.255	.325					.973	1302	1236					

Runs
Stirnweiss-NY 107
Stephens-StL 90
Cullenbine-Cle-Det . . . 83

Hits
Stirnweiss-NY 195
Moses-Chi 168
Stephens-StL 165
Hall-Phi 161
Etten-NY 161

Doubles
Moses-Chi 35
Stirnweiss-NY 32
Binks-Was 32
McQuinn-StL 31

Triples
Stirnweiss-NY 22
Moses-Chi 15
Kuhel-Was 13
Dickshot-Chi 10
Peck-Phi 9

Home Runs
Stephens-StL 24
Cullenbine-Cle-Det . . 18
York-Det 18
Etten-NY 18
Heath-Cle 15

Total Bases
Stirnweiss-NY 301
Stephens-StL 270
Etten-NY 247
York-Det 246
Moses-Chi 239

Runs Batted In
Etten-NY 111
Cullenbine-Cle-Det . . 93
Stephens-StL 89
York-Det 87
Binks-Was 81

Runs Produced
Etten-NY 170
Stirnweiss-NY 161
Cullenbine-Cle-Det . . 158
Stephens-StL 155
Kuhel-Was 146

Bases On Balls
Cullenbine-Cle-Det . . 113
Lake-Bos 106
Grimes-NY 97
Etten-NY 90
Kuhel-Was 79

Batting Average
Stirnweiss-NY 309
Dickshot-Chi 302
Estalella-Phi 299
Myatt-Was 296
Moses-Chi 295

On Base Percentage
Lake-Bos 412
Cullenbine-Cle-Det . .402
Estalella-Phi 399
Grimes-NY 395
Etten-NY 387

Slugging Average
Stirnweiss-NY 476
Stephens-StL 473
Cullenbine-Cle-Det . .444
Etten-NY 437
Estalella-Phi 435

Production
Stirnweiss-NY 862
Cullenbine-Cle-Det . .846
Estalella-Phi 834
Stephens-StL 825
Etten-NY 824

Adjusted Production
Stirnweiss-NY 143
Estalella-Phi 142
Kuhel-Was 137
Cullenbine-Cle-Det . . 137
Lake-Bos 136

Batter Runs
Stirnweiss-NY 39.1
Cullenbine-Cle-Det . . 35.1
Etten-NY 29.9
Heath-Cle 29.4
Lake-Bos 28.7

Adjusted Batter Runs
Stirnweiss-NY 35.8
Heath-Cle 31.3
Cullenbine-Cle-Det . . 31.1
Lake-Bos 27.3
Etten-NY 26.8

Clutch Hitting Index
Schalk-Chi 158
Michaels-Chi 143
Etten-NY 141
Tresh-Chi 135
Kuhel-Was 131

Runs Created
Stirnweiss-NY 121
Cullenbine-Cle-Det . . 106
Etten-NY 98
Stephens-StL 98
Moses-Chi 97

Total Average
Cullenbine-Cle-Det . .888
Stirnweiss-NY . . .855
Lake-Bos 849
Etten-NY 794
Estalella-Phi 789

Stolen Bases
Stirnweiss-NY 33
Myatt-Was 30
Case-Was 30
Metkovich-Bos 19
Dickshot-Chi 18

Stolen Base Average
Dickshot-Chi 85.7
Metkovich-Bos . . . 76.0
Myatt-Was 73.2
Stirnweiss-NY 66.0
Case-Was 65.2

Stolen Base Runs
Dickshot-Chi 3.6
Myatt-Was 2.4
Metkovich-Bos . . . 2.1
Crosetti-NY 1.5
Richards-Det 1.2

Fielding Runs
Hall-Phi 26.1
Stirnweiss-NY 25.5
Webb-Det 23.0
Newsome-Bos 22.2
Kell-Phi 21.7

Total Player Rating
Stirnweiss-NY 7.4
Lake-Bos 5.8
Cullenbine-Cle-Det . . 3.6
Mayo-Det 3.2
Newsome-Bos 2.9

Wins
Newhouser-Det 25
Ferriss-Bos 21
Wolff-Was 20
Gromek-Cle 19

Win Percentage
Newhouser-Det 735
Leonard-Was 708
Gromek-Cle 679
Ferriss-Bos 677
Wolff-Was 667

Games
Berry-Phi 52
Reynolds-Cle 44
Pieretti-Was 44
Trout-Det 41
Newhouser-Det 40

Complete Games
Newhouser-Det 29
Ferriss-Bos 26
Wolff-Was 21
Potter-StL 21
Gromek-Cle 21

Shutouts
Newhouser-Det 8
Ferriss-Bos 5
Benton-Det 5

Saves
Turner-NY 10
Berry-Phi 5

Innings Pitched
Newhouser-Det . . 313.1
Ferriss-Bos 264.2
Newsom-Phi 257.1
Potter-StL 255.1
Gromek-Cle 251.0

Fewest Hits/Game
Newhouser-Det . . . 6.86
Wolff-Was 7.20
Potter-StL 7.47
Lee-Chi 8.20
Niggeling-Was 8.20

Fewest BB/Game
Bonham-NY 1.10
Leonard-Was 1.46
Wolff-Was 1.91
Overmire-Det 2.33
Gromek-Cle 2.37

Strikeouts
Newhouser-Det . . . 212
Potter-StL 129
Newsom-Phi 127
Reynolds-Cle 112

Strikeouts/Game
Newhouser-Det . . . 6.09
Kramer-StL 4.62
Niggeling-Was 4.58
Potter-StL 4.55
Newsom-Phi 4.44

Ratio
Wolff-Was 9.14
Potter-StL 9.90
Newhouser-Det . . . 10.02
Leonard-Was 10.21
Bonham-NY 10.41

Earned Run Average
Newhouser-Det . . . 1.81
Benton-Det 2.02
Wolff-Was 2.12
Leonard-Was 2.13
Lee-Chi 2.44

Adjusted ERA
Newhouser-Det . . . 194
Benton-Det 174
Wolff-Was 146
Leonard-Was 146
Potter-StL 143

Opponents' Batting Avg.
Newhouser-Det 211
Wolff-Was 215
Potter-StL 226
Niggeling-Was 240
Benton-Det 241

Opponents' On Base Pct.
Wolff-Was 258
Potter-StL 279
Leonard-Was 279
Newhouser-Det 281
Bonham-NY 288

Starter Runs
Newhouser-Det . . . 54.1
Wolff-Was 34.5
Leonard-Was 29.8
Benton-Det 28.7
Potter-StL 25.5

Adjusted Starter Runs
Newhouser-Det . . . 59.4
Benton-Det 31.9
Potter-StL 29.8
Wolff-Was 27.2
Leonard-Was 23.5

Clutch Pitching Index
Benton-Det 139
Lee-Chi 121
Shirley-StL 116
Hollingsworth-StL . . 116
Ferriss-Bos 114

Relief Runs
Berry-Phi 14.7
Holcombe-NY 9.7
Barrett-Bos 7.2
Zoldak-StL 0

Adjusted Relief Runs
Berry-Phi 15.7
Holcombe-NY 10.3
Barrett-Bos 7.5
Zoldak-StL 1.2

Relief Ranking
Berry-Phi 17.6
Holcombe-NY 10.0
Barrett-Bos 6.1
Zoldak-StL 8

Total Pitcher Index
Newhouser-Det 8.0
Potter-StL 3.8
Ferriss-Bos 3.2
Benton-Det 3.1
Leonard-Was 2.8

Total Baseball Ranking
Newhouser-Det 8.0
Stirnweiss-NY 7.4
Lake-Bos 5.8
Potter-StL 3.8
Cullenbine-Cle-Det . . . 3.6

TEAM	G	W	L	PCT	GB	R	OR	AB	H	2B	3B	HR	BB	SO	AVG	OBP	SLG	PRO	PRO+	BR	/A	PF	CHI	RC	SB	CS	SBA	SBR
STL	156	98	58	.628		712	545	5372	1426	265	56	81	530	537	.265	.334	.381	.715	105	54	27	104	105	702	58			
BRO	157	96	60	.615	2	701	570	5285	1376	233	66	55	691	575	.260	.348	.361	.709	106	60	54	101	101	699	100			
CHI	155	82	71	.536	14.5	626	581	5298	1344	223	50	56	586	599	.254	.331	.346	.677	100	-9	3	98	102	622	43			
BOS	154	81	72	.529	15.5	630	592	5225	1377	238	48	44	558	468	.264	.337	.353	.690	101	16	9	101	100	641	60			
PHI	155	69	85	.448	28	560	705	5233	1351	209	40	80	417	590	.258	.315	.359	.674	100	-30	-13	97	99	598	41			
CIN	156	67	87	.435	30	523	570	5291	1262	206	33	65	493	604	.239	.307	.327	.634	88	-101	-78	96	102	546	82			
PIT	155	63	91	.409	34	552	668	5199	1300	202	52	60	592	555	.250	.328	.344	.672	95	-18	-33	103	93	602	48			
NY	154	61	93	.396	36	612	685	5191	1326	176	37	121	532	546	.255	.328	.374	.702	104	27	23	101	97	644	46			
TOT	621					4916		42094	10762	1752	382	562	4399	4474	.256	.329	.355	.684						478				

TEAM	CG	SH	SV	IP	H	H/G	HR	BB	SO	RAT	ERA	ERA+	OAV	OOB	PR	/A	PF	CPI	FA	E	DP	FW	PW	BW	SBW	DIF
STL	75	18	15	1397	1326	8.5	63	493	607	11.9	3.01	115	.254	.322	63	70	101	108	.980	124	167	2.1	7.4	2.9		7.6
BRO	52	14	28	1418	1280	8.1	58	671	647	12.5	3.05	111	.243	.331	58	52	99	107	.972	174	154	-.9	5.5	5.7		7.6
CHI	59	15	11	1393	1370	8.9	58	527	619	12.4	3.24	102	.256	.325	26	15	97	102	.976	146	119	.7	1.6	.3		2.9
BOS	73	10	12	1371	1291	8.5	76	478	566	11.7	3.35	102	.249	.314	10	13	101	93	.972	169	129	-.8	1.4	1.0		2.9
PHI	55	11	23	1369	1442	9.5	73	542	490	13.3	3.99	86	.273	.344	-88	-85	101	98	.975	148	144	.6	-9.0	-1.4		1.8
CIN	69	17	11	1413¹	1334	8.5	70	467	506	11.6	3.08	109	.252	.314	53	42	98	101	.975	155	192	.2	4.5	-8.3		-6.4
PIT	61	10	6	1370	1406	9.2	50	561	458	13.1	3.72	95	.269	.342	-46	-29	103	99	.970	184	127	-1.6	-3.1	-3.5		-5.8
NY	47	8	13	1353¹	1313	8.7	114	660	581	13.2	3.92	88	.256	.343	-76	-71	101	100	.973	159	121	-.2	-7.5	2.4		-10.7
TOT	491	103	119	11084²		8.7				12.5	3.41		.256	.329					.974	1259	1153					

Runs
Musial-StL 124
Slaughter-StL 100
Stanky-Bro 98
Schoendienst-StL . . 94
Cavarretta-Chi 89

Hits
Musial-StL 228
Walker-Bro 184
Slaughter-StL 183
Holmes-Bos 176
Schoendienst-StL . . 170

Doubles
Musial-StL 50
Holmes-Bos 35
Kurowski-StL 32
Herman-Bro-Bos . . 31

Triples
Musial-StL 20
Reese-Bro 10
Cavarretta-Chi 10
Walker-Bro 9

Home Runs
Kiner-Pit 23
Mize-NY 22
Slaughter-StL 18
Ennis-Phi 17

Total Bases
Musial-StL 366
Slaughter-StL 283
Ennis-Phi 262
Walker-Bro 258
Holmes-Bos 241

Runs Batted In
Slaughter-StL 130
Walker-Bro 116
Musial-StL 103
Kurowski-StL 89
Kiner-Pit 81

Runs Produced
Slaughter-StL 212
Musial-StL 211
Walker-Bro 187
Cavarretta-Chi 159
Holmes-Bos 153

Bases On Balls
Stanky-Bro 137
Fletcher-Pit 111
Cavarretta-Chi 88
Reese-Bro 87
Hack-Chi 83

Batting Average
Musial-StL 365
Hopp-Bos 333
Walker-Bro 319
Ennis-Phi 313
Holmes-Bos 310

On Base Percentage
Stanky-Bro 436
Musial-StL 434
Cavarretta-Chi 401
Herman-Bro-Bos . . .395
Walker-Bro 391

Slugging Average
Musial-StL 587
Ennis-Phi 485
Slaughter-StL 465
Kurowski-StL 462
Walker-Bro 448

Production
Musial-StL 1.021
Kurowski-StL 853
Ennis-Phi 849
Walker-Bro 839
Slaughter-StL 838

Adjusted Production
Musial-StL 180
Ennis-Phi 144
Cavarretta-Chi 140
Walker-Bro 136
Kurowski-StL 136

Batter Runs
Musial-StL 70.9
Mize-NY 43.6
Kurowski-StL 29.1
Walker-Bro 28.9
Slaughter-StL 28.6

Adjusted Batter Runs
Musial-StL 67.7
Mize-NY 43.3
Cavarretta-Chi 29.0
Walker-Bro 28.2
Ennis-Phi 27.2

Clutch Hitting Index
Walker-Bro 161
Slaughter-StL 152
Elliott-Pit 137
Reiser-Bro 130
Cavarretta-Chi 125

Runs Created
Musial-StL 164
Slaughter-StL 110
Walker-Bro 104
Kurowski-StL 97
Ennis-Phi 96

Total Average
Musial-StL 1.114
Stanky-Bro 890
Reiser-Bro 877
Kurowski-StL 855
Walker-Bro 848

Stolen Bases
Reiser-Bro 34
Haas-Cin 22
Hopp-Bos 21
Adams-Cin 16
Walker-Bro 14

Stolen Base Average

Stolen Base Runs

Fielding Runs
Marion-StL 18.8
Wyrostek-Phi 17.2
Ennis-Phi 13.6
Handley-Pit 13.2
Mueller-Cin 9.8

Total Player Rating
Musial-StL 6.0
Mize-NY 4.4
Ennis-Phi 3.6
Stanky-Bro 3.1
Kurowski-StL 3.0

Wins
Pollet-StL 21
Sain-Bos 20
Higbe-Bro 17
Dickson-StL 15
Brecheen-StL 15

Win Percentage
Dickson-StL 714
Higbe-Bro 680
Pollet-StL 677
Sain-Bos 588
Brecheen-StL 500

Games
Trinkle-NY 48
Dickson-StL 47
Behrman-Bro 47
Casey-Bro 46

Complete Games
Sain-Bos 24
Pollet-StL 22
Koslo-NY 17
Ostermueller-Pit . . 16
Cooper-Bos 15

Shutouts
Brecheen-StL 5
Blackwell-Cin 5
VanderMeer-Cin . . . 4
Pollet-StL 4
Cooper-Bos 4

Saves
Raffensberger-Phi . . 6
Pollet-StL 5
Karl-Phi 5
Herring-Bro 5
Casey-Bro 5

Innings Pitched
Pollet-StL 266.0
Koslo-NY 265.1
Sain-Bos 265.0
Brecheen-StL 231.1
Schmitz-Chi 224.1

Fewest Hits/Game
Kennedy-NY 7.38
Schmitz-Chi 7.38
Blackwell-Cin 7.41
Higbe-Bro 7.60
Sain-Bos 7.64

Fewest BB/Game
Cooper-Bos 1.76
Raffensberger-Phi . 1.79
Beggs-Cin 1.85
Heusser-Cin 2.09
Strincevich-Pit . . . 2.25

Strikeouts
Schmitz-Chi 135
Higbe-Bro 134
Sain-Bos 129
Koslo-NY 121
Brecheen-StL 117

Strikeouts/Game
Higbe-Bro 5.72
Schmitz-Chi 5.42
Blackwell-Cin 4.63
Brecheen-StL 4.55
Voiselle-NY 4.50

Ratio
Cooper-Bos 9.95
Beggs-Cin 10.18
Sain-Bos 10.66
Dickson-StL 10.74
Pollet-StL 10.79

Earned Run Average
Pollet-StL 2.10
Sain-Bos 2.21
Beggs-Cin 2.32
Blackwell-Cin 2.45
Brecheen-StL 2.49

Adjusted ERA
Pollet-StL 165
Sain-Bos 155
Beggs-Cin 144
Brecheen-StL 139
Blackwell-Cin 136

Opponents' Batting Avg.
Schmitz-Chi 221
Kennedy-NY 224
Blackwell-Cin 226
Higbe-Bro 229
Sain-Bos 230

Opponents' On Base Pct.
Cooper-Bos 276
Beggs-Cin 287
Sain-Bos 294
Dickson-StL 295
Pollet-StL 300

Starter Runs
Pollet-StL 38.9
Sain-Bos 35.5
Brecheen-StL 23.7
Beggs-Cin 23.1
Blackwell-Cin 20.7

Adjusted Starter Runs
Pollet-StL 40.1
Sain-Bos 36.0
Brecheen-StL 24.8
Beggs-Cin 21.6
Rowe-Phi 19.9

Clutch Pitching Index
Hatten-Bro 129
Pollet-StL 127
Beggs-Cin 124
Wyse-Chi 117
Ostermueller-Pit . . 110

Relief Runs
Casey-Bro 15.8
Thompson-NY 14.8
Malloy-Cin 5.3
Budnick-NY 2.5
Herring-Bro 6

Adjusted Relief Runs
Casey-Bro 15.5
Thompson-NY 15.0
Malloy-Cin 4.8
Budnick-NY 2.8
Wilks-StL 5

Relief Ranking
Casey-Bro 24.1
Thompson-NY . . . 23.7
Malloy-Cin 4.5
Budnick-NY 1.6
Wilks-StL 4

Total Pitcher Index
Sain-Bos 5.1
Pollet-StL 4.6
Beggs-Cin 2.8
Brecheen-StL 2.5
Rowe-Phi 2.3

Total Baseball Ranking
Musial-StL 6.0
Sain-Bos 5.1
Pollet-StL 4.6
Mize-NY 4.4
Ennis-Phi 3.6

TEAM	G	W	L	PCT	GB	R	OR	AB	H	2B	3B	HR	BB	SO	AVG	OBP	SLG	PRO	PRO+	BR	/A	PF	CHI	RC	SB	CS	SBA	SBR
BOS	156	104	50	.675		792	594	5318	1441	268	50	109	687	661	.271	.356	.402	.758	113	136	100	106	101	790	45	36	56	-8
DET	155	92	62	.597	12	704	567	5318	1373	212	41	108	622	616	.258	.337	.374	.711	100	42	3	106	103	698	65	41	61	-5
NY	154	87	67	.565	17	684	547	5139	1275	208	50	136	627	706	.248	.334	.387	.721	107	55	47	101	101	695	48	35	58	-7
WAS	155	76	78	.494	28	608	706	5337	1388	260	63	60	511	641	.260	.327	.366	.693	106	1	39	94	96	653	51	50	50	-15
CHI	155	74	80	.481	30	562	595	5312	1364	206	44	37	501	600	.257	.323	.333	.656	94	-64	-40	96	100	579	78	64	55	-15
CLE	156	68	86	.442	36	537	638	5242	1285	233	56	79	506	697	.245	.313	.356	.669	99	-49	-9	94	94	596	57	49	54	-12
STL	156	66	88	.429	38	621	710	5373	1350	220	46	84	465	713	.251	.313	.356	.669	89	-53	-84	105	108	601	23	35	40	-14
PHI	155	49	105	.318	55	529	680	5200	1317	220	51	40	482	594	.253	.328	.338	.656	91	-68	-64	99	97	574	39	30	57	-6
TOT	621					5037		42239	10793	1827	401	653	4401	5228	.256	.328	.364	.692							406	340	54	-82

TEAM	CG	SH	SV	IP	H	H/G	HR	BB	SO	RAT	ERA	ERA+	OAV	OOB	PR	/A	PF	CPI	FA	E	DP	FW	PW	BW	SBW	DIF
BOS	79	15	20	1396²	1359	8.8	89	501	667	12.1	3.38	108	.254	.319	19	44	105	100	.977	139	163	1.5	4.6	10.5	.2	10.2
DET	94	18	15	1402	1277	8.2	97	497	896	11.5	3.22	114	.241	.307	45	68	104	95	.974	155	155	.5	7.1	.3	.6	6.5
NY	68	17	17	1361	1232	8.1	66	552	653	11.9	3.13	110	.243	.319	56	48	99	100	.975	150	174	.7	5.0	4.9	.3	-1.0
WAS	71	8	10	1396¹	1459	9.4	81	547	537	13.1	3.74	89	.269	.339	-36	-61	96	103	.966	211	162	-2.8	-6.4	4.1	-.5	4.6
CHI	62	9	16	1392¹	1348	8.7	80	508	550	12.1	3.10	110	.255	.323	63	49	97	110	.972	175	170	-.7	5.1	-4.2	-.5	-2.7
CLE	63	16	13	1388²	1282	8.3	84	649	789	12.6	3.62	91	.245	.331	-17	-48	94	96	.975	147	147	1.0	-5.0	-.9	-.2	-3.8
STL	63	13	12	1382¹	1465	9.5	73	573	574	13.3	3.95	94	.272	.343	-69	-34	107	99	.974	159	157	.3	-3.6	-8.8	-.4	1.5
PHI	61	10	5	1342²	1371	9.2	83	577	562	13.2	3.90	91	.264	.340	-59	-53	101	98	.971	167	141	-.2	-5.6	-6.7	.4	-15.9
TOT	561	106	108	11062		8.8				12.5	3.50		.256	.328					.973	1303	1252					

Runs
Williams-Bos 142
Pesky-Bos 115
Lake-Det 105
Keller-NY 98
Doerr-Bos 95

Hits
Pesky-Bos 208
Vernon-Was 207
Appling-Chi 180
Williams-Bos 176
Lewis-Was 170

Doubles
Vernon-Was 51
Spence-Was 50
Pesky-Bos 43
Williams-Bos 37
Doerr-Bos 34

Triples
Edwards-Cle 16
Lewis-Was 13
Kell-Phi-Det 10
Spence-Was 10
Keller-NY 10

Home Runs
Greenberg-Det 44
Williams-Bos 38
Keller-NY 30
Seerey-Cle 26
DiMaggio-NY 25

Total Bases
Williams-Bos 343
Greenberg-Det ... 316
Vernon-Was 298
Spence-Was 287
Keller-NY 287

Runs Batted In
Greenberg-Det ... 127
Williams-Bos 123
York-Bos 119
Doerr-Bos 116
Keller-NY 101

Runs Produced
Williams-Bos 227
Doerr-Bos 193
York-Bos 180
Greenberg-Det ... 174
Keller-NY 169

Bases On Balls
Williams-Bos 156
Keller-NY 113
Lake-Det 103
Cullenbine-Det.... 88
Henrich-NY 87

Batting Average
Vernon-Was ..... .353
Williams-Bos ..... .342
Pesky-Bos .... .335
Kell-Phi-Det ..... .322
DiMaggio-Bos .... .316

On Base Percentage
Williams-Bos ..... .497
Keller-NY .... .405
Vernon-Was ..... .403
Pesky-Bos .... .401
DiMaggio-Bos .... .393

Slugging Average
Williams-Bos 667
Greenberg-Det ...604
Keller-NY .... .533
DiMaggio-NY ... .511
Edwards-Cle ..... .509

Production
Williams-Bos ... 1.164
Greenberg-Det ... .977
Keller-NY .... .938
Vernon-Was 910
DiMaggio-NY 878

Adjusted Production
Williams-Bos 211
Vernon-Was 163
Greenberg-Det ... 160
Keller-NY 158
Edwards-Cle 151

Batter Runs
Williams-Bos 94.2
Greenberg-Det ... 46.1
Keller-NY 45.9
Cullenbine-Det.... 42.2
Vernon-Was 40.3

Adjusted Batter Runs
Williams-Bos 90.2
Keller-NY 45.0
Vernon-Was 44.4
Greenberg-Det ... 42.2
Cullenbine-Det.... 39.5

Clutch Hitting Index
York-Bos 158
Doerr-Bos 147
Travis-Was 141
Berardino-StL 123
DiMaggio-Bos 118

Runs Created
Williams-Bos 188
Keller-NY 127
Vernon-Was 120
Greenberg-Det ... 119
Pesky-Bos 111

Total Average
Williams-Bos 1.431
Greenberg-Det .. 1.010
Keller-NY 1.005
Vernon-Was 873
DiMaggio-NY 862

Stolen Bases
Case-Cle 28
Stirnweiss-NY 18
Lake-Det 15

Stolen Base Average
Stirnweiss-NY ... 75.0
Case-Cle 71.8

Stolen Base Runs
Stirnweiss-NY 1.8
Dillinger-StL 1.8
Case-Cle 1.8
Philley-Chi 1.5
Evers-Det 1.5

Fielding Runs
Doerr-Bos 26.8
Gordon-NY 21.5
Boudreau-Cle ... 16.2
Rizzuto-NY 13.1
Pesky-Bos 12.0

Total Player Rating
Williams-Bos 8.4
Doerr-Bos 4.8
Pesky-Bos 4.3
Greenberg-Det 3.8
Cullenbine-Det..... 3.8

Wins
Newhouser-Det ... 26
Feller-Cle 26
Ferriss-Bos 25
Hughson-Bos 20
Chandler-NY 20

Win Percentage
Ferriss-Bos 806
Newhouser-Det ... .743
Chandler-NY ..... .714
Harris-Bos 654
Hughson-Bos ..... .645

Games
Feller-Cle 48
Savage-Phi 40
Ferriss-Bos 40
Hughson-Bos 39
Caldwell-Chi 39

Complete Games
Feller-Cle 36
Newhouser-Det ... 29
Ferriss-Bos 26
Trout-Det 23
Hughson-Bos 21

Shutouts
Feller-Cle 10
Newhouser-Det ... 6
Hughson-Bos 6
Ferriss-Bos 6
Chandler-NY 6

Saves
Klinger-Bos 9
Caldwell-Chi 8
Murphy-NY 7
Ferrick-Cle-StL ... 6

Innings Pitched
Feller-Cle 371.1
Newhouser-Det .. 292.2
Hughson-Bos ... 278.0
Trout-Det 276.1
Ferriss-Bos 274.0

Fewest Hits/Game
Newhouser-Det ... 6.61
Feller-Cle 6.71
Chandler-NY 6.99
Embree-Cle 7.65
Bevens-NY....... 7.68

Fewest BB/Game
Hughson-Bos 1.65
Lopat-Chi 1.87
Leonard-Was 2.00
Flores-Phi 2.21
Ferriss-Bos 2.33

Strikeouts
Feller-Cle 348
Newhouser-Det ... 275
Hughson-Bos 172
Trucks-Det 161
Trout-Det 151

Strikeouts/Game
Newhouser-Det ... 8.46
Feller-Cle 8.43
Trucks-Det 6.12
Hutchinson-Det ... 6.00
Hughson-Bos 5.57

Ratio
Newhouser-Det ... 9.66
Hughson-Bos 9.87
Chandler-NY 10.18
Lopat-Chi 10.32
Feller-Cle 10.49

Earned Run Average
Newhouser-Det ... 1.94
Chandler-NY 2.10
Feller-Cle 2.18
Bevens-NY....... 2.23
Flores-Phi 2.32

Adjusted ERA
Newhouser-Det ... 189
Chandler-NY 164
Trout-Det 156
Bevens-NY....... 154
Flores-Phi 153

Opponents' Batting Avg.
Newhouser-Det ... .201
Feller-Cle .... .208
Chandler-NY ..... .218
Embree-Cle ...... .227
Bevens-NY........ .232

Opponents' On Base Pct.
Newhouser-Det ... .269
Hughson-Bos ..... .274
Chandler-NY ..... .288
Lopat-Chi .... .288
Feller-Cle .... .291

Starter Runs
Feller-Cle 54.5
Newhouser-Det ... 50.9
Chandler-NY 40.2
Trout-Det 35.6
Bevens-NY....... 35.2

Adjusted Starter Runs
Newhouser-Det ... 55.8
Feller-Cle 46.5
Trout-Det 40.2
Chandler-NY 38.7
Bevens-NY....... 33.7

Clutch Pitching Index
Grove-Chi 126
Flores-Phi 121
Trout-Det 119
Haynes-Chi 118
Bevens-NY....... 115

Relief Runs
Caldwell-Chi 14.3
Lemon-Cle 10.6
Klinger-Bos 7.2
Kinder-StL 1.7

Adjusted Relief Runs
Caldwell-Chi 13.4
Lemon-Cle 8.5
Klinger-Bos 8.2
Kinder-StL 3.9

Relief Ranking
Caldwell-Chi 25.2
Klinger-Bos 9.4
Lemon-Cle 7.6
Kinder-StL 2.5

Total Pitcher Index
Newhouser-Det 6.5
Trout-Det 5.3
Feller-Cle 4.9
Chandler-NY 4.8
Bevens-NY........ 2.8

Total Baseball Ranking
Williams-Bos 8.4
Newhouser-Det 6.5
Trout-Det 5.3
Feller-Cle 4.9
Doerr-Bos 4.8

TEAM	G	W	L	PCT	GB	R	OR	AB	H	2B	3B	HR	BB	SO	AVG	OBP	SLG	PRO	PRO+	BR	/A	PF	CHI	RC	SB	CS	SBA	SBR
BRO	155	94	60	.610		774	668	5249	1428	241	50	83	**732**	561	.272	**.364**	.384	.748	102	62	34	104	98	781	**88**			
STL	156	89	65	.578	5	780	634	5422	**1462**	235	**65**	115	612	511	.270	.347	.401	.748	101	41	9	104	102	762	28			
BOS	154	86	68	.558	8	701	**622**	5253	1444	**265**	42	85	558	**500**	**.275**	.346	.390	.736	105	19	36	98	97	717	58			
NY	155	81	73	.526	13	**830**	761	5343	1446	220	48	**221**	494	568	.271	.335	**.454**	**.789**	**114**	**95**	**91**	101	**104**	**809**	29			
CIN	154	73	81	.474	21	681	755	5299	1372	242	43	95	539	530	.259	.330	.375	.705	95	-48	-43	99	103	672	46			
CHI	155	69	85	.448	25	567	722	5305	1373	231	48	71	471	578	.259	.321	.361	.682	91	-93	-65	96	94	620	22			
PIT	156	62	92	.403	32	744	817	5307	1385	216	44	156	607	687	.261	.340	.406	.746	102	31	11	103	100	738	30			
PHI	155	62	92	.403	32	589	687	5256	1354	210	52	60	464	594	.258	.321	.352	.673	88	-108	-82	96	101	597	60			
TOT	620					5666		42434	11264	1860	392	886	4477	4529	.265	.338	.390	.729							361			

TEAM	CG	SH	SV	IP	H	H/G	HR	BB	SO	RAT	ERA	ERA+	OAV	OOB	PR	/A	PF	CPI	FA	E	DP	FW	PW	BW	SBW	DIF
BRO	47	**14**	**34**	1375	**1299**	8.5	104	626	592	12.8	3.82	108	.251	.336	37	49	102	100	.978	129	**169**	.9	4.8	3.3		7.9
STL	65	12	20	1397²	1417	9.1	106	495	**642**	12.4	3.53	117	.266	.330	83	94	102	110	**.979**	128	**169**	1.1	9.2	.9		.8
BOS	**74**	**14**	13	1362²	1342	8.9	**93**	453	494	11.9	3.62	108	.255	**.316**	67	41	96	95	.974	153	124	-.6	4.0	3.5		2.0
NY	58	6	14	1363²	1428	9.4	122	590	553	13.4	4.44	92	.267	.342	-58	-56	100	94	.974	155	136	-.7	-5.5	**9.0**		1.2
CIN	54	13	13	1365¹	1442	9.5	102	589	633	13.5	4.41	93	.274	.349	-53	-46	101	98	.977	138	134	.3	-4.5	-4.2		4.4
CHI	46	8	15	1367	1449	9.5	106	618	571	13.7	4.04	98	.274	.353	4	-13	97	109	.975	150	159	-.4	-1.3	-6.4		.0
PIT	44	9	13	1374	1488	9.7	155	592	530	13.9	4.68	90	.278	.354	-95	-71	104	101	.975	149	131	-.2	-7.0	1.1		-8.9
PHI	70	8	14	1362	1399	9.2	98	513	514	12.8	3.96	101	.276	.346	15	7	99	108	.974	152	140	-.5	.7	-8.1		-7.1
TOT	458	84	136	10967¹		9.2				13.1	4.06		.265	.338					.976	1154	1162					

Runs
Mize-NY 137
Robinson-Bro 125
Kiner-Pit 118
Musial-StL 113
Kurowski-StL 108

Hits
Holmes-Bos 191
Walker-StL-Phi .. 186
Musial-StL 183
Gustine-Pit 183
Baumholtz-Cin ... 182

Doubles
Miller-Cin 38
R.Elliott-Bos 35
Ryan-Bos 33
Holmes-Bos 33
Baumholtz-Cin ... 32

Triples
Walker-StL-Phi 16
Slaughter-StL 13
Musial-StL 13
Schoendienst-StL ... 9
Baumholtz-Cin 9

Home Runs
Mize-NY 51
Kiner-Pit 51
Marshall-NY 36
W.Cooper-NY 35
Thomson-NY 29

Total Bases
Kiner-Pit 361
Mize-NY 360
Marshall-NY 310
W.Cooper-NY 302
Musial-StL 296

Runs Batted In
Mize-NY 138
Kiner-Pit 127
W.Cooper-NY 122
R.Elliott-Bos 113
Marshall-NY 107

Runs Produced
Mize-NY 224
Kiner-Pit 194
Musial-StL 189
Kurowski-StL..... 185
R.Elliott-Bos 184

Bases On Balls
Reese-Bro 104
Greenberg-Pit 104
Stanky-Bro....... 103
Kiner-Pit 98
Walker-Bro 97

Batting Average
Walker-StL-Phi....363
R.Elliott-Bos 317
Galan-Cin 314
Cavarretta-Chi 314
Kiner-Pit 313

On Base Percentage
Galan-Cin 449
Walker-StL-Phi....436
Kurowski-StL......420
Kiner-Pit 417
Walker-Bro 415

Slugging Average
Kiner-Pit 639
Mize-NY 614
W.Cooper-NY 586
Kurowski-StL......544
Marshall-NY.......528

Production
Kiner-Pit 1.055
Mize-NY .... .998
Kurowski-StL......964
R.Elliott-Bos 927
W.Cooper-NY 926

Adjusted Production
Kiner-Pit 172
Mize-NY 160
Walker-StL-Phi... 150
R.Elliott-Bos 148
Kurowski-StL..... 148

Batter Runs
Kiner-Pit 61.4
Mize-NY 48.3
Kurowski-StL..... 41.8
R.Elliott-Bos 36.8
Walker-StL-Phi.... 35.4

Adjusted Batter Runs
Kiner-Pit 59.1
Mize-NY 47.8
R.Elliott-Bos 38.6
Kurowski-StL..... 38.5
Walker-StL-Phi.... 37.6

Clutch Hitting Index
Walker-Bro 146
Marion-StL 138
Haas-Cin 135
Edwards-Bro 135
Cavarretta-Chi ... 131

Runs Created
Kiner-Pit 154
Mize-NY 143
R.Elliott-Bos 120
Kurowski-StL..... 118
Musial-StL 118

Total Average
Kiner-Pit 1.155
Mize-NY 1.060
Kurowski-StL.... 1.019
Walker-StL-Phi....979
Torgeson-Bos 973

Stolen Bases
Robinson-Bro 29
Reiser-Bro 14
Walker-StL-Phi.... 13
Hopp-Bos 13
Torgeson-Bos 11

Stolen Base Average

Stolen Base Runs

Fielding Runs
Marion-StL........ 20.1
Verban-Phi 16.9
Gustine-Pit 14.8
Kiner-Pit 13.2
Kerr-NY 12.1

Total Player Rating
Kiner-Pit 6.2
Mize-NY 4.9
Walker-StL-Phi... 4.1
R.Elliott-Bos 3.6
Marshall-NY....... 3.0

Wins
Blackwell-Cin...... 22
Spahn-Bos 21
Sain-Bos 21
Jansen-NY 21
Branca-Bro 21

Win Percentage
Jansen-NY 808
Munger-StL 762
Blackwell-Cin.....733
Hatten-Bro 680
Spahn-Bos 677

Games
Trinkle-NY 62
Higbe-Bro-Pit 50
Behrman-Bro-Pit-Bro . 50
Kush-Chi 47
Dickson-StL...... 47

Complete Games
Blackwell-Cin..... 23
Spahn-Bos 22
Sain-Bos 22
Jansen-NY 20
Leonard-Phi 19

Shutouts
Spahn-Bos 7
Munger-StL 6
Blackwell-Cin..... 6
Dickson-StL...... 4
Branca-Bro 4

Saves
Casey-Bro 18
Trinkle-NY 10
Gumbert-Cin 10
Behrman-Bro-Pit-Bro .. 8

Innings Pitched
Spahn-Bos 289.2
Branca-Bro 280.0
Blackwell-Cin... 273.0
Sain-Bos 266.0
Jansen-NY 248.0

Fewest Hits/Game
Taylor-Bro 7.22
Blackwell-Cin..... 7.48
Spahn-Bos....... 7.61
Lombardi-Bro 8.04
Branca-Bro 8.07

Fewest BB/Game
Jansen-NY 2.07
Rowe-Phi 2.07
Leonard-Phi 2.18
Barrett-Bos 2.26
Brazle-StL 2.57

Strikeouts
Blackwell-Cin..... 193
Branca-Bro 148
Sain-Bos 132
Spahn-Bos 123
Munger-StL 123

Strikeouts/Game
Blackwell-Cin..... 6.36
Munger-StL 4.93
Branca-Bro 4.76
Brazle-StL 4.55
Sain-Bos 4.47

Ratio
Spahn-Bos 10.25
Blackwell-Cin.... 10.75
Leonard-Phi 10.84
Jansen-NY 10.85
Barrett-Bos 10.89

Earned Run Average
Spahn-Bos 2.33
Blackwell-Cin.... 2.47
Branca-Bro 2.67
Leonard-Phi 2.68
Brazle-StL 2.84

Adjusted ERA
Spahn-Bos 167
Blackwell-Cin.... 166
Branca-Bro 155
Leonard-Phi 149
Brazle-StL 146

Opponents' Batting Avg.
Taylor-Bro 225
Spahn-Bos.......226
Blackwell-Cin.....234
Branca-Bro 240
Lombardi-Bro 241

Opponents' On Base Pct.
Spahn-Bos.......283
Barrett-Bos 292
Blackwell-Cin.....304
Leonard-Phi 306
Jansen-NY 306

Starter Runs
Spahn-Bos 55.7
Blackwell-Cin.... 48.2
Branca-Bro 43.3
Leonard-Phi 36.0
Dickson-StL..... 25.5

Adjusted Starter Runs
Spahn-Bos 50.3
Blackwell-Cin.... 49.5
Branca-Bro 45.6
Leonard-Phi 34.6
Dickson-StL..... 27.4

Clutch Pitching Index
Brazle-StL 139
Leonard-Phi 123
Branca-Bro 122
Blackwell-Cin.... 115
Jansen-NY 114

Relief Runs
Lanfranconi-Bos ... 7.9
Kush-Chi 7.1
Trinkle-NY 3.3
Gumbert-Cin 1.8
Casey-Bro 6

Adjusted Relief Runs
Lanfranconi-Bos ... 6.7
Kush-Chi 5.9
Trinkle-NY 3.4
Gumbert-Cin 2.2
Casey-Bro 1.2

Relief Ranking
Lanfranconi-Bos ... 7.8
Kush-Chi 7.2
Gumbert-Cin 4.9
Trinkle-NY 4.7
Casey-Bro 2.6

Total Pitcher Index
Blackwell-Cin..... 5.3
Spahn-Bos 5.1
Branca-Bro 4.0
Leonard-Phi 3.9
Dickson-StL...... 2.9

Total Baseball Ranking
Kiner-Pit 6.2
Blackwell-Cin.... 5.3
Spahn-Bos 5.1
Mize-NY 4.9
Walker-StL-Phi... 4.1

TEAM	G	W	L	PCT	GB	R	OR	AB	H	2B	3B	HR	BB	SO	AVG	OBP	SLG	PRO	PRO+	BR	/A	PF	CHI	RC	SB	CS	SBA	SBR
NY	155	97	57	.630		794	568	5308	1439	230	72	115	610	581	.271	.349	.407	.756	117	110	117	99	104	780	27	23	54	-6
DET	158	85	69	.552	12	714	642	5276	1363	234	42	103	762	565	.258	.353	.377	.730	106	77	58	103	96	735	52	60	46	-20
BOS	157	83	71	.539	14	720	669	5322	1412	206	54	103	666	590	.265	.349	.382	.731	102	71	22	107	98	734	29	25	54	-9
CLE	157	80	74	.519	17	687	588	5367	1392	234	51	112	502	609	.259	.324	.385	.709	106	9	26	97	105	687	37	33	53	-9
PHI	156	78	76	.506	19	633	614	5198	1311	218	52	61	605	563	.252	.333	.349	.682	94	-24	-37	102	102	635	37	33	53	-9
CHI	155	70	84	.455	27	553	661	5274	1350	211	41	53	492	527	.256	.321	.342	.663	93	-69	-46	96	98	584	91	57	61	-7
WAS	154	64	90	.416	33	496	675	5112	1234	186	48	42	525	534	.241	.313	.321	.634	84	-118	-101	97	99	523	53	51	51	-15
STL	154	59	95	.383	38	564	744	5145	1238	189	52	90	583	664	.241	.320	.350	.670	90	-55	-67	102	98	596	69	49	58	-9
TOT	623					5161		42002	10739	1708	412	679	4745	4633	.256	.333	.364	.698							399	333	55	-80

TEAM	CG	SH	SV	IP	H	H/G	HR	BB	SO	RAT	ERA	ERA+	OAV	OOB	PR	/A	PF	CPI	FA	E	DP	FW	PW	BW	SBW	DIF
NY	73	14	21	1374^1	1221	8.0	95	628	691	12.2	3.39	104	.238	.323	48	22	95	100	.981	109	151	1.5	2.3	12.1	.4	3.7
DET	77	15	18	1398^2	1382	8.9	79	531	648	12.4	3.57	106	.258	.326	21	31	102	100	.975	155	142	-1.0	3.2	6.0	-1.0	.8
BOS	64	13	19	1391^1	1383	8.9	84	575	586	12.8	3.81	102	.261	.335	-16	12	105	100	.977	137	172	-.0	1.2	2.3	.1	2.4
CLE	55	13	29	1402^1	1244	8.0	94	628	590	12.2	3.44	101	.240	.325	41	7	94	100	.983	104	178	1.9	.7	2.7	.4	-2.7
PHI	70	12	15	1391^1	1291	8.4	85	597	493	12.3	3.51	109	.247	.326	30	46	103	99	.976	143	161	-.4	4.8	-3.8	.1	.4
CHI	47	11	27	1391	1384	9.0	76	603	522	13.0	3.64	100	.261	.339	11	3	99	105	.975	155	180	-1.2	.3	-4.8	.3	-1.7
WAS	67	15	12	1362	1408	9.3	63	579	551	13.2	3.97	94	.267	.342	-40	-37	101	98	.976	143	151	-.5	-3.8	-10.5	-.5	2.3
STL	50	7	13	1365	1426	9.4	103	604	552	13.4	4.33	90	.272	.348	-94	-68	105	98	.977	134	169	.0	-7.0	-6.9	.1	-4.1
TOT	503	100	154	11076		8.7				12.7	3.71		.256	.333					.977	1080	1304					

Runs
Williams-Bos	125
Henrich-NY	109
Pesky-Bos	106
Stirnweiss-NY	102
DiMaggio-NY	97

Hits
Pesky-Bos	207
Kell-Det	188
Williams-Bos	181
McCosky-Phi	179

Doubles
Boudreau-Cle	45
Williams-Bos	40
Henrich-NY	35
DiMaggio-NY	31

Triples
Henrich-NY	13
Vernon-Was	12
Philley-Chi	11

Home Runs
Williams-Bos	32
Gordon-Cle	29
Heath-StL	27
Cullenbine-Det	24
York-Bos-Chi	21

Total Bases
Williams-Bos	335
Gordon-Cle	279
DiMaggio-NY	279
Henrich-NY	267
Pesky-Bos	250

Runs Batted In
Williams-Bos	114
Henrich-NY	98
DiMaggio-NY	97
Jones-Chi-Bos	96

Runs Produced
Williams-Bos	207
Henrich-NY	191
DiMaggio-NY	174
Kell-Det	163
Doerr-Bos	157

Bases On Balls
Williams-Bos	162
Cullenbine-Det	137
Lake-Det	120
Joost-Phi	114
Fain-Phi	95

Batting Average
Williams-Bos	.343
McCosky-Phi	.328
Pesky-Bos	.324
Kell-Det	.320
Mitchell-Cle	.316

On Base Percentage
Williams-Bos	.499
Fain-Phi	.414
Cullenbine-Det	.401
McCosky-Phi	.395
McQuinn-NY	.395

Slugging Average
Williams-Bos	.634
DiMaggio-NY	.522
Gordon-Cle	.496
Henrich-NY	.485
Heath-StL	.485

Production
Williams-Bos	1.133
DiMaggio-NY	.913
Henrich-NY	.857
Heath-StL	.850
Gordon-Cle	.842

Adjusted Production
Williams-Bos	199
DiMaggio-NY	154
Henrich-NY	139
Gordon-Cle	136
Heath-StL	133

Batter Runs
Williams-Bos	91.1
DiMaggio-NY	36.5
Henrich-NY	26.4
Fain-Phi	24.7
Cullenbine-Det	23.8

Adjusted Batter Runs
Williams-Bos	85.5
DiMaggio-NY	37.2
Henrich-NY	27.1
McQuinn-NY	24.0
Fain-Phi	23.5

Clutch Hitting Index
W.Johnson-NY	151
Kell-Det	141
Vernon-Was	130
Jones-Chi-Bos	129
Chapman-Phi	129

Runs Created
Williams-Bos	186
DiMaggio-NY	112
Henrich-NY	104
Pesky-Bos	103
McQuinn-NY	97

Total Average
Williams-Bos	1.391
DiMaggio-NY	.918
Cullenbine-Det	.898
Heath-StL	.856
Henrich-NY	.849

Stolen Bases
Dillinger-StL	34
Philley-Chi	21
Vernon-Was	12
Pesky-Bos	12

Stolen Base Average
Dillinger-StL	72.3
Philley-Chi	56.8

Stolen Base Runs
Dillinger-StL	2.4
Valo-Phi	1.5
Binks-Phi	1.2

Fielding Runs
Doerr-Bos	23.8
DiMaggio-Bos	19.0
Baker-Chi	18.3
Kell-Det	17.9
Boudreau-Cle	16.7

Total Player Rating
Williams-Bos	7.8
Boudreau-Cle	4.7
Doerr-Bos	3.4
Cullenbine-Det	3.3
Kell-Det	3.1

Wins
Feller-Cle	20
Reynolds-NY	19
Marchildon-Phi	19
Hutchinson-Det	18
Dobson-Bos	18

Win Percentage
Reynolds-NY	.704
Dobson-Bos	.692
Marchildon-Phi	.679
Feller-Cle	.645
Hutchinson-Det	.643

Games
Klieman-Cle	58
Page-NY	56
Johnson-Bos	45
Savage-Phi	44
Christopher-Phi	44

Complete Games
Newhouser-Det	24
Wynn-Was	22
Lopat-Chi	22
Marchildon-Phi	21
Feller-Cle	20

Shutouts
Feller-Cle	5
Reynolds-NY	4
Masterson-Was	4
Haefner-Was	4

Saves
Page-NY	17
Klieman-Cle	17
Christopher-Phi	12
Ferrick-Was	9

Innings Pitched
Feller-Cle	299.0
Newhouser-Det	285.0
Marchildon-Phi	276.2
Masterson-Was	253.0
Lopat-Chi	252.2

Fewest Hits/Game
Shea-NY	6.40
Feller-Cle	6.92
Marchildon-Phi	7.42
Embree-Cle	7.58
Masterson-Was	7.65

Fewest BB/Game
Galehouse-StL-Bos	2.48
Hutchinson-Det	2.50
Lopat-Chi	2.60
Muncrief-StL	2.60
Dobson-Bos	2.87

Strikeouts
Feller-Cle	196
Newhouser-Det	176
Masterson-Was	135
Reynolds-NY	129
Marchildon-Phi	128

Strikeouts/Game
Feller-Cle	5.90
Hughson-Bos	5.66
Newhouser-Det	5.56
Trucks-Det	5.38
Kinder-StL	5.09

Ratio
Feller-Cle	10.87
Dobson-Bos	10.90
Shea-NY	11.08
Masterson-Was	11.17
Hutchinson-Det	11.23

Earned Run Average
Haynes-Chi	2.42
Feller-Cle	2.68
Fowler-Phi	2.81
Lopat-Chi	2.81
Newhouser-Det	2.87

Adjusted ERA
Haynes-Chi	151
Fowler-Phi	136
Dobson-Bos	132
Newhouser-Det	131
Feller-Cle	130

Opponents' Batting Avg.
Shea-NY	.200
Feller-Cle	.215
Marchildon-Phi	.224
Reynolds-NY	.227
Embree-Cle	.233

Opponents' On Base Pct.
Dobson-Bos	.299
Feller-Cle	.300
Shea-NY	.303
Hutchinson-Det	.304
Lopat-Chi	.307

Starter Runs
Feller-Cle	34.1
Newhouser-Det	26.3
Haynes-Chi	25.9
Lopat-Chi	25.0
Fowler-Phi	22.6

Adjusted Starter Runs
Newhouser-Det	28.3
Feller-Cle	26.7
Fowler-Phi	25.3
Haynes-Chi	24.9
Dobson-Bos	23.8

Clutch Pitching Index
Haynes-Chi	124
Fowler-Phi	119
Lopat-Chi	116
Ferriss-Bos	114
Newsom-Was-NY	112

Relief Runs
Page-NY	19.2
Christopher-Phi	7.2
Klieman-Cle	6.9
Murphy-Bos	5.5
Ferrick-Was	3.7

Adjusted Relief Runs
Page-NY	16.5
Christopher-Phi	8.2
Murphy-Bos	6.6
Klieman-Cle	4.6
Ferrick-Was	3.8

Relief Ranking
Page-NY	27.6
Christopher-Phi	18.2
Klieman-Cle	6.0
Ferrick-Was	5.9
Maltzberger-Chi	1.6

Total Pitcher Index
Newhouser-Det	3.7
Hutchinson-Det	3.4
Feller-Cle	3.2
Haynes-Chi	3.0
Chandler-NY	2.5

Total Baseball Ranking
Williams-Bos	7.8
Boudreau-Cle	4.7
Newhouser-Det	3.7
Hutchinson-Det	3.4
Doerr-Bos	3.4

TEAM	G	W	L	PCT	GB	R	OR	AB	H	2B	3B	HR	BB	SO	AVG	OBP	SLG	PRO	PRO+	BR	/A	PF	CHI	RC	SB	CS	SBA	SBR
BOS	154	91	62	.595		739	584	5297	1458	272	49	95	671	536	.275	.359	.399	.758	114	95	107	98	92	784	43			
STL	155	85	69	.552	6.5	742	646	5302	1396	238	58	105	594	521	.263	.340	.389	.729	98	31	-8	106	103	713	24			
BRO	155	84	70	.545	7.5	744	667	5328	1393	256	54	91	601	684	.261	.338	.381	.719	98	13	-11	103	105	709	114			
PIT	156	83	71	.539	8.5	706	699	5286	1388	191	54	108	580	578	.263	.338	.380	.718	99	10	-4	102	101	698	68			
NY	155	78	76	.506	13.5	780	704	5277	1352	210	49	164	599	648	.256	.334	.408	.742	106	46	42	101	106	731	51			
PHI	155	66	88	.429	25.5	591	729	5287	1367	227	39	91	440	598	.259	.318	.368	.686	94	-63	-51	98	97	625	68			
CIN	153	64	89	.418	27	588	752	5127	1266	221	37	104	478	586	.247	.313	.365	.678	92	-76	-54	97	101	587	42			
CHI	155	64	90	.416	27.5	597	706	5352	1402	225	44	87	443	578	.262	.322	.369	.691	97	-52	-25	96	95	641	39			
TOT	619					5487		42256	11022	1840	384	845	4406	4729	.261	.333	.383	.715						449				

TEAM	CG	SH	SV	IP	H	H/G	HR	BB	SO	RAT	ERA	ERA+	OAV	OOB	PR	/A	PF	CPI	FA	E	DP	FW	PW	BW	SBW	DIF
BOS	70	10	17	1389¹	1354	8.8	93	430	579	11.6	3.37	114	.249	.306	89	71	97	96	.976	143	132	.7	7.1	10.7		-4.0
STL	60	13	18	1368	1392	9.2	103	476	625	12.4	3.91	105	.262	.324	7	28	103	97	.980	119	138	2.1	2.8	-.8		3.9
BRO	52	9	22	1392²	1328	8.6	119	633	670	12.9	3.75	106	.253	.337	31	37	101	107	.973	161	151	-.2	3.7	-1.1		4.6
PIT	65	5	19	1371²	1373	9.0	120	564	543	12.9	4.15	98	.261	.335	-29	-12	103	98	.977	137	150	1.2	-1.2	-.4		6.4
NY	54	15	21	1373	1425	9.3	122	556	527	13.2	3.93	100	.269	.342	4	0	100	109	.974	156	134	.1	.0	4.2		-3.3
PHI	61	6	15	1362¹	1385	9.1	95	556	550	13.0	4.08	97	.262	.335	-18	-20	100	97	.964	210	126	-2.8	-2.0	-5.1		-1.1
CIN	40	8	20	1343¹	1410	9.4	104	572	599	13.4	4.47	87	.270	.344	-77	-85	99	95	.973	158	135	-.1	-8.5	-5.4		1.5
CHI	51	7	10	1355¹	1355	9.0	89	619	636	13.2	4.00	97	.261	.342	-7	-15	99	101	.972	172	152	-.7	-1.5	-2.5		-8.3
TOT	453	73	142	10955²		9.1				12.8	3.95		.261	.333					.974	1256	1118					

Runs
Musial-StL 135
Lockman-NY 117
Mize-NY 110
Robinson-Bro . . . 108
Kiner-Pit 104

Hits
Musial-StL 230
Holmes-Bos 190
Rojek-Pit 186
Slaughter-StL 176
Dark-Bos 175

Doubles
Musial-StL 46
Ennis-Phi 40
Dark-Bos 39
Robinson-Bro 38
Holmes-Bos 35

Triples
Musial-StL 18
Hopp-Pit 12
Slaughter-StL 11
Waitkus-Chi 10
Lockman-NY 10

Home Runs
Mize-NY 40
Kiner-Pit 40
Musial-StL 39
Sauer-Cin 35

Total Bases
Musial-StL 429
Mize-NY 316
Ennis-Phi 309
Kiner-Pit 296
Pafko-Chi 283

Runs Batted In
Musial-StL 131
Mize-NY 125
Kiner-Pit 123
Gordon-NY 107
Pafko-Chi 101

Runs Produced
Musial-StL 227
Mize-NY 195
Kiner-Pit 187
Robinson-Bro . . . 181
Gordon-NY 177

Bases On Balls
R.Elliott-Bos 131
Kiner-Pit 112
Mize-NY 94

Batting Average
Musial-StL 376
Ashburn-Phi 333
Holmes-Bos 325
Dark-Bos 322
Slaughter-StL 321

On Base Percentage
Musial-StL 450
R.Elliott-Bos 423
Ashburn-Phi 410
Slaughter-StL 409
Mize-NY 395

Slugging Average
Musial-StL 702
Mize-NY 564
Gordon-NY 537
Kiner-Pit 533
Ennis-Phi 525

Production
Musial-StL 1.152
Mize-NY 959
Gordon-NY 927
Kiner-Pit 924
R.Elliott-Bos 897

Adjusted Production
Musial-StL 196
Mize-NY 156
Gordon-NY 148
Kiner-Pit 145
R.Elliott-Bos 145

Batter Runs
Musial-StL 90.2
Mize-NY 44.6
Kiner-Pit 38.5
R.Elliott-Bos 37.8
Gordon-NY 35.1

Adjusted Batter Runs
Musial-StL 85.7
Mize-NY 44.1
R.Elliott-Bos . . . 39.1
Kiner-Pit 37.0
Gordon-NY 34.6

Clutch Hitting Index
Murtaugh-Pit 146
Jones-StL 140
Stallcup-Cin 139
Lowrey-Chi 128
Marshall-NY 128

Runs Created
Musial-StL 191
Mize-NY 131
Kiner-Pit 120
R.Elliott-Bos 117
Slaughter-StL 110

Total Average
Musial-StL 1.298
Mize-NY 1.032
R.Elliott-Bos 980
Kiner-Pit 974
Gordon-NY 953

Stolen Bases
Ashburn-Phi 32
Reese-Bro 25
Rojek-Pit 24
Robinson-Bro . . . 22
Torgeson-Bos 19

Stolen Base Average

Stolen Base Runs

Fielding Runs
Ashburn-Phi 17.8
Pafko-Chi 12.8
Reese-Bro 10.3
Marion-StL 9.4
Gustine-Pit 9.0

Total Player Rating
Musial-StL 6.8
Mize-NY 4.6
Pafko-Chi 4.2
Kiner-Pit 3.5
Ashburn-Phi 2.8

Wins
Sain-Bos 24
Brecheen-StL 20
Schmitz-Chi 18
Jansen-NY 18
VanderMeer-Cin . . 17

Win Percentage
Brecheen-StL 741
Jones-NY 667
Sain-Bos 615
Jansen-NY 600
Schmitz-Chi 581

Games
Gumbert-Cin 61
Wilks-StL 57
Higbe-Pit 56
Jones-NY 55
Dobernic-Chi 54

Complete Games
Sain-Bos 28
Brecheen-StL 21
Schmitz-Chi 18
Spahn-Bos 16
Leonard-Phi 16

Shutouts
Brecheen-StL 7
Sain-Bos 4
Raffensberger-Cin . . 4
Jansen-NY 4
Barney-Bro 4

Saves
Gumbert-Cin 17
Wilks-StL 13
Higbe-Pit 10
Trinkle-NY 7
Behrman-Bro 7

Innings Pitched
Sain-Bos 314.2
Jansen-NY 277.0
Spahn-Bos 257.0
Dickson-StL 252.1
Barney-Bro 246.2

Fewest Hits/Game
Schmitz-Chi 6.92
Barney-Bro 7.04
Brecheen-StL 7.44
Branca-Bro 7.89
Roe-Bro 7.90

Fewest BB/Game
Roe-Bro 1.67
Jansen-NY 1.75
Raffensberger-Cin 1.85
Brecheen-StL . . . 1.89
Leonard-Phi 2.15

Strikeouts
Brecheen-StL 149
Barney-Bro 138
Sain-Bos 137
Jansen-NY 126
Branca-Bro 122

Strikeouts/Game
Brecheen-StL . . . 5.75
Branca-Bro 5.09
Barney-Bro 5.04
Higbe-Pit 4.90
Meyer-Chi 4.86

Ratio
Brecheen-StL 9.41
Roe-Bro 9.68
Schmitz-Chi 10.60
Sain-Bos 11.01
Spahn-Bos 11.03

Earned Run Average
Brecheen-StL 2.24
Leonard-Phi 2.51
Sain-Bos 2.60
Roe-Bro 2.63
Schmitz-Chi 2.64

Adjusted ERA
Brecheen-StL 183
Leonard-Phi 157
Roe-Bro 152
Schmitz-Chi 148
Sain-Bos 147

Opponents' Batting Avg.
Schmitz-Chi 215
Barney-Bro 217
Brecheen-StL 222
Branca-Bro 232
Roe-Bro 233

Opponents' On Base Pct.
Brecheen-StL 265
Roe-Bro 271
Schmitz-Chi 295
Sain-Bos 296
Raffensberger-Cin .296

Starter Runs
Sain-Bos 47.3
Brecheen-StL . . . 44.5
Leonard-Phi 36.2
Schmitz-Chi 35.3
Roe-Bro 26.1

Adjusted Starter Runs
Brecheen-StL 48.0
Sain-Bos 43.0
Leonard-Phi 35.9
Schmitz-Chi 34.0
Roe-Bro 26.8

Clutch Pitching Index
Leonard-Phi 134
Jones-NY 126
Hatten-Bro 124
Voiselle-Bos 120
Sain-Bos 115

Relief Runs
Wilks-StL 19.4
Hansen-NY 10.9
Minner-Bro 10.5
Higbe-Pit 10.4
Dobernic-Chi 7.6

Adjusted Relief Runs
Wilks-StL 21.4
Higbe-Pit 12.4
Minner-Bro 10.8
Hansen-NY 10.7
Dobernic-Chi 7.2

Relief Ranking
Wilks-StL 22.4
Higbe-Pit 12.4
Minner-Bro 11.3
Gumbert-Cin 9.7
Trinkle-NY 8.1

Total Pitcher Index
Brecheen-StL 5.2
Sain-Bos 4.6
Schmitz-Chi 4.0
Leonard-Phi 3.9
Roe-Bro 2.5

Total Baseball Ranking
Musial-StL 6.8
Brecheen-StL 5.2
Sain-Bos 4.6
Mize-NY 4.6
Pafko-Chi 4.2

TEAM	G	W	L	PCT	GB	R	OR	AB	H	2B	3B	HR	BB	SO	AVG	OBP	SLG	PRO	PRO+	BR	/A	PF	CHI	RC	SB	CS	SBA	SBR
CLE	156	97	58	.626		840	568	5446	1534	242	54	155	646	575	.282	.360	.431	.791	119	112	131	97	97	868	54	44	55	-10
BOS	155	96	59	.619	1	907	720	5363	1471	277	40	121	823	552	.274	.374	.409	.783	109	116	78	105	104	869	38	17	69	1
NY	154	94	60	.610	2.5	857	633	5324	1480	251	75	139	623	478	.278	.356	.432	.788	116	99	106	99	103	838	24	24	50	-7
PHI	154	84	70	.545	12.5	729	735	5181	1345	231	47	68	726	523	.260	.353	.362	.715	96	-20	-21	100	102	699	40	32	56	-7
DET	154	78	76	.506	18.5	700	726	5235	1396	219	58	78	671	504	.267	.353	.375	.728	96	0	-20	103	95	723	22	32	41	-13
STL	155	59	94	.386	37	671	849	5303	1438	251	62	63	578	572	.271	.345	.378	.723	96	-21	-40	103	95	711	63	46	59	-8
WAS	154	56	97	.366	40	578	796	5111	1245	203	75	31	568	572	.244	.322	.331	.653	81	-151	-131	97	105	566	76	48	61	-6
CHI	154	51	101	.336	44.5	559	814	5192	1303	172	39	55	595	528	.251	.329	.331	.660	84	-134	-110	97	97	588	46	47	49	-14
TOT	618					5841		42155	11212	1846	450	710	5230	4304	.266	.349	.382	.731							363	288	56	-64

TEAM	CG	SH	SV	IP	H	H/G	HR	BB	SO	RAT	ERA	ERA+	OAV	OOB	PR	/A	PF	CPI	FA	E	DP	FW	PW	BW	SBW	DIF
CLE	66	26	30	1409[1]	1246	8.0	82	628	595	12.1	3.22	126	.239	.323	167	130	95	108	.982	114	183	1.4	12.6	12.7	-.2	-7.0
BOS	70	11	13	1379[1]	1445	9.4	83	592	513	13.4	4.26	103	.270	.345	4	21	102	99	.981	116	174	1.2	2.0	7.6	.9	6.8
NY	62	16	24	1365[2]	1289	8.5	94	641	654	12.9	3.75	109	.250	.336	82	51	95	104	.979	120	161	.9	4.9	10.3	.0	.7
PHI	74	7	18	1368[2]	1456	9.6	86	638	486	13.9	4.43	97	.275	.355	-21	-20	100	101	.981	113	180	1.3	-1.9	-2.0	-.9	9.6
DET	60	5	22	1377	1367	8.9	92	589	678	12.9	4.15	105	.259	.371	21	33	102	95	.974	155	143	-.9	3.2	-1.9	-.5	1.2
STL	35	4	20	1373[1]	1513	9.9	103	737	531	14.9	5.01	91	.281	.371	-109	-69	106	99	.972	168	190	-1.6	-6.7	-3.9	.0	-5.3
WAS	42	4	22	1357[1]	1439	9.5	81	734	446	14.6	4.65	93	.273	.364	-55	-47	101	99	.974	154	144	-.9	-4.6	-12.7	.2	-2.6
CHI	35	2	23	1345[2]	1454	9.7	89	673	403	14.4	4.89	87	.280	.365	-90	-94	99	97	.974	160	176	-1.2	-9.1	-10.7	-.6	-3.4
TOT	444	75	172	10976[1]		9.2				13.6	4.29		.266	.349					.977	1100	1351					

Runs
Henrich-NY 138
DiMaggio-Bos .. 127
Williams-Bos 124
Pesky-Bos 124
Boudreau-Cle .. 116

Hits
Dillinger-StL 207
Mitchell-Cle 204
Boudreau-Cle .. 199
DiMaggio-NY ... 190
Williams-Bos 188

Doubles
Williams-Bos 44
Henrich-NY 42
Majeski-Phi 41
Priddy-StL 40
DiMaggio-Bos ... 40

Triples
Henrich-NY 14
Stewart-NY-Was . 13
Yost-Was 11
Mullin-Det 11
DiMaggio-NY 11

Home Runs
DiMaggio-NY 39
Gordon-Cle 32
Keltner-Cle 31
Stephens-Bos 29
Doerr-Bos 27

Total Bases
DiMaggio-NY 355
Henrich-NY 326
Williams-Bos 313
Stephens-Bos ... 299
Boudreau-Cle ... 299

Runs Batted In
DiMaggio-NY 155
Stephens-Bos ... 137
Williams-Bos 127
Gordon-Cle 124
Majeski-Phi 120

Runs Produced
Williams-Bos 226
DiMaggio-NY 226
Stephens-Bos ... 222
Henrich-NY 213
DiMaggio-Bos ... 205

Bases On Balls
Williams-Bos 126
Joost-Phi 119
Fain-Phi 113
DiMaggio-Bos ... 101
Pesky-Bos 99

Batting Average
Williams-Bos .... .369
Boudreau-Cle ...355
Mitchell-Cle 336
Zarilla-StL 329
McCosky-Phi 326

On Base Percentage
Williams-Bos 497
Boudreau-Cle ...453
Appling-Chi 423
Goodman-Bos ...414
Fain-Phi 412

Slugging Average
Williams-Bos 615
DiMaggio-NY 598
Henrich-NY 554
Boudreau-Cle ...534
Keltner-Cle.......522

Production
Williams-Bos 1.112
DiMaggio-NY 994
Boudreau-Cle ...987
Henrich-NY 945
Keltner-Cle.......917

Adjusted Production
Williams-Bos 185
Boudreau-Cle .. 166
DiMaggio-NY 164
Henrich-NY 151
Keltner-Cle....... 146

Batter Runs
Williams-Bos .. 75.7
Boudreau-Cle .. 52.7
DiMaggio-NY ... 48.6
Henrich-NY 38.9
Keltner-Cle 33.0

Adjusted Batter Runs
Williams-Bos ... 71.8
Boudreau-Cle .. 54.8
DiMaggio-NY ... 49.4
Henrich-NY 39.7
Keltner-Cle 35.1

Clutch Hitting Index
Majeski-Phi 141
Fain-Phi 139
Platt-StL 136
Evers-Det 134
Goodman-Bos 130

Runs Created
Williams-Bos 172
Boudreau-Cle ... 143
DiMaggio-NY 140
Henrich-NY 130
Keltner-Cle...... 116

Total Average
Williams-Bos 1.347
Boudreau-Cle .. 1.058
DiMaggio-NY 1.012
Henrich-NY 955
Keltner-Cle.......918

Stolen Bases
Dillinger-StL 28
Coan-Was 23
Vernon-Was 15
Mitchell-Cle 13

Stolen Base Average
Coan-Was 71.9
Dillinger-StL 71.8

Stolen Base Runs
Robertson-Was 2.4
Tucker-Cle 2.1
DiMaggio-Bos ... 1.8
Dillinger-StL 1.8

Fielding Runs
Pellagrini-StL 24.0
Priddy-StL 23.5
Hegan-Cle 21.3
DiMaggio-Bos .. 15.8
Philley-Chi 15.1

Total Player Rating
Boudreau-Cle 6.8
Williams-Bos 6.2
Priddy-StL 4.5
DiMaggio-NY 4.3
Doerr-Bos 3.7

Wins
Newhouser-Det 21
Lemon-Cle 20
Bearden-Cle 20
Raschi-NY 19
Feller-Cle 19

Win Percentage
Kramer-Bos 783
Bearden-Cle 741
Raschi-NY 704
Reynolds-NY 696

Games
Page-NY 55
Widmar-StL 49
Biscan-StL 47
Thompson-Was.... 46

Complete Games
Lemon-Cle 20
Newhouser-Det .. 19
Raschi-NY 18
Feller-Cle 18

Shutouts
Lemon-Cle 10
Raschi-NY 6
Bearden-Cle 6
Dobson-Bos 5

Saves
Christopher-Cle 17
Page-NY 16
Houtteman-Det ... 10
Ferrick-Was 10
Judson-Chi 8

Innings Pitched
Lemon-Cle 293.2
Feller-Cle 280.1
Newhouser-Det .. 272.1
Dobson-Bos ... 245.1
Reynolds-NY 236.1

Fewest Hits/Game
Shea-NY 6.76
Lemon-Cle 7.08
Bearden-Cle 7.33
Scarborough-Was . 8.06
Trucks-Det 8.08

Fewest BB/Game
Hutchinson-Det ... 1.95
Zoldak-StL-Cle .. 2.42
Lopat-NY 2.62
Kramer-Bos 2.81
Houtteman-Det .. 2.85

Strikeouts
Feller-Cle 164
Lemon-Cle 147
Newhouser-Det ... 143
Brissie-Phi 127
Raschi-NY 124

Strikeouts/Game
Brissie-Phi 5.89
Feller-Cle 5.27
Trucks-Det 5.23
Raschi-NY 5.01
Newhouser-Det ... 4.73

Ratio
Hutchinson-Det .. 11.08
Lemon-Cle 11.12
Raschi-NY 11.52
Newhouser-Det .. 11.53
Bearden-Cle 11.60

Earned Run Average
Bearden-Cle 2.43
Scarborough-Was . 2.82
Lemon-Cle 2.82
Newhouser-Det .. 3.01
Parnell-Bos 3.14

Adjusted ERA
Bearden-Cle 167
Scarborough-Was . 154
Newhouser-Det ... 145
Lemon-Cle 144
Parnell-Bos 140

Opponents' Batting Avg.
Shea-NY 208
Lemon-Cle 216
Bearden-Cle 229
Scarborough-Was..233
Trucks-Det 240

Opponents' On Base Pct.
Hutchinson-Det 297
Lemon-Cle 302
Scarborough-Was .307
Newhouser-Det ...309
Raschi-NY 310

Starter Runs
Lemon-Cle 48.0
Bearden-Cle 47.5
Newhouser-Det .. 38.8
Scarborough-Was . 30.3
Parnell-Bos 27.1

Adjusted Starter Runs
Bearden-Cle 41.6
Newhouser-Det ... 41.1
Lemon-Cle 40.4
Scarborough-Was . 31.5
Parnell-Bos 29.5

Clutch Pitching Index
Bearden-Cle 132
Garver-StL 129
Fowler-Phi 119
Lopat-NY 118
Reynolds-NY 117

Relief Runs
Klieman-Cle 15.0
Christopher-Cle ... 9.1
Thompson-Was .. 6.6
Hiller-NY 1.7
Harris-Phi......... 1.6

Adjusted Relief Runs
Klieman-Cle 12.9
Christopher-Cle ... 7.6
Thompson-Was ... 7.4
Harris-Phi......... 1.6
Ferrick-Was 1.6

Relief Ranking
Christopher-Cle ... 10.7
Klieman-Cle 8.8
Thompson-Was ... 8.6
Ferrick-Was 1.8
Harris-Phi......... 1.3

Total Pitcher Index
Lemon-Cle 6.5
Bearden-Cle 5.2
Newhouser-Det .. 4.5
Scarborough-Was . 3.4
Garver-StL 3.1

Total Baseball Ranking
Boudreau-Cle 6.8
Lemon-Cle 6.5
Williams-Bos 6.2
Bearden-Cle 5.2
Priddy-StL 4.5

1949 National League

TEAM	G	W	L	PCT	GB	R	OR	AB	H	2B	3B	HR	BB	SO	AVG	OBP	SLG	PRO	PRO+	BR	/A	PF	CHI	RC	SB	CS	SBA	SBR
BRO	156	97	57	.630		879	651	5400	1477	236	47	152	638	570	.274	.354	.419	.773	110	103	73	104	106	815	117			
STL	157	96	58	.623	1	766	616	5463	1513	281	54	102	569	482	.277	.348	.404	.752	103	61	28	105	98	777	17			
PHI	154	81	73	.526	16	662	668	5307	1349	232	55	122	528	670	.254	.325	.388	.713	100	-27	-8	97	99	674	27			
BOS	157	75	79	.487	22	706	719	5336	1376	246	33	103	684	656	.258	.345	.374	.719	105	6	44	95	97	710	28			
NY	156	73	81	.474	24	736	693	5308	1383	203	52	147	613	523	.261	.340	.401	.741	105	36	37	100	99	735	43			
PIT	154	71	83	.461	26	681	760	5214	1350	191	41	126	548	554	.259	.332	.384	.716	96	-14	-32	103	101	682	48			
CIN	156	62	92	.403	35	627	770	5469	1423	264	35	86	429	559	.260	.316	.368	.684	88	-84	-92	101	101	636	31			
CHI	154	61	93	.396	36	593	773	5214	1336	212	53	97	396	573	.256	.312	.373	.685	91	-83	-65	97	100	601	53			
TOT	622					5650		42711	11207	1865	370	935	4405	4587	.262	.334	.389	.723						364				

TEAM	CG	SH	SV	IP	H	H/G	HR	BB	SO	RAT	ERA	ERA+	OAV	OOB	PR	/A	PF	CPI	FA	E	DP	FW	PW	BW	SBW	DIF
BRO	62	15	17	1408²	1306	8.3	132	582	743	12.2	3.80	108	.246	.324	37	46	102	99	.980	122	162	1.5	4.6	7.2		6.7
STL	64	13	19	1407²	1356	8.7	87	507	606	12.1	3.44	121	.252	.319	94	113	103	101	.976	146	149	.3	11.2	2.8		4.8
PHI	58	12	15	1391²	1389	9.0	104	502	495	12.4	3.89	101	.268	.335	23	8	98	105	.974	156	141	-.5	.8	-.8		4.5
BOS	68	12	11	1400	1466	9.4	110	520	589	12.9	3.99	95	.268	.334	8	-32	94	102	.976	148	144	.1	-3.2	4.4		-3.3
NY	68	10	9	1374¹	1328	8.7	132	544	516	12.4	3.82	104	.249	.321	33	24	99	97	.973	161	134	-.6	2.4	3.7		-9.4
PIT	53	9	15	1356	1452	9.6	142	535	556	13.4	4.57	92	.274	.344	-79	-55	104	99	.978	132	173	.9	-5.5	-3.2		1.7
CIN	55	10	6	1401²	1423	9.1	124	640	538	13.4	4.34	96	.264	.345	-47	-24	104	99	.977	138	150	.6	-2.4	-9.1		-4.1
CHI	44	8	17	1357²	1487	9.9	104	575	544	13.8	4.50	90	.279	.351	-70	-71	100	100	.970	186	160	-2.1	-7.0	-6.4		-.4
TOT	472	89	109	11097²		9.1				12.8	4.04		.262	.334					.975	1189	1213					

Runs		Hits		Doubles		Triples		Home Runs		Total Bases	
Reese-Bro	132	Musial-StL	207	Musial-StL	41	Slaughter-StL	13	Kiner-Pit	54	Musial-StL	382
Musial-StL	128	Robinson-Bro	203	Ennis-Phi	39	Musial-StL	13	Musial-StL	36	Kiner-Pit	361
Robinson-Bro	122	Thomson-NY	198	Robinson-Bro	38	Robinson-Bro	12	Sauer-Cin-Chi	31	Thomson-NY	332
Kiner-Pit	116	Slaughter-StL	191	Hatton-Cin	38	Ennis-Phi	11	Thomson-NY	27	Ennis-Phi	320
Schoendienst-StL	102	Schoendienst-StL	190			Ashburn-Phi	11	Gordon-NY	26	Robinson-Bro	313

Runs Batted In		Runs Produced		Bases On Balls		Batting Average		On Base Percentage		Slugging Average	
Kiner-Pit	127	Robinson-Bro	230	Kiner-Pit	117	Robinson-Bro	.342	Musial-StL	.438	Kiner-Pit	.658
Robinson-Bro	124	Musial-StL	215	Reese-Bro	116	Musial-StL	.338	Robinson-Bro	.432	Musial-StL	.624
Musial-StL	123	Reese-Bro	189	Stanky-Bos	113	Slaughter-StL	.336	Kiner-Pit	.432	Robinson-Bro	.528
Hodges-Bro	115	Kiner-Pit	189	Musial-StL	107	Furillo-Bro	.322	Slaughter-StL	.418	Ennis-Phi	.525
Ennis-Phi	110	Hodges-Bro	186	Gordon-NY	95	Kiner-Pit	.310	Stanky-Bos	.417	Thomson-NY	.518

Production		Adjusted Production		Batter Runs		Adjusted Batter Runs		Clutch Hitting Index		Runs Created	
Kiner-Pit	1.089	Kiner-Pit	183	Musial-StL	72.4	Musial-StL	68.5	Marion-StL	136	Musial-StL	173
Musial-StL	1.062	Musial-StL	174	Kiner-Pit	70.0	Kiner-Pit	68.0	Hodges-Bro	135	Kiner-Pit	163
Robinson-Bro	.960	Robinson-Bro	150	Robinson-Bro	49.9	Robinson-Bro	46.5	Robinson-Bro	124	Robinson-Bro	135
Slaughter-StL	.929	Gordon-NY	142	Slaughter-StL	40.1	Slaughter-StL	36.6	Cooper-NY-Cin	124	Slaughter-StL	127
Gordon-NY	.909	Slaughter-StL	141	Gordon-NY	31.6	Gordon-NY	31.7	Furillo-Bro	123	Ennis-Phi	118

Total Average		Stolen Bases		Stolen Base Average		Stolen Base Runs		Fielding Runs		Total Player Rating	
Kiner-Pit	1.247	Robinson-Bro	37					Ashburn-Phi	24.7	Kiner-Pit	5.8
Musial-StL	1.185	Reese-Bro	26					Schoendienst-StL	24.0	Robinson-Bro	5.1
Robinson-Bro	1.078							Thomson-NY	19.5	Musial-StL	4.1
Slaughter-StL	.971							Marion-StL	16.6	Thomson-NY	3.6
Gordon-NY	.925							Reich-Chi	14.1	R.Elliott-Bos	3.4

Wins		Win Percentage		Games		Complete Games		Shutouts		Saves	
Spahn-Bos	21	Roe-Bro	.714	Wilks-StL	59	Spahn-Bos	25	Raffensberger-Cin	5	Wilks-StL	9
Pollet-StL	20	Pollet-StL	.690	Konstanty-Phi	53	Raffensberger-Cin	20	Pollet-StL	5	Potter-Bos	7
Raffensberger-Cin	18	Newcombe-Bro	.680	Palica-Bro	49	Newcombe-Bro	19	Newcombe-Bro	5	Konstanty-Phi	7
		Meyer-Phi	.680	Banta-NY	48	Pollet-StL	17	Heintzelman-Phi	5	Staley-StL	6
		Munger-StL	.652	Muncrief-Pit-Chi	47	Jansen-NY	17			Palica-Bro	6

Innings Pitched		Fewest Hits/Game		Fewest BB/Game		Strikeouts		Strikeouts/Game		Ratio	
Spahn-Bos	302.1	Staley-StL	8.09	Koslo-NY	1.83	Spahn-Bos	151	Newcombe-Bro	5.49	Koslo-NY	10.02
Raffensberger-Cin	284.0	Koslo-NY	8.19	Roe-Bro	1.86	Newcombe-Bro	149	Branca-Bro	5.26	Staley-StL	10.40
Jansen-NY	259.2	Newcombe-Bro	8.21	Werle-Pit	2.08	Jansen-NY	113	Chambers-Pit	4.72	Roe-Bro	10.45
Heintzelman-Phi	250.0	Kennedy-NY	8.38	Jansen-NY	2.15	Roe-Bro	109	Roe-Bro	4.61	Newcombe-Bro	11.01
Newcombe-Bro	244.1	Meyer-Phi	8.41	Leonard-Chi	2.15	Branca-Bro	109	Spahn-Bos	4.50	Spahn-Bos	11.07

Earned Run Average		Adjusted ERA		Opponents' Batting Avg.		Opponents' On Base Pct.		Starter Runs		Adjusted Starter Runs	
Koslo-NY	2.50	Koslo-NY	159	Staley-StL	.238	Koslo-NY	.278	Koslo-NY	36.2	Pollet-StL	35.7
Staley-StL	2.73	Staley-StL	152	Koslo-NY	.239	Staley-StL	.286	Spahn-Bos	32.7	Koslo-NY	34.8
Pollet-StL	2.77	Pollet-StL	150	Kennedy-NY	.242	Roe-Bro	.293	Pollet-StL	32.6	Roe-Bro	30.9
Roe-Bro	2.79	Roe-Bro	147	Newcombe-Bro	.243	Spahn-Bos	.299	Roe-Bro	29.5	Staley-StL	27.2
Heintzelman-Phi	3.02	Brazle-StL	131	Spahn-Bos	.245	Newcombe-Bro	.301	Heintzelman-Phi	28.2	Heintzelman-Phi	25.5

Clutch Pitching Index		Relief Runs		Adjusted Relief Runs		Relief Ranking		Total Pitcher Index		Total Baseball Ranking	
Roe-Bro	126	Erautt-Cin	8.6	Erautt-Cin	10.3	Erautt-Cin	12.6	Koslo-NY	3.7	Kiner-Pit	5.8
Heintzelman-Phi	123	Konstanty-Phi	8.5	Konstanty-Phi	7.5	Konstanty-Phi	11.0	Pollet-StL	3.7	Robinson-Bro	5.1
Brazle-StL	121	Hogue-Bos	7.3	Wilks-StL	5.7	Palica-Bro	8.9	Staley-StL	3.1	Musial-StL	4.1
Jones-NY	116	Palica-Bro	4.5	Hogue-Bos	5.2	Wilks-StL	6.6	Newcombe-Bro	3.0	Koslo-NY	3.7
Dickson-Pit	113	Wilks-StL	4.1	Palica-Bro	5.2	Hogue-Bos	3.1	Dickson-Pit	2.9	Pollet-StL	3.7

TEAM	G	W	L	PCT	GB	R	OR	AB	H	2B	3B	HR	BB	SO	AVG	OBP	SLG	PRO	PRO+	BR	/A	PF	CHI	RC	SB	CS	SBA	SBR
NY	155	97	57	.630		829	637	5196	1396	215	60	115	731	539	.269	.362	.400	.762	108	58	58	100	106	790	58	30	66	-1
BOS	155	96	58	.623	1	896	667	5320	1500	272	36	131	835	510	.282	.381	.420	.801	111	147	93	107	100	890	43	25	63	-2
CLE	154	89	65	.578	8	675	574	5221	1358	194	58	112	601	534	.260	.339	.384	.723	99	-30	-16	98	99	696	44	40	52	-11
DET	155	87	67	.565	10	751	655	5259	1405	215	51	88	751	502	.267	.361	.378	.739	102	20	19	100	99	739	36	25	59	-4
PHI	154	81	73	.526	16	726	725	5123	1331	214	49	82	783	493	.260	.361	.369	.730	104	6	31	97	99	719	62	55	53	-14
CHI	154	63	91	.409	34	648	737	5204	1340	207	66	43	702	596	.257	.339	.347	.694	93	-41	-70	104	101	670	38	39	49	-12
STL	155	53	101	.344	44	667	913	5112	1301	213	30	117	631	700	.254	.339	.377	.716	92	-66	-43	97	99	657	46	33	58	-6
WAS	154	50	104	.325	47	584	868	5234	1330	207	41	81	593	495	.254	.333	.356	.689	90	-93	-77	98	95	640	39	52	43	-20
TOT	618					5776		41669	10961	1737	391	769	5627	4369	.263	.353	.379	.732							366	299	55	-70

TEAM	CG	SH	SV	IP	H	H/G	HR	BB	SO	RAT	ERA	ERA+	OAV	OOB	PR	/A	PF	CPI	FA	E	DP	FW	PW	BW	SBW	DIF
NY	59	12	36	1371[1]	1231	8.1	98	812	671	13.6	3.69	110	.242	.351	77	54	96	107	.977	138	195	.0	5.3	5.6	.7	8.3
BOS	84	16	16	1377	1375	9.0	82	661	598	13.5	3.97	110	.262	.347	34	59	104	101	.980	120	207	1.1	5.7	9.1	.7	2.5
CLE	65	10	19	1383[2]	1275	8.3	82	611	594	12.4	3.36	119	.247	.329	129	98	95	104	.983	103	192	2.1	9.5	-1.6	-.2	2.2
DET	70	19	12	1393[2]	1338	8.6	102	628	631	12.8	3.77	110	.254	.335	66	60	99	100	.976	140	217	-.1	-1.8	3.0	.5	2.5
PHI	85	9	11	1365	1359	9.0	105	758	490	14.1	4.23	97	.263	.360	-5	-19	98	103	.977	131	174	.4	5.8	1.8	-1.1	3.0
CHI	57	10	17	1363[1]	1362	9.0	108	693	502	13.7	4.30	97	.264	.353	-15	-19	99	99	.977	141	180	-.2	-1.8	-4.2	-.5	-7.2
STL	43	3	16	1341[1]	1583	10.6	113	685	432	15.4	5.21	87	.294	.377	-151	-102	108	98	.971	166	154	-1.6	-9.9	-6.8	-.3	-5.3
WAS	44	9	9	1345[2]	1438	9.6	79	779	451	15.0	5.10	84	.276	.373	-134	-126	101	91	.973	161	168	-1.4	-12.3	-7.5	.3	-6.1
TOT	507	88	136	10941		9.0				13.8	4.20		.263	.353					.977	1100	1487					

Runs
Williams-Bos 150
Joost-Phi 128
DiMaggio-Bos 126
Stephens-Bos 113
Pesky-Bos 111

Hits
Mitchell-Cle 203
Williams-Bos 194
DiMaggio-Bos 186
Wertz-Det 185
Pesky-Bos 185

Doubles
Williams-Bos 39
Kell-Det 38
DiMaggio-Bos 34
Zarilla-StL-Bos 33
Stephens-Bos 31

Triples
Mitchell-Cle 23
Dillinger-StL 13
Valo-Phi 12

Home Runs
Williams-Bos 43
Stephens-Bos 39

Total Bases
Williams-Bos 368
Stephens-Bos 329
Wertz-Det 283
Mitchell-Cle 274
Doerr-Bos 269

Runs Batted In
Williams-Bos 159
Stephens-Bos 159
Wertz-Det 133
Doerr-Bos 109
Chapman-Phi..... 108

Runs Produced
Williams-Bos 266
Stephens-Bos 233
Wertz-Det 209
Joost-Phi 186
Doerr-Bos 182

Bases On Balls
Williams-Bos 162
Joost-Phi 149
Fain-Phi 136
Appling-Chi 121
Valo-Phi 119

Batting Average
Kell-Det .... .343
Williams-Bos ..... .343
Dillinger-StL ...... .324
Mitchell-Cle ...... .317
Doerr-Bos .... .309

On Base Percentage
Williams-Bos .... .490
Appling-Chi ...... .439
Joost-Phi .... .429
Kell-Det .... .424
Michaels-Chi ..... .417

Slugging Average
Williams-Bos ..... .650
Stephens-Bos .... .539
Henrich-NY ...... .526
Doerr-Bos .... .497
Sievers-StL ...... .471

Production
Williams-Bos 1.141
Henrich-NY ...... .942
Stephens-Bos .... .930
Kell-Det .... .892
Doerr-Bos .... .890

Adjusted Production
Williams-Bos 187
Henrich-NY 148
Joost-Phi 138
Kell-Det 136
Stephens-Bos 135

Batter Runs
Williams-Bos 88.9
Stephens-Bos 36.9
Joost-Phi 31.9
DiMaggio-NY 31.7
Henrich-NY 29.7

Adjusted Batter Runs
Williams-Bos 82.6
Joost-Phi 34.6
DiMaggio-NY 31.7
Stephens-Bos 30.8
Henrich-NY 29.7

Clutch Hitting Index
Wertz-Det........ 141
Fain-Phi 137
Lipon-Det 134
Stephens-Bos 129
Doerr-Bos 123

Runs Created
Williams-Bos 193
Stephens-Bos 132
Joost-Phi 119
DiMaggio-Bos 110
Wertz-Det........ 110

Total Average
Williams-Bos 1.347
Henrich-NY 1.017
Joost-Phi .... .995
Stephens-Bos .... .947
Kell-Det .... .877

Stolen Bases
Dillinger-StL 20
Rizzuto-NY 18
Valo-Phi 14
Philley-Chi 13

Stolen Base Average
Rizzuto-NY 75.0
Dillinger-StL 58.8

Stolen Base Runs
Tebbetts-Bos 1.8
Rizzuto-NY 1.8
Mapes-NY 1.8
Fain-Phi 1.8
Philley-Chi 1.5

Fielding Runs
Doerr-Bos 27.8
Pesky-Bos 21.4
Vernon-Cle 18.8
DiMaggio-Bos 14.3
Baker-Chi........ 11.8

Total Player Rating
Williams-Bos 7.3
Doerr-Bos 5.2
Joost-Phi 5.1
Stephens-Bos 4.3
Michaels-Chi 3.9

Wins
Parnell-Bos 25
Kinder-Bos 23
Lemon-Cle 22
Raschi-NY 21
Kellner-Phi 20

Win Percentage
Kinder-Bos 793
Parnell-Bos 781
Reynolds-NY 739
Lemon-Cle 688

Games
Page-NY 60
Welteroth-Was 52
Ferrick-StL 50
Kennedy-StL 48
Surkont-Chi 44

Complete Games
Parnell-Bos 27
Newhouser-Det ... 22
Lemon-Cle 22
Raschi-NY 21

Shutouts
Trucks-Det 6
Kinder-Bos 6
Garcia-Cle 5

Saves
Page-NY 27
Benton-Cle 10
Ferrick-StL 6
Paige-Cle 5

Innings Pitched
Parnell-Bos 295.1
Newhouser-Det . 292.0
Lemon-Cle 279.2
Trucks-Det 275.0
Raschi-NY 274.2

Fewest Hits/Game
Byrne-NY 5.74
Lemon-Cle 6.79
Trucks-Det 6.84
Gray-Det 7.52
Pierce-Chi 7.60

Fewest BB/Game
Hutchinson-Det ... 2.48
Houtteman-Det ... 2.61
Lopat-NY 2.88
Garcia-Cle 3.07
Wynn-Cle 3.12

Strikeouts
Trucks-Det 153
Newhouser-Det ... 144
Lemon-Cle 138
Kinder-Bos 138
Byrne-NY 129

Strikeouts/Game
Byrne-NY 5.92
Trucks-Det 5.01
Pierce-Chi 4.98
Kinder-Bos 4.93
Garcia-Cle 4.82

Ratio
Hutchinson-Det .. 10.49
Trucks-Det 11.03
Garcia-Cle 11.07
Lemon-Cle 11.39
Gumpert-Chi 11.81

Earned Run Average
Garcia-Cle 2.36
Parnell-Bos 2.77
Trucks-Det 2.81
Hutchinson-Det ... 2.96
Lemon-Cle 2.99

Adjusted ERA
Garcia-Cle 169
Parnell-Bos 157
Trucks-Det 148
Hutchinson-Det ... 141
Lemon-Cle 133

Opponents' Batting Avg.
Byrne-NY .... .183
Lemon-Cle ...... .211
Trucks-Det ...... .211
Gray-Det .... .227
Pierce-Chi .... .228

Opponents' On Base Pct.
Hutchinson-Det ... .290
Trucks-Det ...... .301
Garcia-Cle ...... .308
Lemon-Cle .... .309
Gumpert-Chi ..... .318

Starter Runs
Parnell-Bos 46.7
Trucks-Det 42.3
Lemon-Cle 37.4
Garcia-Cle 35.9
Benton-Cle 31.3

Adjusted Starter Runs
Parnell-Bos 52.1
Trucks-Det 41.1
Garcia-Cle 31.9
Lemon-Cle 31.0
Benton-Cle 28.2

Clutch Pitching Index
Garcia-Cle 123
Lopat-NY 122
Wight-Chi 118
Houtteman-Det ... 115
Kinder-Bos 114

Relief Runs
Page-NY 24.1
Paige-Cle 10.7
Papish-Cle 6.9
Ferrick-StL 3.7

Adjusted Relief Runs
Page-NY 21.8
Paige-Cle 8.8
Ferrick-StL 7.5
Papish-Cle 5.5
Starr-StL 1.9

Relief Ranking
Page-NY 40.3
Paige-Cle 11.7
Ferrick-StL 7.4
Starr-StL 1.7
Papish-Cle 1.0

Total Pitcher Index
Parnell-Bos 5.6
Lemon-Cle 5.5
Garcia-Cle 3.6
Hutchinson-Det ... 3.2
Trucks-Det 3.2

Total Baseball Ranking
Williams-Bos 7.3
Parnell-Bos 5.6
Lemon-Cle 5.5
Doerr-Bos 5.2
Joost-Phi 5.1

TEAM	G	W	L	PCT	GB	R	OR	AB	H	2B	3B	HR	BB	SO	AVG	OBP	SLG	PRO	PRO+	BR	/A	PF	CHI	RC	SB	CS	SBA	SBR
PHI	157	91	63	.591		722	624	5426	1440	225	55	125	535	569	.265	.334	.396	.730	100	-14	-2	98	101	714	33			
BRO	155	89	65	.578	2	847	724	5364	1461	247	46	194	607	632	.272	.349	.444	.793	113	107	92	102	101	833	77			
NY	154	86	68	.558	5	735	643	5238	1352	204	50	133	627	629	.258	.342	.392	.734	100	4	0	101	101	726	42			
BOS	156	83	71	.539	8	785	736	5363	1411	246	36	148	615	616	.263	.342	.405	.747	110	24	71	94	104	750	71			
STL	153	78	75	.510	12.5	693	670	5215	1353	255	50	102	606	604	.259	.339	.386	.725	93	-15	-49	105	99	696	23			
CIN	153	66	87	.431	24.5	654	734	5253	1366	257	27	99	504	497	.260	.327	.376	.703	91	-65	-67	100	102	643	37			
CHI	154	64	89	.418	26.5	643	694	5230	1298	224	47	161	479	767	.248	.315	.401	.716	95	-53	-45	99	100	658	46			
PIT	154	57	96	.373	33.5	681	857	5327	1404	227	59	138	564	693	.264	.338	.406	.744	99	13	-11	103	93	729	43			
TOT	618					5760		42416	11085	1885	370	1100	4537	5007	.261	.336	.401	.737							372			

TEAM	CG	SH	SV	IP	H	H/G	HR	BB	SO	RAT	ERA	ERA+	OAV	OOB	PR	/A	PF	CPI	FA	E	DP	FW	PW	BW	SBW	DIF
PHI	57	13	27	1406	1324	8.5	122	530	620	12.0	3.50	116	.250	.320	101	86	98	105	.975	151	155	.1	8.4	-.2		5.7
BRO	62	10	21	1389²	1397	9.0	163	591	772	13.0	4.28	96	.263	.339	-22	-29	99	102	.979	127	183	1.4	-2.8	9.0		4.5
NY	70	19	15	1375	1268	8.3	140	536	596	12.0	3.71	110	.246	.320	66	59	99	100	.977	137	181	.8	5.8	.0		2.5
BOS	88	7	10	1385¹	1411	9.2	129	554	615	13.0	4.14	93	.263	.336	0	-45	93	99	.970	182	146	-1.7	-4.4	6.9		5.1
STL	58	10	14	1356	1398	9.4	119	535	603	13.0	3.97	108	.268	.339	26	49	104	105	.978	130	172	1.1	4.8	-4.8		.4
CIN	67	7	13	1357²	1363	9.0	145	582	686	13.2	4.32	98	.259	.338	-26	-13	102	97	.976	140	132	.5	-1.3	-6.5		-3.2
CHI	55	9	19	1371¹	1452	9.5	130	593	559	13.6	4.28	98	.271	.347	-21	-11	101	103	.968	201	169	-2.8	-1.1	-4.4		-4.2
PIT	42	6	16	1368²	1472	9.7	152	616	556	13.9	4.96	88	.275	.353	-124	-88	106	95	.977	136	165	.8	-8.6	-1.1		-10.6
TOT	498	81	135	11009²		9.1				13.0	4.14		.261	.336					.975	1204	1303					

Runs
Torgeson-Bos 120
Stanky-NY 115
Kiner-Pit 112
Snider-Bro 109
Musial-StL 105

Hits
Snider-Bro 199
Musial-StL 192
Furillo-Bro 189
Ennis-Phi 185
Waitkus-Phi 182

Doubles
Schoendienst-StL .. 43
Musial-StL 41
Robinson-Bro 39
Kluszewski-Cin ... 37
Dark-NY 36

Triples
Ashburn-Phi....... 14
Bell-Pit 11
Snider-Bro 10
Smalley-Chi 9
Schoendienst-StL ... 9

Home Runs
Kiner-Pit 47
Pafko-Chi 36
Sauer-Chi 32
Hodges-Bro 32

Total Bases
Snider-Bro 343
Musial-StL 331
Ennis-Phi 328
Kiner-Pit 323
Pafko-Chi 304

Runs Batted In
Ennis-Phi 126
Kiner-Pit 118
Hodges-Bro 113
Kluszewski-Cin ... 111
Musial-StL 109

Runs Produced
Furillo-Bro 187
Ennis-Phi 187
Musial-StL 186
Snider-Bro 185
Torgeson-Bos 184

Bases On Balls
Stanky-NY 144
Kiner-Pit 122
Torgeson-Bos 119
Westrum-NY 92
Reese-Bro 91

Batting Average
Musial-StL 346
Robinson-Bro 328
Snider-Bro 321
Ennis-Phi 311
Kluszewski-Cin ...307

On Base Percentage
Stanky-NY 460
Musial-StL 437
Robinson-Bro 423
Glaviano-StL 421
Torgeson-Bos 412

Slugging Average
Musial-StL 596
Pafko-Chi 591
Kiner-Pit 590
Gordon-Bos 557
Snider-Bro 553

Production
Musial-StL 1.034
Kiner-Pit .... .998
Pafko-Chi .... .989
Gordon-Bos ...... .960
Snider-Bro ...... .932

Adjusted Production
Musial-StL 161
Gordon-Bos 160
Pafko-Chi 158
Kiner-Pit 154
Elliott-Bos 143

Batter Runs
Musial-StL 57.3
Kiner-Pit 48.7
Pafko-Chi 41.5
Snider-Bro 35.6
Gordon-Bos 35.3

Adjusted Batter Runs
Musial-StL 53.5
Kiner-Pit 46.1
Pafko-Chi 42.3
Gordon-Bos 39.6
Torgeson-Bos 36.5

Clutch Hitting Index
Slaughter-StL 158
D.Mueller-NY 149
Wyrostek-Cin 131
Kluszewski-Cin .. 129
Furillo-Bro 128

Runs Created
Musial-StL 149
Kiner-Pit 133
Snider-Bro 131
Pafko-Chi 124
Torgeson-Bos 121

Total Average
Musial-StL 1.139
Kiner-Pit 1.071
Pafko-Chi 1.057
Stanky-NY 1.013
Gordon-Bos 1.003

Stolen Bases
Jethroe-Bos 35
Reese-Bro 17
Snider-Bro 16
Torgeson-Bos 15
Ashburn-Phi 14

Stolen Base Average

Stolen Base Runs

Fielding Runs
Smalley-Chi 21.3
Cox-Bro 12.0
Ryan-Bos-Cin ... 11.6
Robinson-Bro ... 10.6
Westrum-NY 10.4

Total Player Rating
Robinson-Bro 4.7
Stanky-NY 4.2
Gordon-Bos 3.8
Snider-Bro 3.5
Kiner-Pit 3.5

Wins
Spahn-Bos 21
Sain-Bos 20
Roberts-Phi 20

Win Percentage
Maglie-NY 818
Konstanty-Phi ...696
Simmons-Phi 680
Roberts-Phi 645

Games
Konstanty-Phi ... 74
Dickson-Pit 51
Werle-Pit 48
Maglie-NY 47
Brazle-StL 46

Complete Games
Bickford-Bos 27
Spahn-Bos 25
Sain-Bos 25
Roberts-Phi 21
Jansen-NY 21

Shutouts
Hearn-StL-NY 5
Roberts-Phi 5
Maglie-NY 5
Jansen-NY 5

Saves
Konstanty-Phi 22
Werle-Pit 8
Hogue-Bos 7
Branca-Bro 7

Innings Pitched
Bickford-Bos 311.2
Roberts-Phi 304.1
Spahn-Bos 293.0
Sain-Bos 278.1
Jansen-NY 275.0

Fewest Hits/Game
Blackwell-Cin 7.00
Maglie-NY 7.38
Simmons-Phi 7.46
Spahn-Bos 7.62
Jansen-NY 7.79

Fewest BB/Game
Raffensberger-Cin 1.51
Jansen-NY 1.80
Sain-Bos 2.26
Roberts-Phi 2.28
Roe-Bro 2.37

Strikeouts
Blackwell-Cin 191
Blackwell-Cin 188
Jansen-NY 161
Simmons-Phi 146
Roberts-Phi 146

Strikeouts/Game
Blackwell-Cin 6.48
Simmons-Phi 6.12
Spahn-Bos 5.87
Palica-Bro 5.86
Jansen-NY 5.27

Ratio
Jansen-NY 9.62
Roberts-Phi 10.68
Brecheen-StL ... 10.97
Spahn-Bos 11.06
Simmons-Phi ... 11.24

Earned Run Average
Maglie-NY 2.71
Blackwell-Cin 2.97
Jansen-NY 3.01
Roberts-Phi 3.02
Lanier-StL 3.13

Adjusted ERA
Maglie-NY 151
Blackwell-Cin 143
Lanier-StL 137
Jansen-NY 136
Roberts-Phi 134

Opponents' Batting Avg.
Blackwell-Cin 210
Simmons-Phi 223
Maglie-NY 226
Spahn-Bos 227
Jansen-NY 232

Opponents' On Base Pct.
Jansen-NY 271
Roberts-Phi 297
Brecheen-StL 298
Spahn-Bos 299
Blackwell-Cin ...301

Starter Runs
Roberts-Phi 38.0
Jansen-NY 34.5
Blackwell-Cin ... 34.1
Maglie-NY 32.8
Spahn-Bos 31.8

Adjusted Starter Runs
Blackwell-Cin 36.7
Roberts-Phi 34.8
Jansen-NY 33.1
Maglie-NY 31.7
Pollet-StL 25.9

Clutch Pitching Index
Brazle-StL 125
Roe-Bro 118
Maglie-NY 116
Ramsdell-Bro-Cin . 115
Minner-Chi 113

Relief Runs
Konstanty-Phi ... 24.9
Kramer-NY 5.9
Leonard-Chi 3.1
VanderMeer-Chi .. 2.9
Smith-Cin 2.7

Adjusted Relief Runs
Konstanty-Phi ... 23.3
Kramer-NY 5.4
Smith-Cin 3.6
Leonard-Chi 3.5
VanderMeer-Chi .. 3.4

Relief Ranking
Konstanty-Phi ... 39.4
Kramer-NY 5.2
Smith-Cin 3.5
Leonard-Chi 3.2
VanderMeer-Chi .. 3.0

Total Pitcher Index
Blackwell-Cin 3.7
Jansen-NY 3.5
Maglie-NY 3.4
Roberts-Phi 3.2
Spahn-Bos 2.7

Total Baseball Ranking
Robinson-Bro 4.7
Stanky-NY 4.2
Gordon-Bos 3.8
Blackwell-Cin ... 3.7
Jansen-NY 3.5

TEAM	G	W	L	PCT	GB	R	OR	AB	H	2B	3B	HR	BB	SO	AVG	OBP	SLG	PRO	PRO+	BR	/A	PF	CHI	RC	SB	CS	SBA	SBR
NY	155	98	56	.636		914	691	5361	1511	234	70	159	687	463	.282	.367	.441	.808	116	92	115	97	104	902	41	28	59	-5
DET	157	95	59	.617	3	837	713	5381	1518	285	50	114	722	480	.282	.369	.417	.786	104	60	34	103	97	846	23	40	37	-17
BOS	154	94	60	.610	4	1027	804	5516	1665	287	61	161	719	582	.302	.385	.464	.849	112	185	106	110	103	1014	40	34	65	-1
CLE	155	92	62	.597	6	806	654	5263	1417	222	46	164	693	624	.269	.358	.422	.780	109	39	65	97	98	820	42	25	63	-2
WAS	155	67	87	.435	31	690	813	5251	1365	190	53	76	671	606	.260	.347	.360	.707	91	-93	-56	95	101	690	40	34	54	-8
CHI	156	60	94	.390	38	625	749	5260	1368	172	47	77	551	566	.260	.337	.364	.697	86	-125	-104	97	98	648	19	22	46	-8
STL	154	58	96	.377	40	684	916	5163	1269	235	43	106	690	744	.246	.337	.370	.707	84	-102	-131	104	103	667	39	40	49	-12
PHI	154	52	102	.338	46	670	913	5212	1361	204	53	100	685	493	.261	.349	.378	.727	94	-56	-41	98	94	708	42	25	63	-2
TOT	620					6253		42407	11474	1829	423	973	5418	4558	.271	.356	.402	.759							278	231	55	-55

TEAM	CG	SH	SV	IP	H	H/G	HR	BB	SO	RAT	ERA	ERA+	OAV	OOB	PR	/A	PF	CPI	FA	E	DP	FW	PW	BW	SBW	DIF
NY	66	12	31	1372²	1322	8.7	118	708	712	13.5	4.15	103	.255	.348	65	22	94	102	.980	119	188	1.3	2.1	10.8	.2	6.7
DET	72	9	20	1407¹	1444	9.2	141	553	576	13.0	4.12	114	.267	.339	71	88	102	105	.981	120	194	1.3	8.2	3.2	-.9	6.2
BOS	66	6	28	1362¹	1413	9.3	121	748	630	14.4	4.88	100	.270	.364	-46	3	107	97	.981	111	181	1.7	.3	9.9	.6	4.6
CLE	69	11	16	1378²	1289	8.4	120	647	674	12.8	3.75	115	.248	.333	126	88	95	103	.978	129	160	.7	8.2	6.1	-.1	.0
WAS	59	7	18	1364²	1479	9.8	99	648	486	14.2	4.66	96	.278	.359	-12	-25	98	99	.977	140	181	.2	1.1	-9.7	-.1	-8.5
CHI	62	7	9	1365²	1370	9.0	107	734	566	14.0	4.41	102	.263	.356	26	12	98	100	.972	167	181	-1.4	-2.3	-5.2	.5	-1.5
STL	56	7	14	1365¹	1629	10.7	129	651	448	15.2	5.20	95	.295	.372	-94	-38	108	100	.967	196	155	-3.1	-3.6	-12.3	-.5	.4
PHI	50	3	18	1346¹	1528	10.2	138	729	466	15.3	5.49	83	.287	.376	-136	-140	99	96	.974	155	208	-.8	-13.1	-3.8	.5	-7.7
TOT	500	62	154	10963		9.4				14.0	4.58		.271	.356					.976	1137	1448					

Runs
DiMaggio-Bos 131
Stephens-Bos 125
Rizzuto-NY 125
Berra-NY 116

Hits
Kell-Det 218
Rizzuto-NY 200
DiMaggio-Bos 193
Berra-NY 192
Stephens-Bos 185

Doubles
Kell-Det 56
Wertz-Det 37
Rizzuto-NY 36
Evers-Det 35
Stephens-Bos 34

Triples
Evers-Det 11
Doerr-Bos 11
DiMaggio-Bos 11

Home Runs
Rosen-Cle 37
Dropo-Bos 34
DiMaggio-NY 32
Stephens-Bos 30
Zernial-Chi 29

Total Bases
Dropo-Bos 326
Stephens-Bos 321
Berra-NY 318
Kell-Det 310
DiMaggio-NY 307

Runs Batted In
Stephens-Bos 144
Dropo-Bos 144
Berra-NY 124
Wertz-Det 123
DiMaggio-NY 122

Runs Produced
Stephens-Bos 239
Berra-NY 212
Dropo-Bos 211
Kell-Det 207
DiMaggio-NY 204

Bases On Balls
Yost-Was 141
Fain-Phi 133
Pesky-Bos 104
Joost-Phi 103
Rosen-Cle 100

Batting Average
Goodman-Bos ..... .354
Kell-Det .... .340
DiMaggio-Bos .... .328
Doby-Cle .... .326
Zarilla-Bos ...... .325

On Base Percentage
Doby-Cle .... .442
Yost-Was .... .440
Pesky-Bos .... .437
Fain-Phi .... .430
Goodman-Bos ..... .427

Slugging Average
DiMaggio-NY ..... .585
Dropo-Bos .... .583
Evers-Det .... .551
Doby-Cle .... .545
Rosen-Cle .... .543

Production
Doby-Cle .... .986
DiMaggio-NY ..... .979
Dropo-Bos .... .961
Evers-Det .... .959
Rosen-Cle .... .948

Adjusted Production
Doby-Cle 156
DiMaggio-NY 152
Rosen-Cle 146
Evers-Det 139
Berra-NY 136

Batter Runs
Doby-Cle 41.7
Williams-Bos 40.9
DiMaggio-NY 35.4
Rosen-Cle 34.3
Evers-Det 33.5

Adjusted Batter Runs
Doby-Cle 44.3
DiMaggio-NY 37.7
Rosen-Cle 37.2
Williams-Bos 35.7
Evers-Det 31.0

Clutch Hitting Index
Vernon-Cle-Was .. 136
Mele-Was 135
Stephens-Bos 128
Fain-Phi 126
Dropo-Bos 123

Runs Created
Doby-Cle 130
Wertz-Det 128
DiMaggio-NY 125
Berra-NY 125
Rizzuto-NY 124

Total Average
Doby-Cle 1.073
DiMaggio-NY 1.018
Wertz-Det .... .978
Zarilla-Bos ...... .954
Rosen-Cle .... .953

Stolen Bases
DiMaggio-Bos 15
Valo-Phi 12
Rizzuto-NY 12
Coan-Was 10
Lipon-Det 9

Stolen Base Average

Stolen Base Runs
DiMaggio-Bos 2.1
Vernon-Cle-Was .. 1.8
Collins-NY 1.5
Avila-Cle 1.5
Jensen-NY 1.2

Fielding Runs
Priddy-Det 31.3
Hegan-Cle 24.2
Pesky-Bos 21.5
Noren-Was 15.9
Carrasquel-Chi ... 11.2

Total Player Rating
Rizzuto-NY 4.1
Berra-NY 3.4
DiMaggio-NY 3.0
Rosen-Cle 3.0
Priddy-Det 3.0

Wins
R.Lemon-Cle 23
Raschi-NY 21
Houtteman-Det ... 19

Win Percentage
Raschi-NY .... .724
Wynn-Cle .... .692
Lopat-NY .... .692
Hutchinson-Det ... .680
R.Lemon-Cle ..... .676

Games
Harris-Was 53
Kinder-Bos 48
Ferrick-StL-NY ... 46
Judson-Chi 46
Brissie-Phi 46

Complete Games
R.Lemon-Cle 22
Garver-StL 22
Parnell-Bos 21
Houtteman-Det ... 21

Shutouts
Houtteman-Det ... 4

Saves
Harris-Was 15
Page-NY 13
Ferrick-StL-NY ... 11
Kinder-Bos 9
Brissie-Phi 8

Innings Pitched
R.Lemon-Cle 288.0
Houtteman-Det ... 274.2
Garver-StL 260.0
Raschi-NY 256.2
Parnell-Bos 249.0

Fewest Hits/Game
Wynn-Cle 6.99
Pierce-Chi 7.76
Cain-Chi 8.02
Reynolds-NY 8.04
Raschi-NY 8.14

Fewest BB/Game
Hutchinson-Det ... 1.86
Lopat-NY 2.48
Overmire-StL 2.52
Trout-Det 3.12
Houtteman-Det ... 3.24

Strikeouts
R.Lemon-Cle 170
Reynolds-NY 160
Raschi-NY 155
Wynn-Cle 143
Feller-Cle 119

Strikeouts/Game
Wynn-Cle 6.02
Reynolds-NY 5.98
Raschi-NY 5.44
R.Lemon-Cle 5.31
Byrne-NY 5.22

Ratio
Wynn-Cle 11.41
Lopat-NY 11.92
Houtteman-Det ... 11.93
Raschi-NY 12.31
Feller-Cle 12.32

Earned Run Average
Wynn-Cle 3.20
Garver-StL 3.39
Feller-Cle 3.43
Lopat-NY 3.47
Houtteman-Det ... 3.54

Adjusted ERA
Garver-StL 146
Parnell-Bos 136
Wynn-Cle 135
Houtteman-Det ... 132
Feller-Cle 126

Opponents' Batting Avg.
Wynn-Cle .... .212
Pierce-Chi .... .228
Reynolds-NY ..... .242
Raschi-NY .... .243
Cain-Chi .... .244

Opponents' On Base Pct.
Wynn-Cle .... .305
Lopat-NY .... .317
Houtteman-Det ... .322
Feller-Cle .... .325
Raschi-NY .... .327

Starter Runs
Garver-StL 34.3
Wynn-Cle 32.7
Houtteman-Det ... 31.7
Feller-Cle 31.7
Lopat-NY 29.2

Adjusted Starter Runs
Garver-StL 45.0
Parnell-Bos 35.5
Houtteman-Det ... 35.1
Wynn-Cle 26.8
Feller-Cle 24.9

Clutch Pitching Index
Garver-StL 119
Hudson-Was 113
R.Lemon-Cle 111
Houtteman-Det ... 110
Parnell-Bos 110

Relief Runs
Judson-Chi 8.0
Aloma-Chi 7.6
Benton-Cle 7.0
Ferrick-StL-NY ... 7.0
Flores-Cle 5.0

Adjusted Relief Runs
Judson-Chi 6.8
Aloma-Chi 6.7
Ferrick-StL-NY ... 6.2
Benton-Cle 5.3
Flores-Cle 3.5

Relief Ranking
Ferrick-StL-NY ... 13.0
Aloma-Chi 6.9
Benton-Cle 5.3
Flores-Cle 4.2
Judson-Chi 2.7

Total Pitcher Index
Garver-StL 5.4
Parnell-Bos 3.8
R.Lemon-Cle 3.5
Houtteman-Det ... 3.4
Wynn-Cle 3.3

Total Baseball Ranking
Garver-StL 5.4
Rizzuto-NY 4.1
Parnell-Bos 3.8
R.Lemon-Cle 3.5
Berra-NY 3.4

TEAM	G	W	L	PCT	GB	R	OR	AB	H	2B	3B	HR	BB	SO	AVG	OBP	SLG	PRO	PRO+	BR	/A	PF	CHI	RC	SB	CS	SBA	SBR
NY	157	98	59	.624		781	641	5360	1396	201	53	179	671	624	.260	.347	.418	.765	111	91	85	101	97	812	55	34	62	-4
BRO	158	97	60	.618	1	855	672	5492	1511	249	37	184	603	649	.275	.352	.434	.786	116	130	116	102	101	843	89	70	56	-15
STL	155	81	73	.526	15.5	683	671	5317	1404	230	57	95	569	492	.264	.339	.382	.721	99	7	3	101	97	705	30	30	50	-9
BOS	155	76	78	.494	20.5	723	662	5293	1385	234	37	130	565	617	.262	.336	.375	.730	111	20	68	93	102	719	80	34	70	4
PHI	154	73	81	.474	23.5	648	644	5332	1384	199	47	108	505	525	.260	.326	.375	.701	96	-38	-28	99	99	676	63	28	69	2
CIN	155	68	86	.442	28.5	559	667	5285	1309	215	33	88	415	577	.248	.304	.351	.655	81	-134	-144	102	104	562	44	40	52	-11
PIT	155	64	90	.416	32.5	689	845	5318	1372	218	56	137	557	615	.258	.331	.397	.728	99	11	-9	103	98	712	29	27	52	-8
CHI	155	62	92	.403	34.5	614	750	5307	1327	200	47	103	477	647	.250	.315	.364	.679	86	-86	-98	102	103	613	63	30	68	1
TOT	622					5552		42704	11088	1746	367	1024	4362	4746	.260	.331	.390	.721							453	293	61	-40

TEAM	CG	SH	SV	IP	H	H/G	HR	BB	SO	RAT	ERA	ERA+	OAV	OOB	PR	/A	PF	CPI	FA	E	DP	FW	PW	BW	SBW	DIF
NY	64	9	18	1412²	1334	8.5	148	482	625	11.7	3.48	113	.248	.313	75	69	99	104	.972	171	175	-1.0	6.9	8.5	.0	5.0
BRO	64	10	13	1423¹	1360	8.6	150	549	693	12.2	3.88	101	.253	.326	13	8	99	101	.979	129	192	1.3	.8	11.6	-1.0	5.8
STL	58	9	23	1387²	1391	9.0	119	568	546	12.8	3.95	100	.264	.338	1	2	100	103	.980	125	187	1.3	.2	.3	-.4	2.6
BOS	73	16	12	1389	1378	8.9	96	595	604	13.0	3.75	98	.259	.337	33	-11	93	104	.976	145	157	.3	-1.1	6.8	.9	-7.9
PHI	57	19	15	1384²	1373	8.9	110	497	570	12.3	3.81	101	.258	.324	23	6	97	98	.977	138	146	.6	.6	-2.8	.7	-3.1
CIN	55	14	23	1390²	1357	8.8	119	490	584	12.2	3.70	110	.255	.323	40	58	103	100	.977	140	141	.5	5.8	-14.4	-.6	-.3
PIT	40	9	22	1380¹	1479	9.6	157	609	580	13.8	4.79	88	.274	.350	-128	-88	107	97	.972	170	178	-1.1	-8.8	-.9	-.3	-1.9
CHI	48	10	10	1385²	1416	9.2	125	572	544	13.1	4.34	94	.265	.340	-58	-38	103	96	.971	181	161	-1.7	-3.8	-9.8	.6	-.3
TOT	459	96	136	11154		8.9				12.6	3.96		.260	.331					.975	1199	1337					

Runs
Musial-StL 124
Kiner-Pit 124
Hodges-Bro 118
Dark-NY 114
Robinson-Bro 106

Hits
Ashburn-Phi 221
Musial-StL 205
Furillo-Bro 197
Dark-NY 196
Robinson-Bro 185

Doubles
Dark-NY 41
Kluszewski-Cin . . . 35
Robinson-Bro 33
Campanella-Bro . . 33

Triples
Musial-StL 12
Bell-Pit 12
Irvin-NY 11
Jethroe-Bos 10
Baumholtz-Chi . . . 10

Home Runs
Kiner-Pit 42
Hodges-Bro 40
Campanella-Bro . . . 33
Thomson-NY 32
Musial-StL 32

Total Bases
Musial-StL 355
Kiner-Pit 333
Hodges-Bro 307
Campanella-Bro . . 298

Runs Batted In
Irvin-NY 121
Kiner-Pit 109
Gordon-Bos 109
Musial-StL 108
Campanella-Bro . . 108

Runs Produced
Musial-StL 200
Kiner-Pit 191
Irvin-NY 191
Hodges-Bro 181
Gordon-Bos 176

Bases On Balls
Kiner-Pit 137
Stanky-NY 127
Westrum-NY 104
Torgeson-Bos . . . 102
Musial-StL 98

Batting Average
Musial-StL 355
Ashburn-Phi 344
Robinson-Bro 338
Campanella-Bro . . .325
Irvin-NY 312

On Base Percentage
Kiner-Pit 452
Musial-StL 449
Robinson-Bro 429
Irvin-NY 415
Stanky-NY 401

Slugging Average
Kiner-Pit 627
Musial-StL 614
Campanella-Bro . . .590
Thomson-NY 562
Hodges-Bro 527

Production
Kiner-Pit 1.079
Musial-StL 1.063
Campanella-Bro . . .983
Robinson-Bro 957
Thomson-NY 947

Adjusted Production
Musial-StL 182
Kiner-Pit 182
Campanella-Bro . . 158
Robinson-Bro . . . 153
Thomson-NY 150

Batter Runs
Kiner-Pit 70.8
Musial-StL 70.1
Robinson-Bro 45.8
Campanella-Bro . . 41.7
Irvin-NY 40.7

Adjusted Batter Runs
Musial-StL 69.6
Kiner-Pit 68.5
Robinson-Bro 44.3
Campanella-Bro . . 40.4
Irvin-NY 40.1

Clutch Hitting Index
Slaughter-StL 147
Irvin-NY 138
Gordon-Bos 123
Westlake-Pit-StL . . 121
Hamner-Phi 118

Runs Created
Musial-StL 169
Kiner-Pit 165
Robinson-Bro 133
Irvin-NY 127
Hodges-Bro 119

Total Average
Kiner-Pit 1.251
Musial-StL 1.180
Robinson-Bro 1.034
Irvin-NY 985
Campanella-Bro . . .978

Stolen Bases
Jethroe-Bos 35
Ashburn-Phi 29
Robinson-Bro . . . 25
Torgeson-Bos 20
Reese-Bro 20

Stolen Base Average
Jethroe-Bos 87.5
Ashburn-Phi 82.9
Robinson-Bro 75.8
Torgeson-Bos 64.5
Reese-Bro 58.8

Stolen Base Runs
Jethroe-Bos 7.5
Ashburn-Phi 5.1
Robinson-Bro 2.7
Jackson-Chi 2.4
Irvin-NY 2.4

Fielding Runs
Ashburn-Phi 32.3
Robinson-Bro 16.5
Furillo-Bro 16.1
Schoendienst-StL . 15.5
Hemus-StL 13.4

Total Player Rating
Robinson-Bro 6.9
Musial-StL 6.4
Kiner-Pit 5.6
Campanella-Bro . . . 5.3
Ashburn-Phi 5.1

Wins
Maglie-NY 23
Jansen-NY 23
Spahn-Bos 22
Roe-Bro 22
Roberts-Phi 21

Win Percentage
Roe-Bro 880
Maglie-NY 793
Newcombe-Bro . . .690
Jansen-NY 676
Hearn-NY 654

Games
Wilks-StL-Pit 65
Werle-Pit 59
Konstanty-Phi 58
Spencer-NY 57
Brazle-StL 56

Complete Games
Spahn-Bos 26
Roberts-Phi 22
Maglie-NY 22
Roe-Bro 19
Dickson-Pit 19

Shutouts
Spahn-Bos 7
Roberts-Phi 6
Raffensberger-Cin . . 5

Saves
Wilks-StL-Pit 13
Smith-Cin 11
Konstanty-Phi 9
Brazle-StL 7

Innings Pitched
Roberts-Phi 315.0
Spahn-Bos 310.2
Maglie-NY 298.0
Dickson-Pit 288.2
Jansen-NY 278.2

Fewest Hits/Game
Maglie-NY 7.67
Newcombe-Bro . . 7.78
Blackwell-Cin 7.89
Branca-Bro 7.94
Queen-Pit 7.97

Fewest BB/Game
Raffensberger-Cin 1.38
Jansen-NY 1.81
Roberts-Phi 1.83
Roe-Bro 2.24
Sain-Bos 2.53

Strikeouts
Spahn-Bos 164
Newcombe-Bro . . 164
Maglie-NY 146
Jansen-NY 145
Rush-Chi 129

Strikeouts/Game
Queen-Pit 6.58
Rush-Chi 5.49
Newcombe-Bro . . 5.43
Branca-Bro 5.21
Spahn-Bos 4.75

Ratio
Raffensberger-Cin 9.99
Roberts-Phi 10.03
Jansen-NY 10.11
Maglie-NY 10.45
Roe-Bro 10.86

Earned Run Average
Nichols-Bos 2.88
Maglie-NY 2.93
Spahn-Bos 2.98
Roberts-Phi 3.03
Jansen-NY 3.04

Adjusted ERA
Maglie-NY 134
Roe-Bro 129
Jansen-NY 129
Nichols-Bos 127
Roberts-Phi 127

Opponents' Batting Avg.
Maglie-NY 230
Newcombe-Bro . . .230
Blackwell-Cin 233
Queen-Pit 233
Branca-Bro 237

Opponents' On Base Pct.
Roberts-Phi 278
Jansen-NY 279
Raffensberger-Cin .279
Maglie-NY 289
Newcombe-Bro . . .297

Starter Runs
Maglie-NY 34.1
Spahn-Bos 33.7
Roberts-Phi 32.6
Jansen-NY 28.6
Roe-Bro 26.4

Adjusted Starter Runs
Maglie-NY 32.7
Roberts-Phi 28.7
Jansen-NY 27.2
Roe-Bro 25.3
Spahn-Bos 23.8

Clutch Pitching Index
Roe-Bro 122
Sain-Bos 113
Nichols-Bos 112
Minner-Chi 111
Bickford-Bos 108

Relief Runs
Brazle-StL 14.9
Kennedy-NY 12.9
Perkowski-Cin . . . 12.9
Wilks-StL-Pit 12.3
Leonard-Chi 11.9

Adjusted Relief Runs
Brazle-StL 15.0
Wilks-StL-Pit 14.7
Perkowski-Cin . . . 14.2
Leonard-Chi 13.1
Kennedy-NY 12.6

Relief Ranking
Leonard-Chi 24.3
Wilks-StL-Pit 14.8
Perkowski-Cin . . . 11.6
Smith-Cin 11.2
Brazle-StL 11.1

Total Pitcher Index
Maglie-NY 3.3
Roberts-Phi 3.2
Spahn-Bos 2.7
Jansen-NY 2.6
Newcombe-Bro . . . 2.6

Total Baseball Ranking
Robinson-Bro 6.9
Musial-StL 6.4
Kiner-Pit 5.6
Campanella-Bro . . . 5.3
Ashburn-Phi 5.1

TEAM	G	W	L	PCT	GB	R	OR	AB	H	2B	3B	HR	BB	SO	AVG	OBP	SLG	PRO	PRO+	BR	/A	PF	CHI	RC	SB	CS	SBA	SBR
NY	154	98	56	.636		798	621	5194	1395	208	48	140	605	547	.269	.349	.408	.757	113	62	88	96	104	762	78	39	67	0
CLE	155	93	61	.604	5	696	594	5250	1346	208	35	140	606	632	.256	.336	.389	.725	106	0	40	94	98	710	52	35	60	-5
BOS	154	87	67	.565	11	804	725	5378	1428	233	35	127	756	594	.266	.349	.392	.750	98	64	-8	110	100	778	20	21	49	-7
CHI	155	81	73	.526	17	714	644	5378	1453	229	64	86	596	524	.265	.349	.385	.734	105	23	38	98	95	745	99	70	59	-12
DET	154	73	81	.474	25	685	741	5336	1413	231	35	104	568	525	.265	.338	.380	.718	99	-14	-17	100	98	697	37	34	52	-9
PHI	154	70	84	.455	28	736	745	5277	1381	262	43	102	677	565	.262	.349	.386	.735	101	29	14	102	98	745	47	36	57	-8
WAS	154	62	92	.403	36	672	764	5329	1399	242	45	54	560	515	.263	.336	.355	.691	93	-60	-47	98	103	648	45	38	54	-9
STL	154	52	102	.338	46	611	882	5219	1288	223	47	86	521	693	.247	.317	.357	.674	84	-102	-122	103	103	592	35	38	48	-12
TOT	617					5716		42361	11103	1836	349	839	4889	4595	.262	.342	.381	.723							413	311	57	-63

TEAM	CG	SH	SV	IP	H	H/G	HR	BB	SO	RAT	ERA	ERA+	OAV	OOB	PR	/A	PF	CPI	FA	E	DP	FW	PW	BW	SBW	DIF
NY	66	24	22	1367	1290	8.5	92	562	664	12.4	3.56	107	.250	.328	85	41	93	103	.975	144	190	.3	4.0	8.7	.8	7.2
CLE	76	10	19	1391¹	1287	8.3	86	577	642	12.2	3.38	112	.245	.323	114	63	92	103	.978	134	151	.9	6.2	3.9	.3	4.7
BOS	46	7	24	1399	1413	9.1	100	599	658	13.2	4.14	108	.264	.342	-2	50	108	100	.977	141	184	.5	4.9	-.8	.0	5.3
CHI	74	11	14	1418¹	1353	8.6	109	549	572	12.2	3.50	115	.252	.323	97	84	98	105	.975	151	176	.0	8.3	3.7	-.4	-7.6
DET	51	8	17	1384	1385	9.0	102	602	597	13.2	4.29	97	.262	.342	-26	-18	101	96	.973	163	166	-.7	-1.8	-1.7	-.1	.2
PHI	52	7	22	1358	1421	9.4	109	569	437	13.4	4.47	96	.272	.347	-52	-29	104	98	.978	136	204	.8	-2.9	1.4	-.0	-6.3
WAS	58	6	13	1366¹	1429	9.4	110	630	475	13.7	4.49	91	.269	.348	-55	-59	99	97	.973	160	148	-.5	-5.8	-4.6	-.1	-3.9
STL	56	5	9	1370¹	1525	10.0	131	801	550	15.5	5.18	85	.282	.379	-160	-119	107	101	.971	172	179	-1.2	-11.7	-12.0	-.4	.3
TOT	479	78	140	11054¹		9.0				13.2	4.12		.262	.342					.975	1201	1398					

Runs
DiMaggio-Bos 113
Minoso-Cle-Chi ... 112
Yost-Was 109
Williams-Bos 109
Joost-Phi 107

Hits
Kell-Det 191
Fox-Chi 189
DiMaggio-Bos ... 189
Minoso-Cle-Chi ... 173
Williams-Bos ... 169

Doubles
Yost-Was 36
Mele-Was 36
Kell-Det 36

Triples
Minoso-Cle-Chi ... 14
Coleman-StL-Chi ... 12
Fox-Chi 12
Young-StL 9

Home Runs
Zernial-Chi-Phi ... 33
Williams-Bos 30
Robinson-Chi 29

Total Bases
Williams-Bos 295
Zernial-Chi-Phi ... 292
Robinson-Chi ... 279
Berra-NY 269
DiMaggio-Bos 267

Runs Batted In
Zernial-Chi-Phi ... 129
Williams-Bos ... 126
Robinson-Chi 117
Easter-Cle 103
Rosen-Cle 102

Runs Produced
Williams-Bos 205
Zernial-Chi-Phi ... 188
Minoso-Cle-Chi ... 178
Robinson-Chi 173
DiMaggio-Bos 173

Bases On Balls
Williams-Bos 144
Yost-Was 126
Joost-Phi 106
Doby-Cle 101
Rosen-Cle 85

Batting Average
Fain-Phi 344
Minoso-Cle-Chi ...326
Kell-Det 319
Williams-Bos 318
Fox-Chi 313

On Base Percentage
Williams-Bos 464
Fain-Phi 451
Doby-Cle 428
Yost-Was 423
Minoso-Cle-Chi ...422

Slugging Average
Williams-Bos 556
Doby-Cle 512
Zernial-Chi-Phi ...511
Wertz-Det 511
Minoso-Cle-Chi ...500

Production
Williams-Bos 1.019
Doby-Cle 941
Minoso-Cle-Chi ...922
Fain-Phi 921
Wertz-Det........894

Adjusted Production
Doby-Cle 163
Williams-Bos 159
Minoso-Cle-Chi ... 152
Fain-Phi 146
Wertz-Det 140

Batter Runs
Williams-Bos 62.8
Minoso-Cle-Chi .. 38.2
Doby-Cle 37.0
Fain-Phi 33.8
Joost-Phi 30.5

Adjusted Batter Runs
Williams-Bos 55.0
Doby-Cle 40.7
Minoso-Cle-Chi .. 39.9
Fain-Phi 32.5
Yost-Was 31.7

Clutch Hitting Index
Mele-Was 147
Noren-Was 140
Busby-Chi 132
Vernon-Was 128
Williams-Bos 124

Runs Created
Williams-Bos 152
Minoso-Cle-Chi ... 120
Yost-Was 117
Joost-Phi 115
Doby-Cle 108

Total Average
Williams-Bos 1.177
Doby-Cle 1.031
Minoso-Cle-Chi ...987
Fain-Phi 959
Yost-Was 909

Stolen Bases
Minoso-Cle-Chi 31
Busby-Chi 26
Rizzuto-NY 18

Stolen Base Average
Rizzuto-NY 85.7
Minoso-Cle-Chi .. 75.6
Busby-Chi 70.3

Stolen Base Runs
Rizzuto-NY 3.6
Minoso-Cle-Chi ... 3.3
Carrasquel-Chi 1.8

Fielding Runs
Coan-Was 22.0
Noren-Was 21.1
Stephens-Bos 14.1
Fain-Phi 12.6
Carrasquel-Chi ... 12.5

Total Player Rating
Williams-Bos 5.1
Joost-Phi 3.9
Fain-Phi 3.7
Doby-Cle 3.4
Berra-NY 3.2

Wins
Feller-Cle 22
Raschi-NY 21
Lopat-NY 21

Win Percentage
Feller-Cle 733
Lopat-NY 700
Reynolds-NY 680
Raschi-NY 677
Shantz-Phi 643

Games
Kinder-Bos 63
Brissie-Phi-Cle 56
Garcia-Cle 47
Scheib-Phi 46

Complete Games
Garver-StL 24
Wynn-Cle 21
Lopat-NY 20
Pierce-Chi 18

Shutouts
Reynolds-NY 7
Raschi-NY 4
Lopat-NY 4
Feller-Cle 4

Saves
Kinder-Bos 14
Scheib-Phi 10
Brissie-Phi-Cle 9
Reynolds-NY 7
Garcia-Cle 6

Innings Pitched
Wynn-Cle 274.1
Lemon-Cle 263.1
Raschi-NY 258.1
Garcia-Cle 254.0
Feller-Cle 249.2

Fewest Hits/Game
Reynolds-NY 6.96
McDermott-Bos ... 7.38
Wynn-Cle 7.45
Rogovin-Det-Chi .. 7.85
Lopat-NY 8.02

Fewest BB/Game
Hutchinson-Det ... 1.29
Lopat-NY 2.72
Pierce-Chi 2.73
Hooper-Phi 2.90
Garcia-Cle 2.91

Strikeouts
Raschi-NY 164
Wynn-Cle 133
Lemon-Cle 132
Gray-Det 131
McDermott-Bos.... 127

Strikeouts/Game
McDermott-Bos... 6.65
Gray-Det 5.97
Raschi-NY 5.71
Reynolds-NY 5.13
Lemon-Cle 4.51

Ratio
Lopat-NY 10.85
Rogovin-Det-Chi . 10.97
Wynn-Cle 11.06
Hutchinson-Det .. 11.13
Reynolds-NY 11.24

Earned Run Average
Rogovin-Det-Chi .. 2.78
Lopat-NY 2.91
Wynn-Cle 3.02
Pierce-Chi 3.03
Reynolds-NY 3.05

Adjusted ERA
Rogovin-Det-Chi .. 146
Parnell-Bos 137
McDermott-Bos... 133
Pierce-Chi 133
Lopat-NY 131

Opponents' Batting Avg.
Reynolds-NY 213
Wynn-Cle 225
McDermott-Bos....226
Rogovin-Det-Chi ..235
Lopat-NY 239

Opponents' On Base Pct.
Lopat-NY 298
Rogovin-Det-Chi ..301
Wynn-Cle 301
Hutchinson-Det ...302
Reynolds-NY 304

Starter Runs
Wynn-Cle 33.6
Rogovin-Det-Chi . 32.2
Lopat-NY 31.5
Pierce-Chi 29.1
Garcia-Cle 27.3

Adjusted Starter Runs
Rogovin-Det-Chi . 30.5
Parnell-Bos 29.5
Pierce-Chi 26.7
Lopat-NY 23.8
Wynn-Cle 23.4

Clutch Pitching Index
Parnell-Bos 119
Pierce-Chi 113
Rogovin-Det-Chi .. 111
Feller-Cle 109
Raschi-NY 108

Relief Runs
Kinder-Bos....... 22.2
Aloma-Chi 17.7
Brissie-Phi-Cle 7.5
Ostrowski-NY 6.7
Masterson-Bos ... 5.2

Adjusted Relief Runs
Kinder-Bos 26.9
Aloma-Chi 17.1
Masterson-Bos 7.4
Brissie-Phi-Cle 3.6
Ostrowski-NY 3.6

Relief Ranking
Kinder-Bos....... 31.5
Aloma-Chi 15.0
Harris-Was 4.3
Masterson-Bos ... 3.9
Ostrowski-NY 3.8

Total Pitcher Index
Parnell-Bos 3.5
Rogovin-Det-Chi . 3.2
Garver-StL....... 2.8
Lopat-NY 2.6
Pierce-Chi 2.6

Total Baseball Ranking
Williams-Bos 5.1
Joost-Phi 3.9
Fain-Phi 3.7
Parnell-Bos 3.5
Doby-Cle 3.4

TEAM	G	W	L	PCT	GB	R	OR	AB	H	2B	3B	HR	BB	SO	AVG	OBP	SLG	PRO	PRO+	BR	/A	PF	CHI	RC	SB	CS	SBA	SBR
BRO	155	96	57	.627		775	603	5266	1380	199	32	153	663	699	.262	.348	.399	.747	113	107	100	101	100	754	90	49	65	-2
NY	154	92	62	.597	4.5	722	639	5229	1337	186	56	151	536	672	.256	.329	.399	.728	107	56	51	101	103	712	30	31	49	-10
STL	154	88	66	.571	8.5	677	630	5200	1386	247	54	97	537	479	.267	.340	.391	.731	110	68	67	100	95	708	33	32	51	-9
PHI	154	87	67	.565	9.5	657	552	5205	1353	237	45	93	540	534	.260	.332	.376	.708	104	26	33	99	98	671	60	41	59	-7
CHI	155	77	77	.500	19.5	628	631	5330	1408	223	45	107	422	712	.264	.321	.383	.704	101	5	-3	101	97	652	50	40	56	-9
CIN	154	69	85	.448	27.5	615	659	5234	1303	212	45	104	480	709	.249	.314	.366	.680	95	-36	-34	100	102	610	32	42	43	-16
BOS	155	64	89	.418	32	569	651	5221	1214	187	31	110	483	711	.233	.301	.343	.644	88	-102	-80	97	106	555	58	34	63	-3
PIT	155	42	112	.273	54.5	515	793	5193	1201	181	30	92	486	724	.231	.300	.331	.631	79	-125	-142	103	101	530	43	41	51	-12
TOT	618					5158		41878	10582	1672	338	907	4147	5240	.253	.323	.374	.697							396	310	56	-67

TEAM	CG	SH	SV	IP	H	H/G	HR	BB	SO	RAT	ERA	ERA+	OAV	OOB	PR	/A	PF	CPI	FA	E	DP	FW	PW	BW	SBW	DIF
BRO	45	11	24	1399[1]	1295	8.3	121	544	773	12.0	3.53	103	.247	.321	31	17	98	103	.982	106	169	2.0	1.8	10.3	.7	4.7
NY	49	12	31	1371	1282	8.4	121	538	655	12.2	3.59	103	.248	.323	22	17	99	103	.974	158	175	-.8	1.8	5.3	-.2	8.9
STL	49	12	27	1361[1]	1274	8.4	119	501	712	11.9	3.66	101	.247	.317	11	8	100	98	.977	141	159	.1	.8	6.9	-.0	3.2
PHI	80	17	16	1386[2]	1306	8.5	95	373	609	11.0	3.07	119	.249	.301	102	90	98	104	.975	150	145	-.4	9.3	3.4	.1	-2.5
CHI	59	15	15	1386[1]	1265	8.2	101	534	661	11.9	3.58	107	.240	.314	23	41	103	94	.976	146	123	-.1	4.2	-.3	-.0	-3.8
CIN	56	11	12	1363[1]	1377	9.1	111	517	579	12.8	4.01	94	.267	.338	-43	-36	101	103	.982	107	145	1.9	-3.7	-3.5	-.8	-1.9
BOS	63	11	13	1396	1388	8.9	106	525	687	12.5	3.78	96	.259	.329	-7	-26	97	102	.975	154	143	-.5	-2.7	-8.3	.6	-1.6
PIT	43	5	8	1363[2]	1395	9.2	133	615	564	13.4	4.65	86	.265	.345	-139	-99	107	94	.970	182	167	-2.0	-10.2	-14.7	-.4	-7.7
TOT	444	94	146	11027[2]		8.6				12.2	3.73		.253	.323					.976	1144	1226					

Runs
Musial-StL 105
Hemus-StL 105
Robinson-Bro ... 104
Lockman-NY 99
Reese-Bro 94

Hits
Musial-StL 194
Schoendienst-StL . 188
Adams-Cin 180
Dark-NY 177
Lockman-NY ... 176

Doubles
Musial-StL 42
Schoendienst-StL . 40
McMillan-Cin ... 32
Sauer-Chi 31
Ashburn-Phi...... 31

Triples
Thomson-NY 14
Slaughter-StL ... 12
Kluszewski-Cin ... 11
Ennis-Phi 10

Home Runs
Sauer-Chi 37
Kiner-Pit 37
Hodges-Bro 32
Mathews-Bos 25
Gordon-Bos 25

Total Bases
Musial-StL 311
Sauer-Chi 301
Thomson-NY 293
Ennis-Phi 281
Snider-Bro 264

Runs Batted In
Sauer-Chi 121
Thomson-NY ... 108
Ennis-Phi 107
Hodges-Bro ... 102
Slaughter-StL ... 101

Runs Produced
Ennis-Phi 177
Musial-StL 175
Thomson-NY 173
Sauer-Chi 173
Slaughter-StL ... 163

Bases On Balls
Kiner-Pit 110
Hodges-Bro 107
Robinson-Bro ... 106
Musial-StL 96
Hemus-StL 96

Batting Average
Musial-StL 336
Kluszewski-Cin ..320
Robinson-Bro 308
Snider-Bro 303
Schoendienst-StL ..303

On Base Percentage
Robinson-Bro 440
Musial-StL 432
Hemus-StL.......392
Hodges-Bro 386
Slaughter-StL 386

Slugging Average
Musial-StL 538
Sauer-Chi 531
Kluszewski-Cin ...509
Kiner-Pit 500
Hodges-Bro 500

Production
Musial-StL 970
Robinson-Bro ...904
Kluszewski-Cin ...892
Sauer-Chi.......892
Hodges-Bro 886

Adjusted Production
Musial-StL 167
Robinson-Bro ... 149
Kluszewski-Cin ... 146
Gordon-Bos 144
Sauer-Chi 143

Batter Runs
Musial-StL 55.7
Robinson-Bro ... 41.9
Sauer-Chi........32.8
Kiner-Pit 32.7
Hodges-Bro 32.4

Adjusted Batter Runs
Musial-StL 55.6
Robinson-Bro ... 41.1
Sauer-Chi........31.9
Hodges-Bro 31.6
Kiner-Pit 30.8

Clutch Hitting Index
Slaughter-StL ... 161
Hatton-Cin 140
Campanella-Bro . 139
Ennis-Phi 130
Thomson-NY 122

Runs Created
Musial-StL 141
Robinson-Bro ... 116
Sauer-Chi 111
Kiner-Pit 111
Hodges-Bro 106

Total Average
Musial-StL 1.017
Robinson-Bro 995
Kiner-Pit 955
Hodges-Bro 921
Sauer-Chi........886

Stolen Bases
Reese-Bro 30
Jethroe-Bos 28
Robinson-Bro ... 24
Ashburn-Phi 16

Stolen Base Average
Reese-Bro 85.7
Robinson-Bro ... 77.4
Jethroe-Bos 75.7
Ashburn-Phi 59.3

Stolen Base Runs
Reese-Bro 6.0
Robinson-Bro ... 3.0
Jethroe-Bos 3.0
Davis-Pit 1.5
Slaughter-StL 1.2

Fielding Runs
Schoendienst-StL . 32.9
Logan-Bos 17.6
Sauer-Chi 16.6
Ashburn-Phi 15.1
McMillan-Cin 10.6

Total Player Rating
Robinson-Bro 5.6
Schoendienst-StL . 4.9
Sauer-Chi 4.2
Musial-StL 4.2
Hemus-StL........ 3.8

Wins
Roberts-Phi 28
Maglie-NY 18
Staley-StL 17
Rush-Chi 17
Raffensberger-Cin . 17

Win Percentage
Wilhelm-NY 833
Roberts-Phi 800
Black-Bro 789
Maglie-NY 692
Hacker-Chi.......625

Games
Wilhelm-NY 71
Black-Bro 56
Yuhas-StL 54
Smith-Cin 53
Main-Pit 48

Complete Games
Roberts-Phi 30
Dickson-Pit 21
Spahn-Bos........ 19
Raffensberger-Cin . 18
Rush-Chi 17

Shutouts
Simmons-Phi...... 6
Raffensberger-Cin . 6

Saves
Brazle-StL 16
Black-Bro 15
Wilhelm-NY 11
Leonard-Chi...... 11

Innings Pitched
Roberts-Phi 330.0
Spahn-Bos 290.0
Dickson-Pit 277.2
Rush-Chi 250.1
Raffensberger-Cin 247.0

Fewest Hits/Game
Hacker-Chi.......7.01
Wilhelm-NY 7.17
Erskine-Bro 7.27
Rush-Chi 7.37
Loes-Bro 7.40

Fewest BB/Game
Roberts-Phi 1.23
Hacker-Chi...... 1.51
Raffensberger-Cin 1.64
Staley-StL 1.95
Drews-Phi 2.05

Strikeouts
Spahn-Bos 183
Rush-Chi 157
Roberts-Phi 148
Mizell-StL....... 146
Simmons-Phi ... 141

Strikeouts/Game
Mizell-StL........ 6.92
Simmons-Phi 6.30
Wilhelm-NY 6.10
Wade-Bro 5.90
Erskine-Bro 5.70

Ratio
Hacker-Chi....... 8.56
Roberts-Phi 9.33
Erskine-Bro 10.45
Rush-Chi 10.50
Drews-Phi 10.59

Earned Run Average
Wilhelm-NY 2.43
Hacker-Chi 2.58
Roberts-Phi 2.59
Loes-Bro 2.69
Rush-Chi 2.70

Adjusted ERA
Wilhelm-NY 152
Hacker-Chi 149
Rush-Chi 143
Roberts-Phi 141
Loes-Bro 135

Opponents' Batting Avg.
Hacker-Chi.......212
Rush-Chi .... .216
Wilhelm-NY ..... .220
Erskine-Bro ..... .220
Loes-Bro .... .224

Opponents' On Base Pct.
Hacker-Chi....... .247
Roberts-Phi ..... .263
Rush-Chi .... .282
Erskine-Bro ..... .289
Spahn-Bos....... .291

Starter Runs
Roberts-Phi 41.8
Rush-Chi 28.8
Drews-Phi 25.8
Raffensberger-Cin 25.4
Spahn-Bos...... 24.3

Adjusted Starter Runs
Roberts-Phi 39.0
Rush-Chi 32.1
Raffensberger-Cin 26.6
Hacker-Chi...... 26.2
Drews-Phi 23.8

Clutch Pitching Index
Roe-Bro 127
Church-Phi-Cin .. 119
Wilhelm-NY 119
Raffensberger-Cin 117
Maglie-NY 116

Relief Runs
Black-Bro 25.0
Wilhelm-NY 23.1
Brazle-StL 12.3
Leonard-Chi 11.6
Yuhas-StL 11.2

Adjusted Relief Runs
Black-Bro 23.5
Wilhelm-NY 22.5
Leonard-Chi.... 12.5
Brazle-StL 12.1
Yuhas-StL 11.0

Relief Ranking
Black-Bro 33.9
Wilhelm-NY 26.4
Brazle-StL 20.9
Yuhas-StL 15.4
Leonard-Chi...... 11.4

Total Pitcher Index
Rush-Chi 4.7
Roberts-Phi 4.1
Spahn-Bos 2.6
Erskine-Bro 2.5
Wilhelm-NY 2.4

Total Baseball Ranking
Robinson-Bro 5.6
Schoendienst-StL . 4.9
Rush-Chi 4.7
Sauer-Chi 4.2
Musial-StL 4.2

TEAM	G	W	L	PCT	GB	R	OR	AB	H	2B	3B	HR	BB	SO	AVG	OBP	SLG	PRO	PRO+	BR	/A	PF	CHI	RC	SB	CS	SBA	SBR
NY	154	95	59	.617		727	557	5294	1411	221	56	129	566	652	.267	.341	.403	.744	121	89	128	94	99	758	52	42	55	-10
CLE	155	93	61	.604	2	763	606	5330	1399	211	49	148	626	749	.262	.342	.404	.746	122	95	138	94	102	759	46	39	54	-10
CHI	156	81	73	.526	14	610	568	5316	1337	199	38	80	541	654	.252	.327	.348	.675	93	-35	-40	101	99	633	61	38	62	-5
PHI	155	79	75	.513	16	664	723	5163	1305	212	35	89	683	561	.253	.343	.359	.702	96	26	-15	106	99	659	52	43	55	-10
WAS	157	78	76	.506	17	598	608	5357	1282	225	44	50	580	607	.239	.317	.326	.643	88	-98	-76	97	107	572	48	37	56	-8
BOS	154	76	78	.494	19	668	658	5246	1338	233	34	113	542	739	.255	.328	.377	.705	96	14	-36	108	103	659	59	47	56	-11
STL	155	64	90	.416	31	604	733	5353	1340	225	46	82	540	720	.250	.322	.356	.678	92	-39	-57	103	99	631	30	34	47	-11
DET	156	50	104	.325	45	557	738	5258	1278	190	37	103	553	605	.243	.318	.352	.670	92	-52	-57	101	95	594	27	38	42	-15
TOT	621					5191		42317	10690	1716	339	794	4631	5154	.253	.330	.365	.695							375	318	54	-78

TEAM	CG	SH	SV	IP	H	H/G	HR	BB	SO	RAT	ERA	ERA+	OAV	OOB	PR	/A	PF	CPI	FA	E	DP	FW	PW	BW	SBW	DIF
NY	72	21	27	1381	1240	8.1	94	581	666	12.1	3.14	106	.243	.324	82	28	90	110	.979	127	199	.8	2.9	13.3	-.0	1.1
CLE	80	19	18	1407	1278	8.2	94	556	671	11.9	3.32	101	.241	.316	55	4	91	99	.975	155	141	-.8	.4	14.3	-.0	2.1
CHI	53	15	28	1416[1]	1251	7.9	86	578	774	11.7	3.25	112	.238	.316	66	62	99	98	.980	123	158	1.1	6.4	-4.2	.5	.1
PHI	73	11	16	1384[1]	1402	9.1	113	526	562	12.8	4.15	95	.263	.333	-74	-30	108	94	.977	140	148	.0	-3.1	-1.6	-.0	6.6
WAS	75	10	15	1429[2]	1405	8.8	78	577	574	12.7	3.37	105	.258	.332	48	29	97	108	.978	132	152	.6	3.0	-7.9	.2	5.1
BOS	53	7	24	1372[1]	1332	8.7	107	623	624	13.1	3.80	104	.256	.340	-20	21	107	104	.976	145	181	-.3	2.2	-3.7	-.1	1.0
STL	48	6	18	1399	1388	8.9	111	598	581	13.0	4.12	95	.260	.339	-69	-32	107	97	.974	155	176	-.8	-3.3	-5.9	-.1	-2.8
DET	51	10	14	1388[1]	1394	9.0	111	591	702	13.0	4.25	90	.262	.338	-89	-69	104	94	.975	152	145	-.6	-7.2	-5.9	-.5	-12.8
TOT	505	99	160	11178[1]		8.6				12.5	3.67		.253	.330					.977	1129	1300					

Runs
Doby-Cle 104
Avila-Cle 102
Rosen-Cle 101
Berra-NY 97
Minoso-Chi 96

Hits
Fox-Chi 192
Avila-Cle 179
Robinson-Chi 176
Fain-Phi 176

Doubles
Fain-Phi 43
Mantle-NY 37
Vernon-Was 33
Robinson-Chi 33

Triples
Avila-Cle 11
Simpson-Cle 10
Rizzuto-NY 10
Fox-Chi 10

Home Runs
Doby-Cle 32
Easter-Cle 31
Berra-NY 30
Dropo-Bos-Det ... 29
Zernial-Phi 29

Total Bases
Rosen-Cle 297
Mantle-NY 291
Dropo-Bos-Det ... 282
Doby-Cle 281
Robinson-Chi 277

Runs Batted In
Rosen-Cle 105
Robinson-Chi 104
Doby-Cle 104
Zernial-Phi 100
Berra-NY 98

Runs Produced
Rosen-Cle 178
Doby-Cle 176
Berra-NY 165
Robinson-Chi 161
Mantle-NY 158

Bases On Balls
Yost-Was 129
Joost-Phi 122
Fain-Phi 105
Valo-Phi 101
Doby-Cle 90

Batting Average
Fain-Phi .... .327
Mitchell-Cle ...... .323
Mantle-NY .... .311
Kell-Det-Bos ..... .311
Goodman-Bos .... .306

On Base Percentage
Fain-Phi 438
Valo-Phi 432
Mantle-NY .... .394
Joost-Phi 388
Rosen-Cle .... .387

Slugging Average
Doby-Cle 541
Mantle-NY 530
Rosen-Cle ...... .524
Easter-Cle ...... .513
Wertz-Det-StL .... .506

Production
Mantle-NY .... .924
Doby-Cle .... .924
Rosen-Cle .... .911
Wertz-Det-StL ... .887
Fain-Phi .... .867

Adjusted Production
Doby-Cle 166
Mantle-NY 166
Rosen-Cle 162
Easter-Cle 144
Wertz-Det-StL ... 143

Batter Runs
Mantle-NY 40.3
Rosen-Cle 38.6
Doby-Cle 37.9
Fain-Phi 36.3
Robinson-Chi 28.3

Adjusted Batter Runs
Mantle-NY 44.4
Rosen-Cle 43.2
Doby-Cle 42.2
Fain-Phi 31.9
Robinson-Chi 27.7

Clutch Hitting Index
Runnels-Was 130
McDougald-NY ... 125
Vernon-Was 125
Jensen-NY-Was... 121
Robinson-Chi 120

Runs Created
Mantle-NY 123
Doby-Cle 116
Rosen-Cle 115
Robinson-Chi 113
Fain-Phi 107

Total Average
Doby-Cle .... .974
Mantle-NY .... .961
Wertz-Det-StL ... .912
Rosen-Cle .... .900
Valo-Phi .... .873

Stolen Bases
Minoso-Chi 22
Rivera-StL-Chi 21
Jensen-NY-Was.... 18
Rizzuto-NY 17
Throneberry-Bos .. 16

Stolen Base Average
Jensen-NY-Was... 75.0
Rizzuto-NY 73.9
Rivera-StL-Chi 70.0
Throneberry-Bos . 69.6
Minoso-Chi 57.9

Stolen Base Runs
Jensen-NY-Was ... 1.8
Rizzuto-NY 1.5
Michaels-Was-StL-Phi 1.2
Porter-StL 1.2
Goodman-Bos 1.2

Fielding Runs
Goodman-Bos 20.1
Rizzuto-NY 18.9
Martin-NY 18.3
Hatfield-Bos-Det .. 17.8
Fain-Phi 16.0

Total Player Rating
Doby-Cle 4.8
Mantle-NY 4.3
Fain-Phi 4.2
Berra-NY 3.4
Goodman-Bos 3.1

Wins
Shantz-Phi 24
Wynn-Cle 23
Lemon-Cle 22
Garcia-Cle 22
Reynolds-NY 20

Win Percentage
Shantz-Phi 774
Raschi-NY 727
Reynolds-NY 714
Lemon-Cle ...... .667
Garcia-Cle .... .667

Games
Kennedy-Chi 47
Paige-StL 46
Garcia-Cle 46
Hooper-Phi 43

Complete Games
Lemon-Cle 28
Shantz-Phi 27
Reynolds-NY 24
Wynn-Cle 19
Garcia-Cle 19

Shutouts
Reynolds-NY 6
Garcia-Cle 6
Shantz-Phi 5
Lemon-Cle 5

Saves
Dorish-Chi 11
Paige-StL 10
Sain-NY 7

Innings Pitched
Lemon-Cle 309.2
Garcia-Cle 292.1
Wynn-Cle 285.2
Shantz-Phi 279.2
Pierce-Chi 255.1

Fewest Hits/Game
Lemon-Cle 6.86
Raschi-NY 7.02
Reynolds-NY 7.15
Dobson-Chi 7.36
Shantz-Phi 7.40

Fewest BB/Game
Shantz-Phi 2.03
Pillette-StL 2.41
Marrero-Was 2.59
Houtteman-Det ... 2.65
Garcia-Cle 2.68

Strikeouts
Reynolds-NY 160
Wynn-Cle 153
Shantz-Phi 152
Pierce-Chi 144
Garcia-Cle 143

Strikeouts/Game
McDermott-Bos... 6.50
Reynolds-NY 5.89
Trucks-Det 5.89
Gray-Det 5.54
Grissom-Chi 5.26

Ratio
Shantz-Phi 9.56
Dobson-Chi 10.05
Lemon-Cle 10.09
Pierce-Chi 10.43
Raschi-NY 10.94

Earned Run Average
Reynolds-NY 2.06
Garcia-Cle 2.37
Shantz-Phi 2.48
Lemon-Cle 2.50
Dobson-Chi 2.51

Adjusted ERA
Reynolds-NY 161
Shantz-Phi 160
Dobson-Chi 145
Pierce-Chi 142
Garcia-Cle 141

Opponents' Batting Avg.
Lemon-Cle ...... .208
Raschi-NY ...... .216
Reynolds-NY .... .218
Dobson-Chi ..... .222
Shantz-Phi ..... .225

Opponents' On Base Pct.
Shantz-Phi ..... .272
Lemon-Cle ..... .279
Dobson-Chi .... .280
Pierce-Chi ..... .289
Reynolds-NY .... .300

Starter Runs
Reynolds-NY 43.8
Garcia-Cle 42.4
Lemon-Cle 40.4
Shantz-Phi 37.2
Pierce-Chi 31.3

Adjusted Starter Runs
Shantz-Phi 46.0
Reynolds-NY 34.2
Garcia-Cle 31.6
Pierce-Chi 30.5
Lemon-Cle 29.1

Clutch Pitching Index
Garcia-Cle 127
Byrd-Phi 126
Reynolds-NY 125
Porterfield-Was ... 120
Hudson-Was-Bos . 117

Relief Runs
Dorish-Chi 12.2
Kennedy-Chi 6.9
Consuegra-Was ... 5.1
Brissie-Cle 1.8
Littlefield-Det-StL .. 1.4

Adjusted Relief Runs
Dorish-Chi 11.9
Kennedy-Chi 6.7
Consuegra-Was ... 4.1
Littlefield-Det-StL .. 3.3
White-Det 8

Relief Ranking
Dorish-Chi 17.4
Kennedy-Chi 4.4
Consuegra-Was ... 3.6
Littlefield-Det-StL .. 2.6
White-Det 1.1

Total Pitcher Index
Shantz-Phi 5.6
Lemon-Cle 4.6
Reynolds-NY 3.6
Garcia-Cle 3.4
Pierce-Chi 3.3

Total Baseball Ranking
Shantz-Phi 5.6
Doby-Cle 4.8
Lemon-Cle 4.6
Mantle-NY 4.3
Fain-Phi 4.2

TEAM	G	W	L	PCT	GB	R	OR	AB	H	2B	3B	HR	BB	SO	AVG	OBP	SLG	PRO	PRO+	BR	/A	PF	CHI	RC	SB	CS	SBA	SBR
BRO	155	105	49	.682		955	689	5373	1529	274	59	208	655	686	.285	.366	.474	.840	121	188	171	102	101	963	90	47	66	-1
MIL	157	92	62	.597	13	738	589	5349	1422	227	52	156	439	637	.266	.325	.415	.740	104	-22	23	94	104	727	46	27	63	-2
STL	157	83	71	.539	22	768	713	5397	1474	281	56	140	574	617	.273	.347	.424	.771	107	53	54	100	95	806	18	22	45	-8
PHI	156	83	71	.539	22	716	666	5290	1400	228	62	115	530	597	.265	.335	.396	.731	97	-25	-21	99	101	727	42	21	67	0
NY	155	70	84	.455	35	768	747	5362	1452	195	45	176	499	608	.271	.336	.422	.758	101	20	7	102	101	771	31	21	60	-3
CIN	155	68	86	.442	37	714	788	5343	1396	190	34	166	485	701	.261	.325	.403	.728	94	-42	-47	101	103	711	25	20	56	-5
CHI	155	65	89	.422	40	633	835	5272	1372	204	57	137	514	746	.260	.328	.399	.727	93	-41	-57	102	92	697	49	21	70	2
PIT	154	50	104	.325	55	622	887	5253	1297	178	49	99	524	715	.247	.319	.356	.675	82	-130	-126	99	103	614	41	39	51	-11
TOT	622					5914		42639	11342	1777	414	1197	4220	5307	.266	.335	.411	.747							342	218	61	-28

TEAM	CG	SH	SV	IP	H	H/G	HR	BB	SO	RAT	ERA	ERA+	OAV	OOB	PR	/A	PF	CPI	FA	E	DP	FW	PW	BW	SBW	DIF
BRO	51	11	29	1380²	1337	8.7	169	509	817	12.1	4.10	104	.253	.320	29	25	99	97	.980	118	161	1.7	2.4	16.5	.2	7.2
MIL	72	14	15	1387	1282	8.3	107	539	738	12.0	3.30	119	.245	.318	153	96	92	106	.976	143	169	.4	9.2	2.2	.1	3.0
STL	51	11	36	1386²	1406	9.1	139	533	732	12.9	4.23	101	.262	.333	9	5	99	98	.977	138	161	.7	.5	5.2	-.4	.0
PHI	76	13	15	1369²	1410	9.3	138	410	637	12.1	3.80	111	.265	.320	74	62	98	104	.975	147	161	.0	6.0	-2.0	.3	1.6
NY	46	10	20	1365²	1403	9.2	146	610	647	13.4	4.25	101	.264	.343	5	6	100	103	.975	151	151	-.2	.6	.7	.0	-8.1
CIN	47	7	15	1365	1484	9.8	179	488	506	13.2	4.64	94	.279	.343	-53	-43	102	102	.978	129	176	1.1	-4.1	-4.5	-.1	-1.2
CHI	38	3	22	1359	1491	9.9	151	554	623	13.8	4.79	93	.276	.347	-76	-51	104	97	.967	193	141	-2.5	-4.9	-5.5	.5	.4
PIT	49	4	10	1358	1529	10.1	168	577	607	14.1	5.22	86	.285	.356	-141	-113	104	96	.973	163	139	-.9	-10.9	-12.1	-.7	-2.4
TOT	430	73	162	10971²		9.3				12.9	4.29		.266	.335					.975	1182	1259					

Runs		Hits		Doubles		Triples		Home Runs		Total Bases	
Snider-Bro	132	Ashburn-Phi	205	Musial-StL	53	Gilliam-Bro	17	Mathews-Mil	47	Snider-Bro	370
Musial-StL	127	Musial-StL	200	Dark-NY	41	Bruton-Mil	14	Snider-Bro	42	Mathews-Mil	363
Dark-NY	126	Snider-Bro	198	Snider-Bro	38	Hemus-StL	11	Campanella-Bro	41	Musial-StL	361
Gilliam-Bro	125	Dark-NY	194	Furillo-Bro	38	Fondy-Chi	11	Kluszewski-Cin	40	Kluszewski-Cin	325
		Schoendienst-StL	193	Bell-Cin	37			Kiner-Pit-Chi	35	Bell-Cin	320

Runs Batted In		Runs Produced		Bases On Balls		Batting Average		On Base Percentage		Slugging Average	
Campanella-Bro	142	Snider-Bro	216	Musial-StL	105	Furillo-Bro	.344	Musial-StL	.437	Snider-Bro	.627
Mathews-Mil	135	Musial-StL	210	Kiner-Pit-Chi	100	Schoendienst-StL	.342	Robinson-Bro	.425	Mathews-Mil	.627
Snider-Bro	126	Campanella-Bro	204	Gilliam-Bro	100	Musial-StL	.337	Snider-Bro	.419	Campanella-Bro	.611
Ennis-Phi	125	Mathews-Mil	198	Mathews-Mil	99	Snider-Bro	.336	Irvin-NY	.406	Musial-StL	.609
Hodges-Bro	122			Hemus-StL	86	Mueller-NY	.333	Mathews-Mil	.406	Furillo-Bro	.580

Production		Adjusted Production		Batter Runs		Adjusted Batter Runs		Clutch Hitting Index		Runs Created	
Snider-Bro	1.046	Mathews-Mil	175	Musial-StL	62.7	Musial-StL	62.8	Slaughter-StL	153	Musial-StL	166
Musial-StL	1.046	Musial-StL	169	Snider-Bro	59.3	Mathews-Mil	60.2	Ennis-Phi	141	Snider-Bro	161
Mathews-Mil	1.033	Snider-Bro	165	Mathews-Mil	54.9	Snider-Bro	57.4	Jablonski-StL	139	Mathews-Mil	157
Campanella-Bro	1.006	Campanella-Bro	154	Campanella-Bro	42.9	Campanella-Bro	41.3	Robinson-Bro	135	Campanella-Bro	128
Furillo-Bro	.973	Furillo-Bro	146	Kluszewski-Cin	35.0	Kluszewski-Cin	34.4	Campanella-Bro	128	Kluszewski-Cin	126

Total Average		Stolen Bases		Stolen Base Average		Stolen Base Runs		Fielding Runs		Total Player Rating	
Musial-StL	1.143	Bruton-Mil	26	Robinson-Bro	81.0	Reese-Bro	3.0	Ashburn-Phi	25.7	Schoendienst-StL	5.8
Snider-Bro	1.134	Reese-Bro	22	Reese-Bro	78.6	Robinson-Bro	2.7	Schoendienst-StL	25.3	Mathews-Mil	5.5
Mathews-Mil	1.119	Gilliam-Bro	21	Bruton-Mil	70.3	Torgeson-Phi	1.5	Logan-Mil	20.6	Campanella-Bro	4.8
Campanella-Bro	1.048	Robinson-Bro	17	Snider-Bro	69.6	Miksis-Chi	1.5	Crandall-Mil	14.8	Snider-Bro	4.7
Robinson-Bro	.988	Snider-Bro	16	Gilliam-Bro	60.0	Jeffcoat-Chi	1.5	Bell-Cin	13.7	Musial-StL	4.4

Wins		Win Percentage		Games		Complete Games		Shutouts		Saves	
Spahn-Mil	23	Erskine-Bro	.769	Wilhelm-NY	68	Roberts-Phi	33	Haddix-StL	6	Brazle-StL	18
Roberts-Phi	23	Spahn-Mil	.767	Brazle-StL	60	Spahn-Mil	24	Spahn-Mil	5	Wilhelm-NY	15
Haddix-StL	20	Meyer-Bro	.750	Hetki-Pit	54	Simmons-Phi	19	Roberts-Phi	5	Hughes-Bro	9
Erskine-Bro	20	Burdette-Mil	.750	Smith-Cin	50	Haddix-StL	19	Simmons-Phi	4	Leonard-Chi	8
Staley-StL	18	Haddix-StL	.690			Erskine-Bro	16	Erskine-Bro	4	Burdette-Mil	8

Innings Pitched		Fewest Hits/Game		Fewest BB/Game		Strikeouts		Strikeouts/Game		Ratio	
Roberts-Phi	346.2	Spahn-Mil	7.15	Roberts-Phi	1.58	Roberts-Phi	198	Mizell-StL	6.94	Spahn-Mil	9.55
Spahn-Mil	265.2	Gomez-NY	7.32	Raffensberger-Cin	1.71	Erskine-Bro	187	Erskine-Bro	6.82	Roberts-Phi	10.05
Haddix-StL	253.0	Mizell-StL	7.74	Minner-Chi	1.79	Mizell-StL	173	Antonelli-Mil	6.72	Haddix-StL	10.42
Erskine-Bro	246.2	Erskine-Bro	7.77	Staley-StL	2.11	Haddix-StL	163	Klippstein-Chi	6.07	Simmons-Phi	11.19
Simmons-Phi	238.0	Haddix-StL	7.83	Hacker-Chi	2.19	Spahn-Mil	148	Haddix-StL	5.80	Erskine-Bro	11.35

Earned Run Average		Adjusted ERA		Opponents' Batting Avg.		Opponents' On Base Pct.		Starter Runs		Adjusted Starter Runs	
Spahn-Mil	2.10	Spahn-Mil	187	Spahn-Mil	.217	Spahn-Mil	.270	Spahn-Mil	64.5	Roberts-Phi	56.1
Roberts-Phi	2.75	Roberts-Phi	153	Gomez-NY	.218	Roberts-Phi	.276	Roberts-Phi	59.1	Spahn-Mil	53.8
Haddix-StL	3.06	Haddix-StL	139	Mizell-StL	.227	Haddix-StL	.287	Haddix-StL	34.5	Haddix-StL	33.6
Antonelli-Mil	3.18	Simmons-Phi	131	Erskine-Bro	.230	Hacker-Chi	.299	Simmons-Phi	28.3	Simmons-Phi	26.3
Simmons-Phi	3.21	Gomez-NY	126	Haddix-StL	.232	Simmons-Phi	.302	Buhl-Mil	22.5	Gomez-NY	20.2

Clutch Pitching Index		Relief Runs		Adjusted Relief Runs		Relief Ranking		Total Pitcher Index		Total Baseball Ranking	
Raffensberger-Cin	115	Wilhelm-NY	20.1	Wilhelm-NY	20.1	Labine-Bro	27.9	Spahn-Mil	6.3	Spahn-Mil	6.3
Dickson-Pit	112	Labine-Bro	18.5	Labine-Bro	18.2	Wilhelm-NY	23.4	Roberts-Phi	5.9	Roberts-Phi	5.9
Drews-Phi	112	Johnson-Mil	14.6	White-StL	12.0	White-StL	16.3	Haddix-StL	4.6	Schoendienst-StL	5.8
Burdette-Mil	110	White-StL	12.3	Johnson-Mil	11.3	Johnson-Mil	8.8	Gomez-NY	2.2	Mathews-Mil	5.5
Roe-Bro	108	Hughes-Bro	7.8	Hughes-Bro	7.6	Hughes-Bro	7.3	Simmons-Phi	2.1	Campanella-Bro	4.8

TEAM	G	W	L	PCT	GB	R	OR	AB	H	2B	3B	HR	BB	SO	AVG	OBP	SLG	PRO	PRO+	BR	/A	PF	CHI	RC	SB	CS	SBA	SBR
NY	151	99	52	.656		801	547	5194	1420	226	52	139	656	644	.273	.359	.417	.776	120	113	137	97	100	809	34	44	44	-16
CLE	155	92	62	.597	8.5	770	627	5285	1426	201	29	160	609	683	.270	.349	.410	.759	114	77	96	97	100	780	33	29	53	-8
CHI	156	89	65	.578	11.5	716	592	5212	1345	226	53	74	601	530	.258	.341	.364	.705	93	-17	-38	103	106	666	73	55	57	-11
BOS	153	84	69	.549	16	656	632	5246	1385	255	37	101	496	601	.264	.332	.384	.716	94	-10	-46	105	98	683	33	45	42	-17
WAS	152	76	76	.500	23.5	687	614	5149	1354	230	53	69	596	604	.263	.343	.368	.711	100	-6	10	98	103	675	65	36	64	-2
DET	158	60	94	.390	40.5	695	923	5553	1479	259	44	108	506	603	.266	.331	.387	.718	100	-10	-1	99	99	716	30	35	46	-12
PHI	157	59	95	.383	41.5	632	799	5455	1398	205	38	116	498	602	.256	.321	.372	.693	89	-61	-87	104	100	658	41	24	63	-2
STL	154	54	100	.351	46.5	555	778	5264	1310	214	25	112	507	644	.249	.317	.363	.680	87	-83	-96	102	93	606	17	34	33	-15
TOT	618					5512		42358	11117	1816	331	879	4469	4911	.262	.336	.383	.720							326	302	52	-83

TEAM	CG	SH	SV	IP	H	H/G	HR	BB	SO	RAT	ERA	ERA+	OAV	OOB	PR	/A	PF	CPI	FA	E	DP	FW	PW	BW	SBW	DIF
NY	50	18	39	1358[1]	1286	8.5	94	500	604	12.1	3.20	115	.251	.321	120	74	92	110	.979	126	182	.3	7.4	13.7	-.6	2.6
CLE	81	11	15	1373	1311	8.6	92	519	586	12.2	3.64	103	.253	.325	53	16	94	99	.979	127	197	.4	1.6	9.6	.2	3.1
CHI	57	17	33	1403[2]	1299	8.3	113	583	714	12.2	3.41	118	.246	.324	91	95	101	105	.980	125	144	.6	9.5	-3.8	-.0	5.8
BOS	41	15	37	1373	1333	8.7	92	584	642	12.7	3.58	118	.254	.331	63	96	105	104	.975	148	173	-.9	9.6	-4.6	-.7	4.0
WAS	76	16	10	1344[2]	1313	8.8	112	478	515	12.2	3.66	106	.258	.324	50	35	98	103	.979	120	173	.7	3.5	1.0	.8	-6.0
DET	50	2	16	1415	1633	10.4	154	585	645	14.4	5.25	77	.291	.363	-198	-187	102	96	.978	135	149	.1	-18.7	-.1	-.2	1.9
PHI	51	7	11	1409	1475	9.4	121	594	566	13.6	4.67	92	.271	.349	-106	-60	107	93	.977	137	161	-.0	-6.0	-8.7	.8	-4.1
STL	28	10	24	1383[2]	1467	9.5	101	626	639	13.8	4.48	94	.273	.351	-74	-43	105	97	.974	152	165	-1.0	-4.3	-9.6	-.5	-7.6
TOT	434	96	185	11060[1]		9.0				12.9	3.99		.262	.336					.978	1070	1344					

Runs
Rosen-Cle 115
Yost-Was 107
Mantle-NY 105
Minoso-Chi 104
Vernon-Was 101

Hits
Kuenn-Det 209
Vernon-Was 205
Rosen-Cle 201
Philley-Phi 188
Busby-Was 183

Doubles
Vernon-Was 43
Kell-Bos 41
White-Bos 34
Kuenn-Det 33
Goodman-Bos 33

Triples
Rivera-Chi 16
Vernon-Was 11
Piersall-Bos 9
Philley-Phi 9

Home Runs
Rosen-Cle 43
Zernial-Phi 42
Doby-Cle 29
Berra-NY 27
Boone-Cle-Det 26

Total Bases
Rosen-Cle 367
Vernon-Was 315
Zernial-Phi 311
Philley-Phi 263
Berra-NY 263

Runs Batted In
Rosen-Cle 145
Vernon-Was 115
Boone-Cle-Det ... 114
Zernial-Phi 108
Berra-NY 108

Runs Produced
Rosen-Cle 217
Vernon-Was 201
Minoso-Chi 193
Boone-Cle-Det ... 182
Mantle-NY 176

Bases On Balls
Yost-Was 123
Fain-Chi 108
Doby-Cle 96
Gernert-Bos 88
Rosen-Cle 85

Batting Average
Vernon-Was ...... .337
Rosen-Cle .... .336
Goodman-Bos .... .313
Minoso-Chi ...... .313
Busby-Was .... .312

On Base Percentage
Woodling-NY ..... .429
Rosen-Cle .... .422
Minoso-Chi ...... .410
Fain-Chi .... .405
Yost-Was .... .403

Slugging Average
Rosen-Cle .... .613
Zernial-Phi .... .559
Berra-NY .... .523
Boone-Cle-Det ... .519
Vernon-Was ...... .518

Production
Rosen-Cle 1.034
Vernon-Was ...... .921
Zernial-Phi .... .914
Boone-Cle-Det ... .909
Woodling-NY ..... .898

Adjusted Production
Rosen-Cle 181
Vernon-Was 151
Woodling-NY 147
Boone-Cle-Det ... 146
Mantle-NY 145

Batter Runs
Rosen-Cle 63.3
Vernon-Was 39.7
Minoso-Chi 30.6
Boone-Cle-Det ... 30.5
Zernial-Phi 30.4

Adjusted Batter Runs
Rosen-Cle 65.5
Vernon-Was 41.5
Boone-Cle-Det ... 31.5
Mantle-NY 29.4
Woodling-NY 29.2

Clutch Hitting Index
Dropo-Det 143
Minoso-Chi 134
Boone-Cle-Det ... 133
Rizzuto-NY 133
Jensen-Was 129

Runs Created
Rosen-Cle 155
Vernon-Was 127
Zernial-Phi 113
Boone-Cle-Det ... 106
Minoso-Chi 106

Total Average
Rosen-Cle 1.078
Mantle-NY .... .943
Boone-Cle-Det ... .925
Zernial-Phi .... .917
Doby-Cle .... .912

Stolen Bases
Minoso-Chi 25
Rivera-Chi 22
Jensen-Was 18
Philley-Phi 13
Busby-Was 13

Stolen Base Average
Jensen-Was 69.2
Minoso-Chi 61.0
Rivera-Chi 59.5

Stolen Base Runs
Michaels-Phi 2.1
Coan-Was 2.1
Zernial-Phi 1.2
Souchock-Det 9
Philley-Phi 9

Fielding Runs
Busby-Was 18.9
Groth-StL 17.1
Piersall-Bos 16.1
Strickland-Cle 15.6
Hunter-StL 14.6

Total Player Rating
Rosen-Cle 6.0
Zernial-Phi 3.6
Berra-NY 3.3
Boone-Cle-Det ... 3.1
Vernon-Was 3.0

Wins
Porterfield-Was ... 22
Parnell-Bos 21
R.Lemon-Cle 21
Trucks-StL-Chi ... 20

Win Percentage
Lopat-NY .... .800
Ford-NY .... .750
Parnell-Bos ...... .724
Porterfield-Was ... .688

Games
Kinder-Bos 69
Stuart-StL 60
Martin-Phi 58
Paige-StL 57
Dorish-Chi 55

Complete Games
Porterfield-Was ... 24
R.Lemon-Cle 23
Garcia-Cle 21
Pierce-Chi 19
Trucks-StL-Chi ... 17

Shutouts
Porterfield-Was 9
Pierce-Chi 7
Trucks-StL-Chi 5
Parnell-Bos 5
R.Lemon-Cle 5

Saves
Kinder-Bos 27
Dorish-Chi 18
Reynolds-NY 13
Paige-StL 11
Sain-NY 9

Innings Pitched
R.Lemon-Cle 286.2
Garcia-Cle 271.2
Pierce-Chi 271.1
Trucks-StL-Chi .. 264.1
Porterfield-Was .. 255.0

Fewest Hits/Game
Pierce-Chi 7.16
McDermott-Bos ... 7.37
Raschi-NY 7.46
Masterson-Was ... 7.85
Trucks-StL-Chi ... 7.97

Fewest BB/Game
Lopat-NY 1.61
Sain-NY 2.14
A.Kellner-Phi 2.28
Porterfield-Was ... 2.58
Hoeft-Det 2.64

Strikeouts
Pierce-Chi 186
Trucks-StL-Chi ... 149
Wynn-Cle 138
Parnell-Bos 136
Garcia-Cle 134

Strikeouts/Game
Pierce-Chi 6.17
Gray-Det 5.88
Masterson-Was ... 5.14
Parnell-Bos 5.08
Trucks-StL-Chi ... 5.07

Ratio
Raschi-NY 10.24
Lopat-NY 10.35
Pierce-Chi 10.65
Porterfield-Was .. 11.19
Sain-NY 11.29

Earned Run Average
Lopat-NY 2.42
Pierce-Chi 2.72
Trucks-StL-Chi ... 2.93
Sain-NY 3.00
Ford-NY 3.00

Adjusted ERA
Lopat-NY 152
Pierce-Chi 148
McDermott-Bos ... 140
Trucks-StL-Chi ... 139
Parnell-Bos 137

Opponents' Batting Avg.
Pierce-Chi .... .218
McDermott-Bos ... .224
Raschi-NY .... .224
Masterson-Was ... .232
Trucks-StL-Chi ... .238

Opponents' On Base Pct.
Raschi-NY .... .283
Lopat-NY .... .288
Pierce-Chi .... .292
Masterson-Was ... .304
Garcia-Cle .... .307

Starter Runs
Pierce-Chi 38.4
Trucks-StL-Chi ... 31.3
Lopat-NY 31.2
Parnell-Bos 25.0
Ford-NY 22.9

Adjusted Starter Runs
Pierce-Chi 39.3
Trucks-StL-Chi ... 33.9
Parnell-Bos 30.6
McDermott-Bos ... 27.4
Lopat-NY 25.1

Clutch Pitching Index
Ford-NY 127
Lopat-NY 123
Sain-NY 118
R.Lemon-Cle 113
Parnell-Bos 112

Relief Runs
Kinder-Bos 25.5
Dorish-Chi 9.7
Kuzava-NY 7.0
Bearden-Chi 6.9
Paige-StL 6.1

Adjusted Relief Runs
Kinder-Bos 28.0
Dorish-Chi 10.1
Paige-StL 8.7
Bearden-Chi 7.1
Kuzava-NY 3.9

Relief Ranking
Kinder-Bos 53.6
Dorish-Chi 12.8
Paige-StL 9.9
Bearden-Chi 6.5
Kuzava-NY 4.5

Total Pitcher Index
McDermott-Bos 3.7
Trucks-StL-Chi 3.7
Pierce-Chi 3.4
Kinder-Bos 3.2
Parnell-Bos 3.1

Total Baseball Ranking
Rosen-Cle 6.0
McDermott-Bos 3.7
Trucks-StL-Chi 3.7
Zernial-Phi 3.6
Pierce-Chi 3.4

TEAM	G	W	L	PCT	GB	R	OR	AB	H	2B	3B	HR	BB	SO	AVG	OBP	SLG	PRO	PRO+	BR	/A	PF	CHI	RC	SB	CS	SBA	SBR
NY	154	97	57	.630		732	550	5245	1386	194	42	186	522	561	.264	.335	.424	.759	102	17	14	101	102	747	30	23	57	-5
BRO	154	92	62	.597	5	778	740	5251	1418	246	56	186	634	625	.270	.353	.444	.797	110	100	78	103	96	821	46	39	54	-10
MIL	154	89	65	.578	8	670	556	5261	1395	217	41	139	471	619	.265	.330	.401	.731	103	-33	12	94	101	697	54	31	64	-2
PHI	154	75	79	.487	22	659	614	5184	1384	243	58	102	604	620	.267	.345	.395	.740	99	-2	-1	100	95	707	30	27	53	-7
CIN	154	74	80	.481	23	729	634	5234	1369	221	46	147	557	645	.262	.336	.406	.742	96	-8	-28	103	105	726	47	30	61	-4
STL	154	72	82	.468	25	799	790	5405	1518	285	58	119	582	586	.281	.354	.421	.775	107	65	59	101	102	807	63	46	58	-9
CHI	154	64	90	.416	33	700	766	5359	1412	229	45	159	478	693	.263	.327	.412	.739	97	-21	-29	101	103	717	46	31	60	-5
PIT	154	53	101	.344	44	557	845	5088	1260	181	57	76	566	737	.248	.326	.350	.676	83	-119	-109	99	98	596	21	13	62	-2
TOT	616					5624		42027	11142	1816	403	1114	4414	5086	.265	.338	.407	.745							337	240	58	-43

TEAM	CG	SH	SV	IP	H	H/G	HR	BB	SO	RAT	ERA	ERA+	OAV	OOB	PR	/A	PF	CPI	FA	E	DP	FW	PW	BW	SBW	DIF
NY	45	19	33	1390	1258	8.1	113	613	692	12.3	3.09	130	.243	.328	151	145	99	113	.975	154	172	-.5	14.4	1.4	.0	4.8
BRO	39	8	36	1393²	1399	9.0	164	533	762	12.6	4.31	95	.261	.330	-36	-35	100	93	.978	129	138	.8	-3.5	7.7	-.5	10.4
MIL	63	13	21	1394²	1296	8.4	106	553	698	12.1	3.19	117	.250	.326	137	83	92	110	.981	116	171	1.5	8.2	1.2	.3	.7
PHI	78	14	12	1365¹	1329	8.8	133	450	570	11.8	3.59	112	.256	.318	73	68	99	100	.975	145	133	-.0	6.7	-.0	-.2	-8.4
CIN	34	8	27	1367¹	1491	9.8	169	547	537	13.6	4.50	93	.282	.354	-65	-47	103	.105	.977	137	194	.4	-4.7	-2.8	.1	3.9
STL	40	11	18	1390¹	1484	9.6	170	535	680	13.4	4.50	91	.275	.346	-66	-60	101	100	.976	146	178	-.0	-5.9	5.8	-.4	-4.4
CHI	41	6	19	1374¹	1375	9.0	131	619	622	13.2	4.51	93	.264	.345	-66	-46	103	92	.974	154	164	-.5	-4.6	-2.9	.0	-5.1
PIT	37	4	15	1346	1510	10.1	128	564	525	14.0	4.92	85	.287	.359	-127	-109	103	95	.971	173	136	-1.6	-10.8	-10.8	.3	-1.2
TOT	377	83	181	11021²		9.1				12.9	4.07		.265	.338					.976	1154	1286					

Runs		Hits		Doubles		Triples		Home Runs		Total Bases	
Snider-Bro	120	Mueller-NY	212	Musial-StL	41	Mays-NY	13	Kluszewski-Cin	49	Snider-Bro	378
Musial-StL	120	Snider-Bro	199	Snider-Bro	39	Hamner-Phi	11	Hodges-Bro	42	Mays-NY	377
Mays-NY	119	Musial-StL	195	Repulski-StL	39	Snider-Bro	10	Sauer-Chi	41	Kluszewski-Cin	368
Ashburn-Phi	111	Mays-NY	195	Hamner-Phi	39			Mays-NY	41	Musial-StL	359
Gilliam-Bro	107	Moon-StL	193							Hodges-Bro	335

Runs Batted In		Runs Produced		Bases On Balls		Batting Average		On Base Percentage		Slugging Average	
Kluszewski-Cin	141	Musial-StL	211	Ashburn-Phi	125	Mays-NY	.345	Ashburn-Phi	.442	Mays-NY	.667
Snider-Bro	130	Snider-Bro	210	Mathews-Mil	113	Mueller-NY	.342	Musial-StL	.433	Snider-Bro	.647
Hodges-Bro	130	Kluszewski-Cin	196	Musial-StL	103	Snider-Bro	.341	Mathews-Mil	.428	Kluszewski-Cin	.642
Musial-StL	126	Hodges-Bro	194	Thompson-NY	90	Musial-StL	.330	Snider-Bro	.427	Musial-StL	.607
Ennis-Phi	119			Reese-Bro	90	Kluszewski-Cin	.326	Mays-NY	.415	Mathews-Mil	.603

Production		Adjusted Production		Batter Runs		Adjusted Batter Runs		Clutch Hitting Index		Runs Created	
Mays-NY	1.083	Mathews-Mil	177	Snider-Bro	64.6	Snider-Bro	62.1	Ennis-Phi	154	Snider-Bro	161
Snider-Bro	1.074	Mays-NY	176	Mays-NY	61.8	Mays-NY	61.4	Jablonski-StL	148	Mays-NY	155
Kluszewski-Cin	1.052	Snider-Bro	170	Musial-StL	60.7	Musial-StL	60.1	Post-Cin	131	Musial-StL	153
Musial-StL	1.040	Musial-StL	166	Kluszewski-Cin	57.1	Kluszewski-Cin	54.9	Furillo-Bro	128	Kluszewski-Cin	151
Mathews-Mil	1.031	Kluszewski-Cin	165	Mathews-Mil	48.6	Mathews-Mil	53.2	Hodges-Bro	118	Mathews-Mil	131

Total Average		Stolen Bases		Stolen Base Average		Stolen Base Runs		Fielding Runs		Total Player Rating	
Mathews-Mil	1.169	Bruton-Mil	34	Fondy-Chi	80.0	Fondy-Chi	3.0	Schoendienst-StL	32.9	Mays-NY	6.8
Mays-NY	1.158	Temple-Cin	21	Temple-Cin	75.0	Bruton-Mil	2.4	Grammas-StL	29.8	Mathews-Mil	4.8
Snider-Bro	1.156	Fondy-Chi	20	Bruton-Mil	72.3	Temple-Cin	2.1	Ashburn-Phi	17.2	Snider-Bro	4.8
Kluszewski-Cin	1.117	Moon-StL	18	Moon-StL	64.3	Torgeson-Phi	1.5	Mays-NY	15.5	Schoendienst-StL	4.8
Musial-StL	1.087	Ashburn-Phi	11					Logan-Mil	14.4	Musial-StL	4.7

Wins		Win Percentage		Games		Complete Games		Shutouts		Saves	
Roberts-Phi	23	Antonelli-NY	.750	Hughes-Bro	60	Roberts-Phi	29	Antonelli-NY	6	Hughes-Bro	24
Spahn-Mil	21	Lawrence-StL	.714	Hetki-Pit	58	Spahn-Mil	23			Smith-Cin	20
Antonelli-NY	21	Gomez-NY	.654	Brazle-StL	58	Simmons-Phi	21			Grissom-NY	19
Haddix-StL	18	Spahn-Mil	.636	Wilhelm-NY	57	Antonelli-NY	18			Jolly-Mil	10
Erskine-Bro	18	Roberts-Phi	.605	Grissom-NY	56					Hetki-Pit	9

Innings Pitched		Fewest Hits/Game		Fewest BB/Game		Strikeouts		Strikeouts/Game		Ratio	
Roberts-Phi	336.2	Antonelli-NY	7.27	Roberts-Phi	1.50	Roberts-Phi	185	Haddix-StL	6.38	Roberts-Phi	9.36
Spahn-Mil	283.1	Roberts-Phi	7.73	Minner-Chi	2.06	Haddix-StL	184	Erskine-Bro	5.74	Antonelli-NY	10.72
Erskine-Bro	260.1	Conley-Mil	7.92	Hacker-Chi	2.10	Erskine-Bro	166	Littlefield-Pit	5.34	Burdette-Mil	10.97
Haddix-StL	259.2	Lawrence-StL	8.00	Burdette-Mil	2.34	Antonelli-NY	152	Antonelli-NY	5.29	Spahn-Mil	11.09
Antonelli-NY	258.2	Wehmeier-Cin-Phi	8.02	Meyer-Bro	2.45	Spahn-Mil	136	Conley-Mil	5.23	Hacker-Chi	11.23

Earned Run Average		Adjusted ERA		Opponents' Batting Avg.		Opponents' On Base Pct.		Starter Runs		Adjusted Starter Runs	
Antonelli-NY	2.30	Antonelli-NY	176	Antonelli-NY	.219	Roberts-Phi	.267	Antonelli-NY	51.0	Antonelli-NY	50.0
Burdette-Mil	2.76	Simmons-Phi	144	Roberts-Phi	.231	Antonelli-NY	.293	Roberts-Phi	41.3	Roberts-Phi	40.1
Simmons-Phi	2.81	Gomez-NY	140	Simmons-Phi	.239	Spahn-Mil	.302	Simmons-Phi	35.5	Simmons-Phi	34.6
Gomez-NY	2.88	Roberts-Phi	136	Littlefield-Pit	.239	Burdette-Mil	.302	Burdette-Mil	34.7	Gomez-NY	28.4
Conley-Mil	2.96	Burdette-Mil	135	Wehmeier-Cin-Phi	.239	Hacker-Chi	.304	Gomez-NY	29.3	Burdette-Mil	25.5

Clutch Pitching Index		Relief Runs		Adjusted Relief Runs		Relief Ranking		Total Pitcher Index		Total Baseball Ranking	
Gomez-NY	130	Wilhelm-NY	24.4	Wilhelm-NY	23.9	Grissom-NY	36.6	Antonelli-NY	5.5	Mays-NY	6.8
Dickson-Phi	123	Grissom-NY	23.4	Grissom-NY	22.9	Wilhelm-NY	34.3	Roberts-Phi	3.5	Antonelli-NY	5.5
Fowler-Cin	116	Jolly-Mil	20.4	Jolly-Mil	16.1	Smith-Cin	27.5	Simmons-Phi	3.1	Mathews-Mil	4.8
Conley-Mil	116	Johnson-Mil	13.9	Smith-Cin	13.7	Jolly-Mil	25.4	Gomez-NY	3.0	Snider-Bro	4.8
Antonelli-NY	115	Smith-Cin	12.7	Johnson-Mil	10.1	Hughes-Bro	15.6	Spahn-Mil	2.6	Schoendienst-StL	4.8

TEAM	G	W	L	PCT	GB	R	OR	AB	H	2B	3B	HR	BB	SO	AVG	OBP	SLG	PRO	PRO+	BR	/A	PF	CHI	RC	SB	CS	SBA	SBR
CLE	156	111	43	.721		746	504	5222	1368	188	39	156	637	668	.262	.345	.403	.748	109	76	65	102	102	739	30	33	48	-11
NY	155	103	51	.669	8	805	563	5226	1400	215	59	133	650	632	.268	.351	.408	.759	118	101	124	97	106	768	34	41	45	-14
CHI	155	94	60	.610	17	711	521	5168	1382	203	47	94	604	536	.267	.350	.379	.729	103	51	29	103	101	700	98	58	63	-5
BOS	156	69	85	.448	42	700	728	5399	1436	244	41	123	654	660	.266	.348	.395	.743	99	-37	-25	98	97	749	51	30	63	-3
DET	155	68	86	.442	43	584	664	5233	1351	215	41	90	492	603	.258	.324	.367	.691	97	-37	-25	98	97	609	48	44	52	-12
WAS	155	66	88	.429	45	632	680	5249	1292	188	69	81	610	719	.246	.328	.355	.683	98	-44	-8	95	104	631	37	21	64	-2
BAL	154	54	100	.351	57	483	668	5206	1309	195	49	52	468	634	.251	.316	.338	.654	92	-104	-56	93	91	553	30	31	49	-10
PHI	156	51	103	.331	60	542	875	5206	1228	191	41	94	504	677	.236	.307	.342	.649	84	-117	-119	100	105	553	30	29	51	-8
TOT	621					5203		41909	10766	1639	386	823	4619	5129	.257	.334	.373	.707							358	287	56	-65

TEAM	CG	SH	SV	IP	H	H/G	HR	BB	SO	RAT	ERA	ERA+	OAV	OOB	PR	/A	PF	CPI	FA	E	DP	FW	PW	BW	SBW	DIF
CLE	77	12	36	1419¹	1220	7.7	89	486	678	10.9	2.78	132	.232	.299	148	141	99	100	.979	128	148	.7	14.6	6.7	-.3	12.3
NY	51	16	37	1379¹	1284	8.4	86	552	655	12.2	3.26	105	.251	.328	71	27	92	107	.979	126	198	.8	2.8	12.8	-.6	10.2
CHI	60	23	33	1383	1255	8.2	94	517	701	11.6	3.05	122	.244	.314	103	105	100	105	.982	108	149	1.8	10.8	3.0	.3	1.0
BOS	41	10	22	1412¹	1434	9.1	118	612	707	13.3	4.01	102	.265	.344	-46	15	110	101	.972	176	163	-2.0	1.5	-.1	.5	-8.0
DET	58	13	13	1383	1375	8.9	138	506	603	12.5	3.81	97	.261	.330	-13	-17	99	103	.978	129	131	.6	-1.8	-2.6	-.4	-4.9
WAS	69	10	7	1383¹	1396	9.1	79	573	562	13.0	3.84	93	.265	.340	-18	-43	96	99	.977	137	172	.2	-4.4	-4.8	.6	-6.5
BAL	58	6	8	1373¹	1279	8.4	78	688	668	13.0	3.88	92	.250	.341	-24	-45	96	94	.975	147	152	-.4	-4.6	-5.8	-.2	-11.9
PHI	49	3	13	1371¹	1523	10.0	141	685	555	14.7	5.18	75	.285	.370	-222	-194	105	95	.972	169	163	-1.6	-20.0	-12.3	.0	7.9
TOT	463	93	169	11105		8.7				12.6	3.72		.257	.334					.977	1120	1276					

Runs
Mantle-NY	129
Minoso-Chi	119
Avila-Cle	112
Fox-Chi	111
Carrasquel-Chi	106

Hits
Kuenn-Det	201
Fox-Chi	201
Avila-Cle	189
Busby-Was	187
Minoso-Chi	182

Doubles
Vernon-Was	33
Smith-Cle	29
Minoso-Chi	29

Triples
Minoso-Chi	18
Runnels-Was	15
Vernon-Was	14
Mantle-NY	12
Tuttle-Det	11

Home Runs
Doby-Cle	32
Williams-Bos	29
Mantle-NY	27
Jensen-Bos	25

Total Bases
Minoso-Chi	304
Vernon-Was	294
Mantle-NY	285
Berra-NY	285
Doby-Cle	279

Runs Batted In
Doby-Cle	126
Berra-NY	125
Jensen-Bos	117
Minoso-Chi	116

Runs Produced
Minoso-Chi	216
Mantle-NY	204
Berra-NY	191
Doby-Cle	188
Jensen-Bos	184

Bases On Balls
Williams-Bos	136
Yost-Was	131
Mantle-NY	102
Smith-Cle	88

Batting Average
Williams-Bos	.345
Avila-Cle	.341
Minoso-Chi	.320
Noren-NY	.319
Fox-Chi	.319

On Base Percentage
Williams-Bos	.516
Minoso-Chi	.416
Rosen-Cle	.412
Mantle-NY	.411
Yost-Was	.406

Slugging Average
Williams-Bos	.635
Minoso-Chi	.535
Mantle-NY	.525
Rosen-Cle	.506
Vernon-Was	.492

Production
Williams-Bos	1.151
Minoso-Chi	.951
Mantle-NY	.936
Rosen-Cle	.918
Avila-Cle	.882

Adjusted Production
Williams-Bos	193
Mantle-NY	160
Minoso-Chi	154
Rosen-Cle	148
Noren-NY	140

Batter Runs
Williams-Bos	70.9
Minoso-Chi	47.3
Mantle-NY	42.8
Rosen-Cle	34.2
Avila-Cle	31.5

Adjusted Batter Runs
Williams-Bos	64.6
Mantle-NY	45.2
Minoso-Chi	44.8
Rosen-Cle	33.2
Avila-Cle	30.3

Clutch Hitting Index
Berra-NY	143
Sievers-Was	136
Doby-Cle	135
Jensen-Bos	135
Rosen-Cle	128

Runs Created
Williams-Bos	139
Mantle-NY	127
Minoso-Chi	125
Avila-Cle	109
Doby-Cle	108

Total Average
Williams-Bos	1.452
Mantle-NY	1.013
Minoso-Chi	.969
Rosen-Cle	.959
Doby-Cle	.862

Stolen Bases
Jensen-Bos	22
Rivera-Chi	18
Minoso-Chi	18
Jacobs-Phi	17
Busby-Was	17

Stolen Base Average
Busby-Was	89.5
Jacobs-Phi	85.0
Jensen-Bos	75.9
Rivera-Chi	64.3
Fox-Chi	64.0

Stolen Base Runs
Busby-Was	3.9
Jacobs-Phi	3.3
Jensen-Bos	2.4
Cavarretta-Chi	1.2

Fielding Runs
Coleman-NY	17.9
Carey-NY	16.7
Lepcio-Bos	16.1
Bolling-Bos	15.3
Minoso-Chi	13.4

Total Player Rating
Williams-Bos	5.7
Minoso-Chi	5.1
Avila-Cle	4.7
Mantle-NY	3.9
Berra-NY	3.5

Wins
Wynn-Cle	23
Lemon-Cle	23
Grim-NY	20
Trucks-Chi	19
Garcia-Cle	19

Win Percentage
Consuegra-Chi	.842
Grim-NY	.769
Lemon-Cle	.767
Garcia-Cle	.704
Houtteman-Cle	.682

Games
Dixon-Was-Phi	54
Martin-Phi-Chi	48
Pascual-Was	48
Kinder-Bos	48

Complete Games
Porterfield-Was	21
Lemon-Cle	21
Wynn-Cle	20
Gromek-Det	17

Shutouts
Trucks-Chi	5
Garcia-Cle	5

Saves
Sain-NY	22
Kinder-Bos	15
Narleski-Cle	13

Innings Pitched
Wynn-Cle	270.2
Trucks-Chi	264.2
Garcia-Cle	258.2
Lemon-Cle	258.1
Gromek-Det	252.2

Fewest Hits/Game
Turley-Bal	6.48
Ford-NY	7.26
Wynn-Cle	7.48
Coleman-Bal	7.48
Reynolds-NY	7.61

Fewest BB/Game
Lopat-NY	1.75
Gromek-Det	2.03
Garver-Det	2.27
Garcia-Cle	2.47
Zuverink-Det	2.75

Strikeouts
Turley-Bal	185
Wynn-Cle	155
Trucks-Chi	152
Pierce-Chi	148
Harshman-Chi	134

Strikeouts/Game
Pierce-Chi	7.06
Harshman-Chi	6.81
Turley-Bal	6.73
Hoeft-Det	5.86
Reynolds-NY	5.72

Ratio
Garcia-Cle	10.19
Wynn-Cle	10.24
Garver-Det	10.30
Gromek-Det	10.86
Trucks-Chi	10.88

Earned Run Average
Garcia-Cle	2.64
Lemon-Cle	2.72
Wynn-Cle	2.73
Gromek-Det	2.74
Trucks-Chi	2.79

Adjusted ERA
Garcia-Cle	139
Lemon-Cle	135
Wynn-Cle	135
Gromek-Det	135
Trucks-Chi	134

Opponents' Batting Avg.
Turley-Bal	.203
Wynn-Cle	.225
Ford-NY	.227
Trucks-Chi	.228
Garcia-Cle	.229

Opponents' On Base Pct.
Garcia-Cle	.284
Wynn-Cle	.284
Garver-Det	.287
Gromek-Det	.297
Trucks-Chi	.297

Starter Runs
Garcia-Cle	31.0
Wynn-Cle	30.0
Lemon-Cle	28.9
Gromek-Det	27.5
Trucks-Chi	27.5

Adjusted Starter Runs
Garcia-Cle	29.6
Wynn-Cle	28.5
Trucks-Chi	27.8
Lemon-Cle	27.5
Gromek-Det	26.7

Clutch Pitching Index
Keegan-Chi	126
Gromek-Det	116
Houtteman-Cle	114
Lopat-NY	114
Harshman-Chi	114

Relief Runs
Mossi-Cle	18.5
Narleski-Cle	14.8
Dorish-Chi	12.1
Miller-Det	9.8
Sain-NY	4.9

Adjusted Relief Runs
Mossi-Cle	18.0
Narleski-Cle	14.3
Dorish-Chi	12.2
Miller-Det	9.6
Kinder-Bos	5.9

Relief Ranking
Mossi-Cle	15.2
Narleski-Cle	13.4
Dorish-Chi	11.6
Kinder-Bos	9.7
Sain-NY	4.9

Total Pitcher Index
Lemon-Cle	4.0
Garcia-Cle	2.9
Trucks-Chi	2.9
Wynn-Cle	2.8
Garver-Det	2.7

Total Baseball Ranking
Williams-Bos	5.7
Minoso-Chi	5.1
Avila-Cle	4.7
Lemon-Cle	4.0
Mantle-NY	3.9

TEAM	G	W	L	PCT	GB	R	OR	AB	H	2B	3B	HR	BB	SO	AVG	OBP	SLG	PRO	PRO+	BR	/A	PF	CHI	RC	SB	CS	SBA	SBR
BRO	154	98	55	.641		857	650	5193	1406	230	44	201	674	718	.271	.359	.448	.807	116	142	122	103	100	834	79	56	59	-10
MIL	154	85	69	.552	13.5	743	668	5277	1377	219	55	182	504	735	.261	.329	.427	.756	109	27	62	95	102	733	42	27	61	-4
NY	154	80	74	.519	18.5	702	673	5288	1377	173	34	169	497	581	.260	.328	.402	.730	98	-15	-16	100	102	699	38	22	63	-2
PHI	154	77	77	.500	21.5	675	666	5092	1300	214	50	132	652	673	.255	.343	.425	.738	103	14	26	98	95	692	44	32	58	-6
CIN	154	75	79	.487	23.5	761	684	5270	1424	216	28	181	556	657	.270	.344	.425	.769	103	63	22	106	99	773	51	36	59	-6
CHI	154	72	81	.471	26	626	713	5214	1287	187	55	164	428	806	.247	.307	.398	.705	91	-75	-72	100	103	623	37	35	51	-10
STL	154	68	86	.442	30.5	654	757	5266	1375	228	36	143	458	597	.261	.324	.400	.724	96	-30	-29	100	99	662	64	59	52	-16
PIT	154	60	94	.390	38.5	560	767	5173	1262	210	60	91	471	652	.244	.310	.361	.671	84	-127	-117	99	100	567	22	22	50	-7
TOT	616					5578		41773	10808	1677	362	1263	4240	5419	.259	.330	.407	.737							377	289	57	-60

TEAM	CG	SH	SV	IP	H	H/G	HR	BB	SO	RAT	ERA	ERA+	OAV	OOB	PR	/A	PF	CPI	FA	E	DP	FW	PW	BW	SBW	DIF
BRO	46	11	37	1378	1296	8.5	168	483	773	11.7	3.68	110	.248	.314	54	58	101	100	.978	133	156	.5	5.8	12.1	-.2	3.4
MIL	61	5	12	1383	1339	8.7	138	591	654	12.7	3.85	98	.256	.333	29	-14	93	102	.975	152	155	-.6	-1.4	6.2	.4	3.5
NY	52	6	14	1386²	1347	8.7	155	560	721	12.7	3.77	107	.257	.334	41	39	100	107	.976	142	165	.0	3.9	-1.6	.5	.2
PHI	58	11	21	1356²	1291	8.6	161	477	657	11.9	3.93	101	.251	.318	17	6	98	96	.981	110	117	1.8	.6	2.6	.2	-5.1
CIN	38	12	22	1363	1373	9.1	161	443	576	12.1	3.95	107	.264	.324	13	43	105	102	.977	139	169	.2	4.3	2.2	.2	-8.8
CHI	47	10	23	1378¹	1306	8.5	153	601	686	12.6	4.17	98	.251	.332	-21	-13	101	95	.975	147	147	-.3	-1.3	-7.1	-.2	4.5
STL	42	10	15	1376²	1376	9.0	185	549	730	12.9	4.56	89	.262	.337	-80	-77	101	95	.975	146	152	-.2	-7.6	-2.9	-.8	2.6
PIT	41	5	16	1362	1480	9.8	142	536	622	13.5	4.39	94	.281	.350	-54	-42	102	104	.972	166	175	-1.4	-4.2	-11.6	.0	.0
TOT	385	70	160	10984¹		8.9				12.5	4.04		.259	.330					.976	1135	1236					

Runs
Snider-Bro 126
Mays-NY 123
Post-Cin 116
Kluszewski-Cin ... 116
Gilliam-Bro 110

Hits
Kluszewski-Cin ... 192
Aaron-Mil 189
Bell-Cin 188
Post-Cin 186

Doubles
Logan-Mil 37
Aaron-Mil 37
Snider-Bro 34
Post-Cin 33
Ashburn-Phi 32

Triples
Mays-NY 13
Long-Pit 13
Bruton-Mil 12
Clemente-Pit 11

Home Runs
Mays-NY 51
Kluszewski-Cin ... 47
Banks-Chi 44
Snider-Bro 42
Mathews-Mil 41

Total Bases
Mays-NY 382
Kluszewski-Cin ... 358
Banks-Chi 355
Post-Cin 345
Snider-Bro 338

Runs Batted In
Snider-Bro 136
Mays-NY 127
Ennis-Phi 120
Banks-Chi 117
Kluszewski-Cin ... 113

Runs Produced
Snider-Bro 220
Mays-NY 199
Post-Cin 185
Aaron-Mil 184
Kluszewski-Cin ... 182

Bases On Balls
Mathews-Mil 109
Ashburn-Phi 105
Snider-Bro 104
Thompson-NY 84

Batting Average
Ashburn-Phi 338
Mays-NY 319
Musial-StL 319
Campanella-Bro ..318
Aaron-Mil 314

On Base Percentage
Ashburn-Phi 449
Snider-Bro 421
Mathews-Mil 417
Musial-StL 411
Mays-NY 404

Slugging Average
Mays-NY 659
Snider-Bro 628
Mathews-Mil 601
Banks-Chi 596
Kluszewski-Cin ...585

Production
Mays-NY 1.063
Snider-Bro 1.050
Mathews-Mil 1.018
Campanella-Bro ..985
Musial-StL 977

Adjusted Production
Mays-NY 176
Mathews-Mil 175
Snider-Bro 169
Musial-StL 156
Campanella-Bro . 153

Batter Runs
Mays-NY 62.3
Snider-Bro 58.9
Mathews-Mil 50.0
Musial-StL 46.5
Kluszewski-Cin . 44.9

Adjusted Batter Runs
Mays-NY 62.2
Snider-Bro 56.8
Mathews-Mil 53.6
Musial-StL 46.5
Kluszewski-Cin . 40.2

Clutch Hitting Index
Jones-Phi 136
Mueller-NY 136
Ennis-Phi 136
Snider-Bro 126
Campanella-Bro . 124

Runs Created
Mays-NY 157
Snider-Bro 145
Kluszewski-Cin . 136
Musial-StL 131
Mathews-Mil 131

Total Average
Mays-NY 1.180
Snider-Bro 1.147
Mathews-Mil ... 1.124
Musial-StL 1.020
Campanella-Bro . 1.000

Stolen Bases
Bruton-Mil 25
Mays-NY 24
Boyer-StL 22
Temple-Cin 19
Gilliam-Bro 15

Stolen Base Average
Mays-NY 85.7
Temple-Cin 82.6
Bruton-Mil 69.4
Boyer-StL 56.4

Stolen Base Runs
Mays-NY 4.8
Temple-Cin 3.3
Robinson-Bro 1.8
Blaylock-Phi 1.2

Fielding Runs
Mays-NY 19.8
McMillan-Cin ... 16.6
O'Connell-Mil .. 15.8
Groat-Pit 15.4
Bruton-Mil 14.7

Total Player Rating
Mays-NY 7.7
Banks-Chi 5.3
Snider-Bro 4.8
Mathews-Mil 4.7
Ashburn-Phi 4.0

Wins
Roberts-Phi 23
Newcombe-Bro 20
Spahn-Mil 17
Nuxhall-Cin 17

Win Percentage
Newcombe-Bro 800
Roberts-Phi 622
Nuxhall-Cin 586
Spahn-Mil 548

Games
Labine-Bro 60
Wilhelm-NY 59
LaPalme-StL 56
Grissom-NY 55
Freeman-Cin 52

Complete Games
Roberts-Phi 26
Newcombe-Bro 17
Spahn-Mil 16

Shutouts
Nuxhall-Cin 5
Jones-Chi......... 4
Dickson-Phi 4

Saves
Meyer-Phi 16
Roebuck-Bro 12
Labine-Bro 11
Freeman-Cin 11
Grissom-NY 8

Innings Pitched
Roberts-Phi 305.0
Nuxhall-Cin 257.0
Spahn-Mil 245.2
Jones-Chi....... 241.2
Antonelli-NY ... 235.1

Fewest Hits/Game
Jones-Chi 6.52
Buhl-Mil 7.50
Rush-Chi 7.85
Antonelli-NY ... 7.88
Dickson-Phi 7.92

Fewest BB/Game
Newcombe-Phi ... 1.46
Roberts-Phi 1.56
Hacker-Chi 1.82
Friend-Pit 2.34
Spahn-Mil 2.38

Strikeouts
Jones-Chi....... 198
Roberts-Phi 160
Haddix-StL 150
Newcombe-Bro ... 143
Antonelli-NY ... 143

Strikeouts/Game
Jones-Chi....... 7.37
Haddix-StL 6.49
Podres-Bro 6.44
Conley-Mil 6.09
Newcombe-Bro ... 5.51

Ratio
Newcombe-Bro ... 10.05
Roberts-Phi 10.24
Friend-Pit 10.42
Hacker-Chi 10.44
Rush-Chi 10.73

Earned Run Average
Friend-Pit 2.83
Newcombe-Bro ... 3.20
Buhl-Mil 3.21
Spahn-Mil 3.26
Roberts-Phi 3.28

Adjusted ERA
Friend-Pit 145
Newcombe-Bro ... 127
Nuxhall-Cin 122
Roberts-Phi 121
Antonelli-NY ... 121

Opponents' Batting Avg.
Jones-Chi........206
Buhl-Mil 227
Rush-Chi 234
Antonelli-NY 234
Dickson-Phi 238

Opponents' On Base Pct.
Roberts-Phi 280
Newcombe-Bro 280
Hacker-Chi 285
Friend-Pit 294
Rush-Chi 295

Starter Runs
Friend-Pit 26.9
Roberts-Phi 25.8
Newcombe-Bro 21.8
Spahn-Mil 21.2
Antonelli-NY 18.6

Adjusted Starter Runs
Friend-Pit 28.6
Roberts-Phi 23.5
Newcombe-Bro 22.5
Nuxhall-Cin 21.9
Schmidt-StL 18.5

Clutch Pitching Index
Minner-Chi 122
Spahn-Mil 114
Jackson-StL 113
Law-Pit 109
Friend-Pit 109

Relief Runs
Freeman-Cin 19.1
Miller-Phi 16.2
LaPalme-StL 13.1
Labine-Bro 12.8
Jeffcoat-Chi ... 12.2

Adjusted Relief Runs
Freeman-Cin 21.1
Miller-Phi 15.5
LaPalme-StL 13.4
Labine-Bro 13.1
Jeffcoat-Chi ... 12.7

Relief Ranking
Freeman-Cin 28.5
Miller-Phi 19.1
Jeffcoat-Chi ... 17.6
Labine-Bro 17.0
Bessent-Bro 13.3

Total Pitcher Index
Newcombe-Bro 4.3
Roberts-Phi 3.4
Friend-Pit 3.1
Nuxhall-Cin 2.4
Freeman-Cin 2.3

Total Baseball Ranking
Mays-NY 7.7
Banks-Chi 5.3
Snider-Bro 4.8
Mathews-Mil 4.7
Newcombe-Bro 4.3

TEAM	G	W	L	PCT	GB	R	OR	AB	H	2B	3B	HR	BB	SO	AVG	OBP	SLG	PRO	PRO+	BR	/A	PF	CHI	RC	SB	CS	SBA	SBR
NY	154	96	58	.623		762	569	5161	1342	179	55	175	609	658	.260	.343	.418	.761	113	71	82	98	101	759	55	25	69	2
CLE	154	93	61	.604	3	698	601	5146	1325	195	31	148	723	715	.257	.353	.394	.747	104	60	34	104	93	741	28	24	54	-6
CHI	155	91	63	.591	5	725	557	5220	1401	204	36	116	567	595	.268	.347	.388	.735	101	31	12	103	101	712	69	45	61	-6
BOS	154	84	70	.545	12	755	652	5273	1392	241	39	137	707	733	.264	.354	.402	.756	101	77	14	97	97	773	43	17	72	3
DET	154	79	75	.513	17	775	658	5283	1407	211	38	130	641	583	.266	.348	.394	.742	108	46	62	98	104	736	41	22	65	-1
KC	155	63	91	.409	33	638	911	5335	1395	189	46	121	463	725	.261	.323	.382	.705	95	-40	-47	101	100	637	22	36	38	-15
BAL	156	57	97	.370	39	540	754	5257	1263	177	39	54	560	742	.240	.316	.320	.636	83	-159	-111	93	104	532	34	46	43	-17
WAS	154	53	101	.344	43	598	789	5142	1277	178	54	80	538	654	.248	.324	.351	.675	93	-86	-50	95	103	586	25	32	44	-12
TOT	618						5491	41817	10802	1574	338	961	4808	5405	.258	.339	.381	.720							317	247	56	-53

TEAM	CG	SH	SV	IP	H	H/G	HR	BB	SO	RAT	ERA	ERA+	OAV	OOB	PR	/A	PF	CPI	FA	E	DP	FW	PW	BW	SBW	DIF
NY	52	19	33	1372¹	1163	7.6	108	688	731	12.3	3.23	116	.232	.328	111	78	95	107	.978	128	180	.5	7.8	8.2	.9	1.6
CLE	45	15	36	1386¹	1285	8.3	111	558	877	12.1	3.39	118	.245	.320	88	92	101	101	.981	108	152	1.7	9.2	3.4	.0	1.7
CHI	55	20	23	1378	1301	8.5	111	497	720	11.9	3.37	117	.251	.319	90	89	100	103	.981	111	147	1.5	8.9	1.2	.0	2.3
BOS	44	9	34	1384¹	1333	8.7	128	582	674	12.7	3.72	115	.253	.331	37	88	108	102	.977	136	140	.0	8.8	1.4	1.0	-4.2
DET	66	16	12	1380¹	1381	9.0	126	517	629	12.6	3.79	101	.261	.331	26	7	97	102	.976	139	159	-.2	.7	6.2	.6	-5.3
KC	29	9	22	1382	1486	9.7	175	707	572	14.6	5.35	78	.278	.367	-214	-181	100	94	.976	146	174	-.5	-18.1	-4.7	-.8	10.2
BAL	35	10	20	1388²	1403	9.1	103	625	595	13.4	4.21	91	.266	.348	-39	-61	96	98	.972	167	159	-1.7	-6.1	-11.1	-1.0	-.0
WAS	37	10	16	1354²	1450	9.6	99	634	607	14.2	4.62	83	.279	.362	-100	-119	97	98	.974	154	170	-1.0	-11.9	-5.0	-.5	-5.5
TOT	363	108	196	11026²		8.8				13.0	3.96		.258	.339					.977	1089	1281					

Runs
Smith-Cle 123
Mantle-NY 121
Kaline-Det 121
Tuttle-Det 102
Kuenn-Det 101

Hits
Kaline-Det 200
Fox-Chi 198
Power-KC 190
Kuenn-Det 190
Smith-Cle 186

Doubles
Kuenn-Det 38
Power-KC 34
Goodman-Bos 31
White-Bos 30
Finigan-KC 30

Triples
Mantle-NY 11
Carey-NY 11
Power-KC 10

Home Runs
Mantle-NY 37
Zernial-KC 30
Williams-Bos 28

Total Bases
Kaline-Det 321
Mantle-NY 316
Power-KC 301
Smith-Cle 287
Jensen-Bos 275

Runs Batted In
Jensen-Bos 116
Boone-Det 116
Berra-NY 108
Sievers-Was 106
Kaline-Det 102

Runs Produced
Kaline-Det 196
Jensen-Bos 185
Mantle-NY 183
Smith-Cle 178
Tuttle-Det 166

Bases On Balls
Mantle-NY 113
Goodman-Bos 99
Yost-Was 95
Fain-Det-Cle 94
Smith-Cle 93

Batting Average
Kaline-Det .... .340
Power-KC .... .319
Kell-Chi .... .312
Fox-Chi .... .311
Kuenn-Det .... .306

On Base Percentage
Mantle-NY .... .433
Kaline-Det .... .425
Smith-Cle .... .411
Yost-Was .... .410
Goodman-Bos ...... .397

Slugging Average
Mantle-NY .... .611
Kaline-Det .... .546
Doby-Cle .... .505
Power-KC .... .505
Sievers-Was ...... .489

Production
Mantle-NY 1.044
Kaline-Det .... .971
Smith-Cle .... .884
Doby-Cle .... .877
Power-KC .... .862

Adjusted Production
Mantle-NY 181
Kaline-Det 163
Sievers-Was 136
Vernon-Was 133
Smith-Cle 132

Batter Runs
Williams-Bos 59.3
Mantle-NY 59.0
Kaline-Det 50.2
Smith-Cle 34.7
Valo-KC 24.8

Adjusted Batter Runs
Mantle-NY 60.2
Williams-Bos 55.0
Kaline-Det 52.0
Smith-Cle 31.7
Valo-KC 24.4

Clutch Hitting Index
Kell-Chi 148
Boone-Det 148
Jensen-Bos 130
Sievers-Was 129
Berra-NY 127

Runs Created
Mantle-NY 148
Kaline-Det 135
Smith-Cle 128
Power-KC 103
Jensen-Bos 102

Total Average
Mantle-NY 1.206
Kaline-Det .... .993
Smith-Cle .... .928
Doby-Cle .... .884
Jensen-Bos .... .849

Stolen Bases
Rivera-Chi 25
Minoso-Chi 19
Jensen-Bos 16
Busby-Was-Chi 12
Smith-Cle 11

Stolen Base Average
Minoso-Chi 70.4
Jensen-Bos 69.6
Rivera-Chi 61.0

Stolen Base Runs
Torgeson-Det 2.7
Busby-Was-Chi 1.8
Mantle-NY 1.8
Klaus-Bos 1.8

Fielding Runs
Fox-Chi 26.9
McDougald-NY 19.4
Miranda-Bal 19.0
Lopez-KC 15.1
Tuttle-Det 14.9

Total Player Rating
Mantle-NY 6.2
Kaline-Det 4.9
Williams-Bos 4.9
Fox-Chi 3.9
McDougald-NY 3.5

Wins
F.Sullivan-Bos ... 18
Lemon-Cle 18
Ford-NY 18
Wynn-Cle 17
Turley-NY 17

Win Percentage
Byrne-NY .... .762
Ford-NY .... .720
Hoeft-Det .... .696
Lemon-Cle .... .643
Donovan-Chi ...... .625

Games
Narleski-Cle 60
Mossi-Cle 57
Gorman-KC 57
Dorish-Chi-Bal ... 48
Moore-Bal 46

Complete Games
Ford-NY 18
Hoeft-Det 17

Shutouts
Hoeft-Det 7
Wynn-Cle 6
Turley-NY 6
Pierce-Chi 6

Saves
Narleski-Cle 19
Kinder-Bos 18
Gorman-KC 18
Konstanty-NY 11
Morgan-NY 10

Innings Pitched
F.Sullivan-Bos ... 260.0
Ford-NY 253.2
Turley-NY 246.2
Wilson-Bal 235.1
Lary-Det 235.0

Fewest Hits/Game
Turley-NY 6.13
Score-Cle 6.26
Ford-NY 6.67
Pierce-Chi 7.09
Harshman-Chi 7.23

Fewest BB/Game
Gromek-Det 1.84
Donovan-Chi 2.31
Garcia-Cle 2.39
Garver-Det 2.61
Porterfield-Was .. 2.73

Strikeouts
Score-Cle 245
Turley-NY 210
Pierce-Chi 157
Ford-NY 137
Hoeft-Det 133

Strikeouts/Game
Score-Cle 9.70
Turley-NY 7.66
Pierce-Chi 6.87
Harshman-Chi 5.82
Hoeft-Det 5.44

Ratio
Pierce-Chi 10.02
Ford-NY 10.71
Hoeft-Det 10.96
Wilson-Bal 11.13
Wynn-Cle 11.35

Earned Run Average
Pierce-Chi 1.97
Ford-NY 2.63
Wynn-Cle 2.82
Score-Cle 2.85
F.Sullivan-Bos ... 2.91

Adjusted ERA
Pierce-Chi 201
F.Sullivan-Bos ... 148
Ford-NY 143
Wynn-Cle 142
Score-Cle 140

Opponents' Batting Avg.
Turley-NY .... .193
Score-Cle .... .194
Ford-NY .... .208
Pierce-Chi .... .213
Harshman-Chi ..... .224

Opponents' On Base Pct.
Pierce-Chi .... .277
Ford-NY .... .297
Hoeft-Det .... .298
Wilson-Bal .... .300
Wynn-Cle .... .307

Starter Runs
Pierce-Chi 45.5
Ford-NY 37.6
F.Sullivan-Bos ... 30.4
Wynn-Cle 29.2
Score-Cle 28.1

Adjusted Starter Runs
Pierce-Chi 45.2
F.Sullivan-Bos ... 39.9
Ford-NY 31.5
Wynn-Cle 29.9
Score-Cle 28.8

Clutch Pitching Index
Pierce-Chi 119
Byrne-NY 119
F.Sullivan-Bos ... 116
Lary-Det 115
Schmitz-Was 115

Relief Runs
Consuegra-Chi 18.6
Mossi-Cle 13.9
Konstanty-NY 13.4
Kiely-Bos 11.6
Dorish-Chi-Bal ... 10.4

Adjusted Relief Runs
Consuegra-Chi 18.4
Kiely-Bos 14.9
Mossi-Cle 14.2
Konstanty-NY 11.6
Hurd-Bos 11.4

Relief Ranking
Kinder-Bos 21.1
Hurd-Bos 19.5
Consuegra-Chi 16.7
Konstanty-NY 16.7
Mossi-Cle 14.5

Total Pitcher Index
Pierce-Chi 4.7
F.Sullivan-Bos ... 3.8
Ford-NY 3.4
Wynn-Cle 3.0
Wight-Cle-Bal 2.4

Total Baseball Ranking
Mantle-NY 6.2
Kaline-Det 4.9
Williams-Bos 4.9
Pierce-Chi 4.7
Fox-Chi 3.9

TEAM	G	W	L	PCT	GB	R	OR	AB	H	2B	3B	HR	BB	SO	AVG	OBP	SLG	PRO	PRO+	BR	/A	PF	CHI	RC	SB	CS	SBA	SBR
BRO	154	93	61	.604		720	601	5098	1315	212	36	179	649	738	.258	.344	.419	.763	103	81	29	108	97	728	65	37	64	-3
MIL	155	92	62	.597	1	709	569	5207	1350	212	54	177	486	714	.259	.325	.423	.748	113	38	78	94	101	714	29	20	59	-3
CIN	155	91	63	.591	2	775	658	5291	1406	201	32	221	528	760	.266	.338	.441	.779	107	103	60	106	100	789	45	22	67	0
STL	156	76	78	.494	17	678	698	5378	1443	234	49	124	503	622	.268	.335	.399	.734	103	25	25	100	97	707	41	35	54	-9
PHI	154	71	83	.461	22	668	738	5204	1313	207	49	121	585	673	.252	.331	.381	.712	99	-12	1	98	103	658	45	23	66	0
NY	154	67	87	.435	26	540	650	5190	1268	192	45	145	402	659	.244	.301	.382	.683	89	-85	-81	99	97	586	67	34	66	0
PIT	157	66	88	.429	27	588	653	5221	1340	199	57	110	383	752	.257	.310	.380	.690	93	-70	-55	98	102	594	24	33	42	-13
CHI	157	60	94	.390	33	597	708	5260	1281	202	50	142	446	776	.244	.304	.382	.686	91	-79	-67	98	103	606	55	38	59	-6
TOT	621					5275		41849	10716	1659	372	1219	3982	5694	.256	.324	.401	.725							371	242	61	-34

TEAM	CG	SH	SV	IP	H	H/G	HR	BB	SO	RAT	ERA	ERA+	OAV	OOB	PR	/A	PF	CPI	FA	E	DP	FW	PW	BW	SBW	DIF
BRO	46	12	30	1368²	1251	8.2	171	441	772	11.3	3.57	111	.244	.307	31	60	105	97	.981	111	149	1.4	6.1	3.0	.1	5.3
MIL	64	12	27	1393¹	1295	8.4	133	467	639	11.5	3.11	111	.247	.311	102	54	92	107	.979	130	159	.3	5.5	8.0	.1	1.0
CIN	47	4	29	1389	1406	9.1	141	458	653	12.3	3.85	103	.265	.327	-12	20	106	101	.981	113	147	1.3	2.0	6.1	.4	4.0
STL	41	12	30	1388²	1339	8.7	155	546	709	12.3	3.97	95	.257	.329	-30	-28	100	98	.978	134	172	.1	-2.9	2.6	-.5	-.3
PHI	57	4	15	1377¹	1407	9.2	172	437	750	12.2	4.20	89	.266	.325	-66	-73	99	95	.975	144	140	-.6	-7.5	.1	.4	1.5
NY	31	9	28	1378	1287	8.4	144	551	765	12.2	3.78	100	.250	.326	-1	1	100	98	.976	144	143	-.6	.1	-8.3	.4	-1.7
PIT	37	8	24	1376¹	1406	9.2	142	469	662	12.4	3.74	101	.267	.329	5	5	100	105	.973	162	140	-1.5	.5	-5.6	-.9	-3.5
CHI	37	6	17	1392	1325	8.6	161	613	744	12.7	3.96	95	.252	.334	-29	-29	100	100	.976	144	141	-.4	-3.0	-6.9	-.2	-6.6
TOT	360	67	200	11063¹		8.7				12.1	3.77		.256	.324					.977	1082	1191					

Runs
Robinson-Cin 122
Snider-Bro 112
Aaron-Mil 106
Mathews-Mil 103
Gilliam-Bro 102

Hits
Aaron-Mil 200
Ashburn-Phi 190
Virdon-StL-Pit ... 185
Musial-StL 184
Boyer-StL 182

Doubles
Aaron-Mil 34
Snider-Bro 33
Musial-StL 33
Lopata-Phi 33
Bell-Cin 31

Triples
Bruton-Mil 15
Aaron-Mil 14
Walls-Pit 11
Moon-StL 11
Virdon-StL-Pit 10

Home Runs
Snider-Bro 43
Robinson-Cin 38
Adcock-Mil 38
Mathews-Mil 37

Total Bases
Aaron-Mil 340
Snider-Bro 324
Mays-NY 322
Robinson-Cin 319
Musial-StL 310

Runs Batted In
Musial-StL 109
Adcock-Mil 103
Kluszewski-Cin ... 102
Snider-Bro 101
Boyer-StL 98

Runs Produced
Aaron-Mil 172
Snider-Bro 170
Musial-StL 169
Robinson-Cin 167
Boyer-StL 163

Bases On Balls
Snider-Bro 99
Gilliam-Bro 95
Jones-Phi 92
Mathews-Mil 91
Moon-StL 80

Batting Average
Aaron-Mil .... .328
Virdon-StL-Pit ... .319
Clemente-Pit ..... .311
Musial-StL .... .310
Boyer-StL .... .306

On Base Percentage
Snider-Bro .... .402
Gilliam-Bro ...... .400
Musial-StL .... .390
Moon-StL .... .390
Jones-Phi .... .387

Slugging Average
Snider-Bro .... .598
Adcock-Mil .... .597
Aaron-Mil .... .558
Robinson-Cin ..... .558
Mays-NY .... .557

Production
Snider-Bro 1.000
Robinson-Cin ..... .939
Adcock-Mil .... .936
Mays-NY .... .928
Aaron-Mil .... .927

Adjusted Production
Adcock-Mil 154
Aaron-Mil 154
Snider-Bro 152
Mays-NY 146
Mathews-Mil 146

Batter Runs
Snider-Bro 50.5
Robinson-Cin 39.1
Aaron-Mil 36.3
Musial-StL 36.3
Mays-NY 35.9

Adjusted Batter Runs
Snider-Bro 44.7
Aaron-Mil 40.7
Mays-NY 36.4
Musial-StL 36.3
Robinson-Cin 34.3

Clutch Hitting Index
McMillan-Cin 151
Thomson-Mil 128
Jones-Phi 127
Musial-StL 125
Long-Pit 118

Runs Created
Snider-Bro 128
Robinson-Cin 121
Musial-StL 119
Mays-NY 118
Aaron-Mil 115

Total Average
Snider-Bro 1.052
Mays-NY .... .972
Robinson-Cin ..... .960
Mathews-Mil ...... .946
Adcock-Mil .... .916

Stolen Bases
Mays-NY 40
Gilliam-Bro 21
White-NY 15
Temple-Cin 14
Reese-Bro 13

Stolen Base Average
Mays-NY 80.0
Gilliam-Bro 70.0

Stolen Base Runs
Mays-NY 6.0
Ashburn-Phi 2.4
Temple-Cin 1.8
Post-Cin 1.8
Mathews-Mil 1.8

Fielding Runs
McMillan-Cin 29.9
Ashburn-Phi 25.3
Blasingame-StL ... 21.9
Gilliam-Bro 17.7
Baker-Chi 17.2

Total Player Rating
Mays-NY 4.7
Aaron-Mil 4.1
McMillan-Cin 3.7
Snider-Bro 3.6
Gilliam-Bro 3.5

Wins
Newcombe-Bro 27
Spahn-Mil 20
Antonelli-NY 20

Win Percentage
Newcombe-Bro .... .794
Buhl-Mil .... .692
Lawrence-Cin .... .655
Burdette-Mil .... .655
Spahn-Mil .... .645

Games
Face-Pit 68
Wilhelm-NY 64
Freeman-Cin 64
Labine-Bro 62
Lown-Chi 61

Complete Games
Roberts-Phi 22
Spahn-Mil 20
Friend-Pit 19
Newcombe-Bro 18
Burdette-Mil 16

Shutouts
Burdette-Mil 6
Newcombe-Bro 5
Antonelli-NY 5
Friend-Pit 4

Saves
Labine-Bro 19
Freeman-Cin 18
Lown-Chi 13
Jackson-StL 9
Bessent-Bro 9

Innings Pitched
Friend-Pit 314.1
Roberts-Phi 297.1
Spahn-Mil 281.1
Newcombe-Bro ... 268.0
Kline-Pit 264.0

Fewest Hits/Game
Maglie-Bro 7.26
Newcombe-Bro ... 7.35
Jones-Chi 7.39
Mizell-StL 7.42
Craig-Bro 7.64

Fewest BB/Game
Roberts-Phi 1.21
Newcombe-Bro ... 1.54
Spahn-Mil 1.66
Fowler-Cin 1.77
Burdette-Mil ... 1.83

Strikeouts
Jones-Chi 176
Haddix-StL-Phi ... 170
Friend-Pit 166
Roberts-Phi 157
Mizell-StL 153

Strikeouts/Game
Jones-Chi 8.40
Haddix-StL-Phi .. 6.64
Mizell-StL 6.60
Nuxhall-Cin 5.38
Worthington-NY .. 5.16

Ratio
Newcombe-Bro ... 9.00
Spahn-Mil 9.73
Maglie-Bro 9.94
Burdette-Mil ... 10.15
Rush-Chi 10.18

Earned Run Average
Burdette-Mil 2.70
Spahn-Mil 2.78
Antonelli-NY 2.86
Maglie-Bro 2.87
Newcombe-Bro ... 3.06

Adjusted ERA
Maglie-Bro 138
Antonelli-NY 132
Newcombe-Bro 130
Burdette-Mil 128
Spahn-Mil 124

Opponents' Batting Avg.
Newcombe-Bro ... .221
Jones-Chi .... .221
Mizell-StL ...... .222
Maglie-Bro ...... .222
Craig-Bro .... .231

Opponents' On Base Pct.
Newcombe-Bro ... .257
Spahn-Mil .... .276
Maglie-Bro ...... .281
Burdette-Mil .... .282
Rush-Chi .... .282

Starter Runs
Spahn-Mil 30.9
Burdette-Mil 30.4
Antonelli-NY 26.3
Newcombe-Bro ... 21.3
Maglie-Bro 19.0

Adjusted Starter Runs
Newcombe-Bro ... 27.1
Antonelli-NY 26.6
Maglie-Bro 23.2
Burdette-Mil 21.6
Spahn-Mil 21.2

Clutch Pitching Index
Conley-Mil 127
Klippstein-Cin ... 111
Kline-Pit 110
Poholsky-StL 108
Jeffcoat-Cin 105

Relief Runs
Grissom-NY 19.8
Acker-Cin 13.1
Bessent-Bro 11.2
R.Miller-Phi 7.3
Labine-Bro 5.5

Adjusted Relief Runs
Grissom-NY 19.9
Acker-Cin 15.0
Bessent-Bro 13.0
Labine-Bro 8.0
Freeman-Cin 7.0

Relief Ranking
Freeman-Cin 13.7
Bessent-Bro 13.6
Labine-Bro 12.9
Acker-Cin 11.7
Grissom-NY 8.3

Total Pitcher Index
Newcombe-Bro 3.9
Antonelli-NY 3.1
Spahn-Mil 2.8
Burdette-Mil 2.5
Dickson-Phi-StL . 2.2

Total Baseball Ranking
Mays-NY 4.7
Aaron-Mil 4.1
Newcombe-Bro ... 3.9
McMillan-Cin 3.7
Snider-Bro 3.6

TEAM	G	W	L	PCT	GB	R	OR	AB	H	2B	3B	HR	BB	SO	AVG	OBP	SLG	PRO	PRO+	BR	/A	PF	CHI	RC	SB	CS	SBA	SBR
NY	154	97	57	.630		857	631	5312	1433	193	55	190	615	755	.270	.349	.434	.783	116	80	104	97	106	814	51	37	58	-7
CLE	155	88	66	.571	9	712	581	5148	1256	199	23	153	681	764	.244	.337	.381	.718	93	-35	-51	102	105	681	40	32	56	-7
CHI	154	85	69	.552	12	776	634	5286	1412	218	43	128	619	660	.267	.352	.397	.749	102	30	20	101	102	756	70	33	68	1
BOS	155	84	70	.545	13	780	751	5349	1473	261	45	139	727	687	.275	.365	.419	.784	101	100	10	112	93	826	28	19	60	-3
DET	155	82	72	.532	15	789	699	5364	1494	209	50	150	644	618	.279	.359	.420	.779	111	84	83	100	97	816	43	26	62	-3
BAL	154	69	85	.448	28	571	705	5090	1242	198	34	91	563	725	.244	.322	.350	.672	90	-123	-70	92	101	572	39	42	48	-14
WAS	155	59	95	.383	38	652	924	5202	1302	198	62	112	690	877	.250	.343	.377	.720	96	-27	-26	100	94	681	37	34	52	-9
KC	154	52	102	.338	45	619	831	5256	1325	204	41	112	480	727	.252	.317	.370	.687	86	-108	-110	100	105	610	40	30	57	-6
TOT	618					5756		42007	10937	1680	353	1075	5019	5813	.260	.343	.394	.737							348	253	58	-47

TEAM	CG	SH	SV	IP	H	H/G	HR	BB	SO	RAT	ERA	ERA+	OAV	OOB	PR	/A	PF	CPI	FA	E	DP	FW	PW	BW	SBW	DIF
NY	50	10	35	1382	1285	8.4	114	652	732	12.9	3.63	107	.249	.337	82	37	93	105	.977	136	214	.6	3.6	10.2	-.1	5.7
CLE	67	17	24	1384	1233	8.0	116	564	845	11.9	3.32	127	.238	.316	129	136	101	100	.978	129	130	1.0	13.3	-5.0	-.1	1.8
CHI	65	11	13	1389	1351	8.8	118	524	722	12.3	3.73	110	.255	.325	67	58	99	99	.979	122	160	1.3	5.7	2.0	.7	-1.6
BOS	50	8	20	1398	1354	8.7	130	668	712	13.3	4.17	111	.254	.342	-1	71	111	96	.972	169	168	-1.2	7.0	1.0	.3	-.0
DET	62	10	15	1379	1389	9.1	140	655	788	13.6	4.06	101	.264	.351	15	9	99	108	.976	140	151	.4	.9	8.1	.3	-4.7
BAL	38	10	24	1360²	1362	9.0	99	547	715	12.8	4.20	93	.263	.337	-6	-42	94	93	.977	137	142	.5	-4.1	-6.9	-.8	3.2
WAS	36	1	18	1368²	1539	10.1	171	730	663	15.1	5.33	81	.287	.376	-179	-153	104	99	.972	171	173	-1.3	-15.0	-2.5	-.3	1.1
KC	30	3	18	1370¹	1424	9.4	187	679	636	14.1	4.86	89	.271	.359	-107	-81	104	101	.973	166	187	-1.1	-7.9	-10.8	.0	-5.2
TOT	398	70	167	11031²		8.9				13.2	4.16		.260	.343					.975	1170	1325					

Runs		Hits		Doubles		Triples		Home Runs		Total Bases	
Mantle-NY	132	Kuenn-Det	196	Piersall-Bos	40	Simpson-KC	11	Mantle-NY	52	Mantle-NY	376
Fox-Chi	109	Kaline-Det	194	Kuenn-Det	32	Minoso-Chi	11	Wertz-Cle	32	Kaline-Det	327
Minoso-Chi	106	Fox-Chi	192	Kaline-Det	32	Lemon-Was	11	Berra-NY	30	Jensen-Bos	287
		Mantle-NY	188			Jensen-Bos	11	Sievers-Was	29	Minoso-Chi	286
		Jensen-Bos	182					Maxwell-Det	28		

Runs Batted In		Runs Produced		Bases On Balls		Batting Average		On Base Percentage		Slugging Average	
Mantle-NY	130	Mantle-NY	210	Yost-Was	151	Mantle-NY	.353	Williams-Bos	.479	Mantle-NY	.705
Kaline-Det	128	Kaline-Det	197	Mantle-NY	112	Williams-Bos	.345	Mantle-NY	.467	Williams-Bos	.605
Wertz-Cle	106	Minoso-Chi	173	Williams-Bos	102	Kuenn-Det	.332	Nieman-Chi-Bal	.438	Maxwell-Det	.534
Simpson-KC	105	Kuenn-Det	172	Doby-Chi	102	Maxwell-Det	.326	Minoso-Chi	.430	Berra-NY	.534
Berra-NY	105	Berra-NY	168	Sievers-Was	100	Nieman-Chi-Bal	.320	Maxwell-Det	.420	Kaline-Det	.530

Production		Adjusted Production		Batter Runs		Adjusted Batter Runs		Clutch Hitting Index		Runs Created	
Mantle-NY	1.172	Mantle-NY	213	Mantle-NY	83.3	Mantle-NY	85.8	Doby-Chi	131	Mantle-NY	188
Williams-Bos	1.084	Williams-Bos	164	Williams-Bos	54.1	Williams-Bos	46.7	Simpson-KC	126	Minoso-Chi	130
Minoso-Chi	.954	Nieman-Chi-Bal	156	Minoso-Chi	43.2	Minoso-Chi	42.1	Triandos-Bal	123	Kaline-Det	129
Maxwell-Det	.954	Maxwell-Det	150	Maxwell-Det	37.5	Maxwell-Det	37.4	Lollar-Chi	122	Williams-Bos	121
Nieman-Chi-Bal	.934	Minoso-Chi	149	Kaline-Det	33.4	Nieman-Chi-Bal	36.5	Wertz-Cle	118	Maxwell-Det	118

Total Average		Stolen Bases		Stolen Base Average		Stolen Base Runs		Fielding Runs		Total Player Rating	
Mantle-NY	1.426	Aparicio-Chi	21	Aparicio-Chi	84.0	Aparicio-Chi	3.9	Piersall-Bos	17.6	Mantle-NY	8.4
Williams-Bos	1.255	Rivera-Chi	20	Avila-Cle	81.0	Avila-Cle	2.7	Kaline-Det	17.3	Kaline-Det	4.2
Minoso-Chi	1.031	Avila-Cle	17	Rivera-Chi	69.0	Mantle-NY	2.4	Hegan-Cle	15.6	Maxwell-Det	4.2
Maxwell-Det	1.015	Minoso-Chi	12					Buddin-Bos	13.9	Berra-NY	4.1
Nieman-Chi-Bal	.955							Maxwell-Det	13.1	Minoso-Chi	3.7

Wins		Win Percentage		Games		Complete Games		Shutouts		Saves	
Lary-Det	21	Ford-NY	.760	Zuverink-Bal	62	Pierce-Chi	21	Score-Cle	5	Zuverink-Bal	16
		Wynn-Cle	.690	Crimian-KC	54	Lemon-Cle	21			Mossi-Cle	11
		Score-Cle	.690	Gorman-KC	52	Lary-Det	20			Morgan-NY	11
		Pierce-Chi	.690	Mossi-Cle	48					Shantz-KC	9
		Brewer-Bos	.679	Delock-Bos	48					Delock-Bos	9

Innings Pitched		Fewest Hits/Game		Fewest BB/Game		Strikeouts		Strikeouts/Game		Ratio	
Lary-Det	294.0	Score-Cle	5.85	Stobbs-Was	2.03	Score-Cle	263	Score-Cle	9.49	Score-Cle	10.58
Wynn-Cle	277.2	Larsen-NY	6.66	Donovan-Chi	2.26	Pierce-Chi	192	Pascual-Was	7.73	Donovan-Chi	10.62
Pierce-Chi	276.1	Harshman-Chi	7.27	Kucks-NY	2.89	Foytack-Det	184	Foytack-Det	6.47	Wynn-Cle	10.66
Foytack-Det	256.0	Brewer-Bos	7.37	Wynn-Cle	2.95	Hoeft-Det	172	Pierce-Chi	6.25	Sturdivant-NY	10.80
Lemon-Cle	255.1	Foytack-Det	7.42	Sturdivant-NY	2.96	Lary-Det	165	Sturdivant-NY	6.25	Ford-NY	10.97

Earned Run Average		Adjusted ERA		Opponents' Batting Avg.		Opponents' On Base Pct.		Starter Runs		Adjusted Starter Runs	
Ford-NY	2.47	Score-Cle	166	Score-Cle	.186	Sturdivant-NY	.291	Score-Cle	45.2	Score-Cle	46.5
Score-Cle	2.53	Ford-NY	156	Larsen-NY	.204	Donovan-Chi	.292	Wynn-Cle	44.3	Wynn-Cle	45.7
Wynn-Cle	2.72	Wynn-Cle	154	Brewer-Bos	.220	Score-Cle	.292	Ford-NY	42.3	Ford-NY	35.0
Lemon-Cle	3.03	Lemon-Cle	139	Harshman-Chi	.221	Wynn-Cle	.294	Lary-Det	32.9	Lemon-Cle	33.3
Harshman-Chi	3.10	Sullivan-Bos	135	Sturdivant-NY	.224	Ford-NY	.303	Lemon-Cle	32.0	Sullivan-Bos	32.2

Clutch Pitching Index		Relief Runs		Adjusted Relief Runs		Relief Ranking		Total Pitcher Index		Total Baseball Ranking	
Lary-Det	117	Narleski-Cle	17.4	Narleski-Cle	17.7	Narleski-Cle	16.1	Wynn-Cle	5.3	Mantle-NY	8.4
Sullivan-Bos	116	Grim-NY	11.5	Grim-NY	9.1	Byerly-Was	9.6	Score-Cle	4.6	Wynn-Cle	5.3
Hoeft-Det	116	Byrne-NY	9.7	Byerly-Was	7.9	Delock-Bos	9.2	Ford-NY	4.5	Score-Cle	4.6
Ford-NY	114	Byerly-Was	6.9	Byrne-NY	6.1	Grim-NY	9.0	Lemon-Cle	4.4	Ford-NY	4.5
Stobbs-Was	114	Mossi-Cle	5.5	Mossi-Cle	6.0	Mossi-Cle	8.4	Brewer-Bos	4.1	Lemon-Cle	4.4

TEAM	G	W	L	PCT	GB	R	OR	AB	H	2B	3B	HR	BB	SO	AVG	OBP	SLG	PRO	PRO+	BR	/A	PF	CHI	RC	SB	CS	SBA	SBR
MIL	155	95	59	.617		772	613	5458	1469	221	62	199	461	729	.269	.329	.442	.771	121	82	131	93	101	787	35	16	69	1
STL	154	87	67	.565	8	737	666	5472	1497	235	43	132	493	672	.274	.336	.405	.741	103	36	22	102	102	731	58	44	57	-9
BRO	154	84	70	.545	11	690	591	5242	1325	188	38	147	550	848	.253	.328	.387	.715	89	-11	-76	110	104	664	60	34	64	-2
CIN	154	80	74	.519	15	747	781	5389	1452	251	33	187	546	752	.269	.341	.432	.773	106	97	49	107	95	794	51	36	59	-6
PHI	156	77	77	.500	18	623	646	5241	1311	213	44	117	534	758	.250	.325	.375	.700	97	-39	-18	97	99	635	57	26	69	2
NY	154	69	85	.448	26	643	701	5346	1349	171	54	157	447	669	.252	.313	.393	.706	95	-42	-40	100	103	646	64	38	63	-4
PIT	155	62	92	.403	33	586	696	5402	1447	231	60	92	374	733	.268	.318	.384	.702	97	-46	-26	97	93	649	46	35	57	-7
CHI	156	62	92	.403	33	628	722	5369	1312	223	31	147	461	989	.244	.307	.380	.687	91	-78	-67	98	105	623	28	25	53	-7
TOT	619					5426		42919	11162	1733	365	1178	3866	6150	.260	.325	.400	.724							399	254	61	-33

TEAM	CG	SH	SV	IP	H	H/G	HR	BB	SO	RAT	ERA	ERA+	OAV	OOB	PR	/A	PF	CPI	FA	E	DP	FW	PW	BW	SBW	DIF
MIL	60	9	24	1411	1347	8.6	124	570	693	12.3	3.47	101	.253	.327	64	4	90	107	.981	120	173	1.0	.4	13.3	.5	2.7
STL	46	11	29	1413[1]	1385	8.8	140	506	778	12.2	3.78	105	.257	.324	16	29	102	100	.979	131	168	.4	2.9	2.2	-.5	5.0
BRO	44	18	29	1399	1285	8.3	144	456	891	11.4	3.35	124	.244	.307	82	127	107	101	.979	127	136	.6	12.9	-7.7	.2	1.0
CIN	40	5	29	1395[2]	1486	9.6	179	429	707	12.7	4.62	89	.275	.334	-116	-79	106	95	.982	107	139	1.7	-8.0	5.0	-.2	4.6
PHI	54	9	23	1401[2]	1363	8.8	139	412	858	11.5	3.79	100	.254	.310	13	1	98	92	.976	136	117	.2	.1	-1.8	.6	.9
NY	35	9	20	1398[2]	1436	9.2	150	471	701	12.5	4.01	98	.267	.330	-20	-12	101	101	.974	161	180	-1.3	-1.2	-4.1	.0	-1.4
PIT	47	9	15	1395	1463	9.4	158	421	663	12.3	3.88	98	.270	.325	0	-14	98	105	.972	170	143	-1.7	-1.4	-2.6	-.3	-8.9
CHI	30	5	26	1403[1]	1397	9.0	144	601	859	13.0	4.13	94	.261	.339	-39	-40	100	100	.975	149	140	-.5	-4.1	-6.8	-.3	-3.3
TOT	356	75	195	11217[2]		9.0				12.2	3.88		.260	.325					.977	1101	1196					

Runs
Aaron-Mil 118
Banks-Chi 113
Mays-NY 112
Mathews-Mil 109
Blasingame-StL 108

Hits
Schoendienst-NY-Mil 200
Aaron-Mil 198
Robinson-Cin 197
Mays-NY 195
Ashburn-Phi 186

Doubles
Hoak-Cin 39
Musial-StL 38
Bouchee-Phi 35
Banks-Chi 34
Moryn-Chi 33

Triples
Mays-NY 20
Virdon-Pit 11
Mathews-Mil 9
Bruton-Mil 9

Home Runs
Aaron-Mil 44
Banks-Chi 43
Snider-Bro 40
Mays-NY 35
Mathews-Mil 32

Total Bases
Aaron-Mil 369
Mays-NY 366
Banks-Chi 344
Robinson-Cin 323
Mathews-Mil 309

Runs Batted In
Aaron-Mil 132
Ennis-StL 105
Musial-StL 102
Banks-Chi 102
Hodges-Bro 98

Runs Produced
Aaron-Mil 206
Mays-NY 174
Banks-Chi 172
Mathews-Mil 171
Hodges-Bro 165

Bases On Balls
Temple-Cin 94
Ashburn-Phi 94
Mathews-Mil 90
Bouchee-Phi 84
Snider-Bro 77

Batting Average
Musial-StL 351
Mays-NY 333
Robinson-Cin 322
Aaron-Mil 322
Groat-Pit 315

On Base Percentage
Musial-StL 428
Mays-NY 411
Bouchee-Phi 396
Ashburn-Phi 392
Temple-Cin 391

Slugging Average
Mays-NY 626
Musial-StL 612
Aaron-Mil 600
Snider-Bro 587
Banks-Chi 579

Production
Musial-StL . . . 1.040
Mays-NY 1.037
Aaron-Mil 979
Snider-Bro 957
Banks-Chi 942

Adjusted Production
Mays-NY 174
Musial-StL 172
Aaron-Mil 170
Mathews-Mil 157
Banks-Chi 150

Batter Runs
Mays-NY 60.5
Musial-StL 54.1
Aaron-Mil 48.3
Banks-Chi 38.6
Mathews-Mil 38.3

Adjusted Batter Runs
Mays-NY 60.8
Aaron-Mil 53.8
Musial-StL 52.8
Mathews-Mil 43.7
Banks-Chi 39.9

Clutch Hitting Index
Ennis-StL 141
McMillan-Cin 140
Hamner-Phi 134
Moryn-Chi 124
Hoak-Cin 121

Runs Created
Mays-NY 145
Aaron-Mil 136
Musial-StL 129
Mathews-Mil 126
Banks-Chi 123

Total Average
Musial-StL 1.103
Mays-NY 1.092
Aaron-Mil 988
Mathews-Mil 973
Snider-Bro 962

Stolen Bases
Mays-NY 38
Gilliam-Bro 26
Blasingame-StL . . 21
Temple-Cin 19
Fernandez-Phi . . . 18

Stolen Base Average
Temple-Cin 79.2
Fernandez-Phi . . . 78.3
Gilliam-Bro 72.2
Blasingame-StL . . 70.0
Mays-NY 66.7

Stolen Base Runs
Temple-Cin 2.7
Fernandez-Phi . . . 2.4
Robinson-Cin 1.8
Gilliam-Bro 1.8

Fielding Runs
Ashburn-Phi 32.4
Blasingame-StL . . 25.8
Logan-Mil 23.9
Robinson-Cin . . . 18.7
Campanella-Bro . . 16.0

Total Player Rating
Mays-NY 6.3
Aaron-Mil 4.7
Musial-StL 4.6
Mathews-Mil 4.5
Robinson-Cin 4.1

Wins
Spahn-Mil 21
Sanford-Phi 19
Buhl-Mil 18
Drysdale-Bro 17
Burdette-Mil 17

Win Percentage
Buhl-Mil 720
Sanford-Phi 704
Spahn-Mil 656
Drysdale-Bro 654
Burdette-Mil 654

Games
Lown-Chi 67
Face-Pit 59
Labine-Bro 58
Worthington-NY . . 55
Grissom-NY 55

Complete Games
Spahn-Mil 18
Friend-Pit 17
Gomez-NY 16
Sanford-Phi 15

Shutouts
Podres-Bro 6
Spahn-Mil 4
Newcombe-Bro . . . 4
Drysdale-Bro 4

Saves
Labine-Bro 17
Grissom-NY 14
Lown-Chi 12
Wilhelm-StL 11

Innings Pitched
Friend-Pit 277.0
Spahn-Mil 271.0
Burdette-Mil 256.2
Lawrence-Cin . . . 250.1
Roberts-Phi 249.2

Fewest Hits/Game
Sanford-Phi 7.38
Podres-Bro 7.71
Drott-Chi 7.86
Buhl-Mil 7.93
Worthington-NY . . 7.99

Fewest BB/Game
Newcombe-Bro . . . 1.49
Roberts-Phi 1.55
Law-Pit 1.67
Purkey-Pit 1.90
Jeffcoat-Cin 2.00

Strikeouts
Sanford-Phi 188
Drott-Chi 170
Drabowsky-Chi . . . 170
Jones-StL 154
Drysdale-Bro 148

Strikeouts/Game
Jones-StL 7.59
Haddix-Phi 7.17
Sanford-Phi 7.15
Drott-Chi 6.68
Drabowsky-Chi . . . 6.38

Ratio
Podres-Bro 9.78
Roberts-Phi 10.45
Newcombe-Bro . . 10.56
Spahn-Mil 10.66
Law-Pit 10.74

Earned Run Average
Podres-Bro 2.66
Drysdale-Bro 2.69
Spahn-Mil 2.69
Buhl-Mil 2.74
Law-Pit 2.87

Adjusted ERA
Podres-Bro 156
Drysdale-Bro 155
Law-Pit 132
Spahn-Mil 130
Buhl-Mil 128

Opponents' Batting Avg.
Sanford-Phi 221
Podres-Bro 230
Drott-Chi 234
Drysdale-Bro 236
Spahn-Mil 237

Opponents' On Base Pct.
Podres-Bro 274
Roberts-Phi 284
Newcombe-Bro 290
Law-Pit 291
Spahn-Mil 293

Starter Runs
Spahn-Mil 35.8
Drysdale-Bro 29.2
Buhl-Mil 27.4
Podres-Bro 26.5
Sanford-Phi 21.0

Adjusted Starter Runs
Drysdale-Bro 36.3
Podres-Bro 32.7
Spahn-Mil 24.3
Sanford-Phi 19.0
Buhl-Mil 18.2

Clutch Pitching Index
Buhl-Mil 135
Barclay-NY 117
Law-Pit 113
Spahn-Mil 109
Antonelli-NY 108

Relief Runs
Farrell-Phi 13.9
Roebuck-Bro 12.5
Grissom-NY 11.6
Face-Pit 8.4
Miller-Phi 8.0

Adjusted Relief Runs
Roebuck-Bro 15.6
Farrell-Phi 13.2
Grissom-NY 12.1
Labine-Bro 8.4
Miller-Phi 7.5

Relief Ranking
Farrell-Phi 20.7
Roebuck-Bro 17.5
Grissom-NY 15.2
Labine-Bro 11.8
Miller-Phi 9.5

Total Pitcher Index
Drysdale-Bro 4.5
Podres-Bro 3.6
Spahn-Mil 2.7
Newcombe-Bro . . . 2.2
Roebuck-Bro 2.2

Total Baseball Ranking
Mays-NY 6.3
Aaron-Mil 4.7
Musial-StL 4.6
Drysdale-Bro 4.5
Mathews-Mil 4.5

TEAM	G	W	L	PCT	GB	R	OR	AB	H	2B	3B	HR	BB	SO	AVG	OBP	SLG	PRO	PRO+	BR	/A	PF	CHI	RC	SB	CS	SBA	SBR
NY	154	98	56	.636		723	534	5271	1412	200	54	145	562	709	.268	.341	.409	.750	113	76	87	98	99	729	49	38	56	-8
CHI	155	90	64	.584	8	707	566	5265	1369	208	41	106	633	745	.260	.347	.375	.722	103	40	37	101	100	708	109	51	68	2
BOS	154	82	72	.532	16	721	668	5267	1380	231	32	153	624	739	.262	.343	.405	.748		76	38	106	98	725	29	21	58	-4
DET	154	78	76	.506	20	614	614	5348	1376	224	37	116	504	643	.257	.324	.378	.702	96	-18	-35	103	96	644	36	47	43	-17
BAL	154	76	76	.500	21	597	588	5264	1326	191	39	87	504	699	.252	.321	.353	.674	96	-66	-25	94	101	600	57	35	62	-4
CLE	153	76	77	.497	21.5	682	722	5171	1304	199	26	140	591	786	.252	.332	.382	.714	102	10	16	99	103	661	40	47	46	-16
KC	154	59	94	.386	38.5	563	710	5170	1262	195	40	166	364	760	.244	.297	.353	.691	92	-60	-71	102	100	578	35	27	56	-6
WAS	154	55	99	.357	43	603	808	5231	1274	215	38	111	527	733	.244	.318	.363	.681	93	-56	-48	99	102	592	13	38	25	-19
TOT	616					5210		41987	10703	1663	307	1024	4309	5814	.255	.328	.382	.710							368	304	55	-72

TEAM	CG	SH	SV	IP	H	H/G	HR	BB	SO	RAT	ERA	ERA+	OAV	OOB	PR	/A	PF	CPI	FA	E	DP	FW	PW	BW	SBW	DIF
NY	41	13	42	1395[1]	1198	7.7	110	580	810	11.7	3.00	120	.234	.317	122	91	95	109	.980	123	183	.2	9.4	9.0	.1	2.3
CHI	59	16	27	1401[2]	1305	8.4	124	470	665	11.6	3.35	112	.248	.313	69	61	99	102	.982	107	169	1.1	6.3	3.8	1.1	.6
BOS	55	9	23	1376[2]	1391	9.1	116	498	692	12.6	3.88	103	.264	.331	-14	17	105	100	.976	149	179	-1.2	1.8	3.9	.5	-.0
DET	52	9	21	1417[2]	1330	8.4	147	505	756	11.9	3.56	108	.250	.320	37	47	102	104	.980	121	151	.3	4.9	-3.6	-.8	.3
BAL	44	13	25	1408	1272	8.1	95	493	767	11.5	3.46	104	.243	.312	51	20	95	92	.981	112	159	.8	2.1	-2.6	.5	-.8
CLE	46	7	23	1380[2]	1381	9.0	130	618	807	13.3	4.06	92	.261	.343	-42	-53	98	101	.974	153	154	-1.4	-5.5	1.7	-.7	5.5
KC	26	6	19	1369[2]	1344	8.8	153	565	626	12.7	4.19	94	.260	.336	-61	-35	104	99	.979	125	162	.1	-3.6	-7.3	.3	-7.0
WAS	31	5	16	1377	1482	9.7	149	580	691	13.7	4.85	80	.278	.353	-162	-146	103	95	.979	128	159	-.0	-15.1	-5.0	-1.0	-.9
TOT	354	78	196	11126[2]		8.7				12.4	3.79		.255	.328					.979	1018	1316					

Runs
Mantle-NY 121
Fox-Chi 110
Piersall-Bos 103
Sievers-Was 99

Hits
Fox-Chi 196
Malzone-Bos 185
Minoso-Chi 176
Mantle-NY 173
Kuenn-Det 173

Doubles
Minoso-Chi 36
Gardner-Bal 36
Malzone-Bos 31
Kuenn-Det 30

Triples
Simpson-KC-NY 9
McDougald-NY 9
Bauer-NY 9
Fox-Chi........... 8
Boyd-Bal 8

Home Runs
Sievers-Was 42
Williams-Bos 38
Mantle-NY 34
Wertz-Cle 28
Zernial-KC 27

Total Bases
Sievers-Was 331
Mantle-NY 315
Williams-Bos 307
Kaline-Det 276
Malzone-Bos 271

Runs Batted In
Sievers-Was 114
Wertz-Cle 105
Minoso-Chi 103
Malzone-Bos 103
Jensen-Bos 103

Runs Produced
Minoso-Chi 187
Mantle-NY 181
Sievers-Was 171
Malzone-Bos 170
Fox-Chi.......... 165

Bases On Balls
Mantle-NY 146
Williams-Bos 119
Smith-Cle 79
Minoso-Chi 79
Wertz-Cle 78

Batting Average
Williams-Bos 388
Mantle-NY 365
Woodling-Cle 321
Boyd-Bal 318
Fox-Chi...........317

On Base Percentage
Williams-Bos 528
Mantle-NY 515
Minoso-Chi 413
Woodling-Cle 412
Fox-Chi.........404

Slugging Average
Williams-Bos 731
Mantle-NY 665
Sievers-Was 579
Woodling-Cle 521
Wertz-Cle 485

Production
Williams-Bos 1.259
Mantle-NY 1.179
Sievers-Was 968
Woodling-Cle 933
Minoso-Chi 867

Adjusted Production
Williams-Bos 227
Mantle-NY 223
Sievers-Was 163
Woodling-Cle 155
Minoso-Chi 136

Batter Runs
Williams-Bos 89.9
Mantle-NY 88.9
Sievers-Was 47.3
Woodling-Cle 33.0
Minoso-Chi 32.7

Adjusted Batter Runs
Mantle-NY 90.0
Williams-Bos 86.4
Sievers-Was 48.1
Woodling-Cle 33.6
Minoso-Chi 32.3

Clutch Hitting Index
Minoso-Chi 147
Malzone-Bos 136
Doby-Chi 135
Skowron-NY 133
Jensen-Bos 133

Runs Created
Mantle-NY 178
Williams-Bos 167
Sievers-Was 131
Fox-Chi.......... 109
Minoso-Chi 106

Total Average
Williams-Bos 1.599
Mantle-NY ... 1.534
Sievers-Was 1.010
Woodling-Cle 944
Maxwell-Det.......876

Stolen Bases
Aparicio-Chi 28
Rivera-Chi 18
Minoso-Chi 18
Mantle-NY 16

Stolen Base Average
Rivera-Chi 90.0
Mantle-NY 84.2
Aparicio-Chi 77.8
Minoso-Chi 54.5

Stolen Base Runs
Rivera-Chi 4.2
Aparicio-Chi 3.6
Mantle-NY 3.0
Landis-Chi 1.8
Martin-NY-KC 1.5

Fielding Runs
Bridges-Was 29.3
Fox-Chi 20.9
Berra-NY 15.6
Phillips-Chi 15.5
McDougald-NY ... 15.1

Total Player Rating
Mantle-NY 8.5
Williams-Bos 7.5
Fox-Chi........... 5.6
Sievers-Was 4.3
McDougald-NY 4.2

Wins
Pierce-Chi 20
Bunning-Det 20
Sturdivant-NY 16
Donovan-Chi 16
Brewer-Bos 16

Win Percentage
Sturdivant-NY 727
Donovan-Chi 727
Bunning-Det 714
Wilson-Chi 652
Pierce-Chi 625

Games
Zuverink-Bal 56
Hyde-Was 52
Clevenger-Was 52
Delock-Bos 49
Trucks-KC 48

Complete Games
Pierce-Chi 16
Donovan-Chi 16
Brewer-Bos 15

Shutouts
Wilson-Chi 5
Turley-NY 4
Pierce-Chi 4

Saves
Grim-NY 19
Narleski-Cle 16
Delock-Bos 11
Zuverink-Bal 9
Clevenger-Was 8

Innings Pitched
Bunning-Det 267.1
Wynn-Cle 263.0
Pierce-Chi 257.0
Johnson-Bal ... 242.0
F.Sullivan-Bos ... 240.2

Fewest Hits/Game
Turley-NY 6.12
Bunning-Det 7.20
Foytack-Det 7.43
Sturdivant-NY 7.59
F.Sullivan-Bos ... 7.70

Fewest BB/Game
F.Sullivan-Bos 1.80
Donovan-Chi 1.84
Shantz-NY 2.08
Loes-Bal......... 2.14
Bunning-Det 2.42

Strikeouts
Wynn-Cle 184
Bunning-Det 182
Johnson-Bal 177
Pierce-Chi 171
Turley-NY 152

Strikeouts/Game
Turley-NY 7.76
Johnson-Bal 6.58
Wynn-Cle 6.30
Bunning-Det 6.13
Pierce-Chi 5.99

Ratio
F.Sullivan-Bos 9.76
Bunning-Det 10.00
Donovan-Chi 10.44
Johnson-Bal 10.45
Pierce-Chi 10.51

Earned Run Average
Shantz-NY 2.45
Sturdivant-NY 2.54
Bunning-Det 2.69
Turley-NY 2.71
F.Sullivan-Bos 2.73

Adjusted ERA
Shantz-NY 147
F.Sullivan-Bos 146
Bunning-Det 143
Sturdivant-NY 141
Donovan-Chi 135

Opponents' Batting Avg.
Turley-NY 194
Bunning-Det 218
Foytack-Det 226
F.Sullivan-Bos 230
Sturdivant-NY 232

Opponents' On Base Pct.
F.Sullivan-Bos 275
Bunning-Det 279
Pierce-Chi 287
Johnson-Bal 289
Donovan-Chi 293

Starter Runs
Bunning-Det 32.5
F.Sullivan-Bos ... 28.3
Sturdivant-NY 27.9
Shantz-NY 25.8
Donovan-Chi 24.9

Adjusted Starter Runs
Bunning-Det 34.5
F.Sullivan-Bos ... 33.6
Donovan-Chi 23.6
Sturdivant-NY ... 23.4
Shantz-NY 22.0

Clutch Pitching Index
Shantz-NY 131
Sturdivant-NY 121
Narleski-Cle 112
Kemmerer-Bos-Was 110
Donovan-Chi 108

Relief Runs
Staley-Chi 20.2
Zuverink-Bal 16.4
Trucks-KC 9.8
Grim-NY 9.3
Lehman-Bal 7.6

Adjusted Relief Runs
Staley-Chi 19.6
Zuverink-Bal 14.0
Trucks-KC 12.0
Byerly-Was 8.1
Grim-NY 7.7

Relief Ranking
Grim-NY 23.8
Zuverink-Bal 20.3
Trucks-KC 16.5
Staley-Chi 13.0
Byerly-Was 10.4

Total Pitcher Index
F.Sullivan-Bos 3.7
Bunning-Det 3.5
Shantz-NY 3.3
Donovan-Chi 2.8
Sturdivant-NY 2.4

Total Baseball Ranking
Mantle-NY 8.5
Williams-Bos 7.5
Fox-Chi........... 5.6
Sievers-Was 4.3
McDougald-NY 4.2

TEAM	G	W	L	PCT	GB	R	OR	AB	H	2B	3B	HR	BB	SO	AVG	OBP	SLG	PRO	PRO+	BR	/A	PF	CHI	RC	SB	CS	SBA	SBR
MIL	154	92	62	.597		675	541	5225	1388	221	21	167	478	646	.266	.331	.412	.743	111	14	71	92	98	705	26	8	76	3
PIT	154	84	70	.545	8	662	607	5247	1386	229	68	134	396	753	.264	.319	.410	.729	101	-21	-3	97	103	669	30	15	67	0
SF	154	80	74	.519	12	727	698	5318	1399	250	42	170	531	817	.263	.334	.422	.756	107	37	53	98	100	747	64	29	69	2
CIN	154	76	78	.494	16	695	621	5273	1359	242	40	123	572	765	.258	.333	.389	.722	92	-19	-55	105	104	690	61	38	62	-5
STL	154	72	82	.468	20	619	704	5255	1371	216	39	111	533	637	.261	.331	.380	.711	90	-38	-64	104	97	638	44	43	51	-13
CHI	154	72	82	.468	20	709	725	5289	1402	207	49	182	487	853	.265	.332	.426	.758	108	39	50	98	99	737	39	23	63	-2
LA	154	71	83	.461	21	668	761	5173	1297	166	50	172	495	850	.251	.319	.402	.721	93	-32	-53	103	106	650	73	47	61	-6
PHI	154	69	85	.448	23	664	762	5363	1424	238	56	124	573	871	.266	.341	.400	.741	103	20	30	99	93	729	51	33	61	-5
TOT	616					5419		42143	11026	1769	365	1183	4065	6192	.262	.330	.405	.735							388	236	62	-25

TEAM	CG	SH	SV	IP	H	H/G	HR	BB	SO	RAT	ERA	ERA+	OAV	OOB	PR	/A	PF	CPI	FA	E	DP	FW	PW	BW	SBW	DIF
MIL	72	16	17	1376	1261	8.2	125	426	773	11.2	3.21	110	.244	.305	113	47	89	99	.980	120	152	.8	4.7	7.2	.6	1.7
PIT	43	10	41	1367	1344	8.8	123	470	679	12.1	3.56	109	.261	.325	59	46	98	105	.978	133	173	.1	4.6	-.3	.3	2.2
SF	38	7	25	1389[1]	1400	9.1	166	512	775	12.6	3.98	96	.263	.332	-4	-25	97	103	.975	152	156	-.9	-2.5	5.3	.5	.6
CIN	50	7	20	1385[1]	1422	9.2	148	419	705	12.1	3.73	111	.267	.324	34	64	105	105	.983	100	148	1.9	6.5	-5.5	-.2	-3.6
STL	45	6	25	1381[2]	1398	9.1	158	567	822	13.1	4.12	100	.264	.340	-25	2	105	102	.974	153	163	-.9	.2	-6.5	-1.0	3.2
CHI	27	5	24	1361	1322	8.7	142	619	805	13.1	4.22	93	.254	.338	-40	-46	99	94	.975	150	161	-.8	-4.6	5.0	.1	-4.7
LA	30	7	31	1368[1]	1399	9.2	173	606	855	13.4	4.47	92	.267	.347	-79	-57	104	100	.975	146	198	-.6	-5.7	-5.3	-.3	6.0
PHI	51	6	15	1397	1480	9.5	148	446	778	12.5	4.32	92	.272	.329	-58	-56	100	93	.978	129	136	.3	-5.6	3.0	-.2	-5.5
TOT	356	64	198	11025[2]		9.0				12.5	3.95		.262	.330					.977	1083	1287					

Runs		Hits		Doubles		Triples		Home Runs		Total Bases	
Mays-SF	121	Ashburn-Phi	215	Cepeda-SF	38	Ashburn-Phi	13	Banks-Chi	47	Banks-Chi	379
Banks-Chi	119	Mays-SF	208	Groat-Pit	36	Virdon-Pit	11	Thomas-Pit	35	Mays-SF	350
Aaron-Mil	109	Aaron-Mil	196	Musial-StL	35	Mays-SF	11	Robinson-Cin	31	Aaron-Mil	328
Boyer-StL	101	Banks-Chi	193	H.Anderson-Phi	34	Banks-Chi	11	Mathews-Mil	31	Cepeda-SF	309
Ashburn-Phi	98	Cepeda-SF	188	Aaron-Mil	34			Aaron-Mil	30	Thomas-Pit	297

Runs Batted In		Runs Produced		Bases On Balls		Batting Average		On Base Percentage		Slugging Average	
Banks-Chi	129	Banks-Chi	201	Ashburn-Phi	97	Ashburn-Phi	.350	Ashburn-Phi	.441	Banks-Chi	.614
Thomas-Pit	109	Mays-SF	188	Temple-Cin	91	Mays-SF	.347	Musial-StL	.426	Mays-SF	.583
H.Anderson-Phi	97	Aaron-Mil	174	Mathews-Mil	85	Musial-StL	.337	Mays-SF	.423	Aaron-Mil	.546
Mays-SF	96	Boyer-StL	168	Cunningham-StL	82	Aaron-Mil	.326	Temple-Cin	.406	Thomas-Pit	.528
Cepeda-SF	96	Thomas-Pit	163			Skinner-Pit	.321	Skinner-Pit	.390	Musial-StL	.528

Production		Adjusted Production		Batter Runs		Adjusted Batter Runs		Clutch Hitting Index		Runs Created	
Mays-SF	1.006	Mays-SF	167	Mays-SF	55.3	Mays-SF	57.1	H.Anderson-Phi	121	Mays-SF	152
Banks-Chi	.984	Banks-Chi	157	Banks-Chi	45.7	Banks-Chi	47.0	Spencer-SF	120	Banks-Chi	135
Musial-StL	.953	Aaron-Mil	157	Aaron-Mil	37.0	Aaron-Mil	43.5	Thomas-Pit	119	Ashburn-Phi	129
Aaron-Mil	.933	Musial-StL	145	Musial-StL	36.7	Ashburn-Phi	37.7	Groat-Pit	117	Aaron-Mil	121
H.Anderson-Phi	.900	H.Anderson-Phi	137	Ashburn-Phi	36.5	Musial-StL	34.2	Fernandez-Phi	115	Skinner-Pit	102

Total Average		Stolen Bases		Stolen Base Average		Stolen Base Runs		Fielding Runs		Total Player Rating	
Mays-SF	1.110	Mays-SF	31	Mays-SF	83.8	Mays-SF	5.7	Zimmer-LA	32.6	Mays-SF	7.0
Banks-Chi	.984	Ashburn-Phi	30	Blasingame-StL	80.0	Zimmer-LA	3.0	Clemente-Pit	25.2	Banks-Chi	5.7
Musial-StL	.970	A.Taylor-Chi	21	A.Taylor-Chi	77.8	Blasingame-StL	3.0	Boyer-StL	23.4	Ashburn-Phi	5.3
Ashburn-Phi	.929	Blasingame-StL	20	Ashburn-Phi	71.4	A.Taylor-Chi	2.7	Ashburn-Phi	22.1	Boyer-StL	4.1
Aaron-Mil	.916	Gilliam-LA	18	Gilliam-LA	62.1	Robinson-Cin	2.4	Flood-StL	19.3	Aaron-Mil	3.7

Wins		Win Percentage		Games		Complete Games		Shutouts		Saves	
Spahn-Mil	22	Spahn-Mil	.667	Elston-Chi	69	Spahn-Mil	23	Willey-Mil	4	Face-Pit	20
Friend-Pit	22	Burdette-Mil	.667	Klippstein-Cin-LA	57	Roberts-Phi	21	Witt-Pit	3	Labine-LA	14
Burdette-Mil	20	Friend-Pit	.611	Face-Pit	57	Burdette-Mil	19	Purkey-Cin	3	Farrell-Phi	11
Roberts-Phi	17	Purkey-Cin	.607	Hobbie-Chi	55	Purkey-Cin	17	Jay-Mil	3		
Purkey-Cin	17	Antonelli-SF	.552			Friend-Pit	16	Burdette-Mil	3		

Innings Pitched		Fewest Hits/Game		Fewest BB/Game		Strikeouts		Strikeouts/Game		Ratio	
Spahn-Mil	290.0	Jones-StL	7.34	Burdette-Mil	1.63	Jones-StL	225	Jones-StL	8.10	Spahn-Mil	10.40
Burdette-Mil	275.1	Koufax-LA	7.49	Roberts-Phi	1.70	Spahn-Mil	150	Koufax-LA	7.43	Miller-SF	10.43
Friend-Pit	274.0	Miller-SF	7.91	Law-Pit	1.73	Podres-LA	143	Drott-Chi	6.83	Roberts-Phi	10.78
Roberts-Phi	269.2	Spahn-Mil	7.98	Purkey-Cin	1.76	Antonelli-SF	143	Podres-LA	6.12	Burdette-Mil	10.92
		Brosnan-Chi-StL	7.99	Newcombe-LA-Cin	1.93	Friend-Pit	135	Miller-SF	5.88	Purkey-Cin	11.23

Earned Run Average		Adjusted ERA		Opponents' Batting Avg.		Opponents' On Base Pct.		Starter Runs		Adjusted Starter Runs	
Miller-SF	2.47	Miller-SF	154	Koufax-LA	.220	Miller-SF	.286	Burdette-Mil	31.9	Jones-StL	34.7
Jones-StL	2.88	Jones-StL	143	Jones-StL	.223	Spahn-Mil	.288	Miller-SF	29.9	Miller-SF	27.1
Burdette-Mil	2.91	Roberts-Phi	122	Miller-SF	.233	Roberts-Phi	.294	Jones-StL	29.8	Witt-Pit	26.5
Spahn-Mil	3.07	Brosnan-Chi-StL	121	Spahn-Mil	.237	Burdette-Mil	.301	Spahn-Mil	28.3	Roberts-Phi	21.6
Roberts-Phi	3.24	Burdette-Mil	121	Antonelli-SF	.239	Purkey-Cin	.306	Witt-Pit	27.5	Burdette-Mil	18.7

Clutch Pitching Index		Relief Runs		Adjusted Relief Runs		Relief Ranking		Total Pitcher Index		Total Baseball Ranking	
Haddix-Cin	116	Elston-Chi	11.6	Elston-Chi	11.2	Elston-Chi	20.3	Spahn-Mil	3.6	Mays-SF	7.0
Newcombe-LA-Cin	115	Face-Pit	9.9	Schmidt-Cin	9.9	Farrell-Phi	12.0	Burdette-Mil	3.0	Banks-Chi	5.7
Mizell-StL	114	Henry-Chi	9.7	Henry-Chi	9.4	Face-Pit	11.7	Jones-StL	3.0	Ashburn-Phi	5.3
Miller-SF	110	Schmidt-Cin	8.4	Face-Pit	9.1	Henry-Chi	10.9	Miller-SF	3.0	Boyer-StL	4.1
Podres-LA	109	Porterfield-Pit	6.5	Farrell-Phi	6.4	Schmidt-Cin	10.3	Witt-Pit	2.7	Aaron-Mil	3.7

TEAM	G	W	L	PCT	GB	R	OR	AB	H	2B	3B	HR	BB	SO	AVG	OBP	SLG	PRO	PRO+	BR	/A	PF	CHI	RC	SB	CS	SBA	SBR
NY	155	92	62	.597		759	577	5294	1418	212	39	164	537	822	.268	.338	.416	.754	117	88	112	96	102	746	48	32	60	-5
CHI	155	82	72	.532	10	634	615	5249	1348	191	42	101	518	669	.257	.329	.367	.696	99	-13	0	98	99	647	101	33	75	11
BOS	155	79	75	.513	13	697	691	5218	1335	229	30	155	638	820	.256	.340	.400	.740	102	70	25	107	96	708	29	22	57	-5
CLE	153	77	76	.503	14.5	694	635	5201	1340	210	31	161	494	819	.258	.327	.403	.730	109	38	54	98	102	677	50	49	51	-14
DET	154	77	77	.500	15	659	606	5194	1384	229	41	109	463	678	.266	.329	.389	.718	96	20	-27	107	100	657	48	32	60	-5
BAL	154	74	79	.484	17.5	521	575	5111	1233	195	19	108	483	731	.241	.310	.350	.660	92	-85	-52	95	96	546	33	35	49	-11
KC	156	73	81	.474	19	642	713	5261	1297	196	50	138	452	747	.247	.309	.381	.690	93	-40	-52	102	106	601	22	36	38	-15
WAS	156	61	93	.396	31	553	747	5156	1240	161	38	121	477	751	.240	.309	.357	.666	91	-78	-66	98	99	555	22	41	35	-18
TOT	619					5159		41684	10595	1623	290	1057	4062	6037	.254	.324	.383	.707							353	280	56	-62

TEAM	CG	SH	SV	IP	H	H/G	HR	BB	SO	RAT	ERA	ERA+	OAV	OOB	PR	/A	PF	CPI	FA	E	DP	FW	PW	BW	SBW	DIF
NY	53	21	33	1379	1201	7.8	116	557	796	11.8	3.22	110	.235	.315	85	48	94	103	.978	128	182	-.1	5.0	11.6	.3	-1.7
CHI	55	15	25	1389[2]	1296	8.4	152	515	751	11.8	3.61	101	.250	.320	25	5	97	104	.981	114	160	.7	.5	.0	1.9	1.9
BOS	44	5	28	1380	1396	9.1	121	521	695	12.7	3.92	102	.264	.334	-23	13	106	101	.976	145	172	-1.1	1.3	2.6	.3	-1.2
CLE	51	2	20	1373[1]	1283	8.4	123	604	766	12.5	3.73	98	.249	.331	6	-12	97	101	.974	152	171	-1.5	-1.2	5.6	-.6	-1.7
DET	59	8	19	1357[1]	1294	8.6	133	437	797	11.8	3.59	112	.252	.316	26	67	107	101	.982	106	140	1.1	6.9	-2.8	.3	-5.5
BAL	55	15	28	1369[1]	1277	8.4	106	403	749	11.3	3.40	106	.249	.308	57	30	95	97	.980	114	159	.6	3.1	-5.4	-.3	-.5
KC	42	9	25	1398[1]	1405	9.0	150	467	721	12.2	4.15	94	.262	.324	-59	-38	104	95	.979	125	166	.1	-3.9	-5.4	-.7	5.9
WAS	28	6	28	1376[2]	1443	9.4	156	558	762	13.3	4.53	84	.272	.344	-116	-110	101	98	.980	118	163	.5	-11.4	-6.8	-1.1	2.8
TOT	387	81	206	11024		8.6				12.2	3.77		.254	.324					.979	1002	1313					

Runs
Mantle-NY	127
Runnels-Bos	103
Power-KC-Cle	98
Minoso-Cle	94
Cerv-KC	93

Hits
Fox-Chi	187
Malzone-Bos	185
Power-KC-Cle	184
Runnels-Bos	183
Kuenn-Det	179

Doubles
Kuenn-Det	39
Power-KC-Cle	37
Kaline-Det	34
Runnels-Bos	32
Jensen-Bos	31

Triples
Power-KC-Cle	10
Tuttle-KC	9
Lemon-Was	9
Aparicio-Chi	9
Harris-Det	8

Home Runs
Mantle-NY	42
Colavito-Cle	41
Sievers-Was	39
Cerv-KC	38
Jensen-Bos	35

Total Bases
Mantle-NY	307
Cerv-KC	305
Colavito-Cle	303
Sievers-Was	299
Jensen-Bos	293

Runs Batted In
Jensen-Bos	122
Colavito-Cle	113
Sievers-Was	108
Cerv-KC	104
Mantle-NY	97

Runs Produced
Mantle-NY	182
Jensen-Bos	170
Power-KC-Cle	162
Cerv-KC	159

Bases On Balls
Mantle-NY	129
Jensen-Bos	99
Williams-Bos	98
Runnels-Bos	87
Colavito-Cle	84

Batting Average
Williams-Bos	.328
Runnels-Bos	.322
Kuenn-Det	.319
Kaline-Det	.313
Power-KC-Cle	.312

On Base Percentage
Williams-Bos	.462
Mantle-NY	.445
Runnels-Bos	.418
Colavito-Cle	.407
Jensen-Bos	.398

Slugging Average
Colavito-Cle	.620
Cerv-KC	.592
Mantle-NY	.592
Williams-Bos	.584
Sievers-Was	.544

Production
Williams-Bos	1.046
Mantle-NY	1.036
Colavito-Cle	1.027
Cerv-KC	.964
Jensen-Bos	.933

Adjusted Production
Mantle-NY	189
Colavito-Cle	183
Williams-Bos	174
Cerv-KC	158
Sievers-Was	148

Batter Runs
Mantle-NY	64.2
Williams-Bos	53.6
Colavito-Cle	52.8
Jensen-Bos	42.7
Cerv-KC	40.7

Adjusted Batter Runs
Mantle-NY	66.8
Colavito-Cle	54.4
Williams-Bos	49.7
Cerv-KC	39.5
Jensen-Bos	37.8

Clutch Hitting Index
Courtney-Was	142
Lollar-Chi	137
Jensen-Bos	130
Skowron-NY	125
Harris-Det	120

Runs Created
Mantle-NY	147
Colavito-Cle	122
Jensen-Bos	120
Williams-Bos	112
Runnels-Bos	107

Total Average
Mantle-NY	1.208
Williams-Bos	1.163
Colavito-Cle	1.078
Jensen-Bos	.980
Cerv-KC	.947

Stolen Bases
Aparicio-Chi	29
Rivera-Chi	21
Landis-Chi	19
Mantle-NY	18
Minoso-Cle	14

Stolen Base Average
Rivera-Chi	87.5
Mantle-NY	85.7
Aparicio-Chi	82.9
Landis-Chi	73.1

Stolen Base Runs
Aparicio-Chi	5.1
Rivera-Chi	4.5
Mantle-NY	3.6
Wilson-Det	3.0

Fielding Runs
Kaline-Det	23.0
Kubek-NY	20.0
Cerv-KC	20.0
Malzone-Bos	16.6
Kuenn-Det	15.1

Total Player Rating
Mantle-NY	6.3
Cerv-KC	5.2
Colavito-Cle	4.9
Runnels-Bos	4.0
Kaline-Det	3.8

Wins
Turley-NY	21
Pierce-Chi	17
McLish-Cle	16
Lary-Det	16

Win Percentage
Turley-NY	.750
McLish-Cle	.667
Pierce-Chi	.607
Portocarrero-Bal	.577
Foytack-Det	.536

Games
Clevenger-Was	55
Tomanek-Cle-KC	54
Hyde-Was	53
Wall-Bos	52

Complete Games
Turley-NY	19
Pierce-Chi	19
Lary-Det	19
Harshman-Bal	17

Shutouts
Ford-NY	7
Turley-NY	6
Wynn-Chi	4
Ramos-Was	4
Donovan-Chi	4

Saves
Duren-NY	20
Hyde-Was	18
Kiely-Bos	12
Wall-Bos	10

Innings Pitched
Lary-Det	260.1
Ramos-Was	259.1
Donovan-Chi	248.0
Turley-NY	245.1
Pierce-Chi	245.0

Fewest Hits/Game
Turley-NY	6.53
Bell-Cle	6.97
Ford-NY	7.14
Pierce-Chi	7.49
Portocarrero-Bal	7.61

Fewest BB/Game
Donovan-Chi	1.92
O'Dell-Bal	2.07
Sullivan-Bos	2.21
Lary-Det	2.35
Pierce-Chi	2.42

Strikeouts
Wynn-Chi	179
Bunning-Det	177
Turley-NY	168
Harshman-Bal	161
Pascual-Was	146

Strikeouts/Game
Pascual-Was	7.41
Bunning-Det	7.25
Wynn-Chi	6.72
Turley-NY	6.16
Harshman-Bal	6.13

Ratio
Ford-NY	9.81
Pierce-Chi	9.96
Portocarrero-Bal	10.25
O'Dell-Bal	10.41
Harshman-Bal	10.74

Earned Run Average
Ford-NY	2.01
Pierce-Chi	2.68
Harshman-Bal	2.89
Lary-Det	2.90
O'Dell-Bal	2.97

Adjusted ERA
Ford-NY	176
Lary-Det	139
Pierce-Chi	136
Harshman-Bal	124
McLish-Cle	122

Opponents' Batting Avg.
Turley-NY	.206
Bell-Cle	.213
Ford-NY	.217
Pierce-Chi	.227
Grant-Cle	.228

Opponents' On Base Pct.
Ford-NY	.276
Pierce-Chi	.280
Portocarrero-Bal	.286
O'Dell-Bal	.288
Harshman-Bal	.294

Starter Runs
Ford-NY	42.9
Pierce-Chi	29.6
Lary-Det	25.0
Harshman-Bal	23.0
Turley-NY	21.7

Adjusted Starter Runs
Ford-NY	37.1
Lary-Det	32.8
Pierce-Chi	26.0
Wilhelm-Cle-Bal	18.9
Harshman-Bal	18.4

Clutch Pitching Index
McLish-Cle	120
Ford-NY	117
Pierce-Chi	114
Lary-Det	113
Wilson-Chi	110

Relief Runs
Hyde-Was	23.1
Duren-NY	14.7
Kiely-Bos	6.9
Staley-Chi	5.7
Morgan-Det	4.2

Adjusted Relief Runs
Hyde-Was	23.7
Duren-NY	12.7
Kiely-Bos	9.1
Morgan-Det	6.1
Wall-Bos	4.9

Relief Ranking
Hyde-Was	36.2
Duren-NY	22.6
Kiely-Bos	10.1
Wall-Bos	7.5
Morgan-Det	6.4

Total Pitcher Index
Ford-NY	4.5
Lary-Det	3.3
Harshman-Bal	3.2
Pierce-Chi	2.7
Hyde-Was	2.5

Total Baseball Ranking
Mantle-NY	6.3
Cerv-KC	5.2
Colavito-Cle	5.0
Ford-NY	4.5
Runnels-Bos	4.0

TEAM	G	W	L	PCT	GB	R	OR	AB	H	2B	3B	HR	BB	SO	AVG	OBP	SLG	PRO	PRO+	BR	/A	PF	CHI	RC	SB	CS	SBA	SBR
LA	156	88	68	.564		705	670	5282	1360	196	46	148	591	891	.257	.335	.396	.731	94	17	-33	107	99	706	84	51	62	-5
MIL	157	86	70	.551	2	724	623	5388	1426	216	36	177	488	765	.265	.329	.417	.746	115	32	90	92	100	729	41	14	75	4
SF	154	83	71	.539	4	705	613	5281	1377	239	35	167	473	875	.261	.324	.414	.738	105	16	32	98	101	711	81	34	70	4
PIT	155	78	76	.506	9	651	680	5369	1414	230	42	112	442	715	.263	.322	.384	.706	95	-39	-33	99	101	653	32	26	55	-6
CIN	154	74	80	.481	13	764	738	5288	1448	258	34	161	499	763	.274	.340	.427	.767	108	76	56	103	101	764	65	28	70	3
CHI	155	74	80	.481	13	673	688	5296	1321	209	44	163	498	911	.249	.319	.398	.717	98	-23	-15	99	102	673	32	19	63	-2
STL	154	71	83	.461	16	641	725	5317	1432	244	49	118	485	747	.269	.333	.400	.733	96	14	-30	106	92	699	65	53	55	-12
PHI	155	64	90	.416	23	599	725	5109	1237	196	38	113	498	858	.242	.314	.362	.676	86	-92	-103	102	105	574	39	46	46	-16
TOT	620					5462		42330	11015	1788	324	1159	3974	6525	.260	.327	.400	.727							439	271	62	-31

TEAM	CG	SH	SV	IP	H	H/G	HR	BB	SO	RAT	ERA	ERA+	OAV	OOB	PR	/A	PF	CPI	FA	E	DP	FW	PW	BW	SBW	DIF
LA	43	14	26	1411²	1317	8.4	157	614	1077	12.6	3.79	111	.247	.331	24	68	107	103	.981	114	154	1.5	6.8	-3.3	-.1	5.1
MIL	69	18	18	1400²	1406	9.0	128	429	775	11.9	3.51	101	.260	.317	68	5	90	104	.979	127	138	.8	.5	9.1	.8	-3.1
SF	52	12	23	1376¹	1279	8.4	139	500	873	11.8	3.47	110	.246	.316	74	52	97	103	.974	152	118	-.8	5.2	3.2	.8	-2.5
PIT	48	7	17	1393¹	1432	9.2	134	418	730	12.1	3.90	99	.267	.323	7	-5	98	100	.975	154	165	-.8	-.5	-3.3	-.2	5.9
CIN	44	7	26	1357¹	1460	9.7	162	456	690	12.9	4.31	94	.275	.337	-55	-39	103	102	.978	126	157	.7	-3.9	5.6	.7	-6.1
CHI	30	11	25	1391	1337	8.7	152	519	765	12.2	4.01	98	.254	.323	-10	-10	100	96	.977	140	142	-.0	-1.0	-1.5	.2	-.6
STL	36	8	21	1363	1427	9.4	137	564	846	13.3	4.34	94	.271	.344	-59	-15	107	100	.975	146	158	-.4	-1.5	-3.0	-.8	-.2
PHI	54	8	15	1354	1357	9.0	150	474	769	12.4	4.27	96	.261	.326	-49	-25	104	93	.973	154	132	-.8	-2.5	-10.4	-1.2	1.9
TOT	376	85	171	11047¹		9.0				12.4	3.95		.260	.327					.977	1113	1164					

Runs		Hits		Doubles		Triples		Home Runs		Total Bases	
Pinson-Cin	131	Aaron-Mil	223	Pinson-Cin	47	Neal-LA	11	Mathews-Mil	46	Aaron-Mil	400
Mays-SF	125	Pinson-Cin	205	Aaron-Mil	46	Moon-LA	11	Banks-Chi	45	Mathews-Mil	352
Mathews-Mil	118	Cepeda-SF	192	Mays-SF	43	White-StL	9	Aaron-Mil	39	Banks-Chi	351
Aaron-Mil	116	Temple-Cin	186	Cimoli-StL	40	Pinson-Cin	9	Robinson-Cin	36	Mays-SF	335
Robinson-Cin	106	Mathews-Mil	182			Dark-Chi	9	Mays-SF	34	Pinson-Cin	330

Runs Batted In		Runs Produced		Bases On Balls		Batting Average		On Base Percentage		Slugging Average	
Banks-Chi	143	Aaron-Mil	200	Gilliam-LA	96	Aaron-Mil	.355	Cunningham-StL	.456	Aaron-Mil	.636
Robinson-Cin	125	Robinson-Cin	195	Cunningham-StL	88	Cunningham-StL	.345	Aaron-Mil	.406	Banks-Chi	.596
Aaron-Mil	123	Pinson-Cin	195	Moon-LA	81	Cepeda-SF	.317	Robinson-Cin	.397	Mathews-Mil	.593
Bell-Cin	115	Mays-SF	195	Mathews-Mil	80	Pinson-Cin	.316	Moon-LA	.396	Robinson-Cin	.583
Mathews-Mil	114	Banks-Chi	195	Ashburn-Phi	79	Mays-SF	.313	Mathews-Mil	.391	Mays-SF	.583

Production		Adjusted Production		Batter Runs		Adjusted Batter Runs		Clutch Hitting Index		Runs Created	
Aaron-Mil	1.042	Aaron-Mil	188	Aaron-Mil	62.8	Aaron-Mil	69.5	Bell-Cin	156	Aaron-Mil	156
Mathews-Mil	.984	Mathews-Mil	172	Mathews-Mil	48.4	Mathews-Mil	55.0	Post-Phi	138	Mathews-Mil	143
Robinson-Cin	.980	Mays-SF	157	Banks-Chi	44.4	Banks-Chi	45.3	Mazeroski-Pit	129	Mays-SF	131
Banks-Chi	.975	Banks-Chi	156	Robinson-Cin	44.0	Mays-SF	44.3	Robinson-Cin	127	Banks-Chi	126
Mays-SF	.967	Robinson-Cin	152	Mays-SF	42.6	Robinson-Cin	41.9	Banks-Chi	126	Pinson-Cin	124

Total Average		Stolen Bases		Stolen Base Average		Stolen Base Runs		Fielding Runs		Total Player Rating	
Aaron-Mil	1.089	Mays-SF	27	Mays-SF	87.1	Mays-SF	5.7	Virdon-Pit	23.5	Banks-Chi	6.2
Mathews-Mil	1.041	A.Taylor-Chi	23	Pinson-Cin	77.8	Pinson-Cin	2.7	Blasingame-StL	20.5	Aaron-Mil	6.1
Mays-SF	1.037	Gilliam-LA	23	Neal-LA	73.9	Temple-Cin	2.4	Neal-LA	20.0	Mathews-Mil	5.7
Robinson-Cin	1.015	Cepeda-SF	23	A.Taylor-Chi	71.9	Aaron-Mil	2.4	Pinson-Cin	19.7	Mays-SF	4.9
Cunningham-StL	.978	Pinson-Cin	21	Cepeda-SF	71.9	Cimoli-StL	2.1	H.Anderson-Phi	18.3	Pinson-Cin	4.0

Wins		Win Percentage		Games		Complete Games		Shutouts		Saves	
Spahn-Mil	21	Face-Pit	.947	Henry-Chi	65	Spahn-Mil	21	Spahn-Mil	4	McMahon-Mil	15
S.Jones-SF	21	Law-Pit	.667	Elston-Chi	65	Law-Pit	20	S.Jones-SF	4	McDaniel-StL	15
Burdette-Mil	21	Antonelli-SF	.655	McDaniel-StL	62	Burdette-Mil	20	Drysdale-LA	4	Elston-Chi	13
Antonelli-SF	19	Buhl-Mil	.625	McMahon-Mil	60	Roberts-Phi	19	Craig-LA	4	Henry-Chi	12
				Miller-SF	59			Burdette-Mil	4		
								Buhl-Mil	4		
								Antonelli-SF	4		

Innings Pitched		Fewest Hits/Game		Fewest BB/Game		Strikeouts		Strikeouts/Game		Ratio	
Spahn-Mil	292.0	Haddix-Pit	7.58	Newcombe-Cin	1.09	Drysdale-LA	242	Drysdale-LA	8.05	Haddix-Pit	9.63
Burdette-Mil	289.2	S.Jones-SF	7.71	Burdette-Mil	1.18	S.Jones-SF	209	S.Jones-SF	6.95	Newcombe-Cin	10.05
Antonelli-SF	282.0	Hobbie-Chi	7.85	Roberts-Phi	1.22	Koufax-LA	173	Podres-LA	6.69	Conley-Phi	10.15
S.Jones-SF	270.2	Drysdale-LA	7.88	Purkey-Cin	1.78	Antonelli-SF	165	Broglio-StL	6.60	Law-Pit	10.15
Drysdale-LA	270.2	Antonelli-SF	7.88	Law-Pit	1.79	McCormick-SF	151	McCormick-SF	6.02	Antonelli-SF	10.40

Earned Run Average		Adjusted ERA		Opponents' Batting Avg.		Opponents' On Base Pct.		Starter Runs		Adjusted Starter Runs	
S.Jones-SF	2.83	Conley-Phi	137	S.Jones-SF	.228	Haddix-Pit	.273	S.Jones-SF	33.7	Craig-LA	36.7
Miller-SF	2.84	S.Jones-SF	135	Haddix-Pit	.228	Newcombe-Cin	.280	Spahn-Mil	32.1	S.Jones-SF	29.6
Buhl-Mil	2.86	Miller-SF	134	Antonelli-SF	.233	Conley-Phi	.281	Craig-LA	32.0	Jackson-StL	26.6
Spahn-Mil	2.96	Law-Pit	130	Drysdale-LA	.233	Law-Pit	.282	Law-Pit	28.7	Law-Pit	26.3
Law-Pit	2.98	Jackson-StL	128	Conley-Phi	.235	Antonelli-SF	.286	Antonelli-SF	26.7	Drysdale-LA	23.1

Clutch Pitching Index		Relief Runs		Adjusted Relief Runs		Relief Ranking		Total Pitcher Index		Total Baseball Ranking	
Miller-SF	134	Miller-SF	20.5	Henry-Chi	18.9	Henry-Chi	25.3	Newcombe-Cin	3.9	Banks-Chi	6.2
Buhl-Mil	120	Henry-Chi	18.9	Miller-SF	18.0	Face-Pit	25.1	Craig-LA	3.4	Aaron-Mil	6.1
Spahn-Mil	105	Face-Pit	12.9	Face-Pit	12.1	Miller-SF	16.4	Law-Pit	3.0	Mathews-Mil	5.7
Jackson-StL	104	McMahon-Mil	12.4	McMahon-Mil	8.7	Elston-Chi	13.4	Drysdale-LA	3.0	Mays-SF	4.9
S.Jones-SF	104	Elston-Chi	6.8	Meyer-Phi	7.7	McDaniel-StL	12.5	S.Jones-SF	2.7	Pinson-Cin	4.0

TEAM	G	W	L	PCT	GB	R	OR	AB	H	2B	3B	HR	BB	SO	AVG	OBP	SLG	PRO	PRO+	BR	/A	PF	CHI	RC	SB	CS	SBA	SBR
CHI	156	94	60	.610		669	588	5297	1325	220	**46**	97	580	634	.250	.330	.364	.694	97	-20	-11	99	100	653	**113**	53	68	2
CLE	154	89	65	.578	5	**745**	646	5288	1390	216	25	**167**	433	721	**.263**	.323	**.408**	.731	**110**	32	**57**	96	**107**	682	33	36	48	-12
NY	155	79	75	.513	15	687	647	5379	**1397**	224	40	153	457	828	.260	.321	.402	.723	107	17	40	97	98	695	45	22	67	0
DET	154	76	78	.494	18	713	732	5211	1346	196	30	160	580	737	.258	**.338**	.400	**.738**	102	**57**	20	105	97	**720**	34	17	67	0
BOS	154	75	79	.487	19	726	696	5225	1335	**248**	28	125	**626**	810	.256	**.338**	.385	.723	99	36	5	105	101	697	68		**73**	**5**
BAL	155	74	80	.481	20	551	621	5208	1240	182	23	109	536	690	.238	.312	.345	.657	88	-96	-81	98	96	563	36	24	60	-4
KC	154	66	88	.429	28	681	760	5264	1383	231	43	117	481	780	**.263**	.328	.390	.718	100	16	4	102	99	669	34	24	59	-4
WAS	154	63	91	.409	31	619	701	5092	1205	179	32	163	517	881	.237	.310	.379	.689	94	-43	-40	100	101	594	51	34	60	-5
TOT	618					5391		41964	10621	1690	267	1091	4210	6081	.253	.325	.384	.709							414	235	64	-17

TEAM	CG	SH	SV	IP	H	H/G	HR	BB	SO	RAT	ERA	ERA+	OAV	OOB	PR	/A	PF	CPI	FA	E	DP	FW	PW	BW	SBW	DIF
CHI	44	13	36	1425.1	1297	8.2	129	525	761	11.7	**3.29**	114	.242	**.313**	91	74	97	106	**.979**	130	141	.6	**7.5**	-1.1	.4	9.6
CLE	58	7	23	1383.2	1230	8.0	148	635	799	12.3	3.75	98	**.239**	.325	18	-10	95	101	.978	127	138	.7	-1.0	5.8	-1.0	7.5
NY	38	**15**	28	1399	1281	8.2	120	594	**836**	12.2	3.60	101	.244	.324	40	7	94	102	.978	131	160	.5	.7	4.0	.2	-3.5
DET	53	9	24	1360	1327	8.8	177	**432**	829	11.9	4.20	97	.254	.316	-52	-21	105	94	.978	**124**	131	**.9**	-2.1	2.0	.2	-2.0
BOS	38	9	25	1364	1386	9.1	135	589	724	13.2	4.17	97	.266	.343	-47	-17	105	104	.978	131	**167**	.5	-1.7	.5	**.7**	-2.0
BAL	45	**15**	30	1400.1	1290	8.3	**111**	476	735	**11.5**	3.56	106	.246	**.313**	47	35	98	96	.976	146	163	-.4	3.5	-8.2	-.2	2.2
KC	44	8	21	1360.2	1452	9.6	148	492	703	13.2	4.35	92	.274	.341	-74	-52	104	102	.973	160	156	-1.2	-5.3	.4	-.2	-4.7
WAS	46	10	21	1360	1358	9.0	123	467	694	12.3	4.01	98	.259	.324	-23	-14	101	96	.973	162	140	-1.4	-1.4	-4.0	-.3	-6.9
TOT	366	86	208	11053		8.6				12.3	3.86		.253	.325					.977	1111	1196					

Runs
Yost-Det 115
Mantle-NY 104
Power-Cle 102
Jensen-Bos 101
Kuenn-Det 99

Hits
Kuenn-Det 198
Fox-Chi 191
Runnels-Bos 176
Power-Cle 172
Minoso-Cle 172

Doubles
Kuenn-Det 42
Malzone-Bos 34
Fox-Chi 34
Williams-KC 33
Runnels-Bos 33

Triples
Allison-Was 9
McDougald-NY 8

Home Runs
Killebrew-Was 42
Colavito-Cle 42
Lemon-Was 33
Maxwell-Det 31
Mantle-NY 31

Total Bases
Colavito-Cle 301
Killebrew-Was 282
Kuenn-Det 281
Mantle-NY 278
Allison-Was 275

Runs Batted In
Jensen-Bos 112
Colavito-Cle 111
Killebrew-Was 105
Lemon-Was 100
Maxwell-Det....... 95

Runs Produced
Jensen-Bos 185
Minoso-Cle 163
Malzone-Bos 163
Kuenn-Det 161
Killebrew-Was 161

Bases On Balls
Yost-Det 135
Runnels-Bos 95
Mantle-NY 93
Buddin-Bos 92
Killebrew-Was 90

Batting Average
Kuenn-Det .... .353
Kaline-Det .... .327
Runnels-Bos ...... .314
Fox-Chi .... .306
Minoso-Cle ...... .302

On Base Percentage
Yost-Det 437
Runnels-Bos ..... .415
Kaline-Det .... .414
Woodling-Bal ..... .405
Kuenn-Det .... .405

Slugging Average
Kaline-Det 530
Killebrew-Was .... .516
Mantle-NY .... .514
Colavito-Cle ..... .512
Lemon-Was ...... .510

Production
Kaline-Det .... .944
Kuenn-Det .... .906
Mantle-NY .... .905
Yost-Det .... .873
Killebrew-Was .... .873

Adjusted Production
Mantle-NY 152
Kaline-Det 149
Kuenn-Det 140
Woodling-Bal 139
Killebrew-Was 137

Batter Runs
Kaline-Det 41.6
Yost-Det 37.9
Francona-Cle..... 36.6
Kuenn-Det 36.2
Mantle-NY 36.0

Adjusted Batter Runs
Francona-Cle 38.5
Mantle-NY 38.5
Kaline-Det 38.0
Yost-Det 33.7
Kuenn-Det 32.4

Clutch Hitting Index
Strickland-Cle 136
Jensen-Bos 135
Woodling-Bal 125
Cerv-KC 124
Williams-KC 120

Runs Created
Mantle-NY 117
Kuenn-Det 117
Yost-Det 115
Kaline-Det 114
Killebrew-Was 103

Total Average
Yost-Det .... .992
Mantle-NY .... .985
Kaline-Det .... .983
Kuenn-Det .... .903
Jensen-Bos ...... .888

Stolen Bases
Aparicio-Chi 56
Mantle-NY 21
Landis-Chi 20
Jensen-Bos 20
Allison-Was 13

Stolen Base Average
Mantle-NY 87.5
Aparicio-Chi 81.2
Jensen-Bos 80.0
Landis-Chi 69.0

Stolen Base Runs
Aparicio-Chi 9.0
Mantle-NY 4.5
Jensen-Bos 3.0
Malzone-Bos 1.8
Yost-Det 1.5

Fielding Runs
Gardner-Bal...... 30.5
Minoso-Cle 16.2
Landis-Chi 15.8
Jensen-Bos 15.1
Colavito-Cle 11.6

Total Player Rating
Mantle-NY 4.4
Kaline-Det 4.2
Jensen-Bos 3.5
Runnels-Bos 3.5
Minoso-Cle 3.3

Wins
Wynn-Chi 22
McLish-Cle 19
Shaw-Chi 18

Win Percentage
Shaw-Chi .... .750
McLish-Cle .... .704
Wynn-Chi .... .688
Mossi-Det .... .654

Games
Staley-Chi 67
Lown-Chi 60
Clevenger-Was 50
Shaw-Chi 47

Complete Games
Pascual-Was 17
Pappas-Bal 15
Mossi-Det 15
Wynn-Chi 14
Bunning-Det 14

Shutouts
Pascual-Was 6
Wynn-Chi 5
Pappas-Bal 4

Saves
Lown-Chi 15
Staley-Chi 14
Loes-Bal.......... 14
Duren-NY 14
Fornieles-Bos 11

Innings Pitched
Wynn-Chi 255.2
Bunning-Det ... 249.2
Foytack-Det 240.1
Pascual-Was ... 238.2
McLish-Cle 235.1

Fewest Hits/Game
Score-Cle 6.89
Ditmar-NY 6.95
Wilhelm-Bal 7.09
Wynn-Chi 7.11
O'Dell-Bal 7.36

Fewest BB/Game
Brown-Bal 1.76
Lary-Det 1.86
Garver-KC 1.88
Mossi-Det 1.93
Ramos-Was 2.00

Strikeouts
Bunning-Det 201
Pascual-Was 185
Wynn-Chi 179
Score-Cle 147
Wilhelm-Bal 139

Strikeouts/Game
Score-Cle 8.23
Bunning-Det 7.25
Pascual-Was 6.98
Turley-NY 6.47
Wynn-Chi 6.30

Ratio
Ditmar-NY 9.62
Pascual-Was 10.33
Mossi-Det 10.34
O'Dell-Bal....... 10.43
Brown-Bal 10.48

Earned Run Average
Wilhelm-Bal 2.19
Pascual-Was 2.64
Shaw-Chi 2.69
Ditmar-NY 2.90
Walker-Bal 2.92

Adjusted ERA
Wilhelm-Bal 173
Pascual-Was 148
Shaw-Chi 140
Walker-Bal 130
O'Dell-Bal 129

Opponents' Batting Avg.
Score-Cle .... .210
Ditmar-NY .... .211
Wynn-Chi .... .216
O'Dell-Bal........ .220
Wilhelm-Bal ...... .224

Opponents' On Base Pct.
Ditmar-NY .... .270
Pascual-Was ...... .284
O'Dell-Bal........ .286
Mossi-Det .... .286
Brown-Bal .... .290

Starter Runs
Wilhelm-Bal 42.0
Pascual-Was 32.4
Shaw-Chi 30.0
Ditmar-NY 21.7
Perry-Cle 20.6

Adjusted Starter Runs
Wilhelm-Bal 40.0
Pascual-Was 33.8
Shaw-Chi 27.3
Daley-KC 20.2
O'Dell-Bal 18.8

Clutch Pitching Index
Wilhelm-Bal 132
Daley-KC 122
Ford-NY 119
Shaw-Chi 114
McLish-Cle 114

Relief Runs
Staley-Chi 20.9
Duren-NY 16.9
Shantz-NY 15.6
Coates-NY 11.0
Lown-Chi 10.0

Adjusted Relief Runs
Staley-Chi 19.6
Duren-NY 15.0
Shantz-NY 13.3
Stobbs-Was 9.4
Fornieles-Bos 9.0

Relief Ranking
Staley-Chi 25.0
Duren-NY 22.1
Shantz-NY 13.6
Lown-Chi 12.7
Fornieles-Bos 10.6

Total Pitcher Index
Pascual-Was 5.0
Wilhelm-Bal 3.6
Shaw-Chi 2.7
Daley-KC 2.6
Wynn-Chi 2.5

Total Baseball Ranking
Pascual-Was 5.0
Mantle-NY 4.4
Kaline-Det 4.2
Wilhelm-Bal 3.6
Jensen-Bos 3.5

TEAM	G	W	L	PCT	GB	R	OR	AB	H	2B	3B	HR	BB	SO	AVG	OBP	SLG	PRO	PRO+	BR	/A	PF	CHI	RC	SB	CS	SBA	SBR
PIT	155	95	59	.617		734	593	5406	1493	236	56	120	486	747	.276	.338	.407	.745	109	72	68	101	99	737	34	24	59	-4
MIL	154	88	66	.571	7	724	658	5263	1393	198	48	170	463	793	.265	.327	.417	.744	118	60	109	93	102	714	69	37	65	-2
STL	155	86	68	.558	9	639	616	5187	1317	213	48	138	501	792	.254	.323	.393	.716	94	13	-43	109	97	652	48	35	58	-7
LA	154	82	72	.532	13	662	593	5227	1333	216	38	126	529	837	.255	.327	.383	.710	94	6	-36	106	99	659	95	53	64	-3
SF	156	79	75	.513	16	671	631	5324	1357	220	62	130	467	846	.255	.319	.393	.712	106	1	41	94	102	663	86	45	66	-1
CIN	154	67	87	.435	28	640	692	5289	1324	230	40	140	512	858	.250	.320	.388	.708	98	-1	-12	102	97	661	73	37	66	0
CHI	156	60	94	.390	35	634	776	5311	1293	213	48	119	531	897	.243	.314	.369	.683	94	-48	-40	99	103	617	51	34	60	-5
PHI	154	59	95	.383	36	546	691	5169	1235	196	44	99	448	1054	.239	.304	.351	.655	85	-102	-103	100	102	546	45	48	48	-15
TOT	619					5250		42176	10745	1722	384	1042	3937	6824	.255	.322	.388	.710							501	313	62	-38

TEAM	CG	SH	SV	IP	H	H/G	HR	BB	SO	RAT	ERA	ERA+	OAV	OOB	PR	/A	PF	CPI	FA	E	DP	FW	PW	BW	SBW	DIF
PIT	47	11	33	1399²	1363	8.8	105	386	811	11.3	3.49	107	.257	.309	42	40	100	99	.979	128	163	.7	4.1	7.0	.0	6.1
MIL	55	13	28	1387¹	1327	8.6	130	518	807	12.2	3.76	91	.251	.322	0	-52	91	99	.976	141	137	-.0	-5.4	11.2	.3	4.9
STL	37	11	30	1371	1316	8.6	127	511	906	12.1	3.64	112	.253	.322	18	69	109	103	.976	141	152	.0	7.1	-4.4	-.2	6.5
LA	46	13	20	1398	1218	7.8	154	564	1122	11.7	3.40	117	.234	.312	56	89	106	103	.979	125	142	.9	9.2	-3.7	.2	-1.5
SF	55	16	26	1396	1288	8.3	107	512	897	11.8	3.44	101	.245	.315	50	6	93	99	.972	166	117	-1.3	.6	4.2	.4	-1.9
CIN	33	8	35	1390¹	1417	9.2	134	442	740	12.3	4.00	96	.267	.328	-37	-27	102	101	.979	125	155	.9	-2.8	-1.2	.5	-7.3
CHI	36	6	25	1402²	1393	8.9	152	565	805	12.8	4.35	87	.260	.335	-92	-89	100	96	.977	143	133	-.0	-9.2	-4.1	-.0	-3.7
PHI	45	6	16	1375¹	1423	9.3	133	439	736	12.3	4.01	97	.270	.328	-38	-20	103	101	.974	155	129	-.8	-2.1	-10.6	-1.1	-3.5
TOT	354	84	213	11120¹		8.7				12.1	3.76		.255	.322					.977	1124	1128					

Runs
Bruton-Mil 112
Mathews-Mil 108
Pinson-Cin 107
Mays-SF 107
Aaron-Mil 102

Hits
Mays-SF 190
Pinson-Cin 187
Groat-Pit 186
Bruton-Mil 180
Clemente-Pit 179

Doubles
Pinson-Cin 37
Cepeda-SF 36
Skinner-Pit 33
Robinson-Cin 33
Banks-Chi 32

Triples
Bruton-Mil 13
Pinson-Cin 12
Mays-SF 12
Aaron-Mil 11

Home Runs
Banks-Chi 41
Aaron-Mil 40
Mathews-Mil 39
Boyer-StL 32
Robinson-Cin 31

Total Bases
Aaron-Mil 334
Banks-Chi 331
Mays-SF 330
Boyer-StL 310
Pinson-Cin 308

Runs Batted In
Aaron-Mil 126
Mathews-Mil 124
Banks-Chi 117
Mays-SF 103
Boyer-StL 97

Runs Produced
Mathews-Mil 193
Aaron-Mil 188
Mays-SF 181
Banks-Chi 170
Clemente-Pit 167

Bases On Balls
Ashburn-Chi 116
Mathews-Mil 111
Gilliam-LA 96
Robinson-Cin 82
Spencer-StL 81

Batting Average
Groat-Pit .... .325
Larker-LA .... .323
Mays-SF .... .319
Clemente-Pit .... .314
Boyer-StL .... .304

On Base Percentage
Ashburn-Chi .... .416
Robinson-Cin .... .413
Mathews-Mil .... .401
Moon-LA .... .387
Mays-SF .... .386

Slugging Average
Robinson-Cin .... .595
Aaron-Mil .... .566
Boyer-StL .... .562
Mays-SF .... .555
Banks-Chi .... .554

Production
Robinson-Cin 1.007
Mathews-Mil .... .952
Mays-SF .... .941
Boyer-StL .... .934
Aaron-Mil .... .925

Adjusted Production
Mathews-Mil 170
Robinson-Cin 169
Mays-SF 164
Aaron-Mil 161
Banks-Chi 145

Batter Runs
Robinson-Cin 47.8
Mathews-Mil 46.0
Mays-SF 43.5
Boyer-StL 37.9
Aaron-Mil 37.4

Adjusted Batter Runs
Mathews-Mil 51.6
Mays-SF 48.0
Robinson-Cin 46.8
Aaron-Mil 42.9
Banks-Chi 35.2

Clutch Hitting Index
Larker-LA 155
Clemente-Pit 131
Skinner-Pit 127
Bailey-Cin 125
Stuart-Pit 123

Runs Created
Mathews-Mil 128
Mays-SF 124
Aaron-Mil 119
Banks-Chi 113
Robinson-Cin 113

Total Average
Robinson-Cin 1.069
Mathews-Mil 1.029
Mays-SF .... .953
Aaron-Mil .... .935
Boyer-StL .... .918

Stolen Bases
Wills-LA 50
Pinson-Cin 32
A.Taylor-Chi-Phi 26
Mays-SF 25
Bruton-Mil 22

Stolen Base Average
Javier-StL 82.6
Wills-LA 80.6
Ashburn-Chi 80.0
Pinson-Cin 72.7
Mays-SF 71.4

Stolen Base Runs
Wills-LA 7.8
Javier-StL 3.3
Blasingame-SF 3.0
Pinson-Cin 2.4
Ashburn-Chi 2.4

Fielding Runs
Mazeroski-Pit 25.4
Wills-LA 20.5
Grammas-StL 19.8
Smith-StL 18.0
Mays-SF 13.7

Total Player Rating
Banks-Chi 5.7
Mays-SF 5.6
Robinson-Cin 4.6
Aaron-Mil 4.5
Boyer-StL 4.3

Wins
Spahn-Mil 21
Broglio-StL 21
Law-Pit 20
Burdette-Mil 19

Win Percentage
Broglio-StL .... .700
Law-Pit .... .690
Spahn-Mil .... .677
Buhl-Mil .... .640
Purkey-Cin .... .607

Games
Face-Pit 68
McDaniel-StL 65
Elston-Chi 60
Farrell-Phi 59
Roebuck-LA 58

Complete Games
Spahn-Mil 18
Law-Pit 18
Burdette-Mil 18
Hobbie-Chi 16
Friend-Pit 16

Shutouts
Sanford-SF 6
Drysdale-LA 5

Saves
McDaniel-StL 26
Face-Pit 24
Henry-Cin 17
Brosnan-Cin 12

Innings Pitched
Jackson-StL 282.0
Friend-Pit 275.2
Burdette-Mil 275.2
Law-Pit 271.2
Drysdale-LA 269.0

Fewest Hits/Game
Broglio-StL 6.84
Koufax-LA 6.84
Williams-LA 7.03
Drysdale-LA 7.16
Buhl-Mil 7.62

Fewest BB/Game
Burdette-Mil 1.14
Roberts-Phi 1.29
Law-Pit 1.33
Friend-Pit 1.47
Haddix-Pit 1.98

Strikeouts
Drysdale-LA 246
Koufax-LA 197
S.Jones-SF 190
Broglio-StL 188
Friend-Pit 183

Strikeouts/Game
Koufax-LA 10.13
Drysdale-LA 8.23
Williams-LA 7.60
Broglio-StL 7.48
S.Jones-SF 7.31

Ratio
Drysdale-LA 9.90
Friend-Pit 10.15
Law-Pit 10.27
Burdette-Mil 10.35
Williams-LA 10.37

Earned Run Average
McCormick-SF 2.70
Broglio-StL 2.74
Drysdale-LA 2.84
Williams-LA 3.00
Friend-Pit 3.00

Adjusted ERA
Broglio-StL 149
Drysdale-LA 140
Simmons-Phi-StL 134
Williams-LA 133
Podres-LA 129

Opponents' Batting Avg.
Koufax-LA .... .207
Williams-LA .... .210
Broglio-StL .... .213
Drysdale-LA .... .215
Buhl-Mil .... .229

Opponents' On Base Pct.
Drysdale-LA .... .275
Friend-Pit .... .281
Williams-LA .... .282
Law-Pit .... .287
Burdette-Mil .... .287

Starter Runs
McCormick-SF 29.8
Drysdale-LA 27.5
Broglio-StL 25.6
Friend-Pit 23.2
Law-Pit 20.6

Adjusted Starter Runs
Broglio-StL 34.0
Drysdale-LA 33.6
Friend-Pit 22.9
Williams-LA 22.4
Podres-LA 22.4

Clutch Pitching Index
Simmons-Phi-StL 121
Podres-LA 117
O'Dell-SF 110
Sadecki-StL 109
Buhl-Mil 108

Relief Runs
McDaniel-StL 21.6
Brosnan-Cin 15.4
Roebuck-LA 12.8
Farrell-Phi 12.2
Face-Pit 10.9

Adjusted Relief Runs
McDaniel-StL 26.0
Brosnan-Cin 16.1
Roebuck-LA 15.5
Farrell-Phi 13.6
Face-Pit 10.8

Relief Ranking
McDaniel-StL 45.2
Farrell-Phi 22.2
Face-Pit 20.3
Brosnan-Cin 17.5
Roebuck-LA 15.5

Total Pitcher Index
Drysdale-LA 4.4
Broglio-StL 4.1
McDaniel-StL 2.9
McCormick-SF 2.7
Law-Pit 2.6

Total Baseball Ranking
Banks-Chi 5.7
Mays-SF 5.6
Robinson-Cin 4.6
Aaron-Mil 4.5
Drysdale-LA 4.4

TEAM	G	W	L	PCT	GB	R	OR	AB	H	2B	3B	HR	BB	SO	AVG	OBP	SLG	PRO	PRO+	BR	/A	PF	CHI	RC	SB	CS	SBA	SBR
NY	155	97	57	.630		746	627	5290	1377	215	40	193	537	818	.260	.332	.426	.758	117	63	101	94	100	747	37	23	62	-3
BAL	154	89	65	.578	8	682	606	5170	1307	206	33	123	596	801	.253	.334	.377	.711	99	-8	1	99	103	659	37	24	61	-3
CHI	154	87	67	.565	10	741	617	5191	1402	242	38	112	567	648	.270	.348	.396	.744	108	57	64	99	101	726	58	25	70	8
CLE	154	76	78	.494	21	667	693	5296	1415	218	20	127	444	573	.267	.328	.388	.716	102	-11	10	97	101	673	58	25	70	2
WAS	154	73	81	.474	24	672	696	5248	1283	205	43	147	584	883	.244	.326	.384	.710	99	-18	-11	99	101	656	52	43	55	-10
DET	154	71	83	.461	26	633	644	5202	1243	188	34	150	636	728	.239	.326	.375	.701	93	-32	-50	103	97	651	66	32	67	1
BOS	154	65	89	.422	32	658	775	5215	1359	234	32	124	570	798	.261	.336	.389	.725	99	16	-8	104	95	674	34	28	55	-7
KC	155	58	96	.377	39	615	756	5226	1303	212	34	110	513	744	.249	.318	.366	.684	90	-68	-72	101	103	598	16	11	59	-2
TOT	617					5414		41838	10689	1720	274	1086	4447	5993	.255	.331	.388	.718							422	234	64	-14

TEAM	CG	SH	SV	IP	H	H/G	HR	BB	SO	RAT	ERA	ERA+	OAV	OOB	PR	/A	PF	CPI	FA	E	DP	FW	PW	BW	SBW	DIF
NY	38	16	42	1398	1225	7.9	123	609	712	12.0	3.52	102	.238	.322	55	10	93	98	.979	129	162	.2	1.0	10.2	-.1	8.7
BAL	48	11	22	1375²	1222	8.0	117	552	785	11.8	3.52	108	.241	.320	54	44	98	98	.982	108	172	1.4	4.5	.1	-.1	6.2
CHI	42	11	26	1381	1338	8.7	127	533	695	12.3	3.60	105	.258	.329	41	27	98	106	.982	109	175	1.4	2.7	6.5	1.0	-1.5
CLE	32	10	30	1382¹	1308	8.5	161	636	771	12.8	3.95	95	.252	.336	-12	-33	97	103	.978	128	165	.2	-3.3	1.0	.4	.8
WAS	34	10	35	1405¹	1392	8.9	130	538	775	12.6	3.77	103	.260	.331	16	18	100	103	.973	165	159	-2.1	1.8	-1.1	-.8	-1.7
DET	40	7	25	1405²	1336	8.6	141	474	824	11.9	3.64	109	.251	.317	37	50	102	99	.977	138	138	-.5	5.1	-5.1	.3	-5.8
BOS	34	6	23	1361	1440	9.5	127	580	767	13.6	4.62	87	.273	.349	-113	-88	104	94	.976	141	156	-.6	-8.9	-.8	-.5	-1.1
KC	44	4	14	1374	1428	9.4	160	525	664	13.1	4.38	91	.271	.342	-77	-60	103	100	.979	127	149	.3	-6.1	-7.3	-.0	-5.9
TOT	312	75	217	11083		8.7				12.5	3.87		.255	.331					.978	1045	1276					

Runs
Mantle-NY 119
Maris-NY 98
Minoso-Chi 89
Landis-Chi 89
Sievers-Chi 87

Hits
Minoso-Chi 184
Robinson-Bal 175
Fox-Chi 175
Smith-Chi 169
Runnels-Bos 169

Doubles
Francona-Cle 36
Skowron-NY 34
Minoso-Chi 32
Freese-Chi 32

Triples
Fox-Chi 10
Robinson-Bal 9

Home Runs
Mantle-NY 40
Maris-NY 39
Lemon-Was 38
Colavito-Det 35
Killebrew-Was 31

Total Bases
Mantle-NY 294
Maris-NY 290
Skowron-NY 284
Minoso-Chi 284
Lemon-Was 268

Runs Batted In
Maris-NY 112
Minoso-Chi 105
Wertz-Bos 103
Lemon-Was 100
Gentile-Bal 98

Runs Produced
Minoso-Chi 174
Mantle-NY 173
Maris-NY 171
Sievers-Chi 152
Robinson-Bal 148

Bases On Balls
Yost-Det 125
Mantle-NY 111
Allison-Was 92
Woodling-Bal 84
Landis-Chi 80

Batting Average
Runnels-Bos ...... .320
Smith-Chi .... .315
Minoso-Chi .... .311
Skowron-NY .... .309
Kuenn-Cle .... .308

On Base Percentage
Yost-Det .... .416
Woodling-Bal ..... .403
Runnels-Bos ...... .403
Mantle-NY .... .402
Sievers-Chi ...... .399

Slugging Average
Maris-NY .... .581
Mantle-NY .... .558
Killebrew-Was .... .534
Sievers-Chi ...... .534
Skowron-NY .... .528

Production
Mantle-NY .... .960
Maris-NY .... .955
Sievers-Chi ...... .933
Killebrew-Was .... .911
Skowron-NY .... .884

Adjusted Production
Mantle-NY 166
Maris-NY 164
Sievers-Chi 152
Killebrew-Was 145
Skowron-NY 144

Batter Runs
Mantle-NY 43.9
Williams-Bos 43.5
Maris-NY 36.5
Sievers-Chi 32.1
Killebrew-Was 26.9

Adjusted Batter Runs
Mantle-NY 48.0
Williams-Bos 41.9
Maris-NY 40.2
Sievers-Chi 32.7
Skowron-NY 28.3

Clutch Hitting Index
Wertz-Bos 155
Power-Cle 135
Minoso-Chi 127
Robinson-Bal 120
Aparicio-Chi 119

Runs Created
Mantle-NY 125
Maris-NY 111
Minoso-Chi 104
Lemon-Was 99
Francona-Cle 96

Total Average
Mantle-NY 1.053
Maris-NY .... .992
Sievers-Chi ...... .960
Killebrew-Was .... .936
Lemon-Was .... .871

Stolen Bases
Aparicio-Chi 51
Landis-Chi 23
Green-Was 21
Kaline-Det 19
Piersall-Cle 18

Stolen Base Average
Aparicio-Chi 86.4
Kaline-Det 82.6
Landis-Chi 79.3
Piersall-Cle 78.3
Green-Was 72.4

Stolen Base Runs
Aparicio-Chi 10.5
Landis-Chi 3.3
Kaline-Det 3.3
Piersall-Cle 2.4
Mantle-NY 2.4

Fielding Runs
Aparicio-Chi 30.4
Boyer-NY 27.6
Power-Cle 21.0
Tuttle-KC 17.1
Landis-Chi 12.9

Total Player Rating
Mantle-NY 4.2
Aparicio-Chi 3.8
Maris-NY 3.6
Williams-Bos 3.5
Runnels-Bos 3.2

Wins
Perry-Cle 18
Estrada-Bal 18
L.Daley-KC 16

Win Percentage
Perry-Cle .... .643
Ditmar-NY .... .625
Estrada-Bal ...... .621
Pappas-Bal .... .577

Games
Fornieles-Bos 70
Staley-Chi 64
Clevenger-Was 53
Moore-Chi-Was 51
Kutyna-KC 51

Complete Games
Lary-Det 15
Ramos-Was 14
Herbert-KC 14
Wynn-Chi 13
L.Daley-KC 13

Shutouts
Wynn-Chi 4
Perry-Cle 4
Ford-NY 4

Saves
Klippstein-Cle ... 14
Fornieles-Bos 14
Moore-Chi-Was 13
R.Shantz-NY 11

Innings Pitched
Lary-Det 274.1
Ramos-Was 274.0
Perry-Cle 261.1
Herbert-KC 252.2
Bunning-Det 252.0

Fewest Hits/Game
Estrada-Bal 6.99
Turley-NY 7.17
Barber-Bal 7.33
Bunning-Det 7.75
Ford-NY 7.85

Fewest BB/Game
Brown-Bal 1.25
Mossi-Det 1.82
Hall-KC 1.88
Lary-Det 2.03
Pierce-Chi 2.11

Strikeouts
Bunning-Det 201
Ramos-Was 160
Wynn-Chi 158
Lary-Det 149
Estrada-Bal 144

Strikeouts/Game
Bunning-Det 7.18
Bell-Cle 6.34
Estrada-Bal 6.21
Wynn-Chi 5.99
Monbouquette-Bos . 5.61

Ratio
Brown-Bal 10.08
Bunning-Det 10.43
Baumann-Chi 10.83
Mossi-Det 10.86
Ford-NY 10.93

Earned Run Average
Baumann-Chi 2.67
Bunning-Det 2.79
Brown-Bal 3.06
Ditmar-NY 3.06
Ford-NY 3.08

Adjusted ERA
Bunning-Det 142
Baumann-Chi 141
Brown-Bal 125
Herbert-KC 121
Barber-Bal 118

Opponents' Batting Avg.
Estrada-Bal ...... .218
Turley-NY .... .222
Barber-Bal .... .226
Ford-NY .... .235
Bunning-Det ...... .236

Opponents' On Base Pct.
Brown-Bal .... .286
Bunning-Det ...... .293
Mossi-Det .... .296
Ford-NY .... .299
Terry-NY .... .300

Starter Runs
Bunning-Det 30.4
Baumann-Chi 24.7
Ditmar-NY 18.0
Ford-NY 16.9
Herbert-KC 16.7

Adjusted Starter Runs
Bunning-Det 32.8
Baumann-Chi 22.8
Herbert-KC 19.7
Pascual-Was 14.5
Kralick-Was 14.2

Clutch Pitching Index
Ditmar-NY 121
Perry-Cle 113
Lee-Was 113
Baumann-Chi 113
Herbert-KC 111

Relief Runs
Staley-Chi 18.6
Fornieles-Bos 14.9
Sisler-Det 12.4
Aguirre-Det 10.7
R.Shantz-NY 8.1

Adjusted Relief Runs
Staley-Chi 17.4
Fornieles-Bos 17.0
Sisler-Det 13.2
Aguirre-Det 11.6
Stobbs-Was 7.5

Relief Ranking
Staley-Chi 32.0
Fornieles-Bos 25.9
Sisler-Det 20.0
Aguirre-Det 11.6
Klippstein-Cle ... 11.2

Total Pitcher Index
Bunning-Det 3.0
Herbert-KC 2.4
Baumann-Chi 2.2
Staley-Chi 2.2
Fornieles-Bos 2.0

Total Baseball Ranking
Mantle-NY 4.2
Aparicio-Chi 3.8
Maris-NY 3.6
Williams-Bos 3.5
Runnels-Bos 3.2

TEAM	G	W	L	PCT	GB	R	OR	AB	H	2B	3B	HR	BB	SO	AVG	OBP	SLG	PRO	PRO+	BR	/A	PF	CHI	RC	SB	CS	SBA	SBR
CIN	154	93	61	.604		710	653	5243	1414	247	35	158	423	761	.270	.328	.421	.749	102	19	10	101	101	713	70	33	68	1
LA	154	89	65	.578	4	735	697	5189	1358	193	40	157	596	796	.262	.340	.405	.745	95	29	-32	109	100	722	86	45	66	-1
SF	155	85	69	.552	8	773	655	5233	1379	219	32	183	506	764	.264	.332	.423	.755	109	35	61	96	106	719	79	54	59	-9
MIL	155	83	71	.539	10	712	656	5288	1365	199	34	188	534	880	.258	.330	.415	.745	110	19	62	94	98	714	70	43	62	-5
STL	155	80	74	.519	13	703	668	5307	1436	236	51	103	494	745	.271	.336	.393	.729	90	-3	-3	100	100	702	46	28	62	-3
PIT	154	75	79	.487	18	694	675	5311	1448	232	57	128	428	721	.273	.330	.410	.740	101	8	6	100	99	694	26	30	46	-10
CHI	156	64	90	.416	29	689	800	5344	1364	238	51	176	539	1027	.255	.327	.418	.745	101	16	7	101	95	726	35	25	58	-5
PHI	155	47	107	.305	46	584	796	5213	1265	185	50	103	475	928	.243	.311	.357	.668	84	-123	-113	99	102	577	56	30	65	-1
TOT	619					5600		42128	11029	1749	350	1196	3995	6622	.262	.329	.405	.735							468	288	62	-32

TEAM	CG	SH	SV	IP	H	H/G	HR	BB	SO	RAT	ERA	ERA+	OAV	OOB	PR	/A	PF	CPI	FA	E	DP	FW	PW	BW	SBW	DIF
CIN	46	12	40	1370	1300	8.5	147	500	829	12.0	3.78	107	.250	.320	38	43	101	98	.977	134	124	.7	4.3	1.0	.5	9.6
LA	40	10	35	1378¹	1346	8.8	167	544	1105	12.7	4.04	107	.256	.331	-2	46	108	101	.975	144	162	.1	4.6	-3.2	.3	10.2
SF	39	9	30	1388	1306	8.5	152	502	924	11.9	3.77	101	.249	.318	40	6	95	98	.977	133	126	.8	.6	6.1	-.5	1.1
MIL	57	8	16	1391¹	1357	8.8	153	493	652	12.1	3.89	96	.258	.324	21	-24	93	101	.982	111	152	2.0	-2.4	6.2	-.0	.3
STL	49	10	24	1368²	1334	8.8	136	570	823	12.7	3.74	118	.256	.333	44	100	109	106	.972	166	165	-1.1	9.9	-7.2	.1	1.3
PIT	34	9	29	1362	1442	9.5	121	400	759	12.3	3.92	102	.274	.328	17	10	99	102	.975	150	187	-.2	1.0	.6	-.6	-2.8
CHI	34	6	25	1385	1492	9.7	165	465	755	12.9	4.48	93	.277	.338	-70	-47	104	99	.970	183	175	-2.0	-4.7	.7	-.0	-7.0
PHI	29	9	13	1383¹	1452	9.4	155	521	775	13.1	4.61	88	.273	.342	-88	-82	101	96	.976	146	179	.0	-8.1	-11.2	.3	-11.0
TOT	328	73	212	11026²		9.0				12.5	4.03		.262	.329					.976	1167	1270					

Runs
Mays-SF 129
Robinson-Cin 117
Aaron-Mil 115
Boyer-StL 109

Hits
Pinson-Cin 208
Clemente-Pit 201
Aaron-Mil 197
Boyer-StL 194
Cepeda-SF 182

Doubles
Aaron-Mil 39
Pinson-Cin 34
Santo-Chi 32
Robinson-Cin 32
Mays-SF 32

Triples
Altman-Chi 12
White-StL 11
Callison-Phi 11
Boyer-StL 11

Home Runs
Cepeda-SF 46
Mays-SF 40
Robinson-Cin 37
Stuart-Pit 35
Adcock-Mil 35

Total Bases
Aaron-Mil 358
Cepeda-SF 356
Mays-SF 334
Robinson-Cin 333
Clemente-Pit 320

Runs Batted In
Cepeda-SF 142
Robinson-Cin 124
Mays-SF 123
Aaron-Mil 120
Stuart-Pit 117

Runs Produced
Mays-SF 212
Robinson-Cin 204
Cepeda-SF 201
Aaron-Mil 201
Boyer-StL 180

Bases On Balls
Mathews-Mil 93
Moon-LA 89
Mays-SF 81
Gilliam-LA 79

Batting Average
Clemente-Pit .... .351
Pinson-Cin .... .343
Boyer-StL .... .329
Moon-LA .... .328
Aaron-Mil .... .327

On Base Percentage
Moon-LA .... .438
Robinson-Cin .... .411
Mathews-Mil .... .405
Boyer-StL .... .400
Mays-SF .... .395

Slugging Average
Robinson-Cin .... .611
Cepeda-SF .... .609
Aaron-Mil .... .594
Mays-SF .... .584
Stuart-Pit .... .581

Production
Robinson-Cin 1.022
Aaron-Mil .... .979
Mays-SF .... .979
Cepeda-SF .... .972
Clemente-Pit .... .951

Adjusted Production
Aaron-Mil 165
Robinson-Cin 164
Mays-SF 162
Cepeda-SF 158
Mathews-Mil 156

Batter Runs
Robinson-Cin 52.4
Aaron-Mil 46.0
Mays-SF 45.8
Cepeda-SF 40.7
Mathews-Mil 40.4

Adjusted Batter Runs
Robinson-Cin 51.5
Aaron-Mil 50.8
Mays-SF 48.7
Mathews-Mil 45.2
Cepeda-SF 43.5

Clutch Hitting Index
Moon-LA 132
Cepeda-SF 123
Stuart-Pit 121
Robinson-Cin 119
Mays-SF 116

Runs Created
Robinson-Cin 137
Aaron-Mil 132
Mays-SF 130
Mathews-Mil 128
Boyer-StL 126

Total Average
Robinson-Cin 1.119
Mays-SF 1.017
Moon-LA 1.003
Aaron-Mil .... .993
Mathews-Mil .... .981

Stolen Bases
Wills-LA 35
Pinson-Cin 23
Robinson-Cin 22
Aaron-Mil 21
Mays-SF 18

Stolen Base Average
Robinson-Cin 88.0
Wills-LA 70.0
Aaron-Mil 70.0
Pinson-Cin 69.7
Mays-SF 66.7

Stolen Base Runs
Robinson-Cin 4.8
Maye-Mil 2.4
Williams-Chi 1.8
Wills-LA 1.5
Gonzalez-Phi 1.5

Fielding Runs
Mazeroski-Pit 30.5
Malkmus-Phi 16.3
Amaro-Phi 14.1
Boyer-StL 13.3
Clemente-Pit 13.0

Total Player Rating
Robinson-Cin 5.4
Boyer-StL 4.4
Clemente-Pit 4.3
Mays-SF 4.2
Aaron-Mil 4.2

Wins
Spahn-Mil 21
Jay-Cin 21
O'Toole-Cin 19

Win Percentage
Podres-LA .... .783
O'Toole-Cin .... .679
Jay-Cin .... .677
Burdette-Mil .... .621
Spahn-Mil .... .618

Games
Baldschun-Phi 65
Miller-SF 63
Face-Pit 62
Elston-Chi 58
Anderson-Chi 57

Complete Games
Spahn-Mil 21
Koufax-LA 15
Jay-Cin 14
Burdette-Mil 14

Shutouts
Spahn-Mil 4
Jay-Cin 4

Saves
Miller-SF 17
Face-Pit 17
Henry-Cin 16
Brosnan-Cin 16
L.Sherry-LA 15

Innings Pitched
Burdette-Mil 272.1
Spahn-Mil 262.2
Cardwell-Chi 259.1
Koufax-LA 255.2
O'Toole-Cin 252.2

Fewest Hits/Game
Koufax-LA 7.46
Jay-Cin 7.90
Gibson-StL 7.92
Sadecki-StL 7.92
Spahn-Mil 8.09

Fewest BB/Game
Burdette-Mil 1.09
Friend-Pit 1.72
Purkey-Cin 1.86
Spahn-Mil 2.19
Ellsworth-Chi 2.31

Strikeouts
Koufax-LA 269
Williams-LA 205
Drysdale-LA 182
O'Toole-Cin 178
Gibson-StL 166

Strikeouts/Game
Koufax-LA 9.47
Williams-LA 7.84
Gibson-StL 7.07
Drysdale-LA 6.71
Gibbon-Pit 6.68

Ratio
Spahn-Mil 10.42
Burdette-Mil 10.94
Koufax-LA 10.95
Purkey-Cin 11.03
Jackson-StL 11.22

Earned Run Average
Spahn-Mil 3.02
O'Toole-Cin 3.10
Simmons-StL 3.13
McCormick-SF 3.20
Gibson-StL 3.24

Adjusted ERA
Simmons-StL 141
Gibson-StL 136
O'Toole-Cin 131
Spahn-Mil 124
Koufax-LA 123

Opponents' Batting Avg.
Koufax-LA .... .222
Jay-Cin .... .236
Sadecki-StL .... .238
Gibson-StL .... .239
O'Toole-Cin .... .240

Opponents' On Base Pct.
Spahn-Mil .... .293
Koufax-LA .... .295
Burdette-Mil .... .296
Purkey-Cin .... .297
Jackson-StL .... .303

Starter Runs
Spahn-Mil 29.7
O'Toole-Cin 26.2
McCormick-SF 23.0
Simmons-StL 19.6
Gibson-StL 18.7

Adjusted Starter Runs
Simmons-StL 27.6
Gibson-StL 27.3
O'Toole-Cin 27.1
Koufax-LA 23.3
Spahn-Mil 21.2

Clutch Pitching Index
Simmons-StL 122
Ellsworth-Chi 121
Podres-LA 116
McCormick-SF 115
Gibson-StL 114

Relief Runs
Miller-SF 18.6
Perranoski-LA 14.1
McMahon-Mil 12.2
Henry-Cin 10.9
Schultz-Chi 9.9

Adjusted Relief Runs
Perranoski-LA 17.2
Miller-SF 15.6
Henry-Cin 11.1
Schultz-Chi 11.0
McMahon-Mil 9.2

Relief Ranking
Miller-SF 26.8
Perranoski-LA 22.8
Schultz-Chi 21.8
Brosnan-Cin 18.5
Henry-Cin 13.1

Total Pitcher Index
Simmons-StL 3.5
Spahn-Mil 3.5
Gibson-StL 3.1
O'Toole-Cin 2.7
Drysdale-LA 2.2

Total Baseball Ranking
Robinson-Cin 5.4
Boyer-StL 4.4
Clemente-Pit 4.3
Mays-SF 4.2
Aaron-Mil 4.2

TEAM	G	W	L	PCT	GB	R	OR	AB	H	2B	3B	HR	BB	SO	AVG	OBP	SLG	PRO	PRO+	BR	/A	PF	CHI	RC	SB	CS	SBA	SBR
NY	163	109	53	.673		827	612	5559	1461	194	40	240	543	785	.263	.332	.442	.774	118	82	120	95	101	811	28	18	61	-2
DET	163	101	61	.623	8	841	671	5561	1481	215	53	180	673	867	.266	.349	.421	.770	109	96	75	103	99	835	98	36	73	8
BAL	163	95	67	.586	14	691	588	5481	1393	227	36	149	581	902	.254	.328	.390	.718	100	-16	-1	98	97	699	100	40	71	6
CHI	163	86	76	.531	23	765	726	5556	1475	216	46	138	550	612	.265	.338	.395	.733	104	1	29	98	101	754	39	30	57	-6
CLE	161	78	83	.484	30.5	737	752	5609	1493	257	39	150	492	720	.266	.328	.406	.734	105	9	29	97	99	743	34	11	76	4
BOS	163	76	86	.469	33	729	792	5508	1401	251	37	112	647	847	.254	.336	.374	.710	94	-22	-40	102	101	704	56	36	61	-5
MIN	161	70	90	.438	38	707	778	5417	1353	215	40	167	597	840	.250	.328	.397	.725	95	-5	-45	106	98	698	47	43	52	-12
LA	162	70	91	.435	38.5	744	784	5424	1331	218	22	189	681	1068	.245	.333	.398	.731	91	12	-71	111	99	734	37	28	57	-6
WAS	161	61	100	.379	47.5	618	776	5366	1307	217	44	119	558	917	.244	.317	.367	.684	90	-83	-72	99	98	625	81	47	63	-4
KC	162	61	100	.379	47.5	683	863	5423	1342	216	47	90	580	772	.247	.323	.354	.677	87	-90	-91	100	107	642	58	22	73	4
TOT	811					7342		54904	14037	2226	404	1534	5902	8330	.256	.331	.395	.726							578	311	65	-13

TEAM	CG	SH	SV	IP	H	H/G	HR	BB	SO	RAT	ERA	ERA+	OAV	OOB	PR	/A	PF	CPI	FA	E	DP	FW	PW	BW	SBW	DIF
NY	47	14	39	1451	1288	8.0	137	542	866	11.5	3.46	107	.239	.312	91	42	92	99	.980	124	180	1.6	4.2	11.9	-.0	10.4
DET	62	12	30	1459¹	1404	8.7	170	469	836	11.7	3.55	116	.252	.313	78	90	102	106	.976	146	147	.3	8.9	7.4	.9	2.4
BAL	54	21	33	1471¹	1226	7.5	109	617	926	11.5	3.22	121	.227	.310	132	113	97	97	.980	128	173	1.4	11.2	-.0	-.5	2.0
CHI	39	3	33	1448²	1491	9.3	158	498	814	12.4	4.06	97	.268	.329	-5	-23	97	102	.980	128	138	1.4	-2.3	2.9	.7	2.3
CLE	35	12	23	1443¹	1426	8.9	178	599	801	12.8	4.15	95	.258	.334	-20	-34	98	102	.977	139	142	.6	-3.4	2.9	.5	-3.2
BOS	35	6	30	1442²	1472	9.2	167	679	831	13.5	4.29	97	.266	.348	-43	-20	104	105	.977	144	170	.4	-2.0	-4.0	-.4	.9
MIN	49	14	23	1432¹	1415	8.7	163	570	914	12.8	4.28	99	.254	.331	-41	-6	105	95	.972	174	150	-1.4	-.6	-4.5	-1.1	-2.5
LA	25	5	34	1438	1391	8.7	180	713	973	13.4	4.31	105	.254	.343	-46	32	112	101	.969	192	154	-2.4	3.2	-7.0	-.5	-3.7
WAS	39	8	21	1425	1405	8.9	131	586	666	12.8	4.23	95	.260	.336	-33	-34	100	96	.975	156	171	-.4	-3.4	-7.1	-.3	-8.4
KC	32	5	23	1415	1519	9.7	141	629	703	14.0	4.74	87	.275	.355	-113	-99	102	97	.972	175	160	-1.4	-9.8	-9.0	.5	.2
TOT	417	100	289	14426²		8.8				12.6	4.02		.256	.331					.976	1506	1585					

Runs
Maris-NY 132
Mantle-NY 132
Colavito-Det 129
Cash-Det 119
Kaline-Det 116

Hits
Cash-Det 193
B.Robinson-Bal . . . 192
Kaline-Det 190
Francona-Cle 178
Richardson-NY . . . 173

Doubles
Kaline-Det 41
B.Robinson-Bal . . . 38
Kubek-NY 38
Siebern-KC 36
Power-Cle 34

Triples
Wood-Det 14
Lumpe-KC 9
Keough-Was 9

Home Runs
Maris-NY 61
Mantle-NY 54
Killebrew-Min 46
Gentile-Bal 46
Colavito-Det 45

Total Bases
Maris-NY 366
Cash-Det 354
Mantle-NY 353
Colavito-Det 338
Killebrew-Min 328

Runs Batted In
Maris-NY 142
Gentile-Bal 141
Colavito-Det 140
Cash-Det 132
Mantle-NY 128

Runs Produced
Colavito-Det 224
Maris-NY 213
Cash-Det 210
Mantle-NY 206
Gentile-Bal 191

Bases On Balls
Mantle-NY 126
Cash-Det 124
Colavito-Det 113
Killebrew-Min 107
Allison-Min 103

Batting Average
Cash-Det 361
Kaline-Det 324
Piersall-Cle 322
Mantle-NY 317
Gentile-Bal 302

On Base Percentage
Cash-Det 488
Mantle-NY 452
Gentile-Bal 428
Pearson-LA 422
Killebrew-Min 409

Slugging Average
Mantle-NY 687
Cash-Det 662
Gentile-Bal 646
Maris-NY 620
Killebrew-Min 606

Production
Cash-Det 1.150
Mantle-NY 1.138
Gentile-Bal 1.074
Killebrew-Min . . . 1.015
Maris-NY 997

Adjusted Production
Mantle-NY 210
Cash-Det 198
Gentile-Bal 187
Maris-NY 170
Killebrew-Min 159

Batter Runs
Cash-Det 86.1
Mantle-NY 76.3
Gentile-Bal 59.1
Killebrew-Min . . . 52.9
Colavito-Det 51.5

Adjusted Batter Runs
Cash-Det 83.9
Mantle-NY 80.2
Gentile-Bal 60.6
Maris-NY 53.8
Colavito-Det 49.2

Clutch Hitting Index
Malzone-Bos 134
Allison-Min 129
Siebern-KC 127
Minoso-Chi 126
Yastrzemski-Bos . . 126

Runs Created
Cash-Det 178
Mantle-NY 174
Colavito-Det 141
Gentile-Bal 138
Maris-NY 138

Total Average
Mantle-NY 1.384
Cash-Det 1.358
Gentile-Bal 1.196
Killebrew-Min . . . 1.098
Colavito-Det 1.051

Stolen Bases
Aparicio-Chi 53
Howser-KC 37
Wood-Det 30
Hinton-Was 22
Bruton-Det 22

Stolen Base Average
Hinton-Was 81.5
Howser-KC 80.4
Aparicio-Chi 80.3
Geiger-Bos 80.0
Landis-Chi 79.2

Stolen Base Runs
Aparicio-Chi 8.1
Howser-KC 5.7
Wood-Det 3.6
Kaline-Det 3.6
Hinton-Was 3.6

Fielding Runs
Boyer-NY 30.3
Landis-Chi 19.3
Power-Cle 18.1
Cottier-Det-Was . . 16.9
Lumpe-KC 16.0

Total Player Rating
Mantle-NY 7.6
Cash-Det 7.3
Gentile-Bal 5.0
Colavito-Det 4.8
Howard-NY 4.1

Wins
Ford-NY 25
Lary-Det 23
Barber-Bal 18
Bunning-Det 17
Terry-NY 16

Win Percentage
Ford-NY 862
Terry-NY 842
Arroyo-NY 750
Lary-Det 719

Games
Arroyo-NY 65
Morgan-LA 59
Lown-Chi 59
Kunkel-KC 58
Fornieles-Bos 57

Complete Games
Lary-Det 22
Pascual-Min 15
Barber-Bal 14

Shutouts
Pascual-Min 8
Barber-Bal 8
Pappas-Bal 4
Lary-Det 4
Bunning-Det 4

Saves
Arroyo-NY 29
Wilhelm-Bal 18
Fornieles-Bos 15
Moore-Min 14
Fox-Det 12

Innings Pitched
Ford-NY 283.0
Lary-Det 275.1
Bunning-Det 268.0
Ramos-Min 264.1
Pascual-Min 252.1

Fewest Hits/Game
Estrada-Bal 6.75
Pappas-Bal 6.79
Barber-Bal 7.03
Pascual-Min 7.31
Donovan-Was 7.36

Fewest BB/Game
Mossi-Det 1.76
Brown-Bal 1.78
Donovan-Was 1.87
Terry-NY 2.01
McClain-Was 2.04

Strikeouts
Pascual-Min 221
Ford-NY 209
Bunning-Det 194
Pizarro-Chi 188
McBride-LA 180

Strikeouts/Game
Pizarro-Chi 8.69
Pascual-Min 7.88
Estrada-Bal 6.79
McBride-LA 6.70
Ford-NY 6.65

Ratio
Donovan-Was 9.39
Terry-NY 9.80
Brown-Bal 10.10
Bunning-Det 10.48
Lary-Det 10.59

Earned Run Average
Donovan-Was 2.40
Stafford-NY 2.68
Mossi-Det 2.96
Pappas-Bal 3.04
Pizarro-Chi 3.05

Adjusted ERA
Donovan-Was 167
Stafford-NY 139
Mossi-Det 139
Schwall-Bos 129
Archer-KC 129

Opponents' Batting Avg.
Estrada-Bal 207
Pappas-Bal 208
Pascual-Min 217
Barber-Bal 218
Donovan-Was 224

Opponents' On Base Pct.
Donovan-Was 269
Terry-NY 277
Bunning-Det 285
Brown-Bal 286
Ford-NY 292

Starter Runs
Hoeft-Bal 30.7
Donovan-Was 30.4
Stafford-NY 29.2
Mossi-Det 28.5
Ford-NY 25.5

Adjusted Starter Runs
Mossi-Det 30.5
Donovan-Was 30.3
Hoeft-Bal 28.9
Bunning-Det 27.1
Lary-Det 26.5

Clutch Pitching Index
Schwall-Bos 131
Mossi-Det 119
Shaw-Chi-KC 115
Monbouquette-Bos 115
McBride-LA 112

Relief Runs
Arroyo-NY 24.2
Wilhelm-Bal 21.0
Morgan-LA 17.0
Fox-Det 16.6
Lown-Chi 14.2

Adjusted Relief Runs
Morgan-LA 21.9
Arroyo-NY 20.2
Wilhelm-Bal 19.6
Fox-Det 17.1
Lown-Chi 12.9

Relief Ranking
Arroyo-NY 41.6
Wilhelm-Bal 33.0
Morgan-LA 26.9
Fox-Det 26.9
Lown-Chi 17.0

Total Pitcher Index
Lary-Det 3.6
Donovan-Was 3.4
Mossi-Det 3.3
Hoeft-Bal 3.2
Stafford-NY 2.4

Total Baseball Ranking
Mantle-NY 7.6
Cash-Det 7.3
Gentile-Bal 5.0
Colavito-Det 4.8
Howard-NY 4.1

TEAM	G	W	L	PCT	GB	R	OR	AB	H	2B	3B	HR	BB	SO	AVG	OBP	SLG	PRO	PRO+	BR	/A	PF	CHI	RC	SB	CS	SBA	SBR
SF	165	103	62	.624		878	690	5588	1552	235	32	204	523	822	.278	.344	.441	.785	119	123	135	98	102	838	73	50	59	-8
LA	165	102	63	.618	1	842	697	5628	1510	192	65	140	572	886	.268	.339	.400	.739	112	41	86	94	107	783	198	43	82	34
CIN	162	98	64	.605	3.5	802	685	5645	1523	252	40	167	498	903	.270	.333	.417	.750	104	54	30	103	103	779	66	39	63	-4
PIT	161	93	68	.578	8	706	685	5483	1468	240	65	108	432	836	.268	.323	.394	.717	99	-15	-16	100	102	682	50	39	56	-8
MIL	162	86	76	.531	15.5	730	665	5458	1376	204	38	181	581	975	.252	.328	.403	.731	105	16	35	97	99	720	57	27	68	1
STL	163	84	78	.519	17.5	774	664	5643	1528	221	31	137	515	846	.271	.337	.394	.731	94	22	-49	110	102	747	86	41	68	1
PHI	161	81	80	.503	20	705	759	5420	1410	199	39	142	531	923	.260	.332	.390	.722	103	4	26	97	98	705	79	42	65	-2
HOU	162	64	96	.400	36.5	592	717	5558	1370	170	47	105	493	806	.246	.312	.351	.663	91	-117	-63	93	97	605	42	30	58	-5
CHI	162	59	103	.364	42.5	632	827	5534	1398	196	56	126	504	1044	.253	.319	.377	.696	90	-53	-79	104	94	657	78	50	61	-7
NY	161	40	120	.250	60.5	617	948	5492	1318	166	40	139	616	991	.240	.320	.361	.681	88	-75	-87	102	94	640	59	48	55	-11
TOT	812					7278		55449	14453	2075	453	1449	5265	9032	.261	.329	.393	.722							788	409	66	-9

TEAM	CG	SH	SV	IP	H	H/G	HR	BB	SO	RAT	ERA	ERA+	OAV	OOB	PR	/A	PF	CPI	FA	E	DP	FW	PW	BW	SBW	DIF
SF	62	10	39	1461²	1399	8.6	148	503	886	11.9	3.79	100	.251	.316	24	0	96	95	.977	142	153	1.0	.0	13.5	-.7	6.8
LA	44	8	46	1488²	1386	8.4	115	588	1104	12.1	3.62	100	.245	.319	54	2	92	94	.970	193	144	-2.1	.2	8.6	3.5	9.3
CIN	51	13	35	1460²	1397	8.6	149	567	964	12.4	3.75	107	.254	.329	31	44	102	104	.977	145	144	.6	4.4	3.0	-.3	9.3
PIT	40	13	41	1432¹	1433	9.0	118	466	897	12.1	3.37	117	.262	.322	90	89	100	110	.976	152	177	.2	8.9	-1.6	-.7	5.8
MIL	59	10	24	1434²	1443	9.1	151	407	802	11.8	3.68	103	.262	.317	42	19	96	103	.980	124	154	1.9	1.9	3.5	.2	-2.5
STL	53	17	25	1463¹	1394	8.6	149	517	914	11.9	3.55	120	.252	.319	64	117	108	104	.979	132	170	1.5	11.7	-4.9	.2	-5.4
PHI	43	7	24	1426²	1469	9.3	155	574	863	13.2	4.28	90	.268	.343	-53	-65	98	102	.977	138	167	1.0	-6.5	2.6	-.1	3.5
HOU	34	9	19	1453²	1446	9.0	113	471	1047	12.1	3.83	98	.259	.321	19	-15	95	95	.973	173	149	-1.0	-1.5	-6.3	-.4	-6.8
CHI	29	4	26	1438¹	1509	9.4	159	601	783	13.5	4.54	91	.272	.348	-95	-62	105	99	.977	146	171	.6	-6.2	-7.9	-.6	-7.9
NY	43	4	10	1430	1577	9.9	192	571	772	13.8	5.04	83	.281	.352	-175	-137	106	96	.967	210	167	-3.3	-13.7	-8.7	-1.0	-13.3
TOT	458	95	289	14490		9.0				12.5	3.94		.261	.329					.975	1555	1596					

Runs		Hits		Doubles		Triples		Home Runs		Total Bases	
Robinson-Cin	134	H.Davis-LA	230	Robinson-Cin	51	Wills-LA	10	Mays-SF	49	Mays-SF	382
Wills-LA	130	Wills-LA	208	Mays-SF	36	Virdon-Pit	10	H.Aaron-Mil	45	Robinson-Cin	380
Mays-SF	130	Robinson-Cin	208	Groat-Pit	34	W.Davis-LA	10	Robinson-Cin	39	H.Aaron-Mil	366
H.Aaron-Mil	127	White-StL	199			Callison-Phi	10	Banks-Chi	37	H.Davis-LA	356
H.Davis-LA	120	Groat-Pit	199					Cepeda-SF	35	Cepeda-SF	324

Runs Batted In		Runs Produced		Bases On Balls		Batting Average		On Base Percentage		Slugging Average	
H.Davis-LA	153	H.Davis-LA	246	Mathews-Mil	101	H.Davis-LA	.346	Robinson-Cin	.424	Robinson-Cin	.624
Mays-SF	141	Robinson-Cin	231	Gilliam-LA	93	Robinson-Cin	.342	Musial-StL	.420	H.Aaron-Mil	.618
Robinson-Cin	136	Mays-SF	222	Ashburn-NY	81	Musial-StL	.330	Skinner-Pit	.397	Mays-SF	.615
H.Aaron-Mil	128	H.Aaron-Mil	210	Mays-SF	78	White-StL	.324	Altman-Chi	.394	Howard-LA	.560
Howard-LA	119					H.Aaron-Mil	.323	H.Aaron-Mil	.393	H.Davis-LA	.535

Production		Adjusted Production		Batter Runs		Adjusted Batter Runs		Clutch Hitting Index		Runs Created	
Robinson-Cin	1.048	Robinson-Cin	172	Robinson-Cin	66.6	Robinson-Cin	64.0	H.Davis-LA	146	Robinson-Cin	160
H.Aaron-Mil	1.012	H.Aaron-Mil	171	Mays-SF	54.1	H.Aaron-Mil	56.1	Santo-Chi	130	Mays-SF	146
Mays-SF	1.001	Mays-SF	167	H.Aaron-Mil	54.0	Mays-SF	55.5	Howard-LA	127	H.Aaron-Mil	140
Musial-StL	.928	H.Davis-LA	151	H.Davis-LA	37.2	H.Davis-LA	42.2	White-StL	120	H.Davis-LA	129
H.Davis-LA	.914	Howard-LA	149	Altman-Chi	31.5	Skinner-Pit	30.1	Kuenn-SF	118	White-StL	114

Total Average		Stolen Bases		Stolen Base Average		Stolen Base Runs		Fielding Runs		Total Player Rating	
Robinson-Cin	1.125	Wills-LA	104	Mays-SF	90.0	Wills-LA	23.4	Mazeroski-Pit	41.1	Robinson-Cin	6.2
Mays-SF	1.060	W.Davis-LA	32	Wills-LA	88.9	W.Davis-LA	5.4	Callison-Phi	25.4	Mays-SF	5.5
H.Aaron-Mil	1.050	Pinson-Cin	26	W.Davis-LA	82.1	Mays-SF	4.2	Kanehl-NY	18.2	Mazeroski-Pit	5.0
Musial-StL	.957	Javier-StL	26	Clendenon-Pit	80.0	Pinson-Cin	3.0	Burright-LA	14.2	H.Aaron-Mil	4.1
Skinner-Pit	.930	Taylor-Phi	20	Pinson-Cin	76.5			Groat-Pit	13.9	Callison-Phi	4.1

Wins		Win Percentage		Games		Complete Games		Shutouts		Saves	
Drysdale-LA	25	Purkey-Cin	.821	Perranoski-LA	70	Spahn-Mil	22	Gibson-StL	5	Face-Pit	28
Sanford-SF	24	Sanford-SF	.774	Baldschun-Phi	67	O'Dell-SF	20	Friend-Pit	5	Perranoski-LA	20
Purkey-Cin	23	Drysdale-LA	.735	Roebuck-LA	64	Mahaffey-Phi	20			Miller-SF	19
Jay-Cin	21	Pierce-SF	.727	Face-Pit	63	Drysdale-LA	19			McDaniel-StL	14
		Shaw-Mil	.625	Olivo-Pit	62						

Innings Pitched		Fewest Hits/Game		Fewest BB/Game		Strikeouts		Strikeouts/Game		Ratio	
Drysdale-LA	314.1	Koufax-LA	6.54	Shaw-Mil	1.76	Drysdale-LA	232	Koufax-LA	10.55	Koufax-LA	9.42
Purkey-Cin	288.1	Gibson-StL	6.70	Friend-Pit	1.82	Koufax-LA	216	Johnson-Hou	8.13	Farrell-Hou	10.06
O'Dell-SF	280.2	Bennett-Phi	7.42	Spahn-Mil	1.84	Gibson-StL	208	Gibson-StL	8.01	Spahn-Mil	10.23
Mahaffey-Phi	274.0	Drysdale-LA	7.79	Pierce-SF	1.94	Farrell-Hou	203	Bennett-Phi	7.68	Pierce-SF	10.26
Jay-Cin	273.0	Broglio-StL	7.81	Purkey-Cin	2.00	O'Dell-SF	195	Farrell-Hou	7.56	Drysdale-LA	10.34

Earned Run Average		Adjusted ERA		Opponents' Batting Avg.		Opponents' On Base Pct.		Starter Runs		Adjusted Starter Runs	
Koufax-LA	2.54	Gibson-StL	150	Koufax-LA	.197	Koufax-LA	.261	Drysdale-LA	38.6	Purkey-Cin	38.9
Shaw-Mil	2.80	Purkey-Cin	143	Gibson-StL	.204	Farrell-Hou	.280	Purkey-Cin	36.3	Gibson-StL	36.8
Purkey-Cin	2.81	Koufax-LA	143	Bennett-Phi	.224	Drysdale-LA	.283	Koufax-LA	28.7	Broglio-StL	31.4
Drysdale-LA	2.83	Broglio-StL	142	Drysdale-LA	.230	Pierce-SF	.284	Shaw-Mil	28.5	Drysdale-LA	27.8
Gibson-StL	2.85	Shaw-Mil	136	Farrell-Hou	.233	Spahn-Mil	.287	Gibson-StL	28.3	Friend-Pit	25.4

Clutch Pitching Index		Relief Runs		Adjusted Relief Runs		Relief Ranking		Total Pitcher Index		Total Baseball Ranking	
Shaw-Mil	123	Face-Pit	20.8	Face-Pit	20.8	Face-Pit	45.2	Gibson-StL	4.7	Robinson-Cin	6.2
Friend-Pit	119	McMahon-Mil-Hou	19.9	Shantz-Hou-StL	18.9	McMahon-Mil-Hou	26.6	Purkey-Cin	4.1	Mays-SF	5.5
Broglio-StL	116	Shantz-Hou-StL	17.3	McMahon-Mil-Hou	18.1	Shantz-Hou-StL	23.9	Drysdale-LA	3.4	Mazeroski-Pit	5.0
McBean-Pit	114	Umbricht-Hou	14.3	Umbricht-Hou	12.8	Elston-Chi	23.9	Broglio-StL	3.1	Gibson-StL	4.7
Koonce-Chi	111	Perranoski-LA	13.0	Elston-Chi	12.6	Baldschun-Phi	20.3	Spahn-Mil	2.9	H.Aaron-Mil	4.1

TEAM	G	W	L	PCT	GB	R	OR	AB	H	2B	3B	HR	BB	SO	AVG	OBP	SLG	PRO	PRO+	BR	/A	PF	CHI	RC	SB	CS	SBA	SBR
NY	162	96	66	.593		817	680	5644	1509	240	29	199	584	842	.267	.339	.426	.765	116	87	111	97	99	816	42	29	59	-5
MIN	163	91	71	.562	5	798	713	5561	1445	215	39	185	649	823	.260	.340	.412	.752	104	67	40	104	100	789	33	20	62	-2
LA	162	86	76	.531	10	718	706	5499	1377	232	35	137	602	917	.250	.328	.380	.708	100	-23	0	97	103	698	46	27	63	-2
DET	161	85	76	.528	10.5	758	692	5456	1352	191	36	209	651	894	.248	.332	.411	.743	102	41	16	104	100	757	69	21	77	8
CHI	162	85	77	.525	11	707	658	5514	1415	250	56	92	620	674	.257	.336	.372	.708	97	-13	-9	100	99	701	76	40	66	-1
CLE	162	80	82	.494	16	682	745	5484	1341	202	22	180	502	939	.245	.314	.388	.702	97	-46	-24	97	103	671	35	16	69	1
BAL	162	77	85	.475	19	652	680	5491	1363	225	34	156	516	931	.248	.316	.387	.703	100	-42	-8	95	98	665	45	32	58	-6
BOS	160	76	84	.475	19	707	756	5530	1429	257	53	146	525	923	.258	.326	.403	.729	99	9	-14	103	98	716	39	33	54	-8
KC	162	72	90	.444	24	745	837	5576	1467	220	58	116	556	803	.263	.334	.386	.720	97	3	-19	103	102	738	76	21	78	10
WAS	162	60	101	.373	35.5	599	716	5484	1370	206	38	132	466	789	.250	.310	.373	.683	90	-82	-76	99	97	623	99	53	65	-2
TOT	809					7183		55239	14068	2238	400	1552	5671	8535	.255	.328	.394	.722							560	292	66	-7

TEAM	CG	SH	SV	IP	H	H/G	HR	BB	SO	RAT	ERA	ERA+	OAV	OOB	PR	/A	PF	CPI	FA	E	DP	FW	PW	BW	SBW	DIF
NY	33	10	42	1470[1]	1375	8.4	146	499	838	11.6	3.70	101	.247	.312	44	7	94	96	.979	131	151	.4	.7	11.2	-.4	3.2
MIN	53	11	27	1463[1]	1400	8.6	166	493	948	11.9	3.89	105	.253	.319	13	31	103	99	.980	129	173	.5	3.1	4.0	-.1	2.5
LA	23	15	47	1466	1412	8.7	118	616	858	12.8	3.70	104	.253	.332	45	27	97	104	.973	175	153	-2.2	2.7	.0	-.1	4.6
DET	46	8	35	1443[2]	1452	9.1	169	503	873	12.4	3.81	107	.259	.323	26	42	103	105	.974	156	114	-1.1	4.2	1.6	.9	-1.1
CHI	50	13	28	1451[2]	1380	8.6	123	537	821	12.0	3.73	105	.251	.320	38	28	98	97	.982	110	153	1.6	2.8	-.9	-.0	.6
CLE	45	12	31	1441	1410	8.8	174	594	780	12.7	4.14	94	.258	.334	-27	-43	98	102	.978	139	168	-.1	-4.3	-2.4	.2	5.7
BAL	32	8	33	1462[1]	1373	8.5	147	549	898	12.0	3.69	102	.249	.320	45	11	95	101	.980	122	152	.9	1.1	-.8	-.5	-4.6
BOS	34	12	40	1437[2]	1416	8.9	159	502	923	13.1	4.22	98	.258	.339	-40	-14	104	101	.979	131	152	.3	-1.4	-1.4	-.7	-.7
KC	32	4	33	1434	1450	9.1	199	655	825	13.5	4.79	87	.263	.346	-131	-101	105	97	.979	132	131	.3	-10.2	-1.9	1.1	1.7
WAS	38	11	13	1445	1400	8.7	151	593	771	12.5	4.04	100	.256	.331	-12	-1	102	100	.978	139	160	-.1	-.1	-7.6	-.1	-12.5
TOT	386	104	329	14515		8.7				12.4	3.97		.255	.328					.978	1364	1507					

Runs

Pearson-LA	115
Siebern-KC	114
Allison-Min	102
Yastrzemski-Bos	99
Richardson-NY	99

Hits

Richardson-NY	209
Lumpe-KC	193
B.Robinson-Bal	192
Yastrzemski-Bos	191
Robinson-Chi	187

Doubles

Robinson-Chi	45
Yastrzemski-Bos	43
Bressoud-Bos	40
Richardson-NY	38

Triples

Cimoli-KC	15
Robinson-Chi	10
Lumpe-KC	10
Clinton-Bos	10

Home Runs

Killebrew-Min	48
Cash-Det	39
Wagner-LA	37
Colavito-Det	37

Total Bases

Colavito-Det	309
B.Robinson-Bal	308
Wagner-LA	306
Yastrzemski-Bos	303
Killebrew-Min	301

Runs Batted In

Killebrew-Min	126
Siebern-KC	117
Colavito-Det	112
Robinson-Chi	109
Wagner-LA	107

Runs Produced

Siebern-KC	206
Robinson-Chi	187
Rollins-Min	176
Allison-Min	175
Yastrzemski-Bos	174

Bases On Balls

Mantle-NY	122
Siebern-KC	110
Killebrew-Min	106
Cash-Det	104
Cunningham-Chi	101

Batting Average

Runnels-Bos	.326
Mantle-NY	.321
Robinson-Chi	.312
Hinton-Was	.310
Siebern-KC	.308

On Base Percentage

Mantle-NY	.488
Siebern-KC	.416
Cunningham-Chi	.415
Runnels-Bos	.411
Robinson-Chi	.387

Slugging Average

Mantle-NY	.605
Killebrew-Min	.545
Colavito-Det	.514
Cash-Det	.513
Allison-Min	.511

Production

Mantle-NY	1.093
Killebrew-Min	.914
Siebern-KC	.911
Cash-Det	.897
Colavito-Det	.889

Adjusted Production

Mantle-NY	198
Siebern-KC	140
Killebrew-Min	137
Cash-Det	134
Colavito-Det	132

Batter Runs

Mantle-NY	57.3
Siebern-KC	41.1
Killebrew-Min	33.1
Colavito-Det	31.4
Kaline-Det	30.7

Adjusted Batter Runs

Mantle-NY	59.1
Siebern-KC	38.6
Killebrew-Min	30.2
Kaline-Det	28.9
Colavito-Det	28.5

Clutch Hitting Index

Robinson-Chi	144
Howard-NY	124
Malzone-Bos	122
J.Thomas-LA	120
Siebern-KC	120

Runs Created

Siebern-KC	129
Mantle-NY	126
Colavito-Det	117
Killebrew-Min	113
Robinson-Chi	113

Total Average

Mantle-NY	1.385
Siebern-KC	.956
Cash-Det	.950
Killebrew-Min	.945
Allison-Min	.901

Stolen Bases

Aparicio-Chi	31
Hinton-Was	28
Wood-Det	24
Charles-KC	20

Stolen Base Average

Howser-KC	90.5
Wood-Det	88.9
Charles-KC	83.3
Tartabull-KC	79.2
Hinton-Was	73.7

Stolen Base Runs

Wood-Det	5.4
Howser-KC	4.5
Charles-KC	3.6
Tartabull-KC	2.7
Mantle-NY	2.7

Fielding Runs

Boyer-NY	36.2
Versalles-Min	31.6
Bressoud-Bos	24.5
Kindall-Cle	20.7
Cottier-Was	20.5

Total Player Rating

Mantle-NY	4.8
Boyer-NY	4.0
Bressoud-Bos	3.8
Colavito-Det	3.7
Kaline-Det	3.5

Wins

Terry-NY	23
Pascual-Min	20
Herbert-Chi	20
Donovan-Cle	20
Bunning-Det	19

Win Percentage

Herbert-Chi	.690
Ford-NY	.680
Donovan-Cle	.667
Aguirre-Det	.667
Terry-NY	.657

Games

Radatz-Bos	62
Wyatt-KC	59

Complete Games

Pascual-Min	18
Kaat-Min	16
Donovan-Cle	16
Terry-NY	14

Shutouts

Pascual-Min	5
Kaat-Min	5
Donovan-Cle	5
Monbouquette-Bos	4
McBride-LA	4

Saves

Radatz-Bos	24
Bridges-NY	18
Fox-Det	16
Wilhelm-Bal	15
Bell-Cle	12

Innings Pitched

Terry-NY	298.2
Kaat-Min	269.0
Bunning-Det	258.0
Pascual-Min	257.2
Ford-NY	257.2

Fewest Hits/Game

Aguirre-Det	6.75
Cheney-Was	6.96
Belinsky-LA	7.16
Wilson-Bos	7.67
Stenhouse-Was	7.72

Fewest BB/Game

Donovan-Cle	1.69
Terry-NY	1.72
Mossi-Det	1.80
Roberts-Bal	1.93
Pascual-Min	2.06

Strikeouts

Pascual-Min	206
Bunning-Det	184
Terry-NY	176
Pizarro-Chi	173
Kaat-Min	173

Strikeouts/Game

Pizarro-Chi	7.66
Cheney-Was	7.63
Pascual-Min	7.20
Belinsky-LA	6.97
Estrada-Bal	6.65

Ratio

Terry-NY	9.55
Aguirre-Det	9.67
Pascual-Min	10.37
Roberts-Bal	10.40
Fisher-Chi	10.59

Earned Run Average

Aguirre-Det	2.21
Roberts-Bal	2.78
Ford-NY	2.90
Chance-LA	2.96
Fisher-Chi	3.10

Adjusted ERA

Aguirre-Det	184
Roberts-Bal	135
Chance-LA	130
Kaat-Min	130
Ford-NY	129

Opponents' Batting Avg.

Aguirre-Det	.205
Cheney-Was	.213
Belinsky-LA	.216
Terry-NY	.231
Wilson-Bos	.231

Opponents' On Base Pct.

Aguirre-Det	.269
Terry-NY	.270
Pascual-Min	.286
Roberts-Bal	.289
Fisher-Chi	.293

Starter Runs

Aguirre-Det	42.3
Ford-NY	30.7
Terry-NY	25.8
Roberts-Bal	25.4
Kaat-Min	24.7

Adjusted Starter Runs

Aguirre-Det	44.7
Kaat-Min	28.1
Ford-NY	24.3
Pascual-Min	22.0
Monbouquette-Bos	21.0

Clutch Pitching Index

Chance-LA	114
Roberts-Bal	111
Ramos-Cle	110
Ford-NY	110
Perry-Cle	109

Relief Runs

Radatz-Bos	24.0
Hall-Bal	22.2
Wilhelm-Bal	21.0
Fox-Det	14.6
Fowler-LA	10.0

Adjusted Relief Runs

Radatz-Bos	26.2
Hall-Bal	19.4
Wilhelm-Bal	18.9
Fox-Det	15.2
Fowler-LA	9.0

Relief Ranking

Radatz-Bos	39.7
Wilhelm-Bal	37.9
Hall-Bal	20.0
Fox-Det	18.9
Bridges-NY	10.0

Total Pitcher Index

Kaat-Min	3.9
Aguirre-Det	3.5
Pascual-Min	3.2
Ford-NY	2.9
Herbert-Chi	2.6

Total Baseball Ranking

Mantle-NY	4.8
Boyer-NY	4.0
Kaat-Min	3.9
Bressoud-Bos	3.8
Colavito-Det	3.7

TEAM	G	W	L	PCT	GB	R	OR	AB	H	2B	3B	HR	BB	SO	AVG	OBP	SLG	PRO	PRO+	BR	/A	PF	CHI	RC	SB	CS	SBA	SBR
LA	163	99	63	.611		640	550	5428	1361	178	34	110	453	867	.251	.311	.357	.668	106	-3	39	93	105	596	124	70	64	-5
STL	162	93	69	.574	6	747	628	5678	1540	231	66	128	458	915	.271	.328	.403	.731	107	119	60	109	99	751	77	42	65	-2
SF	162	88	74	.543	11	725	641	5579	1442	206	35	197	441	889	.258	.318	.414	.732	118	111	118	99	98	712	55	49	53	-13
PHI	162	87	75	.537	12	642	578	5524	1390	228	54	126	403	955	.252	.308	.381	.689	106	28	35	99	99	640	56	39	59	-7
CIN	162	86	76	.531	13	648	594	5416	1333	225	44	122	474	960	.246	.312	.371	.683	100	25	7	103	101	630	92	58	61	-7
MIL	163	84	78	.519	15	677	603	5518	1345	204	39	139	525	954	.244	.314	.370	.684	105	30	37	99	102	643	75	52	59	-9
CHI	162	82	80	.506	17	570	578	5404	1286	205	44	127	439	1049	.238	.300	.363	.663	92	-21	-54	105	97	573	68	60	53	-16
PIT	162	74	88	.457	25	567	595	5536	1385	181	49	108	454	940	.250	.310	.359	.669	80	-2	-6	101	92	603	57	41	58	-8
HOU	162	66	96	.407	33	464	640	5384	1184	170	39	62	456	938	.220	.284	.301	.585	80	-159	-121	94	103	461	39	30	57	-6
NY	162	51	111	.315	48	501	774	5336	1168	156	35	96	457	1078	.219	.286	.315	.601	79	-129	-139	102	106	477	41	52	44	-19
TOT	811					6181		54803	13434	1984	439	1215	4560	9545	.245	.307	.364	.671							684	493	58	-91

TEAM	CG	SH	SV	IP	H	H/G	HR	BB	SO	RAT	ERA	ERA+	OAV	OOB	PR	/A	PF	CPI	FA	E	DP	FW	PW	BW	SBW	DIF
LA	51	24	29	1469²	1329	8.1	111	402	1095	10.8	2.85	106	.239	.294	71	27	92	103	.975	159	129	-.0	2.9	4.2	.4	10.4
STL	49	17	32	1463	1329	8.2	124	463	978	11.3	3.32	107	.241	.305	-5	37	108	97	.976	147	136	.6	4.0	6.5	.8	.0
SF	46	9	30	1469	1380	8.5	126	464	954	11.5	3.35	96	.246	.307	-9	-24	97	99	.975	156	113	.1	-2.6	12.8	-.4	-2.9
PHI	45	12	31	1457¹	1262	7.8	113	553	1052	11.4	3.09	105	.235	.311	32	23	98	104	.978	142	147	.9	2.5	3.8	.2	-1.4
CIN	55	22	36	1439²	1307	8.2	117	425	1048	11.1	3.29	102	.242	.302	-1	8	102	96	.978	135	127	1.3	.9	.8	.2	1.8
MIL	56	18	25	1471²	1327	8.1	149	489	924	11.3	3.27	99	.241	.306	4	-8	98	103	.980	129	161	1.8	-.9	4.0	.0	-1.9
CHI	45	15	28	1457	1357	8.4	119	400	851	11.0	3.08	114	.249	.303	34	70	107	105	.976	155	172	.2	7.6	-5.9	-.8	-.1
PIT	34	16	33	1448	1350	8.4	99	457	900	11.5	3.10	107	.249	.313	31	33	100	107	.972	182	195	-1.4	3.6	-.7	.1	-8.6
HOU	36	16	20	1450¹	1341	8.3	95	378	937	10.9	3.44	92	.245	.298	-24	-46	96	87	.974	162	100	-.3	-5.0	-13.1	.3	3.0
NY	42	5	12	1427²	1452	9.2	162	529	806	12.8	4.12	85	.263	.332	-132	-101	106	100	.967	210	151	-3.1	-11.0	-15.1	-1.1	.2
TOT	459	154	276	14553¹		8.3				11.4	3.29		.245	.307					.975	1577	1431					

Runs		Hits		Doubles		Triples		Home Runs		Total Bases	
H.Aaron-Mil	121	Pinson-Cin	204	Groat-StL	43	Pinson-Cin	14	McCovey-SF	44	H.Aaron-Mil	370
Mays-SF	115	Groat-StL	201	Pinson-Cin	37	Gonzalez-Phi	12	H.Aaron-Mil	44	Mays-SF	347
Flood-StL	112	H.Aaron-Mil	201	Williams-Chi	36	Groat-StL	11	Mays-SF	38	Pinson-Cin	335
White-StL	106	White-StL	200	Gonzalez-Phi	36	Callison-Phi	11	Cepeda-SF	34	Cepeda-SF	326
McCovey-SF	103	Flood-StL	200	Callison-Phi	36	Brock-Chi	11	Howard-LA	28	White-StL	323

Runs Batted In		Runs Produced		Bases On Balls		Batting Average		On Base Percentage		Slugging Average	
H.Aaron-Mil	130	H.Aaron-Mil	207	Mathews-Mil	124	H.Davis-LA	.326	Mathews-Mil	.400	H.Aaron-Mil	.586
Boyer-StL	111	White-StL	188	Robinson-Cin	81	Clemente-Pit	.320	H.Aaron-Mil	.394	Mays-SF	.582
White-StL	109	Pinson-Cin	180	H.Aaron-Mil	78	Groat-StL	.319	Mays-SF	.384	McCovey-SF	.566
Pinson-Cin	106	Mays-SF	180	Boyer-StL	70	H.Aaron-Mil	.319	Robinson-Cin	.381	Cepeda-SF	.563
Mays-SF	103	Boyer-StL	173	Schofield-Pit	69	Cepeda-SF	.316	Groat-StL	.380	Pinson-Cin	.514

Production		Adjusted Production		Batter Runs		Adjusted Batter Runs		Clutch Hitting Index		Runs Created	
H.Aaron-Mil	.980	H.Aaron-Mil	180	H.Aaron-Mil	63.0	H.Aaron-Mil	63.8	Robinson-Cin	147	H.Aaron-Mil	149
Mays-SF	.966	Mays-SF	176	Mays-SF	55.8	Mays-SF	56.5	Fairly-LA	146	Mays-SF	131
Cepeda-SF	.930	Cepeda-SF	166	Cepeda-SF	45.4	Cepeda-SF	46.1	Sievers-Phi	141	White-StL	117
McCovey-SF	.916	McCovey-SF	161	McCovey-SF	41.1	McCovey-SF	41.8	Boyer-StL	140	Cepeda-SF	113
Pinson-Cin	.864	Mathews-Mil	147	Mathews-Mil	37.4	Mathews-Mil	38.2	Edwards-Cin	130	Pinson-Cin	113

Total Average		Stolen Bases		Stolen Base Average		Stolen Base Runs		Fielding Runs		Total Player Rating	
H.Aaron-Mil	1.063	Wills-LA	40	H.Aaron-Mil	86.1	H.Aaron-Mil	6.3	Mazeroski-Pit	56.7	H.Aaron-Mil	6.1
Mays-SF	.984	H.Aaron-Mil	31	Gilliam-LA	79.2	Pinson-Cin	3.3	Callison-Phi	20.9	Mays-SF	6.0
McCovey-SF	.911	Pinson-Cin	27	Pinson-Cin	77.1	Maye-Mil	3.0	Hubbs-Chi	20.1	Mazeroski-Pit	6.0
Cepeda-SF	.906	Robinson-Cin	26	Robinson-Cin	72.2	Harper-Cin	3.0	Harkness-NY	16.4	Mathews-Mil	5.0
Mathews-Mil	.894	W.Davis-LA	25	Taylor-Phi	71.9	Gilliam-LA	2.7	Wine-Phi	14.6	Callison-Phi	4.6

Wins		Win Percentage		Games		Complete Games		Shutouts		Saves	
Marichal-SF	25	Perranoski-LA	.842	Perranoski-LA	69	Spahn-Mil	22	Koufax-LA	11	McDaniel-Chi	22
Koufax-LA	25	Koufax-LA	.833	Baldschun-Phi	65	Koufax-LA	20	Spahn-Mil	7	Perranoski-LA	21
Spahn-Mil	23	Spahn-Mil	.767	Bearnarth-NY	58	Ellsworth-Chi	19	Simmons-StL	6	Face-Pit	16
Maloney-Cin	23	Maloney-Cin	.767	Sisk-Pit	57	Marichal-SF	18	Maloney-Cin	6	Baldschun-Phi	16
Ellsworth-Chi	22	Marichal-SF	.758	McDaniel-Chi	57	Drysdale-LA	17			Henry-Cin	14

Innings Pitched		Fewest Hits/Game		Fewest BB/Game		Strikeouts		Strikeouts/Game		Ratio	
Marichal-SF	321.1	Koufax-LA	6.19	Friend-Pit	1.47	Koufax-LA	306	Maloney-Cin	9.53	Koufax-LA	7.96
Drysdale-LA	315.1	Culp-Phi	6.55	Farrell-Hou	1.56	Maloney-Cin	265	Koufax-LA	8.86	Farrell-Hou	8.81
Koufax-LA	311.0	Maloney-Cin	6.58	Nuxhall-Cin	1.62	Drysdale-LA	251	Culp-Phi	7.79	Marichal-SF	9.02
Ellsworth-Chi	290.2	Ellsworth-Chi	6.90	Drysdale-LA	1.63	Marichal-SF	248	Short-Phi	7.27	Ellsworth-Chi	9.29
Sanford-SF	284.1	Farrell-Hou	7.16	Koufax-LA	1.68	Gibson-StL	204	Lemaster-Mil	7.22	Friend-Pit	9.55

Earned Run Average		Adjusted ERA		Opponents' Batting Avg.		Opponents' On Base Pct.		Starter Runs		Adjusted Starter Runs	
Koufax-LA	1.88	Ellsworth-Chi	167	Koufax-LA	.189	Koufax-LA	.230	Koufax-LA	48.6	Ellsworth-Chi	45.3
Ellsworth-Chi	2.11	Koufax-LA	161	Maloney-Cin	.202	Marichal-SF	.256	Ellsworth-Chi	38.2	Koufax-LA	39.4
Friend-Pit	2.34	Simmons-StL	143	Culp-Phi	.206	Farrell-Hou	.256	Marichal-SF	31.4	Jackson-Chi	29.2
Marichal-SF	2.41	Friend-Pit	141	Ellsworth-Chi	.210	Ellsworth-Chi	.263	Friend-Pit	28.2	Friend-Pit	28.5
Simmons-StL	2.48	Jackson-Chi	137	Broglio-StL	.216	Friend-Pit	.269	Drysdale-LA	23.2	Marichal-SF	28.2

Clutch Pitching Index		Relief Runs		Adjusted Relief Runs		Relief Ranking		Total Pitcher Index		Total Baseball Ranking	
Schwall-Pit	118	Perranoski-LA	23.1	Veale-Pit	19.5	Perranoski-LA	32.7	Ellsworth-Chi	5.3	H.Aaron-Mil	6.1
Spahn-Mil	115	Veale-Pit	19.4	Perranoski-LA	19.3	Woodeshick-Hou	26.5	Jackson-Chi	3.9	Mays-SF	6.0
Short-Phi	111	Klippstein-Phi	16.9	Klippstein-Phi	16.2	Baldschun-Phi	20.6	Koufax-LA	3.7	Mazeroski-Pit	6.0
Cardwell-Pit	110	Woodeshick-Hou	16.6	Woodeshick-Hou	14.9	Veale-Pit	17.5	Spahn-Mil	3.1	Ellsworth-Chi	5.3
Buhl-Chi	109	Baldschun-Phi	12.5	Baldschun-Phi	11.8	Klippstein-Phi	16.9	Marichal-SF	3.1	Mathews-Mil	5.0

TEAM	G	W	L	PCT	GB	R	OR	AB	H	2B	3B	HR	BB	SO	AVG	OBP	SLG	PRO	PRO+	BR	/A	PF	CHI	RC	SB	CS	SBA	SBR
NY	161	104	57	.646		714	547	5506	1387	197	35	188	434	808	.252	.310	.403	.713	106	27	33	99	105	686	42	26	62	-3
CHI	162	94	68	.580	10.5	683	544	5508	1379	208	40	114	571	896	.250	.325	.365	.690	101	4	15	98	101	675	64	28	70	2
MIN	161	91	70	.565	13	767	602	5531	1408	223	35	225	547	912	.255	.326	.430	.756	115	116	103	102	98	777	32	14	70	1
BAL	162	86	76	.531	18.5	644	621	5448	1359	207	32	146	469	940	.249	.312	.380	.692	101	-7	-9	100	100	645	97	34	74	9
DET	162	79	83	.488	25.5	700	703	5500	1388	195	36	148	592	908	.252	.329	.382	.711	102	43	20	103	98	699	73	32	70	3
CLE	162	79	83	.488	25.5	635	702	5496	1314	214	29	169	469	1102	.239	.304	.381	.685	98	-26	-20	99	100	634	59	36	62	-4
BOS	161	76	85	.472	28	666	704	5575	1403	247	34	171	475	954	.252	.313	.400	.713	102	31	10	103	96	684	27	16	63	-2
KC	162	73	89	.451	31.5	615	704	5495	1356	225	38	95	529	829	.247	.316	.353	.669	89	-41	-67	104	99	616	47	26	64	-2
LA	161	70	91	.435	34	597	660	5506	1378	208	38	95	448	916	.250	.312	.354	.666	98	-53	-14	94	99	608	43	30	59	-5
WAS	162	56	106	.346	48.5	578	812	5446	1237	190	35	138	497	963	.227	.295	.351	.646	86	-95	-93	100	104	569	68	28	71	4
TOT	808					6599		55011	13609	2114	352	1489	5031	9228	.247	.314	.380	.694							552	270	67	4

TEAM	CG	SH	SV	IP	H	H/G	HR	BB	SO	RAT	ERA	ERA+	OAV	OOB	PR	/A	PF	CPI	FA	E	DP	FW	PW	BW	SBW	DIF
NY	59	19	31	1449	1239	7.7	115	476	965	10.8	3.07	114	.232	.297	89	71	97	98	.982	110	162	1.4	7.5	3.5	-.4	11.5
CHI	49	21	39	1469	1311	8.0	100	440	932	10.9	2.97	118	.239	.299	107	87	97	102	.979	131	163	.3	9.1	1.6	.2	1.9
MIN	58	13	30	1446¹	1322	8.2	162	459	941	11.2	3.28	111	.242	.303	56	59	100	105	.976	144	140	-.5	6.2	10.8	.0	-6.0
BAL	35	8	43	1452	1353	8.4	137	507	913	11.7	3.45	102	.248	.316	29	12	97	104	.984	99	157	2.1	1.3	.7	.9	.0
DET	42	7	28	1456¹	1407	8.7	195	477	930	11.9	3.90	96	.253	.317	-44	-25	103	102	.982	113	124	1.3	-2.6	2.1	.3	-3.0
CLE	40	14	25	1469	1390	8.5	176	478	1018	11.6	3.79	95	.249	.311	-27	-28	100	98	.977	143	129	-.4	-2.9	-2.1	-.5	3.9
BOS	29	7	32	1449²	1367	8.5	152	539	1009	12.0	3.97	95	.248	.318	-55	-30	104	93	.978	135	119	-.0	-3.2	1.1	-.2	-2.1
KC	35	11	29	1458	1417	8.7	156	540	887	12.4	3.92	98	.246	.327	-47	-12	106	101	.980	127	131	.5	-1.3	-7.0	-.2	.0
LA	30	13	31	1455¹	1317	8.1	120	578	889	12.3	3.52	97	.242	.320	17	-16	94	100	.974	163	155	-1.6	-1.7	-1.5	-.6	-5.2
WAS	29	8	25	1447	1486	9.2	176	537	744	12.8	4.42	84	.266	.334	-126	-114	102	98	.971	182	165	-2.6	-12.0	-9.8	.4	-1.0
TOT	406	121	313	14551²		8.4				11.7	3.63		.247	.314					.978	1347	1445					

Runs
Allison-Min 99
Pearson-LA 92
Yastrzemski-Bos . . . 91
Tresh-NY 91
Colavito-Det 91

Hits
Yastrzemski-Bos . . 183
Ward-Chi 177
Pearson-LA 176
Kaline-Det 172
Fregosi-LA 170

Doubles
Yastrzemski-Bos . . . 40
Ward-Chi 34
Torres-LA 32
Causey-KC 32
Alvis-Cle 32

Triples
Versalles-Min 13
Hinton-Was 12
Fregosi-LA 12
Cimoli-KC 11

Home Runs
Killebrew-Min 45
Stuart-Bos 42
Allison-Min 35
Hall-Min 33
Howard-NY 28

Total Bases
Stuart-Bos 319
Ward-Chi 289
Killebrew-Min 286
Kaline-Det 283
Allison-Min 281

Runs Batted In
Stuart-Bos 118
Kaline-Det 101
Killebrew-Min 96
Colavito-Det 91
Allison-Min 91

Runs Produced
Kaline-Det 163
Colavito-Det 160
Stuart-Bos 157
Allison-Min 155
Siebern-KC 147

Bases On Balls
Yastrzemski-Bos . . . 95
Pearson-LA 92
Allison-Min 90
Cash-Det 89
Colavito-Det 84

Batting Average
Yastrzemski-Bos . . .321
Kaline-Det 312
Rollins-Min 307
Pearson-LA 304
Ward-Chi 295

On Base Percentage
Yastrzemski-Bos . . .419
Pearson-LA 403
Cash-Det 388
Allison-Min 381
Kaline-Det 378

Slugging Average
Killebrew-Min 555
Allison-Min 533
Howard-NY 528
Stuart-Bos 521
Hall-Min 521

Production
Allison-Min 914
Killebrew-Min 908
Yastrzemski-Bos . . .894
Kaline-Det 891
Howard-NY 871

Adjusted Production
Allison-Min 150
Killebrew-Min 147
Yastrzemski-Bos . . 145
Kaline-Det 142
Howard-NY 141

Batter Runs
Yastrzemski-Bos . . 42.0
Allison-Min 38.6
Kaline-Det 34.3
Killebrew-Min 33.5
Cash-Det 28.7

Adjusted Batter Runs
Yastrzemski-Bos . . 39.7
Allison-Min 37.3
Killebrew-Min 32.3
Kaline-Det 32.0
Tresh-NY 29.2

Clutch Hitting Index
Hansen-Chi 137
Siebern-KC 133
Charles-KC 124
Colavito-Det 123
Kaline-Det 123

Runs Created
Yastrzemski-Bos . . 118
Allison-Min 113
Kaline-Det 105
Ward-Chi 104
Pearson-LA 100

Total Average
Allison-Min 967
Yastrzemski-Bos . . .916
Killebrew-Min 907
Tresh-NY 879
Cash-Det 876

Stolen Bases
Aparicio-Bal 40
Hinton-Was 25
Wood-Det 18
Snyder-Bal 18
Pearson-LA 17

Stolen Base Average
Tartabull-KC 94.1
Aparicio-Bal 87.0
Wood-Det 78.3
Snyder-Bal 78.3
Hinton-Was 73.5

Stolen Base Runs
Aparicio-Bal 8.4
Tartabull-KC 4.2
Weis-Chi 3.9
Richardson-NY 3.9
Smith-Bal 2.7

Fielding Runs
Hansen-Chi 27.0
Boyer-NY 22.3
Moran-LA 15.2
Lock-Was 14.8
Geiger-Bos 13.7

Total Player Rating
Yastrzemski-Bos . . . 4.6
Allison-Min 4.3
Hansen-Chi 3.6
Battey-Min 3.1
Moran-LA 2.8

Wins
Ford-NY 24
Pascual-Min 21
Bouton-NY 21
Monbouquette-Bos . 20
Barber-Bal 20

Win Percentage
Ford-NY 774
Bouton-NY 750
Radatz-Bos 714
Peters-Chi 704
Pascual-Min 700

Games
S.Miller-Bal 71
Radatz-Bos 66
Dailey-Min 66
Lamabe-Bos 65
Wyatt-KC 63

Complete Games
Terry-NY 18
Pascual-Min 18
Stigman-Min 15
Herbert-Chi 14
Aguirre-Det 14

Shutouts
Herbert-Chi 7
Bouton-NY 6

Saves
S.Miller-Bal 27
Radatz-Bos 25
Wyatt-KC 21
Wilhelm-Chi 21
Dailey-Min 21

Innings Pitched
Ford-NY 269.1
Terry-NY 268.0
Monbouquette-Bos . . . .
 . . . . 266.2
Barber-Bal 258.2
Roberts-Bal 251.1

Fewest Hits/Game
Downing-NY 5.84
Bouton-NY 6.89
Drabowsky-KC 6.97
Morehead-Bos 7.06
McBride-LA 7.10

Fewest BB/Game
Donovan-Cle 1.22
Terry-NY 1.31
Herbert-Chi 1.40
Monbouquette-Bos 1.42
Roberts-Bal 1.43

Strikeouts
Pascual-Min 202
Bunning-Det 196
Stigman-Min 193
Peters-Chi 189
Ford-NY 189

Strikeouts/Game
Downing-NY 8.76
Ramos-Cle 8.24
Pascual-Min 7.32
Stigman-Min 7.21
Bunning-Det 7.10

Ratio
Terry-NY 9.71
Roberts-Bal 9.78
Ramos-Cle 9.80
Peters-Chi 9.93
Downing-NY 9.94

Earned Run Average
Peters-Chi 2.33
Pizarro-Chi 2.39
Pascual-Min 2.46
Bouton-NY 2.53
Downing-NY 2.56

Adjusted ERA
Peters-Chi 150
Pascual-Min 148
Pizarro-Chi 147
Bouton-NY 139
Stange-Min 139

Opponents' Batting Avg.
Downing-NY 184
Morehead-Bos 211
Bouton-NY 212
Drabowsky-KC 214
Peters-Chi 216

Opponents' On Base Pct.
Roberts-Bal 272
Terry-NY 273
Ramos-Cle 273
Downing-NY 277
Peters-Chi 278

Starter Runs
Peters-Chi 35.0
Pascual-Min 32.2
Bouton-NY 30.6
Pizarro-Chi 29.6
Ford-NY 26.6

Adjusted Starter Runs
Pascual-Min 32.6
Peters-Chi 31.7
Bouton-NY 27.3
Pizarro-Chi 26.6
Ford-NY 23.2

Clutch Pitching Index
Barber-Bal 126
Osteen-Was 120
Stange-Min 120
Segui-KC 115
Pascual-Min 115

Relief Runs
Radatz-Bos 24.4
Dailey-Min 19.8
S.Miller-Bal 17.3
Wilhelm-Chi 15.0
Fowler-LA 12.0

Adjusted Relief Runs
Radatz-Bos 26.7
Dailey-Min 20.0
S.Miller-Bal 16.0
Wilhelm-Chi 13.1
Lamabe-Bos 10.7

Relief Ranking
Radatz-Bos 49.4
S.Miller-Bal 25.4
Dailey-Min 23.6
Wilhelm-Chi 15.8
Kline-Was 14.1

Total Pitcher Index
Peters-Chi 4.4
Pascual-Min 4.3
Pizarro-Chi 2.9
Dailey-Min 2.6
Barber-Bal 2.6

Total Baseball Ranking
Yastrzemski-Bos . . . 4.6
Peters-Chi 4.4
Allison-Min 4.3
Pascual-Min 4.3
Hansen-Chi 3.6

TEAM	G	W	L	PCT	GB	R	OR	AB	H	2B	3B	HR	BB	SO	AVG	OBP	SLG	PRO	PRO+	BR	/A	PF	CHI	RC	SB	CS	SBA	SBR
STL	162	93	69	.574	–	715	652	5625	1531	240	53	109	427	925	.272	.326	.392	.718	100	62	5	109	99	711	73	51	59	-9
PHI	162	92	70	.568	1	693	632	5493	1415	241	51	130	440	924	.258	.317	.391	.708	107	41	49	99	100	672	30	35	46	-12
CIN	163	92	70	.568	1	660	566	5561	1383	220	38	130	457	974	.249	.310	.372	.682	96	-10	-34	104	102	642	90	36	71	5
SF	162	90	72	.556	3	656	587	5535	1360	185	38	165	505	900	.246	.313	.382	.695	100	16	2	102	97	657	64	35	65	-2
MIL	162	88	74	.543	5	803	744	5591	1522	274	32	159	486	825	.272	.335	.418	.753	118	132	128	101	101	764	53	41	56	-9
PIT	162	80	82	.494	13	663	636	5566	1469	225	54	121	408	970	.264	.317	.389	.706	105	35	36	100	97	668	39	33	54	-8
LA	164	80	82	.494	13	614	549	5499	1375	180	39	79	438	893	.250	.308	.340	.648	96	-70	-23	93	105	581	141	60	70	6
CHI	162	76	86	.469	17	649	724	5545	1391	239	50	145	499	1041	.251	.316	.390	.706	101	37	10	104	94	679	70	49	59	-8
HOU	162	66	96	.407	27	495	628	5303	1214	162	41	70	381	872	.229	.287	.315	.602	81	-158	-122	94	106	469	40	48	45	-17
NY	163	53	109	.327	40	569	776	5566	1372	195	31	103	353	932	.246	.297	.348	.645	90	-84	-69	98	102	552	36	31	54	-8
TOT	812					6517		55284	14032	2161	427	1211	4394	9256	.254	.313	.374	.687							636	419	60	-61

TEAM	CG	SH	SV	IP	H	H/G	HR	BB	SO	RAT	ERA	ERA+	OAV	OOB	PR	/A	PF	CPI	FA	E	DP	FW	PW	BW	SBW	DIF
STL	47	10	38	1445¹	1405	8.7	133	410	877	11.5	3.43	111	.255	.310	17	60	108	104	.973	172	147	-.7	6.3	.5	-.3	6.2
PHI	37	17	41	1461	1402	8.6	129	440	1009	11.7	3.36	103	.252	.313	28	17	98	106	.975	157	150	.0	1.8	5.2	-.6	4.6
CIN	54	14	35	1467	1306	8.0	112	436	1122	10.9	3.07	118	.238	.298	75	88	102	100	.979	130	137	1.6	9.3	-3.6	1.2	2.5
SF	48	17	30	1476¹	1348	8.2	118	480	1023	11.4	3.19	112	.241	.306	57	61	101	102	.975	159	136	-.0	6.4	.2	.4	1.9
MIL	45	14	39	1434²	1411	8.9	160	452	906	11.8	4.12	88	.257	.316	-92	-95	100	94	.977	143	139	.8	-10.0	13.5	-.3	3.0
PIT	42	14	29	1443²	1429	8.9	92	476	951	12.1	3.52	100	.260	.322	2	-2	99	103	.972	177	179	-1.0	-.2	3.8	-.2	-3.4
LA	47	19	27	1483²	1289	7.8	88	458	1062	10.8	2.95	110	.232	.294	96	47	92	95	.973	170	126	-.5	5.0	-2.4	1.3	-4.3
CHI	58	11	19	1445	1510	9.4	144	423	737	12.1	4.08	91	.270	.323	-87	-59	105	98	.975	162	147	-.2	-6.2	1.1	-.2	.6
HOU	30	9	31	1428	1421	9.0	105	353	852	11.4	3.41	100	.260	.309	20	1	97	102	.976	149	124	.5	.1	-12.9	-1.2	-1.6
NY	40	10	15	1438²	1511	9.5	130	466	717	12.7	4.25	84	.272	.334	-115	-108	101	98	.974	167	154	-.4	-11.4	-7.3	-.2	-8.7
TOT	448	135	304	14523¹		8.7				11.6	3.54		.254	.313					.975	1586	1439					

Runs
Allen-Phi 125
Mays-SF 121
Brock-Chi-StL 111
Robinson-Cin 103
Aaron-Mil 103

Hits
Flood-StL 211
Clemente-Pit 211
Williams-Chi 201
Allen-Phi 201
Brock-Chi-StL 200

Doubles
Maye-Mil 44
Clemente-Pit 40
Williams-Chi 39
Robinson-Cin 38
Allen-Phi 38

Triples
Santo-Chi 13
Allen-Phi 13
Brock-Chi-StL 11
Pinson-Cin 11

Home Runs
Mays-SF 47
Williams-Chi 33
Hart-SF 31
Cepeda-SF 31
Callison-Phi 31

Total Bases
Allen-Phi 352
Mays-SF 351
Williams-Chi 343
Santo-Chi 334
Callison-Phi 322

Runs Batted In
Boyer-StL 119
Santo-Chi 114
Mays-SF 111
Torre-Mil 109
Callison-Phi 104

Runs Produced
Boyer-StL 195
Allen-Phi 187
Mays-SF 185
Santo-Chi 178
Torre-Mil 176

Bases On Balls
Santo-Chi 86
Mathews-Mil 85
Mays-SF 82
Robinson-Cin 79
Boyer-StL 70

Batting Average
Clemente-Pit 339
Carty-Mil 330
Aaron-Mil 328
Torre-Mil 321
Allen-Phi 318

On Base Percentage
Santo-Chi 401
Robinson-Cin 399
Aaron-Mil 394
Carty-Mil 391
Clemente-Pit 391

Slugging Average
Mays-SF 607
Santo-Chi 564
Allen-Phi 557
Carty-Mil 554
Robinson-Cin 548

Production
Mays-SF 992
Santo-Chi 966
Robinson-Cin 947
Carty-Mil 945
Allen-Phi 940

Adjusted Production
Mays-SF 171
Allen-Phi 163
Santo-Chi 162
Carty-Mil 162
Robinson-Cin 158

Batter Runs
Mays-SF 56.5
Santo-Chi 55.1
Allen-Phi 50.5
Robinson-Cin 49.5
Williams-Chi 42.5

Adjusted Batter Runs
Santo-Chi 55.0
Mays-SF 52.1
Allen-Phi 51.5
Robinson-Cin 47.0
Aaron-Mil 40.4

Clutch Hitting Index
Fairly-LA 148
Boyer-StL 136
H.Davis-LA 135
Torre-Mil 132
Bond-Hou 128

Runs Created
Mays-SF 136
Santo-Chi 135
Allen-Phi 135
Robinson-Cin 127
Williams-Chi 125

Total Average
Mays-SF 1.059
Robinson-Cin 1.012
Santo-Chi 998
Allen-Phi 944
Carty-Mil 920

Stolen Bases
Wills-LA 53
Brock-Chi-StL 43
W.Davis-LA 42
Harper-Cin 24
Robinson-Cin 23

Stolen Base Average
Harper-Cin 88.9
Aaron-Mil 84.6
Robinson-Cin 82.1
Mays-SF 79.2
W.Davis-LA 76.4

Stolen Base Runs
Wills-LA 5.7
Harper-Cin 5.4
W.Davis-LA 4.8
Aaron-Mil 4.2
Robinson-Cin 3.9

Fielding Runs
Mazeroski-Pit 33.9
Edwards-Cin 22.6
Rodgers-Chi 19.4
W.Davis-LA 19.2
Callison-Phi 17.6

Total Player Rating
Santo-Chi 6.7
Mays-SF 6.0
Allen-Phi 5.7
Robinson-Cin 4.9
Aaron-Mil 4.9

Wins
Jackson-Chi 24
Marichal-SF 21
Sadecki-StL 20

Win Percentage
Koufax-LA 792
Marichal-SF 724
O'Toole-Cin 708
Bunning-Phi 704
Jackson-Chi 686

Games
R.Miller-LA 74
Perranoski-LA 72
Baldschun-Phi 71
Taylor-StL 63
McDaniel-Chi 63

Complete Games
Marichal-SF 22
Drysdale-LA 21
Jackson-Chi 19
Gibson-StL 17
Ellsworth-Chi 16

Shutouts
Koufax-LA 7
Law-Pit 5
Fischer-Mil 5
Drysdale-LA 5
Bunning-Phi 5

Saves
Woodeshick-Hou . . . 23
McBean-Pit 22
Baldschun-Phi 21
McDaniel-Chi 15

Innings Pitched
Drysdale-LA 321.1
Jackson-Chi 297.2
Gibson-StL 287.1
Bunning-Phi 284.1
Veale-Pit 279.2

Fewest Hits/Game
Koufax-LA 6.22
Drysdale-LA 6.78
Short-Phi 7.10
Veale-Pit 7.14
Maloney-Cin 7.29

Fewest BB/Game
Bunning-Phi 1.46
Bruce-Hou 1.47
Law-Pit 1.50
Marichal-SF 1.74
Jackson-Chi 1.75

Strikeouts
Veale-Pit 250
Gibson-StL 245
Drysdale-LA 237
Koufax-LA 223
Bunning-Phi 219

Strikeouts/Game
Koufax-LA 9.00
Maloney-Cin 8.92
Veale-Pit 8.05
Gibson-StL 7.67
Lemaster-Mil 7.53

Ratio
Koufax-LA 8.35
Drysdale-LA 8.96
Short-Phi 9.34
Bunning-Phi 9.75
Jackson-Chi 9.80

Earned Run Average
Koufax-LA 1.74
Drysdale-LA 2.18
Short-Phi 2.20
Marichal-SF 2.48
Bunning-Phi 2.63

Adjusted ERA
Koufax-LA 187
Short-Phi 157
Drysdale-LA 148
Marichal-SF 144
O'Toole-Cin 136

Opponents' Batting Avg.
Koufax-LA 191
Drysdale-LA 207
Veale-Pit 217
Short-Phi 217
Bolin-SF 220

Opponents' On Base Pct.
Koufax-LA 241
Drysdale-LA 256
Short-Phi 268
Jackson-Chi 273
Marichal-SF 273

Starter Runs
Drysdale-LA 48.2
Koufax-LA 44.6
Short-Phi 32.7
Marichal-SF 31.7
Bunning-Phi 28.7

Adjusted Starter Runs
Drysdale-LA 37.6
Koufax-LA 37.2
Marichal-SF 32.5
Short-Phi 31.0
Bunning-Phi 26.6

Clutch Pitching Index
Craig-StL 122
D.Bennett-Phi 119
Farrell-Hou 115
Tsitouris-Cin 115
Hendley-SF 110

Relief Runs
McBean-Pit 16.2
R.Miller-LA 14.1
Ellis-Cin 13.1
Roebuck-Phi 11.4
McCool-Cin 11.1

Adjusted Relief Runs
McBean-Pit 16.0
Ellis-Cin 14.1
McCool-Cin 11.9
Roebuck-Phi 10.8
R.Miller-LA 9.5

Relief Ranking
McBean-Pit 26.5
Ellis-Cin 17.1
McCool-Cin 15.2
Roebuck-Phi 13.8
Woodeshick-Hou . . 11.0

Total Pitcher Index
Drysdale-LA 4.9
Koufax-LA 3.7
Marichal-SF 3.5
Short-Phi 3.2
Jackson-Chi 2.8

Total Baseball Ranking
Santo-Chi 6.7
Mays-SF 6.0
Allen-Phi 5.7
Drysdale-LA 4.9
Robinson-Cin 4.9

TEAM	G	W	L	PCT	GB	R	OR	AB	H	2B	3B	HR	BB	SO	AVG	OBP	SLG	PRO	PRO+	BR	/A	PF	CHI	RC	SB	CS	SBA	SBR
NY	164	99	63	.611		730	577	5705	1442	208	35	162	520	976	.253	.319	.387	.706	100	13	2	102	105	705	54	18	75	5
CHI	162	98	64	.605	1	642	501	5491	1356	184	40	106	562	902	.247	.323	.353	.676	98	-32	-14	97	101	643	75	39	66	-1
BAL	163	97	65	.599	2	679	567	5463	1357	229	20	162	517	1019	.248	.319	.387	.706	102	14	17	100	101	671	78	38	67	1
DET	163	85	77	.525	14	699	678	5513	1394	199	57	157	517	912	.253	.321	.395	.716	103	35	25	102	100	707	60	27	69	2
LA	162	82	80	.506	17	544	551	5362	1297	186	27	102	472	920	.242	.306	.344	.650	97	-89	-26	90	99	552	49	39	56	-9
MIN	163	79	83	.488	20	737	678	5610	1413	227	46	221	553	1019	.252	.324	.427	.751	113	98	93	101	95	775	46	22	68	1
CLE	164	79	83	.488	20	689	693	5603	1386	208	22	164	500	1063	.247	.315	.380	.695	100	-8	-3	99	104	666	79	51	61	-7
BOS	162	72	90	.444	27	688	793	5513	1425	253	29	186	504	917	.258	.324	.416	.740	106	76	44	105	94	725	18	16	53	-4
WAS	162	62	100	.383	37	578	733	5396	1246	199	28	125	514	1124	.231	.301	.348	.649	86	-95	-92	100	105	566	47	30	61	-4
KC	163	57	105	.352	42	621	836	5524	1321	216	29	166	548	1104	.239	.313	.379	.692	95	-14	-34	103	96	645	34	20	63	-2
TOT	814					6607		55180	13637	2109	333	1551	5227	9956	.247	.316	.382	.698							540	300	64	-18

TEAM	CG	SH	SV	IP	H	H/G	HR	BB	SO	RAT	ERA	ERA+	OAV	OOB	PR	/A	PF	CPI	FA	E	DP	FW	PW	BW	SBW	DIF
NY	46	18	45	1506²	1312	7.8	129	504	989	11.0	3.15	115	.234	.300	79	78	100	97	.983	109	158	1.1	8.2	.2	.7	7.8
CHI	44	20	45	1467²	1216	7.5	124	401	955	10.1	2.72	127	.226	.283	147	119	95	100	.981	122	164	.2	12.5	-1.5	.0	5.6
BAL	44	17	41	1458²	1292	8.0	129	456	939	11.0	3.16	113	.239	.302	76	67	99	100	.985	95	159	1.9	7.0	1.8	.3	5.0
DET	35	11	35	1453	1343	8.3	164	536	993	12.0	3.84	95	.244	.317	-35	-29	101	95	.982	111	137	1.0	-3.0	2.6	.4	3.1
LA	30	28	41	1450²	1273	7.9	100	530	965	11.5	2.91	113	.236	.310	115	60	91	107	.978	138	168	-.7	6.3	-2.7	-.8	-1.1
MIN	47	4	29	1477²	1361	8.3	181	545	1099	11.8	3.58	100	.243	.314	8	1	99	102	.977	145	131	-1.1	.1	9.8	.3	-11.1
CLE	37	16	37	1487²	1443	8.7	154	565	1162	12.3	3.75	96	.255	.326	-21	-25	99	103	.981	118	149	.6	-2.6	-.3	-.5	.9
BOS	21	9	38	1422	1464	9.3	178	571	1094	13.1	4.50	86	.266	.339	-138	-102	106	97	.977	138	123	-.7	-10.7	4.6	-.2	-2.0
WAS	27	5	26	1435¹	1417	8.9	172	505	794	12.2	3.98	93	.259	.324	-57	-45	102	100	.979	127	145	-.0	-4.7	-9.7	-.2	-4.3
KC	18	6	27	1455²	1516	9.4	220	614	966	13.5	4.71	81	.269	.346	-175	-144	105	101	.975	158	152	-1.9	-15.1	-3.6	-.0	-3.4
TOT	349	134	364	14615		8.4				11.8	3.63		.247	.316					.980	1261	1486					

Runs
Oliva-Min 109
Howser-Cle 101
Killebrew-Min 95
Wagner-Cle 94
Versalles-Min 94

Hits
Oliva-Min 217
B.Robinson-Bal . . . 194
Richardson-NY 181
Howard-NY 172
Versalles-Min 171

Doubles
Oliva-Min 43
Bressoud-Bos 41
B.Robinson-Bal . . . 35
Versalles-Min 33

Triples
Versalles-Min 10
Rollins-Min 10
Yastrzemski-Bos . . . 9
Oliva-Min 9
Fregosi-LA 9

Home Runs
Killebrew-Min 49
Powell-Bal 39
Mantle-NY 35
Colavito-KC 34
Stuart-Bos 33

Total Bases
Oliva-Min 374
B.Robinson-Bal . . . 319
Killebrew-Min 316
Colavito-KC 298
Stuart-Bos 296

Runs Batted In
B.Robinson-Bal . . . 118
Stuart-Bos 114
Mantle-NY 111
Killebrew-Min 111
Colavito-KC 102

Runs Produced
B.Robinson-Bal . . . 172
Oliva-Min 171
Mantle-NY 168
Wagner-Cle 163

Bases On Balls
Siebern-Bal 106
Mantle-NY 99
Killebrew-Min 93
Allison-Min 92
Causey-KC 88

Batting Average
Oliva-Min 323
B.Robinson-Bal 317
Howard-NY 313
Mantle-NY 303
Robinson-Chi 301

On Base Percentage
Mantle-NY 426
Allison-Min 406
Powell-Bal 400
Robinson-Chi 388
Kaline-Det 385

Slugging Average
Powell-Bal 606
Mantle-NY 591
Oliva-Min 557
Allison-Min 553
Killebrew-Min 548

Production
Mantle-NY 1.017
Powell-Bal 1.007
Allison-Min 959
Killebrew-Min 927
Oliva-Min 918

Adjusted Production
Mantle-NY 177
Powell-Bal 176
Allison-Min 163
Killebrew-Min 153
Oliva-Min 150

Batter Runs
Mantle-NY 53.0
Allison-Min 45.0
Powell-Bal 44.1
Killebrew-Min 43.1
Oliva-Min 43.0

Adjusted Batter Runs
Mantle-NY 52.0
Allison-Min 44.5
Powell-Bal 44.3
Killebrew-Min 42.6
Oliva-Min 42.5

Clutch Hitting Index
Rodgers-LA 135
B.Robinson-Bal . . . 131
Ward-Chi 130
Stuart-Bos 130
Pepitone-NY 127

Runs Created
Oliva-Min 132
Killebrew-Min 122
Mantle-NY 121
Allison-Min 119
B.Robinson-Bal . . . 115

Total Average
Mantle-NY 1.122
Powell-Bal 1.081
Allison-Min 1.058
Killebrew-Min 956
Oliva-Min 894

Stolen Bases
Aparicio-Bal 57
Weis-Chi 22
Davalillo-Cle 21
Howser-Cle 20
Hinton-Was 17

Stolen Base Average
Aparicio-Bal 77.0
Weis-Chi 75.9
Howser-Cle 74.1
Hinton-Was 73.9
Davalillo-Cle 65.6

Stolen Base Runs
Aparicio-Bal 6.9
Tresh-NY 3.9
Wagner-Cle 3.0
Weis-Chi 2.4
Allison-Min 2.4

Fielding Runs
Knoop-LA 37.2
Yastrzemski-Bos . . 27.7
Boyer-NY 19.3
Green-KC 16.5
Brandt-Bal 16.1

Total Player Rating
Powell-Bal 4.4
Hansen-Chi 4.2
Oliva-Min 4.1
Fregosi-LA 4.1
Yastrzemski-Bos . . . 4.0

Wins
Peters-Chi 20
Chance-LA 20
Wickersham-Det . . . 19
Pizarro-Chi 19
Bunker-Bal 19

Win Percentage
Bunker-Bal 792
Ford-NY 739
Peters-Chi 714
Pappas-Bal 696
Chance-LA 690

Games
Wyatt-KC 81
Radatz-Bos 79
Wilhelm-Chi 73
McMahon-Cle 70
Miller-Bal 66

Complete Games
Chance-LA 15
Pascual-Min 14
Pappas-Bal 13
Osteen-Was 13
Kaat-Min 13

Shutouts
Chance-LA 11
Ford-NY 8
Pappas-Bal 7
Lolich-Det 6
Monbouquette-Bos . . 5

Saves
Radatz-Bos 29
Wilhelm-Chi 27
Miller-Bal 23
Wyatt-KC 20
R.Lee-LA 19

Innings Pitched
Chance-LA 278.1
Peters-Chi 273.2
Bouton-NY 271.1
Pascual-Min 267.1
Osteen-Was 257.0

Fewest Hits/Game
Horlen-Chi 6.07
Chance-LA 6.27
Bunker-Bal 6.77
Peters-Chi 7.14
Pizarro-Chi 7.27

Fewest BB/Game
Monbouquette-Bos 1.54
Pappas-Bal 1.72
Newman-LA 1.85
Bouton-NY 1.99
Pizarro-Chi 2.07

Strikeouts
Downing-NY 217
Pascual-Min 213
Chance-LA 207
Peters-Chi 205
Lolich-Det 192

Strikeouts/Game
McDowell-Cle 9.19
Downing-NY 8.00
Pena-KC 7.55
Stigman-Min 7.53
Morehead-Bos . . . 7.51

Ratio
Horlen-Chi 8.59
Chance-LA 9.12
Pizarro-Chi 9.45
Bunker-Bal 9.50
Bouton-NY 9.72

Earned Run Average
Chance-LA 1.65
Horlen-Chi 1.88
Ford-NY 2.13
Peters-Chi 2.50
Pizarro-Chi 2.56

Adjusted ERA
Chance-LA 199
Horlen-Chi 184
Ford-NY 170
Peters-Chi 138
Pizarro-Chi 135

Opponents' Batting Avg.
Horlen-Chi 190
Chance-LA 195
Bunker-Bal 207
Peters-Chi 219
Pizarro-Chi 219

Opponents' On Base Pct.
Horlen-Chi 250
Chance-LA 261
Pizarro-Chi 267
Bunker-Bal 269
Bouton-NY 273

Starter Runs
Chance-LA 61.1
Horlen-Chi 40.9
Ford-NY 40.6
Peters-Chi 34.2
Pizarro-Chi 28.3

Adjusted Starter Runs
Chance-LA 50.6
Ford-NY 40.5
Horlen-Chi 36.9
Peters-Chi 29.1
Pizarro-Chi 23.7

Clutch Pitching Index
McDowell-Cle 123
Roberts-Bal 121
Kralick-Cle 118
Grant-Cle-Min 112
Peters-Chi 111

Relief Runs
R.Lee-LA 32.2
Wilhelm-Chi 23.9
Radatz-Bos 23.2
Worthington-Min . . 18.1
Hall-Bal 17.3

Adjusted Relief Runs
Radatz-Bos 27.3
R.Lee-LA 27.0
Wilhelm-Chi 21.4
Stock-Bal-KC 18.6
Worthington-Min . . 17.8

Relief Ranking
Radatz-Bos 50.4
Wilhelm-Chi 40.7
Worthington-Min . . 32.0
Kline-Was 28.2
R.Lee-LA 27.9

Total Pitcher Index
Chance-LA 4.9
Ford-NY 4.9
Horlen-Chi 4.5
Peters-Chi 4.1
Pizarro-Chi 2.9

Total Baseball Ranking
Chance-LA 4.9
Ford-NY 4.9
Horlen-Chi 4.5
Powell-Bal 4.4
Hansen-Chi 4.2

TEAM	G	W	L	PCT	GB	R	OR	AB	H	2B	3B	HR	BB	SO	AVG	OBP	SLG	PRO	PRO+	BR	/A	PF	CHI	RC	SB	CS	SBA	SBR
LA	162	97	65	.599		608	**521**	5425	1329	193	32	78	492	891	.245	.314	.335	.649	96	-61	-18	93	103	593	**172**	77	69	**5**
SF	163	95	67	.586	2	682	593	5495	1384	169	43	159	476	**844**	.252	.315	.385	.700	101	24	6	103	101	649	47	27	64	-2
PIT	163	90	72	.556	7	675	580	5686	1506	217	57	111	419	1008	.265	.319	.382	.701	103	27	24	101	97	671	51	38	57	-8
CIN	162	89	73	.549	8	**825**	704	5658	**1544**	268	61	183	419	1003	**.273**	**.341**	**.439**	**.780**	118	**188**	**141**	107	95	**842**	82	40	67	1
MIL	162	86	76	.531	11	708	633	5542	1419	243	28	**196**	408	976	.256	.311	.416	.727	110	67	64	101	99	699	64	37	63	-3
PHI	162	85	76	.528	11.5	654	667	5528	1380	205	53	144	494	1091	.250	.315	.384	.699	105	24	36	98	96	665	46	32	59	-5
STL	162	80	81	.497	16.5	707	674	5579	1415	234	46	109	477	882	.254	.316	.371	.687	91	3	-59	109	**107**	659	100	52	66	-1
CHI	164	72	90	.444	25	635	723	5540	1316	202	33	134	**532**	948	.238	.309	.358	.667	92	-34	-50	102	101	613	65	47	58	-9
HOU	162	65	97	.401	32	569	711	5483	1299	188	42	97	502	877	.237	.306	.340	.646	96	-73	-20	93	98	574	90	37	**71**	5
NY	164	50	112	.309	47	495	752	5441	1202	203	27	107	392	1129	.221	.278	.327	.605	79	-164	-141	96	105	480	28	42	40	-17
TOT	813					6558		55377	13794	2122	422	1318	4730	9649	.249	.313	.374	.687							745	429	63	-34

TEAM	CG	SH	SV	IP	H	H/G	HR	BB	SO	RAT	ERA	ERA+	OAV	OOB	PR	/A	PF	CPI	FA	E	DP	FW	PW	BW	SBW	DIF
LA	**58**	**23**	34	1476	**1223**	7.5	127	425	1079	10.3	**2.81**	116	**.224**	**.284**	119	74	92	99	.979	134	135	.8	7.8	-1.9	**.9**	8.4
SF	42	17	**42**	1465¹	1325	8.1	137	408	1060	10.9	3.20	112	.238	.295	55	65	102	98	.976	148	124	.0	6.9	.6	.1	6.3
PIT	49	17	27	1479	1324	8.1	**89**	469	882	11.2	3.01	**117**	.241	.306	87	**82**	99	103	.977	152	**189**	-.1	**8.7**	2.5	-.5	-1.6
CIN	43	9	34	1457¹	1355	8.4	136	587	**1113**	12.3	3.88	100	.247	.325	-56	-22	106	96	**.981**	117	142	**1.8**	-2.3	**14.9**	.5	-6.8
MIL	43	4	38	1447²	1336	8.3	123	541	966	11.8	3.52	100	.246	.318	3	1	100	101	.978	140	145	.5	.1	6.8	.0	-2.4
PHI	50	18	21	1468²	1426	8.7	116	466	1071	12.0	3.53	98	.256	.320	2	-12	98	104	.975	157	153	-.5	-1.3	3.8	-.2	2.6
STL	40	11	35	1461¹	1414	8.7	166	467	916	11.8	3.77	102	.255	.317	-37	12	109	102	.979	130	152	1.1	1.3	-6.2	.3	3.2
CHI	33	9	35	1472	1470	9.0	154	481	855	12.1	3.78	98	.260	.321	-39	-15	104	104	.974	171	166	-1.2	-1.6	-5.3	-.6	-.4
HOU	29	7	26	1461	1459	9.0	123	**388**	931	11.6	3.84	87	.260	.312	-49	-79	95	94	.974	166	130	-1.0	-8.3	-3.0	.9	-4.6
NY	29	11	14	1454²	1462	9.0	147	498	776	12.4	4.06	87	.262	.328	-84	-86	100	99	.974	171	153	-1.2	-9.1	-14.9	-1.4	-4.4
TOT	416	126	306	14643		8.5				11.6	3.54		.249	.313					.977	1486	1489					

Runs
Harper-Cin 126
Mays-SF 118
Rose-Cin 117
Williams-Chi 115

Hits
Rose-Cin 209
Pinson-Cin 204
Williams-Chi 203
Clemente-Pit 194
Flood-StL 191

Doubles
H.Aaron-Mil 40
Williams-Chi 39
Rose-Cin 35
Brock-StL 35
Pinson-Cin 34

Triples
Callison-Phi 16
Clendenon-Pit 14
Clemente-Pit 14
Allen-Phi 14
Morgan-Hou 12

Home Runs
Mays-SF 52
McCovey-SF 39
Williams-Chi 34
Santo-Chi 33
Robinson-Cin 33

Total Bases
Mays-SF 360
Williams-Chi 356
Pinson-Cin 324
H.Aaron-Mil 319
Johnson-Cin 317

Runs Batted In
Johnson-Cin 130
Robinson-Cin 113
Mays-SF 112
Williams-Chi 108
Stargell-Pit 107

Runs Produced
Johnson-Cin 190
Williams-Chi 189
Robinson-Cin 189
Rose-Cin 187
Mays-SF 178

Bases On Balls
Morgan-Hou 97
Santo-Chi 88
McCovey-SF 88
Wynn-Hou 84
Harper-Cin 78

Batting Average
Clemente-Pit ..... .329
H.Aaron-Mil ...... .318
Mays-SF .... .317
Williams-Chi ..... .315
Rose-Cin .... .312

On Base Percentage
Mays-SF .... .399
Robinson-Cin .... .388
H.Aaron-Mil ...... .384
McCovey-SF ...... .383
Rose-Cin .... .383

Slugging Average
Mays-SF .... .645
H.Aaron-Mil ...... .560
Williams-Chi ..... .552
Robinson-Cin .... .540
McCovey-SF ...... .539

Production
Mays-SF 1.044
H.Aaron-Mil ...... .943
Williams-Chi ..... .932
Robinson-Cin .... .928
McCovey-SF ...... .922

Adjusted Production
Mays-SF 184
H.Aaron-Mil 161
Williams-Chi 155
McCovey-SF 152
Robinson-Cin 148

Batter Runs
Mays-SF 64.7
Williams-Chi 49.3
H.Aaron-Mil 45.9
Robinson-Cin 45.9
McCovey-SF 41.8

Adjusted Batter Runs
Mays-SF 62.9
Williams-Chi 47.5
H.Aaron-Mil 45.6
Robinson-Cin 40.9
McCovey-SF 40.0

Clutch Hitting Index
Johnson-Cin 138
Boyer-StL 138
Fairly-LA 130
Stargell-Pit 130
Banks-Chi 129

Runs Created
Mays-SF 143
Williams-Chi 132
H.Aaron-Mil 122
Santo-Chi 121
Robinson-Cin 120

Total Average
Mays-SF 1.114
H.Aaron-Mil ...... .980
McCovey-SF ...... .945
Robinson-Cin .... .938
Williams-Chi ..... .935

Stolen Bases
Wills-LA 94
Brock-StL 63
Wynn-Hou 43
Harper-Cin 35
W.Davis-LA 25

Stolen Base Average
Wynn-Hou 91.5
H.Aaron-Mil 85.7
Harper-Cin 85.4
Wills-LA 75.2
W.Davis-LA 73.5

Stolen Base Runs
Wynn-Hou 10.5
Wills-LA 9.6
Harper-Cin 6.9
H.Aaron-Mil 4.8
Allen-Phi 3.3

Fielding Runs
Alley-Pit 29.5
Mazeroski-Pit 25.6
Wine-Phi 21.7
Wills-LA 21.2
Santo-Chi 18.5

Total Player Rating
Mays-SF 6.9
Santo-Chi 5.5
H.Aaron-Mil 5.5
Wynn-Hou 5.2
Williams-Chi 4.4

Wins
Koufax-LA 26
Cloninger-Mil 24
Drysdale-LA 23
Marichal-SF 22
Ellis-Cin 22

Win Percentage
Koufax-LA .... .765
Maloney-Cin ..... .690
Ellis-Cin .... .688
Cloninger-Mil .... .686
Bunning-Phi ..... .679

Games
Abernathy-Chi 84
Woodeshick-Hou-StL .. 78
McDaniel-Chi 71
Baldschun-Phi 65

Complete Games
Koufax-LA 27
Marichal-SF 24
Gibson-StL 20
Drysdale-LA 20
Cloninger-Mil 16

Shutouts
Marichal-SF 10
Koufax-LA 8
Veale-Pit 7
Drysdale-LA 7
Bunning-Phi 7

Saves
Abernathy-Chi 31
McCool-Cin 21
Linzy-SF 21

Innings Pitched
Koufax-LA 335.2
Drysdale-LA 308.1
Gibson-StL 299.0
Short-Phi 297.1
Marichal-SF 295.1

Fewest Hits/Game
Koufax-LA 5.79
Maloney-Cin 6.66
Marichal-SF 6.83
Bolin-SF 6.90
Gibson-StL 7.31

Fewest BB/Game
Marichal-SF 1.40
Law-Pit 1.45
Bruce-Hou 1.49
Farrell-Hou 1.51
Johnson-Hou-Mil . 1.87

Strikeouts
Koufax-LA 382
Veale-Pit 276
Gibson-StL 270
Bunning-Phi 268
Maloney-Cin 244

Strikeouts/Game
Koufax-LA 10.24
Veale-Pit 9.34
Maloney-Cin 8.60
Bunning-Phi 8.29
Gibson-StL 8.13

Ratio
Koufax-LA 7.83
Marichal-SF 8.35
Law-Pit 9.11
Bunning-Phi ... 10.11
Drysdale-LA ... 10.16

Earned Run Average
Koufax-LA 2.04
Marichal-SF 2.13
Law-Pit 2.15
Maloney-Cin 2.54
Bunning-Phi 2.60

Adjusted ERA
Marichal-SF 169
Law-Pit 163
Koufax-LA 160
Maloney-Cin 148
Shaw-SF 136

Opponents' Batting Avg
Koufax-LA .... .179
Marichal-SF ..... .205
Maloney-Cin ..... .206
Bolin-SF .... .214
Gibson-StL ...... .222

Opponents' On Base Pct.
Koufax-LA .... .228
Marichal-SF ..... .240
Law-Pit .... .264
Drysdale-LA ..... .280
Shaw-SF .... .280

Starter Runs
Koufax-LA 56.0
Marichal-SF 46.1
Law-Pit 33.5
Bunning-Phi 30.4
Maloney-Cin 28.4

Adjusted Starter Runs
Marichal-SF 48.1
Koufax-LA 45.7
Maloney-Cin 34.3
Law-Pit 32.8
Bunning-Phi 27.8

Clutch Pitching Index
Law-Pit 115
Koonce-Chi 112
Culp-Phi 108
Spahn-NY-SF 107
Buhl-Chi 107

Relief Runs
Linzy-SF 19.1
O'Dell-Mil 16.8
McBean-Pit 15.8
Perranoski-LA ... 15.2
Abernathy-Chi ... 14.6

Adjusted Relief Runs
Linzy-SF 19.7
Abernathy-Chi ... 16.8
O'Dell-Mil 16.6
McDaniel-Chi 15.7
McBean-Pit 15.5

Relief Ranking
Linzy-SF 37.4
O'Dell-Mil 27.4
Woodeshick-Hou-StL 23.5
McBean-Pit 20.2
Abernathy-Chi ... 19.7

Total Pitcher Index
Marichal-SF 5.6
Koufax-LA 5.4
Maloney-Cin 4.6
Law-Pit 4.3
Drysdale-LA 4.2

Total Baseball Ranking
Mays-SF 6.9
Marichal-SF 5.6
Santo-Chi 5.5
H.Aaron-Mil 5.5
Koufax-LA 5.4

TEAM	G	W	L	PCT	GB	R	OR	AB	H	2B	3B	HR	BB	SO	AVG	OBP	SLG	PRO	PRO+	BR	/A	PF	CHI	RC	SB	CS	SBA	SBR
MIN	162	102	60	.630		774	600	5488	1396	257	42	150	554	969	.254	.327	.399	.726	107	84	55	104	106	730	92	33	74	8
CHI	162	95	67	.586	7	647	555	5509	1354	200	38	125	533	916	.246	.317	.364	.681	106	1	41	94	99	636	50	33	60	-5
BAL	162	94	68	.580	8	641	578	5450	1299	227	38	125	529	907	.238	.309	.363	.672	95	-21	-34	102	103	607	67	31	68	2
DET	162	89	73	.549	13	680	602	5368	1278	190	27	162	554	952	.238	.314	.374	.688	101	10	3	101	106	628	57	41	58	-8
CLE	162	87	75	.537	15	663	613	5469	1367	198	21	156	506	857	.250	.317	.379	.696	103	26	21	101	99	667	109	46	70	5
NY	162	77	85	.475	25	611	604	5470	1286	196	31	149	489	951	.235	.300	.364	.664	95	-42	-38	99	103	593	35	20	64	-2
CAL	162	75	87	.463	27	527	569	5354	1279	200	36	92	443	973	.239	.300	.341	.641	90	-81	-67	98	97	549	107	59	64	-3
WAS	162	70	92	.432	32	591	721	5374	1227	179	33	136	570	1125	.228	.306	.350	.656	94	-47	-37	99	101	586	30	19	61	-3
BOS	162	62	100	.383	40	669	791	5487	1378	244	40	165	607	964	.251	.329	.400	.729	107	95	56	106	90	715	47	24	66	0
KC	162	59	103	.364	43	585	755	5393	1294	186	59	110	521	1020	.240	.311	.358	.669	97	-25	-16	99	96	604	110	51	68	2
TOT	810					6388		54362	13158	2077	365	1370	5306	9634	.242	.313	.369	.682							704	357	66	-3

TEAM	CG	SH	SV	IP	H	H/G	HR	BB	SO	RAT	ERA	ERA+	OAV	OOB	PR	/A	PF	CPI	FA	E	DP	FW	PW	BW	SBW	DIF
MIN	32	12	45	1457¹	1278	7.9	166	503	934	11.2	3.14	113	.235	.303	52	68	103	107	.973	172	158	-2.3	7.3	5.9	.9	9.3
CHI	21	14	53	1481²	1261	7.7	122	460	946	10.6	2.99	107	.231	.294	76	33	92	98	.980	127	156	.6	3.5	4.4	-.5	6.0
BAL	32	15	41	1477²	1268	7.7	120	510	939	11.0	2.98	116	.233	.302	78	80	100	104	.980	126	152	.6	8.5	-3.6	.2	7.2
DET	45	14	31	1455	1283	7.9	137	509	1069	11.4	3.35	104	.237	.308	17	20	101	99	.981	116	126	1.3	2.1	.3	-.8	5.1
CLE	41	13	41	1458¹	1254	7.7	129	500	1156	11.0	3.30	106	.232	.300	26	30	101	94	.981	114	127	1.4	3.2	2.2	.6	-1.4
NY	41	11	31	1459²	1337	8.2	126	511	1001	11.6	3.28	104	.245	.313	29	20	98	104	.978	137	166	-.0	2.1	-4.1	-.2	-1.8
CAL	39	14	33	1441²	1259	7.9	91	563	847	11.5	3.17	107	.237	.313	46	37	98	100	.981	123	149	.8	3.9	-7.1	-.3	-3.3
WAS	21	8	40	1435²	1376	8.6	160	633	867	12.8	3.93	88	.254	.336	-75	-73	101	105	.977	143	148	-.4	-7.8	-3.9	-.2	1.4
BOS	33	9	25	1439¹	1443	9.0	158	543	993	12.6	4.24	88	.260	.329	-125	-82	108	95	.974	162	129	-1.6	-8.7	6.0	.0	-14.6
KC	18	7	32	1433	1399	8.8	161	574	882	12.6	4.24	82	.256	.331	-124	-119	101	96	.977	139	142	-.2	-12.7	-1.7	.2	-7.6
TOT	323	117	372	14539¹		8.1				11.6	3.46		.242	.313					.978	1359	1453					

Runs
Versalles-Min 126
Oliva-Min 107
Tresh-NY 94
Buford-Chi 93
Colavito-Cle 92

Hits
Oliva-Min 185
Versalles-Min 182
Colavito-Cle 170
Tresh-NY 168
Fregosi-Cal 167

Doubles
Yastrzemski-Bos ... 45
Versalles-Min 45
Oliva-Min 40
Tresh-NY 29
Richardson-NY 28

Triples
Versalles-Min 12
Campaneris-KC ... 12
Aparicio-Bal 10
W.Smith-Cal 9

Home Runs
Conigliaro-Bos 32
Cash-Det 30
Horton-Det 29
Wagner-Cle 28

Total Bases
Versalles-Min 308
Tresh-NY 287
Oliva-Min 283
Colavito-Cle 277
Conigliaro-Bos ... 267

Runs Batted In
Colavito-Cle 108
Horton-Det 104
Oliva-Min 98
Mantilla-Bos 92
Whitfield-Cle 90

Runs Produced
Oliva-Min 189
Versalles-Min 184
Colavito-Cle 174
Hall-Min 147
Horton-Det 144

Bases On Balls
Colavito-Cle 93
Blefary-Bal 88
Mantilla-Bos 79
Cash-Det 77
Robinson-Chi 76

Batting Average
Oliva-Min .... .321
Yastrzemski-Bos ... .312
Davalillo-Cle ...... .301
Robinson-Bal ..... .297
Wagner-Cle ...... .294

On Base Percentage
Yastrzemski-Bos .. .398
Colavito-Cle ...... .387
Oliva-Min .... .384
Blefary-Bal .... .382
Mantilla-Bos ..... .377

Slugging Average
Yastrzemski-Bos .. .536
Conigliaro-Bos ... .512
Cash-Det .... .512
Wagner-Cle ...... .495
Oliva-Min .... .491

Production
Yastrzemski-Bos .. .935
Cash-Det .... .886
Oliva-Min .... .876
Wagner-Cle ...... .866
Colavito-Cle ...... .855

Adjusted Production
Yastrzemski-Bos .. 154
Cash-Det 147
Wagner-Cle 143
Oliva-Min 141
Colavito-Cle 140

Batter Runs
Yastrzemski-Bos .. 41.6
Oliva-Min 35.3
Colavito-Cle 34.6
Cash-Det 31.0
Wagner-Cle 29.6

Adjusted Batter Runs
Yastrzemski-Bos .. 38.0
Colavito-Cle 34.0
Oliva-Min 32.3
Cash-Det 30.4
Wagner-Cle 29.1

Clutch Hitting Index
Mantilla-Bos 146
Colavito-Cle 134
Horton-Det 130
Oliva-Min 130
Powell-Bal 125

Runs Created
Colavito-Cle 110
Oliva-Min 109
Yastrzemski-Bos .. 102
Versalles-Min 102
Tresh-NY 101

Total Average
Yastrzemski-Bos .. .931
Cash-Det .... .894
Wagner-Cle ...... .882
Blefary-Bal .... .876
Oliva-Min .... .863

Stolen Bases
Campaneris-KC 51
Cardenal-Cal 37
Versalles-Min 27
Davalillo-Cle 26
Aparicio-Bal 26

Stolen Base Average
Hinton-Cle 85.0
Versalles-Min 84.4
Howser-Cle 81.0
Davalillo-Cle 78.8
Aparicio-Bal 78.8

Stolen Base Runs
Versalles-Min 5.1
Campaneris-KC ... 3.9
Davalillo-Cle 3.6
Aparicio-Bal 3.6
Hinton-Cle 3.3

Fielding Runs
Boyer-NY 25.9
Hansen-Chi 16.7
Davalillo-Cle 14.7
Conigliaro-Bos ... 13.5
Knoop-Cal 12.8

Total Player Rating
Yastrzemski-Bos ... 3.9
Oliva-Min 3.4
Weis-Chi 3.4
Buford-Chi 3.2
Colavito-Cle 3.2

Wins
Grant-Min 21
Stottlemyre-NY 20
Kaat-Min 18
McDowell-Cle 17

Win Percentage
Grant-Min .... .750
McLain-Det ...... .727
Stottlemyre-NY ... .690
Fisher-Chi .... .682
Siebert-Cle ...... .667

Games
Fisher-Chi 82
Kline-Was 74
R.Lee-Cal 69
Dickson-KC 68
S.Miller-Bal 67

Complete Games
Stottlemyre-NY 18
McDowell-Cle 14
Grant-Min 14
McLain-Det 13

Shutouts
Grant-Min 6
Stottlemyre-NY 4
McLain-Det 4
Horlen-Chi 4
Chance-Cal 4

Saves
Kline-Was 29
S.Miller-Bal 24
Fisher-Chi 24
R.Lee-Cal 23
Radatz-Bos 22

Innings Pitched
Stottlemyre-NY .. 291.0
McDowell-Cle ... 273.0
Grant-Min 270.1
Kaat-Min 264.1
Newman-Cal 260.2

Fewest Hits/Game
McDowell-Cle ... 5.87
Fisher-Chi 6.42
Siebert-Cle 6.63
Richert-Was 6.77
Brunet-Cal 6.81

Fewest BB/Game
Terry-Cle 1.25
Monbouquette-Bos 1.57
Horlen-Chi 1.60
Ford-NY 1.84
Grant-Min 2.03

Strikeouts
McDowell-Cle 325
Lolich-Det 226
McLain-Det 192
Siebert-Cle 191
Downing-NY 179

Strikeouts/Game
McDowell-Cle ... 10.71
Siebert-Cle 9.11
Lolich-Det 8.35
McLain-Det 7.84
Morehead-Bos ... 7.61

Ratio
Fisher-Chi 8.87
Siebert-Cle 9.06
Terry-Cle 9.67
McLain-Det 9.72
Newman-Cal 10.01

Earned Run Average
McDowell-Cle 2.18
Fisher-Chi 2.40
Siebert-Cle 2.43
Brunet-Cal 2.56
Richert-Was 2.60

Adjusted ERA
McDowell-Cle 160
Siebert-Cle 143
Perry-Min 135
Richert-Was 134
Pappas-Bal 133

Opponents' Batting Avg.
McDowell-Cle .... .185
Fisher-Chi .... .205
Siebert-Cle ...... .206
Brunet-Cal ...... .209
Richert-Was ..... .210

Opponents' On Base Pct.
Siebert-Cle ...... .262
Fisher-Chi .... .262
Terry-Cle .... .269
McLain-Det ...... .273
Pappas-Bal ...... .281

Starter Runs
McDowell-Cle 38.9
Stottlemyre-NY ... 26.8
Siebert-Cle 21.5
Pappas-Bal 21.1
McLain-Det 20.7

Adjusted Starter Runs
McDowell-Cle 39.5
Stottlemyre-NY ... 25.0
Siebert-Cle 21.9
Kaat-Min 21.4
Pappas-Bal 21.3

Clutch Pitching Index
Kaat-Min 123
Perry-Min 117
Peters-Chi 113
Richert-Was 110
Pappas-Bal 110

Relief Runs
Wilhelm-Chi 26.3
R.Lee-Cal 22.5
S.Miller-Bal 20.9
Fisher-Chi 19.5
Hamilton-NY 13.4

Adjusted Relief Runs
Wilhelm-Chi 22.1
R.Lee-Cal 21.6
S.Miller-Bal 21.0
Fisher-Chi 14.6
Hamilton-NY 13.1

Relief Ranking
S.Miller-Bal 42.7
R.Lee-Cal 32.2
Worthington-Min . 31.7
Wilhelm-Chi 26.2
Fisher-Chi 22.3

Total Pitcher Index
McDowell-Cle 4.3
Stottlemyre-NY ... 3.5
Kaat-Min 3.5
Newman-Cal 2.4
Siebert-Cle 2.4

Total Baseball Ranking
McDowell-Cle 4.3
Yastrzemski-Bos ... 3.9
Stottlemyre-NY ... 3.5
Kaat-Min 3.5
Oliva-Min 3.4

TEAM	G	W	L	PCT	GB	R	OR	AB	H	2B	3B	HR	BB	SO	AVG	OBP	SLG	PRO	PRO+	BR	/A	PF	CHI	RC	SB	CS	SBA	SBR
LA	162	95	67	.586		606	490	5471	1399	201	27	108	430	830	.256	.316	.362	.678	103	-37	15	92	98	615	94	64	59	-10
SF	161	93	68	.578	1.5	675	626	5539	1373	195	31	181	414	860	.248	.304	.392	.696	96	-14	-33	103	105	633	29	30	49	-9
PIT	162	92	70	.568	3	759	641	5676	1586	238	66	158	405	1011	.279	.331	.428	.759	116	117	116	100	96	779	64	60	52	-17
PHI	162	87	75	.537	8	696	640	5607	1448	224	49	117	510	969	.258	.323	.378	.701	101	12	11	100	101	683	56	42	57	-8
ATL	163	85	77	.525	10	782	683	5617	1476	220	32	207	512	913	.263	.329	.424	.753	113	106	96	102	100	775	59	47	56	-11
STL	162	83	79	.512	12	571	577	5480	1377	196	61	108	345	977	.251	.300	.368	.668	91	-66	-69	101	99	592	144	61	70	7
CIN	160	76	84	.475	18	692	702	5521	1434	232	33	149	394	877	.260	.311	.395	.706	94	7	-51	109	105	658	70	50	58	-9
HOU	163	72	90	.444	23	612	695	5511	1405	203	35	112	491	885	.255	.320	.365	.685	104	-19	26	93	94	640	90	47	66	-1
NY	161	66	95	.410	28.5	587	761	5371	1286	187	35	98	446	992	.239	.303	.342	.645	87	-99	-84	98	108	546	55	46	54	-11
CHI	162	59	103	.364	36	644	809	5592	1418	203	43	140	457	998	.254	.315	.380	.695	98	-6	-14	101	97	665	76	47	62	-5
TOT	809					6624		55385	14202	2099	412	1378	4404	9312	.256	.315	.384	.699							737	494	60	-75

TEAM	CG	SH	SV	IP	H	H/G	HR	BB	SO	RAT	ERA	ERA+	OAV	OOB	PR	/A	PF	CPI	FA	E	DP	FW	PW	BW	SBW	DIF
LA	52	20	35	1458	1287	7.9	84	356	1084	10.3	2.62	126	.237	.288	159	109	91	102	.979	133	128	.9	11.4	1.6	-.3	.4
SF	52	14	27	1476²	1370	8.3	140	359	973	10.7	3.24	113	.244	.294	61	71	102	96	.974	168	131	-1.2	7.4	-3.5	-.2	9.8
PIT	35	12	43	1463¹	1445	8.9	125	463	898	12.0	3.52	101	.261	.322	13	8	99	105	.978	141	215	.4	.8	12.2	-1.0	-1.4
PHI	52	15	23	1459¹	1439	8.9	137	412	928	11.8	3.57	101	.258	.316	6	4	100	102	.982	113	147	2.0	.4	1.2	-.0	2.5
ATL	37	10	36	1469¹	1430	8.8	129	485	884	11.9	3.68	99	.257	.319	-12	-7	101	98	.976	154	139	-.3	-.7	10.1	-.4	-4.7
STL	47	19	32	1459²	1345	8.3	130	448	892	11.3	3.11	115	.246	.307	80	77	100	107	.977	145	166	.2	8.1	-7.2	1.5	-.6
CIN	28	10	35	1436	1408	8.8	153	490	1043	12.2	4.08	96	.258	.324	-76	-28	108	94	.980	154	133	1.4	-2.9	-5.3	-.2	3.0
HOU	34	13	26	1443²	1468	9.2	130	391	929	11.8	3.76	91	.262	.314	-24	-54	95	96	.972	174	126	-1.4	-5.7	2.7	.7	-5.4
NY	37	9	22	1427	1497	9.4	166	521	773	12.9	4.17	87	.272	.339	-89	-85	101	104	.975	159	171	-.6	-8.9	-8.8	-.4	-8.7
CHI	28	6	24	1458	1513	9.3	184	479	908	12.5	4.33	85	.268	.328	-118	-106	102	97	.974	166	132	-1.0	-11.1	-1.5	.3	-8.7
TOT	402	128	303	14551¹		8.8				11.7	3.61		.256	.315					.977	1475	1488					

Runs
Alou-Atl	122
Aaron-Atl	117
Allen-Phi	112
Clemente-Pit	105
Williams-Chi	100

Hits
Alou-Atl	218
Rose-Cin	205
Clemente-Pit	202
Beckert-Chi	188

Doubles
Callison-Phi	40
Rose-Cin	38
Pinson-Cin	35
Alou-Atl	32

Triples
McCarver-StL	13
Brock-StL	12
Clemente-Pit	11

Home Runs
Aaron-Atl	44
Allen-Phi	40
Mays-SF	37
Torre-Atl	36
McCovey-SF	36

Total Bases
Alou-Atl	355
Clemente-Pit	342
Allen-Phi	331
Aaron-Atl	325
Mays-SF	307

Runs Batted In
Aaron-Atl	127
Clemente-Pit	119
Allen-Phi	110
White-Phi	103
Mays-SF	103

Runs Produced
Aaron-Atl	200
Clemente-Pit	195
Allen-Phi	182
White-Phi	166

Bases On Balls
Santo-Chi	95
Morgan-Hou	89
McCovey-SF	76
Aaron-Atl	76
Menke-Atl	71

Batting Average
Alou-Pit	.342
Alou-Atl	.327
Carty-Atl	.326
Allen-Phi	.317
Clemente-Pit	.317

On Base Percentage
Santo-Chi	.417
Morgan-Hou	.412
Allen-Phi	.398
Carty-Atl	.396
McCovey-SF	.394

Slugging Average
Allen-Phi	.632
McCovey-SF	.586
Stargell-Pit	.581
Torre-Atl	.560
Mays-SF	.556

Production
Allen-Phi	1.030
McCovey-SF	.979
Stargell-Pit	.965
Santo-Chi	.955
Torre-Atl	.945

Adjusted Production
Allen-Phi	181
Stargell-Pit	164
McCovey-SF	163
Santo-Chi	161
Torre-Atl	157

Batter Runs
Allen-Phi	56.8
Santo-Chi	51.2
McCovey-SF	46.9
Torre-Atl	43.0
Stargell-Pit	41.1

Adjusted Batter Runs
Allen-Phi	56.8
Santo-Chi	50.3
McCovey-SF	45.1
Torre-Atl	42.0
Stargell-Pit	41.1

Clutch Hitting Index
White-Phi	135
Staub-Hou	135
Flood-StL	135
Aaron-Atl	124
Woodward-Atl	121

Runs Created
Allen-Phi	131
Santo-Chi	127
Alou-Atl	123
McCovey-SF	119
Clemente-Pit	119

Total Average
Allen-Phi	1.088
McCovey-SF	1.039
Santo-Chi	.988
Stargell-Pit	.980
Mays-SF	.941

Stolen Bases
Brock-StL	74
Jackson-Hou	49
Wills-LA	38
Phillips-Phi-Chi	32
Harper-Cin	29

Stolen Base Average
Aaron-Atl	87.5
Brock-StL	80.4
Jackson-Hou	77.8
Harper-Cin	74.4
White-Phi	72.7

Stolen Base Runs
Brock-StL	11.4
Jackson-Hou	6.3
Aaron-Atl	4.5
Harper-Cin	2.7

Fielding Runs
Mazeroski-Pit	40.8
Santo-Chi	28.8
Lanier-SF	28.2
Maxvill-StL	24.0
Clemente-Pit	15.6

Total Player Rating
Santo-Chi	7.6
Clemente-Pit	4.6
Aaron-Atl	4.5
Mazeroski-Pit	4.5
Allen-Phi	4.3

Wins
Koufax-LA	27
Marichal-SF	25
Perry-SF	21
Gibson-StL	21
Short-Phi	20

Win Percentage
Marichal-SF	.806
Koufax-LA	.750
Perry-SF	.724
Short-Phi	.667
Maloney-Cin	.667

Games
Carroll-Phi	73
Mikkelsen-Pit	71
Knowles-Phi	69
Regan-LA	65
McDaniel-SF	64

Complete Games
Koufax-LA	27
Marichal-SF	25
Gibson-StL	20
Short-Phi	19
Bunning-Phi	16

Shutouts
L.Jackson-Chi-Phi	5
Maloney-Cin	5
Koufax-LA	5
Jaster-StL	5
Gibson-StL	5
Bunning-Phi	5

Saves
Regan-LA	21
McCool-Cin	18
Face-Pit	18
Raymond-Hou	16
Linzy-SF	16

Innings Pitched
Koufax-LA	323.0
Bunning-Phi	314.0
Marichal-SF	307.1
Gibson-StL	280.1
Drysdale-LA	273.2

Fewest Hits/Game
Marichal-SF	6.68
Koufax-LA	6.72
Gibson-StL	6.74
Maloney-Cin	6.97
Bolin-SF	6.98

Fewest BB/Game
Marichal-SF	1.05
Law-Pit	1.22
Perry-SF	1.41
Drysdale-LA	1.48
Bunning-Phi	1.58

Strikeouts
Koufax-LA	317
Bunning-Phi	252
Veale-Pit	229
Gibson-StL	225
Marichal-SF	222

Strikeouts/Game
Koufax-LA	8.83
Maloney-Cin	8.65
Sutton-LA	8.34
Veale-Pit	7.68
Jenkins-Phi-Chi	7.32

Ratio
Marichal-SF	7.88
Koufax-LA	8.86
Gibson-StL	9.41
Bunning-Phi	9.57
Cuellar-Hou	9.70

Earned Run Average
Koufax-LA	1.73
Cuellar-Hou	2.22
Marichal-SF	2.23
Bunning-Phi	2.41
Gibson-StL	2.44

Adjusted ERA
Koufax-LA	191
Marichal-SF	165
Cuellar-Hou	154
Bunning-Phi	149
Gibson-StL	147

Opponents' Batting Avg.
Marichal-SF	.202
Koufax-LA	.205
Gibson-StL	.207
Bolin-SF	.211
Maloney-Cin	.214

Opponents' On Base Pct.
Marichal-SF	.230
Koufax-LA	.253
Gibson-StL	.267
Bunning-Phi	.270
Cuellar-Hou	.274

Starter Runs
Koufax-LA	67.4
Marichal-SF	47.2
Bunning-Phi	41.8
Gibson-StL	36.3
Cuellar-Hou	35.1

Adjusted Starter Runs
Koufax-LA	56.3
Marichal-SF	49.2
Bunning-Phi	41.4
Gibson-StL	35.8
Cuellar-Hou	30.5

Clutch Pitching Index
Jackson-StL	117
L.Jackson-Chi-Phi	110
Ellsworth-Chi	108
Johnson-Atl	108
Osteen-LA	107

Relief Runs
Regan-LA	25.8
Carroll-Atl	19.8
Hoerner-StL	17.5
McCool-Cin	13.2
Woodeshick-StL	13.2

Adjusted Relief Runs
Regan-LA	21.7
Carroll-Atl	20.4
Hoerner-StL	17.3
McCool-Cin	16.7
McDaniel-SF	13.6

Relief Ranking
Regan-LA	33.9
McCool-Cin	29.2
Carroll-Atl	22.5
Hoerner-StL	19.0
McDaniel-SF	16.6

Total Pitcher Index
Marichal-SF	6.4
Koufax-LA	5.4
Bunning-Phi	4.3
Gibson-StL	4.2
Jackson-StL	3.9

Total Baseball Ranking
Santo-Chi	7.6
Marichal-SF	6.4
Koufax-LA	5.4
Clemente-Pit	4.6
Aaron-Atl	4.5

TEAM	G	W	L	PCT	GB	R	OR	AB	H	2B	3B	HR	BB	SO	AVG	OBP	SLG	PRO	PRO+	BR	/A	PF	CHI	RC	SB	CS	SBA	SBR
BAL	160	97	63	.606		755	601	5529	1426	243	35	175	514	926	.258	.325	.409	.734	119	114	124	98	100	727	55	43	56	-9
MIN	162	89	73	.549	9	663	581	5390	1341	219	33	144	513	844	.249	.319	.382	.701	101	49	9	106	98	643	67	42	61	-5
DET	162	88	74	.543	10	719	698	5507	1383	224	45	179	551	987	.251	.323	.406	.729	112	102	87	102	96	714	41	34	55	-8
CHI	163	83	79	.512	15	574	517	5348	1235	193	40	87	476	872	.231	.299	.331	.630	93	-83	-41	93	106	539	153	78	66	-1
CLE	162	81	81	.500	17	574	586	5474	1300	156	25	155	450	914	.237	.299	.360	.659	95	-38	-38	100	97	579	53	41	56	-9
CAL	162	80	82	.494	18	604	643	5360	1244	179	54	122	525	1062	.232	.305	.354	.659	98	-29	-12	97	101	582	80	54	60	-8
KC	160	74	86	.463	23	564	648	5328	1259	212	56	70	421	982	.236	.295	.337	.632	90	-84	-64	97	107	535	132	50	73	10
WAS	159	71	88	.447	25.5	557	659	5318	1245	185	40	126	450	1069	.234	.296	.355	.651	94	-50	-44	99	99	548	53	37	59	-6
BOS	162	72	90	.444	26	655	731	5498	1318	228	44	145	542	1020	.240	.312	.376	.688	93	24	-42	110	98	640	35	24	59	-4
NY	160	70	89	.440	26.5	611	612	5330	1254	182	36	162	485	817	.235	.302	.374	.676	104	-5	18	96	100	598	49	29	63	-3
TOT	806					6276		54082	13005	2021	408	1365	4927	9493	.240	.308	.369	.676							718	432	62	-44

TEAM	CG	SH	SV	IP	H	H/G	HR	BB	SO	RAT	ERA	ERA+	OAV	OOB	PR	/A	PF	CPI	FA	E	DP	FW	PW	BW	SBW	DIF
BAL	23	13	51	1466¹	1267	7.8	127	514	1070	11.1	3.32	100	.233	.303	19	2	97	97	.981	115	142	1.3	.2	13.3	-.5	2.7
MIN	52	11	28	1438²	1246	7.8	139	392	1015	10.4	3.13	115	.232	.287	48	74	105	97	.977	139	118	.0	8.0	1.0	-.0	-.9
DET	36	11	38	1454¹	1356	8.4	185	520	1026	11.9	3.85	90	.247	.317	-67	-60	101	102	.980	120	142	1.1	-6.4	9.3	-.4	3.4
CHI	38	22	34	1475¹	1229	7.5	101	403	896	10.2	2.68	118	.226	.283	123	80	92	100	.976	159	149	-1.1	8.6	-4.4	.4	-1.5
CLE	49	15	28	1467¹	1260	7.7	129	489	1111	10.9	3.23	107	.232	.299	34	35	100	98	.978	138	132	.0	3.8	-4.1	-.5	.7
CAL	31	12	40	1457¹	1364	8.4	136	511	836	11.8	3.56	94	.251	.320	-21	-33	98	105	.979	136	186	.2	-3.5	-1.3	-.4	4.0
KC	19	11	47	1435	1281	8.0	106	630	854	12.2	3.56	96	.241	.326	-19	-25	99	101	.977	139	154	-.0	-2.7	-6.9	1.5	2.1
WAS	25	6	35	1419	1282	8.1	154	448	866	11.1	3.70	93	.242	.304	-42	-39	101	95	.977	142	139	-.3	-4.2	-4.7	-.2	.9
BOS	32	10	31	1463²	1402	8.6	164	577	977	12.4	3.92	97	.253	.327	-78	-18	111	103	.975	155	153	-.9	-1.9	-4.5	.0	-1.7
NY	29	7	32	1415²	1318	8.4	124	443	842	11.3	3.41	97	.248	.308	3	-14	97	102	.977	142	142	-.3	-1.5	1.9	.1	-9.8
TOT	334	118	364	14492²		8.1				11.3	3.44		.240	.308					.978	1385	1457					

Runs
F.Robinson-Bal ... 122
Oliva-Min ... 99
Cash-Det ... 98
Agee-Chi ... 98

Hits
Oliva-Min ... 191
F.Robinson-Bal ... 182
Aparicio-Bal ... 182
Agee-Chi ... 172
Cash-Det ... 168

Doubles
Yastrzemski-Bos ... 39
B.Robinson-Bal ... 35
F.Robinson-Bal ... 34
Oliva-Min ... 32
Fregosi-Cal ... 32

Triples
Knoop-Cal ... 11
Campaneris-KC ... 10
Brinkman-Was ... 9

Home Runs
F.Robinson-Bal ... 49
Killebrew-Min ... 39
Powell-Bal ... 34
Cash-Det ... 32
Pepitone-NY ... 31

Total Bases
F.Robinson-Bal ... 367
Oliva-Min ... 312
Killebrew-Min ... 306
Cash-Det ... 288
Agee-Chi ... 281

Runs Batted In
F.Robinson-Bal ... 122
Killebrew-Min ... 110
Powell-Bal ... 109
B.Robinson-Bal ... 100
Horton-Det ... 100

Runs Produced
F.Robinson-Bal ... 195
B.Robinson-Bal ... 168
Agee-Chi ... 162
Oliva-Min ... 161
Killebrew-Min ... 160

Bases On Balls
Killebrew-Min ... 103
Foy-Bos ... 91
F.Robinson-Bal ... 87
Tresh-NY ... 86
Yastrzemski-Bos ... 84

Batting Average
F.Robinson-Bal ... .316
Oliva-Min ... .307
Kaline-Det ... .288
Powell-Bal ... .287
Killebrew-Min ... .281

On Base Percentage
F.Robinson-Bal ... .415
Kaline-Det ... .396
Killebrew-Min ... .393
McAuliffe-Det ... .375
Powell-Bal ... .374

Slugging Average
F.Robinson-Bal ... .637
Killebrew-Min ... .538
Kaline-Det ... .534
Powell-Bal ... .532
McAuliffe-Det ... .509

Production
F.Robinson-Bal ... 1.052
Killebrew-Min ... .931
Kaline-Det ... .931
Powell-Bal ... .905
McAuliffe-Det ... .884

Adjusted Production
F.Robinson-Bal ... 200
Kaline-Det ... 161
Powell-Bal ... 159
Killebrew-Min ... 155
McAuliffe-Det ... 148

Batter Runs
F.Robinson-Bal ... 73.6
Killebrew-Min ... 49.9
Kaline-Det ... 42.1
Powell-Bal ... 36.3
Oliva-Min ... 33.2

Adjusted Batter Runs
F.Robinson-Bal ... 74.7
Killebrew-Min ... 45.4
Kaline-Det ... 40.7
Powell-Bal ... 37.2
Mantle-NY ... 30.3

Clutch Hitting Index
Hershberger-KC ... 134
Wert-Det ... 130
B.Robinson-Bal ... 129
Powell-Bal ... 129
Horton-Det ... 128

Runs Created
F.Robinson-Bal ... 146
Killebrew-Min ... 122
Oliva-Min ... 106
Kaline-Det ... 105
Cash-Det ... 101

Total Average
F.Robinson-Bal ... 1.104
Kaline-Det ... .969
Killebrew-Min ... .967
Powell-Bal ... .898
McAuliffe-Det ... .877

Stolen Bases
Campaneris-KC ... 52
Buford-Chi ... 51
Agee-Chi ... 44
Aparicio-Bal ... 25
Cardenal-Cal ... 24

Stolen Base Average
Campaneris-KC ... 83.9
Tartabull-KC-Bos ... 82.6
Tovar-Min ... 72.7
Agee-Chi ... 71.0
Buford-Chi ... 69.9

Stolen Base Runs
Campaneris-KC ... 9.6
Tartabull-KC-Bos ... 3.3
Salmon-Cle ... 2.4
Agee-Chi ... 2.4

Fielding Runs
Weis-Chi ... 36.9
Tresh-NY ... 27.7
Boyer-NY ... 19.9
Yastrzemski-Bos ... 16.6
Knoop-Cal ... 16.5

Total Player Rating
F.Robinson-Bal ... 6.6
Tresh-NY ... 4.1
Kaline-Det ... 4.0
Fregosi-Cal ... 3.9
Oliva-Min ... 3.7

Wins
Kaat-Min ... 25
McLain-Det ... 20
Wilson-Bos-Det ... 18
Siebert-Cle ... 16
Palmer-Bal ... 15

Win Percentage
Siebert-Cle ... .667
Kaat-Min ... .658
Wilson-Bos-Det ... .621
Palmer-Bal ... .600
McLain-Det ... .588

Games
Fisher-Chi-Bal ... 67
Cox-Was ... 66
Aker-KC ... 66
Worthington-Min ... 65
Kline-Was ... 63

Complete Games
Kaat-Min ... 19
McLain-Det ... 14
Wilson-Bos-Det ... 13
Bell-Cle ... 12

Shutouts
Tiant-Cle ... 5
McDowell-Cle ... 5
John-Chi ... 5

Saves
Aker-KC ... 32
Kline-Was ... 23
Sherry-Det ... 20
Fisher-Chi-Bal ... 19
S.Miller-Bal ... 18

Innings Pitched
Kaat-Min ... 304.2
McLain-Det ... 264.1
Wilson-Bos-Det ... 264.0
Chance-Cal ... 259.2
Bell-Cle ... 254.1

Fewest Hits/Game
McDowell-Cle ... 6.02
Boswell-Min ... 6.38
Peters-Chi ... 6.86
McLain-Det ... 6.98
Chance-Cal ... 7.14

Fewest BB/Game
Kaat-Min ... 1.62
Peterson-NY ... 1.67
Grant-Min ... 1.77
Peters-Chi ... 1.98
Hargan-Cle ... 2.11

Strikeouts
McDowell-Cle ... 225
Kaat-Min ... 205
Wilson-Bos-Det ... 200
Richert-Was ... 195
Bell-Cle ... 194

Strikeouts/Game
McDowell-Cle ... 10.42
Boswell-Min ... 9.19
Lolich-Det ... 7.64
Richert-Was ... 7.14
Bell-Cle ... 6.87

Ratio
Peters-Chi ... 8.97
Kaat-Min ... 9.72
Richert-Was ... 9.74
Siebert-Cle ... 9.75
Ortega-Was ... 9.85

Earned Run Average
Peters-Chi ... 1.98
Horlen-Chi ... 2.43
Hargan-Cle ... 2.48
Perry-Min ... 2.54
John-Chi ... 2.62

Adjusted ERA
Peters-Chi ... 160
Perry-Min ... 142
Hargan-Cle ... 138
Kaat-Min ... 131
Horlen-Chi ... 130

Opponents' Batting Avg.
McDowell-Cle ... .188
Boswell-Min ... .197
Peters-Chi ... .212
McLain-Det ... .214
Richert-Was ... .215

Opponents' On Base Pct.
Peters-Chi ... .261
Richert-Was ... .271
Kaat-Min ... .271
Ortega-Was ... .276
Siebert-Cle ... .278

Starter Runs
Peters-Chi ... 33.1
Horlen-Chi ... 23.5
Kaat-Min ... 23.3
Hargan-Cle ... 20.3
John-Chi ... 20.1

Adjusted Starter Runs
Kaat-Min ... 28.8
Peters-Chi ... 27.1
Perry-Min ... 21.7
Hargan-Cle ... 20.4
Nash-KC ... 18.9

Clutch Pitching Index
McNally-Bal ... 118
Horlen-Chi ... 114
Brunet-Cal ... 114
Perry-Min ... 113
Hargan-Cle ... 110

Relief Runs
Aker-KC ... 18.1
Wilhelm-Chi ... 16.0
S.Miller-Bal ... 12.1
Fisher-Chi-Bal ... 10.8
Lines-Was ... 10.7

Adjusted Relief Runs
Aker-KC ... 17.7
Wilhelm-Chi ... 13.7
Worthington-Min ... 11.5
S.Miller-Bal ... 11.1
Lines-Was ... 10.9

Relief Ranking
Aker-KC ... 28.1
McMahon-Cle-Bos ... 20.8
S.Miller-Bal ... 18.9
Kline-Was ... 16.8
Worthington-Min ... 14.7

Total Pitcher Index
Peters-Chi ... 4.0
Kaat-Min ... 3.7
Wilson-Bos-Det ... 3.4
Perry-Min ... 2.8
Horlen-Chi ... 2.3

Total Baseball Ranking
F.Robinson-Bal ... 6.6
Tresh-NY ... 4.1
Kaline-Det ... 4.0
Peters-Chi ... 4.0
Fregosi-Cal ... 3.9

1967 National League

TEAM	G	W	L	PCT	GB	R	OR	AB	H	2B	3B	HR	BB	SO	AVG	OBP	SLG	PRO	PRO+	BR	/A	PF	CHI	RC	SB	CS	SBA	SBR
STL	161	101	60	.627		695	557	5566	1462	225	40	115	443	919	.263	.322	.379	.701	109	52	60	99	103	676	102	54	65	-2
SF	162	91	71	.562	10.5	652	551	5524	1354	201	39	140	520	978	.245	.315	.372	.687	104	24	33	99	100	641	22	30	42	-11
CHI	162	87	74	.540	14	702	624	5463	1373	211	49	128	509	912	.251	.319	.378	.697	101	44	15	105	105	654	63	50	56	-11
CIN	162	87	75	.537	14.5	604	563	5519	1366	251	54	109	372	969	.248	.299	.372	.671	88	-20	-90	111	102	592	92	63	59	-10
PHI	162	82	80	.506	19.5	612	581	5401	1306	221	47	103	545	1033	.242	.314	.357	.671	98	-1	-7	101	99	604	79	62	56	-14
PIT	163	81	81	.500	20.5	679	693	5724	1585	193	62	91	387	914	.277	.327	.380	.707	108	63	60	101	97	693	79	37	68	2
ATL	162	77	85	.475	24.5	631	640	5450	1307	191	29	158	512	947	.240	.309	.372	.681	102	10	19	99	100	615	55	45	55	-11
LA	162	73	89	.451	28.5	519	595	5456	1285	203	38	82	485	881	.236	.303	.332	.635	97	-74	-23	92	95	541	56	47	54	-11
HOU	162	69	93	.426	32.5	626	742	5506	1372	259	46	93	537	934	.249	.319	.364	.683	107	20	41	97	97	640	88	38	70	4
NY	162	61	101	.377	40.5	498	672	5417	1288	178	23	83	362	981	.238	.290	.325	.615	83	-118	-108	98	103	500	58	44	57	-9
TOT	810					6218		55026	13698	2133	427	1102	4672	9468	.249	.312	.363	.675							694	470	60	-74

TEAM	CG	SH	SV	IP	H	H/G	HR	BB	SO	RAT	ERA	ERA+	OAV	OOB	PR	/A	PF	CPI	FA	E	DP	FW	PW	BW	SBW	DIF
STL	44	17	45	1465	1313	8.1	97	431	956	10.9	3.05	108	.239	.299	54	39	97	98	.978	140	127	.0	4.2	6.5	.6	9.2
SF	64	17	25	1474¹	1283	7.8	113	453	990	10.8	2.92	113	.234	.296	75	61	97	101	.979	134	149	.4	6.6	3.6	-.4	-.2
CHI	47	7	28	1457	1352	8.4	142	463	888	11.4	3.48	102	.246	.308	-17	10	105	99	.981	121	143	1.1	1.1	1.6	-.4	3.0
CIN	34	18	39	1468	1328	8.1	101	498	1065	11.5	3.05	123	.241	.309	54	115	111	104	.980	121	121	1.1	12.5	-9.7	-.3	2.4
PHI	46	17	23	1453²	1372	8.5	86	403	967	11.2	3.10	110	.250	.306	44	50	101	102	.978	137	174	.2	5.4	-.8	-.7	-3.2
PIT	35	5	35	1458¹	1439	8.9	108	561	820	12.5	3.74	90	.261	.332	-59	-61	100	103	.978	141	186	.0	-6.6	6.5	1.0	-.9
ATL	35	5	32	1454	1377	8.5	118	449	862	11.6	3.47	96	.251	.313	-16	-24	98	100	.978	138	148	.2	-2.6	2.1	-.4	-3.2
LA	41	17	24	1473	1421	8.7	93	393	967	11.3	3.21	96	.254	.308	27	-19	92	102	.975	160	144	-1.1	-2.1	-2.5	-.4	-2.0
HOU	35	8	21	1445²	1444	9.0	120	485	1060	12.3	4.03	82	.260	.324	-105	-115	98	93	.974	159	120	-1.0	-12.5	4.4	1.2	-4.2
NY	36	10	19	1433³	1369	8.6	124	536	893	12.1	3.73	91	.253	.323	-56	-54	100	99	.975	157	147	-.9	-5.8	-11.7	-.2	-1.4
TOT	417	121	291	14582²		8.5				11.6	3.38		.249	.312					.978	1408	1462					

Runs
Brock-StL 113
Aaron-Atl 113
Santo-Chi 107
Clemente-Pit 103
Wynn-Hou 102

Hits
Clemente-Pit 209
Brock-StL 206
Pinson-Cin 187
Wills-Pit 186
Alou-Pit 186

Doubles
Staub-Hou 44
Cepeda-StL 37
Aaron-Atl 37

Triples
Pinson-Cin 13
Williams-Chi 12
Brock-StL 12
Morgan-Hou 11

Home Runs
Aaron-Atl 39
Wynn-Hou 37
Santo-Chi 31
McCovey-SF 31
Hart-SF 29

Total Bases
Aaron-Atl 344
Brock-StL 325
Clemente-Pit 324
Williams-Chi 305
Santo-Chi 300

Runs Batted In
Cepeda-StL 111
Clemente-Pit 110
Aaron-Atl 109
Wynn-Hou 107
Perez-Cin 102

Runs Produced
Clemente-Pit 190
Aaron-Atl 183
Cepeda-StL 177
Santo-Chi 174
Wynn-Hou 172

Bases On Balls
Santo-Chi 96
Morgan-Hou 81
Phillips-Chi 80
Hart-SF 77
Allen-Phi 75

Batting Average
Clemente-Pit 357
Gonzalez-Phi 339
Alou-Pit 338
Flood-StL 335
Staub-Hou 333

On Base Percentage
Allen-Phi 404
Cepeda-StL 403
Staub-Hou 402
Clemente-Pit 402
Santo-Chi 401

Slugging Average
Aaron-Atl 573
Allen-Phi 566
Clemente-Pit 554
McCovey-SF 535
Cepeda-StL 524

Production
Allen-Phi 970
Clemente-Pit 956
Aaron-Atl 946
Cepeda-StL 927
McCovey-SF 916

Adjusted Production
Allen-Phi 173
Clemente-Pit 170
Aaron-Atl 169
Cepeda-StL 166
McCovey-SF 162

Batter Runs
Clemente-Pit 52.1
Aaron-Atl 50.1
Santo-Chi 47.9
Cepeda-StL 47.3
Allen-Phi 46.1

Adjusted Batter Runs
Clemente-Pit 51.8
Aaron-Atl 51.0
Cepeda-StL 48.1
Allen-Phi 45.5
Santo-Chi 44.6

Clutch Hitting Index
Shannon-StL 152
Mazeroski-Pit 134
Cepeda-StL 132
Lanier-SF 130
Boyer-Atl 127

Runs Created
Clemente-Pit 126
Aaron-Atl 126
Santo-Chi 120
Cepeda-StL 118
Hart-SF 111

Total Average
Allen-Phi 1.054
Aaron-Atl .... .965
Clemente-Pit ..... .959
Cepeda-StL ...... .950
McCovey-SF ..... .941

Stolen Bases
Brock-StL 52
Wills-Pit 29
Morgan-Hou 29
Pinson-Cin 26
Phillips-Chi 24

Stolen Base Average
Morgan-Hou 85.3
Wynn-Hou 80.0
Allen-Phi 80.0
Davis-LA 76.9
Pinson-Cin 76.5

Stolen Base Runs
Morgan-Hou 5.7
Brock-StL 4.8
Pinson-Cin 3.0
Allen-Phi 3.0
Wills-Pit 2.7

Fielding Runs
Santo-Chi 30.6
Lanier-SF 28.9
Wine-Phi 28.9
Fuentes-SF 24.5
Mazeroski-Pit 16.7

Total Player Rating
Santo-Chi 7.5
Aaron-Atl 6.0
Clemente-Pit 5.8
Allen-Phi 4.4
Cepeda-StL 4.3

Wins
McCormick-SF 22
Jenkins-Chi 20
Osteen-LA 17
Bunning-Phi 17

Win Percentage
Hughes-StL 727
McCormick-SF ...688
Veale-Pit 667
Jenkins-Chi 606
Jarvis-Atl 600

Games
Perranoski-LA 70
Abernathy-Cin 70
Willis-StL 65
Face-Pit 61

Complete Games
Jenkins-Chi 20
Seaver-NY 18
Perry-SF 18
Marichal-SF 18

Shutouts
Bunning-Phi 6
Osteen-LA 5
Nolan-Cin 5
McCormick-SF 5
L.Jackson-Phi 4

Saves
Abernathy-Cin 28
Linzy-SF 17
Face-Pit 17
Perranoski-LA 16
Hoerner-StL 15

Innings Pitched
Bunning-Phi 302.1
Perry-SF 293.0
Jenkins-Chi 289.1
Osteen-LA 288.1
Drysdale-LA 282.0

Fewest Hits/Game
Hughes-StL 6.64
Wilson-Hou 6.90
Perry-SF 7.10
Queen-Cin 7.13
Niekro-Atl 7.13

Fewest BB/Game
Pappas-Cin 1.57
Osteen-LA 1.62
Johnson-Atl 1.63
Niekro-Atl 1.70
L.Jackson-Phi 1.86

Strikeouts
Bunning-Phi 253
Jenkins-Chi 236
Perry-SF 230
Nolan-Cin 206
Cuellar-Hou 203

Strikeouts/Game
Nolan-Cin 8.18
Veale-Pit 7.94
Carlton-StL 7.83
Wilson-Hou 7.78
Gibson-StL 7.55

Ratio
Hughes-StL 8.78
Bunning-Phi 9.73
Queen-Cin 9.80
Perry-SF 9.80
Niekro-Atl 9.83

Earned Run Average
Niekro-Atl 1.87
Bunning-Phi 2.29
Short-Phi 2.39
Nolan-Cin 2.58
Perry-SF 2.61

Adjusted ERA
Niekro-Atl 178
Bunning-Phi 149
Nolan-Cin 145
Short-Phi 142
Queen-Cin 136

Opponents' Batting Avg.
Hughes-StL 203
Wilson-Hou 209
Perry-SF 214
Queen-Cin 215
Bunning-Phi 217

Opponents' On Base Pct.
Hughes-StL 252
Bunning-Phi 273
Queen-Cin 273
Perry-SF 274
Jenkins-Chi 277

Starter Runs
Bunning-Phi 36.4
Niekro-Atl 34.6
Perry-SF 24.9
Short-Phi 21.8
Nolan-Cin 20.0

Adjusted Starter Runs
Bunning-Phi 37.5
Niekro-Atl 33.4
Nolan-Cin 29.5
Jenkins-Chi 24.0
Short-Phi 22.5

Clutch Pitching Index
Ellis-Cin 123
Niekro-Atl 121
Seaver-NY 114
Marichal-SF 114
Short-Phi 114

Relief Runs
Abernathy-Cin 24.9
Linzy-SF 19.9
Nottebart-Cin 12.8
McBean-Pit 12.1
Farrell-Hou-Phi ... 11.9

Adjusted Relief Runs
Abernathy-Cin 29.3
Linzy-SF 19.0
Nottebart-Cin 16.1
Farrell-Hou-Phi ... 12.1
McBean-Pit 12.0

Relief Ranking
Abernathy-Cin 39.7
Linzy-SF 32.5
Hall-Phi 24.2
Farrell-Hou-Phi ... 20.0
Face-Pit 15.3

Total Pitcher Index
Bunning-Phi 4.3
Niekro-Atl 3.9
Abernathy-Cin 3.3
Nolan-Cin 3.1
Jenkins-Chi 3.1

Total Baseball Ranking
Santo-Chi 7.5
Aaron-Atl 6.0
Clemente-Pit 5.8
Allen-Phi 4.4
Cepeda-StL 4.3

TEAM	G	W	L	PCT	GB	R	OR	AB	H	2B	3B	HR	BB	SO	AVG	OBP	SLG	PRO	PRO+	BR	/A	PF	CHI	RC	SB	CS	SBA	SBR
BOS	162	92	70	.568		722	614	5471	1394	216	39	158	522	1020	.255	.323	.395	.718	109	118	69	108	100	694	68	59	54	-15
MIN	164	91	71	.562	1	671	590	5458	1309	216	48	131	512	976	.240	.310	.369	.679	99	44	-5	108	104	625	55	37	60	-6
DET	163	91	71	.562	1	683	587	5410	1315	192	36	152	626	994	.243	.293	.376	.670	111	100	83	103	96	681	37	21	64	-2
CHI	162	89	73	.549	3	531	491	5383	1209	181	34	89	480	849	.225	.293	.320	.613	90	-80	-58	96	104	504	124	82	60	-12
CAL	161	84	77	.522	7.5	567	587	5307	1265	170	37	114	453	1021	.238	.302	.349	.651	102	-12	10	96	99	553	40	36	53	-10
WAS	161	76	85	.472	15.5	550	637	5441	1211	168	25	115	472	1037	.223	.289	.326	.615	92	-81	-58	96	107	512	53	37	59	-6
BAL	161	76	85	.472	15.5	654	592	5456	1312	215	44	138	531	1002	.240	.313	.372	.685	110	54	59	99	99	639	54	37	59	-6
CLE	162	75	87	.463	17	559	613	5461	1282	213	35	131	413	984	.235	.295	.359	.654	98	-15	-20	101	96	563	53	65	45	-23
NY	163	72	90	.444	20	522	621	5443	1225	166	17	100	532	1043	.225	.298	.317	.615	91	-74	-52	96	98	522	63	37	63	-3
KC	161	62	99	.385	29.5	533	660	5349	1244	212	50	69	452	1019	.233	.297	.330	.627	94	-54	-35	97	100	539	132	59	69	4
TOT	810					5992		54179	12766	1949	365	1197	4993	9945	.236	.305	.351	.656							679	470	59	-78

TEAM	CG	SH	SV	IP	H	H/G	HR	BB	SO	RAT	ERA	ERA+	OAV	OOB	PR	/A	PF	CPI	FA	E	DP	FW	PW	BW	SBW	DIF
BOS	41	9	44	1459[1]	1307	8.1	142	477	1010	11.3	3.36	104	.239	.306	-21	20	108	101	.977	142	142	-.6	2.2	7.6	-.8	2.6
MIN	58	18	24	1461	1336	8.2	115	396	1089	10.9	3.14	110	.243	.298	15	53	107	101	.978	132	123	.1	5.9	-.6	.2	4.4
DET	46	17	40	1443[2]	1230	7.7	151	472	1038	10.8	3.32	98	.230	.297	-14	-9	101	97	.978	132	126	.0	-1.0	9.2	.6	1.1
CHI	36	24	39	1490[1]	1197	7.2	87	465	927	10.4	2.45	127	.219	.288	129	108	96	106	.979	138	149	-.3	11.9	-6.4	-.5	3.3
CAL	19	14	46	1430[1]	1246	7.8	118	525	892	11.4	3.19	98	.237	.311	6	-8	97	105	.982	111	135	1.3	-.9	1.1	-.2	2.2
WAS	24	14	39	1473[1]	1334	8.1	113	495	878	11.4	3.38	93	.242	.309	-25	-36	98	98	.978	144	167	-.8	-4.0	-6.4	.2	6.4
BAL	29	17	36	1457[1]	1218	7.5	116	566	1034	11.2	3.32	95	.228	.305	-15	-27	98	95	.980	124	144	.5	-3.0	6.5	.2	-8.7
CLE	49	14	27	1477[2]	1258	7.7	120	559	1189	11.3	3.25	101	.231	.307	-3	3	101	99	.981	116	138	1.0	.3	-2.2	-1.7	-3.5
NY	37	16	27	1480[2]	1375	8.4	110	480	898	11.5	3.24	97	.249	.313	-2	-19	97	106	.976	154	144	-1.3	-2.1	-5.7	.5	-.4
KC	26	10	34	1428	1265	8.0	125	558	990	11.7	3.68	87	.238	.315	-71	-79	99	94	.978	132	120	-.0	-8.7	-3.9	1.3	-7.2
TOT	365	153	356	14601[2]		7.9				11.2	3.23		.236	.305					.979	1325	1388					

Runs	Hits	Doubles	Triples	Home Runs	Total Bases
Yastrzemski-Bos .. 112	Yastrzemski-Bos .. 189	Oliva-Min 34	Blair-Bal 12	Yastrzemski-Bos ... 44	Yastrzemski-Bos .. 360
Killebrew-Min 105	Tovar-Min 173	Tovar-Min 32	Buford-Chi 9	Killebrew-Min 44	Killebrew-Min 305
Tovar-Min 98	Scott-Bos 171	Yastrzemski-Bos .. 31		Howard-Was 36	F.Robinson-Bal ... 276
Kaline-Det 94	Fregosi-Cal 171	D.Johnson-Bal 30		F.Robinson-Bal ... 30	B.Robinson-Bal ... 265
McAuliffe-Det 92	B.Robinson-Bal ... 164	Campaneris-KC 29			Howard-Was 265

Runs Batted In	Runs Produced	Bases On Balls	Batting Average	On Base Percentage	Slugging Average
Yastrzemski-Bos .. 121	Yastrzemski-Bos .. 189	Killebrew-Min 131	Yastrzemski-Bos ...326	Yastrzemski-Bos ...421	Yastrzemski-Bos ...622
Killebrew-Min 113	Killebrew-Min 174	Mantle-NY 107	F.Robinson-Bal 311	Kaline-Det 415	F.Robinson-Bal 576
F.Robinson-Bal ... 94	F.Robinson-Bal ... 147	McAuliffe-Det 105	Kaline-Det 308	Killebrew-Min 413	Killebrew-Min 558
Howard-Was 89	Kaline-Det 147	Yastrzemski-Bos .. 91	Scott-Bos 303	F.Robinson-Bal 408	Kaline-Det 541
Oliva-Min 83	B.Robinson-Bal ... 143	Kaline-Det 83	Blair-Bal 293	Mantle-NY 394	Howard-Was 511

Production	Adjusted Production	Batter Runs	Adjusted Batter Runs	Clutch Hitting Index	Runs Created
Yastrzemski-Bos .1.043	Yastrzemski-Bos .. 189	Yastrzemski-Bos .. 76.4	Yastrzemski-Bos .. 71.0	Hershberger-KC ... 134	Yastrzemski-Bos .. 155
F.Robinson-Bal 984	F.Robinson-Bal ... 189	Killebrew-Min 62.3	Killebrew-Min 56.8	Pepitone-NY 124	Killebrew-Min 131
Killebrew-Min 970	Kaline-Det 176	F.Robinson-Bal ... 53.3	F.Robinson-Bal ... 53.8	D.Johnson-Bal 123	F.Robinson-Bal ... 113
Kaline-Det 957	Killebrew-Min 170	Kaline-Det 48.4	Kaline-Det 46.9	Blefary-Bal 121	Kaline-Det 104
Mincher-Cal 855	Mincher-Cal 156	Scott-Bos 33.8	Mincher-Cal 33.4	Oliva-Min 119	Scott-Bos 97

Total Average	Stolen Bases	Stolen Base Average	Stolen Base Runs	Fielding Runs	Total Player Rating
Yastrzemski-Bos .1.134	Campaneris-KC 55	Valentine-Was 85.0	Campaneris-KC 6.9	B.Robinson-Bal ... 30.8	Yastrzemski-Bos ... 7.9
Killebrew-Min ...1.058	Buford-Chi 34	Clarke-NY 84.0	Clarke-NY 3.9	Blair-Bal 20.9	Kaline-Det 5.3
F.Robinson-Bal ..1.029	Agee-Chi 28	Aparicio-Bal 78.3	Valentine-Was 3.3	Smith-Bos 16.5	B.Robinson-Bal ... 5.0
Kaline-Det 1.009	McCraw-Chi 24	Campaneris-KC 77.5		Monday-KC 15.2	F.Robinson-Bal ... 4.8
Mantle-NY 874	Clarke-NY 21	Agee-Chi 73.7		Clarke-NY 15.2	Killebrew-Min 4.3

Wins	Win Percentage	Games	Complete Games	Shutouts	Saves
Wilson-Det 22	Horlen-Chi 731	Locker-Chi 77	Chance-Min 18	McGlothlin-Cal ... 6	Rojas-Cal 27
Lonborg-Bos 22	Lonborg-Bos 710	Rojas-Cal 72	Lonborg-Bos 15	Lolich-Det 6	Wyatt-Bos 20
Chance-Min 20	Wilson-Det 667	Kelso-Cal 69	Hargan-Cle 15	John-Chi 6	Locker-Chi 20
Horlen-Chi 19	Sparma-Chi 640	Womack-NY 65		Horlen-Chi 6	Womack-NY 18
McLain-Det 17	Peters-Chi 593	McMahon-Bos-Chi .. 63		Hargan-Cle 6	Worthington-Min ... 16

Innings Pitched	Fewest Hits/Game	Fewest BB/Game	Strikeouts	Strikeouts/Game	Ratio
Chance-Min 283.2	Peters-Chi 6.47	Merritt-Min 1.19	Lonborg-Bos 246	Tiant-Cle 9.22	Horlen-Chi 8.72
Lonborg-Bos 273.1	Boswell-Min 6.55	Kaat-Min 1.44	McDowell-Cle 236	McDowell-Cle 8.99	Merritt-Min 9.21
Wilson-Det 264.0	Horlen-Chi 6.56	Stange-Bos 1.59	Chance-Min 220	Boswell-Min 8.25	Siebert-Cle 9.52
Kaat-Min 263.1	Siebert-Cle 6.60	Horlen-Chi 2.02	Tiant-Cle 219	Lonborg-Bos 8.10	John-Chi 9.84
Peters-Chi 260.0	Downing-NY 7.05	Peterson-NY 2.13	Peters-Chi 215	Phoebus-Bal 7.75	Peters-Chi 10.00

Earned Run Average	Adjusted ERA	Opponents' Batting Avg.	Opponents' On Base Pct.	Starter Runs	Adjusted Starter Runs
Horlen-Chi 2.06	Horlen-Chi 151	Peters-Chi 199	Horlen-Chi 253	Horlen-Chi 33.6	Horlen-Chi 30.0
Peters-Chi 2.28	Siebert-Cle 137	Boswell-Min 202	Merritt-Min 262	Peters-Chi 27.3	Peters-Chi 23.7
Siebert-Cle 2.38	Merritt-Min 137	Siebert-Cle 202	Siebert-Cle 268	Merritt-Min 17.7	Merritt-Min 23.5
John-Chi 2.47	Peters-Chi 136	Horlen-Chi 203	John-Chi 277	Siebert-Cle 17.5	Chance-Min 23.0
Merritt-Min 2.53	Chance-Min 127	Downing-NY 217	Peters-Chi 277	Chance-Min 15.8	Siebert-Cle 18.3

Clutch Pitching Index	Relief Runs	Adjusted Relief Runs	Relief Ranking	Total Pitcher Index	Total Baseball Ranking
Clark-Cal 121	Wilhelm-Chi 18.9	Wilhelm-Chi 17.7	Wilhelm-Chi 25.1	Horlen-Chi 3.9	Yastrzemski-Bos ... 7.9
Stottlemyre-NY ... 117	Drabowsky-Bal 17.2	Drabowsky-Bal 16.4	Drabowsky-Bal ... 23.2	Peters-Chi 3.8	Kaline-Det 5.3
Kaat-Min 108	Locker-Chi 15.7	McMahon-Bos-Chi 14.5	Wyatt-Bos 19.4	Merritt-Min 2.5	B.Robinson-Bal ... 5.0
Tiant-Cle 107	McMahon-Bos-Chi 15.2	Locker-Chi 14.0	Rojas-Cal 17.3	Drabowsky-Bal ... 2.2	F.Robinson-Bal ... 4.8
Stange-Bos 105	Baldwin-Was 11.6	Baldwin-Was 11.1	Locker-Chi 17.2	Hargan-Cle 2.1	Killebrew-Min 4.3

TEAM	G	W	L	PCT	GB	R	OR	AB	H	2B	3B	HR	BB	SO	AVG	OBP	SLG	PRO	PRO+	BR	/A	PF	CHI	RC	SB	CS	SBA	SBR
STL	162	97	65	.599		583	472	5561	1383	227	48	73	378	897	.249	.300	.346	.646	102	2	9	99	104	581	110	45	71	6
SF	163	88	74	.543	9	599	529	5441	1301	162	33	108	508	904	.239	.310	.341	.651	103	20	21	100	103	577	50	37	57	-7
CHI	163	84	78	.519	13	612	611	5458	1319	203	43	130	415	854	.242	.300	.366	.666	100	36	-2	107	104	593	41	30	58	-6
CIN	163	83	79	.512	14	690	673	5767	1573	281	36	106	379	938	.273	.322	.389	.711	114	130	93	106	98	688	59	55	52	-15
ATL	163	81	81	.500	16	514	549	5552	1399	179	31	80	414	782	.252	.308	.339	.647	101	9	7	100	90	564	83	44	65	-2
PIT	163	80	82	.494	17	583	532	5569	1404	180	44	80	422	953	.252	.309	.343	.652	105	19	27	99	100	580	130	59	69	4
PHI	162	76	86	.469	21	543	615	5372	1253	178	30	100	462	1003	.233	.297	.333	.630	96	-24	-24	100	104	527	58	51	53	-13
LA	162	76	86	.469	21	470	509	5354	1234	202	36	67	439	980	.230	.291	.319	.610	97	-61	-20	92	97	501	57	43	57	-9
NY	163	73	89	.451	24	473	499	5503	1252	178	30	81	379	1203	.228	.283	.315	.598	86	-91	-94	101	102	486	72	45	62	-5
HOU	162	72	90	.444	25	510	588	5336	1233	205	28	66	479	988	.231	.300	.317	.617	94	-41	-30	98	100	505	44	51	46	-17
TOT	813					5577		54913	13351	1995	359	891	4275	9502	.243	.302	.341	.643							704	460	60	-65

TEAM	CG	SH	SV	IP	H	H/G	HR	BB	SO	RAT	ERA	ERA+	OAV	OOB	PR	/A	PF	CPI	FA	E	DP	FW	PW	BW	SBW	DIF
STL	63	30	32	1479¹	1282	7.8	82	375	971	10.3	2.49	116	.234	.286	82	67	97	105	.978	140	135	-.0	7.7	1.0	1.4	5.9
SF	77	20	16	1469	1302	8.0	86	344	942	10.2	2.71	109	.236	.283	45	38	99	96	.975	162	125	-1.3	4.4	2.4	-.0	1.6
CHI	46	12	32	1453²	1399	8.7	138	392	894	11.3	3.41	93	.254	.306	-69	-40	106	100	.981	119	149	1.2	-4.6	-.2	.0	6.6
CIN	24	16	38	1490¹	1399	8.4	114	573	963	12.2	3.56	89	.250	.324	-96	-66	106	100	.978	144	144	-.2	-7.6	10.7	-1.0	.1
ATL	44	16	29	1474²	1326	8.1	87	362	871	10.5	2.92	103	.241	.292	11	13	100	96	.980	125	139	.9	1.5	.8	.5	-3.7
PIT	42	19	30	1487	1322	8.0	73	485	897	11.2	2.74	107	.240	.306	40	31	98	107	.979	139	162	.0	3.6	3.1	1.2	-8.9
PHI	42	12	27	1448¹	1416	8.8	91	421	935	11.7	3.36	89	.257	.315	-61	-57	101	100	.980	127	163	.7	-6.5	-2.8	-.7	4.3
LA	38	23	31	1448²	1293	8.0	65	414	994	10.8	2.69	103	.241	.305	48	12	93	104	.977	144	144	-.3	1.4	-2.3	-.3	-3.5
NY	45	25	32	1483¹	1250	7.6	87	430	1014	10.5	2.72	111	.230	.292	43	49	101	98	.979	133	142	.4	5.6	-10.8	.2	-3.4
HOU	50	12	23	1446²	1362	8.5	68	479	1021	11.7	3.26	91	.249	.313	-44	-49	99	96	.975	156	129	-1.0	-5.6	-3.4	-1.2	2.3
TOT	471	185	290	14681		8.2				11.0	2.99		.243	.302					.978	1389	1432					

Runs		Hits		Doubles		Triples		Home Runs		Total Bases	
Beckert-Chi	98	Rose-Cin	210	Brock-StL	46	Brock-StL	14	McCovey-SF	36	Williams-Chi	321
Rose-Cin	94	Alou-Atl	210	Rose-Cin	42	Clemente-Pit	12	Allen-Phi	33	H.Aaron-Atl	302
Perez-Cin	93	Beckert-Chi	189	Bench-Cin	40	Davis-LA	10	Banks-Chi	32	Rose-Cin	294
Brock-StL	92	A.Johnson-Cin	188	Staub-Hou	37	Allen-Phi	9	Williams-Chi	30	Alou-Atl	290
Williams-Chi	91	Flood-StL	186	Alou-Atl	37	Williams-Chi	8	H.Aaron-Atl	29	McCovey-SF	285

Runs Batted In		Runs Produced		Bases On Balls		Batting Average		On Base Percentage		Slugging Average	
McCovey-SF	105	Perez-Cin	167	Santo-Chi	96	Rose-Cin	.335	Rose-Cin	.394	McCovey-SF	.545
Williams-Chi	98	Williams-Chi	159	Wynn-Hou	90	Alou-Pit	.332	McCovey-SF	.383	Allen-Phi	.520
Santo-Chi	98	Santo-Chi	158	Hunt-SF	78	Alou-Atl	.317	Wynn-Hou	.378	Williams-Chi	.500
Perez-Cin	92	McCovey-SF	150	Allen-Phi	74	A.Johnson-Cin	.312	Mays-SF	.376	H.Aaron-Atl	.498
Allen-Phi	90	Allen-Phi	144	Staub-Hou	73	Flood-StL	.301	Staub-Hou	.376	Mays-SF	.488

Production		Adjusted Production		Batter Runs		Adjusted Batter Runs		Clutch Hitting Index		Runs Created	
McCovey-SF	.928	McCovey-SF	176	McCovey-SF	48.8	McCovey-SF	48.9	Hundley-Chi	145	Rose-Cin	113
Allen-Phi	.876	Allen-Phi	160	Rose-Cin	44.5	Rose-Cin	40.5	Santo-Chi	136	McCovey-SF	110
Mays-SF	.864	Mays-SF	158	H.Aaron-Atl	39.0	Wynn-Hou	39.6	Clendenon-Pit	132	Williams-Chi	107
Rose-Cin	.863	Wynn-Hou	158	Wynn-Hou	38.4	H.Aaron-Atl	38.8	Perez-Cin	127	H.Aaron-Atl	104
H.Aaron-Atl	.855	H.Aaron-Atl	154	Allen-Phi	38.0	Allen-Phi	38.0	Swoboda-NY	126	Alou-Atl	103

Total Average		Stolen Bases		Stolen Base Average		Stolen Base Runs		Fielding Runs		Total Player Rating	
McCovey-SF	.953	Brock-StL	62	H.Aaron-Atl	84.8	Brock-StL	11.4	Mazeroski-Pit	25.7	H.Aaron-Atl	5.5
Allen-Phi	.869	Wills-Pit	52	Brock-StL	83.8	H.Aaron-Atl	5.4	Alley-Pit	25.6	Wynn-Hou	4.6
Mays-SF	.853	Davis-LA	36	Taylor-Phi	81.5	Davis-LA	4.8	Kessinger-Chi	17.9	McCovey-SF	4.6
H.Aaron-Atl	.852	H.Aaron-Atl	28	Davis-LA	78.3	Taylor-Phi	3.6	Santo-Chi	17.3	Rose-Cin	4.3
Wynn-Hou	.826	Jones-NY	23			Wills-Pit	3.0	Wynn-Hou	16.7	Santo-Chi	4.2

Wins		Win Percentage		Games		Complete Games		Shutouts		Saves	
Marichal-SF	26	Blass-Pit	.750	Abernathy-Cin	78	Marichal-SF	30	Gibson-StL	13	Regan-LA-Chi	25
Gibson-StL	22	Marichal-SF	.743	Regan-LA-Chi	73	Gibson-StL	28	Drysdale-LA	8	Carroll-Atl-Cin	17
Jenkins-Chi	20	Gibson-StL	.710	Carroll-Atl-Cin	68	Jenkins-Chi	20	Koosman-NY	7	Hoerner-StL	17
		Briles-StL	.633	Taylor-NY	58	Perry-SF	19	Blass-Pit	7	Brewer-LA	14
				Linzy-SF	57	Koosman-NY	17				

Innings Pitched		Fewest Hits/Game		Fewest BB/Game		Strikeouts		Strikeouts/Game		Ratio	
Marichal-SF	326.0	Gibson-StL	5.85	Hands-Chi	1.25	Gibson-StL	268	Singer-LA	7.97	Gibson-StL	7.89
Jenkins-Chi	308.0	Bolin-SF	6.52	Marichal-SF	1.27	Jenkins-Chi	260	Gibson-StL	7.92	Jarvis-Atl	8.93
Gibson-StL	304.2	Veale-Pit	6.86	Seaver-NY	1.56	Singer-LA	227	Maloney-Cin	7.87	Bolin-SF	9.07
Perry-SF	291.0	Jarvis-Atl	7.10	Pappas-Cin-Atl	1.57	Marichal-SF	218	Jenkins-Chi	7.60	Seaver-NY	9.08
Seaver-NY	277.2	Moose-Pit	7.14	Niekro-Atl	1.58	Sadecki-SF	206	Wilson-Hou	7.55	Hands-Chi	9.15

Earned Run Average		Adjusted ERA		Opponents' Batting Avg.		Opponents' On Base Pct.		Starter Runs		Adjusted Starter Runs	
Gibson-StL	1.12	Gibson-StL	258	Gibson-StL	.184	Gibson-StL	.233	Gibson-StL	63.1	Gibson-StL	60.0
Bolin-SF	1.99	Bolin-SF	148	Bolin-SF	.200	Jarvis-Atl	.255	Koosman-NY	26.5	Koosman-NY	27.5
Veale-Pit	2.05	Koosman-NY	145	Veale-Pit	.211	Bolin-SF	.258	Veale-Pit	25.4	Seaver-NY	25.2
Koosman-NY	2.08	Veale-Pit	142	Jarvis-Atl	.214	Seaver-NY	.262	Seaver-NY	24.1	Veale-Pit	23.8
Blass-Pit	2.12	Blass-Pit	138	Moose-Pit	.218	Hands-Chi	.264	Drysdale-LA	22.3	Blass-Pit	19.6

Clutch Pitching Index		Relief Runs		Adjusted Relief Runs		Relief Ranking		Total Pitcher Index		Total Baseball Ranking	
Blass-Pit	125	Kline-Pit	16.4	Kline-Pit	15.6	Kline-Pit	23.4	Gibson-StL	8.1	Gibson-StL	8.1
Briles-StL	124	Regan-LA-Chi	10.7	Regan-LA-Chi	13.0	Regan-LA-Chi	20.1	Seaver-NY	3.3	H.Aaron-Atl	5.5
Koosman-NY	123	Linzy-SF	9.4	Abernathy-Cin	10.3	Linzy-SF	17.0	Koosman-NY	2.8	Wynn-Hou	4.6
Lemaster-Hou	122	Grant-LA	9.4	Linzy-SF	9.0	Abernathy-Cin	13.9	Marichal-SF	2.8	McCovey-SF	4.6
Drysdale-LA	117	Abernathy-Cin	7.7	Carroll-Atl-Cin	7.2	Upshaw-Atl	9.6	Drysdale-LA	2.4	Rose-Cin	4.3

TEAM	G	W	L	PCT	GB	R	OR	AB	H	2B	3B	HR	BB	SO	AVG	OBP	SLG	PRO	PRO+	BR	/A	PF	CHI	RC	SB	CS	SBA	SBR
DET	164	103	59	.636		671	492	5490	1292	190	39	185	521	964	.235	.309	.385	.694	114	102	85	103	100	646	26	32	45	-11
BAL	162	91	71	.562	12	579	497	5275	1187	215	28	133	570	1019	.225	.306	.352	.658	106	41	40	100	97	585	78	32	71	4
CLE	162	86	75	.534	16.5	516	504	5416	1266	210	36	75	427	858	.234	.294	.327	.621	96	-34	-26	99	100	525	76	62	55	-2
BOS	162	86	76	.531	17	614	611	5303	1253	207	17	125	582	974	.236	.352	.352	.668	102	62	25	107	99	590	90	50	64	-14
NY	164	83	79	.512	20	536	531	5310	1137	154	34	109	566	958	.214	.293	.318	.611	95	-46	-29	97	106	507	90	50	64	-3
OAK	163	82	80	.506	21	569	544	5406	1300	192	40	94	472	1022	.240	.306	.343	.649	108	19	46	95	99	580	147	61	71	8
MIN	162	79	83	.488	24	562	546	5373	1274	207	41	105	445	966	.237	.301	.350	.651	99	20	-7	105	99	564	98	54	64	-3
CAL	162	67	95	.414	36	498	615	5331	1209	170	33	83	397	1080	.227	.293	.318	.611	96	-51	-31	96	100	498	62	50	55	-11
CHI	162	67	95	.414	36	463	527	5405	1233	169	33	71	397	840	.228	.286	.311	.597	86	-82	-87	101	99	480	90	50	64	-3
WAS	161	65	96	.404	37.5	524	665	5400	1208	160	37	124	454	960	.224	.289	.336	.625	99	-31	-13	97	101	518	29	19	60	-3
TOT	812					5532		53709	12359	1874	338	1104	4881	9641	.230	.299	.339	.639							811	471	63	-39

TEAM	CG	SH	SV	IP	H	H/G	HR	BB	SO	RAT	ERA	ERA+	OAV	OOB	PR	/A	PF	CPI	FA	E	DP	FW	PW	BW	SBW	DIF
DET	59	19	29	1489²	1180	7.1	129	486	1115	10.3	2.71	111	.217	.285	44	49	101	100	.983	105	133	2.0	5.6	9.7	-.8	5.4
BAL	53	16	31	1451¹	1111	6.9	101	502	1044	10.3	2.66	110	.212	.287	51	43	98	96	.981	120	131	1.0	4.9	4.6	.9	-1.5
CLE	48	23	32	1464¹	1087	6.7	98	540	1157	10.3	2.66	111	.206	.286	53	49	99	93	.979	127	130	.6	5.6	-3.0	.2	2.0
BOS	55	17	31	1447	1303	8.1	115	523	972	11.7	3.33	95	.241	.313	-57	-28	106	100	.979	128	147	.6	-3.2	2.9	-1.2	5.9
NY	45	14	27	1467¹	1308	8.0	99	424	831	10.8	2.79	104	.240	.298	31	18	97	108	.977	139	142	.0	2.1	-3.3	.1	3.2
OAK	45	18	29	1455²	1220	7.5	124	505	997	10.9	2.94	96	.227	.297	6	-20	95	101	.977	145	136	-.4	-2.3	5.3	1.4	-2.9
MIN	46	14	29	1433¹	1224	7.7	92	414	996	10.5	2.89	107	.229	.290	13	31	104	94	.977	170	117	-2.0	3.6	-.8	.1	-2.9
CAL	29	11	31	1437	1234	7.7	131	519	869	11.2	3.43	85	.233	.306	-72	-83	98	94	.977	140	156	-.2	-9.5	-3.6	-.8	.0
CHI	20	11	40	1468	1290	7.9	97	451	834	11.1	2.75	110	.236	.303	38	46	102	110	.977	151	152	-.8	5.3	-10.0	.1	-8.6
WAS	26	11	28	1439²	1402	8.8	118	517	826	12.3	3.64	80	.258	.327	-106	-116	98	104	.976	148	144	-.7	-13.3	-1.5	.1	-.1
TOT	426	154	307	14553¹		7.6				10.9	2.98		.230	.299					.978	1373	1388					

Runs		Hits		Doubles		Triples		Home Runs		Total Bases	
McAuliffe-Det	95	Campaneris-Oak	177	Smith-Bos	37	Fregosi-Cal	13	F.Howard-Was	44	F.Howard-Was	330
Yastrzemski-Bos	90	Tovar-Min	167	B.Robinson-Bal	36	McCraw-Chi	12	Horton-Det	36	Horton-Det	278
White-NY	89	F.Howard-Was	164	Yastrzemski-Bos	32	Stroud-Was	10	Harrelson-Bos	35	Harrelson-Bos	277
Tovar-Min	89	Aparicio-Chi	164	Tovar-Min	31	McAuliffe-Det	10	Jackson-Oak	29	Yastrzemski-Bos	267
Stanley-Det	88	Yastrzemski-Bos	162			Campaneris-Oak	9			Northrup-Det	259

Runs Batted In		Runs Produced		Bases On Balls		Batting Average		On Base Percentage		Slugging Average	
Harrelson-Bos	109	Harrelson-Bos	153	Yastrzemski-Bos	119	Yastrzemski-Bos	.301	Yastrzemski-Bos	.429	F.Howard-Was	.552
F.Howard-Was	106	Northrup-Det	145	Mantle-NY	106	Cater-Oak	.290	F.Robinson-Bal	.391	Horton-Det	.543
Northrup-Det	90	Yastrzemski-Bos	141	Foy-Bos	84	Oliva-Min	.289	Mantle-NY	.387	Harrelson-Bos	.518
Powell-Bal	85	F.Howard-Was	141	McAuliffe-Det	82	Horton-Det	.285	Monday-Oak	.373	Yastrzemski-Bos	.495
Horton-Det	85	Stanley-Det	137	Andrews-Bos	81	Uhlaender-Min	.283	Andrews-Bos	.369	Oliva-Min	.477

Production		Adjusted Production		Batter Runs		Adjusted Batter Runs		Clutch Hitting Index		Runs Created	
Yastrzemski-Bos	.924	F.Howard-Was	172	Yastrzemski-Bos	57.5	Yastrzemski-Bos	53.5	Foy-Bos	137	Yastrzemski-Bos	121
Horton-Det	.900	Yastrzemski-Bos	168	F.Howard-Was	45.1	F.Howard-Was	47.0	Powell-Bal	132	F.Howard-Was	110
F.Howard-Was	.892	Horton-Det	165	Horton-Det	41.1	Horton-Det	39.5	Harrelson-Bos	129	Horton-Det	95
Harrelson-Bos	.877	Harrelson-Bos	153	Harrelson-Bos	40.2	Harrelson-Bos	36.4	Northrup-Det	127	Harrelson-Bos	94
Oliva-Min	.837	F.Robinson-Bal	153	Freehan-Det	32.7	Freehan-Det	30.9	Bando-Oak	126	Freehan-Det	94

Total Average		Stolen Bases		Stolen Base Average		Stolen Base Runs		Fielding Runs		Total Player Rating	
Yastrzemski-Bos	1.000	Campaneris-Oak	62	McCraw-Chi	80.0	Campaneris-Oak	5.4	Clarke-NY	29.5	Yastrzemski-Bos	7.0
F.Howard-Was	.872	Cardenal-Cle	40	Nelson-Cle	76.7	McCraw-Chi	3.0	Aparicio-Chi	24.7	Freehan-Det	4.9
Horton-Det	.867	Tovar-Min	35	Foy-Bos	76.5	Foy-Bos	3.0	Unser-Was	18.8	F.Howard-Was	4.5
F.Robinson-Bal	.865	Buford-Bal	27	Clarke-NY	74.1	Tovar-Min	2.7	Yastrzemski-Bos	17.3	Campaneris-Oak	3.8
Harrelson-Bos	.835	Foy-Bos	26	Campaneris-Oak	73.8	Nelson-Cle	2.7	B.Robinson-Bal	16.6	Harrelson-Bos	3.8

Wins		Win Percentage		Games		Complete Games		Shutouts		Saves	
McLain-Det	31	McLain-Det	.838	Wood-Chi	88	McLain-Det	28	Tiant-Cle	9	Worthington-Min	18
McNally-Bal	22	Culp-Bos	.727	Wilhelm-Chi	72	Tiant-Cle	19			Wood-Chi	16
Tiant-Cle	21	Tiant-Cle	.700	Locker-Chi	70	Stottlemyre-NY	19			Higgins-Was	13
Stottlemyre-NY	21	Ellsworth-Bos	.696	Perranoski-Min	66	McNally-Bal	18				
Hardin-Bal	18	McNally-Bal	.688			Hardin-Bal	16				

Innings Pitched		Fewest Hits/Game		Fewest BB/Game		Strikeouts		Strikeouts/Game		Ratio	
McLain-Det	336.0	Tiant-Cle	5.30	Peterson-NY	1.23	McDowell-Cle	283	McDowell-Cle	9.47	McNally-Bal	7.91
Chance-Min	292.0	McNally-Bal	5.77	McLain-Det	1.69	McLain-Det	280	Tiant-Cle	9.20	Tiant-Cle	7.98
Stottlemyre-NY	278.2	McDowell-Cle	6.06	Ellsworth-Bos	1.70	Tiant-Cle	264	Lolich-Det	8.06	McLain-Det	8.30
McNally-Bal	273.0	Siebert-Bos	6.33	Kaat-Min	1.73	Chance-Min	234	Culp-Bos	7.90	Chance-Min	9.15
McDowell-Cle	269.0	McLain-Det	6.46	McNally-Bal	1.81	McNally-Bal	202	McLain-Det	7.50	Peterson-NY	9.32

Earned Run Average		Adjusted ERA		Opponents' Batting Avg.		Opponents' On Base Pct.		Starter Runs		Adjusted Starter Runs	
Tiant-Cle	1.60	Tiant-Cle	185	Tiant-Cle	.168	Tiant-Cle	.233	Tiant-Cle	39.5	McLain-Det	39.3
McDowell-Cle	1.81	McDowell-Cle	164	McNally-Bal	.182	McNally-Bal	.234	McLain-Det	38.2	Tiant-Cle	38.9
McNally-Bal	1.95	McLain-Det	154	McDowell-Cle	.189	McLain-Det	.243	McDowell-Cle	35.0	McDowell-Cle	34.4
McLain-Det	1.96	John-Chi	153	Siebert-Cle	.198	Chance-Min	.261	McNally-Bal	31.4	McNally-Bal	29.7
John-Chi	1.98	McNally-Bal	150	McLain-Det	.200	Nash-Oak	.270	Bahnsen-NY	27.5	Bahnsen-NY	25.2

Clutch Pitching Index		Relief Runs		Adjusted Relief Runs		Relief Ranking		Total Pitcher Index		Total Baseball Ranking	
Horlen-Chi	133	Wood-Chi	19.6	Wood-Chi	20.5	Wood-Chi	33.6	McLain-Det	4.9	Yastrzemski-Bos	7.0
John-Chi	119	Wilhelm-Chi	13.0	Wilhelm-Chi	13.5	Romo-Cle	14.7	McDowell-Cle	4.2	Freehan-Det	4.9
Fisher-Chi	116	Romo-Cle	12.6	Romo-Cle	12.4	Wilhelm-Chi	14.3	Tiant-Cle	4.0	McLain-Det	4.9
McDowell-Cle	113	McMahon-Chi-Det	9.0	McMahon-Chi-Det	9.4	Drabowsky-Bal	9.9	McNally-Bal	3.7	F.Howard-Was	4.5
Bahnsen-NY	111	Drabowsky-Bal	7.3	Locker-Chi	7.4	Locker-Chi	8.5	John-Chi	3.5	McDowell-Cle	4.2

TEAM	G	W	L	PCT	GB	R	OR	AB	H	2B	3B	HR	BB	SO	AVG	OBP	SLG	PRO	PRO+	BR	/A	PF	CHI	RC	SB	CS	SBA	SBR
EAST																												
NY	162	100	62	.617		632	541	5427	1311	184	41	109	527	1089	.242	.313	.351	.664	91	-52	-66	102	105	601	66	43	61	-6
CHI	163	92	70	.568	8	720	611	5530	1400	215	40	142	559	928	.253	.326	.384	.710	94	37	-49	113	102	693	30	32	48	-10
PIT	162	88	74	.543	12	725	652	5626	1557	220	52	119	454	944	.277	.336	.398	.734	115	84	98	98	97	742	74	34	69	2
STL	162	87	75	.537	13	595	540	5536	1403	228	44	90	503	876	.253	.318	.359	.677	96	-25	-27	100	94	632	87	49	64	-3
PHI	162	63	99	.389	37	645	745	5408	1304	227	35	137	549	1130	.241	.314	.372	.686	102	-12	6	97	101	629	73	49	60	-8
MON	162	52	110	.321	48	582	791	5419	1300	202	33	125	529	962	.240	.312	.359	.671	94	-40	-42	100	96	596	52	52	50	-16
WEST																												
ATL	162	93	69	.574		691	631	5460	1411	195	22	141	485	665	.258	.323	.380	.703	104	20	18	100	103	655	59	48	55	-11
SF	162	90	72	.556	3	713	636	5474	1325	187	28	136	711	1054	.242	.336	.361	.697	104	32	44	98	100	690	71	32	69	2
CIN	163	89	73	.549	4	798	768	5634	1558	224	42	171	474	1042	.277	.338	.422	.760	114	133	99	105	99	791	79	56	59	-10
LA	162	85	77	.525	8	645	561	5532	1405	185	52	97	484	823	.254	.316	.359	.675	103	-31	16	93	103	626	80	51	61	-7
HOU	162	81	81	.500	12	676	668	5348	1284	208	40	104	699	972	.240	.332	.352	.684	101	7	20	98	101	649	101	58	64	-5
SD	162	52	110	.321	41	468	746	5357	1203	180	42	99	423	1143	.225	.286	.329	.615	81	-153	-128	96	98	491	45	44	51	-13
TOT	973					7890		65751	16461	2455	471	1470	6397	11628	.250	.321	.369	.690							817	548	60	-84

TEAM	CG	SH	SV	IP	H	H/G	HR	BB	SO	RAT	ERA	ERA+	OAV	OOB	PR	/A	PF	CPI	FA	E	DP	FW	PW	BW	SBW	DIF
EAST																										
NY	51	28	35	1468¹	1217	7.5	119	517	1012	10.8	2.99	122	.227	.298	99	109	102	99	.980	122	146	1.4	11.4	-6.9	.1	13.0
CHI	58	22	27	1454¹	1366	8.5	118	475	1017	11.6	3.34	120	.248	.311	41	110	112	101	.979	136	149	.6	11.5	-5.1	-.3	4.3
PIT	39	9	33	1445²	1348	8.4	96	553	1124	12.1	3.61	97	.248	.322	-3	-20	97	95	.975	155	169	-.5	-2.1	10.3	.9	-1.6
STL	63	12	26	1460¹	1289	7.9	99	511	1004	11.3	2.94	121	.237	.307	106	102	99	105	.978	138	144	.5	10.7	-2.8	.4	-2.8
PHI	47	14	21	1434	1494	9.4	134	570	921	13.2	4.14	86	.270	.342	-88	-96	99	102	.978	137	157	.5	-10.1	.6	-.1	-9.0
MON	26	8	21	1426	1429	9.0	145	702	973	13.8	4.33	85	.263	.353	-117	-104	102	102	.971	184	179	-2.1	-10.9	-4.4	-.9	-10.6
WEST																										
ATL	38	7	42	1445	1334	8.3	144	438	893	11.2	3.53	102	.245	.304	11	13	100	95	.981	115	114	1.8	1.4	1.9	-.4	7.4
SF	71	15	17	1473²	1381	8.4	120	461	906	11.5	3.26	108	.248	.309	55	40	97	102	.974	169	155	-1.3	4.2	4.6	.9	.5
CIN	23	11	44	1465	1478	9.1	149	611	818	13.2	4.11	92	.262	.340	-84	-57	105	102	.974	167	158	-1.1	-6.0	10.4	-.3	5.0
LA	47	20	31	1457	1324	8.2	122	420	975	11.0	3.08	108	.242	.301	83	39	93	102	.980	126	130	1.2	4.1	1.7	.0	-2.9
HOU	52	11	34	1435²	1347	8.4	111	547	1221	12.1	3.60	98	.247	.319	-1	-9	99	96	.975	153	136	-.4	-.9	2.1	.2	-1.0
SD	16	9	25	1422¹	1454	9.2	113	592	764	13.2	4.24	83	.267	.343	-102	-111	98	97	.975	156	140	-.5	-11.7	-13.4	-.6	-2.7
TOT	531	166	356	17387¹		8.5				12.1	3.59		.250	.321					.977	1758	1777					

Runs
Rose-Cin 120
Bonds-SF 120
Wynn-Hou 113
Kessinger-Chi 109
Alou-Pit 105

Hits
Alou-Pit 231
Rose-Cin 218
Brock-StL 195
Tolan-Cin 194
Williams-Chi 188

Doubles
Alou-Pit 41
Kessinger-Chi 38
Williams-Chi 33
Rose-Cin 33
Brock-StL 33

Triples
Clemente-Pit 12
Rose-Cin 11
Williams-Chi 10
Tolan-Cin 10
Brock-StL 10

Home Runs
McCovey-SF 45
H.Aaron-Atl 44
May-Cin 38
Perez-Cin 37
Wynn-Hou 33

Total Bases
H.Aaron-Atl 332
Perez-Cin 331
McCovey-SF 322
Rose-Cin 321
May-Cin 321

Runs Batted In
McCovey-SF 126
Santo-Chi 123
Perez-Cin 122
May-Cin 110
Banks-Chi 106

Runs Produced
Santo-Chi 191
Perez-Cin 188
Rose-Cin 186
McCovey-SF 182
Bonds-SF 178

Bases On Balls
Wynn-Hou 148
McCovey-SF 121
Staub-Mon 110
Morgan-Hou 110
Santo-Chi 96

Batting Average
Rose-Cin .... .348
Clemente-Pit ..... .345
Jones-NY .... .340
Alou-Pit .... .331
McCovey-SF ..... .320

On Base Percentage
McCovey-SF ..... .458
Wynn-Hou .... .440
Rose-Cin .... .432
Staub-Mon ...... .427
Jones-NY .... .424

Slugging Average
McCovey-SF ..... .656
H.Aaron-Atl ...... .607
Allen-Phi .... .573
Stargell-Pit ...... .556
Clemente-Pit ..... .544

Production
McCovey-SF 1.114
H.Aaron-Atl 1.005
Clemente-Pit ..... .958
Staub-Mon ...... .953
Allen-Phi .... .952

Adjusted Production
McCovey-SF 212
H.Aaron-Atl 177
Clemente-Pit 170
Wynn-Hou 168
Allen-Phi 168

Batter Runs
McCovey-SF 76.1
H.Aaron-Atl 56.3
Rose-Cin 56.0
Staub-Mon 52.6
Wynn-Hou 51.0

Adjusted Batter Runs
McCovey-SF 77.3
H.Aaron-Atl 56.1
Staub-Mon 52.4
Wynn-Hou 52.4
Rose-Cin 52.0

Clutch Hitting Index
Menke-Hou 157
Rader-Hou 143
Santo-Chi 143
Banks-Chi 143
Pinson-StL 135

Runs Created
McCovey-SF 151
Rose-Cin 138
Staub-Mon 128
H.Aaron-Atl 128
Wynn-Hou 126

Total Average
McCovey-SF 1.296
Wynn-Hou 1.118
H.Aaron-Atl 1.032
Staub-Mon 1.018
Allen-Phi .... .988

Stolen Bases
Brock-StL 53
Morgan-Hou 49
Bonds-SF 45
Wills-Mon-LA 40
Tolan-Cin 26

Stolen Base Average
Bonds-SF 91.8
Brock-StL 79.1
Morgan-Hou 77.8
Wynn-Hou 76.7
Alou-Pit 73.3

Stolen Base Runs
Bonds-SF 11.1
Brock-StL 7.5
Morgan-Hou 6.3
Wynn-Hou 2.7
Millan-Atl 2.4

Fielding Runs
Lanier-SF 28.6
Kessinger-Chi 24.6
Maxvill-StL 21.1
Grote-NY 19.3
Money-Phi 17.3

Total Player Rating
McCovey-SF 6.2
Wynn-Hou 5.3
H.Aaron-Atl 5.0
Staub-Mon 4.8
Rose-Cin 4.8

Wins
Seaver-NY 25
Niekro-Atl 23
Marichal-SF 21
Jenkins-Chi 21

Win Percentage
Seaver-NY .... .781
Marichal-SF ...... .656
Merritt-Cin .... .654
Koosman-NY ..... .654
Reed-Atl .... .643

Games
Granger-Cin 90
McGinn-Mon 74
Regan-Chi 71
Carroll-Cin 71
Reberger-SD 67

Complete Games
Gibson-StL 28
Marichal-SF 27
Perry-SF 26
Jenkins-Chi 23
Niekro-Atl 21

Shutouts
Marichal-SF 8
Osteen-LA 7
Jenkins-Chi 7
Koosman-NY 6
Holtzman-Chi 6

Saves
Gladding-Hou 29
Upshaw-Atl 27
Granger-Cin 27
Brewer-LA 20
Regan-Chi 17

Innings Pitched
Perry-SF 325.1
Osteen-LA 321.0
Singer-LA 315.2
Gibson-StL 314.0
Jenkins-Chi 311.1

Fewest Hits/Game
Seaver-NY 6.65
Maloney-Cin 6.80
Singer-LA 6.96
Koosman-NY 6.98
Carlton-StL 7.05

Fewest BB/Game
Marichal-SF 1.62
Niekro-Atl 1.80
Jenkins-Chi 2.05
Niekro-Chi-SD 2.07
Osteen-LA 2.07

Strikeouts
Jenkins-Chi 273
Gibson-StL 269
Singer-LA 247
Wilson-Hou 235
Perry-SF 233

Strikeouts/Game
Griffin-Hou 9.56
Wilson-Hou 9.40
Moose-Pit 8.74
Selma-SD-Chi 8.54
Veale-Pit 8.49

Ratio
Marichal-SF 9.13
Dierker-Hou 9.23
Singer-LA 9.35
Niekro-Atl 9.40
Seaver-NY 9.58

Earned Run Average
Marichal-SF 2.10
Carlton-StL 2.17
Gibson-StL 2.18
Seaver-NY 2.21
Koosman-NY 2.28

Adjusted ERA
Marichal-SF 166
Seaver-NY 166
Carlton-StL 165
Gibson-StL 164
Hands-Chi 162

Opponents' Batting Avg.
Seaver-NY .... .207
Maloney-Cin ..... .208
Singer-LA .... .210
Dierker-Hou ...... .214
Carlton-StL ...... .216

Opponents' On Base Pct.
Dierker-Hou ...... .262
Marichal-SF ...... .263
Singer-LA .... .263
Niekro-Atl .... .264
Seaver-NY .... .273

Starter Runs
Marichal-SF 49.6
Gibson-StL 49.3
Singer-LA 44.0
Dierker-Hou 42.9
Seaver-NY 42.1

Adjusted Starter Runs
Hands-Chi 51.1
Gibson-StL 48.6
Marichal-SF 46.5
Seaver-NY 44.0
Dierker-Hou 41.1

Clutch Pitching Index
Carlton-StL 122
Perry-SF 117
Veale-Pit 114
Robertson-Mon ... 113
Hands-Chi 111

Relief Runs
McGraw-NY 15.1
Granger-Cin 12.8
Brewer-LA 10.3
Gibbon-SF-Pit 9.5
DiLauro-NY 8.4

Adjusted Relief Runs
McGraw-NY 15.7
Granger-Cin 15.5
DiLauro-NY 8.8
Gibbon-SF-Pit 8.7
Upshaw-Atl 8.2

Relief Ranking
McGraw-NY 21.2
Granger-Cin 20.9
Taylor-NY 15.1
Brewer-LA 14.0
Gibbon-SF-Pit 13.9

Total Pitcher Index
Gibson-StL 6.3
Marichal-SF 5.7
Hands-Chi 5.3
Seaver-NY 5.3
Carlton-StL 4.6

Total Baseball Ranking
Gibson-StL 6.3
McCovey-SF 6.2
Marichal-SF 5.7
Wynn-Hou 5.3
Hands-Chi 5.3

TEAM	G	W	L	PCT	GB	R	OR	AB	H	2B	3B	HR	BB	SO	AVG	OBP	SLG	PRO	PRO+	BR	/A	PF	CHI	RC	SB	CS	SBA	SBR
EAST																												
BAL	162	109	53	.673		779	**517**	5518	1465	234	29	175	634	**806**	.265	**.346**	.414	**.760**	118	135	129	101	96	791	82	45	65	-2
DET	162	90	72	.556	19	701	601	5441	1316	188	29	182	578	922	.242	.318	.387	.705	99	17	-11	104	104	674	35	28	56	-6
BOS	162	87	75	.537	22	743	736	5494	1381	234	37	**197**	**658**	923	.251	.335	**.415**	.750	110	110	74	105	95	761	41	47	47	-16
WAS	162	86	76	.531	23	694	644	5447	1365	171	40	148	630	900	.251	.332	.378	.710	111	38	73	105	99	675	52	40	57	-8
NY	162	80	81	.497	28.5	562	587	5308	1247	210	**44**	94	565	840	.235	.310	.344	.654	92	-74	-50	96	99	572	119	74	62	-9
CLE	161	62	99	.385	46.5	573	717	5365	1272	173	24	119	535	906	.237	.309	.345	.654	86	-77	-98	103	101	568	85	37	70	3
WEST																												
MIN	162	97	65	.599		**790**	618	5677	**1520**	246	32	163	599	906	**.268**	.342	.408	.750	114	118	104	102	98	**794**	115	70	62	-8
OAK	162	88	74	.543	9	740	678	5614	1400	210	28	148	516	953	.249	.330	.376	.706	109	32	62	96	103	712	100	39	72	7
CAL	163	71	91	.438	26	528	652	5316	1221	151	29	88	516	929	.230	.302	.319	.621	87	-137	-105	95	**105**	518	54	39	58	-7
KC	163	69	93	.426	28	586	688	5462	1311	179	32	98	522	901	.240	.311	.338	.649	87	-84	-88	101	102	577	129	70	65	-3
CHI	162	68	94	.420	29	625	723	5450	1346	210	27	112	552	844	.247	.322	.357	.679	92	-25	-57	105	98	638	54	22	71	3
SEA	163	64	98	.395	33	639	799	5444	1276	179	27	125	626	1015	.234	.317	.346	.663	94	-53	-42	98	104	622	**167**	59	**74**	**15**
TOT	973					7960		65536	16120	2385	378	1649	7032	10845	.246	.323	.369	.693							1033	570	64	-32

TEAM	CG	SH	SV	IP	H	H/G	HR	BB	SO	RAT	ERA	ERA+	OAV	OOB	PR	/A	PF	CPI	FA	E	DP	FW	PW	BW	SBW	DIF
EAST																										
BAL	50	**20**	36	1473²	**1194**	7.3	117	498	897	10.5	**2.83**	126	**.223**	.291	130	121	98	97	**.984**	101	145	2.2	12.7	13.5	.0	-.5
DET	**55**	**20**	28	1455¹	1250	7.7	128	586	**1032**	11.6	3.31	113	.232	.312	50	67	103	98	.979	130	130	.5	7.0	-1.2	-.3	2.9
BOS	30	7	41	1466²	1423	8.7	155	685	935	13.2	3.92	97	.256	.343	-49	-19	105	106	.975	157	**178**	-1.0	-2.0	7.8	-1.4	2.6
WAS	28	10	41	1447¹	1310	8.1	135	656	835	12.4	3.49	99	.244	.330	22	-4	96	**107**	.978	140	159	-.0	-.4	7.7	-.6	-1.6
NY	53	13	20	1440²	1258	7.9	118	522	801	11.2	3.23	108	.236	.306	63	40	96	97	.979	131	158	.5	4.2	-5.2	-.7	.7
CLE	35	7	22	1437	1330	8.3	134	681	1000	12.9	3.94	96	.248	.338	-51	-27	104	99	.976	145	153	-.4	-2.8	-10.3	.6	-5.6
WEST																										
MIN	41	8	**43**	1497²	1388	8.3	119	524	906	11.7	3.24	113	.246	.315	64	69	101	104	.977	150	177	-.6	7.2	10.9	-1.0	-1.0
OAK	42	14	36	1480²	1356	8.2	163	586	887	12.0	3.71	93	.245	.322	-15	-45	95	100	.979	136	162	.2	-4.7	6.5	1.0	4.0
CAL	25	9	39	1438¹	1294	8.1	126	517	885	11.7	3.54	98	.242	.315	13	-9	96	96	.978	136	164	.2	-.9	-11.0	-.5	2.2
KC	42	10	25	1464²	1357	8.3	136	560	894	11.9	3.72	99	.246	.319	-15	-5	102	95	.975	157	114	-1.0	-.5	-9.2	-.0	-1.3
CHI	29	10	25	1437²	1470	9.2	146	564	810	12.9	4.21	92	.267	.339	-93	-56	107	99	.981	122	163	1.0	-5.9	-6.0	.6	-2.7
SEA	21	6	33	1463²	1490	9.2	172	653	963	13.5	4.35	84	.264	.345	-118	-116	100	101	.974	167	149	-1.5	-12.2	-4.4	1.9	-.7
TOT	451	134	389	17503¹		8.3				12.1	3.62		.246	.323					.978	1672	1852					

Runs		Hits		Doubles		Triples		Home Runs		Total Bases	
Jackson-Oak	123	Oliva-Min	197	Oliva-Min	39	Unser-Was	8	Killebrew-Min	49	Howard-Was	340
F.Robinson-Bal	111	Clarke-NY	183	Jackson-Oak	36	Smith-Bos	7	Howard-Was	48	Jackson-Oak	334
Howard-Was	111	Blair-Bal	178	Johnson-Bal	34	Clarke-NY	7	Jackson-Oak	47	Killebrew-Min	324
Killebrew-Min	106	Howard-Was	175	Petrocelli-Bos	32			Yastrzemski-Bos	40	Oliva-Min	316
Bando-Oak	106	Horton-Cle	174	Blair-Bal	32			Petrocelli-Bos	40	Petrocelli-Bos	315

Runs Batted In		Runs Produced		Bases On Balls		Batting Average		On Base Percentage		Slugging Average	
Killebrew-Min	140	Killebrew-Min	197	Killebrew-Min	145	Carew-Min	.332	Killebrew-Min	.430	Jackson-Oak	.608
Powell-Bal	121	Jackson-Oak	194	Jackson-Oak	114	Smith-Bos	.309	F.Robinson-Bal	.417	Petrocelli-Bos	.589
Jackson-Oak	118	Bando-Oak	188	Bando-Oak	111	Oliva-Min	.309	Jackson-Oak	.410	Killebrew-Min	.584
Bando-Oak	113	F.Robinson-Bal	179	Howard-Was	102	F.Robinson-Bal	.308	Petrocelli-Bos	.407	Howard-Was	.574
				Yastrzemski-Bos	101	Powell-Bal	.304	Howard-Was	.403	Powell-Bal	.559

Production		Adjusted Production		Batter Runs		Adjusted Batter Runs		Clutch Hitting Index		Runs Created	
Jackson-Oak	1.019	Jackson-Oak	190	Killebrew-Min	65.6	Jackson-Oak	65.1	White-NY	149	Killebrew-Min	146
Killebrew-Min	1.014	Howard-Was	180	Jackson-Oak	62.0	Killebrew-Min	64.0	Foy-KC	135	Jackson-Oak	144
Petrocelli-Bos	.996	Killebrew-Min	177	Howard-Was	56.8	Howard-Was	60.7	Reichardt-Cal	131	Howard-Was	132
Howard-Was	.978	Petrocelli-Bos	167	Petrocelli-Bos	54.8	Petrocelli-Bos	51.1	Cater-Oak	130	Petrocelli-Bos	129
F.Robinson-Bal	.957	F.Robinson-Bal	164	F.Robinson-Bal	49.9	F.Robinson-Bal	49.3	Killebrew-Min	127	F.Robinson-Bal	126

Total Average		Stolen Bases		Stolen Base Average		Stolen Base Runs		Fielding Runs		Total Player Rating	
Killebrew-Min	1.143	Harper-Sea	73	Campaneris-Oak	88.6	Campaneris-Oak	13.8	Cardenas-Min	33.5	Petrocelli-Bos	7.2
Jackson-Oak	1.139	Campaneris-Oak	62	Alomar-Cal	87.0	Harper-Sea	11.1	Aparicio-Chi	29.3	Jackson-Oak	6.3
Tovar-Min	1.048	Cardenal-Cle	45	Cardenal-Cle	85.7	Cardenal-Cle	7.2	Blair-Bal	24.8	Cardenas-Min	5.6
F.Robinson-Bal	1.026	Kelly-KC	40	Aparicio-Chi	85.7	Tovar-Min	6.3	Knoop-Cal-Chi	24.5	Aparicio-Chi	5.1
Howard-Was	1.004	Foy-KC	37	Davis-Sea	82.6	Aparicio-Chi	4.8	Quilici-Min	24.2	F.Robinson-Bal	4.2

Wins		Win Percentage		Games		Complete Games		Shutouts		Saves	
McLain-Det	24	Palmer-Bal	.800	Wood-Chi	76	Stottlemyre-NY	24	McLain-Det	9	Perranoski-Min	31
Cuellar-Bal	23	Perry-Min	.769	Perranoski-Min	75	McLain-Det	23	Palmer-Bal	6	K.Tatum-Cal	22
		McNally-Bal	.741	Lyle-Bos	71	McDowell-Cle	18	Cuellar-Bal	5	Lyle-Bos	17
		McLain-Det	.727	Locker-Chi-Sea	68	Cuellar-Bal	18			Watt-Bal	16
		Odom-Oak	.714	Segui-Sea	66	Peterson-NY	16			Higgins-Was	16

Innings Pitched		Fewest Hits/Game		Fewest BB/Game		Strikeouts		Strikeouts/Game		Ratio	
McLain-Det	325.0	Messersmith-Cal	6.08	Peterson-NY	1.42	McDowell-Cle	279	McDowell-Cle	8.81	Peterson-NY	9.07
Stottlemyre-NY	303.0	Palmer-Bal	6.51	Bosman-Was	1.82	Lolich-Det	271	Lolich-Det	8.69	Cuellar-Bal	9.07
Cuellar-Bal	290.2	Cuellar-Bal	6.60	McLain-Det	1.86	Messersmith-Cal	211	Messersmith-Cal	7.60	Bosman-Was	9.19
McDowell-Cle	285.0	Lolich-Det	6.86	Perry-Min	2.27	Boswell-Min	190	Butler-KC	7.25	Palmer-Bal	9.75
Lolich-Det	280.2	Odom-Oak	6.96	Cuellar-Bal	2.45			Williams-Cle	7.01	Messersmith-Cal	9.86

Earned Run Average		Adjusted ERA		Opponents' Batting Avg.		Opponents' On Base Pct.		Starter Runs		Adjusted Starter Runs	
Bosman-Was	2.19	Bosman-Was	158	Messersmith-Cal	.190	Cuellar-Bal	.261	Cuellar-Bal	40.0	Cuellar-Bal	38.1
Palmer-Bal	2.34	Palmer-Bal	153	Palmer-Bal	.200	Bosman-Was	.262	Peterson-NY	32.5	McLain-Det	33.7
Cuellar-Bal	2.38	Cuellar-Bal	150	Cuellar-Bal	.204	Peterson-NY	.263	Bosman-Was	30.7	Peterson-NY	28.1
Messersmith-Cal	2.52	Messersmith-Cal	138	Lolich-Det	.210	Palmer-Bal	.272	Messersmith-Cal	30.6	Bosman-Was	27.3
Peterson-NY	2.55	Peterson-NY	136	McDowell-Cle	.213	Messersmith-Cal	.276	McLain-Det	29.8	Messersmith-Cal	26.8

Clutch Pitching Index		Relief Runs		Adjusted Relief Runs		Relief Ranking		Total Pitcher Index		Total Baseball Ranking	
Cox-Was	128	K.Tatum-Cal	21.7	Perranoski-Min	20.6	Perranoski-Min	41.3	Cuellar-Bal	3.8	Petrocelli-Bos	7.2
Nagy-Bos	119	Perranoski-Min	20.2	K.Tatum-Cal	20.4	K.Tatum-Cal	30.9	Stottlemyre-NY	3.8	Jackson-Oak	6.3
Tiant-Cle	118	Watt-Bal	15.6	Watt-Bal	15.1	Watt-Bal	21.1	Peterson-NY	3.4	Cardenas-Min	5.6
John-Chi	114	Roland-Oak	13.7	Lyle-Bos	14.4	Wood-Chi	21.0	Messersmith-Cal	3.0	Aparicio-Chi	5.1
Wilson-Det	112	Knowles-Was	12.9	Hall-Bal	12.0	Lyle-Bos	19.2	Bosman-Was	3.0	F.Robinson-Bal	4.2

TEAM	G	W	L	PCT	GB	R	OR	AB	H	2B	3B	HR	BB	SO	AVG	OBP	SLG	PRO	PRO+	BR	/A	PF	CHI	RC	SB	CS	SBA	SBR
EAST																												
PIT	162	89	73	.549		729	664	5637	**1522**	235	**70**	130	444	871	**.270**	.328	.406	.734	105	12	27	98	99	740	66	34	66	-1
CHI	162	84	78	.519	5	806	679	5491	1424	228	44	179	607	844	.259	.335	.415	.750	95	49	-39	112	**104**	773	39	16	71	2
NY	162	83	79	.512	6	695	**630**	5443	1358	211	42	120	684	1062	.249	.336	.370	.706	96	-23	-24	100	98	689	118	54	69	3
STL	162	76	86	.469	13	744	747	5689	1497	218	51	113	569	961	.263	.333	.379	.712	95	-20	-36	102	103	719	117	47	71	7
PHI	161	73	88	.453	15.5	594	730	5456	1299	224	58	101	519	1066	.238	.307	.356	.663	85	-125	-105	97	101	582	72	64	53	-17
MON	162	73	89	.451	16	687	807	5411	1284	211	35	136	659	972	.237	.324	.365	.689	91	-62	-61	100	103	658	65	45	59	-8
WEST																												
CIN	162	102	60	.630		775	681	5540	1498	253	45	**191**	547	984	**.270**	.339	**.436**	**.775**	113	94	92	100	94	814	115	52	69	3
LA	161	87	74	.540	14.5	749	684	5606	1515	233	67	87	541	841	**.270**	.337	.382	.719	104	-4	28	96	102	730	**138**	57	71	7
SF	162	86	76	.531	16	**831**	729	5578	1460	**257**	35	165	**729**	1005	.262	**.353**	.409	.762	112	92	**101**	99	98	**821**	83	27	**75**	9
HOU	162	79	83	.488	23	744	763	5574	1446	250	47	129	598	911	.259	.334	.391	.725	104	5	36	96	100	728	114	41	74	10
ATL	162	76	86	.469	26	736	772	5546	1495	215	24	160	522	**736**	**.270**	.337	.404	.741	99	32	-11	106	97	742	58	34	63	-3
SD	162	63	99	.389	39	681	788	5494	1353	208	36	172	500	1164	.246	.314	.391	.705	98	-49	-20	96	102	669	60	45	57	-9
TOT	971					8771		66465	17151	2743	554	1683	6919	11417	.258	.332	.392	.724							1045	516	67	4

TEAM	CG	SH	SV	IP	H	H/G	HR	BB	SO	RAT	ERA	ERA+	OAV	OOB	PR	/A	PF	CPI	FA	E	DP	FW	PW	BW	SBW	DIF
EAST																										
PIT	36	13	43	1453²	1386	8.6	106	625	990	12.7	3.70	106	.255	.336	56	33	96	**106**	.979	137	**195**	.3	3.3	2.7	-.1	1.9
CHI	59	9	25	1435	1402	8.8	143	**475**	1000	11.9	3.76	**120**	.256	.318	46	**118**	111	101	.978	137	146	.3	**11.8**	-3.9	.2	-5.3
NY	47	10	32	1459²	**1260**	7.8	135	575	**1064**	11.5	3.45	117	**.233**	.310	97	93	99	98	.979	124	136	1.0	9.3	-2.4	.3	-6.2
STL	51	11	20	1475²	1483	9.0	102	632	960	13.0	4.06	101	.263	.340	-2	10	102	100	.977	150	159	-.4	1.0	-3.6	.7	-2.7
PHI	24	8	36	1461	1483	9.1	132	538	1047	12.7	4.17	96	.265	.333	-20	-29	99	98	**.981**	114	134	1.5	-2.9	-10.5	-1.7	6.1
MON	29	10	32	1438²	1434	9.0	162	716	914	13.8	4.50	91	.261	.351	-73	-63	102	101	.977	141	193	.0	-6.3	-6.1	-.8	5.1
WEST																										
CIN	32	15	**60**	1444²	1370	8.5	118	592	843	12.4	3.69	109	.251	.327	57	55	100	102	.976	151	173	-.5	5.5	9.2	.3	6.6
LA	37	**17**	42	1458²	1394	8.6	164	496	880	11.9	3.82	100	.250	.316	37	2	95	99	.978	135	135	.4	.2	2.8	.7	2.5
SF	50	7	30	1457²	1514	9.3	156	604	931	13.3	4.50	88	.267	.341	-74	-86	98	98	.973	170	153	-1.5	-8.6	**10.1**	.9	4.2
HOU	36	6	35	1456	1491	9.2	131	577	942	13.0	4.23	92	.265	.338	-30	-58	96	99	.978	140	144	.1	-5.8	3.6	**1.0**	-.9
ATL	45	9	24	1430²	1451	9.1	185	478	960	12.3	4.33	99	.261	.322	-45	-6	106	96	.977	141	118	.0	-.6	-1.1	-.3	-3.1
SD	24	9	32	1440¹	1483	9.3	149	611	886	13.3	4.36	91	.267	.344	-50	-61	98	102	.975	158	159	-.9	-6.1	-2.0	-.9	-8.1
TOT	470	124	411	17411²		8.9				12.6	4.05		.258	.332					.977	1698	1845					

Runs
Williams-Chi	137
Bonds-SF	134
Rose-Cin	120
Brock-StL	114
Tolan-Cin	112

Hits
Williams-Chi	205
Rose-Cin	205
Torre-StL	203
Brock-StL	202
Alou-Pit	201

Doubles
Parker-LA	47
McCovey-SF	39
Rose-Cin	37
Dietz-SF	36
Bonds-SF	36

Triples
Davis-LA	16
Kessinger-Chi	14
Clemente-Pit	10
Bonds-SF	10

Home Runs
Bench-Cin	45
Williams-Chi	42
Perez-Cin	40
McCovey-SF	39

Total Bases
Williams-Chi	373
Bench-Cin	355
Perez-Cin	346
Bonds-SF	334
Gaston-SD	317

Runs Batted In
Bench-Cin	148
Williams-Chi	129
Perez-Cin	129
McCovey-SF	126
H.Aaron-Atl	118

Runs Produced
Williams-Chi	224
Bench-Cin	200
Perez-Cin	196
Bonds-SF	186

Bases On Balls
McCovey-SF	137
Staub-Mon	112
Dietz-SF	109
Wynn-Hou	106
Morgan-Hou	102

Batting Average
Carty-Atl	.366
Torre-StL	.325
Sanguillen-Pit	.325
Williams-Chi	.322
Parker-LA	.319

On Base Percentage
Carty-Atl	.456
McCovey-SF	.446
Dietz-SF	.430
Hickman-Chi	.421
Perez-Cin	.405

Slugging Average
McCovey-SF	.612
Perez-Cin	.589
Bench-Cin	.587
Williams-Chi	.586
Carty-Atl	.584

Production
McCovey-SF	1.058
Carty-Atl	1.040
Hickman-Chi	1.003
Perez-Cin	.994
Williams-Chi	.979

Adjusted Production
McCovey-SF	183
Carty-Atl	167
Perez-Cin	162
Dietz-SF	154
Hickman-Chi	148

Batter Runs
McCovey-SF	62.0
Carty-Atl	54.4
Perez-Cin	52.1
Williams-Chi	51.1
Hickman-Chi	49.5

Adjusted Batter Runs
McCovey-SF	62.9
Perez-Cin	51.8
Carty-Atl	50.6
Dietz-SF	41.7
Williams-Chi	41.0

Clutch Hitting Index
Parker-LA	147
Santo-Chi	137
Davis-LA	135
Dietz-SF	132
Menke-Hou	132

Runs Created
Williams-Chi	147
McCovey-SF	140
Perez-Cin	140
Bonds-SF	134
Hickman-Chi	129

Total Average
McCovey-SF	1.214
Carty-Atl	1.102
Hickman-Chi	1.080
Perez-Cin	1.045
Williams-Chi	1.018

Stolen Bases
Tolan-Cin	57
Brock-StL	51
Bonds-SF	48
Morgan-Hou	42
Davis-LA	38

Stolen Base Average
Henderson-SF	87.0
Harrelson-NY	85.2
Wynn-Hou	82.8
Bonds-SF	82.8
Cedeno-Hou	81.0

Stolen Base Runs
Bonds-SF	8.4
Brock-StL	6.3
Tolan-Cin	5.1
Morgan-Hou	4.8
Harrelson-NY	4.5

Fielding Runs
Maxvill-StL	37.5
Alley-Pit	33.7
Mazeroski-Pit	23.9
Rader-Hou	23.8
Wine-Mon	19.7

Total Player Rating
McCovey-SF	6.1
Bench-Cin	4.8
Perez-Cin	4.3
Bonds-SF	4.2
Morgan-Hou	4.1

Wins
Perry-SF	23
Gibson-StL	23
Jenkins-Chi	22
Merritt-Cin	20

Win Percentage
Gibson-StL	.767
Nolan-Cin	.720
Walker-Pit	.714
Perry-SF	.639
Merritt-Cin	.625

Games
Herbel-SD-NY	76
Selma-Phi	73
Linzy-SF-StL	67
Granger-Cin	67
Giusti-Pit	66

Complete Games
Jenkins-Chi	24
Perry-SF	23
Gibson-StL	23
Seaver-NY	19
Dierker-Hou	17

Shutouts
Perry-SF	5
Sutton-LA	4
Osteen-LA	4
Morton-Mon	4
Ellis-Pit	4

Saves
Granger-Cin	35
Giusti-Pit	26
Brewer-LA	24
Raymond-Mon	23
Selma-Phi	22

Innings Pitched
Perry-SF	328.2
Jenkins-Chi	313.0
Gibson-StL	294.0
Seaver-NY	290.2
Holtzman-Chi	287.2

Fewest Hits/Game
Simpson-Cin	6.39
Seaver-NY	7.12
Walker-Pit	7.12
Gentry-NY	7.41
Jenkins-Chi	7.62

Fewest BB/Game
Jenkins-Chi	1.73
Marichal-SF	1.78
Osteen-LA	1.81
McAndrew-NY	1.86
Merritt-Cin	2.04

Strikeouts
Seaver-NY	283
Jenkins-Chi	274
Gibson-StL	274
Perry-SF	214
Holtzman-Chi	202

Strikeouts/Game
Seaver-NY	8.76
Gibson-StL	8.39
Veale-Pit	7.93
Jenkins-Chi	7.88
Stoneman-Mon	7.63

Ratio
Jenkins-Chi	9.55
Seaver-NY	9.82
McAndrew-NY	10.06
Perry-SF	10.52
Gibson-StL	10.84

Earned Run Average
Seaver-NY	2.82
Simpson-Cin	3.02
Walker-Pit	3.04
Gibson-StL	3.12
Koosman-NY	3.14

Adjusted ERA
Seaver-NY	143
Simpson-Cin	134
Pappas-Atl-Chi	133
Holtzman-Chi	133
Jenkins-Chi	133

Opponents' Batting Avg.
Simpson-Cin	.198
Seaver-NY	.214
Walker-Pit	.219
Jenkins-Chi	.224
Gentry-NY	.224

Opponents' On Base Pct.
Jenkins-Chi	.265
Seaver-NY	.273
McAndrew-NY	.281
Perry-SF	.290
Gibson-StL	.296

Starter Runs
Seaver-NY	39.7
Perry-SF	30.7
Gibson-StL	30.2
Jenkins-Chi	22.7
Nolan-Cin	21.7

Adjusted Starter Runs
Seaver-NY	38.9
Jenkins-Chi	38.5
Holtzman-Chi	35.8
Gibson-StL	32.4
Perry-SF	28.1

Clutch Pitching Index
Ellis-Pit	119
Morton-Mon	118
Coombs-SD	113
Pappas-Atl-Chi	109
Dobson-SD	108

Relief Runs
Selma-Phi	19.4
Carroll-Cin	16.9
Gullett-Cin	13.9
Granger-Cin	13.1
C.Taylor-StL	12.9

Adjusted Relief Runs
Selma-Phi	18.5
Carroll-Cin	16.8
C.Taylor-StL	13.8
Gullett-Cin	13.8
Granger-Cin	12.9

Relief Ranking
Selma-Phi	27.9
Granger-Cin	27.2
Carroll-Cin	24.6
Hoerner-Phi	21.7
McMahon-SF	19.0

Total Pitcher Index
Seaver-NY	4.8
Gibson-StL	4.6
Holtzman-Chi	3.9
Jenkins-Chi	3.6
Perry-SF	3.1

Total Baseball Ranking
McCovey-SF	6.1
Seaver-NY	4.8
Bench-Cin	4.8
Gibson-StL	4.6
Perez-Cin	4.3

TEAM	G	W	L	PCT	GB	R	OR	AB	H	2B	3B	HR	BB	SO	AVG	OBP	SLG	PRO	PRO+	BR	/A	PF	CHI	RC	SB	CS	SBA	SBR
EAST																												
BAL	162	108	54	.667		792	574	5545	1424	213	25	179	717	952	.257	.346	.401	.747	112	101	93	101	99	795	84	39	68	2
NY	163	93	69	.574	15	680	612	5492	1381	208	41	111	588	808	.251	.327	.365	.692	102	-18	17	95	103	662	50	61	63	-5
BOS	162	87	75	.537	21	786	722	5535	1450	252	28	203	594	855	.262	.338	.428	.766	109	119	71	107	98	786	50	48	51	-14
DET	162	79	83	.488	29	666	731	5377	1282	207	38	148	656	825	.238	.325	.374	.699	98	-4	-9	101	99	658	29	30	49	-9
CLE	162	76	86	.469	32	649	675	5463	1358	197	23	183	503	909	.249	.316	.394	.710	96	3	-30	105	97	670	25	36	41	-14
WAS	162	70	92	.432	38	626	689	5460	1302	184	28	138	635	989	.238	.323	.358	.681	99	-36	-3	95	97	638	72	42	63	-4
WEST																												
MIN	162	98	64	.605		744	605	5483	1438	230	41	153	501	905	.262	.329	.403	.732	107	50	41	101	103	709	57	52	52	-14
OAK	162	89	73	.549	9	678	593	5376	1338	208	24	171	584	977	.249	.327	.392	.719	108	28	52	96	98	689	131	68	66	-2
CAL	162	86	76	.531	12	631	630	5532	1391	197	40	114	447	922	.251	.311	.363	.674	95	-64	-41	97	104	622	69	27	72	5
MIL	163	65	97	.401	33	613	751	5395	1305	202	24	126	592	985	.242	.321	.358	.679	92	-42	-47	101	97	618	91	73	55	-17
KC	162	65	97	.401	33	611	705	5503	1341	202	41	97	514	958	.244	.311	.348	.659	88	-88	-87	100	105	593	97	53	65	-3
CHI	162	56	106	.346	42	633	822	5514	1394	192	20	123	477	872	.253	.317	.362	.679	90	-50	-75	104	102	627	53	33	62	-4
TOT	973					8109		65675	16404	2492	373	1746	6808	10957	.250	.324	.379	.703							863	562	61	-78

TEAM	CG	SH	SV	IP	H	H/G	HR	BB	SO	RAT	ERA	ERA+	OAV	OOB	PR	/A	PF	CPI	FA	E	DP	FW	PW	BW	SBW	DIF
EAST																										
BAL	60	12	31	1478²	1317	8.0	139	469	941	11.0	3.15	116	.240	.302	93	82	98	102	.981	117	148	1.1	8.5	9.6	.9	6.9
NY	36	6	49	1471²	1386	8.5	130	451	777	11.4	3.24	108	.249	.308	77	45	95	103	.974	130	146	-1.2	4.7	1.8	.2	5.0
BOS	38	8	44	1446¹	1391	8.7	156	594	1003	12.6	3.87	102	.251	.329	-25	14	107	100	.974	156	131	-1.2	1.5	7.4	-.8	-.9
DET	33	9	39	1447¹	1443	9.0	153	623	1045	13.1	4.09	91	.260	.338	-61	-59	100	100	.978	133	142	.2	-6.1	-.9	-.3	5.2
CLE	34	8	35	1451¹	1333	8.3	163	689	1076	12.8	3.91	101	.247	.337	-31	8	107	103	.979	133	168	.2	.8	-3.1	-.8	-2.1
WAS	20	11	40	1457²	1375	8.5	139	611	823	12.4	3.80	94	.252	.330	-13	-39	96	100	.982	116	173	1.1	-4.0	-.3	.3	-8.0
WEST																										
MIN	26	12	58	1448¹	1329	8.3	130	486	940	11.5	3.23	115	.244	.310	78	79	100	103	.980	123	130	.7	8.2	4.3	-.8	4.6
OAK	33	15	40	1442²	1253	7.8	134	542	858	11.4	3.30	107	.234	.308	66	38	95	98	.977	141	152	-.3	3.9	5.4	.5	-1.5
CAL	21	10	49	1462¹	1280	7.9	154	559	922	11.6	3.48	104	.237	.313	37	21	97	99	.980	127	169	.5	2.2	-4.3	1.2	5.4
MIL	31	2	27	1446²	1397	8.7	146	587	895	12.6	4.21	90	.255	.332	-79	-67	102	93	.978	136	142	.0	-6.9	-4.9	-1.1	-3.1
KC	30	11	25	1463²	1346	8.3	138	641	915	12.4	3.78	99	.247	.331	-11	-7	101	99	.976	152	162	-.9	-.7	-9.0	.4	-5.7
CHI	20	6	30	1430¹	1554	9.8	164	556	762	13.6	4.54	86	.280	.350	-132	-103	105	101	.975	165	187	-1.7	-10.7	-7.8	.3	-5.1
TOT	382	110	467	17447		8.5				12.2	3.71		.250	.324					.978	1629	1850					

Runs
Yastrzemski-Bos .. 125
Tovar-Min 120
White-NY 109
Smith-Bos 109
Harper-Mil 104

Hits
Oliva-Min 204
Johnson-Cal 202
Tovar-Min 195
Yastrzemski-Bos .. 186
White-NY 180

Doubles
Tovar-Min 36
Otis-KC 36
Oliva-Min 36
Harper-Mil 35
Cardenas-Min 34

Triples
Tovar-Min 13
Stanley-Det 11
Otis-KC 9

Home Runs
Howard-Was 44
Killebrew-Min 41
Yastrzemski-Bos .. 40
A.Conigliaro-Bos... 36
Powell-Bal 35

Total Bases
Yastrzemski-Bos .. 335
Oliva-Min 323
Harper-Mil 315
Howard-Was 309
Powell-Bal 289

Runs Batted In
Howard-Was 126
A.Conigliaro-Bos .. 116
Powell-Bal 114
Killebrew-Min 113
Oliva-Min 107

Runs Produced
Yastrzemski-Bos .. 187
White-NY 181
Oliva-Min 180
Howard-Was 172
A.Conigliaro-Bos .. 169

Bases On Balls
Howard-Was 132
Yastrzemski-Bos .. 128
Killebrew-Min 128
Bando-Oak 118
Buford-Bal 109

Batting Average
Johnson-Cal 329
Yastrzemski-Bos ..329
Oliva-Min 325
Aparicio-Chi 313
F.Robinson-Bal ...306

On Base Percentage
Yastrzemski-Bos ..453
Howard-Was 420
Powell-Bal 417
Killebrew-Min 416
Buford-Bal 409

Slugging Average
Yastrzemski-Bos ..592
Powell-Bal 549
Killebrew-Min 546
Howard-Was 546
Harper-Mil 522

Production
Yastrzemski-Bos . 1.045
Powell-Bal 967
Howard-Was 966
Killebrew-Min 962
F.Robinson-Bal ...922

Adjusted Production
Yastrzemski-Bos .. 174
Howard-Was 173
Powell-Bal 163
Killebrew-Min 161
F.Robinson-Bal .. 151

Batter Runs
Yastrzemski-Bos .. 71.7
Howard-Was 54.1
Killebrew-Min 49.5
Powell-Bal 49.2
Harper-Mil 37.5

Adjusted Batter Runs
Yastrzemski-Bos .. 66.4
Howard-Was 57.8
Killebrew-Min 48.5
Powell-Bal 48.4
Harper-Mil 36.9

Clutch Hitting Index
Piniella-KC 138
A.Conigliaro-Bos.. 128
Cater-NY 127
McMullen-Was-Cal 125
B.Robinson-Bal ... 123

Runs Created
Yastrzemski-Bos .. 157
Howard-Was 130
Powell-Bal 123
Harper-Mil 122
Killebrew-Min 116

Total Average
Yastrzemski-Bos . 1.170
Powell-Bal 1.034
Howard-Was 1.026
Killebrew-Min ... 1.000
F.Robinson-Bal ...944

Stolen Bases
Campaneris-Oak... 42
Harper-Mil 38
Alomar-Cal 35
Kelly-KC 34
Otis-KC 33

Stolen Base Average
Otis-KC 94.3
Johnson-Cal 89.5
Campaneris-Oak .. 80.8
Stroud-Was 78.4
Kenney-NY 76.9

Stolen Base Runs
Otis-KC 8.7
Campaneris-Oak .. 6.6
Stroud-Was 3.9
Johnson-Cal 3.9
Alomar-Cal 3.3

Fielding Runs
Knoop-Chi 35.1
Brinkman-Was ... 31.1
Nettles-Cle 27.8
Cullen-Was 26.5
Mitterwald-Min .. 24.3

Total Player Rating
Yastrzemski-Bos ... 5.6
Aparicio-Chi 4.6
Oliva-Min 4.3
Fregosi-Cal 4.2
Howard-Was 3.9

Wins
Perry-Min 24
McNally-Bal 24
Cuellar-Bal 24
Wright-Cal 22

Win Percentage
Cuellar-Bal 750
McNally-Bal 727
Perry-Min 667
Palmer-Bal 667
Siebert-Bos 652

Games
Wood-Chi 77
Grant-Oak 72
Knowles-Was 71
Williams-Min 68

Complete Games
Cuellar-Bal 21
McDowell-Cle 19
Palmer-Bal 17
McNally-Bal 16
Culp-Bos 15

Shutouts
Palmer-Bal 5
Dobson-Oak 5
Peters-Bos 4
Perry-Min 4
Cuellar-Bal 4

Saves
Perranoski-Min 34
McDaniel-NY 29
Timmermann-Det .. 27
Knowles-Was 27
Grant-Oak 24

Innings Pitched
Palmer-Bal 305.0
McDowell-Cle ... 305.0
Cuellar-Bal 297.2
McNally-Bal 296.0
Perry-Min 278.2

Fewest Hits/Game
Messersmith-Cal . 6.66
McDowell-Cle ... 6.96
Segui-Oak 7.22
Johnson-KC 7.49
Culp-Bos 7.56

Fewest BB/Game
Peterson-NY 1.38
Perry-Min 1.84
Cox-Was 2.06
Cuellar-Bal 2.09
Horlen-Chi 2.14

Strikeouts
McDowell-Cle 304
Lolich-Det 230
Johnson-KC 206
Palmer-Bal 199
Culp-Bos 197

Strikeouts/Game
McDowell-Cle 8.97
Johnson-KC 8.66
Cain-Det 7.77
Lolich-Det 7.59
Messersmith-Cal . 7.49

Ratio
Peterson-NY 10.03
Cuellar-Bal 10.37
Perry-Min 10.46
Blyleven-Min 10.54
Messersmith-Cal . 10.54

Earned Run Average
Segui-Oak 2.56
Palmer-Bal 2.71
Wright-Cal 2.83
Peterson-NY 2.90
McDowell-Cle 2.92

Adjusted ERA
Segui-Oak 139
McDowell-Cle ... 136
Palmer-Bal 134
Culp-Bos 130
Wright-Cal 128

Opponents' Batting Avg.
Messersmith-Cal ..205
McDowell-Cle 213
Segui-Oak 222
Culp-Bos 224
Johnson-KC 228

Opponents' On Base Pct.
Peterson-NY 280
Cuellar-Bal 286
Perry-Min 287
Blyleven-Min 289
Messersmith-Cal ..290

Starter Runs
Palmer-Bal 33.9
McDowell-Cle ... 26.9
Wright-Cal 25.6
Peterson-NY 23.4
Perry-Min 21.0

Adjusted Starter Runs
McDowell-Cle ... 35.2
Palmer-Bal 31.6
Culp-Bos 25.6
Wright-Cal 22.7
Perry-Min 21.2

Clutch Pitching Index
Stottlemyre-NY ... 113
Kaat-Min 112
Bahnsen-NY 109
Segui-Oak 108
Wright-Cal 107

Relief Runs
Grant-Oak 25.9
Knowles-Was..... 22.2
Williams-Min 21.8
McDaniel-NY 21.1
Sanders-Mil 20.1

Adjusted Relief Runs
Grant-Oak 23.5
Williams-Min 21.9
Sanders-Mil 20.9
Hall-Min 20.2
Knowles-Was 20.1

Relief Ranking
Knowles-Was..... 34.5
McDaniel-NY 31.8
Perranoski-Min .. 30.3
Wood-Chi 29.6
Williams-Min 25.6

Total Pitcher Index
Palmer-Bal 3.3
McDowell-Cle 3.2
Perry-Min 2.9
Grant-Oak 2.7
Peterson-NY 2.7

Total Baseball Ranking
Yastrzemski-Bos .. 5.6
Aparicio-Chi 4.6
Oliva-Min 4.3
Fregosi-Cal 4.2
Howard-Was 3.9

TEAM	G	W	L	PCT	GB	R	OR	AB	H	2B	3B	HR	BB	SO	AVG	OBP	SLG	PRO	PRO+	BR	/A	PF	CHI	RC	SB	CS	SBA	SBR
EAST																												
PIT	162	97	65	.599		**788**	599	5674	**1555**	223	**61**	**154**	469	919	.274	.333	**.416**	**.749**	119	121	**124**	100	103	**776**	65	31	68	1
STL	163	90	72	.556	7	739	699	5610	1542	225	54	95	543	757	**.275**	**.342**	.385	.727	108	91	66	104	100	736	**124**	53	70	5
NY	162	83	79	.512	14	588	**550**	5477	1365	203	29	98	547	958	.249	.321	.351	.672	98	-20	-10	99	95	614	89	43	67	1
CHI	162	83	79	.512	14	637	648	5438	1401	202	34	128	527	772	.258	.327	.378	.705	93	41	-51	115	95	663	44	32	58	-6
MON	162	71	90	.441	25.5	622	729	5335	1312	197	29	88	543	800	.246	.325	.343	.668	96	-20	-23	100	102	598	51	43	54	-11
PHI	162	67	95	.414	30	558	688	5538	1289	209	35	123	499	1031	.233	.300	.350	.650	90	-74	-73	100	99	586	63	39	62	-5
WEST																												
SF	162	90	72	.556		706	644	5461	1348	224	36	140	**654**	1042	.247	.331	.378	.709	109	57	67	98	101	699	101	36	**74**	9
LA	162	89	73	.549	1	663	587	5523	1469	213	38	95	489	755	.266	.328	.370	.698	111	28	66	94	100	661	76	40	66	-1
ATL	162	82	80	.506	8	643	699	5575	1434	192	30	153	434	**747**	.257	.314	.385	.699	98	18	-22	106	98	658	57	46	55	-11
HOU	162	79	83	.488	11	585	567	5492	1319	203	52	71	478	888	.240	.304	.340	.644	90	-81	-65	97	**107**	573	101	51	66	0
CIN	162	79	83	.488	11	586	581	5414	1306	203	28	138	438	907	.241	.301	.366	.667	96	-45	-32	98	103	580	59	33	64	-2
SD	161	61	100	.379	28.5	486	610	5366	1250	184	31	96	438	966	.233	.294	.332	.626	89	-117	-75	93	98	513	70	45	61	-6
TOT	972					7601		65903	16590	2505	457	1379	6059	10542	.252	.318	.366	.685							900	492	65	-25

TEAM	CG	SH	SV	IP	H	H/G	HR	BB	SO	RAT	ERA	ERA+	OAV	OOB	PR	/A	PF	CPI	FA	E	DP	FW	PW	BW	SBW	DIF
EAST																										
PIT	43	15	**48**	1461	1426	8.8	108	470	813	11.9	3.31	102	.257	.318	26	12	98	105	.979	133	164	.0	1.3	**13.3**	.3	1.0
STL	56	14	22	1467	1482	9.1	104	576	911	12.9	3.85	93	.263	.336	-63	-41	104	99	.978	142	155	-.4	-4.4	7.1	.8	5.9
NY	42	13	22	1466[1]	**1227**	7.5	100	529	**1157**	11.0	**2.99**	**114**	**.227**	**.300**	**78**	**68**	98	94	.981	114	135	1.2	**7.3**	-1.1	.3	-5.7
CHI	**75**	17	13	1444	1458	9.1	132	411	900	11.8	3.61	109	.262	.316	-23	52	114	101	.980	126	150	.5	5.6	-5.5	-.4	1.8
MON	49	8	25	1434[1]	1418	8.9	133	658	829	13.2	4.12	86	.260	.344	-104	-94	102	100	.976	150	164	-.9	-10.1	-2.5	-1.0	4.9
PHI	31	10	25	1470[2]	1396	8.5	132	525	838	12.0	3.71	95	.254	.323	-41	-31	102	98	.981	122	158	.7	-3.3	-7.8	-.3	-3.3
WEST																										
SF	45	14	30	1454[2]	1324	8.2	128	471	831	11.3	3.32	102	.242	.306	24	13	98	97	.972	179	153	-2.6	1.4	7.2	**1.2**	1.8
LA	48	**18**	33	1449[2]	1363	8.5	110	**399**	853	11.1	3.23	100	.250	.304	37	-1	93	98	.979	131	159	.2	-.1	7.1	.1	.7
ATL	40	11	31	1474[2]	1529	9.3	152	485	823	12.5	3.75	99	.269	.330	-44	-6	107	**108**	.977	146	180	-.7	-.6	-2.4	-1.0	5.6
HOU	43	10	25	1471[1]	1318	8.1	**75**	475	914	11.7	3.13	107	.241	.309	55	38	97	95	.983	106	152	1.6	4.1	-7.0	.2	-1.0
CIN	27	11	38	1444	1298	8.1	112	501	750	11.4	3.35	100	.243	.311	18	0	97	97	**.984**	**103**	174	1.8	.0	-3.4	.0	-.4
SD	47	10	17	1438	1351	8.5	93	559	923	12.1	3.22	102	.249	.323	39	12	95	106	.974	161	144	-1.6	1.3	-8.0	-.4	-10.7
TOT	546	151	329	17475[2]		8.5				11.9	3.47		.252	.318					.979	1613	1888					

Runs		Hits		Doubles		Triples		Home Runs		Total Bases	
Brock-StL	126	Torre-StL	230	Cedeno-Hou	40	Morgan-Hou	11	Stargell-Pit	48	Torre-StL	352
Bonds-SF	110	Garr-Atl	219	Brock-StL	37	Metzger-Hou	11	H.Aaron-Atl	47	H.Aaron-Atl	331
Stargell-Pit	104	Brock-StL	200	Torre-StL	34	Davis-LA	10	May-Cin	39	Stargell-Pit	321
Garr-Atl	101	Davis-LA	198	Staub-Mon	34	Gaston-SD	9	Johnson-Phi	34	Bonds-SF	317
Torre-StL	97			Davis-LA	33					Williams-Chi	300

Runs Batted In		Runs Produced		Bases On Balls		Batting Average		On Base Percentage		Slugging Average	
Torre-StL	137	Torre-StL	210	Mays-SF	112	Torre-StL	.363	Mays-SF	.429	H.Aaron-Atl	.669
Stargell-Pit	125	Stargell-Pit	181	Dietz-SF	97	Garr-Atl	.343	Torre-StL	.424	Stargell-Pit	.628
H.Aaron-Atl	118	Brock-StL	180	Bailey-Mon	97	Beckert-Chi	.342	H.Aaron-Atl	.414	Torre-StL	.555
Bonds-SF	102	Bonds-SF	179	Allen-LA	93	Clemente-Pit	.341	Hunt-Mon	.403	May-Cin	.532
Montanez-Phi	99	Staub-Mon	172	Morgan-Hou	88	H.Aaron-Atl	.327	Stargell-Pit	.401	Bonds-SF	.512

Production		Adjusted Production		Batter Runs		Adjusted Batter Runs		Clutch Hitting Index		Runs Created	
H.Aaron-Atl	1.082	H.Aaron-Atl	190	H.Aaron-Atl	65.2	H.Aaron-Atl	61.5	Bailey-Mon	143	Torre-StL	145
Stargell-Pit	1.029	Stargell-Pit	188	Torre-StL	62.5	Torre-StL	59.6	Simmons-StL	140	H.Aaron-Atl	137
Torre-StL	.979	Torre-StL	169	Stargell-Pit	58.7	Stargell-Pit	59.0	Torre-StL	139	Stargell-Pit	131
Mays-SF	.911	Mays-SF	160	Williams-Chi	39.4	Allen-LA	38.9	Sanguillen-Pit	136	Bonds-SF	115
Williams-Chi	.889	Allen-LA	154	Staub-Mon	38.5	Mays-SF	38.5	Fairly-Mon	134	Brock-StL	114

Total Average		Stolen Bases		Stolen Base Average		Stolen Base Runs		Fielding Runs		Total Player Rating	
H.Aaron-Atl	1.178	Brock-StL	64	Mays-SF	88.5	Brock-StL	7.8	Maxvill-StL	29.2	Stargell-Pit	4.9
Stargell-Pit	1.117	Morgan-Hou	40	Henderson-SF	85.7	Morgan-Hou	7.2	Robertson-Pit	15.2	H.Aaron-Atl	4.5
Mays-SF	1.067	Garr-Atl	30	Morgan-Hou	83.3	Mays-SF	5.1	Helms-Cin	14.4	Torre-StL	4.4
Torre-StL	.998			Agee-NY	82.4	Agee-NY	4.8	Barton-SD	14.0	Bonds-SF	3.9
Bonds-SF	.876			Hernandez-SD	80.8	Harrelson-NY	4.2	Harrelson-NY	10.7	Morgan-Hou	3.4

Wins		Win Percentage		Games		Complete Games		Shutouts		Saves	
Jenkins-Chi	24	Gullett-Cin	.727	Granger-Cin	70	Jenkins-Chi	30	Pappas-Chi	5	Giusti-Pit	30
Seaver-NY	20	Downing-LA	.690	J.Johnson-SF	67	Seaver-NY	21	Gibson-StL	5	Marshall-Mon	23
Downing-LA	20	Carlton-StL	.690	Marshall-Mon	66	Stoneman-Mon	20	Downing-LA	5	Brewer-LA	22
Carlton-StL	20	Ellis-Pit	.679	McMahon-SF	61	Gibson-StL	20	Blass-Pit	5	J.Johnson-SF	18
Ellis-Pit	19	Seaver-NY	.667	Carroll-Cin	61					Upshaw-Atl	17

Innings Pitched		Fewest Hits/Game		Fewest BB/Game		Strikeouts		Strikeouts/Game		Ratio	
Jenkins-Chi	325.0	Wilson-Hou	6.55	Jenkins-Chi	1.02	Seaver-NY	289	Seaver-NY	9.08	Seaver-NY	8.64
Stoneman-Mon	294.2	Seaver-NY	6.60	Marichal-SF	1.81	Jenkins-Chi	263	Kirby-SD	7.78	Wilson-Hou	9.44
Seaver-NY	286.1	Kirby-SD	7.17	Stone-Atl	1.82	Stoneman-Mon	251	Stoneman-Mon	7.67	Jenkins-Chi	9.58
Perry-SF	280.0	Gentry-NY	7.39	Hands-Chi	1.86	Kirby-SD	231	Jenkins-Chi	7.28	Marichal-SF	9.77
Marichal-SF	279.0	Stoneman-Mon	7.42	Sutton-LA	1.87	Sutton-LA	194	Gentry-NY	6.86	Sutton-LA	9.87

Earned Run Average		Adjusted ERA		Opponents' Batting Avg.		Opponents' On Base Pct.		Starter Runs		Adjusted Starter Runs	
Seaver-NY	1.76	Seaver-NY	194	Wilson-Hou	.202	Seaver-NY	.253	Seaver-NY	54.3	Seaver-NY	52.4
Roberts-SD	2.10	Roberts-SD	157	Seaver-NY	.206	Wilson-Hou	.268	Roberts-SD	40.9	Jenkins-Chi	42.1
Wilson-Hou	2.45	Jenkins-Chi	142	Kirby-SD	.216	Jenkins-Chi	.271	Wilson-Hou	30.2	Roberts-SD	35.8
Forsch-Hou	2.53	Wilson-Hou	137	Cumberland-SF	.223	Marichal-SF	.274	Sutton-LA	27.2	Wilson-Hou	27.2
Sutton-LA	2.54	Forsch-Hou	133	Gentry-NY	.224	Nolan-Cin	.275	Jenkins-Chi	25.2	Niekro-Atl	21.8

Clutch Pitching Index		Relief Runs		Adjusted Relief Runs		Relief Ranking		Total Pitcher Index		Total Baseball Ranking	
Roberts-SD	120	McGraw-NY	21.7	McGraw-NY	21.0	McGraw-NY	29.0	Seaver-NY	6.8	Seaver-NY	6.8
Downing-LA	115	Miller-Chi-SD-Pit	20.0	Miller-Chi-SD-Pit	18.9	Miller-Chi-SD-Pit	26.7	Jenkins-Chi	6.5	Jenkins-Chi	6.5
Short-Phi	115	Frisella-NY	14.9	Frisella-NY	14.3	Frisella-NY	22.7	Roberts-SD	4.4	Stargell-Pit	4.9
Johnson-Pit	112	Ray-Hou	14.6	Ray-Hou	13.5	Brewer-LA	22.3	Wise-Phi	3.4	H.Aaron-Atl	4.5
Wise-Phi	112	Brewer-LA	14.3	Hoerner-Phi	12.6	Ray-Hou	18.4	Wilson-Hou	2.6	Roberts-SD	4.4

TEAM	G	W	L	PCT	GB	R	OR	AB	H	2B	3B	HR	BB	SO	AVG	OBP	SLG	PRO	PRO+	BR	/A	PF	CHI	RC	SB	CS	SBA	SBR
EAST																												
BAL	158	101	57	.639		**742**	**530**	5303	1382	207	25	158	**672**	844	**.261**	**.349**	.398	**.747**	120	**133**	**139**	99	97	**750**	66	38	63	-3
DET	162	91	71	.562	12	701	645	5502	1399	214	38	**179**	540	854	.254	.327	**.405**	.732	110	88	63	104	97	715	35	43	45	-15
BOS	162	85	77	.525	18	691	667	5401	1360	**246**	28	161	552	871	.252	.325	.397	.722	104	68	24	107	100	686	51	34	60	-5
NY	162	82	80	.506	21	648	641	5413	1377	195	**43**	97	581	**717**	.254	.331	.360	.691	109	22	61	94	99	643	75	55	58	-11
WAS	159	63	96	.396	38.5	537	660	5290	1219	189	30	86	575	956	.230	.309	.326	.635	91	-86	-51	94	102	538	68	45	60	-7
CLE	162	60	102	.370	43	543	747	5467	1303	200	20	109	467	868	.238	.302	.342	.644	81	-83	-140	109	101	558	57	37	61	-5
WEST																												
OAK	161	101	60	.627		691	564	5494	1383	195	25	160	542	1018	.252	.323	.384	.707	109	42	55	98	102	681	80	53	60	-8
KC	161	85	76	.528	16	603	566	5295	1323	225	40	80	490	819	.250	.316	.353	.669	97	-28	-23	99	**104**	594	**130**	46	**74**	11
CHI	162	79	83	.488	22.5	617	597	5382	1346	185	30	138	562	870	.250	.327	.373	.700	102	33	14	103	94	661	83	65	56	-14
CAL	162	76	86	.469	25.5	511	576	5495	1271	213	18	96	441	827	.231	.292	.329	.621	88	-131	-86	93	**104**	518	72	34	68	1
MIN	160	74	86	.463	26.5	654	670	5414	**1406**	197	31	116	512	846	.260	.326	.372	.698	101	28	9	103	101	641	66	44	60	-7
MIL	161	69	92	.429	32	534	609	5185	1188	160	23	104	543	924	.229	.306	.329	.635	87	-88	-81	99	103	534	82	53	61	-7
TOT	966					7472		64641	15957	2426	351	1484	6477	10414	.247	.320	.364	.684							865	547	61	-69

TEAM	CG	SH	SV	IP	H	H/G	HR	BB	SO	RAT	ERA	ERA+	OAV	OOB	PR	/A	PF	CPI	FA	E	DP	FW	PW	BW	SBW	DIF
EAST																										
BAL	71	15	22	1415¹	1257	8.0	125	**416**	793	**10.8**	2.99	112	.239	**.297**	**74**	57	97	101	.981	112	148	.7	6.1	**15.0**	.3	-.0
DET	53	11	32	1468¹	1355	8.3	126	609	**1000**	12.3	3.63	99	.247	.327	-28	-7	104	99	**.983**	**106**	156	**1.2**	-.8	6.8	-1.0	3.8
BOS	44	11	35	1443	1424	8.9	136	535	871	12.5	3.80	97	.259	.329	-55	-18	107	100	.981	116	149	.6	-1.9	2.6	.0	2.6
NY	67	15	12	1452	1382	8.6	126	423	707	11.3	3.43	94	.252	.308	4	-33	93	97	.981	125	159	.1	-3.5	6.6	-.6	-1.5
WAS	30	10	26	1418²	1376	8.7	132	554	762	12.5	3.70	89	.258	.333	-37	-62	96	105	.977	141	170	-1.0	-6.7	-5.5	-.1	-3.2
CLE	21	7	32	1440	1352	8.4	154	770	937	13.6	4.28	89	.252	.351	-130	-72	111	99	.981	116	159	.6	-7.7	-15.1	.0	1.1
WEST																										
OAK	57	18	36	1469¹	**1229**	**7.5**	131	501	999	**10.8**	3.05	109	**.228**	.298	67	46	96	97	.981	117	157	.5	4.9	5.9	-.2	9.4
KC	34	15	**44**	1420¹	1301	8.2	**84**	496	775	11.6	3.25	106	.247	.316	33	28	99	98	.979	132	**178**	-.4	3.0	-2.5	**1.8**	2.5
CHI	46	19	32	1450¹	1348	8.4	100	468	976	11.4	3.12	**115**	.247	.309	55	**75**	104	101	.975	160	128	-1.9	**8.1**	1.5	-.9	-8.7
CAL	39	11	32	1481	1246	7.6	101	607	904	11.5	3.10	104	.230	.312	60	23	94	98	.980	131	159	-.2	2.5	-9.3	.7	1.3
MIN	43	9	25	1416²	1384	8.8	139	529	895	12.4	3.81	93	.257	.328	-55	-41	103	100	.980	118	134	.4	-4.4	1.0	-.1	-2.8
MIL	32	**23**	32	1416¹	1303	8.3	130	569	795	12.1	3.38	103	.247	.324	13	14	100	**106**	.977	138	152	-.7	1.5	-8.7	-.1	-3.5
TOT	537	164	360	17291¹		8.3				11.9	3.46		.247	.320					.980	1512	1849					

Runs
Buford-Bal	99
Tovar-Min	94
Murcer-NY	94
Carew-Min	88
Jackson-Oak	87

Hits
Tovar-Min	204
Alomar-Cal	179
Carew-Min	177
Smith-Bos	175
Murcer-NY	175

Doubles
Smith-Bos	33
Schaal-KC	31
Rodriguez-Det	30
Oliva-Min	30

Triples
Patek-KC	11
Carew-Min	10
Blair-Bal	8

Home Runs
Melton-Chi	33
Jackson-Oak	32
Cash-Det	32
Smith-Bos	30

Total Bases
Smith-Bos	302
Jackson-Oak	288
Murcer-NY	287
Melton-Chi	267
Oliva-Min	266

Runs Batted In
Killebrew-Min	119
F.Robinson-Bal	99
Smith-Bos	96
Murcer-NY	94
Bando-Oak	94

Runs Produced
Murcer-NY	163
F.Robinson-Bal	153
Killebrew-Min	152
White-NY	151
Smith-Bos	151

Bases On Balls
Killebrew-Min	114
Yastrzemski-Bos	106
Schaal-KC	103
Petrocelli-Bos	91
Murcer-NY	91

Batting Average
Oliva-Min	.337
Murcer-NY	.331
Rettenmund-Bal	.318
Tovar-Min	.311
Carew-Min	.307

On Base Percentage
Murcer-NY	.429
Rettenmund-Bal	.424
Kaline-Det	.421
Buford-Bal	.415
White-NY	.399

Slugging Average
Oliva-Min	.546
Murcer-NY	.543
Cash-Det	.531
F.Robinson-Bal	.510
Jackson-Oak	.508

Production
Murcer-NY	.972
Oliva-Min	.918
Cash-Det	.905
F.Robinson-Bal	.900
Buford-Bal	.891

Adjusted Production
Murcer-NY	185
White-NY	155
F.Robinson-Bal	154
Buford-Bal	153
Oliva-Min	152

Batter Runs
Murcer-NY	53.7
Rettenmund-Bal	34.8
Buford-Bal	34.5
White-NY	33.7
Oliva-Min	33.6

Adjusted Batter Runs
Murcer-NY	57.6
White-NY	37.7
Rettenmund-Bal	35.3
Buford-Bal	35.0
F.Robinson-Bal	33.5

Clutch Hitting Index
Killebrew-Min	163
Powell-Bal	148
Alou-Oak	133
B.Robinson-Bal	131
F.Robinson-Bal	130

Runs Created
Murcer-NY	126
Smith-Bos	106
Jackson-Oak	103
White-NY	103
Rettenmund-Bal	99

Total Average
Murcer-NY	1.035
Buford-Bal	.970
Cash-Det	.933
F.Robinson-Bal	.905
Rettenmund-Bal	.904

Stolen Bases
Otis-KC	52
Patek-KC	49
Alomar-Cal	39
Campaneris-Oak	34

Stolen Base Average
Harper-Mil	89.3
Otis-KC	86.7
Campaneris-Oak	82.9
Pinson-Cle	80.6
Alomar-Cal	79.6

Stolen Base Runs
Otis-KC	10.8
Patek-KC	6.3
Campaneris-Oak	6.0
Harper-Mil	5.7
Alomar-Cal	5.7

Fielding Runs
Nettles-Cle	42.3
Melton-Chi	27.0
Alomar-Cal	21.4
Cullen-Was	20.5
Otis-KC	19.8

Total Player Rating
Nettles-Cle	5.5
Murcer-NY	5.2
Melton-Chi	5.1
White-NY	4.3
Otis-KC	4.2

Wins
Lolich-Det	25
Blue-Oak	24
Wood-Chi	22
McNally-Bal	21
Hunter-Oak	21

Win Percentage
McNally-Bal	.808
Dobson-Oak	.750
Blue-Oak	.750
Dobson-Bal	.714

Games
Sanders-Mil	83
Scherman-Det	69
Burgmeier-KC	67
Abernathy-KC	63

Complete Games
Lolich-Det	29
Blue-Oak	24
Wood-Chi	22
Cuellar-Bal	21
Palmer-Bal	20

Shutouts
Blue-Oak	8
Wood-Chi	7
Stottlemyre-NY	7
Bradley-Chi	6

Saves
Sanders-Mil	31
Abernathy-KC	23
Scherman-Det	20
Fingers-Oak	17
Burgmeier-KC	17

Innings Pitched
Lolich-Det	376.0
Wood-Chi	334.0
Blue-Oak	312.0
Cuellar-Bal	292.1
Coleman-Det	286.0

Fewest Hits/Game
Blue-Oak	6.03
McDowell-Cle	6.71
May-Cal	6.91
Messersmith-Cal	7.29
Wright-Chi	7.32

Fewest BB/Game
Peterson-NY	1.38
Kline-NY	1.50
Kaat-Min	1.62
Wood-Chi	1.67
Drago-KC	1.72

Strikeouts
Lolich-Det	308
Blue-Oak	301
Coleman-Det	236
Blyleven-Min	224
Wood-Chi	210

Strikeouts/Game
Blue-Oak	8.68
McDowell-Cle	8.05
Johnson-Chi	7.74
Coleman-Det	7.43
Lolich-Det	7.37

Ratio
Blue-Oak	8.68
Wood-Chi	9.19
Kline-NY	9.84
Dobson-Bal	9.98
McNally-Bal	10.07

Earned Run Average
Blue-Oak	1.82
Wood-Chi	1.91
Palmer-Bal	2.68
Hedlund-KC	2.71
Blyleven-Min	2.81

Adjusted ERA
Wood-Chi	188
Blue-Oak	183
Siebert-Bos	127
Hedlund-KC	126
Blyleven-Min	126

Opponents' Batting Avg.
Blue-Oak	.189
McDowell-Cle	.207
May-Cal	.213
Messersmith-Cal	.218
Palmer-Bal	.221

Opponents' On Base Pct.
Blue-Oak	.252
Wood-Chi	.264
Kline-NY	.276
Dobson-Bal	.279
Hunter-Oak	.282

Starter Runs
Wood-Chi	57.5
Blue-Oak	57.0
Palmer-Bal	24.5
Lolich-Det	22.6
Blyleven-Min	20.0

Adjusted Starter Runs
Wood-Chi	62.2
Blue-Oak	52.6
Lolich-Det	28.0
Blyleven-Min	22.8
Palmer-Bal	21.0

Clutch Pitching Index
Drago-KC	119
Krausse-Mil	118
Johnson-Chi	117
Bosman-Was	112
Wood-Chi	112

Relief Runs
Sanders-Mil	23.4
Burgmeier-KC	17.0
Mingori-Cle	12.8
Queen-Cal	12.3
Grzenda-Was	12.0

Adjusted Relief Runs
Sanders-Mil	23.5
Burgmeier-KC	16.7
Mingori-Cle	15.1
Scherman-Det	11.1
Lee-Bos	10.9

Relief Ranking
Sanders-Mil	41.6
Burgmeier-KC	34.4
Scherman-Det	19.4
Abernathy-KC	13.8
Grzenda-Was	11.4

Total Pitcher Index
Wood-Chi	7.0
Blue-Oak	5.4
Siebert-Bos	3.6
Lolich-Det	2.8
Sanders-Mil	2.7

Total Baseball Ranking
Wood-Chi	7.0
Nettles-Cle	5.5
Blue-Oak	5.4
Murcer-NY	5.2
Melton-Chi	5.1

TEAM	G	W	L	PCT	GB	R	OR	AB	H	2B	3B	HR	BB	SO	AVG	OBP	SLG	PRO	PRO+	BR	/A	PF	CHI	RC	SB	CS	SBA	SBR
EAST																												
PIT	155	96	59	.619		691	512	5490	**1505**	251	47	110	404	871	**.274**	.327	**.397**	.724	114	74	87	98	100	**701**	49	30	62	-3
CHI	156	85	70	.548	11	685	567	5247	1346	206	40	133	565	815	.257	.332	.387	.719	100	74	9	111	100	670	69	47	59	-8
NY	156	83	73	.532	13.5	528	578	5135	1154	175	31	105	589	990	.225	.309	.332	.641	91	-68	-52	97	99	530	41	41	50	-12
STL	156	75	81	.481	21.5	568	600	5326	1383	214	42	70	437	793	.260	.319	.355	.674	99	-14	-6	99	99	591	104	48	68	2
MON	156	70	86	.449	26.5	513	609	5156	1205	156	22	91	474	828	.234	.304	.325	.629	84	-92	-102	102	102	513	68	66	51	-19
PHI	156	59	97	.378	37.5	503	635	5248	1240	200	36	98	487	930	.236	.304	.344	.648	88	-65	-80	103	94	545	42	50	46	-17
WEST																												
CIN	154	95	59	.617		707	557	5241	1317	214	44	124	**606**	914	.251	**.333**	.380	.713	**116**	67	**103**	94	104	676	**140**	63	69	4
HOU	153	84	69	.549	10.5	708	636	5267	1359	233	38	134	524	907	.258	.329	.393	.722	114	75	88	98	103	686	111	56	66	0
LA	155	85	70	.548	10.5	584	527	5270	1349	178	39	98	480	786	.256	.321	.360	.681	102	1	16	98	96	610	82	39	68	1
ATL	155	70	84	.455	25	628	649	5278	1363	186	17	144	532	770	.258	.308	.382	.712	100	60	4	109	94	661	47	35	57	-7
SF	155	69	86	.445	26.5	662	649	5245	1281	211	36	**150**	480	964	.244	.311	.384	.695	102	17	9	101	**107**	630	123	45	**73**	10
SD	153	58	95	.379	36.5	488	665	5213	1181	168	38	102	407	976	.227	.284	.332	.616	87	-130	-88	93	106	489	78	46	63	-4
TOT	930					7265		63116	15683	2392	430	1359	5985	10544	.248	.317	.365	.682							954	566	63	-53

TEAM	CG	SH	SV	IP	H	H/G	HR	BB	SO	RAT	ERA	ERA+	OAV	OOB	PR	/A	PF	CPI	FA	E	DP	FW	PW	BW	SBW	DIF
EAST																										
PIT	39	15	48	1414.1	1282	8.2	90	433	838	11.1	2.81	118	.243	.304	102	81	96	**108**	.978	136	171	-.0	8.7	9.4	.2	.3
CHI	54	19	32	1398.2	1329	8.6	112	**421**	824	11.5	3.22	118	.251	.311	37	**92**	110	105	.979	132	148	.2	**9.9**	1.0	-.4	-3.2
NY	32	12	41	1414.2	1263	8.0	118	486	**1059**	11.3	3.26	103	.240	.308	30	15	97	99	.980	116	122	1.1	1.6	-5.6	-.8	8.7
STL	**64**	13	13	1399.2	1290	8.3	87	531	912	11.8	3.42	99	.247	.319	5	-3	99	97	.977	141	146	-.3	-.3	-.6	.7	-2.4
MON	39	11	23	1401.1	1281	8.2	103	579	888	12.1	3.59	99	.245	.323	-21	-6	103	97	.978	134	141	.0	-.6	-11.0	-1.6	5.1
PHI	43	13	15	1400	1318	8.5	117	536	927	12.1	3.66	98	.251	.324	-33	-11	104	99	.981	116	142	1.1	-1.2	-8.6	-1.3	-8.9
WEST																										
CIN	25	15	**60**	1412.2	1313	8.4	129	435	806	11.3	3.21	100	.247	.307	38	0	93	104	**.982**	110	143	**1.3**	.0	11.1	.9	4.7
HOU	38	14	31	1385.1	1340	8.7	114	498	971	12.2	3.77	89	.256	.325	-48	-62	97	98	.980	116	151	.9	-6.7	9.5	.5	3.3
LA	50	**23**	29	1403	**1196**	7.7	83	429	856	10.6	2.78	120	.230	.292	104	85	97	96	.974	162	145	-1.5	9.1	1.7	.6	-2.5
ATL	40	4	27	1377	1412	9.2	155	512	732	12.7	4.27	89	.266	.333	-126	-74	110	97	.974	156	130	-1.1	-8.0	.4	-.3	1.9
SF	44	8	23	1386.1	1309	8.5	130	507	771	12.0	3.69	94	.250	.320	-37	-32	101	98	.974	156	121	-1.1	-3.4	1.0	**1.6**	-6.4
SD	39	17	19	1403.2	1350	8.7	121	618	960	12.9	3.78	87	.255	.337	-50	-76	95	103	.976	144	146	-.6	-8.2	-9.5	.0	-.3
TOT	507	164	361	16796.2		8.4				11.8	3.45		.248	.317					.978	1619	1706					

Runs		Hits		Doubles		Triples		Home Runs		Total Bases	
Morgan-Cin	122	Rose-Cin	198	Montanez-Phi	39	Bowa-Phi	13	Bench-Cin	40	Williams-Chi	348
Bonds-SF	118	Brock-StL	193	Cedeno-Hou	39	Rose-Cin	11	Colbert-SD	38	Cedeno-Hou	300
Wynn-Hou	117	Williams-Chi	191	Simmons-StL	36	Sanguillen-Pit	8	Williams-Chi	37	Bench-Cin	291
Rose-Cin	107	Simmons-StL	180	Williams-Chi	34	Cedeno-Hou	8	Aaron-Atl	34	May-Hou	290
Cedeno-Hou	103	Garr-Atl	180			Brock-StL	8	Stargell-Pit	33	Colbert-SD	286

Runs Batted In		Runs Produced		Bases On Balls		Batting Average		On Base Percentage		Slugging Average	
Bench-Cin	125	Wynn-Hou	183	Morgan-Cin	115	Williams-Chi	.333	Morgan-Cin	.419	Williams-Chi	.606
Williams-Chi	122	Williams-Chi	180	Wynn-Hou	103	Garr-Atl	.325	Williams-Chi	.403	Stargell-Pit	.558
Stargell-Pit	112	Morgan-Cin	179	Bench-Cin	100	Baker-Atl	.321	Santo-Chi	.397	Bench-Cin	.541
Colbert-SD	111	Bonds-SF	172	Aaron-Atl	92	Cedeno-Hou	.320	Aaron-Atl	.391	Cedeno-Hou	.537
May-Hou	98	Bench-Cin	172	Evans-Atl	90	Watson-Hou	.312	Wynn-Hou	.391	Aaron-Atl	.514

Production		Adjusted Production		Batter Runs		Adjusted Batter Runs		Clutch Hitting Index		Runs Created	
Williams-Chi	1.010	Bench-Cin	171	Williams-Chi	61.1	Williams-Chi	54.0	Parker-LA	152	Williams-Chi	137
Stargell-Pit	.935	Stargell-Pit	166	Bench-Cin	44.0	Bench-Cin	47.9	Oliver-Pit	137	Morgan-Cin	117
Bench-Cin	.927	Williams-Chi	166	Cedeno-Hou	42.9	Cedeno-Hou	44.3	Torre-StL	135	Cedeno-Hou	115
Cedeno-Hou	.924	Cedeno-Hou	163	Stargell-Pit	39.6	Morgan-Cin	41.3	Evans-Atl	133	Bench-Cin	110
Aaron-Atl	.906	Hebner-Pit	155	Morgan-Cin	37.2	Stargell-Pit	40.8	Bench-Cin	132	Rose-Cin	109

Total Average		Stolen Bases		Stolen Base Average		Stolen Base Runs		Fielding Runs		Total Player Rating	
Williams-Chi	1.050	Brock-StL	63	Hernandez-SD	88.9	Bonds-SF	9.6	Helms-Hou	26.5	Morgan-Cin	5.3
Morgan-Cin	.973	Morgan-Cin	58	Bonds-SF	88.0	Brock-StL	8.1	Money-Phi	20.3	Cedeno-Hou	4.9
Cedeno-Hou	.959	Cedeno-Hou	55	Davis-LA	87.0	Morgan-Cin	7.2	Rader-Hou	18.0	Bench-Cin	4.9
Stargell-Pit	.958	Bonds-SF	44	Brock-StL	77.8	Hernandez-SD	5.4	Russell-LA	16.5	Williams-Chi	4.3
Aaron-Atl	.945	Tolan-Cin	42	Morgan-Cin	77.3	Davis-LA	4.2	Rose-Cin	12.1	Rose-Cin	3.7

Wins		Win Percentage		Games		Complete Games		Shutouts		Saves	
Carlton-Phi	27	Nolan-Cin	.750	Marshall-Mon	65	Carlton-Phi	30	Sutton-LA	9	Carroll-Cin	37
Seaver-NY	21	Carlton-Phi	.730	Carroll-Cin	65	Jenkins-Chi	23	Carlton-Phi	8	McGraw-NY	27
Osteen-LA	20	Pappas-Chi	.708	Borbon-Cin	62	Gibson-StL	23	Norman-SD	6	Giusti-Pit	22
Jenkins-Chi	20	Blass-Pit	.704	Ross-SD	60	Wise-StL	20	Jenkins-Chi	5	Marshall-Mon	18
		Ellis-Pit	.682			Sutton-LA	18	Dierker-Hou	5		

Innings Pitched		Fewest Hits/Game		Fewest BB/Game		Strikeouts		Strikeouts/Game		Ratio	
Carlton-Phi	346.1	Sutton-LA	6.14	Pappas-Chi	1.34	Carlton-Phi	310	Seaver-NY	8.55	Sutton-LA	8.35
Jenkins-Chi	289.1	Carlton-Phi	6.68	Nolan-Cin	1.53	Seaver-NY	249	Reuss-Hou	8.16	Carlton-Phi	8.97
Niekro-Atl	282.1	Gibson-StL	7.32	Niekro-Atl	1.69	Gibson-StL	208	Koosman-NY	8.12	Nolan-Cin	9.10
Gibson-StL	278.0	Seaver-NY	7.39	Ellis-Pit	1.82	Sutton-LA	207	Carlton-Phi	8.06	McAndrew-NY	9.86
Sutton-LA	272.2	Bryant-SF	7.40	Moose-Pit	1.87	Jenkins-Chi	184	Norman-SD	7.10	Niekro-Atl	9.95

Earned Run Average		Adjusted ERA		Opponents' Batting Avg.		Opponents' On Base Pct.		Starter Runs		Adjusted Starter Runs	
Carlton-Phi	1.97	Carlton-Phi	182	Sutton-LA	.189	Sutton-LA	.240	Carlton-Phi	56.9	Carlton-Phi	62.2
Nolan-Cin	1.99	Nolan-Cin	161	Carlton-Phi	.206	Carlton-Phi	.259	Sutton-LA	41.6	Sutton-LA	38.0
Sutton-LA	2.08	Sutton-LA	160	Gibson-StL	.224	Nolan-Cin	.262	Gibson-StL	30.7	Gibson-StL	29.1
Matlack-NY	2.32	Matlack-NY	145	Seaver-NY	.224	Niekro-Atl	.275	Matlack-NY	30.6	Matlack-NY	28.1
Gibson-StL	2.46	Gibson-StL	138	Bryant-SF	.224	McAndrew-NY	.278	Nolan-Cin	28.5	Hooton-Chi	24.4

Clutch Pitching Index		Relief Runs		Adjusted Relief Runs		Relief Ranking		Total Pitcher Index		Total Baseball Ranking	
Blass-Pit	131	Marshall-Mon	21.5	Marshall-Mon	22.8	Marshall-Mon	46.8	Carlton-Phi	7.8	Carlton-Phi	7.8
Nolan-Cin	115	McGraw-NY	20.7	McGraw-NY	19.6	Brewer-LA	39.8	Gibson-StL	4.3	Morgan-Cin	5.3
Hooton-Chi	115	Brewer-LA	19.1	Brewer-LA	18.0	McGraw-NY	34.5	Sutton-LA	4.2	Cedeno-Hou	4.9
Matlack-NY	115	R.Hernandez-Pit	13.9	R.Hernandez-Pit	12.8	Giusti-Pit	23.0	Osteen-LA	3.2	Bench-Cin	4.9
Downing-LA	115	Carroll-Cin	12.8	Giusti-Pit	11.6	Carroll-Cin	18.5	Matlack-NY	3.2	Williams-Chi	4.3

TEAM	G	W	L	PCT	GB	R	OR	AB	H	2B	3B	HR	BB	SO	AVG	OBP	SLG	PRO	PRO+	BR	/A	PF	CHI	RC	SB	CS	SBA	SBR
EAST																												
DET	156	86	70	.551		558	514	5099	1206	179	32	122	483	793	.237	.306	.356	.662	100	18	1	103	101	549	17	21	45	-8
BOS	155	85	70	.548	0.5	**640**	620	5208	1289	**229**	**34**	124	522	858	.248	.320	**.376**	**.696**	108	**83**	53	106	102	**634**	66	30	**69**	**2**
BAL	154	80	74	.519	5	519	**430**	5028	1153	193	29	100	507	935	.229	.304	.339	.643	96	-12	-26	103	100	523	78	41	66	-1
NY	155	79	76	.510	6.5	557	527	5168	1288	201	24	103	491	**689**	.249	.318	.357	.675	111	45	63	97	95	588	71	42	63	-4
CLE	156	72	84	.462	14	472	519	5207	1220	187	18	91	420	762	.234	.295	.330	.625	89	-54	-72	103	98	495	49	53	48	-17
MIL	156	65	91	.417	21	493	595	5124	1204	167	22	88	472	868	.235	.303	.328	.631	96	-35	-25	98	99	495	64	57	53	-15
WEST																												
OAK	155	93	62	.600		604	457	5200	1248	195	29	**134**	463	886	.240	.308	.366	.674	**113**	37	65	95	104	584	87	48	64	-3
CHI	154	87	67	.565	5.5	566	538	5083	1208	170	28	108	511	991	.238	.311	.346	.657	100	14	3	102	103	550	100	52	66	-1
MIN	154	77	77	.500	15.5	537	535	5234	1277	182	31	93	478	905	.244	.311	.344	.655	96	9	-18	105	97	554	53	41	56	-9
KC	154	76	78	.494	16.5	580	545	5167	1317	220	26	78	**534**	711	**.255**	**.329**	.353	.682	111	65	**68**	100	95	601	85	44	66	-1
CAL	155	75	80	.484	18	454	533	5165	1249	171	26	78	358	850	.242	.294	.330	.624	98	-55	-25	94	97	487	57	37	61	-5
TEX	154	54	100	.351	38.5	461	628	5029	1092	166	17	56	503	926	.217	.292	.290	.582	83	-115	-92	96	111	438	**126**	73	63	-6
TOT	929					6441		61712	14751	2260	316	1175	5742	10174	.239	.308	.343	.651							853	539	61	-68

TEAM	CG	SH	SV	IP	H	H/G	HR	BB	SO	RAT	ERA	ERA+	OAV	OOB	PR	/A	PF	CPI	FA	E	DP	FW	PW	BW	SBW	DIF
EAST																										
DET	46	11	33	1388[1]	1212	7.9	101	465	952	11.2	2.96	106	.236	.306	15	28	103	102	**.984**	**96**	137	**1.9**	3.2	.1	-.3	3.0
BOS	48	20	25	1382[2]	1309	8.5	101	512	918	12.1	3.47	93	.251	.323	-63	-39	105	100	.978	130	141	-.0	-4.4	6.0	**.9**	5.1
BAL	62	20	21	1371[2]	1116	7.3	**85**	395	788	10.0	**2.53**	**121**	.224	**.283**	81	82	100	97	.983	100	150	1.6	**9.3**	-3.0	.5	-5.5
NY	35	19	39	1373[1]	1306	8.6	87	419	625	11.5	3.05	97	.252	.312	2	-15	96	105	.978	134	**179**	-.3	-1.7	7.2	.2	-3.8
CLE	47	13	24	1410	1232	7.9	123	534	846	11.5	2.92	110	.237	.313	23	47	105	**112**	.981	116	157	.8	5.3	-8.2	-1.3	-2.6
MIL	37	14	32	1391[2]	1289	8.3	116	486	740	11.7	3.45	88	.247	.315	-61	-65	99	97	.977	139	145	-.5	-7.4	-2.8	-1.1	-1.2
WEST																										
OAK	42	**23**	**43**	1417[2]	1170	7.4	.96	418	862	10.2	2.58	110	.226	.286	76	42	93	99	.979	130	146	-.0	4.8	7.4	.3	3.1
CHI	36	14	42	1385[1]	1269	8.2	94	431	936	11.2	3.12	100	.245	.307	-9	-1	102	99	.977	135	136	-.4	.1	.3	.5	9.4
MIN	37	17	34	1188[1]	1188	7.6	105	444	838	10.7	2.84	113	.230	.296	35	58	105	99	.974	159	133	-1.8	6.6	-2.0	-.4	-2.4
KC	44	16	29	1381[1]	1293	8.4	85	405	801	11.3	3.24	94	.251	.309	-27	-32	99	97	.981	116	164	.7	-3.6	**7.7**	.5	-6.3
CAL	57	18	16	1377[2]	**1109**	**7.2**	90	620	**1000**	11.5	3.06	95	**.222**	.312	0	-23	95	96	.981	114	135	.8	-2.6	-2.8	.0	2.0
TEX	11	8	34	1374[2]	1258	8.2	92	613	868	12.6	3.53	85	.246	.332	-71	-79	98	99	.972	166	147	-2.2	-9.0	-10.5	-.0	-1.3
TOT	502	193	372	16653[2]		8.0				11.3	3.06		.239	.308					.979	1535	1770					

Runs		Hits		Doubles		Triples		Home Runs		Total Bases	
Murcer-NY	102	Rudi-Oak	181	Piniella-KC	33	Rudi-Oak	9	R.Allen-Chi	37	Murcer-NY	314
Rudi-Oak	94	Piniella-KC	179	Rudi-Oak	32	Fisk-Bos	9	Murcer-NY	33	R.Allen-Chi	305
Harper-Bos	92	Murcer-NY	171	Murcer-NY	30	Blair-Bal	8	Killebrew-Min	26	Rudi-Oak	288
R.Allen-Chi	90	Carew-Min	170	White-NY	29	Murcer-NY	7	Epstein-Oak	26	Mayberry-KC	255
Tovar-Min	86	May-Chi	161	Harper-Bos	29	Kelly-Chi	7			Piniella-KC	253

Runs Batted In		Runs Produced		Bases On Balls		Batting Average		On Base Percentage		Slugging Average	
R.Allen-Chi	113	R.Allen-Chi	166	White-NY	99	Carew-Min	.318	R.Allen-Chi	.422	R.Allen-Chi	.603
Mayberry-KC	100	Murcer-NY	165	R.Allen-Chi	99	Piniella-KC	.312	May-Chi	.408	Fisk-Bos	.538
Murcer-NY	96	Rudi-Oak	150	Killebrew-Min	94	R.Allen-Chi	.308	Mayberry-KC	.396	Murcer-NY	.537
Scott-Mil	88	Mayberry-KC	140	May-Chi	79	May-Chi	.308	White-NY	.385	Mayberry-KC	.507
Powell-Bal	81					Rudi-Oak	.305	Scheinblum-KC	.385	Epstein-Oak	.490

Production		Adjusted Production		Batter Runs		Adjusted Batter Runs		Clutch Hitting Index		Runs Created	
R.Allen-Chi	1.025	R.Allen-Chi	199	R.Allen-Chi	66.1	R.Allen-Chi	64.9	Billings-Tex	149	R.Allen-Chi	131
Fisk-Bos	.909	Murcer-NY	171	Murcer-NY	44.9	Murcer-NY	47.0	Petrocelli-Bos	142	Murcer-NY	114
Mayberry-KC	.903	Mayberry-KC	168	Mayberry-KC	43.0	Mayberry-KC	43.3	Bando-Oak	141	Mayberry-KC	101
Murcer-NY	.900	Epstein-Oak	166	Fisk-Bos	37.1	Epstein-Oak	35.8	Yastrzemski-Bos	141	May-Chi	96
Epstein-Oak	.868	Fisk-Bos	159	May-Chi	36.7	May-Chi	35.5	Rojas-KC	133	Rudi-Oak	95

Total Average		Stolen Bases		Stolen Base Average		Stolen Base Runs		Fielding Runs		Total Player Rating	
R.Allen-Chi	1.121	Campaneris-Oak	52	Baylor-Bal	92.3	Campaneris-Oak	7.2	Patek-KC	29.5	R.Allen-Chi	5.5
Mayberry-KC	.910	Nelson-Tex	51	Patek-KC	82.5	Baylor-Bal	6.0	Rodriguez-Det	24.0	Murcer-NY	5.3
Fisk-Bos	.908	Patek-KC	33	Scott-Mil	80.0	Patek-KC	5.7	Michael-NY	23.7	Fisk-Bos	4.6
Murcer-NY	.888	Kelly-Chi	32	Campaneris-Oak	78.8	Nelson-Tex	5.1	Belanger-Bal	20.8	Patek-KC	3.8
Epstein-Oak	.885	Otis-KC	28	Harper-Bos	78.1	Kelly-Chi	4.2	May-Mil	14.9	White-NY	3.3

Wins		Win Percentage		Games		Complete Games		Shutouts		Saves	
Wood-Chi	24	Hunter-Oak	.750	Lindblad-Tex	66	Perry-Cle	29	Ryan-Cal	9	Lyle-NY	35
Perry-Cle	24	Tiant-Bos	.714	Fingers-Oak	65	Lolich-Det	23	Wood-Chi	8	Forster-Chi	29
Lolich-Det	22	Odom-Oak	.714	Granger-Min	63	Wood-Chi	20	Stottlemyre-NY	7	Fingers-Oak	21
		Palmer-Bal	.677			Ryan-Cal	20			Granger-Min	19
		Kline-NY	.640			Palmer-Bal	18			Sanders-Mil	17

Innings Pitched		Fewest Hits/Game		Fewest BB/Game		Strikeouts		Strikeouts/Game		Ratio	
Wood-Chi	376.2	Ryan-Cal	5.26	Peterson-NY	1.58	Ryan-Cal	329	Ryan-Cal	10.43	Nelson-KC	7.89
Perry-Cle	342.2	Hunter-Oak	6.09	Nelson-KC	1.61	Lolich-Det	250	Messersmith-Cal	7.53	Hunter-Oak	8.32
Lolich-Det	327.1	Nelson-KC	6.23	Kline-NY	1.68	Perry-Cle	234	May-Cal	7.41	Perry-Cle	9.11
Hunter-Oak	295.1	Tiant-Bos	6.44	Holtzman-Oak	1.76	Blyleven-Min	228	Bradley-Chi	7.23	Palmer-Bal	9.51
Blyleven-Min	287.1	Messersmith-Cal	6.63	Wood-Chi	1.77	Coleman-Det	222	Blyleven-Min	7.14	Wood-Chi	9.70

Earned Run Average		Adjusted ERA		Opponents' Batting Avg.		Opponents' On Base Pct.		Starter Runs		Adjusted Starter Runs	
Tiant-Bos	1.91	Tiant-Bos	168	Ryan-Cal	.171	Nelson-KC	.236	Perry-Cle	43.5	Perry-Cle	49.5
Perry-Cle	1.92	Perry-Cle	168	Hunter-Oak	.189	Hunter-Oak	.242	Hunter-Oak	33.4	Palmer-Bal	30.7
Hunter-Oak	2.04	Palmer-Bal	149	Nelson-KC	.196	Perry-Cle	.261	Palmer-Bal	30.3	Hunter-Oak	26.3
Palmer-Bal	2.07	Nelson-KC	146	Tiant-Bos	.202	Palmer-Bal	.269	Ryan-Cal	24.6	Tiant-Bos	25.9
Nelson-KC	2.08	Hunter-Oak	139	Perry-Cle	.205	Tiant-Bos	.277	Wood-Chi	23.1	Wood-Chi	25.8

Clutch Pitching Index		Relief Runs		Adjusted Relief Runs		Relief Ranking		Total Pitcher Index		Total Baseball Ranking	
Paul-Tex	128	Lyle-NY	13.6	Lyle-NY	12.3	Lyle-NY	23.3	Perry-Cle	6.6	Perry-Cle	6.6
Odom-Oak	124	Knowles-Oak	12.3	Bell-Mil	10.8	Forster-Chi	16.0	Palmer-Bal	4.1	R.Allen-Chi	5.5
Wilcox-Cle	119	Bell-Mil	11.0	Knowles-Oak	10.7	Knowles-Oak	12.9	Wood-Chi	3.2	Murcer-NY	5.3
Lonborg-Mil	112	Forster-Chi	9.0	Forster-Chi	9.7	Abernathy-KC	11.0	Hunter-Oak	3.1	Fisk-Bos	4.6
Lolich-Det	111	Abernathy-KC	8.8	Abernathy-KC	8.6	Fingers-Oak	8.5	Tiant-Bos	2.7	Palmer-Bal	4.1

TEAM	G	W	L	PCT	GB	R	OR	AB	H	2B	3B	HR	BB	SO	AVG	OBP	SLG	PRO	PRO+	BR	/A	PF	CHI	RC	SB	CS	SBA	SBR
EAST																												
NY	161	82	79	.509		608	588	5457	1345	198	24	85	540	805	.246	.317	.338	.655	89	-81	-70	98	104	583	27	22	55	-5
STL	162	81	81	.500	1.5	643	603	5478	1418	240	35	75	531	796	.259	.328	.357	.685	96	-24	-22	100	100	635	100	46	68	2
PIT	162	80	82	.494	2.5	704	693	5608	1465	257	44	154	432	842	.261	.317	.405	.722	109	30	47	97	101	697	23	30	43	-11
MON	162	79	83	.488	3.5	668	702	5369	1345	190	23	125	695	777	.251	.341	.364	.705	98	30	6	104	94	672	77	68	53	-18
CHI	161	77	84	.478	5	614	655	5363	1322	201	21	117	575	855	.247	.322	.357	.679	88	-35	-84	107	99	605	65	58	53	-15
PHI	162	71	91	.438	11.5	642	717	5546	1381	218	29	134	476	979	.249	.312	.371	.683	93	-40	-57	103	102	641	51	47	52	-13
WEST																												
CIN	162	99	63	.611		741	621	5505	1398	232	34	137	639	947	.254	.335	.383	.718	**111**	43	79	95	102	724	148	55	73	11
LA	162	95	66	.590	3.5	675	**565**	5604	1473	219	29	110	497	795	.263	.326	.371	.697	104	-5	25	96	100	676	109	50	69	3
SF	162	88	74	.543	11	739	702	5537	1452	212	**52**	161	590	913	.262	.337	.407	.744	108	87	59	104	96	765	112	52	68	2
HOU	162	82	80	.506	17	681	672	5532	1391	216	35	134	469	962	.251	.314	.376	.690	97	-28	-26	100	107	639	92	48	66	-1
ATL	162	76	85	.472	22.5	**799**	774	5631	**1497**	219	34	**206**	608	870	**.266**	**.341**	**.427**	**.768**	111	134	82	108	97	826	84	40	68	1
SD	162	60	102	.370	39	548	770	5457	1330	198	26	112	401	966	.244	.298	.351	.649	92	-110	-57	92	102	566	88	36	71	5
TOT	971						8062		66087	16817	2600	386	1550	6453	10507	.254	.324	.376	.700						976	552	64	-38

TEAM	CG	SH	SV	IP	H	H/G	HR	BB	SO	RAT	ERA	ERA+	OAV	OOB	PR	/A	PF	CPI	FA	E	DP	FW	PW	BW	SBW	DIF
EAST																										
NY	47	15	40	1465	1345	8.3	127	490	**1027**	11.4	3.26	111	.245	.309	65	58	99	101	.980	126	140	1.1	6.0	-7.3	-.2	1.8
STL	42	14	36	1460²	1366	8.4	**105**	486	867	11.6	3.25	112	.248	.312	66	63	100	100	.975	159	149	-.7	6.6	-2.3	.5	-4.1
PIT	26	11	**44**	1450²	1426	8.8	110	564	839	12.6	3.73	94	.258	.331	-12	-35	96	100	.976	151	156	-.3	-3.6	4.9	-.8	-1.2
MON	26	6	38	1451²	1356	8.4	128	681	866	12.8	3.71	103	.250	.337	-9	16	104	103	.974	163	156	-.9	1.7	.6	-1.5	-1.8
CHI	27	13	40	1437²	1471	9.2	128	**438**	885	12.1	3.66	108	.267	.325	1	46	108	104	.975	157	155	-.7	4.8	-8.7	-1.2	2.3
PHI	**49**	11	22	1447¹	1435	8.9	131	632	919	13.1	3.99	95	.263	.343	-53	-31	104	103	.979	134	**179**	.7	-3.2	-5.9	-1.0	-.5
WEST																										
CIN	39	**17**	43	1473	1389	8.5	135	518	801	11.8	3.40	100	.252	.319	42	0	93	**105**	**.982**	115	162	**1.8**	.0	8.2	**1.5**	6.5
LA	45	15	38	1491	**1270**	**7.7**	129	461	961	10.6	**3.00**	115	**.231**	**.294**	109	72	94	97	.981	125	166	1.2	**7.5**	2.6	.6	2.5
SF	33	8	**44**	1452²	1442	8.9	145	485	787	12.1	3.79	101	.257	.320	-21	4	104	97	.974	163	138	-.9	.4	6.1	.5	.8
HOU	45	14	26	1460²	1389	8.6	111	575	907	12.3	3.75	97	.252	.325	-14	-19	99	95	.981	116	140	1.7	-2.0	-2.7	.2	3.7
ATL	34	9	35	1462	1467	9.0	144	575	803	12.7	4.25	93	.263	.335	-95	-51	107	95	.974	166	142	-1.1	-5.3	**8.5**	.4	-7.0
SD	34	10	23	1430	1461	9.2	157	548	845	12.8	4.16	83	.267	.336	-79	-110	95	100	.973	170	152	-1.3	-11.5	-5.9	.9	-3.1
TOT	447	143	429	17482		8.7				12.2	3.66		.254	.324					.977	1745	1835					

Runs
Bonds-SF 131
Morgan-Cin 116
Rose-Cin 115
Evans-Atl 114
Brock-StL 110

Hits
Rose-Cin 230
Garr-Atl 200
Brock-StL 193
Simmons-StL 192
Oliver-Pit 191

Doubles
Stargell-Pit 43
Oliver-Pit 38
Staub-NY 36
Simmons-StL 36
Rose-Cin 36

Triples
Metzger-Hou 14
Matthews-SF 10
Maddox-SF 10
Davis-LA 9

Home Runs
Stargell-Pit 44
Johnson-Atl 43
Evans-Atl 41
Aaron-Atl 40
Bonds-SF 39

Total Bases
Bonds-SF 341
Stargell-Pit 337
Evans-Atl 331
Johnson-Atl 305
Oliver-Pit 303

Runs Batted In
Stargell-Pit 119
May-Hou 105
Evans-Atl 104
Bench-Cin 104
Singleton-Mon 103

Runs Produced
Bonds-SF 188
Stargell-Pit 181
Singleton-Mon 180
Baker-Atl 179
Evans-Atl 177

Bases On Balls
Evans-Atl 124
Singleton-Mon 123
Morgan-Cin 111
McCovey-SF 105
Monday-Chi 92

Batting Average
Rose-Cin 338
Cedeno-Hou 320
Maddox-SF 319
Perez-Cin 314
Watson-Hou 312

On Base Percentage
Singleton-Mon 429
Fairly-Mon 422
Morgan-Cin 408
Evans-Atl 407
Watson-Hou 405

Slugging Average
Stargell-Pit 646
Evans-Atl 556
Johnson-Atl 546
Cedeno-Hou 537
Bonds-SF 530

Production
Stargell-Pit 1.041
Evans-Atl .... .964
Perez-Cin .... .923
Johnson-Atl ..... .917
Cedeno-Hou ..... .914

Adjusted Production
Stargell-Pit 189
Perez-Cin 162
Morgan-Cin 157
Evans-Atl 153
Cedeno-Hou 151

Batter Runs
Stargell-Pit 57.8
Evans-Atl 54.8
Aaron-Atl 45.5
Singleton-Mon 44.8
Morgan-Cin 41.6

Adjusted Batter Runs
Stargell-Pit 59.5
Evans-Atl 48.8
Morgan-Cin 45.5
Perez-Cin 44.9
Singleton-Mon 42.1

Clutch Hitting Index
Bench-Cin 141
Cey-LA 137
Watson-Hou 131
Singleton-Mon 130
Speier-SF 129

Runs Created
Evans-Atl 143
Stargell-Pit 136
Bonds-SF 130
Morgan-Cin 128
Rose-Cin 119

Total Average
Stargell-Pit 1.129
Evans-Atl 1.048
Morgan-Cin 1.034
Cedeno-Hou .... .949
Johnson-Atl .... .947

Stolen Bases
Brock-StL 70
Morgan-Cin 67
Cedeno-Hou 56
Bonds-SF 43
Lopes-LA 36

Stolen Base Average
Baker-Atl 88.9
Morgan-Cin 81.7
Concepcion-Cin .. 81.5
Cedeno-Hou 78.9
Brock-StL 77.8

Stolen Base Runs
Morgan-Cin 11.1
Brock-StL 9.0
Cedeno-Hou 7.8
Baker-Atl 5.4
Garr-Atl 3.9

Fielding Runs
Schmidt-Phi 21.2
Kessinger-Chi 17.0
Cey-LA 16.2
Menke-Cin 16.2
Unser-Phi 11.9

Total Player Rating
Morgan-Cin 5.9
Evans-Atl 5.6
Stargell-Pit 5.5
Cedeno-Hou 4.7
Bonds-SF 4.2

Wins
Bryant-SF 24
Seaver-NY 19
Billingham-Cin 19
Sutton-LA 18
Gullett-Cin 18

Win Percentage
John-LA 696
Gullett-Cin 692
Bryant-SF 667
Seaver-NY 655
Billingham-Cin 655

Games
Marshall-Mon 92
Borbon-Cin 80
Sosa-SF 71
Giusti-Pit 67
Segui-StL 65

Complete Games
Seaver-NY 18
Carlton-Phi........ 18
Billingham-Cin 16

Shutouts
Billingham-Cin 7
Roberts-Hou 6
Wise-StL 5
Twitchell-Phi 5

Saves
Marshall-Mon 31
McGraw-NY 25
Giusti-Pit 20
Brewer-LA 20

Innings Pitched
Carlton-Phi...... 293.1
Billingham-Cin ... 293.1
Seaver-NY 290.0
Reuss-Hou 279.1
Jenkins-Chi 271.0

Fewest Hits/Game
Seaver-NY 6.80
Sutton-LA 6.88
Twitchell-Phi 6.93
Wilson-Hou 7.03
Messersmith-LA .. 7.07

Fewest BB/Game
Marichal-SF 1.61
Jenkins-Chi 1.89
Barr-SF 1.91
Sutton-LA 1.97
Seaver-NY 1.99

Strikeouts
Seaver-NY 251
Carlton-Phi....... 223
Matlack-NY 205
Sutton-LA 200

Strikeouts/Game
Seaver-NY 7.79
Moore-Mon 7.71
Matlack-NY 7.62
Sutton-LA 7.02
Carlton-Phi....... 6.84

Ratio
Seaver-NY 8.91
Sutton-LA 9.02
Messersmith-LA . 10.06
Gibson-StL 10.11
Rooker-Pit 10.41

Earned Run Average
Seaver-NY 2.08
Sutton-LA 2.42
Twitchell-Phi 2.50
Marshall-Mon 2.66
Messersmith-LA .. 2.70

Adjusted ERA
Seaver-NY 174
Twitchell-Phi 152
Marshall-Mon 143
Sutton-LA 142
Renko-Mon 136

Opponents' Batting Avg.
Seaver-NY 206
Sutton-LA 209
Wilson-Hou 213
Messersmith-LA ..214
Renko-Mon 218

Opponents' On Base Pct.
Seaver-NY 254
Sutton-LA 258
Messersmith-LA ..279
Gibson-StL 284
Briles-Pit 288

Starter Runs
Seaver-NY 51.0
Sutton-LA 35.3
Rogers-Mon 31.5
Twitchell-Phi 28.8
Messersmith-LA .. 26.6

Adjusted Starter Runs
Seaver-NY 49.5
Rogers-Mon 33.8
Twitchell-Phi..... 32.2
Sutton-LA 28.9
Renko-Mon 27.8

Clutch Pitching Index
Marshall-Mon 134
Roberts-Hou 122
Twitchell-Phi 121
Grimsley-Cin 116
Moose-Pit 113

Relief Runs
Borbon-Cin 20.2
Marshall-Mon 19.8
Giusti-Pit 14.1
Moffitt-SF 13.8
Locker-Chi 13.3

Adjusted Relief Runs
Marshall-Mon 22.9
Borbon-Cin 16.8
Locker-Chi 16.6
Moffitt-SF 15.6
Giusti-Pit 12.6

Relief Ranking
Marshall-Mon 37.7
Locker-Chi 28.8
Borbon-Cin 23.1
Giusti-Pit 18.3
Scarce-Phi 16.5

Total Pitcher Index
Seaver-NY 6.0
Rogers-Mon 4.1
Renko-Mon 3.8
Sutton-LA 2.9
Marshall-Mon 2.9

Total Baseball Ranking
Seaver-NY 6.0
Morgan-Cin 5.9
Evans-Atl 5.6
Stargell-Pit 5.5
Cedeno-Hou 4.7

TEAM	G	W	L	PCT	GB	R	OR	AB	H	2B	3B	HR	BB	SO	AVG	OBP	SLG	PRO	PRO+	BR	/A	PF	CHI	RC	SB	CS	SBA	SBR
EAST																												
BAL	162	97	65	.599		754	**561**	5537	1474	229	**48**	119	**648**	752	.266	**.348**	.389	.737	108	**61**	**67**	99	98	**765**	**146**	64	70	5
BOS	162	89	73	.549	8	738	647	5513	1472	235	30	147	581	799	.267	.340	**.401**	**.741**	102	58	17	106	98	751	114	45	**72**	**7**
DET	162	85	77	.525	12	642	674	5508	1400	213	32	157	509	722	.254	.322	.390	.712	94	-9	-54	107	95	674	28	30	48	-10
NY	162	80	82	.494	17	641	610	5492	1435	212	17	131	489	**680**	.261	.324	.378	.702	101	-25	-1	97	98	655	47	43	52	-12
MIL	162	74	88	.457	23	708	731	5526	1399	229	40	145	563	977	.253	.327	.388	.715	103	2	17	98	101	702	110	66	63	-7
CLE	162	71	91	.438	26	680	826	5592	1429	205	29	**158**	471	793	.256	.317	.387	.704	95	-27	-39	102	103	666	60	68	47	-23
WEST																												
OAK	162	94	68	.580		**758**	615	5507	1431	216	28	147	595	919	.260	.336	.389	.725	**110**	28	64	95	**104**	730	128	57	69	4
KC	162	88	74	.543	6	755	752	5508	1440	239	40	114	644	696	.261	.342	.381	.723	96	31	-23	108	103	720	105	69	60	-10
MIN	162	81	81	.500	13	738	692	5625	**1521**	**240**	44	120	598	954	**.270**	.344	.393	.737	103	56	28	104	97	756	87	46	65	-2
CAL	162	79	83	.488	15	629	657	5505	1395	183	29	93	509	816	.253	.320	.348	.668	95	-84	-31	92	**104**	609	59	47	56	-11
CHI	162	77	85	.475	17	652	705	5475	1400	228	38	111	537	952	.256	.326	.372	.698	93	-28	-51	103	99	647	83	73	53	-19
TEX	162	57	105	.352	37	619	844	5488	1397	195	29	110	503	791	.255	.320	.361	.681	95	-63	-34	96	100	629	91	53	63	-5
TOT	972					8314		66276	17193	2624	404	1552	6647	9851	.259	.331	.381	.712							1058	661	62	-79

TEAM	CG	SH	SV	IP	H	H/G	HR	BB	SO	RAT	ERA	ERA+	OAV	OOB	PR	/A	PF	CPI	FA	E	DP	FW	PW	BW	SBW	DIF
EAST																										
BAL	67	14	26	1461^2	**1297**	**8.0**	124	475	715	**11.0**	**3.07**	**122**	**.240**	**.303**	**122**	**108**	98	102	.981	119	184	1.3	**11.0**	**6.9**	1.2	-4.4
BOS	67	10	33	1440^1	1417	8.9	158	499	808	12.2	3.65	110	.259	.325	27	59	105	**106**	.979	127	162	.8	6.0	1.7	**1.4**	-2.0
DET	39	11	**46**	1447^2	1468	9.1	154	493	911	12.4	3.90	105	.265	.328	-13	30	107	101	**.982**	**112**	144	**1.7**	3.1	-5.5	-.3	5.1
NY	47	16	39	1427^2	1379	8.7	109	**457**	708	11.7	3.34	110	.254	.315	75	51	96	102	.976	156	172	-.8	5.2	-.1	-.6	-4.8
MIL	50	11	28	1454	1476	9.1	119	623	671	13.2	3.98	94	.265	.342	-27	-36	99	101	.977	145	167	-.2	-3.7	1.7	-.0	-4.8
CLE	55	9	21	1464^2	1532	9.4	172	602	883	13.4	4.58	85	.271	.345	-125	-108	103	96	.978	139	174	.2	-11.0	-4.0	-1.7	6.6
WEST																										
OAK	46	16	41	1457^1	1311	8.1	143	494	797	11.3	3.29	108	.241	.308	86	42	93	100	.978	137	170	.3	4.3	6.5	1.1	.8
KC	40	7	41	1449^1	1521	9.4	114	617	790	13.5	4.19	98	.273	.349	-60	-13	108	100	.974	167	**192**	-1.4	-1.3	-2.4	-.3	12.4
MIN	48	**18**	34	1451^2	1443	8.9	115	519	879	12.4	3.77	105	.259	.327	7	30	104	97	.978	139	147	.2	3.1	2.9	.5	-6.6
CAL	**72**	13	19	1456^1	1351	8.3	**104**	614	**1010**	12.4	3.53	100	.246	.326	46	3	93	98	.975	156	153	-.8	.3	-3.2	-.5	2.1
CHI	48	15	35	1456	1484	9.2	110	574	848	13.0	3.86	102	.266	.338	-8	15	104	101	.977	144	165	-.1	1.5	-5.2	-1.3	1.1
TEX	35	10	27	1430	1514	9.5	130	680	831	14.1	4.64	80	.273	.357	-131	-146	98	96	.974	161	164	-1.1	-14.9	-3.5	.2	-4.7
TOT	614	150	390	17396^2		8.9				12.5	3.82		.259	.331					.977	1702	1994					

Runs		Hits		Doubles		Triples		Home Runs		Total Bases	
Jackson-Oak	99	Carew-Min	203	Garcia-Mil	32	Carew-Min	11	Jackson-Oak	32	Scott-Mil	295
Scott-Mil	98	May-Mil	189	Bando-Oak	32	Bumbry-Bal	11	Robinson-Cal	30	May-Mil	295
North-Oak	98	Murcer-NY	187	Scott-Mil	30	Orta-Chi	10	Burroughs-Tex	30	Bando-Oak	295
Carew-Min	98	Scott-Mil	185	Chambliss-Cle	30	Coggins-Bal	9	Bando-Oak	29	Murcer-NY	286
Bando-Oak	97	Johnson-Tex	179	Carew-Min	30	Coluccio-Mil	8			Jackson-Oak	286

Runs Batted In		Runs Produced		Bases On Balls		Batting Average		On Base Percentage		Slugging Average	
Jackson-Oak	117	Jackson-Oak	184	Mayberry-KC	122	Carew-Min	.350	Mayberry-KC	.420	Jackson-Oak	.531
Scott-Mil	107	Scott-Mil	181	Grich-Bal	107	Scott-Mil	.306	Carew-Min	.415	Bando-Oak	.498
Mayberry-KC	100	Bando-Oak	166	Yastrzemski-Bos	105	Davis-Bal	.306	Yastrzemski-Bos	.411	Robinson-Cal	.489
Bando-Oak	98	May-Mil	164	Tenace-Oak	101	Murcer-NY	.304	Tenace-Oak	.391	Scott-Mil	.488
Robinson-Cal	97	Mayberry-KC	161	Briggs-Mil	87	May-Mil	.303	Jackson-Oak	.387	Munson-NY	.487

Production		Adjusted Production		Batter Runs		Adjusted Batter Runs		Clutch Hitting Index		Runs Created	
Jackson-Oak	.918	Jackson-Oak	165	Mayberry-KC	41.0	Jackson-Oak	44.2	Davis-Bal	156	Bando-Oak	113
Mayberry-KC	.898	Robinson-Cal	153	Jackson-Oak	40.5	Bando-Oak	39.5	May-Chi	139	Carew-Min	113
Carew-Min	.885	Bando-Oak	153	Carew-Min	38.9	Carew-Min	36.0	Darwin-Min	137	Mayberry-KC	113
Bando-Oak	.876	Scott-Mil	144	Yastrzemski-Bos	36.8	Robinson-Cal	35.6	Oliva-Min	136	Jackson-Oak	112
Yastrzemski-Bos	.874	Carew-Min	143	Bando-Oak	35.5	Mayberry-KC	35.6	Robinson-Bal	134	Scott-Mil	106

Total Average		Stolen Bases		Stolen Base Average		Stolen Base Runs		Fielding Runs		Total Player Rating	
Mayberry-KC	.995	Harper-Bos	54	Rojas-KC	81.8	Harper-Bos	7.8	Patek-KC	35.3	Carew-Min	5.5
Jackson-Oak	.953	North-Oak	53	Money-Mil	81.5	Campaneris-Oak	4.2	Nettles-NY	26.0	Grich-Bal	4.6
Carew-Min	.885	Nelson-Tex	43	Harper-Bos	79.4	Baylor-Bal	4.2	Bell-Cle	24.3	Jackson-Oak	4.4
Yastrzemski-Bos	.879	Carew-Min	41	Baylor-Bal	78.0	North-Oak	3.9	North-Oak	23.6	Robinson-Cal	3.8
Bando-Oak	.876	Patek-KC	36	Campaneris-Oak	77.3	Money-Mil	3.6	Grich-Bal	21.0	Munson-NY	3.7

Wins		Win Percentage		Games		Complete Games		Shutouts		Saves	
Wood-Chi	24	Hunter-Oak	.808	Hiller-Det	65	Perry-Cle	29	Blyleven-Min	9	Hiller-Det	38
Coleman-Det	23	Palmer-Bal	.710	Fingers-Oak	62	Ryan-Cal	26	Perry-Cle	7	Lyle-NY	27
Palmer-Bal	22	Blue-Oak	.690	Bird-KC	54	Blyleven-Min	25	Palmer-Bal	6	Fingers-Oak	22
		Splittorff-KC	.645	Knowles-Oak	52	Tiant-Bos	23			Bird-KC	20
		Colborn-Mil	.625			Colborn-Mil	22			Acosta-Chi	18

Innings Pitched		Fewest Hits/Game		Fewest BB/Game		Strikeouts		Strikeouts/Game		Ratio	
Wood-Chi	359.1	Bibby-Tex	6.04	Kaat-Min-Chi	1.73	Ryan-Cal	383	Ryan-Cal	10.57	Tiant-Bos	9.99
Perry-Cle	344.0	Ryan-Cal	6.57	Blyleven-Min	1.86	Blyleven-Min	258	Bibby-Tex	7.74	Hunter-Oak	10.25
Ryan-Cal	326.0	Palmer-Bal	6.83	Holtzman-Oak	2.00	Singer-Cal	241	Blyleven-Min	7.14	Blyleven-Min	10.30
Blyleven-Min	325.0	Tiant-Bos	7.18	Wood-Chi	2.28	Perry-Cle	238	Stone-Chi	7.04	Palmer-Bal	10.36
Singer-Cal	315.2	Blue-Oak	7.30	Lolich-Det	2.30	Lolich-Det	214	Singer-Cal	6.87	Holtzman-Oak	10.44

Earned Run Average		Adjusted ERA		Opponents' Batting Avg.		Opponents' On Base Pct.		Starter Runs		Adjusted Starter Runs	
Palmer-Bal	2.40	Blyleven-Min	157	Bibby-Tex	.192	Tiant-Bos	.281	Blyleven-Min	46.8	Blyleven-Min	51.9
Blyleven-Min	2.52	Palmer-Bal	156	Ryan-Cal	.203	Hunter-Oak	.284	Palmer-Bal	46.6	Palmer-Bal	43.9
Lee-Bos	2.75	Lee-Bos	146	Palmer-Bal	.211	Blyleven-Min	.287	Ryan-Cal	34.2	Lee-Bos	40.1
Ryan-Cal	2.87	Medich-NY	124	Tiant-Bos	.219	Holtzman-Oak	.287	Lee-Bos	33.7	Ryan-Cal	24.4
Medich-NY	2.95	Ryan-Cal	123	Blue-Oak	.224	Palmer-Bal	.289	Holtzman-Oak	28.1	Perry-Cle	20.8

Clutch Pitching Index		Relief Runs		Adjusted Relief Runs		Relief Ranking		Total Pitcher Index		Total Baseball Ranking	
Lee-Bos	119	Hiller-Det	33.1	Hiller-Det	36.9	Hiller-Det	64.9	Blyleven-Min	5.6	Blyleven-Min	5.6
Forster-Chi	116	Fingers-Oak	26.7	Fingers-Oak	22.9	Acosta-Chi	35.5	Palmer-Bal	4.7	Carew-Min	5.5
Curtis-Bos	113	Reynolds-Bal	23.1	Reynolds-Bal	22.0	Fingers-Oak	33.3	Lee-Bos	4.5	Palmer-Bal	4.7
Drago-KC	112	Acosta-Chi	17.1	Acosta-Chi	18.6	Reynolds-Bal	25.5	Hiller-Det	3.6	Grich-Bal	4.6
Bahnsen-Chi	112	Jackson-Bal	17.1	Jackson-Bal	16.3	Lyle-NY	23.8	Ryan-Cal	2.8	Lee-Bos	4.5

2072 1974 National League

TEAM	G	W	L	PCT	GB	R	OR	AB	H	2B	3B	HR	BB	SO	AVG	OBP	SLG	PRO	PRO+	BR	/A	PF	CHI	RC	SB	CS	SBA	SBR
EAST																												
PIT	162	88	74	.543		751	657	5702	**1560**	238	46	114	514	828	**.274**	.338	.391	.729	114	66	91	96	100	745	55	31	64	-2
STL	161	86	75	.534	1.5	677	643	5620	1492	216	46	83	531	752	.265	.334	.365	.699	102	9	15	99	98	687	**172**	62	74	**14**
PHI	162	80	82	.494	8	676	701	5494	1434	233	**50**	95	469	822	.261	.322	.373	.695	96	-7	-34	104	**104**	658	115	58	66	0
MON	161	79	82	.491	8.5	662	657	5343	1355	201	29	86	652	812	.254	.338	.350	.688	93	2	-35	106	99	657	124	49	72	8
NY	162	71	91	.438	17	572	646	5468	1286	183	22	96	597	**735**	.235	.314	.329	.643	86	-99	-88	98	100	571	43	23	65	-1
CHI	162	66	96	.407	22	669	826	5574	1397	221	42	110	621	857	.251	.329	.365	.694	96	-1	-29	104	98	668	78	73	52	-20
WEST																												
LA	162	102	60	.630		**798**	**561**	5557	1511	231	34	**139**	597	820	.272	**.346**	**.401**	**.747**	**120**	**103**	**131**	96	102	774	149	75	67	0
CIN	163	98	64	.605	4	776	631	5535	1437	**271**	35	135	**693**	940	.260	.345	.394	.739	115	95	105	99	99	**776**	146	49	**75**	**14**
ATL	163	88	74	.543	14	661	563	5533	1375	202	37	120	571	772	.249	.321	.363	.684	93	-23	-52	104	101	649	72	44	62	-5
HOU	162	81	81	.500	21	653	632	5489	1441	222	41	110	471	864	.263	.324	.378	.702	107	6	34	96	98	663	108	65	62	-7
SF	162	72	90	.444	30	634	723	5482	1380	228	38	93	548	869	.252	.323	.358	.681	92	-28	-59	105	100	642	107	51	68	2
SD	162	60	102	.370	42	541	830	5415	1239	196	27	99	564	900	.229	.304	.330	.634	87	-122	-94	96	101	555	85	45	65	-2
TOT	972					8070		66212	16907	2642	447	1280	6828	9971	.255	.328	.367	.695							1254	625	67	1

TEAM	CG	SH	SV	IP	H	H/G	HR	BB	SO	RAT	ERA	ERA+	OAV	OOB	PR	/A	PF	CPI	FA	E	DP	FW	PW	BW	SBW	DIF
EAST																										
PIT	**51**	9	17	1466	1428	8.8	93	543	721	12.3	3.49	99	.256	.326	21	-7	95	100	.975	162	154	-.5	-.7	9.5	-.2	-1.1
STL	37	13	20	1473^1	1399	8.5	97	616	794	12.5	3.48	103	.254	.331	22	15	99	**104**	.977	147	**192**	.4	1.6	1.6	**1.4**	.6
PHI	46	4	19	1447^1	1394	8.7	111	682	892	13.1	3.91	97	.257	.343	-47	-22	104	101	.976	148	168	.4	-2.3	-3.5	-.0	4.5
MON	35	8	**27**	1429	1340	8.4	99	544	822	12.0	3.60	107	.249	.321	3	38	106	94	.976	153	157	.0	4.0	-3.6	.8	-2.6
NY	46	15	14	1470^1	1433	8.8	99	504	908	12.0	3.42	104	.257	.322	33	24	99	102	.975	158	150	-.2	2.5	-9.2	-.1	-3.0
CHI	23	6	26	1466^1	1593	9.8	122	576	895	13.6	4.28	89	.277	.347	-108	-76	105	100	.969	199	141	-2.6	-7.9	-3.0	-2.1	.7
WEST																										
LA	33	19	23	1465^1	**1272**	**7.8**	112	**464**	**943**	**10.8**	**2.97**	114	**.233**	**.296**	**105**	70	94	96	.975	157	122	-.2	7.3	**13.6**	-.0	.3
CIN	34	11	**27**	1466^1	1364	8.4	126	536	875	11.8	3.41	102	.247	.316	33	12	96	100	.979	134	151	1.2	1.2	10.9	**1.4**	2.1
ATL	46	**21**	22	1474^1	1343	8.2	97	488	772	11.3	3.05	**124**	.244	.309	93	**119**	104	102	.979	132	161	1.3	**12.4**	-5.4	-.5	-.8
HOU	36	18	18	1450^2	1396	8.7	**84**	601	738	12.6	3.46	100	.255	.333	25	0	96	**104**	**.982**	**113**	161	**2.4**	.0	3.5	-.7	-5.2
SF	27	11	25	1439	1409	8.8	116	559	756	12.5	3.78	101	.257	.328	-26	3	105	97	.972	175	153	-1.2	.3	-6.1	.2	-2.1
SD	25	7	19	1445^2	1536	9.6	124	715	855	14.3	4.58	78	.275	.362	-155	-165	98	99	.973	170	126	-.9	-17.2	-9.8	-.2	7.1
TOT	439	142	257	17493^2		8.7				12.4	3.62		.255	.328					.976	1848	1836					

Runs	Hits	Doubles	Triples	Home Runs	Total Bases
Rose-Cin 110	Garr-Atl 214	Rose-Cin 45	Garr-Atl 17	Schmidt-Phi 36	Bench-Cin 315
Schmidt-Phi 108	Cash-Phi 206	Oliver-Pit 38	Oliver-Pit 12	Bench-Cin 33	Schmidt-Phi 310
Bench-Cin 108	Garvey-LA 200	Bench-Cin 38	Cash-Phi 11	Wynn-LA 32	Garr-Atl 305
Morgan-Cin 107	Oliver-Pit 198	Stargell-Pit 37	Metzger-Hou 10	Perez-Cin 28	Garvey-LA 301
Brock-StL 105	Stennett-Pit 196		Bowa-Phi 10	Cedeno-Hou 26	Oliver-Pit 293

Runs Batted In	Runs Produced	Bases On Balls	Batting Average	On Base Percentage	Slugging Average
Bench-Cin 129	Bench-Cin 204	Evans-Atl 126	Garr-Atl 353	Morgan-Cin 430	Schmidt-Phi 546
Schmidt-Phi 116	Schmidt-Phi 188	Morgan-Cin 120	Oliver-Pit 321	Stargell-Pit 409	Stargell-Pit 537
Garvey-LA 111	Garvey-LA 185	Wynn-LA 108	Gross-Hou 314	Bailey-Mon 400	Smith-StL 528
Wynn-LA 108	Wynn-LA 180	Schmidt-Phi 106	Buckner-LA 314	Schmidt-Phi 398	Bench-Cin 507
Simmons-StL 103	Cedeno-Hou 171	Rose-Cin 106	Madlock-Chi 313	Smith-StL 394	Garr-Atl 503

Production	Adjusted Production	Batter Runs	Adjusted Batter Runs	Clutch Hitting Index	Runs Created
Stargell-Pit 947	Stargell-Pit 169	Schmidt-Phi 48.3	Stargell-Pit 46.8	Cey-LA 140	Schmidt-Phi 130
Schmidt-Phi 944	Morgan-Cin 160	Morgan-Cin 45.2	Morgan-Cin 46.2	Singleton-Mon 133	Morgan-Cin 125
Morgan-Cin 924	Smith-StL 158	Stargell-Pit 44.4	Schmidt-Phi 45.3	Montanez-Phi 131	Stargell-Pit 115
Smith-StL 922	Schmidt-Phi 156	Smith-StL 38.5	Wynn-LA 39.3	Zisk-Pit 129	Bench-Cin 114
Wynn-LA 891	Wynn-LA 154	Wynn-LA 36.4	Smith-StL 39.1	Simmons-StL 128	Garr-Atl 113

Total Average	Stolen Bases	Stolen Base Average	Stolen Base Runs	Fielding Runs	Total Player Rating
Morgan-Cin 1.108	Brock-StL 118	Lintz-Mon 87.7	Brock-StL 15.6	Cash-Phi 29.1	Schmidt-Phi 7.1
Schmidt-Phi 1.017	Lopes-LA 59	Concepcion-Cin .. 87.2	Lintz-Mon 10.8	Schmidt-Phi 26.3	Morgan-Cin 5.1
Stargell-Pit 997	Morgan-Cin 58	Morgan-Cin 82.9	Morgan-Cin 10.2	Foli-Mon 19.4	Concepcion-Cin ... 4.3
Smith-StL 920	Cedeno-Hou 57	Bonds-SF 78.8	Concepcion-Cin ... 8.7	Milbourne-Hou ... 17.9	Cash-Phi 4.0
Wynn-LA 915	Lintz-Mon 50	Hernandez-SD 78.7		Cey-LA 17.2	Smith-StL 3.9

Wins	Win Percentage	Games	Complete Games	Shutouts	Saves
P.Niekro-Atl 20	Messersmith-LA ...769	Marshall-LA 106	P.Niekro-Atl 18	Matlack-NY 7	Marshall-LA 21
Messersmith-LA ... 20	Sutton-LA 679	Hardy-SD 76	Carlton-Phi 17	P.Niekro-Atl 6	Moffitt-SF 15
Sutton-LA 19	Capra-Atl 667	Borbon-Cin 73	Lonborg-Phi 16		Borbon-Cin 14
Billingham-Cin 19	Torrez-Mon 652	Forsch-Hou 70	Rooker-Pit 15		Giusti-Pit 12
	Billingham-Cin 633	Sosa-SF 68			

Innings Pitched	Fewest Hits/Game	Fewest BB/Game	Strikeouts	Strikeouts/Game	Ratio
P.Niekro-Atl 302.1	Capra-Atl 6.76	Barr-SF 1.76	Carlton-Phi 240	Seaver-NY 7.67	Messersmith-LA .. 9.97
Messersmith-LA . 292.1	Messersmith-LA .. 6.99	Reed-Atl 1.98	Messersmith-LA .. 221	Carlton-Phi 7.42	P.Niekro-Atl 10.21
Carlton-Phi 291.0	P.Niekro-Atl 7.41	Ellis-Pit 2.09	Seaver-NY 201	Bonham-Chi 7.08	Barr-SF 10.21
Lonborg-Phi 283.0	Gullett-Cin 7.44	Lonborg-Phi 2.23	P.Niekro-Atl 195	D'Acquisto-SF 6.99	Matlack-NY 10.24
Sutton-LA 276.0	Wilson-Hou 7.48	Marshall-LA 2.42	Matlack-NY 195	Norman-Cin 6.81	Reed-Atl 10.35

Earned Run Average	Adjusted ERA	Opponents' Batting Avg.	Opponents' On Base Pct.	Starter Runs	Adjusted Starter Runs
Capra-Atl 2.28	Capra-Atl 166	Capra-Atl 208	Messersmith-LA ...278	P.Niekro-Atl 41.5	P.Niekro-Atl 46.9
P.Niekro-Atl 2.38	P.Niekro-Atl 159	Messersmith-LA ..212	Matlack-NY 285	Matlack-NY 35.6	Capra-Atl 36.1
Matlack-NY 2.41	Matlack-NY 148	Gullett-Cin 222	P.Niekro-Atl 286	Messersmith-LA .. 33.5	Matlack-NY 34.0
Marshall-LA 2.42	Marshall-LA 141	P.Niekro-Atl 225	Reed-Atl 286	Capra-Atl 32.2	Barr-SF 28.1
Messersmith-LA .. 2.59	Barr-SF 139	Matlack-NY 226	Capra-Atl 287	Rooker-Pit 24.6	Messersmith-LA .. 26.4

Clutch Pitching Index	Relief Runs	Adjusted Relief Runs	Relief Ranking	Total Pitcher Index	Total Baseball Ranking
Caldwell-SF 117	Marshall-LA 27.7	Marshall-LA 22.7	Marshall-LA 31.6	P.Niekro-Atl 5.3	Schmidt-Phi 7.1
Morton-Atl 117	Murray-Mon 20.0	Murray-Mon 21.7	C.Carroll-Cin 24.8	Messersmith-LA ... 3.9	P.Niekro-Atl 5.3
Marshall-LA 116	House-Atl 19.3	House-Atl 21.1	House-Atl 19.9	Capra-Atl 3.7	Morgan-Cin 5.1
Schueler-Phi 113	Taylor-Mon 17.3	Taylor-Mon 19.9	Taylor-Mon 17.9	Barr-SF 3.7	Concepcion-Cin ... 4.3
McGlothen-StL ... 112	C.Carroll-Cin 16.5	C.Carroll-Cin 15.0	Leon-Atl 13.4	Rooker-Pit 3.4	Cash-Phi 4.0

TEAM	G	W	L	PCT	GB	R	OR	AB	H	2B	3B	HR	BB	SO	AVG	OBP	SLG	PRO	PRO+	BR	/A	PF	CHI	RC	SB	CS	SBA	SBR
EAST																												
BAL	162	91	71	.562		659	612	5535	1418	226	27	116	509	770	.256	.325	.370	.695	103	-2	19	97	98	671	145	58	**71**	**9**
NY	162	89	73	.549	2	671	623	5524	1451	220	30	101	515	**690**	.263	.328	.368	.696	103	1	20	97	100	666	53	35	60	-5
BOS	162	84	78	.519	7	**696**	661	5499	1449	**236**	31	109	569	811	.264	.336	.377	.713	98	39	-8	107	98	699	104	58	64	-4
CLE	162	77	85	.475	14	662	694	5474	1395	201	19	131	432	756	.255	.312	.370	.682	97	-36	-30	99	**108**	610	79	68	54	-17
MIL	162	76	86	.469	15	647	660	5472	1335	228	**49**	120	500	909	.244	.310	.369	.679	96	-41	-37	99	105	622	106	75	59	-13
DET	162	72	90	.444	19	620	768	5568	1375	200	35	131	436	784	.247	.304	.366	.670	89	-64	-87	104	104	607	67	38	64	-3
WEST																												
OAK	162	90	72	.556		689	**551**	5331	1315	205	37	132	568	876	.247	.324	.373	.697	107	1	43	94	105	648	**164**	93	64	-7
TEX	161	84	76	.525	5	690	698	5449	1482	198	39	99	508	710	**.272**	**.338**	.377	.715	**108**	42	**59**	98	98	677	113	80	59	-14
MIN	163	82	80	.506	8	673	669	5632	**1530**	190	37	111	520	791	**.272**	**.338**	.378	.716	102	44	17	104	93	**707**	74	45	62	-5
CHI	163	80	80	.500	9	684	721	5577	1492	225	23	**135**	519	858	.268	.333	**.389**	**.722**	104	49	33	102	95	701	64	53	55	-13
KC	162	77	85	.475	13	667	662	5582	1448	232	42	89	550	768	.259	.329	.364	.693	94	-2	-41	106	99	668	146	76	66	-2
CAL	163	68	94	.420	22	618	657	5401	1372	203	31	95	509	801	.254	.323	.356	.679	101	-30	7	94	99	615	119	79	60	-12
TOT	973					7976		66044	17062	2564	400	1369	6135	9524	.258	.325	.371	.697							1234	758	62	-85

TEAM	CG	SH	SV	IP	H	H/G	HR	BB	SO	RAT	ERA	ERA+	OAV	OOB	PR	/A	PF	CPI	FA	E	DP	FW	PW	BW	SBW	DIF
EAST																										
BAL	57	**16**	25	1474	1393	8.5	101	480	701	11.6	3.27	105	.253	.316	56	29	95	102	**.980**	128	174	1.0	3.0	2.0	**1.7**	2.3
NY	53	13	24	1455¹	1402	8.7	104	528	829	12.1	3.31	105	.256	.325	50	29	96	**107**	.977	142	158	.2	3.0	2.1	.2	2.5
BOS	**71**	12	18	1455¹	1462	9.0	126	463	751	12.1	3.72	103	.262	.322	-16	20	106	99	.977	145	156	.0	2.1	-.8	.3	1.4
CLE	45	9	27	1445²	1419	8.8	138	479	650	12.0	3.80	95	.260	.323	-30	-31	100	98	.977	146	157	-.0	-3.2	-3.1	-1.0	3.4
MIL	43	11	24	1457²	1476	9.1	126	493	621	12.3	3.76	96	.266	.329	-23	-23	100	102	**.980**	**127**	168	1.1	-2.4	-3.9	-.6	.8
DET	54	7	15	1455²	1443	8.9	148	621	869	13.0	4.16	91	.262	.341	-88	-58	105	99	.975	158	155	-.7	-6.1	-9.1	.4	6.5
WEST																										
OAK	49	12	28	1439²	**1322**	8.3	90	430	755	11.1	2.95	112	.246	.305	107	59	92	103	.977	141	154	.3	**6.2**	4.5	.0	-1.9
TEX	62	**16**	12	1433²	1423	8.9	126	449	871	12.0	3.82	93	.260	.321	-33	-41	99	95	.974	163	164	-1.1	-4.3	**6.2**	-.7	3.9
MIN	43	11	**29**	1455¹	1436	8.9	115	513	934	12.3	3.64	103	.260	.327	-4	18	104	101	.976	151	164	-.3	1.9	1.8	.2	-2.6
CHI	55	11	**29**	1465²	1470	9.0	103	548	826	12.7	3.94	95	.263	.334	-52	-34	103	96	.977	147	**188**	-.0	-3.6	3.5	-.6	.8
KC	54	13	17	1471²	1477	9.0	91	482	731	12.2	3.51	109	.263	.325	17	50	106	101	.976	152	166	-.4	5.2	-4.3	.5	-5.1
CAL	64	13	12	1439	1339	8.4	101	649	**986**	12.7	3.52	98	.248	.334	15	-14	95	102	.976	147	150	-.0	-1.5	.7	-.5	-11.7
TOT	650	144	260	17448²		8.8				12.2	3.62		.258	.325					.977	1747	1954					

Runs
Yastrzemski-Bos ... 93
Grich-Bal ... 92
Jackson-Oak ... 90
Otis-KC ... 87
Carew-Min ... 86

Hits
Carew-Min ... 218
Davis-Bal ... 181
Money-Mil ... 178
K.Henderson-Chi ... 176
Rudi-Oak ... 174

Doubles
Rudi-Oak ... 39
Scott-Mil ... 36
McRae-KC ... 36
K.Henderson-Chi ... 35
Burroughs-Tex ... 33

Triples
Rivers-Cal ... 11
Otis-KC ... 9

Home Runs
R.Allen-Chi ... 32
Jackson-Oak ... 29
Tenace-Oak ... 26
Darwin-Min ... 25
Burroughs-Tex ... 25

Total Bases
Rudi-Oak ... 287
K.Henderson-Chi ... 281
Burroughs-Tex ... 279
Carew-Min ... 267

Runs Batted In
Burroughs-Tex ... 118
Bando-Oak ... 103
Rudi-Oak ... 99
K.Henderson-Chi ... 95
Darwin-Min ... 94

Runs Produced
Burroughs-Tex ... 177
Bando-Oak ... 165
Yastrzemski-Bos ... 157
Grich-Bal ... 155
Jackson-Oak ... 154

Bases On Balls
Tenace-Oak ... 110
Yastrzemski-Bos ... 104
Burroughs-Tex ... 91
Grich-Bal ... 90

Batting Average
Carew-Min ... .364
Orta-Chi ... .316
McRae-KC ... .310
Piniella-NY ... .305
Maddox-NY ... .303

On Base Percentage
Carew-Min ... .435
Yastrzemski-Bos ... .421
Burroughs-Tex ... .405
Maddox-NY ... .397
Jackson-Oak ... .396

Slugging Average
R.Allen-Chi ... .563
Jackson-Oak ... .514
Burroughs-Tex ... .504
Rudi-Oak ... .484
Freehan-Det ... .479

Production
R.Allen-Chi ... .942
Jackson-Oak ... .910
Burroughs-Tex ... .908
Carew-Min ... .880
Yastrzemski-Bos ... .866

Adjusted Production
Jackson-Oak ... 171
Burroughs-Tex ... 164
R.Allen-Chi ... 164
Carew-Min ... 148
Robinson-Cal-Cle ... 143

Batter Runs
Burroughs-Tex ... 45.3
Carew-Min ... 44.7
Jackson-Oak ... 41.0
R.Allen-Chi ... 39.3
Yastrzemski-Bos ... 38.1

Adjusted Batter Runs
Burroughs-Tex ... 47.1
Jackson-Oak ... 45.2
Carew-Min ... 41.8
R.Allen-Chi ... 37.9
Yastrzemski-Bos ... 33.3

Clutch Hitting Index
Bando-Oak ... 154
Davis-Bal ... 130
Petrocelli-Bos ... 129
Murcer-NY ... 128
Burroughs-Tex ... 126

Runs Created
Carew-Min ... 118
Burroughs-Tex ... 113
Jackson-Oak ... 109
Yastrzemski-Bos ... 102
K.Henderson-Chi ... 100

Total Average
Jackson-Oak ... .992
R.Allen-Chi ... .953
Burroughs-Tex ... .919
Yastrzemski-Bos ... .900
Carew-Min ... .879

Stolen Bases
North-Oak ... 54
Carew-Min ... 38
Lowenstein-Cle ... 36
Campaneris-Oak ... 34
Patek-KC ... 33

Stolen Base Average
Jackson-Oak ... 83.3
Coggins-Bal ... 81.3
Pinson-KC ... 80.8
Otis-KC ... 78.3
Money-Mil ... 76.0

Stolen Base Runs
Jackson-Oak ... 4.5
Coggins-Bal ... 4.2
Pinson-KC ... 3.3
Miller-Bos ... 2.7
Blair-Bal ... 2.7

Fielding Runs
Terrell-Min ... 23.3
Rodriguez-Det ... 21.6
Robinson-Bal ... 20.5
North-Oak ... 18.4
Doyle-Cal ... 16.4

Total Player Rating
Carew-Min ... 6.1
Jackson-Oak ... 5.4
Grich-Bal ... 4.7
Burroughs-Tex ... 3.2
Robinson-Bal ... 3.1

Wins
Jenkins-Tex ... 25
Hunter-Oak ... 25

Win Percentage
Cuellar-Bal ... .688
Jenkins-Tex ... .676
Hunter-Oak ... .676
Tiant-Bos ... .629

Games
Fingers-Oak ... 76
Murphy-Mil ... 70
Foucault-Tex ... 69
Lyle-NY ... 66
Campbell-Min ... 63

Complete Games
Jenkins-Tex ... 29
G.Perry-Cle ... 28
Lolich-Det ... 27
Ryan-Cal ... 26
Tiant-Bos ... 25

Shutouts
Tiant-Bos ... 7
Jenkins-Tex ... 6
Hunter-Oak ... 6
Cuellar-Bal ... 5
Bibby-Tex ... 5

Saves
Forster-Chi ... 24
Murphy-Mil ... 20
Campbell-Min ... 19
Buskey-NY-Cle ... 18
Fingers-Oak ... 18

Innings Pitched
Ryan-Cal ... 332.2
Jenkins-Tex ... 328.1
G.Perry-Cle ... 322.1
Wood-Chi ... 320.1
Hunter-Oak ... 318.1

Fewest Hits/Game
Ryan-Cal ... 5.98
G.Perry-Cle ... 6.42
DalCanton-KC ... 6.93
Hassler-Cal ... 7.33
Hunter-Oak ... 7.58

Fewest BB/Game
Jenkins-Tex ... 1.23
Hunter-Oak ... 1.30
Holtzman-Oak ... 1.80
Kaat-Chi ... 2.04
Wright-Mil ... 2.09

Strikeouts
Ryan-Cal ... 367
Blyleven-Min ... 249
Jenkins-Tex ... 225
G.Perry-Cle ... 216
Lolich-Det ... 202

Strikeouts/Game
Ryan-Cal ... 9.93
Blyleven-Min ... 7.98
Jenkins-Tex ... 6.17
Busby-KC ... 6.10
G.Perry-Cle ... 6.03

Ratio
Hunter-Oak ... 8.99
Jenkins-Tex ... 9.29
G.Perry-Cle ... 9.35
Grimsley-Bal ... 10.53
Blyleven-Min ... 10.57

Earned Run Average
Hunter-Oak ... 2.49
G.Perry-Cle ... 2.51
Hassler-Cal ... 2.61
Blyleven-Min ... 2.66
Fitzmorris-KC ... 2.79

Adjusted ERA
G.Perry-Cle ... 144
Blyleven-Min ... 141
Fitzmorris-KC ... 137
Hunter-Oak ... 133
Hassler-Cal ... 132

Opponents' Batting Avg.
Ryan-Cal ... .190
G.Perry-Cle ... .204
DalCanton-KC ... .211
Hassler-Cal ... .225
Hunter-Oak ... .229

Opponents' On Base Pct.
Hunter-Oak ... .260
Jenkins-Tex ... .264
G.Perry-Cle ... .272
Blyleven-Min ... .292
Tiant-Bos ... .293

Starter Runs
Hunter-Oak ... 39.9
G.Perry-Cle ... 39.6
Blyleven-Min ... 29.9
Jenkins-Tex ... 29.0
Ryan-Cal ... 26.7

Adjusted Starter Runs
G.Perry-Cle ... 39.4
Blyleven-Min ... 34.1
Tiant-Bos ... 31.9
Hunter-Oak ... 29.3
Jenkins-Tex ... 27.0

Clutch Pitching Index
Goltz-Min ... 124
Hassler-Cal ... 121
Lee-Bos ... 119
Fitzmorris-KC ... 116
Tanana-Cal ... 113

Relief Runs
Lyle-NY ... 24.8
Murphy-Mil ... 23.4
Foucault-Tex ... 22.0
Lindblad-Oak ... 17.5
Hiller-Det ... 16.3

Adjusted Relief Runs
Murphy-Mil ... 23.4
Lyle-NY ... 23.2
Foucault-Tex ... 21.1
Hiller-Det ... 19.4
Campbell-Min ... 15.2

Relief Ranking
Murphy-Mil ... 42.9
Hiller-Det ... 39.8
Lyle-NY ... 28.8
Foucault-Tex ... 26.4
Campbell-Min ... 22.4

Total Pitcher Index
G.Perry-Cle ... 4.6
Blyleven-Min ... 3.7
Jenkins-Tex ... 3.0
Tiant-Bos ... 3.0
Hunter-Oak ... 2.9

Total Baseball Ranking
Carew-Min ... 6.1
Jackson-Oak ... 5.4
Grich-Bal ... 4.7
G.Perry-Cle ... 4.6
Blyleven-Min ... 3.7

TEAM	G	W	L	PCT	GB	R	OR	AB	H	2B	3B	HR	BB	SO	AVG	OBP	SLG	PRO	PRO+	BR	/A	PF	CHI	RC	SB	CS	SBA	SBR
EAST																												
PIT	161	92	69	.571		712	565	5489	1444	255	47	**138**	468	832	.263	.325	**.402**	.727	109	44	50	99	102	709	49	28	64	-2
PHI	162	86	76	.531	6.5	735	694	5592	1506	**283**	42	125	610	960	.269	.344	**.402**	.746	109	98	71	104	94	785	126	57	69	4
NY	162	82	80	.506	10.5	646	625	5587	1430	217	34	101	501	805	.256	.321	.361	.682	100	-36	-5	95	102	639	32	26	55	-6
STL	163	82	80	.506	10.5	662	689	5597	**1527**	239	46	81	444	**649**	.273	.329	.375	.704	99	7	-16	104	99	683	116	49	70	5
MON	162	75	87	.463	17.5	601	690	5518	1346	216	31	98	579	954	.244	.319	.348	.667	87	-63	-92	104	99	623	108	58	65	-2
CHI	162	75	87	.463	17.5	712	827	5470	1419	229	41	95	650	802	.259	.341	.368	.709	99	33	3	104	100	702	67	55	55	-13
WEST																												
CIN	162	108	54	.667		**840**	586	5581	1515	278	37	124	**691**	916	.271	**.355**	.401	**.756**	**114**	128	116	102	103	**829**	168	36	**82**	**29**
LA	162	88	74	.543	20	648	**534**	5453	1355	217	31	118	611	825	.248	.328	.365	.693	103	-10	19	96	98	667	138	52	73	10
SF	161	80	81	.497	27.5	659	671	5447	1412	235	45	84	604	775	.259	.336	.365	.701	97	11	-17	104	99	673	99	47	68	2
SD	162	71	91	.438	37	552	580	5429	1324	215	22	78	506	754	.244	.313	.335	.648	92	-100	-59	94	99	571	85	50	63	-5
ATL	161	67	94	.416	40.5	583	739	5424	1323	179	28	107	543	759	.244	.315	.346	.661	86	-75	-99	104	101	587	55	38	59	-6
HOU	162	64	97	.398	43.5	664	711	5515	1401	218	**54**	84	523	762	.254	.322	.359	.681	102	-36	12	93	**106**	643	133	62	68	3
TOT	971					8014		66102	17002	2781	458	1233	6730	9793	.257	.329	.369	.698							1176	558	68	18

TEAM	CG	SH	SV	IP	H	H/G	HR	BB	SO	RAT	ERA	ERA+	OAV	OOB	PR	/A	PF	CPI	FA	E	DP	FW	PW	BW	SBW	DIF
EAST																										
PIT	43	14	31	1437¹	1302	8.2	**79**	551	768	11.7	3.01	**118**	.243	.315	98	**85**	98	103	.976	151	147	.2	**8.9**	5.2	-.4	-2.4
PHI	33	11	30	1455	1353	8.4	111	546	897	11.9	3.82	98	.249	.320	-33	-15	103	89	.976	152	156	.2	-1.6	7.4	.3	-1.3
NY	40	14	31	1466	1344	8.3	99	580	**989**	12.0	3.39	102	.246	.321	38	10	95	98	.976	151	144	.3	1.0	-.5	-.8	1.0
STL	33	13	36	1454²	1452	9.0	98	571	824	12.7	3.57	105	.260	.331	8	30	104	102	.973	171	140	-.8	3.1	-1.7	-.4	-.0
MON	30	12	25	1480	1448	8.8	102	665	831	13.1	3.72	103	.259	.341	-17	17	106	103	.973	180	**179**	-1.3	1.8	-9.6	-.4	3.5
CHI	27	8	33	1444¹	1587	9.9	130	551	850	13.6	4.49	86	.281	.349	-140	-105	106	98	.972	179	152	-1.3	-11.0	.3	-1.5	7.4
WEST																										
CIN	22	8	**50**	1459	1422	8.8	112	487	663	12.0	3.37	107	.257	.321	41	36	99	105	**.984**	102	173	**3.0**	3.8	12.1	**2.9**	5.3
LA	51	18	21	1469²	**1215**	7.4	104	**448**	894	**10.4**	2.92	116	**.225**	**.287**	114	78	94	88	.979	127	106	1.6	8.1	2.0	.9	-5.6
SF	37	9	24	1432²	1406	8.8	92	612	856	12.9	3.74	102	.259	.339	-19	10	105	101	.979	146	164	.5	1.0	-1.8	.0	-.3
SD	40	12	20	1463¹	1494	9.2	99	521	713	12.5	3.48	100	.266	.331	23	-1	96	**107**	.971	188	163	-1.8	-.1	-6.2	-.7	-1.3
ATL	32	4	24	1430	1543	9.7	101	519	669	13.3	3.91	96	.278	.344	-47	-23	104	105	.972	175	147	-1.1	-2.4	-10.3	-.8	1.1
HOU	39	6	25	1458¹	1436	8.9	106	679	839	13.3	4.04	83	.262	.347	-67	-108	93	99	.979	137	166	1.1	-11.3	1.3	.2	-7.7
TOT	427	129	350	17450¹		8.8				12.4	3.62		.257	.329					.976	1859	1837					

Runs		Hits		Doubles		Triples		Home Runs		Total Bases	
Rose-Cin	112	Cash-Phi	213	Rose-Cin	47	Garr-Atl	11	Schmidt-Phi	38	Luzinski-Phi	322
Cash-Phi	111	Rose-Cin	210	Cash-Phi	40	Parker-Pit	10	Kingman-NY	36	Garvey-LA	314
Lopes-LA	108	Garvey-LA	210	Oliver-Pit	39	Kessinger-Chi	10	Luzinski-Phi	34	Parker-Pit	302
Morgan-Cin	107	Simmons-StL	193	Bench-Cin	39	Joshua-SF	10	Bench-Cin	28	Schmidt-Phi	294
Thomas-SF	99	Millan-NY	191	Garvey-LA	38	Gross-Hou	10			Rose-Cin	286

Runs Batted In		Runs Produced		Bases On Balls		Batting Average		On Base Percentage		Slugging Average	
Luzinski-Phi	120	Morgan-Cin	184	Morgan-Cin	132	Madlock-Chi	.354	Morgan-Cin	.471	Parker-Pit	.541
Bench-Cin	110	Staub-NY	179	Wynn-LA	110	Simmons-StL	.332	Wynn-LA	.407	Luzinski-Phi	.540
Perez-Cin	109	Rose-Cin	179	Evans-Atl	105	Sanguillen-Pit	.328	Rose-Cin	.407	Schmidt-Phi	.523
Staub-NY	105	Luzinski-Phi	171	Schmidt-Phi	101	Morgan-Cin	.327	Madlock-Chi	.406	Bench-Cin	.519
		Bench-Cin	165			Watson-Hou	.324	Murcer-SF	.404	Foster-Cin	.518

Production		Adjusted Production		Batter Runs		Adjusted Batter Runs		Clutch Hitting Index		Runs Created	
Morgan-Cin	.979	Morgan-Cin	168	Morgan-Cin	57.1	Morgan-Cin	55.9	Montanez-Phi-SF	148	Morgan-Cin	145
Luzinski-Phi	.939	Luzinski-Phi	152	Luzinski-Phi	47.5	Luzinski-Phi	44.5	Perez-Cin	144	Luzinski-Phi	128
Parker-Pit	.899	Watson-Hou	152	Simmons-StL	35.7	Simmons-StL	33.3	Morales-Chi	144	Rose-Cin	120
Stargell-Pit	.894	Parker-Pit	148	Thornton-Chi	35.4	Thornton-Chi	33.2	Murcer-SF	143	Schmidt-Phi	113
Schmidt-Phi	.890	Stargell-Pit	147	Schmidt-Phi	33.7	Parker-Pit	32.2	Trillo-Chi	143	Simmons-StL	108

Total Average		Stolen Bases		Stolen Base Average		Stolen Base Runs		Fielding Runs		Total Player Rating	
Morgan-Cin	1.279	Lopes-LA	77	Morgan-Cin	87.0	Lopes-LA	15.9	Schmidt-Phi	24.0	Morgan-Cin	7.2
Luzinski-Phi	.956	Morgan-Cin	67	Lopes-LA	86.5	Morgan-Cin	14.1	Evans-Atl	23.4	Schmidt-Phi	5.8
Schmidt-Phi	.943	Brock-StL	56	Maddox-SF-Phi	86.2	Brock-StL	7.2	Mackanin-Mon	18.2	Bench-Cin	4.1
Bench-Cin	.901	Cedeno-Hou	50	Winfield-SD	85.2	Concepcion-Cin	6.3	Maddox-SF-Phi	18.1	Evans-Atl	3.5
Stargell-Pit	.895	Cardenal-Chi	34	Concepcion-Cin	84.6	Maddox-SF-Phi	5.1	Trillo-Chi	16.0	Simmons-StL	3.3

Wins		Win Percentage		Games		Complete Games		Shutouts		Saves	
Seaver-NY	22	Gullett-Cin	.789	Garber-Phi	71	Messersmith-LA	19	Messersmith-LA	7	Hrabosky-StL	22
Jones-SD	20	Seaver-NY	.710	McEnaney-Cin	70	Jones-SD	18	Reuss-Pit	6	Eastwick-Cin	22
Messersmith-LA	19	Hooton-Chi-LA	.667	Tomlin-SD	67	Seaver-NY	15	Jones-SD	6	Giusti-Pit	17
Hooton-Chi-LA	18	Murray-Mon	.652	Borbon-Cin	67	Reuss-Pit	15	Seaver-NY	5	McEnaney-Cin	15
Reuss-Pit	18			Garman-StL	66					Knowles-Chi	15

Innings Pitched		Fewest Hits/Game		Fewest BB/Game		Strikeouts		Strikeouts/Game		Ratio	
Messersmith-LA	321.2	Messersmith-LA	6.83	Nolan-Cin	1.24	Seaver-NY	243	Montefusco-SF	7.94	Jones-SD	9.41
Jones-SD	285.0	Seaver-NY	6.97	Jones-SD	1.77	Montefusco-SF	215	Richard-Hou	7.80	Sutton-LA	9.45
Seaver-NY	280.1	Warthen-Mon	6.98	Reed-Atl-StL	1.91	Messersmith-LA	213	Seaver-NY	7.80	Messersmith-LA	9.65
Morton-Atl	277.2	Sutton-LA	7.15	Rau-LA	2.13	Carlton-Phi	192	Warthen-Mon	6.87	Hooton-Chi-LA	9.89
Niekro-Atl	275.2	Hooton-Chi-LA	7.29	Barr-SF	2.14	Richard-Hou	176	Carlton-Phi	6.77	Nolan-Cin	9.91

Earned Run Average		Adjusted ERA		Opponents' Batting Avg.		Opponents' On Base Pct.		Starter Runs		Adjusted Starter Runs	
Jones-SD	2.24	Jones-SD	155	Messersmith-LA	.213	Sutton-LA	.264	Messersmith-LA	47.4	Messersmith-LA	39.5
Messersmith-LA	2.29	Messersmith-LA	148	Sutton-LA	.213	Jones-SD	.271	Jones-SD	43.7	Jones-SD	39.0
Seaver-NY	2.38	Seaver-NY	145	Seaver-NY	.214	Hooton-Chi-LA	.276	Seaver-NY	38.8	Seaver-NY	33.5
Reuss-Pit	2.54	Reuss-Pit	139	Warthen-Mon	.217	Messersmith-LA	.276	Reuss-Pit	28.5	Reuss-Pit	26.4
Forsch-StL	2.86	Montefusco-SF	132	Hooton-Chi-LA	.219	Nolan-Cin	.278	Sutton-LA	21.3	Montefusco-SF	24.8

Clutch Pitching Index		Relief Runs		Adjusted Relief Runs		Relief Ranking		Total Pitcher Index		Total Baseball Ranking	
Reuss-Pit	122	Hrabosky-StL	21.2	Hrabosky-StL	22.6	Hrabosky-StL	44.9	Jones-SD	4.9	Morgan-Cin	7.2
Niekro-Atl	122	Apodaca-NY	20.1	Apodaca-NY	18.5	Apodaca-NY	20.1	Messersmith-LA	4.4	Schmidt-Phi	5.8
Blair-Mon	114	Hilgendorf-Phi	15.9	Hilgendorf-Phi	17.1	Garman-StL	18.4	Seaver-NY	4.3	Jones-SD	4.9
Koosman-NY	113	McEnaney-Cin	11.6	Garman-StL	12.0	Hilgendorf-Phi	15.9	Forsch-StL	3.8	Messersmith-LA	4.4
Barr-SF	110	Garman-StL	10.8	McEnaney-Cin	11.3	McGraw-Phi	13.9	Reuss-Pit	3.4	Seaver-NY	4.3

TEAM	G	W	L	PCT	GB	R	OR	AB	H	2B	3B	HR	BB	SO	AVG	OBP	SLG	PRO	PRO+	BR	/A	PF	CHI	RC	SB	CS	SBA	SBR
EAST
BOS	160	95	65	.594		**796**	709	5448	**1500**	284	44	134	565	741	**.275**	**.347**	**.417**	**.764**	106	**108**	49	109	99	**776**	66	58	53	-15
BAL	159	90	69	.566	4.5	682	**553**	5474	1382	224	33	124	580	834	.252	.328	.373	.701	105	-14	31	94	100	680	104	55	65	-2
NY	160	83	77	.519	12	681	588	5415	1430	230	39	110	486	710	.264	.328	.382	.710	103	-3	16	97	101	665	102	59	63	-5
CLE	159	79	80	.497	15.5	688	703	5404	1409	201	25	**153**	525	**667**	.261	.329	.392	.721	103	17	18	100	99	672	106	89	54	-22
MIL	162	68	94	.420	28	675	792	5378	1343	242	34	146	553	922	.250	.323	.389	.712	100	-2	-5	101	99	663	65	64	50	-19
DET	159	57	102	.358	37.5	570	786	5366	1338	171	39	125	383	872	.249	.303	.366	.669	84	-94	-123	104	101	573	63	57	53	-15
WEST
OAK	162	98	64	.605		758	606	5415	1376	220	33	151	609	846	.254	.335	.391	.726	**107**	34	**50**	98	104	725	183	82	**69**	**6**
KC	162	91	71	.562	7	710	649	5491	1431	263	**58**	118	591	675	.261	.336	.394	.730	103	40	22	103	96	736	155	75	67	2
TEX	162	79	83	.488	19	714	733	5599	1431	208	17	134	613	863	.256	.332	.371	.703	99	-10	-4	99	102	693	102	62	62	-7
MIN	159	76	83	.478	20.5	724	736	5514	1497	215	28	121	563	746	.271	.343	.386	.729	104	46	31	102	97	732	81	48	63	-5
CHI	161	75	86	.466	22.5	655	703	5490	1400	209	38	94	611	800	.255	.334	.358	.692	95	-24	-34	101	97	659	101	54	65	-2
CAL	161	72	89	.447	25.5	628	723	5377	1324	195	41	55	593	811	.246	.324	.328	.652	91	-99	-51	93	**106**	596	**220**	108	67	1
TOT	963					8281		65371	16861	2662	429	1465	6672	9487	.258	.330	.379	.709							1348	811	62	-82

TEAM	CG	SH	SV	IP	H	H/G	HR	BB	SO	RAT	ERA	ERA+	OAV	OOB	PR	/A	PF	CPI	FA	E	DP	FW	PW	BW	SBW	DIF
EAST
BOS	62	11	31	1436²	1463	9.2	145	**490**	720	12.4	3.98	102	.265	.327	-33	14	108	99	.977	139	142	.9	1.4	5.0	-.8	8.5
BAL	**70**	**19**	21	1451	1285	8.0	110	500	717	11.1	**3.17**	**111**	.242	**.308**	98	55	93	100	**.983**	**107**	175	**2.6**	5.6	3.2	.5	-1.4
NY	**70**	11	20	1424	1325	8.4	104	502	809	11.7	3.29	111	.249	.317	78	56	96	103	.978	135	148	1.1	5.7	1.6	.2	-5.6
CLE	37	6	33	1435¹	1395	8.7	136	599	800	12.7	3.84	98	.258	.335	-10	-10	100	99	.978	134	156	1.1	-1.0	1.8	-1.5	-.9
MIL	36	10	34	1431²	1496	9.4	133	624	643	13.7	4.34	88	.271	.351	-89	-81	101	100	.971	180	162	-1.4	-8.3	-.5	-1.2	-1.6
DET	52	10	17	1396	1496	9.6	137	533	787	13.3	4.27	94	.275	.343	-77	-40	106	100	.972	173	141	-1.1	-4.1	-12.6	-.8	-3.9
WEST
OAK	36	10	**44**	1448	**1267**	7.9	102	523	784	11.4	3.27	111	**.236**	.308	82	58	96	94	.977	143	140	.7	5.9	**5.1**	**1.3**	3.9
KC	52	11	25	1456²	1422	8.8	108	498	815	12.0	3.47	111	.258	.322	50	62	102	102	.976	155	151	.0	**6.3**	2.4	.9	.5
TEX	60	16	17	1465²	1456	8.9	123	518	792	12.4	3.86	97	.261	.329	-14	-17	99	98	.971	191	173	-2.0	-1.7	-.4	-.0	2.1
MIN	57	7	22	1423	1381	8.7	137	617	846	12.9	4.05	95	.257	.337	-43	-31	102	98	.973	170	147	-.9	-3.2	3.2	.2	-2.7
CHI	34	7	39	1452¹	1489	9.2	107	655	799	13.5	3.93	99	.268	.349	-24	-9	103	105	.978	140	155	.9	-.9	-3.5	.5	-2.5
CAL	59	**19**	16	1453¹	1386	8.6	123	613	**975**	12.6	3.89	91	.253	.333	-18	-55	94	97	.971	184	164	-1.6	-5.6	-5.2	.8	3.2
TOT	625	137	319	17273²		8.8				12.5	3.78		.258	.330					.975	1851	1854					

Runs
Lynn-Bos 103
Mayberry-KC 95
Bonds-NY 93
Rice-Bos 92

Hits
Brett-KC 195
Carew-Min 192
Munson-NY 190
C.Washington-Oak 182

Doubles
Lynn-Bos 47
Jackson-Oak 39
McRae-KC 38
Mayberry-KC 38
Chambliss-NY 38

Triples
Rivers-Cal 13
Brett-KC 13
Orta-Chi 10
Cowens-KC 8

Home Runs
Scott-Mil 36
Jackson-Oak 36
Mayberry-KC 34
Bonds-NY 32

Total Bases
Scott-Mil 318
Mayberry-KC 303
Jackson-Oak 303
Lynn-Bos 299
Brett-KC 289

Runs Batted In
Scott-Mil 109
Mayberry-KC 106
Lynn-Bos 105
Jackson-Oak 104

Runs Produced
Lynn-Bos 187
Munson-NY 173
Rice-Bos 172
Mayberry-KC 167
Brett-KC 162

Bases On Balls
Mayberry-KC 119
Singleton-Bal 118
Grich-Bal 107
Tenace-Oak 106
Harrah-Tex 98

Batting Average
Carew-Min .... .359
Lynn-Bos .... .331
Munson-NY .... .318
Rice-Bos .... .309
C.Washington-Oak .308

On Base Percentage
Carew-Min .... .428
Mayberry-KC ..... .419
Singleton-Bal .... .418
Harrah-Tex ...... .406
Lynn-Bos .... .405

Slugging Average
Lynn-Bos .... .566
Mayberry-KC ..... .547
Powell-Cle .... .524
Scott-Mil .... .515
Bonds-NY .... .512

Production
Lynn-Bos .... .971
Mayberry-KC ..... .966
Carew-Min .... .926
Powell-Cle .... .906
Bonds-NY .... .891

Adjusted Production
Mayberry-KC 167
Lynn-Bos 158
Carew-Min 158
Singleton-Bal 156
Bonds-NY 154

Batter Runs
Mayberry-KC 56.0
Lynn-Bos 49.4
Carew-Min 44.4
Singleton-Bal 41.3
Bonds-NY 35.4

Adjusted Batter Runs
Mayberry-KC 54.0
Singleton-Bal 46.4
Lynn-Bos 43.6
Carew-Min 43.0
Bonds-NY 37.3

Clutch Hitting Index
Munson-NY 142
Stanton-Cal 140
Robinson-Bal..... 136
May-Bal 132
McRae-KC 127

Runs Created
Mayberry-KC 135
Lynn-Bos 120
Singleton-Bal 118
Carew-Min 118
Harrah-Tex 105

Total Average
Mayberry-KC ... 1.059
Lynn-Bos 1.000
Carew-Min .... .986
Tenace-Oak ...... .919
Harrah-Tex ...... .914

Stolen Bases
Rivers-Cal 70
C.Washington-Oak . 40
Otis-KC 39
Carew-Min 35
Remy-Cal 34

Stolen Base Average
Hisle-Min 85.0
Bumbry-Bal 84.2
Rivers-Cal 83.3
Alomar-NY 82.4
Patek-KC 82.1

Stolen Base Runs
Rivers-Cal 12.6
Patek-KC 5.4
Otis-KC 5.1
Carew-Min 5.1
Alomar-NY 4.8

Fielding Runs
Belanger-Bal 28.0
Dent-Chi 27.2
Grich-Bal 24.0
Rodriguez-Det ... 20.7
North-Oak 19.6

Total Player Rating
Harrah-Tex 6.2
Carew-Min 5.7
Grich-Bal 5.7
Lynn-Bos 5.1
Mayberry-KC 4.8

Wins
Palmer-Bal 23
Hunter-NY 23
Blue-Oak 22
Torrez-Bal 20
Kaat-Chi 20

Win Percentage
Torrez-Bal ...... .690
Leonard-KC ...... .682
Palmer-Bal ...... .676
Blue-Oak .... .667
Lee-Bos .... .654

Games
Fingers-Oak 75
Lindblad-Oak 68
Gossage-Chi 62
LaRoche-Cle 61
Foucault-Tex 59

Complete Games
Hunter-NY 30
G.Perry-Cle-Tex ... 25
Palmer-Bal 25
Jenkins-Tex 22
Blyleven-Min 20

Shutouts
Palmer-Bal 10
Hunter-NY 7

Saves
Gossage-Chi 26
Fingers-Oak 24
Murphy-Mil 20
LaRoche-Cle 17
Drago-Bos 15

Innings Pitched
Hunter-NY 328.0
Palmer-Bal 323.0
G.Perry-Cle-Tex . 305.2
Kaat-Chi 303.2
Wood-Chi 291.1

Fewest Hits/Game
Hunter-NY 6.80
Ryan-Cal 6.91
Palmer-Bal 7.05
Eckersley-Cle ... 7.09
Blyleven-Min ... 7.15

Fewest BB/Game
Jenkins-Tex 1.87
G.Perry-Cle-Tex .. 2.06
Grimsley-Bal 2.15
Palmer-Bal 2.23
Hunter-NY 2.28

Strikeouts
Tanana-Cal 269
G.Perry-Cle-Tex .. 233
Blyleven-Min 233
Palmer-Bal 193
Blue-Oak 189

Strikeouts/Game
Tanana-Cal 9.41
Ryan-Cal 8.45
Blyleven-Min 7.61
Eckersley-Cle ... 7.33
G.Perry-Cle-Tex . 6.86

Ratio
Hunter-NY 9.22
Palmer-Bal 9.33
Blyleven-Min ... 10.02
Tanana-Cal 10.18
G.Perry-Cle-Tex . 10.33

Earned Run Average
Palmer-Bal 2.09
Hunter-NY 2.58
Eckersley-Cle ... 2.60
Tanana-Cal 2.62
Figueroa-Cal ... 2.91

Adjusted ERA
Palmer-Bal 168
Eckersley-Cle ... 145
Hunter-NY 141
Tanana-Cal 135
Blyleven-Min ... 128

Opponents' Batting Avg.
Hunter-NY ..... .208
Ryan-Cal ...... .213
Eckersley-Cle ... .215
Palmer-Bal ..... .216
Blyleven-Min ... .219

Opponents' On Base Pct.
Hunter-NY ..... .263
Palmer-Bal ..... .267
Blyleven-Min ... .283
G.Perry-Cle-Tex . .284
Tanana-Cal ..... .288

Starter Runs
Palmer-Bal 60.6
Hunter-NY 43.7
Tanana-Cal 33.0
Eckersley-Cle ... 24.4
Blyleven-Min ... 23.7

Adjusted Starter Runs
Palmer-Bal 51.0
Hunter-NY 38.7
Tanana-Cal 26.4
Blyleven-Min ... 26.0
Kaat-Chi 25.7

Clutch Pitching Index
Kaat-Chi 119
Eckersley-Cle ... 116
Torrez-Bal 111
Osteen-Chi 110
Hargan-Tex 108

Relief Runs
Gossage-Chi ... 30.5
Todd-Oak 20.2
LaRoche-Cle ... 14.6
Lindblad-Oak ... 14.4
Hiller-Det 12.7

Adjusted Relief Runs
Gossage-Chi 32.0
Todd-Oak 18.2
LaRoche-Cle ... 14.6
Hiller-Det 14.5
Lindblad-Oak ... 12.3

Relief Ranking
Gossage-Chi 47.7
LaRoche-Cle 19.5
Todd-Oak 16.6
Hiller-Det 15.7
Fingers-Oak 14.1

Total Pitcher Index
Palmer-Bal 6.4
Hunter-NY 3.7
Tanana-Cal 3.6
Gossage-Chi 3.5
Blyleven-Min ... 3.0

Total Baseball Ranking
Palmer-Bal 6.4
Harrah-Tex 6.2
Carew-Min 5.7
Grich-Bal 5.7
Lynn-Bos 5.1

TEAM	G	W	L	PCT	GB	R	OR	AB	H	2B	3B	HR	BB	SO	AVG	OBP	SLG	PRO	PRO+	BR	/A	PF	CHI	RC	SB	CS	SBA	SBR
EAST																												
PHI	162	101	61	.623		770	557	5528	1505	259	45	110	542	793	.272	.342	.395	.737	112	106	86	103	101	746	127	70	64	-4
PIT	162	92	70	.568	9	708	630	5604	1499	249	56	110	433	807	.267	.323	.391	.714	107	50	45	101	102	700	130	45	74	12
NY	162	86	76	.531	15	615	538	5415	1334	198	34	102	561	797	.246	.320	.352	.672	103	-19	18	94	99	608	66	58	53	-15
CHI	162	75	87	.463	26	611	728	5519	1386	216	24	105	490	834	.251	.316	.356	.672	89	-27	-85	109	99	605	74	74	50	-22
STL	162	72	90	.444	29	629	671	5516	1432	243	57	63	512	860	.260	.325	.359	.684	99	1	-5	101	97	644	123	55	69	4
MON	162	55	107	.340	46	531	734	5428	1275	224	32	94	433	841	.235	.293	.340	.633	82	-109	-135	104	102	539	86	44	66	-1
WEST																												
CIN	162	102	60	.630		857	633	5702	1599	271	63	141	681	902	.280	.360	.424	.784	126	214	198	102	95	907	210	57	79	29
LA	162	92	70	.568	10	608	543	5472	1371	200	34	91	486	744	.251	.315	.349	.664	96	-39	-27	98	101	604	144	55	72	10
HOU	162	80	82	.494	22	625	657	5464	1401	195	50	66	530	719	.256	.325	.347	.672	107	-20	38	91	101	622	150	57	72	11
SF	162	74	88	.457	28	595	686	5452	1340	211	37	85	518	778	.246	.314	.345	.659	90	-48	-67	103	100	591	88	55	62	-7
SD	162	73	89	.451	29	570	662	5369	1327	216	37	64	488	716	.247	.313	.337	.650	98	-65	-14	92	100	570	92	46	67	0
ATL	162	70	92	.432	32	620	700	5345	1309	170	30	82	589	811	.245	.322	.334	.656	87	-44	-84	106	104	579	74	61	55	-14
TOT	972					7739		65814	16778	2652	499	1113	6263	9602	.255	.323	.361	.684							1364	677	67	3

TEAM	CG	SH	SV	IP	H	H/G	HR	BB	SO	RAT	ERA	ERA+	OAV	OOB	PR	/A	PF	CPI	FA	E	DP	FW	PW	BW	SBW	DIF
EAST																										
PHI	34	9	44	1459	1377	8.5	98	397	918	11.1	3.08	115	.250	.303	69	76	101	102	.981	115	148	1.7	8.1	9.1	-.5	1.5
PIT	45	12	35	1466¹	1402	8.6	95	460	762	11.5	3.36	104	.253	.313	22	20	100	99	.975	163	142	-1.0	2.1	4.8	1.2	3.9
NY	53	18	25	1449	1248	7.8	97	419	1025	10.5	2.94	112	.233	.292	91	57	94	95	.979	131	116	.8	6.1	1.9	-1.6	-2.2
CHI	27	12	33	1471¹	1511	9.2	123	490	850	12.4	3.93	98	.268	.330	-71	-12	110	100	.978	140	145	.3	-1.3	-9.0	-2.4	6.4
STL	35	15	26	1453²	1416	8.8	91	581	731	12.5	3.60	98	.258	.332	-16	-11	101	103	.973	174	163	-1.7	-1.2	-.5	.4	-6.0
MON	26	10	21	1440	1442	9.0	89	659	783	13.4	3.99	93	.266	.350	-79	-44	106	102	.976	155	179	-.6	-4.7	-14.3	-.1	-6.3
WEST																										
CIN	33	12	45	1471	1436	8.8	100	491	790	11.9	3.51	100	.258	.321	-1	0	100	101	.984	102	157	2.5	.0	21.0	3.1	-5.6
LA	47	17	28	1470²	1330	8.1	97	479	747	11.2	3.02	112	.243	.307	79	60	97	104	.980	128	154	1.0	6.4	-2.9	1.0	5.5
HOU	42	17	29	1444¹	1349	8.4	82	662	780	12.7	3.56	90	.250	.335	-9	-59	91	101	.978	140	155	.3	-6.3	4.0	1.1	-.2
SF	27	18	31	1461²	1464	9.0	68	518	746	12.3	3.53	103	.263	.328	-4	16	104	100	.971	186	153	-2.4	1.7	-7.1	-.8	1.5
SD	47	11	18	1432¹	1368	8.6	87	543	652	12.1	3.65	90	.253	.323	-24	-61	93	95	.978	141	148	.2	-6.5	-1.5	-.0	-.2
ATL	33	13	27	1438	1435	9.0	86	564	818	12.8	3.86	98	.261	.335	-58	-12	108	97	.973	167	151	-1.3	-1.3	-8.9	-1.5	2.0
TOT	449	164	362	17457¹		8.6				12.0	3.50		.255	.323					.977	1742	1811					

Runs		Hits		Doubles		Triples		Home Runs		Total Bases	
Rose-Cin	130	Rose-Cin	215	Rose-Cin	42	Cash-Phi	12	Schmidt-Phi	38	Schmidt-Phi	306
Morgan-Cin	113	Montanez-SF-Atl	206	Johnstone-Phi	38	Geronimo-Cin	11	Kingman-NY	37	Rose-Cin	299
Schmidt-Phi	112	Garvey-LA	200	Maddox-Phi	37	Parker-Pit	10	Monday-Chi	32	Foster-Cin	298
Griffey-Cin	111	Buckner-LA	193	Garvey-LA	37	W.Davis-SD	10	Foster-Cin	29	Garvey-LA	284
Monday-Chi	107							Morgan-Cin	27		

Runs Batted In		Runs Produced		Bases On Balls		Batting Average		On Base Percentage		Slugging Average	
Foster-Cin	121	Morgan-Cin	197	Wynn-Atl	127	Madlock-Chi	.339	Morgan-Cin	.453	Morgan-Cin	.576
Morgan-Cin	111	Rose-Cin	183	Morgan-Cin	114	Griffey-Cin	.336	Madlock-Chi	.415	Foster-Cin	.530
Schmidt-Phi	107	Schmidt-Phi	181	Schmidt-Phi	100	Maddox-Phi	.330	Rose-Cin	.406	Schmidt-Phi	.524
Watson-Hou	102	Griffey-Cin	179	Cey-LA	89	Rose-Cin	.323	Griffey-Cin	.403	Monday-Chi	.507
Luzinski-Phi	95	Foster-Cin	178	Rose-Cin	86	Morgan-Cin	.320	Cey-LA	.389	Kingman-NY	.506

Production		Adjusted Production		Batter Runs		Adjusted Batter Runs		Clutch Hitting Index		Runs Created	
Morgan-Cin	1.029	Morgan-Cin	186	Morgan-Cin	61.4	Morgan-Cin	59.9	Simmons-StL	133	Morgan-Cin	144
Madlock-Chi	.915	Watson-Hou	151	Schmidt-Phi	42.7	Schmidt-Phi	40.4	Watson-Hou	132	Rose-Cin	123
Schmidt-Phi	.904	Schmidt-Phi	150	Madlock-Chi	40.6	Rose-Cin	37.7	Cruz-StL	128	Schmidt-Phi	121
Foster-Cin	.899	Foster-Cin	149	Rose-Cin	39.6	Watson-Hou	35.4	Brock-StL	127	Foster-Cin	111
Rose-Cin	.855	Madlock-Chi	146	Foster-Cin	36.7	Foster-Cin	35.2	Milner-NY	126	Griffey-Cin	109

Total Average		Stolen Bases		Stolen Base Average		Stolen Base Runs		Fielding Runs		Total Player Rating	
Morgan-Cin	1.319	Lopes-LA	63	Morgan-Cin	87.0	Lopes-LA	12.9	Schmidt-Phi	24.7	Schmidt-Phi	6.5
Schmidt-Phi	.944	Morgan-Cin	60	Lopes-LA	86.3	Morgan-Cin	12.6	Trillo-Chi	18.3	Morgan-Cin	6.0
Foster-Cin	.911	Taveras-Pit	58	Foster-Cin	85.0	Taveras-Pit	10.8	Maddox-Phi	17.8	Foster-Cin	4.3
Madlock-Chi	.882	Cedeno-StL	58	Taveras-Pit	84.1	Cedeno-Hou	8.4	Stennett-Pit	17.4	Concepcion-Cin	4.1
Griffey-Cin	.876	Brock-StL	56	Geronimo-Cin	81.5	Cabell-Hou	5.7	Royster-Atl	16.6	Cey-LA	4.0

Wins		Win Percentage		Games		Complete Games		Shutouts		Saves	
Jones-SD	22	Carlton-Phi	.741	Murray-Mon	81	Jones-SD	25	Montefusco-SF	6	Eastwick-Cin	26
Sutton-LA	21	Candelaria-Pit	.696	Metzger-SD	77	Koosman-NY	17	Matlack-NY	6	Lockwood-NY	19
Koosman-NY	21	Sutton-LA	.677	Hough-LA	77	Matlack-NY	16	Seaver-NY	5	Forsch-Hou	19
Richard-Hou	20	Koosman-NY	.677	Eastwick-Cin	71	Sutton-LA	15	Jones-SD	5	Hough-LA	18
Carlton-Phi	20	Rooker-Pit	.652	Borbon-Cin	69	Richard-Hou	14			Metzger-SD	16

Innings Pitched		Fewest Hits/Game		Fewest BB/Game		Strikeouts		Strikeouts/Game		Ratio	
Jones-SD	315.1	Richard-Hou	6.84	Nolan-Cin	1.02	Seaver-NY	235	Seaver-NY	7.80	Jones-SD	9.36
Richard-Hou	291.0	Seaver-NY	7.01	Kaat-Phi	1.27	Richard-Hou	214	Koosman-NY	7.28	Candelaria-Pit	9.61
Seaver-NY	271.0	Candelaria-Pit	7.08	Jones-SD	1.43	Koosman-NY	200	Carlton-Phi	6.95	Seaver-NY	9.70
Niekro-Atl	270.2	Messersmith-Atl	7.21	Matlack-NY	1.96	Carlton-Phi	195	Richard-Hou	6.62	Nolan-Cin	9.78
Sutton-LA	267.2	Falcone-StL	7.34	Lonborg-Phi	2.03	Niekro-Atl	173	Zachry-Cin	6.31	Koosman-NY	9.90

Earned Run Average		Adjusted ERA		Opponents' Batting Avg.		Opponents' On Base Pct.		Starter Runs		Adjusted Starter Runs	
Denny-StL	2.52	Denny-StL	140	Richard-Hou	.212	Jones-SD	.267	Seaver-NY	27.4	Denny-StL	23.3
Rau-LA	2.57	Rau-LA	132	Seaver-NY	.213	Candelaria-Pit	.273	Jones-SD	26.7	Montefusco-SF	22.1
Seaver-NY	2.59	Zachry-Cin	128	Candelaria-Pit	.216	Seaver-NY	.273	Richard-Hou	24.2	Seaver-NY	21.2
Koosman-NY	2.69	Montefusco-SF	128	Messersmith-Atl	.219	Nolan-Cin	.276	Rau-LA	23.9	Rau-LA	20.8
Zachry-Cin	2.74	Seaver-NY	127	Falcone-StL	.222	Koosman-NY	.279	Denny-StL	22.5	Burris-Chi	20.8

Clutch Pitching Index		Relief Runs		Adjusted Relief Runs		Relief Ranking		Total Pitcher Index		Total Baseball Ranking	
Rau-LA	139	Hough-LA	20.5	Hough-LA	18.6	Eastwick-Cin	31.8	Denny-StL	3.0	Schmidt-Phi	6.5
Denny-StL	129	Eastwick-Cin	16.9	Eastwick-Cin	16.9	Hough-LA	28.8	Barr-SF	2.9	Morgan-Cin	6.0
Burris-Chi	118	Reed-Phi	14.8	Moffitt-SF	15.5	Moffitt-SF	21.0	Jones-SD	2.3	Foster-Cin	4.3
Christenson-Phi	112	Moffitt-SF	14.1	Reed-Phi	15.4	Reed-Phi	20.1	Rau-LA	2.3	Concepcion-Cin	4.1
Fryman-Mon	112	Forsch-Hou	13.8	Twitchell-Phi	12.3	Lavelle-SF	17.8	Seaver-NY	2.3	Cey-LA	4.0

TEAM	G	W	L	PCT	GB	R	OR	AB	H	2B	3B	HR	BB	SO	AVG	OBP	SLG	PRO	PRO+	BR	/A	PF	CHI	RC	SB	CS	SBA	SBR
EAST																												
NY	159	97	62	.610		730	**575**	5555	1496	231	36	120	470	**616**	.269	.330	.389	.719	111	64	**70**	99	103	723	163	65	71	10
BAL	162	88	74	.543	10.5	619	598	5457	1326	213	28	119	519	883	.243	.311	.358	.669	102	-33	7	94	102	612	150	61	71	8
BOS	162	83	79	.512	15.5	716	660	5511	1448	257	53	**134**	500	832	.263	.327	**.402**	**.729**	101	**80**	1	112	98	709	95	70	58	-14
CLE	159	81	78	.509	16	615	615	5412	1423	189	38	85	479	631	.263	.324	.359	.683	101	-2	5	99	97	611	75	69	52	-19
DET	161	74	87	.460	24	609	709	5441	1401	207	38	101	450	730	.257	.318	.365	.683	96	-7	-32	104	97	611	107	59	64	-3
MIL	161	66	95	.410	32	570	655	5396	1326	170	38	88	511	909	.246	.314	.340	.654	93	-57	-45	98	98	575	62	61	50	-18
WEST																												
KC	162	90	72	.556		713	611	5540	1490	**259**	**57**	65	484	650	.269	.331	.371	.702	104	37	32	101	103	687	218	106	67	2
OAK	161	87	74	.540	2.5	686	598	5353	1319	208	33	113	**592**	818	.246	.327	.361	.688	105	13	39	96	**105**	663	**341**	123	**73**	29
MIN	162	85	77	.525	5	**743**	704	5574	**1526**	222	51	81	550	714	**.274**	**.343**	.375	.718	107	78	59	103	100	**727**	146	75	66	-1
TEX	162	76	86	.469	14	616	652	5555	1390	213	26	80	568	809	.250	.323	.341	.664	99	-32	-46	102	98	616	87	45	66	-1
CAL	162	76	86	.469	14	550	631	5385	1265	210	23	63	534	812	.235	.309	.318	.627	90	-105	-65	94	102	531	126	80	61	-10
CHI	161	64	97	.398	25.5	586	745	5532	1410	209	46	73	471	739	.255	.317	.349	.666	94	-36	-40	101	96	622	120	53	69	4
TOT	967					7753		65711	16820	2588	467	1122	6128	9143	.256	.323	.361	.684							1690	867	66	-13

TEAM	CG	SH	SV	IP	H	H/G	HR	BB	SO	RAT	ERA	ERA+	OAV	OOB	PR	/A	PF	CPI	FA	E	DP	FW	PW	BW	SBW	DIF
EAST																										
NY	62	15	37	1455	**1300**	8.0	97	448	674	10.9	3.19	107	**.241**	**.301**	53	36	97	95	.980	126	141	.9	3.8	**7.4**	1.2	4.2
BAL	59	16	23	1468²	1396	8.6	**80**	489	678	11.7	3.32	99	.255	.318	33	-7	93	101	**.982**	118	157	**1.5**	-.7	.7	1.0	4.5
BOS	49	13	27	1458	1495	9.2	109	**409**	673	12.0	3.52	111	.267	.320	-1	62	111	104	.978	141	148	.2	**6.6**	-.1	-1.4	-3.5
CLE	30	**17**	**46**	1432	1361	8.6	**80**	533	928	12.1	3.47	101	.255	.326	8	3	99	101	.980	121	159	1.2	.3	.5	-1.9	1.4
DET	55	12	20	1431¹	1426	9.0	101	550	738	12.6	3.87	96	.263	.334	-56	-25	105	99	.974	168	161	-1.4	-2.7	-3.4	-.2	1.2
MIL	45	10	27	1435¹	1406	8.8	99	567	677	12.6	3.64	96	.260	.334	-20	-24	99	104	.975	152	160	-.5	-2.5	-4.8	-1.8	-4.9
WEST																										
KC	41	12	35	1472¹	1356	8.3	83	493	735	11.5	3.21	109	.247	.312	51	48	100	99	.978	139	147	.3	5.1	3.4	.3	-.1
OAK	39	15	29	1459¹	1412	8.7	96	415	711	11.5	3.26	103	.255	.310	42	16	95	101	.977	144	130	-.0	1.7	4.1	**3.2**	-2.5
MIN	29	11	23	1459	1421	8.8	69	610	762	12.8	3.69	97	.259	.337	-29	-16	102	102	.973	172	**182**	-1.6	-1.7	6.3	.0	1.0
TEX	63	15	15	1472	1464	9.0	106	461	773	12.0	3.45	104	.262	.322	10	21	102	**105**	.976	156	142	-.7	2.2	-4.9	.0	-1.7
CAL	**64**	15	17	1477¹	1323	8.1	95	553	**992**	11.7	3.36	99	**.241**	.315	26	-5	95	96	.977	150	139	-.3	-.5	-6.9	-.9	3.7
CHI	54	10	22	1448	1460	9.1	87	600	802	13.0	4.25	84	.266	.342	-118	-111	101	92	.979	130	155	.7	-11.8	-4.2	.5	-1.8
TOT	590	161	321	17468¹		8.7				12.0	3.52		.256	.323					.977	1717	1821					

Runs		Hits		Doubles		Triples		Home Runs		Total Bases	
White-NY	104	Brett-KC	215	Otis-KC	40	Brett-KC	14	Nettles-NY	32	Brett-KC	298
Carew-Min	97	Carew-Min	200	McRae-KC	34	Garner-Oak	12	R.Jackson-Bal	27	Chambliss-NY	283
Rivers-NY	95	Chambliss-NY	188	Evans-Cle	34	Carew-Min	12	Bando-Oak	27	Rice-Bos	280
Brett-KC	94	Munson-NY	186	Carty-Cle	34	Poquette-KC	10			Carew-Min	280
		Rivers-NY	184	Brett-KC	34	Bostock-Min	9			Nettles-NY	277

Runs Batted In		Runs Produced		Bases On Balls		Batting Average		On Base Percentage		Slugging Average	
L.May-Bal	109	Carew-Min	178	Hargrove-Tex	97	Brett-KC	.333	McRae-KC	.412	R.Jackson-Bal	.502
Munson-NY	105	Munson-NY	167	Harrah-Tex	91	McRae-KC	.332	Hargrove-Tex	.401	Rice-Bos	.482
Yastrzemski-Bos	102	Hisle-Min	163	Grich-Bal	86	Carew-Min	.331	Carew-Min	.398	Nettles-NY	.475
		Otis-KC	161	White-NY	83	Bostock-Min	.323	Staub-Det	.392	Lynn-Bos	.467
				Staub-Det	83	LeFlore-Det	.316	Carty-Cle	.384	Carew-Min	.463

Production		Adjusted Production		Batter Runs		Adjusted Batter Runs		Clutch Hitting Index		Runs Created	
McRae-KC	.873	R.Jackson-Bal	158	Carew-Min	40.0	McRae-KC	38.4	Mayberry-KC	160	Brett-KC	114
Carew-Min	.861	McRae-KC	154	McRae-KC	38.8	Carew-Min	37.9	Rudi-Oak	152	Carew-Min	111
R.Jackson-Bal	.855	Tenace-Oak	150	Brett-KC	36.2	Brett-KC	35.7	Hisle-Min	144	McRae-KC	101
Brett-KC	.843	Carew-Min	147	Staub-Det	33.2	R.Jackson-Bal	32.4	Randle-Tex	138	Staub-Det	99
Lynn-Bos	.842	Brett-KC	145	Carty-Cle	29.8	Carty-Cle	30.5	L.May-Bal	137	White-NY	98

Total Average		Stolen Bases		Stolen Base Average		Stolen Base Runs		Fielding Runs		Total Player Rating	
McRae-KC	.862	North-Oak	75	Rivers-NY	86.0	Campaneris-Oak	9.0	White-KC	21.1	Nettles-NY	4.1
R.Jackson-Bal	.857	LeFlore-Det	58	Campaneris-Oak	81.8	Rivers-NY	8.7	Kuiper-Cle	20.0	Brett-KC	4.0
Tenace-Oak	.855	Campaneris-Oak	54	Baylor-Oak	81.3	Baylor-Oak	8.4	Beniquez-Tex	19.5	McRae-KC	3.8
Carew-Min	.854	Baylor-Oak	52	Bumbry-Bal	80.8	Bumbry-Bal	6.6	Brohamer-Chi	18.0	Grich-Bal	3.7
Brett-KC	.797	Patek-KC	51	R.Jackson-Bal	80.0	Patek-KC	6.3	Nettles-NY	17.2	LeFlore-Det	3.6

Wins		Win Percentage		Games		Complete Games		Shutouts		Saves	
Palmer-Bal	22	Campbell-Min	.773	Campbell-Min	78	Fidrych-Det	24	Ryan-Cal	7	Lyle-NY	23
Tiant-Bos	21	Garland-Bal	.741	Fingers-Oak	70	Tanana-Cal	23	Blyleven-Min-Tex	6	LaRoche-Cle	21
Garland-Bal	20	Ellis-NY	.680	Lindblad-Oak	65	Palmer-Bal	23	Palmer-Bal	6	Fingers-Oak	20
		Fidrych-Det	.679	Lyle-NY	64			Blue-Oak	6	Campbell-Min	20
				LaRoche-Cle	61					Littell-KC	16

Innings Pitched		Fewest Hits/Game		Fewest BB/Game		Strikeouts		Strikeouts/Game		Ratio	
Palmer-Bal	315.0	Ryan-Cal	6.11	Bird-KC	1.41	Ryan-Cal	327	Ryan-Cal	10.35	Tanana-Cal	9.18
Hunter-NY	298.2	Tanana-Cal	6.62	Jenkins-Bos	1.85	Tanana-Cal	261	Eckersley-Cle	9.03	Fidrych-Det	9.81
Blue-Oak	298.1	Eckersley-Cle	7.00	Perry-Tex	1.87	Blyleven-Min-Tex	219	Tanana-Cal	8.15	Palmer-Bal	9.91
Blyleven-Min-Tex	297.2	Palmer-Bal	7.29	Blue-Oak	1.90	Eckersley-Cle	200	Blyleven-Min-Tex	6.62	Blue-Oak	10.02
Slaton-Mil	292.2	Brett-NY-Chi	7.67	Fidrych-Det	1.91	Hunter-NY	173	Campbell-Min	6.17	Perry-Tex	10.21

Earned Run Average		Adjusted ERA		Opponents' Batting Avg.		Opponents' On Base Pct.		Starter Runs		Adjusted Starter Runs	
Fidrych-Det	2.34	Fidrych-Det	159	Ryan-Cal	.195	Tanana-Cal	.261	Blue-Oak	38.6	Fidrych-Det	38.1
Blue-Oak	2.35	Blue-Oak	142	Tanana-Cal	.203	Fidrych-Det	.279	Palmer-Bal	35.1	Blue-Oak	33.1
Tanana-Cal	2.43	Tanana-Cal	137	Eckersley-Cle	.214	Blue-Oak	.280	Tanana-Cal	34.7	Tanana-Cal	28.5
Torrez-Oak	2.50	Torrez-Oak	134	Palmer-Bal	.224	Palmer-Bal	.282	Fidrych-Det	32.8	Palmer-Bal	26.5
Palmer-Bal	2.51	Palmer-Bal	130	Brett-NY-Chi	.233	Bird-KC	.283	Torrez-Oak	30.1	Tiant-Bos	26.2

Clutch Pitching Index		Relief Runs		Adjusted Relief Runs		Relief Ranking		Total Pitcher Index		Total Baseball Ranking	
Hartzell-Cal	124	Littell-KC	16.7	Hiller-Det	17.9	Hiller-Det	30.9	Fidrych-Det	5.0	Fidrych-Det	5.0
Travers-Mil	120	Fingers-Oak	15.6	Littell-KC	16.4	Fingers-Oak	25.5	Palmer-Bal	3.6	Nettles-NY	4.1
Umbarger-Tex	118	Hiller-Det	15.3	Kern-Cle	14.6	Lyle-NY	24.0	Tanana-Cal	3.5	Brett-KC	4.0
Garland-Bal	116	Kern-Cle	15.0	Burgmeier-Min	14.1	Kern-Cle	23.2	Blue-Oak	3.3	McRae-KC	3.8
Torrez-Oak	115	Lyle-NY	14.5	Thomas-Cle	11.6	Littell-KC	22.8	Torrez-Oak	2.9	Grich-Bal	3.7

2078 1977 National League

TEAM	G	W	L	PCT	GB	R	OR	AB	H	2B	3B	HR	BB	SO	AVG	OBP	SLG	PRO	PRO+	BR	/A	PF	CHI	RC	SB	CS	SBA	SBR
EAST																												
PHI	162	101	61	.623		**847**	668	5546	1548	266	56	186	573	806	**.279**	**.351**	**.448**	**.799**	**114**	**143**	**111**	104	98	**865**	135	68	67	0
PIT	162	96	66	.593	5	734	665	5662	**1550**	278	57	133	474	878	.274	.334	.413	.747	102	37	18	103	98	776	**260**	120	68	6
STL	162	83	79	.512	18	737	688	5527	1490	252	56	96	489	823	.270	.332	.388	.720	100	-13	0	98	**107**	690	134	112	54	-27
CHI	162	81	81	.500	20	692	739	5604	1489	271	37	111	534	**796**	.266	.333	.387	.720	88	-11	-91	111	98	709	64	45	59	-8
MON	162	75	87	.463	26	665	736	5675	1474	**294**	50	138	478	877	.260	.320	.402	.722	101	-20	1	97	95	715	88	50	64	-4
NY	162	64	98	.395	37	587	663	5410	1319	227	30	88	529	887	.244	.315	.346	.661	87	-125	-92	95	103	577	98	81	55	-19
WEST																												
LA	162	98	64	.605		769	**582**	5589	1484	223	28	**191**	588	896	.266	.338	.418	.756	109	58	62	100	98	794	114	62	65	-3
CIN	162	88	74	.543	10	802	725	5524	1513	269	42	181	600	911	.274	.348	.436	.784	113	115	102	102	97	847	170	64	**73**	**13**
HOU	162	81	81	.500	17	680	650	5530	1405	263	**60**	114	515	839	.254	.322	.385	.707	104	-41	22	91	102	697	187	72	72	**13**
SF	162	75	87	.463	23	673	711	5497	1392	227	41	134	568	842	.253	.326	.383	.709	95	-35	-32	100	100	683	90	59	60	-8
SD	162	69	93	.426	29	692	834	5602	1397	245	49	120	**602**	1057	.249	.325	.375	.700	104	-49	26	90	102	700	133	57	70	6
ATL	162	61	101	.377	37	678	895	5534	1404	218	20	139	537	876	.254	.322	.376	.698	82	-58	-142	112	104	660	82	53	61	-7
TOT	972					8556		66700	17465	3033	526	1631	6487	10488	.262	.330	.396	.727							1555	843	65	-39

TEAM	CG	SH	SV	IP	H	H/G	HR	BB	SO	RAT	ERA	ERA+	OAV	OOB	PR	/A	PF	CPI	FA	E	DP	FW	PW	BW	SBW	DIF
EAST																										
PHI	31	7	**47**	1455^{2}	1451	9.0	134	482	856	12.1	3.71	108	.263	.325	32	47	102	103	.981	120	168	1.3	4.8	**11.2**	.3	2.4
PIT	25	**15**	39	1481^{2}	1406	**8.5**	149	485	890	11.6	3.61	110	.252	.314	50	62	102	99	.977	145	137	-.0	6.3	1.8	.9	6.0
STL	26	10	31	1446	1420	8.8	139	532	768	12.3	3.81	101	.260	.329	16	6	98	102	.978	139	**174**	.3	.6	.0	-2.4	3.5
CHI	16	10	44	1468	1500	9.2	128	489	**942**	12.3	4.01	109	.266	.327	-16	61	112	96	.977	153	147	-.5	6.2	-9.2	-.5	4.0
MON	31	11	33	1481	1426	8.7	135	579	856	12.3	4.01	95	.255	.327	-17	-34	97	94	.980	129	128	.8	-3.4	.1	-.0	-3.4
NY	27	12	28	1433^{2}	**1378**	8.7	118	490	911	11.9	3.77	99	.254	.319	22	-6	96	94	.978	134	132	.5	-.6	-9.3	-1.6	-6.0
WEST																										
LA	34	13	39	1475^{1}	1393	**8.5**	119	**438**	930	**11.3**	**3.22**	**119**	**.251**	**.309**	**113**	**99**	98	104	.981	124	160	1.1	**10.0**	6.3	.0	-.4
CIN	33	12	32	1437^{1}	1469	9.2	156	544	868	12.8	4.21	93	.267	.337	-49	-46	101	100	**.984**	**95**	154	**2.7**	-4.7	10.3	**1.6**	-3.0
HOU	**37**	11	28	1465^{2}	1384	**8.5**	**110**	545	871	12.0	3.54	101	**.251**	.321	61	5	91	99	.978	142	136	.0	.5	2.2	**1.6**	-4.5
SF	27	10	33	1459	1501	9.3	114	529	854	12.7	3.75	104	.267	.333	26	26	100	104	.972	179	136	-2.0	2.6	-3.2	-.5	-2.9
SD	6	5	44	1466^{1}	1556	9.6	160	673	827	13.8	4.43	80	.276	.355	-85	-146	91	**105**	.971	189	142	-2.5	-14.8	2.6	.9	1.7
ATL	28	5	31	1445^{1}	1581	9.8	169	701	915	14.5	4.85	92	.279	.363	-151	-65	114	101	.972	175	127	-1.7	-6.6	-14.4	-.4	3.1
TOT	321	121	429	17515		9.0				12.5	3.91		.262	.330					.977	1724	1741					

Runs
Foster-Cin 124
Griffey-Cin 117
Schmidt-Phi 114
Morgan-Cin 113
Parker-Pit 107

Hits
Parker-Pit 215
Rose-Cin 204
Templeton-StL 200
Foster-Cin 197
Garvey-LA 192

Doubles
Parker-Pit 44
Cash-Mon 42
Hernandez-StL 41
Cromartie-Mon 41

Triples
Templeton-StL 18
Schmidt-Phi 11
Richards-SD 11
Almon-SD 11

Home Runs
Foster-Cin 52
Burroughs-Atl 41
Luzinski-Phi 39
Schmidt-Phi 38
Garvey-LA 33

Total Bases
Foster-Cin 388
Parker-Pit 338
Luzinski-Phi 329
Garvey-LA 322
Schmidt-Phi 312

Runs Batted In
Foster-Cin 149
Luzinski-Phi 130
Garvey-LA 115
Burroughs-Atl 114

Runs Produced
Foster-Cin 221
Luzinski-Phi 190
Schmidt-Phi 177
Parker-Pit 174
Garvey-LA 173

Bases On Balls
Tenace-SD 125
Morgan-Cin 117
Smith-LA 104
Schmidt-Phi 104
Cey-LA 93

Batting Average
Parker-Pit .... .338
Templeton-StL ...... .322
Foster-Cin .... .320
Griffey-Cin .... .318
Simmons-StL ...... .318

On Base Percentage
Smith-LA .... .432
Morgan-Cin .... .420
Tenace-SD .... .417
Simmons-StL ...... .410
Parker-Pit .... .399

Slugging Average
Foster-Cin .... .631
Luzinski-Phi .... .594
Smith-LA .... .576
Schmidt-Phi .... .574
Bench-Cin .... .540

Production
Foster-Cin 1.017
Smith-LA 1.008
Luzinski-Phi .... .993
Schmidt-Phi .... .972
Parker-Pit .... .929

Adjusted Production
Smith-LA 168
Foster-Cin 165
Luzinski-Phi 155
Schmidt-Phi 151
Hendrick-SD 148

Batter Runs
Foster-Cin 56.0
Smith-LA 50.3
Luzinski-Phi 48.6
Schmidt-Phi 45.8
Parker-Pit 42.0

Adjusted Batter Runs
Foster-Cin 54.6
Smith-LA 50.6
Luzinski-Phi 45.3
Schmidt-Phi 42.4
Parker-Pit 39.8

Clutch Hitting Index
Cey-LA 136
Watson-Hou 131
Bench-Cin 124
Luzinski-Phi 124
Robinson-Pit 123

Runs Created
Foster-Cin 144
Luzinski-Phi 132
Parker-Pit 130
Schmidt-Phi 129
Smith-LA 129

Total Average
Smith-LA 1.121
Morgan-Cin 1.054
Schmidt-Phi 1.046
Luzinski-Phi 1.043
Foster-Cin 1.039

Stolen Bases
Taveras-Pit 70
Cedeno-Hou 61
Richards-SD 56
Moreno-Pit 53
Morgan-Cin 49

Stolen Base Average
Bowa-Phi 91.4
McBride-StL-Phi .. 83.7
Morgan-Cin 83.1
Richards-SD 82.4
Cedeno-Hou 81.3

Stolen Base Runs
Taveras-Pit 10.2
Cedeno-Hou 9.9
Richards-SD 9.6
Morgan-Cin 8.7
Bowa-Phi 7.8

Fielding Runs
DeJesus-Chi 35.8
Trillo-Chi 30.1
Schmidt-Phi 28.8
Parker-Pit 28.1
Tyson-StL 22.0

Total Player Rating
Schmidt-Phi 6.8
Foster-Cin 6.0
Parker-Pit 5.5
Smith-LA 3.6
Morgan-Cin 3.5

Wins
Carlton-Phi 23
Seaver-NY-Cin 21

Win Percentage
Candelaria-Pit ..... .800
Seaver-NY-Cin ..... .778
Christenson-Phi ... .760
John-LA .... .741
Forsch-StL .... .741

Games
Fingers-SD 78
Tomlin-SD 76
Spillner-SD 76
Metzger-SD-StL ... 75

Complete Games
Niekro-Atl 20
Seaver-NY-Cin 19
Rogers-Mon 17
Carlton-Phi 17
Richard-Hou 13

Shutouts
Seaver-NY-Cin 7
Rogers-Mon 4
R.Reuschel-Chi 4

Saves
Fingers-SD 35
Sutter-Chi 31
Gossage-Pit 26
Hough-LA 22

Innings Pitched
Niekro-Atl 330.1
Rogers-Mon 301.2
Carlton-Phi 283.0
Richard-Hou 267.0
Seaver-NY-Cin ... 261.1

Fewest Hits/Game
Seaver-NY-Cin 6.85
Richard-Hou 7.15
Carlton-Phi 7.28
Hooton-LA 7.41
Candelaria-Pit 7.69

Fewest BB/Game
Candelaria-Pit 1.95
John-LA 2.04
Rau-LA 2.08
Barr-SF 2.15
Lemongello-Hou .. 2.18

Strikeouts
Niekro-Atl 262
Richard-Hou 214
Rogers-Mon 206
Carlton-Phi 198
Seaver-NY-Cin 196

Strikeouts/Game
Koosman-NY 7.62
Richard-Hou 7.21
Niekro-Atl 7.14
Seaver-NY-Cin 6.75
Matlack-NY 6.55

Ratio
Seaver-NY-Cin 9.13
Candelaria-Pit 9.72
Hooton-LA 9.95
Carlton-Phi 10.24
Sutton-LA 10.45

Earned Run Average
Candelaria-Pit 2.34
Seaver-NY-Cin 2.58
Hooton-LA 2.62
Carlton-Phi 2.64
John-LA 2.78

Adjusted ERA
Candelaria-Pit 170
R.Reuschel-Chi ... 157
Carlton-Phi 151
Seaver-NY-Cin 149
Hooton-LA 146

Opponents' Batting Avg.
Seaver-NY-Cin ..... .209
Richard-Hou .... .218
Carlton-Phi .... .223
Hooton-LA .... .225
Koosman-NY ...... .232

Opponents' On Base Pct.
Seaver-NY-Cin ..... .260
Candelaria-Pit ..... .276
Hooton-LA .... .281
Carlton-Phi .... .287
Sutton-LA .... .291

Starter Runs
Candelaria-Pit 40.2
Carlton-Phi 39.9
Seaver-NY-Cin 38.5
Hooton-LA 32.0
R.Reuschel-Chi ... 31.4

Adjusted Starter Runs
R.Reuschel-Chi ... 44.8
Carlton-Phi 42.7
Candelaria-Pit 42.1
Seaver-NY-Cin 37.0
Hooton-LA 29.9

Clutch Pitching Index
Candelaria-Pit 126
John-LA 120
Rooker-Pit 118
Lemongello-Hou .. 116
Rau-LA 114

Relief Runs
Gossage-Pit 33.8
Sutter-Chi 30.6
Lavelle-SF 24.4
Garber-Phi 17.9
Reed-Phi 16.0

Adjusted Relief Runs
Sutter-Chi 36.3
Gossage-Pit 34.9
Lavelle-SF 24.4
Garber-Phi 18.9
Reed-Phi 17.2

Relief Ranking
Gossage-Pit 62.5
Sutter-Chi 54.0
Lavelle-SF 35.3
Garber-Phi 30.9
G.Hernandez-Chi . 21.7

Total Pitcher Index
Carlton-Phi 5.7
R.Reuschel-Chi 5.5
Candelaria-Pit 4.8
Seaver-NY-Cin 4.4
Sutter-Chi 3.9

Total Baseball Ranking
Schmidt-Phi 6.8
Foster-Cin 6.0
Carlton-Phi 5.7
Parker-Pit 5.5
R.Reuschel-Chi 5.5

TEAM	G	W	L	PCT	GB	R	OR	AB	H	2B	3B	HR	BB	SO	AVG	OBP	SLG	PRO	PRO+	BR	/A	PF	CHI	RC	SB	CS	SBA	SBR
EAST																												
NY	162	100	62	.617		831	651	5605	1576	267	47	184	533	681	.281	.347	.444	.791	115	104	112	99	98	853	93	57	62	-6
BAL	161	97	64	.602	2.5	719	653	5494	1433	231	25	148	560	945	.261	.332	.393	.725	103	-23	22	94	102	711	90	51	64	-4
BOS	161	97	64	.602	2.5	859	712	5510	1551	258	56	213	528	905	.281	.349	.465	.814	107	144	58	112	98	875	66	47	58	-8
DET	162	74	88	.457	26	714	751	5604	1480	228	45	166	452	764	.264	.321	.410	.731	93	-25	-64	105	101	717	60	46	57	-10
CLE	161	71	90	.441	28.5	676	739	5491	1476	221	46	100	531	688	.269	.337	.380	.717	98	-31	-8	97	96	682	87	87	50	-26
MIL	162	67	95	.414	33	639	765	5517	1425	255	46	125	443	862	.258	.316	.389	.705	91	-73	-72	100	99	660	85	67	56	-15
TOR	161	54	107	.335	45.5	605	822	5418	1367	230	41	100	499	819	.252	.318	.365	.683	85	-106	-116	101	99	610	65	55	54	-14
WEST																												
KC	162	102	60	.630		822	651	5594	1549	299	77	146	522	687	.277	.343	.436	.779	110	82	76	101	100	835	170	87	66	-1
TEX	162	94	68	.580	8	767	657	5541	1497	265	39	135	596	904	.270	.345	.405	.750	103	34	26	101	98	780	154	85	64	-5
CHI	162	90	72	.556	12	844	771	5633	1568	254	52	192	559	666	.278	.347	.444	.791	114	107	108	100	99	858	42	44	49	-14
MIN	161	84	77	.522	17.5	867	776	5639	1588	273	60	123	563	754	.282	.351	.417	.768	110	71	82	99	105	827	105	65	62	-8
CAL	162	74	88	.457	28	675	695	5410	1380	233	40	131	542	880	.255	.327	.386	.713	97	-47	-18	96	100	681	159	89	64	-6
SEA	162	64	98	.395	38	624	855	5460	1398	218	33	133	426	769	.256	.314	.381	.695	89	-91	-84	99	100	643	110	67	62	-7
OAK	161	63	98	.391	38.5	605	749	5358	1284	176	37	117	516	910	.240	.311	.352	.663	81	-145	-134	99	107	589	176	89	66	-1
TOT	1131					10247		77274	20572	3408	644	2013	7270	11234	.266	.333	.405	.738							1462	936	61	-123

TEAM	CG	SH	SV	IP	H	H/G	HR	BB	SO	RAT	ERA	ERA+	OAV	OOB	PR	/A	PF	CPI	FA	E	DP	FW	PW	BW	SBW	DIF
EAST																										
NY	52	16	34	1449¹	1395	8.7	139	486	758	11.8	3.61	109	.254	.318	73	54	97	101	.979	132	151	.6	5.4	11.1	.3	1.6
BAL	65	11	23	1451	1414	8.8	124	494	737	12.0	3.74	101	.260	.325	51	8	93	101	.983	106	189	2.0	.8	2.2	.5	11.0
BOS	40	13	40	1428	1555	9.8	158	378	758	12.3	4.11	109	.278	.327	-8	60	111	102	.978	133	162	.5	6.0	5.8	.0	4.2
DET	44	3	23	1457	1526	9.4	162	470	784	12.5	4.13	104	.271	.329	-11	26	106	100	.978	142	153	.0	2.6	-6.4	-.1	-3.1
CLE	45	8	30	1452¹	1441	8.9	136	550	876	12.5	4.10	96	.261	.331	-6	-25	97	96	.979	130	145	.7	-2.5	-.8	-1.7	-5.2
MIL	38	6	25	1431	1461	9.2	136	566	719	13.0	4.32	94	.268	.341	-42	-40	100	97	.978	139	165	.2	-4.0	-7.2	-.6	-2.5
TOR	40	3	20	1428¹	1538	9.7	152	623	771	13.7	4.57	92	.278	.354	-81	-59	103	101	.974	164	133	-1.2	-5.9	-11.5	-.5	-7.3
WEST																										
KC	41	15	42	1460²	1377	8.5	110	499	850	11.8	3.52	115	.251	.318	88	84	99	98	.978	137	145	.3	8.3	7.5	.8	4.0
TEX	49	17	31	1472¹	1412	8.6	134	471	864	11.7	3.56	114	.255	.317	81	84	101	101	.982	117	156	1.5	8.3	2.6	.4	.2
CHI	34	3	40	1444²	1557	9.7	136	516	842	13.2	4.25	96	.277	.342	-31	-27	101	101	.974	159	125	-.9	-2.7	10.7	-.5	2.4
MIN	34	5	25	1442	1546	9.6	151	507	737	13.0	4.36	91	.278	.342	-48	-60	98	101	.978	143	184	-.0	-6.0	8.1	.0	1.3
CAL	53	13	26	1437²	1383	8.7	136	572	965	12.5	3.72	105	.256	.333	54	31	96	105	.976	147	137	-.2	3.1	-1.8	.3	-8.3
SEA	18	1	31	1433	1508	9.5	194	578	785	13.5	4.83	85	.272	.347	-123	-114	101	96	.976	147	162	-.2	-11.3	-8.3	.2	2.7
OAK	32	4	26	1436²	1459	9.1	145	560	788	12.8	4.04	100	.265	.336	3	-3	99	102	.970	190	136	-2.7	-.3	-13.3	.8	-1.9
TOT	586	117	416	20224		9.2				12.6	4.06		.266	.333					.977	1986	2143					

Runs		Hits		Doubles		Triples		Home Runs		Total Bases	
Carew-Min	128	Carew-Min	239	McRae-KC	54	Carew-Min	16	Rice-Bos	39	Rice-Bos	382
Fisk-Bos	106	LeFlore-Det	212	Jackson-NY	39	Rice-Bos	15	Nettles-NY	37	Carew-Min	351
Brett-KC	105	Rice-Bos	206	Lemon-Chi	38	Cowens-KC	14	Bonds-Cal	37	McRae-KC	330
		Bostock-Min	199	Carew-Min	38	Brett-KC	13	Scott-Bos	33	Cowens-KC	318
		Burleson-Bos	194			Bostock-Min	12	Jackson-NY	32	LeFlore-Det	310

Runs Batted In		Runs Produced		Bases On Balls		Batting Average		On Base Percentage		Slugging Average	
Hisle-Min	119	Carew-Min	214	Harrah-Tex	109	Carew-Min	.388	Carew-Min	.452	Rice-Bos	.593
Bonds-Cal	115	Cowens-KC	187	Singleton-Bal	107	Bostock-Min	.336	Singleton-Bal	.442	Carew-Min	.570
Rice-Bos	114	Hisle-Min	186	Hargrove-Tex	103	Singleton-Bal	.328	Hargrove-Tex	.424	Jackson-NY	.550
Hobson-Bos	112	Fisk-Bos	182	Gross-Oak	86	Rivers-NY	.326	Fisk-Bos	.408	Hisle-Min	.533
Cowens-KC	112	Bonds-Cal	181	Mayberry-KC	83	LeFlore-Det	.325	Page-Oak	.407	Brett-KC	.532

Production		Adjusted Production		Batter Runs		Adjusted Batter Runs		Clutch Hitting Index		Runs Created	
Carew-Min	1.022	Carew-Min	179	Carew-Min	67.0	Carew-Min	68.2	Wynegar-Min	141	Carew-Min	160
Rice-Bos	.972	Singleton-Bal	168	Rice-Bos	51.4	Singleton-Bal	53.3	Hisle-Min	133	Rice-Bos	136
Singleton-Bal	.949	Page-Oak	153	Singleton-Bal	48.5	Rice-Bos	41.6	Doyle-Bos	133	Singleton-Bal	124
Fisk-Bos	.929	Jackson-NY	151	Fisk-Bos	39.9	Page-Oak	38.4	Sundberg-Tex	133	McRae-KC	119
Page-Oak	.928	Thornton-Cle	149	Hargrove-Tex	37.8	Hargrove-Tex	37.0	Carty-Cle	133	Page-Oak	117

Total Average		Stolen Bases		Stolen Base Average		Stolen Base Runs		Fielding Runs		Total Player Rating	
Carew-Min	1.093	Patek-KC	53	Page-Oak	89.4	Page-Oak	9.6	Lemon-Chi	34.9	Carew-Min	6.2
Page-Oak	1.064	Page-Oak	42	Jackson-NY	85.0	Patek-KC	8.1	Sundberg-Tex	22.9	Page-Oak	4.8
Singleton-Bal	1.011	Remy-Cal	41	Harrah-Tex	84.4	Harrah-Tex	5.1	R.Jones-Sea	22.0	Singleton-Bal	4.6
Jackson-NY	.997	Bonds-Cal	41	White-KC	82.1	White-KC	3.9	Belanger-Bal	20.7	Brett-KC	4.5
Harrah-Tex	.964	LeFlore-Det	39	Patek-KC	80.3			Smalley-Min	18.7	Lemon-Chi	4.0

Wins		Win Percentage		Games		Complete Games		Shutouts		Saves	
Palmer-Bal	20	Splittorff-KC	.727	Lyle-NY	72	Ryan-Cal	22	Tanana-Cal	7	Campbell-Bos	31
Leonard-KC	20	T.Johnson-Min	.696	T.Johnson-Min	71	Palmer-Bal	22	Leonard-KC	5	Lyle-NY	26
Goltz-Min	20	Guidry-NY	.696	Campbell-Bos	69	Leonard-KC	21	Guidry-NY	5	LaGrow-Chi	25
Ryan-Cal	19	Rozema-Det	.682	McClure-Mil	68	Garland-Cle	21	Blyleven-Tex	5	Kern-Cle	18
				LaGrow-Chi	66	Tanana-Cal	20			LaRoche-Cle-Cal	17

Innings Pitched		Fewest Hits/Game		Fewest BB/Game		Strikeouts		Strikeouts/Game		Ratio	
Palmer-Bal	319.0	Ryan-Cal	5.96	Rozema-Det	1.40	Ryan-Cal	341	Ryan-Cal	10.26	Blyleven-Tex	9.86
Goltz-Min	303.0	Blyleven-Tex	6.94	Jenkins-Bos	1.68	Leonard-KC	244	Tanana-Cal	7.65	Eckersley-Cle	10.01
Ryan-Cal	299.0	Palmer-Bal	7.42	Hartzell-Cal	1.81	Tanana-Cal	205	Guidry-NY	7.52	Guidry-NY	10.21
Leonard-KC	292.2	Guidry-NY	7.43	Eckersley-Cle	1.96	Palmer-Bal	193	Leonard-KC	7.50	Tanana-Cal	10.22
Garland-Cle	282.2	Tanana-Cal	7.50	Cleveland-Bos	2.03	Eckersley-Cle	191	Blyleven-Tex	6.98	Leonard-KC	10.24

Earned Run Average		Adjusted ERA		Opponents' Batting Avg.		Opponents' On Base Pct.		Starter Runs		Adjusted Starter Runs	
Tanana-Cal	2.54	Tanana-Cal	154	Ryan-Cal	.193	Eckersley-Cle	.278	Ryan-Cal	42.8	Ryan-Cal	38.0
Blyleven-Tex	2.72	Blyleven-Tex	150	Blyleven-Tex	.214	Blyleven-Tex	.279	Palmer-Bal	40.8	Tanana-Cal	36.9
Ryan-Cal	2.77	Ryan-Cal	141	Guidry-NY	.224	Guidry-NY	.284	Tanana-Cal	40.8	Blyleven-Tex	35.3
Guidry-NY	2.82	Guidry-NY	140	Tanana-Cal	.227	Leonard-KC	.285	Blyleven-Tex	34.8	Leonard-KC	32.2
Palmer-Bal	2.91	Rozema-Det	139	Leonard-KC	.227	Tanana-Cal	.286	Leonard-KC	33.0	Palmer-Bal	31.3

Clutch Pitching Index		Relief Runs		Adjusted Relief Runs		Relief Ranking		Total Pitcher Index		Total Baseball Ranking	
Slaton-Mil	118	Lyle-NY	28.8	Lyle-NY	27.0	Campbell-Bos	45.6	Tanana-Cal	4.2	Carew-Min	6.2
Rozema-Det	116	Torrealba-Oak	18.6	Campbell-Bos	23.8	Lyle-NY	43.4	Ryan-Cal	4.0	Page-Oak	4.8
Grimsley-Bal	110	LaGrow-Chi	17.5	Torrealba-Oak	18.1	Romo-Sea	28.1	Blyleven-Tex	3.8	Singleton-Bal	4.6
Splittorff-KC	108	Campbell-Bos	17.1	LaGrow-Chi	17.8	LaGrow-Chi	26.3	Palmer-Bal	3.8	Brett-KC	4.5
Tanana-Cal	106	Coleman-Oak	15.6	Romo-Sea	16.2	T.Johnson-Min	22.8	Rozema-Det	3.1	Tanana-Cal	4.2

TEAM	G	W	L	PCT	GB	R	OR	AB	H	2B	3B	HR	BB	SO	AVG	OBP	SLG	PRO	PRO+	BR	/A	PF	CHI	RC	SB	CS	SBA	SBR
EAST																												
PHI	162	90	72	.556		708	586	5448	1404	248	32	133	552	866	.258	.331	.388	.719	106	49	43	101	101	715	152	58	72	11
PIT	161	88	73	.547	1.5	684	637	5406	1390	239	**54**	115	480	874	.257	.323	.385	.708	100	21	-8	105	104	676	**213**	90	70	10
CHI	162	79	83	.488	11	664	724	5532	**1461**	224	48	72	562	746	**.264**	.334	.361	.695	90	11	-69	112	99	673	110	58	65	-2
MON	162	76	86	.469	14	633	611	5530	1404	269	31	121	396	881	.254	.308	.379	.687	98	-27	-19	99	103	629	80	42	66	-1
STL	162	69	93	.426	21	600	657	5415	1351	263	44	79	420	**713**	.249	.306	.358	.664	92	-66	-57	99	106	583	97	42	70	4
NY	162	66	96	.407	24	607	690	5433	1332	227	47	86	549	829	.245	.317	.352	.669	96	-47	-24	96	101	600	100	77	56	-16
WEST																												
LA	162	95	67	.586		**727**	573	5437	1435	251	27	**149**	610	818	**.264**	**.340**	**.402**	**.742**	114	98	101	100	96	763	137	52	72	10
CIN	161	92	69	.571	2.5	710	688	5392	1378	270	32	136	**636**	899	.256	.337	.393	.730	110	75	75	100	97	730	137	58	70	6
SF	162	89	73	.549	6	613	594	5364	1331	240	41	117	564	814	.248	.320	.374	.694	104	-1	24	96	95	647	87	54	62	-6
SD	162	84	78	.519	11	591	598	5360	1349	208	42	75	536	848	.252	.323	.348	.671	102	-37	13	92	98	624	152	70	68	4
HOU	162	74	88	.457	21	605	634	5458	1408	231	45	70	434	743	.258	.315	.355	.670	101	-49	-1	93	103	608	178	59	**75**	**18**
ATL	162	69	93	.426	26	600	750	5381	1313	191	39	123	550	874	.244	.317	.363	.680	86	-28	-100	111	98	608	90	65	58	-12
TOT	971					7742		65156	16556	2861	482	1276	6279	9905	.254	.323	.372	.694							1533	725	68	25

TEAM	CG	SH	SV	IP	H	H/G	HR	BB	SO	RAT	ERA	ERA+	OAV	OOB	PR	/A	PF	CPI	FA	E	DP	FW	PW	BW	SBW	DIF
EAST																										
PHI	38	9	29	1436.1	1343	8.4	118	**393**	813	11.0	3.33	107	.251	**.305**	39	37	100	99	**.983**	104	156	2.0	3.9	4.5	.9	-2.4
PIT	30	13	44	1444.2	1366	8.5	103	499	880	11.8	3.41	108	.249	.315	26	46	104	98	.973	167	133	-1.4	4.9	-.8	.8	4.1
CHI	24	7	38	1455.1	1475	9.1	125	539	768	12.7	4.05	99	.265	.333	-77	-4	113	98	.978	144	154	-.2	-.4	-7.3	-.4	6.3
MON	42	13	32	1446	1332	8.3	117	572	740	11.8	3.42	103	.249	.325	24	16	99	106	.979	134	150	.4	1.7	-2.0	-.3	-4.7
STL	32	13	22	1437.2	**1300**	8.1	94	600	859	12.1	3.58	98	**.245**	.326	-1	-11	98	97	.978	136	155	.3	-1.2	-6.0	.2	-5.3
NY	21	7	26	1455.1	1447	8.9	114	531	775	12.4	3.87	90	.265	.334	-48	-62	98	101	.979	132	160	.5	-6.6	-2.5	-1.9	-4.5
WEST																										
LA	46	16	38	1440.1	1362	8.5	107	440	800	11.4	**3.12**	112	.250	.309	73	62	98	106	.978	140	138	.0	6.6	10.7	.8	-4.1
CIN	16	10	46	1448.1	1437	8.9	122	567	908	12.6	3.81	93	.261	.332	-38	-42	99	102	.978	134	120	.3	-4.4	7.9	.4	7.3
SF	42	17	29	1455.2	1377	8.5	84	453	840	11.5	3.30	104	.252	.311	44	23	96	98	.977	146	118	-.3	2.4	2.5	-.9	4.1
SD	21	10	**55**	1433.2	1385	8.7	**74**	483	744	11.8	3.28	101	.257	.320	47	8	93	104	.975	160	171	-1.0	.8	1.4	.2	1.6
HOU	**48**	**17**	23	1440.1	1328	8.3	86	578	**930**	12.1	3.63	91	.247	.323	-9	-52	93	94	.978	133	109	.4	-5.5	-.1	**1.7**	-3.5
ATL	29	12	32	1440.1	1404	8.8	132	624	848	12.9	4.08	99	.257	.337	-81	-5	113	98	.975	153	126	-.6	-.5	-10.6	-1.5	1.2
TOT	389	144	414	17333.1		8.6				12.0	3.57		.254	.323					.978	1683	1690					

Runs		Hits		Doubles		Triples		Home Runs		Total Bases	
DeJesus-Chi	104	Garvey-LA	202	Rose-Cin	51	Templeton-StL	13	Foster-Cin	40	Parker-Pit	340
Rose-Cin	103	Rose-Cin	198	Clark-SF	46	Richards-SD	12	Luzinski-Phi	35	Foster-Cin	330
Parker-Pit	102	Cabell-Hou	195	Simmons-StL	40	Parker-Pit	12	Parker-Pit	30	Garvey-LA	319
Foster-Cin	97	Parker-Pit	194	Parrish-Mon	39			Smith-LA	29	Clark-SF	318
Moreno-Pit	95	Bowa-Phi	192	Perez-Mon	38					Winfield-SD	293

Runs Batted In		Runs Produced		Bases On Balls		Batting Average		On Base Percentage		Slugging Average	
Foster-Cin	120	Parker-Pit	189	Burroughs-Atl	117	Parker-Pit	.334	Burroughs-Atl	.436	Parker-Pit	.585
Parker-Pit	117	Garvey-LA	181	Evans-SF	105	Garvey-LA	.316	Parker-Pit	.395	Smith-LA	.559
Garvey-LA	113	Foster-Cin	177	Tenace-SD	101	Cruz-Hou	.315	Tenace-SD	.394	Foster-Cin	.546
Luzinski-Phi	101	Clark-SF	163	Luzinski-Phi	100	Madlock-SF	.309	Smith-LA	.392	Clark-SF	.537
Clark-SF	98	Winfield-SD	161	Cey-LA	96	Winfield-SD	.308	Luzinski-Phi	.390	Burroughs-Atl	.529

Production		Adjusted Production		Batter Runs		Adjusted Batter Runs		Clutch Hitting Index		Runs Created	
Parker-Pit	.981	Smith-LA	164	Parker-Pit	52.9	Parker-Pit	49.9	Morgan-Cin	145	Parker-Pit	134
Burroughs-Atl	.965	Parker-Pit	163	Burroughs-Atl	50.1	Burroughs-Atl	42.8	Montanez-NY	139	Burroughs-Atl	116
Smith-LA	.951	Clark-SF	155	Luzinski-Phi	40.9	Luzinski-Phi	40.3	W.Robinson-Pit	136	Foster-Cin	115
Luzinski-Phi	.916	Winfield-SD	153	Foster-Cin	39.2	Foster-Cin	39.2	Reitz-StL	136	Luzinski-Phi	114
Foster-Cin	.909	Luzinski-Phi	152	Smith-LA	37.8	Clark-SF	38.5	Watson-Hou	128	Clark-SF	109

Total Average		Stolen Bases		Stolen Base Average		Stolen Base Runs		Fielding Runs		Total Player Rating	
Burroughs-Atl	1.042	Moreno-Pit	71	Cedeno-Hou	92.0	Lopes-LA	11.1	Trillo-Chi	28.9	Parker-Pit	5.2
Parker-Pit	1.025	Taveras-Pit	46	Lopes-LA	91.8	Moreno-Pit	8.1	Smith-SD	25.6	Clark-SF	4.2
Smith-LA	1.009	Lopes-LA	45	McBride-Phi	90.3	McBride-Phi	6.6	Templeton-StL	22.9	Lopes-LA	4.0
Luzinski-Phi	.957	DeJesus-Chi	41	Sexton-Hou	88.9			Thomas-SD	21.6	Templeton-StL	3.8
Foster-Cin	.893	Smith-SD	40	Bowa-Phi	84.4			Puhl-Hou	19.5	Smith-SD	3.8

Wins		Win Percentage		Games		Complete Games		Shutouts		Saves	
Perry-SD	21	Perry-SD	.778	Tekulve-Pit	91	Niekro-Atl	22	Knepper-SF	6	Fingers-SD	37
Grimsley-Mon	20	Hooton-LA	.655	Littell-StL	72	Grimsley-Mon	19	Niekro-Atl	4	Tekulve-Pit	31
Niekro-Atl	19	Grimsley-Mon	.645	Moore-Chi	71	Richard-Hou	16	Halicki-SF	4	Bair-Cin	28
Hooton-LA	19	Blue-SF	.643	Moffitt-SF	70	Knepper-SF	16	Blyleven-Pit	4	Sutter-Chi	27
		John-LA	.630	Bair-Cin	70			Blue-SF	4	Garber-Phi-Atl	25

Innings Pitched		Fewest Hits/Game		Fewest BB/Game		Strikeouts		Strikeouts/Game		Ratio	
Niekro-Atl	334.1	Richard-Hou	6.28	Christenson-Phi	1.86	Richard-Hou	303	Richard-Hou	9.90	Swan-NY	9.72
Richard-Hou	275.1	Swan-NY	7.12	Barr-SF	1.93	Niekro-Atl	248	Seaver-Cin	7.83	Hooton-LA	9.80
Grimsley-Mon	263.0	Hooton-LA	7.47	R.Reuschel-Chi	2.00	Seaver-Cin	226	Vuckovich-StL	6.76	Halicki-SF	9.86
Perry-SD	260.2	Halicki-SF	7.51	Halicki-SF	2.04	Blyleven-Pit	182	Blyleven-Pit	6.72	Christenson-Phi	10.14
Knepper-SF	260.0	Knepper-SF	7.55	Sutton-LA	2.04	Montefusco-SF	177	Niekro-Atl	6.68	Rogers-Mon	10.36

Earned Run Average		Adjusted ERA		Opponents' Batting Avg.		Opponents' On Base Pct.		Starter Runs		Adjusted Starter Runs	
Swan-NY	2.43	Swan-NY	143	Richard-Hou	.196	Halicki-SF	.271	Knepper-SF	27.3	Niekro-Atl	43.3
Rogers-Mon	2.47	Rogers-Mon	143	Swan-NY	.219	Swan-NY	.277	Rogers-Mon	27.0	Rogers-Mon	25.7
Vuckovich-StL	2.54	Niekro-Atl	140	Halicki-SF	.221	Hooton-LA	.277	Swan-NY	26.4	Swan-NY	24.3
Knepper-SF	2.63	Vuckovich-StL	138	Hooton-LA	.226	Christenson-Phi	.284	Niekro-Atl	25.8	Knepper-SF	23.6
Hooton-LA	2.71	Knepper-SF	131	Seaver-Cin	.227	D.Robinson-Pit	.286	Perry-SD	24.5	Vuckovich-StL	21.4

Clutch Pitching Index		Relief Runs		Adjusted Relief Runs		Relief Ranking		Total Pitcher Index		Total Baseball Ranking	
Rau-LA	134	Tekulve-Pit	18.6	Garber-Phi-Atl	22.5	Bair-Cin	31.5	Niekro-Atl	5.7	Niekro-Atl	5.7
Vuckovich-StL	124	Garber-Phi-Atl	18.5	Tekulve-Pit	20.5	Tekulve-Pit	31.1	Carlton-Phi	3.2	Parker-Pit	5.2
Carlton-Phi	121	Bair-Cin	17.9	Bair-Cin	17.5	Garber-Phi-Atl	29.9	Rogers-Mon	2.8	Clark-SF	4.2
Jones-SD	114	Reed-Phi	16.2	Reed-Phi	16.1	Forster-LA	22.9	Swan-NY	2.8	Lopes-LA	4.0
Rogers-Mon	113	D'Acquisto-SD	14.9	D'Acquisto-SD	12.4	Fingers-SD	22.9	Denny-StL	2.7	Templeton-StL	3.8

TEAM	G	W	L	PCT	GB	R	OR	AB	H	2B	3B	HR	BB	SO	AVG	OBP	SLG	PRO	PRO+	BR	/A	PF	CHI	RC	SB	CS	SBA	SBR
EAST																												
NY	163	100	63	.613		735	582	5583	1489	228	38	125	505	695	.267	.332	.388	.720	105	14	31	98	105	720	98	42	70	4
BOS	163	99	64	.607	1	796	657	5587	1493	270	46	172	582	835	.267	.339	.424	.763	102	96	21	111	100	793	74	51	59	-8
MIL	162	93	69	.574	6.5	804	650	5536	1530	265	38	173	520	805	.276	.342	.432	.774	116	114	112	100	100	822	95	53	64	-3
BAL	161	90	71	.559	9	659	633	5422	1397	248	19	154	552	864	.258	.329	.396	.725	110	18	60	94	95	691	75	61	55	-14
DET	162	86	76	.531	13.5	714	653	5601	1520	218	34	129	563	695	.271	.341	.392	.733	103	45	25	103	96	748	90	38	70	4
CLE	159	69	90	.434	29	639	644	5365	1400	223	45	106	498	698	.261	.326	.379	.705	99	-19	-11	99	99	649	64	63	50	-19
TOR	161	59	102	.366	40	590	775	5430	1358	217	39	98	448	645	.250	.310	.359	.669	86	-93	-106	102	103	587	28	52	35	-23
WEST																												
KC	162	92	70	.568		743	634	5474	1469	305	59	98	498	644	.268	.333	.399	.732	102	34	16	103	104	739	216	84	72	14
TEX	162	87	75	.537	5	692	632	5347	1353	216	36	132	624	779	.253	.335	.381	.716	101	11	10	100	100	696	196	91	68	4
CAL	162	87	75	.537	5	691	666	5472	1417	226	28	108	539	682	.259	.333	.370	.703	101	-14	12	96	103	669	86	69	55	-16
MIN	162	73	89	.451	19	666	678	5522	1472	259	47	82	604	684	.267	.342	.375	.717	99	21	8	102	92	715	99	56	64	-4
CHI	161	71	90	.441	20.5	634	731	5393	1423	221	41	106	409	625	.264	.320	.379	.699	95	-35	-41	101	102	635	83	68	55	-16
OAK	162	69	93	.426	23	532	690	5321	1304	200	31	100	433	800	.245	.305	.351	.656	89	-117	-83	95	99	552	144	117	55	-27
SEA	160	56	104	.350	35	614	834	5358	1327	229	37	97	522	702	.248	.317	.359	.676	91	-73	-69	99	103	620	123	47	72	9
TOT	1131					9509		76411	19952	3325	538	1680	7287	10153	.261	.329	.385	.714							1471	892	62	-94

TEAM	CG	SH	SV	IP	H	H/G	HR	BB	SO	RAT	ERA	ERA+	OAV	OOB	PR	/A	PF	CPI	FA	E	DP	FW	PW	BW	SBW	DIF
EAST																										
NY	39	16	36	1460²	1321	8.1	111	478	817	11.3	3.18	114	.243	.308	95	72	96	99	.982	113	134	1.5	7.4	3.2	1.1	5.2
BOS	57	15	26	1472²	1530	9.4	137	464	706	12.4	3.54	116	.270	.329	37	94	109	111	.977	146	171	-.3	9.7	2.2	-.1	6.1
MIL	62	19	24	1436	1442	9.0	109	398	577	11.8	3.65	103	.262	.316	17	17	100	95	.977	150	144	-.6	1.8	11.5	.4	-1.0
BAL	65	16	33	1429	1340	8.4	107	509	754	11.7	3.56	98	.251	.318	32	-11	93	95	.982	110	166	1.6	-1.1	6.2	-.8	3.6
DET	60	12	21	1455²	1441	8.9	135	503	684	12.2	3.64	106	.263	.329	20	36	103	106	.981	118	177	1.2	3.7	2.6	1.1	-3.6
CLE	36	6	28	1407¹	1397	8.9	100	568	739	12.7	3.97	94	.261	.335	-33	-37	99	95	.980	123	142	.8	-3.8	-1.1	-1.3	-5.1
TOR	35	5	23	1429¹	1529	9.6	149	614	758	13.6	4.54	86	.279	.353	-123	-98	104	100	.979	131	163	.4	-10.1	-10.9	-1.7	.8
WEST																										
KC	53	14	33	1439	1350	8.4	108	478	657	11.6	3.44	111	.251	.316	52	61	102	98	.976	150	153	-.6	6.3	1.6	2.1	1.6
TEX	54	12	25	1456¹	1431	8.8	108	421	776	11.6	3.36	112	.259	.315	66	63	100	102	.976	153	140	-.8	6.5	1.0	1.1	-1.8
CAL	44	13	33	1455²	1382	8.5	125	599	892	12.4	3.65	99	.253	.330	19	-6	96	102	.978	136	136	.2	-.6	1.2	-1.0	6.2
MIN	48	9	26	1459²	1468	9.1	102	520	703	12.5	3.69	103	.266	.333	11	20	102	102	.977	146	171	-.4	2.1	.8	.3	-10.8
CHI	38	9	33	1409¹	1380	8.8	128	586	710	12.6	4.21	90	.259	.337	-71	-65	101	94	.977	139	130	-.0	-6.7	-4.2	-1.0	2.4
OAK	26	11	29	1433¹	1401	8.8	106	582	750	12.6	3.62	100	.259	.333	22	3	97	103	.971	179	145	-2.3	.3	-8.5	-2.1	.6
SEA	28	4	20	1419¹	1540	9.8	155	567	630	13.6	4.67	81	.280	.352	-144	-136	101	98	.978	141	174	-.2	-14.0	-7.1	1.6	-4.3
TOT	645	161	390	20163¹		8.9				12.4	3.76		.261	.329					.978	1935	2146					

Runs		Hits		Doubles		Triples		Home Runs		Total Bases	
LeFlore-Det	126	Rice-Bos	213	Brett-KC	45	Rice-Bos	15	Rice-Bos	46	Rice-Bos	406
Rice-Bos	121	LeFlore-Det	198	McRae-KC	39	Ford-Min	10	Hisle-Mil	34	Murray-Bal	293
Baylor-Cal	103	Carew-Min	188	Fisk-Bos	39	Carew-Min	10	Baylor-Cal	34	Staub-Det	279
Thornton-Cle	97	Munson-NY	183	DeCinces-Bal	37	Yount-Mil	9	Thornton-Cle	33	Baylor-Cal	279
Hisle-Mil	96	Staub-Det	175	Ford-Min	36	Garr-Chi	9	Thomas-Mil	32	Thompson-Det	278

Runs Batted In		Runs Produced		Bases On Balls		Batting Average		On Base Percentage		Slugging Average	
Rice-Bos	139	Rice-Bos	214	Hargrove-Tex	107	Carew-Min	.333	Carew-Min	.415	Rice-Bos	.600
Staub-Det	121	Hisle-Mil	177	Singleton-Bal	98	Oliver-Tex	.324	Singleton-Bal	.410	Hisle-Mil	.533
Hisle-Mil	115	LeFlore-Det	176	Kemp-Det	97	Rice-Bos	.315	Hargrove-Tex	.391	DeCinces-Bal	.526
Thornton-Cle	105	Staub-Det	172	Thornton-Cle	93	Piniella-NY	.314	Otis-KC	.387	Otis-KC	.525
		Thornton-Cle	169	Smalley-Min	85	Oglivie-Mil	.303	Randolph-NY	.385	Thornton-Cle	.516

Production		Adjusted Production		Batter Runs		Adjusted Batter Runs		Clutch Hitting Index		Runs Created	
Rice-Bos	.973	Singleton-Bal	154	Rice-Bos	58.7	Rice-Bos	49.8	L.Johnson-Chi	137	Rice-Bos	147
Otis-KC	.911	Rice-Bos	153	Hisle-Mil	36.3	Singleton-Bal	38.2	Chambliss-NY	137	LeFlore-Det	105
Hisle-Mil	.909	Hisle-Mil	153	Thornton-Cle	35.6	Thornton-Cle	36.4	Staub-Det	131	Carew-Min	105
Thornton-Cle	.898	Thornton-Cle	152	Otis-KC	35.2	Hisle-Mil	36.1	Bostock-Cal	129	Thompson-Det	104
Roberts-Sea	.881	DeCinces-Bal	152	Singleton-Bal	34.0	Otis-KC	33.5	Whitaker-Det	128	Murray-Bal	104

Total Average		Stolen Bases		Stolen Base Average		Stolen Base Runs		Fielding Runs		Total Player Rating	
Rice-Bos	.973	LeFlore-Det	68	Cruz-Sea	85.5	Cruz-Sea	11.7	Belanger-Bal	33.8	Rice-Bos	5.5
Otis-KC	.972	Cruz-Sea	59	Campaneris-Tex	84.6	LeFlore-Det	10.8	Bell-Cle	28.3	Smalley-Min	5.3
Hisle-Mil	.907	Wills-Tex	52	Lowenstein-Tex	84.2	Wills-Tex	7.2	Bosetti-Tor	25.1	Yount-Mil	4.5
Singleton-Bal	.900	Dilone-Oak	50	Randolph-NY	83.7	Wilson-KC	6.6	Yount-Mil	21.9	Otis-KC	4.3
Thornton-Cle	.897	Wilson-KC	46	Rivers-NY	83.3	Randolph-NY	6.6	Wills-Tex	21.3	DeCinces-Bal	3.8

Wins		Win Percentage		Games		Complete Games		Shutouts		Saves	
Guidry-NY	25	Guidry-NY	.893	Lacey-Oak	74	Caldwell-Mil	23	Guidry-NY	9	Gossage-NY	27
Caldwell-Mil	22	Stanley-Bos	.882	Heaverlo-Oak	69	Leonard-KC	20	Palmer-Bal	6	LaRoche-Cal	25
Palmer-Bal	21	Gura-KC	.800	Sosa-Oak	68	Palmer-Bal	19	Caldwell-Mil	6	Stanhouse-Bal	24
Leonard-KC	21	Eckersley-Bos	.714	Gossage-NY	63	Matlack-Tex	18	Tiant-Bos	5	Marshall-Min	21
		Caldwell-Mil	.710							Hrabosky-KC	20

Innings Pitched		Fewest Hits/Game		Fewest BB/Game		Strikeouts		Strikeouts/Game		Ratio	
Palmer-Bal	296.0	Guidry-NY	6.15	Jenkins-Tex	1.48	Ryan-Cal	260	Ryan-Cal	9.97	Guidry-NY	8.55
Leonard-KC	294.2	Ryan-Cal	7.02	Sorensen-Mil	1.60	Guidry-NY	248	Guidry-NY	8.16	Caldwell-Mil	9.79
Caldwell-Mil	293.1	Gura-KC	7.43	Caldwell-Mil	1.66	Leonard-KC	183	Kravec-Chi	6.83	Jenkins-Tex	9.83
Flanagan-Bal	281.1	Palmer-Bal	7.48	Matlack-Tex	1.70	Flanagan-Bal	167	Underwood-Tor	6.33	Gura-KC	10.03
Sorensen-Mil	280.2	Tiant-Bos	7.84	Rozema-Det	1.76	Eckersley-Bos	162	Knapp-Chi	6.02	Matlack-Tex	10.23

Earned Run Average		Adjusted ERA		Opponents' Batting Avg.		Opponents' On Base Pct.		Starter Runs		Adjusted Starter Runs	
Guidry-NY	1.74	Guidry-NY	208	Guidry-NY	.193	Guidry-NY	.250	Guidry-NY	61.4	Guidry-NY	57.1
Matlack-Tex	2.27	Matlack-Tex	165	Ryan-Cal	.220	Caldwell-Mil	.274	Caldwell-Mil	45.7	Caldwell-Mil	45.5
Caldwell-Mil	2.36	Caldwell-Mil	159	Palmer-Bal	.227	Jenkins-Tex	.279	Matlack-Tex	44.9	Matlack-Tex	44.3
Palmer-Bal	2.46	Goltz-Min	153	Gura-KC	.229	Matlack-Tex	.284	Palmer-Bal	42.8	Palmer-Bal	34.0
Goltz-Min	2.49	Palmer-Bal	142	Tiant-Bos	.234	Gura-KC	.286	Goltz-Min	31.1	Eckersley-Bos	33.6

Clutch Pitching Index		Relief Runs		Adjusted Relief Runs		Relief Ranking		Total Pitcher Index		Total Baseball Ranking	
Lee-Bos	130	Gossage-NY	26.2	Gossage-NY	24.0	Gossage-NY	44.7	Guidry-NY	6.8	Guidry-NY	6.8
Zahn-Min	129	Stanley-Bos	18.2	Stanley-Bos	23.7	Marshall-Min	37.2	Caldwell-Mil	5.2	Rice-Bos	5.5
Goltz-Min	125	Hiller-Det	14.6	Hiller-Det	15.7	Stanley-Bos	29.4	Matlack-Tex	5.0	Smalley-Min	5.3
Gale-KC	115	Marshall-Min	14.4	Marshall-Min	15.0	Hiller-Det	25.6	Palmer-Bal	4.3	Caldwell-Mil	5.2
Eckersley-Bos	115	Sosa-Oak	13.6	Sosa-Oak	12.1	LaRoche-Cal	19.9	Goltz-Min	3.6	Matlack-Tex	5.0

1979 National League

TEAM	G	W	L	PCT	GB	R	OR	AB	H	2B	3B	HR	BB	SO	AVG	OBP	SLG	PRO	PRO+	BR	/A	PF	CHI	RC	SB	CS	SBA	SBR
EAST																												
PIT	163	98	64	.605		775	643	5661	1541	264	52	148	483	855	.272	.333	.416	.749	105	68	35	105	101	781	180	66	73	14
MON	160	95	65	.594	2	701	581	5465	1445	273	42	143	432	890	.264	.321	.408	.729	105	23	29	99	102	701	121	56	68	3
STL	163	86	76	.531	12	731	693	5734	1594	279	63	100	460	838	.278	.335	.401	.736	106	46	40	101	98	757	116	69	63	-7
PHI	163	84	78	.519	14	683	718	5463	1453	250	53	119	602	764	.266	.343	.396	.739	105	63	41	103	91	743	128	76	63	-7
CHI	162	80	82	.494	18	706	707	5550	1494	250	43	135	478	762	.269	.331	.403	.734	97	40	-25	110	98	726	73	52	58	-9
NY	163	63	99	.389	35	593	706	5591	1399	255	41	74	498	817	.250	.315	.350	.665	90	-90	-65	96	99	615	135	79	63	-7
WEST																												
CIN	161	90	71	.559		731	644	5477	1445	266	31	132	614	902	.264	.340	.396	.736	106	55	51	101	99	741	99	47	68	2
HOU	162	89	73	.549	1.5	583	582	5394	1382	224	52	49	461	745	.256	.317	.344	.661	91	-93	-54	94	102	591	190	95	67	0
LA	162	79	83	.488	11.5	739	717	5490	1443	220	24	183	516	834	.263	.333	.412	.745	111	62	72	99	99	743	106	46	70	4
SF	162	71	91	.438	19.5	672	751	5395	1328	192	36	125	580	925	.246	.322	.365	.687	100	-46	0	93	106	644	140	73	66	-2
SD	161	68	93	.422	22	603	681	5446	1316	193	53	93	534	770	.242	.313	.348	.661	91	-97	-56	94	103	600	100	58	63	-5
ATL	160	66	94	.413	23.5	669	763	5422	1389	220	28	126	490	818	.256	.320	.377	.697	89	-31	-80	107	105	654	98	50	66	-1
TOT	971					8186		66088	17229	2886	518	1427	6188	9920	.261	.327	.385	.712						1486	767	66	-14

TEAM	CG	SH	SV	IP	H	H/G	HR	BB	SO	RAT	ERA	ERA+	OAV	OOB	PR	/A	PF	CPI	FA	E	DP	FW	PW	BW	SBW	DIF
EAST																										
PIT	24	7	52	1493[1]	1424	8.6	125	504	904	11.8	3.41	114	.254	.318	53	77	104	103	.979	134	163	.4	7.9	3.6	1.6	3.5
MON	33	18	39	1447[1]	1379	8.6	116	450	813	11.5	3.14	117	.253	.312	95	84	98	107	.979	131	123	.4	8.7	3.0	.4	2.5
STL	38	10	25	1486[2]	1449	8.8	127	501	788	11.9	3.72	101	.258	.321	1	6	101	97	.980	132	166	.5	.6	4.1	-.6	.3
PHI	33	14	29	1441[1]	1455	9.1	135	477	787	12.2	4.16	92	.266	.328	-69	-54	103	94	.983	106	148	2.1	-5.6	4.2	-.6	2.9
CHI	20	11	44	1446[2]	1500	9.3	127	521	933	12.8	3.88	106	.270	.338	-24	37	110	105	.975	159	163	-1.1	3.8	-2.6	-.8	-.3
NY	16	10	36	1482[2]	1486	9.0	120	607	819	12.9	3.84	95	.266	.341	-18	-34	98	105	.978	140	168	.0	-3.5	-6.7	-.6	-7.2
WEST																										
CIN	27	10	40	1440[1]	1415	8.8	103	485	773	12.0	3.58	104	.260	.322	24	24	100	99	.980	124	152	.9	2.5	5.3	.3	.5
HOU	55	19	31	1447[2]	1278	7.9	90	504	854	11.2	3.20	110	.237	.306	86	51	94	93	.978	138	146	.1	5.3	-5.6	.1	8.1
LA	30	6	34	1444	1425	8.9	101	555	811	12.5	3.83	95	.260	.325	-15	-31	97	97	.981	118	123	1.3	-3.2	7.4	.5	-8.1
SF	25	6	34	1436	1484	9.3	143	577	880	13.1	4.16	84	.269	.341	-69	-107	94	101	.974	163	138	-1.4	-11.0	.0	.0	2.5
SD	29	7	25	1453	1438	8.9	108	513	779	12.2	3.69	96	.263	.328	6	-27	95	101	.978	141	154	-.1	-2.8	-5.8	-.4	-3.4
ATL	32	3	34	1407[2]	1496	9.6	132	494	779	13.0	4.18	97	.272	.337	-70	-21	109	99	.970	183	139	-2.7	-2.2	-8.3	.0	-.9
TOT	362	121	423	17426[2]		8.9				12.3	3.73		.261	.327					.978	1669	1783					

Leader Categories

Runs		Hits		Doubles		Triples		Home Runs		Total Bases	
Hernandez-StL	116	Templeton-StL	211	Hernandez-StL	48	Templeton-StL	19	Kingman-Chi	48	Winfield-SD	333
Moreno-Pit	110	Hernandez-StL	210	Cromartie-Mon	46	Moreno-Pit	12	Schmidt-Phi	45	Parker-Pit	327
Schmidt-Phi	109	Rose-Phi	208	Parker-Pit	45	McBride-Phi	12	Winfield-SD	34	Kingman-Chi	326
Parker-Pit	109	Garvey-LA	204	Reitz-StL	41	Dawson-Mon	12	Horner-Atl	33	Garvey-LA	322
Lopes-LA	109	Moreno-Pit	196	Rose-Phi	40			Stargell-Pit	32	Matthews-Atl	317

Runs Batted In		Runs Produced		Bases On Balls		Batting Average		On Base Percentage		Slugging Average	
Winfield-SD	118	Hernandez-StL	210	Schmidt-Phi	120	Hernandez-StL	.344	Hernandez-StL	.421	Kingman-Chi	.613
Kingman-Chi	115	Winfield-SD	181	Tenace-SD	105	Rose-Phi	.331	Rose-Phi	.421	Schmidt-Phi	.564
Schmidt-Phi	114	Schmidt-Phi	178	Lopes-LA	97	Knight-Cin	.318	Tenace-SD	.407	Foster-Cin	.561
Garvey-LA	110	Parker-Pit	178	North-SF	96	Garvey-LA	.315	Mazzilli-NY	.397	Winfield-SD	.558
Hernandez-StL	105	Garvey-LA	174	Rose-Phi	95	Horner-Atl	.314	Winfield-SD	.396	Horner-Atl	.552

Production		Adjusted Production		Batter Runs		Adjusted Batter Runs		Clutch Hitting Index		Runs Created	
Kingman-Chi	.960	Winfield-SD	167	Winfield-SD	47.4	Winfield-SD	52.0	Hebner-NY	148	Hernandez-StL	135
Schmidt-Phi	.955	Foster-Cin	155	Hernandez-StL	47.1	Hernandez-StL	46.5	Foli-NY-Pit	134	Winfield-SD	132
Winfield-SD	.954	Schmidt-Phi	153	Schmidt-Phi	44.9	Schmidt-Phi	42.5	Luzinski-Phi	132	Parker-Pit	131
Foster-Cin	.950	Hernandez-StL	152	Parker-Pit	39.3	Parker-Pit	35.6	Flynn-NY	129	Schmidt-Phi	123
Hernandez-StL	.934	Parrish-Mon	146	Kingman-Chi	37.8	Foster-Cin	33.3	Hernandez-StL	127	Matthews-Atl	118

Total Average		Stolen Bases		Stolen Base Average		Stolen Base Runs		Fielding Runs		Total Player Rating	
Schmidt-Phi	1.024	Moreno-Pit	77	Lopes-LA	91.7	Lopes-LA	10.8	Evans-SF	22.4	Schmidt-Phi	6.0
Winfield-SD	.988	North-SF	58	Parker-Pit	83.3	Moreno-Pit	10.5	Smith-SD	20.4	Winfield-SD	5.6
Kingman-Chi	.972	Taveras-Pit-NY	44	Morgan-Cin	82.4	Royster-Atl	5.7	Maddox-Phi	20.2	Hernandez-StL	5.6
Hernandez-StL	.961	Lopes-LA	44	Royster-Atl	81.4	Morgan-Cin	4.8	Hernandez-StL	18.8	Templeton-StL	4.6
Foster-Cin	.959	Scott-Mon	39	Smith-SD	80.0			Schmidt-Phi	18.4	Parker-Pit	4.2

Wins		Win Percentage		Games		Complete Games		Shutouts		Saves	
Niekro-Atl	21	Seaver-Cin	.727	Tekulve-Pit	94	Niekro-Atl	23	Seaver-Cin	5	Sutter-Chi	37
Niekro-Hou	21	Niekro-Hou	.656	Romo-Pit	84	Richard-Hou	19	Rogers-Mon	5	Tekulve-Pit	31
Richard-Hou	18	Martinez-StL	.652	Jackson-Pit	72	Rogers-Mon	13	Niekro-Hou	5	Garber-Atl	25
Reuschel-Chi	18	Sutcliffe-LA	.630	Lavelle-SF	70	Carlton-Phi	13	Richard-Hou	4	Sambito-Hou	22
Carlton-Phi	18	Carlton-Phi	.621	Garber-Atl	68	Hooton-LA	12	Carlton-Phi	4	Lavelle-SF	20

Innings Pitched		Fewest Hits/Game		Fewest BB/Game		Strikeouts		Strikeouts/Game		Ratio	
Niekro-Atl	342.0	Richard-Hou	6.77	Forsch-Hou	1.77	Richard-Hou	313	Richard-Hou	9.64	Forsch-Hou	9.62
Richard-Hou	292.1	Carlton-Phi	7.24	Candelaria-Pit	1.78	Carlton-Phi	213	Carlton-Phi	7.64	Richard-Hou	9.88
Niekro-Hou	263.2	Niekro-Hou	7.54	Lee-Mon	1.82	Niekro-Atl	208	Sanderson-Mon	7.39	Seaver-Cin	10.38
Jones-SD	263.0	Schatzeder-Mon	7.56	Lee-Mon	1.86	Blyleven-Pit	172	Blyleven-Pit	6.52	Sutton-LA	10.47
Swan-NY	251.1	Andujar-Hou	7.79	Swan-NY	2.04	McGlothen-Chi	147	Krukow-Chi	6.50	Carlton-Phi	10.61

Earned Run Average		Adjusted ERA		Opponents' Batting Avg.		Opponents' On Base Pct.		Starter Runs		Adjusted Starter Runs	
Richard-Hou	2.71	Hume-Cin	135	Richard-Hou	.209	Forsch-Hou	.275	Richard-Hou	33.2	Richard-Hou	26.0
Hume-Cin	2.76	Richard-Hou	130	Carlton-Phi	.219	Richard-Hou	.278	Niekro-Hou	21.3	Niekro-Atl	24.8
Schatzeder-Mon	2.83	Schatzeder-Mon	129	Schatzeder-Mon	.225	Seaver-Cin	.291	Rogers-Mon	20.1	Fulgham-StL	20.0
Hooton-LA	2.97	Hooton-LA	122	Niekro-Hou	.228	Sutton-LA	.291	Fulgham-StL	19.5	Rogers-Mon	18.2
Niekro-Hou	3.00	Rogers-Mon	122	Andujar-Hou	.233	Carlton-Phi	.292	Hooton-LA	17.9	Bibby-Pit	16.3

Clutch Pitching Index		Relief Runs		Adjusted Relief Runs		Relief Ranking		Total Pitcher Index		Total Baseball Ranking	
Hume-Cin	117	Sambito-Hou	19.9	Sutter-Chi	21.3	Sutter-Chi	40.3	Niekro-Atl	3.2	Schmidt-Phi	6.0
Lamp-Chi	114	Sosa-Mon	19.1	Sosa-Mon	18.4	Sambito-Hou	35.6	Richard-Hou	2.7	Winfield-SD	5.6
Lee-Mon	113	Hume-Cin	17.6	Sambito-Hou	17.6	Sosa-Mon	33.3	Sutter-Chi	2.4	Hernandez-StL	5.6
Kobel-NY	112	Minton-SF	17.0	Hume-Cin	17.6	Tekulve-Pit	29.1	Rogers-Mon	2.3	Templeton-StL	4.6
Blyleven-Pit	112	Sutter-Chi	17.0	Tekulve-Pit	16.9	Littell-StL	25.6	Sambito-Hou	2.2	Parker-Pit	4.2

TEAM	G	W	L	PCT	GB	R	OR	AB	H	2B	3B	HR	BB	SO	AVG	OBP	SLG	PRO	PRO+	BR	/A	PF	CHI	RC	SB	CS	SBA	SBR
EAST																												
BAL	159	102	57	.642		757	**582**	5371	1401	258	24	181	608	847	.261	.339	.419	.758	107	25	53	96	98	758	99	49	67	0
MIL	161	95	66	.590	8	807	722	5536	1552	291	41	185	549	745	.280	.347	.448	.795	113	95	95	100	94	**850**	100	53	65	-2
BOS	160	91	69	.569	11.5	841	711	5538	1567	**310**	34	**194**	512	708	**.283**	.347	**.456**	**.803**	109	**108**	66	106	97	848	60	43	58	-8
NY	160	89	71	.556	13.5	734	672	5421	1443	226	40	150	509	**590**	.266	.331	.406	.737	100	-21	-5	98	102	708	65	46	59	-8
DET	161	85	76	.528	18	770	738	5375	1446	221	35	164	575	814	.269	.342	.415	.757	100	24	0	103	101	754	176	86	67	1
CLE	161	81	80	.503	22	760	805	5376	1388	206	29	138	**657**	786	.258	.344	.384	.728	96	-21	-24	100	103	720	143	90	61	-11
TOR	162	53	109	.327	50.5	613	862	5423	1362	253	34	95	448	663	.251	.313	.363	.676	81	-142	-150	101	104	602	75	56	57	-11
WEST																												
CAL	162	88	74	.543		**866**	768	5550	1563	242	43	164	589	843	.282	**.354**	.429	.783	**114**	83	**109**	97	101	842	100	53	65	-2
KC	162	85	77	.525	3	851	816	5653	**1596**	286	**79**	116	528	675	.282	.347	.422	.769	104	51	36	102	103	836	**207**	76	**73**	**17**
TEX	162	83	79	.512	5	750	698	5562	1549	252	26	140	461	607	.278	.337	.409	.746	101	-1	8	99	99	750	79	51	61	-7
MIN	162	82	80	.506	6	764	725	5544	1544	256	46	112	526	693	.278	.344	.402	.746	96	7	-22	104	99	770	66	45	59	-7
CHI	160	73	87	.456	14	730	748	5463	1505	290	33	127	454	668	.275	.335	.410	.745	100	-4	-4	100	99	726	97	62	61	-8
SEA	162	67	95	.414	21	711	820	5544	1490	250	52	132	515	725	.269	.334	.404	.738	96	-17	-30	102	96	733	126	52	71	7
OAK	162	54	108	.333	34	573	860	5348	1276	188	32	108	482	751	.239	.304	.346	.650	79	-189	-150	95	**106**	552	104	69	60	-10
TOT	1128					10527		76704	20682	3529	548	2006	7413	10115	.270	.337	.408	.746							1497	831	64	-50

TEAM	CG	SH	SV	IP	H	H/G	HR	BB	SO	RAT	ERA	ERA+	OAV	OOB	PR	/A	PF	CPI	FA	E	DP	FW	PW	BW	SBW	DIF
EAST																										
BAL	52	**12**	30	1434^1	**1279**	**8.0**	133	467	786	**11.0**	**3.26**	**123**	**.241**	**.304**	**152**	**119**	95	100	.980	125	161	.8	**11.6**	5.2	.3	4.6
MIL	**61**	**12**	23	1439^2	1563	9.8	162	**381**	580	12.3	4.03	103	.279	.327	29	21	99	105	.980	127	153	.7	2.0	9.3	.1	2.3
BOS	47	11	29	1431^1	1487	9.4	133	463	731	12.5	4.03	110	.270	.330	29	61	105	100	.977	142	166	-.2	6.0	6.4	-.4	-.8
NY	43	10	37	1432^1	1446	9.1	123	455	731	12.0	3.83	106	.268	.326	61	38	97	102	**.981**	122	183	1.0	3.7	-.5	-.4	5.2
DET	25	5	37	1423^1	1429	9.0	167	547	802	12.8	4.27	101	.265	.338	-9	8	103	101	**.981**	**120**	184	**1.1**	.8	.0	.4	2.1
CLE	28	7	32	1431^2	1502	9.4	138	570	781	13.2	4.57	93	.272	.343	-56	-50	101	94	.978	134	149	.3	-4.9	-2.3	-.7	8.1
TOR	44	7	11	1417	1537	9.8	165	594	613	13.8	4.82	90	.281	.356	-95	-75	103	100	.975	159	187	-1.0	-7.3	-14.6	-.7	-4.3
WEST																										
CAL	46	9	33	1436	1463	9.2	131	573	**820**	13.0	4.34	94	.267	.340	-19	-42	97	96	.978	135	172	.3	-4.1	**10.6**	.1	-.0
KC	42	7	27	1448^1	1477	9.2	165	536	640	12.7	4.45	96	.267	.335	-38	-30	101	95	.977	146	160	-.3	-2.9	3.5	**2.0**	1.7
TEX	26	10	**42**	1437	1371	8.6	135	532	773	12.1	3.86	107	.253	.323	56	45	98	97	.979	130	151	.6	4.4	.8	-.3	-3.5
MIN	31	6	33	1444^1	1590	9.9	128	452	721	12.8	4.13	106	.285	.340	14	40	104	**106**	.979	134	**203**	.4	3.9	-2.1	-.3	-.8
CHI	28	9	37	1409	1365	8.7	**114**	618	675	12.9	4.10	104	.256	.338	18	23	101	96	.972	173	142	-1.9	2.2	-.4	-.4	-6.5
SEA	37	7	26	1438	1567	9.8	165	571	736	13.6	4.58	95	.281	.351	-57	-34	103	103	.978	141	170	.0	-3.3	-2.9	1.0	-8.8
OAK	41	4	20	1429^1	1606	10.1	147	654	726	14.5	4.75	85	.288	.367	-84	-112	96	105	.972	174	137	-1.9	-10.9	-14.6	-.6	1.1
TOT	551	116	417	20051^2		9.3				12.8	4.22		.270	.337					.978	1962	2318					

Runs
Baylor-Cal 120
Brett-KC 119
Rice-Bos 117
Lynn-Bos 116
Lansford-Cal 114

Hits
Brett-KC 212
Rice-Bos 201
Bell-Tex 200
Molitor-Mil 188
Lansford-Cal 188

Doubles
Lemon-Chi 44
Cooper-Mil 44
Lynn-Bos 42
Brett-KC 42
Bell-Tex 42

Triples
Brett-KC 20
Molitor-Mil 16
Wilson-KC 13
Randolph-NY 13

Home Runs
Thomas-Mil 45
Rice-Bos 39
Lynn-Bos 39
Baylor-Cal 36
Singleton-Bal 35

Total Bases
Rice-Bos 369
Brett-KC 363
Lynn-Bos 338
Baylor-Cal 333
Singleton-Bal 304

Runs Batted In
Baylor-Cal 139
Rice-Bos 130
Thomas-Mil 123
Lynn-Bos 122
Porter-KC 112

Runs Produced
Baylor-Cal 223
Rice-Bos 208
Brett-KC 203
Lynn-Bos 199
Porter-KC 193

Bases On Balls
Porter-KC 121
Singleton-Bal 109
Thomas-Mil 98
Randolph-NY 95
Thornton-Cle 90

Batting Average
Lynn-Bos 333
Brett-KC 329
Downing-Cal 326
Rice-Bos 325
Oliver-Tex 323

On Base Percentage
Porter-KC 429
Lynn-Bos 426
Downing-Cal 420
Lezcano-Mil 420
Singleton-Bal 409

Slugging Average
Lynn-Bos 637
Rice-Bos 596
Lezcano-Mil 573
Brett-KC 563
Jackson-NY 544

Production
Lynn-Bos 1.063
Lezcano-Mil 992
Rice-Bos 981
Kemp-Det 946
Singleton-Bal 942

Adjusted Production
Lynn-Bos 173
Lezcano-Mil 165
Singleton-Bal 158
Rice-Bos 152
Jackson-NY 151

Batter Runs
Lynn-Bos 62.1
Rice-Bos 50.2
Lezcano-Mil 44.6
Singleton-Bal 44.4
Brett-KC 42.8

Adjusted Batter Runs
Lynn-Bos 58.0
Singleton-Bal 47.5
Rice-Bos 45.6
Lezcano-Mil 44.6
Brett-KC 41.2

Clutch Hitting Index
Porter-KC 143
Bochte-Sea 127
Cerone-Tor 127
Ford-Cal 126
Sundberg-Tex 125

Runs Created
Lynn-Bos 147
Rice-Bos 138
Brett-KC 134
Singleton-Bal 127
Baylor-Cal 126

Total Average
Lynn-Bos 1.162
Lezcano-Mil 1.051
Rice-Bos 993
Singleton-Bal 993
Porter-KC 982

Stolen Bases
Wilson-KC 83
LeFlore-Det 78
Cruz-Sea 49
Bumbry-Bal 37
Wills-Tex 35

Stolen Base Average
Wilson-KC 87.4
Otis-KC 85.7
LeFlore-Det 84.8
Cruz-Sea 84.5
Lowenstein-Bal ... 80.0

Stolen Base Runs
Wilson-KC 17.7
LeFlore-Det 15.0
Cruz-Sea 9.3
Otis-KC 6.0
Manning-Cle 4.2

Fielding Runs
Smalley-Min 33.1
Dent-NY 32.0
Mendoza-Sea 28.0
Burleson-Bos 22.1
Wilfong-Min 20.7

Total Player Rating
Smalley-Min 5.7
Lynn-Bos 5.5
Brett-KC 5.0
Grich-Cal 4.2
Rice-Bos 4.1

Wins
Flanagan-Bal 23
John-NY 21
Koosman-Min 20
Guidry-NY 18

Win Percentage
Caldwell-Mil 727
Flanagan-Bal 719
Morris-Det 708
John-NY 700
Guidry-NY 692

Games
Marshall-Min 90
Monge-Cle 76
Kern-Tex 71
Lyle-Tex 67
Heaverlo-Oak 62

Complete Games
J.Martinez-Bal 18
Ryan-Cal 17
John-NY 17
Eckersley-Bos 17

Shutouts
Ryan-Cal 5
Leonard-KC 5
Flanagan-Bal 5
Stanley-Bos 4
Caldwell-Mil 4

Saves
Marshall-Min 32
Kern-Tex 29
Stanhouse-Bal 21
Lopez-Det 21
Monge-Cle 19

Innings Pitched
J.Martinez-Bal ... 292.1
John-NY 276.1
Flanagan-Bal 265.2
Koosman-Min ... 263.2
Jenkins-Tex 259.0

Fewest Hits/Game
Ryan-Cal 6.83
Kravec-Chi 7.49
Guidry-NY 7.73
Morris-Det 8.15
Baumgarten-Chi .. 8.26

Fewest BB/Game
McGregor-Bal 1.19
Caldwell-Mil 1.49
Sorensen-Mil 1.61
Stanley-Bos 1.83
John-NY 2.12

Strikeouts
Ryan-Cal 223
Guidry-NY 201
Flanagan-Bal 190
Jenkins-Tex 164
Koosman-Min 157

Strikeouts/Game
Ryan-Cal 9.01
Guidry-NY 7.65
Flanagan-Bal 6.44
Jenkins-Tex 5.70
Bannister-Sea 5.68

Ratio
McGregor-Bal 9.79
Guidry-NY 10.43
Flanagan-Bal ... 10.77
Leonard-KC 10.83
Eckersley-Bos ... 10.91

Earned Run Average
Guidry-NY 2.78
John-NY 2.96
Eckersley-Bos 2.99
Flanagan-Bal 3.08
Morris-Det 3.28

Adjusted ERA
Eckersley-Bos 148
Guidry-NY 146
John-NY 137
Morris-Det 132
Flanagan-Bal 130

Opponents' Batting Avg.
Ryan-Cal 212
Kravec-Chi 233
Guidry-NY 236
Baumgarten-Chi ...243
Morris-Det 244

Opponents' On Base Pct.
McGregor-Bal 275
Guidry-NY 294
Flanagan-Bal 297
Eckersley-Bos 298
Leonard-KC 299

Starter Runs
John-NY 38.4
Guidry-NY 37.7
Eckersley-Bos 33.5
Flanagan-Bal 33.4
Koosman-Min 24.5

Adjusted Starter Runs
Eckersley-Bos 39.0
John-NY 34.0
Guidry-NY 33.9
Koosman-Min 29.3
Flanagan-Bal 27.4

Clutch Pitching Index
Eckersley-Bos 115
Keough-Oak 114
McCatty-Oak 114
Travers-Mil 113
Koosman-Min 112

Relief Runs
Kern-Tex 42.0
Monge-Cle 26.4
Lopez-Det 25.5
Marshall-Min 24.8
Stoddard-Bal 16.2

Adjusted Relief Runs
Kern-Tex 40.9
Marshall-Min 27.4
Lopez-Det 27.0
Monge-Cle 26.9
Burgmeier-Bos ... 16.5

Relief Ranking
Kern-Tex 65.0
Marshall-Min 57.1
Monge-Cle 49.5
Lopez-Det 38.8
Drago-Bos 26.6

Total Pitcher Index
Kern-Tex 4.1
Eckersley-Bos 4.1
John-NY 3.9
Guidry-NY 3.5
Koosman-Min 3.2

Total Baseball Ranking
Smalley-Min 5.7
Lynn-Bos 5.5
Brett-KC 5.0
Grich-Cal 4.2
Kern-Tex 4.1

TEAM	G	W	L	PCT	GB	R	OR	AB	H	2B	3B	HR	BB	SO	AVG	OBP	SLG	PRO	PRO+	BR	/A	PF	CHI	RC	SB	CS	SBA	SBR
EAST																												
PHI	162	91	71	.562		728	639	5625	1517	272	54	117	472	**708**	.270	.330	**.400**	.730	103	61	24	106	100	736	140	62	69	5
MON	162	90	72	.556	1	694	629	5465	1407	250	61	114	547	865	.257	.327	.388	.715	105	36	35	100	101	709	237	82	74	22
PIT	162	83	79	.512	8	666	646	5517	1469	249	38	116	452	760	.266	.325	.388	.713	102	27	17	102	98	686	209	102	67	2
STL	162	74	88	.457	17	**738**	710	5608	**1541**	300	49	101	451	781	**.275**	**.331**	**.400**	**.731**	106	**63**	43	103	102	724	117	54	68	3
NY	162	67	95	.414	24	611	702	5478	1407	218	41	61	501	840	.257	.322	.345	.667	95	-52	-34	97	102	601	158	99	61	-12
CHI	162	64	98	.395	27	614	728	5619	1411	251	35	107	471	912	.251	.311	.365	.676	88	-47	-96	107	100	627	93	64	59	-11
WEST																												
HOU	163	93	70	.571		637	**589**	5566	1455	231	**67**	75	540	755	.261	.328	.367	.695	**109**	2	**54**	92	96	688	194	74	72	14
LA	163	92	71	.564	1	663	591	5568	1462	209	24	**148**	492	846	.263	.325	.388	.713	106	29	42	98	96	699	123	72	63	-6
CIN	163	89	73	.549	3.5	707	670	5516	1445	256	45	113	537	852	.262	.330	.386	.716	105	39	39	100	101	716	156	43	**78**	21
ATL	161	81	80	.503	11	630	660	5402	1352	226	22	144	434	899	.250	.308	.380	.688	94	-27	-48	103	**104**	616	73	52	58	-9
SF	161	75	86	.466	17	573	634	5368	1310	199	44	80	509	840	.244	.311	.342	.653	90	-82	-67	98	102	571	100	58	63	-5
SD	163	73	89	.451	19.5	591	654	5540	1410	195	43	67	**563**	791	.255	.326	.342	.668	98	-48	-10	94	96	641	**239**	73	77	**28**
TOT	973					7852		66272	17186	2856	523	1243	5969	9849	.259	.323	.374	.697							1839	835	69	51

TEAM	CG	SH	SV	IP	H	H/G	HR	BB	SO	RAT	ERA	ERA+	OAV	OOB	PR	/A	PF	CPI	FA	E	DP	FW	PW	BW	SBW	DIF
EAST																										
PHI	25	8	40	1480	1419	8.6	87	530	889	12.0	3.43	110	.255	.322	28	**59**	105	100	.979	136	136	.2	**6.2**	2.5	.0	.9
MON	33	15	36	1456²	1447	8.9	100	460	823	11.9	3.48	102	.261	.321	20	14	99	102	.977	144	126	-.2	1.5	3.7	1.9	2.1
PIT	25	8	**43**	1458¹	1422	8.8	110	**451**	832	11.7	3.58	102	.259	.318	4	10	101	99	.978	137	154	.2	1.1	1.8	-.2	-.8
STL	**34**	9	27	1447	1454	9.0	90	495	664	12.3	3.93	94	.265	.329	-53	-39	103	94	.981	122	174	1.0	-4.1	4.5	-.1	-8.3
NY	17	9	33	1451¹	1473	9.1	140	510	886	12.4	3.85	92	.267	.331	-40	-48	99	104	.975	154	132	-.7	-5.1	-3.6	-1.7	-2.9
CHI	13	6	35	1479	1525	9.3	109	589	923	13.0	3.89	101	.263	.344	-47	4	109	**106**	.974	174	149	-1.7	.4	-10.1	-1.6	-3.9
WEST																										
HOU	31	18	41	1482²	1367	**8.3**	**69**	466	**929**	11.3	**3.10**	106	**.246**	.307	**82**	31	91	96	.978	140	145	.0	3.3	**5.7**	1.0	1.4
LA	24	**19**	42	1472²	**1358**	**8.3**	100	480	835	11.3	3.25	108	.247	.309	58	41	97	100	.981	123	149	1.0	4.3	4.4	-1.1	1.8
CIN	30	12	37	1459¹	1404	8.7	113	**506**	833	11.9	3.85	93	.255	.319	-40	-44	99	92	**.983**	106	144	**1.9**	-4.6	4.1	1.8	4.9
ATL	29	9	37	1428	1397	8.8	131	454	696	11.8	3.77	99	.258	.318	-27	-4	104	97	.975	162	156	-1.2	-.4	-5.1	-1.4	8.6
SF	27	10	35	1448¹	1446	9.0	92	492	811	12.2	3.46	102	.261	.325	24	13	98	104	.975	159	124	-1.0	1.4	-7.1	-1.0	2.2
SD	19	9	39	1466¹	1474	9.0	97	536	728	12.4	3.65	94	.267	.333	-8	-36	95	105	.980	132	157	.5	-3.8	-1.1	**2.5**	-6.2
TOT	307	132	445	17529²		8.8				12.0	3.60		.259	.323					.978	1689	1746					

Runs
Hernandez-StL ... 111
Schmidt-Phi ... 104
Murphy-Atl ... 98
Dawson-Mon ... 96

Hits
Garvey-LA ... 200
Richards-SD ... 193
Hernandez-StL ... 191
Buckner-Chi ... 187

Doubles
Rose-Phi ... 42
Dawson-Mon ... 41
Buckner-Chi ... 41
Knight-Cin ... 39
Hernandez-StL ... 39

Triples
Scott-Mon ... 13
Moreno-Pit ... 13
LeFlore-Mon ... 11
Herndon-SF ... 11

Home Runs
Schmidt-Phi ... 48
Horner-Atl ... 35
Murphy-Atl ... 33
Carter-Mon ... 29
Baker-LA ... 29

Total Bases
Schmidt-Phi ... 342
Garvey-LA ... 307
Hernandez-StL ... 294
Baker-LA ... 291
Murphy-Atl ... 290

Runs Batted In
Schmidt-Phi ... 121
Hendrick-StL ... 109
Garvey-LA ... 106
Carter-Mon ... 101
Hernandez-StL ... 99

Runs Produced
Hernandez-StL ... 194
Schmidt-Phi ... 177
Dawson-Mon ... 166
Simmons-StL ... 161
Griffey-Cin ... 161

Bases On Balls
Morgan-Hou ... 93
Driessen-Cin ... 93
Tenace-SD ... 92
Schmidt-Phi ... 89
Hernandez-StL ... 86

Batting Average
Buckner-Chi ... .324
Hernandez-StL ... .321
Templeton-StL ... .319
McBride-Phi ... .309
Cedeno-Hou ... .309

On Base Percentage
Hernandez-StL ... .410
Cedeno-Hou ... .390
Clark-SF ... .390
Schmidt-Phi ... .388
Driessen-Cin ... .382

Slugging Average
Schmidt-Phi ... .624
Clark-SF ... .517
Murphy-Atl ... .510
Simmons-StL ... .505
Baker-LA ... .503

Production
Schmidt-Phi ... 1.012
Clark-SF ... .907
Hernandez-StL ... .904
Simmons-StL ... .885
Murphy-Atl ... .859

Adjusted Production
Schmidt-Phi ... 169
Clark-SF ... 155
Cedeno-Hou ... 150
Hernandez-StL ... 147
Simmons-StL ... 140

Batter Runs
Schmidt-Phi ... 56.5
Hernandez-StL ... 43.3
Easler-Pit ... 37.2
Clark-SF ... 31.1
Simmons-StL ... 29.6

Adjusted Batter Runs
Schmidt-Phi ... 52.7
Hernandez-StL ... 41.0
Easler-Pit ... 36.5
Clark-SF ... 32.4
Cedeno-Hou ... 31.3

Clutch Hitting Index
Concepcion-Cin ... 135
Montanez-SD-Mon ... 135
McBride-Phi ... 131
Cruz-Hou ... 130
Youngblood-NY ... 127

Runs Created
Schmidt-Phi ... 137
Hernandez-StL ... 122
Dawson-Mon ... 105
Murphy-Atl ... 101
Griffey-Cin ... 99

Total Average
Schmidt-Phi ... 1.095
Hernandez-StL ... .915
Clark-SF ... .906
Cedeno-Hou ... .890
Simmons-StL ... .872

Stolen Bases
LeFlore-Mon ... 97
Moreno-Pit ... 96
Collins-Cin ... 79
Scott-Mon ... 63
Richards-SD ... 61

Stolen Base Average
Griffey-Cin ... 95.8
Mumphrey-SD ... 91.2
LeFlore-Mon ... 83.6
Maddox-Phi ... 83.3
Scott-Mon ... 82.9

Stolen Base Runs
LeFlore-Mon ... 17.7
Mumphrey-SD ... 12.6
Scott-Mon ... 11.1
Collins-Cin ... 11.1
Moreno-Pit ... 9.0

Fielding Runs
Smith-SD ... 40.8
Templeton-StL ... 27.6
Schmidt-Phi ... 23.2
Hubbard-Atl ... 19.2
Youngblood-NY ... 18.9

Total Player Rating
Schmidt-Phi ... 7.6
Smith-SD ... 4.8
Templeton-StL ... 4.7
Carter-Mon ... 3.9
Dawson-Mon ... 3.9

Wins
Carlton-Phi ... 24
Niekro-Hou ... 20
Bibby-Pit ... 19
Reuss-LA ... 18
Ruthven-Phi ... 17

Win Percentage
Bibby-Pit ... .760
Reuss-LA ... .750
Carlton-Phi ... .727
Ruthven-Phi ... .630
Niekro-Hou ... .625

Games
Tidrow-Chi ... 84
Tekulve-Pit ... 78
Hume-Cin ... 78
Camp-Atl ... 77
Romo-Pit ... 74

Complete Games
Rogers-Mon ... 14
Carlton-Phi ... 13
Niekro-Atl ... 11
Niekro-Hou ... 11

Shutouts
Reuss-LA ... 6
Rogers-Mon ... 4
Richard-Hou ... 4

Saves
Sutter-Chi ... 28
Hume-Cin ... 25
Fingers-SD ... 23
Camp-Atl ... 22
Allen-NY ... 22

Innings Pitched
Carlton-Phi ... 304.0
Rogers-Mon ... 281.0
Niekro-Atl ... 275.0
Reuschel-Chi ... 257.0
Niekro-Hou ... 256.0

Fewest Hits/Game
Soto-Cin ... 5.96
Sutton-LA ... 6.91
Carlton-Phi ... 7.19
Seaver-Cin ... 7.50
Reuss-LA ... 7.57

Fewest BB/Game
Forsch-StL ... 1.38
Reuss-LA ... 1.57
Forsch-Hou ... 1.66
Candelaria-Pit ... 1.93
Sutton-LA ... 1.99

Strikeouts
Carlton-Phi ... 286
Ryan-Hou ... 200
Soto-Cin ... 182
Niekro-Atl ... 176
Blyleven-Pit ... 168

Strikeouts/Game
Soto-Cin ... 8.61
Carlton-Phi ... 8.47
Ryan-Hou ... 7.70
Blyleven-Pit ... 6.98
Welch-LA ... 5.94

Ratio
Sutton-LA ... 8.99
Reuss-LA ... 9.14
Pastore-Cin ... 9.89
Carlton-Phi ... 9.92
Soto-Cin ... 10.02

Earned Run Average
Sutton-LA ... 2.20
Carlton-Phi ... 2.34
Reuss-LA ... 2.51
Blue-SF ... 2.97
Rogers-Mon ... 2.98

Adjusted ERA
Carlton-Phi ... 162
Sutton-LA ... 159
Reuss-LA ... 139
Rogers-Mon ... 120
Blue-SF ... 119

Opponents' Batting Avg.
Soto-Cin ... .187
Sutton-LA ... .211
Carlton-Phi ... .218
Seaver-Cin ... .225
Reuss-LA ... .227

Opponents' On Base Pct.
Sutton-LA ... .258
Reuss-LA ... .261
Pastore-Cin ... .277
Carlton-Phi ... .278
Soto-Cin ... .279

Starter Runs
Carlton-Phi ... 42.6
Sutton-LA ... 33.0
Reuss-LA ... 27.8
Ruhle-Hou ... 21.8
Richard-Hou ... 21.5

Adjusted Starter Runs
Carlton-Phi ... 49.0
Sutton-LA ... 30.5
Reuss-LA ... 25.1
Rogers-Mon ... 18.3
Richard-Hou ... 17.5

Clutch Pitching Index
Reuschel-Chi ... 119
Bomback-NY ... 116
Zachry-NY ... 114
Ruthven-Phi ... 112
Sanderson-Mon ... 111

Relief Runs
McGraw-Phi ... 21.9
Camp-Atl ... 20.3
Caudill-Chi ... 20.1
Smith-Hou ... 19.1
Holland-SF ... 16.9

Adjusted Relief Runs
Caudill-Chi ... 24.5
McGraw-Phi ... 23.9
Camp-Atl ... 22.0
Holland-SF ... 16.4
Smith-Hou ... 15.5

Relief Ranking
McGraw-Phi ... 32.6
Camp-Atl ... 28.4
Hume-Cin ... 25.6
Sutter-Chi ... 25.5
Fryman-Mon ... 20.1

Total Pitcher Index
Carlton-Phi ... 5.4
Sutton-LA ... 2.9
Camp-Atl ... 2.8
Camp-Atl ... 2.7
McGraw-Phi ... 2.6

Total Baseball Ranking
Schmidt-Phi ... 7.6
Carlton-Phi ... 5.4
Smith-SD ... 4.8
Templeton-StL ... 4.7
Carter-Mon ... 3.9

TEAM	G	W	L	PCT	GB	R	OR	AB	H	2B	3B	HR	BB	SO	AVG	OBP	SLG	PRO	PRO+	BR	/A	PF	CHI	RC	SB	CS	SBA	SBR
EAST																												
NY	162	103	59	.636		820	662	5553	1484	239	34	189	643	739	.267	.346	.425	.771	112	79	92	98	100	820	86	36	70	4
BAL	162	100	62	.617	3	805	**640**	5585	1523	258	29	156	587	766	.273	.344	.413	.757	107	52	59	99	102	788	111	38	74	11
MIL	162	86	76	.531	17	811	682	5653	1555	**298**	36	**203**	455	745	.275	.332	**.448**	**.780**	**116**	78	**101**	97	100	**834**	131	56	70	6
BOS	160	83	77	.519	19	757	767	5603	1588	297	36	162	475	720	.283	.343	.436	.779	107	**86**	49	105	93	810	79	48	62	-5
DET	163	84	78	.519	19	**830**	757	5648	1543	232	53	143	**645**	844	.273	.351	.409	.760	106	66	49	102	101	804	75	68	52	-18
CLE	160	79	81	.494	23	738	807	5470	1517	221	40	89	617	625	.277	**.355**	.381	.736	102	26	23	100	97	739	118	58	67	1
TOR	162	67	95	.414	36	624	762	5571	1398	249	53	126	448	813	.251	.310	.383	.693	85	-92	-125	105	99	640	67	72	48	-23
WEST																												
KC	162	97	65	.599		809	694	5714	**1633**	266	**59**	115	508	709	**.286**	.348	.413	.761	107	62	56	101	100	826	**185**	43	**81**	**30**
OAK	162	83	79	.512	14	686	642	5495	1424	212	35	137	506	824	.259	.324	.385	.709	100	-51	-1	93	102	680	175	82	68	3
MIN	161	77	84	.478	19.5	670	724	5530	1468	252	46	99	436	703	.265	.322	.381	.703	86	-65	-117	107	103	655	62	46	57	-9
TEX	163	76	85	.472	20.5	756	752	5690	1616	263	27	124	480	**589**	.284	.342	.405	.747	107	30	52	97	98	768	91	49	65	-2
CHI	162	70	90	.438	26	587	722	5444	1408	255	38	91	399	670	.259	.314	.370	.684	87	-104	-100	100	98	608	68	54	56	-12
CAL	160	65	95	.406	31	698	797	5443	1442	236	32	106	539	889	.265	.335	.378	.713	97	-33	-15	98	102	681	91	63	59	-11
SEA	163	59	103	.364	38	610	793	5489	1359	211	35	104	483	727	.248	.311	.356	.667	81	-136	-142	101	**105**	598	116	62	65	-2
TOT	1132					10201		77888	20958	3489	553	1844	7221	10363	.269	.334	.399	.733							1455	775	65	-29

TEAM	CG	SH	SV	IP	H	H/G	HR	BB	SO	RAT	ERA	ERA+	OAV	OOB	PR	/A	PF	CPI	FA	E	DP	FW	PW	BW	SBW	DIF
EAST																										
NY	29	**15**	**50**	1464^{1}	1433	8.8	**102**	463	845	11.8	3.58	109	.259	.319	73	55	97	98	.978	138	160	.0	5.5	9.2	.6	6.7
BAL	42	10	41	1460	1438	8.9	134	507	789	12.1	3.64	109	.261	.325	63	50	98	104	**.985**	**95**	178	**2.4**	5.0	5.9	1.3	4.4
MIL	48	14	30	1450	1530	9.5	137	**420**	575	12.3	3.71	104	.273	.326	53	26	96	**107**	.977	147	189	-.5	2.6	**10.1**	.8	-8.0
BOS	30	8	43	1441^{1}	1557	9.7	129	481	696	12.9	4.38	96	.279	.340	-55	-26	105	97	.977	149	**206**	-.7	-2.6	4.9	-.3	1.7
DET	40	9	30	1467^{1}	1505	9.2	152	558	741	12.8	4.25	97	.267	.336	-35	-23	102	98	.979	133	165	.3	-2.3	4.9	-1.6	1.7
CLE	35	8	32	1428	1519	9.6	137	552	843	13.3	4.68	87	.275	.344	-103	-97	101	92	.983	105	143	1.8	-9.7	2.3	.3	4.3
TOR	39	9	23	1466	1523	9.3	135	635	705	13.4	4.19	103	.274	.351	-26	17	107	105	.979	133	**206**	.3	1.7	-12.5	-2.1	-1.4
WEST																										
KC	37	10	42	1459^{1}	1496	9.2	129	465	614	12.2	3.83	106	.267	.325	33	36	100	100	.978	141	150	-.2	3.6	5.6	**3.2**	3.8
OAK	**94**	9	13	1471^{2}	**1347**	**8.2**	142	521	769	**11.6**	**3.46**	109	**.244**	**.312**	**94**	50	93	99	.979	130	115	.5	5.0	-.0	.5	-3.8
MIN	35	9	30	1451	1502	9.3	120	468	744	12.4	3.93	**111**	.272	.331	16	**68**	108	100	.977	148	192	-.6	**6.8**	-11.7	-.7	2.7
TEX	35	6	25	1451^{2}	1561	9.7	119	519	**890**	13.1	4.02	97	.277	.342	2	-21	97	104	.977	147	169	-.5	-2.1	5.2	.0	-7.1
CHI	32	12	42	1435^{1}	1434	9.0	108	563	724	12.8	3.92	103	.263	.337	18	17	100	99	.973	171	162	-1.9	1.7	-10.0	-1.0	1.1
CAL	22	6	30	1428^{1}	1548	9.8	141	529	725	13.3	4.52	87	.278	.345	-77	-94	97	97	.978	134	144	.1	-9.4	-1.5	-.9	-3.4
SEA	31	7	26	1457^{1}	1565	9.7	159	540	703	13.2	4.38	94	.278	.344	-56	-40	102	101	.977	149	189	-.6	-4.0	-14.2	.0	-3.3
TOT	549	132	457	20331^{2}		9.3				12.7	4.03		.269	.334					.978	1920	2368					

Runs
Wilson-KC 133
Yount-Mil 121
Bumbry-Bal 118
Henderson-Oak ... 111
Trammell-Det 107

Hits
Wilson-KC 230
Cooper-Mil 219
Rivers-Tex 210
Oliver-Tex 209
Bumbry-Bal 205

Doubles
Yount-Mil 49
Oliver-Tex 43
Morrison-Chi 40
McRae-KC 39
Evans-Bos 37

Triples
Wilson-KC 15
Griffin-Tor 15
Washington-KC ... 11
Landreaux-Min 11
Yount-Mil 10

Home Runs
Oglivie-Mil 41
Jackson-NY 41
Thomas-Mil 38
Armas-Oak 35
Murray-Bal 32

Total Bases
Cooper-Mil 335
Oglivie-Mil 333
Murray-Bal 322
Yount-Mil 317
Oliver-Tex 315

Runs Batted In
Cooper-Mil 122
Oglivie-Mil 118
G.Brett-KC 118
Oliver-Tex 117
Murray-Bal 116

Runs Produced
Oliver-Tex 194
Cooper-Mil 193
Yount-Mil 185
Murray-Bal 184
G.Brett-KC 181

Bases On Balls
Randolph-NY 119
Henderson-Oak ... 117
Hargrove-Cle 111
Murphy-Oak 102
Harrah-Cle 98

Batting Average
G.Brett-KC .... .390
Cooper-Mil .... .352
Dilone-Cle .... .341
Rivers-Tex .... .333
Carew-Cal .... .331

On Base Percentage
G.Brett-KC .... .461
Randolph-NY ...... .429
Henderson-Oak .... .422
Hargrove-Cle ...... .421
Thompson-Det-Cal .402

Slugging Average
G.Brett-KC .... .664
Jackson-NY .... .597
Oglivie-Mil .... .563
Cooper-Mil .... .539
Yount-Mil .... .519

Production
G.Brett-KC 1.124
Jackson-NY .... .996
Cooper-Mil .... .931
Oglivie-Mil .... .930
Singleton-Bal ..... .885

Adjusted Production
G.Brett-KC 202
Jackson-NY 172
Cooper-Mil 157
Oglivie-Mil 156
Singleton-Bal 143

Batter Runs
G.Brett-KC 64.8
Jackson-NY 49.1
Cooper-Mil 42.9
Oglivie-Mil 39.2
Singleton-Bal 35.4

Adjusted Batter Runs
G.Brett-KC 64.3
Jackson-NY 50.3
Cooper-Mil 45.5
Oglivie-Mil 41.7
Singleton-Bal 36.2

Clutch Hitting Index
Kemp-Det 137
Manning-Cle 135
Aikens-KC 132
G.Brett-KC 132
Oliver-Tex 130

Runs Created
G.Brett-KC 135
Cooper-Mil 126
Jackson-NY 125
Oglivie-Mil 121
Henderson-Oak ... 120

Total Average
G.Brett-KC 1.258
Jackson-NY 1.060
Henderson-Oak ... .973
Randolph-NY ..... .952
Oglivie-Mil .... .925

Stolen Bases
Henderson-Oak ... 100
Wilson-KC 79
Dilone-Cle 61
Cruz-Sea 45
Bumbry-Bal 44

Stolen Base Average
Otis-KC 94.1
Harrah-Cle 89.5
Kelly-Bal 88.9
Wilson-KC 88.8
Cruz-Sea 86.5

Stolen Base Runs
Wilson-KC 17.7
Henderson-Oak ... 14.4
Cruz-Sea 9.3
Dilone-Cle 7.5
Bumbry-Bal 6.6

Fielding Runs
Castino-Min 27.8
Burleson-Bos 25.5
DeCinces-Bal 24.5
Murphy-Oak 23.9
Henderson-Oak ... 23.3

Total Player Rating
G.Brett-KC 6.5
Henderson-Oak 6.4
Oglivie-Mil 5.3
Bell-Tex 4.6
Wilson-KC 4.3

Wins
Stone-Bal 25
Norris-Oak 22
John-NY 22
McGregor-Bal 20
Leonard-KC 20

Win Percentage
Stone-Bal .... .781
May-NY .... .750
McGregor-Bal ..... .714
Norris-Oak .... .710
John-NY .... .710

Games
Quisenberry-KC ... 75
Corbett-Min 73
Monge-Cle 67
Lopez-Det 67

Complete Games
Langford-Oak 28
Norris-Oak 24
Keough-Oak 20
John-NY 16
Gura-KC 16

Shutouts
John-NY 6
Zahn-Min 5
Stieb-Tor 4
McGregor-Bal 4
Gura-KC 4

Saves
Quisenberry-KC ... 33
Gossage-NY 33
Farmer-Chi 30
Stoddard-Bal 26
Burgmeier-Bos 24

Innings Pitched
Langford-Oak .. 290.0
Norris-Oak 284.1
Gura-KC 283.1
Leonard-KC 280.1
John-NY 265.1

Fewest Hits/Game
Norris-Oak 6.81
May-NY 7.39
Clancy-Tor 7.79
Underwood-NY ... 7.84
Keough-Oak 7.85

Fewest BB/Game
Matlack-Tex 1.84
Splittorff-KC 1.90
John-NY 1.90
Tanana-Cal 1.99
Langford-Oak 1.99

Strikeouts
Barker-Cle 187
Norris-Oak 180
Guidry-NY 166
Leonard-KC 155
Bannister-Sea 155

Strikeouts/Game
Barker-Cle 6.83
May-NY 6.83
Guidry-NY 6.80
Bannister-Sea 6.41
Perry-Tex-NY 5.91

Ratio
May-NY 9.39
Norris-Oak 9.62
Langford-Oak ... 10.58
Burns-Chi 10.59
Eckersley-Bos ... 10.65

Earned Run Average
May-NY 2.46
Norris-Oak 2.53
Burns-Chi 2.84
Keough-Oak 2.92
Gura-KC 2.95

Adjusted ERA
May-NY 159
Norris-Oak 149
Burns-Chi 142
Gura-KC 137
Erickson-Min 134

Opponents' Batting Avg.
Norris-Oak .... .209
May-NY .... .224
Clancy-Tor .... .233
Keough-Oak ...... .236
Underwood-NY ... .237

Opponents' On Base Pct.
May-NY .... .268
Norris-Oak .... .272
Eckersley-Bos .... .291
Burns-Chi .... .295
Bannister-Sea .... .296

Starter Runs
Norris-Oak 47.4
Gura-KC 34.0
Burns-Chi 31.7
Keough-Oak 31.0
May-NY 30.6

Adjusted Starter Runs
Norris-Oak 39.0
Gura-KC 34.5
Burns-Chi 31.5
May-NY 28.4
Clancy-Tor 27.8

Clutch Pitching Index
Sorensen-Mil 126
Stanley-Bos 117
Keough-Oak 113
Trout-Chi 113
Perry-Tex-NY 112

Relief Runs
Corbett-Min 31.1
Burgmeier-Bos ... 22.4
Gossage-NY 19.4
Darwin-Tex 17.1
Garvin-Tor 16.0

Adjusted Relief Runs
Corbett-Min 36.0
Burgmeier-Bos ... 24.4
Garvin-Tor 18.5
Gossage-NY 18.1
Proly-Chi 15.6

Relief Ranking
Corbett-Min 46.9
Burgmeier-Bos ... 33.2
Gossage-NY 26.8
Quisenberry-KC .. 26.3
Garvin-Tor 26.2

Total Pitcher Index
Norris-Oak 4.8
Gura-KC 3.7
Corbett-Min 3.4
Burns-Chi 3.3
May-NY 3.0

Total Baseball Ranking
G.Brett-KC 6.5
Henderson-Oak 6.4
Oglivie-Mil 5.3
Norris-Oak 4.8
Bell-Tex 4.6

1981 National League

TEAM	G	W	L	PCT	GB	R	OR	AB	H	2B	3B	HR	BB	SO	AVG	OBP	SLG	PRO	PRO+	BR	/A	PF	CHI	RC	SB	CS	SBA	SBR
EAST																												
Split Season: First-half Winner PHI (34-21); Second-half Winner MON (30-23)																												
STL	103	59	43	.578		464	417	3537	936	158	45	50	379	495	.265	.339	.377	.716	106	43	32	103	102	454	88	45	66	-1
MON	108	60	48	.556	2	443	394	3591	883	146	28	81	368	498	.246	.319	.370	.689	100	3	-2	101	105	435	138	40	78	17
PHI	107	59	48	.551	2.5	491	472	3665	1002	165	25	69	372	432	.273	.344	.389	.733	109	66	47	104	100	495	103	46	69	3
PIT	103	46	56	.451	13	407	425	3576	920	176	30	55	278	494	.257	.314	.369	.683	96	-9	-22	103	102	417	122	52	70	5
NY	105	41	62	.398	18.5	348	432	3493	868	136	35	57	304	603	.248	.311	.356	.667	96	-26	-20	98	93	387	103	42	71	6
CHI	106	38	65	.369	21.5	370	483	3546	838	138	29	57	342	611	.236	.306	.340	.646	84	-52	-70	104	104	368	72	41	64	-3
WEST																												
Split Season: First-half Winner LA (36-21); Second-half Winner HOU (33-20)																												
CIN	108	66	42	.611		464	440	3637	972	190	24	64	375	553	.267	.339	.385	.724	109	53	46	102	97	469	58	37	61	-5
LA	110	63	47	.573	4	450	356	3751	984	133	20	82	331	550	.262	.325	.374	.699	108	16	31	96	101	450	73	46	61	-6
HOU	110	61	49	.555	6	394	331	3693	948	160	35	45	340	488	.257	.321	.356	.677	100	-12	-9	95	95	425	81	43	65	-2
SF	111	56	55	.505	11.5	427	414	3766	941	161	26	63	386	543	.250	.322	.357	.679	100	-8	0	98	99	431	89	50	64	-3
ATL	107	50	56	.472	15	395	416	3642	886	148	22	64	321	540	.243	.308	.349	.657	90	-41	-52	103	105	391	98	39	72	6
SD	110	41	69	.373	26	382	455	3757	963	170	35	32	311	525	.256	.316	.346	.662	100	-33	-2	93	96	400	83	62	57	-12
TOT	644					5035		43654	11141	1881	354	719	4107	6332	.255	.322	.364	.686							1108	543	67	7

TEAM	CG	SH	SV	IP	H	H/G	HR	BB	SO	RAT	ERA	ERA+	OAV	OOB	PR	/A	PF	CPI	FA	E	DP	FW	PW	BW	SBW	DIF
EAST																										
STL	11	5	33	943	902	8.6	52	290	388	11.5	3.63	98	.255	.314	-14	-7	102	91	.981	82	108	.6	-.8	3.4	-.2	4.8
MON	20	12	23	975	902	8.3	58	268	520	11.0	3.30	106	.247	.302	21	21	100	92	.980	81	88	.9	2.3	-.2	1.8	1.3
PHI	19	5	23	960¹	967	9.1	72	347	580	12.4	4.05	90	.267	.333	-60	-45	104	97	.980	86	90	.6	-4.8	5.1	.3	4.4
PIT	11	5	29	942	953	9.1	60	346	492	12.6	3.56	101	.266	.333	-8	3	103	107	.979	86	106	.4	.3	-2.4	.5	-3.9
NY	7	3	24	926¹	906	8.8	74	336	490	12.2	3.55	98	.259	.326	-6	-7	100	105	.968	130	89	-1.6	-.8	-2.1	.6	-6.5
CHI	6	2	20	956²	983	9.2	58	388	532	13.1	4.01	92	.270	.344	-55	-33	106	101	.974	113	103	-.8	-3.5	-7.5	-.4	-1.3
WEST																										
CIN	25	14	20	965²	863	8.0	67	393	593	11.8	3.73	95	.241	.318	-26	-19	102	90	.981	80	99	1.0	-2.0	4.9	-.6	8.7
LA	26	19	24	997	904	8.2	54	302	603	11.0	3.01	110	.245	.304	54	35	95	100	.980	87	101	.7	3.8	3.3	-.7	.9
HOU	23	19	25	990	842	7.7	40	300	610	10.5	2.66	124	.231	.291	91	69	94	96	.980	87	81	.7	7.4	1.0	-.3	-2.8
SF	8	9	33	1009¹	970	8.6	57	393	561	12.4	3.28	105	.256	.330	23	17	98	109	.977	102	102	.0	1.8	.0	-.4	-1.0
ATL	11	4	24	968	936	8.7	62	330	471	11.9	3.45	104	.257	.321	4	14	103	102	.976	102	93	-.2	1.5	-5.6	.6	.7
SD	9	6	23	1002	1013	9.1	64	414	492	13.0	3.72	88	.268	.343	-25	-51	93	108	.977	102	117	-.0	-5.5	-.2	-1.3	-6.9
TOT	176	103	301	11635¹		8.6				11.9	3.49		.255	.322					.978	1138	1177					

Runs		Hits		Doubles		Triples		Home Runs		Total Bases	
Schmidt-Phi	78	Rose-Phi	140	Buckner-Chi	35	Richards-SD	12	Schmidt-Phi	31	Schmidt-Phi	228
Rose-Phi	73	Buckner-Chi	131	Jones-SD	34	Reynolds-Hou	12	Dawson-Mon	24	Dawson-Mon	218
Dawson-Mon	71	Concepcion-Cin	129	Concepcion-Cin	28	Herr-StL	9	Kingman-NY	22	Foster-Cin	215
Hendrick-StL	67	Baker-LA	128	Hernandez-StL	27			Foster-Cin	22	Buckner-Chi	202
		Griffey-Cin	123	Chambliss-Atl	25			Hendrick-StL	18	Hendrick-StL	191

Runs Batted In		Runs Produced		Bases On Balls		Batting Average		On Base Percentage		Slugging Average	
Schmidt-Phi	91	Schmidt-Phi	138	Schmidt-Phi	73	Madlock-Pit	.341	Madlock-Pit	.439	Schmidt-Phi	.644
Foster-Cin	90	Foster-Cin	132	Morgan-SF	66	Rose-Phi	.325	Schmidt-Phi	.418	Dawson-Mon	.553
Buckner-Chi	75	Matthews-Phi	120	Hernandez-StL	61	Baker-LA	.320	Hernandez-StL	.405	Foster-Cin	.519
Carter-Mon	68	Concepcion-Cin	119	Thompson-Pit	59	Schmidt-Phi	.316	Matthews-Phi	.404	Madlock-Pit	.495
		Garvey-LA	117	Matthews-Phi	59	Buckner-Chi	.311	Raines-Mon	.394	Hendrick-StL	.485

Production		Adjusted Production		Batter Runs		Adjusted Batter Runs		Clutch Hitting Index		Runs Created	
Schmidt-Phi	1.083	Schmidt-Phi	195	Schmidt-Phi	50.1	Schmidt-Phi	48.1	Matthews-Phi	147	Schmidt-Phi	102
Dawson-Mon	.923	Dawson-Mon	157	Dawson-Mon	28.8	Dawson-Mon	28.3	Concepcion-Cin	135	Dawson-Mon	83
Madlock-Pit	.912	Madlock-Pit	153	Foster-Cin	27.7	Foster-Cin	26.9	Buckner-Chi	134	Foster-Cin	81
Foster-Cin	.895	Foster-Cin	150	Hernandez-StL	24.6	Hernandez-StL	23.4	Carter-Mon	132	Hernandez-StL	73
Hernandez-StL	.868	Cey-LA	145	Matthews-Phi	22.0	Madlock-Pit	21.0	Scott-Mon	129	Matthews-Phi	71

Total Average		Stolen Bases		Stolen Base Average		Stolen Base Runs		Fielding Runs		Total Player Rating	
Schmidt-Phi	1.227	Raines-Mon	71	Lopes-LA	90.9	Raines-Mon	14.7	Smith-SD	25.9	Schmidt-Phi	7.2
Raines-Mon	1.034	Moreno-Pit	39	Lacy-Pit	88.9	Lacy-Pit	5.4	Schmidt-Phi	22.5	Dawson-Mon	4.5
Dawson-Mon	.989	Scott-Mon	30	Dawson-Mon	86.7	Dawson-Mon	5.4	Dawson-Mon	13.4	Foster-Cin	3.0
Madlock-Pit	.959			Raines-Mon	86.6	Scott-Mon	4.8	Flynn-NY	12.2	Raines-Mon	2.8
Matthews-Phi	.908			Puhl-Hou	84.6	Lopes-LA	4.8	Trillo-Phi	10.8	Hernandez-StL	2.6

Wins		Win Percentage		Games		Complete Games		Shutouts		Saves	
Seaver-Cin	14	Seaver-Cin	.875	Lucas-SD	57	Valenzuela-LA	11	Valenzuela-LA	8	Sutter-StL	25
Valenzuela-LA	13	Carlton-Phi	.765	Minton-SF	55	Soto-Cin	10	Knepper-Hou	5	Minton-SF	21
Carlton-Phi	13	Ryan-Hou	.688	Tidrow-Chi	51	Carlton-Phi	10	Hooton-LA	4	Allen-NY	18
		Valenzuela-LA	.650	Hume-Cin	51	Reuss-LA	8			Camp-Atl	17
		Hooton-LA	.647	Sambito-Hou	49	Rogers-Mon	7				

Innings Pitched		Fewest Hits/Game		Fewest BB/Game		Strikeouts		Strikeouts/Game		Ratio	
Valenzuela-LA	192.1	Ryan-Hou	5.98	Perry-Atl	1.43	Valenzuela-LA	180	Carlton-Phi	8.48	Sutton-Hou	9.19
Carlton-Phi	190.0	Seaver-Cin	6.49	Reuss-LA	1.59	Carlton-Phi	179	Ryan-Hou	8.46	Valenzuela-LA	9.45
Soto-Cin	175.0	Valenzuela-LA	6.55	Sutton-Hou	1.64	Soto-Cin	151	Valenzuela-LA	8.42	Knepper-Hou	9.77
Seaver-Cin	166.1	Berenyi-Cin	6.93	Sorensen-StL	1.67	Ryan-Hou	140	Soto-Cin	7.77	Reuss-LA	9.96
Niekro-Hou	166.0	Blue-SF	7.00	Solomon-Pit	1.91	Gullickson-Mon	115	Berenyi-Cin	7.57	Hooton-LA	10.05

Earned Run Average		Adjusted ERA		Opponents' Batting Avg.		Opponents' On Base Pct.		Starter Runs		Adjusted Starter Runs	
Ryan-Hou	1.69	Ryan-Hou	195	Ryan-Hou	.188	Sutton-Hou	.268	Ryan-Hou	29.8	Ryan-Hou	26.5
Knepper-Hou	2.18	Knepper-Hou	151	Valenzuela-LA	.205	Valenzuela-LA	.271	Knepper-Hou	22.8	Carlton-Phi	25.6
Hooton-LA	2.28	Carlton-Phi	150	Seaver-Cin	.205	Knepper-Hou	.280	Carlton-Phi	22.7	Knepper-Hou	19.4
Reuss-LA	2.30	Hooton-LA	146	Berenyi-Cin	.211	Sanderson-Mon	.281	Valenzuela-LA	21.6	Seaver-Cin	18.7
Carlton-Phi	2.42	Reuss-LA	144	Blue-SF	.217	Ryan-Hou	.281	Reuss-LA	20.2	Valenzuela-LA	17.9

Clutch Pitching Index		Relief Runs		Adjusted Relief Runs		Relief Ranking		Total Pitcher Index		Total Baseball Ranking	
Mahler-Atl	124	Lucas-SD	14.9	Camp-Atl	15.2	Camp-Atl	29.3	Ryan-Hou	3.4	Schmidt-Phi	7.2
Solomon-Pit	124	Camp-Atl	14.5	Lucas-SD	12.6	Lucas-SD	21.7	Carlton-Phi	2.8	Dawson-Mon	4.5
Alexander-SF	122	Holland-SF	12.0	Holland-SF	11.4	Sambito-Hou	18.2	Valenzuela-LA	2.6	Ryan-Hou	3.4
Blue-SF	112	Sambito-Hou	11.7	Sambito-Hou	10.3	Fryman-Mon	15.7	Seaver-Cin	2.4	Foster-Cin	3.0
Zachry-NY	111	Reardon-NY-Mon	10.3	Reardon-NY-Mon	10.3	Holland-SF	14.0	Reuss-LA	2.3	Raines-Mon	2.8

TEAM	G	W	L	PCT	GB	R	OR	AB	H	2B	3B	HR	BB	SO	AVG	OBP	SLG	PRO	PRO+	BR	/A	PF	CHI	RC	SB	CS	SBA	SBR
EAST																												
Split Season: First-half Winner NY (34-22); Second-half Winner MIL (31-22)																												
MIL	109	62	47	.569		493	459	3743	961	173	20	96	300	461	.257	.317	.391	.708	109	9	32	95	108	451	39	36	52	-10
BAL	105	59	46	.562	1	429	437	3516	883	165	11	88	**404**	454	.251	.331	.379	.710	104	22	23	100	95	431	41	34	55	-8
NY	107	59	48	.551	2	421	**343**	3529	889	148	22	100	391	434	.252	.328	.391	.719	108	29	35	99	92	445	47	30	61	-4
DET	109	60	49	.550	2	427	404	3600	922	148	29	65	**404**	500	.256	.334	.368	.702	98	14	-2	104	94	442	61	37	62	-4
BOS	108	59	49	.546	2.5	**519**	481	3820	**1052**	168	17	90	378	520	**.275**	**.343**	**.399**	**.742**	107	**65**	37	106	99	**514**	32	31	51	-9
CLE	103	52	51	.505	7	431	442	3507	922	150	21	39	343	**379**	.263	.331	.351	.682	98	-11	-5	99	104	414	**119**	37	**76**	**14**
TOR	106	37	69	.349	23.5	329	466	3521	797	137	23	61	284	556	.226	.288	.330	.618	73	-103	-130	106	105	326	66	57	54	-14
WEST																												
Split Season: First-half Winner OAK (37-23); Second-half Winner KC (30-23)																												
OAK	109	64	45	.587		458	403	3677	910	119	26	**104**	342	647	.247	.314	.379	.693	104	-8	13	95	106	438	98	47	68	1
TEX	105	57	48	.543	5	452	389	3581	968	**178**	15	49	295	396	.270	.329	.369	.698	107	5	28	95	105	425	46	41	53	-11
CHI	106	54	52	.509	8.5	476	423	3615	982	135	27	76	322	518	.272	.338	.387	.725	**110**	41	**50**	98	100	471	86	44	66	-1
KC	103	50	53	.485	11	397	405	3560	952	169	29	61	301	419	.267	.327	.383	.710	105	17	21	99	90	437	100	53	65	-2
CAL	110	51	59	.464	13.5	476	453	3688	944	134	16	97	393	571	.256	.332	.380	.712	105	26	26	100	100	463	44	33	57	-7
SEA	110	44	65	.404	20	426	521	3780	950	148	13	89	329	553	.251	.316	.368	.684	93	-19	-37	104	98	441	100	50	67	0
MIN	110	41	68	.376	23	378	486	3676	884	147	**36**	47	275	497	.240	.295	.338	.633	77	-87	-116	107	**109**	355	34	27	56	-6
TOT	750					6112		50813	13016	2119	305	1062	4761	6905	.256	.323	.373	.696							913	557	62	-60

TEAM	CG	SH	SV	IP	H	H/G	HR	BB	SO	RAT	ERA	ERA+	OAV	OOB	PR	/A	PF	CPI	FA	E	DP	FW	PW	BW	SBW	DIF
EAST																										
MIL	11	4	**35**	986	994	9.1	72	352	448	12.4	3.91	88	.266	.331	-27	-53	94	99	.982	79	**135**	.5	-5.6	3.4	-.6	9.8
BAL	25	10	23	940	923	8.8	83	347	489	12.3	3.70	98	.260	.328	-4	-7	99	**104**	.983	68	114	1.0	-.7	2.4	-.4	4.2
NY	16	**13**	30	948	**827**	7.9	**64**	287	**606**	**10.7**	**2.90**	**123**	**.235**	**.295**	**80**	**71**	98	99	.982	72	100	.8	**7.5**	3.7	.0	-6.5
DET	33	**13**	22	969^1	840	**7.8**	83	373	476	11.5	3.53	107	.236	.313	14	26	103	94	**.984**	**67**	109	**1.2**	2.7	-.2	.0	1.7
BOS	19	4	24	987^1	983	9.0	90	354	536	12.4	3.81	102	.262	.330	-17	7	106	103	.979	91	108	-.2	.7	3.9	-.5	1.1
CLE	33	10	13	931	989	9.6	67	311	569	12.7	3.88	94	.274	.333	-23	-26	99	102	.978	87	91	-.2	-2.7	-.5	**1.9**	2.0
TOR	20	4	18	953^1	908	8.6	72	377	451	12.5	3.81	103	.252	.329	-17	13	108	97	.975	105	102	-1.1	1.4	-13.6	-1.0	-1.6
WEST																										
OAK	**60**	11	10	993	883	8.0	80	370	505	11.6	3.30	105	.240	.314	40	20	95	101	.980	81	74	.4	2.1	1.4	.6	5.1
TEX	23	**13**	18	940^1	851	8.1	67	322	488	11.4	3.40	102	.243	.310	27	7	95	95	**.984**	69	102	.9	.7	2.9	-.7	.6
CHI	20	8	23	940^2	891	8.5	73	336	529	12.0	3.47	103	.252	.321	19	11	98	102	.979	87	113	-.0	1.2	**5.2**	.3	-5.7
KC	24	8	24	922^1	909	8.9	75	**273**	404	11.7	3.56	101	.260	.317	10	5	99	101	.982	72	94	.7	.5	2.2	.2	-5.1
CAL	27	8	19	971^1	958	8.9	81	323	426	12.1	3.70	99	.261	.324	-4	-5	100	102	.977	101	120	-.7	-.5	2.7	-.3	-5.2
SEA	10	5	23	997^1	1039	9.4	76	360	478	12.8	4.23	91	.271	.336	-64	-42	105	95	.979	91	122	-.1	-4.4	-3.9	.5	-2.5
MIN	13	6	22	979^2	1021	9.4	79	376	500	13.0	3.98	99	.272	.341	-35	-3	108	**104**	.978	96	103	-.4	-.3	-12.2	-.2	-.4
TOT	334	117	304	13459^2		8.7				12.1	3.66		.256	.323					.980	1166	1487					

Runs
Henderson-Oak.... 89
Evans-Bos........ 84
Cooper-Mil........ 70
Harrah-Cle........ 64
Rivers-Tex........ 62

Hits
Henderson-Oak... 135
Lansford-Bos 134
Wilson-KC 133
Cooper-Mil....... 133
Paciorek-Sea..... 132

Doubles
Cooper-Mil........ 35
Oliver-Tex......... 29
Paciorek-Sea...... 28
Dauer-Bal......... 27
G.Brett-KC........ 27

Triples
Castino-Min........ 9
Wilson-KC......... 7
Henderson-Oak..... 7
G.Brett-KC......... 7
Baines-Chi.......... 7

Home Runs
Murray-Bal........ 22
Grich-Cal......... 22
Evans-Bos........ 22
Armas-Oak....... 22

Total Bases
Evans-Bos....... 215
Armas-Oak...... 211
Paciorek-Sea..... 206
Cooper-Mil....... 206
Murray-Bal....... 202

Runs Batted In
Murray-Bal........ 78
Armas-Oak....... 76
Oglivie-Mil........ 72
Evans-Bos........ 71
Winfield-NY....... 68

Runs Produced
Evans-Bos....... 133
Henderson-Oak... 118
Cooper-Mil....... 118
Murray-Bal....... 113
Oglivie-Mil....... 111

Bases On Balls
Evans-Bos........ 85
Murphy-Oak...... 73
Kemp-Det......... 70
Henderson-Oak.... 64
Aikens-KC........ 62

Batting Average
Lansford-Bos.....336
Paciorek-Sea.....326
Cooper-Mil........320
Henderson-Oak....319
Hargrove-Cle......317

On Base Percentage
Hargrove-Cle......432
Evans-Bos........418
Henderson-Oak....411
Kemp-Det.........393
Lansford-Bos.....391

Slugging Average
Grich-Cal.........543
Murray-Bal........534
Evans-Bos........522
Paciorek-Sea......509
Cooper-Mil........495

Production
Evans-Bos........940
Grich-Cal.........924
Murray-Bal........897
Paciorek-Sea......894
Lemon-Chi........879

Adjusted Production
Grich-Cal........ 164
Evans-Bos....... 160
Murray-Bal....... 156
Lemon-Chi....... 155
Cooper-Mil....... 154

Batter Runs
Evans-Bos.......39.8
Paciorek-Sea.....28.4
Grich-Cal........28.3
Henderson-Oak...26.9
Murray-Bal.......25.9

Adjusted Batter Runs
Evans-Bos.......36.5
Henderson-Oak...29.5
Grich-Cal........28.3
Paciorek-Sea.....26.4
Cooper-Mil.......26.1

Clutch Hitting Index
Hargrove-Cle..... 150
Yastrzemski-Bos.. 150
Oglivie-Mil....... 149
Bell-Tex......... 144
Simmons-Mil..... 137

Runs Created
Evans-Bos........ 95
Henderson-Oak.... 81
Paciorek-Sea...... 76
Grich-Cal......... 73
Murray-Bal........ 70

Total Average
Evans-Bos......1.007
Grich-Cal.........917
Henderson-Oak....899
Murray-Bal........864
Paciorek-Sea......846

Stolen Bases
Henderson-Oak.... 56
Cruz-Sea......... 43
LeFlore-Chi....... 36
Wilson-KC........ 34
Dilone-Cle........ 29

Stolen Base Average
Manning-Cle......89.3
Bannister-Cle.....88.9
Cruz-Sea........84.3
Wilson-KC.......81.0
Gibson-Det.......77.3

Stolen Base Runs
Cruz-Sea..........8.1
Manning-Cle......5.7
Wilson-KC........5.4
LeFlore-Chi.......4.2

Fielding Runs
Bell-Tex.........30.0
Yount-Mil........27.5
Wilson-KC........22.1
Burleson-Cal.....21.0
Henderson-Oak...20.1

Total Player Rating
Henderson-Oak....5.0
Evans-Bos........4.7
Bell-Tex..........4.5
Grich-Cal.........4.5
Yount-Mil.........4.5

Wins
Vuckovich-Mil..... 14
Morris-Det........ 14
McCatty-Oak...... 14
J.Martinez-Bal..... 14

Win Percentage
Vuckovich-Mil.....778
J.Martinez-Bal.....737
McGregor-Bal.....722
Guidry-NY........688

Games
Corbett-Min....... 54
Fingers-Mil........ 47
Rawley-Sea....... 46
Easterly-Mil....... 44

Complete Games
Langford-Oak..... 18
McCatty-Oak...... 16
Morris-Det........ 15
Norris-Oak........ 12
Gura-KC.......... 12

Shutouts
Medich-Tex........ 4
McCatty-Oak....... 4
Forsch-Cal......... 4
Dotson-Chi........ 4

Saves
Fingers-Mil........ 28
Gossage-NY...... 20
Quisenberry-KC... 18
Corbett-Min....... 17
Saucier-Det....... 13

Innings Pitched
Leonard-KC.....201.2
Morris-Det......198.0
Langford-Oak....195.1
McCatty-Oak....185.2
Stieb-Tor.......183.2

Fewest Hits/Game
Righetti-NY......6.41
McCatty-Oak.....6.79
Morris-Det.......6.95
Guidry-NY.......7.09
Darwin-Tex.......7.09

Fewest BB/Game
Honeycutt-Tex....1.20
Forsch-Cal.......1.59
Gura-KC.........1.83
Leonard-KC.......1.83
Guidry-NY.......1.84

Strikeouts
Barker-Cle....... 127
Burns-Chi........ 108
Leonard-KC...... 107
Blyleven-Cle..... 107
Guidry-NY....... 104

Strikeouts/Game
Righetti-NY......7.60
Barker-Cle.......7.41
Guidry-NY.......7.37
Bannister-Sea....6.30
Burns-Chi........6.20

Ratio
Guidry-NY.......9.00
Gura-KC.........9.30
Righetti-NY......9.66
Honeycutt-Tex....9.66
McCatty-Oak.....9.84

Earned Run Average
Righetti-NY......2.05
Stewart-Bal......2.32
McCatty-Oak.....2.33
Lamp-Chi........2.41
John-NY.........2.63

Adjusted ERA
Righetti-NY...... 174
Stewart-Bal...... 156
McCatty-Oak..... 149
Lamp-Chi........ 148
John-NY......... 136

Opponents' Batting Avg.
Righetti-NY.......196
McCatty-Oak......211
Guidry-NY........214
Darwin-Tex........218
Morris-Det........218

Opponents' On Base Pct.
Guidry-NY........257
Gura-KC..........269
Righetti-NY.......269
Honeycutt-Tex.....272
McCatty-Oak......279

Starter Runs
McCatty-Oak.....27.5
Righetti-NY......18.8
Gura-KC.........18.0
Burns-Chi........17.7
Lamp-Chi........17.6

Adjusted Starter Runs
McCatty-Oak.....23.8
Righetti-NY......17.8
Gura-KC.........17.1
Lamp-Chi........16.5
Burns-Chi........16.3

Clutch Pitching Index
Stewart-Bal...... 145
John-NY......... 129
Burns-Chi........ 121
Denny-Cle....... 119
McGregor-Bal.... 116

Relief Runs
Fingers-Mil......22.7
Gossage-NY.....15.0
Quisenberry-KC..13.3
Saucier-Det......10.9
Corbett-Min......10.6

Adjusted Relief Runs
Fingers-Mil......20.7
Gossage-NY.....14.5
Corbett-Min......13.4
Quisenberry-KC..13.0
Saucier-Det......11.5

Relief Ranking
Fingers-Mil......38.2
Gossage-NY......28.0
Saucier-Det......19.6
Quisenberry-KC..17.8
Corbett-Min......16.9

Total Pitcher Index
McCatty-Oak......2.8
Fingers-Mil........2.3
Righetti-NY........2.0
Gura-KC...........1.9
Lamp-Chi..........1.9

Total Baseball Ranking
Henderson-Oak....5.0
Evans-Bos........4.7
Bell-Tex..........4.5
Grich-Cal.........4.5
Yount-Mil.........4.5

1982 National League

TEAM	G	W	L	PCT	GB	R	OR	AB	H	2B	3B	HR	BB	SO	AVG	OBP	SLG	PRO	PRO+	BR	/A	PF	CHI	RC	SB	CS	SBA	SBR
EAST																												
STL	162	92	70	.568		685	609	5455	1439	239	52	67	569	805	.264	**.337**	.364	.701	101	24	17	101	99	682	**200**	91	69	5
PHI	162	89	73	.549	3	664	654	5454	1417	245	25	112	506	831	.260	.325	.376	.701	100	14	0	102	99	654	128	76	63	-7
MON	162	86	76	.531	6	697	616	5557	1454	270	38	133	503	816	.262	.327	.396	.723	106	52	39	102	97	725	156	56	**74**	13
PIT	162	84	78	.519	8	724	696	5614	**1535**	**272**	40	134	447	862	**.273**	.330	**.408**	**.738**	109	80	60	103	97	**745**	161	75	68	3
CHI	162	73	89	.451	19	676	709	5531	1436	239	46	102	460	869	.260	.319	.375	.694	97	-4	-22	103	103	662	132	70	65	-2
NY	162	65	97	.401	27	609	723	5510	1361	227	26	97	456	1005	.247	.307	.350	.657	90	-75	-70	99	105	595	137	58	70	6
WEST																												
ATL	162	89	73	.549		739	702	5507	1411	215	22	**146**	554	869	.256	.327	.383	.710	100	33	6	104	105	697	151	77	66	-1
LA	162	88	74	.543	1	691	612	5642	1487	222	32	138	528	804	.264	.330	.388	.718	110	47	**64**	98	95	735	151	56	73	12
SF	162	87	75	.537	2	673	687	5499	1393	213	30	133	**607**	915	.253	.329	.376	.705	103	27	28	100	97	685	130	56	70	5
SD	162	81	81	.500	8	675	658	5575	1435	217	52	81	429	877	.257	.313	.359	.672	99	-49	-14	95	110	626	165	77	68	3
HOU	162	77	85	.475	12	569	620	5440	1342	236	48	74	435	830	.247	.305	.349	.654	95	-84	-35	92	102	578	140	61	70	5
CIN	162	61	101	.377	28	545	661	5479	1375	228	34	82	470	817	.251	.313	.350	.663	89	-63	-76	102	92	588	131	69	66	2
TOT	972					7947		66263	17085	2823	445	1299	5964	10300	.258	.322	.373	.695							1782	822	68	41

TEAM	CG	SH	SV	IP	H	H/G	HR	BB	SO	RAT	ERA	ERA+	OAV	OOB	PR	/A	PF	CPI	FA	E	DP	FW	PW	BW	SBW	DIF
EAST																										
STL	25	10	47	1465.1	1420	8.7	94	502	689	11.9	3.37	107	.258	.322	37	40	101	105	**.981**	124	169	.9	4.2	1.8	.2	3.9
PHI	**38**	13	33	1456.1	1395	8.6	86	472	**1002**	11.7	3.61	102	.255	.317	-1	9	102	93	**.981**	121	138	1.1	.9	.0	-1.1	7.0
MON	34	10	43	1460.2	1371	8.4	110	**448**	936	11.3	3.31	**110**	.250	.309	46	**53**	101	99	.980	122	117	1.1	5.6	4.1	1.0	-6.7
PIT	19	7	39	1466.2	1434	8.8	118	521	933	12.2	3.81	97	.257	.324	-34	-17	103	96	.977	145	133	-.3	-1.8	6.3	-.0	-1.2
CHI	9	7	43	1447.1	1510	9.4	125	452	764	12.4	3.92	95	.272	.330	-51	-30	104	102	.979	132	110	.5	-3.2	-2.3	-.6	-2.4
NY	15	5	37	1447.1	1508	9.4	119	582	759	13.1	3.88	94	.273	.344	-45	-40	101	**109**	.972	175	134	-2.0	-4.2	-7.4	.3	-2.7
WEST																										
ATL	15	11	**51**	1463	1484	9.1	126	502	813	12.2	3.82	98	.267	.331	-36	-15	104	103	.979	137	**186**	.2	-1.6	.6	-.5	9.2
LA	37	**16**	28	1488.1	1356	**8.2**	81	468	932	**11.2**	3.26	106	**.244**	**.305**	56	34	96	92	.979	139	131	.0	3.6	**6.7**	.9	-4.3
SF	18	4	45	1465.1	1507	9.3	109	466	810	12.3	3.64	99	.270	.329	-6	-7	100	106	.973	173	125	-1.9	-.7	2.9	.2	5.5
SD	20	11	41	1476	1348	8.2	139	502	765	11.4	3.52	97	**.244**	.310	13	-16	95	96	.976	152	142	-.7	-1.7	-1.5	-.0	3.9
HOU	37	**16**	31	1446.2	**1338**	8.3	87	479	899	11.5	3.42	97	.247	.312	30	-16	92	94	.978	136	154	.3	-1.7	-3.7	.2	.9
CIN	22	7	31	1460.1	1414	8.7	105	570	998	12.6	3.66	101	.258	.330	-10	6	103	102	.980	128	158	.7	.6	-8.0	-.6	-12.8
TOT	289	117	469	17543.1		8.8				12.0	3.60		.258	.322					.978	1684	1697					

Runs
L.Smith-StL 120
Murphy-Atl 113
Schmidt-Phi 108
Dawson-Mon 107
Sandberg-Chi 103

Hits
Oliver-Mon 204
Buckner-Chi 201
Dawson-Mon 183
L.Smith-StL 182
Ray-Pit 182

Doubles
Oliver-Mon 43
Kennedy-SD 42
Dawson-Mon 37
Knight-Hou 36

Triples
Thon-Hou 10
Wilson-NY 9
Puhl-Hou 9
Moreno-Pit 9

Home Runs
Kingman-NY 37
Murphy-Atl 36
Schmidt-Phi 35
Horner-Atl 32
Guerrero-LA 32

Total Bases
Oliver-Mon 317
Guerrero-LA 308
Murphy-Atl 303
Dawson-Mon 303
Buckner-Chi 290

Runs Batted In
Oliver-Mon 109
Murphy-Atl 109
Buckner-Chi 105
Hendrick-StL 104
Clark-SF 103

Runs Produced
Murphy-Atl 186
Buckner-Chi 183
L.Smith-StL 181
Oliver-Mon 177
Madlock-Pit 168

Bases On Balls
Schmidt-Phi 107
Thompson-Pit 101
Hernandez-StL ... 100
Murphy-Atl 93
Clark-SF 90

Batting Average
Oliver-Mon .... .331
Madlock-Pit ...... .319
Durham-Chi ...... .312
L.Smith-StL ...... .307
Buckner-Chi ...... .306

On Base Percentage
Schmidt-Phi ...... .407
Hernandez-StL .... .404
Morgan-SF .... .402
Thompson-Pit .... .397
Oliver-Mon .... .394

Slugging Average
Schmidt-Phi ...... .547
Guerrero-LA ...... .536
Durham-Chi ...... .521
Oliver-Mon .... .514
Thompson-Pit ..... .511

Production
Schmidt-Phi ..... .954
Guerrero-LA ...... .915
Durham-Chi ...... .910
Oliver-Mon .... .908
Thompson-Pit ..... .908

Adjusted Production
Schmidt-Phi 161
Guerrero-LA 157
Oliver-Mon 149
Lezcano-SD 149
Durham-Chi 148

Batter Runs
Schmidt-Phi 47.2
Oliver-Mon 42.7
Thompson-Pit 40.7
Guerrero-LA 40.3
Murphy-Atl 37.8

Adjusted Batter Runs
Schmidt-Phi 45.7
Guerrero-LA 42.0
Oliver-Mon 41.3
Thompson-Pit 38.5
Durham-Chi 36.0

Clutch Hitting Index
Hernandez-StL ... 150
Hendrick-StL 149
DeJesus-Phi 133
Lezcano-SD 124
Salazar-SD 124

Runs Created
Oliver-Mon 125
Guerrero-LA 120
Murphy-Atl 118
Schmidt-Phi 118
Thompson-Pit 117

Total Average
Schmidt-Phi 1.026
Guerrero-LA ...... .959
Thompson-Pit ..... .951
Morgan-SF .... .923
Durham-Chi ...... .917

Stolen Bases
Raines-Mon 78
L.Smith-StL 68
Moreno-Pit 60
Wilson-NY 58
S.Sax-LA 49

Stolen Base Average
Bailor-NY 87.0
Morgan-SF 85.7
Wiggins-SD 84.6
Matthews-Phi 84.0
O.Smith-StL 83.3

Stolen Base Runs
Raines-Mon 13.8
Wilson-NY 7.8
Wiggins-SD 6.3
Thon-Hou 6.3
Dawson-Mon 5.7

Fielding Runs
O.Smith-StL 33.1
Hubbard-Atl 19.9
Schmidt-Phi 18.8
Ramirez-Atl 16.5
Salazar-SD 16.2

Total Player Rating
Schmidt-Phi 6.2
Carter-Mon 5.5
Guerrero-LA 4.9
O.Smith-StL 4.4
Dawson-Mon 4.0

Wins
Carlton-Phi 23
Valenzuela-LA 19
Rogers-Mon 19
Reuss-LA 18

Win Percentage
Niekro-Atl .... .810
Rogers-Mon .... .704
Carlton-Phi .... .676
Lollar-SD .... .640
Forsch-StL .... .625

Games
Tekulve-Pit 85
Minton-SF 78
Scurry-Pit 76
Reardon-Mon 75
Hernandez-Chi 75

Complete Games
Carlton-Phi 19
Valenzuela-LA 18
Niekro-Hou 16
Rogers-Mon 14
Soto-Cin 13

Shutouts
Carlton-Phi 6
Niekro-Hou 5
Andujar-StL 5

Saves
Sutter-StL 36
Minton-SF 30
Garber-Atl 30
Reardon-Mon 26
Tekulve-Pit 20

Innings Pitched
Carlton-Phi 295.2
Valenzuela-LA 285.0
Rogers-Mon 277.0
Niekro-Hou 270.0
Andujar-StL 265.2

Fewest Hits/Game
Ryan-Hou 7.05
Soto-Cin 7.06
Lea-Mon 7.35
Lollar-SD 7.43
Niekro-Hou 7.47

Fewest BB/Game
Bird-Chi 1.41
Hammaker-SF 1.44
Andujar-StL 1.69
Reuss-LA 1.77
Candelaria-Pit 1.91

Strikeouts
Carlton-Phi 286
Soto-Cin 274
Ryan-Hou 245
Valenzuela-LA 199
Rogers-Mon 179

Strikeouts/Game
Soto-Cin 9.57
Ryan-Hou 8.81
Carlton-Phi 8.71
Candelaria-Pit 6.85
Welch-LA 6.72

Ratio
Soto-Cin 9.68
Niekro-Hou 9.77
Andujar-StL 9.96
Sutton-Hou 9.97
Reuss-LA 10.04

Earned Run Average
Rogers-Mon 2.40
Niekro-Hou 2.47
Andujar-StL 2.47
Soto-Cin 2.79
Valenzuela-LA ... 2.87

Adjusted ERA
Rogers-Mon 151
Andujar-StL 146
Niekro-Hou 134
Soto-Cin 132
Candelaria-Pit ... 126

Opponents' Batting Avg.
Ryan-Hou .... .213
Soto-Cin .... .215
Lea-Mon .... .222
Lollar-SD .... .224
Niekro-Hou .... .229

Opponents' On Base Pct.
Soto-Cin .... .273
Reuss-LA .... .278
Sutton-Hou .... .279
Niekro-Hou .... .279
Andujar-StL ...... .282

Starter Runs
Rogers-Mon 36.8
Niekro-Hou 34.0
Andujar-StL 33.3
Soto-Cin 23.1
Valenzuela-LA ... 23.0

Adjusted Starter Runs
Rogers-Mon 38.0
Andujar-StL 33.8
Soto-Cin 25.9
Niekro-Hou 25.5
Valenzuela-LA ... 18.8

Clutch Pitching Index
Camp-Atl 124
Jenkins-Chi 121
Krukow-Phi 120
Gale-SF 114
Mura-StL 110

Relief Runs
Minton-SF 24.2
Scurry-Pit 21.5
Reardon-Mon 18.6
Bedrosian-Atl ... 18.1
DeLeon-SD 17.8

Adjusted Relief Runs
Minton-SF 24.1
Scurry-Pit 21.7
Bedrosian-Atl ... 20.1
Reardon-Mon 19.1
Garber-Atl 18.5

Relief Ranking
Minton-SF 37.9
Garber-Atl 35.5
Reardon-Mon 27.6
DeLeon-SD 24.8
Scurry-Pit 24.6

Total Pitcher Index
Rogers-Mon 4.3
Andujar-StL 3.8
Soto-Cin 2.9
Minton-SF 2.7
Valenzuela-LA ... 2.7

Total Baseball Ranking
Schmidt-Phi 6.2
Carter-Mon 5.5
Guerrero-LA 4.9
O.Smith-StL 4.4
Rogers-Mon 4.3

TEAM	G	W	L	PCT	GB	R	OR	AB	H	2B	3B	HR	BB	SO	AVG	OBP	SLG	PRO	PRO+	BR	/A	PF	CHI	RC	SB	CS	SBA	SBR
EAST																												
MIL	163	95	67	.586		**891**	717	5733	1599	277	41	**216**	484	714	.279	.337	**.455**	**.792**	**123**	**109**	**155**	94	105	**865**	84	52	62	-6
BAL	163	94	68	.580	1	774	687	5557	1478	259	27	179	634	796	.266	.344	.419	.763	108	67	70	100	96	795	49	38	56	-8
BOS	162	89	73	.549	6	753	713	5596	1536	271	31	136	547	736	.274	.342	.407	.749	99	39	-3	106	98	755	42	39	52	-11
DET	162	83	79	.512	12	729	685	5590	1489	237	40	177	470	807	.266	.326	.418	.744	103	15	12	100	99	752	93	66	58	-12
NY	162	79	83	.488	16	709	716	5526	1417	225	37	161	590	719	.256	.331	.398	.729	101	-5	7	98	98	716	69	45	61	-6
TOR	162	78	84	.481	17	651	701	5526	1447	262	45	106	415	749	.262	.317	.383	.700	83	-70	-135	109	102	655	118	81	59	-13
CLE	162	78	84	.481	17	683	748	5559	1458	225	32	109	**651**	**625**	.262	.343	.373	.716	97	-13	-9	100	94	723	151	68	69	5
WEST																												
CAL	162	93	69	.574		814	**670**	5532	1518	268	26	186	613	760	.274	**.350**	.433	.783	114	108	108	100	96	834	55	53	51	-15
KC	162	90	72	.556	3	784	717	5629	**1603**	**295**	**58**	132	442	758	**.285**	.340	.428	.768	109	67	66	100	99	802	133	48	**73**	11
CHI	162	87	75	.537	6	786	710	5575	1523	266	52	136	533	866	.273	.340	.413	.753	106	43	43	100	102	784	136	58	70	6
SEA	162	76	86	.469	17	651	712	5626	1431	259	33	130	456	806	.254	.313	.381	.694	87	-84	-104	103	102	657	131	82	62	-10
OAK	162	68	94	.420	25	691	819	5448	1286	211	27	149	582	948	.236	.312	.367	.679	90	-106	-74	96	**113**	644	**232**	87	**73**	**17**
TEX	162	64	98	.395	29	590	749	5445	1354	204	26	115	447	750	.249	.309	.359	.668	87	-128	-93	95	103	593	63	45	58	-8
MIN	162	60	102	.370	33	657	819	5544	1427	234	44	148	474	887	.257	.319	.396	.715	93	-43	-62	103	98	676	38	33	54	-8
TOT	1135					10163		77886	20566	3493	519	2080	7338	10921	.264	.330	.402	.733							1394	795	64	-59

TEAM	CG	SH	SV	IP	H	H/G	HR	BB	SO	RAT	ERA	ERA+	OAV	OOB	PR	/A	PF	CPI	FA	E	DP	FW	PW	BW	SBW	DIF
EAST																										
MIL	34	6	**47**	1467[1]	1514	9.3	152	511	717	12.5	3.98	95	.270	.333	15	-32	93	106	.980	125	**185**	.1	-3.2	**15.5**	-.2	1.8
BAL	38	8	34	1462[1]	1436	8.8	147	488	719	**12.0**	3.99	101	.257	**.320**	14	7	99	95	**.984**	**101**	140	**1.4**	.7	7.0	-.4	4.3
BOS	23	11	33	1453	1557	9.6	155	478	816	12.8	4.03	107	.276	.336	7	44	106	**108**	.981	121	172	.3	4.4	-.3	-.7	4.3
DET	**45**	5	27	1451	**1371**	**8.5**	172	554	740	12.1	**3.80**	107	**.251**	.323	**44**	42	100	104	.981	117	165	.5	4.2	1.2	-.8	-3.1
NY	24	8	39	1459	1471	9.1	113	491	939	12.2	3.99	100	.264	.326	13	-1	98	95	.979	128	158	-.0	-.1	.7	-.2	-2.3
TOR	41	**13**	25	1443[2]	1428	8.9	147	493	776	12.1	3.95	**113**	.257	.321	20	**85**	110	97	.978	136	146	-.5	**8.5**	-13.5	-.9	3.4
CLE	31	9	30	1468[1]	1433	8.8	122	589	882	12.5	4.11	99	.257	.330	-5	-5	100	94	.980	123	129	.2	-.5	-.9	.9	-2.7
WEST																										
CAL	40	10	27	1464	1436	8.8	124	482	728	**12.0**	3.82	106	.259	.322	42	38	100	98	.983	108	171	1.0	3.8	10.8	-1.1	-2.5
KC	16	12	45	1431	1443	9.1	163	471	650	12.2	4.08	100	.262	.323	-1	0	100	98	.979	127	140	-.0	.0	6.6	1.5	.9
CHI	30	10	41	1439	1502	9.4	**99**	**460**	753	12.4	3.87	104	.270	.329	33	27	99	100	.976	154	173	-1.5	2.7	4.3	1.0	-.5
SEA	23	11	39	1476[1]	1431	8.7	173	547	**1002**	12.2	3.88	109	.256	.325	32	60	104	104	.978	139	158	-.7	6.0	-10.4	-.6	.7
OAK	42	6	22	1456	1506	9.3	177	648	697	13.5	4.54	86	.268	.346	-76	-103	96	100	.974	160	140	-1.8	-10.3	-7.4	2.1	4.4
TEX	32	5	24	1431	1554	9.8	128	483	690	13.1	4.28	90	.280	.342	-33	-66	95	102	.981	121	169	.3	-6.6	-9.3	-.4	-1.0
MIN	26	7	30	1433	1484	9.3	208	643	812	13.4	4.72	90	.269	.347	-103	-77	104	101	.982	108	162	1.0	-7.7	-6.2	-.4	-7.7
TOT	445	121	463	20335		9.1				12.5	4.07		.264	.330					.980	1768	2208					

Runs
Molitor-Mil 136
Yount-Mil 129
Evans-Bos 122
Henderson-Oak ... 119
Downing-Cal 109

Hits
Yount-Mil 210
Cooper-Mil 205
Molitor-Mil 201
Wilson-KC 194
McRae-KC 189

Doubles
Yount-Mil 46
McRae-KC 46
White-KC 45
DeCinces-Cal 42
Cowens-Sea 39

Triples
Wilson-KC 15
Herndon-Det 13
Yount-Mil 12
Mumphrey-NY 10

Home Runs
Thomas-Mil 39
R.Jackson-Cal 39
Winfield-NY 37
Oglivie-Mil 34

Total Bases
Yount-Mil 367
Cooper-Mil 345
McRae-KC 332
Evans-Bos 325
DeCinces-Cal 315

Runs Batted In
McRae-KC 133
Cooper-Mil 121
Thornton-Cle 116
Yount-Mil 114
Thomas-Mil 112

Runs Produced
Yount-Mil 214
McRae-KC 197
Cooper-Mil 193
Molitor-Mil 188
Evans-Bos 188

Bases On Balls
Henderson-Oak ... 116
Evans-Bos 112
Thornton-Cle 109
Hargrove-Cle 101
Murphy-Oak 94

Batting Average
Wilson-KC .... .332
Yount-Mil .... .331
Carew-Cal .... .319
Murray-Bal .... .316
Cooper-Mil .... .313

On Base Percentage
Evans-Bos .... .403
Harrah-Cle .... .400
Henderson-Oak .... .399
Carew-Cal .... .399
Murray-Bal .... .395

Slugging Average
Yount-Mil .... .578
Winfield-NY .... .560
Murray-Bal .... .549
DeCinces-Cal ..... .548
McRae-KC .... .542

Production
Yount-Mil .... .962
Murray-Bal .... .944
Evans-Bos .... .937
DeCinces-Cal ..... .922
McRae-KC .... .912

Adjusted Production
Yount-Mil 170
Murray-Bal 157
DeCinces-Cal 149
R.Jackson-Cal 147
McRae-KC 146

Batter Runs
Yount-Mil 50.3
Evans-Bos 48.5
Murray-Bal 42.5
DeCinces-Cal 38.1
Harrah-Cle 38.0

Adjusted Batter Runs
Yount-Mil 55.4
Evans-Bos 43.6
Murray-Bal 42.8
Harrah-Cle 38.4
DeCinces-Cal 38.1

Clutch Hitting Index
Otis-KC 160
Foli-Cal 143
Wathan-KC 138
McRae-KC 136
Luzinski-Chi 136

Runs Created
Yount-Mil 136
Evans-Bos 134
Harrah-Cle 123
McRae-KC 123
Cooper-Mil 118

Total Average
Evans-Bos .... .976
Yount-Mil .... .969
Murray-Bal .... .957
Henderson-Oak .... .934
Harrah-Cle .... .931

Stolen Bases
Henderson-Oak ... 130
Garcia-Tor 54
J.Cruz-Sea 46
Molitor-Mil 41
Wilson-KC 37

Stolen Base Average
Sexton-Oak 100.0
Fisk-Chi 89.5
Dilone-Cle 86.8
Harrah-Cle 85.0
Brown-Sea 82.4

Stolen Base Runs
Henderson-Oak ... 13.8
Molitor-Mil 6.9
Dilone-Cle 6.9
J.Cruz-Sea 6.0
Wathan-KC 5.4

Fielding Runs
Bell-Tex 34.4
Bernazard-Chi 24.6
Murphy-Oak 21.8
DeCinces-Cal 20.6
Almon-Chi 20.0

Total Player Rating
Yount-Mil 6.7
DeCinces-Cal 5.3
Bell-Tex 5.0
Evans-Bos 4.4
Henderson-Oak 4.3

Wins
Hoyt-Chi 19
Zahn-Cal 18
Vuckovich-Mil 18
Gura-KC 18

Win Percentage
Vuckovich-Mil ..... .750
Palmer-Bal .... .750
Zahn-Cal .... .692
Petry-Det .... .625
Gura-KC .... .600

Games
VandeBerg-Sea 78
F.Martinez-Bal 76
Quisenberry-KC ... 72
Caudill-Sea 70
Spillner-Cle 65

Complete Games
Stieb-Tor 19
Morris-Det 17
Langford-Oak 15
Hoyt-Chi 14

Shutouts
Stieb-Tor 5
Zahn-Cal 4
Forsch-Cal 4

Saves
Quisenberry-KC ... 35
Gossage-NY 30
Fingers-Mil 29
Caudill-Sea 26
Davis-Min 22

Innings Pitched
Stieb-Tor 288.1
Clancy-Tor 266.2
Morris-Det 266.1
Caldwell-Mil 258.0
J.Martinez-Bal ... 252.0

Fewest Hits/Game
Sutcliffe-Cle 7.25
Ujdur-Det 7.58
Righetti-NY 7.62
Palmer-Bal 7.73
Barker-Cle 7.76

Fewest BB/Game
John-NY-Cal 1.58
Eckersley-Bos 1.73
Hoyt-Chi 1.80
Haas-Mil 1.82
Langford-Oak 1.86

Strikeouts
Bannister-Sea 209
Barker-Cle 187
Righetti-NY 163
Guidry-NY 162
Tudor-Bos 146

Strikeouts/Game
Righetti-NY 8.02
Bannister-Sea 7.62
Beattie-Sea 7.31
Barker-Cle 6.88
Tudor-Bos 6.72

Ratio
Palmer-Bal 10.39
Eckersley-Bos ... 10.95
Stieb-Tor 10.96
Barker-Cle 11.11
Bannister-Sea ... 11.11

Earned Run Average
Sutcliffe-Cle 2.96
Stanley-Bos 3.10
Palmer-Bal 3.13
Petry-Det 3.22
Stieb-Tor 3.25

Adjusted ERA
Stanley-Bos 139
Stieb-Tor 138
Sutcliffe-Cle 138
Palmer-Bal 129
Beattie-Sea 127

Opponents' Batting Avg.
Sutcliffe-Cle ...... .226
Righetti-NY .... .229
Ujdur-Det .... .230
Palmer-Bal .... .231
Barker-Cle .... .232

Opponents' On Base Pct.
Palmer-Bal .... .287
Eckersley-Bos .... .297
Stieb-Tor .... .299
Barker-Cle .... .301
Clancy-Tor .... .302

Starter Runs
Sutcliffe-Cle 26.8
Stieb-Tor 26.5
Palmer-Bal 23.7
Petry-Det 23.3
Vuckovich-Mil 18.2

Adjusted Starter Runs
Stieb-Tor 39.4
Sutcliffe-Cle 26.9
Petry-Det 23.0
Palmer-Bal 22.7
Clancy-Tor 22.6

Clutch Pitching Index
Vuckovich-Mil 131
Tudor-Bos 121
Dotson-Chi 118
Wilcox-Det 113
Stanley-Bos 110

Relief Runs
Spillner-Cle 23.5
Quisenberry-KC .. 22.9
Burgmeier-Bos ... 20.3
Gossage-NY 19.1
Caudill-Sea 18.3

Adjusted Relief Runs
Spillner-Cle 23.6
Quisenberry-KC .. 23.0
Burgmeier-Bos ... 23.0
Stanley-Bos 22.5
Caudill-Sea 20.1

Relief Ranking
Caudill-Sea 51.9
Spillner-Cle 43.2
Quisenberry-KC .. 37.4
Clear-Bos 34.6
Gossage-NY 29.0

Total Pitcher Index
Stieb-Tor 4.4
Quisenberry-KC ... 3.0
Sutcliffe-Cle 2.9
Petry-Det 2.9
Stanley-Bos 2.6

Total Baseball Ranking
Yount-Mil 6.7
DeCinces-Cal 5.3
Bell-Tex 5.0
Evans-Bos 4.4
Stieb-Tor 4.4

TEAM	G	W	L	PCT	GB	R	OR	AB	H	2B	3B	HR	BB	SO	AVG	OBP	SLG	PRO	PRO+	BR	/A	PF	CHI	RC	SB	CS	SBA	SBR
EAST																												
PHI	163	90	72	.556		696	635	5426	1352	209	45	125	**640**	906	.249	.331	.373	.704	102	17	25	99	101	676	143	75	66	-2
PIT	162	84	78	.519	6	659	648	5531	1460	238	29	121	497	873	.264	.327	.383	.710	100	17	0	103	96	682	124	77	62	-9
MON	163	82	80	.506	8	677	646	5611	1482	**297**	41	102	509	**733**	.264	.329	.386	.715	105	30	34	99	95	716	138	44	**76**	**15**
STL	162	79	83	.488	11	679	710	5550	**1496**	262	**63**	83	543	879	.270	.337	.384	.721	**106**	47	**47**	100	94	725	**207**	89	70	9
CHI	162	71	91	.438	19	701	719	5512	1436	272	42	140	470	868	.261	.322	**.401**	.723	101	35	3	105	100	707	84	40	68	1
NY	162	68	94	.420	22	575	680	5444	1314	172	26	112	436	1031	.241	.301	.344	.645	85	-112	-106	99	107	562	141	64	69	4
WEST																												
LA	163	91	71	.562		654	**609**	5440	1358	197	34	**146**	541	925	.250	.320	.379	.699	100	-6	-2	99	100	663	166	76	69	4
ATL	162	88	74	.543	3	**746**	640	5472	1489	218	45	130	582	847	**.272**	**.344**	.400	**.744**	104	**91**	41	107	98	**744**	146	88	62	-9
HOU	162	85	77	.525	6	643	646	5502	1412	239	60	97	517	869	.257	.323	.375	.698	**106**	-7	34	94	97	673	164	95	63	-8
SD	163	81	81	.500	10	653	653	5527	1384	207	34	93	482	822	.250	.313	.351	.664	93	-74	-51	97	**110**	609	179	67	73	14
SF	162	79	83	.488	12	687	697	5369	1324	206	30	142	619	990	.247	.328	.375	.703	104	11	32	97	102	662	140	78	64	-5
CIN	162	74	88	.457	17	623	710	5333	1274	236	35	107	588	1006	.239	.317	.356	.673	89	-49	-72	104	103	606	154	77	67	0
TOT	974					7993		65717	16781	2753	484	1398	6424	10749	.255	.324	.376	.700							1786	870	67	14

TEAM	CG	SH	SV	IP	H	H/G	HR	BB	SO	RAT	ERA	ERA+	OAV	OOB	PR	/A	PF	CPI	FA	E	DP	FW	PW	BW	SBW	DIF
EAST																										
PHI	20	10	41	1461^2	1429	8.8	111	**464**	**1092**	11.8	3.34	107	.256	.316	47	37	98	103	.976	152	117	-.7	3.9	2.6	-.3	3.6
PIT	25	14	41	1462^1	1378	8.5	109	563	1061	12.1	3.55	104	.252	.323	12	25	102	99	**.982**	115	165	1.4	2.6	.0	-1.1	.0
MON	**38**	**15**	34	1471	1406	8.6	120	479	899	11.7	3.58	100	.254	.317	8	1	99	98	.981	116	130	1.4	.1	3.6	**1.4**	-5.5
STL	22	10	27	1460^2	1479	9.1	115	525	709	12.5	3.79	96	.266	.332	-26	-28	100	102	.976	152	173	-.8	-2.9	**4.9**	.8	-4.0
CHI	9	10	42	1428^2	1496	9.4	117	498	807	12.7	4.08	93	.274	.337	-71	-45	105	100	**.982**	115	164	1.4	-4.7	.3	-.0	-7.0
NY	18	7	33	1451	1384	8.6	97	615	717	12.5	3.68	99	.256	.334	-8	-8	100	100	.976	151	171	-.7	-.8	-11.1	.3	-.7
WEST																										
LA	27	12	40	1464	1336	8.2	97	495	1000	**11.4**	**3.10**	**116**	.244	**.309**	**85**	**79**	99	101	.974	168	132	-1.7	**8.3**	-.2	.3	3.3
ATL	18	4	**48**	1440^2	1412	8.8	132	540	895	12.3	3.67	106	.260	.329	-7	33	107	**105**	.978	137	**176**	.1	3.4	4.3	-1.1	.2
HOU	22	14	**48**	1466^1	**1276**	**7.8**	**94**	570	904	11.5	3.45	99	**.236**	.312	29	-8	94	90	.977	147	165	-.5	-.8	3.6	-1.0	2.7
SD	23	5	44	1467^2	1389	8.5	144	528	850	11.9	3.62	96	.253	.322	1	-22	96	102	.979	129	135	.6	-2.3	-5.3	1.3	5.6
SF	20	9	47	1445^2	1431	8.9	127	520	881	12.3	3.70	96	.259	.326	-11	-27	97	101	.973	171	109	-1.9	-2.8	3.3	-.6	.0
CIN	34	5	29	1441^1	1365	8.5	135	627	934	12.6	3.98	95	.253	.333	-57	-29	105	97	.981	**114**	121	**1.5**	-3.0	-7.5	-.1	2.2
TOT	276	115	474	17461		8.6				12.1	3.63		.255	.324					.978	1667	1758					

Runs
Raines-Mon 133
Murphy-Atl 131
Schmidt-Phi 104
Dawson-Mon 104

Hits
Dawson-Mon 189
Cruz-Hou 189
Ramirez-Atl 185
Oliver-Mon 184
Raines-Mon 183

Doubles
Ray-Pit 38
Oliver-Mon 38
Buckner-Chi 38
Carter-Mon 37

Triples
Butler-Atl 13
Moreno-Hou 11
Green-StL 10
Dawson-Mon 10

Home Runs
Schmidt-Phi 40
Murphy-Atl 36
Guerrero-LA 32
Dawson-Mon 32
Evans-SF 30

Total Bases
Dawson-Mon 341
Murphy-Atl 318
Guerrero-LA 310
Thon-Hou 283
Schmidt-Phi 280

Runs Batted In
Murphy-Atl 121
Dawson-Mon 113
Schmidt-Phi 109
Guerrero-LA 103
Kennedy-SD 98

Runs Produced
Murphy-Atl 216
Raines-Mon 193
Dawson-Mon 185
Schmidt-Phi 173
Cruz-Hou 163

Bases On Balls
Schmidt-Phi 128
Thompson-Pit 99
Raines-Mon 97
Murphy-Atl 90
Morgan-Phi 89

Batting Average
Madlock-Pit 323
L.Smith-StL 321
Cruz-Hou 318
Hendrick-StL 318
Knight-Hou 304

On Base Percentage
Schmidt-Phi 402
Hernandez-StL-NY .398
Murphy-Atl 396
Raines-Mon 395
Madlock-Pit 389

Slugging Average
Murphy-Atl 540
Dawson-Mon 539
Guerrero-LA 531
Schmidt-Phi 524
Evans-SF 516

Production
Murphy-Atl 936
Schmidt-Phi 926
Guerrero-LA 908
Evans-SF 896
Dawson-Mon 886

Adjusted Production
Schmidt-Phi 156
Evans-SF 151
Guerrero-LA 150
Murphy-Atl 146
Cruz-Hou 143

Batter Runs
Murphy-Atl 46.2
Schmidt-Phi 43.2
Guerrero-LA 37.8
Evans-SF 33.0
Dawson-Mon 32.4

Adjusted Batter Runs
Schmidt-Phi 44.1
Murphy-Atl 40.7
Guerrero-LA 38.2
Evans-SF 35.1
Dawson-Mon 32.8

Clutch Hitting Index
Kennedy-SD 142
Garner-Hou 134
McGee-StL 131
Concepcion-Cin .. 130
Oliver-Mon 128

Runs Created
Murphy-Atl 131
Raines-Mon 120
Guerrero-LA 118
Schmidt-Phi 117
Dawson-Mon 113

Total Average
Murphy-Atl 1.014
Schmidt-Phi 986
Raines-Mon 959
Guerrero-LA 935
Evans-SF 908

Stolen Bases
Raines-Mon 90
Wiggins-SD 66
S.Sax-LA 56
Wilson-NY 54
L.Smith-StL 43

Stolen Base Average
Morgan-Phi 90.0
Murphy-Atl 88.2
Raines-Mon 86.5
Bailor-NY 85.7
Wiggins-SD 83.5

Stolen Base Runs
Raines-Mon 18.6
Wiggins-SD 12.0
McGee-StL 6.9
Wilson-NY 6.6
Murphy-Atl 6.6

Fielding Runs
Sandberg-Chi 41.1
Schmidt-Phi 23.3
Hubbard-Atl 21.6
Thon-Hou 20.8
Buckner-Chi 20.6

Total Player Rating
Schmidt-Phi 6.4
Thon-Hou 5.8
Raines-Mon 5.4
Guerrero-LA 4.6
Murphy-Atl 4.1

Wins
Denny-Phi 19
Soto-Cin 17
Rogers-Mon 17
Gullickson-Mon 17
Lea-Mon 16

Win Percentage
Denny-Phi 760
Perez-Atl 652
McWilliams-Pit.....652
Candelaria-Pit 652
McMurtry-Atl 625

Games
Campbell-Chi 82
Tekulve-Pit 76
Hernandez-Chi-Phi . 74
Scherrer-Cin 73
Minton-SF 73

Complete Games
Soto-Cin 18
Rogers-Mon 13
Gullickson-Mon 10

Shutouts
Rogers-Mon 5
Valenzuela-LA 4
McWilliams-Pit 4
Lea-Mon 4

Saves
Smith-Chi 29
Holland-Phi 25
Minton-SF 22
Sutter-StL 21
Reardon-Mon 21

Innings Pitched
Carlton-Phi 283.2
Soto-Cin 273.2
Rogers-Mon 273.0
Niekro-Hou 263.2
Valenzuela-LA ... 257.0

Fewest Hits/Game
Ryan-Hou 6.14
Soto-Cin 6.81
Welch-LA 7.24
Hammaker-SF 7.68
Pena-LA 7.73

Fewest BB/Game
Hammaker-SF 1.67
Ruthven-Phi-Chi .. 1.87
Denny-Phi 1.97
Reuss-LA 2.01
Candelaria-Pit 2.05

Strikeouts
Carlton-Phi 275
Soto-Cin 242
McWilliams-Pit 199
Valenzuela-LA 189
Ryan-Hou 183

Strikeouts/Game
Carlton-Phi 8.73
Ryan-Hou 8.39
Soto-Cin 7.96
McWilliams-Pit 7.53
Berenyi-Cin 7.29

Ratio
Hammaker-SF 9.50
Soto-Cin 10.10
Pena-LA 10.37
Welch-LA 10.54
Denny-Phi 10.61

Earned Run Average
Hammaker-SF 2.25
Denny-Phi 2.37
Welch-LA 2.65
Soto-Cin 2.70
Pena-LA 2.75

Adjusted ERA
Hammaker-SF 157
Denny-Phi 150
Soto-Cin 141
Welch-LA 136
Pena-LA 131

Opponents' Batting Avg.
Ryan-Hou 195
Soto-Cin 208
Welch-LA 222
Hammaker-SF 228
Pena-LA 229

Opponents' On Base Pct.
Hammaker-SF 267
Soto-Cin 280
Pena-LA 285
Welch-LA 294
Denny-Phi 294

Starter Runs
Denny-Phi 33.8
Soto-Cin 28.3
Hammaker-SF 26.4
Welch-LA 22.2
Smith-Mon 19.6

Adjusted Starter Runs
Soto-Cin 33.7
Denny-Phi 32.1
Hammaker-SF 24.6
Welch-LA 21.4
McMurtry-Atl 19.8

Clutch Pitching Index
Rhoden-Pit 119
Niekro-Atl 117
Reuss-LA 116
Denny-Phi 115
Knepper-Hou 111

Relief Runs
Orosco-NY 26.3
Smith-Chi 22.6
Tekulve-Pit 21.9
Niedenfuer-LA 18.1
Howe-LA 16.7

Adjusted Relief Runs
Orosco-NY 26.3
Smith-Chi 24.5
Tekulve-Pit 22.7
Niedenfuer-LA 17.8
Howe-LA 16.4

Relief Ranking
Orosco-NY 52.2
Smith-Chi 45.4
Tekulve-Pit 34.1
Howe-LA 33.3
Holland-Phi 23.8

Total Pitcher Index
Denny-Phi 3.8
Soto-Cin 3.3
Orosco-NY 3.0
Reuss-LA 2.8
Hammaker-SF 2.7

Total Baseball Ranking
Schmidt-Phi 6.4
Thon-Hou 5.8
Raines-Mon 5.4
Guerrero-LA 4.6
Murphy-Atl 4.1

TEAM	G	W	L	PCT	GB	R	OR	AB	H	2B	3B	HR	BB	SO	AVG	OBP	SLG	PRO	PRO+	BR	/A	PF	CHI	RC	SB	CS	SBA	SBR
EAST																												
BAL	162	98	64	.605		799	652	5546	1492	283	27	**168**	601	800	.269	**.343**	.421	.764	111	70	84	98	99	794	61	33	65	-2
DET	162	92	70	.568	6	789	679	5592	1530	283	53	156	508	831	.274	.338	.427	.765	112	67	86	97	99	799	93	53	64	-4
NY	162	91	71	.562	7	770	703	5631	1535	269	40	153	533	686	.273	.339	.416	.755	110	52	79	96	98	783	84	42	67	0
TOR	162	89	73	.549	9	795	726	5581	1546	268	**58**	167	510	810	**.277**	.341	**.436**	**.777**	106	**89**	45	106	97	**818**	131	72	65	-4
MIL	162	87	75	.537	11	764	708	5620	**1556**	281	57	132	475	**665**	**.277**	.336	.418	.754	**115**	44	**100**	92	98	774	101	49	67	1
BOS	162	78	84	.481	20	724	775	5590	1512	**287**	32	142	536	758	.270	.337	.409	.746	97	35	-18	107	94	749	30	26	54	-7
CLE	162	70	92	.432	28	704	785	5476	1451	249	31	86	**605**	691	.265	.341	.369	.710	92	-23	-51	104	100	687	109	71	61	-10
WEST																												
CHI	162	99	63	.611		**800**	650	5484	1439	270	42	157	527	888	.262	.332	.413	.745	100	26	-1	104	**107**	762	165	50	77	20
KC	163	79	83	.488	20	696	767	5598	1515	273	54	109	397	722	.271	.322	.397	.719	97	-31	-32	100	102	711	182	47	**79**	**26**
TEX	163	77	85	.475	22	639	**609**	5610	1429	242	33	106	442	767	.255	.312	.366	.678	88	-108	-94	98	104	633	119	60	66	0
OAK	162	74	88	.457	25	708	782	5516	1447	237	28	121	524	872	.262	.330	.381	.711	101	-34	9	94	102	694	**235**	98	71	12
CAL	162	70	92	.432	29	722	779	5640	1467	241	22	154	509	835	.260	.325	.393	.718	98	-29	-22	99	102	702	41	39	51	-11
MIN	162	70	92	.432	29	709	822	5601	1463	280	41	141	467	802	.261	.321	.401	.722	94	-23	-49	104	101	701	44	29	60	-4
SEA	162	60	102	.370	39	558	740	5336	1280	247	31	111	460	840	.240	.303	.360	.663	79	-135	-161	104	100	574	144	80	64	-5
TOT	1135					10177		77821	20662	3710	549	1903	7094	10967	.266	.330	.401	.731							1539	749	67	12

TEAM	CG	SH	SV	IP	H	H/G	HR	BB	SO	RAT	ERA	ERA+	OAV	OOB	PR	/A	PF	CPI	FA	E	DP	FW	PW	BW	SBW	DIF
EAST																										
BAL	36	**15**	38	1452^{1}	1451	9.0	130	452	774	11.9	3.63	109	.261	.318	70	53	97	104	.981	121	159	.5	5.3	8.4	-.3	3.1
DET	42	9	28	1451	**1318**	**8.2**	170	522	875	11.6	3.80	103	**.242**	.312	42	17	96	96	.980	125	142	.3	1.7	8.6	-.5	.9
NY	**47**	12	32	1456^{2}	1449	9.0	116	455	892	11.9	3.86	101	.260	.318	33	6	96	95	.978	139	157	-.5	.6	7.9	-.0	2.1
TOR	43	8	32	1445^{1}	1434	8.9	145	517	835	12.4	4.12	104	.259	.327	-10	29	106	97	.981	115	148	.9	2.9	4.5	-.5	.2
MIL	35	10	43	1454	1513	9.4	133	491	689	12.6	4.02	93	.270	.332	6	-46	92	103	**.982**	**113**	162	**1.0**	-4.6	**10.0**	.0	-.4
BOS	29	7	42	1446^{1}	1572	9.8	158	493	767	13.0	4.34	100	.279	.340	-44	2	107	104	.979	130	168	.0	.2	-1.8	-.8	-.7
CLE	34	8	25	1441^{2}	1531	9.6	120	529	794	13.1	4.43	96	.275	.342	-60	-32	104	97	.980	122	174	.5	-3.2	-5.1	-1.1	-2.1
WEST																										
CHI	35	12	48	1445^{1}	1355	8.4	128	**447**	877	**11.4**	3.67	114	.248	**.309**	63	83	103	94	.981	120	158	.6	8.3	-.0	1.9	7.3
KC	19	8	**49**	1437^{2}	1535	9.6	133	471	593	12.7	4.25	96	.274	.333	-30	-28	100	99	.974	165	178	-1.9	-2.8	-3.2	**2.5**	3.4
TEX	43	11	32	1466^{2}	1392	8.5	**97**	471	826	11.7	**3.31**	**121**	.252	.315	**122**	**113**	99	104	**.982**	**113**	151	**1.0**	**11.3**	-9.4	-.0	-6.8
OAK	22	12	33	1454^{1}	1462	9.0	135	626	719	13.1	4.34	89	.263	.340	-46	-79	95	97	.974	157	157	-1.5	-7.9	.9	1.1	.3
CAL	39	7	23	1474	1636	10.0	130	496	668	13.2	4.31	93	.284	.344	-41	-49	99	104	.977	154	**190**	-1.3	-4.9	-2.2	-1.2	-1.4
MIN	20	5	39	1437^{1}	1559	9.8	163	580	748	13.6	4.66	91	.280	.351	-96	-67	105	102	.980	121	170	.5	-6.7	-4.9	-.5	.5
SEA	25	9	39	1418^{1}	1455	9.2	145	544	**910**	12.9	4.12	103	.268	.339	-9	22	105	**105**	.978	136	159	-.3	2.2	-16.1	-.6	-6.2
TOT	469	133	503	20281		9.2				12.5	4.06		.266	.330					.979	1831	2273					

Runs
Ripken-Bal 121
Murray-Bal 115
Cooper-Mil 106
Henderson-Oak ... 105
Moseby-Tor 104

Hits
Ripken-Bal 211
Boggs-Bos 210
Whitaker-Det 206
Cooper-Mil 203
Rice-Bos 191

Doubles
Ripken-Bal 47
Boggs-Bos 44
Yount-Mil 42
Parrish-Det 42

Triples
Yount-Mil 10
Herndon-Det 9
Griffin-Tor 9
Gibson-Det 9

Home Runs
Rice-Bos 39
Armas-Bos 36
Kittle-Chi 35
Murray-Bal 33

Total Bases
Rice-Bos 344
Ripken-Bal 343
Cooper-Mil 336
Murray-Bal 313
Winfield-NY 307

Runs Batted In
Rice-Bos 126
Cooper-Mil 126
Winfield-NY 116
Parrish-Det 114
Murray-Bal 111

Runs Produced
Cooper-Mil 202
Ripken-Bal 196
Murray-Bal 193
Winfield-NY 183
Rice-Bos 177

Bases On Balls
Henderson-Oak ... 103
Singleton-Bal 99
Boggs-Bos 92
Thornton-Cle 87
Murray-Bal 86

Batting Average
Boggs-Bos .... .361
Carew-Cal .... .339
Whitaker-Det ..... .320
Trammell-Det ..... .319
Ripken-Bal .... .318

On Base Percentage
Boggs-Bos .... .449
Henderson-Oak ... .415
Carew-Cal .... .411
Murray-Bal .... .398
Singleton-Bal ..... .395

Slugging Average
Brett-KC .... .563
Rice-Bos .... .550
Murray-Bal .... .538
Fisk-Chi .... .518
Ripken-Bal .... .517

Production
Brett-KC .... .949
Murray-Bal .... .936
Boggs-Bos .... .935
Rice-Bos .... .914
Upshaw-Tor ...... .891

Adjusted Production
Murray-Bal 158
Brett-KC 157
Yount-Mil 155
Boggs-Bos 147
Ripken-Bal 145

Batter Runs
Boggs-Bos 50.6
Murray-Bal 44.9
Rice-Bos 38.7
Ripken-Bal 37.1
Brett-KC 36.3

Adjusted Batter Runs
Murray-Bal 46.5
Boggs-Bos 44.8
Yount-Mil 40.8
Ripken-Bal 38.7
Brett-KC 36.1

Clutch Hitting Index
Simmons-Mil 145
Murphy-Oak 135
Franco-Cle 132
Hargrove-Cle 130
Parrish-Det 127

Runs Created
Murray-Bal 133
Boggs-Bos 130
Ripken-Bal 120
Yount-Mil 115
Whitaker-Det 114

Total Average
Henderson-Oak .. 1.048
Murray-Bal 1.000
Boggs-Bos .... .964
Brett-KC .... .964
Yount-Mil .... .897

Stolen Bases
Henderson-Oak ... 108
R.Law-Chi 77
Wilson-KC 59
J.Cruz-Sea-Chi 57
Sample-Tex 44

Stolen Base Average
Wilson-KC 88.1
R.Law-Chi 86.5
Washington-KC ... 85.1
Henderson-Oak ... 85.0

Stolen Base Runs
Henderson-Oak ... 21.0
R.Law-Chi 15.9
Wilson-KC 12.9
J.Cruz-Sea-Chi 9.9
Sample-Tex 8.4

Fielding Runs
Ward-Min 25.9
T.Cruz-Sea-Bal ... 25.4
Dempsey-Bal 20.6
Fletcher-Chi 18.2
Brunansky-Min ... 17.8

Total Player Rating
Ripken-Bal 6.6
Henderson-Oak 5.5
Yount-Mil 4.9
Boggs-Bos 4.9
Grich-Cal 4.5

Wins
Hoyt-Chi 24
Dotson-Chi 22
Guidry-NY 21
Morris-Det 20
Petry-Det 19

Win Percentage
Dotson-Chi ...... .759
McGregor-Bal .... .720
Hoyt-Chi .... .706
Guidry-NY .... .700
Boddicker-Bal .... .667

Games
Quisenberry-KC ... 69
VandeBerg-Sea 68
Davis-Min 66
F.Martinez-Bal 65
Stanley-Bos 64

Complete Games
Guidry-NY 21
Morris-Det 20
Stieb-Tor 14
Rawley-NY 13
McGregor-Bal 12

Shutouts
Boddicker-Bal 5
Stieb-Tor 4
Burns-Chi 4

Saves
Quisenberry-KC ... 45
Stanley-Bos 33
Davis-Min 30
Caudill-Sea 26
Ladd-Mil 25

Innings Pitched
Morris-Det 293.2
Stieb-Tor 278.0
Petry-Det 266.1
Hoyt-Chi 260.2
McGregor-Bal ... 260.0

Fewest Hits/Game
Boddicker-Bal 7.09
Stieb-Tor 7.22
Conroy-Oak 7.82
Hough-Tex 7.82
Dotson-Chi 7.84

Fewest BB/Game
Hoyt-Chi 1.07
McGregor-Bal 1.56
John-Cal 1.88
Honeycutt-Tex 1.91
Eckersley-Bos 1.99

Strikeouts
Morris-Det 232
Bannister-Chi 193
Stieb-Tor 187
Righetti-NY 169
Sutcliffe-Cle 160

Strikeouts/Game
Bannister-Chi 7.99
Morris-Det 7.11
Righetti-NY 7.01
Conroy-Oak 6.21
Gott-Tor 6.16

Ratio
Hoyt-Chi 9.25
Boddicker-Bal 9.70
Morris-Det 10.51
Guidry-NY 10.57
Stieb-Tor 10.68

Earned Run Average
Honeycutt-Tex 2.42
Boddicker-Bal 2.77
Stieb-Tor 3.04
Hough-Tex 3.18
McGregor-Bal 3.18

Adjusted ERA
Honeycutt-Tex 165
Boddicker-Bal 143
Stieb-Tor 141
Young-Sea 130
Dotson-Chi 130

Opponents' Batting Avg.
Boddicker-Bal .... .216
Stieb-Tor .... .219
Conroy-Oak ...... .232
Bannister-Chi .... .233
Morris-Det .... .233

Opponents' On Base Pct.
Hoyt-Chi .... .262
Boddicker-Bal .... .274
Morris-Det .... .289
Guidry-NY .... .291
Stieb-Tor .... .293

Starter Runs
Honeycutt-Tex 31.8
Stieb-Tor 31.4
Boddicker-Bal 25.8
McGregor-Bal 25.3
Hough-Tex 24.7

Adjusted Starter Runs
Stieb-Tor 38.8
Honeycutt-Tex 30.7
Dotson-Chi 25.6
Boddicker-Bal 23.6
Hough-Tex 23.1

Clutch Pitching Index
Honeycutt-Tex 139
Zahn-Cal 118
Hurst-Bos 113
Dotson-Chi 113
McGregor-Bal 113

Relief Runs
Quisenberry-KC .. 32.7
F.Martinez-Bal ... 19.6
Stanley-Bos 19.6
Gossage-NY 17.4
Lopez-Det 16.0

Adjusted Relief Runs
Quisenberry-KC .. 32.9
Stanley-Bos 24.2
F.Martinez-Bal ... 18.4
Barojas-Chi 16.6
Gossage-NY 15.8

Relief Ranking
Quisenberry-KC .. 41.0
Stanley-Bos 39.4
Gossage-NY 38.1
F.Martinez-Bal ... 27.6
Lopez-Det 23.6

Total Pitcher Index
Stieb-Tor 4.2
Honeycutt-Tex 3.8
Quisenberry-KC ... 3.5
Dotson-Chi 3.1
Hough-Tex 2.9

Total Baseball Ranking
Ripken-Bal 6.6
Henderson-Oak 5.5
Yount-Mil 4.9
Boggs-Bos 4.9
Grich-Cal 4.5

TEAM	G	W	L	PCT	GB	R	OR	AB	H	2B	3B	HR	BB	SO	AVG	OBP	SLG	PRO	PRO+	BR	/A	PF	CHI	RC	SB	CS	SBA	SBR
EAST																												
CHI	161	96	65	.596		**762**	658	5437	1415	240	47	136	**567**	967	.260	.333	.397	.730	102	78	18	109	104	729	154	66	70	7
NY	162	90	72	.556	6.5	652	676	5438	1400	235	25	107	500	1001	.257	.322	.369	.691	102	1	11	99	100	645	149	54	73	12
STL	162	84	78	.519	12.5	652	645	5433	1369	225	44	75	516	924	.252	.319	.351	.670	97	-35	-18	97	**106**	623	**220**	71	76	**23**
PHI	162	81	81	.500	15.5	720	690	5614	1494	**248**	51	**147**	555	1084	**.266**	**.335**	**.407**	**.742**	**112**	**102**	**91**	102	93	**766**	186	60	76	20
MON	161	78	83	.484	18	593	585	5439	1367	242	36	96	470	**782**	.251	.314	.362	.676	101	-32	-3	96	96	630	131	38	**78**	17
PIT	162	75	87	.463	21.5	615	**567**	5537	1412	237	33	98	438	841	.255	.312	.363	.675	95	-37	-37	100	99	611	96	62	61	-8
WEST																												
SD	162	92	70	.568		686	634	5504	1425	207	42	109	472	810	.259	.320	.371	.691	100	-1	0	100	105	645	152	68	69	5
HOU	162	80	82	.494	12	693	630	5548	1465	222	**67**	79	494	837	.264	.326	.371	.697	110	14	62	93	102	679	105	61	63	-5
ATL	162	80	82	.494	12	632	655	5422	1338	234	27	111	555	896	.247	.319	.361	.680	90	-18	-65	107	99	623	140	85	62	-9
LA	162	79	83	.488	13	580	600	5399	1316	213	23	102	488	829	.244	.308	.348	.656	91	-68	-61	99	100	573	109	69	61	-9
CIN	162	70	92	.432	22	627	747	5498	1342	238	30	106	566	978	.244	.316	.356	.672	91	-34	-64	105	100	635	160	63	72	10
SF	162	66	96	.407	26	682	807	5650	**1499**	229	26	112	528	980	.265	.330	.375	.705	108	31	53	97	97	686	126	76	62	-8
TOT	971					7894		65919	16842	2770	451	1278	6149	10929	.255	.321	.369	.691							1728	773	69	55

TEAM	CG	SH	SV	IP	H	H/G	HR	BB	SO	RAT	ERA	ERA+	OAV	OOB	PR	/A	PF	CPI	FA	E	DP	FW	PW	BW	SBW	DIF
EAST																										
CHI	19	8	50	1434	1458	9.2	99	**442**	879	12.1	3.75	104	.267	.324	-26	25	109	99	.981	121	137	1.1	2.6	1.9	.3	9.6
NY	12	15	50	1442[2]	1371	8.6	104	573	1028	12.3	3.60	98	.252	.326	-2	-10	99	101	.979	129	154	.7	-1.1	1.2	.8	7.4
STL	19	12	**51**	1449	1427	8.9	94	494	808	12.1	3.58	97	.262	.326	1	-18	97	103	**.982**	**118**	**184**	**1.3**	-1.9	-1.9	**1.9**	3.5
PHI	11	6	35	1458[1]	1416	8.7	101	448	904	11.6	3.62	100	.253	**.310**	-5	2	101	92	.975	161	112	-1.2	.2	**9.6**	1.6	-10.2
MON	19	10	48	1431	1333	8.4	114	474	861	11.5	3.31	103	.249	.312	45	18	95	103	.978	132	147	.4	1.9	-.3	1.3	-5.8
PIT	27	13	34	1470	1344	**8.2**	102	502	995	**11.4**	**3.11**	**116**	.246	**.310**	**78**	**80**	100	**105**	.980	128	142	.7	**8.4**	-3.9	-1.3	-9.9
WEST																										
SD	13	**17**	44	1460[1]	**1327**	**8.2**	122	563	812	11.8	3.48	102	**.244**	.317	17	14	99	99	.978	138	144	.1	1.5	.0	.0	9.3
HOU	24	13	29	1449[1]	1350	8.4	91	502	950	11.6	3.32	100	.248	.314	44	0	93	99	.979	133	160	.4	.0	6.5	-1.0	-6.9
ATL	17	7	49	1447	1401	8.7	122	525	859	12.1	3.57	108	.257	.324	3	46	107	**105**	.978	139	153	.0	4.8	-6.8	-1.4	2.3
LA	**39**	16	27	1460[2]	1381	8.5	**76**	499	**1033**	11.7	3.17	111	.250	.314	68	59	98	102	.975	163	146	-1.3	6.2	-6.4	-1.4	1.0
CIN	25	6	25	1461[1]	1445	8.9	128	578	946	12.6	4.16	91	.259	.330	-92	-62	105	94	.977	139	116	.0	-6.5	-6.7	.6	1.6
SF	9	7	38	1461	1589	9.8	125	549	854	13.4	4.39	80	.278	.345	-131	-143	98	99	.973	173	134	-1.9	-15.0	5.6	-1.3	-2.3
TOT	234	130	480	17424[2]		8.7				12.0	3.59		.255	.321					.978	1674	1729					

Runs
Sandberg-Chi 114
Wiggins-SD 106
Raines-Mon 106
Samuel-Phi 105
Matthews-Chi 101

Hits
Gwynn-SD 213
Sandberg-Chi 200
Raines-Mon 192
Samuel-Phi 191
Cruz-Hou 187

Doubles
Ray-Pit 38
Raines-Mon 38
Sandberg-Chi 36
Samuel-Phi 36

Triples
Sandberg-Chi 19
Samuel-Phi 19
Cruz-Hou 13

Home Runs
Schmidt-Phi 36
Murphy-Atl 36
Carter-Mon 27
Strawberry-NY 26
Cey-Chi 25

Total Bases
Murphy-Atl 332
Sandberg-Chi 331
Samuel-Phi 310
Carter-Mon 290
Schmidt-Phi 283

Runs Batted In
Schmidt-Phi 106
Carter-Mon 106
Murphy-Atl 100
Strawberry-NY 97
Cey-Chi 97

Runs Produced
Sandberg-Chi 179
Cruz-Hou 179
Matthews-Chi 169
Schmidt-Phi 163
Hernandez-NY 162

Bases On Balls
Matthews-Chi 103
Hernandez-NY 97
Schmidt-Phi 92
Thompson-Pit 87
Raines-Mon 87

Batting Average
Gwynn-SD .... .351
Lacy-Pit .... .321
C.Davis-SF .... .315
Sandberg-Chi ..... .314
Ray-Pit .... .312

On Base Percentage
Matthews-Chi ..... .417
Hernandez-NY ..... .415
Gwynn-SD .... .411
Raines-Mon .... .395
Schmidt-Phi .... .388

Slugging Average
Murphy-Atl .... .547
Schmidt-Phi .... .536
Sandberg-Chi ..... .520
C.Davis-SF .... .507
Durham-Chi .... .505

Production
Schmidt-Phi ...... .924
Murphy-Atl .... .920
Sandberg-Chi ..... .889
Durham-Chi .... .877
C.Davis-SF .... .876

Adjusted Production
Schmidt-Phi 155
C.Davis-SF 149
Cruz-Hou 148
Murphy-Atl 145
Hernandez-NY 145

Batter Runs
Murphy-Atl 43.8
Schmidt-Phi 41.2
Sandberg-Chi 37.9
Hernandez-NY 35.5
Gwynn-SD 33.9

Adjusted Batter Runs
Schmidt-Phi 40.1
Murphy-Atl 38.4
Hernandez-NY 36.5
Cruz-Hou 36.0
Gwynn-SD 34.0

Clutch Hitting Index
Mumphrey-Hou ... 143
Davis-Chi 136
Garvey-SD 135
Matthews-Chi 135
Hernandez-NY 134

Runs Created
Sandberg-Chi 126
Raines-Mon 124
Murphy-Atl 123
Cruz-Hou 111
Carter-Mon 108

Total Average
Raines-Mon .... .953
Murphy-Atl .... .942
Schmidt-Phi .... .933
Sandberg-Chi ..... .913
Matthews-Chi ..... .888

Stolen Bases
Raines-Mon 75
Samuel-Phi 72
Wiggins-SD 70
L.Smith-StL 50

Stolen Base Average
Dilone-Mon 93.1
Raines-Mon 88.2
Cedeno-Cin 86.4
VanSlyke-StL 84.8
Stone-Phi 84.4

Stolen Base Runs
Raines-Mon 16.5
Samuel-Phi 12.6
Wilson-NY 8.4
Wiggins-SD 8.4
Redus-Cin 7.8

Fielding Runs
O.Smith-StL 26.2
Sandberg-Chi 23.3
Garner-Hou 23.1
Martinez-SD 20.6
Hubbard-Atl 19.6

Total Player Rating
Sandberg-Chi 6.7
Raines-Mon 5.7
Schmidt-Phi 4.9
Cruz-Hou 4.7
Hernandez-NY 4.5

Wins
Andujar-StL 20
Soto-Cin 18
Gooden-NY 17
Sutcliffe-Chi 16
Niekro-Hou 16

Win Percentage
Sutcliffe-Chi .... .941
Soto-Cin .... .720
Gooden-NY .... .654
Show-SD .... .625

Games
Power-Cin 78
Lavelle-SF 77
Minton-SF 74
Tekulve-Pit 72
Sutter-StL 71

Complete Games
Soto-Cin 13
Valenzuela-LA 12
Andujar-StL 12
Knepper-Hou 11
Mahler-Atl 9

Shutouts
Pena-LA 4
Hershiser-LA 4
Andujar-StL 4

Saves
Sutter-StL 45
Smith-Chi 33
Orosco-NY 31
Holland-Phi 29
Gossage-SD 25

Innings Pitched
Andujar-StL 261.1
Valenzuela-LA ... 261.0
Niekro-Hou 248.1
Rhoden-Pit 238.1
Soto-Cin 237.1

Fewest Hits/Game
Gooden-NY 6.65
Soto-Cin 6.86
DeLeon-Pit 6.88
Ryan-Hou 7.01
Andujar-StL 7.51

Fewest BB/Game
Gullickson-Mon ... 1.47
Candelaria-Pit ... 1.65
Whitson-SD 2.00
Pena-LA 2.08
Knepper-Hou 2.12

Strikeouts
Gooden-NY 276
Valenzuela-LA 240
Ryan-Hou 197
Soto-Cin 185
Carlton-Phi 163

Strikeouts/Game
Gooden-NY 11.39
Ryan-Hou 9.65
Valenzuela-LA 8.28
Berenyi-Cin-NY ... 7.27
DeLeon-Pit 7.16

Ratio
Gooden-NY 9.74
Hershiser-LA 10.15
Andujar-StL 10.16
Soto-Cin 10.35
Candelaria-Pit ... 10.39

Earned Run Average
Pena-LA 2.48
Gooden-NY 2.60
Hershiser-LA 2.66
Rhoden-Pit 2.72
Candelaria-Pit 2.72

Adjusted ERA
Pena-LA 142
Gooden-NY 136
Hershiser-LA 133
Rhoden-Pit 132
Candelaria-Pit 132

Opponents' Batting Avg.
Gooden-NY .... .202
Soto-Cin .... .209
Ryan-Hou .... .211
DeLeon-Pit .... .214
Hershiser-LA ...... .225

Opponents' On Base Pct.
Gooden-NY .... .270
Hershiser-LA ...... .279
Soto-Cin .... .286
Andujar-StL .... .286
Ryan-Hou .... .288

Starter Runs
Pena-LA 24.5
Gooden-NY 23.9
Rhoden-Pit 23.0
Hershiser-LA 19.6
Denny-Phi 19.5

Adjusted Starter Runs
Rhoden-Pit 23.3
Pena-LA 23.2
Gooden-NY 22.6
Sutcliffe-Chi 20.3
Denny-Phi 20.3

Clutch Pitching Index
McWilliams-Pit 130
Terrell-NY 124
Candelaria-Pit 122
Honeycutt-LA 117
Trout-Chi 117

Relief Runs
Sutter-StL 27.9
Dawley-Hou 18.1
Lefferts-SD 17.1
Sisk-NY 13.0
Andersen-Phi 12.1

Adjusted Relief Runs
Sutter-StL 26.3
Lefferts-SD 16.9
Dawley-Hou 15.1
Bedrosian-Atl 13.8
Andersen-Phi 12.6

Relief Ranking
Sutter-StL 44.8
Bedrosian-Atl 26.4
Dawley-Hou 22.6
Orosco-NY 22.5
Power-Cin 18.0

Total Pitcher Index
Rhoden-Pit 3.9
Mahler-Atl 2.8
Sutter-StL 2.8
Sutcliffe-Chi 2.8
Denny-Phi 2.8

Total Baseball Ranking
Sandberg-Chi 6.7
Raines-Mon 5.7
Schmidt-Phi 4.9
Cruz-Hou 4.7
Hernandez-NY 4.5

TEAM	G	W	L	PCT	GB	R	OR	AB	H	2B	3B	HR	BB	SO	AVG	OBP	SLG	PRO	PRO+	BR	/A	PF	CHI	RC	SB	CS	SBA	SBR
EAST																												
DET	162	104	58	.642		829	643	5644	1529	254	46	187	602	941	.271	.345	.432	.777	114	103	108	99	99	843	106	68	61	-9
TOR	163	89	73	.549	15	750	696	5687	1555	275	68	143	460	816	.273	.333	.421	.754	103	52	26	104	96	808	193	67	74	18
NY	162	87	75	.537	17	758	679	5661	1560	275	32	130	534	673	.276	.342	.404	.746	110	47	76	96	97	773	62	38	62	-4
BOS	162	86	76	.531	18	810	764	5648	1598	259	45	181	500	842	.283	.343	.441	.784	110	113	80	105	97	832	38	25	60	-4
BAL	162	85	77	.525	19	681	667	5456	1374	234	23	160	620	884	.252	.331	.391	.722	101	-4	12	98	96	705	51	36	59	-6
CLE	163	75	87	.463	29	761	766	5643	1498	222	39	123	600	815	.265	.339	.384	.723	98	4	-9	102	103	732	126	77	62	-8
MIL	161	67	94	.416	36.5	641	734	5511	1446	232	36	96	432	673	.262	.319	.370	.689	94	-75	-47	96	103	621	52	57	48	-19
WEST																												
KC	162	84	78	.519		673	686	5543	1487	269	52	117	400	832	.268	.320	.399	.719	97	-23	-29	101	99	685	106	64	62	-7
CAL	162	81	81	.500	3	696	697	5470	1363	211	30	150	556	928	.249	.322	.381	.703	95	-46	-41	99	105	663	80	51	61	-7
MIN	162	81	81	.500	3	673	675	5562	1473	259	33	114	437	735	.265	.321	.385	.706	90	-45	-77	105	102	669	39	30	57	-6
OAK	162	77	85	.475	7	738	796	5457	1415	257	29	158	568	871	.259	.332	.404	.736	109	18	66	93	101	736	145	64	69	5
SEA	162	74	88	.457	10	682	774	5546	1429	244	34	129	519	871	.258	.326	.384	.710	97	-32	-23	99	100	700	116	62	65	-2
CHI	162	74	88	.457	10	679	736	5513	1360	225	38	172	523	883	.247	.316	.395	.711	91	-37	-69	105	101	690	109	49	69	3
TEX	161	69	92	.429	14.5	656	714	5569	1452	227	29	120	420	807	.261	.315	.377	.692	88	-75	-98	103	104	643	81	50	62	-6
TOT	1134					10027		77910	20539	3443	534	1980	7171	11571	.264	.329	.398	.727							1304	738	64	-52

TEAM	CG	SH	SV	IP	H	H/G	HR	BB	SO	RAT	ERA	ERA+	OAV	OOB	PR	/A	PF	CPI	FA	E	DP	FW	PW	BW	SBW	DIF
EAST																										
DET	19	8	51	1464	1358	8.3	130	489	914	11.5	3.49	112	.246	.311	81	70	98	98	.979	127	162	.3	7.0	10.9	-.5	5.3
TOR	34	10	33	1464	1433	8.8	140	528	875	12.3	3.86	106	.257	.325	21	38	103	99	.980	123	166	.6	3.8	2.6	2.2	-1.2
NY	15	12	43	1465¹	1485	9.1	120	518	992	12.4	3.78	100	.264	.328	35	2	95	102	.977	142	177	-.5	.2	7.6	-.0	-1.3
BOS	40	12	32	1442	1524	9.5	141	517	927	12.9	4.18	100	.270	.334	-29	-2	104	99	.977	143	166	-.6	-.2	8.0	-.0	-2.2
BAL	48	13	32	1439¹	1393	8.7	137	512	714	12.1	3.71	104	.256	.323	44	25	97	102	.981	123	166	.5	2.5	1.2	-.2	-.0
CLE	21	7	35	1467²	1523	9.3	141	545	803	13.1	4.26	96	.269	.336	-43	-27	102	98	.977	146	163	-.7	-2.7	-.9	-.4	-1.2
MIL	13	7	41	1433	1532	9.6	137	480	785	12.8	4.06	95	.274	.334	-10	-33	96	103	.978	136	156	-.3	-3.3	-4.7	-1.5	-3.7
WEST																										
KC	18	9	50	1444	1426	8.9	136	433	724	11.8	3.92	103	.258	.315	11	17	101	93	.979	131	157	.0	1.7	-2.9	-.3	4.5
CAL	36	12	26	1458	1526	9.4	143	474	754	12.5	3.96	100	.271	.331	6	2	99	104	.980	128	170	.2	.2	-4.1	-.3	4.0
MIN	32	9	38	1437²	1489	8.9	159	463	713	12.1	3.85	109	.260	.321	23	56	105	101	.980	120	134	.7	5.6	-7.7	-.2	1.7
OAK	15	6	44	1430	1554	9.8	155	592	695	13.7	4.48	84	.278	.351	-78	-117	94	103	.975	146	159	-.8	-11.8	6.6	.9	1.0
SEA	26	4	35	1442	1497	9.3	138	619	972	13.5	4.31	93	.270	.348	-50	-51	100	94	.979	128	143	.2	-5.1	-2.3	-.2	.0
CHI	43	9	32	1454¹	1416	8.8	155	483	840	12.0	4.13	101	.256	.320	-23	4	104	93	.981	122	160	.6	.4	-6.9	.7	-1.7
TEX	38	6	21	1438²	1443	9.0	148	518	863	12.5	3.91	106	.260	.327	13	38	104	101	.977	138	138	-.4	3.8	-9.9	-.2	-4.9
TOT	398	124	513	20280		9.1				12.5	3.99		.264	.329					.979	1853	2179					

Runs		Hits		Doubles		Triples		Home Runs		Total Bases	
Evans-Bos	121	Mattingly-NY	207	Mattingly-NY	44	Moseby-Tor	15	Armas-Bos	43	Armas-Bos	339
Henderson-Oak	113	Boggs-Bos	203	Parrish-Tex	42	Collins-Tor	15	Kingman-Oak	35	Evans-Bos	335
Boggs-Bos	109	Ripken-Bal	195	Bell-Tor	39	Gibson-Det	10	Thornton-Cle	33	Ripken-Bal	327
Butler-Cle	108	Winfield-NY	193	Ripken-Bal	37	Baines-Chi	10	Parrish-Det	33	Mattingly-NY	324
Armas-Bos	107			Evans-Bos	37			Murphy-Oak	33	Easler-Bos	310

Runs Batted In		Runs Produced		Bases On Balls		Batting Average		On Base Percentage		Slugging Average	
Armas-Bos	123	Evans-Bos	193	Murray-Bal	107	Mattingly-NY	.343	Murray-Bal	.415	Baines-Chi	.541
Rice-Bos	122	Rice-Bos	192	Davis-Sea	97	Winfield-NY	.340	Boggs-Bos	.409	Mattingly-NY	.537
Kingman-Oak	118	Winfield-NY	187	Evans-Bos	96	Boggs-Bos	.325	Henderson-Oak	.401	Evans-Bos	.532
Davis-Sea	116	Armas-Bos	187	Thornton-Cle	91	Bell-Tex	.315	Winfield-NY	.397	Armas-Bos	.531
				Boggs-Bos	89	Trammell-Det	.314	Davis-Sea	.395	Hrbek-Min	.522

Production		Adjusted Production		Batter Runs		Adjusted Batter Runs		Clutch Hitting Index		Runs Created	
Evans-Bos	.924	Mattingly-NY	159	Murray-Bal	46.8	Murray-Bal	48.6	Simmons-Mil	131	Evans-Bos	132
Mattingly-NY	.923	Murray-Bal	157	Evans-Bos	46.6	Mattingly-NY	44.3	Kingman-Oak	130	Murray-Bal	130
Murray-Bal	.923	Winfield-NY	156	Mattingly-NY	41.3	Evans-Bos	42.7	Franco-Cle	127	Ripken-Bal	122
Winfield-NY	.912	Henderson-Oak	147	Winfield-NY	38.4	Winfield-NY	41.3	Bell-Tex	123	Mattingly-NY	120
Hrbek-Min	.909	Davis-Sea	147	Davis-Sea	37.5	Davis-Sea	38.5	Davis-Sea	122	Easler-Bos	118

Total Average		Stolen Bases		Stolen Base Average		Stolen Base Runs		Fielding Runs		Total Player Rating	
Murray-Bal	.993	Henderson-Oak	66	Wilson-KC	90.4	Wilson-KC	11.1	Ripken-Bal	38.8	Ripken-Bal	9.1
Henderson-Oak	.971	Collins-Tor	60	Tolleson-Tex	84.6	Collins-Tor	9.6	Puckett-Min	30.1	Yount-Mil	5.0
Evans-Bos	.942	Butler-Cle	52	Perconte-Sea	82.9	Henderson-Oak	9.0	Cruz-Chi	22.1	Murray-Bal	4.8
Davis-Sea	.928	Pettis-Cal	48	Moseby-Tor	81.3	Garcia-Tor	6.6	Boggs-Bos	21.0	Mattingly-NY	4.7
Gibson-Det	.926	Wilson-KC	47	Collins-Tor	81.1	Moseby-Tor	6.3	Murphy-Oak	21.0	Henderson-Oak	4.5

Wins		Win Percentage		Games		Complete Games		Shutouts		Saves	
Boddicker-Bal	20	Alexander-Tor	.739	Hernandez-Det	80	Hough-Tex	17	Zahn-Cal	5	Quisenberry-KC	44
Morris-Det	19	Blyleven-Cle	.731	Quisenberry-KC	72	Boddicker-Bal	16	Ojeda-Bos	5	Caudill-Oak	36
Blyleven-Cle	19	Petry-Det	.692	Lopez-Det	71	Dotson-Chi	14			Hernandez-Det	32
Viola-Min	18	Wilcox-Det	.680	Camacho-Cle	69	Blyleven-Cle	12			Righetti-NY	31
Petry-Det	18			Caudill-Oak	68	Beattie-Sea	12			Davis-Min	29

Innings Pitched		Fewest Hits/Game		Fewest BB/Game		Strikeouts		Strikeouts/Game		Ratio	
Stieb-Tor	267.0	Stieb-Tor	7.25	Hoyt-Chi	1.64	Langston-Sea	204	Langston-Sea	8.16	Black-KC	10.30
Hough-Tex	266.0	Blyleven-Cle	7.49	Smithson-Min	1.93	Stieb-Tor	198	Witt-Cal	7.15	Alexander-Tor	10.32
Alexander-Tor	261.2	Boddicker-Bal	7.51	Guidry-NY	2.02	Witt-Cal	196	Moore-Sea	6.71	Mason-Tex	10.35
Boddicker-Bal	261.1	Langston-Sea	7.52	Alexander-Tor	2.03	Blyleven-Cle	170	Stieb-Tor	6.67	Blyleven-Cle	10.43
Viola-Min	257.2	Mason-Tex	7.76	Haas-Mil	2.04	Hough-Tex	164	Berenguer-Det	6.31	Boddicker-Bal	10.47

Earned Run Average		Adjusted ERA		Opponents' Batting Avg.		Opponents' On Base Pct.		Starter Runs		Adjusted Starter Runs	
Boddicker-Bal	2.79	Stieb-Tor	145	Stieb-Tor	.221	Black-KC	.283	Boddicker-Bal	34.9	Stieb-Tor	37.5
Stieb-Tor	2.83	Blyleven-Cle	143	Blyleven-Cle	.224	Blyleven-Cle	.287	Stieb-Tor	34.4	Blyleven-Cle	33.3
Blyleven-Cle	2.87	Boddicker-Bal	139	Boddicker-Bal	.228	Alexander-Tor	.287	Blyleven-Cle	30.7	Boddicker-Bal	31.4
Niekro-NY	3.09	Alexander-Tor	131	Langston-Sea	.230	Mason-Tex	.288	Alexander-Tor	25.0	Viola-Min	28.3
Zahn-Cal	3.12	Viola-Min	131	Berenguer-Det	.232	Seaver-Chi	.290	Black-KC	25.0	Alexander-Tor	28.1

Clutch Pitching Index		Relief Runs		Adjusted Relief Runs		Relief Ranking		Total Pitcher Index		Total Baseball Ranking	
Niekro-NY	125	Hernandez-Det	32.2	Hernandez-Det	31.1	Hernandez-Det	39.9	Stieb-Tor	4.1	Ripken-Bal	9.1
Fontenot-NY	119	Quisenberry-KC	19.4	Quisenberry-KC	19.9	Camacho-Cle	32.7	Boddicker-Bal	4.0	Yount-Mil	5.0
Cocanower-Mil	114	Righetti-NY	17.7	Camacho-Cle	18.4	Quisenberry-KC	27.7	Blyleven-Cle	3.6	Murray-Bal	4.8
Hurst-Bos	113	Corbett-Cal	17.7	Corbett-Cal	17.5	Righetti-NY	27.3	Hernandez-Det	3.1	Mattingly-NY	4.7
Burris-Oak	112	Camacho-Cle	17.3	Righetti-NY	15.6	Caudill-Oak	25.9	Black-KC	3.0	Henderson-Oak	4.5

TEAM	G	W	L	PCT	GB	R	OR	AB	H	2B	3B	HR	BB	SO	AVG	OBP	SLG	PRO	PRO+	BR	/A	PF	CHI	RC	SB	CS	SBA	SBR
EAST																												
STL	162	101	61	.623		**747**	572	5467	1446	245	**59**	87	**586**	853	**.264**	**.338**	.379	**.717**	108	52	58	99	**105**	733	314	96	77	37
NY	162	98	64	.605	3	695	**568**	5549	1425	239	35	134	546	872	.257	.326	.385	.711	108	31	48	98	99	691	117	53	69	3
MON	161	84	77	.522	16.5	633	636	5429	1342	242	49	118	492	880	.247	.313	.375	.688	104	-19	19	94	101	633	169	77	69	5
CHI	162	77	84	.478	23.5	686	729	5492	1397	239	28	**150**	562	937	.254	.326	**.390**	.716	95	40	-33	111	98	710	182	49	**79**	25
PHI	162	75	87	.463	26	667	673	5477	1343	238	47	141	527	1095	.245	.314	.383	.697	97	0	-18	103	102	657	122	51	71	6
PIT	161	57	104	.354	43.5	568	708	5436	1340	251	28	80	514	842	.247	.313	.347	.660	91	-64	-57	99	97	587	110	60	65	-3
WEST																												
LA	162	95	67	.586		682	579	5502	1434	226	28	129	539	846	.261	.330	.382	.712	108	38	**58**	97	97	704	136	58	70	6
CIN	162	89	72	.553	5.5	677	666	5431	1385	249	34	114	576	856	.255	.329	.376	.705	98	26	-7	105	99	672	159	70	69	6
SD	162	83	79	.512	12	650	622	5507	1405	241	28	109	513	**809**	.255	.321	.368	.689	101	-9	1	99	100	645	60	39	61	-5
HOU	162	83	79	.512	12	706	691	5582	**1457**	261	42	121	477	873	.261	.322	.388	.710	107	25	44	97	103	684	96	56	63	-5
ATL	162	66	96	.407	29	632	781	5526	1359	213	28	126	553	849	.246	.317	.363	.680	91	-28	-68	106	99	622	72	52	58	-10
SF	162	62	100	.383	33	556	674	5420	1263	217	31	115	488	962	.233	.301	.348	.649	91	-93	-61	95	100	564	99	55	64	-3
TOT	971					7899		65818	16596	2861	437	1424	6373	10674	.252	.321	.374	.695							1636	716	70	61

TEAM	CG	SH	SV	IP	H	H/G	HR	BB	SO	RAT	ERA	ERA+	OAV	OOB	PR	/A	PF	CPI	FA	E	DP	FW	PW	BW	SBW	DIF
EAST																										
STL	**37**	20	44	1464	1343	8.3	**98**	453	798	11.2	3.10	114	.246	.307	79	70	98	102	**.983**	108	166	1.7	7.4	**6.1**	**3.4**	1.5
NY	32	19	37	1488	1306	**7.9**	111	515	**1039**	11.1	3.11	111	.237	.304	80	57	96	99	.982	115	138	1.3	6.0	5.0	-.2	4.9
MON	13	13	**53**	1457	1346	8.3	99	509	870	11.6	3.55	96	.247	.313	7	-25	94	93	.981	121	152	.8	-2.6	2.0	-.0	3.3
CHI	20	8	42	1442¹	1492	9.3	156	519	820	12.7	4.16	96	.271	.336	-91	-27	111	103	.979	134	150	.1	-2.8	-3.5	2.1	.6
PHI	24	9	30	1447	1424	8.9	115	596	892	12.7	3.68	100	.259	.334	-15	0	103	105	.978	139	142	-.2	-.0	-1.9	.0	-4.0
PIT	15	6	29	1445¹	1406	8.8	107	584	962	12.6	3.97	90	.255	.330	-61	-64	100	94	.979	133	127	.1	-6.7	-6.0	-.9	-10.0
WEST																										
LA	**37**	21	36	1465	**1280**	**7.9**	102	462	979	**10.8**	**2.96**	117	**.234**	**.296**	102	84	97	98	.974	166	131	-1.8	8.8	6.1	.0	.8
CIN	24	11	45	1451¹	1347	8.4	131	535	910	11.8	3.71	102	.248	.317	-19	12	105	96	.980	122	142	.8	1.3	-.7	.0	7.0
SD	26	19	44	1451¹	1399	8.7	127	**443**	727	11.6	3.40	104	.257	.316	30	21	98	106	.980	124	158	.7	2.2	.1	-1.1	.0
HOU	17	9	42	1458	1393	8.6	119	543	909	12.1	3.66	95	.254	.324	-11	-32	96	100	.976	152	159	-1.0	-3.4	4.6	-1.1	2.8
ATL	9	9	29	1457¹	1512	9.3	134	642	776	13.5	4.19	92	.271	.349	-98	-56	107	104	.976	159	**197**	-1.4	-5.9	-7.2	-1.6	1.0
SF	13	5	24	1448	1348	8.4	125	572	985	12.1	3.61	95	.247	.321	-3	-28	96	99	.976	148	134	-.7	-2.9	-6.4	-.9	-8.1
TOT	267	149	455	17474²		8.5				12.0	3.59		.252	.321					.979	1621	1796					

Runs		Hits		Doubles		Triples		Home Runs		Total Bases	
Murphy-Atl	118	McGee-StL	216	Parker-Cin	42	McGee-StL	18	Murphy-Atl	37	Parker-Cin	350
Raines-Mon	115	Parker-Cin	198	Wilson-Phi	39	Samuel-Phi	13	Parker-Cin	34	Murphy-Atl	332
McGee-StL	114	Gwynn-SD	197	Herr-StL	38	Raines-Mon	13	Schmidt-Phi	33	McGee-StL	308
Sandberg-Chi	113	Sandberg-Chi	186	Wallach-Mon	36	Garner-Hou	10	Guerrero-LA	33	Sandberg-Chi	307
Coleman-StL	107	Murphy-Atl	185			Coleman-StL	10	Carter-NY	32	Schmidt-Phi	292

Runs Batted In		Runs Produced		Bases On Balls		Batting Average		On Base Percentage		Slugging Average	
Parker-Cin	125	Herr-StL	199	Murphy-Atl	90	McGee-StL	.353	Guerrero-LA	.425	Guerrero-LA	.577
Murphy-Atl	111	Murphy-Atl	192	Schmidt-Phi	87	Guerrero-LA	.320	Scioscia-LA	.409	Parker-Cin	.551
Herr-StL	110	McGee-StL	186	Martinez-SD	87	Raines-Mon	.320	Raines-Mon	.407	Murphy-Atl	.539
Moreland-Chi	106	Parker-Cin	179	Rose-Cin	86	Gwynn-SD	.317	Rose-Cin	.398	Schmidt-Phi	.532
Wilson-Phi	102	Sandberg-Chi	170	Law-Mon	86	Parker-Cin	.312	Clark-StL	.397	Marshall-LA	.515

Production		Adjusted Production		Batter Runs		Adjusted Batter Runs		Clutch Hitting Index		Runs Created	
Guerrero-LA	1.002	Guerrero-LA	183	Guerrero-LA	52.8	Guerrero-LA	54.7	Herr-StL	155	Murphy-Atl	131
Murphy-Atl	.929	Raines-Mon	155	Murphy-Atl	47.6	Murphy-Atl	43.0	Pendleton-StL	151	Raines-Mon	124
Parker-Cin	.918	Clark-StL	151	Parker-Cin	42.5	Raines-Mon	41.6	Moreland-Chi	149	McGee-StL	123
Schmidt-Phi	.911	McGee-StL	148	Schmidt-Phi	38.5	Parker-Cin	38.8	Brooks-Mon	146	Guerrero-LA	121
Clark-StL	.899	Murphy-Atl	148	Raines-Mon	37.5	McGee-StL	37.3	Rose-Cin	144	Sandberg-Chi	117

Total Average		Stolen Bases		Stolen Base Average		Stolen Base Runs		Fielding Runs		Total Player Rating	
Guerrero-LA	1.086	Coleman-StL	110	Lopes-Chi	92.2	Coleman-StL	18.0	Hubbard-Atl	61.8	Raines-Mon	6.4
Raines-Mon	1.022	Raines-Mon	70	Herr-StL	91.2	Raines-Mon	15.6	Wallach-Mon	36.7	Guerrero-LA	6.2
Murphy-Atl	.960	McGee-StL	56	Raines-Mon	88.6	Lopes-Chi	11.7	McReynolds-SD	23.1	McGee-StL	5.4
Schmidt-Phi	.927	Sandberg-Chi	54	VanSlyke-StL	85.0	Sandberg-Chi	9.6	Pendleton-StL	22.7	Hubbard-Atl	5.3
McGee-StL	.920	Samuel-Phi	53	Davis-Cin	84.2	Herr-StL	7.5	Wilson-Phi	20.4	Sandberg-Chi	4.9

Wins		Win Percentage		Games		Complete Games		Shutouts		Saves	
Gooden-NY	24	Hershiser-LA	.864	Burke-Mon	78	Gooden-NY	16	Tudor-StL	10	Reardon-Mon	41
Tudor-StL	21	Gooden-NY	.857	M.Davis-SF	77	Valenzuela-LA	14	Gooden-NY	8	Smith-Chi	33
Andujar-StL	21	Smith-Mon	.783	Garrelts-SF	74	Tudor-StL	14	Valenzuela-LA	5	Smith-Hou	27
Browning-Cin	20	Darling-NY	.727	Carman-Phi	71	Cox-StL	10	Hershiser-LA	5	Power-Cin	27
Hershiser-LA	19	Tudor-StL	.724	Minton-SF	68	Andujar-StL	10			Gossage-SD	26

Innings Pitched		Fewest Hits/Game		Fewest BB/Game		Strikeouts		Strikeouts/Game		Ratio	
Gooden-NY	276.2	Fernandez-NY	5.71	Hoyt-SD	.86	Gooden-NY	268	Fernandez-NY	9.51	Tudor-StL	8.61
Tudor-StL	275.0	Gooden-NY	6.44	Eckersley-Chi	1.01	Soto-Cin	214	Gooden-NY	8.72	Gooden-NY	8.75
Valenzuela-LA	272.1	Hershiser-LA	6.72	Lynch-NY	1.27	Ryan-Hou	209	DeLeon-Pit	8.24	Eckersley-Chi	8.88
Andujar-StL	269.2	Tudor-StL	6.84	Tudor-StL	1.60	Valenzuela-LA	208	Ryan-Hou	8.11	Hershiser-LA	9.50
Mahler-Atl	266.2	Soto-Cin	6.87	Smith-Mon	1.66	Fernandez-NY	180	Soto-Cin	7.50	Smith-Mon	9.51

Earned Run Average		Adjusted ERA		Opponents' Batting Avg.		Opponents' On Base Pct.		Starter Runs		Adjusted Starter Runs	
Gooden-NY	1.53	Gooden-NY	226	Fernandez-NY	.181	Tudor-StL	.249	Gooden-NY	63.4	Gooden-NY	59.2
Tudor-StL	1.93	Tudor-StL	183	Gooden-NY	.201	Gooden-NY	.254	Tudor-StL	50.7	Tudor-StL	48.9
Hershiser-LA	2.03	Hershiser-LA	171	Hershiser-LA	.206	Eckersley-Chi	.255	Hershiser-LA	41.6	Hershiser-LA	38.5
Reuschel-Pit	2.27	Reuschel-Pit	157	Tudor-StL	.209	Hershiser-LA	.268	Valenzuela-LA	34.6	Valenzuela-LA	31.2
Welch-LA	2.31	Welch-LA	150	Soto-Cin	.211	Smith-Mon	.269	Reuschel-Pit	28.4	Reuschel-Pit	28.1

Clutch Pitching Index		Relief Runs		Adjusted Relief Runs		Relief Ranking		Total Pitcher Index		Total Baseball Ranking	
Darling-NY	120	Burke-Mon	16.0	Franco-Cin	17.6	Franco-Cin	28.8	Gooden-NY	8.0	Gooden-NY	8.0
Hawkins-SD	119	Gossage-SD	15.5	Carman-Phi	15.3	Gossage-SD	24.8	Tudor-StL	5.8	Raines-Mon	6.4
Show-SD	119	Franco-Cin	15.5	Gossage-SD	15.0	Smith-Hou	24.7	Hershiser-LA	5.7	Guerrero-LA	6.2
Reuss-LA	115	Garrelts-SF	15.2	Garrelts-SF	13.3	Carman-Phi	23.5	Valenzuela-LA	4.0	Tudor-StL	5.8
Gooden-NY	115	Carman-Phi	14.4	Burke-Mon	13.3	Power-Cin	22.5	Reuschel-Pit	3.9	McGee-StL	5.4

TEAM	G	W	L	PCT	GB	R	OR	AB	H	2B	3B	HR	BB	SO	AVG	OBP	SLG	PRO	PRO+	BR	/A	PF	CHI	RC	SB	CS	SBA	SBR
EAST																												
TOR	161	99	62	.615		759	588	5508	1482	281	53	158	503	807	.269	.334	.425	.759	103	43	25	103	98	767	144	77	65	-3
NY	161	97	64	.602	2	839	660	5458	1458	272	31	176	620	771	.267	.347	.425	.772	113	82	100	98	102	821	155	53	75	15
DET	161	84	77	.522	15	729	688	5575	1413	254	45	202	526	926	.253	.321	.424	.745	103	8	13	99	97	765	75	41	65	-2
BAL	161	83	78	.516	16	818	764	5517	1451	234	22	214	604	908	.263	.338	.430	.768	112	64	84	97	102	794	69	43	62	-5
BOS	163	81	81	.500	18.5	800	720	5720	1615	292	31	162	562	816	.282	.350	.429	.779	108	96	65	104	93	844	66	27	71	4
MIL	161	71	90	.441	28	690	802	5568	1467	250	44	101	462	746	.263	.322	.379	.701	91	-68	-64	100	103	666	69	34	67	0
CLE	162	60	102	.370	39.5	729	861	5527	1465	254	31	116	492	817	.265	.327	.385	.712	95	-44	-38	99	106	681	132	72	65	-4
WEST																												
KC	162	91	71	.562		687	639	5500	1384	261	49	154	473	840	.252	.315	.401	.716	94	-47	-49	100	101	687	128	48	73	10
CAL	162	90	72	.556	1	732	703	5442	1364	215	31	153	648	902	.251	.335	.386	.721	97	-17	-13	100	100	710	106	51	68	1
CHI	163	85	77	.525	6	736	720	5470	1386	247	37	146	471	843	.253	.318	.392	.710	90	-55	-83	104	110	674	108	56	66	-1
MIN	162	77	85	.475	14	705	782	5509	1453	282	41	141	502	779	.264	.327	.407	.736	95	-1	43	106	97	729	68	44	61	-6
OAK	162	77	85	.475	14	757	787	5581	1475	230	34	155	508	861	.264	.327	.401	.728	106	-15	40	93	104	725	117	58	67	0
SEA	162	74	88	.457	17	719	818	5521	1410	277	38	171	564	942	.255	.328	.412	.740	100	7	3	101	96	739	94	35	73	7
TEX	161	62	99	.385	28.5	617	785	5361	1359	213	41	129	530	819	.253	.324	.381	.705	91	-54	-63	101	93	652	130	76	63	-7
TOT	1132					10317		77257	20182	3562	528	2178	7465	11777	.261	.330	.406	.735							1461	715	67	9

TEAM	CG	SH	SV	IP	H	H/G	HR	BB	SO	RAT	ERA	ERA+	OAV	OOB	PR	/A	PF	CPI	FA	E	DP	FW	PW	BW	SBW	DIF
EAST																										
TOR	18	9	47	1448	1312	8.2	147	484	823	11.3	3.31	127	.243	.308	135	145	102	107	.980	125	164	.2	14.3	2.5	-.4	1.8
NY	25	9	49	1440[1]	1373	8.6	157	518	907	11.9	3.69	109	.251	.318	74	50	97	104	.979	126	172	.2	4.9	9.9	1.4	.0
DET	31	11	40	1456	1313	8.1	141	556	943	11.7	3.78	108	.240	.313	59	47	98	94	.977	143	152	-.8	4.6	1.3	-.3	-1.4
BAL	32	6	33	1427[1]	1480	9.3	160	568	793	13.1	4.38	92	.270	.341	-36	-55	97	102	.979	129	168	-.0	-5.4	8.3	-.6	.2
BOS	35	8	29	1461[1]	1487	9.2	130	540	913	12.7	4.06	106	.265	.333	14	37	103	101	.977	145	161	-.8	3.7	6.4	.3	-9.6
MIL	34	5	37	1437	1510	9.5	175	499	777	12.8	4.39	95	.271	.334	-39	-36	100	101	.977	142	153	-.7	-3.6	-6.3	-.0	1.2
CLE	24	7	28	1421	1556	9.9	170	547	702	13.6	4.91	84	.281	.350	-121	-123	100	98	.977	141	161	-.6	-12.2	-3.8	-.5	-4.0
WEST																										
KC	27	11	41	1461	1433	8.8	103	463	846	11.9	3.49	119	.257	.317	107	109	100	103	.980	127	160	.1	10.8	-4.8	.9	3.0
CAL	22	8	41	1457[1]	1453	9.0	171	514	767	12.3	3.91	105	.263	.328	38	32	99	108	.982	112	202	1.0	3.2	-1.3	.0	6.1
CHI	20	8	39	1451[2]	1411	8.7	161	569	1023	12.5	4.07	106	.263	.330	13	40	104	101	.982	111	152	1.1	4.0	-8.2	-.2	7.3
MIN	41	7	34	1426[1]	1468	9.3	154	462	767	12.4	4.48	98	.268	.329	-53	-11	106	95	.980	120	139	.5	-1.1	-4.3	-.7	1.5
OAK	10	6	41	1453	1451	9.0	172	607	785	12.9	4.41	87	.259	.334	-43	-89	93	97	.977	140	137	-.6	-8.8	4.0	-.0	1.5
SEA	23	8	30	1432	1456	9.2	154	637	868	13.4	4.68	93	.265	.346	-84	-74	102	96	.980	122	156	.4	-7.3	.3	.6	-1.0
TEX	18	5	33	1411[2]	1479	9.4	173	501	863	12.9	4.56	93	.269	.334	-65	-52	102	97	.980	120	145	.5	-5.1	-6.2	-.8	-6.9
TOT	360	108	522	20184		9.0				12.5	4.15		.261	.330					.979	1803	2222					

Runs
Henderson-NY ... 146
Ripken-Bal ... 116
Murray-Bal ... 111
Evans-Bos ... 110
Brett-KC ... 108

Hits
Boggs-Bos ... 240
Mattingly-NY ... 211
Buckner-Bos ... 201
Puckett-Min ... 199
Baines-Chi ... 198

Doubles
Mattingly-NY ... 48
Buckner-Bos ... 46
Boggs-Bos ... 42
Cooper-Mil ... 39

Triples
Wilson-KC ... 21
Butler-Cle ... 14
Puckett-Min ... 13
Fernandez-Tor ... 10

Home Runs
Evans-Det ... 40
Fisk-Chi ... 37
Balboni-KC ... 36
Mattingly-NY ... 35
J.Thomas-Sea ... 32

Total Bases
Mattingly-NY ... 370
Brett-KC ... 322
Bradley-Sea ... 319
Boggs-Bos ... 312
Murray-Bal ... 305

Runs Batted In
Mattingly-NY ... 145
Murray-Bal ... 124
Winfield-NY ... 114
Baines-Chi ... 113
Brett-KC ... 112

Runs Produced
Mattingly-NY ... 217
Murray-Bal ... 204
Ripken-Bal ... 200
Henderson-NY ... 194
Winfield-NY ... 193

Bases On Balls
Evans-Bos ... 114
Harrah-Tex ... 113
Brett-KC ... 103
Henderson-NY ... 99
Boggs-Bos ... 96

Batting Average
Boggs-Bos ... .368
Brett-KC ... .335
Mattingly-NY ... .324
Henderson-NY ... .314
Butler-Cle ... .311

On Base Percentage
Boggs-Bos ... .452
Brett-KC ... .442
Harrah-Tex ... .437
Henderson-NY ... .422
Murray-Bal ... .387

Slugging Average
Brett-KC ... .585
Mattingly-NY ... .567
Barfield-Tor ... .536
Murray-Bal ... .523
Evans-Det ... .519

Production
Brett-KC ... 1.028
Mattingly-NY ... .946
Henderson-NY ... .938
Boggs-Bos ... .929
Murray-Bal ... .910

Adjusted Production
Brett-KC ... 178
Henderson-NY ... 159
Mattingly-NY ... 159
Murray-Bal ... 150
Boggs-Bos ... 149

Batter Runs
Brett-KC ... 63.4
Boggs-Bos ... 54.8
Mattingly-NY ... 47.5
Henderson-NY ... 45.5
Murray-Bal ... 38.4

Adjusted Batter Runs
Brett-KC ... 63.2
Boggs-Bos ... 51.1
Mattingly-NY ... 49.6
Henderson-NY ... 47.3
Murray-Bal ... 40.5

Clutch Hitting Index
Thornton-Cle ... 146
Meacham-NY ... 142
Boone-Cal ... 136
Baylor-NY ... 134
Buckner-Bos ... 132

Runs Created
Brett-KC ... 146
Boggs-Bos ... 143
Henderson-NY ... 138
Mattingly-NY ... 136
Murray-Bal ... 122

Total Average
Henderson-NY ... 1.155
Brett-KC ... 1.150
Gibson-Det ... .953
Boggs-Bos ... .952
Murray-Bal ... .938

Stolen Bases
Henderson-NY ... 80
Pettis-Cal ... 56
Butler-Cle ... 47
Wilson-KC ... 43
Smith-KC ... 40

Stolen Base Average
Perconte-Sea ... 93.9
Henderson-NY ... 88.9
Gibson-Det ... 88.2
Pettis-Cal ... 86.2
Smith-KC ... 85.1

Stolen Base Runs
Henderson-NY ... 18.0
Pettis-Cal ... 11.4
Perconte-Sea ... 8.1
Smith-KC ... 7.8
Gibson-Det ... 6.6

Fielding Runs
Owen-Sea ... 30.3
Buckner-Bos ... 25.4
Barfield-Tor ... 21.9
Butler-Cle ... 21.8
Puckett-Min ... 21.2

Total Player Rating
Henderson-NY ... 7.3
Brett-KC ... 7.2
Boggs-Bos ... 5.5
Barfield-Tor ... 4.8
Murray-Bal ... 4.3

Wins
Guidry-NY ... 22
Saberhagen-KC ... 20
Viola-Min ... 18
Burns-Chi ... 18

Win Percentage
Guidry-NY ... .786
Saberhagen-KC ... .769
Leibrandt-KC ... .654
Higuera-Mil ... .652

Games
Quisenberry-KC ... 84
VandeBerg-Sea ... 76
Righetti-NY ... 74
Hernandez-Det ... 74
Nunez-Sea ... 70

Complete Games
Blyleven-Cle-Min ... 24
Moore-Sea ... 14
Hough-Tex ... 14
Morris-Det ... 13
Boyd-Bos ... 13

Shutouts
Blyleven-Cle-Min ... 5
Morris-Det ... 4
Burns-Chi ... 4

Saves
Quisenberry-KC ... 37
James-Chi ... 32
Moore-Cal ... 31
Hernandez-Det ... 31

Innings Pitched
Blyleven-Cle-Min ... 293.2
Boyd-Bos ... 272.1
Stieb-Tor ... 265.0
Alexander-Tor ... 260.2
Guidry-NY ... 259.0

Fewest Hits/Game
Stieb-Tor ... 7.00
Hough-Tex ... 7.12
Petry-Det ... 7.16
Morris-Det ... 7.42
Higuera-Mil ... 7.88

Fewest BB/Game
Haas-Mil ... 1.39
Saberhagen-KC ... 1.45
Guidry-NY ... 1.46
Butcher-Min ... 1.86
Key-Tor ... 2.12

Strikeouts
Blyleven-Cle-Min ... 206
Bannister-Chi ... 198
Morris-Det ... 191
Hurst-Bos ... 189
Witt-Cal ... 180

Strikeouts/Game
Bannister-Chi ... 8.46
Hurst-Bos ... 7.42
Burns-Chi ... 6.82
Morris-Det ... 6.69
Tanana-Tex-Det ... 6.66

Ratio
Saberhagen-KC ... 9.56
Guidry-NY ... 9.90
Key-Tor ... 10.16
Petry-Det ... 10.33
Hough-Tex ... 10.35

Earned Run Average
Stieb-Tor ... 2.48
Leibrandt-KC ... 2.69
Saberhagen-KC ... 2.87
Key-Tor ... 3.00
Blyleven-Cle-Min ... 3.16

Adjusted ERA
Stieb-Tor ... 170
Leibrandt-KC ... 155
Saberhagen-KC ... 145
Key-Tor ... 140
Seaver-Chi ... 136

Opponents' Batting Avg.
Stieb-Tor ... .213
Hough-Tex ... .215
Petry-Det ... .217
Morris-Det ... .225
Higuera-Mil ... .235

Opponents' On Base Pct.
Saberhagen-KC ... .273
Guidry-NY ... .279
Key-Tor ... .284
Hough-Tex ... .285
Petry-Det ... .285

Starter Runs
Stieb-Tor ... 49.1
Leibrandt-KC ... 38.5
Saberhagen-KC ... 33.4
Blyleven-Cle-Min ... 32.3
Key-Tor ... 27.0

Adjusted Starter Runs
Stieb-Tor ... 50.9
Leibrandt-KC ... 38.8
Blyleven-Cle-Min ... 35.4
Saberhagen-KC ... 33.8
Seaver-Chi ... 30.5

Clutch Pitching Index
Leibrandt-KC ... 121
Romanick-Cal ... 117
Boddicker-Bal ... 115
Alexander-Tor ... 114
Stieb-Tor ... 112

Relief Runs
Moore-Cal ... 25.5
Quisenberry-KC ... 25.4
James-Chi ... 24.7
Cliburn-Cal ... 22.6
Harris-Tex ... 21.1

Adjusted Relief Runs
James-Chi ... 26.8
Quisenberry-KC ... 25.6
Moore-Cal ... 25.0
Cliburn-Cal ... 22.2
Harris-Tex ... 22.1

Relief Ranking
Moore-Cal ... 51.9
James-Chi ... 50.4
Quisenberry-KC ... 46.9
Hernandez-Det ... 35.3
Righetti-NY ... 32.2

Total Pitcher Index
Stieb-Tor ... 6.0
Leibrandt-KC ... 4.6
Saberhagen-KC ... 3.8
Blyleven-Cle-Min ... 3.6
Seaver-Chi ... 3.4

Total Baseball Ranking
Henderson-NY ... 7.3
Brett-KC ... 7.2
Stieb-Tor ... 6.0
Boggs-Bos ... 5.5
Barfield-Tor ... 4.8

TEAM	G	W	L	PCT	GB	R	OR	AB	H	2B	3B	HR	BB	SO	AVG	OBP	SLG	PRO	PRO+	BR	/A	PF	CHI	RC	SB	CS	SBA	SBR
EAST																												
NY	162	108	54	.667		783	578	5558	1462	261	31	148	631	968	.263	.341	.401	.742	114	84	104	97	101	773	118	48	71	7
PHI	161	86	75	.534	21.5	739	713	5483	1386	266	39	154	589	1154	.253	.330	.400	.730	103	50	26	104	101	739	153	59	72	11
STL	161	79	82	.491	28.5	601	611	5378	1270	216	48	58	568	905	.236	.311	.327	.638	83	-119	-113	99	109	584	262	78	77	32
MON	161	78	83	.484	29.5	637	688	5508	1401	255	50	110	537	1016	.254	.324	.379	.703	101	-1	5	99	94	676	193	95	67	1
CHI	160	70	90	.438	37	680	781	5499	1409	258	27	155	508	966	.256	.321	.398	.719	96	21	-31	108	98	697	132	62	68	2
PIT	162	64	98	.395	44	663	700	5456	1366	273	33	111	569	929	.250	.323	.374	.697	96	-12	-27	102	100	654	152	84	64	-5
WEST																												
HOU	162	96	66	.593		654	569	5441	1388	244	32	125	536	916	.255	.325	.381	.706	104	3	22	97	98	668	163	75	75	4
CIN	162	86	76	.531	10	732	717	5536	1404	237	35	144	568	920	.254	.327	.387	.714	99	21	-8	104	104	712	177	53	77	21
SF	162	83	79	.512	13	698	618	5501	1394	269	29	114	536	1087	.253	.324	.375	.699	104	-9	25	95	104	674	148	93	61	-11
SD	162	74	88	.457	22	656	723	5515	1442	239	25	136	484	917	.261	.323	.388	.711	104	9	23	98	97	671	96	68	59	-12
LA	162	73	89	.451	23	638	679	5471	1373	232	14	130	478	966	.251	.315	.370	.685	102	-42	5	93	102	639	155	67	70	6
ATL	161	72	89	.447	23.5	615	719	5384	1348	241	24	138	538	904	.250	.321	.381	.702	94	-5	-42	106	93	646	93	76	55	-18
TOT	969					8096		65730	16643	2991	387	1523	6560	11648	.253	.324	.380	.704							1842	858	68	38

TEAM	CG	SH	SV	IP	H	H/G	HR	BB	SO	RAT	ERA	ERA+	OAV	OOB	PR	/A	PF	CPI	FA	E	DP	FW	PW	BW	SBW	DIF
EAST																										
NY	27	11	46	1484	1304	7.9	103	509	1083	11.2	3.11	114	.236	.304	100	70	95	98	.978	138	145	.1	7.3	10.8	.4	8.4
PHI	22	11	39	1451²	1473	9.1	130	553	874	12.1	3.85	100	.265	.334	-22	0	104	105	.978	137	157	.1	.0	2.7	.8	1.9
STL	17	4	46	1466¹	1364	8.4	135	485	761	11.5	3.37	108	.250	.314	56	44	98	106	.981	123	178	.9	4.6	-11.7	3.0	1.8
MON	15	9	50	1466¹	1350	8.3	119	566	1051	12.0	3.78	98	.246	.320	-11	-15	99	93	.979	133	132	.3	-1.5	.5	-.2	-1.6
CHI	11	6	42	1445	1546	9.6	143	557	962	13.2	4.49	90	.279	.346	-124	-72	109	100	.980	124	147	.8	-7.5	-3.2	-.1	.0
PIT	17	9	30	1450²	1397	8.7	138	570	924	12.4	3.90	98	.255	.329	-30	-11	103	100	.978	143	134	-.2	-1.1	-2.8	-.8	-12.0
WEST																										
HOU	18	19	51	1456¹	1203	7.4	116	523	1160	10.8	3.15	114	.225	.297	92	73	97	93	.979	130	108	.6	7.6	2.3	.0	4.5
CIN	14	8	45	1468	1465	9.0	136	524	924	12.3	3.91	99	.264	.329	-32	-7	104	101	.978	140	160	.0	-.7	-.8	1.9	4.7
SF	18	10	35	1460¹	1264	7.8	121	591	992	11.6	3.33	106	.236	.316	62	30	95	101	.977	143	149	-.2	3.1	2.6	-1.5	-2.1
SD	13	7	32	1443¹	1406	8.8	150	607	934	12.7	3.99	92	.258	.335	-44	-54	98	102	.978	137	135	.2	-5.6	2.4	-1.6	-2.4
LA	35	14	25	1454²	1428	8.8	115	499	1051	12.1	3.76	92	.256	.320	-7	-51	93	96	.971	181	118	-2.2	-5.3	.5	.3	-1.3
ATL	17	5	39	1424²	1443	9.1	117	576	932	12.9	3.97	100	.266	.340	-41	0	107	103	.978	141	181	-.1	.0	-4.4	-2.2	-1.8
TOT	224	113	480	17471		8.6				12.1	3.72		.253	.324					.978	1670	1744					

Runs		Hits		Doubles		Triples		Home Runs		Total Bases	
Hayes-Phi	107	Gwynn-SD	211	Hayes-Phi	46	Webster-Mon	13	Schmidt-Phi	37	Parker-Cin	304
Gwynn-SD	107	Sax-LA	210	Sax-LA	43	Samuel-Phi	12	Parker-Cin	31	Schmidt-Phi	302
Schmidt-Phi	97	Raines-Mon	194	Dunston-Chi	37	Raines-Mon	10	Davis-Hou	31	Gwynn-SD	300
Davis-Cin	97	Hayes-Phi	186	Bream-Pit	37	Coleman-StL	8	Murphy-Atl	29	Murphy-Atl	293
		Bass-Hou	184	Samuel-Phi	36					Hayes-Phi	293

Runs Batted In		Runs Produced		Bases On Balls		Batting Average		On Base Percentage		Slugging Average	
Schmidt-Phi	119	Hayes-Phi	186	Hernandez-NY	94	Raines-Mon	.334	Raines-Mon	.415	Schmidt-Phi	.547
Parker-Cin	116	Schmidt-Phi	179	Schmidt-Phi	89	Sax-LA	.332	Hernandez-NY	.414	Strawberry-NY	.507
Carter-NY	105	Parker-Cin	174	C.Davis-SF	84	Gwynn-SD	.329	Schmidt-Phi	.395	McReynolds-SD	.504
Davis-Hou	101	Hernandez-NY	164	Oberkfell-Atl	83	Bass-Hou	.311	Sax-LA	.391	Davis-Hou	.493
Hayes-Phi	98	Carter-NY	162	Doran-Hou	81	Hernandez-NY	.310	Gwynn-SD	.382	Bass-Hou	.486

Production		Adjusted Production		Batter Runs		Adjusted Batter Runs		Clutch Hitting Index		Runs Created	
Schmidt-Phi	.942	Schmidt-Phi	152	Schmidt-Phi	44.0	Schmidt-Phi	41.5	Carter-NY	154	Raines-Mon	130
Raines-Mon	.891	Raines-Mon	146	Raines-Mon	38.0	Raines-Mon	38.7	Herr-StL	135	Schmidt-Phi	122
Strawberry-NY	.871	Strawberry-NY	142	Hernandez-NY	32.2	Hernandez-NY	34.3	Pendleton-StL	133	Gwynn-SD	113
McReynolds-SD	.867	Hernandez-NY	141	Hayes-Phi	30.3	Sax-LA	31.4	Ray-Pit	132	Hayes-Phi	111
Hayes-Phi	.861	McReynolds-SD	140	Gwynn-SD	28.4	Gwynn-SD	30.0	Cruz-Hou	131	Sax-LA	110

Total Average		Stolen Bases		Stolen Base Average		Stolen Base Runs		Fielding Runs		Total Player Rating	
Raines-Mon	1.040	Coleman-StL	107	Dernier-Chi	93.1	Coleman-StL	23.7	Hubbard-Atl	41.0	Raines-Mon	6.2
Schmidt-Phi	.988	Davis-Cin	80	Raines-Mon	88.6	Davis-Cin	17.4	Pendleton-StL	24.2	Gwynn-SD	5.2
Strawberry-NY	.910	Raines-Mon	70	Coleman-StL	88.4	Raines-Mon	15.6	Bream-Pit	22.8	Hernandez-NY	4.3
Hernandez-NY	.873	Duncan-LA	48	Davis-Cin	87.9	Dernier-Chi	6.9	Wilson-Phi	20.6	Sax-LA	3.6
McReynolds-SD	.848			Leonard-SF	84.2			Dunston-Chi	20.3	Hubbard-Atl	3.5

Wins		Win Percentage		Games		Complete Games		Shutouts		Saves	
Valenzuela-LA	21	Ojeda-NY	.783	Lefferts-SD	83	Valenzuela-LA	20	Scott-Hou	5	Worrell-StL	36
Krukow-SF	20	Gooden-NY	.739	McDowell-NY	75	Rhoden-Pit	12	Knepper-Hou	5	Reardon-Mon	35
Scott-Hou	18	Fernandez-NY	.727	Worrell-StL	74	Gooden-NY	12	Welch-LA	3	Smith-Hou	33
Ojeda-NY	18	Darling-NY	.714	Franco-Cin	74	Krukow-SF	12	Valenzuela-LA	3	Smith-Chi	31
		Krukow-SF	.690	Tekulve-Phi	73						

Innings Pitched		Fewest Hits/Game		Fewest BB/Game		Strikeouts		Strikeouts/Game		Ratio	
Scott-Hou	275.1	Scott-Hou	5.95	Eckersley-Chi	1.93	Scott-Hou	306	Scott-Hou	10.00	Scott-Hou	8.37
Valenzuela-LA	269.1	Youmans-Mon	5.96	Sanderson-Chi	1.96	Valenzuela-LA	242	Ryan-Hou	9.81	Krukow-SF	9.66
Knepper-Hou	258.0	Ryan-Hou	6.02	Krukow-SF	2.02	Youmans-Mon	202	Fernandez-NY	8.81	Ojeda-NY	9.90
Rhoden-Pit	253.2	Fernandez-NY	7.09	Welch-LA	2.10	Gooden-NY	200	Youmans-Mon	8.30	Gooden-NY	10.12
Gooden-NY	250.0	Gooden-NY	7.09	Ojeda-NY	2.15	Fernandez-NY	200	Valenzuela-LA	8.09	Rhoden-Pit	10.25

Earned Run Average		Adjusted ERA		Opponents' Batting Avg.		Opponents' On Base Pct.		Starter Runs		Adjusted Starter Runs	
Scott-Hou	2.22	Scott-Hou	162	Scott-Hou	.186	Scott-Hou	.244	Scott-Hou	45.7	Scott-Hou	42.1
Ojeda-NY	2.57	Ojeda-NY	138	Ryan-Hou	.188	Krukow-SF	.271	Ojeda-NY	27.7	Rhoden-Pit	28.0
Darling-NY	2.81	Rhoden-Pit	135	Youmans-Mon	.188	Ojeda-NY	.279	Rhoden-Pit	24.7	Ojeda-NY	23.3
Rhoden-Pit	2.84	Darling-NY	126	Gooden-NY	.215	Gooden-NY	.280	Gooden-NY	24.2	Ruffin-Phi	22.6
Gooden-NY	2.84	Cox-StL	125	Fernandez-NY	.216	Ryan-Hou	.285	Darling-NY	23.9	Gooden-NY	19.2

Clutch Pitching Index		Relief Runs		Adjusted Relief Runs		Relief Ranking		Total Pitcher Index		Total Baseball Ranking	
Dravecky-SD	115	Worrell-StL	18.8	Worrell-StL	17.9	Worrell-StL	43.5	Scott-Hou	4.8	Raines-Mon	6.2
Darling-NY	113	McGaffigan-Mon	16.9	McGaffigan-Mon	16.5	Smith-Chi	24.5	Rhoden-Pit	4.2	Gwynn-SD	5.2
Garrelts-SF	110	Horton-StL	16.4	Tekulve-Phi	16.1	Orosco-NY	23.1	Ojeda-NY	2.3	Scott-Hou	4.8
Tudor-StL	109	Tekulve-Phi	14.4	Horton-StL	15.6	Garber-Atl	22.9	Darling-NY	2.2	Hernandez-NY	4.3
Gullickson-Cin	109	McCullers-SD	14.2	McCullers-SD	13.2	Tekulve-Phi	22.3	Gooden-NY	2.0	Rhoden-Pit	4.2

TEAM	G	W	L	PCT	GB	R	OR	AB	H	2B	3B	HR	BB	SO	AVG	OBP	SLG	PRO	PRO+	BR	/A	PF	CHI	RC	SB	CS	SBA	SBR
EAST																												
BOS	161	95	66	.590		794	696	5498	1488	320	21	144	595	707	.271	.349	.415	.764	107	59	57	100	98	792	41	34	55	-8
NY	162	90	72	.556	5.5	797	738	5570	1512	275	23	188	645	911	.271	.350	.430	.780	112	89	98	99	94	843	139	48	74	13
DET	162	87	75	.537	8.5	798	714	5512	1447	234	30	198	613	885	.263	.341	.424	.765	107	52	55	100	99	814	138	58	70	7
TOR	163	86	76	.531	9.5	809	733	5716	1540	285	35	181	496	848	.269	.331	.427	.758	102	29	11	102	103	796	110	59	65	-2
CLE	163	84	78	.519	11.5	831	841	5702	1620	270	45	157	456	944	.284	.344	.430	.770	110	57	71	98	102	822	141	54	72	10
MIL	161	77	84	.478	18	667	734	5461	1393	255	38	127	530	986	.255	.324	.385	.709	89	-59	-82	103	98	682	100	50	67	0
BAL	162	73	89	.451	22.5	708	760	5524	1425	223	13	169	563	862	.258	.330	.395	.725	97	-28	-17	99	99	708	64	34	65	-1
WEST																												
CAL	162	92	70	.568		786	684	5433	1387	236	36	167	671	860	.255	.341	.404	.745	103	22	31	99	101	765	109	42	72	8
TEX	162	87	75	.537	5	771	743	5529	1479	248	43	184	511	1088	.267	.333	.428	.761	103	37	19	102	99	761	103	85	55	-20
KC	162	76	86	.469	16	654	673	5561	1403	264	45	137	474	919	.252	.315	.390	.705	88	-77	-91	102	99	683	97	46	68	2
OAK	162	76	86	.469	16	731	760	5435	1370	213	25	163	553	983	.252	.325	.390	.715	101	-48	7	103	106	700	139	61	70	5
CHI	162	72	90	.444	20	644	699	5406	1335	197	34	121	487	940	.247	.313	.363	.676	81	-125	-147	103	107	614	115	54	68	2
MIN	162	71	91	.438	21	741	839	5531	1446	257	39	196	501	977	.261	.327	.428	.755	100	21	2	103	97	756	81	61	57	-12
SEA	162	67	95	.414	25	718	835	5498	1392	243	41	158	572	1148	.253	.327	.399	.726	95	-28	-33	101	100	706	93	76	55	-18
TOT	1134					10449		77376	20237	3520	468	2290	7667	13058	.262	.332	.408	.740							1470	762	66	-16

TEAM	CG	SH	SV	IP	H	H/G	HR	BB	SO	RAT	ERA	ERA+	OAV	OOB	PR	/A	PF	CPI	FA	E	DP	FW	PW	BW	SBW	DIF
EAST																										
BOS	36	6	41	1429²	1469	9.2	167	474	1033	12.4	3.93	106	.266	.327	38	36	100	106	.979	129	146	-.2	3.5	5.6	-.7	6.2
NY	13	8	58	1443¹	1461	9.1	175	492	878	12.3	4.11	99	.263	.325	11	-3	98	100	.979	127	153	.0	-.3	9.6	1.4	-1.7
DET	33	12	38	1443²	1374	8.6	183	571	880	12.3	4.02	102	.251	.325	25	16	99	100	.982	108	163	1.1	1.6	5.4	.8	-2.9
TOR	16	12	44	1476	1467	8.9	164	487	1002	12.2	4.08	103	.261	.325	16	23	101	99	.984	100	150	1.7	2.3	1.1	-.0	.0
CLE	31	7	34	1447²	1548	9.6	167	605	744	13.7	4.58	91	.273	.349	-64	-70	99	101	.975	157	148	-1.7	-6.9	7.0	1.1	3.5
MIL	29	12	32	1431²	1478	9.3	158	494	952	12.6	4.01	108	.267	.330	26	50	104	104	.976	146	146	-1.2	4.9	-8.1	.1	.7
BAL	17	6	39	1436²	1451	9.1	177	535	954	12.6	4.30	96	.263	.330	-20	-27	99	98	.978	135	163	-.5	-2.7	-1.7	.0	-3.2
WEST																										
CAL	29	12	40	1456	1356	8.4	153	478	955	11.5	3.84	107	.248	.311	54	44	98	94	.983	107	156	1.2	4.3	3.0	.9	1.5
TEX	15	8	41	1450¹	1356	8.4	145	736	1059	13.2	4.11	105	.249	.342	11	31	103	100	.980	122	160	.3	3.0	1.9	-1.9	2.6
KC	24	13	31	1440²	1413	8.8	121	479	888	12.1	3.82	111	.258	.322	56	68	102	98	.980	123	153	.2	6.7	-8.9	.3	-3.3
OAK	22	8	37	1433	1334	8.4	166	667	937	12.8	4.31	90	.247	.333	-21	-70	93	94	.978	135	120	-.5	-6.9	.7	.6	1.1
CHI	18	8	38	1442¹	1361	8.5	143	561	895	12.2	3.93	110	.251	.325	39	61	103	97	.981	117	142	.6	6.0	-14.5	.3	-1.5
MIN	39	6	24	1432²	1579	9.9	200	503	937	13.4	4.77	90	.281	.345	-94	-74	103	101	.980	118	168	.5	-7.3	.2	-1.1	-2.4
SEA	33	5	27	1439²	1590	9.9	171	585	944	13.9	4.65	91	.283	.355	-76	-65	102	105	.975	156	191	-1.7	-6.4	-3.2	-1.7	-1.0
TOT	355	123	524	20203¹		9.0				12.7	4.18		.262	.332					.979	1780	2159					

Runs		Hits		Doubles		Triples		Home Runs		Total Bases	
Henderson-NY	130	Mattingly-NY	238	Mattingly-NY	53	Butler-Cle	14	Barfield-Tor	40	Mattingly-NY	388
Puckett-Min	119	Puckett-Min	223	Boggs-Bos	47	Sierra-Tex	10	Kingman-Oak	35	Puckett-Min	365
Mattingly-NY	117	Fernandez-Tor	213	Rice-Bos	39	Fernandez-Tor	9	Gaetti-Min	34	Carter-Cle	341
Carter-Cle	108	Boggs-Bos	207	Buckner-Bos	39	Carter-Cle	9	Deer-Mil	33	Bell-Tor	341
				Barrett-Bos	39			Canseco-Oak	33	Barfield-Tor	329

Runs Batted In		Runs Produced		Bases On Balls		Batting Average		On Base Percentage		Slugging Average	
Carter-Cle	121	Carter-Cle	200	Boggs-Bos	105	Boggs-Bos	.357	Boggs-Bos	.455	Mattingly-NY	.573
Canseco-Oak	117	Mattingly-NY	199	Evans-Bos	97	Mattingly-NY	.352	P.Bradley-Sea	.406	Barfield-Tor	.559
Mattingly-NY	113	Rice-Bos	188	Randolph-NY	94	Puckett-Min	.328	Brett-KC	.404	Puckett-Min	.537
Rice-Bos	110	Puckett-Min	184	Jackson-Cal	92	Tabler-Cle	.326	Murray-Bal	.400	Bell-Tor	.532
		Bell-Tor	178	Evans-Det	91	Rice-Bos	.324	Mattingly-NY	.399	Gaetti-Min	.518

Production		Adjusted Production		Batter Runs		Adjusted Batter Runs		Clutch Hitting Index		Runs Created	
Mattingly-NY	.973	Mattingly-NY	163	Mattingly-NY	55.6	Mattingly-NY	56.7	Downing-Cal	132	Mattingly-NY	150
Boggs-Bos	.942	Boggs-Bos	156	Boggs-Bos	51.6	Boggs-Bos	51.3	Winfield-NY	132	Boggs-Bos	133
Barfield-Tor	.929	Barfield-Tor	145	Barfield-Tor	39.0	Barfield-Tor	37.1	Rice-Bos	128	Puckett-Min	127
Puckett-Min	.903	Puckett-Min	138	Puckett-Min	37.1	Puckett-Min	35.0	Murray-Bal	127	Barfield-Tor	122
Brett-KC	.885	Rice-Bos	137	Rice-Bos	32.6	Rice-Bos	32.4	Joyner-Cal	125	Carter-Cle	116

Total Average		Stolen Bases		Stolen Base Average		Stolen Base Runs		Fielding Runs		Total Player Rating	
Boggs-Bos	.987	Henderson-NY	87	Felder-Mil	88.9	Henderson-NY	15.3	Owen-Sea-Bos	31.9	Barfield-Tor	4.9
Mattingly-NY	.969	Pettis-Cal	50	Davis-Oak	87.1	Pettis-Cal	7.2	Reynolds-Sea	29.0	Ripken-Bal	4.3
Gibson-Det	.950	Cangelosi-Chi	50	Gibson-Det	85.0	Gibson-Det	6.6	Barfield-Tor	20.9	Boggs-Bos	4.3
Barfield-Tor	.931	Wilson-KC	34	Henderson-NY	82.9	Davis-Oak	5.7	Pettis-Cal	20.7	Rice-Bos	4.2
Henderson-NY	.931	Gibson-Det	34			Wilson-KC	5.4	Buckner-Bos	20.1	Henderson-NY	4.2

Wins		Win Percentage		Games		Complete Games		Shutouts		Saves	
Clemens-Bos	24	Clemens-Bos	.857	Williams-Tex	80	Candiotti-Cle	17	Morris-Det	6	Righetti-NY	46
Morris-Det	21	Rasmussen-NY	.750	Righetti-NY	74	Blyleven-Min	16	Hurst-Bos	4	Aase-Bal	34
Higuera-Mil	20	Morris-Det	.724	Harris-Tex	73	Morris-Det	15	Higuera-Mil	4	Henke-Tor	27
Witt-Cal	18	Higuera-Mil	.645	Eichhorn-Tor	69	Higuera-Mil	15			Hernandez-Det	24
Rasmussen-NY	18	Witt-Cal	.643			Witt-Cal	14			Moore-Cal	21

Innings Pitched		Fewest Hits/Game		Fewest BB/Game		Strikeouts		Strikeouts/Game		Ratio	
Blyleven-Min	271.2	Clemens-Bos	6.34	Guidry-NY	1.78	Langston-Sea	245	Langston-Sea	9.21	Clemens-Bos	8.86
Witt-Cal	269.0	Rasmussen-NY	7.13	Boyd-Bos	1.89	Clemens-Bos	238	Hurst-Bos	8.62	Witt-Cal	9.84
Morris-Det	267.0	Witt-Cal	7.29	Blyleven-Min	1.92	Morris-Det	223	Clemens-Bos	8.43	Morris-Det	10.48
Moore-Sea	266.0	Hough-Tex	7.35	Wegman-Mil	1.95	Blyleven-Min	215	Correa-Tex	8.41	Rasmussen-NY	10.51
Clemens-Bos	254.0	Cowley-Chi	7.37	Sutton-Cal	2.13	Witt-Cal	208	Rijo-Oak	8.18	Sutton-Cal	10.61

Earned Run Average		Adjusted ERA		Opponents' Batting Avg.		Opponents' On Base Pct.		Starter Runs		Adjusted Starter Runs	
Clemens-Bos	2.48	Clemens-Bos	168	Clemens-Bos	.195	Clemens-Bos	.253	Clemens-Bos	47.8	Clemens-Bos	47.5
Higuera-Mil	2.79	Higuera-Mil	155	Rasmussen-NY	.217	Witt-Cal	.277	Witt-Cal	39.8	Higuera-Mil	42.4
Witt-Cal	2.84	Witt-Cal	144	Witt-Cal	.221	Morris-Det	.287	Higuera-Mil	38.2	Witt-Cal	37.8
Hurst-Bos	2.99	Hurst-Bos	139	Hough-Tex	.221	Sutton-Cal	.288	Morris-Det	26.9	Morris-Det	25.3
D.Jackson-KC	3.20	D.Jackson-KC	133	Correa-Tex	.223	Rasmussen-NY	.290	Hurst-Bos	22.9	Hurst-Bos	22.6

Clutch Pitching Index		Relief Runs		Adjusted Relief Runs		Relief Ranking		Total Pitcher Index		Total Baseball Ranking	
Hurst-Bos	123	Eichhorn-Tor	42.8	Eichhorn-Tor	43.6	Eichhorn-Tor	56.2	Clemens-Bos	5.0	Clemens-Bos	5.0
D.Jackson-KC	121	Righetti-NY	20.5	Righetti-NY	19.4	Righetti-NY	45.1	Eichhorn-Tor	4.4	Barfield-Tor	4.9
Higuera-Mil	119	Harris-Tex	16.7	Harris-Tex	18.2	Harris-Tex	33.8	Witt-Cal	4.3	Eichhorn-Tor	4.4
Stieb-Tor	119	Clear-Mil	16.2	Clear-Mil	17.4	Clear-Mil	29.8	Higuera-Mil	4.2	Ripken-Bal	4.3
Niekro-Cle	117	Mohorcic-Tex	14.7	Mohorcic-Tex	15.8	Plesac-Mil	27.9	Morris-Det	2.6	Boggs-Bos	4.3

TEAM	G	W	L	PCT	GB	R	OR	AB	H	2B	3B	HR	BB	SO	AVG	OBP	SLG	PRO	PRO+	BR	/A	PF	CHI	RC	SB	CS	SBA	SBR
EAST																												
STL	162	95	67	.586		798	693	5500	1449	252	49	94	**644**	933	.263	**.343**	.378	.721	95	-9	-23	102	**109**	740	**248**	72	78	**31**
NY	162	92	70	.568	3	**823**	698	5601	**1499**	287	34	192	592	1012	.268	.341	.434	**.775**	117	81	120	95	100	**848**	159	49	76	18
MON	162	91	71	.562	4	741	720	5527	1467	**310**	39	120	501	918	.265	.330	.401	.731	96	-6	-28	103	103	734	166	74	69	5
PIT	162	80	82	.494	15	723	744	5536	1464	282	45	131	535	914	.264	.332	.403	.735	99	3	-1	101	98	741	140	58	71	7
PHI	162	80	82	.494	15	702	749	5475	1390	248	**51**	169	587	1109	.254	.329	.410	.739	98	8	-15	103	95	736	111	49	69	4
CHI	161	76	85	.472	18.5	720	801	5583	1475	244	33	**209**	504	1064	.264	.327	.432	.759	102	40	12	104	94	785	109	48	69	4
WEST																												
SF	162	90	72	.556		783	**669**	5608	1458	274	32	205	511	1094	.260	.326	.430	.756	110	33	68	95	102	768	126	97	57	-20
CIN	162	84	78	.519	6	783	752	5560	1478	262	29	192	514	928	.266	.331	.427	.758	102	42	10	104	102	786	169	46	**79**	23
HOU	162	76	86	.469	14	648	678	5485	1386	238	28	122	526	936	.253	.321	.373	.694	94	-78	-51	96	100	669	162	46	78	21
LA	162	73	89	.451	17	635	675	5517	1389	236	23	125	445	923	.252	.311	.371	.682	88	-108	-89	97	104	627	128	59	68	3
ATL	161	69	92	.429	20.5	747	829	5428	1401	284	24	152	641	**834**	.258	.341	.403	.744	98	28	-8	105	98	747	135	68	67	0
SD	162	65	97	.401	25	668	763	5456	1419	209	48	113	577	992	.260	.334	.378	.712	99	-34	-8	96	96	693	198	91	69	5
TOT	971					8771		66276	17275	3126	435	1824	6577	11657	.261	.331	.404	.734							1851	757	71	101

TEAM	CG	SH	SV	IP	H	H/G	HR	BB	SO	RAT	ERA	ERA+	OAV	OOB	PR	/A	PF	CPI	FA	E	DP	FW	PW	BW	SBW	DIF
EAST																										
STL	10	7	48	1466	1484	9.1	**129**	533	873	12.5	3.91	106	.265	.332	28	40	102	103	**.982**	**116**	172	.9	4.0	-2.3	**2.2**	9.2
NY	16	7	**51**	1454	1407	8.7	135	510	1032	12.1	3.84	98	.254	.321	38	-11	93	97	.978	137	137	-.3	-1.1	**11.9**	1.0	-.5
MON	16	8	50	1450¹	1428	8.9	145	**446**	1012	**11.8**	3.92	**107**	.257	**.315**	26	**46**	103	95	.976	147	122	-.9	**4.6**	-2.8	-.3	9.4
PIT	**25**	**13**	39	1445	1377	8.6	164	562	914	12.2	4.20	98	.253	.326	-19	-14	101	95	.980	123	147	.5	-1.4	-.0	-.1	-1.2
PHI	13	7	48	1448¹	1453	9.0	167	587	877	12.9	4.18	101	.263	.338	-16	9	104	103	.980	121	137	.6	.9	-1.5	-.4	-.6
CHI	11	5	48	1434²	1524	9.6	159	628	1024	13.7	4.55	94	.275	.352	-76	-44	105	103	.979	130	154	.0	-4.4	1.2	-.4	-.9
WEST																										
SF	19	10	38	1471	1407	8.6	146	547	1038	12.1	**3.68**	105	.255	.325	66	27	94	**106**	.980	129	**183**	.1	2.7	6.8	-2.8	2.2
CIN	7	6	44	1452¹	1486	9.2	170	485	919	12.4	4.24	100	.267	.328	-27	-0	104	99	.979	130	137	.0	.0	1.0	1.5	.5
HOU	13	13	33	1441¹	**1363**	8.5	141	525	**1137**	12.0	3.84	102	**.250**	.319	38	12	96	96	.981	116	113	.9	1.2	-5.1	1.3	-3.2
LA	**29**	8	32	1455	1415	8.8	130	565	1097	12.4	3.72	107	.255	.327	59	40	97	103	.975	155	144	-1.3	4.0	-8.9	-.5	-1.2
ATL	16	4	32	1427²	1529	9.6	163	587	837	13.6	4.63	94	.276	.350	-87	-45	107	101	**.982**	116	170	.8	-4.5	-.8	-.8	-6.2
SD	14	10	33	1433¹	1402	8.8	175	602	897	12.8	4.27	93	.256	.334	-30	-50	97	98	.976	147	135	-.9	-5.0	-.8	-.3	-9.0
TOT	189	98	496	17379		8.9				12.5	4.08		.261	.331					.979	1567	1751					

Runs		Hits		Doubles		Triples		Home Runs		Total Bases	
Raines-Mon	123	Gwynn-SD	218	Wallach-Mon	42	Samuel-Phi	15	Dawson-Chi	49	Dawson-Chi	353
Coleman-StL	121	Guerrero-LA	184	Smith-StL	40	Gwynn-SD	13	Murphy-Atl	44	Samuel-Phi	329
Davis-Cin	120	Smith-StL	182	Galarraga-Mon	40	VanSlyke-Pit	11	Strawberry-NY	39	Murphy-Atl	328
Gwynn-SD	119	Coleman-StL	180			McGee-StL	11	Davis-Cin	37	Strawberry-NY	310
Murphy-Atl	115					Coleman-StL	10	Johnson-NY	36	Clark-SF	307

Runs Batted In		Runs Produced		Bases On Balls		Batting Average		On Base Percentage		Slugging Average	
Dawson-Chi	137	Wallach-Mon	186	Clark-StL	136	Gwynn-SD	.370	Clark-StL	.461	Clark-StL	.597
Wallach-Mon	123	Samuel-Phi	185	Hayes-Phi	121	Guerrero-LA	.338	Gwynn-SD	.450	Davis-Cin	.593
Schmidt-Phi	113	Davis-Cin	183	Murphy-Atl	115	Raines-Mon	.330	Raines-Mon	.431	Strawberry-NY	.583
Clark-StL	106	Smith-StL	179	Strawberry-NY	97	Kruk-SD	.313	Guerrero-LA	.421	Clark-SF	.580
		Dawson-Chi	178	Raines-Mon	90	James-Atl	.312	Murphy-Atl	.420	Murphy-Atl	.580

Production		Adjusted Production		Batter Runs		Adjusted Batter Runs		Clutch Hitting Index		Runs Created	
Clark-StL	1.058	Clark-StL	174	Clark-StL	54.3	Clark-StL	53.0	Herr-StL	200	Murphy-Atl	143
Murphy-Atl	1.000	Strawberry-NY	165	Murphy-Atl	53.3	Gwynn-SD	52.4	McGee-StL	147	Gwynn-SD	143
Davis-Cin	.994	Gwynn-SD	160	Gwynn-SD	49.6	Murphy-Atl	49.3	Pendleton-StL	142	Strawberry-NY	132
Strawberry-NY	.984	Guerrero-LA	156	Strawberry-NY	44.7	Strawberry-NY	48.6	Wallach-Mon	136	Raines-Mon	132
Gwynn-SD	.961	Clark-SF	155	Raines-Mon	43.2	Guerrero-LA	44.5	Kruk-SD	133	Clark-StL	127

Total Average		Stolen Bases		Stolen Base Average		Stolen Base Runs		Fielding Runs		Total Player Rating	
Clark-StL	1.258	Coleman-StL	109	Sandberg-Chi	91.3	Coleman-StL	19.5	Hubbard-Atl	28.2	Davis-Cin	7.1
Davis-Cin	1.182	Gwynn-SD	56	Raines-Mon	90.9	Raines-Mon	12.0	Davis-Cin	28.1	Gwynn-SD	6.4
Raines-Mon	1.133	Hatcher-Hou	53	Davis-Cin	89.3	Davis-Cin	11.4	Bonds-Pit	19.7	Raines-Mon	6.2
Murphy-Atl	1.106	Raines-Mon	50	Hatcher-Hou	85.5	Hatcher-Hou	10.5	Smith-StL	19.3	Murphy-Atl	5.6
Strawberry-NY	1.103	Davis-Cin	50	Coleman-StL	83.2	Gwynn-SD	9.6	Hernandez-NY	17.7	Strawberry-NY	4.8

Wins		Win Percentage		Games		Complete Games		Shutouts		Saves	
Sutcliffe-Chi	18	Gooden-NY	.682	Tekulve-Phi	90	Reuschel-Pit-SF	12	Reuschel-Pit-SF	4	Bedrosian-Phi	40
Rawley-Phi	17	Sutcliffe-Chi	.643	Murphy-Cin	87	Valenzuela-LA	12	Welch-LA	4	Smith-Chi	36
Scott-Hou	16	Welch-LA	.625	Williams-Cin	85	Hershiser-LA	10			Worrell-StL	33
Hershiser-LA	16	Rawley-Phi	.607	J.Robinson-SF-Pit	81	Z.Smith-Atl	9			Franco-Cin	32
		Z.Smith-Atl	.600	McCullers-SD	78	Scott-Hou	8			McDowell-NY	25

Innings Pitched		Fewest Hits/Game		Fewest BB/Game		Strikeouts		Strikeouts/Game		Ratio	
Hershiser-LA	264.2	Ryan-Hou	6.55	Reuschel-Pit-SF	1.67	Ryan-Hou	270	Ryan-Hou	11.48	Reuschel-Pit-SF	10.19
Welch-LA	251.2	Scott-Hou	7.23	Heaton-Mon	1.72	Scott-Hou	233	Scott-Hou	8.47	Scott-Hou	10.25
Valenzuela-LA	251.0	Welch-LA	7.30	Gullickson-Cin	2.13	Sebra-Mon	196	Sebra-Mon	7.92	Ryan-Hou	10.42
Scott-Hou	247.2	Dunne-Pit	7.88	Forsch-StL	2.26	Valenzuela-LA	190	Gooden-NY	7.41	Welch-LA	10.51
Z.Smith-Atl	242.0	Darling-NY	7.93	Drabek-Pit	2.35	Hershiser-LA	190	Darling-NY	7.24	Drabek-Pit	10.77

Earned Run Average		Adjusted ERA		Opponents' Batting Avg.		Opponents' On Base Pct.		Starter Runs		Adjusted Starter Runs	
Ryan-Hou	2.76	Ryan-Hou	142	Ryan-Hou	.199	Scott-Hou	.282	Ryan-Hou	30.9	Ryan-Hou	27.1
Dunne-Pit	3.03	Dunne-Pit	136	Scott-Hou	.217	Ryan-Hou	.284	Hershiser-LA	30.0	Hershiser-LA	26.6
Hershiser-LA	3.06	Reuschel-Pit-SF	131	Welch-LA	.221	Reuschel-Pit-SF	.284	Reuschel-Pit-SF	24.9	Reuschel-Pit-SF	24.1
Reuschel-Pit-SF	3.09	Hershiser-LA	130	Darling-NY	.233	Welch-LA	.291	Welch-LA	24.1	Welch-LA	20.9
Gooden-NY	3.21	Welch-LA	123	Dunne-Pit	.240	Drabek-Pit	.296	Scott-Hou	23.3	Dunne-Pit	19.6

Clutch Pitching Index		Relief Runs		Adjusted Relief Runs		Relief Ranking		Total Pitcher Index		Total Baseball Ranking	
LaCoss-SF	124	Burke-Mon	29.3	Burke-Mon	30.5	Franco-Cin	36.1	Hershiser-LA	3.3	Davis-Cin	7.1
Cox-StL	120	McGaffigan-Mon	22.5	McGaffigan-Mon	24.2	Burke-Mon	34.7	Burke-Mon	3.1	Gwynn-SD	6.4
Dravecky-SD-SF	113	Williams-Cin	20.9	Williams-Cin	22.8	Worrell-StL	33.2	Reuschel-Pit-SF	2.8	Raines-Mon	6.2
Ruffin-Phi	112	J.Robinson-SF-Pit	16.9	Worrell-StL	15.7	Smith-Chi	26.6	Welch-LA	2.5	Murphy-Atl	5.6
Grant-SF-SD	111	Smith-Hou	16.2	Franco-Cin	15.7	Bedrosian-Phi	25.3	Ryan-Hou	2.4	Strawberry-NY	4.8

TEAM	G	W	L	PCT	GB	R	OR	AB	H	2B	3B	HR	BB	SO	AVG	OBP	SLG	PRO	PRO+	BR	/A	PF	CHI	RC	SB	CS	SBA	SBR
EAST																												
DET	162	98	64	.605		**896**	735	5649	1535	274	32	**225**	**653**	913	.272	.352	**.451**	**.803**	**116**	**91**	**127**	96	98	**910**	106	50	68	2
TOR	162	96	66	.593	2	845	**655**	5635	1514	277	38	215	555	970	.269	.338	.446	.784	103	42	27	102	100	841	126	50	72	8
MIL	162	91	71	.562	7	862	817	5625	1552	272	46	163	598	1040	.276	.349	.428	.777	102	40	18	103	101	852	**176**	74	70	8
NY	162	89	73	.549	9	788	758	5511	1445	239	16	196	604	949	.262	.338	.418	.756	100	-6	3	99	100	773	105	43	71	6
BOS	162	78	84	.481	20	842	825	5586	**1554**	273	26	174	606	**825**	**.278**	**.355**	.430	.785	104	61	40	103	97	855	77	45	63	-4
BAL	162	67	95	.414	31	729	880	5576	1437	219	20	211	524	939	.258	.324	.418	.742	98	-47	-26	97	99	736	69	45	61	-6
CLE	162	61	101	.377	37	742	957	5606	1476	267	30	187	489	977	.263	.326	.422	.748	95	-35	-40	101	98	772	140	54	72	10
WEST																												
MIN	162	85	77	.525		786	806	5441	1422	258	35	196	523	898	.261	.330	.430	.760	96	-8	-35	104	103	757	113	65	63	-5
KC	162	83	79	.512	2	715	691	5499	1443	239	40	168	523	1034	.262	.330	.412	.742	93	-40	-59	102	97	747	125	43	**74**	**12**
OAK	162	81	81	.500	4	806	789	5511	1432	263	33	199	593	1056	.260	.336	.428	.764	108	4	58	93	101	796	140	63	69	4
SEA	162	78	84	.481	7	760	801	5508	1499	282	**48**	161	500	863	.272	.337	.428	.765	96	9	-31	105	96	788	174	73	70	8
CHI	162	77	85	.475	8	748	746	5538	1427	**283**	36	173	487	971	.258	.321	.415	.736	91	-57	-75	102	103	737	138	52	73	10
TEX	162	75	87	.463	10	823	849	5564	1478	264	35	194	567	1081	.266	.336	.430	.766	101	9	8	100	102	798	120	71	63	-7
CAL	162	75	87	.463	10	770	803	5570	1406	257	26	172	590	926	.252	.328	.401	.729	95	-65	-37	97	**105**	744	125	44	**74**	11
TOT	1134					11112		77819	20620	3667	461	2634	7812	13442	.265	.336	.425	.761							1734	772	69	57

TEAM	CG	SH	SV	IP	H	H/G	HR	BB	SO	RAT	ERA	ERA+	OAV	OOB	PR	/A	PF	CPI	FA	E	DP	FW	PW	BW	SBW	DIF
EAST																										
DET	33	10	31	1456	1430	8.8	180	563	976	12.5	4.02	105	.256	.328	70	32	95	103	.980	122	147	.1	3.1	**12.1**	-.2	1.9
TOR	18	8	43	1454	**1323**	**8.2**	158	567	1064	**11.8**	**3.74**	**120**	**.244**	**.318**	**115**	**121**	101	100	.982	111	148	.8	**11.5**	2.6	.4	-.3
MIL	28	6	45	1464	1548	9.5	169	529	1039	12.9	4.62	99	.271	.336	-27	-8	103	96	.976	145	155	-1.3	-.8	1.7	.4	10.0
NY	19	10	**47**	1446^{1}	1475	9.2	179	542	900	12.8	4.36	101	.266	.334	16	5	98	101	.983	102	155	1.3	.5	.3	.2	5.7
BOS	**47**	**13**	16	1436	1584	9.9	190	517	1034	13.4	4.77	95	.282	.346	-50	-37	102	102	.982	110	158	.8	-3.5	3.8	-.8	-3.4
BAL	17	6	30	1439^{2}	1555	9.7	226	547	870	13.3	5.01	88	.276	.343	-88	-97	99	98	.982	111	**174**	.8	-9.2	-2.5	-1.0	-2.1
CLE	24	8	25	1422^{2}	1566	9.9	219	606	849	14.1	5.28	86	.278	.354	-131	-120	102	97	.975	153	128	-1.8	-11.4	-3.8	.6	-3.5
WEST																										
MIN	16	4	39	1427^{1}	1465	9.2	210	564	990	13.1	4.63	100	.266	.339	-27	-2	104	100	**.984**	**98**	147	**1.6**	-.2	-3.3	-.9	6.8
KC	44	11	26	1424	1424	9.0	**128**	548	923	12.7	3.86	118	.261	.333	95	111	102	**105**	.979	131	151	-.5	10.6	-5.6	**.8**	-3.3
OAK	18	6	40	1445^{2}	1442	9.0	176	531	1042	12.5	4.32	96	.258	.327	22	-31	93	96	.977	142	122	-1.1	-3.0	5.5	.0	-1.4
SEA	39	10	33	1430^{2}	1503	9.5	199	**497**	919	12.8	4.49	105	.272	.335	-5	37	106	102	.980	122	150	.1	3.5	-3.0	.4	-4.0
CHI	29	12	37	1447^{2}	1436	8.9	189	537	792	12.5	4.30	107	.259	.329	26	46	103	99	.981	116	**174**	.5	4.4	-7.1	.6	-2.3
TEX	20	3	27	1444^{1}	1388	8.6	199	760	**1103**	13.7	4.63	97	.253	.350	-28	-25	100	100	.976	151	148	-1.7	-2.4	.8	-1.1	-1.6
CAL	20	7	36	1457^{1}	1481	9.1	212	504	941	12.5	4.38	98	.264	.329	13	-13	97	101	.981	117	162	.4	-1.2	-3.5	.7	-2.3
TOT	372	114	475	20195^{2}		9.2				12.9	4.46		.265	.336					.980	1731	2119					

Runs
Molitor-Mil 114
Bell-Tor 111
Whitaker-Det 110
Downing-Cal 110

Hits
Seitzer-KC 207
Puckett-Min 207
Trammell-Det 205
Boggs-Bos 200
Yount-Mil 198

Doubles
Molitor-Mil 41
Boggs-Bos 40

Triples
Wilson-KC 15
Polonia-Oak 10
P.Bradley-Sea 10
Yount-Mil 9

Home Runs
McGwire-Oak 49
Bell-Tor 47

Total Bases
Bell-Tor 369
McGwire-Oak 344
Puckett-Min 333
Trammell-Det 329
Boggs-Bos 324

Runs Batted In
Bell-Tor 134
Evans-Bos 123
McGwire-Oak 118
Joyner-Cal 117
Mattingly-NY 115

Runs Produced
Evans-Bos 198
Bell-Tor 198
Trammell-Det 186
Joyner-Cal 183
Yount-Mil 181

Bases On Balls
Evans-Bos 106
Downing-Cal 106
Boggs-Bos 105
Evans-Det 100
Butler-Cle 91

Batting Average
Boggs-Bos .... .363
Molitor-Mil .... .353
Trammell-Det ...... .343
Puckett-Min .... .332
Mattingly-NY ...... .327

On Base Percentage
Boggs-Bos .... .467
Molitor-Mil .... .438
Evans-Bos .... .422
Randolph-NY ...... .415
Trammell-Det ...... .406

Slugging Average
McGwire-Oak ..... .618
Bell-Tor .... .605
Boggs-Bos .... .588
Evans-Bos .... .569
Molitor-Mil .... .566

Production
Boggs-Bos 1.055
Molitor-Mil 1.004
McGwire-Oak ..... .992
Evans-Bos .... .991
Bell-Tor .... .962

Adjusted Production
Boggs-Bos 173
McGwire-Oak 168
Molitor-Mil 159
Trammell-Det 157
Evans-Bos 155

Batter Runs
Boggs-Bos 66.6
Evans-Bos 49.6
Molitor-Mil 44.8
McGwire-Oak 44.2
Trammell-Det 43.7

Adjusted Batter Runs
Boggs-Bos 64.4
McGwire-Oak 49.8
Trammell-Det 47.4
Evans-Bos 47.4
Molitor-Mil 43.0

Clutch Hitting Index
Griffin-Oak 132
Brock-Mil 132
Baines-Chi 130
Braggs-Mil 127
Tabler-Cle 127

Runs Created
Boggs-Bos 154
Trammell-Det 137
Evans-Bos 134
McGwire-Oak 131
Molitor-Mil 125

Total Average
Molitor-Mil 1.171
Boggs-Bos 1.169
Evans-Bos 1.059
McGwire-Oak ... 1.042
Trammell-Det 1.015

Stolen Bases
Reynolds-Sea 60
Wilson-KC 59
Redus-Chi 52
Molitor-Mil 45
Henderson-NY 41

Stolen Base Average
McDowell-Tex 92.3
Trammell-Det 91.3
Schofield-Cal 86.4
Moseby-Tor 84.8
Wilson-KC 84.3

Stolen Base Runs
Wilson-KC 11.1
Redus-Chi 9.0
Moseby-Tor 7.5
Molitor-Mil 7.5
Henderson-NY 7.5

Fielding Runs
Barrett-Bos 32.3
Salazar-KC 21.8
Manrique-Chi 18.9
Reynolds-Sea 18.8
Gagne-Min 16.9

Total Player Rating
Boggs-Bos 6.0
Trammell-Det 5.2
Molitor-Mil 3.8
Henderson-NY 3.6
Bell-Tor 3.2

Wins
Stewart-Oak 20
Clemens-Bos 20
Langston-Sea 19

Win Percentage
Clemens-Bos ...... .690
Key-Tor .... .680
Saberhagen-KC ... .643
Higuera-Mil .... .643

Games
Eichhorn-Tor 89
Williams-Tex 85
Mohorcic-Tex 74
Henke-Tor 72
Musselman-Tor 68

Complete Games
Clemens-Bos 18
Saberhagen-KC ... 15
Hurst-Bos 15
Langston-Sea 14
Higuera-Mil 14

Shutouts
Clemens-Bos 7
Saberhagen-KC 4

Saves
Henke-Tor 34
Righetti-NY 31
Reardon-Min 31
Plesac-Mil 23
Buice-Cal 17

Innings Pitched
Hough-Tex 285.1
Clemens-Bos 281.2
Langston-Sea ... 272.0
Blyleven-Min 267.0
Morris-Det 266.0

Fewest Hits/Game
Key-Tor 7.24
Hough-Tex 7.51
Morris-Det 7.68
Stewart-Oak 7.71
DeLeon-Chi 7.73

Fewest BB/Game
Long-Chi 1.49
Saberhagen-KC .. 1.86
Sutton-Cal 1.93
Bannister-Chi 1.93
Young-Oak 1.95

Strikeouts
Langston-Sea 262
Clemens-Bos 256
Higuera-Mil 240
Hough-Tex 223
Morris-Det 208

Strikeouts/Game
Langston-Sea 8.67
Higuera-Mil 8.25
Clemens-Bos 8.18
Bosio-Mil 7.94
Nieves-Mil 7.50

Ratio
Key-Tor 9.59
Bannister-Chi ... 10.43
Saberhagen-KC . 10.68
Young-Oak 10.68
Viola-Min 10.80

Earned Run Average
Key-Tor 2.76
Viola-Min 2.90
Clemens-Bos 2.97
Saberhagen-KC .. 3.36
Morris-Det 3.38

Adjusted ERA
Key-Tor 163
Viola-Min 159
Clemens-Bos 153
Saberhagen-KC .. 135
Leibrandt-KC 134

Opponents' Batting Avg.
Key-Tor .... .221
Hough-Tex .... .223
Morris-Det .... .228
Stewart-Oak ...... .229
DeLeon-Chi .... .230

Opponents' On Base Pct.
Key-Tor .... .273
Bannister-Chi ..... .286
Viola-Min .... .294
Morris-Det .... .294
Young-Oak .... .295

Starter Runs
Key-Tor 49.2
Clemens-Bos 46.5
Viola-Min 43.6
Morris-Det 31.7
Saberhagen-KC .. 31.2

Adjusted Starter Runs
Key-Tor 50.3
Clemens-Bos 49.0
Viola-Min 48.1
Saberhagen-KC .. 34.0
Leibrandt-KC 30.6

Clutch Pitching Index
Viola-Min 115
Rhoden-NY 112
Terrell-Det 110
Blyleven-Min 109
Gubicza-KC 107

Relief Runs
Henke-Tor 20.5
Eckersley-Oak ... 18.3
Eichhorn-Tor 18.2
Thigpen-Chi 17.1
Plesac-Mil 16.3

Adjusted Relief Runs
Henke-Tor 20.9
Eichhorn-Tor 18.7
Thigpen-Chi 18.3
Plesac-Mil 17.3
Mohorcic-Tex 16.4

Relief Ranking
Plesac-Mil 32.9
Thigpen-Chi 29.6
Henke-Tor 29.0
Mohorcic-Tex 25.2
Eichhorn-Tor 22.4

Total Pitcher Index
Key-Tor 5.2
Viola-Min 4.8
Clemens-Bos 4.8
Leibrandt-KC 3.5
Saberhagen-KC ... 3.5

Total Baseball Ranking
Boggs-Bos 6.0
Key-Tor 5.2
Trammell-Det 5.2
Viola-Min 4.8
Clemens-Bos 4.8

TEAM	G	W	L	PCT	GB	R	OR	AB	H	2B	3B	HR	BB	SO	AVG	OBP	SLG	PRO	PRO+	BR	/A	PF	CHI	RC	SB	CS	SBA	SBR
EAST																												
NY	160	100	60	.625		**703**	532	5408	1387	251	24	**152**	544	842	.256	**.328**	**.396**	**.724**	120	95	126	95	97	**717**	140	51	73	11
PIT	160	85	75	.531	15	651	616	5379	1327	240	45	110	**553**	947	.247	.321	.369	.690	105	33	42	99	99	648	119	60	66	0
MON	163	81	81	.500	20	628	592	5573	1400	260	**48**	107	454	1053	.251	.311	.373	.684	98	12	-17	105	97	636	189	89	68	3
CHI	163	77	85	.475	24	660	694	5675	**1481**	262	46	113	403	910	**.261**	.312	.383	.695	100	31	2	105	99	673	120	46	72	8
STL	162	76	86	.469	25	578	633	5518	1373	207	33	71	484	**827**	.249	.312	.337	.649	92	-47	-53	101	98	601	**234**	64	**79**	32
PHI	162	65	96	.404	35.5	597	734	5403	1294	246	31	106	489	981	.239	.308	.355	.663	94	-22	-35	102	100	599	112	49	70	4
WEST																												
LA	162	94	67	.584		628	544	5431	1346	217	25	99	437	947	.248	.308	.352	.660	99	-32	-13	97	**107**	590	131	46	74	12
CIN	161	87	74	.540	7	641	596	5426	1334	246	25	122	479	922	.246	.311	.368	.679	97	6	-19	104	102	639	207	56	**79**	29
SD	161	83	78	.516	11	594	583	5366	1325	205	35	94	494	892	.247	.313	.351	.664	99	-19	-8	98	99	594	123	50	71	7
SF	162	83	79	.512	11.5	670	626	5450	1353	227	44	113	550	1023	.248	.321	.368	.689	99	32	59	96	101	642	121	78	61	-11
HOU	162	82	80	.506	12.5	617	631	5494	1338	239	31	96	474	840	.244	.308	.351	.659	99	-32	-7	96	103	604	198	71	74	17
ATL	160	54	106	.338	39.5	555	741	5440	1319	228	28	96	432	848	.242	.301	.348	.649	88	-56	-87	105	99	549	95	69	58	-13
TOT	969					7522		65563	16277	2828	415	1279	5793	11032	.248	.313	.363	.675							1789	729	71	99

TEAM	CG	SH	SV	IP	H	H/G	HR	BB	SO	RAT	ERA	ERA+	OAV	OOB	PR	/A	PF	CPI	FA	E	DP	FW	PW	BW	SBW	DIF
EAST																										
NY	31	22	46	1439	**1253**	7.8	78	404	**1100**	10.6	2.91	111	**.235**	.293	86	50	93	97	**.981**	115	127	.9	5.4	**13.6**	.3	-.2
PIT	12	11	46	1440²	1349	8.4	108	469	790	11.6	3.47	98	.250	.314	-3	-10	99	101	.980	125	128	.3	-1.1	4.5	-.9	2.1
MON	18	12	43	1482²	1310	8.0	122	476	923	11.1	3.08	**117**	.238	.303	60	84	104	**105**	.978	142	145	-.5	**9.1**	-1.8	-.6	-6.2
CHI	30	10	29	1464¹	1494	9.2	115	490	897	12.4	3.84	94	.265	.327	-64	-38	105	102	.980	125	128	.5	-4.1	.2	-.0	-.5
STL	17	14	42	1470²	1387	8.5	91	486	881	11.6	3.47	100	.252	.314	-4	1	101	99	**.981**	121	131	.6	.1	-5.7	**2.6**	-2.6
PHI	16	6	36	1433	1447	9.1	118	628	859	13.3	4.14	86	.265	.344	-110	-92	103	102	.976	145	139	-.7	-9.9	-3.8	-.5	-.6
WEST																										
LA	**32**	**24**	**49**	1463¹	1291	7.9	84	473	1029	11.0	2.96	112	.237	.301	78	59	97	102	.977	142	126	-.5	6.4	-1.4	.4	8.7
CIN	24	13	43	1455	1271	7.9	121	504	934	11.1	3.35	107	.237	.306	16	38	104	98	.980	125	131	.4	4.1	-2.0	2.2	1.9
SD	30	9	39	1449	1332	8.3	112	439	885	11.1	3.28	104	.247	.306	27	19	99	102	**.981**	120	**147**	.6	2.0	-.9	-.1	.8
SF	25	13	42	1462¹	1323	8.1	99	422	875	10.9	3.39	96	.242	.300	10	-20	95	93	.980	129	145	.2	-2.2	6.4	-2.1	-.3
HOU	21	15	40	1474²	1339	8.2	123	478	1049	11.3	3.41	97	.242	.307	7	-14	96	99	.978	138	124	-.3	-1.5	-.8	.9	2.6
ATL	14	4	25	1446	1481	9.2	108	524	810	12.7	4.09	90	.268	.336	-103	-67	107	100	.976	151	138	-1.1	-7.2	-9.4	-2.3	-6.0
TOT	270	153	480	17480²		8.4				11.6	3.45		.248	.313					.979	1578	1609					

Runs		Hits		Doubles		Triples		Home Runs		Total Bases	
Butler-SF	109	Galarraga-Mon	184	Galarraga-Mon	42	VanSlyke-Pit	15	Strawberry-NY	39	Galarraga-Mon	329
Gibson-LA	106	Dawson-Chi	179	Palmeiro-Chi	41	Coleman-StL	10	Davis-Hou	30	Dawson-Chi	298
Clark-SF	102	Palmeiro-Chi	178	Sabo-Cin	40	Young-Hou	9	Galarraga-Mon	29	VanSlyke-Pit	297
VanSlyke-Pit	101	Sax-LA	175	Bream-Pit	37	Samuel-Phi	9	Clark-SF	29	Strawberry-NY	296
Strawberry-NY	101	Larkin-Cin	174			Butler-SF	9	McReynolds-NY	27	Clark-SF	292

Runs Batted In		Runs Produced		Bases On Balls		Batting Average		On Base Percentage		Slugging Average	
Clark-SF	109	Clark-SF	182	Clark-SF	100	Gwynn-SD	.313	Daniels-Cin	.400	Strawberry-NY	.545
Strawberry-NY	101	VanSlyke-Pit	176	Butler-SF	97	Palmeiro-Chi	.307	Butler-SF	.395	Galarraga-Mon	.540
VanSlyke-Pit	100	Strawberry-NY	163	Daniels-Cin	87	Perry-Atl	.303	Clark-SF	.392	Clark-SF	.508
Bonilla-Pit	100	Bonilla-Pit	163	Johnson-NY	86	Galarraga-Mon	.302	Gibson-LA	.381	VanSlyke-Pit	.506
		Galarraga-Mon	162			Perry-Atl	.300	Gwynn-SD	.374	Dawson-Chi	.504

Production		Adjusted Production		Batter Runs		Adjusted Batter Runs		Clutch Hitting Index		Runs Created	
Strawberry-NY	.916	Strawberry-NY	168	Clark-SF	44.3	Clark-SF	47.3	Moreland-SD	142	Clark-SF	120
Clark-SF	.900	Clark-SF	163	Strawberry-NY	42.0	Strawberry-NY	45.3	Perry-Atl	129	Galarraga-Mon	114
Galarraga-Mon	.894	Gibson-LA	151	Galarraga-Mon	39.2	Galarraga-Mon	36.1	Doran-Hou	124	Strawberry-NY	111
Gibson-LA	.864	Bonds-Pit	147	Gibson-LA	33.8	Gibson-LA	35.8	Maldonado-SF	124	Gibson-LA	107
Daniels-Cin	.863	Galarraga-Mon	147	Daniels-Cin	33.2	Bonilla-Pit	33.2	Davis-Cin	123	VanSlyke-Pit	107

Total Average		Stolen Bases		Stolen Base Average		Stolen Base Runs		Fielding Runs		Total Player Rating	
Strawberry-NY	.957	Coleman-StL	81	McReynolds-NY	100.0	Smith-StL	11.7	Smith-StL	22.9	Smith-StL	5.1
Clark-SF	.955	Young-Hou	65	Davis-Cin	92.1	McGee-StL	8.7	Bream-Pit	20.9	VanSlyke-Pit	5.1
Gibson-LA	.929	Smith-StL	57	Gibson-LA	88.6	Davis-Cin	8.7	Sabo-Cin	18.8	Strawberry-NY	5.0
Davis-Cin	.927	Sabo-Cin	46	McGee-StL	87.2	Coleman-StL	8.1	Murphy-Atl	17.5	Gibson-LA	4.9
Daniels-Cin	.924	Nixon-Mon	46	Smith-StL	86.4	Larkin-Cin	7.8	VanSlyke-Pit	16.7	Larkin-Cin	4.6

Wins		Win Percentage		Games		Complete Games		Shutouts		Saves	
Jackson-Cin	23	Cone-NY	.870	Murphy-Cin	76	Jackson-Cin	15	Hershiser-LA	8	Franco-Cin	39
Hershiser-LA	23	Browning-Cin	.783	Robinson-Pit	75	Hershiser-LA	15	Leary-LA	6	Gott-Pit	34
Cone-NY	20	Jackson-Cin	.742	Agosto-Hou	75	Show-SD	13	Jackson-Cin	6	Worrell-StL	32
Reuschel-SF	19	Hershiser-LA	.742	Tekulve-Phi	75	Sutcliffe-Chi	12	Scott-Hou	5	Davis-SD	28
		Maddux-Chi	.692	Franco-Cin	70	Gooden-NY	10	Ojeda-NY	5	Bedrosian-Phi	28

Innings Pitched		Fewest Hits/Game		Fewest BB/Game		Strikeouts		Strikeouts/Game		Ratio	
Hershiser-LA	267.0	Fernandez-NY	6.11	B.Smith-Mon	1.45	Ryan-Hou	228	Ryan-Hou	9.33	Perez-Mon	8.81
Jackson-Cin	260.2	Perez-Mon	6.37	Mahler-Atl	1.52	Cone-NY	213	Fernandez-NY	9.10	Scott-Hou	9.18
Browning-Cin	250.2	Rijo-Cin	6.67	Reuschel-SF	1.54	DeLeon-StL	208	Rijo-Cin	8.89	Ojeda-NY	9.22
Mahler-Atl	249.0	Scott-Hou	6.67	Ojeda-NY	1.56	Scott-Hou	190	DeLeon-StL	8.31	Hershiser-LA	9.61
Maddux-Chi	249.0	Cone-NY	6.93	Tudor-StL-LA	1.87	Fernandez-NY	189	Cone-NY	8.29	Jackson-Cin	9.63

Earned Run Average		Adjusted ERA		Opponents' Batting Avg.		Opponents' On Base Pct.		Starter Runs		Adjusted Starter Runs	
Magrane-StL	2.18	Magrane-StL	160	Fernandez-NY	.191	Perez-Mon	.253	Hershiser-LA	35.3	Hershiser-LA	31.8
Cone-NY	2.22	Rijo-Cin	150	Perez-Mon	.196	Scott-Hou	.261	Cone-NY	31.6	Cone-NY	25.8
Hershiser-LA	2.26	Tudor-StL-LA	148	Scott-Hou	.204	Ojeda-NY	.264	Tudor-StL-LA	24.7	Jackson-Cin	24.7
Tudor-StL-LA	2.32	Hershiser-LA	147	Rijo-Cin	.209	Hershiser-LA	.271	Magrane-StL	23.3	Tudor-StL-LA	24.5
Rijo-Cin	2.39	Perez-Mon	147	Cone-NY	.213	Fernandez-NY	.274	Perez-Mon	21.0	Perez-Mon	24.1

Clutch Pitching Index		Relief Runs		Adjusted Relief Runs		Relief Ranking		Total Pitcher Index		Total Baseball Ranking	
Tudor-StL-LA	135	Franco-Cin	17.9	Franco-Cin	19.2	Franco-Cin	43.8	Hershiser-LA	4.3	Smith-StL	5.1
Rawley-Phi	122	Holton-LA	16.4	Holton-LA	15.3	Davis-SD	30.4	Magrane-StL	3.2	VanSlyke-Pit	5.1
Moyer-Chi	118	Pena-LA	16.1	Davis-SD	15.1	Myers-NY	24.7	Jackson-Cin	2.9	Strawberry-NY	5.0
Robinson-SF	113	Davis-SD	15.7	Pena-LA	14.9	Pena-LA	24.7	Cone-NY	2.8	Gibson-LA	4.9
J.Martinez-Mon	112	Myers-NY	13.0	Harris-Phi	14.3	Holton-LA	16.7	J.Martinez-Mon	2.8	Larkin-Cin	4.6

TEAM	G	W	L	PCT	GB	R	OR	AB	H	2B	3B	HR	BB	SO	AVG	OBP	SLG	PRO	PRO+	BR	/A	PF	CHI	RC	SB	CS	SBA	SBR
EAST																												
BOS	162	89	73	.549		**813**	689	5545	**1569**	**310**	39	124	**623**	**728**	**.283**	**.360**	.420	**.780**	**113**	**140**	**110**	104	94	**842**	65	36	64	-2
DET	162	88	74	.543	1	703	658	5433	1358	213	28	143	588	841	.250	.326	.378	.704	100	-20	7	96	103	673	87	42	67	1
TOR	162	87	75	.537	2	763	680	5557	1491	271	**47**	**158**	521	935	.268	.334	.419	.753	109	68	65	100	98	771	107	36	75	11
MIL	162	87	75	.537	2	682	**616**	5488	1409	258	26	113	439	911	.257	.316	.375	.691	92	-56	-62	101	**107**	648	**159**	55	74	15
NY	161	85	76	.528	3.5	772	748	5592	1469	272	12	148	588	935	.263	.336	.395	.731	105	33	39	99	102	754	146	39	**79**	**20**
CLE	162	78	84	.481	11	666	731	5505	1435	235	28	134	416	866	.261	.317	.387	.704	94	-35	-53	103	101	667	97	50	66	-1
BAL	161	54	107	.335	34.5	550	789	5358	1275	199	20	137	504	869	.238	.307	.359	.666	88	-101	-82	97	94	581	69	44	61	-6
WEST																												
OAK	162	104	58	.642		800	620	5602	1474	251	22	156	580	926	.263	.339	.399	.738	110	50	75	97	103	763	129	54	70	6
MIN	162	91	71	.562	13	759	672	5510	1508	294	31	151	528	832	.274	.343	**.421**	.764	110	94	73	103	95	785	107	63	63	-6
KC	161	84	77	.522	19.5	704	648	5469	1419	275	40	121	486	944	.259	.324	.391	.715	98	-9	-15	101	102	696	137	54	72	9
CAL	162	75	87	.463	29	714	771	5582	1458	258	31	124	469	819	.261	.324	.385	.709	101	-18	1	97	103	690	86	52	62	-5
CHI	161	71	90	.441	32.5	631	757	5449	1327	224	35	132	446	908	.244	.305	.370	.675	88	-92	-89	100	105	609	98	46	68	2
TEX	161	70	91	.435	33.5	637	735	5479	1378	227	39	112	542	1022	.252	.323	.368	.691	91	-47	-64	102	97	661	130	57	70	5
SEA	161	68	93	.422	35.5	664	744	5436	1397	271	27	148	461	787	.257	.319	.398	.717	95	-7	-37	104	97	673	95	61	61	-8
TOT	1131					9858		77005	19967	3558	425	1901	7191	12323	.259	.327	.391	.718							1512	689	69	40

TEAM	CG	SH	SV	IP	H	H/G	HR	BB	SO	RAT	ERA	ERA+	OAV	OOB	PR	/A	PF	CPI	FA	E	DP	FW	PW	BW	SBW	DIF
EAST																										
BOS	26	14	37	1426^{1}	1415	8.9	143	493	**1085**	12.3	3.97	104	.259	.324	-1	23	104	99	.984	93	123	1.6	2.3	**11.1**	-.5	-6.5
DET	34	8	36	1445^{2}	1361	8.5	150	497	890	11.8	3.71	103	.248	.314	41	17	96	99	.982	109	129	.6	1.7	.7	-.2	4.1
TOR	16	**17**	47	1449	1404	8.7	143	528	904	12.4	3.80	104	.256	.328	27	22	99	**105**	.982	110	170	.6	2.2	6.6	.8	-4.2
MIL	30	8	51	1449^{1}	1355	8.4	125	**437**	832	**11.2**	3.45	**115**	.248	**.306**	84	**85**	100	99	.981	120	146	-.0	**8.6**	-6.3	1.2	2.5
NY	16	5	43	1456	1512	9.3	157	487	861	12.7	4.26	92	.267	.331	-48	-52	99	99	.978	134	161	-.9	-5.3	3.9	**1.7**	5.0
CLE	35	10	46	1434	1501	9.4	120	442	812	12.4	4.16	99	.270	.328	-31	-8	104	97	.980	124	131	-.3	-.8	-5.4	-.4	3.8
BAL	20	7	26	1416	1506	9.6	153	523	709	13.2	4.54	86	.274	.342	-90	-100	98	99	.980	119	172	.0	-10.1	-8.3	-.9	-7.2
WEST																										
OAK	22	9	**64**	1489^{1}	1376	8.3	116	553	983	11.8	**3.44**	110	.247	.318	**87**	56	95	104	.983	105	151	.9	5.7	7.6	.3	8.6
MIN	18	9	52	1431^{2}	1457	9.2	146	453	897	12.3	3.93	104	.266	.327	6	22	103	104	**.986**	**84**	155	**2.1**	2.2	7.4	-.9	-.8
KC	29	12	32	1428^{1}	1415	8.9	**102**	465	886	12.1	3.65	109	.258	.320	49	52	101	100	.980	124	147	-.3	5.3	-1.5	.6	-.6
CAL	26	9	33	1455^{2}	1503	9.3	135	568	817	13.1	4.32	89	.270	.342	-57	-74	97	101	.979	135	175	-.9	-7.5	.1	-.8	3.1
CHI	11	9	43	1439	1467	9.2	138	533	754	12.7	4.12	96	.266	.334	-25	-24	100	101	.976	154	**177**	-2.1	-2.4	-9.0	-.0	4.1
TEX	**41**	11	31	1438^{2}	**1310**	**8.2**	129	654	912	12.6	4.05	101	**.244**	.332	-13	5	103	95	.979	131	145	-.7	.5	-6.5	.2	-4.0
SEA	28	11	28	1428	1385	8.7	144	558	981	12.5	4.15	100	.256	.330	-30	1	105	97	.980	123	168	-.2	.1	-3.7	-1.1	-7.5
TOT	352	139	569	20187		8.9				12.4	3.97		.259	.327					.981	1665	2150					

Runs
Boggs-Bos....... 128
Canseco-Oak 120
Henderson-NY ... 118
Molitor-Mil 115
Puckett-Min 109

Hits
Puckett-Min 234
Boggs-Bos....... 214
Greenwell-Bos.... 192
Yount-Mil 190
Molitor-Mil 190

Doubles
Boggs-Bos......... 45
Ray-Cal 42
Puckett-Min 42
Brett-KC.......... 42
Fernandez-Tor..... 41

Triples
Yount-Mil 11
Wilson-KC 11
Reynolds-Sea 11
Greenwell-Bos...... 8

Home Runs
Canseco-Oak 42
McGriff-Tor........ 34
McGwire-Oak 32
Murray-Bal........ 28
Gaetti-Min 28

Total Bases
Puckett-Min 358
Canseco-Oak 347
Greenwell-Bos.... 313
Brett-KC.......... 300
Carter-Cle 297

Runs Batted In
Canseco-Oak 124
Puckett-Min 121
Greenwell-Bos.... 119
Evans-Bos 111
Winfield-NY 107

Runs Produced
Puckett-Min 206
Canseco-Oak 202
Evans-Bos 186
Greenwell-Bos.... 183
Boggs-Bos....... 181

Bases On Balls
Boggs-Bos....... 125
Clark-NY 113
C.Ripken-Bal 102
Davis-Sea 95
Greenwell-Bos..... 87

Batting Average
Boggs-Bos........366
Puckett-Min 356
Greenwell-Bos.....325
Winfield-NY 322
Molitor-Mil 312

On Base Percentage
Boggs-Bos........480
Greenwell-Bos.....420
Davis-Sea 416
Winfield-NY 398
Henderson-NY 397

Slugging Average
Canseco-Oak 569
McGriff-Tor........552
Gaetti-Min 551
Puckett-Min 545
Greenwell-Bos.....531

Production
Boggs-Bos.........970
Canseco-Oak 963
Greenwell-Bos.....950
McGriff-Tor........930
Winfield-NY 928

Adjusted Production
Canseco-Oak 172
Boggs-Bos....... 165
Winfield-NY 159
Greenwell-Bos.... 158
McGriff-Tor....... 156

Batter Runs
Boggs-Bos........ 65.8
Canseco-Oak 54.1
Greenwell-Bos.... 53.4
Puckett-Min 45.5
Winfield-NY 43.4

Adjusted Batter Runs
Boggs-Bos........ 62.3
Canseco-Oak 57.0
Greenwell-Bos.... 50.1
Winfield-NY 44.0
Puckett-Min 43.2

Clutch Hitting Index
Evans-Bos 139
Greenwell-Bos..... 132
Larkin-Min 131
Hall-Cle 128
Clark-NY 127

Runs Created
Boggs-Bos........ 140
Canseco-Oak 136
Greenwell-Bos.... 134
Puckett-Min 126
Brett-KC.......... 119

Total Average
Boggs-Bos...... 1.043
Canseco-Oak ... 1.011
Greenwell-Bos... 1.000
McGriff-Tor........958
Henderson-NY 955

Stolen Bases
Henderson-NY 93
Pettis-Det......... 44
Molitor-Mil 41
Canseco-Oak 40

Stolen Base Average
Javier-Oak 95.2
Redus-Chi 92.9
Cotto-Sea........ 90.0
Henderson-NY ... 87.7
Yount-Mil 84.6

Stolen Base Runs
Henderson-NY .. 20.1
Pettis-Det 7.2
Redus-Chi 6.6

Fielding Runs
Guillen-Chi 42.6
Gruber-Tor 25.1
Schofield-Cal...... 23.2
Puckett-Min 19.5
Gladden-Min 16.3

Total Player Rating
Canseco-Oak 6.2
Boggs-Bos......... 5.5
Puckett-Min 5.5
Greenwell-Bos...... 5.2
Henderson-NY 4.7

Wins
Viola-Min 24
Stewart-Oak 21
Gubicza-KC 20

Win Percentage
Viola-Min 774
Hurst-Bos 750
Gubicza-KC 714
Davis-Oak 696
Stieb-Tor 667

Games
Crim-Mil 70
Thigpen-Chi 68
Williams-Tex....... 67
Henneman-Det 65

Complete Games
Stewart-Oak 14
Clemens-Bos 14
Witt-Tex 13
Witt-Cal 12
Swindell-Cle........ 12

Shutouts
Clemens-Bos 8
Swindell-Cle......... 4
Stieb-Tor 4
Gubicza-KC 4

Saves
Eckersley-Oak 45
Reardon-Min 42
Jones-Cle.......... 37
Thigpen-Chi 34
Plesac-Mil 30

Innings Pitched
Stewart-Oak 275.2
Gubicza-KC 269.2
Clemens-Bos....264.0
Langston-Sea ...261.1
Saberhagen-KC .260.2

Fewest Hits/Game
Robinson-Det 6.33
Higuera-Mil 6.65
Stieb-Tor 6.82
Witt-Tex 6.92
Hough-Tex 7.21

Fewest BB/Game
Anderson-Min 1.65
Swindell-Cle...... 1.67
Alexander-Det..... 1.81
Bosio-Mil 1.88
Viola-Min 1.90

Strikeouts
Clemens-Bos...... 291
Langston-Sea 235
Viola-Min 193
Stewart-Oak 192
Higuera-Mil 192

Strikeouts/Game
Clemens-Bos..... 9.92
Langston-Sea 8.09
Witt-Tex 7.64
Higuera-Mil 7.60
Moore-Sea........ 7.16

Ratio
Higuera-Mil 9.22
Clemens-Bos...... 9.72
Robinson-Det ... 10.26
Moore-Sea....... 10.31
Viola-Min 10.33

Earned Run Average
Anderson-Min 2.45
Higuera-Mil 2.45
Viola-Min 2.64
Gubicza-KC 2.70
Clemens-Bos..... 2.93

Adjusted ERA
Anderson-Min 166
Higuera-Mil 162
Viola-Min 154
Gubicza-KC 147
Clemens-Bos..... 140

Opponents' Batting Avg.
Robinson-Det 197
Higuera-Mil 207
Stieb-Tor 210
Witt-Tex 216
Clemens-Bos.......220

Opponents' On Base Pct.
Higuera-Mil 265
Clemens-Bos.......270
Robinson-Det 284
Moore-Sea.........287
Swindell-Cle........287

Starter Runs
Higuera-Mil 38.2
Gubicza-KC 37.8
Viola-Min 37.5
Anderson-Min 34.1
Clemens-Bos..... 30.3

Adjusted Starter Runs
Viola-Min 40.4
Higuera-Mil 38.5
Gubicza-KC 38.4
Anderson-Min 36.5
Clemens-Bos..... 34.6

Clutch Pitching Index
Anderson-Min 138
Davis-Oak 121
Candiotti-Cle 116
Leibrandt-KC..... 116
Viola-Min 115

Relief Runs
Henneman-Det ... 21.2
Jones-Cle......... 15.7
Harvey-Cal 15.5
Mirabella-Mil 15.4
Jackson-Sea 14.8

Adjusted Relief Runs
Henneman-Det ... 19.7
Jones-Cle......... 17.1
Jackson-Sea 16.9
Mirabella-Mil 15.5
Harvey-Cal 14.6

Relief Ranking
Henneman-Det ... 39.8
Jones-Cle......... 30.0
Harvey-Cal 28.1
Reardon-Min 26.4
Eckersley-Oak.... 24.6

Total Pitcher Index
Gubicza-KC 4.5
Higuera-Mil 4.3
Viola-Min 4.2
Anderson-Min 4.1
Clemens-Bos...... 3.2

Total Baseball Ranking
Canseco-Oak 6.2
Boggs-Bos......... 5.5
Puckett-Min 5.5
Greenwell-Bos...... 5.2
Henderson-NY 4.7

TEAM	G	W	L	PCT	GB	R	OR	AB	H	2B	3B	HR	BB	SO	AVG	OBP	SLG	PRO	PRO+	BR	/A	PF	CHI	RC	SB	CS	SBA	SBR
EAST																												
CHI	162	93	69	.574		**702**	623	5513	**1438**	235	45	124	472	921	**.261**	.322	.387	**.709**	101	54	7	107	101	**685**	136	57	70	7
NY	162	87	75	.537	6	683	595	5489	1351	**280**	21	**147**	504	934	.246	.313	.385	.698	110	30	61	95	102	676	158	53	**75**	**16**
STL	164	86	76	.531	7	632	608	5492	1418	263	47	73	507	848	.258	**.323**	.363	.686	99	16	-4	103	97	652	155	54	74	14
MON	162	81	81	.500	12	632	630	5482	1353	267	30	100	**572**	958	.247	.322	.361	.683	100	13	4	101	96	645	**160**	70	70	6
PIT	164	74	88	.457	19	637	680	5539	1334	263	**53**	95	563	914	.241	.314	.359	.673	102	-13	10	97	100	629	155	69	69	5
PHI	163	67	95	.414	26	629	735	5447	1324	215	36	123	558	926	.243	.316	.364	.680	100	1	1	100	99	634	106	50	68	2
WEST																												
SF	162	92	70	.568		699	600	5469	1365	241	52	141	508	1071	.250	.318	**.390**	.708	**111**	50	**68**	97	102	683	87	54	62	-6
SD	162	89	73	.549	3	642	626	5422	1360	215	32	120	552	1013	.251	.321	.369	.690	103	22	21	100	98	644	136	67	67	1
HOU	162	86	76	.531	6	647	646	5516	1316	239	28	97	530	885	.239	.308	.345	.653	95	-50	-27	97	109	606	144	62	70	6
LA	160	77	83	.481	14	554	**536**	5465	1313	241	17	89	507	885	.240	.308	.339	.647	93	-61	-50	98	96	576	81	54	60	-8
CIN	162	75	87	.463	17	632	691	5520	1362	243	28	128	493	1028	.247	.312	.370	.682	97	1	-21	103	99	639	128	71	64	-4
ATL	161	63	97	.394	28	584	680	5463	1281	201	22	128	485	996	.234	.300	.350	.650	89	-64	-80	103	103	575	83	54	61	-8
TOT	973					7673		65817	16215	2903	411	1365	6251	11354	.246	.315	.365	.680							1529	715	68	30

TEAM	CG	SH	SV	IP	H	H/G	HR	BB	SO	RAT	ERA	ERA+	OAV	OOB	PR	/A	PF	CPI	FA	E	DP	FW	PW	BW	SBW	DIF
EAST																										
CHI	18	10	**55**	1460¹	1369	8.4	106	532	918	11.9	3.43	110	.250	.319	11	54	108	104	.980	124	130	.6	5.8	.7	.5	4.4
NY	24	12	38	1454¹	**1260**	**7.8**	115	532	**1108**	11.3	3.29	99	**.231**	**.303**	33	-5	93	95	.976	144	110	-.6	-.5	6.5	**1.4**	-.9
STL	18	18	43	1461	1330	8.2	**84**	482	844	11.3	3.36	108	.243	.308	21	43	104	95	**.982**	112	114	1.4	4.6	-.4	1.2	-1.8
MON	20	13	35	1468¹	1344	8.2	120	519	1059	11.6	3.48	104	.245	.314	3	9	101	101	.979	136	126	-.1	1.0	.4	.4	-1.7
PIT	20	9	40	1487²	1394	8.4	121	539	827	11.9	3.64	92	.248	.317	-24	-47	96	98	.975	160	130	-1.4	-5.0	1.1	.3	-1.9
PHI	10	10	33	1433¹	1408	8.8	127	613	899	12.9	4.04	88	.259	.337	-87	-80	101	101	.979	133	136	.1	-8.6	.1	-.0	-5.6
WEST																										
SF	12	16	47	1457	1320	8.2	120	471	802	11.2	3.30	102	.243	.307	31	11	97	102	**.982**	114	135	1.2	1.2	**7.3**	-.9	2.3
SD	21	11	52	1457¹	1359	8.4	133	481	933	11.5	3.38	103	.249	.312	19	19	100	106	.976	154	147	-1.1	2.0	2.2	-.2	5.0
HOU	19	12	38	1479¹	1379	8.4	105	551	965	11.9	3.64	99	.247	.318	-25	-42	97	96	.977	142	121	-.4	-4.5	.4	.4	12.4
LA	**25**	**19**	36	1463¹	1278	7.9	95	504	1052	11.1	**2.95**	**116**	.237	.306	**89**	**76**	98	**107**	.981	118	**153**	.8	**8.1**	-5.3	-1.1	-5.5
CIN	16	9	37	1464¹	1404	8.6	125	559	981	12.3	3.73	96	.253	.326	-38	-21	103	102	.980	121	108	.8	-2.2	-2.2	-.7	-1.6
ATL	15	8	33	1447²	1370	8.5	114	**468**	966	11.5	3.70	99	.250	.311	-33	-8	104	94	.976	152	124	-1.1	-.9	-8.6	-1.1	-5.4
TOT	218	147	487	17534		8.3				11.7	3.49		.246	.315					.978	1610	1554					

Runs		Hits		Doubles		Triples		Home Runs		Total Bases	
Sandberg-Chi	104	Gwynn-SD	203	Wallach-Mon	42	Thompson-SF	11	Mitchell-SF	47	Mitchell-SF	345
Johnson-NY	104	Clark-SF	196	Guerrero-StL	42	Bonilla-Pit	10	Johnson-NY	36	Clark-SF	321
Clark-SF	104	R.Alomar-SD	184	Johnson-NY	41	VanSlyke-Pit	9	Davis-Hou	34	Johnson-NY	319
Mitchell-SF	100	Guerrero-StL	177	Clark-SF	38	Coleman-StL	9	Davis-Cin	34	Bonilla-Pit	302
Butler-SF	100	Sandberg-Chi	176	Bonilla-Pit	37	Clark-SF	9	Sandberg-Chi	30	Sandberg-Chi	301

Runs Batted In		Runs Produced		Bases On Balls		Batting Average		On Base Percentage		Slugging Average	
Mitchell-SF	125	Clark-SF	192	J.Clark-SD	132	Gwynn-SD	.336	L.Smith-Atl	.420	Mitchell-SF	.635
Guerrero-StL	117	Mitchell-SF	178	V.Hayes-Phi	101	Clark-SF	.333	J.Clark-SD	.413	Johnson-NY	.559
Clark-SF	111	Johnson-NY	169	Raines-Mon	93	L.Smith-Atl	.315	Clark-SF	.412	Clark-SF	.546
Johnson-NY	101	Guerrero-StL	160	Bonds-Pit	93	Grace-Chi	.314	Grace-Chi	.407	Davis-Cin	.541
Davis-Cin	101	Bonilla-Pit	158			Guerrero-StL	.311	Guerrero-StL	.398	L.Smith-Atl	.533

Production		Adjusted Production		Batter Runs		Adjusted Batter Runs		Clutch Hitting Index		Runs Created	
Mitchell-SF	1.027	Mitchell-SF	194	Mitchell-SF	62.1	Mitchell-SF	64.0	Guerrero-StL	154	Clark-SF	136
Clark-SF	.958	Clark-SF	177	Clark-SF	55.6	Clark-SF	57.6	J.Clark-SD	140	Mitchell-SF	136
L.Smith-Atl	.953	Johnson-NY	171	L.Smith-Atl	47.0	Johnson-NY	49.0	Murphy-Atl	134	Johnson-NY	127
Johnson-NY	.932	L.Smith-Atl	166	Johnson-NY	45.7	L.Smith-Atl	45.4	Hatcher-Hou-Pit	131	L.Smith-Atl	113
Davis-Cin	.916	Davis-Cin	154	Guerrero-StL	38.3	Guerrero-StL	36.1	Doran-Hou	127	Guerrero-StL	109

Total Average		Stolen Bases		Stolen Base Average		Stolen Base Runs		Fielding Runs		Total Player Rating	
Mitchell-SF	1.099	Coleman-StL	65	Doran-Hou	88.0	Coleman-StL	13.5	Pendleton-StL	30.2	Mitchell-SF	6.8
Johnson-NY	1.026	Samuel-Phi-NY	42	Biggio-Hou	87.5	Johnson-NY	7.5	Young-Hou	26.3	L.Smith-Atl	5.3
L.Smith-Atl	1.023	R.Alomar-SD	42	Coleman-StL	86.7	Raines-Mon	6.9	Oquendo-StL	20.4	Clark-SF	4.8
Clark-SF	1.010	Raines-Mon	41	D.Martinez-Mon	85.2	Samuel-Phi-NY	5.4	Foley-Mon	19.8	Bonds-Pit	4.2
J.Clark-SD	.969	Johnson-NY	41	Johnson-NY	83.7	Doran-Hou	4.8	Bonds-Pit	19.7	Bonilla-Pit	4.1

Wins		Win Percentage		Games		Complete Games		Shutouts		Saves	
Scott-Hou	20	Bielecki-Chi	.720	Williams-Chi	76	Hurst-SD	10	Belcher-LA	8	Davis-SD	44
Maddux-Chi	19	J.Martinez-Mon	.696	Dibble-Cin	74	Belcher-LA	10	Drabek-Pit	5	Williams-Chi	36
Magrane-StL	18	Reuschel-SF	.680	Parrett-Phi	72	Scott-Hou	9	Langston-Mon	4	Franco-Cin	32
Bielecki-Chi	18	Scott-Hou	.667	Dayley-StL	71	Magrane-StL	9	Hershiser-LA	4	Howell-LA	28
Reuschel-SF	17	Magrane-StL	.667	Agosto-Hou	71	Browning-Cin	9	Glavine-Atl	4	Burke-Mon	28

Innings Pitched		Fewest Hits/Game		Fewest BB/Game		Strikeouts		Strikeouts/Game		Ratio	
Hershiser-LA	256.2	DeLeon-StL	6.36	Robinson-SF	1.69	DeLeon-StL	201	Langston-Mon	8.92	Garrelts-SF	9.08
Browning-Cin	249.2	Fernandez-NY	6.44	Lilliquist-Atl	1.85	Belcher-LA	200	Fernandez-NY	8.12	DeLeon-StL	9.53
Hurst-SD	244.2	Howell-Phi	6.84	J.Martinez-Mon	1.90	Fernandez-NY	198	Belcher-LA	7.83	Scott-Hou	9.63
DeLeon-StL	244.2	Smoltz-Atl	6.92	Whitson-SD	1.90	Cone-NY	190	Cone-NY	7.78	Fernandez-NY	9.77
Drabek-Pit	244.1	Garrelts-SF	6.94	Glavine-Atl	1.94	Hurst-SD	179	DeLeon-StL	7.39	B.Smith-Mon	9.81

Earned Run Average		Adjusted ERA		Opponents' Batting Avg.		Opponents' On Base Pct.		Starter Runs		Adjusted Starter Runs	
Garrelts-SF	2.28	Garrelts-SF	148	DeLeon-StL	.197	Garrelts-SF	.260	Hershiser-LA	33.7	Hershiser-LA	31.4
Hershiser-LA	2.31	Hershiser-LA	148	Fernandez-NY	.198	Scott-Hou	.268	Garrelts-SF	26.1	Garrelts-SF	23.4
Langston-Mon	2.39	Langston-Mon	147	Smoltz-Atl	.212	DeLeon-StL	.269	Hurst-SD	22.0	Langston-Mon	22.3
Whitson-SD	2.66	Whitson-SD	132	Garrelts-SF	.212	Fernandez-NY	.272	Langston-Mon	21.6	Hurst-SD	22.0
Hurst-SD	2.69	Hurst-SD	130	Scott-Hou	.212	Smiley-Pit	.276	Whitson-SD	21.2	Maddux-Chi	21.5

Clutch Pitching Index		Relief Runs		Adjusted Relief Runs		Relief Ranking		Total Pitcher Index		Total Baseball Ranking	
Langston-Mon	135	Andersen-Hou	19.0	Lancaster-Chi	19.3	Davis-SD	29.7	Hershiser-LA	4.4	Mitchell-SF	6.8
Hershiser-LA	124	Lancaster-Chi	17.2	Andersen-Hou	18.0	Howell-LA	27.5	Maddux-Chi	3.0	L.Smith-Atl	5.3
Lilliquist-Atl	117	Davis-SD	17.0	Davis-SD	17.0	McDowell-NY-Phi	26.3	Garrelts-SF	2.6	Clark-SF	4.8
Maddux-Chi	115	Howell-LA	16.9	Dibble-Cin	16.6	Dibble-Cin	23.4	Langston-Mon	2.5	Hershiser-LA	4.4
Drabek-Pit	113	Landrum-Pit	16.5	Howell-LA	16.2	Landrum-Pit	19.4	Hurst-SD	2.4	Bonds-Pit	4.2

TEAM	G	W	L	PCT	GB	R	OR	AB	H	2B	3B	HR	BB	SO	AVG	OBP	SLG	PRO	PRO+	BR	/A	PF	CHI	RC	SB	CS	SBA	SBR
EAST																												
TOR	162	89	73	.549		731	651	5581	1449	265	40	142	521	923	.260	.326	.398	.724	105	18	31	98	102	724	144	58	71	8
BAL	162	87	75	.537	2	708	686	5440	1369	238	33	129	593	957	.252	.329	.379	.708	102	-6	16	97	102	678	118	55	68	2
BOS	162	83	79	.512	6	774	735	5666	**1571**	326	30	108	643	755	.277	.355	.403	.758	106	106	61	106	93	802	56	35	62	-4
MIL	162	81	81	.500	8	707	679	5473	1415	235	32	126	455	791	.259	.321	.382	.703	98	-22	-15	99	106	677	**165**	62	73	12
NY	161	74	87	.460	14.5	698	792	5458	1470	229	23	130	502	831	.269	.334	.391	.725	105	26	34	99	98	709	137	60	70	5
CLE	162	73	89	.451	16	604	654	5463	1340	221	26	127	499	934	.245	.312	.365	.677	89	-72	-83	102	98	622	74	51	59	-8
DET	162	59	103	.364	30	617	816	5432	1315	198	24	116	585	899	.242	.320	.351	.671	91	-74	-58	98	100	616	103	50	67	1
WEST																												
OAK	162	99	63	.611		712	**576**	5416	1414	220	25	127	562	855	.261	.334	.381	.715	105	12	37	96	101	687	157	55	74	14
KC	162	92	70	.568	7	690	635	5475	1428	227	41	101	554	897	.261	.332	.373	.705	98	-9	-6	100	101	682	154	51	**75**	**16**
CAL	162	91	71	.562	8	669	578	5545	1422	208	37	**145**	429	1011	.256	.313	.386	.699	98	-38	-26	98	103	663	89	40	69	3
TEX	162	83	79	.512	16	695	714	5458	1433	260	**46**	122	503	989	.263	.329	.394	.723	101	18	7	102	98	694	101	49	67	1
MIN	162	80	82	.494	19	740	738	5581	1542	278	35	117	483	**743**	.276	.340	.402	.740	101	53	6	107	98	751	111	53	68	2
SEA	162	73	89	.451	26	694	728	5512	1417	237	29	134	489	838	.257	.323	.384	.707	95	-16	-38	103	103	699	81	55	60	-9
CHI	161	69	92	.429	29.5	693	750	5504	1493	262	36	94	464	873	.271	.331	.383	.714	103	4	21	98	100	696	97	52	65	-2
TOT	1133					9732		77004	20078	3404	457	1718	7277	12296	.261	.328	.384	.712							1587	726	69	41

TEAM	CG	SH	SV	IP	H	H/G	HR	BB	SO	RAT	ERA	ERA+	OAV	OOB	PR	/A	PF	CPI	FA	E	DP	FW	PW	BW	SBW	DIF
EAST																										
TOR	12	12	38	1467	1408	8.6	99	478	849	11.8	3.58	105	.255	.320	49	31	97	99	.980	127	164	-.1	3.2	3.2	.5	1.3
BAL	16	7	44	1448¹	1518	9.4	134	486	676	12.6	4.00	95	.272	.333	-19	-33	98	104	**.986**	**87**	163	**2.3**	-3.4	1.6	-.0	5.5
BOS	14	9	42	1460	1448	8.9	131	548	1054	12.5	4.01	102	.261	.331	-20	15	106	99	.980	127	162	-.1	1.5	**6.2**	-.7	-4.9
MIL	16	8	45	1432¹	1463	9.2	129	457	812	12.2	3.80	101	.265	.324	14	7	99	102	.975	155	164	-1.8	.7	-1.5	.9	1.7
NY	15	9	44	1414²	1550	9.9	150	521	787	13.4	4.50	86	.281	.347	-98	-100	100	102	.980	122	**183**	.1	-10.2	3.5	.2	-.1
CLE	23	13	38	1453	1423	8.8	107	**452**	844	11.8	3.65	109	.257	.315	38	50	102	96	.981	118	126	.4	5.1	-8.5	-1.1	-4.0
DET	24	4	26	1427¹	1514	9.5	150	652	831	13.9	4.53	84	.274	.355	-103	-114	98	103	.979	130	153	-.3	-11.6	-5.9	-.2	-4.0
WEST																										
OAK	17	**20**	**57**	1448¹	1287	**8.0**	103	510	930	**11.3**	3.09	119	.238	**.307**	128	95	95	103	.979	129	159	-.2	**9.7**	3.8	1.1	3.7
KC	27	13	38	1451²	1415	8.8	**86**	455	978	11.7	3.55	109	.257	.316	54	49	99	97	.982	114	139	.7	5.0	-.6	**1.3**	4.6
CAL	**32**	**20**	38	1454¹	1384	8.6	113	465	897	11.6	3.28	116	.253	.315	97	86	98	**107**	.985	96	173	1.7	8.8	-2.6	.0	2.1
TEX	26	7	44	1434¹	**1279**	**8.0**	119	654	**1112**	12.4	3.91	101	.239	.327	-4	9	102	92	.978	136	137	-.6	.9	.7	-.2	1.2
MIN	19	8	38	1429¹	1495	9.4	139	500	851	12.8	4.28	97	.269	.334	-63	-23	107	97	.982	107	141	1.1	-2.3	.6	-.0	-.3
SEA	15	10	44	1438	1422	8.9	114	560	897	12.7	4.00	101	.259	.333	-19	4	104	98	.977	143	168	-1.1	.4	-3.9	-1.2	-2.3
CHI	9	5	46	1422	1472	9.3	144	539	778	12.9	4.23	90	.269	.338	-54	-67	98	101	.975	151	176	-1.6	-6.8	2.1	-.5	-4.7
TOT	265	145	582	20181		9.0				12.4	3.88		.261	.328					.980	1742	2208					

Runs		Hits		Doubles		Triples		Home Runs		Total Bases	
R.Henderson-NY-Oak	113	Puckett-Min	215	Boggs-Bos	51	Sierra-Tex	14	McGriff-Tor	36	Sierra-Tex	344
Boggs-Bos	113	Sax-NY	205	Puckett-Min	45	White-Cal	13	Carter-Cle	35	Yount-Mil	314
Yount-Mil	101	Boggs-Bos	205	Reed-Bos	42	Bradley-Bal	10	McGwire-Oak	33	Carter-Cle	303
Sierra-Tex	101	Yount-Mil	195	Bell-Tor	41			Jackson-KC	32	Mattingly-NY	301
McGriff-Tor	98			Yount-Mil	38			Esasky-Bos	30	Puckett-Min	295

Runs Batted In		Runs Produced		Bases On Balls		Batting Average		On Base Percentage		Slugging Average	
Sierra-Tex	119	Sierra-Tex	191	R.Henderson-NY-Oak	126	Puckett-Min	.339	Boggs-Bos	.434	Sierra-Tex	.543
Mattingly-NY	113	Yount-Mil	183	McGriff-Tor	119	Lansford-Oak	.336	Davis-Sea	.428	McGriff-Tor	.525
Esasky-Bos	108	Bell-Tor	174	Boggs-Bos	107	Boggs-Bos	.330	R.Henderson-NY-Oak	.413	Yount-Mil	.511
Jackson-KC	105	Mattingly-NY	169	Seitzer-KC	102	Yount-Mil	.318	McGriff-Tor	.402	Esasky-Bos	.500
Carter-Cle	105	Greenwell-Bos	168	Davis-Sea	101	Franco-Tex	.316	Evans-Bos	.402	Davis-Sea	.496

Production		Adjusted Production		Batter Runs		Adjusted Batter Runs		Clutch Hitting Index		Runs Created	
McGriff-Tor	.927	McGriff-Tor	162	McGriff-Tor	46.8	McGriff-Tor	48.2	Brett-KC	141	Yount-Mil	125
Davis-Sea	.924	Davis-Sea	155	Boggs-Bos	46.6	Davis-Sea	42.0	Evans-Bos	132	Boggs-Bos	122
Yount-Mil	.898	Yount-Mil	152	Davis-Sea	44.2	Yount-Mil	41.9	Greenwell-Bos	131	Sierra-Tex	122
Sierra-Tex	.895	Sierra-Tex	146	Yount-Mil	41.2	Boggs-Bos	41.4	Parker-Oak	131	McGriff-Tor	121
Boggs-Bos	.883	Baines-Chi-Tex	144	Sierra-Tex	37.4	Sierra-Tex	36.2	Franco-Tex	130	R.Henderson-NY-Oak	110

Total Average		Stolen Bases		Stolen Base Average		Stolen Base Runs		Fielding Runs		Total Player Rating	
McGriff-Tor	.986	R.Henderson-NY-Oak	77	Thurman-KC	100.0	R.Henderson-NY-Oak	14.7	Reynolds-Sea	27.0	R.Henderson-NY-Oak	5.2
R.Henderson-NY-Oak	.983	Espy-Tex	45	Franco-Tex	87.5	Thurman-KC	4.8	Howell-Cal	22.5	Yount-Mil	4.6
Davis-Sea	.975	White-Cal	44	Yount-Mil	86.4	Felder-Mil	4.8	Gruber-Tor	19.2	Puckett-Min	4.0
Yount-Mil	.926	Sax-NY	43	Finley-Bal	85.0	Franco-Tex	4.5	Snyder-Cle	18.6	Sierra-Tex	3.9
Boggs-Bos	.882	Pettis-Det	43	R.Henderson-NY-Oak	84.6			Puckett-Min	18.4	Boggs-Bos	3.6

Wins		Win Percentage		Games		Complete Games		Shutouts		Saves	
Saberhagen-KC	23	Saberhagen-KC	.793	Crim-Mil	76	Saberhagen-KC	12	Blyleven-Cal	5	Russell-Tex	38
Stewart-Oak	21	Blyleven-Cal	.773	Murphy-Bos	74	Morris-Det	10	Saberhagen-KC	4	Thigpen-Chi	34
Moore-Oak	19	Davis-Oak	.731	Rogers-Tex	73	Finley-Cal	9	McCaskill-Cal	4	Schooler-Sea	33
Davis-Oak	19	Stewart-Oak	.700	Russell-Tex	71					Plesac-Mil	33
Ballard-Bal	18	Ballard-Bal	.692	Guetterman-NY	70					Eckersley-Oak	33

Innings Pitched		Fewest Hits/Game		Fewest BB/Game		Strikeouts		Strikeouts/Game		Ratio	
Saberhagen-KC	262.1	Ryan-Tex	6.09	Key-Tor	1.13	Ryan-Tex	301	Ryan-Tex	11.32	Saberhagen-KC	8.71
Stewart-Oak	257.2	Gordon-KC	6.74	Saberhagen-KC	1.48	Clemens-Bos	230	Gordon-KC	8.45	Ryan-Tex	10.12
Gubicza-KC	255.0	Stieb-Tor	7.14	Blyleven-Cal	1.64	Saberhagen-KC	193	Clemens-Bos	8.17	Blyleven-Cal	10.34
Clemens-Bos	253.1	Saberhagen-KC	7.17	Bosio-Mil	1.84	Gubicza-KC	173	Witt-Tex	7.69	Moore-Oak	10.35
Milacki-Bal	243.0	Moore-Oak	7.19	Witt-Cal	1.96	Bosio-Mil	173	Viola-Min	7.07	Key-Tor	10.67

Earned Run Average		Adjusted ERA		Opponents' Batting Avg.		Opponents' On Base Pct.		Starter Runs		Adjusted Starter Runs	
Saberhagen-KC	2.16	Saberhagen-KC	178	Ryan-Tex	.187	Saberhagen-KC	.252	Saberhagen-KC	50.2	Saberhagen-KC	49.2
Finley-Cal	2.57	Finley-Cal	148	Gordon-KC	.210	Ryan-Tex	.276	Moore-Oak	34.3	Blyleven-Cal	29.1
Moore-Oak	2.61	Moore-Oak	141	Saberhagen-KC	.217	Moore-Oak	.288	Blyleven-Cal	31.0	Moore-Oak	28.8
Blyleven-Cal	2.73	Blyleven-Cal	140	Stieb-Tor	.219	Blyleven-Cal	.289	Finley-Cal	29.1	Finley-Cal	27.6
McCaskill-Cal	2.93	Clemens-Bos	131	Moore-Oak	.219	Bosio-Mil	.291	Bosio-Mil	24.2	Clemens-Bos	27.4

Clutch Pitching Index		Relief Runs		Adjusted Relief Runs		Relief Ranking		Total Pitcher Index		Total Baseball Ranking	
Cerutti-Tor	130	Montgomery-KC	25.7	Montgomery-KC	25.3	Jones-Cle	40.4	Saberhagen-KC	5.5	Saberhagen-KC	5.5
Ballard-Bal	123	Olson-Bal	20.7	Lamp-Bos	22.2	Russell-Tex	38.7	Moore-Oak	3.6	R.Henderson-NY-Oak	5.2
Finley-Cal	123	Lamp-Bos	19.5	Olson-Bal	19.8	Montgomery-KC	35.9	Blyleven-Cal	3.2	Yount-Mil	4.6
McCaskill-Cal	116	Henke-Tor	19.4	Henke-Tor	18.3	Henke-Tor	29.6	Gubicza-KC	2.7	Puckett-Min	4.0
Davis-Oak	113	Burns-Oak	17.6	Orosco-Cle	16.3	Olson-Bal	28.9	Clemens-Bos	2.6	Sierra-Tex	3.9

TEAM	G	W	L	PCT	GB	R	OR	AB	H	2B	3B	HR	BB	SO	AVG	OBP	SLG	PRO	PRO+	BR	/A	PF	CHI	RC	SB	CS	SBA	SBR
EAST																												
PIT	162	95	67	.586		733	619	5388	1395	**288**	42	138	582	914	.259	**.334**	.405	**.739**	113	64	**90**	96	99	738	137	52	72	10
NY	162	91	71	.562	4	**775**	613	5504	1410	278	21	**172**	536	851	.256	.326	**.408**	.734	107	48	50	100	**106**	748	110	33	**77**	13
MON	162	85	77	.525	10	662	598	5453	1363	227	**43**	114	576	1024	.250	.325	.370	.695	101	-18	8	96	99	672	**235**	99	70	11
PHI	162	77	85	.475	18	646	729	5535	1410	237	27	103	**582**	915	.255	.329	.363	.692	96	-19	-17	100	96	675	108	35	76	11
CHI	162	77	85	.475	18	690	774	5600	**1474**	240	36	136	406	869	.263	.316	.392	.708	93	-7	-57	107	103	695	151	50	75	15
STL	162	70	92	.432	25	599	698	5462	1398	255	41	73	517	**844**	.256	.323	.358	.681	93	-46	-49	100	95	650	221	74	75	**22**
WEST																												
CIN	162	91	71	.562		693	**597**	5525	1466	284	40	125	466	913	**.265**	.327	.399	.726	101	35	6	104	97	726	166	66	72	10
LA	162	86	76	.531	5	728	685	5491	1436	222	27	129	538	952	.262	.331	.382	.713	105	17	36	97	104	699	141	65	68	3
SF	162	85	77	.525	6	719	710	5573	1459	221	35	152	498	973	.262	.325	.396	.721	108	24	49	96	101	724	109	56	66	-1
SD	162	75	87	.463	16	673	673	5554	1429	243	35	123	509	902	.257	.323	.380	.703	98	-8	-13	101	99	682	138	59	70	6
HOU	162	75	87	.463	16	573	656	5379	1301	209	32	94	548	997	.242	.315	.345	.660	90	-83	-64	97	97	596	179	83	68	1
ATL	162	65	97	.401	26	682	821	5504	1376	263	26	162	473	1010	.250	.312	.396	.708	95	-8	-47	106	103	675	92	55	63	-5
TOT	972					8173		65968	16917	2967	405	1521	6221	11164	.256	.324	.383	.707							1787	727	71	100

TEAM	CG	SH	SV	IP	H	H/G	HR	BB	SO	RAT	ERA	ERA+	OAV	OOB	PR	/A	PF	CPI	FA	E	DP	FW	PW	BW	SBW	DIF
EAST																										
PIT	18	8	43	1447	1367	8.5	135	**413**	848	11.3	3.40	106	.251	.307	63	35	95	103	.979	134	125	-.4	3.6	**9.3**	.2	1.4
NY	18	**14**	41	1440	1339	8.4	119	444	**1217**	11.3	3.42	109	.246	**.306**	59	51	99	97	.978	132	107	-.3	5.3	5.2	.5	-.6
MON	18	11	50	1473[1]	1349	**8.2**	127	510	991	11.6	3.37	108	.245	.313	70	46	96	103	.982	110	134	.9	4.7	.8	.3	-2.8
PHI	18	7	35	1449	1381	8.6	124	651	840	12.8	4.07	94	.253	.336	-45	-40	101	97	.981	117	**150**	.5	-4.1	-1.8	.3	1.1
CHI	13	7	42	1442[2]	1510	9.4	121	572	877	13.2	4.34	94	.271	.342	-87	-42	108	98	.980	124	136	.1	-4.4	-5.9	.7	5.4
STL	8	13	39	1443[1]	1432	8.9	**98**	475	833	12.1	3.87	98	.261	.324	-13	-9	101	95	.979	130	114	-.2	-.9	-5.1	**1.4**	-6.2
WEST																										
CIN	14	12	50	1456[1]	**1338**	8.3	124	543	1029	11.8	3.39	**116**	.246	.318	64	**89**	104	105	**.983**	**102**	126	**1.4**	**9.2**	.6	.2	-1.4
LA	**29**	12	29	1442	1364	8.5	137	478	1021	11.7	3.72	98	.249	.313	11	-10	97	96	.979	130	123	-.2	-1.0	3.7	-.5	3.1
SF	14	6	45	1446[1]	1477	9.2	131	553	788	12.8	4.08	89	.267	.335	-46	-70	96	101	**.983**	107	148	1.1	-7.2	5.1	-1.0	6.0
SD	21	12	35	1461[2]	1437	8.8	147	507	928	12.1	3.68	104	.258	.322	19	24	101	**106**	.977	141	141	-.8	2.5	-1.3	-.2	-6.0
HOU	12	6	37	1450	1396	8.7	130	496	854	12.0	3.61	103	.255	.321	30	17	98	104	.978	131	124	-.3	1.8	-6.6	-.4	-.4
ATL	17	8	30	1429[2]	1527	9.6	128	579	938	13.4	4.58	88	.275	.346	-125	-86	106	97	.974	158	133	-1.8	-8.9	-4.8	-1.4	.9
TOT	200	116	476	17381[1]		8.8				12.2	3.79		.256	.324					.980	1516	1561					

Runs		Hits		Doubles		Triples		Home Runs		Total Bases	
Sandberg-Chi	116	Dykstra-Phi	192	Jefferies-NY	40	Duncan-Cin	11	Sandberg-Chi	40	Sandberg-Chi	344
Bonilla-Pit	112	Butler-SF	192	Bonilla-Pit	39	Gwynn-SD	10	Strawberry-NY	37	Bonilla-Pit	324
Butler-SF	108	Sandberg-Chi	188	Sabo-Cin	38	L.Smith-Atl	9	Mitchell-SF	35	Gant-Atl	310
Gant-Atl	107	Wallach-Mon	185	Wallach-Mon	37	Coleman-StL	9	Williams-SF	33	Williams-SF	301
Dykstra-Phi	106	Larkin-Cin	185	Johnson-NY	37	Butler-SF	9	Bonds-Pit	33	Wallach-Mon	295

Runs Batted In		Runs Produced		Bases On Balls		Batting Average		On Base Percentage		Slugging Average	
Williams-SF	122	Bonilla-Pit	200	J.Clark-SD	104	McGee-StL	.335	Magadan-NY	.425	Bonds-Pit	.565
Bonilla-Pit	120	Bonds-Pit	185	Bonds-Pit	93	Murray-LA	.330	Dykstra-Phi	.420	Sandberg-Chi	.559
Carter-SD	115	Williams-SF	176	Butler-SF	90	Magadan-NY	.328	Murray-LA	.417	Mitchell-SF	.544
Bonds-Pit	114	Sandberg-Chi	176	Dykstra-Phi	89	Dykstra-Phi	.325	Bonds-Pit	.410	Gant-Atl	.539
Strawberry-NY	108	Carter-SD	170	V.Hayes-Phi	87	Dawson-Chi	.310	Butler-SF	.401	Justice-Atl	.535

Production		Adjusted Production		Batter Runs		Adjusted Batter Runs		Clutch Hitting Index		Runs Created	
Bonds-Pit	.974	Bonds-Pit	172	Bonds-Pit	48.1	Bonds-Pit	50.7	Carter-SD	151	Bonds-Pit	128
Murray-LA	.936	Murray-LA	160	Murray-LA	44.7	Murray-LA	46.7	O.Smith-StL	132	Sandberg-Chi	124
Daniels-LA	.923	Daniels-LA	156	Sandberg-Chi	37.9	J.Clark-SD	36.1	Guerrero-StL	129	Dykstra-Phi	121
Sandberg-Chi	.918	Mitchell-SF	151	J.Clark-SD	36.5	Dykstra-Phi	34.5	Williams-SF	128	Murray-LA	118
Justice-Atl	.909	Magadan-NY	143	Dykstra-Phi	34.3	Daniels-LA	33.9	Grace-Chi	128	Gant-Atl	109

Total Average		Stolen Bases		Stolen Base Average		Stolen Base Runs		Fielding Runs		Total Player Rating	
Bonds-Pit	1.115	Coleman-StL	77	Gibson-LA	92.9	Coleman-StL	12.9	Thompson-SF	27.7	Bonds-Pit	7.1
Daniels-LA	.945	Yelding-Hou	64	Grissom-Mon	91.7	Bonds-Pit	7.8	Grace-Chi	26.7	Dykstra-Phi	5.8
Murray-LA	.945	Bonds-Pit	52	Dawson-Chi	88.9	Nixon-Mon	7.2	C.Hayes-Phi	23.6	Sandberg-Chi	4.6
Justice-Atl	.941	Butler-SF	51	Davis-Cin	87.5	Dykstra-Phi	6.9	Dykstra-Phi	20.1	Larkin-Cin	4.3
Dykstra-Phi	.941	Nixon-Mon	50	Dykstra-Phi	86.8			Larkin-Cin	19.9	Murray-LA	3.9

Wins		Win Percentage		Games		Complete Games		Shutouts		Saves	
Drabek-Pit	22	Drabek-Pit	.786	Agosto-Hou	82	Martinez-LA	12	Morgan-LA	4	Franco-NY	33
Viola-NY	20	Martinez-LA	.769	Assenmacher-Chi	74	Hurst-SD	9	Hurst-SD	4	Myers-Cin	31
Martinez-LA	20	Gooden-NY	.731	Harris-SD	73	Drabek-Pit	9			L.Smith-StL	27
Gooden-NY	19	Viola-NY	.625	McDowell-Phi	72	Maddux-Chi	8			Smith-Hou	23
		Browning-Cin	.625	Akerfelds-Phi	71					Lefferts-SD	23

Innings Pitched		Fewest Hits/Game		Fewest BB/Game		Strikeouts		Strikeouts/Game		Ratio	
Viola-NY	249.2	Fernandez-NY	6.52	Darwin-Hou	1.72	Cone-NY	233	Cone-NY	9.91	Darwin-Hou	9.46
Maddux-Chi	237.0	Rijo-Cin	6.90	Whitson-SD	1.85	Martinez-LA	223	Fernandez-NY	9.08	Drabek-Pit	9.69
Martinez-LA	234.1	Martinez-LA	7.34	Leibrandt-Atl	1.94	Gooden-NY	223	Gooden-NY	8.63	J.Martinez-Mon	9.80
Gooden-NY	232.2	Drabek-Pit	7.39	J.Martinez-Mon	1.95	Viola-NY	182	Martinez-LA	8.56	Martinez-LA	10.06
		Darwin-Hou	7.52	Browning-Cin	2.06	Fernandez-NY	181	DeLeon-StL	8.08	Fernandez-NY	10.14

Earned Run Average		Adjusted ERA		Opponents' Batting Avg.		Opponents' On Base Pct.		Starter Runs		Adjusted Starter Runs	
Darwin-Hou	2.21	Darwin-Hou	168	Fernandez-NY	.200	Darwin-Hou	.267	Viola-NY	31.2	Whitson-SD	31.1
Smith-Mon-Pit	2.55	Whitson-SD	147	Rijo-Cin	.212	Drabek-Pit	.275	Whitson-SD	30.3	Viola-NY	29.8
Whitson-SD	2.60	Rijo-Cin	146	Martinez-LA	.220	J.Martinez-Mon	.275	Smith-Mon-Pit	29.7	Rijo-Cin	27.3
Viola-NY	2.67	Smith-Mon-Pit	143	Drabek-Pit	.225	Martinez-LA	.279	Darwin-Hou	28.5	Darwin-Hou	27.1
Rijo-Cin	2.70	Viola-NY	140	Darwin-Hou	.225	Fernandez-NY	.280	Drabek-Pit	26.4	Smith-Mon-Pit	26.0

Clutch Pitching Index		Relief Runs		Adjusted Relief Runs		Relief Ranking		Total Pitcher Index		Total Baseball Ranking	
Gullickson-Hou	121	Dibble-Cin	22.3	Dibble-Cin	23.9	Myers-Cin	33.1	Whitson-SD	3.8	Bonds-Pit	7.1
Smith-Mon-Pit	118	Brantley-SF	21.5	Charlton-Cin	20.6	Dibble-Cin	30.2	Drabek-Pit	3.1	Dykstra-Phi	5.8
Whitson-SD	115	Harris-SD	19.4	Brantley-SF	20.1	Harris-SD	27.7	Rijo-Cin	3.1	Sandberg-Chi	4.6
Rasmussen-SD	114	Charlton-Cin	18.0	Harris-SD	19.8	Brantley-SF	26.6	Viola-NY	3.1	Larkin-Cin	4.3
Darwin-Hou	107	Myers-Cin	16.5	Myers-Cin	18.0	Charlton-Cin	25.8	Smith-Mon-Pit	3.1	Murray-LA	3.9

TEAM	G	W	L	PCT	GB	R	OR	AB	H	2B	3B	HR	BB	SO	AVG	OBP	SLG	PRO	PRO+	BR	/A	PF	CHI	RC	SB	CS	SBA	SBR
EAST																												
BOS	162	88	74	.543		699	664	5516	**1502**	298	31	106	598	795	**.272**	**.346**	.395	.741	102	57	25	105	92	733	53	52	50	-15
TOR	162	86	76	.531	2	**767**	661	5589	1479	263	**50**	167	526	970	.265	.331	**.419**	**.750**	106	56	43	102	101	**769**	111	52	68	2
DET	162	79	83	.488	9	750	754	5479	1418	241	32	**172**	634	952	.259	.339	.409	.748	107	**62**	57	101	98	754	82	57	59	-10
CLE	162	77	85	.475	11	732	737	5485	1465	266	41	110	458	836	.267	.327	.391	.718	101	-5	-2	100	107	694	107	52	67	1
BAL	161	76	85	.472	11.5	669	698	5410	1328	234	22	132	**660**	962	.245	.332	.370	.702	99	-21	1	97	98	676	94	52	64	-3
MIL	162	74	88	.457	14	732	760	5503	1408	247	36	128	519	821	.256	.324	.384	.708	98	-24	-18	99	**109**	692	**164**	72	69	6
NY	162	67	95	.414	21	603	749	5483	1322	208	19	147	427	1027	.241	.302	.366	.668	86	-109	-112	100	105	605	119	45	**73**	9
WEST																												
OAK	162	103	59	.636		733	**570**	5433	1379	209	22	164	651	992	.254	.339	.391	.730	**108**	31	**60**	96	100	739	141	54	72	**10**
CHI	162	94	68	.580	9	682	633	5402	1393	251	44	106	478	903	.258	.322	.379	.701	97	-35	-20	98	105	651	140	90	61	-12
TEX	162	83	79	.512	20	676	696	5469	1416	257	27	110	575	1054	.259	.333	.376	.709	98	-11	-12	100	98	688	115	48	71	6
CAL	162	80	82	.494	23	690	706	5570	1448	237	27	147	566	1000	.260	.331	.391	.722	103	10	24	98	96	715	69	43	62	-5
SEA	162	77	85	.475	26	640	680	5474	1419	251	26	107	596	**749**	.259	.336	.373	.709	97	-7	-15	101	92	691	105	51	67	1
KC	161	75	86	.466	27.5	707	709	5488	1465	**316**	44	100	498	879	.267	.331	.395	.726	104	14	25	98	101	706	107	62	63	-5
MIN	162	74	88	.457	29	666	729	5499	1458	281	39	100	445	**749**	.265	.326	.385	.711	92	-17	-62	107	99	673	96	53	64	-3
TOT	1133					9746		76800	19900	3559	460	1796	7631	12689	.259	.330	.388	.718							1503	783	66	-19

TEAM	CG	SH	SV	IP	H	H/G	HR	BB	SO	RAT	ERA	ERA+	OAV	OOB	PR	/A	PF	CPI	FA	E	DP	FW	PW	BW	SBW	DIF
EAST																										
BOS	15	13	44	1442	1439	9.0	**92**	519	997	12.5	3.72	110	.261	.329	30	57	104	100	.980	123	154	-.2	5.8	2.5	-1.4	.3
TOR	6	9	48	1454	1434	8.9	143	**445**	892	11.9	3.84	103	.260	.319	11	17	101	99	**.986**	**86**	144	**2.0**	1.7	4.4	.3	-3.5
DET	15	12	45	1430[1]	1401	8.8	154	661	856	13.3	4.39	90	.259	.345	-76	-68	101	98	.979	131	178	-.7	-6.9	5.8	-.9	.7
CLE	12	10	47	1427[1]	1491	9.4	163	518	860	12.9	4.26	92	.270	.337	-57	-55	100	102	.981	117	146	.2	-5.6	-.2	.2	1.4
BAL	10	5	43	1435[1]	1445	9.1	161	537	776	12.5	4.04	94	.264	.331	-21	-39	97	103	.985	93	151	1.6	-4.0	.1	-.2	-2.0
MIL	23	13	42	1445	1558	9.7	121	469	771	12.9	4.08	95	.275	.335	-28	-34	99	101	.976	149	152	-1.8	-3.5	-1.8	.7	-.7
NY	15	6	41	1444[2]	1430	8.9	144	618	909	12.9	4.21	94	.261	.339	-49	-39	102	99	.980	126	164	-.4	-4.0	-11.4	1.1	.7
WEST																										
OAK	18	**16**	64	1456	**1287**	**8.0**	123	494	831	**11.2**	**3.18**	**117**	**.238**	**.305**	**118**	**87**	95	101	**.986**	87	152	**2.0**	**8.9**	**6.1**	**1.2**	3.9
CHI	17	10	**68**	1449[1]	1313	8.2	106	548	914	11.8	3.61	106	.244	.318	48	34	98	95	.980	124	169	-.3	3.5	-2.0	-1.1	12.9
TEX	**25**	9	36	1444[2]	1343	8.4	113	623	997	12.5	3.83	102	.248	.330	12	14	100	97	.979	133	161	-.8	1.4	-1.2	.7	1.9
CAL	21	13	42	1454	1482	9.2	106	544	944	12.8	3.79	101	.267	.337	18	3	98	**105**	.978	142	**186**	-1.4	.3	2.4	-.4	-2.0
SEA	21	7	41	1443[1]	1319	8.2	120	606	**1064**	12.3	3.69	107	.243	.324	34	42	101	97	.979	130	152	-.6	4.3	-1.5	.2	-6.4
KC	18	8	33	1420[2]	1449	9.2	116	560	1006	13.0	3.93	97	.264	.337	-5	-16	98	102	.980	122	161	-.2	-1.6	2.5	-.4	-5.9
MIN	13	13	43	1435[2]	1509	9.5	134	489	872	12.7	4.12	101	.273	.335	-35	4	106	101	.983	101	161	1.1	.4	-6.3	-.2	-2.1
TOT	229	144	637	20182[1]		8.9				12.5	3.91		.259	.330					.981	1664	2231					

Runs
R.Henderson-Oak . 119
Fielder-Det 104
Reynolds-Sea 100
Yount-Mil 98
Phillips-Det 97

Hits
Palmeiro-Tex 191
Boggs-Bos 187
Kelly-NY 183
Greenwell-Bos 181

Doubles
J.Reed-Bos 45
Brett-KC 45
Calderon-Chi 44
Boggs-Bos 44
Harper-Min 42

Triples
Fernandez-Tor 17
Sosa-Chi 10
Polonia-NY-Cal 9
Liriano-Tor-Min 9
Johnson-Chi 9

Home Runs
Fielder-Det 51
McGwire-Oak 39
J.Canseco-Oak 37
McGriff-Tor 35
Gruber-Tor 31

Total Bases
Fielder-Det 339
Gruber-Tor 303
McGriff-Tor 295
K.GriffeyJr-Sea 287
Burks-Bos 286

Runs Batted In
Fielder-Det 132
Gruber-Tor 118
McGwire-Oak 108
J.Canseco-Oak . . . 101
Sierra-Tex 96

Runs Produced
Fielder-Det 185
Gruber-Tor 179
Yount-Mil 158
Burks-Bos 157
McGwire-Oak 156

Bases On Balls
McGwire-Oak 110
Tettleton-Bal 106
Phillips-Det 99
R.Henderson-Oak . . 97
McGriff-Tor 94

Batting Average
Brett-KC 329
R.Henderson-Oak . .325
Palmeiro-Tex 319
Trammell-Det 304
Boggs-Bos 302

On Base Percentage
R.Henderson-Oak . .441
McGriff-Tor 403
E.Martinez-Sea 399
Davis-Sea 393
Brett-KC 392

Slugging Average
Fielder-Det 592
R.Henderson-Oak . . .577
J.Canseco-Oak 543
McGriff-Tor 530
Brett-KC 515

Production
R.Henderson-Oak 1.017
Fielder-Det 972
McGriff-Tor 932
J.Canseco-Oak 917
Brett-KC 906

Adjusted Production
R.Henderson-Oak . 190
Fielder-Det 167
J.Canseco-Oak . . . 160
McGriff-Tor 156
Brett-KC 154

Batter Runs
R.Henderson-Oak . 57.5
Fielder-Det 51.3
McGriff-Tor 45.5
Brett-KC 37.0
J.Canseco-Oak 34.3

Adjusted Batter Runs
R.Henderson-Oak . 60.3
Fielder-Det 50.8
McGriff-Tor 44.2
Brett-KC 38.1
J.Canseco-Oak 36.9

Clutch Hitting Index
Leonard-Sea 150
Fletcher-Chi 131
Sierra-Tex 130
Gaetti-Min 128
Guillen-Chi 127

Runs Created
R.Henderson-Oak . 137
Fielder-Det 129
McGriff-Tor 124
Brett-KC 106
K.GriffeyJr-Sea . . . 103

Total Average
R.Henderson-Oak 1.241
Fielder-Det 1.007
McGriff-Tor 983
J.Canseco-Oak 943
McGwire-Oak 903

Stolen Bases
R.Henderson-Oak . . 65
Sax-NY 43
Kelly-NY 42
Cole-Cle 40
Pettis-Tex 38

Stolen Base Average
Cotto-Sea 87.5
R.Henderson-Oak . 86.7
Molitor-Mil 85.7
Gantner-Mil 85.7
Wilson-Tor 85.2

Stolen Base Runs
R.Henderson-Oak . 13.5
Sax-NY 7.5
Cole-Cle 6.6
Wilson-Tor 4.5
Cotto-Sea 4.5

Fielding Runs
Espinoza-NY 21.1
Reynolds-Sea 15.5
Quintana-Bos 14.5
Gaetti-Min 13.8
Gallego-Oak 13.7

Total Player Rating
R.Henderson-Oak . . 8.1
Fielder-Det 4.2
McGriff-Tor 4.2
J.Canseco-Oak 3.9
Fisk-Chi 3.5

Wins
Welch-Oak 27
Stewart-Oak 22
Clemens-Bos 21

Win Percentage
Welch-Oak 818
Clemens-Bos 778
Stieb-Tor 750
Boddicker-Bos 680

Games
Thigpen-Chi 77
Ward-Tor 73
Montgomery-KC . . . 73
Rogers-Tex 69
Henneman-Det 69

Complete Games
Stewart-Oak 11
Morris-Det 11

Shutouts
Stewart-Oak 4
Clemens-Bos 4
Perez-Chi 3
Morris-Det 3
Appier-KC 3

Saves
Thigpen-Chi 57
Eckersley-Oak 48
Jones-Cle 43
Olson-Bal 37
Righetti-NY 36

Innings Pitched
Stewart-Oak 267.0
Morris-Det 249.2
Welch-Oak 238.0
Hanson-Sea 236.0
Finley-Cal 236.0

Fewest Hits/Game
Ryan-Tex 6.04
Johnson-Sea 7.13
Clemens-Bos 7.61
Stewart-Oak 7.62
Stieb-Tor 7.72

Fewest BB/Game
Anderson-Min 1.86
Swindell-Cle 1.97
Clemens-Bos 2.13
Knudson-Mil 2.14
Wells-Tor 2.14

Strikeouts
Ryan-Tex 232
Witt-Tex 221
Hanson-Sea 211
Clemens-Bos 209
Langston-Cal 195

Strikeouts/Game
Ryan-Tex 10.24
Witt-Tex 8.96
Clemens-Bos 8.24
Gordon-KC 8.06
Hanson-Sea 8.05

Ratio
Ryan-Tex 9.62
Clemens-Bos 10.01
Wells-Tor 10.10
Hanson-Sea 10.49
Stewart-Oak 10.58

Earned Run Average
Clemens-Bos 1.93
Finley-Cal 2.40
Stewart-Oak 2.56
Appier-KC 2.76
Stieb-Tor 2.93

Adjusted ERA
Clemens-Bos 211
Finley-Cal 159
Stewart-Oak 145
Appier-KC 139
Stieb-Tor 134

Opponents' Batting Avg.
Ryan-Tex 188
Johnson-Sea 216
Clemens-Bos 228
Stieb-Tor 230
Stewart-Oak 231

Opponents' On Base Pct.
Ryan-Tex 269
Clemens-Bos 280
Wells-Tor 283
Hanson-Sea 289
Black-Cle-Tor 293

Starter Runs
Clemens-Bos 50.1
Stewart-Oak 39.9
Finley-Cal 39.4
Welch-Oak 25.3
Appier-KC 23.6

Adjusted Starter Runs
Clemens-Bos 54.3
Finley-Cal 37.1
Stewart-Oak 34.2
Stieb-Tor 23.4
Appier-KC 22.0

Clutch Pitching Index
Finley-Cal 136
Appier-KC 121
Clemens-Bos 118
Welch-Oak 117
Johnson-Bal 113

Relief Runs
Farr-KC 27.1
Eckersley-Oak 26.8
Swift-Sea 21.5
Thigpen-Chi 20.5
Nelson-Oak 19.4

Adjusted Relief Runs
Farr-KC 26.1
Eckersley-Oak 25.3
Swift-Sea 22.3
Thigpen-Chi 19.6
Nelson-Oak 17.8

Relief Ranking
Eckersley-Oak 55.8
Thigpen-Chi 48.3
Farr-KC 37.4
Jones-Cle 28.1
Olson-Bal 27.8

Total Pitcher Index
Clemens-Bos 6.2
Finley-Cal 4.0
Stewart-Oak 3.7
Farr-KC 2.9
Stieb-Tor 2.8

Total Baseball Ranking
R.Henderson-Oak . . 8.1
Clemens-Bos 6.2
Fielder-Det 4.2
McGriff-Tor 4.2
Finley-Cal 4.0

TEAM	G	W	L	PCT	GB	R	OR	AB	H	2B	3B	HR	BB	SO	AVG	OBP	SLG	PRO	PRO+	BR	/A	PF	CHI	RC	SB	CS	SBA	SBR
EAST																												
PIT	162	98	64	.605		**768**	632	5449	**1433**	**259**	50	126	**620**	901	**.263**	**.342**	.398	**.740**	116	104	**115**	98	98	**762**	124	46	73	**10**
STL	162	84	78	.519	14	651	648	5362	1366	239	**53**	68	532	857	.255	.324	.357	.681	96	-13	-18	101	102	628	202	110	65	-5
PHI	162	78	84	.481	20	629	680	5521	1332	248	33	111	490	1026	.241	.306	.358	.664	93	-60	-52	99	**104**	609	92	30	**75**	10
CHI	160	77	83	.481	20	695	734	5522	1395	232	26	159	442	879	.253	.312	.390	.702	97	11	-20	105	103	675	123	64	66	-2
NY	161	77	84	.478	20.5	640	646	5359	1305	250	24	117	578	**789**	.244	.320	.365	.685	99	-9	-4	99	99	641	153	70	69	4
MON	161	71	90	.441	26.5	579	655	5412	1329	236	42	95	484	1056	.246	.311	.357	.668	94	-47	-37	99	95	607	221	100	69	6
WEST																												
ATL	162	94	68	.580		749	644	5456	1407	255	30	141	563	906	.258	.331	.393	.724	103	65	25	106	102	719	165	76	68	4
LA	162	93	69	.574	1	665	**565**	5408	1366	191	29	108	583	957	.253	.328	.359	.687	101	1	16	98	100	650	126	68	65	-3
SD	162	84	78	.519	19	636	646	5408	1321	204	36	121	501	1069	.244	.312	.362	.674	92	-35	-55	103	102	605	101	64	61	-8
SF	162	75	87	.463	19	649	697	5463	1345	215	48	141	471	973	.246	.311	.381	.692	103	-9	13	97	100	647	95	57	63	-6
CIN	162	74	88	.457	20	689	691	5501	1419	250	27	**164**	488	1006	.258	.322	**.403**	.725	105	57	32	104	96	721	124	56	69	4
HOU	162	65	97	.401	29	605	717	5504	1345	240	43	79	502	1027	.244	.312	.347	.659	97	-64	-25	94	101	606	125	68	65	-3
TOT	970					7955		65365	16363	2819	441	1430	6254	11446	.250	.319	.373	.692							1651	809	67	10

TEAM	CG	SH	SV	IP	H	H/G	HR	BB	SO	RAT	ERA	ERA+	OAV	OOB	PR	/A	PF	CPI	FA	E	DP	FW	PW	BW	SBW	DIF
EAST																										
PIT	**18**	11	**51**	1456²	1411	8.7	117	**401**	919	11.4	3.44	104	.256	.309	39	21	97	103	.981	120	134	.4	2.2	**12.0**	1.0	1.5
STL	9	5	**51**	1435¹	1367	8.6	114	454	822	11.7	3.69	101	.255	.318	0	5	101	100	**.982**	**107**	133	**1.1**	.5	-1.9	-.6	3.9
PHI	16	11	35	1463	1346	8.3	111	670	988	12.7	3.86	95	.246	.332	-29	-32	100	99	.981	119	111	.4	-3.3	-5.4	**1.0**	4.4
CHI	12	4	40	1456²	1415	8.7	117	542	927	12.3	4.03	96	.257	.327	-57	-24	105	96	.982	113	120	.7	-2.5	-2.1	-.3	1.2
NY	12	11	39	1437¹	1403	8.8	108	410	1028	11.5	3.56	102	.257	.311	20	13	99	100	.977	143	112	-1.0	1.4	-.4	.3	-3.7
MON	12	**14**	39	1440¹	**1304**	**8.1**	111	584	909	12.0	3.64	99	.244	.322	7	-4	98	100	.979	133	128	-.4	-.4	-3.9	.5	-5.3
WEST																										
ATL	**18**	7	48	1452²	**1304**	**8.1**	118	481	969	**11.2**	3.49	111	**.240**	.305	32	64	106	95	.978	138	122	-.7	6.7	2.6	.3	4.1
LA	15	**14**	40	1458	1312	**8.1**	**96**	500	1028	11.4	**3.06**	**117**	.241	.308	**101**	**86**	98	**107**	.980	123	126	.2	**9.0**	1.7	-.4	1.6
SD	14	11	47	1452²	1385	8.6	139	457	921	11.5	3.57	106	.252	.311	18	30	103	102	**.982**	113	130	.8	3.8	-5.7	-.9	5.1
SF	10	10	45	1442	1397	8.7	143	544	905	12.3	4.03	89	.257	.329	-56	-72	97	100	**.982**	109	151	1.0	-7.5	1.4	-.7	-.1
CIN	7	11	43	1440	1372	8.6	127	560	997	12.3	3.83	99	.253	.326	-24	-5	103	101	.979	125	131	.0	-.5	3.3	.3	-10.2
HOU	7	13	36	1453	1347	8.3	129	651	**1033**	12.6	4.00	88	.247	.330	-51	-80	95	97	.974	161	129	-2.0	-8.4	-2.6	-.4	-2.6
TOT	150	122	514	17387²		8.5				11.9	3.68		.250	.319					.980	1504	1527					

Runs
Butler-LA 112
Johnson-NY 108
Sandberg-Chi 104
Bonilla-Pit 102
Gant-Atl 101

Hits
Pendleton-Atl 187
Butler-LA 182
Sabo-Cin 175
Bonilla-Pit 174
Jose-StL 173

Doubles
Bonilla-Pit 44
Jose-StL 40
Zeile-StL 36
O'Neill-Cin 36

Triples
Lankford-StL 15
Gwynn-SD 11
Finley-Hou 10
Grissom-Mon 9
Gonzalez-Hou 9

Home Runs
Johnson-NY 38
Williams-SF 34
Gant-Atl 32
McGriff-SD 31
Dawson-Chi 31

Total Bases
Pendleton-Atl 303
Clark-SF 303
Johnson-NY 302
Williams-SF 294
Sabo-Cin 294

Runs Batted In
Johnson-NY 117
Clark-SF 116
Bonds-Pit 116
McGriff-SD 106
Gant-Atl 105

Runs Produced
Johnson-NY 187
Bonds-Pit 186
Bonilla-Pit 184
Sandberg-Chi 178
Gant-Atl 174

Bases On Balls
Butler-LA 108
Bonds-Pit 107
McGriff-SD 105
DeShields-Mon 95
Bonilla-Pit 90

Batting Average
Pendleton-Atl 319
Morris-Cin .... .318
Gwynn-SD .... .317
McGee-SF .... .312
Jose-StL .... .305

On Base Percentage
Bonds-Pit .... .419
Butler-LA .... .402
McGriff-SD ...... .400
Bonilla-Pit ...... .398
Bagwell-Hou ..... .391

Slugging Average
Clark-SF .... .536
Johnson-NY ..... .535
Pendleton-Atl ... .517
Bonds-Pit .... .514
Larkin-Cin .... .506

Production
Bonds-Pit .... .932
Clark-SF .... .897
McGriff-SD .... .894
Bonilla-Pit ...... .890
Larkin-Cin .... .886

Adjusted Production
Bonds-Pit 163
Clark-SF 154
Bonilla-Pit 151
Johnson-NY 147
McGriff-SD 146

Batter Runs
Bonds-Pit 45.5
Bonilla-Pit 39.5
McGriff-SD 38.4
Sandberg-Chi ... 34.8
Clark-SF 34.7

Adjusted Batter Runs
Bonds-Pit 46.6
Bonilla-Pit 40.6
Clark-SF 36.9
McGriff-SD 36.3
Johnson-NY 33.2

Clutch Hitting Index
Murray-LA 138
Bonds-Pit 138
Magadan-NY 137
Pagnozzi-StL 134
Wallach-Mon 131

Runs Created
Bonds-Pit 118
Sandberg-Chi 114
Bonilla-Pit 114
Clark-SF 110
Pendleton-Atl 107

Total Average
Bonds-Pit 1.055
McGriff-SD ...... .937
Larkin-Cin .... .923
Johnson-NY ..... .902
Sandberg-Chi .... .896

Stolen Bases
Grissom-Mon 76
Nixon-Atl 72
DeShields-Mon ... 56
Lankford-StL 44
Bonds-Pit 43

Stolen Base Average
Dykstra-Phi 85.7
Redus-Pit 85.0
Landrum-Chi 84.4
Jefferies-NY 83.9
Grissom-Mon 81.7

Stolen Base Runs
Grissom-Mon 12.6
Nixon-Atl 9.0
O.Smith-StL 5.1
Landrum-Chi 5.1
Bonds-Pit 5.1

Fielding Runs
Pendleton-Atl 27.9
Belliard-Atl 26.1
Lind-Pit 22.6
Grissom-Mon 20.4
Grace-Chi 20.0

Total Player Rating
Bonds-Pit 6.4
Pendleton-Atl 6.1
Larkin-Cin 5.9
Sandberg-Chi 4.9
Bonilla-Pit 4.1

Wins
Smiley-Pit 20
Glavine-Atl 20
Avery-Atl 18
Martinez-LA 17

Win Percentage
Smiley-Pit .... .714
Rijo-Cin .... .714
Avery-Atl .... .692
Hurst-SD .... .652
Glavine-Atl ...... .645

Games
Jones-Mon 77
Assenmacher-Chi .. 75
Stanton-Atl 74
Burke-Mon-NY 72
Agosto-StL 72

Complete Games
J.Martinez-Mon 9
Glavine-Atl 9
Mulholland-Phi 8
Maddux-Chi 7

Shutouts
J.Martinez-Mon 5
Martinez-LA 4
Smith-Pit 3
Mulholland-Phi 3
Black-SF 3

Saves
L.Smith-StL 47
Dibble-Cin 31
Williams-Phi 30
Franco-NY 30
Righetti-SF 24

Innings Pitched
Maddux-Chi 263.0
Glavine-Atl 246.2
Morgan-LA 236.1
Drabek-Pit 234.2
Cone-NY 232.2

Fewest Hits/Game
Harnisch-Hou 7.02
Rijo-Cin 7.27
DeJesus-Phi 7.28
Hill-StL 7.30
Glavine-Atl 7.33

Fewest BB/Game
Smith-Pit 1.14
Tewksbury-StL ... 1.79
Mulholland-Phi ... 1.90
Smiley-Pit 1.91
B.Smith-StL 2.04

Strikeouts
Cone-NY 241
Maddux-Chi 198
Glavine-Atl 192
Rijo-Cin 172
Harnisch-Hou 172

Strikeouts/Game
Cone-NY 9.32
Rijo-Cin 7.58
Harnisch-Hou 7.14
Gooden-NY 7.11
Glavine-Atl 7.01

Ratio
Rijo-Cin 9.82
Glavine-Atl 9.92
Morgan-LA 9.94
J.Martinez-Mon .. 10.26
Benes-SD 10.37

Earned Run Average
J.Martinez-Mon ... 2.39
Rijo-Cin 2.51
Glavine-Atl 2.55
Belcher-LA 2.62
Harnisch-Hou 2.70

Adjusted ERA
Glavine-Atl 152
Rijo-Cin 151
J.Martinez-Mon ... 151
DeLeon-StL 137
Belcher-LA 137

Opponents' Batting Avg.
Harnisch-Hou ... .212
Rijo-Cin .... .219
Glavine-Atl ..... .222
Hill-StL .... .224
DeJesus-Phi .... .224

Opponents' On Base Pct.
Rijo-Cin .... .274
Glavine-Atl ..... .279
Morgan-LA ...... .279
J.Martinez-Mon .. .283
Benes-SD .... .286

Starter Runs
J.Martinez-Mon .. 31.9
Glavine-Atl 31.0
Rijo-Cin 26.6
Belcher-LA 24.7
Morgan-LA 23.7

Adjusted Starter Runs
Glavine-Atl 36.5
J.Martinez-Mon .. 30.2
Rijo-Cin 29.3
Harris-SD 23.1
Belcher-LA 22.6

Clutch Pitching Index
DeLeon-StL 131
Drabek-Pit 127
Tewksbury-StL ... 121
Ojeda-LA 121
Belcher-LA 118

Relief Runs
McElroy-Chi 19.5
Maddux-SD 13.4
Williams-Phi 13.2
Brantley-SF 12.0
Pena-NY-Atl 11.7

Adjusted Relief Runs
McElroy-Chi 21.7
Maddux-SD 14.6
Williams-Phi 13.0
Brantley-SF 11.9
Pena-NY-Atl 11.8

Relief Ranking
Williams-Phi 32.4
L.Smith-StL 28.5
McElroy-Chi 16.9
Pena-NY-Atl 16.5
Franco-NY 15.3

Total Pitcher Index
Glavine-Atl 4.9
J.Martinez-Mon ... 3.9
Rijo-Cin 3.3
Maddux-Chi 2.6
McElroy-Chi 2.4

Total Baseball Ranking
Bonds-Pit 6.4
Pendleton-Atl 6.1
Larkin-Cin 5.9
Glavine-Atl 4.9
Sandberg-Chi 4.9

TEAM	G	W	L	PCT	GB	R	OR	AB	H	2B	3B	HR	BB	SO	AVG	OBP	SLG	PRO	PRO+	BR	/A	PF	CHI	RC	SB	CS	SBA	SBR
EAST																												
TOR	162	91	71	.562		684	**622**	5489	1412	295	45	133	499	1043	.257	.326	.400	.726	96	-7	-34	104	96	724	148	53	74	**13**
DET	162	84	78	.519	7	817	794	5547	1372	259	26	**209**	**699**	1185	.247	.335	.416	.751	105	50	40	101	103	800	109	47	70	5
BOS	162	84	78	.519	7	731	712	5530	1486	**305**	25	126	593	820	.269	.343	.401	.744	100	42	6	105	95	756	59	39	60	-6
MIL	162	83	79	.512	8	799	744	5611	1523	247	**53**	116	556	802	.271	.340	.396	.736	106	24	42	98	105	745	106	68	61	-9
NY	162	71	91	.438	20	674	777	5541	1418	249	19	147	473	861	.256	.319	.387	.706	94	-47	-48	100	101	683	109	36	**75**	11
BAL	162	67	95	.414	24	686	796	5604	1421	256	29	170	528	974	.254	.321	.401	.722	102	-17	13	96	96	707	50	33	60	-5
CLE	162	57	105	.352	34	576	759	5470	1390	236	26	79	449	888	.254	.316	.350	.666	83	-118	-122	101	98	591	84	58	59	-10
WEST																												
MIN	162	95	67	.586		776	652	5556	**1557**	270	42	140	526	**747**	**.280**	**.347**	.420	**.767**	106	82	49	105	96	786	107	68	61	-9
CHI	162	87	75	.537	8	758	681	5594	1464	226	39	139	610	896	.262	.338	.391	.729	103	12	30	98	101	741	134	74	64	-4
TEX	162	85	77	.525	10	**829**	814	5703	1539	288	31	177	596	1039	.270	.343	**.424**	**.767**	**113**	**85**	**99**	98	99	**831**	102	50	67	1
OAK	162	84	78	.519	11	760	776	5410	1342	246	19	159	642	981	.248	.333	.389	.722	105	-2	39	94	**106**	711	**151**	64	70	7
SEA	162	83	79	.512	12	702	674	5494	1400	268	29	126	588	811	.255	.331	.383	.714	97	-21	-22	100	99	698	97	44	69	3
KC	162	82	80	.506	13	727	722	5584	1475	290	41	117	523	969	.264	.331	.394	.725	100	-4	-7	100	101	720	119	68	64	-5
CAL	162	81	81	.500	14	653	649	5470	1396	245	29	115	448	928	.255	.316	.374	.690	90	-78	-77	100	104	640	94	56	63	-5
TOT	1134					10172		77603	20195	3680	453	1953	7730	12944	.260	.331	.395	.726							1469	758	66	-14

TEAM	CG	SH	SV	IP	H	H/G	HR	BB	SO	RAT	ERA	ERA+	OAV	OOB	PR	/A	PF	CPI	FA	E	DP	FW	PW	BW	SBW	DIF
EAST																										
TOR	10	**16**	**60**	1462^{2}	**1301**	8.0	121	523	971	**11.5**	**3.50**	**120**	**.238**	**.309**	**96**	**114**	103	96	.980	127	115	-.6	**11.4**	-3.4	**1.4**	1.2
DET	18	8	38	1450^{1}	1570	9.7	148	593	739	13.6	4.51	92	.280	.352	-66	-57	101	105	.983	104	171	.7	-5.7	4.0	.6	3.4
BOS	15	13	45	1439^{2}	1405	8.8	147	530	999	12.3	4.01	107	.257	.326	13	46	105	100	.981	116	165	.0	4.6	.6	-.5	-1.7
MIL	23	11	41	1463^{2}	1498	9.2	147	527	859	12.7	4.14	96	.266	.334	-8	-28	97	102	.981	118	176	-.0	-2.8	4.2	-.8	1.5
NY	3	11	37	1444	1510	9.4	152	506	936	12.8	4.42	94	.271	.336	-52	-45	101	99	.979	133	181	-.9	-4.5	-4.8	1.2	-1.0
BAL	8	8	42	1457^{2}	1534	9.5	147	504	868	12.8	4.59	86	.273	.335	-80	-103	97	95	**.985**	**91**	172	**1.4**	-10.3	1.3	-.4	-6.0
CLE	22	8	33	1441^{1}	1551	9.7	110	**441**	862	12.7	4.23	98	.276	.333	-22	-13	101	98	.976	149	150	-1.8	-1.3	-12.2	-.9	-7.8
WEST																										
MIN	21	12	53	1449^{1}	1402	8.7	139	488	876	11.9	3.69	115	.255	.319	64	92	104	104	**.985**	95	161	1.2	9.2	4.9	-.8	-.5
CHI	**28**	8	40	1478	1302	**7.9**	154	601	923	11.8	3.79	105	.239	.318	50	30	97	98	.982	116	151	.0	3.0	3.0	-.3	.3
TEX	9	10	41	1479	1486	9.0	151	662	**1022**	13.3	4.47	90	.262	.344	-61	-72	98	98	.979	134	138	-1.0	-7.2	**9.9**	.2	2.1
OAK	14	10	49	1444^{1}	1425	8.9	155	655	892	13.3	4.57	84	.260	.345	-77	-119	94	97	.982	107	150	.5	-11.9	3.9	.8	9.7
SEA	10	13	48	1464^{1}	1387	8.5	136	628	1003	12.7	3.79	109	.253	.335	50	54	101	**107**	.983	110	**187**	.3	5.4	-2.2	.4	-1.9
KC	17	12	41	1466	1473	9.0	**105**	529	1004	12.6	3.92	105	.261	.329	28	32	101	99	.980	125	141	-.5	3.2	-.7	-.4	-.6
CAL	18	10	50	1441^{2}	1351	8.4	141	543	990	12.1	3.69	111	.250	.323	65	66	100	105	.984	102	156	.8	6.6	-7.7	-.4	.7
TOT	216	150	618	20382		8.9				12.6	4.09		.260	.331					.981	1627	2214					

Runs	Hits	Doubles	Triples	Home Runs	Total Bases
Molitor-Mil 133	Molitor-Mil 216	Palmeiro-Tex 49	Molitor-Mil 13	Fielder-Det 44	C.Ripken-Bal 368
Palmeiro-Tex 115	C.Ripken-Bal 210	C.Ripken-Bal 46	Johnson-Chi 13	Canseco-Oak 44	Palmeiro-Tex 336
Canseco-Oak 115	Sierra-Tex 203	Sierra-Tex 44	Alomar-Tor 11	C.Ripken-Bal 34	Sierra-Tex 332
White-Tor 110	Palmeiro-Tex 203		White-Tor 10	Carter-Tor 33	Molitor-Mil 325
Sierra-Tex 110	Franco-Tex 201		Devereaux-Bal 10	Thomas-Chi 32	Carter-Tor 321

Runs Batted In	Runs Produced	Bases On Balls	Batting Average	On Base Percentage	Slugging Average
Fielder-Det 133	Sierra-Tex 201	Thomas-Chi 138	Franco-Tex .... .341	Thomas-Chi .... .454	Tartabull-KC .... .593
Canseco-Oak 122	Canseco-Oak 193	Tettleton-Det 101	Boggs-Bos .... .332	Randolph-Mil .... .427	C.Ripken-Bal ...... .566
Sierra-Tex 116	Molitor-Mil 191	R.Henderson-Oak .. 98	Randolph-Mil ...... .327	Boggs-Bos .... .425	Canseco-Oak ...... .556
C.Ripken-Bal 114	Fielder-Det 191	Clark-Bos 96	K.GriffeyJr-Sea .... .327	Franco-Tex .... .409	Thomas-Chi .... .553
Thomas-Chi 109	Thomas-Chi 181	Davis-Min 95	Molitor-Mil .... .325	E.Martinez-Sea .... .407	Palmeiro-Tex ...... .532

Production	Adjusted Production	Batter Runs	Adjusted Batter Runs	Clutch Hitting Index	Runs Created
Thomas-Chi 1.007	Thomas-Chi 181	Thomas-Chi 65.9	Thomas-Chi 67.8	Yount-Mil 144	Thomas-Chi 145
Tartabull-KC .... .993	Tartabull-KC 170	C.Ripken-Bal 48.5	C.Ripken-Bal 51.9	Davis-Sea 140	C.Ripken-Bal 134
C.Ripken-Bal ...... .945	C.Ripken-Bal 164	Tartabull-KC 46.4	Palmeiro-Tex 47.1	Randolph-Mil 132	Molitor-Mil 132
K.GriffeyJr-Sea .... .932	Canseco-Oak 159	Palmeiro-Tex 45.6	Tartabull-KC 46.1	Surhoff-Mil 130	Palmeiro-Tex 129
Palmeiro-Tex ...... .925	Palmeiro-Tex 156	K.GriffeyJr-Sea ... 42.3	Molitor-Mil 43.6	Hrbek-Min 129	K.GriffeyJr-Sea ... 118

Total Average	Stolen Bases	Stolen Base Average	Stolen Base Runs	Fielding Runs	Total Player Rating
Thomas-Chi 1.109	R.Henderson-Oak .. 58	Cotto-Sea 84.2	Alomar-Tor 9.3	Gaetti-Cal 24.6	C.Ripken-Bal 8.1
Tartabull-KC 1.044	Alomar-Tor 53	Knoblauch-Min ... 83.3	R.Henderson-Oak .. 6.6	Vizquel-Sea 24.2	Thomas-Chi 5.8
K.GriffeyJr-Sea .... .969	Raines-Chi 51	Alomar-Tor 82.8	Raines-Chi 6.3	Espinoza-NY 20.3	K.GriffeyJr-Sea 4.9
Canseco-Oak ..... .962	Polonia-Cal 48	Gibson-KC 81.8	Cuyler-Det 6.3	Buechele-Tex 20.1	Canseco-Oak 4.1
Whitaker-Det ...... .942	Cuyler-Det 41	Canseco-Oak 81.3	Franco-Tex 5.4	Sojo-Cal 20.1	R.Henderson-Oak .. 4.0

Wins	Win Percentage	Games	Complete Games	Shutouts	Saves
Gullickson-Det 20	Erickson-Min ...... .714	R.Ward-Tor 81	McDowell-Chi 15	Clemens-Bos 4	Harvey-Cal 46
Erickson-Min 20	Langston-Cal ...... .704	Olson-Bal 72	Clemens-Bos 13	McDowell-Chi 3	Eckersley-Oak 43
Langston-Cal 19	Gullickson-Det ..... .690	Jackson-Sea 72	Navarro-Mil 10	Holman-Sea 3	Aguilera-Min 42
	Wegman-Mil .... .682	Swift-Sea 71	Morris-Min 10	Erickson-Min 3	Reardon-Bos 40
	Moore-Oak .... .680		Terrell-Det 8	Appier-KC 3	Montgomery-KC ... 33

Innings Pitched	Fewest Hits/Game	Fewest BB/Game	Strikeouts	Strikeouts/Game	Ratio
Clemens-Bos 271.1	Ryan-Tex 5.31	Swindell-Cle 1.17	Clemens-Bos 241	Ryan-Tex 10.56	Ryan-Tex 9.31
McDowell-Chi ... 253.2	Johnson-Sea 6.75	Sanderson-NY 1.25	Johnson-Sea 228	Johnson-Sea 10.19	Clemens-Bos 9.59
Morris-Min 246.2	Langston-Cal 6.94	Tapani-Min 1.48	Ryan-Tex 203	Clemens-Bos 7.99	Tapani-Min 9.85
Langston-Cal 246.1	Clemens-Bos 7.26	Gullickson-Det 1.75	McDowell-Chi 191	Hanson-Sea 7.37	Sanderson-NY ... 10.04
Tapani-Min 244.0	McDowell-Chi 7.52	Wegman-Mil 1.86	Langston-Cal 183	Appier-KC 6.85	Saberhagen-KC . 10.04

Earned Run Average	Adjusted ERA	Opponents' Batting Avg.	Opponents' On Base Pct.	Starter Runs	Adjusted Starter Runs
Clemens-Bos 2.62	Clemens-Bos 164	Ryan-Tex .... .172	Ryan-Tex .... .267	Clemens-Bos 44.4	Clemens-Bos 50.6
Candiotti-Cle-Tor .. 2.65	Candiotti-Cle-Tor .. 158	Johnson-Sea ...... .213	Clemens-Bos ...... .272	Candiotti-Cle-Tor .. 38.3	Candiotti-Cle-Tor .. 40.6
Wegman-Mil 2.84	Tapani-Min 143	Langston-Cal ...... .215	Tapani-Min .... .278	J.Abbott-Cal 32.5	Tapani-Min 34.7
J.Abbott-Cal 2.89	J.Abbott-Cal 142	Clemens-Bos ...... .221	Sanderson-NY ..... .281	Langston-Cal 30.1	J.Abbott-Cal 32.8
Ryan-Tex 2.91	Wegman-Mil 140	Candiotti-Cle-Tor .. .228	Saberhagen-KC ... .281	Tapani-Min 30.0	Langston-Cal 30.3

Clutch Pitching Index	Relief Runs	Adjusted Relief Runs	Relief Ranking	Total Pitcher Index	Total Baseball Ranking
Krueger-Sea 130	Frohwirth-Bal 23.8	Frohwirth-Bal 22.3	Harvey-Cal 43.8	Clemens-Bos 5.3	C.Ripken-Bal 8.1
Holman-Sea 117	Harvey-Cal 21.8	Harvey-Cal 21.9	Aguilera-Min 37.4	Candiotti-Cle-Tor ... 4.3	Thomas-Chi 5.8
Terrell-Det 117	Swift-Sea 21.1	Swift-Sea 21.3	Farr-NY 30.8	J.Abbott-Cal 3.8	Clemens-Bos 5.3
Guzman-Tex 116	Eichhorn-Cal 19.2	Eichhorn-Cal 19.2	R.Ward-Tor 27.0	Tapani-Min 3.6	K.GriffeyJr-Sea ... 4.9
Tanana-Det 115	Flanagan-Bal 18.7	Habyan-NY 18.4	Radinsky-Chi 23.4	Langston-Cal 3.2	Candiotti-Cle-Tor ... 4.3

TEAM	G	W	L	PCT	GB	R	OR	AB	H	2B	3B	HR	BB	SO	AVG	OBP	SLG	PRO	PRO+	BR	/A	PF	CHI	RC	SB	CS	SBA	SBR
EAST																												
PIT	162	96	66	.593		**693**	595	5527	1409	272	**54**	106	569	872	.255	.327	.381	.708	**107**	48	**56**	99	101	**699**	110	53	67	1
MON	162	87	75	.537	9	648	581	5477	1381	263	37	102	463	976	.252	.315	.370	.685	101	-4	-1	100	104	651	196	63	76	**21**
STL	162	83	79	.512	13	631	604	5594	**1464**	262	44	94	495	996	**.262**	.325	.375	.700	106	30	40	99	94	680	**208**	118	64	-8
CHI	162	78	84	.481	18	593	624	5590	1420	221	41	104	417	**816**	.254	.309	.364	.673	94	-31	-46	102	99	617	77	51	60	-8
NY	162	72	90	.444	24	599	653	5340	1254	259	17	93	**572**	956	.235	.312	.342	.654	92	-54	-50	99	**106**	583	129	52	71	8
PHI	162	70	92	.432	26	686	717	5500	1392	255	36	118	509	1059	.253	.322	.377	.699	105	27	32	99	104	684	127	31	**80**	20
WEST																												
ATL	162	98	64	.605		682	**569**	5480	1391	223	48	**138**	493	924	.254	.318	**.388**	.706	97	34	-18	108	103	686	126	60	68	2
CIN	162	90	72	.556	8	660	609	5460	1418	**281**	44	99	563	888	.260	**.331**	.382	**.713**	103	**58**	27	105	96	689	125	65	66	-2
SD	162	82	80	.506	16	617	636	5476	1396	255	30	135	453	864	.255	.315	.386	.701	101	22	1	103	96	648	69	52	57	-11
HOU	162	81	81	.500	17	608	668	5480	1350	255	38	96	506	1025	.246	.316	.359	.675	103	-20	16	94	100	636	139	54	72	9
SF	162	72	90	.444	26	574	647	5456	1330	220	36	105	435	1067	.244	.304	.355	.659	97	-57	-25	95	102	584	112	64	64	-5
LA	162	63	99	.389	35	548	636	5368	1333	201	34	72	503	899	.248	.316	.339	.655	93	-54	-45	99	97	579	142	78	65	-4
TOT	972					7539		65748	16538	2967	459	1262	5978	11342	.252	.318	.368	.686							1560	741	68	23

TEAM	CG	SH	SV	IP	H	H/G	HR	BB	SO	RAT	ERA	ERA+	OAV	OOB	PR	/A	PF	CPI	FA	E	DP	FW	PW	BW	SBW	DIF
EAST																										
PIT	20	20	43	1479^2	1410	8.6	101	455	844	11.5	3.35	102	.254	.314	25	9	97	103	.984	101	142	.9	1.0	**6.0**	-.1	7.2
MON	11	14	49	1468	**1296**	**7.9**	92	525	1014	11.5	3.25	107	**.238**	.310	41	38	100	97	.980	124	113	-.4	4.1	-.1	**2.1**	.4
STL	10	9	47	1480	1405	8.5	118	**400**	842	**11.2**	3.38	102	.252	**.305**	20	10	98	99	**.985**	**94**	146	**1.3**	1.1	4.3	-1.1	-3.6
CHI	16	11	37	1469	1337	8.2	107	575	901	12.0	3.39	106	.246	.323	18	34	103	104	.982	114	142	.2	3.7	-5.0	-1.1	-.8
NY	17	13	34	1446^2	1404	8.7	98	482	1025	12.0	3.66	95	.256	.321	-25	-27	100	98	.981	116	134	.0	-2.9	-5.4	.7	-1.4
PHI	**27**	7	34	1428	1387	8.7	113	549	851	12.4	4.11	85	.257	.328	-96	-97	100	92	.978	131	128	-.8	-10.5	3.4	1.9	-5.1
WEST																										
ATL	26	**24**	41	1460	1321	8.1	89	489	948	11.3	**3.14**	**119**	.242	.307	**58**	**97**	107	99	.982	109	121	.4	**10.5**	-1.9	.0	8.0
CIN	9	11	**55**	1449^2	1362	8.5	109	470	**1060**	11.5	3.46	106	.251	.314	6	32	105	100	.984	96	128	1.2	3.4	2.9	-.4	1.9
SD	9	11	46	1461^1	1444	8.9	111	439	971	11.7	3.56	102	.261	.318	-9	11	104	102	.982	115	127	.0	1.2	.1	-1.4	1.0
HOU	5	12	45	1459^1	1386	8.5	114	539	978	12.1	3.72	90	.252	.323	-35	-61	95	98	.981	114	125	.2	-6.6	1.7	.8	3.9
SF	9	12	30	1461	1385	8.5	128	502	927	11.8	3.61	93	.253	.320	-17	-42	96	102	.982	113	**174**	.2	-4.5	-2.7	-.7	-1.2
LA	18	13	29	1438	1401	8.8	**82**	553	981	12.4	3.41	101	.257	.328	15	7	99	**106**	.972	174	136	-3.2	.8	-4.8	-.6	-10.1
TOT	177	157	490	17500^2		8.5				11.8	3.50		.252	.318					.981	1401	1616					

Runs	Hits	Doubles	Triples	Home Runs	Total Bases
Bonds-Pit 109	VanSlyke-Pit 199	VanSlyke-Pit 45	Sanders-Atl 14	McGriff-SD 35	Sheffield-SD 323
Hollins-Phi 104	Pendleton-Atl 199	Lankford-StL 40	Finley-Hou 13	Bonds-Pit 34	Sandberg-Chi 312
VanSlyke-Pit 103	Sandberg-Chi 186	Duncan-Phi 40	VanSlyke-Pit 12	Sheffield-SD 33	VanSlyke-Pit 310
Sandberg-Chi 100	Grace-Chi 185	Clark-SF 40	Butler-LA 11	Hollins-Phi 27	Pendleton-Atl 303
Grissom-Mon 99	Sheffield-SD 184		Alicea-StL 11	Daulton-Phi 27	

Runs Batted In	Runs Produced	Bases On Balls	Batting Average	On Base Percentage	Slugging Average
Daulton-Phi 109	Pendleton-Atl 182	Bonds-Pit 127	Sheffield-SD .330	Bonds-Pit .461	Bonds-Pit .624
Pendleton-Atl 105	VanSlyke-Pit 178	McGriff-SD 96	VanSlyke-Pit .324	Kruk-Phi .428	Sheffield-SD .580
McGriff-SD 104	Bonds-Pit 178	Butler-LA 95	Kruk-Phi .323	Butler-LA .413	McGriff-SD .556
Bonds-Pit 103	Hollins-Phi 170	Biggio-Hou 94	Roberts-Cin .323	McGriff-SD .396	Daulton-Phi .524
Sheffield-SD 100	Bagwell-Hou 165	Kruk-Phi 92	Gwynn-SD .317	Roberts-Cin .396	Sandberg-Chi .510

Production	Adjusted Production	Batter Runs	Adjusted Batter Runs	Clutch Hitting Index	Runs Created
Bonds-Pit 1.085	Bonds-Pit 207	Bonds-Pit 71.8	Bonds-Pit 72.7	Murray-NY 136	Bonds-Pit 148
Sheffield-SD .969	Sheffield-SD 166	Sheffield-SD 50.1	Sheffield-SD 48.0	Daulton-Phi 134	VanSlyke-Pit 122
McGriff-SD .952	McGriff-SD 161	McGriff-SD 48.1	McGriff-SD 45.9	Bagwell-Hou 131	Sheffield-SD 118
Daulton-Phi .912	Daulton-Phi 157	VanSlyke-Pit 40.2	VanSlyke-Pit 41.1	Lind-Pit 125	Sandberg-Chi 117
VanSlyke-Pit .891	VanSlyke-Pit 152	Kruk-Phi 38.6	Kruk-Phi 39.1	Karros-LA 124	McGriff-SD 116

Total Average	Stolen Bases	Stolen Base Average	Stolen Base Runs	Fielding Runs	Total Player Rating
Bonds-Pit 1.335	Grissom-Mon 78	Davis-LA 95.0	Grissom-Mon 15.6	Belliard-Atl 26.6	Bonds-Pit 9.0
Daulton-Phi .994	DeShields-Mon 46	Alou-Mon 88.9	Finley-Hou 7.8	Jackson-SD 24.0	Sheffield-SD 5.9
McGriff-SD .987	Roberts-Cin 44	Duncan-Phi 88.5	O.Smith-StL 7.5	Thompson-SF 20.3	Sandberg-Chi 5.8
Sheffield-SD .945	Finley-Hou 44		Bonds-Pit 6.9	Wallach-Mon 18.5	VanSlyke-Pit 5.3
Kruk-Phi .900	O.Smith-StL 43		Dykstra-Phi 6.0	Harris-LA 16.7	Larkin-Cin 4.7

Wins	Win Percentage	Games	Complete Games	Shutouts	Saves
Maddux-Chi 20	Tewksbury-StL .762	Boever-Hou 81	Mulholland-Phi 12	Glavine-Atl 5	L.Smith-StL 43
Glavine-Atl 20	Glavine-Atl .714	D.Jones-Hou 80	Schilling-Phi 10	Cone-NY 5	Myers-SD 38
	Leibrandt-Atl .682	Perez-StL 77	Drabek-Pit 10		Wetteland-Mon 37
	Morgan-Chi .667	Hernandez-Hou 77	Smoltz-Atl 9		D.Jones-Hou 36
	Maddux-Chi .645	Innis-NY 76	Maddux-Chi 9		M.Williams-Phi 29

Innings Pitched	Fewest Hits/Game	Fewest BB/Game	Strikeouts	Strikeouts/Game	Ratio
Maddux-Chi 268.0	Schilling-Phi 6.56	Tewksbury-StL .77	Smoltz-Atl 215	Cone-NY 9.79	Schilling-Phi 8.95
Drabek-Pit 256.2	Maddux-Chi 6.75	Cormier-StL 1.60	Cone-NY 214	Fernandez-NY 8.09	Tewksbury-StL 9.27
Smoltz-Atl 246.2	Fernandez-NY 6.79	Swindell-Cin 1.73	Maddux-Chi 199	Smoltz-Atl 7.84	Maddux-Chi 9.57
Morgan-Chi 240.0	Martinez-Mon 6.84	Mulholland-Phi 1.81	Fernandez-NY 193	Rijo-Cin 7.29	Martinez-Mon 9.58
Avery-Atl 233.2	Cone-NY 7.41	Tomlin-Pit 1.81	Drabek-Pit 177	Harnisch-Hou 7.14	Drabek-Pit 9.75

Earned Run Average	Adjusted ERA	Opponents' Batting Avg.	Opponents' On Base Pct.	Starter Runs	Adjusted Starter Runs
Swift-SF 2.08	Maddux-Chi 165	Schilling-Phi .201	Schilling-Phi .256	Maddux-Chi 39.3	Maddux-Chi 42.3
Tewksbury-StL 2.16	Swift-SF 161	Maddux-Chi .210	Tewksbury-StL .267	Tewksbury-StL 34.7	Tewksbury-StL 33.1
Maddux-Chi 2.18	Tewksbury-StL 159	Fernandez-NY .210	Martinez-Mon .273	Schilling-Phi 29.1	Schilling-Phi 28.9
Schilling-Phi 2.35	Schilling-Phi 149	Martinez-Mon .211	Maddux-Chi .273	Swift-SF 26.1	Morgan-Chi 28.1
Martinez-Mon 2.47	Rijo-Cin 143	Cone-NY .223	Drabek-Pit .277	Martinez-Mon 26.1	Rijo-Cin 25.9

Clutch Pitching Index	Relief Runs	Adjusted Relief Runs	Relief Ranking	Total Pitcher Index	Total Baseball Ranking
Swift-SF 131	Rojas-Mon 23.2	Rojas-Mon 23.0	D.Jones-Hou 41.7	Maddux-Chi 6.0	Bonds-Pit 9.0
Tewksbury-StL 120	D.Jones-Hou 20.5	D.Jones-Hou 18.5	Rojas-Mon 21.6	Tewksbury-StL 3.6	Maddux-Chi 6.0
Swindell-Cin 119	Beck-SF 17.8	Perez-StL 16.6	Perez-StL 19.3	Martinez-Mon 3.3	Sheffield-SD 5.9
Morgan-Chi 115	Hernandez-Hou 17.2	Beck-SF 16.2	Beck-SF 16.3	Glavine-Atl 3.3	Sandberg-Chi 5.8
Ojeda-LA 113	Perez-StL 17.2	Hernandez-Hou 15.2	Hernandez-Hou 14.5	Rijo-Cin 3.2	VanSlyke-Pit 5.3

TEAM	G	W	L	PCT	GB	R	OR	AB	H	2B	3B	HR	BB	SO	AVG	OBP	SLG	PRO	PRO+	BR	/A	PF	CHI	RC	SB	CS	SBA	SBR
EAST																												
TOR	162	96	66	.593		780	682	5536	1458	265	40	163	561	933	.263	.336	**.414**	**.750**	104	**63**	31	105	102	**779**	129	39	**77**	**15**
MIL	162	92	70	.568	4	740	**604**	5504	1477	272	35	82	511	779	.268	.334	.375	.709	100	-10	5	98	108	700	**256**	115	69	8
BAL	162	89	73	.549	7	705	656	5485	1423	243	36	148	647	827	.259	.343	.398	.741	107	56	59	100	92	754	89	48	65	-2
NY	162	76	86	.469	20	733	746	5593	1462	281	18	163	536	903	.261	.331	.406	.737	103	33	18	102	99	742	78	37	68	1
CLE	162	76	86	.469	20	674	746	5620	1495	227	24	127	448	885	.266	.325	.383	.708	97	-22	-30	101	99	686	144	67	68	3
DET	162	75	87	.463	21	**791**	794	5515	1411	256	16	**182**	675	1055	.256	.340	.407	.747	107	**63**	54	101	102	769	66	45	59	-7
BOS	162	73	89	.451	23	599	669	5461	1343	259	21	84	591	865	.246	.323	.347	.670	84	-84	-119	105	98	617	44	48	48	-16
WEST																												
OAK	162	96	66	.593		745	672	5387	1389	219	24	142	**707**	831	.258	**.349**	.386	.735	**110**	54	**82**	96	98	748	143	59	71	8
MIN	162	90	72	.556	6	747	653	5582	**1544**	275	27	104	527	834	**.277**	.345	.391	.736	103	46	23	103	99	748	123	74	62	-8
CHI	162	86	76	.531	10	738	690	5498	1434	269	36	110	622	784	.261	.339	.383	.722	105	19	36	98	102	728	160	57	74	14
TEX	162	77	85	.475	19	682	753	5537	1387	266	23	159	550	1036	.250	.324	.393	.717	103	-5	18	97	98	708	81	44	65	-2
KC	162	72	90	.444	24	610	667	5501	1411	**284**	**42**	75	439	**741**	.256	.317	.364	.681	89	-73	-79	101	99	629	131	71	65	-3
CAL	162	72	90	.444	24	579	671	5364	1306	202	20	88	416	882	.243	.303	.338	.641	80	-152	-143	99	**112**	529	160	101	61	-13
SEA	162	64	98	.395	32	679	799	5564	1466	278	24	149	474	841	.263	.326	.402	.728	102	13	7	101	96	708	100	55	65	-3
TOT	1134					9802		77147	20006	3596	386	1776	7704	12196	.259	.331	.385	.716							1704	860	66	-5

TEAM	CG	SH	SV	IP	H	H/G	HR	BB	SO	RAT	ERA	ERA+	OAV	OOB	PR	/A	PF	CPI	FA	E	DP	FW	PW	BW	SBW	DIF
EAST																										
TOR	18	14	49	1440^2	1346	8.4	124	541	954	12.1	3.91	104	.248	.321	5	27	104	93	.985	93	109	1.4	2.7	3.2	**1.6**	6.1
MIL	19	14	39	1457	**1344**	**8.3**	127	**435**	793	**11.3**	**3.43**	111	**.246**	**.307**	**82**	61	97	98	**.986**	**89**	146	**1.6**	6.2	.5	.8	1.8
BAL	20	**16**	48	1464	1419	8.7	124	518	846	12.1	3.79	103	.256	.324	25	19	99	99	.985	93	168	1.4	1.9	6.0	-.2	-1.2
NY	20	9	44	1452^2	1453	9.0	129	612	851	13.0	4.21	96	.263	.341	-43	-26	103	99	.982	114	165	.2	-2.6	1.8	.1	-4.6
CLE	13	7	46	1470	1507	9.2	159	566	890	12.9	4.11	98	.268	.339	-28	-13	102	106	.978	141	**176**	-1.3	-1.3	-3.1	.3	.3
DET	10	4	36	1435^2	1534	9.6	155	564	693	13.3	4.60	87	.277	.346	-105	-97	101	99	.981	116	164	.1	-9.9	5.5	-.7	-1.1
BOS	22	13	39	1448^2	1403	8.7	107	535	943	12.3	3.58	**116**	.255	.326	57	**91**	105	103	.978	139	170	-1.2	**9.3**	-12.1	-1.6	-2.4
WEST																										
OAK	8	9	**58**	1447	1396	8.7	129	601	843	12.7	3.73	101	.256	.335	34	8	96	**107**	.979	125	158	-.4	.8	**8.4**	.8	5.4
MIN	16	13	50	1453	1391	8.6	121	479	923	11.8	3.70	109	.254	.318	38	52	102	98	.985	95	155	1.3	5.3	2.3	-.8	.8
CHI	21	5	52	1461^2	1400	8.6	123	550	810	12.3	3.82	100	.252	.326	19	0	97	98	.979	129	134	-.6	.0	3.7	1.5	.5
TEX	19	3	42	1460^1	1471	9.1	113	598	**1034**	13.0	4.09	94	.264	.341	-24	-43	97	100	.975	154	153	-2.0	-4.4	1.8	-.2	.7
KC	9	12	44	1447^1	1426	8.9	**106**	512	834	12.3	3.81	104	.259	.327	21	28	101	98	.980	122	164	-.2	2.9	-8.0	-.3	-3.3
CAL	**26**	13	42	1446	1449	9.0	130	532	888	12.6	3.84	102	.264	.333	16	11	99	106	.979	134	172	-.9	1.1	-14.6	-1.3	6.6
SEA	21	9	30	1445	1467	9.1	129	661	894	13.6	4.55	88	.266	.351	-97	-89	101	96	.982	112	170	.3	-9.1	.7	-.3	-8.7
TOT	242	141	619	20329		8.9				12.5	3.94		.259	.331					.981	1656	2204					

Runs
Phillips-Det 114
Thomas-Chi 108
Alomar-Tor 105
Puckett-Min 104
Knoblauch-Min ... 104

Hits
Puckett-Min 210
Baerga-Cle 205
Molitor-Mil 195
Mack-Min 189
Thomas-Chi 185

Doubles
Thomas-Chi 46
E.Martinez-Sea 46
Yount-Mil 40
Mattingly-NY 40
Griffey-Sea 39

Triples
Johnson-Chi 12
Devereaux-Bal 11
Anderson-Bal 10
Raines-Chi 9

Home Runs
Gonzalez-Tex 43
McGwire-Oak 42
Fielder-Det 35
Carter-Tor 34
Belle-Cle 34

Total Bases
Puckett-Min 313
Carter-Tor 310
Gonzalez-Tex 309
Thomas-Chi 307
Devereaux-Bal 303

Runs Batted In
Fielder-Det 124
Carter-Tor 119
Thomas-Chi 115
Belle-Cle 112
Bell-Chi 112

Runs Produced
Thomas-Chi 199
Puckett-Min 195
Carter-Tor 182
Baerga-Cle 177
Winfield-Tor 174

Bases On Balls
Thomas-Chi 122
Tettleton-Det 122
Phillips-Det 114
Milligan-Bal 106
Tartabull-NY 103

Batting Average
E.Martinez-Sea ... .343
Puckett-Min ...... .329
Thomas-Chi ...... .323
Molitor-Mil ...... .320
Mack-Min ...... .315

On Base Percentage
Thomas-Chi ...... .446
Tartabull-NY ...... .410
E.Martinez-Sea ... .408
Alomar-Tor ...... .406
Molitor-Mil ...... .396

Slugging Average
McGwire-Oak ..... .585
E.Martinez-Sea ... .544
Thomas-Chi ...... .536
Griffey-Sea ...... .535
Gonzalez-Tex ...... .529

Production
Thomas-Chi ...... .981
McGwire-Oak ..... .976
E.Martinez-Sea ... .951
Tartabull-NY ...... .900
Griffey-Sea ...... .898

Adjusted Production
Thomas-Chi 178
McGwire-Oak 177
E.Martinez-Sea ... 163
Tartabull-NY 148
Griffey-Sea 147

Batter Runs
Thomas-Chi 62.4
E.Martinez-Sea ... 44.9
McGwire-Oak 44.4
Griffey-Sea 34.2
Mack-Min 33.8

Adjusted Batter Runs
Thomas-Chi 64.4
McGwire-Oak 46.9
E.Martinez-Sea ... 44.4
Molitor-Mil 35.1
Griffey-Sea 33.6

Clutch Hitting Index
Surhoff-Mil 148
Lansford-Oak 145
Felix-Cal 140
Seitzer-Mil 137
Bell-Chi 136

Runs Created
Thomas-Chi 142
Anderson-Bal 118
E.Martinez-Sea ... 116
Molitor-Mil 116
Mack-Min 114

Total Average
Thomas-Chi 1.066
McGwire-Oak ... 1.040
Tartabull-NY ...... .972
E.Martinez-Sea ... .970
Alomar-Tor ...... .915

Stolen Bases
Lofton-Cle 66
Listach-Mil 54
Anderson-Bal 53
Polonia-Cal 51
Alomar-Tor 49

Stolen Base Average
Cotto-Sea 92.0
White-Tor 90.2
Raines-Chi 88.2
R.Kelly-NY 84.8
Lofton-Cle 84.6

Stolen Base Runs
Lofton-Cle 12.6
Raines-Chi 9.9
Alomar-Tor 9.3
White-Tor 8.7
R.Henderson-Oak .. 7.8

Fielding Runs
Reed-Bos 23.8
Ventura-Chi 23.7
Gagne-Min 20.9
Lofton-Cle 16.6
White-Tor 15.1

Total Player Rating
E.Martinez-Sea 4.8
Ventura-Chi 4.8
Anderson-Bal 4.5
R.Henderson-Oak .. 4.4
Thomas-Chi 4.4

Wins
Morris-Tor 21
Brown-Tex 21
McDowell-Chi 20
Mussina-Bal 18
Clemens-Bos 18

Win Percentage
Mussina-Bal ...... .783
Morris-Tor ...... .778
Guzman-Tor ...... .762
Bosio-Mil ...... .727
McDowell-Chi ..... .667

Games
Rogers-Tex 81
R.Ward-Tor 79
Olin-Cle 72
Lilliquist-Cle 71
Harris-Bos 70

Complete Games
McDowell-Chi 13
Clemens-Bos 11
Brown-Tex 11
Perez-NY 10
Nagy-Cle 10

Shutouts
Clemens-Bos 5
Mussina-Bal 4
Fleming-Sea 4

Saves
Eckersley-Oak 51
Aguilera-Min 41
Montgomery-KC 39
Olson-Bal 36
Henke-Tor 34

Innings Pitched
Brown-Tex 265.2
Wegman-Mil 261.2
McDowell-Chi 260.2
Nagy-Cle 252.0
Perez-NY 247.2

Fewest Hits/Game
Johnson-Sea 6.59
Guzman-Tor 6.73
Appier-KC 7.21
Clemens-Bos 7.41
Smiley-Min 7.66

Fewest BB/Game
Bosio-Mil 1.71
Mussina-Bal 1.79
Wegman-Mil 1.89
Tapani-Min 1.96
Gullickson-Det 2.03

Strikeouts
Johnson-Sea 241
Perez-NY 218
Clemens-Bos 208
Guzman-Tex 179
McDowell-Chi 178

Strikeouts/Game
Johnson-Sea 10.31
Guzman-Tor 8.22
Perez-NY 7.92
Clemens-Bos 7.59
Guzman-Tex 7.19

Ratio
Mussina-Bal 9.78
Clemens-Bos 10.00
Appier-KC 10.24
Smiley-Min 10.31
Guzman-Tor 10.36

Earned Run Average
Clemens-Bos 2.41
Appier-KC 2.46
Mussina-Bal 2.54
Guzman-Tor 2.64
Abbott-Cal 2.77

Adjusted ERA
Clemens-Bos 172
Appier-KC 162
Guzman-Tor 155
Mussina-Bal 154
Abbott-Cal 141

Opponents' Batting Avg.
Johnson-Sea ...... .206
Guzman-Tor ...... .207
Appier-KC ...... .217
Clemens-Bos ...... .224
Smiley-Min ...... .231

Opponents' On Base Pct.
Mussina-Bal ...... .279
Clemens-Bos ...... .280
Appier-KC ...... .282
Guzman-Tor ...... .287
Smiley-Min ...... .288

Starter Runs
Clemens-Bos 42.0
Mussina-Bal 37.5
Appier-KC 34.2
Perez-NY 29.4
Abbott-Cal 27.4

Adjusted Starter Runs
Clemens-Bos 47.7
Mussina-Bal 36.5
Appier-KC 35.2
Perez-NY 32.3
Nagy-Cle 29.8

Clutch Pitching Index
Abbott-Cal 132
Finley-Cal 124
Erickson-Min 113
Perez-NY 110
Moore-Oak 108

Relief Runs
R.Ward-Tor 22.4
Hernandez-Chi ... 18.1
Eckersley-Oak ... 18.0
Frohwirth-Bal 17.4
Harris-Bos 17.1

Adjusted Relief Runs
R.Ward-Tor 24.0
Harris-Bos 19.6
Hernandez-Chi ... 17.1
Frohwirth-Bal 17.0
Montgomery-KC .. 16.6

Relief Ranking
Eckersley-Oak 38.7
Olin-Cle 34.2
J.Russell-Tex-Oak . 31.7
Montgomery-KC 30.2
R.Ward-Tor 29.8

Total Pitcher Index
Clemens-Bos 5.3
Mussina-Bal 4.0
Appier-KC 3.8
Nagy-Cle 3.5
Perez-NY 3.3

Total Baseball Ranking
Clemens-Bos 5.3
E.Martinez-Sea 4.8
Ventura-Chi 4.8
Anderson-Bal 4.5
R.Henderson-Oak .. 4.4

The All-Time Leaders

This section is divided into two parts: lifetime leaders and single-season leaders. Both groups command our attention and convey the pleasures of the game, which lie as much in contemplation of the past as in experiencing the present: Henry Aaron, 755; Babe Ruth, 714; Willie Mays, 660—this is no mere aggregation of names and numbers, as in a telephone directory . . . it comprises the romance and lore of the home run, and of baseball itself. Jack Chesbro, 41, 1904; Bob Gibson, 1.12, 1968; Nolan Ryan, 373, 1973 . . . you can fill in the blanks that tell the story of pitching's most glorious seasons.

What follows are the all-time great achievements in 219 categories, both the traditional statistics and the new. For most of these we will give not the top 10 or 20 but the top 100, because some categories would otherwise be dominated by players of a certain era (for example, slugging average by batters of the 1920s and 1930s, earned run average by pitchers of 1900–1919). And for many stats we will offer a second kind of ranking, broken down into the five distinct eras of baseball, with the top 10 or 15 leaders in each. For example, breaking down single-season home runs this way would produce lists topped by these men:

> 1876–1892: Ned Williamson, 27, 1884
> 1893–1919: Babe Ruth, 29, 1919
> 1920–1941: Babe Ruth, 60, 1927
> 1942–1960: Ralph Kiner, 54, 1949
> 1961–1992: Roger Maris, 61, 1961

And for single-season Adjusted ERA (normalized to league average and adjusted for home-park factor), we get:

> 1876–1892: Tim Keefe, 294
>   (adjusted from actual 0.80), 1880
> 1893–1919: Dutch Leonard, 280
>   (adjusted from actual 0.96), 1914
> 1920–1941: Lefty Grove, 218
>   (adjusted from actual 2.06), 1931
> 1942–1960: Billy Pierce, 201
>   (adjusted from actual 1.97), 1955
> 1961–1992: Bob Gibson, 258
>   (adjusted from actual 1.12), 1968

This is quite a different lineup from the traditional list of ERA leaders (which relegates pre-1900 pitching to the shadows), where of the 15 top spots, 14 are accorded to pitchers active from 1905 to 1918. Is there a baseball fan alive who thinks that all the great pitchers were created in that 14-year span and that the mold was then broken?

But enough expostulation and fulmination. Let's set some ground rules, define some terms that may still be unfamiliar after you've browsed through the Player and Pitcher registers, and get on with the show.

To be eligible for a lifetime pitching category that is stated as an average, a man must have pitched 1,500 or more innings, or 750 or more innings if he is a relief pitcher, in the major leagues; for a counting statistic, he must simply have attained the necessary quantity to crack the list. For a single-season category expressed as an average, he must have pitched one inning per league scheduled game or have attained the necessary quantity (wins, strikeouts, saves) to head a counted list.

To be eligible for a lifetime batting category that is stated as an average, a man must have played in 1,000 or more games; for counting stats such as strikeouts, a Rob Deer earned his place on the list before he played his 1,000th game. For Pitcher Batting Average, the criterion is 1,500 innings pitched or 100 hits. And to reach the single-season batting lists, a man must have 3.1 plate appearances per scheduled game.

We provide tables of the top fielding performances, too, sorted by position as you would expect (and, in this second edition, including only games played at the position, rather than combining data from secondary positions under the dominant postion). But we go one step further and rank several *batting* categories by position, thus recognizing and illustrating the greater demands for fielding skill at such positions as shortstop, catcher, and second base, and the comparatively plentiful supply of batting talent in the outfield and at first base. As we establish a 1,000-game minimum for inclusion in all but a few batting and baserunning categories, we likewise establish for these positional rankings a minimum of 1,000 games played at the position.

For the three principal categories—Total Player Rating, Total Pitcher Index, and Total Baseball Ranking—we have introduced several variations. For example, TPR and TBR are shown 500 deep for lifetime leaders—sorted first by highest value; then alphabetically so that the reader may find a particular player without scanning 500 names; and last by the above-named eras, the top 25 in each. Total Pitcher Index is also sorted this way, but because far fewer pitchers than position players meet the longevity criteria, the lifetime groupings go 300 and 200 deep rather than 500 and 300. Ties are calculated to as many decimal places as needed to break them, but averages are shown to only three places. When two or more players are tied in an averaged category with a narrow base of data, such as a season's won-lost percentage, the reader can presume a numerical dead heat (and obviously

this goes for counting stats, too—one man's 39 doubles are as good as another's). But where there is a tie for batting average, earned run average, or any of the sabermetric measures, the reader may assume that the man listed above the other(s) has the minutely higher average.

Here are the few stats carried in this section that are not carried in the Annual Record or Registers, with definitions where the terms are not self-explanatory (see Glossary for formulas):

Batting, Baserunning, Fielding

Runs (Scored) Per Game   Broken down by era
Home Run Percentage   Home runs per 100 at bats
Bases on Balls Percentage   Walks (most) per 100 at bats
At-Bats Per Strikeout   Broken down by era
Relative Batting Average   Normalized to league average
Isolated Power   Slugging average minus batting average
Extra Base Hits
Pinch Hits
Pinch Hit Batting Average
Pinch Hit Home Runs
Strikeout Percentage
Total Player Rating Per 150 Games   A category highlighting the achievements of modern players and those with comparatively short careers (though at least 1,000 games)
Total Chances Per Game   Broken down by position
Chances Accepted Per Game   Broken down by position
Putouts   Broken down by position
Putouts Per Game   Broken down by position
Assists   Broken down by position
Assists Per Game   Broken down by position
Double Plays   Broken down by position

Pitching

Wins Above Team   How many wins a pitcher garnered beyond those expected of an average pitcher for that team; the formula is weighted so that a pitcher on a good team has a chance to compete with pitchers on poor teams who otherwise would benefit from the larger potential spread between their team's won-lost percentage and their own; see Glossary for more information.
Wins Above League   A pitcher's won-lost record restated by adding his Pitching Wins above the league average to the record that a league-average pitcher would have had with the same number of decisions (for example, Tom Seaver goes 20–10 with 7 Pitching Wins; applying the 7 wins to a 15–15 mark in the same 30 decisions results in a WAL of 22–8).
Percentage of Team Wins
Relief Games
Pitchers' Batting Runs
Pitchers' Fielding Runs
Relief Wins   This statistic, like the relief stats below, includes only games in relief.
Relief Losses
Relief Innings Pitched
Relief Points   Relief wins plus saves minus losses

Games

1	Pete Rose	3562
2	Carl Yastrzemski	3308
3	Hank Aaron	3298
4	Ty Cobb	3035
5	Stan Musial	3026
6	Willie Mays	2992
7	Rusty Staub	2951
8	Brooks Robinson	2896
9	Al Kaline	2834
10	Eddie Collins	2826
11	Reggie Jackson	2820
12	Frank Robinson	2808
13	Honus Wagner	2792
14	Tris Speaker	2789
15	Tony Perez	2777
16	Mel Ott	2730
17	Robin Yount	2729
18	Dave Winfield	2707
19	Graig Nettles	2700
20	Darrell Evans	2687
21	Rabbit Maranville	2670
22	Joe Morgan	2649
23	Lou Brock	2616
24	Dwight Evans	2606
25	Luis Aparicio	2599
26	Willie McCovey	2588
27	George Brett	2562
28	Paul Waner	2549
29	Ernie Banks	2528
30	Bill Buckner	2517
	Sam Crawford	2517
32	Babe Ruth	2503
33	Dave Concepcion	2488
	Billy Williams	2488
35	Nap Lajoie	2480
36	Max Carey	2476
37	Carlton Fisk	2474
38	Rod Carew	2469
	Vada Pinson	2469
40	Dave Parker	2466
41	Ted Simmons	2456
42	Eddie Murray	2444
43	Bill Dahlen	2443
44	Ron Fairly	2442
45	Harmon Killebrew	2435
46	Roberto Clemente	2433
47	Willie Davis	2429
48	Luke Appling	2422
49	Zack Wheat	2410
50	Mickey Vernon	2409
51	Buddy Bell	2405
52	Sam Rice	2404
	Mike Schmidt	2404
54	Mickey Mantle	2401
55	Eddie Mathews	2391
56	Jake Beckley	2386
57	Bobby Wallace	2383
58	Enos Slaughter	2380
59	George Davis	2368
	Al Oliver	2368
61	Nellie Fox	2367
62	Willie Stargell	2360
63	Jose Cruz	2353
64	Brian Downing	2344
65	Steve Garvey	2332
66	Bert Campaneris	2328
67	Frank White	2324
68	Charlie Gehringer	2323
69	Jimmie Foxx	2317
70	Frankie Frisch	2311
71	Andre Dawson	2310
72	Harry Hooper	2309
73	Gary Carter	2296
74	Don Baylor	2292
	Ted Williams	2292
76	Goose Goslin	2287
77	Jimmy Dykes	2282
78	Cap Anson	2276
79	Lave Cross	2275
80	Bob Boone	2264
81	Chris Speier	2260
82	Rogers Hornsby	2259
83	Larry Bowa	2247
84	Ron Santo	2243
85	Fred Clarke	2242
86	Doc Cramer	2239
87	Red Schoendienst	2216
88	Al Simmons	2215
89	Joe Torre	2209
90	Ozzie Smith	2208
91	Willie Randolph	2202
92	Tommy Corcoran	2200
93	Tony Taylor	2195
94	Richie Ashburn	2189
95	Bill Russell	2181
96	Chris Chambliss	2175
97	Joe Judge	2171
98	Charlie Grimm	2166
	Pee Wee Reese	2166
100	Lou Gehrig	2164

At Bats

1	Pete Rose	14053
2	Hank Aaron	12364
3	Carl Yastrzemski	11988
4	Ty Cobb	11434
5	Stan Musial	10972
6	Willie Mays	10881
7	Brooks Robinson	10654
8	Robin Yount	10554
9	Honus Wagner	10430
10	Lou Brock	10332
11	Luis Aparicio	10230
12	Tris Speaker	10195
13	Al Kaline	10116
14	Rabbit Maranville	10078
15	Dave Winfield	10047
16	Frank Robinson	10006
17	Eddie Collins	9949
18	Reggie Jackson	9864
19	George Brett	9789
20	Tony Perez	9778
21	Rusty Staub	9720
22	Vada Pinson	9645
23	Nap Lajoie	9589
24	Sam Crawford	9570
25	Jake Beckley	9526
26	Paul Waner	9459
27	Mel Ott	9456
28	Roberto Clemente	9454
29	Ernie Banks	9421
30	Bill Buckner	9397
31	Max Carey	9363
32	Dave Parker	9358
33	Billy Williams	9350
34	Rod Carew	9315
35	Joe Morgan	9277
36	Sam Rice	9269
37	Nellie Fox	9232
38	Willie Davis	9174
39	Doc Cramer	9140
40	Eddie Murray	9124
41	Frankie Frisch	9112
42	Zack Wheat	9106
43	Cap Anson	9101
44	Lave Cross	9072
45	Al Oliver	9049
46	Bill Dahlen	9031
	George Davis	9031
48	Dwight Evans	8996
49	Buddy Bell	8995
50	Graig Nettles	8986
51	Darrell Evans	8973
52	Andre Dawson	8890
53	Charlie Gehringer	8860
54	Luke Appling	8856
55	Steve Garvey	8835
56	Tommy Corcoran	8804
57	Harry Hooper	8785
58	Al Simmons	8759
59	Mickey Vernon	8731
60	Dave Concepcion	8723
61	Carlton Fisk	8703
62	Bert Campaneris	8684
63	Ted Simmons	8680
64	Goose Goslin	8656
65	Bobby Wallace	8618
66	Willie Keeler	8591
67	Fred Clarke	8568
68	Eddie Mathews	8537
69	Red Schoendienst	8479
70	Jesse Burkett	8421
71	Larry Bowa	8418
72	Babe Ruth	8399
73	Richie Ashburn	8365
74	Mike Schmidt	8352
75	Bid McPhee	8291
76	George Sisler	8267
77	Jim Rice	8225
78	Don Baylor	8198
79	Willie McCovey	8197
80	Rogers Hornsby	8173
81	Jimmy Ryan	8164
82	Harmon Killebrew	8147
83	Ron Santo	8143
84	Jimmie Foxx	8134
85	Mickey Mantle	8102
86	Ozzie Smith	8087
87	Pee Wee Reese	8058
88	Jimmy Dykes	8046
89	George Van Haltren	8021
90	Willie Randolph	8018
91	Lou Gehrig	8001
92	Joe Kuhel	7984
93	Gary Carter	7971
94	Tommy Leach	7959
95	Enos Slaughter	7946
96	Orlando Cepeda	7927
	Willie Stargell	7927
98	Dale Murphy	7918
99	Jose Cruz	7917
	Charlie Grimm	7917

Runs

1	Ty Cobb	2246
2	Hank Aaron	2174
	Babe Ruth	2174
4	Pete Rose	2165
5	Willie Mays	2062
6	Stan Musial	1949
7	Lou Gehrig	1888
8	Tris Speaker	1882
9	Mel Ott	1859
10	Frank Robinson	1829
11	Eddie Collins	1821
12	Carl Yastrzemski	1816
13	Ted Williams	1798
14	Charlie Gehringer	1774
15	Jimmie Foxx	1751
16	Honus Wagner	1736
17	Jesse Burkett	1720
18	Cap Anson	1719
	Willie Keeler	1719
20	Billy Hamilton	1690
21	Bid McPhee	1678
22	Mickey Mantle	1677
23	Joe Morgan	1650
24	Jimmy Ryan	1642
25	George Van Haltren	1639
26	Paul Waner	1627
27	Al Kaline	1622
28	Roger Connor	1620
29	Fred Clarke	1619
30	Lou Brock	1610
31	Jake Beckley	1600
32	Ed Delahanty	1599
33	Bill Dahlen	1589
34	Rogers Hornsby	1579
35	Robin Yount	1570
36	Hugh Duffy	1552
37	Reggie Jackson	1551
	Dave Winfield	1551
39	Max Carey	1545
40	George Davis	1539
41	Frankie Frisch	1532
42	Dan Brouthers	1523
43	Tom Brown	1521
44	George Brett	1514
	Sam Rice	1514
46	Eddie Mathews	1509
47	Al Simmons	1507
48	Mike Schmidt	1506
49	Nap Lajoie	1504
50	Harry Stovey	1492
51	Goose Goslin	1483
52	Arlie Latham	1478
53	Rickey Henderson	1472
54	Dwight Evans	1470
55	Herman Long	1455
56	Jim O'Rourke	1446
57	Harry Hooper	1429
58	Dummy Hoy	1426
59	Rod Carew	1424
60	Joe Kelley	1421
61	Roberto Clemente	1416
62	Billy Williams	1410
63	John Ward	1408
64	Mike Griffin	1405
65	Sam Crawford	1391
66	Joe DiMaggio	1390
67	Vada Pinson	1366
68	Doc Cramer	1357
	King Kelly	1357
70	Tommy Leach	1355
71	Darrell Evans	1344
72	Eddie Murray	1343
73	Pee Wee Reese	1338
74	Luis Aparicio	1335
75	Lave Cross	1333
76	George Gore	1327
77	Richie Ashburn	1322
78	Luke Appling	1319
79	Patsy Donovan	1318
80	Mike Tiernan	1313
81	Ernie Banks	1305
82	Jimmy Sheckard	1296
83	Kiki Cuyler	1295
84	Harry Heilmann	1291
85	Zack Wheat	1289
86	Heinie Manush	1287
87	George Sisler	1284
88	Harmon Killebrew	1283
89	Donie Bush	1280
90	Nellie Fox	1279
91	Fred Tenney	1278
92	Paul Molitor	1275
93	Carlton Fisk	1274
94	Dave Parker	1272
	Tony Perez	1272
96	Andre Dawson	1259
	Duke Snider	1259
98	Bobby Bonds	1258
99	Sam Thompson	1256
100	Rabbit Maranville	1255

Runs per Game (by era)

1876-1892

1	George Gore	1.01
2	Harry Stovey	1.00
3	King Kelly	.93
4	Dan Brouthers	.91
5	Arlie Latham	.91
6	Sam Thompson	.89
7	Buck Ewing	.86
8	Tom Brown	.85
9	Hardy Richardson	.84
10	Tommy McCarthy	.84
11	Tip O'Neill	.83
12	Denny Lyons	.83
13	Curt Welch	.83
14	Jim O'Rourke	.82
15	Roger Connor	.81

1893-1919

1	Billy Hamilton	1.06
2	John McGraw	.93
3	Mike Griffin	.93
4	Hugh Duffy	.89
5	Mike Tiernan	.89
6	Ed Delahanty	.87
7	Cupid Childs	.83
8	Jesse Burkett	.83
9	George Van Haltren	.83
10	Jimmy Ryan	.82
11	Willie Keeler	.81
12	Dummy Hoy	.79
13	Herman Long	.78
14	Hughie Jennings	.77
15	Joe Kelley	.77

1920-1941

1	Lou Gehrig	.87
2	Babe Ruth	.87
3	Earle Combs	.82
4	Red Rolfe	.80
5	Charlie Gehringer	.76
6	Jimmie Foxx	.76
7	Hank Greenberg	.75
8	Earl Averill	.73
9	Max Bishop	.72
10	Lu Blue	.71
11	Mickey Cochrane	.70
12	Rogers Hornsby	.70
13	Kiki Cuyler	.69
14	Mel Ott	.68
15	Al Simmons	.68

1942-1960

1	Joe DiMaggio	.80
2	Ted Williams	.78
3	Dom DiMaggio	.75
4	Tommy Henrich	.70
5	Mickey Mantle	.70
6	Jackie Robinson	.69
7	Johnny Pesky	.68
8	Ralph Kiner	.66
9	Eddie Stanky	.64
10	Stan Musial	.64
11	George Case	.64
12	Eddie Mathews	.63
13	Larry Doby	.63
14	Charlie Keller	.62
15	Minnie Minoso	.62

1961-1992

1	Rickey Henderson	.79
2	Willie Mays	.69
3	Paul Molitor	.69
4	Bobby Bonds	.68
5	Tim Raines	.67
6	Barry Bonds	.67
7	Ron LeFlore	.67
8	Hank Aaron	.66
9	Wade Boggs	.66
10	Frank Robinson	.65
11	Vince Coleman	.63
12	Ryne Sandberg	.63
13	Dick Allen	.63
14	Mike Schmidt	.63
15	Brett Butler	.62

Hits

1	Pete Rose	4256
2	Ty Cobb	4189
3	Hank Aaron	3771
4	Stan Musial	3630
5	Tris Speaker	3514
6	Carl Yastrzemski	3419
7	Honus Wagner	3415
8	Eddie Collins	3312
9	Willie Mays	3283
10	Nap Lajoie	3242
11	Paul Waner	3152
12	Rod Carew	3053
13	Robin Yount	3025
14	Lou Brock	3023
15	Al Kaline	3007
16	George Brett	3005
17	Roberto Clemente	3000
18	Cap Anson	2995
19	Sam Rice	2987
20	Sam Crawford	2961
21	Frank Robinson	2943
22	Willie Keeler	2932
23	Jake Beckley	2930
	Rogers Hornsby	2930
25	Al Simmons	2927
26	Zack Wheat	2884
27	Frankie Frisch	2880
28	Mel Ott	2876
29	Babe Ruth	2873
30	Dave Winfield	2866
31	Jesse Burkett	2850
32	Brooks Robinson	2848
33	Charlie Gehringer	2839
34	George Sisler	2812
35	Vada Pinson	2757
36	Luke Appling	2749
37	Al Oliver	2743
38	Goose Goslin	2735
39	Tony Perez	2732
40	Lou Gehrig	2721
41	Rusty Staub	2716
42	Bill Buckner	2715
43	Dave Parker	2712
44	Billy Williams	2711
45	Doc Cramer	2705
46	Luis Aparicio	2677
47	Fred Clarke	2672
48	Max Carey	2665
49	Nellie Fox	2663
50	George Davis	2660
	Harry Heilmann	2660
52	Ted Williams	2654
53	Jimmie Foxx	2646
	Eddie Murray	2646
55	Lave Cross	2645
56	Rabbit Maranville	2605
57	Steve Garvey	2599
58	Ed Delahanty	2597
59	Reggie Jackson	2584
60	Ernie Banks	2583
61	Richie Ashburn	2574
62	Willie Davis	2561
63	George Van Haltren	2532
64	Heinie Manush	2524
65	Joe Morgan	2517
66	Buddy Bell	2514
67	Andre Dawson	2504
68	Jimmy Ryan	2502
69	Mickey Vernon	2495
70	Ted Simmons	2472
71	Joe Medwick	2471
72	Roger Connor	2467
73	Harry Hooper	2466
74	Lloyd Waner	2459
75	Bill Dahlen	2457
76	Jim Rice	2452
77	Red Schoendienst	2449
78	Dwight Evans	2446
79	Pie Traynor	2416
80	Mickey Mantle	2415
81	Stuffy McInnis	2405
82	Enos Slaughter	2383
83	Edd Roush	2376
84	Joe Judge	2352
85	Orlando Cepeda	2351
86	Carlton Fisk	2346
87	Billy Herman	2345
88	Joe Torre	2342
89	Dave Concepcion	2326
	Jake Daubert	2326
91	Eddie Mathews	2315
92	Jim Bottomley	2313
93	Bobby Wallace	2309
94	Jim O'Rourke	2304
95	Kiki Cuyler	2299
	Charlie Grimm	2299
97	Dan Brouthers	2296
98	Joe Cronin	2285
99	Hugh Duffy	2282
100	Paul Molitor	2281

Doubles

1	Tris Speaker	792
2	Pete Rose	746
3	Stan Musial	725
4	Ty Cobb	724
5	Nap Lajoie	657
6	Carl Yastrzemski	646
7	Honus Wagner	640
8	George Brett	634
9	Hank Aaron	624
10	Paul Waner	605
11	Charlie Gehringer	574
12	Robin Yount	558
13	Harry Heilmann	542
14	Rogers Hornsby	541
15	Joe Medwick	540
16	Al Simmons	539
17	Lou Gehrig	534
18	Al Oliver	529
19	Cap Anson	528
	Frank Robinson	528
21	Dave Parker	526
22	Ted Williams	525
23	Willie Mays	523
24	Ed Delahanty	522
25	Joe Cronin	515
26	Babe Ruth	506
27	Tony Perez	505
28	Goose Goslin	500
29	Rusty Staub	499
30	Bill Buckner	498
	Al Kaline	498
	Sam Rice	498
33	Dave Winfield	493
34	Heinie Manush	491
35	Mickey Vernon	490
36	Mel Ott	488
37	Lou Brock	486
	Billy Herman	486
39	Vada Pinson	485
40	Hal McRae	484
41	Dwight Evans	483
	Ted Simmons	483
43	Brooks Robinson	482
44	Zack Wheat	476
45	Jake Beckley	473
46	Frankie Frisch	466
47	Jim Bottomley	465
48	Reggie Jackson	463
49	Eddie Murray	462
50	Dan Brouthers	460
51	Sam Crawford	458
	Jimmie Foxx	458
53	Jimmy Dykes	453
54	George Davis	451
	Jimmy Ryan	451
56	Joe Morgan	449
57	Rod Carew	445
58	George Burns	444
	Andre Dawson	444
60	Dick Bartell	442
61	Roger Connor	441
62	Luke Appling	440
	Roberto Clemente	440
	Steve Garvey	440
65	Eddie Collins	438
66	Cesar Cedeno	436
	Joe Sewell	436
68	Wally Moses	435
69	Billy Williams	434
70	Joe Judge	433
71	Red Schoendienst	427
72	Keith Hernandez	426
73	Buddy Bell	425
	Sherry Magee	425
	George Sisler	425
76	Willie Stargell	423
77	Wade Boggs	422
78	Carlton Fisk	421
79	Max Carey	419
80	Orlando Cepeda	417
81	Cecil Cooper	415
82	Jim O'Rourke	414
83	Bill Dahlen	413
	Enos Slaughter	413
85	Joe Kuhel	412
86	Lave Cross	411
87	Mike Schmidt	408
88	Ernie Banks	407
	Ben Chapman	407
	Frank White	407
91	Paul Molitor	405
92	Earl Averill	401
	Marty McManus	401
94	Babe Herman	399
	Gee Walker	399
96	Chuck Klein	398
97	Doc Cramer	396
	Gabby Hartnett	396
	Bob Johnson	396
	Chet Lemon	396

Triples

1	Sam Crawford	309
2	Ty Cobb	295
3	Honus Wagner	252
4	Jake Beckley	243
5	Roger Connor	233
6	Tris Speaker	222
7	Fred Clarke	220
8	Dan Brouthers	205
9	Joe Kelley	194
10	Paul Waner	191
11	Bid McPhee	188
12	Eddie Collins	186
13	Ed Delahanty	185
14	Sam Rice	184
15	Jesse Burkett	182
	Edd Roush	182
17	Ed Konetchy	181
18	Buck Ewing	178
19	Rabbit Maranville	177
	Stan Musial	177
21	Harry Stovey	174
22	Goose Goslin	173
23	Tommy Leach	172
	Zack Wheat	172
25	Rogers Hornsby	169
26	Joe Jackson	168
27	Roberto Clemente	166
	Sherry Magee	166
29	Jake Daubert	165
30	Elmer Flick	164
	George Sisler	164
	Pie Traynor	164
33	Bill Dahlen	163
	George Davis	163
	Lou Gehrig	163
	Nap Lajoie	163
37	Mike Tiernan	162
38	George Van Haltren	161
39	Harry Hooper	160
	Heinie Manush	160
	Sam Thompson	160
42	Max Carey	159
	Joe Judge	159
44	Ed McKean	158
45	Kiki Cuyler	157
	Jimmy Ryan	157
47	Tommy Corcoran	155
48	Earle Combs	154
49	Jim Bottomley	151
	Harry Heilmann	151
51	Kip Selbach	149
	Al Simmons	149
53	Wally Pipp	148
	Enos Slaughter	148
55	Bobby Veach	147
56	Charlie Gehringer	146
57	Harry Davis	145
	Willie Keeler	145
59	Bobby Wallace	143
60	Willie Wilson	142
61	Lou Brock	141
62	Willie Mays	140
63	John Reilly	139
64	Tom Brown	138
	Willie Davis	138
	Frankie Frisch	138
	Jimmy Williams	138
68	Babe Ruth	136
	Jimmy Sheckard	136
	Elmer Smith	136
71	Lave Cross	135
	Pete Rose	135
73	George Brett	134
74	Shano Collins	133
75	Jim O'Rourke	132
	George Wood	132
77	Joe DiMaggio	131
	Buck Freeman	131
79	Buddy Myer	130
80	Oyster Burns	129
	Larry Gardner	129
82	Earl Averill	128
	Arky Vaughan	128
84	Vada Pinson	127
85	Hardy Richardson	126
86	Jimmie Foxx	125
87	John Anderson	124
	Cap Anson	124
	Hal Chase	124
	Frank Schulte	124
91	Larry Doyle	123
	Duke Farrell	123
	Robin Yount	123
94	Dummy Hoy	121
95	Mickey Vernon	120
96	Hugh Duffy	119
	Fred Pfeffer	119
98	Joe Cronin	118
	Chick Stahl	118
	Lloyd Waner	118

Triples (by era)

1876-1892

1	Roger Connor	233
2	Dan Brouthers	205
3	Bid McPhee	188
4	Buck Ewing	178
5	Harry Stovey	174
6	Sam Thompson	160
7	John Reilly	139
8	Tom Brown	138
9	Jim O'Rourke	132
	George Wood	132
11	Oyster Burns	129
12	Hardy Richardson	126
13	Cap Anson	124
14	Fred Pfeffer	119
15	Bill Kuehne	115

1893-1919

1	Sam Crawford	309
2	Ty Cobb	295
3	Honus Wagner	252
4	Jake Beckley	243
5	Tris Speaker	222
6	Fred Clarke	220
7	Joe Kelley	194
8	Eddie Collins	186
9	Ed Delahanty	185
10	Jesse Burkett	182
11	Ed Konetchy	181
12	Tommy Leach	172
	Zack Wheat	172
14	Joe Jackson	168
15	Sherry Magee	166

1920-1941

1	Paul Waner	191
2	Sam Rice	184
3	Edd Roush	182
4	Rabbit Maranville	177
5	Goose Goslin	173
6	Rogers Hornsby	169
7	George Sisler	164
	Pie Traynor	164
9	Lou Gehrig	163
10	Heinie Manush	160
11	Max Carey	159
	Joe Judge	159
13	Kiki Cuyler	157
14	Earle Combs	154
15	2 players tied	151

1942-1960

1	Stan Musial	177
2	Enos Slaughter	148
3	Joe DiMaggio	131
4	Mickey Vernon	120
5	Nellie Fox	112
6	Wally Moses	110
7	Richie Ashburn	109
8	Bill Bruton	102
	Jeff Heath	102
10	Phil Cavarretta	99
11	Dixie Walker	96
12	Bob Elliott	94
13	Bobby Doerr	89
14	Duke Snider	85
15	2 players tied	83

1961-1992

1	Roberto Clemente	166
2	Willie Wilson	142
3	Lou Brock	141
4	Willie Mays	140
5	Willie Davis	138
6	Pete Rose	135
7	George Brett	134
8	Vada Pinson	127
9	Robin Yount	123
10	Rod Carew	112
11	Garry Templeton	106
12	Larry Bowa	99
	Brett Butler	99
14	Hank Aaron	98
15	2 players tied	96

Home Runs

1	Hank Aaron	755
2	Babe Ruth	714
3	Willie Mays	660
4	Frank Robinson	586
5	Harmon Killebrew	573
6	Reggie Jackson	563
7	Mike Schmidt	548
8	Mickey Mantle	536
9	Jimmie Foxx	534
10	Willie McCovey	521
	Ted Williams	521
12	Ernie Banks	512
	Eddie Mathews	512
14	Mel Ott	511
15	Lou Gehrig	493
16	Stan Musial	475
	Willie Stargell	475
18	Carl Yastrzemski	452
19	Dave Kingman	442
20	Dave Winfield	432
21	Billy Williams	426
22	Darrell Evans	414
	Eddie Murray	414
24	Duke Snider	407
25	Andre Dawson	399
	Al Kaline	399
27	Dale Murphy	398
28	Graig Nettles	390
29	Johnny Bench	389
30	Dwight Evans	385
31	Frank Howard	382
	Jim Rice	382
33	Orlando Cepeda	379
	Tony Perez	379
35	Norm Cash	377
36	Carlton Fisk	375
37	Rocky Colavito	374
38	Gil Hodges	370
39	Ralph Kiner	369
40	Joe DiMaggio	361
41	Johnny Mize	359
42	Yogi Berra	358
43	Lee May	354
44	Dick Allen	351
45	George Foster	348
46	Ron Santo	342
47	Jack Clark	340
48	Dave Parker	339
	Boog Powell	339
50	Don Baylor	338
51	Joe Adcock	336
52	Bobby Bonds	332
53	Hank Greenberg	331
54	Willie Horton	325
55	Gary Carter	324
56	Roy Sievers	318
57	Ron Cey	316
	Lance Parrish	316
59	Reggie Smith	314
60	Greg Luzinski	307
	Al Simmons	307
62	Fred Lynn	306
63	Rogers Hornsby	301
64	Chuck Klein	300
65	George Brett	298
66	Rusty Staub	292
67	Jim Wynn	291
68	Del Ennis	288
	Bob Johnson	288
	Hank Sauer	288
71	Frank Thomas	286
72	Darryl Strawberry	285
73	Ken Boyer	282
74	Ted Kluszewski	279
75	Rudy York	277
76	Brian Downing	275
	Roger Maris	275
78	Cal Ripken	273
79	Steve Garvey	272
80	George Scott	271
81	Joe Morgan	268
	Brooks Robinson	268
	Gorman Thomas	268
84	George Hendrick	267
85	Vic Wertz	266
86	Bobby Thomson	264
87	Kent Hrbek	258
88	Bob Allison	256
	Larry Parrish	256
	Vada Pinson	256
91	Tom Brunansky	255
	John Mayberry	255
93	Larry Doby	253
	Joe Gordon	253
	Andy Thornton	253
96	George Bell	252
	Bobby Murcer	252
	Joe Torre	252
99	Tony Armas	251
	Cy Williams	251

Home Runs (by era)

1876-1892

1	Roger Connor	138
2	Sam Thompson	127
3	Harry Stovey	122
4	Dan Brouthers	106
5	Cap Anson	97
6	Fred Pfeffer	94
7	Jack Clements	77
8	Jerry Denny	74
9	Buck Ewing	71
10	Hardy Richardson	70
11	King Kelly	69
	John Reilly	69
13	George Wood	68
14	Oyster Burns	65
	Bug Holliday	65

1893-1919

1	Zack Wheat	132
2	Gavvy Cravath	119
3	Jimmy Ryan	118
	Tilly Walker	118
5	Ty Cobb	117
	Tris Speaker	117
7	Hugh Duffy	106
	Mike Tiernan	106
9	Ed Delahanty	101
	Honus Wagner	101
11	Sam Crawford	97
12	Frank Baker	96
13	Herman Long	92
	Frank Schulte	92
15	Jake Beckley	86

1920-1941

1	Babe Ruth	714
2	Jimmie Foxx	534
3	Mel Ott	511
4	Lou Gehrig	493
5	Hank Greenberg	331
6	Al Simmons	307
7	Rogers Hornsby	301
8	Chuck Klein	300
9	Bob Johnson	288
10	Cy Williams	251
11	Goose Goslin	248
12	Hack Wilson	244
13	Wally Berger	242
14	Dolph Camilli	239
15	Earl Averill	238

1942-1960

1	Mickey Mantle	536
2	Ted Williams	521
3	Eddie Mathews	512
4	Stan Musial	475
5	Duke Snider	407
6	Gil Hodges	370
7	Ralph Kiner	369
8	Joe DiMaggio	361
9	Johnny Mize	359
10	Yogi Berra	358
11	Joe Adcock	336
12	Roy Sievers	318
13	Del Ennis	288
	Hank Sauer	288
15	Frank Thomas	286

1961-1992

1	Hank Aaron	755
2	Willie Mays	660
3	Frank Robinson	586
4	Harmon Killebrew	573
5	Reggie Jackson	563
6	Mike Schmidt	548
7	Willie McCovey	521
8	Ernie Banks	512
9	Willie Stargell	475
10	Carl Yastrzemski	452
11	Dave Kingman	442
12	Dave Winfield	432
13	Billy Williams	426
14	Darrell Evans	414
	Eddie Murray	414

Home Run Percentage

1	Babe Ruth	8.50
2	Ralph Kiner	7.09
3	Harmon Killebrew	7.03
4	Ted Williams	6.76
5	Dave Kingman	6.62
6	Mickey Mantle	6.62
7	Jimmie Foxx	6.57
8	Mike Schmidt	6.56
9	Hank Greenberg	6.37
10	Willie McCovey	6.36
11	Darryl Strawberry	6.24
12	Lou Gehrig	6.16
13	Hank Aaron	6.11
14	Rob Deer	6.09
15	Willie Mays	6.07
16	Hank Sauer	6.01
17	Eddie Mathews	6.00
18	Willie Stargell	5.99
19	Frank Howard	5.89
20	Frank Robinson	5.86
21	Bob Horner	5.77
22	Roy Campanella	5.76
23	Rocky Colavito	5.75
24	Gus Zernial	5.74
25	Gorman Thomas	5.73
26	Reggie Jackson	5.71
27	Dick Stuart	5.70
28	Duke Snider	5.68
29	Norm Cash	5.62
30	Johnny Mize	5.57
31	Dick Allen	5.54
32	Ernie Banks	5.43
33	Mel Ott	5.40
34	Roger Maris	5.39
35	Joe DiMaggio	5.29
36	Gil Hodges	5.26
37	Wally Post	5.24
38	Al Rosen	5.15
39	Hack Wilson	5.13
40	Bob Allison	5.09
41	Joe Adcock	5.09
42	Johnny Bench	5.08
43	Boog Powell	5.07
44	Jesse Barfield	5.06
45	Nate Colbert	5.06
46	Dale Murphy	5.03
47	Charlie Keller	4.99
48	Roy Sievers	4.98
49	Cliff Johnson	4.97
50	Don Mincher	4.97
51	Jack Clark	4.97
52	George Foster	4.96
53	Barry Bonds	4.91
54	Tony Armas	4.86
55	Andy Thornton	4.78
56	Orlando Cepeda	4.78
57	Leon Wagner	4.77
58	Jim Lemon	4.76
59	Yogi Berra	4.74
60	Howard Johnson	4.73
61	Don Demeter	4.73
62	Larry Doby	4.73
63	Greg Luzinski	4.72
64	Bobby Bonds	4.71
65	Ted Kluszewski	4.71
66	Rudy York	4.70
67	Wally Berger	4.69
68	Lance Parrish	4.69
69	John Mayberry	4.68
70	Kent Hrbek	4.67
71	Joe Carter	4.65
72	Lee May	4.65
73	Jim Rice	4.64
74	Chuck Klein	4.63
75	Darrell Evans	4.61
76	Gene Tenace	4.58
77	Charlie Maxwell	4.56
78	Billy Williams	4.56
79	Frank Thomas	4.55
80	Eddie Murray	4.54
81	Jim Ray Hart	4.49
82	Andre Dawson	4.49
83	Gary Roenicke	4.47
84	Dolph Camilli	4.46
85	Reggie Smith	4.46
86	Woodie Held	4.45
87	Willie Horton	4.45
88	Oscar Gamble	4.44
89	Joe Gordon	4.43
90	Fred Lynn	4.42
91	Hal Trosky	4.42
92	Ron Cey	4.41
93	George Bell	4.41
94	Wes Covington	4.40
95	Jim Wynn	4.37
96	Dale Long	4.37
97	Vic Wertz	4.36
98	Tom Brunansky	4.35
99	Kirk Gibson	4.34
100	Graig Nettles	4.34

Home Run Pctg. (by era)

1876-1892

1	Sam Thompson	2.12
2	Harry Stovey	1.99
3	Jack Clements	1.80
4	Roger Connor	1.77
5	Dan Brouthers	1.58
6	Jerry Denny	1.50
7	John Reilly	1.47
8	Denny Lyons	1.44
9	Charlie Bennett	1.44
10	Fred Pfeffer	1.43
11	Ned Williamson	1.41
12	Oyster Burns	1.40
13	Buck Ewing	1.32
14	George Wood	1.27
15	Hardy Richardson	1.24

1893-1919

1	Gavvy Cravath	3.01
2	Tilly Walker	2.33
3	Buck Freeman	1.95
4	Mike Tiernan	1.79
5	Fred Luderus	1.73
6	Frank Baker	1.60
7	Hugh Duffy	1.51
8	Charlie Hickman	1.48
9	Zack Wheat	1.45
10	Jimmy Ryan	1.45
11	Frank Schulte	1.41
12	Casey Stengel	1.40
13	Ed Delahanty	1.35
14	Mike Donlin	1.32
15	Chief Wilson	1.28

1920-1941

1	Babe Ruth	8.50
2	Jimmie Foxx	6.57
3	Hank Greenberg	6.37
4	Lou Gehrig	6.16
5	Mel Ott	5.40
6	Hack Wilson	5.13
7	Wally Berger	4.69
8	Chuck Klein	4.63
9	Dolph Camilli	4.46
10	Hal Trosky	4.42
11	Bob Johnson	4.16
12	Ken Williams	4.03
13	Earl Averill	3.75
14	Cy Williams	3.70
15	Rogers Hornsby	3.68

1942-1960

1	Ralph Kiner	7.09
2	Ted Williams	6.76
3	Mickey Mantle	6.62
4	Hank Sauer	6.01
5	Eddie Mathews	6.00
6	Roy Campanella	5.76
7	Gus Zernial	5.74
8	Duke Snider	5.68
9	Johnny Mize	5.57
10	Joe DiMaggio	5.29
11	Gil Hodges	5.26
12	Wally Post	5.24
13	Al Rosen	5.15
14	Joe Adcock	5.09
15	Charlie Keller	4.99

1961-1992

1	Harmon Killebrew	7.03
2	Dave Kingman	6.62
3	Mike Schmidt	6.56
4	Willie McCovey	6.36
5	Darryl Strawberry	6.24
6	Hank Aaron	6.11
7	Rob Deer	6.09
8	Willie Mays	6.07
9	Willie Stargell	5.99
10	Frank Howard	5.89
11	Frank Robinson	5.86
12	Bob Horner	5.77
13	Rocky Colavito	5.75
14	Gorman Thomas	5.73
15	Reggie Jackson	5.71

Total Bases

1	Hank Aaron	6856
2	Stan Musial	6134
3	Willie Mays	6066
4	Ty Cobb	5854
5	Babe Ruth	5793
6	Pete Rose	5752
7	Carl Yastrzemski	5539
8	Frank Robinson	5373
9	Tris Speaker	5101
10	Lou Gehrig	5060
11	Mel Ott	5041
12	Jimmie Foxx	4956
13	Ted Williams	4884
14	Honus Wagner	4862
15	Al Kaline	4852
16	Reggie Jackson	4834
17	Dave Winfield	4821
18	George Brett	4801
19	Rogers Hornsby	4712
20	Ernie Banks	4706
21	Al Simmons	4685
22	Billy Williams	4599
23	Robin Yount	4558
24	Tony Perez	4532
25	Mickey Mantle	4511
26	Roberto Clemente	4492
27	Paul Waner	4478
28	Nap Lajoie	4474
29	Eddie Murray	4414
30	Dave Parker	4405
31	Mike Schmidt	4404
32	Eddie Mathews	4349
33	Andre Dawson	4333
34	Sam Crawford	4328
35	Goose Goslin	4325
36	Brooks Robinson	4270
37	Vada Pinson	4264
38	Eddie Collins	4263
39	Charlie Gehringer	4257
40	Lou Brock	4238
41	Dwight Evans	4230
42	Willie McCovey	4219
43	Willie Stargell	4190
44	Rusty Staub	4185
45	Jake Beckley	4147
46	Harmon Killebrew	4143
47	Jim Rice	4129
48	Zack Wheat	4100
49	Al Oliver	4083
50	Cap Anson	4062
51	Harry Heilmann	4053
52	Rod Carew	3998
53	Carlton Fisk	3986
54	Joe Morgan	3962
55	Orlando Cepeda	3959
56	Sam Rice	3955
57	Joe DiMaggio	3948
58	Steve Garvey	3941
59	Frankie Frisch	3937
60	George Sisler	3871
61	Darrell Evans	3866
62	Duke Snider	3865
63	Joe Medwick	3852
64	Bill Buckner	3833
65	Ted Simmons	3793
66	Ed Delahanty	3792
67	Roger Connor	3788
68	Graig Nettles	3779
	Ron Santo	3779
70	Willie Davis	3778
71	Jesse Burkett	3759
72	Mickey Vernon	3741
73	Jim Bottomley	3737
74	Dale Murphy	3726
75	Fred Clarke	3674
76	Heinie Manush	3665
77	George Davis	3656
78	Buddy Bell	3654
79	Johnny Bench	3644
80	Yogi Berra	3643
81	Johnny Mize	3621
	Jimmy Ryan	3621
83	Max Carey	3612
84	Enos Slaughter	3599
85	Don Baylor	3571
86	Willie Keeler	3562
87	Joe Torre	3560
88	Joe Cronin	3546
89	Luke Appling	3528
90	Chuck Klein	3522
91	Luis Aparicio	3504
92	Bob Johnson	3501
93	Gary Carter	3497
94	Lee May	3495
95	Dan Brouthers	3484
96	Lave Cross	3467
97	Bill Dahlen	3448
98	Ken Boyer	3443
99	Reggie Smith	3439
100	Doc Cramer	3430

Runs Batted In

1	Hank Aaron	2297
2	Babe Ruth	2213
3	Lou Gehrig	1995
4	Stan Musial	1951
5	Ty Cobb	1937
6	Jimmie Foxx	1922
7	Willie Mays	1903
8	Cap Anson	1879
9	Mel Ott	1860
10	Carl Yastrzemski	1844
11	Ted Williams	1839
12	Al Simmons	1827
13	Frank Robinson	1812
14	Honus Wagner	1732
15	Dave Winfield	1710
16	Reggie Jackson	1702
17	Tony Perez	1652
18	Ernie Banks	1636
19	Goose Goslin	1609
20	Nap Lajoie	1599
21	Mike Schmidt	1595
22	Rogers Hornsby	1584
	Harmon Killebrew	1584
24	Al Kaline	1583
25	Jake Beckley	1575
26	Eddie Murray	1562
27	Willie McCovey	1555
28	Willie Stargell	1540
29	Harry Heilmann	1539
30	Joe DiMaggio	1537
31	Tris Speaker	1529
32	Sam Crawford	1525
33	George Brett	1520
34	Mickey Mantle	1509
35	Dave Parker	1493
36	Billy Williams	1475
37	Rusty Staub	1466
38	Ed Delahanty	1464
39	Eddie Mathews	1453
40	Jim Rice	1451
41	George Davis	1437
42	Yogi Berra	1430
43	Charlie Gehringer	1427
44	Andre Dawson	1425
45	Joe Cronin	1424
46	Jim Bottomley	1422
47	Ted Simmons	1389
48	Dwight Evans	1384
49	Joe Medwick	1383
50	Johnny Bench	1376
51	Orlando Cepeda	1365
52	Brooks Robinson	1357
53	Robin Yount	1355
54	Darrell Evans	1354
55	Johnny Mize	1337
56	Duke Snider	1333
57	Ron Santo	1331
58	Carlton Fisk	1326
	Al Oliver	1326
60	Roger Connor	1322
61	Graig Nettles	1314
	Pete Rose	1314
63	Mickey Vernon	1311
64	Paul Waner	1309
65	Steve Garvey	1308
66	Roberto Clemente	1305
67	Enos Slaughter	1304
68	Hugh Duffy	1302
69	Eddie Collins	1300
70	Sam Thompson	1299
71	Dan Brouthers	1296
72	Del Ennis	1284
73	Bob Johnson	1283
74	Don Baylor	1276
	Hank Greenberg	1276
76	Gil Hodges	1274
77	Pie Traynor	1273
78	Dale Murphy	1259
79	Zack Wheat	1248
80	Bobby Doerr	1247
81	Frankie Frisch	1244
	Lee May	1244
83	George Foster	1239
84	Bill Dahlen	1233
85	Gary Carter	1225
86	Dave Kingman	1210
87	Bill Dickey	1209
88	Bill Buckner	1208
89	Chuck Klein	1201
90	Bob Elliott	1195
91	Joe Kelley	1194
92	Tony Lazzeri	1191
93	Boog Powell	1187
94	Joe Torre	1185
95	Heinie Manush	1183
96	Jack Clark	1180
97	Gabby Hartnett	1179
98	Vic Wertz	1178
99	Sherry Magee	1176
100	George Sisler	1175

Runs Batted In (by era)

1876-1892

1	Cap Anson	1879
2	Roger Connor	1322
3	Sam Thompson	1299
4	Dan Brouthers	1296
5	Fred Pfeffer	1019
6	Jim O'Rourke	1010
7	King Kelly	950
8	Buck Ewing	883
9	John Ward	867
10	Hardy Richardson	822
11	Deacon White	756
12	Paul Hines	751
13	Tom Burns	683
14	Sam Wise	672
15	2 players tied	667

1893-1919

1	Ty Cobb	1937
2	Honus Wagner	1732
3	Nap Lajoie	1599
4	Jake Beckley	1575
5	Tris Speaker	1529
6	Sam Crawford	1525
7	Ed Delahanty	1464
8	George Davis	1437
9	Hugh Duffy	1302
10	Eddie Collins	1300
11	Zack Wheat	1248
12	Bill Dahlen	1233
13	Joe Kelley	1194
14	Sherry Magee	1176
15	Bobby Veach	1166

1920-1941

1	Babe Ruth	2213
2	Lou Gehrig	1995
3	Jimmie Foxx	1922
4	Mel Ott	1860
5	Al Simmons	1827
6	Goose Goslin	1609
7	Rogers Hornsby	1584
8	Harry Heilmann	1539
9	Charlie Gehringer	1427
10	Joe Cronin	1424
11	Jim Bottomley	1422
12	Joe Medwick	1383
13	Paul Waner	1309
14	Bob Johnson	1283
15	Hank Greenberg	1276

1942-1960

1	Stan Musial	1951
2	Ted Williams	1839
3	Joe DiMaggio	1537
4	Mickey Mantle	1509
5	Eddie Mathews	1453
6	Yogi Berra	1430
7	Johnny Mize	1337
8	Duke Snider	1333
9	Mickey Vernon	1311
10	Enos Slaughter	1304
11	Del Ennis	1284
12	Gil Hodges	1274
13	Bobby Doerr	1247
14	Bob Elliott	1195
15	Vic Wertz	1178

1961-1992

1	Hank Aaron	2297
2	Willie Mays	1903
3	Carl Yastrzemski	1844
4	Frank Robinson	1812
5	Dave Winfield	1710
6	Reggie Jackson	1702
7	Tony Perez	1652
8	Ernie Banks	1636
9	Mike Schmidt	1595
10	Harmon Killebrew	1584
11	Al Kaline	1583
12	Eddie Murray	1562
13	Willie McCovey	1555
14	Willie Stargell	1540
15	George Brett	1520

Runs Batted In per Game

1	Sam Thompson	.92
2	Lou Gehrig	.92
3	Hank Greenberg	.92
4	Joe DiMaggio	.89
5	Babe Ruth	.88
6	Jimmie Foxx	.83
7	Cap Anson	.83
8	Al Simmons	.82
9	Ted Williams	.80
10	Ed Delahanty	.80
11	Hack Wilson	.79
12	Dan Brouthers	.77
13	Bob Meusel	.76
14	Hal Trosky	.75
15	Hugh Duffy	.75
16	Rudy York	.72
17	Harry Heilmann	.72
18	Jim Bottomley	.71
19	Johnny Mize	.71
20	Roy Campanella	.70
21	Goose Goslin	.70
22	Rogers Hornsby	.70
23	Earl Averill	.70
24	Joe Medwick	.70
25	Hank Aaron	.70
26	Jim Rice	.69
27	Ralph Kiner	.69
28	Bob Johnson	.69
29	Al Rosen	.69
30	Chuck Klein	.69
31	Tony Lazzeri	.68
32	Vern Stephens	.68
33	Mel Ott	.68
34	Bill Dickey	.68
35	Del Ennis	.67
36	Yogi Berra	.67
37	Bob Horner	.67
38	Buck Ewing	.67
39	Joe Cronin	.67
40	Bobby Doerr	.67
41	Dick Stuart	.67
42	Wally Berger	.67
43	Darryl Strawberry	.66
44	Mike Schmidt	.66
45	Roger Connor	.66
46	Jake Beckley	.66
47	Pie Traynor	.66
48	Hughie Jennings	.65
49	Ken Williams	.65
50	King Kelly	.65
51	Willie Stargell	.65
52	Harmon Killebrew	.65
53	Charlie Keller	.65
54	Joe Carter	.65
55	Chick Hafey	.65
56	Ernie Banks	.65
57	Glenn Wright	.65
58	Jackie Jensen	.65
59	Frank Robinson	.65
60	Nap Lajoie	.64
61	Stan Musial	.64
62	Joe Kelley	.64
63	Orlando Cepeda	.64
64	Babe Herman	.64
65	Jeff Heath	.64
66	Bobby Veach	.64
67	Don Mattingly	.64
68	Dick Allen	.64
69	Eddie Murray	.64
70	Ty Cobb	.64
71	Johnny Bench	.64
72	Dolph Camilli	.64
73	Willie Mays	.64
74	Irish Meusel	.64
75	Ruben Sierra	.63
76	Buck Freeman	.63
77	Larry Doby	.63
78	Vic Wertz	.63
79	Dave Winfield	.63
80	George Bell	.63
81	Patsy Tebeau	.63
82	Rocky Colavito	.63
83	George Kelly	.63
84	Gus Zernial	.63
85	Mickey Mantle	.63
86	George Foster	.63
87	Frank Baker	.63
88	Bill Terry	.63
89	Steve Brodie	.63
90	Hank Sauer	.63
91	Dave Kingman	.62
92	Joe Gordon	.62
93	Duke Snider	.62
94	Honus Wagner	.62
95	Frank McCormick	.62
96	Greg Luzinski	.62
97	Tommy Henrich	.62
98	Will Clark	.62
99	Joe Vosmik	.62
100	Hardy Richardson	.62

Walks

1	Babe Ruth	2056
2	Ted Williams	2019
3	Joe Morgan	1865
4	Carl Yastrzemski	1845
5	Mickey Mantle	1733
6	Mel Ott	1708
7	Eddie Yost	1614
8	Darrell Evans	1605
9	Stan Musial	1599
10	Pete Rose	1566
11	Harmon Killebrew	1559
12	Lou Gehrig	1508
13	Mike Schmidt	1507
14	Eddie Collins	1499
15	Willie Mays	1464
16	Jimmie Foxx	1452
17	Eddie Mathews	1444
18	Frank Robinson	1420
19	Hank Aaron	1402
20	Dwight Evans	1391
21	Tris Speaker	1381
22	Reggie Jackson	1375
23	Willie McCovey	1345
24	Luke Appling	1302
25	Rickey Henderson	1286
26	Al Kaline	1277
27	Ken Singleton	1263
28	Jack Clark	1262
29	Rusty Staub	1255
30	Ty Cobb	1249
31	Willie Randolph	1243
32	Jim Wynn	1224
33	Pee Wee Reese	1210
34	Richie Ashburn	1198
35	Brian Downing	1197
36	Billy Hamilton	1187
37	Charlie Gehringer	1186
38	Donie Bush	1158
39	Max Bishop	1153
	Toby Harrah	1153
41	Eddie Murray	1147
42	Harry Hooper	1136
43	Jimmy Sheckard	1135
44	Dave Winfield	1126
45	Ron Santo	1108
46	Lu Blue	1092
	Stan Hack	1092
48	Paul Waner	1091
49	Graig Nettles	1088
50	Bobby Grich	1087
51	Bob Johnson	1075
52	Harlond Clift	1070
	Keith Hernandez	1070
54	Bill Dahlen	1064
55	Joe Cronin	1059
56	George Brett	1057
57	Ron Fairly	1052
58	Lou Whitaker	1047
59	Billy Williams	1045
60	Norm Cash	1043
	Eddie Joost	1043
62	Roy Thomas	1042
63	Max Carey	1040
64	Rogers Hornsby	1038
65	Jim Gilliam	1036
66	Sal Bando	1031
67	Jesse Burkett	1029
68	Rod Carew	1018
	Enos Slaughter	1018
70	Ron Cey	1012
71	Ralph Kiner	1011
72	Wade Boggs	1004
	Dummy Hoy	1004
74	Miller Huggins	1003
75	Roger Connor	1002
76	Boog Powell	1001
77	Eddie Stanky	996
78	Cupid Childs	991
79	Gene Tenace	984
80	Bid McPhee	981
	Dale Murphy	981
82	Joe Kuhel	980
	Earl Torgeson	980
84	Augie Galan	979
85	Duke Snider	971
86	Bob Elliott	967
87	Mike Hargrove	965
	Joe Judge	965
	Buddy Myer	965
90	Honus Wagner	963
91	Jimmy Dykes	958
92	Mickey Vernon	955
93	Cap Anson	952
94	Rocky Colavito	951
95	Goose Goslin	949
	Ozzie Smith	949
97	Dolph Camilli	947
98	Gil Hodges	943
99	Elmer Valo	942
100	Gary Matthews	940

Walk Percentage

1	Ted Williams	20.76
2	Max Bishop	20.42
3	Babe Ruth	19.67
4	Eddie Stanky	18.80
5	Ferris Fain	18.70
6	Gene Tenace	18.31
7	Roy Cullenbine	18.03
8	Eddie Yost	18.01
9	Mickey Mantle	17.62
10	John McGraw	17.56
11	Charlie Keller	17.14
12	Joe Morgan	16.74
13	Earl Torgeson	16.47
14	Bernie Carbo	16.45
15	Roy Thomas	16.44
16	Ralph Kiner	16.26
17	Harmon Killebrew	16.06
18	Billy Hamilton	15.92
19	Lou Gehrig	15.86
20	Elmer Valo	15.78
21	Joe Ferguson	15.77
22	Rickey Henderson	15.75
23	Harlond Clift	15.74
24	Eddie Joost	15.69
25	Lu Blue	15.61
26	Jack Clark	15.56
27	Jim Wynn	15.54
28	Mel Ott	15.30
29	Miller Huggins	15.29
30	Mike Schmidt	15.29
31	Darrell Evans	15.17
32	Jimmie Foxx	15.15
33	Joe Cunningham	15.12
34	Dolph Camilli	15.03
35	Cupid Childs	14.99
36	Ken Singleton	14.94
37	Elbie Fletcher	14.85
38	Merv Rettenmund	14.83
39	Mike Hargrove	14.78
40	Topsy Hartsel	14.72
41	Dwayne Murphy	14.66
42	Wayne Garrett	14.59
43	Barry Bonds	14.56
44	Jason Thompson	14.52
45	Eddie Mathews	14.47
46	Mickey Cochrane	14.22
47	Andy Thornton	14.20
48	Augie Galan	14.16
49	Gene Woodling	14.15
50	Willie McCovey	14.10
51	Hank Greenberg	14.09
52	Darrell Porter	14.04
53	Larry Doby	14.01
54	John Mayberry	13.92
55	Wade Boggs	13.91
56	Alvin Davis	13.91
57	John Briggs	13.87
58	Billy North	13.85
59	Donie Bush	13.84
60	Wally Schang	13.79
61	Roger Bresnahan	13.74
62	Paul Radford	13.71
63	Steve Braun	13.69
64	Norm Siebern	13.64
65	Bob Allison	13.64
66	Bobby Grich	13.63
67	Al Rosen	13.61
68	Toby Harrah	13.48
69	Lee Mazzilli	13.47
70	Norm Cash	13.46
71	Mike Jorgensen	13.46
72	Bob Johnson	13.45
73	Willie Randolph	13.42
74	Tommy Henrich	13.40
75	Dwight Evans	13.39
76	Rick Ferrell	13.38
77	Wayne Gross	13.36
78	Carl Yastrzemski	13.34
79	Grady Hatton	13.31
80	Lyn Lary	13.28
81	Brian Downing	13.23
82	Ed Bailey	13.21
83	Jackie Robinson	13.17
84	Jack Graney	13.14
85	Eddie Collins	13.09
86	Rick Monday	13.09
87	Don Mincher	13.08
88	Pee Wee Reese	13.06
89	Jeff Burroughs	13.05
90	Stan Hack	13.05
91	Gary Roenicke	13.04
92	Boog Powell	13.03
93	Rob Deer	13.00
94	Jimmy Sheckard	12.99
95	Charlie Maxwell	12.98
96	Gorman Thomas	12.97
97	Andy Seminick	12.92
98	Darryl Strawberry	12.87
99	Don Buford	12.86
100	Luke Appling	12.82

Strikeouts

1	Reggie Jackson	2597
2	Willie Stargell	1936
3	Mike Schmidt	1883
4	Tony Perez	1867
5	Dave Kingman	1816
6	Bobby Bonds	1757
7	Dale Murphy	1733
8	Lou Brock	1730
9	Mickey Mantle	1710
10	Harmon Killebrew	1699
11	Dwight Evans	1697
12	Lee May	1570
13	Dick Allen	1556
14	Willie McCovey	1550
15	Dave Parker	1537
16	Frank Robinson	1532
17	Willie Mays	1526
18	Rick Monday	1513
19	Dave Winfield	1503
20	Greg Luzinski	1495
21	Eddie Mathews	1487
22	Frank Howard	1460
23	Lance Parrish	1442
24	Jack Clark	1441
25	Jim Wynn	1427
26	Jim Rice	1423
27	George Foster	1419
28	George Scott	1418
29	Darrell Evans	1410
30	Carl Yastrzemski	1393
31	Hank Aaron	1383
32	Carlton Fisk	1375
33	Larry Parrish	1359
34	Andre Dawson	1349
35	Ron Santo	1343
36	Gorman Thomas	1339
37	Babe Ruth	1330
38	Deron Johnson	1318
39	Willie Horton	1313
40	Jimmie Foxx	1311
41	Johnny Bench	1278
	Bobby Grich	1278
43	Claudell Washington	1266
44	Robin Yount	1257
45	Ken Singleton	1246
46	Duke Snider	1237
47	Ernie Banks	1236
48	Ron Cey	1235
49	Jesse Barfield	1234
50	Roberto Clemente	1230
51	Boog Powell	1226
52	Eddie Murray	1224
53	Rob Deer	1210
54	Graig Nettles	1209
55	Juan Samuel	1208
56	Tony Armas	1201
57	Vada Pinson	1196
58	Dave Concepcion	1186
59	Orlando Cepeda	1169
60	Pete Rose	1143
61	Bert Campaneris	1142
62	Donn Clendenon	1140
63	Gil Hodges	1137
64	Jeff Burroughs	1135
	Leo Cardenas	1135
	Lloyd Moseby	1135
67	Brian Downing	1127
68	Bob Bailey	1126
69	Gary Matthews	1125
70	Darryl Strawberry	1119
71	Fred Lynn	1116
72	Willie Wilson	1098
73	Jim Fregosi	1097
74	Joe Torre	1094
75	Garry Templeton	1092
76	Norm Cash	1091
77	Chili Davis	1087
78	Tony Taylor	1083
79	Tommy Harper	1080
80	Tom Brunansky	1071
81	Don Baylor	1069
82	Kirk Gibson	1068
83	Johnny Callison	1064
84	Gary Gaetti	1060
85	Joe Adcock	1059
86	Doug Rader	1055
87	Billy Williams	1046
88	Frank White	1035
89	Bob Allison	1033
90	Jose Cruz	1031
91	Reggie Smith	1030
92	Rod Carew	1028
93	Darrell Porter	1025
94	Chet Lemon	1024
95	Al Kaline	1020
96	Harold Baines	1017
	Ken Boyer	1017
98	Joe Morgan	1015
99	George Hendrick	1013
100	Keith Hernandez	1012

At Bats per Strikeout

1	Joe Sewell	62.6
2	Lloyd Waner	44.9
3	Nellie Fox	42.7
4	Tommy Holmes	40.9
5	Andy High	33.8
6	Sam Rice	33.7
7	Frankie Frisch	33.5
8	Dale Mitchell	33.5
9	Johnny Cooney	31.5
10	Frank McCormick	30.3
11	Don Mueller	29.9
12	Billy Southworth	29.5
13	Rip Radcliff	28.9
14	Edd Roush	28.3
15	Pie Traynor	27.2
16	Doc Cramer	26.5
17	Carson Bigbee	26.0
18	Hank Severeid	25.5
19	George Sisler	25.3
20	Paul Waner	25.2
21	Sparky Adams	24.9
22	Lou Finney	24.9
23	Deacon White	24.8
24	Jack Rowe	24.8
25	Irish Meusel	24.6
26	Ezra Sutton	24.6
27	Red Schoendienst	24.5
28	Vic Power	24.5
29	Arky Vaughan	24.0
30	Felix Millan	23.9
31	Mickey Cochrane	23.8
32	Charlie Gehringer	23.8
33	John Ward	23.5
34	George Kell	23.4
35	George Cutshaw	23.2
36	Jack Tobin	23.1
37	Taffy Wright	23.1
38	Hughie Critz	23.1
39	Mark Koenig	22.5
40	Ernie Lombardi	22.3
41	Heinie Manush	22.2
42	Bobby Richardson	22.2
43	Jo-Jo Moore	22.0
44	Earl Sheely	21.8
45	Bill Dickey	21.8
46	Johnny Pesky	21.8
47	Rick Ferrell	21.8
48	Glenn Beckert	21.4
49	Dick Siebert	21.2
50	Eddie Waitkus	20.9
51	Max Flack	20.8
52	Bill Buckner	20.7
53	Dixie Walker	20.7
54	Everett Scott	20.7
55	Earle Combs	20.7
56	Paul Hines	20.6
57	Freddy Lindstrom	20.3
58	Mickey Owen	20.2
59	Joe Vosmik	20.1
60	Tony Gwynn	19.6
61	Lou Boudreau	19.5
62	Milt Stock	19.5
63	Willard Marshall	19.3
64	Debs Garms	19.3
65	Charlie Grimm	19.3
66	Harry Rice	19.3
67	Skeeter Newsome	19.2
68	Curt Walker	19.1
69	Peanuts Lowrey	19.1
70	Charlie Jamieson	19.0
71	Muddy Ruel	19.0
72	Tommy Griffith	18.9
73	Tommy Thevenow	18.8
74	Joe Stripp	18.6
75	Joe DiMaggio	18.5
76	Bob Fothergill	18.5
77	Bing Miller	18.3
78	Riggs Stephenson	18.3
79	Yogi Berra	18.2
80	Billy Herman	18.0
81	Lee Magee	18.0
82	Dave Cash	18.0
83	Elmer Valo	17.7
84	Heinie Groh	17.6
85	Luke Sewell	17.5
86	Rich Dauer	17.5
87	Buddy Lewis	17.4
88	Billy Goodman	17.2
89	Jim Gilliam	17.1
90	Harvey Kuenn	17.1
91	Gus Mancuso	17.1
92	Jimmie Wilson	17.1
93	Billy Cox	17.0
94	Ken Williams	16.9
95	George Case	16.9
96	Cecil Travis	16.9
97	Luke Appling	16.8
98	Jackie Hayes	16.8
99	Jackie Robinson	16.8
100	Bibb Falk	16.7

Batting Average

1	Ty Cobb	.366
2	Rogers Hornsby	.358
3	Joe Jackson	.356
4	Ed Delahanty	.346
5	Tris Speaker	.345
6	Ted Williams	.344
7	Billy Hamilton	.344
8	Dan Brouthers	.342
9	Babe Ruth	.342
10	Harry Heilmann	.342
11	Pete Browning	.341
12	Willie Keeler	.341
13	Bill Terry	.341
14	George Sisler	.340
15	Lou Gehrig	.340
16	Jesse Burkett	.338
17	Nap Lajoie	.338
18	Wade Boggs	.338
19	Riggs Stephenson	.336
20	Al Simmons	.334
21	John McGraw	.334
22	Paul Waner	.333
23	Eddie Collins	.333
24	Mike Donlin	.333
25	Stan Musial	.331
26	Sam Thompson	.331
27	Heinie Manush	.330
28	Cap Anson	.329
29	Rod Carew	.328
30	Honus Wagner	.327
31	Tony Gwynn	.327
32	Tip O'Neill	.326
33	Bob Fothergill	.325
34	Jimmie Foxx	.325
35	Earle Combs	.325
36	Joe DiMaggio	.325
37	Babe Herman	.324
38	Hugh Duffy	.324
39	Joe Medwick	.324
40	Edd Roush	.323
41	Sam Rice	.322
42	Ross Youngs	.322
43	Kiki Cuyler	.321
44	Kirby Puckett	.321
45	Charlie Gehringer	.320
46	Chuck Klein	.320
47	Pie Traynor	.320
48	Mickey Cochrane	.320
49	Ken Williams	.319
50	Earl Averill	.318
51	Arky Vaughan	.318
52	Roberto Clemente	.317
53	Chick Hafey	.317
54	Joe Kelley	.317
55	Zack Wheat	.317
56	Roger Connor	.317
57	Lloyd Waner	.316
58	Frankie Frisch	.316
59	Goose Goslin	.316
60	George Van Haltren	.316
61	Bibb Falk	.314
62	Cecil Travis	.314
63	Hank Greenberg	.313
64	Jack Fournier	.313
65	Elmer Flick	.313
66	Bill Dickey	.313
67	Dale Mitchell	.312
68	Johnny Mize	.312
69	Joe Sewell	.312
70	Fred Clarke	.312
71	Barney McCosky	.312
72	Bing Miller	.312
73	Hughie Jennings	.311
74	Freddy Lindstrom	.311
75	Jackie Robinson	.311
76	Baby Doll Jacobson	.311
77	Taffy Wright	.311
78	Rip Radcliff	.311
79	Don Mattingly	.311
80	Ginger Beaumont	.311
81	Mike Tiernan	.311
82	Denny Lyons	.310
83	Luke Appling	.310
84	Irish Meusel	.310
85	Elmer Smith	.310
86	Bobby Veach	.310
87	Jim O'Rourke	.310
88	Jim Bottomley	.310
89	John Stone	.310
90	Sam Crawford	.309
91	Bob Meusel	.309
92	Jack Tobin	.309
93	Spud Davis	.308
94	Richie Ashburn	.308
95	King Kelly	.308
96	Jake Beckley	.308
97	Stuffy McInnis	.307
98	Joe Vosmik	.307
99	Frank Baker	.307
100	George Burns	.307

Batting Average (by era)

1876-1892

1	Dan Brouthers	.342
2	Pete Browning	.341
3	Sam Thompson	.331
4	Cap Anson	.329
5	Tip O'Neill	.326
6	Roger Connor	.317
7	Denny Lyons	.310
8	Jim O'Rourke	.310
9	King Kelly	.308
10	Deacon White	.303
11	Henry Larkin	.303
12	Buck Ewing	.303
13	George Gore	.301
14	Paul Hines	.301
15	Oyster Burns	.300

1893-1919

1	Ty Cobb	.366
2	Joe Jackson	.356
3	Ed Delahanty	.346
4	Tris Speaker	.345
5	Billy Hamilton	.344
6	Willie Keeler	.341
7	Jesse Burkett	.338
8	Nap Lajoie	.338
9	John McGraw	.334
10	Eddie Collins	.333
11	Mike Donlin	.333
12	Honus Wagner	.327
13	Hugh Duffy	.324
14	Joe Kelley	.317
15	Zack Wheat	.317

1920-1941

1	Rogers Hornsby	.358
2	Babe Ruth	.342
3	Harry Heilmann	.342
4	Bill Terry	.341
5	George Sisler	.340
6	Lou Gehrig	.340
7	Riggs Stephenson	.336
8	Al Simmons	.334
9	Paul Waner	.333
10	Heinie Manush	.330
11	Bob Fothergill	.325
12	Jimmie Foxx	.325
13	Earle Combs	.325
14	Babe Herman	.324
15	Joe Medwick	.324

1942-1960

1	Ted Williams	.344
2	Stan Musial	.331
3	Joe DiMaggio	.325
4	Dale Mitchell	.312
5	Johnny Mize	.312
6	Barney McCosky	.312
7	Jackie Robinson	.311
8	Taffy Wright	.311
9	Richie Ashburn	.308
10	Johnny Pesky	.307
11	George Kell	.306
12	Dixie Walker	.306
13	Harvey Kuenn	.303
14	Tommy Holmes	.302
15	Enos Slaughter	.300

1961-1992

1	Wade Boggs	.338
2	Rod Carew	.328
3	Tony Gwynn	.327
4	Kirby Puckett	.321
5	Roberto Clemente	.317
6	Don Mattingly	.311
7	George Brett	.307
8	Matty Alou	.307
9	Ralph Garr	.306
10	Hank Aaron	.305
11	Bill Madlock	.305
12	Tony Oliva	.304
13	Manny Mota	.304
14	Paul Molitor	.303
15	Al Oliver	.303

Batting Average (by position)

First Base

1	Dan Brouthers	.342
2	Bill Terry	.341
3	George Sisler	.340
4	Lou Gehrig	.340
5	Cap Anson	.329
6	Rod Carew	.328
7	Jimmie Foxx	.325
8	Roger Connor	.317
9	Hank Greenberg	.313
10	Jack Fournier	.313

Second Base

1	Rogers Hornsby	.358
2	Nap Lajoie	.338
3	Eddie Collins	.333
4	Charlie Gehringer	.320
5	Frankie Frisch	.316
6	Cupid Childs	.306
7	Billy Herman	.304
8	Buddy Myer	.303
9	Del Pratt	.292
10	Tony Lazzeri	.292

Shortstop

1	Honus Wagner	.327
2	Arky Vaughan	.318
3	Joe Sewell	.312
4	Luke Appling	.310
5	Ed McKean	.302
6	Joe Cronin	.301
7	Lou Boudreau	.295
8	George Davis	.295
9	Glenn Wright	.294
10	Travis Jackson	.291

Third Base

1	Wade Boggs	.338
2	Pie Traynor	.320
3	Denny Lyons	.310
4	Frank Baker	.307
5	George Brett	.307
6	George Kell	.306
7	Bill Madlock	.305
8	Stan Hack	.301
9	Pinky Whitney	.295
10	Jimmy Collins	.294

Outfield

1	Ty Cobb	.366
2	Joe Jackson	.356
3	Ed Delahanty	.346
4	Tris Speaker	.345
5	Ted Williams	.344
6	Billy Hamilton	.344
7	Babe Ruth	.342
8	Harry Heilmann	.342
9	Willie Keeler	.341
10	Jesse Burkett	.338

Catcher

1	Mickey Cochrane	.320
2	Bill Dickey	.313
3	Spud Davis	.308
4	Ernie Lombardi	.306
5	Gabby Hartnett	.297
6	Manny Sanguillen	.296
7	Smoky Burgess	.295
8	Thurman Munson	.292
9	Hank Severeid	.289
10	Jack Clements	.286

Relative Batting Average

1	Ty Cobb	134.7
2	Joe Jackson	133.1
3	Pete Browning	131.6
4	Wade Boggs	129.0
5	Ted Williams	128.1
6	Dan Brouthers	127.8
7	Nap Lajoie	127.3
8	Rod Carew	127.0
9	Rogers Hornsby	126.2
10	Tris Speaker	125.4
11	Tip O'Neill	125.3
12	Tony Gwynn	125.3
13	Willie Keeler	124.5
14	Stan Musial	123.9
15	Mike Donlin	123.6
16	Honus Wagner	123.1
17	Kirby Puckett	123.0
18	Billy Hamilton	122.7
19	Ed Delahanty	122.7
20	Cap Anson	122.7
21	Jesse Burkett	121.7
22	Eddie Collins	121.6
23	Sam Thompson	121.1
24	Roberto Clemente	120.7
25	Tony Oliva	120.4
26	Harry Heilmann	119.4
27	Babe Ruth	119.2
28	George Sisler	118.9
29	Don Mattingly	118.9
30	Sam Crawford	118.8
31	King Kelly	118.2
32	Jim O'Rourke	118.1
33	Matty Alou	117.9
34	Joe Medwick	117.8
35	Paul Waner	117.8
36	Elmer Flick	117.4
37	Roger Connor	117.4
38	George Brett	117.3
39	Bill Terry	117.3
40	Lou Gehrig	117.2
41	Joe DiMaggio	117.1
42	Ginger Beaumont	117.0
43	Ralph Garr	116.7
44	Manny Mota	116.4
45	Dale Mitchell	116.3
46	Henry Larkin	116.2
47	John McGraw	116.2
48	Deacon White	116.0
49	Hank Aaron	116.0
50	Will Clark	115.9
51	Paul Hines	115.8
52	George Gore	115.7
53	Jackie Robinson	115.7
54	Paul Molitor	115.6
55	Pete Rose	115.6
56	Al Simmons	115.4
57	Frank Baker	115.4
58	Al Kaline	115.4
59	Bill Madlock	115.2
60	Arky Vaughan	115.1
61	Edd Roush	115.1
62	Al Oliver	115.1
63	Riggs Stephenson	115.0
64	Mickey Mantle	115.0
65	Julio Franco	115.0
66	Johnny Mize	115.0
67	Zack Wheat	114.9
68	Hugh Duffy	114.8
69	George Kell	114.8
70	Barney McCosky	114.7
71	Richie Ashburn	114.6
72	Hardy Richardson	114.6
73	Pedro Guerrero	114.5
74	Johnny Pesky	114.5
75	Harvey Kuenn	114.5
76	Rico Carty	114.4
77	Willie Mays	114.3
78	Fred Clarke	114.0
79	Heinie Manush	114.0
80	Cy Seymour	113.9
81	Willie McGee	113.9
82	Jimmie Foxx	113.8
83	Joe Torre	113.8
84	Tim Raines	113.6
85	Denny Lyons	113.6
86	Cecil Cooper	113.5
87	Jim Rice	113.5
88	Frank Robinson	113.4
89	Tommy Davis	113.4
90	Taffy Wright	113.4
91	Minnie Minoso	113.1
92	Jimmy Wolf	113.0
93	Tommy Holmes	113.0
94	Joe Kelley	112.9
95	Orlando Cepeda	112.9
96	Mickey Rivers	112.9
97	Bake McBride	112.9
98	Manny Sanguillen	112.8
99	Thurman Munson	112.8
100	John Reilly	112.7

On Base Percentage

1	Ted Williams	.483
2	Babe Ruth	.474
3	John McGraw	.465
4	Billy Hamilton	.455
5	Lou Gehrig	.447
6	Rogers Hornsby	.434
7	Ty Cobb	.433
8	Wade Boggs	.432
9	Jimmie Foxx	.428
	Tris Speaker	.428
11	Ferris Fain	.425
12	Eddie Collins	.424
13	Max Bishop	.423
	Dan Brouthers	.423
	Joe Jackson	.423
	Mickey Mantle	.423
17	Mickey Cochrane	.419
18	Stan Musial	.418
19	Cupid Childs	.416
20	Jesse Burkett	.415
21	Mel Ott	.414
22	Roy Thomas	.413
23	Ed Delahanty	.412
	Hank Greenberg	.412
25	Harry Heilmann	.410
	Charlie Keller	.410
	Jackie Robinson	.410
	Eddie Stanky	.410
29	Roy Cullenbine	.408
30	Denny Lyons	.407
	Riggs Stephenson	.407
32	Joe Cunningham	.406
	Rickey Henderson	.406
	Arky Vaughan	.406
35	Charlie Gehringer	.404
	Paul Waner	.404
37	Pete Browning	.403
38	Lu Blue	.402
39	Joe Kelley	.401
40	Mike Hargrove	.400
41	Luke Appling	.399
	Elmer Valo	.399
	Ross Youngs	.399
44	Joe DiMaggio	.398
	Ralph Kiner	.398
46	Richie Ashburn	.397
	Earle Combs	.397
	Roger Connor	.397
	Johnny Mize	.397
	Elmer Smith	.397
51	Cap Anson	.395
	Earl Averill	.395
	Rod Carew	.395
	Joe Morgan	.395
	Hack Wilson	.395
	Eddie Yost	.395
57	Frank Chance	.394
	Stan Hack	.394
	Johnny Pesky	.394
60	Bob Johnson	.393
	Wally Schang	.393
	Bill Terry	.393
	Ken Williams	.393
64	Jack Fournier	.392
	George Grantham	.392
	Tip O'Neill	.392
	Frank Robinson	.392
	Mike Tiernan	.392
69	Minnie Minoso	.391
	Joe Sewell	.391
	Ken Singleton	.391
	Gene Tenace	.391
73	Harlond Clift	.390
	Joe Cronin	.390
	Augie Galan	.390
	Hughie Jennings	.390
	Honus Wagner	.390
78	Bernie Carbo	.389
	Elmer Flick	.389
	Buddy Myer	.389
	Tim Raines	.389
82	Dolph Camilli	.388
	Mike Griffin	.388
	Keith Hernandez	.388
	Gene Woodling	.388
86	Larry Doby	.387
	Goose Goslin	.387
	Willie Keeler	.387
	Willie Mays	.387
	Earl Torgeson	.387
91	Fred Clarke	.386
	Kiki Cuyler	.386
	George Gore	.386
	Barney McCosky	.386
	Al Rosen	.386
96	Roger Bresnahan	.385
	Mike Donlin	.385
	Dummy Hoy	.385
	George Van Haltren	.385
100	5 players tied	.384

Slugging Average

1	Babe Ruth	.690
2	Ted Williams	.634
3	Lou Gehrig	.632
4	Jimmie Foxx	.609
5	Hank Greenberg	.605
6	Joe DiMaggio	.579
7	Rogers Hornsby	.577
8	Johnny Mize	.562
9	Stan Musial	.559
10	Willie Mays	.557
11	Mickey Mantle	.557
12	Hank Aaron	.555
13	Ralph Kiner	.548
14	Hack Wilson	.545
15	Chuck Klein	.543
16	Duke Snider	.540
17	Frank Robinson	.537
18	Al Simmons	.535
19	Dick Allen	.534
20	Earl Averill	.534
21	Mel Ott	.533
22	Babe Herman	.532
23	Ken Williams	.530
24	Willie Stargell	.529
25	Mike Schmidt	.527
26	Chick Hafey	.526
27	Hal Trosky	.522
28	Wally Berger	.522
29	Harry Heilmann	.520
30	Dan Brouthers	.519
31	Charlie Keller	.518
32	Joe Jackson	.517
33	Willie McCovey	.515
34	Ty Cobb	.512
35	Darryl Strawberry	.512
36	Eddie Mathews	.509
37	Jeff Heath	.509
38	Harmon Killebrew	.509
39	Will Clark	.507
40	Bob Johnson	.506
41	Bill Terry	.506
42	Ed Delahanty	.505
43	Sam Thompson	.505
44	Joe Medwick	.505
45	Barry Bonds	.503
46	Jim Rice	.502
47	Tris Speaker	.500
48	Jim Bottomley	.500
49	Goose Goslin	.500
50	Roy Campanella	.500
51	Ernie Banks	.500
52	Orlando Cepeda	.499
53	Bob Horner	.499
54	Frank Howard	.499
55	Ted Kluszewski	.498
56	Bob Meusel	.497
57	Hank Sauer	.496
58	Al Rosen	.495
59	Billy Williams	.492
60	Ripper Collins	.492
61	Dolph Camilli	.492
62	Tommy Henrich	.491
63	George Brett	.490
64	Larry Doby	.490
65	Reggie Jackson	.490
66	Dick Stuart	.489
67	Reggie Smith	.489
68	Gabby Hartnett	.489
69	Rocky Colavito	.489
70	Norm Cash	.488
71	Andre Dawson	.487
72	Gil Hodges	.487
73	Bill Dickey	.486
74	Roger Connor	.486
75	Gus Zernial	.486
76	Joe Adcock	.485
77	Wally Post	.485
78	Kent Hrbek	.485
79	Fred Lynn	.484
80	Eddie Murray	.484
81	Jack Fournier	.483
82	Rudy York	.483
83	Don Mattingly	.483
84	Yogi Berra	.482
85	Charlie Gehringer	.480
86	Pedro Guerrero	.480
87	George Foster	.480
88	Dave Winfield	.480
89	Al Kaline	.480
90	Heinie Manush	.479
91	Gavvy Cravath	.478
92	Dave Kingman	.478
93	Mickey Cochrane	.478
94	Greg Luzinski	.478
95	George Bell	.477
96	Tony Oliva	.476
97	Roger Maris	.476
98	Johnny Bench	.476
99	Jack Clark	.476
100	Leon Durham	.475

Production

1	Babe Ruth	1.163
2	Ted Williams	1.116
3	Lou Gehrig	1.080
4	Jimmie Foxx	1.038
5	Hank Greenberg	1.017
6	Rogers Hornsby	1.010
7	Mickey Mantle	.979
8	Joe DiMaggio	.977
	Stan Musial	.977
10	Johnny Mize	.959
11	Mel Ott	.947
12	Ralph Kiner	.946
13	Ty Cobb	.945
14	Willie Mays	.944
15	Dan Brouthers	.942
16	Joe Jackson	.940
	Hack Wilson	.940
18	Hank Aaron	.932
19	Harry Heilmann	.930
20	Frank Robinson	.929
21	Earl Averill	.928
	Charlie Keller	.928
	Tris Speaker	.928
24	Ken Williams	.924
25	Chuck Klein	.922
26	Duke Snider	.921
27	Ed Delahanty	.917
28	Babe Herman	.915
	Al Simmons	.915
30	Dick Allen	.914
31	Mike Schmidt	.912
32	Bob Johnson	.899
	Bill Terry	.899
34	Chick Hafey	.898
35	Mickey Cochrane	.897
36	Wade Boggs	.893
37	Willie McCovey	.892
	Willie Stargell	.892
	Hal Trosky	.892
40	Eddie Mathews	.888
	Sam Thompson	.888
42	Barry Bonds	.887
	Goose Goslin	.887
	Billy Hamilton	.887
	Harmon Killebrew	.887
46	Will Clark	.886
47	Charlie Gehringer	.884
48	Roger Connor	.883
	Jackie Robinson	.883
50	Al Rosen	.882
51	Wally Berger	.881
52	Dolph Camilli	.880
	Riggs Stephenson	.880
54	Jeff Heath	.879
55	Paul Waner	.878
56	Larry Doby	.877
57	Jack Fournier	.875
	John McGraw	.875
59	Tommy Henrich	.873
60	Darryl Strawberry	.872
61	Jim Bottomley	.869
	Pete Browning	.869
63	Bill Dickey	.868
64	George Brett	.867
	Joe Medwick	.867
66	Norm Cash	.865
67	Jesse Burkett	.861
	Roy Campanella	.861
69	Kiki Cuyler	.860
70	Earle Combs	.859
	Al Kaline	.859
	Reggie Smith	.859
	Arky Vaughan	.859
74	Jack Clark	.858
	Gavvy Cravath	.858
	Gabby Hartnett	.858
	Jim Rice	.858
78	Joe Cronin	.857
79	Kent Hrbek	.856
	Heinie Manush	.856
	Honus Wagner	.856
	Billy Williams	.856
83	Mike Donlin	.854
	George Grantham	.854
	Pedro Guerrero	.854
	Eddie Murray	.854
	Mike Tiernan	.854
88	Eddie Collins	.853
	Frank Howard	.853
90	Orlando Cepeda	.852
	Ripper Collins	.852
	Joe Kelley	.852
	Ted Kluszewski	.852
	Bob Meusel	.852
95	Rocky Colavito	.851
	Minnie Minoso	.851
97	Denny Lyons	.850
	Tip O'Neill	.850
99	Bob Nieman	.849
100	3 players tied	.848

Adjusted Production

1	Babe Ruth	209
2	Ted Williams	186
3	Lou Gehrig	182
4	Rogers Hornsby	176
5	Mickey Mantle	173
6	Dan Brouthers	171
7	Joe Jackson	169
8	Ty Cobb	167
9	Pete Browning	166
10	Jimmie Foxx	161
11	Hank Greenberg	157
	Willie Mays	157
	Johnny Mize	157
	Stan Musial	157
15	Hank Aaron	156
	Dick Allen	156
	Joe DiMaggio	156
	Tris Speaker	156
19	Roger Connor	155
	Mel Ott	155
21	Ed Delahanty	154
	Frank Robinson	154
23	Charlie Keller	152
24	Will Clark	151
25	Nap Lajoie	150
	Honus Wagner	150
27	Gavvy Cravath	149
	Elmer Flick	149
29	Harry Heilmann	148
	Ralph Kiner	148
	Willie McCovey	148
	Sam Thompson	148
33	Barry Bonds	147
	Mike Schmidt	147
	Willie Stargell	147
36	Eddie Mathews	145
	Hack Wilson	145
38	Henry Larkin	144
	Darryl Strawberry	144
40	Sam Crawford	143
	Jack Fournier	143
	Frank Howard	143
	Harry Stovey	143
44	Eddie Collins	142
	Mike Donlin	142
	Harmon Killebrew	142
	Tip O'Neill	142
48	Jesse Burkett	141
	Billy Hamilton	141
	Babe Herman	141
	Denny Lyons	141
52	Wally Berger	140
	Wade Boggs	140
	Jeff Heath	140
	Reggie Jackson	140
	Mike Tiernan	140
57	Cap Anson	139
	Rickey Henderson	139
	Bob Johnson	139
60	Oyster Burns	138
	Norm Cash	138
	Jack Clark	138
	Pedro Guerrero	138
	Al Rosen	138
	Duke Snider	138
66	George Brett	137
	Larry Doby	137
	King Kelly	137
	Sherry Magee	137
	Eddie Murray	137
	Gene Tenace	137
	Bill Terry	137
73	Frank Baker	136
	George Gore	136
	John McGraw	136
	Reggie Smith	136
	Arky Vaughan	136
	Ken Williams	136
79	Frank Chance	135
	Chuck Klein	135
81	Dolph Camilli	134
	Charlie Hickman	134
	Paul Hines	134
	Al Kaline	134
	Jim O'Rourke	134
	Boog Powell	134
	Dave Winfield	134
88	Orlando Cepeda	133
	Chick Hafey	133
	Joe Kelley	133
	Joe Medwick	133
	Joe Morgan	133
	Bill Nicholson	133
	Paul Waner	133
95	10 players tied	132

Batting Runs

1	Babe Ruth	1322
2	Ted Williams	1166
3	Ty Cobb	1032
4	Stan Musial	983
5	Lou Gehrig	918
6	Hank Aaron	878
7	Rogers Hornsby	844
8	Tris Speaker	843
9	Willie Mays	827
10	Jimmie Foxx	803
	Mickey Mantle	803
12	Frank Robinson	773
13	Mel Ott	767
14	Honus Wagner	661
15	Dan Brouthers	648
16	Carl Yastrzemski	617
17	Eddie Collins	605
18	Mike Schmidt	592
19	Roger Connor	563
20	Cap Anson	562
21	Nap Lajoie	558
22	Ed Delahanty	539
23	Harmon Killebrew	532
24	Willie McCovey	524
25	Johnny Mize	520
26	Harry Heilmann	517
27	Jesse Burkett	514
28	George Brett	513
	Al Kaline	513
30	Joe DiMaggio	507
31	Sam Crawford	494
32	Paul Waner	491
33	Billy Hamilton	484
34	Willie Stargell	483
35	Eddie Mathews	480
36	Dick Allen	470
37	Hank Greenberg	468
38	Reggie Jackson	466
39	Billy Williams	463
40	Joe Jackson	452
41	Wade Boggs	445
42	Duke Snider	441
43	Joe Morgan	438
44	Rod Carew	431
45	Eddie Murray	427
46	Dwight Evans	418
47	Pete Rose	416
48	Al Simmons	399
49	Dave Winfield	393
50	Ralph Kiner	391
51	Norm Cash	390
52	Fred Clarke	383
53	Joe Kelley	382
54	Reggie Smith	379
55	Charlie Gehringer	376
	Sam Thompson	376
57	Chuck Klein	375
58	Rickey Henderson	374
59	Pete Browning	368
60	Jack Clark	367
	Jim Rice	367
62	Bob Johnson	366
63	Arky Vaughan	361
64	Harry Stovey	360
65	Roberto Clemente	354
	Joe Medwick	354
67	Willie Keeler	345
	Ron Santo	345
69	Elmer Flick	342
70	Goose Goslin	341
71	Orlando Cepeda	337
72	Earl Averill	334
	Zack Wheat	334
74	Ken Singleton	332
75	Sherry Magee	331
76	Frank Howard	324
77	King Kelly	321
78	Dolph Camilli	319
79	Rusty Staub	318
	Bill Terry	318
81	Keith Hernandez	310
82	Fred Lynn	309
83	Jimmy Ryan	306
	Enos Slaughter	306
85	Boog Powell	305
	Mike Tiernan	305
	Hack Wilson	305
88	Babe Herman	304
89	Jim O'Rourke	303
90	Minnie Minoso	299
91	Joe Torre	298
92	Rocky Colavito	297
	George Gore	297
94	Tony Perez	292
95	Greg Luzinski	291
96	Jake Beckley	289
	John McGraw	289
98	Ernie Banks	288
99	Charlie Keller	287
100	Jack Fournier	285

Adjusted Batting Runs

1	Babe Ruth	1355
2	Ted Williams	1093
3	Ty Cobb	1017
4	Lou Gehrig	966
5	Stan Musial	930
6	Hank Aaron	902
7	Rogers Hornsby	859
8	Mickey Mantle	838
	Willie Mays	838
10	Tris Speaker	813
11	Mel Ott	773
12	Jimmie Foxx	768
13	Frank Robinson	754
14	Honus Wagner	644
15	Dan Brouthers	631
16	Eddie Collins	614
17	Roger Connor	564
18	Nap Lajoie	561
	Mike Schmidt	561
20	Ed Delahanty	551
21	Willie McCovey	538
22	Eddie Mathews	531
23	Harry Heilmann	527
24	Joe DiMaggio	522
25	Carl Yastrzemski	515
26	Johnny Mize	505
27	Reggie Jackson	503
28	Harmon Killebrew	500
29	George Brett	499
30	Jesse Burkett	493
31	Willie Stargell	485
32	Al Kaline	481
33	Sam Crawford	475
34	Paul Waner	474
35	Cap Anson	470
	Joe Morgan	470
37	Dick Allen	469
38	Eddie Murray	457
39	Billy Hamilton	441
40	Hank Greenberg	440
	Joe Jackson	440
42	Dave Winfield	438
43	Rod Carew	414
44	Rickey Henderson	412
45	Wade Boggs	407
46	Duke Snider	405
47	Billy Williams	401
48	Pete Browning	388
49	Bob Johnson	381
50	Fred Clarke	379
51	Pete Rose	378
	Al Simmons	378
53	Jack Clark	374
54	Ralph Kiner	373
55	Norm Cash	366
56	Roberto Clemente	362
	Sam Thompson	362
58	Arky Vaughan	356
59	Dwight Evans	351
	Reggie Smith	351
61	Elmer Flick	350
	Ken Singleton	350
63	Goose Goslin	348
64	Frank Howard	344
65	Joe Kelley	340
66	Charlie Gehringer	339
67	Orlando Cepeda	337
68	Zack Wheat	335
69	Rusty Staub	333
70	Bill Terry	332
71	Chuck Klein	330
72	Sherry Magee	328
73	Mike Tiernan	324
74	Joe Medwick	322
75	Harry Stovey	320
76	Keith Hernandez	319
77	Babe Herman	318
78	Jake Beckley	311
79	Hack Wilson	310
80	Boog Powell	309
81	Earl Averill	305
82	Jack Fournier	302
	Joe Torre	302
84	Willie Keeler	300
	Jim O'Rourke	300
	Jim Rice	300
87	Minnie Minoso	298
88	Charlie Keller	291
89	Rocky Colavito	290
90	Ron Santo	284
91	Jim Wynn	281
92	Fred Lynn	280
93	Larry Doby	278
94	Dolph Camilli	277
95	Bobby Bonds	276
96	Pedro Guerrero	273
97	Tony Perez	272
98	Brian Downing	271
	John McGraw	271
100	2 players tied	270

Batting Wins

1	Babe Ruth	127.5
2	Ted Williams	115.9
3	Ty Cobb	106.4
4	Stan Musial	99.7
5	Hank Aaron	91.1
6	Tris Speaker	86.1
7	Willie Mays	85.5
8	Lou Gehrig	85.4
9	Rogers Hornsby	84.9
10	Mickey Mantle	82.9
11	Frank Robinson	80.7
12	Mel Ott	76.2
13	Jimmie Foxx	75.3
14	Honus Wagner	68.2
15	Carl Yastrzemski	64.3
16	Eddie Collins	62.1
17	Mike Schmidt	61.8
18	Nap Lajoie	57.2
19	Dan Brouthers	56.6
20	Harmon Killebrew	55.8
21	Willie McCovey	54.9
22	Al Kaline	53.4
23	Sam Crawford	52.5
24	Johnny Mize	52.2
25	George Brett	51.7
26	Willie Stargell	51.0
27	Harry Heilmann	50.8
28	Dick Allen	50.0
29	Cap Anson	49.7
30	Roger Connor	49.2
31	Eddie Mathews	49.2
32	Joe DiMaggio	48.6
33	Billy Williams	48.6
34	Paul Waner	48.6
35	Reggie Jackson	47.9
36	Ed Delahanty	47.5
37	Joe Jackson	47.4
38	Jesse Burkett	47.1
39	Joe Morgan	45.9
40	Rod Carew	44.7
41	Hank Greenberg	44.5
42	Wade Boggs	44.5
43	Duke Snider	44.4
44	Pete Rose	43.9
45	Eddie Murray	43.2
46	Billy Hamilton	42.2
47	Dwight Evans	42.2
48	Norm Cash	41.1
49	Reggie Smith	40.3
50	Dave Winfield	40.0
51	Ralph Kiner	39.1
52	Jack Clark	38.0
53	Rickey Henderson	37.5
54	Al Simmons	37.4
55	Fred Clarke	37.4
56	Jim Rice	36.9
57	Roberto Clemente	36.8
58	Chuck Klein	36.7
59	Arky Vaughan	36.4
60	Ron Santo	36.3
61	Sherry Magee	35.8
62	Joe Medwick	35.8
63	Bob Johnson	35.2
64	Joe Kelley	35.1
65	Charlie Gehringer	35.1
66	Orlando Cepeda	35.1
67	Elmer Flick	34.8
68	Frank Howard	34.4
69	Zack Wheat	34.4
70	Ken Singleton	34.0
71	Rusty Staub	33.3
72	Willie Keeler	33.3
73	Sam Thompson	32.6
74	Boog Powell	32.4
75	Keith Hernandez	32.4
76	Dolph Camilli	32.2
77	Pete Browning	32.1
78	Goose Goslin	31.9
79	Harry Stovey	31.7
80	Joe Torre	31.4
81	Fred Lynn	31.1
82	Enos Slaughter	30.9
83	Earl Averill	30.8
84	Rocky Colavito	30.8
85	Bill Terry	30.8
86	Tony Perez	30.6
87	Minnie Minoso	30.3
88	Greg Luzinski	30.1
89	Ernie Banks	29.8
90	Gavvy Cravath	29.7
91	Hack Wilson	29.5
92	Babe Herman	29.5
93	Tony Oliva	28.9
94	King Kelly	28.8
95	Jack Fournier	28.8
96	Charlie Keller	28.6
97	Dale Murphy	28.5
98	Bobby Bonds	28.4
99	Cy Williams	28.4
100	Pedro Guerrero	27.9

Adjusted Batting Wins

1	Babe Ruth	130.7
2	Ted Williams	108.6
3	Ty Cobb	104.9
4	Stan Musial	94.3
5	Hank Aaron	93.6
6	Lou Gehrig	89.9
7	Willie Mays	86.6
8	Mickey Mantle	86.5
9	Rogers Hornsby	86.4
10	Tris Speaker	83.0
11	Frank Robinson	78.7
12	Mel Ott	76.8
13	Jimmie Foxx	72.0
14	Honus Wagner	66.4
15	Eddie Collins	63.0
16	Mike Schmidt	58.6
17	Nap Lajoie	57.5
18	Willie McCovey	56.4
19	Dan Brouthers	55.1
20	Eddie Mathews	54.4
21	Carl Yastrzemski	53.7
22	Harmon Killebrew	52.4
23	Harry Heilmann	51.7
24	Reggie Jackson	51.7
25	Willie Stargell	51.2
26	Johnny Mize	50.7
27	Sam Crawford	50.5
28	George Brett	50.3
29	Al Kaline	50.1
30	Joe DiMaggio	50.1
31	Dick Allen	49.8
32	Roger Connor	49.3
33	Joe Morgan	49.2
34	Ed Delahanty	48.6
35	Paul Waner	46.9
36	Eddie Murray	46.2
37	Joe Jackson	46.1
38	Jesse Burkett	45.2
39	Dave Winfield	44.6
40	Rod Carew	43.0
41	Billy Williams	42.1
42	Hank Greenberg	41.8
43	Cap Anson	41.6
44	Rickey Henderson	41.3
45	Duke Snider	40.8
46	Wade Boggs	40.7
47	Pete Rose	39.9
48	Jack Clark	38.8
49	Norm Cash	38.6
50	Billy Hamilton	38.5
51	Roberto Clemente	37.7
52	Reggie Smith	37.3
53	Ralph Kiner	37.3
54	Fred Clarke	37.0
55	Bob Johnson	36.6
56	Frank Howard	36.6
57	Arky Vaughan	35.9
58	Ken Singleton	35.8
59	Elmer Flick	35.6
60	Sherry Magee	35.5
61	Al Simmons	35.4
62	Dwight Evans	35.4
63	Orlando Cepeda	35.1
64	Rusty Staub	34.9
65	Zack Wheat	34.5
66	Pete Browning	33.8
67	Keith Hernandez	33.3
68	Boog Powell	32.8
69	Goose Goslin	32.6
70	Joe Medwick	32.6
71	Chuck Klein	32.3
72	Bill Terry	32.1
73	Joe Torre	31.8
74	Charlie Gehringer	31.7
75	Sam Thompson	31.4
76	Joe Kelley	31.3
77	Babe Herman	30.9
78	Jack Fournier	30.5
79	Minnie Minoso	30.2
80	Jim Rice	30.2
81	Rocky Colavito	30.1
82	Hack Wilson	30.0
83	Ron Santo	29.9
84	Jim Wynn	29.7
85	Willie Keeler	29.0
86	Charlie Keller	29.0
87	Bobby Bonds	28.6
88	Pedro Guerrero	28.6
89	Tony Perez	28.5
90	Jake Beckley	28.4
91	Harry Stovey	28.2
92	Fred Lynn	28.2
93	Earl Averill	28.2
94	Tim Raines	28.1
95	Mike Tiernan	28.1
96	Dolph Camilli	28.0
97	Greg Luzinski	27.9
98	Larry Doby	27.7
99	Darrell Evans	27.5
100	Darryl Strawberry	27.4

Runs Created

1	Babe Ruth	2838
2	Ty Cobb	2803
3	Stan Musial	2625
4	Hank Aaron	2550
5	Ted Williams	2538
6	Willie Mays	2372
7	Tris Speaker	2321
8	Lou Gehrig	2312
9	Mel Ott	2235
10	Honus Wagner	2231
11	Pete Rose	2220
12	Jimmie Foxx	2189
13	Carl Yastrzemski	2147
14	Frank Robinson	2126
15	Rogers Hornsby	2074
16	Mickey Mantle	2069
17	Eddie Collins	2056
18	Nap Lajoie	1907
19	Paul Waner	1853
20	Al Kaline	1846
21	Ed Delahanty	1833
22	George Brett	1807
23	Joe Morgan	1804
24	Jesse Burkett	1803
25	Charlie Gehringer	1781
26	Reggie Jackson	1772
27	Al Simmons	1771
28	Mike Schmidt	1757
29	Cap Anson	1756
30	Eddie Mathews	1738
31	Sam Crawford	1715
32	Billy Hamilton	1705
33	Goose Goslin	1700
34	Harry Heilmann	1690
35	Dave Winfield	1689
36	Willie Keeler	1685
37	Jake Beckley	1684
38	Fred Clarke	1678
39	Billy Williams	1671
40	Roger Connor	1648
41	Willie McCovey	1638
42	George Davis	1634
43	Eddie Murray	1632
44	Dan Brouthers	1624
45	Dwight Evans	1611
46	Harmon Killebrew	1609
47	Joe DiMaggio	1606
48	Robin Yount	1598
49	Rod Carew	1595
50	George Van Haltren	1566
51	Jimmy Ryan	1562
52	Roberto Clemente	1557
53	Zack Wheat	1539
54	Rusty Staub	1534
55	Joe Kelley	1533
56	Willie Stargell	1531
57	Tony Perez	1523
58	Ernie Banks	1513
59	Lou Brock	1512
60	Hugh Duffy	1508
61	Bill Dahlen	1505
62	Johnny Mize	1502
63	Darrell Evans	1499
64	Sam Rice	1495
65	Luke Appling	1493
66	George Sisler	1490
67	Duke Snider	1487
68	Max Carey	1472
69	Frankie Frisch	1464
70	Dave Parker	1452
71	Enos Slaughter	1432
72	Rickey Henderson	1428
73	Joe Cronin	1426
74	Bob Johnson	1418
75	Andre Dawson	1396
76	Vada Pinson	1394
77	Mickey Vernon	1387
78	Richie Ashburn	1386
79	Jim Bottomley	1384
80	Heinie Manush	1383
81	Jim Rice	1382
82	Ron Santo	1379
83	Chuck Klein	1378
84	Carlton Fisk	1372
	Joe Medwick	1372
86	Earl Averill	1358
	Brooks Robinson	1358
88	Harry Hooper	1349
89	Al Oliver	1348
90	Bid McPhee	1345
91	Orlando Cepeda	1338
92	Kiki Cuyler	1336
93	Hank Greenberg	1331
94	Sherry Magee	1327
95	Arky Vaughan	1323
96	Jimmy Sheckard	1314
97	Dale Murphy	1306
98	Lave Cross	1304
	Joe Judge	1304
100	Dummy Hoy	1300

Total Average

1	Babe Ruth	1.399
2	Ted Williams	1.320
3	Lou Gehrig	1.229
4	Billy Hamilton	1.191
5	John McGraw	1.152
6	Jimmie Foxx	1.143
7	Hank Greenberg	1.105
	Rogers Hornsby	1.105
9	Mickey Mantle	1.091
10	Ty Cobb	1.066
11	Dan Brouthers	1.061
12	Ed Delahanty	1.036
	Mel Ott	1.036
14	Stan Musial	1.028
15	Joe DiMaggio	1.012
	Tris Speaker	1.012
17	Joe Jackson	1.008
18	Ralph Kiner	1.006
19	Johnny Mize	1.005
	Hack Wilson	1.005
21	Charlie Keller	1.000
22	Rickey Henderson	.989
23	Willie Mays	.982
24	Mike Tiernan	.970
25	Harry Heilmann	.963
26	Barry Bonds	.962
27	Frank Robinson	.961
28	Joe Kelley	.959
29	Earl Averill	.957
30	Denny Lyons	.955
31	Mike Schmidt	.954
32	Roger Connor	.952
33	Mickey Cochrane	.947
34	Pete Browning	.946
35	Honus Wagner	.945
36	Chuck Klein	.944
37	Ken Williams	.943
38	Jesse Burkett	.942
	Babe Herman	.942
40	Eddie Collins	.941
41	Hank Aaron	.940
42	Jackie Robinson	.939
	Sam Thompson	.939
44	Duke Snider	.933
45	Dick Allen	.930
	Hugh Duffy	.930
47	Dolph Camilli	.928
48	Harry Stovey	.923
49	Frank Chance	.920
	Bob Johnson	.920
51	Eddie Mathews	.916
52	Elmer Flick	.914
53	Mike Donlin	.913
54	Willie McCovey	.912
55	Charlie Gehringer	.910
	Harmon Killebrew	.910
	Joe Morgan	.910
	Elmer Smith	.910
59	Chick Hafey	.908
	Tim Raines	.908
61	Gavvy Cravath	.905
	Mike Griffin	.905
63	Al Simmons	.904
64	Wade Boggs	.902
65	Kiki Cuyler	.901
	Goose Goslin	.901
	Darryl Strawberry	.901
68	Cupid Childs	.900
	Riggs Stephenson	.900
70	Bill Terry	.899
71	Tip O'Neill	.897
72	Arky Vaughan	.894
73	Larry Doby	.893
	Tommy Henrich	.893
75	Willie Stargell	.889
	Hal Trosky	.889
77	Paul Waner	.888
78	Fred Clarke	.884
	Jack Fournier	.884
80	Will Clark	.883
	Hughie Jennings	.883
82	George Grantham	.882
83	Roy Cullenbine	.881
	George Van Haltren	.881
85	Norm Cash	.875
	Al Rosen	.875
87	Oyster Burns	.873
88	Wally Berger	.870
	Jimmy Ryan	.870
90	Jeff Heath	.869
91	Cap Anson	.867
	Jack Clark	.867
93	Dummy Hoy	.865
94	Jim Bottomley	.862
95	King Kelly	.861
	Nap Lajoie	.861
97	Joe Cronin	.859
98	Harlond Clift	.858
	Tony Lazzeri	.858
100	Bill Dickey	.857

Runs Produced

1	Ty Cobb	4066
2	Hank Aaron	3716
3	Babe Ruth	3673
4	Cap Anson	3501
5	Stan Musial	3425
6	Lou Gehrig	3390
7	Honus Wagner	3367
8	Pete Rose	3319
9	Willie Mays	3305
10	Tris Speaker	3294
11	Mel Ott	3208
	Carl Yastrzemski	3208
13	Jimmie Foxx	3139
14	Ted Williams	3116
15	Jake Beckley	3089
16	Eddie Collins	3074
17	Frank Robinson	3055
18	Al Simmons	3027
19	Nap Lajoie	3020
20	Charlie Gehringer	3017
21	Ed Delahanty	2962
22	George Davis	2903
23	Rogers Hornsby	2862
24	Goose Goslin	2844
25	Dave Winfield	2829
26	Paul Waner	2823
27	Sam Crawford	2819
28	Al Kaline	2806
29	Roger Connor	2804
30	Hugh Duffy	2748
31	Bill Dahlen	2738
32	George Brett	2736
33	Dan Brouthers	2713
34	Reggie Jackson	2690
35	Robin Yount	2682
36	Frankie Frisch	2671
37	Mickey Mantle	2650
38	Harry Heilmann	2647
39	Jimmy Ryan	2617
40	Jesse Burkett	2597
41	George Van Haltren	2584
42	Fred Clarke	2567
43	Joe DiMaggio	2566
44	Sam Rice	2558
45	Mike Schmidt	2553
46	Joe Kelley	2550
47	Tony Perez	2545
48	Joe Morgan	2515
49	Willie Keeler	2496
50	Eddie Murray	2491
51	Joe Cronin	2487
52	Roberto Clemente	2481
53	Dwight Evans	2469
54	Billy Williams	2459
55	Eddie Mathews	2450
56	Ernie Banks	2429
57	Sam Thompson	2428
58	Dave Parker	2426
59	Herman Long	2418
60	Jim O'Rourke	2406
61	Zack Wheat	2405
62	Pie Traynor	2398
63	Luke Appling	2390
64	Billy Hamilton	2386
65	Enos Slaughter	2382
66	Jim Bottomley	2380
67	Joe Medwick	2376
68	Rusty Staub	2363
69	Lou Brock	2361
70	Heinie Manush	2360
71	George Sisler	2357
72	Rod Carew	2347
73	Mickey Vernon	2335
74	Brooks Robinson	2321
75	Jim Rice	2318
76	Al Oliver	2296
77	Harmon Killebrew	2294
78	Tommy Corcoran	2285
	Andre Dawson	2285
80	Darrell Evans	2284
81	Vada Pinson	2280
82	Max Carey	2275
83	Willie McCovey	2263
84	Willie Stargell	2260
85	John Ward	2249
86	Yogi Berra	2247
87	King Kelly	2238
88	Bob Johnson	2234
89	Kiki Cuyler	2232
90	Carlton Fisk	2225
91	Ted Simmons	2215
92	Sherry Magee	2205
93	Duke Snider	2185
94	Steve Garvey	2179
95	Don Baylor	2174
96	Harry Hooper	2171
97	Doc Cramer	2162
98	Joe Kuhel	2154
99	Earl Averill	2150
100	2 players tied	2147

Clutch Hitting Index

1	Cap Anson	138
2	Earl Sheely	136
	Pie Traynor	136
4	Duffy Lewis	135
	Bobby Veach	135
6	Sherry Magee	133
7	Kitty Bransfield	132
8	Sam Mertes	131
	Tommy Thevenow	131
10	Tommy Davis	130
	Chick Gandil	130
	Possum Whitted	130
13	Larry Gardner	129
	Stuffy McInnis	129
	Pinky Whitney	129
	Heinie Zimmerman	129
17	Terry Pendleton	128
	Red Smith	128
19	Frank Chance	127
	Bob Elliott	127
	Ted Simmons	127
	Harry Steinfeldt	127
	Pat Tabler	127
	Patsy Tebeau	127
25	Rube Bressler	126
	Frank LaPorte	126
	Glenn Wright	126
28	Frank McCormick	125
	Dots Miller	125
	Enos Slaughter	125
	Gus Suhr	125
32	Joe Cronin	124
	George Cutshaw	124
	Bob Fothergill	124
	Cookie Lavagetto	124
	Red Murray	124
	Fred Pfeffer	124
	Lee Tannehill	124
	Bobby Wallace	124
	Ned Williamson	124
	Taffy Wright	124
42	Tom Burns	123
	Gavvy Cravath	123
	Del Ennis	123
	Ferris Fain	123
	Art Fletcher	123
	Jackie Jensen	123
	Keith Moreland	123
	Luke Sewell	123
	Billy Sullivan	123
	Vic Wertz	123
52	Frank Baker	122
	Frank Bowerman	122
	Roy Campanella	122
	Tony Cuccinello	122
	Harry Heilmann	122
	Solly Hofman	122
	Willie Kamm	122
	Sam Mele	122
	Willie Montanez	122
	Muddy Ruel	122
	Deacon White	122
	Jimmy Williams	122
64	Lou Criger	121
	Kid Elberfeld	121
	Ron Fairly	121
	Carl Furillo	121
	Hughie Jennings	121
	Steve Kemp	121
	Tony Perez	121
	Boog Powell	121
	Ray Schalk	121
	Joe Sewell	121
	Riggs Stephenson	121
	Joe Tinker	121
	Honus Wagner	121
77	John Anderson	120
	Walt Dropo	120
	Bibb Falk	120
	Pinky Higgins	120
	George Kelly	120
	Tony Lazzeri	120
	Dan McGann	120
	Irish Meusel	120
	Mike Mowrey	120
	Del Pratt	120
	Elmer Smith	120
	Dick Stuart	120
	Bob Watson	120
90	13 players tied	119

Isolated Power

1	Babe Ruth	.348
2	Lou Gehrig	.292
3	Hank Greenberg	.292
4	Ted Williams	.289
5	Jimmie Foxx	.284
6	Ralph Kiner	.269
7	Mike Schmidt	.260
8	Mickey Mantle	.259
9	Willie Mays	.256
10	Joe DiMaggio	.254
11	Harmon Killebrew	.252
12	Johnny Mize	.250
13	Darryl Strawberry	.250
14	Hank Aaron	.250
15	Willie Stargell	.247
16	Willie McCovey	.245
17	Duke Snider	.244
18	Frank Robinson	.243
19	Dave Kingman	.242
20	Dick Allen	.242
21	Eddie Mathews	.238
22	Hack Wilson	.238
23	Charlie Keller	.231
24	Hank Sauer	.230
25	Mel Ott	.229
26	Barry Bonds	.229
27	Stan Musial	.228
28	Reggie Jackson	.228
29	Rob Deer	.228
30	Dick Stuart	.225
31	Ernie Banks	.225
32	Frank Howard	.225
33	Roy Campanella	.224
34	Chuck Klein	.223
35	Gorman Thomas	.223
36	Rocky Colavito	.223
37	Bob Horner	.222
38	Wally Berger	.221
39	Gus Zernial	.221
40	Wally Post	.220
41	Hal Trosky	.219
42	Rogers Hornsby	.218
43	Norm Cash	.217
44	Bob Allison	.217
45	Roger Maris	.216
46	Earl Averill	.216
47	Jeff Heath	.216
48	Dolph Camilli	.215
49	Gil Hodges	.214
50	Ken Williams	.211
51	Jesse Barfield	.210
52	Al Rosen	.210
53	Bob Johnson	.210
54	Tommy Henrich	.209
55	Chick Hafey	.209
56	Jack Clark	.209
57	Johnny Bench	.208
58	Roy Sievers	.208
59	Rudy York	.208
60	Joe Adcock	.208
61	Nate Colbert	.207
62	Babe Herman	.207
63	Larry Doby	.207
64	Will Clark	.206
65	George Foster	.206
66	Andre Dawson	.206
67	Dale Murphy	.205
68	Jim Rice	.204
69	Joe Carter	.203
70	Bobby Bonds	.203
71	Orlando Cepeda	.203
72	Howard Johnson	.202
73	Billy Williams	.202
74	Greg Luzinski	.202
75	Cliff Johnson	.202
76	Reggie Smith	.202
77	Fred Lynn	.201
78	Al Simmons	.201
79	Don Mincher	.201
80	Tony Armas	.200
81	Ted Kluszewski	.200
82	Leon Durham	.199
83	Kent Hrbek	.199
84	Dwight Evans	.198
85	Jim Lemon	.198
86	Andy Thornton	.198
87	Bill Nicholson	.198
88	Dale Long	.198
89	Yogi Berra	.198
90	Joe Gordon	.197
91	Boog Powell	.196
92	Ripper Collins	.196
93	Don Demeter	.195
94	Dave Winfield	.195
95	George Bell	.194
96	Eddie Murray	.194
97	Kirk Gibson	.192
98	Lee May	.192
99	Vic Wertz	.192
100	Mack Jones	.192

Extra Base Hits

1	Hank Aaron	1477
2	Stan Musial	1377
3	Babe Ruth	1356
4	Willie Mays	1323
5	Lou Gehrig	1190
6	Frank Robinson	1186
7	Carl Yastrzemski	1157
8	Ty Cobb	1136
9	Tris Speaker	1131
10	Jimmie Foxx	1117
	Ted Williams	1117
12	Reggie Jackson	1075
13	Mel Ott	1071
14	George Brett	1066
15	Pete Rose	1041
16	Mike Schmidt	1015
17	Rogers Hornsby	1011
18	Ernie Banks	1009
19	Dave Winfield	1008
20	Al Simmons	995
21	Honus Wagner	993
22	Al Kaline	972
23	Tony Perez	963
24	Willie Stargell	953
25	Mickey Mantle	952
26	Billy Williams	948
27	Dwight Evans	941
28	Dave Parker	940
29	Eddie Mathews	938
30	Andre Dawson	937
31	Robin Yount	924
32	Goose Goslin	921
33	Willie McCovey	920
34	Paul Waner	909
35	Eddie Murray	908
36	Charlie Gehringer	904
37	Nap Lajoie	903
38	Harmon Killebrew	887
39	Joe DiMaggio	881
40	Harry Heilmann	876
41	Vada Pinson	868
42	Sam Crawford	864
43	Joe Medwick	858
44	Duke Snider	850
45	Roberto Clemente	846
46	Carlton Fisk	843
47	Rusty Staub	838
48	Jim Bottomley	835
49	Jim Rice	834
50	Al Oliver	825
51	Orlando Cepeda	823
52	Brooks Robinson	818
53	Joe Morgan	813
54	Roger Connor	812
55	Johnny Mize	809
56	Ed Delahanty	808
57	Joe Cronin	803
58	Jake Beckley	802
59	Johnny Bench	794
60	Dale Murphy	786
61	Mickey Vernon	782
62	Hank Greenberg	781
63	Zack Wheat	780
64	Darrell Evans	779
	Bob Johnson	779
66	Ted Simmons	778
67	Lou Brock	776
68	Ron Santo	772
69	Chuck Klein	772
70	Dan Brouthers	771
71	Earl Averill	767
72	Heinie Manush	761
73	Steve Garvey	755
74	Dick Allen	750
75	Cap Anson	749
76	Graig Nettles	746
77	Hal McRae	741
78	Fred Lynn	737
79	Reggie Smith	734
80	Don Baylor	732
81	Enos Slaughter	730
82	Yogi Berra	728
83	Gary Carter	726
	Jimmy Ryan	726
85	Lee May	725
86	Bill Buckner	721
87	Sam Rice	716
88	Willie Davis	715
	Del Ennis	715
90	Gil Hodges	713
91	Jack Clark	711
92	Frankie Frisch	709
93	Dave Kingman	707
94	Cecil Cooper	703
95	George Foster	702
96	Bobby Bonds	700
97	Gabby Hartnett	696
98	Cesar Cedeno	695
99	Bobby Doerr	693
100	George Sisler	691

Pinch Hits

1	Manny Mota	150
2	Smoky Burgess	145
3	Greg Gross	143
4	Jose Morales	123
5	Jerry Lynch	116
6	Red Lucas	114
7	Steve Braun	113
8	Terry Crowley	108
	Denny Walling	108
10	Gates Brown	107
11	Mike Lum	103
12	Jim Dwyer	102
13	Rusty Staub	100
14	Larry Biittner	95
	Vic Davalillo	95
16	Jerry Hairston	94
17	Dave Philley	93
	Joel Youngblood	93
19	Jay Johnstone	92
20	Ed Kranepool	90
	Elmer Valo	90
22	Dave Collins	85
23	Jesus Alou	82
	Thad Bosley	82
	Kurt Bevacqua	82
	Tim McCarver	82

Pinch Hit Average

1	Tommy Davis	.320
2	Frenchy Bordagaray	.312
3	Frankie Baumholtz	.307
4	Red Schoendienst	.303
5	Bob Fothergill	.300
6	Dave Philley	.299
7	Ken Griffey Sr.	.299
8	Manny Mota	.297
9	Ted Easterly	.296
10	Harvey Hendrick	.295
11	Milt Thompson	.295
12	Larry Herndon	.294
13	Rance Mulliniks	.292
14	Terry Puhl	.289
15	Manny Sanguillen	.288
16	Smoky Burgess	.286
17	Rick Miller	.286
18	Johnny Mize	.283
19	Bubba Morton	.281
20	Steve Braun	.281
21	Don Mueller	.280
22	Rusty Staub	.279
23	Mickey Vernon	.279
24	Herm Winningham	.279
25	Thad Bosley	.278
26	Gene Woodling	.278

Pinch Hit Home Runs

1	Cliff Johnson	20
2	Jerry Lynch	18
3	Gates Brown	16
	Smoky Burgess	16
	Willie McCovey	16
6	George Crowe	14
7	Joe Adcock	12
	Bob Cerv	12
	Jose Morales	12
	Graig Nettles	12
11	Jeff Burroughs	11
	Jay Johnstone	11
	Fred Whitfield	11
	Cy Williams	11
15	Jim Dwyer	10
	Mike Lum	10
	Ken McMullen	10
	Don Mincher	10
	Wally Post	10
	Champ Summers	10
	Jerry Turner	10
	Gus Zernial	10

Total Player Rating / 150g

1	Babe Ruth	6.30
2	Ted Williams	6.05
3	Nap Lajoie	5.74
4	Rickey Henderson	5.41
5	Rogers Hornsby	5.30
6	Barry Bonds	5.15
7	Mike Schmidt	5.01
8	Tris Speaker	4.76
9	Mickey Mantle	4.60
10	Ty Cobb	4.59
11	Honus Wagner	4.44
12	Willie Mays	4.33
13	Joe Jackson	4.30
14	Lou Gehrig	4.29
15	Tim Raines	4.15
16	Joe DiMaggio	4.02
17	Dan Brouthers	3.92
18	Hank Aaron	3.85
19	Frank Robinson	3.76
20	Pete Browning	3.75
21	Eddie Collins	3.68
22	Wade Boggs	3.68
23	Lou Boudreau	3.68
24	Ed Delahanty	3.66
25	Jimmie Foxx	3.59
26	Stan Musial	3.55
27	Jackie Robinson	3.54
28	Ryne Sandberg	3.52
29	Buck Ewing	3.49
30	Mel Ott	3.43
31	Hank Greenberg	3.41
32	Roger Connor	3.34
33	George Davis	3.29
34	Arky Vaughan	3.28
35	Jack Glasscock	3.27
36	Mickey Cochrane	3.26
37	Bobby Grich	3.23
38	Bill Dahlen	3.22
39	Cal Ripken	3.22
40	Cupid Childs	3.21
41	Bobby Doerr	3.20
42	Hardy Richardson	3.20
43	Hughie Jennings	3.20
44	Sam Thompson	3.20
45	Frank Baker	3.19
46	Tony Gwynn	3.18
47	Joe Morgan	3.15
48	Darryl Strawberry	3.10
49	Eddie Mathews	3.05
50	Ralph Kiner	3.05
51	Gabby Hartnett	3.02
52	Johnny Mize	3.00
53	Charlie Keller	2.99
54	Bid McPhee	2.97
55	Bill Dickey	2.92
56	Charlie Gehringer	2.91
57	Elmer Flick	2.89
58	Dick Allen	2.87
59	Ozzie Smith	2.86
60	Denny Lyons	2.85
61	Bob Johnson	2.83
62	Joe Cronin	2.82
63	Ron Santo	2.79
64	King Kelly	2.78
65	Dave Bancroft	2.78
66	Joe Sewell	2.77
67	Charlie Bennett	2.77
68	Billy Hamilton	2.71
69	Roy Campanella	2.70
70	Joe Gordon	2.65
71	Bobby Bonds	2.65
72	Kirby Puckett	2.64
73	Reggie Smith	2.63
74	Art Fletcher	2.57
75	Roberto Clemente	2.56
76	Bill Mazeroski	2.54
77	Luke Appling	2.53
78	Gavvy Cravath	2.52
79	Frankie Frisch	2.52
80	Yogi Berra	2.51
81	Billy Herman	2.50
82	Will Clark	2.50
83	George Brett	2.46
84	Frank Chance	2.46
85	Paul Molitor	2.46
86	Al Kaline	2.46
87	Keith Hernandez	2.45
88	Harry Stovey	2.40
89	Ferris Fain	2.40
90	Heinie Groh	2.39
	Tony Oliva	2.39
92	Cap Anson	2.39
93	Robin Yount	2.36
94	Roy Cullenbine	2.35
95	John McGraw	2.35
96	Art Devlin	2.32
97	Bobby Wallace	2.32
98	Wally Berger	2.31
99	Roy Thomas	2.31
100	Carl Yastrzemski	2.30

Stolen Bases

Rank	Player	Total
1	Rickey Henderson	1042
2	Lou Brock	938
3	Billy Hamilton	912
4	Ty Cobb	891
5	Eddie Collins	744
6	Arlie Latham	739
7	Max Carey	738
8	Tim Raines	730
9	Honus Wagner	722
10	Joe Morgan	689
11	Willie Wilson	660
12	Tom Brown	657
13	Bert Campaneris	649
14	George Davis	616
15	Vince Coleman	610
16	Dummy Hoy	594
17	Maury Wills	586
18	George Van Haltren	583
19	Hugh Duffy	574
20	Bid McPhee	568
21	Davey Lopes	557
22	Cesar Cedeno	550
23	Bill Dahlen	547
24	Ozzie Smith	542
25	John Ward	540
26	Herman Long	534
27	Patsy Donovan	518
28	Jack Doyle	516
29	Harry Stovey	509
30	Luis Aparicio	506
	Fred Clarke	506
32	Willie Keeler	495
	Clyde Milan	495
34	Omar Moreno	487
35	Mike Griffin	473
36	Tommy McCarthy	468
37	Jimmy Sheckard	465
38	Bobby Bonds	461
39	Ed Delahanty	455
	Ron LeFlore	455
41	Curt Welch	453
42	Joe Kelley	443
43	Sherry Magee	441
44	Brett Butler	437
	Steve Sax	437
46	John McGraw	436
47	Tris Speaker	434
48	Mike Tiernan	428
49	Bob Bescher	427
50	Charlie Comiskey	419
	Frankie Frisch	419
52	Jimmy Ryan	418
53	Paul Molitor	412
54	Tommy Harper	408
55	Donie Bush	403
56	Frank Chance	401
57	Bill Lange	399
58	Willie Davis	398
59	Sam Mertes	396
60	Dave Collins	395
	Billy North	395
62	Jesse Burkett	389
63	Tommy Corcoran	387
64	Tom Daly	385
	Freddie Patek	385
66	George Burns	383
	Hugh Nicol	383
68	Fred Pfeffer	382
69	Walt Wilmot	381
70	Nap Lajoie	380
71	Harry Hooper	375
	George Sisler	375
73	Jack Glasscock	372
74	King Kelly	368
75	Sam Crawford	366
	Tommy Dowd	366
77	Hal Chase	363
78	Tommy Leach	361
79	Lonnie Smith	360
80	Hughie Jennings	359
	Fielder Jones	359
82	Buck Ewing	354
	Gary Pettis	354
84	Rod Carew	353
85	Tommy Tucker	352
86	Sam Rice	351
87	George Case	349
	Juan Samuel	349
89	Paul Radford	346
90	Julio Cruz	343
91	Amos Otis	341
92	John Anderson	338
	Willie Mays	338
94	Joe Tinker	336
95	Kip Selbach	334
96	Elmer Flick	330
97	Jose Cardenal	329
	Ned Hanlon	329
99	3 players tied	328

Stolen Base Average

Rank	Player	Avg
1	Eric Davis	87.5
2	Tim Raines	85.2
3	Henry Cotto	84.4
4	Willie Wilson	83.3
5	Davey Lopes	83.0
6	Barry Larkin	81.8
7	Vince Coleman	81.6
8	Lenny Dykstra	81.5
9	Julio Cruz	81.5
10	Rickey Henderson	81.3
11	Joe Morgan	81.0
12	Ozzie Smith	80.8
13	Mickey Mantle	80.1
14	Gary Redus	80.1
15	Kirk Gibson	79.8
16	Enzo Hernandez	79.6
17	Mike Felder	79.4
18	Andy Van Slyke	79.4
19	Roberto Alomar	79.3
20	R. J. Reynolds	79.0
21	Luis Aparicio	78.8
22	Amos Otis	78.6
23	Mariano Duncan	78.2
24	Paul Molitor	78.2
25	Tommy Harper	77.9
26	Rudy Law	77.8
27	Ryne Sandberg	77.7
28	Barry Bonds	77.7
29	Bob Dernier	77.6
30	Devon White	77.5
31	Miguel Dilone	77.4
32	Joe Carter	77.4
33	Gary Pettis	77.3
34	Milt Thompson	77.0
35	Mookie Wilson	76.9
36	Hank Aaron	76.7
37	Willie Mays	76.6
38	Bert Campaneris	76.5
39	Dick Schofield	76.2
40	Ron LeFlore	76.2
41	George Case	76.2
42	Dick Howser	75.5
43	Howard Johnson	75.5
44	Cesar Cedeno	75.4
45	Willie McGee	75.4
46	Lou Brock	75.3
47	Lloyd Moseby	75.3
48	Oddibe McDowell	75.2
49	Willie Davis	75.2
50	Larry Bowa	75.2

Stolen Base Runs

Rank	Player	Runs
1	Rickey Henderson	169
2	Tim Raines	143
3	Willie Wilson	119
4	Joe Morgan	110
5	Vince Coleman	100
6	Davey Lopes	99
7	Lou Brock	97
8	Ozzie Smith	85
9	Bert Campaneris	75
10	Luis Aparicio	70
11	Cesar Cedeno	58
12	Eric Davis	57
13	Julio Cruz	56
14	Paul Molitor	55
15	Tommy Harper	53
16	Ron LeFlore	51
	Maury Wills	51
18	Gary Redus	48
19	Amos Otis	47
20	Gary Pettis	44
21	Willie Davis	41
22	Willie Mays	40
	Ryne Sandberg	40
24	George Case	39
	Mookie Wilson	39
26	Kirk Gibson	38
27	Bobby Bonds	37
	Omar Moreno	37
	Freddie Patek	37
30	Lenny Dykstra	36
31	Dave Collins	35
32	Juan Samuel	34
33	Miguel Dilone	33
34	Barry Bonds	32
	Larry Bowa	32
	Willie McGee	32
	Andy Van Slyke	32
38	Dave Concepcion	31
39	Otis Nixon	30
40	Andre Dawson	29
	Rudy Law	29
	Lloyd Moseby	29
43	Hank Aaron	28
	Roberto Alomar	28
	Bob Dernier	28
46	Mickey Rivers	26
	Steve Sax	26
	Lonnie Smith	26
	Frank Taveras	26
50	2 players tied	25

Stolen Base Wins

Rank	Player	Wins
1	Rickey Henderson	16.9
2	Tim Raines	14.9
3	Willie Wilson	11.9
4	Joe Morgan	11.5
5	Vince Coleman	10.5
6	Davey Lopes	10.2
7	Lou Brock	10.2
8	Ozzie Smith	8.9
9	Bert Campaneris	7.9
10	Luis Aparicio	7.3
11	Cesar Cedeno	6.1
12	Eric Davis	6.0
13	Tommy Harper	5.6
14	Julio Cruz	5.6
15	Paul Molitor	5.5
16	Maury Wills	5.3
17	Ron LeFlore	5.2
18	Gary Redus	5.0
19	Amos Otis	4.9
20	Gary Pettis	4.4
21	Willie Davis	4.3
22	Ryne Sandberg	4.2
23	Willie Mays	4.1
24	Mookie Wilson	4.1
25	George Case	3.9
26	Freddie Patek	3.8
27	Omar Moreno	3.8
28	Bobby Bonds	3.8
29	Kirk Gibson	3.8
30	Lenny Dykstra	3.8
31	Dave Collins	3.6
32	Juan Samuel	3.6
33	Miguel Dilone	3.4
34	Andy Van Slyke	3.4
35	Barry Bonds	3.4
36	Larry Bowa	3.3
37	Willie McGee	3.3
38	Dave Concepcion	3.2
39	Otis Nixon	3.1
40	Andre Dawson	3.0
41	Bob Dernier	2.9
42	Rudy Law	2.9
43	Roberto Alomar	2.9
44	Hank Aaron	2.9
45	Lloyd Moseby	2.9
46	Frank Taveras	2.7
47	Lonnie Smith	2.7
48	Steve Sax	2.7
49	Mickey Rivers	2.7
50	Barry Larkin	2.6

Games

First Base
1. Jake Beckley 2377
2. Mickey Vernon 2237
3. Eddie Murray 2214
4. Lou Gehrig 2137
5. Charlie Grimm 2131
6. Joe Judge 2084
7. Ed Konetchy 2073
8. Steve Garvey 2059
9. Cap Anson 2058
10. Joe Kuhel 2057

Second Base
1. Eddie Collins 2650
2. Joe Morgan 2527
3. Nellie Fox 2295
4. Charlie Gehringer 2206
5. Willie Randolph 2152
6. Frank White 2150
7. Bid McPhee 2126
8. Bill Mazeroski 2094
9. Lou Whitaker 2052
10. Nap Lajoie 2035

Shortstop
1. Luis Aparicio 2581
2. Larry Bowa 2222
3. Luke Appling 2218
4. Ozzie Smith 2188
5. Dave Concepcion 2178
6. Rabbit Maranville 2153
7. Bill Dahlen 2132
8. Bert Campaneris 2097
9. Tommy Corcoran 2073
10. Roy McMillan 2028

Third Base
1. Brooks Robinson 2870
2. Graig Nettles 2412
3. Mike Schmidt 2212
4. Buddy Bell 2183
5. Eddie Mathews 2181
6. Ron Santo 2130
7. Eddie Yost 2008
8. Ron Cey 1989
9. Aurelio Rodriguez 1983
10. Sal Bando 1896

Outfield
1. Ty Cobb 2935
2. Willie Mays 2843
3. Hank Aaron 2760
4. Tris Speaker 2698
5. Lou Brock 2507
6. Al Kaline 2488
7. Dave Winfield 2437
8. Max Carey 2421
9. Vada Pinson 2403
10. Roberto Clemente 2370

Catcher
1. Bob Boone 2225
2. Carlton Fisk 2204
3. Gary Carter 2056
4. Jim Sundberg 1927
5. Al Lopez 1918
6. Rick Ferrell 1806
7. Gabby Hartnett 1793
8. Ted Simmons 1771
9. Johnny Bench 1742
10. Ray Schalk 1727

Pitcher
1. Hoyt Wilhelm 1070
2. Kent Tekulve 1050
3. Lindy McDaniel 987
4. Rollie Fingers 944
5. Gene Garber 931
6. Rich Gossage 927
7. Cy Young 906
8. Sparky Lyle 899
9. Jim Kaat 898
10. Don McMahon 874

Fielding Average

First Base
1. Steve Garvey .... .996
2. Wes Parker .... .996
3. Don Mattingly .... .996
4. Dan Driessen .... .995
5. Mark McGwire .... .995
6. Jim Spencer .... .995
7. Frank McCormick ..... .995
8. Keith Hernandez ..... .994
9. Vic Power .... .994
10. Pete Rose .... .994

Second Base
1. Ryne Sandberg .... .990
2. Tom Herr .... .989
3. Rich Dauer .... .987
4. Doug Flynn .... .986
5. Marty Barrett .... .986
6. Jerry Adair .... .985
7. Jim Gantner .... .985
8. Lou Whitaker .... .984
9. Frank White .... .984
10. Bobby Grich .... .984

Shortstop
1. Tony Fernandez ...... .980
2. Larry Bowa .... .980
3. Ozzie Smith .... .979
4. Cal Ripken .... .978
5. Spike Owen .... .978
6. Frank Duffy .... .977
7. Alan Trammell ...... .977
8. Mark Belanger ...... .977
9. Dick Schofield ...... .977
10. Bucky Dent .... .976

Third Base
1. Brooks Robinson ...... .971
2. Ken Reitz .... .970
3. George Kell .... .969
4. Don Money .... .968
5. Steve Buechele ...... .968
6. Hank Majeski .... .968
7. Don Wert .... .968
8. Willie Kamm .... .967
9. Heinie Groh .... .967
10. Carney Lansford ..... .966

Outfield
1. Terry Puhl .... .993
2. Brett Butler .... .992
3. Pete Rose .... .991
4. Amos Otis .... .991
5. Joe Rudi .... .991
6. Mickey Stanley ...... .991
7. Don Demeter .... .990
8. Jim Piersall .... .990
9. Robin Yount .... .990
10. Jim Landis .... .989

Catcher
1. Bill Freehan .... .993
2. Elston Howard ...... .993
3. Ron Hassey .... .993
4. Jim Sundberg .... .993
5. Joe Azcue .... .992
6. Sherm Lollar .... .992
7. Buddy Rosar .... .992
8. Johnny Edwards ..... .992
9. Tom Haller .... .992
10. Lance Parrish ...... .991

Pitcher
1. Don Mossi .... .990
2. Gary Nolan .... .990
3. Rick Rhoden .... .989
4. Lon Warneke .... .988
5. Jim Wilson .... .988
6. Woodie Fryman ..... .988
7. Larry Gura .... .986
8. Pete Alexander ..... .985
9. General Crowder ..... .984
10. Bill Monbouquette ..... .984

Total Chances per Game

First Base
1. Tom Jones 11.38
2. George Stovall 11.30
3. George Kelly 11.09
4. Candy LaChance 11.05
5. Wally Pipp 11.05
6. Ed Konetchy 11.04
7. George Burns 10.92
8. Bill Terry 10.91
9. Cap Anson 10.86
10. Walter Holke 10.83
11. Bill Phillips 10.83
12. Fred Tenney 10.83
13. Phil Todt 10.83

Second Base
1. Joe Gerhardt 7.11
2. Fred Pfeffer 6.95
3. Fred Dunlap 6.83
4. Bid McPhee 6.70
5. Cub Stricker 6.59
6. Lou Bierbauer 6.50
7. Jack Burdock 6.50
8. Cupid Childs 6.32
9. Al Myers 6.22
10. Ski Melillo 6.16

Shortstop
1. Hughie Jennings 6.69
2. Herman Long 6.38
3. Dave Bancroft 6.33
4. Bill Dahlen 6.26
5. George Davis 6.22
6. Rabbit Maranville 6.10
7. Bobby Wallace 6.10
8. Tommy Corcoran 6.09
9. Kid Elberfeld 6.07
10. Monte Cross 6.06
11. Bones Ely 6.06

Third Base
1. Jerry Denny 4.21
2. Billy Shindle 4.15
3. Billy Nash 4.07
4. Arlie Latham 4.04
5. Tommy Leach 3.98
6. Denny Lyons 3.98
7. Jimmy Collins 3.89
8. Art Whitney 3.82
9. Hick Carpenter 3.81
10. Jimmy Austin 3.74
11. Joe Mulvey 3.74

Outfield
1. Taylor Douthit 3.16
2. Richie Ashburn 3.04
3. Johnny Mostil 3.03
4. Dom DiMaggio 2.99
5. Mike Kreevich 2.95
6. Dwayne Murphy 2.92
7. Sam Chapman 2.91
8. Sam West 2.88
9. Max Carey 2.87
10. Kirby Puckett 2.84
11. Fred Schulte 2.84
12. Devon White 2.84

Catcher
1. Johnny Edwards 6.98
2. Charlie Bennett 6.87
3. Johnny Roseboro 6.83
4. Bill Freehan 6.79
5. Joe Azcue 6.72
6. John Bateman 6.61
7. Mike Scioscia 6.59
8. Jerry Grote 6.53
9. Tony Pena 6.47
10. Tim McCarver 6.41

Pitcher
1. Nick Altrock 3.72
2. Harry Howell 3.61
3. Addie Joss 3.60
4. Ed Walsh 3.49
5. Nixey Callahan 3.47
6. Willie Sudhoff 3.31
7. George Mullin 3.20
8. Barney Pelty 3.20
9. Chick Fraser 3.12
10. Red Donahue 2.95
11. Ed Willett 2.95

Chances Accepted per Game

First Base
1. Tom Jones 11.21
2. George Stovall 11.15
3. George Kelly 11.00
4. Wally Pipp 10.96
5. Ed Konetchy 10.93
6. Candy LaChance 10.87
7. Bill Terry 10.82
8. George Burns 10.77
9. Walter Holke 10.75
10. Phil Todt 10.74

Second Base
1. Joe Gerhardt 6.49
2. Fred Pfeffer 6.39
3. Bid McPhee 6.33
4. Fred Dunlap 6.32
5. Lou Bierbauer 6.07
6. Ski Melillo 6.00
7. Cub Stricker 5.97
8. Jack Burdock 5.93
9. Hughie Critz 5.91
10. Frankie Frisch 5.89

Shortstop
1. Hughie Jennings 6.16
2. Dave Bancroft 5.98
3. George Davis 5.85
4. Rabbit Maranville 5.81
5. Bill Dahlen 5.80
6. Herman Long 5.78
7. Bobby Wallace 5.73
8. Travis Jackson 5.67
9. Dick Bartell 5.64
10. Tommy Corcoran 5.63
11. Honus Wagner 5.63

Third Base
1. Jerry Denny 3.72
2. Billy Shindle 3.70
3. Billy Nash 3.65
4. Tommy Leach 3.62
5. Jimmy Collins 3.61
6. Arlie Latham 3.52
7. Denny Lyons 3.51
8. Lave Cross 3.50
9. Jimmy Austin 3.49
10. Ossie Vitt 3.45

Outfield
1. Taylor Douthit 3.07
2. Richie Ashburn 2.98
3. Johnny Mostil 2.94
4. Dom DiMaggio 2.92
5. Mike Kreevich 2.89
6. Dwayne Murphy 2.88
7. Sam Chapman 2.83
8. Sam West 2.83
9. Kirby Puckett 2.81
10. Devon White 2.80

Catcher
1. Johnny Edwards 6.92
2. Johnny Roseboro 6.76
3. Bill Freehan 6.75
4. Joe Azcue 6.67
5. Mike Scioscia 6.51
6. John Bateman 6.49
7. Charlie Bennett 6.47
8. Jerry Grote 6.47
9. Tony Pena 6.40
10. Tim McCarver 6.35

Pitcher
1. Nick Altrock 3.59
2. Addie Joss 3.47
3. Harry Howell 3.46
4. Ed Walsh 3.36
5. Nixey Callahan 3.25
6. Willie Sudhoff 3.11
7. George Mullin 3.03
8. Barney Pelty 3.00
9. Chick Fraser 2.90
10. Red Donahue 2.81
11. Christy Mathewson 2.81

Putouts

First Base
1	Jake Beckley	23709
2	Ed Konetchy	21361
3	Cap Anson	20794
4	Charlie Grimm	20711
5	Stuffy McInnis	19962
6	Mickey Vernon	19808
7	Jake Daubert	19634
8	Eddie Murray	19523
9	Lou Gehrig	19510
10	Joe Kuhel	19386

Second Base
1	Bid McPhee	6545
2	Eddie Collins	6526
3	Nellie Fox	6090
4	Joe Morgan	5742
5	Nap Lajoie	5496
6	Charlie Gehringer	5369
7	Bill Mazeroski	4974
8	Bobby Doerr	4928
9	Willie Randolph	4859
10	Billy Herman	4780

Shortstop
1	Rabbit Maranville	5139
2	Bill Dahlen	4850
3	Dave Bancroft	4623
4	Honus Wagner	4576
5	Tommy Corcoran	4550
6	Luis Aparicio	4548
7	Luke Appling	4398
8	Herman Long	4225
9	Bobby Wallace	4142
10	Pee Wee Reese	4040

Third Base
1	Brooks Robinson	2697
2	Jimmy Collins	2372
3	Eddie Yost	2356
4	Lave Cross	2306
5	Pie Traynor	2289
6	Billy Nash	2219
7	Frank Baker	2154
8	Willie Kamm	2151
9	Eddie Mathews	2049
10	Willie Jones	2045

Outfield
1	Willie Mays	7095
2	Tris Speaker	6787
3	Max Carey	6363
4	Ty Cobb	6361
5	Richie Ashburn	6089
6	Hank Aaron	5539
7	Willie Davis	5449
8	Doc Cramer	5412
9	Vada Pinson	5097
10	Andre Dawson	5037

Catcher
1	Gary Carter	11785
2	Carlton Fisk	11294
3	Bob Boone	11260
4	Bill Freehan	9941
5	Jim Sundberg	9767
6	Johnny Roseboro	9291
7	Tony Pena	9270
8	Johnny Bench	9249
9	Lance Parrish	9029
10	Johnny Edwards	8925

Pitcher
1	Phil Niekro	386
2	Jack Morris	364
3	Fergie Jenkins	363
4	Gaylord Perry	349
5	Don Sutton	334
6	Tony Mullane	328
	Rick Reuschel	328
	Tom Seaver	328
9	Jim Galvin	324
10	Robin Roberts	316

Putouts per Game

First Base
1	Tom Jones	10.53
2	Candy LaChance	10.48
3	George Stovall	10.45
4	George Kelly	10.37
5	Wally Pipp	10.33
6	Ed Konetchy	10.31
7	Bill Phillips	10.22
8	Walter Holke	10.20
9	Charlie Comiskey	10.15
10	Sid Farrar	10.13

Second Base
1	Joe Gerhardt	3.15
2	Bid McPhee	3.08
3	Fred Pfeffer	3.07
4	Fred Dunlap	3.03
5	Cub Stricker	3.02
6	Jack Burdock	2.82
7	Lou Bierbauer	2.74
8	Jerry Priddy	2.74
9	Bucky Harris	2.73
10	Nap Lajoie	2.71

Shortstop
1	Hughie Jennings	2.66
2	Dave Bancroft	2.47
3	Honus Wagner	2.43
4	Rabbit Maranville	2.39
5	Monte Cross	2.38
6	Heinie Wagner	2.38
7	George Davis	2.36
8	Herman Long	2.36
9	Kid Elberfeld	2.32
10	Dick Bartell	2.31
11	Ray Chapman	2.31

Third Base
1	Jerry Denny	1.61
2	Denny Lyons	1.55
3	Billy Nash	1.52
4	Jimmy Austin	1.43
5	Billy Shindle	1.43
6	Charlie Irwin	1.42
7	Jimmy Collins	1.41
8	Frank Baker	1.40
9	Tommy Leach	1.39
10	Hick Carpenter	1.37

Outfield
1	Taylor Douthit	3.01
2	Richie Ashburn	2.90
3	Johnny Mostil	2.83
4	Dom DiMaggio	2.82
5	Dwayne Murphy	2.82
6	Mike Kreevich	2.81
7	Sam Chapman	2.74
8	Sam West	2.74
9	Kirby Puckett	2.73
10	Devon White	2.73

Catcher
1	Johnny Edwards	6.42
2	Johnny Roseboro	6.30
3	Bill Freehan	6.29
4	Joe Azcue	6.14
5	Jerry Grote	6.00
6	Mike Scioscia	5.98
7	John Bateman	5.97
8	Tim McCarver	5.92
9	Tom Haller	5.85
10	Tony Pena	5.84

Pitcher
1	Nick Altrock	0.78
2	Dave Foutz	0.78
3	Mike Boddicker	0.73
4	Chick Fraser	0.73
5	Jack Morris	0.73
6	Carl Morton	0.72
7	Dan Petry	0.69
8	Mel Stottlemyre	0.68
9	Orel Hershiser	0.67
10	Nixey Callahan	0.66
11	Larry Corcoran	0.66

Assists

First Base
1	Eddie Murray	1717
2	Keith Hernandez	1682
3	George Sisler	1529
4	Mickey Vernon	1448
5	Fred Tenney	1363
6	Bill Buckner	1351
	Chris Chambliss	1351
8	Norm Cash	1317
9	Jake Beckley	1315
10	Joe Judge	1301

Second Base
1	Eddie Collins	7630
2	Charlie Gehringer	7068
3	Joe Morgan	6967
4	Bid McPhee	6905
5	Bill Mazeroski	6685
6	Nellie Fox	6373
7	Willie Randolph	6336
8	Nap Lajoie	6262
9	Frank White	6250
10	Frankie Frisch	6026

Shortstop
1	Luis Aparicio	8016
2	Bill Dahlen	7500
3	Rabbit Maranville	7354
4	Ozzie Smith	7342
5	Luke Appling	7218
6	Tommy Corcoran	7106
7	Larry Bowa	6857
8	Dave Concepcion	6594
9	Dave Bancroft	6561
10	Roger Peckinpaugh	6337

Third Base
1	Brooks Robinson	6205
2	Graig Nettles	5279
3	Mike Schmidt	5045
4	Buddy Bell	4925
5	Ron Santo	4581
6	Eddie Mathews	4322
7	Aurelio Rodriguez	4150
8	Ron Cey	4018
9	Sal Bando	3720
10	Lave Cross	3706

Outfield
1	Tris Speaker	448
2	Ty Cobb	392
3	Jimmy Ryan	375
4	Tom Brown	348
	George VanHaltren	348
6	Harry Hooper	344
7	Max Carey	339
8	Jimmy Sheckard	307
9	Clyde Milan	294
10	Orator Shaffer	289

Catcher
1	Deacon McGuire	1859
2	Ray Schalk	1811
3	Steve O'Neill	1698
4	Red Dooin	1590
5	Chief Zimmer	1580
6	Johnny Kling	1552
7	Ivey Wingo	1487
8	Wilbert Robinson	1454
9	Bill Bergen	1444
10	Wally Schang	1420

Pitcher
1	Cy Young	2014
2	Christy Mathewson	1503
3	Pete Alexander	1419
4	Jim Galvin	1382
5	Walter Johnson	1351
6	Burleigh Grimes	1252
7	George Mullin	1244
8	Jack Quinn	1240
9	Ed Walsh	1208
10	Eppa Rixey	1195

Assists per Game

First Base
1	Darrell Evans	0.88
2	Bill Buckner	0.87
3	Sid Bream	0.84
4	Ferris Fain	0.84
5	Keith Hernandez	0.84
6	Vic Power	0.83
7	Wally Joyner	0.79
8	Dick Siebert	0.79
9	Eddie Murray	0.78
10	Pete O'Brien	0.78
11	George Sisler	0.78

Second Base
1	Hughie Critz	3.54
2	Frankie Frisch	3.42
3	Ski Melillo	3.38
4	Joe Gerhardt	3.35
5	Lou Bierbauer	3.34
6	Glenn Hubbard	3.34
7	Fred Pfeffer	3.33
8	Rogers Hornsby	3.31
9	Fred Dunlap	3.30
10	Jackie Hayes	3.30

Shortstop
1	Germany Smith	3.70
2	Art Fletcher	3.55
3	Bill Dahlen	3.52
4	Dave Bancroft	3.51
5	Hughie Jennings	3.51
6	Bones Ely	3.50
7	Travis Jackson	3.50
8	George Davis	3.49
9	Jack Glasscock	3.46
10	Bobby Wallace	3.46

Third Base
1	Terry Pendleton	2.32
2	Mike Schmidt	2.29
3	Bill Melton	2.27
4	Billy Shindle	2.27
5	Buddy Bell	2.26
6	Arlie Latham	2.26
7	Clete Boyer	2.24
8	Tommy Leach	2.23
9	Ossie Vitt	2.22
10	Jimmy Collins	2.20

Outfield
1	Orator Shaffer	0.35
2	Hugh Nicol	0.28
3	Paul Radford	0.25
4	Tommy McCarthy	0.23
5	Pop Corkhill	0.22
6	Jimmy Wolf	0.22
7	Sam Thompson	0.21
8	Tom Brown	0.20
9	Pete Hotaling	0.20
10	Jimmy Ryan	0.20
11	George VanHaltren	0.20
12	Curt Welch	0.20

Catcher
1	Bill Bergen	1.54
2	Duke Farrell	1.42
3	Lou Criger	1.37
4	Red Dooin	1.34
5	Johnny Kling	1.33
6	Bill Killefer	1.32
7	Bill Rariden	1.30
8	Oscar Stanage	1.29
9	Frank Bowerman	1.28
10	Chief Zimmer	1.28

Pitcher
1	Addie Joss	2.96
2	Harry Howell	2.84
3	Nick Altrock	2.81
4	Ed Walsh	2.81
5	Willie Sudhoff	2.73
6	Nixey Callahan	2.60
7	George Mullin	2.56
8	Ed Willett	2.54
9	Barney Pelty	2.51
10	Red Donahue	2.46

Double Plays

First Base

1	Mickey Vernon	2044
2	Eddie Murray	1878
3	Joe Kuhel	1769
4	Charlie Grimm	1733
5	Chris Chambliss	1687
6	Keith Hernandez	1654
7	Gil Hodges	1614
8	Lou Gehrig	1575
9	Jim Bottomley	1562
10	Jimmie Foxx	1528

Second Base

1	Bill Mazeroski	1706
2	Nellie Fox	1619
3	Willie Randolph	1547
4	Bobby Doerr	1507
5	Joe Morgan	1505
6	Charlie Gehringer	1444
7	Frank White	1382
8	Lou Whitaker	1377
9	Red Schoendienst	1368
10	Bobby Grich	1302

Shortstop

1	Luis Aparicio	1553
2	Luke Appling	1424
3	Ozzie Smith	1361
4	Roy McMillan	1304
5	Dave Concepcion	1290
6	Larry Bowa	1265
7	Pee Wee Reese	1246
8	Dick Groat	1237
9	Phil Rizzuto	1217
10	Alan Trammell	1190

Third Base

1	Brooks Robinson	618
2	Graig Nettles	470
3	Mike Schmidt	450
4	Buddy Bell	430
5	Aurelio Rodriguez	408
6	Ron Santo	395
7	Eddie Mathews	369
8	Ken Boyer	355
9	Sal Bando	345
	Eddie Yost	345

Outfield

1	Tris Speaker	139
2	Ty Cobb	107
3	Max Carey	86
4	Tom Brown	85
5	Harry Hooper	81
6	Jimmy Sheckard	80
7	Mike Griffin	75
8	Dummy Hoy	72
9	Jimmy Ryan	71
10	Fielder Jones	70

Catcher

1	Ray Schalk	226
2	Yogi Berra	175
	Steve O'Neill	175
4	Gabby Hartnett	163
5	Bob Boone	154
6	Jimmie Wilson	153
7	Gary Carter	149
	Wally Schang	149
9	Carlton Fisk	147
10	Jim Sundberg	145

Pitcher

1	Phil Niekro	83
2	Warren Spahn	82
3	Freddie Fitzsimmons	79
4	Bob Lemon	78
5	Bucky Walters	76
6	Burleigh Grimes	74
7	Walter Johnson	72
8	Tommy John	69
9	Jim Kaat	65
10	Dizzy Trout	63

Fielding Runs

1	Nap Lajoie	369
2	Bill Mazeroski	362
3	Bill Dahlen	349
4	Bid McPhee	315
5	Fred Pfeffer	266
6	Mike Schmidt	265
7	George Davis	250
8	Tris Speaker	247
9	Jack Glasscock	242
10	Richie Ashburn	234
11	Clete Boyer	233
12	Glenn Hubbard	229
13	Ozzie Smith	219
14	Bobby Wallace	212
15	Joe Tinker	204
16	Max Carey	199
17	Dave Bancroft	198
18	Buddy Bell	191
19	Aurelio Rodriguez	184
20	Bobby Doerr	181
21	Dick Bartell	178
22	Mickey Doolan	177
23	Joe Gerhardt	173
24	George McBride	170
25	Mark Belanger	169
26	Art Fletcher	166
	Lee Tannehill	166
28	Roberto Clemente	162
29	Darrell Evans	161
	Dal Maxvill	161
	Terry Pendleton	161
32	Rabbit Maranville	158
33	Rickey Henderson	157
34	Germany Smith	155
35	Danny Richardson	153
36	Lou Bierbauer	151
	Hughie Jennings	151
	Ski Melillo	151
	Brooks Robinson	151
40	Frankie Frisch	150
	Bobby Knoop	150
42	Jim Hegan	149
	Keith Hernandez	149
	Carl Yastrzemski	149
45	Lave Cross	147
	Pop Snyder	147
47	Jimmy Collins	140
	Billy Jurges	140
49	Bobby Wine	138
50	Fred Dunlap	137
	Bill Killefer	137
	Ron Santo	137
53	Lou Boudreau	134
54	Hal Lanier	132
	Graig Nettles	132
	John Ward	132
57	Lou Criger	131
	Willie Mays	131
	Ryne Sandberg	131
60	Manny Trillo	129
61	Harold Reynolds	126
62	Gene Alley	125
63	Kirby Puckett	124
	Fred Tenney	124
65	Vic Power	123
66	Al Weis	121
67	Bill Bergen	117
	Everett Scott	117
69	Gary Gaetti	116
	Chet Lemon	116
71	Tony Gwynn	115
72	Jesse Barfield	114
73	Hobe Ferris	113
	Tommy Leach	113
	Hardy Richardson	113
76	Hughie Critz	111
77	Jerry Denny	110
78	Joe Sewell	109
79	Tommy Corcoran	107
	Curt Welch	107
81	Bill Buckner	106
82	Johnny Logan	105
83	Brett Butler	104
	Travis Jackson	104
85	Buck Ewing	103
	Al Kaline	103
	Chief Zimmer	103
88	Johnny Callison	102
	Eddie Miller	102
	Dwayne Murphy	102
91	Dom DiMaggio	101
	Honus Wagner	101
93	Barry Bonds	99
	Roger Peckinpaugh	99
	Tim Wallach	99
96	Jim Fogarty	98
97	Johnny Edwards	97
	Ozzie Guillen	97
	Herman Long	97
	Jim Sundberg	97

Fielding Runs (by position)

First Base

1	Keith Hernandez	150
2	Fred Tenney	129
3	Vic Power	124
4	Bill Buckner	121
5	George Sisler	89
6	Darrell Evans	76
7	Sid Bream	69
8	Bill Terry	67
9	Eddie Murray	63
10	Ed Konetchy	60

Second Base

1	Nap Lajoie	370
2	Bill Mazeroski	363
3	Bid McPhee	315
4	Fred Pfeffer	258
5	Glenn Hubbard	229
6	Bobby Doerr	180
7	Joe Gerhardt	160
8	Lou Bierbauer	152
9	Bobby Knoop	150
10	Ski Melillo	148

Shortstop

1	Bill Dahlen	302
2	Jack Glasscock	244
3	Ozzie Smith	218
4	Joe Tinker	206
5	Dave Bancroft	200
6	George Davis	187
7	Rabbit Maranville	177
8	George McBride	173
9	Mark Belanger	166
	Mickey Doolan	166

Third Base

1	Mike Schmidt	265
2	Clete Boyer	201
3	Buddy Bell	199
4	Aurelio Rodriguez	185
5	Terry Pendleton	162
6	Brooks Robinson	152
7	Jimmy Collins	139
8	Graig Nettles	136
9	Ron Santo	135
10	Lave Cross	132

Outfield

1	Tris Speaker	246
2	Richie Ashburn	234
3	Max Carey	202
4	Roberto Clemente	162
5	Rickey Henderson	158
6	Carl Yastrzemski	143
7	Willie Mays	136
8	Kirby Puckett	125
9	Chet Lemon	119
10	Tony Gwynn	115

Catcher

1	Jim Hegan	149
2	Bill Killefer	137
3	Lou Criger	135
4	Bill Bergen	115
5	Chief Zimmer	105
6	Jim Sundberg	99
7	Johnny Edwards	97
8	Duke Farrell	93
9	Steve Yeager	91
10	Rollie Hemsley	89

Pitcher

1	Ed Walsh	84
2	Carl Mays	74
3	Christy Mathewson	69
4	Freddie Fitzsimmons	61
5	Bob Lemon	59
6	Burleigh Grimes	58
7	Tommy John	56
8	Harry Gumbert	51
9	Harry Howell	50
10	John Clarkson	45

Fielding Wins

1	Nap Lajoie	37.9
2	Bill Mazeroski	37.7
3	Bill Dahlen	33.2
4	Mike Schmidt	27.7
5	Bid McPhee	27.4
6	Tris Speaker	25.2
7	Clete Boyer	24.2
8	Glenn Hubbard	23.8
9	George Davis	23.5
10	Richie Ashburn	23.4
11	Fred Pfeffer	23.2
12	Ozzie Smith	23.0
13	Joe Tinker	21.5
14	Jack Glasscock	21.5
15	Bobby Wallace	21.4
16	Max Carey	20.4
17	Dave Bancroft	20.2
18	Buddy Bell	19.6
19	Aurelio Rodriguez	19.2
20	Mickey Doolan	18.9
21	George McBride	18.3
22	Lee Tannehill	18.0
23	Bobby Doerr	17.8
24	Art Fletcher	17.7
25	Mark Belanger	17.7
26	Dick Bartell	17.5
27	Dal Maxvill	17.1
28	Terry Pendleton	16.9
29	Roberto Clemente	16.9
30	Darrell Evans	16.6
31	Bobby Knoop	16.2
32	Rabbit Maranville	16.0
33	Brooks Robinson	15.9
34	Rickey Henderson	15.7
35	Keith Hernandez	15.6
36	Carl Yastrzemski	15.5
37	Joe Gerhardt	15.5
38	Jim Hegan	14.9
39	Bill Killefer	14.8
40	Frankie Frisch	14.7
41	Bobby Wine	14.5
42	Ron Santo	14.4
43	Billy Jurges	14.2
44	Ski Melillo	14.1
45	Hal Lanier	14.1
46	Ryne Sandberg	13.7
47	Graig Nettles	13.7
48	Willie Mays	13.5
49	Jimmy Collins	13.5
50	Lave Cross	13.5
51	Lou Boudreau	13.5
52	Manny Trillo	13.5
53	Germany Smith	13.3
54	Danny Richardson	13.3
55	Hughie Jennings	13.3
56	Gene Alley	13.3
57	Lou Criger	13.2
58	Pop Snyder	13.1
59	Al Weis	12.9
60	Lou Bierbauer	12.8
61	Harold Reynolds	12.6
62	Vic Power	12.6
63	Fred Dunlap	12.4
64	Bill Bergen	12.4
65	Kirby Puckett	12.4
66	Fred Tenney	12.3
67	Tony Gwynn	12.0
68	Hobe Ferris	12.0
69	Everett Scott	11.9
70	Tommy Leach	11.8
71	John Ward	11.6
72	Chet Lemon	11.6
73	Gary Gaetti	11.6
74	Jesse Barfield	11.4
75	Bill Buckner	10.9
76	Hughie Critz	10.7
77	Al Kaline	10.7
78	Johnny Callison	10.7
79	Brett Butler	10.7
80	Johnny Logan	10.6
81	Honus Wagner	10.4
82	Eddie Miller	10.4
83	Tim Wallach	10.4
84	Barry Bonds	10.4
85	Joe Sewell	10.3
86	Dwayne Murphy	10.2
87	Johnny Edwards	10.2
88	Hardy Richardson	10.1
89	Travis Jackson	10.0
90	Roger Peckinpaugh	10.0
91	Dom DiMaggio	10.0
92	Ed Brinkman	10.0
93	Jim Sundberg	9.8
94	Tommy Corcoran	9.8
95	Jerry Denny	9.8
96	Amos Otis	9.7
97	Ozzie Guillen	9.7
98	Tim Raines	9.6
99	Rocky Bridges	9.6
100	Ron Hansen	9.5

Total Player Rating

Rank	Player	Rating
1	Babe Ruth	105.2
2	Nap Lajoie	94.9
3	Ty Cobb	92.8
4	Ted Williams	92.4
5	Tris Speaker	88.5
6	Willie Mays	86.4
7	Hank Aaron	84.6
8	Honus Wagner	82.6
9	Mike Schmidt	80.3
10	Rogers Hornsby	79.8
11	Mickey Mantle	73.6
12	Stan Musial	71.7
13	Frank Robinson	70.3
14	Eddie Collins	69.4
15	Rickey Henderson	67.0
16	Mel Ott	62.4
17	Lou Gehrig	61.9
18	Joe Morgan	55.7
19	Jimmie Foxx	55.4
20	Bill Dahlen	52.4
21	George Davis	52.0
22	Carl Yastrzemski	50.8
23	Eddie Mathews	48.6
24	Tim Raines	47.1
25	Joe DiMaggio	46.5
26	Al Kaline	46.4
27	Charlie Gehringer	45.1
28	Ed Delahanty	44.8
29	Roger Connor	44.4
30	Dan Brouthers	43.7
31	Bobby Grich	43.3
32	Robin Yount	43.0
33	Reggie Jackson	42.7
34	Bid McPhee	42.3
35	George Brett	42.1
	Ozzie Smith	42.1
37	Ron Santo	41.7
38	Roberto Clemente	41.5
39	Luke Appling	40.9
40	Lou Boudreau	40.4
41	Dave Winfield	40.3
42	Gabby Hartnett	40.1
43	Ryne Sandberg	40.0
44	Wade Boggs	39.9
	Joe Cronin	39.9
46	Bobby Doerr	39.8
47	Arky Vaughan	39.7
48	Frankie Frisch	38.8
49	Cal Ripken	38.6
50	Joe Jackson	38.2
51	Jack Glasscock	37.8
52	Johnny Mize	37.7
53	Eddie Murray	37.5
54	Paul Waner	37.0
55	Bobby Wallace	36.8
56	Bill Mazeroski	36.6
57	Cap Anson	36.2
58	Yogi Berra	35.5
59	Dave Bancroft	35.4
60	Darrell Evans	35.2
	Joe Sewell	35.2
62	Bob Johnson	35.1
	Willie McCovey	35.1
64	Bill Dickey	34.8
	Reggie Smith	34.8
66	Barry Bonds	34.7
67	Keith Hernandez	34.1
68	Dick Allen	33.5
	Frank Robinson	33.5
70	Dwight Evans	32.8
71	Bobby Bonds	32.7
72	Jackie Robinson	32.6
73	Rod Carew	32.5
74	Mickey Cochrane	32.2
75	Billy Herman	32.0
76	Harry Heilmann	31.9
77	Hank Greenberg	31.7
78	Cupid Childs	31.2
	Sam Crawford	31.2
80	Tony Gwynn	31.0
81	Jim Rice	30.9
82	Richie Ashburn	30.7
83	Buck Ewing	30.6
84	Jesse Burkett	30.4
	Paul Molitor	30.4
86	Fred Clarke	30.1
87	Sam Thompson	30.0
88	Ralph Kiner	29.9
89	Pete Browning	29.6
90	Gary Carter	29.5
	Fred Dunlap	29.5
92	Jack Clark	29.0
	Andre Dawson	29.0
94	Billy Hamilton	28.7
	Harmon Killebrew	28.7
96	Norm Cash	28.6
	Elmer Flick	28.6
98	Hardy Richardson	28.4
	Jim Wynn	28.4
100	Joe Medwick	28.0

Total Player Rating

Rank	Player	Rating
101	Dick Bartell	27.7
	Joe Gordon	27.7
103	Hughie Jennings	27.4
104	Sherry Magee	27.2
	Al Simmons	27.2
106	Stan Hack	27.1
	Rusty Staub	27.1
	Billy Williams	27.1
109	King Kelly	27.0
110	Heinie Groh	26.7
	Tony Oliva	26.7
	Darryl Strawberry	26.7
113	Carlton Fisk	26.6
114	Art Fletcher	26.3
115	Willie Stargell	26.1
116	Goose Goslin	26.0
117	Minnie Minoso	25.8
118	Ernie Banks	25.7
119	Rocky Colavito	25.6
120	Johnny Bench	25.2
121	Zack Wheat	24.7
122	Chuck Klein	24.6
123	Jake Beckley	24.5
124	Bill Terry	24.4
125	Kirby Puckett	24.3
	Joe Tinker	24.3
127	Jimmy Collins	24.2
	Duke Snider	24.2
129	Travis Jackson	24.0
130	Harry Stovey	23.8
131	Fred Lynn	23.7
132	Max Carey	23.4
	Jack Fournier	23.4
	Ed Konetchy	23.4
135	Charlie Keller	23.3
	Barry Larkin	23.3
	Alan Trammell	23.3
138	Fred Pfeffer	23.0
	Willie Randolph	23.0
	George Sisler	23.0
141	Buddy Bell	22.9
	Harlond Clift	22.9
143	George Foster	22.8
144	Jose Cruz	22.7
145	Roy Thomas	22.6
146	Chet Lemon	22.0
	Dave Parker	22.0
148	Roy Campanella	21.9
	Joe Kelley	21.9
150	Ron Cey	21.7
151	Graig Nettles	21.5
152	Charley Jones	21.4
	Fred Tenney	21.4
154	Denny Lyons	21.3
155	Frank Chance	21.1
	Mike Griffin	21.1
157	Ken Singleton	21.0
158	Pie Traynor	20.9
	Andy Van Slyke	20.9
160	Wally Berger	20.8
	Roy White	20.8
162	Amos Otis	20.7
163	Brian Downing	20.6
	Vern Stephens	20.6
165	Gavvy Cravath	20.5
166	Ken Boyer	20.3
	Art Devlin	20.3
	Larry Doby	20.3
169	Cesar Cedeno	20.2
	Del Pratt	20.2
171	Jim Fregosi	20.1
	Joe Torre	20.1
173	Glenn Hubbard	20.0
174	Eric Davis	19.9
	Frank Howard	19.9
176	Brooks Robinson	19.8
177	Charlie Bennett	19.6
	Roger Bresnahan	19.6
	Jose Canseco	19.6
	Jimmy Sheckard	19.6
181	Lou Whitaker	19.5
182	Pete Rose	19.4
183	Bill Joyce	19.3
184	Dale Murphy	18.8
185	George Gore	18.6
186	Brett Butler	18.5
	Roy Cullenbine	18.5
	Bob Elliott	18.5
	Eddie Stanky	18.5
190	Ferris Fain	18.4
	Bill Nicholson	18.4
192	Earl Averill	18.3
	Ken Williams	18.3
194	Gene Alley	18.2
	Miller Huggins	18.2
196	Johnny Logan	18.1
	Wally Schang	18.1
198	Paul Hines	17.8
	Tommy Leach	17.8
200	Enos Slaughter	17.7

Total Player Rating

Rank	Player	Rating
201	Ted Simmons	17.5
202	Pedro Guerrero	17.4
203	Benny Kauff	17.2
	John McGraw	17.2
	Jim O'Rourke	17.2
206	Orlando Cepeda	17.1
	Will Clark	17.1
	Ernie Lombardi	17.1
	Jocko Milligan	17.1
210	Henry Larkin	16.8
211	Babe Herman	16.7
	Gil McDougald	16.7
	Chief Zimmer	16.7
214	Lenny Dykstra	16.6
215	Jesse Barfield	16.5
	Jimmy Williams	16.5
217	Kiki Cuyler	16.3
	Hal McRae	16.3
219	Tony Lazzeri	16.1
	Fred McGriff	16.1
221	Lave Cross	16.0
	Dwayne Murphy	16.0
223	Ray Chapman	15.9
	Phil Rizzuto	15.9
225	Davey Johnson	15.8
226	Mark Belanger	15.7
	Jeff Heath	15.7
	Jimmy Ryan	15.7
229	Rico Carty	15.6
	Duke Farrell	15.6
	Mike Hargrove	15.6
	Hack Wilson	15.6
233	Kirk Gibson	15.4
234	Bobby Knoop	15.3
235	Kevin McReynolds	15.2
236	Thurman Munson	15.1
237	Bob Allison	14.9
238	Bobby Veach	14.8
239	Augie Galan	14.7
	Boog Powell	14.7
	Mike Scioscia	14.7
242	Billy Nash	14.6
	Pee Wee Reese	14.6
244	Harold Baines	14.5
	Ron Hansen	14.5
	Edd Roush	14.5
	Roy Smalley	14.5
248	Dolph Camilli	14.4
	Danny Tartabull	14.4
250	Tony Fernandez	14.3
	Sid Gordon	14.3
	Chief Meyers	14.3
253	Tommy Henrich	14.2
	Gil Hodges	14.2
255	Kip Selbach	14.1
	Andy Thornton	14.1
257	Jack Clements	14.0
	Gene Tenace	14.0
259	Dave Orr	13.9
260	Don Baylor	13.8
	Willie Kamm	13.8
	Roger Peckinpaugh	13.8
	Mike Tiernan	13.8
	Richie Zisk	13.8
265	Fred Carroll	13.7
266	Johnny Evers	13.6
	Kevin Mitchell	13.6
268	Rabbit Maranville	13.5
	Tip O'Neill	13.5
270	Ben Chapman	13.4
	Bill Freehan	13.4
	Tommy Holmes	13.4
	Deacon McGuire	13.4
	Terry Pendleton	13.4
275	Orator Shaffer	13.3
276	Chick Hafey	13.2
	Johnny Pesky	13.2
278	Sixto Lezcano	13.1
279	Kal Daniels	13.0
280	Clete Boyer	12.9
	George Stone	12.9
282	Johnny Callison	12.8
	Doug DeCinces	12.8
284	Riggs Stephenson	12.7
	John Titus	12.7
286	Harry Hooper	12.6
	Darrell Porter	12.6
	Roy Sievers	12.6
	Red Smith	12.6
290	Lonnie Smith	12.5
291	Kid Elberfeld	12.4
292	Jackie Jensen	12.3
293	Bobby Murcer	12.2
294	Jake Daubert	12.1
	Lefty O'Doul	12.1
	Curt Welch	12.1
297	Luis Aparicio	12.0
	Lou Criger	12.0
	Lonny Frey	12.0
	Jerry Priddy	12.0

Total Player Rating

Rank	Player	Rating
	Ossee Schreckengost	12.0
	George Van Haltren	12.0
303	Harry Davis	11.9
	Nellie Fox	11.9
	Johnny Kling	11.9
	Al Rosen	11.9
	Ed Swartwood	11.9
308	Mike Donlin	11.8
	Robby Thompson	11.8
310	Bobby Bonilla	11.7
	Buck Herzog	11.7
	Lance Parrish	11.7
	Cy Seymour	11.7
314	Rick Burleson	11.6
	Don Mattingly	11.6
316	Dom DiMaggio	11.5
	Willie Keeler	11.5
	Danny Murphy	11.5
	Deacon White	11.5
	Jimmy Wolf	11.5
	Rudy York	11.5
322	Toby Harrah	11.4
	Ken Keltner	11.4
	Ned Williamson	11.4
325	Joe Harris	11.3
	Roger Maris	11.3
327	Tom Daly	11.1
	Tom Haller	11.1
	Monte Irvin	11.1
	Dan McGann	11.1
	Ben Oglivie	11.1
332	Freddy Lindstrom	11.0
	Andy Seminick	11.0
	Dixie Walker	11.0
	Maury Wills	11.0
	Heinie Zimmerman	11.0
337	Earl Battey	10.9
	Earle Combs	10.9
	Jack Crooks	10.9
	Jim Gentile	10.9
	Rico Petrocelli	10.9
	Hank Sauer	10.9
	Stan Spence	10.9
344	Tony Cuccinello	10.8
	Kent Hrbek	10.8
	Whitey Kurowski	10.8
	Greg Luzinski	10.8
	Bill Melton	10.8
349	Jerry Denny	10.7
	Ed McFarland	10.7
	Red Schoendienst	10.7
352	Billy Jurges	10.6
353	Ken Griffey	10.5
	Ross Youngs	10.5
355	Oyster Burns	10.3
	Rick Ferrell	10.3
	Oscar Gamble	10.3
358	Cecil Travis	10.2
359	Al Oliver	10.1
	Tony Perez	10.1
361	Chili Davis	10.0
	Elmer Smith	10.0
363	Mike Greenwell	9.9
364	Bill Lange	9.8
	Buddy Myer	9.8
	Doug Rader	9.8
	Vic Wertz	9.8
368	Bill Bradley	9.6
	Larry Hisle	9.6
370	Cliff Johnson	9.5
	Cy Williams	9.5
372	Hank Gowdy	9.4
	Sherm Lollar	9.4
	Claude Ritchey	9.4
	Bob Watson	9.4
	Bump Wills	9.4
377	Dave Concepcion	9.3
	Walker Cooper	9.3
	Jimmy Dykes	9.3
	Charlie Hickman	9.3
381	Johnny Romano	9.2
	Harry Steinfeldt	9.2
	Wes Westrum	9.2
384	Mark Grace	9.1
	Marty McManus	9.1
386	Don Buford	9.0
387	Bert Campaneris	8.9
	John Kruk	8.9
	Fred Luderus	8.9
	Willie McGee	8.9
	Tim Wallach	8.9
392	Sam Rice	8.8
	Pinky Whitney	8.8
394	Happy Felsch	8.7
	Frank Fennelly	8.7
	Steve Kemp	8.7
	Dal Maxvill	8.7
	Mark McGwire	8.7
399	John Ward	8.6
400	Del Ennis	8.5

Total Player Rating

	Snuffy Stirnweiss	8.5
402	Del Crandall	8.4
	Topsy Hartsel	8.4
	Bob Nieman	8.4
	Danny Richardson	8.4
406	Eddie Joost	8.3
	Herman Long	8.3
	Rafael Palmeiro	8.3
409	Cecil Cooper	8.2
	Jim McTamany	8.2
411	Julio Franco	8.1
	Bill Sweeney	8.1
413	Elbie Fletcher	8.0
	Gary Matthews	8.0
	Mike Mitchell	8.0
	Ruben Sierra	8.0
	Dickie Thon	8.0
	Al Weis	8.0
	Art Wilson	8.0
	Gene Woodling	8.0
421	Donie Bush	7.9
	Hugh Duffy	7.9
	Solly Hemus	7.9
	Willie Horton	7.9
	Jim Sundberg	7.9
	Lee Tannehill	7.9
427	Alvin Davis	7.8
	Joe Gerhardt	7.8
	George Selkirk	7.8
	Billy Werber	7.8
431	Sal Bando	7.7
	Johnny Bassler	7.7
	Johnny Bates	7.7
	Spud Davis	7.7
	Socks Seybold	7.7
	Pop Snyder	7.7
	Ernie Whitt	7.7
	Sam Wise	7.7
439	Jimmy Barrett	7.6
	Ken Phelps	7.6
	Harold Reynolds	7.6
	George Wood	7.6
443	Jim Fogarty	7.5
444	Phil Bradley	7.4
	Bernie Carbo	7.4
	Phil Garner	7.4
	Mickey Tettleton	7.4
448	Roberto Alomar	7.3
	George Bell	7.3
	Johnny Mostil	7.3
451	Matty McIntyre	7.2
	Pete Reiser	7.2
453	Charlie Maxwell	7.1
	Ray Schalk	7.1
455	Glenn Davis	7.0
	Ken McMullen	7.0
	Johnny Ray	7.0
458	Dave Cash	6.9
	Ival Goodman	6.9
	Bill Killefer	6.9
	Rick Monday	6.9
462	Julio Cruz	6.8
	Harry Danning	6.8
	Elston Howard	6.8
	Tim McCarver	6.8
	Ezra Sutton	6.8
467	Tom Brunansky	6.7
	Ivan Calderon	6.7
	Charlie Hollocher	6.7
	Buddy Lewis	6.7
	Spike Owen	6.7
472	Lou Bierbauer	6.6
	Larry Gardner	6.6
	Odell Hale	6.6
	Stan Lopata	6.6
	Tony Pena	6.6
477	Rob Deer	6.5
478	Von Hayes	6.4
	Alex Kampouris	6.4
	George Kell	6.4
	Don Mincher	6.4
	Freddie Patek	6.4
	Norm Siebern	6.4
484	Joe Adcock	6.3
	Heinie Peitz	6.3
	Hank Thompson	6.3
	Willie Wilson	6.3
488	John Briggs	6.2
	Lyn Lary	6.2
	Bob O'Farrell	6.2
	Earl Torgeson	6.2
	Elmer Valo	6.2
493	Johnny Edwards	6.1
	Kelly Gruber	6.1
	Wally Joyner	6.1
	Wally Moses	6.1
	Mickey Rivers	6.1
498	5 players tied	6.0

Total Player Rating (alpha.)

Hank Aaron	84.6
Joe Adcock	6.3
Dick Allen	33.5
Gene Alley	18.2
Bob Allison	14.9
Roberto Alomar	7.3
Cap Anson	36.2
Luis Aparicio	12.0
Luke Appling	40.9
Richie Ashburn	30.7
Earl Averill	18.3
Harold Baines	14.5
Frank Baker	33.5
Dave Bancroft	35.4
Sal Bando	7.7
Ernie Banks	25.7
Jesse Barfield	16.5
Jimmy Barrett	7.6
Dick Bartell	27.7
Johnny Bassler	7.7
Johnny Bates	7.7
Earl Battey	10.9
Don Baylor	13.8
Jake Beckley	24.5
Mark Belanger	15.7
Buddy Bell	22.9
George Bell	7.3
Johnny Bench	25.2
Charlie Bennett	19.6
Wally Berger	20.8
Yogi Berra	35.5
Lou Bierbauer	6.6
Wade Boggs	39.9
Barry Bonds	34.7
Bobby Bonds	32.7
Bobby Bonilla	11.7
Lou Boudreau	40.4
Clete Boyer	12.9
Ken Boyer	20.3
Phil Bradley	7.4
Bill Bradley	9.6
Roger Bresnahan	19.6
George Brett	42.1
John Briggs	6.2
Dan Brouthers	43.7
Pete Browning	29.6
Tom Brunansky	6.7
Don Buford	9.0
Jesse Burkett	30.4
Rick Burleson	11.6
Oyster Burns	10.3
Donie Bush	7.9
Brett Butler	18.5
Ivan Calderon	6.7
Johnny Callison	12.8
Dolph Camilli	14.4
Roy Campanella	21.9
Bert Campaneris	8.9
Jose Canseco	19.6
Bernie Carbo	7.4
Rod Carew	32.5
Max Carey	23.4
Fred Carroll	13.7
Gary Carter	29.5
Rico Carty	15.6
Dave Cash	6.9
Norm Cash	28.6
Cesar Cedeno	20.2
Orlando Cepeda	17.1
Ron Cey	21.7
Frank Chance	21.1
Ray Chapman	15.9
Ben Chapman	13.4
Cupid Childs	31.2
Jack Clark	29.0
Will Clark	17.1
Fred Clarke	30.1
Roberto Clemente	41.5
Jack Clements	14.0
Harlond Clift	22.9
Ty Cobb	92.8
Mickey Cochrane	32.2
Rocky Colavito	25.6
Eddie Collins	69.4
Jimmy Collins	24.2
Earle Combs	10.9
Dave Concepcion	9.3
Roger Connor	44.4
Cecil Cooper	8.2
Walker Cooper	9.3
Del Crandall	8.4
Gavvy Cravath	20.5
Sam Crawford	31.2
Lou Criger	12.0
Joe Cronin	39.9
Jack Crooks	10.9
Lave Cross	16.0
Jose Cruz	22.7
Julio Cruz	6.8
Tony Cuccinello	10.8

Total Player Rating (alpha.)

Roy Cullenbine	18.5
Kiki Cuyler	16.3
Bill Dahlen	52.4
Tom Daly	11.1
Kal Daniels	13.0
Harry Danning	6.8
Jake Daubert	12.1
Alvin Davis	7.8
Chili Davis	10.0
Eric Davis	19.9
George Davis	52.0
Glenn Davis	7.0
Harry Davis	11.9
Spud Davis	7.7
Andre Dawson	29.0
Doug DeCinces	12.8
Rob Deer	6.5
Ed Delahanty	44.8
Jerry Denny	10.7
Art Devlin	20.3
Bill Dickey	34.8
Dom DiMaggio	11.5
Joe DiMaggio	46.5
Larry Doby	20.3
Bobby Doerr	39.8
Mike Donlin	11.8
Brian Downing	20.6
Hugh Duffy	7.9
Fred Dunlap	29.5
Jimmy Dykes	9.3
Lenny Dykstra	16.6
Johnny Edwards	6.1
Kid Elberfeld	12.4
Bob Elliott	18.5
Del Ennis	8.5
Darrell Evans	35.2
Dwight Evans	32.8
Johnny Evers	13.6
Buck Ewing	30.6
Ferris Fain	18.4
Duke Farrell	15.6
Happy Felsch	8.7
Frank Fennelly	8.7
Tony Fernandez	14.3
Rick Ferrell	10.3
Carlton Fisk	26.6
Art Fletcher	26.3
Elbie Fletcher	8.0
Elmer Flick	28.6
Jim Fogarty	7.5
George Foster	22.8
Jack Fournier	23.4
Nellie Fox	11.9
Jimmie Foxx	55.4
Julio Franco	8.1
Bill Freehan	13.4
Jim Fregosi	20.1
Lonny Frey	12.0
Frankie Frisch	38.8
Augie Galan	14.7
Oscar Gamble	10.3
Larry Gardner	6.6
Phil Garner	7.4
Lou Gehrig	61.9
Charlie Gehringer	45.1
Jim Gentile	10.9
Joe Gerhardt	7.8
Kirk Gibson	15.4
Jack Glasscock	37.8
Ival Goodman	6.9
Joe Gordon	27.7
Sid Gordon	14.3
George Gore	18.6
Goose Goslin	26.0
Hank Gowdy	9.4
Mark Grace	9.1
Hank Greenberg	31.7
Mike Greenwell	9.9
Bobby Grich	43.3
Ken Griffey	10.5
Mike Griffin	21.1
Heinie Groh	26.7
Kelly Gruber	6.1
Pedro Guerrero	17.4
Tony Gwynn	31.0
Stan Hack	27.1
Chick Hafey	13.2
Odell Hale	6.6
Tom Haller	11.1
Billy Hamilton	28.7
Ron Hansen	14.5
Mike Hargrove	15.6
Toby Harrah	11.4
Joe Harris	11.3
Gabby Hartnett	40.1
Topsy Hartsel	8.4
Von Hayes	6.4
Jeff Heath	15.7
Harry Heilmann	31.9
Solly Hemus	7.9

Total Player Rating (alpha.)

Rickey Henderson	67.0
Tommy Henrich	14.2
Babe Herman	16.7
Billy Herman	32.0
Keith Hernandez	34.1
Buck Herzog	11.7
Charlie Hickman	9.3
Paul Hines	17.8
Larry Hisle	9.6
Gil Hodges	14.2
Charlie Hollocher	6.7
Tommy Holmes	13.4
Harry Hooper	12.6
Rogers Hornsby	79.8
Willie Horton	7.9
Elston Howard	6.8
Frank Howard	19.9
Kent Hrbek	10.8
Glenn Hubbard	20.0
Miller Huggins	18.2
Monte Irvin	11.1
Joe Jackson	38.2
Reggie Jackson	42.7
Travis Jackson	24.0
Hughie Jennings	27.4
Jackie Jensen	12.3
Cliff Johnson	9.5
Davey Johnson	15.8
Bob Johnson	35.1
Charley Jones	21.4
Eddie Joost	8.3
Bill Joyce	19.3
Wally Joyner	6.1
Billy Jurges	10.6
Al Kaline	46.4
Willie Kamm	13.8
Alex Kampouris	6.4
Benny Kauff	17.2
Willie Keeler	11.5
George Kell	6.4
Charlie Keller	23.3
Joe Kelley	21.9
King Kelly	27.0
Ken Keltner	11.4
Steve Kemp	8.7
Harmon Killebrew	28.7
Bill Killefer	6.9
Ralph Kiner	29.9
Chuck Klein	24.6
Johnny Kling	11.9
Bobby Knoop	15.3
Ed Konetchy	23.4
John Kruk	8.9
Whitey Kurowski	10.8
Nap Lajoie	94.9
Bill Lange	9.8
Barry Larkin	23.3
Henry Larkin	16.8
Lyn Lary	6.2
Tony Lazzeri	16.1
Tommy Leach	17.8
Chet Lemon	22.0
Buddy Lewis	6.7
Sixto Lezcano	13.1
Freddy Lindstrom	11.0
Johnny Logan	18.1
Sherm Lollar	9.4
Ernie Lombardi	17.1
Herman Long	8.3
Stan Lopata	6.6
Fred Luderus	8.9
Greg Luzinski	10.8
Fred Lynn	23.7
Denny Lyons	21.3
Sherry Magee	27.2
Mickey Mantle	73.6
Rabbit Maranville	13.5
Roger Maris	11.3
Eddie Mathews	48.6
Gary Matthews	8.0
Don Mattingly	11.6
Dal Maxvill	8.7
Charlie Maxwell	7.1
Willie Mays	86.4
Bill Mazeroski	36.6
Tim McCarver	6.8
Willie McCovey	35.1
Gil McDougald	16.7
Ed McFarland	10.7
Dan McGann	11.1
Willie McGee	8.9
John McGraw	17.2
Fred McGriff	16.1
Deacon McGuire	13.4
Mark McGwire	8.7
Matty McIntyre	7.2
Marty McManus	9.1
Ken McMullen	7.0
Bid McPhee	42.3
Hal McRae	16.3

Total Player Rating (alpha.)

Kevin McReynolds	15.2
Jim McTamany	8.2
Joe Medwick	28.0
Bill Melton	10.8
Chief Meyers	14.3
Jocko Milligan	17.1
Don Mincher	6.4
Minnie Minoso	25.8
Kevin Mitchell	13.6
Mike Mitchell	8.0
Johnny Mize	37.7
Paul Molitor	30.4
Rick Monday	6.9
Joe Morgan	55.7
Wally Moses	6.1
Johnny Mostil	7.3
Thurman Munson	15.1
Bobby Murcer	12.2
Dale Murphy	18.8
Danny Murphy	11.5
Dwayne Murphy	16.0
Eddie Murray	37.5
Stan Musial	71.7
Buddy Myer	9.8
Billy Nash	14.6
Graig Nettles	21.5
Bill Nicholson	18.4
Bob Nieman	8.4
Lefty O'Doul	12.1
Bob O'Farrell	6.2
Ben Oglivie	11.1
Tony Oliva	26.7
Al Oliver	10.1
Tip O'Neill	13.5
Jim O'Rourke	17.2
Dave Orr	13.9
Amos Otis	20.7
Mel Ott	62.4
Spike Owen	6.7
Rafael Palmeiro	8.3
Dave Parker	22.0
Lance Parrish	11.7
Freddie Patek	6.4
Roger Peckinpaugh	13.8
Heinie Peitz	6.3
Tony Pena	6.6
Terry Pendleton	13.4
Tony Perez	10.1
Johnny Pesky	13.2
Rico Petrocelli	10.9
Fred Pfeffer	23.0
Ken Phelps	7.6
Darrell Porter	12.6
Boog Powell	14.7
Del Pratt	20.2
Jerry Priddy	12.0
Kirby Puckett	24.3
Doug Rader	9.8
Tim Raines	47.1
Willie Randolph	23.0
Johnny Ray	7.0
Pee Wee Reese	14.6
Pete Reiser	7.2
Harold Reynolds	7.6
Sam Rice	8.8
Jim Rice	30.9
Hardy Richardson	28.4
Danny Richardson	8.4
Cal Ripken	38.6
Claude Ritchey	9.4
Mickey Rivers	6.1
Phil Rizzuto	15.9
Brooks Robinson	19.8
Frank Robinson	70.3
Jackie Robinson	32.6
Johnny Romano	9.2
Pete Rose	19.4
Al Rosen	11.9
Edd Roush	14.5
Babe Ruth	105.2
Jimmy Ryan	15.7
Ryne Sandberg	40.0
Ron Santo	41.7
Hank Sauer	10.9
Ray Schalk	7.1
Wally Schang	18.1
Mike Schmidt	80.3
Red Schoendienst	10.7
Ossee Schreckengost	12.0
Mike Scioscia	14.7
Kip Selbach	14.1
George Selkirk	7.8
Andy Seminick	11.0
Joe Sewell	35.2
Socks Seybold	7.7
Cy Seymour	11.7
Orator Shaffer	13.3
Jimmy Sheckard	19.6
Norm Siebern	6.4
Ruben Sierra	8.0

Total Player Rating (alpha.)

Roy Sievers	12.6
Al Simmons	27.2
Ted Simmons	17.5
Ken Singleton	21.0
George Sisler	23.0
Enos Slaughter	17.7
Roy Smalley	14.5
Reggie Smith	34.8
Elmer Smith	10.0
Red Smith	12.6
Lonnie Smith	12.5
Ozzie Smith	42.1
Duke Snider	24.2
Pop Snyder	7.7
Tris Speaker	88.5
Stan Spence	10.9
Eddie Stanky	18.5
Willie Stargell	26.1
Rusty Staub	27.1
Harry Steinfeldt	9.2
Vern Stephens	20.6
Riggs Stephenson	12.7
Snuffy Stirnweiss	8.5
George Stone	12.9
Harry Stovey	23.8
Darryl Strawberry	26.7
Jim Sundberg	7.9
Ezra Sutton	6.8
Ed Swartwood	11.9
Bill Sweeney	8.1
Lee Tannehill	7.9
Danny Tartabull	14.4
Gene Tenace	21.4
Fred Tenney	21.4
Bill Terry	24.4
Mickey Tettleton	7.4
Roy Thomas	22.6
Hank Thompson	6.3
Robby Thompson	11.8
Sam Thompson	30.0
Dickie Thon	8.0
Andy Thornton	14.1
Mike Tiernan	13.8
Joe Tinker	24.3
John Titus	12.7
Earl Torgeson	6.2
Joe Torre	20.1
Alan Trammell	23.3
Cecil Travis	10.2
Pie Traynor	20.9
Elmer Valo	6.2
George Van Haltren	12.0
Andy Van Slyke	20.9
Arky Vaughan	39.7
Bobby Veach	14.8
Honus Wagner	82.6
Dixie Walker	11.0
Bobby Wallace	36.8
Tim Wallach	8.9
Paul Waner	37.0
John Ward	8.6
Bob Watson	9.4
Al Weis	8.0
Curt Welch	12.1
Billy Werber	7.8
Vic Wertz	9.8
Wes Westrum	9.2
Zack Wheat	24.7
Lou Whitaker	19.5
Deacon White	11.5
Roy White	20.8
Pinky Whitney	8.8
Ernie Whitt	7.7
Billy Williams	27.1
Cy Williams	9.5
Jimmy Williams	16.5
Ken Williams	18.3
Ted Williams	92.4
Ned Williamson	11.4
Bump Wills	9.4
Maury Wills	11.0
Art Wilson	8.0
Hack Wilson	15.6
Willie Wilson	6.3
Dave Winfield	40.3
Sam Wise	7.7
Jimmy Wolf	11.5
George Wood	7.6
Gene Woodling	8.0
Jim Wynn	28.4
Carl Yastrzemski	50.8
Rudy York	11.5
Ross Youngs	10.5
Robin Yount	43.0
Chief Zimmer	16.7
Heinie Zimmerman	11.0
Richie Zisk	13.8

Total Player Rating (by era)

1876-1892

1	Roger Connor	44.4
2	Dan Brouthers	43.7
3	Bid McPhee	42.3
4	Jack Glasscock	37.8
5	Cap Anson	36.2
6	Buck Ewing	30.6
7	Sam Thompson	30.0
8	Pete Browning	29.6
9	Fred Dunlap	29.5
10	Hardy Richardson	28.4
11	King Kelly	27.0
12	Harry Stovey	23.8
13	Fred Pfeffer	23.0
14	Charley Jones	21.4
15	Denny Lyons	21.3
16	Charlie Bennett	19.6
17	George Gore	18.6
18	Paul Hines	17.8
19	Jim O'Rourke	17.2
20	Jocko Milligan	17.1
21	Henry Larkin	16.8
22	Billy Nash	14.6
23	Jack Clements	14.0
24	Dave Orr	13.9
25	Fred Carroll	13.7

1893-1919

1	Nap Lajoie	94.9
2	Ty Cobb	92.8
3	Tris Speaker	88.5
4	Honus Wagner	82.6
5	Eddie Collins	69.4
6	Bill Dahlen	52.4
7	George Davis	52.0
8	Ed Delahanty	44.8
9	Joe Jackson	38.2
10	Bobby Wallace	36.8
11	Frank Baker	33.5
12	Cupid Childs	31.2
	Sam Crawford	31.2
14	Jesse Burkett	30.4
15	Fred Clarke	30.1
16	Billy Hamilton	28.7
17	Elmer Flick	28.6
18	Hughie Jennings	27.4
19	Sherry Magee	27.2
20	Heinie Groh	26.7
21	Art Fletcher	26.3
22	Zack Wheat	24.7
23	Jake Beckley	24.5
24	Joe Tinker	24.3
25	Jimmy Collins	24.2

1920-1941

1	Babe Ruth	105.2
2	Rogers Hornsby	79.8
3	Mel Ott	62.4
4	Lou Gehrig	61.9
5	Jimmie Foxx	55.4
6	Charlie Gehringer	45.1
7	Luke Appling	40.9
8	Gabby Hartnett	40.1
9	Joe Cronin	39.9
10	Arky Vaughan	39.7
11	Frankie Frisch	38.8
12	Paul Waner	37.0
13	Dave Bancroft	35.4
14	Joe Sewell	35.2
15	Bob Johnson	35.1
16	Bill Dickey	34.8
17	Mickey Cochrane	32.2
18	Billy Herman	32.0
19	Harry Heilmann	31.9
20	Hank Greenberg	31.7
21	Joe Medwick	28.0
22	Dick Bartell	27.7
23	Al Simmons	27.2
24	Stan Hack	27.1
25	Goose Goslin	26.0

Total Player Rating (by era)

1942-1960

1	Ted Williams	92.4
2	Mickey Mantle	73.6
3	Stan Musial	71.7
4	Eddie Mathews	48.6
5	Joe DiMaggio	46.5
6	Lou Boudreau	40.4
7	Bobby Doerr	39.8
8	Johnny Mize	37.7
9	Yogi Berra	35.5
10	Jackie Robinson	32.6
11	Richie Ashburn	30.7
12	Ralph Kiner	29.9
13	Joe Gordon	27.7
14	Minnie Minoso	25.8
15	Duke Snider	24.2
16	Charlie Keller	23.3
17	Roy Campanella	21.9
18	Vern Stephens	20.6
19	Larry Doby	20.3
20	Roy Cullenbine	18.5
	Bob Elliott	18.5
	Eddie Stanky	18.5
23	Ferris Fain	18.4
	Bill Nicholson	18.4
25	Johnny Logan	18.1

1961-1992

1	Willie Mays	86.4
2	Hank Aaron	84.6
3	Mike Schmidt	80.3
4	Frank Robinson	70.3
5	Rickey Henderson	67.0
6	Joe Morgan	55.7
7	Carl Yastrzemski	50.8
8	Tim Raines	47.1
9	Al Kaline	46.4
10	Bobby Grich	43.3
11	Robin Yount	43.0
12	Reggie Jackson	42.7
13	George Brett	42.1
	Ozzie Smith	42.1
15	Ron Santo	41.7
16	Roberto Clemente	41.5
17	Dave Winfield	40.3
18	Ryne Sandberg	40.0
19	Wade Boggs	39.9
20	Cal Ripken	38.6
21	Eddie Murray	37.5
22	Bill Mazeroski	36.6
23	Darrell Evans	35.2
24	Willie McCovey	35.1
25	Reggie Smith	34.8

Wins

1	Cy Young	511
2	Walter Johnson	417
3	Pete Alexander	373
	Christy Mathewson	373
5	Warren Spahn	363
6	Kid Nichols	361
7	Jim Galvin	360
8	Tim Keefe	342
9	Steve Carlton	329
10	John Clarkson	328
11	Eddie Plank	326
12	Don Sutton	324
13	Nolan Ryan	319
14	Phil Niekro	318
15	Gaylord Perry	314
16	Tom Seaver	311
17	Charley Radbourn	309
18	Mickey Welch	307
19	Lefty Grove	300
	Early Wynn	300
21	Tommy John	288
22	Bert Blyleven	287
23	Robin Roberts	286
24	Fergie Jenkins	284
	Tony Mullane	284
26	Jim Kaat	283
27	Red Ruffing	273
28	Burleigh Grimes	270
29	Jim Palmer	268
30	Bob Feller	266
	Eppa Rixey	266
32	Jim McCormick	265
33	Gus Weyhing	264
34	Ted Lyons	260
35	Red Faber	254
36	Carl Hubbell	253
37	Bob Gibson	251
38	Vic Willis	249
39	Jack Quinn	247
40	Joe McGinnity	246
41	Jack Powell	245
	Amos Rusie	245
43	Juan Marichal	243
44	Herb Pennock	240
45	Mordecai Brown	239
46	Clark Griffith	237
	Waite Hoyt	237
	Jack Morris	237
49	Whitey Ford	236
50	Charlie Buffinton	233
	Frank Tanana	233
52	Sam Jones	229
	Luis Tiant	229
	Will White	229
55	George Mullin	228
56	Jim Bunning	224
	Catfish Hunter	224
58	Paul Derringer	223
	Mel Harder	223
60	Hooks Dauss	222
	Jerry Koosman	222
62	Joe Niekro	221
63	Jerry Reuss	220
64	Bob Caruthers	218
	Earl Whitehill	218
66	Freddie Fitzsimmons	217
	Mickey Lolich	217
68	Wilbur Cooper	216
69	Stan Coveleski	215
	Jim Perry	215
71	Rick Reuschel	214
72	Chief Bender	212
73	Bobo Newsom	211
	Billy Pierce	211
75	Jesse Haines	210
76	Vida Blue	209
	Don Drysdale	209
	Milt Pappas	209
79	Eddie Cicotte	208
80	Bob Lemon	207
	Carl Mays	207
	Hal Newhouser	207
83	Silver King	204
	Al Orth	204
85	Lew Burdette	203
	Jack Stivetts	203
87	Charlie Hough	202
88	Rube Marquard	201
	Charlie Root	201
90	George Uhle	200
91	Bob Welch	199
92	Jack Chesbro	198
	Bucky Walters	198
94	Larry French	197
	Bob Friend	197
	Jesse Tannehill	197
	Adonis Terry	197
	Dazzy Vance	197
99	Claude Osteen	196
	Bob Shawkey	196

Losses

1	Cy Young	316
2	Jim Galvin	308
3	Nolan Ryan	287
4	Walter Johnson	279
5	Phil Niekro	274
6	Gaylord Perry	265
7	Don Sutton	256
8	Jack Powell	254
9	Eppa Rixey	251
10	Bert Blyleven	250
11	Robin Roberts	245
	Warren Spahn	245
13	Steve Carlton	244
	Early Wynn	244
15	Jim Kaat	237
16	Gus Weyhing	232
17	Tommy John	231
18	Bob Friend	230
	Ted Lyons	230
20	Fergie Jenkins	226
21	Tim Keefe	225
	Red Ruffing	225
23	Bobo Newsom	222
24	Tony Mullane	220
25	Frank Tanana	219
26	Jack Quinn	218
27	Sam Jones	217
28	Jim McCormick	214
29	Red Faber	213
30	Paul Derringer	212
	Chick Fraser	212
	Burleigh Grimes	212
33	Mickey Welch	210
34	Jerry Koosman	209
35	Pete Alexander	208
	Kid Nichols	208
37	Tom Seaver	205
	Vic Willis	205
39	Joe Niekro	204
	Jim Whitney	204
41	George Mullin	196
	Adonis Terry	196
43	Claude Osteen	195
	Charley Radbourn	195
45	Eddie Plank	194
46	Charlie Hough	191
	Mickey Lolich	191
	Rick Reuschel	191
	Jerry Reuss	191
	Tom Zachary	191
51	Al Orth	189
52	Christy Mathewson	188
53	Mel Harder	186
54	Earl Whitehill	185
55	Jim Bunning	184
56	Joe Bush	183
	Larry Jackson	183
	Curt Simmons	183
59	Hooks Dauss	182
	Waite Hoyt	182
61	Murry Dickson	181
	Dutch Leonard	181
	Rick Wise	181
64	Lee Meadows	180
65	Pink Hawley	179
	Dolf Luque	179
67	John Clarkson	178
	Wilbur Cooper	178
69	Bill Dinneen	177
	Rube Marquard	177
71	Red Donahue	175
	Tom Hughes	175
73	Doyle Alexander	174
	Bob Gibson	174
	Jim Perry	174
	Amos Rusie	174
77	Luis Tiant	172
78	Larry French	171
79	Ted Breitenstein	170
	Camilo Pascual	170
81	Billy Pierce	169
82	Jack Morris	168
83	Red Ames	167
	Jim Clancy	167
	Bert Cunningham	167
	Red Ehret	167
87	Don Drysdale	166
	Howard Ehmke	166
	Catfish Hunter	166
	George Uhle	166
	Will White	166
92	Mark Baldwin	165
	Bump Hadley	165
	Si Johnson	165
95	Milt Gaston	164
	Win Mercer	164
	Milt Pappas	164
98	Bill Hutchison	163
99	Bob Feller	162
	Herb Pennock	162

Winning Percentage

1	Dave Foutz	.690
2	Whitey Ford	.690
3	Bob Caruthers	.688
4	Dwight Gooden	.683
5	Lefty Grove	.680
6	Roger Clemens	.679
7	Vic Raschi	.667
8	Larry Corcoran	.665
9	Christy Mathewson	.665
10	Sam Leever	.660
11	Sal Maglie	.657
12	Sandy Koufax	.655
13	Johnny Allen	.654
14	Ron Guidry	.651
15	Lefty Gomez	.649
16	John Clarkson	.648
17	Mordecai Brown	.648
18	Dizzy Dean	.644
19	Pete Alexander	.642
20	Jim Palmer	.638
21	Kid Nichols	.634
22	Deacon Phillippe	.634
23	Joe McGinnity	.634
24	Ed Reulbach	.632
25	Juan Marichal	.631
26	Mort Cooper	.631
27	Allie Reynolds	.630
28	Jesse Tannehill	.629
29	Ray Kremer	.627
30	Firpo Marberry	.627
31	Eddie Plank	.627
32	Tommy Bond	.627
33	Chief Bender	.625
34	Don Newcombe	.623
35	Nig Cuppy	.623
36	Addie Joss	.623
37	Fred Goldsmith	.622
38	Doc Crandall	.622
39	Carl Hubbell	.622
	Carl Mays	.622
41	Bob Feller	.621
42	Mel Parnell	.621
43	John Tudor	.619
44	Clark Griffith	.619
45	Bob Lemon	.618
46	Cy Young	.618
47	John Ward	.617
48	Urban Shocker	.615
49	Jeff Tesreau	.615
50	Jim Maloney	.615
51	Lon Warneke	.613
52	Charley Radbourn	.613
53	Gary Nolan	.611
54	Schoolboy Rowe	.610
55	Carl Erskine	.610
56	Ed Walsh	.607
57	Charlie Ferguson	.607
58	Dave McNally	.607
59	Hooks Wiltse	.607
60	Bob Welch	.607
61	Jack Stivetts	.606
62	Art Nehf	.605
63	Charlie Buffinton	.605
64	Orval Overall	.603
65	Tim Keefe	.603
66	Tom Seaver	.603
67	Stan Coveleski	.602
68	Preacher Roe	.602
69	Wes Ferrell	.601
70	J.R. Richard	.601
71	Jack Chesbro	.600
72	Walter Johnson	.599
73	John Candelaria	.598
74	Freddie Fitzsimmons	.598
75	Ed Lopat	.597
76	Warren Spahn	.597
77	Herb Pennock	.597
78	Rip Sewell	.596
79	Mike Garcia	.594
80	Mickey Welch	.594
81	Pat Malone	.593
82	General Crowder	.592
83	Harry Brecheen	.591
84	Jim Bagby	.591
85	Bob Gibson	.591
86	Dutch Ruether	.591
87	Denny McLain	.590
88	Eddie Rommel	.590
89	Jack Coombs	.590
90	Jimmy Key	.589
91	Tiny Bonham	.589
92	Mike Cuellar	.587
93	Bill Bernhard	.586
	Orel Hershiser	.586
95	Tom Browning	.585
96	Jack Morris	.585
	Jeff Pfeffer	.585
98	Lew Burdette	.585
99	Amos Rusie	.585
100	Dazzy Vance	.585

Games

1	Hoyt Wilhelm	1070
2	Kent Tekulve	1050
3	Lindy McDaniel	987
4	Rollie Fingers	944
5	Gene Garber	931
6	Rich Gossage	927
7	Cy Young	906
8	Sparky Lyle	899
9	Jim Kaat	898
10	Don McMahon	874
11	Phil Niekro	864
12	Roy Face	848
13	Tug McGraw	824
14	Jeff Reardon	811
15	Charlie Hough	803
16	Walter Johnson	802
17	Nolan Ryan	794
18	Lee Smith	787
19	Gaylord Perry	777
20	Don Sutton	774
21	Darold Knowles	765
22	Tommy John	760
23	Jack Quinn	756
24	Ron Reed	751
25	Warren Spahn	750
26	Tom Burgmeier	745
	Gary Lavelle	745
28	Willie Hernandez	744
29	Steve Carlton	741
30	Dennis Eckersley	740
31	Ron Perranoski	737
32	Ron Kline	736
33	Clay Carroll	731
34	Mike Marshall	723
35	Johnny Klippstein	711
36	Greg Minton	710
37	Stu Miller	704
38	Joe Niekro	702
39	Bill Campbell	700
40	Jim Galvin	697
41	Pete Alexander	696
42	Bob Miller	694
43	Bert Blyleven	692
	Grant Jackson	692
	Eppa Rixey	692
46	Early Wynn	691
47	Eddie Fisher	690
48	Bob McClure	684
49	Ted Abernathy	681
50	Robin Roberts	676
51	Waite Hoyt	674
	Dan Quisenberry	674
53	Red Faber	669
54	Dave Giusti	668
55	Fergie Jenkins	664
56	Bruce Sutter	661
57	Jesse Orosco	657
58	Tom Seaver	656
59	Paul Lindblad	655
60	Wilbur Wood	651
61	Sam Jones	647
	Dave LaRoche	647
63	Dutch Leonard	640
	Gerry Staley	640
65	Dennis Lamp	639
	Diego Segui	639
67	Dave Righetti	637
	Bob Stanley	637
69	Christy Mathewson	635
70	Charlie Root	632
71	Jim Perry	630
72	Jerry Reuss	628
73	Lew Burdette	626
74	Murry Dickson	625
	Woodie Fryman	625
76	Red Ruffing	624
77	Eddie Plank	623
78	Kid Nichols	620
	Dick Tidrow	620
80	Herb Pennock	617
81	Burleigh Grimes	616
	Lefty Grove	616
83	Terry Forster	614
	Craig Lefferts	614
85	Jerry Koosman	612
86	Dave Smith	609
87	Steve Bedrosian	608
88	Larry Andersen	606
	Frank Tanana	606
90	Bob Friend	602
	Al Worthington	602
92	Elias Sosa	601
93	Bobo Newsom	600
94	Tim Keefe	599
95	Ted Lyons	594
96	Pedro Borbon	593
97	Jim Bunning	591
98	Turk Farrell	590
99	Moe Drabowsky	589
100	Rick Honeycutt	588

Games Started

1	Cy Young	815
2	Nolan Ryan	760
3	Don Sutton	756
4	Phil Niekro	716
5	Steve Carlton	709
6	Tommy John	700
7	Gaylord Perry	690
8	Bert Blyleven	685
9	Jim Galvin	682
10	Walter Johnson	666
11	Warren Spahn	665
12	Tom Seaver	647
13	Jim Kaat	625
14	Early Wynn	612
15	Robin Roberts	609
16	Pete Alexander	598
17	Fergie Jenkins	594
18	Tim Keefe	593
19	Frank Tanana	584
20	Kid Nichols	561
21	Eppa Rixey	552
22	Christy Mathewson	551
23	Mickey Welch	549
24	Jerry Reuss	547
25	Red Ruffing	536
26	Eddie Plank	529
	Rick Reuschel	529
28	Jerry Koosman	527
29	Jim Palmer	521
30	Jim Bunning	519
31	John Clarkson	518
32	Jack Powell	516
33	Tony Mullane	504
34	Charley Radbourn	503
	Gus Weyhing	503
36	Joe Niekro	500
37	Bob Friend	497
38	Mickey Lolich	496
39	Burleigh Grimes	495
40	Claude Osteen	488
41	Sam Jones	487
42	Jim McCormick	485
43	Bob Feller	484
	Ted Lyons	484
	Luis Tiant	484
46	Red Faber	483
	Bobo Newsom	483
48	Bob Gibson	482
49	Jack Morris	477
50	Catfish Hunter	476
51	Vida Blue	473
	Earl Whitehill	473
53	Vic Willis	471
54	Don Drysdale	465
	Milt Pappas	465
56	Doyle Alexander	464
57	Curt Simmons	461
58	Mike Torrez	458
59	Lefty Grove	457
	Juan Marichal	457
61	Rick Wise	455
62	Jim Perry	447
63	Paul Derringer	445
64	Jack Quinn	444
65	Dennis Martinez	442
66	Whitey Ford	438
67	Mel Harder	433
68	Billy Pierce	432
69	Carl Hubbell	431
70	Larry Jackson	429
71	George Mullin	428
72	Amos Rusie	427
73	Freddie Fitzsimmons	426
	Bob Welch	426
75	Waite Hoyt	423
76	Bob Forsch	422
77	Herb Pennock	420
78	Bob Knepper	413
79	Ken Holtzman	410
80	Tom Zachary	409
81	Wilbur Cooper	408
82	Adonis Terry	406
83	Dave Stieb	405
84	Mike Flanagan	404
	Lee Meadows	404
	Camilo Pascual	404
87	Rube Marquard	403
88	Will White	401
89	Bucky Walters	398
90	Charlie Buffinton	396
	Dave McNally	396
	Jim Whitney	396
93	Al Orth	394
94	Steve Rogers	393
95	Paul Splittorff	392
96	Chick Fraser	389
97	Hooks Dauss	388
	Jesse Haines	388
99	Stan Coveleski	385
	Charlie Hough	385

Games Started (by era)

1876-1892

1	Jim Galvin	682
2	Tim Keefe	593
3	Mickey Welch	549
4	John Clarkson	518
5	Tony Mullane	504
6	Charley Radbourn	503
	Gus Weyhing	503
8	Jim McCormick	485
9	Adonis Terry	406
10	Will White	401
11	Charlie Buffinton	396
	Jim Whitney	396
13	Silver King	371
14	Bill Hutchison	347
15	Jack Stivetts	333

1893-1919

1	Cy Young	815
2	Walter Johnson	666
3	Pete Alexander	598
4	Kid Nichols	561
5	Christy Mathewson	551
6	Eddie Plank	529
7	Jack Powell	516
8	Vic Willis	471
9	George Mullin	428
10	Amos Rusie	427
11	Rube Marquard	403
12	Al Orth	394
13	Chick Fraser	389
14	Hooks Dauss	388
15	Joe McGinnity	381

1920-1941

1	Eppa Rixey	552
2	Red Ruffing	536
3	Burleigh Grimes	495
4	Sam Jones	487
5	Ted Lyons	484
6	Red Faber	483
	Bobo Newsom	483
8	Earl Whitehill	473
9	Lefty Grove	457
10	Paul Derringer	445
11	Jack Quinn	444
12	Mel Harder	433
13	Carl Hubbell	431
14	Freddie Fitzsimmons	426
15	Waite Hoyt	423

1942-1960

1	Warren Spahn	665
2	Early Wynn	612
3	Robin Roberts	609
4	Bob Friend	497
5	Bob Feller	484
6	Curt Simmons	461
7	Whitey Ford	438
8	Billy Pierce	432
9	Dutch Leonard	375
10	Hal Newhouser	374
11	Lew Burdette	373
12	Bob Buhl	369
13	Vern Law	364
14	Bob Lemon	350

1961-1992

1	Nolan Ryan	760
2	Don Sutton	756
3	Phil Niekro	716
4	Steve Carlton	709
5	Tommy John	700
6	Gaylord Perry	690
7	Bert Blyleven	685
8	Tom Seaver	647
9	Jim Kaat	625
10	Fergie Jenkins	594
11	Frank Tanana	584
12	Jerry Reuss	547
13	Rick Reuschel	529
14	Jerry Koosman	527
15	Jim Palmer	521

Complete Games

1	Cy Young	749
2	Jim Galvin	639
3	Tim Keefe	554
4	Walter Johnson	531
	Kid Nichols	531
6	Mickey Welch	525
7	Charley Radbourn	489
8	John Clarkson	485
9	Tony Mullane	468
10	Jim McCormick	466
11	Gus Weyhing	448
12	Pete Alexander	437
13	Christy Mathewson	434
14	Jack Powell	422
15	Eddie Plank	410
16	Will White	394
17	Amos Rusie	392
18	Vic Willis	388
19	Warren Spahn	382
20	Jim Whitney	377
21	Adonis Terry	367
22	Ted Lyons	356
23	George Mullin	353
24	Charlie Buffinton	351
25	Chick Fraser	342
26	Clark Griffith	337
27	Red Ruffing	335
28	Silver King	329
29	Al Orth	324
30	Bill Hutchison	321
31	Burleigh Grimes	314
	Joe McGinnity	314
33	Red Donahue	313
34	Guy Hecker	310
35	Bill Dinneen	306
36	Robin Roberts	305
37	Gaylord Perry	303
38	Ted Breitenstein	300
39	Bob Caruthers	298
	Lefty Grove	298
41	Pink Hawley	297
	Ed Morris	297
43	Mark Baldwin	296
44	Tommy Bond	294
45	Brickyard Kennedy	293
46	Eppa Rixey	290
	Early Wynn	290
48	Bill Donovan	289
	Bobby Mathews	289
50	Bert Cunningham	286
51	Wilbur Cooper	279
	Bob Feller	279
	Sadie McMahon	279
54	Jack Stivetts	278
	Jack Taylor	278
56	Charlie Getzien	277
57	Red Faber	273
58	Mordecai Brown	271
59	Frank Dwyer	270
	Jouett Meekin	270
61	Fergie Jenkins	267
62	Elton Chamberlain	264
	Matt Kilroy	264
64	Jesse Tannehill	263
65	Doc White	262
66	Rube Waddell	261
67	Jack Chesbro	260
	Red Ehret	260
	Carl Hubbell	260
70	Larry Corcoran	256
71	Chief Bender	255
	Bob Gibson	255
73	Steve Carlton	254
74	Frank Killen	253
75	Paul Derringer	251
	Win Mercer	251
77	Sam Jones	250
	Ed Walsh	250
79	Eddie Cicotte	249
	Stump Weidman	249
81	Herb Pennock	247
82	Bobo Newsom	246
83	George Bradley	245
	Hooks Dauss	245
	Phil Niekro	245
86	Harry Howell	244
	Juan Marichal	244
	John Ward	244
89	Jack Quinn	243
90	Bert Blyleven	242
	Deacon Phillippe	242
	Bucky Walters	242
93	Sam Leever	241
94	Kid Gleason	240
95	Addie Joss	234
96	George Uhle	232
97	Carl Mays	231
	Tom Seaver	231
	Harry Staley	231
100	Earl Moore	230

Complete Games (by era)

1876-1892

1	Jim Galvin	639
2	Tim Keefe	554
3	Mickey Welch	525
4	Charley Radbourn	489
5	John Clarkson	485
6	Tony Mullane	468
7	Jim McCormick	466
8	Gus Weyhing	448
9	Will White	394
10	Jim Whitney	377
11	Adonis Terry	367
12	Charlie Buffinton	351
13	Silver King	329
14	Bill Hutchison	321
15	Guy Hecker	310

1893-1919

1	Cy Young	749
2	Walter Johnson	531
	Kid Nichols	531
4	Pete Alexander	437
5	Christy Mathewson	434
6	Jack Powell	422
7	Eddie Plank	410
8	Amos Rusie	392
9	Vic Willis	388
10	George Mullin	353
11	Chick Fraser	342
12	Clark Griffith	337
13	Al Orth	324
14	Joe McGinnity	314
15	Red Donahue	313

1920-1941

1	Ted Lyons	356
2	Red Ruffing	335
3	Burleigh Grimes	314
4	Lefty Grove	298
5	Eppa Rixey	290
6	Wilbur Cooper	279
7	Red Faber	273
8	Carl Hubbell	260
9	Paul Derringer	251
10	Sam Jones	250
11	Herb Pennock	247
12	Bobo Newsom	246
13	Jack Quinn	243
14	Bucky Walters	242
15	George Uhle	232

1942-1960

1	Warren Spahn	382
2	Robin Roberts	305
3	Early Wynn	290
4	Bob Feller	279
5	Hal Newhouser	212
6	Billy Pierce	193
7	Dutch Leonard	192
8	Bob Lemon	188
9	Ed Lopat	164
10	Bob Friend	163
	Curt Simmons	163
12	Lew Burdette	158
	Dizzy Trout	158
14	Whitey Ford	156
	Jim Tobin	156

1961-1992

1	Gaylord Perry	303
2	Fergie Jenkins	267
3	Bob Gibson	255
4	Steve Carlton	254
5	Phil Niekro	245
6	Juan Marichal	244
7	Bert Blyleven	242
8	Tom Seaver	231
9	Nolan Ryan	222
10	Jim Palmer	211
11	Mickey Lolich	195
12	Luis Tiant	187
13	Catfish Hunter	181
14	Jim Kaat	180
15	Don Sutton	178

Shutouts

1	Walter Johnson	110
2	Pete Alexander	90
3	Christy Mathewson	79
4	Cy Young	76
5	Eddie Plank	69
6	Warren Spahn	63
7	Nolan Ryan	61
	Tom Seaver	61
9	Bert Blyleven	60
10	Don Sutton	58
11	Ed Walsh	57
12	Jim Galvin	56
	Bob Gibson	56
14	Mordecai Brown	55
	Steve Carlton	55
16	Jim Palmer	53
	Gaylord Perry	53
18	Juan Marichal	52
19	Rube Waddell	50
	Vic Willis	50
21	Don Drysdale	49
	Fergie Jenkins	49
	Luis Tiant	49
	Early Wynn	49
25	Kid Nichols	48
26	Tommy John	46
	Jack Powell	46
28	Whitey Ford	45
	Addie Joss	45
	Phil Niekro	45
	Robin Roberts	45
	Red Ruffing	45
	Doc White	45
34	Babe Adams	44
	Bob Feller	44
36	Milt Pappas	43
37	Catfish Hunter	42
	Bucky Walters	42
39	Mickey Lolich	41
	Hippo Vaughn	41
	Mickey Welch	41
42	Chief Bender	40
	Jim Bunning	40
	Larry French	40
	Sandy Koufax	40
	Claude Osteen	40
	Ed Reulbach	40
	Mel Stottlemyre	40
49	Tim Keefe	39
	Sam Leever	39
	Jerry Reuss	39
52	Stan Coveleski	38
	Billy Pierce	38
	Nap Rucker	38
55	Vida Blue	37
	John Clarkson	37
	Larry Jackson	37
	Eppa Rixey	37
	Steve Rogers	37
60	Mike Cuellar	36
	Bob Friend	36
	Carl Hubbell	36
	Sam Jones	36
	Camilo Pascual	36
	Allie Reynolds	36
	Curt Simmons	36
	Will White	36
68	Tommy Bond	35
	Joe Bush	35
	Jack Chesbro	35
	Eddie Cicotte	35
	Jack Coombs	35
	Wilbur Cooper	35
	Bill Donovan	35
	Burleigh Grimes	35
	Lefty Grove	35
	George Mullin	35
	Herb Pennock	35
	Charley Radbourn	35
80	Roger Clemens	34
	Bill Doak	34
	Earl Moore	34
	Frank Tanana	34
	Jesse Tannehill	34
85	Tommy Bridges	33
	Lew Burdette	33
	Dean Chance	33
	Mort Cooper	33
	Jerry Koosman	33
	Lefty Leifield	33
	Dutch Leonard	33
	Jim McCormick	33
	Dave McNally	33
	Hal Newhouser	33
	Bob Shawkey	33
	Virgil Trucks	33
97	Paul Derringer	32
	Joe McGinnity	32
	Jim Perry	32
100	6 players tied	31

Saves

1	Jeff Reardon	357
2	Lee Smith	355
3	Rollie Fingers	341
4	Rich Gossage	308
5	Bruce Sutter	300
6	Dave Righetti	251
7	Dan Quisenberry	244
8	Dennis Eckersley	239
9	Sparky Lyle	238
10	Hoyt Wilhelm	227
11	John Franco	226
12	Tom Henke	220
13	Gene Garber	218
14	Dave Smith	216
15	Bobby Thigpen	200
16	Roy Face	193
17	Mike Marshall	188
18	Steve Bedrosian	184
	Kent Tekulve	184
20	Tug McGraw	180
21	Ron Perranoski	179
22	Lindy McDaniel	172
23	Doug Jones	164
24	Stu Miller	154
25	Jay Howell	153
	Don McMahon	153
27	Greg Minton	150
28	Roger McDowell	149
29	Ted Abernathy	148
30	Willie Hernandez	147
31	Dave Giusti	145
32	Clay Carroll	143
	Darold Knowles	143
	Mitch Williams	143
35	Gary Lavelle	136
36	Dan Plesac	133
37	Jim Brewer	132
	Bob Stanley	132
39	Randy Myers	131
	Gregg Olson	131
41	Ron Davis	130
42	Todd Worrell	129
43	Terry Forster	127
44	Bill Campbell	126
	Bryan Harvey	126
	Dave LaRoche	126
47	John Hiller	125
48	Jack Aker	123
49	Rick Aguilera	122
	Jesse Orosco	122
	Dick Radatz	122
52	Tippy Martinez	115
	Jeff Montgomery	115
54	Jeff Russell	113
55	Frank Linzy	111
56	Al Worthington	110
57	Fred Gladding	109
58	Wayne Granger	108
	Ron Kline	108
60	Johnny Murphy	107
61	Bill Caudill	104
62	Mike Henneman	104
63	Steve Farr	103
	Ron Reed	103
	John Wyatt	103
66	Tom Burgmeier	102
	Tim Burke	102
	Ellis Kinder	102
69	Firpo Marberry	101
70	Craig Lefferts	100
71	Joe Hoerner	99
72	Mike Schooler	98
73	Al Hrabosky	97
	Tom Niedenfuer	97
75	Clem Labine	96
	Randy Moffitt	96
77	Bob Locker	95
78	Aurelio Lopez	93
79	Mark Davis	92
	Tom Hume	92
	Phil Regan	92
82	Bill Henry	90
83	Donnie Moore	89
84	Jim Kern	88
85	Ken Sanders	86
	Cecil Upshaw	86
87	Joe Sambito	84
88	Mark Clear	83
	Turk Farrell	83
	Claude Raymond	83
	Elias Sosa	83
92	Don Aase	82
	Larry Sherry	82
94	Doug Bair	81
	Eddie Fisher	81
96	Pedro Borbon	80
	Eddie Watt	80
98	Grant Jackson	79
99	Al Holland	78
100	3 players tied	76

Innings Pitched

1	Cy Young	7354.2
2	Jim Galvin	5941.1
3	Walter Johnson	5923.2
4	Phil Niekro	5404.1
5	Gaylord Perry	5350.1
6	Nolan Ryan	5319.2
7	Don Sutton	5282.1
8	Warren Spahn	5243.2
9	Steve Carlton	5217.1
10	Pete Alexander	5189.1
11	Kid Nichols	5056.1
12	Tim Keefe	5047.1
13	Bert Blyleven	4970.0
14	Mickey Welch	4802.0
15	Tom Seaver	4782.2
16	Christy Mathewson	4780.2
17	Tommy John	4710.1
18	Robin Roberts	4688.2
19	Early Wynn	4564.0
20	John Clarkson	4536.1
21	Charley Radbourn	4535.1
22	Tony Mullane	4531.1
23	Jim Kaat	4530.1
24	Fergie Jenkins	4500.2
25	Eddie Plank	4495.2
26	Eppa Rixey	4494.2
27	Jack Powell	4389.0
28	Red Ruffing	4344.0
29	Gus Weyhing	4324.1
30	Jim McCormick	4275.2
31	Burleigh Grimes	4179.2
32	Ted Lyons	4161.0
33	Red Faber	4086.2
34	Vic Willis	3996.0
35	Frank Tanana	3985.2
36	Jim Palmer	3948.0
37	Lefty Grove	3940.2
38	Jack Quinn	3920.1
39	Bob Gibson	3884.1
40	Sam Jones	3883.0
41	Jerry Koosman	3839.1
42	Bob Feller	3827.0
43	Amos Rusie	3769.2
44	Waite Hoyt	3762.1
45	Jim Bunning	3760.1
46	Bobo Newsom	3759.1
47	George Mullin	3686.2
48	Jerry Reuss	3669.2
49	Paul Derringer	3645.0
50	Mickey Lolich	3638.1
51	Bob Friend	3611.0
52	Carl Hubbell	3590.1
53	Joe Niekro	3584.0
54	Herb Pennock	3571.2
55	Earl Whitehill	3564.2
56	Rick Reuschel	3548.1
57	Will White	3542.2
58	Jack Morris	3530.0
59	Adonis Terry	3514.0
60	Juan Marichal	3507.1
61	Jim Whitney	3496.1
62	Luis Tiant	3486.1
63	Charlie Hough	3483.1
64	Wilbur Cooper	3480.0
65	Claude Osteen	3460.1
66	Catfish Hunter	3449.1
67	Joe McGinnity	3441.1
68	Don Drysdale	3432.0
69	Mel Harder	3426.1
70	Charlie Buffinton	3404.0
71	Hooks Dauss	3390.2
72	Clark Griffith	3385.2
73	Doyle Alexander	3367.2
74	Chick Fraser	3356.0
75	Al Orth	3354.2
76	Curt Simmons	3348.1
77	Vida Blue	3343.1
78	Rube Marquard	3306.2
	Billy Pierce	3306.2
80	Jim Perry	3285.2
81	Larry Jackson	3262.2
82	Freddie Fitzsimmons	3223.2
83	Eddie Cicotte	3223.1
84	Dolf Luque	3220.1
85	Dutch Leonard	3218.1
86	Jesse Haines	3208.2
87	Red Ames	3198.0
88	Charlie Root	3197.1
89	Silver King	3190.2
90	Milt Pappas	3186.0
91	Mordecai Brown	3172.1
92	Whitey Ford	3170.1
93	Lee Meadows	3160.2
94	Dennis Martinez	3159.1
95	Larry French	3152.0
96	Rick Wise	3127.0
97	Tom Zachary	3126.1
98	George Uhle	3119.2
99	Bucky Walters	3104.2
100	Joe Bush	3087.1

Innings Pitched (by era)

1876-1892

1	Jim Galvin	5941.1
2	Tim Keefe	5047.1
3	Mickey Welch	4802.0
4	John Clarkson	4536.1
5	Charley Radbourn	4535.1
6	Tony Mullane	4531.1
7	Gus Weyhing	4324.1
8	Jim McCormick	4275.2
9	Will White	3542.2
10	Adonis Terry	3514.0
11	Jim Whitney	3496.1
12	Charlie Buffinton	3404.0
13	Silver King	3190.2
14	Bill Hutchison	3083.0
15	Guy Hecker	2906.0

1893-1919

1	Cy Young	7354.2
2	Walter Johnson	5923.2
3	Pete Alexander	5189.1
4	Kid Nichols	5056.1
5	Christy Mathewson	4780.2
6	Eddie Plank	4495.2
7	Jack Powell	4389.0
8	Vic Willis	3996.0
9	Amos Rusie	3769.2
10	George Mullin	3686.2
11	Joe McGinnity	3441.1
12	Hooks Dauss	3390.2
13	Clark Griffith	3385.2
14	Chick Fraser	3356.0
15	Al Orth	3354.2

1920-1941

1	Eppa Rixey	4494.2
2	Red Ruffing	4344.0
3	Burleigh Grimes	4179.2
4	Ted Lyons	4161.0
5	Red Faber	4086.2
6	Lefty Grove	3940.2
7	Jack Quinn	3920.1
8	Sam Jones	3883.0
9	Waite Hoyt	3762.1
10	Bobo Newsom	3759.1
11	Paul Derringer	3645.0
12	Carl Hubbell	3590.1
13	Herb Pennock	3571.2
14	Earl Whitehill	3564.2
15	Wilbur Cooper	3480.0

1942-1960

1	Warren Spahn	5243.2
2	Robin Roberts	4688.2
3	Early Wynn	4564.0
4	Bob Feller	3827.0
5	Bob Friend	3611.0
6	Curt Simmons	3348.1
7	Billy Pierce	3306.2
8	Dutch Leonard	3218.1
9	Whitey Ford	3170.1
10	Lew Burdette	3067.1
11	Murry Dickson	3052.1
12	Hal Newhouser	2993.0
13	Bob Lemon	2850.0
14	Dizzy Trout	2725.2
15	Virgil Trucks	2682.1

1961-1992

1	Phil Niekro	5404.1
2	Gaylord Perry	5350.1
3	Nolan Ryan	5319.2
4	Don Sutton	5282.1
5	Steve Carlton	5217.1
6	Bert Blyleven	4970.0
7	Tom Seaver	4782.2
8	Tommy John	4710.1
9	Jim Kaat	4530.1
10	Fergie Jenkins	4500.2
11	Frank Tanana	3985.2
12	Jim Palmer	3948.0
13	Bob Gibson	3884.1
14	Jerry Koosman	3839.1
15	Jim Bunning	3760.1

Hits per Game

#	Player	HG
1	Nolan Ryan	6.55
2	Sandy Koufax	6.79
3	J.R. Richard	6.88
4	Andy Messersmith	6.94
5	Hoyt Wilhelm	7.01
6	Sam McDowell	7.03
7	Ed Walsh	7.12
8	Bob Turley	7.18
9	Orval Overall	7.22
10	Jeff Tesreau	7.24
11	Ed Reulbach	7.24
12	Mario Soto	7.26
13	Addie Joss	7.30
14	Rich Gossage	7.37
15	Jim Maloney	7.39
16	Jose DeLeon	7.41
17	Walter Johnson	7.47
18	Tom Seaver	7.47
19	Rube Waddell	7.48
20	Roger Clemens	7.55
21	Bob Gibson	7.60
22	Don Wilson	7.61
23	Jim Palmer	7.63
24	Charlie Hough	7.66
25	Larry Cheney	7.68
26	Mordecai Brown	7.68
27	Sam Jones	7.68
28	Bob Feller	7.69
29	Johnny Vander Meer	7.69
30	Catfish Hunter	7.72
31	Al Downing	7.72
32	Jim Scott	7.73
33	Bobby Bolin	7.79
34	Stan Williams	7.79
35	Rollie Fingers	7.80
36	Dwight Gooden	7.80
37	Dean Chance	7.81
38	Frank Smith	7.82
39	Tug McGraw	7.83
40	Barney Pelty	7.84
41	Whitey Ford	7.85
42	Denny McLain	7.85
43	Bob Veale	7.87
44	Mark Langston	7.89
45	Chief Bender	7.89
46	George McQuillan	7.89
47	Jack Coombs	7.89
48	Moe Drabowsky	7.90
49	Vida Blue	7.91
50	Tim Keefe	7.91
51	Orel Hershiser	7.91
52	Nap Rucker	7.92
53	Allie Reynolds	7.92
54	Eddie Plank	7.92
55	Dave Stieb	7.93
56	Luis Tiant	7.94
57	Christy Mathewson	7.94
58	Rudy May	7.94
59	Ray Culp	7.95
60	Bill Donovan	7.99
61	Howie Camnitz	7.99
62	Don Sutton	7.99
63	Juan Pizarro	7.99
64	Gary Bell	8.01
65	Earl Moore	8.02
66	Sonny Siebert	8.03
67	Lefty Tyler	8.03
68	Hal Newhouser	8.04
69	Claude Hendrix	8.06
70	Steve Carlton	8.06
71	Hooks Wiltse	8.06
72	Willie Mitchell	8.07
73	Fernando Valenzuela	8.07
74	Larry Corcoran	8.08
75	Amos Rusie	8.08
76	Bill Singer	8.08
77	Bob Lemon	8.08
78	Mike Scott	8.08
79	Stu Miller	8.09
80	Don Drysdale	8.09
81	Gary Nolan	8.09
82	Eddie Cicotte	8.09
83	Juan Marichal	8.09
84	Virgil Trucks	8.11
85	Hippo Vaughn	8.11
86	Doc White	8.12
87	Blue Moon Odom	8.12
88	Kirby Higbe	8.13
89	Jim Shaw	8.13
90	Mike Cuellar	8.13
91	Billy Pierce	8.14
92	Mort Cooper	8.15
93	Red Ames	8.15
94	Vic Willis	8.16
95	Harry Brecheen	8.17
96	Earl Wilson	8.17
97	Jim Bibby	8.18
98	Eddie Fisher	8.18
99	Steve Barber	8.19
100	Gary Peters	8.19

Home Runs Allowed

#	Player	HR
1	Robin Roberts	505
2	Fergie Jenkins	484
3	Phil Niekro	482
4	Don Sutton	472
5	Warren Spahn	434
6	Bert Blyleven	430
7	Frank Tanana	420
8	Steve Carlton	414
9	Gaylord Perry	399
10	Jim Kaat	395
11	Tom Seaver	380
12	Catfish Hunter	374
13	Jim Bunning	372
14	Jack Morris	357
15	Mickey Lolich	347
16	Charlie Hough	346
	Luis Tiant	346
18	Early Wynn	338
19	Doyle Alexander	324
20	Juan Marichal	320
21	Nolan Ryan	316
22	Pedro Ramos	315
23	Jim Perry	308
24	Dennis Eckersley	307
25	Jim Palmer	303
26	Murry Dickson	302
	Tommy John	302
28	Milt Pappas	298
29	Mudcat Grant	292
30	Floyd Bannister	291
31	Jerry Koosman	290
32	Lew Burdette	289
33	Bob Friend	286
	Dennis Martinez	286
35	Billy Pierce	284
36	Don Drysdale	280
37	Jim Slaton	277
38	Joe Niekro	276
39	Frank Viola	271
40	Vern Law	268
41	Vida Blue	263
42	Rick Wise	261
43	Larry Jackson	259
44	Bob Gibson	257
45	Camilo Pascual	256
46	Mike McCormick	255
	Curt Simmons	255
48	Red Ruffing	254
49	Don Newcombe	252
50	Mike Flanagan	251
51	Ken Holtzman	249
	Bruce Hurst	249
	Claude Osteen	249
54	Steve Renko	248
55	Jerry Reuss	245
56	Jim Clancy	244
57	John Candelaria	243
58	Denny McLain	242
	Johnny Podres	242
60	Harvey Haddix	240
	Ray Sadecki	240
62	Scott Sanderson	239
63	Bob Buhl	238
64	Earl Wilson	236
65	Scott McGregor	235
66	Joe Coleman	234
67	Jim Lonborg	233
68	Bob Welch	232
69	Bill Gullickson	230
	Dave McNally	230
71	Whitey Ford	228
	Bob Knepper	228
73	Carl Hubbell	227
74	Ron Guidry	226
75	Don Cardwell	225
76	Bob Feller	224
77	Stan Bahnsen	223
	Ted Lyons	223
	Mike Torrez	223
80	Mike Cuellar	222
81	Ray Burris	221
	Rick Reuschel	221
83	Mike Caldwell	218
	Ron Kline	218
	Dan Petry	218
	Dave Stieb	218
87	Bob Forsch	216
	Ralph Terry	216
89	Ned Garver	213
90	Tom Browning	211
	Bill Monbouquette	211
	Ed Whitson	211
93	Herm Wehmeier	210
94	Joe Nuxhall	209
	Marty Pattin	209
	Wilbur Wood	209
97	Gary Bell	206
	Bobo Newsom	206
99	Mike Moore	205
100	4 players tied	204

Home Runs Allowed (by era)

1876-1892

#	Player	HR
1	John Clarkson	161
2	Jack Stivetts	131
3	Jim Galvin	122
4	Gus Weyhing	120
5	Charley Radbourn	117
6	Mickey Welch	106
7	Bill Hutchison	104
8	Tony Mullane	98
9	Charlie Getzien	95
10	Harry Staley	92
11	Charlie Buffinton	87
12	Jim McCormick	84
13	Mark Baldwin	82
14	Jim Whitney	79
15	Adonis Terry	76

1893-1919

#	Player	HR
1	Pete Alexander	164
2	Kid Nichols	156
3	Cy Young	138
4	Jack Powell	110
5	Frank Dwyer	109
6	Rube Marquard	107
7	Walter Johnson	97
8	Brickyard Kennedy	93
9	Christy Mathewson	91
10	Hooks Dauss	87
11	Ad Gumbert	81
12	Kid Carsey	80
13	Ted Breitenstein	79
14	Bill Dinneen	78
15	2 players tied	76

1920-1941

#	Player	HR
1	Red Ruffing	254
2	Carl Hubbell	227
3	Ted Lyons	223
4	Bobo Newsom	206
5	Earl Whitehill	192
6	Charlie Root	187
7	Freddie Fitzsimmons	186
8	Tommy Bridges	181
9	Lon Warneke	175
10	George Blaeholder	173
	Syl Johnson	173
12	Bump Hadley	167
13	Jesse Haines	165
14	Larry French	164
15	Rube Walberg	163

1942-1960

#	Player	HR
1	Robin Roberts	505
2	Warren Spahn	434
3	Early Wynn	338
4	Pedro Ramos	315
5	Murry Dickson	302
6	Lew Burdette	289
7	Bob Friend	286
8	Billy Pierce	284
9	Vern Law	268
10	Curt Simmons	255
11	Don Newcombe	252
12	Johnny Podres	242
13	Harvey Haddix	240
14	Bob Buhl	238
15	Whitey Ford	228

1961-1992

#	Player	HR
1	Fergie Jenkins	484
2	Phil Niekro	482
3	Don Sutton	472
4	Bert Blyleven	430
5	Frank Tanana	420
6	Steve Carlton	414
7	Gaylord Perry	399
8	Jim Kaat	395
9	Tom Seaver	380
10	Catfish Hunter	374
11	Jim Bunning	372
12	Jack Morris	357
13	Mickey Lolich	347
14	Charlie Hough	346
	Luis Tiant	346

Walks

#	Player	BB
1	Nolan Ryan	2755
2	Steve Carlton	1833
3	Phil Niekro	1809
4	Early Wynn	1775
5	Bob Feller	1764
6	Bobo Newsom	1732
7	Amos Rusie	1704
8	Gus Weyhing	1566
9	Charlie Hough	1542
10	Red Ruffing	1541
11	Bump Hadley	1442
12	Warren Spahn	1434
13	Earl Whitehill	1431
14	Tony Mullane	1408
15	Sam Jones	1396
16	Tom Seaver	1390
17	Gaylord Perry	1379
18	Mike Torrez	1371
19	Walter Johnson	1363
20	Don Sutton	1343
21	Bob Gibson	1336
22	Chick Fraser	1332
23	Bert Blyleven	1322
24	Sam McDowell	1312
25	Jim Palmer	1311
26	Mark Baldwin	1307
27	Adonis Terry	1298
28	Mickey Welch	1297
29	Burleigh Grimes	1295
30	Kid Nichols	1268
31	Joe Bush	1263
32	Joe Niekro	1262
33	Allie Reynolds	1261
34	Tommy John	1259
35	Jack Morris	1258
36	Bob Lemon	1251
37	Hal Newhouser	1249
38	George Mullin	1238
39	Tim Keefe	1224
40	Cy Young	1219
41	Red Faber	1213
42	Vic Willis	1212
43	Ted Breitenstein	1203
44	Brickyard Kennedy	1201
45	Frank Tanana	1200
46	Jerry Koosman	1198
47	Tommy Bridges	1192
48	John Clarkson	1191
49	Lefty Grove	1187
50	Vida Blue	1185
51	Billy Pierce	1178
52	Jack Stivetts	1155
53	Johnny Vander Meer	1132
54	Bill Hutchison	1129
55	Jerry Reuss	1127
56	Ted Lyons	1121
	Bucky Walters	1121
58	Mel Harder	1118
59	Earl Moore	1108
60	Bob Buhl	1105
61	Luis Tiant	1104
62	Mickey Lolich	1099
63	Lefty Gomez	1095
64	Virgil Trucks	1088
65	Whitey Ford	1086
66	Jim Kaat	1083
67	Eppa Rixey	1082
68	Eddie Plank	1072
69	Camilo Pascual	1069
70	Bob Turley	1068
71	Hooks Dauss	1067
72	Elton Chamberlain	1065
73	Bert Cunningham	1064
74	Curt Simmons	1063
75	Bill Donovan	1059
76	Murry Dickson	1058
	Jouett Meekin	1058
78	Vern Kennedy	1049
79	Dizzy Trout	1046
80	Howard Ehmke	1042
81	Wes Ferrell	1040
82	Tommy Byrne	1037
83	Red Ames	1034
84	Rube Walberg	1031
85	Jack Powell	1021
86	Bob Shawkey	1018
87	Steve Renko	1010
88	Jim Slaton	1004
89	Joe Coleman	1003
	Waite Hoyt	1003
	Dave Stieb	1003
92	Jim Bunning	1000
93	Jim Perry	998
94	Fergie Jenkins	997
95	Kirby Higbe	979
96	Doyle Alexander	978
	Johnny Klippstein	978
98	Rick Sutcliffe	975
99	Pink Hawley	974
100	Silver King	970

Fewest Walks per Game

1876-1892

1	Tommy Bond	0.58
2	George Bradley	0.67
3	Terry Larkin	0.71
4	John Ward	0.92
5	Fred Goldsmith	0.96
6	Jim Whitney	1.06
7	Bobby Mathews	1.11
8	Jim Galvin	1.13
9	Will White	1.26
10	Jack Lynch	1.38
11	Guy Hecker	1.51
12	Lee Richmond	1.53
13	Jim McCormick	1.58
14	Jumbo McGinnis	1.65
15	Ed Morris	1.67

1893-1919

1	Deacon Phillippe	1.25
2	Babe Adams	1.29
3	Addie Joss	1.41
4	Cy Young	1.49
5	Jesse Tannehill	1.56
6	Christy Mathewson	1.59
7	Nick Altrock	1.62
8	Pete Alexander	1.65
9	Noodles Hahn	1.69
10	Dick Rudolph	1.77
11	Al Orth	1.77
12	Slim Sallee	1.83
13	Bill Bernhard	1.83
14	Ed Siever	1.86
15	Ed Walsh	1.87

1920-1941

1	Red Lucas	1.61
2	Pete Donohue	1.80
3	Jesse Barnes	1.80
4	Carl Hubbell	1.82
5	Curt Davis	1.85
6	Paul Derringer	1.88
7	Bill Swift	1.93
8	Sherry Smith	1.93
9	Watty Clark	1.97
10	Jack Quinn	1.97
11	Syl Johnson	2.03
12	Dizzy Dean	2.07
13	Art Nehf	2.13
14	Sloppy Thurston	2.15
15	Eppa Rixey	2.17

1942-1960

1	Tiny Bonham	1.67
2	Robin Roberts	1.73
3	Lew Burdette	1.84
4	Ken Raffensberger	1.88
5	Vern Law	2.01
6	Don Newcombe	2.05
7	Dutch Leonard	2.06
8	Hal Brown	2.08
9	Larry Jansen	2.09
10	Bob Purkey	2.17
11	Dick Donovan	2.21
12	Bob Friend	2.23
13	Don Mossi	2.24
14	Preacher Roe	2.37
15	Ed Lopat	2.40

1961-1992

1	Fritz Peterson	1.73
2	Juan Marichal	1.82
3	Bret Saberhagen	1.83
4	Fergie Jenkins	1.99
5	Jim Barr	2.04
6	Dennis Eckersley	2.06
7	Lary Sorensen	2.08
8	John Candelaria	2.09
9	Bill Monbouquette	2.12
10	Ken Johnson	2.14
11	Jimmy Key	2.14
12	Bryn Smith	2.15
13	Jim Kaat	2.15
14	Ralph Terry	2.17
15	Bill Gullickson	2.18

Strikeouts

1	Nolan Ryan	5668
2	Steve Carlton	4136
3	Bert Blyleven	3701
4	Tom Seaver	3640
5	Don Sutton	3574
6	Gaylord Perry	3534
7	Walter Johnson	3509
8	Phil Niekro	3342
9	Fergie Jenkins	3192
10	Bob Gibson	3117
11	Jim Bunning	2855
12	Mickey Lolich	2832
13	Cy Young	2800
14	Frank Tanana	2657
15	Warren Spahn	2583
16	Bob Feller	2581
17	Jerry Koosman	2556
18	Tim Keefe	2545
19	Christy Mathewson	2502
20	Don Drysdale	2486
21	Jim Kaat	2461
22	Sam McDowell	2453
23	Luis Tiant	2416
24	Sandy Koufax	2396
25	Robin Roberts	2357
26	Early Wynn	2334
27	Rube Waddell	2316
28	Juan Marichal	2303
29	Jack Morris	2275
30	Lefty Grove	2266
31	Eddie Plank	2246
32	Tommy John	2245
33	Jim Palmer	2212
34	Pete Alexander	2198
35	Vida Blue	2175
36	Charlie Hough	2171
37	Camilo Pascual	2167
38	Dennis Eckersley	2118
39	Bobo Newsom	2082
40	Dazzy Vance	2045
41	Rick Reuschel	2015
42	Catfish Hunter	2012
43	Billy Pierce	1999
44	Red Ruffing	1987
45	John Clarkson	1978
46	Whitey Ford	1956
47	Amos Rusie	1934
48	Jerry Reuss	1907
49	Roger Clemens	1873
50	Kid Nichols	1868
51	Bob Welch	1862
52	Mickey Welch	1850
53	Charley Radbourn	1830
54	Mark Langston	1805
55	Tony Mullane	1803
56	Jim Galvin	1799
57	Hal Newhouser	1796
58	Ron Guidry	1778
59	Fernando Valenzuela	1764
60	Rudy May	1760
61	Joe Niekro	1747
62	Ed Walsh	1736
63	Bob Friend	1734
64	Joe Coleman	1728
	Milt Pappas	1728
66	Floyd Bannister	1723
67	Frank Viola	1722
68	Chief Bender	1711
69	Larry Jackson	1709
70	Jim McCormick	1704
71	Bob Veale	1703
72	Red Ames	1702
73	Charlie Buffinton	1700
74	Curt Simmons	1697
75	Dennis Martinez	1693
76	Dwight Gooden	1686
77	Carl Hubbell	1677
78	Tommy Bridges	1674
79	Gus Weyhing	1665
80	John Candelaria	1656
	Bruce Hurst	1656
82	Vic Willis	1651
83	Rick Wise	1647
84	Al Downing	1639
85	Mike Cuellar	1632
86	Dave Stieb	1631
87	Chris Short	1629
88	Andy Messersmith	1625
89	Jack Powell	1621
	Steve Rogers	1621
91	Ray Sadecki	1614
92	Claude Osteen	1612
93	Hoyt Wilhelm	1610
94	Jim Maloney	1605
95	Ken Holtzman	1601
96	Rube Marquard	1593
97	Woodie Fryman	1587
98	Jim Perry	1576
99	Harvey Haddix	1575
100	Rick Sutcliffe	1573

Strikeouts per Game

1	Nolan Ryan	9.59
2	Sandy Koufax	9.28
3	Sam McDowell	8.86
4	J.R. Richard	8.37
5	Roger Clemens	8.30
6	Bob Veale	7.96
7	Dwight Gooden	7.90
8	Mark Langston	7.84
9	Jim Maloney	7.81
10	Jose DeLeon	7.54
11	Mario Soto	7.54
12	Sam Jones	7.54
13	Rich Gossage	7.52
14	Bob Gibson	7.22
15	Steve Carlton	7.13
16	Rube Waddell	7.04
17	Mickey Lolich	7.01
18	Rollie Fingers	6.87
19	Tom Seaver	6.85
20	Jim Bunning	6.83
21	Fernando Valenzuela	6.74
22	Juan Pizarro	6.73
23	Bobby Bolin	6.71
24	Bert Blyleven	6.70
25	Ron Guidry	6.69
26	Ray Culp	6.69
27	Stan Williams	6.66
28	Camilo Pascual	6.65
29	Bob Turley	6.65
30	Don Wilson	6.60
31	Tug McGraw	6.59
32	Denny Lemaster	6.57
33	Andy Messersmith	6.56
34	Don Drysdale	6.52
35	Al Downing	6.50
36	Floyd Bannister	6.49
37	Toad Ramsey	6.49
38	Diego Segui	6.46
39	Dean Chance	6.43
40	Hoyt Wilhelm	6.43
41	Dennis Eckersley	6.42
42	Mike Scott	6.39
43	Fergie Jenkins	6.38
44	Moe Drabowsky	6.37
45	Earl Wilson	6.37
46	Harvey Haddix	6.34
47	Sonny Siebert	6.32
48	Chris Short	6.31
49	Bruce Hurst	6.30
50	Kevin Gross	6.28
51	Bill Singer	6.27
52	Luis Tiant	6.24
53	Turk Farrell	6.21
54	Dazzy Vance	6.20
55	Stu Miller	6.18
56	Ron Darling	6.18
57	Clay Kirby	6.17
58	Gary Bell	6.15
59	Gary Peters	6.14
60	Orel Hershiser	6.13
61	Denny McLain	6.12
62	Don Sutton	6.09
63	Mike Krukow	6.07
64	Bob Feller	6.07
65	Joe Coleman	6.05
66	Fred Norman	6.05
67	Rudy May	6.04
68	Frank Viola	6.01
69	Danny Darwin	6.01
70	Bret Saberhagen	6.01
71	Frank Tanana	6.00
72	Jerry Koosman	5.99
73	John Candelaria	5.95
74	Mark Gubicza	5.94
75	Gaylord Perry	5.94
76	Woodie Fryman	5.92
77	Juan Marichal	5.91
78	Dave Stewart	5.90
79	Steve Barber	5.89
80	John Montefusco	5.89
81	Bob Welch	5.87
82	Vida Blue	5.85
83	Mike Witt	5.85
84	Scott Sanderson	5.83
85	Joey Jay	5.81
86	Ray Sadecki	5.81
87	Jack Morris	5.80
88	Jim O'Toole	5.79
89	Dave Giusti	5.78
90	Jon Matlack	5.77
91	Tom Candiotti	5.76
92	Larry Dierker	5.76
93	Don Robinson	5.75
94	Rick Sutcliffe	5.75
95	Lindy McDaniel	5.73
96	Tony Cloninger	5.70
97	Johnny Podres	5.70
98	Mike Boddicker	5.68
99	Jim Bibby	5.64
100	Billy O'Dell	5.61

Ratio

1	Addie Joss	8.9
2	Ed Walsh	9.2
3	John Ward	9.4
4	Christy Mathewson	9.6
5	Tommy Bond	9.8
	Mordecai Brown	9.8
	Walter Johnson	9.8
8	George Bradley	9.9
9	Babe Adams	10.0
	Larry Corcoran	10.0
	Sandy Koufax	10.0
	Juan Marichal	10.0
13	Charlie Ferguson	10.1
	Terry Larkin	10.1
	Deacon Phillippe	10.1
16	Pete Alexander	10.2
	Roger Clemens	10.2
	Jim McCormick	10.2
	Ed Morris	10.2
	Tom Seaver	10.2
	Will White	10.2
22	Chief Bender	10.3
	Catfish Hunter	10.3
	Tim Keefe	10.3
	Rube Waddell	10.3
26	Nick Altrock	10.4
	Tiny Bonham	10.4
	Fred Goldsmith	10.4
	Noodles Hahn	10.4
	George McQuillan	10.4
	Gary Nolan	10.4
	Eddie Plank	10.4
	Charley Radbourn	10.4
	Bret Saberhagen	10.4
	Don Sutton	10.4
	Jim Whitney	10.4
	Hoyt Wilhelm	10.4
	Hooks Wiltse	10.4
	Cy Young	10.4
41	Eddie Cicotte	10.5
	Andy Messersmith	10.5
	Dick Rudolph	10.5
	Jeff Tesreau	10.5
	Doc White	10.5
46	Dennis Eckersley	10.6
	Rollie Fingers	10.6
	Dwight Gooden	10.6
	Carl Hubbell	10.6
	Sam Leever	10.6
	Denny McLain	10.6
	Robin Roberts	10.6
	Frank Smith	10.6
54	John Candelaria	10.7
	Bob Caruthers	10.7
	Jack Chesbro	10.7
	Don Drysdale	10.7
	Ron Guidry	10.7
	Guy Hecker	10.7
	Jumbo McGinnis	10.7
	Orval Overall	10.7
	Jim Palmer	10.7
	Ed Reulbach	10.7
	Slim Sallee	10.7
	George Winter	10.7
66	Mike Cuellar	10.8
	Bob Ewing	10.8
	Jim Galvin	10.8
	Orel Hershiser	10.8
	Barney Pelty	10.8
	Gaylord Perry	10.8
	Nap Rucker	10.8
	Dupee Shaw	10.8
	Mario Soto	10.8
	Warren Spahn	10.8
	Ralph Terry	10.8
77	Harry Brecheen	10.9
	Phil Douglas	10.9
	Eddie Fisher	10.9
	Dave Foutz	10.9
	Bob Gibson	10.9
	Claude Hendrix	10.9
	Jimmy Key	10.9
	Fritz Peterson	10.9
	Jim Scott	10.9
	Jack Taylor	10.9
	Luis Tiant	10.9
	Fred Toney	10.9
	John Tudor	10.9
	Carl Weilman	10.9
91	Henry Boyle	11.0
	Jim Bunning	11.0
	John Clarkson	11.0
	Dizzy Dean	11.0
	Whitey Ford	11.0
	Joe Horlen	11.0
	Don Mossi	11.0
	Don Newcombe	11.0
	Mike Scott	11.0
	Bryn Smith	11.0

Earned Run Average

1	Ed Walsh	1.82
2	Addie Joss	1.89
3	Mordecai Brown	2.06
4	John Ward	2.10
5	Christy Mathewson	2.13
6	Walter Johnson	2.16
	Rube Waddell	2.16
8	Orval Overall	2.23
9	Tommy Bond	2.25
10	Ed Reulbach	2.28
	Will White	2.28
12	Jim Scott	2.30
13	Eddie Plank	2.35
14	Larry Corcoran	2.36
15	Eddie Cicotte	2.38
	Ed Killian	2.38
	George McQuillan	2.38
18	Doc White	2.39
19	Nap Rucker	2.42
20	Terry Larkin	2.43
	Jim McCormick	2.43
	Jeff Tesreau	2.43
23	Chief Bender	2.46
24	Sam Leever	2.47
	Lefty Leifield	2.47
	Hooks Wiltse	2.47
27	Bob Ewing	2.49
	Hippo Vaughn	2.49
29	George Bradley	2.50
30	Hoyt Wilhelm	2.52
31	Noodles Hahn	2.55
32	Pete Alexander	2.56
	Slim Sallee	2.56
34	Deacon Phillippe	2.59
	Frank Smith	2.59
36	Ed Siever	2.60
37	Bob Rhoads	2.61
38	Tim Keefe	2.62
39	Red Ames	2.63
	Barney Pelty	2.63
	Vic Willis	2.63
	Cy Young	2.63
43	Claude Hendrix	2.65
44	Joe McGinnity	2.66
	Dick Rudolph	2.66
	Jack Taylor	2.66
47	Nick Altrock	2.67
	Charlie Ferguson	2.67
	Charley Radbourn	2.67
	Carl Weilman	2.67
51	Jack Chesbro	2.68
	Cy Falkenberg	2.68
53	Bill Donovan	2.69
	Fred Toney	2.69
55	Larry Cheney	2.70
56	Mickey Welch	2.71
57	Fred Goldsmith	2.73
58	Harry Howell	2.74
59	Howie Camnitz	2.75
	Whitey Ford	2.75
	Dummy Taylor	2.75
62	Babe Adams	2.76
	Sandy Koufax	2.76
	Dutch Leonard	2.76
65	Jeff Pfeffer	2.77
66	Jack Coombs	2.78
	Earl Moore	2.78
68	Tully Sparks	2.79
	Jesse Tannehill	2.79
70	Roger Clemens	2.80
	Phil Douglas	2.80
72	John Clarkson	2.81
73	Ray Fisher	2.82
	Ed Morris	2.82
	George Mullin	2.82
76	Bob Caruthers	2.83
77	Dave Foutz	2.84
78	Andy Messersmith	2.86
	Jim Palmer	2.86
	Tom Seaver	2.86
81	Jim Galvin	2.87
	Orel Hershiser	2.87
	George Winter	2.87
84	Willie Mitchell	2.88
85	Wilbur Cooper	2.89
	Stan Coveleski	2.89
	Juan Marichal	2.89
88	Rollie Fingers	2.90
89	Bob Gibson	2.91
90	Harry Brecheen	2.92
	Dean Chance	2.92
	Doc Crandall	2.92
	Guy Hecker	2.92
	Carl Mays	2.92
95	Dave Davenport	2.93
	Rich Gossage	2.93
97	Don Drysdale	2.95
	Jumbo McGinnis	2.95
	Kid Nichols	2.95
	Lefty Tyler	2.95

Earned Run Average (by era)

1876-1892

1	John Ward	2.10
2	Tommy Bond	2.25
3	Will White	2.28
4	Larry Corcoran	2.36
5	Terry Larkin	2.43
	Jim McCormick	2.43
7	George Bradley	2.50
8	Tim Keefe	2.62
9	Charlie Ferguson	2.67
	Charley Radbourn	2.67
11	Mickey Welch	2.71
12	Fred Goldsmith	2.73
13	John Clarkson	2.81
14	Ed Morris	2.82
15	Bob Caruthers	2.83

1893-1919

1	Ed Walsh	1.82
2	Addie Joss	1.89
3	Mordecai Brown	2.06
4	Christy Mathewson	2.13
5	Walter Johnson	2.16
	Rube Waddell	2.16
7	Orval Overall	2.23
8	Ed Reulbach	2.28
9	Jim Scott	2.30
10	Eddie Plank	2.35
11	Eddie Cicotte	2.38
	Ed Killian	2.38
	George McQuillan	2.38
14	Doc White	2.39
15	Nap Rucker	2.42

1920-1941

1	Wilbur Cooper	2.89
	Stan Coveleski	2.89
3	Carl Mays	2.92
4	Carl Hubbell	2.98
5	Dizzy Dean	3.02
6	Lefty Grove	3.06
7	Bob Shawkey	3.09
8	Red Faber	3.15
	Eppa Rixey	3.15
10	Urban Shocker	3.17
11	Lon Warneke	3.18
12	Art Nehf	3.20
13	Jesse Barnes	3.22
14	George Mogridge	3.23
15	2 players tied	3.24

1942-1960

1	Hoyt Wilhelm	2.52
2	Whitey Ford	2.75
3	Harry Brecheen	2.92
4	Mort Cooper	2.97
5	Max Lanier	3.01
6	Tiny Bonham	3.06
	Hal Newhouser	3.06
8	Warren Spahn	3.09
9	Sal Maglie	3.15
10	Ed Lopat	3.21
11	Bob Lemon	3.23
	Dizzy Trout	3.23
13	Stu Miller	3.24
14	Bob Feller	3.25
	Dutch Leonard	3.25

1961-1992

1	Sandy Koufax	2.76
2	Roger Clemens	2.80
3	Andy Messersmith	2.86
	Jim Palmer	2.86
	Tom Seaver	2.86
6	Orel Hershiser	2.87
7	Juan Marichal	2.89
8	Rollie Fingers	2.90
9	Bob Gibson	2.91
10	Dean Chance	2.92
11	Rich Gossage	2.93
12	Don Drysdale	2.95
13	Mel Stottlemyre	2.97
14	Dwight Gooden	2.99
15	Bob Veale	3.07

Adjusted Earned Run Average

1	Roger Clemens	151
2	Lefty Grove	148
3	Walter Johnson	147
4	Hoyt Wilhelm	146
5	Ed Walsh	145
6	Addie Joss	142
7	Mordecai Brown	139
	Kid Nichols	139
9	Cy Young	138
10	Christy Mathewson	136
11	Pete Alexander	135
	Rube Waddell	135
13	John Clarkson	134
14	Harry Brecheen	133
	Whitey Ford	133
	Noodles Hahn	133
17	Sandy Koufax	131
18	Dizzy Dean	130
	Carl Hubbell	130
	Hal Newhouser	130
	Amos Rusie	130
22	Stan Coveleski	128
23	Nig Cuppy	127
	Bob Gibson	127
	Rich Gossage	127
	Sal Maglie	127
	Tom Seaver	127
28	Tommy Bridges	126
	Bret Saberhagen	126
30	Lefty Gomez	125
	Tim Keefe	125
	Max Lanier	125
	Jim Palmer	125
	Mel Parnell	125
	Dazzy Vance	125
36	Dave Foutz	124
	Urban Shocker	124
	Dizzy Trout	124
39	Bob Caruthers	123
	Eddie Cicotte	123
	Mort Cooper	123
	Orel Hershiser	123
	Sam Leever	123
	Orval Overall	123
	Ed Reulbach	123
	Dave Stieb	123
	John Tudor	123
48	Larry Corcoran	122
	Bob Feller	122
	Charlie Ferguson	122
	Silver King	122
	Juan Marichal	122
	Eddie Plank	122
	Eddie Rommel	122
55	Don Drysdale	121
	Clark Griffith	121
	Jimmy Key	121
	Andy Messersmith	121
	Jack Stivetts	121
60	Tiny Bonham	120
	Joe McGinnity	120
	Deacon Phillippe	120
	Charley Radbourn	120
	Jim Scott	120
	Hippo Vaughn	120
	Will White	120
67	Dean Chance	119
	Red Faber	119
	Rollie Fingers	119
	Ron Guidry	119
	Thornton Lee	119
	Bob Lemon	119
	Dutch Leonard	119
	Carl Mays	119
	Jim McCormick	119
	Billy Pierce	119
	Nap Rucker	119
	Bobby Shantz	119
	Lon Warneke	119
80	Babe Adams	118
	Dwight Gooden	118
	Ted Lyons	118
	Sadie McMahon	118
	Tony Mullane	118
	Warren Spahn	118
	John Ward	118
	Vic Willis	118
88	Bert Blyleven	117
	Tom Candiotti	117
	Dennis Eckersley	117
	Wes Ferrell	117
	Mike Garcia	117
	Dolf Luque	117
	Gaylord Perry	117
	Toad Ramsey	117
	Bob Stanley	117
	Virgil Trucks	117
98	15 players tied	116

Adjusted ERA (by era)

1876-1892

1	John Clarkson	134
2	Tim Keefe	125
3	Dave Foutz	124
4	Bob Caruthers	123
5	Larry Corcoran	122
	Charlie Ferguson	122
	Silver King	122
8	Jack Stivetts	121
9	Charley Radbourn	120
	Will White	120
11	Jim McCormick	119
12	Sadie McMahon	118
	Tony Mullane	118
	John Ward	118
15	Toad Ramsey	117

1893-1919

1	Walter Johnson	147
2	Ed Walsh	145
3	Addie Joss	142
4	Mordecai Brown	139
	Kid Nichols	139
6	Cy Young	138
7	Christy Mathewson	136
8	Pete Alexander	135
	Rube Waddell	135
10	Noodles Hahn	133
11	Amos Rusie	130
12	Nig Cuppy	127
13	4 players tied	123

1920-1941

1	Lefty Grove	148
2	Dizzy Dean	130
	Carl Hubbell	130
4	Stan Coveleski	128
5	Tommy Bridges	126
6	Lefty Gomez	125
	Dazzy Vance	125
8	Urban Shocker	124
9	Eddie Rommel	122
10	Red Faber	119
	Thornton Lee	119
	Carl Mays	119
	Lon Warneke	119
14	Ted Lyons	118
15	2 players tied	117

1942-1960

1	Hoyt Wilhelm	146
2	Harry Brecheen	133
	Whitey Ford	133
4	Hal Newhouser	130
5	Sal Maglie	127
6	Max Lanier	125
	Mel Parnell	125
8	Dizzy Trout	124
9	Mort Cooper	123
10	Bob Feller	122
11	Tiny Bonham	120
12	Bob Lemon	119
	Dutch Leonard	119
	Billy Pierce	119
	Bobby Shantz	119

1961-1992

1	Roger Clemens	151
2	Sandy Koufax	131
3	Bob Gibson	127
	Rich Gossage	127
	Tom Seaver	127
6	Bret Saberhagen	126
7	Jim Palmer	125
8	Orel Hershiser	123
	Dave Stieb	123
	John Tudor	123
11	Juan Marichal	122
12	Don Drysdale	121
	Jimmy Key	121
	Andy Messersmith	121
15	3 players tied	119

Pitching Runs

#	Player	Runs
1	Cy Young	753
2	Walter Johnson	709
3	Lefty Grove	595
4	Kid Nichols	531
5	Pete Alexander	484
6	Warren Spahn	470
7	Christy Mathewson	420
8	Tom Seaver	419
9	Amos Rusie	416
10	Tim Keefe	404
11	Carl Hubbell	393
12	Whitey Ford	386
13	Bob Feller	385
14	Jim Palmer	374
15	John Clarkson	371
16	Lefty Gomez	322
17	Ted Lyons	313
	Nolan Ryan	313
19	Gaylord Perry	311
20	Ed Walsh	310
	Hoyt Wilhelm	310
22	Charley Radbourn	302
23	Mordecai Brown	295
24	Red Faber	294
25	Bob Gibson	290
26	Roger Clemens	287
27	Dazzy Vance	281
28	Red Ruffing	272
29	Bert Blyleven	271
30	Dutch Leonard	267
	Eddie Plank	267
32	Don Drysdale	266
33	Robin Roberts	264
34	Juan Marichal	262
35	Stan Coveleski	259
	Don Sutton	259
37	Hal Newhouser	257
38	Tommy Bridges	256
39	Bob Lemon	251
40	Billy Pierce	250
	Eppa Rixey	250
42	Dolf Luque	245
	Tony Mullane	245
44	Sandy Koufax	243
45	Rube Waddell	241
46	Steve Carlton	236
47	Clark Griffith	233
48	Carl Mays	217
49	Addie Joss	216
	Mickey Welch	216
51	Jim McCormick	215
52	Bob Caruthers	214
	Tommy John	214
54	Waite Hoyt	210
	Urban Shocker	210
56	Silver King	207
57	Dave Stieb	204
58	Nig Cuppy	201
	Ron Guidry	201
60	Eddie Cicotte	200
61	Will White	198
62	Harry Brecheen	194
63	Phil Niekro	192
64	Mel Harder	190
65	Lon Warneke	188
66	Dizzy Dean	187
67	Ed Lopat	186
	Joe McGinnity	186
69	Jim Bunning	179
	Ed Morris	179
	Eddie Rommel	179
72	Larry French	178
73	Dizzy Trout	177
74	Spud Chandler	176
75	Sam Leever	175
76	Freddie Fitzsimmons	174
	Mike Garcia	174
78	Sadie McMahon	172
	Andy Messersmith	172
	Vic Willis	172
81	Early Wynn	170
82	Thornton Lee	169
83	Wilbur Cooper	168
	Ed Reulbach	168
85	Charlie Buffinton	162
	Jack Quinn	162
87	Babe Adams	161
	Noodles Hahn	161
	Bret Saberhagen	161
	Bob Welch	161
91	Jim Galvin	160
92	Fergie Jenkins	157
93	Rich Gossage	156
	Sal Maglie	156
	Firpo Marberry	156
96	Dennis Eckersley	154
	Guy Hecker	154
	Orel Hershiser	154
99	Deacon Phillippe	153
100	2 players tied	152

Adjusted Pitching Runs

#	Player	Runs
1	Cy Young	819
2	Walter Johnson	671
3	Kid Nichols	653
4	Lefty Grove	643
5	Pete Alexander	522
6	John Clarkson	480
7	Tom Seaver	411
8	Christy Mathewson	403
9	Amos Rusie	381
10	Tim Keefe	373
11	Carl Hubbell	355
12	Bob Gibson	335
13	Warren Spahn	330
14	Roger Clemens	320
15	Bert Blyleven	318
16	Whitey Ford	315
	Jim Palmer	315
18	Hal Newhouser	305
	Gaylord Perry	305
20	Ted Lyons	302
21	Bob Feller	301
22	Phil Niekro	299
23	Tommy Bridges	291
24	Hoyt Wilhelm	289
25	Mordecai Brown	283
26	Steve Carlton	277
27	Stan Coveleski	276
28	Red Faber	274
29	Tony Mullane	270
	Ed Walsh	270
31	Charley Radbourn	267
32	Clark Griffith	266
	Dazzy Vance	266
34	Eddie Plank	263
35	Fergie Jenkins	254
36	Silver King	253
37	Eppa Rixey	248
	Rube Waddell	248
39	Juan Marichal	247
	Jack Stivetts	247
41	Dave Stieb	245
42	Nig Cuppy	239
	Robin Roberts	239
44	Dizzy Trout	232
45	Don Drysdale	230
46	Lefty Gomez	229
	Billy Pierce	229
48	Urban Shocker	226
49	Dutch Leonard	224
	Nolan Ryan	224
51	Sandy Koufax	221
52	Eddie Rommel	217
53	Jim McCormick	215
54	Vic Willis	208
55	Addie Joss	207
	Joe McGinnity	207
57	Bob Caruthers	206
58	Harry Brecheen	205
59	Jack Quinn	204
60	Dizzy Dean	201
61	Dolf Luque	200
62	Dennis Eckersley	196
	Mickey Welch	196
64	Eddie Cicotte	195
	Wes Ferrell	195
66	Bob Lemon	193
67	Jim Bunning	192
68	Carl Mays	189
69	Lon Warneke	188
70	Noodles Hahn	187
71	Rick Reuschel	183
72	Mel Harder	182
	Sadie McMahon	182
74	Wilbur Cooper	180
75	Tommy John	179
	Will White	179
77	Frank Dwyer	177
78	Red Ruffing	174
79	Waite Hoyt	173
	Luis Tiant	173
81	Thornton Lee	172
82	Larry French	171
83	Mel Parnell	170
84	Sam Leever	169
85	Bucky Walters	168
86	Ron Guidry	167
	Virgil Trucks	167
88	Bret Saberhagen	164
89	Jim Galvin	162
90	Babe Adams	161
	Charlie Buffinton	161
92	Sal Maglie	160
93	Larry Jackson	155
	Ed Reulbach	155
95	Steve Rogers	154
96	Rich Gossage	152
	Hippo Vaughn	152
98	Deacon Phillippe	150
	Joe Wood	150
100	Spud Chandler	149

Pitching Wins

#	Player	Wins
1	Walter Johnson	73.5
2	Cy Young	70.7
3	Lefty Grove	55.5
4	Pete Alexander	49.7
5	Warren Spahn	47.4
6	Kid Nichols	47.1
7	Christy Mathewson	44.2
8	Tom Seaver	43.8
9	Whitey Ford	39.3
10	Jim Palmer	38.8
11	Carl Hubbell	38.7
12	Bob Feller	37.5
13	Tim Keefe	36.3
14	Amos Rusie	35.7
15	Ed Walsh	33.4
16	John Clarkson	33.1
17	Gaylord Perry	32.6
18	Nolan Ryan	32.5
19	Hoyt Wilhelm	31.9
20	Mordecai Brown	31.4
21	Bob Gibson	30.5
22	Lefty Gomez	29.9
23	Ted Lyons	29.4
24	Red Faber	28.9
25	Roger Clemens	28.7
26	Eddie Plank	28.3
27	Bert Blyleven	27.8
28	Don Drysdale	27.7
29	Juan Marichal	27.6
30	Dazzy Vance	27.0
31	Don Sutton	26.9
32	Charley Radbourn	26.9
33	Robin Roberts	26.6
34	Dutch Leonard	26.4
35	Hal Newhouser	26.0
36	Stan Coveleski	25.9
37	Red Ruffing	25.6
38	Rube Waddell	25.3
39	Sandy Koufax	25.1
40	Eppa Rixey	25.1
41	Billy Pierce	25.1
42	Bob Lemon	25.0
43	Steve Carlton	24.7
44	Tommy Bridges	24.1
45	Dolf Luque	23.9
46	Addie Joss	23.4
47	Tommy John	22.1
48	Carl Mays	22.0
49	Tony Mullane	21.5
50	Eddie Cicotte	21.4
51	Clark Griffith	20.8
52	Urban Shocker	20.5
53	Dave Stieb	20.4
54	Waite Hoyt	20.2
55	Ron Guidry	20.1
56	Phil Niekro	20.0
57	Mickey Welch	19.7
58	Jim McCormick	19.6
59	Harry Brecheen	19.6
60	Lon Warneke	18.9
61	Bob Caruthers	18.8
62	Ed Lopat	18.8
63	Jim Bunning	18.6
64	Joe McGinnity	18.6
65	Dizzy Dean	18.6
66	Will White	18.2
67	Andy Messersmith	18.2
68	Ed Reulbach	18.1
69	Mel Harder	18.1
70	Dizzy Trout	17.9
71	Silver King	17.8
72	Sam Leever	17.8
73	Vic Willis	17.6
74	Spud Chandler	17.6
75	Larry French	17.6
76	Wilbur Cooper	17.5
77	Mike Garcia	17.4
78	Early Wynn	17.2
79	Nig Cuppy	17.1
80	Freddie Fitzsimmons	17.1
81	Eddie Rommel	17.0
82	Babe Adams	16.7
83	Bob Welch	16.6
84	Fergie Jenkins	16.4
85	Thornton Lee	16.3
86	Orel Hershiser	16.2
87	Jack Quinn	16.1
88	Rich Gossage	16.1
89	Bret Saberhagen	16.1
90	Ed Morris	16.0
91	Vida Blue	15.9
92	Noodles Hahn	15.8
93	Joe Wood	15.7
94	Dennis Eckersley	15.6
95	Sal Maglie	15.6
96	Bucky Walters	15.4
97	Deacon Phillippe	15.4
98	Steve Rogers	15.2
99	Bob Shawkey	15.2
100	Rollie Fingers	15.1

Adjusted Pitching Wins

#	Player	Wins
1	Cy Young	77.0
2	Walter Johnson	69.6
3	Lefty Grove	59.9
4	Kid Nichols	57.9
5	Pete Alexander	53.6
6	Tom Seaver	43.0
7	John Clarkson	42.8
8	Christy Mathewson	42.7
9	Bob Gibson	35.2
10	Carl Hubbell	35.0
11	Tim Keefe	33.5
12	Warren Spahn	33.3
13	Amos Rusie	32.7
14	Jim Palmer	32.7
15	Bert Blyleven	32.7
16	Whitey Ford	32.1
17	Gaylord Perry	32.0
18	Roger Clemens	32.0
19	Phil Niekro	31.2
20	Hal Newhouser	30.9
21	Mordecai Brown	30.1
22	Hoyt Wilhelm	29.7
23	Bob Feller	29.3
24	Ed Walsh	29.1
25	Steve Carlton	29.0
26	Ted Lyons	28.4
27	Eddie Plank	27.9
28	Stan Coveleski	27.6
29	Tommy Bridges	27.4
30	Red Faber	27.0
31	Fergie Jenkins	26.5
32	Rube Waddell	26.1
33	Juan Marichal	26.0
34	Dazzy Vance	25.6
35	Eppa Rixey	24.9
36	Dave Stieb	24.5
37	Robin Roberts	24.1
38	Don Drysdale	24.0
39	Clark Griffith	23.8
40	Charley Radbourn	23.7
41	Tony Mullane	23.7
42	Dizzy Trout	23.5
43	Nolan Ryan	23.3
44	Billy Pierce	23.0
45	Sandy Koufax	22.9
46	Addie Joss	22.4
47	Dutch Leonard	22.1
48	Urban Shocker	22.1
49	Silver King	21.8
50	Vic Willis	21.3
51	Lefty Gomez	21.3
52	Jack Stivetts	20.9
53	Eddie Cicotte	20.8
54	Harry Brecheen	20.7
55	Joe McGinnity	20.7
56	Eddie Rommel	20.6
57	Nig Cuppy	20.4
58	Jack Quinn	20.3
59	Dizzy Dean	20.0
60	Jim Bunning	19.9
61	Dennis Eckersley	19.9
62	Jim McCormick	19.6
63	Dolf Luque	19.5
64	Bob Lemon	19.2
65	Rick Reuschel	19.1
66	Carl Mays	19.1
67	Lon Warneke	18.9
68	Wilbur Cooper	18.7
69	Tommy John	18.5
70	Noodles Hahn	18.3
71	Luis Tiant	18.2
72	Bob Caruthers	18.1
73	Wes Ferrell	18.0
74	Mickey Welch	17.9
75	Mel Harder	17.3
76	Sam Leever	17.2
77	Bucky Walters	17.1
78	Virgil Trucks	16.9
79	Larry French	16.9
80	Mel Parnell	16.8
81	Babe Adams	16.7
82	Ron Guidry	16.7
83	Ed Reulbach	16.7
84	Waite Hoyt	16.6
85	Thornton Lee	16.6
86	Hippo Vaughn	16.5
87	Will White	16.5
88	Bret Saberhagen	16.4
89	Red Ruffing	16.4
90	Larry Jackson	16.1
91	Steve Rogers	16.1
92	Sal Maglie	16.0
93	Joe Wood	15.7
94	Rich Gossage	15.7
95	Sadie McMahon	15.5
96	Andy Messersmith	15.3
97	Don Sutton	15.2
98	Deacon Phillippe	15.1
99	John Tudor	15.1
100	Frank Dwyer	15.0

Opponents' Batting Average

1	Nolan Ryan	.203
2	Sandy Koufax	.205
3	Andy Messersmith	.212
	J.R. Richard	.212
5	Sam McDowell	.215
6	Hoyt Wilhelm	.216
7	Ed Walsh	.218
8	Mario Soto	.220
	Bob Turley	.220
10	Addie Joss	.223
	Orval Overall	.223
	Jeff Tesreau	.223
13	Jim Maloney	.224
	Ed Reulbach	.224
15	Jose DeLeon	.225
16	Roger Clemens	.226
	Larry Corcoran	.226
	Tim Keefe	.226
	Tom Seaver	.226
20	Rich Gossage	.227
	Walter Johnson	.227
22	Bob Gibson	.228
	Rube Waddell	.228
	Don Wilson	.228
25	Charlie Hough	.230
	Sam Jones	.230
	Jim Palmer	.230
28	Bobby Bolin	.231
	Bob Feller	.231
	Catfish Hunter	.231
31	Al Downing	.232
	Johnny Vander Meer	.232
	Stan Williams	.232
34	Mordecai Brown	.233
	Charlie Ferguson	.233
	Dwight Gooden	.233
37	Dean Chance	.234
	Larry Cheney	.234
	Denny McLain	.234
	Toad Ramsey	.234
	Amos Rusie	.234
42	Ray Culp	.235
	Rollie Fingers	.235
	Whitey Ford	.235
	Dave Foutz	.235
	Orel Hershiser	.235
	Ed Morris	.235
	Tony Mullane	.235
	John Ward	.235
50	Moe Drabowsky	.236
	Christy Mathewson	.236
	Don Sutton	.236
	Luis Tiant	.236
	Bob Veale	.236
55	Vida Blue	.237
	Mark Langston	.237
	Juan Marichal	.237
	Tug McGraw	.237
	Juan Pizarro	.237
	Frank Smith	.237
61	Rudy May	.238
	Allie Reynolds	.238
	Jim Scott	.238
	Sonny Siebert	.238
	Dave Stieb	.238
66	Gary Bell	.239
	Chief Bender	.239
	Bill Donovan	.239
	Don Drysdale	.239
	Hal Newhouser	.239
	Gary Nolan	.239
	Barney Pelty	.239
	Eddie Plank	.239
	Dupee Shaw	.239
	Will White	.239
76	Steve Carlton	.240
	Bob Caruthers	.240
	John Clarkson	.240
	Mort Cooper	.240
	Billy Pierce	.240
	Mike Scott	.240
	Bill Singer	.240
	Virgil Trucks	.240
84	Jack Coombs	.241
	Kirby Higbe	.241
	Bob Lemon	.241
	George McQuillan	.241
	Earl Moore	.241
	Charley Radbourn	.241
	Fernando Valenzuela	.241
	Hooks Wiltse	.241
92	10 players tied	.242

Opponents' On Base Pctg.

1	John Ward	.254
2	Addie Joss	.260
3	George Bradley	.262
4	Terry Larkin	.263
5	Larry Corcoran	.264
	Ed Walsh	.264
7	Tommy Bond	.267
8	Will White	.268
9	Charlie Ferguson	.270
10	Christy Mathewson	.273
	Ed Morris	.273
12	Jim McCormick	.274
13	Fred Goldsmith	.275
	Tim Keefe	.275
	Jim Whitney	.275
16	Sandy Koufax	.276
17	Mordecai Brown	.278
	Juan Marichal	.278
	Charley Radbourn	.278
20	Walter Johnson	.279
	Dupee Shaw	.279
22	Guy Hecker	.281
	Jumbo McGinnis	.281
24	Roger Clemens	.283
	Deacon Phillippe	.283
26	Babe Adams	.284
	Jim Galvin	.284
28	Bob Caruthers	.285
	Bobby Mathews	.285
	Tom Seaver	.285
31	Dave Foutz	.286
32	Catfish Hunter	.287
	Gary Nolan	.287
	Don Sutton	.287
	Cy Young	.287
36	Pete Alexander	.288
	Bret Saberhagen	.288
	Rube Waddell	.288
39	Tiny Bonham	.289
	Henry Boyle	.289
	Noodles Hahn	.289
	Fergie Jenkins	.289
	Jack Lynch	.289
	Andy Messersmith	.289
45	Chief Bender	.290
	Dennis Eckersley	.290
	Hoyt Wilhelm	.290
	Hooks Wiltse	.290
49	Nick Altrock	.291
	John Clarkson	.291
	Carl Hubbell	.291
52	Charlie Buffinton	.292
	Denny McLain	.292
	Eddie Plank	.292
	Mickey Welch	.292
	Doc White	.292
57	Dwight Gooden	.293
	Sam Leever	.293
	Robin Roberts	.293
60	Don Drysdale	.294
	Ron Guidry	.294
	George McQuillan	.294
63	Rollie Fingers	.295
	Toad Ramsey	.295
	Jeff Tesreau	.295
66	Jack Chesbro	.296
	Orel Hershiser	.296
	Jim Palmer	.296
	Mario Soto	.296
	Ralph Terry	.296
71	John Candelaria	.297
	Gaylord Perry	.297
	Frank Smith	.297
	Warren Spahn	.297
	George Winter	.297
76	Harry Brecheen	.298
	Eddie Cicotte	.298
	Dizzy Dean	.298
	Jimmy Key	.298
	Tony Mullane	.298
	Orval Overall	.298
	Lee Richmond	.298
	Dick Rudolph	.298
	Jack Taylor	.298
	Luis Tiant	.298
86	Jim Bunning	.299
	Mike Cuellar	.299
	Eddie Fisher	.299
	Bob Gibson	.299
	Don Mossi	.299
	Don Newcombe	.299
	Ed Reulbach	.299
	Slim Sallee	.299
94	Mort Cooper	.300
	Joe Horlen	.300
	Kid Nichols	.300
	Fritz Peterson	.300
	Mike Scott	.300
	Bryn Smith	.300
100	4 players tied	.301

Wins Above Team

1	Cy Young	99.7
2	Walter Johnson	90.0
3	Pete Alexander	81.6
4	Christy Mathewson	64.9
5	Lefty Grove	62.9
6	Tom Seaver	58.9
7	Jim McCormick	56.3
8	Jim Galvin	53.7
9	Charley Radbourn	50.3
10	Warren Spahn	45.8
11	Clark Griffith	45.6
12	Whitey Ford	44.4
13	Will White	43.5
14	Roger Clemens	41.6
15	Juan Marichal	38.7
16	Bob Feller	36.8
	Mickey Welch	36.8
18	Ted Lyons	36.2
	Phil Niekro	36.2
20	Amos Rusie	35.9
21	Tony Mullane	35.8
	Eddie Plank	35.8
23	Jesse Tannehill	35.6
24	Charlie Buffinton	35.0
25	Wes Ferrell	34.8
26	Carl Hubbell	34.6
27	Kid Nichols	34.4
28	Steve Carlton	33.5
29	Dazzy Vance	33.2
30	Jim Devlin	32.5
31	Joe McGinnity	32.4
32	Dwight Gooden	31.8
33	Ed Walsh	31.5
34	Bob Gibson	31.0
35	Ed Morris	30.8
	Eddie Rommel	30.8
37	Sandy Koufax	30.6
38	Bob Caruthers	30.4
39	Jim Palmer	30.2
	Urban Shocker	30.2
41	Robin Roberts	30.0
42	Guy Hecker	29.5
	Sadie McMahon	29.5
44	Fergie Jenkins	29.3
45	Ron Guidry	29.1
46	Mordecai Brown	29.0
47	Addie Joss	28.7
48	Dizzy Dean	27.6
49	Bobby Mathews	26.7
50	Schoolboy Rowe	26.5
51	Sam Leever	25.7
52	John Candelaria	25.4
	Rip Sewell	25.4
54	Frank Killen	25.1
55	Jack Chesbro	24.8
56	Nap Rucker	24.7
57	Red Lucas	24.5
58	Russ Ford	24.3
59	Herb Pennock	23.9
60	Charlie Ferguson	23.6
61	Red Faber	23.5
62	Johnny Allen	23.4
	Chief Bender	23.4
64	John Clarkson	23.2
65	Gaylord Perry	23.1
	Rick Reuschel	23.1
67	Joe Wood	23.0
68	Noodles Hahn	22.9
	Firpo Marberry	22.9
70	Orel Hershiser	22.7
	Sal Maglie	22.7
72	Gus Weyhing	22.6
73	Tim Keefe	22.5
	Bob Welch	22.5
75	Tommy John	22.2
	Jack Morris	22.2
77	Carl Mays	21.6
78	Burleigh Grimes	21.3
	Claude Passeau	21.3
	Hippo Vaughn	21.3
81	Spud Chandler	21.2
82	Dutch Leonard	21.1
	J.R. Richard	21.1
84	John Tudor	21.0
	George Uhle	21.0
	Bucky Walters	21.0
87	Jim Maloney	20.9
88	Slim Sallee	20.6
89	Vida Blue	20.4
	Hal Newhouser	20.4
91	Bert Blyleven	20.3
	Freddie Fitzsimmons	20.3
	Teddy Higuera	20.3
	Dave Stieb	20.3
95	Babe Adams	20.2
	Allie Reynolds	20.2
97	Ted Breitenstein	20.1
	Stan Coveleski	20.1
99	Art Nehf	20.0
100	2 players tied	19.9

Wins Above League

1	Cy Young	413.5
2	Walter Johnson	348.0
3	Jim Galvin	334.0
4	Warren Spahn	304.0
5	Nolan Ryan	303.0
6	Phil Niekro	296.0
7	Pete Alexander	290.5
8	Don Sutton	290.0
9	Gaylord Perry	289.5
10	Steve Carlton	286.5
11	Kid Nichols	284.5
12	Tim Keefe	283.5
13	Christy Mathewson	280.5
14	Early Wynn	272.0
15	Bert Blyleven	268.5
16	Robin Roberts	265.5
17	Jim Kaat	260.0
	Eddie Plank	260.0
19	Tommy John	259.5
20	Eppa Rixey	258.5
	Mickey Welch	258.5
22	Tom Seaver	258.0
23	Fergie Jenkins	255.0
24	John Clarkson	253.0
25	Tony Mullane	252.0
	Charley Radbourn	252.0
27	Jack Powell	249.5
28	Red Ruffing	249.0
29	Gus Weyhing	248.0
30	Ted Lyons	245.0
31	Burleigh Grimes	241.0
32	Jim McCormick	239.5
33	Red Faber	233.5
34	Jack Quinn	232.5
35	Vic Willis	227.0
36	Frank Tanana	226.0
37	Sam Jones	223.0
38	Lefty Grove	220.5
39	Paul Derringer	217.5
40	Bobo Newsom	216.5
41	Jerry Koosman	215.5
42	Bob Feller	214.0
43	Bob Friend	213.5
44	Bob Gibson	212.5
	Joe Niekro	212.5
46	George Mullin	212.0
47	Jim Palmer	210.0
48	Waite Hoyt	209.5
	Amos Rusie	209.5
50	Jerry Reuss	205.5
51	Mel Harder	204.5
52	Jim Bunning	204.0
	Mickey Lolich	204.0
54	Carl Hubbell	203.5
55	Jack Morris	202.5
	Rick Reuschel	202.5
57	Hooks Dauss	202.0
58	Earl Whitehill	201.5
59	Herb Pennock	201.0
60	Luis Tiant	200.5
61	Will White	197.5
	Jim Whitney	197.5
63	Wilbur Cooper	197.0
64	Charlie Hough	196.5
	Al Orth	196.5
	Adonis Terry	196.5
67	Claude Osteen	195.5
68	Catfish Hunter	195.0
69	Jim Perry	194.5
70	Joe McGinnity	194.0
71	Chick Fraser	193.5
72	Charlie Buffinton	192.5
	Juan Marichal	192.5
74	Clark Griffith	191.5
75	Billy Pierce	190.0
76	Joe Bush	189.0
	Rube Marquard	189.0
78	Larry Jackson	188.5
	Tom Zachary	188.5
80	Curt Simmons	188.0
81	Don Drysdale	187.5
82	Dolf Luque	186.5
	Milt Pappas	186.5
84	Dutch Leonard	186.0
85	Vida Blue	185.0
86	Mordecai Brown	184.5
	Rick Wise	184.5
88	Doyle Alexander	184.0
	Larry French	184.0
	Jesse Haines	184.0
	Lee Meadows	184.0
92	George Uhle	183.0
93	Freddie Fitzsimmons	181.5
94	Charlie Root	180.5
95	Bucky Walters	179.0
96	Eddie Cicotte	178.5
	Stan Coveleski	178.5
	Silver King	178.5
	Hal Newhouser	178.5
100	Murry Dickson	176.5

Relief Games

1	Kent Tekulve	1050
2	Hoyt Wilhelm	1018
3	Gene Garber	922
4	Lindy McDaniel	913
5	Rollie Fingers	907
6	Sparky Lyle	899
7	Rich Gossage	890
8	Don McMahon	872
9	Roy Face	821
10	Jeff Reardon	811
11	Tug McGraw	785
12	Lee Smith	781
13	Darold Knowles	757
14	Tom Burgmeier	742
	Gary Lavelle	742
16	Ron Perranoski	736
17	Willie Hernandez	733
18	Clay Carroll	703
	Greg Minton	703
20	Mike Marshall	699
21	Bill Campbell	691
22	Dan Quisenberry	674
23	Bruce Sutter	661
24	Jesse Orosco	653
25	Ted Abernathy	647
26	Dave LaRoche	632
27	Eddie Fisher	627
28	Paul Lindblad	623
29	Bob McClure	611
	Stu Miller	611
31	Grant Jackson	609
32	Dave Smith	608
33	Larry Andersen	605
34	Elias Sosa	598
35	Bob Miller	595
36	Pedro Borbon	589
37	Doug Bair	579
38	Craig Lefferts	577
39	Bob Locker	576
40	Terry Forster	575
41	Steve Bedrosian	562
42	Dave Righetti	557
43	Bob Stanley	552
44	Johnny Klippstein	550
45	Jim Brewer	549
46	Al Hrabosky	544
	Tippy Martinez	544
48	Juan Agosto	535
	Dave Giusti	535
50	3 players tied	533

Relief Wins

1	Hoyt Wilhelm	124
2	Lindy McDaniel	119
3	Rich Gossage	108
4	Rollie Fingers	107
5	Sparky Lyle	99
6	Roy Face	96
7	Gene Garber	94
	Kent Tekulve	94
9	Mike Marshall	92
10	Don McMahon	90
11	Tug McGraw	89
12	Clay Carroll	88
13	Bob Stanley	85
14	Bill Campbell	80
	Gary Lavelle	80
16	Tom Burgmeier	79
	Stu Miller	79
	Ron Perranoski	79
19	Johnny Murphy	73
20	John Hiller	72
21	Mark Clear	71
	Dick Hall	71
23	Willie Hernandez	70
24	Pedro Borbon	69
25	Jeff Reardon	68
	Bruce Sutter	68
27	Lee Smith	65
28	Al Hrabosky	64
29	Darold Knowles	63
	Clem Labine	63
	Dave LaRoche	63
	Jesse Orosco	63
33	Jim Brewer	62
	Turk Farrell	62
	Eddie Fisher	62
	Grant Jackson	62
	Paul Lindblad	62
	Frank Linzy	62
39	Joe Heving	60
40	Steve Bedrosian	59
	Johnny Klippstein	59
	Elias Sosa	59
43	John Franco	58
	Aurelio Lopez	58
	Phil Regan	58
46	Ted Abernathy	57
	Bob Locker	57
	Roger McDowell	57
	Greg Minton	57
50	2 players tied	56

Relief Losses

1	Gene Garber	108
2	Hoyt Wilhelm	103
3	Rollie Fingers	101
4	Mike Marshall	98
5	Kent Tekulve	90
6	Lindy McDaniel	88
7	Roy Face	82
8	Rich Gossage	80
9	Sparky Lyle	76
10	Gary Lavelle	75
11	Ron Perranoski	74
12	Darold Knowles	71
	Jeff Reardon	71
	Bruce Sutter	71
15	Tug McGraw	69
	Lee Smith	69
17	Stu Miller	67
18	Clay Carroll	66
	Don McMahon	66
20	Bill Campbell	65
21	Greg Minton	62
22	Bob Stanley	61
23	John Hiller	60
24	Roger McDowell	58
25	Frank Linzy	57
26	Jesse Orosco	56
27	Steve Bedrosian	55
	Willie Hernandez	55
29	Tom Burgmeier	53
	Ron Davis	53
	Dave Smith	53
32	Jim Kern	52
	Randy Moffitt	52
34	Turk Farrell	51
	Eddie Fisher	51
	Dave LaRoche	51
	Claude Raymond	51
38	Dale Murray	50
	Dave Righetti	50
	Al Worthington	50
41	Jim Brewer	49
	Craig Lefferts	49
	Elias Sosa	49
44	Ted Abernathy	48
	Mark Clear	48
46	Don Elston	47
	Ron Kline	47
48	4 players tied	46

Relief Innings Pitched

1	Hoyt Wilhelm	1871.0
2	Lindy McDaniel	1694.0
3	Rollie Fingers	1500.1
4	Rich Gossage	1461.2
5	Gene Garber	1452.2
6	Kent Tekulve	1436.1
7	Sparky Lyle	1390.1
8	Tug McGraw	1301.1
9	Don McMahon	1297.0
10	Mike Marshall	1259.1
11	Tom Burgmeier	1248.2
12	Roy Face	1212.1
13	Clay Carroll	1204.2
14	Eddie Fisher	1186.0
15	Bill Campbell	1177.1
16	Ron Perranoski	1170.2
17	Bob Stanley	1157.0
18	Stu Miller	1095.2
19	Greg Minton	1087.1
20	Gary Lavelle	1077.2
21	Jeff Reardon	1061.0
22	Darold Knowles	1052.1
23	Paul Lindblad	1043.1
24	Dan Quisenberry	1043.1
25	Bruce Sutter	1042.1
26	Johnny Klippstein	1039.2
27	Lee Smith	1029.2
28	Pedro Borbon	1016.1
29	Willie Hernandez	994.1
30	Bob Miller	992.2
31	Dave LaRoche	975.3
32	Ted Abernathy	970.0
33	John Hiller	962.2
34	Elias Sosa	905.0
35	Dale Murray	901.1
36	Larry Andersen	896.1
37	Doug Bair	889.1
38	Terry Forster	888.0
39	Bob Locker	879.0
40	Dennis Lamp	876.0
41	Jim Brewer	861.0
42	Aurelio Lopez	860.0
43	Dick Tidrow	857.2
44	Jesse Orosco	857.2
45	Dave Giusti	854.2
46	Clem Labine	854.0
47	Grant Jackson	848.1
48	Al Worthington	838.0
49	Diego Segui	829.0
50	Ron Kline	827.2

Relief Points

1	Rollie Fingers	795
2	Jeff Reardon	779
3	Lee Smith	771
4	Rich Gossage	752
5	Bruce Sutter	665
6	Hoyt Wilhelm	599
7	Sparky Lyle	598
8	Dan Quisenberry	554
9	Dave Righetti	542
10	John Franco	524
11	Gene Garber	516
12	Roy Face	496
13	Lindy McDaniel	494
14	Dave Smith	485
15	Tom Henke	474
16	Tug McGraw	469
17	Kent Tekulve	466
18	Mike Marshall	462
19	Ron Perranoski	442
20	Steve Bedrosian	431
21	Bobby Thigpen	423
22	Don McMahon	420
23	Stu Miller	399
24	Clay Carroll	396
25	Willie Hernandez	379
26	Bob Stanley	373
27	Dave Giusti	363
28	Ted Abernathy	362
29	Doug Jones	357
	Gary Lavelle	357
31	Jay Howell	355
32	Roger McDowell	354
33	Greg Minton	352
34	Bill Campbell	347
35	Darold Knowles	341
36	Jim Brewer	339
37	John Hiller	336
38	Dave LaRoche	327
39	Mitch Williams	324
40	Johnny Murphy	317
41	Jesse Orosco	314
42	Tom Burgmeier	309
43	Dick Radatz	305
44	Terry Forster	302
45	Ron Davis	301
46	Tippy Martinez	300
47	Jack Aker	295
48	Todd Worrell	291
49	Frank Linzy	289
50	Al Hrabosky	287

Relief Ranking

1	Hoyt Wilhelm	334
2	Rich Gossage	289
3	Lee Smith	245
4	Bruce Sutter	215
5	Rollie Fingers	211
6	Dan Quisenberry	207
7	John Franco	204
	Kent Tekulve	204
9	Sparky Lyle	179
10	Mike Marshall	175
11	John Hiller	173
12	Tom Henke	170
	Jeff Reardon	170
14	Bob Stanley	168
15	Tug McGraw	159
16	Gary Lavelle	152
17	Gene Garber	148
18	Lindy McDaniel	143
19	Clay Carroll	138
	Jesse Orosco	138
21	Doug Jones	136
	Dave Righetti	136
23	Dave Smith	131
24	Ron Perranoski	128
25	Stu Miller	125
26	Willie Hernandez	123
27	Don McMahon	114
28	Jeff Montgomery	112
29	Johnny Murphy	111
30	Todd Worrell	110
31	Steve Farr	109
32	Bobby Thigpen	105
33	Dan Plesac	104
34	Gregg Olson	103
35	Roy Face	102
36	Tom Burgmeier	99
37	Tim Burke	98
	Terry Forster	98
	Mike Henneman	98
	Greg Minton	98
41	Jay Howell	97
	Frank Linzy	97
43	Bryan Harvey	96
44	Mark Eichhorn	93
	Steve Howe	93
46	Greg Harris	92
47	Dick Hall	90
48	Steve Bedrosian	89
49	Rick Aguilera	88
50	Dick Radatz	85

Relievers' Runs

1	Hoyt Wilhelm	261
2	Rich Gossage	182
3	Rollie Fingers	156
4	Dan Quisenberry	144
5	Kent Tekulve	128
6	Sparky Lyle	121
7	Tug McGraw	110
8	Lee Smith	104
9	Clay Carroll	100
	Mike Marshall	100
	Ron Perranoski	100
12	Tom Henke	99
	John Hiller	99
	Gary Lavelle	99
	Don McMahon	99
16	Stu Miller	96
17	Lindy McDaniel	94
18	Jesse Orosco	93
	Bob Stanley	93
20	Bruce Sutter	91
21	John Franco	89
	Dave Smith	89
23	Mark Eichhorn	88
	Greg Minton	88
25	Johnny Murphy	85
26	Jeff Reardon	84
27	Dave Righetti	80
28	Greg Harris	79
29	Tom Burgmeier	78
30	Steve Farr	77
31	Willie Hernandez	74
32	Jim Brewer	73
33	Tim Burke	72
34	Terry Forster	71
	Jeff Montgomery	71
36	Bob Miller	70
37	Jay Howell	67
38	Dick Hall	66
	Doug Jones	66
40	Bob Locker	64
41	Larry Andersen	63
	Roy Face	63
43	Gene Garber	62
	Marv Grissom	62
	Sammy Stewart	62
46	Frank Linzy	60
47	Mike Henneman	59
	Darold Knowles	59
49	Steve Howe	58
50	3 players tied	57

Adjusted Relievers' Runs

1	Hoyt Wilhelm	245
2	Rich Gossage	177
3	Dan Quisenberry	147
4	Kent Tekulve	141
5	Lee Smith	126
6	Bob Stanley	121
7	Rollie Fingers	120
8	Sparky Lyle	119
9	Bruce Sutter	116
10	John Hiller	115
11	Tug McGraw	113
12	Lindy McDaniel	108
13	Mike Marshall	103
14	Tom Henke	101
15	John Franco	98
16	Clay Carroll	97
17	Gary Lavelle	96
18	Gene Garber	93
19	Mark Eichhorn	90
20	Greg Harris	88
	Jesse Orosco	88
22	Tom Burgmeier	87
	Jeff Reardon	87
24	Don McMahon	85
25	Willie Hernandez	84
	Ron Perranoski	84
27	Stu Miller	83
28	Steve Farr	80
29	Terry Forster	78
30	Greg Minton	75
31	Dave Righetti	73
	Dave Smith	73
33	Jeff Montgomery	71
34	Tim Burke	70
35	Doug Jones	67
36	Johnny Murphy	66
37	Larry Andersen	63
	Rob Dibble	63
39	Bill Campbell	61
	Roy Face	61
	Marv Grissom	61
42	Dick Hall	60
43	Frank Linzy	59
44	Bob Locker	58
45	Dan Plesac	57
46	Mike Henneman	56
47	Jim Brewer	55
	Bill Henry	55
	Steve Howe	55
50	3 players tied	54

Clutch Pitching Index

1	Ed Killian	117
2	Bob Rhoads	116
	Ed Siever	116
4	Win Mercer	115
5	Ron Kline	113
	Bill Lee	113
	Will White	113
8	Al Benton	112
	Ed Lopat	112
	Bob Stanley	112
	Tom Zachary	112
12	Whitey Ford	111
	Preacher Roe	111
14	Frank Dwyer	110
	Max Lanier	110
	Bob Miller	110
	Gerry Staley	110
	Bill Wight	110
19	Steve Blass	109
	Bob Buhl	109
	Max Butcher	109
	Dan Casey	109
	Lefty Leifield	109
	Sal Maglie	109
	Mel Parnell	109
	Bob Shaw	109
	Geoff Zahn	109
28	Steve Barber	108
	Sheriff Blake	108
	Lefty Grove	108
	Carl Morton	108
	George Mullin	108
	Dizzy Trout	108
	Bob Veale	108
35	Nelson Briles	107
	Lloyd Brown	107
	Nixey Callahan	107
	Nig Cuppy	107
	Larry French	107
	Clark Griffith	107
	Claude Osteen	107
	Togie Pittinger	107
	Eddie Rommel	107
	Dutch Ruether	107
	Eddie Smith	107
	Dummy Taylor	107
	Steve Trout	107
	Mickey Welch	107
49	Jim Bagby	106
	Mark Baldwin	106
	Roger Craig	106
	Red Donahue	106
	Red Faber	106
	Dave Foutz	106
	Mel Harder	106
	Joe Haynes	106
	Guy Hecker	106
	Tommy John	106
	Jim McCormick	106
	Cal McLish	106
	Jeff Pfeffer	106
	Howie Pollet	106
	Nap Rucker	106
	Jim Scott	106
	Sherry Smith	106
	Sloppy Thurston	106
	John Tudor	106
	Rube Waddell	106
	Bucky Walters	106
70	Jack Curtis	105
	Murry Dickson	105
	Bill Dugglesby	105
	Dick Ellsworth	105
	Wes Ferrell	105
	Fred Frankhouse	105
	Gene Garber	105
	Mike Garcia	105
	Ken Heintzelman	105
	Johnny Klippstein	105
	Frank Lary	105
	Thornton Lee	105
	Dutch Leonard	105
	Ted Lyons	105
	Bobby Mathews	105
	Tug McGraw	105
	Stu Miller	105
	Clarence Mitchell	105
	George Mogridge	105
	Shane Rawley	105
	Allie Reynolds	105
	Lee Richmond	105
	Johnny Sain	105
	Jim Slaton	105
	Al Smith	105
	George Suggs	105
	Jesse Tannehill	105
	Hippo Vaughn	105
	Lon Warneke	105
	Wilbur Wood	105
100	35 players tied	104

Pitcher Batting Runs

1	Red Ruffing	135
2	Bob Caruthers	110
3	Wes Ferrell	105
4	Walter Johnson	97
	Red Lucas	97
6	George Uhle	93
7	George Mullin	89
	Jim Whitney	89
9	Guy Hecker	86
	Bob Lemon	86
11	Warren Spahn	82
12	Don Newcombe	81
13	Schoolboy Rowe	76
14	Babe Ruth	75
15	Jack Stivetts	72
16	Early Wynn	70
17	Bob Gibson	68
18	Al Orth	64
19	Carl Mays	62
20	Earl Wilson	60
21	Don Drysdale	59
22	Bucky Walters	58
23	Doc Crandall	57
	Gary Peters	57
25	Christy Mathewson	55
26	Jim Tobin	54
27	Jesse Tannehill	53
28	Burleigh Grimes	52
	Claude Hendrix	52
30	Steve Carlton	50
	Ad Gumbert	50
32	Joe Bush	49
	Charlie Ferguson	49
	Bob Forsch	49
35	Tony Mullane	47
36	Dave Foutz	46
	Rick Rhoden	46
	Scott Stratton	46
39	Vern Law	45
	Dutch Ruether	45
	Adonis Terry	45
42	Don Larsen	44
43	Jim Kaat	43
	Jack Scott	43
45	Frank Killen	42
46	Don Robinson	41
47	Tommy Byrne	40
	Wilbur Cooper	40
	Fred Hutchinson	40
50	Johnny Sain	38
51	Mickey McDermott	37
	Claude Osteen	37
	Charley Radbourn	37
	Sloppy Thurston	37
55	Ken Brett	36
	Doc White	36
57	Jack Coombs	35
	Harvey Haddix	35
	Dolf Luque	35
60	Clark Griffith	34
	Robin Roberts	34
	Rick Wise	34
63	Chief Bender	33
	Win Mercer	33
	Art Nehf	33
	Ben Sanders	33
	Frank Smith	33
	Jack Taylor	33
69	Ray Caldwell	32
	Hooks Dauss	32
	Catfish Hunter	32
	Ted Lyons	32
	Dizzy Trout	32
74	Joe Wood	31
75	Al Maul	30
	Camilo Pascual	30
	John Ward	30
78	Ed Brandt	29
	Lew Burdette	29
	Jack Harshman	29
	Jouett Meekin	29
	Joe Nuxhall	29
	Urban Shocker	29
	Lefty Tyler	29
85	Brickyard Kennedy	28
	Ed Lopat	28
	Jim Maloney	28
	Juan Pizarro	28
	Tom Seaver	28
	Fernando Valenzuela	28
	Lon Warneke	28
92	Charlie Buffinton	27
	Clarence Mitchell	27
	Bill Sherdel	27
95	Murry Dickson	26
	Ned Garver	26
	Johnny Marcum	26
	Joe Shaute	26
	Elmer Smith	26
100	6 players tied	25

Pitcher Fielding Runs

1	Ed Walsh	83
2	Carl Mays	74
3	Christy Mathewson	68
4	Freddie Fitzsimmons	60
	Bob Lemon	60
6	Burleigh Grimes	58
7	Tommy John	55
8	Harry Howell	51
9	Harry Gumbert	50
10	John Clarkson	45
11	Bill Doak	43
12	Willis Hudlin	42
	Eddie Rommel	42
14	Jack Quinn	40
15	Jim Galvin	39
	Rick Reuschel	39
	Bobby Shantz	39
18	Hooks Dauss	38
	Dizzy Trout	38
20	Jack Russell	36
	Mel Stottlemyre	36
22	Charlie Buffinton	35
	Johnny Schmitz	35
24	Nick Altrock	34
	Willie Sudhoff	34
26	Tony Mullane	33
27	Red Ames	32
	Murry Dickson	32
	Howard Ehmke	32
	Randy Jones	32
31	Pete Alexander	31
	Curt Davis	31
	John Denny	31
	Greg Maddux	31
	Dennis Martinez	31
36	Tommy Bond	30
	Addie Joss	30
	Hal Schumacher	30
	Dave Stieb	30
40	Chick Fraser	29
	Gerry Staley	29
42	Mike Boddicker	28
	Ben Cantwell	28
	Sid Hudson	28
	Matt Kilroy	28
	George Mullin	28
	Phil Niekro	28
	Ed Willett	28
49	Ted Abernathy	27
	Tom Burgmeier	27
	Spud Chandler	27
	Amos Rusie	27
	Frank Smith	27
	Fernando Valenzuela	27
	Bucky Walters	27
	Vic Willis	27
57	Nixey Callahan	26
	Whitey Ford	26
	Sherry Smith	26
60	Don Drysdale	25
	Larry Jackson	25
	Dan Quisenberry	25
63	Mike Caldwell	24
	Frank Corridon	24
	Ned Garvin	24
	Guy Hecker	24
	Dutch Leonard	24
	John Ward	24
	Doc White	24
70	Jean Dubuc	23
	Lindy McDaniel	23
	Cy Seymour	23
73	Tom Brewer	22
	Bill Hart	22
	Joe Horlen	22
	Carl Hubbell	22
	Jim McCormick	22
	Stu Miller	22
	Hal Newhouser	22
	Dan Petry	22
	Ed Reulbach	22
	Bob Stanley	22
	Kent Tekulve	22
84	Eldon Auker	21
	Joe Bush	21
	Benny Frey	21
	Sadie McMahon	21
	Frank Owen	21
	Gaylord Perry	21
	Bob Purkey	21
	Jack Taylor	21
	Lefty Tyler	21
93	13 players tied	20

Pitcher Batting Average

1	Jack Stivetts	.297
2	George Uhle	.289
3	Charlie Ferguson	.288
4	Win Mercer	.286
5	Doc Crandall	.285
6	Guy Hecker	.283
7	Bob Caruthers	.282
8	Red Lucas	.281
9	Wes Ferrell	.280
10	Dave Foutz	.276
11	Jack Scott	.275
	John Ward	.275
13	Scott Stratton	.274
14	Nixey Callahan	.273
	Ad Gumbert	.273
	Al Orth	.273
17	Don Newcombe	.271
18	Sloppy Thurston	.270
19	Red Ruffing	.269
20	Carl Mays	.268
21	Schoolboy Rowe	.263
22	George Mullin	.262
23	Kid Gleason	.261
	Brickyard Kennedy	.261
	Jim Whitney	.261
26	Dutch Ruether	.258
	Joe Shaute	.258
28	Lee Richmond	.257
29	Jesse Tannehill	.256
30	Joe Bush	.253
31	Clarence Mitchell	.252
	Jack Taylor	.252
33	Adonis Terry	.249
34	Ray Caldwell	.248
	Burleigh Grimes	.248
36	Amos Rusie	.247
37	Pete Donohue	.246
38	Charlie Buffinton	.245
	Johnny Sain	.245
40	Vern Kennedy	.244
41	Jouett Meekin	.243
	Tony Mullane	.243
	Elam Vangilder	.243
	Bucky Walters	.243
45	Don Larsen	.242
	Bob Smith	.242
47	Duke Esper	.241
	Pink Hawley	.241
	Claude Hendrix	.241
	Frank Killen	.241
51	Frank Kitson	.240
52	Wilbur Cooper	.239
53	Ed Crane	.238
	Rick Rhoden	.238
55	Tommy Bond	.236
	Ed Brandt	.236
	Jim McCormick	.236
58	Jack Coombs	.235
	Walter Johnson	.235
	Terry Larkin	.235
	Charley Radbourn	.235
62	Fritz Ostermueller	.234
63	Nig Cuppy	.233
	Clark Griffith	.233
	Ted Lyons	.233
	Sherry Smith	.233
67	Bob Lemon	.232
68	Ben Cantwell	.231
	Murry Dickson	.231
	Don Robinson	.231
71	Frank Dwyer	.230
	George Earnshaw	.230
	Jim Tobin	.230
74	Vic Aldridge	.229
75	George Bradley	.228
	Nels Potter	.228
77	George Haddock	.227
	Dolf Luque	.227
	Bill Swift	.227
80	Jim Bagby	.226
	Catfish Hunter	.226
	Kid Nichols	.226
	Ed Stein	.226
	Tom Zachary	.226
85	Dizzy Dean	.225
86	Fred Foreman	.224
	Fred Goldsmith	.224
	Mickey Welch	.224
89	Hal Carlson	.223
	Larry Corcoran	.223
	George Hemming	.223
	Bill Sherdel	.223
	Jack Taylor	.223
	Lon Warneke	.223
95	Matt Kilroy	.222
	Gary Peters	.222
97	Van Mungo	.221
98	Sid Hudson	.220
99	3 players tied	.219

Total Pitcher Index

1	Walter Johnson	84.1
2	Cy Young	78.8
3	Pete Alexander	63.9
4	Kid Nichols	59.9
5	Christy Mathewson	59.3
6	Lefty Grove	58.7
7	Tom Seaver	51.1
8	John Clarkson	49.2
9	Bob Gibson	45.1
10	Warren Spahn	43.7
11	Ed Walsh	42.1
12	Whitey Ford	38.7
13	Carl Hubbell	38.4
	Jim Palmer	38.4
15	Hal Newhouser	37.9
16	Amos Rusie	37.3
17	Tim Keefe	37.1
18	Phil Niekro	36.0
19	Bob Lemon	35.6
20	Steve Carlton	35.3
	Gaylord Perry	35.3
22	Ted Lyons	35.2
23	Carl Mays	34.9
24	Don Drysdale	34.8
25	Mordecai Brown	33.6
26	Roger Clemens	33.2
	Tony Mullane	33.2
28	Bert Blyleven	33.1
29	Dizzy Trout	32.6
30	Wes Ferrell	30.8
31	Fergie Jenkins	30.3
32	Juan Marichal	30.1
33	Bob Caruthers	30.0
34	Bucky Walters	29.0
35	Dave Stieb	28.9
36	Charley Radbourn	28.8
	Hoyt Wilhelm	28.8
38	Clark Griffith	28.4
39	Jack Stivetts	28.1
40	Bob Feller	27.8
41	Tommy Bridges	27.4
42	Tommy John	26.8
	Eddie Plank	26.8
44	Red Ruffing	26.5
45	Stan Coveleski	26.2
46	Red Faber	25.8
	Dazzy Vance	25.8
48	Addie Joss	25.5
	Rick Reuschel	25.5
	Robin Roberts	25.5
51	Dolf Luque	25.3
52	Eppa Rixey	24.7
53	Urban Shocker	24.6
	Rube Waddell	24.6
55	Eddie Rommel	24.4
56	Burleigh Grimes	24.3
57	Guy Hecker	24.1
58	Eddie Cicotte	23.9
59	Jack Quinn	23.7
60	Silver King	23.5
	Dutch Leonard	23.5
62	Harry Brecheen	23.4
63	Jim McCormick	22.6
64	Lon Warneke	22.5
65	Nig Cuppy	22.4
	Freddie Fitzsimmons	22.4
67	Billy Pierce	22.3
68	Joe Wood	21.7
69	Nolan Ryan	21.6
	Vic Willis	21.6
71	Spud Chandler	21.0
72	Charlie Buffinton	20.7
73	Wilbur Cooper	20.3
	Jesse Tannehill	20.3
75	Bobby Shantz	20.2
76	Dizzy Dean	20.1
77	Don Newcombe	20.0
78	Sandy Koufax	19.8
79	Orel Hershiser	19.1
	Joe McGinnity	19.1
81	Dave Foutz	19.0
	Larry Jackson	19.0
83	Jim Kaat	18.9
84	Dennis Eckersley	18.8
85	Curt Davis	18.7
86	Ed Reulbach	18.6
	Bret Saberhagen	18.6
88	Murry Dickson	18.5
89	Andy Messersmith	18.4
90	Steve Rogers	18.3
91	Red Lucas	18.2
	Hippo Vaughn	18.2
	Doc White	18.2
94	Ron Guidry	18.1
95	Lefty Gomez	18.0
96	Ed Lopat	17.7
97	Dan Quisenberry	17.5
	Schoolboy Rowe	17.5
	Mel Stottlemyre	17.5
100	Ned Garver	17.3

Total Pitcher Index

	Mel Harder	17.3
	Thornton Lee	17.3
	Babe Ruth	17.3
	Early Wynn	17.3
105	Noodles Hahn	17.2
106	Claude Hendrix	17.1
	Mel Parnell	17.1
108	Jim Bunning	17.0
	Dwight Gooden	17.0
110	Babe Adams	16.9
111	Larry French	16.8
	Jack Taylor	16.8
113	Claude Passeau	16.7
	Kent Tekulve	16.7
115	Luis Tiant	16.3
116	Harry Howell	16.2
	Hal Schumacher	16.2
118	John Tudor	16.1
119	George Mullin	16.0
120	Sam Leever	15.3
121	Sadie McMahon	15.2
122	Frank Dwyer	15.1
123	Jim Whitney	15.0
124	John Candelaria	14.9
	Waite Hoyt	14.9
	George Uhle	14.9
127	Max Lanier	14.8
	Frank Tanana	14.8
129	Don Sutton	14.7
	Mickey Welch	14.7
131	Chief Bender	14.6
	Rich Gossage	14.6
	Jimmy Key	14.6
	Sal Maglie	14.6
	Virgil Trucks	14.6
	John Ward	14.6
137	Charlie Ferguson	14.4
138	Larry Corcoran	14.3
139	Jim Devlin	14.2
	Wilbur Wood	14.2
141	Mort Cooper	14.1
142	Johnny Antonelli	13.9
	Mike Garcia	13.9
	Fred Hutchinson	13.9
145	Bill Hutchison	13.8
146	Jim Galvin	13.7
147	Greg Maddux	13.6
148	Deacon Phillippe	13.5
149	Charlie Hough	13.3
150	Nap Rucker	13.2
	Bob Shawkey	13.2
152	Jim Maloney	13.1
	Jon Matlack	13.1
	Howie Pollet	13.1
	Curt Simmons	13.1
	Bob Stanley	13.1
157	Jerry Koosman	12.8
	Sparky Lyle	12.8
	Jim Tobin	12.8
160	Bob Welch	12.7
161	Tom Candiotti	12.6
162	Frank Killen	12.5
	Frank Lary	12.5
	Bruce Sutter	12.5
	Will White	12.5
166	Rollie Fingers	12.4
167	John Hiller	12.2
168	Ted Breitenstein	12.1
169	Russ Ford	12.0
	Claude Osteen	12.0
	Milt Pappas	12.0
172	Fernando Valenzuela	11.9
173	Ewell Blackwell	11.8
	Harvey Haddix	11.8
	Jack Morris	11.8
176	Stu Miller	11.7
	Gary Peters	11.7
178	Jake Weimer	11.6
179	Frank Viola	11.5
180	Sam McDowell	11.4
	Van Mungo	11.4
182	Matt Kilroy	11.3
183	Orval Overall	11.2
	Sherry Smith	11.2
185	Dean Chance	11.1
	Gene Garber	11.1
	Mike Marshall	11.1
	Sonny Siebert	11.1
	Lee Smith	11.1
190	Nixey Callahan	11.0
	John Franco	11.0
	Firpo Marberry	11.0
	Camilo Pascual	11.0
194	Clay Carroll	10.9
	Teddy Higuera	10.9
	Jose Rijo	10.9
197	Mike Boddicker	10.8
198	Jim Perry	10.7
	Ben Sanders	10.7
200	Bob Ewing	10.6

Total Pitcher Index

	Charlie Leibrandt	10.6
	Hooks Wiltse	10.6
203	Jack Chesbro	10.5
	Tex Hughson	10.5
205	Lefty Leifield	10.4
	Bob Rush	10.4
	Tom Zachary	10.4
208	Hooks Dauss	10.3
	Dennis Martinez	10.3
210	Ellis Kinder	10.2
	Lindy McDaniel	10.2
	Art Nehf	10.2
213	Frank Sullivan	10.1
214	Al Brazle	10.0
	Elton Chamberlain	10.0
	Fritz Ostermueller	10.0
217	Vida Blue	9.9
	Charlie Root	9.9
	Adonis Terry	9.9
220	Tom Burgmeier	9.8
	Doug Drabek	9.8
	Tug McGraw	9.8
	Ed Morris	9.8
224	Jeff Pfeffer	9.7
225	Mark Langston	9.6
	Win Mercer	9.6
	Greg Minton	9.6
228	Johnny Allen	9.5
	Ned Garvin	9.5
	Tom Henke	9.5
	Joe Horlen	9.5
	Monte Pearson	9.5
	Johnny Sain	9.5
234	Tommy Bond	9.4
	Gary Lavelle	9.4
236	Mark Baldwin	9.3
	Mike Cuellar	9.3
	Mark Eichhorn	9.3
	Bill Hands	9.3
	Gary Nolan	9.3
241	Red Ames	9.2
	Doc Crandall	9.2
243	Harry Coveleski	9.1
	Terry Forster	9.1
	Jesse Orosco	9.1
	Dave Righetti	9.1
	Rip Sewell	9.1
248	Rick Rhoden	9.0
	Johnny Rigney	9.0
250	Danny Darwin	8.9
	Joe Dobson	8.9
	Larry Jansen	8.9
253	Gerry Staley	8.8
254	Watty Clark	8.7
	Pink Hawley	8.7
	Don Mossi	8.7
	Jeff Tesreau	8.7
258	Mark Gubicza	8.6
	Ron Perranoski	8.6
260	Don McMahon	8.5
	Jim Scott	8.5
262	Frank Linzy	8.4
	Al Orth	8.4
264	Clint Brown	8.3
	Steve Farr	8.3
266	Tim Burke	8.2
	Dutch Ruether	8.2
	Slim Sallee	8.2
269	Preacher Roe	8.1
270	John Denny	8.0
	Willie Hernandez	8.0
	Bob Locker	8.0
	Johnny Schmitz	8.0
	Frank Smith	8.0
	Lefty Tyler	8.0
276	Howard Ehmke	7.9
	Toad Ramsey	7.9
	Billy Rhines	7.9
	Dave Rozema	7.9
280	George Mogridge	7.8
281	Bill Doak	7.7
	Sam Jones	7.7
	Mickey McDermott	7.7
284	Bob Friend	7.5
	Greg Harris	7.5
	Bill Lee	7.5
287	Lady Baldwin	7.4
	Joe Benz	7.4
	Tiny Bonham	7.4
	Joe Bush	7.4
	Burt Hooton	7.4
	Willis Hudlin	7.4
	Vern Law	7.4
	Reb Russell	7.4
295	Jack Harshman	7.3
	Darold Knowles	7.3
	Johnny Murphy	7.3
	Herb Pennock	7.3
299	3 players tied	7.2

Total Pitcher Index (alpha.)

Babe Adams	16.9
Pete Alexander	63.9
Johnny Allen	9.5
Red Ames	9.2
Johnny Antonelli	13.9
Lady Baldwin	7.4
Mark Baldwin	9.3
Chief Bender	14.6
Joe Benz	7.4
Ewell Blackwell	11.8
Vida Blue	9.9
Bert Blyleven	33.1
Mike Boddicker	10.8
Tommy Bond	9.4
Tiny Bonham	7.4
Al Brazle	10.0
Harry Brecheen	23.4
Ted Breitenstein	12.1
Tommy Bridges	27.4
Clint Brown	8.3
Mordecai Brown	33.6
Charlie Buffinton	20.7
Jim Bunning	17.0
Tom Burgmeier	9.8
Tim Burke	8.2
Joe Bush	7.4
Nixey Callahan	11.0
John Candelaria	14.9
Tom Candiotti	12.6
Steve Carlton	35.3
Clay Carroll	10.9
Bob Caruthers	30.0
Elton Chamberlain	10.0
Dean Chance	11.1
Spud Chandler	21.0
Jack Chesbro	10.5
Eddie Cicotte	23.9
Watty Clark	8.7
John Clarkson	49.2
Roger Clemens	33.2
Wilbur Cooper	20.3
Mort Cooper	14.1
Larry Corcoran	14.3
Harry Coveleski	9.1
Stan Coveleski	26.2
Doc Crandall	9.2
Mike Cuellar	9.3
Nig Cuppy	22.4
Danny Darwin	8.9
Hooks Dauss	10.3
Curt Davis	18.7
Dizzy Dean	20.1
John Denny	8.0
Jim Devlin	14.2
Murry Dickson	18.5
Bill Doak	7.7
Joe Dobson	8.9
Doug Drabek	9.8
Don Drysdale	34.8
Frank Dwyer	15.1
Dennis Eckersley	18.8
Howard Ehmke	7.9
Mark Eichhorn	9.3
Bob Ewing	10.6
Red Faber	25.8
Steve Farr	8.3
Bob Feller	27.8
Charlie Ferguson	14.4
Wes Ferrell	30.8
Rollie Fingers	12.4
Freddie Fitzsimmons	22.4
Whitey Ford	38.7
Russ Ford	12.0
Terry Forster	9.1
Dave Foutz	19.0
John Franco	11.0
Larry French	16.8
Bob Friend	7.5
Jim Galvin	13.7
Gene Garber	11.1
Mike Garcia	13.9
Ned Garver	17.3
Ned Garvin	9.5
Bob Gibson	45.1
Lefty Gomez	18.0
Dwight Gooden	17.0
Rich Gossage	14.6
Clark Griffith	28.4
Burleigh Grimes	24.3
Lefty Grove	58.7
Mark Gubicza	8.6
Ron Guidry	18.1
Harvey Haddix	11.8
Noodles Hahn	17.2
Bill Hands	9.3
Mel Harder	17.3
Greg Harris	7.5
Jack Harshman	7.3
Pink Hawley	8.7
Guy Hecker	24.1

Total Pitcher Index (alpha.)

Claude Hendrix	17.1
Tom Henke	9.5
Willie Hernandez	8.0
Orel Hershiser	19.1
Teddy Higuera	10.9
John Hiller	12.2
Burt Hooton	7.4
Joe Horlen	9.5
Charlie Hough	13.3
Harry Howell	16.2
Waite Hoyt	14.9
Carl Hubbell	38.4
Willis Hudlin	7.4
Tex Hughson	10.5
Fred Hutchinson	13.9
Bill Hutchison	13.8
Larry Jackson	19.0
Larry Jansen	8.9
Fergie Jenkins	30.3
Tommy John	26.8
Walter Johnson	84.1
Sam Jones	7.7
Addie Joss	25.5
Jim Kaat	18.9
Tim Keefe	37.1
Jimmy Key	14.6
Frank Killen	12.5
Matt Kilroy	11.3
Ellis Kinder	10.2
Silver King	23.5
Darold Knowles	7.3
Jerry Koosman	12.8
Sandy Koufax	19.8
Mark Langston	9.6
Max Lanier	14.8
Frank Lary	12.5
Gary Lavelle	9.4
Vern Law	7.4
Thornton Lee	17.3
Bill Lee	7.5
Sam Leever	15.3
Charlie Leibrandt	10.6
Lefty Leifield	10.4
Bob Lemon	35.6
Dutch Leonard	23.5
Frank Linzy	8.4
Bob Locker	8.0
Ed Lopat	17.7
Red Lucas	18.2
Dolf Luque	25.3
Sparky Lyle	12.8
Ted Lyons	35.2
Greg Maddux	13.6
Sal Maglie	14.6
Jim Maloney	13.1
Firpo Marberry	11.0
Juan Marichal	30.1
Mike Marshall	11.1
Dennis Martinez	10.3
Christy Mathewson	59.3
Jon Matlack	13.1
Carl Mays	34.9
Jim McCormick	22.6
Lindy McDaniel	10.2
Mickey McDermott	7.7
Sam McDowell	11.4
Joe McGinnity	19.1
Tug McGraw	9.8
Don McMahon	8.5
Sadie McMahon	15.2
Win Mercer	9.6
Andy Messersmith	18.4
Stu Miller	11.7
Greg Minton	9.6
George Mogridge	7.8
Ed Morris	9.8
Jack Morris	11.8
Don Mossi	8.7
Tony Mullane	33.2
George Mullin	16.0
Van Mungo	11.4
Johnny Murphy	7.3
Art Nehf	10.2
Don Newcombe	20.0
Hal Newhouser	37.9
Kid Nichols	59.9
Phil Niekro	36.0
Gary Nolan	9.3
Jesse Orosco	9.1
Al Orth	8.4
Claude Osteen	12.0
Fritz Ostermueller	10.0
Orval Overall	11.2
Jim Palmer	38.4
Milt Pappas	12.0
Mel Parnell	17.1
Camilo Pascual	11.0
Claude Passeau	16.7
Monte Pearson	9.5
Herb Pennock	7.3

Total Pitcher Index (alpha.)

Ron Perranoski	8.6
Gaylord Perry	35.3
Jim Perry	10.7
Gary Peters	11.7
Jeff Pfeffer	9.7
Deacon Phillippe	13.5
Billy Pierce	22.3
Eddie Plank	26.8
Howie Pollet	13.1
Jack Quinn	23.7
Dan Quisenberry	17.5
Charley Radbourn	28.8
Toad Ramsey	7.9
Ed Reulbach	18.6
Rick Reuschel	25.5
Billy Rhines	7.9
Rick Rhoden	9.0
Dave Righetti	9.1
Johnny Rigney	9.0
Jose Rijo	10.9
Eppa Rixey	24.7
Robin Roberts	25.5
Preacher Roe	8.1
Steve Rogers	18.3
Eddie Rommel	24.4
Charlie Root	9.9
Schoolboy Rowe	17.5
Dave Rozema	7.9
Nap Rucker	13.2
Dutch Ruether	8.2
Red Ruffing	26.5
Bob Rush	10.4
Amos Rusie	37.3
Reb Russell	7.4
Babe Ruth	17.3
Nolan Ryan	21.6
Bret Saberhagen	18.6
Johnny Sain	9.5
Slim Sallee	8.2
Ben Sanders	10.7
Johnny Schmitz	8.0
Hal Schumacher	16.2
Jim Scott	8.5
Tom Seaver	51.1
Rip Sewell	9.1
Bobby Shantz	20.2
Bob Shawkey	13.2
Urban Shocker	24.6
Sonny Siebert	11.1
Curt Simmons	13.1
Frank Smith	8.0
Lee Smith	11.1
Sherry Smith	11.2
Warren Spahn	43.7
Gerry Staley	8.8
Bob Stanley	13.1
Dave Stieb	28.9
Jack Stivetts	28.1
Mel Stottlemyre	17.5
Frank Sullivan	10.1
Bruce Sutter	12.5
Don Sutton	14.7
Frank Tanana	14.8
Jesse Tannehill	20.3
Jack Taylor	16.8
Kent Tekulve	16.7
Adonis Terry	9.9
Jeff Tesreau	8.7
Luis Tiant	16.3
Jim Tobin	12.8
Dizzy Trout	32.6
Virgil Trucks	14.6
John Tudor	16.1
Lefty Tyler	8.0
George Uhle	14.9
Fernando Valenzuela	11.9
Dazzy Vance	25.8
Hippo Vaughn	18.2
Frank Viola	11.5
Rube Waddell	24.6
Ed Walsh	42.1
Bucky Walters	29.0
John Ward	14.6
Lon Warneke	22.5
Jake Weimer	11.6
Mickey Welch	14.7
Bob Welch	12.7
Doc White	18.2
Will White	12.5
Jim Whitney	15.0
Hoyt Wilhelm	28.8
Vic Willis	21.6
Hooks Wiltse	10.6
Joe Wood	21.7
Wilbur Wood	14.2
Early Wynn	17.3
Cy Young	78.8
Tom Zachary	10.4

Total Pitcher Index (by era)

Total Baseball Ranking

Rank	Name	Value
1	Babe Ruth	122.5
2	Nap Lajoie	94.9
3	Ty Cobb	92.8
4	Ted Williams	92.4
5	Tris Speaker	88.5
6	Willie Mays	86.4
7	Hank Aaron	84.6
8	Walter Johnson	83.7
9	Honus Wagner	82.9
10	Mike Schmidt	80.3
11	Rogers Hornsby	79.8
12	Cy Young	78.8
13	Mickey Mantle	73.6
14	Stan Musial	71.7
15	Frank Robinson	70.3
16	Eddie Collins	69.4
17	Rickey Henderson	67.0
18	Pete Alexander	63.9
19	Mel Ott	62.4
20	Lou Gehrig	61.9
21	Kid Nichols	59.9
22	Christy Mathewson	59.3
23	Lefty Grove	58.7
24	Jimmie Foxx	56.2
25	Joe Morgan	55.7
26	Bill Dahlen	52.4
27	George Davis	51.5
28	Tom Seaver	51.1
29	Carl Yastrzemski	50.8
30	John Clarkson	49.2
31	Eddie Mathews	48.6
32	Tim Raines	47.1
33	Joe DiMaggio	46.5
34	Al Kaline	46.4
35	Bob Gibson	45.1
	Charlie Gehringer	45.1
37	Ed Delahanty	44.8
38	Roger Connor	44.4
39	Warren Spahn	43.7
40	Bobby Grich	43.3
41	Robin Yount	43.0
42	Dan Brouthers	42.7
	Reggie Jackson	42.7
44	Bid McPhee	42.3
45	Ed Walsh	42.1
	George Brett	42.1
	Ozzie Smith	42.1
48	Ron Santo	41.7
49	Roberto Clemente	41.5
50	Luke Appling	40.9
51	Bobby Wallace	40.5
52	Lou Boudreau	40.4
53	Dave Winfield	40.3
54	Gabby Hartnett	40.1
55	Ryne Sandberg	40.0
56	Wade Boggs	39.9
	Joe Cronin	39.9
58	Bobby Doerr	39.8
59	Arky Vaughan	39.7
60	Frankie Frisch	38.8
61	Whitey Ford	38.7
62	Cal Ripken	38.6
63	Carl Hubbell	38.4
	Jim Palmer	38.4
65	Joe Jackson	38.2
66	Hal Newhouser	37.9
67	Johnny Mize	37.7
68	Jack Glasscock	37.5
	Eddie Murray	37.5
70	Amos Rusie	37.3
71	Tim Keefe	37.1
72	Paul Waner	37.0
73	Bill Mazeroski	36.6
74	Cap Anson	36.2
75	Phil Niekro	36.0
76	Yogi Berra	35.5
77	Dave Bancroft	35.4
78	Steve Carlton	35.3
	Gaylord Perry	35.3
80	Ted Lyons	35.2
	Darrell Evans	35.2
	Joe Sewell	35.2
83	Bob Lemon	35.1
	Bob Johnson	35.1
	Willie McCovey	35.1
86	Carl Mays	34.9
87	Don Drysdale	34.8
	Bill Dickey	34.8
	Reggie Smith	34.8
90	Barry Bonds	34.7
91	Keith Hernandez	34.1
92	Mordecai Brown	33.6
93	Dick Allen	33.5
	Frank Baker	33.5
95	Roger Clemens	33.2
96	Bert Blyleven	33.1
97	Dwight Evans	32.8
98	Bobby Bonds	32.7
99	Bob Caruthers	32.6
	Dizzy Trout	32.6

Total Baseball Ranking

Rank	Name	Value
	Jackie Robinson	32.6
102	Rod Carew	32.5
103	Mickey Cochrane	32.2
104	Tony Mullane	32.0
	Billy Herman	32.0
106	Harry Heilmann	31.9
107	Hank Greenberg	31.7
108	Cupid Childs	31.2
	Sam Crawford	31.2
110	Tony Gwynn	31.0
111	Wes Ferrell	30.9
	Buck Ewing	30.9
	Jim Rice	30.9
114	Richie Ashburn	30.7
115	Paul Molitor	30.4
116	Fergie Jenkins	30.3
117	Juan Marichal	30.1
	Fred Clarke	30.1
119	Sam Thompson	30.0
120	Ralph Kiner	29.9
121	Pete Browning	29.5
	Gary Carter	29.5
123	Fred Dunlap	29.4
124	Jack Clark	29.0
	Andre Dawson	29.0
126	Dave Stieb	28.9
127	Hoyt Wilhelm	28.8
128	Billy Hamilton	28.7
	Harmon Killebrew	28.7
130	Jesse Burkett	28.6
	Norm Cash	28.6
	Elmer Flick	28.6
133	Hardy Richardson	28.4
	Jim Wynn	28.4
135	Joe Medwick	28.0
136	Bob Feller	27.8
137	Clark Griffith	27.7
	Dick Bartell	27.7
	Joe Gordon	27.7
140	Tommy Bridges	27.4
	Hughie Jennings	27.4
142	Sherry Magee	27.2
	Al Simmons	27.2
144	Stan Hack	27.1
	Rusty Staub	27.1
	Billy Williams	27.1
147	King Kelly	26.9
148	Tommy John	26.8
	Eddie Plank	26.8
150	Bucky Walters	26.7
	Heinie Groh	26.7
	Tony Oliva	26.7
	Darryl Strawberry	26.7
154	Carlton Fisk	26.6
155	Charley Radbourn	26.4
	Red Ruffing	26.4
157	Art Fletcher	26.3
158	Stan Coveleski	26.2
159	Jack Stivetts	26.1
	Willie Stargell	26.1
161	Goose Goslin	26.0
162	Rocky Colavito	25.9
163	Red Faber	25.8
	Dazzy Vance	25.8
	Minnie Minoso	25.8
166	Ernie Banks	25.7
167	Addie Joss	25.5
	Rick Reuschel	25.5
	Robin Roberts	25.5
170	Dolf Luque	25.3
171	Johnny Bench	25.2
172	Eppa Rixey	24.7
	Zack Wheat	24.7
174	Urban Shocker	24.6
	Rube Waddell	24.6
	Chuck Klein	24.6
177	Eddie Rommel	24.4
	Jake Beckley	24.4
	Bill Terry	24.4
180	Burleigh Grimes	24.3
	Kirby Puckett	24.3
	Joe Tinker	24.3
183	Jimmy Collins	24.2
	George Sisler	24.2
	Duke Snider	24.2
186	Travis Jackson	24.0
187	Eddie Cicotte	23.9
188	Jack Quinn	23.7
	Fred Lynn	23.7
190	Silver King	23.5
	Dutch Leonard	23.5
	Jack Fournier	23.5
	Harry Stovey	23.5
194	Harry Brecheen	23.4
	Max Carey	23.4
	Fred Pfeffer	23.4
197	Charlie Keller	23.3
	Barry Larkin	23.3
	Alan Trammell	23.3
200	Ed Konetchy	23.2

Total Baseball Ranking

Rank	Name	Value
	John Ward	23.2
202	Willie Randolph	23.0
203	Buddy Bell	22.9
	Harlond Clift	22.9
205	George Foster	22.8
206	Jose Cruz	22.7
207	Jim McCormick	22.6
	Roy Thomas	22.6
209	Lon Warneke	22.5
210	Nig Cuppy	22.4
	Freddie Fitzsimmons	22.4
212	Guy Hecker	22.3
	Billy Pierce	22.3
214	Chet Lemon	22.0
	Dave Parker	22.0
216	Roy Campanella	21.9
	Joe Kelley	21.9
218	Ron Cey	21.7
219	Nolan Ryan	21.6
	Vic Willis	21.6
221	Graig Nettles	21.5
222	Charley Jones	21.4
	Fred Tenney	21.4
224	Denny Lyons	21.3
225	Frank Chance	21.1
	Mike Griffin	21.1
227	Spud Chandler	21.0
	Ken Singleton	21.0
229	Pie Traynor	20.9
	Andy Van Slyke	20.9
231	Wally Berger	20.8
	Roy White	20.8
233	Amos Otis	20.7
234	Brian Downing	20.6
	Vern Stephens	20.6
236	Gavvy Cravath	20.5
237	Joe Wood	20.4
238	Wilbur Cooper	20.3
	Ken Boyer	20.3
	Art Devlin	20.3
	Larry Doby	20.3
242	Bobby Shantz	20.2
	Cesar Cedeno	20.2
	Del Pratt	20.2
245	Dizzy Dean	20.1
	Jim Fregosi	20.1
	Joe Torre	20.1
248	Don Newcombe	20.0
	Glenn Hubbard	20.0
250	Roger Bresnahan	19.9
	Eric Davis	19.9
	Frank Howard	19.9
253	Sandy Koufax	19.8
	Brooks Robinson	19.8
255	Charlie Bennett	19.6
	Jose Canseco	19.6
	Jimmy Sheckard	19.6
258	Lou Whitaker	19.5
259	Pete Rose	19.4
260	Bill Joyce	19.3
261	Jesse Tannehill	19.2
262	Orel Hershiser	19.1
	Joe McGinnity	19.1
264	Larry Jackson	19.0
265	Jim Kaat	18.9
266	Dennis Eckersley	18.8
	Dale Murphy	18.8
268	Curt Davis	18.7
269	Ed Reulbach	18.6
	Bret Saberhagen	18.6
	George Gore	18.6
272	Murry Dickson	18.5
	Brett Butler	18.5
	Roy Cullenbine	18.5
	Bob Elliott	18.5
	Eddie Stanky	18.5
277	Andy Messersmith	18.4
	Ferris Fain	18.4
	Bill Nicholson	18.4
280	Steve Rogers	18.3
	Earl Averill	18.3
	Ken Williams	18.3
283	Hippo Vaughn	18.2
	Gene Alley	18.2
	Miller Huggins	18.2
286	Ron Guidry	18.1
	Johnny Logan	18.1
	Wally Schang	18.1
289	Lefty Gomez	18.0
290	Paul Hines	17.8
	Tommy Leach	17.8
292	Ed Lopat	17.7
	Enos Slaughter	17.7
294	Red Lucas	17.6
295	Dan Quisenberry	17.5
	Schoolboy Rowe	17.5
	Mel Stottlemyre	17.5
	Ted Simmons	17.5
299	Pedro Guerrero	17.4
300	Ned Garver	17.3

Total Baseball Ranking

Rank	Name	Value
	Mel Harder	17.3
	Thornton Lee	17.3
	Early Wynn	17.3
304	Noodles Hahn	17.2
	Benny Kauff	17.2
	John McGraw	17.2
307	Claude Hendrix	17.1
	Mel Parnell	17.1
	Orlando Cepeda	17.1
	Will Clark	17.1
	Ernie Lombardi	17.1
	Jocko Milligan	17.1
	Jim O'Rourke	17.1
314	Jim Bunning	17.0
	Dwight Gooden	17.0
316	Babe Adams	16.9
317	Larry French	16.8
	Jack Taylor	16.8
	Doc White	16.8
	Henry Larkin	16.8
321	Claude Passeau	16.7
	Kent Tekulve	16.7
	Babe Herman	16.7
	Gil McDougald	16.7
	Chief Zimmer	16.7
326	Lenny Dykstra	16.6
	Jimmy Ryan	16.6
328	Jesse Barfield	16.5
	Jimmy Williams	16.5
330	Luis Tiant	16.3
	Kiki Cuyler	16.3
	Hal McRae	16.3
333	Hal Schumacher	16.2
334	John Tudor	16.1
	Tony Lazzeri	16.1
	Fred McGriff	16.1
337	Lave Cross	16.0
	Dwayne Murphy	16.0
339	Ray Chapman	15.9
	Phil Rizzuto	15.9
	Cy Seymour	15.9
342	Davey Johnson	15.8
343	Mark Belanger	15.7
	Jeff Heath	15.7
345	Rico Carty	15.6
	Duke Farrell	15.6
	Mike Hargrove	15.6
	Hack Wilson	15.6
349	George Mullin	15.5
350	Charlie Buffinton	15.4
	Kirk Gibson	15.4
	Elmer Smith	15.4
353	Sam Leever	15.3
	Bobby Knoop	15.3
355	Sadie McMahon	15.2
	Kevin McReynolds	15.2
357	Frank Dwyer	15.1
	Thurman Munson	15.1
359	John Candelaria	14.9
	Waite Hoyt	14.9
	George Uhle	14.9
	Bob Allison	14.9
363	Max Lanier	14.8
	Frank Tanana	14.8
365	Don Sutton	14.7
	Mickey Welch	14.7
	Augie Galan	14.7
	Boog Powell	14.7
	Mike Scioscia	14.7
	Bobby Veach	14.7
371	Chief Bender	14.6
	Rich Gossage	14.6
	Jimmy Key	14.6
	Sal Maglie	14.6
	Virgil Trucks	14.6
	Billy Nash	14.6
	Pee Wee Reese	14.6
378	Harold Baines	14.5
	Ron Hansen	14.5
	Edd Roush	14.5
	Roy Smalley	14.5
382	Charlie Ferguson	14.4
	Dolph Camilli	14.4
	Danny Tartabull	14.4
385	Tony Fernandez	14.3
	Sid Gordon	14.3
	Chief Meyers	14.3
388	Jim Devlin	14.2
	Wilbur Wood	14.2
	Tommy Henrich	14.2
	Gil Hodges	14.2
392	Mort Cooper	14.1
	Dave Foutz	14.1
	Kip Selbach	14.1
	Andy Thornton	14.1
396	Jack Clements	14.0
	Gene Tenace	14.0
398	Johnny Antonelli	13.9
	Mike Garcia	13.9
400	Fred Hutchinson	13.8

Total Baseball Ranking

	Bill Hutchison	13.8
	Don Baylor	13.8
	Willie Kamm	13.8
	Roger Peckinpaugh	13.8
	Richie Zisk	13.8
406	Jim Galvin	13.7
	Harry Howell	13.7
	Fred Carroll	13.7
409	Greg Maddux	13.6
	Johnny Evers	13.6
	Kevin Mitchell	13.6
412	Deacon Phillippe	13.5
	Rabbit Maranville	13.5
	Dave Orr	13.5
415	Bill Freehan	13.4
	Tommy Holmes	13.4
	Terry Pendleton	13.4
418	Charlie Hough	13.3
	Jim Whitney	13.3
	Deacon McGuire	13.3
	Tip O'Neill	13.3
	Orator Shaffer	13.3
423	Nap Rucker	13.2
	Bob Shawkey	13.2
	Chick Hafey	13.2
	Johnny Pesky	13.2
	George Van Haltren	13.2
428	Jim Maloney	13.1
	Jon Matlack	13.1
	Howie Pollet	13.1
	Curt Simmons	13.1
	Bob Stanley	13.1
	Sixto Lezcano	13.1
434	Kal Daniels	13.0
	Mike Tiernan	13.0
436	Clete Boyer	12.9
	George Stone	12.9
438	Jerry Koosman	12.8
	Sparky Lyle	12.8
	Jim Tobin	12.8
	Johnny Callison	12.8
	Doug DeCinces	12.8
443	Bob Welch	12.7
	Ben Chapman	12.7
	Harry Hooper	12.7
	Riggs Stephenson	12.7
	John Titus	12.7
448	Tom Candiotti	12.6
	Darrell Porter	12.6
	Roy Sievers	12.6
	Red Smith	12.6
452	Larry Corcoran	12.5
	Frank Killen	12.5
	Frank Lary	12.5
	Bruce Sutter	12.5
	Will White	12.5
	Lonnie Smith	12.5
458	Rollie Fingers	12.4
	Kid Elberfeld	12.4
460	Jackie Jensen	12.3
461	John Hiller	12.2
	Bobby Murcer	12.2
463	Ted Breitenstein	12.1
	Jake Daubert	12.1
465	Russ Ford	12.0
	Claude Osteen	12.0
	Milt Pappas	12.0
	Luis Aparicio	12.0
	Lou Criger	12.0
	Lonny Frey	12.0
	Jerry Priddy	12.0
	Ossee Schreckengost	12.0
473	Fernando Valenzuela	11.9
	Harry Davis	11.9
	Nellie Fox	11.9
	Johnny Kling	11.9
	Al Rosen	11.9
478	Ewell Blackwell	11.8
	Harvey Haddix	11.8
	Jack Morris	11.8
	Robby Thompson	11.8
482	Stu Miller	11.7
	Gary Peters	11.7
	Bobby Bonilla	11.7
	Buck Herzog	11.7
	Lance Parrish	11.7
	Ed Swartwood	11.7
	Curt Welch	11.7
489	Jake Weimer	11.6
	Rick Burleson	11.6
	Don Mattingly	11.6
492	Frank Viola	11.5
	Dom DiMaggio	11.5
	Willie Keeler	11.5
	Danny Murphy	11.5
	Rudy York	11.5
497	6 players tied	11.4

Total Baseball Rank (alpha.)

Hank Aaron	84.6
Babe Adams	16.9
Pete Alexander	63.9
Dick Allen	33.5
Gene Alley	18.2
Bob Allison	14.9
Cap Anson	36.2
Johnny Antonelli	13.9
Luis Aparicio	12.0
Luke Appling	40.9
Richie Ashburn	30.7
Earl Averill	18.3
Harold Baines	14.5
Frank Baker	33.5
Dave Bancroft	35.4
Ernie Banks	25.7
Jesse Barfield	16.5
Dick Bartell	27.7
Don Baylor	13.8
Jake Beckley	24.4
Mark Belanger	15.7
Buddy Bell	22.9
Johnny Bench	25.2
Chief Bender	14.6
Charlie Bennett	19.6
Wally Berger	20.8
Yogi Berra	35.5
Ewell Blackwell	11.8
Bert Blyleven	33.1
Wade Boggs	39.9
Barry Bonds	34.7
Bobby Bonds	32.7
Bobby Bonilla	11.7
Lou Boudreau	40.4
Clete Boyer	12.9
Ken Boyer	20.3
Harry Brecheen	23.4
Ted Breitenstein	12.1
Roger Bresnahan	19.9
George Brett	42.1
Tommy Bridges	27.4
Dan Brouthers	42.7
Mordecai Brown	33.6
Pete Browning	29.5
Charlie Buffinton	15.4
Jim Bunning	17.0
Jesse Burkett	28.6
Rick Burleson	11.6
Brett Butler	18.5
Johnny Callison	12.8
Dolph Camilli	14.4
Roy Campanella	21.9
John Candelaria	14.9
Tom Candiotti	12.6
Jose Canseco	19.6
Rod Carew	32.5
Max Carey	23.4
Steve Carlton	35.3
Fred Carroll	13.7
Gary Carter	29.5
Rico Carty	15.6
Bob Caruthers	32.6
Norm Cash	28.6
Cesar Cedeno	20.2
Orlando Cepeda	17.1
Ron Cey	21.7
Frank Chance	21.1
Spud Chandler	21.0
Ray Chapman	15.9
Ben Chapman	12.7
Cupid Childs	31.2
Eddie Cicotte	23.9
Jack Clark	29.0
Will Clark	17.1
Fred Clarke	30.1
John Clarkson	49.2
Roger Clemens	33.2
Roberto Clemente	41.5
Jack Clements	14.0
Harlond Clift	22.9
Ty Cobb	92.8
Mickey Cochrane	32.2
Rocky Colavito	25.9
Eddie Collins	69.4
Jimmy Collins	24.2
Roger Connor	44.4
Wilbur Cooper	20.3
Mort Cooper	14.1
Larry Corcoran	12.5
Stan Coveleski	26.2
Gavvy Cravath	20.5
Sam Crawford	31.2
Lou Criger	12.0
Joe Cronin	39.9
Lave Cross	16.0
Jose Cruz	22.7
Roy Cullenbine	18.5
Nig Cuppy	22.4
Kiki Cuyler	16.3
Bill Dahlen	52.4

Total Baseball Rank (alpha.)

Kal Daniels	13.0
Jake Daubert	12.1
Curt Davis	18.7
Eric Davis	19.9
George Davis	51.5
Harry Davis	11.9
Andre Dawson	29.0
Dizzy Dean	20.1
Doug DeCinces	12.8
Ed Delahanty	44.8
Jim Devlin	14.2
Art Devlin	20.3
Bill Dickey	34.8
Murry Dickson	18.5
Dom DiMaggio	11.5
Joe DiMaggio	46.5
Larry Doby	20.3
Bobby Doerr	39.8
Brian Downing	20.6
Don Drysdale	34.8
Fred Dunlap	29.4
Frank Dwyer	15.1
Lenny Dykstra	16.6
Dennis Eckersley	18.8
Kid Elberfeld	12.4
Bob Elliott	18.5
Darrell Evans	35.2
Dwight Evans	32.8
Johnny Evers	13.6
Buck Ewing	30.9
Red Faber	25.8
Ferris Fain	18.4
Duke Farrell	15.6
Bob Feller	27.8
Charlie Ferguson	14.4
Tony Fernandez	14.3
Wes Ferrell	30.9
Rollie Fingers	12.4
Carlton Fisk	26.6
Freddie Fitzsimmons	22.4
Art Fletcher	26.3
Elmer Flick	28.6
Whitey Ford	38.7
Russ Ford	12.0
George Foster	22.8
Jack Fournier	23.5
Dave Foutz	14.1
Nellie Fox	11.9
Jimmie Foxx	56.2
Bill Freehan	13.4
Jim Fregosi	20.1
Larry French	16.8
Lonny Frey	12.0
Frankie Frisch	38.8
Augie Galan	14.7
Jim Galvin	13.7
Mike Garcia	13.9
Ned Garver	17.3
Lou Gehrig	61.9
Charlie Gehringer	45.1
Bob Gibson	45.1
Kirk Gibson	15.4
Jack Glasscock	37.5
Lefty Gomez	18.0
Dwight Gooden	17.0
Joe Gordon	27.7
Sid Gordon	14.3
George Gore	18.6
Goose Goslin	26.0
Rich Gossage	14.6
Hank Greenberg	31.7
Bobby Grich	43.3
Mike Griffin	21.1
Clark Griffith	27.7
Burleigh Grimes	24.3
Heinie Groh	26.7
Lefty Grove	58.7
Pedro Guerrero	17.4
Ron Guidry	18.1
Tony Gwynn	31.0
Stan Hack	27.1
Harvey Haddix	11.8
Chick Hafey	13.2
Noodles Hahn	17.2
Billy Hamilton	28.7
Ron Hansen	14.5
Mel Harder	17.3
Mike Hargrove	15.6
Gabby Hartnett	40.1
Jeff Heath	15.7
Guy Hecker	22.3
Harry Heilmann	31.9
Rickey Henderson	67.0
Claude Hendrix	17.1
Tommy Henrich	14.2
Babe Herman	16.7
Billy Herman	32.0
Keith Hernandez	34.1
Orel Hershiser	19.1
Buck Herzog	11.7

Total Baseball Rank (alpha.)

John Hiller	12.2
Paul Hines	17.8
Gil Hodges	14.2
Tommy Holmes	13.4
Harry Hooper	12.7
Rogers Hornsby	79.8
Charlie Hough	13.3
Frank Howard	19.9
Harry Howell	13.7
Waite Hoyt	14.9
Glenn Hubbard	20.0
Carl Hubbell	38.4
Miller Huggins	18.2
Fred Hutchinson	13.8
Bill Hutchison	13.8
Larry Jackson	19.0
Joe Jackson	38.2
Reggie Jackson	42.7
Travis Jackson	24.0
Fergie Jenkins	30.3
Hughie Jennings	27.4
Jackie Jensen	12.3
Tommy John	26.8
Walter Johnson	83.7
Davey Johnson	15.8
Bob Johnson	35.1
Charley Jones	21.4
Addie Joss	25.5
Bill Joyce	19.3
Jim Kaat	18.9
Al Kaline	46.4
Willie Kamm	13.8
Benny Kauff	17.2
Tim Keefe	37.1
Willie Keeler	11.5
Charlie Keller	23.3
Joe Kelley	21.9
King Kelly	26.9
Jimmy Key	14.6
Harmon Killebrew	28.7
Frank Killen	12.5
Ralph Kiner	29.9
Silver King	23.5
Chuck Klein	24.6
Johnny Kling	11.9
Bobby Knoop	15.3
Ed Konetchy	23.2
Jerry Koosman	12.8
Sandy Koufax	19.8
Nap Lajoie	94.9
Max Lanier	14.8
Barry Larkin	23.3
Henry Larkin	16.8
Frank Lary	12.5
Tony Lazzeri	16.1
Tommy Leach	17.8
Thornton Lee	17.3
Sam Leever	15.3
Bob Lemon	35.1
Chet Lemon	22.0
Dutch Leonard	23.5
Sixto Lezcano	13.1
Johnny Logan	18.1
Ernie Lombardi	17.1
Ed Lopat	17.7
Red Lucas	17.6
Dolf Luque	25.3
Sparky Lyle	12.8
Fred Lynn	23.7
Ted Lyons	35.2
Denny Lyons	21.3
Greg Maddux	13.6
Sherry Magee	27.2
Sal Maglie	14.6
Jim Maloney	13.1
Mickey Mantle	73.6
Rabbit Maranville	13.5
Juan Marichal	30.1
Eddie Mathews	48.6
Christy Mathewson	59.3
Jon Matlack	13.1
Don Mattingly	11.6
Carl Mays	34.9
Willie Mays	86.4
Bill Mazeroski	36.6
Jim McCormick	22.6
Willie McCovey	35.1
Gil McDougald	16.7
Joe McGinnity	19.1
John McGraw	17.2
Fred McGriff	16.1
Deacon McGuire	13.3
Sadie McMahon	15.2
Bid McPhee	42.3
Hal McRae	16.3
Kevin McReynolds	15.2
Joe Medwick	28.0
Andy Messersmith	18.4
Chief Meyers	14.3
Stu Miller	11.7

Total Baseball Rank (alpha.)

Jocko Milligan	17.1
Minnie Minoso	25.8
Kevin Mitchell	13.6
Johnny Mize	37.7
Paul Molitor	30.4
Joe Morgan	55.7
Jack Morris	11.8
Tony Mullane	32.0
George Mullin	15.5
Thurman Munson	15.1
Bobby Murcer	12.2
Dale Murphy	18.8
Danny Murphy	11.5
Dwayne Murphy	16.0
Eddie Murray	37.5
Stan Musial	71.7
Billy Nash	14.6
Graig Nettles	21.5
Don Newcombe	20.0
Hal Newhouser	37.9
Kid Nichols	59.9
Bill Nicholson	18.4
Phil Niekro	36.0
Tony Oliva	26.7
Tip O'Neill	13.3
Jim O'Rourke	17.1
Dave Orr	13.5
Claude Osteen	12.0
Amos Otis	20.7
Mel Ott	62.4
Jim Palmer	38.4
Milt Pappas	12.0
Dave Parker	22.0
Mel Parnell	17.1
Lance Parrish	11.7
Claude Passeau	16.7
Roger Peckinpaugh	13.8
Terry Pendleton	13.4
Gaylord Perry	35.3
Johnny Pesky	13.2
Gary Peters	11.7
Fred Pfeffer	23.4
Deacon Phillippe	13.5
Billy Pierce	22.3
Eddie Plank	26.8
Howie Pollet	13.1
Darrell Porter	12.6
Boog Powell	14.7
Del Pratt	20.2
Jerry Priddy	12.0
Kirby Puckett	24.3
Jack Quinn	23.7
Dan Quisenberry	17.5
Charley Radbourn	26.4
Tim Raines	47.1
Willie Randolph	23.0
Pee Wee Reese	14.6
Ed Reulbach	18.6
Rick Reuschel	25.5
Jim Rice	30.9
Hardy Richardson	28.4
Cal Ripken	38.6
Eppa Rixey	24.7
Phil Rizzuto	15.9
Robin Roberts	25.5
Brooks Robinson	19.8
Frank Robinson	70.3
Jackie Robinson	32.6
Steve Rogers	18.3
Eddie Rommel	24.4
Pete Rose	19.4
Al Rosen	11.9
Edd Roush	14.5
Schoolboy Rowe	17.5
Nap Rucker	13.2
Red Ruffing	26.4
Amos Rusie	37.3
Babe Ruth	122.5
Nolan Ryan	21.6
Jimmy Ryan	16.6
Bret Saberhagen	18.6
Ryne Sandberg	40.0
Ron Santo	41.7
Wally Schang	18.1
Mike Schmidt	80.3
Ossee Schreckengost	12.0
Hal Schumacher	16.2
Mike Scioscia	14.7
Tom Seaver	51.1
Kip Selbach	14.1
Joe Sewell	35.2
Cy Seymour	15.9
Orator Shaffer	13.3
Bobby Shantz	20.2
Bob Shawkey	13.2
Jimmy Sheckard	19.6
Urban Shocker	24.6
Roy Sievers	12.6
Curt Simmons	13.1
Al Simmons	27.2

Total Baseball Rank (alpha.)

Ted Simmons	17.5
Ken Singleton	21.0
George Sisler	24.2
Enos Slaughter	17.7
Roy Smalley	14.5
Reggie Smith	34.8
Elmer Smith	15.4
Red Smith	12.6
Lonnie Smith	12.5
Ozzie Smith	42.1
Duke Snider	24.2
Warren Spahn	43.7
Tris Speaker	88.5
Eddie Stanky	18.5
Bob Stanley	13.1
Willie Stargell	26.1
Rusty Staub	27.1
Vern Stephens	20.6
Riggs Stephenson	12.7
Dave Stieb	28.9
Jack Stivetts	26.1
George Stone	12.9
Mel Stottlemyre	17.5
Harry Stovey	23.5
Darryl Strawberry	26.7
Bruce Sutter	12.5
Don Sutton	14.7
Ed Swartwood	11.7
Frank Tanana	14.8
Jesse Tannehill	19.2
Danny Tartabull	14.4
Jack Taylor	16.8
Kent Tekulve	16.7
Gene Tenace	14.0
Fred Tenney	21.4
Bill Terry	24.4
Roy Thomas	22.6
Robby Thompson	11.8
Sam Thompson	30.0
Andy Thornton	14.1
Luis Tiant	16.3
Mike Tiernan	13.0
Joe Tinker	24.3
John Titus	12.7
Jim Tobin	12.8
Joe Torre	20.1
Alan Trammell	23.3
Pie Traynor	20.9
Dizzy Trout	32.6
Virgil Trucks	14.6
John Tudor	16.1
George Uhle	14.9
Fernando Valenzuela	11.9
Dazzy Vance	25.8
George Van Haltren	13.2
Andy Van Slyke	20.9
Arky Vaughan	39.7
Hippo Vaughn	18.2
Bobby Veach	14.7
Frank Viola	11.5
Rube Waddell	24.6
Honus Wagner	82.9
Bobby Wallace	40.5
Ed Walsh	42.1
Bucky Walters	26.7
Paul Waner	37.0
John Ward	23.2
Lon Warneke	22.5
Jake Weimer	11.6
Mickey Welch	14.7
Bob Welch	12.7
Curt Welch	11.7
Zack Wheat	24.7
Lou Whitaker	19.5
Doc White	16.8
Will White	12.5
Roy White	20.8
Jim Whitney	13.3
Hoyt Wilhelm	28.8
Billy Williams	27.1
Jimmy Williams	16.5
Ken Williams	18.3
Ted Williams	92.4
Vic Willis	21.6
Hack Wilson	15.6
Dave Winfield	40.3
Joe Wood	20.4
Wilbur Wood	14.2
Early Wynn	17.3
Jim Wynn	28.4
Carl Yastrzemski	50.8
Rudy York	11.5
Cy Young	78.8
Robin Yount	43.0
Chief Zimmer	16.7
Richie Zisk	13.8

Total Baseball Rank (by era)

1876-1892

1	John Clarkson	49.2
2	Roger Connor	44.4
3	Dan Brouthers	42.7
4	Bid McPhee	42.3
5	Jack Glasscock	37.5
6	Tim Keefe	37.1
7	Cap Anson	36.2
8	Bob Caruthers	32.6
9	Tony Mullane	32.0
10	Buck Ewing	30.9
11	Sam Thompson	30.0
12	Pete Browning	29.5
13	Fred Dunlap	29.4
14	Hardy Richardson	28.4
15	King Kelly	26.9
16	Charley Radbourn	26.4
17	Jack Stivetts	26.1
18	Silver King	23.5
	Harry Stovey	23.5
20	Fred Pfeffer	23.4
21	John Ward	23.2
22	Jim McCormick	22.6
23	Guy Hecker	22.3
24	Charley Jones	21.4
25	Denny Lyons	21.3

1893-1919

1	Nap Lajoie	94.9
2	Ty Cobb	92.8
3	Tris Speaker	88.5
4	Walter Johnson	83.7
5	Honus Wagner	82.9
6	Cy Young	78.8
7	Eddie Collins	69.4
8	Pete Alexander	63.9
9	Kid Nichols	59.9
10	Christy Mathewson	59.3
11	Bill Dahlen	52.4
12	George Davis	51.5
13	Ed Delahanty	44.8
14	Ed Walsh	42.1
15	Bobby Wallace	40.5
16	Joe Jackson	38.2
17	Amos Rusie	37.3
18	Mordecai Brown	33.6
19	Frank Baker	33.5
20	Cupid Childs	31.2
	Sam Crawford	31.2
22	Fred Clarke	30.1
23	Billy Hamilton	28.7
24	Jesse Burkett	28.6
	Elmer Flick	28.6

1920-1941

1	Babe Ruth	122.5
2	Rogers Hornsby	79.8
3	Mel Ott	62.4
4	Lou Gehrig	61.9
5	Lefty Grove	58.7
6	Jimmie Foxx	56.2
7	Charlie Gehringer	45.1
8	Luke Appling	40.9
9	Gabby Hartnett	40.1
10	Joe Cronin	39.9
11	Arky Vaughan	39.7
12	Frankie Frisch	38.8
13	Carl Hubbell	38.4
14	Paul Waner	37.0
15	Dave Bancroft	35.4
16	Ted Lyons	35.2
	Joe Sewell	35.2
18	Bob Johnson	35.1
19	Carl Mays	34.9
20	Bill Dickey	34.8
21	Mickey Cochrane	32.2
22	Billy Herman	32.0
23	Harry Heilmann	31.9
24	Hank Greenberg	31.7
25	Wes Ferrell	30.9

Total Baseball Rank (by era)

1942-1960

1	Ted Williams	92.4
2	Mickey Mantle	73.6
3	Stan Musial	71.7
4	Eddie Mathews	48.6
5	Joe DiMaggio	46.5
6	Warren Spahn	43.7
7	Lou Boudreau	40.4
8	Bobby Doerr	39.8
9	Whitey Ford	38.7
10	Hal Newhouser	37.9
11	Johnny Mize	37.7
12	Yogi Berra	35.5
13	Bob Lemon	35.1
14	Dizzy Trout	32.6
	Jackie Robinson	32.6
16	Richie Ashburn	30.7
17	Ralph Kiner	29.9
18	Hoyt Wilhelm	28.8
19	Bob Feller	27.8
20	Joe Gordon	27.7
21	Minnie Minoso	25.8
22	Robin Roberts	25.5
23	Duke Snider	24.2
24	Dutch Leonard	23.5
25	Harry Brecheen	23.4

1961-1992

1	Willie Mays	86.4
2	Hank Aaron	84.6
3	Mike Schmidt	80.3
4	Frank Robinson	70.3
5	Rickey Henderson	67.0
6	Joe Morgan	55.7
7	Tom Seaver	51.1
8	Carl Yastrzemski	50.8
9	Tim Raines	47.1
10	Al Kaline	46.4
11	Bob Gibson	45.1
12	Bobby Grich	43.3
13	Robin Yount	43.0
14	Reggie Jackson	42.7
15	George Brett	42.1
	Ozzie Smith	42.1
17	Ron Santo	41.7
18	Roberto Clemente	41.5
19	Dave Winfield	40.3
20	Ryne Sandberg	40.0
21	Wade Boggs	39.9
22	Cal Ripken	38.6
23	Jim Palmer	38.4
24	Eddie Murray	37.5
25	Bill Mazeroski	36.6

At Bats

1	Willie Wilson, 1980	705
2	Juan Samuel, 1984	701
3	Dave Cash, 1975	699
4	Matty Alou, 1969	698
5	Woody Jensen, 1936	696
6	Maury Wills, 1962	695
	Omar Moreno, 1979	695
8	Bobby Richardson, 1962	692
9	Kirby Puckett, 1985	691
10	Lou Brock, 1967	689
	Sandy Alomar, 1971	689
12	Dave Cash, 1974	687
	Tony Fernandez, 1986	687
14	Horace Clarke, 1970	686
15	Lloyd Waner, 1931	681
	Jo-Jo Moore, 1935	681
17	Pete Rose, 1973	680
	Frank Taveras, 1979	680
	Kirby Puckett, 1986	680
20	Harvey Kuenn, 1953	679
	Curt Flood, 1964	679
	Bobby Richardson, 1964	679
23	Dick Groat, 1962	678
24	Matty Alou, 1970	677
	Jim Rice, 1978	677
	Don Mattingly, 1986	677
27	Felix Millan, 1975	676
	Omar Moreno, 1980	676
29	Rennie Stennett, 1974	673
	Bill Buckner, 1985	673
31	Rabbit Maranville, 1922	672
	Tony Oliva, 1964	672
	Sandy Alomar, 1970	672
	Garry Templeton, 1979	672
35	Jack Tobin, 1921	671
36	Al Simmons, 1932	670
	Pete Rose, 1965	670
	Buddy Bell, 1979	670
39	Vada Pinson, 1965	669
	Larry Bowa, 1974	669
41	Buddy Lewis, 1937	668
	Brooks Robinson, 1961	668
	Ralph Garr, 1973	668
44	Carl Furillo, 1951	667
45	Billy Herman, 1935	666
	Zoilo Versalles, 1965	666
	Felipe Alou, 1966	666
	Dave Cash, 1976	666
	Ron LeFlore, 1978	666
	Paul Molitor, 1982	666
51	Tommy Davis, 1962	665
	Pete Rose, 1976	665
	Paul Molitor, 1991	665
54	Taylor Douthit, 1930	664
	Bobby Richardson, 1965	664
	Don Kessinger, 1969	664
	Lou Brock, 1970	664
58	Jake Wood, 1961	663
	Bill Virdon, 1962	663
	Bobby Bonds, 1970	663
	Rick Burleson, 1977	663
	Cal Ripken, 1983	663
	Juan Samuel, 1985	663
	Joe Carter, 1986	663
65	Lloyd Waner, 1929	662
	Hughie Critz, 1930	662
	Richie Ashburn, 1949	662
	Granny Hamner, 1949	662
	Bobby Richardson, 1961	662
	Curt Flood, 1963	662
	Felipe Alou, 1968	662
	Pete Rose, 1975	662
73	Doc Cramer, 1933	661
	Doc Cramer, 1940	661
	Ken Hubbs, 1962	661
	Cecil Cooper, 1983	661
	Ruben Sierra, 1991	661
78	Tom Brown, 1892	660
	Doc Cramer, 1941	660
	Lou Brock, 1968	660
	Enos Cabell, 1978	660
82	Lloyd Waner, 1928	659
	Hughie Critz, 1932	659
	Red Schoendienst, 1947	659
	Billy Moran, 1962	659
	Zoilo Versalles, 1964	659
	Luis Aparicio, 1966	659
	Steve Garvey, 1975	659
	Warren Cromartie, 1979	659
	Travis Fryman, 1992	659
91	Heinie Manush, 1933	658
	Doc Cramer, 1938	658
	Bill White, 1963	658
	Dave Cash, 1978	658
	Steve Garvey, 1980	658
	Julio Franco, 1984	658
97	5 players tied	657

Runs

1	Billy Hamilton, 1894	192
2	Tom Brown, 1891	177
	Babe Ruth, 1921	177
4	Tip O'Neill, 1887	167
	Lou Gehrig, 1936	167
6	Billy Hamilton, 1895	166
7	Willie Keeler, 1894	165
	Joe Kelley, 1894	165
9	Arlie Latham, 1887	163
	Babe Ruth, 1928	163
	Lou Gehrig, 1931	163
12	Willie Keeler, 1895	162
13	Hugh Duffy, 1890	161
14	Fred Dunlap, 1884	160
	Hugh Duffy, 1894	160
	Jesse Burkett, 1896	160
17	Hughie Jennings, 1895	159
18	Bobby Lowe, 1894	158
	Babe Ruth, 1920	158
	Babe Ruth, 1927	158
	Chuck Klein, 1930	158
22	John McGraw, 1894	156
	Rogers Hornsby, 1929	156
24	King Kelly, 1886	155
	Kiki Cuyler, 1930	155
26	Dan Brouthers, 1887	153
	Jesse Burkett, 1895	153
	Willie Keeler, 1896	153
29	Arlie Latham, 1886	152
	Mike Griffin, 1889	152
	Harry Stovey, 1889	152
	Billy Hamilton, 1896	152
	Billy Hamilton, 1897	152
	Lefty O'Doul, 1929	152
	Woody English, 1930	152
	Al Simmons, 1930	152
	Chuck Klein, 1932	152
38	Babe Ruth, 1923	151
	Jimmie Foxx, 1932	151
	Joe DiMaggio, 1937	151
41	George Gore, 1886	150
	Babe Ruth, 1930	150
	Ted Williams, 1949	150
44	Herman Long, 1893	149
	Bill Dahlen, 1894	149
	Ed Delahanty, 1895	149
	Lou Gehrig, 1927	149
	Babe Ruth, 1931	149
49	Hub Collins, 1890	148
	Jake Stenzel, 1894	148
	Joe Kelley, 1895	148
	Joe Kelley, 1896	148
53	Mike Tiernan, 1889	147
	Hugh Duffy, 1893	147
	Ed Delahanty, 1894	147
	Ty Cobb, 1911	147
57	Darby O'Brien, 1889	146
	Tom Brown, 1890	146
	Hack Wilson, 1930	146
	Rickey Henderson, 1985	146
61	Jesse Burkett, 1893	145
	Cupid Childs, 1893	145
	Ed Delahanty, 1893	145
	Patsy Donovan, 1894	145
	Willie Keeler, 1897	145
	Nap Lajoie, 1901	145
	Harland Clift, 1936	145
68	Hugh Duffy, 1889	144
	Billy Hamilton, 1889	144
	Ty Cobb, 1915	144
	Kiki Cuyler, 1925	144
	Charlie Gehringer, 1930	144
	Al Simmons, 1932	144
	Charlie Gehringer, 1936	144
	Hank Greenberg, 1938	144
76	Cupid Childs, 1894	143
	John McGraw, 1898	143
	Babe Ruth, 1924	143
	Babe Herman, 1930	143
	Lou Gehrig, 1930	143
	Earle Combs, 1932	143
	Red Rolfe, 1937	143
83	Mike Griffin, 1887	142
	Harry Stovey, 1889	142
	Jesse Burkett, 1901	142
	Paul Waner, 1928	142
	Ted Williams, 1946	142
88	Billy Hamilton, 1891	141
	Rogers Hornsby, 1922	141
	Ted Williams, 1942	141
91	Tom Poorman, 1887	140
	Jimmy Ryan, 1889	140
	Jim McTamany, 1890	140
	Mike Griffin, 1895	140
	Willie Keeler, 1899	140
	John McGraw, 1899	140
	Max Carey, 1922	140
	Earl Averill, 1931	140
99	9 players tied	139

Runs per Game

1876-1892

1	Ross Barnes, 1876	1.91
2	Fred Dunlap, 1884	1.58
3	George Gore, 1890	1.42
4	Tip O'Neill, 1887	1.35
5	King Kelly, 1886	1.31
6	Tom Brown, 1891	1.29
7	George Gore, 1886	1.27
8	Dan Brouthers, 1887	1.24
9	Orator Shaffer, 1884	1.23
10	Mike Tiernan, 1889	1.20
11	Harry Stovey, 1890	1.20
12	Arlie Latham, 1887	1.20
13	Harry Stovey, 1884	1.19
14	George Gore, 1882	1.18
15	George Gore, 1881	1.18

1893-1919

1	Billy Hamilton, 1894	1.49
2	Billy Hamilton, 1895	1.35
3	Billy Hamilton, 1893	1.34
4	Herman Long, 1894	1.31
5	Ed Delahanty, 1894	1.29
6	Ed Delahanty, 1895	1.28
7	Hugh Duffy, 1894	1.28
8	Willie Keeler, 1894	1.28
	Joe Kelley, 1894	1.28
10	John McGraw, 1894	1.26
11	Willie Keeler, 1895	1.24
12	Bill Dahlen, 1894	1.23
13	Jimmy Ryan, 1894	1.22
14	Willie Keeler, 1896	1.21
15	Hughie Jennings, 1895	1.21

1920-1941

1	Babe Ruth, 1921	1.16
2	Babe Ruth, 1920	1.11
3	Al Simmons, 1930	1.10
4	Lou Gehrig, 1936	1.08
5	Babe Ruth, 1928	1.06
6	Lou Gehrig, 1931	1.05
7	Jimmie Foxx, 1939	1.05
8	Babe Ruth, 1927	1.05
9	Babe Ruth, 1930	1.03
10	Babe Ruth, 1931	1.03
11	Chuck Klein, 1930	1.01
12	Rogers Hornsby, 1929	1.00
	Joe DiMaggio, 1937	1.00
14	Kiki Cuyler, 1930	.99
15	Babe Ruth, 1923	.99

1942-1960

1	Ted Williams, 1949	.97
2	Ted Williams, 1946	.95
3	Tommy Henrich, 1948	.95
4	Ted Williams, 1942	.94
5	Dom DiMaggio, 1950	.93
6	Ted Williams, 1941	.91
7	Johnny Mize, 1947	.89
8	Eddie Joost, 1949	.89
9	Mickey Mantle, 1954	.88
10	Johnny Pesky, 1950	.88
11	Mickey Mantle, 1956	.88
12	Stan Musial, 1948	.87
13	Goody Rosen, 1945	.87
	Dom DiMaggio, 1949	.87
15	Johnny Pesky, 1948	.87

1961-1992

1	Rickey Henderson, 1985	1.02
2	Paul Molitor, 1987	.97
3	Eric Davis, 1987	.93
4	Tim Raines, 1987	.88
5	Rickey Henderson, 1990	.88
6	Mickey Mantle, 1961	.86
7	Bobby Bonds, 1970	.85
8	Tim Raines, 1983	.85
9	Billy Williams, 1970	.85
10	Paul Molitor, 1982	.85
11	Rickey Henderson, 1986	.85
12	Robin Yount, 1980	.85
13	Rickey Henderson, 1988	.84
14	Paul Molitor, 1991	.84
15	Willie Mays, 1961	.84

Hits

1	George Sisler, 1920	257
2	Lefty O'Doul, 1929	254
	Bill Terry, 1930	254
4	Al Simmons, 1925	253
5	Rogers Hornsby, 1922	250
	Chuck Klein, 1930	250
7	Ty Cobb, 1911	248
8	George Sisler, 1922	246
9	Heinie Manush, 1928	241
	Babe Herman, 1930	241
11	Jesse Burkett, 1896	240
	Wade Boggs, 1985	240
13	Willie Keeler, 1897	239
	Rod Carew, 1977	239
15	Ed Delahanty, 1899	238
	Don Mattingly, 1986	238
17	Hugh Duffy, 1894	237
	Harry Heilmann, 1921	237
	Paul Waner, 1927	237
	Joe Medwick, 1937	237
21	Jack Tobin, 1921	236
22	Rogers Hornsby, 1921	235
23	Lloyd Waner, 1929	234
	Kirby Puckett, 1988	234
25	Joe Jackson, 1911	233
26	Nap Lajoie, 1901	232
	Earl Averill, 1936	232
28	Earle Combs, 1927	231
	Freddy Lindstrom, 1928	231
	Freddy Lindstrom, 1930	231
	Matty Alou, 1969	231
32	Stan Musial, 1948	230
	Tommy Davis, 1962	230
	Joe Torre, 1971	230
	Pete Rose, 1973	230
	Willie Wilson, 1980	230
37	Rogers Hornsby, 1929	229
38	Kiki Cuyler, 1930	228
	Stan Musial, 1946	228
40	Nap Lajoie, 1910	227
	Rogers Hornsby, 1924	227
	Jim Bottomley, 1925	227
	Sam Rice, 1925	227
	Billy Herman, 1935	227
	Charlie Gehringer, 1936	227
46	Jesse Burkett, 1901	226
	Joe Jackson, 1912	226
	Ty Cobb, 1912	226
	Bill Terry, 1929	226
	Chuck Klein, 1932	226
51	Tip O'Neill, 1887	225
	Jesse Burkett, 1895	225
	Ty Cobb, 1917	225
	Harry Heilmann, 1925	225
	Johnny Hodapp, 1930	225
	Bill Terry, 1932	225
57	Eddie Collins, 1920	224
	George Sisler, 1925	224
	Joe Medwick, 1935	224
	Tommy Holmes, 1945	224
61	Frankie Frisch, 1923	223
	Lloyd Waner, 1927	223
	Paul Waner, 1928	223
	Chuck Klein, 1933	223
	Joe Medwick, 1936	223
	Hank Aaron, 1959	223
	Kirby Puckett, 1986	223
68	Sam Thompson, 1893	222
	Tris Speaker, 1912	222
	Charlie Jamieson, 1923	222
71	Jesse Burkett, 1899	221
	Zach Wheat, 1925	221
	Lloyd Waner, 1928	221
	Heinie Manush, 1933	221
	Richie Ashburn, 1951	221
76	Pete Browning, 1887	220
	Billy Hamilton, 1894	220
	Kiki Cuyler, 1925	220
	Lou Gehrig, 1930	220
	Stan Musial, 1943	220
81	Ed Delahanty, 1893	219
	Willie Keeler, 1894	219
	Jimmy Williams, 1899	219
	Cy Seymour, 1905	219
	Chuck Klein, 1929	219
	Lefty O'Doul, 1932	219
	Paul Waner, 1937	219
	Ralph Garr, 1971	219
	Cecil Cooper, 1980	219
90	12 players tied	218

Doubles

1	Earl Webb, 1931	67
2	George Burns, 1926	64
	Joe Medwick, 1936	64
4	Hank Greenberg, 1934	63
5	Paul Waner, 1932	62
6	Charlie Gehringer, 1936	60
7	Tris Speaker, 1923	59
	Chuck Klein, 1930	59
9	Billy Herman, 1935	57
	Billy Herman, 1936	57
11	Joe Medwick, 1937	56
	George Kell, 1950	56
13	Ed Delahanty, 1899	55
	Gee Walker, 1936	55
15	Hal McRae, 1977	54
16	Tris Speaker, 1912	53
	Al Simmons, 1926	53
	Paul Waner, 1936	53
	Stan Musial, 1953	53
	Don Mattingly, 1986	53
21	Tip O'Neill, 1887	52
	Tris Speaker, 1921	52
	Tris Speaker, 1926	52
	Lou Gehrig, 1927	52
	Johnny Frederick, 1929	52
	Enos Slaughter, 1939	52
27	Hugh Duffy, 1894	51
	Nap Lajoie, 1910	51
	Baby Doll Jacobson, 1926	51
	George Burns, 1927	51
	Johnny Hodapp, 1930	51
	Beau Bell, 1937	51
	Joe Cronin, 1938	51
	Stan Musial, 1944	51
	Mickey Vernon, 1946	51
	Frank Robinson, 1962	51
	Pete Rose, 1978	51
	Wade Boggs, 1989	51
39	Tris Speaker, 1920	50
	Harry Heilmann, 1927	50
	Paul Waner, 1928	50
	Kiki Cuyler, 1930	50
	Chuck Klein, 1932	50
	Charlie Gehringer, 1934	50
	Odell Hale, 1936	50
	Ben Chapman, 1936	50
	Hank Greenberg, 1940	50
	Stan Musial, 1946	50
	Stan Spence, 1946	50
50	Ned Williamson, 1883	49
	Ed Delahanty, 1895	49
	Nap Lajoie, 1904	49
	George Sisler, 1920	49
	Heinie Manush, 1930	49
	Riggs Stephenson, 1932	49
	Hank Greenberg, 1937	49
	Robin Yount, 1980	49
	Rafael Palmeiro, 1991	49
59	Joe Kelley, 1894	48
	Nap Lajoie, 1901	48
	Nap Lajoie, 1906	48
	Tris Speaker, 1922	48
	Joe Sewell, 1927	48
	Babe Herman, 1930	48
	Dick Bartell, 1932	48
	Earl Averill, 1934	48
	Wally Moses, 1937	48
	Joe Medwick, 1939	48
	Stan Musial, 1943	48
	Keith Hernandez, 1979	48
	Don Mattingly, 1985	48
72	Harry Davis, 1905	47
	Ty Cobb, 1911	47
	George Burns, 1923	47
	Lou Gehrig, 1926	47
	Bob Meusel, 1927	47
	Lou Gehrig, 1928	47
	Heinie Manush, 1928	47
	Rogers Hornsby, 1929	47
	Chick Hafey, 1929	47
	Adam Comorosky, 1930	47
	Ed Morgan, 1930	47
	Charlie Gehringer, 1930	47
	Dale Alexander, 1931	47
	Eric McNair, 1932	47
	Joe Vosmik, 1935	47
	Joe Vosmik, 1937	47
	Joe Medwick, 1938	47
	Tommy Holmes, 1945	47
	Vada Pinson, 1959	47
	Wes Parker, 1970	47
	Pete Rose, 1975	47
	Fred Lynn, 1975	47
	Cal Ripken, 1983	47
	Wade Boggs, 1986	47
96	27 players tied	46

Triples

1	Chief Wilson, 1912	36
2	Dave Orr, 1886	31
	Heinie Reitz, 1894	31
4	Perry Werden, 1893	29
5	Harry Davis, 1897	28
6	George Davis, 1893	27
	Sam Thompson, 1894	27
	Jimmy Williams, 1899	27
9	John Reilly, 1890	26
	George Treadway, 1894	26
	Joe Jackson, 1912	26
	Sam Crawford, 1914	26
	Kiki Cuyler, 1925	26
14	Roger Connor, 1894	25
	Buck Freeman, 1899	25
	Sam Crawford, 1903	25
	Larry Doyle, 1911	25
	Tom Long, 1915	25
19	Ed McKean, 1893	24
	Ty Cobb, 1911	24
	Ty Cobb, 1917	24
22	Harry Stovey, 1884	23
	Sam Thompson, 1887	23
	Elmer Smith, 1893	23
	Dan Brouthers, 1894	23
	Nap Lajoie, 1897	23
	Ty Cobb, 1912	23
	Sam Crawford, 1913	23
	Earle Combs, 1927	23
	Adam Comorosky, 1930	23
	Dale Mitchell, 1949	23
32	Roger Connor, 1887	22
	Bid McPhee, 1890	22
	Jake Beckley, 1890	22
	Joe Visner, 1890	22
	Willie Keeler, 1894	22
	Kip Selbach, 1895	22
	Anderson, 1898	22
	Honus Wagner, 1900	22
	Tommy Leach, 1902	22
	Sam Crawford, 1902	22
	Bill Bradley, 1903	22
	Elmer Flick, 1906	22
	Mike Mitchell, 1911	22
	Birdie Cree, 1911	22
	Tris Speaker, 1913	22
	Hi Myers, 1920	22
	Jake Daubert, 1922	22
	Paul Waner, 1926	22
	Earle Combs, 1930	22
	Snuffy Stirnweiss, 1945	22
52	Dave Orr, 1885	21
	Mike Tiernan, 1890	21
	Billy Shindle, 1890	21
	Tom Brown, 1891	21
	Ed Delahanty, 1892	21
	Sam Thompson, 1895	21
	Mike Tiernan, 1895	21
	Tom McCreery, 1896	21
	George Van Haltren, 1896	21
	Bobby Wallace, 1897	21
	Jimmy Williams, 1901	21
	Bill Keister, 1901	21
	Jimmy Williams, 1902	21
	Cy Seymour, 1905	21
	Frank Schulte, 1911	21
	Frank Baker, 1912	21
	Sam Crawford, 1912	21
	Vic Saier, 1913	21
	Joe Jackson, 1916	21
	Edd Roush, 1924	21
	Earle Combs, 1928	21
	Willie Wilson, 1985	21
74	36 players tied	20

Triples (by era)

1876-1892

1	Dave Orr, 1886	31
2	John Reilly, 1890	26
3	Harry Stovey, 1884	23
	Sam Thompson, 1887	23
5	Roger Connor, 1887	22
	Bid McPhee, 1890	22
	Jake Beckley, 1890	22
	Joe Visner, 1890	22
9	Dave Orr, 1885	21
	Mike Tiernan, 1890	21
	Billy Shindle, 1890	21
	Tom Brown, 1891	21
	Ed Delahanty, 1892	21
14	10 players tied	20

1893-1919

1	Chief Wilson, 1912	36
2	Heinie Reitz, 1894	31
3	Perry Werden, 1893	29
4	Harry Davis, 1897	28
5	George Davis, 1893	27
	Sam Thompson, 1894	27
	Jimmy Williams, 1899	27
8	George Treadway, 1894	26
	Joe Jackson, 1912	26
	Sam Crawford, 1914	26
11	Roger Connor, 1894	25
	Buck Freeman, 1899	25
	Sam Crawford, 1903	25
	Larry Doyle, 1911	25
	Tom Long, 1915	25

1920-1941

1	Kiki Cuyler, 1925	26
2	Earle Combs, 1927	23
	Adam Comorosky, 1930	23
4	Hi Myers, 1920	22
	Jake Daubert, 1922	22
	Paul Waner, 1926	22
	Earle Combs, 1930	22
8	Edd Roush, 1924	21
	Earle Combs, 1928	21
10	12 players tied	20

1942-1960

1	Dale Mitchell, 1949	23
2	Snuffy Stirnweiss, 1945	22
3	Stan Musial, 1943	20
	Stan Musial, 1946	20
	Willie Mays, 1957	20
6	Johnny Barrett, 1944	19
7	Stan Musial, 1948	18
	Minnie Minoso, 1954	18
9	Enos Slaughter, 1942	17
	Jim Gilliam, 1953	17
11	6 players tied	16

1961-1992

1	Willie Wilson, 1985	21
2	George Brett, 1979	20
3	Garry Templeton, 1979	19
	Juan Samuel, 1984	19
	Ryne Sandberg, 1984	19
6	Garry Templeton, 1977	18
	Willie McGee, 1985	18
8	Ralph Garr, 1974	17
	Tony Fernandez, 1990	17
10	Johnny Callison, 1965	16
	Willie Davis, 1970	16
	Rod Carew, 1977	16
	Paul Molitor, 1979	16
14	12 players tied	15

Home Runs

1	Roger Maris, 1961	61
2	Babe Ruth, 1927	60
3	Babe Ruth, 1921	59
4	Jimmie Foxx, 1932	58
	Hank Greenberg, 1938	58
6	Hack Wilson, 1930	56
7	Babe Ruth, 1920	54
	Babe Ruth, 1928	54
	Ralph Kiner, 1949	54
	Mickey Mantle, 1961	54
11	Mickey Mantle, 1956	52
	Willie Mays, 1965	52
	George Foster, 1977	52
14	Ralph Kiner, 1947	51
	Johnny Mize, 1947	51
	Willie Mays, 1955	51
	Cecil Fielder, 1990	51
18	Jimmie Foxx, 1938	50
19	Babe Ruth, 1930	49
	Lou Gehrig, 1934	49
	Lou Gehrig, 1936	49
	Ted Kluszewski, 1954	49
	Willie Mays, 1962	49
	Harmon Killebrew, 1964	49
	Frank Robinson, 1966	49
	Harmon Killebrew, 1969	49
	Andre Dawson, 1987	49
	Mark McGwire, 1987	49
29	Jimmie Foxx, 1933	48
	Harmon Killebrew, 1962	48
	Frank Howard, 1969	48
	Willie Stargell, 1971	48
	Dave Kingman, 1979	48
	Mike Schmidt, 1980	48
35	Babe Ruth, 1926	47
	Lou Gehrig, 1927	47
	Ralph Kiner, 1950	47
	Eddie Mathews, 1953	47
	Ted Kluszewski, 1955	47
	Ernie Banks, 1958	47
	Willie Mays, 1964	47
	Reggie Jackson, 1969	47
	Hank Aaron, 1971	47
	George Bell, 1987	47
	Kevin Mitchell, 1989	47
46	Babe Ruth, 1924	46
	Babe Ruth, 1929	46
	Babe Ruth, 1931	46
	Lou Gehrig, 1931	46
	Joe DiMaggio, 1937	46
	Eddie Mathews, 1959	46
	Orlando Cepeda, 1961	46
	Jim Gentile, 1961	46
	Harmon Killebrew, 1961	46
	Jim Rice, 1978	46
56	Ernie Banks, 1959	45
	Rocky Colavito, 1961	45
	Hank Aaron, 1962	45
	Harmon Killebrew, 1963	45
	Willie McCovey, 1969	45
	Johnny Bench, 1970	45
	Mike Schmidt, 1979	45
	Gorman Thomas, 1979	45
64	Jimmie Foxx, 1934	44
	Hank Greenberg, 1946	44
	Ernie Banks, 1955	44
	Hank Aaron, 1957	44
	Hank Aaron, 1963	44
	Willie McCovey, 1963	44
	Hank Aaron, 1966	44
	Harmon Killebrew, 1967	44
	Carl Yastrzemski, 1967	44
	Frank Howard, 1968	44
	Hank Aaron, 1969	44
	Frank Howard, 1970	44
	Willie Stargell, 1973	44
	Dale Murphy, 1987	44
	Jose Canseco, 1991	44
	Cecil Fielder, 1991	44
80	Chuck Klein, 1929	43
	Johnny Mize, 1940	43
	Ted Williams, 1949	43
	Al Rosen, 1953	43
	Duke Snider, 1956	43
	Ernie Banks, 1957	43
	Dave Johnson, 1973	43
	Tony Armas, 1984	43
	Juan Gonzalez, 1992	43
89	16 players tied	42

Home Runs (by era)

1876-1892

1	Ned Williamson, 1884	27
2	Fred Pfeffer, 1884	25
3	Abner Dalrymple, 1884	22
4	Cap Anson, 1884	21
5	Sam Thompson, 1889	20
6	Billy O'Brien, 1887	19
	Bug Holliday, 1889	19
	Harry Stovey, 1889	19
9	Jerry Denny, 1889	18
10	Roger Connor, 1887	17
	Jimmy Ryan, 1889	17
12	Fred Pfeffer, 1887	16
	Jimmy Ryan, 1888	16
	Harry Stovey, 1891	16
	Mike Tiernan, 1891	16

1893-1919

1	Babe Ruth, 1919	29
2	Buck Freeman, 1899	25
3	Gavvy Cravath, 1915	24
4	Frank Schulte, 1911	21
5	Ed Delahanty, 1893	19
	Gavvy Cravath, 1913	19
	Gavvy Cravath, 1914	19
8	Hugh Duffy, 1894	18
	Sam Thompson, 1895	18
	Fred Luderus, 1913	18
	Vic Saier, 1914	18
12	5 players tied	17

1920-1941

1	Babe Ruth, 1927	60
2	Babe Ruth, 1921	59
3	Jimmie Foxx, 1932	58
	Hank Greenberg, 1938	58
5	Hack Wilson, 1930	56
6	Babe Ruth, 1920	54
	Babe Ruth, 1928	54
8	Jimmie Foxx, 1938	50
9	Babe Ruth, 1930	49
	Lou Gehrig, 1934	49
	Lou Gehrig, 1936	49
12	Jimmie Foxx, 1933	48
13	Babe Ruth, 1926	47
	Lou Gehrig, 1927	47
15	5 players tied	46

1942-1960

1	Ralph Kiner, 1949	54
2	Mickey Mantle, 1956	52
3	Ralph Kiner, 1947	51
	Johnny Mize, 1947	51
	Willie Mays, 1955	51
6	Ted Kluszewski, 1954	49
7	Ralph Kiner, 1950	47
	Eddie Mathews, 1953	47
	Ted Kluszewski, 1955	47
	Ernie Banks, 1958	47
11	Eddie Mathews, 1959	46
12	Ernie Banks, 1959	45
13	Hank Greenberg, 1946	44
	Ernie Banks, 1955	44
	Hank Aaron, 1957	44

1961-1992

1	Roger Maris, 1961	61
2	Mickey Mantle, 1961	54
3	Willie Mays, 1965	52
	George Foster, 1977	52
5	Cecil Fielder, 1990	51
6	Willie Mays, 1962	49
	Harmon Killebrew, 1964	49
	Frank Robinson, 1966	49
	Harmon Killebrew, 1969	49
	Andre Dawson, 1987	49
	Mark McGwire, 1987	49
12	5 players tied	48

Home Run Percentage

1	Babe Ruth, 1920	11.79
2	Babe Ruth, 1927	11.11
3	Babe Ruth, 1921	10.93
4	Mickey Mantle, 1961	10.51
5	Hank Greenberg, 1938	10.43
6	Roger Maris, 1961	10.34
7	Babe Ruth, 1928	10.07
8	Jimmie Foxx, 1932	9.91
9	Ralph Kiner, 1949	9.84
10	Mickey Mantle, 1956	9.76
11	Hack Wilson, 1930	9.57
12	Babe Ruth, 1926	9.49
	Hank Aaron, 1971	9.49
14	Jim Gentile, 1961	9.47
15	Babe Ruth, 1930	9.46
16	Willie Stargell, 1971	9.39
17	Willie Mays, 1965	9.32
18	Babe Ruth, 1929	9.22
19	Boog Powell, 1964	9.20
20	Willie McCovey, 1969	9.16
21	Ted Williams, 1957	9.05
22	Ralph Kiner, 1947	9.03
23	Dave Kingman, 1979	9.02
24	Mark McGwire, 1992	8.99
25	Babe Ruth, 1932	8.97
26	Cecil Fielder, 1990	8.90
27	Jimmie Foxx, 1938	8.85
28	Harmon Killebrew, 1969	8.83
29	Mark McGwire, 1987	8.80
30	Willie Mays, 1955	8.79
31	Mike Schmidt, 1980	8.76
32	Mike Schmidt, 1981	8.76
33	Harmon Killebrew, 1963	8.74
34	Johnny Mize, 1947	8.70
35	Babe Ruth, 1924	8.70
	Harmon Killebrew, 1962	8.70
37	Kevin Mitchell, 1989	8.66
38	Babe Ruth, 1922	8.62
39	Babe Ruth, 1931	8.61
40	Ralph Kiner, 1950	8.59
41	Reggie Jackson, 1969	8.56
42	Ted Kluszewski, 1954	8.55
43	Frank Robinson, 1966	8.51
44	Harmon Killebrew, 1961	8.50
45	Harmon Killebrew, 1964	8.49
46	Lou Gehrig, 1934	8.46
	Lou Gehrig, 1936	8.46
48	George Foster, 1977	8.46
49	Willie Stargell, 1973	8.43
50	Hank Greenberg, 1946	8.41
51	Eddie Mathews, 1954	8.40
52	Rocky Colavito, 1958	8.38
53	Jimmie Foxx, 1933	8.38
54	Joe Adcock, 1956	8.37
55	Jack Clark, 1987	8.35
56	Mike Schmidt, 1979	8.32
57	Eddie Mathews, 1955	8.22
58	Jimmie Foxx, 1934	8.16
59	Willie Mays, 1964	8.13
60	Eddie Mathews, 1953	8.12
61	Ted Williams, 1941	8.11
62	Frank Howard, 1969	8.11
63	Mickey Mantle, 1958	8.09
64	Gorman Thomas, 1979	8.08
65	Lou Gehrig, 1927	8.05
66	Harmon Killebrew, 1967	8.04
	Hank Aaron, 1969	8.04
68	Reggie Jackson, 1980	7.98
69	Mickey Mantle, 1962	7.96
70	Duke Snider, 1956	7.93
71	Darrell Evans, 1985	7.92
72	Ralph Kiner, 1951	7.91
73	Roy Campanella, 1953	7.90
74	Willie Mays, 1962	7.89
	Andre Dawson, 1987	7.89
76	Hank Sauer, 1954	7.88
77	Willie McCovey, 1970	7.88
78	Duke Snider, 1957	7.87
79	Orlando Cepeda, 1961	7.86
80	Babe Ruth, 1923	7.85
81	Roger Maris, 1960	7.82
82	Duke Snider, 1955	7.81
83	Dave Kingman, 1976	7.81
	Eric Davis, 1987	7.81
85	Willie McCovey, 1963	7.80
86	Harmon Killebrew, 1970	7.78
87	Frank Howard, 1970	7.77
	Dale Murphy, 1987	7.77
89	Eddie Mathews, 1959	7.74
90	Rogers Hornsby, 1925	7.74
91	Rocky Colavito, 1961	7.72
92	Mel Ott, 1929	7.71
93	George Bell, 1987	7.70
94	Harmon Killebrew, 1959	7.69
	Norm Cash, 1962	7.69
	Dave Johnson, 1973	7.69
	Jose Canseco, 1990	7.69
	Jose Canseco, 1991	7.69
99	Ted Kluszewski, 1955	7.68
100	2 players tied	7.66

Home Run Pctg.(by era)

1876-1892

1	Ned Williamson, 1884	6.47
2	Fred Pfeffer, 1884	5.35
3	Cap Anson, 1884	4.42
4	Abner Dalrymple, 1884	4.22
5	Billy O'Brien, 1887	4.19
6	Sam Thompson, 1889	3.75
7	Roger Connor, 1887	3.61
8	Dan Brouthers, 1884	3.52
9	Harry Stovey, 1889	3.42
10	Bug Holliday, 1889	3.37
11	Fred Pfeffer, 1887	3.34
12	Harry Stovey, 1883	3.33
13	Jerry Denny, 1889	3.11
14	Dan Brouthers, 1881	2.96
15	Mike Tiernan, 1891	2.95

1893-1919

1	Babe Ruth, 1919	6.71
2	Bill Joyce, 1894	4.79
3	Gavvy Cravath, 1915	4.60
4	Jack Clements, 1893	4.52
5	Buck Freeman, 1899	4.25
6	Gavvy Cravath, 1914	3.81
7	Jim Canavan, 1894	3.65
8	Frank Schulte, 1911	3.64
9	Gavvy Cravath, 1913	3.62
10	Bill Joyce, 1895	3.59
11	Sherry Magee, 1911	3.37
12	Vic Saier, 1914	3.35
13	Sam Thompson, 1895	3.35
14	Hugh Duffy, 1894	3.34
15	Ed Delahanty, 1893	3.19

1920-1941

1	Babe Ruth, 1920	11.79
2	Babe Ruth, 1927	11.11
3	Babe Ruth, 1921	10.93
4	Hank Greenberg, 1938	10.43
5	Babe Ruth, 1928	10.07
6	Jimmie Foxx, 1932	9.91
7	Hack Wilson, 1930	9.57
8	Babe Ruth, 1926	9.49
9	Babe Ruth, 1930	9.46
10	Babe Ruth, 1929	9.22
11	Babe Ruth, 1932	8.97
12	Jimmie Foxx, 1938	8.85
13	Babe Ruth, 1924	8.70
14	Babe Ruth, 1922	8.62
15	Babe Ruth, 1931	8.61

1942-1960

1	Ralph Kiner, 1949	9.84
2	Mickey Mantle, 1956	9.76
3	Ted Williams, 1957	9.05
4	Ralph Kiner, 1947	9.03
5	Willie Mays, 1955	8.79
6	Johnny Mize, 1947	8.70
7	Ralph Kiner, 1950	8.59
8	Ted Kluszewski, 1954	8.55
9	Hank Greenberg, 1946	8.41
10	Eddie Mathews, 1954	8.40
11	Rocky Colavito, 1958	8.38
12	Joe Adcock, 1956	8.37
13	Eddie Mathews, 1955	8.22
14	Eddie Mathews, 1953	8.12
15	Mickey Mantle, 1958	8.09

1961-1992

1	Mickey Mantle, 1961	10.51
2	Roger Maris, 1961	10.34
3	Hank Aaron, 1971	9.49
4	Jim Gentile, 1961	9.47
5	Willie Stargell, 1971	9.39
6	Willie Mays, 1965	9.32
7	Boog Powell, 1964	9.20
8	Willie McCovey, 1969	9.16
9	Dave Kingman, 1979	9.02
10	Mark McGwire, 1992	8.99
11	Cecil Fielder, 1990	8.90
12	Harmon Killebrew, 1969	8.83
13	Mark McGwire, 1987	8.80
14	Mike Schmidt, 1980	8.76
15	Mike Schmidt, 1981	8.76

Total Bases

1	Babe Ruth, 1921	457
2	Rogers Hornsby, 1922	450
3	Lou Gehrig, 1927	447
4	Chuck Klein, 1930	445
5	Jimmie Foxx, 1932	438
6	Stan Musial, 1948	429
7	Hack Wilson, 1930	423
8	Chuck Klein, 1932	420
9	Lou Gehrig, 1930	419
10	Joe DiMaggio, 1937	418
11	Babe Ruth, 1927	417
12	Babe Herman, 1930	416
13	Lou Gehrig, 1931	410
14	Rogers Hornsby, 1929	409
	Lou Gehrig, 1934	409
16	Joe Medwick, 1937	406
	Jim Rice, 1978	406
18	Chuck Klein, 1929	405
	Hal Trosky, 1936	405
20	Jimmie Foxx, 1933	403
	Lou Gehrig, 1936	403
22	Hank Aaron, 1959	400
23	George Sisler, 1920	399
	Babe Ruth, 1923	399
25	Jimmie Foxx, 1938	398
26	Lefty O'Doul, 1929	397
	Hank Greenberg, 1937	397
28	Al Simmons, 1925	392
	Bill Terry, 1930	392
	Al Simmons, 1930	392
31	Babe Ruth, 1924	391
32	Hank Greenberg, 1935	389
33	Babe Ruth, 1920	388
	George Foster, 1977	388
	Don Mattingly, 1986	388
36	Earl Averill, 1936	385
37	Hank Greenberg, 1940	384
38	Stan Musial, 1949	382
	Willie Mays, 1955	382
	Willie Mays, 1962	382
	Jim Rice, 1977	382
42	Rogers Hornsby, 1925	381
43	Babe Ruth, 1928	380
	Hank Greenberg, 1938	380
	Frank Robinson, 1962	380
46	Babe Ruth, 1930	379
	Ernie Banks, 1958	379
48	Rogers Hornsby, 1921	378
	Duke Snider, 1954	378
50	Willie Mays, 1954	377
51	Mickey Mantle, 1956	376
52	Hugh Duffy, 1894	374
	Babe Ruth, 1931	374
	Hal Trosky, 1934	374
	Tony Oliva, 1964	374
56	Rogers Hornsby, 1924	373
	Al Simmons, 1929	373
	Bill Terry, 1932	373
	Billy Williams, 1970	373
60	Lou Gehrig, 1932	370
	Duke Snider, 1953	370
	Hank Aaron, 1963	370
	Don Mattingly, 1985	370
64	Kiki Cuyler, 1925	369
	Ripper Collins, 1934	369
	Jimmie Foxx, 1936	369
	Hank Aaron, 1957	369
	Jim Rice, 1979	369
	George Bell, 1987	369
70	Johnny Mize, 1940	368
	Ted Williams, 1949	368
	Ted Kluszewski, 1954	368
	Cal Ripken, 1991	368
74	Ty Cobb, 1911	367
	Ken Williams, 1922	367
	Heinie Manush, 1928	367
	Al Simmons, 1932	367
	Joe Medwick, 1936	367
	Joe DiMaggio, 1936	367
	Tommy Holmes, 1945	367
	Al Rosen, 1953	367
	Frank Robinson, 1966	367
	Robin Yount, 1982	367
84	Lou Gehrig, 1937	366
	Stan Musial, 1946	366
	Willie Mays, 1957	366
	Roger Maris, 1961	366
	Hank Aaron, 1962	366
89	Harry Heilmann, 1921	365
	Babe Ruth, 1926	365
	Chuck Klein, 1933	365
	Joe Medwick, 1935	365
	Kirby Puckett, 1986	365
94	Lou Gehrig, 1928	364
95	Dale Alexander, 1929	363
	Eddie Mathews, 1953	363
	George Brett, 1979	363
98	Jim Bottomley, 1928	362
99	4 players tied	361

Runs Batted In

1	Hack Wilson, 1930	190
2	Lou Gehrig, 1931	184
3	Hank Greenberg, 1937	183
4	Lou Gehrig, 1927	175
	Jimmie Foxx, 1938	175
6	Lou Gehrig, 1930	174
7	Babe Ruth, 1921	171
8	Chuck Klein, 1930	170
	Hank Greenberg, 1935	170
10	Jimmie Foxx, 1932	169
11	Joe DiMaggio, 1937	167
12	Sam Thompson, 1887	166
13	Sam Thompson, 1895	165
	Al Simmons, 1930	165
	Lou Gehrig, 1934	165
16	Babe Ruth, 1927	164
17	Babe Ruth, 1931	163
	Jimmie Foxx, 1933	163
19	Hal Trosky, 1936	162
20	Hack Wilson, 1929	159
	Lou Gehrig, 1937	159
	Ted Williams, 1949	159
	Vern Stephens, 1949	159
24	Al Simmons, 1929	157
25	Jimmie Foxx, 1930	156
26	Ken Williams, 1922	155
	Joe DiMaggio, 1948	155
28	Babe Ruth, 1929	154
	Joe Medwick, 1937	154
30	Babe Ruth, 1930	153
	Tommy Davis, 1962	153
32	Rogers Hornsby, 1922	152
	Lou Gehrig, 1936	152
34	Mel Ott, 1929	151
	Lou Gehrig, 1932	151
	Al Simmons, 1932	151
37	Hank Greenberg, 1940	150
38	Rogers Hornsby, 1929	149
	George Foster, 1977	149
40	Johnny Bench, 1970	148
41	Cap Anson, 1886	147
42	Hardy Richardson, 1890	146
	Ed Delahanty, 1893	146
	Babe Ruth, 1926	146
	Hank Greenberg, 1938	146
46	Hugh Duffy, 1894	145
	Chuck Klein, 1929	145
	Ted Williams, 1939	145
	Al Rosen, 1953	145
	Don Mattingly, 1985	145
51	Walt Dropo, 1950	144
	Vern Stephens, 1950	144
53	Rogers Hornsby, 1925	143
	Earl Averill, 1931	143
	Don Hurst, 1932	143
	Jimmie Foxx, 1936	143
	Ernie Banks, 1959	143
58	Lou Gehrig, 1928	142
	Babe Ruth, 1928	142
	Hal Trosky, 1934	142
	Roy Campanella, 1953	142
	Orlando Cepeda, 1961	142
	Roger Maris, 1961	142
64	Sam Thompson, 1894	141
	Ted Kluszewski, 1954	141
	Jim Gentile, 1961	141
	Willie Mays, 1962	141
68	Joe DiMaggio, 1938	140
	Rocky Colavito, 1961	140
	Harmon Killebrew, 1969	140
71	Harry Heilmann, 1921	139
	Lou Gehrig, 1933	139
	Hank Greenberg, 1934	139
	Jim Rice, 1978	139
	Don Baylor, 1979	139
76	Bob Meusel, 1925	138
	Goose Goslin, 1930	138
	Joe Medwick, 1936	138
	Zeke Bonura, 1936	138
	Johnny Mize, 1947	138
81	Ed Delahanty, 1899	137
	Babe Ruth, 1920	137
	Jim Bottomley, 1929	137
	Dale Alexander, 1929	137
	Chuck Klein, 1932	137
	Babe Ruth, 1932	137
	Johnny Mize, 1940	137
	Ted Williams, 1942	137
	Vern Stephens, 1948	137
	Joe Torre, 1971	137
	Andre Dawson, 1987	137
92	George Davis, 1897	136
	George Kelly, 1924	136
	Jim Bottomley, 1928	136
	Ed Morgan, 1930	136
	Duke Snider, 1955	136
	Frank Robinson, 1962	136
98	5 players tied	135

Runs Batted In per Game

1	Sam Thompson, 1894	1.42
2	Sam Thompson, 1895	1.39
3	Sam Thompson, 1887	1.31
4	Hack Wilson, 1930	1.23
5	Al Simmons, 1930	1.20
6	Hank Greenberg, 1937	1.19
7	Lou Gehrig, 1931	1.19
8	Cap Anson, 1886	1.18
9	Jimmie Foxx, 1938	1.17
10	Hugh Duffy, 1894	1.16
11	Dave Orr, 1890	1.16
12	Ed Delahanty, 1894	1.15
13	Babe Ruth, 1929	1.14
14	Lou Gehrig, 1930	1.13
15	Lou Gehrig, 1927	1.13
16	Babe Ruth, 1921	1.13
17	Babe Ruth, 1931	1.12
18	Hardy Richardson, 1890	1.12
19	Hank Greenberg, 1935	1.12
20	Ed Delahanty, 1893	1.11
21	Joe DiMaggio, 1937	1.11
22	Al Simmons, 1929	1.10
23	Jimmie Foxx, 1932	1.10
24	Jimmie Foxx, 1933	1.09
25	Chuck Klein, 1930	1.09
26	Babe Ruth, 1927	1.09
27	Oyster Burns, 1890	1.08
28	Hal Trosky, 1936	1.07
29	Lou Gehrig, 1934	1.07
30	Ed McKean, 1893	1.06
31	Hack Wilson, 1929	1.06
32	Walt Dropo, 1950	1.06
33	Babe Ruth, 1930	1.06
34	Buck Ewing, 1893	1.05
35	Lave Cross, 1894	1.05
36	Joe DiMaggio, 1939	1.05
37	George Davis, 1897	1.05
38	Dan Brouthers, 1894	1.04
39	Rogers Hornsby, 1925	1.04
40	Jim O'Rourke, 1890	1.04
41	Babe Ruth, 1932	1.03
42	Ted Williams, 1949	1.03
	Vern Stephens, 1949	1.03
44	Ed Delahanty, 1896	1.02
45	Steve Brodie, 1895	1.02
	Joe Kelley, 1895	1.02
47	Jimmie Foxx, 1930	1.02
48	Hank Greenberg, 1940	1.01
49	Ken Williams, 1922	1.01
	Joe DiMaggio, 1948	1.01
51	Lou Gehrig, 1937	1.01
52	Cap Anson, 1882	1.01
53	George Decker, 1894	1.01
54	George Brett, 1980	1.01
55	Joe DiMaggio, 1940	1.01
56	Mel Ott, 1929	1.01
57	Nap Lajoie, 1897	1.00
	Al Simmons, 1931	1.00
59	Roger Connor, 1889	.99
60	Tommy McCarthy, 1894	.99
61	Jake Beckley, 1890	.99
62	Dan Brouthers, 1883	.99
63	Joe Medwick, 1937	.99
64	Rogers Hornsby, 1922	.99
65	Roy Campanella, 1953	.99
66	Jimmy Collins, 1897	.99
67	Ed McKean, 1894	.98
68	Bug Holliday, 1894	.98
69	Lou Gehrig, 1936	.98
70	Al Simmons, 1932	.98
71	Walt Wilmot, 1894	.98
72	Cap Anson, 1881	.98
73	Chuck Klein, 1929	.97
	Ted Williams, 1939	.97
75	Heinie Reitz, 1894	.97
76	Lou Gehrig, 1932	.97
77	Vern Stephens, 1950	.97
78	Joe DiMaggio, 1938	.97
79	Babe Ruth, 1920	.96
80	Cap Anson, 1885	.96
81	Hugh Duffy, 1897	.96
82	Sam Thompson, 1893	.96
83	Billy Nash, 1893	.96
84	Babe Ruth, 1926	.96
85	Harry Heilmann, 1929	.96
86	Tommy McCarthy, 1893	.96
87	Rogers Hornsby, 1929	.96
88	Hughie Jennings, 1895	.95
	Nap Lajoie, 1901	.95
90	Don Hurst, 1932	.95
91	Jim Gentile, 1961	.95
92	Jack Doyle, 1894	.95
93	Bill Dickey, 1937	.95
94	Ted Kluszewski, 1954	.95
95	George Kelly, 1924	.94
96	George Foster, 1977	.94
97	Hank Greenberg, 1938	.94
98	Rudy York, 1938	.94
99	Tommy Davis, 1962	.94
100	2 players tied	.94

Walks

1	Babe Ruth, 1923	170
2	Ted Williams, 1947	162
	Ted Williams, 1949	162
4	Ted Williams, 1946	156
5	Eddie Yost, 1956	151
6	Eddie Joost, 1949	149
7	Babe Ruth, 1920	148
	Eddie Stanky, 1945	148
	Jim Wynn, 1969	148
10	Jimmy Sheckard, 1911	147
11	Mickey Mantle, 1957	146
12	Ted Williams, 1941	145
	Ted Williams, 1942	145
	Harmon Killebrew, 1969	145
15	Babe Ruth, 1921	144
	Babe Ruth, 1926	144
	Eddie Stanky, 1950	144
	Ted Williams, 1951	144
19	Babe Ruth, 1924	142
20	Eddie Yost, 1950	141
21	Babe Ruth, 1927	138
	Frank Thomas, 1991	138
23	Eddie Stanky, 1946	137
	Roy Cullenbine, 1947	137
	Ralph Kiner, 1951	137
	Willie McCovey, 1970	137
27	Jack Crooks, 1892	136
	Babe Ruth, 1930	136
	Ferris Fain, 1949	136
	Ted Williams, 1954	136
	Jack Clark, 1987	136
32	Babe Ruth, 1928	135
	Eddie Yost, 1959	135
34	Ferris Fain, 1950	133
35	Lou Gehrig, 1935	132
	Frank Howard, 1970	132
	Joe Morgan, 1975	132
	Jack Clark, 1989	132
39	Bob Elliott, 1948	131
	Eddie Yost, 1954	131
	Harmon Killebrew, 1967	131
42	Babe Ruth, 1932	130
	Lou Gehrig, 1936	130
44	Eddie Yost, 1952	129
	Mickey Mantle, 1958	129
46	Max Bishop, 1929	128
	Max Bishop, 1930	128
	Babe Ruth, 1931	128
	Harmon Killebrew, 1970	128
	Carl Yastrzemski, 1970	128
	Mike Schmidt, 1983	128
52	Lu Blue, 1931	127
	Lou Gehrig, 1937	127
	Eddie Stanky, 1951	127
	Jim Wynn, 1976	127
	Barry Bonds, 1992	127
57	Billy Hamilton, 1894	126
	Lu Blue, 1929	126
	Ted Williams, 1948	126
	Eddie Yost, 1951	126
	Mickey Mantle, 1961	126
	Darrell Evans, 1974	126
	Rickey Henderson, 1989	126
64	Richie Ashburn, 1954	125
	Eddie Yost, 1960	125
	Gene Tenace, 1977	125
	Wade Boggs, 1988	125
68	John McGraw, 1899	124
	Norm Cash, 1961	124
	Eddie Mathews, 1963	124
	Darrell Evans, 1973	124
72	Bill Joyce, 1890	123
	Eddie Yost, 1953	123
	Ken Singleton, 1973	123
75	Jimmy Sheckard, 1912	122
	Lou Gehrig, 1929	122
	Luke Appling, 1935	122
	Ralph Kiner, 1950	122
	Eddie Joost, 1952	122
	Mickey Mantle, 1962	122
	John Mayberry, 1973	122
	Mickey Tettleton, 1992	122
	Frank Thomas, 1992	122
84	Jack Crooks, 1893	121
	Topsy Hartsel, 1905	121
	Roy Cullenbine, 1941	121
	Luke Appling, 1949	121
	Willie McCovey, 1969	121
	Darrell Porter, 1979	121
	Von Hayes, 1987	121
91	Cupid Childs, 1893	120
	Eddie Lake, 1947	120
	Joe Morgan, 1974	120
	Mike Schmidt, 1979	120
95	14 players tied	119

Strikeouts

1	Bobby Bonds, 1970	189
2	Bobby Bonds, 1969	187
3	Rob Deer, 1987	186
4	Pete Incaviglia, 1986	185
5	Cecil Fielder, 1990	182
6	Mike Schmidt, 1975	180
7	Rob Deer, 1986	179
8	Dave Nicholson, 1963	175
	Gorman Thomas, 1979	175
	Jose Canseco, 1986	175
	Rob Deer, 1991	175
12	Jim Presley, 1986	172
	Bo Jackson, 1989	172
14	Reggie Jackson, 1968	171
15	Gorman Thomas, 1980	170
16	Andres Galarraga, 1990	169
17	Juan Samuel, 1984	168
	Pete Incaviglia, 1987	168
19	Gary Alexander, 1978	166
	Steve Balboni, 1985	166
	Cory Snyder, 1987	166
22	Donn Clendenon, 1968	163
23	Butch Hobson, 1977	162
	Juan Samuel, 1987	162
25	Dick Allen, 1968	161
	Reggie Jackson, 1971	161
27	Mickey Tettleton, 1990	160
28	Bo Jackson, 1987	158
	Andres Galarraga, 1989	158
	Rob Deer, 1989	158
	Jose Canseco, 1990	158
32	Dan Tartabull, 1986	157
	Jose Canseco, 1987	157
	Jim Presley, 1987	157
35	Tommie Agee, 1970	156
	Dave Kingman, 1982	156
	Reggie Jackson, 1982	156
	Tony Armas, 1984	156
39	Frank Howard, 1967	155
	Jeff Burroughs, 1975	155
41	Willie Stargell, 1971	154
	Larry Parrish, 1987	154
	Dean Palmer, 1992	154
44	Dave Kingman, 1975	153
	Andres Galarraga, 1988	153
	Rob Deer, 1988	153
	Pete Incaviglia, 1988	153
48	George Scott, 1966	152
	Larry Hisle, 1969	152
	Jose Canseco, 1991	152
51	Don Lock, 1963	151
	Greg Luzinski, 1975	151
	Juan Samuel, 1988	151
	Delino DeShields, 1991	151
	Cecil Fielder, 1991	151
	Cecil Fielder, 1992	151
57	Dick Allen, 1965	150
	Nate Colbert, 1970	150
	Ron Kittle, 1983	150
	Jesse Barfield, 1989	150
	Jesse Barfield, 1990	150
	Sammy Sosa, 1990	150
63	Billy Grabarkewitz, 1970	149
	Mike Schmidt, 1976	149
	Fred McGriff, 1988	149
	Travis Fryman, 1991	149
67	Bobby Bonds, 1973	148
	Mike Schmidt, 1983	148
	Gorman Thomas, 1983	148
	Roberto Kelly, 1990	148
71	Rob Deer, 1990	147
	Ray Lankford, 1992	147
73	Deron Johnson, 1971	146
	Nate Colbert, 1973	146
	Steve Balboni, 1986	146
	Jesse Barfield, 1986	146
	Bo Jackson, 1988	146
	Pete Incaviglia, 1990	146
	Jay Buhner, 1992	146
80	Lee May, 1972	145
	Bobby Darwin, 1972	145
	Dale Murphy, 1978	145
	Jack Clark, 1989	145
84	Dick Stuart, 1963	144
	Bobby Knoop, 1966	144
	Dick Allen, 1969	144
	Travis Fryman, 1992	144
88	Nelson Mathews, 1964	143
	Byron Browne, 1966	143
	Rick Monday, 1968	143
	Gorman Thomas, 1982	143
	Jesse Barfield, 1985	143
	Juan Gonzalez, 1992	143
94	8 players tied	142

At Bats per Strikeout

1876-1892

1 Mike McGeary, 1876 ...... 276.0
2 Cap Anson, 1878 .... 261.0
3 John Peters, 1876 .... 158.0
4 John Clapp, 1876 .... 149.0
5 Joe Start, 1877 .... 135.5
6 Joe Start, 1876 .... 132.0
7 Levi Meyerle, 1876 ...... 128.0
8 Jim Holdsworth, 1876 .... 120.5
9 Lon Knight, 1876 .... 120.0
10 Ezra Sutton, 1876 ...... 118.0
11 Bobby Mathews, 1876 ... 109.0
12 Paul Hines, 1876 .... 101.7
13 Deacon White, 1876 .... 101.0
14 Al Spalding, 1876 .... 97.3
15 Davy Force, 1876 .... 95.7

1893-1919

1 Jack Doyle, 1894 .... 140.7
2 Monte Ward, 1893 ...... 117.6
3 Willie Keeler, 1894 ...... 98.3
4 Joe Quinn, 1895 .... 90.5
5 Monte Ward, 1894 ...... 90.0
6 Joe Quinn, 1893 .... 78.1
7 Lave Cross, 1894 .... 75.6
8 Steve Brodie, 1894 ..... 71.6
9 Jack Glasscock, 1893 ... 69.7
10 Lave Cross, 1895 ...... 66.9
11 Ed McKean, 1896 ...... 63.4
12 Dummy Hoy, 1893 ...... 62.7
13 Patsy Donovan, 1893 ... 62.4
14 Farmer Vaughn, 1896 ... 61.9
15 Willie Keeler, 1896 ..... 60.4

1920-1941

1 Joe Sewell, 1932 .... 167.7
2 Joe Sewell, 1925 .... 152.0
3 Joe Sewell, 1929 ...... 144.5
4 Joe Sewell, 1933 ...... 131.0
5 Charlie Hollocher, 1922 ... 118.4
6 Stuffy McInnis, 1922 .... 107.4
7 Stuffy McInnis, 1924 .... 96.8
8 Joe Sewell, 1926 ...... 96.3
9 Joe Sewell, 1927 ...... 81.3
10 Pie Traynor, 1929 ...... 77.1
11 Sam Rice, 1929 .... 68.4
12 Tris Speaker, 1927 ..... 65.4
13 Joe Sewell, 1928 ...... 65.3
14 Sam Rice, 1925 .... 64.9
15 Stuffy McInnis, 1921 .... 64.9

1942-1960

1 Tommy Holmes, 1945 .... 70.7
2 Emil Verban, 1947 ...... 67.5
3 Lou Boudreau, 1948 .... 62.2
4 Dale Mitchell, 1949 ..... 58.2
5 Tommy Holmes, 1944 ... 57.4
6 Dale Mitchell, 1952 ..... 56.8
7 Nellie Fox, 1958 .... 56.6
8 Tommy Holmes, 1942 ... 55.8
9 Jimmy Brown, 1942 ..... 55.1
10 Nellie Fox, 1951 .... 54.9
11 Lou Boudreau, 1947 .... 53.8
12 Nellie Fox, 1954 ...... 52.6
13 Harvey Kuenn, 1954 .... 50.5
14 Don Mueller, 1955 ...... 50.4
15 Yogi Berra, 1950 .... 49.8

1961-1992

1 Nellie Fox, 1962 .... 51.8
2 Dave Cash, 1976 .... 51.2
3 Nellie Fox, 1961 .... 50.5
4 Tim Foli, 1979 .... 38.0
5 Matty Alou, 1970 ...... 37.6
6 Felix Millan, 1974 ...... 37.0
7 Vic Power, 1961 .... 35.2
8 Nellie Fox, 1964 .... 34.0
9 Tony Gwynn, 1992 ..... 32.5
10 Glenn Beckert, 1968 ... 32.2
11 Bill Buckner, 1980 ..... 32.1
12 Nellie Fox, 1963 .... 31.7
13 Tim Foli, 1981 .... 31.6
14 Bob Bailor, 1978 .... 29.6
15 Rich Dauer, 1980 ...... 29.3

Strikeout Percentage

1876-1892

1 Frank Meinke, 1884 ..... 26.10
2 Jim Galvin, 1883 .... 24.53
3 Sam Wise, 1884 .... 24.41
4 Jim Galvin, 1879 ...... 21.13
5 Charlie Bastian, 1885 ... 21.08
6 Will White, 1878 .... 20.81
7 Silver Flint, 1883 ...... 20.78
8 John Morrill, 1884 ..... 19.86
9 John Morrill, 1885 ..... 19.80
10 Charlie Bastian, 1886 ... 19.57
11 Jim Lillie, 1886 .... 19.23
12 Will White, 1879 ...... 19.05
13 John Morrill, 1886 ..... 18.84
14 Sam Wise, 1883 ...... 18.23
15 Bill Crowley, 1884 ..... 18.18

1893-1919

1 Gus Williams, 1914 .... 24.05
2 Grover Gilmore, 1914 .... 20.38
3 Gavvy Cravath, 1916 .... 19.87
4 Ed McDonald, 1912 .... 19.83
5 Art Wilson, 1914 ...... 18.18
6 Gavvy Cravath, 1912 .... 17.66
7 Cozy Dolan, 1914 ..... 17.58
8 Max Carey, 1911 ...... 17.56
9 Danny Moeller, 1913 ... 17.49
10 Doug Baird, 1915 ..... 17.19
11 Al Boucher, 1914 ..... 17.05
12 Wally Pipp, 1915 ..... 16.91
13 Joe Agler, 1914 ...... 16.85
14 Ray Powell, 1919 ..... 16.81
15 Cy Williams, 1917 .... 16.67

1920-1941

1 Vince DiMaggio, 1938 .... 24.81
2 Vince DiMaggio, 1937 .... 22.52
3 Chet Ross, 1940 ...... 22.32
4 Dolph Camilli, 1941 .... 21.74
5 Joe Orengo, 1940 ..... 21.69
6 Jimmie Foxx, 1941 .... 21.15
7 Boze Berger, 1935 .... 21.04
8 Jimmie Foxx, 1936 .... 20.34
9 Dolph Camilli, 1938 .... 19.84
10 Babe Ruth, 1922 ..... 19.70
11 Babe Ruth, 1933 ..... 19.61
12 Jimmy Dykes, 1922 ... 19.56
13 Hank Greenberg, 1939 ... 19.00
14 Vince DiMaggio, 1941 .... 18.94
15 Dolph Camilli, 1939 .... 18.94

1942-1960

1 Pancho Herrera, 1960 .... 26.56
2 Jim Lemon, 1956 ...... 25.65
3 Dick Stuart, 1960 ..... 24.43
4 Frank Howard, 1960 ... 24.11
5 Harmon Killebrew, 1960 ... 23.98
6 Jim Lemon, 1958 ...... 23.95
7 Mickey Mantle, 1960 ... 23.72
8 Larry Doby, 1953 ..... 23.59
9 Pat Seerey, 1945 ..... 23.43
10 Mickey Mantle, 1959 ... 23.29
11 Mickey Mantle, 1958 ... 23.12
12 Wally Post, 1956 ..... 23.01
13 Woodie Held, 1959 .... 22.48
14 Gil Hodges, 1959 ..... 22.28
15 Norm Zauchin, 1955 ... 22.01

1961-1992

1 Rob Deer, 1987 .... 39.24
2 Rob Deer, 1991 .... 39.06
3 Dave Nicholson, 1963 .... 38.98
4 Rob Deer, 1986 ...... 38.41
5 Mickey Tettleton, 1990 ... 36.04
6 Pete Incaviglia, 1986 ... 34.26
7 Rob Deer, 1989 ...... 33.91
8 Rob Deer, 1990 ...... 33.41
9 Bo Jackson, 1989 ..... 33.40
10 Gary Alexander, 1978 .... 33.33
11 Jack Clark, 1987 ...... 33.17
12 Pete Incaviglia, 1987 ... 33.01
13 Dick Allen, 1969 ...... 32.88
14 Jose Canseco, 1990 ... 32.85
15 Mike Schmidt, 1975 ... 32.03

Batting Average

1 Hugh Duffy, 1894 ...... .440
2 Tip O'Neill, 1887 ...... .435
3 Ross Barnes, 1876 ..... .429
4 Nap Lajoie, 1901 ...... .426
5 Willie Keeler, 1897 .... .424
6 Rogers Hornsby, 1924 ... .424
7 George Sisler, 1922 .... .420
8 Ty Cobb, 1911 .... .420
9 Fred Dunlap, 1884 ..... .412
10 Ed Delahanty, 1899 .... .410
11 Jesse Burkett, 1896 .... .410
12 Jesse Burkett, 1895 .... .409
13 Ty Cobb, 1912 .... .409
14 Joe Jackson, 1911 ..... .408
15 Sam Thompson, 1894 ... .407
16 George Sisler, 1920 .... .407
17 Ed Delahanty, 1894 .... .407
18 Ted Williams, 1941 .... .406
19 Billy Hamilton, 1894 ... .404
20 Ed Delahanty, 1895 .... .404
21 Rogers Hornsby, 1925 ... .403
22 Harry Heilmann, 1923 ... .403
23 Pete Browning, 1887 ... .402
24 Rogers Hornsby, 1922 ... .401
25 Bill Terry, 1930 ...... .401
26 Hughie Jennings, 1896 ... .401
27 Ty Cobb, 1922 .... .401
28 Cap Anson, 1881 ..... .399
29 Lefty O'Doul, 1929 .... .398
30 Harry Heilmann, 1927 ... .398
31 Rogers Hornsby, 1921 ... .397
32 Ed Delahanty, 1896 .... .397
33 Jesse Burkett, 1899 .... .396
34 Joe Jackson, 1912 .... .395
35 Harry Heilmann, 1921 ... .394
36 Babe Ruth, 1923 ..... .393
37 Harry Heilmann, 1925 ... .393
38 Babe Herman, 1930 ... .393
39 Joe Kelley, 1894 ..... .393
40 Sam Thompson, 1895 ... .392
41 John McGraw, 1899 ... .391
42 Ty Cobb, 1913 .... .390
43 Fred Clarke, 1897 .... .390
44 Al Simmons, 1931 .... .390
45 George Brett, 1980 ... .390
46 Tris Speaker, 1925 .... .389
47 Bill Lange, 1895 ..... .389
48 Billy Hamilton, 1895 ... .389
49 Ty Cobb, 1921 ...... .389
50 Ted Williams, 1957 .... .388
51 King Kelly, 1886 ..... .388
52 Rod Carew, 1977 .... .388
53 Luke Appling, 1936 ... .388
54 Tris Speaker, 1920 .... .388
55 Deacon White, 1877 ... .387
56 Al Simmons, 1925 .... .387
57 Rogers Hornsby, 1928 ... .387
58 Tris Speaker, 1916 .... .386
59 Willie Keeler, 1896 .... .386
60 Chuck Klein, 1930 .... .386
61 Lave Cross, 1894 .... .386
   Hughie Jennings, 1895 ... .386
63 Willie Keeler, 1898 .... .385
64 Arky Vaughan, 1935 ... .385
65 Rogers Hornsby, 1923 ... .384
66 Ty Cobb, 1924 ...... .384
67 Nap Lajoie, 1910 .... .384
68 Ty Cobb, 1910 ...... .383
69 Jesse Burkett, 1897 ... .383
70 Tris Speaker, 1912 .... .383
71 Ty Cobb, 1917 ...... .383
72 Lefty O'Doul, 1930 .... .383
73 Joe Jackson, 1920 .... .382
74 Ty Cobb, 1918 ...... .382
75 Honus Wagner, 1900 ... .381
76 Babe Herman, 1929 ... .381
77 Joe DiMaggio, 1939 ... .381
78 Al Simmons, 1930 .... .381
79 Paul Waner, 1927 .... .380
80 Rogers Hornsby, 1929 ... .380
81 Billy Hamilton, 1893 ... .380
82 Tris Speaker, 1923 .... .380
83 Goose Goslin, 1928 ... .379
84 Freddy Lindstrom, 1930 ... .379
85 Willie Keeler, 1899 .... .379
86 Lou Gehrig, 1930 .... .379
87 John Cassidy, 1877 ... .378
88 Pete Browning, 1882 ... .378
89 Ty Cobb, 1925 ...... .378
90 Babe Ruth, 1924 ..... .378
91 Sam Crawford, 1911 ... .378
92 Tris Speaker, 1922 .... .378
93 Earl Averill, 1936 .... .378
94 Babe Ruth, 1921 ..... .378
95 Heinie Manush, 1928 ... .378
96 Heinie Manush, 1926 ... .378
97 Ed Delahanty, 1897 ... .377
98 Willie Keeler, 1895 .... .377
99 Ty Cobb, 1909 ...... .377
100 Cy Seymour, 1905 .... .377

Batting Average (by era)

1876-1892

1 Tip O'Neill, 1887 .... .435
2 Ross Barnes, 1876 ..... .429
3 Fred Dunlap, 1884 ..... .412
4 Pete Browning, 1887 ... .402
5 Cap Anson, 1881 ..... .399
6 King Kelly, 1886 ...... .388
7 Deacon White, 1877 ... .387
8 John Cassidy, 1877 ... .378
9 Pete Browning, 1882 ... .378
10 Dan Brouthers, 1883 ... .374
11 Pete Browning, 1890 ... .373
12 Dan Brouthers, 1889 ... .373
13 Dave Orr, 1890 .... .373
14 Sam Thompson, 1887 ... .372
15 Tommy Tucker, 1889 ... .372

1893-1919

1 Hugh Duffy, 1894 ...... .440
2 Nap Lajoie, 1901 ...... .426
3 Willie Keeler, 1897 .... .424
4 Ty Cobb, 1911 .... .420
5 Ed Delahanty, 1899 .... .410
6 Jesse Burkett, 1896 .... .410
7 Jesse Burkett, 1895 .... .409
8 Ty Cobb, 1912 .... .409
9 Joe Jackson, 1911 ..... .408
10 Sam Thompson, 1894 ... .407
11 Ed Delahanty, 1894 .... .407
12 Billy Hamilton, 1894 ... .404
13 Ed Delahanty, 1895 .... .404
14 Hughie Jennings, 1896 ... .401
15 Ed Delahanty, 1896 .... .397

1920-1941

1 Rogers Hornsby, 1924 ... .424
2 George Sisler, 1922 .... .420
3 George Sisler, 1920 .... .407
4 Ted Williams, 1941 .... .406
5 Rogers Hornsby, 1925 ... .403
6 Harry Heilmann, 1923 ... .403
7 Rogers Hornsby, 1922 ... .401
8 Bill Terry, 1930 ...... .401
9 Ty Cobb, 1922 .... .401
10 Lefty O'Doul, 1929 .... .398
11 Harry Heilmann, 1927 ... .398
12 Rogers Hornsby, 1921 ... .397
13 Harry Heilmann, 1921 ... .394
14 Babe Ruth, 1923 ..... .393
15 Harry Heilmann, 1925 ... .393

1942-1960

1 Ted Williams, 1957 ...... .388
2 Stan Musial, 1948 ..... .376
3 Ted Williams, 1948 .... .369
4 Stan Musial, 1946 .... .365
5 Mickey Mantle, 1957 ... .365
6 Harry Walker, 1947 ... .363
7 Dixie Walker, 1944 ... .357
8 Stan Musial, 1943 .... .357
9 Ted Williams, 1942 ... .356
10 Phil Cavarretta, 1945 ... .355
11 Lou Boudreau, 1948 ... .355
12 Stan Musial, 1951 .... .355
13 Hank Aaron, 1959 .... .355
14 Billy Goodman, 1950 ... .354
15 Harvey Kuenn, 1959 ... .353

1961-1992

1 George Brett, 1980 ...... .390
2 Rod Carew, 1977 ..... .388
3 Tony Gwynn, 1987 .... .370
4 Wade Boggs, 1985 .... .368
5 Wade Boggs, 1988 .... .366
6 Rico Carty, 1970 ..... .366
7 Rod Carew, 1974 .... .364
8 Wade Boggs, 1987 .... .363
9 Joe Torre, 1971 ..... .363
10 Wade Boggs, 1983 ... .361
11 Norm Cash, 1961 .... .361
12 Rod Carew, 1975 .... .359
13 Roberto Clemente, 1967 .. .357
14 Wade Boggs, 1986 ... .357
15 Kirby Puckett, 1988 .... .356

Batting Average (by position)

First Base
1	George Sisler, 1922	.420
2	George Sisler, 1920	.407
3	Bill Terry, 1930	.401
4	Cap Anson, 1881	.399
5	Rod Carew, 1977	.388
6	Lou Gehrig, 1930	.379
7	Dan Brouthers, 1883	.374
8	Lou Gehrig, 1928	.374
9	Lou Gehrig, 1927	.373
10	Dan Brouthers, 1889	.373

Second Base
1	Ross Barnes, 1876	.429
2	Nap Lajoie, 1901	.426
3	Rogers Hornsby, 1924	.424
4	Fred Dunlap, 1884	.412
5	Rogers Hornsby, 1925	.403
6	Rogers Hornsby, 1922	.401
7	Rogers Hornsby, 1921	.397
8	Rogers Hornsby, 1928	.387
9	Nap Lajoie, 1910	.384
10	Rogers Hornsby, 1929	.380

Shortstop
1	Hughie Jennings, 1896	.401
2	Luke Appling, 1936	.388
3	Hughie Jennings, 1895	.386
4	Arky Vaughan, 1935	.385
5	Honus Wagner, 1905	.363
6	Hughie Jennings, 1897	.355
7	Honus Wagner, 1903	.355
8	Honus Wagner, 1908	.354
9	Honus Wagner, 1907	.350
10	Honus Wagner, 1904	.349

Third Base
1	John McGraw, 1899	.391
2	George Brett, 1980	.390
3	Lave Cross, 1894	.386
4	Freddy Lindstrom, 1930	.379
5	Heinie Zimmerman, 1912	.372
6	John McGraw, 1895	.369
7	Wade Boggs, 1985	.368
8	Denny Lyons, 1887	.367
9	Wade Boggs, 1988	.366
10	Pie Traynor, 1930	.366

Outfield
1	Hugh Duffy, 1894	.440
2	Tip O'Neill, 1887	.435
3	Willie Keeler, 1897	.424
4	Ty Cobb, 1911	.420
5	Ty Cobb, 1912	.410
6	Ed Delahanty, 1899	.410
7	Jesse Burkett, 1896	.410
8	Jesse Burkett, 1895	.409
9	Joe Jackson, 1911	.408
10	Sam Thompson, 1894	.407

Catcher
1	Cal McVey, 1877	.368
2	Mickey Cochrane, 1930	.357
3	Wilbert Robinson, 1894	.353
4	Spud Davis, 1933	.349
5	Mickey Cochrane, 1931	.349
6	Ernie Lombardi, 1938	.342
7	Gabby Hartnett, 1930	.339
8	Mickey Cochrane, 1932	.338
9	Ted Simmons, 1975	.332
10	Bill Dickey, 1937	.332

Relative Batting Average

1	Fred Dunlap, 1884	1.667
2	Ross Barnes, 1876	1.608
3	Tip O'Neill, 1887	1.564
4	Nap Lajoie, 1910	1.537
5	Ty Cobb, 1910	1.534
6	Pete Browning, 1882	1.526
7	Cap Anson, 1881	1.512
8	King Kelly, 1886	1.508
9	Roger Connor, 1885	1.506
10	Tris Speaker, 1916	1.506
11	Ty Cobb, 1917	1.501
12	Ty Cobb, 1912	1.501
13	Nap Lajoie, 1901	1.501
14	Nap Lajoie, 1904	1.499
15	Ty Cobb, 1911	1.493
16	Ty Cobb, 1909	1.492
17	Ted Williams, 1957	1.476
18	Ty Cobb, 1913	1.475
19	Ted Williams, 1941	1.472
20	Ty Cobb, 1918	1.469
21	George Gore, 1880	1.462
22	Rogers Hornsby, 1924	1.461
23	Rod Carew, 1977	1.458
24	Orator Shaffer, 1884	1.455
25	Dan Brouthers, 1885	1.455
26	Joe Jackson, 1911	1.452
27	Joe Jackson, 1912	1.451
28	Dan Brouthers, 1882	1.449
29	Dave Orr, 1884	1.448
30	George Brett, 1980	1.448
31	Ty Cobb, 1915	1.448
32	Pete Browning, 1887	1.446
33	Ty Cobb, 1916	1.445
34	Cap Anson, 1886	1.442
35	Pete Browning, 1885	1.439
36	Dan Brouthers, 1886	1.439
37	Honus Wagner, 1908	1.434
38	George Sisler, 1922	1.433
39	Cap Anson, 1882	1.428
40	Cy Seymour, 1905	1.425
41	Willie Keeler, 1897	1.422
42	Ed Delahanty, 1899	1.414
43	Wade Boggs, 1988	1.413
44	King Kelly, 1884	1.411
45	Joe Jackson, 1913	1.411
46	Rod Carew, 1974	1.408
47	Wade Boggs, 1985	1.407
48	Tris Speaker, 1912	1.406
49	Deacon White, 1877	1.405
50	Dan Brouthers, 1883	1.402
51	Jimmy Wolf, 1890	1.401
52	Stan Musial, 1948	1.400
53	George Stone, 1906	1.400
54	Cap Anson, 1888	1.399
55	George Sisler, 1920	1.398
56	Joe Torre, 1971	1.397
57	Hugh Duffy, 1894	1.395
58	Stan Musial, 1946	1.393
59	Ty Cobb, 1919	1.392
60	Rod Carew, 1975	1.391
61	Tommy Tucker, 1889	1.391
62	Nap Lajoie, 1906	1.390
63	John Reilly, 1884	1.389
64	Ed Swartwood, 1883	1.389
65	Harry Heilmann, 1923	1.389
66	Mickey Mantle, 1957	1.388
67	Willie Keeler, 1898	1.387
68	Honus Wagner, 1907	1.387
69	Roberto Clemente, 1967	1.385
70	George Sisler, 1917	1.383
71	Jim O'Rourke, 1884	1.383
72	Pete Browning, 1886	1.382
73	Tris Speaker, 1917	1.380
74	Ezra Sutton, 1884	1.380
75	Ty Cobb, 1907	1.379
76	Hick Carpenter, 1882	1.379
77	Roger Connor, 1886	1.378
78	Jesse Burkett, 1896	1.378
79	Paul Hines, 1879	1.377
80	Tony Gwynn, 1987	1.375
81	Pete Browning, 1884	1.374
82	Tris Speaker, 1913	1.374
83	Kirby Puckett, 1988	1.374
84	John Cassidy, 1877	1.373
85	Honus Wagner, 1905	1.372
86	Dave Orr, 1886	1.372
87	Rico Carty, 1970	1.372
88	George Hall, 1876	1.372
89	Eddie Collins, 1909	1.370
90	Tip O'Neill, 1888	1.370
91	Wade Boggs, 1987	1.370
92	Ty Cobb, 1922	1.370
93	Dan Brouthers, 1889	1.370
94	Cap Anson, 1880	1.368
95	Norm Cash, 1961	1.368
96	Jesse Burkett, 1899	1.367
97	Jesse Burkett, 1901	1.365
98	Hardy Richardson, 1886	1.365
99	Willie Keeler, 1904	1.365
100	Wade Boggs, 1986	1.365

On Base Percentage

1	Ted Williams, 1941	.551
2	John McGraw, 1899	.547
3	Babe Ruth, 1923	.545
4	Babe Ruth, 1920	.530
5	Ted Williams, 1957	.528
6	Billy Hamilton, 1894	.523
7	Ted Williams, 1954	.516
8	Babe Ruth, 1926	.516
9	Mickey Mantle, 1957	.515
10	Babe Ruth, 1924	.513
11	Babe Ruth, 1921	.512
12	Rogers Hornsby, 1924	.507
13	John McGraw, 1900	.503
14	Joe Kelley, 1894	.502
15	Hugh Duffy, 1894	.502
16	Ed Delahanty, 1895	.500
17	Ted Williams, 1942	.499
18	Ted Williams, 1947	.499
19	Rogers Hornsby, 1928	.498
20	Ted Williams, 1946	.497
21	Ted Williams, 1948	.497
22	Bill Joyce, 1894	.496
23	Babe Ruth, 1931	.495
24	Babe Ruth, 1930	.493
25	Arky Vaughan, 1935	.491
26	Ted Williams, 1949	.490
27	Billy Hamilton, 1895	.490
28	Billy Hamilton, 1893	.490
29	Tip O'Neill, 1887	.490
30	Rogers Hornsby, 1925	.489
	Babe Ruth, 1932	.489
32	Norm Cash, 1961	.488
33	Mickey Mantle, 1962	.488
34	Babe Ruth, 1927	.487
35	Ty Cobb, 1915	.486
36	Jesse Burkett, 1895	.486
37	Tris Speaker, 1920	.483
38	King Kelly, 1886	.483
39	Harry Heilmann, 1923	.481
40	Wade Boggs, 1988	.480
41	Billy Hamilton, 1898	.480
42	Tris Speaker, 1925	.479
	Ted Williams, 1956	.479
44	Ed Delahanty, 1894	.478
45	Lou Gehrig, 1936	.478
46	Billy Hamilton, 1896	.477
47	Cupid Childs, 1894	.475
48	John McGraw, 1898	.475
49	Harry Heilmann, 1927	.475
50	Tris Speaker, 1922	.474
51	Lou Gehrig, 1927	.474
52	Luke Appling, 1936	.474
53	Lou Gehrig, 1930	.473
54	Lou Gehrig, 1937	.473
55	Hughie Jennings, 1896	.472
56	Ed Delahanty, 1896	.472
57	John McGraw, 1897	.471
58	Joe Morgan, 1975	.471
59	Dan Brouthers, 1891	.471
60	Tris Speaker, 1916	.470
61	Bill Joyce, 1896	.470
62	Joe Kelley, 1896	.469
63	Tris Speaker, 1923	.469
64	Jimmie Foxx, 1932	.469
65	Jesse Burkett, 1897	.468
66	Ty Cobb, 1925	.468
67	Joe Jackson, 1911	.468
68	Lou Gehrig, 1928	.467
69	Ty Cobb, 1913	.467
70	George Sisler, 1922	.467
71	Mike Griffin, 1894	.467
72	Cupid Childs, 1896	.467
73	Mickey Mantle, 1956	.467
74	Wade Boggs, 1987	.467
75	Ty Cobb, 1911	.467
76	Dan Brouthers, 1890	.466
77	Lou Gehrig, 1935	.466
78	Lou Gehrig, 1934	.465
79	Lefty O'Doul, 1929	.465
80	Jimmie Foxx, 1939	.464
81	Tris Speaker, 1912	.464
82	Ed Delahanty, 1899	.464
83	Pete Browning, 1887	.464
84	Ted Williams, 1951	.464
85	Willie Keeler, 1897	.464
86	Bob Caruthers, 1887	.463
87	Cupid Childs, 1893	.463
88	Jimmie Foxx, 1929	.463
89	Hughie Jennings, 1897	.463
90	Nap Lajoie, 1901	.463
91	Jesse Burkett, 1899	.463
92	Ross Barnes, 1876	.462
	Jimmie Foxx, 1938	.462
	Ted Williams, 1958	.462
95	Dan Brouthers, 1889	.462
96	Fred Clarke, 1897	.462
97	Ty Cobb, 1922	.462
98	Babe Ruth, 1928	.461
99	Jack Clark, 1987	.461
100	Eddie Collins, 1925	.461

Slugging Average

1	Babe Ruth, 1920	.847
2	Babe Ruth, 1921	.846
3	Babe Ruth, 1927	.772
4	Lou Gehrig, 1927	.765
5	Babe Ruth, 1923	.764
6	Rogers Hornsby, 1925	.756
7	Jimmie Foxx, 1932	.749
8	Babe Ruth, 1924	.739
9	Babe Ruth, 1926	.737
10	Ted Williams, 1941	.735
11	Babe Ruth, 1930	.732
12	Ted Williams, 1957	.731
13	Hack Wilson, 1930	.723
14	Rogers Hornsby, 1922	.722
15	Lou Gehrig, 1930	.721
16	Babe Ruth, 1928	.709
17	Al Simmons, 1930	.708
18	Lou Gehrig, 1934	.706
19	Mickey Mantle, 1956	.705
20	Jimmie Foxx, 1938	.704
21	Jimmie Foxx, 1933	.703
22	Stan Musial, 1948	.702
23	Babe Ruth, 1931	.700
24	Babe Ruth, 1929	.697
25	Lou Gehrig, 1936	.696
26	Rogers Hornsby, 1924	.696
27	Hugh Duffy, 1894	.694
28	Jimmie Foxx, 1939	.694
29	Tip O'Neill, 1887	.691
30	Mickey Mantle, 1961	.687
31	Chuck Klein, 1930	.687
32	Sam Thompson, 1894	.686
33	Hank Greenberg, 1938	.683
34	Rogers Hornsby, 1929	.679
35	Babe Herman, 1930	.678
36	Joe DiMaggio, 1937	.673
37	Babe Ruth, 1922	.672
38	Joe DiMaggio, 1939	.671
39	Hank Greenberg, 1940	.670
40	Hank Aaron, 1971	.669
41	Hank Greenberg, 1937	.668
42	Ted Williams, 1946	.667
43	Willie Mays, 1954	.667
44	Mickey Mantle, 1957	.665
45	George Brett, 1980	.664
46	Lou Gehrig, 1931	.662
47	Norm Cash, 1961	.662
48	Babe Ruth, 1932	.661
49	Willie Mays, 1955	.659
50	Ralph Kiner, 1949	.658
51	Chuck Klein, 1929	.657
52	Babe Ruth, 1919	.657
53	Willie McCovey, 1969	.656
54	Sam Thompson, 1895	.654
55	Jimmie Foxx, 1934	.653
56	Chick Hafey, 1930	.652
57	Ted Williams, 1949	.650
58	Bill Joyce, 1894	.648
59	Lou Gehrig, 1928	.648
60	Ted Williams, 1942	.648
61	Duke Snider, 1954	.647
62	Chuck Klein, 1932	.646
63	Jim Gentile, 1961	.646
64	Willie Stargell, 1973	.646
65	Willie Mays, 1965	.645
66	Mike Schmidt, 1981	.644
67	Hal Trosky, 1936	.644
68	Nap Lajoie, 1901	.643
69	Joe DiMaggio, 1941	.643
70	Lou Gehrig, 1937	.643
71	Ted Kluszewski, 1954	.642
72	Al Simmons, 1929	.642
73	Joe Medwick, 1937	.641
74	Al Simmons, 1931	.641
75	Ralph Kiner, 1947	.639
76	Rogers Hornsby, 1921	.639
77	Frank Robinson, 1966	.637
78	Jimmie Foxx, 1930	.637
79	Fred Lynn, 1979	.637
80	Hank Aaron, 1959	.636
81	Johnny Mize, 1940	.636
82	Jimmie Foxx, 1935	.636
83	Kevin Mitchell, 1989	.635
84	Mel Ott, 1929	.635
85	Ted Williams, 1954	.635
86	Ted Williams, 1947	.634
87	Chick Hafey, 1929	.632
88	George Sisler, 1920	.632
89	Rogers Hornsby, 1928	.632
90	Harry Heilmann, 1923	.632
	Dick Allen, 1966	.632
92	Ed Delahanty, 1896	.631
93	George Foster, 1977	.631
94	Jimmie Foxx, 1936	.631
95	Gabby Hartnett, 1930	.630
96	Jim Bottomley, 1928	.628
97	Hank Greenberg, 1935	.628
98	Duke Snider, 1955	.628
99	Willie Stargell, 1971	.628
100	Rogers Hornsby, 1923	.627

Production

1	Babe Ruth, 1920	1.378
2	Babe Ruth, 1921	1.358
3	Babe Ruth, 1923	1.309
4	Ted Williams, 1941	1.286
5	Babe Ruth, 1927	1.259
6	Ted Williams, 1957	1.259
7	Babe Ruth, 1926	1.253
8	Babe Ruth, 1924	1.252
9	Rogers Hornsby, 1925	1.245
10	Lou Gehrig, 1927	1.240
11	Babe Ruth, 1930	1.225
12	Jimmie Foxx, 1932	1.218
13	Rogers Hornsby, 1924	1.203
14	Hugh Duffy, 1894	1.196
15	Babe Ruth, 1931	1.195
16	Lou Gehrig, 1930	1.194
17	Rogers Hornsby, 1922	1.181
18	Tip O'Neill, 1887	1.180
19	Mickey Mantle, 1957	1.179
20	Hack Wilson, 1930	1.177
21	Lou Gehrig, 1936	1.174
22	Mickey Mantle, 1956	1.172
23	Lou Gehrig, 1934	1.172
24	Babe Ruth, 1928	1.170
25	Jimmie Foxx, 1938	1.166
26	Ted Williams, 1946	1.164
27	Jimmie Foxx, 1939	1.158
28	Jimmie Foxx, 1933	1.153
29	Stan Musial, 1948	1.152
30	Ted Williams, 1954	1.151
31	Babe Ruth, 1932	1.150
32	Norm Cash, 1961	1.150
33	Ted Williams, 1942	1.147
34	Sam Thompson, 1894	1.145
35	Bill Joyce, 1894	1.143
36	Ted Williams, 1949	1.141
37	Rogers Hornsby, 1929	1.139
38	Mickey Mantle, 1961	1.138
39	Ted Williams, 1947	1.133
40	Babe Herman, 1930	1.132
41	Al Simmons, 1930	1.130
42	Rogers Hornsby, 1928	1.130
43	Babe Ruth, 1929	1.128
44	George Brett, 1980	1.124
45	Chuck Klein, 1930	1.123
46	Hank Greenberg, 1938	1.122
47	Joe DiMaggio, 1939	1.119
48	Ed Delahanty, 1895	1.117
49	Lou Gehrig, 1937	1.116
50	Lou Gehrig, 1928	1.115
51	Babe Ruth, 1919	1.114
52	Willie McCovey, 1969	1.114
53	Harry Heilmann, 1923	1.113
54	Ted Williams, 1948	1.112
55	Lou Gehrig, 1931	1.108
56	Nap Lajoie, 1901	1.106
57	Babe Ruth, 1922	1.106
58	Hank Greenberg, 1937	1.105
59	Joe Kelley, 1894	1.104
60	Hank Greenberg, 1940	1.103
61	Ed Delahanty, 1896	1.103
62	Jimmie Foxx, 1934	1.102
63	Arky Vaughan, 1935	1.098
64	Rogers Hornsby, 1921	1.097
65	Jimmie Foxx, 1935	1.096
66	Mickey Mantle, 1962	1.093
67	Harry Heilmann, 1927	1.091
68	Ralph Kiner, 1949	1.089
69	Jimmie Foxx, 1929	1.088
70	Ty Cobb, 1911	1.088
71	Lefty O'Doul, 1929	1.087
72	Rogers Hornsby, 1923	1.086
73	Al Simmons, 1931	1.085
74	Barry Bonds, 1992	1.085
75	Joe DiMaggio, 1937	1.085
76	Sam Thompson, 1895	1.085
77	Ted Williams, 1956	1.084
78	Mel Ott, 1929	1.084
79	Joe DiMaggio, 1941	1.083
80	Willie Mays, 1954	1.083
81	Mike Schmidt, 1981	1.083
82	Hank Aaron, 1971	1.082
83	George Sisler, 1920	1.082
84	Tris Speaker, 1922	1.080
85	Ralph Kiner, 1951	1.079
86	Tris Speaker, 1923	1.079
87	Jim Gentile, 1961	1.074
88	Duke Snider, 1954	1.074
89	Lou Gehrig, 1932	1.072
90	Bill Terry, 1930	1.071
91	Jimmie Foxx, 1936	1.071
92	Johnny Mize, 1939	1.070
93	Fred Dunlap, 1884	1.069
94	Jimmie Foxx, 1930	1.066
95	Ty Cobb, 1925	1.066
96	Earl Averill, 1936	1.065
97	Chuck Klein, 1929	1.065
98	Ed Delahanty, 1894	1.063
99	Stan Musial, 1951	1.063
100	Willie Mays, 1955	1.063

Adjusted Production

1	Babe Ruth, 1920	252
2	Fred Dunlap, 1884	249
3	Babe Ruth, 1923	238
4	Babe Ruth, 1921	236
5	Ted Williams, 1941	232
6	Babe Ruth, 1927	229
7	Pete Browning, 1882	229
8	Babe Ruth, 1926	228
9	Ted Williams, 1957	227
10	Lou Gehrig, 1927	224
11	Babe Ruth, 1919	224
12	Babe Ruth, 1931	223
13	Mickey Mantle, 1957	223
14	Rogers Hornsby, 1924	223
15	Ross Barnes, 1876	222
16	Babe Ruth, 1924	221
17	Babe Ruth, 1930	216
18	Ted Williams, 1942	214
19	Lou Gehrig, 1934	213
20	Mickey Mantle, 1956	213
21	Willie McCovey, 1969	212
22	Ted Williams, 1946	211
23	Mickey Mantle, 1961	210
24	Babe Ruth, 1928	210
25	Rogers Hornsby, 1922	210
26	Ty Cobb, 1917	210
27	George Hall, 1876	208
28	Rogers Hornsby, 1925	208
29	Tip O'Neill, 1887	208
30	Lou Gehrig, 1930	207
31	Barry Bonds, 1992	207
32	Babe Ruth, 1932	206
33	Nap Lajoie, 1904	205
34	Honus Wagner, 1908	205
35	Rogers Hornsby, 1928	204
36	Dan Brouthers, 1886	204
37	Ty Cobb, 1912	203
38	Jimmie Foxx, 1932	203
39	Roger Connor, 1885	203
40	George Brett, 1980	203
41	Ty Cobb, 1910	202
42	Dave Orr, 1885	201
43	Frank Robinson, 1966	200
44	Jimmie Foxx, 1933	199
45	Dave Orr, 1884	199
46	Ted Williams, 1947	199
47	Lou Gehrig, 1931	199
48	Dan Brouthers, 1885	199
49	Babe Ruth, 1929	199
50	Dick Allen, 1972	199
51	Norm Cash, 1961	198
52	Mickey Mantle, 1962	198
53	Dan Brouthers, 1882	198
54	Nap Lajoie, 1910	198
55	Ed Swartwood, 1882	197
56	Lou Gehrig, 1928	197
57	Stan Musial, 1948	196
58	Ty Cobb, 1918	196
59	Ty Cobb, 1913	196
60	Nap Lajoie, 1901	196
61	Orator Shaffer, 1878	196
62	Orator Shaffer, 1884	195
63	George Stone, 1906	195
64	Mike Schmidt, 1981	195
65	Harry Heilmann, 1923	195
66	Kevin Mitchell, 1989	194
67	Ed Delahanty, 1896	194
68	Pete Browning, 1885	193
69	Lou Gehrig, 1936	193
70	Cupid Childs, 1890	193
71	Ed Delahanty, 1899	193
72	Ty Cobb, 1911	193
73	Ted Williams, 1954	193
74	Joe Jackson, 1911	192
75	Rogers Hornsby, 1921	191
76	Ty Cobb, 1909	190
77	Rickey Henderson, 1990	190
78	Hank Aaron, 1971	190
79	Joe Jackson, 1913	190
80	Reggie Jackson, 1969	190
81	Deacon White, 1877	190
82	Rogers Hornsby, 1920	190
83	John Reilly, 1884	190
84	Joe Jackson, 1912	190
85	Cap Anson, 1881	189
86	Carl Yastrzemski, 1967	189
87	Mickey Mantle, 1958	189
88	Frank Robinson, 1967	189
89	Ed Delahanty, 1895	189
90	Willie Stargell, 1973	189
91	Willie Stargell, 1971	188
92	King Kelly, 1879	188
93	Jimmie Foxx, 1934	188
94	Hank Aaron, 1959	188
95	Dan Brouthers, 1891	188
96	Roger Connor, 1882	188
97	Rogers Hornsby, 1923	188
98	Dave Orr, 1886	188
99	Arky Vaughan, 1935	187
100	Ted Williams, 1949	187

Batting Runs

1	Babe Ruth, 1921	119
2	Babe Ruth, 1923	119
3	Babe Ruth, 1920	113
4	Ted Williams, 1941	102
5	Lou Gehrig, 1927	101
6	Babe Ruth, 1924	101
7	Babe Ruth, 1927	101
8	Babe Ruth, 1926	97
9	Jimmie Foxx, 1932	97
10	Ted Williams, 1946	94
11	Rogers Hornsby, 1924	94
12	Ted Williams, 1942	93
13	Babe Ruth, 1931	92
14	Ted Williams, 1947	91
15	Stan Musial, 1948	90
16	Rogers Hornsby, 1922	90
17	Ted Williams, 1957	90
18	Babe Ruth, 1930	90
19	Mickey Mantle, 1957	89
20	Ted Williams, 1949	89
21	Lou Gehrig, 1930	88
22	Tip O'Neill, 1887	88
23	Rogers Hornsby, 1925	87
24	Norm Cash, 1961	86
25	Lou Gehrig, 1934	86
26	Babe Ruth, 1928	84
27	Mickey Mantle, 1956	83
28	Jimmie Foxx, 1933	83
29	Lou Gehrig, 1936	82
30	Lou Gehrig, 1931	80
31	Ty Cobb, 1911	78
32	Jimmie Foxx, 1938	78
33	Hugh Duffy, 1894	77
34	Carl Yastrzemski, 1967	76
35	Mickey Mantle, 1961	76
36	Willie McCovey, 1969	76
37	Lou Gehrig, 1928	76
38	Ted Williams, 1948	76
39	Hack Wilson, 1930	75
40	Rogers Hornsby, 1921	74
41	Ty Cobb, 1917	74
42	Rogers Hornsby, 1929	74
43	Nap Lajoie, 1901	74
44	Frank Robinson, 1966	74
45	Lou Gehrig, 1937	73
46	George Sisler, 1920	73
47	Tris Speaker, 1912	73
48	Rogers Hornsby, 1928	72
49	Fred Dunlap, 1884	72
50	Stan Musial, 1949	72
51	Arky Vaughan, 1935	72
52	Barry Bonds, 1992	72
53	Joe Jackson, 1911	72
54	Carl Yastrzemski, 1970	72
55	Ty Cobb, 1915	72
56	Babe Ruth, 1932	71
57	Ted Williams, 1954	71
58	Tris Speaker, 1923	71
59	Stan Musial, 1946	71
60	Ralph Kiner, 1951	71
61	Harry Heilmann, 1923	71
62	Joe Jackson, 1912	70
63	Stan Musial, 1951	70
64	Ralph Kiner, 1949	70
65	Chuck Klein, 1933	69
66	Joe Medwick, 1937	69
67	Hank Greenberg, 1940	69
68	Johnny Mize, 1939	69
69	Babe Herman, 1930	69
70	Lou Gehrig, 1932	69
71	Lefty O'Doul, 1929	69
72	Nap Lajoie, 1910	68
73	Chuck Klein, 1932	68
74	Ed Delahanty, 1895	68
75	Ed Delahanty, 1899	68
76	Ty Cobb, 1910	68
77	Chuck Klein, 1930	67
78	Jimmie Foxx, 1935	67
79	Hank Greenberg, 1937	67
80	Ty Cobb, 1912	67
81	Rod Carew, 1977	67
82	Frank Robinson, 1962	67
83	Wade Boggs, 1987	67
84	Babe Ruth, 1919	67
85	Jimmie Foxx, 1934	66
86	Ed Delahanty, 1396	66
87	Jimmie Foxx, 1939	66
88	Dick Allen, 1972	66
89	Hank Greenberg, 1938	66
90	Dan Brouthers, 1886	66
91	Frank Thomas, 1991	66
92	Wade Boggs, 1988	66
93	Tris Speaker, 1920	66
94	Harmon Killebrew, 1969	66
95	Joe Jackson, 1913	66
96	Stan Musial, 1943	66
97	Honus Wagner, 1908	65
98	Hank Aaron, 1971	65
99	George Brett, 1980	65
100	Willie Mays, 1965	65

Adjusted Batting Runs

1	Babe Ruth, 1923	118
2	Babe Ruth, 1921	117
3	Babe Ruth, 1920	110
4	Lou Gehrig, 1927	104
5	Babe Ruth, 1927	103
6	Babe Ruth, 1924	101
7	Ted Williams, 1941	100
8	Babe Ruth, 1926	99
9	Babe Ruth, 1931	96
10	Rogers Hornsby, 1924	95
11	Rogers Hornsby, 1922	94
12	Babe Ruth, 1930	94
13	Jimmie Foxx, 1932	93
14	Lou Gehrig, 1930	93
15	Lou Gehrig, 1934	92
16	Ted Williams, 1946	90
17	Ted Williams, 1942	90
18	Mickey Mantle, 1957	90
19	Babe Ruth, 1928	87
20	Ted Williams, 1957	86
21	Mickey Mantle, 1956	86
22	Lou Gehrig, 1936	86
23	Stan Musial, 1948	86
24	Ted Williams, 1947	86
25	Rogers Hornsby, 1925	85
26	Lou Gehrig, 1931	85
27	Norm Cash, 1961	84
28	Ted Williams, 1949	83
29	Jimmie Foxx, 1933	82
30	Mickey Mantle, 1961	80
31	Lou Gehrig, 1928	79
32	Tip O'Neill, 1887	78
33	Willie McCovey, 1969	77
34	Rogers Hornsby, 1928	76
35	Rogers Hornsby, 1921	76
36	Babe Ruth, 1932	75
37	Frank Robinson, 1966	75
38	Ty Cobb, 1917	75
39	Hack Wilson, 1930	75
40	Ty Cobb, 1911	74
41	Rogers Hornsby, 1929	74
42	Jimmie Foxx, 1938	74
43	Lou Gehrig, 1932	73
44	Lou Gehrig, 1937	73
45	Barry Bonds, 1992	73
46	Harry Heilmann, 1923	72
47	Ted Williams, 1948	72
48	Tris Speaker, 1923	71
49	Ed Delahanty, 1899	71
50	Carl Yastrzemski, 1967	71
51	Joe Jackson, 1911	71
52	George Sisler, 1920	71
53	Nap Lajoie, 1901	71
54	Babe Ruth, 1919	70
55	Fred Dunlap, 1884	70
56	Babe Herman, 1930	70
57	Stan Musial, 1951	70
58	Jimmie Foxx, 1934	70
59	Hank Aaron, 1959	70
60	Ty Cobb, 1912	70
61	Arky Vaughan, 1935	70
62	Tris Speaker, 1912	69
63	Ralph Kiner, 1951	69
64	Stan Musial, 1949	68
65	Hugh Duffy, 1894	68
66	Rod Carew, 1977	68
67	Ralph Kiner, 1949	68
68	Jimmie Foxx, 1935	68
69	Frank Thomas, 1991	68
70	Ty Cobb, 1915	68
71	Joe Jackson, 1912	68
72	Stan Musial, 1946	68
73	Ed Delahanty, 1895	68
74	Ed Delahanty, 1896	67
75	Nap Lajoie, 1910	67
76	Joe Medwick, 1937	67
77	Babe Ruth, 1929	67
78	Mickey Mantle, 1958	67
79	Carl Yastrzemski, 1970	66
80	Lou Gehrig, 1935	66
81	Al Rosen, 1953	65
82	Joe DiMaggio, 1941	65
83	Honus Wagner, 1908	65
84	Rogers Hornsby, 1920	65
85	Hank Greenberg, 1937	65
86	Reggie Jackson, 1969	65
87	Dick Allen, 1972	65
88	Billy Hamilton, 1894	65
89	Lou Gehrig, 1933	65
90	Ted Williams, 1954	65
91	Frank Thomas, 1992	64
92	Wade Boggs, 1987	64
93	George Brett, 1980	64
94	Frank Robinson, 1962	64
95	Kevin Mitchell, 1989	64
96	Harmon Killebrew, 1969	64
97	Johnny Mize, 1939	64
98	Ty Cobb, 1910	64
99	Hank Aaron, 1963	64
100	Dan Brouthers, 1886	64

Batting Wins

1	Babe Ruth, 1923	11.5
2	Babe Ruth, 1921	11.1
3	Babe Ruth, 1920	11.0
4	Ted Williams, 1941	9.9
5	Ted Williams, 1946	9.9
6	Lou Gehrig, 1927	9.6
7	Babe Ruth, 1927	9.6
8	Babe Ruth, 1924	9.5
9	Ted Williams, 1942	9.5
10	Ted Williams, 1947	9.4
11	Babe Ruth, 1926	9.4
12	Rogers Hornsby, 1924	9.3
13	Ted Williams, 1957	9.3
14	Mickey Mantle, 1957	9.2
15	Stan Musial, 1948	9.0
16	Jimmie Foxx, 1932	8.9
17	Ted Williams, 1949	8.6
18	Norm Cash, 1961	8.5
19	Babe Ruth, 1931	8.5
20	Rogers Hornsby, 1922	8.5
21	Carl Yastrzemski, 1967	8.4
22	Ty Cobb, 1917	8.3
23	Rogers Hornsby, 1925	8.2
24	Mickey Mantle, 1956	8.2
25	Babe Ruth, 1928	8.1
26	Babe Ruth, 1930	8.1
27	Lou Gehrig, 1930	8.0
28	Willie McCovey, 1969	8.0
29	Lou Gehrig, 1934	8.0
30	Frank Robinson, 1966	7.9
31	Jimmie Foxx, 1933	7.8
32	Barry Bonds, 1992	7.7
33	Ty Cobb, 1911	7.7
34	Ty Cobb, 1915	7.6
35	Nap Lajoie, 1910	7.6
36	Mickey Mantle, 1961	7.6
37	Honus Wagner, 1908	7.6
38	Ty Cobb, 1910	7.5
39	Stan Musial, 1946	7.5
40	Dick Allen, 1972	7.5
41	Carl Yastrzemski, 1970	7.4
42	Lou Gehrig, 1931	7.4
43	Rogers Hornsby, 1921	7.3
44	Lou Gehrig, 1928	7.3
45	Ted Williams, 1948	7.3
46	Ted Williams, 1954	7.3
47	Chuck Klein, 1933	7.3
48	Tris Speaker, 1912	7.3
49	Lou Gehrig, 1936	7.3
50	Ty Cobb, 1909	7.2
51	Stan Musial, 1949	7.2
52	Tris Speaker, 1916	7.1
53	Tip O'Neill, 1887	7.1
54	Ralph Kiner, 1951	7.1
55	George Sisler, 1920	7.1
56	Rogers Hornsby, 1928	7.1
57	Jimmie Foxx, 1938	7.1
58	Joe Jackson, 1911	7.1
59	Joe Jackson, 1912	7.0
60	Stan Musial, 1951	7.0
61	Hank Aaron, 1971	7.0
62	Stan Musial, 1943	7.0
63	Nap Lajoie, 1904	7.0
64	Arky Vaughan, 1935	7.0
65	Joe Jackson, 1913	7.0
66	Babe Ruth, 1919	7.0
67	Ralph Kiner, 1949	6.9
68	Harmon Killebrew, 1967	6.9
69	Harmon Killebrew, 1969	6.9
70	Johnny Mize, 1939	6.9
71	Tris Speaker, 1923	6.9
72	Willie Mays, 1965	6.8
73	Harry Heilmann, 1923	6.8
74	Hank Aaron, 1963	6.8
75	Joe Medwick, 1937	6.8
76	Chuck Klein, 1932	6.7
77	Rogers Hornsby, 1929	6.7
78	Lou Gehrig, 1937	6.7
79	Ty Cobb, 1912	6.7
80	Cy Seymour, 1905	6.7
81	Rogers Hornsby, 1920	6.7
82	Joe Torre, 1971	6.7
83	Nap Lajoie, 1901	6.7
84	Hack Wilson, 1930	6.7
85	Rod Carew, 1977	6.7
86	Wade Boggs, 1988	6.7
87	Frank Robinson, 1962	6.6
88	Kevin Mitchell, 1989	6.6
89	Mickey Mantle, 1958	6.6
90	Carl Yastrzemski, 1968	6.6
91	Frank Thomas, 1991	6.6
92	Babe Ruth, 1932	6.6
93	Billy Williams, 1972	6.6
94	Joe Morgan, 1976	6.5
95	Reggie Jackson, 1969	6.5
96	Hank Greenberg, 1940	6.5
97	Johnny Mize, 1940	6.5
98	George Brett, 1980	6.5
99	Duke Snider, 1954	6.4
100	Ty Cobb, 1916	6.4

Adjusted Batting Wins

1	Babe Ruth, 1923	11.4
2	Babe Ruth, 1921	11.0
3	Babe Ruth, 1920	10.7
4	Lou Gehrig, 1927	9.8
5	Babe Ruth, 1927	9.8
6	Ted Williams, 1941	9.7
7	Babe Ruth, 1926	9.6
8	Babe Ruth, 1924	9.5
9	Rogers Hornsby, 1924	9.5
10	Ted Williams, 1946	9.5
11	Mickey Mantle, 1957	9.3
12	Ted Williams, 1942	9.2
13	Babe Ruth, 1931	9.0
14	Ted Williams, 1957	8.9
15	Rogers Hornsby, 1922	8.9
16	Ted Williams, 1947	8.9
17	Jimmie Foxx, 1932	8.6
18	Stan Musial, 1948	8.6
19	Lou Gehrig, 1934	8.5
20	Babe Ruth, 1930	8.5
21	Mickey Mantle, 1956	8.4
22	Lou Gehrig, 1930	8.4
23	Babe Ruth, 1928	8.4
24	Norm Cash, 1961	8.3
25	Ty Cobb, 1917	8.3
26	Willie McCovey, 1969	8.1
27	Ted Williams, 1949	8.0
28	Frank Robinson, 1966	8.0
29	Rogers Hornsby, 1925	8.0
30	Mickey Mantle, 1961	8.0
31	Lou Gehrig, 1931	7.9
32	Carl Yastrzemski, 1967	7.8
33	Barry Bonds, 1992	7.8
34	Jimmie Foxx, 1933	7.8
35	Lou Gehrig, 1928	7.6
36	Lou Gehrig, 1936	7.6
37	Honus Wagner, 1908	7.6
38	Rogers Hornsby, 1921	7.5
39	Nap Lajoie, 1910	7.5
40	Rogers Hornsby, 1928	7.5
41	Dick Allen, 1972	7.4
42	Babe Ruth, 1919	7.3
43	Ty Cobb, 1911	7.3
44	Ty Cobb, 1915	7.2
45	Stan Musial, 1946	7.2
46	Ty Cobb, 1910	7.1
47	Nap Lajoie, 1904	7.0
48	Hank Aaron, 1959	7.0
49	Harry Heilmann, 1923	7.0
50	Rogers Hornsby, 1920	7.0
51	Stan Musial, 1951	7.0
52	Ted Williams, 1948	7.0
53	Babe Ruth, 1932	7.0
54	Joe Jackson, 1911	7.0
55	Ty Cobb, 1912	7.0
56	Hank Aaron, 1963	6.9
57	Mickey Mantle, 1958	6.9
58	Carl Yastrzemski, 1970	6.9
59	Ty Cobb, 1909	6.9
60	Tris Speaker, 1923	6.9
61	Tris Speaker, 1912	6.9
62	Ralph Kiner, 1951	6.9
63	Kevin Mitchell, 1989	6.8
64	George Sisler, 1920	6.8
65	Reggie Jackson, 1969	6.8
66	Lou Gehrig, 1932	6.8
67	Frank Thomas, 1991	6.8
68	Stan Musial, 1949	6.8
69	Rod Carew, 1977	6.8
70	Joe Jackson, 1912	6.8
71	Joe Jackson, 1913	6.8
72	Arky Vaughan, 1935	6.8
73	Ralph Kiner, 1949	6.7
74	Rogers Hornsby, 1929	6.7
75	Tris Speaker, 1916	6.7
76	Harmon Killebrew, 1969	6.7
77	Ted Williams, 1954	6.7
78	Lou Gehrig, 1937	6.7
79	Jimmie Foxx, 1938	6.7
80	Joe Medwick, 1937	6.7
81	George Stone, 1906	6.7
82	Stan Musial, 1943	6.7
83	Willie Mays, 1965	6.6
84	Hank Aaron, 1971	6.6
85	Hack Wilson, 1930	6.6
86	Al Rosen, 1953	6.6
87	Frank Thomas, 1992	6.6
88	Jimmie Foxx, 1934	6.5
89	Ed Delahanty, 1899	6.4
90	George Brett, 1980	6.4
91	Johnny Mize, 1939	6.4
92	Joe Torre, 1971	6.4
93	Frank Robinson, 1962	6.4
94	Chuck Klein, 1933	6.4
95	Nap Lajoie, 1901	6.4
96	Frank Howard, 1969	6.4
97	Joe Morgan, 1976	6.4
98	Jimmie Foxx, 1935	6.4
99	Joe DiMaggio, 1941	6.3
100	Willie Stargell, 1971	6.3

Runs Created

1	Babe Ruth, 1921	238
2	Babe Ruth, 1923	223
3	Hugh Duffy, 1894	217
4	Babe Ruth, 1920	211
5	Jimmie Foxx, 1932	207
6	Billy Hamilton, 1894	207
7	Ty Cobb, 1911	207
8	Babe Ruth, 1924	205
9	Lou Gehrig, 1927	203
10	Ted Williams, 1941	202
11	Rogers Hornsby, 1922	200
12	Babe Ruth, 1927	200
13	Lou Gehrig, 1936	199
14	Babe Ruth, 1926	196
15	Lou Gehrig, 1930	195
16	Lou Gehrig, 1934	195
17	Tip O'Neill, 1887	194
18	Ted Williams, 1949	193
19	Babe Ruth, 1931	192
20	Babe Ruth, 1930	191
21	Pete Browning, 1887	191
22	Stan Musial, 1948	191
23	Hack Wilson, 1930	189
24	Jimmie Foxx, 1938	189
25	Ted Williams, 1946	188
26	Mickey Mantle, 1956	188
27	Rogers Hornsby, 1925	187
28	Ted Williams, 1947	186
29	Rogers Hornsby, 1924	186
30	Chuck Klein, 1930	186
31	Lou Gehrig, 1931	185
32	Ted Williams, 1942	185
33	Jimmie Foxx, 1933	184
34	Rogers Hornsby, 1929	183
35	Babe Herman, 1930	183
36	Joe Kelley, 1894	182
37	Babe Ruth, 1928	182
38	Lou Gehrig, 1937	181
39	Lefty O'Doul, 1929	180
40	Nap Lajoie, 1901	179
41	Mickey Mantle, 1957	178
42	Billy Hamilton, 1895	178
43	Joe Kelley, 1896	178
44	Norm Cash, 1961	178
45	Hank Greenberg, 1937	178
46	Ed Delahanty, 1895	176
47	George Sisler, 1920	176
48	Willie Keeler, 1897	176
49	Ed Delahanty, 1899	175
50	Benny Kauff, 1914	175
51	Tris Speaker, 1912	175
52	Joe Jackson, 1911	175
53	Mickey Mantle, 1961	174
54	Stan Musial, 1949	173
55	Joe DiMaggio, 1937	173
56	Ty Cobb, 1912	173
57	Hank Greenberg, 1938	172
58	Ted Williams, 1948	172
59	Chuck Klein, 1932	171
60	Hank Greenberg, 1940	171
61	Ed Delahanty, 1896	170
62	Joe Medwick, 1937	170
63	Bill Terry, 1930	170
64	Stan Musial, 1951	169
65	Lou Gehrig, 1928	169
66	Rogers Hornsby, 1921	169
67	Earl Averill, 1936	168
68	Jimmie Foxx, 1936	168
69	Lou Gehrig, 1932	168
70	Sam Thompson, 1895	167
71	Ted Williams, 1957	167
72	Ed Delahanty, 1893	167
73	Jesse Burkett, 1896	166
74	Stan Musial, 1953	166
75	Joe Jackson, 1912	166
76	Tris Speaker, 1923	166
77	Jimmie Foxx, 1934	165
78	Ralph Kiner, 1951	165
79	Jake Stenzel, 1894	165
80	Jesse Burkett, 1895	165
81	Ty Cobb, 1917	164
82	Stan Musial, 1946	164
83	Ralph Kiner, 1949	163
84	Arky Vaughan, 1935	163
85	Jimmie Foxx, 1935	163
86	Al Simmons, 1930	163
87	Johnny Mize, 1939	162
88	Chuck Klein, 1933	162
89	George Sisler, 1922	162
90	Joe DiMaggio, 1941	162
91	Duke Snider, 1954	161
92	Hank Greenberg, 1935	161
93	Duke Snider, 1953	161
94	Bill Lange, 1895	160
95	Rod Carew, 1977	160
96	Denny Lyons, 1887	160
97	Frank Robinson, 1962	160
98	Billy Hamilton, 1896	160
99	Harry Heilmann, 1923	159
100	Ty Cobb, 1909	159

Total Average

1	Babe Ruth, 1920	1.797
2	Babe Ruth, 1921	1.745
3	Ted Williams, 1941	1.688
4	Babe Ruth, 1923	1.683
5	Hugh Duffy, 1894	1.619
6	Babe Ruth, 1926	1.606
7	Billy Hamilton, 1894	1.605
8	John McGraw, 1899	1.601
9	Ted Williams, 1957	1.599
10	Babe Ruth, 1927	1.571
11	Babe Ruth, 1924	1.558
12	Rogers Hornsby, 1925	1.539
13	Mickey Mantle, 1957	1.534
14	Bill Joyce, 1894	1.528
15	Ed Delahanty, 1895	1.517
16	Tip O'Neill, 1887	1.514
17	Babe Ruth, 1930	1.509
18	Joe Kelley, 1894	1.503
19	Lou Gehrig, 1927	1.500
20	Babe Ruth, 1931	1.487
21	Ty Cobb, 1911	1.464
22	Ted Williams, 1954	1.452
23	Jimmie Foxx, 1932	1.451
24	Billy Hamilton, 1895	1.443
25	Babe Ruth, 1932	1.432
26	Ted Williams, 1946	1.431
27	Joe Kelley, 1896	1.430
28	Lou Gehrig, 1936	1.426
29	Mickey Mantle, 1956	1.426
30	Rogers Hornsby, 1924	1.424
31	Pete Browning, 1887	1.422
32	Hack Wilson, 1930	1.411
33	Rogers Hornsby, 1928	1.409
34	Sam Thompson, 1894	1.409
35	Ed Delahanty, 1896	1.405
36	Babe Ruth, 1928	1.405
37	Lou Gehrig, 1934	1.401
38	Ted Williams, 1942	1.394
39	Jimmie Foxx, 1938	1.392
40	Ted Williams, 1947	1.391
41	Lou Gehrig, 1930	1.389
42	Billy Hamilton, 1893	1.386
43	Mickey Mantle, 1962	1.385
44	Mickey Mantle, 1961	1.384
45	Bill Lange, 1895	1.373
46	Bob Caruthers, 1887	1.368
47	King Kelly, 1886	1.366
48	Babe Ruth, 1919	1.358
49	Norm Cash, 1961	1.358
50	Rogers Hornsby, 1922	1.353
51	Babe Herman, 1930	1.351
52	Jimmie Foxx, 1933	1.348
53	Ted Williams, 1948	1.347
54	Ted Williams, 1949	1.347
55	Lou Gehrig, 1937	1.339
56	Rogers Hornsby, 1929	1.338
57	Barry Bonds, 1992	1.335
58	Nap Lajoie, 1901	1.327
59	Ty Cobb, 1912	1.321
60	Ty Cobb, 1910	1.321
61	Jake Stenzel, 1894	1.320
62	Joe Morgan, 1976	1.319
63	Arky Vaughan, 1935	1.317
64	Billy Hamilton, 1896	1.316
65	Ty Cobb, 1913	1.310
66	Jimmie Foxx, 1934	1.310
67	Tris Speaker, 1912	1.310
68	Joe Jackson, 1911	1.308
69	Bill Joyce, 1896	1.306
70	Hank Greenberg, 1938	1.306
71	Jimmie Foxx, 1939	1.304
72	Stan Musial, 1948	1.298
73	Willie McCovey, 1969	1.296
74	Ed Delahanty, 1894	1.290
75	Joe Kelley, 1895	1.289
76	Jimmie Foxx, 1935	1.288
77	Babe Ruth, 1929	1.288
78	Mel Ott, 1929	1.287
79	Harry Heilmann, 1923	1.284
80	Joe Morgan, 1975	1.279
81	Benny Kauff, 1914	1.278
82	Hank Greenberg, 1937	1.277
83	Chuck Klein, 1930	1.274
84	Al Simmons, 1930	1.272
85	Tris Speaker, 1922	1.272
86	Fred Clarke, 1897	1.272
87	Billy Hamilton, 1891	1.270
88	Sam Thompson, 1895	1.269
89	Lou Gehrig, 1931	1.267
90	Harry Heilmann, 1927	1.265
91	Jesse Burkett, 1895	1.265
92	Hughie Jennings, 1896	1.263
93	Billy Hamilton, 1898	1.262
94	Willie Keeler, 1897	1.262
95	Jimmie Foxx, 1929	1.261
96	Jack Clark, 1987	1.258
97	George Brett, 1980	1.258
98	Lou Gehrig, 1928	1.256
99	John McGraw, 1900	1.256
100	Ted Williams, 1956	1.255

Runs Produced

1	Lou Gehrig, 1931	301
2	Babe Ruth, 1921	289
3	Chuck Klein, 1930	288
4	Hugh Duffy, 1894	287
5	Al Simmons, 1930	281
6	Hughie Jennings, 1895	280
	Hack Wilson, 1930	280
	Hank Greenberg, 1937	280
9	Sam Thompson, 1895	278
10	Lou Gehrig, 1927	277
11	Kiki Cuyler, 1930	276
	Lou Gehrig, 1930	276
13	Billy Hamilton, 1894	275
14	Ed Delahanty, 1894	274
15	Sam Thompson, 1887	273
16	Ed Delahanty, 1893	272
	Joe Kelley, 1895	272
	Joe DiMaggio, 1937	272
19	Joe Kelley, 1894	270
	Lou Gehrig, 1936	270
21	Ty Cobb, 1911	266
	Rogers Hornsby, 1929	266
	Babe Ruth, 1931	266
	Ted Williams, 1949	266
25	Jimmie Foxx, 1938	264
26	Ed Delahanty, 1899	263
27	Babe Ruth, 1927	262
	Jimmie Foxx, 1932	262
29	Al Simmons, 1932	260
	Lou Gehrig, 1937	260
31	Hardy Richardson, 1890	259
	Hugh Duffy, 1893	259
	Walt Wilmot, 1894	259
34	Dan Brouthers, 1894	256
	Bobby Lowe, 1894	256
	Jake Stenzel, 1894	256
	Nap Lajoie, 1901	256
38	Hack Wilson, 1929	255
	Lou Gehrig, 1932	255
	Hank Greenberg, 1935	255
41	Cap Anson, 1886	254
	Willie Keeler, 1894	254
	Lou Gehrig, 1928	254
	Babe Ruth, 1930	254
45	Harry Stovey, 1889	252
46	Rogers Hornsby, 1922	251
	Babe Ruth, 1928	251
	Earl Averill, 1931	251
	Chuck Klein, 1932	251
50	Charlie Gehringer, 1934	250
51	Hugh Duffy, 1897	248
52	John McGraw, 1894	247
	Mel Ott, 1929	247
54	Hughie Jennings, 1896	246
	Tris Speaker, 1923	246
	Jimmie Foxx, 1930	246
	Zeke Bonura, 1936	246
	Tommy Davis, 1962	246
59	Sam Thompson, 1893	245
	Bill Terry, 1930	245
	Lou Gehrig, 1933	245
	Charlie Gehringer, 1936	245
	Ted Williams, 1939	245
64	Steve Brodie, 1894	244
	Ed Delahanty, 1895	244
	Ed Delahanty, 1896	244
	Ken Williams, 1922	244
	Lou Gehrig, 1934	244
	Hal Trosky, 1936	244
70	Tom Brown, 1891	243
71	Dan Brouthers, 1887	242
	Ed McKean, 1895	242
	Lefty O'Doul, 1929	242
	Ted Williams, 1942	242
75	Lave Cross, 1894	241
	Bill Dahlen, 1894	241
	Babe Ruth, 1920	241
	Babe Ruth, 1923	241
79	Dan Brouthers, 1892	240
	Joe Kelley, 1896	240
	Ty Cobb, 1915	240
	George Sisler, 1920	240
	Joe Cronin, 1930	240
	Jimmie Foxx, 1933	240
85	Hughie Jennings, 1894	239
	Vern Stephens, 1950	239
87	George Davis, 1897	238
	Babe Ruth, 1926	238
	Babe Herman, 1930	238
	Hank Greenberg, 1940	238
91	Rogers Hornsby, 1925	237
	Al Simmons, 1929	237
	Joe DiMaggio, 1938	237
94	8 players tied	236

Clutch Hitting Index

1	Tom Herr, 1987	200
2	Ed Abbaticchio, 1907	194
3	Bill McClellan, 1878	193
4	George Davis, 1906	180
5	Sam Crawford, 1910	178
6	Frank LaPorte, 1914	176
7	Possum Whitted, 1920	176
8	Jack Barry, 1913	176
9	Heinie Reitz, 1896	176
10	George Stovall, 1911	176
11	John Sullivan, 1943	175
12	Cy Seymour, 1908	175
13	Fred Hartman, 1902	173
14	Cookie Lavagetto, 1941	173
15	Cap Anson, 1893	172
16	Farmer Vaughn, 1893	172
17	Pie Traynor, 1928	172
18	Larry Kopf, 1920	172
19	Stuffy McInnis, 1914	171
20	Cap Anson, 1880	171
21	Heinie Zimmerman, 1917	171
22	Sherry Magee, 1918	171
23	Bill Dahlen, 1904	170
24	Ned Williamson, 1885	170
	Clyde Barnhart, 1925	170
26	Cap Anson, 1881	169
27	Cap Anson, 1885	169
28	Joe Kelley, 1898	169
29	Larry Gardner, 1920	168
30	John Gochnauer, 1903	168
31	Lave Cross, 1903	168
32	Cap Anson, 1882	167
33	Maurice Van Robays, 1940	167
34	Jim O'Rourke, 1887	167
35	Monte Ward, 1881	167
36	Frank LaPorte, 1910	166
37	Bill Hague, 1878	166
38	Ross Youngs, 1921	166
39	Bob Ferguson, 1877	165
40	Deacon White, 1876	165
41	Johnny Berardino, 1941	165
42	Cap Anson, 1896	165
43	King Kelly, 1880	165
44	Larry Gardner, 1921	164
45	Bernie Friberg, 1924	164
46	Fred Pfeffer, 1886	164
47	Mike Higgins, 1938	164
48	Russ McKelvy, 1878	164
49	Steve Brodie, 1895	163
50	Earl Sheely, 1931	163
	Harmon Killebrew, 1971	163
52	Kid Gleason, 1897	163
53	John Ganzel, 1901	163
54	Joe Gerhardt, 1879	162
	Mike Dorgan, 1886	162
	Sam Mertes, 1905	162
57	Tom Burns, 1888	162
	Sherry Magee, 1910	162
59	Art Croft, 1877	162
60	Dixie Walker, 1946	161
61	Joe Tinker, 1906	161
62	Enos Slaughter, 1952	161
63	Ed Konetchy, 1918	160
64	Wally Pipp, 1923	160
65	Harry Swacina, 1914	160
66	Amos Otis, 1982	160
67	John Mayberry, 1976	160
68	Bill Brubaker, 1936	160
69	Tommy Corcoran, 1904	159
70	George Davis, 1902	159
71	Fred Pfeffer, 1885	159
	Stuffy McInnis, 1918	159
	Milt Stock, 1923	159
74	Fred Pfeffer, 1882	159
75	Ed McKean, 1892	159
76	Del Pratt, 1916	158
77	Charlie Dexter, 1901	158
	Enos Slaughter, 1950	158
79	Steve Evans, 1910	158
80	Rudy York, 1946	158
81	Billy Nash, 1892	158
	Bobby Veach, 1915	158
	Irish Meusel, 1924	158
	Roy Schalk, 1945	158
85	Fred Hartman, 1898	158
86	Dixie Walker, 1945	157
87	Red Smith, 1918	157
	Glenn Wright, 1927	157
	Bob Elliott, 1945	157
90	Jack Burdock, 1883	157
	Mike Mowrey, 1916	157
92	Bill Johnson, 1943	157
93	Denis Menke, 1969	157
94	Jim Nealon, 1906	156
95	Bid McPhee, 1896	156
	Gus Bell, 1959	156
	Tommy Davis, 1973	156
98	Art Fletcher, 1915	156
	Ray Bates, 1917	156
100	Sherry Magee, 1916	156

Isolated Power

1	Babe Ruth, 1920	.472
2	Babe Ruth, 1921	.469
3	Babe Ruth, 1927	.417
4	Lou Gehrig, 1927	.392
5	Babe Ruth, 1928	.386
6	Jimmie Foxx, 1932	.385
7	Babe Ruth, 1930	.373
8	Babe Ruth, 1923	.372
9	Mickey Mantle, 1961	.370
10	Hank Greenberg, 1938	.369
11	Hack Wilson, 1930	.368
12	Babe Ruth, 1926	.366
13	Babe Ruth, 1924	.361
14	Babe Ruth, 1922	.357
15	Jimmie Foxx, 1938	.356
16	Rogers Hornsby, 1925	.353
17	Mickey Mantle, 1956	.353
18	Babe Ruth, 1929	.353
19	Roger Maris, 1961	.351
20	Ralph Kiner, 1949	.348
21	Jimmie Foxx, 1933	.347
22	Willie Stargell, 1973	.347
23	Kevin Mitchell, 1989	.344
24	Lou Gehrig, 1934	.344
25	Jim Gentile, 1961	.344
26	Ted Williams, 1957	.343
27	Lou Gehrig, 1930	.343
28	Lou Gehrig, 1936	.342
29	Hank Aaron, 1971	.341
30	Willie Mays, 1955	.340
31	Mike Schmidt, 1980	.338
32	Willie McCovey, 1969	.336
33	Babe Ruth, 1919	.336
34	Jimmie Foxx, 1939	.334
35	Reggie Jackson, 1969	.333
36	Willie Stargell, 1971	.333
37	Hank Greenberg, 1937	.332
38	Hank Greenberg, 1940	.330
39	Ted Williams, 1941	.329
40	Mark McGwire, 1987	.329
41	Willie Mays, 1965	.328
42	Babe Ruth, 1931	.328
43	Mike Schmidt, 1981	.328
44	Hank Greenberg, 1946	.327
45	Joe DiMaggio, 1937	.327
46	Al Simmons, 1930	.327
47	Stan Musial, 1948	.326
48	Ralph Kiner, 1947	.326
49	Dave Kingman, 1979	.325
50	Ted Williams, 1946	.325
51	Eddie Mathews, 1953	.325
52	Willie McCovey, 1970	.323
53	Willie Mays, 1954	.322
54	Lou Gehrig, 1931	.321
55	Johnny Mize, 1940	.321
56	Frank Robinson, 1966	.321
57	Rogers Hornsby, 1922	.321
58	Duke Snider, 1955	.320
59	Babe Ruth, 1932	.319
60	Jimmie Foxx, 1934	.319
61	Ralph Kiner, 1951	.318
62	Ralph Kiner, 1950	.318
63	Harmon Killebrew, 1961	.318
64	Rocky Colavito, 1958	.317
65	Mark McGwire, 1992	.317
66	Chick Hafey, 1930	.316
67	Boog Powell, 1964	.316
68	Ted Kluszewski, 1954	.316
69	Dick Allen, 1966	.315
70	Cecil Fielder, 1990	.314
71	Eddie Mathews, 1954	.313
72	Duke Snider, 1957	.313
73	Barry Bonds, 1992	.313
74	Eddie Mathews, 1955	.313
75	Johnny Mize, 1947	.312
76	Willie Mays, 1964	.311
77	Willie Mays, 1962	.311
78	George Foster, 1977	.311
79	Mike Schmidt, 1979	.311
80	Jack Clark, 1987	.310
81	Hank Greenberg, 1939	.310
82	Harmon Killebrew, 1969	.308
83	Ted Williams, 1949	.307
84	Hank Aaron, 1969	.307
85	Duke Snider, 1954	.307
86	Mel Ott, 1929	.306
87	Duke Snider, 1956	.306
88	Joe Adcock, 1956	.306
89	Mickey Mantle, 1955	.306
90	Wally Berger, 1930	.305
91	Jim Bottomley, 1928	.304
92	Fred Lynn, 1979	.303
93	Harmon Killebrew, 1962	.303
94	Jimmie Foxx, 1930	.302
95	Chuck Klein, 1929	.302
96	Ernie Banks, 1958	.301
97	Norm Cash, 1961	.301
98	Chuck Klein, 1930	.301
99	Hank Greenberg, 1935	.300
100	Hal Trosky, 1936	.300

Extra Base Hits

1	Babe Ruth, 1921	119
2	Lou Gehrig, 1927	117
3	Chuck Klein, 1930	107
4	Chuck Klein, 1932	103
	Hank Greenberg, 1937	103
	Stan Musial, 1948	103
7	Rogers Hornsby, 1922	102
8	Lou Gehrig, 1930	100
	Jimmie Foxx, 1932	100
10	Babe Ruth, 1920	99
	Babe Ruth, 1923	99
	Hank Greenberg, 1940	99
13	Hank Greenberg, 1935	98
14	Babe Ruth, 1927	97
	Hack Wilson, 1930	97
	Joe Medwick, 1937	97
17	Hank Greenberg, 1934	96
	Hal Trosky, 1936	96
	Joe DiMaggio, 1937	96
20	Lou Gehrig, 1934	95
	Joe Medwick, 1936	95
22	Rogers Hornsby, 1929	94
	Chuck Klein, 1929	94
	Babe Herman, 1930	94
	Jimmie Foxx, 1933	94
26	Jim Bottomley, 1928	93
	Al Simmons, 1930	93
	Lou Gehrig, 1936	93
29	Babe Ruth, 1924	92
	Lou Gehrig, 1931	92
	Jimmie Foxx, 1938	92
	Stan Musial, 1953	92
	Hank Aaron, 1959	92
	Frank Robinson, 1962	92
35	Babe Ruth, 1928	91
36	Rogers Hornsby, 1925	90
	Stan Musial, 1949	90
	Willie Mays, 1962	90
	Willie Stargell, 1973	90
40	Hal Trosky, 1934	89
	Duke Snider, 1954	89
42	Joe DiMaggio, 1936	88
43	Tris Speaker, 1923	87
	Kiki Cuyler, 1925	87
	Lou Gehrig, 1928	87
	Ripper Collins, 1934	87
	Charlie Gehringer, 1936	87
	Johnny Mize, 1940	87
	Willie Mays, 1954	87
	Robin Yount, 1982	87
	Kevin Mitchell, 1989	87
52	George Sisler, 1920	86
	Babe Ruth, 1930	86
	Wally Moses, 1937	86
	Johnny Mize, 1939	86
	Ted Williams, 1939	86
	Stan Musial, 1946	86
	Eddie Mathews, 1953	86
	Reggie Jackson, 1969	86
	Hal McRae, 1977	86
	Jim Rice, 1978	86
	Don Mattingly, 1985	86
	Don Mattingly, 1986	86
64	Tip O'Neill, 1887	85
	Hugh Duffy, 1894	85
	Chick Hafey, 1929	85
	Goose Goslin, 1930	85
	Lou Gehrig, 1932	85
	Lou Gehrig, 1933	85
	Earl Averill, 1934	85
	Hank Greenberg, 1938	85
	Rudy York, 1940	85
	Ted Williams, 1949	85
	Stan Musial, 1954	85
	Frank Robinson, 1966	85
	George Foster, 1977	85
	George Brett, 1979	85
	Cal Ripken, 1991	85
79	Sam Thompson, 1895	84
	Ken Williams, 1922	84
	Al Simmons, 1929	84
	Ed Morgan, 1930	84
	Earl Webb, 1931	84
	Joe DiMaggio, 1941	84
	Duke Snider, 1953	84
	Tony Oliva, 1964	84
	Johnny Bench, 1970	84
	Jim Rice, 1979	84
89	Rogers Hornsby, 1921	83
	Lou Gehrig, 1926	83
	Dale Alexander, 1929	83
	Jimmie Foxx, 1930	83
	Earl Averill, 1932	83
	Lou Gehrig, 1937	83
	Ted Williams, 1946	83
	Ernie Banks, 1957	83
	Hank Aaron, 1961	83
	Jim Rice, 1977	83
	George Bell, 1987	83
100	14 players tied	82

Pinch Hits

1	Jose Morales, 1976	25
2	Dave Philley, 1961	24
	Vic Bavalillo, 1970	24
	Rusty Staub, 1983	24
5	Sam Leslie, 1932	22
	Red Schoendienst, 1962	22
	Wallace Johnson, 1988	22
8	Doc Miller, 1913	21
	Peanuts Lowrey, 1953	21
	Smoky Burgess, 1966	21
	Merv Rettenmund, 1977	21
12	Ed Coleman, 1936	20
	Frenchy Bordagaray, 1938	20
	Joe Frazier, 1954	20
	Smoky Burgess, 1965	20
	Ken Boswell, 1976	20
	Jerry Turner, 1978	20
	Thad Bosley, 1985	20
	Chris Chambliss, 1986	20
20	many players tied	19

Pinch Hit Average
(30 at-bats minimum)

1	Ed Kranepool, 1974	.486
2	Smead Jolley, 1931	.467
3	Frenchy Bordagaray, 1938	.465
4	Rick Miller, 1983	.457
5	Jose Pagan, 1969	.452
6	Elmer Valo, 1955	.452
7	Gates Brown, 1968	.450
8	Ted Easterly, 1912	.433
	Milt Thompson, 1985	.433
	Randy Bush, 1986	.433
11	Joe Cronin, 1943	.429
	Don Dillard, 1961	.429
13	Candy Maldonado, 1986	.425
14	Richie Ashburn, 1962	.419
	Dick Williams, 1962	.419
16	Merritt Ranew, 1963	.415
	Carl Taylor, 1969	.415
18	Kurt Bevacqua, 1983	.412
19	Jerry Turner, 1978	.408
20	Bob Bowman, 1958	.406
	Harry Spilman, 1986	.406
	Chico Walker, 1991	.406
23	Frankie Baumholtz, 1955	.405
24	6 players tied	.400

Pinch Hit Home Runs

1	Johnny Frederick, 1932	6
2	Joe Cronin, 1943	5
	Butch Nieman, 1945	5
	Gene Freese, 1959	5
	Jerry Lynch, 1961	5
	Cliff Johnson, 1974	5
	Lee Lacy, 1978	5
	Jerry Turner, 1978	5
9	Ernie Lombardi, 1946	4
	Del Wilber, 1953	4
	Bill Taylor, 1955	4
	Bob Thurman, 1957	4
	Rip Repulski, 1958	4
	George Crowe, 1959	4
	George Crowe, 1960	4
	Johnny Blanchard, 1961	4
	Carl Sawatski, 1961	4
	Jerry Lynch, 1963	4
	Don Mincher, 1964	4
	Hal Breeden, 1973	4
	Mike Ivie, 1978	4
	Del Unser, 1979	4
	Jeff Burroughs, 1982	4
	Danny Heep, 1983	4
	Candy Maldonado, 1986	4
	Mark Carreon, 1989	4
	Tommy Gregg, 1990	4
	Ernest Riles, 1990	4

Total Player Rating / 150g

1	Fred Dunlap, 1884	12.77
2	Babe Ruth, 1923	10.66
3	Mike Schmidt, 1981	10.59
4	Nap Lajoie, 1901	10.53
5	Pete Browning, 1882	10.00
6	Nap Lajoie, 1903	9.96
7	Barry Bonds, 1992	9.64
8	Ross Barnes, 1876	9.55
9	Babe Ruth, 1921	9.47
10	Babe Ruth, 1920	9.40
11	Rickey Henderson, 1990	8.93
12	Mickey Mantle, 1957	8.85
13	Babe Ruth, 1927	8.84
14	Rogers Hornsby, 1924	8.81
15	Ted Williams, 1957	8.52
16	Ted Williams, 1941	8.50
17	Fred Pfeffer, 1884	8.44
18	Cal Ripken, 1984	8.43
19	Ted Williams, 1942	8.40
	Ted Williams, 1946	8.40
	Mickey Mantle, 1956	8.40
22	Nap Lajoie, 1906	8.39
	Ty Cobb, 1917	8.39
24	Babe Ruth, 1924	8.33
	George Brett, 1980	8.33
26	Eric Davis, 1987	8.26
27	Nap Lajoie, 1910	8.21
28	Babe Ruth, 1926	8.09
29	Hughie Jennings, 1896	7.96
30	Rogers Hornsby, 1920	7.95
31	Rogers Hornsby, 1922	7.89
32	Tris Speaker, 1913	7.87
33	Rogers Hornsby, 1917	7.86
34	Tris Speaker, 1912	7.84
35	Cupid Childs, 1896	7.84
36	Honus Wagner, 1906	7.82
37	George Sisler, 1920	7.79
38	Nap Lajoie, 1904	7.71
	Ty Cobb, 1910	7.71
40	Lou Boudreau, 1944	7.70
41	Rickey Henderson, 1985	7.66
42	Cupid Childs, 1890	7.62
43	Ty Cobb, 1911	7.60
44	Mike Schmidt, 1980	7.60
	Willie Mays, 1955	7.60
46	Honus Wagner, 1905	7.55
47	Lou Gehrig, 1927	7.55
48	Ted Williams, 1947	7.50
	Cal Ripken, 1991	7.50
50	Nap Lajoie, 1908	7.45
51	Mickey Mantle, 1961	7.45
52	Honus Wagner, 1903	7.44
53	Ed Delahanty, 1896	7.44
54	King Kelly, 1879	7.40
55	Joe Morgan, 1975	7.40
56	Carl Yastrzemski, 1967	7.36
57	Ron Santo, 1966	7.35
58	Nap Lajoie, 1900	7.35
59	Nap Lajoie, 1907	7.34
60	Jack Glasscock, 1882	7.32
61	Ted Williams, 1954	7.31
62	Snuffy Stirnweiss, 1945	7.30
63	Ed Delahanty, 1893	7.27
64	Babe Ruth, 1930	7.24
65	Tris Speaker, 1914	7.22
66	Barry Larkin, 1991	7.20
67	George Sisler, 1922	7.18
68	Frankie Frisch, 1927	7.16
69	Dick Bartell, 1937	7.15
70	Bob Ferguson, 1878	7.13
71	Hughie Jennings, 1895	7.10
72	Ted Williams, 1949	7.06
73	Benny Kauff, 1915	7.06
74	Barry Bonds, 1990	7.05
75	Babe Ruth, 1931	7.03
76	Robin Yount, 1981	7.03
77	Lou Gehrig, 1934	7.01
	Snuffy Stirnweiss, 1944	7.01
	Rico Petrocelli, 1969	7.01
80	Joe DiMaggio, 1939	7.00
81	Ron Santo, 1967	6.99
82	Harland Clift, 1937	6.97
	George Brett, 1985	6.97
84	Eddie Collins, 1910	6.96
85	Buddy Bell, 1981	6.96
86	Honus Wagner, 1908	6.95
87	Rickey Henderson, 1981	6.94
88	Joe Jackson, 1911	6.94
89	Hughie Jennings, 1897	6.92
	Babe Ruth, 1919	6.92
	Rogers Hornsby, 1929	6.92
92	Joe Jackson, 1912	6.92
93	Willie Mays, 1958	6.91
94	Arky Vaughan, 1935	6.90
95	Norm Cash, 1961	6.89
96	Ned Williamson, 1884	6.87
97	W Jones, 1877	6.84
98	Bill Dahlen, 1896	6.84
99	Bobby Wallace, 1901	6.83
100	Honus Wagner, 1912	6.83

Stolen Bases

1	Hugh Nicol, 1887	138
2	Rickey Henderson, 1982	130
3	Arlie Latham, 1887	129
4	Lou Brock, 1974	118
5	Charlie Comiskey, 1887	117
6	Monte Ward, 1887	111
	Billy Hamilton, 1889	111
	Billy Hamilton, 1891	111
9	Vince Coleman, 1985	110
10	Arlie Latham, 1888	109
	Vince Coleman, 1987	109
12	Rickey Henderson, 1983	108
13	Vince Coleman, 1986	107
14	Tom Brown, 1891	106
15	Maury Wills, 1962	104
16	Pete Browning, 1887	103
	Hugh Nicol, 1888	103
18	Jim Fogarty, 1887	102
	Billy Hamilton, 1890	102
20	Rickey Henderson, 1980	100
21	Jim Fogarty, 1889	99
22	Billy Hamilton, 1894	98
23	Harry Stovey, 1890	97
	Billy Hamilton, 1895	97
	Ron LeFlore, 1980	97
26	Ty Cobb, 1915	96
	Omar Moreno, 1980	96
28	Bid McPhee, 1887	95
	Curt Welch, 1888	95
30	Mike Griffin, 1887	94
	Maury Wills, 1965	94
32	Tommy McCarthy, 1888	93
	Rickey Henderson, 1988	93
34	Darby O'Brien, 1889	91
35	Tim Raines, 1983	90
36	Curt Welch, 1887	89
	Herman Long, 1889	89
38	Tom Poorman, 1887	88
	Blondie Purcell, 1887	88
	Monte Ward, 1892	88
	Clyde Milan, 1912	88
42	Harry Stovey, 1888	87
	Arlie Latham, 1891	87
	Joe Kelley, 1896	87
	Rickey Henderson, 1986	87
46	Cub Stricker, 1887	86
47	Tommy Tucker, 1887	85
	Hub Collins, 1890	85
	Hugh Duffy, 1891	85
50	King Kelly, 1887	84
	Chippy McGarr, 1887	84
	Billy Sunday, 1890	84
	Bill Lange, 1896	84
54	Tommy McCarthy, 1890	83
	Billy Hamilton, 1896	83
	Ty Cobb, 1911	83
	Willie Wilson, 1979	83
58	Dummy Hoy, 1888	82
	John Reilly, 1888	82
60	Eddie Collins, 1910	81
	Vince Coleman, 1988	81
62	Emmett Seery, 1888	80
	Hugh Nicol, 1889	80
	Bob Bescher, 1911	80
	Rickey Henderson, 1985	80
	Eric Davis, 1986	80
67	Tom Brown, 1890	79
	Dave Collins, 1980	79
	Willie Wilson, 1980	79
70	Hugh Duffy, 1890	78
	Tom Brown, 1892	78
	John McGraw, 1894	78
	Ron LeFlore, 1979	78
	Tim Raines, 1982	78
	Marquis Grissom, 1992	78
76	Ted Scheffler, 1890	77
	Jimmy Sheckard, 1899	77
	Davey Lopes, 1975	77
	Omar Moreno, 1979	77
	Rudy Law, 1983	77
	Rickey Henderson, 1989	77
	Vince Coleman, 1990	77
83	Ed McKean, 1887	76
	Walt Wilmot, 1890	76
	Dusty Miller, 1896	76
	Ty Cobb, 1909	76
	Marquis Grissom, 1991	76
88	Yank Robinson, 1887	75
	George Van Haltren, 1891	75
	Clyde Milan, 1913	75
	Benny Kauff, 1914	75
	Bill North, 1976	75
	Tim Raines, 1984	75
94	Frank Fennelly, 1887	74
	Harry Stovey, 1887	74
	Walt Wilmot, 1894	74
	Fritz Maisel, 1914	74
	Lou Brock, 1966	74
99	7 players tied	73

Stolen Base Average

1	Kevin McReynolds, 1988	100.0
2	Max Carey, 1922	96.2
3	Ken Griffey, 1980	95.8
4	Stan Javier, 1988	95.2
5	Amos Otis, 1970	94.3
6	Jack Perconte, 1985	93.9
7	Miguel Dilone, 1984	93.1
	Bob Dernier, 1986	93.1
9	Kirk Gibson, 1990	92.9
10	Don Baylor, 1972	92.3
	Oddibe McDowell, 1987	92.3
12	Davey Lopes, 1985	92.2
13	Eric Davis, 1988	92.1
14	Henry Cotto, 1992	92.0
15	Bobby Bonds, 1969	91.8
	Davey Lopes, 1978	91.8
17	Davey Lopes, 1979	91.7
	Marquis Grissom, 1990	91.7
19	Jim Wynn, 1965	91.5
20	Larry Bowa, 1977	91.4
21	Ryne Sandberg, 1987	91.3
	Alan Trammell, 1987	91.3
23	Jerry Mumphrey, 1980	91.2
24	Tom Herr, 1985	91.2
25	Jack Smith, 1925	90.9
	Davey Lopes, 1981	90.9
	Tim Raines, 1987	90.9
28	Willie Wilson, 1984	90.4
29	Bake McBride, 1978	90.3
30	Devon White, 1992	90.2
31	Henry Cotto, 1988	90.0
32	Mitchell Page, 1977	89.4
33	Tommy Harper, 1971	89.3
	Rick Manning, 1981	89.3
	Eric Davis, 1987	89.3
36	Maury Wills, 1962	88.9
	Jake Wood, 1962	88.9
	Tommy Harper, 1964	88.9
	Enzo Hernandez, 1972	88.9
	Dusty Baker, 1973	88.9
	Leon Lacy, 1981	88.9
	Rickey Henderson, 1985	88.9
43	Willie Wilson, 1980	88.8
44	Tim Raines, 1985	88.6
	Tim Raines, 1986	88.6
46	Bert Campaneris, 1969	88.6
	Kirk Gibson, 1988	88.6
48	Willie Mays, 1971	88.5
	Mariano Duncan, 1992	88.5
50	Vince Coleman, 1986	88.4

Stolen Base Runs

1	Vince Coleman, 1986	24
2	Maury Wills, 1962	23
3	Rickey Henderson, 1983	21
4	Rickey Henderson, 1988	20
5	Vince Coleman, 1987	20
6	Tim Raines, 1983	19
7	Vince Coleman, 1985	18
	Rickey Henderson, 1985	18
9	Willie Wilson, 1979	18
	Ron LeFlore, 1980	18
	Willie Wilson, 1980	18
12	Eric Davis, 1986	17
13	Tim Raines, 1984	17
14	Davey Lopes, 1975	16
	Rudy Law, 1983	16
16	Lou Brock, 1974	16
	Tim Raines, 1985	16
	Tim Raines, 1986	16
	Marquis Grissom, 1992	16
20	Rickey Henderson, 1986	15
21	Ron LeFlore, 1979	15
22	Tim Raines, 1981	15
	Rickey Henderson, 1989	15
24	Rickey Henderson, 1980	14
25	Max Carey, 1922	14
	Joe Morgan, 1975	14
27	Bert Campaneris, 1969	14
	Tim Raines, 1982	14
	Rickey Henderson, 1982	14
30	Vince Coleman, 1989	14
	Rickey Henderson, 1990	14
32	Davey Lopes, 1976	13
	Willie Wilson, 1983	13
	Vince Coleman, 1990	13
35	Mickey Rivers, 1975	13
	Joe Morgan, 1976	13
	Jerry Mumphrey, 1980	13
	Juan Samuel, 1984	13
	Marquis Grissom, 1991	13
	Kenny Lofton, 1992	13
41	Fritz Maisel, 1914	12
	Al Wiggins, 1983	12
	Tim Raines, 1987	12
44	Julio Cruz, 1978	12
	Davey Lopes, 1985	12
	Ozzie Smith, 1988	12
47	Lou Brock, 1966	11
	Lou Brock, 1968	11
	Gary Pettis, 1985	11
	Eric Davis, 1987	11

Stolen Base Wins

1	Vince Coleman, 1986	2.5
2	Maury Wills, 1962	2.3
3	Rickey Henderson, 1983	2.1
4	Rickey Henderson, 1988	2.0
5	Tim Raines, 1983	1.9
6	Vince Coleman, 1987	1.9
7	Vince Coleman, 1985	1.9
8	Ron LeFlore, 1980	1.9
9	Eric Davis, 1986	1.8
10	Rickey Henderson, 1985	1.8
11	Willie Wilson, 1980	1.8
12	Tim Raines, 1984	1.7
13	Willie Wilson, 1979	1.7
14	Marquis Grissom, 1992	1.7
15	Davey Lopes, 1975	1.7
16	Tim Raines, 1985	1.6
17	Lou Brock, 1974	1.6
18	Tim Raines, 1986	1.6
19	Rudy Law, 1983	1.6
20	Tim Raines, 1981	1.6
21	Rickey Henderson, 1986	1.5
22	Rickey Henderson, 1989	1.5
23	Joe Morgan, 1975	1.5
24	Ron LeFlore, 1979	1.5
25	Tim Raines, 1982	1.4
26	Bert Campaneris, 1969	1.4
27	Vince Coleman, 1989	1.4
28	Rickey Henderson, 1980	1.4
29	Rickey Henderson, 1982	1.4
30	Rickey Henderson, 1990	1.4
31	Davey Lopes, 1976	1.4
32	Joe Morgan, 1976	1.3
33	Jerry Mumphrey, 1980	1.3
34	Max Carey, 1922	1.3
35	Vince Coleman, 1990	1.3
36	Fritz Maisel, 1914	1.3
37	Juan Samuel, 1984	1.3
38	Marquis Grissom, 1991	1.3
39	Lou Brock, 1968	1.3
40	Willie Wilson, 1983	1.3
41	Mickey Rivers, 1975	1.3
42	Kenny Lofton, 1992	1.3
43	Ozzie Smith, 1988	1.3
44	Al Wiggins, 1983	1.3
45	Davey Lopes, 1985	1.2
46	Julio Cruz, 1978	1.2
47	Lou Brock, 1966	1.2
48	Tim Raines, 1987	1.2
49	Davey Lopes, 1978	1.2
50	2 players tied	1.2

Fielding Average

First Base

1	Steve Garvey, 1984	1.000
2	Stuffy McInnis, 1921	.999
3	Frank McCormick, 1946	.999
4	Steve Garvey, 1981	.999
5	Jim Spencer, 1973	.999
6	Wes Parker, 1968	.999
7	Eddie Murray, 1981	.999
8	Hal Morris, 1992	.999
9	Jim Spencer, 1976	.998
10	Jim Spencer, 1981	.998

Second Base

1	Bobby Grich, 1985	.997
2	Jose Oquendo, 1990	.996
3	Ryne Sandberg, 1991	.995
4	Rob Wilfong, 1980	.995
5	Bobby Grich, 1973	.995
6	Frank White, 1988	.994
7	Jose Oquendo, 1989	.994
8	Jerry Adair, 1964	.994
9	Ryne Sandberg, 1986	.994
10	Tim Cullen, 1970	.994

Shortstop

1	Cal Ripken, 1990	.996
2	Tony Fernandez, 1989	.992
3	Larry Bowa, 1979	.991
4	Ed Brinkman, 1972	.990
5	Cal Ripken, 1989	.990
6	Spike Owen, 1990	.989
7	Omar Vizquel, 1992	.989
8	Tony Fernandez, 1990	.989
9	Dick Schofield, 1992	.988
10	Ozzie Smith, 1991	.987

Third Base

1	Steve Buechele, 1991	.991
2	Don Money, 1974	.989
3	Hank Majeski, 1947	.988
4	Aurelio Rodriguez, 1978	.987
5	Willie Kamm, 1933	.984
6	George Kell, 1946	.983
7	Heinie Groh, 1924	.983
8	Carney Lansford, 1979	.983
9	George Kell, 1950	.982
10	Pinky Whitney, 1937	.982

Outfield

1	Danny Litwhiler, 1942	1.000
	Willard Marshall, 1951	1.000
	Tony Gonzalez, 1962	1.000
	Don Demeter, 1963	1.000
	Rocky Colavito, 1965	1.000
	Curt Flood, 1966	1.000
	Johnny Callison, 1968	1.000
	Mickey Stanley, 1968	1.000
	Ken Harrelson, 1968	1.000
	Ken Berry, 1969	1.000
	Mickey Stanley, 1970	1.000
	Roy White, 1971	1.000
	Al Kaline, 1971	1.000
	Ken Berry, 1972	1.000
	Carl Yastrzemski, 1977	1.000
	Terry Puhl, 1979	1.000
	Gary Roenicke, 1980	1.000
	Ken Landreaux, 1981	1.000
	Terry Puhl, 1981	1.000
	Ken Singleton, 1981	1.000
	Brian Downing, 1982	1.000
	John Lowenstein, 1982	1.000
	Brian Downing, 1984	1.000
	Brett Butler, 1991	1.000
	Darryl Hamilton, 1992	1.000

Catcher

1	Spud Davis, 1939	1.000
	Buddy Rosar, 1946	1.000
	Lou Berberet, 1957	1.000
	Pete Daley, 1957	1.000
	Yogi Berra, 1958	1.000
	Rick Cerone, 1988	1.000
7	Tom Pagnozzi, 1992	.999
8	Joe Azcue, 1967	.999
9	Wes Westrum, 1950	.999
10	Thurman Munson, 1971	.998

Pitcher (92 chances accepted)

1	Kid Nichols, 1896	1.000
	Frank Owen, 1904	1.000
	Mordecai Brown, 1908	1.000
	Pete Alexander, 1913	1.000
	Walter Johnson, 1913	1.000
	Eppa Rixey, 1917	1.000
	Walter Johnson, 1917	1.000
	Hal Schumacher, 1935	1.000
	Larry Jackson, 1964	1.000
	Randy Jones, 1976	1.000
	Greg Maddux, 1990	1.000

Total Chances per Game

First Base

1	Joe Gerhardt, 1876	13.28
2	Jiggs Donahue, 1907	12.73
3	Oscar Walker, 1879	12.60
4	Joe Start, 1878	12.54
5	Tim Murnane, 1878	12.52
6	Joe Start, 1879	12.49
7	Jake Goodman, 1878	12.45
8	Herman Dehlman, 1876	12.36
9	Phil Todt, 1926	12.36
10	Joe Start, 1877	12.35

Second Base

1	Thorny Hawkes, 1879	8.44
2	Chick Fulmer, 1879	8.34
3	Jack Burdock, 1878	8.30
4	Ed Somerville, 1876	8.28
5	Joe Gerhardt, 1877	8.12
6	Fred Pfeffer, 1884	8.08
7	Jack Burdock, 1879	7.88
8	Joe Quest, 1878	7.81
9	Pop Smith, 1885	7.74
10	Joe Quest, 1879	7.73

Shortstop

1	Herman Long, 1889	7.27
2	Hughie Jennings, 1895	7.16
3	Dave Bancroft, 1918	7.14
4	Phil Tomney, 1889	7.12
5	George Davis, 1899	7.08
6	Hughie Jennings, 1896	7.07
7	Hughie Jennings, 1897	7.03
8	Bobby Wallace, 1901	6.97
9	Monte Cross, 1897	6.97
10	Bill Dahlen, 1895	6.93

Third Base

1	Al Nichols, 1876	5.81
2	Bob Ferguson, 1877	5.61
3	Jumbo Davis, 1888	5.13
4	Cap Anson, 1876	5.03
5	George Bradley, 1880	4.93
6	Billy Shindle, 1892	4.93
7	Jack Gleason, 1882	4.90
8	Bill Bradley, 1900	4.87
9	Will Foley, 1877	4.79
10	Levi Meyerle, 1876	4.78

Outfield

1	Fred Treacey, 1876	4.39
2	Redleg Snyder, 1876	3.84
3	Charley Jones, 1877	3.77
4	Taylor Douthit, 1928	3.68
5	Mike Mansell, 1879	3.64
6	Richie Ashburn, 1951	3.64
7	Chet Lemon, 1977	3.60
8	Thurman Tucker, 1944	3.58
9	Kirby Puckett, 1984	3.57
10	Irv Noren, 1951	3.53

Catcher

1	Bill Holbert, 1883	10.63
2	Sam Trott, 1884	10.35
3	Bill Holbert, 1884	9.51
4	Jocko Milligan, 1884	9.40
5	Mert Hackett, 1884	9.35
6	Barney Gilligan, 1884	9.30
7	Mike Hines, 1883	9.27
8	George Baker, 1884	8.99
9	Jocko Milligan, 1885	8.82
10	Lew Brown, 1877	8.65

Pitcher

1	Harry Howell, 1905	5.42
2	Harry Howell, 1904	5.12
3	Will White, 1882	4.76
4	Ed Walsh, 1907	4.75
5	George Mullin, 1904	4.53
6	Tony Mullane, 1882	4.38
7	Red Donahue, 1902	4.37
8	Nick Altrock, 1905	4.37
9	Harry Howell, 1906	4.34
10	John Katoll, 1902	4.31

Chances Accepted per Game

First Base
1 Jiggs Donahue, 1907 . . . . 12.65
2 Joe Gerhardt, 1876 . . . . . . 12.54
3 Phil Todt, 1926 . . . . 12.21
4 Joe Start, 1879 . . . . 12.15
5 George Burns, 1914 . . . . . 12.10
6 Stuffy McInnis, 1918 . . . . . 12.10
7 George Stovall, 1908 . . . . . 12.08
8 George Kelly, 1920 . . . . . . 12.01
9 Joe Start, 1878 . . . . 12.00
10 Oscar Walker, 1879 . . . . . . 11.92

Second Base
1 Jack Burdock, 1878 . . . . . . 7.62
2 Thorny Hawkes, 1879 . . . 7.56
3 Chick Fulmer, 1879 . . . . . 7.55
4 Fred Pfeffer, 1884 . . . . 7.29
5 Joe Gerhardt, 1877 . . . . . . 7.21
6 Ed Somerville, 1876 . . . . . 7.20
7 Jack Burdock, 1879 . . . . . 7.18
8 Joe Quest, 1879 . . . . 7.16
9 Pop Smith, 1885 . . . . 7.13
10 Bid McPhee, 1886 . . . . 7.09

Shortstop
1 Hughie Jennings, 1895 . . . 6.73
2 George Davis, 1899 . . . . . . 6.69
3 Dave Bancroft, 1918 . . . . . 6.62
4 Hughie Jennings, 1896 . . . 6.56
5 Hughie Jennings, 1897 . . . 6.55
6 Rabbit Maranville, 1919 . . 6.48
7 Bobby Wallace, 1901 . . . . . 6.48
8 Monte Cross, 1897 . . . . . . 6.41
9 Dave Bancroft, 1920 . . . . . 6.40
10 George Davis, 1900 . . . . . . 6.39

Third Base
1 Bob Ferguson, 1877 . . . . . 4.71
2 Al Nichols, 1876 . . . . 4.53
3 Billy Shindle, 1892 . . . . . . 4.34
4 Jumbo Davis, 1888 . . . . . . 4.33
5 Bill Bradley, 1900 . . . . 4.29
6 Cap Anson, 1876 . . . . 4.27
7 George Bradley, 1880 . . . . 4.23
8 Joe Battin, 1883 . . . . 4.17
9 Bill Hague, 1878 . . . . 4.16
10 Billy Shindle, 1888 . . . . . . 4.13

Outfield
1 Fred Treacey, 1876 . . . . . . 3.70
2 Taylor Douthit, 1928 . . . . . 3.62
3 Richie Ashburn, 1951 . . . 3.59
4 Thurman Tucker, 1944 . . . . 3.55
5 Kirby Puckett, 1984 . . . . . 3.55
6 Chet Lemon, 1977 . . . . . . 3.52
7 Irv Noren, 1951 . . . . 3.45
8 Richie Ashburn, 1949 . . . . 3.42
9 Carden Gillenwater, 1945 . 3.39
10 Sam West, 1935 . . . . 3.38

Catcher
1 Bill Holbert, 1883 . . . . 9.78
2 Sam Trott, 1884 . . . . 9.63
3 Jocko Milligan, 1884 . . . . 8.83
4 Bill Holbert, 1884 . . . . 8.75
5 Mert Hackett, 1884 . . . . . . 8.68
6 Barney Gilligan, 1884 . . . . 8.63
7 Duffy Dyer, 1972 . . . . 8.25
8 Jocko Milligan, 1885 . . . . 8.25
9 Mike Hines, 1883 . . . . 8.22
10 George Baker, 1884 . . . . . 8.06

Pitcher
1 Harry Howell, 1905 . . . . . . 5.24
2 Harry Howell, 1904 . . . . . . 4.97
3 Ed Walsh, 1907 . . . . 4.68
4 Will White, 1882 . . . . 4.56
5 Nick Altrock, 1905 . . . . . . 4.32
6 George Mullin, 1904 . . . . . 4.24
7 Tony Mullane, 1882 . . . . . 4.20
8 Willie Sudhoff, 1904 . . . . . 4.19
9 Red Donahue, 1902 . . . . . . 4.14
10 Nick Altrock, 1904 . . . . . . 4.13

Putouts

First Base
1 Jiggs Donahue, 1907 1846
2 George Kelly, 1920 1759
3 Phil Todt, 1926 1755
4 Wally Pipp, 1926 1710
5 Jiggs Donahue, 1906 1697
6 Candy LaChance, 1904 . . . 1691
7 Tom Jones, 1907 1687
8 Ernie Banks, 1965 1682
9 Wally Pipp, 1922 1667
10 Lou Gehrig, 1927 1662

Second Base
1 Bid McPhee, 1886 529
2 Bobby Grich, 1974 484
3 Bucky Harris, 1922 483
4 Nellie Fox, 1956 478
5 Lou Bierbauer, 1889 472
6 Billy Herman, 1933 466
7 Bill Wambsganss, 1924 . . . 463
8 Cub Stricker, 1887 461
9 Buddy Myer, 1935 460
10 Bill Sweeney, 1912 459

Shortstop
1 Hughie Jennings, 1895 . . . 425
   Donie Bush, 1914 425
3 Joe Cassidy, 1905 408
4 Rabbit Maranville, 1914 . . 407
5 Dave Bancroft, 1922 405
   Eddie Miller, 1940 405
7 Monte Cross, 1898 404
8 Dave Bancroft, 1921 396
9 Mickey Doolan, 1906 395
10 Buck Weaver, 1913 392

Third Base
1 Denny Lyons, 1887 255
2 Jimmy Williams, 1899 251
   Jimmy Collins, 1900 251
4 Jimmy Collins, 1898 243
   Willie Kamm, 1928 243
6 Willie Kamm, 1927 236
7 Frank Baker, 1913 233
8 Bill Coughlin, 1901 232
9 Ernie Courtney, 1905 229
10 Jimmy Austin, 1911 228

Outfield
1 Taylor Douthit, 1928 547
2 Richie Ashburn, 1951 538
3 Richie Ashburn, 1949 514
4 Chet Lemon, 1977 512
5 Dwayne Murphy, 1980 . . . 507
6 Dom DiMaggio, 1948 503
   Richie Ashburn, 1956 503
8 Richie Ashburn, 1957 502
9 Richie Ashburn, 1953 496
10 Richie Ashburn, 1958 495

Catcher
1 Johnny Edwards, 1969 . . . 1135
2 Johnny Edwards, 1963 . . . 1008
3 Randy Hundley, 1969 978
4 Tony Pena, 1983 976
5 Bill Freehan, 1968 971
6 Gary Carter, 1985 956
7 Gary Carter, 1982 954
8 Bill Freehan, 1967 950
9 Johnny Bench, 1968 942
10 Elston Howard, 1964 939

Pitcher
1 Dave Foutz, 1886 57
2 Tony Mullane, 1882 54
3 George Bradley, 1876 50
   Guy Hecker, 1884 50
5 Mike Boddicker, 1984 49
6 Larry Corcoran, 1884 47
7 Al Spalding, 1876 45
   Ted Breitenstein, 1895 45
9 Jim Devlin, 1876 44
   Dave Foutz, 1887 44
   Bill Hutchinson, 1890 44

Putouts per Game

First Base
1 Joe Gerhardt, 1876 . . . . . . 12.30
2 Joe Start, 1879 . . . . 11.98
3 Joe Start, 1878 . . . . 11.79
4 Jiggs Donahue, 1907 . . . . . 11.76
5 Joe Start, 1877 . . . . 11.73
6 Herman Dehlman, 1876 . . 11.72
7 Joe Start, 1880 . . . . 11.63
8 Jake Goodman, 1878 . . . . . 11.55
9 George Burns, 1914 . . . . . . 11.53
10 Oscar Walker, 1879 . . . . . . 11.50

Second Base
1 Jack Burdock, 1878 . . . . . . 4.08
2 Jack Burdock, 1880 . . . . . . 3.81
3 Bid McPhee, 1886 . . . . 3.78
4 Bid McPhee, 1884 . . . . 3.71
5 Joe Quest, 1878 . . . . 3.68
6 Cub Stricker, 1887 . . . . . . 3.66
7 Lou Bierbauer, 1889 . . . . . 3.63
8 Jack Burdock, 1879 . . . . . . 3.61
9 Chick Fulmer, 1879 . . . . . . 3.59
10 Bob Ferguson, 1880 . . . . . . 3.59

Shortstop
1 Hughie Jennings, 1895 . . . 3.24
2 Dave Bancroft, 1918 . . . . . 2.97
3 Hughie Jennings, 1896 . . . 2.90
4 Hughie Jennings, 1897 . . . 2.89
5 George Davis, 1898 . . . . . . 2.88
6 George Davis, 1899 . . . . . . 2.88
7 Rabbit Maranville, 1919 . . 2.76
8 Honus Wagner, 1913 . . . . . 2.75
9 Kid Elberfeld, 1901 . . . . . . 2.74
10 Buck Weaver, 1914 . . . . . . 2.74

Third Base
1 Al Nichols, 1876 . . . . 2.16
2 Cap Anson, 1876 . . . . 2.05
3 Hick Carpenter, 1880 . . . . 2.03
4 Bob Ferguson, 1877 . . . . . 1.95
5 Denny Lyons, 1887 . . . . . . 1.86
6 Patsy Tebeau, 1890 . . . . . . 1.85
7 Cap Anson, 1877 . . . . 1.85
8 Joe Battin, 1876 . . . . 1.83
9 Jerry Denny, 1883 . . . . 1.82
10 Frank Hankinson, 1881 . . . 1.80

Outfield
1 Taylor Douthit, 1928 . . . . . 3.55
2 Fred Treacey, 1876 . . . . . . 3.54
3 Richie Ashburn, 1951 . . . . 3.49
4 Thurman Tucker, 1944 . . . 3.45
5 Chet Lemon, 1977 . . . . 3.44
6 Kirby Puckett, 1984 . . . . . 3.42
7 Richie Ashburn, 1949 . . . . 3.34
8 Irv Noren, 1951 . . . . 3.33
9 Sam West, 1935 . . . . 3.33
10 Jim Busby, 1952 . . . . 3.28

Catcher
1 Sam Trott, 1884 . . . . 8.18
2 Bill Holbert, 1883 . . . . 7.75
3 Duffy Dyer, 1972 . . . . 7.58
4 Johnny Edwards, 1969 . . . 7.52
5 Barney Gilligan, 1884 . . . . 7.47
6 John Romano, 1964 . . . . . . 7.44
7 Johnny Edwards, 1964 . . . 7.42
8 Joe Azcue, 1967 . . . . 7.40
9 John Roseboro, 1960 . . . . . 7.36
10 Jerry Grote, 1971 . . . . 7.31

Pitcher
1 Mike Boddicker, 1984 . . . . 1.44
2 Oil Can Boyd, 1985 . . . . . . 1.20
3 Nick Altrock, 1904 . . . . . . 1.13
4 Greg Maddux, 1990 . . . . . . 1.11
5 Dave Foutz, 1887 . . . . 1.10
6 Dwight Gooden, 1986 . . . . 1.09
7 Dan Petry, 1984 . . . . 1.09
8 Nat Hudson, 1888 . . . . 1.08
   Al Nipper, 1986 . . . . 1.08
10 John Harkins, 1885 . . . . . . 1.06
   Dan Petry, 1985 . . . . 1.06

Assists

First Base
1 Bill Buckner, 1985 184
2 Mark Grace, 1990 180
3 Mark Grace, 1991 167
4 Sid Bream, 1986 166
5 Bill Buckner, 1983 161
6 Bill Buckner, 1982 159
7 Bill Buckner, 1986 157
8 Mickey Vernon, 1949 155
9 Fred Tenney, 1905 152
   Eddie Murray, 1985 152

Second Base
1 Frankie Frisch, 1927 641
2 Hughie Critz, 1926 588
3 Rogers Hornsby, 1927 582
4 Ski Melillo, 1930 572
5 Ryne Sandberg, 1983 571
6 Rabbit Maranville, 1924 . . 568
7 Frank Parkinson, 1922 . . . 562
8 Tony Cuccinello, 1936 . . . 559
9 Johnny Hodapp, 1930 557
10 Lou Bierbauer, 1892 555

Shortstop
1 Ozzie Smith, 1980 621
2 Glenn Wright, 1924 601
3 Dave Bancroft, 1920 598
4 Tommy Thevenow, 1926 . . 597
5 Ivan DeJesus, 1977 595
6 Cal Ripken, 1984 583
7 Whitey Wietelmann, 1943 . 581
8 Dave Bancroft, 1922 579
9 Rabbit Maranville, 1914 . . 574
10 Don Kessinger, 1968 573

Third Base
1 Graig Nettles, 1971 412
2 Graig Nettles, 1973 410
   Brooks Robinson, 1974 . . 410
4 Harlond Clift, 1937 405
   Brooks Robinson, 1967 . . 405
6 Mike Schmidt, 1974 404
7 Doug DeCinces, 1982 399
8 Clete Boyer, 1962 396
   Mike Schmidt, 1977 396
   Buddy Bell, 1982 396

Outfield
1 Orator Shaffer, 1879 50
2 Hugh Nicol, 1884 48
3 Hardy Richardson, 1881 . . 45
4 Tommy McCarthy, 1888 . . . 44
   Chuck Klein, 1930 44
6 Charlie Duffee, 1889 43
   Jimmy Bannon, 1894 43
8 Jim Fogarty, 1889 42
9 Orator Shaffer, 1883 41
   Jim Lillie, 1884 41

Catcher
1 Bill Rariden, 1915 238
2 Bill Rariden, 1914 215
3 Pat Moran, 1903 214
4 Oscar Stanage, 1911 212
   Art Wilson, 1914 212
6 Gabby Street, 1909 210
7 Frank Snyder, 1915 204
8 George Gibson, 1910 203
9 Bill Bergen, 1909 202
   Claude Berry, 1914 202

Pitcher
1 Ed Walsh, 1907 227
2 Will White, 1882 223
3 Ed Walsh, 1908 190
4 Harry Howell, 1905 178
5 Tony Mullane, 1882 177
6 John Clarkson, 1885 174
7 John Clarkson, 1889 172
8 Jack Chesbro, 1904 166
9 George Mullin, 1904 163
10 Ed Walsh, 1911 160

Assists per Game

First Base
1	Mark Grace, 1990	1.18
2	Bill Buckner, 1986	1.14
3	Bill Buckner, 1985	1.14
4	Bill Buckner, 1983	1.12
5	Sid Bream, 1986	1.08
6	Ferris Fain, 1951	1.05
7	Mark Grace, 1991	1.04
8	Ferris Fain, 1952	1.04
9	Fred Tenney, 1905	1.03
10	Keith Hernandez, 1983	1.02

Second Base
1	Joe Gerhardt, 1877	4.28
2	Frankie Frisch, 1927	4.19
3	Thorny Hawkes, 1879	4.13
4	Hughie Critz, 1933	4.07
5	Frank Parkinson, 1922	4.04
6	Joe Quest, 1879	3.99
7	Chick Fulmer, 1879	3.96
8	Ed Somerville, 1876	3.92
9	Ski Melillo, 1930	3.86
10	Glenn Hubbard, 1985	3.85

Shortstop
1	Germany Smith, 1885	4.21
2	Arthur Irwin, 1880	4.13
3	Art Fletcher, 1919	4.10
4	Bill Dahlen, 1895	4.09
5	Phil Tomney, 1889	4.05
6	Bobby Wallace, 1901	4.04
7	Jack Glasscock, 1887	4.04
8	Germany Smith, 1892	4.04
9	Henry Easterday, 1888	3.99
10	Dave Bancroft, 1920	3.99

Third Base
1	Jumbo Davis, 1888	2.96
2	Buddy Bell, 1981	2.93
3	George Bradley, 1880	2.89
4	Bill Hague, 1878	2.85
5	Billy Shindle, 1892	2.85
6	Bob Ferguson, 1877	2.77
7	Ned Williamson, 1879	2.76
8	Arlie Latham, 1884	2.75
9	Bill Bradley, 1900	2.75
10	Arlie Latham, 1891	2.74

Outfield
1	Orator Shaffer, 1879	0.69
2	Hardy Richardson, 1881	0.57
3	Hugh Nicol, 1884	0.55
4	King Kelly, 1878	0.51
5	John Cassidy, 1878	0.50
	King Kelly, 1880	0.50
7	King Kelly, 1883	0.46
8	Jake Evans, 1882	0.46
9	Orator Shaffer, 1878	0.44
10	Dick Higham, 1878	0.44

Catcher
1	Bill Holbert, 1884	2.41
2	Tom Daly, 1887	2.31
3	Bill Holbert, 1882	2.14
4	Pop Snyder, 1884	2.08
5	Bill Holbert, 1883	2.03
6	Buck Ewing, 1881	2.02
7	Pat Moran, 1903	2.00
	Charlie Reipschlager, 1885	1.98
9	Connie Mack, 1888	1.92
10	King Kelly, 1888	1.92

Pitcher
1	Harry Howell, 1905	4.68
2	Harry Howell, 1904	4.21
3	Will White, 1882	4.13
4	Ed Walsh, 1907	4.05
5	Willie Sudhoff, 1904	3.85
6	Red Donahue, 1902	3.71
7	George Mullin, 1904	3.62
8	Frank Owen, 1904	3.51
9	Carl Mays, 1918	3.49
10	Nick Altrock, 1905	3.47

Double Plays

First Base
1	Ferris Fain, 1949	194
2	Ferris Fain, 1950	192
3	Donn Clendenon, 1966	182
4	Ron Jackson, 1979	175
5	Gil Hodges, 1951	171
6	Mickey Vernon, 1949	168
7	Ted Kluszewski, 1954	166
8	Rudy York, 1944	163
9	Donn Clendenon, 1965	161
	Rod Carew, 1977	161

Second Base
1	Bill Mazeroski, 1966	161
2	Jerry Priddy, 1950	150
3	Bill Mazeroski, 1961	144
4	Nellie Fox, 1957	141
	Dave Cash, 1974	141
6	Buddy Myer, 1935	138
	Bill Mazeroski, 1962	138
	Carlos Baerga, 1992	138
9	Jerry Coleman, 1950	137
	Jackie Robinson, 1951	137
	Red Schoendienst, 1954	137

Shortstop
1	Rick Burleson, 1980	147
2	Roy Smalley, 1979	144
3	Bobby Wine, 1970	137
4	Lou Boudreau, 1944	134
5	Spike Owen, 1986	133
6	Rafael Ramirez, 1982	130
7	Roy McMillan, 1954	129
8	Hod Ford, 1928	128
	Vern Stephens, 1949	128
	Gene Alley, 1966	128

Third Base
1	Graig Nettles, 1971	54
2	Harlond Clift, 1937	50
3	Johnny Pesky, 1949	48
	Paul Molitor, 1982	48
5	Sammy Hale, 1927	46
	Clete Boyer, 1965	46
	Gary Gaetti, 1983	46
8	Eddie Yost, 1950	45
	Frank Malzone, 1961	45
	Darrell Evans, 1974	45

Outfield
1	Happy Felsch, 1919	15
2	Jimmy Sheckard, 1899	14
3	Tom Brown, 1893	13
4	Tom Brown, 1886	12
	Tommy McCarthy, 1888	12
	Jimmy Bannon, 1894	12
	Mike Griffin, 1895	12
	Danny Green, 1899	12
	Cy Seymour, 1905	12
	Ginger Beaumont, 1907	12
	Ty Cobb, 1907	12
	Tris Speaker, 1909	12
	Jimmy Sheckard, 1911	12
	Tris Speaker, 1914	12
	Mel Ott, 1929	12

Catcher
1	Steve O'Neill, 1916	36
2	Frankie Hayes, 1945	29
3	Ray Schalk, 1916	25
	Yogi Berra, 1951	25
5	Jack Lapp, 1915	23
	Muddy Ruel, 1924	23
	Tom Haller, 1968	23
8	Steve O'Neill, 1914	22
	Bob O'Farrell, 1922	22
10	Gabby Hartnett, 1927	21
	Wes Westrum, 1950	21

Pitcher
1	Bob Lemon, 1953	15
2	Eddie Rommel, 1924	12
	Curt Davis, 1934	12
	Randy Jones, 1976	12
5	Scott Perry, 1919	11
	Tom Rogers, 1919	11
	Art Nehf, 1920	11
	Burleigh Grimes, 1925	11
	Gene Bearden, 1948	11
10	Nick Altrock, 1905	10
	Carl Mays, 1926	10
	Willis Hudlin, 1931	10
	Freddie Fitzsimmons, 1932	10
	Freddie Fitzsimmons, 1934	10
	Bucky Walters, 1939	10
	Dave Ferriss, 1945	10
	Bob Hooper, 1950	10
	Don Drysdale, 1958	10
	Dan Petry, 1983	10

Fielding Runs

1	Glenn Hubbard, 1985	61.8
2	Danny Richardson, 1892	57.6
3	Bill Mazeroski, 1963	56.7
4	Rabbit Maranville, 1914	51.8
5	Freddie Maguire, 1928	50.5
6	Nap Lajoie, 1908	49.3
7	Danny Richardson, 1891	49.1
8	Frankie Frisch, 1927	48.6
9	Hughie Critz, 1933	46.5
10	George Davis, 1899	46.3
11	Fred Pfeffer, 1884	45.5
12	Nap Lajoie, 1907	45.0
13	Dick Bartell, 1936	44.8
14	Ozzie Guillen, 1988	42.6
15	Dave Shean, 1910	42.5
	Lee Tannehill, 1911	42.5
17	Graig Nettles, 1971	42.3
18	Cupid Childs, 1896	42.2
19	Joe Gerhardt, 1890	41.5
20	Bid McPhee, 1889	41.1
	Bill Mazeroski, 1962	41.1
	Ryne Sandberg, 1983	41.1
23	Harlond Clift, 1937	41.0
	Glenn Hubbard, 1986	41.0
25	Bill Mazeroski, 1966	40.8
	Ozzie Smith, 1980	40.8
27	Nap Lajoie, 1903	40.1
28	Germany Smith, 1885	39.9
29	Lee Tannehill, 1906	39.6
30	Arlie Latham, 1884	39.5
31	John Kerins, 1886	39.1
32	Dave Bancroft, 1920	39.0
33	Cal Ripken, 1984	38.8
34	Bob Allen, 1890	38.6
35	Fred Pfeffer, 1888	38.3
	Bobby Wallace, 1899	38.3
37	Everett Scott, 1921	38.1
38	Bill Dahlen, 1908	37.5
	Dick Bartell, 1937	37.5
	Dal Maxvill, 1970	37.5
41	Bobby Knoop, 1964	37.2
42	Al Weis, 1966	36.9
43	Billy Shindle, 1888	36.8
44	Tim Wallach, 1985	36.7
45	Lou Bierbauer, 1889	36.6
46	Miller Huggins, 1905	36.2
	Clete Boyer, 1962	36.2
48	Harry Steinfeldt, 1900	35.9
49	George Davis, 1898	35.8
	Tommy Leach, 1904	35.8
	Ivan DeJesus, 1977	35.8
52	Jack Glasscock, 1889	35.7
	Hughie Jennings, 1895	35.7
54	Billy Shindle, 1892	35.5
	Eddie Collins, 1910	35.5
56	Bill Holbert, 1883	35.3
	Freddie Patek, 1973	35.3
58	Bill Dahlen, 1895	35.2
59	Bobby Knoop, 1970	35.1
60	Jack Glasscock, 1887	35.0
61	Chet Lemon, 1977	34.9
62	Jimmy Bloodworth, 1941	34.7
63	Hughie Jennings, 1896	34.4
	Buddy Bell, 1982	34.4
65	Shorty Fuller, 1895	34.2
	Doc Lavan, 1916	34.2
67	Art Fletcher, 1915	34.1
68	Bid McPhee, 1893	34.0
69	Bill Mazeroski, 1964	33.9
70	Mark Belanger, 1978	33.8
71	Gene Alley, 1970	33.7
72	Donie Bush, 1914	33.6
73	Buck Weaver, 1913	33.5
	Leo Cardenas, 1969	33.5
75	Lave Cross, 1895	33.4
76	John Farrell, 1902	33.3
77	Pop Smith, 1885	33.2
78	Hughie Jennings, 1894	33.1
	Joe Cassidy, 1905	33.1
	Ski Melillo, 1931	33.1
	Roy Smalley, 1979	33.1
	Ozzie Smith, 1982	33.1
83	Lave Cross, 1899	32.9
	Red Schoendienst, 1952	32.9
	Red Schoendienst, 1954	32.9
86	Tom Daly, 1887	32.8
	George McBride, 1908	32.8
88	Don Zimmer, 1958	32.6
89	Richie Ashburn, 1957	32.4
90	Richie Ashburn, 1951	32.3
	Marty Barrett, 1987	32.3
92	Herman Long, 1889	32.2
93	Mickey Doolan, 1915	32.1
94	Germany Smith, 1887	32.0
	Wally Gerber, 1928	32.0
	Bucky Dent, 1979	32.0
97	Nap Lajoie, 1906	31.9
	Spike Owen, 1986	31.9
99	Pep Young, 1938	31.8
100	4 players tied	31.7

Fielding Runs

First Base
1	Mark Grace, 1990	27
2	Bill Buckner, 1985	25
3	Chick Gandil, 1914	24
4	Sid Bream, 1986	24
5	Fred Tenney, 1905	22
6	Bill Buckner, 1983	22
7	Vic Power, 1960	21
8	Sid Bream, 1988	21
9	Jiggs Donahue, 1907	21
10	Jake Beckley, 1892	21

Second Base
1	Glenn Hubbard, 1985	62
2	Bill Mazeroski, 1963	57
3	Freddie Maguire, 1928	50
4	Frankie Frisch, 1927	49
5	Nap Lajoie, 1908	48
6	Hughie Critz, 1933	46
7	Fred Pfeffer, 1884	46
8	Danny Richardson, 1891	44
9	Nap Lajoie, 1907	43
10	Dave Shean, 1910	42

Shortstop
1	Rabbit Maranville, 1914	52
2	George Davis, 1899	46
3	Dick Bartell, 1936	45
4	Ozzie Guillen, 1988	43
5	Ozzie Smith, 1980	41
6	Germany Smith, 1885	40
7	Dave Bancroft, 1920	39
8	Cal Ripken, 1984	39
9	Bob Allen, 1890	39
10	Everett Scott, 1921	38

Third Base
1	Graig Nettles, 1971	42
2	Harlond Clift, 1937	41
3	Arlie Latham, 1884	40
4	Billy Shindle, 1892	38
5	Billy Shindle, 1888	37
6	Tim Wallach, 1985	37
7	Clete Boyer, 1962	36
8	Tommy Leach, 1904	36
9	Buddy Bell, 1982	35
10	Lave Cross, 1895	33

Outfield
1	Chet Lemon, 1977	35
2	Richie Ashburn, 1957	32
3	Richie Ashburn, 1951	32
4	Jim Fogarty, 1887	32
5	Kirby Puckett, 1984	30
6	Tommy McCarthy, 1888	30
7	Max Carey, 1916	30
8	Dave Parker, 1977	28
9	Eric Davis, 1987	28
10	Tris Speaker, 1914	27

Catcher
1	Bill Holbert, 1883	37
2	Tom Daly, 1887	32
3	Duke Farrell, 1894	30
4	Pop Snyder, 1884	26
5	Connie Mack, 1892	25
6	Pop Snyder, 1879	25
	Ossee Schreckengost, 1902	24
8	George Mitterwald, 1970	24
9	Jim Hegan, 1950	24
10	Duke Farrell, 1890	24

Pitcher
1	Ed Walsh, 1907	22
2	Harry Howell, 1905	18
3	Ed Walsh, 1911	15
4	Ed Walsh, 1908	14
5	Will White, 1882	13
6	John Clarkson, 1889	11
7	Tony Mullane, 1882	11
8	Sadie McMahon, 1890	11
9	Carl Mays, 1926	10
10	Frank Smith, 1909	10

Fielding Wins

1	Glenn Hubbard, 1985	6.5
2	Bill Mazeroski, 1963	6.2
3	Nap Lajoie, 1908	5.6
4	Rabbit Maranville, 1914	5.6
5	Danny Richardson, 1892	5.3
6	Nap Lajoie, 1907	5.0
7	Freddie Maguire, 1928	4.9
8	Hughie Critz, 1933	4.9
9	Frankie Frisch, 1927	4.8
10	Graig Nettles, 1971	4.6
11	Dave Shean, 1910	4.5
12	Danny Richardson, 1891	4.4
13	Dick Bartell, 1936	4.4
14	Lee Tannehill, 1906	4.4
15	Bill Dahlen, 1908	4.3
16	Ozzie Smith, 1980	4.3
17	Ozzie Guillen, 1988	4.3
18	Ryne Sandberg, 1983	4.3
19	Bill Mazeroski, 1966	4.3
20	Glenn Hubbard, 1986	4.3
21	George Davis, 1899	4.2
22	Dave Bancroft, 1920	4.2
23	Lee Tannehill, 1911	4.2
24	Nap Lajoie, 1903	4.2
25	Bill Mazeroski, 1962	4.1
26	Fred Pfeffer, 1884	4.1
27	Al Weis, 1966	4.0
28	Eddie Collins, 1910	3.9
29	Bobby Knoop, 1964	3.9
30	Cal Ripken, 1984	3.9
31	Tim Wallach, 1985	3.9
32	Doc Lavan, 1916	3.8
33	Art Fletcher, 1915	3.8
34	Tommy Leach, 1904	3.8
35	Harland Clift, 1937	3.8
36	Fred Pfeffer, 1888	3.8
37	Miller Huggins, 1905	3.8
38	Dal Maxvill, 1970	3.7
39	George McBride, 1908	3.7
40	Dick Bartell, 1937	3.7
41	Donie Bush, 1914	3.7
42	Joe Gerhardt, 1890	3.6
43	Bobby Knoop, 1970	3.6
44	Clete Boyer, 1962	3.6
45	Joe Cassidy, 1905	3.6
46	Ivan DeJesus, 1977	3.6
47	Freddie Patek, 1973	3.6
48	Heinie Wagner, 1908	3.6
49	Arlie Latham, 1884	3.6
50	Germany Smith, 1885	3.6
51	Bill Mazeroski, 1964	3.6
52	Cupid Childs, 1896	3.6
53	Buck Weaver, 1913	3.6
54	Everett Scott, 1921	3.6
55	Joe Tinker, 1908	3.5
56	Leo Cardenas, 1969	3.5
57	John Farrell, 1902	3.5
58	Nap Lajoie, 1906	3.5
59	Mark Belanger, 1978	3.5
60	Ozzie Smith, 1982	3.5
61	Bid McPhee, 1889	3.5
62	Bobby Wallace, 1899	3.5
63	Chet Lemon, 1977	3.5
64	Mickey Doolan, 1915	3.5
65	Buddy Bell, 1982	3.4
66	John Kerins, 1886	3.4
67	Buck Herzog, 1915	3.4
68	Bob Allen, 1890	3.4
69	Max Carey, 1916	3.4
70	Red Schoendienst, 1952	3.4
71	Brooks Robinson, 1967	3.4
72	Billy Shindle, 1888	3.4
73	Horace Clarke, 1968	3.4
74	Nap Lajoie, 1916	3.4
75	Jimmy Bloodworth, 1941	3.4
76	Gene Alley, 1970	3.4
77	Freddie Patek, 1972	3.4
78	George Davis, 1898	3.3
79	Ron Santo, 1967	3.3
80	Johnny Evers, 1907	3.3
81	Johnny Evers, 1904	3.3
82	Buck Herzog, 1914	3.3
83	Richie Ashburn, 1957	3.3
84	Don Zimmer, 1958	3.3
85	Billy Shindle, 1892	3.3
86	Harry Steinfeldt, 1900	3.3
87	Red Schoendienst, 1954	3.3
88	Bruno Betzel, 1916	3.2
89	Richie Ashburn, 1951	3.2
90	Roy Smalley, 1979	3.2
91	Terry Pendleton, 1989	3.2
92	Ed Brinkman, 1970	3.2
93	Pep Young, 1938	3.2
94	Rabbit Maranville, 1919	3.2
95	Zoilo Versalles, 1962	3.2
96	Dave Bancroft, 1917	3.2
97	Buddy Bell, 1981	3.1
98	Spike Owen, 1986	3.1
99	Billy Jurges, 1932	3.1
100	Dal Maxvill, 1971	3.1

Total Player Rating

1	Babe Ruth, 1923	10.8
2	Babe Ruth, 1921	9.6
3	Nap Lajoie, 1901	9.2
4	Cal Ripken, 1984	9.1
5	Barry Bonds, 1992	9.0
6	Babe Ruth, 1920	8.9
	Babe Ruth, 1927	8.9
8	Nap Lajoie, 1910	8.7
9	Fred Dunlap, 1884	8.6
10	Nap Lajoie, 1906	8.5
	Ty Cobb, 1917	8.5
	Babe Ruth, 1924	8.5
	Mickey Mantle, 1957	8.5
14	Rogers Hornsby, 1924	8.4
	Ted Williams, 1942	8.4
	Ted Williams, 1946	8.4
	Mickey Mantle, 1956	8.4
18	Nap Lajoie, 1903	8.3
19	Babe Ruth, 1926	8.2
20	Rogers Hornsby, 1922	8.1
	Ted Williams, 1941	8.1
	Rickey Henderson, 1990	8.1
	Cal Ripken, 1991	8.1
24	Tris Speaker, 1912	8.0
	George Sisler, 1920	8.0
26	Rogers Hornsby, 1920	7.9
	Carl Yastrzemski, 1967	7.9
28	Nap Lajoie, 1908	7.8
	Lou Gehrig, 1927	7.8
	Ted Williams, 1947	7.8
31	Lou Boudreau, 1944	7.7
	Willie Mays, 1955	7.7
33	Tris Speaker, 1914	7.6
	Rogers Hornsby, 1917	7.6
	Mickey Mantle, 1961	7.6
	Ron Santo, 1966	7.6
	Mike Schmidt, 1980	7.6
38	Ted Williams, 1957	7.5
	Ron Santo, 1967	7.5
40	Honus Wagner, 1905	7.4
	Honus Wagner, 1906	7.4
	Ty Cobb, 1911	7.4
	Tris Speaker, 1913	7.4
	Snuffy Stirnweiss, 1945	7.4
45	Frankie Frisch, 1927	7.3
	Ted Williams, 1949	7.3
	Norm Cash, 1961	7.3
	Rickey Henderson, 1985	7.3
49	Nap Lajoie, 1904	7.2
	Ty Cobb, 1910	7.2
	Rogers Hornsby, 1929	7.2
	Lou Gehrig, 1934	7.2
	Harland Clift, 1937	7.2
	Snuffy Stirnweiss, 1944	7.2
	Rico Petrocelli, 1969	7.2
	Joe Morgan, 1975	7.2
	Mike Schmidt, 1981	7.2
	George Brett, 1985	7.2
59	Eddie Collins, 1910	7.1
	Joe Jackson, 1912	7.1
	Mike Schmidt, 1974	7.1
	Eric Davis, 1987	7.1
	Barry Bonds, 1990	7.1
64	Honus Wagner, 1908	7.0
	Rogers Hornsby, 1921	7.0
	Babe Ruth, 1930	7.0
	Willie Mays, 1958	7.0
	Carl Yastrzemski, 1968	7.0
69	Cupid Childs, 1896	6.9
	Hughie Jennings, 1896	6.9
	Rogers Hornsby, 1927	6.9
	Jackie Robinson, 1951	6.9
	Willie Mays, 1965	6.9
74	Joe Jackson, 1911	6.8
	George Sisler, 1922	6.8
	Babe Ruth, 1928	6.8
	Babe Ruth, 1931	6.8
	Jimmie Foxx, 1932	6.8
	Stan Musial, 1948	6.8
	Lou Boudreau, 1948	6.8
	Willie Mays, 1954	6.8
	Mike Schmidt, 1977	6.8
	Kevin Mitchell, 1989	6.8
84	Nap Lajoie, 1907	6.7
	Joe Cronin, 1930	6.7
	Jimmie Foxx, 1933	6.7
	Stan Musial, 1943	6.7
	Ron Santo, 1964	6.7
	Robin Yount, 1982	6.7
	Ryne Sandberg, 1984	6.7
91	Honus Wagner, 1912	6.6
	Ty Cobb, 1915	6.6
	Frank Robinson, 1966	6.6
	Cal Ripken, 1983	6.6
95	7 players tied	6.5

Total Player Rating (alpha.)

Barry Bonds, 1990	7.1
Barry Bonds, 1992	9.0
Lou Boudreau, 1944	7.7
Lou Boudreau, 1948	6.8
George Brett, 1985	7.2
Norm Cash, 1961	7.3
Cupid Childs, 1896	6.9
Harlond Clift, 1937	7.2
Ty Cobb, 1910	7.2
Ty Cobb, 1911	7.4
Ty Cobb, 1915	6.6
Ty Cobb, 1917	8.5
Eddie Collins, 1910	7.1
Joe Cronin, 1930	6.7
Eric Davis, 1987	7.1
Fred Dunlap, 1884	8.6
Jimmie Foxx, 1932	6.8
Jimmie Foxx, 1933	6.7
Frankie Frisch, 1927	7.3
Lou Gehrig, 1927	7.8
Lou Gehrig, 1934	7.2
Rickey Henderson, 1985	7.3
Rickey Henderson, 1990	8.1
Rogers Hornsby, 1917	7.6
Rogers Hornsby, 1920	7.9
Rogers Hornsby, 1921	7.0
Rogers Hornsby, 1922	8.1
Rogers Hornsby, 1924	8.4
Rogers Hornsby, 1927	6.9
Rogers Hornsby, 1929	7.2
Joe Jackson, 1911	6.8
Joe Jackson, 1912	7.1
Hughie Jennings, 1896	6.9
Nap Lajoie, 1901	9.2
Nap Lajoie, 1903	8.3
Nap Lajoie, 1904	7.2
Nap Lajoie, 1906	8.5
Nap Lajoie, 1907	6.7
Nap Lajoie, 1908	7.8
Nap Lajoie, 1910	8.7
Mickey Mantle, 1956	8.4
Mickey Mantle, 1957	8.5
Mickey Mantle, 1961	7.6
Willie Mays, 1954	6.8
Willie Mays, 1955	7.7
Willie Mays, 1958	7.0
Willie Mays, 1965	6.9
Kevin Mitchell, 1989	6.8
Joe Morgan, 1975	7.2
Stan Musial, 1943	6.7
Stan Musial, 1948	6.8
Rico Petrocelli, 1969	7.2
Cal Ripken, 1983	6.6
Cal Ripken, 1984	9.1
Cal Ripken, 1991	8.1
Jackie Robinson, 1951	6.9
Frank Robinson, 1966	6.6
Babe Ruth, 1920	8.9
Babe Ruth, 1921	9.6
Babe Ruth, 1923	10.8
Babe Ruth, 1924	8.5
Babe Ruth, 1926	8.2
Babe Ruth, 1927	8.9
Babe Ruth, 1928	6.8
Babe Ruth, 1930	7.0
Babe Ruth, 1931	6.8
Ryne Sandberg, 1984	6.7
Ron Santo, 1964	6.7
Ron Santo, 1966	7.6
Ron Santo, 1967	7.5
Mike Schmidt, 1974	7.1
Mike Schmidt, 1977	6.8
Mike Schmidt, 1980	7.6
Mike Schmidt, 1981	7.2
George Sisler, 1920	8.0
George Sisler, 1922	6.8
Tris Speaker, 1912	8.0
Tris Speaker, 1913	7.4
Tris Speaker, 1914	7.6
Snuffy Stirnweiss, 1944	7.2
Snuffy Stirnweiss, 1945	7.4
Honus Wagner, 1905	7.4
Honus Wagner, 1906	7.4
Honus Wagner, 1908	7.0
Honus Wagner, 1912	6.6
Ted Williams, 1941	8.1
Ted Williams, 1942	8.4
Ted Williams, 1946	8.4
Ted Williams, 1947	7.8
Ted Williams, 1949	7.3
Ted Williams, 1957	7.5
Carl Yastrzemski, 1967	7.9
Carl Yastrzemski, 1968	7.0
Robin Yount, 1982	6.7

Total Player Rating (by era)

1876-1892

1	Fred Dunlap, 1884	8.6
2	Cupid Childs, 1890	6.4
3	Fred Pfeffer, 1884	6.3
4	Dan Brouthers, 1892	6.1
5	Jack Glasscock, 1889	6.0
6	Tip O'Neill, 1887	5.5
7	King Kelly, 1886	5.3
8	Jack Glasscock, 1890	5.1
9	Billy Nash, 1888	5.0
	Harry Stovey, 1889	5.0
11	Ned Williamson, 1884	4.9
	Hardy Richardson, 1886	4.9
	Denny Lyons, 1890	4.9
14	John Kerins, 1886	4.8
15	3 players tied	4.7

1893-1919

1	Nap Lajoie, 1901	9.2
2	Nap Lajoie, 1910	8.7
3	Nap Lajoie, 1906	8.5
	Ty Cobb, 1917	8.5
5	Nap Lajoie, 1903	8.3
6	Tris Speaker, 1912	8.0
7	Nap Lajoie, 1908	7.8
8	Tris Speaker, 1914	7.6
	Rogers Hornsby, 1917	7.6
10	Honus Wagner, 1905	7.4
	Honus Wagner, 1906	7.4
	Ty Cobb, 1911	7.4
	Tris Speaker, 1913	7.4
14	Nap Lajoie, 1904	7.2
	Ty Cobb, 1910	7.2

1920-1941

1	Babe Ruth, 1923	10.8
2	Babe Ruth, 1921	9.6
3	Babe Ruth, 1920	8.9
	Babe Ruth, 1927	8.9
5	Babe Ruth, 1924	8.5
6	Rogers Hornsby, 1924	8.4
7	Babe Ruth, 1926	8.2
8	Rogers Hornsby, 1922	8.1
	Ted Williams, 1941	8.1
10	George Sisler, 1920	8.0
11	Rogers Hornsby, 1920	7.9
12	Lou Gehrig, 1927	7.8
13	Frankie Frisch, 1927	7.3
14	3 players tied	7.2

1942-1960

1	Mickey Mantle, 1957	8.5
2	Ted Williams, 1942	8.4
	Ted Williams, 1946	8.4
	Mickey Mantle, 1956	8.4
5	Ted Williams, 1947	7.8
6	Lou Boudreau, 1944	7.7
	Willie Mays, 1955	7.7
8	Ted Williams, 1957	7.5
9	Snuffy Stirnweiss, 1945	7.4
10	Ted Williams, 1949	7.3
11	Snuffy Stirnweiss, 1944	7.2
12	Willie Mays, 1958	7.0
13	Jackie Robinson, 1951	6.9
14	3 players tied	6.8

1961-1992

1	Cal Ripken, 1984	9.1
2	Barry Bonds, 1992	9.0
3	Rickey Henderson, 1990	8.1
	Cal Ripken, 1991	8.1
5	Carl Yastrzemski, 1967	7.9
6	Mickey Mantle, 1961	7.6
	Ron Santo, 1966	7.6
	Mike Schmidt, 1980	7.6
9	Ron Santo, 1967	7.5
10	Norm Cash, 1961	7.3
	Rickey Henderson, 1985	7.3
12	Rico Petrocelli, 1969	7.2
	Joe Morgan, 1975	7.2
	Mike Schmidt, 1981	7.2
	George Brett, 1985	7.2

Wins

1	Charley Radbourn, 1884	59
2	John Clarkson, 1885	53
3	Guy Hecker, 1884	52
4	John Clarkson, 1889	49
5	Charley Radbourn, 1883	48
	Charlie Buffinton, 1884	48
7	Al Spalding, 1876	47
	Monte Ward, 1879	47
9	Jim Galvin, 1883	46
	Jim Galvin, 1884	46
	Matt Kilroy, 1887	46
12	George Bradley, 1876	45
	Jim McCormick, 1880	45
	Silver King, 1888	45
15	Mickey Welch, 1885	44
	Bill Hutchinson, 1891	44
17	Tommy Bond, 1879	43
	Will White, 1879	43
	Larry Corcoran, 1880	43
	Will White, 1883	43
21	Lady Baldwin, 1886	42
	Tim Keefe, 1886	42
	Bill Hutchinson, 1890	42
24	Tim Keefe, 1883	41
	Dave Foutz, 1886	41
	Ed Morris, 1886	41
	Jack Chesbro, 1904	41
28	Tommy Bond, 1877	40
	Tommy Bond, 1878	40
	Will White, 1882	40
	Bill Sweeney, 1884	40
	Bob Caruthers, 1885	40
	Bob Caruthers, 1889	40
	Ed Walsh, 1908	40
35	Monte Ward, 1880	39
	Mickey Welch, 1884	39
	Ed Morris, 1885	39
38	Toad Ramsey, 1886	38
	John Clarkson, 1887	38
	Kid Gleason, 1890	38
41	Jim Galvin, 1879	37
	Jim Whitney, 1883	37
	Tim Keefe, 1884	37
	Jack Lynch, 1884	37
	Toad Ramsey, 1887	37
	Bill Hutchinson, 1892	37
	Christy Mathewson, 1908	37
48	Jim McCormick, 1882	36
	Tony Mullane, 1884	36
	John Clarkson, 1886	36
	Sadie McMahon, 1890	36
	Cy Young, 1892	36
	Frank Killen, 1893	36
	Amos Rusie, 1894	36
	Walter Johnson, 1913	36
56	Jim Devlin, 1877	35
	Tony Mullane, 1883	35
	Larry Corcoran, 1884	35
	Tim Keefe, 1887	35
	Tim Keefe, 1888	35
	Ed Seward, 1888	35
	Silver King, 1889	35
	Sadie McMahon, 1891	35
	Kid Nichols, 1892	35
	Jack Stivetts, 1892	35
	Cy Young, 1895	35
	Joe McGinnity, 1904	35
68	Mickey Welch, 1880	34
	Larry Corcoran, 1883	34
	Ed Morris, 1884	34
	Will White, 1884	34
	Elmer Smith, 1887	34
	Scott Stratton, 1890	34
	Mark Baldwin, 1890	34
	George Haddock, 1891	34
	Kid Nichols, 1893	34
	Cy Young, 1893	34
	Joe Wood, 1912	34
79	Charley Radbourn, 1882	33
	Dave Foutz, 1885	33
	Henry Porter, 1885	33
	Mickey Welch, 1886	33
	Tony Mullane, 1886	33
	John Clarkson, 1888	33
	John Clarkson, 1891	33
	Amos Rusie, 1891	33
	Jack Stivetts, 1891	33
	Amos Rusie, 1893	33
	Jouett Meekin, 1894	33
	Cy Young, 1901	33
	Christy Mathewson, 1904	33
	Walter Johnson, 1912	33
	Pete Alexander, 1916	33
94	9 players tied	32

Wins (by era)

1876-1892

1	Charley Radbourn, 1884	59
2	John Clarkson, 1885	53
3	Guy Hecker, 1884	52
4	John Clarkson, 1889	49
5	Charley Radbourn, 1883	48
	Charlie Buffinton, 1884	48
7	Al Spalding, 1876	47
	Monte Ward, 1879	47
9	Jim Galvin, 1883	46
	Jim Galvin, 1884	46
	Matt Kilroy, 1887	46
12	George Bradley, 1876	45
	Jim McCormick, 1880	45
	Silver King, 1888	45
15	2 players tied	44

1893-1919

1	Jack Chesbro, 1904	41
2	Ed Walsh, 1908	40
3	Christy Mathewson, 1908	37
4	Frank Killen, 1893	36
	Amos Rusie, 1894	36
	Walter Johnson, 1913	36
7	Cy Young, 1895	35
	Joe McGinnity, 1904	35
9	Kid Nichols, 1893	34
	Cy Young, 1893	34
	Joe Wood, 1912	34
12	6 players tied	33

1920-1941

1	Jim Bagby, 1920	31
	Lefty Grove, 1931	31
3	Dizzy Dean, 1934	30
4	Dazzy Vance, 1924	28
	Lefty Grove, 1930	28
	Dizzy Dean, 1935	28
7	Pete Alexander, 1920	27
	Carl Mays, 1921	27
	Urban Shocker, 1921	27
	Eddie Rommel, 1922	27
	Dolf Luque, 1923	27
	George Uhle, 1926	27
	Bucky Walters, 1939	27
	Bob Feller, 1940	27
15	7 players tied	26

1942-1960

1	Hal Newhouser, 1944	29
2	Robin Roberts, 1952	28
3	Dizzy Trout, 1944	27
	Don Newcombe, 1956	27
5	Hal Newhouser, 1946	26
	Bob Feller, 1946	26
7	Hal Newhouser, 1945	25
	Dave Ferriss, 1946	25
	Mel Parnell, 1949	25
10	Johnny Sain, 1948	24
	Bobby Shantz, 1952	24
12	13 players tied	23

1961-1992

1	Denny McLain, 1968	31
2	Sandy Koufax, 1966	27
	Steve Carlton, 1972	27
	Bob Welch, 1990	27
5	Sandy Koufax, 1965	26
	Juan Marichal, 1968	26
7	12 players tied	25

Losses

1	John Coleman, 1883	48
2	Will White, 1880	42
3	Larry McKeon, 1884	41
4	George Bradley, 1879	40
	Jim McCormick, 1879	40
6	Henry Porter, 1888	37
	Kid Carsey, 1891	37
	George Cobb, 1892	37
9	Stump Weidman, 1886	36
	Bill Hutchinson, 1892	36
11	Jim Devlin, 1876	35
	Jim Galvin, 1880	35
	Fleury Sullivan, 1884	35
	Adonis Terry, 1884	35
	Hardie Henderson, 1885	35
	Red Donahue, 1897	35
17	Bobby Mathews, 1876	34
	Bob Barr, 1884	34
	Matt Kilroy, 1886	34
	Al Mays, 1887	34
	Mark Baldwin, 1889	34
	Amos Rusie, 1890	34
23	Harry McCormick, 1879	33
	Jim Whitney, 1881	33
	Lee Richmond, 1882	33
	Frank Mountain, 1883	33
	Jersey Bakely, 1888	33
28	Lee Richmond, 1880	32
	Hardie Henderson, 1883	32
	John Harkins, 1884	32
	Jim Whitney, 1885	32
	Jim Whitney, 1886	32
33	Sam Weaver, 1878	31
	Will White, 1879	31
	Charley Radbourn, 1886	31
	Dupee Shaw, 1886	31
	Billy Crowell, 1887	31
	Amos Rusie, 1892	31
39	Mickey Welch, 1880	30
	Jim McCormick, 1881	30
	Jim McCormick, 1882	30
	Bakely, 1884	30
	Jack Lynch, 1886	30
	Phenomenal Smith, 1887	30
	Toad Ramsey, 1888	30
	John Ewing, 1889	30
	Ed Beatin, 1890	30
	Ted Breitenstein, 1895	30
	Jim Hughey, 1899	30
50	Tommy Bond, 1880	29
	Jim Galvin, 1883	29
	John Healy, 1887	29
	Hank O'Day, 1888	29
	Bert Cunningham, 1888	29
	Red Ehret, 1889	29
	Silver King, 1891	29
	Bill Hart, 1896	29
	Jack Taylor, 1898	29
	Vic Willis, 1905	29
60	Jim McCormick, 1880	28
	Doc Landis, 1882	28
	Hank O'Day, 1884	28
	Hugh Daily, 1884	28
	Al Mays, 1886	28
	Gus Weyhing, 1887	28
	Mark Baldwin, 1891	28
	Duke Esper, 1893	28
	Bill Hill, 1896	28
69	Jim Galvin, 1879	27
	Tim Keefe, 1881	27
	Tim Keefe, 1883	27
	Charlie Buffinton, 1885	27
	Tony Mullane, 1886	27
	Toad Ramsey, 1886	27
	Toad Ramsey, 1887	27
	Park Swartzel, 1889	27
	Phil Knell, 1891	27
	Mark Baldwin, 1892	27
	Pink Hawley, 1894	27
	Chick Fraser, 1896	27
	Bill Hart, 1897	27
	Willie Sudhoff, 1898	27
	Bill Carrick, 1899	27
	Dummy Taylor, 1901	27
	George Bell, 1910	27
	Paul Derringer, 1933	27
87	19 players tied	26

Winning Percentage

1	Roy Face, 1959	.947
2	Rick Sutcliffe, 1984	.941
3	Ron Guidry, 1978	.893
4	Freddie Fitzsimmons, 1940	.889
5	Lefty Grove, 1931	.886
6	Preacher Roe, 1951	.880
7	Fred Goldsmith, 1880	.875
	Jim McCormick, 1884	.875
9	Joe Wood, 1912	.872
10	David Cone, 1988	.870
11	Orel Hershiser, 1985	.864
12	Billy Taylor, 1884	.862
	Bill Donovan, 1907	.862
	Whitey Ford, 1961	.862
15	Dwight Gooden, 1985	.857
	Roger Clemens, 1986	.857
17	Chief Bender, 1914	.850
18	Lefty Grove, 1930	.848
19	Tom Hughes, 1916	.842
	Emil Yde, 1924	.842
	Schoolboy Rowe, 1940	.842
	Sandy Consuegra, 1954	.842
	Ralph Terry, 1961	.842
	Ron Perranoski, 1963	.842
25	Lefty Gomez, 1934	.839
26	Bill Hoffer, 1895	.838
	Denny McLain, 1968	.838
28	Walter Johnson, 1913	.837
29	King Cole, 1910	.833
	Spud Chandler, 1943	.833
	Sandy Koufax, 1963	.833
32	Charley Radbourn, 1884	.831
33	Ed Reulbach, 1906	.826
	Elmer Riddle, 1941	.826
35	Jim Hughes, 1899	.824
	Jack Chesbro, 1902	.824
	Dazzy Vance, 1924	.824
38	Chief Bender, 1910	.821
	Bob Purkey, 1962	.821
40	Sal Maglie, 1950	.818
	Bob Welch, 1990	.818
42	Joe McGinnity, 1904	.814
43	Mordecai Brown, 1906	.813
	Russ Ford, 1910	.813
	Eddie Plank, 1912	.813
	Carl Hubbell, 1936	.813
47	Dizzy Dean, 1934	.811
48	Ed Reulbach, 1907	.810
	Doc Crandall, 1910	.810
	Johnny Allen, 1932	.810
	Ted Wilks, 1944	.810
	Phil Niekro, 1982	.810
53	General Crowder, 1928	.808
	Bobo Newsom, 1940	.808
	Tiny Bonham, 1942	.808
	Larry Jansen, 1947	.808
	Dave McNally, 1971	.808
	Jim Hunter, 1973	.808
59	Christy Mathewson, 1909	.806
	Howie Camnitz, 1909	.806
	Dave Ferriss, 1946	.806
	Juan Marichal, 1966	.806
63	Eddie Cicotte, 1919	.806
64	Mickey Welch, 1885	.800
	Ed Doheny, 1902	.800
	Sam Leever, 1905	.800
	Bert Humphries, 1913	.800
	Stan Coveleski, 1925	.800
	Firpo Marberry, 1931	.800
	Robin Roberts, 1952	.800
	Eddie Lopat, 1953	.800
	Don Newcombe, 1955	.800
	Jim Palmer, 1969	.800
	John Candelaria, 1977	.800
	Larry Gura, 1978	.800
76	Al Spalding, 1876	.797
77	Don Newcombe, 1956	.794
78	Jocko Flynn, 1886	.793
	Ellis Kinder, 1949	.793
	Sal Maglie, 1951	.793
	Bret Saberhagen, 1989	.793
82	Dutch Leonard, 1914	.792
	Sandy Koufax, 1964	.792
	Wally Bunker, 1964	.792
85	Fred Klobedanz, 1897	.788
	Bill James, 1914	.788
	Joe Bush, 1922	.788
88	Jouett Meekin, 1894	.786
	Lon Warneke, 1932	.786
	Tex Hughson, 1942	.786
	Ron Guidry, 1985	.786
	Doug Drabek, 1990	.786
93	Bob Caruthers, 1889	.784
94	George Mullin, 1909	.784
95	9 players tied	.783

Winning Percentage (by era)

1876-1892

1	Fred Goldsmith, 1880	.875
	Jim McCormick, 1884	.875
3	Billy Taylor, 1884	.862
4	Charley Radbourn, 1884	.831
5	Mickey Welch, 1885	.800
6	Al Spalding, 1876	.797
7	Jocko Flynn, 1886	.793
8	Bob Caruthers, 1889	.784
9	Jack Manning, 1876	.783
10	Charlie Sweeney, 1884	.774
11	Will White, 1882	.769
	Charlie Ferguson, 1886	.769
13	John Clarkson, 1885	.768
14	Lady Baldwin, 1886	.764
15	2 players tied	.763

1893-1919

1	Joe Wood, 1912	.872
2	Bill Donovan, 1907	.862
3	Chief Bender, 1914	.850
4	Tom Hughes, 1916	.842
5	Bill Hoffer, 1895	.838
6	Walter Johnson, 1913	.837
7	King Cole, 1910	.833
8	Ed Reulbach, 1906	.826
9	Jim Hughes, 1899	.824
	Jack Chesbro, 1902	.824
11	Chief Bender, 1910	.821
12	Joe McGinnity, 1904	.814
13	Mordecai Brown, 1906	.813
	Russ Ford, 1910	.813
	Eddie Plank, 1912	.813

1920-1941

1	Freddie Fitzsimmons, 1940	.889
2	Lefty Grove, 1931	.886
3	Lefty Grove, 1930	.848
4	Emil Yde, 1924	.842
	Schoolboy Rowe, 1940	.842
6	Lefty Gomez, 1934	.839
7	Elmer Riddle, 1941	.826
8	Dazzy Vance, 1924	.824
9	Carl Hubbell, 1936	.813
10	Dizzy Dean, 1934	.811
11	Johnny Allen, 1932	.810
12	General Crowder, 1928	.808
	Bobo Newsom, 1940	.808
14	Stan Coveleski, 1925	.800
	Firpo Marberry, 1931	.800

1942-1960

1	Roy Face, 1959	.947
2	Preacher Roe, 1951	.880
3	Sandy Consuegra, 1954	.842
4	Spud Chandler, 1943	.833
5	Sal Maglie, 1950	.818
6	Ted Wilks, 1944	.810
7	Tiny Bonham, 1942	.808
	Larry Jansen, 1947	.808
9	Dave Ferriss, 1946	.806
10	Robin Roberts, 1952	.800
	Eddie Lopat, 1953	.800
	Don Newcombe, 1955	.800
13	Don Newcombe, 1956	.794
14	Ellis Kinder, 1949	.793
	Sal Maglie, 1951	.793

1961-1992

1	Rick Sutcliffe, 1984	.941
2	Ron Guidry, 1978	.893
3	David Cone, 1988	.870
4	Orel Hershiser, 1985	.864
5	Whitey Ford, 1961	.862
6	Dwight Gooden, 1985	.857
	Roger Clemens, 1986	.857
8	Ralph Terry, 1961	.842
	Ron Perranoski, 1963	.842
10	Denny McLain, 1968	.838
11	Sandy Koufax, 1963	.833
12	Bob Purkey, 1962	.821
13	Bob Welch, 1990	.818
14	Phil Niekro, 1982	.810
15	2 players tied	.808

Games

1	Mike Marshall, 1974	106
2	Kent Tekulve, 1979	94
3	Mike Marshall, 1973	92
4	Kent Tekulve, 1978	91
5	Wayne Granger, 1969	90
	Mike Marshall, 1979	90
	Kent Tekulve, 1987	90
8	Mark Eichhorn, 1987	89
9	Wilbur Wood, 1968	88
10	Rob Murphy, 1987	87
11	Kent Tekulve, 1982	85
	Frank Williams, 1987	85
	Mitch Williams, 1987	85
14	Ted Abernathy, 1965	84
	Enrique Romo, 1979	84
	Dick Tidrow, 1980	84
	Dan Quisenberry, 1985	84
18	Ken Sanders, 1971	83
	Craig Lefferts, 1986	83
20	Eddie Fisher, 1965	82
	Bill Campbell, 1983	82
	Juan Agosto, 1990	82
23	John Wyatt, 1964	81
	Dale Murray, 1976	81
	Jeff Robinson, 1987	81
	Duane Ward, 1991	81
	Joe Boever, 1992	81
	Kenny Rogers, 1992	81
29	Pedro Borbon, 1973	80
	Willie Hernandez, 1984	80
	Mitch Williams, 1986	80
	Doug Jones, 1992	80
33	Dick Radatz, 1964	79
	Duane Ward, 1992	79
35	Hal Woodeshick, 1965	78
	Ted Abernathy, 1968	78
	Bill Campbell, 1976	78
	Rollie Fingers, 1977	78
	Tom Hume, 1980	78
	Kent Tekulve, 1980	78
	Greg Minton, 1982	78
	Ed Vande Berg, 1982	78
	Ted Power, 1984	78
	Tim Burke, 1985	78
	Lance McCullers, 1987	78
46	Bob Locker, 1967	77
	Wilbur Wood, 1970	77
	Charlie Hough, 1976	77
	Butch Metzger, 1976	77
	Rick Camp, 1980	77
	Gary Lavelle, 1984	77
	Mark Davis, 1985	77
	Craig Lefferts, 1987	77
	Bobby Thigpen, 1990	77
	Barry Jones, 1991	77
	Xavier Hernandez, 1992	77
	Mike Perez, 1992	77
58	Will White, 1879	76
	Jim Galvin, 1883	76
	Charley Radbourn, 1883	76
	Wilbur Wood, 1969	76
	Ron Herbel, 1970	76
	Larry Hardy, 1974	76
	Rollie Fingers, 1974	76
	Dan Spillner, 1977	76
	Dave Tomlin, 1977	76
	Sid Monge, 1979	76
	Rod Scurry, 1982	76
	Tippy Martinez, 1982	76
	Kent Tekulve, 1983	76
	Ed Vande Berg, 1985	76
	Rob Murphy, 1988	76
	Mitch Williams, 1989	76
	Chuck Crim, 1989	76
	Jeff Innis, 1992	76
76	Charley Radbourn, 1884	75
	Guy Hecker, 1884	75
	Bill Hutchinson, 1892	75
	Ron Perranoski, 1969	75
	Rollie Fingers, 1975	75
	Butch Metzger, 1975	75
	Dan Quisenberry, 1980	75
	Willie Hernandez, 1982	75
	Jeff Reardon, 1982	75
	Roger McDowell, 1986	75
	Todd Worrell, 1987	75
	Juan Agosto, 1988	75
	Jeff Robinson, 1988	75
	Paul Assenmacher, 1991	75
90	21 players tied	74

Games (by era)

1876-1892

1	Will White, 1879	76
	Jim Galvin, 1883	76
	Charley Radbourn, 1883	76
4	Charley Radbourn, 1884	75
	Guy Hecker, 1884	75
	Bill Hutchinson, 1892	75
7	Jim McCormick, 1880	74
	Lee Richmond, 1880	74
9	John Clarkson, 1889	73
10	Jim Galvin, 1884	72
11	Bill Hutchinson, 1890	71
12	Monte Ward, 1879	70
	Monte Ward, 1880	70
	John Clarkson, 1885	70
15	Matt Kilroy, 1887	69

1893-1919

1	Ed Walsh, 1908	66
2	Ed Walsh, 1912	62
3	Dave Davenport, 1916	59
4	Amos Rusie, 1893	56
	Ted Breitenstein, 1894	56
	Pink Hawley, 1895	56
	Ed Walsh, 1907	56
	Christy Mathewson, 1908	56
	Ed Walsh, 1911	56
	Reb Russell, 1916	56
11	Frank Killen, 1893	55
	Joe McGinnity, 1903	55
	Jack Chesbro, 1904	55
	Dave Davenport, 1915	55
15	3 players tied	54

1920-1941

1	Firpo Marberry, 1926	64
2	Clint Brown, 1939	61
3	Garland Braxton, 1927	58
	Russ Van Atta, 1935	58
5	Eddie Rommel, 1923	56
	Firpo Marberry, 1927	56
	Hugh Mulcahy, 1937	56
8	Firpo Marberry, 1925	55
	Bump Hadley, 1931	55
	Jim Walkup, 1935	55
11	George Uhle, 1923	54
	Firpo Marberry, 1932	54
	Jack Russell, 1934	54
	Chubby Dean, 1939	54
	Clyde Shoun, 1940	54

1942-1960

1	Jim Konstanty, 1950	74
2	Hoyt Wilhelm, 1952	71
3	Ace Adams, 1943	70
	Mike Fornieles, 1960	70
5	Ellis Kinder, 1953	69
	Don Elston, 1958	69
7	Hoyt Wilhelm, 1953	68
	Roy Face, 1956	68
	Roy Face, 1960	68
10	Andy Karl, 1945	67
	Turk Lown, 1957	67
	Gerry Staley, 1959	67
13	6 players tied	65

1961-1992

1	Mike Marshall, 1974	106
2	Kent Tekulve, 1979	94
3	Mike Marshall, 1973	92
4	Kent Tekulve, 1978	91
5	Wayne Granger, 1969	90
	Mike Marshall, 1979	90
	Kent Tekulve, 1987	90
8	Mark Eichhorn, 1987	89
9	Wilbur Wood, 1968	88
10	Rob Murphy, 1987	87
11	Kent Tekulve, 1982	85
	Frank Williams, 1987	85
	Mitch Williams, 1987	85
14	4 players tied	84

Games Started

1	Will White, 1879	75
	Jim Galvin, 1883	75
3	Jim McCormick, 1880	74
4	Charley Radbourn, 1884	73
	Guy Hecker, 1884	73
6	Jim Galvin, 1884	72
	John Clarkson, 1889	72
8	Bill Hutchinson, 1892	71
9	John Clarkson, 1885	70
10	Matt Kilroy, 1887	69
11	Jim Devlin, 1876	68
	Charley Radbourn, 1883	68
	Tim Keefe, 1883	68
	Matt Kilroy, 1886	68
15	Monte Ward, 1880	67
	Jim McCormick, 1882	67
	Charlie Buffinton, 1884	67
	Toad Ramsey, 1886	67
19	Jim Galvin, 1879	66
	Lee Richmond, 1880	66
	Bill Hutchinson, 1890	66
22	Mickey Welch, 1884	65
	Tony Mullane, 1884	65
	Silver King, 1888	65
25	George Bradley, 1876	64
	Tommy Bond, 1879	64
	Mickey Welch, 1880	64
	Will White, 1883	64
	Tim Keefe, 1886	64
	Toad Ramsey, 1887	64
31	Jim Whitney, 1881	63
	Ed Morris, 1885	63
	Ed Morris, 1886	63
	Amos Rusie, 1890	63
35	Will White, 1880	62
36	Jim Devlin, 1877	61
	John Coleman, 1883	61
	Hardie Henderson, 1885	61
	Jersey Bakely, 1888	61
	Amos Rusie, 1892	61
41	Al Spalding, 1876	60
	Jim McCormick, 1879	60
	Monte Ward, 1879	60
	Larry Corcoran, 1880	60
	Larry McKeon, 1884	60
	Bill Sweeney, 1884	60
47	Tommy Bond, 1878	59
	Frank Mountain, 1883	59
	Larry Corcoran, 1884	59
	Mickey Welch, 1886	59
	John Clarkson, 1887	59
	Mark Baldwin, 1889	59
53	Tommy Bond, 1877	58
	Terry Larkin, 1879	58
	Jim McCormick, 1881	58
	Hugh Daily, 1884	58
	Charley Radbourn, 1886	58
	Bill Hutchinson, 1891	58
	Sadie McMahon, 1891	58
60	Tommy Bond, 1880	57
	Tim Keefe, 1884	57
	Dave Foutz, 1886	57
	Ed Seward, 1888	57
	Sadie McMahon, 1890	57
	Mark Baldwin, 1890	57
	Amos Rusie, 1891	57
67	Bobby Mathews, 1876	56
	Terry Larkin, 1877	56
	Terry Larkin, 1878	56
	Jim Whitney, 1883	56
	Lady Baldwin, 1886	56
	Tony Mullane, 1886	56
	Tim Keefe, 1887	56
	Matt Kilroy, 1889	56
	Silver King, 1890	56
	Jack Stivetts, 1891	56
77	George Derby, 1881	55
	Tony Mullane, 1882	55
	Adonis Terry, 1884	55
	Mickey Welch, 1885	55
	John Clarkson, 1886	55
	Phenomenal Smith, 1887	55
	Gus Weyhing, 1887	55
	Ed Morris, 1888	55
	Kid Gleason, 1890	55
86	George Bradley, 1879	54
	Harry McCormick, 1879	54
	Jim Galvin, 1880	54
	Will White, 1882	54
	Jack Lynch, 1884	54
	Henry Porter, 1885	54
	John Clarkson, 1888	54
	Henry Porter, 1888	54
	Ed Beatin, 1890	54
	Bob Barr, 1890	54
96	8 players tied	53

Games Started (by era)

1876-1892

1	Will White, 1879	75
	Jim Galvin, 1883	75
3	Jim McCormick, 1880	74
4	Charley Radbourn, 1884	73
	Guy Hecker, 1884	73
6	Jim Galvin, 1884	72
	John Clarkson, 1889	72
8	Bill Hutchinson, 1892	71
9	John Clarkson, 1885	70
10	Matt Kilroy, 1887	69
11	Jim Devlin, 1876	68
	Charley Radbourn, 1883	68
	Tim Keefe, 1883	68
	Matt Kilroy, 1886	68
15	4 players tied	67

1893-1919

1	Amos Rusie, 1893	52
2	Jack Chesbro, 1904	51
3	Ted Breitenstein, 1894	50
	Amos Rusie, 1894	50
	Ted Breitenstein, 1895	50
	Pink Hawley, 1895	50
	Frank Killen, 1896	50
8	Ed Walsh, 1908	49
9	Frank Killen, 1893	48
	Jouett Meekin, 1894	48
	Joe McGinnity, 1903	48
12	Cy Young, 1894	47
	Amos Rusie, 1895	47
	Jack Taylor, 1898	47
15	8 players tied	46

1920-1941

1	George Uhle, 1923	44
2	Pete Alexander, 1920	40
	Stan Coveleski, 1921	40
	George Uhle, 1922	40
	George Caster, 1938	40
	Bobo Newsom, 1938	40
	Bob Feller, 1941	40
8	Red Faber, 1920	39
	Red Faber, 1921	39
	Hooks Dauss, 1923	39
	Howard Ehmke, 1923	39
	George Earnshaw, 1930	39
	General Crowder, 1932	39
	Kirby Higbe, 1941	39
15	24 players tied	38

1942-1960

1	Bob Feller, 1946	42
	Bob Friend, 1956	42
3	Bill Voiselle, 1944	41
	Robin Roberts, 1953	41
5	Dizzy Trout, 1944	40
6	Johnny Sain, 1948	39
	Robin Roberts, 1950	39
	Warren Spahn, 1950	39
	Vern Bickford, 1950	39
	Robin Roberts, 1951	39
	Ron Kline, 1956	39
	Lew Burdette, 1959	39
13	10 players tied	38

1961-1992

1	Wilbur Wood, 1972	49
2	Wilbur Wood, 1973	48
3	Mickey Lolich, 1971	45
4	Phil Niekro, 1979	44
5	Wilbur Wood, 1975	43
	Phil Niekro, 1977	43
7	10 players tied	42

Complete Games

1	Will White, 1879	75
2	Charley Radbourn, 1884	73
3	Jim McCormick, 1880	72
	Jim Galvin, 1883	72
	Guy Hecker, 1884	72
6	Jim Galvin, 1884	71
7	Tim Keefe, 1883	68
	John Clarkson, 1885	68
	John Clarkson, 1889	68
10	Bill Hutchinson, 1892	67
11	Jim Devlin, 1876	66
	Charley Radbourn, 1883	66
	Matt Kilroy, 1886	66
	Toad Ramsey, 1886	66
	Matt Kilroy, 1887	66
16	Jim Galvin, 1879	65
	Jim McCormick, 1882	65
	Bill Hutchinson, 1890	65
19	Mickey Welch, 1880	64
	Will White, 1883	64
	Tony Mullane, 1884	64
	Silver King, 1888	64
23	George Bradley, 1876	63
	Charlie Buffinton, 1884	63
	Ed Morris, 1885	63
	Ed Morris, 1886	63
27	Mickey Welch, 1884	62
	Tim Keefe, 1886	62
29	Jim Devlin, 1877	61
	Toad Ramsey, 1887	61
31	Jersey Bakely, 1888	60
32	Tommy Bond, 1879	59
	Jim McCormick, 1879	59
	Monte Ward, 1880	59
	John Coleman, 1883	59
	Larry McKeon, 1884	59
	Hardie Henderson, 1885	59
38	Tommy Bond, 1877	58
	Monte Ward, 1879	58
	Will White, 1880	58
	Bill Sweeney, 1884	58
	Amos Rusie, 1892	58
43	Tommy Bond, 1878	57
	Terry Larkin, 1879	57
	Larry Corcoran, 1880	57
	Lee Richmond, 1880	57
	Jim McCormick, 1881	57
	Jim Whitney, 1881	57
	Frank Mountain, 1883	57
	Larry Corcoran, 1884	57
	Charley Radbourn, 1886	57
	Ed Seward, 1888	57
53	Terry Larkin, 1878	56
	Tim Keefe, 1884	56
	Hugh Daily, 1884	56
	Mickey Welch, 1886	56
	John Clarkson, 1887	56
	Amos Rusie, 1890	56
	Bill Hutchinson, 1891	56
60	Bobby Mathews, 1876	55
	Terry Larkin, 1877	55
	George Derby, 1881	55
	Mickey Welch, 1885	55
	Lady Baldwin, 1886	55
	Dave Foutz, 1886	55
	Tony Mullane, 1886	55
	Matt Kilroy, 1889	55
	Sadie McMahon, 1890	55
69	Jim Whitney, 1883	54
	Jack Lynch, 1884	54
	Adonis Terry, 1884	54
	Tim Keefe, 1887	54
	Phenomenal Smith, 1887	54
	Ed Morris, 1888	54
	Mark Baldwin, 1889	54
	Kid Gleason, 1890	54
	Mark Baldwin, 1890	54
78	Al Spalding, 1876	53
	George Bradley, 1879	53
	Bob Caruthers, 1885	53
	Henry Porter, 1885	53
	Gus Weyhing, 1887	53
	John Clarkson, 1888	53
	Henry Porter, 1888	53
	Ed Beatin, 1890	53
	Sadie McMahon, 1891	53
87	Will White, 1878	52
	Will White, 1882	52
	Will White, 1884	52
	Ed Seward, 1887	52
	Bob Barr, 1890	52
	Amos Rusie, 1891	52
93	Charley Radbourn, 1882	51
	Tony Mullane, 1882	51
	Larry Corcoran, 1883	51
	Fleury Sullivan, 1884	51
	Guy Hecker, 1885	51
	Gus Weyhing, 1891	51
99	10 players tied	50

Complete Games (by era)

1876-1892

1	Will White, 1879	75
2	Charley Radbourn, 1884	73
3	Jim McCormick, 1880	72
	Jim Galvin, 1883	72
	Guy Hecker, 1884	72
6	Jim Galvin, 1884	71
7	Tim Keefe, 1883	68
	John Clarkson, 1885	68
	John Clarkson, 1889	68
10	Bill Hutchinson, 1892	67
11	Jim Devlin, 1876	66
	Charley Radbourn, 1883	66
	Matt Kilroy, 1886	66
	Toad Ramsey, 1886	66
	Matt Kilroy, 1887	66

1893-1919

1	Amos Rusie, 1893	50
2	Jack Chesbro, 1904	48
3	Ted Breitenstein, 1894	46
	Ted Breitenstein, 1895	46
5	Amos Rusie, 1894	45
	Vic Willis, 1902	45
7	Cy Young, 1894	44
	Pink Hawley, 1895	44
	Frank Killen, 1896	44
	Joe McGinnity, 1903	44
11	Kid Nichols, 1893	43
12	7 players tied	42

1920-1941

1	Pete Alexander, 1920	33
	Burleigh Grimes, 1923	33
3	Red Faber, 1921	32
	George Uhle, 1926	32
5	Red Faber, 1922	31
	Wes Ferrell, 1935	31
	Bobo Newsom, 1938	31
	Bucky Walters, 1939	31
	Bob Feller, 1940	31
10	8 players tied	30

1942-1960

1	Bob Feller, 1946	36
2	Dizzy Trout, 1944	33
	Robin Roberts, 1953	33
4	Robin Roberts, 1952	30
5	Hal Newhouser, 1945	29
	Hal Newhouser, 1946	29
	Robin Roberts, 1954	29
8	Jim Tobin, 1942	28
	Jim Tobin, 1944	28
	Johnny Sain, 1948	28
	Bob Lemon, 1952	28
12	Bucky Walters, 1944	27
	Mel Parnell, 1949	27
	Vern Bickford, 1950	27
	Bobby Shantz, 1952	27

1961-1992

1	Juan Marichal, 1968	30
	Fergie Jenkins, 1971	30
	Steve Carlton, 1972	30
	Jim Hunter, 1975	30
5	Mickey Lolich, 1971	29
	Gaylord Perry, 1972	29
	Gaylord Perry, 1973	29
	Fergie Jenkins, 1974	29
9	Bob Gibson, 1968	28
	Denny McLain, 1968	28
	Bob Gibson, 1969	28
	Gaylord Perry, 1974	28
	Rick Langford, 1980	28
14	4 players tied	27

Shutouts

1	George Bradley, 1876	16
	Pete Alexander, 1916	16
3	Jack Coombs, 1910	13
	Bob Gibson, 1968	13
5	Jim Galvin, 1884	12
	Ed Morris, 1886	12
	Pete Alexander, 1915	12
8	Tommy Bond, 1879	11
	Charley Radbourn, 1884	11
	Dave Foutz, 1886	11
	Christy Mathewson, 1908	11
	Ed Walsh, 1908	11
	Walter Johnson, 1913	11
	Sandy Koufax, 1963	11
	Dean Chance, 1964	11
16	John Clarkson, 1885	10
	Cy Young, 1904	10
	Ed Walsh, 1906	10
	Joe Wood, 1912	10
	Dave Davenport, 1915	10
	Carl Hubbell, 1933	10
	Mort Cooper, 1942	10
	Bob Feller, 1946	10
	Bob Lemon, 1948	10
	Juan Marichal, 1965	10
	Jim Palmer, 1975	10
	John Tudor, 1985	10
28	Tommy Bond, 1878	9
	George Derby, 1881	9
	Cy Young, 1892	9
	Joe McGinnity, 1904	9
	Mordecai Brown, 1906	9
	Addie Joss, 1906	9
	Mordecai Brown, 1908	9
	Addie Joss, 1908	9
	Orval Overall, 1909	9
	Pete Alexander, 1913	9
	Walter Johnson, 1914	9
	Cy Falkenberg, 1914	9
	Babe Ruth, 1916	9
	Stan Coveleski, 1917	9
	Pete Alexander, 1919	9
	Bill Lee, 1938	9
	Bob Porterfield, 1953	9
	Luis Tiant, 1968	9
	Denny McLain, 1969	9
	Don Sutton, 1972	9
	Nolan Ryan, 1972	9
	Bert Blyleven, 1973	9
	Ron Guidry, 1978	9
51	Al Spalding, 1876	8
	Monte Ward, 1880	8
	Will White, 1882	8
	Charlie Buffinton, 1884	8
	Tim Keefe, 1888	8
	Ben Sanders, 1888	8
	John Clarkson, 1889	8
	Christy Mathewson, 1902	8
	Jack Chesbro, 1902	8
	Rube Waddell, 1904	8
	Christy Mathewson, 1905	8
	Ed Killian, 1905	8
	Lefty Leifield, 1906	8
	Rube Waddell, 1906	8
	Orval Overall, 1907	8
	Christy Mathewson, 1907	8
	Eddie Plank, 1907	8
	Mordecai Brown, 1909	8
	Christy Mathewson, 1909	8
	Ed Walsh, 1909	8
	Russ Ford, 1910	8
	Walter Johnson, 1910	8
	Reb Russell, 1913	8
	Jeff Tesreau, 1914	8
	Al Mamaux, 1915	8
	Jeff Tesreau, 1915	8
	Joe Bush, 1916	8
	Pete Alexander, 1917	8
	Jim Bagby, 1917	8
	Walter Johnson, 1917	8
	Hippo Vaughn, 1918	8
	Walter Johnson, 1918	8
	Carl Mays, 1918	8
	Babe Adams, 1920	8
	Hal Newhouser, 1945	8
	Steve Barber, 1961	8
	Camilo Pascual, 1961	8
	Whitey Ford, 1964	8
	Sandy Koufax, 1965	8
	Don Drysdale, 1968	8
	Juan Marichal, 1969	8
	Vida Blue, 1971	8
	Steve Carlton, 1972	8
	Wilbur Wood, 1972	8
	Fernando Valenzuela, 1981	8
	Dwight Gooden, 1985	8
	Orel Hershiser, 1988	8
	Roger Clemens, 1988	8
	Tim Belcher, 1989	8
100	88 players tied	7

Saves

1	Bobby Thigpen, 1990	57
2	Dennis Eckersley, 1992	51
3	Dennis Eckersley, 1990	48
4	Lee Smith, 1991	47
5	Dave Righetti, 1986	46
	Bryan Harvey, 1991	46
7	Dan Quisenberry, 1983	45
	Bruce Sutter, 1984	45
	Dennis Eckersley, 1988	45
10	Dan Quisenberry, 1984	44
	Mark Davis, 1989	44
12	Doug Jones, 1990	43
	Dennis Eckersley, 1991	43
	Lee Smith, 1992	43
15	Jeff Reardon, 1988	42
	Rick Aguilera, 1991	42
17	Jeff Reardon, 1985	41
	Rick Aguilera, 1992	41
19	Steve Bedrosian, 1987	40
	Jeff Reardon, 1991	40
21	Johnny Franco, 1988	39
	Jeff Montgomery, 1992	39
23	John Hiller, 1973	38
	Jeff Russell, 1989	38
	Randy Myers, 1992	38
26	Clay Carroll, 1972	37
	Rollie Fingers, 1978	37
	Bruce Sutter, 1979	37
	Dan Quisenberry, 1985	37
	Doug Jones, 1988	37
	Gregg Olson, 1990	37
	John Wetteland, 1992	37
33	Bruce Sutter, 1982	36
	Bill Caudill, 1984	36
	Todd Worrell, 1986	36
	Lee Smith, 1987	36
	Mitch Williams, 1989	36
	Dave Righetti, 1990	36
	Doug Jones, 1992	36
	Gregg Olson, 1992	36
41	Wayne Granger, 1970	35
	Sparky Lyle, 1972	35
	Rollie Fingers, 1977	35
	Dan Quisenberry, 1982	35
	Jeff Reardon, 1986	35
46	Ron Perranoski, 1970	34
	Don Aase, 1986	34
	Tom Henke, 1987	34
	Jim Gott, 1988	34
	Bobby Thigpen, 1988	34
	Bobby Thigpen, 1989	34
	Tom Henke, 1992	34
53	Rich Gossage, 1980	33
	Dan Quisenberry, 1980	33
	Bob Stanley, 1983	33
	Lee Smith, 1984	33
	Lee Smith, 1985	33
	Dave Smith, 1986	33
	Todd Worrell, 1987	33
	Dennis Eckersley, 1989	33
	Dan Plesac, 1989	33
	Mike Schooler, 1989	33
	Johnny Franco, 1990	33
	Jeff Montgomery, 1991	33
65	Jack Aker, 1966	32
	Mike Marshall, 1979	32
	Willie Hernandez, 1984	32
	Bob James, 1985	32
	Johnny Franco, 1987	32
	Todd Worrell, 1988	32
	Johnny Franco, 1989	32
	Doug Jones, 1989	32
	Rick Aguilera, 1990	32
	Tom Henke, 1990	32
	Tom Henke, 1991	32
76	Ted Abernathy, 1965	31
	Ron Perranoski, 1969	31
	Ken Sanders, 1971	31
	Mike Marshall, 1973	31
	Bruce Sutter, 1977	31
	Bill Campbell, 1977	31
	Kent Tekulve, 1978	31
	Kent Tekulve, 1979	31
	Jesse Orosco, 1984	31
	Dave Righetti, 1984	31
	Willie Hernandez, 1985	31
	Donnie Moore, 1985	31
	Lee Smith, 1986	31
	Jeff Reardon, 1987	31
	Dave Righetti, 1987	31
	Jeff Reardon, 1989	31
	Randy Myers, 1990	31
	Rob Dibble, 1991	31
	Gregg Olson, 1991	31
95	14 players tied	30

Innings Pitched

1	Will White, 1879	680.0
2	Charley Radbourn, 1884	678.2
3	Guy Hecker, 1884	670.2
4	Jim McCormick, 1880	657.2
5	Jim Galvin, 1883	656.1
6	Jim Galvin, 1884	636.1
7	Charley Radbourn, 1883	632.1
8	Bill Hutchinson, 1892	627.0
9	John Clarkson, 1885	623.0
10	Jim Devlin, 1876	622.0
11	John Clarkson, 1889	620.0
12	Tim Keefe, 1883	619.0
13	Bill Hutchinson, 1890	603.0
14	Jim McCormick, 1882	595.2
15	Monte Ward, 1880	595.0
16	Jim Galvin, 1879	593.0
17	Lee Richmond, 1880	590.2
18	Matt Kilroy, 1887	589.1
19	Toad Ramsey, 1886	588.2
20	Monte Ward, 1879	587.0
	Charlie Buffinton, 1884	587.0
22	Silver King, 1888	585.2
23	Matt Kilroy, 1886	583.0
24	Ed Morris, 1885	581.0
25	Will White, 1883	577.0
26	Mickey Welch, 1880	574.0
27	George Bradley, 1876	573.0
28	Tony Mullane, 1884	567.0
29	Toad Ramsey, 1887	561.0
	Bill Hutchinson, 1891	561.0
31	Jim Devlin, 1877	559.0
32	Mickey Welch, 1884	557.1
33	Tommy Bond, 1879	555.1
	Ed Morris, 1886	555.1
35	Jim Whitney, 1881	552.1
36	Amos Rusie, 1890	548.2
37	Jim McCormick, 1879	546.1
38	Hardie Henderson, 1885	539.1
39	John Coleman, 1883	538.1
40	Bill Sweeney, 1884	538.0
41	Larry Corcoran, 1880	536.1
42	Tim Keefe, 1886	535.0
43	Tommy Bond, 1878	532.2
	Jersey Bakely, 1888	532.2
45	Amos Rusie, 1892	532.0
46	Tony Mullane, 1886	529.2
47	Al Spalding, 1876	528.2
48	Jim McCormick, 1881	526.0
49	John Clarkson, 1887	523.0
50	Tommy Bond, 1877	521.0
51	Ed Seward, 1888	518.2
52	Will White, 1880	517.1
53	Larry Corcoran, 1884	516.2
54	Bobby Mathews, 1876	516.0
55	Jim Whitney, 1883	514.0
56	Mark Baldwin, 1889	513.2
57	Terry Larkin, 1879	513.1
58	Larry McKeon, 1884	512.0
59	Charley Radbourn, 1886	509.1
60	Sadie McMahon, 1890	509.0
61	Terry Larkin, 1878	506.0
	Kid Gleason, 1890	506.0
63	Dave Foutz, 1886	504.0
64	Frank Mountain, 1883	503.0
	Sadie McMahon, 1891	503.0
66	Terry Larkin, 1877	501.0
	Mark Baldwin, 1890	501.0
68	Hugh Daily, 1884	500.2
69	Amos Rusie, 1891	500.1
70	Mickey Welch, 1886	500.0
71	Jack Lynch, 1884	496.0
72	George Derby, 1881	494.2
73	Bob Barr, 1890	493.1
74	Tommy Bond, 1880	493.0
75	Mickey Welch, 1885	492.0
76	Phenomenal Smith, 1887	491.1
77	George Bradley, 1879	487.0
	Lady Baldwin, 1886	487.0
79	John Clarkson, 1888	483.1
80	Tim Keefe, 1884	482.2
81	Bob Caruthers, 1885	482.1
82	Amos Rusie, 1893	482.0
83	Henry Porter, 1885	481.2
84	Matt Kilroy, 1889	480.2
85	Will White, 1882	480.0
	Guy Hecker, 1885	480.0
	Ed Morris, 1888	480.0
88	Tim Keefe, 1887	476.2
89	Adonis Terry, 1884	476.0
90	Ed Beatin, 1890	474.1
91	Jim Galvin, 1881	474.0
	Charley Radbourn, 1882	474.0
	Henry Porter, 1888	474.0
94	Larry Corcoran, 1883	473.2
95	Ed Seward, 1887	470.2
96	Gus Weyhing, 1892	469.2
97	Will White, 1878	468.0
98	John Clarkson, 1886	466.2
99	Gus Weyhing, 1887	466.1
100	Ed Walsh, 1908	464.0

Innings Pitched (by era)

1876-1892

1	Will White, 1879	680.0
2	Charley Radbourn, 1884	678.2
3	Guy Hecker, 1884	670.2
4	Jim McCormick, 1880	657.2
5	Jim Galvin, 1883	656.1
6	Jim Galvin, 1884	636.1
7	Charley Radbourn, 1883	632.1
8	Bill Hutchinson, 1892	627.0
9	John Clarkson, 1885	623.0
10	Jim Devlin, 1876	622.0
11	John Clarkson, 1889	620.0
12	Tim Keefe, 1883	619.0
13	Bill Hutchinson, 1890	603.0
14	Jim McCormick, 1882	595.2
15	Monte Ward, 1880	595.0

1893-1919

1	Amos Rusie, 1893	482.0
2	Ed Walsh, 1908	464.0
3	Jack Chesbro, 1904	454.2
4	Ted Breitenstein, 1894	447.1
5	Pink Hawley, 1895	444.1
6	Amos Rusie, 1894	444.0
7	Joe McGinnity, 1903	434.0
8	Frank Killen, 1896	432.1
9	Ted Breitenstein, 1895	429.2
10	Kid Nichols, 1893	425.0
11	Cy Young, 1893	422.2
12	Ed Walsh, 1907	422.1
13	Frank Killen, 1893	415.0
14	Cy Young, 1896	414.1
15	Vic Willis, 1902	410.0

1920-1941

1	Pete Alexander, 1920	363.1
2	George Uhle, 1923	357.2
3	Red Faber, 1922	352.0
4	Urban Shocker, 1922	348.0
5	Bob Feller, 1941	343.0
6	Jim Bagby, 1920	339.2
7	Carl Mays, 1921	336.2
8	Red Faber, 1921	330.2
	Burleigh Grimes, 1928	330.2
10	Bobo Newsom, 1938	329.2
11	Wilbur Cooper, 1920	327.0
	Wilbur Cooper, 1921	327.0
	Burleigh Grimes, 1923	327.0
	General Crowder, 1932	327.0
15	Urban Shocker, 1921	326.2

1942-1960

1	Bob Feller, 1946	371.1
2	Dizzy Trout, 1944	352.1
3	Robin Roberts, 1953	346.2
4	Robin Roberts, 1954	336.2
5	Robin Roberts, 1952	330.0
6	Robin Roberts, 1951	315.0
7	Johnny Sain, 1948	314.2
8	Bob Friend, 1956	314.1
9	Hal Newhouser, 1945	313.1
10	Bill Voiselle, 1944	312.2
11	Hal Newhouser, 1944	312.1
12	Vern Bickford, 1950	311.2
13	Warren Spahn, 1951	310.2
14	Bob Lemon, 1952	309.2
15	Robin Roberts, 1955	305.0

1961-1992

1	Wilbur Wood, 1972	376.2
2	Mickey Lolich, 1971	376.0
3	Wilbur Wood, 1973	359.1
4	Steve Carlton, 1972	346.1
5	Gaylord Perry, 1973	344.0
6	Gaylord Perry, 1972	342.2
7	Phil Niekro, 1979	342.0
8	Denny McLain, 1968	336.0
9	Sandy Koufax, 1965	335.2
10	Phil Niekro, 1978	334.1
11	Wilbur Wood, 1971	334.0
12	Nolan Ryan, 1974	332.2
13	Phil Niekro, 1977	330.1
14	Gaylord Perry, 1970	328.2
15	Fergie Jenkins, 1974	328.1

Hits per Game

1	Nolan Ryan, 1972	5.26
2	Luis Tiant, 1968	5.30
3	Nolan Ryan, 1991	5.31
4	Ed Reulbach, 1906	5.33
5	Dutch Leonard, 1914	5.57
6	Carl Lundgren, 1907	5.65
7	Sid Fernandez, 1985	5.71
8	Tommy Byrne, 1949	5.74
9	Dave McNally, 1968	5.77
10	Sandy Koufax, 1965	5.79
11	Russ Ford, 1910	5.83
12	Al Downing, 1963	5.84
13	Herb Score, 1956	5.85
14	Bob Gibson, 1968	5.85
15	Sam McDowell, 1965	5.87
16	Ed Walsh, 1910	5.89
17	Mike Scott, 1986	5.95
18	Mario Soto, 1980	5.96
19	Floyd Youmans, 1986	5.96
20	Nolan Ryan, 1977	5.96
21	Nolan Ryan, 1974	5.98
22	Nolan Ryan, 1981	5.98
23	Nolan Ryan, 1986	6.02
24	Sam McDowell, 1966	6.02
25	Vida Blue, 1971	6.03
26	Walter Johnson, 1913	6.03
27	Jim Bibby, 1973	6.04
28	Nolan Ryan, 1990	6.04
29	Pete Alexander, 1915	6.05
30	Sam McDowell, 1968	6.06
31	Joe Horlen, 1964	6.07
32	Andy Messersmith, 1969	6.08
33	Tim Keefe, 1880	6.09
34	Nolan Ryan, 1989	6.09
35	Stan Coveleski, 1917	6.09
36	Jim Hunter, 1972	6.09
37	Nolan Ryan, 1976	6.11
38	Sid Fernandez, 1988	6.11
39	Bob Turley, 1957	6.12
40	Bob Turley, 1955	6.13
41	Don Sutton, 1972	6.14
42	Nolan Ryan, 1983	6.14
43	Ron Guidry, 1978	6.15
44	Mordecai Brown, 1908	6.17
45	Sandy Koufax, 1963	6.19
46	Jack Pfiester, 1906	6.21
47	Sandy Koufax, 1964	6.22
48	Charlie Sweeney, 1884	6.23
	Roger Nelson, 1972	6.23
50	Herb Score, 1955	6.26
51	Cy Morgan, 1909	6.26
52	Dean Chance, 1964	6.27
53	Christy Mathewson, 1909	6.28
	J.R. Richard, 1978	6.28
55	Art Fromme, 1909	6.28
56	Jack Coombs, 1910	6.32
57	Rube Waddell, 1905	6.33
58	Vean Gregg, 1911	6.33
59	Jeff Robinson, 1988	6.33
60	Larry Cheney, 1916	6.33
61	Walter Johnson, 1912	6.33
62	Sonny Siebert, 1968	6.33
63	Allie Reynolds, 1943	6.34
64	Roger Clemens, 1986	6.34
65	Willie Mitchell, 1913	6.35
66	Jose DeLeon, 1989	6.36
67	Pascual Perez, 1988	6.37
68	Dave Boswell, 1966	6.38
69	Harry Krause, 1909	6.38
70	Dutch Leonard, 1915	6.38
71	Eddie Cicotte, 1917	6.39
72	Wayne Simpson, 1970	6.39
73	Babe Ruth, 1916	6.40
74	Spec Shea, 1947	6.40
75	Ed Reulbach, 1905	6.42
76	Gaylord Perry, 1974	6.42
77	Eddie Fisher, 1965	6.42
78	Addie Joss, 1908	6.42
79	Mordecai Brown, 1906	6.43
80	Luis Tiant, 1972	6.44
81	Frank Smith, 1908	6.44
82	Dwight Gooden, 1985	6.44
83	Orval Overall, 1909	6.44
84	Sid Fernandez, 1989	6.44
85	Denny McLain, 1968	6.46
86	Mordecai Brown, 1909	6.46
87	Ray Caldwell, 1914	6.46
88	Fred Toney, 1915	6.47
89	Jim McCormick, 1884	6.47
90	Dupee Shaw, 1884	6.47
91	Gary Peters, 1967	6.47
92	Walter Johnson, 1910	6.47
93	Bob Turley, 1954	6.48
94	Ed Walsh, 1909	6.49
95	Guy Hecker, 1882	6.49
96	Frank Smith, 1910	6.49
97	Tom Seaver, 1981	6.49
98	Al Mamaux, 1915	6.51
99	Claude Hendrix, 1914	6.51
	Jim Palmer, 1969	6.51

Hits per Game (by era)

1876-1892

1	Tim Keefe, 1880	6.09
2	Charlie Sweeney, 1884	6.23
3	Jim McCormick, 1884	6.47
4	Dupee Shaw, 1884	6.47
5	Guy Hecker, 1882	6.49
6	Tim Keefe, 1888	6.57
7	Adonis Terry, 1888	6.69
8	Silver King, 1888	6.72
9	Frank Knauss, 1890	6.73
10	Ed Seward, 1888	6.73
11	Tim Keefe, 1885	6.75
12	Tony Mullane, 1892	6.77
13	Larry Corcoran, 1880	6.78
14	Mickey Welch, 1885	6.80
15	Cannonball Titcomb, 1888	6.81

1893-1919

1	Ed Reulbach, 1906	5.33
2	Dutch Leonard, 1914	5.57
3	Carl Lundgren, 1907	5.65
4	Russ Ford, 1910	5.83
5	Ed Walsh, 1910	5.89
6	Walter Johnson, 1913	6.03
7	Pete Alexander, 1915	6.05
8	Stan Coveleski, 1917	6.09
9	Mordecai Brown, 1908	6.17
10	Jack Pfiester, 1906	6.21
11	Cy Morgan, 1909	6.26
12	Christy Mathewson, 1909	6.28
13	Art Fromme, 1909	6.28
14	Jack Coombs, 1910	6.32
15	Rube Waddell, 1905	6.33

1920-1941

1	Johnny Vander Meer, 1941	6.84
2	Bob Feller, 1940	6.88
3	Bob Feller, 1939	6.89
4	Hal Schumacher, 1933	6.92
5	Dazzy Vance, 1924	6.94
6	Whit Wyatt, 1941	6.96
7	Bucky Walters, 1939	7.05
8	Johnny Vander Meer, 1938	7.07
9	Bucky Walters, 1940	7.11
10	Lefty Gomez, 1934	7.13
11	Ernie White, 1941	7.24
12	Dazzy Vance, 1928	7.26
13	Bump Hadley, 1931	7.26
14	Dolf Luque, 1920	7.28
15	Bob Feller, 1938	7.29

1942-1960

1	Tommy Byrne, 1949	5.74
2	Herb Score, 1956	5.85
3	Bob Turley, 1957	6.12
4	Bob Turley, 1955	6.13
5	Herb Score, 1955	6.26
6	Allie Reynolds, 1943	6.34
7	Spec Shea, 1947	6.40
8	Bob Turley, 1954	6.48
9	Sam Jones, 1955	6.52
10	Bob Turley, 1958	6.53
11	Hal Newhouser, 1946	6.61
12	Johnny Niggeling, 1943	6.66
13	Don Larsen, 1956	6.66
14	Whitey Ford, 1955	6.67
15	Mort Cooper, 1942	6.69

1961-1992

1	Nolan Ryan, 1972	5.26
2	Luis Tiant, 1968	5.30
3	Nolan Ryan, 1991	5.31
4	Sid Fernandez, 1985	5.71
5	Dave McNally, 1968	5.77
6	Sandy Koufax, 1965	5.79
7	Al Downing, 1963	5.84
8	Bob Gibson, 1968	5.85
9	Sam McDowell, 1965	5.87
10	Mike Scott, 1986	5.95
11	Mario Soto, 1980	5.96
12	Floyd Youmans, 1986	5.96
13	Nolan Ryan, 1977	5.96
14	Nolan Ryan, 1974	5.98
15	Nolan Ryan, 1981	5.98

Home Runs Allowed

1	Bert Blyleven, 1986	50
2	Robin Roberts, 1956	46
	Bert Blyleven, 1987	46
4	Pedro Ramos, 1957	43
5	Denny McLain, 1966	42
6	Robin Roberts, 1955	41
	Phil Niekro, 1979	41
8	Robin Roberts, 1957	40
	Ralph Terry, 1962	40
	Orlando Pena, 1964	40
	Phil Niekro, 1970	40
	Fergie Jenkins, 1979	40
	Jack Morris, 1986	40
14	Murry Dickson, 1948	39
	Pedro Ramos, 1961	39
	Jim Perry, 1971	39
	Jim Hunter, 1973	39
	Jack Morris, 1987	39
19	Warren Hacker, 1955	38
	Pedro Ramos, 1958	38
	Lew Burdette, 1959	38
	Jim Bunning, 1963	38
	Don Sutton, 1970	38
	Mickey Lolich, 1971	38
	Matt Keough, 1982	38
	Floyd Bannister, 1987	38
	Don Sutton, 1987	38
	Curt Young, 1987	38
29	Jim Bunning, 1959	37
	Earl Wilson, 1964	37
	Luis Tiant, 1969	37
	Fergie Jenkins, 1975	37
	Jack Morris, 1982	37
	Dan Petry, 1983	37
	Frank Viola, 1986	37
36	Larry Jansen, 1949	36
	Art Mahaffey, 1962	36
	Pete Richert, 1966	36
	Mickey Lolich, 1971	36
	Eddie Whitson, 1987	36
	Charlie Hough, 1987	36
	Tom Browning, 1988	36
43	Larry Corcoran, 1884	35
	Warren Hacker, 1953	35
	Robin Roberts, 1954	35
	Don Newcombe, 1955	35
	Jim Perry, 1960	35
	Roger Craig, 1962	35
	Robin Roberts, 1963	35
	Sammy Ellis, 1966	35
	Denny McLain, 1967	35
	Fergie Jenkins, 1973	35
	Mickey Lolich, 1973	35
	Mike Caldwell, 1983	35
	Mike Smithson, 1984	35
	Scott McGregor, 1986	35
	Scott Bankhead, 1987	35
	Bruce Hurst, 1987	35
	Bill Gullickson, 1992	35
60	Preacher Roe, 1950	34
	Johnny Sain, 1950	34
	Ken Raffensberger, 1950	34
	Robin Roberts, 1959	34
	Paul Foytack, 1959	34
	Juan Marichal, 1962	34
	Dick Ellsworth, 1964	34
	Bill Monbouquette, 1964	34
	Bob Gibson, 1965	34
	Jim Grant, 1965	34
	Earl Wilson, 1967	34
	Jim Hunter, 1969	34
	Mike Cuellar, 1970	34
	Gaylord Perry, 1973	34
	Rick Wise, 1975	34
	Frank Viola, 1983	34
	Danny Darwin, 1985	34
	Scott McGregor, 1985	34
	Ken Schrom, 1986	34
	Don Carman, 1987	34
	Mike Witt, 1987	34
81	Don Newcombe, 1956	33
	Camilo Pascual, 1956	33
	Jim Bunning, 1957	33
	Billy Pierce, 1958	33
	Mike McCormick, 1961	33
	Gene Conley, 1961	33
	Phil Regan, 1963	33
	Phil Ortega, 1965	33
	Jim Merritt, 1969	33
	Lew Krausse, 1970	33
	Jerry Garvin, 1977	33
	Dennis Leonard, 1979	33
	Bill Travers, 1979	33
	Rick Langford, 1982	33
	Ken Dixon, 1986	33
	Bill Gullickson, 1987	33
	Willie Fraser, 1988	33
98	28 players tied	32

Home Runs Allowed (by era)

1876-1892

1	Larry Corcoran, 1884	35
2	Charlie Getzien, 1889	27
3	Bill Hutchinson, 1891	26
4	Charlie Getzien, 1887	24
	John Healy, 1887	24
6	Jim Galvin, 1884	23
	Mark Baldwin, 1887	23
	Lev Shreve, 1888	23
9	Billy Serad, 1884	21
	John Clarkson, 1885	21
	Park Swartzel, 1889	21
	George Cobb, 1892	21
13	7 players tied	20

1893-1919

1	Frank Dwyer, 1894	27
	Jack Stivetts, 1894	27
3	Kid Nichols, 1894	23
4	Harry Staley, 1893	22
	Kid Carsey, 1894	22
6	Ted Breitenstein, 1894	21
7	Jack Stivetts, 1896	20
8	Tom Parrott, 1894	19
	Cy Young, 1894	19
10	Kid Gleason, 1893	18
	Al Orth, 1902	18
12	5 players tied	17

1920-1941

1	Lon Warneke, 1937	32
2	Phil Collins, 1934	30
	Bobo Newsom, 1938	30
4	Ray Kremer, 1930	29
	Lynn Nelson, 1938	29
6	George Earnshaw, 1932	28
	George Earnshaw, 1934	28
8	Roy Mahaffey, 1932	27
	Carl Hubbell, 1935	27
	Luke Hamlin, 1939	27
	Lynn Nelson, 1939	27
	Johnny Marcum, 1939	27
	Freddie Fitzsimmons, 1930	26
13	Gordon Rhodes, 1936	26
	Nels Potter, 1939	26

1942-1960

1	Robin Roberts, 1956	46
2	Pedro Ramos, 1957	43
3	Robin Roberts, 1955	41
4	Robin Roberts, 1957	40
5	Murry Dickson, 1948	39
6	Warren Hacker, 1955	38
	Pedro Ramos, 1958	38
	Lew Burdette, 1959	38
9	Jim Bunning, 1959	37
10	Larry Jansen, 1949	36
11	Warren Hacker, 1953	35
	Robin Roberts, 1954	35
	Don Newcombe, 1955	35
	Jim Perry, 1960	35
15	5 players tied	34

1961-1992

1	Bert Blyleven, 1986	50
2	Bert Blyleven, 1987	46
3	Denny McLain, 1966	42
4	Phil Niekro, 1979	41
5	Ralph Terry, 1962	40
	Orlando Pena, 1964	40
	Phil Niekro, 1970	40
	Fergie Jenkins, 1979	40
	Jack Morris, 1986	40
10	Pedro Ramos, 1961	39
	Jim Perry, 1971	39
	Jim Hunter, 1973	39
	Jack Morris, 1987	39
14	7 players tied	38

Walks

1	Amos Rusie, 1890	289
2	Mark Baldwin, 1889	274
3	Amos Rusie, 1892	267
4	Amos Rusie, 1891	262
5	Mark Baldwin, 1890	249
6	Jack Stivetts, 1891	232
7	Mark Baldwin, 1891	227
8	Phil Knell, 1891	226
9	Bob Barr, 1890	219
10	Amos Rusie, 1893	218
11	Cy Seymour, 1898	213
12	Gus Weyhing, 1889	212
13	Ed Crane, 1890	210
14	Bob Feller, 1938	208
15	Toad Ramsey, 1886	207
16	Elton Chamberlain, 1891	206
17	Mike Morrison, 1887	205
18	Henry Gruber, 1890	204
	Nolan Ryan, 1977	204
20	John Clarkson, 1889	203
21	Nolan Ryan, 1974	202
22	Bert Cunningham, 1890	201
23	Amos Rusie, 1894	200
24	Bill Hutchinson, 1890	199
25	Mark Baldwin, 1892	194
	Bob Feller, 1941	194
27	Bobo Newsom, 1938	192
28	Ted Breitenstein, 1894	191
29	Ed Crane, 1892	189
	Tony Mullane, 1893	189
31	Tony Mullane, 1891	187
	Bill Hutchinson, 1892	187
	Kid Gleason, 1893	187
34	Ed Beatin, 1890	186
35	Sam Jones, 1955	185
36	Tom Vickery, 1890	184
37	Nolan Ryan, 1976	183
38	Matt Kilroy, 1886	182
	Frank Killen, 1892	182
40	Willie McGill, 1893	181
	Bob Harmon, 1911	181
	Bob Turley, 1954	181
43	Jack Stivetts, 1890	179
	Gus Weyhing, 1890	179
	Tommy Byrne, 1949	179
46	Bill Hutchinson, 1891	178
	Ted Breitenstein, 1895	178
48	Bob Turley, 1955	177
49	Phenomenal Smith, 1887	176
	George Hemming, 1893	176
51	Silver King, 1892	174
52	Jack Stivetts, 1892	171
	Jouett Meekin, 1894	171
	Bump Hadley, 1932	171
55	Elton Chamberlain, 1892	170
	Ed Stein, 1894	170
	Cy Seymour, 1899	170
58	Willie McGill, 1891	168
	Gus Weyhing, 1892	168
	Brickyard Kennedy, 1893	168
	Elmer Myers, 1916	168
62	Toad Ramsey, 1887	167
	Gus Weyhing, 1887	167
	Darby O'Brien, 1889	167
	Kid Gleason, 1890	167
	Bill Daley, 1890	167
	Bobo Newsom, 1937	167
68	Tony Mullane, 1886	166
	Sadie McMahon, 1890	166
	Phil Knell, 1890	166
	Chick Fraser, 1896	166
72	Elton Chamberlain, 1889	165
	Dan Casey, 1890	165
	Kid Gleason, 1891	165
	John Wyckoff, 1915	165
76	Cy Seymour, 1897	164
	Earl Moore, 1911	164
	Phil Niekro, 1977	164
79	Mickey Welch, 1886	163
	Silver King, 1890	163
	Hank O'Day, 1890	163
	George Haddock, 1892	163
83	Johnny Vander Meer, 1943	162
	Nolan Ryan, 1973	162
85	John Sowders, 1890	161
	Kid Carsey, 1891	161
	Gus Weyhing, 1891	161
88	Tommy Byrne, 1950	160
89	George Hemming, 1894	159
	Amos Rusie, 1895	159
	Marty O'Toole, 1912	159
92	Joe Coleman, 1974	158
93	Matt Kilroy, 1887	157
	Bert Cunningham, 1888	157
	Pink Hawley, 1896	157
	Grover Lowdermilk, 1915	157
	Nolan Ryan, 1972	157
98	5 players tied	156

Fewest Walks/Game (by era)

1876-1892
1	George Zettlein, 1876	0.23
2	Cherokee Fisher, 1876	0.24
3	George Bradley, 1880	0.28
4	Tommy Bond, 1876	0.29
5	Tommy Bond, 1879	0.39
6	Bobby Mathews, 1876	0.42
7	Charlie Sweeney, 1884	0.43
8	Guy Hecker, 1882	0.43
9	Dale Williams, 1876	0.43
10	Al Spalding, 1876	0.44
11	Jim Galvin, 1879	0.47
12	George Bradley, 1879	0.48
13	Sam Weaver, 1878	0.49
14	Terry Larkin, 1879	0.53
15	Jim Devlin, 1876	0.54

1893-1919
1	Christy Mathewson, 1913	0.62
2	Christy Mathewson, 1914	0.66
3	Cy Young, 1904	0.69
4	Cy Young, 1906	0.78
5	Babe Adams, 1919	0.79
6	Slim Sallee, 1919	0.79
7	Slim Sallee, 1918	0.82
8	Addie Joss, 1908	0.83
9	Cy Young, 1905	0.84
10	Deacon Phillippe, 1902	0.86
11	Cy Young, 1901	0.90
12	Deacon Phillippe, 1903	0.90
13	Christy Mathewson, 1908	0.97
14	Christy Mathewson, 1915	0.97
15	Jesse Tannehill, 1902	0.97

1920-1941
1	Babe Adams, 1920	0.62
2	Red Lucas, 1933	0.74
3	Babe Adams, 1922	0.79
4	Pete Alexander, 1923	0.89
5	Babe Adams, 1921	1.01
6	Paul Derringer, 1939	1.05
7	Carl Hubbell, 1934	1.06
8	Bill Swift, 1932	1.09
9	Pete Alexander, 1925	1.11
10	Herb Pennock, 1930	1.15
11	Red Lucas, 1932	1.17
12	Pete Alexander, 1921	1.18
13	Watty Clark, 1935	1.22
14	Pete Donohue, 1926	1.23
15	Pete Alexander, 1922	1.25

1942-1960
1	Tiny Bonham, 1942	0.96
2	Don Newcombe, 1959	1.09
3	Tiny Bonham, 1945	1.10
4	Lew Burdette, 1960	1.14
5	Lew Burdette, 1959	1.18
6	Robin Roberts, 1956	1.21
7	Robin Roberts, 1959	1.22
8	Robin Roberts, 1952	1.23
9	Hal Brown, 1960	1.25
10	Ray Prim, 1945	1.25
11	Robin Roberts, 1960	1.29
12	Fred Hutchinson, 1951	1.29
13	Ted Lyons, 1942	1.30
14	Schoolboy Rowe, 1943	1.31
15	Vern Law, 1960	1.33

1961-1992
1	Bob Tewksbury, 1992	0.77
2	La Marr Hoyt, 1985	0.86
3	Dennis Eckersley, 1985	1.01
4	Gary Nolan, 1976	1.02
5	Fergie Jenkins, 1971	1.02
6	Juan Marichal, 1966	1.05
7	La Marr Hoyt, 1983	1.07
8	Lew Burdette, 1961	1.09
9	Jimmy Key, 1989	1.13
10	Zane Smith, 1991	1.14
11	Greg Swindell, 1991	1.17
12	Scott McGregor, 1979	1.19
13	Jim Merritt, 1967	1.19
14	Rick Honeycutt, 1981	1.20
15	Vern Law, 1966	1.22

Strikeouts

1	Matt Kilroy, 1886	513
2	Toad Ramsey, 1886	499
3	Hugh Daily, 1884	483
4	Charley Radbourn, 1884	441
5	Charlie Buffinton, 1884	417
6	Guy Hecker, 1884	385
7	Nolan Ryan, 1973	383
8	Sandy Koufax, 1965	382
9	Bill Sweeney, 1884	374
10	Jim Galvin, 1884	369
11	Mark Baldwin, 1889	368
12	Nolan Ryan, 1974	367
13	Tim Keefe, 1883	361
14	Toad Ramsey, 1887	355
15	Rube Waddell, 1904	349
16	Bob Feller, 1946	348
17	Hardie Henderson, 1884	346
18	Jim Whitney, 1883	345
	Mickey Welch, 1884	345
20	Amos Rusie, 1890	341
	Nolan Ryan, 1977	341
22	Amos Rusie, 1891	337
23	Tim Keefe, 1888	335
24	Nolan Ryan, 1972	329
25	Nolan Ryan, 1976	327
26	Ed Morris, 1886	326
27	Tony Mullane, 1884	325
	Sam McDowell, 1965	325
29	Lady Baldwin, 1886	323
30	Tim Keefe, 1884	317
	Sandy Koufax, 1966	317
32	Bill Hutchinson, 1892	316
33	Charley Radbourn, 1883	315
34	John Clarkson, 1886	313
	Walter Johnson, 1910	313
	J.R. Richard, 1979	313
37	Steve Carlton, 1972	310
38	Dupee Shaw, 1884	309
39	Larry McKeon, 1884	308
	John Clarkson, 1885	308
	Mickey Lolich, 1971	308
42	Sandy Koufax, 1963	306
	Mike Scott, 1986	306
44	Sam McDowell, 1970	304
45	Walter Johnson, 1912	303
	J.R. Richard, 1978	303
47	Ed Morris, 1884	302
	Rube Waddell, 1903	302
49	Vida Blue, 1971	301
	Nolan Ryan, 1989	301
51	Ed Morris, 1885	298
52	Tim Keefe, 1886	297
53	Jack Lynch, 1884	292
54	Sadie McMahon, 1890	291
	Roger Clemens, 1988	291
56	Bill Hutchinson, 1890	289
	Jack Stivetts, 1890	289
	Tom Seaver, 1971	289
59	Amos Rusie, 1892	288
60	Rube Waddell, 1905	287
61	Bobby Mathews, 1884	286
	Bobby Mathews, 1885	286
	Steve Carlton, 1980	286
	Steve Carlton, 1982	286
65	John Clarkson, 1889	284
66	Dave Foutz, 1886	283
	Sam McDowell, 1968	283
	Tom Seaver, 1970	283
69	Denny McLain, 1968	280
70	Jim Galvin, 1883	279
	Sam McDowell, 1969	279
72	Bob Veale, 1965	276
	Dwight Gooden, 1984	276
74	Hal Newhouser, 1946	275
	Steve Carlton, 1983	275
76	Bob Gibson, 1970	274
	Fergie Jenkins, 1970	274
	Mario Soto, 1982	274
79	Fergie Jenkins, 1969	273
80	Larry Corcoran, 1884	272
	Mickey Welch, 1886	272
	Ed Seward, 1888	272
83	Mickey Lolich, 1969	271
84	Jim Whitney, 1884	270
	Bob Gibson, 1965	270
	Nolan Ryan, 1987	270
87	Ed Walsh, 1908	269
	Sandy Koufax, 1961	269
	Bob Gibson, 1969	269
	Frank Tanana, 1975	269
91	Larry Corcoran, 1880	268
	Bill Wise, 1884	268
	Jim Bunning, 1965	268
	Bob Gibson, 1968	268
	Dwight Gooden, 1985	268
96	Christy Mathewson, 1903	267
97	Jim Maloney, 1963	265
98	Bob Emslie, 1884	264
	Luis Tiant, 1968	264
100	3 players tied	263

Strikeouts (by era)

1876-1892
1	Matt Kilroy, 1886	513
2	Toad Ramsey, 1886	499
3	Hugh Daily, 1884	483
4	Charley Radbourn, 1884	441
5	Charlie Buffinton, 1884	417
6	Guy Hecker, 1884	385
7	Bill Sweeney, 1884	374
8	Jim Galvin, 1884	369
9	Mark Baldwin, 1889	368
10	Tim Keefe, 1883	361
11	Toad Ramsey, 1887	355
12	Hardie Henderson, 1884	346
13	Jim Whitney, 1883	345
	Mickey Welch, 1884	345
15	Amos Rusie, 1890	341

1893-1919
1	Rube Waddell, 1904	349
2	Walter Johnson, 1910	313
3	Walter Johnson, 1912	303
4	Rube Waddell, 1903	302
5	Rube Waddell, 1905	287
6	Ed Walsh, 1908	269
7	Christy Mathewson, 1903	267
8	Christy Mathewson, 1908	259
9	Ed Walsh, 1910	258
	Joe Wood, 1912	258
11	Ed Walsh, 1911	255
12	Ed Walsh, 1912	254
13	Walter Johnson, 1913	243
14	Pete Alexander, 1915	241

1920-1941
1	Dazzy Vance, 1924	262
2	Bob Feller, 1940	261
3	Bob Feller, 1941	260
4	Bob Feller, 1939	246
5	Bob Feller, 1938	240
6	Van Mungo, 1936	238
7	Bobo Newsom, 1938	226
8	Dazzy Vance, 1925	221
9	Lefty Grove, 1930	209
10	Johnny Vander Meer, 1941	202
11	Dazzy Vance, 1928	200
12	Dizzy Dean, 1933	199
13	Dazzy Vance, 1923	197
14	Dizzy Dean, 1934	195
	Dizzy Dean, 1936	195

1942-1960
1	Bob Feller, 1946	348
2	Hal Newhouser, 1946	275
3	Herb Score, 1956	263
4	Don Drysdale, 1960	246
5	Herb Score, 1955	245
6	Don Drysdale, 1959	242
7	Sam Jones, 1958	225
8	Hal Newhouser, 1945	212
9	Bob Turley, 1955	210
10	Sam Jones, 1959	209
11	Jim Bunning, 1959	201
	Jim Bunning, 1960	201
13	Robin Roberts, 1953	198
	Sam Jones, 1955	198
15	Sandy Koufax, 1960	197

1961-1992
1	Nolan Ryan, 1973	383
2	Sandy Koufax, 1965	382
3	Nolan Ryan, 1974	367
4	Nolan Ryan, 1977	341
5	Nolan Ryan, 1972	329
6	Nolan Ryan, 1976	327
7	Sam McDowell, 1965	325
8	Sandy Koufax, 1966	317
9	J.R. Richard, 1979	313
10	Steve Carlton, 1972	310
11	Mickey Lolich, 1971	308
12	Sandy Koufax, 1963	306
	Mike Scott, 1986	306
14	Sam McDowell, 1970	304
15	J.R. Richard, 1978	303

Strikeouts per Game

1	Nolan Ryan, 1987	11.48
2	Dwight Gooden, 1984	11.39
3	Nolan Ryan, 1989	11.32
4	Sam McDowell, 1965	10.71
5	Nolan Ryan, 1973	10.57
6	Nolan Ryan, 1991	10.56
7	Sandy Koufax, 1962	10.55
8	Nolan Ryan, 1972	10.43
9	Sam McDowell, 1966	10.42
10	Nolan Ryan, 1976	10.35
11	Randy Johnson, 1992	10.31
12	Nolan Ryan, 1977	10.26
13	Sandy Koufax, 1965	10.24
14	Nolan Ryan, 1990	10.24
15	Randy Johnson, 1991	10.19
16	Sandy Koufax, 1960	10.13
17	Mike Scott, 1986	10.00
18	Nolan Ryan, 1978	9.97
19	Nolan Ryan, 1974	9.93
20	Roger Clemens, 1988	9.92
21	David Cone, 1990	9.91
22	J.R. Richard, 1978	9.90
23	Nolan Ryan, 1986	9.81
24	David Cone, 1992	9.79
25	Herb Score, 1955	9.70
26	Nolan Ryan, 1984	9.65
27	J.R. Richard, 1979	9.64
28	Mario Soto, 1982	9.57
29	Tom Griffin, 1969	9.56
30	Jim Maloney, 1963	9.53
31	Sid Fernandez, 1985	9.51
32	Herb Score, 1956	9.49
33	Sandy Koufax, 1961	9.47
34	Sam McDowell, 1968	9.47
35	Frank Tanana, 1975	9.41
36	Don Wilson, 1969	9.40
37	Bob Veale, 1965	9.34
38	Nolan Ryan, 1988	9.33
39	David Cone, 1991	9.32
40	Luis Tiant, 1967	9.22
41	Mark Langston, 1986	9.21
42	Luis Tiant, 1968	9.20
43	Dave Boswell, 1966	9.19
44	Sam McDowell, 1964	9.19
45	Sonny Siebert, 1965	9.11
46	Sid Fernandez, 1988	9.10
47	Tom Seaver, 1971	9.08
48	Sid Fernandez, 1990	9.08
49	Dennis Eckersley, 1976	9.03
50	Nolan Ryan, 1979	9.01
51	Sandy Koufax, 1964	9.00
52	Sam McDowell, 1967	8.99
53	Sam McDowell, 1970	8.97
54	Bobby Witt, 1990	8.96
55	Jim Maloney, 1964	8.92
56	Mark Langston, 1989	8.92
57	Jose Rijo, 1988	8.89
58	Sandy Koufax, 1963	8.86
59	Sandy Koufax, 1966	8.83
60	Sam McDowell, 1969	8.81
61	Dupee Shaw, 1884	8.81
62	Sid Fernandez, 1986	8.81
63	Nolan Ryan, 1982	8.81
64	Tom Seaver, 1970	8.76
65	Al Downing, 1963	8.76
66	Bob Moose, 1969	8.74
67	Steve Carlton, 1983	8.73
68	Dwight Gooden, 1985	8.72
69	Steve Carlton, 1982	8.71
70	Juan Pizarro, 1961	8.69
71	Mickey Lolich, 1969	8.69
72	Vida Blue, 1971	8.68
73	Hugh Daily, 1884	8.68
74	Mark Langston, 1987	8.67
75	Bob Johnson, 1970	8.66
76	Jim Maloney, 1966	8.65
77	Dwight Gooden, 1990	8.63
78	Bruce Hurst, 1986	8.62
79	Mario Soto, 1980	8.61
80	Jim Maloney, 1965	8.60
81	Ramon Martinez, 1990	8.56
82	Tom Seaver, 1972	8.55
83	Dick Selma, 1969	8.54
84	Bob Veale, 1969	8.49
85	Steve Carlton, 1981	8.48
86	Steve Carlton, 1980	8.47
87	Mike Scott, 1987	8.47
88	Floyd Bannister, 1985	8.46
89	Hal Newhouser, 1946	8.46
90	Nolan Ryan, 1981	8.46
91	Nolan Ryan, 1975	8.45
92	Tom Gordon, 1989	8.45
93	Bob Feller, 1946	8.43
94	Roger Clemens, 1986	8.43
95	Fernando Valenzuela, 1981	8.42
96	Ed Correa, 1986	8.41
97	Sam Jones, 1956	8.40
98	Rube Waddell, 1903	8.39
99	Nolan Ryan, 1983	8.39
100	Bob Gibson, 1970	8.39

Strikeouts per Game (by era)

1876-1892
1	Dupee Shaw, 1884	8.81
2	Hugh Daily, 1884	8.68
3	Matt Kilroy, 1886	7.92
4	Charlie Gagus, 1884	7.92
5	John Clarkson, 1884	7.78
6	Toad Ramsey, 1886	7.63
7	Jim Whitney, 1884	7.23
8	Mike Dorgan, 1884	7.17
9	Walter Burke, 1884	7.13
10	Hardie Henderson, 1884	7.09
11	Tim Keefe, 1888	6.94
12	Jim McCormick, 1884	6.90
13	Bob Black, 1884	6.80
14	Lady Baldwin, 1885	6.78
15	Jack Stivetts, 1889	6.71

1893-1919
1	Rube Waddell, 1903	8.39
2	Rube Waddell, 1904	8.20
3	Rube Waddell, 1905	7.86
4	Rube Marquard, 1911	7.68
5	Joe Wood, 1911	7.54
6	Walter Johnson, 1910	7.53
7	Walter Johnson, 1912	7.41
8	Rube Waddell, 1907	7.33
9	Rube Waddell, 1908	7.31
10	Dutch Leonard, 1914	7.05
11	Red Ames, 1906	6.90
12	Rube Waddell, 1902	6.84
13	Red Ames, 1905	6.78
14	Joe Wood, 1912	6.75
15	Orval Overall, 1908	6.68

1920-1941
1	Johnny Vander Meer, 1941	8.03
2	Bob Feller, 1938	7.78
3	Dazzy Vance, 1924	7.64
4	Dazzy Vance, 1925	7.50
5	Bob Feller, 1939	7.46
6	Dazzy Vance, 1926	7.46
7	Bob Feller, 1940	7.33
8	Van Mungo, 1936	6.87
9	Bob Feller, 1941	6.82
10	Van Mungo, 1937	6.82
11	Lefty Grove, 1926	6.77
12	Bill Hallahan, 1930	6.71
13	George Earnshaw, 1928	6.65
14	Red Ruffing, 1932	6.60
15	Lefty Grove, 1930	6.46

1942-1960
1	Sandy Koufax, 1960	10.13
2	Herb Score, 1955	9.70
3	Herb Score, 1956	9.49
4	Hal Newhouser, 1946	8.46
5	Bob Feller, 1946	8.43
6	Sam Jones, 1956	8.40
7	Herb Score, 1959	8.23
8	Don Drysdale, 1960	8.23
9	Sam Jones, 1958	8.10
10	Don Drysdale, 1959	8.05
11	Bob Turley, 1957	7.76
12	Camilo Pascual, 1956	7.73
13	Bob Turley, 1955	7.66
14	Stan Williams, 1960	7.60
15	Sam Jones, 1957	7.59

1961-1992
1	Nolan Ryan, 1987	11.48
2	Dwight Gooden, 1984	11.39
3	Nolan Ryan, 1989	11.32
4	Sam McDowell, 1965	10.71
5	Nolan Ryan, 1973	10.57
6	Nolan Ryan, 1991	10.56
7	Sandy Koufax, 1962	10.55
8	Nolan Ryan, 1972	10.43
9	Sam McDowell, 1966	10.42
10	Nolan Ryan, 1976	10.35
11	Randy Johnson, 1992	10.31
12	Nolan Ryan, 1977	10.26
13	Sandy Koufax, 1965	10.24
14	Nolan Ryan, 1990	10.24
15	Randy Johnson, 1991	10.19

Ratio

1	Guy Hecker, 1882	6.92
2	Jim McCormick, 1884	7.07
3	Walter Johnson, 1913	7.26
4	Charlie Sweeney, 1884	7.31
5	Addie Joss, 1908	7.31
6	Charlie Sweeney, 1884	7.41
7	Christy Mathewson, 1909	7.45
8	Ed Walsh, 1910	7.47
9	Dupee Shaw, 1884	7.53
10	George Bradley, 1880	7.53
11	Tim Keefe, 1880	7.54
12	Christy Mathewson, 1908	7.60
13	Henry Boyle, 1884	7.68
14	Mordecai Brown, 1908	7.72
15	Denny Driscoll, 1882	7.79
16	Pete Alexander, 1915	7.82
17	Sandy Koufax, 1965	7.83
18	Juan Marichal, 1966	7.88
19	Bob Gibson, 1968	7.89
20	Roger Nelson, 1972	7.89
21	Dave McNally, 1968	7.91
22	Ed Walsh, 1908	7.91
23	Sandy Koufax, 1963	7.96
24	Luis Tiant, 1968	7.98
25	George Bradley, 1876	7.98
26	Jim Whitney, 1884	8.01
27	Guy Hecker, 1884	8.02
28	Mordecai Brown, 1909	8.04
29	Cy Young, 1908	8.07
30	Cy Young, 1905	8.08
31	Tommy Bond, 1876	8.12
32	Babe Adams, 1919	8.17
33	Russ Ford, 1910	8.17
34	Monte Ward, 1880	8.26
35	Lady Baldwin, 1885	8.28
36	Eddie Cicotte, 1917	8.28
37	Dutch Leonard, 1914	8.29
38	Charley Radbourn, 1884	8.30
39	Denny McLain, 1968	8.30
40	Jim Hunter, 1972	8.32
41	Doc White, 1906	8.33
42	Silver King, 1888	8.34
43	Pete Alexander, 1919	8.35
44	Juan Marichal, 1965	8.35
45	Don Sutton, 1972	8.35
46	Sandy Koufax, 1964	8.35
47	Ed Morris, 1884	8.36
48	Mike Scott, 1986	8.37
49	Christy Mathewson, 1905	8.42
50	Larry Corcoran, 1880	8.44
51	Addie Joss, 1906	8.49
52	Tim Keefe, 1883	8.49
53	Reb Russell, 1916	8.51
54	Cy Young, 1904	8.53
55	Mordecai Brown, 1906	8.53
56	Ron Guidry, 1978	8.55
57	Claude Hendrix, 1914	8.55
58	Warren Hacker, 1952	8.56
59	Bill Burns, 1908	8.56
60	Jack Lynch, 1884	8.56
61	Jack Chesbro, 1904	8.57
62	John Clarkson, 1885	8.58
63	Walter Johnson, 1912	8.58
64	Joe Horlen, 1964	8.59
65	Ed Walsh, 1909	8.60
66	Perry Werden, 1884	8.60
67	Chief Bender, 1910	8.60
68	John Tudor, 1985	8.61
69	Walter Johnson, 1910	8.61
70	Addie Joss, 1909	8.64
71	Tom Seaver, 1971	8.64
72	Russ Ford, 1914	8.66
73	Bill Bernhard, 1902	8.68
74	Tim Keefe, 1888	8.68
75	Vida Blue, 1971	8.68
76	Charlie Buffinton, 1888	8.70
77	Lady Baldwin, 1886	8.70
78	Larry Corcoran, 1882	8.70
79	Frank Smith, 1908	8.71
80	Tony Mullane, 1883	8.71
81	Bret Saberhagen, 1989	8.71
82	Christy Mathewson, 1907	8.71
83	Joe Horlen, 1967	8.72
84	Jim Devlin, 1876	8.73
85	Tim Keefe, 1884	8.73
86	Frank Smith, 1909	8.73
87	Mordecai Brown, 1907	8.73
88	Charlie Getzien, 1884	8.74
89	Dwight Gooden, 1985	8.75
90	Fred Anderson, 1917	8.78
91	Charlie Ferguson, 1886	8.78
92	Dick Hughes, 1967	8.78
93	Ray Caldwell, 1914	8.79
94	Turk Farrell, 1963	8.81
95	Pascual Perez, 1988	8.81
96	Charley Radbourn, 1883	8.81
97	Walter Johnson, 1918	8.83
98	Addie Joss, 1903	8.85
99	Dick Rudolph, 1916	8.86
100	Chief Bender, 1909	8.86

Earned Run Average

1	Tim Keefe, 1880	0.86
2	Dutch Leonard, 1914	0.96
3	Mordecai Brown, 1906	1.04
4	Bob Gibson, 1968	1.12
5	Christy Mathewson, 1909	1.14
6	Walter Johnson, 1913	1.14
7	Jack Pfiester, 1907	1.15
8	Addie Joss, 1908	1.16
9	Carl Lundgren, 1907	1.17
10	Denny Driscoll, 1882	1.21
11	Pete Alexander, 1915	1.22
12	George Bradley, 1876	1.23
13	Cy Young, 1908	1.26
14	Ed Walsh, 1910	1.27
15	Walter Johnson, 1918	1.27
16	Christy Mathewson, 1905	1.28
17	Guy Hecker, 1882	1.30
18	Jack Coombs, 1910	1.30
19	Mordecai Brown, 1909	1.31
20	Jack Taylor, 1902	1.33
21	Walter Johnson, 1910	1.35
22	George Bradley, 1880	1.38
23	Charley Radbourn, 1884	1.38
24	Mordecai Brown, 1907	1.39
25	Walter Johnson, 1912	1.39
26	Harry Krause, 1909	1.39
27	Ed Walsh, 1909	1.41
28	Ed Walsh, 1908	1.42
29	Ed Reulbach, 1905	1.42
30	Orval Overall, 1909	1.42
31	Christy Mathewson, 1908	1.43
32	Fred Anderson, 1917	1.44
33	Mordecai Brown, 1908	1.47
34	Rube Waddell, 1905	1.48
35	Joe Wood, 1915	1.49
36	Walter Johnson, 1919	1.49
37	Jack Pfiester, 1906	1.51
38	Monte Ward, 1878	1.51
39	Harry McCormick, 1882	1.52
40	Doc White, 1906	1.52
41	George McQuillan, 1908	1.53
42	Dwight Gooden, 1985	1.53
43	Eddie Cicotte, 1917	1.53
44	Will White, 1882	1.54
45	Jim McCormick, 1884	1.54
46	Charlie Sweeney, 1884	1.55
47	Cy Morgan, 1910	1.55
48	Walter Johnson, 1915	1.55
49	Pete Alexander, 1916	1.55
50	Howie Camnitz, 1908	1.56
51	Jim Devlin, 1876	1.56
52	Tim Keefe, 1885	1.58
53	Fred Toney, 1915	1.58
54	Eddie Cicotte, 1913	1.58
55	Rube Marquard, 1916	1.58
56	Chief Bender, 1910	1.58
57	Barney Pelty, 1906	1.59
58	Addie Joss, 1904	1.59
59	Ed Walsh, 1907	1.60
60	Luis Tiant, 1968	1.60
61	Joe McGinnity, 1904	1.61
62	Ray Collins, 1910	1.62
63	Rube Waddell, 1904	1.62
64	Howie Camnitz, 1909	1.62
65	Cy Young, 1901	1.62
66	Spud Chandler, 1943	1.64
67	Ernie Shore, 1915	1.64
68	Walter Johnson, 1908	1.64
69	Silver King, 1888	1.64
70	Ed Summers, 1908	1.64
71	Dean Chance, 1964	1.65
72	Ed Reulbach, 1906	1.65
73	Russ Ford, 1910	1.65
74	Chief Bender, 1909	1.66
75	Sam Leever, 1907	1.66
76	Carl Hubbell, 1933	1.66
77	Mickey Welch, 1885	1.66
78	Candy Cummings, 1876	1.67
79	Joe Wood, 1910	1.68
80	Tommy Bond, 1876	1.68
81	Billy Taylor, 1884	1.68
82	Orval Overall, 1907	1.68
83	Ned Garvin, 1904	1.68
84	Ed Reulbach, 1907	1.69
85	Claude Hendrix, 1914	1.69
86	Bill Burns, 1908	1.69
87	Nolan Ryan, 1981	1.69
88	Jim McCormick, 1878	1.69
89	Rube Foster, 1914	1.70
90	Addie Joss, 1909	1.71
91	Ed Killian, 1909	1.71
92	Walter Johnson, 1914	1.72
93	Doc White, 1909	1.72
94	Bill Doak, 1914	1.72
95	Addie Joss, 1906	1.72
	Pete Alexander, 1919	1.72
97	Sandy Koufax, 1966	1.73
98	Bob Ewing, 1907	1.73
99	Vic Willis, 1906	1.73
100	Sandy Koufax, 1964	1.74

Earned Run Average (by era)

1876-1892
1	Tim Keefe, 1880	0.86
2	Denny Driscoll, 1882	1.21
3	George Bradley, 1876	1.23
4	Guy Hecker, 1882	1.30
5	George Bradley, 1880	1.38
6	Charley Radbourn, 1884	1.38
7	Monte Ward, 1878	1.51
8	Harry McCormick, 1882	1.52
9	Will White, 1882	1.54
10	Jim McCormick, 1884	1.54
11	Charlie Sweeney, 1884	1.55
12	Jim Devlin, 1876	1.56
13	Tim Keefe, 1885	1.58
14	Silver King, 1888	1.64
15	Mickey Welch, 1885	1.66

1893-1919
1	Dutch Leonard, 1914	0.96
2	Mordecai Brown, 1906	1.04
3	Christy Mathewson, 1909	1.14
4	Walter Johnson, 1913	1.14
5	Jack Pfiester, 1907	1.15
6	Addie Joss, 1908	1.16
7	Carl Lundgren, 1907	1.17
8	Pete Alexander, 1915	1.22
9	Cy Young, 1908	1.26
10	Ed Walsh, 1910	1.27
11	Walter Johnson, 1918	1.27
12	Christy Mathewson, 1905	1.28
13	Jack Coombs, 1910	1.30
14	Mordecai Brown, 1909	1.31
15	Jack Taylor, 1902	1.33

1920-1941
1	Carl Hubbell, 1933	1.66
2	Pete Alexander, 1920	1.91
3	Dolf Luque, 1923	1.93
4	Lon Warneke, 1933	2.00
5	Lefty Grove, 1931	2.06
6	Dazzy Vance, 1928	2.09
7	Babe Adams, 1920	2.16
8	Hal Schumacher, 1933	2.16
9	Dazzy Vance, 1924	2.16
10	Burleigh Grimes, 1920	2.22
11	Elmer Riddle, 1941	2.24
12	Bill Walker, 1931	2.26
13	Wilcy Moore, 1927	2.28
14	Bucky Walters, 1939	2.29
15	Carl Hubbell, 1934	2.30

1942-1960
1	Spud Chandler, 1943	1.64
2	Mort Cooper, 1942	1.78
3	Hal Newhouser, 1945	1.81
4	Max Lanier, 1943	1.90
5	Hal Newhouser, 1946	1.94
6	Billy Pierce, 1955	1.97
7	Whitey Ford, 1958	2.01
8	Al Benton, 1945	2.02
9	Allie Reynolds, 1952	2.06
10	Ted Lyons, 1942	2.10
11	Howie Pollet, 1946	2.10
12	Spud Chandler, 1946	2.10
13	Warren Spahn, 1953	2.10
14	Dizzy Trout, 1944	2.12
15	Roger Wolff, 1945	2.12

1961-1992
1	Bob Gibson, 1968	1.12
2	Dwight Gooden, 1985	1.53
3	Luis Tiant, 1968	1.60
4	Dean Chance, 1964	1.65
5	Nolan Ryan, 1981	1.69
6	Sandy Koufax, 1966	1.73
7	Sandy Koufax, 1964	1.74
8	Ron Guidry, 1978	1.74
9	Tom Seaver, 1971	1.76
10	Sam McDowell, 1968	1.81
11	Vida Blue, 1971	1.82
12	Phil Niekro, 1967	1.87
13	Joe Horlen, 1964	1.88
14	Sandy Koufax, 1963	1.88
15	Luis Tiant, 1972	1.91

Adjusted Earned Run Average

1	Tim Keefe, 1880	294
2	Dutch Leonard, 1914	280
3	Walter Johnson, 1913	258
4	Bob Gibson, 1968	258
5	Mordecai Brown, 1906	254
6	Walter Johnson, 1912	239
7	Christy Mathewson, 1905	230
8	Dwight Gooden, 1985	226
9	Pete Alexander, 1915	225
10	Christy Mathewson, 1909	224
11	Lefty Grove, 1931	218
12	Cy Young, 1901	217
13	Jack Pfiester, 1907	216
14	Denny Driscoll, 1882	216
15	Walter Johnson, 1919	216
16	Walter Johnson, 1918	214
17	Carl Lundgren, 1907	213
18	Roger Clemens, 1990	211
19	Ed Reulbach, 1905	210
20	Ron Guidry, 1978	208
21	Addie Joss, 1908	206
22	Jim McCormick, 1884	205
23	Charley Radbourn, 1884	205
24	Jack Taylor, 1902	203
25	Billy Pierce, 1955	201
26	Dolf Luque, 1923	200
27	Dean Chance, 1964	199
28	Silver King, 1888	198
29	Spud Chandler, 1943	197
30	Al Maul, 1895	196
31	Cy Young, 1908	195
32	Nolan Ryan, 1981	195
33	Hal Newhouser, 1945	194
34	Mordecai Brown, 1909	194
35	Tom Seaver, 1971	194
36	Carl Hubbell, 1933	193
37	Mort Cooper, 1942	193
38	Walter Johnson, 1915	191
39	Monty Stratton, 1937	191
40	Guy Hecker, 1882	191
41	Lefty Gomez, 1937	191
42	Sandy Koufax, 1966	191
43	Ed Siever, 1902	191
44	Clark Griffith, 1898	191
45	Dazzy Vance, 1928	190
46	Vean Gregg, 1911	189
47	Lefty Grove, 1936	189
48	Ed Walsh, 1910	189
49	Amos Rusie, 1894	189
50	Hal Newhouser, 1946	189
51	Dazzy Vance, 1930	188
52	Billy Rhines, 1896	188
53	Wilbur Wood, 1971	188
54	Jack Stivetts, 1889	188
55	Joe Wood, 1915	187
56	Warren Spahn, 1953	187
57	Sandy Koufax, 1964	187
58	Lefty Grove, 1939	186
59	Eddie Cicotte, 1913	185
60	Walter Johnson, 1910	185
61	Luis Tiant, 1968	185
62	Lefty Grove, 1930	184
63	Hank Aguirre, 1962	184
64	Joe Horlen, 1964	184
65	Henry Boyle, 1886	184
66	Vida Blue, 1971	183
67	John Tudor, 1985	183
68	Harry Brecheen, 1948	183
69	Jack Coombs, 1910	183
70	Charlie Sweeney, 1884	182
71	Billy Rhines, 1890	182
72	Steve Carlton, 1972	182
73	Fred Toney, 1915	182
74	Russ Ford, 1914	181
75	Johnny Allen, 1937	181
76	Rube Waddell, 1905	180
77	Mordecai Brown, 1907	179
78	Orval Overall, 1909	179
79	Rube Waddell, 1902	179
80	Joe Wood, 1912	178
81	Bret Saberhagen, 1989	178
82	Phil Niekro, 1967	178
83	Max Lanier, 1943	177
84	Fred Anderson, 1917	177
85	Billy Taylor, 1884	177
86	Cy Young, 1892	176
87	Johnny Antonelli, 1954	176
88	Whitey Ford, 1958	176
89	Lefty Grove, 1935	176
90	Jack Pfiester, 1906	175
91	Eddie Cicotte, 1919	175
92	Claude Hendrix, 1914	175
93	Mel Harder, 1934	174
94	Lefty Gomez, 1934	174
95	Harry McCormick, 1882	174
96	Al Benton, 1945	174
97	George Bradley, 1876	174
98	Tom Seaver, 1973	174
99	Jim Devlin, 1876	174
100	Dazzy Vance, 1924	174

Adjusted ERA (by era)

1876-1892

1	Tim Keefe, 1880	294
2	Denny Driscoll, 1882	216
3	Jim McCormick, 1884	205
4	Charley Radbourn, 1884	205
5	Silver King, 1888	198
6	Guy Hecker, 1882	191
7	Jack Stivetts, 1889	188
8	Henry Boyle, 1886	184
9	Charlie Sweeney, 1884	182
10	Billy Rhines, 1890	182
11	Billy Taylor, 1884	177
12	Cy Young, 1892	176
13	Harry McCormick, 1882	174
14	George Bradley, 1876	174
15	Jim Devlin, 1876	174

1893-1919

1	Dutch Leonard, 1914	280
2	Walter Johnson, 1913	258
3	Mordecai Brown, 1906	254
4	Walter Johnson, 1912	239
5	Christy Mathewson, 1905	230
6	Pete Alexander, 1915	225
7	Christy Mathewson, 1909	224
8	Cy Young, 1901	217
9	Jack Pfiester, 1907	216
10	Walter Johnson, 1919	216
11	Walter Johnson, 1918	214
12	Carl Lundgren, 1907	213
13	Ed Reulbach, 1905	210
14	Addie Joss, 1908	206
15	Jack Taylor, 1902	203

1920-1941

1	Lefty Grove, 1931	218
2	Dolf Luque, 1923	200
3	Carl Hubbell, 1933	193
4	Monty Stratton, 1937	191
5	Lefty Gomez, 1937	191
6	Dazzy Vance, 1928	190
7	Lefty Grove, 1936	189
8	Dazzy Vance, 1930	188
9	Lefty Grove, 1939	186
10	Lefty Grove, 1930	184
11	Johnny Allen, 1937	181
12	Lefty Grove, 1935	176
13	Mel Harder, 1934	174
14	Lefty Gomez, 1934	174
15	Dazzy Vance, 1924	174

1942-1960

1	Billy Pierce, 1955	201
2	Spud Chandler, 1943	197
3	Hal Newhouser, 1945	194
4	Mort Cooper, 1942	193
5	Hal Newhouser, 1946	189
6	Warren Spahn, 1953	187
7	Harry Brecheen, 1948	183
8	Max Lanier, 1943	177
9	Johnny Antonelli, 1954	176
10	Whitey Ford, 1958	176
11	Al Benton, 1945	174
12	Hoyt Wilhelm, 1959	173
13	Ted Lyons, 1942	172

1961-1992

1	Bob Gibson, 1968	258
2	Dwight Gooden, 1985	226
3	Roger Clemens, 1990	211
4	Ron Guidry, 1978	208
5	Dean Chance, 1964	199
6	Nolan Ryan, 1981	195
7	Tom Seaver, 1971	194
8	Sandy Koufax, 1966	191
9	Wilbur Wood, 1971	188
10	Sandy Koufax, 1964	187
11	Luis Tiant, 1968	185
12	Hank Aguirre, 1962	184
13	Joe Horlen, 1964	184
14	Vida Blue, 1971	183
15	John Tudor, 1985	183

Pitching Runs

1	Amos Rusie, 1894	125.7
2	Charley Radbourn, 1884	120.9
3	Guy Hecker, 1884	108.0
4	Silver King, 1888	92.3
5	John Clarkson, 1889	88.7
6	Cy Young, 1901	84.2
7	Matt Kilroy, 1887	80.4
8	Pink Hawley, 1895	79.1
9	Silver King, 1890	78.9
10	Walter Johnson, 1912	78.7
11	Will White, 1883	77.7
12	Amos Rusie, 1893	76.9
13	Charley Radbourn, 1883	76.5
14	Dave Foutz, 1886	75.2
15	Lefty Grove, 1931	74.5
16	Dolf Luque, 1923	74.2
17	Jouett Meekin, 1894	73.9
18	Scott Stratton, 1890	72.3
19	Billy Rhines, 1890	72.2
20	Lefty Gomez, 1937	70.9
21	Jim Galvin, 1884	69.8
22	Walter Johnson, 1913	68.8
23	George Bradley, 1876	68.8
24	Cy Young, 1892	68.5
25	Kid Nichols, 1897	68.4
26	Lefty Grove, 1930	68.4
27	Dazzy Vance, 1930	67.9
28	Lefty Gomez, 1934	67.7
29	Elmer Smith, 1887	67.6
30	Sandy Koufax, 1966	67.5
31	John Clarkson, 1885	67.1
32	Red Faber, 1921	66.4
33	Toad Ramsey, 1886	65.7
34	Christy Mathewson, 1905	65.0
35	Warren Spahn, 1953	64.5
36	Pete Alexander, 1915	64.1
37	Kid Nichols, 1898	63.5
38	Amos Rusie, 1897	63.5
39	Kid Nichols, 1896	63.5
40	Ted Breitenstein, 1893	63.4
41	Dwight Gooden, 1985	63.4
42	Kid Nichols, 1890	63.2
43	Mickey Welch, 1885	63.1
44	Bob Gibson, 1968	63.1
45	Bob Caruthers, 1885	63.1
46	Bob Feller, 1940	63.0
47	Lefty Grove, 1936	62.8
48	Cy Young, 1894	62.7
49	Clark Griffith, 1898	62.6
50	Cy Young, 1895	62.5
51	Ed Morris, 1886	61.9
52	Amos Rusie, 1890	61.6
53	Ron Guidry, 1978	61.4
54	Carl Hubbell, 1934	61.3
55	Will White, 1882	61.3
56	Cy Young, 1893	61.1
57	Dean Chance, 1964	61.1
58	Tim Keefe, 1883	61.1
59	Claude Hendrix, 1914	61.0
60	Cy Young, 1902	60.8
61	Jim Palmer, 1975	60.6
62	Ed Seward, 1888	60.5
63	Thornton Lee, 1941	59.4
64	Dazzy Vance, 1928	59.2
65	Robin Roberts, 1953	59.1
66	Dazzy Vance, 1924	58.6
67	Charlie Ferguson, 1886	58.6
68	Bob Feller, 1939	58.3
69	Bill Hutchinson, 1890	58.2
70	Lady Baldwin, 1886	58.2
71	Bucky Walters, 1939	57.8
72	Kid Nichols, 1895	57.8
73	Carl Hubbell, 1936	57.8
74	John Clarkson, 1887	57.7
75	Ed Morris, 1885	57.7
76	Jesse Duryea, 1889	57.5
77	Carl Hubbell, 1933	57.5
78	Wilbur Wood, 1971	57.4
79	Guy Hecker, 1885	57.2
80	Tony Mullane, 1883	57.0
81	Vida Blue, 1971	57.0
82	Steve Carlton, 1972	56.9
83	Walter Johnson, 1919	56.1
84	Sandy Koufax, 1965	56.0
85	Warren Spahn, 1947	55.7
86	Tim Keefe, 1885	55.3
87	Win Mercer, 1894	55.0
88	Bill Hoffer, 1895	54.9
89	Bob Feller, 1946	54.5
90	Charlie Buffinton, 1884	54.5
91	Kid Nichols, 1893	54.3
92	Walter Johnson, 1918	54.3
93	Tom Seaver, 1971	54.3
94	Hal Newhouser, 1945	54.2
95	Joe Wood, 1912	53.9
96	Toad Ramsey, 1887	53.8
97	Mel Harder, 1934	53.6
98	Matt Kilroy, 1889	53.6
99	Tim Keefe, 1888	53.5
100	Red Ehret, 1890	53.4

Adjusted Pitching Runs

1	Amos Rusie, 1894	121.7
2	Charley Radbourn, 1884	108.9
3	Silver King, 1888	105.2
4	John Clarkson, 1889	98.9
5	Guy Hecker, 1884	95.9
6	Silver King, 1890	84.5
7	John Clarkson, 1885	82.2
8	Jim Galvin, 1884	81.9
9	John Clarkson, 1887	81.8
10	Jim Devlin, 1876	79.7
11	Walter Johnson, 1912	79.3
12	Cy Young, 1901	78.6
13	Lefty Grove, 1931	78.2
14	Toad Ramsey, 1886	78.1
15	Amos Rusie, 1893	76.4
16	Kid Nichols, 1897	74.9
17	Dave Foutz, 1886	74.6
18	Will White, 1883	74.1
19	Cy Young, 1892	73.7
20	Charley Radbourn, 1883	72.7
21	Kid Nichols, 1890	71.8
22	Billy Rhines, 1890	71.7
23	Cy Young, 1893	71.4
24	Scott Stratton, 1890	71.4
25	Kid Nichols, 1895	71.3
26	Cy Young, 1895	70.9
27	Kid Nichols, 1896	70.9
28	Lefty Grove, 1936	70.6
29	Jouett Meekin, 1894	70.3
30	Elmer Smith, 1887	69.9
31	Walter Johnson, 1913	69.6
32	Dolf Luque, 1923	69.3
33	Lefty Grove, 1930	69.1
34	Cy Young, 1894	69.0
35	Matt Kilroy, 1887	67.4
36	Kid Nichols, 1898	67.3
37	Kid Nichols, 1893	67.1
38	Tony Mullane, 1883	66.3
39	Dazzy Vance, 1930	66.2
40	Ted Breitenstein, 1893	66.2
41	Pink Hawley, 1895	66.2
42	Jack Stivetts, 1891	65.7
43	Lefty Gomez, 1937	65.5
44	Jim Devlin, 1877	65.5
45	Red Faber, 1921	64.6
46	Bob Caruthers, 1885	64.3
47	Bill Hutchinson, 1890	64.2
48	John Clarkson, 1886	64.0
49	Pete Alexander, 1915	63.7
50	Vic Willis, 1899	63.4
51	Tim Keefe, 1883	62.7
52	Christy Mathewson, 1905	62.3
53	Wilbur Wood, 1971	62.2
54	Steve Carlton, 1972	62.2
55	Lefty Grove, 1935	61.9
56	Clark Griffith, 1898	61.6
57	Cy Young, 1902	60.8
58	Jesse Duryea, 1889	60.1
59	Bob Gibson, 1968	60.0
60	Cy Young, 1896	59.9
61	Kid Nichols, 1891	59.8
62	Toad Ramsey, 1887	59.7
63	Dan Casey, 1887	59.5
64	Hal Newhouser, 1945	59.4
65	Dwight Gooden, 1985	59.2
66	Elton Chamberlain, 1889	59.0
67	Will White, 1882	58.8
68	Matt Kilroy, 1889	58.7
69	Dazzy Vance, 1928	58.7
70	Lady Baldwin, 1886	58.3
71	Charlie Ferguson, 1886	58.1
72	Ed Morris, 1886	58.0
73	Amos Rusie, 1897	57.9
74	Mark Baldwin, 1890	57.8
75	George Bradley, 1876	57.8
76	Thornton Lee, 1941	57.7
77	Kid Gleason, 1890	57.5
78	Amos Rusie, 1890	57.5
79	Cy Young, 1899	57.4
80	Ron Guidry, 1978	57.1
81	Bob Feller, 1940	57.1
82	Joe Wood, 1912	57.0
83	Nig Cuppy, 1895	56.7
84	Dizzy Trout, 1944	56.6
85	Bobo Newsom, 1940	56.5
86	Nig Cuppy, 1896	56.5
87	Sandy Koufax, 1966	56.3
88	Ed Seward, 1888	56.2
89	Robin Roberts, 1953	56.1
90	Tony Mullane, 1884	56.1
91	Guy Hecker, 1885	56.0
92	Hal Newhouser, 1946	55.8
93	Ed Morris, 1885	55.8
94	Walter Johnson, 1919	55.5
95	Silver King, 1889	55.1
96	Mel Harder, 1934	55.0
97	Mickey Welch, 1885	54.8
98	Bucky Walters, 1939	54.8
99	Lefty Grove, 1932	54.6
100	Carl Hubbell, 1934	54.5

Pitching Wins

1	Charley Radbourn, 1884	10.8
2	Guy Hecker, 1884	9.9
3	Amos Rusie, 1894	9.6
4	Silver King, 1888	8.5
5	Walter Johnson, 1912	7.9
6	John Clarkson, 1889	7.7
7	Cy Young, 1901	7.6
8	Walter Johnson, 1913	7.3
9	Bob Gibson, 1968	7.2
10	Dolf Luque, 1923	7.1
11	Pete Alexander, 1915	7.1
12	Sandy Koufax, 1966	7.1
13	Lefty Grove, 1931	6.9
14	Will White, 1883	6.8
15	Christy Mathewson, 1905	6.7
16	Charley Radbourn, 1883	6.7
17	Dwight Gooden, 1985	6.7
18	Dave Foutz, 1886	6.6
19	Lefty Gomez, 1937	6.5
20	Matt Kilroy, 1887	6.5
21	Dean Chance, 1964	6.4
22	Billy Rhines, 1890	6.4
23	Pink Hawley, 1895	6.4
24	Scott Stratton, 1890	6.4
25	Cy Young, 1892	6.3
26	Claude Hendrix, 1914	6.3
27	Ron Guidry, 1978	6.3
28	John Clarkson, 1885	6.3
29	Amos Rusie, 1893	6.3
30	Lefty Gomez, 1934	6.3
31	Silver King, 1890	6.3
32	Jim Galvin, 1884	6.2
33	Warren Spahn, 1953	6.2
34	Red Faber, 1921	6.2
35	Jim Palmer, 1975	6.2
36	Lefty Grove, 1930	6.2
37	Wilbur Wood, 1971	6.2
38	Vida Blue, 1971	6.1
39	Steve Carlton, 1972	6.1
40	Carl Hubbell, 1933	6.1
41	Walter Johnson, 1918	6.1
42	George Bradley, 1876	6.1
43	Dazzy Vance, 1930	6.0
44	Carl Hubbell, 1934	6.0
45	Bob Feller, 1940	5.9
46	Kid Nichols, 1898	5.9
47	Mickey Welch, 1885	5.9
48	Sandy Koufax, 1965	5.9
49	Walter Johnson, 1919	5.9
50	Kid Nichols, 1897	5.9
51	Clark Griffith, 1898	5.8
52	Tom Seaver, 1971	5.8
53	Dazzy Vance, 1924	5.8
54	Hal Newhouser, 1945	5.8
55	Bucky Walters, 1939	5.8
56	Dazzy Vance, 1928	5.8
57	Cy Young, 1902	5.8
58	Toad Ramsey, 1886	5.8
59	Thornton Lee, 1941	5.8
60	Ed Walsh, 1908	5.8
61	Ed Walsh, 1910	5.7
62	Bob Feller, 1946	5.7
63	Robin Roberts, 1953	5.7
64	Bob Caruthers, 1885	5.7
65	Jouett Meekin, 1894	5.7
66	Carl Hubbell, 1936	5.6
67	Will White, 1882	5.6
68	Kid Nichols, 1890	5.6
69	Ed Seward, 1888	5.6
70	Lefty Grove, 1936	5.5
71	Jack Taylor, 1902	5.5
72	Walter Johnson, 1915	5.5
73	Warren Spahn, 1947	5.5
74	Amos Rusie, 1890	5.5
75	Elmer Smith, 1887	5.5
76	Mordecai Brown, 1906	5.5
77	Amos Rusie, 1897	5.4
78	Ed Morris, 1886	5.4
79	Mordecai Brown, 1909	5.4
80	Walter Johnson, 1910	5.4
81	Joe McGinnity, 1904	5.4
82	Dizzy Trout, 1944	5.4
83	Joe Wood, 1912	5.4
84	Kid Nichols, 1896	5.4
85	Tim Keefe, 1883	5.4
86	Bob Feller, 1939	5.4
87	Hal Newhouser, 1946	5.3
88	John Tudor, 1985	5.3
89	Ed Reulbach, 1905	5.3
90	Jack Coombs, 1910	5.3
91	Tom Seaver, 1973	5.3
92	Pete Alexander, 1920	5.3
93	Charlie Ferguson, 1886	5.3
94	Sandy Koufax, 1963	5.3
95	Pete Alexander, 1916	5.3
96	Lady Baldwin, 1886	5.3
97	Tim Keefe, 1888	5.2
98	Juan Marichal, 1969	5.2
99	Tim Keefe, 1885	5.2
100	Ted Breitenstein, 1893	5.2

Adjusted Pitching Wins

1	Charley Radbourn, 1884	9.7
2	Silver King, 1888	9.7
3	Amos Rusie, 1894	9.3
4	Guy Hecker, 1884	8.8
5	John Clarkson, 1889	8.6
6	Walter Johnson, 1912	7.9
7	John Clarkson, 1885	7.7
8	Walter Johnson, 1913	7.4
9	Jim Galvin, 1884	7.3
10	Lefty Grove, 1931	7.3
11	Cy Young, 1901	7.1
12	Pete Alexander, 1915	7.1
13	Jim Devlin, 1876	7.0
14	John Clarkson, 1887	6.9
15	Bob Gibson, 1968	6.9
16	Toad Ramsey, 1886	6.8
17	Cy Young, 1892	6.8
18	Silver King, 1890	6.7
19	Wilbur Wood, 1971	6.7
20	Steve Carlton, 1972	6.7
21	Dolf Luque, 1923	6.7
22	Dave Foutz, 1886	6.5
23	Will White, 1883	6.5
24	Christy Mathewson, 1905	6.5
25	Kid Nichols, 1897	6.4
26	Kid Nichols, 1890	6.4
27	Billy Rhines, 1890	6.4
28	Hal Newhouser, 1945	6.4
29	Charley Radbourn, 1883	6.3
30	Kid Nichols, 1898	6.3
31	Scott Stratton, 1890	6.3
32	Amos Rusie, 1893	6.3
33	Lefty Grove, 1930	6.3
34	Lefty Grove, 1936	6.2
35	Dwight Gooden, 1985	6.2
36	Red Faber, 1921	6.0
37	Kid Nichols, 1896	6.0
38	Lefty Gomez, 1937	6.0
39	Dizzy Trout, 1944	6.0
40	Sandy Koufax, 1966	5.9
41	Ron Guidry, 1978	5.9
42	Walter Johnson, 1918	5.9
43	Cy Young, 1893	5.9
44	Hal Newhouser, 1946	5.8
45	Dazzy Vance, 1930	5.8
46	Tony Mullane, 1883	5.8
47	Jim Devlin, 1877	5.8
48	Walter Johnson, 1919	5.8
49	Lefty Grove, 1935	5.8
50	John Clarkson, 1886	5.8
51	Bob Caruthers, 1885	5.8
52	Kid Nichols, 1895	5.8
53	Cy Young, 1902	5.8
54	Clark Griffith, 1898	5.8
55	Vic Willis, 1899	5.7
56	Cy Young, 1895	5.7
57	Dazzy Vance, 1928	5.7
58	Joe Wood, 1912	5.7
59	Bill Hutchinson, 1890	5.7
60	Elmer Smith, 1887	5.7
61	Jack Stivetts, 1891	5.7
62	Vida Blue, 1971	5.7
63	Walter Johnson, 1915	5.6
64	Gaylord Perry, 1972	5.6
65	Carl Hubbell, 1933	5.6
66	Tom Seaver, 1971	5.6
67	Pete Alexander, 1920	5.6
68	Thornton Lee, 1941	5.6
69	Roger Clemens, 1990	5.5
70	Tim Keefe, 1883	5.5
71	Kid Nichols, 1893	5.5
72	Bucky Walters, 1939	5.5
73	Mordecai Brown, 1906	5.5
74	Mort Cooper, 1942	5.5
75	Matt Kilroy, 1887	5.5
76	Cy Falkenberg, 1914	5.4
77	Pete Alexander, 1916	5.4
78	Ted Breitenstein, 1893	5.4
79	Dazzy Vance, 1924	5.4
80	Robin Roberts, 1953	5.4
81	Will White, 1882	5.4
82	Bob Feller, 1940	5.4
83	Jouett Meekin, 1894	5.4
84	Bill Hands, 1969	5.4
85	Pink Hawley, 1895	5.4
86	Joe McGinnity, 1904	5.3
87	Kid Nichols, 1891	5.3
88	Bobo Newsom, 1940	5.3
89	Dean Chance, 1964	5.3
90	Carl Hubbell, 1934	5.3
91	Bert Blyleven, 1973	5.3
92	Dizzy Dean, 1934	5.3
93	Cy Young, 1894	5.3
94	Ed Walsh, 1908	5.3
95	Walter Johnson, 1910	5.3
96	Claude Hendrix, 1914	5.3
97	Lady Baldwin, 1886	5.3
98	Curt Davis, 1934	5.3
99	Ed Reulbach, 1905	5.3
100	Charlie Ferguson, 1886	5.3

Opponents' Batting Average

1	Luis Tiant, 1968	.168
2	Nolan Ryan, 1972	.171
3	Nolan Ryan, 1991	.172
4	Ed Reulbach, 1906	.175
5	Sandy Koufax, 1965	.179
6	Dutch Leonard, 1914	.180
7	Sid Fernandez, 1985	.181
8	Dave McNally, 1968	.182
9	Tommy Byrne, 1949	.183
10	Al Downing, 1963	.184
11	Bob Gibson, 1968	.184
12	Sam McDowell, 1965	.185
13	Carl Lundgren, 1907	.185
14	Herb Score, 1956	.186
15	Mike Scott, 1986	.186
16	Tim Keefe, 1880	.187
17	Nolan Ryan, 1989	.187
18	Ed Walsh, 1910	.187
19	Mario Soto, 1980	.187
20	Walter Johnson, 1913	.187
21	Charlie Sweeney, 1884	.187
22	Nolan Ryan, 1981	.188
23	Russ Ford, 1910	.188
24	Nolan Ryan, 1986	.188
25	Jim McCormick, 1884	.188
26	Dupee Shaw, 1884	.188
27	Nolan Ryan, 1990	.188
28	Guy Hecker, 1882	.188
29	Floyd Youmans, 1986	.188
30	Sam McDowell, 1966	.188
31	Sandy Koufax, 1963	.189
32	Sam McDowell, 1968	.189
33	Don Sutton, 1972	.189
34	Jim Hunter, 1972	.189
35	Vida Blue, 1971	.189
36	Nolan Ryan, 1974	.190
37	Andy Messersmith, 1969	.190
38	Joe Horlen, 1964	.190
39	Sid Fernandez, 1988	.191
40	Pete Alexander, 1915	.191
41	Sandy Koufax, 1964	.191
42	Jim Bibby, 1973	.192
43	Bob Turley, 1955	.193
44	Nolan Ryan, 1977	.193
45	Fred Beebe, 1908	.193
46	Ron Guidry, 1978	.193
47	Stan Coveleski, 1917	.194
48	Bob Turley, 1957	.194
49	Herb Score, 1955	.194
50	Jack Pfiester, 1906	.194
51	Mordecai Brown, 1908	.195
52	Nolan Ryan, 1976	.195
53	Nolan Ryan, 1983	.195
54	Dean Chance, 1964	.195
55	Roger Clemens, 1986	.195
56	Tim Keefe, 1888	.196
57	Walter Johnson, 1912	.196
58	Roger Nelson, 1972	.196
59	J.R. Richard, 1978	.196
60	Pascual Perez, 1988	.196
61	Jeff Robinson, 1988	.197
62	Lady Baldwin, 1885	.197
63	Jose DeLeon, 1989	.197
64	Dave Boswell, 1966	.197
65	Sandy Koufax, 1962	.197
66	Charlie Sweeney, 1884	.197
67	Addie Joss, 1908	.197
68	Sonny Siebert, 1968	.198
69	Sid Fernandez, 1989	.198
70	Toad Ramsey, 1886	.198
71	Larry Cheney, 1916	.198
72	Wayne Simpson, 1970	.198
73	Orval Overall, 1909	.198
74	Gary Peters, 1967	.199
75	Larry Corcoran, 1880	.199
76	Willie Mitchell, 1913	.199
77	Rube Waddell, 1905	.199
78	Adonis Terry, 1888	.199
79	Nolan Ryan, 1987	.199
80	Mordecai Brown, 1904	.199
81	Christy Mathewson, 1909	.200
82	Denny McLain, 1968	.200
83	Larry Corcoran, 1882	.200
84	Bobby Bolin, 1968	.200
	Jim Palmer, 1969	.200
	Sid Fernandez, 1990	.200
87	Silver King, 1888	.200
88	Christy Mathewson, 1908	.200
89	Spec Shea, 1947	.200
90	Ed Seward, 1888	.200
91	Tony Mullane, 1892	.201
92	Art Fromme, 1909	.201
93	Babe Ruth, 1916	.201
94	Dwight Gooden, 1985	.201
95	Cannonball Titcomb, 1888	.201
96	Curt Schilling, 1992	.201
97	Hal Newhouser, 1946	.201
98	Ed Reulbach, 1905	.201
99	Jack Coombs, 1910	.201
100	Frank Knauss, 1890	.201

Opponents' On Base Pctg.

1	Guy Hecker, 1882	.198
2	Jim McCormick, 1884	.202
3	Charlie Sweeney, 1884	.207
4	Dupee Shaw, 1884	.212
5	Charlie Sweeney, 1884	.215
6	Henry Boyle, 1884	.215
7	George Bradley, 1880	.217
8	Walter Johnson, 1913	.217
9	Denny Driscoll, 1882	.218
10	Addie Joss, 1908	.218
11	Tim Keefe, 1880	.222
12	Jim Whitney, 1884	.223
13	George Bradley, 1876	.224
14	Christy Mathewson, 1908	.225
15	Guy Hecker, 1884	.226
16	Ed Walsh, 1910	.226
17	Tommy Bond, 1876	.227
18	Lady Baldwin, 1885	.228
19	Sandy Koufax, 1965	.228
20	Christy Mathewson, 1909	.228
21	Sandy Koufax, 1963	.230
22	Juan Marichal, 1966	.230
23	Monte Ward, 1880	.232
24	Mordecai Brown, 1908	.232
25	Ed Walsh, 1908	.232
26	Tim Keefe, 1883	.233
27	Luis Tiant, 1968	.233
28	Bob Gibson, 1968	.233
29	Pete Alexander, 1915	.234
30	Dave McNally, 1968	.234
31	Larry Corcoran, 1882	.234
32	Charley Radbourn, 1884	.234
33	Ed Morris, 1884	.234
34	Jim Devlin, 1876	.235
35	Perry Werden, 1884	.235
36	Jack Lynch, 1884	.236
37	Larry Corcoran, 1880	.236
38	Roger Nelson, 1972	.236
39	Charlie Getzien, 1884	.237
40	Silver King, 1888	.237
41	Tony Mullane, 1883	.238
42	John Clarkson, 1885	.239
43	Mordecai Brown, 1909	.239
44	Fred Corey, 1880	.239
45	Juan Marichal, 1965	.240
46	Tim Keefe, 1884	.240
47	Cy Young, 1908	.240
48	Don Sutton, 1972	.240
49	Babe Adams, 1919	.241
50	Sandy Koufax, 1964	.241
51	Cy Young, 1905	.241
52	Jim Hunter, 1972	.242
53	Billy Taylor, 1884	.243
54	Pete Conway, 1888	.243
55	Harry McCormick, 1882	.243
56	Denny McLain, 1968	.243
57	Tim Keefe, 1888	.243
58	Lady Baldwin, 1886	.243
59	Mike Scott, 1986	.244
60	Will White, 1883	.244
61	Charley Radbourn, 1883	.244
62	Charlie Ferguson, 1886	.244
63	Charlie Buffinton, 1888	.244
64	Will White, 1882	.244
65	Charlie Buffinton, 1884	.244
66	Russ Ford, 1910	.245
67	Pete Alexander, 1919	.245
68	Christy Mathewson, 1905	.245
69	Dutch Leonard, 1914	.246
70	Bobby Mathews, 1882	.246
71	Jim Galvin, 1884	.246
72	Charley Radbourn, 1882	.246
73	Sam Weaver, 1878	.247
74	Christy Mathewson, 1907	.247
75	Charlie Gagus, 1884	.247
76	Warren Hacker, 1952	.247
77	Jim McCormick, 1880	.247
78	Ed Morris, 1885	.247
79	Fred Goldsmith, 1880	.247
80	Eddie Cicotte, 1917	.248
81	Walter Johnson, 1912	.248
82	Doc White, 1906	.249
83	John Clarkson, 1884	.249
84	Jumbo McGinnis, 1883	.249
85	John Tudor, 1985	.249
86	Henry Gruber, 1888	.249
87	Ron Guidry, 1978	.250
88	Hugh Daily, 1884	.250
89	Joe Horlen, 1964	.250
90	Terry Larkin, 1879	.250
91	Monte Ward, 1879	.250
92	Monte Ward, 1878	.251
93	Candy Cummings, 1876	.251
94	Jim Whitney, 1883	.251
95	Cy Young, 1904	.251
96	Claude Hendrix, 1914	.251
97	Dick Burns, 1884	.252
98	Jack Chesbro, 1904	.252
99	Vida Blue, 1971	.252
100	Mordecai Brown, 1906	.252

Wins Above Team

1	George Bradley, 1876	22.5
2	Will White, 1879	21.5
3	Charley Radbourn, 1884	20.1
4	Jim McCormick, 1880	19.4
5	Guy Hecker, 1884	18.0
6	Jim Galvin, 1883	17.6
7	Jim Devlin, 1877	17.5
8	Charley Radbourn, 1883	15.7
9	Matt Kilroy, 1887	15.4
10	Jim Galvin, 1884	15.1
11	Jim Devlin, 1876	15.0
12	Charlie Buffinton, 1884	14.9
13	Walter Johnson, 1913	14.7
14	Jack Chesbro, 1904	14.0
15	Tony Mullane, 1884	13.9
16	Sadie McMahon, 1890	13.4
17	Will White, 1882	13.1
18	Ed Morris, 1885	12.9
19	Joe Wood, 1912	12.8
20	Bill Sweeney, 1884	12.7
	Ed Walsh, 1908	12.7
22	John Clarkson, 1889	12.1
23	Tommy Bond, 1879	12.0
24	Lefty Grove, 1931	11.8
25	Steve Carlton, 1972	11.7
26	Cy Young, 1901	11.6
27	Bill Hutchinson, 1891	11.4
	Denny McLain, 1968	11.4
29	Terry Larkin, 1878	11.2
	Mickey Welch, 1884	11.2
	Bob Caruthers, 1889	11.2
32	Henry Porter, 1885	11.0
	Bill Hoffer, 1895	11.0
	Christy Mathewson, 1908	11.0
35	Cy Young, 1902	10.9
36	Cy Young, 1895	10.7
37	Dazzy Vance, 1924	10.6
	Robin Roberts, 1952	10.6
	Ron Guidry, 1978	10.6
40	Bobby Mathews, 1876	10.5
	Dizzy Dean, 1934	10.5
42	Toad Ramsey, 1886	10.2
	Cy Young, 1892	10.2
	Joe McGinnity, 1904	10.2
	Eddie Rommel, 1922	10.2
46	Lefty Grove, 1930	10.1
47	Ed Morris, 1886	10.0
	Bill Donovan, 1907	10.0
49	Frank Mountain, 1883	9.9
	Eddie Cicotte, 1919	9.9
	Lefty Gomez, 1934	9.9
52	Kid Gleason, 1890	9.8
	Pete Alexander, 1915	9.8
	Hal Newhouser, 1944	9.8
55	Bobby Mathews, 1885	9.7
	Russ Ford, 1910	9.7
	Roger Clemens, 1986	9.7
58	Charlie Ferguson, 1886	9.6
	Pete Conway, 1888	9.6
	Eddie Plank, 1912	9.6
61	Pete Alexander, 1916	9.5
	Carl Hubbell, 1936	9.5
	Dwight Gooden, 1985	9.5
64	Jouett Meekin, 1894	9.4
	Walter Johnson, 1912	9.4
	Claude Hendrix, 1914	9.4
67	Joe McGinnity, 1900	9.3
	Sandy Koufax, 1963	9.3
69	Bert Cunningham, 1898	9.2
	Walter Johnson, 1911	9.2
	Bobby Shantz, 1952	9.2
	Don Newcombe, 1956	9.2
	Juan Marichal, 1966	9.2
	Bob Gibson, 1970	9.2
	Bob Welch, 1990	9.2
76	Tim Keefe, 1888	9.1
	Whitey Ford, 1961	9.1
78	Jim McCormick, 1882	9.0
	Cy Young, 1893	9.0
	Preacher Roe, 1951	9.0
81	Frank Killen, 1892	8.9
	Red Faber, 1921	8.9
83	Tim Keefe, 1883	8.8
	Tim Keefe, 1887	8.8
	Christy Mathewson, 1909	8.8
	Dolf Luque, 1923	8.8
87	Lee Richmond, 1881	8.7
	Frank Killen, 1893	8.7
	Jim Hughes, 1899	8.7
	Juan Marichal, 1963	8.7
	Juan Marichal, 1968	8.7
92	Jim McCormick, 1883	8.6
	Lefty Grove, 1933	8.6
	Bob Feller, 1946	8.6
	Roy Face, 1959	8.6
96	7 players tied	8.5

Wins Above League

1	Charley Radbourn, 1884	45.2
2	Guy Hecker, 1884	44.8
3	Charley Radbourn, 1883	42.8
4	Silver King, 1888	42.7
5	John Clarkson, 1889	42.6
6	John Clarkson, 1885	42.2
7	Jim Galvin, 1884	41.3
8	Jim Galvin, 1883	40.4
9	Bill Hutchinson, 1892	40.3
10	Jim McCormick, 1880	40.1
11	Tim Keefe, 1883	39.5
12	Jim Devlin, 1876	39.5
13	Will White, 1879	39.4
14	Toad Ramsey, 1886	39.3
15	Bill Hutchinson, 1890	39.2
16	Will White, 1883	39.0
17	Matt Kilroy, 1887	38.0
18	George Bradley, 1876	37.1
19	Toad Ramsey, 1887	36.8
20	Amos Rusie, 1890	36.6
21	Ed Morris, 1885	36.5
22	John Clarkson, 1887	36.4
23	Charlie Buffinton, 1884	36.3
24	Tony Mullane, 1884	36.1
25	Jim Devlin, 1877	35.8
26	Ed Morris, 1886	35.6
27	Jim McCormick, 1882	35.6
28	Dave Foutz, 1886	35.0
29	Lee Richmond, 1880	34.9
30	Tim Keefe, 1886	34.5
31	Monte Ward, 1880	34.5
32	Bill Hutchinson, 1891	34.4
33	Bill Sweeney, 1884	34.3
34	Monte Ward, 1879	34.3
35	Jim Galvin, 1879	34.0
36	Sadie McMahon, 1891	34.0
37	Tommy Bond, 1879	34.0
38	Amos Rusie, 1894	33.8
39	Mark Baldwin, 1890	33.6
40	Jim Whitney, 1883	33.3
41	Amos Rusie, 1893	33.3
42	Jack Stivetts, 1891	33.2
43	Al Spalding, 1876	33.1
44	Jim Whitney, 1881	33.0
45	Amos Rusie, 1892	32.9
46	Ed Walsh, 1908	32.8
47	Lady Baldwin, 1886	32.8
48	Larry Corcoran, 1884	32.7
49	Silver King, 1890	32.7
50	Mickey Welch, 1885	32.7
51	Mickey Welch, 1884	32.6
52	Kid Gleason, 1890	32.6
53	John Clarkson, 1886	32.3
54	Bob Caruthers, 1885	32.3
55	Ed Seward, 1888	32.2
56	Tommy Bond, 1877	32.1
57	Matt Kilroy, 1889	32.0
58	Will White, 1880	31.9
59	Mickey Welch, 1880	31.9
60	Pink Hawley, 1895	31.9
61	Matt Kilroy, 1886	31.8
62	Guy Hecker, 1885	31.5
63	Jack Chesbro, 1904	31.5
64	Sadie McMahon, 1890	31.5
65	Will White, 1882	31.4
66	Larry Corcoran, 1880	31.2
67	Tim Keefe, 1884	31.2
68	George Derby, 1881	31.2
69	Tommy Bond, 1878	31.2
70	Elmer Smith, 1887	31.2
71	Hugh Daily, 1884	30.9
72	Cy Young, 1893	30.9
73	Tony Mullane, 1883	30.8
74	Cy Young, 1892	30.8
75	Jesse Duryea, 1889	30.6
76	Mark Baldwin, 1889	30.6
77	Jim McCormick, 1879	30.4
78	Walter Johnson, 1912	30.4
79	Hardie Henderson, 1885	30.4
80	Scott Stratton, 1890	30.3
81	Larry Corcoran, 1883	30.2
82	Silver King, 1889	30.2
83	Charley Radbourn, 1886	30.0
84	Charley Radbourn, 1882	30.0
85	John Clarkson, 1891	29.9
86	Tim Keefe, 1887	29.9
87	Phil Knell, 1891	29.9
88	Tony Mullane, 1882	29.8
89	Joe McGinnity, 1903	29.8
90	Amos Rusie, 1891	29.7
91	Jersey Bakely, 1888	29.6
92	Kid Nichols, 1893	29.5
93	Henry Porter, 1885	29.5
94	Kid Nichols, 1890	29.4
95	Gus Weyhing, 1892	29.3
96	Tony Mullane, 1886	29.1
97	Gus Weyhing, 1889	29.0
98	Christy Mathewson, 1908	29.0
99	Jim McCormick, 1881	28.9
100	Walter Johnson, 1913	28.9

Relief Games

1	Mike Marshall, 1974	106
2	Kent Tekulve, 1979	94
3	Mike Marshall, 1973	92
4	Kent Tekulve, 1978	91
5	Wayne Granger, 1969	90
	Kent Tekulve, 1987	90
7	Mike Marshall, 1979	89
	Mark Eichhorn, 1987	89
9	Rob Murphy, 1987	87
10	Wilbur Wood, 1968	86
11	Kent Tekulve, 1982	85
	Frank Williams, 1987	85
13	Ted Abernathy, 1965	84
	Enrique Romo, 1979	84
	Dick Tidrow, 1980	84
	Dan Quisenberry, 1985	84
	Mitch Williams, 1987	84
18	Ken Sanders, 1971	83
	Craig Lefferts, 1986	83
20	Eddie Fisher, 1965	82
	Bill Campbell, 1983	82
	Juan Agosto, 1990	82
23	John Wyatt, 1964	81
	Dale Murray, 1976	81
	Jeff Robinson, 1987	81
	Duane Ward, 1991	81
	Joe Boever, 1992	81
	Kenny Rogers, 1992	81
29	Pedro Borbon, 1973	80
	Willie Hernandez, 1984	80
	Mitch Williams, 1986	80
	Doug Jones, 1992	80
33	Dick Radatz, 1964	79
	Duane Ward, 1992	79
35	Hal Woodeshick, 1965	78
	Ted Abernathy, 1968	78
	Bill Campbell, 1976	78
	Rollie Fingers, 1977	78
	Tom Hume, 1980	78
	Kent Tekulve, 1980	78
	Greg Minton, 1982	78
	Ed Vande Berg, 1982	78
	Ted Power, 1984	78
	Tim Burke, 1985	78
	Lance McCullers, 1987	78
46	11 players tied	77

Relief Wins

1	Roy Face, 1959	18
2	John Hiller, 1974	17
	Bill Campbell, 1976	17
4	Jim Konstanty, 1950	16
	Ron Perranoski, 1963	16
	Dick Radatz, 1964	16
	Tom Johnson, 1977	16
8	Mace Brown, 1938	15
	Hoyt Wilhelm, 1952	15
	Luis Arroyo, 1961	15
	Dick Radatz, 1963	15
	Eddie Fisher, 1965	15
	Mike Marshall, 1974	15
	Dale Murray, 1975	15
15	Joe Page, 1947	14
	Joe Black, 1952	14
	Hersh Freeman, 1956	14
	Stu Miller, 1961	14
	Stu Miller, 1965	14
	Phil Regan, 1966	14
	Frank Linzy, 1969	14
	Mike Marshall, 1972	14
	Mike Marshall, 1973	14
	Ron Davis, 1979	14
	Mark Clear, 1982	14
	Jim Slaton, 1983	14
	Roger McDowell, 1986	14
	Mark Eichhorn, 1986	14
29	Earl Caldwell, 1946	13
	Joe Page, 1949	13
	Clyde King, 1951	13
	Lindy McDaniel, 1959	13
	Larry Sherry, 1960	13
	Gerry Staley, 1960	13
	Lindy McDaniel, 1963	13
	Al Hrabosky, 1975	13
	Rollie Fingers, 1976	13
	Bill Campbell, 1977	13
	Sparky Lyle, 1977	13
	Gary Lavelle, 1978	13
	Bob Stanley, 1978	13
	Ron Reed, 1979	13
	Jim Kern, 1979	13
	Aurelio Lopez, 1980	13
	Jesse Orosco, 1983	13
	Rich Gossage, 1983	13
47	30 players tied	12

Relief Losses

1	Gene Garber, 1979	16
2	Darold Knowles, 1970	14
	John Hiller, 1974	14
	Mike Marshall, 1975	14
	Mike Marshall, 1979	14
6	Wilbur Wood, 1970	13
	Rollie Fingers, 1978	13
	Skip Lockwood, 1978	13
9	Roy Face, 1956	12
	Roy Face, 1961	12
	Ken Sanders, 1971	12
	Mike Marshall, 1974	12
	Gene Garber, 1975	12
	Jim Willoughby, 1976	12
	Charlie Hough, 1977	12
	Mike Marshall, 1978	12
	Kent Tekulve, 1980	12
	Ken Howell, 1986	12
19	Nels Potter, 1949	11
	Frank Funk, 1961	11
	Dick Radatz, 1965	11
	Frank Linzy, 1966	11
	Wilbur Wood, 1968	11
	Wilbur Wood, 1969	11
	Mike Marshall, 1973	11
	Rollie Fingers, 1976	11
	Rich Gossage, 1978	11
	Dave Heaverlo, 1979	11
	Mark Clear, 1980	11
	Greg Minton, 1983	11
	Ron Davis, 1984	11
	Mark Davis, 1985	11
	Joe Boever, 1989	11
34	44 players tied	10

Relief Innings Pitched

1	Mike Marshall, 1974	208.1
2	Allan Russell, 1923	181.1
3	Mike Marshall, 1973	179.0
4	Bob Stanley, 1982	168.1
5	Bill Campbell, 1976	167.2
6	Andy Karl, 1945	166.2
7	Eddie Fisher, 1965	165.1
8	Lindy McDaniel, 1973	160.1
9	Hoyt Wilhelm, 1952	159.1
10	Dick Radatz, 1964	157.0
	Mark Eichhorn, 1986	157.0
12	Jim Konstanty, 1950	152.0
13	John Hiller, 1974	150.0
14	Tom Johnson, 1977	146.2
15	Garland Braxton, 1927	146.0
16	Bob Stanley, 1983	145.1
17	Hoyt Wilhelm, 1953	145.0
	Wilbur Wood, 1968	145.0
19	Wayne Granger, 1969	144.2
20	Steve Foucault, 1974	144.1
21	Hoyt Wilhelm, 1965	144.0
22	Jim Kern, 1979	143.0
23	Charlie Hough, 1976	142.2
24	Rich Gossage, 1975	141.2
25	Mike Marshall, 1979	140.2
26	Sammy Stewart, 1983	140.1
	Willie Hernandez, 1984	140.1
28	Bill Campbell, 1977	140.0
29	Jack Lamabe, 1963	139.2
30	Pedro Borbon, 1974	139.0
	Dan Quisenberry, 1983	139.0
32	Aurelio Lopez, 1984	137.2
33	Clay Carroll, 1966	137.1
34	Sparky Lyle, 1977	137.0
	Tom Hume, 1980	137.0
36	Dan Quisenberry, 1982	136.2
37	Ted Abernathy, 1965	136.1
	Ken Sanders, 1971	136.1
	Doug Corbett, 1980	136.1
40	Joe Page, 1949	135.1
41	Clay Carroll, 1968	135.0
	Kent Tekulve, 1978	135.0
43	Ted Abernathy, 1968	134.2
	Phil Regan, 1968	134.2
	Rollie Fingers, 1976	134.2
46	Bill Henry, 1959	134.1
	Dick Selma, 1970	134.1
	Rich Gossage, 1978	134.1
	Kent Tekulve, 1979	134.1
50	2 players tied	134.0

Relief Points

1	Bobby Thigpen, 1990	116
2	Dennis Eckersley, 1992	115
3	Lee Smith, 1991	103
4	Dennis Eckersley, 1990	102
5	Dave Righetti, 1986	100
6	Dan Quisenberry, 1983	97
	Dan Quisenberry, 1984	97
8	Dennis Eckersley, 1988	96
9	Bruce Sutter, 1984	93
	Mark Davis, 1989	93
11	Dennis Eckersley, 1991	92
	Bryan Harvey, 1991	92
13	John Hiller, 1973	91
	Doug Jones, 1990	91
15	Steve Bedrosian, 1987	87
	Rick Aguilera, 1991	87
17	Doug Jones, 1992	86
18	Lee Smith, 1992	85
19	Johnny Franco, 1988	84
	Jeff Reardon, 1988	84
	Jeff Russell, 1989	84
22	Luis Arroyo, 1961	83
	Sparky Lyle, 1972	83
	Dan Quisenberry, 1980	83
	Bill Caudill, 1984	83
26	Clay Carroll, 1972	82
	Bruce Sutter, 1982	82
28	Dick Radatz, 1964	81
	Dan Quisenberry, 1982	81
	Dan Quisenberry, 1985	81
	Gregg Olson, 1990	81
32	Bruce Sutter, 1979	80
	Todd Worrell, 1986	80
	Rick Aguilera, 1992	80
35	Mike Marshall, 1973	79
	Bill Campbell, 1977	79
	Jim Kern, 1979	79
	Willie Hernandez, 1984	79
	Mitch Williams, 1991	79
40	Jeff Reardon, 1985	78
	Jeff Reardon, 1988	78
	John Wetteland, 1992	78
43	Wayne Granger, 1970	77
	Rollie Fingers, 1977	77
	Lee Smith, 1984	77
46	9 players tied	76

Relief Ranking

1	Jim Kern, 1979	65.0
2	John Hiller, 1973	64.9
3	Rich Gossage, 1977	62.5
4	Lindy McDaniel, 1960	57.5
5	Mike Marshall, 1979	56.2
6	Mark Eichhorn, 1986	56.2
7	Dennis Eckersley, 1990	55.8
8	Bruce Sutter, 1977	54.0
9	Ellis Kinder, 1953	53.6
10	Jesse Orosco, 1983	52.2
11	Donnie Moore, 1985	51.9
12	Bill Caudill, 1982	51.9
13	Dick Radatz, 1964	50.4
14	Bob James, 1985	50.4
15	Sid Monge, 1979	49.5
16	Dick Radatz, 1963	49.4
17	Bobby Thigpen, 1990	48.3
18	Rich Gossage, 1975	47.7
19	Doug Corbett, 1980	46.9
20	Dan Quisenberry, 1985	46.9
21	Mike Marshall, 1972	46.8
22	Bill Campbell, 1977	45.5
23	Lee Smith, 1983	45.4
24	Roy Face, 1962	45.2
25	Dave Righetti, 1986	45.1
26	Al Hrabosky, 1975	44.9
27	Bruce Sutter, 1984	44.8
28	Rich Gossage, 1978	44.7
29	Bryan Harvey, 1991	43.8
30	Johnny Franco, 1988	43.8
31	Todd Worrell, 1986	43.5
32	Sparky Lyle, 1977	43.4
33	Dan Spillner, 1982	43.2
34	Tom Murphy, 1974	42.9
35	Stu Miller, 1965	42.7
36	Doug Jones, 1992	41.7
37	Ken Sanders, 1971	41.6
38	Luis Arroyo, 1961	41.6
39	Ron Perranoski, 1969	41.3
40	Dan Quisenberry, 1983	41.0
41	Hoyt Wilhelm, 1964	40.7
42	Doug Jones, 1989	40.4
43	Joe Page, 1949	40.3
44	Bruce Sutter, 1979	40.3
45	Willie Hernandez, 1984	39.9
46	Jim Brewer, 1972	39.8
47	Mike Henneman, 1988	39.8
48	John Hiller, 1974	39.8
49	Dick Radatz, 1962	39.7
50	Ted Abernathy, 1967	39.7

Relievers' Runs

1	Mark Eichhorn, 1986	42.8
2	Jim Kern, 1979	42.0
3	Rich Gossage, 1977	33.8
4	John Hiller, 1973	33.1
5	Dan Quisenberry, 1983	32.7
6	Willie Hernandez, 1984	32.2
7	Doug Corbett, 1980	31.1
8	Bruce Sutter, 1977	30.6
9	Rich Gossage, 1975	30.5
10	Tim Burke, 1987	29.3
11	Sparky Lyle, 1977	28.8
12	Lindy McDaniel, 1960	28.6
13	Bob Lee, 1964	28.4
14	Garland Braxton, 1927	28.2
15	Bruce Sutter, 1984	27.9
16	Mike Marshall, 1974	27.7
17	Dennis Eckersley, 1990	26.8
18	Sid Monge, 1979	26.4
19	Jesse Orosco, 1983	26.3
20	Hoyt Wilhelm, 1965	26.3
21	Rich Gossage, 1978	26.2
22	Jim Grant, 1970	25.9
23	Phil Regan, 1966	25.8
24	Jeff Montgomery, 1989	25.7
25	Ellis Kinder, 1953	25.5
26	Aurelio Lopez, 1979	25.5
27	Donnie Moore, 1985	25.5
28	Dan Quisenberry, 1985	25.4
29	Ellis Kinder, 1951	25.1
30	Jim Konstanty, 1950	25.0
31	Ted Abernathy, 1967	24.9
32	Mike Marshall, 1979	24.9
33	Sparky Lyle, 1974	24.8
34	Bob James, 1985	24.7
35	Rollie Fingers, 1973	24.5
36	Gary Lavelle, 1977	24.4
37	Dick Radatz, 1963	24.4
38	Hoyt Wilhelm, 1954	24.4
39	Joe Black, 1952	24.2
40	Greg Minton, 1982	24.2
41	Luis Arroyo, 1961	24.2
42	Joe Page, 1949	24.1
43	Dick Radatz, 1962	24.0
44	Hoyt Wilhelm, 1964	23.9
45	Todd Frohwirth, 1991	23.8
46	Dan Spillner, 1982	23.5
47	Tom Murphy, 1974	23.4
48	Ken Sanders, 1971	23.4
49	Dick Radatz, 1964	23.2
50	Joe Heving, 1933	23.2

Adjusted Relievers' Runs

1	Mark Eichhorn, 1986	43.6
2	Jim Kern, 1979	40.9
3	John Hiller, 1973	36.9
4	Bruce Sutter, 1977	36.3
5	Doug Corbett, 1980	36.0
6	Rich Gossage, 1977	34.9
7	Dan Quisenberry, 1983	32.9
8	Lindy McDaniel, 1960	32.5
9	Rich Gossage, 1975	32.0
10	Willie Hernandez, 1984	31.1
11	Tim Burke, 1987	30.5
12	Ellis Kinder, 1951	29.3
13	Ted Abernathy, 1967	29.3
14	Ellis Kinder, 1953	28.0
15	Mike Marshall, 1979	27.4
16	Dick Radatz, 1964	27.3
17	Aurelio Lopez, 1979	27.0
18	Sparky Lyle, 1977	27.0
19	Sid Monge, 1979	26.9
20	Bob James, 1985	26.8
21	Dick Radatz, 1963	26.7
22	Jesse Orosco, 1983	26.3
23	Bruce Sutter, 1984	26.3
24	Dick Radatz, 1962	26.2
25	Dan Quisenberry, 1985	25.6
26	Jeff Montgomery, 1989	25.3
27	Dennis Eckersley, 1990	25.3
28	Donnie Moore, 1985	25.0
29	Lee Smith, 1983	24.5
30	Gary Lavelle, 1977	24.4
31	Tom Burgmeier, 1980	24.4
32	Bob Lee, 1964	24.3
33	Bob Stanley, 1983	24.2
34	Andy McGaffigan, 1987	24.2
35	Greg Minton, 1982	24.1
36	Rich Gossage, 1978	24.0
37	Duane Ward, 1992	24.0
38	Rob Dibble, 1990	23.9
39	Hoyt Wilhelm, 1954	23.9
40	Tug McGraw, 1980	23.9
41	Bill Campbell, 1977	23.8
42	Dick Hyde, 1958	23.7
43	Dan Spillner, 1982	23.6
44	Ken Sanders, 1971	23.5
45	Clay Carroll, 1966	23.5
46	Jim Grant, 1970	23.5
47	Tom Murphy, 1974	23.4
48	Jim Konstanty, 1950	23.4
49	Bill Caudill, 1980	23.3
50	Sparky Lyle, 1974	23.2

Percent of Team Wins (by era)

1876-1892

1	Will White, 1879	100.0
	Bobby Mathews, 1876	100.0
	Jim Devlin, 1877	100.0
	Jim Devlin, 1876	100.0
	George Bradley, 1876	100.0
6	Tommy Bond, 1878	97.6
7	Terry Larkin, 1878	96.7
8	Jim McCormick, 1880	95.7
9	Tommy Bond, 1877	95.2
10	Terry Larkin, 1877	93.5
11	Al Spalding, 1876	90.4
	Jim Galvin, 1883	88.5
13	Will White, 1880	85.7
	Jim McCormick, 1882	85.7
15	Mickey Welch, 1880	82.9

1893-1919

1	Ted Breitenstein, 1895	48.7
2	Amos Rusie, 1893	48.5
3	Ted Breitenstein, 1894	48.2
4	Cy Young, 1893	46.6
5	Ed Walsh, 1908	45.5
	Frank Killen, 1896	45.5
7	Ted Breitenstein, 1896	45.0
8	Jack Chesbro, 1904	44.6
9	Frank Killen, 1893	44.4
10	Pink Hawley, 1895	43.7
11	Win Mercer, 1896	43.1
12	Noodles Hahn, 1901	42.3
13	Cy Young, 1901	41.8
14	Cy Young, 1895	41.6
15	Cy Young, 1902	41.6

1920-1941

1	Eddie Rommel, 1922	41.5
2	Red Faber, 1921	40.3
3	Buck Newsom, 1938	36.4
4	Jimmy Ring, 1923	36.0
	Pete Alexander, 1920	36.0
6	Ted Lyons, 1930	35.5
7	Curt Davis, 1934	33.9
8	Urban Shocker, 1921	33.3
	Bob Feller, 1941	33.3
	Ed Morris, 1928	33.3
11	Howard Ehmke, 1923	32.8
12	Dazzy Vance, 1925	32.4
	Paul Derringer, 1935	32.4
14	Wes Ferrell, 1935	32.1
15	George Uhle, 1923	31.7

1942-1960

1	Ned Garver, 1951	38.5
2	Bob Feller, 1946	38.2
3	Murry Dickson, 1952	33.3
4	Robin Roberts, 1952	32.2
5	Bill Voiselle, 1944	31.3
6	Murry Dickson, 1951	31.3
7	Phil Marchildon, 1942	30.9
8	Dizzy Trout, 1944	30.7
9	Robin Roberts, 1954	30.7
10	Bobby Shantz, 1952	30.4
11	Ewell Blackwell, 1947	30.1
12	Robin Roberts, 1955	29.9
13	Johnny Antonelli, 1956	29.9
14	Dave Ferriss, 1945	29.6
15	2 players tied	29.0

1961-1992

1	Steve Carlton, 1972	45.8
2	Gaylord Perry, 1972	33.3
3	Nolan Ryan, 1974	32.4
4	Phil Niekro, 1979	31.8
5	Larry Jackson, 1964	31.6
6	Wilbur Wood, 1973	31.2
7	Bob Gibson, 1970	30.3
8	Randy Jones, 1976	30.1
9	Denny McLain, 1968	30.1
10	Fergie Jenkins, 1974	29.8
11	Dave Stieb, 1981	29.7
12	Juan Marichal, 1968	29.5
13	Sam McDowell, 1969	29.0
14	Fergie Jenkins, 1971	28.9
	Fernando Valenzuela,	
15	1986	28.8

Clutch Pitching Index

1	Ned Garvin, 1904	154.0
2	Mordecai Brown, 1903	153.5
3	Doc White, 1904	153.1
4	Jim McCormick, 1878	152.3
5	Max Lanier, 1943	150.8
6	Ed Killian, 1907	147.1
7	Pete Schneider, 1917	145.4
8	Sammy Stewart, 1981	144.8
9	Carl Lundgren, 1902	143.9
10	Bill Burns, 1909	142.4
11	Ed Summers, 1908	142.3
12	Andy Coakley, 1905	142.1
	Cy Morgan, 1910	142.1
14	Fred Olmstead, 1910	141.6
	Ben Tincup, 1914	141.6
16	Dick Rudolph, 1919	141.2
17	Sherry Smith, 1919	141.1
18	Fred Blanding, 1913	140.8
19	Mal Eason, 1902	140.4
20	Vic Willis, 1906	139.9
21	Ed Poole, 1902	139.7
	Ed Willett, 1908	139.7
23	Bert Humphries, 1915	139.5
24	Rick Honeycutt, 1983	139.3
25	Doug Rau, 1976	139.2
26	Sloppy Thurston, 1923	139.0
27	Al Benton, 1945	138.7
	Al Brazle, 1947	138.7
29	Charlie Hodnett, 1884	138.6
30	Allan Anderson, 1988	137.8
31	Mark Baldwin, 1888	137.4
32	Al Maul, 1895	137.0
	Bob Rhoads, 1908	137.0
34	Mike Sullivan, 1892	136.3
35	Spud Chandler, 1942	136.2
	Chuck Finley, 1990	136.2
37	Red Faber, 1917	135.9
38	King Cole, 1910	135.8
39	Clark Griffith, 1898	135.6
40	Bob Buhl, 1957	134.8
	John Tudor, 1988	134.8
42	Mark Langston, 1989	134.7
43	Doug Rau, 1978	134.5
44	Andy Coakley, 1908	134.4
	Stu Miller, 1959	134.4
46	Win Mercer, 1894	134.3
47	Joe McGinnity, 1908	134.2
	Ken Chase, 1940	134.2
	Dutch Leonard, 1948	134.2
50	Ed Siever, 1904	134.1
51	Mike Marshall, 1973	133.7
52	Charlie Chech, 1905	133.2
53	Andy Coakley, 1907	133.1
	Joe Horlen, 1968	133.1
55	Eddie Plank, 1911	132.8
56	Art Nehf, 1928	132.7
57	Gene Bearden, 1948	132.3
	Hoyt Wilhelm, 1959	132.3
59	Mike O'Neill, 1904	132.2
60	Win Mercer, 1897	132.1
	Stan Baumgartner, 1924	132.1
62	Ed Killian, 1909	131.9
	Bump Hadley, 1939	131.9
64	Lew Brockett, 1909	131.8
65	Jim Abbott, 1992	131.7
66	Jose DeLeon, 1991	131.5
67	Steve Blass, 1972	131.3
68	Don Schwall, 1961	131.1
69	Chick Fraser, 1900	131.0
70	Ted Lyons, 1942	130.9
	Bobby Shantz, 1957	130.9
72	Tony Mullane, 1890	130.7
73	Lon Warneke, 1933	130.6
	Pete Vuckovich, 1982	130.6
	Bill Swift, 1992	130.6
76	Bill Lee, 1978	130.5
77	Bill Bernhard, 1904	130.3
	Hal McKain, 1929	130.3
	Bill Krueger, 1991	130.3
80	Larry Pape, 1911	130.2
	Hi Bithorn, 1942	130.2
	John Cerutti, 1989	130.2
83	Brickyard Kennedy, 1899	130.0
	Vean Gregg, 1913	130.0
85	Rollie Naylor, 1920	129.9
86	Earl Moore, 1911	129.6
	Ruben Gomez, 1954	129.6
	Larry McWilliams, 1984	129.6
89	Jim Galvin, 1886	129.5
90	Lefty Weinert, 1922	129.4
91	Tom Hughes, 1912	129.3
	Harry Moran, 1915	129.3
	Ned Garver, 1948	129.3
94	Jim Pastorius, 1907	129.2
	Clarence Mitchell, 1929	129.2
	Atley Donald, 1944	129.2
	Joe Hatten, 1946	129.2
98	Buttons Briggs, 1904	129.1
	Bill Walker, 1929	129.1
	John Denny, 1976	129.1

Pitcher Batting Runs

1	Guy Hecker, 1884	26.0
2	Bob Caruthers, 1886	24.5
3	Jim Whitney, 1882	22.3
4	Wes Ferrell, 1935	21.5
5	Don Drysdale, 1965	20.2
6	Don Newcombe, 1955	20.1
7	Bob Caruthers, 1887	19.6
8	Guy Hecker, 1886	19.1
9	Jim Whitney, 1883	18.1
10	Wes Ferrell, 1931	17.8
11	Billy Taylor, 1884	17.4
12	Tony Mullane, 1884	16.9
13	Charlie Ferguson, 1885	16.8
14	Schoolboy Rowe, 1943	16.7
15	George Uhle, 1923	16.4
16	Babe Ruth, 1917	16.3
17	Warren Spahn, 1958	16.0
18	Walter Johnson, 1925	15.9
19	Scott Stratton, 1890	15.8
20	Bob Caruthers, 1889	15.7
21	Red Ruffing, 1930	15.6
22	Bob Lemon, 1950	15.6
23	Jack Stivetts, 1890	15.3
24	Jack Stivetts, 1892	15.1
25	Don Newcombe, 1959	15.1
26	Doc Crandall, 1915	14.9
27	Jack Bentley, 1923	14.8
28	Monte Ward, 1879	14.7
29	Bob Lemon, 1949	14.7
30	Red Lucas, 1930	14.7
31	Claude Hendrix, 1912	14.6
32	Babe Ruth, 1915	14.5
33	Dave Foutz, 1887	14.3
34	Frank Killen, 1893	14.2
35	Charlie Ferguson, 1887	14.1
36	Jim Tobin, 1942	14.0
37	Red Ruffing, 1936	13.8
38	Red Lucas, 1932	13.7
39	Robin Roberts, 1955	13.6
40	Terry Larkin, 1878	13.6
41	Elam Vangilder, 1922	13.4
42	Pete Conway, 1888	13.1
43	Babe Ruth, 1916	13.1
44	Joe Bush, 1924	13.0
45	Jack Coombs, 1911	13.0
46	Adonis Terry, 1890	12.9
47	Clark Griffith, 1901	12.8
48	Bucky Walters, 1939	12.7
49	Pink Hawley, 1895	12.7
50	Bob Lemon, 1948	12.6
51	Red Lucas, 1933	12.5
52	Schoolboy Rowe, 1935	12.5
53	Red Ruffing, 1932	12.5
54	Cy Young, 1903	12.3
55	Curt Davis, 1939	12.3
56	Scott Stratton, 1888	12.3
57	Red Ruffing, 1935	12.2
58	Bob Gibson, 1970	12.2
59	Red Ruffing, 1928	12.2
60	Jim Hunter, 1971	12.1
61	Wes Ferrell, 1936	11.9
62	Dizzy Trout, 1944	11.9
63	Joe Bowman, 1939	11.8
64	Charley Radbourn, 1883	11.8
65	Fergie Jenkins, 1971	11.7
66	Johnny Sain, 1947	11.7
67	Jouett Meekin, 1896	11.7
68	Adonis Terry, 1889	11.7
69	Dutch Ruether, 1921	11.6
70	Erv Brame, 1929	11.5
71	Babe Ruth, 1918	11.5
72	Jack Stivetts, 1896	11.5
73	Ad Gumbert, 1891	11.4
74	Claude Hendrix, 1915	11.4
75	George Mullin, 1904	11.3
76	George Van Haltren, 1888	11.3
77	Charlie Ferguson, 1886	11.2
78	Schoolboy Rowe, 1934	11.2
79	Tim Keefe, 1884	11.0
80	Bob Caruthers, 1891	11.0
81	Tom Parrott, 1895	11.0
82	Jim Whitney, 1887	11.0
83	Carl Mays, 1921	11.0
84	Jim Whitney, 1881	11.0
85	Jack Stivetts, 1894	11.0
86	Mickey Welch, 1880	10.9
87	Red Lucas, 1931	10.9
88	Dave Ferriss, 1945	10.9
89	Charlie Buffinton, 1884	10.8
90	Red Ruffing, 1941	10.8
91	Erv Brame, 1930	10.8
92	Red Lucas, 1929	10.7
93	Ad Gumbert, 1889	10.7
94	Fred Hutchinson, 1947	10.7
95	Joe Wood, 1912	10.6
96	Bill Phillips, 1902	10.6
97	Burleigh Grimes, 1928	10.6
98	Burleigh Grimes, 1920	10.5
99	Guy Hecker, 1887	10.5
100	Dick Burns, 1884	10.5

Pitcher Fielding Runs

1	Ed Walsh, 1907	21.6
2	Harry Howell, 1905	17.7
3	Ed Walsh, 1911	14.8
4	Ed Walsh, 1908	13.6
5	Will White, 1882	12.9
6	John Clarkson, 1889	11.3
7	Tony Mullane, 1882	10.8
8	Sadie McMahon, 1890	10.7
9	Carl Mays, 1926	10.1
10	Frank Smith, 1909	10.0
11	Tommy Bond, 1880	9.8
12	Mike Morrison, 1887	9.7
	Ed Walsh, 1910	9.7
14	Christy Mathewson, 1908	9.6
15	Tony Mullane, 1884	9.5
	Matt Kilroy, 1887	9.5
	Charlie Buffinton, 1888	9.5
18	Harry Howell, 1904	9.4
19	Ed Scott, 1900	9.1
	Elmer Stricklett, 1906	9.1
	Carl Mays, 1916	9.1
	Carl Mays, 1918	9.1
	Curt Davis, 1934	9.1
24	John Clarkson, 1887	9.0
	Elmer Stricklett, 1905	9.0
26	Hooks Dauss, 1915	8.9
27	Addie Joss, 1907	8.6
	Gene Packard, 1914	8.6
29	Park Swartzel, 1889	8.5
	Bucky Walters, 1936	8.5
31	Jack Taylor, 1898	8.4
	Nick Altrock, 1905	8.4
	Hooks Dauss, 1920	8.4
	Wilcy Moore, 1927	8.4
	Bob Lemon, 1948	8.4
36	Cy Seymour, 1898	8.3
	Randy Jones, 1976	8.3
38	Harry Howell, 1907	8.2
	Burleigh Grimes, 1925	8.2
40	Matt Kilroy, 1889	8.1
	George Mullin, 1904	8.1
	Carl Mays, 1924	8.1
	Eddie Rommel, 1924	8.1
44	Fred Newman, 1965	8.0
45	Cy Young, 1895	7.9
	Cy Young, 1896	7.9
	Bob Lemon, 1953	7.9
	Mel Stottlemyre, 1969	7.9
49	Jim Galvin, 1887	7.8
	Carl Mays, 1917	7.8
	Freddie Fitzsimmons, 1931	7.8
	Harry Gumbert, 1938	7.8
	John Denny, 1978	7.8
54	John Clarkson, 1885	7.7
	Amos Rusie, 1894	7.7
	Joe Wood, 1912	7.7
	Mel Harder, 1933	7.7
	Harry Gumbert, 1937	7.7
	Russ Christopher, 1943	7.7
60	Larry McKeon, 1884	7.6
	Cy Seymour, 1897	7.6
	Ed Walsh, 1906	7.6
63	Willie Sudhoff, 1898	7.5
	Christy Mathewson, 1901	7.5
	Ned Garvin, 1903	7.5
	Jean Dubuc, 1913	7.5
	Greg Maddux, 1990	7.5
68	Harry Howell, 1906	7.4
	Christy Mathewson, 1911	7.4
	Carl Hubbell, 1933	7.4
71	Tommy Bond, 1879	7.3
	Charlie Buffinton, 1887	7.3
	Bob Caruthers, 1887	7.3
	Bill Doak, 1915	7.3
75	Jim Galvin, 1881	7.2
	Eddie Cicotte, 1913	7.2
	Russ Christopher, 1945	7.2
78	Jim Galvin, 1884	7.1
	Ed Walsh, 1912	7.1
	Harry Coveleski, 1914	7.1
81	George Mullin, 1905	7.0
	Doc White, 1908	7.0
	Red Ames, 1909	7.0
	Hal Schumacher, 1935	7.0
85	Guy Hecker, 1884	6.9
	Dave Foutz, 1885	6.9
	Red Donahue, 1902	6.9
	Elmer Stricklett, 1907	6.9
	Lefty Tyler, 1913	6.9
	Gene Krapp, 1915	6.9
	Larry Jackson, 1964	6.9
92	Jim McCormick, 1883	6.8
	Larry Corcoran, 1884	6.8
	Cy Young, 1894	6.8
	Vic Willis, 1904	6.8
	Christy Mathewson, 1910	6.8
	Pete Alexander, 1915	6.8
	Ted Wingfield, 1925	6.8
	Jim Tobin, 1944	6.8
100	7 players tied	6.7

Total Pitcher Index

1	Guy Hecker, 1884	12.9
2	Silver King, 1888	11.4
3	Amos Rusie, 1894	11.0
4	Charley Radbourn, 1884	10.4
5	John Clarkson, 1889	10.2
6	Walter Johnson, 1912	10.0
7	Walter Johnson, 1913	9.7
8	Christy Mathewson, 1905	9.0
9	John Clarkson, 1885	8.9
	Scott Stratton, 1890	8.9
11	Dizzy Trout, 1944	8.8
12	Pete Alexander, 1915	8.6
13	Joe Wood, 1912	8.5
14	John Clarkson, 1887	8.3
15	Charley Radbourn, 1883	8.1
	Bob Gibson, 1968	8.1
17	Dave Foutz, 1886	8.0
	Bucky Walters, 1939	8.0
	Hal Newhouser, 1945	8.0
	Dwight Gooden, 1985	8.0
21	Jim Devlin, 1876	7.9
	Tony Mullane, 1884	7.9
	Cy Young, 1901	7.9
24	Steve Carlton, 1972	7.8
25	Will White, 1882	7.5
	Ed Walsh, 1908	7.5
	Dolf Luque, 1923	7.5
	Lefty Grove, 1931	7.5
29	Walter Johnson, 1918	7.4
30	Matt Kilroy, 1887	7.3
	Ed Walsh, 1910	7.3
32	Jim Galvin, 1884	7.1
	Charlie Ferguson, 1886	7.1
	Jack Stivetts, 1891	7.1
	Amos Rusie, 1893	7.1
	Walter Johnson, 1915	7.1
	Carl Hubbell, 1933	7.1
38	Matt Kilroy, 1889	7.0
	Silver King, 1890	7.0
	Cy Young, 1892	7.0
	Kid Nichols, 1897	7.0
	Claude Hendrix, 1914	7.0
	Pete Alexander, 1916	7.0
	Wilbur Wood, 1971	7.0
45	Kid Nichols, 1890	6.9
	Pink Hawley, 1895	6.9
	Christy Mathewson, 1909	6.9
	Wes Ferrell, 1935	6.9
49	Bob Caruthers, 1886	6.8
	Amos Rusie, 1890	6.8
	Kid Nichols, 1898	6.8
	Ed Walsh, 1907	6.8
	Pete Alexander, 1920	6.8
	Tom Seaver, 1971	6.8
	Ron Guidry, 1978	6.8
56	Bob Caruthers, 1885	6.7
	Guy Hecker, 1885	6.7
	Cy Young, 1896	6.7
	Jack Chesbro, 1904	6.7
	Walter Johnson, 1919	6.7
61	Tim Keefe, 1883	6.6
	Toad Ramsey, 1886	6.6
	Jack Taylor, 1902	6.6
	Christy Mathewson, 1908	6.6
	Walter Johnson, 1914	6.6
	Dazzy Vance, 1928	6.6
	Lefty Grove, 1930	6.6
	Lefty Grove, 1936	6.6
	Thornton Lee, 1941	6.6
	Spud Chandler, 1943	6.6
	Gaylord Perry, 1972	6.6
72	Will White, 1883	6.5
	Hal Newhouser, 1946	6.5
	Bob Lemon, 1948	6.5
	Fergie Jenkins, 1971	6.5
76	John Clarkson, 1886	6.4
	Bob Caruthers, 1887	6.4
	Billy Rhines, 1890	6.4
	Cy Young, 1895	6.4
	Mordecai Brown, 1906	6.4
	Curt Davis, 1934	6.4
	Juan Marichal, 1966	6.4
	Jim Palmer, 1975	6.4
84	Jim Devlin, 1877	6.3
	Tony Mullane, 1883	6.3
	Red Faber, 1921	6.3
	Lon Warneke, 1933	6.3
	Warren Spahn, 1953	6.3
	Bob Gibson, 1969	6.3
90	Kid Nichols, 1896	6.2
	Clark Griffith, 1898	6.2
	Ed Walsh, 1912	6.2
	Lefty Gomez, 1937	6.2
	Roger Clemens, 1990	6.2
95	Addie Joss, 1908	6.1
96	11 players tied	6.0

Total Pitcher Index (alpha.)

Pete Alexander, 1915	8.6
Pete Alexander, 1916	7.0
Pete Alexander, 1920	6.8
Mordecai Brown, 1906	6.4
Steve Carlton, 1972	7.8
Bob Caruthers, 1885	6.7
Bob Caruthers, 1886	6.8
Bob Caruthers, 1887	6.4
Spud Chandler, 1943	6.6
Jack Chesbro, 1904	6.7
John Clarkson, 1885	8.9
John Clarkson, 1886	6.4
John Clarkson, 1887	8.3
John Clarkson, 1889	10.2
Roger Clemens, 1990	6.2
Curt Davis, 1934	6.4
Jim Devlin, 1876	7.9
Jim Devlin, 1877	6.3
Red Faber, 1921	6.3
Charlie Ferguson, 1886	7.1
Wes Ferrell, 1935	6.9
Dave Foutz, 1886	8.0
Jim Galvin, 1884	7.1
Bob Gibson, 1968	8.1
Bob Gibson, 1969	6.3
Lefty Gomez, 1937	6.2
Dwight Gooden, 1985	8.0
Clark Griffith, 1898	6.2
Lefty Grove, 1930	6.6
Lefty Grove, 1931	7.5
Lefty Grove, 1936	6.6
Ron Guidry, 1978	6.8
Pink Hawley, 1895	6.9
Guy Hecker, 1884	12.9
Guy Hecker, 1885	6.7
Claude Hendrix, 1914	7.0
Carl Hubbell, 1933	7.1
Fergie Jenkins, 1971	6.5
Walter Johnson, 1912	10.0
Walter Johnson, 1913	9.7
Walter Johnson, 1914	6.6
Walter Johnson, 1915	7.1
Walter Johnson, 1918	7.4
Walter Johnson, 1919	6.7
Addie Joss, 1908	6.1
Tim Keefe, 1883	6.6
Matt Kilroy, 1887	7.3
Matt Kilroy, 1889	7.0
Silver King, 1888	11.4
Silver King, 1890	7.0
Thornton Lee, 1941	6.6
Bob Lemon, 1948	6.5
Dolf Luque, 1923	7.5
Juan Marichal, 1966	6.4
Christy Mathewson, 1905	9.0
Christy Mathewson, 1908	6.6
Christy Mathewson, 1909	6.9
Tony Mullane, 1883	6.3
Tony Mullane, 1884	7.9
Hal Newhouser, 1945	8.0
Hal Newhouser, 1946	6.5
Kid Nichols, 1890	6.9
Kid Nichols, 1896	6.2
Kid Nichols, 1897	7.0
Kid Nichols, 1898	6.8
Jim Palmer, 1975	6.4
Gaylord Perry, 1972	6.6
Charley Radbourn, 1883	8.1
Charley Radbourn, 1884	10.4
Toad Ramsey, 1886	6.6
Billy Rhines, 1890	6.4
Amos Rusie, 1890	6.8
Amos Rusie, 1893	7.1
Amos Rusie, 1894	11.0
Tom Seaver, 1971	6.8
Warren Spahn, 1953	6.3
Jack Stivetts, 1891	7.1
Scott Stratton, 1890	8.9
Jack Taylor, 1902	6.6
Dizzy Trout, 1944	8.8
Dazzy Vance, 1928	6.6
Ed Walsh, 1907	6.8
Ed Walsh, 1908	7.5
Ed Walsh, 1910	7.3
Ed Walsh, 1912	6.2
Bucky Walters, 1939	8.0
Lon Warneke, 1933	6.3
Will White, 1882	7.5
Will White, 1883	6.5
Joe Wood, 1912	8.5
Wilbur Wood, 1971	7.0
Cy Young, 1892	7.0
Cy Young, 1895	6.4
Cy Young, 1896	6.7
Cy Young, 1901	7.9

Total Pitcher Index (by era)

1876-1892
1	Guy Hecker, 1884	12.9
2	Silver King, 1888	11.4
3	Charley Radbourn, 1884	10.4
4	John Clarkson, 1889	10.2
5	John Clarkson, 1885	8.9
	Scott Stratton, 1890	8.9
7	John Clarkson, 1887	8.3
8	Charley Radbourn, 1883	8.1
9	Dave Foutz, 1886	8.0
10	Jim Devlin, 1876	7.9
	Tony Mullane, 1884	7.9
12	Will White, 1882	7.5
13	Matt Kilroy, 1887	7.3
14	3 players tied	7.1

1893-1919
1	Amos Rusie, 1894	11.0
2	Walter Johnson, 1912	10.0
3	Walter Johnson, 1913	9.7
4	Christy Mathewson, 1905	9.0
5	Pete Alexander, 1915	8.6
6	Joe Wood, 1912	8.5
7	Cy Young, 1901	7.9
8	Ed Walsh, 1908	7.5
9	Walter Johnson, 1918	7.4
10	Ed Walsh, 1910	7.3
11	Amos Rusie, 1893	7.1
	Walter Johnson, 1915	7.1
13	Kid Nichols, 1897	7.0
	Claude Hendrix, 1914	7.0
	Pete Alexander, 1916	7.0

1920-1941
1	Bucky Walters, 1939	8.0
2	Dolf Luque, 1923	7.5
	Lefty Grove, 1931	7.5
4	Carl Hubbell, 1933	7.1
5	Wes Ferrell, 1935	6.9
6	Pete Alexander, 1920	6.8
7	Dazzy Vance, 1928	6.6
	Lefty Grove, 1930	6.6
	Lefty Grove, 1936	6.6
	Thornton Lee, 1941	6.6
11	Curt Davis, 1934	6.4
12	Red Faber, 1921	6.3
	Lon Warneke, 1933	6.3
14	Lefty Gomez, 1937	6.2
15	Carl Hubbell, 1934	6.0

1942-1960
1	Dizzy Trout, 1944	8.8
2	Hal Newhouser, 1945	8.0
3	Spud Chandler, 1943	6.6
4	Hal Newhouser, 1946	6.5
	Bob Lemon, 1948	6.5
6	Warren Spahn, 1953	6.3
7	Hal Newhouser, 1944	5.9
	Robin Roberts, 1953	5.9
9	Mel Parnell, 1949	5.6
	Bobby Shantz, 1952	5.6
11	Bob Lemon, 1949	5.5
	Johnny Antonelli, 1954	5.5
13	Mort Cooper, 1942	5.4
	Ned Garver, 1950	5.4
15	3 players tied	5.3

1961-1992
1	Bob Gibson, 1968	8.1
2	Dwight Gooden, 1985	8.0
3	Steve Carlton, 1972	7.8
4	Wilbur Wood, 1971	7.0
5	Tom Seaver, 1971	6.8
	Ron Guidry, 1978	6.8
7	Gaylord Perry, 1972	6.6
8	Fergie Jenkins, 1971	6.5
9	Juan Marichal, 1966	6.4
	Jim Palmer, 1975	6.4
11	Bob Gibson, 1969	6.3
12	Roger Clemens, 1990	6.2
13	Tom Seaver, 1973	6.0
	Dave Stieb, 1985	6.0
	Greg Maddux, 1992	6.0

Total Baseball Ranking

1	Guy Hecker, 1884	12.9
2	Silver King, 1888	11.4
3	Amos Rusie, 1894	11.0
4	Babe Ruth, 1923	10.8
5	Charley Radbourn, 1884	10.4
6	John Clarkson, 1889	10.2
7	Walter Johnson, 1912	10.0
8	Walter Johnson, 1913	9.7
9	Babe Ruth, 1921	9.6
10	Nap Lajoie, 1901	9.2
11	Cal Ripken, 1984	9.1
12	Christy Mathewson, 1905	9.0
	Barry Bonds, 1992	9.0
14	John Clarkson, 1885	8.9
	Scott Stratton, 1890	8.9
	Babe Ruth, 1920	8.9
	Babe Ruth, 1927	8.9
18	Dizzy Trout, 1944	8.8
19	Nap Lajoie, 1910	8.7
20	Pete Alexander, 1915	8.6
	Fred Dunlap, 1884	8.6
22	Joe Wood, 1912	8.5
	Nap Lajoie, 1906	8.5
	Ty Cobb, 1917	8.5
	Babe Ruth, 1924	8.5
	Mickey Mantle, 1957	8.5
27	Rogers Hornsby, 1924	8.4
	Ted Williams, 1942	8.4
	Ted Williams, 1946	8.4
	Mickey Mantle, 1956	8.4
31	John Clarkson, 1887	8.3
	Nap Lajoie, 1903	8.3
33	Babe Ruth, 1926	8.2
34	Charley Radbourn, 1883	8.1
	Bob Gibson, 1968	8.1
	Rogers Hornsby, 1922	8.1
	Ted Williams, 1941	8.1
	Rickey Henderson, 1990	8.1
	Cal Ripken, 1991	8.1
40	Dave Foutz, 1886	8.0
	Bucky Walters, 1939	8.0
	Hal Newhouser, 1945	8.0
	Dwight Gooden, 1985	8.0
	Tris Speaker, 1912	8.0
	George Sisler, 1920	8.0
46	Jim Devlin, 1876	7.9
	Tony Mullane, 1884	7.9
	Cy Young, 1901	7.9
	Rogers Hornsby, 1920	7.9
	Carl Yastrzemski, 1967	7.9
51	Steve Carlton, 1972	7.8
	Nap Lajoie, 1908	7.8
	Lou Gehrig, 1927	7.8
	Ted Williams, 1947	7.8
55	Lou Boudreau, 1944	7.7
	Willie Mays, 1955	7.7
57	Tris Speaker, 1914	7.6
	Rogers Hornsby, 1917	7.6
	Mickey Mantle, 1961	7.6
	Ron Santo, 1966	7.6
	Mike Schmidt, 1980	7.6
62	Will White, 1882	7.5
	Ed Walsh, 1908	7.5
	Dolf Luque, 1923	7.5
	Lefty Grove, 1931	7.5
	Ted Williams, 1957	7.5
	Ron Santo, 1967	7.5
68	Walter Johnson, 1918	7.4
	Honus Wagner, 1905	7.4
	Honus Wagner, 1906	7.4
	Ty Cobb, 1911	7.4
	Tris Speaker, 1913	7.4
	Snuffy Stirnweiss, 1945	7.4
74	Matt Kilroy, 1887	7.3
	Ed Walsh, 1910	7.3
	Frankie Frisch, 1927	7.3
	Ted Williams, 1949	7.3
	Norm Cash, 1961	7.3
	Rickey Henderson, 1985	7.3
80	Nap Lajoie, 1904	7.2
	Ty Cobb, 1910	7.2
	Rogers Hornsby, 1929	7.2
	Lou Gehrig, 1934	7.2
	Harlond Clift, 1937	7.2
	Snuffy Stirnweiss, 1944	7.2
	Rico Petrocelli, 1969	7.2
	Joe Morgan, 1975	7.2
	Mike Schmidt, 1981	7.2
	George Brett, 1985	7.2
90	Jim Galvin, 1884	7.1
	Charlie Ferguson, 1886	7.1
	Jack Stivetts, 1891	7.1
	Amos Rusie, 1893	7.1
	Walter Johnson, 1915	7.1
	Carl Hubbell, 1933	7.1
	Eddie Collins, 1910	7.1
	Joe Jackson, 1912	7.1
	Mike Schmidt, 1974	7.1
	Eric Davis, 1987	7.1
	Barry Bonds, 1990	7.1

Total Baseball Rank (alpha.)

Pete Alexander, 1915	8.6
Barry Bonds, 1990	7.1
Barry Bonds, 1992	9.0
Lou Boudreau, 1944	7.7
George Brett, 1985	7.2
Steve Carlton, 1972	7.8
Norm Cash, 1961	7.3
John Clarkson, 1885	8.9
John Clarkson, 1887	8.3
John Clarkson, 1889	10.2
Harlond Clift, 1937	7.2
Ty Cobb, 1910	7.2
Ty Cobb, 1911	7.4
Ty Cobb, 1917	8.5
Eddie Collins, 1910	7.1
Eric Davis, 1987	7.1
Jim Devlin, 1876	7.9
Fred Dunlap, 1884	8.6
Charlie Ferguson, 1886	7.1
Dave Foutz, 1886	8.0
Frankie Frisch, 1927	7.3
Jim Galvin, 1884	7.1
Lou Gehrig, 1927	7.8
Lou Gehrig, 1934	7.2
Bob Gibson, 1968	8.1
Dwight Gooden, 1985	8.0
Lefty Grove, 1931	7.5
Guy Hecker, 1884	12.9
Rickey Henderson, 1985	7.3
Rickey Henderson, 1990	8.1
Rogers Hornsby, 1917	7.6
Rogers Hornsby, 1920	7.9
Rogers Hornsby, 1922	8.1
Rogers Hornsby, 1924	8.4
Rogers Hornsby, 1929	7.2
Carl Hubbell, 1933	7.1
Joe Jackson, 1912	7.1
Walter Johnson, 1912	10.0
Walter Johnson, 1913	9.7
Walter Johnson, 1915	7.1
Walter Johnson, 1918	7.4
Matt Kilroy, 1887	7.3
Silver King, 1888	11.4
Nap Lajoie, 1901	9.2
Nap Lajoie, 1903	8.3
Nap Lajoie, 1904	7.2
Nap Lajoie, 1906	8.5
Nap Lajoie, 1908	7.8
Nap Lajoie, 1910	8.7
Dolf Luque, 1923	7.5
Mickey Mantle, 1956	8.4
Mickey Mantle, 1957	8.5
Mickey Mantle, 1961	7.6
Christy Mathewson, 1905	9.0
Willie Mays, 1955	7.7
Joe Morgan, 1975	7.2
Tony Mullane, 1884	7.9
Hal Newhouser, 1945	8.0
Rico Petrocelli, 1969	7.2
Charley Radbourn, 1883	8.1
Charley Radbourn, 1884	10.4
Cal Ripken, 1984	9.1
Cal Ripken, 1991	8.1
Amos Rusie, 1893	7.1
Amos Rusie, 1894	11.0
Babe Ruth, 1920	8.9
Babe Ruth, 1921	9.6
Babe Ruth, 1923	10.8
Babe Ruth, 1924	8.5
Babe Ruth, 1926	8.2
Babe Ruth, 1927	8.9
Ron Santo, 1966	7.6
Ron Santo, 1967	7.5
Mike Schmidt, 1974	7.1
Mike Schmidt, 1980	7.6
Mike Schmidt, 1981	7.2
George Sisler, 1920	8.0
Tris Speaker, 1912	8.0
Tris Speaker, 1913	7.4
Tris Speaker, 1914	7.6
Snuffy Stirnweiss, 1944	7.2
Snuffy Stirnweiss, 1945	7.4
Jack Stivetts, 1891	7.1
Scott Stratton, 1890	8.9
Dizzy Trout, 1944	8.8
Honus Wagner, 1905	7.4
Honus Wagner, 1906	7.4
Ed Walsh, 1908	7.5
Ed Walsh, 1910	7.3
Bucky Walters, 1939	8.0
Will White, 1882	7.5
Ted Williams, 1941	8.1
Ted Williams, 1942	8.4
Ted Williams, 1946	8.4
Ted Williams, 1947	7.8
Ted Williams, 1949	7.3
Ted Williams, 1957	7.5
Joe Wood, 1912	8.5
Carl Yastrzemski, 1967	7.9
Cy Young, 1901	7.9

Total Baseball Rank (by era)

1876-1892
1	Guy Hecker, 1884	12.9
2	Silver King, 1888	11.4
3	Charley Radbourn, 1884	10.4
4	John Clarkson, 1889	10.2
5	John Clarkson, 1885	8.9
	Scott Stratton, 1890	8.9
7	Fred Dunlap, 1884	8.6
8	John Clarkson, 1887	8.3
9	Charley Radbourn, 1883	8.1
10	Dave Foutz, 1886	8.0
11	Jim Devlin, 1876	7.9
	Tony Mullane, 1884	7.9
13	Will White, 1882	7.5
14	Matt Kilroy, 1887	7.3
15	3 players tied	7.1

1893-1919
1	Amos Rusie, 1894	11.0
2	Walter Johnson, 1912	10.0
3	Walter Johnson, 1913	9.7
4	Nap Lajoie, 1901	9.2
5	Christy Mathewson, 1905	9.0
6	Nap Lajoie, 1910	8.7
7	Pete Alexander, 1915	8.6
8	Joe Wood, 1912	8.5
	Nap Lajoie, 1906	8.5
	Ty Cobb, 1917	8.5
11	Nap Lajoie, 1903	8.3
12	Tris Speaker, 1912	8.0
13	Cy Young, 1901	7.9
14	Nap Lajoie, 1908	7.8
15	2 players tied	7.6

1920-1941
1	Babe Ruth, 1923	10.8
2	Babe Ruth, 1921	9.6
3	Babe Ruth, 1920	8.9
	Babe Ruth, 1927	8.9
5	Babe Ruth, 1924	8.5
6	Rogers Hornsby, 1924	8.4
7	Babe Ruth, 1926	8.2
8	Rogers Hornsby, 1922	8.1
	Ted Williams, 1941	8.1
10	Bucky Walters, 1939	8.0
	George Sisler, 1920	8.0
12	Rogers Hornsby, 1920	7.9
13	Lou Gehrig, 1927	7.8
14	Dolf Luque, 1923	7.5
	Lefty Grove, 1931	7.5

1942-1960
1	Dizzy Trout, 1944	8.8
2	Mickey Mantle, 1957	8.5
3	Ted Williams, 1942	8.4
	Ted Williams, 1946	8.4
	Mickey Mantle, 1956	8.4
6	Hal Newhouser, 1945	8.0
7	Ted Williams, 1947	7.8
8	Lou Boudreau, 1944	7.7
	Willie Mays, 1955	7.7
10	Ted Williams, 1957	7.5
11	Snuffy Stirnweiss, 1945	7.4
12	Ted Williams, 1949	7.3
13	Snuffy Stirnweiss, 1944	7.2
14	Willie Mays, 1958	7.0
15	Jackie Robinson, 1951	6.9

1961-1992
1	Cal Ripken, 1984	9.1
2	Barry Bonds, 1992	9.0
3	Bob Gibson, 1968	8.1
	Rickey Henderson, 1990	8.1
	Cal Ripken, 1991	8.1
6	Dwight Gooden, 1985	8.0
7	Carl Yastrzemski, 1967	7.9
8	Steve Carlton, 1972	7.8
9	Mickey Mantle, 1961	7.6
	Ron Santo, 1966	7.6
	Mike Schmidt, 1980	7.6
12	Ron Santo, 1967	7.5
13	Norm Cash, 1961	7.3
	Rickey Henderson, 1985	7.3
15	4 players tied	7.2

Managers and Coaches

Fred Stein

Baseball, established as a "gentleman's sport" by the 1840s, attained a degree of commercial success by the end of the 1860s. Within this transition from a participatory, upper-class social game to an organized professional, spectator sport there developed a need for accountability, both as a sporting endeavor and as a money-making enterprise.

Harry Wright was the first important manager, and his functions in the 1860s were typical of the workload carried by managers of that period. A former professional cricket player, Wright saw his first baseball game at age twenty-two, and it was love at first sight. A decade later, he helped organize the famous Cincinnati Red Stockings, the first all-salaried team, which won 84 consecutive games in 1869–1870. Wright's duties included the following: field manager, center fielder, relief pitcher, team trainer, tracker of team baseballs and field equipment, disciplinarian, scheduler of games and travel arrangements, checker of gate receipts, and bursar.

Wright continued his managing career with the advent of "organized baseball" in 1871, winning four straight pennants with the Boston Red Stockings from 1872 through 1875. He managed National League entries through 1893. The highly moral, immensely popular Wright is credited with playing the dominant role in establishing the integrity of professional baseball in its critical, formative years.

It bothered Wright to hear that other managers felt they could do as well as he had done with his players. He felt that managing a team effectively involved handling players with proper recognition of their human frailties as well as capitalization of their physical skills.

The baseball manager's role became more clearly defined in the 1870–1900 period, as increased revenues permitted clubs to hire people—"managers" akin to today's general managers—to handle such administrative functions as monitoring gate receipts, paying salaries, and supervising equipment and stadium operations. But these business managers, twenty-eight of whom have been carried in the Macmillan Encyclopedia as managers, never filled out a lineup card or accompanied the team on a road trip. The research of Rich Topp and Bob Tiemann has set the matter straight in this volume. Scheduling of games became the function of league offices, relieving the manager of this responsibility. Still, for economic reasons, the on-field manager (or "captain," as he was often designated) usually was expected to perform double duty—serving as a player as well as the field boss. He was also responsible for disciplining players, keeping them in condition, and, depending on circumstances, handling player transactions. The 1890s in particular featured increased emphasis on scientific baseball, and the strategies employed by managers became a matter of increased interest and importance.

Adrian "Cap" Anson was the most prominent manager and player of the 1880s and '90s. The massive (for the time) first baseman hit .336 for his full twenty-seven-year career, and was the first National League player with more than 3,000 career hits. The gruff, no-nonsense type, Anson ranked high on the all-time managers list with a .578 won-and-lost percentage over twenty-one seasons as a manager. He directed Chicago to five pennants in his first eight seasons.

The outspoken Iowa native was a stern taskmaster who ruled his club with an iron hand. He was an innovative manager—he utilized spring training for conditioning purposes, encouraged base stealing, rotated pitchers with contrasting styles, used signals, and employed the hit-and-run play. On the down side, Anson played an important role in barring black players from organized baseball. He had little of the philosophical concern for the game which characterized the gentle, high-minded Harry Wright. Yet Anson, not Wright, became the principal hero of the era.

Ned Hanlon was an important manager in the 1890s, a prime exponent of the rough-and-ready, anything-to-win approach typical of the play of that decade. Hanlon's famed Baltimore Orioles won three successive pennants in 1894-1896, then finished in second place twice before Hanlon moved to the Brooklyn club, which he led to pennant wins in 1899 and 1900. The bookish-appearing Hanlon headed a Baltimore cast which included such legendary players as McGraw, Keller, Robinson, Kelley, and Jennings. Even allowing for hyperbole, the club was noted for its "inside baseball" and rowdy antics. Scholars differ as to who invented strategies like the squeeze play, the "Baltimore chop," and judicious doctoring of the baseball diamond, but there is little doubt that the Orioles, under Hanlon, perfected these techniques.

Managing in the 1900–1920 period was marked by continuing emphasis on scientific baseball, in a dead-ball era when runs were hard to come by. During these two decades, the game reached new popularity, and some managers, along with players, became national heroes.

Connie Mack and John McGraw were the towering managerial figures of the period. Mack was a journeyman catcher whose managing career began with Pittsburgh of the National League in 1894. After three seasons, he managed Milwaukee of the Western League until 1901, when he and Benjamin Shibe were awarded the Philadelphia franchise in the new American League.

Nicknamed "The Tall Tactician," Mack put together, and then took apart, dominating teams in two different eras. Between 1910 and 1914, his Athletics won four pennants before, feeling the need for financial retrench-

ment, he began shedding such high-priced stars as second baseman Eddie Collins and pitchers Jack Coombs, Eddie Plank, and Chief Bender. As a result, the A's finished dead last from 1915 through 1921.

Beginning in the mid-1920s, Mack gathered several future Hall of Famers—Cochrane, Simmons, Foxx, and Grove—and the A's won three straight pennants starting in 1929. However, with the Depression deepening and attendance dropping drastically, Mack again was forced to sell his stars. It was all downhill for the cash-poor Mack as the A's finished in the second division from 1934 through 1950, his last year as manager.

During Mack's fifty-three-year managerial career, he won and lost more games (3,731 and 3,948) than any other major league pilot. In addition to his records, he is remembered for managing from the bench in street clothes and for deploying his fielders (usually with remarkable precision) with a wave of his ever-present scorecard. Many felt he remained at the helm for too long, simply because he couldn't be fired. They pointed to the Athletics' ineffectual showing over his last seventeen years and his tendency to nod off on the bench. Regardless, baseball men respected his shrewd judgment of talent, his ability to manage unlettered eccentrics and college men with equal effectiveness, his skill in building great teams in both the dead- and live-ball eras, and his entrepreneurial skill in keeping afloat on a financial shoestring. Mack's players revered the dignified old man with the New England accent—a link between them and when baseball was barely beyond its infancy.

John McGraw shared Connie Mack's Irish background and his acumen, but they were direct opposites in most other respects. "The Little Napoleon" was a scrappy little third baseman whose .334 lifetime average, fielding skill, and driving aggressiveness would have justified Hall of Fame recognition if his managing had not done so. McGraw was the ringleader of Ned Hanlon's Orioles. After moving to St. Louis of the National League in 1900, he went to the new American League, accepting Ban Johnson's offer to manage the Baltimore club in 1901.

Unable to get along with Johnson, McGraw jumped at the chance to manage the New York Giants in July 1902. The Giants became the most successful team for the next thirty years, with McGraw engendering high emotions. As Grantland Rice wrote, "His very walk across the field in a hostile town is a challenge to the multitude." McGraw is credited with stimulating the growth of baseball during the 1900–1920 period, just before the lively-ball era.

Most experts consider McGraw the greatest ever. He ranks second only to Mack in games managed (4,845) and in games won (2,816). His teams captured ten pennants in thirty years with only two second-division finishes. McGraw's genius produced strategic and tactical innovations, and attracted and developed many superb players. His career evoked continuous arguments, fistfights, and controversies with league presidents, owners, umpires, managers and players, and off-the-field acquaintances. However, this bon vivant and man of varied nonbaseball interests was also famous for helping downtrodden former players.

Clark Griffith, Fred Clarke, and Frank Chance were three other prominent managers of the 1900–1920 period.

Griffith had pitching credentials (240–141) which would have justified his election to the Hall of Fame as a player as well as a manager. The pocket-sized righthander, nicknamed "The Old Fox," relied upon control, guile, and uncanny skill at nicking or otherwise doctoring the ball to fool the hitters.

At the request of President Ban Johnson, Griffith managed the New York Highlanders from 1903 through 1908. He managed Cincinnati in 1909–1911 before purchasing a 10 percent interest in Washington. During his managerial tenure with the Senators from 1912 to 1920, Griffith operated with little capital, as evidenced by only two first-division finishes during the period, both largely attributable to the superhuman efforts of speedballing Walter Johnson. Griffith gained controlling interest in the Senators in 1920 and vacated the manager's slot to become club president.

Fred Clarke, another outstanding player, was a field manager in nineteen of his twenty-one major league seasons. The compact outfielder had a .315 batting average while collecting 2,708 hits. He hit a career high .406 in 1897, stole over 30 bases in seven seasons, and was a superb left fielder.

Clarke managed Louisville from 1897 to 1899 and Pittsburgh for the next sixteen years, ranking among the top managers with 1,602 wins and a .576 winning percentage. Led by Clarke himself, shortstop Honus Wagner, and center fielder Ginger Beaumont, the Pirates won consecutive pennants in 1901–1903, then won the World Championship in 1909. Hallmarks of the energetic Clarke's teams were their excellent physical condition and tight discipline, both on and off the field.

Clubs managed by Frank Chance, along with McGraw and Clarke, won every National League pennant from 1901 through 1913. Chance is best remembered as the first baseman of the famous "Tinker to Evers to Chance" double-play combination of the Chicago Cubs, as the Cubs won three straight pennants in 1906–1908 and added another in 1910.

Chance, a smart, natural leader, took over the Cubs in midseason of 1905 from Frank Selee, himself a great but little-remembered pilot, and remained through the 1912 season. During his seven-and-a-half-year tenure, the "Peerless Leader's" clubs won 753 games and lost only 379, for a remarkable .665 percentage. Handicapped by recurring headaches attributable to several beanings, Chance withdrew from active play and later managed the Highlanders in 1913–1914 and the Red Sox in 1923, but with none of his earlier success.

The lively ball changed major league baseball and managerial strategy after 1920. Such offensive baseball tactics as the stolen base, the sacrifice bunt in early innings, and the squeeze play were virtually ignored as the long ball came into vogue. "Big bang" baseball became the rule rather than the exception, with only occasional aberrations. Big-inning baseball strategies had largely replaced those of the dead-ball era, and baseball managers were forced to adapt to the changes.

Connie Mack successfully shifted his managerial focus to the new offensive game, and the Athletics won pennants in 1929–1931. John McGraw won four successive pennants in the early twenties, largely on the strength of strong, well-balanced teams rather than offensive

powerhouses. After 1924 McGraw's failure to adapt to the power game prevented him from winning any more pennants before he left the game in 1932.

The powerful Yankees of the twenties, thirties, and early forties were famed for power hitting complemented by exemplary pitching and fielding. Yankee managers Miller Huggins and Joe McCarthy were the beneficiaries of crushing offenses led by Ruth, Gehrig, Meusel, Combs, Lazzeri, and Dickey, then later by DiMaggio, Henrich, Gordon and Keller.

Miller Huggins was a tiny second baseman, considered an excellent fielder but a weak hitter (.265 lifetime average with little power), whose offensive forte was drawing walks and stealing bases. The bright "Mighty Mite," a law school graduate, managed the St. Louis Cardinals in 1913–1917 with modest success. He was then hired by Yankee owner Col. Jacob Ruppert against the wishes of co-owner Col. Tillinghast Huston, who was overseas in World War One action at the time.

Huggins's masterstroke was in convincing the Yankees to purchase Babe Ruth from the financially troubled Red Sox. Ruth was largely responsible for the Yankees' developing dynasty, which brought Huggins six pennants in twelve seasons. Ruth was important to Huggins in another respect: maintaining player discipline. Ruth regularly broke club rules until Huggins fined him $5,000 (a lot of money in 1925) and suspended him. Management strongly supported Huggins, and Ruth and his fellow recalcitrants bowed to Huggins's authority.

Huggins died unexpectedly at fifty in 1929, and Joe McCarthy took over as the Yankees' manager a year later. Another weak-hitting infielder, "Marse Joe" never made it to the majors as a player. After gaining recognition as one of the leading minor league managers, McCarthy managed the Chicago Cubs from 1926 to 1930, winning the pennant in 1929. McCarthy went on to win eight pennants and seven World Championships in fifteen full seasons as Yankees' manager, with only one finish as low as fourth. Under McCarthy the Yankees did not merely outshine the competition, they annihilated them, winning the 1936 flag by a record 19½ games and winning the 1932, 1938, and 1939 World Series in four games straight.

McCarthy's teams were noted for their attention to detail and their teamwork, as well as their overpowering talent. McCarthy was a strict, if undemonstrative, disciplinarian (ties and jackets were compulsory, and even pipe smoking was discouraged) and was adept at maintaining the defensive excellence which undergirded his teams' successes. McCarthy ranks first among all managers with a .614 winning percentage.

Charles Dillon "Casey" Stengel was the third in a line of great Yankee managers. He was a sometimes comic journeyman outfielder (.284 career batting average) whose playing career is best remembered for his sparkling hitting in the 1923 World Series, when he won two games for the Giants against the Yankees with home runs.

The lovable "Old Perfessor" with the great sense of humor, total recall of game situations, and gift of gab (he specialized in long-winded non sequiturs) began his fabled major league managerial career with Brooklyn in 1934. After three mediocre seasons with the Dodgers and one season (1937) when he was paid not to manage the Dodg-

ers, Stengel spent six seasons managing the Braves, still unable to rise into the first division.

After managing in the high minors from 1944 to 1948, Stengel signed with the Yankees for 1949. He took the club to an unprecedented five consecutive pennants, finished in second place in 1954 (despite 103 wins), then won four more consecutive pennants before falling to third place in 1959. He closed out with another pennant in 1960, a total of ten pennants and seven World Championships in twelve seasons. Dismissed as "too old," Stengel managed the fledgling Mets from 1962 to 1965, finishing in last place each season, before retiring two-thirds into the 1965 season. Stengel had a won-lost percentage of .508 for twenty-five seasons, ranking fourth in games managed and seventh in games won.

Huggins and McCarthy were essentially orthodox, conservative managers who consistently turned out magnificent teams with magnificent players. Stengel, also gifted with great players—DiMaggio, Berra, Rizzuto, Ford, Mantle—added another dimension to managing. He rose above crushing injuries to his stars and obtained high performance from unexpected sources. Even more remarkable, he played with and *against* the percentages with outstanding success. In addition, he had unparalleled rapport with writers, thereby helping in the press as well as on the field. Stengel was, in his own word, "amazin'!"

Leo Durocher was another interesting, if more controversial, manager. The brash, street-smart "Lippy Leo" was a weak-hitting but great-fielding shortstop for the Yankees, Reds, "Gas House Gang" Cardinals, and Dodgers. Durocher became the Dodgers' player-manager in 1939, just as President Larry MacPhail was beginning to raise the club from its long-standing doldrums. In 1941, they won Brooklyn's first pennant in twenty-one years. Durocher just barely lost out to St. Louis in 1942 and 1946. Sparked by rookie Jackie Robinson, the Dodgers won the pennant in 1947, but Durocher was not on hand—he had been suspended for "conduct detrimental to baseball" for the entire 1947 season. Leo returned in 1948, but with the Dodgers doing poorly, he moved in midseason across town to the New York Giants. It was a shock for Giants' fans—idolized Mel Ott replaced by the hated Durocher.

Durocher's revamped Giants, 13½ games off the pace in August 1951, came back to beat the Dodgers on Bobby Thomson's "Miracle at Coogan's Bluff" home run. In many respects this was Durocher's finest season. Although Durocher went on to win the World Championship in 1954, the Polo Grounders slipped, and Durocher, never completely accepted by Giants' fans, was let out after the 1955 season. He returned to manage the Cubs from 1966 through midseason 1972 but was unable to win a pennant. His career ended after he piloted Houston unsuccessfully through the 1973 season.

Durocher was a knowledgeable, aggressive manager who could inspire a team with winning potential but seemed to lose interest with lesser teams. Leo tended to find himself in unsavory company, the basic reason for his suspension in 1947. Although respected as a strategist and competitor, he was disliked intensely by many who resented his beanball orders and by umpires and fans offended by his rowdy tactics. Over his career, Durocher ranks fifth in games managed and sixth in wins.

Walter "Smokey" Alston was the antithesis of Durocher—a quiet, unassuming, stable man who at first won with power-packed teams, then with speedy clubs. A hard-hitting first baseman in the minors, the Ohio strongman had only a cup of coffee in the majors—in 1936 he struck out in his only at bat. He was installed as manager at Brooklyn in 1954 after they fired pennant-winning pilot Charlie Dressen, who wanted a multiyear contract. Alston, who never received more than a single-year contract in his twenty-three Dodger seasons, responded with seven pennants and four World Championships. He led the famous "Boys of Summer" Dodgers to pennants in 1955–1956. His 1965–1966 flags were sparked by the herculean pitching of Sandy Koufax and the base-stealing heroics of Maury Wills. Only two men, Connie Mack and John McGraw, managed the same team for a longer period. He ranks fifth in games won with a .558 winning percentage.

The role (some would say the importance) of the manager has changed significantly over the past two decades, in terms of both strategy and the maintenance of discipline. The designated hitter rule has changed the game drastically, giving the manager either more or fewer options, depending on the viewpoint. Pitching strategy has shifted to a decreased emphasis on going the route and an increased emphasis on a dominant relief pitcher. Artificial turf requires different strategies and playing styles from play on natural grass. Base stealing has changed strategies. Platooning, which has been around for at least seventy years, has been refined to an art.

Maintaining discipline has become much more difficult over the years. Until the 1960s, the manager ruled completely. But today most players are paid more than managers, implying that a higher-paid star is more valuable than the manager. As a result, fining highly paid players is a relatively ineffective disciplinary tactic. Today air travel has telescoped travel time, and players spend more time away from their teammates. The resulting reduced team discipline and togetherness have made it more difficult for managers to weld their players into cohesive units.

Drug abuse presents an extremely difficult managerial problem. Excessive drinking has been a common difficulty from the early days of professional baseball. But its impact upon performance is usually readily determined. However, the use of drugs is extremely difficult to detect, and its impact is long term and virtually impossible to judge.

Managers have been laid off, sacrifices on the altars of second-division finishes or general discontent, since the game began. But over the last two decades there is evidence that managers have become an increasingly endangered species. From 1970 through 1981, for example, National League managers enjoyed a mere 2.4-year average tenure, while their American League counterparts lasted only 1.9 years on the average.

On the positive side, today's manager has a multitude of helpers, sufficient to give his job a chairman-of-the-board aura. He now has hitting instructors, base-stealing coaches, specialists in playing each position, pitching coaches, conditioning and medical specialists, motivation experts, and, yes, someone to check on the inventory of baseballs.

Several managers have been adept at dealing with these emerging changes, most prominently Sparky Anderson, Earl Weaver, Dick Williams, and Billy Martin.

George "Sparky" Anderson fits the classic pattern of the successful manager—a brainy, hustling, good-field-no-hit infielder. After hitting .218 for the Phillies in his only major league season, Anderson managed in the minors from 1964 to 1968, then coached for the fledgling Padres in 1969.

Appointed to manage the Reds in 1970, Anderson was an immediate success, winning the pennant by 14½ games. Anderson's clubs won again in 1972, 1975, and 1976, powered by Johnny Bench, Tony Perez, Pete Rose, and Joe Morgan. Many experts rate his 1976 powerhouse with the great Yankee teams. Despite Anderson's brilliant tenure at Cincinnati (four pennants and two World Championships in nine years), the Reds released him after a second-place finish in 1978. The Tigers hired him immediately, and he improved the club steadily, guiding them to a World Championship in 1984.

The garrulous Anderson is one of the most popular men in the game, frequently broadcasting postseason games despite lamentable diction. Nicknamed "Captain Hook" because of crisp yanking of struggling pitchers, Anderson is highly respected for diligence, ready availability to the press, and fairness and loyalty to his players.

The inimitable Earl Weaver is considered by many experts to be the top manager of the last twenty years. Another ex-minor league infielder who never made it to the majors, Weaver managed in the minors from 1956 through 1967, then took over Baltimore in midseason 1968. He led the Orioles through 1982, then stepped down voluntarily for the 1983–1984 campaigns. Summoned back as the Orioles faltered in 1985, Weaver managed through the 1986 season before retiring to Florida.

Weaver ranks among the ten best managers statistically, with a .583 winning percentage. During his seventeen seasons, he won four pennants and one World Championship, but was remarkably consistent, finishing out of the first division only once.

Weaver's style combined those of John McGraw and Casey Stengel. He was the most frequently ejected manager of his era, with ninety-one ejections and four suspensions. His explosive debates with umpires (many precipitated by Weaver for his own strategic purposes) are unforgettable—the stocky little manager cheek to cheek with the umpire, his cap turned around to prevent contact, and his violent outbursts punctuated by vigorous hand slaps against his ever-present rule book.

The innovative Weaver set up an instruction plan in the early 1960s, still used throughout the Orioles organization, permitting future stars to move from the lowest farm club to the parent club with a minimum of adjustment. Weaver made unprecedented use of charts and computers, although he never abandoned his fundamental reliance upon three-run homers, a relatively walk-free pitching staff, and a tight, well-disciplined defense.

Weaver was a realist in recognizing players' capabilities and limitations. Accordingly he used his entire roster to maximize player strengths and minimize weaknesses, accomplishing this by extensive analysis of scouting reports and past performances of players against individual opponents. Weaver was the supreme strategist of his time.

Dick Williams has been one of the most successful

managers since the late 1960s. He was a journeyman outfielder-infielder, hitting .260 over his injury-plagued thirteen-year playing career. After managing the Red Sox's Triple A Toronto farm team in 1965–1966, Williams led the parent club to a pennant in 1967. Released after failing to repeat in 1968–1969, Williams was hired by Charles Finley to manage the Athletics in 1971.

Williams won two straight pennants and World Championships in three boisterous seasons in Oakland. He had an imposing aggregation of young players, as well as the unpredictable—and unignorable—Finley as his boss. Tiring of meddling, Williams quit after his second straight World Championship in 1973. He managed California in 1974–1976, but with little success, then managed the Montreal Expos from 1977 to 1981 without winning a pennant. Williams piloted San Diego from 1982 to 1985, winning the 1984 flag. He left the Padres before the 1986 season to take over the youthful Mariners for a brief while.

Especially effective with younger players, Williams ran a no-nonsense, well-disciplined ship—no simple task in these times. He retired with 1,571 victories.

Billy Martin was the most combative figure in the game from the time he joined the Yankees as a twenty-two-year-old second baseman in 1950 until his death in 1989. A fair fielder and an average hitter (.257 lifetime average) who enhanced his value by his razor-sharp baseball instincts and aggressiveness, Martin was best known for his many brawls with other players, club officials, and miscellaneous bystanders. He attributed much of his bellicosity to a rough childhood in Berkeley.

Martin produced winning teams everywhere he managed, but off-field troubles with owners and other incidents resulted in his string of firings and resignations. He began managing at Denver in 1968 and in the majors with Minnesota in 1969, where his club won the AL West. Fired "for ignoring Twins policies," Martin was hired at Detroit in 1971. After a second-place finish, he led the Tigers to the Eastern Division title in 1972. He left the Tigers near the end of the 1973 season and finished out the season managing Texas. Martin was fired by the Rangers on July 21, 1975, then took over as Yankees manager on August 2, 1975. Hired by owner George Steinbrenner to restore the Yankee former glory, Martin produced a pennant in 1976. Reggie Jackson joined the Yankees in 1977, contributing to a World Championship in a tumultuous season remembered for a highly publicized feud (and a nationally televised dugout confrontation and near fight) between Jackson and Martin.

In 1978 Steinbrenner fired Martin in midseason. Then, in a dramatic announcement preceding the Yankees' Old Timers' Game in July 1978, Steinbrenner promised to rehire Martin. Billy returned in 1979 but was fired again in midseason because of an off-field incident. Martin managed Oakland in 1980 and, with the last-place club of the previous year playing spirited "Billy Ball," he lifted the Athletics to second place in 1980 and a division title in 1981. The A's deteriorated in 1982 and Martin was dismissed at the end of the season.

In a familiar scenario, Martin returned to the Yankees in 1983 but was replaced after finishing third. Incredibly he was rehired for a fourth time in 1985, but replaced by Lou Piniella. He had a career percentage of .552, five

divisional championships, two pennants, and a World Championship.

Martin served the Yankees in the broadcasting booth and other capacities in 1986–1987. Then, as Steinbrenner's opinion of Piniella soured (while others were recommending him as a candidate for Manager of the Year!), the by now monotonous announcement came over the wires: Martin would manage the Yankees again in 1988. The other shoe dropped in early summer, as Martin was let go in favor of Piniella.

Similar to his mentor Casey Stengel, Martin's success in large part stemmed from his intense concentration on the game and his ability to motivate players of average talent. However, unlike Stengel, Martin's greatest problem was handling young players. He also had difficulties with established players, especially stars such as Reggie Jackson and Don Baylor, who made no bones of their intense dislike for Martin. He had tremendous success in attaining immediate improvement in team performance. However, he tended to wear out his welcome within a short time. He had a tendency to burn out starting pitchers, particularly evident during his tenure at Oakland.

Managerial Styles

As John McGraw—with simple directness—put it, "The idea [in managing] is to win." No argument there, but it is interesting to consider the widely different approaches major league managers have brought to the task.

First, there are the autocrats, the "you'll do it my way or else" types. Some prime examples are Cap Anson, John McGraw, Rogers Hornsby, Leo Durocher, Charlie Dressen, Earl Weaver, Gene Mauch, Dick Williams, and Billy Martin.

Cap Anson was a strong disciplinarian who did not allow his players to smoke (apparently chewing tobacco was permitted) or to drink alcohol in a notably heavy-drinking era. Anson was the largest player on his team and was known to exert brute strength to carry out his edicts.

McGraw was the most notorious autocrat of them all. He demanded that his players submit to his will unconditionally. This included strict curfews and long hours of sliding, fielding, hitting, and bunting practice. Christy Mathewson told of games during which McGraw called every pitch: ". . . McGraw . . . plans every move, most of the hitters going to the plate with definite instructions from him as to what to try to do. In order to make this system efficient, absolute discipline must be assured. If a player has other ideas than McGraw, . . . the invariable answer to him is "You do what I tell you, and I'll take the responsibility if we lose."

The success of the stifling McGraw approach continued as long as players followed his orders without question. But Fred Lindstrom described its effect on the club in McGraw's later years. Lindstrom said, "With the advent of fellows like Bill Terry, Mel Ott, Carl Hubbell, Travis Jackson, and me, we were a different breed. We didn't need someone hitting us over the head to keep us in shape. In fact, we wouldn't take it—at least Terry and I wouldn't. I don't think McGraw was able to adapt his methods of handling . . . the more modern-style players.

And after 1924 he never won another pennant."

McGraw's postgame "meetings" were noted for their length (sometimes as long as three hours) and for McGraw's vicious harangues. (Pete Reiser reported that Leo Durocher, another absolute ruler, forbade his Brooklyn Dodger players from taking off their uniforms after losing a game until the Lippy One gave his permission.)

Rogers Hornsby, a blunt, humorless man, was another imperious manager. Hall of Famer Billy Herman, who joined the Chicago Cubs as a rookie at the end of the 1931 season, later described Hornsby as follows:

> He ran the clubhouse like a gestapo camp. You couldn't smoke, drink a soft drink, eat a sandwich. Couldn't read a paper . . . no more kidding around, no joking, no laughing . . . It still burns me up just a little bit to remember some of his sarcastic remarks.

Billy Martin acted like a Marine drill sergeant. Graig Nettles played for Martin in 1968 at Denver. In his book *Balls*, Nettles reports that Martin would scream from the dugout at an errant player as the player came in from the field. Martin held his players in contempt, thought they had not "scuffled around." Nettles concluded gamely that "on a Billy Martin team, there is only one boss: Billy Martin. And if you do it his way, you'll win."

Then there are the managers who downplay their own importance in deference to their players. They have been likened to school guidance counselors. Typical members of this group include Connie Mack, Wilbert Robinson, Bill McKechnie, Miller Huggins, Bucky Harris, Eddie Sawyer, Walter Alston, Danny Murtaugh, Ralph Houk, Tom Lasorda, and Sparky Anderson.

Connie Mack was an unobtrusive figure who never upstaged his players. He preferred not to wear a uniform and, therefore, was forbidden from stepping onto the field. As a result, he did not project himself into the public eye during a game. According to Jimmy Dykes, nothing ever seemed to bother Mack, who was perfectly content to yield the spotlight to his players. He was the same placid man sitting on the bench, whether his Athletics were in last or a World Series. To Dykes's knowledge, Mack never fined a player, although he was known to express his displeasure when a player violated the midnight curfew without permission. The saintly Mack never used profanity; Dykes said that if Mack used the word "damn," he was deeply disturbed.

Eddie Sawyer was perfect for the pennant-winning 1950 Phillies "Whiz Kids," a group of youngsters more in need of friendly encouragement and understanding than of a domineering boss. The unassuming, fatherly Sawyer made it a point to involve himself in the personal problems of his players. He played his father-confessor role to the hilt during one season when nine of his players were expectant fathers.

John McGraw's old Orioles teammate, Wilbert Robinson, had a much more relaxed approach to managing than the intense McGraw. His players loved Robinson for his down-to-earth approach and his reluctance to exaggerate his own considerable store of baseball knowledge.

Walter Alston, a strong, silent man, had a simple philosophy. "Be your own self. To me that's probably the most important part of it, more so than the strategy part. If you know yourself, you'll know your players—how to handle them, . . . which ones to pat on the back, which ones to give a kick in the ass now and then . . . the winning of the ballgame and the good of the team come first." With that simple credo, Alston lasted twenty-three seasons as Dodgers' manager, the classic "faceless" manager whose records did the talking for him.

Then there's the "I'm just one of the boys" managing school. Some who come readily to mind are Pie Traynor, Rabbit Maranville, Charlie Grimm, Yogi Berra, Billy Herman, and Harvey Kuenn. Unfortunately, with some exceptions, this group tends to be comprised of "nice guys" who have been known to finish last.

By his own admission, Billy Herman was not a good manager in his rookie season as boss of the Pirates in 1946: "I could run the game as well as anybody. But I was terrible with the men. I was too easy with them, letting them have too much latitude . . . I was determined not to change, and that's where I was wrong." The Pirates finished tied for last and Herman was fired.

Yet there have been pleasant, relaxed "one of the boys" managers who have done well. Laid-back Harvey Kuenn was the perfect leader for the pennant-winning Milwaukee Brewers in 1982, and relaxed Joe Altobelli replaced overwrought Earl Weaver in 1983 and led the Baltimore Orioles to the World Championship. Charlie Grimm was one of the most successful of the easygoing managers. "Jolly Cholly" replaced the forbidding Rogers Hornsby as manager of the Chicago Cubs in midseason of 1932 and managed the Cubs to the pennant. Grimm permitted his players to do things their own way, with no rules or curfews. He ran the club on the field, but he was a happy-go-lucky man off the field, singing and dancing in the clubhouse and playing his banjo after the games.

And then there was vest-pocket-sized Walter "Rabbit" Maranville, renowned for basket catches and world-class carousing. Informed of his appointment to manage the Cubs in midseason of 1925 while on a train with his teammates, the well-oiled Rabbit celebrated by waking up all hands, shouting, "There will be no sleeping on this train under Maranville management." Not surprisingly, Maranville lasted only fifty-three games, with the Cubs resolutely on their way to last.

Pitcher-author Jim Brosnan has identified another category of managers whose central goal is to weld players into tightly knit communities. Adherents of this style tend to insist on conformity to team standards and to unload troublemakers. Of the great managers, Brosnan lumps Joe McCarthy, Casey Stengel, and Al Lopez in this category. Bill Terry and more recently Tony Larussa and Jim Leyland, among others, can also be included in this group.

Joe McCarthy's skills as a builder of unified teams, well developed during his pre-New York Yankees managerial years, were honed during the 1931–1934 seasons, when he had to deal with a fractious, aging Babe Ruth. The Bambino made no bones about his goal: he wanted to replace McCarthy without even managing in the minor leagues (Ruth had turned down Colonel Ruppert's offer of the managership of the Yankees' farm at Newark). McCarthy managed to keep his club in the running, and the team from splitting pro- and anti-Ruth factions, until the disillusioned Babe left after the 1934 season.

McCarthy, a quiet disciplinarian, attained tight control by requiring model behavior both on and off the field. He traded established regulars, righthander Johnny Allen and outfielder Ben Chapman, whose hot tempers did not fit the Yankee mold. McCarthy's demands that players dress formally led baseball men to anticipate a confrontation between McCarthy and Ted Williams when Marse Joe took over as Red Sox manager in 1948. Williams was the embodiment of the nonconformist, as witness his refusal to wear a necktie. The first morning of spring training, Williams appeared at breakfast with an open-neck sport shirt. Said the surprisingly flexible Marse Joe, "Any manager who can't get along with a .400 hitter is out of his mind."

Bill Terry's New York Giants of the 1930s built their success on close teamwork and a tight defense, as Terry scratched for runs in the best early 1900s style. He frequently had Mel Ott, the club's only authentic home run threat, bunt runners along as early as the first inning of a game.

Terry had little use for most writers, whom he referred to scornfully as "a bunch of twenty-five-dollar-a-week clerks." Terry refused to talk with them on his own time, and he discouraged his players from talking to writers, probably feeling that these contacts could well break down the tight unity among the Giant players.

Whitey Herzog resembled Terry in mental toughness, the *esprit de corps* he engendered in his players, and in his reliance on defensive strength to keep competitive. Herzog's executive capacity and competence were also reminiscent of Terry in that both served simultaneously and successfully as general field manager. But unlike Memphis Bill, Whitey talked to the media willingly.

Managing a ballclub is a crazy business, mainly because the human element is so unpredictable. Many years ago, when Casey Stengel was managing in the minors, he walked into a hotel lobby with a writer and saw his star pitcher sprawled out fast asleep on a divan, mouth open and a silly, moronic look on his face. "This is what drives managers nuts," Casey growled. "As a manager, you work hard, analyze the game, study your players, learn the weaknesses of every team in the league, and think and sweat all day long. And once every four or five days you have to trust your job and reputation to a lunkhead like that."

The Coaches

The first coaches were managers and players assigned to direct traffic on the base paths and to pass along signs, not the nonplaying, full-time coaches as we know them today. Another primary function of the pre-1910 coaches was to distract the opposing pitcher. This was frequently accomplished by running up and down the baselines to divert his attention, a practice curtailed in 1887 with the establishment of coaching boxes in foul territory off first and third bases.

Many early-day coaches were especially adept at heckling pitchers to reduce their effectiveness. Often this was a matter of screaming obscenities or insults. Hall of Fame outfielder "King" Kelly, coaching at third base for the Boston Beaneaters in the late 1880s, threw in a new varia-

tion. With Boston and Pittsburgh tied in the ninth inning and two Beaneaters on base, Kelly called authoritatively to the rookie Pittsburgh pitcher, "Let's see the ball, son." The youngster obliged guilelessly, tossing the ball to Kelly. Mike stepped aside to let it bounce past him, and the game-winning run scored.

Arlie Latham was the first full-time coach. John McGraw hired Latham in 1909, presumably without any illusions that Latham would be a character builder. Latham was a favorite of the more hardboiled fans, recognized as a relentless heckler who could stir opponents' ire; not for nothing was he known as "The Freshest Man Alive." A former infielder, he had been a troublemaker to his managers during his seventeen-year major league career. Moreover, Latham's private life was a disaster. His first wife had attempted suicide, and his second wife divorced him, charging "perversion, assault, desertion, and infidelity."

In 1911 McGraw hired the majors' second full-time coach, Wilbert Robinson. Uncle Robby was the first pitching coach, a man who aided the entire pitching staff, but most particularly lefthander Rube Marquand, whom Robinson converted from a "$11,000 lemon" to a Hall of Famer. The rotund, jovial Robinson remained with the Giants until 1913, when he left the club after a quarrel with McGraw.

Nick Altrock, hired by the Washington's Clark Griffith, was the best known coach over the next twenty years. A former pitcher, Altrock was a competent coach, but his forte was as a clown. He was a master mimic, imitating the mannerisms of players and umpires, throwing and catching baseballs in impossible positions, and acting out elaborate shadow boxing routines. In his later years he teamed with Al Schacht, the "Clown Prince of Baseball," to entertain at a number of World Series. Altrock coached for the Senators for forty years.

Altrock was the only full-time nonplaying major league coach from 1914 until 1920, when the Giants hired Johnny Evers and the Phillies picked up former lefthander Jesse Tannehill. By the end of the decade, most clubs employed at least one nonplaying coach. Just before World War Two, each employed at least one full-time coach, and there were a total of forty coaches, an average of 2.5 per team.

The number increased after World War Two as baseball became more complex and increasing attendance and broadcasting revenues made it more feasible to hire bigger staffs. Teams routinely employed at least three coaches, two for the bases and one to oversee the bullpen. In addition, from the 1960s to the present, almost all teams have had a full-time pitching coach. Many have employed batting coaches, rotating them from the parent club to the organization's farm teams.

The third base coach is the quarterback of the team. He relays signs from the manager, and he directs offensive strategy on the field. "Coaching at third base," Al Simmons, the Hall of Famer who was one of the top third base coaches, once remarked, "is the toughest job on the club. The coach on third gets all the blame when things go wrong, and he gets none of the credit when things go right. Yet a good coach can win a dozen or more games a season. A bad coach can lose that many—except, he doesn't last that long."

Two celebrated incidents involving third base coaches illustrate Simmons's point. First there was Enos "Country" Slaughter's famous World Series-winning score from first base in the 1946 fall classic. Slaughter tallied on a routine hit to left center, which was generously scored as a double. Enos, breaking into full stride even before the ball was hit, rounded second and headed for third. Standing in the coaching box, in full view of the charging Slaughter, stood Mike Gonzales. Mike raised both arms in the classic "stop" gesture, all the time screaming, "No! No! No!" But Enos ignored Gonzales. He rounded third and slid home with the winning run in one of the most unforgettable plays of Series history. Technically the play should never have been attempted. Gonzales was right, and Slaughter was wrong—except that the determined Enos made it work.

Then there was the Mike Ferraro incident. Ferraro was the hapless Yankee third base coach who, in Game Two of the 1980 American League Championship Series, waved home a Yankee runner on a two-out hit. The runner was thrown out, and the Yankees lost to Kansas City, 3–2. George Steinbrenner, who had been unhappy with Ferraro's coaching before the incident, precipitated an ugly public argument with the late Dick Howser, the Yankees' manager. At Steinbrenner's insistence, Ferraro coached at first base in 1981, constantly bedeviled by taunts from the stands to "Send him home, Mike" when a batter approached first base on a weak hit to the outfield.

The first base coach has less burdensome duties. A runner traveling from second to third cannot see what's happening behind him and has to use the third base traffic cop as his eyes. But the hitter running toward first base has the field spread out in front of him. The responsibility of going for the extra base is his, not the coach's.

The first base coach is responsible for helping the runner avoid a pickoff play and, elementary as it may seem, being sure that the runner touches first base en route to an extra-base hit.

The bullpen coach gets the relief pitchers ready to enter the game and sometimes recommends their selection to the manager. Ten minutes before Thomson's historic home run, Dodger manager Charlie Dressen phoned bullpen coach Clyde Sukeforth. "Who's got the best stuff out there, Sukey?" asked Dressen. "[Ralph] Branca," replied Sukeforth. "[Carl] Erskine's bouncing 'em in the dirt." So Dressen brought in Branca, and Thomson ended the game dramatically. When Dressen attempted to place the blame for the defeat on Sukeforth, the angry Sukey understandably quit. It was the manager's decision, not the coach's, and there was no way that Dressen could escape that basic truth.

There have been many well-publicized pitching coaches. Jim Turner was credited for much of the effectiveness of the Yankee pitching staff during the 1949–1959 period. Johnny Sain has been an independent-minded, exemplary pitching coach for six different teams over the last thirty years. Art Fowler, Billy Martin's ever present alter ego in several major league jobs, has long been accused of teaching Martin's pitchers to throw the spitball. George Bamberger and Ray Miller were given much of the credit for the Orioles' pitching excellence over the 1968–1985 period. And Roger Craig has been a highly respected pitching mentor, largely responsible for widespread use of the devastating split-fingered fastball.

Batting coaches have come into vogue over the last twenty years. Wally Moses, one of the first, was the hitting specialist for the Philadelphia Athletics as early as 1952. The late Charlie Lau and Walter Hriniak, both former catchers, have been the most celebrated batting coaches over the last several years. Lau developed a revolutionary style of hitting which has gained wide use throughout baseball—especially with star pupil George Brett and other players Lau has coached. Interestingly, Lau hit a mere .255 over his eleven-year career, and Hriniak hit .253 (without an extra-base hit) in 47 career games. These are two classic examples of "Do as I say, not as I do."

Over the last forty years, there has been a noticeable improvement in the quality of coaching. There was a time when most coaches were thought to be old pensioners or drinking companions of the manager. Or maybe they were, as Casey Stengel once commented, "relatives of the manager's wife." In contrast, today's coaches are primarily teachers with established expertise in specific areas.

There was one circumstance where coaches had a touch of managing. After the Chicago Cubs finished seventh (in an eight-team league) in 1960, owner Philip K. Wrigley pondered how best to utilize his field supervisory team. He hit upon a novel idea. In 1961 he launched a grand experiment, called the "College of Coaches," in which a staff of coaches shared equally in managing, coaching, and player development. Wrigley hired no less than eight coaches to rotate as the supervisory "manager." The result: the player-poor Cubs finished seventh again in 1961 and did not rise above that level during the following four seasons while the unique arrangement remained in place. Needless to say, there has been no interest since in rotating coaches in the manager's job.

The Manager Roster

This section details the managerial record of every man who ever held the reins of a major league club from 1871 through 1992. For many years, the assignment of wins and losses was thought a relatively simple task—almost as simple as identifying the managers themselves. In recent years, however, Richard Topp and Robert Tiemann wondered how it was that "managers" who never set foot on the field to lead their charges or even accompanied their clubs on road trips could be regarded as managers at all, at least in the commonly understood sense of field manager rather than business manager. Topp and Tiemann wondered how John McGraw, for example, could be credited as manager of the New York Giants for all of 1924 when a knee injury kept him from the bench for seven weeks: Somebody else must have run the team, they figured, so why not credit that man as interim manager?

That there were record-keeping errors in the 1870s or even the early 1900s may strike the average fan as unsurprising, but the incorrect assignment of decisions to helmsmen has been characteristic of every decade, up to and including the 1980s. Tiemann and Topp undertook a complete review of managerial records dating back to the National Association and found that the records published in previous baseball encyclopedias were wrong—so wrong that they had to be refigured from scratch. Here are the criteria they established for their groundbreaking study:

1. *Definition* A manager is the person designated by the club ownership to run the club on the field.

2. *Absences* When the regular manager is unable to be with the team for 30 or more days, the assistant in charge during his absence should be credited with the team's record from the time the absence begins until the regular manager returns to active duty.

3. *Interim manager* When a manager is removed, either by resignation or by being fired, and his designated replacement is not present to replace him, the assistant temporarily in charge of the team shall be credited with the team's record during the interim.

4. *Head coaches* From 1961 through 1964, the Chicago Cubs had a "panel of coaches" rather than a single manager. One of these coaches was designated *head coach* for a period of time; and that coach is credited with the team's record during his term as head coach.

5. *Captains* During the early years of professional baseball, the man who had the title of "manager" often served merely as the club's business manager, while the captain (a player) was responsible for the team on the field. Some captains were also managers. Each ambiguous situation is judged according to its particular circumstances, but in general the captain, rather than the manager, is credited with the team's record if the manager did not travel with the team or did not have previous baseball experience.

6. *Suspended games* If a game was suspended when one man was managing the team and was completed on a later date when another man was managing, the second manager is credited if the game was suspended before five innings were completed. If the game was suspended after five or more innings were played, then:

(a) credit the first manager with a win if the team was leading at the point of suspension and maintained the lead to win the game; or

(b) credit the first manager with a loss if the team was losing at the point of suspension and remained behind to lose the game; or

(c) credit the second manager with a win (or tie) if the team was losing at the point of suspension but came back to tie the score or win the game; or

(d) credit the second manager with a loss if the team was winning at the point of suspension but then lost the lead and/or game; or

(e) credit the second manager with the win or loss if the score was tied at the point of suspension.

7. *Protested games* If a protest was granted and the game was ordered resumed from the point of protest, then the same rules used for suspended games apply. If a protested game of at least five innings' duration was ordered replayed in its entirety, then no win or loss is credited, but both managers are credited with a no-decision game.

8. *Forfeited games* All forfeited games are counted as games managed, even if the game did not start or if it did not go five innings.

9. *Split seasons* In 1892 the National League played a split season, the winners meeting for the championship. In 1981, because of a players' strike, the National and American Leagues played split seasons. The managers' totals will have entries for each half-season.

10. *Replacement clubs* In the American Association (1882–1891), there were three instances in which one club dropped out and was replaced by another club. In 1884 Richmond replaced Washington; in 1890 Baltimore replaced Brooklyn; and in 1891 Milwaukee replaced Cincinnati. In each case, the new club inherited the old club's record. Therefore, the manager of the new club is credited with starting in the position (standing) in which the old club finished.

In the Union Association (1884), when a new club

replaced an old one, the new club started with a 0–0 record rather than inheriting the old club's record, except in the case of the Chicago franchise, which moved to Pittsburgh. Therefore, all such Union Association managers are credited with a finish as if their teams had begun their season at the beginning of the league season. The finish for each manager is his club's standing in the eight-team league when (a) he left the job, (b) his club dropped out of the league, or (c) his club finished the season. The clubs that dropped out were Altoona (replaced by Kansas City); Philadelphia (replaced by Wilmington); Wilmington (replaced by St. Paul); and Pittsburgh (replaced by Milwaukee).

In a typical entry in the Manager Roster (a hypothetical entry has been created below), the column marked STANDING will, in cases where a team has had only one manager throughout the year, show the team's final standing (in the example below, see the entry for 1972). In the case of a manager who began the season but was replaced midway, however, the figure on the left of the column shows the team's standing when he departed and the figure on the right shows the team's final standing (in the example below, see the entry for 1976). In the case of a manager who finished the season but did not begin it, the team's standing when he took over is shown on the left and the final standing on the right (see the entry for 1978). In the case of a manager who began when the season was already under way but who failed to finish, the figure on the left of the column shows the team's standing when he took over; the middle figure shows the team's standing when he departed; and a third figure shows the team's final standing (see the entry for 1977). The figure in the next column represents the number of wins predicted by the team's runs scored and runs allowed, with about ten extra runs being required for each win beyond .500. Last, the number of wins in the A-E column, which may be a positive figure or a negative figure, reflects the extent to which a manager may have stretched (or hindered) his available talent. The bottom line of a manager's entry provides his career totals, beginning at the left with the number of years, full or partial, in which he managed a major league club. The symbols shown in the sample entry are explained after the example.

Whenever a manager served two or more teams in the same year, the totals for each club are shown separately (see the entry above for 1973). The split seasons of 1892 and 1981 are indicated with separate records for each half. A figure to the right of the year indicates first half or second half (see entry above for 1981).

TM/L	Team and League
G	Games managed (including ties)
W	Wins
L	Losses
PCT	Percentage of games won
M/Y	Manager/Year (The latter figure indicates how many managers the team employed that year, while the former indicates the chronological position of the manager whose entry it is; "2/5," for example, would mean that this manager was the second of the team's five managers during that year.)
W-EXP	Expected Wins Calculated for the team based on its actual runs scored and allowed, not its predicted runs scored and runs allowed. A team that allows exactly as many runs as it scores is predicted to play .500 ball. The equation for expected wins is:

$$\frac{\text{Runs Scored} - \text{Runs Allowed} + 81}{\text{Runs Per Win}}$$

A-E	Actual Wins Minus Expected Wins (A measure of the extent to which a team outperformed or underperformed its talent; for a single season or two a high figure may be attributable to chance, but over time one must credit good managing.)
E	Eastern Division
W	Western Division
*	Indicates playing manager; for vital statistics, consult the player or pitcher register
▲	Tied for first place, involved in league or division playoff
●	Tied for position in standings
◆	League Championship Series win
★	World Series win

The team and league abbreviations used in this section are found on the final pages of this book. For a prose account of the history of managers (and coaches), see the feature article by Fred Stein.

YEAR	TM/L	G	W	L	PCT	STANDING			M/Y	W-EXP	A-E
Blow, Josiah H. "Joe"											
1969	Det-A*	134	71	63	.530	3 E	3 E		1/2	66.8	4.2
1971	Tex-A*	23	9	14	.391	6 W	6 W		3/3	12.0	-3.0
1972	Tex-A	161	84	76	.525	2 W				79.1	4.9
1973	Tex-A	95	44	51	.463	4 W	3 W		1/2	44.2	-0.2
1973	NY-A	56	30	26	.535	3 E	3 E		2/2	28.7	1.3
1974	NY-A	159	97	62	.610	★◆1 E				82.8	14.2
1975	NY-A	162	100	62	.617	◆1 E				90.0	10.0
1976	NY-A	94	52	42	.553	3 E	▲◆1E		1/3	53.8	-1.8
1977	Bos-A	95	55	40	.579	4 E	4 E	2 E	2/3	50.4	4.6
1978	Oak-A	152	83	69	.546	5 W	●2 W		2/2	75.2	7.8
1979	Oak-A	60	37	23	.617	1 W	2 W		1/2	33.0	4.0
1980	Oak-A	49	27	22	.551	2 W	3 W		2/2	27.4	-0.4
1981(1)	Oak-A	62	24	38	.387	6 W				32.4	-7.6
1981(2)	Oak-A	100	44	56	.440	5 W				57.0	-13.0
1982	NY-A	162	91	71	.562	3 E				81.5	10.5
1983	NY-A	145	91	54	.628	7 E	2 E		2/2	84.0	7.0
	14	1709	939	769	.550					898.3	42.5

YEAR	TM/L	G	W	L	PCT	STANDING			M/Y	W-EXP	A-E
Adair, Marion Danne "Bill"											
1970	Chi-A	10	4	6	.400	6 W	6 W	6 W	2/3	3.8	0.2
Adcock, Joseph Wilbur "Joe"											
1967	Cle-A	162	75	87	.463	8				75.0	0.0
Addy, Robert Edward "Bob"											
1875	Phi-n*	7	3	4	.429	4	5		2/2	4.3	-1.3
1877	Cin-N*	24	5	19	.208	6	6	6	2/3	5.3	-0.3
	2	31	8	23	.258						-1.6
Allen, Robert Gilman "Bob"											
1890	Phi-N*	35	25	10	.714	3	2	3	4/5	20.2	4.8
1900	Cin-N*	144	62	77	.446	7				65.5	-3.5
	2	179	87	87	.500						1.3
Alou, Felipe Rojas											
1992	Mon-N	125	70	55	.560	4 E	2 E		2/2	68.1	1.9
Alston, Walter Emmons											
1954	Bro-N	154	92	62	.597	2				80.6	11.4
1955	Bro-N	154	98	55	.641	★1				96.4	1.6
1956	Bro-N	154	93	61	.604	1				89.2	3.8
1957	Bro-N	154	84	70	.545	3				87.3	-3.3
1958	LA-N	154	71	83	.461	7				67.8	3.2
1959	LA-N	156	88	68	.564	▲★1				81.5	6.5
1960	LA-N	154	82	72	.532	4				84.3	-2.3
1961	LA-N	154	89	65	.578	2				80.7	8.3
1962	LA-N	165	102	63	.618	▲2				96.7	5.3
1963	LA-N	163	99	63	.611	★1				91.0	8.0
1964	LA-N	164	80	82	.494	•6				85.7	-5.7
1965	LA-N	162	97	65	.599	★1				90.9	6.1
1966	LA-N	162	95	67	.586	1				94.4	0.6
1967	LA-N	162	73	89	.451	8				72.3	0.7
1968	LA-N	162	76	86	.469	•7				76.2	-0.2
1969	LA-N	162	85	77	.525	4 W				90.2	-5.2
1970	LA-N	161	87	74	.540	2 W				87.0	-0.0
1971	LA-N	162	89	73	.549	2 W				89.2	-0.2
1972	LA-N	155	85	70	.548	3 W				83.9	1.1
1973	LA-N	162	95	66	.590	2 W				92.4	2.6
1974	LA-N	162	102	60	.630	♦1 W				105.6	-3.6
1975	LA-N	162	88	74	.543	2 W				93.7	-5.7
1976	LA-N	158	90	68	.570	2 W	2 W		1/2	86.1	3.9
	23	3658	2040	1613	.558						36.8
Altobelli, Joseph "Joe"											
1977	SF-N	162	75	87	.463	4 W				77.1	-2.1
1978	SF-N	162	89	73	.549	3 W				83.1	5.9
1979	SF-N	140	61	79	.436	4 W	4 W		1/2	63.1	-2.1
1983	Bal-A	162	98	64	.605	★1 E				95.7	2.3
1984	Bal-A	162	85	77	.525	5 E				82.5	2.5
1985	Bal-A	55	29	26	.527	4 E	4 E		1/3	29.3	-0.3
1991	Chi-N	1	0	1	.000	4 E	5 E	4 E	2/3	0.5	-0.5
	7	844	437	407	.518						5.8
Amalfitano, John Joseph "Joey"											
1979	Chi-N	7	2	5	.286	5 E	5 E		2/2	3.5	-1.5
1980	Chi-N	72	26	46	.361	6 E	6 E		2/2	30.7	-4.7
1981(1)	Chi-N	54	15	37	.288	6 E					
(2)	Chi-N	52	23	28	.451	5 E				39.5	-1.5
	3	185	66	116	.363						-7.8
Anderson, George Lee "Sparky"											
1970	Cin-N	162	102	60	.630	♦1 W				90.4	11.6
1971	Cin-N	162	79	83	.488	•4 W				81.6	-2.6
1972	Cin-N	154	95	59	.617	♦1 W				92.7	2.3
1973	Cin-N	162	99	63	.611	1 W				93.4	5.6
1974	Cin-N	163	98	64	.605	2 W				95.8	2.2
1975	Cin-N	162	108	54	.667	★1 W				106.7	1.3
1976	Cin-N	162	102	60	.630	★1 W				103.2	-1.2
1977	Cin-N	162	88	74	.543	2 W				88.5	-0.5
1978	Cin-N	161	92	69	.571	2 W				82.7	9.3
1979	Det-A	106	56	50	.528	5 E	5 E		3/3	55.1	0.9
1980	Det-A	163	84	78	.519	5 E				88.0	-4.0
1981(1)	Det-A	57	31	26	.544	4 E					
(2)	Det-A	52	29	23	.558	•2 E				57.0	3.0
1982	Det-A	162	83	79	.512	4 E				85.5	-2.5
1983	Det-A	162	92	70	.568	2 E				92.0	0.0
1984	Det-A	162	104	58	.642	★1 E				99.5	4.5
1985	Det-A	161	84	77	.522	3 E				84.6	-0.6
1986	Det-A	162	87	75	.537	3 E				89.2	-2.2
1987	Det-A	162	98	64	.605	1 E				96.2	1.8
1988	Det-A	162	88	74	.543	2 E				85.7	2.3
1989	Det-A	162	59	103	.364	7 E				60.9	-1.9
1990	Det-A	162	79	83	.488	3 E				80.6	-1.6
1991	Det-A	162	84	78	.519	•2 E				83.2	0.8
1992	Det-A	162	75	87	.463	6 E				80.7	-5.7
	23	3609	1996	1611	.553						22.8
Anson, Adrian Constantine "Cap"											
1875	Ath-n*	8	4	2	.667	2	2		2/2	4.9	-0.9
1879	Chi-N*	64	41	21	.661	2	4		1/2	32.9	8.1
1880	Chi-N*	86	67	17	.798	1				63.0	4.0
1881	Chi-N*	84	56	28	.667	1				57.4	-1.4
1882	Chi-N*	84	55	29	.655	1				64.3	-9.3
1883	Chi-N*	98	59	39	.602	2				60.8	-1.8
1884	Chi-N*	113	62	50	.554	•4				71.5	-9.5
1885	Chi-N*	113	87	25	.777	1				88.1	-1.1
1886	Chi-N*	126	90	34	.726	1				92.5	-2.5
1887	Chi-N*	127	71	50	.587	3				68.9	2.1
1888	Chi-N*	136	77	58	.570	2				74.5	2.5
1889	Chi-N*	136	67	65	.508	3				70.5	-3.5
1890	Chi-N*	139	84	53	.613	2				82.5	1.5
1891	Chi-N*	137	82	53	.607	2				76.6	5.4
1892(1)	Chi-N*	71	31	39	.443	8					
(2)	Chi-N*	76	39	37	.513	7				63.2	6.8
1893	Chi-N*	128	56	71	.441	9				59.8	-3.8
1894	Chi-N*	137	57	75	.432	8				64.1	-7.1
1895	Chi-N*	133	72	58	.554	4				66.0	6.0
1896	Chi-N*	132	71	57	.555	5				65.4	5.6
1897	Chi-N*	138	59	73	.447	9				60.7	-1.7
1898	NY-N	22	9	13	.409	6	7	7	2/3	11.5	-2.5
	21	2288	1296	947	.578						-3.2
Appling, Lucius Benjamin "Luke"											
1967	KC-A	40	10	30	.250	10	10		2/2	16.5	-6.5
Armour, William Clark "Bill"											
1902	Cle-A	137	69	67	.507	5				69.8	-0.8
1903	Cle-A	140	77	63	.550	3				76.1	0.9
1904	Cle-A	154	86	65	.570	4				93.8	-7.8
1905	Det-A	154	79	74	.516	3				66.5	12.5
1906	Det-A	151	71	78	.477	6				65.6	5.4
	5	736	382	347	.524						10.3
Aspromonte, Kenneth Joseph "Ken"											
1972	Cle-A	156	72	84	.462	5 E				72.4	-0.4
1973	Cle-A	162	71	91	.438	6 E				66.6	4.4
1974	Cle-A	162	77	85	.475	4 E				77.7	-0.7
	3	480	220	260	.458						3.3
Austin, James Philip "Jimmy"											
1913	StL-A*	8	2	6	.250	7	7	8	2/3	3.3	-1.3
1918	StL-A*	16	7	9	.438	6	6	5	2/3	7.7	-0.7
1923	StL-A*	51	22	29	.431	3	5		2/2	24.4	-2.4
	3	75	31	44	.413						-4.5
Baker, Delmer David "Del"											
1933	Det-A	2	2	0	1.000	5	5		2/2	1.0	1.0
1936	Det-A	34	18	16	.529	3	4	2	2/3	18.0	0.0
1937	Det-A	54	34	20	.630	3	3	2	2/5	29.9	4.1
	Det-A	10	7	3	.700	2	2	2	4/5	5.5	1.5
1938	Det-A	57	37	19	.661	5	4		2/2	30.2	6.8
1939	Det-A	155	81	73	.526	5				85.1	-4.1
1940	Det-A	155	90	64	.584	1				92.9	-2.9
1941	Det-A	155	75	79	.487	•4				71.4	3.6
1942	Det-A	156	73	81	.474	5				77.2	-4.2
1960	Bos-A	7	2	5	.286	8	8	7	2/3	3.0	-1.0
	9	785	419	360	.538						4.7
Bamberger, George Irvin											
1978	Mil-A	162	93	69	.574	3 E				96.4	-3.4
1979	Mil-A	161	95	66	.590	2 E				88.8	6.2
1980	Mil-A	92	47	45	.511	2 E	4 E	3 E	2/3	53.2	-6.2
1982	NY-N	162	65	97	.401	6 E				69.1	-4.1
1983	NY-N	46	16	30	.348	6 E	6 E		1/2	19.8	-3.8
1985	Mil-A	161	71	90	.441	6 E				69.5	1.5
1986	Mil-A	152	71	81	.467	6 E	6 E		1/2	69.6	1.4
	7	936	458	478	.489						-8.3
Bancroft, David James "Dave"											
1924	Bos-N*	154	53	100	.346	8				47.8	5.2
1925	Bos-N*	153	70	83	.458	5				67.5	2.5
1926	Bos-N*	153	66	86	.434	7				66.4	-0.4
1927	Bos-N*	155	60	94	.390	7				65.1	-5.1
	4	615	249	363	.407						2.2
Bancroft, Frank Carter											
1880	Wor-N	85	40	43	.482	5				45.7	-5.7
1881	Det-N	84	41	43	.488	4				42.9	-1.9
1882	Det-N	86	42	41	.506	6				34.0	8.0
1883	Cle-N	100	55	42	.567	4				51.8	3.2
1884	Pro-N	114	84	28	.750	1				83.3	0.7
1885	Pro-N	110	53	57	.482	4				46.0	7.0
1887	Phi-a	55	26	29	.473	6	5		1/2	27.6	-1.6
1889	Ind-N	68	25	43	.368	7	7		1/2	30.8	-5.8
1902	Cin-N	16	9	7	.563	6	6	4	2/3	8.8	0.2
	9	718	375	333	.530						4.1
Barkley, Samuel E. "Sam"											
1888	KC-a*	58	21	36	.368	8	8	8	2/3	16.2	4.8
Barnie, William Harrison "Billy"											
1883	Bal-a*	96	28	68	.292	8				25.1	2.9
1884	Bal-a	109	63	43	.594	6				64.1	-1.1
1885	Bal-a	110	41	68	.376	8				41.7	-0.7
1886	Bal-a	139	48	83	.366	8				42.4	5.6
1887	Bal-a	141	77	58	.570	3				77.0	0.0
1888	Bal-a	139	57	80	.416	5				56.8	0.2
1889	Bal-a	139	70	65	.519	5				67.1	2.9
1890	Bal-a	38	15	19	.441	8				16.0	-1.0
1891	Bal-a	139	71	64	.526	3				72.0	-1.0
1892(1)	Was-N	2	0	2	.000	•11	7		1/2	0.8	-0.8

YEAR	TM/L	G	W	L	PCT	STANDING			M/Y	W-EXP	A-E
1893	Lou-N	126	50	75	.400	11				47.6	2.4
1894	Lou-N	131	36	94	.277	12				39.3	-3.3
1897	Bro-N	136	61	71	.462	●6				62.3	-1.3
1898	Bro-N	35	15	20	.429	9	10		1/3	13.5	1.5
	14	1480	632	810	.438						6.1
Barrow, Edward Grant "Ed"											
1903	Det-A	137	65	71	.478	5				71.0	-6.0
1904	Det-A	84	32	46	.410	7	7		1/2	31.9	0.1
1918	Bos-A	126	75	51	.595	★1				73.8	1.2
1919	Bos-A	138	66	71	.482	6				69.8	-3.8
1920	Bos-A	154	72	81	.471	5				71.6	0.4
	5	639	310	320	.492						-8.1
Barry, John Joseph "Jack"											
1917	Bos-A*	157	90	62	.592	2				88.0	2.0
Battin, Joseph V. "Joe"											
1883	Pit-a*	13	2	11	.154	7	7		3/3	4.2	-2.2
1884	Pit-a*	13	6	7	.462	11	10	10	3/5	2.9	3.1
	Pit-U*	6	1	5	.167	5	5		1/2	2.7	-1.7
	2	32	9	23	.281						-0.9
Bauer, Henry Albert "Hank"											
1961	KC-A*	102	35	67	.343	8	●9		2/2	39.9	-4.9
1962	KC-A	162	72	90	.444	9				72.2	-0.2
1964	Bal-A	163	97	65	.599	3				93.2	3.8
1965	Bal-A	162	94	68	.580	3				87.9	6.1
1966	Bal-A	160	97	63	.606	★1				95.9	1.1
1967	Bal-A	161	76	85	.472	●6				87.2	-11.2
1968	Bal-A	80	43	37	.538	3	2		1/2	44.7	-1.7
1969	Oak-A	149	80	69	.537	2 W	2 W		1/2	80.3	-0.3
	8	1139	594	544	.522						-7.2
Benjamin, John W.											
1873	Res-n	23	2	21	.087	8				-3.0	5.0
Benson, Vernon Adair "Vern"											
1977	Atl-N	1	1	0	1.000	6 W	6 W	6 W	3/4	0.4	0.6
Berra, Lawrence Peter "Yogi"											
1964	NY-A	164	99	63	.611	1				97.3	1.7
1972	NY-N	156	83	73	.532	3 E				72.4	10.6
1973	NY-N	161	82	79	.509	♦1 E				82.7	-0.7
1974	NY-N	162	71	91	.438	5 E				72.9	-1.9
1975	NY-N	109	56	53	.514	3 E	●3 E		1/2	56.0	-0.0
1984	NY-A	162	87	75	.537	3 E				89.0	-2.0
1985	NY-A	16	6	10	.375	7 E	2 E		1/2	9.7	-3.7
	7	930	484	444	.522						4.0
Bezdek, Hugo Frank											
1917	Pit-N	91	30	59	.337	8	8		3/3	35.8	-5.8
1918	Pit-N	126	65	60	.520	4				68.6	-3.6
1919	Pit-N	139	71	68	.511	4				70.2	0.8
	3	356	166	187	.470						-8.6
Bickerson											
1884	Was-a	1	0	1	.000	12	12		2/2	0.2	-0.2
Birmingham, Joseph Leo "Joe"											
1912	Cle-A*	28	21	7	.750	6	5		2/2	13.9	7.1
1913	Cle-A*	155	86	66	.566	3				86.6	-0.6
1914	Cle-A*	157	51	102	.333	8				58.3	-7.3
1915	Cle-A	28	12	16	.429	6	7		1/2	11.4	0.6
	4	368	170	191	.471						-0.2
Bissonette, Adelphia Louis "Del"											
1945	Bos-N	60	25	34	.424	7	6		2/2	29.2	-4.2
Blackburne, Russell Aubrey "Lena"											
1928	Chi-A	80	40	40	.500	6	5		2/2	36.4	3.6
1929	Chi-A*	152	59	93	.388	7				59.8	-0.8
	2	232	99	133	.427						2.8
Blades, Francis Raymond "Ray"											
1939	StL-N	155	92	61	.601	2				91.0	1.0
1940	StL-N	39	14	24	.368	6	3		1/3	20.2	-6.2
1948	Bro-N	1	1	0	1.000	5	5	3	2/3	0.5	0.5
	3	195	107	85	.557						-4.7
Blair, Walter Allen "Walter"											
1915	Buf-F*	2	1	1	.500	8	8	6	2/3	0.9	0.1
Bluege, Oswald Louis "Ossie"											
1943	Was-A	153	84	69	.549	2				83.9	0.1
1944	Was-A	154	64	90	.416	8				69.4	-5.4
1945	Was-A	156	87	67	.565	2				83.5	3.5
1946	Was-A	155	76	78	.494	4				66.9	9.1
1947	Was-A	154	64	90	.416	7				57.5	6.5
	5	772	375	394	.488						13.7
Bond, Thomas Henry "Tommy"											
1882	Wor-N*	6	2	4	.333	8	8	8	2/3	1.3	0.7
Boros, Stephen "Steve"											
1983	Oak-A	162	74	88	.457	4 W				73.7	0.3
1984	Oak-A	44	20	24	.455	5 W	4 W		1/2	20.5	-0.5
1986	SD-N	162	74	88	.457	4 W				74.1	-0.1
	3	368	168	200	.457						-0.3
Bottomley, James Leroy "Jim"											
1937	StL-A*	78	21	56	.273	7	8		2/2	24.7	-3.7

YEAR	TM/L	G	W	L	PCT	STANDING			M/Y	W-EXP	A-E
Boudreau, Louis "Lou"											
1942	Cle-A*	156	75	79	.487	4				69.7	5.3
1943	Cle-A*	153	82	71	.536	3				79.0	3.0
1944	Cle-A*	155	72	82	.468	●5				73.5	-1.5
1945	Cle-A*	147	73	72	.503	5				73.5	-0.5
1946	Cle-A*	156	68	86	.442	6				66.0	2.0
1947	Cle-A*	157	80	74	.519	4				87.4	-7.4
1948	Cle-A*	156	97	58	.626	▲★1				104.7	-7.7
1949	Cle-A*	154	89	65	.578	3				87.6	1.4
1950	Cle-A*	155	92	62	.597	4				91.9	0.1
1952	Bos-A*	154	76	78	.494	6				78.0	-2.0
1953	Bos-A	153	84	69	.549	4				79.0	5.0
1954	Bos-A	156	69	85	.448	4				74.2	-5.2
1955	KC-A	155	63	91	.409	6				51.1	11.9
1956	KC-A	154	52	102	.338	8				56.3	-4.3
1957	KC-A	104	36	67	.350	8	7		1/2	41.2	-5.2
1960	Chi-N	139	54	83	.394	7	7		2/2	55.9	-1.9
	16	2404	1162	1224	.487						-6.9
Bowa, Lawrence Robert "Larry"											
1987	SD-N	162	65	97	.401	6 W				71.4	-6.4
1988	SD-N	46	16	30	.348	5 W	3 W		1/2	23.3	-7.3
	2	208	81	127	.389						-13.8
Bowerman, Frank Eugene "Frank"											
1909	Bos-N*	76	22	54	.289	8	8		1/2	24.2	-2.2
Boyd, William J. "Bill"											
1875	Atl-n*	2	0	2	.000	12	12		2/2	-0.2	0.2
Boyer, Kenton Lloyd "Ken"											
1978	StL-N	143	62	81	.434	6 E	5 E		3/3	66.1	-4.1
1979	StL-N	163	86	76	.531	3 E				84.9	1.1
1980	StL-N	51	18	33	.353	6 E	4 E		1/4	26.4	-8.4
	3	357	166	190	.466						-11.3
Bradley, William Joseph "Bill"											
1905	Cle-A*	41	20	21	.488	●1	2	5	2/3	19.9	0.1
1914	Bro-F*	157	77	77	.500	5				75.5	1.5
	2	198	97	98	.497						1.6
Bragan, Robert Randall "Bobby"											
1956	Pit-N	157	66	88	.429	7				70.1	-4.1
1957	Pit-N	104	36	67	.350	7	●7		1/2	43.8	-7.8
1958	Cle-A	67	31	36	.463	6	4		1/2	36.1	-5.1
1963	Mil-N	163	84	78	.519	6				88.9	-4.9
1964	Mil-N	162	88	74	.543	5				86.7	1.3
1965	Mil-N	162	86	76	.531	5				88.8	-2.8
1966	Atl-N	112	52	59	.468	7	5		1/2	62.3	-10.3
	7	927	443	478	.481						-33.8
Bresnahan, Roger Philip											
1909	StL-N*	154	54	98	.355	7				60.8	-6.8
1910	StL-N*	153	63	90	.412	7				68.5	-5.5
1911	StL-N*	158	75	74	.503	5				67.1	7.9
1912	StL-N*	153	63	90	.412	6				60.1	2.9
1915	Chi-N*	157	73	80	.477	4				71.1	1.9
	5	775	328	432	.432						0.5
Bristol, James David "Dave"											
1966	Cin-N	77	39	38	.506	8	7		2/2	38.0	1.0
1967	Cin-N	162	87	75	.537	4				85.6	1.4
1968	Cin-N	163	83	79	.512	4				82.8	0.2
1969	Cin-N	163	89	73	.549	3 W				83.9	5.1
1970	Mil-A	163	65	97	.401	●4 W				66.7	-1.7
1971	Mil-A	161	69	92	.429	6 W				72.1	-3.1
1972	Mil-A	30	10	20	.333	6 E	6 E		1/3	12.8	-2.8
1976	Atl-N	162	70	92	.432	6 W				72.6	-2.6
1977	Atl-N	29	8	21	.276	6 W	6 W		1/4	10.8	-2.8
	Atl-N	131	52	79	.397	6 W	6 W		4/4	48.6	3.4
1979	SF-N	22	10	12	.455	4 W	4 W		2/2	9.9	0.1
1980	SF-N	161	75	86	.466	5 W				73.8	1.2
	11	1424	657	764	.462						-0.5
Brown, Freeman											
1882	Wor-N	41	9	32	.220	8	8		1/3	9.1	-0.1
Brown, Mordecai Peter Centennial "Three Finger"											
1914	StL-F*	114	50	63	.442	7	8		1/2	46.1	3.9
Brown, Thomas T. "Tom"											
1897	Was-N*	99	52	46	.531	11	●6		2/2	48.2	3.8
1898	Was-N*	38	12	26	.316	11	11		1/4	13.6	-1.6
	2	137	64	72	.471						2.2
Brucker, Earle Francis Sr											
1952	Cin-N	5	3	2	.600	7	7	6	2/3	2.4	0.6
Buckenberger, Albert C. "Al"											
1889	Col-a	140	60	78	.435	6				56.5	3.5
1890	Col-a	80	39	41	.488	5	2		1/3	51.9	-12.9
1892(1)	Pit-N	29	15	14	.517	7	6		1/2		
(2)	Pit-N	66	38	27	.585	10	4		2/2	47.3	5.7
1893	Pit-N	131	81	48	.628	2				81.3	-0.3
1894	Pit-N	110	53	55	.491	7	7		1/2	52.9	0.1
1895	StL-N	50	16	34	.320	11	11		1/4	16.0	-0.0
1902	Bos-N	142	73	64	.533	3				74.6	-1.6
1903	Bos-N	140	58	80	.420	6				57.0	1.0
1904	Bos-N	155	55	98	.359	7				49.1	5.9

YEAR	TM/L	G	W	L	PCT	STANDING			M/Y	W-EXP	A-E
	9	1043	488	539	.475						1.3
Buffinton, Charles G. "Charlie"											
1890	Phi-P*	116	61	54	.530	5	5		2/2	63.6	-2.6
Burdock, John Joseph "Jack"											
1883	Bos-N*	54	30	24	.556	4	1		1/2	37.4	-7.4
Burke, James Timothy "Jimmy"											
1905	StL-N*	90	34	56	.378	7	6	6	2/3	32.8	1.2
1918	StL-A	61	29	31	.483	6	5		3/3	28.8	0.2
1919	StL-A	140	67	72	.482	5				65.9	1.1
1920	StL-A	154	76	77	.497	4				79.4	-3.4
	4	445	206	236	.466						-0.9
Burnham, George Walter "Watch"											
1887	Ind-N	28	6	22	.214	8	8		1/3	7.7	-1.7
Burns, Thomas Everett "Tom"											
1892(1)	Pit-N*	47	22	25	.468	7	6		2/2		
(2)	Pit-N*	13	5	7	.417	10	4		1/2	29.7	-2.7
1898	Chi-N	152	85	65	.567	4				89.2	-4.2
1899	Chi-N	152	75	73	.507	8				78.6	-3.6
	3	364	187	170	.524						-10.5
Burwell, William Edwin "Bill"											
1947	Pit-N	1	1	0	1.000	8	•7		2/2	0.5	0.5
Bush, Owen Joseph "Donie"											
1923	Was-A*	155	75	78	.490	4				73.9	1.1
1927	Pit-N	156	94	60	.610	1				92.4	1.6
1928	Pit-N	152	85	67	.559	4				88.5	-3.5
1929	Pit-N	119	67	51	.568	2	2		1/2	67.7	-0.7
1930	Chi-A	154	62	92	.403	7				62.6	-0.6
1931	Chi-A	156	56	97	.366	8				54.8	1.2
1933	Cin-N	153	58	94	.382	8				59.8	-1.8
	7	1045	497	539	.480						-2.7
Butler, Ormond Hook											
1883	Pit-a	53	17	36	.321	6	6	7	2/3	17.3	-0.3
Byrne, Charles H. "Charlie"											
1885	Bro-a	75	38	37	.507	7	•5		2/2	36.0	2.0
1886	Bro-a	141	76	61	.555	3				68.5	7.5
1887	Bro-a	138	60	74	.448	6				65.8	-5.8
	3	354	174	172	.503						3.7
Callahan, James Joseph "Jim"											
1903	Chi-A*	138	60	77	.438	7				58.3	1.7
1904	Chi-A*	42	23	18	.561	4	3		1/2	24.1	-1.1
1912	Chi-A*	158	78	76	.506	4				76.1	1.9
1913	Chi-A*	153	78	74	.513	5				74.8	3.2
1914	Chi-A	157	70	84	.455	•6				68.5	1.5
1916	Pit-N	157	65	89	.422	6				65.3	-0.3
1917	Pit-N	61	20	40	.333	8	8		1/3	24.1	-4.1
	7	866	394	458	.462						2.8
Cammeyer, William Henry "Bill"											
1876	NY-N	57	21	35	.375	6				14.7	6.3
Campau, Charles Columbus "Count"											
1890	StL-a*	42	27	14	.659	5	2	3	4/6	24.1	2.9
Cantillon, Joseph D. "Joe"											
1907	Was-A	154	49	102	.325	8				55.6	-6.6
1908	Was-A	155	67	85	.441	7				69.0	-2.0
1909	Was-A	156	42	110	.276	8				43.9	-1.9
	3	465	158	297	.347						-10.4
Carey, Max George											
1932	Bro-N	154	81	73	.526	3				77.5	3.5
1933	Bro-N	157	65	88	.425	6				68.4	-3.4
	2	311	146	161	.476						0.1
Carey, Thomas John "Tom"											
1873	Bal-n*	24	14	9	.609	3	3		2/2	16.9	-2.9
1874	Mut-n*	25	13	12	.520	2	2		1/2	16.4	-3.4
	2	49	27	21	.563						-6.3
Carrigan, William Francis "Bill"											
1913	Bos-A*	70	40	30	.571	5	4		2/2	36.0	4.0
1914	Bos-A*	159	91	62	.595	2				85.5	5.5
1915	Bos-A*	155	101	50	.669	★1				94.1	6.9
1916	Bos-A*	156	91	63	.591	★1				85.2	5.8
1927	Bos-A	154	51	103	.331	8				51.7	-0.7
1928	Bos-A	154	57	96	.373	8				58.2	-1.2
1929	Bos-A	155	58	96	.377	8				57.3	0.7
	7	1003	489	500	.494						21.0
Caruthers, Robert Lee "Bob"											
1892(2)	StL-N*	50	16	32	.333	12	11		3/3	17.5	-1.5
Cavarretta, Philip Joseph "Phil"											
1951	Chi-N*	74	27	47	.365	7	8		2/2	30.4	-3.4
1952	Chi-N*	155	77	77	.500	5				76.7	0.3
1953	Chi-N*	155	65	89	.422	7				57.3	7.7
	3	384	169	213	.442						4.6
Caylor, Oliver Perry "O.P."											
1885	Cin-a	112	63	49	.563	2				62.1	0.9
1886	Cin-a	141	65	73	.471	5				70.5	-5.5
1887	NY-a	100	35	60	.368	7	7		3/3	27.6	7.4
	3	353	163	182	.472						2.7

YEAR	TM/L	G	W	L	PCT	STANDING			M/Y	W-EXP	A-E
Chance, Frank Leroy											
1905	Chi-N*	90	55	33	.625	4	3		2/2	58.5	-3.5
1906	Chi-N*	155	116	36	.763	1				112.7	3.3
1907	Chi-N*	155	107	45	.704	★1				98.1	8.9
1908	Chi-N*	158	99	55	.643	★1				95.7	3.3
1909	Chi-N*	155	104	49	.680	2				105.1	-1.1
1910	Chi-N*	154	104	50	.675	1				99.8	4.2
1911	Chi-N*	158	92	62	.597	2				92.3	-0.3
1912	Chi-N*	153	91	59	.607	3				83.6	7.4
1913	NY-A*	153	57	94	.377	7				60.6	-3.6
1914	NY-A*	137	60	74	.448	7	•6		1/2	65.7	-5.7
1923	Bos-A	154	61	91	.401	8				53.6	7.4
	11	1622	946	648	.593						20.3
Chapman, John Curtis "Jack"											
1876	Lou-N*	69	30	36	.455	5				26.6	3.4
1877	Lou-N	61	35	25	.583	2				34.8	0.2
1878	Mil-N	61	15	45	.250	6				18.0	-3.0
1882	Wor-N	37	7	30	.189	8	8		3/3	8.2	-1.2
1883	Det-N	101	40	58	.408	7				37.9	2.1
1884	Det-N	114	28	84	.250	8				28.9	-0.9
1885	Buf-N	88	31	57	.352	7	7		2/2	25.3	5.7
1889	Lou-a	7	1	6	.143	8	8		4/4	1.5	-0.5
1890	Lou-a	136	88	44	.667	1				87.5	0.5
1891	Lou-a	141	55	84	.396	7				53.7	1.3
1892(1)	Lou-N	54	21	33	.389	10	11		1/2		
	11	869	351	502	.411						7.6
Chapman, William Benjamin "Ben"											
1945	Phi-N*	85	28	57	.329	8	8		2/2	25.2	2.8
1946	Phi-N*	155	69	85	.448	5				61.8	7.2
1947	Phi-N	155	62	92	.403	•7				66.8	-4.8
1948	Phi-N	79	37	42	.468	7	6		1/3	32.2	4.8
	4	474	196	276	.415						10.1
Chase, Harold Homer "Hal"											
1910	NY-A*	14	10	4	.714	3	2		2/2	7.7	2.3
1911	NY-A*	153	76	76	.500	6				72.0	4.0
	2	167	86	80	.518						6.3
Clapp, John Edgar											
1872	Man-n*	24	5	19	.208	8				4.1	0.9
1878	Ind-N*	63	24	36	.400	5				26.7	-2.7
1879	Buf-N*	79	46	32	.590	3				41.8	4.2
1880	Cin-N*	82	21	59	.262	8				22.6	-1.6
1881	Cle-N*	74	32	41	.438	6	7		2/2	34.6	-2.6
1883	NY-N*	98	46	50	.479	6				43.8	2.2
	6	420	174	237	.423						0.3
Clarke, Fred Clifford											
1897	Lou-N*	92	35	54	.393	9	11		2/2	32.9	2.1
1898	Lou-N*	154	70	81	.464	9				65.6	4.4
1899	Lou-N*	156	75	77	.493	9				80.9	-5.9
1900	Pit-N*	140	79	60	.568	2				81.2	-2.2
1901	Pit-N*	140	90	49	.647	1				93.2	-3.2
1902	Pit-N*	142	103	36	.741	1				103.9	-0.9
1903	Pit-N*	141	91	49	.650	1				87.1	3.9
1904	Pit-N*	156	87	66	.569	4				85.2	1.8
1905	Pit-N*	155	96	57	.627	2				89.3	6.7
1906	Pit-N*	154	93	60	.608	3				93.7	-0.7
1907	Pit-N*	157	91	63	.591	2				90.8	0.2
1908	Pit-N*	155	98	56	.636	•2				90.3	7.7
1909	Pit-N*	154	110	42	.724	★1				103.6	6.4
1910	Pit-N*	154	86	67	.562	3				84.9	1.1
1911	Pit-N*	156	85	69	.552	3				96.4	-11.4
1912	Pit-N	153	93	58	.616	2				94.5	-1.5
1913	Pit-N*	155	78	71	.523	4				83.8	-5.8
1914	Pit-N*	158	69	85	.448	7				72.7	-3.7
1915	Pit-N*	157	73	81	.474	5				81.2	-8.2
	19	2829	1602	1181	.576						-9.3
Clements, John J. "Jack"											
1890	Phi-N*	19	13	6	.684	1	2	3	2/5	11.0	2.0
Clinton, James Lawrence "Jim"											
1872	Eck-n*	11	0	11	.000	10	9		1/2	-1.2	1.2
Cobb, Tyrus Raymond "Ty"											
1921	Det-A*	154	71	82	.464	6				79.3	-8.3
1922	Det-A*	155	79	75	.513	3				80.4	-1.4
1923	Det-A*	155	83	71	.539	2				85.5	-2.5
1924	Det-A*	156	86	68	.558	3				81.9	4.1
1925	Det-A*	156	81	73	.526	4				83.7	-2.7
1926	Det-A*	157	79	75	.513	6				73.5	5.5
	6	933	479	444	.519						-5.3
Cochrane, Gordon Stanley "Mickey"											
1934	Det-A*	154	101	53	.656	1				99.8	1.2
1935	Det-A*	152	93	58	.616	★1				99.1	-6.1
1936	Det-A*	53	29	24	.547	3	2		1/3	28.0	1.0
	Det-A*	67	36	31	.537	4	2		3/3	35.4	0.6
1937	Det-A*	29	16	13	.552	3	2		1/5	16.1	-0.1
	Det-A*	47	26	20	.565	3	2	2	3/5	25.5	0.5
1938	Det-A	98	47	51	.480	5	4		1/2	52.9	-5.9
	5	600	348	250	.582						-8.8

YEAR	TM/L	G	W	L	PCT	STANDING			M/Y	W-EXP	A-E
Cohen, Andrew Howard "Andy"											
1960	Phi-N	1	1	0	1.000	●6	●4	8	2/3	0.4	0.6
Coleman, Gerald Francis "Jerry"											
1980	SD-N	163	73	89	.451	6 W				74.2	-1.2
Coleman, Robert Hunter "Bob"											
1943	Bos-N	46	21	25	.457	6	6		1/2	18.0	3.0
1944	Bos-N	155	65	89	.422	6				68.5	-3.5
1945	Bos-N	94	42	51	.452	7	6		1/2	46.1	-4.1
	3	295	128	165	.437						-4.6
Collins, Edward Trowbridge Sr. "Eddie"											
1924	Chi-A*	27	14	13	.519	6			3/4	12.4	1.6
1925	Chi-A*	154	79	75	.513	5				80.8	-1.8
1926	Chi-A*	155	81	72	.529	5				83.0	-2.0
	3	336	174	160	.521						-2.3
Collins, James Joseph "Jimmy"											
1901	Bos-A*	138	79	57	.581	2				82.4	-3.4
1902	Bos-A*	138	77	60	.562	3				74.8	2.2
1903	Bos-A*	141	91	47	.659	★1				89.9	1.1
1904	Bos-A*	157	95	59	.617	1				93.3	1.7
1905	Bos-A*	153	78	74	.513	4				77.6	0.4
1906	Bos-A*	115	35	79	.307	8	8		1/2	37.3	-2.3
	6	842	455	376	.548						-0.4
Collins, John Francis "Shano"											
1931	Bos-A	153	62	90	.408	6				58.8	3.2
1932	Bos-A	55	11	44	.200	8	8		1/2	15.4	-4.4
	2	208	73	134	.353						-1.2
Comiskey, Charles Albert "Charlie"											
1883	StL-a*	19	12	7	.632	2	2		2/2	12.1	-0.1
1884	StL-a*	25	16	7	.696	5	4		2/2	13.8	2.2
1885	StL-a*	112	79	33	.705	1				76.3	2.7
1886	StL-a*	139	93	46	.669	1				101.3	-8.3
1887	StL-a*	138	95	40	.704	1				97.5	-2.5
1888	StL-a*	137	92	43	.681	1				95.7	-3.7
1889	StL-a*	141	89	46	.659	2				91.9	-1.9
1890	Chi-P*	138	75	62	.547	4				78.5	-3.5
1891	StL-a*	141	86	52	.623	2				88.1	-2.1
1892(1)	Cin-N*	77	44	31	.587	4					
(2)	Cin-N*	78	38	37	.507	8				78.4	3.6
1893	Cin-N*	131	65	63	.508	●6				59.2	5.8
1894	Cin-N*	134	55	75	.423	10				51.5	3.5
	12	1410	839	542	.608						-4.3
Connor, Roger											
1896	StL-N*	46	8	37	.178	11	11	11	4/5	12.3	-4.3
Cooke, Allen Lindsey "Dusty"											
1948	Phi-N	13	6	6	.500	7	6	6	2/3	4.9	1.1
Coombs, John Wesley "Jack"											
1919	Phi-N	63	18	44	.290	8	8		1/2	22.3	-4.3
Cooney, John Walter "Johnny"											
1949	Bos-N	46	20	25	.444	4	4		2/2	22.1	-2.1
Corrales, Patrick "Pat"											
1978	Tex-A	1	1	0	1.000	●2 W	●2 W		2/2	0.5	0.5
1979	Tex-A	162	83	79	.512	3 W				86.2	-3.2
1980	Tex-A	163	76	85	.472	4 W				80.9	-4.9
1982	Phi-N	162	89	73	.549	2 E				82.1	6.9
1983	Phi-N	86	43	42	.506	1 E	♦1E		1/2	45.9	-2.9
	Cle-A	62	30	32	.484	7 E	7 E		2/2	27.9	2.1
1984	Cle-A	163	75	87	.463	6 E				80.5	-5.5
1985	Cle-A	162	60	102	.370	7 E				68.4	-8.4
1986	Cle-A	163	84	78	.519	5 E				80.1	3.9
1987	Cle-A	87	31	56	.356	7 E	7 E		1/2	32.8	-1.8
	9	1211	572	634	.474						-13.2
Corriden, John Michael Sr. "Red"											
1950	Chi-A	125	52	72	.419	8	6		2/2	51.9	0.1
Cottier, Charles Keith "Chuck"											
1984	Sea-A	27	15	12	.556	7 W	●5 W		2/2	12.0	3.0
1985	Sea-A	162	74	88	.457	6 W				71.4	2.6
1986	Sea-A	28	9	19	.321	6 W	7 W		1/3	12.0	-3.0
	3	217	98	119	.452						2.6
Cox, Robert Joseph "Bobby"											
1978	Atl-N	162	69	93	.426	6 W				65.4	3.6
1979	Atl-N	160	66	94	.412	6 W				70.6	-4.6
1980	Atl-N	161	81	80	.503	4 W				77.3	3.7
1981(1)	Atl-N	55	25	29	.463	4 W					
(2)	Atl-N	52	25	27	.481	5 W				50.7	-0.7
1982	Tor-A	162	78	84	.481	●6 E				75.8	2.2
1983	Tor-A	162	89	73	.549	4 E				87.8	1.2
1984	Tor-A	163	89	73	.549	2 E				86.4	2.6
1985	Tor-A	161	99	62	.615	1 E				98.2	0.8
1990	Atl-N	97	40	57	.412	6 W	6 W		2/2	40.3	-0.3
1991	Atl-N	162	94	68	.580	♦1 W				91.7	2.3
1992	Atl-N	162	98	64	.605	1 W				93.2	4.8
	11	1659	853	804	.515						15.5
Craft, Harry Francis											
1957	KC-A	50	23	27	.460	8	7		2/2	20.0	3.0
1958	KC-A	156	73	81	.474	7				69.8	3.2

YEAR	TM/L	G	W	L	PCT	STANDING			M/Y	W-EXP	A-E
1959	KC-A	154	66	88	.429	7				69.3	-3.3
1961	Chi-N	12	4	8	.333	●6	7	7	2/9	5.2	-1.2
	Chi-N	4	3	1	.750	7	7	7	5/9	1.7	1.3
1962	Hou-N	162	64	96	.400	8				66.8	-2.8
1963	Hou-N	162	66	96	.407	9				60.8	5.2
1964	Hou-N	149	61	88	.409	9	9		1/2	60.6	0.4
	7	849	360	485	.426						6.0
Craig, Roger Lee											
1978	SD-N	162	84	78	.519	4 W				80.2	3.8
1979	SD-N	161	68	93	.422	5 W				72.2	-4.2
1985	SF-N	18	6	12	.333	6 W	6 W		2/2	7.6	-1.6
1986	SF-N	162	83	79	.512	3 W				89.4	-6.4
1987	SF-N	162	90	72	.556	1 W				92.4	-2.4
1988	SF-N	162	83	79	.512	4 W				85.7	-2.7
1989	SF-N	162	92	70	.568	♦1 W				91.5	0.5
1990	SF-N	162	85	77	.525	3 W				81.9	3.1
1991	SF-N	162	75	87	.463	4 W				76.0	-1.0
1992	SF-N	162	72	90	.444	5 W				73.0	-1.0
	10	1475	738	737	.500						-11.9
Crandall, Delmar Wesley "Del"											
1972	Mil-A	124	54	70	.435	6 E	6 E		3/3	52.8	1.2
1973	Mil-A	162	74	88	.457	5 E				78.7	-4.7
1974	Mil-A	162	76	86	.469	5 E				79.6	-3.6
1975	Mil-A	161	67	94	.416	5 E	5 E		1/2	68.9	-1.9
1983	Sea-A	89	34	55	.382	7 W	7 W		2/2	33.9	0.1
1984	Sea-A	135	59	76	.437	7 W	●5 W		1/2	59.8	-0.8
	6	833	364	469	.437						-9.7
Crane, Samuel Newhall "Sam"											
1880	Buf-N*	84	24	58	.293	7				24.6	-0.6
1884	Cin-U*	70	49	21	.700	5	3		2/2	49.2	-0.2
	2	154	73	79	.480						-0.8
Cravath, Clifford Carlton "Gavvy"											
1919	Phi-N*	75	29	46	.387	8	8		2/2	27.0	2.0
1920	Phi-N*	153	62	91	.405	8				61.0	1.0
	2	228	91	137	.399						2.9
Craver, William H. "Bill"											
1871	Tro-n*	25	12	12	.500	7	6		2/2	11.4	0.6
1872	Bal-n*	41	27	13	.675	2	2		1/2	29.6	-2.6
1874	Phi-n*	58	29	29	.500	4				32.6	-3.6
1875	Cen-n*	14	2	12	.143	11				1.7	0.3
	4	138	70	66	.515						-5.3
Creamer, George W.											
1884	Pit-a*	8	0	8	.000	10	10	10	4/5	1.8	-1.8
Cronin, Joseph Edward "Joe"											
1933	Was-A*	153	99	53	.651	1				93.6	5.4
1934	Was-A*	155	66	86	.434	7				68.7	-2.7
1935	Bos-A*	154	78	75	.510	4				75.1	2.9
1936	Bos-A*	155	74	80	.481	6				78.0	-4.0
1937	Bos-A*	154	80	72	.526	5				80.3	-0.3
1938	Bos-A*	150	88	61	.591	2				88.1	-0.1
1939	Bos-A*	152	89	62	.589	2				84.1	4.9
1940	Bos-A*	154	82	72	.532	●4				81.2	0.8
1941	Bos-A*	155	84	70	.545	2				87.7	-3.7
1942	Bos-A*	152	93	59	.612	2				92.8	0.2
1943	Bos-A*	155	68	84	.447	7				71.2	-3.2
1944	Bos-A*	156	77	77	.500	4				83.3	-6.3
1945	Bos-A*	157	71	83	.461	7				69.1	1.9
1946	Bos-A	156	104	50	.675	1				96.9	7.1
1947	Bos-A	157	83	71	.539	3				82.1	0.9
	15	2315	1236	1055	.540						3.7
Crooks, John Charles											
1892(1)	StL-N*	47	24	22	.522	11	9		3/3		
(2)	StL-N*	15	3	11	.214	12	11		1/3	21.9	5.1
Cross, Lafayette Napoleon "Lave"											
1899	Cle-N*	38	8	30	.211	12	12		1/2	3.3	4.7
Cubbage, Michael Lee "Mike"											
1991	NY-N	7	3	4	.429	3 E	5 E		2/2	3.5	-0.5
Curtis, Edwin R. "Ed"											
1884	Alt-U	25	6	19	.240	6				1.7	4.3
Cushman, Charles H. "Charlie"											
1891	Mil-a	36	21	15	.583	5				24.5	-3.5
Cuthbert, Edgar Edward "Ned"											
1882	StL-a*	80	37	43	.463	5				31.3	5.7
Dahlen, William Frederick "Bill"											
1910	Bro-N*	156	64	90	.416	6				62.9	1.1
1911	Bro-N*	154	64	86	.427	7				62.1	1.9
1912	Bro-N	153	58	95	.379	7				66.3	-8.3
1913	Bro-N	152	65	84	.436	6				72.6	-7.6
	4	615	251	355	.414						-12.9
Dark, Alvin Ralph											
1961	SF-N	155	85	69	.552	3				88.7	-3.7
1962	SF-N	165	103	62	.624	▲1				100.8	2.2
1963	SF-N	162	88	74	.543	3				89.7	-1.7
1964	SF-N	162	90	72	.556	4				88.5	1.5
1966	KC-A	160	74	86	.463	7				70.8	3.2

YEAR	TM/L	G	W	L	PCT	STANDING			M/Y	W-EXP	A-E
1967	KC-A	121	52	69	.430	10	10		1/2	50.0	2.0
1968	Cle-A	162	86	75	.534	3				81.9	4.1
1969	Cle-A	161	62	99	.385	6 E				65.2	-3.2
1970	Cle-A	162	76	86	.469	5 E				78.3	-2.3
1971	Cle-A	103	42	61	.408	6 E	6 E		1/2	37.7	4.3
1974	Oak-A	162	90	72	.556	★1 W				96.0	-6.0
1975	Oak-A	162	98	64	.605	1 W				96.7	1.3
1977	SD-N	113	48	65	.425	4 W	5 W		3/3	46.8	1.2
	13	1950	994	954	.510						2.9
Davenport, James Houston "Jim"											
1985	SF-N	144	56	88	.389	6 W	6 W		1/2	60.6	-4.6
Davidson, Mordecai H.											
1888	Lou-a	3	1	2	.333	8	8	7	2/4	1.1	-0.1
	Lou-a	90	34	52	.395	8	7		4/4	32.7	1.3
Davis, George Stacey											
1895	NY-N*	33	16	17	.485	8	9		1/3	16.9	-0.9
1900	NY-N*	78	39	37	.513	8	8		2/2	32.5	6.5
1901	NY-N*	141	52	85	.380	7				47.6	4.4
	3	252	107	139	.435						10.0
Davis, Harry H											
1912	Cle-A*	127	54	71	.432	6	5		1/2	62.2	-8.2
Davis, Virgil Lawrence "Spud"											
1946	Pit-N	3	1	2	.333	7	7		2/2	1.3	-0.3
Day, John B.											
1899	NY-N	66	29	35	.453	9	10		1/2	26.9	2.1
Deane, John Henry "Harry"											
1871	Kek-n*	5	2	3	.400	7	8		2/2	0.6	1.4
Dent, Russell Earl "Bucky"											
1989	NY-A	40	18	22	.450	6 E	5 E		2/2	17.7	0.3
1990	NY-A	49	18	31	.367	7 E	7 E		1/2	19.9	-1.9
	2	89	36	53	.404						-1.6
Dickey, William Malcolm "Bill"											
1946	NY-A*	105	57	48	.543	2	3	3	2/3	62.4	-5.4
Diddlebock, Henry H. "Harry"											
1896	StL-N	17	7	10	.412	10	11		1/5	4.6	2.4
Doby, Lawrence Eugene "Larry"											
1978	Chi-A	87	37	50	.425	5 W	5 W		2/2	38.1	-1.1
Donovan, Patrick Joseph "Patsy"											
1897	Pit-N*	135	60	71	.458	8				51.2	8.8
1899	Pit-N*	131	69	58	.543	10	7		2/2	69.0	0.0
1901	StL-N*	142	76	64	.543	4				79.6	-3.6
1902	StL-N*	140	56	78	.418	6				48.8	7.2
1903	StL-N*	139	43	94	.314	8				40.0	3.0
1904	Was-A*	139	37	97	.276	8	8		2/2	37.3	-0.3
1906	Bro-N*	153	66	86	.434	5				61.7	4.3
1907	Bro-N*	153	65	83	.439	5				64.9	0.1
1908	Bro-N	154	53	101	.344	7				59.7	-6.7
1910	Bos-A	158	81	72	.529	4				84.5	-3.5
1911	Bos-A	153	78	75	.510	5				80.3	-2.3
	11	1597	684	879	.438						6.9
Donovan, William Edward "Bill"											
1915	NY-A*	154	69	83	.454	5				75.6	-6.6
1916	NY-A*	156	80	74	.519	4				78.8	1.2
1917	NY-A	155	71	82	.464	6				72.6	-1.6
1921	Phi-N	87	25	62	.287	8	8		1/2	27.3	-2.3
	4	552	245	301	.449						-9.3
Dooin, Charles Sebastian "Red"											
1910	Phi-N*	157	78	75	.510	4				80.1	-2.1
1911	Phi-N*	153	79	73	.520	4				74.9	4.1
1912	Phi-N*	152	73	79	.480	5				74.2	-1.2
1913	Phi-N*	159	88	63	.583	2				81.4	6.6
1914	Phi-N*	154	74	80	.481	6				73.3	0.7
	5	775	392	370	.514						8.0
Dorgan, Michael Cornelius "Mike"											
1879	Syr-N*	43	17	26	.395	6	7		1/3	10.9	6.1
1880	Pro-N*	39	26	12	.684	3	2		3/3	24.7	1.3
1881	Wor-N*	56	24	32	.429	7	8		1/2	22.9	1.1
	3	138	67	70	.489						8.6
Dowd, Thomas Jefferson "Tom"											
1896	StL-N*	63	25	38	.397	11	11		5/5	17.2	7.8
1897	StL-N*	29	6	22	.214	12	12		1/4	5.1	0.9
	2	92	31	60	.341						8.8
Doyle, John Joseph "Jack"											
1895	NY-N*	64	32	31	.508	8	9	9	2/3	32.2	-0.2
1898	Was-N*	17	8	9	.471	11	10	11	2/4	6.1	1.9
	2	81	40	40	.500						1.7
Dressen, Charles Walter "Chuck"											
1934	Cin-N	60	21	39	.350	8	8		3/3	21.7	-0.7
1935	Cin-N	154	68	85	.444	6				64.0	4.0
1936	Cin-N	154	74	80	.481	5				73.3	0.7
1937	Cin-N	130	51	78	.395	8	8		1/2	56.3	-5.3
1951	Bro-N	158	97	60	.618	▲2				96.2	0.8
1952	Bro-N	155	96	57	.627	1				93.8	2.2
1953	Bro-N	155	105	49	.682	1				101.5	3.5

YEAR	TM/L	G	W	L	PCT	STANDING			M/Y	W-EXP	A-E
1955	Was-A	154	53	101	.344	8				57.9	-4.9
1956	Was-A	155	59	95	.383	7				51.4	7.6
1957	Was-A	20	4	16	.200	8	8		1/2	7.4	-3.4
1960	Mil-N	154	88	66	.571	2				83.6	4.4
1961	Mil-N	130	71	58	.550	3	4		1/2	69.2	1.8
1963	Det-A	102	55	47	.539	9	•5		2/2	50.8	4.2
1964	Det-A	163	85	77	.525	4				83.2	1.8
1965	Det-A	120	65	55	.542	3	4		2/2	66.2	-1.2
1966	Det-A	26	16	10	.615	3	3		1/3	13.3	2.7
	16	1990	1008	973	.509						18.2
Duffy, Hugh											
1901	Mil-A*	139	48	89	.350	8				51.2	-3.2
1904	Phi-N*	155	52	100	.342	8				54.4	-2.4
1905	Phi-N*	155	83	69	.546	4				86.9	-3.9
1906	Phi-N*	154	71	82	.464	4				72.4	-1.4
1910	Chi-A	156	68	85	.444	6				73.8	-5.8
1911	Chi-A	154	77	74	.510	4				85.2	-8.2
1921	Bos-A	154	75	79	.487	5				74.2	0.8
1922	Bos-A	154	61	93	.396	8				59.8	1.2
	8	1221	535	671	.444						-22.9
Dunlap, Frederick C. "Fred"											
1882	Cle-N*	80	42	36	.538	8	5		2/2	38.2	3.8
1884	StL-U*	83	66	16	.805	1	1		2/2	70.3	-4.3
1885	StL-N*	50	21	29	.420	5	8		1/3	15.5	5.5
	StL-N*	22	9	11	.450	8	8		3/3	6.2	2.8
1889	Pit-N*	17	7	10	.412	6	7	5	2/3	7.6	-0.6
	4	252	145	102	.587						7.1
Durocher, Leo Ernest											
1939	Bro-N*	157	84	69	.549	3				82.9	1.1
1940	Bro-N*	156	88	65	.575	2				84.3	3.7
1941	Bro-N*	157	100	54	.649	1				99.2	0.8
1942	Bro-N	155	104	50	.675	2				101.5	2.5
1943	Bro-N*	153	81	72	.529	3				80.7	0.3
1944	Bro-N	155	63	91	.409	7				63.4	-0.4
1945	Bro-N*	155	87	67	.565	3				83.8	3.2
1946	Bro-N	157	96	60	.615	▲2				91.8	4.2
1948	Bro-N	73	35	37	.486	5	3		1/3	39.6	-4.6
	NY-N	79	41	38	.519	4	5		2/2	43.3	-2.3
1949	NY-N	156	73	81	.474	5				81.3	-8.3
1950	NY-N	154	86	68	.558	3				86.2	-0.2
1951	NY-N	157	98	59	.624	▲1				92.5	5.5
1952	NY-N	154	92	62	.597	2				85.4	6.6
1953	NY-N	155	70	84	.455	5				79.0	-9.0
1954	NY-N	154	97	57	.630	★1				95.9	1.1
1955	NY-N	154	80	74	.519	3				79.9	0.1
1966	Chi-N	162	59	103	.364	10				64.5	-5.5
1967	Chi-N	162	87	74	.540	3				88.7	-1.7
1968	Chi-N	163	84	78	.519	3				81.1	2.9
1969	Chi-N	163	92	70	.568	2 E				92.4	-0.4
1970	Chi-N	162	84	78	.519	2 E				93.6	-9.6
1971	Chi-N	162	83	79	.512	•3 E				79.8	3.2
1972	Chi-N	91	46	44	.511	4 E	2 E		1/2	52.3	-6.3
	Hou-N	31	16	15	.516	2 W	2 W		3/3	17.0	-1.0
1973	Hou-N	162	82	80	.506	4 W				81.9	0.1
	24	3739	2008	1709	.540						-14.0
Dwyer, John Francis "Frank"											
1902	Det-A	137	52	83	.385	7				58.4	-6.4
Dyer, Edwin Hawley "Eddie"											
1946	StL-N	156	98	58	.628	▲★1				95.7	2.3
1947	StL-N	156	89	65	.578	2				91.5	-2.5
1948	StL-N	155	85	69	.552	2				86.6	-1.6
1949	StL-N	157	96	58	.623	2				92.2	3.8
1950	StL-N	153	78	75	.510	5				78.8	-0.8
	5	777	446	325	.578						1.2
Dykes, James Joseph "Jimmy"											
1934	Chi-A*	138	49	88	.358	8	8		2/2	48.6	0.4
1935	Chi-A*	153	74	78	.487	5				74.8	-0.8
1936	Chi-A*	153	81	70	.536	3				79.6	1.4
1937	Chi-A*	154	86	68	.558	3				81.8	4.2
1938	Chi-A*	149	65	83	.439	6				69.9	-4.9
1939	Chi-A*	155	85	69	.552	4				78.7	6.3
1940	Chi-A	155	82	72	.532	•4				83.3	-1.3
1941	Chi-A	156	77	77	.500	3				75.9	1.1
1942	Chi-A	148	66	82	.446	6				66.3	-0.3
1943	Chi-A	155	82	72	.532	4				74.7	7.3
1944	Chi-A	154	71	83	.461	7				64.2	6.8
1945	Chi-A	150	71	78	.477	6				70.6	0.4
1946	Chi-A	30	10	20	.333	7	5		1/2	14.3	-4.3
1951	Phi-A	154	70	84	.455	6				76.1	-6.1
1952	Phi-A	155	79	75	.513	4				71.1	7.9
1953	Phi-A	157	59	95	.383	7				60.4	-1.4
1954	Bal-A	154	54	100	.351	7				56.7	-2.7
1958	Cin-N	41	24	17	.585	8	4		2/2	22.5	1.5
1959	Det-A	137	74	63	.540	8	4		2/2	66.8	7.2
1960	Det-A	96	44	52	.458	6	6		1/3	47.3	-3.3
	Cle-A	58	26	32	.448	4	4		3/3	28.0	-2.0
1961	Cle-A	160	77	83	.481	5	5		1/2	78.5	-1.5
	21	2962	1406	1541	.477						15.7

YEAR	TM/L	G	W	L	PCT	STANDING			M/Y	W-EXP	A-E
Ebbets, Charles Hercules "Charlie"											
1898	Bro-N	110	38	68	.358	9	10		3/3	40.8	-2.8
Edwards, Howard Rodney "Doc"											
1987	Cle-A	75	30	45	.400	7 E	7 E		2/2	28.3	1.7
1988	Cle-A	162	78	84	.481	6 E				74.4	3.6
1989	Cle-A	143	65	78	.455	6 E	6 E		1/2	66.7	-1.7
	3	380	173	207	.455						3.6
Elberfeld, Norman Arthur "Kid"											
1908	NY-A*	98	27	71	.276	6	8		2/2	31.4	-4.4
Elia, Lee Constantine											
1982	Chi-N	162	73	89	.451	5 E				77.6	-4.6
1983	Chi-N	123	54	69	.439	5 E	5 E		1/2	60.1	-6.1
1987	Phi-N	101	51	50	.505	5 E	•4 E		2/2	47.6	3.4
1988	Phi-N	153	60	92	.395	6 E	6 E		1/2	62.5	-2.5
	4	539	238	300	.442						-9.8
Ellick, Joseph J. "Joe"											
1884	Pit-U*	13	6	6	.500	5	5		2/2	5.4	0.6
Elliott, Robert Irving "Bob"											
1960	KC-A	155	58	96	.377	8				62.8	-4.8
Ens, Jewel Winklemeyer											
1929	Pit-N	35	21	14	.600	2	2		2/2	20.1	0.9
1930	Pit-N	154	80	74	.519	5				73.8	6.2
1931	Pit-N	155	75	79	.487	5				71.4	3.6
	3	344	176	167	.513						10.8
Ermer, Calvin Coolidge "Cal"											
1967	Min-A	114	66	46	.589	6	•2		2/2	62.1	3.9
1968	Min-A	162	79	83	.488	7				82.8	-3.8
	2	276	145	129	.529						0.1
Essian, James Sarkis "Jim"											
1991	Chi-N	122	59	63	.484	5 E	4 E		3/3	58.0	1.0
Esterbrook, Thomas Jefferson "Dude"											
1889	Lou-a*	10	2	8	.200	7	8		1/4	2.2	-0.2
Evers, John Joseph "Johnny"											
1913	Chi-N*	155	88	65	.575	3				85.6	2.4
1921	Chi-N	96	41	55	.427	6	7		1/2	41.6	-0.6
1924	Chi-A	21	10	11	.476	6			1/4	9.7	0.3
	Chi-A	103	41	61	.402	8			4/4	47.0	-6.0
	3	375	180	192	.484						-3.9
Ewing, William "Buck"											
1890	NY-P*	132	74	57	.565	3				76.8	-2.8
1895	Cin-N*	132	66	64	.508	8				69.0	-3.0
1896	Cin-N*	128	77	50	.606	3				78.3	-1.3
1897	Cin-N*	134	76	56	.576	4				71.3	4.7
1898	Cin-N	157	92	60	.605	3				84.6	7.4
1899	Cin-N	157	83	67	.553	6				83.0	0.0
1900	NY-N	63	21	41	.339	8	8		1/2	26.5	-5.5
	7	903	489	395	.553						-0.5
Faatz, Jayson S. "Jay"											
1890	Buf-P*	34	9	24	.273	8	8	8	2/3	8.6	0.4
Falk, Bibb August											
1933	Cle-A	1	1	0	1.000	5	5	4	2/3	0.5	0.5
Fanning, William James "Jim"											
1981(2)	Mon-N	27	16	11	.593	2 E	1 E		2/2	14.8	1.2
1982	Mon-N	162	86	76	.531	3 E				89.5	-3.5
1984	Mon-N	30	14	16	.467	5 E	5 E		2/2	15.2	-1.2
	3	219	116	103	.530						-3.5
Farrell, John A. "Jack"											
1881	Pro-N*	51	24	27	.471	4	2		1/2	26.7	-2.7
Farrell, Major Kerby "Kerby"											
1957	Cle-A	153	76	77	.497	6				72.5	3.5
Felske, John Frederick											
1985	Phi-N	162	75	87	.463	5 E				80.4	-5.4
1986	Phi-N	161	86	75	.534	2 E				83.1	2.9
1987	Phi-N	61	29	32	.475	5 E	•4 E		1/2	28.7	0.3
	3	384	190	194	.495						-2.2
Ferguson, Robert V. "Bob"											
1871	Mut-n*	33	16	17	.485	4				15.7	0.3
1872	Atl-n*	37	9	28	.243	6				2.3	6.7
1873	Atl-n*	55	17	37	.315	6				13.5	3.5
1874	Atl-n*	56	22	33	.400	6				15.4	6.6
1875	Har-n*	86	54	28	.659	3				60.8	-6.8
1876	Har-N*	69	47	21	.691	3				49.9	-2.9
1877	Har-N*	60	31	27	.534	3				31.7	-0.7
1878	Chi-N*	61	30	30	.500	4				33.5	-3.5
1879	Tro-N*	30	7	22	.241	8	8		2/2	6.8	0.2
1880	Tro-N*	83	41	42	.494	4				37.1	3.9
1881	Tro-N*	85	39	45	.464	5				39.1	-0.1
1882	Tro-N*	85	35	48	.422	7				33.3	1.7
1883	Phi-N*	17	4	13	.235	8	8		1/2	2.1	1.9
1884	Pit-a*	42	11	31	.262	9	11	10	2/5	9.4	1.6
1886	NY-a	120	48	70	.407	8	7		2/2	47.7	0.3
1887	NY-a	30	6	24	.200	8	7		1/3	8.7	-2.7
	16	949	417	516	.447						9.8

YEAR	TM/L	G	W	L	PCT	STANDING			M/Y	W-EXP	A-E
Ferraro, Michael Dennis "Mike"											
1983	Cle-A	100	40	60	.400	7 E	7 E		1/2	45.1	-5.1
1986	KC-A	74	36	38	.486	4 W	•3 W		2/2	36.1	-0.1
	2	174	76	98	.437						-5.1
Fessenden, Wallace Clifton											
1890	Syr-a	11	4	7	.364	7	7	6	2/3	4.5	-0.5
Fitzsimmons, Frederick Landis "Freddie"											
1943	Phi-N	65	26	38	.406	7	7		2/2	27.4	-1.4
1944	Phi-N	154	61	92	.399	8				63.7	-2.7
1945	Phi-N	69	18	51	.261	8	8		1/2	20.4	-2.4
	3	288	105	181	.367						-6.5
Fletcher, Arthur "Art"											
1923	Phi-N	155	50	104	.325	8				53.8	-3.8
1924	Phi-N	152	55	96	.364	7				59.1	-4.1
1925	Phi-N	153	68	85	.444	•6				66.0	2.0
1926	Phi-N	152	58	93	.384	8				55.7	2.3
1929	NY-A	11	6	5	.545	2	2		2/2	6.3	-0.3
	5	623	237	383	.382						-4.0
Flint, Frank Sylvester "Silver"											
1879	Chi-N*	19	5	12	.294	2	4		2/2	9.0	-4.0
Fogarty, James G. "Jim"											
1890	Phi-P*	16	7	9	.438	5	5		1/2	8.9	-1.9
Fogel, Horace S.											
1887	Ind-N	70	20	49	.290	8	8		3/3	18.9	1.1
1902	NY-N	44	18	23	.439	4	8		1/3	14.1	3.9
	2	114	38	72	.345						5.0
Fohl, Leo Alexander "Lee"											
1915	Cle-A	127	45	79	.363	6	7		2/2	50.6	-5.6
1916	Cle-A	157	77	77	.500	6				80.0	-3.0
1917	Cle-A	156	88	66	.571	3				81.6	6.4
1918	Cle-A	129	73	54	.575	2				69.8	3.2
1919	Cle-A	78	44	34	.564	3	2		1/2	44.7	-0.7
1921	StL-A	154	81	73	.526	3				76.1	4.9
1922	StL-A	154	93	61	.604	2				98.5	-5.5
1923	StL-A	103	52	49	.515	3	5		1/2	48.4	3.6
1924	Bos-A	157	67	87	.435	7				70.4	-3.4
1925	Bos-A	152	47	105	.309	8				49.5	-2.5
1926	Bos-A	154	46	107	.301	8				49.3	-3.3
	11	1521	713	792	.474						-5.8
Fonseca, Lewis Albert "Lew"											
1932	Chi-A*	152	49	102	.325	7				54.0	-5.0
1933	Chi-A*	151	67	83	.447	6				62.5	4.5
1934	Chi-A	15	4	11	.267	8	8		1/2	5.3	-1.3
	3	318	120	196	.380						-1.8
Foutz, David Luther "Dave"											
1893	Bro-N*	130	65	63	.508	•6				58.1	6.9
1894	Bro-N*	135	70	61	.534	5				66.6	3.4
1895	Bro-N*	134	71	60	.542	•5				68.3	2.7
1896	Bro-N*	133	58	73	.443	•9				59.0	-1.0
	4	532	264	257	.507						12.1
Fox, Charles Francis "Charlie"											
1970	SF-N	120	67	53	.558	4 W	3 W		2/2	60.3	6.7
1971	SF-N	162	90	72	.556	1 W				87.4	2.6
1972	SF-N	155	69	86	.445	5 W				78.8	-9.8
1973	SF-N	162	88	74	.543	3 W				84.7	3.3
1974	SF-N	76	34	42	.447	5 W	5 W		1/2	33.7	0.3
1976	Mon-N	34	12	22	.353	6 E	6 E		2/2	12.4	-0.4
1983	Chi-N	39	17	22	.436	5 E	5 E		2/2	19.1	-2.1
	7	748	377	371	.504						0.5
Franks, Herman Louis											
1965	SF-N	163	95	67	.586	2				90.5	4.5
1966	SF-N	161	93	68	.578	2				85.7	7.3
1967	SF-N	162	91	71	.562	2				92.1	-1.1
1968	SF-N	163	88	74	.543	2				89.0	-1.0
1977	Chi-N	162	81	81	.500	4 E				76.3	4.7
1978	Chi-N	162	79	83	.488	3 E				74.8	4.2
1979	Chi-N	155	78	77	.503	5 E	5 E		1/2	77.4	0.6
	7	1128	605	521	.537						19.2
Frazer, George Kasson											
1890	Syr-a	71	31	40	.437	7	6		1/3	29.0	2.0
	Syr-a	46	20	25	.444	7	6		3/3	18.4	1.6
Frazier, Joseph Filmore "Joe"											
1976	NY-N	162	86	76	.531	3 E				89.7	-3.7
1977	NY-N	45	15	30	.333	6 E	6 E		1/2	20.2	-5.2
	2	207	101	106	.488						-8.9
Fregosi, James Louis "Jim"											
1978	Cal-A	117	62	55	.530	3 W	•2 W		2/2	60.4	1.6
1979	Cal-A	162	88	74	.543	1 W				90.3	-2.3
1980	Cal-A	160	65	95	.406	6 W				70.3	-5.3
1981(1)	Cal-A	47	22	25	.468	4 W	4 W		1/2	24.5	-2.5
1986	Chi-A	96	45	51	.469	5 W	5 W		3/3	44.6	0.4
1987	Chi-A	162	77	85	.475	5 W				81.2	-4.2
1988	Chi-A	161	71	90	.441	5 W				67.6	3.4
1991	Phi-N	149	74	75	.497	6 E	3 E		2/2	69.5	4.5
1992	Phi-N	162	70	92	.432	6 E				77.8	-7.8
	9	1216	574	642	.472						-12.2

YEAR	TM/L	G	W	L	PCT	STANDING			M/Y	W-EXP	A-E
Frey, James Gottfried "Jim"											
1980	KC-A	162	97	65	.599	♦1 W				92.3	4.7
1981(1)	KC-A	50	20	30	.400	5 W					
(2)	KC-A	20	10	10	.500	●2 W	1 W		1/2	34.4	-4.4
1984	Chi-N	161	96	65	.596	1 E				91.0	5.0
1985	Chi-N	162	77	84	.478	4 E				76.1	0.9
1986	Chi-N	56	23	33	.411	5 E	5 E		1/3	24.5	-1.5
	5	611	323	287	.530						4.6
Frisch, Frank Francis "Frankie"											
1933	StL-N*	63	36	26	.581	5	5		2/2	34.3	1.7
1934	StL-N*	154	95	58	.621	★1				90.5	4.5
1935	StL-N*	154	96	58	.623	2				96.9	-0.9
1936	StL-N*	155	87	67	.565	●2				77.1	9.9
1937	StL-N*	157	81	73	.526	4				82.4	-1.4
1938	StL-N	139	63	72	.467	6	6		1/2	67.9	-4.9
1940	Pit-N	156	78	76	.506	4				79.4	-1.4
1941	Pit-N	156	81	73	.526	4				81.8	-0.8
1942	Pit-N	151	66	81	.449	5				68.6	-2.6
1943	Pit-N	157	80	74	.519	4				83.7	-3.7
1944	Pit-N	158	90	63	.588	2				84.7	5.3
1945	Pit-N	155	82	72	.532	4				83.6	-1.6
1946	Pit-N	152	62	89	.411	7	7		1/2	63.3	-1.3
1949	Chi-N	104	42	62	.404	7	8		2/2	39.8	2.2
1950	Chi-N	154	64	89	.418	7				63.7	0.3
1951	Chi-N	81	35	45	.438	7	8		1/2	32.9	2.1
	16	2246	1138	1078	.514						7.3
Fuchs, Emil Edmund "Judge"											
1929	Bos-N	154	56	98	.364	8				56.2	-0.2
Gaffney, John H.											
1886	Was-N	43	15	25	.375	8			2/2	9.0	6.0
1887	Was-N	126	46	76	.377	7				41.6	4.4
	2	169	61	101	.377						10.4
Galvin, James Francis "Jim"											
1885	Buf-N*	24	7	17	.292	7	7		1/2	6.9	0.1
Ganzel, John Henry											
1908	Cin-N*	155	73	81	.474	5				70.6	2.4
1915	Bro-F	35	17	18	.486	7	7		2/2	16.9	0.1
	2	190	90	99	.476						2.5
Garcia, David "Dave"											
1977	Cal-A	81	35	46	.432	5 W	5 W		2/2	39.5	-4.5
1978	Cal-A	45	25	20	.556	3 W	●2 W		1/2	23.2	1.8
1979	Cle-A	66	38	28	.576	6 E	6 E		2/2	31.2	6.8
1980	Cle-A	160	79	81	.494	6 E				73.3	5.7
1981(1)	Cle-A	50	26	24	.520	6 E					
(2)	Cle-A	53	26	27	.491	5 E				50.4	1.6
1982	Cle-A	162	78	84	.481	●6 E				74.4	3.6
	6	617	307	310	.498						14.9
Gardner, William Frederick "Billy"											
1981(1)	Min-A	20	6	14	.300	6 W	7 W		2/2		
(2)	Min-A	53	24	29	.453	4 W				28.8	1.2
1982	Min-A	162	60	102	.370	7 W				64.9	-4.9
1983	Min-A	162	70	92	.432	5 W				70.0	0.0
1984	Min-A	162	81	81	.500	2 W				80.8	0.2
1985	Min-A	62	27	35	.435	6 W	4 W		1/2	28.1	-1.1
1987	KC-A	126	62	64	.492	4 W	2 W		1/2	64.9	-2.9
	6	747	330	417	.442						-7.4
Garner, Philip Mason "Phil"											
1992	Mil-A	162	92	70	.568	2 E				95.2	-3.2
Gaston, Clarence Edwin "Cito"											
1989	Tor-A	126	77	49	.611	6 E	1 E		2/2	69.4	7.6
1990	Tor-A	162	86	76	.531	2 E				91.7	-5.7
1991	Tor-A	120	66	54	.550	1 E	1 E		1/3	64.9	1.1
	Tor-A	9	6	3	.667	1 E	1 E		3/3	4.9	1.1
1992	Tor-A	162	96	66	.593	1 E				90.8	5.2
	4	579	331	248	.572						9.4
Gerhardt, John Joseph "Joe"											
1883	Lou-a*	98	52	45	.536	5				48.7	3.3
1890	StL-a*	38	20	16	.556	2	3		6/6	21.1	-1.1
	2	136	72	61	.541						2.2
Gessler, Harry Homer "Doc"											
1914	Pit-F	11	3	8	.273	8	7		1/2	4.8	-1.8
Gibson, George C. "Moon"											
1920	Pit-N	155	79	75	.513	4				74.5	4.5
1921	Pit-N	154	90	63	.588	2				86.6	3.4
1922	Pit-N	65	32	33	.492	5	●3		1/2	37.6	-5.6
1925	Chi-N	26	12	14	.462	5	7	8	3/3	12.2	-0.2
1932	Pit-N	154	86	68	.558	2				76.0	10.0
1933	Pit-N	154	87	67	.565	2				82.0	5.0
1934	Pit-N	51	27	24	.529	4	5		1/2	26.2	0.8
	7	759	413	344	.546						17.9
Gifford, James H. "Jim"											
1884	Ind-a	87	25	60	.294	10	11		1/2	21.5	3.5
1885	NY-a	108	44	64	.407	7				39.5	4.5
1886	NY-a	17	5	12	.294	8	7		1/2	6.9	-1.9
	3	212	74	136	.352						6.1
Glasscock, John Wesley "Jack"											
1889	Ind-N*	67	34	32	.515	7	7		2/2	29.9	4.1
1892(1)	StL-N*	4	1	3	.250	10	9		1/3		
	2	71	35	35	.500						4.1
Gleason, William J. "Kid"											
1919	Chi-A	140	88	52	.629	1				83.6	4.4
1920	Chi-A	154	96	58	.623	2				89.6	6.4
1921	Chi-A	154	62	92	.403	7				60.4	1.6
1922	Chi-A	155	77	77	.500	5				77.0	0.0
1923	Chi-A	156	69	85	.448	7				72.1	-3.1
	5	759	392	364	.519						9.3
Gomez, Pedro W. "Preston"											
1969	SD-N	162	52	110	.321	6 W				50.5	1.5
1970	SD-N	162	63	99	.389	6 W				70.3	-7.3
1971	SD-N	161	61	100	.379	6 W				66.2	-5.2
1972	SD-N	11	4	7	.364	4 W	6 W		1/2	4.1	-0.1
1974	Hou-N	162	81	81	.500	4 W				83.2	-2.2
1975	Hou-N	127	47	80	.370	6 W	6 W		1/2	59.7	-12.7
1980	Chi-N	90	38	52	.422	6 E	6 E		1/2	38.4	-0.4
	7	875	346	529	.395						-26.5
Gonzalez, Miguel Angel "Mike"											
1938	StL-N	17	8	8	.500	6	6		2/2	8.0	-0.0
1940	StL-N	6	1	5	.167	6	7	3	2/3	3.2	-2.2
	2	23	9	13	.409						-2.2
Gordon, Joseph Lowell "Joe"											
1958	Cle-A	86	46	40	.535	6	4		2/2	46.4	-0.4
1959	Cle-A	154	89	65	.578	2				86.9	2.1
1960	Cle-A	95	49	46	.516	4	4		1/3	45.9	3.1
	Det-A	57	26	31	.456	6	6		3/3	28.1	-2.1
1961	KC-A	60	26	33	.441	8	●9		1/2	23.1	2.9
1969	KC-A	163	69	93	.426	4 W				70.1	-1.1
	5	615	305	308	.498						4.6
Gore, George F.											
1892(2)	StL-N*	16	6	9	.400	12	12	11	2/3	5.5	0.5
Goryl, John Albert "Johnny"											
1980	Min-A	36	23	13	.639	4 W	3 W		2/2	16.8	6.2
1981(1)	Min-A	37	11	25	.306	6 W	7 W		1/2		
	2	73	34	38	.472						6.2
Gould, Charles Harvey "Charlie"											
1875	NH-n*	23	2	21	.087	11	8		1/3	1.9	0.1
1876	Cin-N*	65	9	56	.138	8				3.6	5.4
	2	88	11	77	.125						5.5
Gowdy, Henry Morgan "Hank"											
1946	Cin-N	4	3	1	.750	6	6		2/2	1.9	1.1
Graffen, Samuel Mason "Mase"											
1876	StL-N	56	39	17	.696	2	2		1/2	41.3	-2.3
Grammas, Alexander Peter "Alex"											
1969	Pit-N	5	4	1	.800	3 E	3 E		2/2	2.7	1.3
1976	Mil-A	161	66	95	.410	6 E				71.3	-5.3
1977	Mil-A	162	67	95	.414	6 E				68.2	-1.2
	3	328	137	191	.418						-5.1
Green, George Dallas "Dallas"											
1979	Phi-N	30	19	11	.633	5 E	4 E		2/2	14.3	4.7
1980	Phi-N	162	91	71	.562	★1 E				90.2	0.8
1981(1)	Phi-N	55	34	21	.618	1 E					
(2)	Phi-N	52	25	27	.481	3 E				55.4	3.6
1989	NY-A	121	56	65	.463	6 E	5 E			53.5	2.5
	4	420	225	195	.536						11.5
Griffin, Michael Joseph "Mike"											
1898	Bro-N*	4	1	3	.250	9	9	10	2/3	1.5	-0.5
Griffin, Tobias Charles "Sandy"											
1891	Was-a*	6	2	4	.333	8	8		4/4	1.6	0.4
Griffith, Clark Calvin											
1901	Chi-A*	137	83	53	.610	1				85.3	-2.3
1902	Chi-A	138	74	60	.552	4				74.2	-0.2
1903	NY-A	136	72	62	.537	4				67.6	4.4
1904	NY-A*	155	92	59	.609	2				83.5	8.5
1905	NY-A*	152	71	78	.477	6				70.7	0.3
1906	NY-A*	155	90	61	.596	2				86.5	3.5
1907	NY-A*	152	70	78	.473	5				67.8	2.2
1908	NY-A	57	24	32	.429	6	8		1/2	17.9	6.1
1909	Cin-N*	157	77	76	.503	4				77.3	-0.3
1910	Cin-N*	156	75	79	.487	5				70.4	4.6
1911	Cin-N	159	70	83	.458	6				74.1	-4.1
1912	Was-A*	154	91	61	.599	2				88.3	2.7
1913	Was-A*	155	90	64	.584	2				80.8	9.2
1914	Was-A*	158	81	73	.526	3				83.1	-2.1
1915	Was-A	155	85	68	.556	4				85.4	-0.4
1916	Was-A	159	76	77	.497	7				75.7	0.3
1917	Was-A	158	74	79	.484	5				73.9	0.1
1918	Was-A	130	72	56	.563	3				69.7	2.3
1919	Was-A	142	56	84	.400	7				66.0	-10.0
1920	Was-A	153	68	84	.447	6				68.5	-0.5
	20	2918	1491	1367	.522						24.4

YEAR	TM/L	G	W	L	PCT	STANDING			M/Y	W-EXP	A-E
Grimes, Burleigh Arland											
1937	Bro-N	155	62	91	.405	6				60.9	1.1
1938	Bro-N	151	69	80	.463	7				73.9	-4.9
	2	306	131	171	.434						-3.8
Grimm, Charles John "Charlie"											
1932	Chi-N*	55	37	18	.673	2	1		2/2	30.6	6.4
1933	Chi-N*	154	86	68	.558	3				88.9	-2.9
1934	Chi-N*	152	86	65	.570	3				82.2	3.8
1935	Chi-N*	154	100	54	.649	1				101.5	-1.5
1936	Chi-N*	154	87	67	.565	•2				92.4	-5.4
1937	Chi-N	154	93	61	.604	2				89.4	3.6
1938	Chi-N	81	45	36	.556	3	1		1/2	46.8	-1.8
1944	Chi-N	146	74	69	.517	8	4		3/3	74.6	-0.6
1945	Chi-N	155	98	56	.636	1				98.3	-0.3
1946	Chi-N	155	82	71	.536	3				81.3	0.7
1947	Chi-N	155	69	85	.448	6				60.9	8.1
1948	Chi-N	155	64	90	.416	8				65.7	-1.7
1949	Chi-N	50	19	31	.380	7	8		1/2	19.1	-0.1
1952	Bos-N	120	51	67	.432	7	7		2/2	52.2	-1.2
1953	Mil-N	157	92	62	.597	2				92.4	-0.4
1954	Mil-N	154	89	65	.578	3				89.1	-0.1
1955	Mil-N	154	85	69	.552	2				84.4	0.6
1956	Mil-N	46	24	22	.522	5	2		1/2	27.4	-3.4
1960	Chi-N	17	6	11	.353	7	7		1/2	6.9	-0.9
	19	2368	1287	1067	.547						2.8
Groh, Henry Knight "Heinie"											
1918	Cin-N*	10	7	3	.700	4	3		2/2	5.3	1.7
Gutteridge, Donald Joseph "Don"											
1969	Chi-A	145	60	85	.414	4 W	5 W		2/2	63.4	-3.4
1970	Chi-A	136	49	87	.360	6 W	6 W		1/3	52.1	-3.1
	2	281	109	172	.388						-6.5
Haas, George Edwin "Eddie"											
1985	Atl-N	121	50	71	.413	5 W	5 W		1/2	49.2	0.8
Hack, Stanley Camfield "Stan"											
1954	Chi-N	154	64	90	.416	7				70.6	-6.6
1955	Chi-N	154	72	81	.471	6				67.6	4.4
1956	Chi-N	157	60	94	.390	8				65.4	-5.4
1958	StL-N	10	3	7	.300	5	•5		2/2	4.4	-1.4
	4	475	199	272	.423						-9.1
Hackett, Charles M. "Charlie"											
1884	Cle-N	113	35	77	.313	7				32.0	3.0
1885	Bro-a	37	15	22	.405	7	•5		1/2	17.7	-2.7
	2	150	50	99	.336						0.3
Hallman, William Wilson "Bill"											
1897	StL-N*	50	13	36	.265	12	12	12	3/4	8.9	4.1
Haney, Fred Girard											
1939	StL-A	156	43	111	.279	8				50.1	-7.1
1940	StL-A	156	67	87	.435	6				65.4	1.6
1941	StL-A	44	15	29	.341	7	•6		1/2	20.4	-5.4
1953	Pit-N	154	50	104	.325	8				51.6	-1.6
1954	Pit-N	154	53	101	.344	8				48.4	4.6
1955	Pit-N	154	60	94	.390	8				55.8	4.2
1956	Mil-N	109	68	40	.630	5	2		2/2	64.3	3.7
1957	Mil-N	155	95	59	.617	★1				93.0	2.0
1958	Mil-N	154	92	62	.597	1				91.3	0.7
1959	Mil-N	157	86	70	.551	▲2				88.3	-2.3
	10	1393	629	757	.454						0.4
Hanlon, Edward Hugh "Ned"											
1889	Pit-N*	46	26	18	.591	7	5		3/3	19.8	6.2
1890	Pit-P*	131	60	68	.469	6				59.3	0.7
1891	Pit-N*	78	31	47	.397	8	8		1/2	35.5	-4.5
1892(1)	Bal-N*	56	17	39	.304	12	12		3/3		
(2)	Bal-N*	77	26	46	.361	10				45.7	-2.7
1893	Bal-N	130	60	70	.462	8				59.0	1.0
1894	Bal-N	129	89	39	.695	1				90.9	-1.9
1895	Bal-N	132	87	43	.669	1				95.8	-8.8
1896	Bal-N	132	90	39	.698	1				92.7	-2.7
1897	Bal-N	136	90	40	.692	2				90.1	-0.1
1898	Bal-N	154	96	53	.644	2				103.8	-7.8
1899	Bro-N	150	101	47	.682	1				95.8	5.2
1900	Bro-N	142	82	54	.603	1				76.6	5.4
1901	Bro-N	137	79	57	.581	3				81.8	-2.8
1902	Bro-N	141	75	63	.543	2				73.9	1.1
1903	Bro-N	139	70	66	.515	5				66.6	3.4
1904	Bro-N	154	56	97	.366	6				63.4	-7.4
1905	Bro-N	155	48	104	.316	8				45.0	3.0
1906	Cin-N	155	64	87	.424	6				70.0	-6.0
1907	Cin-N	156	66	87	.431	6				77.3	-11.3
	19	2530	1313	1164	.530						-29.8
Harder, Melvin Leroy "Mel"											
1961	Cle-A	1	1	0	1.000	5	5		2/2	0.5	0.5
1962	Cle-A	2	2	0	1.000	6	6		2/2	0.9	1.1
	2	3	3	0	1.000						1.6
Hargrove, Dudley Michael "Mike"											
1991	Cle-A	85	32	53	.376	7 E	7 E		2/2	32.5	-0.5
1992	Cle-A	162	76	86	.469	•4 E				73.7	2.3
	2	247	108	139	.437						1.8

YEAR	TM/L	G	W	L	PCT	STANDING			M/Y	W-EXP	A-E
Harrah, Colbert Dale "Toby"											
1992	Tex-A	76	32	44	.421	3 W	4 W		2/2	34.6	-2.6
Harrelson, Derrel Mc Kinley "Bud"											
1990	NY-N	120	71	49	.592	4 E	2 E		2/2	72.3	-1.3
1991	NY-N	154	74	80	.481	3 E	5 E		1/2	76.4	-2.4
	2	274	145	129	.529						-3.7
Harris, Chalmer Luman "Lum"											
1961	Bal-A	27	17	10	.630	3	3		2/2	15.3	1.7
1964	Hou-N	13	5	8	.385	9	9		2/2	5.3	-0.3
1965	Hou-N	162	65	97	.401	9				65.8	-0.8
1968	Atl-N	163	81	81	.500	5				76.9	4.1
1969	Atl-N	162	93	69	.574	1 W				87.3	5.7
1970	Atl-N	162	76	86	.469	5 W				77.5	-1.5
1971	Atl-N	162	82	80	.506	3 W				75.2	6.8
1972	Atl-N	105	47	57	.452	4 W	4 W		1/2	45.0	2.0
	8	956	466	488	.488						17.7
Harris, Stanley Raymond "Bucky"											
1924	Was-A*	156	92	62	.597	★1				91.4	0.6
1925	Was-A*	152	96	55	.636	1				90.7	5.3
1926	Was-A*	152	81	69	.540	4				78.8	2.2
1927	Was-A*	157	85	69	.552	3				82.0	3.0
1928	Was-A*	155	75	79	.487	4				78.3	-3.3
1929	Det-A*	155	70	84	.455	6				76.8	-6.8
1930	Det-A	154	75	79	.487	5				72.4	2.6
1931	Det-A*	154	61	93	.396	7				59.1	1.9
1932	Det-A	153	76	75	.503	5				76.6	-0.6
1933	Det-A	153	73	79	.480	5	5		1/2	74.9	-1.9
1934	Bos-A	153	76	76	.500	4				80.2	-4.2
1935	Was-A	154	67	86	.438	6				69.3	-2.3
1936	Was-A	153	82	71	.536	4				84.6	-2.6
1937	Was-A	158	73	80	.477	6				68.6	4.4
1938	Was-A	152	75	76	.497	5				70.2	4.8
1939	Was-A	153	65	87	.428	6				66.9	-1.9
1940	Was-A	154	64	90	.416	7				62.9	1.1
1941	Was-A	156	70	84	.455	•6				70.3	-0.3
1942	Was-A	151	62	89	.411	7				59.7	2.3
1943	Phi-N	92	38	52	.422	7	7		1/2	38.5	-0.5
1947	NY-A	155	97	57	.630	★1				99.9	-2.9
1948	NY-A	154	94	60	.610	3				98.6	-4.6
1950	Was-A	155	67	87	.435	5				65.1	1.9
1951	Was-A	154	62	92	.403	7				68.0	-6.0
1952	Was-A	157	78	76	.506	5				75.9	2.1
1953	Was-A	152	76	76	.500	5				83.5	-7.5
1954	Was-A	155	66	88	.429	6				72.1	-6.1
1955	Det-A	154	79	75	.513	5				88.5	-9.5
1956	Det-A	155	82	72	.532	5				85.7	-3.7
	29	4408	2157	2218	.493						-32.5
Hart, James Aristotle "Jim"											
1885	Lou-a	112	53	59	.473	•5				52.8	0.2
1886	Lou-a	138	66	70	.485	4				70.4	-4.4
1889	Bos-N	133	83	45	.648	2				82.2	0.8
	3	383	202	174	.537						-3.4
Hart, John Henry											
1989	Cle-A	19	8	11	.421	6 E	6 E		2/2	8.9	-0.9
Hartnett, Charles Leo "Gabby"											
1938	Chi-N*	73	44	27	.620	3	1		2/2	41.0	3.0
1939	Chi-N*	156	84	70	.545	4				81.6	2.4
1940	Chi-N*	154	75	79	.487	5				81.6	-6.6
	3	383	203	176	.536						-1.2
Hartsfield, Roy Thomas											
1977	Tor-A	161	54	107	.335	7 E				58.6	-4.6
1978	Tor-A	161	59	102	.366	7 E				61.4	-2.4
1979	Tor-A	162	53	109	.327	7 E				56.2	-3.2
	3	484	166	318	.343						-10.3
Hastings, Winfield Scott "Scott"											
1871	Rok-n*	25	4	21	.160	9				8.8	-4.8
1872	Cle-n*	20	6	14	.300	5	7		1/2	5.1	0.9
	2	45	10	35	.222						-3.9
Hatfield, John Van Buren											
1872	Mut-n*	40	24	14	.632	4	3		2/2	27.6	-3.6
1873	Mut-n*	28	11	17	.393	5	4		1/2	15.6	-4.6
	2	68	35	31	.530						-8.1
Hatton, Grady Edgebert											
1966	Hou-N	163	72	90	.444	8				72.2	-0.2
1967	Hou-N	162	69	93	.426	9				69.0	-0.0
1968	Hou-N	61	23	38	.377	10	10		1/2	27.1	-4.1
	3	386	164	221	.426						-4.3
Hecker, Guy Jackson											
1890	Pit-N*	138	23	113	.169	8				15.5	7.5
Heffner, Donald Henry "Don"											
1966	Cin-N	83	37	46	.446	8	7		1/2	41.0	-4.0
Heilbroner, Louis Wilbur "Louie"											
1900	StL-N	50	23	25	.479	7	•5		2/2	23.9	-0.9
Helms, Tommy Vann											
1988	Cin-N	27	12	15	.444	4 W	4 W	2 W	2/3	14.3	-2.3
1989	Cin-N	37	16	21	.432	•4 W	5 W		2/2	17.1	-1.1

YEAR	TM/L	G	W	L	PCT	STANDING			M/Y	W-EXP	A-E
	2	64	28	36	.438						-3.4
Hemus, Solomon Joseph "Solly"											
1959	StL-N*	154	71	83	.461	7				68.5	2.5
1960	StL-N	155	86	68	.558	3				79.4	6.6
1961	StL-N	75	33	41	.446	6	5		1/2	38.7	-5.7
	3	384	190	192	.497						3.3
Henderson, William C. "Bill"											
1884	Bal-U	106	58	47	.552	4				55.5	2.5
Hendricks, John Charles "Jack"											
1918	StL-N	133	51	78	.395	8				56.5	-5.5
1924	Cin-N	153	83	70	.542	4				83.9	-0.9
1925	Cin-N	153	80	73	.523	3				81.3	-1.3
1926	Cin-N	157	87	67	.565	2				86.7	0.3
1927	Cin-N	153	75	78	.490	5				75.5	-0.5
1928	Cin-N	153	78	74	.513	5				72.1	5.9
1929	Cin-N	155	66	88	.429	7				69.7	-3.7
	7	1057	520	528	.496						-5.7
Hengle, Edward S. "Ed"											
1884	Chi-U	74	34	39	.466	5				41.3	-0.3
Herman, William Jennings Bryan "Billy"											
1947	Pit-N*	155	61	92	.399	8	•7		1/2	69.6	-8.6
1964	Bos-A	2	2	0	1.000	8	8		2/2	0.9	1.1
1965	Bos-A	162	62	100	.383	9				68.8	-6.8
1966	Bos-A	146	64	82	.438	9	9		1/2	66.0	-2.0
	4	465	189	274	.408						-16.3
Herzog, Charles Lincoln "Buck"											
1914	Cin-N*	157	60	94	.390	8				63.8	-3.8
1915	Cin-N*	160	71	83	.461	7				69.1	1.9
1916	Cin-N*	84	34	49	.410	8	•7		1/3	34.7	-0.7
	3	401	165	226	.422						-2.6
Herzog, Dorrel Norman Elvert "Whitey"											
1973	Tex-A	138	47	91	.341	6 W	6 W		1/3	49.9	-2.9
1974	Cal-A	4	2	2	.500	6 W	6 W	6 W	2/3	1.9	0.1
1975	KC-A	66	41	25	.621	2 W	2 W		2/2	35.6	5.4
1976	KC-A	162	90	72	.556	1 W				91.7	-1.7
1977	KC-A	162	102	60	.630	1 W				98.0	4.0
1978	KC-A	162	92	70	.568	1 W				92.2	-0.2
1979	KC-A	162	85	77	.525	2 W				84.3	0.7
1980	StL-N	73	38	35	.521	6 E	5 E	4 E	3/4	37.8	0.2
1981(1)	StL-N	51	30	20	.600	2 E					
(2)	StL-N	52	29	23	.558	2 E				55.8	3.2
1982	StL-N	162	92	70	.568	★1 E				89.1	2.9
1983	StL-N	162	79	83	.488	4 E				77.8	1.2
1984	StL-N	162	84	78	.519	3 E				81.7	2.3
1985	StL-N	162	101	61	.623	♦1 E				99.4	1.6
1986	StL-N	161	79	82	.491	3 E				79.4	-0.4
1987	StL-N	162	95	67	.586	♦1 E				91.4	3.6
1988	StL-N	162	76	86	.469	5 E				75.0	1.0
1989	StL-N	164	86	76	.531	3 E				83.6	2.4
1990	StL-N	80	33	47	.412	6 E	6 E		1/3	34.8	-1.8
	18	2409	1281	1125	.532						21.6
Hewett, Walter F.											
1888	Was-N	40	10	29	.256	8	8		1/2	12.2	-2.2
Hicks, Nathaniel Woodhull "Nat"											
1875	Mut-n*	71	30	38	.441	7				25.1	4.9
Higgins, Michael Franklin "Pinky"											
1955	Bos-A	154	84	70	.545	4				87.2	-3.2
1956	Bos-A	155	84	70	.545	4				79.8	4.2
1957	Bos-A	154	82	72	.532	3				82.3	-0.3
1958	Bos-A	155	79	75	.513	3				77.6	1.4
1959	Bos-A	73	31	42	.425	8	8		1/3	37.9	-6.9
1960	Bos-A	105	48	57	.457	8	7		3/3	44.7	3.3
1961	Bos-A	163	76	86	.469	6				74.8	1.2
1962	Bos-A	160	76	84	.475	8				75.1	0.9
	8	1119	560	556	.502						0.6
Higham, Richard "Dick"											
1874	Mut-n*	40	29	11	.725	2	2		2/2	26.2	2.8
Himsl, Avitus Bernard "Vedie"											
1961	Chi-N	11	5	6	.455	6	•6		1/9	4.7	0.3
	Chi-N	17	5	12	.294	7	7	7	3/9	7.3	-2.3
	Chi-N	4	0	3	.000	7	7	7	6/9	1.3	-1.3
Hitchcock, William Clyde "Billy"											
1960	Det-A	1	1	0	1.000	6	6	6	2/3	0.5	0.5
1962	Bal-A	162	77	85	.475	7				78.1	-1.1
1963	Bal-A	162	86	76	.531	4				83.5	2.5
1966	Atl-N	51	33	18	.647	7	5		2/2	28.6	4.4
1967	Atl-N	159	77	82	.484	7	7		1/2	78.6	-1.6
	5	535	274	261	.512						4.8
Hobson, Clell Lavern "Butch"											
1992	Bos-A	162	73	89	.451	7 E				73.5	-0.5
Hodges, Gilbert Raymond "Gil"											
1963	Was-A	121	42	79	.347	10	10		3/3	42.6	-0.6
1964	Was-A	162	62	100	.383	9				64.7	-2.7
1965	Was-A	162	70	92	.432	8				67.3	2.7
1966	Was-A	159	71	88	.447	8				68.4	2.6

YEAR	TM/L	G	W	L	PCT	STANDING			M/Y	W-EXP	A-E
1967	Was-A	161	76	85	.472	•6				70.9	5.1
1968	NY-N	163	73	89	.451	9				77.8	-4.8
1969	NY-N	162	100	62	.617	★1 E				91.1	8.9
1970	NY-N	162	83	79	.512	3 E				87.8	-4.8
1971	NY-N	162	83	79	.512	•3 E				85.3	-2.3
	9	1414	660	753	.467						4.1
Hoey, Frederick C. "Fred"											
1899	NY-N	87	31	55	.360	9	10		2/2	36.2	-5.2
Holbert, William H. "Bill"											
1879	Syr-N*	1	0	1	.000	6	6	7	2/3	0.3	-0.3
Hollingshead, John Samuel "Holly"											
1875	Was-n*	20	4	16	.200	8	10		1/2	-2.4	6.4
1884	Was-a	62	12	50	.194	12	12		1/2	10.8	1.2
	2	82	16	66	.195						7.6
Holmes, Thomas Francis "Tommy"											
1951	Bos-N*	95	48	47	.505	5	4		2/2	51.3	-3.3
1952	Bos-N	35	13	22	.371	7	7		1/2	15.5	-2.5
	2	130	61	69	.469						-5.8
Hornsby, Rogers											
1925	StL-N*	115	64	51	.557	8	4		2/2	62.0	2.0
1926	StL-N*	156	89	65	.578	★1				90.5	-1.5
1927	NY-N*	33	22	10	.688	4	3		2/2	17.9	4.1
1928	Bos-N*	122	39	83	.320	7	7		2/2	42.2	-3.2
1930	Chi-N*	4	4	0	1.000	2	2		2/2	2.3	1.7
1931	Chi-N*	156	84	70	.545	3				88.3	-4.3
1932	Chi-N*	99	53	46	.535	2	1		1/2	55.2	-2.2
1933	StL-A*	54	19	33	.365	8	8		3/3	21.0	-2.0
1934	StL-A*	154	67	85	.441	6				63.8	3.2
1935	StL-A*	155	65	87	.428	7				56.5	8.5
1936	StL-A*	155	57	95	.375	7				53.5	3.5
1937	StL-A*	78	25	52	.325	7	8		1/2	24.7	0.3
1952	StL-A	51	22	29	.431	8	7		1/2	21.1	0.9
	Cin-N	51	27	24	.529	7	6		3/3	24.0	3.0
1953	Cin-N	147	64	82	.438	6	6		1/2	66.2	-2.2
	14	1530	701	812	.463						11.9
Houk, Ralph George "Ralph"											
1961	NY-A	163	109	53	.673	★1				102.7	6.3
1962	NY-A	162	96	66	.593	★1				94.5	1.5
1963	NY-A	161	104	57	.646	1				98.4	5.6
1966	NY-A	140	66	73	.475	10	10		2/2	69.4	-3.4
1967	NY-A	163	72	90	.444	9				69.8	2.2
1968	NY-A	164	83	79	.512	5				81.6	1.4
1969	NY-A	162	80	81	.497	5 E				77.7	2.3
1970	NY-A	163	93	69	.574	2 E				88.2	4.8
1971	NY-A	162	82	80	.506	4 E				81.7	0.3
1972	NY-A	155	79	76	.510	4 E				80.9	-1.9
1973	NY-A	162	80	82	.494	4 E				84.3	-4.3
1974	Det-A	162	72	90	.444	6 E				65.8	6.2
1975	Det-A	159	57	102	.358	6 E				57.3	-0.3
1976	Det-A	161	74	87	.460	5 E				70.0	4.0
1977	Det-A	162	74	88	.457	4 E				77.3	-3.3
1978	Det-A	162	86	76	.531	5 E				87.3	-1.3
1981(1)	Bos-A	56	30	26	.536	5 E					
(2)	Bos-A	52	29	23	.558	•2 E				57.7	1.3
1982	Bos-A	162	89	73	.549	3 E				85.0	4.0
1983	Bos-A	162	78	84	.481	6 E				76.0	2.0
1984	Bos-A	162	86	76	.531	4 E				85.4	0.6
	20	3157	1619	1531	.514						27.8
Howard, Frank Oliver											
1981(1)	SD-N	56	23	33	.411	6 W					
(2)	SD-N	54	18	36	.333	6 W				47.1	-6.1
1983	NY-N	116	52	64	.448	6 E	6 E		2/2	49.9	2.1
	2	226	93	133	.412						-4.0
Howe, Arthur Henry "Art"											
1989	Hou-N	162	86	76	.531	3 W				78.7	7.3
1990	Hou-N	162	75	87	.463	•4 W				72.0	3.0
1991	Hou-N	162	65	97	.401	6 W				69.2	-4.2
1992	Hou-N	162	81	81	.500	4 W				74.6	6.4
	4	648	307	341	.474						12.5
Howley, Daniel Philip "Dan"											
1927	StL-A	155	59	94	.386	7				59.8	-0.8
1928	StL-A	154	82	72	.532	3				79.9	2.1
1929	StL-A	154	79	73	.520	4				78.0	1.0
1930	Cin-N	154	59	95	.383	7				58.7	0.3
1931	Cin-N	154	58	96	.377	8				61.7	-3.7
1932	Cin-N	155	60	94	.390	8				62.4	-2.4
	6	926	397	524	.431						-3.5
Howser, Richard Dalton "Dick"											
1978	NY-A	1	0	1	.000	3 E	4 E	▲★1 E	2/3	0.6	-0.6
1980	NY-A	162	103	59	.636	1 E				96.7	6.3
1981(2)	KC-A	33	20	13	.606	•2 W	1 W		2/2	16.2	3.8
1982	KC-A	162	90	72	.556	2 W				87.6	2.4
1983	KC-A	163	79	83	.488	2 W				73.9	5.1
1984	KC-A	162	84	78	.519	1 W				79.7	4.3
1985	KC-A	162	91	71	.562	★1 W				86.0	5.0
1986	KC-A	88	40	48	.455	4 W	•3 W		1/2	42.9	-2.9
	8	933	507	425	.544						23.4

YEAR	TM/L	G	W	L	PCT	STANDING			M/Y	W-EXP	A-E
Huff, George A.											
1907	Bos-A	8	2	6	.250	•4	6	7	2/4	3.4	-1.4
Huggins, Miller James											
1913	StL-N*	153	51	99	.340	8				51.5	-0.5
1914	StL-N*	157	81	72	.529	3				78.5	2.5
1915	StL-N*	157	72	81	.471	6				75.3	-3.3
1916	StL-N*	153	60	93	.392	•7				59.4	0.6
1917	StL-N	154	82	70	.539	3				72.0	10.0
1918	NY-A	126	60	63	.488	4				63.4	-3.4
1919	NY-A	141	80	59	.576	3				77.3	2.7
1920	NY-A	154	95	59	.617	3				97.3	-2.3
1921	NY-A	153	98	55	.641	1				98.4	-0.4
1922	NY-A	154	94	60	.610	1				91.1	2.9
1923	NY-A	152	98	54	.645	★1				95.6	2.4
1924	NY-A	153	89	63	.586	2				88.7	0.3
1925	NY-A	156	69	85	.448	7				70.4	-1.4
1926	NY-A	155	91	63	.591	1				89.7	1.3
1927	NY-A	155	110	44	.714	★1				112.4	-2.4
1928	NY-A	154	101	53	.656	★1				96.6	4.4
1929	NY-A	143	82	61	.573	2	2		1/2	82.0	0.0
	17	2570	1413	1134	.555						13.5
Hunter, Gordon William "Billy"											
1977	Tex-A	93	60	33	.645	5 W	2 W		4/4	52.9	7.1
1978	Tex-A	161	86	75	.534	•2 W	•2 W		1/2	86.8	-0.8
	2	254	146	108	.575						6.4
Hurst, Timothy Carroll "Tim"											
1898	StL-N	154	39	111	.260	12				40.6	-1.6
Hutchinson, Frederick Charles "Fred"											
1952	Det-A*	83	27	55	.329	8	8		2/2	31.0	-4.0
1953	Det-A*	158	60	94	.390	6				55.6	4.4
1954	Det-A	155	68	86	.442	5				68.5	-0.5
1956	StL-N	156	76	78	.494	4				75.0	1.0
1957	StL-N	154	87	67	.565	2				84.1	2.9
1958	StL-N	144	69	75	.479	5	•5		1/2	63.9	5.1
1959	Cin-N	74	39	35	.527	7	•5		2/2	38.2	0.8
1960	Cin-N	154	67	87	.435	6				71.7	-4.7
1961	Cin-N	154	93	61	.604	1				82.7	10.3
1962	Cin-N	162	98	64	.605	3				92.6	5.4
1963	Cin-N	162	86	76	.531	5				86.9	-0.9
1964	Cin-N	100	54	45	.545	3	•2		1/4	55.8	-1.8
	Cin-N	10	6	4	.600	4	3	•2	3/4	5.6	0.4
	12	1666	830	827	.501						18.5
Irwin, Arthur Albert											
1889	Was-N*	76	28	45	.384	8	8		2/2	23.2	4.8
1891	Bos-a*	139	93	42	.689	1				97.8	-4.8
1892(1)	Was-N	74	35	39	.473	•11	7		2/2		
(2)	Was-N	34	11	21	.344	11	12		1/2	44.0	2.0
1894	Phi-N*	132	71	57	.555	4				77.1	-6.1
1895	Phi-N	133	78	53	.595	3				74.0	4.0
1896	NY-N	90	36	53	.404	10	7		1/2	45.0	-9.0
1898	Was-N	30	10	19	.345	11	11		4/4	10.4	-0.4
1899	Was-N	155	54	98	.355	11				54.4	-0.4
	8	863	416	427	.493						-9.9
Jennings, Hugh Ambrose "Hughie"											
1907	Det-A*	153	92	58	.613	1				92.2	-0.2
1908	Det-A	154	90	63	.588	1				87.3	2.7
1909	Det-A*	158	98	54	.645	1				95.2	2.8
1910	Det-A	155	86	68	.558	3				87.2	-1.2
1911	Det-A	154	89	65	.578	2				82.1	6.9
1912	Det-A*	154	69	84	.451	6				71.0	-2.0
1913	Det-A	153	66	87	.431	6				67.2	-1.2
1914	Det-A	157	80	73	.523	4				76.2	3.8
1915	Det-A	156	100	54	.649	2				95.3	4.7
1916	Det-A	155	87	67	.565	3				84.9	2.1
1917	Det-A	155	78	75	.510	4				83.1	-5.1
1918	Det-A*	128	55	71	.437	7				54.4	0.6
1919	Det-A	140	80	60	.571	4				74.1	5.9
1920	Det-A	155	61	93	.396	7				59.5	1.5
1924	NY-N	44	32	12	.727	3	1		2/3	28.0	4.0
	15	2171	1163	984	.542						25.4
Johnson, Darrell Dean											
1974	Bos-A	162	84	78	.519	3 E				84.6	-0.6
1975	Bos-A	160	95	65	.594	♦1 E				88.5	6.5
1976	Bos-A	86	41	45	.477	5 E	3 E		1/2	46.1	-5.1
1977	Sea-A	162	64	98	.395	6 W				58.1	5.9
1978	Sea-A	160	56	104	.350	7 W				58.1	-2.1
1979	Sea-A	162	67	95	.414	6 W				70.4	-3.4
1980	Sea-A	105	39	65	.375	6 W	7 W		1/2	40.0	-1.0
1982	Tex-A	66	26	40	.394	6 W	6 W		2/2	26.2	-0.2
	8	1063	472	590	.444						0.1
Johnson, David Allen "Davey"											
1984	NY-N	162	90	72	.556	2 E				78.5	11.5
1985	NY-N	162	98	64	.605	2 E				94.6	3.4
1986	NY-N	162	108	54	.667	★1 E				102.2	5.8
1987	NY-N	162	92	70	.568	2 E				93.2	-1.2
1988	NY-N	160	100	60	.625	1 E				98.5	1.5
1989	NY-N	162	87	75	.537	2 E				90.4	-3.4
1990	NY-N	42	20	22	.476	4 E	2 E		1/2	25.3	-5.3

YEAR	TM/L	G	W	L	PCT	STANDING			M/Y	W-EXP	A-E
	7	1012	595	417	.588						12.2
Johnson, Roy J											
1944	Chi-N	1	0	1	.000	8	8	4	2/3	0.5	-0.5
Johnson, Walter Perry											
1929	Was-A	153	71	81	.467	5				71.6	-0.6
1930	Was-A	154	94	60	.610	2				96.0	-2.0
1931	Was-A	156	92	62	.597	3				91.5	0.5
1932	Was-A	154	93	61	.604	3				88.7	4.3
1933	Cle-A	99	48	51	.485	5	4		3/3	48.5	-0.5
1934	Cle-A	154	85	69	.552	3				81.8	3.2
1935	Cle-A	96	46	48	.489	5	3		1/2	49.2	-3.2
	7	966	529	432	.550						1.7
Jones, Fielder Allison											
1904	Chi-A*	114	66	47	.584	4	3		2/2	66.4	-0.4
1905	Chi-A*	158	92	60	.605	2				94.6	-2.6
1906	Chi-A*	154	93	58	.616	★1				88.3	4.7
1907	Chi-A*	157	87	64	.576	3				88.7	-1.7
1908	Chi-A*	156	88	64	.579	3				83.9	4.1
1914	StL-F*	40	12	26	.316	7	8		2/2	15.5	-3.5
1915	StL-F*	159	87	67	.565	2				88.9	-1.9
1916	StL-A	158	79	75	.513	5				81.8	-2.8
1917	StL-A	155	57	97	.370	7				57.9	-0.9
1918	StL-A	46	22	24	.478	6	5		1/3	22.1	-0.1
	10	1297	683	582	.540						-5.0
Joost, Edwin David "Eddie"											
1954	Phi-A*	156	51	103	.331	8				43.8	7.2
Joyce, William Michael "Bill"											
1896	NY-N*	43	28	14	.667	10	7		2/2	21.2	6.8
1897	NY-N*	138	83	48	.634	3				83.1	-0.1
1898	NY-N*	43	22	21	.512	6	7		1/3	22.5	-0.5
	NY-N*	92	46	39	.541	7	7		3/3	44.4	1.6
	3	316	179	122	.595						7.7
Jurges, William Frederick "Billy"											
1959	Bos-A	80	44	36	.550	8	5		3/3	41.5	2.5
1960	Bos-A	42	15	27	.357	8	7		1/3	17.9	-2.9
	2	122	59	63	.484						-0.4
Kasko, Edward Michael "Eddie"											
1970	Bos-A	162	87	75	.537	3 E				87.3	-0.3
1971	Bos-A	162	85	77	.525	3 E				83.5	1.5
1972	Bos-A	155	85	70	.548	2 E				79.6	5.4
1973	Bos-A	161	88	73	.547	2 E	2 E		1/2	89.8	-1.8
	4	640	345	295	.539						4.8
Keane, John Joseph "Johnny"											
1961	StL-N	80	47	33	.587	6	5		2/2	41.8	5.2
1962	StL-N	163	84	78	.519	6				92.1	-8.1
1963	StL-N	162	93	69	.574	2				93.3	-0.3
1964	StL-N	162	93	69	.574	★1				87.5	5.5
1965	NY-A	162	77	85	.475	6				81.8	-4.8
1966	NY-A	20	4	16	.200	10	10		1/2	10.0	-6.0
	6	749	398	350	.532						-8.5
Kelley, Joseph James "Joe"											
1902	Cin-N*	60	34	26	.567	6	4		3/3	33.0	1.0
1903	Cin-N*	141	74	65	.532	4				79.8	-5.8
1904	Cin-N*	157	88	65	.575	3				92.3	-4.3
1905	Cin-N*	155	79	74	.516	5				80.2	-1.2
1908	Bos-N*	156	63	91	.409	6				67.6	-4.6
	5	669	338	321	.513						-14.8
Kelly, Jay Thomas "Tom"											
1986	Min-A	23	12	11	.522	7 W	6 W		2/2	10.2	1.8
1987	Min-A	162	85	77	.525	★1 W				79.1	5.9
1988	Min-A	162	91	71	.562	2 W				89.8	1.2
1989	Min-A	162	80	82	.494	5 W				81.2	-1.2
1990	Min-A	162	74	88	.457	7 W				74.6	-0.6
1991	Min-A	162	95	67	.586	★1 W				93.5	1.5
1992	Min-A	162	90	72	.556	2 W				90.6	-0.6
	7	995	527	468	.530						8.1
Kelly, John O.											
1887	Lou-a	139	76	60	.559	4				76.5	-0.5
1888	Lou-a	39	10	29	.256	8	7		1/4	14.8	-4.8
	2	178	86	89	.491						-5.3
Kelly, Michael Joseph "King"											
1887	Bos-N*	95	49	43	.533	5	5		1/2	48.5	0.5
1890	Bos-P*	133	81	48	.628	1				82.9	-1.9
1891	Cin-a*	102	43	57	.430	6				41.7	1.3
	3	330	173	148	.539						-0.1
Kennedy, James C. "Jim"											
1890	Bro-a	100	26	73	.263	8				28.8	-2.8
Kennedy, Robert Daniel "Bob"											
1963	Chi-N	162	82	80	.506	7				80.1	1.9
1964	Chi-N	162	76	86	.469	8				73.3	2.7
1965	Chi-N	58	24	32	.429	9	8		1/2	24.8	-0.8
1968	Oak-A	163	82	80	.506	6				83.9	-1.9
	4	545	264	278	.487						1.9
Kerins, John Nelson											
1888	Lou-a*	7	3	4	.429	8	8	7	3/4	2.7	0.3

YEAR	TM/L	G	W	L	PCT	STANDING			M/Y	W-EXP	A-E
1890	StL-a*	17	9	8	.529	4	4	3	2/6	10.0	-1.0
	2	24	12	12	.500						-0.6
Kessinger, Donald Eulon "Don"											
1979	Chi-A	106	46	60	.434	5 W	5 W		1/2	51.8	-5.8
Killefer, William Lavier "Bill"											
1921	Chi-N*	57	23	34	.404	6	7		2/2	24.7	-1.7
1922	Chi-N	156	80	74	.519	5				73.5	6.5
1923	Chi-N	154	83	71	.539	4				82.1	0.9
1924	Chi-N	154	81	72	.529	5				76.4	4.6
1925	Chi-N	75	33	42	.440	7	8		1/3	35.2	-2.2
1930	StL-A	154	64	90	.416	6				64.6	-0.6
1931	StL-A	154	63	91	.409	5				63.2	-0.2
1932	StL-A	154	63	91	.409	6				62.1	0.9
1933	StL-A	91	34	57	.374	8	8		1/3	36.7	-2.7
	9	1149	524	622	.457						5.6
King, Clyde Edward											
1969	SF-N	162	90	72	.556	2 W				89.0	1.0
1970	SF-N	42	19	23	.452	4 W	3 W		1/2	21.1	-2.1
1974	Atl-N	64	38	25	.603	4 W	3 W		2/2	35.7	2.3
1975	Atl-N	134	58	76	.433	5 W	5 W		1/2	53.4	4.6
1982	NY-A	62	29	33	.468	●5 E	5 E		3/3	30.7	-1.7
	5	464	234	229	.505						4.1
Kittridge, Malachi J.											
1904	Was-A*	18	1	16	.059	8	8		1/2	4.7	-3.7
Klein, Louis Frank "Lou"											
1961	Chi-N	11	5	6	.455	7	7	7	8/9	4.7	0.3
1962	Chi-N	30	12	18	.400	9	9	9	2/3	11.4	0.6
1965	Chi-N	106	48	58	.453	9	8		2/2	47.0	1.0
	3	147	65	82	.442						1.9
Kling, John "Johnny"											
1912	Bos-N*	155	52	101	.340	8				60.6	-8.6
Knabe, Franz Otto "Otto"											
1914	Bal-F*	160	84	70	.545	3				78.8	5.2
1915	Bal-F*	155	47	107	.305	8				55.4	-8.4
	2	315	131	177	.425						-3.2
Knight, Alonzo P. "Lon"											
1883	Phi-a*	98	66	32	.673	1				63.4	2.6
1884	Phi-a*	109	61	46	.570	7				67.1	-6.1
	2	207	127	78	.620						-3.5
Krol, John Thomas "Jack"											
1978	StL-N	2	1	1	.500	6 E	6 E	5 E	2/3	0.9	0.1
1980	StL-N	1	0	1	.000	6 E	6 E	4 E	2/4	0.5	-0.5
	2	3	1	2	.333						-0.4
Kuehl, Karl Otto											
1976	Mon-N	128	43	85	.336	6 E	6 E		1/2	46.8	-3.8
Kuenn, Harvey Edward											
1975	Mil-A	1	1	0	1.000	5 E	5 E		2/2	0.4	0.6
1982	Mil-A	116	72	43	.626	5 E	♦1 E		2/2	69.3	2.7
1983	Mil-A	162	87	75	.537	5 E				86.6	0.4
	3	279	160	118	.576						3.7
Kuhel, Joseph Anthony "Joe"											
1948	Was-A	154	56	97	.366	7				54.6	1.4
1949	Was-A	154	50	104	.325	8				49.3	0.7
	2	308	106	201	.345						2.1
Lachemann, Rene George											
1981 (1)	Sea-A	33	15	18	.455	7 W	6 W		2/2		
(2)	Sea-A	52	23	29	.442	5 W				34.9	3.1
1982	Sea-A	162	76	86	.469	4 W				74.7	1.3
1983	Sea-A	73	26	47	.356	7 W	7 W		1/2	27.8	-1.8
1984	Mil-A	161	67	94	.416	7 E				71.0	-4.0
	4	481	207	274	.430						-1.4
Lajoie, Napoleon "Nap"											
1905	Cle-A*	58	37	21	.638	●1	5		1/3	28.2	8.8
	Cle-A*	56	19	36	.345	2	5		3/3	26.7	-7.7
1906	Cle-A*	157	89	64	.582	3				96.6	-7.6
1907	Cle-A*	158	85	67	.559	4				76.6	8.4
1908	Cle-A*	157	90	64	.584	2				90.0	-0.0
1909	Cle-A*	114	57	57	.500	4	6		1/2	53.6	3.4
	5	700	377	309	.550						5.3
Lake, Frederick Lovett "Fred"											
1908	Bos-A	40	22	17	.564	6	5		2/2	21.0	1.0
1909	Bos-A	152	88	63	.583	3				80.6	7.4
1910	Bos-N*	157	53	100	.346	8				54.1	-1.1
	3	349	163	180	.475						7.3
Lamont, Gene William											
1992	Chi-A	162	86	76	.531	3 W				85.9	0.1
Lanier, Harold Clifton "Hal"											
1986	Hou-N	162	96	66	.593	1 W				90.3	5.7
1987	Hou-N	162	76	86	.469	3 W				77.9	-1.9
1988	Hou-N	162	82	80	.506	5 W				79.5	2.5
	3	486	254	232	.523						6.4
Larkin, Henry E. "Ted"											
1890	Cle-P*	79	34	45	.430	7	7		1/2	30.9	3.1

YEAR	TM/L	G	W	L	PCT	STANDING			M/Y	W-EXP	A-E
LaRussa, Anthony "Tony"											
1979	Chi-A	54	27	27	.500	5 W	5 W		2/2	26.4	0.6
1980	Chi-A	162	70	90	.438	5 W				65.8	4.2
1981 (1)	Chi-A	53	31	22	.585	3 W					
(2)	Chi-A	53	23	30	.434	6 W				58.5	-4.5
1982	Chi-A	162	87	75	.537	3 W				88.5	-1.5
1983	Chi-A	162	99	63	.611	1 W				96.0	3.0
1984	Chi-A	162	74	88	.457	●5 W				75.2	-1.2
1985	Chi-A	163	85	77	.525	3 W				82.6	2.4
1986	Chi-A	64	26	38	.406	6 W	5 W		1/3	29.7	-3.7
	Oak-A	79	45	34	.570	7 W	●3 W		3/3	38.1	6.9
1987	Oak-A	162	81	81	.500	3 W				82.6	-1.6
1988	Oak-A	162	104	58	.642	♦1 W				99.2	4.8
1989	Oak-A	162	99	63	.611	★1 W				95.5	3.5
1990	Oak-A	162	103	59	.636	♦1 W				98.2	4.8
1991	Oak-A	162	84	78	.519	4 W				79.4	4.6
1992	Oak-A	162	96	66	.593	1 W				88.4	7.6
	14	2086	1134	949	.544						29.8
Lasorda, Thomas Charles "Tom"											
1976	LA-N	4	2	2	.500	2 W	2 W		2/2	2.2	-0.2
1977	LA-N	162	98	64	.605	♦1 W				100.4	-2.4
1978	LA-N	162	95	67	.586	♦1 W				97.3	-2.3
1979	LA-N	162	79	83	.488	3 W				83.2	-4.2
1980	LA-N	163	92	71	.564	▲2 W				89.3	2.7
1981 (1)	LA-N	57	36	21	.632	★1 W					
(2)	LA-N	53	27	26	.509	4 W				65.4	-2.4
1982	LA-N	162	88	74	.543	2 W				89.4	-1.4
1983	LA-N	163	91	71	.562	1 W				85.9	5.1
1984	LA-N	162	79	83	.488	4 W				78.8	0.2
1985	LA-N	162	95	67	.586	1 W				92.1	2.9
1986	LA-N	162	73	89	.451	5 W				76.7	-3.7
1987	LA-N	162	73	89	.451	4 W				76.8	-3.8
1988	LA-N	162	94	67	.584	★1 W				89.9	4.1
1989	LA-N	160	77	83	.481	4 W				82.1	-5.1
1990	LA-N	162	86	76	.531	2 W				85.4	0.6
1991	LA-N	162	93	69	.574	2 W				91.9	1.1
1992	LA-N	162	63	99	.389	6 W				71.2	-8.2
	17	2544	1341	1201	.528						-16.8
Latham, George Warren "Juice"											
1875	NH-n*	18	4	14	.222	11	8	8	2/3	1.5	2.5
1882	Phi-a*	75	41	34	.547	2				39.1	1.9
	2	93	45	48	.484						4.4
Latham, Walter Arlington "Arlie"											
1896	StL-N*	3	0	3	.000	10	10	11	2/5	0.8	-0.8
Lavagetto, Harry Arthur "Cookie"											
1957	Was-A	134	51	83	.381	8	8		2/2	49.3	1.7
1958	Was-A	156	61	93	.396	8				56.8	4.2
1959	Was-A	154	63	91	.409	8				68.6	-5.6
1960	Was-A	154	73	81	.474	5				74.6	-1.6
1961	Min-A	49	19	30	.388	8	7		1/4	22.4	-3.4
	Min-A	10	4	6	.400	9	9	7	3/4	4.6	-0.6
	5	657	271	384	.414						-5.3
Leadley, Robert H. "Bob"											
1888	Det-N	40	19	19	.500	3	5		2/2	21.5	-2.5
1890	Cle-N	58	23	33	.411	7	7		2/2	20.2	2.8
1891	Cle-N	68	34	34	.500	4	5		1/2	31.8	2.2
	3	166	76	86	.469						2.5
Lefebvre, James Kenneth "Jim"											
1989	Sea-A	162	73	89	.451	6 W				77.6	-4.6
1990	Sea-A	162	77	85	.475	5 W				76.8	0.2
1991	Sea-A	162	83	79	.512	5 W				83.9	-0.9
1992	Chi-N	162	78	84	.481	4 E				77.6	0.4
	4	648	311	337	.480						-4.8
Lemon, James Robert "Jim"											
1968	Was-A	161	65	96	.404	10				64.9	0.1
Lemon, Robert Granville "Bob"											
1970	KC-A	110	46	64	.418	5 W	●4 W		2/2	48.3	-2.3
1971	KC-A	161	85	76	.528	2 W				84.6	0.4
1972	KC-A	154	76	78	.494	4 W				80.9	-4.9
1977	Chi-A	162	90	72	.556	3 W				87.9	2.1
1978	Chi-A	74	34	40	.459	5 W	5 W		1/2	32.4	1.6
	NY-A	68	48	20	.706	4 E	▲★E		3/3	40.7	7.3
1979	NY-A	65	34	31	.523	4 E	4 E		1/2	35.0	-1.0
1981 (2)	NY-A	25	11	14	.440	4 E	6 E		2/2	14.5	-3.5
1982	NY-A	14	6	8	.429	●4 E	5 E		1/3	6.9	-0.9
	8	833	430	403	.516						-1.4
Lennon, William F. "Bill"											
1871	Kek-n*	14	5	9	.357	7	8		1/2	1.8	3.2
Leyland, James Richard "Jim"											
1986	Pit-N	162	64	98	.395	6 E				77.2	-13.2
1987	Pit-N	162	80	82	.494	●4 E				78.9	1.1
1988	Pit-N	160	85	75	.531	2 E				83.7	1.3
1989	Pit-N	164	74	88	.457	5 E				76.4	-2.4
1990	Pit-N	162	95	67	.586	1 E				92.8	2.2
1991	Pit-N	162	98	64	.605	1 E				94.9	3.1
1992	Pit-N	162	96	66	.593	1 E				91.4	4.6
	7	1134	592	540	.523						-3.4

YEAR	TM/L	G	W	L	PCT	STANDING			M/Y	W-EXP	A-E
Leyva, Nicolas Tomas "Nick"											
1989	Phi-N	163	67	95	.414	6 E				70.0	-3.0
1990	Phi-N	162	77	85	.475	•4 E				72.5	4.5
1991	Phi-N	13	4	9	.308	6 E	3 E		1/2	6.1	-2.1
	3	338	148	189	.439						-0.5
Lillis, Robert Perry "Bob"											
1982	Hou-N	51	28	23	.549	5 W	5 W		2/2	23.7	4.3
1983	Hou-N	162	85	77	.525	3 W				80.7	4.3
1984	Hou-N	162	80	82	.494	•2 W				87.6	-7.6
1985	Hou-N	162	83	79	.512	•3 W				82.5	0.5
	4	537	276	261	.514						1.5
Lipon, John Joseph "Johnny"											
1971	Cle-A	59	18	41	.305	6 E	6 E		2/2	21.6	-3.6
Lobert, John Bernard "Hans"											
1938	Phi-N	2	0	2	.000	8	8		2/2	0.6	-0.6
1942	Phi-N	151	42	109	.278	8				40.8	1.2
	2	153	42	111	.275						0.6
Lockman, Carroll Walter "Whitey"											
1972	Chi-N	65	39	26	.600	4 E	2 E		2/2	37.7	1.3
1973	Chi-N	161	77	84	.478	5 E				76.1	0.9
1974	Chi-N	93	41	52	.441	5 E	6 E		1/2	37.6	3.4
	3	319	157	162	.492						5.5
Loftus, Thomas Joseph "Tom"											
1884	Mil-U	12	8	4	.667	2				8.1	-0.1
1888	Cle-a	71	30	38	.441	8	6		2/2	25.3	4.7
1889	Cle-N	136	61	72	.459	6				60.5	0.5
1890	Cin-N	134	77	55	.583	4				77.2	-0.2
1891	Cin-N	138	56	81	.409	7				55.1	0.9
1900	Chi-N	146	65	75	.464	•5				58.7	6.3
1901	Chi-N	140	53	86	.381	6				57.5	-4.5
1902	Was-A	138	61	75	.449	6				60.4	0.6
1903	Was-A	140	43	94	.314	8				41.7	1.3
	9	1055	454	580	.439						9.6
Lopat, Edmund Walter "Ed"											
1963	KC-A	162	73	89	.451	8				71.6	1.4
1964	KC-A	52	17	35	.327	10	10		1/2	19.1	-2.1
	2	214	90	124	.421						-0.7
Lopez, Alfonso Ramon "Al"											
1951	Cle-A	155	93	61	.604	2				87.6	5.4
1952	Cle-A	155	93	61	.604	2				92.8	0.2
1953	Cle-A	155	92	62	.597	2				91.3	0.7
1954	Cle-A	156	111	43	.721	1				102.7	8.3
1955	Cle-A	154	93	61	.604	2				87.0	6.0
1956	Cle-A	155	88	66	.571	2				90.6	-2.6
1957	Chi-A	155	90	64	.584	2				91.8	-1.8
1958	Chi-A	155	82	72	.532	2				79.0	3.0
1959	Chi-A	156	94	60	.610	1				85.6	8.4
1960	Chi-A	154	87	67	.565	3				89.5	-2.5
1961	Chi-A	163	86	76	.531	4				84.9	1.1
1962	Chi-A	162	85	77	.525	5				86.1	-1.1
1963	Chi-A	162	94	68	.580	2				96.2	-2.2
1964	Chi-A	162	98	64	.605	2				96.9	1.1
1965	Chi-A	162	95	67	.586	2				91.1	3.9
1968	Chi-A	11	6	5	.545	9	9	•8	3/5	5.0	1.0
	Chi-A	36	15	21	.417	9	•8		5/5	16.3	-1.3
1969	Chi-A	17	8	9	.471	4 W	5 W		1/2	7.4	0.6
	17	2425	1410	1004	.584						28.3
Lord, Harry Donald											
1915	Buf-F*	110	60	49	.550	8	6		3/3	49.9	10.1
Lowe, Robert Lincoln "Bobby"											
1904	Det-A*	78	30	44	.405	7	7		2/2	30.3	-0.3
Lucchesi, Frank Joseph											
1970	Phi-N	161	73	88	.453	5 E				66.3	6.7
1971	Phi-N	162	67	95	.414	6 E				66.9	0.1
1972	Phi-N	76	26	50	.342	6 E	6 E		1/2	30.9	-4.9
1975	Tex-A	67	35	32	.522	4 W	3 W		2/2	32.7	2.3
1976	Tex-A	162	76	86	.469	•4 W				77.1	-1.1
1977	Tex-A	62	31	31	.500	•3 W	2 W		1/4	35.3	-4.3
1987	Chi-N	25	8	17	.320	5 E	6 E		2/2	11.3	-3.3
	7	715	316	399	.442						-4.4
Lumley, Harry G											
1909	Bro-N*	155	55	98	.359	6				55.6	-0.6
Lyons, Theodore Amar "Ted"											
1946	Chi-A	125	64	60	.516	7	5		2/2	59.1	4.9
1947	Chi-A	155	70	84	.455	6				65.4	4.6
1948	Chi-A	154	51	101	.336	8				50.4	0.6
	3	434	185	245	.430						10.1
Mack, Cornelius Alexander "Connie"											
1894	Pit-N*	23	12	10	.545	7	7		2/2	10.8	1.2
1895	Pit-N*	135	71	61	.538	7				68.1	2.9
1896	Pit-N*	131	66	63	.512	6				68.5	-2.5
1901	Phi-A	137	74	62	.544	4				71.9	2.1
1902	Phi-A	137	83	53	.610	1				81.0	2.0
1903	Phi-A	137	75	60	.556	2				75.7	-0.7
1904	Phi-A	155	81	70	.536	5				81.7	-0.7
1905	Phi-A	152	92	56	.622	1				88.5	3.5
1906	Phi-A	149	78	67	.538	4				74.5	3.5
1907	Phi-A	150	88	57	.607	2				80.4	7.6
1908	Phi-A	157	68	85	.444	6				67.7	0.3
1909	Phi-A	153	95	58	.621	2				99.5	-4.5
1910	Phi-A	155	102	48	.680	★1				101.0	1.0
1911	Phi-A	152	101	50	.669	★1				100.7	0.3
1912	Phi-A	153	90	62	.592	3				87.8	2.2
1913	Phi-A	153	96	57	.627	★1				96.6	-0.6
1914	Phi-A	158	99	53	.651	1				99.2	-0.2
1915	Phi-A	154	43	109	.283	8				42.3	0.7
1916	Phi-A	154	36	117	.235	8				41.5	-5.5
1917	Phi-A	154	55	98	.359	8				59.2	-4.2
1918	Phi-A	130	52	76	.406	8				50.0	2.0
1919	Phi-A	140	36	104	.257	8				40.8	-4.8
1920	Phi-A	156	48	106	.312	8				49.3	-1.3
1921	Phi-A	155	53	100	.346	8				54.0	-1.0
1922	Phi-A	155	65	89	.422	7				65.1	-0.1
1923	Phi-A	153	69	83	.454	6				66.2	2.8
1924	Phi-A	152	71	81	.467	5				67.0	4.0
1925	Phi-A	153	88	64	.579	2				87.1	0.9
1926	Phi-A	150	83	67	.553	3				86.1	-3.1
1927	Phi-A	155	91	63	.591	2				87.9	3.1
1928	Phi-A	153	98	55	.641	2				97.4	0.6
1929	Phi-A	151	104	46	.693	★1				102.1	1.9
1930	Phi-A	154	102	52	.662	★1				95.0	7.0
1931	Phi-A	153	107	45	.704	1				98.4	8.6
1932	Phi-A	154	94	60	.610	2				97.5	-3.5
1933	Phi-A	152	79	72	.523	3				77.5	1.5
1934	Phi-A	153	68	82	.453	5				68.1	-0.1
1935	Phi-A	149	58	91	.389	8				59.8	-1.8
1936	Phi-A	154	53	100	.346	8				47.1	5.9
1937	Phi-A	120	39	80	.328	7	7		1/2	48.0	-9.0
1938	Phi-A	154	53	99	.349	8				55.1	-2.1
1939	Phi-A	62	25	37	.403	6	7		1/2	19.7	5.3
1940	Phi-A	154	54	100	.351	8				55.9	-1.9
1941	Phi-A	154	64	90	.416	8				65.0	-1.0
1942	Phi-A	154	55	99	.357	8				51.5	3.5
1943	Phi-A	155	49	105	.318	8				53.4	-4.4
1944	Phi-A	155	72	82	.468	•5				69.3	2.7
1945	Phi-A	153	52	98	.347	8				59.1	-7.1
1946	Phi-A	155	49	105	.318	8				60.8	-11.8
1947	Phi-A	156	78	76	.506	5				79.0	-1.0
1948	Phi-A	154	84	70	.545	4				76.4	7.6
1949	Phi-A	154	81	73	.526	5				77.1	3.9
1950	Phi-A	154	52	102	.338	8				54.3	-2.3
	53	7755	3731	3948	.486						13.6
Mack, Dennis Joseph "Denny"											
1882	Lou-a*	80	42	38	.525	3				48.7	-6.7
Mack, Earle Thaddeus											
1937	Phi-A	34	15	17	.469	7	7		2/2	12.9	2.1
1939	Phi-A	91	30	60	.333	6	7		2/2	28.6	1.4
	2	125	45	77	.369						3.5
Macullar, James F. "Jimmy"											
1879	Syr-N*	27	5	21	.192	6	7		3/3	6.6	-1.6
Magee, Leo Christopher "Lee"											
1915	Bro-F*	118	53	64	.453	7	7		1/2	56.5	-3.5
Malone, Ferguson G. "Fergy"											
1873	Phi-n*	10	8	2	.800	2	2		1/2	6.8	1.2
1874	Chi-n*	36	18	18	.500	4	5		1/2	15.1	2.9
1884	Phi-U*	67	21	46	.313	7				23.1	-2.1
	3	113	47	66	.416						2.0
Manning, James H. "Jimmy"											
1901	Was-A	138	61	73	.455	6				58.3	2.7
Manning, John E. "Jack"											
1877	Cin-N*	20	7	12	.368	6	6		3/3	4.2	2.8
Maranville, Walter James Vincent "Rabbit"											
1925	Chi-N*	53	23	30	.434	7	7	8	2/3	24.8	-1.8
Marion, Martin Whitford "Marty"											
1951	StL-N	155	81	73	.526	3				78.2	2.8
1952	StL-A*	104	42	61	.408	8	7		2/2	42.7	-0.7
1953	StL-A*	154	54	100	.351	8				54.3	-0.3
1954	Chi-A	9	3	6	.333	3	3		2/2	5.7	-2.7
1955	Chi-A	155	91	63	.591	3				94.5	-3.5
1956	Chi-A	154	85	69	.552	3				91.1	-6.1
	6	731	356	372	.489						-10.5
Marshall, Rufus James "Jim"											
1974	Chi-N	69	25	44	.362	5 E	6 E		2/2	27.9	-2.9
1975	Chi-N	162	75	87	.463	•5 E				69.8	5.2
1976	Chi-N	162	75	87	.463	4 E				68.8	6.2
1979	Oak-A	162	54	108	.333	7 W				52.0	2.0
	4	555	229	326	.413						10.5
Martin, Alfred Manuel "Billy"											
1969	Min-A	162	97	65	.599	1 W				98.5	-1.5
1971	Det-A	162	91	71	.562	2 E				86.8	4.2
1972	Det-A	156	86	70	.551	1 E				83.0	3.0
1973	Det-A	134	71	63	.530	3 E	3 E		1/2	64.2	6.8
	Tex-A	23	9	14	.391	6 W	6 W		3/3	8.3	0.7

YEAR	TM/L	G	W	L	PCT	STANDING			M/Y	W-EXP	A-E
1974	Tex-A	161	84	76	.525	2 W				79.2	4.8
1975	Tex-A	95	44	51	.463	4 W	3 W		1/2	46.4	-2.4
	NY-A	56	30	26	.536	3 E	3 E		2/2	31.5	-1.5
1976	NY-A	159	97	62	.610	♦1 E				95.7	1.3
1977	NY-A	162	100	62	.617	★1 E				98.9	1.1
1978	NY-A	94	52	42	.553	3 E	▲★1E		1/3	56.3	-4.3
1979	NY-A	95	55	40	.579	4 E	4 E		2/2	51.2	3.8
1980	Oak-A	162	83	79	.512	2 W				85.6	-2.6
1981(1)	Oak-A	60	37	23	.617	1 W					
(2)	Oak-A	49	27	22	.551	2 W				60.4	3.6
1982	Oak-A	162	68	94	.420	5 W				68.4	-0.4
1983	NY-A	162	91	71	.562	3 E				87.7	3.3
1985	NY-A	145	91	54	.628	7 E	2 E		2/2	88.4	2.6
1988	NY-A	68	40	28	.588	2 E	5 E		1/2	35.0	5.0
	16	2267	1253	1013	.553						27.5
Martinez, Orlando iva] "Marty"											
1986	Sea-A	1	0	1	.000	6 W	6 W	7 W	2/3	0.4	-0.4
Mason, Charles E. "Charlie"											
1887	Phi-a	82	38	40	.487	6	5		2/2	39.1	-1.1
Mathews, Edwin Lee "Eddie"											
1972	Atl-N	50	23	27	.460	4 W	4 W		2/2	21.6	1.4
1973	Atl-N	162	76	85	.472	5 W				82.9	-6.9
1974	Atl-N	99	50	49	.505	4 W	3 W		1/2	56.1	-6.1
	3	311	149	161	.481						-11.6
Mathewson, Christopher "Christy"											
1916	Cin-N*	69	25	43	.368	8	•7		3/3	28.4	-3.4
1917	Cin-N	157	78	76	.506	4				75.9	2.1
1918	Cin-N	120	61	57	.517	4	3		1/2	62.3	-1.3
	3	346	164	176	.482						-2.7
Mattick, Robert James "Bobby"											
1980	Tor-A	162	67	95	.414	7 E				66.8	0.2
1981(1)	Tor-A	58	16	42	.276	7 E					
(2)	Tor-A	48	21	27	.438	7 E				38.0	-1.0
	2	268	104	164	.388						-0.8
Mauch, Gene William											
1960	Phi-N	152	58	94	.382	•4	8		3/3	60.8	-2.8
1961	Phi-N	155	47	107	.305	8				55.7	-8.7
1962	Phi-N	161	81	80	.503	7				75.1	5.9
1963	Phi-N	162	87	75	.537	4				88.0	-1.0
1964	Phi-N	162	92	70	.568	•2				87.4	4.6
1965	Phi-N	162	85	76	.528	6				79.1	5.9
1966	Phi-N	162	87	75	.537	4				86.9	0.1
1967	Phi-N	162	82	80	.506	5				84.4	-2.4
1968	Phi-N	54	27	27	.500	•6	•7		1/3	24.3	2.7
1969	Mon-N	162	52	110	.321	6 E				59.5	-7.5
1970	Mon-N	162	73	89	.451	6 E				69.1	3.9
1971	Mon-N	162	71	90	.441	5 E				69.4	1.6
1972	Mon-N	156	70	86	.449	5 E				67.3	2.7
1973	Mon-N	162	79	83	.488	4 E				77.5	1.5
1974	Mon-N	161	79	82	.491	4 E				81.0	-2.0
1975	Mon-N	162	75	87	.463	•5 E				71.5	3.5
1976	Min-A	162	85	77	.525	3 W				84.9	0.1
1977	Min-A	161	84	77	.522	4 W				89.0	-5.0
1978	Min-A	162	73	89	.451	4 W				79.8	-6.8
1979	Min-A	162	82	80	.506	4 W				84.9	-2.9
1980	Min-A	125	54	71	.432	4 W	3 W		1/2	58.2	-4.2
1981(1)	Cal-A	13	9	4	.692	4 W	4 W		2/2		
(2)	Cal-A	50	20	30	.400	7 W				32.9	-3.9
1982	Cal-A	162	93	69	.574	1 W				95.3	-2.3
1985	Cal-A	162	90	72	.556	2 W				83.9	6.1
1986	Cal-A	162	92	70	.568	1 W				91.2	0.8
1987	Cal-A	162	75	87	.463	•6 W				77.8	-2.8
	26	3942	1902	2037	.483						-12.9
McAleer, James Robert "Jimmy"											
1901	Cle-A*	138	55	82	.401	7				53.1	0.9
1902	StL-A*	140	78	58	.574	2				69.2	8.8
1903	StL-A	139	65	74	.468	6				66.7	-1.7
1904	StL-A	156	65	87	.428	6				62.0	3.0
1905	StL-A	156	54	99	.353	8				65.6	-11.6
1906	StL-A	154	76	73	.510	5				81.4	-5.4
1907	StL-A*	155	69	83	.454	6				74.5	-5.5
1908	StL-A	155	83	69	.546	4				83.1	-0.1
1909	StL-A	154	61	89	.407	7				59.3	1.7
1910	Was-A	157	66	85	.437	7				69.8	-3.8
1911	Was-A	154	64	90	.416	7				62.9	1.1
	11	1658	736	889	.453						-12.8
McBride, George Florian											
1921	Was-A	154	80	73	.523	4				73.2	6.8
McBride, James Dickson "Dick"											
1871	Ath-n*	28	21	7	.750	1				20.9	0.1
1872	Ath-n*	47	30	14	.682	4				35.1	-5.1
1873	Ath-n*	52	28	23	.549	5				30.7	-2.7
1874	Ath-n*	56	33	23	.589	3				35.2	-2.2
1875	Ath-n*	69	49	18	.731	2	2		1/2	55.1	-6.1
	5	252	161	85	.654						-16.0
McCallister, John "Jack"											
1927	Cle-A	153	66	87	.431	6				66.9	-0.9

YEAR	TM/L	G	W	L	PCT	STANDING			M/Y	W-EXP	A-E
McCarthy, Joseph Vincent "Joe"											
1926	Chi-N	155	82	72	.532	4				85.3	-3.3
1927	Chi-N	153	85	68	.556	4				85.3	-0.3
1928	Chi-N	154	91	63	.591	3				87.1	3.9
1929	Chi-N	156	98	54	.645	1				96.1	1.9
1930	Chi-N	152	86	64	.573	2	2		1/2	85.8	0.2
1931	NY-A	155	94	59	.614	2				103.3	-9.3
1932	NY-A	156	107	47	.695	★1				102.1	4.9
1933	NY-A	152	91	59	.607	2				89.3	1.7
1934	NY-A	154	94	60	.610	2				93.6	0.4
1935	NY-A	149	89	60	.597	2				92.4	-3.4
1936	NY-A	155	102	51	.667	★1				105.9	-3.9
1937	NY-A	157	102	52	.662	★1				105.5	-3.5
1938	NY-A	157	99	53	.651	★1				99.5	-0.5
1939	NY-A	152	106	45	.702	★1				114.5	-8.5
1940	NY-A	155	88	66	.571	3				91.1	-3.1
1941	NY-A	156	101	53	.656	★1				96.5	4.5
1942	NY-A	154	103	51	.669	1				107.3	-4.3
1943	NY-A	155	98	56	.636	★1				90.6	7.4
1944	NY-A	154	83	71	.539	3				82.9	0.1
1945	NY-A	152	81	71	.533	4				83.2	-2.2
1946	NY-A	35	22	13	.629	2	3		1/3	20.8	1.2
1948	Bos-A	155	96	59	.619	▲2				94.8	1.2
1949	Bos-A	155	96	58	.623	2				98.6	-2.6
1950	Bos-A	59	31	28	.525	4	3		1/2	36.9	-5.9
	24	3487	2125	1333	.615						-23.6
McCarthy, Thomas Francis "Tommy"											
1890	StL-a*	22	11	11	.500	4	3		1/6	12.9	-1.9
	StL-a*	5	4	1	.800	2	2	3	5/6	2.9	1.1
McCloskey, John Joseph											
1895	Lou-N	133	35	96	.267	12				33.4	1.6
1896	Lou-N	19	2	17	.105	12	12		1/2	5.2	-3.2
1906	StL-N	154	52	98	.347	7				59.5	-7.5
1907	StL-N	155	52	101	.340	8				54.5	-2.5
1908	StL-N	154	49	105	.318	8				46.9	2.1
	5	615	190	417	.313						-9.5
McCormick, James "Jim"											
1879	Cle-N*	82	27	55	.329	6				27.5	-0.5
1880	Cle-N*	85	47	37	.560	3				47.1	-0.1
1882	Cle-N*	4	0	4	.000	8	5		1/2	2.0	-2.0
	3	171	74	96	.435						-2.6
McGaha, Fred Melvin "Mel"											
1962	Cle-A	160	78	82	.488	6	6		1/2	73.7	4.3
1964	KC-A	111	40	70	.364	10	10		2/2	40.3	-0.3
1965	KC-A	26	5	21	.192	10	10		1/2	10.2	-5.2
	3	297	123	173	.416						-1.2
McGeary, Michael Henry "Mike"											
1875	Phi-n*	63	34	27	.557	4	5		1/2	37.8	-3.8
1880	Pro-N*	16	8	7	.533	4	2		1/3	9.7	-1.7
1881	Cle-N*	11	4	7	.364	6	7		1/2	5.2	-1.2
	3	90	46	41	.529						-6.7
McGraw, John Joseph											
1899	Bal-N*	152	86	62	.581	4				86.9	-0.9
1901	Bal-A*	135	68	65	.511	5				67.4	0.6
1902	Bal-A*	58	26	31	.456	7	8		1/2	23.5	2.5
	NY-N*	65	25	38	.397	8	8		3/3	21.7	3.3
1903	NY-N*	142	84	55	.604	2				85.6	-1.6
1904	NY-N*	158	106	47	.693	1				105.4	0.6
1905	NY-N*	155	105	48	.686	★1				105.2	-0.2
1906	NY-N*	153	96	56	.632	2				88.7	7.3
1907	NY-N	155	82	71	.536	4				83.8	-1.8
1908	NY-N	157	98	56	.636	•2				99.1	-1.1
1909	NY-N	158	92	61	.601	3				85.0	7.0
1910	NY-N	155	91	63	.591	2				92.4	-1.4
1911	NY-N	154	99	54	.647	1				98.6	0.4
1912	NY-N	154	103	48	.682	1				100.6	2.4
1913	NY-N	156	101	51	.664	1				94.3	6.7
1914	NY-N	156	84	70	.545	2				87.2	-3.2
1915	NY-N	155	69	83	.454	8				71.1	-2.1
1916	NY-N	155	86	66	.566	4				86.5	-0.5
1917	NY-N	158	98	56	.636	1				97.3	0.7
1918	NY-N	124	71	53	.573	2				69.3	1.7
1919	NY-N	140	87	53	.621	2				84.6	2.4
1920	NY-N	155	86	68	.558	2				91.8	-5.8
1921	NY-N	153	94	59	.614	★1				96.1	-2.1
1922	NY-N	156	93	61	.604	★1				95.7	-2.7
1923	NY-N	153	95	58	.621	1				93.1	1.9
1924	NY-N	29	16	13	.552	3	1		1/3	18.4	-2.4
	NY-N	81	45	35	.563	1	1		3/3	40.9	-5.9
1925	NY-N	152	86	66	.566	2				79.3	6.7
1926	NY-N	151	74	77	.490	5				75.0	-1.0
1927	NY-N	122	70	52	.574	4	3		1/2	68.3	1.7
1928	NY-N	155	93	61	.604	2				92.1	0.9
1929	NY-N	152	84	67	.556	3				92.9	-8.9
1930	NY-N	154	87	67	.565	3				89.8	-2.8
1931	NY-N	153	87	65	.572	2				93.0	-6.0
1932	NY-N	40	17	23	.425	8	•6		1/2	21.2	-4.2
	33	4801	2784	1959	.587						-7.7

YEAR	TM/L	G	W	L	PCT	STANDING			M/Y	W-EXP	A-E
McGuire, James Thomas "Deacon"											
1898	Was-N*	70	21	47	.309	10	11	11	3/4	24.3	-3.3
1907	Bos-A*	112	45	61	.425	8	7		4/4	45.2	-0.2
1908	Bos-A*	115	53	62	.461	6	5		1/2	61.8	-8.8
1909	Cle-A	41	14	25	.359	4	6		2/2	18.3	-4.3
1910	Cle-A*	161	71	81	.467	5				64.0	7.0
1911	Cle-A	17	6	11	.353	7	3		1/2	8.3	-2.3
	6	516	210	287	.423						-12.0
McGunnigle, William Henry "Bill"											
1888	Bro-a	143	88	52	.629	2				87.0	1.0
1889	Bro-a	140	94	43	.686	1				93.4	-0.4
1890	Bro-N	129	86	43	.667	1				87.7	-1.7
1891	Pit-N	59	24	33	.421	8	8		2/2	25.9	-1.9
1896	Lou-N	115	36	76	.321	12	12		2/2	30.9	5.1
	5	586	328	247	.570						2.1
McInnis, John Phalen "Stuffy"											
1927	Phi-N*	155	51	103	.331	8				55.9	-4.9
McKechnie, William Boyd "Bill"											
1915	New-F*	102	54	45	.545	6	5		2/2	51.2	2.8
1922	Pit-N	90	53	36	.596	5	●3		2/2	51.5	1.5
1923	Pit-N	154	87	67	.565	3				85.7	1.3
1924	Pit-N	153	90	63	.588	3				90.4	-0.4
1925	Pit-N	153	95	58	.621	★1				94.6	0.4
1926	Pit-N	157	84	69	.549	3				84.4	-0.4
1928	StL-N	154	95	59	.617	1				93.8	1.2
1929	StL-N	63	34	29	.540	4	4		3/3	32.5	1.5
1930	Bos-N	154	70	84	.455	6				63.5	6.5
1931	Bos-N	156	64	90	.416	7				61.2	2.8
1932	Bos-N	155	77	77	.500	5				76.4	0.6
1933	Bos-N	156	83	71	.539	4				79.4	3.6
1934	Bos-N	152	78	73	.517	4				72.4	5.6
1935	Bos-N	153	38	115	.248	8				49.3	-11.3
1936	Bos-N	157	71	83	.461	6				68.4	2.6
1937	Bos-N	152	79	73	.520	5				78.5	0.5
1938	Cin-N	151	82	68	.547	4				83.9	-1.9
1939	Cin-N	156	97	57	.630	1				94.5	2.5
1940	Cin-N	155	100	53	.654	★1				95.5	4.5
1941	Cin-N	154	88	66	.571	3				82.6	5.4
1942	Cin-N	154	76	76	.500	4				74.0	2.0
1943	Cin-N	155	87	67	.565	2				84.2	2.8
1944	Cin-N	155	89	65	.578	3				81.0	8.0
1945	Cin-N	154	61	93	.396	7				60.2	0.8
1946	Cin-N	152	64	86	.427	6	6		1/2	69.8	-5.8
	25	3647	1896	1723	.524						37.3
McKeon, John Aloysius "Jack"											
1973	KC-A	162	88	74	.543	2 W				81.3	6.7
1974	KC-A	162	77	85	.475	5 W				81.5	-4.5
1975	KC-A	96	50	46	.521	2 W	2 W		1/2	51.7	-1.7
1977	Oak-A	53	26	27	.491	●5 W	7 W		1/2	21.6	4.4
1978	Oak-A	123	45	78	.366	1 W	6 W		2/2	48.4	-3.4
1988	SD-N	115	67	48	.583	5 W	3 W		2/2	58.4	8.6
1989	SD-N	162	89	73	.549	2 W				82.7	6.3
1990	SD-N	80	37	43	.463	4 W	5 W		1/2	40.0	-3.0
	8	953	479	474	.503						13.4
McKinnon, Alexander J. "Alex"											
1885	StL-N*	39	6	32	.158	5	8	8	2/3	11.8	-5.8
McKnight, Dennis Hamar "Denny"											
1884	Pit-a	12	4	8	.333	9	10		1/5	2.7	1.3
McManus, George											
1876	StL-N	8	6	2	.750	2	2		2/2	5.9	0.1
1877	StL-N	60	28	32	.467	4				26.8	1.2
	2	68	34	34	.500						1.3
McManus, Martin Joseph "Marty"											
1932	Bos-A*	99	32	67	.323	8	8		2/2	27.8	4.2
1933	Bos-A*	149	63	86	.423	7				68.9	-5.9
	2	248	95	153	.383						-1.7
McMillan, Roy David											
1972	Mil-A	2	1	1	.500	6 E	6 E	6 E	2/3	0.9	0.1
1975	NY-N	53	26	27	.491	3 E	●3 E		2/2	27.2	-1.2
	2	55	27	28	.491						-1.1
McNamara, John Francis											
1969	Oak-A	13	8	5	.615	2 W	2 W		2/2	7.0	1.0
1970	Oak-A	162	89	73	.549	2 W				90.1	-1.1
1974	SD-N	162	60	102	.370	6 W				51.2	8.8
1975	SD-N	162	71	91	.438	4 W				66.8	4.2
1976	SD-N	162	73	89	.451	5 W				71.0	2.0
1977	SD-N	48	20	28	.417	4 W	5 W		1/3	19.9	0.1
1979	Cin-N	161	90	71	.559	1 W				89.4	0.6
1980	Cin-N	163	89	73	.549	3 W				84.8	4.2
1981(1)	Cin-N	56	35	21	.625	2 W					
(2)	Cin-N	52	31	21	.596	2 W				56.5	9.5
1982	Cin-N	92	34	58	.370	6 W	6 W		1/2	38.8	-4.8
1983	Cal-A	162	70	92	.432	●5 W				75.4	-5.4
1984	Cal-A	162	81	81	.500	●2 W				80.9	0.1
1985	Bos-A	163	81	81	.500	5 E				88.9	-7.9
1986	Bos-A	161	95	66	.590	♦1 E				90.2	4.8
1987	Bos-A	162	78	84	.481	5 E				82.6	-4.6
1988	Bos-A	85	43	42	.506	4 E	1 E		1/2	48.9	-5.9
1990	Cle-A	162	77	85	.475	4 E				80.5	-3.5
1991	Cle-A	77	25	52	.325	7 E	7 E		1/2	29.4	-4.4
	18	2367	1150	1215	.486						-2.2
McPhee, John Alexander "Bid"											
1901	Cin-N	142	52	87	.374	8				44.8	7.2
1902	Cin-N	65	27	37	.422	6	4		1/3	35.2	-8.2
	2	207	79	124	.389						-0.9
McRae, Harold Abraham "Hal"											
1991	KC-A	124	66	58	.532	7 W	6 W		3/3	62.4	3.6
1992	KC-A	162	72	90	.444	●5 W				74.9	-2.9
	2	286	138	148	.483						0.7
McVey, Calvin Alexander "Cal"											
1873	Bal-n*	32	19	13	.594	2	3		1/2	23.5	-4.5
1878	Cin-N*	61	37	23	.617	2				34.9	2.1
1879	Cin-N*	63	34	28	.548	4	5		2/2	32.4	1.6
	3	156	90	64	.584						-0.9
Mele, Sabath Anthony "Sam"											
1961	Min-A	7	2	5	.286	8	9	7	2/4	3.2	-1.2
	Min-A	95	45	49	.479	9	7		4/4	42.9	2.1
1962	Min-A	163	91	71	.562	2				89.4	1.6
1963	Min-A	161	91	70	.565	3				97.5	-6.5
1964	Min-A	163	79	83	.488	●6				87.0	-8.0
1965	Min-A	162	102	60	.630	1				98.9	3.1
1966	Min-A	162	89	73	.549	2				89.9	-0.9
1967	Min-A	50	25	25	.500	6	●2		1/2	27.7	-2.7
	7	963	524	436	.546						-12.4
Melillo, Oscar Donald "Ski"											
1938	StL-A	10	2	7	.222	7	7		2/2	3.4	-1.4
Merrill, Carl Harrison "Stump"											
1990	NY-A	113	49	64	.434	7 E	7 E		2/2	45.9	3.1
1991	NY-A	162	71	91	.438	5 E				70.7	0.3
	2	275	120	155	.436						3.4
Metro, Charles "Charlie"											
1962	Chi-N	112	43	69	.384	9	9		3/3	42.5	0.5
1970	KC-A	52	19	33	.365	5 W	●4 W		1/2	22.8	-3.8
	2	164	62	102	.378						-3.3
Meyer, William Adam "Billy"											
1948	Pit-N	156	83	71	.539	4				77.7	5.3
1949	Pit-N	154	71	83	.461	6				69.3	1.7
1950	Pit-N	154	57	96	.373	8				59.8	-2.8
1951	Pit-N	155	64	90	.416	7				62.1	1.9
1952	Pit-N	155	42	112	.273	8				48.3	-6.3
	5	774	317	452	.412						-0.2
Michael, Eugene Richard "Gene"											
1981(1)	NY-A	56	34	22	.607	♦1 E					
(2)	NY-A	26	14	12	.538	4 E	6 E		1/2	47.7	0.3
1982	NY-A	86	44	42	.512	●4 E	●5 E	5 E	2/3	42.6	1.4
1986	Chi-N	102	46	56	.451	5 E	5 E		3/3	44.6	1.4
1987	Chi-N	136	68	68	.500	5 E	6 E		1/2	61.3	6.7
	4	406	206	200	.507						9.7
Milan, Jesse Clyde "Clyde"											
1922	Was-A*	154	69	85	.448	6				71.3	-2.3
Miller, George Frederick											
1894	StL-N*	133	56	76	.424	9				50.8	5.2
Miller, Joseph Wick "Joe"											
1872	Nat-n*	11	0	11	.000	11				-1.2	1.2
Miller, Raymond Roger "Ray"											
1985	Min-A	100	50	50	.500	6 W	4 W		2/2	45.3	4.7
1986	Min-A	139	59	80	.424	7 W	6 W		1/2	61.4	-2.4
	2	239	109	130	.456						2.3
Mills, Colonel Buster "Buster"											
1953	Cin-N	8	4	4	.500	6	6		2/2	3.6	0.4
Mills, Everett											
1872	Bal-n*	17	8	6	.571	2	2		2/2	10.3	-2.3
Mitchell, Frederick Francis "Fred"											
1917	Chi-N	157	74	80	.481	5				75.3	-1.3
1918	Chi-N	131	84	45	.651	1				80.8	3.2
1919	Chi-N	140	75	65	.536	3				75.7	-0.7
1920	Chi-N	154	75	79	.487	●5				75.3	-0.3
1921	Bos-N	153	79	74	.516	4				78.9	0.1
1922	Bos-N	154	53	100	.346	8				54.2	-1.2
1923	Bos-N	155	54	100	.351	7				61.0	-7.0
	7	1044	494	543	.476						-7.2
Moore, Jackie Spencer											
1984	Oak-A	118	57	61	.483	5 W	4 W		2/2	54.9	2.1
1985	Oak-A	162	77	85	.475	●4 W				78.1	-1.1
1986	Oak-A	73	29	44	.397	●6 W	●3 W		1/3	35.2	-6.2
	3	353	163	190	.462						-5.2
Moore, Terry Bluford											
1954	Phi-N	77	35	42	.455	3	4		2/2	40.8	-5.8
Moran, Patrick Joseph "Pat"											
1915	Phi-N	153	90	62	.592	1				90.4	-0.4
1916	Phi-N	154	91	62	.595	2				87.0	4.0

YEAR	TM/L	G	W	L	PCT	STANDING			M/Y	W-EXP	A-E
1917	Phi-N	155	87	65	.572	2				84.8	2.2
1918	Phi-N	125	55	68	.447	6				53.1	1.9
1919	Cin-N	140	96	44	.686	★1				90.0	6.0
1920	Cin-N	154	82	71	.536	3				84.0	-2.0
1921	Cin-N	153	70	83	.458	6				73.3	-3.3
1922	Cin-N	156	86	68	.558	2				85.8	0.2
1923	Cin-N	154	91	63	.591	2				85.0	6.0
	9	1344	748	586	.561						14.6

Morgan, Joseph Michael "Joe"

YEAR	TM/L	G	W	L	PCT	STANDING			M/Y	W-EXP	A-E
1988	Bos-A	77	46	31	.597	4 E	1 E		2/2	44.3	1.7
1989	Bos-A	162	83	79	.512	3 E				84.8	-1.8
1990	Bos-A	162	88	74	.543	1 E				84.6	3.4
1991	Bos-A	162	84	78	.519	●2 E				82.9	1.1
	4	563	301	262	.535						4.3

Moriarty, George Joseph

1927	Det-A	156	82	71	.536	4				80.2	1.8
1928	Det-A	154	68	86	.442	6				71.3	-3.3
	2	310	150	157	.489						-1.5

Morrill, John Francis

1882	Bos-N*	85	45	39	.536	●3				47.4	-2.4
1883	Bos-N*	44	33	11	.750	4	1		2/2	30.5	2.5
1884	Bos-N*	116	73	38	.658	2				76.1	-3.1
1885	Bos-N*	113	46	66	.411	5				50.2	-4.2
1886	Bos-N*	118	56	61	.479	5				58.1	-2.1
1887	Bos-N*	32	12	17	.414	5	5		2/2	15.3	-3.3
1888	Bos-N*	137	70	64	.522	4				71.9	-1.9
1889	Was-N*	51	13	38	.255	8	8		1/2	16.2	-3.2
	8	696	348	334	.510						-17.7

Morton, Charles Hazen "Charlie"

1884	Tol-a*	110	46	58	.442	8				41.4	4.6
1885	Det-N*	38	7	31	.184	8	6		1/2	16.7	-9.7
1890	Tol-a	134	68	64	.515	4				70.6	-2.6
	3	282	121	153	.442						-7.8

Moses, Felix I.

1884	Ric-a	46	12	30	.286	12				11.8	0.2

Moss, John Lester "Les"

1968	Chi-A	2	0	2	.000	9	9	●8	2/5	0.9	-0.9
	Chi-A	34	12	22	.353	9	9	●8	4/5	15.4	-3.4
1979	Det-A	53	27	26	.509	5 E	5 E		1/3	27.5	-0.5
	2	89	39	50	.438						-4.8

Murnane, Timothy Hayes "Tim"

1884	Bos-U*	111	58	51	.532	5				61.6	-3.6

Murray, William Jeremiah "Billy"

1907	Phi-N	149	83	64	.565	3				77.7	5.3
1908	Phi-N	155	83	71	.539	4				84.2	-1.2
1909	Phi-N	154	74	79	.484	5				76.3	-2.3
	3	458	240	214	.529						1.9

Murtaugh, Daniel Edward "Danny"

1957	Pit-N	51	26	25	.510	7	●7		2/2	21.7	4.3
1958	Pit-N	154	84	70	.545	2				82.7	1.3
1959	Pit-N	155	78	76	.506	4				74.0	4.0
1960	Pit-N	155	95	59	.617	★1				91.5	3.5
1961	Pit-N	154	75	79	.487	6				78.9	-3.9
1962	Pit-N	161	93	68	.578	4				88.8	4.2
1963	Pit-N	162	74	88	.457	8				77.9	-3.9
1964	Pit-N	162	80	82	.494	●6				83.9	-3.9
1967	Pit-N	79	39	39	.500	6	6		2/2	38.3	0.7
1970	Pit-N	162	89	73	.549	1 E				87.7	1.3
1971	Pit-N	162	97	65	.599	★1 E				100.4	-3.4
1973	Pit-N	26	13	13	.500	2 E	3 E		2/2	13.2	-0.2
1974	Pit-N	162	88	74	.543	1 E				90.6	-2.6
1975	Pit-N	161	92	69	.571	1 E				96.2	-4.2
1976	Pit-N	162	92	70	.568	2 E				89.1	2.9
	15	2068	1115	950	.540						0.2

Mutrie, James J. "Jim"

1883	NY-a	97	54	42	.563	4				57.1	-3.1
1884	NY-a	112	75	32	.701	1				82.5	-7.5
1885	NY-N	112	85	27	.759	2				87.3	-2.3
1886	NY-N	124	75	44	.630	3				72.2	2.8
1887	NY-N	129	68	55	.553	4				69.6	-1.6
1888	NY-N	138	84	47	.641	1				84.3	-0.3
1889	NY-N	131	83	43	.659	1				82.2	0.8
1890	NY-N	135	63	68	.481	6				66.9	-3.9
1891	NY-N	136	71	61	.538	3				69.9	1.1
	9	1114	658	419	.611						-14.1

Myatt, George Edward "George"

1968	Phi-N	1	1	0	1.000	●6	5	●7	2/3	0.5	0.5
1969	Phi-N	54	19	35	.352	5 E	5 E		2/2	23.6	-4.6
	2	55	20	35	.364						-4.0

Myers, Henry C.

1882	Bal-a*	74	19	54	.260	6				14.2	4.8

Nash, William Mitchell "Billy"

1896	Phi-N*	130	62	68	.477	8				64.9	-2.9

Neun, John Henry "Johnny"

1946	NY-A	14	8	6	.571	3	3		3/3	8.3	-0.3
1947	Cin-N	154	73	81	.474	5				69.7	3.3
1948	Cin-N	100	44	56	.440	7	7		1/2	39.1	4.9
	3	268	125	143	.466						7.8

Newman, Jeffrey Lynn "Jeff"

1986	Oak-A	10	2	8	.200	●6 W	7 W	●3 W	2/3	4.8	-2.8

Nichols, Charles Augustus "Kid"

1904	StL-N*	155	75	79	.487	5				77.8	-2.8
1905	StL-N*	14	5	9	.357	7	6		1/3	5.1	-0.1
	2	169	80	88	.476						-2.9

Nicol, Hugh

1897	StL-N	40	8	32	.200	12	12	12	2/4	7.3	0.7

Nixon, Russell Eugene "Russ"

1982	Cin-N	70	27	43	.386	6 W	6 W		2/2	29.5	-2.5
1983	Cin-N	162	74	88	.457	6 W				71.9	2.1
1988	Atl-N	121	42	79	.347	6 W	6 W		2/2	45.7	-3.7
1989	Atl-N	161	63	97	.394	6 W				69.7	-6.7
1990	Atl-N	65	25	40	.385	6 W	6 W		1/2	27.0	-2.0
	5	579	231	347	.400						-12.8

Norman, Henry Willis Patrick "Bill"

1958	Det-A	105	56	49	.533	8	5		2/2	56.3	-0.3
1959	Det-A	17	2	15	.118	8	4		1/2	8.3	-6.3
	2	122	58	64	.475						-6.6

Oakes, Ennis Telfair "Rebel"

1914	Pit-F*	143	61	78	.439	8	7		2/2	60.6	0.4
1915	Pit-F*	156	86	67	.562	3				84.1	1.9
	2	299	147	145	.503						2.3

Oates, Johnny Lane

1991	Bal-A	125	54	71	.432	7 E	6 E		2/2	54.1	-0.1
1992	Bal-A	162	89	73	.549	3 E				86.1	2.9
	2	287	143	144	.498						2.8

O'Connor, John Joseph "Jack"

1910	StL-A*	158	47	107	.305	8				45.1	1.9

O'Day, Henry Francis "Hank"

1912	Cin-N	155	75	78	.490	4				69.9	5.1
1914	Chi-N	156	78	76	.506	4				73.5	4.5
	2	311	153	154	.498						9.6

O'Farrell, Robert Arthur "Bob"

1927	StL-N*	153	92	61	.601	2				85.3	6.7
1934	Cin-N*	91	30	60	.333	8	8		1/3	32.5	-2.5
	2	244	122	121	.502						4.2

O'Leary, Daniel "Dan"

1884	Cin-U*	35	20	15	.571	5	3		1/2	24.6	-4.6

O'Neill, Stephen Francis "Steve"

1935	Cle-A	60	36	23	.610	5	3		2/2	30.9	5.1
1936	Cle-A	157	80	74	.519	5				82.3	-2.3
1937	Cle-A	156	83	71	.539	4				81.6	1.4
1943	Det-A	155	78	76	.506	5				84.8	-6.8
1944	Det-A	156	88	66	.571	2				85.2	2.8
1945	Det-A	155	88	65	.575	★1				83.8	4.2
1946	Det-A	155	92	62	.597	2				91.4	0.6
1947	Det-A	158	85	69	.552	2				84.4	0.6
1948	Det-A	154	78	76	.506	5				74.4	3.6
1950	Bos-A	95	63	32	.663	4	3		2/2	59.5	3.5
1951	Bos-A	154	87	67	.565	3				84.5	2.5
1952	Phi-N	91	59	32	.648	6	4		2/2	52.1	6.9
1953	Phi-N	156	83	71	.539	●3				82.0	1.0
1954	Phi-N	77	40	37	.519	3	4		1/2	40.8	-0.8
	14	1879	1040	821	.559						22.2

Onslow, John James "Jack"

1949	Chi-A	154	63	91	.409	6				68.1	-5.1
1950	Chi-A	31	8	22	.267	8	6		1/2	12.6	-4.6
	2	185	71	113	.386						-9.7

O'Rourke, James Henry "Jim"

1881	Buf-N*	83	45	38	.542	3				40.9	4.1
1882	Buf-N*	84	45	39	.536	●3				45.5	-0.5
1883	Buf-N*	98	52	45	.536	5				51.8	0.2
1884	Buf-N*	115	64	47	.577	3				62.0	0.2
1893	Was-N*	130	40	89	.310	12				39.2	0.8
	5	510	246	258	.488						6.7

Orr, David L. "Dave"

1887	NY-a*	8	3	5	.375	8	7	7	2/3	2.3	0.7

Ott, Melvin Thomas "Mel"

1942	NY-N*	154	85	67	.559	3				83.8	1.2
1943	NY-N*	156	55	98	.359	8				60.2	-5.2
1944	NY-N*	155	67	87	.435	5				68.1	-1.1
1945	NY-N*	154	78	74	.513	5				72.8	5.2
1946	NY-N*	154	61	93	.396	8				69.5	-8.5
1947	NY-N*	155	81	73	.526	4				83.5	-2.5
1948	NY-N	76	37	38	.493	4	5		1/2	41.1	-4.1
	7	1004	464	530	.467						-14.9

Owens, Paul Francis

1972	Phi-N	80	33	47	.412	6 E	6 E		2/2	32.5	0.5
1983	Phi-N	77	47	30	.610	1 E	◆1 E		2/2	41.5	5.5
1984	Phi-N	162	81	81	.500	4 E				84.1	-3.1
	3	319	161	158	.505						2.9

YEAR	TM/L	G	W	L	PCT	STANDING			M/Y	W-EXP	A-E
Ozark, Daniel Leonard "Danny"											
1973	Phi-N	162	71	91	.438	6 E				73.2	-2.2
1974	Phi-N	162	80	82	.494	3 E				78.4	1.6
1975	Phi-N	162	86	76	.531	2 E				85.1	0.9
1976	Phi-N	162	101	61	.623	1 E				103.3	-2.3
1977	Phi-N	162	101	61	.623	1 E				98.6	2.4
1978	Phi-N	162	90	72	.556	1 E				94.0	-4.0
1979	Phi-N	133	65	67	.492	5 E	4 E		1/2	63.1	1.9
1984	SF-N	56	24	32	.429	6 W	6 W		2/2	23.7	0.3
	8	1161	618	542	.533						-1.4
Pabor, Charles Henry "Charlie"											
1871	Cle-n*	29	10	19	.345	7				8.4	1.6
1875	Atl-n*	42	2	40	.048	12	12		1/2	-3.3	5.3
	NH-n*	6	1	5	.167	8	8		3/3	0.5	0.5
	2	77	13	64	.169						7.5
Parker, Francis James "Salty"											
1967	NY-N	11	4	7	.364	10	10		2/2	4.2	-0.2
1972	Hou-N	1	1	0	1.000	2 W	2 W		2/3	0.5	0.5
	2	12	5	7	.417						0.3
Parks, William Robert "Bill"											
1875	Was-n*	8	1	7	.125	8	10		2/2	-1.0	2.0
Pearce, Richard J. "Dickey"											
1872	Mut-n*	16	10	6	.625	4	3		1/2	11.6	-1.6
1875	StL-n*	72	39	29	.574	4				35.6	3.4
	2	88	49	35	.583						1.8
Peckinpaugh, Roger Thorpe											
1914	NY-A*	20	10	10	.500	7	●6		2/2	9.8	0.2
1928	Cle-A	155	62	92	.403	7				62.0	0.0
1929	Cle-A	152	81	71	.533	3				74.2	6.8
1930	Cle-A	154	81	73	.526	4				74.8	6.2
1931	Cle-A	155	78	76	.506	4				81.7	-3.7
1932	Cle-A	153	87	65	.572	4				85.1	1.9
1933	Cle-A	51	26	25	.510	5	4		1/3	25.0	1.0
1941	Cle-A	155	75	79	.487	●4				77.9	-2.9
	8	995	500	491	.505						9.5
Perkins, Ralph Foster "Cy"											
1937	Det-A	15	6	9	.400	2	2		5/5	8.3	-2.3
Pesky, John Michael "Johnny"											
1963	Bos-A	161	76	85	.472	7				76.6	-0.6
1964	Bos-A	160	70	90	.438	8	8		1/2	69.7	0.3
1980	Bos-A	5	1	4	.200	3 E	4 E		2/2	2.5	-1.5
	3	326	147	179	.451						-1.8
Pfeffer, Nathaniel Frederick "Fred"											
1892(1)	Lou-N*	23	9	14	.391	10	11		2/2		
(2)	Lou-N*	77	33	42	.440	9				39.2	2.8
Phelan, Lewis G. "Lew"											
1895	StL-N	45	11	30	.268	11	11		4/4	13.1	-2.1
Phillips, Harold Ross "Lefty"											
1969	Cal-A	124	60	63	.488	6 W	3 W		2/2	51.0	9.0
1970	Cal-A	162	86	76	.531	3 W				81.1	4.9
1971	Cal-A	162	76	86	.469	4 W				73.5	2.5
	3	448	222	225	.497						16.4
Phillips, Horace B.											
1879	Tro-N	47	12	34	.261	8	8		1/2	10.8	1.2
1883	Col-a	97	32	65	.330	6				32.4	-0.4
1884	Pit-a	35	9	24	.273	10	10		5/5	7.4	1.6
1885	Pit-a	111	56	55	.505	3				56.3	-0.3
1886	Pit-a	140	80	57	.584	2				83.7	-3.7
1887	Pit-N	125	55	69	.444	6				50.3	4.7
1888	Pit-N	139	66	68	.493	6				62.1	3.9
1889	Pit-N	71	28	43	.394	6	5		1/3	31.9	-3.9
	8	765	338	415	.449						3.1
Phillips, William Corcoran "Bill"											
1914	Ind-F	157	88	65	.575	1				90.6	-2.6
1915	New-F	53	26	27	.491	6	5		1/2	27.4	-1.4
	2	210	114	92	.553						-4.0
Pike, Lipman Emanuel "Lip"											
1871	Tro-n*	4	1	3	.250	7	6		1/2	1.9	-0.9
1874	Har-n*	54	17	37	.315	7				19.0	-3.0
1877	Cin-N*	14	3	11	.214	6	6		1/3	3.1	-0.1
	3	72	21	51	.292						-4.0
Piniella, Louis Victor "Lou"											
1986	NY-A	162	90	72	.556	2 E				86.8	3.2
1987	NY-A	162	89	73	.549	4 E				83.9	5.1
1988	NY-A	93	45	48	.484	2 E	5 E		2/2	47.9	-2.9
1990	Cin-N	162	91	71	.562	★1 W				91.2	-0.2
1991	Cin-N	162	74	88	.457	5 W				80.8	-6.8
1992	Cin-N	162	90	72	.556	2 W				86.5	3.5
	6	903	479	424	.530						2.0
Plummer, William Francis "Bill"											
1992	Sea-A	162	64	98	.395	7 W				69.1	-5.1
Popowski, Edward Joseph "Eddie"											
1969	Bos-A	9	5	4	.556	3 E	3 E		2/2	4.5	0.5
1973	Bos-A	1	1	0	1.000	2 E	2 E		2/2	0.6	0.4
	2	10	6	4	.600						0.9

YEAR	TM/L	G	W	L	PCT	STANDING			M/Y	W-EXP	A-E
Porter, Matthew S. "Matt"											
1884	KC-U*	16	3	13	.188	8	8	8	2/3	2.5	0.5
Powers, Patrick Thomas "Pat"											
1890	Roc-a	133	63	63	.500	5				62.8	0.2
1892(1)	NY-N	74	31	43	.419	10					
(2)	NY-N	79	40	37	.519	6				74.1	-3.1
	2	286	134	143	.484						-2.9
Pratt, Albert George "Al"											
1882	Pit-a	79	39	39	.500	4				39.9	-0.9
1883	Pit-a	32	12	20	.375	6	7		1/3	10.4	1.6
	2	111	51	59	.464						0.6
Price, James L. "Jim"											
1884	NY-N	100	56	42	.571	4	●4		1/2	54.5	1.5
Prothro, James Thompson "Doc"											
1939	Phi-N	152	45	106	.298	8				45.6	-0.6
1940	Phi-N	153	50	103	.327	8				49.6	0.4
1941	Phi-N	155	43	111	.279	8				46.7	-3.7
	3	460	138	320	.301						-3.9
Purcell, William Aloysius "Blondie"											
1883	Phi-N*	82	13	68	.160	8	8		2/2	10.0	3.0
Quilici, Francis Ralph "Frank"											
1972	Min-A	84	41	43	.488	3 W	3 W		2/2	42.1	-1.1
1973	Min-A	162	81	81	.500	3 W				85.6	-4.6
1974	Min-A	163	82	80	.506	3 W				81.4	0.6
1975	Min-A	159	76	83	.478	4 W				78.3	-2.3
	4	568	280	287	.494						-7.5
Quinn, Joseph J. "Joe"											
1895	StL-N*	40	11	28	.282	11	11	11	3/4	12.5	-1.5
1899	Cle-N*	116	12	104	.103	12	12		2/2	10.0	2.0
	2	156	23	132	.148						0.6
Rader, Douglas Lee "Doug"											
1983	Tex-A	163	77	85	.475	3 W				84.3	-7.3
1984	Tex-A	161	69	92	.429	7 W				74.5	-5.5
1985	Tex-A	32	9	23	.281	7 W	7 W		1/2	12.6	-3.6
1986	Chi-A	2	1	1	.500	6 W	5 W	5 W	2/3	0.9	0.1
1989	Cal-A	162	91	71	.562	3 W				90.8	0.2
1990	Cal-A	162	80	82	.494	4 W				79.4	0.6
1991	Cal-A	124	61	63	.492	7 W	7 W		1/2	62.3	-1.3
	7	806	388	417	.482						-16.9
Rapp, Vernon Fred "Vern"											
1977	StL-N	162	83	79	.512	3 E				86.0	-3.0
1978	StL-N	17	6	11	.353	6 E	5 E		1/3	7.9	-1.9
1984	Cin-N	121	51	70	.421	5 W	5 W		1/2	51.3	-0.3
	3	300	140	160	.467						-5.1
Reach, Alfred James "Al"											
1890	Phi-N	11	4	7	.364	2	3	3	3/5	6.4	-2.4
Rice, Delbert "Del"											
1972	Cal-A	155	75	80	.484	5 W				68.1	6.9
Richards, Paul Rapier											
1951	Chi-A	155	81	73	.526	4				84.1	-3.1
1952	Chi-A	156	81	73	.526	3				81.6	-0.6
1953	Chi-A	156	89	65	.578	3				89.8	-0.8
1954	Chi-A	146	91	54	.628	3	3		1/2	91.5	-0.5
1955	Bal-A	156	57	97	.370	7				54.7	2.3
1956	Bal-A	154	69	85	.448	6				63.0	6.0
1957	Bal-A	154	76	76	.500	5				77.0	-1.0
1958	Bal-A	154	74	79	.484	6				70.4	3.6
1959	Bal-A	155	74	80	.481	6				69.4	4.6
1960	Bal-A	154	89	65	.578	2				84.9	4.1
1961	Bal-A	136	78	57	.578	3	3		1/2	76.7	1.3
1976	Chi-A	161	64	97	.398	6 W				63.9	0.1
	12	1837	923	901	.506						15.9
Richardson, Daniel "Danny"											
1892(2)	Was-N*	43	12	31	.279	11	12		2/2	17.9	-5.9
Rickey, Wesley Branch "Branch"											
1913	StL-A	12	5	6	.455	7	8		3/3	4.6	0.4
1914	StL-A*	159	71	82	.464	5				66.2	4.8
1915	StL-A	159	63	91	.409	6				59.6	3.4
1919	StL-N	138	54	83	.394	7				58.7	-4.7
1920	StL-N	155	75	79	.487	●5				76.3	-1.3
1921	StL-N	154	87	66	.569	3				88.8	-1.8
1922	StL-N	154	85	69	.552	●3				81.0	4.0
1923	StL-N	154	79	74	.516	5				77.9	1.1
1924	StL-N	154	65	89	.422	6				76.0	-11.0
1925	StL-N	38	13	25	.342	8	4		1/2	20.5	-7.5
	10	1277	597	664	.473						-12.6
Riddoch, Gregory Lee "Greg"											
1990	SD-N	82	38	44	.463	4 W	5 W		2/2	41.0	-3.0
1991	SD-N	162	84	78	.519	3 W				79.9	4.1
1992	SD-N	150	78	72	.520	3 W	3 W		1/2	73.1	4.9
	3	394	200	194	.508						6.0
Riggleman, James David "Jim"											
1992	SD-N	12	4	8	.333	3 W	3 W		2/2	5.8	-1.8
Rigney, William Joseph "Bill"											
1956	NY-N	154	67	87	.435	6				65.1	1.9

YEAR	TM/L	G	W	L	PCT	STANDING			M/Y	W-EXP	A-E
1957	NY-N	154	69	85	.448	6				71.1	-2.1
1958	SF-N	154	80	74	.519	3				79.9	0.1
1959	SF-N	154	83	71	.539	3				86.4	-3.4
1960	SF-N	58	33	25	.569	2	5		1/2	30.6	2.4
1961	LA-A	162	70	91	.435	8				76.6	-6.6
1962	LA-A	162	86	76	.531	3				82.2	3.8
1963	LA-A	161	70	91	.435	9				73.7	-3.7
1964	LA-A	162	82	80	.506	5				80.2	1.8
1965	Cal-A	162	75	87	.463	7				76.2	-1.2
1966	Cal-A	162	80	82	.494	6				76.8	3.2
1967	Cal-A	161	84	77	.522	5				78.3	5.7
1968	Cal-A	162	67	95	.414	8				67.6	-0.6
1969	Cal-A	39	11	28	.282	6 W	3 W		1/2	16.2	-5.2
1970	Min-A	162	98	64	.605	1 W				95.5	2.5
1971	Min-A	160	74	86	.463	5 W				78.3	-4.3
1972	Min-A	70	36	34	.514	3 W	3 W		1/2	35.1	0.9
1976	SF-N	162	74	88	.457	4 W				71.3	2.7
	18	2561	1239	1321	.484						-2.0
Ripken, Calvin Edwin Sr. "Cal"											
1985	Bal-A	1	1	0	1.000	4 E	4 E	4 E	2/3	0.5	0.5
1987	Bal-A	162	67	95	.414	6 E				66.6	0.4
1988	Bal-A	6	0	6	.000	7 E	7 E		1/2	2.1	-2.1
	3	169	68	101	.402						-1.2
Robinson, Frank											
1975	Cle-A*	159	79	80	.497	4 E				78.0	1.0
1976	Cle-A*	159	81	78	.509	4 E				79.5	1.5
1977	Cle-A	57	26	31	.456	5 E	5 E		1/2	26.2	-0.2
1981(1)	SF-N	59	27	32	.458	5 W					
(2)	SF-N	52	29	23	.558	3 W				56.9	-0.9
1982	SF-N	162	87	75	.537	3 W				79.6	7.4
1983	SF-N	162	79	83	.488	5 W				80.0	-1.0
1984	SF-N	106	42	64	.396	6 W	6 W		1/2	44.9	-2.9
1988	Bal-A	155	54	101	.348	7 E	7 E		2/2	53.6	0.4
1989	Bal-A	162	87	75	.537	2 E				83.3	3.7
1990	Bal-A	162	76	85	.472	5 E				77.5	-1.5
1991	Bal-A	37	13	24	.351	7 E	6 E		1/2	16.0	-3.0
	11	1432	680	751	.475						4.6
Robinson, Wilbert											
1902	Bal-A*	83	24	57	.296	7	8		2/2	33.5	-9.5
1914	Bro-N	154	75	79	.487	5				77.4	-2.4
1915	Bro-N	154	80	72	.526	3				73.3	6.7
1916	Bro-N	156	94	60	.610	1				90.1	3.9
1917	Bro-N	156	70	81	.464	7				70.0	-0.0
1918	Bro-N	127	57	69	.452	5				50.9	6.1
1919	Bro-N	141	69	71	.493	5				71.3	-2.3
1920	Bro-N	155	93	61	.604	1				91.3	1.7
1921	Bro-N	152	77	75	.507	5				74.6	2.4
1922	Bro-N	155	76	78	.494	6				75.9	0.1
1923	Bro-N	155	76	78	.494	6				78.2	-2.2
1924	Bro-N	154	92	62	.597	2				81.2	10.8
1925	Bro-N	153	68	85	.444	●6				69.2	-1.2
1926	Bro-N	155	71	82	.464	6				68.1	2.9
1927	Bro-N	154	65	88	.425	6				68.0	-3.0
1928	Bro-N	155	77	76	.503	6				79.1	-2.1
1929	Bro-N	153	70	83	.458	6				64.3	5.7
1930	Bro-N	154	86	68	.558	4				89.3	-3.3
1931	Bro-N	153	79	73	.520	4				76.8	2.2
	19	2819	1399	1398	.500						16.4
Robison, Matthew Stanley "Stanley"											
1905	StL-N	50	19	31	.380	6	6		3/3	18.2	0.8
Rodgers, Robert Leroy "Bob"											
1980	Mil-A	47	26	21	.553	2 E	3 E		1/3	27.2	-1.2
	Mil-A	23	13	10	.565	4 E	3 E		3/3	13.3	-0.3
1981(1)	Mil-A	56	31	25	.554	3 E					
(2)	Mil-A	53	31	22	.585	1 E				58.0	4.0
1982	Mil-A	47	23	24	.489	5 E	♦1E		1/2	28.3	-5.3
1985	Mon-N	161	84	77	.522	3 E				80.2	3.8
1986	Mon-N	161	78	83	.484	4 E				75.2	2.8
1987	Mon-N	162	91	71	.562	3 E				83.1	7.9
1988	Mon-N	163	81	81	.500	3 E				84.9	-3.9
1989	Mon-N	162	81	81	.500	4 E				81.2	-0.2
1990	Mon-N	162	85	77	.525	3 E				87.9	-2.9
1991	Mon-N	49	20	29	.408	6 E	6 E		1/2	22.0	-2.0
	Cal-A	38	20	18	.526	7 W	7 W		2/2	19.1	0.9
1992	Cal-A	39	19	20	.487	5 W	●5 W		1/3	17.1	1.9
	Cal-A	34	14	20	.412	5 W	●5 W		3/3	14.9	-0.9
	11	1357	697	659	.514						4.6
Rogers, James F. "Jim"											
1897	Lou-N*	44	17	24	.415	9	11		1/2	15.2	1.8
Rojas, Octavio Victor "Cookie"											
1988	Cal-A	154	75	79	.487	4 W	4 W		1/2	71.6	3.4
Rolfe, Robert Abial "Red"											
1949	Det-A	155	87	67	.565	4				86.6	0.4
1950	Det-A	157	95	59	.617	2				88.8	6.2
1951	Det-A	154	73	81	.474	5				71.5	1.5
1952	Det-A	73	23	49	.319	8	8		1/2	27.2	-4.2
	4	539	278	256	.521						3.9

YEAR	TM/L	G	W	L	PCT	STANDING			M/Y	W-EXP	A-E
Rose, Peter Edward "Pete"											
1984	Cin-N*	41	19	22	.463	5 W	5 W		2/2	17.4	1.6
1985	Cin-N*	162	89	72	.553	2 W				81.6	7.4
1986	Cin-N*	162	86	76	.531	2 W				82.5	3.5
1987	Cin-N	162	84	78	.519	2 W				84.0	-0.0
1988	Cin-N	23	11	12	.478	4 W	2 W		1/3	12.2	-1.2
	Cin-N	111	64	47	.577	4 W	2 W		3/3	58.9	5.1
1989	Cin-N	125	59	66	.472	●4 W	5 W		1/2	57.7	1.3
	6	786	412	373	.525						17.7
Roseman, James John "Chief"											
1890	StL-a*	15	7	8	.467	4	5	3	3/6	8.8	-1.8
Rowe, David E. "Dave"											
1886	KC-N*	126	30	91	.248	7				26.1	3.9
1888	KC-a*	50	14	36	.280	8	8		1/3	14.2	-0.2
	2	176	44	127	.257						3.7
Rowe, John Charles "Jack"											
1890	Buf-P*	81	22	58	.275	8	8		1/3	20.9	1.1
	Buf-P*	19	5	14	.263	8	8		3/3	5.0	0.0
Rowland, Clarence Henry "Pants"											
1915	Chi-A	156	93	61	.604	3				99.2	-6.2
1916	Chi-A	155	89	65	.578	2				88.7	0.3
1917	Chi-A	156	100	54	.649	★1				98.5	1.5
1918	Chi-A	124	57	67	.460	6				63.2	-6.2
	4	591	339	247	.578						-10.6
Ruel, Herold Dominic "Muddy"											
1947	StL-A	154	59	95	.383	8				58.5	0.5
Runnells, Thomas William "Tom"											
1991	Mon-N	112	51	61	.455	6 E	6 E		2/2	50.3	0.7
1992	Mon-N	37	17	20	.459	4 E	2 E		1/2	20.2	-3.2
	2	149	68	81	.456						-2.4
Runnels, James Edward "Pete"											
1966	Bos-A	16	8	8	.500	9	9		2/2	7.2	0.8
Ryan, Cornelius Joseph "Connie"											
1975	Atl-N	27	9	18	.333	5 W	5 W		2/2	10.8	-1.8
1977	Tex-A	6	2	4	.333	3 W	5 W	2 W	3/4	3.4	-1.4
	2	33	11	22	.333						-3.2
Sawyer, Edwin Milby "Eddie"											
1948	Phi-N	63	23	40	.365	6	6		3/3	25.7	-2.7
1949	Phi-N	154	81	73	.526	3				76.4	4.6
1950	Phi-N	157	91	63	.591	1				87.0	4.0
1951	Phi-N	154	73	81	.474	5				77.4	-4.4
1952	Phi-N	63	28	35	.444	6	4		1/2	36.1	-8.1
1958	Phi-N	70	30	40	.429	8	8		2/2	30.6	-0.6
1959	Phi-N	155	64	90	.416	8				64.1	-0.1
1960	Phi-N	1	0	1	.000	●6	8		1/3	0.4	-0.4
	8	817	390	423	.480						-7.7
Scanlon, Michael B. "Mike"											
1884	Was-U	114	47	65	.420	6				46.3	0.7
1886	Was-N	82	13	67	.162	8	8		1/2	18.0	-5.0
	2	196	60	132	.313						-4.3
Schaefer, Robert Wald "Bob"											
1991	KC-A	1	1	0	1.000	7 W	7 W	6 W	2/3	0.5	0.5
Schalk, Raymond William "Ray"											
1927	Chi-A*	153	70	83	.458	5				71.9	-1.9
1928	Chi-A*	75	32	42	.432	6	5		1/2	33.7	-1.7
	2	228	102	125	.449						-3.6
Scheffing, Robert Boden "Bob"											
1957	Chi-N	156	62	92	.403	●7				67.4	-5.4
1958	Chi-N	154	72	82	.468	●5				75.4	-3.4
1959	Chi-N	155	74	80	.481	●5				75.5	-1.5
1961	Det-A	163	101	61	.623	2				97.7	3.3
1962	Det-A	161	85	76	.528	4				87.1	-2.1
1963	Det-A	60	24	36	.400	9	●5		1/2	29.9	-5.9
	6	849	418	427	.495						-15.1
Schlafly, Harry Linton "Larry"											
1914	Buf-F*	156	80	71	.530	4				77.4	2.6
1915	Buf-F	41	13	28	.317	8	6		1/3	18.8	-5.8
	2	197	93	99	.484						-3.2
Schmelz, Gustavius Heinrich "Gus"											
1884	Col-a	110	69	39	.639	2				66.3	2.7
1886	StL-N	126	43	79	.352	6				45.3	-2.3
1887	Cin-a	136	81	54	.600	2				80.2	0.8
1888	Cin-a	137	80	54	.597	4				78.1	1.9
1889	Cin-a	141	76	63	.547	4				80.7	-4.7
1890	Cle-N	78	21	55	.276	7	7		1/2	27.4	-6.4
	Col-a	57	38	13	.745	5	2		2/3	33.1	4.9
1891	Col-a	138	61	76	.445	6				61.6	-0.6
1894	Was-N	132	45	87	.341	11				47.5	-2.5
1895	Was-N	133	43	85	.336	10				47.2	-4.2
1896	Was-N	133	58	73	.443	●9				57.0	1.0
1897	Was-N	36	9	25	.265	11	●6		1/2	16.7	-7.7
	11	1357	624	703	.470						-17.2
Schoendienst, Albert Fred "Red"											
1965	StL-N	162	80	81	.497	7				83.9	-3.9
1966	StL-N	162	83	79	.512	6				80.3	2.7

YEAR	TM/L	G	W	L	PCT	STANDING			M/Y	W-EXP	A-E
1967	StL-N	161	101	60	.627	★1				95.3	5.7
1968	StL-N	162	97	65	.599	1				94.1	2.9
1969	StL-N	162	87	75	.537	4 E				87.2	-0.2
1970	StL-N	162	76	86	.469	4 E				80.7	-4.7
1971	StL-N	163	90	72	.556	2 E				85.0	5.0
1972	StL-N	156	75	81	.481	4 E				74.5	0.5
1973	StL-N	162	81	81	.500	2 E				85.3	-4.3
1974	StL-N	161	86	75	.534	2 E				84.1	1.9
1975	StL-N	163	82	80	.506	●3 E				78.2	3.8
1976	StL-N	162	72	90	.444	5 E				76.6	-4.6
1980	StL-N	37	18	19	.486	5 E	4 E		4/4	19.1	-1.1
1990	StL-N	24	13	11	.542	6 E	6 E	6 E	2/3	10.4	2.6
	14	1999	1041	955	.522						6.2
Schultz, Joseph Charles Jr. "Joe"											
1969	Sea-A	163	64	98	.395	6 W				64.8	-0.8
1973	Det-A	28	14	14	.500	3 E	3 E		2/2	13.4	0.6
	2	191	78	112	.411						-0.3
Selee, Frank Gibson											
1890	Bos-N	134	76	57	.571	5				82.5	-6.5
1891	Bos-N	140	87	51	.630	1				86.3	0.7
1892(1)	Bos-N	75	52	22	.703	1					
(2)	Bos-N	77	50	26	.658	2				95.3	6.7
1893	Bos-N	131	86	43	.667	1				81.7	4.3
1894	Bos-N	133	83	49	.629	3				82.0	1.0
1895	Bos-N	133	71	60	.542	●5				72.2	-1.2
1896	Bos-N	132	74	57	.565	4				74.0	0.0
1897	Bos-N	135	93	39	.705	1				96.5	-3.5
1898	Bos-N	152	102	47	.685	1				99.3	2.7
1899	Bos-N	153	95	57	.625	2				96.4	-1.4
1900	Bos-N	142	66	72	.478	4				72.6	-6.6
1901	Bos-N	140	69	69	.500	5				66.3	2.7
1902	Chi-N	143	68	69	.496	5				71.7	-3.7
1903	Chi-N	139	82	56	.594	3				78.4	3.6
1904	Chi-N	156	93	60	.608	2				85.7	7.3
1905	Chi-N	65	37	28	.569	4	3		1/2	43.2	-6.2
	16	2180	1284	862	.598						-0.1
Sewell, James Luther "Luke"											
1941	StL-A	113	55	55	.500	7	●6		2/2	51.1	3.9
1942	StL-A*	151	82	69	.543	3				84.8	-2.8
1943	StL-A	153	72	80	.474	6				75.1	-3.1
1944	StL-A	154	89	65	.578	1				87.1	1.9
1945	StL-A	154	81	70	.536	3				80.9	0.1
1946	StL-A	125	53	71	.427	7	7		1/2	54.6	-1.6
1949	Cin-N	3	1	2	.333	7	7		2/2	1.2	-0.2
1950	Cin-N	153	66	87	.431	6				68.5	-2.5
1951	Cin-N	155	68	86	.442	6				65.5	2.5
1952	Cin-N	98	39	59	.398	7	6		1/3	46.1	-7.1
	10	1259	606	644	.485						-9.0
Shannon, Daniel W. "Dan"											
1889	Lou-a*	58	10	46	.179	8	8	8	3/4	12.1	-2.1
1891	Was-a*	51	15	34	.306	7	8	8	3/4	13.0	2.0
	2	109	25	80	.238						-0.1
Sharsig, William A. "Bill"											
1886	Phi-a	41	22	17	.564	6	6		2/2	15.3	6.7
1888	Phi-a	137	81	52	.609	3				88.1	-7.1
1889	Phi-a	138	75	58	.564	3				74.5	0.5
1890	Phi-a	132	54	78	.409	7				45.4	8.6
1891	Phi-a	18	6	11	.353	7	4		1/2	8.8	-2.8
	5	466	238	216	.524						5.9
Shawkey, James Robert "Bob"											
1930	NY-A	154	86	68	.558	3				90.8	-4.8
Sheehan, Thomas Clancy "Tom"											
1960	SF-N	98	46	50	.479	2	5		2/2	50.6	-4.6
Shepard, Lawrence William "Larry"											
1968	Pit-N	163	80	82	.494	6				86.9	-6.9
1969	Pit-N	157	84	73	.535	3 E	3 E		1/2	85.8	-1.8
	2	320	164	155	.514						-8.6
Sherry, Norman Burt "Norm"											
1976	Cal-A	66	37	29	.561	6 W	●4 W		2/2	29.3	7.7
1977	Cal-A	81	39	42	.481	5 W	5 W		1/2	39.5	-0.5
	2	147	76	71	.517						7.2
Shettsline, William Joseph "Bill"											
1898	Phi-N	104	59	44	.573	●8	6		2/2	54.0	5.0
1899	Phi-N	154	94	58	.618	3				91.8	2.2
1900	Phi-N	141	75	63	.543	3				70.6	4.4
1901	Phi-N	140	83	57	.593	2				82.8	0.2
1902	Phi-N	138	56	81	.409	7				51.2	4.8
	5	677	367	303	.548						16.6
Shotton, Burton Edwin "Burt"											
1928	Phi-N	152	43	109	.283	8				48.7	-5.7
1929	Phi-N	154	71	82	.464	5				65.1	5.9
1930	Phi-N	156	52	102	.338	8				56.4	-4.4
1931	Phi-N	155	66	88	.429	6				63.2	2.8
1932	Phi-N	154	78	76	.506	4				81.4	-3.4
1933	Phi-N	152	60	92	.395	7				60.7	-0.7
1934	Cin-N	1	1	0	1.000	8	8	8	2/3	0.4	0.6
1947	Bro-N	153	92	60	.605	●1	1		2/2	86.3	5.7

YEAR	TM/L	G	W	L	PCT	STANDING			M/Y	W-EXP	A-E
1948	Bro-N	81	48	33	.593	5	3		3/3	44.5	3.5
1949	Bro-N	156	97	57	.630	1				98.8	-1.8
1950	Bro-N	155	89	65	.578	2				88.6	0.4
	11	1469	697	764	.477						3.0
Showalter, William Nathaniel "Buck"											
1992	NY-A	162	76	86	.469	●4 E				79.7	-3.7
Silvestri, Kenneth Joseph "Ken"											
1967	Atl-N	3	0	3	.000	7	7		2/2	1.5	-1.5
Simmons, Joseph S. "Joe"											
1875	Wes-n*	13	1	12	.077	13				2.5	-1.5
1884	Wil-U	18	2	16	.111	8				0.8	1.2
	2	31	3	28	.097						-0.2
Simmons, Lewis "Lew"											
1886	Phi-a	98	41	55	.427	6	6		1/2	37.7	3.3
Sisler, George Harold											
1924	StL-A*	153	74	78	.487	4				72.3	1.7
1925	StL-A*	154	82	71	.536	3				76.0	6.0
1926	StL-A*	155	62	92	.403	7				61.4	0.6
	3	462	218	241	.475						8.3
Sisler, Richard Allan "Dick"											
1964	Cin-N	6	3	3	.500	3	4	●2	2/4	3.4	-0.4
	Cin-N	47	29	18	.617	3	●2		4/4	26.5	2.5
1965	Cin-N	162	89	73	.549	4				92.8	-3.8
	2	215	121	94	.563						-1.7
Skaff, Francis Michael "Frank"											
1966	Det-A	79	40	39	.506	2	3		3/3	40.5	-0.5
Skinner, Robert Ralph "Bob"											
1968	Phi-N	107	48	59	.449	5	●7		3/3	48.2	-0.2
1969	Phi-N	108	44	64	.407	5 E	5 E		1/2	47.2	-3.2
1977	SD-N	1	1	0	1.000	4 W	4 W	5 W	2/3	0.4	0.6
	3	216	93	123	.431						-2.7
Slattery, John Terrence "Jack"											
1928	Bos-N	31	11	20	.355	7	7		1/2	10.7	0.3
Smith, Edward Mayo "Mayo"											
1955	Phi-N	154	77	77	.500	4				77.9	-0.9
1956	Phi-N	154	71	83	.461	5				70.0	1.0
1957	Phi-N	156	77	77	.500	5				73.5	3.5
1958	Phi-N	84	39	45	.464	8	8		1/2	36.7	2.3
1959	Cin-N	80	35	45	.438	7	●5		1/2	41.3	-6.3
1967	Det-A	163	91	71	.562	●2				91.3	-0.3
1968	Det-A	164	103	59	.636	★1				101.2	1.8
1969	Det-A	162	90	72	.556	2 E				91.6	-1.6
1970	Det-A	162	79	83	.488	4 E				74.4	4.6
	9	1279	662	612	.520						4.0
Smith, George Henry "Heinie"											
1902	NY-N*	32	5	27	.156	4	8	8	2/3	11.0	-6.0
Smith, Harry Thomas											
1909	Bos-N*	79	23	54	.299	8	8		2/2	24.6	-1.6
Smith, William J. "Bill"											
1873	Mar-n*	5	0	5	.000	9				-3.9	3.9
Snyder, Charles N. "Pop"											
1882	Cin-a*	80	55	25	.688	1				61.6	-6.6
1883	Cin-a*	98	61	37	.622	3				71.6	-10.6
1884	Cin-a*	40	24	14	.632	5	5		2/2	26.5	-2.5
1891	Was-a*	70	23	46	.333	6	7	8	2/4	18.3	4.7
	4	288	163	122	.572						-14.9
Snyder, James Robert "Jim"											
1988	Sea-A	105	45	60	.429	6 W	7 W		2/2	47.2	-2.2
Sothoron, Allen Sutton											
1933	StL-A	8	2	6	.250	8	8	8	2/3	3.2	-1.2
Southworth, William Harrison "Billy"											
1929	StL-N*	90	43	45	.489	4	4		1/3	45.3	-2.3
1940	StL-N	111	69	40	.633	7	3		3/3	57.9	11.1
1941	StL-N	155	97	56	.634	2				91.4	5.6
1942	StL-N	156	106	48	.688	★1				106.1	-0.1
1943	StL-N	157	105	49	.682	1				99.6	5.4
1944	StL-N	157	105	49	.682	★1				106.8	-1.8
1945	StL-N	155	95	59	.617	2				94.7	0.3
1946	Bos-N	154	81	72	.529	4				80.5	0.5
1947	Bos-N	154	86	68	.558	3				85.1	0.9
1948	Bos-N	154	91	62	.595	1				92.4	-1.4
1949	Bos-N	111	55	54	.505	4	4		1/2	53.6	1.4
1950	Bos-N	156	83	71	.539	4				81.7	1.3
1951	Bos-N	60	28	31	.475	5	4		1/2	31.8	-3.8
	13	1770	1044	704	.597						17.1
Spalding, Albert Goodwill "Al"											
1876	Chi-N*	66	52	14	.788	1				63.1	-11.1
1877	Chi-N*	60	26	33	.441	5				28.7	-2.7
	2	126	78	47	.624						-13.9
Speaker, Tristram E "Tris"											
1919	Cle-A*	61	40	21	.656	3	2		2/2	35.0	5.0
1920	Cle-A*	154	98	56	.636	★1				97.7	0.3
1921	Cle-A*	154	94	60	.610	2				96.6	-2.6
1922	Cle-A*	155	78	76	.506	4				72.4	5.6

YEAR	TM/L	G	W	L	PCT	STANDING			M/Y	W-EXP	A-E
1923	Cle-A*	153	82	71	.536	3				89.5	-7.5
1924	Cle-A*	153	67	86	.438	6				71.0	-4.0
1925	Cle-A*	155	70	84	.455	6				73.7	-3.7
1926	Cle-A*	154	88	66	.571	2				89.8	-1.8
	8	1139	617	520	.543						-8.7

Spence, Harrison L. "Harry"

YEAR	TM/L	G	W	L	PCT	STANDING			M/Y	W-EXP	A-E
1888	Ind-N	136	50	85	.370	7				55.2	-5.2

Stahl, Charles Sylvester "Chick"

1906	Bos-A*	40	14	26	.350	8	8		2/2	13.1	0.9

Stahl, Garland "Jake"

1905	Was-A*	154	64	87	.424	7				68.6	-4.6
1906	Was-A*	151	55	95	.367	7				59.3	-4.3
1912	Bos-A*	154	105	47	.691	★1				101.9	3.1
1913	Bos-A*	81	39	41	.488	5	4		1/2	41.2	-2.2
	4	540	263	270	.493						-8.0

Stallings, George Tweedy

1897	Phi-N*	134	55	77	.417	10				62.5	-7.5
1898	Phi-N*	46	19	27	.413	●8	6		1/2	24.1	-5.1
1901	Det-A	136	74	61	.548	3				71.8	2.2
1909	NY-A	153	74	77	.490	5				75.8	-1.8
1910	NY-A	142	78	59	.569	3	2		1/2	75.3	2.7
1913	Bos-N	154	69	82	.457	5				70.5	-1.5
1914	Bos-N	158	94	59	.614	★1				88.3	5.7
1915	Bos-N	157	83	69	.546	2				80.1	2.9
1916	Bos-N	158	89	63	.586	3				86.6	2.4
1917	Bos-N	158	72	81	.471	6				74.7	-2.7
1918	Bos-N	124	53	71	.427	7				57.0	-4.0
1919	Bos-N	140	57	82	.410	6				58.6	-1.6
1920	Bos-N	153	62	90	.408	7				60.2	1.8
	13	1813	879	898	.495						-6.7

Stanky, Edward Raymond "Eddie"

1952	StL-N*	154	88	66	.571	3				81.8	6.2
1953	StL-N*	157	83	71	.539	●3				82.4	0.6
1954	StL-N	154	72	82	.468	6				77.8	-5.8
1955	StL-N	36	17	19	.472	5	7		1/2	15.6	1.4
1966	Chi-A	163	83	79	.512	4				87.6	-4.6
1967	Chi-A	162	89	73	.549	4				85.8	3.2
1968	Chi-A	79	34	45	.430	9	8		1/5	35.7	-1.7
1977	Tex-A	1	1	0	1.000	●3 W	3 W	2 W	2/4	0.6	0.4
	8	906	467	435	.518						-0.3

Start, Joseph "Joe"

1873	Mut-n*	25	18	7	.720	5	4		2/2	13.9	4.1

Stengel, Charles Dillon "Casey"

1934	Bro-N	153	71	81	.467	6				71.6	-0.6
1935	Bro-N	154	70	83	.458	5				71.1	-1.1
1936	Bro-N	156	67	87	.435	7				68.0	-1.0
1938	Bos-N	153	77	75	.507	'5				69.8	7.2
1939	Bos-N	152	63	88	.417	7				66.3	-3.3
1940	Bos-N	152	65	87	.428	7				63.8	1.2
1941	Bos-N	156	62	92	.403	7				63.8	-1.8
1942	Bos-N	150	59	89	.399	7				60.0	-1.0
1943	Bos-N	107	47	60	.439	6	6		2/2	41.9	5.1
1949	NY-A	155	97	57	.630	★1				95.7	1.3
1950	NY-A	155	98	56	.636	★1				97.8	0.2
1951	NY-A	154	98	56	.636	★1				94.5	3.5
1952	NY-A	154	95	59	.617	★1				94.7	0.3
1953	NY-A	151	99	52	.656	★1				101.0	-2.0
1954	NY-A	155	103	51	.669	2				101.4	1.6
1955	NY-A	154	96	58	.623	1				96.7	-0.7
1956	NY-A	154	97	57	.630	★1				98.8	-1.8
1957	NY-A	154	98	56	.636	1				96.8	1.2
1958	NY-A	155	92	62	.597	★1				95.6	-3.6
1959	NY-A	155	79	75	.513	3				81.1	-2.1
1960	NY-A	155	97	57	.630	1				89.0	8.0
1962	NY-N	161	40	120	.250	10				48.1	-8.1
1963	NY-N	162	51	111	.315	10				51.8	-0.8
1964	NY-N	163	53	109	.327	10				59.4	-6.4
1965	NY-N	96	31	64	.326	10	10		1/2	31.1	-0.1
	25	3766	1905	1842	.508						-4.8

Stovall, George Thomas

1911	Cle-A*	139	74	62	.544	7	3		2/2	66.1	7.9
1912	StL-A*	117	41	74	.357	8	7		2/2	41.1	-0.1
1913	StL-A*	135	50	84	.373	7	8		1/3	56.1	-6.1
1914	KC-F*	154	67	84	.444	6				71.5	-4.5
1915	KC-F*	153	81	72	.529	4				76.1	4.9
	5	698	313	376	.454						2.1

Stovey, Harry Duffield

1881	Wor-N*	27	8	18	.308	7	8		2/2	10.6	-2.6
1885	Phi-a*	113	55	57	.491	4				62.1	-7.1
	2	140	63	75	.457						-9.7

Street, Charles Evard "Gabby"

1929	StL-N	1	1	0	1.000	4	4	4	2/3	0.5	0.5
1930	StL-N	154	92	62	.597	1				96.4	-4.4
1931	StL-N*	154	101	53	.656	★1				96.8	4.2
1932	StL-N	156	72	82	.468	●6				73.7	-1.7
1933	StL-N	91	46	45	.505	5	5		1/2	50.3	-4.3
1938	StL-A	146	53	90	.371	7	7		1/2	53.9	-0.9

YEAR	TM/L	G	W	L	PCT	STANDING			M/Y	W-EXP	A-E
	6	702	365	332	.524						-6.6

Stricker, John A. "Cub"

1892(1)	StL-N*	23	6	17	.261	10	11	9	2/3	8.4	-2.4

Strickland, George Bevan

1964	Cle-A	73	33	39	.458	8	●6		1/2	35.8	-2.8
1966	Cle-A	39	15	24	.385	3	5		2/2	19.2	-4.2
	2	112	48	63	.432						-7.0

Stubing, Lawrence George "Moose"

1988	Cal-A	8	0	8	.000	4 W	4 W		2/2	3.7	-3.7

Sukeforth, Clyde Leroy

1947	Bro-N	2	2	0	1.000	●1	1		1/2	1.1	0.9

Sullivan, Haywood Cooper

1965	KC-A	136	54	82	.397	10	10		2/2	53.1	0.9

Sullivan, James Patrick "Pat"

1890	Col-a	3	2	1	.667	5	5	2	3/3	1.9	0.1

Sullivan, Timothy Paul "Ted"

1883	StL-a	79	53	26	.671	2	2		1/2	50.3	2.7
1884	StL-U	31	28	3	.903	1	1		1/2	26.6	1.4
	KC-U*	62	13	46	.220	8	8		3/3	9.1	3.9
1888	Was-N	96	38	57	.400	8	8		2/2	29.8	8.2
	3	268	132	132	.500						16.2

Sullivan, William Joseph Sr. "Billy"

1909	Chi-A*	159	78	74	.513	4				79.6	-1.6

Sweasy, Charles James "Charlie"

1875	RS-n*	19	4	15	.211	9				0.6	3.4

Swift, Robert Virgil "Bob"

1965	Det-A	42	24	18	.571	3	4		1/2	23.2	0.8
1966	Det-A	57	32	25	.561	3	2	3	2/3	29.2	2.8
	2	99	56	43	.566						3.6

Tanner, Charles William "Chuck"

1970	Chi-A	16	3	13	.188	6 W	6 W		3/3	6.1	-3.1
1971	Chi-A	162	79	83	.488	3 W				83.2	-4.2
1972	Chi-A	154	87	67	.565	2 W				80.1	6.9
1973	Chi-A	162	77	85	.475	5 W				75.5	1.5
1974	Chi-A	163	80	80	.500	4 W				76.2	3.8
1975	Chi-A	161	75	86	.466	5 W				75.5	-0.5
1976	Oak-A	161	87	74	.540	2 W				89.8	-2.8
1977	Pit-N	162	96	66	.593	2 E				88.0	8.0
1978	Pit-N	161	88	73	.547	2 E				85.4	2.6
1979	Pit-N	163	98	64	.605	★1 E				94.4	3.6
1980	Pit-N	162	83	79	.512	3 E				83.1	-0.1
1981(1)	Pit-N	49	25	23	.521	4 E					
(2)	Pit-N	54	21	33	.389	6 E				49.1	-3.1
1982	Pit-N	162	84	78	.519	4 E				83.8	0.2
1983	Pit-N	162	84	78	.519	2 E				82.2	1.8
1984	Pit-N	162	75	87	.463	6 E				86.3	-11.3
1985	Pit-N	161	57	104	.354	6 E				65.6	-8.6
1986	Atl-N	161	72	89	.447	6 W				69.7	2.3
1987	Atl-N	161	69	92	.429	5 W				72.6	-3.6
1988	Atl-N	39	12	27	.308	6 W	6 W		1/2	14.7	-2.7
	19	2738	1352	1381	.495						-9.6

Tappe, Elvin Walter "El"

1961	Chi-N	2	2	0	1.000	7	7	7	4/9	0.9	1.1
	Chi-N	79	35	43	.449	7	7	7	7/9	33.5	1.5
	Chi-N	16	5	11	.313	7	7		9/9	6.9	-1.9
1962	Chi-N	20	4	16	.200	9	9		1/3	7.6	-3.6
	2	117	46	70	.397						-2.9

Taylor, George J.

1884	Bro-a	109	40	64	.385	9				36.3	3.7

Taylor, James Wren "Zack"

1946	StL-A	31	13	17	.433	7	7		2/2	13.2	-0.2
1948	StL-A	155	59	94	.386	6				59.4	-0.4
1949	StL-A	155	53	101	.344	7				53.9	-0.9
1950	StL-A	154	58	96	.377	7				55.4	2.6
1951	StL-A	154	52	102	.338	8				50.9	1.1
	5	649	235	410	.364						2.2

Tebbetts, George Robert "Birdie"

1954	Cin-N	154	74	80	.481	5				73.7	0.3
1955	Cin-N	154	75	79	.487	5				84.5	-9.5
1956	Cin-N	155	91	63	.591	3				88.5	2.5
1957	Cin-N	154	80	74	.519	4				73.8	6.2
1958	Cin-N	113	52	61	.460	8	4		1/2	62.1	-10.1
1961	Mil-N	25	12	13	.480	3	4		2/2	13.4	-1.4
1962	Mil-N	162	86	76	.531	5				87.6	-1.6
1963	Cle-A	162	79	83	.488	●5				74.0	5.0
1964	Cle-A	91	46	44	.511	8	●6		2/2	44.8	1.2
1965	Cle-A	162	87	75	.537	5				86.3	0.7
1966	Cle-A	123	66	57	.537	3	5		1/2	60.5	5.5
	11	1455	748	705	.515						-1.3

Tebeau, Oliver Wendell "Patsy"

1890	Cle-P*	52	21	30	.412	7	7		2/2	20.0	1.0
1891	Cle-N*	73	31	40	.437	4	5		2/2	33.2	-2.2
1892(1)	Cle-N*	74	40	33	.548	5					
(2)	Cle-N*	79	53	23	.697	1				97.9	-4.9
1893	Cle-N*	129	73	55	.570	3				75.0	-2.0

YEAR	TM/L	G	W	L	PCT	STANDING			M/Y	W-EXP	A-E
1894	Cle-N*	130	68	61	.527	6				67.4	0.6
1895	Cle-N*	132	84	46	.646	2				81.7	2.3
1896	Cle-N*	135	80	48	.625	2				81.2	-1.2
1897	Cle-N*	132	69	62	.527	5				73.9	-4.9
1898	Cle-N*	156	81	68	.544	5				79.2	1.8
1899	StL-N*	155	84	67	.556	5				83.1	0.9
1900	StL-N*	92	42	50	.457	7	•5		1/2	45.8	-3.8
	11	1339	726	583	.555						-12.2
Tenace, Fury Gene "Gene"											
1991	Tor-A	33	19	14	.576	1 E	1 E	1 E	2/3	17.8	1.2
Tenney, Frederick "Fred"											
1905	Bos-N*	156	51	103	.331	7				48.3	2.7
1906	Bos-N*	152	49	102	.325	8				48.1	0.9
1907	Bos-N*	152	58	90	.392	7				57.7	0.3
1911	Bos-N*	156	44	107	.291	8				46.4	-2.4
	4	616	202	402	.334						1.5
Terry, William Harold "Bill"											
1932	NY-N*	114	55	59	.482	8	•6		2/2	60.5	-5.5
1933	NY-N*	156	91	61	.599	★1				89.4	1.6
1934	NY-N*	153	93	60	.608	2				94.4	-1.4
1935	NY-N*	156	91	62	.595	3				85.9	5.1
1936	NY-N*	154	92	62	.597	1				89.2	2.8
1937	NY-N	152	95	57	.625	1				89.2	5.8
1938	NY-N	152	83	67	.553	3				81.9	1.1
1939	NY-N	151	77	74	.510	5				77.3	-0.3
1940	NY-N	152	72	80	.474	6				76.4	-4.4
1941	NY-N	156	74	79	.484	5				72.6	1.4
	10	1496	823	661	.555						6.3
Thomas, Frederick L. "Fred"											
1887	Ind-N	29	11	18	.379	8	8	8	2/3	7.9	3.1
Thompson, Andrew M. "A. M."											
1884	Stp-U	9	2	6	.250	7				0.7	1.3
Tighe, John Thomas "Jack"											
1957	Det-A	154	78	76	.506	4				77.0	1.0
1958	Det-A	49	21	28	.429	8	5		1/2	26.3	-5.3
	2	203	99	104	.488						-4.3
Tinker, Joseph Bert "Joe"											
1913	Cin-N*	156	64	89	.418	7				65.2	-1.2
1914	Chi-F*	158	87	67	.565	2				88.6	-1.6
1915	Chi-F*	156	86	66	.566	1				87.1	-1.1
1916	Chi-N*	156	67	86	.438	5				74.1	-7.1
	4	626	304	308	.497						-10.9
Torborg, Jeffrey Allen "Jeff"											
1977	Cle-A	104	45	59	.433	5 E	5 E		2/2	47.9	-2.9
1978	Cle-A	159	69	90	.434	6 E				73.8	-4.8
1979	Cle-A	95	43	52	.453	6 E	6 E		1/2	44.9	-1.9
1989	Chi-A	161	69	92	.429	7 W				74.8	-5.8
1990	Chi-A	162	94	68	.580	2 W				86.2	7.8
1991	Chi-A	162	87	75	.537	2 W				88.8	-1.8
1992	NY-N	162	72	90	.444	5 E				75.2	-3.2
	7	1005	479	526	.477						-12.5
Torre, Joseph Paul "Joe"											
1977	NY-N*	117	49	68	.419	6 E	6 E		2/2	52.6	-3.6
1978	NY-N	162	66	96	.407	6 E				72.2	-6.2
1979	NY-N	163	63	99	.389	6 E				69.0	-6.0
1980	NY-N	162	67	95	.414	5 E				71.4	-4.4
1981(1)	NY-N	52	17	34	.333	5 E					
(2)	NY-N	53	24	28	.462	4 E				42.3	-1.3
1982	Atl-N	162	89	73	.549	1 W				84.7	4.3
1983	Atl-N	162	88	74	.543	2 W				91.9	-3.9
1984	Atl-N	162	80	82	.494	•2 W				78.6	1.4
1990	StL-N	58	24	34	.414	6 E	6 E		3/3	25.2	-1.2
1991	StL-N	162	84	78	.519	2 E				81.3	2.7
1992	StL-N	162	83	79	.512	3 E				83.9	-0.9
	11	1577	734	840	.466						-19.1
Tracewski, Richard Joseph "Dick"											
1979	Det-A	2	2	0	1.000	5 E	5 E	5 E	2/3	1.0	1.0
Traynor, Harold Joseph "Pie"											
1934	Pit-N*	100	47	52	.475	4	5		2/2	50.9	-3.9
1935	Pit-N*	153	86	67	.562	4				86.1	-0.1
1936	Pit-N	156	84	70	.545	4				85.3	-1.3
1937	Pit-N*	154	86	68	.558	3				82.9	3.1
1938	Pit-N	152	86	64	.573	2				82.8	3.2
1939	Pit-N	153	68	85	.444	6				71.0	-3.0
	6	868	457	406	.530						-1.9
Trebelhorn, Thomas Lynn "Tom"											
1986	Mil-A	9	6	3	.667	6 E	6 E		2/2	4.1	1.9
1987	Mil-A	162	91	71	.562	3 E				85.2	5.8
1988	Mil-A	162	87	75	.537	•3 E				88.0	-1.0
1989	Mil-A	162	81	81	.500	4 E				83.9	-2.9
1990	Mil-A	162	74	88	.457	6 E				78.2	-4.2
1991	Mil-A	162	83	79	.512	3 E				86.3	-3.3
	6	819	422	397	.515						-3.8
Trott, Samuel W. "Sam"											
1891	Was-a	12	4	7	.364	6	9		1/4	2.9	1.1

YEAR	TM/L	G	W	L	PCT	STANDING			M/Y	W-EXP	A-E
Turner, Robert Edward "Ted"											
1977	Atl-N	1	0	1	.000	6 W	6 W	6 W	2/4	0.4	-0.4
Unglaub, Robert Alexander "Bob"											
1907	Bos-A*	29	9	20	.310	6	8	7	3/4	12.4	-3.4
Valentine, Robert John "Bobby"											
1985	Tex-A	129	53	76	.411	7 W	7 W		2/2	50.8	2.2
1986	Tex-A	162	87	75	.537	2 W				83.7	3.3
1987	Tex-A	162	75	87	.463	•6 W				78.6	-3.6
1988	Tex-A	161	70	91	.435	6 W				70.4	-0.4
1989	Tex-A	162	83	79	.512	4 W				79.1	3.9
1990	Tex-A	162	83	79	.512	3 W				78.9	4.1
1991	Tex-A	162	85	77	.525	3 W				82.4	2.6
1992	Tex-A	86	45	41	.523	3 W	4 W		1/2	39.2	5.8
	8	1186	581	605	.490						17.8
Van Haltren, George Edward											
1892(1)	Bal-N*	11	1	10	.091	12	12		1/3	3.9	-2.9
Vernon, James Barton "Mickey"											
1961	Was-A	161	61	100	.379	•9				64.4	-3.4
1962	Was-A	162	60	101	.373	10				68.2	-8.2
1963	Was-A	40	14	26	.350	10	10		1/3	14.1	-0.1
	3	363	135	227	.373						-11.7
Virdon, William Charles "Bill"											
1972	Pit-N	155	96	59	.619	1 E				96.8	-0.8
1973	Pit-N	136	67	69	.493	2 E	3 E		1/2	68.9	-1.9
1974	NY-A	162	89	73	.549	2 E				86.1	2.9
1975	NY-A	104	53	51	.510	3 E	3 E		1/2	58.4	-5.4
	Hou-N	35	17	17	.500	6 W	6 W		2/2	16.0	1.0
1976	Hou-N	162	80	82	.494	3 W				77.6	2.4
1977	Hou-N	162	81	81	.500	3 W				84.1	-3.1
1978	Hou-N	162	74	88	.457	5 W				77.9	-3.9
1979	Hou-N	162	89	73	.549	2 W				81.1	7.9
1980	Hou-N	163	93	70	.571	▲1 W				86.8	6.2
1981(1)	Hou-N	57	28	29	.491	3 W					
(2)	Hou-N	53	33	20	.623	1 W				62.4	-1.4
1982	Hou-N	111	49	62	.441	5 W	5 W		1/2	51.6	-2.6
1983	Mon-N	163	82	80	.506	3 E				84.3	-2.3
1984	Mon-N	131	64	67	.489	5 E	5 E		1/2	66.2	-2.2
	13	1918	995	921	.519						-3.2
Vitt, Oscar Joseph "Ossie"											
1938	Cle-A	153	86	66	.566	3				82.0	4.0
1939	Cle-A	154	87	67	.565	3				86.3	0.7
1940	Cle-A	155	89	65	.578	2				84.4	4.6
	3	462	262	198	.570						9.3
Von Der Ahe, Christian Frederick Wilhelm "Chris"											
1895	StL-N	1	1	0	1.000	11	11	11	2/4	0.3	0.7
1896	StL-N	2	0	2	.000	10	11	11	3/5	0.5	-0.5
1897	StL-N	14	2	12	.143	12	12		4/4	2.5	-0.5
	3	17	3	14	.176						-0.4
Vukovich, John Christopher											
1986	Chi-N	2	1	1	.500	5 E	5 E	5 E	2/3	0.9	0.1
1988	Phi-N	9	5	4	.556	6 E	6 E		2/2	3.7	1.3
	2	11	6	5	.545						1.4
Wagner, Charles F. "Heinie"											
1930	Bos-A	154	52	102	.338	8				57.1	-5.1
Wagner, John Peter "Honus"											
1917	Pit-N*	5	1	4	.200	8	8	8	2/3	2.0	-1.0
Walker, Harry William											
1955	StL-N*	118	51	67	.432	5	7		2/2	51.2	-0.2
1965	Pit-N	163	90	72	.556	3				91.3	-1.3
1966	Pit-N	162	92	70	.568	3				93.0	-1.0
1967	Pit-N	84	42	42	.500	6	6		1/2	41.2	0.8
1968	Hou-N	101	49	52	.485	10	10		2/2	44.9	4.1
1969	Hou-N	162	81	81	.500	5 W				81.8	-0.8
1970	Hou-N	162	79	83	.488	4 W				79.1	-0.1
1971	Hou-N	162	79	83	.488	•4 W				83.0	-4.0
1972	Hou-N	121	67	54	.554	2 W	2 W		1/3	66.3	0.7
	9	1235	630	604	.511						-1.9
Wallace, Roderick John "Bobby"											
1911	StL-A*	152	45	107	.296	8				51.6	-6.6
1912	StL-A*	40	12	27	.308	8	7		1/2	13.9	-1.9
1937	Cin-N	25	5	20	.200	8	8		2/2	10.9	-5.9
	3	217	62	154	.287						-14.4
Walsh, Edward Augustine "Ed"											
1924	Chi-A	3	1	2	.333	6			2/4	1.4	-0.4
Walsh, Michael John "Mike"											
1884	Lou-a	110	68	40	.630	3				68.7	-0.7
Walters, William Henry "Bucky"											
1948	Cin-N*	53	20	33	.377	7	7		2/2	20.7	-0.7
1949	Cin-N	153	61	90	.404	7	7		1/2	61.4	-0.4
	2	206	81	123	.397						-1.2
Waltz, John J.											
1892(1)	Bal-N	8	2	6	.250	12	12	12	2/3	2.9	-0.9
Ward, John Montgomery "Monte"											
1880	Pro-N*	32	18	13	.581	4	3	2	2/3	20.1	-2.1
1884	NY-N*	16	6	8	.429	4	•4		2/2	7.8	-1.8

YEAR	TM/L	G	W	L	PCT	STANDING	M/Y	W-EXP	A-E
1890	Bro-P*	133	76	56	.576	2		71.7	4.3
1891	Bro-N*	137	61	76	.445	6		63.6	-2.6
1892(1)	Bro-N*	78	51	26	.662	2			
(2)	Bro-N*	80	44	33	.571	3		95.7	-0.7
1893	NY-N*	136	68	64	.515	5		73.9	-5.9
1894	NY-N*	139	88	44	.667	2		78.8	9.2
	7	751	412	320	.563				0.4
Wathan, John David									
1987	KC-A	36	21	15	.583	4 W 2 W	2/2	18.5	2.5
1988	KC-A	161	84	77	.522	3 W		86.3	-2.3
1989	KC-A	162	92	70	.568	2 W		86.8	5.2
1990	KC-A	161	75	86	.466	6 W		80.3	-5.3
1991	KC-A	37	15	22	.405	7 W 6 W	1/3	18.6	-3.6
1992	Cal-A	89	39	50	.438	5 W 5 W ●5 W	2/3	39.0	-0.0
	6	646	326	320	.505				-3.6
Watkins, Harvey L.									
1895	NY-N	35	18	17	.514	9 9	3/3	17.9	0.1
Watkins, William Henry "Bill"									
1884	Ind-a*	23	4	18	.182	10 11	2/2	5.6	-1.6
1885	Det-N	70	34	36	.486	8 6	2/2	30.8	3.2
1886	Det-N	126	87	36	.707	2		88.0	-1.0
1887	Det-N	127	79	45	.637	1		83.0	-4.0
1888	Det-N	94	49	44	.527	3 5	1/2	52.7	-3.7
	KC-a	25	8	17	.320	8 8	3/3	7.1	0.9
1889	KC-a	139	55	82	.401	7		53.9	1.1
1893	StL-N	135	57	75	.432	10		58.6	-1.6
1898	Pit-N	151	72	76	.486	8		67.9	4.1
1899	Pit-N	24	7	15	.318	10 7	1/2	11.9	-4.9
	9	914	452	444	.504				-7.6
Weaver, Earl Sidney									
1968	Bal-A	82	48	34	.585	3 2	2/2	45.8	2.2
1969	Bal-A	162	109	53	.673	♦1 E		108.8	0.2
1970	Bal-A	162	108	54	.667	★1 E		103.5	4.5
1971	Bal-A	158	101	57	.639	♦1 E		101.4	-0.4
1972	Bal-A	154	80	74	.519	3 E		87.8	-7.8
1973	Bal-A	162	97	65	.599	1 E		101.3	-4.3
1974	Bal-A	162	91	71	.562	1 E		86.0	5.0
1975	Bal-A	159	90	69	.566	2 E		93.4	-3.4
1976	Bal-A	162	88	74	.543	2 E		83.3	4.7
1977	Bal-A	161	97	64	.602	●2 E		87.3	9.7
1978	Bal-A	161	90	71	.559	4 E		83.3	6.7
1979	Bal-A	159	102	57	.642	♦1 E		97.6	4.4
1980	Bal-A	162	100	62	.617	2 E		97.6	2.4
1981(1)	Bal-A	54	31	23	.574	2 E			
(2)	Bal-A	51	28	23	.549	4 E		51.7	7.3
1982	Bal-A	163	94	68	.580	2 E		89.7	4.3
1985	Bal-A	105	53	52	.505	4 E 4 E	3/3	55.9	-2.9
1986	Bal-A	162	73	89	.451	7 E		75.8	-2.8
	17	2541	1480	1060	.583				29.9
Westrum, Wesley Noreen "Wes"									
1965	NY-N	68	19	48	.284	10 10	2/2	21.9	-2.9
1966	NY-N	161	66	95	.410	9		62.5	3.5
1967	NY-N	151	57	94	.377	10 10	1/2	57.4	-0.4
1974	SF-N	86	38	48	.442	5 W 5 W	2/2	38.1	-0.1
1975	SF-N	161	80	81	.497	3 W		79.2	0.8
	5	627	260	366	.415				0.9
Wheeler, Harry Eugene									
1884	KC-U*	4	0	4	.000	8 8	1/3	0.6	-0.6
White, James Laurie "Deacon"									
1872	Cle-n*	2	0	2	.000	5 7	2/2	0.5	-0.5
1879	Cin-N*	18	9	9	.500	4 5	1/2	9.4	-0.4
	2	20	9	11	.450				-0.9
White, Joyner Clifford "Jo-Jo"									
1960	Cle-A	1	1	0	1.000	4 4 4	2/3	0.5	0.5
White, William Henry "Will"									
1884	Cin-a*	72	44	27	.620	5	1/2	49.6	-5.6
White, William Warren "Warren"									
1874	Bal-n*	47	9	38	.191	8		2.4	6.6
Wilber, Delbert Quentin "Del"									
1973	Tex-A	1	1	0	1.000	6 W 6 W 6 W	2/3	0.4	0.6
Wilhelm, Irvin Key "Kaiser"									
1921	Phi-N*	67	26	41	.388	8 8	2/2	21.0	5.0
1922	Phi-N	154	57	96	.373	7		59.9	-2.9
	2	221	83	137	.377				2.1
Williams, James A. "Jimmy"									
1884	StL-a	85	51	33	.607	5 4	1/2	50.5	0.5
1887	Cle-a	133	39	92	.298	8		34.6	4.4
1888	Cle-a	64	20	44	.313	8 6	1/2	23.8	-3.8
	3	282	110	169	.394				1.1
Williams, James Francis "Jimy"									
1986	Tor-A	163	86	76	.531	4 E		88.4	-2.4
1987	Tor-A	162	96	66	.593	2 E		99.7	-3.7
1988	Tor-A	162	87	75	.537	●3 E		89.3	-2.3
1989	Tor-A	36	12	24	.333	6 E 1 E	1/2	19.8	-7.8
	4	523	281	241	.538				-16.3

YEAR	TM/L	G	W	L	PCT	STANDING	M/Y	W-EXP	A-E
Williams, Richard Hirschfeld "Dick"									
1967	Bos-A	162	92	70	.568	1		92.3	-0.3
1968	Bos-A	162	86	76	.531	4		81.3	4.7
1969	Bos-A	153	82	71	.536	3 E 3 E	1/2	77.2	4.8
1971	Oak-A	161	101	60	.627	1 W		94.1	6.9
1972	Oak-A	155	93	62	.600	★1 W		94.4	-1.4
1973	Oak-A	162	94	68	.580	★1 W		95.7	-1.7
1974	Cal-A	84	36	48	.429	6 W 6 W	3/3	39.8	-3.8
1975	Cal-A	161	72	89	.447	6 W		70.7	1.3
1976	Cal-A	96	39	57	.406	6 W ●4 W	1/2	42.7	-3.7
1977	Mon-N	162	75	87	.463	5 E		73.8	1.2
1978	Mon-N	162	76	86	.469	4 E		83.4	-7.4
1979	Mon-N	160	95	65	.594	2 E		92.7	2.3
1980	Mon-N	162	90	72	.556	2 E		87.8	2.2
1981(1)	Mon-N	55	30	25	.545	3 E			
(2)	Mon-N	26	14	12	.538	2 E 1 E	1/2	44.5	-0.5
1982	SD-N	162	81	81	.500	4 W		82.8	-1.8
1983	SD-N	163	81	81	.500	4 W		81.0	0.0
1984	SD-N	162	92	70	.568	♦1 W		86.5	5.5
1985	SD-N	162	83	79	.512	●3 W		84.0	-1.0
1986	Sea-A	133	58	75	.436	6 W 7 W	3/3	57.2	0.8
1987	Sea-A	162	78	84	.481	4 W		77.0	1.0
1988	Sea-A	56	23	33	.411	6 W 7 W	1/2	25.2	-2.2
	21	3023	1571	1451	.520				7.0
Williams, Theodore Samuel "Ted"									
1969	Was-A	162	86	76	.531	4 E		86.2	-0.2
1970	Was-A	162	70	92	.432	6 E		74.4	-4.4
1971	Was-A	159	63	96	.396	5 E		66.1	-3.1
1972	Tex-A	154	54	100	.351	6 W		58.2	-4.2
	4	637	273	364	.429				-11.8
Wills, Maurice Morning "Maury"									
1980	Sea-A	58	20	38	.345	6 W 7 W	2/2	22.3	-2.3
1981(1)	Sea-A	25	6	18	.250	7 W 6 W	1/2		
	2	83	26	56	.317				-2.3
Wilson, James "Jimmie"									
1934	Phi-N*	149	56	93	.376	7		63.1	-7.1
1935	Phi-N*	156	64	89	.418	7		58.8	5.2
1936	Phi-N*	154	54	100	.351	8		63.2	-9.2
1937	Phi-N*	155	61	92	.399	7		62.9	-1.9
1938	Phi-N*	149	45	103	.304	8 8	1/2	45.7	-0.7
1941	Chi-N	155	70	84	.455	6		76.6	-6.6
1942	Chi-N	155	68	86	.442	6		69.2	-1.2
1943	Chi-N	154	74	79	.484	5		79.9	-5.9
1944	Chi-N	10	1	9	.100	8 4	1/3	5.2	-4.2
	9	1237	493	735	.401				-31.7
Wine, Robert Paul Sr. "Bobby"									
1985	Atl-N	41	16	25	.390	5 W 5 W	2/2	16.7	-0.7
Wingo, Ivey Brown									
1916	Cin-N*	2	1	1	.500	8 8 ●7	2/3	0.8	0.2
Winkles, Bobby Brooks									
1973	Cal-A	162	79	83	.488	4 W		78.0	1.0
1974	Cal-A	75	30	44	.405	6 W 6 W	1/3	35.1	-5.1
1977	Oak-A	108	37	71	.343	●5 W 7 W	2/2	44.0	-7.0
1978	Oak-A	39	24	15	.615	1 W 6 W	1/2	15.3	8.7
	4	384	170	213	.444				-2.5
Wolf, William Van Winkle "Chicken"									
1889	Lou-a*	65	14	51	.215	8 8 8	2/4	14.0	-0.0
Wolverton, Harry Sterling									
1912	NY-A*	153	50	102	.329	8		55.5	-5.5
Wood, George A.									
1891	Phi-a*	125	67	55	.549	7 4	2/2	62.8	4.2
Wood, James Leon "Jimmy"									
1871	Chi-n*	28	19	9	.679	2		18.2	0.8
1872	Tro-n*	25	15	10	.600	5		18.2	-3.2
	Eck-n*	18	3	15	.167	10 9	2/2	-2.0	5.0
1873	Phi-n*	43	28	15	.651	2 2	2/2	29.1	-1.1
1874	Chi-n	23	10	13	.435	4 5	2/2	9.6	0.4
1875	Chi-n	69	30	37	.448	6		30.2	-0.2
	5	206	105	99	.515				1.7
Wright, Alfred Hector "Al"									
1876	Phi-N	60	14	45	.237	7		17.5	-3.5
Wright, George									
1879	Pro-N*	85	59	25	.702	1		64.9	-5.9
Wright, William Henry "Harry"									
1871	Bos-n*	31	20	10	.667	3		21.2	-1.2
1872	Bos-n*	48	39	8	.830	1		45.0	-6.0
1873	Bos-n*	60	43	16	.729	1		48.2	-5.2
1874	Bos-n*	71	52	18	.743	1		58.9	-6.9
1875	Bos-n*	82	71	8	.899	1		78.2	-7.2
1876	Bos-N*	70	39	31	.557	4		36.7	2.3
1877	Bos-N*	61	42	18	.700	1		44.0	-2.0
1878	Bos-N	60	41	19	.683	1		35.7	5.3
1879	Bos-N	84	54	30	.643	2		61.5	-7.5
1880	Bos-N	86	40	44	.476	6		38.2	1.8
1881	Bos-N	83	38	45	.458	6		35.4	2.6
1882	Pro-N	84	52	32	.619	2		52.3	-0.3

YEAR	TM/L	G	W	L	PCT	STANDING			M/Y	W-EXP	A-E
1883	Pro-N	98	58	40	.592	3				67.1	-9.1
1884	Phi-N	113	39	73	.348	6				32.3	6.7
1885	Phi-N	111	56	54	.509	3				55.2	0.8
1886	Phi-N	119	71	43	.623	4				69.0	2.0
1887	Phi-N	128	75	48	.610	2				78.4	-3.4
1888	Phi-N	132	69	61	.531	3				67.8	1.2
1889	Phi-N	130	63	64	.496	3				63.0	0.0
1890	Phi-N	22	14	8	.636	1	3		1/5	12.7	1.3
	Phi-N	46	22	23	.489	2	3		5/5	26.0	-4.0
1891	Phi-N	138	68	69	.496	4				67.0	1.0
1892(1)	Phi-N	77	46	30	.605	3					
(2)	Phi-N	78	41	36	.532	5				92.6	-5.6
1893	Phi-N	133	72	57	.558	4				78.2	-6.2
	23	2145	1225	885	.581						-39.7

York, Preston Rudolph "Rudy"

YEAR	TM/L	G	W	L	PCT	STANDING			M/Y	W-EXP	A-E
1959	Bos-A	1	0	1	.000	8	8	5	2/3	0.5	-0.5

York, Thomas J. "Tom"

YEAR	TM/L	G	W	L	PCT	STANDING			M/Y	W-EXP	A-E
1878	Pro-N*	62	33	27	.550	3				31.4	1.6
1881	Pro-N*	34	23	10	.697	4	2		2/2	17.3	5.7
	2	96	56	37	.602						7.3

Yost, Edward Frederick "Eddie"

YEAR	TM/L	G	W	L	PCT	STANDING			M/Y	W-EXP	A-E
1963	Was-A	1	0	1	.000	10	10	10	2/3	0.4	-0.4

Young, Denton True "Cy"

YEAR	TM/L	G	W	L	PCT	STANDING			M/Y	W-EXP	A-E
1907	Bos-A*	6	3	3	.500	●4	7		1/4	2.6	0.4

Young, Nicholas Ephraim "Nick"

YEAR	TM/L	G	W	L	PCT	STANDING			M/Y	W-EXP	A-E
1871	Oly-n	32	15	15	.500	5				15.5	-0.5
1872	Oly-n	9	2	7	.222	10				-1.1	3.1
1873	Was-n	39	8	31	.205	7				5.8	2.2
	3	80	25	53	.321						4.7

Zimmer, Charles Louis "Chief"

YEAR	TM/L	G	W	L	PCT	STANDING			M/Y	W-EXP	A-E
1903	Phi-N*	139	49	86	.363	7				55.9	-6.9

Zimmer, Donald William "Don"

YEAR	TM/L	G	W	L	PCT	STANDING			M/Y	W-EXP	A-E
1972	SD-N	142	54	88	.380	4 W	6 W		2/2	53.0	1.0
1973	SD-N	162	60	102	.370	6 W				57.6	2.4
1976	Bos-A	76	42	34	.553	5 E	3 E		2/2	40.7	1.3
1977	Bos-A	161	97	64	.602	●2 E				94.6	2.4
1978	Bos-A	163	99	64	.607	▲2 E				95.5	3.5
1979	Bos-A	160	91	69	.569	3 E				92.5	-1.5
1980	Bos-A	155	82	73	.529	3 E	4 E		1/2	76.6	5.4
1981(1)	Tex-A	55	33	22	.600	2 W					
(2)	Tex-A	50	24	26	.480	3 W				59.2	-2.2
1982	Tex-A	96	38	58	.396	6 W	6 W		1/2	38.2	-0.2
1988	Chi-N	163	77	85	.475	4 E				77.5	-0.5
1989	Chi-N	162	93	69	.574	1 E				89.3	3.7
1990	Chi-N	162	77	85	.475	●4 E				72.6	4.4
1991	Chi-N	37	18	19	.486	4 E	4 E		1/3	17.6	0.4
	13	1744	885	858	.508						20.1

Biographical Data for Managers Not Appearing in the Player/Pitcher Registers

BILL ADAIR   Adair, Marion Danne   b: 2/10/13, Mobile, Ala.
BILL ARMOUR   Armour, William Clark   b: 9/3/1869, Homestead, Pa.   d: 12/2/22, Minneapolis, Minn.
FRANK BANCROFT   Bancroft, Frank Carter   b: 5/9/1846, Lancaster, Mass.   d: 3/30/21, Cincinnati, Ohio
ED BARROW   Barrow, Edward Grant "Cousin Ed"   b: 5/10/1868, Springfield, Ill.   d: 12/15/53, Port Chester, N.Y.
JOHN BENJAMIN   Benjamin, John W.   b: 1835, Elizabeth, N.J.   d: 11/14/1895, Elizabeth, N.J.
HUGO BEZDEK   Bezdek, Hugo Frank   b: 4/1/1884, Prague, Czech'Kia   d: 9/19/52, Atlantic City, N.J.
BICKERSON   Bickerson
DAVE BRISTOL   Bristol, James David   b: 6/23/33, Macon, Ga.
FREEMAN BROWN   Brown, Freeman   b: 1/31/1845, Hubbardstown, Mass   d: 12/27/16, Worcester, Mass.
AL BUCKENBERGER   Buckenberger, Albert C.   b: 1/31/1861, Detroit, Mich.   d: 7/1/17, Syracuse, N.Y.
GEORGE BURNHAM   Burnham, George Walter "Watch"   b: 5/20/1860, Albion, Mich.   d: 11/18/02, Detroit, Mich.
ORMOND BUTLER   Butler, Ormond Hook   b: 11/1854, West Virginia   d: 9/12/15, Mt.Hope, Md.
CHARLIE BYRNE   Byrne, Charles H.   b: 9/1843, New York, N.Y.   d: 1/4/1898, New York, N.Y.
BILL CAMMEYER   Cammeyer, William Henry   b: 3/20/1821, New York, N.Y.   d: 9/4/1898, New York, N.Y.
JOE CANTILLON   Cantillon, Joseph D. "Pongo Joe"   b: 8/19/1861, Janesville, Wis.   d: 1/31/30, Hickman, Ky.
O. P. CAYLOR   Caylor, Oliver Perry   b: 12/17/1849, Near Dayton, Ohio   d: 10/19/1897, Winona, Minn.
ED CURTIS   Curtis, Edwin R.
CHARLIE CUSHMAN   Cushman, Charles H.   b: 5/25/1850, New York, N.Y.   d: 6/29/09, Milwaukee, Wis.
MORDECAI DAVIDSON   Davidson, Mordecai H.   b: 11/30/1846, Port Washington, O   d: 9/6/40, Louisville, Ky.
JOHN DAY   Day, John B.   b: 9/23/47, Colchester, Mass.   d: 1/25/25, Cliffside, N.J.
HARRY DIDDLEBOCK   Diddlebock, Henry H.   b: 6/27/1854, Philadelphia, Pa.   d: 2/5/1900, Philadelphia, Pa.
CHARLIE EBBETS   Ebbets, Charles Hercules   b: 10/29/1859, New York, N.Y.   d: 4/18/25, New York, N.Y.
WALLACE FESSENDEN   Fessenden, Wallace Clifton   b: Watertown, Mass.
HORACE FOGEL   Fogel, Horace S.   b: 3/2/1861, Macungie, Pa.   d: 11/15/28, Philadelphia, Pa.
GEORGE FRAZER   Frazer, George Kasson   b: 1/7/1861, Syracuse, N.Y.   d: 2/5/13, Philadelphia, Pa.
JIM FREY   Frey, James Gottfried   b: 5/26/31, Cleveland, Ohio
JUDGE FUCHS   Fuchs, Emil Edmund   b: 4/17/1878, Hamburg, Germany   d: 12/5/61, Boston, Mass.
JOHN GAFFNEY   Gaffney, John H.   b: 6/29/1855, Roxbury, Mass.   d: 8/8/13, New York, N.Y.
DAVE GARCIA   Garcia, David   b: 9/15/20, E.St.Louis, Mo.
JIM GIFFORD   Gifford, James H.   b: 10/18/1845, Warren, N.Y.   d: 12/19/01, Columbus, Ohio
MASE GRAFFEN   Graffen, Samuel Mason   b: 1845, Philadelphia, Pa.   d: 11/18/1883, Silver City, N.Mex
CHARLIE HACKETT   Hackett, Charles M.   b: 1855, Lee, Mass.   d: 8/1/1898, Holyoke, Mass.
JIM HART   Hart, James Aristotle   b: 7/10/1855, Fairview, Pa.   d: 7/18/19, Chicago, Ill.
JOHN HART   Hart, John Henry (born John Henry Reen)   b: 7/21/48, Tampa, Fla.
LOUIE HEILBRONER   Heilbroner, Louis Wilbur   b: 7/4/1861, Ft.Wayne, Ind.   d: 12/21/33, Ft.Wayne, Ind.
BILL HENDERSON   Henderson, William C.
ED HENGLE   Hengle, Edward Siegfried   b: Chicago, Ill.   d: 11/4/27, Norwich, England
WALTER HEWETT   Hewett, Walter F.   b: 1861, Washington, D.C.   d: 10/7/44, Washington, D.C.
VEDIE HIMSL   Himsl, Avitus Bernard   b: 4/2/17, Plevna, Mont.
FRED HOEY   Hoey, Frederick C.   b: New York, N.Y.   d: 12/7/33, Paris, France
GEORGE HUFF   Huff, George A. "Gee"   b: 6/11/1872, Cahmpaign, Ill.   d: 10/1/36, Champaign, Ill.
TIM HURST   Hurst, Timothy Carroll   b: 6/30/1865, Ashland, Pa.   d: 6/4/15, Pottsville, Pa.
JOHNNY KEANE   Keane, John Joseph   b: 11/3/11, St.Louis, Mo.   d: 1/6/67, Houston, Tex.
JIM KENNEDY   Kennedy, James C.   b: 1867, New York, N.Y.   d: 4/20/04, Brighton Beach, N.Y.
JACK KROL   Krol, John Thomas   b: 7/5/36, Chicago, Ill.
KARL KUEHL   Kuehl, Karl Otto   b: 9/9/37, Monterey Park, Cal.
BOB LEADLEY   Leadley, Robert H.   b: 1858, Brooklyn, N.Y.
JIM LEYLAND   Leyland, James Richard   b: 12/15/44, Toledo, Ohio
NICK LEYVA   Leyva, Nicolas Tomas   b: 8/16/53, Ontario, Cal.
FRANK LUCCHESI   Lucchesi, Frank Joseph   b: 4/24/27, San Francisco, Cal.
JACK McCALLISTER   McCallister, John   b: 1/19/1879, Marietta, Ohio   d: 10/18/46, Columbus, Ohio
JOE McCARTHY   McCarthy, Joseph Vincent "Marse Joe"   b: 4/21/1887, Philadelphia, Pa.   d: 1/13/78, Buffalo, N.Y.
JOHN McCLOSKEY   McCloskey, John Joseph "Honest John"   b: 4/4/1862, Louisville, Ky.   d: 11/17/40, Louisville, Ky.
MEL McGAHA   McGaha, Fred Melvin   b: 9/26/26, Bastrop, La.
JACK McKEON   McKeon, John Aloysius   b: 11/23/30, South Amboy, N.J.
DENNY McKNIGHT   McKnight, Dennis Hamar   b: 1847, Pittsburgh, Pa.   d: 5/5/1900, Pittsburgh, Pa.
GEORGE McMANUS   McManus, George   b: 1846, Ireland   d: 10/2/18, New York, N.Y.
JOHN McNAMARA   McNamara, John Francis   b: 6/4/32, Sacramento, Cal.
STUMP MERRILL   Merrill, Carl Harrison   b: 2/25/44, Brunswick, Me.
RAY MILLER   Miller, Raymond Roger   b: 4/30/45, Takoma Park, Md.

FELIX MOSES   Moses, Felix I.   b: Richmond, Va.
BILLY MURRAY   Murray, William Jeremiah   b: 4/13/1864, Peabody, Mass.   d: 3/25/37, Youngstown, Ohio
JIM MUTRIE   Mutrie, James J. "Truthful Jim"   b: 6/13/1851, Chelsea, Mass.   d: 1/24/38, New York, N.Y.
PAUL OWENS   Owens, Paul Francis   b: 2/7/24, Salamanca, N.Y.
DANNY OZARK   Ozark, Daniel Leonard (born Daniel Leonard Orzechowski)   b: 11/26/23, Buffalo, N.Y.
LEW PHELAN   Phelan, Lewis G.
LEFTY PHILLIPS   Phillips, Harold Ross   b: 6/16/19, Los Angeles, Cal.   d: 6/12/72, Fullerton, Cal.
HORACE PHILLIPS   Phillips, Horace B.   b: 5/14/1853, Salem, Ohio
EDDIE POPOWSKI   Popowski, Edward Joseph   b: 8/20/13, Sayerville, N.J.
PAT POWERS   Powers, Patrick Thomas   b: 6/27/1860, Trenton, N.J.   d: 8/29/25, Belmar, N.J.
JIM PRICE   Price, James L.   b: 1847, New York, N.Y.   d: 10/6/31, Chicago, Ill.
VERN RAPP   Rapp, Vernon Fred   b: 5/11/28, St.Louis, Mo.
GREG RIDDOCH   Riddoch, Gregory Lee   b: 7/17/45, Greeley, Colo.
JIM RIGGLEMAN   Riggleman, James David   b: 11/9/52, Fort Dix, N.J.
CAL RIPKEN   Ripken, Calvin Edwin Sr.   b: 12/17/35, Aberdeen, Md.
STAN ROBISON   Robison, Matthew Stanley   b: 3/30/1859, Pittsburgh, Pa.   d: 3/24/11, Cleveland, Ohio
PANTS ROWLAND   Rowland, Clarence Henry   b: 2/12/1879, Platteville, Wis.   d: 5/17/69, Chicago, Ill.
EDDIE SAWYER   Sawyer, Edwin Milby   b: 9/10/10, Westerly, R.I.
MIKE SCANLON   Scanlon, Michael B.   b: 1847, Cork, Ireland   d: 1/18/29, Washington, D.C.
BOB SCHAEFER   Schaefer, Robert Wald   b: 5/22/44, Putnam, Conn.   5'11", 180 lbs.   Deb: 5/22/91   M
GUS SCHMELZ   Schmelz, Gustavius Heinrich   b: 9/26/1850, Columbus, Ohio   d: 10/13/25, Columbus, Ohio
FRANK SELEE   Selee, Frank Gibson   b: 10/26/1859, Amherst, N.Y.   d: 7/5/09, Denver, Colo.
BILL SHARSIG   Sharsig, William A.   b: 1855, Philadelphia, Pa.   d: 2/1/02, Philadelphia, Pa.
LARRY SHEPARD   Shepard, Lawrence William   b: 4/3/19, Lakewood, Ohio
BILL SHETTSLINE   Shettsline, William Joseph   b: 10/25/1863, Philadelphia, Pa.   d: 2/22/33, Philadelphia, Pa.
BUCK SHOWALTER   Showalter, William Nathaniel   b: 5/23/57, DeFuniak Springs, Fla.
LEW SIMMONS   Simmons, Lewis   b: 8/27/1838, New Castle, Pa.   d: 9/2/11, Jamestown, Pa.
HARRY SPENCE   Spence, Harrison L.   b: 1858, Virginia   d: 5/17/08, Chicago, Ill.
PAT SULLIVAN   Sullivan, James Patrick   d: 5/22/1898.
GEORGE TAYLOR   Taylor, George J.   b: 11/22/1853, New York
FRED THOMAS   Thomas, Frederick L.   b: Indiana
JACK TIGHE   Tighe, John Thomas   b: 8/9/13, Kearny, N.J.
TOM TREBELHORN   Trebelhorn, Thomas Lynn   b: 1/27/48, Portland, Ore.
TED TURNER   Turner, Robert Edward   b: 11/19/38, Cincinnati, Ohio
CHRIS VonDER AHE   Von Der Ahe, Christian Frederick Wilhelm   b: 11/7/1851, Hille, Germany   d: 6/7/13, St.Louis, Mo.
MIKE WALSH   Walsh, Michael John   b: 4/29/1850, Ireland   d: 2/2/29, Louisville, Ky.
JOHN WALTZ   Waltz, John J.
HARVEY WATKINS   Watkins, Harvey L.
EARL WEAVER   Weaver, Earl Sidney   b: 8/14/30, St.Louis, Mo.
JIMMY WILLIAMS   Williams, James Andrews   b: 1/3/1848, Columbus, Ohio   d: 10/24/18, N.Hempstead, N.Y.
BOBBY WINKLES   Winkles, Bobby Brooks   b: 3/11/30, Tuckerman, Ark.
AL WRIGHT   Wright, Alfred Hector   b: 3/30/1842, Cedar Grove, N.J.   d: 4/20/05, New York, N.Y.
NICK YOUNG   Young, Nicholas Ephraim   b: 9/12/1840, Amsterdam, N.Y.   d: 10/31/16, Washington, D.C.

The Coach Roster

In an age of ever greater specialization in baseball, coaches have become increasingly important to the successful management of a team. The need for such assistance did not occur to any manager until John McGraw took on Arlie Latham as baseball's first full-time coach in 1909; today, teams employ separate coaches for first base, third base, pitching, the bullpen, hitting, baserunning, strength, conditioning, and more. Some coaches, like Charlie Lau and Roger Craig, have achieved fame exceeding that of the managers under whom they served. But coaches leave no statistical trail by which to track them. Players and pitchers have official records, and so do managers, but the accomplishments of coaches (and umpires) have until now resided largely in memory.

In the first edition of *Total Baseball,* the Coach Roster that follows represented a first attempt in a baseball encyclopedia to recognize these foot soldiers, who too often serve as scapegoats when a team fails but are invisible when it succeeds. We offered the roster in full knowledge that there were gaps and probably gaffes in our research; we hoped that our readers would advise us of omissions so that we could improve this roster in future editions of *Total Baseball*—and they have. A new feature is the addition of not only many names, but also full biographical data for all coaches who did not play at the major-league level and so are absent from the Registers.

The principal sources of the data herein are, for 1921–1939, the *Baseball Blue Book*; for 1940–1981, the *Baseball Register*, and for years since 1982, the *American League Red Book* and the *National League Green Book*. We have done our best to reconcile the many differences among the lists. The team and league abbreviations used in the Coach Roster are found on the final pages of this book.

For a prose account of the history of coaches (and managers), see the preceding article by Fred Stein.

Aaron, Tommie Lee   Atl-N 1979-83
Abbott, Spencer   Was-A 1935
Adair, James A. "Jimmy"   Chi-A 1951-52,
   Bal-A 1957-61, Hou-N 1962-65
Adair, K. Jerry   Oak-A 1972-74, Cal-A 1975
Adair, Marion D. "Bill"   Mil-N 1962, Atl-N 1967,
   Chi-A 1970, Mon-N 1976
Adair, M. Richard "Rick"   Cle-A 1992
Adams, Charles D. "Red"   LA-N 1969-80
Adams, Robert H. "Bobby"   Chi-N 1961-64
Aguirre, Henry J. "Hank"   Chi-N 1972-74
Aker, Jackie D. "Jack"   Cle-A 1985-87
Alfonso, Carlos   SF-N 1992
Allenson, Gary M.   Bos-A 1992
Alomar, Santos C. "Sandy"   SD-N 1986-90
Alou, Felipe R.   Mon-N 1979-80, 1984, 1992
Alou, Jesus M. R.   Hou-N 1979
Altobelli, Joseph S. "Joe"   NY-A 1981-82, 1986,
   Chi-N 1988-91
Altrock, Nicholas "Nick"   Was-A 1912-53
Amalfitano, J. Joseph "Joey"   Chi-N 1967-71,
   SF-N 1972-75, Chi-N 1976-77, Chi-N 1978-80,
   Cin-N 1982, LA-N 1983-92
Amaro, Ruben   Phi-N 1980-81, Chi-N 1983-86
Anderson, George L. "Sparky"   SD-N 1969
Appling, Lucius B. "Luke"   Det-A 1960,
   Cle-A 1960-61, Bal-A 1963, KC-A 1964-67,
   Chi-A 1970-71
Auferio, Anthony P. "Tony"   StL-N 1973
Austin, James P. "Jimmy"   StL-A 1923-32,
   Chi-A 1933-40
Babe, Loren R.   NY-A 1967, Chi-A 1980-81,
   1983
Bader, Lore V.   Bos-N 1926
Bailor, Robert M. "Bob"   Tor-A 1992
Baker, Delmer D. "Del"   Det-A 1933-38,
   Cle-A 1943-44, Bos-A 1945-48, 1953-60
Baker, Eugene H. "Gene"   Pit-N 1963
Baker, Floyd W.   Min-A 1961-64
Baker, Johnnie B "Dusty"   SF-N 1988-92
Baker, William P. "Bill"   Chi-N 1950
Bamberger, George I.   Bal-A 1968-77
Bancroft, David J. "Dave"   NY-N 1930-32
Bando, Salvatore L. "Sal"   Mil-N 1980-81
Banks, Ernest "Ernie"   Chi-N 1967-69, 1972-73
Bartell, Richard W. "Dick"   Det-A 1949-52,
   Cin-N 1954-55
Bartirome, Anthony J. "Tony"   Atl-N 1986-88
Basgall, Romanus "Monty"   LA-N 1973-86
Bassler, John L. "Johnny"   Cle-A 1938-40,
   StL-A 1941
Baylor, Don E.   Mil-A 1990-91, StL-N 1992
Bauer, Henry A. "Hank"   Bal-A 1963
Beauchamp, James E. "Jim"   Atl-N 1991-92
Bearnarth, Lawrence D. "Larry"   Mon-N 1976,
   1985-91
Beck, Walter W. "Boom-Boom"   Was-A 1957-59
Becker, Joseph E. "Joe"   Bro-N 1955-57,
   LA-N 1958-64, StL-N 1965-66, Chi-N 1967-70
Bedell, Howard W. "Howie"   KC-A 1984,
   SE-A 1988
Bender, Charles A. "Chief"   Cin-N 1919,
   Chi-N 1925-26, NY-N 1931, Phi-A 1951-53
Bengough, Bernard O. "Benny"
   Was-A 1940-43, Bos-N 1945, Phi-N 1946-58
Benson, Vernon A. "Vern"   Chi-N 1961-64,
   NY-A 1965-66, Cin-N 1966-69, StL-N 1970-75,
   Atl-N 1976-77, SF-N 1980
Berardino, Richard J. "Dick"   Bos-A 1989-91
Berg, Morris "Moe"   Bos-A 1940-41
Beringer, Carroll J. "C. B."   LA-N 1967-72,
   Phi-N 1973-78
Berra, Lawrence P. "Yogi"   NY-A 1963,
   NY-N 1965-71, NY-A 1976-83, Hou-N 1986-89
Berres, Raymond F. "Ray"   Chi-N 1949-66,
   1968-69
Berry, Charles F. "Charlie"   Phi-A 1936-40
Bevington, Terry Paul   Chi-A 1989-92
Biagini, Gregory P. "Greg"   Bal-A 1992
Bissonette, Adelphia L. "Del"   Bos-N 1945,
   Pit-N 1946
Blackburn, Wayne C.   Det-A 1963-64
Blackburne, Russell A. "Lena"   Chi-A 1927-28,
   StL-A 1930, Phi-A 1933-40, 1942-43
Blades, F. Raymond "Ray"   StL-N 1930-32,
   Cin-N 1942, Bro-N 1947-48, StL-N 1951,
   Chi-N 1953-56
Blaylock, Gary N.   KC-A 1984-87
Bloomfield, Gordon L. "Jack"   SD-N 1974,
   Chi-N 1975-76
Bluege, Oswald L. "Ossie"   Was-A 1940-42
Bonds, Bobby L.   Cle-A 1984-87
Boros, Stephen "Steve"   KC-A 1975-79,
   Mon-N 1981-82

Bosman, Richard A. "Dick"   Chi-A 1986-87,
   Bal-A 1992
Bottomley, James L. "Jim"   StL-A 1937
Bowa, Lawrence R. "Larry"   Phi-N 1988-92
Boyer, Cletis L. "Clete"   Oak-A 1980-85,
   NY-A 1988, 1992
Boyer, Cloyd V.   NY-A 1977, Atl-N 1978-81,
   KC-A 1982-83
Boyer, Kenton L. "Ken"   StL-N 1971-72
Bragan, James A. "Jimmy"   Cin-N 1967-69,
   Mon-N 1970-72, Mil-A 1976-77
Bragan, Robert R. "Bobby"   LA-N 1960,
   Hou-N 1962
Braun, Stephen R. "Steve"   StL-N 1990
Brecheen, Harry D.   Bal-A 1954-67
Breeden, H. Scott   Cin-N 1986-89
Brenly, Robert E. "Bob"   SF-N 1992
Bresnahan, Roger P.   NY-N 1925-28,
   Det-A 1930-31
Brewer, James T. "Jim"   Mon-N 1977-79
Bridges, Everett L. "Rocky"   LA-N 1962-63,
   Cal-A 1968-71, SF-N 1985
Bridges, Thomas J. "Tommy"   Det-A 1946,
   Cin-N 1951
Brinkman, Edwin A. "Ed"   Det-A 1979,
   SD-N 1981, Chi-A 1983-88
Bristol, J. David "Dave"   Cin-N 1966,
   Mon-N 1973-75, SF-N 1978-79, Phi-N 1982-85,
   1988, Cin-N 1989
Brown, Jackie G.   Tex-A 1979-82, Chi-A 1992
Brown, James R. "Jimmy"   Bos-N 1949-51
Brown, Mace S.   Bos-A 1965
Brown, William J. "Gates"   Det-A 1978-84
Brucker, Earle F., Sr.   Phi-A 1941-49,
   StL-A 1950, Cin-N 1952
Bryant, Claiborne H. "Clay"   LA-N 1961,
   Cle-A 1967, 1974
Bryant, Donald R. "Don"   Bos-A 1974-76,
   Sea-A 1977-80
Buford, Donald A. "Don"   SF-N 1981-84
Bumbry, Alonza B. "Al"   Bos-A 1988-92
Burdette, S. Lewis "Lew"   Atl-N 1972-73
Burgess, Thomas R. "Tom"   NY-N 1977,
   Atl-N 1978
Burgmeier, Thomas H. "Tom"   KC-A 1991
Burke, James T. "Jimmy"   Bos-A 1921-23,
   Chi-N 1926-30, NY-A 1931-33
Burkett, Jesse C.   NY-N 1921
Burleson, Richard P. "Rick"   Oak-A 1991,
   Bos-A 1992
Burns, George J.   NY-N 1931
Burns, John I. "Jack"   Bos-A 1955-59
Burris, B. Ray   Mil-A 1990-91, Tex-A 1992
Burwell, William E. "Bill"   Bos-A 1944,
   Pit-N 1947-48, 1958-62
Busby, James F. "Jim"   Bal-A 1961,
   Hou-N 1962, 1963-67, Atl-N 1968-75,
   Chi-A 1976, Sea-A 1977-78
Butler, John S. "Johnny"   Chi-A 1932
Camacho, Joseph G. "Joe"   Was-A 1969-71,
   Tex-A 1972
Camilli, Douglas J. "Doug"   Was-A 1968-69,
   Bos-A 1970-73
Cannizzaro,
   Christopher J. "Chris"   Atl-N 1976-78
Carew, Rodney C. "Rod"   Cal-A 1992
Carey, Max G.   Pit-N 1930
Carey, Thomas F. "Tom"   Bos-A 1946-47
Carisch, Frederick B. "Fred"   Det-A 1923-24
Carnevale, Daniel J. "Danny"   KC-A 1970
Carrion, Leonel S,   Mon-N 1988
Carter, Richard J. "Dick"   Phi-N 1959-60
Case, George W.   Was-A 1961-63, Min-A 1968
Castro, William R. "Bill"   Mil-A 1992
Cavarretta, Philip J. "Phil"   Det-A 1961-63,
   NY-N 1978
Cepeda, Orlando M.   Chi-A 1980
Chambliss, C. Christopher "Chris"   NY-A 1988
Chandler, Spurgeon F. "Spud"   KC-A 1957-58
Chapman, W. Benjamin "Ben"   Cin-N 1952
Chesbro, John D. "Jack"   Was-A 1924
Chiti, H. Dominic "Dom"   Cle-A 1991-92
Cisco, Galen B.   KC-A 1971-79,
   Mon-N 1980-84, SD-N 1985-87, Tor-A 1988,
   1990-92
Clark, Ronald B. "Ron"   Chi-A 1988-90,
   Sea-A 1991, Cle-A 1992
Clarke, Thomas A. "Tommy"   NY-N 1932-35,
   1938
Clary, Ellis   Was-A 1955-60, Tor-A 1989
Clear, E. Robert "Bob"   Cal-A 1976-87
Clines, Eugene A. "Gene"   Chi-N 1979-81,
   Hou-N 1988, Sea-A 1989-92
Cloninger, Tony L.   NY-A 1992
Cluck, Robert A. "Bob"   Hou-N 1979, 1990-92

Clymer, William J. "Bill"   Cin-N 1925
Cochrane, Gordon S. "Mickey"   Phi-A 1950
Cohen, Andrew H. "Andy"   Phi-N 1960
Colavito, Rocco D. "Rocky"   Cle-A 1973,
   1976-78, KC-A 1982-83
Cole, Richard R. "Dick"   Chi-N 1961
Coleman, Joseph H. "Joe"   Cal-A 1988-90,
   StL-N 1991-92
Coleman, Robert H. "Bob"   Bos-A 1926,
   Det-A 1932, Bos-N 1943
Collins, David S "Dave"   StL-N 1991-92
Collins, Edward T. "Eddie"   Phi-A 1931-32
Collins, James A. "Ripper"   Chi-N 1961-63
Collins, Terry L.   Pit-N 1992
Combs, Earle B.   NY-A 1936-44, StL-A 1947,
   Bos-A 1948-52, Phi-N 1954
Combs, Merrill R. "Merl"   Tex-A 1974-75
Comer, Stephen M. "Steve"   Cle-A 1987
Connor, Mark P.   NY-A 1984-85, 1986-87,
   1990-92
Connors, William J. "Billy"   KC-A 1980-81,
   Chi-N 1982-86, Sea-A 1987-88, NY-A 1989-90,
   Chi-N 1991-92
Conroy, William E. "Wid"   Phi-N 1922
Consolo, William A. "Billy"   Det-A 1979-92
Cooke, Allen L. "Dusty"   Phi-N 1948-52
Coombs, John W. "Jack"   Det-A 1920
Cooney, John W. "Johnny"   Bos-N 1940-42,
   1946-49, 1950-52, Mil-N 1953-55,
   Chi-A 1957-64
Cooper, W. Walker   StL-N 1957, KC-A 1960
Corrales, Patrick "Pat"   Tex-A 1975-78,
   NY-A 1989, Atl-N 1990-92
Corriden, John M., Sr "Red"   Chi-N 1932-40,
   Bro-N 1941-46, NY-A 1947-48, Chi-A 1950
Cottier, Charles K. "Chuck"   NY-N 1979-81,
   Sea-A 1982-84, Chi-N 1988-92
Courtney, Clinton D. "Clint"   Hou-N 1965
Cox, Larry E.   Chi-N 1988-89
Cox, Robert J. "Bobby"   NY-A 1977
Crabtree, Estel C.   Cin-N 1943-44
Craft, Harry F.   KC-A 1955-57, Chi-N 1960-61
Craig, Roger L.   SD-N 1969-72, Hou-N 1974-75,
   SD-N 1976-77, Det-A 1980-84
Cramer, Roger M. "Doc"   Det-A 1948,
   Chi-A 1951-53
Crandall, Delmar W. "Del"   Cal-A 1977
Crandall, J. Otis "Doc"   Pit-N 1931-34
Cravath, Clifford C. "Gavvy"   Phi-N 1923
Cresse, Mark E.   LA-N 1977-92
Crosetti, Frank P. J. "Frankie"   NY-A 1947-68,
   Sea-A 1969, Min-A 1970-71
Crowley, Terrence M. "Terry"   Bal-A 1985-88,
   Min-A 1991-92
Cubbage, Michael L. "Mike"   NY-N 1990-91,
   1992
Cuccinello, Anthony F. "Tony"   Cin-N 1949-51,
   Cle-A 1952-56, Chi-A 1957-66, Det-A 1967-68,
   Chi-A 1969
Culp, Benjamin B. "Benny"   Phi-N 1946-47
Cunningham, Joseph R. "Joe"   StL-N 1982
Cunningham, William A. "Bill"   Chi-A 1932
Cuyler, Hazen S. "Kiki"   Chi-N 1941-43,
   Bos-A 1949
Dahlgren, Ellsworth T. "Babe"   KC-A 1964
Dal Canton, J. Bruce   Chi-A 1978, Atl-N 1987-90
Daly, Thomas D. "Tom"   Bos-A 1933-46
Dark, Alvin R.   Chi-N 1965, 1977
Dauer, Richard F. "Rich"   Cle-A 1990-91
Davenport, James H. "Jim"   SF-N 1970,
   SD-N 1974-75, SF-N 1976-82, 1984,
   Phi-N 1986-87, Cle-A 1989
Davis, Harry H.   Phi-A 1913-19
Davis, H. Thomas "Tommy"   Sea-A 1981
Davis, R. Brandon "Brandy"   Phi-N 1972
Davis, Virgil L. "Spud"   Pit-N 1942-46,
   Chi-N 1950-53
Deal, Ellis F. "Cot"   Cin-N 1959-60,
   Hou-N 1962-64, NY-A 1965, KC-A 1966-67,
   Cle-A 1970-71, Det-A 1973-74, Hou-N 1983-85
DeMars, William L. "Billy"   Phi-N 1969-81,
   Mon-N 1982-84, Cin-N 1985-87
Dean, Jay H. "Dizzy"   Chi-N 1941
DeMerritt, Martin G. "Marty"   SF-N 1989
Demeter, Stephen "Steve"   Pit-N 1985
Dent, Russell E. "Bucky"   StL-N 1991-92
Devlin, Arthur M. "Art"   Bos-N 1926, 1928
Dews, Robert W. "Bobby"   Atl-N 1979-81, 1985
Dickey, William M. "Bill"   NY-A 1949-57, 1960
Didier, Robert D. "Bob"   Oak-A 1984-86,
   Sea-A 1989-90
DiMaggio, Joseph P. "Joe"   Oak-A 1968-69
Dobson, Patrick E. "Pat"   Mil-A 1982-84,
   SD-N 1988-90, KC-A 1991

Doby, Lawrence E. "Larry"   Mon-N 1971-73,
   Cle-A 1974, Mon-N 1976, Chi-A 1977-78
Doerr, Robert P. "Bobby"   Bos-A 1967-69,
   Tor-A 1977-81
Dolan, Albert J. "Cozy"   NY-N 1922-24
Donnelly, Richard F. "Rich"   Tex-A 1980,
   1983-85, Pit-N 1986-92
Doolan, Michael J. "Mickey"   Chi-N 1926-28,
   Cin-N 1930-32
Dorish, Harry "Fritz"   Bos-A 1963,
   Atl-N 1968-71
Douglas, Otis W.   Cin-N 1961-62
Down, Richard J. "Rick"   Cal-A 1987-88
Drabowsky, Myron W. "Moe"   Chi-A 1986
Dressen, Charles W. "Chuck"   Bro-N 1939-42,
   1943-46, NY-A 1947-48, LA-N 1958-59
Dubuc, Jean J.   Det-A 1930-31
Duffy, Hugh   Bos-A 1932
Dugey, Oscar J.   Chi-N 1921-24
Duncan, David E. "Dave"   Cle-A 1978-81,
   Sea-A 1982, Chi-A 1983-86, Oak-A 1986-92
Dunlop, Harry A.   KC-A 1969-75, Chi-N 1976,
   Cin-N 1979-82, SD-N 1983-86
Durocher, Leo E.   LA-N 1961-64
Dusan, Eugene P. "Gene"   NY-N 1983
Dyer, Don R. "Duffy"   Chi-N 1983,
   Mil-A 1989-92
Dykes, James J. "Jimmy"   Phi-A 1949-50,
   Cin-N 1955-58, Pit-N 1959, Mil-N 1962,
   KC-A 1963-64
Earnshaw, George L.   Phi-N 1949-50
Easler, Michael A. "Mike"   Mil-A 1992
Easter, L. Luke   Cle-A 1969
Edwards, Howard R. "Doc"   Phi-N 1970-72,
   Cle-A 1985-87, NY-N 1990-91
Egan, Arthur A. "Ben"   Bro-N 1925, Chi-A 1926
Egan, Richard W. "Dick"   Tex-A 1988-89
Elia, Lee C.   Phi-N 1980-81, 1985-87,
   NY-A 1989
Elliott, Robert I. "Bob"   LA-A 1961
Ellis, Samuel J. "Sammy"   NY-A 1982, 1983-84,
   1986, Chi-A 1989-91, Chi-N 1992
Emery, Calvin W. "Cal"   Chi-A 1988
Ens, Jewel W.   Pit-N 1926-29, Det-A 1932,
   Cin-N 1933, Bos-N 1934, Pit-N 1935-39,
   Cin-N 1941
Ermer, Calvin C. "Cal"   Bal-A 1962,
   Mil-A 1970-71, Oak-A 1977
Estrada, Charles L. "Chuck"   Tex-A 1973,
   SD-N 1978-81, Cle-A 1983
Etchebarren, Andrew A. "Andy"   Cal-A 1977,
   Mil-A 1985-91
Evans, Darrell W.   NY-A 1990
Evers, John J. "Johnny"   NY-N 1920,
   Chi-A 1922-23, Bos-N 1929-32
Evers, Walter A. "Hoot"   Cle-A 1970
Ezell, Glenn W.   Tex-A 1983-85, KC-A 1989-92
Faber, Urban C. "Red"   Chi-A 1946-48
Fahey, William R. "Bill"   SF-N 1986-91
Falk, Bibb A.   Cle-A 1933, Bos-A 1934
Fanning, W. James "Jim"   Atl-N 1967
Farrell, M. Kerby   Chi-A 1966-69, Cle-A 1970-71
Felske, John F.   Tor-A 1980-81, Phi-N 1984
Ferguson, Joseph V. "Joe"   Tex-A 1986-87,
   LA-N 1988-89, 1992
Ferraro, Michael D. "Mike"   NY-A 1979-82,
   KC-A 1984-86, NY-A 1987-88, 1989-91
Ferrell, Richard B. "Rick"   Was-A 1946-49,
   Det-A 1950-53
Ferrick, Thomas J. "Tom"   Cin-N 1954-58,
   Phi-N 1959, Det-A 1960-63, KC-A 1964-65
Ferriss, David M. "Dave"   Bos-A 1955-59
Fischer, William C. "Bill"   Cin-N 1979-83,
   Bos-A 1985-91
Fitzgerald, Edward R. "Ed"   Cle-A 1960,
   KC-A 1961, Min-A 1962-64
Fitzgerald, Joseph P. "Joe"   Was-A 1947-56
Fitzpatrick, John A.   Pit-N 1953-56,
   Mil-N 1958-59
Fitzsimmons, Frederick "Freddie"   Bro-N 1942,
   Bos-N 1948, NY-N 1949-53, 1954-55,
   Chi-N 1957-59, KC-A 1960, Chi-N 1966
Fletcher, Arthur "Art"   NY-A 1927-45
Flowers, D'Arcy R. "Jake"   Pit-N 1940-45,
   Bos-A 1946, Cle-A 1951-52
Foli, Timothy J. "Tim"   Tex-A 1986-87,
   Mil-A 1992
Foote, Barry C.   Chi-A 1991, NY-N 1992
Ford, Edward C. "Whitey"   NY-A 1968, 1974-75
Fowler, J. Arthur "Art"   LA-A 1964, Min-A 1969,
   Det-A 1971-73, Tex-A 1973-75, NY-A 1977-79,
   Oak-A 1980-82, NY-A 1983, 1988
Fox, Charles F. "Charlie"   SF-N 1965-68,
   NY-A 1989

Fox, J. Nelson "Nellie"   Hou-N 1965, 1966-67,
   Was-A 1968-71, Tex-A 1972
Franks, Herman L.   NY-N 1949-55, SF-N 1958,
   1964, Chi-N 1970
Fraser, Charles C. "Chick"   Pit-N 1923
Frey, James G. "Jim"   Bal-A 1970-79,
   NY-N 1982-83
Friend, Owen L.   KC-A 1969
Frisch, Frank F. "Frankie"   NY-N 1949
Funk, Franklin R. "Frank"   SF-N 1976,
   Sea-A 1980-81, 1983-84, KC-A 1988-90
Galan, August J. "Augie"   Phi-A 1954
Galante, Matthew "Matt"   Hou-N 1985-92
Gale, Richard B. "Rich"   Bos-A 1992
Garcia, David "Dave"   SD-N 1970-73,
   Cle-A 1975-76, Cal-A 1977, Cle-A 1979,
   Mil-A 1983-84
Gardenhire, Ronald C. "Ron"   Min-A 1991-92
Gardner, William F. "Billy"   Bos-A 1965-66,
   Mon-A 1977-78, Min-A 1981
Garner, Philip M. "Phil"   Hou-N 1989-91
Garrett, H. Adrian   KC-A 1988-92
Garrison, R. Ford   Cin-N 1953
Gaston, Clarence E. "Cito"   Tor-A 1982-89
Gebhard, Robert H. "Bob"   Mon-N 1982
Gehringer, Charles L. "Charlie"   Det-A 1942
Gernert, Richard E. "Dick"   Tex-A 1975-76
Gharrity, E. Patrick "Patsy"   Was-A 1929-32,
   Cle-A 1933-35
Gibson, George C.   Was-A 1923, Chi-N 1925
Gibson, Robert "Bob"   NY-N 1981,
   Atl-N 1982-84
Gilbert, Andrew "Andy"   SF-N 1972-75
Gilliam, James W. "Jim"   LA-N 1965-78
Gladding, Fred E.   Det-A 1976-78
Gleason, William J. "Kid"   Phi-N 1908-11,
   Chi-A 1912-17, Phi-A 1926-32
Gleeson, James J. "Jim"   KC-A 1957,
   NY-A 1964
Gomez, Juan A. "Orlando"   Tex-A 1991-92
Gomez, Pedro "Preston"   LA-N 1965-68,
   Hou-N 1973, StL-N 1976, LA-N 1977-79,
   Cal-N 1981-84
Gonzalez, Miguel A. "Mike"   StL-N 1934-46
Gooch, John B. "Johnny"   Pit-N 1937-39
Goodman, William D. "Billy"   Atl-N 1968-70
Gordon, Joseph L. "Joe"   Det-A 1956
Goryl, John A. "Johnny"   Min-A 1968-69,
   1979-80, Cle-A 1982-88
Gowdy, Henry M. "Hank"   Bos-N 1929-37,
   Cin-N 1938-42, 1945-46, NY-N 1947-48
Graff, Milton E. "Milt"   Pit-N 1985
Grammas, Alexander P. "Alex"   Pit-N 1965-69,
   Cin-N 1970-75, 1978, Atl-N 1979,
   Det-A 1980-91
Grimes, Burleigh A.   KC-A 1955
Grimm, Charles J. "Charlie"   Chi-N 1941,
   1961-62
Grissom, Marvin E. "Marv"   LA-A 1961-65,
   Cal-A 1966, Chi-A 1967-68, Cal-A 1969,
   Min-A 1970-71, Chi-N 1975-76, Cal-A 1977-78
Grodzicki, John "Johnny"   Det-A 1979
Guerrero, Epifanio O. "Epy"   Tor-A 1981
Gutteridge, Donald J. "Don"   Chi-A 1955-66,
   1968-69
Haas, G. Edward "Eddie"   Atl-N 1974-77, 1984
Haas, George W. "Mule"   Chi-A 1940-46
Hack, Stanley C. "Stan"   StL-N 1957-58
Hacker, Richard W. "Rich"   StL-N 1986-90,
   Tor-A 1991-92
Haddix, Harvey   NY-N 1966-67, Cin-N 1969,
   Bos-A 1971, Cle-A 1975-78, Pit-N 1979-84
Haines, Jesse J.   Bro-N 1938
Hairston, Samuel "Sammy"   Chi-A 1978
Haller, Thomas F. "Tom"   SF-N 1977-79
Hamilton, Steve A.   Det-A 1975
Hancken, Morris Jean "Buddy"   Hou-N 1968-72
Haney, Fred G.   Mil-N 1956
Haney, W. Larry   Mil-A 1978-91
Hansen, Guy C.   KC-A 1991-92
Hansen, Roger C.   Sea-A 1992
Hansen, Ronald L. "Ron"   Mil-A 1980-83,
   Mon-N 1985-89
Harder, Melvin L. "Mel"   Cle-A 1947, 1949-63,
   NY-N 1964, Chi-N 1965, Cin-N 1966-68,
   KC-A 1969
Hargrove, D. Michael "Mike"   Cle-A 1990-91
Harmon, Thomas "Tom"   Chi-N 1982
Harper, Tommy   Bos-A 1980-84,
   Mon-N 1990-92
Harrah, Colbert D. "Toby"   Tex-A 1989-92
Harrelson, Derrel M. "Bud"   NY-N 1982,
   1985-90
Harris, C. Luman "Lum"   Chi-A 1951-54,
   Bal-A 1955-61, Hou-N 1962-64

Hart, John H.   Bal-A 1988
Hartenstein, Charles O. "Chuck"   Cle-A 1979,
   Mil-A 1987-89
Hartley, Grover A.   Cle-A 1928-30,
   Pit-N 1931-33, StL-A 1934-36, NY-N 1946
Hartnett, Charles L. "Gabby"   Chi-N 1938,
   NY-N 1941, KC-A 1965
Hartsfield, Roy T.   LA-N 1969-72, Atl-N 1973
Hatfield, Fred J.   Det-A 1977-78
Hatton, Grady E.   Chi-N 1960, Hou-N 1973-74
Haynes, Joseph W. "Joe"   Was-A 1953-55
Hayworth, Raymond H. "Ray"   Bro-N 1945
Hebner, Richard J. "Richie"   Bos-A 1989-91
Heffner, Donald H. "Don"   KC-A 1958-60,
   Det-A 1961, NY-N 1964-65, Cal-A 1967-68
Hegan, James E. "Jim"   NY-A 1960-73,
   Det-A 1974-78, NY-A 1979-80
Heilmann, Harry E.   Cin-N 1932
Heist, Alfred M. "Al"   Hou-N 1966-67,
   SD-N 1980
Helms, Tommy V.   Tex-A 1981-82,
   Cin-N 1983-89
Hemsley, Ralston B. "Rollie"   Phi-A 1954,
   Was-A 1961-62
Hemus, Solomon J. "Solly"   NY-N 1962-63,
   Cle-A 1964-65
Hendricks, Elrod J.   Bal-A 1978-92
Henrich, Thomas D. "Tommy"   NY-A 1951,
   NY-N 1957, Det-A 1958-59
Herman, Floyd C. "Babe"   Pit-N 1951
Herman, William J. "Billy"   Bro-N 1952-57,
   Mil-N 1958-59, Bos-A 1960-64, Cal-A 1967,
   SD-N 1978-79
Hernandez, Carlo A "Chuck"   Cal-A 1992
Herndon, Larry D.   Det-A 1992
Herzog, Dorrel N. "Whitey"   KC-A 1965,
   NY-N 1966, Cal-A 1974-75
Hiatt, Jack E   Chi-N 1981
High, Andrew A. "Andy"   Bro-N 1937-38
Hill, Marc K.   Hou-N 1988, NY-A 1991
Hill, Perry   Tex-A 1992
Hiller, Charles J. "Chuck"   Tex-A 1973,
   KC-A 1976-79, StL-N 1981-83, SF-N 1985,
   NY-N 1990
Hilton, J. David "Dave"   Mil-A 1987-88
Himsl, Avitus B. "Vedie"   Chi-N 1960-64
Hinchman, William W. "Bill"   Pit-N 1923
Hines, Benjamin T. "Ben"   Sea-A 1984,
   LA-N 1986, 1988-92
Hines, Bruce E.   Cal-A 1991
Hisle, Larry E.   Tor-A 1992
Hitchcock, William C. "Billy"   Det-A 1955-60,
   Atl-N 1966
Hoak, Donald A. "Don"   Phi-N 1967
Hofman, Robert G. "Bobby"   KC-A 1966-67,
   Was-A 1968, Oak-A 1969-70, Cle-A 1971-72,
   Oak-A 1974-75, 1978
Hofmann, Fred   StL-A 1938-49
Holke, Walter H.   StL-A 1940
Hollingsworth, Albert W. "Al"   StL-N 1957-58
Holt, Golden D. "Goldie"   Pit-N 1948-50,
   Chi-N 1961-64
Holmquist, Douglas L. "Doug"   NY-A 1984,
   1985
Hopp, John L. "Johnny"   Det-A 1954,
   StL-N 1956
Hornsby, Rogers   Chi-N 1958-59, NY-N 1962
Horton, Willie W.   NY-A 1985, Chi-A 1986
Hoscheit, Vernard A. "Vern"   Bal-A 1968,
   Oak-A 1969-74, Cal-A 1976, NY-N 1984-87
Houk, Ralph G.   NY-A 1954, 1958-60
House, Thomas R. "Tom"   Tex-A 1985-92
Howard, Elston G.   NY-A 1969-79
Howard, Frank O.   Mil-A 1977-80,
   NY-N 1982-83, 1984, Mil-A 1985-86,
   Sea-A 1987-88, NY-A 1989, 1991-92
Howe, Arthur H. "Art"   Tex-A 1985-88
Howley, Daniel P. "Dan"   Bos-A 1919,
   Det-A 1921-22
Howser, Richard D. "Dick"   NY-A 1969-78
Hriniak, Walter J. "Walt"   Mon-N 1974-75,
   Bos-A 1977-88, Chi-A 1989-92
Hudlin, G. Willis   Det-A 1957-59
Hudson, Sidney C. "Sid"   Was-A 1961-65,
   1968-71, Tex-A 1972, 1977-78
Hulswitt, Rudolph E. "Rudy"   Bos-A 1931-33
Hundley, C. Randolph "Randy"   Chi-N 1977
Hunter, Frederick C. "Newt"   Phi-N 1928-31,
   1933
Hunter, G. William "Billy"   Bal-A 1964-77
Isaac, Luis   Cle-A 1987-91
Jackson, Alvin N. "Al"   Bos-A 1977-79,
   Bal-A 1989-91
Jackson, Grant D.   Pit-N 1984-85
Jackson, Roland T. "Sonny"   Atl-N 1982-83

Jackson, Travis C. NY-N 1939-40, 1947-48
Jansen, Lawrence J. "Larry" NY-N 1954,
 SF-N 1961-71, Chi-N 1972-73
Jaramillo, Rudolph "Rudy" Hou-N 1990-92
Jennings, Hugh A. "Hughie" NY-N 1921-25
Johnson, Darrell D. StL-N 1960-61, Bal-A 1962,
 Bos-A 1968-69, Tex-A 1981-82
Johnson, Deron R. Cal-A 1979-80, NY-N 1981,
 Phi-N 1982-84, Sea-A 1985-86, Chi-A 1987,
 Cal-A 1989-91
Johnson, Roy J Chi-N 1935-39, 1944-53
Johnson, Sylvester W. "Syl" Phi-N 1937-40
Johnston, James H. "Jimmy" Bro-N 1931
Jones, Clarence W. Atl-N 1985, 1988-92
Jones, Gordon B. Hou-N 1966-67
Jones, Grover W. "Deacon" Hou-N 1976-82,
 SD-N 1984-87
Jones, Lynn M. KC-A 1991-92
Jones, Joseph C. "Joe" KC-A 1987, 1992
Jonnard, Clarence J. "Bubber" Phi-N 1935,
 NY-N 1942-46
Judge, Joseph I. "Joe" Was-A 1945-46
Jurges, William F. "Billy" Chi-N 1947-48,
 Was-A 1956-59
Kaat, James L. "Jim" Cin-N 1984-85
Kahn, Louis "Lou" StL-N 1955
Katt, Raymond F. "Ray" StL-N 1959-60,
 Cle-A 1962
Kaufmann, Anthony C. "Tony" StL-N 1947-50
Keane, John J. "Johnny" StL-N 1959-61
Keefe, David E. "Dave" Phi-A 1940-49
Keely, Robert W. "Bob" Bos-N 1946-52,
 Mil-N 1953-57
Kelleher, Michael D. "Mick" Pit-N 1986
Kelley, Joseph J. "Joe" Bro-N 1926
Kelly, Bernard F. "Mike" Chi-A 1930-31,
 Chi-N 1934, Bos-N 1937-39, Pit-N 1940-41
Kelly, George L. Cin-N 1935-37,
 Bos-N 1938-43, Cin-N 1947-48
Kelly, J. Thomas "Tom" Min-A 1983-86
Kennedy, Kevin Mon-N 1992
Kennedy, Robert D. "Bob" Chi-N 1962-64,
 Atl-N 1967
Kerr, John F. Was-A 1935
Kerrigan, Joseph T. "Joe" Mon-N 1983-86,
 1992
Killefer, William L. "Bill" StL-N 1926,
 StL-A 1927-29, Bro-N 1939, Phi-N 1942
Kim, Wendell K. SF-N 1989-92
Kimm, Bruce E. Cin-N 1984-88, Pit-N 1989,
 SD-N 1991-92
King, Clyde E. Cin-N 1959, Pit-N 1965-67,
 NY-A 1981, 1988
Kison, Bruce E. KC-A 1992
Kissell, George M. StL-N 1969-75
Kittle, Hubert M. "Hub" Hou-N 1971-75,
 StL-N 1981-83
Klein, Charles H. "Chuck" Phi-N 1942-45
Klein, Louis F. "Lou" Chi-N 1960-65
Kluszewski, Theodore B. "Ted" Cin-N 1970-78
Knoop, Robert F. "Bobby" Chi-A 1977-78,
 Cal-N 1979-92
Knowles, Darold D. StL-N 1983, Phi-N 1989-90
Koenig, Fred Carl Cal-A 1970-71, StL-N 1976,
 Tex-A 1977-82, Chi-N 1983, Cle-A 1985-86
Kress, Ralph "Red" Det-A 1940,
 NY-N 1946-49, Cle-A 1953-60, LA-A 1961,
 NY-N 1962
Krol, John T. "Jack" StL-N 1977-80,
 SD-N 1981-86
Kuehl, Karl O. Min-A 1977-82
Kuenn, Harvey E. Mil-A 1971-82
Kuntz, Russell J. "Rusty" Sea-A 1989-92
Kusnyer, Arthur L. "Art" Chi-A 1980-87,
 Oak-A 1989-92
Lachemann, Marcel E. Cal-A 1984-92
Lachemann, Rene G. Bos-A 1985-86,
 Oak-A 1987-92
Lakeman, Albert W. "Al" Bos-A 1963-64,
 1967-69
Lamont, Gene W. Pit-N 1986-91
Land, Grover C. Cin-N 1926-28, Chi-N 1929
Landestoy, Rafael S. Mon-N 1989
Landrith, Hobert N. "Hobie" Was-A 1964
Lanier, Harold C. "Hal" StL-N 1981-85,
 Phi-N 1990-91
LaRoche, David E. "Dave" Chi-A 1989-91,
 NY-N 1992
LaRussa, Anthony "Tony" Chi-A 1978
Lasorda, Thomas C. "Tommy" LA-N 1973-76
Latham, W. Arlington "Arlie" Cin-N 1900,
 NY-N 1909
Lau, Charles R. "Charley" Bal-A 1969,
 Oak-A 1970, KC-A 1971-74, 1975-78,
 NY-A 1979-81, Chi-A 1982-83

Lauder, William "Billy" Chi-A 1925
Lavagetto, Harry A. "Cookie" Bro-N 1951-53,
 Was-A 1955-57, NY-N 1962-63, SF-N 1964-67
Law, Vernon S. "Vern" Pit-N 1968-69
Lazzeri, Anthony M. "Tony" Chi-N 1938
Lefebvre, James K. "Jim" LA-N 1978-79,
 SF-N 1980-82, Oak-A 1987-88
Leifield, Albert P. "Lefty" StL-A 1920-23,
 Bos-A 1924-26, Det-A 1927-28
Lemon, James R. "Jim" Min-A 1965-67,
 1981-84
Lemon, Robert G. "Bob" Cle-A 1960,
 Phi-N 1961, Cal-A 1967-68, KC-A 1970,
 NY-A 1976
Lenhardt, Donald E. "Don" Bos-A 1970-73
Leonard, Emil J. "Dutch" Chi-N 1954-56
Leppert, Donald G. "Don" Pit-N 1968-76,
 Tor-A 1977-79, Hou-N 1980-85
Lett, James C. "Jim" Cin-N 1988-89
Levy, Leonard Pit-N 1957-63
Lewis, George E. "Duffy" Bos-N 1931-35
Lewis, Johnny J. StL-N 1973-76, 1985-89
Leyland, James R. "Jim" Chi-A 1982-85
Leyva, Nicolas T. "Nick" StL-N 1984-88
Lillis, Robert P. "Bob" Hou-N 1967, 1973-82,
 SF-N 1986-92
Lipon, John J. "Johnny" Cle-A 1968-71
Litwhiler, Daniel W. "Danny" Cin-N 1951
Llenas, Winston E. Tor-A 1988
Lobe, William C. "Bill" Cle-A 1951-56
Lobert, John B. "Hans" Phi-N 1934-41,
 Cin-N 1943-44
Lockman, Carroll W. "Whitey" Cin-N 1960,
 SF-N 1961-64, Chi-N 1966
Lodigiani, Dario A. KC-A 1961-62
Lollar, J. Sherman "Sherm" Bal-A 1964-67,
 Oak-A 1968
Long, R. Dale NY-A 1963
Lonnett, Joseph P. "Joe" Chi-A 1971-75,
 Oak-A 1976, Pit-N 1977-84
Lopat, Edmund W. "Ed" NY-A 1960,
 Min-A 1961, KC-A 1962
Lopes, David E. "Davey" Tex-A 1988-91,
 Bal-A 1992
Lowe, Q. V. "Q. V." Chi-N 1972
Lowrey, Harry L. "Peanuts" Phi-N 1960-66,
 SF-N 1967-68, Mon-N 1969, Chi-N 1970-71,
 Cal-N 1972, Chi-N 1977-79, 1981
Lucchesi, Frank J. Tex-A 1974-75, 1979-80
Lum, Michael K. "Mike" Chi-A 1985,
 KC-A 1988-89
Lumpe, Jerry D. Oak-A 1971
Lund, Donald A. "Don" Det-A 1957-58
Luque, Adolfo "Dolf" NY-N 1935-38, 1941-45
Lutz, R. Joseph "Joe" Cle-A 1972-73
Lyons, Edward H. "Eddie" Min-A 1976
Lyons, Theodore A. "Ted" Det-A 1949-53,
 Bro-N 1954
Macha, Kenneth E. "Ken" Mon-N 1986-91,
 Cal-A 1992
Mack, Earle T. Phi-A 1924-50
MacKenzie, H. Gordon "Gordy" KC-A 1980-81,
 Chi-N 1983, Pit-N 1986-88, Cle-A 1991
Maglie, Salvatore A. "Sal" Bos-A 1960-62,
 1966-67, Sea-A 1969
Mahoney, James T. "Jim" Chi-A 1972-76,
 Sea-A 1985-86
Majtyka, LeRoy W. "Roy" Atl-N 1988-90
Malmberg, Harry W. Bos-A 1963-64
Maloof, Jack G. SD-N 1990
Maltzberger, Gordon R. Min-A 1962-64
Mancuso, August R. "Gus" Cin-N 1950
Mansolino, Doug Chi-A 1992
Mantle, Mickey C. NY-A 1970
Manuel, Charles F. "Charlie" Cle-A 1988-89
Manuel, Jerry Mon-N 1991-92
Manush, Henry E. "Heinie" Was-A 1953-54
Marion, Martin W. "Marty" StL-A 1952,
 Chi-A 1954
Marshall, R. James "Jim" Chi-N 1974
Martin, Alfred M. "Billy" Min-A 1965-68,
 Tex-A 1974
Martin, Fred T. Chi-N 1961-64, Chi-A 1979
Martin, John L. "Pepper" Chi-N 1956
Martin, Joseph C. "J. C." Chi-N 1974
Martinez, Jose KC-A 1980-87, Chi-N 1988-92
Martinez, Orlando "Marty" Sea-A 1984-86,
 1992
Mathews, Edwin L. "Eddie" Atl-N 1971-72
Mathews, Henry "Harry" Cle-A 1926-27,
 NY-A 1929
Mathewson,
 Christopher "Christy" NY-N 1919-21
Maxvill, C. Dallan "Dal" Oak-A 1975,
 NY-N 1978, StL-N 1979-80, Atl-N 1982-84

May, Lee A. KC-A 1984-86, Cin-N 1988-89,
 KC-A 1992
May, Milton S. "Milt" Pit-N 1987-92
Mayberry, John C. KC-A 1989-90
Mayo, Edward J. "Eddie" Bos-A 1951,
 Phi-N 1952-54
Mays, Willie H. NY-N 1974-79
Mazeroski, William S. "Bill" Pit-N 1973,
 Sea-A 1979-80
Mazzone, Leo D. Atl-N 1985, 1990-92
McBride, George F. Det-A 1925-26, 1929
McBride, Kenneth F. "Ken" Mil-A 1975
McCallister, John "Jack" Cle-A 1920-26,
 Bos-A 1930
McCormick, Frank A. Cin-N 1956-57
McCrabb, Lester W. "Les" Phi-A 1950-54
McCraw, Tommy L. Cle-A 1975, 1979-82,
 SF-N 1983-85, Bal-A 1989-91, NY-N 1992
McCullough, Clyde E. Was-A 1960,
 Min-A 1961, NY-N 1963, SD-N 1982
McDermott, Maurice J. "Mickey" Cal-A 1968
McDonnell, Robert A. "Maje" Phi-N 1951-57
McGaha, F. Melvin "Mel" Cle-A 1961,
 KC-A 1963-64, Hou-N 1968-70
McGinnity, Joseph J. "Joe" Bro-N 1926
McGuire, James T. "Deacon" Det-A 1911-16
McKay, David L. "Dave" Oak-A 1984-92
McKechnie, William B. "Bill" Pit-N 1922,
 StL-N 1927, Cle-A 1947-49, Bos-A 1952-53
McKee, J. R. Pit-N 1947
McKeon, John A. "Jack" Oak-A 1978
McLaren, John L. Tor-A 1986-90, Bos-A 1991,
 Cin-N 1992
McLish, Calvin C. "Cal" Phi-N 1965-66,
 Mon-N 1969-75, Mil-A 1976-82
McMahon, Donald J. "Don" SF-N 1973-75,
 Min-A 1976-77, SF-N 1980-82, Cle-A 1983-85
McMillan, Roy D. Mil-A 1970-72, NY-N 1973-76
McNamara, John F. Oak-A 1968-69,
 SF-N 1971-73, Cal-A 1978
McNeely, G. Earl StL-N 1931, Was-A 1936-37
McNertney, Gerald E. "Jerry" Bos-A 1988
McRae, Harold A. "Hal" KC-A 1987,
 Mon-N 1990-91
Mele, Sabath A. "Sam" Was-A 1959-60,
 Min-A 1961
Melillo, Oscar D. "Ski" StL-A 1938,
 Cle-A 1939-40, 1942, 1945-48, 1950,
 Bos-A 1952-53, KC-A 1955-56
Mendoza, Mario Bal-A 1988
Menke, Denis J. Tor-A 1980-81,
 Hou-N 1983-88, Phi-N 1989-92
Merkle, Frederick C. "Fred" NY-A 1925-26
Merrill, Carl H. "Stump" NY-A 1985, 1986-87
Metro, Charles "Charlie" Chi-N 1962,
 Chi-A 1965, Oak-A 1982
Meusel, Emil F. "Irish" NY-N 1930
Meyer, Bernhard "Benny" Phi-N 1924-26,
 Det-A 1928-30
Meyer, Russell C. "Russ" Or "Monk"
 NY-A 1972
Michael, Eugene R. "Gene" NY-A 1976-77,
 1978, 1984-86, 1988, 1989
Milan, J. Clyde Was-A 1928-29, 1938-52
Miller, Dyar K Chi-A 1987-88
Miller, Edmund J. "Bing" Bos-A 1937,
 Det-A 1938-41, Chi-A 1942-49, Phi-A 1950-53
Miller, L. Otto Bro-N 1926-36
Miller, Raymond R. "Ray" Bal-A 1978-85,
 Pit-N 1987-92
Miller, Robert L. "Bob" Tor-A 1977-79,
 SF-N 1985
Milliken, Robert F. "Bob" StL-N 1965-70, 1976
Mills, Arthur G. "Art" Det-A 1944-48
Mills, C. Buster Cle-A 1946, Chi-A 1947-50,
 Cin-N 1953, Bos-A 1954
Minoso, S. Orestes "Minnie" Chi-A 1976-78,
 1980-81
Mitchell, Clarence E. NY-N 1932-33
Mitterwald, George E. Oak-A 1979-82,
 NY-A 1988
Mize, John R. "Johnny" KC-A 1961
Monbouquette, William C. "Bill" NY-N 1982-83,
 NY-A 1985
Monchak, Alex "Al" Chi-A 1971-75,
 Oak-A 1976, Pit-N 1977-84, Atl-N 1986-88
Moon, Wallace W. "Wally" SD-N 1969
Moore, Jackie S. Mil-A 1970-72,
 Tex-A 1973-74, 1975-76, Tor-A 1977-79,
 Tex-A 1980, Oak-A 1981-84, Mon-N 1987-89,
 Cin-N 1990-92
Moore, Terry B. StL-N 1949-52, 1956-58
Motton, Curtell H. "Curt" Bal-A 1991
Morales, Jose M. SF-N 1986-88, Cle-A 1990-92
Morales, Richard A. "Rich" Atl-N 1986-87

Morgan, Joseph M. "Joe"   Pit-N 1972,
  Bos-A 1985-88
Morgan, Tom S.   Cal-A 1972-74, SD-N 1975,
  NY-A 1979, Cal-A 1981-83
Morgan, Vernon T. "Vern"   Min-A 1969-75
Moses, Wallace "Wally"   Phi-A 1952-54,
  Phi-N 1955-58, Cin-N 1959-60, NY-A 1961-62,
  1966, Det-A 1967-70
Moss, J. Lester "Les"   Chi-A 1967-68, 1970,
  Chi-N 1981, Hou-N 1982-84, 1985-89
Mota, Manuel R. "Manny"   LA-N 1980-89
Mozzali, Maurice J. "Mo"   StL-N 1977-78
Mueller, Ray C.   NY-N 1956, Chi-N 1957
Muffett, Billy A.   StL-N 1967-70, Cal-A 1974-77,
  Det-A 1985-92
Mulcahy, Hugh N.   Chi-A 1970
Mull, Jack L.   SF-N 1985
Mulleavy, Gregory T. "Greg"   Bro-N 1957,
  LA-N 1958-60, 1962-64
Mullin, Patrick J. "Pat"   Det-A 1963-66,
  Cle-A 1967, Mon-N 1979-81
Murphy, Daniel F. "Danny"   Phi-A 1921-24,
  Phi-N 1927
Murtaugh, Daniel E. "Danny"   Pit-N 1956-57
Muser, Anthony J. "Tony"   Mil-A 1985-89
Myatt, George E.   Was-A 1950-54,
  Chi-A 1955-56, Chi-N 1957-59, Mil-N 1960-61,
  Det-A 1962-63, Phi-N 1964-72
Napoleon, Edward G. "Ed"   Cle-A 1983-85,
  KC-A 1987-88, Hou-N 1989, NY-A 1992
Naragon, Harold R. "Hal"   Min-A 1963-66,
  Det-A 1967-69
Narron, Samuel "Sam"   Pit-N 1952-64
Neale, A. Earle "Greasy"   StL-N 1929
Nelson, David E. "Dave"   Chi-A 1981-84,
  Cle-A 1992
Nettles, Graig   NY-A 1991
Neun, John H. "Johnny"   NY-A 1944-46
Newman, Jeffrey L. "Jeff"   Oak-A 1986,
  Cle-A 1992
Niarhos, C. Gus   KC-A 1962-64
Niehoff, J. Albert "Bert"   NY-N 1929
Nixon, Russell E. "Russ"   Cin-N 1976-82,
  Mon-N 1984-85, Atl-N 1986-87, Sea-A 1992
Noren, Irving A. "Irv"   Oak-A 1971-74,
  Chi-N 1975
Norman, H. Willis P. "Bill"   StL-N 1952-53
Northey, Ronald J. "Ron"   Pit-N 1961-63
Nossek, Joseph R. "Joe"   Mil-A 1973-75,
  Min-A 1976, Cle-A 1977-81, KC-A 1982-83,
  Chi-A 1984-85, 1986, 1991-92
Nottle, Edward W. "Ed"   Oak-A 1983
Oates, Johnny L.   Chi-N 1984-87,
  Bal-A 1989-91
O'Brien, Edward J. "Eddie"   Sea-A 1969
Oceak, Frank J.   Pit-N 1958-64, Cin-N 1965,
  Pit-N 1970-72
O'Connell, Daniel F. "Danny"   Was-A 1963-64
Okrie, Leonard J. "Len"   Bos-A 1961-62,
  1965-66, Det-A 1970
Oldis, Robert C. "Bob"   Phi-N 1964-66,
  Min-A 1968, Mon-N 1969
O'Leary, Charles T. "Charley"   StL-N 1913,
  NY-A 1921-30, Chi-N 1931-33, StL-A 1934-37
Oliva, Pedro "Tony"   Min-A 1976-78, 1985-91
Oliver, David J. "Dave"   Tex-A 1987-92
Oliver, Thomas N. "Tom"   Phi-A 1951-53,
  Bal-A 1954
Olson, Ivan M. "Ivy"   Bro-N 1924, 1930-31,
  NY-N 1932
O'Neil, G. Michael "Mickey"   Cle-A 1930
O'Neil, John S. "Buck"   Chi-N 1962
O'Neill, Stephen F. "Steve"   Cle-A 1935,
  Det-A 1941, Cle-A 1949, Bos-A 1950
Onslow, John J. "Jack"   Pit-N 1925-26,
  Was-A 1927, StL-N 1928, Phi-N 1931-32,
  Bos-A 1934
Osborn, Donald E. "Don"   Pit-N 1963-64,
  1970-72, 1974-76
Osteen, Claude W.   StL-N 1977-80,
  Phi-N 1982-88
Otero, Regino J. "Regie"   Cin-N 1959-65,
  Cle-A 1966
Otis, Amos J.   SD-N 1988-90
Ott, N. Edward "Ed"   Hou-N 1989-92
Overmire, Frank "Stubby"   Det-A 1963-66
Owen, Arnold M. "Mickey"   Bos-A 1955-56
Owens, James P. "Jim"   Hou-N 1967-72
Ozark, Daniel L. "Danny"   LA-N 1965-72,
  1980-82, SF-N 1983-84
Pacheco, Antonio A. "Tony"   Cle-A 1974,
  Hou-N 1976-79, 1982
Paepke, Jack   LA-A 1961-64, Cal-A 1965-66
Pafko, Andrew "Andy"   Mil-N 1960-62
Pagan, Jose A.   Pit-N 1974-78

Page, Philippe R. "Phil"   Cin-N 1947-52
Paige, Leroy R. "Satchell"   Atl-N 1968-69
Parker, Francis J. "Salty"   SF-N 1958-61,
  Cle-A 1962, LA-A 1964, Cin-A 1965-66,
  NY-N 1967, Hou-N 1968-72, Cal-A 1973-74
Pascual, Camilo A.   Min-A 1978-80
Patterson, Henry J. C. "Hank"   Bos-A 1932
Pattin, Martin W. "Marty"   Tor-A 1989
Paul, Michael G. "Mike"   Oak-A 1987-88,
  Sea-A 1989-91
Pavlick, Gregory M. "Greg"   NY-N 1985-86,
  1988-91
Peitz, Henry C. "Heinie"   StL-N 1913
Pennock, Herbert J. "Herb"   Bos-A 1936-39
Pepitone, Joseph A. "Joe"   NY-A 1982
Perez, Atanacio R. "Tony"   Cin-N 1987-92
Perkins, Ralph F. "Cy"   NY-A 1932-33,
  Det-A 1934-39, Phi-N 1946-54
Perlozzo, Samuel B. "Sam"   NY-N 1987-89,
  Cin-N 1990-92
Perranoski, Ronald P. "Ron"   LA-N 1981-92
Pesky, John M. "Johnny"   Pit-N 1965-67,
  Bos-A 1975-84
Peterson, Eric H. "Rick"   Pit-N 1984-85
Phillips, Harold R. "Lefty"   LA-N 1965-68,
  Cal-A 1969
Phillips, Richard E. "Dick"   SD-N 1980
Picciolo, Robert M. "Rob"   SD-N 1990-92
Piche, Ronald J. "Ron"   Mon-N 1976
Picinich, Valentine J. "Val"   Cin-N 1934
Piersall, James A. "Jimmy"   Tex-A 1975
Pignatano, Joseph B. "Joe"   Was-A 1965-67,
  NY-N 1968-81, Atl-N 1982-85
Piniella, Louis V. "Lou"   NY-A 1984-85
Pinson, Vada E.   Sea-A 1977-80, Chi-A 1981,
  Sea-A 1982-83, Det-A 1985-91
Pitler, Jacob A. "Jake"   Bro-N 1947-57
Pitts, Gaylen R.   StL-N 1991-92
Plaza, Ronald C. "Ron"   Sea-A 1969,
  Cin-N 1978-83, Oak-A 1986
Plummer, William F. "Bill"   Sea-A 1982-83,
  1988-91
Podres, John J. "Johnny"   SD-N 1973,
  Bos-A 1980, Min-A 1981-85, Phi-N 1991-92
Pole, Richard H. "Dick"   Chi-N 1988-91
Pollet, Howard J. "Howie"   StL-N 1959-64,
  Hou-N 1965
Popowski, Edward J. "Eddie"   Bos-A 1967-76
Posedel, William J. "Bill"   Pit-N 1949-53,
  StL-N 1954-57, Phi-N 1958, SF-N 1959-60,
  Oak-A 1968-72, SD-N 1974
Queen, Melvin D. "Mel"   Cle-A 1982
Quilici, Francis R. "Frank"   Min-A 1971-72
Quirk, James P. "Jamie"   StL-N 1984
Rader, Douglas L. "Doug"   SD-N 1979,
  Chi-A 1986-87, Oak-A 1992
Ragan, D. C. Patrick "Pat"   Phi-N 1924
Randall, Robert L. "Bobby"   Min-A 1980
Rapp, Vernon F. "Vern"   Mon-N 1979-83
Reberger, Frank B.   Cal-A 1991
Reese, Harold H. "Pee Wee"   LA-N 1959
Reese, James H. "Jimmie"   Cal-A 1973-92
Regan, Philip R. "Phil"   Sea-A 1984-86
Reiser, Harold P. "Pete"   LA-N 1960-64,
  Chi-N 1966-69, Cal-A 1970-71, Chi-N 1972-73
Renick, W. Richard "Rick"   KC-A 1981,
  Mon-N 1985-86, Min-A 1987-90
Resinger, Grover S.   Atl-N 1966, Chi-A 1967-68,
  Det-A 1969-70, Cal-A 1975-76
Rettenmund, Mervin W. "Merv"   Cal-A 1980-82,
  Tex-A 1983-85, Oak-A 1989-90, SD-N 1991-92
Reyes, Benjamin "Cananea"   Sea-A 1981
Reynolds, Tommie D   Oak-A 1989-92
Rice, Delbert "Del"   LA-A 1962-64,
  Cal-A 1965-66, Cle-A 1967
Ricketts, David W. "Dave"   Pit-N 1971-73,
  StL-N 1974-75, 1978-91
Riddle, John L. "Johnny"   Pit-N 1948-50,
  StL-N 1952-55, Mil-N 1956-57, Cin-N 1958,
  Phi-N 1959
Riddoch, Gregory L. "Greg"   SD-N 1987-90
Riggleman, James D. "Jim"   StL-N 1989-90
Rigney, William J. "Bill"   SD-N 1975
Ripken, Calvin E., Sr. "Cal"   Bal-A 1976-86,
  1989-92
Rippelmeyer, Raymond R. "Ray"
  Phi-N 1970-78
Roarke, Michael T. "Mike"   Det-A 1965-66,
  Cal-A 1967-69, Det-A 1970, Chi-N 1978-80,
  StL-N 1984-90, SD-N 1991-92
Roberts, David W. "Dave"   Cle-A 1987
Roberts, Melvin H. "Mel"   Phi-N 1992
Robertson, Sherrard A. "Sherry"   Min-N 1970
Robinson, Brooks C.   Bal-A 1977

Robinson, Frank   Cal-A 1977, Bal-A 1978-80,
  1985-87
Robinson, Warren G. "Sheriff"   NY-N 1964,
  1965-67, 1972
Robinson, Wilbert   NY-N 1911-13
Robinson, William H. "Bill"   NY-N 1984-89
Robinson, W. Edward "Eddie"   Bal-A 1957-59
Robson, Thomas J. "Tom"   Tex-A 1986-92
Rodgers, Robert L. "Bob"   Min-A 1970-74,
  SF-N 1976, Mil-A 1978-80
Rojas, Octavio V. "Cookie"   Chi-N 1978-81
Rolfe, Robert A. "Red"   NY-A 1946
Rommel, Edwin A. "Eddie"   Phi-A 1933-34
Roof, Phillip A. "Phil"   SD-N 1978,
  Sea-A 1983-88, Chi-N 1990-91, Det-A 1992
Root, Charles H. "Charlie"   Chi-N 1951-53,
  Mil-N 1956-57, Chi-N 1960
Roseboro, John J.   Was-A 1971, Cal-A 1972-74
Rosenbaum, Glen O.   Chi-A 1973-75, 1986-88
Roth, Francis C. "Frank"   Pit-N 1917,
  NY-A 1921-22, Cle-A 1923-25, Chi-A 1927
Rothschild,
  Lawrence L. "Larry"   Cin-N 1990-92
Roush, Edd J   Cin-N 1938
Rowe, Donald H. "Don"   Chi-A 1988, Mil-A 1992
Rowe, Kenneth D. "Ken"   Bal-A 1985-86
Rowe, Lynwood T. "Schoolboy"   Det-A 1954-55
Rowe, Ralph E.   Min-A 1972-75, Bal-A 1981-84
Ruberto, John E. "Sonny"   StL-N 1977-78
Rudi, Joseph O. "Joe"   Oak-A 1986-87
Rudolph, Richard "Dick"   Bos-N 1921-27
Ruel, Herold D. "Muddy"   Chi-A 1935-45,
  Cle-A 1948-50
Ruffing, Charles H. "Red"   NY-N 1962
Runnels, James E. "Pete"   Bos-A 1965-66
Runnells, Thomas W. "Tom"   Mon-N 1990-91
Russell, William E. "Bill"   LA-N 1987-91
Ruth, George H. "Babe"   Bro-N 1938
Ryan, Cornelius J. "Connie"   Mil-N 1957,
  Atl-N 1971, 1973-75, Tex-A 1977-79
Ryan, John B. "Jack"   Bos-A 1923-27
Ryan, Michael J. "Mike"   Phi-N 1980-89
Ryba, Dominic J. "Mike"   StL-N 1951-54
Sain, John F. "Johnny"   KC-A 1959,
  NY-A 1961-63, Min-A 1965-66, Det-A 1967-69,
  Chi-A 1971-75, Atl-N 1977, 1985-86
Sanford, John A. "Jack"   Cle-A 1968-69
Sandt, Thomas J. "Tommy"   Pit-N 1987-92
Sauer, Henry J. "Hank"   SF-N 1959
Saul, James A. "Jim"   Chi-N 1975-76,
  Oak-A 1979
Scarborough, Ray W.   Bal-A 1968
Schacht, Alexander "Al"   Was-A 1925-34,
  Bos-A 1935-36
Schaefer, Robert W. "Bob"   KC-A 1988-91
Schaffer, Jimmie R. "Jim"   Tex-A 1978,
  KC-A 1980-88
Schalk, Raymond W. "Ray"   Chi-A 1930-31
Schang, Walter H. "Wally"   Cle-A 1936-38
Scheffing, Robert B. "Bob"   StL-N 1952-53,
  Chi-N 1954-55, Mil-N 1960
Scherger, George R.   Cin-N 1970-78, 1982-86
Schoendienst, Albert F. "Red"   StL-N 1963-64,
  Oak-A 1977-78, StL-N 1979-89
Schreiber, Paul F.   NY-A 1942, Bos-A 1947-58
Schueler, Ronald R. "Ron"   Chi-A 1979-82,
  Oak-A 1983-84, Pit-N 1986
Schulte, John C. "Johnny"   Chi-N 1933,
  NY-A 1934-48, Bos-A 1949-50
Schultz, George W. "Barney"   StL-N 1971-75,
  Chi-N 1977
Schultz, Joseph C., Jr. "Joe"   StL-A 1949,
  StL-N 1963-68, KC-A 1970, Det-A 1971-76
Seminick, Andrew W. "Andy"   Phi-N 1957-58,
  1967-69
Sewell, J. Luther "Luke"   Cle-A 1939-41,
  Cin-N 1949
Sewell, Joseph W. "Joe"   NY-A 1934-35
Sewell, Truett B. "Rip"   Pit-N 1948
Shanks, Howard S. "Howie"   Cle-A 1928-32
Shaughnessy, Francis J. "Shag"   Det-A 1928
Shaw, Robert J. "Bob"   Mil-A 1973
Shawkey, J. Robert "Bob"   NY-A 1929
Shea, Mervyn D. "Merv"   Det-A 1939-42,
  Phi-N 1944-45, Chi-N 1949
Sheehan, Thomas C. "Tom"   Cin-N 1935-37,
  Bos-N 1944
Shellenback, Frank V.   StL-A 1939,
  Bos-A 1940-44, Det-A 1946-47, NY-N 1950-55
Shellenback, James P. "Jim"   Min-A 1983
Shepard, Robert E. "Bert"   Was-A 1946
Shepard, Lawrence W. "Larry"   Phi-N 1967,
  Cin-N 1970-78, SF-N 1979
Sherry, Lawrence "Larry"   Pit-N 1977-78,
  Cal-A 1979-80

Sherry, Norman B. "Norm" Cal-A 1970-71, 1976, Mon-N 1978-81, SD-N 1982-84, SF-N 1986-91
Shore, Raymond E. "Ray" Cin-N 1963-67
Shotton, Burton E. "Burt" StL-N 1923-25, Cin-N 1934, Cle-A 1942-45
Showalter, William N. "Buck" NY-A 1990-91
Sievers, Roy L. Cin-N 1966
Silvera, Charles A. "Charlie" Min-A 1969, Det-A 1971-73, Tex-A 1973-75
Silvestri, Kenneth J. "Ken" Phi-N 1959-60, Mil-N 1963-65, Atl-N 1966-75, Chi-A 1976, 1982
Simmons, Aloysius H. "Al" Phi-A 1940-42, 1944-49, Cle-A 1950-51
Sisler, George H. Bos-N 1930
Sisler, Richard A. "Dick" Cin-N 1961-64, StL-N 1966-70, SD-N 1975-76, NY-N 1979-80
Sisti, Sebastian D. "Sibby" Sea-A 1969
Skaff, Francis M. "Frank" Bal-A 1954, Det-A 1965-66, 1971
Skinner, Robert R. "Bob" SD-N 1970-73, Pit-N 1974-76, SD-N 1977, Cal-A 1978, Pit-N 1979-85, Atl-N 1986-88
Slattery, John T. "Jack" Bos-N 1918-19
Slider, Rachel W. "Rac" Bos-N 1987-90
Smith, Alfred J. "Al" NY-N 1933
Smith, Billy F. Tor-A 1984-88
Smith, Harold R. "Hal" StL-N 1962, Pit-N 1965-67, Cin-N 1968-69, Mil-A 1976-77
Smith, Richard P. "Red" Chi-A 1945-48
Snitker, Brian G. Atl-N 1985, 1988-90
Snyder, Francis E. "Frank" NY-N 1933-41
Snyder, James R. "Jim" Chi-N 1987, Sea-A 1988, SD-N 1991-92
Sommers, Dennis J. "Denny" NY-N 1977-78, Cle-A 1980-85, SD-N 1988-90
Sothoron, Allen S. StL-N 1927-28, StL-A 1932-33
Southworth, William H. "Billy" NY-N 1933
Spahn, Warren E. NY-N 1965, Cle-A 1972-73
Spalding, Charles H. "Dick" Phi-N 1934-36, Chi-N 1941-43
Spangler, Albert D. "Al" Chi-N 1970-71, 1974
Sparks, Joseph E. "Joe" Chi-A 1979, Cin-N 1984, Mon-N 1989, NY-A 1990
Spencer, H. Thomas "Tom" Cle-A 1988-89, NY-N 1991, Hou-N 1992
Squires, Michael L. "Mike" Tor-A 1989-91, Chi-A 1992
Staller, George W. Bal-A 1962, 1969-75
Stanage, Oscar H. Pit-N 1927-31
Stange, A. Lee Bos-A 1972-74, Min-A 1975, Oak-A 1977-79, Bos-A 1981-84
Stanky, Edward R. "Eddie" Cle-A 1957-58
Stanley, Frederick B. "Fred" Mil-A 1991
Stargell, Wilver D. "Willie" Pit-N 1985, Atl-N 1986-88
Starrette, Herman P. "Herm" Atl-N 1974-76, SF-N 1977-78, Phi-N 1979-81, SF-N 1983-84, Mil-A 1985-86, Chi-N 1987, Bal-A 1988
Staub, Daniel J. "Rusty" NY-N 1982
Stearns, John H. NY-A 1989
Stelmaszek, Richard F. "Rick" Min-A 1981-92
Stengel, Charles D. "Casey" Bro-N 1932-33
Stevens, Edward L. "Ed" SD-N 1981
Stock, Milton J. "Milt" Chi-N 1944-48, Bro-N 1949-50, Pit-N 1951-52
Stock, Wesley G. "Wes" KC-A 1967, Mil-N 1970-72, Oak-A 1972-76, Sea-A 1977-81, Oak-A 1984-86
Stottlemyre, Melvin L. "Mel" NY-N 1984-92
Stratton, Monty F. Chi-A 1939-41
Street, Charles E. "Gabby" StL-N 1929, StL-A 1937
Strickland, George B. Min-A 1962, Cle-A 1963-69, KC-A 1970-72
Stubing, Lawrence G. "Moose" Cal-A 1985-88, 1989-90
Such, Richard S. "Dick" Tex-A 1983-85, Min-A 1985-92
Sugden, Joseph "Joe" StL-N 1921-25, Phi-N 1926-27

Sukeforth, Clyde L. Bro-N 1943-51, Pit-N 1952-57
Sullivan, John P. KC-A 1979, Atl-N 1980-81, Tor-A 1982-92
Summers, John J. "Champ" NY-A 1989-90
Susce, George C. M. Cle-A 1941-47, 1948-49, Bos-A 1950-54, KC-A 1955-56, Mil-N 1958-59, Was-A 1961-67, 1969-71, Tex-A 1972
Sweeney, William J. "Bill" Det-A 1947-48
Sweet, Ricky J. "Rick" Sea-A 1984
Swift, Robert V. "Bob" Det-A 1953-54, KC-A 1957-59, Was-A 1960, Det-A 1963-66
Tannehill, Jesse N. Phi-N 1920
Tappe, Elvin W. "El" Chi-N 1959-63
Taylor, Antonio N. "Tony" Phi-N 1977-79, 1988-89
Taylor, James W. "Zack" Bro-N 1936, StL-A 1941-46, Pit-N 1947
Temple, John E. "Johnny" Cin-N 1964
Tenace, F. Gene Hou-N 1986-87, Tor-A 1990-92
Terwilliger, W. Wayne Was-A 1969-71, Tex-A 1972, 1981-85, Min-A 1986-92
Testa, Nicholas "Nick" SF-N 1958
Thomas, George E. Bos-A 1970
Thomas, Ira F. Phi-A 1914-17, 1925-26
Thomas, J. Leroy "Lee" StL-N 1972, 1983
Thomas, Roy A. StL-N 1922
Thompson, Charles L. "Tim" StL-N 1981
Tiefenauer, Bobby G. Phi-N 1979
Tighe, John T. "Jack" Det-A 1942, 1955-56
Tincup, A. Ben Bro-N 1940
Tobin, John T. "Jack" StL-A 1949-51
Tolan, Robert "Bobby" SD-N 1980-83, Sea-A 1987
Torborg, Jeffrey A. "Jeff" Cle-A 1975-77, NY-A 1979-88
Torchia, Anthony L. "Tony" Bos-A 1985
Torres, Hector E. Tor-A 1991
Tracewski, Richard J. "Dick" Det-A 1972-92
Trebelhorn, Thomas L. "Tom" Mil-A 1984, 1986, Chi-N 1992
Trucks, Virgil O. Pit-N 1963
Turley, Robert L. "Bob" Bos-A 1964
Turner, James R. "Jim" NY-A 1949-59, Cin-N 1961-65, NY-A 1966-73
Turner, Terrence L. "Terry" StL-N 1924
Uhle, George E. Cle-A 1936-37, Chi-N 1940, Was-A 1944
Unser, Delbert B. "Del" Phi-N 1985-88
Valentine, Robert J. "Bobby" NY-N 1983-85
Valo, Elmer W. Cle-A 1963-64
Van Ornum, John C. SF-N 1981-84
Vernon, James B. "Mickey" Pit-N 1960, 1964, StL-N 1965, Mon-N 1977-78, NY-A 1982
Vincent, Albert L. "Al" Det-A 1943-44, Bal-A 1955-59, Phi-N 1961-63, KC-A 1966-67
Virdon, William C. "Bill" Pit-N 1968-71, 1986
Virgil, Osvaldo Jose Sr. "Ozzie" SF-N 1969-72, 1974-75, Mon-N 1976-81, SD-N 1982-85, Sea-A 1986-88
Vukovich, John C. Chi-N 1982-87, Phi-N 1988, 1989-92
Wagner, Charles F. "Heinie" Bos-A 1916-19, 1927-29
Wagner, Charles T. "Charley" Bos-A 1970
Wagner, John P. "Honus" Pit-N 1933-51
Walker, Albert B. "Rube" LA-N 1958, Was-A 1965-67, NY-N 1968-81, Atl-N 1982-84
Walker, Fred "Dixie" StL-N 1953, 1955, Mil-N 1963-65
Walker, Gerald H. "Gee" Cin-N 1946
Walker, Harry W. StL-N 1959-62
Walker, Jerry A. NY-A 1981-82, Hou-N 1983-85
Walker, Verlon L. Chi-N 1961-70
Wallace, Roderick J. "Bobby" Cin-N 1926
Walls, R. Lee Oak-A 1979-82, NY-A 1983
Walsh, Edward A. "Ed" Chi-A 1923-25, 1928-30
Walters, William H. "Bucky" Bos-N 1950-52, Mil-N 1953-55, NY-N 1956-57
Walton, James R. "Jim" Mil-A 1973-75

Waner, Paul G. Phi-N 1965
Ward, John F. "Jay" NY-A 1987, Mon-N 1991-92
Ward, Peter T. "Pete" Atl-N 1978
Wares, Clyde E. "Buzzy" StL-N 1930-35, 1937-51
Warner, Harry C. Tor-A 1977-79, 1980, Mil-A 1981-82
Warthen, Daniel D. "Dan" Sea-A 1991-92
Wathan, John D. KC-A 1986, Cal-A 1992
Watson, Robert J. "Bob" Oak-A 1986-88
Weaver, Earl S. Bal-A 1968
Webb, William J. "Billy" Chi-A 1935-39
West, Samuel F. "Sam" Was-A 1947-49
Westrum, Wesley N. "Wes" SF-N 1958-63, NY-N 1964-65, SF-N 1968-71
Whisenant, T. Peter "Pete" Cin-N 1961-62
White, Ernest D. "Ernie" Bos-A 1947-48, NY-N 1963
White, Joyner C. "Jo-Jo" Cle-A 1958-60, Det-A 1960, KC-A 1961-62, Mil-N 1963-65, Atl-N 1966, KC-A 1969
White, Roy H. NY-A 1983-84, 1986
Whitehill, Earl O. Cle-A 1941, Phi-N 1943
Whitmer, Daniel C. "Dan" Det-A 1992
Widmar, Albert J. "Al" Phi-N 1962-64, 1968-69, Mil-A 1973-74, Tor-A 1980-88, 1989
Wietelmann, William F. "Whitey" Cin-N 1966-67, SD-N 1969-79
Wilber, Delbert Q. "Del" Chi-A 1955-56, Was-A 1970, Tex-A 1973
Wiley, Mark E. Bal-A 1987, Cle-A 1988-91
Wilhelm, Irvin K. "Kaiser" Phi-N 1921
Wilks, Theodore "Ted" KC-A 1961
Williams, Billy L. Chi-N 1980-82, Oak-A 1983-85, Chi-N 1986-87
Williams, David C. "Davey" NY-N 1956-57
Williams, Donald E. "Don" SD-N 1977-80
Williams, James B. "Jimmy" Hou-N 1975, Bal-A 1981-87
Williams, James F. "Jimy" Tor-A 1980-85, Atl-N 1990-92
Williams, Otto G. Det-A 1925, StL-A 1927, Cin-N 1930
Williams, Richard H. "Dick" Mon-N 1970
Williams, Stanley W. "Stan" Bos-A 1975-76, Chi-A 1977-78, NY-A 1980-81, 1982, Cin-N 1984, NY-A 1987, 1988, Cin-N 1990-91
Williams, Walter A. "Walt" Chi-A 1988
Wilson, James "Jimmy" Cin-N 1939-40, 1944-46
Wiltse, George L. "Hooks" NY-A 1925
Wine, Robert P. Sr. "Bobby" Phi-N 1972-83, Atl-N 1985, 1988-90
Winegarner, Ralph L. StL-A 1948-51
Wingo, Ivey B. Cin-N 1928-29, 1936
Winkles, Bobby B. Cal-A 1972, Oak-A 1974-75, SF-N 1976-77, Chi-A 1979-81, Mon-N 1986-88
Wolgamot, C. Earl Cle-A 1931-33
Woodall, C. Lawrence "Larry" Bos-A 1942-48
Woodling, Eugene F. "Gene" Bal-A 1964-67
Worthington, Allan F. "Al" Min-A 1972-73
Wright, Melvin J. "Mel" Chi-N 1963-64, 1971, Pit-N 1973, NY-A 1974-75, Hou-N 1976-82
Wyatt, J. Whitlow "Whit" Phi-N 1955-57, Mil-N 1958-65, Atl-N 1966-67
Wynn, Early Cle-A 1964-66, Min-A 1967-69
York, P. Rudolph "Rudy" Bos-A 1959-62
Yost, Edward F. "Eddie" LA-A 1962, Was-A 1963-67, NY-A 1968-76, Bos-A 1977-84
Zarilla, Allen L. "Al" Was-A 1971
Zeller, Barton W. "Bart" StL-N 1970
Zimmer, Donald W. "Don" Mon-N 1971, SD-N 1972, Bos-A 1974-76, NY-A 1983, Chi-N 1984-86, NY-A 1986, SF-N 1987, Bos-A 1992
Zimmer, Thomas J. "Tom" StL-N 1976
Zimmerman, Gerald R. "Gerry" Min-A 1967, Mon-N 1969-75, Min-A 1976-80
Zwilling, Edward H. "Dutch" Cle-A 1941

Biographical Data for Coaches Not Appearing in the Player/Pitcher Registers or Manager Roster

SPENCER ABBOTT Abbott, Spencer b: 8/27/1877, Chicago, Ill. d: 12/18/51, Washington, D.C. (1B)
RICK ADAIR Adair, Michael Richard b: 1/19/58, Spartanburg, S.Car. BL/TL, 6', 185 lbs. (P)
CARLOS ALFONSO Alfonso, Carlos b: 12/18/50, Havana, Cuba BR/TR, 6'2", 205 lbs. (P)
TONY AUFERIO Auferio, Anthony Patrick b: 6/13/47, Orange, N.J. BR/TR, 5'10", 185 lbs. (3B)
DICK BERARDINO Berardino, Richard J. b: 7/2/37, Cambridge, Mass. BR/TR, 6'1", 190 lbs. (OF)
C. B. BERINGER Beringer, Carroll James b: 8/14/28, Bellwood, Neb. BR/TR, 6', 195 lbs. (P)
TERRY BEVINGTON Bevington, Terry Paul b: 7/7/56, Akron, Ohio BR/TR, 6'2", 190 lbs. (C)
GREG BIAGINI Biagini, Gregory Peter b: 7/30/44, Chicago, Ill. BB/TR, 6'2", 205 lbs. (1B-OF)

WAYNE BLACKBURN Blackburn, Wayne Clark   b: 7/10/16, My.Joy, Ohio   BL/TR, 5'10", 165 lbs.   (OF-3B-2B)
JACK BLOOMFIELD Bloomfield, Gordon Leigh   b: 8/7/32, Monti Alto, Tex.   BL/TR, 6'2", 185 lbs.   (2B)
JIMMY BRAGAN Bragan, James Alton   b: 3/12/29, Birmingham, Ala.   BR/TR, 6', 198 lbs.   (2B)
SCOTT BREEDEN Breeden, Harold Scott   b: 9/17/37, Charlottesville, Va.   BR/TR, 6'2", 210 lbs.   (P)
JOE CAMACHO Camacho, Joseph Gomes   b: 5/29/28, New Bedford, Mass.   BR/TR, 6', 185 lbs.   (SS-2B)
DANNY CARNEVALE Carnevale, Daniel Joseph   b: 2/8/18, Buffalo, N.Y.   BR/TR, 6', 195 lbs.   (SS)
LEONEL CARRION Carrion, Leonel Santiago (Matheus)   b: 2/15/52, Maracaibo, Venez.   BR/TR, 5'11", 185 lbs.   (OF)
DICK CARTER Carter, Richard Joseph   b: 8/31/16, Philadelphia, Pa.   d: 9/11/69, Philadelphia, Pa.   BR/TR, 5'10", 190 lbs.   (P-OF)
DOM CHITI Chiti, Harry Dominic   b: 12/10/58, Independence, Mo.   BL/TL, 6'2", 200 lbs.   (P)
BOB CLEAR Clear, Elwood Robert   b: 12/14/27, Denver, Colo.   BR/TR, 5'10", 170 lbs.   (P)
BOB CLUCK Cluck, Robert Alton   b: 1/10/46, San Diego, Cal.   BL/TL, 6'2", 195 lbs.   (P)
TERRY COLLINS Collins, Terry Lee   b: 5/7/49, Midland, Mich.   BR/TR, 5'8", 160 lbs.   (2B)
MARK CONNOR Connor, Mark Peter   b: 5/27/49, Brooklyn, N.Y.   BR/TR, 6'3", 195 lbs.   (P)
MARK CRESSE Cresse, Mark Emery   b: 9/21/51, St.Albans, N.Y.   BR/TR, 6'3", 220 lbs.   (C)
MARTY DeMERRITT DeMerritt, Martin Gordon   b: 3/4/53, San Francisco, Cal.   BR/TR, 6'2.5", 205 lbs.   (P)
BOBBY DEWS Dews, Robert Walter   b: 3/23/38, Clinton, Iowa   BR/TR, 6'1", 175 lbs.   (SS)
RICH DONNELLY Donnelly, Richard Francis   b: 8/3/46, Steubenville, Ohio   BL/TR, 6', 185 lbs.   (C)
OTIS DOUGLAS Douglas, Otis W.   b: 7/25/11, Reedville, Va.   d: 3/21/89, Kilmarnock, Va.   BR/TR, 6'1", 230 lbs.   (DNP)
RICK DOWN Down, Richard John   b: 12/14/50, Wyandotte, Mich.   BR/TR, 5'11", 220 lbs.   (OF)
HARRY DUNLOP Dunlop, Harry Alexander   b: 9/6/33, Sacramento, Cal.   BL/TR, 6'3", 200 lbs.   (C)
GENE DUSAN Dusan, Eugene Paul   b: 11/9/49, Los Angeles, Cal.   BB/TR, 6', 200 lbs.   (C)
GLENN EZZELL Ezzell, Glenn Wayne   b: 10/29/44, Kentwood, La.   BR/TR, 6', 190 lbs.   (C)
JOE FITZGERALD Fitzgerald, Joseph Patrick   b: 3/17/1897, Washington, D.C.   d: 8/29/67, Orlando, Fla.   BR/TR, 5'11", 200 lbs.   (C)
JOHN FITZPATRICK Fitzpatrick, John Arthur   b: 3/9/ 19, 04La Salle, Ill.   BR/TR, 6'1.5", 185 lbs.   (C)
MATT GALANTE Galante, Matthew Joseph   b: 3/2/44, Brooklyn, N.Y.   BR/TR, 5'6", 175 lbs.   (2B)
ORLANDO GOMEZ Gomez, Juan Alejandro   b: 6/24/46, Juana Diaz, P.R.   BR/TR, 6', 190 lbs.   (C)
EPY GUERRERO Guerrero, Epifanio Obdulio (Abud)   b: 1/3/42, Santo Domingo, D.R.   BR/TR, 5'11", 168 lbs.   (OF)
GUY HANSEN Hansen, Guy Christopher   b: 11/12/47, Los Angeles, Cal.   BR/TR, 6', 170 lbs.   (P)
ROGER HANSEN Hansen, Roger Christian   b: 8/28/61, Johnstown, Pa.   BR/TR, 6', 200 lbs.   (C)
TOM HARMON Harmon, Thomas Harold   b: 12/16/48, Lubbock, Tex.   BL/TR, 5'11", 185 lbs.   (C)
CHUCK HERNANDEZ Hernandez, Carlo Amado   b: 11/11/60, Tampa, Fla.   BL/TL, 6'3", 200 lbs.   (P)
PERRY HILL Hill, Perry   b: 3/19/52, Euless, Tex.   BR/TR, (2B)
BEN HINES Hines, Benjamin Thortan   b: 11/7/35, Yeager, Okla.   BR/TR, 5'11", 205 lbs.   (3B-C)
BRUCE HINES Hines, Bruce Edwin   b: 11/7/57, Pomona, Cal.   BB/TR, 5'10", 180 lbs.   (2B)
DOUG HOLMQUIST Holmquist, Douglas Leonard   b: 10/4/41, Bridgeport, Conn.   d: 2/27/88, Altamonte Springs, Fla.   BR/TR, 6'2", 195 lbs.   (C)
GOLDIE HOLT Holt, Golden Desmond   b: 3/22/02, Enlo, Tex.   d: 6/11/91, Sherman Oaks, Cal.   BR/TR, 5'7.5", 165 lbs.   (3B-OF-2B)
VERN HOSCHEIT Hoscheit, Vernard Arthur   b: 4/1/22, Brunswick, Neb.   BR/TR, 5'9", 185 lbs.   (C)
LUIS ISAAC Isaac, Luis (Aponte)   b: 6/19/46, Rio Piedras, P.R.   BR/TR, 5'11.5", 195 lbs.   (C)
RUDY JARAMILLO Jaramillo, Rudolph   b: 9/20/50, Beeville, Tex.   BL/TR, 5'11", 180 lbs.   (OF)
JOE JONES Jones, Joseph Carmack   b: 12/13/41, Lebanon, Tenn.   BR/TR, 5'9", 155 lbs.   (2B)
LOU KAHN Kahn, Louis   b: 12/4/16, St.Louis, Mo.   BR/TR, 5'11", 195 lbs.   (C)
MIKE KELLY Kelly, Bernard Francis   b: 5/1/1896, Indianapolis, Ind.   d: 10/23/68, Indianapolis, Ind.   BR/TR, 6', 198 lbs.   (1B)
KEVIN KENNEDY Kennedy, Kevin   b: 53,   BR/TR, (C)
WENDELL KIM Kim, Wendell Kealohapauloe   b: 3/9/51, Honolulu, Hawaii   BR/TR, 5'5", 160 lbs.   (2B)
GEORGE KISSELL Kissell, George Marshall   b: 9/9/21, Watertown, N.Y.   BR/TR, 5'8", 175 lbs.   (3B)
HUB KITTLE Kittle, Hubert Milton   b: 2/19/17, Los Angeles, Cal.   BR/TR, 6'1", 195 lbs.   (P)
FRED KOENIG Koenig, Fred Carl   b: 4/27/31, St.Louis, Mo.   BR/TR, 6'3", 200 lbs.   (1B-3B)
JIM LETT Lett, James Curtis   b: 1/3/51, Charleston, W.Va.   BR/TR, 6'2", 185 lbs.   (3B)
LENNY LEVY Levy, Leonard Howard   b: 6/11/13, Pittsburgh, Pa.   BR/TR, 5'10.5", 190 lbs.   (C)
BILL LOBE Lobe, William Charles   b: 3/24/12, Cleveland, Ohio   d: 1/7/69, Cleveland, Ohio   BR/TR, 5'9.5", 178 lbs.   (C)
Q. V. LOWE Lowe, Q. V.   b: 1/15/45, Red Level, Ala.   BR/TR, 6'1", 185 lbs.   (P)
ROY MAJTYKA Majtyka, Le Roy W.   b: 6/1/39, Buffalo, N.Y.   BR/TR, 5'11", 170 lbs.   (2B)
JACK MALOOF Maloof, Jack Garth   b: 10/12/49, Redlands, Cal.   BL/TL, 6', 175 lbs.   (1B-OF)
DOUG MANSOLINO Mansolino, Douglas   b: 9/20/56, Plainfield, N.J.   BR/TR, 5'7", 155 lbs.   (IF)
HARRY MATHEWS Mathews, Henry
LEO MAZZONE Mazzone, Leo David   b: 10/16/48, Keyser, W.Va.   BL/TL, 5'10", 185 lbs.   (P)
MAJE McDONNELL McDonnell, Robert A.   b: 7/20/20, Philadelphia, Pa.   BR/TR, 5'6", 135 lbs.   (P)
J. R. McKEE McKee, J. R.
JOHN McLAREN McLaren, John Lowell   b: 9/29/51, Galveston, Tex.   BR/TR, 6', 200 lbs.   (C)
MO MOZZALI Mozzali, Maurice Joseph   b: 12/12/22, Louisville, Ky.   d: 3/2/87, Lakeland, Fla.   BL/TL, 5'10", 160 lbs.   (1B)
JACK MULL Mull, Jack Leroy   b: 9/29/43, Chambersburg, Pa.   BR/TR, 5'10", 188 lbs.   (C)
ED NAPOLEON Napoleon, Edward George   b: 9/17/37, Baltimore, Md.   BR/TR, 5'8", 165 lbs.   (OF-3B-1B)
ED NOTTLE Nottle, Edward William   b: 10/22/39, Philadelphia, Pa.   BR/TR, 5'10", 180 lbs.   (P)
FRANK OCEAK Oceak, Frank John "Fez'   b: 9/8/12, Pocahontas, Va.   d: 3/19/83, Johnstown, Pa.   BR/TR, 5'9", 172 lbs.   (2B)
BUCK O'NEIL O'Neil, John Jordan   b: 11/13/11, Carrabelle, Fla.   BR/TR, 6'2", 190 lbs.   (1B)
DON OSBORN Osborn, Donald Edwin   b: 6/3/08, Sandpoint, Idaho   d: 3/23/79, Torrance, Cal.   BR/TR, 6', 185 lbs.   (P)
TONY PACHECO Pacheco, Antonio Aristides   b: 8/9/27, Havana, Cuba   d: 87, Miami, Fla.   BR/TR, 6', 190 lbs.   (2B)
JACK PAEPKE Paepke, Jack   b: 8/8/ 28, 22Provo, Utah   BR/TR, 6'2.5", 220 lbs.   (C-P)
GREG PAVLICK Pavlick, Gregory Michael   b: 3/10/50, Washington, D.C.   BR/TR, 6'3", 205 lbs.   (P)
RICK PETERSON Peterson, Eric Harding   b: 10/30/54, Brunswick, N.J.   BL/TL, 6', 175 lbs.   (P)
RON PLAZA Plaza, Ronald Charles   b: 8/24/34, Passaic, N.J.   BL/TR, 6', 180 lbs.   (3B)
GROVER RESINGER Resinger, Grover S.   b: 10/20/15, St.Louis, Mo.   d: 1/1/86, St.Louis, Mo.   BR/TR, 5'9", 180 lbs.   (3B)
CANANEA REYES Reyes, Benjamin (Chavez)   b: 2/18/37, Nacosari, Sonora, Mexico   d: 11/11/91, Hermosillo, Mexico   BR/TR, 5'10", 180 lbs.   (OF)
MEL ROBERTS Roberts, Melvin Henry   b: 1/18/43, Abington, Pa.   BR/TR, 6', 180 lbs.   (OF)
SHERIFF ROBINSON Robinson, Warren Grant   b: 9/8/21, Cambridge, Md.   BR/TR, 6'1", 195 lbs.   (C)
GLEN ROSENBAUM Rosenbaum, Glen Otis   b: 6/14/36, Union Mills, Ind.   BR/TR, 5'11", 180 lbs.   (P)
RALPH ROWE Rowe, Ralph Emanuel   b: 7/14/24, Newberry, S.C.   BL/TR, 5'6", 160 lbs.   (OF)
JIM SAUL Saul, James Allen   b: 11/24/39, Bristol, Va.   BL/TR, 6'3", 210 lbs.   (C)
GEORGE SCHERGER Scherger, George Richard   b: 11/20/20, Dickinson, N.D.   BR/TR, 5'8", 183 lbs.   (2B)
RAC SLIDER Slider, Rachel W.   b: 12/23/33, Simms, Tex.   BL/TR, 5'8", 160 lbs.   (SS)
BILLY SMITH Smith, Billy Franklin   b: 1/14/30, High Point, N.C.   BL/TL, 5'9", 160 lbs.   (1B-OF)
BRIAN SNITKER Snitker, Brian Gerald   b: 10/17/55, Decatur, Ill.   BR/TR, 6'1", 192 lbs.   (C)
DENNY SOMMERS Sommers, Dennis James   b: 7/12/40, New London, Wis.   BL/TR, 6'2", 205 lbs.   (C)
JOE SPARKS Sparks, Joseph Everett   b: 3/15/38, McComas, W.Va.   BL/TR, 6', 195 lbs.   (3B-2B)
TONY TORCHIA Torchia, Anthony Lewis   b: 12/13/43, Chicago, Ill.   BR/TL, 5'10", 180 lbs.   (1B-OF)
JOHN VanORNUM Van Ornum, John Clayton   b: 10/20/39, Pasadena, Cal.   BR/TR, 5'11", 175 lbs.   (C)
AL VINCENT Vincent, Albert Linder   b: 12/23/06, Birmingham, Ala.   BR/TR, 5'9.5", 170 lbs.   (2B)
VERLON WALKER Walker, Verlon Lee "Rube'   b: 3/7/29, Lenoir, N.C.   d: 3/24/71, Chicago, Ill.   BL/TR, 6', 210 lbs.   (C)
JIM WALTON Walton, James Robert   b: 9/5/35, Shattuck, Okla.   BR/TR, 6'2", 190 lbs.   (P)
HARRY WARNER Warner, Harry Clinton   b: 12/11/28, Reeders, Pa.   BL/TR, 6'2", 215 lbs.   (1B)
DAN WHITMER Whitmer, Daniel C.   b: 11/23/55, Redlands, Cal.   BR/TR, 6'3", 200 lbs.   (C)
DON WILLIAMS Williams, Donald Ellis   b: 12/24/37, Paragould, Ark.   BR/TR, 5'10", 185 lbs.   (SS)
JIMMY WILLIAMS Williams, James Bernard   b: 5/15/26, Toronto, Ont., Can.   BR/TR, 5'10", 180 lbs.   (OF)
EARL WOLGAMOT Wolgamot, Clinton Earl   b: 12/21/1895, Fairbank, Iowa   d: 4/25/70, Independence, Iowa   BR/TR, 5'8", 155 lbs.   (C)

Negro Baseball Roster

Dick Clark and Larry Lester

In 1970 Robert Peterson wrote a pioneering book, *Only the Ball Was White,* that launched the serious study of black baseball in the years before Jackie Robinson broke the color line in 1947. Peterson was followed in that decade by John Holway's *Voices from the Great Black Baseball Leagues* and William Brashler's *Josh Gibson,* and in the 1980s by Jules Tygiel's *Baseball's Great Experiment: Jackie Robinson and His Legacy.* Recent years have produced further interesting work, from television documentaries to lavish pictorials to oral histories. You don't hear much argument anymore, as once was prevalent, about whether black stars like Satchel Paige or Buck Leonard, Oscar Charleston or Judy Johnson, truly belong in Baseball's Hall of Fame.

Underlying much of the good work that has come forth over the last two decades has been the diligent research of unheralded members of the Society for American Baseball Research (SABR), founded in 1971 by L. Robert Davids and fifteen other empassioned students of the game. Their early establishment of a Negro Leagues research committee spurred such valuable efforts as the compilation of team and individual statistics for many seasons of Negro League play; the dedication of a monu-ment in honor of Bud Fowler, the nation's first professional black player; the founding of a Negro League Baseball Museum in Kansas City, Missouri; and the long, steady progress toward an encyclopedic research guide to black baseball, nearing publication by SABR as this third edition of *Total Baseball* goes to press.

Part of that volume, edited by Larry Lester and Dick Clark, co-chairmen of SABR's Negro Leagues Committee, is a massive revision of Robert Peterson's listing of black baseball players and officials. Lester and Clark, aided by other SABR members, have added players, corrected names and team affiliations, ranged earlier and later, broader and deeper, than Peterson's original work, and have provided us with an invaluable reference tool.

From vintage figures like Bud Fowler, Moses Fleetwood Walker and Billy Whyte to more recognizable names like Willie Mays, Henry Aaron, Larry Doby, Monte Irvin, and Ernie Banks; from Hall of Famers like Martin Dihigo and Ray Dandridge to storied figures like Cannonball Dick Redding and Bullet Joe Rogan, Turkey Stearnes and Oliver Marcelle, the shadows of legend are here. They were part of America's game; savor their names.

Aaron, Henry Louis (Hank), 1952 INF,
Indianapolis Clowns
Aballi, —, 1930 P, Cuban Stars
Abbott, —, 1906-1908 P, OF, Cuban Giants,
Genuine Cuban Giants
Abernathy, James, 1946-47 OF, Boston Blues,
Indianapolis Clowns
Abreu, Eufemio [Abreu], 1920-34 C, 1B, OF,
Cuban Stars (NNL), Cuban Stars (ECL)
Acosta, Jose, 1915 P, Long Branch N.J. Cubans
Adams, Emery (Ace), 1932-46 P, Memphis Red
Sox, Baltimore Elite Giants, New York Black
Yankees
Adams, (Packinghouse), 1938 3B, Kansas City
Monarchs
Addison, J., 1910-11 C, Philadelphia Giants
Addison, K., 1911-12 3B, Philadelphia Giants,
Pittsburgh Giants
Addison, T., 1911 SS, Philadelphia Giants
Adkins, Clarence, 1931 OF, Nashville Elite
Giants
Adkins, Stacy, see Stacy Atkins
Agnew, Clyde, 1950 P, Baltimore Elite Giants
Ahrens, —, 1930 OF, P, Cuban Stars
Albrecht, R., 1928-29 P, Bacharach Giants
Albright, Thomas (Pistol Pete), 1936 P, New
York Cubans
Albritton, Alexander (Alex), 1921-25 P,
Baltimore Black Sox, Washington Potomacs,
Hilldale, Bacharach Giants
Alderette, —, 1918 C, Cuban Stars (East)
Alexander, —, 1918-21 OF, 1B, 2B, Dayton
Marcos, Chicago Giants, Columbus Buckeyes
Alexander, Calvin, 1922 P, New Orleans
Crescent Stars
Alexander, (Chuffy), 1927-32 3B, OF, 1B,
Birmingham Black Barons, Monroe Monarchs
Alexander, Freyl, 1912 pres, Homestead Grays
Alexander, Grover Cleveland (Buck), 1923-26 P,
Chicago Giants, Detroit Stars, Indianapolis
ABCs, Cleveland Elites
Alexander, (Hub), 1913 C, Chicago Giants
Alexander, Joe, 1950 C, Kansas City Monarchs
Alexander, Spencer, 1940-41 OF, Newark
Eagles
Alexander, Ted (Red), 1940-49 P, Cleveland
Bears, Chicago American Giants, Kansas City
Monarchs, Birmingham Black Barons,
Homestead Grays, New York Black Yankees
Alfonso, Angel, 1924-30 SS, 3B, 2B, Cuban
Stars (NNL), Cuban Stars (ECL)
Allen, —, 1940,1943 OF, Birmingham Black
Barons, New York Black Yankees
Allen, Clifford (Crooks, Clyde), 1932-38 P,
Hilldale, Baltimore Black Sox, Homestead
Grays, Memphis Red Sox, Philadelphia Stars
Allen, Dave, 1887 C, 1B, UTIL, Trenton Cuban
Giants (Middle States Lg.), Pittsburgh
Keystones
Allen, Homer, 1932 P, Monroe Monarchs
Allen, Hoses (Buster), 1942-47 P, UTIL,
Jacksonville Red Caps, Cincinnati Clowns,
Cincinnati-Indianapolis Clowns, Memphis Red
Sox, Cleveland Buckeyes
Allen, M., 1919-22 2B, Lincoln Giants, Baltimore
Black Sox
Allen, Newton Henry (Newt, Colt), 1922-47 2B,
SS, OF, MGR, All Nations, Kansas City
Monarchs, St. Louis Stars, Homestead Grays,
Indianapolis Clowns
Allen, Todd, 1915-25 3B, MGR, Bowser's
ABCs, Indianapolis ABCs, Chicago American
Giants, Lincoln Giants
Allen, Toussaint L'Ouverture (Tom), 1914-26
1B, Havana Red Sox, Hilldale, Wilmington
Potomacs, Newark Stars
Allen, William 1887 player, Cincinnati Browns
Allison, —, 1915-17,21,25 1B, 2B, C, Chicago
Union Giants, Chicago American Giants,
Nashville Elite Giants, Indianapolis ABCs
Almagro, Jorge, 1945 OF, Pittsburgh Crawfords
Almas, —, 1925 P, Cubans (NNL)
Almenteros, Juan Pablo, 1916 P, Cuban Stars
Almeyda, —, 1905 3B, All Cubans
Alonso, Rogelio, 1927-30 P, OF, Cuban Stars
(NNL)
Alsop, Clifford, 1920-22 P, Kansas City
Monarchs
Alston, Tom, 1948 1B, Greensboro (Nc) Red
Wings
Alvarez, Raul, 1924-33 P, Cuban Stars (NNL),
Cuban Stars (East)

Amoros, Edmundo (Sandy), 1950 1B, OF, New
York Cubans
Anas, A., 1935 P, New York Cubans
Anderson, , 1908,1912 P, 3B, Cuban Giants
Anderson, Lewis , 1930-33 C, Chicago
American Giants, Baltimore Black Sox
Anderson, Ralph, 1927,1932 OF, Nashville Elite
Giants, Indianapolis ABCs, Homestead Grays
Anderson, Robert James (Bobby), 1915-25 SS,
2B, Peters' Union Giants, Chicago American
Giants, Philadelphia Giants, Gilkerson's Union
Giants, Chicago Giants
Anderson, Theodore (Bubbles), 1922-25 2B, C,
Kansas City Monarchs, Birmingham Black
Barons, Washington Potomacs, Wilmington
Potomacs, Indianapolis ABCs
Anderson, William, 1927,1930 OF, Nashville
Elite Giants
Anderson, William (Bill), 1940-47 P, Brooklyn
Royal Giants, Cuban Stars, New York Cubans,
Philadelphia Stars
Andrews, Herman (Jabo), 1930-43 OF, P, 1B,
MGR, Birmingham Black Barons, Memphis
Red Sox, Indianapolis ABCs, Detroit Wolves,
Homestead Grays, Columbus Blue Birds,
Pittsburgh Crawfords, Washington Black
Senators, Chicago American Giants,
Jacksonville Red Caps, Cleveland Bears,
Philadelphia Stars, New York Cubans
Andrews, (Pop), 1906-19 P, OF, 1B, 2B,
Brooklyn Royal Giants, Pittsburgh Stars of
Buffalo, Philadelphia Giants, Havana Red Sox
Anthony, Lavance (Pete), 1950 C, Houston
Eagles, New York Cubans
Anthony, Thad, 1950 C, Baltimore Elite Giants
Arango, Luis, 1925-39 3B, 1B, Cuban Stars
(NNL), New York Cubans
Archer, —, 1919-24 P, C, Lincoln Giants,
Baltimore Black Sox, Philadelphia Giants
Arencibia, Eduardo, 1948 OF, New York Cubans
Arguelles, Martinano, see Garay
Ariosa, Homero Mario, 1947-49 OF, New York
Cubans
Armentero, —, 1916 P, New York Cuban Stars
Armour, —, 1933 P, 3B, Detroit Stars
Armour, Alfred (Buddy), 1936-50 OF, SS, St.
Louis Stars, Indianapolis ABCs, New
Orleans-St. Louis Stars, Harrisburg- St.Louis
Stars, Cleveland Buckeyes, Chicago American
Giants, Homestead Grays
Armstead, James (Jimmie), 1938-49 P, OF,
Indianapolis ABCs, St.Louis Stars, Baltimore
Elite Giants, Philadelphia Stars
Arnet, —, 1921 P, Bacharach Giants
Arnold, Paul, 1926-36 OF, Brooklyn Royal
Giants, Newark Dodgers, Bacharach Giants,
Hilldale
Arthur, Robert, 1946 P, Pittsburgh Crawfords
Arumis, (Arumi), 1920 OF, 2B, Kansas City
Monarchs
Asbury, —, 1918 P, Lincoln Giants
Ascanio, Carlos, 1946 1B, New York Black
Yankees
Ash, Rudolph [Rudolph], 1920,1926 OF, P,
Chicago American Giants, Newark Stars,
Hilldale
Ashby, Earl, 1945-48 C, Cleveland Buckeyes,
Birmingham Black Barons, Homestead Grays,
Newark Eagles
Askew, Jesse, 1936 SS, St. Louis Stars
Ashport, , 1913 3B, Havana Red Sox
Atame, , 1920 P, Kansas City Monarchs
Atkins, Abe, 1923 SS, 3B, Toledo Tigers
Atkins, Joseph O. (Joe, Leroy) , 1946-47 3B,
Pittsburgh Crawfords, Cleveland Buckeyes
Atkins, Stacy, 1950 P, Chicago American Giants
Augustine, Leon, 1923 umpire, NNL
Augustus, —, 1927 P, Memphis Red Sox
Austin, Frank Samuel (Junior), 1944-48 SS,
Philadelphia Stars
Austin, John 1887 player, Cincinnati Browns
Austin, (Tank), 1930-32 P, Nashville Elite Giants,
Birmingham Black Barons, Atlanta Black
Crackers
Averett, —, 1943 OF, New York Black Yankees
Awkard, Russell, 1940-41 OF, Cuban Stars,
Newark Eagles
Aylor, James 1887 player, Philadelphia Pythians
Bagley, —, 1937 C, Cincinnati Tigers
Bailey, —, 1910 C, Chicago Giants
Bailey, Alonza, 1935 P, Newark Dodgers
Bailey, Bob, 1932 OF, Hilldale

Bailey, D., 1916-28 OF, 3B, Lincoln Stars,
Pennsylvania Red Caps of New York
Bailey, Otha William, 1950 C, Cleveland
Buckeyes, Houston Eagles
Bailey, Percy (Bill), 1927-34 P, Baltimore Black
Sox, Nashville Elite Giants, Detroit Stars,
Cole's American Giants, New York Black
Yankees
Baird, Thomas Y., 1938-50 officer, Kansas City
Monarchs; booking agent for NAL exhibition
games
Baker, Edgar, 1945-46 P, Memphis Red Sox,
Cleveland Clippers (USL)
Baker, Eugene Walter (Gene), 1948-50 SS,
Kansas City Monarchs
Baker, Henry, 1925-32 OF, Indianapolis ABCs,
Dayton Marcos
Baker, Howard (Home Run), 1910 player,
Leland Giants
Baker, Lamar, 1950 P, New York Black Yankees
Baker, Norman (Bud), 1937 P, Newark Eagles,
New York Black Yankees
Baker, Rufus (Scoop), 1943-50 INF, C, OF, New
York Black Yankees
Baker, Sammy, 1950 P, Chicago American
Giants
Baker, Tom, 1940 P, Baltimore Elite Giants
Baker, W.B., 1937-38 bus. mgr, Atlanta Black
Crackers
Baldwin, Robert , 1925-26 SS, 2B, Indianapolis
ABCs, Cleveland Elites, Detroit Stars
Ball, George Walter (Georgia Rabbit), 1902-23
P, Cuban X Giants, Augusta, Georgia,
Philadelphia Giants, Leland Giants, Chicago
Giants, Chicago American Giants, St.Louis
Giants, Mohawk Giants, Brooklyn Royal
Giants, Chicago Union Giants, Milwaukee
Giants, Lincoln Stars, Lincoln Giants
Ballard, —, 1910 P, Chicago Giants
Ballesteros, —, 1916 P, Long Branch Cubans
Ballestro, Miguel (Pedro Ballester), 1948 SS,
New York Cubans
Ballew, —, 1930 P, Louisville White Sox
Bames, —, 1937 C, Birmingham Black Barons
Bankes, James, 1950 P, Baltimore Elite Giants
Bankhead, Daniel Robert (Dan), 1940-47 P,
Chicago American Giants, Birmingham Black
Barons, Memphis Red Sox
Bankhead, Fred, 1936-48 2B, 3B, 1B,
Birmingham Black Barons, Memphis Red Sox
Bankhead, Garnett, 1948 P, Homestead Grays
Bankhead, Joe, 1948 P, Birmingham Black
Barons
Bankhead, Samuel Howard (Sam), 1930-50 SS,
OF, 2B, P, MGR, Birmingham Black Barons,
Nashville Elite Giants, Pittsburgh Crawfords,
Toledo Crawfords, Homestead Grays,
Louisville Black Caps, Kansas City Monarchs
Banks, —, 1896 P, Cuban X Giants
Banks, —, 1930 2B, Hilldale
Banks, Earl, 1945 2B, Newark Eagles
Banks, Ernest (Ernie), 1950-53 SS, Kansas City
Monarchs
Banks, G., 1914-17-P, Lincoln Giants,
Philadelphia Giants
Banks, Johnny, 1950 P, Philadelphia Stars
Banks, S., 1915-19 C, Philadelphia Giants,
Lincoln Giants
Banton, —, 1914 P, Chicago American Giants
Bapiste, —, 1923-24 OF, Bacharach Giants,
Philadelphia Giants
Baranda, —, 1915-16 3B, OF, Long Branch N.J.
Cubans, Jersey City Cubans
Barbee, Lamb (Bud, Barboo), 1937-49 P, 1B,
MGR, New York Black Yankees, Cincinnati
Clowns, Cincinnati-Indianapolis Clowns,
Philadelphia Stars, Baltimore Elite Giants,
Raleigh Tigers, Indianapolis Clowns
Barbee, Quincy (Bud), 1949 OF, Louisville
Buckeyes, Kansas City Monarchs
Barber, (Bull), 1920,1925 2B, Hilldale, Kansas
City Monarchs
Barber, John, 1946 OF, Pittsburgh Crawfords
Barber, Sam, 1943-50 P, Cleveland Clippers
(USL), Cleveland Buckeyes
Barbette, —, 1918 1B, Cuban Stars (East)
Barbour, Jess, 1910-1926 OF, 1B, 3B,
Philadelphia Giants, Chicago American Giants,
Bacharach Giants, Detroit Stars, Pittsburgh
Keystones, Harrisburg Giants, St. Louis
Giants, Indianapolis ABCs
Barcelo, —, 1921 P, Cuban Stars (East)

Barker, Marvin (Hack), 1935-50 OF, 2B, 3B, MGR, New York Black Yankees, Philadelphia Stars, Newark Dodgers, Bacharach Giants

Barkins, W.C., 1928 officer, Cleveland Stars

Barlow, Tom 1877 player, Mutuals of Washington

Barnes, —, 1906 3B, Philadelphia Giants

Barnes, —, 1925 P, Kansas City Monarchs

Barnes, Ed, 1937-40 P, Kansas City Monarchs, Baltimore Elite Giants

Barnes, Frank, 1947-50 P, Indianapolis ABCs, Kansas City Monarchs

Barnes, Harry (Tack Head), 1949 C, Memphis Red Sox

Barnes, John (Tubby, Fat), 1921-31,36-38 C, Cleveland Tate Stars, Cleveland Browns, Detroit Stars, St. Louis Stars, Cleveland Hornets, Cleveland Tigers, Memphis Red Sox, Toledo Tigers, Indianapolis ABCs, Birmingham Black Barons

Barnes, O., 1932 officer, New York Black Yankees

Barnes, Tobias, 1937 INF, Chicago American Giants

Barnes, V., 1940 OF, Kansas City Monarchs

Barnes, William (Jimmy, Bill), 1941-47 P, Baltimore Elite Giants, Memphis Red Sox, Indianapolis Clowns

Barnhill, David (Dave, Impo), 1939-49 P, New Orleans-St. Louis Stars, New York Cubans, Ethiopian Clowns

Barnhill, Herbert (Herb), 1938-46 C, Jacksonville Red Caps, Kansas City Monarchs, Chicago American Giants, Cleveland Bears

Baro, Bernardo, 1916-30 OF, 1B, P, Cuban Stars (East), Cuban Stars (NNL), New York Cuban Stars, Kansas City Monarchs

Barr, —, 1921-22 3B, SS, Kansas City Monarchs, Cuban Stars

Barrow, Wesley, 1945-47 MGR, New Orleans Black Pelicans, Nashville Cubs, Baltimore Elite Giants

Bartamino, —, 1904 MGR., All Cubans

Bartlett, Howard (Homer, Hop), 1913-25 P, Indianapolis ABCs, Kansas City Monarchs

Barton, Sherman 1896-1911 OF, 3B, Chicago Unions, Columbia Giants, Quaker Giants of New York, Cuban X Giants, St. Paul Gophers, Chicago Giants, Chicago Union Giants, Leland Giants Adrian (MI) Page Fence Giants, Algona (IA) Brownies

Bashum, —, 1932 C, Indianapolis ABCs

Baskin, William 1890-92 2B, Chicago Unions

Bass, Leroy (Red), 1938-40 C, Homestead Grays, Pittsburgh Crawfords

Bassett, Lloyd P. (Pepper), 1934-50 C, New Orleans Crescent Stars, Philadelphia Stars, Chicago American Giants, Pittsburgh Crawfords, Cincinnati Clowns, Cincinnati-Indianapolis Clowns, Birmingham Black Barons, Toledo Crawfords, Homestead Grays

Batson, —, 1908-09 OF, Genuine Cuban Giants, Philadelphia Giants

Battles, Ray, 1944-45 3B, Homestead Grays

Battle, William (Bill), 1947-49 P, Homestead Grays, Memphis Red Sox

Battles, —, 1924 INF, C, Harrisburg Giants

Batum, G.W. 1885 2B, Brooklyn Remsens

Bauchman, Harry, 1915-23 2B, SS, 1B, Chicago American Giants, Chicago Union Giants, Chicago Giants

Bauza, Marcelino, 1930 SS, Cuban Stars (NNL)

Bayliss, Henry J., 1948-50 INF, C, Chicago American Giants, Baltimore Elite Giants, Birmingham Black Barons

Baynard, Frank, 1917-28 OF, Pennsylvania Red Caps of New York, Newark Stars, Hilldale, Bacharach Giants, Havana Red Sox

Baxter, Al 1898 OF, Celeron Acme Colored Giants (Iron and Oil Lg.)

Bea, Bill, 1940 OF, New York Black Yankees, Philadelphia Stars

Beal, G. (Lefty), 1947 P, Newark Eagles

Bebley, —, 1925 P, Birmingham Black Barons

Bebop, Ralph (Spec), 1950 player, Indianapolis Clowns

Beckwith, John, 1917-38 SS, 3B, C, OF, MGR, Chicago Giants, Chicago American Giants, Baltimore Black Sox, Homestead Grays, Harrisburg Giants, Lincoln Giants, Bacharach Giants, New York Black Yankees, Newark Dodgers, Brooklyn Royal Giants, Newark Browns, Hilldale Daisies

Bejerano, Agustin, 1928-29-OF, Cuban Stars (ECL)

Bell, —, 1918 OF, Baltimore Black Sox

Bell, —, 1946 UTIL, Philadelphia Stars

Bell, Charles (Lefty), 1948 P, Homestead Grays

Bell, Clifford (Cliff, Cherry), 1921-31 P, Kansas City Monarchs, Memphis Red Sox, Cleveland Cubs

Bell, Frank 1888-91-OF, Cuban Giants, New York Gorhams(Middle States Lg.), Ansonia Cuban Giants (Connecticut St.Lg.), Philadelphia Giants

Bell, Fred (Lefty), 1922-27 P, OF, St. Louis Stars, Detroit Stars, Birmingham Black Barons, Toledo Tigers, Harrisburg Giants, Washington Potomacs

Bell, Herman, 1943-50 C, Birmingham Black Barons

Bell, James Thomas (Cool Papa), 1922-46 OF, P, St. Louis Stars, Pittsburgh Crawfords, Detroit Wolves, Kansas City Monarchs, Chicago American Giants, Memphis Red Sox, Homestead Grays

Bell, James (Steel Arm), 1933-40 C, Montgomery Grey Sox, Indianapolis Crawfords, Jacksonville Red Caps

Bell, Julian (Jute), 1923-30 P, Birmingham Black Barons, Memphis Red Sox, Detroit Stars

Bell, William, 1902-04 P, OF, Philadelphia Giants

Bell, William Sr. (W.), 1923-48 P, MGR, Kansas City Monarchs, Detroit Wolves, Homestead Grays, Pittsburgh Crawfords, Newark Dodgers, Newark Eagles, New York Black Yankees

Bell, William R. Jr.(Lefty), 1950 P, Kansas City Monarchs, Birmingham Black Barons

Benjamin, Jerry Charles, 1932-48 OF, Memphis Red Sox, Detroit Stars, Birmingham Black Barons, Homestead Grays, Toledo Crawfords, New York Cubans

Bennett, Bradford, 1940-46 OF, St. Louis Stars, New Orleans-St. Louis Stars, New York Black Yankees, Boston Blues

Bennett, Don, 1926,1932-34 2B, Dayton Marcos, Cleveland Cubs, Memphis Red Sox

Bennett, Frank, 1918 MGR, Bacharach Giants

Bennett, Jim, 1945-48 P, Cincinnati-Indianapolis Clowns, Indianapolis Clowns

Bennett, John, 1932 OF, Louisville Black Colonels

Bennett, Sam, 1911-25 OF, C, St. Louis Giants, St. Louis Stars

Bennette, George Clifford (Jew Baby), 1920-36 OF, C, Columbus Buckeyes, Memphis Red Sox, Indianapolis ABCs, Detroit Stars, Chicago Giants, Chicago Union Giants, Pittsburgh Keystones

Benning, —, 1937 2B, Indianapolis Athletics

Benson, —, 1940 P, Memphis Red Sox

Benson, Eugene (Gene, Spider), 1933-48 OF, Brooklyn Royal Giants Bacharach Giants, Pittsburgh Crawfords, Philadelphia Stars, Newark Eagles

Bention, see Gene Benson

Benton, —, 1950 P, Memphis Red Sox

Benvenuti, Julius, 1939 vice-pres, Chicago American Giants

Berkely, —, 1919 C, Hilldale

Berkley, —, 1941 P, New Orleans-St. Louis Stars

Bernal, Blacedo (Pablo), 1941 P, New York Cuban Stars

Bernard, —, 1911-17-C, OF, Pittsburgh Giants, Lincoln Stars, Cuban Giants, Philadelphia Giants, Lincoln Giants

Bernard, Pablo, 1949-50 2B, SS, Louisville Buckeyes, Cleveland Buckeyes

Berry, E., 1930 SS, 2B, Memphis Red Sox, Detroit Stars

Berry, John Paul, 1935-37,1945 P, 1B, Kansas City Monarchs, St. Louis Stars

Berry, R., 1947 P, Kansas City Monarchs

Bert, —, 1906 P, Cuban Giants

Best, R., 1904-06 P, Brooklyn Royal Giants, Cuban Giants

Betts, —, 1938 OF, Kansas City Monarchs

Betts, Russell B., 1950 P, Kansas City Monarchs

Beverie, —, 1939 3B, Baltimore Elite Giants

Beverly, Charles, 1924-36 P, Cleveland Browns, Birmingham Black Barons, Kansas City Monarchs, Cleveland Stars, Pittsburgh Crawfords, New Orleans Crescent Stars, Newark Eagles, Nash- Ville Elite Giants, Philadelphia Stars

Beverly, William (Fireball), 1950 P, Houston Eagles

Bibbs, Rainey, 1933-44 2B, SS, 3B, Detroit Stars, Cincinnati Tigers, Chicago American Giants, Kansas City Monarchs, Indianapolis Crawfords, Chicago American Giants, Cleveland Buckeyes

Billings, —, 1948 C, Homestead Grays

Billings, William, 1921 P, Nashville Elite Giants

Billingsley, John, 1950 C, Memphis Red Sox

Billingsley, Sam, 1950 P, Memphis Red Sox

Binder, James (Jimmy), 1930-37 3B, 2B, Memphis Red Sox, Brooklyn Eagles, Indianapolis ABCs, Detroit Stars, Homestead Grays, Washington Elite Giants, Pittsburgh Crawfords

Binga, Jess E. 1887 player, Washington Capital Citys

Binga, William 1895-1910 3B, C, Page Fence Giants, Columbia Giants, Philadelphia Giants, St. Paul Gophers, Chicago Union Giants, Kansas City (KS) Giants, Adrian (Michigan State Lg.)

Bingham, (Bingo), 1910-21 OF, Chicago Union Giants, Chicago Giants, West Baden (Ind.) Sprudels

Biot, Charles (Charlie), 1939-41 OF, Newark Eagles, New York Black Yankees, Baltimore Elite Giants, Philadelphia Stars

Biran, —, 1916 INF, Chicago American Giants

Bissant, John, 1934-47 OF, P, 2B, Cole's American Giants, Chicago American Giants, Birmingham Black Barons, Chicago Brown Bombers

Bivins, —, 1948 P, Memphis Red Sox

Bix, —, 1921 P, St. Louis Giants

Black, —, 1926 P, Cleveland Elites

Black, Howard, 1928 INF, Brooklyn Cuban Giants

Black, Joseph (Joe), 1943-50 P, Baltimore Elite Giants

Blackburn, —, 1920 P, Kansas City Monarchs

Blackman, Clifford, 1937-41 P, Chicago American Giants, Birmingham Black Barons, Memphis Red Sox, New York Cubans, Indianapolis ABCs, Homestead Grays, New Orleans-St. Louis Stars

Blackman, Henry, 1920-24 3B, Indianapolis ABCs, Baltimore Black Sox

Blackstone, William 1887 player, Cincinnati Browns

Blackwell, Charles, 1915-29 OF, West Baden, Ind. Sprudels, Bowser's ABCs, Jewell's ABCs, St. Louis Giants, St. Louis Stars, Birmingham Black Barons, Indianapolis ABCs, Detroit Stars, Nashville Elite Giants

Blair, Garnet E. Sr, 1945-46 P, Homestead Grays

Blair, Lonnie J., 1949-50 P, 2B, Homestead Grays

Blake, Frank (Big Red), 1932-35 P, Baltimore Black Sox, New York Black Yankees, New York Cubans

Blakely, Bert, 1934 C, Cincinnati Tigers

Blanchard, Chester, 1926-33 SS, Dayton Marcos

Blanco, Carlos, 1938-41 1B, New York Cubans, Cuban Stars

Blanco, Heberto (Harry, Henny), 1941-42 2B, Cuban Stars, New New Cubans

Blatner, —, 1921 1B, OF, Kansas City Monarchs

Blavis, Fox, 1936 3B, Homestead Grays

Bleach, Larry, 1937 2B, Detroit Stars

Bledsoe, —, 1937 player, St. Louis Stars

Blount, John T. (Tenny), 1919-33 officer, Detroit Stars; vice- pres, NNL

Blueitt, Virgil, 1916-18,1937-49 2B, umpire, Chicago Union Giants, NAL

Blukoi, Frank, 1917,1920 2B, All Nations, Kansas City Monarchs

Boada, Lucas, 1921-24 P, OF, Cuban Stars (NNL) Cuban Stars (ECL)

Bobo, J., see James Leonard

Bobo, Willie, 1923-30 1B, All Nations, Kansas City Monarchs, St. Louis Stars, Nashville Elite Giants

Boggs, G., 1923-34 P, OF, Milwaukee Bears, Detroit Stars, Dayton Marcos, Cleveland Tigers

Bolden, Edward (Ed, Chief), 1910-50 officer, Hilldale, Darby Phantoms, Philadelphia Stars; officer, ECL, Anl, NNL

Bolden, L.W. 1885 player, Brooklyn Remsens

Bolden, Otto, 1910,1920 C, P, Leland Giants, Chicago Giants

Bond, Timothy, 1935-40 SS, 3B, Pittsburgh Crawfords, Newark Dodgers, Chicago American Giants

Bonds, —, 1927 C, Cleveland Hornets

Bonner, Robert, 1921-26 1B, C, 2B, Cleveland Tate Stars, St. Louis Stars, Toledo Stars, Cleveland Browns, Cleveland Elites

Booker, Billy 1898 2B, Celeron (NY) Acme Colored Giants (Iron and Oil Lg.)

Booker, Dan, 1909 P, Kansas City (MO) Royal Giants

Booker, James (Pete), 1905-17 C, 1B, Philadelphia Giants, Leland Giants, Lincoln Giants, Chicago American Giants, Chicago Giants, Mohawk Giants, Brooklyn Royal Giants

Boone, Alonzo D. (Buster), 1929-50 P, MGR, Cleveland Cubs, Birmingham Black Barons, Chicago American Giants, Cincinnati Buckeyes, Cleveland Buckeyes, Louisville Buckeyes, Memphis Red Sox, Cleveland Bears

Boone, Charles (Lefty), 1941-46 P, New Orleans-St. Louis Stars, Harrisburg-St. Louis Stars, Pittsburgh Crawfords, Cincinnati Buckeyes, Jacksonville Red Caps, Cleveland Buckeyes, Philadelphia Stars

Boone, Oscar, 1939-42 C, 1B, Indianapolis ABCs, Chicago American Giants, Birmingham Black Barons

Boone, Robert, 1923-28 umpire, NNL

Boone, Steve (Lefty), 1940 P, Memphis Red Sox

Borden, —, 1912 CF, Pittsburgh Giants

Borden, J., 1932-33 SS, UTIL, Birmingham Black Barons

Bordes, Ed, 1940 UTIL, Cleveland Bears

Borges, —, 1928 INF, Cuban Stars (NNL)

Borselo, [Borotto], 1921 P, C, Cuban Stars (East), All Cubans

Bostick, —, 1924 OF, St. Louis Giants

Bostock, Lyman Wesley Sr., 1940-49 1B, OF, Birmingham Black Barons, Chicago American Giants, New York Cubans

Boston, Bob, 1948 3B, Homestead Grays

Boswell, —, 1939 P, Toledo Crawfords

Bough, —, 1923 P, Milwaukee Bears

Bowe, Randolph (Bob, Lefty), 1938-40 P, Kansas City Monarchs, Chicago American Giants

Bowen, —, 1904 OF, Philadelphia Giants

Bowen, —, 1950 P, Indianapolis Clowns

Bowen, (Chuck), 1937-43 OF, Indianapolis Athletics, Chicago Brown Bombers

Bowers, —, 1887 OF, Philadelphia Pythians

Bowers, —, 1926 P, SS, Baltimore Black Sox

Bowers, Julius (Julie), 1947-1950 C, New York Black Yankees

Bowman, Emmett (Scotty), 1905-12 3B, P, C, SS, OF, Philadelphia Giants, Leland Giants, Brooklyn Royal Giants

Boyd, —, 1933 OF, Kansas City Monarchs

Boyd, Benjamin 1885-91 2B, OF, Argyle Hotel, Cuban Giants, York Cuban Giants (Eastern Interstate Lg.), Trenton Cuban Giants (Middle States Lg.), Ansonia Cuban Giants (Connecticut St.Lg.)

Boyd, Fred 1920-22 OF, Chicago American Giants, Cleveland Tate Stars

Boyd, James, 1946 P, Newark Eagles

Boyd, Lincoln, 1949 OF, Louisville Buckeyes

Boyd, Robert R. (Bob, Rope), 1947-50 1B, Memphis Red Sox

Bracken, Herb (Doc), 1940,1946-47 P, St. Louis Stars, Cleveland Buckeyes

Bradford, Charles, 1910-28 P, OF, 1B, coach, Pittsburgh Giants, Lincoln Giants, Philadelphia Giants

Bradford, William (Bill), 1938-43 OF, 2B, Indianapolis ABCs, St. Louis Stars, Memphis Red Sox, Birmingham Black Barons, New York Black Yankees, Chicago American Giants

Bradley, Frank (Red, Dick), 1937-43 P, Cincinnati Tigers, Kansas City Monarchs, Memphis Red Sox

Bradley, Phil, 1905-27 C, 1B, UTIL, Brooklyn Royal Giants, Lincoln Giants, Smart Set, Pittsburgh Colored Stars, Pittsburgh Stars of Buffalo, Mohawk Giants, Cuban Giants, Philadelphia Giants, Pop Watkins Stars

Brady, John 1887 player, Pittsburgh Keystones

Brady (Lefty), 1921 P, Cleveland Tate Stars

Bragana, Ramon, 1928-37,1947 P, OF, Cuban Stars (ECL), Stars of Cuba, New York Cubans, Cleveland Buckeyes

Bragg, Eugene, 1925 C, Chicago American Giants

Bragg, Jesse, 1908-19 3B, SS, 2B, Genuine Cuban Giants, Cuban Giants, Brooklyn Royal Giants, Mohawk Giants, Lincoln Giants, Philadelphia Giants, Pennsylvania Red Caps of NY

Braithwaite, Alonzo (Archie), 1944-48 OF, Newark Eagles, Philadelphia Stars

Bram, —, 1930 P, Hilldale

Brammell, —, 1932 C, Indianapolis ABCs

Branahan, J. Finis (Slim), 1922-27,1931 P, Cleveland Tate Stars, Harrisburg Giants, Detroit Stars, Cleveland Elites, Cleveland Hornets, St. Louis Stars, Toledo Tigers, Lincoln Giants, Indianapolis ABCs

Branham, (Slim), 1917-23 P, Jewell's ABCs, Toledo Tigers, Dayton Marcos, Cleveland Elites

Branham, Luther, 1949-50 INF, Birmingham Black Barons, Chicago American Giants

Brannigan, George, 1926-27 P, Cleveland Elites, Cleveland Hornets

Brantley, Ollie, 1950 P, Memphis Red Sox

Bray, James, 1922-31 C, OF, Chicago Giants, Chicago American Giants, Chicago Columbia Giants

Brazelton, John Clarkson [Clarkson], 1915-16 C, Chicago American Giants, Chicago Giants

Breda, Bill, 1950 OF, Kansas City Monarchs

Breen, W., 1935 OF, Pittsburgh Crawfords

Bremmer, Eugene (Gene), 1932-48 P, New Orleans Crescent Stars, Cincinnati Tigers, Memphis Red Sox, Kansas City Monarchs, Cincinnati Buckeyes, Cleveland Buckeyes

Brewer, Chester Arthur (Chet), 1925-48 P, Kansas City Monarchs, Washington Pilots, New York Cubans, Philadelphia Stars, Chicago American Giants, Cleveland Buckeyes

Brewer, Luther, 1918-21 1B, OF, Chicago Giants

Brewer, Sherwood (Sherry), 1949-50 OF, SS, Indianapolis Clowns

Brewster, Samuel, 1950 OF, Cleveland Buckeyes

Brewton, —, 1936 P, Birmingham Black Barons

Bridgefort, R., 1932 officer, Cleveland Cubs

Briggery, —, 1932 SS, Atlanta Black Crackers

Briggs, —, 1917 P, Indianapolis ABCs

Briggs, Otto, 1914-34 OF, MGR, West Baden Ind., Sprudels, Dayton Marcos, Hilldale, Quaker Giants, Bacharach Giants

Brigham, —, 1924 P, Harrisburg Giants

Bright, John M. 1888-1909 MGR, Cuban Giants

Brisker, William, 1950 gen mgr, Cleveland Buckeyes

Britt, Charles (Charlie), 1927-33 3B, Homestead Grays

Britt, George (Chippy) [Britton], 1920-44 P, C, INF, Dayton Marcos, Columbus Buckeyes, Baltimore Black Sox, Hilldale, Homestead Grays, Newark Dodgers, Columbus Elite Giants, Washington Black Senators, Jacksonville Red Caps, Brooklyn Royal Giants, Chicago American Giants, Detroit Wolves, Cleveland Buckeyes, Harrisburg Giants

Britton, John (Jack), 1940-50 3B, St. Louis Stars, Cincinnati Clowns, Birmingham Black Barons, Indianapolis Clowns

Broadnax, Willie (Broadway), 1928-29 P, OF, Memphis Red Sox

Brodnax, Maceo (Baby Boy), 1932 P, Kansas City Monarchs

Broiles, see Broyles

Brooks, —, 1887 player, Louisville Falls City

Brooks, Alex (Alvin), 1934-40 OF, New York Black Yankees, Brooklyn Royal Giants, Hilldale

Brooks, Ameal (Macon), 1929-47 C, OF, Chicago American Giants, Cleveland Cubs, Cole's American Giants, Columbus Blue Birds, Cincinnati Clowns, New York Black Yankees, Cuban Stars, New York Cubans, Homestead Grays, Newark Eagles

Brooks, Beattie, 1918-21 INF, C, Lincoln Giants, Brooklyn Royal Giants, Philadelphia Giants

Brooks, Charles, 1919-26 2B, P, OF, St. Louis Giants, St. Louis Stars, Homestead Grays, Dayton Marcos, Detroit Stars

Brooks, Chester, 1918-33 OF, Brooklyn Royal Giants

Brooks, E., 1936 P, Kansas City Monarchs

Brooks, Edward (Eddie), 1949-50 2B, Houston Eagles, Memphis Red Sox

Brooks, Gus 1894-95 OF, Page Fence Giants, Chicago Unions

Brooks, Irvin, 1919-27 P, UTIL, Brooklyn Royal Giants

Brooks, James 1887 player, Baltimore Lord Baltimores

Brooks, Jesse, 1934-37 3B, OF, Cleveland Red Sox, Kansas City Monarchs

Brooks, John O., 1942 P, Memphis Red Sox

Brooks, Moxie, 1945 P, Toledo Cubs (USL)

Brooks, Wallace, 1948 P, Baltimore Elite Giants

Broom, —, 1941-42 P, Jacksonville Red Caps

Broome, J.B., 1947 OF, New York Black Yankees

Browcow, —, 1905-06 2B, Brooklyn Royal Giants

Brown, —, 1890 UTIL, Lincoln (Neb) Giants

Brown, —, 1906-12 OF, Brooklyn Royal Giants

Brown, —, 1910 OF, West Baden (Ind.) Sprudels

Brown, A., 1923 C, Birmingham Black Barons

Brown, Arnold, 1921-22 SS, 2B, Hilldale, Bacharach Giants, Harrisburg Giants, Washington Braves

Brown, B., 1918 OF, Washington Red Caps

Brown, Barney, 1931-49 P, Cuban Stars (East & West), Philadelphia Stars, New York Black Yankees

Brown, Ben 1899-1900 P, OF, Genuine Cuban Giants

Brown, Benny, 1932 SS, Newark Stars

Brown, Charles 1886-87 P, Cuban Giants, Pittsburgh Keystones

Brown, Curtis, 1947,1950 1B, New York Black Yankees

Brown, David (Dave, Lefty), 1918-25 P, Chicago American Giants, Lincoln Giants

Brown, E., 1918 3B, Chicago Union Giants

Brown, Earl, 1923-26 P, OF, Lincoln Giants, Baltimore Black Sox, Harrisburg Giants

Brown, Edward, 1920-21 P, Detroit Stars, Indianapolis ABCs, Chicago Giants

Brown, Elias (Country), 1918-33 3B, 2B, OF, New York Bacharach Giants, Bacharach Giants, Brooklyn Royal Giants, Washington Potomacs, Wilmington Potomacs, Hilldale

Brown, Elmore (Scrappy), 1918-32 SS, Washington Red Caps, Lincoln Giants, Baltimore Black Sox, Brooklyn Royal Giants, Hilldale

Brown, F., 1918 2B, Chicago Union Giants

Brown, G., 1925-27 P, St. Louis Stars

Brown, George, 1915-28 OF, MGR, Jewell's ABCs, Indianapolis ABCs, St. Louis Giants, Dayton Marcos, Detroit Stars, Columbus Buckeyes, West Baden (Ind) Sprudels

Brown, George, 1939-42 OF, Ethiopian Clowns, Cincinnati Buckeyes, Cleveland Buckeyes

Brown, H., 1913-15 P, Mohawk Giants, Brooklyn Royal Giants

Brown, James (Jim), 1918-42 C, 1B, MGR, Chicago American Giants, Louisville Black Caps, Cole's American Giants, Minneapolis - St. Paul Gophers, Chicago Columbia Giants, Cleveland Cubs

Brown, James Phillips, 1939-48 P, of Newark Eagles, Indianapolis Clowns

Brown, Jerome, 1949 INF, Houston Eagles

Brown, Jesse J. (Professor, Lefty), 1938-42 P, New York Black Yankees, Newark Eagles, Baltimore Elite Giants

Brown, Jim, see Willard Brown

Brown, John W., 1942-49 P, St. Louis Giants, Cleveland Buckeyes, Houston Eagles

Brown, L.A., 1926-27 officer, St. Louis Stars

Brown, Larry, 1919-49 C, MGR, Birmingham Black Barons, Pittsburgh Keystones, Indianapolis ABCs, Memphis Red Sox, Detroit Stars, Chicago American Giants, Lincoln Giants, New York Black Yankees, Cole's American Giants, Philadelphia Stars

Brown, Lawrence James (Lefty), 1933-37 P, Memphis Red Sox

Brown, M., 1918 OF, Bacharach Giants

Brown, Maywood, 1921-25 P, Indianapolis ABCs

Brown, Oliver, 1932 bus. mgr, Newark Browns

Brown, Oscar, 1939 C, Indianapolis ABCs, Baltimore Elite Giants

Brown, Ossie, 1934-39 P, OF, Cole's American Giants, Indianapolis Athletics, Indianapolis ABCs, St. Louis Stars

Brown, Ray, 1939-40 C, Brooklyn Royal Giants, Chicago American Giants

Brown, Raymond (Ray), 1930-48 P, OF, Dayton Marcos, Indianapolis ABCs, Detroit Wolves, Homestead Grays

Brown, Robert 1887 player, Boston Resolutes

Brown, Ronnie, 1943 1B, Harrisburg-St. Louis Stars

Brown, Roy, 1928,1931 P, OF, Kansas City Monarchs

Brown, T.J. (Tom), 1939-50 SS, 3B, Memphis Red Sox, Cleveland Buckeyes, Indianapolis Clowns, Harrisburg-St.Louis Stars

Brown, Theo, 1911 3B, Chicago Union Giants

Brown, Tom, 1917-19 P, Brooklyn Royal Giants, Chicago American Giants, Lincoln Giants

Brown, (Tute), 1918 3B, Washington Red Caps

Brown, Ulysses (Buster, Joe), 1937-42 C, OF, Newark Eagles, Jacksonville Red Caps, Cincinnati Buckeyes, Cleveland Buckeyes

Brown, W. (Mike), 1910-15 P, 1B, OF, Mohawk Giants, Philadelphia Giants, Cuban Giants

Brown, Walter S. 1887 MGR, pres, Pittsburgh Keystones, Lg. of Colored Base Ball Clubs

Brown, Willard Jesse, 1934-50 OF, SS, Monroe Monarchs, Kansas City Monarchs

Brown, William, 1906 asst MGR, Leland Giants

Brown, William H. 1887 player, Pittsburgh Keystones

Brown, William M., 1931-32 officer, Montgomery Grey Sox

Browne, (Hap), 1924 P, Cleveland Browns

Broyles, [Broiles], 1925-27 P, St. Louis Stars

Bruce, Clarence, 1947-48 2B, Homestead Grays

Bruce, Lloyd, 1940 P, Chicago American Giants

Bruton, Charles John (Jack) [Burton], 1928-41,1950 P, OF, INF, Cleveland Bears, Philadelphia Stars, New Orleans-St. Louis Stars, Birmingham Black Barons, Cleveland Buckeyes, New York Black Yankees

Bryant, Allen (Lefty), 1937-46 P, All Nations, Kansas City Monarchs, Memphis Red Sox

Bryant, Eddie, 1925-28 2B, Pennsylvania Red Caps of NY Harrisburg Giants

Bryant, Johnnie, 1950 OF, Cleveland Buckeyes

Bryant, R.B., 1937 SS, Memphis Red Sox

Bubbles, —, 1938 P, Atlanta Black Crackers

Buchanan, Chester (Buck), 1936-43 P, Philadelphia Stars, Bacharach Giants

Buchanan, Floyd (Buck), 1914 P, Hilldale

Buck, —, 1923 P, Birmingham Black Barons

Buckner, Harry 1896-1918 P, OF, Chicago Unions, Columbia Giants, Philadelphia Giants, Cuban X Giants, Brooklyn Royal Giants, Quaker Giants, Lincoln Giants, Smart Set, Chicago Giants, Mohawk Giants

Budbill, —, 1950 P, Houston Eagles

Buddles, —, 1925 INF, Chicago American Giants

Buford, (Black Bottom), 1927-34 3B, SS, 2B, Nashville Elite Giants, Cleveland Cubs, Detroit Stars, Louisville Red Caps, Birmingham Black Barons

Bumpus, Earl, 1944-48 P, OF, Kansas City Monarchs, Birmingham Black Barons, Chicago American Giants

Burbage, Knowlington O.(Buddy), 1929-43 OF, Hilldale, Pittsburgh Crawfords, Baltimore Black Sox, Bacharach Giants, Newark Dodgers, Homestead Grays, Washington Black Senators, Brooklyn Royal Giants, Philadelphia Stars

Burch, John Walter, 1931-46 C, 2B, SS, MGR, Bacharach Giants, Baltimore Black Sox, Cleveland Bears, St. Louis Stars, New Orleans-St. Louis Stars, Cincinnati Buckeyes, Cleveland Buckeyes, Chicago American Giants

Burdine, J., 1927-32 P, OF, Birmingham Black Barons, Memphis Red Sox

Burgee, Louis, 1910,1917 P, 2B, Hilldale

Burgess, —, 1942 P, Chicago American Giants

Burgett, —, 1920 OF, St. Louis Giants

Burgin, —, 1913 rf, Havana Red Sox

Burgin, Ralph, 1917-1943 2B, SS, 3B, OF, Hilldale, New York Black Yankees, Philadelphia Stars, Brooklyn Royal Giants Baltimore Black Sox, Pittsburgh Crawfords

Burgos, Jose Antonio, 1949-50 SS, Birmingham Black Barons

Burke, Billy, 1942 3B, Boston Royal Giants

Burke, Charles, 1937 SS, Indianapolis Athletics

Burke, Ernest, 1947-48 P, Baltimore Elite Giants

Burnett, Fred (Tex), 1922-46 C, 1B OF, coach, MGR, Pittsburgh Keystones, Indianapolis ABCs, Lincoln Giants, Harrisburg Giants, Brooklyn Royal Giants, New York Black Yankees, Baltimore Black Sox, Homestead Grays, Brooklyn Eagles, Newark Eagles, Pittsburgh Crawfords, Bacharach Giants, Nashville Cubs

Burnham, Willie (Bee), 1930-34 P, Monroe Monarchs

Burns, Pete 1890-1902 C, OF, Page Fence Giants, Columbia Giants Chicago Unions, Adrian (MI. St. Lg.), Algona (IA) Brownies

Burns, William (Bill, Willie), 1935-44 P, Memphis Red Sox, Cincinnati- Indianapolis Clowns, Newark Dodgers, Philadelphia Stars, Baltimore Elite Giants, Ethiopian Clowns Atlanta Black Crackers

Burrell, George 1884-85 P, C, Baltimore Atlantics

Burrell, —, 1918 OF, Baltimore Black Sox

Burris, Samuel (Speed), 1937-40 P, Memphis Red Sox, Birmingham Black Barons

Burton, see Charles Bruton

Busby, —, 1933 OF, Detroit Stars

Busby, Maurice (Lefty), 1920-21 P, Bacharach Giants, All Cubans, Baltimore Black Sox

Bush, —, 1946 P, Cleveland Buckeyes

Bustamente, Luis, 1905-12 SS, 2B, Cuban Stars, All Cubans

Buster, Herbert, 1943 INF, Chicago American Giants

Butler, —, 1917 OF, Lincoln Giants

Butler, —, 1937 3B, Pittsburgh Crawfords

Butler, Benjamin 1887 manager, New York Gorhams

Butler, (Doc), 1950 C, Memphis Red Sox

Butler, Frank 1894-95 OF, P, Chicago Unions

Butler, J. 1884 Philadelphia Mutual B.B.C.

Butler, (Sol), 1925 P, Kansas City Monarchs

Butts, Harry, 1949-50 P, Indianapolis Clowns

Butts, Thomas (Tommy, Pee Wee), 1938-50 SS, Atlanta Black Crackers, Indianapolis ABCs, Baltimore Elite Giants

Byas, Richard Thomas (Subby), 1931-42 C, 1B, OF, Kansas City Monarchs, Cole's American Giants, Chicago American Giants, Newark Dodgers, Memphis Red Sox

Byatt, see Charles Biot

Byers, Henry [Byus] 1887 2B, Pittsburgh Keystones

Byrd, —, 1921 1B, Chicago Giants

Byrd, James F., 1927-30 officer, Hilldale

Byrd, Prentice, 1934 officer, Cleveland Red Sox

Byrd, William (Bill), 1932-50 P, OF, Columbus Turfs, Columbus Blue Birds, Columbus Elite Giants, Washington Elite Giants, Baltimore Elite Giants, Nashville Elite Giants, Cleveland Red Sox

Caballero, Luis Perez [Luis Perez], 1948-50 3B, Indianapolis Clowns, New York Cubans

Cabrera, —, 1905 1B, All Cubans

Cabrera, Clemente (Sungo) [Carrera], 1938-41 2B, OF, 3B, New York Cubans, Cuban Stars

Cabrera, Lorenzo (Chiquitin), 1947-50 1B, New York Cubans

Cabrera, Luis Raul, 1948 P, Indianapolis Clowns

Cabrera, Rafael Villa, 1944-50 P, OF, Indianapolis Clowns, Birmingham Black Barons

Cade, Joe, 1929 P, OF, Bacharach Giants

Caffie, Joseph Clifford (Joe), 1950 OF, Cleveland Buckeyes

Cain, Marion (Sugar), 1937-49 P, Pittsburgh Crawfords, Brooklyn Royal Giants, Indianapolis Clowns, New York Black Yankees

Calderin, —, 1917-18, 1924 P, OF, Havana Stars, Cuban Stars (East)

Calderon, Benito, 1926-28 C, Cuban Stars (NNL), Homestead Grays

Caldwell, —, 1933 P, Birmingham Black Barons

Caldwell, Frank, 1947 P, Cleveland Buckeyes

Calhan, Rowland, 1938 P, Washington Black Senators

Calhoun, Jim, 1923 2B, Toledo Tigers

Calhoun, Walter (Lefty), 1931-46 P, Birmingham Black Barons, Montgomery Grey Sox, Washington Black Senators, Pittsburgh Crawfords, Indianapolis ABCs, St. Louis Stars, New Orleans- St. Louis Stars, New York Black Yankees, Harrisburg-St. Louis Stars, Cleveland Buckeyes, Philadelphia Stars, Memphis Red Sox, Indianapolis Athletics, Louisville Black Colonels

Calhoun, Wesley, 1950 INF, OF, Cleveland Buckeyes

Call, F. 1884-85 INF, Baltimore Atlantics

Callis, J. Joseph 1887 manager, Baltimore Lord Baltimore

Calvo, Jacinto (Jack), 1913-15 OF, Long Branch, N.J. Cubans

Calvo, T., 1915-16 OF, Long Branch, N.J. Cubans, Jersey City Cubans

Cam, —, 1891 OF, Ansonia Cuban Giants (Connecticut St.Lg.)

Cambria, Joe, 1933 owner, officer, Baltimore Black Sox

Campanella, Roy, 1937-45 C, Baltimore Elite Giants

Campbell, Andrew, 1903-06 C, Leland Giants, Chicago Union Giants

Campbell, David (Dave), 1938-41 2B, New York Black Yankees, Philadelphia Stars

Campbell, Grant 1887-93 2B, OF, Chicago Unions

Campbell, Hunter, 1938-42 MGR, Officer, Ethiopian Clowns, Cincinnati Clowns

Campbell, Joe 1887-93 P, Chicago Unions

Campbell, Joe, 1922 OF, 3B, Pittsburgh Keystones

Campbell, Robert (Buddy), 1932 C, Cole's American Giants

Campbell, William (Zip), 1923-29 P, Washington Potomacs, Philadelphia Giants, Hilldale, Lincoln Giants, Richmond Giants

Campini, Joe, 1948 C, Baltimore Elite Giants

Campos, Manuel, 1905 MGR, Cuban Stars of Santiago

Campos, Tatica, 1915-23 P, OF, 1B, 2B, 3B, Cuban Stars, Cuban Stars (East), Cuban Stars (NNL)

Canada, James (Cat), 1936-45 1B, Birmingham Black Barons, Memphis Red Sox, Baltimore Elite Giants, Jacksonville Red Caps, Atlanta Black Crackers

Canizares, Avelino, 1945 SS, Cleveland Buckeyes

Cannady, Walter (Rev), 1921-45 2B, SS, OF, 3B, 1B, P, MGR, Columbus Buckeyes, Dayton Marcos, Cleveland Tate Stars, Homestead Grays, Harrisburg Giants, Hilldale, Lincoln Giants, Darby Daisies, Pittsburgh Crawfords, New York Black Yankees, Philadelphia Stars, Brooklyn Royal Giants, Chicago American Giants, Cincinnati-Indianapolis Clowns, New York Cubans

Cannon, Richard (Speed Ball), 1928-34 P, St. Louis Stars, Nashville Elite Giants, Birmingham Black Barons, Louisville Red Caps, Cleveland Cubs, Louisville Blacks Caps

Caper, —, 1912 SS, Pittsburgh Giants

Capers, (Lefty), 1930-31 P, Louisville White Sox

Carabello, Esterio, 1939 OF, Cuban Stars

Card, Al 1887 player, Pittsburgh Keystones

Cardenas, P., 1924-27 C, OF, Cuban Stars (ECL), Cuban Stars (NNL)

Carey, [Carry], 1916-1921 3B, 2B, St. Louis Giants, Dayton Marcos

Carlisle, Matthew (Lick), 1931-46 2B, SS, Birmingham Black Barons, Montgomery Grey Sox, Memphis Red Sox, Homestead Grays, New Orleans Crescent Stars

Carlson, —, 1916 C, Chicago American Giants

Carlyle, Sylvester Junius, 1945 INF, Kansas City Monarchs

Carmichael, Luther, 1948 sec'y, NSL

Carpenter, —, 1923,1927 OF, Memphis Red Sox, Nashville Elite Giants

Carpenter, Clay, 1925-26 P, 3B, Baltimore Black Sox, Philadelphia Giants

Carr, —, 1890 OF, Lincoln (Neb) Giants

Carr, George Henry (Tank), 1912-1934 1B, 3B, OF, C, Los Angeles White Sox, Kansas City Monarchs, Hilldale, Bacharach Giants, Philadelphia Stars, Lincoln Giants

Carr, Wayne, 1920-28 P, St. Louis Giants, Indianapolis ABCs, Baltimore Black Sox, Washington Potomacs, Bacharach Giants, Wilmington Potomacs, Newark Stars, Brooklyn Royal Giants, Lincoln Giants

Carrera, see Sungo Cabrera

Carroll, Hal 1887 player, Cincinnati Browns

Carroll, (Sonny), 1950 P, Baltimore Elite Giants

Cary, —, 1927 P, Brooklyn Royal Giants

Carry, see Carey

Carswell, Frank, 1944-46 P, Cleveland Buckeyes

Carter, —, 1897-99 P, Cuban Giants

Carter, —, 1918 2B, Chicago Giants

Carter, Alfred, 1935 40-OF, UTIL, Pittsburgh Crawfords, New York Cuban Stars

Carter, Bill, 1948 P, Newark Eagles

Carter, (Bo), 1931 pres, Chattanooga Black Lookouts

Carter, Charles (Kid), 1902-13 P, Philadelphia Giants, Wilmington Giants, Brooklyn Royal Giants

Carter, Charles, 1943 P, Baltimore Elite Giants, Homestead Grays

Carter, Clifford, 1923-34 P, Baltimore Black Sox, Bacharach Giants, Harrisburg Giants, Philadelphia Tigers, Hilldale, Philadelphia Stars

Carter, Dr. A.B., 1933 vice-pres, NSL

Carter, Elmer (Willie), 1930-32 C, SS, 1B, Birmingham Black Barons

Carter, Ernest C. (Spoon, Whip), 1932-49 P, MGR, Pittsburgh Crawfords, Memphis Red Sox, Cleveland Red Sox, Toledo Crawfords, Indianapolis Crawfords, Newark Eagles, Philadelphia Stars, Homestead Grays, Birmingham Black Barons, Louisville Black Caps, Akron Tyrites, Cleveland Giants, Montgomery Dodgers

Carter, Frank, 1917 P, St. Louis Giants

Carter, Ike 1884 2B, St. Louis Black Stockings

Carter, Jimmy, 1938-39 P, Philadelphia Stars

Carter, Kenneth, 1950 C, Cleveland Buckeyes

Carter, Marlin Theodore (Mel, Pee Wee), 1933-50 3B, 2B, Cincinnati Tigers, Atlanta Black Crackers, Memphis Red Sox, Chicago American Giants

Carter, Paul (Nick), 1924-36 P, Hilldale, Darby Daisies, Philadelphia Stars, New York Black Yankees

Carter, Robert, 1947 P, Homestead Grays

Carter, William, 1920-22 C, Detroit Stars, Kansas City Monarchs

Carter, William, 1937,1943 3B, St. Louis Stars, Harrisburg- St. Louis Stars

Cartmill, Alfred Jr., 1949 2B, Kansas City Monarchs

Casey, Joe, 1920 P, St. Louis Giants

Casey, William (Mickey), 1930-43 C, MGR, Baltimore Black Sox, Bacharach Giants, Philadelphia Stars, Washington Black Senators, New York Cubans, Cuban Stars, Baltimore Grays, New York Black Yankees, Hilldale

Cash, William Walker (Bill, Ready), 1943-50 C, OF, 3B, Philadelphia Stars

Cason, John, 1917-32 C, OF, 2B, SS, Brooklyn Royal Giants, Norfolk Stars, Hilldale, Lincoln Giants, Bacharach Giants, Baltimore Black Sox, Birmingham Black Barons, Havana Red Sox

Castillo, Julian, 1911-12 1B, All Cubans, Cuban Stars

Castone, William 1889-92 P, OF, Lincoln-Kearney (Nebraska State Lg.), Lincoln (Neb) Giants, Aspen (Colorado St.Lg.)

Castro, Antonio, 1929 C, Cuban Stars (East)

Cates, Joe (Rabbit), 1931-34 SS, Louisville White Sox, Louisville Red Caps

Cathey, Willis (Jim, Bill), 1948-50 P, Indianapolis Clowns

Cato, Harry 1887-96 2B, P, OF, SS, Cuban X Giants, Cuban Giants New York Gorhams (Middle States Lg.), Philadelphia Giants, Trenton (NJ) Cuban Giants

Caulfield, Fred, 1926 MGR, New Orleans Ads

Celada, —, 1928-29 SS, Cuban Stars (NNL)

Cepeda, Pedro Anibal (Perucho), 1941 OF, New York Cuban Stars

Cephus, Goldie, 1925-31,1938 OF, SS, Philadelphia Giants, Bacharach Giants, Birmingham Black Barons

Chacon, Pelayo, 1910-31 SS, MGR, Stars of Cuba, Cuban Stars, Havana Stars, Cuban Stars (ECL), Cuban Stars (NNL)

Chamberlain, 1889 1B, New York Gorhams (Middle States Lg.)

Chambers, Arthur (Rube), 1925-27 P, Lincoln Giants, Wilmington Potomacs

Chapman, Edward, 1927,1931 P, Detroit Stars, Chicago Columbia Giants

Chapman, J.W. 1887 player, Cincinnati Browns

Chapman, John 1887 player, Cincinnati Browns

Chapman, Roy Lee (Ray), 1949-50 P, New York Black Yankees

Charleston, —, 1942 C, Cincinnati Buckeyes

Charleston, Benny, 1930 OF, Homestead Grays

Charleston, Oscar Mckinley, 1915-50 OF, 1B, MGR, Bowser's ABCs, Indianapolis ABCs, Lincoln Stars, Chicago American Giants, St. Louis Giants, Harrisburg Giants, Hilldale, Homestead Grays, Pittsburgh Crawfords, Toledo Crawfords, Indianapolis Crawfords, Philadelphia Stars, Brooklyn Brown Dodgers,

Charleston, Porter, 1927-35 P, Hilldale, Darby Daisies, Philadelphia Stars

Charleston, (Red), 1921-32 C, Nashville Elite Giants, Birmingham Black Barons, Memphis Red Sox, Montgomery Grey Sox

Charter, William M.(Baby, Bill), 1933-34,1942-46 OF, 1B, C, 3B, Louisville Red Caps, Chicago American Giants, Detroit Black Sox

Chase, —, 1920,1923 OF, P, Detroit Stars, Chicago Giants, Toledo Tigers

Chatman, —, 1922 P, Cleveland Tate Stars

Chatman, Edgar, 1944-45 P, Memphis Red Sox

Chavous, —, 1895-96 P, OF, Adrian (MI) Page Fence Giants

Cheatham, —, 1930-34 P, Baltimore Black Sox, Pittsburgh Crawfords, Homestead Grays

Cherry, Hugh, 1949 officer, Houston Eagles

Chester, —, 1926 OF, Harrisburg Giants

Chestnut, Henry (Joe), 1950 P, Indianapolis Clowns, Philadelphia Stars

Childs, Andy, 1936-45 2B, P, Indianapolis Athletics, Memphis Red Sox, St. Louis Stars, Indianapolis ABCs

Chirban, Louis, 1950 P, Chicago American Giants

Chism, Elijah (Eli, Little Chis), 1937,1946-47 OF, St. Louis Stars, Birmingham Black Barons, Cleveland Buckeyes

Chretian, Ernest, 1950 OF, INF, Kansas City Monarchs, Philadelphia Stars

Christian, —, 1915 OF, Indianapolis ABCs

Christopher, Ted, 1949 C, New York Black Yankees

Christopher, Thadist (Thad), 1935-45 OF, 1B, Newark Eagles, Pittsburgh Crawfords, New York Black Yankees, Cincinnati Buckeyes, Cincinnati Clowns, Cleveland Buckeyes, Toledo Crawfords, Homestead Grays, Nashville Elite Giants, Cincinnati Buckeyes, Ethiopian Clowns, Jacksonville Red Caps

Cisco, J. 1884 player, Philadelphia Mutual B.B.C.

Clarizio, Louis, 1950 OF, Chicago American Giants

Clark, —, 1887 player, Louisville Falls City

Clark, —, 1908 2B, Brooklyn Colored Giants

Clark, —, 1919 OF, Brooklyn Royal Giants

Clark, —, 1931 OF, Louisville White Sox

Clark, —, 1931 P, Kansas City Monarchs

Clark, Albert, 1919-26 P, Dayton Marcos, Cleveland Tate Stars, Pittsburgh Keystones, Indianapolis ABCs, Cleveland Browns, Memphis Red Sox

Clark, Chifian Cleveland, 1945-50 OF, New York Cubans

Clark, Dell, 1914-23 SS, Brooklyn Royal Giants, Indianapolis ABCs, Lincoln Giants, Washington Potomacs, St. Louis Giants

Clark, Harry (Lefty), 1922-25 P, Brooklyn Royal Giants, Hilldale Bacharach Giants

Clark, John L., 1932-46 bus. mgr, Pittsburgh Crawfords; public relations man, Homestead Grays; sec'y, NNL

Clark, Maceo (Marty), 1923-25 1B, P, Washington Potomacs Wilmington Potomacs, Indianapolis ABCs, Bacharach Giants

Clark, Milton J., Jr., 1937 sec'y, Chicago American Giants

Clark, Morten (Specs), 1910-23 SS, 3B, OF, Indianapolis ABCs, Baltimore Black Sox, West Baden (Ind.) Sprudels

Clark, Roy, 1934-35 P, Newark Dodgers

Clarke, William (Eggie, Biff), 1928 OF, Memphis Red Sox

Clarke, (Allie), 1938 1B, 2B, C, OF, Washington Black Senators

Clarke, Robert (Kike, Eggie), 1922-48 C, MGR, Richmond Giants, Baltimore Black Sox, New York Black Yankees, Philadelphia Stars, Baltimore Elite Giants

Clarke, Vibert Ernesto (Webbo), 1946-50 P, Cleveland Buckeyes, Louisville Buckeyes, Memphis Red Sox

Clarkson, see John Brazelton

Clarkson, James Buster (Bus), 1937-50 SS, OF, 2B, Pittsburgh Crawfords, Toledo Crawfords, Indianapolis Crawfords, Newark Eagles, Philadelphia Stars, Baltimore Elite Giants

Clay, Albert (Alton), 1949-50 OF, New York Black Yankees

Clay, William (Lefty), 1932 P, Kansas City Monarchs

Clayton, Leroy Watkins (Zack), 1934-44 1B, C, Bacharach Giants, Cole's American Giants, Chicago American Giants, New York Black Yankees, Chicago Brown Bombers, Brooklyn Eagles

Claxton, James E., 1916,1932 P, Oakland Oaks (PCL), Cuban Stars

Cleage, Pete, 1936 umpire, NNL

Cleage, Ralph, 1924 OF, St. Louis Stars

Cleveland, Howard (Duke) [Duke], 1938-46 OF, Jacksonville Red Caps, Cleveland Bears, Cincinnati Buckeyes, Cleveland Buckeyes, Indianapolis Clowns

Clifford, Luther, 1948-50 C, OF, Homestead Grays

Clifton, Nat (Sweetwater), 1949 1B, Chicago American Giants

Clinton, —, 1917 3B, Bacharach Giants

Close, Herman 1887 manager, Philadelphia Pythians

Cobb, L.S.N., 1920-34 officer, St. Louis Giants, Birmingham Black Barons, Memphis Red Sox, Cleveland Elites; sec'y, NSL

Cobb, W., 1915-20,1928 C, OF, St. Louis Giants, Lincoln Giants, Jewell's ABCs, Indianapolis ABCs, St. Louis Giants

Cockerell, Phi, see Cockrell

Cockerham, Jimmy, 1939 1B, Indianapolis ABCs

Cockrell, Philip (Phil, Fish), 1913-46 P, OF, Havana Red Sox, Lincoln Giants, Hilldale, Darby Daisies, Bacharach Giants, Philadelphia Stars; umpire, NNL

Coffey, Marshall 1889 2B, Chicago Unions

Coffie, Cliffor, see Joe Caffie

Cohen, James C.(Jim, Fireball), 1948-50 P, Indianapolis Clowns

Coimbre, Francisco (Pancho, Al), 1940-44 OF, 2B, Cuban Stars, New York Cubans

Colas, Carlos (Charlie), 1941,1949-50 C, Cuban Stars, Memphis Red Sox

Colas, Jose Luis, 1947-50 OF, MGR, Memphis Red Sox

Cole, see Coley

Cole, Cecil, 1946 P, Newark Eagles

Cole, Ralph (Punjab, Askari), 1939-46 OF, Jacksonville Red Caps, Cleveland Bears, Cincinnati Clowns

Cole, Robert A., 1932-35 officer, Chicago American Giants; tres, NNL; vice-pres, NSL

Cole, William 1896-99 C, P, Cuban Giants

Coleman, Benny, 1950 P, Chicago American Giants

Coleman, Clarence, 1913-21,1926 P, C, OF, 1B, 2B, Chicago Giants, Chicago Union Giants, Indianapolis ABCs, Cleveland Tate Stars, St. Louis Giants, Columbus Buckeyes, Dayton Marcos, Lincoln Giants, All Nations, Bowser's ABCs

Coleman, Gilbert, 1928,1932 INF, OF, Brooklyn Cuban Giants, Bacharach Giants

Coleman, John 1885 OF, Brooklyn Remsens

Coleman, John, 1950 P, Baltimore Elite Giants

Coleman, Melvin, 1937-39 SS, C, Birmingham Black Barons, Ethiopian Clowns

Coley, —, 1923-24 P, Toledo Tigers, Kansas City Monarchs, Detroit Stars

Coley, —, 1931 OF, Nashville Elite Giants

Collier, —, 1928 C, Bacharach Giants

Colliers, Leonard, 1950 P, Cleveland Buckeyes

Collins, —, 1910-18 C, 1B, New York Black Sox, Brooklyn Royal Giants, Pennsylvania Red Caps of New York, Lincoln Giants, Pittsburgh Giants, Philadelphia Giants, Pittsburgh Stars of Buffalo

Collins, —, 1928 P, Baltimore Black Sox

Collins, —, 1936 P, New York Black Yankees

Collins, Eugene (Gene), 1947-50 P, OF, Kansas City Monarchs

Collins, George, 1921-33 OF, 2B, P, SS, New Orleans Crescent Stars, Milwaukee Bears, Toledo Tigers, Indianapolis ABCs, Nashville Elite Giants, New Orleans Caulfield Ads

Collins, Nat 1888-89 P, New York Gorhams (Middle States Lg.), Philadelphia Giants

Collins, Walter, 1947-48 P, Chicago American Giants, Memphis Red Sox

Collins, Willie, 1933 OF, Nashville Elite Giants

Collins, Willie P. (James), 1950 P, Birmingham Black Barons

Colzie, Jim, 1946-47 P, Cincinnati-Indianapolis Clowns, Indianapolis Clowns

Combs, A. Clark (Jack), 1922-26 P, Detroit Stars

Condon, Lafayette 1887 player, Louisville Falls Citys

Connors, John W., 1904-1922 owner, Officer, Brooklyn Royal Giants, Bacharach Giants

Cook, Howard (Johnny), 1937 P, Indianapolis Athletics

Cook, Walter 1886-88 officer, Cuban Giants

Cooke, James (Jay), 1932-33 P, Baltimore Black Sox, Bacharach Giants

Cooley, Walter, 1931 C, 3B, Birmingham Black Barons

Cooper, Alex, 1928 OF, Philadelphia Tigers, Harrisburg Giants

Cooper, Alfred (Army), 1923-32 P, Kansas City Monarchs, Cleveland Stars

Cooper, Andy (Lefty), 1920-41 P, MGR, Detroit Stars, Chicago American Giants, St. Louis Stars, Kansas City Monarchs

Cooper, Anthony (Ant), 1928-35,1941 SS, 2B, OF, Birmingham Black Barons, Cleveland Stars, Baltimore Black Sox, Cleveland Red Sox, Louisville Red Sox, Pittsburgh Crawfords, Newark Dodgers, Homestead Grays, New York Black Yankees

Cooper, C. 1884 player, Philadelphia Mutual B.B.C.

Cooper, (Chief), 1928 umpire, NNL

Cooper, Daltie 1921-40 P, Nashville Elite Giants, Indianapolis ABCs, Harrisburg Giants, Lincoln Giants, Hilldale, Bacharach Giants, Homestead Grays, Baltimore Black Sox, Newark Eagles, Washington Potomacs

Cooper, E., 1916-1924 1B, OF, Lincoln Stars, Cleveland Tate Stars, St. Louis Giants

Cooper, James, 1938,1946-47 P, Atlanta Black Crackers, New York Black Yankees, Newark Eagles

Cooper, Ray, 1928-29 P, Hilldale

Cooper, Sam, 1926-34 P, Harrisburg Giants, Baltimore Black Sox, Bacharach Giants, Homestead Grays

Cooper, Thomas (Tom), 1947-50 C, OF, 1B, Kansas City Monarchs

Cooper, W.T. (Bill, Thomas), 1938-46 C, Atlanta Black Crackers, Philadelphia Stars, New York Black Yankees

Copeland, L., 1935 INF, Brooklyn Eagles

Corbett, Charles, 1921-28 P, Pittsburgh Keystones, Indianapolis ABCs, Harrisburg Giants, Hilldale

Corcoran, Tom, 1942 P, Homestead Grays

Cordova, (Pete), 1921-23 3B, SS, Kansas City Monarchs, Cleveland Tate Stars, Toledo Tigers

Cornelius, William Mckinley (Willie, Sug), 1928-46 P, Nashville Elite Giants, Memphis Red Sox, Chicago American Giants, Cole's American Giants, Birmingham Black Barons, Cleveland Elites

Cornett, Harry, 1913 C, Indianapolis ABCs

Correa, Marcelino (Cho-Cho Cuco), 1926-36 SS, Cuban Stars (NNL), Cuban Stars (East), New York Cubans

Cortez, Aurelio, 1928-31 C, Cuban Stars (NNL), Cuban Stars (East)

Cosa, —, 1932 OF, Memphis Red Sox

Costello, —, 1911 1B, All Cubans

Cottman, Darby 1887-93 3B, Chicago Unions

Cotton, see Robert A. Williams

Cotton, James, 1945 officer, Chattanooga Choo Choos

Cottrell, —, 1923 C, Hilldale

Cowan, Eddie, 1919 SS, Cleveland Tate Stars

Cowan, Johnnie, 1934-50 3B, 2B, Birmingham Black Barons, Cleveland Buckeyes, Memphis Red Sox, Cincinnati Buckeyes

Cowans, Russ, 1942 sec'y, Negro Baseball Lg. of America

Cox, Comer Lane (Hannibal), 1930-31-OF, Nashville Elite Giants, Cleveland Cubs

Cox, M.D. Alphonse, 1938-43 P, Memphis Red Sox, Jacksonville Red Caps, Cleveland Bears

Cox, Roosevelt, 1937-43 3B, 2B, SS, Detroit Stars, Kansas City Monarchs, New York Cubans, Cuban Stars, Ethiopian Clowns

Cox, Tom (Lefty), 1930-32 P, Lincoln Giants, Cleveland Cubs

Cozart, Haywood (Harry, Big Train), 1939-43 P, Newark Eagles

Craig, Charles, 1926-28 P, Lincoln Giants, Brooklyn Cuban Giants, Harrisburg Giants, Homestead Grays

Craig, Dick, 1940 1B, Indianapolis Crawfords

Craig, Homer, 1935 P, Newark Stars

Craig, John, 1935-46 umpire, NNL

Craig, Joseph (Joe), 1940,1946 1B, OF, Indianapolis Crawfords, Philadelphia Stars

Crain, A.C. 1887 player, Baltimore Lord Baltimores

Crawford, John, 1943 umpire, NNL

Crawford, Sam, 1910-38 P, MGR, coach, New York Black Sox, Chicago Giants, Chicago American Giants, Chicago Union Giants, Detroit Stars, Kansas City Monarchs, Brooklyn Royal Giants, Birmingham Black Barons, Chicago Columbia Giants, Cole's American Giants, Indianapolis Athletics, St. Louis Stars, Cleveland Tate Stars

Crawford, Willie Walker, 1934 OF, Birmingham Black Barons

Creacy, A.D. (Dewey), 1924-40 3B, Kansas City Monarchs, St. Louis Stars, Detroit Wolves, Washington Pilots, Columbus Blue Birds, Cleveland Giants, Philadelphia Stars, Brooklyn Royal Giants

Creek, Willie, 1924,1930-32 C, SS, Washington Potomacs, Brooklyn Royal Giants

Crelin, Wilbur C., 1926 officer, Newark Stars

Crespo, Alejandro Rogelio, 1918-33 2B, 3B, Cuban Stars (East), Cuban Stars of Havana

Crespo, Alejandro (Alex, Home Run), 1940-46 OF, Cuban Stars, New York Cubans

Crockett, Frank, 1916-23 OF, Bacharach Giants, Brooklyn Royal Giants, Norfolk Stars

Cromartie, Leroy, 1945 2B, Cincinnati-Indianapolis Clowns

Cross, Bennie 1887 OF, Boston Resolutes

Cross, Norman, 1932-36 P, Cole's American Giants

Crowder, —, 1920 P, Lincoln Stars

Crowe, George, 1947-49-1B, INF, New York Cubans, New York Black Yankees

Croxton, —, 1908-09 P, C, Cuban Giants

Crudup, Zeke, 1925-26 P, Philadelphia Giants

Crue, Martin (Matty), 1942-48 P, New York Cubans, Homestead Grays

Crumbie, Ralph, 1946 C, Pittsburgh Crawfords

Crumbley, Alex, 1937-38 OF, New York Black Yankees, Atlanta Black Crackers, Pittsburgh Crawfords, Washington Black Senators

Crump, James, 1920-38 2B, Norfolk Giants, Hilldale, Philadelphia Giants, Norfolk Stars; umpire, NNL

Crump, Willis, 1916-23 OF, 2B, Bacharach Giants

Crutchfield, John William (Jimmie), 1930-45 OF, Birmingham Black Barons, Indianapolis ABCs, Pittsburgh Crawfords, Newark Eagles, Toledo Crawfords, Indianapolis Crawfords, Chicago American Giants, Cleveland Buckeyes

Cruz, —, 1930 P, Cuban Stars

Cuella, Jose Luis, 1945 OF, Pittsburgh Crawfords

Cuerira, Basilo, 1921-22 P, OF, All Cubans, Cuban Stars (NNL)

Culver, [Culcra], 1916-22 3B, SS, OF, Pittsburgh Stars of Buffalo Penn Red Caps of NY, Cuban Stars (NNL)

Cumming, Hugh S. 1887 player, Baltimore Lord Baltimores

Cummings, —, 1932 C, Louisville Black Caps

Cummings, Napoleon (Chance), 1916-29 1B, 2B, Bacharach Giants, Hilldale, Norfolk Stars, Madison Stars

Cunningham, —, 1917-20 SS, St. Louis Giants, Dayton Marcos

Cunningham, —, 1926-27 2B, Pennsylvania Red Caps of NY

Cunningham, —, 1934 OF, Baltimore Black Sox

Cunningham, H. (Rounder), 1918-31 SS, Montgomery Grey Sox

Cunningham, Harry (Baby), 1930-37 P, Memphis Red Sox, Birmingham Black Barons

Cunningham, Larry, 1950 OF, Memphis Red Sox, Houston Eagles

Cunningham, Marion (Daddy), 1921-26 1B, MGR, Memphis Red Sox, Montgomery Grey Sox

Cunningham, Robert (Slim), 1950 P, Cleveland Buckeyes

Curley, Earl C., 1925 OF, Memphis Red Sox

Currie, Reuben (Rube, Black Snake), 1919-32 P, Chicago Unions, Kansas City Monarchs, Hilldale, Chicago American Giants, Detroit Stars, Cleveland Red Sox, Baltimore Black Sox

Curry, Homer (Goose), 1928-50 OF, P, MGR, Memphis Red Sox, Washington Elite Giants, New York Black Yankees, Newark Eagles, Baltimore Elite Giants, Philadelphia Stars, Nashville Elite Giants, Cleveland Tigers, Indianapolis Athletics

Curry, Oscar J. 1887 P, Cuban Giants

Curtis, see Curtiss Ricks

Curtis, —, 1932 C, Louisville Black Caps

Curtis, Harry 1898 MGR, Celeron Acme Colored Giants (Iron and Oil Lg.)

Cyrus, Herb, see Herb Souell

Dabney, Milton 1885-96 OF, P, Argyle Hotel, Cuban X Giants, Cuban Giants

Dailey, James, 1948 P, Baltimore Elite Giants

Dallard, William (Eggie), 1920-33 1B, OF, C, 2B, Wilmington Potomacs, Baltimore Black Sox, Bacharach Giants, Hilldale, Quaker Giants, Darby Daisies, Philadelphia Stars, Washington Potomacs, Madison Stars, Pennsylvania Giants

Dallas, Porter (Big Boy), 1929-32 3B, Birmingham Black Barons, Monroe Monarchs

Dalton, Rossie, 1940 UTIL, Chicago American Giants, Birmingham Black Barons

Dandridge, John, 1949 P, Houston Eagles

Dandridge, (Ping) [Dandy], 1917-20 INF, P, Havana Red Sox, Lincoln Giants, St.Louis Giants

Dandridge, Raymond Emmett (Hooks, Squatty), 1933-49 3B, 2B, SS, Detroit Stars, Nashville Elite Giants, Newark Dodgers, Newark Eagles, New York Cubans

Dandridge, Troy Rasmussen (Dan), 1926-29 3B, SS, Chicago Giants, Dayton Marcos

Daniels, Eddie, 1946-47 P, New York Cubans

Daniels, Fred, 1919-28 P, St. Louis Giants, Hilldale, Birmingham Black Barons, Lincoln Giants, Nashville Elite Giants

Daniels, Hammond, 1924-26 officer, Bacharach Giants

Daniels, James George (Jim, Schoolboy), 1943 P, Birmingham Black Barons

Daniels, Leon (Pepper), 1921-35 C, 1B, Detroit Stars, Harrisburg Giants, Cuban Stars, Brooklyn Eagles, Bacharach Giants, Chicago Columbia Giants

Darden, Clarence, 1938 3B, Atlanta Black Crackers

Darden, Floyd, 1950 2B, OF, Baltimore Elite Giants

Davenport, Lloyd (Bear Man, Ducky), 1934-49 OF, MGR, Monroe Monarchs, Philadelphia Stars, Cincinnati Tigers, Memphis Red Sox, Birmingham Black Barons, Chicago American Giants, Cleveland Buckeyes, Pittsburgh Crawfords, Louisville Buckeyes, Jacksonville Red Caps, New Orleans Crescent Stars

Davidson, Charles (Specks), 1939-40,1946-49 P, New York Black Yankees, Brooklyn Royal Giants, Baltimore Elite Giants, Memphis Red Sox

Davis, —, 1934 OF, Kansas City Monarchs

Davis, A. 1886-91 OF, MGR, Boston Resolutes, New York Gorhams

Davis, A.L., 1924-25 SS, OF, Indianapolis ABCs

Davis, Albert, 1927-37 P, Detroit Stars, Baltimore Black Sox

Davis, (Big Boy), 1932 P, Indianapolis ABCs

Davis, Dwight, 1930 P, Detroit Stars

Davis, Earl (Hawk), 1927-36   2B, Indianapolis ABCs, Bacharach Giants, Newark Browns, Hilldale, Philadelphia Giants

Davis, Edward A. (Eddie, Peanuts, Nyasses), 1939-50   P, Ethiopian Clowns, Cincinnati Clowns, Cincinnati-Indianapolis Clowns, Indianapolis Clowns

Davis, (Goldie, Red), 1924-25   P, OF, Indianapolis ABCs

Davis, Hy, 1934   1B, Hilldale, Newark Dodgers

Davis, Jack, 1922-25   3B, Bacharach Giants, Philadelphia Giants

Davis, James, 1920   P, Chicago Giants, Lincoln Giants

Davis, John, 1903-10   P, Leland Giants, Cuban Giants, Philadelphia Giants, Chicago Union Giants, Cuban Giants, Algona (IA) Brownies

Davis, John Howard (Cherokee), 1941-50   OF, P, Newark Eagles, Houston Eagles

Davis, Lee, 1945   P, Kansas City Monarchs

Davis, Lorenzo (Piper), 1942-50   1B, 2B, SS, MGR, Birmingham Black Barons

Davis, Martin Luther, 1945   P, Chicago American Giants

Davis, Nathaniel, 1947-50   1B, New York Black Yankees, Philadelphia Stars

Davis, (Quack), 1913   player, Indianapolis ABCs

Davis, Robert (Butch), 1947-50   OF, Baltimore Elite Giants

Davis, Roosevelt (Rosey, Duro), 1924-45   P, St. Lous Stars, Columbus Blue Birds, Pittsburgh Crawfords, New York Black Yankees, Philadelphia Stars, Memphis Red Sox, Brooklyn Royal Giants, Baltimore Elite Giants, Chicago Brown Bombers, Cincinnati Clowns, Cincinnati-Indianapolis Clowns, Cleveland Buckeyes, Indianapolis ABCs, Newark Eagles

Davis, Ross (Satchel), 1943-47   P, Cleveland Buckeyes, Boston Blues (USL)

Davis, S., 1935   OF, Brooklyn Eagles

Davis, Saul Henry (Rareback), 1921-31   3B, 2B, SS, Birmingham Black Barons, Cleveland Tigers, Memphis Red Sox, Chicago American Giants, Detroit Stars, Columbus Buckeyes

Davis, Spencer (Babe), 1937-48   SS, OF, 3B, MGR, Atlanta Black Crackers, Indianapolis ABCs, New York Black Yankees, Winston-Salem Giants, Memphis Red Sox

Davis, Walter (Steel Arm), 1923-34   OF, 1B, P, Detroit Stars, Chicago American Giants, Chicago Columbia Giants, Cole's American Giants, Nashville Elite Giants

Davis, William, 1937-40   3B, OF, St. Louis Stars, Indianapolis ABCs, Memphis Red Sox, Atlanta Black Crackers

Davis, William N. (Bill), 1945-47   P, Philadelphia Stars

Davis, Willie, 1945   officer, Mobile Black Shippers

Dawson, —, 1908   P, New York Colored Giants

Dawson, Johnny, 1938-42   C, Memphis Red Sox, Kansas City Monarchs Chicago American Giants, Birmingham Black Barons

Dawson, Leroy, 1946   MGR., Philadelphia Stars

Day, Eddie 1898   SS, Celeron Acme Colored Giants (Iron and Oil Lg.)

Day, Guy 1885   C, Argyle Hotel

Day, Leon, 1934-50   P, Bacharach Giants, Brooklyn Eagles, Newark Eagles, Baltimore Elite Giants

Day, Wilson C. (Connie), 1920-32,1939   2B, 3B, SS, manager, Indianapolis ABCs, Baltimore Black Sox, Harrisburg Giants, Bacharach Giants

Dean, Bob, 1937-40   P, St. Louis Stars

Dean, Charlie, 1947   P, New York Black Yankees

Dean, Jimmy, 1949-50   P, Philadelphia Stars

Dean, Nelson, 1925-32   P, Kansas City Monarchs, Cleveland Hornets, Cleveland Tigers, Detroit Stars, Cleveland Stars, Memphis Red Sox, Birmingham Black Barons

Dean, Robert, 1925-33   3B, 2B, Lincoln Giants, Pennsylvania Red Caps of New York

Deane, Alpheus, 1947   P, New York Black Yankees

Deas, James Alvin (Yank), 1916-28   C, Bacharach Giants, Pennsylvania Giants, Lincoln Giants, Hilldale, Richmond Giants, Philadelphia Giants

Deberry, C.I. (Charlie), 1948   MGR, Greensboro Red Wings; vice- pres, Negro American Association

Debran, Roy, 1940   OF, New York Black Yankees

Decker, Charles (Dusty), 1932-38   INF, MGR, Indianapolis ABCs, Montgomery Grey Sox, Detroit Stars, Memphis Red Sox, Louisville Black Colonels

Decuir, Lionel, 1939-40   C, Kansas City Monarchs

Dedeaux, Russ, 1941,1946   P, Newark Eagles, New York Black Yankees

Delgado, Felix Rafael (Felle), 1941   OF, 1B, Cuban Stars

Delugo, —, 1935   P, New York Cubans

Demeza, —, 1905   P, All Cubans

Demoss, Elwood (Bingo), 1905-43   2B, SS, P, MGR, Topeka Giants, Kansas City, Kan., Giants, Oklahoma Giants, Indianapolis ABCs, Chicago American Giants, Detroit Stars, Cleveland Giants, Chicago Brown Bombers, Bowser's ABCs, All Cubans

Dennard, Dick, 1945   player, Toledo Cubs (USL)

Dennis, Wesley L. (Doc), 1943-48   1B, OF, Baltimore Elite Giants, Philadelphia Stars

Dent, Carl J., 1950   SS, Indianapolis Clowns

Derrick, L.B., 1925-26   officer, Detroit Stars

Despert, Denny, 1914-16   OF, Lincoln Giants, Brooklyn Royal Giants, Philadelphia Giants

Devean, —, 1908   C, New York Colored Giants

Devers, —, 1950   P, Houston Eagles

Devoe, —, 1905-18   C, Philadelphia Giants, Chicago Giants

Devoe, J.R., 1922   bus. mgr, Cleveland Tate Stars

Devon, —, 1933   OF, Philadelphia Stars

Dewberry, William, 1904   C, Chicago Union Giants

Dewear, —, 1923   C, Kansas City Monarchs

Dewitt, Fred, 1925-30   1B, INF, Kansas City Monarchs, Memphis Red Sox, Hilldale

Dewitt, S.R. (Eddie), 1917-30   3B, Dayton Giants, Dayton Marcos, Indianapolis ABCs, Columbus Buckeyes, Toledo Tigers, Kansas City Monarchs, Cleveland Tigers, Hilldale

Dial, Kermit, 1933-40   2B, P, Columbus Blue Birds, Cole's American Giants, Detroit Stars, Cincinnati Buckeyes

Dials, Alonzo Odem (Lou), 1925-36   1B, OF, Detroit Stars Chicago American Giants, Memphis Red Sox, Hilldale, Cleveland Giants Homestead Grays, Akron Tyrites, Birmingham Black Barons

Diamond, (Lefty), *see Robert Pipkin*

Diaz, Fernando, *see Fernando Diaz Pedroso*

Diaz, Heliodoro (Yoyo), 1926-39   P, 1B, OF, Cuban Stars (NNL), New York Cubans (East)

Diaz, Pablo Mesa, 1930-35   C, 1B, Cuban Stars (NNL), Cuban Stars (East), New York Cubans

Diaz, Pedro (Manny), *see Fernando Diaz Pedroso*

Dibut, Pedro, 1923   P, Cubans (NNL)

Dickins, —, 1945   P, Cincinnati Clowns

Dickerson, John Fount (Babe), 1950   P, Homestead Grays, Chicago American Giants

Dickerson, Lou, 1921   P, Hilldale

Dickey, John (Steel Arm), 1921-22   P, Montgomery Grey Sox, St. Louis Stars, St. Louis Giants

Dieckert, —, 1943   3B, Cuban Stars

Dihigo, Martin, 1923-1945   2B, P, OF, SS, 3B, 1B, C, MGR, Cuban Stars (East), New York Cubans, Homestead Grays, Hilldale, Darby Daisies

Dillard, —, 1927   P, Lincoln Giants

Dilworth, Arthur, 1916-18   P, OF, C, Bacharach Giants, Hilldale, Lincoln Giants

Dimes, —, 1926,1933   OF, Dayton Marcos, Akron

Direaux, Jimmy [Direux], 1937-39   P, Washington Elite Giants, Baltimore Elite Giants

Dismukes, William (Dizzy), 1910-50   P, MGR, NNL sec'y, club sec'y, Philadelphia Giants, Brooklyn Royal Giants, Mohawk Giants, Indianapolis ABCs, Chicago American Giants, Dayton Marcos, Pittsburgh Keystones, Memphis Red Sox, St. Louis Stars, Cincinnati Dismukes, Detroit Wolves, Homestead Grays, Columbus Blue Birds, Birmingham Black Barons, Kansas City Monarchs, West Baden (Ind.) Sprudels, Lincoln Giants

Dixon, —, 1915-16   P, Chicago American Giants, Chicago Giants

Dixon, Eddie Lee (Ed), 1938-39   P, Atlanta Black Crackers, Indianapolis ABCs, Baltimore Elite Giants

Dixon, George (Tubby), 1917-31   C, Chicago American Giants, Indianapolis ABCs, Birmingham Black Barons, Cleveland Hornets, Cleveland Cubs

Dixon, Glenn, 1937   OF, P, St. Louis Stars

Dixon, Herbert Albert (Rap), 1922-37   OF, MGR., Harrisburg Giants, Baltimore Black Sox, Chicago American Giants, Hilldale Darby Daisies, Pittsburgh Crawfords, Philadelphia Stars, Brooklyn Eagles, Homestead Grays, New York Cubans, Washington Potomacs

Dixon, John Robert (Johnny Bob), 1927-34   SS, Cleveland Tigers, Detroit Stars, Cuban Stars, Cleveland Giants, Cleveland Red Sox, Indianapolis ABCs

Dixon, John, 1950   P, Chicago American Giants, Birmingham Black Barons

Dixon, Paul Perry (Dick), 1931-38   OF, Bacharachs Giants, Baltimore Black Sox, Washington Pilots, New York Cubans, Philadelphia Stars

Dixon, Tom, 1932-36   C, P, Baltimore Black Sox, Bacharach Giants, Hilldale

Dobbins, Nat, 1921   P, SS, Hilldale

Doby, Lawrence Eugene (Larry) [Larry Walker], 1942-47   2B, Newark Eagles

Dominguez, —, 1925   P, Cuban Stars (NNL)

Donaldson, John Wesley, 1916-34   P, OF, All Nations, Los Angeles White Sox, Chicago Giants, Indianapolis ABCs, Kansas City Monarchs, Detroit Stars, Brooklyn Royal Giants, Donaldson All-Stars, Lincoln Giants

Donaldson, W.W. (Billy), 1923-37   umpire, NNL

Donoso, Lino Galata, 1947-49   P, New York Cubans

Dorsey, F.T. 1884-85   OF, Baltimore Lord Baltimore

Dougherty, Charles (Pat), 1909-15   P, Leland Giants, Chicago American Giants, Chicago Giants

Dougherty, Lon, 1935   P, Brooklyn Eagles

Douglas, Eddie, 1922   OF, St. Louis Stars

Douglas, George 1885,1891   OF, P, Brooklyn Remsens, Ansonia Cuban Giants (Connecticut St.Lg.)

Douglas, Jesse Warren, 1937-50   INF, OF, Kansas City Monarchs, Birmingham Black Barons, Chicago American Giants, Memphis Red Sox

Douglass, Edward (Eddie), 1918-29   1B, MGR, Brooklyn Royal Giants, Lincoln Giants

Dow, —, 1911   P, Philadelphia Giants

Downer, Fred, 1921-22   OF, Pittsburgh Keystones, Baltimore Black Sox

Downs, Ellsworth 1887   player, Cincinnati Browns

Downs, Mckinley (Bunny), 1915-43   2B, SS, 3B, MGR, St. Louis Giants, Bacharach Giants, Hilldale, Brooklyn Royal Giants, Brooklyn Cuban Giants, Philadelphia Tigers, Cincinnati Clowns, Indianapolis ABCs, West Baden (Ind.) Sprudels, Louisville Sox, Harris burg Giants, Richmond Giants

Drake, Andrew, 1930-32   C, P, Birmingham Black Barons, Chattanooga Black Lookouts, Cole's American Giants, Nashville Elite Giants, Louisville Red Sox

Drake, Reynaldo Verdes, 1945-50   OF, Cincinnati-Indianapolis Clowns, Indianapolis Clowns

Drake, William P. (Plunk), 1916-30   P, St. Louis Giants, St. Louis Stars, Kansas City Monarchs, Indianapolis ABCs, Detroit Stars

Dreke, Valentin, 1919-28   OF, Cuban Stars of Havana, Cuban Stars (NNL)

Drew, John M., 1931-32   officer, Darby Daisies, Hilldale

Drew, P., 1939   OF, P, Indianapolis ABCs

Drummer, —, 1948   P, Newark Eagles

Duany, Claro, 1944-47   OF, New York Cubans

Dubisson, D.J., 1932   officer; Little Rock Grays

Ducey, —, 1924-26   INF, OF, St. Louis Giants, Dayton Marcos

Duckett, Mahlon Newton (John, Mal), 1940-49   3B, 2B, SS, Philadelphia Stars, Homestead Grays

Ducy, Eddie, 1947   2B, Homestead Grays

Dudley, C.A., 1920-23   OF, St. Louis Giants, St. Louis Stars

Dudley, Edward, 1925-28-P, Lincoln Giants, Brooklyn Royal Giants, Philadelphia Tigers

Duff, Ernest, 1925-32 OF, Indianapolis ABCs, Cleveland Elites, Cleveland Hornets, Cleveland Tigers, Cuban Stars

Duffy, Bill, 1947 C, Kansas City Monarchs

Dukes, Tommy, 1928-45 C, 3B, Chicago American Giants, Memphis Red Sox, Nashville Elite Giants, Columbus Elite Giants, Homestead Grays, Toledo Crawfords, Indianapolis Crawfords Birmingham Black Barons, Cuban Stars (East)

Dula, Louis, 1933-38 P, Cincinnati Tigers, Homestead Grays

Dumas, Jim, 1940-41 P, Memphis Red Sox

Dumpson, Bill, 1950 P, Indianapolis Clowns, Philadelphia Stars

Dunbar, Ashby, 1909-19 OF, Brooklyn Royal Giants, Lincoln Stars, Indianapolis ABCs, Pennsylvania Red Caps of New York, Lincoln Giants, Louisville Sox, Mohawk Giants

Dunbar, Frank, 1908 OF, Philadelphia Giants

Dunbar, (Vet) 1937 INF, C, Memphis Red Sox, Indianapolis Athletics

Duncan, Charlie (Scottie), 1938-40 P, Atlanta Black Crackers, Indianapolis ABCs, St. Louis Stars

Duncan, Frank (Pete), 1909-28 OF, MGR, Philadelphia Giants, Leland Giants, Chicago American Giants, Detroit Stars, Chicago Giants, Toledo Tigers, Cleveland Elites, Cleveland Hornets, Cleveland Tigers, Milwaukee Bears

Duncan, Frank Jr., 1920-48 C, OF, MGR, Chicago Giants, Kansas City Monarchs, New York Black Yankees, Pittsburgh Crawfords, Homestead Grays, New York Cubans, Chicago American Giants

Duncan, Frank, III, 1941,1945-46 P, Kansas City Monarchs, Baltimore Elite Giants

Duncan, Joe, 1927 C, Bacharachs Giants

Duncan, Melvin L., 1949-50 P, Kansas City Monarchs

Duncan, Warren, 1922-1927 C, OF, Bacharach Giants

Dunkin, Ishkooda (Stringbean), 1937 P, Pittsburgh Crawfords

Dunlap, Herman, 1936-39 OF, Chicago American Giants

Dunn, Alphonse (Blue), 1937-43 1B, OF, Detroit Stars, New York Cubans, Birmingham Black Barons, Ethiopian Clowns

Dunn, Joseph (Jake), 1930-41 SS, OF, 2B, MGR, Detroit Stars, Washington Pilots, Nashville Elite Giants, Baltimore Black Sox, Philadelphia Stars

Dunn, Willie, 1942 P, Jacksonville Red Caps

Durant, —, 1932 OF, Washington Pilots, Baltimore Black Sox, Hilldale

Durvant, —, 1923 P, Cuban Stars (NNL)

Dwight, Edward Joseph (Eddie, Pee Wee), 1924-37 OF, Indianapolis ABCs, Kansas City Monarchs, Gilkerson's Union Giants

Dykes, A., 1929 2B, Birmingham Black Barons

Dykes, John, 1932 officer, Washington Pilots

Dyll, Frank R., 1950 SS, Chicago American Giants

Dysoin, Major, 1950 SS, New York Black Yankees

Earle, Charles Babcock (Frank, Peles), 1906-19 OF, P, MGR, Wilmington Giants, Cuban Giants, Philadelphia Giants, Brooklyn Royal Giants, Lincoln Giants, Bacharach Giants, Pennsylvania Red Caps of NY

Easley, —, 1936 OF, Memphis Red Sox

Easte, —, 1923 P, Hilldale

Easter, Luscious (Luke), 1946-48 OF, 1B, Cincinnati Crescents, Homestead Grays

Easterling, Howard, 1936-49 3B, SS, 2B, Cincinnati Tigers, Chicago American Giants, Homestead Grays, New York Cubans

Eatmon, [Eaton], 1937-38 P, Birmingham Black Barons

Echevarria, Rafael, 1938 2B, New York Cubans

Echols, Jim, 1943 P, Atlanta Black Crackers

Echols, Joe, 1939 OF, Newark Eagles

Eckelson, Juan [Ekelson], 1925 P, Cuban Stars (NNL)

Edsall, George 1898 OF, Celeron Acme Colored Giants (Iron and Oil Lg.)

Edwards, Chancellor (Jack, Pep), 1928 C, Cleveland Tigers

Edwards, Frank Nutinous (Teannie)-1936-37 2B, C, St. Louis Stars

Edwards, James, 1919 C, Bacharach Giants

Edwards, Jesse (Johnny), 1923-31 2B, OF, P, Nashville Elite Giants, Birmingham Black Barons, Memphis Red Sox, Detroit Stars

Edwards, Osee, 1950 CF, New York Black Yankees

Edwards, Smokey), 1913-18 P, OF, Mohawk Giants, Lincoln Stars, Pennsylvania Red Caps of New York

Edwards, William, 1944 P, Kansas City Monarchs

Eggleston, Macajah Marchand (Mack, Egg), 1917-34 C, OF, 3B, Dayton Giants, Dayton Marcos, Detroit Stars, Indianapolis ABCs, Washington Potomacs, Columbus Buckeyes, Wilmington Potomacs, Harrisburg Giants, Baltimore Black Sox, Bacharach Giants, New York Black Yankees, Washington Pilots, Homestead Grays, Nashville Elite Giants, Lincoln Giants

Eggleston, William 1885 SS, Argyle Hotel

Ekelson, see Eckelson

Elam, James (Ed) [Elan], 1943 P, INF, Newark Eagles

Ellerbe, Lacey, 1950 UTIL, Baltimore Elite Giants

Ellis, Albert, 1950 P, Cleveland Buckeyes

Ellis, James, 1921-1925 1B, 3B, Memphis Red Sox, Dayton Marcos, Nashville Elite Giants, Cleveland Browns

Ellis, (Rocky, Rube), 1925-42 P, OF, Hilldale, Philadelphia Stars, Homestead Grays, Jacksonville Red Caps, Baltimore Grays Bacharach Giants, Birmingham Black Barons

Else, Harry (Speedy), 1931-40 C, Monroe Monarchs, Kansas City Monarchs, Chicago American Giants, New Orleans Black Creoles

Embry, William R. (Cap), 1923 umpire, NNL

Emery, Jack, 1908-16-P, OF, Brooklyn Colored Giants, Philadelphia Giants, Smart Set, Pittsburgh Colored Stars, Pittsburgh Stars of Buffalo

Emmett, —, 1924 P, Indianapolis ABCs

Emory, —, 1887-89 C, 1B, New York Gorhams (Middle States Lg.), Philadelphia Pythians

English, H.D., 1932 officer, Monroe Monarchs

English, Louis, 1929-34 C, OF, Louisville White Sox, Louisville Black Caps, Louisville Red Caps, Nashville Elite Giants, Detroit Stars

Ervin, Willie, 1948 P, New York Black Yankees

Erye, John, see John Frye

Espenosia, —, 1947 P, Indianapolis Clowns

Estenza, —, 1927-28 P, OF, 3B, C, Cuban Stars (NNL)

Estrada, Oscar, 1924-25,1931 P, OF, Cuban Stars (ECL), Cuban Stars (West)

Etchegoyen, Carlos, 1930-32 OF, 3B, Cuban Stars (East)

Evans, —, 1918 2B, Baltimore Black Sox

Evans, Charles Alexander, 1921-27 P, Bacharach Giants, Penn Red Caps of NY, Baltimore Black Sox

Evans, Clarence, 1949 P, Homestead Grays

Evans, Felix (Chin), 1934-49 P, OF, Atlanta Black Crackers, Indianapolis ABCs, Memphis Red Sox, Birmingham Black Barons Baltimore Elite Giants, St. Louis Stars

Evans, Frank, 1915 player, Kansas City Giants

Evans, Frank, 1950 OF, Cleveland Buckeyes

Evans, George 1887 player, New York Gorhams

Evans, John 1887-88 player, New York Gorhams

Evans, Robert (Bob), 1934-43 P, Newark Dodgers, Newark Eagles, Jacksonville Red Caps, New York Black Yankees, Philadelphia Stars

Evans, Ulysses (Cowboy), 1933,1943 P, Louisville Red Caps, Cincinnati Clowns, Chicago Brown Bombers

Evans, William, 1903 C, OF, Philadelphia Giants

Evans, William Demont II (Bill, Happy, Grey Ghost), 1924-36 OF, SS, 3B, P, Chicago American Giants, Brooklyn Royal Giants, Dayton Marcos, Cleveland Hornets, St. Louis Stars, Indianapolis ABCs, Homestead Grays, Washington Pilots, Detroit Wolves, Cincinnati Tigers, Memphis Red Sox

Evans, W. P., 1920-24 OF, P, Baltimore Black Sox, Chicago American Giants, Lincoln Stars

Everett, —, 1927 SS, Kansas City Monarchs, Detroit Stars

Everett, Curtis, 1950 C, OF, Kansas City Monarchs

Everett, Dean, 1929 P, Lincoln Giants

Everett, James W., 1931-43 P, OF, Pennsylvania Red Caps of New York, Cincinnati Clowns, Newark Browns, Memphis Red Sox

Ewell, Wilmer, 1925-34 C, Indianapolis ABCs, Cincinnati Tigers

Ewing, William Monroe (Buck), 1920-30 C, Chicago American Giants, Columbus Buckeyes, Indianapolis ABCs, Homestead Grays, Lincoln Giants, Cleveland Tate Stars

Eyers, Henry, see Henry Byers

Fabelo, Julian, 1916-23 INF, OF, Cuban Stars (East), Havana Stars, New York Cuban Stars

Fabre, Isidro, 1918-39 P, OF, Cuban Stars (ECL), Cuban Stars (NNL), New York Cubans, All Cubans

Fabors, Thomas, 1942 P, Baltimore Elite Giants

Fagan, Gervis, 1942-43 INF, Memphis Red Sox, Jacksonville Red Caps, Philadelphia Stars

Fagan, R.W. (Bob), 1920-23 2B, Kansas City Monarchs, St. Louis Stars

Falling, John, 1947 P, New York Black Yankees

Fanell, —, 1950 P, Baltimore Elite Giants

Farmer, Greene Jr., 1942-47 OF, Cincinnati Clowns, New York Cubans, New York Black Yankees, Jacksonville Red Caps

Farrell, Jack, 1934 owner, Baltimore Black Sox

Farrell, Luther [Luther], 1920-34 P, OF, Bacharach Giants, Lincoln Giants, New York Black Yankees, Chicago Giants, Chicago American Giants, Lincoln Giants, Hilldale, St. Louis Stars, Gilkerson's Union Giants

Favors, —, 1947 UTIL, Kansas City Monarchs

Felder, James, 1948 SS, Indianapolis Clowns

Felder, Kendall (Buck), 1944-46 3B, Memphis Red Sox, Chicago American Giants, Birmingham Black Barons,

Felder, William (Benny), 1946-48 SS, Newark Eagles, Indianapolis Clowns

Fellows, —, 1937 P, C, Birmingham Black Barons

Fennar, Albertus A. (Al, Cleffie), 1932 SS, Brooklyn Royal Giants

Fern, —, 1920 P, Kansas City Monarchs

Fernandez, Bernard, 1938-39,1948-49 P, Atlanta Black Crackers, Jacksonville Red Caps, New York Cubans, New York Black Yankees

Fernandez, Jose Maria Sr, 1916-50 C, 1B, MGR, Havana Stars, Cuban Stars (East), New York Cubans, Chicago American Giants, New York Cuban Stars

Fernandez, Jose M. Jr. (Pepe), 1948-50 C, New York Cubans

Fernandez, Renaldo, 1950 OF, New York Cubans

Fernandez, Rodolfo, 1916,1923 P, Cuban Stars, Cuban Stars (NNL)

Fernandez, Rodolfo (Rudy, Ven Pordios), 1932-46 P, New York Cubans, Cuban Stars, New York Black Yankees

Fernandez, T., 1941 P, Cuban Stars

Ferrell, Leroy Howard, 1948-50 P, Baltimore Elite Giants

Ferrell, W.E., 1918 1B, Pennsylvania Giants

Ferrell, Willie (Truehart, Red), 1937-43 P, Homestead Grays, Chicago American Giants, Cincinnati Clowns, Birmingham Black Barons, Jacksonville Red Caps, Cleveland Bears

Ferrer, Efigenio (Coco, Al), 1946-48 2B, SS, Indianapolis Clowns

Ferrer, Pedro, 1922-25 2B, Cuban Stars (ECL)

Fiall, George, 1920-29 SS, 3B, Lincoln Giants, Harrisburg Giants, Baltimore Black Sox, Birmingham Black Barons, Penn Red Caps of NY

Fiall, Tom, 1917-25,1931 OF, C, 3B, Cuban Giants, Brooklyn Royal Giants, Lincoln Giants, Hilldale, Pennsylvania Red Caps of New York

Fields, —, 1918-26 P, Chicago American Giants, Cleveland Browns, St. Louis Giants, Dayton Marcos, Cleveland Elites

Fields, Benny, 1930-36 2B, OF, Memphis Red Sox, Cleveland Cubs, Birmingham Black Barons

Fields, Clifford Peter, 1950 OF, Chicago American Giants

Fields, Wilmer Leon Sr.(Red, Bill), 1940-50 P, 3B, OF, Homestead Grays

Fifer, —, 1921 P, Indianapolis ABCs

Figarola, Jose, 1910-16 C, 1B, Stars of Cuba, Cuban Stars

Figueroa, Enrique (Tite), 1946 P, Baltimore Elite Giants

Figueroa, Jose Antonio (Tito), 1940,1946 P,
Baltimore Elite Giants, New York Cubans

Fillmore, Joe, 1941-50 P, Philadelphia Stars,
Baltimore Grays

Fine, Charlie, *see Charles Harmon*

Finch, Rayford, 1949-50 P, Cleveland Buckeyes,
Louisville Buckeyes

Finch, Robert [Fitch], 1926 P, Lincoln Giants

Findell, Thomas 1887 player, Washington
Capital City

Finley, Thomas (Tom), 1923-33 3B, C,
Bacharach Giants, Lincoln Giants, Brooklyn
Royal Giants, Pennsylvania Red Caps of New
York, Darby Daisies, New York Black Yankees,
Baltimore Black Sox, Philadelphia Stars,
Wilmington Potomacs, Washington Potomacs

Finner, John, 1919-25 P, St. Louis Giants, St.
Louis Stars, Milwaukee Bears, Birmingham
Black Barons

Finney, Ed, 1948-50 3B, Baltimore Elite Giants

Fisher, —, 1909-10 P, Philadelphia Giants

Fisher, —, 1932 P, Columbus Turfs

Fisher, A. 1884 player, Philadelphia Mutual
B.B.C.

Fisher, F. 1884 player, Philadelphia Mutual
B.B.C.

Fisher, George, 1922-23 OF, Richmond Giants,
Harrisburg Giants

Fisher, W. —, 1884 player, Philadelphia Mutual
B.B.C.

Fishue, Pete (The Wonder) 1886 C, New York
Gorhams

Fleet, Joseph, 1930 P, Chicago American
Giants

Fleming, Buddy, *see Fleming Reedy*

Flemming, Frank, 1946 P, Cleveland Buckeyes

Flood, Jess, 1919 C, Cleveland Tate Stars

Flourney, —, 1950 P, Cleveland Buckeyes

Fox, Orange 1887 rf, Chicago Unions

Flournoy, Fred, 1928 C, Brooklyn Cuban Giants,
Penn Red Caps of NY

Flournoy, Willis (Pud), 1919-33 P, Hilldale,
Brooklyn Royal Giants, Baltimore Black Sox,
Bacharach Giants

Flowers, Johnny (Jake), 1941-43 INF, New York
Black Yankees

Floyd, —, 1935-37 P, Brooklyn Eagles,
Indianapolis Athletics

Floyd, J.J., 1932 officer, Little Rock Greys

Footes, Robert 1895-1909 C, Chicago Unions,
Philadelphia Giants, Brooklyn Royal Giants,
Chicago Union Giants

Forbes, —, 1886-88 OF, 3B, Cuban Giants,
Philadelphia Pythians

Forbes, Frank, 1929-43 umpire; bus. mgr, New
York Cubans; NNL promoter

Forbes, Joe, 1913-27 SS, 3B, OF, Lincoln
Giants, Pennsylvania Red Caps of New York,
Bacharach Giants, Brooklyn Royal Giants,
Lincoln Stars, Philadelphia Giants

Force, William, 1921-30 P, Detroit Stars,
Baltimore Black Sox, Brooklyn Royal Giants

Ford, (Bubber), 1947 officer, Jacksonville
Eagles

Ford, C., 1918 P, Pennsylvania Giants

Ford, Carl, 1947 officer, Shreveport Tigers

Ford, Frank, 1915-18 C, Pennsylvania Giants,
Hilldale

Ford, James (Jimmy), 1931-45 3B, 2B,
Memphis Red Sox, St. Louis Stars, New
Orleans-St. Louis Stars, New York Black
Yankees, Cincinnati Clowns, Philadelphia
Stars, Baltimore Elite Giants,
Harrisburg-St.Louis Stars, Washington Black
Senators

Ford, Roy, 1918-25 2B, Baltimore Black Sox,
Harrisburg Giants

Foreman, —, 1921 SS, Hilldale

Foreman, F.Slyvester (Hooks), 1921-33 C, P,
Kansas City Monarchs, Indianapolis ABCs,
Washington Pilots, Milwaukee Bears.
Homestead Grays

Foreman, Zack, 1920 P, Kansas City Monarchs

Forest, Charles, 1920 player, St. Louis Giants

Forkins, Marty, 1931 officer, New York Black
Yankees

Formenthal, Pedro, 1947-50 OF, Memphis Red
Sox

Forrest, —, 1917-28 OF, C, Havana Red Sox,
Lincoln Giants, Philadelphia Giants

Forrest, Joe, 1949 P, New York Black Yankees

Forrest, Percy (Pete), 1938-49 P, Chicago
American Giants, Newark Eagles, New York
Black Yankees, Indianapolis Clowns

Foster, Albert (Red), 1910 1B, Kansas City,
Kan., Giants

Foster, Andrew (Rube), 1902-26 P, MGR,
Chicago Union Giants, Cuban X Giants,
Philadelphia Giants, Leland Giants, Chicago
American Giants; founder and pres, tres, NNL

Foster, Jim, 1945 officer, Chicago Brown
Bombers

Foster, Leland, 1932-36 P, Monroe Monarchs

Foster, Leonard, 1938 INF, Atlanta Black
Crackers

Foster, Willie Hendrick (Bill), 1923-37 P, MGR,
Memphis Red Sox, Chicago American Giants,
Homestead Grays, Kansas City Monarchs,
Cole's American Giants, Birmingham Black
Barons, Pittsburgh Crawfords

Foulke, —, 1912 rf, Cuban Giants

Fowler, J.W. (Bud) **(real name John Jackson)**
1872-1899 2B, P, OF, 3B, C, SS, MGR, New
Castle, Pa.; Stillwater (Northwestern Lg.);
Keokuk and Topeka (Western Lg.); Binghamton
(International Lg.); Crawfordsville, Terre Haute,
and Galesburg (Central Interstate league);
Lafayette, Indiana; Greenville (Michigan Lg.);
Sterling and Davenport (Illinois-Iowa Lg.);
Evansville, New York Gorhams, All-American
Black Tourists, Page Fence Giants Adrian
(Michigan St. Lg.), Lansing (Michigan St. Lg.)
Lynn (Int. Ass.), Lincoln-Kearney (Neb. St. Lg.),
Galesburg (Ill-Iowa Lg.), Burlington (Ill-Iowa
Lg.), Pueblo (Colorado Lg.) Worchester (New
England Assn.), Santa Fe (New Mexico Lg.),
Montpelier (Vermont Lg.)

Fowlkes, Erwin, 1947-48 SS, Chicago American
Giants, Homestead Grays

Fowlkes, Samuel, 1950 P, Kansas City
Monarchs, Cleveland Buckeyes

Francis, Del, 1917-20 2B, Indianapolis ABCs

Francis, William (Billy, Brodie), 1906-25 3B, SS,
Wilmington Giants, Cuban Giants, Philadelphia
Giants, Lincoln Giants, Chicago American
Giants, Hilldale, Bacharach Giants, Cleveland
Browns, Chicago Giants

Franklin, —, 1908 SS, Brooklyn Colored Giants

Franklin, William B. 1887 manager, Louisville
Falls City

Frazier, Albert Edwin (Cool Papa), 1932-40 2B,
3B, Montgomery Grey Sox, Jacksonville Red
Caps, Cleveland Bears

Freeman, Bill, 1925,1933 P, Indianapolis ABCs,
Cuban Stars

Freeman, Charlie, 1916,1927-30 player, Officer,
Hilldale

Freeman, William 1888-89 3B, Chicago Unions

Freihofer, William, 1906 pres, International Lg.
of Independent Professional Base Ball Clubs

Friely, —, 1922 2B, Bacharach Giants

Frye, John H. (Jack) 1883-96 1B, C, P, OF,
Cuban Giants, Reading, Pa (Interstate Lg.),
Lewiston (Penn. St. Lg.), York Cuban Giants
(Eastern Interstate Lg.), Trenton Cuban Giants
(Middle States Lg.), Ansonia Cuban Giants
(Connecticut St. Lg.), New York Gorhams

Fulcur, Robert, 1940 P, Chicago American
Giants, Birmingham Black Barons

Fuller, Jimmy, 1912-20 C, Cuban Giants,
Bacharach Giants, Philadelphia Giants

Fuller, W.W. (Chick), 1908-19 SS, 2B,
Bacharach Giants, Cuban Giants, Pennsylvania
Giants, Cleveland Tate Stars, Hilldale Brooklyn
Colored Giants, New York Colored Giants,
Pennsylvania Red Caps of NY

Fumes, —, 1925-30 OF, Cuban Stars (NNL),
Cuban Stars (East)

Gadsden, Gus, 1932 OF, Hilldale

Gaichey, —, 1948 P, Memphis Red Sox

Gaideria, —, 1918 P, Cuban Stars

Gaines, Jonas George (Lefty), 1937-50 P,
Newark Eagles, Baltimore Elite Giants,
Philadelphia Stars, Washington Elite Giants

Gaines, Willie, 1950 P, Philadelphia Stars

Galata, Domingo, 1949 P, New York Cubans

Galata, Raul, 1949-50 P, Indianapolis Clowns,
New York Cubans

Gales, —, 1931 1B, Detroit Stars

Galey, —, 1897 1B, OF, Cuban Giants

Gallardy, —, 1906 OF, Cuban Giants

Galloway, Bill 1899-06 OF, 2B, Cuban X Giants,
Cuban Giants, Woodstock (Canadian Lg.)

Galvez, Cuneo, 1928-32 P, Cuban Stars (NNL),
Cuban Stars (East)

Gamble, —, 1921 P, Columbus Buckeyes

Gans, Robert Edward (Jude, Judy), 1910-38
OF, P, MGR, Cuban Giants, Smart Set, Lincoln
Giants, Chicago American Giants, Chicago
Giants, Lincoln Stars, Mohawk Giants; umpire,
East-West Lg., NNL

Gant, —, 1887 3B, Pittsburgh Keystones

Gantz, *see Domingo Gomez*

Garay, Martiniano Arguelles (Jose) [Arguelles],
1948-50-OF, P, New York Cubans

Garcia, Antonio, 1909-12 C, 1B, Cuban Stars,
All Cubans

Garcia, Atires (Angel), 1945-50 P,
Cincinnati-Indianapolis Clowns, Indianapolis
Clowns

Garcia, John, 1904 C, Cuban Giants

Garcia, Manuel (Cocaina), 1926-36 P, OF,
Cuban Stars (NNL), New York Cubans

Garcia, Romando (Chano), 1926-27 2B,
Bacharach Giants, Lincoln Giants

Garcia, Silvio, 1940-47 INF, Cuban Stars, New
York Cubans

Gardner, —, 1920-23,1926 OF, Toledo Tigers,
St. Louis Stars, Dayton Marcos

Gardner, Floyd (Jelly), 1919-1933 OF, 1B,
Detroit Stars, Chicago American Giants,
Lincoln Giants, Homestead Grays

Gardner, James (Chappy), 1908-17 2B, 3B,
Brooklyn Royal Giants, Havana Red Sox,
Cuban Giants, Brooklyn Colored Giants

Gardner, Kenneth (Ping, Steel Arm), 1918-32 P,
Washington Red Caps, Brooklyn Royal Giants,
Hilldale, Philadelphia Royal Stars, Lincoln
Giants, Harrisburg Giants, Bacharach Giants,
Cleveland Tigers, Baltimore Black Sox, Newark
Browns

Garey, —, 1925 C, Cuban Stars (NNL)

Garmer, 1886 3B, New York Gorhams

Garner, Horace Charles, 1949 OF, Indianapolis
Clowns

Garren, —, 1905 C, All Cubans

Garrett, Al H. 1899-1900 manager, Columbia
Giants

Garrett, Frank 1887 player, Louisville Falls Citys

Garrett, Soloman, 1950 2B, New York Black
Yankees

Garrett, William, 1943 officer, New York Black
Yankees

Garrido, Gil, 1945-46 INF, New York Cubans

Garrison, Robert, 1909 P, St. Paul Gophers

Garrison, Ross 1889-97 SS, 3B, York Cuban
Giants (Eastern Interstate Lg.), New York
Gorhams (Middle States Lg.), Cuban Giants

Garvin, Leedell, 1942 P, Philadelphia Stars

Gary, Charles, 1948-50 3B, Homestead Grays

Gaston, —, 1921 SS, Hilldale

Gaston, Robert (Rab Roy), 1932-49 C,
Homestead Grays

Gatewood, Bill, 1905-28 P, MGR, Cuban X
Giants, Philadelphia Giants, Brooklyn Royal
Giants, Leland Giants, Chicago Giants,
Chicago American Giants, St. Louis Giants,
Detroit Stars, St. Louis Stars, Toledo Tigers,
Albany, Ga. Giants, Birmingham Black Barons,
Memphis Red Sox, Milwaukee Bears, Lincoln
Giants

Gatewood, Ernest, 1914-27 C, 1B, Lincoln
Giants, Brookyn Royal Giants, Bacharach
Giants, Harrisburg Giants, Lincoln Stars

Gavin, —, 1935 P, Brooklyn Eagles

Gay, Herbert, 1929-30 P, OF, Chicago American
Giants, Birmingham Black Barons, Baltimore
Black Sox

Gay, J.J., 1929 P, Chicago American Giants

Gee, Richard (Rich), 1922-29 C, OF, Lincoln
Giants, New Orleans Crescent Stars

Gee, Tom, 1925-26 C, Lincoln Giants, Newark
Stars

George, John, 1921-25 SS, New Orleans
Crescent Stars, Chicago Giants, Harrisburg
Giants, Chicago American Giants, Bacharach
Giants, New Orleans Caulfield Ads

Gerald, Alphonso [Gerrard], 1945-49 OF, INF,
New York Black Yankees, Chicago American
Giants, Indianapolis Clowns

Getty, —, 1936 C, Bacharach Giants

Gholston, Bert E., 1923-43 umpire, NNL,
East-West Lg.

Gibbons, —, 1923 3B, Harrisburg Giants

Gibbons, Walter Lee, 1948-49 P, Indianapolis
Clowns

Gibson, B., 1927 P, Cleveland Hornets

Gibson, Jerry A., 1936-43 OF, P, Cincinnati
Tigers, Cincinnati Clowns, Cincinnati Buckeyes

Gibson, Joshua (Josh) Sr, 1930-46 C, OF, Homestead Grays, Pittsburgh Crawfords

Gibson, Joshua, Jr., 1949-50 INF, Homestead Grays

Gibson, Ted, 1940-41 INF, P, Columbus Buckeyes, Chicago American Giants, Cincinnati Buckeyes

Gibson, Welda H., 1949-50 P, Houston Eagles

Gilcrest, Dennis, 1931-35 C, 2B, Indianapolis ABCs, Columbus Blue Birds, Cleveland Red Sox, Brooklyn Eagles

Gilers, —, 1928 OF, Birmingham Black Barons

Giles, George Franklin, 1927-38 1B, Kansas City Monarchs, St. Louis Stars, Brooklyn Eagles, New York Black Yankees, Philadelphia Stars, Detroit Wolves, Homestead Grays, Pittsburgh Crawfords, Baltimore Black Sox

Gill, William, 1931-37 1B, 3B, OF, Detroit Stars, Louisville Red Caps, Indianapolis Athletics, Homestead Grays

Gillard, (Hamp), 1909-14 P, St. Louis Giants, Chicago American Giants, West Baden (In) Sprudels, Birmingham Giants

Gillard, Luther (Pen) [Gilyard], 1934-42 OF, 1B, Memphis Red Sox, Chicago American Giants, Indianapolis Crawfords, Birmingham Black Barons, St. Louis Stars, Kansas City Monarchs

Gillespie, H. 1887 player, Louisville Falls Citys

Gillespie, Henry, 1917-34 P, OF, Pennsylvania Giants, Hilldale, Lincoln Giants, Bacharach Giants, Philadelphia Tigers, Quaker Giants, New York Black Yankees, Baltimore Black Sox Harrisburg Giants, Madison Stars

Gillespie, Murray (Lefty), 1930-32 P, Memphis Red Sox, Nashville Elite Giants, Monroe Monarchs

Gilliam, James (Junior), 1945-50 2B, Nashville Black Vols, Baltimore Elite Giants

Gilmore, Quincy Jordan, 1922-37 bus MGR, Kansas City Monarchs; sec'y, tres, NNL; pres, Texas-Oklahoma-Louisiana Lg.

Gilmore, (Speed), 1926-28 P, Lincoln Giants

Gilyard, Luther, see Luther Gillard

Gipson, Alvin (Bubber, Skeet), 1941-50 P, Chicago American Giants, Birmingham Black Barons, Houston Eagles

Gisentaner, Willie (Lefty), 1921-36 P, OF, Columbus Buckeyes, Washington Potomacs, Kansas City Monarchs, Harrisburg Giants, Newark Stars, Lincoln Giants, Cuban Stars (East), Louisville White Sox, Pittsburgh Crawfords, Nashville Elite Giants, Louisville Red Caps, Homestead Grays, Louisville Black Caps, Chicago American Giants, Philadelphia Giants

Givens, —, 1927 SS, Cleveland Hornets

Givens, Oscar, 1946-48 SS, Newark Eagles

Gladney, —, 1932 SS, Indianapolis ABCs

Gladstone, Granville, 1950 OF, Indianapolis Clowns

Glass, Carl Lee (Butch), 1923-36 P, MGR, Memphis Red Sox, Cincinnati Tigers, St. Louis Stars, Birmingham Black Barons, Chicago American Giants, Kansas City Monarchs, Louisville White Sox

Glenn, Hubert (Country), 1945-49 P, New York Black Yankees, Brooklyn Brown Dodgers, Indianapolis Clowns

Glenn, Oscar, 1937-38 3B, Atlanta Black Crackers

Glenn, Stanley Rudolf (Doc), 1943-50 C, P, Philadelphia Stars

Glover, Thomas (Lefty), 1934-45 P, Birmingham Black Barons, Cleveland Red Sox, New Orleans Black Pelicans, Washington Elite Giants, Memphis Red Sox, Baltimore Elite Giants, Columbus Elite Giants

Godinez, Manuel, 1946-49 P, Cincinnati-Indianapolis Clowns, Indianapolis Clowns

Goines, Charles, 1915 C, Indianapolis ABCs

Goins, —, 1932 P, Montgomery Grey Sox

Golden, Clyde, 1948-50 P, Newark Eagles, Houston Eagles, Cleveland Buckeyes

Goldie, —, 1926-28 1B, Indianapolis ABCs, Cleveland Tigers, Cleveland Elites, Cleveland Hornets

Goliath, Fred, 1920 OF, Chicago Giants

Gomez, David, 1925-28,1932 P, Cuban Stars (NNL)

Gomez, Domingo (Harry), 1926-29 C, Harrisburg Giants, Philadelphia Tigers, Baltimore Black Sox

Gomez, Joe, 1932-33 P, Bacharach Giants

Gomez, Sijo [Sijo] 1929 C, P, Cuban Stars (East)

Gonzales, A., 1910-12 P, Cuban Stars

Gonzalez, Gervasio (Strike), 1910-17 1B, C, Cuban Stars, Long Branch Cubans

Gonzalez, Luis (Chicho), 1910 P, Cuban Stars

Gonzalez, Miguel Angel Cordero (Mike), 1911-14 C, 1B, Cuban Stars

Gonzalez, Rene, 1950 OF, New York Cubans

Good, —, 1890 OF, York Cuban Giants (Eastern Interstate Lg.)

Good, —, 1916 C, OF, Lincoln Stars

Good, Cleveland, 1937 P, Newark Eagles

Gooden, Ernest (Pud), 1922-23 2B, 3B, Pittsburgh Keystones, Toledo Tigers, Chicago American Giants, Cleveland Tate Stars

Goodgame, John, 1917 P, Chicago Giants

Goodman, —, 1928 OF, Harrisburg Giants

Goodrich, Joe, 1923-26 2B, SS, 3B, Washington Potomacs, Philadelphia Giants, Wilmington Potomacs, Harrisburg Giants

Goodson, M.E., 1932 officer, New York Black Yankees

Gordon, —, 1905-11 SS, 3B, Genuine Cuban Giants, Cuban Giants

Gordon, —, 1915 OF, Indianapolis ABCs

Gordon, Charles William (Charlie, Flash), 1940 OF, New York Black Yankees

Gordon, Harold, 1950 P, Chicago American Giants

Gordon, Herman, 1920-24 P, OF, 2B, Toledo Tigers, Birmingham Black Barons, Kansas City Monarchs, St. Louis Stars, Cleveland Browns

Gorham, —, 1911 rf, Philadelphia Giants

Goshay, Samuel, 1949 OF, Kansas City Monarchs

Gottlieb, Eddie, 1936-50 officer, Philadelphia Stars; sec'y, NNL; promoter and booking agent, Owner

Gould, John (Willie, Hal), 1947-48 P, Philadelphia Stars

Govantes, Manuel, 1909-10 2B, OF, Cuban Stars, Stars of Cuba

Govern, S.K. (Siki) 1887-88,1896 MGR, Cuban Giants

Grace, Arthur 1889 P, 1B, Champaign (Ill.-Ind. Lg.)

Grace, Ellsworth, 1950 2B, New York Black Yankees

Grace, Willie, 1942-50 OF, Cincinnati Buckeyes, Cleveland Buckeyes, Louisville Buckeyes, Houston Eagles

Grady, —, 1924 P, Washington Potomacs

Graham, Dennis, 1918-31 OF, Washington Red Caps, Bacharach Giants St. Louis Stars, Homestead Grays, Pittsburgh Crawfords

Graham, Vasco 1895-99 C, OF, Lansing, Michigan, Colored Capital All-Americans, Page Fence Giants, Adrian (Michigan St. Lg.) Dubuque (IA), Cuban Giants

Gransberry, Bill, 1929 OF, 1B, Chicago American Giants, Chicago Giants

Grant, Art, 1920-22 C, Baltimore Black Sox, Richmond Giants

Grant, Charles 1896-1913 2B, Page Fence Giants, Columbia Giants, Cuban X Giants, Philadelphia Giants, New York Black Sox, Lincoln Giants

Grant, Frank 1886-1905 2B, SS, Meriden (Eastern Lg.); Buffalo (International Lg.); Cuban Giants, Harrisburg (Eastern Interstate Lg.); Lansing, Michigan, Colored Capital All-Americans, New York Gorhams (Middle States Lg.), Ansonia Cuban Giants (Connecticut St.Lg.), Trenton Cuban Giants (Middle States Lg.), Philadelphia Giants

Grant, Leroy, 1911-25 1B, Chicago American Giants, Lincoln Giants, Indianapolis ABCs, Cleveland Browns, Mohawk Giants

Graves, Bob, 1932-37 P, OF, Indianapolis ABCs, Indianapolis Athletics

Graves, Lawrence, 1923 P, Harrisburg Giants

Graves, Whitt, 1950 P, Indianapolis Clowns

Gray, —, 1931 3B, Nashville Elite Giants

Gray, Chesley (Chester), 1940-45 C, St. Louis Stars, New York Black Yankees, Harrisburg-St. Louis Stars, Kansas City Monarchs, Toledo Cubs (USL)

Gray, G.E. (Willie, Dolly) [Grey], 1920-33-OF, P, Cleveland Tate Stars, Homestead Grays, Lincoln Giants, Pennnsylvania Red Caps of New York, Dayton Marcos, Pittsburgh Keystones, Newark Stars

Gray, Roosevelt (Chappy), 1920-23 1B, P, Cleveland Tate Stars, Toledo Tigers, Dayton Marcos, Kansas City Monarchs

Gray, William 1884-87 OF, Baltimore Atlantics, Baltimore Lord Baltimores

Greason, William Henry (Willie, Bill), 1948-50 P, Birmingham Black Barons

Green, —, 1920 P, Detroit Stars

Green, —, 1939-41 P, Cleveland Bears, Memphis Red Sox

Green, —, 1940 2B, Philadelphia Stars

Green, Alvin, 1950 INF, Baltimore Elite Giants

Green, Charles (Joe), 1902-31 MGR, OF, Leland Giants, Chicago Giants, Chicago American Giants, Union Giants, Columbia Giants

Green, Curtis, 1923-26 1B, OF, Birmingham Black Barons, Brooklyn Cuban Giants

Green, Dave, 1950 OF, Baltimore Elite Giants

Green, Henryene P., 1949-50 owner, Baltimore Elite Giants

Green, James [Greene], 1950 3B, New York Black Yankees

Green, Julius, 1929-30 OF, Memphis Red Sox, Detroit Stars

Green, Leslie (Chin), 1939-46 OF, St. Louis Stars, New York Black Yankees, Memphis Red Sox

Green, Peter (Ed), 1908-20 OF, P, Pittsburgh Giants Lincoln Stars, Brooklyn Royal Giants, Brooklyn Colored Giants

Green, Vernon (Fat, Baby), 1921,1942-49 C, officer, Nashville Giants, Baltimore Elite Giants

Green, William, 1915-23 3B, OF, Chicago Giants, Chicago Union Giants

Green, Willie, 1910-12 C, P, Pittsburgh Giants, St. Louis Giants

Greene, James Elbert (Joe) [James Green], 1932-48 C, Kansas City Monarchs, Cleveland Buckeyes, Atlanta Black Crackers, Homestead Grays

Greene, Walter, 1928 OF, 1B, Brooklyn Cuban Giants, Bacharach Giants

Greene, Will, 1912 P, Pittsburgh Giants

Greenidge, Victor (Slicker), 1941-45 P, Cuban Stars, New York Cubans

Greenlee, William Augustus (Gus,Big Red), 1931-45 officer, Pittsburgh Crawfords; founder and pres, second NNL; founder, United States Baseball Lg.

Greer, J.B., 1939-42 officer, Cleveland Bears, Knoxville Red Caps, Jacksonville Red Caps

Gregory, —, 1940 P, Birmingham Black Barons

Grey, William, see G.E. Gray

Greyer, George, 1918-22 1B, Baltimore Black Sox

Grier, Claude (Red), 1924-28 P, Wilmington Potomacs, Bacharach Giants, Washington Potomacs

Griffin, C.B. (Clarence), 1933-35 OF, Columbus Blue Birds, Cleveland Red Sox, Brooklyn Eagles, Columbus Elite Giants

Griffin, James (Horse), 1912-21 2B, Cuban Giants, Nashville Elite Giants, Pittsburgh Giants, Philadelphia Giants

Griffin, Robert, 1931-37 P, Chicago Columbia Giants, St. Louis Stars

Griffith, Robert Lee (Big Bill, Schoolboy), 1934-49 P, Nashville Elite Giants, Columbus Elite Giants, Washington Elite Giants, Baltimore Elite Giants, New York Black Yankees, Philadelphia Stars

Griggs, Wiley Lee (Willie), 1948-50 3B, INF, Birmingham Black Barons, Houston Eagles, Cleveland Buckeyes

Grimes, —, 1943 OF, P, Cleveland Buckeyes, Harrisburg-St. Louis Stars

Grimm, —, 1921 OF, Bacharach Giants

Gross, Ben, Jr. 1887 OF, Pittsburgh Keystones

Guerra, Juan, 1910-24 OF, 1B, C, Stars of Cuba, Cuban Stars (NNL), New York Cuban Stars, Cuban Stars

Guerra, Marcelino, 1916 1B, Cuban Stars

Guilbe, Felix, 1946 OF, Baltimore Elite Giants

Guilbe, Juan, 1940-47 P, OF, Cuban Stars, Baltimore Elite Giants, Indianapolis Clowns

Guiterrez, Luis (Joe), 1926 OF, Cuban Stars (NNL)

Guiwn, Jefferson, 1943-45 C, Cleveland Buckeyes

Gulley, Napoleon, 1943-47 P, Cleveland Buckeyes, Newark Eagles

Gurley, James, 1922-32 OF, P, 1B, St. Louis Stars, Memphis Red Sox, Chicago American Giants, Montgomery Grey Sox, Nashville Elite Giants, Birmingham Black Barons, Indianapolis ABCs, Cleveland Hornets, Harrisburg Giants

Guy, Wesley, 1927-29 P, Chicago Giants

Hackett, —, 1932 P, Washington Pilots

Hackley, Albert 1887-96 OF, INF, Chicago Unions

Haddad, —, 1931 P, OF (House of David) Cubans

Hadley, (Red), 1937-38 C, OF, Atlanta Black Crackers

Haines, —, 1920 P, Indianapolis ABCs

Hairston, Harold (Hal), 1946-47 P, Homestead Grays

Hairston, Napoleon, 1938-40 OF, Pittsburgh Crawfords, Indianapolis Crawfords, Toledo Crawfords

Hairston, (Rap), 1934 player, Newark Dodgers

Hairston, Samuel (Sam), 1945-50 C, 3B, Cincinnati-Indianapolis Clowns, Indianapolis Clowns

Hairstone, J.Burke (J.B.), 1918-22-MGR, OF, C, Baltimore Black Sox, Bacharach Giants

Hale, (Red), 1937-39 SS, Detroit Stars, Chicago American Giants

Haley, —, 1923 P, Detroit Stars

Haley, (Red), 1928 2B, Chicago American Giants, Birmingham Black Barons

Hall, —, 1887 2B, Philadelphia Pythians

Hall, —, 1921-23 P, St. Louis Giants, Milwaukee Bears, Detroit Stars

Hall, (Bad News), 1937-40 3B, Indianapolis Athletics, Indianapolis Crawfords

Hall, Blainey, 1913-25 OF, Mohawk Giants, Lincoln Giants, Philadelphia Giants, Baltimore Black Sox

Hall, Horace G., 1933-42 officer, Chicago American Giants; vice pres, NAL

Hall, Joseph W., 1945 officer, Hilldale Club of Philadelphia

Hall, Perry, 1926-47 3B, OF, Memphis Red Sox, Cleveland Tigers, Chicago Giants, Indianapolis Athletics, Chicago Columbia Giants, Birmingham Black Barons, Detroit Stars

Hall, Sellers Mckee (Sell), 1916-20 P, Pittsburgh Colored Giants, Homestead Grays, Chicago American Giants

Hamilton, —, 1886 2B, New York Gorhams

Hamilton, —, 1921-24 P, Kansas City Monarchs, Cleveland Browns, St. Louis Stars, Bacharach Giants

Hamilton, George, 1923-29 C, Memphis Red Sox, Birmingham Black Barons

Hamilton, J.C. (John, Ed), 1940-42 P, Homestead Grays

Hamilton, J.H. (John), 1924-27 3B, INF, Washington Potomacs, Birmingham Black Barons, Indianapolis ABCs, Cleveland Elites, Wilmington Potomacs

Hamilton, Jim, 1946 SS, Kansas City Monarchs

Hamilton, L., 1923-25 2B, OF, Memphis Red Sox, Birmingham Black Barons

Hamilton, Theron B., 1934 vice pres, Homestead Grays

Hammond, Don, 1923-24 3B, SS, Cleveland Tate Stars, Cleveland Browns, Toledo Tigers

Hampton, Eppie, 1925-38 C, P, Memphis Red Sox, Washington Pilots, New Orleans Crescent Stars, Birmingham Black Barons, Cleveland Tigers

Hampton, Lewis, 1921-28 P, Columbus Buckeyes, Indianapolis ABCs, Bacharach Giants, Washington Potomacs, Lincoln Giants, Detroit Stars

Hampton, Wade, 1918-23 P, Pennsylvania Giants, Hilldale

Hancock, Art, 1926-27 1B, OF, Cleveland Elites, Cleveland Hornets

Hancock, Charles Winston (Charley), 1921 C, St. Louis Giants

Hancock, W. 1885 player, Brooklyn Remsens

Handy, George, 1947-49 INF, Memphis Red Sox, Houston Eagles

Handy, William Oscar (Bill,Buck), 1910-27 2B, SS, 3B, New York Black Sox, Brooklyn Royal Giants, St. Louis Giants, Lincoln Giants, Bacharach Giants, Philadelphia Royal Giants

Hanks, —, 1908 C, Brooklyn Colored Giants

Hannibal, —, 1914-17 OF, Bowser's ABCs, Indianapolis ABCs

Hannibal, Leo Jack, 1932,1937-38 P, Indianapolis ABCs, Indianapolis Athletics, Homestead Grays

Hannon, —, 1908-10 OF, 3B, Pop Watkins Stars, Philadelphia Giants, St.Louis Giants

Hanson, —, 1915 SS, Chicago American Giants

Hanson, Harry, 1926 vice pres, NSL

Harden, James, 1943 P, Homestead Grays

Harden, John H., 1939-48 officer, Atlanta Black Crackers, Indianapolis ABCs, New York Black Yankees; tres, NSL

Harden, Lovell (Big Pitch), 1943-45 P, Cleveland Buckeyes

Hardiman, —, 1937 P, St. Louis Stars

Harding, A. Hallie, 1926-31 SS, 2B, 3B, Indianapolis ABCs, Detroit Stars, Kansas City Monarchs, Chicago Columbia Giants, Bacharach Giants, Baltimore Black Sox

Harding, Roy, 1937 P, Philadelphia Stars

Harding, Tom, 1940 OF, Indianapolis Crawfords

Hardy, Arthur Wesley (Art), 1906-12 P, Topeka Giants, Kansas City, Kansas, Giants

Hardy, (Doc), 1950 INF, Cleveland Buckeyes

Hardy, Paul James, 1931-47 C, Montgomery Grey Sox, Detroit Stars, Birmingham Black Barons, Baltimore Elite Giants, Columbus Elite Giants, Chicago American Giants, Kansas City Monarchs, Memphis Red Sox

Hardy, Walter, 1945-50 SS, 2B, New York Black Yankees, New York Cubans

Hargett, —, 1918 P, Hilldale

Hargett, Yook 1887 player, Philadelphia Pythians

Harland, Bill, 1929 P, Lincoln Giants

Harmon, Charles (Chuck) [Charlie Fine], 1947 OF, Indianapolis Clowns

Harness, Robert Marseilles (O), 1927-28 P, Chicago Giants

Harney, George, 1923-31 P, Chicago Giants, Chicago Columbia Giants, Chicago American Giants

Harper, —, 1910 P, Leland Giants

Harper, (Chick), 1920-25 SS, OF, P, Hilldale, Norfolk Stars, Kansas City Monarchs, Detroit Stars

Harper, David (Dave), 1943-45 OF, P, Kansas City Monarchs, Philadelphia Stars

Harper, John, 1922-26 P, Bacharach Giants, Lincoln Giants, Richmond Giants

Harper, Walter, 1923,1929-31 1B, C, Chicago American Giants, Birmingham Black Barons, Chicago Columbia Giants

Harps, Fred, 1928 INF, Brooklyn Cuban Giants

Harris, —, 1919 OF, Lincoln Giants

Harris, —, 1921 P, Indianapolis ABCs, Columbus Buckeyes, Chicago American Giants

Harris, —, 1927 1B, Lincoln Giants

Harris, Ananias, 1921-23 P, Brooklyn Royal Giants, Hilldale, Harrisburg Giants

Harris, Andy, 1917-26 INF, MGR, Hilldale, Pennsylvania Giants, Pennsylvania Red Caps of New York, Newark Stars, Pittsburgh Stars of Buffalo

Harris, Bill, 1930-32 C, Memphis Red Sox, Indianapolis ABCs, Monroe Monarchs

Harris, Charlie, 1943 INF, Cincinnati Clowns, Chicago Brown Bombers

Harris, Chick (Popsickle, Moocha), 1931-36 OF, 1B, Detroit Wolves, Kansas City Monarchs, New Orleans Crescent Stars

Harris, Curtis (Popeye), 1931-40 2B, SS, 1B, C, Pittsburgh Crawfords, Philadelphia Stars, Kansas City Monarchs

Harris, Dixon, 1932 player, Homestead Grays

Harris, E. 1884 player, Philadelphia Mutual B.B.C.

Harris, Elander Victor (Vic), 1923-50 OF, MGR, coach, Cleveland Tate Stars, Cleveland Browns, Chicago American Giants, Homestead Grays, Pittsburgh Crawfords, Baltimore Elite Giants, Birmingham Black Barons, Toledo Tigers, Detroit Wolves

Harris, Frank 1885 P, Argyle Hotel

Harris, George, 1932-33 2B, Louisville Black Caps, Louisville Red Caps

Harris, H.B., 1919 bus. mgr, Brooklyn Royal Giants

Harris, Henry, 1928-34 SS, Memphis Red Sox, Louisville Black Caps, Baltimore Black Sox

Harris, Isaiah, 1949-50 P, Memphis Red Sox

Harris, J. (Sonny), 1936-1942 OF, INF, Cincinnati Buckeyes, Cincinnati Tigers, Cleveland Buckeyes

Harris, James 1884-87 OF, Baltimore Atlantics, Baltimore Lord Baltimores

Harris, Joseph 1887 player, Boston Resolutes

Harris, (Lefty), 1941 P, Cuban Stars

Harris, Nathan (Nate), 1901-11 2B, OF, Philadelphia Giants, Leland Giants, Chicago Giants, Cuban Giants, Columbia Giants

Harris, Neal (Nate), 1931 OF, 3B, Pittsburgh Crawfords

Harris, Raymond M. (MO), 1916-43 2B, OF, Homestead Grays; umpire, East-West Lg., NNL

Harris, Robert (Bob), 1935 ph., Pittsburgh Crawfords

Harris, Roger, 1942 INF, Birmingham Black Barons

Harris, Sam, 1932 OF, Monroe Monarchs

Harris, Samuel, 1940 P, Chicago American Giants, Birmingham Black Barons

Harris, Tommy, 1946-49 C, Cleveland Buckeyes, Louisville Buckeyes

Harris, Virgil, 1936-37 P, OF, 2B, Cincinnati Tigers

Harris, William (Bill), 1930-31 OF, Pittsburgh Crawfords

Harris, Wilmer, 1945-50 P, Philadelphia Stars

Harris, Win, 1922-28 1B, SS, Homestead Grays

Harrison, —, 1915-16 1B, West Baden (Ind.) Sprudels, Bowser's ABCs

Harrison, Abraham 1885-97 SS, Philadelphia Orions, Argyle Hotel, Cuban Giants, Trenton Cuban Giants (Middle States Lg.), York Cuban Giants (Eastern Interstate Lg.)

Harrison, Tomlini, 1927-30 P, St. Louis Stars, Kansas City Monarchs

Harriston, Clyde, 1944 INF, Birmingham Black Barons, Cincinnati-Indianapolis Clowns

Hart, —, 1887 C, Pittsburgh Keystones

Hart, Frank 1884 SS, St. Louis Black Stockings

Hartley, (Hop), 1925 P, Kansas City Monarchs

Harvey, —, 1937 SS, Philadelphia Stars

Harvey, B.T., 1950 sec'y, NSL

Harvey, Charles, 1950 SS, Cleveland Buckeyes

Harvey, David William (Bill), 1932-45 P, Memphis Red Sox, Pittsburgh Crawfords, Baltimore Elite Giants, Cleveland Red Sox, Toledo Crawfords, Indianapolis Crawfords, Cleveland Giants

Harvey, Frank, 1912-24 P, OF, St. Louis Giants, Brooklyn Royal Giants, Lincoln Stars, Lincoln Giants, Bacharach Giants, Philadelphia Giants

Harvey, Robert A. (Bob), 1943-50 OF, Newark Eagles, Houston Eagles

Haslett, Claude, 1936-37 P, Memphis Red Sox, Indianapolis Athletics

Havis, Chester, 1947 P, Memphis Red Sox

Hawk, —, 1905 C, Brooklyn Royal Giants

Hawks, —, 1913 3B, Philadelphia Giants

Hawkins, Lemuel (Hawk), 1919-28 1B, OF, Los Angeles White Sox, Kansas City Monarchs, Chicago Giants, Chicago American Giants

Hawley, —, 1932 C, Memphis Red Sox

Hayes, —, 1912-13 C, OF, SS, Pittsburgh Giants, Philadelphia Giants, Havana Red Sox

Hayes, Buddy, 1916-24 C, Chicago American Giants, Indianapolis ABCs, Pittsburgh Keystones, Cleveland Browns, St. Louis Giants, Milwaukee Bears, Toledo Tigers

Hayes, Burnalle James (Bun), 1929-35 P, Baltimore Black Sox, Washington Pilots, Chicago American Giants, Newark Dodgers, Brooklyn Eagles

Hayes, Jimmy, 1949 C, Kansas City Monarchs

Hayes, John William, 1934-50 C, Newark Dodgers, Newark Eagles, New York Black Yankees, Boston Blues, Baltimore Elite Giants

Hayes, John W., 1940 SS, 2B, Philadelphia Stars, St. Louis Stars

Hayes, Thomas H. Jr., 1939-50 officer, Birmingham Black Barons; vice pres, NAL

Hayes, Wilbur, 1942-50 off., g.m., Cincinnati Buckeyes, Cleveland Buckeyes; sergeant-at-arms, NAL

Hayman, Charles (Bugs), 1909-16 P, 1B, Philadelphia Giants

Haynes, Sammy, 1943-45 C, Kansas City Monarchs

Haynes, Bill (Willie), 1921-24 P, Dallas Giants, Hilldale, Harrisburg Giants, Baltimore Black Sox, Bacharach Giants

Haywood, Albert (Buster), 1935-50 C, MGR, Birmingham Black Barons, New York Cubans, Cincinnati-Indianapolis Clowns, Indianapolis Clowns, Cincinnati Clowns, Memphis Red Sox, Brooklyn Eagles

Heard, Jehosie, 1947-50 P, Birmingham Black Barons, Memphis Red Sox, Houston Eagles

Heat, —, 1941 P, Cuban Stars

Heffner, Arthur, 1947-49 OF, New York Black Yankees, Philadelphia Stars

Henderson, —, 1925 C, Birmingham Black Barons

Henderson, Armour, 1915 P, Mohawk Giants

Henderson, Arthur Chauncey (Rats), 1922-31 P, Richmond Giants, Bacharach Giants, Detroit Stars

Henderson, Ben, 1936-37 P, St. Louis Stars, Birmingham Black Barons

Henderson, Curtis (Curt), 1936-42 SS, 3B, Philadelphia Stars New York Black Yankees, Washington Black Senators, Toledo Crawfords, Indianapolis Crawfords, Chicago American Giants Homestead Grays

Henderson, George (Rube), 1921-23 OF, 3B, P, Cleveland Tate Stars, Toledo Tigers, Detroit Stars

Henderson, H. (Long), 1932 1B, Nashville Elite Giants

Henderson, Lenon, 1930-33 3B, SS, Nashville Elite Giants, Birmingham Black Barons, Montgomery Grey Sox, Louisville Black Caps, Indianapolis ABCs

Henderson, Louis, 1925 P, OF, Bacharach Giants

Henderson, Neal, 1949 OF, Kansas City Monarchs

Hendricks, —, 1918,1922 P, OF, Lincoln Giants, Baltimore Black Sox

Hendrix, Stokes, 1934 P, Nashville Elite Giants

Henry, Alfred, 1950 OF, Baltimore Elite Giants

Henry, Charles (Charlie), 1922-42 P, MGR, Hilldale, Harrisburg Giants, Detroit Stars, Bacharach Giants, Detroit Black Sox, Louisville Black Colonels

Henry, Joe, 1950 2B, Memphis Red Sox

Henry, Leo (Preacher), 1938-47 P, Jacksonville Red Caps, Cleveland Bears, Cincinnati Clowns, Indianapolis Clowns

Henry, Otis, 1931-37 2B, 3B, Memphis Red Sox, Monroe Monarchs, Indianapolis Athletics

Hensley, Logan (Eggie, Slap), 1923-39 P, St. Louis Stars, Toledo Tigers, Indianapolis ABCs, Detroit Stars, Cleveland Giants, Chicago American Giants, Cleveland Tate Stars, Cleveland Browns

Herbert, 1894 OF, Pawtucket (New England Lg.)

Heredia, Ramon (Napoleon), 1939-45 3B, SS, Cuban Stars, New York Cubans

Herman, see Herman Andrews

Hernandez, Jose, 1920-22 P, OF, Cuban Stars (NNL)

Hernandez, Ramon, 1929-30 3B, Cuban Stars (NNL)

Hernandez, Ricardo (Chico), 1909-14 2B, 3B, Cuban Stars, All Cubans

Herrera, Ramon (Paito), 1916-28 2B, 3B, Jersey City Cubans, Cuban Stars (NNL), Cuban Stars (ECL), Long Branch Cubans

Herring, —, 1920 3B, St. Louis Giants

Herron, Robert Lee, 1950 OF, Houston Eagles

Heslip, Jesse, 1945 pres; Toledo Cubs (USL)

Hewitt, Joe, 1910-32 SS, OF, 2B, MGR, St. Louis Giants, Brooklyn Royal Giants, Lincoln Giants, Philadelphia Giants, Detroit Stars, Chicago American Giants, St. Louis Stars, Cleveland Cubs, Dayton Marcos, Milwaukee Bears, Birmingham Black Barons, Nashville Elite Giants

Heywood, Charlie (Dobie), 1925-26 P, Lincoln Giants

Hicks, Eugene (Jimmy), 1940-41 P, Homestead Grays, New York Cuban Stars

Hicks, Wesley, 1927-31 OF, Chicago American Giants, Memphis Red Sox, Kansas City Monarchs

Hidalgo, Heliodoro, 1910-12 OF, 3B, Stars of Cuba, Cuban Stars, All Cubans

Higdon, Barney, 1943 P, Cincinnati Clowns

Higgins, Robert (Bob) 1887-88 P, Syracuse (International Lg.)

Higgins, N. 1887 C, Columbus (Ohio St. Lg.)

Hightower, —, 1890 1B, Lincoln (Neb) Giants

Hill, Ben, 1943,1946 P, Philadelphia Stars, Pittsburgh Crawfords

Hill, C. (Lefty), 1914-24 OF, P, Chicago Union Giants, Dayton Marcos, Detroit Stars, St. Louis Giants, Chicago American Giants

Hill, Herb, 1949 OF, P, Philadelphia Stars

Hill, J. Preston (Pete), 1904-25 OF, 2B, MGR, bus. mgr, Philadelphia Giants, Leland Giants, Chicago American Giants, Detroit Stars, Milwaukee Bears, Baltimore Black Sox, Cuban X Giants

Hill, Jimmy (Lefty, Squab), 1938-45 P, Newark Eagles

Hill, John, 1900-05 3B, SS, Genuine Cuban Giants, Philadelphia Giants, Cuban X Giants

Hill, Johnson (Fred), 1920-28 2B, 3B, OF, St. Louis Giants, Detroit Stars, Milwaukee Bears, Brooklyn Royal Giants

Hill, Jonathan, 1937 OF, P, Atlanta Black Crackers, St. Louis Stars

Hill, Samuel (Sam), 1937,1947-48 OF, 1B, Detroit Stars, Chicago American Giants,

Hill, W.R., 1885 SS, Brooklyn Remsens

Hines, John, 1924-34 C, OF, Chicago American Giants, Cole's American Giants

Hinson, Frank, 1896 P, Cuban X Giants

Hinton, Roland (Archie, Charlie), 1945-46 P, INF, Baltimore Elite Giants

Hitchman, —, 1925 3B, Indianapolis ABCs

Hoagland, F.B., 1885 sec'y, Brooklyn Remsens

Hoard, —, 1921 P, Kansas City Monarchs

Hobgood, Frederick (Lefty, John) [Hopgood], 1941-46-P, UTIL, Newark Eagles, New York Black Yankees

Hobson, Charles (Johnny [Hopson]), 1922-25 P, SS, OF, Lincoln Giants, Bacharach Giants, Richmond Giants

Hocker, Bruce, 1914-20 1B, OF, Bowser's ABCs, Lincoln Stars Dayton Marcos, Louisville White Sox, Chicago American Giants, Hilldale

Hodges, William (Jimmy), 1918-25 P, Lincoln Giants, Baltimore Black Sox

Hoke, (Bud), 1945 player, Toledo Cubs (USL)

Holcomb, —, 1923 P, Detroit Stars

Holland, —, 1921 1B, Hilldale

Holland, Elvis William (Bill), 1920-41 P, MGR, Detroit Stars, Chicago American Giants, Lincoln Giants, Brooklyn Royal Giants, New York Black Yankees, Philadelphia Stars

Holland, William (Billy) 1894-1908,1923 P, OF, 3B, Page Fence Giants, Chicago Unions, Brooklyn Royal Giants, Leland Giants, Pop Watkins Stars, Algona (IA) Brownies; umpire, NNL

Holliday, Charles Dourcher (Flit), 1938 OF, P, Atlanta Black Crackers

Hollingsworth, Curtis, 1947,1950 P, Birmingham Black Barons

Hollins, —, 1936 P, Birmingham Black Barons

Holloway, Christopher Columbus (Crush), 1921-39 OF, Indianapolis ABCs, Baltimore Black Sox, Hilldale, Detroit Stars, Bacharach Giants, Brooklyn Eagles, New York Black Yankees

Holmes, Benjamin F. (Ben) 1885-89 3B, Argyle Hotel, Cuban Giants, Trenton Cuban Giants (Middle States Lg.)

Holmes, Eddie, 1932 P, Baltimore Black Sox

Holmes, Frank (Sonny), 1929-38 P, Bacharach Giants, Philadelphia Stars, Lincoln Giants, Washington Elite Giants, Washington Black Senators

Holmes, Leroy Thomas (Phillie), 1935-45 SS, Jacksonville Red Caps, Cleveland Bears, Atlanta Black Crackers, Kansas City Monarchs, Cincinnati-Indianapolis Clowns, New York Black Yankees, Brooklyn Eagles

Holsey, Robert J. (Frog), 1928-32 P, Chicago American Giants, Chicago Columbia Giants, Cleveland Stars, Nashville Elite Giants

Holt, Johnny, 1922-23 OF, Pittsburgh Keystones, Toledo Tigers

Holt, Joseph, 1928 OF, Brooklyn Cuban Giants

Holtz, Eddie, 1920-24 2B, SS, St. Louis Giants, Chicago American Giants, St. Louis Stars, Lincoln Giants

Hood, Dozier Charles, 1945 C, Kansas City Monarchs

Hoods, William, see William Woods

Hooker, see Bruce Hocker

Hooker, Leniel Charlie (Len, Elbow), 1940-49 P, Newark Eagles, Houston Eagles

Hopkins, George 1890-99 P, 2B, Chicago Unions, Adrian Page Fence Giants

Hopwood, —, 1928 OF, Kansas City Monarchs

Hordy, J.H. 1887 player, Baltimore Lord Baltimores

Horn, —, 1925 2B, Birmingham Black Barons

Horn, William (Will) 1896-1905 P, Chicago Unions, Philadelphia Giants, Leland Giants

Horne, William (Billie), 1938-46 SS, 2B, Monroe Monarchs, Chicago American Giants, Cincinnati Buckeyes, Cleveland Buckeyes, Harrisburg-St.Louis Stars

Horns, James J. 1887 player, Boston Resolutes

Hoskins, David Taylor (Dave), 1942-49 OF, P, Cincinnati Clowns, Chicago American Giants, Homestead Grays, Louisville Buckeyes

Hoskins, William (Bill), 1937-46 OF, Detroit Stars, Memphis Red Sox, Baltimore Elite Giants, New York Black Yankees, St. Louis Stars, Kansas City Monarchs

House, Charles (Red), 1937,1942 3B, Detroit Stars, Detroit Black Sox

Houston, —, 1910 C, SS, West Baden (Ind) Sprudels

Houston, —, 1920 P, 2B, Indianapolis ABCs, Kansas City Monarchs

Houston, Bill, 1941-42 P, Homestead Grays

Houston, Nathanial (Jess), 1930-39 P, INF, Memphis Red Sox, Cincinnatitigers, Chicago American Giants

Hovley, —, 1932 P, Nashville Elite Giants

Howard, —, 1897-99 UTIL, Cuban Giants, Cuban X Giants

Howard, —, 1921-23,1927 P, 3B, Detroit Stars, Indianapolis ABCs, Memphis Red Sox, Cleveland Hornets

Howard, —, 1920-29 SS, P, Norfolk Giants, Harrisburg Giants, Baltimore Black Sox, Lincoln Giants, Norfolk Stars

Howard, Carl, 1935 OF, Pittsburgh Crawfords

Howard, Carranza (Schoolboy), 1941-50 P, Cuban Stars, New York Cubans, Indianapolis Clowns, New York Black Yankees

Howard, Elston, 1948-50 OF, C, Kansas City Monarchs

Howard, Herb, 1948 P, OF, Kansas City Monarchs

Howard, Herman (Red), 1932-46 P, Atlanta Black Crackers, Memphis Red Sox, Washington Elite Giants, Indianapolis Athletics, Jacksonville Red Caps, Indianapolis ABCs, Chicago American Giants, Birmingham Black Barons, Little Rock Black Travelers, Cleveland Bears

Howard, William (Bill), 1931-33 1B, 3B, Birmingham Black Barons

Howell, —, 1908 OF, Brooklyn Royal Giants

Howell, Henry, 1918-21 P, Pennsylvania Giants, Bacharach Giants, Pennsylvania Red Caps of New York, Brooklyn Royal Giants

Hubbard, Dehart, 1934-37,1942 official, sec'y, Cincinnati Tigers, Cleveland-Cincinnati Buckeyes

Hubbard, Jesse James (Mountain), 1919-34 P, OF, Bacharach Giants, Brooklyn Royal Giants, Baltimore Black Sox, Hilldale, Homestead Grays, New York Black Yankees

Hubbard, Larry, 1946 UTIL, Kansas City Monarchs

Huber, —, 1930-31 C, OF, Memphis Red Sox, Nashville Elite Giants, Birmingham Black Barons

Huber, John Marshall [Hubert], 1939-50 P, C, Ethiopian Clowns, Chicago American Giants, Birmingham Black Barons, Cincinnati Clowns, Memphis Red Sox, Philadelphia Stars

Hubert, Willie (Bubber), 1939-46 P, Newark Eagles, Baltimore Elite Giants, Cincinnati Buckeyes, Baltimore Grays, Homestead Grays, Pittsburgh Crawfords, Brooklyn Brown Dodgers, Philadelphia Stars, Cleveland Buckeyes, New York Black Yankees

Hudson, —, 1908 rf, Brooklyn Colored Giants

Hudson, Charles (Keen Legs), 1923,1930 P, Milwaukee Bears, Louisville White Sox

Hudson, William, 1937-42 P, Cincinnati Tigers, Chicago American Giants

Hudspeth, Robert (Highpockets), 1920-32 1B, Indianapolis ABCs, Columbus Buckeyes, Bacharach Giants, Lincoln Giants, Brooklyn Royal Giants, Hilldale, New York Black Yankees

Hueston, William C., 1926-31 pres, NNL

Huff, Eddie, 1923-32   C, OF, MGR, Bacharach Giants, Dayton Marcos

Hughbanks, [Hubanks] 1890   2B, Lincoln (Neb) Giants

Hughes, A., 1927   OF, Kansas City Monarchs

Hughes, Charley, 1931-38   2B, Cleveland Red Sox, Columbus Blue Birds, Washington Black Senators, Washington Pilots, Pittsburgh Crawfords

Hughes, Frank, 1937   P, Indianapolis Athletics

Hughes, Lee, 1950   P, Kansas City Monarchs

Hughes, Robert, 1931   P, Louisville White Sox

Hughes, Samuel Thomas (Sammy T.), 1930-46   2B, Louisville White Sox, Nashville Elite Giants, Homestead Grays, Columbus Elite Giants, Washington Elite Giants, Baltimore Elite Giants, Washington Pilots

Humber, Tom (Charlie), 1945,1950   2B, Newark Eagles, Baltimore Elite Giants

Humes, John, 1937   P, Newark Eagles

Humphries, —, 1936-37   OF, Atlanta Black Crackers, Memphis Red Sox

Hundley, Johnny Lee, 1943   C, OF, Cleveland Buckeyes

Hungo, —, 1916   1B, Long Branch Cubans

Hunt, Grover, 1946   C, Chicago American Giants

Hunt, Leonard (Len), 1949-50   OF, Kansas City Monarchs

Hunter, Bertrum (Nate), 1931-36   P, St. Louis Stars, Detroit Wolves, Pittsburgh Crawfords, Kansas City Monarchs, Philadelphia Stars, Homestead Grays

Hunter, Eugene, 1924   P, Memphis Red Sox, Cleveland Browns

Hunter, Willie, 1933   P, Akron Black Tyrites

Hutchinson, Fred (Hutch, Puggey), 1910-25   SS, 3B, 2B, Leland Giants, Chicago American Giants, Indianapolis ABCs, Bacharach Giants, Bowser's ABCs

Hutchinson, Willie (Ace), 1939-50   P, Kansas City Monarchs, Memphis Red Sox

Hutt, —, 1920-24   1B, OF, Dayton Marcos, Toledo Tigers, St. Louis Giants

Hyde, —, 1927-30   OF, 2B, Memphis Red Sox, Birmingham Black Barons

Hyde, Cowan F. (Bubba), 1937-50   OF, 2B, Cincinnati Tigers, Memphis Red Sox, Chicago American Giants, Indianapolis Athletics, Houston Eagles

Hyde, Harry 1896-1904   3B, 1B, Chicago Unions, Chicago Union Giants

Ingersoll, —, 1905   2B, Brooklyn Royal Giants

Ingram, Alfred, 1942   P, Jacksonville Red Caps

Irvin, Irwin (Bill), 1906,1919   3B, OF,MGR, Leland Giants, Cleveland Tate Stars

Irvin, Monford Merrill (Monte), 1937-48   OF, SS, 3B, Newark Eagles

Israel, Clarence Charles (Pint), 1940-47   3B, 2B, Newark Eagles, Homestead Grays

Israel, Elbert, 1950   INF, Philadelphia Stars

Ivory, —, 1936   P, 1B, Chicago American Giants

Jackman, Bill (Earl, Cannon Ball), 1925-42   P, Lincoln Giants, Philadelphia Giants, Quaker Giants, Brooklyn Eagles, Boston Royal Giants

Jackson, —, 1915   SS, Chicago Giants

Jackson, —, 1916-26   C, OF, Pennsylvania Red Caps of New York, Lincoln Giants, Newark Stars, Lincoln Stars, Philadelphia Giants

Jackson, —, 1921   P, Indianapolis ABCs

Jackson, —, 1931   P, Brooklyn Royal Giants

Jackson, —, 1932   OF, C, Indianapolis ABCs

Jackson, A. Matthew, 1932-34   3B, SS, Montgomery Grey Sox, Birmingham Black Barons, Cincinnati Tigers

Jackson, Andrew (Andy), 1888-99   3B, New York Gorhams, Cuban Giants, Lansing, (Mi) Colored Capital All-Americans, Cuban X Giants, York Cuban Giants (Eastern Interstate Lg.), New York Gorhams (Middle States Lg.)

Jackson, B. (Bozo), 1945   3B, Homestead Grays

Jackson, C., 1929   3B, Homestead Grays

Jackson, Carlton, 1928   officer, Harrisburg Giants

Jackson, Dallas, 1950   2B, INF, Cleveland Buckeyes

Jackson, Daniel M. (Dan, Hatchet), 1949   OF, Homestead Grays

Jackson, Edgar S., 1937   C, Memphis Red Sox

Jackson, F., 1887   officer, Brooklyn Remsens

Jackson, (Gen) 1947   OF, P, Baltimore Elite Giants

Jackson, George, 1886-87   P, OF, Philadelphia Pythians, Trenton Cuban Giants (Middle States Lg.)

Jackson, George, 1950   INF, New York Black Yankees

Jackson, (Gumbo), 1922   3B, New Orleans Crescent Stars

Jackson, Jack, 1927-28   OF, Bacharach Giants, Baltimore Black Sox

Jackson, Jackie, 1950   OF, Homestead Grays

Jackson, John W. Jr. (Stony), 1950   P, Houston Eagles

Jackson, (Lefty), 1926   P, Philadelphia Giants

Jackson, Lester E., 1938-41   P, OF, Newark Eagles, New York Black Yankees

Jackson, Norman (Jelly), 1934-45   SS, 2B, Cleveland Red Sox, Homestead Grays, Washington Elite Giants

Jackson, Oscar, 1887-96   OF, 1B, New York Gorhams, Cuban Giants, Cuban X Giants, York Cuban Giants (Eastern Interstate Lg.), Philadelphia Giants

Jackson, R.B., 1931-50   pres, vice pres, NSL; officer, owner, Nashville Black Vols, Nashville Cubs

Jackson, R.R. (Major), 1889   manager, Chicago Unions

Jackson, R.T., 1928-31   officer, Birmingham Black Barons; pres, NSL

Jackson, Randolph, 1887   2B, Oswego (International Lg.)

Jackson, Richard, 1921-31   2B, SS, 3B, Bacharach Giants, Harrisburg Giants, Baltimore Black Sox, Hilldale

Jackson, Robert (Bob), 1887-96   C, 1B, OF, New York Gorhams, Cuban X Giants, Ansonia Cuban Giants (Connecticut St. Lg.)

Jackson, Robert, 1897-1900   C, Chicago Unions

Jackson, Robert R.(Major), 1939-42   commissioner, NAL

Jackson, Rufus (Sonnyman), 1934-49   pres, tres, Homestead Grays

Jackson, Sam, 1887   player, Pittsburgh Keystones

Jackson, Sam, 1926   C, Cleveland Elites

Jackson, Samuel, 1942-47   P, 1B, Chicago American Giants

Jackson, Stanford, 1923-31   OF, SS, 3B, 2B, Memphis Red Sox, Chicago American Giants, Chicago Columbia Giants, Birmingham Black Barons

Jackson, Tom, 1924-31   P, St. Louis Stars, Cleveland Tigers, Nashville Elite Giants, Memphis Red Sox, Louisville White Sox

Jackson, Thomas, 1916-28   officer, Bacharach Giants

Jackson, Verdell, 1950   P, Memphis Red Sox

Jackson, W. (Big Train), 1938-40   P, Kansas City Monarchs, Memphis Red Sox

Jackson, William, 1890-1906   OF, C, 2B, Cuban Giants, Cuban X Giants, York Cuban Giants (Eastern Interstate Lg.), Ansonia Cuban Giants (Connecticut St.Lg.)

Jackson, William (Ashes), 1910-17   3B, Kansas City, (KS) Giants, Kansas City Royal Giants

Jamerson, Londell (Tincy), 1950   P, Kansas City Monarchs

James, —, 1896   P, Cuban X Giants

James, —, 1925   P, Cuban Stars (ECL)

James, J., 1912   1B, Smart Set

James, Livingston (Tice, Winky, Tarzan), 1939-42-SS, Ethiopian Clowns, Cincinnati Buckeyes, Cincinnati Clowns, Chicago American Giants, Cleveland Buckeyes

James, W. (Gus, Nux), 1905-20   2B, C, OF, Philadelphia Giants, Smart Set, Mohawk N.Y. Giants, Lincoln Giants, Bacharach Giants, Brooklyn Royal Giants, Pop Watkins Stars, Pittsburgh Stars of Buffalo

James, William, 1887   player, Philadelphia Pythians

Jameson, —, 1932-35   P, Newark Dodgers, Homestead Grays

Jamison, Caesar, 1923-32   umpire, NNL, East-West Lg.

Jamison, Eddie, 1950   C, Cleveland Buckeyes

Jarmon, Don, 1933   P, Columbus Blue Birds

Jasper, —, 1932   P, Birmingham Black Barons

Jauron —, 1928   P, Cleveland Tigers

Jefferson, Edward L. (Eddie), 1945-47   P, Philadelphia Stars

Jefferson, George Leo (Jeff), 1942-50   P, Jacksonville Red Caps, Cleveland Buckeyes, Louisville Buckeyes

Jefferson, R., 1939   3B, P, Indianapolis ABCs

Jefferson, Ralph, 1918-26   OF, Indianapolis ABCs, Bacharach Giants, Philadelphia Royal Stars, Washington Potomacs, Philadelphia Giants, Peter's Chicago Union Giants

Jefferson, Willie, 1937-50   P, Cincinnati Tigers, Memphis Red Sox, Cinciinnati Buckeyes, Cleveland Buckeyes

Jeffreys, Frank, 1917-20   OF, 2B, Chicago Giants

Jeffries, E., 1922   C, Chicago Giants

Jeffries, Harry, 1920-48   3B, C, SS, 1B, MGR, Chicago Giants, Chicago American Giants, Detroit Stars, Cleveland Tigers, Chicago Columbia Giants, Bacharach Giants, Knoxville Giants, Toledo Tigers, Baltimore Black Sox, Harrisburg Giants, Baltimore Panthers, Cleveland Browns

Jeffries, James C., 1914-31   P, OF, Indianapolis ABCs, Baltimore Black Sox, Birmingham Black Barons, Harrisburg Giants

Jeffries, Jeff, 1940   P, Brooklyn Royal Giants

Jeffries, M., 1925,1932   3B, Baltimore Black Sox, Hilldale

Jenkins, —, 1924   P, Washington Potomacs

Jenkins, Clarence (Barney), 1925-29   C, Philadelphia Giants, Detroit Stars

Jenkins, Clarence R. (Fats), 1920-40   OF, MGR, Lincoln Giants, Harrisburg Giants, Bacharach Giants, Baltimore Black Sox, New York Black Yankees, Philadelphia Stars, Brooklyn Eagles, Brooklyn Royal Giants, Pittsburgh Crawfords, Toledo Crawfords, Penn Red Caps of NY

Jenkins, Horace, 1914-25   OF, P, Chicago American Giants, Chicago Giants, Chicago Unions Giants

Jenkins, James Edward (Pee Wee), 1944-50   P, Cincinnati- Indianapolis Clowns, New York Cubans

Jenkins, Tom, 1916,1928   player, sec'y, Hilldale

Jennings, Thurman (Jack), 1915-27   2B, SS, OF, Chicago Giants

Jessie, W., 1887   player, Louisville Falls City

Jessup, Gentry, 1940-49   P, Chicago American Giants, Birmingham Black Barons

Jethroe, Samuel (Sam, The Jet), 1942-48   OF, Cincinnati Buckeyes, Cleveland Buckeyes

Jewell, Warner, 1917-26   owner, Officer, Jewell's ABCs, Indianapolis ABCs

Jimenez, Bienvenido (Hooks), 1915-29   2B, Cuban Stars (NNL), Cuban Stars (ECL), Cuban Stars

Jimenez, E., 1920-21   OF, Philadelphia Giants, Cuban Stars (NNL)

Johnson, —, 1886   OF, New York Gorhams

Johnson, —, 1922   OF, Detroit Stars

Johnson, A., 1914-17   2B, 3B, Lincoln Stars

Johnson, A. (Sampson), 1914-22   C, Bacharach Giants, Pittsburgh Giants, Pennsylvania Giants, Homestead Grays, Philadelphia Giants

Johnson, Al, 1938-40   P, Baltimore Elite Giants, Washington Black Senators

Johnson, Allen, 1942-46   officer, owner, St. Louis Stars, New York Black Yankees, Harrisburg-St. Louis Stars, Boston Blues

Johnson, B. (Monk), 1917-26   1B, 2B, P, OF, Pennsylvania Red Caps of New York, Lincoln Giants

Johnson, B., 1940   SS, Brooklyn Royal Giants

Johnson, Ben, 1916-23   P, Bacharach Giants

Johnson, Bert, see Bert Johnston

Johnson, Bill, 1933   3B, Akron Tyrites

Johnson, Bill (Willie), 1938-39   C, New York Black Yankees, Chicago American Giants

Johnson, Byron (Mex), 1937-39   SS, Kansas City Monarchs

Johnson, C., see G. Claude Johnson

Johnson, Cecil (Sess), 1918-28   1B, 3B, SS, P, Hilldale, Philadelphia Tigers, Philadelphia Royal Stars, Baltimore Black Sox, Newark Stars, Norfolk Stars

Johnson, Charles, 1949-50   3B, Cleveland Buckeyes, Memphis Red Sox

Johnson, Charles B., 1925-26   officer, Bacharach Giants

Johnson, Clifford Jr. (Cliff, Connie), 1940-50   P, Indianapolis Crawfords, Kansas City Monarchs

Johnson, Curtis, 1950   P, Kansas City Monarchs

Johnson, D. (Dud), 1914-19   OF, SS, 2B, Philadelphia Giants, Brooklyn Royal Giants

Johnson, Dan (Shang), 1916-21 P, Bacharach Giants, Brooklyn Royal Giants, Lincoln Giants, Hilldale, Indianapolis ABCs

Johnson, Ernest (Schoolboy), 1949-50 P, OF, Kansas City Monarchs

Johnson, Frank, 1932-37 OF,MGR, Monroe Monarchs, Memphis Red Sox

Johnson, Fred, 1946 P, Pittsburgh Crawfords

Johnson, G. Claude (Hooks), 1921-32 3B, 2B, SS, P, Baltimore Black Sox, Harrisburg Giants, Detroit Stars, Birmingham Black Barons, Memphis Red Sox, Cleveland Tate Stars, Hilldale

Johnson, George (Chappie), 1896-1939 C, 1B, MGR Columbia Giants, Chicago Unions Giants, Brooklyn Royal Giants, Leland Giants, Chicago Giants, St. Louis Giants, Dayton Chappies, Custer's Baseball Club of Columbus, Philadelphia Royal Stars, Norfolk Stars, Algona (IA) Brownies, Adrian Page Fence Giants, Mohawk N.Y. Giants, Philadelphia Giants, Pennsylvania Red Caps of N.Y., Chappie Johnson's Stars

Johnson, George Washington (Dibo), 1909-28 OF, Fort Worth Wonders, Kansas City, Kan., Giants, Brooklyn Royal Giants, Hilldale, Lincoln Giants, Philadelphia Tigers, Bacharach Giants

Johnson, Grant (Home Run), 1894-1921 SS, 2B, MGR, Page Fence Giants, Columbia Giants, Brooklyn Royal Giants, Cuban X Giants, Philadelphia Giants, Lincoln Giants, Lincoln Stars, Philadelphia Colored Stars, Pittsburgh Stars of Buffalo, Chicago Unions, Findlay, Ohio, Mohawk Giants, Brooklyn Colored Giants

Johnson, H. (Hamp), 1933-34,1946 OF, Birmingham Black Barons

Johnson, Harry A., 1886-89 2B, OF, C, Cuban Giants, Trenton Cuban Giants (Middle States Lg.)

Johnson, J. (Lefty), 1929-33 1B, P, OF, Memphis Red Sox

Johnson, Jack (Topeka Jack), 1903-04,1909-10 1B, OF, Philadelphia Giants, Kansas City (Mo.) Royal Giants, Kansas City, Kansas Giants

Johnson, Jack, 1938-40 3B, Homestead Grays, Toledo Crawfords, Cincinnati Buckeyes

Johnson, James, 1898 RF, C, Adrian Page Fence Giants

Johnson, James (J.D.), 1950 P, Philadelphia Stars

Johnson, Jim, 1932-34 SS, Hilldale, Bacharach Giants

Johnson, Jimmy (Slim), 1939-43 P, Toledo Crawfords, Indianapolis Crawfords, Philadelphia Stars

Johnson, Jimmy (Jeep), 1946-47 SS, Pittsburgh Crawfords, Homestead Grays

Johnson, Joe, 1884-85 P, C, Baltimore Atlantics

Johnson, John (Johnny), 1938-46 P, Birmingham Black Barons, Homestead Grays, New York Black Yankees, Newark Eagles, Baltimore Elite Giants

Johnson, John, 1950 UTIL, New York Cubans

Johnson, John B., 1925-28 pres, MGR, Brooklyn Cuban Giants

Johnson, Rev. John H., 1947-48 pres, NNL

Johnson, John Wesley (Smokey), 1922-28 P, Cleveland Tate Stars, Cleveland Elites, Cleveland Browns, Lincoln Giants

Johnson, Johnny, 1943 P, Cleveland Buckeyes

Johnson, Joseph, 1937 officer, Indianapolis Athletics

Johnson, Joshua (Josh, Brute), 1934-42 C, P, OF, Cincinnati Tigers, Homestead Grays, New York Black Yankees, Brooklyn Royal Giants

Johnson, Judy, see Johnson, William J

Johnson, Junior, 1899-1906 1B, C, Columbia Giants, Philadelphia Giants, Quaker Giants, Brooklyn Royal Giants

Johnson, L., 1948 P, Kansas City Monarchs

Johnson, Leaman, 1941-45 SS, INF, Memphis Red Sox, Newark Eagles, Birmingham Black Barons, New York Black Yankees

Johnson, Lee, 1941 C, Birmingham Black Barons

Johnson, Leonard, 1947-48 P, Chicago American Giants

Johnson, Leroy, 1950 P, Birmingham Black Barons

Johnson, Louis (Dicta), 1911-25 P, MGR, coach, Twin City Gophers, Chicago American Giants, Indianapolis ABCs, Detroit Stars, Toledo Tigers, Pittsburgh Keystones, Milwaukee Bears, Bowser's ABCs

Johnson, M., see B. (Monk) Johnson

Johnson, (Monk), see B. (Monk) Johnson

Johnson, Nate, 1922-24 P, Bacharach Giants, Cleveland Browns, Brooklyn Royal Giants, Harrisburg Giants

Johnson, Othello, 1916-22 P, OF, Bacharach Giants, Brooklyn Royal Giants, Philadelphia Giants, Lincoln Giants, Penn Red Caps of NY

Johnson, Oscar (Heavy), 1922-33 OF, C, 2B, Kansas City Monarchs, Baltimore Black Sox, Harrisburg Giants, Cleveland Tigers, Memphis Red Sox, Dayton Marcos

Johnson, (Pee Wee), 1939 2B, Newark Eagles

Johnson, Pearley (Tubby, Peter), 1920-27, 1942 P, OF, INF, Baltimore Black Sox, Boston Royal Giants

Johnson, R., 1932 OF, Washington Pilots

Johnson, Ralph, 1940-41,1945 P, Philadelphia Stars

Johnson, Ralph, 1950 SS, Indianapolis Clowns

Johnson, (Rat), 1909 player, St. Paul Gophers

Johnson, Ray, 1923 OF, St. Louis Stars

Johnson, Richard, 1887-90 C, OF, Zanesville (Ohio State Lg.), Tri-State Lg.), Springfield and Peoria (Central Interstate Lg.)

Johnson, Robert (Bob), 1928 INF, Brooklyn Cuban Giants, Philadelphia Tigers

Johnson, Robert, 1939-40 OF, New York Black Yankees

Johnson, Robert, 1944 P, Kansas City Monarchs

Johnson, Roy (Bubbles), 1920-22 1B, 2B, St. Louis Giants, Kansas City Monarchs

Johnson, Rudolph, 1950 OF, Cleveland Buckeyes

Johnson, S., see Cecil Johnson

Johnson, Tom (Tommy), 1937-42 P, St. Louis Stars, Chicago American Giants

Johnson, Thomas (Tommy), 1914-25 P, Indianapolis ABCs, Chicago American Giants, Pittsburgh Keystones;umpire, NNL

Johnson, Tommy F., 1950 P, Indianapolis Clowns

Johnson, W., 1944-45 P, Memphis Red Sox

Johnson, W., 1925 see William H. Johnson

Johnson, W., 1928 see Wade Johnston

Johnson, William H. (Wise, Bill, Big C.), 1920-33 C, OF, MGR, Homestead Grays, Hilldale, Philadelphia Tigers, Pennsylvania Red Caps of New York, Wilmington Potomacs, Harrisburg Giants, Washington Potomacs, Dayton Marcos

Johnson, William Julius (Judy), 1918-38 3B, SS, MGR, Hilldale, Homestead Grays, Darby Daisies, Pittsburgh Crawfords

Johnston, Bert (Bucky) [Johnson], 1933-38 OF, Newark Dodgers, Baltimore Black Sox, Birmingham Black Barons

Johnston, C., 1916 2B, Lincoln Stars

Johnston, Tom, 1923 umpire, NNL

Johnston, Wade [Johnson], 1920-33 OF, P, Cleveland Tate Stars, Kansas City Monarchs, Baltimore Black Sox, Detroit Stars, Pennsylvania Red Caps of NY

Johnstone, —, 1912-13 C, Pittsburgh Giants, Philadelphia Giants

Jones, —, 1912 P, Cuban Giants

Jones, —, 1920-21 SS, Indianapolis ABCs

Jones, Abe, 1887-94 C, manager, Chicago Unions

Jones, Albert Alonzo, 1944-46 P, Chicago American Giants, Memphis Red Sox

Jones, Alvin, 1928 officer, Harrisburg Giants

Jones, Archie, 1939 P, New York Cubans

Jones, Arthur Brown (Mutt, Dump), 1925,1934 P, Birmingham Black Barons

Jones, B., 1934 OF, C, Cleveland Red Sox

Jones, Ben, 1950 SS, New York Black Yankees

Jones, Bert, 1896-1903 P, OF, Chicago Unions, Atchison (Kansas St. Lg.), Algona (IA) Brownies

Jones, Charles, 1950 3B, Cleveland Buckeyes

Jones, Clinton Jr. (Casey), 1944-50 C, Memphis Red Sox

Jones, Collins (Collis), 1943-44 UTIL, Cincinnati Clowns, Birmingham Black Barons

Jones, (Country), 1932-33 2B, C, Brooklyn Royal Giants

Jones, Curtis, 1946 P, Cleveland Buckeyes

Jones, D., 1884 player, Philadelphia Mutual B.B.C.

Jones, Edward, 1915-29 C, Chicago American Giants, Chicago Giants, Bacharach Giants

Jones, Ernest (Mint), 1937-41 1B, Jacksonville Red Caps, Cleveland Bears, Philadelphia Stars

Jones, Eugene, 1943 P, Homestead Grays, Baltimore Elite Giants

Jones, Fate, 1950 OF, Birmingham Black Barons

Jones, Hurley, 1931 P, Birmingham Black Barons

Jones, James, 1949-50 OF, 1B, Philadelphia Stars

Jones, John, 1922-34 OF, 1B, Detroit Stars, Memphis Red Sox, Indianapolis ABCs

Jones, Lee, 1908-22 OF, Brooklyn Colored Giants, Brooklyn Royal Giants, Dallas Giants

Jones, Ollie, 1919 3B, St. Louis Giants

Jones, Paul, 1949-50 P, Louisville Buckeyes, Cleveland Buckeyes

Jones, Reuben, 1918-49 OF, MGR, Dallas Giants, Birmingham Black Barons, Indianapolis ABCs, Chicago American Giants, Little Rock Black Travelers, Memphis Red Sox, Houston Eagles

Jones, Robert Leo (Fox), 1933-34 OF, Memphis Red Sox

Jones, Sam (Red, Sad Sam), 1946-48 P, Homestead Grays, Cleveland Buckeyes

Jones, Stuart (Slim, Country), 1933-38 P, Baltimore Black Sox, Philadelphia Stars

Jones, Tom (Pete), 1946 C, Philadelphia Stars

Jones, W., 1934 OF, Birmingham Black Barons

Jones, William (Fox), 1915-30 C, P, Chicago American Giants, Chicago Giants, Bacharach Giants, Hilldale, Chicago Union Giants

Jones, Willis (Will), 1895-1911 SS, OF, Chicago Unions, Leland Giants, Chicago Union Giants, Algona (IA) Brownies

Jordan, Henry (Hen), 1921-25 C, OF, Harrisburg Giants, Pittsburg Stars of Buffalo, Baltimore Black Sox

Jordan, Larnie, 1936-42 SS, Philadelphia Stars, New York Black Yankees, Brooklyn Royal Giants, Bacharach Giants

Jordan, Maynard, 1950 OF, Houston Eagles

Jordan, Robert, 1896-1906 C, 1B, Cuban Giants, Cuban X Giants, Philadelphia Giants

Jordan William F., 1899 MGR, Baltimore Giants

Jordan, Willie, 1933,1938 P, Chicago American Giants, Louisville Black Colonels

Joseph, Walter Lee (Newt), 1922-39 3B, 2B, MGR, Kansas City Monarchs, Birmingham Black Barons, Satchel Paige's All- Stars

Josephs, William, 1924-25 SS, Birmingham Black Barons, Cleveland Browns

Joyner, William, 1893-1902 SS, Chicago Unions, Chicago Union Giants

Juanelo, see Juanelo Mirabel

Juillo, —, 1940 P, Cuban Stars

Juncos, Jose, 1912-21 P, Cuban Stars (East)

Jupiter, —, 1887 P, Cuban Giants

Juran, B., 1923 P, Birmingham Black Barons

Juran, Eli, 1923-1926 P,Birmingham Black Barons, Newark Stars

Justice, Charles P. (Charley), 1933,1937 P, Akron Tyrites, Detroit Stars

Kaiser, Cecil, 1945-49 P, Pittsburgh Crawfords, Homestead Grays

Keene, —, 1915 3B, West Baden (Ind.) Sprudels, Bowser's ABCs

Keeton, Eugene, 1921-26 P, Dayton Marcos, Cleveland Tate Stars, Indianapolis ABCs

Keck, D.J., 1948 tres, Negro American Association

Keenan, James J., 1919-30 bus. mgr, Lincoln Giants; sec'y-tres, ECL

Keigeri, —, 1887 player, Louisville Falls City

Kelley, Holland, 1942 gen. sec'y, United States Lg.

Kelley, Palmer, 1916-18 P, Chicago Giants, Chicago Union Giants

Kelley, Richard A. (Charles), 1889-91 1B, 2B, SS, Danville (Illinois- Indiana Lg.); Jamestown (Pennsylvania-New York Lg.)

Kellman, Edric (Leon), 1946-50 3B, Cleveland Buckeyes, Louisville Buckeyes, Memphis Red Sox

Kelly, —, 1900-08 SS, OF, 3B, Genuine Cuban Giants, Famous Cuban Giants, New York Colored Giants

Kelly, —, 1941 P, Jacksonville Red Caps

Kelly, (Lefty), *see Kelly Searcy*

Kelly, Walter, 1950 P, Cleveland Buckeyes

Kelly, William, 1898 3B, Celeron Acme Colored Giants (Iron and Oil Lg.)

Kelly, William, 1945-47-C, New York Black Yankees, Homestead Grays

Kemp, —, 1943 C, New York Black Yankees

Kemp, Ed, 1914-28 OF, Philadelphia Royal Giants, Norfolk Stars, Norfolk Giants, Baltimore Black Sox, Lincoln Giants

Kemp, George, 1917 OF, Hilldale

Kemp, James, 1937-39 2B, Atlanta Black Crackers, Jacksonville Red Caps, Indianpolis ABCs

Kemp, John, 1923-28 OF, Memphis Red Sox, Birmingham Black Barons

Kendall, —, 1920,1925 2B, Lincoln Giants

Kendricks, L.H. (Willie), 1943 P, Atlanta Black Crackers

Kennard, Dan, 1915-25 C, Indianapolis ABCs, Chicago American Giants, St. Louis Giants, Lincoln Giants, St. Louis Stars, Detroit Stars

Kennedy, —, 1926 SS, Lincoln Giants

Kennedy, Ernest D., 1950 INF, Memphis Red Sox

Kennedy, Walter, 1950 OF, Chicago American Giants

Kenner, —, 1921,1928 SS, 2B, Hilldale, Washington Grays

Kent, Richard, 1922-31 officer, St. Louis Stars

Kenyon, Harry C., 1919-29 P, 2B, OF, MGR, Brooklyn Royal Giants, Hilldale, Indianpolis ABCs, Chicago American Giants, Lincoln Giants, Detroit Stars, Kansas City Monarchs, Memphis Red Sox

Kerner, J., 1931-33 OF, Columbus Blue Birds, Detroit Stars, Indianapolis ABCs

Key, Ludie, 1934 pres, Birmingham Black Barons

Keyes, Garvin, 1943 INF, Philadelphia Stars

Keyes, Robert, 1944-46 P, Memphis Red Sox,

Keyes, Steve (Youngie, Zeke, Khora), 1940-48 P, Memphis Red Sox, Philadelphia Stars, Indianapolis Crawfords, Cincinnati Clowns

Keys, —, 1950 P, Houston Eagles

Keys, Dr. George B., 1922-32 officer, St. Louis Stars; officer, NNL

Kimbro, Arthur (Jess, Ted), 1915-18 3B, 2B, Bowser's ABCs, St. Louis Giants, Lincoln Giants, Louisville Sox

Kimbro, Henry Allen (Kimmie), 1937-50 OF, MGR, Washington Elite Giants, Baltimore Elite Giants, New York Black Yankees

Kimbro, (Howdy), 1945 P, Pittsburgh Crawfords

Kimbrough, Jim, 1945-48 P, Philadelphia Stars, Homestead Grays

Kimbrough, Larry Nathaniel (Schoolboy), 1942-46 P, Philadelphia Stars

Kinard, Roosevelt, 1932 3B, Washington Pilots

Kincaide, C.J., 1945-47 officer, NSL

Kincannon, Harry, 1930-39 P, Pittsburgh Crawfords, Philadelphia Stars, New York Black Yankees, Washington Black Senators, Toledo Crawfords

Kindle, William (Bill), 1911-20 SS, 2B, OF, Brooklyn Royal Giants, Indianapolis ABCs, Chicago American Giants, Lincoln Stars, Lincoln Giants

King, Brendan, 1943 P, Cincinnati Clowns

King, Clarence (Charley, Pijo), 1947-50 OF, Birmingham Black Barons

King, Leonard, 1921 OF, Kansas City Monarchs

King, Wilbur, 1944-47 SS, 2B Memphis Red Sox, Cleveland Buckeyes, Chicago American Giants, Homestead Grays

King, William, 1890-92 SS, Chicago Unions

Kinkeide, John, 1887 player, Louisville Falls City

Kirby, —, 1928 P, Cleveland Tigers

Kirksey, —, 1926 C, Dayton Marcos

Klepp, Eddie, 1946 P, Cleveland Buckeyes

Knight, —, 1921 OF, Detroit Stars

Knight, —, 1922 1B, Baltimore Black Sox

Knight, H., 1930 P, Chicago American Giants

Knox, Elwood C., 1920 co-drafter of constitution, NNL

Kranson, Floyd Arthur [Kranston], 1936-41 P, Kansas City Monarchs, Memphis Red Sox, Chicago American Giants

Krider, J. Monroe [Kreiter], 1890 MGR, Cuban Giants (Colored Monarchs of York, Pa., Eastern Interstate Lg.)

Kyle, Andy, 1922 OF, P, Baltimore Black Sox, Bacharach Giants

Lackey, Obie Ezekiel [Obie], 1927-43 SS, 2B, P, 3B, Philadelphia Giants, Hilldale, Bacharach Giants, Pittsburgh Crawfords, Homestead Grays, Baltimore Black Sox, Philadelphia Stars, Brooklyn Royal Giants, New York Black Yankees

Lacy, Raymond, 1949-50 OF, Houston Eagles

Lain, William, 1911 3B, Chicago Giants

Lair, —, 1925 OF, Pennsylvania Red Caps of New York

Lamar, Clarence (Lemon), 1937-42 SS, 2B, St. Louis Stars, Cleveland Bears, Jacksonville Red Caps, Indianapolis ABCs, Birmingham Black Barons

Lamar, E.B., Jr., 1895-1926 MGR, club officer, booker, Cuban X Giants, Cuban Stars, Bacharach Giants, Harrisburg Giants, Brooklyn Cuban Giants

Lamarque, James H.(Jim, Lefty), 1942-50 P, Kansas City Monarchs

Lamberto, —, 1929 OF, Cuban Stars (ECL)

Land, —, 1908-13 OF, 1B, New York Colored Giants, Cuban Giants, Smart Set, Mohawk Giants

Landers, John, 1917 P, Indianapolis ABCs

Landers, Robert Henry, 1949 P, Kansas City Monarchs

Lane, —, 1911 SS, Chicago American Giants

Lane, Alto, 1929-34 P, Memphis Red Sox, Indianapolis ABCs, Cincinnati Tigers, Louisville White Sox, Kansas City Monarchs

Lane, Isaac S., 1917-22 OF, 3B, P, Dayton Giants, Dayton Marcos, Columbus Buckeyes, Detroit Stars

Lang, John F., 1885-86 MGR, Argyle Hotel, Cuban Giants

Langford, (Ad), 1912-20 P, OF, St. Louis Giants, Lincoln Stars, Brooklyn Royal Giants, Pennsylvania Red Caps of New York, Lincoln Giants, Mohawk Giants

Langram, —, 1939 2B, OF, Kansas City Monarchs

Langrum, Dr. E.L., 1934 officer, Cleveland Red Sox

Lanier, A.S., 1921 officer, Cuban Stars (NNL)

Lansing, Wilbur, 1948-49 P, Newark Eagles, Houston Eagles

Lantiqua, Enrique, 1935 C, New York Cubans

Lanuza, Pedro, 1931-32 C, Cuban Stars, House of David Cubans

Larrinago, Perez, 1946 2B, SS, Cleveland Buckeyes

Latimer, —, 1921 P, Indianapolis ABCs

Lattimore, —, 1929-33 C, Baltimore Black Sox, Brooklyn Royal Giants, Columbus Blue Birds

Lau, —, 1927 P, Cubans (ECL)

Laurent, Milfred Stephen (Milt, Rick), 1929-35 3B, 1B, OF, 2B, C, Memphis Red Sox, Cleveland Cubs, Birmingham Black Barons, Nashville Elite Giants, New Orleans Crescent Stars

Lavelle, —, 1908-12 C, 1B, Genuine Cuban Giants, Cuban Giants, Cuban Stars

Lavera, —, 1919 C, Cuban Stars

Lawson, L.B. (Flash), 1940 P, Philadelphia Stars

Lawyer, —, 1913 rf, Mohawk Giants

Layton, Obie, 1931 P, Hilldale

Lazaga, Agipito, 1916-22 OF, P, Cuban Stars (NNL), New York Cuban Stars

Leak, Curtis, A., 1940-48 officer, New York Black Yankees; sec'y, NNL

Leary, —, 1920-25 3B, Dayton Marcos, Penn Red Caps of NY

Lebeaux, —, 1936 SS, 2B, Chicago American Giants

Leblanc, —, 1915 SS, Lincoln Giants

Leblanc, Julio (Jose), 1919-21 P, OF, Cuban Stars (NNL)

Lee, Dick, 1917-18 OF, Chicago Union Giants

Lee, Fred, 1915 OF, Kansas City Giants

Lee, Holsey Scranton (Scrip), 1920-43 P, OF, 1B, Norfolk Stars, Philadelphia Stars, Hilldale, Norfolk Giants, Richmond Giants, Baltimore Black Sox, Bacharach Giants, Cleveland Red Sox, Philadelphia Giants; umpire, NNL

Lee, Lown, 1909 P, Kansas City Royal Giants

Lee, William, 1888 SS, Chicago Unions

Leftwich, John (Hymie), 1945 P, Homestead Grays

Legrove, —, 1937 OF, Indianapolis Athletics

Leland, Frank C., 1887-1912 OF, MGR, Washington Capital Citys, Chicago Union Giants, Leland Giants, Chicago Giants

Lemon, *see Clarence Lamar*

Lenox, —, 1943 1B, New York Black Yankees

Leon, —, 1917-18 OF, P, Cuban Stars (East)

Leon, Isidore, 1948 OF, New York Cubans

Leonard, James (Bobo), 1919-32 P, OF, 1B, Cleveland Tate Stars, Cleveland Browns, Cleveland Tigers, Cleveland Hornets, Toledo Tigers, Chicago American Giants, Bacharach Giants, Lincoln Giants, Baltimore Black Sox, Homestead Grays, Pennsylvania Red Caps of New York

Leonard, Walter Fenner (Buck), 1933-50 1B, OF, Brooklyn Royal Giants, Homestead Grays

Lerue, —, 1921 C, Detroit Stars

Lester, —, 1932 P, Nashville Elite Giants

Lett, Roger, 1943 P, Cincinnati Clowns

Lettlers, George, 1887 player, Washington Capital Citys

Leuschner, W.A. (Bill), 1940-43 booking agent; officer, New York Black Yankees

Levis, Oscar [Oscal], 1921-32 P, Cuban Stars (East), Hilldale, Darby Daisies, Baltimore Black Sox, All Cubans

Lewis, —, 1887 player, Boston Resolutes

Lewis, —, 1923 P, Indianapolis ABCs

Lewis, A.D., 1937-38 1B, Birmingham Black Barons, Louisville Black Colonels

Lewis, Bernard, 1943 P, Atlanta Black Crackers

Lewis, Cary B., 1920 co-drafter, constitution of NNL; sec'y, NNL

Lewis, Charles (Babe), 1926 SS, Lincoln Giants, Philadelphia Giants

Lewis, Clarence (Foots), 1931-37 SS, Memphis Red Sox, Cleveland Red Sox, Nashville Elite Giants, Pittsburgh Crawfords, Akron Tyrites, Cleveland Giants

Lewis, F., 1932 OF, Montgomery Grey Sox

Lewis, George (Peaches), 1917-22 P, Lincoln Giants, Bacharach Giants

Lewis, Grover, 1928 3B, Homestead Grays

Lewis, Henry N., 1943-45 MGR, Officer,owner, Atlanta Black Crackers, Knoxville Black Smokies

Lewis, Ira F., 1922 sec'y, Pittsburgh Keystones

Lewis, Jerome, 1910 1B, West Baden (Ind.) Sprudels

Lewis, Jim (Slim), 1943,1947 P, Chicago Brown Bombers, New York Black Yankees

Lewis, Joseph Herman (Sleepy), 1919-34,1946 C, 3B,MGR, Baltimore Black Sox, Washington Potomacs, Homestead Grays, Hilldale, Lincoln Giants, Quaker Giants, Darby Daisies, Bacharach Giants, Norfolk-Newport News Royals

Lewis, Milton, 1922-28 2B, 1B,UTIL, Wilmington Potomacs, Bacharach Giants, Richmond Giants, Harrisburg Giants, Philadelphia Giants

Lewis, R.S. (Bubbles), 1923-28 officer, Memphis Red Sox; vice pres, NNL

Lewis, Rufus (Lew), 1936-50 P, Pittsburgh Crawfords, Newark Eagles, Houston Eagles

Lewis, (Tuck), 1916 2B, Chicago Giants

Liggons, James, 1932-34 P, OF, Monroe Monarchs, Memphis Red Sox, Little Rock Black Travelers

Lightner, —, 1920,1932 P, Kansas City Monarchs, Cole's American Giants

Ligon, Rufus, 1944-45 P, Memphis Red Sox

Lillard, Joe, 1932-37 P, OF, C, Cole's American Giants, Chicago American Giants, Cincinnati Tigers

Lillie, —, 1925 UTIL, Birmingham Black Barons

Linares, Abel, 1911-12 owner, pres., All Cubans, Cuban Stars

Linares, Rogelio (Ice Cream), 1940-46 1B, OF, Cuban Stars, New York Cubans

Lincoln, —, 1890-95 SS, 3B, Lincoln (Neb) Giants, Adrian Page Fence Giants,

Linder, —, 1922 P, Kansas City Monarchs

Lindsay, Bill, 1910-15 P, Kansas City, Kansas, Giants, Leland Giants, Chicago American Giants

Lindsay, Charles Clarence, 1920-34 SS, Richmond Giants, Bacharach Giants, Baltimore Black Sox, Wilmington Potomacs, Penn Red Caps of New York, Lincoln Giants, Philadelphia Giants

Lindsay, James, 1943 INF, Birmingham Black Barons

Lindsay, Leonard (Yahoodi), 1942-46 1B, P, 3B, Cincinnati Clowns, Birmingham Black Barons, Indianapolis Clowns

Lindsay, Merf, 1910 OF, Kansas City (Kan) Giants

Lindsay, P., 1910 1B, OF, Kansas City (Kan) Giants

Lindsay, Robert (Frog), 1910-17 SS, Kansas City, (Kan.), Giants

Lindsey, —, 1912 OF, Lincoln Giants

Lindsey, Ben, 1929 SS, Bacharach Giants

Lindsey, Bill, 1924-26 SS, 2B, OF, Washington Potomacs, Lincoln Giants, Dayton Marcos

Lindsey, James, 1887 OF, Pittsburgh Keystones

Lindsey, Robert, 1931 P, OF, 1B, Indianapolis ABCs

Linton, Benjamin, 1945 officer, Detroit Giants

Lisby, —, 1934 P, Newark Dodgers, Bacharach Giants

Listach, Nora [Listash], 1940-41 OF, Birmingham Black Barons, Cincinnati Buckeyes

Little, William, 1937-50 officer, Chicago American Giants

Littles, Ben, 1947-50 OF, Homestead Grays, New York Black Yankees, Philadelphia Stars

Livingston, Curtis, 1950 OF, Cleveland Buckeyes

Livingston, L.D. (Lee, Goo Goo), 1928-32 OF, Kansas City Monarchs, New York Black Yankees, Pittsburgh Crawfords, Pennsylvania Red Caps of NY

Lloyd, John Henry (Pop), 1905-32 SS, 1B, 2B, C, MGR, Macon Acmes, Cuban X Giants, Philadelphia Giants, Leland Giants, Lincoln Giants, Chicago American Giants, Brooklyn Royal Giants, Columbus Buckeyes, Bacharach Giants, Hilldale, New York Black Yankees , Lincoln Stars, Kansas City Monarchs

Locke, Clarence Virgil, 1945-48 P, 1B, Chicago American Giants

Locke, Eddie, 1943-50 P, 3B, Cincinnati Clowns, Kansas City Monarchs, New York Black Yankees

Lockett, Lester (Buck), 1937-50 2B, 3B, OF, Chicago American Giants, Birmingham Black Barons, Cincinnati-Indianapolis Clowns, Baltimore Elite Giants, Memphis Red Sox, St.Louis Stars, Cincinnati Buckeyes

Lockett, Monroe, 1938 P, Indianapolis ABCs

Lockett, Willie, 1938 OF, Indianapolis ABCs

Lockhart, A.J., 1925-26 P, 3B, Wilmington Potomacs, Philadelphia Giants

Lockhart, G. Hubert (Joe), 1923-29 P, Bacharach Giants, Chicago American Giants, Wilmington Potomacs

Loftin, Louis Santop, see Santop, Louis

Logan, Carl, 1940 INF, Philadelphia Stars

Logan, Fred, 1950 OF, New York Black Yankees

Logan, Nick, 1920-25 P, Baltimore Black Sox

Londo, Julius, 1909 player, St. Paul Gophers

Long, —, 1920-26 OF, Detroit Stars, Indianapolis ABCs

Long, (Buck), 1950 C, Memphis Red Sox

Long, Emory (Bang), 1932-40,1945 3B, OF, Atlanta Black Crackers, Chicago American Giants, Indianapolis Athletics, Philadelphia Stars, Kansas City Monarchs, Washington Black Senators

Long, Ernest S., 1948-50 P, Cleveland Buckeyes, Louisville Buckeyes

Longest, Bernell, 1942-47 2B, Chicago Brown Bombers, Chicago American Giants

Longest, Jimmy, 1942 1B, Chicago Brown Bombers

Longley, Wayman (Red, Ray), 1932-50 2B, OF, SS, C, 1B, 3B, Memphis Red Sox, Chicago American Giants, Little Rock Black Travelers

Longware, —, 1920 2B, 3B, OF, Detroit Stars

Looney, Charlie, 1933,1938 2B, Akron Tyrites, Louisville Black Colonels

Lopez, Cando, 1920-35 OF, 3B, Cuban Stars (NNL), New York Cubans

Lopez, Justo, 1939 1B, Cuban Stars

Lopez, Pedro, 1938-39 OF, Cuban Stars

Lopez, Raul, 1948-50 P, New York Cubans

Lopez, Vidal, 1923-39 P, Cuban Stars (ECL), Cuban Stars (NNL)

Lorenzo, Jesus, 1928-30 P, Cuban Stars (NNL)

Lott, Benjamin (Benny, Honey), 1949-50-2B, 3B, Indianapolis Clowns, New York Black Yankees

Lott, Raymond (Ray), 1950 OF, Philadelphia Stars

Louden, Louis Oliver (Tommy, Lou), 1942-50 C, New York Cubans, Cuban Stars

Love, William Andy, 1930-31,1945 C, OF, Detroit Stars, Memphis Red Sox, Toledo Cubs (USL)

Loving, J.G., 1887 player, Washington Capital Citys

Lowe, William M., 1921-31 3B, SS, 2B, OF, MGR, Indianapolis ABCs, Detroit Stars, Memphis Red Sox, Chattanooga Black Lookouts, Nashville Elite Giants

Lowell, —, 1924 P, Bacharach Giants

Lucas, Miles (Pepe), 1919-20,1925-27 P, OF, Cuban Stars of Havana, Cuban Stars (East), New Orleans Crescent Stars, Harrisburg Giants

Lucas, (Scotty), 1928 officer, Philadelphia Tigers

Lugo, Levingelo (Leo), 1944-46 OF, Cincinnati-Indianapolis Clowns, Indianapolis Clowns

Lundy, Richard (Dick), 1916-48 SS, 3B, 2B, MGR, Bacharach Giants, Lincoln Giants, Hilldale, Baltimore Black Sox, Philadelphia Stars, Newark Dodgers, New York Cubans, Newark Eagles, Jacksonville Eagles, Brooklyn Royal Giants, Havana Red Sox

Luque, Adolfo (Dolf), 1912-13 P, OF, Cuban Stars, Long Branch (NJ) Cubans

Luther, see Luther Farrell

Lyda, —, 1932 P, Coles American Giants

Lyles, John, 1932-43 OF, SS, 2B, 3B, C, Homestead Grays, Indianapolis ABCs, Cleveland Bears, St. Louis Stars, Chicago American Giants, Cincinnati Buckeyes, Cleveland Buckeyes, Indianapolis Clowns, New Orleans-St. Louis Stars

Lynch, Thomas, 1917-18 OF, Indianapolis ABCs, Dayton Marcos

Lynn, —, 1917 P, Jewell's ABCs

Lyons, —, 1950 P, Cleveland Buckeyes

Lyons, Bennie, 1917-18 1B, Jewell's ABCs, Dayton Marcos

Lyons, Chase, 1899-1905 P, Genuine Cuban Giants, Cuban Giants

Lyons, Granville, 1931-42 1B, P, Nashville Elite Giants, Louisville Black Caps, Detroit Stars, Louisville Red Caps, Philadelphia Stars, Memphis Red Sox, Baltimore Black Sox

Lyons, James (Jimmie), 1910-32 OF, MGR, Lincoln Giants, St. Louis Giants, Chicago Giants, Brooklyn Royal Giants, Indianapolis ABCs, Chicago American Giants, Detroit Stars, Cleveland Browns, Louisville Black Caps, Washington Potomacs Bowser's ABCs

Lytle, Clarence, 1901-06 P, Chicago Union Giants, Leland Giants

Mack, John H., 1945 P, Kansas City Monarchs

Mack, Paul, 1916-17 OF, 3B, Bacharach Giants, Jersey City Colored Giants

Mack, Robert, 1945 P, New York Black Yankees

Mackey, Raleigh (Biz), 1918-47 C, SS, 3B, MGR, San Antonio Giants, Indianapolis ABCs, Hilldale, Darby Daisies, Philadelphia Stars, Washington Elite Giants, Baltimore Elite Giants, Newark Eagles, Newark Dodgers, Nashville Elite Giants

Macklin, —, 1924-29 3B, OF, Chicago Giants

Maddix, Raydell (Ray, Bo), 1949-50 P, Indianapolis Clowns

Maddox, (One Wing), 1923—, P, OF, Birmingham Black Barons

Madert, —, 1917 2B, Chicago Giants

Madison, Robert, 1935-42 P, OF, 3B, Kansas City Monarchs, Memphis Red Sox, Indianapolis Athletics, Birmingham Black Barons

Magrinat, Hector (Kako), 1909-16 OF, Cuban Stars, All Cubans

Mainor, Hank, 1950 P, Baltimore Elite Giants

Mahoney, Tony, 1920-23 P, Norfolk Giants, Indianapolis ABCs, Baltimore Black Sox, Brooklyn Royal Giants, Norfolk Stars

Mahoney, Ulysses, 1944 P, Philadelphia Stars

Maison, J., 1887 player, Pittsburgh Keystones

Makell, Frank, 1944-49 C, Newark Eagles, Baltimore Elite Giants

Malarcher, David Julius (Cap, Gentleman Dave), 1916-34 3B, OF, 2B, MGR, Indianapolis ABCs, Detroit Stars, Chicago American Giants, Cole's American Giants, Chicago Columbia Giants

Malloy, [Mallory], 1918-21 OF, Pennsylvania Red Caps of New York, Nashville Elite Giants

Malone, William H., 1887-97 P, 1B, 3B, OF, Cuban Giants, Pittsburgh Keystones, New York Gorhams (Middle States Lg.), Page Fence Giants, York Cuban Giants (Eastern Interstate Lg.), Trenton Cuban Giants (Middle States Lg.), Philadelphia Pythians

Manella, see Manolo

Manese, E., 1923-26 2B, Detroit Stars, Kansas City Monarchs, Indianapolis ABCs

Mangrum, —, 1948 OF, New York Cubans

Manley, Abraham (Abe), 1935-46 officer, Brooklyn Eagles, Newark Eagles; vice pres, tres, NNL

Manley, Effa (Mrs. Abraham), 1935-48 officer, Brooklyn Eagles, Newark Eagles, sec'y; NNL

Mann, —, 1918 1B, Chicago Union Giants

Manning, —, 1932 1B, Montgomery Grey Sox

Manning, John, 1902 OF, Philadelphia Giants

Manning, Maxwell (Max), 1939-49 P, Newark Eagles, Houston Eagles

Manolo, [Manella, Manno], 1916-24 1B, P, Cuban Stars (East & West)

Manuel, (Clown), 1940 OF, Cleveland Bears

Mapp, Dick, 1942 SS, Boston Royal Giants

Mara, Candido, 1948 3B, Memphis Red Sox

Maravale, —, 1923 P, Cuban Stars (ECL)

Marcel, Everett (Sam, Ziggy, Joe), 1939-48 C, Chicago American Giants, Newark Eagles, Baltimore Elite Giants, New York Black Yankees, Kansas City Monarchs

Marcelle, Oliver H. (Ghost) [Marcel, Marcell], 1918-32 3B, SS, Brooklyn Royal Giants, Bacharach Giants, Lincoln Giants, Detroit Stars, Baltimore Black Sox

Marcello, —, 1921 P, Cuban Stars (NNL)

Markham, John Matthew [Marcum], 1930-45 P, Kansas City Monarchs, Monroe Monarchs, Birmingham Black Barons

Markham, Melvin, 1935-36 P, Brooklyn Eagles, Newark Eagles

Marlotica, —, 1911 OF, All Cubans

Marquez, Luis Angel Canena, 1945-48 SS, 2B, 3B, OF, New York Black Yankees, Homestead Grays, Baltimore Elite Giants

Marsans, Armando, 1923 OF, Cuban Stars

Marsellas, David, Jr., 1941 C, New York Black Yankees

Marsh, Lorenzo, 1950 C, Cleveland Buckeyes

Marshall, Jack, 1920-29 P, Chicago American Giants, Detroit Stars, Kansas City Monarchs

Marshall, Robert W. (Bobby), 1909-11 1B, MGR, St. Paul Gophers, Leland Giants, Twin City Gophers, Chicago Giants

Marshall, William James (Jack, Boisy), 1926-44 2B, 3B, 1B, Dayton Marcos, Gilkerson's Union Giants, Chicago Columbia Giants, Cole's American Giants, Chicago American Giants, Philadelphia Stars, Cincinnati-Indianapolis Clowns, Kansas City Monarchs

Martin, Alexander, 1932 officer, Cleveland Cubs

Martin, Dr. A.T., 1923-50 officer, Memphis Red Sox

Martin, Dr. B.B., 1933-50 officer, Memphis Red Sox; officer, NSL

Martin, Dr. John B., 1929-50 officer, Memphis Red Sox, Chicago American Giants; pres, Negro Dixie Lg., NSL, NAL

Martin, Dr. William S., 1927-50 officer, Memphis Red Sox; pres, NSL, officer, NAL

Martin, R., 1885 P, Argyle Hotel

Martin, William (Stack), 1925-28 OF, 1B, C, Indianapolis ABCs, Detroit Stars, Dayton Marcos, Wilmington Potomacs

Martinez, C., 1928 C, Cubans (NNL)

Martinez, Francisco, 1939 P, Cuban Stars

Martinez, Horacio (Rabbit), 1935-47 SS, 3B, New York Cubans, Cuban Stars

Martinez, Pasquel, 1920-28 P, Cuban Stars (NNL), Cuban Stars (East)

Martini, Jose, 1928 P, Cubans (NNL)

Marvarez, Fernando, 1945 INF, Pittsburgh Crawfords

Marvin, Alfred, 1938 P, Kansas City Monarchs

Marvray, Charles, 1949-50 OF,Louisville Buckeyes, Cleveland Buckeyes

Mason, —, 1927 3B, INF, Baltimore Black Sox

Mason, Charles (Corporal), 1922-29 OF, P, Richmond Giants, Bacharach Giants, Lincoln Giants, Newark Stars, Homestead Grays

Mason, Jim, 1932-34 1B, OF, Cuban Stars (ECL), Cubans (NNL), Memphis Red Sox, Washington Pilots

Massey, —, 1930 OF, Louisville White Sox

Massip, Armando, 1920-30 1B, OF, Cuban Stars (ECL), Washington Pilots, Memphis Red Sox

Matchett, Jack, 1940-45 P, Kansas City Monarchs

Mathew, —, 1946 OF, Memphis Red Sox

Mathis, Verdell Sr. (Lefty), 1940-50 P, OF, 1B, Memphis Red Sox, Philadelphia Stars

Matlock, Leroy, 1929-42 P, St. Louis Stars, Detroit Wolves, Washington Pilots, Homestead Grays, Pittsburgh Crawfords, New York Cubans

Matthews, Clifford, 1945 officer, owner, New Orleans Black Pelicans

Matthews, Dell, 1904-05 P, OF, Chicago Union Giants, Leland Giants

Matthews, Dick, 1932-33 P, Monroe Monarchs, New Orleans Crescent Stars

Matthews, Francis Oliver (Fran), 1938-45 1B, Newark Eagles, Boston Royal Giants, Baltimore Elite Giants, New York Cubans

Matthews, Jack, 1923 3B, Toledo Tigers

Matthews, Jesse, 1942 INF, Birmingham Black Barons

Matthews, John, 1919-33 officer, Dayton Marcos

Matthews, William Clarence, 1905-10 SS, 2B, Burlington (Vermont Lg.); New York Black Sox

Maupin, Frank, 1890-92 C, 3B, Lincoln (Neb) Giants, Plattsmouth (Nebraska St. Lg.)

Maxwell, —, 1914 OF, Chicago American Giants

Maxwell, Zearlee (Jiggs), 1931-38 3B, 2B, Monroe Monarchs, Memphis Red Sox

Mayari, —, 1923 1B, Cuban Stars (ECL)

Mayers, George, *see George Meyers*

Mayfield, Fred, 1887 player, Louisville Falls City

Mayo, George (Hot Stuff), 1911-17,1928 1B, OF, Officier, Pittsburgh Giants, Pittsburgh Colored Stars, Hilldale, Pittsburgh Stars of Buffalo

Mays, —, 1937 P, St. Louis Stars, Memphis Red Sox

Mays, Dave, 1937 OF, Kansas City Monarchs

Mays, Willie, 1948-50 OF, Birmingham Black Barons

Mayweather, Eldridge (Chillie, Ed), 1934-46 1B, Monroe Monarchs, Kansas City Monarchs, St. Louis Stars, New Orleans-St. Louis Stars, New York Black Yankees, Boston Blues, Brooklyn Eagles

Mayweather, Elliott, 1928-29 P, Memphis Red Sox

Maywood, —, 1917-19 P, Lincoln Giants

Mazaar, Robert, 1945 officer, Hilldale Club of Philadelphia

McAdoo, Dudley (Tully), 1907-24 1B, Topeka Giants, Kansas City, Kan., Giants, St. Louis Giants, St. Louis Stars, Cleveland Browns, Chicago American Giants

McAllister, Frank (Chip, Bud), 1938-46 P, Indianapolis ABCs, St. Louis Stars, New Orleans-St. Louis Stars, New York Black Yankees, Harrisburg-St. Louis Stars, Brooklyn Brown Dodgers, Cleveland Clippers (USL)

McAllister, George, 1923-34 1B, Birmingham Black Barons, Chicago American Giants, Indianapolis ABCs, Memphis Red Sox, Homestead Grays, Cleveland Red Sox, Detroit Stars

McAllister, Mike, 1921 OF, Kansas City Monarchs

McBride, Fred, 1931-40 1B, OF, Indianapolis ABCs, Chicago American Giants, Birmingham Black Barons

McCabb, —, 1923 P, St. Louis Stars

McCall, (Butch), 1936-38 1B, Chicago American Giants, Birmingham Black Barons, Indianapolis Athletics

McCall, Henry, 1945 OF, Chicago American Giants

McCall, William (Bill), 1922-31 P, Pittsburgh Keystones, Birmingham Black Barons, Kansas City Monarchs, Chicago American Giants, Indianapolis ABCs, Detroit Stars, Toledo Tigers, Cleveland Tigers

McCampbell, Ernest, 1915 player, Kansas City Giants

McCampbell, Tom, 1915 player, Kansas City Giants

McCarey, Willie, 1943-45 P, Cleveland Buckeyes

McCarthy, C.H., 1921 pres, Southeastern Negro Lg.

McCauley, —, 1930 P, Nashville Elite Giants

McClain, Bill, 1933 P, Columbus Blue Birds

McClain, Edward (Boots) [Mclain], 1920-26 INF, P, Dayton Marcos, Cleveland Tate Stars, Toledo Tigers, Cleveland Browns, Detroit Stars, Indianapolis ABCs, Columbus Buckeyes

McClinic, Nathaniel (Nath), 1946-48 OF, Cleveland Buckeyes

McClellan, Dan, 1903-30 P, MGR, Cuban X Giants, Philadelphia Giants, Smart Set, Lincoln Giants, Quaker Giants, Washington Potomacs, Wilmington Potomacs

McClelland, Dr. J.W., 1922 officer, St. Louis Stars

McClure, Robert (Bob), 1920-30 P, Indianapolis ABCs, Cleveland Tate Stars, Baltimore Black Sox, Bacharach Giants, Brooklyn Royal Giants, Toledo Tigers

McClure, Will, 1947 officer, Chattanooga Choo Choos

McCord, Clinton Hill Jr. (Butch), 1947-50 INF, 1B, Baltimore Elite Giants, Chicago American Giants

McCoy, Frank (Chink), 1931-43 C, Newark Stars, Newark Dodgers, Harrisburg-St.Louis Stars

McCoy, Roy, 1932 officer, Washington Pilots

McCoy, Walter, 1945-48 P, Chicago American Giants

McCrary, George, 1943 P, New York Black Yankees

McCreary, Fred, 1938-49 umpire, NNL

McCurine, James, 1946-48 OF, Chicago American Giants

McDaniels, Booker Taliaferro, 1940-49 P, OF, Kansas City Monarchs, Memphis Red Sox

McDaniels, Fred, 1940-50 OF, Memphis Red Sox, Kansas City Monarchs

McDevitt, John J., 1922 officer, Baltimore Black Sox

McDonald, Earl, 1938 officer, Washington Black Senators

McDonald, Luther (Vet), 1927-37 P, St. Louis Stars, Chicago American Giants, Chicago Columbia Giants, Cole's American Giants, Detroit Stars, Memphis Red Sox

McDonald, Webster (Mac), 1918-45 P, MGR, Philadelphia Giants, Richmond Giants, Chicago American Giants, Hilldale, Darby Daisies, Washington Pilots, Philadelphia Stars, Wilmington Potomacs, Detroit Stars, Homestead Grays, Lincoln Giants, Norfolk Stars

McDonnel, —, 1921 P, Bacharach Giants

McDougal, Lemuel (Lem), 1917-20 P, Chicago American Giants, Indianapolis ABCs, Chicago Giants

McDuffie, Terris, 1930-45 P, Of Birmingham Black Barons, Baltimore Black Sox, New York Black Yankees, Newark Eagles, Homestead Grays, Philadelphia Stars, Newark Dodgers, Brooklyn Eagles, Pennsylvania Red Caps

McFall, —, 1940 OF, Cincinnati Buckeyes

McFarland, John, 1944-47 P, New York Black Yankees

McGee, Horace, 1887 manager, Cincinnati Browns

McGowan, Curtis, 1950 P, Memphis Red Sox

McGowan, Malcolm, 1923-41 owner, officer, Bacharach Giants

McHaskell, J.C., 1927-29 1B, Memphis Red Sox

McHenry, Henry (Cream), 1930-50 . P, Kansas City Monarchs, New York Black Yankees, Philadelphia Stars, Indianapolis Clowns, Pennsylvania Red Caps

McIntosh, Jimmy, 1937 C, Detroit Stars

McIntyre, B., 1924 P, Memphis Red Sox

McKamey, —, 1946 SS, Kansas City Monarchs

McKeg, —, 1897 SS, Cuban Giants

McKelvin, Fred [Mckellam], 1942 P, Cincinnati Buckeyes, Cleveland Buckeyes

McKenzie, Herbert, 1950 C, New York Black Yankees

McKinley, —, 1940 P, Chicago American Giants

McKinnis, Gread (Lefty), 1941-49 P, Birmingham Black Barons, Chicago American Giants, Pittsburgh Crawfords

McLain, *see Edward McClain*

McLaughlin, —, 1917-1919 P, 1B, OF, Jewell's ABCs, Lincoln Giants

McLaurin, Felix, 1942-49 OF, Jacksonville Red Caps, Birmingham Black Barons, New York Black Yankees, Chicago American Giants

McLawn, —, 1948 C, Newark Eagles

McMahon, Jess, 1911-14 officer, Lincoln Giants

McMahon, Rod, 1911-14 officer, Lincoln Giants

McMeans, Willie, 1945 P, Chicago American Giants

McMillan, Earl, 1923 OF, Toledo Tigers

McMullin, Clarence [Mccullin], 1945-49 OF, Kansas City Monarchs, Houston Eagles

McMurray, William, 1909-22 C, St. Paul Gophers, St. Louis Giants

McNair, Hurley Allen (Bugger), 1912-42 OF, Chicago Giants, Gilkerson's Union Giants, Chicago American Giants, Detroit Stars, Chicago Union Giants, Kansas City Monarchs, Cincinnati Tigers, All Nations; umpire, NAL

McNeal, Clyde, 1945-50 SS, Chicago American Giants

McNeil, —, 1918-20 1B, C, Dayton Marcos

McNeil, William (Red), 1930-33 OF, P, Louisville White Sox, Louisville Black Caps, Nashville Elite Giants, Louisville Red Caps

McQueen, Pete, 1932,1937-45 OF, Memphis Red Sox, New York Black Yankees, Little Rock Black Travelers

McReynolds, —, 1916 OF, P, Bowser's ABCs, Indianapolis ABCs

Meade, (Chick), 1916-22 3B, SS, OF, Pittsburgh Colored Stars, Hilldale, Pittsburgh Stars of Buffalo, Bacharach Giants, Baltimore Black Sox, Harrisburg Giants, Indianapolis ABCs

Meadows, Helburn, 1934 OF, Cincinnati Tigers

Means, Lewis, 1920-27 2B, 1B, C, Bacharach Giants, Birmingham Black Barons

Means, Thomas, 1900-04 P, Chicago Unions, Chicago Union Giants

Meckling, S., 1909 C, Kansas City Royal Giants

Mederos, Jesus (Frank), 1911-20 P, OF, All Cubans, Bacharach Giants

Medina, Lazarus (Lazaro) [Chapman], 1944-46 P, Cincinnati- Indianapolis Clowns, Indianapolis Clowns

Medina, Pedro, 1905 C, Cuban Stars of Santiago

Medley, Calvin, 1946 P, New York Black Yankees

Medros, —, 1910 P, Cuban Stars

Mellito, *see Emilio Navarro*

Mellix, George Ralph (Lefty), 1922-34,1946 P, MGR, Homestead Grays, Newark Browns, Brooklyn Brown Dodgers

Mello, Harry, 1946 INF, Chicago American Giants

Melton, —, 1916 P, St. Louis Giants

Melton, Elbert, 1928-29 OF, Brooklyn Cuban Giants, Lincoln Giants, Baltimore Black Sox

Mendez, Jose De La Caridad (Joe), 1908-26 P, SS, 3B, 2B, MGR, Cuban Stars, Stars of Cuba, All Nations, Los Angeles White Sox, Chicago American Giants, Detroit Stars, Kansas City Monarchs

Mendieta, Inocente, 1912-13 2B, Cuban Stars, Long Branch (NJ) Cubans

Meredith, Buford (Geetchie), 1923-31 SS, 2B, Birmingham Black Barons, Nashville Elite Giants, Memphis Red Sox

Merchant, Henry L. (Speed), 1940-50 P, OF, Chicago American Giants, Cincinnati-Indianapolis Clowns, Indianapolis Clowns

Merritt, B., 1905-17 P, Brooklyn Royal Giants, Lincoln Giants

Merritt, Schute, 1934-35 UTIL, Newark Dodgers

Mesa, Andres Anares, 1948 OF, Indianapolis Clowns

Mesa, Pablo, 1921-27 OF, Cuban Stars (ECL)

Metz, —, 1939 player, Kansas City Monarchs

Meyers, C., 1908 LF, Brooklyn Colored Giants

Meyers, George (Deacon) [Myers, Mayers], 1921-26 P, 1B, St. Louis Stars, Dayton Marcos, St. Louis Giants, Toledo Tigers

Meyers, L., 1908 2B, Brooklyn Colored Giants

Miarka, Stanley V., 1950 2B, P, Chicago American Giants

Mickey, James, 1940 SS, 3B, Chicago American Giants, Birmingham Black Barons

Mickey, John, 1898 P, Celeron Acme Colored Giants (Iron and Oil Lg.)

Miles, —, 1940 P, Cincinnati Buckeyes

Miles, John (Jack, Mule, Sonny Boy), 1934-38 OF, 3B, Chicago American Giants, Philadelphia Stars

Miles, Willie, 1923-27 OF, 1B, 3B, Toledo Tigers, Memphis Red Sox Cleveland Tate Stars, Cleveland Browns, Cleveland Elites, Cleveland Hornets, Homestead Grays

Miles, Zell, 1946-49 OF, 3B, Chicago American Giants

Miller, —, 1911-20 C, Pittsburgh Giants, Dayton Marcos

Miller, —, 1934 2B, Cincinnati Tigers

Miller, —, 1934 SS, New Orleans Crescent Stars

Miller, A., 1927 OF, Memphis Red Sox, Birmingham Black Barons

Miller, Bob (Ruby), 1923-28 2B, 3B, Memphis Red Sox, Birmingham Black Barons

Miller, Dempsey (Dimp), 1926-45 P, MGR, Cleveland Hornets, Cleveland Tigers, Nashville Elite Giants, Detroit Stars, Detroit Giants, Cleveland Cubs, Birmingham Black Barons, Memphis Red Sox, Kansas City Monarchs

Miller, Eddie (Buck), 1924-31 P, SS, 3B, Chicago American Giants, Indianapolis ABCs, Homestead Grays, Chicago Columbia Giants

Miller, Eugene, 1909 OF, St. Paul Gophers

Miller, Frank, 1887-97 P, OF, Pittsburgh Keystones, Cuban Giants, Cuban X Giants, New York Gorhams (Middle States Lg.), Philadelphia Giants

Miller, Henry Joseph (Hank), 1938-49 P, Philadelphia Stars

Miller, Jasper, 1930,1940 P, Memphis Red Sox

Miller, Joe, 1895-03 P, OF, Page Fence Giants, Columbia Giants, Adrian (Michigan State Lg), Chicago Union Giants

Miller, L., 1912-23 3B, 2B, Smart Set, Lincoln Giants, Lincoln Stars, Brooklyn Royal Giants, Bacharach Giants, Baltimore Black Sox

Miller, Leroy (Flash), 1935-43 SS, 2B, Newark Dodgers, New York Black Yankees

Miller, Ned, 1937 1B, Indianapolis Athletics

Miller, Percy, 1921-33 P, OF, St. Louis Stars, St. Louis Giants, Nashville Elite Giants, Chicago Giants, Kansas City Monarchs

Miller, Pleas (Hub), 1913-16 P, West Baden, (Ind) Sprudels, St. Louis Giants

Miller, W., 1940 P, Chicago American Giants

Milliner, Eugene J., 1903-10 OF, Chicago Union Giants, St. Paul Gophers, Kansas City Royal Giants

Millon, Herald, 1946-47 UTIL, Chicago American Giants

Mills, Charles A., 1909-24 officer, St. Louis Giants, St. Louis Black Sox

Milton, C., 1933-34 INF, Cleveland Red Sox, Columbus Blue Birds

Milton, Edward, 1926-28 OF, 2B, Cleveland Elites

Milton, Henry, 1932-43 OF, Chicago Giants, Indianapolis ABCs, Chicago American Giants, Brooklyn Royal Giants, Kansas City Monarchs, New York Black Yankees, Brooklyn Eagles

Mimms, —, 1932 P, Columbus Turfs

Mincey, —, 1939 P, Philadelphia Stars

Minor, George, 1944-49 OF, Chicago American Giants, Cleveland Buckeyes, Louisville Buckeyes

Minoso, Saturnino Orestes Arrieta Armas (Minnie), 1945-48 3B, New York Cubans

Mirabel, Juanelo, —, 1922-32,1949-50 P, pres, Cuban Stars (ECL) New York Cubans

Mirable, Autorio, 1939-40 C, New York Cuban Stars

Miraka, Stanley, see Stanley Miarka

Mirall, —, 1930 3B, Brooklyn Royal Giants

Miranda, P., 1916 player, Cuban Stars

Miro, Pedro, 1945-48 2B, New York Cubans

Missouri, Jim, 1937-41 P, Philadelphia Stars

Mitchell, —, 1901 C, Chicago Union Giants

Mitchell, —, 1914 P, Pittsburgh Giants

Mitchell, A., 1884 player, Philadelphia Mutual B.B.C.

Mitchell, Alonzo (Fluke, Hooks), 1921-41 MGR, 1B, P, club officer, Jacksonville Red Caps, Cleveland Bears, Atlanta Black Crackers, Jacksonville Red Caps, Indianapolis ABCs, Baltimore Black Sox, Bacharach Giants, Harrisburg Giants, Birmingham Black Barons, Akron Tyrites

Mitchell, Arthur Harold, 1939 INF, New York Black Yankees

Mitchell, Bob, 1950 P, Cleveland Buckeyes

Mitchell, (Bud), 1929-34 OF, P, C, Hilldale, Darby Daisies, Bacharach Giants

Mitchell, Charlie, 1942 C, Boston Royal Giants

Mitchell, George, 1925-49 P, MGR, bus. mgr, Chicago American Giants, Indianapolis ABCs, Montgomery Grey Sox, Cleveland Cubs, Mounds City, Illinois, Blues (became Indianapolis ABCs), St. Louis Stars, New Orleans-St. Louis Stars, New York Black Yankees, Harrisburg-St. Louis Stars, Houston Eagles, Cleveland Stars, Detroit Stars, Kansas City Monarchs

Mitchell, John, 1932 C, OF, Montgomery Grey Sox

Mitchell, Leonard Otto, 1930-31 2B, Birmingham Black Barons, Louisville White Sox

Mitchell, Robert, 1923-24 C, OF, St. Louis Stars, Birmingham Black Barons

Moles, (Lefty), 1935 P, Philadelphia Stars

Molina, —, 1929-30 P, Cuban Stars (NNL)

Molina, Agustin (Tinti), 1907-31 1B, OF, C, MGR., Officer, Cuban Stars, Cuban Stars (NNL)

Mollett, —, 1913-16 2B, SS, Mohawk Giants, Lincoln Stars

Molloy, —, 1922 P, Bacharach Giants

Mongin, Sam, 1908-27 3B, 2B, Brooklyn Royal Giants, Lincoln Stars, Lincoln Giants, Bacharach Giants, St. Louis Giants Baltimore Black Sox, Philadelphia Giants

Monceville, [Monchile] —, 1930-31 OF, Cuban Stars (East & West)

Monroe, Al, 1937 sec'y, NAL

Monroe, Bill, 1920,1927 3B, SS, Pittsburgh Stars of Buffalo Baltimore Black Sox

Monroe, William (Bill), 1896-1914 2B, 3B, Chicago Unions, Philadelphia Giants, Brooklyn Royal Giants, Chicago American Giants, Cuban X Giants

Montalvo, Estaban, 1923-28 1B, OF, Cuban Stars (NNL), Lincoln Giants

Montgomery, A.G., 1926 sec'y, NSL

Montgomery, Lou, 1942 P, OF, INF, Cincinnati Clowns

Moody, —, 1931 SS, Memphis Red Sox

Moody, —, 1940 P, Birmingham Black Barons

Moody, Lee, 1944-47 1B, Kansas City Monarchs

Moody, Willis, 1921-29 OF, Pittsburgh Keystones, Homestead Grays

Moore, Charles, 1943 umpire, NNL

Moore, Clarence Lee (C.L., Cool Breeze), 1945-48 MGR., Officer, owner, Asheville Blues; pres. Negro American Association

Moore, Excell, 1950 P, Cleveland Buckeyes

Moore, Harry W. (Mike), 1894-1912 OF, 1B, 3B, Chicago Unions, Algona (IA) Brownies, Cuban X Giants, Philadelphia Giants, Leland Giants, Chicago Giants, Lincoln Giants

Moore, Henry L., 1937-38 officer, St. Louis Stars, Birmingham Black Barons

Moore, James (Red), 1936-40 1B, Newark Eagles, Atlanta Black Crackers, Baltimore Elite Giants, Indianapolis ABCs

Moore, John, 1929 SS, Birmingham Black Barons

Moore, L., 1910-20 OF, St. Louis Giants, Bowser's ABCs, West Baden (Ind.) Sprudels, Lincoln Giants, Louisville Sox

Moore, N., 1920-24 OF, Detroit Stars

Moore, P.D., 1932 C, Monroe Monarchs

Moore, Ralph (Squire, Roy, Square), 1921-28 P, 1B, Memphis Red Sox, Kansas City Monarchs, Cleveland Hornets, Cleveland Tigers, Cleveland Tate Stars, Birmingham Black Barons

Moore, Shirley, 1915 P, Bowser's ABCs, Louisville Sox

Moore, Walter (Dobie), 1920-26 SS, OF, Kansas City Monarchs

Moorhead, Albert, 1925-32 C, Chicago Giants, Cleveland Cubs

Morales, Ismael, 1932 OF, Cuban Stars

Moran, Francisco, 1911 OF, Cuban Stars, All Cubans

Morefield, Fred, 1945-46 OF, Pittsburgh Crawfords

Morehead, Albert, 1943 C, Birmingham Black Barons, Chicago Brown Bombers

Moreland, Nate, 1940-45 P, Baltimore Elite Giants, Kansas City Monarchs

Morgan, —, 1928 OF, Birmingham Black Barons

Morgan, John. L. (Pepper), 1937 OF, Memphis Red Sox, Indianapolis Athletics

Morgan, William (Wild Bill), 1945-48 P, Memphis Red Sox, Baltimore Elite Giants, Birmingham Black Barons

Morin, Eugenio, 1910-23 2B, 3B, C, Cuban Stars, Cuban Stars (NNL)

Morney, Leroy, 1931-44 SS, 3B, 2B, Monroe Monarchs, Columbus Blue Birds, Cleveland Giants, Pittsburgh Crawfords, Columbus Elite Giants, Washington Elite Giants, New York Black Yankees, Philadelphia Stars, Chicago American Giants, Birmingham Black Barons, Cincinnati Clowns, Toledo Crawfords, Homestead Grays, Nashville Elite Giants

Morris, Al, 1927-30 OF, 2B, Nashville Elite Giants, Louisville White Sox

Morris, Barney (Big Ad), 1932-48 P, Monroe Monarchs, Pittsburgh Crawfords, Cuban Stars, New York Cubans, Toledo Crawfords, New Orleans Stars

Morris, F.B., 1948 sec'y, Negro American Association

Morris, Harold (Yellowhorse), 1924-36 P, Kansas City Monarchs, Detroit Stars, Chicago American Giants, Monroe Monarchs

Morrison, Jimmy, 1930 UTIL, Memphis Red Sox

Morrison, W., 1925 1B, Cleveland Browns

Mortin, R., 1885 P, Argyle Giants

Morton, —, 1917 2B, Havana Red Sox

Morton, Ferdinand Q., 1935-38 commissioner, NNL

Morton, John, 1935 OF, Brooklyn Eagles

Morton, Sidney Douglas (Sy), 1940-47 SS, 2B, Philadelphia Stars, Pittsburgh Crawfords, Chicago American Giants

Moseley, Beauregard F., 1910-11 officer, Leland Giants

Moses, —, 1938-40 P, Kansas City Monarchs

Mosley, —, 1934-35 P, New Orleans Crescent Stars, Homestead Grays

Mosley, William, 1928-33 officer, Detroit Stars

Moss, Porter (Ankle Ball), 1934-44 P, Cincinnati Tigers, Memphis Red Sox

Mothell, Carroll Ray (Dink), 1920-34 OF, 2B, 1B, SS, C, All Nations, Kansas City Monarchs, Cleveland Stars, Chicago American Giants

Mott, —, 1931 3B, Birmingham Black Barons

Mullen, A., 1928 OF, Birmingham Black Barons

Mungin, J., 1925-27 P, Baltimore Black Sox, Harrisburg Giants

Munoz, Joseito (Joe), 1909-16 P, OF, Cuban Stars, Stars of Cuba, Jersey City Cubans, Long Branch Cubans

Munroe, Elmer, 1942 P, Boston Royal Giants

Munroe, William, see William Monroe

Murdock, —, 1924 P, Indianapolis ABCs

Murphy, —, 1908 CF, Brooklyn Colored Giants

Murphy, —, 1915 OF, Chicago American Giants

Murphy, —, 1922 P, Kansas City Monarchs

Murphy, Al, 1936-37 P, Indianapolis Athletics, Birmingham Black Barons, Cincinnati Tigers

Murray, Charles, 1949-50 player, Cleveland Buckeyes

Murray, Mitchell, 1920-32 C, Indianapolis ABCs, Dayton Marcos, Cleveland Tate Stars, Toledo Tigers, St. Louis Stars, Chicago American Giants

Muse, B., 1922,1934 P, New Orleans Crescent Stars, Hilldale, Monroe Monarchs

Myers, —, 1908-10 SS, Pop Watkins Stars, Brooklyn Royal Giants

Nance, —, 1929 SS, Chicago American Giants

Napier, Euthumn (Eudie), 1935-50 C, Homestead Grays, Pittsburgh Crawfords

Napoleon, Lawrence (Larry), 1946-47 P, Kansas City Monarchs

Naranjo, Pedro, 1950 P, Indianapolis Clowns

Nash, William, 1928-34 P, OF, Birmingham Black Barons, Memphis Red Sox, Nashville Elite Giants

Navarrette, Ramundo, 1950 P, New York Cubans

Navarro, Emilio (Millito), 1928-29 INF, Cuban Stars (East)

Navarro, Raymond Raul, 1945-46 OF, INF, C, Cincinnati-Indianapolis Clowns, Indianapolis Clowns

Neal, George, 1910-11 2B, Chicago Giants, Kansas City Kan. Giants

Nears, (Red), 1940 C, OF, Memphis Red Sox

Neely, —, 1932-33 P, Louisville Black Caps, Cuban Stars

Neil, Ray, 1942-50 2B, Cincinnati Clowns, Indianapolis Clowns

Nelson, Clyde, 1939,1943-49 3B, 2B, 1B, OF, Chicago Brown Bombers, Chicago American Giants, Cleveland Buckeyes, Indianapolis Clowns, Indianapolis ABCs

Nelson, Everett (Ace), 1922,1931-33 P, Montgomery Grey Sox, Detroit Stars

Nelson, John, 1887-1903 P, OF, New York Gorhams, Cuban Giants, Cuban X Giants, Philadelphia Giants, Philadelphia Gorhams, (Middle States Lg.) Ansonia Cuban Giants (Connecticut St. Lg.), Trenton Cuban Giants (Middle States Lg.), Adrian Page Fence Giants

Nesbit, Dr. E.E., 1929 officer, Memphis Red Sox

Nestor, S. Jace, 1926 OF, Lincoln Giants

Newberry, Henry, 1947 P, Chicago American Giants

Newberry, James Lee (Jimmie), 1943-50 P, Birmingham Black Barons

Newberry, Richard, 1947 SS, Chicago American Giants

Newcombe, Donald (Don), 1944-45 P, Newark Eagles

Newkirk, Alexander (Alex), 1946-49 P, New York Black Yankees, New York Cubans

Newman, —, 1940 P, Memphis Red Sox

Newsome, Omer, 1923-29 P, Indianapolis ABCs, Washington Potomacs, Detroit Stars, Dayton Marcos, Memphis Red Sox, Wilmington Potomacs

Newson, —, 1940 OF, Newark Eagles

Nichols, Charles, 1885 OF, Argyle Hotel

Nichols, William, 1936 P, Newark Eagles

Nirsa, —, 1923 OF, Cuban Stars

Nix, —, 1939 P, Brooklyn Royal Giants

Nixon, —, 1940-41 OF, Birmingham Black Barons

Noble, Carlos, 1950 P, New York Cubans

Noble, Juan (John, Gyp), 1949-50 P, New York Cubans

Noble, Rafael Miguel (Ray, Sam), 1945-50 C, New York Cubans

Noel, Eddie, 1921 P, Nashville Elite Giants

Nolan, —, 1916-17 C, St. Louis Giants, Kansas City Colored Giants

Norman, Alton (Ed), 1920-26 SS, Lincoln Giants, Cleveland Elites

Norman, (Bud, Ace), 1940 P, Indianapolis Crawfords

Norman, Garrett, 1923 OF, Memphis Red Sox

Norman, Jim, 1909 INF, Kansas City, Kansas, Giants

Norman, William (Shin), 1906-10 P, Leland Giants, Union Giants

Norris, (Slim), 1930 3B, Louisville White Sox

Norwood, C.H., 1887 player, Philadelphia Pythians

Norwood, Walter, 1933 officer, Detroit Stars

Nunley, Beauford, 1934 1B, Memphis Red Sox

Nuttall, H. (Bill), 1924-26 P, Lincoln Giants, Bacharach Giants

Nutter, Isaac H., 1927-28 officer, Bacharach Giants, pres., Eastern Lg.

O'Bryant, Willie [O'Brien], 1932 SS, OF, Washington Pilots

O'Dell, John Wesley, 1949-50 P, Houston Eagles

Oden, J. Webb, 1927-32 SS, OF, Birmingham Black Barons, Knoxville Giants, Louisville Black Caps, Memphis Red Sox

O'Farrell, Orlando, 1949 SS, Indianapolis Clowns, Philadelphia Stars

Offert, Mose, 1925-26 P, Indianapolis ABCs

Oldham, Jimmy, 1920-23 P, St. Louis Giants, St. Louis Stars

Oliver, James (Pee Wee), 1943-46 SS, Cincinnati-indianapolis Clowns, Birmingham Black Barons, Indianapolis Clowns

Oliver, John, 1885 3B, Brooklyn Remsens

Oliver, John Henry, 1945-46 SS, Memphis Red Sox, Cleveland Buckeyes

Oliver, Leonard E., 1913 SS, Philadelphia Giants

Oliver, Martin, 1930-34 C, OF, Birmingham Black Barons, Louisville Black Caps, Memphis Red Sox

Oms, Alejandro (Walla Walla), 1917-35 OF, Cuban Stars (ECL), New York Cubans, All Cubans

O'Neil, John Jordan (Buck), 1937-55 1B, MGR, Memphis Red Sox, Kansas City Monarchs

O'Neill, —, 1910 P, West Baden (Ind.) Sprudels

O'Neill, Charles, 1921-23 C, Columbus Buckeyes, Bacharach Giants, Toledo Tigers, Chicago American Giants

Ora, Clarence, 1932 OF, Cleveland Cubs

Orange, Grady, 1925-31 SS, 2B, 3B, Birmingham Black Barons, Kansas City Monarchs, Detroit Stars, Cleveland Tigers

Ormes, A.W., 1911 player, Leland Giants

Ortiz, Julio Arango (Ortie, Bill), 1944-45 OF, SS, Cincinnati-Indianapolis Clowns, Kansas City Monarchs

Ortiz, Rafaelito, 1948 P, Chicago American Giants

Osborne, —, 1905 P, Philadelphia Giants

Oscal, see Oscar Levis

Osley, —, 1938 P, Birmingham Black Barons

Osorio, Alberto, 1949 P, Louisville Buckeyes

Otis, Amos, 1921 OF, Nashville Elite Giants

Ousley, Guy C., 1931-32 SS, 2B, 3B, Chicago Columbia Giants, Cleveland Cubs, Memphis Red Sox

Overton, Albert, 1937 P, Philadelphia Stars

Overton, John, 1925 officer, Indianapolis ABCs

Owens, —, 1934,1937 P, Newark Dodgers, Newark Eagles

Owens, A., 1928 SS, Cleveland Tigers

Owens, Albert, 1930-31 P, Nashville Elite Giants

Owens, Aubrey, 1920-25 P, Indianapolis ABCs, Chicago American Giants, New Orleans Caulfield Ads, Chicago Giants

Owens, Dewitt, 1936-39 OF, 2B, Birmingham Black Barons, Indianapolis ABCs

Owens, Jackson, 1950 P, Chicago American Giants

Owens, Raymond (Smokey, Kankol), 1939-42 P, OF, Cleveland Bears, Cleveland Buckeyes, New Orleans-St. Louis Stars, Cincinnati Clowns, Cincinnati Buckeyes, Jacksonville Red Caps

Owens, W.E., 1887 player, Cincinnati Browns

Owens, W. Oscar, 1913-31 P, 1B, OF, Homestead Grays, Indianapolis ABCs, Pittsburgh Keystones

Owens, William John (Willie), 1923-33 SS, 2B, P, Washington Potomacs, Chicago American Giants, Indianapolis ABCs, Dayton Marcos, Birmingham Black Barons, Memphis Red Sox, Detroit Stars, Cleveland Elites, Harrisburg Giants, Brooklyn Royal Giants, Wilmington Potomacs

Pace, —, 1930 OF, Nashville Elite Giants

Pace, Benjamin (Brother), 1922 C, Pittsburgh Keystones, Homestead Grays

Padrone, Juan Luis, 1909-26 P, 2B, OF, Cuban Stars (ECL), Smart Set, Long Branch (NJ) Cubans, Chicago American Giants, Lincoln Giants, Cuban Stars (NNL), Indianapolis ABCs, Brooklyn Royal Giants, Birmingham Black Barons, All Cubans

Page, Allen, 1945-50 vice pres, tres, NSL; officer, New Orleans Creoles; promoter

Page, R., 1925 officer, Indianapolis ABCs

Page, Theodore Roosevelt (Ted), 1926-37 OF, 1B, Newark Stars, Homestead Grays, Pittsburgh Crawfords, New York Black Yankees, Newark Eagles, Philadelphia Stars, Brooklyn Royal Giants, Baltimore Black Sox, Quaker Giants, Brooklyn Eagles

Pages, Pedro, 1939,1947 OF, New York Cubans

Paige, Leroy (Satchel), 1926-50 P, Chattanoogo Black Lookouts, Birmingham Black Barons, Cleveland Cubs, Pittsburgh Crawfords, Kansas City Monarchs, New York Black Yankees, Satchel Paige's All-Stars, Philadelphia Stars, Memphis Red Sox, Baltimore Black Sox

Paine, Henry, 1884 OF, Brooklyn Remsens

Paine, John, 1887 OF, Philadelphia Pythians

Palm, Robert Clarence (Spoony), 1927-46 C, Birmingham Black Barons, St. Louis Stars, Detroit Stars, Cleveland Giants, Homestead Grays, Brooklyh Eagles, New York Black Yankees, Philadelphia Stars, Cole's American Giants, Akron Tyrites, Pittsburgh Crawfords

Palma, —, 1930 P, Cuban Stars (NNL)

Palmer, Earl, 1918-19 OF, Chicago Union Giants, Lincoln Giants

Palmer, Curtis, 1949-50 OF, New York Black Yankees

Palmer, James, 1887 UTIL, New York Gorhams

Palmer, Leon, 1926,1930 OF, Dayton Marcos, Louisville White Sox

Panier, —, 1917-20 P, Cuban Giants, Philadelphia Giants

Pape, Ed, 1946 OF, Homestead Grays

Pardee, —, 1925 C, Birmingham Black Barons

Pareda, H. (Monk, Pastor), 1910-21 P, 1B, Stars of Cuba, Cuban Stars, Cuban Stars (NNL)

Parego, George A. [Parago], 1885-88 P, OF, 1B, Argyle Hotel, Cuban Giants, Trenton Cuban Giants (Middle States Lg.), Cuban Giants

Parker, —, 1890-1908 OF, Genuine Cuban Giants, Chicago Unions, New York Colored Giants

Parker, —, 1921-23 1B, OF, Pittsburgh Stars of Buffalo, Baltimore Black Sox, Memphis Red Sox

Parker, Jack, 1938 INF, Pittsburgh Crawfords

Parker, (Sonny), 1942-43 P, Chicago Brown Bombers, Kansas City Monarchs, Harrisburg-St.Louis Stars

Parker, Thomas (Tom, Big Train), 1929-48 P, OF, MGR, Memphis Red Sox, Indianapolis ABCs, Monroe Monarchs, Homestead Grays, New Orleans-St. Louis Stars, New York Black Yankees, Harrisburg-St. Louis Stars, New York Cubans, Boston Blues, Indianapolis Athletics, Nashville Elite Giants, Columbus Elite Giants

Parker, Willie (Lefty), 1918-20 P, Lincoln Giants, Baltimore Black Sox

Parkinson, (Parky), 1950 P, Houston Eagles

Parks, Charles Edison (Charlie, Hunky), 1940-47 C, Newark Eagles

Parks, John, 1939-47 C, OF, New York Black Yankees, Newark Eagles

Parks, Joseph B., 1909-19 OF, C, SS, Cuban Giants, Philadelphia Giants, Brooklyn Royal Giants, Pennsylvania Red Caps of New York

Parks, Sam, 1945 officer, Memphis Grey Sox

Parks, William (Bubber), 1910-20 SS, 2B, OF, Chicago Giants, Lincoln Giants, Chicago American Giants, Lincoln Stars, Pennsylvania Red Caps of New York, Philadelphia Giants

Parnell, Roy (Red), 1926-50 OF, 1B, MGR, Birmingham Black Barons, Monroe Monarchs, New Orleans Crescent Stars, Columbus Elite Giants, Philadelphia Stars, Pittsburgh Crawfords, Houston Eagles, Nashville Elite Giants, New York Cubans Stars

Parpetti, Augustin, 1909-23 1B, OF, Cuban Stars, Kansas City Monarchs, Bacharach Giants, Richmong Giants

Parris, Jonathan Clyde (The Dude), 1946-49 1B, 3B, OF, New York Black Yankees, Louisville Buckeyes

Parson, —, 1908 P, Genuine Cuban Giants

Parsons, A.S., 1895-97 MGR, Adrian (MI) Page Fence Giants

Partlow, Roy (Silent Roy), 1934-50 P, Cincinnati Tigers, Memphis Red Sox, Homestead Grays, Philadelphia Stars

Passon, Harry, 1934 officer, Bacharach Giants

Pastoria, —, 1924 P, Cuban Stars (NNL)

Pate, Archie, 1909,1917 OF, St. Paul Gophers, Chicago Giants

Patterson, —, 1886 OF, New York Gorhams

Patterson, —, 1941-43 OF, C, New York Black Yankees

Patterson, Andrew L. (Pat), 1934-49 2B, 3B, OF, Pennsylvania Red Caps Cleveland Red Sox, Pittsburgh Crawfords, Kansas City Monarchs, Philadelphia Stars, Newark Eagles, Houston Eagles

Patterson, Gabriel, 1945-50 OF, Pittsburgh Crawfords, Homestead Grays, New York Black Yankees, Philadelphia Stars

Patterson, John W. (Pat), 1890-1906 2B, OF, SS, MGR, Lincoln (Nebraska) Giants, Page Fence Giants, Columbia Giants of Chicago, Philadelphia Giants, Cuban X Giants, Cuban Giants, Quaker Giants, of New York, Brooklyn Royal Giants, Chicago Union Giants, Plattsmouth (Nebraska St. Lg.)

Patterson, Roy (Willie), 1950 C, New York Cubans

Patterson, William B., 1914-25 MGR, Houston Black Buffaloes, Austin Senators, Birmingham Black Barons

Patton, —, 1909 OF, P, Philadelphia Giants

Patton, —, 1926 P, St. Louis Stars

Paul, —, 1908 SS, Brooklyn Colored Giants

Payne, —, 1926-31 2B, P, Brooklyn Royal Giants, Newark Stars, Philadelphia Giants

Payne, —, 1928 OF, Birmingham Black Barons

Payne, Andrew H. (Jap), 1902-22 OF, Philadelphia Giants, Cuban X Giants, Leland Giants, Chicago American Giants, Chicago Union Giants, New York Central Red Caps, Brooklyn Royal Giants, Pennsylvania Red Caps of NY, Lincoln Stars

Payne, Ernest (Rusty), 1937,1940 OF, Cincinnati Tigers, Indianapolis Crawfords

Payne, James, 1887 OF, Baltimore Lord Baltimore, Cuban Giants

Payne, Tom, 1933 OF, Homestead Grays, Baltimore Black Sox

Payne, William (Doc), 1898 OF, Celeron Acme Colored Giants (Iron and Oil Lg.)

Peace, Warren, 1945-48 P, Newark Eagles

Peacock, —, 1933 3B, Homestead Grays

Peak, Rufus, 1931 officer, Detroit Stars

Pearson, Frank (Ivy, Wahoo), 1945-50 P, Memphis Red Sox, Chicago American Giants

Pearson, Jimmy, 1949 P, New York Cubans

Pearson, Leonard Curtis (Lennie, Hoss), 1937-50 OF, 3B, SS, 1B, MGR, Newark Eagles, Baltimore Elite Giants, St. Louis Stars

Peatross, Maurice, 1947 1B, Homestead Grays

Pedemonte, —, 1926 P, 3B, OF, Cuban Stars (NNL)

Pedroso, Eustaquio, 1910-30 P, OF, 1B, C, Cuban Stars, All Cubans, Cuban Stars (ECL), Cuban Stars (NNL)

Pedroso, [Fernando Diaz] (El Bicho), 1945-50-INF, OF, New York Cubans

Peebles, A.J., 1933 officer, Columbus Blue Birds

Peeks, A.J., 1932 officer, Atlanta Black Crackers

Peeples, Nathaniel, 1950 C, Kansas City Monarchs, Indianapolis Clowns

Peete, Charles, 1950 OF, Indianapolis Clowns

Pelham, William (Don), 1933-38 SS, OF, Bacharach Giants, Atlanta Black Crackers

Pellas, —, 1923 P, Cuban Stars (NNL)

Pena, —, 1929 C, 1B, Cuban Stars (NNL)

Pendleton, James (Jim), 1948 SS, Chicago American Giants

Pennington, —, 1929 P, Nashville Elite Giants

Pennington, Arthur David (Art, Superman), 1940-50 OF, 1B, 2B, Chicago American Giants, Pittsburgh Crawfords

Penno, Dan, 1893-1896 P, OF, 2B, Cuban Giants, Cuban X Giants

Penoy, —, 1932 C, Pennsylvania Red Caps

Perdue, Frank M., 1920-34 pres, NSL; officer, Birmingham Black Barons

Pereira, Jose (Pepin), 1947 P, Baltimore Elite Giants

Perez, Javier (Blue), 1942-45 3B, New York Cubans, Cuban Stars

Perez, Jose (Pepin), 1911-37 P, 1B, C, 2B, SS, 3B, Cuban Stars (ECL), Cuban Stars (NNL), Harrisburg Giants, Bacharach Giants, Hilldale, New York Cubans, Homestead Grays, Brooklyn Eagles, Madison Stars

Perez, Luis, *see Luis Perez Caballero*

Perkins, William George (Bill), 1928-48 C, OF, MGR, Birmingham Black Barons, Cleveland Cubs, Pittsburgh Crawfords, Cleveland Stars, Philadelphia Stars, Baltimore Elite Giants, New York Black Yankees, Homestead Grays

Perry, Alonzo Thomas, 1940-50 P, 1B, Homestead Grays, Birmingham Black Barons

Perry, Carlisle (Carl), 1921-26 2B, 3B, SS, Detroit Stars, Bacharach Giants, Washington Potomacs, Lincoln Giants, Cleveland Browns, Baltimore Black Sox, Indianapolis ABCs, Hilldale, Cleveland Tate Stars, Richmond Giants, Norfolk Stars

Perry, Don, 1921-27 1B, Madison Stars, Washington Braves, Harrisburg Giants

Perry, Ed, 1887 player, Washington Capital City

Perry, Hank, 1926,1934 P, Hilldale, Newark Dodgers

Pervis, —, 1932,1937 P, Monroe Monarchs, Birmingham Black Barons

Peters, Frank, 1916-23 SS, Chicago Union Giants, Peters Union Giants

Peters, William S., 1887-1923 1B, owner, MGR, Chicago Unions, Peters Union Giants

Peterson, Harvey (Pete), 1931-36,1946 OF, P, INF, Montgomery Grey Sox, Birmingham Black Barons, Memphis Red Sox, Cincinnati Tigers, Cleveland Clippers(USL)

Peterson, L., 1885 1B, Brooklyn Remsens

Petricola, —, 1924 P, Cuban Stars (NNL)

Pettus, William Thomas (Zack), 1909-23 C, 1B, 2B, SS, MGR, Kansas City Giants, Leland Giants, Chicago Giants, Lincoln Stars, Lincoln Giants, St. Louis Giants, Hilldale, Bacharach Giants, Richmond Giants, Harrisburg Giants, Brooklyn Royal Giants

Petway, —, 1931-32 SS, 2B, Nashville Elite Giants, Birmingham Black Barons, Louisville Black Caps

Petway, Bruce, 1906-25 C, OF, MGR, Leland Giants, Brooklyn Royal Giants, Philadelphia Giants, Chicago American Giants, Detroit Stars

Petway, Howard, 1906 P, Leland Giants

Petway, Sherley (Charlie), 1937-44 C, MGR, Detroit Stars, Chicago Brown Bombers, Cleveland Buckeyes

Pfiffer, —, 1937 3B, St. Louis Stars

Phillips, —, 1923 SS, 2B, Nashville Elite Giants, Detroit Stars

Phillips, —, 1927 P, Birmingham Black Barons

Phillips, John, 1939 P, Baltimore Elite Giants

Phillips, Norris, 1942-43 P, Kansas City Monarchs, Memphis Red Sox

Pierce, Herbert, 1925-26 C, Homestead Grays

Pierce, Leonard, 1924-27 P, Wilmington Potomacs, Philadelphia Giants

Pierce, Steve, 1925-28 officer, Detroit Stars

Pierce, William H. (Bill), 1910-32 1B, C, OF, Philadelphia Giants, Chicago American Giants, Lincoln Stars, Lincoln Giants, Pennsylvania Red Caps of New York, Bacharach Giants, Norfolk Giants, Detroit Stars, Baltimore Black Sox, Homestead Grays, Mohawk Giants; umpire, East-West Lg.

Pierson, 1937, *see Len Pearson*

Pierson, —, 1933 3B, Homestead Grays

Pierre, Joseph, 1950 INF, Kansas City Monarchs

Pierre, Rogers, 1939 P, Chicago American Giants

Pigg, Leonard, 1947-50 C, Indianapolis Clowns, Cleveland Buckeyes

Pillot, Guillermo Luis (Guillo), 1941-43 P, New York Black Yankees, Cincinnati Clowns

Piloto, Jose, 1949-50 P, Memphis Red Sox

Pinder, Eddie (Potato), 1914-16 OF, Hilldale

Pinder, Fred, 1910-17 SS, Hilldale

Pinder, George (Monk), 1910 OF, Hilldale

Pinkston, Al, 1950 1B, St. Louis Stars

Pipkin, Robert (Lefty, Black Diamond), 1928-33, 1942 P, Birmingham Black Barons, Cleveland Cubs, New Orleans Crescent Stars

Pitts, Curtis, 1950 C, Chicago American Giants, Cleveland Buckeyes

Pitts, Ed, 1940 C, Philadelphia Stars

Pla, —, 1933 P, Cuban Stars

Pluno, —, 1887 player, Boston Resolutes

Poindexter, Robert, 1924-29 P, 1B, Birmingham Black Barons, Chicago American Giants, Memphis Red Sox

Poinsette, Robert, 1939 OF, P, New York Black Yankees, Toledo Crawfords

Pointer, Robert Lee, 1950 P, Kansas City Monarchs

Pointter, —, 1887 P, 3B, Binghamton, N.Y. (Int. Lg.)

Polanco, Rafael (Ralph), 1942 P, Philadelphia Stars

Poles, E. (Possum, Googles), 1922-28 SS, 3B, Baltimore Black Sox, Harrisburg Giants

Poles, Spottswood (Spot), 1909-23 OF, Philadelphia Giants, Lincoln Giants, Brooklyn Royal Giants, Lincoln Stars, Hilldale, Bacharach Giants, Richmond Giants

Pollard, —, 1936 OF, St. Louis Stars

Pollard, Nat, 1946-50 P, Birmingham Black Barons

Pollock, Syd, 1926-50 off.,owner, Havana Red Sox, Cuban House of David, Cuban Stars, Ethiopian Clowns, Cincinnati Clowns, Indianapolis Clowns

Pompez, Alexandro (Alex), 1922-50 officer, Cuban Stars (ECL), New York Cubans; vice-pres, NNL

Pontello, —, 1927 P, Cuban Stars (ECL)

Poole, Claude, 1945-46 P, New York Black Yankees

Pope, A., 1948 OF, Homestead Grays

Pope, Dave, 1946 UTIL, Homestead Grays

Pope, Edgar, 1938 OF, Atlanta Black Crackers

Pope, James, 1931-32 P, Louisville White Sox, Montgomery Grey Sox

Pope, Willie (Bill), 1947-48 P, Homestead Grays

Porsee, —, 1921 P, St. Louis Giants

Porter, Andrew (Andy, Pullman), 1932-50 P, Cleveland Cubs, Nashville Elite Giants, Washington Elite Giants, Baltimore Elite Giants, Indianapolis Clowns, Columbus Elite Giants, Louisville White Sox, Newark Eagles

Portuando, Bartolo, 1916-27 3B, 1B, Cuban Stars, Kansas City Monarchs, Cuban Stars (ECL), New York Cuban Stars

Posey, Cumberland Willis (Cum), 1911-46 OF, officer, Homestead Grays, Detroit Wolves; founder, East-West Lg.; sec'y, tres, NNL

Posey, Seward Hayes (See, Sea), 1911-48 officer, bus. mgr, Homestead Grays

Postell, —, 1934 2B, Cincinnati Tigers

Potter, —, 1921 C, Kansas City Monarchs

Potter, D., 1932 OF, Atlanta Black Crackers

Powell, —, 1914-15 P, Lincoln Giants

Powell, Edward D. (Eddie, Big Red, Boche), 1936-38 C, New York Black Yankees, Washington Black Senators, New York Cubans

Powell, Elvin (Shoeless), 1931 2B, Memphis Red Sox

Powell, J.J., 1931 officer, Little Rock Black Travelers

Powell, Melvin (Putt), 1930-43 P, OF, Cole's American Giants, Chicago American Giants, Chicago Brown Bombers, Chicago Columbia Giants

Powell, Richard D. (Dick), 1938-52 officer, owner, Baltimore Elite Giants, Nashville Elite Giants

Powell, Russell, 1914-21 C, 2B, Indianapolis ABCs

Powell, William H. (Bill), 1947-50 P, Birmingham Black Barons

Powell, Willie Ernest (Wee Willie, Piggy), 1925-35 P, Chicago American Giants, Detroit Stars, Cole's American Giants, Cleveland Red Sox, Akron Tyrites

Presby, —, 1945 P, Chicago Brown Bombers

Presswood, Henry, 1948-50 SS, Cleveland Buckeyes

Preston, Albert, 1943-1949 P, New York Black Yankees

Preston, Robert, 1950 P, Baltimore Elite Giants

Price, —, 1922 OF, Pittsburgh Keystones

Price, Marvin, 1950 1B, Cleveland Buckeyes, Chicago American Giants

Prichett, W., 1921 P, Hilldale

Prim, Randolph, 1926 P, Kansas City Monarchs

Prim, William, 1905 C, Leland Giants

Primm, —, 1910 C, St. Louis Giants

Pritchett, Wilbur, 1924-32 P, Harrisburg Giants, Baltimore Black Sox, Brooklyn Royal Giants, Hilldale, Bacharach Giants

Proctor, James (Cub), 1884-87 P, C, Baltimore Atlantics, Baltimore Lord Baltimores

Pryor, —, 1916-17 P, Indianapolis ABCs, St. Louis Giants, Jewell's ABCs, Bowser's ABCs

Pryor, Anderson, 1922-33 2B, SS, Milwaukee Bears, Detroit Stars, Memphis Red Sox, New Orleans Crescent Stars,

Pryor, Bill, 1927-31 P, Memphis Red Sox, Detroit Stars

Pryor, Edward, 1925-27 2B, Lincoln Giants, Penn Red Caps of NY

Pryor, Wes, 1910-13 3B, Leland Giants, Chicago American Giants, St. Louis Giants, Chicago Giants, Mohawk Giants, Brooklyn Royal Giants

Pugh, Johnny, 1912-22 3B, 2B, OF, Mohawk Giants, Brooklyn Royal Giants, Philadelphia Giants, Bacharach Giants, Harrisburg Giants, Lincoln Giants, Lincoln Stars

Pulamino, —, 1905 OF, All Cubans

Pullen, C. Neil, 1920-27 C, Brooklyn Royal Giants, Kansas City Monarchs, Baltimore Black Sox, Lincoln Giants

Pulliam, Arthur (Chick), 1909-15 C, Kansas City (KS) Giants, Kansas City (MO) Royal Giants

Purcell, Herman, 1944-47 3B, P, Cleveland Buckeyes, Memphis Red Sox

Purgen, —, 1920-21 SS, Madison Stars, Hilldale

Quinones, Thomas Plancharon, 1946-47 P, Indianapolis Clowns

Quintana, Busta, 1928-34 INF, Cuban Stars (NNL), Newark Dodgers

Radcliff, Alexander (Alex), 1926-46 SS, 3B, Chicago Giants, Cole's American Giants, Chicago American Giants, New York Cubans, Kansas City Monarchs, Cincinnati-Indianapolis Clowns, Memphis Red Sox, Dayton Marcos, Birmingham Black Barons

Radcliffe, Theodore R. (Double Duty), 1928-50 C, P, MGR, Detroit Stars, St. Louis Stars, Pittsburgh Crawfords, Homestead Grays, Columbus Blue Birds, New York Black Yankees, Brooklyn Eagles, Cincinnati Tigers, Memphis Red Sox, Birmingham Black Barons, Chicago American Giants, Louisville Buckeyes, Kansas City Monarchs

Raggs, Harry, *see Harry Roberts*

Ragland, Hurland, 1920-21 P, Indianapolis ABCs, Kansas City Monarchs, Columbus Buckeyes, Dayton Marcos

Raine, J., 1884-85 OF, Baltimore Atlantics

Ramirez, Ramiro (Rome), 1916-48 OF, MGR, Cuban Stars, Havana Stars, Cuban Stars (East), All Cubans, Bacharach Giants, Baltimore Black Sox, Havana Red Sox, Cuban House of David, Indianapolis Clowns, Brooklyn Royal Giants, New York Cuban Stars, Richmond Giants

Ramos, —, 1912 P, Cuban Stars, Long Branch (NJ) Cubans

Ramos, Jose (Cheo), 1921-29 OF, All Cubans, Cuban Stars (ECL)

Ramsay, William, 1889 OF, Chicago Unions

Randolph, Andrew G., 1882-88 1B, OF, Argyle Hotel, Trenton (NJ) Cuban Giants, Boston Resolutes, Active of Philadelphia

Rankin, Bill (Bullets, Shorty), 1923-27 P, C, Washington Potomacs, Richmond Giants, Philadelphia Giants

Rankin, George, 1887 player, Cincinnati Browns

Ransom, Joe, 1926 C, Cleveland Elites

Rawlins, —, 1905 OF, Cuban Giants

Ray, John, 1932-45 OF, Montgomery Grey Sox, Birmingham Black Barons, Cleveland Bears, Jacksonville Red Caps, Cincinnati-Indianapolis Clowns, Kansas City Monarchs, Pittsburgh Crawfords

Ray, Otto C. (Jaybird), 1920-24 P, C, OF, Kansas City Monarchs, Chicago Giants, St. Louis Stars, Cleveland Tate Stars, Cleveland Browns, Toledo Tigers

Ray, Richard, 1943 INF, OF, Chicago Brown Bombers

Ray, Thomas, 1887 player, New York Gorhams

Reavis, W., 1920-32 P, Lincoln Giants, Pennsylvania Red Caps of New York

Rector, Cornelius (Connie), 1920-44 P, Hilldale, Brooklyn Royal Giants, Lincoln Giants, New York Black Yankees, New York Cubans

Redd, Eugene, 1922-23 3B, Pittsburgh Keystones, Milwaukee Bears New Orleans Crescent Stars, Kansas City Monarchs

Redd, Ulysses A. (Hickey), 1940-41 SS, Chicago American Giants, Birmingham Black Barons

Redding, Richard (Dick, Cannonball), 1911-38 P, OF, MGR, Lincoln Giants, Lincoln Stars, Indianapolis ABCs, Chicago American Giants, Brooklyn Royal Giants, Bacharach Giants

Reddon, Bob, 1919 P, Cleveland Tate Stars

Redmon, Tom, 1911 player, Leland Giants

Redus, Wilson, 1924-40 OF, MGR, coach, St. Louis Stars, Cleveland Stars, Columbus Blue Birds, Cleveland Giants, Kansas City Monarchs, Cleveland Red Sox, Chicago American Giants, Cleveland Browns, Indianapolis ABCs

Redwine, —, 1926 P, Cleveland Elites

Reed, Ambrose, 1922-32 OF, 2B, 1B, 3B, Bacharach Giants, Hilldale, Pittsburgh Crawfords, Atlanta Black Crackers, Homestead Grays

Reed, Andrew, 1917-21 3B, OF, Chicago Union Giants, Detroit Stars, Chicago Giants

Reed, Curtis, 1937 OF, St. Louis Stars

Reed, John, 1934-42 P, Cole's American Giants, Indianapolis ABCs, Chicago American Giants, Chicago Brown Bombers, Atlanta Black Crackers, Indianapolis Athletics, St. Louis Stars

Reedy, Fleming (Buddy), 1950 3B, Baltimore Elite Giants

Reel, Jimmy, 1923 OF, Toledo Tigers

Reese, —, 1910 P, Cuban Giants

Reese, James, 1934-35 P, Cleveland Red Sox, Brooklyn Eagles

Reese, John E., 1918-31 OF, Bacharach Giants, Hilldale, Chicago American Giants, Detroit Stars, Toledo Tigers, St. Louis Stars

Reeves, —, 1908 CF, Brooklyn Colored Giants

Reeves, —, 1929 C, Hilldale

Reeves, Donald, 1937-41 1B, OF, Atlanta Black Crackers, Indianapolis ABCs, Chicago American Giants

Reeves, John, 1890-92 3B, OF, Lincoln (Neb) Giants, Plattsmouth (Nebraska St. Lg.)

Reggie, —, 1921 P, Indianapolis ABCs

Reid, Porter, 1949 OF, Houston Eagles

Rena, *see Pena*

Renfro, William, 1887 P, Binghamton, N.Y. (Int. Lg.)

Renfroe, Othello Nelson Sr. (Chico, Chappy), 1945-50 OF, C, SS, Kansas City Monarchs, Cleveland Buckeyes, Indianapolis Clowns

Reveria, Charlie, 1939 3B, Baltimore Elite Giants

Reynolds, —, 1946 1B, Birmingham Black Barons

Reynolds, Jimmy, 1940,1946 3B, Indianapolis Crawfords, Cleveland Buckeyes

Reynolds, Joe, 1935 P, Philadelphia Stars

Reynolds, Louis Thomas (Lou), 1897-99-OF, 1B, Chicago Columbia Giants, Chicago Unions

Reynolds, William Ernest (Bill), 1948-50 2B, SS, Cleveland Buckeyes, Louisville Buckeyes

Rhoades, Cornelius (Neal), 1910-18-C, OF, Bowser's ABCs, Hilldale

Rhodes, Claude (Dusty), 1931-33 P, Louisville Black Caps, Columbus Blue Birds, Chattanoogna Black Lookouts

Rhodes, Harry, 1942-50 P, 1B, Chicago American Giants

Rice, Miller, 1934-37 OF, Cincinnati Tigers

Rich, —, 1924 3B, St. Louis Giants

Richardson, —, 1908 OF, Brooklyn Colored Giants

Richardson, Bob (Johnny), 1949-50 SS, Homestead Grays

Richardson, Dewey, 1922 C, Hilldale

Richardson, Earl, 1943 SS, Newark Eagles

Richardson, Eugene (Gene), 1947-50 P, Kansas City Monarchs

Richardson, George, 1901-03 SS, Chicago Union Giants, Algona (IA) Brownies

Richardson, George, 1925 officer, Detroit Stars

Richardson, Glemby (Glenn), 1946-49 2B, New York Black Yankees

Richardson, Henry (Long Tom), 1921-38 P, OF, Baltimore Black Sox, Washington Pilots, Bacharach Giants, Washington Black Senators, Pittsburgh Crawfords, Cuban Stars, Richmond Giants

Richardson, Jim, 1939 P, New York Black Yankees

Richardson, John, 1924-25 P, Birmingham Black Barons

Richardson, Vicial, 1946 SS, Cleveland Buckeyes

Ricks, Curtiss, 1921-26-OF, P, 1B, Dayton Marcos, Cleveland Tate Stars, Indianapolis ABCs, Chicago American Giants, Cleveland Browns

Ricks, Napoleon, 1887 player, Louisville Falls City

Ricks, Pender, 1924-28-1B, Philadelphia Giants, Harrisburg Giants

Ricks, William (Bill), 1944-50 P, Philadelphia Stars

Riddick, Vernon, 1939-41 SS, Newark Eagles

Riddle, Marshall Lewis (Jit), 1936-43 2B, SS, Indianapolis ABCs, St. Louis Stars, New Orleans-St. Louis Stars, Cleveland Buckeyes, Jacksonville Red Caps

Ridgely, (Buck), 1919-23 SS, Lincoln Giants, Baltimore Black Sox, Harrisburg Giants

Ridley, Jack, 1927-34 OF, 1B, Nashville Elite Giants, Cleveland Cubs, Louisville Red Caps

Rigal, —, 1922-27 SS, 3B, Cuban Stars (NNL)

Riggins, Orville, 1920-35 SS, 3B, 2B, MGR, Detroit Stars, Cleveland Hornets, Homestead Grays, Lincoln Giants, New York Black Yankees, Brooklyn Royal Giants, Chicago American Giants

Rigney, H.G. (Hank), 1939-45 officer, Toledo Crawfords, Indianapolis Crawfords, Toledo Cubs (USL)

Rile, Edward (Ed, Huck), 1920-33 P, 1B, Indianapolis ABCs, Chicago American Giants, Lincoln Giants, Columbus Buckeyes, Detroit Stars, Cole's American Giants, Brooklyn Royal Giants, Kansas City Monarchs

Riley, Jim (Jack), 1945 2B, Birmingham Black Barons

Rims, —, 1920 P, Bacharach Giants

Rios, Herman, 1915-24 3B, SS, Cuban Stars (NNL), Havana Stars, Cuban Stars

Risley, —, 1922-23 3B, Baltimore Black Sox, Washington Potomacs

Ritchey, John F., 1947 C, Chicago American Giants

Rivas, —, 1917-18 2B, Cuban Stars (East)

Rivera, Nenene Aniceto, 1933 P, INF, Cuban Stars

Rivero, Carlos (Charley), 1939,1943-44 SS, 3B, Cuban Stars, New York Black Yankees, Baltimore Elite Giants

Rivers, Bill (Rivera), 1944 OF, Kansas City Monarchs

Rivers, Dewey(Deep), 1926,1933 OF, Hilldale, Baltimore Black Sox

Roberson, (Charley), 1934 SS, Nashville Elite Giants

Roberts, —, 1931 C, Chicago Columbia Giants

Roberts, Charley, 1938 P, Washington Black Senators

Roberts, Curtis B., 1947-50 3B, 2B, Kansas City Monarchs

Roberts, Elihu, 1916-20 OF, Bacharach Giants, Hilldale

Roberts, Harry (Raggs), 1920-32 OF, C, Norfolk Giants, Baltimore Black Sox, Harrisburg Giants, Homestead Grays, Chicago Columbia Giants, Pittsburgh Crawfords, Norfolk Stars

Roberts, J.D., 1918-24 SS, 3B, 2B, Pennsylvania Giants, Hilldale, Bacharach Giants, Richmond Giants

Roberts, Leroy (Roy, Everready), 1916-34 P, Bacharach Giants, Columbus Buckeyes, Brooklyn Royal Giants, Lincoln Giants, Hilldale, Cleveland Giants, Cleveland Red Sox, Madison Stars

Roberts, P., 1903 2B, Chicago Union Giants

Roberts, Sarah Mutt, 1937-39 P, Philadelphia Stars, Nashville Elite Giants, Baltimore Elite Giants

Roberts, Tom (Speck), 1937-45 P, Homestead Grays, New York Black Yankees, Newark Eagles, Philadelphia Stars, Washington Black Senators

Robertson, Bobbie, *see William Robinson*

Robertson, Charles, 1921-25 P, Birmingham Black Barons, St. Louis Stars, New Orleans Caulfield Ads

Robinson, —, 1943 C, New York Black Yankees

Robinson, Al, 1905-12 1B, P, Brooklyn Royal Giants, New York Black Sox

Robinson, Bill (Bojangles), 1931 officer, New York Stars (Black Yankees)

Robinson, (Black Diamond), 1886 1B, New York Gorhams

Robinson, Bob, 1905 C, Leland Giants

Robinson, Bobby (Robbie), 1939-40,1945 UTIL, 3B, St. Louis Stars, Homestead Grays

Robinson, Charles, 1939 OF, Chicago American Giants

Robinson, Cornelius Randall (Neil), 1936-50 OF, SS, Cincinnati Tigers, Homestead Grays, Memphis Red Sox

Robinson, Edward, 1931 OF, Louisville White Sox

Robinson, George (Sis), 1918 P, Bacharach Giants

Robinson, George, 1924 officer, Washington Potomacs

Robinson, Henry Frazier (Sloe, Hank), 1942-50 C, Homestead Grays, Baltimore Elite Giants, Kansas City Monarchs

Robinson, J., 1905-10 OF, Kansas City, Kan. Giants, Brooklyn Royal Giants

Robinson, J., 1938-39 3B, Indianapolis ABCs, St. Louis Stars

Robinson, Jack Roosevelt (Jackie), 1945 SS, Kansas City Monarchs

Robinson, Jacob, 1946-47 3B, Chicago American Giants

Robinson, James (Black Rusie), 1894-1906 P, Lansing, Michigan, Colored Capital All-Americans, Cuban Giants, Cuban X Giants, Brooklyn Royal Giants, Pawtucket (New Eng. Lg.)

Robinson, Johnny, 1930,1942 INF, OF, Memphis Red Sox, Detroit Black Sox

Robinson, Joshua, 1939 OF, New York Black Yankees

Robinson, Kenneth, 1931,1939 2B, 3B, OF, Brooklyn Royal Giants, Newark Browns

Robinson, Neil, see Cornelius Robinson

Robinson, Newt, see Walter Robinson

Robinson, Norman Wayne (Bobby, Norm), 1939-50 OF, SS, 3B, Baltimore Elite Giants, Birmingham Black Barons

Robinson, Ray (Not Sugar), 1941-47 P, Newark Eagles, Cincinnati Buckeyes, Philadelphia Stars, Cleveland Buckeyes

Robinson, Richmond, 1883-86 OF, St.Louis Black Stockings Trenton (NJ) Cuban Giants,

Robinson, Walter William (Newt, Bill), 1925-31 SS, Hilldale, Lincoln Giants, Harrisburg Giants, New York Black Yankees

Robinson, Walter (Skindown), 1940-42 2B, Cleveland Bears, Jacksonville Red Caps

Robinson, William (Bobbie), 1925-34 3B, SS, Indianapolis ABCs, Cleveland Elites, Memphis Red Sox, Detroit Stars, Cleveland Stars, Cleveland Red Sox, Birmingham Black Barons

Rochelle, Clarence, 1944 P, Kansas City Monarchs

Roddy, B.M., 1926 pres, NSL

Rodgers, Silvester Clifford (Speedie), 1949-50 P, Baltimore Elite Giants

Rodriquez, —, 1915 P, Cuban Stars

Rodriguez, Antonio, 1939 P, Cuban Stars

Rodriguez, Antonio Hector, 1944 3B, New York Cubans

Rodriguez, B.Conrado, 1922,1927-29 P, OF, Cuban Stars (NNL)

Rodriguez, Benvienido, 1948 OF, C, Chicago American Giants

Rodriguez, Herrado, see Antonio Hector Rodriguez

Rodriquez, Jose, 1915-29 C, Cuban Stars, Cuban Stars (East), Detroit Stars, Kansas City Monarchs, Cuban Stars (NNL), All Cubans

Rodriquez, Oscar, 1935 MGR., Havana Red Sox

Rodoud, —, 1921 C, Cuban Stars (East)

Roesink, John, 1925-30 officer, owner, Detroit Stars

Rogan, Wilber (Bullet Joe), 1917-46 P, OF, 1B, 2B, 3B, SS, MGR, Kansas City Colored Giants, All Nations, Los Angeles White Sox, Kansas City Monarchs; umpire, NAL

Rogers, —, 1900 P, Genuine Cuban Giants

Rogers, Pierre, 1934-39 P, Cincinnati Tigers, Chicago American Giants, Ethiopian Clowns

Rogers, Sid, 1887 player, Cincinnati Browns

Rogers, William Nathaniel (Nat), 1923-45 OF, 1B, 3B, C, Harrisburg Giants, Brooklyn Royal Giants, Memphis Red Sox, Chicago Columbia Giants, Cole's American Giants, Chicago American Giants, Birmingham Black Barons, Kansas City Monarchs

Rojo, Julio, 1916-38 C, 3B, Cuban Stars, Havana Stars, Bacharach Giants, Baltimore Black Sox, Cuban Stars of Havana, Lincoln Giants, New York Cuban Stars

Rolls, Charles, 1911 player, Leland Giants

Romanach, —, 1916 SS, Long Branch Cubans

Romby, Robert L. (Bob), 1946-50 P, Baltimore Elite Giants

Ronsell, —, 1928-31 OF, Birmingham Black Barons, Memphis Red Sox, Nashville Elite Giants

Roque, Jacinto (Battling Siki), 1928-29 OF, Cuban Stars (NNL)

Rose, Cecil, 1924 P, St. Louis Stars

Rose, Haywood, 1907 C, Leland Giants

Roselle, Basilio [Rosselle, Rosello], 1926-35 P, Cuban Stars (NNL), Cuban Stars (ECL), New York Cubans

Ross, Alex, 1887-1889 3B, OF, Greenville (Northern Mich. Lg.), and (Michigan St. Lg.)

Ross, —, 1918 P, Indianapolis ABCs

Ross, Arthur, 1903-05 P, Chicago Union Giants, Leland Giants

Ross, Dick, 1925 OF, St. Louis Stars

Ross, Harold, 1922-25 P, Indianapolis ABCs, Washington Potomacs, Chicago American Giants, Cleveland Browns

Ross, Jerry, 1926 P, Cleveland Elites

Ross, Sam, 1923 P, Hilldale, Harrisburg Giants

Ross, William, 1924-30 P, St. Louis Stars, Cleveland Hornets, Chicago American Giants, Homestead Grays

Rossiter, George, 1922-31 officer, owner, Baltimore Black Sox

Roth, Herman Joseph (Bobby), 1921-25 C, New Orleans Crescent Stars, Chicago American Giants, Milwaukee Bears, Detroit Stars, Birmingham Black Barons

Rotoret, —, 1950 P, New York Cubans

Rovira, Jaime, 1911 3B, All Cubans

Rowe, —, 1932 P, Nashville Elite Giants

Rowe, William (Schoolboy), 1943-45 P, Chicago Brown Bombers, Pittsburgh Crawfords, Cleveland Buckeyes

Royall, Joseph John, 1937-42 P, OF, Indianapolis Athletics, Jacksonville Red Caps, New York Black Yankees, Cleveland Bears

Ruffin, Charles Leon (Lassas), 1935-50 C, MGR, Newark Eagles, Pittsburgh Crawfords, Philadelphia Stars, Houston Eagles, Brooklyn Eagles, Toledo Crawfords

Ruiz, Antonio (Perez), 1944 P, Cincinnati-Indianapolis Clowns

Ruiz, Silvino (Poppa), 1928-42 P, Cuban Stars (ECL), New York Cubans

Rush, Joe, 1923-26 officer, Birmingham Black Barons; sec'y, NNL; pres, NSL

Ruson, —, 1931 SS, Brooklyn Royal Giants

Russ, Pythias, 1925-29 C, SS, Chicago American Giants, Memphis Red Sox

Russell, 1929-31, see Ronsell

Russell, —, 1933 P, Brooklyn Royal Giants

Russell, 1940 see Russell Awkard

Russell, Aaron A., 1913-20 3B, Homestead Grays

Russell, Branch L., 1922-33 3B, OF, Kansas City Monarchs, St. Louis Stars, Cleveland Stars, Cleveland Cubs

Russell, E., 1924-26 3B, OF, Harrisburg Giants, Dayton Marcos

Russell, Frank (Junior), 1943-49 2B, OF, Baltimore Elite Giants

Russell, John Henry (Pistol), 1923-34 2B, 3B, Memphis Red Sox, St. Louis Stars, Indianapolis ABCs, Pittsburgh Crawfords, Detroit Wolves, Cleveland Red Sox

Russell, Thomas, 1950 P, Cleveland Buckeyes

Rutledge, —, 1921 P, Dayton Marcos

Ryan, Merven J. (Red), 1915-31 P, Pittsburgh Stars of Buffalo, Brooklyn Royal Giants, Hilldale, Harrisburg Giants, Bacharach Giants, Baltimore Black Sox, Lincoln Stars, Newark Browns, Lincoln Giants, New York Black Yankees

Saabin, —, 1927 P, Cuban Stars (ECL)

Sadler, William A.(Bill, Bubby), 1935-38 SS, Brooklyn Eagles, Washington Black Senators

St. Thomas, Larry, 1943,1947 P, Newark Eagles, New York Black Yankees

Salas, Wilfredo, 1948 P, New York Cubans

Salazar, Lazaro, 1924-36 OF, P, 1B, Cuban Stars (NNL), New York Cubans

Salazar, Santos, 1945 UTIL, New York Cubans

Salmon, Harry, 1923-35 P, Birmingham Black Barons, Homestead Grays, Memphis Red Sox, Detroit Wolves

Salters, Edward, 1937 OF, Detroit Stars

Salvat, —, 1924-25 P, Cuban Stars (ECL)

Sama, Pablo, 1950 3B, Indianapolis Clowns

Sampson, —, 1899-1905 P, OF, Genuine Cuban Giants, Cuban Giants

Sampson, Eddie (Leo), 1941-43 OF, Birmingham Black Barons

Sampson, John, 1942 OF, New York Cubans

Sampson, Ormond Leonard, 1932-38 SS, Atlanta Black Crackers, Brooklyn Royal Giants, Newark Dodgers

Sampson, Sam, 1940-41 2B, OF, Cleveland Bears, Jacksonville Red Caps

Sampson, Thomas (Tommy, Toots), 1938-48 2B, 1B, MGR, Chicago American Giants, Birmingham Black Barons, New York Cubans

Samuels, —, 1940 P, Philadelphia Stars

San, Pedro Alejandro (Eli), 1926-28 P, Cuban Stars (ECL)

Sanchez, —, 1913 OF, 1B, Philadelphia Giants

Sanchez, Amando, 1948 P, Memphis Red Sox

Sanders, Willie, 1936 P, Memphis Red Sox

Sanderson, Johnny, 1947 SS, Kansas City Monarchs

Sands, Sam (Piggy), 1950 SS, Indianapolis Clowns

Santa Cruz, Eugenio (Santa), 1909-10 OF, Cuban Stars

Santaella, Anastacio (Juan, Tacho), 1935-36 2B, SS, New York Cubans

Santiago, Carlos Manuel, 1946 2B, New York Cubans

Santiago, Jose Guillermo, 1947-48 P, SS, New York Cubans

Santop, Louis (Top) (real name Louis Santop Loftin), 1909-26 C, OF, MGR, Fort Worth Wonders, Oklahoma Monarchs, Philadelphia Giants, Lincoln Giants, Chicago American Giants, Lincoln Stars, Brooklyn Royal Giants, Hilldale

Saperstein, A.M. (Abe), 1932-50 booking agent; officer, Cleveland Cubs, Cincinnati Clowns, Chicago American Giants; pres, Negro Midwestern Lg., West Coast Negro Baseball Association

Sarvis, Andrew (Smoky), 1939-42 P, Cleveland Bears, Jacksonville Red Caps

Satterfield, —, 1905-11 2B, SS, Cuban Giants, Genuine Cuban Giants, Brooklyn Royal Giants

Saunders, —, 1925-28 C, 3B, Pennsylvania Red Caps of NY

Saunders, Bob, 1926-37 2B, SS, P, Kansas City Monarchs, Detroit Stars, Bacharach Giants, Monroe Monarchs, Louisville Red Caps, Cleveland Hornets, Memphis Red Sox

Saunders, Leo, 1940 P, SS, Chicago American Giants, Birmingham Black Barons

Saunders, William, 1887 player, Pittsburgh Keystones

Saunders, William, 1950 C, Baltimore Elite Giants

Savage, —, 1925 P, Bacharach Giants, Wilmington Potomacs

Savage, Artie, 1932 officer, Cleveland Stars

Savage, Bill (Junior), 1940 P, Memphis Red Sox

Sawyer, Carl, 1924 2B, Detroit Stars

Saxon, Thomas (Lefty), 1942 P, New York Cubans

Saylor, Alfred (Greyhound), 1940-45 P, 1B, C, Birmingham Black Barons, Cincinnati Buckeyes

Scales, George (Tubby), 1920-48 2B, 3B, OF, SS, MGR, St. Louis Giants, St. Louis Stars, Lincoln Giants, Newark Stars, Homestead Grays, New York Black Yankees, Philadelphia Stars, Baltimore Elite Giants, Pittsburgh Keystones

Scantlebury, Patricio Athelstan (Pat), 1944-50 P, New York Cubans

Schiff, —, 1908 LF, Genuine Cuban Giants

Schlichter, H. Walter, 1902-10 officer,MGR, Philadelphia Giants; pres, National Associaton of Colored Base Ball Clubs of the United States and Cuba

Schorling, John M., 1911-27 officer, Chicago American Giants

Scotland, —, 1914-17 OF, Chicago Union Giants, Indianapolis ABCs, Bowser's ABCs, Louisville Sox

Scott, —, 1916 P, Chicago Giants

Scott, —, 1920 C, Detroit Stars

Scott, —, 1937 P, Birmingham Black Barons

Scott, —, 1940 OF, Cincinnati Buckeyes

Scott, C.L., 1915 player, Mohawk Giants

Scott, Charles, 1919-20 OF, St. Louis Giants

Scott, Elisha, 1920 co-drafter, constitution of NNL

Scott, Frank, 1887-94 2B, SS, Chicago Unions

Scott, Jimmy, 1950 P, Memphis Red Sox

Scott, John, 1944-50 OF, 1B, Birmingham Black Barons, Kansas City Monarchs, Louisville Buckeyes, Chicago American Giants, Philadelphia Stars

Scott, Joseph (Joe), 1947-50 1B, Birmingham Black Barons, Chicago American Giants

Scott, Joseph Burt (Joe), 1944-49 OF, Memphis Red Sox

Scott, Robert, 1920-27 OF, Brooklyn Royal Giants, Lincoln Giants Hilldale

Scott, Robert, 1950 P, New York Black Yankees

Scott, William, 1932 officer, Louisville Black Caps

Scott, William Jr. (Bill), 1950 OF, Philadelphia Stars

Scott, Willie Lee (Joe), 1927-34 1B, Memphis Red Sox, Louisville White Sox, Indianapolis ABCs, Columbus Blue Birds, Homestead Grays, Chicago American Giants
Scragg, Jesse, 1915 P, Philadelphia Giants
Scroggins, John, 1947 P, Kansas City Monarchs
Scruggs, Robert, 1950 P, Cleveland Buckeyes
Scruggs, William C. (Willie), 1949-50 P, Louisville Buckeyes, Cleveland Buckeyes, Houston Eagles, Birmingham Black Barons
Scudder, —, 1887 C, Philadelphia Pythians
Seagraves, —, 1937 OF, Indianapolis Athletics
Seagraves, Samuel, 1946 C, Chicago American Giants
Searcy, Kelly (Lefty), 1950 P, Baltimore Elite Giants, Memphis Red Sox
Seay, Richard William (Dick, Erkie), 1925-47 2B, SS, Pennsylvania Red Caps of New York, Newark Stars, Baltimore Black Sox, Brooklyn Royal Giants, Philadelphia Stars, Pittsburgh Crawfords, Newark Eagles, New York Black Yankees
Segula, —, 1921-23 P, New Orleans Caulfield Ads Milwaukee Bears
Selden, William H., 1887-99 P, OF, Boston Resolutes, Cuban Giants, New York Gorhams (Middle States Lg.), Lansing, Michigan Colored Capital All-Americans, Cuban X Giants, Trenton Cuban Giants (Middle States Lg.), York Cuban Giants (Eastern Interstate Lg.)
Seldom, —, 1910-14 SS, Chicago Giants, Indianapolis ABCs
Seller, see George Suttles
Semler, James (Soldier Boy), 1932-48 officer, New York Black Yankees
Serrell, William C. (Bonnie, Barney), 1942-50 2B, 3B, Kansas City Monarchs
Seruby, —, 1888 OF, Cuban X Giants
Seto, —, 1929 OF, Cuban Stars (ECL)
Shackleford, John G., 1924-45 3B, 2B, Cleveland Browns, Chicago American Giants, Birmingham Black Barons, Harrisburg Giants, pres, United States Lg.
Shamberg, —, 1938 player, Atlanta Black Crackers
Shanks, Hank, 1927 1B, Birmingham Black Barons
Shannon, —, 1932 OF, Pittsburgh Crawfords
Sharpe, —, 1923 SS, St. Louis Stars
Sharpe, Robert (Pepper), 1943-49 P, OF, Memphis Red Sox, Chicago American Giants, Chicago Brown Bombers
Shartz, —, 1911 C, Philadelphia Giants
Shaw, —, 1920 OF, St. Louis Giants
Shaw, R., 1897 P, Page Fence Giants, Chicago Unions
Shaw, Theodore (Ted), 1927-31 P, Chicago American Giants, Detroit Stars, Memphis Red Sox
Shawler, —, 1909 OF, Leland Giants
Sheffey, Doug, 1910 P, Hilldale
Shelby, Hiawatha, 1946 OF, Indianapolis Clowns
Shelton, —, 1920 C, Dayton Marcos
Shelton, —, 1943 OF, Harrisburg-St. Louis Stars
Shepard, Fred, 1945-48 P, UTIL, Birmingham Black Barons, Chicago American Giants
Sheppard, Ray, 1924-32 SS, Birmingham Black Barons, Detroit Wolves, Homestead Grays, Detroit Stars, Kansas City Monarchs Monroe Monarchs, Indianapolis ABCs
Sheppard, Samuel (Sam), 1887-1926 player, New York Gorhams; officer, St. Louis Stars, owner, Cleveland Elites
Sheppard, William, 1922-24 P, Kansas City Monarchs, Memphis Red Sox
Sherkliff, Ed, 1931 P, Hilldale
Shields, —, 1916 P, Lincoln Giants
Shields, Charlie (Lefty), 1941-45 P, Chicago American Giants, Homestead Grays, New York Cubans
Shields, Jimmy, 1928-29 P, Bacharach Giants
Shipp, Jesse, 1908-12 P, Brooklyn Royal Giants, New York Colored Giants
Shirley, —, 1914 OF, Brooklyn Royal Giants
Shively, George, 1914-25 Indianapolis ABCs, Bacharach Giants, Washington Potomacs, Bowser's ABCs, Brooklyn Royal Giants
Shropshire, —, 1937 C, St. Louis Stars
Sibley, —, 1913 P, Indianapolis ABCs
Siebert, —, 1937 OF, St. Louis Stars

Sierra, Felipe, 1921-32 SS, 2B, 3B, OF, All Cubans, Cuban Stars (NNL)
Sigenero, —, 1940 P, Cuban Stars
Sijo, see Sijo Gomez
Siki, Roque, 1931-32 OF, Cuban Stars, Cuban House of David
Silva, Pedro, 1921-22 P, OF, All Cubans, Cuban Stars (NNL)
Silvers, —, 1933 INF, Philadelphia Stars
Simerson, —, 1936 P, St. Louis Stars
Simmons, —, 1926 P, Lincoln Giants
Simmons, Hubert, 1950 P, Baltimore Elite Giants
Simmons, J.R., 1887 player, Baltimore Lord Baltimores
Simmons, R.S., 1943-49 officer, Chicago American Giants; sec'y, NAL
Simms, Willie (Bill, Simmy), 1934-43 OF, Monroe Monarchs, Cincinnati Tigers, Kansas City Monarchs, Chicago American Giants
Simpson, —, 1933 1B, OF, Cleveland Giants, Baltimore Black Sox, Akron Tyrites
Simpson, Harry (Suitcase), 1946-48 OF, Philadelphia Stars
Simpson, Herbert, 1942 OF, Birmingham Black Barons
Simpson, James, 1887 OF, Philadelphia Pythians
Simpson, Lawrence, 1916-20 P, OF, Chicago Union Giants, Chicago Giants, Bowser's ABCs
Sinclair, Harry, 1931 sec'y, NNL
Sinelan, —, 1932 3B, Bacharach Giants
Singer, Orville (Red), 1921-32 OF, INF, Lincoln Giants, Cleveland Browns, Cleveland Tigers, Cleveland Cubs, Cleveland Stars
Singleton, —, 1896 C, Cuban X Giants
Singleton, —, 1946 P, Cleveland Buckeyes
Singlong, —, 1929 2B, OF, Nashville Elite Giants
Sis —, 1934 OF, New Orleans Crescent Stars
Sisco, —, 1913 LF, Philadelphia Giants
Skinner, A., 1910,1917 C, UTIL, Leland Giants, Kansas City Colored Giants
Skinner, —, 1948 C, Newark Eagles
Slaughter, C., 1884-85 INF, Baltimore Atlantics
Slawson, —, 1916 3B, 2B, Lincoln Stars
Sloan, Robert, 1919-21 OF, Brooklyn Royal Giants
Smallwood, Dewitt Mark (Woody), 1950-1952 OF, Philadelphia Stars, New York Black Yankees, Birmingham Black Barons, Indianapolis Clowns.
Smallwood, Louis, 1923-29 2B, Milwaukee Bears, Chicago Giants
Smart, —, 1932 P, Indianapolis ABCs
Smaulding, Owen, 1927-28 P, Kansas City Monarchs, Cleveland Tigers, Chicago American Giants, Birmingham Black Barons
Smith, —, 1897 1B, Cuban Giants
Smith, —, 1908 OF, New York Colored Giants
Smith, —, 1925 C, St. Louis Stars
Smith, —, 1927 OF, Memphis Red Sox
Smith, Alphonse Eugene (Al, Fuzzy), 1946-48 OF, SS, Cleveland Buckeyes
Smith, B.B.H. (Babe), 1887 P, New York Gorhams
Smith, (Buster), 1932-33 P, 1B, Birmingham Black Barons
Smith, C., 1931 1B, Chicago Columbia Giants
Smith, C., 1933-38 C, Birmingham Black Barons
Smith, Charles (Chino), 1924-31 OF, 2B, Philadelphia Giants, Brooklyn Royal Giants, Lincoln Giants
Smith, Charlie, 1938 INF, Washington Black Senators
Smith, Clarence, 1921-33 OF, MGR, Columbus Buckeyes, Detroit Stars, Birmingham Black Barons, Baltimore Black Sox, Cleveland Cubs, Bacharach Giants
Smith, Cleveland (Cleo), 1922-28 2B, 3B, SS, Baltimore Black Sox, Lincoln Giants, Homestead Grays, Philadelphia Tigers, Harrisburg Giants
Smith, Clyde (Carl, Boots), 1938 3B, Pittsburgh Crawfords
Smith, D., 1945-46 P, Philadelphia Stars, Homestead Grays
Smith, Dode, 1942 P, Cincinnati Buckeyes, Cleveland Buckeyes
Smith, Douglas, 1943 officer, Baltimore Elite Giants

Smith, Ed, 1887 player, Boston Resolutes
Smith, Ernest, 1934-40 C, Monroe Monarchs, Chicago American Giants
Smith, Eugene (Genie), 1939-50 P, St. Louis Stars, New Orleans- St. Louis Stars, New York Black Yankees, Homestead Grays, Cleveland Buckeyes, Louisville Buckeyes, Chicago American Giants, Kansas City Monarchs, Ethiopian Clowns
Smith, Eugene, 1942-46 3B, Jacksonville Red Caps, Cincinnati Buckeyes, Cleveland Buckeyes, Indianapolis Clowns
Smith, F (Lefty), 1922-24 P, Richmond Giants, Baltimore Black Sox
Smith, Ford, see John Ford Smith
Smith, Fred, 1946 C, Kansas City Monarchs
Smith, G., 1941 P, Kansas City Monarchs
Smith, George C., 1956-57 2B, Indianapolis Clowns
Smith, H., 1922-32 P, Washington Potomacs, Baltimore Black Sox, Bacharach Giants, Homestead Grays
Smith, Harry, 1902-05 1B, OF, Philadelphia Giants
Smith, Harvey, 1938 P, Pittsburgh Crawfords
Smith, Henry, 1942-47 2B, SS, Jacksonville Red Caps, Chicago American Giants, Cincinnati Clowns, Cincinnati-Indianapolis Clowns, New York Black Yankees, Indianapolis Clowns
Smith, Hilton Lee, 1932-48 P, New Orleans Black Creoles, Monroe Monarchs, Kansas City Monarchs
Smith, Hy, 1885 OF, Brooklyn Remsens
Smith, J., 1922-28 2B, SS, Brooklyn Royal Giants, Harrisburg Giants, Bacharach Giants
Smith, James, 1903-06 3B, INF, Cuban X Giants, Leland Giants, Chicago Union Giants
Smith, James, 1925,1930 SS, Detroit Stars
Smith, John Ford (Lefty, Gerinomo), 1939-50 OF, P, Indianapolis Crawfords, Chicago American Giants, New York Black Yankees, Kansas City Monarchs
Smith, L., 1922-23 OF, Baltimore Black Sox
Smith, L., 1942 C, Jacksonville Red Caps
Smith, (Lefty), 1920-21 P, OF, Kansas City Monarchs
Smith, (Lefty), 1940-43 see John Ford Smith
Smith, Mance, 1944 OF, Kansas City Monarchs
Smith, Marshall (Darknight), 1920-24 P, Baltimore Black Sox, Homestead Grays, Richmond Giants, Madison Stars
Smith, Milt, 1949-50 INF, Philadelphia Stars
Smith, O.H., 1885 P, Brooklyn Remsens
Smith, Oliver (Ollie), 1945 P, Cincinnati-Indianapolis Clowns
Smith, P., 1939 P, St. Louis Stars
Smith, Pete, 1937 OF, Pittsburgh Crawfords
Smith, Quincy, 1943-45 OF, Cleveland Buckeyes, Birmingham Black Barons
Smith, R., 1912-15 P, OF, Lincoln Giants
Smith, Robert (Bob), 1930-44 C, 3B, Birmingham Black Barons, Memphis Red Sox, Cincinnati Tigers, St. Louis Stars, New Orleans-St. Louis Stars, Chicago American Giants, Pittsburgh Crawfords, Cleveland Cubs
Smith, Taylor, 1948-49 P, Chicago American Giants
Smith, Theolic (Fireball), 1936-49 P, Pittsburgh Crawfords, St. Louis Stars, New Orleans-St. Louis Stars, Cleveland Buckeyes, Kansas City Monarchs, Toledo Crawfords, Chicago American Giants
Smith, W., 1921,1925 SS, P, Hilldale, Lincoln Giants
Smith, Wardell, 1946 P, Chicago American Giants
Smith, William, 1938 2B, SS, Newark Eagles
Smith, William T. (Big Bill), 1888-1913 C, OF,MGR, Genuine Cuban Giants, Cuban X Giants, Philadelphia Giants, Brooklyn Royal Giants, Mohawk Giants, Chicago Unions
Smith, Willie D., 1948 P, Homestead Grays
Smith, Wyman, 1920-25 OF, Baltimore Black Sox
Smoot, —, 1886 SS, New York Gorhams
Snaer, Lucian, 1923 umpire, NNL
Snead, Sylvester, 1939-46 OF, 2B, SS, Ethiopian Clowns, Kansas City Monarchs, Cincinnati Clowns, New York Black Yankees
Sneed, Eddie (Lefty), 1940-42 P, Birmingham Black Barons
Sneeden, —, 1894 OF, Cuban Giants

Snow, Felton (Skipper), 1931-47 3B, 2B, MGR, Louisville White Sox, Louisville Black Caps, Nashville Elite Giants, Columbus Elite Giants, Washington Elite Giants, Baltimore Elite Giants, Nashville Cubs, New Orleans Crescent Stars

Snowden, —, 1933 P, Detroit Stars

Snyder, —, 1943 OF, New York Cubans

Sockard, see Stockard

Soldero, —, 1932 P, Cuban Stars

Solis, L., 1928-34 2B, 3B, Cuban Stars (East)

Soss, Ramon, 1948 C, Homestead Grays

Sostre, Francisco, 1947 P, New York Cubans

Souell, Herbert [Herb Cyrus], 1940-50 INF, Kansas City Monarchs

Southall, John, 1898 C, Celeron Acme Colored Giants (Iron and Oil Lg.)

Southy, —, 1921 SS, Lincoln Giants

Sowell, Clyde, 1948 P, Baltimore Elite Giants

Sparks, Joe, 1937-40 2B, SS, St. Louis Stars, Chicago American Giants

Sparrow, Roy W., 1938 officer, Washington Black Senators

Spearman, Alvin, 1950 P, Chicago American Giants

Spearman, Charles, 1919-31 C, 2B, 3B, SS, Brooklyn Royal Giants, Cleveland Elites, Homestead Grays, Lincoln Giants, Pennsylvania Red Caps of New York

Spearman, Clyde (Splo), 1932-46 OF, Pittsburgh Crawfords, New York Black Yankees, New York Cubans, Newark Eagles, Philadelphia Stars, Chicago American Giants, Birmingham Black Barons

Spearman, Henry (Jake, Splo), 1932-46 3B, 1B, Homestead Grays, Pittsburgh Crawfords, Washington Black Senators, New York Black Yankees, Baltimore Elite Giants, Philadelphia Stars, Newark Eagles

Spearman, William, 1923-29 P, Memphis Red Sox, Cleveland Elites, Cleveland Hornets, Nashville Elite Giants, St. Louis Stars

Spedden, Charles P., 1922-31 officer, owner, Baltimore Black Sox

Spencer, —, 1921-22 OF, Pittsburgh Keystones

Spencer, J.C., see Joseph Spencer

Spencer, Joseph B., 1942-48 2B, SS, Birmingham Black Barons, Homestead Grays, Pittsburgh Crawfords, New York Cubans, Baltimore Elite Giants, New York Black Yankees

Spencer, (Pee Wee), 1933-40,1945 C, 3B, Chicago American Giants, Toledo Crawfords, Indianapolis Crawfords, Toledo Cubs (USL)

Spencer, Willie, 1941 OF, Birmingham Black Barons

Spencer, Zack, 1931-33 P, Chicago Columbia Giants, Columbus Blue Birds, Detroit Stars, Cleveland Cubs

Spike, —, 1923 P, Washington Potomacs

Spotsville, Roy (Bill), 1950 P, Houston Eagles

Stamps, Hulan (Lefty), 1924-28 P, Memphis Red Sox, Indianapolis ABCs

Stanley, John Wesley (Neck), 1928-49 P, Bacharach Giants, Lincoln Giants, Quaker Giants, Brooklyn Royal Giants, Baltimore Black Sox, New York Black Yankees, New York Cubans, Philadelphia Stars, Hilldale

Staples, John, 1921 MGR, Montgomery Grey Sox

Starks, James, 1938-46 1B,New York Black Yankees, Harrisburg- St. Louis Stars

Stark, L., 1887 player, Cincinnati Browns

Starks, Leslie, 1927,1934-35 OF, Memphis Red Sox, Kansas City Monarchs, Newark Dodgers

Starks, Otis (Lefty), 1919-1932 P, Hilldale, Chicago American Giants, Brooklyn Royal Giants, Lincoln Giants, Bacharach Giants, Newark Stars, St. Louis Giants

Starmand, —, 1887 OF, Pittsburgh Keystones

Stearnes, Norman Thomas (Turkey), 1920-42,45 OF,Nashville Giants, Montgomery Grey Sox, Detroit Stars, Lincoln Giants, Cole's American Giants, Chicago American Giants, Philadelphia Stars, Kansas City Monarchs, Detroit Black Sox, Toledo Cubs (USL)

Stedgrass, —, 1937 P, Memphis Red Sox

Steel, Harry, 1938 P, Indianapolis ABCs

Steele, Edward (Ed, Stainless), 1941-50 OF, Birmingham Black Barons

Stephens, see Frank Stevens

Stephens, Paul Eugene (Jake) [Stevens], 1921-37 SS, Hilldale, Philadelphia Giants, Homestead Grays, Pittsburgh Crawfords, Philadelphia Stars, New York Black Yankees

Stephens, Joe (Junior), 1949-50 P, New York Black Yankees

Sterman, Tom, 1909,1915 OF, Kansas City Giants

Stevens, —, 1927-29 C, Detroit Stars

Stevens, —, 1929 P, Bacharach Giants

Stevens, —, 1950 P, Houston Eagles

Stevens, Frank, 1921-27 P, OF, 1B, Chicago American Giants, Indianapolis ABCs, Cleveland Hornets, Toledo Tigers, St. Louis Stars

Stevens, (Jake), see Stephens

Stevens, Jim, 1933 2B, Philadelphia Stars

Stevens, L., see Frank Stevens

Stevenson, (Lefty), 1925-28 P, OF, Cleveland Tigers, Indianapolis ABCs, Birmingham Black Barons

Stevenson, Willie, 1940,1943 P, Homestead Grays

Stewart, —, 1920-23 P, SS, St. Louis Giants, St. Louis Stars

Stewart, Artis, 1950 P, Cleveland Buckeyes

Stewart, Frank, 1936-40 P, Washington Elite Giants, Indianapolis ABCs, Memphis Red Sox

Stewart, Leoniel, 1940-42 P, OF, Newark Eagles, Birmingham Black Barons

Stewart, Leslie, 1922 C, Philadelphia Giants

Stewart, Manuel, 1946-47 3B, Baltimore Elite Giants

Stewart, Riley A. Sr., 1947-50 P, Chicago American Giants, New York Cubans

Stewart, W., 1946 P, Memphis Red Sox

Stiles, Norris, 1950 P, Cleveland Buckeyes

Still, Bobby, 1887 player, Philadelphia Pythians

Still, Joe, 1887 player, Philadelphia Pythians

Stinson, C.P., 1887 player, Philadelphia Pythians

Stitler, —, 1922 P, Bacharach Giants

Stockard, Theodore, 1927-28-SS, 3B, Cleveland Hornets, Cleveland Tigers

Stockley, Lawrence, 1950 OF, New York Black Yankees

Stone, Ed, 1931-50 OF, Bacharach Giants, Brooklyn Eagles, Newark Eagles, Philadelphia Stars, Pittsburgh Crawfords, New York Black Yankees

Stovall, —, 1924 P, Cleveland Browns

Stovall, Fred, 1930-35 officer, Monroe Monarchs

Stovey, George Washington, 1886-96 P, OF, Jersey City (Eastern Lg.); Newark (International Lg.); Cuban Giants, New York Gorhams (Middle States Lg.), Cuban X Giants, Worcester (Northeastern Lg.), Ansonia Cuban Giants Connecticut St. Lg.), Troy (NY St. Lg.), York Cuban Giants (Eastern Interstate Lg.), Trenton Cuban Giants (Middle States Lg.)

Stratton, Felton, 1930 C, Hilldale

Stratton, Leroy, 1920-33 SS, 3B, 2B, MGR, Nashville Giants, Milwaukee Bears, Birmingham Black Barons, Chicago American Giants, Nashville Elite Giants

Streeter, Samuel (Sam, Lefty), 1920-35 P, Montgomery Grey Sox, Atlanta Black Crackers, Chicago American Giants, Bacharach Giants, Lincoln Giants, Birmingham Black Barons, Homestead Grays, Cleveland Cubs, Pittsburgh Crawfords

Streets, Albert, 1925 INF, Chicago American Giants

Strickland, —, 1924 P, Indianapolis ABCs

Strong, Fulton, 1922-23 P, Cleveland Tate Stars, Chicago American Giants New Orleans Crescent Stars, Milwaukee Bears

Strong, Henry, 1936 SS, Chicago American Giants

Strong, Joseph Talton (Joe, Baby Face, J.T.), 1922-37 P, Hilldale, St. Louis Stars, Homestead Grays, Baltimore Black Sox

Strong, Nathanial Colvin (Nat), 1908-34 booking agent; officer, Brooklyn Royal Giants, New York Black Yankees, Cuban Stars

Strong, Othello L., 1949-50 P, Chicago American Giants

Strong, T.R. (Ted), 1937-48 OF, INF, MGR, Indianapolis Athletics, Indianapolis ABCs, Kansas City Monarchs, Indianapolis Clowns

Strothers, C.W., 1924-27 officer, Harrisburg Giants

Strothers, Tim Samuel (Sam), 1908-18 C, 1B, 2B, Leland Giants, Chicago American Giants, Chicago Giants, Chicago Union Giants, West Baden (Ind.) Sprudels

Stuart, —, 1900 SS, Cuban X Giants

Stuart, Joe, 1884-85 P, C, Brooklyn Atlantics

Stubblefield, —, 1948 P, Kansas City Monarchs

Sturdeven, Mark, 1916,1928 player, treasurer, Hilldale

Suarez, —, 1916-21 P, Cuban Stars, Havana Stars, Cuban Stars of Havana, Cuban Stars (NNL), New York Cuban Stars

Sullivan, —, 1918 OF, Chicago Union Giants

Sullivan, —, 1937 P, Birmingham Black Barons

Summerall, William (Big, Red), 1936-40 P, St. Louis Stars, Memphis Red Sox

Summers, Lonnie, 1938-49 OF, C, Baltimore Elite Giants, Chicago American Giants

Summers, Smith (Tack), 1923-29 OF, Toledo Tigers, Cleveland Browns, Cleveland Elites, Cleveland Hornets, Cleveland Tigers, Chicago American Giants

Susini, Antonio, 1921 2B, SS, All Cubans

Sunkett, Pete (Golden), 1943-45 P, Philadelphia Stars

Suttles, Earl, 1950 1B, Cleveland Buckeyes

Suttles, George (Mule), 1918-48 1B, OF, Birmingham Black Barons, St. Louis Stars, Detroit Wolves, Washington Pilots, Chicago American Giants, Cole's American Giants, Newark Eagles, New York Black Yankees, Bacharach Giants Baltimore Black Sox; umpire

Sutton, Leroy, 1941-45 P, New Orleans-St. Louis Stars, Chicago American Giants, Cincinnati-Indianapolis Clowns

Swan, —, 1933 SS, Akron

Swancy, —, 1924 P, Indianapolis ABCs

Sweatt, George Alexander (Never, Sharkey), 1921-28 3B, 2B, OF, Chicago Giants, Kansas City Monarchs, Chicago American Giants

Sykes, Franklin J.(Doc), 1915-26 P, Lincoln Stars, Hilldale, Baltimore Black Sox, Brooklyn Royal Giants

Sykes, Melvin, 1926 OF, Hilldale

Sykes, Joe (Siki), 1942 OF, Cincinnati Clowns

Taborn, Earl, 1946-50 C, Kansas City Monarchs

Talbert, Dangerfield, 1900-11 3B, Leland Giants, Chicago Giants Cuban X Giants, Chicago Unions, Algona, (IA) Brownies

Talbert, James, 1947-48 C, Chicago American Giants

Talley, —, 1934 P, New York Black Yankees

Tapley, John R., 1933 3B, Akron Tyrites

Tapley, Townsend, 1933 SS, Akron Tyrites

Tate, —, 1914 P, Lincoln Giants

Tate, George, 1918-22 officer, Cleveland Tate Stars; vice pres, NNL

Tate, Roosevelt (Speed), 1931-37 OF, Birmingham Black Barons, Nashville Elite Giants, Memphis Red Sox, Cincinnati Tigers, Knoxville, Louisville White Sox, Chicago American Giants

Tatum, Reece (Goose), 1941-49 OF, 1B, Birmingham Black Barons, Minneapolis-St. Paul Gophers, Cincinnati Clowns, Cincinnati-Indianapolis Clowns, Indianapolis Clowns

Taylor, Alfred, 1933 1B, Akron Tyrites

Taylor, Benjamin, 1947 P, New York Black Yankees

Taylor, Benjamin H. (Ben), 1910-40 1B, MGR, Chicago American Giants, Indianapolis ABCs, St. Louis Giants, Bacharach Giants, Washington Potomacs, Harrisburg Giants, Baltimore Black Sox, Baltimore Stars, Brooklyn Eagles, Washington Black Senators, New York Cubans, West Baden (Ind.) Sprudels, Washington Pilots, Hilldale, Lincoln Giants

Taylor, (Big), see John Taylor

Taylor, Charles Ishum (C.I.), 1904-22 MGR, Birmingham Giants, West Baden (Ind.) Sprudels, Indianapolis ABCs; vice pres, NNL

Taylor, Mrs. C.I., 1922-24 officer, Indianapolis ABCs

Taylor, Cyrus G., 1924-25 OF, Lincoln Giants, Harrisburg Giants

Taylor, George, 1889-06 1B, C, INF, OF, Aspen (Colo. St. Lg.), Denver (Colorado St. Lg.)Page Fence Giants, Chicago Union Giants, Leland Giants, Beatrice (Neb. St. Lg.), Lincoln (Neb) Giants

Taylor, H.C., 1887 player, Boston Resolutes

Taylor, James Allen (Candy Jim), 1904-48 3B, 2B, MGR, Birmingham Giants, St. Paul Gophers, Leland Giants, Indianapolis ABCs, St. Louis Giants, Chicago American Giants, Dayton Marcos, Cleveland Tate Stars, St. Louis Stars, Cleveland Elites, Memphis Red Sox, Detroit Stars, Nashville Elite Giants, Columbus Elite Giants, Homestead Grays, Baltimore Elite Giants, Bowser's ABCs, Toledo Tigers, Louisville Sox, Chicago Giants; vice chairman, NNL

Taylor, Jim, 1896 OF, Cuban Giants

Taylor, John (Big, Red), 1920-28 Chicago Giants, Lincoln Giants, Kansas City Monarchs, Penn Red Caps of NY

Taylor, John (Johnny, Schoolboy), 1935-45 P, New York Cubans, Cuban Stars, Pittsburgh Crawfords, Toledo Crawfords, Homestead Grays

Taylor, Johnathan Boyce (Steel Arm Johnny), 1903-21 P, St. Paul Gophers, Leland Giants, Chicago Giants, St. Louis Giants, Lincoln Giants, Indianapolis ABCs, Bowser's ABCs, West Baden (Ind.) Sprudels, Birmingham Giants, Louisville Sox, Bacharach Giants, Hilldale

Taylor, Johnny, 1943-45 OF, Birmingham Black Barons

Taylor, Joe C., 1949-50 C, Chicago American Giants

Taylor, Leroy R., 1925-36 OF, Chicago American Giants, Indianapolis ABCs, Kansas City Monarchs, Detroit Wolves, Homestead Grays, Cleveland Red Sox, Detroit Stars

Taylor, O., 1935 P, Columbus Elite Giants

Taylor, Olan (Jelly), 1934-46 1B, C, MGR, Cincinnati Tigers, Memphis Red Sox, Birmingham Black Barons

Taylor, Raymond, 1931-46 C, Memphis Red Sox, Cincinnati Tigers Columbus Buckeyes, Kansas City Monarchs, Cleveland Clippers (USL), New York Black Yankees, New Orleans-St. Louis Stars, Cleveland Buckeyes

Taylor, (Rip), 1931 player, Hilldale

Taylor, Robert (Lightning), 1938-42 C, Indianapolis ABCs, St. Louis Stars, New York Black Yankees

Taylor, S., 1912-31 P, MGR, St. Louis Giants, Little Rock Black Travelers

Taylor, (Shine), 1939 OF, Toledo Crawfords

Taylor, Zachary, 1937 P, Memphis Red Sox

Teasley, Ron, 1945 OF, 1B, Toledo Cubs (USL)

Tenney, William, 1910 C, Kansas City, (KS) Giants

Teran, Recurvon (Julio), 1916-24 2B, 3B, Cuban Stars (East), Cuban Stars of Havana, Cuban Stars (NNL), New York Cuban Stars

Terrell, Lawrence, 1924-25 P, Detroit Stars

Terrell, S.M., 1928 officer, Cleveland Stars

Terrill, Windsor W., 1887-96 SS, UTIL, Boston Resolutes, Cuban X Giants, York Cuban Giants (Eastern Interstate Lg.), Ansonia Cuban Giants (Connecticut St. Lg.)

Terry, John, 1931-36 2B, 3B, Indianapolis ABCs, Homestead Grays, Cincinnati Tigers

Tevera, —, 1924 2B, Cuban Stars (NNL)

Thomas, —, 1904,1911 1B, P, Philadelphia Giants

Thomas, —, 1919-20 1B, Pennsylvania Red Caps of NY

Thomas, A., 1909-11 P, OF, Brooklyn Royal Giants

Thomas, Alfred (Buck), 1944-49 P, Chicago American Giants

Thomas, Arthur, 1886-91 C, 1B, OF, Cuban Giants, New York Gorhams, Trenton Cuban Giants (Middle States Lg.), York Cuban Giants (Eastern Interstate Lg.)

Thomas, (Boy), see Herb Thomas

Thomas, Charley, 1918-22 C, Baltimore Black Sox

Thomas, Clinton Cyrus (Clint, Hawk), 1920-38 OF, 2B, Brooklyn Royal Giants, Columbus Buckeyes, Detroit Stars, Hilldale, Bacharach Giants, Lincoln Giants, Darby Daisies, New York Black Yankees, Newark Eagles, Philadelphia Stars

Thomas, Dan, 1921-28 2B, Indianapolis ABCs, St. Louis Stars, Kansas City Monarchs, Cleveland Hornets, Memphis Red Sox

Thomas, Dan, 1936-40 OF, P, Jacksonville Red Caps, Chicago American Giants, Birmingham Black Barons, Cincinnati Tigers

Thomas, David (Showboat), 1923-46 1B, OF, MGR, Montgomery Grey Sox, Birmingham Black Barons, Baltimore Black Sox, New York Black Yankees, New York Cubans, Washington Black Senators, Brooklyn Royal Giants

Thomas, Hazel, 1935 P, Chicago American Giants

Thomas, Henry, 1931 OF, New York Black Yankees

Thomas, Herb (Boy, Lefty), 1929-30 P, Lincoln Giants, Hilldale

Thomas, J., 1887 player, Louisville Falls City

Thomas, J., 1932,1937 SS, Indianapolis ABCs, Detroit Stars

Thomas, J., 1946-47 OF, Birmingham Black Barons

Thomas, Jack (Jules), 1911-31 OF, Brooklyn Royal Giants, Lincoln Giants, Pennsylvania Red Caps of New York

Thomas, Jerome, 1887 player, Washington Capital City

Thomas, John, 1950 P, Cleveland Buckeyes

Thomas, L., 1928-30 C, OF, 1B, Birmingham Black Barons, Nashville Elite Giants

Thomas, Lacey, 1934-39-P, OF, Jacksonville Red Caps, Cleveland Bears

Thomas, M., 1919 P, Lincoln Giants

Thomas, Nelson, 1947 P, Newark Eagles

Thomas, Orel (Little Dean), 1937 P, Detroit Stars

Thomas, Walter Lewis, 1937-47 P, OF, Detroit Stars, Kansas City Monarchs, Memphis Red Sox, Birmingham Black Barons

Thomas, William, 1943 OF, Chicago Brown Bombers

Thomason, Charles (Charlie), 1941-44 OF, Newark Eagles

Tompkins, —, 1920 OF, Dayton Marcos

Thompson, —, 1906 P, Cuban Giants

Thompson, —, 1916-20 P, 1B, Lincoln Stars, Pittsburgh Starsqs of Buffalo, Detroit Stars, Lincoln Giants, Penn Red Caps of NY

Thompson —, 1917 1B, Cuban Giants, Pittsburgh Stars of Buffalo

Thompson, —, 1933 P, Cuban Stars

Thompson, (Buddy), 1942 C, Chicago Brown Bombers

Thompson, (Copperknee), 1942 INF, Cincinnati Clowns, Minneapolis-St. Paul Gophers

Thompson, Frank, 1885 organizer, Argyle Hotel, Cuban Giants

Thompson, Frank (Groundhog), 1945-50 P, Birmingham Black Barons, Homestead Grays, Memphis Red Sox

Thompson, Harold, 1949 P, Kansas City Monarchs

Thompson, Henry Curtis, 1943-48 OF, 2B, SS, Kansas City Monarchs

Thompson, James (Sandy), 1920-32 OF, C, 1B, Dayton Marcos, Milwaukee Bears, Birmingham Black Barons, Chicago American Giants, Chicago Columbia Giants, Cole's American Giants

Thompson, Jimmy, 1945 umpire, NAL

Thompson, Lloyd P., 1910-16,1922-30 OF, SS, Officer, Hilldale

Thompson, Marshall, 1887 manager, Boston Resolutes

Thompson, Samuel Tommy (Sad Sam, Long Tom), 1931-42 P, Kansas City Monarchs, Indianapolis ABCs, Detroit Stars, Columbus Elite Giants, Philadelphia Stars, Chicago American Giants, Monroe Monarchs, Nashville Elite Giants

Thompson, Sammy (Runt), 1931-38 2B,Memphis Red Sox, Little Rock Black Travelers, Cleveland Bears, Atlanta Black Crackers

Thompson, Wade, 1923-26 P, Harrisburg Giants, Richmond Giants

Thompson, Will, 1949-50 P, Philadelphia Stars

Thompson, William, 1887-1900 C, Louisville Falls City, Genuine Cuban Giants

Thornton, Charles, 1887 player, Pittsburgh Keystones

Thornton, H., 1931 OF, Memphis Red Sox

Thornton, Jack, 1932-37 P, 2B, 1B, Atlanta Black Crackers

Thornton, Jesse, 1937 officer, Indianapolis Athletics

Thorpe, Clarence Jim, 1928 P, Hilldale

Thurman, —, 1937 1B, St. Louis Stars

Thurman, Jim, 1932-33-P, OF, Louisville Black Caps, Columbus Blue Birds

Thurman, Robert Burns, 1946-49 P, Homestead Grays, Kansas City Monarchs

Thurston, —, 1938 P, Birmingham Black Barons

Thurston, Bobby, 1911 OF, Chicago Giants

Tiant, Luis Sr. (Lefty), 1930-47 P, Cuban Stars (NNL), New York Cubans, Cuban House of David

Tindle, Levy, 1933 officer, Detroit Stars

Tinker, Harold (Hooks), 1931 OF, Pittsburgh Crawfords

Titus, James, 1937 officer, Detroit Stars

Tolbert, —, 1946 P, New York Black Yankees

Toles, Ted (Lefty), 1946 P, Pittsburgh Crawfords

Tomm, —, 1917-18 P, OF, Brooklyn Royal Giants, Philadelphia Giants, Bacharach Giants

Toney, Albert, 1901-16 SS, 2B, OF, Chicago Union Giants, Leland Giants, Chicago American Giants, Chicago Giants, Algona (IA) Brownies

Torres, —, 1916 C, Long Branch Cubans

Torres, Armando, 1939 P, Cuban Stars

Torriente, Christobel; see below

Torriente, Cristobal (Carlos) [Torrienti], 1914-32 OF, P, Cuban Stars, Chicago American Giants, Kansas City Monarchs, Detroit Stars, Gilkerson's Union Giants, Atlanta Black Crackers, Cleveland Cubs

Torrin, —, 1920 P, St. Louis Giants

Town, see Tomm

Trabue, —, 1924 P, Indianapolis ABCs

Trammel, Nat, 1930-32 1B, Birmingham Black Barons, Brooklyn Royal Giants

Trawick, Joe, 1950 2B, Cleveland Buckeyes

Treadwell, Harold, 1919-28 P, Brooklyn Royal Giants, Bacharach Giants, Harrisburg Giants, Chicago American Giants, Indianapolis ABCs, Dayton Marcos, Detroit Stars, Cleveland Browns, Lincoln Giants

Treadway, —, 1939-40 P, Kansas City Monarchs, Toledo Crawfords

Trealkill, Clarence, Harvey [Trilkill], 1929-31 SS, OF, Nashville Elite Giants

Trent, Theodore (Ted), 1927-39 P, St. Louis Stars, Detroit Wolves, Homestead Grays, Cole's American Giants, Chicago American Giants, Washington Pilots, New York Black Yankees

Trice, Robert (Bill), 1948-50 P, OF, Homestead Grays

Trimble, William E., 1927-32 officer, Chicago American Giants

Triplett, —, 1917-18 OF, Hilldale

Trouppe, Quincy Thomas (Big Train), 1930-49 C, OF, P, MGR, St. Louis Stars, Detroit Wolves, Homestead Grays, Kansas City Monarchs, Chicago American Giants, Indianapolis ABCs, Cleveland Buckeyes, New York Cubans

Troy, Donald, 1944-45 P, Baltimore Elite Giants

Trusty, Job, 1896 3B, Cuban Giants

Trusty, Shepard (Shep), 1885-89 P, OF, Philadelphia Orions, Argyle Hotel, Cuban Giants, Trenton Cuban Giants (Middle States Lg.)

Tucker, Henry, 1916-22 OF, officer, Bacharach Giants

Tucker, Orval, 1930,1942 2B, Baltimore Black Sox, Hilldale, Boston Royal Giants

Tugerson, Leander, 1950 P, Indianapolis Clowns

Turner, —, 1908 2B, New York Colored Giants

Turner, —, 1930 1B, Kansas City Monarchs

Turner, B., 1916-17 1B, Chicago Union Giants, Chicago Giants, All Nations

Turner, Bob, 1946,1950 C, Kansas City Monarchs, Houston Eagles

Turner, E.C. (Pop), 1925-37 3B, SS, Brooklyn Royal Giants, Homestead Grays, Birmingham Black Barons, Cleveland Cubs, Cole's American Giants New York Black Yankees; umpire, NNL

Turner, Etwood, 1923 OF, Toledo Tigers

Turner, Henry (Flash), 1938-43 C, 2B, 1B, OF, Jacksonville Red Caps, Cleveland Bears, Harrisburg-St. Louis Stars

Turner, J.O., 1887 player, Philadelphia Pythians

Turner, (Little Lefty), 1940-42 1B, Indianapolis Crawfords, Baltimore Elite Giants

Turner, Oliver, 1943 P, Chicago Brown Bombers

Turner, Thomas, 1947 1B, Chicago American Giants

Turner, (Tuck), 1919,1923,1928 P, Chicago American Giants, St. Louis Stars

Turnstall, Willie, 1950 P, Cleveland Buckeyes

Tut, Richard (King), 1943-50 1B, Cincinnati Clowns, Indianapolis Clowns

Tye, Dan, 1930-36 3B, SS, P, Memphis Red Sox, Cincinnati Tigers

Tyler, Charles H., 1934-35 officer, Newark Dodgers

Tyler, Edward, 1926-28 P, Brooklyn Cuban Giants, Hilldale, St.Louis Stars

Tyler, Eugene, 1942-43 C, INF, Chicago Brown Bombers, Kansas City Monarchs

Tyler, Roy, 1925-27 P, OF, Chicago American Giants, Cleveland Hornets

Tyler, William (Steel Arm), 1925-32 P, Memphis Red Sox, Detroit Stars, Kansas City Monarchs, Cole's American Giants

Tyms, —, 1923 OF, Chicago American Giants

Tyree, Ruby, 1916-24 P, All Nations, Chicago American Giants, Chicago Brown Bombers, Cleveland Browns

Tyson, Armand Cupree (Cap), 1936-40 C, Birmingham Black Barons

Tyus, Julius Jr, 1947 P, Philadelphia Stars

Underhill, Bob, 1924 P, Hilldale

Underwood, Ely, 1937 OF, Detroit Stars

Underwood, Ray, 1937 P, Detroit Stars

Vactor, John, 1887-88 player, Philadelphia Pythians, New York Gorhams

Valdes, Fermin, 1944 2B, Cincinnati-Indianapolis Clowns

Valdes, Rogelio, 1911 OF, All Cubans

Valdez, Strico (Swat), 1931-39 2B, SS, Cuban Stars, Atlanta Black Crackers, New York Cubans

Valdez, Tony, 1910-20 OF, P, Stars of Cuba, Cuban Stars (NNL)

Valentine, —, 1915-18 OF, Hilldale, Philadelphia Giants

Valos, —, 1917 3B, Cuban Giants

Van Buren, —, 1931 OF, Memphis Red Sox

Vance, Columbus, 1927-34 P, Birmingham Black Barons, Homestead Grays, Detroit Wolves, Detroit Stars, Indianapolis ABCs

Vandever, Bobby, 1944 INF, Kansas City Monarchs

Van Dyke, Fred, 1895-97 P, OF, Page Fence Giants

Vargas, —, 1927-31 SS, Cuban Stars (ECL), Cuban Stars (West)

Vargas, Juan Esteban (Tetelo) [Jose], 1927-44 OF, SS, Cuban Stars (ECL) Cuban Stars (NNL), Cuban Stars, New York Cubans

Vargas, Guillermo, 1949 OF, New York Cubans

Vargas, Roberto Enrique, 1948 P, Chicago American Giants

Varona, Gilberto, 1950 1B, Memphis Red Sox

Varona, Orlando Clemente [Verona], 1948-50 SS, Memphis Red Sox

Vasquez, Armando, 1944-48 UTIL, Cincinnati-Indianapolis Clowns, Indianapolis Clowns, New York Cubans

Vaughn, Harold, 1926-27 OF, Kansas City Monarchs

Vaughn, Joe, 1931 sec'y, NSL

Vaughn, Ray (Slim), 1934 P, Newark Dodgers, Newark Browns

Veal, —, 1931 P, OF, Birmingham Black Barons

Velasquez, Jose Luis, 1948 P, Indianapolis Clowns

Velasquez, Laru, 1948-50 P, Indianapolis Clowns

Veney, Jerome, 1908-17 OF, MGR, Homestead Grays

Ventura, —, 1929 P, Cuban Stars (NNL)

Vernal, (Sleepy), 1941 P, New York Cuban Stars

Verona, Orlando, see Orlando Varona

Victory, George M., 1919-20 officer, Pennsylvania Giants

Vierira, Chris, 1949 OF, New York Black Yankees

Villa, Roberto (Bobby), 1910-22 OF, 2B, Stars of Cuba, Cuban Stars, All Cubans, Cuban Stars (NNL)

Villafane, Vicente, 1947 UTIL, Indianapolis Clowns

Villodas, Luis, 1946-47 C, Baltimore Elite Giants

Vincent, Irving B. (Lefty), 1934-35 P, Pittsburgh Crawfords

Vines, Eddie, 1940 P, 3B, Chicago American Giants, Birmingham Black Barons

Vivens, —, 1929 P, St. Louis Stars

Waddy, Irving (Lefty), 1932-33 P, Indianapolis ABCs, Detroit Stars

Wade, Lee, 1909-19 P, OF, 1B, Cuban Giants, Philadelphia Giants, St. Louis Giants, Lincoln Giants, Chicago American Giants, Lincoln Stars, Brooklyn Royal Giants, Pennsylvania Red Caps of New York

Wagner, Bill, 1921-27 SS, 2B, MGR, Lincoln Giants, Brooklyn Royal Giants

Wagner, J., 1927 2B, 1B, Bacharach Giants, Hilldale

Waite, Arnold, 1936-37 P, Homestead Grays, Washington Elite Giants

Wakefield, Bert, 1895-1902,1915 1B, 2B, Chicago Unions, Kansas City Giants, Salina and Emporia (Kansas St. Lg.), Algona (IA) Brownies

Waldon, (Allie, Ollie), 1944 OF, Chicago American Giants

Walker, —, 1904 C, Brooklyn Royal Giants

Walker, A., 1923,1927 P, Milwaukee Bears, Kansas City Monarchs

Walker, A.M., 1937 MGR, Birmingham Black Barons

Walker, Casey, 1935-37-C, Newark Dodgers, Indianapolis Athletics

Walker, Charlie, 1930-34 officer, Homestead Grays

Walker, Edsall (Big), 1936-45 P, Homestead Grays, Philadelphia Stars

Walker, George T. (Little, Schoolboy), 1937-50 P, Homestead Grays, Kansas City Monarchs

Walker, H., 1932 C, Monroe Monarchs

Walker, Jack, 1940-43 P, Newark Eagles, Philadelphia Stars, Harrisburg-St. Louis Stars

Walker, Jesse (Hoss, Deuce, Aussa), 1929-50 SS, 3B, MGR, Officer Bacharach Giants, Cleveland Cubs, Nashville Elite Giants, Washington Elite Giants, Baltimore Elite Giants, New York Black Yankees, Birmingham Black Barons, Cincinnati Clowns, Cincinnati-Indianapolis Clowns, Nashville Cubs, Indianapolis Clowns, Columbus Elite Giants

Walker, Larry, see Larry Doby

Walker, Moses Fleetwood (Fleet), 1883-89 C, OF, 1B, Toledo (Northwestern Lg. and American Association); Cleveland (Western Lg.); Waterbury southern New England and Eastern Lg.s); Newark and Syracuse (International Lg.)

Walker, Moses L., 1928-31 officer, Detroit Stars

Walker, Pete (Lottie), 1923-26 P, OF, 2B, 3B, Homestead Grays

Walker, R.A., 1887 player, Boston Resolutes

Walker, Robert Taylor (R.T.), 1945-49 P, Homestead Grays

Walker, Tom (Tony), 1945 P, Baltimore Elite Giants

Walker, W., 1931-32 OF, Monroe Monarchs

Walker, Weldy Wilberforce, 1884-87 OF, C, 2B, Toledo (American Association); Akron (Ohio State Lg.); Pittsburgh Keystones, Cleveland (Western Lg.)

Wallace, —, 1940 2B, Cincinnati Buckeyes

Wallace, Felix (Dick), 1906-21 SS, 2B, 3B, MGR, St. Paul Gophers, Leland Giants, St. Louis Giants, Bacharach Giants, Lincoln Giants, Cuban Giants, Hilldale

Wallace, Jack, 1926-31 3B, 2B, Bacharach Giants, Cleveland Cubs, Philadelphia Giants

Wallace, James, 1949 C, Houston Eagles

Waller, —, 1906 SS, Cuban Giants

Waller, George, 1943 INF, Chicago Brown Bombers

Walls, Eddie [Wall], 1925-26 P, St. Louis Stars, Cleveland Hornets, Cleveland Elites

Walls, (Greenie), 1941-42 umpire

Walsh, —, 1916 2B, Bacharach Giants

Walters, —, 1923-24 P, Milwaukee Bears, Cleveland Browns

Walton, —, 1948 UTIL, Indianapolis Clowns

Walton, (Fuzzy), 1938 OF, Pittsburgh Crawfords

Ward, Britt, 1944 C, Kansas City Monarchs

Ward, C. (Pinky), 1924-35 OF, Memphis Red Sox, Chicago Columbia Giants, Louisville Black Caps, Cincinnati Tigers, Birmingham Black Barons, Brooklyn Eagles, Indianapolis ABCs Bacharach Giants

Ward, Ira, 1922-27 SS, 1B, Chicago Giants

Ware, Joe (Showboat), 1921,1932-36 OF, Nashville Elite Giants Cleveland Stars, Cleveland Giants, Memphis Red Sox, Akron Tyrites, Pittsburgh Crawfords, Newark Dodgers

Ware, Archie V., 1940-50 1B, Chicago American Giants, Kansas City Monarchs, Cleveland Buckeyes, Louisville Buckeyes, Indianapolis Clowns, Cincinnati Buckeyes

Ware, William, 1924-26 1B, Chicago American Giants

Warfield, Francis Xavier (Frank), 1915-32 2B, SS, 3B, MGR, St. Louis Giants, Indianapolis ABCs, Kansas City Monarchs, Detroit Stars, Hilldale, Baltimore Black Sox, Washington Pilots, Bowser's ABCs

Warmack, —, 1910 1B, St. Louis Giants

Warmack, Sam, 1922-38 OF, Richmond Giants, Hilldale, Bacharach Giants, Louisville Black Colonels

Warren, Cicero, 1946-47 P, Homestead Grays

Warren, Jesse, 1940-47 2B, 3B, P, Memphis Red Sox, New Orleans- St. Louis Stars, Birmingham Black Barons, Chicago American Giants

Warrick, —, 1905 P, Brooklyn Royal Giants

Washington, —, 1929 C, Nashville Elite Giants

Washington, Edgar (Ed, Blue), 1915-20 P, 1B, Chicago American Giants, Kansas City Monarchs

Washington, I. (Jap), 1922-37 3B, 1B, OF, Pittsburgh Keystones, Homestead Grays, Pittsburgh Crawfords, Newark Browns; umpire, NNL

Washington, Isaac, 1928 officer, Bacharach Giants

Washington, John G. (Johnny), 1933-50 1B, 3B, Montgomery Grey Sox, Birmingham Black Barons, Pittsburgh Crawfords, New York Black Yankees, Baltimore Elite Giants, Houston Eagles

Washington, L., 1884-85 SS, Baltimore Atlantics

Washington, Lafayette (Fay), 1940-45 P, Chicago American Giants, Birmingham Black Barons, Cincinnati-Indianapolis Clowns, Kansas City Monarchs, St. Louis Stars, New Orleans-St. Louis Stars

Washington, Lawrence, 1945 1B, New York Black Yankees

Washington, Namon, 1920-31 OF, SS, C, Indianapolis ABCs, Hilldale, Brooklyn Cuban Giants, Philadelphia Tigers, Lincoln Giants, Brooklyn Royal Giants

Washington, Peter (Pete), 1923-35 OF, Washington Potomacs, Wilmington Potomacs, Baltimore Black Sox, Philadelphia Stars, Lincoln Giants

Washington, Tom, 1904-10 C, OF, Philadelphia Giants, Chicago Giants, Pittsburgh Giants

Waters, —, 1887 player, Boston Resolutes

Waters, Dick, 1916 MGR, St. Louis Giants

Waters, Theodore (Ted), 1920-1928-P, OF, Chicago Giants, Hilldale, Philadelphia Tigers

Watkins, F. (Pop), 1899-1922 1B, C, MGR, Genuine Cuban Giants, Cuban Giants, Havana Red Sox, Pop Watkins Stars

Watkins, G.C., 1937 officer, Indianapolis Athletics

Watkins, Murray (Skeeter), 1943-50 3B, Newark Eagles, Philadelphia Stars

Watkins, Richard, 1950 INF, Memphis Red Sox

Watson, Amos, 1945-50 P, Cincinnati-Indianapolis Clowns, Baltimore Elite Giants, New York Cubans, Indianapolis Clowns, Kansas City Monarchs

Watson, David, 1923 P, Birmingham Black Barons

Watson, Everett, 1931 officer, Detroit Stars

Watson, George Johnny, 1922-26 OF, Detroit Stars

Watson, Jimmy, 1950 P, New York Cubans

Watson, William, 1925-26,1931 OF, Brooklyn Royal Giants, Bacharach Giants, Penn Red Caps of NY

Watters, —, 1916 INF, Chicago Giants

Watts, Andrew (Sonny, Big Six), 1946-50 INF, Cleveland Buckeyes, Birmingham Black Barons

Watts, Eddie, 1924-27 2B, 1B, St. Louis Stars, Cleveland Hornets, Cleveland Elites

Watts, Herman (Lefty), 1941-42 P, Jacksonville Red Caps, Cincinnati Buckeyes, Cleveland Buckeyes, New York Black Yankees

Watts, Jack, 1913-19 C, Louisville Cubs, Chicago American Giants, Indianapolis ABCs, Dayton Marcos, Bowser's ABCs

Watts, Richard (Dick), 1949-50 P, Birmingham Black Barons

Webb, —, 1917-19 P, Lincoln Giants

Webb, James (Baby), 1910 C, Leland Giants

Webb, Normal (Tweed), 1926,1931 INF, Ft. Wayne Pirates, St.Louis Pullmans

Webster, Charles, 1950 OF, Birmingham Black Barons

Webster, Daniel Jim (Double Duty), 1933-37 C, P, Detroit Stars, Kansas City Monarchs

Webster, William (West, Specks), 1912-26 C, 1B, OF, St. Louis Giants, Chicago Giants, Brooklyn Royal Giants, Mohawk Giants, Lincoln Giants, Hilldale, Detroit Stars, Dayton Marcos, Brooklyn Cuban Giants, Jewell's ABCs, Bacharach Giants

Weeks, E., 1918-24 2B, 3B, Pennsylvania Giants, Harrisburg Giants, Pittsburgh Stars of Buffalo, Brooklyn Royal Giants, Hilldale

Weeks, William, 1922 officer, Bacharach Giants

Weems, —, 1936 OF, Memphis Red Sox

Welch, Wingfield Scott (Moe), 1918-49 MGR, player, New Orleans Black Pelicans, Monroe Monarchs, Shreveport Giants, Cincinnati Buckeyes, Birmingham Black Barons, Cincinnati Crescents, New York Cubans, Chicago American Giants

Wells, —, 1918 2B, C, Lincoln Giants, Pennsylvania Giants

Wells, I., 1948 P, Memphis Red Sox

Wells, Willie Brooks, 1944-50 SS, Memphis Red Sox

Wells, Willie James (The Devil, Chico), 1924-49 SS, 3B, MGR, St. Louis Stars, Detroit Wolves, Kansas City Monarchs, Chicago American Giants, Cole's American Giants, Newark Eagles, Memphis Red Sox, New York Black Yankees, Baltimore Elite Giants, Indianapolis Clowns, Homestead Grays

Welmaker, Roy Horace (Snook), 1932-45 P, Atlanta Black Crackers, Homestead Grays, Philadelphia Stars

Wesley, Charles (Connie), 1921-30 OF, 2B, manager, Columbus Buckeyes, Pittsburgh Keystones, Indianapolis ABCs, Memphis Red Sox, Birmingham Black Barons, St. Louis Stars, Louisville White Sox, Louisville Red Caps

Wesley, Edgar, 1918-31 1B, Detroit Stars, Cleveland Hornets, Bacharach Giants, Chicago American Giants, Harrisburg Giants

Wesson, Les, 1949 P, New York Black Yankees

West, C., see James West

West, Charlie, 1942 OF, Birmingham Black Barons

West, James (Jim), 1930-47 1B, Birmingham Black Barons, Cleveland Cubs, Memphis Red Sox, Nashville Elite Giants, Columbus Elite Giants, Washington Elite Giants, Baltimore Elite Giants, Philadelphia Stars, New York Black Yankees

West, Ollie Ernest, 1942-46 P, Chicago American Giants, Pittsburgh Crawfords, Birmingham Black Barons, Homestead Grays

Weston, —, 1930 P, Hilldale

Weston, Issac (Deacon), 1949 P, Louisville Buckeyes

Weyman, J.B., 1887 player, Baltimore Lord Baltimores

Wharton, —, 1923 OF, Kansas City Monarchs

Whatley, David (Speed), 1936-46 OF, Birmingham Black Barons, Homestead Grays, Pittsburgh Crawfords, Cleveland Bears, Jacksonville Red Caps

Wheeler, Joe (Jodie), 1922-28 P, Bacharach Giants, Baltimore Black Sox, Brooklyn Cuban Giants, Wilmington Potomacs

Wheeler, Sam, 1948 OF, New York Cubans

White, —, 1913 P, Mohawk Giants

White, Artemis (Art), 1948 P, Indianapolis Clowns

White, Arthur, 1934 P, Newark Dodgers

White, Burlin, 1915-42 C, MGR, West Baden (Ind.) Sprudels, Bacharach Giants, Lincoln Giants, Philadelphia Royal Stars, Harrisburg Giants, Philadelphia Giants, Quaker Giants, Cuban Stars, Boston Royal Giants, Bowser's ABCs, Hilldale, Madison Stars

White, Butler, 1920-23 1B, Chicago Giants

White, Chaney, 1920-36 OF, Hilldale, Bacharach Giants, Wilmington Potomacs, Quaker Giants, Homestead Grays, Darby Daisies, Philadelphia Stars, Baltimore Black Sox, New York Cubans

White, Charles, 1950 3B, Philadelphia Stars

White, Clarence (Red), 1928-32 P, Nashville Elite Giants, Memphis Red Sox, Louisville White Sox, Monroe Monarchs

White, Edward, 1944 P, Homestead Grays

White, Eugene, 1935-36 3B, Brooklyn Eagles, Newark Eagles

White, Henry (Lefty), 1940 P, Cleveland Bears

White, (Ladd), 1947-48 P, Memphis Red Sox

White, Lawrence (Eugene), 1950 INF, Chicago American Giants

White, M., 1886-87 P, New York Gorhams

White, R.W., 1887 player, Washington Capital Citys, Cuban Giants

White, (Red), see Clarence White

White, Robert, 1922-23 2B, 3B, Pittsburgh Keystones, Toledo Tigers, St. Louis Stars

White, Sol, 1887-1926 2B, 3B, OF, 1B, MGR, coach, bus. mgr, Pittsburgh Keystones, Washington Capital Citys, Wheeling (Ohio State Lg.); New York Gorhams (Middle States Lg.), York Monarchs (Eastern Interstate Lg.), York Cuban Giants (Eastern Interstate Lg.), Genuine Cuban Giants, Fort Wayne (Western Interstate Lg.), Page Fence Giants, Cuban X Giants, Columbia Giants, Philadelphia Giants, Lincoln Giants, Quaker Giants, Cleveland Browns, Newark Stars, Philadelphia Gorhams, Ansonia Cuban Giants (Connecticut St. Lg.)

White, Zarlie, 1934 OF, Monroe Monarchs

Whitfield, (Lefty), 1950 P, Baltimore Elite Giants

Whitlock, —, 1926 1B, Dayton Marcos

Whitney, —, 1942 P, OF, New York Black Yankees

Whitworth, Richard, 1915-24 P, Chicago American Giants, Chicago Giants, Hilldale

Whyte, William T. (Billy), 1883-1894 P, OF, Cuban Giants, York Cuban Giants (Eastern Interstate Lg.), Trenton Cuban Giants (Middle States Lg.), St.Louis Black Stockings, Boston Resolutes

Wickware, Frank (Smiley, Smokey), 1910-25 P, Leland Giants, St. Louis Giants, Philadelphia Giants, Mohawk Giants, Lincoln Stars, Chicago American Giants, Chicago Giants, Brooklyn Royal Giants, Detroit Stars, Norfolk Stars, Lincoln Giants, Jewell ABCs, Indianapolis ABCs

Wiggins, —, 1920 SS, Chicago American Giants

Wiggins, Bob, 1942 SS, Chicago Brown Bombers

Wiggins, Joe, 1930-34 3B, Nashville Elite Giants, Bacharach Giants, Baltimore Black Sox

Wigware, —, 1930 SS, 3B, Nashville Elite Giants

Wilbert, Art (Mofike), 1942 OF, Cincinnati Clowns, Minneapolis- St. Paul Gophers

Wilds, —, 1892 C, Stockton (California Lg.)

Wiley, F., 1920-27 3B, OF, Lincoln Giants, Pennsylvania Red Caps of New York

Wiley, Joe, 1947-50 3B, 2B, Baltimore Elite Giants, Memphis Red Sox

Wiley, Wabishaw Spencer (Doc), 1910-23 C, 1B, OF, Brooklyn Royal Giants, Lincoln Giants, Philadelphia Giants, West Baden (Ind.) Sprudels, Mohawk Giants

Wilkes, Barron D., 1919 officer, New York Bacharach Giants

Wilkes, James E. (Jimmy), 1945-50 OF, Newark Eagles, Houston Eagles

Wilkins, Wesley, 1910-15 OF, Kansas City, Kansas, Giants

Wilkinson, James Leslie (J.L.), 1909-48 officer, All Nations, Kansas City Monarchs; sec'y, NNL; tres, NAL

Willas, S., 1887 player, New York Gorhams

Willburn, —, 1926 P, Baltimore Black Sox

Willett, Pete, 1923-28 SS, OF, Lincoln Giants, Cleveland Browns, Cleveland Tigers, Homestead Grays

Williams, —, 1939 C, Indianapolis ABCs

Williams, A., 1916-18 P, OF, 2B, Brooklyn Royal Giants

Williams, A.D., 1925 officer, Indianapolis ABCs

Williams, A.N., 1922 officer, Pittsburgh Keystones

Williams, Albert, 1943-45 P, Newark Eagles

Williams, Andrew (Stringbean), 1915-25 P, MGR, St. Louis Giants, Pennsylvania Red Caps of New York, Indianapolis ABCs, Chicago American Giants, Dayton Marcos, Bacharach Giants, Brooklyn Royal Giants, Washington Potomacs

Williams, B., 1931-32,1939 OF, Montgomery Grey Sox, Indianapolis ABCs

Williams, Bert, 1923 officer, Philadelphia Giants

Williams, Bilbo (Biggie), 1942-43 OF, Chicago Brown Bombers, Baltimore Elite Giants

Williams, Bill, 1894-1900 P, Genuine Cuban Giants, Cuban X Giants

Williams, C., 1885 MGR, Brooklyn Remsens

Williams, Charles, 1887 player, Boston Resolutes

Williams, Charles Arthur, 1924-31 SS, 2B, Memphis Red Sox, Chicago American Giants, Indianapolis ABCs, Chicago Columbia Giants

Williams, Charles Henry (Lefty), 1915-34 P, Homestead Grays

Williams, Charley, 1945 P, Toledo Cubs (USL)

Williams, Chester, Arthur, 1930-43 SS, 2B, Memphis Red Sox, Pittsburgh Crawfords, Homestead Grays, Philadelphia Stars, Chicago American Giants, Toledo Crawfords

Williams, Clarence, 1886-1912 C, SS, 3B, OF,MGR, Cuban Giants, New York Gorhams, Cuban X Giants, Philadelphia Giants, Lansing, Michigan Colored Capital All-Americans, Smart Set, Ansonia Cuban Giants (Connecticut St. Lg.), Trenton Cuban Giants, (Middle States Lg.) Harrisburg (Eastern Interstate Lg.)

Williams, Clarence, 1938-40 P, OF, Baltimore Elite Giants, Washington Black Senators

Williams, Clyde (Lefty), 1947-50 P, Cleveland Buckeyes

Williams, (Cotton), see Robert Williams

Williams, Craig (Stringbean), 1928 P, Brooklyn Cuban Giants

Williams, (Curly), see Willie Williams

Williams, E.J., 1887 player, Washington Capital Citys

Williams, Elbert, 1931-34 P, Louisville White Sox, Monroe Monarchs

Williams, Eli (Eddie), 1943-45 OF, Harrisburg-St. Louis Stars, Kansas City Monarchs

Williams, F., 1927 OF, Birmingham Black Barons

Williams, Felix (Jeff), 1950 2B, Houston Eagles, Kansas City Monarchs

Williams, Frank (Shorty), 1942-46 OF, Homestead Grays

Williams, Fred, 1922-25 C, Washington Potomacs, Harrisburg Giants, Brooklyn Royal Giants, Indianapolis ABCs

Williams, G., 1939 UTIL, Baltimore Elite Giants

Williams, George, 1885-1902 2B, 1B, 3B Philadelphia Orions, Argyle Hotel, Cuban Giants, New York Gorhams, Cuban X Giants, York Cuban Giants (Eastern Interstate Lg.), Trenton Cuban Giants (Middle States Lg.)

Williams, George, 1928 SS, 3B, Cleveland Tigers

Williams, Gerard, 1921-25 SS, Indianapolis ABCs, Homestead Grays, Lincoln Giants

Williams, Graham H., 1929-34 P, Homestead Grays, Monroe Monarchs, New Orleans Crescent Stars

Williams, Hank, 1911-13 3B, 2B, 1B, Mohawk Giants, Brooklyn Royal Giants

Williams, Harry, 1918-22 3B, Baltimore Black Sox

Williams, Harry, 1931-50 3B, 2B, SS, MGR, Pittsburgh Crawfords, Toledo Crawfords, Baltimore Black Sox, Homestead Grays, Brooklyn Eagles, Newark Eagles, New York Black Yankees, Harrisburg-St. Louis Stars, Baltimore Elite Giants, New York Cubans, New Orleans Creoles

Williams, Henry (Flick), 1922-31 C, Kansas City Monarchs, St. Louis Stars, Indianapolis ABCs

Williams, James, 1885 C, Brooklyn Remsens

Williams, James (Jim), 1937-48 OF, MGR, Homestead Grays, Toledo Crawfords, Cleveland Bears, New York Black Yankees, New York Cubans, Birmingham Black Barons, Durham Eagles, Atlanta Black Crackers

Williams, Jesse, 1942-47 C, UTIL, Cleveland Buckeyes

Williams, Jesse Horace (Bill), 1939-50 SS, 3B, Kansas City Monarchs, Indianapolis Clowns

Williams, Jim (Bullet), 1929-32 P, Nashville Elite Giants, Cleveland Cubs, Detroit Wolves

Williams, Jim, 1934-37 OF, 1B, Newark Dodgers, New York Black Yankees, Philadelphia Stars

Williams, Joe, 1941 SS, Homestead Grays

Williams, Joe, 1946 OF, New York Black Yankees

Williams, John (Big Boy), 1926-38 OF, P, 1B, St. Louis Stars, Indianapolis ABCs, Detroit Stars, Homestead Grays, Dayton Marcos, Columbus Elite Giants, Jacksonville Red Caps

Williams, John, 1948 1B, Chicago American Giants

Williams, Johnny, 1943-48 P, Chicago Brown Bombers, Cincinnati- Indianapolis Clowns, Indianapolis Clowns

Williams, Joseph (Cyclone, Smokey Joe), 1905-1932 P, MGR, San Antonio Bronchos, Leland Giants, Chicago Giants, Lincoln Giants, Chicago American Giants, Bacharach Giants, Brooklyn Royal Giants, Homestead Grays, Detroit Wolves, Hilldale, Mohawk Giants

Williams, L., 1905-09 OF, Cuban Giants

Williams, L.C., 1939-42 OF, Ethiopian Clowns, New York Cubans

Williams, L.R., 1931 officer, Cleveland Stars

Williams, Lem, 1923 umpire, NNL

Williams, Lemuel, 1937-39 P, St.Louis Stars, Chicago American Giants

Williams, Len, 1950 INF, OF, Indianapolis Clowns

Williams, Leroy, 1947-50 SS, 2B, Newark Eagles, Kansas City Monarchs

Williams, M., 1931 SS, Pittsburgh Crawfords

Williams, M., 1939 P, Baltimore Elite Giants

Williams, Marvin, 1943-50 2B, Philadelphia Stars

Williams, Mathis (Matt), 1921-23 SS, 3B, Pittsburgh Keystones, Cleveland Tate Stars

Williams, Morris, 1920-21 P, Indianapolis ABCs

Williams, Nish (Zeke, Nate), 1927-39 C, OF, 3B, 1B, Nashville Elite Giants, Cleveland Cubs, Columbus Elite Giants, Washington Elite Giants, Birmingham Black Barons, Indianapolis ABCs, Atlanta Black Crackers

Williams, Norm, 1930 OF, Nashville Elite Giants

Williams, Phil (Pete), 1931-39 2B, Baltimore Black Sox, Toledo Crawfords, Jacksonville Red Caps

Williams, Poindexter, 1920-33 C, MGR, Chicago American Giants, Detroit Stars, Kansas City Monarchs, Birmingham Black Barons, Louisville White Sox, Nashville Elite Giants, Homestead Grays

Williams, Ray, 1933-39 P, New York Black Yankees

Williams, Ray, 1950 P, OF, New York Black Yankees

Williams, (Red), 1926 SS, Indianapolis ABCs

Williams, Robert A. (Cotton), 1943-50 P, INF, Newark Eagles, Houston Eagles

Williams, Robert Lawns (Bobby), 1918-45 SS, 2B, 3B, MGR, Chicago American Giants, Indianapolis ABCs, Homestead Grays, Pittsburgh Crawfords, Cleveland Red Sox, Cleveland Tigers, Columbus Blue Birds, Akron, Cleveland Giants

Williams, Roy K., 1931-41 P, Pittsburgh Crawfords, Columbus Blue Birds, Baltimore Black Sox, Brooklyn Royal Giants, Brooklyn Eagles, Philadelphia Stars, New York Black Yankees, Baltimore Elite Giants, Homestead Grays

Williams, S., 1914-18 P, Brooklyn Royal Giants, Philadelphia Giants

Williams, S. (Al), 1945 P, Newark Eagles

Williams, Samuel C. (Sam), 1947-50 P, Birmingham Black Barons

Williams, Solomon (Sol), 1884-85 OF, Baltimore Atlantics

Williams, Stuart, 1950 2B, Cleveland Buckeyes

Williams, T., 1896-05 C, OF, Cuban X Giants

Williams, Thomas (Tom), 1916-25 P, Bacharach Giants, Chicago American Giants, Lincoln Giants, Brooklyn Royal Giants, Hilldale, Chicago Giants, Detroit Stars

Williams, V., 1929 C, St.Louis Stars

Williams, Walter, 1898 P, Celeron Acme Colored Giants (Iron and Oil Lg.)

Williams, Walter, 1939 P, Newark Eagles

Williams, Wil, 1902 1B, St. Cloud, (Minn.)

Williams, (Willie), 1929-33 SS, 2B, Bacharach Giants, Brooklyn Royal Giants

Williams, Willie, 1934-41 P, Washington Elite Giants, Baltimore Elite Giants, Birmingham Black Barons

Williams, Willie C. (Curley), 1945-50 3B, SS, Newark Eagles, Houston Eagles

Williams, Wilmore, 1943 OF, Newark Eagles

Williams, Woodrow, 1933 P, Akron Tyrites

Williams, (Zeke), see Nish Williams

Willis, Jim (Cannonball), 1927-39 P, Birmingham Black Barons, Nashville Elite Giants, Cleveland Cubs, Philadelphia Stars, Columbus Elite Giants, Washington Elite Giants, Baltimore Elite Giants

Willis, S., 1887 player, New York Gorhams

Wills, —, 1911 3B, Brooklyn Royal Giants

Wilmore, Alfred (Apple), 1947-50 P, Philadelphia Stars, Baltimore Elite Giants

Wilson, —, 1917 SS, Bacharach Giants

Wilson, —, 1927 C, Harrisburg Giants

Wilson, —, 1950 P, Cleveland Buckeyes

Wilson, Alec, 1939 OF, New York Black Yankees

Wilson, Andrew, 1922-27 OF, P, New Orleans Crescent Stars, Milwaukee Bears, Chicago Giants

Wilson, Arthur Lee (Artie), 1940,1944-48 SS, Birmingham Black Barons

Wilson, Benjamin (Benny), 1923-28 OF, Lincoln Giants, Pennsylvania Red Caps of New York

Wilson, Bill, 1948 3B, Newark Eagles

Wilson, Carter (Coltie), 1920-23 OF, Gilkerson's Union Giants, Peters' Union Giants, Chicago Giants

Wilson, Charles, 1917-22 P, OF, Dayton Giants, Dayton Marcos Columbus Buckeyes, Detroit Stars

Wilson, Charles, 1948-49 OF, 3B, Indianapolis Clowns

Wilson, Daniel Richard (Dan), 1937-47 OF, 3B, 2B, SS, Pittsburgh Crawfords, St. Louis Stars, New Orleans-St. Louis Stars, New York Black Yankees, Harrisburg-St. Louis Stars, Homestead Grays, Philadelphia Stars

Wilson, Ed, 1896-1905 1B, OF, Cuban X Giants, Lansing, Michigan, Colored Capital All-Americans, Adrian (MI) Page Fence Giants

Wilson, Edward, 1898 P, Celeron Acme Colored Giants (Iron and Oil Lg.)

Wilson, Elmer, 1921-26 2B, 3B, Dayton Marcos, Detroit Stars, St. Louis Stars

Wilson, Emmett Dabney, 1937-46 OF, Pittsburgh Crawfords, Cincinnati Buckeyes, Cleveland Buckeyes, Cincinnati Clowns, Boston Blues

Wilson, Felton, 1937 C, Detroit Stars

Wilson, Fietman, 1932-33 P, C, Akron Tyrites, Cleveland Stars

Wilson, Fred (Sardo),1938-45 OF, P, MGR, New York Black Yankees, Newark Eagles, Cincinnati Clowns, Cincinnati-Indianapolis Clowns

Wilson, George H., 1895-1905 P, OF, Page Fence Giants, Columbia Giants, Chicago Union Giants, Adrian (Michigan St. Lg.)

Wilson, George, 1922 OF, New Orleans Crescent Stars

Wilson, Harvey, 1939 INF, Toledo Crawfords

Wilson, Herb, 1928-29 P, Kansas City Monarchs

Wilson, J.H., 1887 player, Baltimore Lord Baltimore

Wilson, James (Chubby), 1929 OF, Bacharach Giants

Wilson, James, 1940 OF, 2B, Indianapolis Crawfords

Wilson, James, 1947 P, Memphis Red Sox

Wilson, Jay, 1945-1948 SS, Birmingham Black Barons

Wilson, John E. (Johnny), 1948-49 OF, Chicago American Giants

Wilson, Joseph, 1887 player, Washington Capital Citys

Wilson, Judson Ernest (Jud, Bojum), 1922-45 3B, 1B, 2B, MGR, Baltimore Black Sox, Homestead Grays, Philadelphia Stars, Pittsburgh Crawfords

Wilson, (Lefty), see Woodrow Wilson

Wilson, Percy Lawrance, 1922-24 1B, OF, New Orleans Crescent Stars, Milwaukee Bears

Wilson, Pete, 1924 1B, Baltimore Black Sox

Wilson, Ray, 1902-10 1B, Cuban X Giants, Philadelphia Giants

Wilson, Robert (Bob), 1947-50 3B, Newark Eagles, Houston Eagles

Wilson, Thomas T. (Tom), 1918-47 officer, Nashville Standard Giants, Nashville Elite Giants, Cleveland Cubs, Baltimore Elite Giants; vice-chairman, tres, pres, NNL; sec'y, pres, NSL

Wilson, W. Rollo, 1929-34 sec'y, Anl; commissioner, NNL

Wilson, William H., 1887 SS, Pittsburgh Keystones

Wilson, Woodrow (Lefty), 1931,1936-40 P, Kansas City Monarchs, Memphis Red Sox, Baltimore Elite Giants, New York Cubans

Wingfield, —, 1920-23,1931 2B, OF, SS, P, Dayton Marcos Detroit Stars, Toledo Tigers, Memphis Red Sox

Wingo, (Doc), 1944 C, Kansas City Monarchs

Winkle, —, 1946 3B, Indianapolis Clowns

Winston, —, 1929-32 P, OF, Chicago Giants, Chicago Columbia Giants, Atlanta Black Crackers, Detroit Stars

Winston, Clarence (Bobby), 1905-23 OF, Philadelphia Giants, Leland Giants, Chicago Giants, Cuban X Giants

Winters, Jesse (Nip), 1919-33 P, Norfolk Stars, Bacharach Giants, Norfolk Giants, Hilldale, Philadelphia Stars, Harrisburg Giants, Lincoln Giants, Darby Daisies, Newark Browns, Washington Pilots, Baltimore Black Sox

Wise, Russell, 1940 1B, Indianapolis Crawfords

Wisher, —, 1923 OF, Harrisburg Giants

Witherspoon, Lester, 1948-49 P, OF, Indianapolis Clowns, Homestead Grays

Wolfolk, Lewis, 1923-24 P, Chicago American Giants

Womack, James, 1923-33 1B, Cleveland Tigers, Indianapolis ABCs, Cuban Stars (NNL), Columbus Turfs, Columbus Blue Birds, Baltimore Black Sox, Richmond Giants

Woodard, —, 1928 INF, Cleveland Tigers

Wood, —, 1897 OF, Adrian Page Fence Giants

Woods, —, 1916 P, Chicago American Giants

Woods, (Doggy), 1904 P, Gray Eagle (Minn.)

Woods, Ed, 1891-98 P, 1B, Ansonia Cuban Giants (Connecticut St. Lg.), Chicago Unions

Woods, Parnell, 1933-49 3B, MGR, Birmingham Black Barons, Cleveland Bears, Jacksonville Red Caps, Cincinnati Buckeyes, Cleveland Buckeyes, Louisville Buckeyes, Philadelphia Stars

Woods, Sam (Buddy), 1946-50 P, Cleveland Buckeyes, Memphis Red Sox

Woods, William, 1887 SS, Philadelphia Pythians

Woods, William J., 1919-26 OF, Brooklyn Royal Giants, Indianapolis ABCs, Columbus Buckeyes, St. Louis Stars, Washington Potomacs, Bacharach Giants, Chicago American Giants, St. Louis Giants

Woolridge, Edward, 1926-28 SS, 1B, OF, Cleveland Elites, Cleveland Tigers

Wright, —, 1908 1B, Brooklyn Colored Giants

Wright, —, 1915 C, Chicago American Giants

Wright, —, 1946 3B, New York Cubans

Wright, Burnis (Bill), 1932-45 OF, Nashville Elite Giants, Columbus Elite Giants, Washington Elite Giants, Baltimore Elite Giants, Philadelphia Stars

Wright, Charley, 1931 P, Birmingham Black Barons

Wright, Clarence (Buggy), 1898 1B, Celeron Acme Colored Giants (Iron and Oil Lg.)

Wright, Ernest (Ernie), 1941-49 off,owner, Cleveland White Sox, Cincinnati Buckeyes, Cleveland Buckeyes; vice-pres, NAL

Wright, George (Ed), 1905-13 SS, 2B, Quaker Giants, Brooklyn Royal Giants, Leland Giants, Chicago Giants, Lincoln Giants

Wright, Henry, 1928-35 P, Nashville Elite Giants, Cleveland Cubs, Columbus Elite Giants, Birmingham Black Barons

Wright, Henry L. Jr. (Red), 1948 C, Baltimore Elite Giants

Wright, Howard, 1933   P, Nashville Elite Giants

Wright, John Richard (Needle Nose), 1937-48   P, Newark Eagles, Indianapolis Crawfords, Pittsburgh Crawfords, Homestead Grays, Toledo Crawfords

Wright, L., 1932   OF, Nashville Elite Giants

Wright, Zollie, 1931-43   OF, Memphis Red Sox, Monroe Monarchs, New Orleans Crescent Stars, Columbus Elite Giants, Washington Elite Giants, Washington Black Senators, New York Black Yankees, Philadelphia Stars

Wyatt, —, 1929   C, Detroit Stars

Wyatt, David (Dave), 1896-1920   OF, 2B, SS, Chicago Unions, Chicago Union Giants; co-drafter, constitution of NNL

Wyatt, Ralph Arthur (Pepper), 1941-46   SS, Chicago American Giants, Homestead Grays, Cleveland Buckeyes

Wylie, Ensloe, 1944-47   P, Kansas City Monarchs, Memphis Red Sox

Wynder, Clarence, 1950   C, Cleveland Buckeyes

Wynn, Calvin, 1949   OF, Louisville Buckeyes

Wynn, Willie, 1944-50   C, Newark Eagles, New York Cubans

Yancy, —, 1911   CF, Philadelphia Giants

Yancey, William James (Bill, Yank), 1923-36   SS, Philadelphia Giants, Hilldale, Philadelphia Tigers, Lincoln Giants, Darby Daisies, New York Black Yankees, Brooklyn Eagles, Philadelphia Stars, New York Cubans, Bacharach Giants

Yarbrough, —, 1932   C, Atlanta Black Crackers

Yokeley, Laymon Samuel (Norman), 1926-38   P, Baltimore Black Sox, Bacharach Giants, Philadelphia Stars, Washington Black Senators, Brooklyn Eagles

Yokum, —, 1922   P, Kansas City Monarchs

York, Jim, 1919-23   C, OF, Norfolk Stars, Hilldale, Bacharach Giants

Young, Berdell, 1922-28   OF, Bacharach Giants, Lincoln Giants

Young, Bob, 1950   INF, Cleveland Buckeyes

Young, Edward (Pep), 1936-47   C, 1B, 3B, Chicago American Giants, Kansas City Monarchs, Homestead Grays

Young, Frank A. (Fay), 1939-48   sec'y, NAL

Young, John, 1923-24-P, St. Louis Stars, Memphis Red Sox

Young, Leandy, 1944-45   OF, Birmingham Black Barons, Kansas City Monarchs

Young, Maurice (Doolittle), 1927   P, Kansas City Monarchs

Young, Norman Harvey, 1941-44   SS, Baltimore Elite Giants, Cleveland Buckeyes, New York Black Yankees

Young, Roy, 1942-45   umpire, NAL

Young, Thomas Jefferson (T.J., Tom), 1926-41   C, Kansas City Monarchs, St. Louis Stars, Detroit Wolves, New York Cubans, Pittsburgh Crawfords, Homestead Grays, Newark Eagles

Young, Dr. W.H., 1949-50   officer, Houston Eagles

Young, Wilbur, 1945   P, Birmingham Black Barons

Young, William P. (Pep), 1919-34   C, Homestead Grays

Young, William, 1927   P, Kansas City Monarchs

Yvanes, Armando, 1949-50   SS, New York Cubans

Zapp, James (Zipper), 1948-50   OF, Birmingham Black Barons, Baltimore Elite Giants

Zapp, Stephen, 1946   INF, Baltimore Elite Giants

Ziegler, William (Doc), 1927-29   OF, Chicago Giants

Zimmerman, George, 1887   player, Pittsburgh Keystones

Zomphier, Charles (Zomp), 1926-31   2B, 3B, SS, Cleveland Elites, Cleveland Hornets, Cleveland Tigers, Memphis Red Sox, Cleveland Cubs, Birmingham Black Barons, St. Louis Stars, Cuban Stars (NNL); umpire NAL

Umpires

Larry R. Gerlach

Traditionally regarded as villains by fans, adversarial autocrats by players, and invisible men by the press, umpires have been, as Furman Bisher put it, "submerged in the history of baseball like idiot children in a family album." Yet the umpire is baseball's indispensable man, for the arbiter transformed baseball from a recreational activity to a competitive sport and has personified the integrity of the professional game. Since attorney William R. Wheaton officiated the first recorded "modern" game on October 6, 1845, umpires have made important contributions to the National Pastime. Indeed, the history of the umpire mirrors the distinctive eras and developments of the game itself.

From the creation of the modern game in the 1840s through the Civil War, the umpire was the personification of base ball (two words then) as an amateur sport played by gentlemen. According to the September 23, 1845, rules of the Knickerbocker Club of New York, which created modern baseball, the president of the club "shall appoint an Umpire, who shall keep the game in a book provided for that purpose, and note all violations of the Bylaws and Rules." As "match" games between clubs became more frequent, three officials were commonly used—one umpire chosen by each team and a neutral "referee" to decide the often partisan split decisions. In 1858 the National Association of Base Ball Players sanctioned a single umpire, sometimes a spectator or even a player, chosen by the home team with the consent of the rival captain. There was no dress code, but contemporary prints depict the idealized portrait of the gentleman arbiter—a distinguished-looking gentleman resplendent in top hat, Prince Albert coat, and cane, who stood, kneeled, or sat on a stool in foul territory along the first base line. Although the attire became less formal by the Civil War, the volunteer arbiters continued to receive no remuneration for their services other than the "honor" of being chosen "the sole judge of fair and unfair play."

The nationwide popularity of the game after the Civil War led to the professionalization of baseball and, in turn, to professional umpires. In 1871 the newly formed National Association of Professional Base Ball Players continued the tradition of unpaid volunteers by allowing the home team to choose the umpire from a list of five names submitted by the visiting club, but gave the arbiter greater authority by limiting appeals to decisions involving rules interpretation, not judgment. In 1878 the National League of Professional Base Ball Clubs, organized two years earlier, instructed home teams to pay umpires $5 per game, and in 1879 National League president William A. Hulbert appointed baseball's first umpire staff—a group of twenty men from which teams could

chose an arbiter. The approved list and compensation did not free the umpires from the "homer" syndrome (ruling in favor of the home team as a civic gesture) or suspicion of collusion with gamblers. Indeed, in 1882 Richard Higham of Troy, New York, former manager and National League player, was banished from the league for advising gamblers how to bet on games he umpired, thus earning the infamous distinction of being the only umpire ever judged guilty of dishonesty on the field. That same year a new professional circuit, the American Association, pioneered in the creation of an umpiring staff that was hired, paid, and assigned to games by the league itself. Paid $140 a month and $3 per diem for expenses while on the road, American Association umpires were required to wear blue flannel coats and caps while working games. The next year the National League adopted its own permanent paid and uniformed staff, thus completing the professionalization of major league "men in blue."

Despite increased status, umpiring in the major leagues was an uncertain, stressful, and even dangerous occupation through the end of the century. Frequent revisions in the rules and innovations in playing techniques made the umpire's job exceedingly difficult, while the physical and verbal abuse from fans and players alike often made an umpire's life intolerable. Umpires were routinely spiked, kicked, cursed, and spat upon by players, while fans hurled vile epithets and all manner of debris at the arbiters. Mobbings and physical assaults were frequent, so much so that police escorts were familiar and welcome sights to the men in blue. The transformation of the umpire from esteemed arbitrator to despised villain was largely deliberate. As club owners and league officials recognized that umpire baiting boosted gate receipts, they refused to support the umpires's field decisions, dismissed or paid player's fines, did little to curb rowdiness, and even joined sportswriters in depicting umpires as scoundrels and scapegoats. Occasionally umpires retaliated by hurling objects back into the stands or by punching players and reporters—and were summarily punished for so doing. But most found other jobs. In an era when "Kill the umpire!" was not mere rhetoric, there was a high turnover rate in umpires as few men were willing to endure such trials and tribulations for paltry pay and poor working conditions.

Nonetheless, baseball's tumultuous era produced several umpires of historical importance. William B. "Billy" McLean, part-time pugilist from Philadelphia, was the first professional umpire. So great was his ability and reputation for fairness that National League officials in 1876 not only agreed to his demands for the unheard of $5 per game but also sent him on a expense-paid tour of every city in the league. The most famous early exponents

of the two basic styles of umpiring were Robert V. Ferguson and John H. Gaffney. Ferguson, known during his playing days as "Robert the Great" and "Death to Flying Things," ruled as an iron-fisted autocrat, while Gaffney, dubbed "The King of the Umpires," controlled the game through tact and diplomacy. Gaffney also popularized the technique of working behind home plate until a player reached base and then moving behind the pitcher. (Before this the umpire worked either behind the batter or behind the pitcher and did not shift.) In 1888 Gaffney was the highest-paid umpire in baseball, earning $2,500 a year, plus expenses on the road. Other umpires of note include John O. "Honest John" Kelly, who appeared in more World Series (five) than any other umpire of the day; fiesty Timothy Hurst, quick and handy with curses, quips, and fists; Benjamin F. Young, killed in a railroad accident en route to a game, who in 1887 drew up a professional code of ethics for umpires as well as a ten-point proposal to improve their status; John F. Sheridan, the prototype of the modern umpire; and John A. Heydler and Thomas J. Lynch, each of whom later became president of the National League.

With the 1903 peace agreement between the National League and the new American League, major league baseball entered the modern era and brought stature and stability for umpires. Byron Bancroft "Ban" Johnson, president of the upstart American League, led in providing the strong support from league officials that was essential to the morale and effectiveness of the umpires. Noted for his backing of umpires when he had been the head of the Western League, Johnson insisted that umpires be respected and backed up his words by supporting their decisions and suspending players who were guilty of flagrant misconduct. In turn, he insisted upon tactfulness in contrast to the combativeness of the previous era. The National League followed suit, especially under ex-umps Lynch and Heydler, and by World War One, major league umpires enjoyed "unprecedented authority, dignity, and security." As umpire, manager, and baseball executive, Clarence "Pants" Rowland later remarked: "All umpires ought to tip their hats whenever Ban Johnson's name is mentioned."

Johnson also took the lead in dealing with the obvious handicaps presented by the single-umpire system. The game had long since become too fast and the players too devious for a lone arbiter to follow the action, let alone control the contest; moreover, in case of illness or injury clubs had to use a player to officiate the game. A three-umpire system, suggested in 1885 and actually used in the World Series that year, was an aberration, but a two-umpire system was much discussed in the 1880s and 1890s. Although the Players League of 1890 employed two umpires and in 1898 the two-umpire system was sanctioned in the rules, club owners continued to resist the expense of a second arbiter. After Johnson added a fifth umpire in 1902, the use of two arbiters became frequent, common, and then standard—an umpire-in-chief to call balls and strikes and a field umpire to make decisions on the bases. Again, the National League followed apace and in 1912 both leagues had ten-man staffs—two umpires per game and two replacements in reserve.

While front office support and the two-man system contributed greatly to the effectiveness of the umpire on the field, the enhanced stature of umpires was due perhaps as much to the personalities and contributions of the men who served in the first two decades of the twentieth century. That so many of the umpires who loom large in baseball history (and mythology) hail from the early decades of the century is partly the result of the extraordinary skill required to manage the game during the dead-ball era, when the bunt, stolen base, and hit-and-run were primary offensive tactics, and partly because of the media attention lavished on major league baseball at the time.

Ban Johnson, who personally selected his umpires with an exacting eye for ability and character, assembled an imposing staff for the American League. The senior umpire was John F. "Jack" Sheridan, veteran from the nineteenth century, who served as the acknowledged model for the younger men in both leagues and popularized working from a crouch position behind the plate. Another holdover was Franklin O'Loughlin, nicknamed "Silk" as a boy because of his long, curly hair, who successfully matched wits and words with players. College-educated William G. "Billy" Evans, who in 1906 became, at twenty-two, the youngest major league umpire in history, wrote nationally syndicated sports columns while working as an umpire, and went on to be a baseball executive. A fastidious dresser, Evans set the standard for the appearance of umpires on the field. English-born Thomas H. "Tommy" Connolly umpired the American League's first game in 1901 and thirty years later became the Junior Circuit's first umpire-in-chief (1931–54); patient and reserved yet firm, he established the league's tradition of ejecting players only as a last resort and once went ten years without a banishment.

The National League had its own illustrious arbiters. Outstanding were Canadian Bob Emslie, who for years umpired wearing a wig because his frazzled nerves caused premature baldness; hulking Cy Rigler, who while in the minors in 1905 started the tradition of raising his right hand on called strikes; Hank O'Day, stickler for technicalities, whose controversial Merkle decision in 1908 is a staple of baseball lore; and William J. "Lord" Byron, "The Singing Umpire," who periodically announced his decisions in melodious (if not poetical) singsong verse. But it was William G. "Bill" Klem, generally regarded as the greatest umpire in history, who dominated the league staff and set the style for Senior Circuit arbiters. Self-righteous and autocratic, Klem boasted of his scrupulous honesty and encyclopedic knowledge of the rules, intimidated players with threats of fines, and dramatically illustrated his insistence upon discipline and authority during arguments by drawing a mark in the dirt and warning antagonists, "Don't cross the line!" He also popularized the inside chest protector, the over-the-shoulder position for calling balls and strikes, emphatic arm signals for calls, and straddling the lines instead of standing in foul territory. Sharp-tongued and tough-minded, the highly publicized "Old Arbitrator," who for sixteen consecutive years worked every game behind the plate (instead of rotating with the base umpire as had become the norm) and vowed, "I never missed one [call] in my life," was for most of his thirty-six-year career the public's personification of the major league umpire. Upon retiring in 1941, Klem served as the league's first modern chief of umpires until his death in 1951.

Between World Wars One and Two, when baseball dominated the nation's sport consciousness as the National Pastime, umpiring became a career vocation instead of a limited occupational opportunity. Expanded schedules meant seven months of employment, and umpires received better salaries and more recognition. Staff stability became the norm: an umpire who passed muster the first two or three years could look forward to a long career. Umpires continued to be vexed by arguments with players, insults from fans, and occasional flying objects, but the vicious rowdiness declined. The physical abuse was curtailed significantly because of the stiff penalties imposed for fighting and bottle tossing, while the verbal abuse abated as league officials and the press did an about-face after the infamous Black Sox Scandal by proclaiming the umpire the personification the game's integrity. To underscore their role as independent arbitrators, umpires had to make travel arrangements separate from players and patronize different bars, hotels, and restaurants.

Umpiring had become a desirable and respectable vocation, but the odds against a major league career were far greater for umpires than for players. Competition was keen, as normally only one or two of the some two dozen umpiring positions came open each year. And the low pay, primitive working conditions, wearisome travel, and vicious abuse from players and fans that characterized the life of the minor league umpire drove out those who would or could pursue other employment. Moreover, there was no prescribed system of career development. Becoming a professional umpire was a matter of chance opportunity or personal contacts; there was no systematic evaluation or supervision of minor league arbiters; and advancement, even to the major leagues, was sometimes more a matter of politics and personalities than merit or ability. Nonetheless, those who persevered as "men of the cloth" and proved their mettle in the big time enjoyed a secure and esteemed career. Where Tim Hurst justified working as an umpire by saying, "You can't beat the hours," Bill Klem would declare, "Baseball to me is not a game; it is a religion."

Still, major league umpires received far greater recognition than remuneration. The pay scales for umpires were the same in both leagues. In the early 1900s the annual salary for major league umpires ranged from $1,500 to $2,000; by 1910 the top salary in the National League was $3,000, with only four of the seven umpires earning more than $2,000. Umpires who worked the World Series received $400 until Bill Klem demanded and received $650 in 1917; the next year Klem received $1,000 for the Fall Classic, but the pay for all other umpires remained $650. In 1937 salaries ranged from $4,000 for new umpires to $10,000 for the most veteran arbiters; umpires could expect an extra $2,500 from the World Series. Five years later the pay scale rose to $5,000 and $12,000, but compensation for the Series remained the same. Although the salaries for men at the top of the pay scale seem good for a 154-game, seven-month season, umpires had to pay all their expenses except railroad fares while on the road until 1940, when they received a $750 allowance for travel, a sum that most umpires argued covered only about one-half of their expenses. Moreover, they had to buy and maintain their own clothing and

equipment, including ball-strike indicators, masks, and chest protectors. Nonetheless, better pay, working conditions, and status translated into more attractive and thus longer careers; twenty years' service was not uncommon. Consequently, both major leagues established a pension plan for retired umpires, but they were restricted to those who had served more than fifteen years and limited to $100 per year with maximum lifetime benefits of $2,400.

The size of umpiring staffs was also increased. The two-umpire system was the norm during the 1920s, but it became common practice to assign one of the reserve umpires to critical games or series; by 1933 three umpires were assigned routinely to regular-season games. The four-man crew was instituted in 1952. In the World Series the two-man crew, one umpire from each league, was used until 1908, when a pair of two-man teams alternated games. In the third game of the 1909 Series, all four umpires were on the field at the same time, thus establishing the four-umpire tradition that continued through 1946; in 1947 an "alternate" umpire from each league was stationed along a foul line in the outfield, thus creating the current six-umpire crew. Four umpires worked the All-Star Game from 1933 to 1948; the following year it conformed to the World Series format in putting the alternates on the field.

Although major league umpires, save for a few short-lived experiments, wore blue serge suits and officiated according to the same rule book, subtle and not-so-subtle differences in the style and technique of umpiring developed between the two leagues. Inasmuch as league presidents from the beginning hired, assigned, and instructed their umpires, personal preferences were reflected in the umpiring staffs early in the century. Then interleague chauvinism sustained and accentuated the distinctiveness. Under Ban Johnson's leadership, the American League soon boasted an overall staff that was superior to the National League, just as the Junior Circuit had more star players, stronger teams, and more successful managers during the same period. Because Johnson believed that all of his umpires were good enough to work the World Series, the prestigious (and lucrative) assignment was rotated among his staff, whereas postseason honors in the National League went selectively to the best (or most favored) umpires. In return for backing his umpires to the hilt, Johnson demanded reserve and restraint on the field, whereas National League presidents adopted a more laissez-faire attitude toward their umpires.

As a result, arbiters in the Senior Circuit were far more colorful, pugnacious, and individualistic than their American League counterparts, just as National League players and managers were freer and higher spirited than those in the Junior Circuit. It was a volatile mix, and there were many more rhubarbs, fines, and suspensions in the National League, where arbiters had to be courageous in fending off mean-spirited players and managers. And because Johnson liked his umpires to display a strong physical presence, a preference shared by Tommy Connolly, American League umpires were generally "big" men, whereas most National League arbiters, because of the dominant role of the five-foot-seven-inch Bill Klem, were shorter and slight of build.

More important than general differences in style and appearance were the specific differences in technique be-

tween the two leagues. At first umpires in both leagues held large inflated chest protectors in front of their bodies when behind the plate. Consequently, they called balls and strikes by crouching directly behind the catcher and looking over his head. The American League continued to use the "balloon" or "mattress" as favored by Tommy Connolly, but it became *de rigueur* in the National League to follow Bill Klem's preference for wearing a more compact chest protector under his coat and calling balls and strikes by viewing the plate from just over the catcher's shoulder nearest the batter. Here, form had great effect: the American League umpires became known for calling more "high" strikes and the National League for calling more "low" strikes.

Not as well known as the flamboyant umpires of the formative years, the men who worked between the World Wars were collectively better umpires and included some of the game's greatest arbiters. Along with Emslie, Klem, O'Day, and Rigler, the National League staff boasted George Barr, Lee Ballanfant, Larry Goetz, George Magerkurth, "Uncle Charley" Moran, Ralph "Babe" Pinelli, Ernie Quigley, and John "Beans" Reardon. Joining Connolly and Bill Dinneen in the American League were such illuminaries as Harry Geisel, Cal Hubbard, George Moriarty, Bill McGowan, Emmett "Red" Ormsby, and Clarence "Brick" Owens. Perhaps the best was McGowan, who for thirty years received universal praise from his peers and ranks as one of the premier umpires in history.

Sociologically, the umpires of the Golden Age represented both change and continuity. Like their predecessors, the majority hailed from the Northeast, the Midwest, and the South; and many were former athletes for whom umpiring was a way of staying in baseball. Some were ex-major leaguers— Charlie Berry, Bill Dinneen, George Hildebrand, Charlie Moran, George Moriarty, Hank O'Day, Al Orth, Babe Pinelli, George Pipgras, and Eddie Rommel. There were, however, important changes. Ethnically, the umpires reflected a pattern of cultural assimilation similar to that evident in the rosters of players. Initially umpires were overwhelmingly English in origin, but then the Irish by the 1890s and Germans by World War One became conspicuous and were followed by Jews in the 1920s and Italians and Slavs in the 1930s. And where collegian Billy Evans was unique among the mostly unlettered arbiters early in the century, college-educated (or graduated) umpires were increasingly common. Essentially, umpires between the wars had become a reasonable cross section of the white working-class American population.

Spurred by war-induced prosperity, continental expansion, and television revenue, baseball led the transformation of professional sport from a commercial business to an entertainment industry. Moreover, baseball, like all organized sport, felt the impact of the social and cultural changes that swept over America. After World War Two umpiring truly became a profession, and by the end of the 1980s major league umpires were not only far better trained and organized than ever before but also a forceful and independent voice in baseball affairs.

Umpiring, like baseball itself, was enormously popular in the days following World War Two. By 1949 some fifty-nine minor leagues provided extensive on-the-job training for an unprecedented number of aspiring arbiters, but it was the umpire training school that was responsible for postwar umpires being so much better prepared than their predecessors. George Barr of the National League opened the first umpire training school in 1935, and in 1939 Bill McGowan of the American League established a second school. In 1946 Bill McKinley, who attended both the Barr and McGowan schools, became the first graduate of a training school to reach the major leagues. By the mid-1950s training school graduates were common, and by the 1960s it was virtually impossible to become a professional umpire without attending one of several training schools.

The umpire schools had profound effects on umpiring. First, graduates of the training schools were more knowledgeable of rules and more skilled in techniques than the earlier "self-taught" umpires. Second, formal training had the predictable effect of imposing uniformity of style and personality, as students were instructed "by the book" and maverick characters were weeded out. Finally—and most significantly—the umpire school was the catalyst that transformed umpiring from vocation to profession.

The professionalization of umpiring had profound effects. Formalized instruction and systematic career development attracted more middle-class college men, as umpiring was increasingly viewed less as a way of staying in professional sport than as a desirable career choice. And, reflecting the demographic shifts that prompted continental expansion, most umpires, like players, now hailed from the Sun Belt or the Pacific Coast. The lone area in which umpires lagged far behind players in mirroring the social changes of society at large was race. It was not until 1966, twenty years after Jackie Robinson broke the color line, that Emmett Ashford joined the American League and became the first black major league umpire. (He was also the first black professional umpire, breaking in with the Southwestern International League in 1951.) In 1973 Art Williams integrated the National League. Despite the strong presence of Latino players since the 1940s, Armando Rodriguez (1974) and Rich Garcia (1975), both in the American League, were the first Hispanic umpires in the majors.

Umpires also adopted a more professional attitude. They candidly admitted errors and portrayed themselves not as omnipotent enforcers of the law who demanded respect but as impartial judges who deserved respect. That umpires were skilled but fallible men became clearly visible in 1956, when Ed Rommel and Frank Umont broke a long-standing taboo by wearing eyeglasses on the field. But the most important effect of growing professionalization was that umpires increasingly viewed themselves as deserving the pay and perquisites of professionals.

In contrast with the strong support from league headquarters for their actions on the field, umpires historically were unable to protect themselves from monetary and personnel injustices because they negotiated individually instead of collectively with the leagues. Umpires repeatedly were dismissed arbitrarily, and in 1953, for the first time in fifteen years, umpires received a modest salary increase—a salary range of $6,000 to $16,000 and an increase in World Series pay to $3,000. Early efforts at organizing were to no avail, and in 1945 Ernie Stewart of the American League was fired for alleged unionizing

activity. But in 1963, led by Augie Donatelli, umpires in the Senior Circuit organized the National League Umpires Association, headed by Chicago labor attorney John J. Reynolds. After Reynolds's success in raising salaries, American League umpires became unionists. When Bill Valentine and Al Salerno were dismissed in 1968, allegedly for incompetence but patently for unionizing activities, an appeal to the National Labor Relations Board resulted in umpires in both leagues being organized into the Major League Umpires Association. A one-day strike of the first game of the championship playoffs on October 3, 1970, the first by umpires in major league history, prompted the league presidents to recognize the Association and negotiate a labor contract that set a minimum salary of $11,000 and raised the average salary to $21,000.

Eight years later the Umpires Association made major advances under the new leadership of Richard G. "Richie" Phillips, a Philadelphia lawyer who also represented National Basketball Association referees. A second umpire's strike on August 25, 1978, lasted only one day, owing to a court injunction against the Association, but a third strike from Opening Day to May 18, 1979, won major concessions for the union, including a salary schedule of $22,000 to $55,000, based on years of service; annual no-cut contracts; $77 per diem while traveling; and two weeks' midseason vacation. The aftermath of the prolonged strike, which demonstrated the power of the Association and the inadequacy of replacement umpires, was marked by ill will between the union umpires and "the Class of '79"—the four "scab" umpires retained on each league's staff. A fourth strike of seven of the eight 1984 playoff games was settled by the intercession of new Commissioner Peter Ueberroth, who granted the umpires a sizable increase for playoff and World Series games as well as providing that the money go into a pool that would be distributed in part to umpires not working postseason contests. A fifth strike was averted in 1985 when an arbitrator—former President Richard M. Nixon—awarded umpires a 40 percent pay increase for the expanded best-of-seven playoff series. An MLUA strike appeared certain in 1991 until prodding of both sides by Commissioner Fay Vincent produced an eleventh-hour settlement. The new four-year contract called for a salary scale ranging from $61,000 to $175,000 and a third week of in-season vacation, in exchange for a return to a "merit" instead of "rotation" system for postseason assignments. However, agreement on the pact came too late to avoid using substitute umpires for games on Opening Day.

By the early 1990s the MLUA had transformed the umpiring profession as well as the role of umpires in major league baseball. Although most attention has been focused on contract negotiations, umpires have also successfully used the power of the Association to seek from league presidents and the commissioner the impositions of fines and suspensions on players, managers, and even owners for objectionable conduct and comments.

Most significant, the press and the public increasingly viewed umpires in a critical, even cynical manner. It was charged that umpires, because of the protection afforded by the MLUA, had unilaterally created a strike zone much smaller than that prescribed by the rules, had become belligerent and confrontational in dealing with play-

ers and managers, and had assumed too large a role in games through quick ejection and exaggerated motions when making calls. To many, plate umpire Terry Cooney's ejection of Boston Red Sox star pitcher Roger Clemens in the 1990 American League Championship Series symbolized the aggressive action and arrogant attitude of the "new" umpire. That such perceptions did not square with reality was secondary to the fact that umpires no longer enjoyed the unqualified respect of fans and journalists. (On the other hand, admiration for umpires as individuals increased after one of the American League's top arbiters, Steve Palermo, suffered a career-ending gunshot wound in 1991 while attempting to prevent the robbery of two waitresses in a restaurant parking lot.)

The growth and success of the umpire's union was made possible by two factors. First, with the expansion of franchises from the traditional sixteen (8 in each league) to twenty in 1961-1962, twenty-four in 1969, and twenty-six in 1977, umpires became a numerically significant force. Second—and far more important—was television, which not only brought unprecedented publicity to umpires but also generated the enormous revenue that made it possible for major league baseball to meet the monetary demands of umpires as well as players.

Finances aside, television was a mixed blessing for umpires. If heightened visibility underscored the umpire's skill and central role in the game, it also glaringly exposed errors to millions of viewers. The photographer's camera had occasionally exposed an incorrect call, but television's instant replay both emphasized mistakes and encouraged second-guessing. When slow-motion replays began to be shown on scoreboard screens, one crew in 1975 left the field and refused to return until the practice stopped. Television also affected performance and appearance. It had once been axiomatic for umpires to develop a subdued, even somber appearance, and take pride in anonymity. But in the Age of Television, arbiters began to project themselves into leading roles. From the time televised games became popular in the early 1950s, some umpires played to the camera through flamboyant, demonstrative motions when making calls. While a few like Emmett Ashford and Ron Luciano subsequently developed "showboating" to a fine art, umpires no longer shunned the spotlight of publicity; Luciano even parlayed his popularity for comedic calls on the field into a career in the telecast booth and as a writer.

In contrast to increased tolerance regarding on-field behavior, the personal lives of umpires received unprecedented scrutiny. In November 1988 Commissioner A. Bartlett Giamatti, acting on behalf of club owners, released ten-year National League umpire Dave Pallone because of the fear that the arbiter's homosexuality might compromise his on-field performance and baseball's image. NL president Bill White suspended Bob Engel in April 1990 after he was charged with two misdemeanor counts of shoplifting baseball cards; baseball's insistence upon the unquestioned integrity of umpires prompted the twenty-five-year veteran to retire immediately upon his conviction in July. And in 1991 two unidentified umpires, one in each league, were placed on a year's "probation" because of alleged association with bookmakers even though there was no indication that they had ever bet on baseball games.

The physical appearance of umpires was also tailored for the public eye. Increased emphasis was placed on size, as taller and more muscular men were in vogue—perhaps to personify the umpire's authority in an antiauthoritarian age. The American League's adoption of gray slacks in 1968 and maroon blazers in 1971 was part of an effort to project a distinctive "sporty" image, as was the case later when umpires in both leagues began wearing numerals on their sleeves and baseball caps with letters designating league affiliation. By the early 1990s the "casual look" was completed when umpires wore short-sleeved shirts without jackets during hot weather and satin warmup jackets on cool nights. Contact lenses were favored over glasses until 1991 when Al Clark (AL) and Frank Pulli (NL) wore spectacles while umpiring behind the plate as well as on the bases. In 1988 obese umpires were put on weight-reduction programs during the offseason; by 1991 those who failed to lose prescribed poundage were subject to suspension pending compliance.

Aside from the superficialities of cap insignia and jacket color, there was little to distinguish the two umpire staffs in appearance. Training in umpire schools and minor league supervision by the Umpire Development Program had the effect of imposing uniformity of style and technique on umpires and thus on the leagues. Moreover, by the 1970s American League arbiters had adopted the inside chest protector, while the National League mimicked the preference for "big" men. However, a reversal in league images also occurred: just as the players in the Senior Circuit were widely regarded as superior to those in the Junior, National League umpires were similarly perceived as better in the 1960s and 1970s; meanwhile, the American League, with umpires like Ashford and Luciano and fiery managers like Billy Martin and Earl Weaver, became more volatile than the now staid National League.

Despite television exposure, heightened after 1969 by intraleague championship playoffs, umpires as a group were more personally anonymous than before. Exceptions like Luciano notwithstanding, the individuality of umpires was submerged by the four-member crew, the numerical expansion of staffs, the frequent rotation among cities, the standardization of styles and techniques, the decline in the frequency of rhubarbs, and the attempt to project a more staid professional image. Few umpires stood out as demonstrably superior to their col-

leagues, partly because systematic training and preparation had increased generally the competence of all arbiters and partly because professional basketball and football now offered competition for outstanding officials. Nonetheless, there were some premier umpires in the postwar era, chief among them Nestor Chylak and John Stevens of the American and Al Barlick and Doug Harvey of the National League.

During the course of a century of major league baseball, the umpire became transformed from a despised, untrained, semiprofessional "necessary evil" to a respected, skilled professional who epitomizes the integrity of the game itself. In the process some arbiters became immortalized in record books for notable achievements and distinctions. J. L. Boake umpired the first professional league game (1871), Billy McLean the first National League game (1876), and Tommy Connolly the first American League game (1901). Hank O'Day and Connolly umpired the first modern World Series (1903), while Bill Dinneen, Bill Klem, Bill McGowan, and Cy Rigler worked the first All-Star Game (1933). Bill Klem holds the record for most seasons in the majors (thirty-seven), most World Series (eighteen) and most World Series games (one hundred-eight). Al Barlick and Bill Summers worked the most All-Star Games (seven). Doug Harvey has umpired the most League Championship Series (nine) and LCS games (thirty-eight). George Hildebrand holds the record for most consecutive games umpired (3,510). (Babe Pinelli has claimed that he did not miss a regulation game in his twenty-two-year career.) Emmett Ashford was the first black professional umpire in both the minor (1951) and major leagues (1966), while Armando Rodriguez (1974) was the first Hispanic umpire in the majors. Bernice Gera was the first female professional umpire (1972), although she worked only one game in the Class A New York-Penn League; Pam Postema's bid to become the first woman to umpire in the major leagues ended with her release from the Triple-A Alliance after spending thirteen years in the minors. Evans was the youngest (twenty-two) and Klem the oldest (sixty-eight) to umpire a major league game. Seven umpires are enshrined in the Baseball Hall of Fame: Jocko Conlan (1974), Tommy Connolly (1953), Bill Klem (1953), Billy Evans (1973), Cal Hubbard (1976), Al Barlick (1989), and Bill McGowan (1992).

The Umpire Roster

The men in blue have been rebuked and scorned since the Knickerbockers cavorted on the Elysian Fields of Hoboken. The first to incur an umpire's wrath in return was Knickerbocker player Davis, fined six cents for swearing, perhaps understandably since his team was being trounced by the New York Club, 23–1. The name of the umpire in that historic game of June 19, 1846—the first match game under Alexander Cartwright's new rules—was not recorded. Ever since, a handful of researchers have scrambled to find out who umpired the league games of baseball's early history.

Larry Gerlach, who knows more about umpires and umpiring than anybody (see his preceding feature article), has created the Umpire Roster that follows. The basis of his roster is the list compiled by S. C. Thompson in the 1930s and 1940s, but his research has corrected several errors and omissions in that list and has scrupulously brought the umpire roster up to date. In *Total Baseball 1* he hoped that "by the next edition we will have finished a complete re-study of the umpire roster.... I am going to try to fashion a biographical encyclopedia of major league umpires—vital statistics; minor and major league service; All-Star, World Series, Playoff games; special achievements; and so on. One of the more frustrating things about the Turkin/Thompson roster (and even ours) is how years of service are noted in terms of seasons; it really is misleading to identify someone as working from 1980–1987 when he may have broken into the majors on September 24, 1980."

The data presented here does not meet those lofty goals, but it is vastly increased and improved, as well as reorganized. Umpires are now divided not only by league but also by: regular, league-employed umpires; substitutes; player-umpires, pressed into emergency service; and those subs used during the recent strikes. New leads continue to flow in, especially about the early days, when umpires were not assigned by the leagues but were supplied by the teams, recruited from among the fans in attendance (this explains why so many given names are lacking for pre-1900 arbiters), or, not infrequently, plucked from the team's reserve players. In this third edition of *Total Baseball,* an innovation is the identification of substitute umpires in the National Association years 1871–1875. An instance of this last practice occurred as late as 1935, when Chicago White Sox outfielder Jocko Conlan was recruited to fill in for umpire Red Ormsby in a game between the Sox and the St. Louis Browns. Conlan, of course, went on to a Hall of Fame career as a man in blue.

But the story of umpires and umpiring is better told in Gerlach's essay. Let's call the roll.

REGULAR UMPIRES

National Association (1871-75)

Avery, C. Hamilton 1875
Beardslee, John J. 1871
Blodgett, C. W. 1875
Boardman, Frederick "Fred" 1875
Bomeisler, Theodore 1871-73
Boyd, William J. "Bill" 1875
Burdock, John J. "Jack" 1872-74
Carey, Thomas J. "Tom" 1874
Clapp, John E. 1874-75
Cone, J. Frederick "Fred" 1875
Daniels, Charles F. 1874-75
Dehlman, Herman J. 1874
Dole, Lester C. 1875
Ferguson, Robert V. "Bob" 1872-73, 1875
Fulmer, Charles J. "Chick" 1873
Heubel, George A. 1875
Hodges, Amory G. 1874-75
Holly, Samuel J. "Sam" 1871
Lennon, William F. "Bill" 1871-72, 1873-74
Mack, Dennis J. "Denny" 1875
Martin, Alphonse C. "Phonney" 1875
Mathews, Robert T. "Bobby" 1873-75
McLean, William H. "Billy" 1874-75
Mills, Charles "Charlie" 1872-73
Patterson, Daniel T. "Dan" 1874
Rogers, M. Mortimer "Mort" 1871
Sensenderfer, John P. J. "Count" 1874
Swandell, J. Martin "Marty" 1872-73
Tate, William 1874
Walsh, Michael F. "Mike" 1875
Young, Nicholas E. "Nick" 1871-75

National League (1876-)

Andrews, G. Edward "Ed" 1895, 1898-99
Baker, William F. "Bill" 1957
Ballanfant, E. Lee 1936-57
Barlick, Albert J. "Al" 1940-43, 1946-55, 1958-71
Barnes, Ronald "Ron" 1990-92
Barnie, William S. "Billy" 1892
Barr, George M. 1932-49
Barron, Mark E. 1992
Battin, Joseph V. "Joe" 1891
Bausewine, George 1905
Behle, Frank 1901
Bell, Wally 1992
Betts, William G. 1894-96, 1898-99
Betz, Edwin J. 1961
Boggess, Lynton R. "Dusty" 1944-48, 1950-62
Boles, Charles 1877
Bond, Thomas H. "Tommy" 1883, 1885
Bonin, Gregory "Greg" 1986-92
Bradley, George H. "Foghorn" 1879-83
Brady, Jackson 1887
Bransfield, William E. "Kitty" 1917
Bredburg, George W. 1877

Brennan, John E. "Jack" 1899
Brennan, William T. "Bill" 1909-13, 1921
Brocklander, Fred W. 1979-90
Brown, Thomas T. "Tom" 1898-99, 1901-02
Bunce, Joshua 1877
Burkhart, W. Kenneth "Ken" 1957-73
Burnham, George W. 1883, 1889, 1895
Burns, John S. 1884
Burns, Thomas E. "Tom" 1892
Burns, Thomas P. "Oyster" 1899
Burtis, L. W. 1876-77
Bush, Garner C. 1911-12
Byron, William J. "Bill" or "Lord" 1913-19
Callahan, Edward J. 1881
Campbell, Daniel "Dan" 1894-96
Campbell, William M. "Bick" 1939-40
Cantillon, Joseph D. "Joe" 1902
Carpenter, William B. "Bill" 1897, 1904, 1906-07
Chapman, John C. "Jack" 1880
Chipman, Harry F. 1883, 1885
Clarke, Robert M. "Bob" 1930-31
Cockill, George W. 1915
Colgan, Harry W. 1901
Colosi, Nicholas "Nick" 1968-82
Conahan, — 1896
Cone, J. F. "Fred" 1877
Conlan, John B. "Jocko" 1941-64
Connolly, John M. 1886
Connolly, Thomas H. "Tommy" 1898-1900
Conway, John H. 1906
Crandall, Robert 1877
Crawford, Gerald J. "Jerry" 1976-92
Crawford, Henry C. "Shag" 1956-75
Cross, John A. 1878
Cunningham, Elmer E. "Bert" 1901
Curry, Wesley "Wes" 1885-86, 1889, 1898
Cusack, Stephen P. 1909
Cushman, Charles H. "Charley" 1885, 1898
Cuzzi, Phil 1991-92
Dailey, John J. 1882
Dale, Jerry R. 1970-85
Daniels, Charles F. 1876, 1878-80, 1887-88
Danley, Kerwin 1991-92
Darling, Gary R. 1988-92
Dascoli, Frank 1948-62
Davidson, David L. "Satch" 1969-84
Davidson, Robert A. "Bob" 1983-92
Davis, Gerald "Gerry" 1985-92
Decker, Stewart M. 1883-85, 1888
Delmore, Victor "Vic" 1956-59
DeMuth, Dana A. 1986-92
Devinney, P. H. "Dan" 1877
Dezelan, Frank J. 1966-68, 1969-71
Dixon, Hal H. 1953-59
Donatelli, August J. "Augie" 1950-73
Donnelly, Charles H. 1931-32
Donohue, Michael R. 1930
Doscher, John H. Sr. "Herm" 1880-81, 1887
Doyle, John J. "Jack" 1911
Ducharme, — 1876-77

Dunn, Thomas P. "Tom" 1939-46
Dunnigan, Joseph 1881-82
Dwyer, J. Francis "Frank" 1899, 1901
Eagan, John J. 1878, 1886
Eason, Malcolm W. "Mal" 1902, 1910-15
Ellick, Joseph J. "Joe" 1886
Emslie, Robert D. "Bob" 1891-1924
Engel, Robert A. "Bob" 1965-90
Engeln, William R. "Bill" 1952-56
Ferguson, Robert V. "Bob" 1879, 1884-85
Fessenden, Wallace C. "Wally" 1889-90
Fields, Stephen H. "Steve" 1979-82
Finneran, William F. 1911-12, 1924
Forman, Allen S. "Al" 1962-65
Fountain, Edward G. 1879
Frary, Ralph 1911
Froemming, Bruce N. 1971-92
Fulmer, Charles J. "Chick" 1886
Furlong, William E. 1878-79, 1883-84
Fyfe, Lee C. 1920
Gaffney, John H. 1884-86, 1891-94, 1899-1900
Galvin, James F. "Jim" 1895
Gillean, Thomas 1879-80
Goetz, Lawrence J. "Larry" 1936-57
Gore, Arthur J. "Artie" 1947-56
Gorman, Brian 1991-92
Gorman, Thomas D. "Tom" 1951-76
Gregg, Eric E. 1977-91
Guglielmo, A. Augie 1952
Gunning, Thomas F. "Tom" 1887
Guthrie, William J. "Bill" 1913-15
Hallion, Thomas F. "Tom" 1986-92
Harris, Lannie D. 1979-85
Harrison, Peter A. "Pete" 1916-20
Hart, Eugene F. "Bob" 1920-28
Hart, William F. "Bill" 1914-15
Harvey, H. Douglas "Doug" 1962-77, 1979-92
Hautz, Charles A. 1876, 1879
Henderson, J. Harding "Hardie" 1895-96
Hengle, Edward S. "Ed" 1887
Henline, Walter J. "Butch" 1945-48
Hernandez, Angel 1991-92
Heuble, George A. 1876
Heydler, John A. 1898
Higham, Richard "Dick" 1881-82
Hirschbeck, Mark 1988-92
Hoagland, Willard A. 1894
Hodges, A. D. 1876
Hohn, William J. "Bill" 1987-92
Holland, John A. 1887
Holliday, James W. "Bug" 1903
Hornung, M. Joseph "Joe" 1893, 1896
Hunt, John T. 1895, 1898-99
Hurst, Timothy C. "Tim" 1891-97, 1900, 1903
Irwin, Arthur A. 1902
Jackowski, William A. "Bill" 1952-68
Jeffers, W. W. 1881

Jevne, Frederick "Fred" 1895
Johnson, Harry S. 1914
Johnstone, James E. "Jim" 1903-12
Jorda, Louis D. "Lou" 1927-31, 1940-52
Julian, Joseph O. 1878
Kane, Stephen J. 1909-10
Keefe, Timothy J. "Tim" 1894-96
Kellogg, Jeffery "Jeff" 1991-92
Kelly, John O. 1882, 1888, 1897
Kennedy, Charles 1904
Kenney, John 1877
Kibler, John W. 1963-89
Klem, William J. "Bill" 1905-41
Knight, Alonzo P. "Lon" 1889
Landes, Stanley A. "Stan" 1955-72
Lane, Frank H. 1883
Latham, W. Arlington "Arlie" 1899, 1902
Layne, Jerry B. 1989-92
Libby, Stephen A. 1880
Lincoln, Frederick H. 1914, 1917
Long, "Robert "Bob" 1992
Long, William H. "Billy" 1895
Lynch, Thomas J. "Tom" 1888-99
Macullar, James F. "Jimmy" 1892
Magee, Sherwood R. "Sherry" 1928
Magerkurth, George L. 1929-47
Mahoney, Michael J. 1892
Malone, Ferguson G. "Fergy" 1884
Manassau, Alfred S. "Al" 1899
Marsh, Randall G. "Randy" 1983-92
Mathews, Robert T. "Bobby" 1880
McCormick, William J. "Barry" 1919-29
McDermott, Michael J. "Sandy" 1890, 1897
McDonald, James F. 1895, 1897-99
McElwee, Harvey 1877
McFarland, Horace 1896-97
McGarr, James B. "Chippy" 1899
McGrew, Harry T. "Ted" 1930-31, 1933-34
McLaughlin, Edward J. 1929
McLaughlin, Michael 1893
McLaughlin, Peter J. 1924-28
McLean, William B. "Billy" 1876, 1878-80, 1882-84
McQuaid, John H. 1889-94
McSherry, John P. 1971-92
Miller, George E. 1879
Mitchell, Charles 1892
Montague, Edward M. "Ed" 1976-92
Moran, August "Augie" 1903-04, 1910, 1918
Moran, Charles B. "Charlie" 1917-39
Mullin, John 1909
Nash, William M. "Billy" 1901
O'Connor, Arthur 1914
O'Day, Henry F. "Hank" 1895, 1897-1911, 1913, 1915-27
Odlin, Albert F. 1883
O'Hara, — 1915
Olsen, Andrew H. "Andy" 1968-81
O'Rourke, James H. "Jim" 1894
Orth, Albert L. "Al" 1912-17

O'Sullivan, John J. 1922
Owens, Clarence B. "Brick" 1908, 1912-13
Pallone, David M. "Dave" 1979-88
Parker, George L. 1936-38
Pearce, Richard J. "Dicky" 1878, 1882
Pears, Frank 1897, 1905
Pelekoudas, Christos G. "Chris" 1960-75
Pfirman, Charles H. "Cy" 1922-36
Pierce, Grayson S. "Gracie" 1886-87
Pinelli, Ralph A. "Babe" 1935-56
Poncino, Larry L. 1986-88, 1991-92
Potter, Scott 1991-92
Powell, Jack 1923-24, 1933
Power, Charles B. 1902
Powers, Philip J. "Phil" 1879, 1881, 1886-91
Pratt, Albert G. "Al" 1879
Pratt, Thomas J. "Tom" 1886
Pryor, J. Paul 1961-81
Pulli, Frank V. 1972-92
Quest, Joseph L. "Joe" 1886-87
Quick, James E. "Jim" 1976-92
Quigley, Ernest C. "Ernie" 1913-37
Quinn, Joseph C. "Joe" 1882
Rapuano, Edward "Ed" 1990-92
Reardon, John E. "Beans" 1926-49
Reliford, Charles "Charlie" 1989-92
Rennert, Laurence H. "Dutch" 1973-92
Rieker, Richard "Rich" 1992
Rigler, Charles "Cy" 1906-22, 1924-35
Riley, William J. 1880
Rippley, T. Steven "Steve" 1985-92
Robb, Douglas W. "Scotty" 1948-52
Roberts, Leonard W. "Lenny" 1953-55
Rudderham, John E. 1908
Runge, Paul E. 1973-92
Ryan, Walter 1946
Scott, James "Jim" 1930-31
Sears, John W. "Ziggy" 1934-45
Secory, Frank E. 1952-70
Sentelle, Leopold T. "Paul" 1922-23
Seward, Edward W. "Ed" 1893
Seward, George E. 1876, 1878
Sheridan, John F. "Jack" 1892, 1896-97
Smith, Vincent A. "Vinnie" 1957-65
Smith, William W. "Billy" 1898-99
Snyder, Charles N. "Pop" 1892-93, 1898-1901
Stage, Charles W. "Billy" 1894
Stambaugh, Calvin G. 1877-78
Stark, Albert D. "Dolly" 1928-35, 1937-39, 1942
Steiner, Melvin J. "Mel" 1961-72
Steinfeldt, Harry M. 1905
Stello, Richard J. "Dick" 1969-87
Sternburg, Paul 1909
Stewart, William J. "Bill" 1933-54
Stockdale, M. J. 1915
Strief, George A. 1890

Sudol, Edward L. "Ed" 1957-77
Sullivan, David F. "Dave" 1882, 1885
Sullivan, Jeremiah "Jerry" 1887
Sullivan, T. P. 1880
Summer, James G. 1877
Swartwood, C. Edward "Ed" 1894, 1898-1900
Sweeney, James M. "Jim" 1924-26
Tata, Terry A. 1973-92
Terry, William H. "Adonis" 1900
Tilden, Otis 1880
Tremblay, Richard H. "Dick" 1971
Truby, Harry G. 1909
Valentine, John G. 1887-88
Van Court, Eugene 1884
Vanover, Larry 1991
Vargo, Edward P. "Ed" 1960-83
Venzon, Anthony "Tony" 1957-71
Walker, William E. 1876-77
Walsh, Francis D. "Frank" 1961-63
Walsh, Michael F. "Mike" 1876, 1878, 1880
Warneke, Lonnie "Lon" 1949-55
Warner, Albert "Al" 1898-1900
Weidman, George E. "Stump" 1896
Wendelstedt, Harry H. 1966-92
West, Joseph H. "Joe" 1976, 1978-92
Westervelt, Frederick E. 1922
Weyer, Lee H. 1961, 1963-88
White, Gideon F. 1878
Wickham, Daniel "Dan" 1990-92
Wilbur, Charles E. 1879
Williams, Arthur "Art" 1972-77
Williams, Charles H. "Charlie" 1978, 1983-92
Williams, William G. "Bill" 1963-87
Wilson, Frank 1923-28
Wilson, John A. 1887
Winters, Michael J. "Mike" 1990-92
Wise, Samuel W. "Sam" 1889, 1893
Wood, George A. 1898
York, Thomas J. "Tom" 1886
Young, Joseph 1879
Zacharias, Thomas 1890
Zimmer, Charles L. "Chief" 1904

American Association (1882-91)

Barnum, George W. 1890
Bauers, Albert J. "Al" 1887
Becannon, William H. 1883
Bradley, George H. "Foghorn" 1886
Brennan, John E. 1884
Butler, Ormond H. 1883
Carey, Thomas J. "Tom" 1882
Clinton, James L. "Jim" 1886
Connell, Terence G. 1884, 1890
Connelly, John M. 1885, 1887
Connelly, William 1884
Curry, Wesley "Wes" 1887, 1890
Cuthbert, Edgar E. "Ned" 1887
Dailey, John J. 1884
Daniels, Charles F. 1883-85, 1889

Davis, James J. "Jumbo" 1891
DeVinney, P. H. "Dan" 1884
Doscher, John H. Sr. "Herm" 1888, 1890
Dyler, John F. 1884
Emslie, Robert D. "Bob" 1890
Ferguson, Robert V. "Bob" 1886-89, 1891
Gaffney, John H. 1888-89
Gleason, William G. "Bill" 1891
Goldsmith, Frederick E. "Fred" 1888-89
Griffith, E. A. 1884
Hautz, Charles A. "Charlie" 1882
Hecker, Guy J. 1889
Holland, John A. 1884
Holland, Willard A. 1889
Hurley, Daniel "Dan" 1887
Jennings, Alfred "Al" 1887
Jones, Charles W. "Charley" 1891
Kelly, John O. 1883-86
Kerins, John A. "Jack" 1889-91
Knight, Alonzo P. "Lon" 1887
Lawler, John F. 1884
Macullar, James F. "Jimmy" 1891
Mack, Dennis J. "Denny" 1886
Magner, John T. 1883
Mahoney, M. J. 1891
Mathews, Robert T. "Bobby" 1891
McLaughlin, Thomas 1891
McLean, William B. "Billy" 1885
McNichol, Robert T. 1883
McQuade, John H. 1886-88
Morton, Charles H. "Charlie" 1886
O'Brien, Frank 1890
Peoples, James E. "Jimmy" 1890
Pike, Lipman. E. "Lip" 1889
Pratt, Albert G. "Al" 1883
Quinn, A. J. 1886
Riley, William J. 1882
Ross, Robert T. 1882
Seward, George E. 1884
Simmons, Joseph S. "Joe" 1882
Snyder, Charles N. "Pop" 1891
Sommer, Benjamin F. 1883
Sullivan, Jeremiah "Jerry" 1887
Sullivan, Theodore P. "Ted" 1887
Taylor, Walter 1890
Toole, Stephen J. "Steve" 1890
Tunnison, William 1885-86
Valentine, John G. 1884-87
Walsh, Michael F. "Mike" 1882-83, 1885-86
York, Thomas J. "Tom" 1886
Young, Benjamin F. "Ben" 1886

Union Association (1884)

Crawford, Alexander 1884
DeVinney, P. H. "Dan" 1884
Dutton, Patrick J. 1884
Hengle, Emory J. "Moxie" 1884
Holland, John A. 1884
Hooper, Michael H. 1884
Jennings, Alfred "Al" 1884
Jordan, — 1884
Mapledoram, Blake A. 1884
McCaffrey, Harry 1884
Seward, George E. 1884
Stearns, D. Eckford "Ecky" 1884

Sullivan, David F. "Dave" 1884

Players League (1890)

Barnes, Roscoe C. "Ross" 1890
Ferguson, Robert V. "Bob" 1890
Gaffney, John H. 1890
Gunning, Thomas F. "Tom" 1890
Holbert, William H. "Bill" 1890
Jones, Charles W. "Charley" 1890
Knight, Alonzo P. "Lon" 1890
Leach, Henry 1890
Matthews, John 1890
Pierce, Grayson S. "Gracie" 1890
Sheridan, John F. 1890
Snyder, Charles N. "Pop" 1890

American League (1901-)

Adams, John H. 1903
Anthony, G. Merlyn 1969-75
Ashford, Emmett L. 1966-70
Avants, Nick R. 1969-71
Barnett, Lawrence R. "Larry" 1968-92
Barry, Daniel "Dan" 1928
Basil, Stephen J. "Steve" 1936-42
Berry, Charles F. "Charlie" 1942-62
Betts, William G. 1901
Boyer, James M. "Jim" 1944-50
Bremigan, Nicholas G. "Nick" 1974-88
Brinkman, Joseph N. "Joe" 1973-92
Campbell, William M. "Bick" 1928-31
Cantillon, Joseph "Joe" 1901
Carrigan, H. Sam 1961-65
Carpenter, William B. 1904
Caruthers, Robert L. "Bob" 1902-03
Cederstrom, Gary 1989-92
Chill, Oliver P. "Ollie" 1914-16, 1919-22
Chylak, Nestor L. 1954-78
Clark, Alan M. "Al" 1976-92
Coble, G. Drew 1983-92
Colliflower, James H. 1910
Connolly, Thomas H. "Tommy" 1901-31
Connor, Thomas "Tom" 1905-06
Cooney, Terrance L. "Terry" 1975-92
Cousins, Derryl 1979-92
Craft, Terry 1989-92
Deegan, William E. J. "Bill" 1970-80
Denkinger, Donald A. "Don" 1968-92
DiMuro, Louis J. "Lou" 1963-80
Dinneen, William H. "Bill" 1909-37
Donnelly, Charles H. 1934-35
Doyle, Walter J. 1963
Drummond, Calvin T. "Cal" 1960-69
Duffy, James F. "Jim" 1951-55
Dwyer, J. Francis "Frank" 1904
Egan, John J. "Rip" 1903, 1908-14
Eldridge, Clarence E. 1914-15
Evans, James B. "Jim" 1971-92

Evans, William G. "Billy" 1906-27
Ferguson, Charles A. 1913
Flaherty, John F. "Red" 1953-73
Ford, R. Dale 1975-92
Frantz, Arthur F. "Art" 1969-77
Friel, William E. "Bill" 1920
Froese, Grover A. 1952-53
Garcia, Richard R. "Rich" 1975-92
Geisel, Harry C. 1925-42
Goetz, Russell L. "Russ" 1968-83
Grieve, William T. T. "Bill" 1938-55
Guthrie, William J. "Bill" 1922, 1928-32
Haller, William E. "Bill" 1961, 1963-82
Hart, Robert F. "Bertie" 1912-13
Hart, William F. "Bill" 1901
Haskell, John E. 1901
Hassett, James E. 1903
Hayes, Gerald 1925-26
Hendry, Eugene "Ted" 1978-92
Hickox, Edward "Ed" 1990-92
Hildebrand, George A. 1912-34
Hirschbeck, John F. 1984-92
Holmes, Howard E. "Ducky" 1923-24
Honochick, G. James "Jim" 1949-73
Hubbard, R. Cal 1936-51, 1954-62
Hurley, Edwin H. "Eddie" 1947-65
Hurst, Timothy C. "Tim" 1905-09
Johnson, Mark S. 1984-92
Johnston, Charles E. 1936-37
Johnstone, James E. "Jim" 1902
Jones, Nicholas I. "Red" 1944-49
Joyce, James A. "Jim" 1989-92
Kaiser, Kenneth J. "Ken" 1977-92
Kelly, Thomas B. 1905
Kerin, John 1909-10
King, Charles F. 1904
Kinnamon, William E. "Bill" 1960-69
Kolls, Louis C. "Lou" 1933-40
Kosc, Gregory J. "Greg" 1976-92
Kunkel, William G. "Bill" 1968-84
Linsalata, Joseph N. "Joe" 1961-62
Luciano, Ronald M. "Ron" 1968-80
Maloney, George P. 1969-83
Mannassau, Alfred S. 1901
Marberry, Frederick "Firpo" 1935
McCarthy, John "Jack" 1905
McClelland, Timothy R. "Tim" 1984-92
McCormick, William J. "Barry" 1917
McCoy, Larry S. 1970-92
McGowan, William A. "Bill" 1925-54
McGreevy, Edward 1912-13
McKean, James G. "Jim" 1974-92
McKinley, William F. "Bill" 1946-65
Meriwether, Julius "Chuck" 1988-92
Merrill, E. Durwood 1977-92

Morgenweck, Henry C. "Hank" 1972-75
Moriarty, George J. 1917-26, 1929-40
Morrison, Daniel G. "Dan" 1984-92
Mullaney, Dominic J. 1915
Mullin, John 1911-12
Nallin, Richard F. "Dick" 1915-32
Napp, Larry A. 1951-74
Neudecker, Jerome A. "Jerry" 1965-85
O'Brien, Joseph "Joe" 1912, 1914
Odom, James C. "Jim" 1965-74
O'Donnell, James M. "Jake" 1968-71
O'Loughlin, Frank H. "Silk" 1902-18
O'Nora, Brian 1992
Ormsby, Emmett T. "Red" 1923-41
Owens, Clarence B. "Brick" 1916-37
Palermo, Stephen M. "Steve" 1977-91
Paparella, Joseph J. "Joe" 1946-65
Parker, Harley P. 1911
Parks, Dallas F. 1979-83
Passarella, Arthur M. "Art" 1941-42, 1945-53
Perrine, Fred "Bull" 1909-12
Phillips, David R. "Dave" 1971-92
Pipgras, George W. 1938-46
Quinn, John A. 1935-42
Reed, Rick A. 1984-92
Reilly, Michael E. "Mike" 1978-92
Rice, John L. 1955-73
Robb, Douglas W. "Scotty" 1952-53
Rodriguez, Armando H. 1974-75
Roe, John "Rocky" 1982-92
Rommel, Edwin A. "Eddie" 1938-59
Rowland, Clarence H. "Pants" 1923-27
Rue, Joseph W. "Joe" 1938-47
Runge, Edward P. "Ed" 1954-70
Salerno, Alexander J. "Al" 1961-68
Schwarts, Harry C. 1960-62
Scott, Dale A. 1986-92
Sheridan, John F. "Jack" 1901-14
Shulock, John R. 1979-92
Smith, W. Alaric "Al" 1960-65
Soar, A. Henry "Hank" 1950-73
Spenn, Frederick C. "Fred" 1979-80
Springstead, Martin J. "Marty" 1965-86
Stafford, John H. 1907
Stevens, John W. "Johnny" 1948-71
Stewart, Ernest D. 1941-45
Stewart, Robert W. "Bob" 1959-70
Summers, William R. "Bill" 1933-59
Tabacchi, Frank T. 1956-59
Tschida, Timothy J. "Tim" 1986-92
Umont, Frank W. 1954-73
Valentine, William T. "Bill" 1963-68
Van Graflan, Roy 1927-33
Voltaggio, Vito H. "Vic" 1977-92
Wallace, Roderick J. "Bobby" 1915-16

Walsh, Edward A. "Ed" 1922
Weafer, Harold L. "Hal" 1943-47
Welke, Timothy J. "Tim" 1985-92
Westervelt, Frederick E. 1911-12
Wilson, Frank 1921-22
Young, Larry E. 1985-92

Federal League (1914-15)

Anderson, Oliver O. "Ollie" 1914
Brennan, William T. "Bill" 1914-15
Bush, Garnet C. 1914
Corcoran, Thomas W. "Tommy" 1915
Cross, Montford M. "Monte" 1914
Cusack, Stephen P. 1914
Finneran, William E. 1915
Fyfe, Louis 1915
Goeckel, E. 1914
Howell, H. Harry 1915
Johnstone, James E. "Jim" 1915
Kane, Stephen J. 1914
Langden, Joseph 1915
Mannassau, Alfred S. "Al" 1914
McCormick, William J. "Barry" 1914-15
Mullin, John 1915
O'Brien, Joseph "Joe" 1915
Quisser, —, 1914
Shannon, William P. "Spike" 1914-15
Stocksdale, Otis H. 1915
Van Sickle, Charles F. 1914
Westervelt, Frederick E. 1915
Wilhelm, Irving K. "Kaiser" 1915

SUBSTITUTE UMPIRES

National Association (1871-75)

Addy, Robert E. "Bob" 1875
Allison, Andrew K. "Andy" 1872, 1874
Allison, Arthur A. "Art" 1872
Allison, Douglas L. "Doug" 1872-73, 1875
Alston, David 1871-72, 1875
Annan, William H. 1873
Arnold, Willis S. "Billy" 1875
Avery, C. Hamilton 1874
Barlow, Thomas H. "Tom" 1875
Barnes, Roscoe C. "Ross" 1874
Barrett, William "Bill" 1872, 1874
Barron, James "Jim" 1875
Barrows, Franklin L. "Frank" 1872
Battin, Joseph V. "Joe" 1874
Beals, Thomas L. "Tommy" 1872, 1874-75
Beardslee, John J. 1872-73
Bechtel, George A. 1874
Beck, W. S. 1872
Berthrong, Hnery W. "Harry" 1872
Bielaski, Oscar 1874-75
Bigelow, W. J. 1875
Birdsall, David S. "Dave" 1873-74
Blair, William J. 1873
Boake, John L. 1871
Bomeisler, Theodore 1874-75

Bond, Thomas H. "Tommy" 1875
Bonse, Nicholas 1871
Boyd, William J. "Bill" 1873
Bradley, George H. "Foghorn" 1875
Brainard, Asa 1872, 1875
Briggs, W. R. 1874
Brown, William 1872, 1875
Bruce, D. W. 1875
Buck, William F. 1871
Bunce, Frederick L. "Fred" 1874
Bunce, H. C. 1872
Bush, Archibald M. "Archie" 1871
Carey, Thomas J. "Tom" 1873, 1875
Carpenter, — 1874
Cassidy, John P. 1875
Cavanaugh, J. H. "Harry" 1875
Chandler, Moses E. 1872-1875
Chapman, John C. "Jack" 1871, 1873-74
Clifton, — 1872
Clinton, James L. "Jim" 1873, 1875
Colby, — 1873
Collins, Daniel T. "Dan" 1875
Cone, J. Frederick "Fred" 1873-74
Cope, Elias 1871
Craver, William H. "Bill" 1873
Cuthbert, Edgar E. "Ned" 1875
Daubney, Thomas 1871
David, L. N. 1874
Dawson, Mort 1871
Deane, J. Henry "Harry" 1871, 1874
Dehlman, Herman J. 1873, 1875
Demorest, D. P. 1872-73
Dobson, H. A. 1871
Dornlach, D. E. 1872
Draper, John H. 1871
Ellis, William R. 1871-72, 1875
English, John W. 1874-75
Erby, Frederick 1872
Evans, George 1872
Fellows, T. E. 1871
Ferguson, Robert V. "Bob" 1871, 1874
Fisher, William C. "Cherokee" 1871, 1875
Foley, Thomas J. "Tom" 1874-75
Force, David W. "Davy" 1873
Fulmer, Charles J. "Chick" 1872, 1874-75
Garrigan, Charles 1873
Geer, William H. "Billy" 1874-75
Gerhardt, Joseph J. "Joe" 1875
Glenn, John W. 1874
Glover, Frank 1873
Goodwin, J. Cheever 1871-72
Gould, Charles H. "Charlie" 1874-75
Graham, J. S. 1871-72
Halback, A. C. N. 1871, 1873-74
Hall, George W. 1873-75
Hall, James "Jim" 1872-73
Hall, N. Samuel 1873
Hanna, Dr. 1872
Hastings, W. Scott 1871-74
Hatfield, John V. B. 1872-73
Hayhurst, E. Hicks 1875
Haynie, James L. 1871
Hegeman, William H. 1871
Helm, J. 1871-72
Higham, Richard "Dick" 1872-75
Hodes, Charles "Charlie" 1874

Hooper, Michael H. "Mike" 1872-74
Hosworth, —, 1872-74
Hough, Pliny 1875
Howard, Charles 1872
Jennings, Alfred J. "Al" 1873
Johns, William R. 1873
Kahn, S. L. 1875
Keerl, George W. 1872
Kenney, John 1872
Kent, John 1875
Knight, George H. 1875
Kohler, Henry C. 1873
Lamb, Henry W. "Harry" 1875
Laughlin, Benjamin "Ben" 1873
Leonard, Andrew J. "Andy" 1872, 1873-74
Leonard, J. 1872
Leroy, Isaac 1871
Locke, Marshall 1873-74
Lovett, James D. 1871
Lowell, John A. 1872-73
Lush, M. R. 1873
MacDiarmed, Thomas 1872
Mack, Dennis J. "Denny" 1873-74
Malone, — 1875
Malone, Ferguson G. "Fergy" 1875
Martin, Alphonse C. "Phonney" 1871, 1873
Martin, Lewis G. 1871, 1873-74
Mathews, Robert T. "Bobby" 1871
Mawny, J. H. 1871
Maxwell, Cortez "Corty" 1875
Mays, — 1871
McCrea, — 1872
McDonald, James F. 1872
McGeary, Michael H. 1872, 1875
McLean, Harry C. 1871, 1873
McLean, William H. "Billy" 1872-73
McMahon, William 1871
McMullin, John F. 1874
McVey, Calvin A. "Cal" 1871, 1873, 1875
Meacham, — 1875
Miller, Joseph W. "Joe" 1872-73
Mills, Charles "Charlie" 1871
Mincher, Edward J. "Ed" 1872, 1875
Mincher, William E. 1875
Mitchell, C. L. 1874
Mitchell, F. B. 1875
Murnane, Timothy H. "Tim" 1873-75
Nelson, John W. "Candy" 1872
Nichols, A. N. 1871
Norton, Frank P. 1872
O'Brien, P. 1875
Pabor, Charles H. "Charlie" 1875
Parks, William R. "Bill" 1875
Patterson, Daniel T. "Dan" 1872
Peak, Frank 1871
Pearson, S. W. 1872
Phelps, Cornelius C. "Neal" 1874
Pike, Jacob Emanuel "Jay" 1875
Porter, — 1874
Powers, W. 1872-73, 1875
Pratt, Thomas J. "Tom" 1871-73
Quinn, — 1875
Radcliff, John Y. 1873
Ramsey, R. 1875
Rastall, Joseph H. 1872
Reach, Albert J. 1872-75
Reed, Hugh 1871, 1873-74

Remsen, John J. "Jack" 1873-74
Robinson, A. Valentine "Val" 1872
Robinson, Miley 1873
Rogers, George R. 1871-72
Ryan, John J. 1872, 1875
Sawyer, Dent 1871
Schafer, Harry C. 1875
Schrader, Louis 1875
Schuester, John A. 1874-75
Scofield, John W. 1871
Sears, John K. 1873
Selman, Frank C. 1873
Sensenderfer, John P. J. "Count" 1872-73, 1875
Simmons, Joseph S. "Joe" 1871, 1873-74
Smith, Eb 1872
Smith, George 1872
Snyder, Charles N. "Pop" 1875
Stahl, George 1875
Stanwood, —, 1872-73
Stires, Garrett "Gat" 1875
Stophlet, J. 1871
Sutton, Ezra B. 1875
Swandell, J. Martin "Marty" 1871, 1874
Sweasy, Charles J. "Charlie" 1871, 1873-74
Tighe, Edward 1871
Treacey, Frederick S. "Fred" 1871, 1873, 1875
Tyler, Columbus T. 1871-74
Urell, M. E. 1873
Van Delft, —, 1875
Voltz, Edward "Ed" 1871-72
Walk, Frank 1871
Wardell, — 1874
Waterman, Frederick A. "Fred" 1873
Weaver, Charles 1873
Weigel, William H. 1873-74
White, Horatio S. 1873
White, W. Warren 1874
White, William H. "Will" 1875
Wiggins, — 1875
Wildey, John 1871
Willard, Gardner 1871
Wirth, Adam 1872, 1875
Wood, James B. "Jimmy" 1871
Wright, W. Harrison "Harry" 1875
York, Thomas J. "Tom" 1874

National League (1876-)

Allen, Hezekiah "Ham" 1876
Ayers, — 1876
Baker, Charles 1884
Barker, Alfred L. 1881
Barnie, William S. "Billy" 1882
Barnum, George W. 1896
Barton, — 1876
Battin, Joseph V. "Joe" 1895
Beard, Oliver P. "Ollie" 1894
Becannon, James M. 1885
Behle, Frank 1895-96
Berger, Frederick 1886
Bigelow, — 1877
Bittman, Henry "Red" 1892, 1894-95, 1897
Blakiston, Robert J. "Bob" 1884
Blodgett, C. W. 1876
Bradley, George H. "Foghorn" 1877
Brady, — 1877
Bredburg, George W. 1878-79
Brennan, John E. "Jack" 1887
Brockway, John 1877, 1879

Brown, Samuel W. 1907
Bullymore, Charles L. 1882
Burke, — 1892
Burlingame, Frank A. 1878
Burnham, George W. 1886-87
Campbell, Al 1886
Campbell, Daniel "Dan" 1897
Carsey, Wilfred "Kid" 1901
Caruthers, Robert L. "Bob" 1886, 1893
Chandler, Moses E. 1877
Chapman, John C. "Jack" 1876, 1882
Chill, Oliver P. "Ollie" 1916
Cheppy, John T. 1876
Chipman, Harry F. 1886
Clack, Robert H. "Bobby" 1897
Cohen, — 1893
Colgan, Harry W. 1899
Collins, Daniel T. "Dan" 1876
Cone, J. F. "Fred" 1876
Connell, Terence G. 1885, 1887
Connolly, John M. 1885, 1887, 1892-93
Cook, W. H. 1879
Crandall, Robert 1876, 1878
Crane, Edward N. "Ed" 1893
Crane, Samuel N. "Sam" 1879, 1887
Cray, P. C. 1893
Cross, John A. 1876
Cudworth, Al 1880
Curren, Peter 1876
Cushman, Charles H. "Charley" 1894
Daniels, — 1885
Deane, J. Henry "Harry" 1876, 1878
Devinney, P. H. "Dan" 1876
Doscher, John H. Sr. "Herm" 1879
Draper, John H. 1877
Dunlap, Frederick C. "Fred" 1879
Dyler, John F. 1892, 1897
Eagan, John J. 1879
Earle, William M. "Billy" 1892
Eason, Malcolm W. "Mal" 1901
Eustace, — 1904
Evans, Jacob "Jake" 1886
Fenno, Norman 1876
Fisher, William C. "Cherokee" 1876
Flaherty, — 1882
Flaherty, Patrick J. "Patsy" 06-07
Flynn, John A. "Jocko" 1893
Fouser, William C. 1876
Fulmer, Charles J. "Chick" 1881
Furlong, William E. 1877, 1880, 1888
Gaffney, John H. 1887, 1898
Galvin, James F. "Jim" 1886
Ganzel, Charles W. "Charlie" 1901
Gifford, James H. 1881
Gillean, Thomas 1881
Gleason, John D. 1877
Gleason, William G. "Bill" 1877
Glenn, John W. 1880
Goldsmith, Frederick E. "Fred" 1886
Graves, Frank M. 1895
Griffiths, — 1884
Gross, Edward M. 1881
Guinney, Daniel 1882
Hardie, Louis W. "Lou" 1887
Hartley, John "Jack" 1894
Hastings, W. Scott 1877
Hatfield, John V. B. 1876

Hawes, William A. 1880-82
Hegeman, William H. 1881
Hernon, Thomas H. "Tom" 1894
Heydler, John A. 1895-97
Hickey, James L. 1882
Hodges, A. D. 1877
Hogan, — 1897
Hogriever, George C. 1893
Hornung, M. Joseph "Joe" 1892
Howard, C. F. 1884
Hurll, George 1876
Hurst, Timothy C. "Tim" 1904
Jevne, Frederick "Fred" 1892, 1894
Jose, — 1889
Joyce, C. E. 1879
Kane, Stephen J. 1906
Kecher, W. H. 1910
Keefe, Timothy J. "Tim" 1893
Keenan, James W. "Jim" 1893
Kelley, J. P. 1879
Kelley, W. W. 1877
Kelly, John O. 1884-85
Kennedy, — 1893
Kennedy, Michael J. 1884
Kenney, John 1876
Kerins, John A. "Jack" 1888
Kipp, Eden 1881
Kling, William "Bill" 1892
Klusman, William F. "Billy" 1893
Knight, Alonzo P. "Lon" 1876, 1888
Lally, Bud 1896
Lanigan, Charles 1908
Latham, W. Arlington "Arlie" 1900
Laughlin, —, 1876
Lawler, Michael H. 1882
Leary, — 1879
Libby, Stephen A. 1879
Long, William H. "Billy" 1893, 1897
Lynch, F. G. 1892
Lynch, Thomas J. "Tom" 1902
Maddox, Charles 1882
Malone, Ferguson G. "Fergy" 1892
Maloney, James "Jim" 1893
Manning, James H. "Jim" 1893
Manning, John E. "Jack" 1881
Mapledoram, Blake A. 1886
Martin, Alphonse C. "Phonney" 1876
Mason, Charles E. "Charlie" 1876
Mathews, Robert T. "Bobby" 1876
Mayer, — 1893
McCaffrey, Harry 1885-86
McCrum, — 1892
McGee, — 1876
McGinnis, —, 1910
McGinty, — 1897
McKinney, — 1883
McLeod, — 1895
McMullen, John F. 1876
Meagher, John 1877
Meals, Gerald W. "Jerry" 1992
Mears, Charles W. 1894
Medart, William 1876-77
Megrue, Cliff 1876
Mills, Abraham G. 1877
Montague, — 1877
Morrill, John F. 1891, 1896
Morris, Edward 1895, 1897
Morris, John S. 1876
Muir, Thomas 1876
Mullane, Anthony J. "Tony" 1897
Mullen, Peter C. 1893
Murnane, Timothy H. "Tim" 1886

Murphy, Henry 1880
Murphy, Martin W. 1886
Murray, Jeremiah J. "Miah" 1894, 1900, 1905, 1910
Myers, Henry C. 1890
Nicol, Hugh N. 1894
O'Brien, William 1876
O'Day, Henry F. "Hank" 1896
Orr, David L. "Dave" 1891
Osborne, William 1876
Pfeffer, Nathaniel F. "Nate" 1897
Phelan, — 1896
Pierce, — 1893
Pierce, Grayson S. "Gracie" 1892
Pike, Lipman E. "Lip" 1890
Power, Charles B. 1893-95
Pratt, Albert G. "Al" 1880, 1887
Quincy, W. 1893
Quinn, Joseph C. "Joe" 1881
Quinn, P. J. 1876
Quinn, William H. "Billy" 1887, 1889
Redheffer, — 1895
Reid, William A. 1882
Reilly, Charles 1880
Remsen, John J. "Jack" 1880
Rhodes, Eugene A. 1887
Richards, J. E. 1880
Ritchie, F. 1876
Rocap, Adam 1876
Roll, — 1876
Rowe, John C. "Jack" 1881
Rudderham, Francis F. "Frank" 1907
Say, Louis I. "Lou" 1879
Schofield, J. W. 1879
Schurer, — 1896
Seward, Edward W. "Ed" 1892
Seward, George E. 1877
Shepard, W. L. 1879
Sheridan, John F. "Jack" 1893
Sick, — 1884
Simmons, Joseph S. "Joe" 1876
Skelly, — 1880
Skinner, S. A. 1886
Smith, — 1876
Sneeden, — 1895
Snodd, Carey 1877
Snyder, Charles N. "Pop" 1895
Sommers, Joseph A. "Joe" 1893
Stafford, John H. "Jack" 1906
Stage, Charles W. "Billy" 1895
Stambaugh, Calvin G. 1879
Strief, George A. 1880
Sullivan, — 1889
Sullivan, David F. "Dave" 1883, 1887-88
Summer, James G. 1876, 1878
Supple, — 1906
Sutton, Ezra B. 1876
Sweasy, Charles J. "Charlie" 1879
Tilden, Otis 1876
Tindall, — 1890
Toole, Stephen J. "Steve" 1888
Tuthill, Benjamin "Ben" 1895
Twitchell, Lawrence G. "Larry" 1894
Wade, Ben F. 1879-80
Walker, William E. 1878
Walsh, Michael F. "Mike" 1879
Walters, —, 1892-93
Walton, G. W. 1876
Warren, L. B. 1876
Wash, Frank 1877
Weeden, —, 1889-90
West, — 1885
West, George 1878

West, Milton D. "Buck" 1890
White, Gideon F. 1876-77
White, W. Warren 1876
Williams, Elisha A. "Dale" 1876
Wilson, William G. "Bill" 1892-93
Witham, C. B. 1879
Wolf, William V. "Jimmy" 1893, 1895-97
Wood, George A. 1899
Wood, James B. "Jimmy" 1876
Wright, William H. "Harry" 1885
Wycoff, — 1892

American Association (1882-91)

Arnold, Frank W. 1889
Austin, Ed 1890
Barnie, William S. "Billy" 1882, 1884, 1887
Battin, Joseph V. "Joe" 1882, 1886
Bauers, Albert J. "Al" 1890
Bell, Frank G. 1889
Bittman, Henry P. "Red" 1889
Blogg, Wesley C. "Wes" 1886
Bloom, — 1887
Bond, Thomas H. "Tommy" 1891
Burdock, John J. "Jack" 1887
Burkalow, Isaac 1888
Burns, — 1882
Butler, Charles 1889
Butler, Ormond H. 1886
Campbell, Daniel "Dan" 1890
Carlin, William J. "Billy" 1885, 1888-89
Connell, J. 1885
Connell, Terence G. 1885-86, 1889
Cornell, — 1884
Crandall, Robert 1882
Creighton, — 1889-90
Critchley, Morris A. "Morrie" 1884-85
Curry, Frank 1884, 1886
Cuthbert, Edgar E. "Ned" 1888
Dailey, John J. 1889
Daniels, Lawrence 1887
Devine, W. James "Jim" 1890
DeVinney, P. H. "Dan" 1887
Devlin, Charles "Charlie" 1888
Dolan, Thomas J. "Tom" 1890-91
Dow, Clarence 1891
Dugan, — 1887
Duke, Martin F. 1890
Dunlevy, Hugh 1887
Dyler, John F. 1883, 1885-86
Ellick, Joseph J. "Joe" 1888-89
Ewing, William "Buck" 1882
Fell, — 1885
Fountain, Henry V. 1888
Galvin, James F. "Jim" 1885
Geer, William H. "Billy" 1887
Gill, Thomas H. "Tommy" 1886
Helburn, Hugo 1887
Henderson, J. Harding "Hardie" 1889
Hengle, Edward S. "Ed" 1889
Hicks, Nathaniel W. "Nat" 1885
Holliday, James W. "Bug" 1889
Irwin, — 1882
Irwin, John 1885

Jennings, Alfred "Al" 1882, 1884-85, 1889
Julian, Joseph O. 1888
Kelly, John O. 1887
Kelly, William 1884
Kleinbacker, —, 1886
Levis, Charles H. "Charlie" 1882
Lilly, J. 1884
Little, — 1884
Loughlin, —, 1885
Loughlin, William 1882
Lyons, Toby A. 1891
Lyston, William E. 1890
Magner, John T. 1882, 1884, 1887
Malone, J. R. 1888
Marshall, — 1887
Mathews, Robert T. "Bobby" 1888
McCartney, Joseph 1882
McCormick, —, 1888
McGee, Patrick 1882, 1884
McGinnis, George W. "Jumbo" 1888-89
McIntosh, — 1882
McLaughlin, William 1882
McLean, William B. "Billy" 1882, 1889-90
McQuade, James H. 1891
McSorley, John B. "Trick" 1888
Medart, William 1887
Miller, Charles A. 1884
Mitchell, — 1887
Morgan, Henry W. 1884
Morton, Charles H. "Charlie" 1884
Mullen, Peter C. 1891
O'Dea, Lawrence 1890
Paasch, William 1887-89
Parker, — 1887
Phillips, Horace B. 1882
Pierce, Grayson S. "Gracie" 1884
Pike, Lipman. E. "Lip" 1887
Pratt, Albert G. "Al" 1886
Quinn, William H. 1884-85
Ramsey, Dick 1887
Reeder, James E. 1884
Reising, Charles 1882
Rice, — 1885
Riley, William J. 1885
Robb, John 1886
Ross, Robert T. 1884
Ruhl, Gus 1882
Ryan, John 1882
Selman, Frank C. 1882
Sherman, Sharon L. "Shang" 1890
Simpson, Lew 1882
Skinner, —, 1884, 1886
Smith, George 1887
Sneed, Jonathon L. 1885
Sullivan, David F. "Dave" 1884
Talbot, — 1887
Tinney, — 1882
Walsh, Michael F. "Mike" 1887-88
West, —, 1885, 1887
Wood, George A. 1886
Wright, — 1884
Young, Benjamin F. "Ben" 1887
Young, Joseph 1890

Union Association (1884)

Adler, — 1884
Burlingame, F. A. 1884
Donovan, E. S. 1884
Furlong, William E. "Bill" 1884
Hudson, Vincent D. 1884
Lee, Thomas F. 1884
McGunnigle, William H. "Bill" 1884
McManaway, D. 1884
McMinimum, Dennis 1884
Montgomery, — 1884
Powers, Charles B. 1884
Timblin, — 1884
Torry, — 1884

American League (1901-)

Betts, William G. 1903
Brown, Thomas T. "Tom" 1907
Egan, John J. "Rip" 1907
Kerin, John 1908
Kerins, John A. 1903
Mace, Harry L. 1903
Pears, Frank 1903
Quigley, Ernest C. "Ernie" 1906
Terry, William H. "Adonis" 1901

Federal League (1914-15)

Murphy, J. A. 1914

ACTIVE PLAYERS WHO UMPIRED

National League (1876-)

Abbey, Charles S. "Charlie" 1897
Abbott, Frederick H. "Fred" 1905
Andrews, G. Edward "Ed" 1889
Arundel, John T. "Tug" 1888
Baker, Philip "Phil" 1889
Baldwin, Marcus E. "Mark" 1892
Bannon, James H. "Jimmy" 1894
Beatin, Ebenezer "Ed" 1889
Beck, Erwin T. "Erve" 1902
Beckley, Jacob P. "Jake" 1906
Beebe, Fred L. 1907
Berger, John H. "Tun" 1891
Bonner, Frank J. 1894
Boyle, Henry J. 1886
Boyle, John A. "Jack" 1892, 1897
Breitenstein, Theodore P. "Ted" 1900
Briody, Charles F. "Fatty" 1881
Brown, Willard 1891
Buelow, Charles J. "Charlie" 1901
Buffinton, Charles G. "Charlie" 1883, 1888-89, 1892
Burdock, John J. "Jack" 1881
Burns, Thomas P. "Oyster" 1895
Bushong, Albert J. "Doc" 1880, 1890
Butler, Richard H. "Dick" 1897
Carrick, William M. "Bill" 1900
Carroll, Frederick H. "Fred" 1887
Carsey, Wilfred "Kid" 1894, 1896
Caruthers, Robert L. "Bob" 1891
Casey, Daniel M. "Dan" 1888
Caskin, Edward J. "Ed" 1884
Cassidy, John P. 1882
Chamberlain, Elton P. 1894
Chance, Frank L. 1902
Clack, Robert H. "Bobby" 1876
Clarke, Arthur F. "Artie" 1890
Clarke, William J. "Boileryard" 1893-94, 1896
Clarkson, Arthur H. "Dad" 1893-96
Clarkson, John G. 1888, 1892-93
Clements, John J. "Jack" 1892
Coleman, John F. 1884

Coogan, Daniel G. "Dan" 1895
Cooney, John W. "Johnny" 1941
Crane, Edward N. "Ed" 1892
Crane, Samuel N. "Sam" 1886, 1890
Crolius, Frederick J. "Fred" 1901
Cronin, John J. "Jack" 1902-03
Cross, Lafayette N. "Lave" 1892
Cunningham, Elmer E. "Bert" 1896-97, 1900
Cuppy, George M. 1894
Cusick, Andrew D. "Tony" 1886-87
Daily, Cornelius F. "Con" 1886, 1891, 1894, 1896
Daly, Thomas P. "Tom" 1901
Darling, Conrad "Dell" 1887
Dealy, Patrick E. "Pat" 1886
Dexter, Charles D. "Charlie" 1896-97
Donahue, Francis R. "Red" 1897
Donahue, Timothy C. "Tim" 1895-96
Donlin, Michael J. "Mike" 1900
Donnelly, James B. "Jim" 1896
Donovan, William E. "Bill" 1902
Dooin, Charles S. "Red" 1904
Douglass, William B. "Klondike" 1903
Dowse, Thomas J. "Tom" 1890
Duggleby, William J. "Bill" 1905
Dwyer, J. Francis "Frank" 1889, 1893-94, 1896-97
Earle, William M. "Billy" 1894
Ehret, Philip S. "Phil" 1892, 1895-97
Farrell, Charles A. "Duke" 1901-02
Ferguson, Charles J. "Charlie" 1886
Fitzsimmons, Frederick "Freddie" 1941
Flaherty, Patrick J. "Patsy" 1904
Force, David W. "Davy" 1881
Foreman, Frank I. 1895
Foreman, John D. "Brownie" 1896
Foster, Clarence F. "Pop" 1900
Freeman, John F. "Buck" 1900
Galvin, James F. "Jim" 1881, 1887, 1889
Gardner, James A. "Jim" 1899
George, William M. "Bill" 1889
German, Lester S. "Les" 1895
Gleason, William J. "Kid" 1890, 1892
Grady, Michael W. "Mike" 1895
Graves, Frank M. 1886
Griffith, Clark C. 1894-95
Grim, John H. 1892, 1895-96
Gruber, Henry J. 1889
Gumbert, Addison C. "Ad" 1892, 1895
Gunning, Thomas F. "Tom" 1884-85
Gunson, Joseph B. "Joe" 1892
Hackett, Mortimer M. "Mert" 1886
Haddock, George S. 1889

Hallman, William W. "Bill" 1903
Hanlon, Edward H. "Ned" 1892
Hart, William F. "Bill" 1896
Hatfield, Gilbert "Gil" 1889
Healy, John J. 1887
Hemming, George E. 1895-96
Hines, Michael P. "Mike" 1884
Holliday, James W. "Bug" 1897
Howe, John "Shorty" 1890
Hurst, Timothy C. "Tim" 1898
Hyatt, R. Hamilton "Ham" 1912
Irwin, Arthur A. 1881
Jacklitsch, Fred L. 1901
Jennings, Hugh A. "Hughie" 1893, 1900
Jones, Henry M. 1890
Kahoe, Michael J. "Mike" 1905
Karger, Edwin "Ed" 1906
Keefe, Timothy J. "Tim" 1880-82, 1884-85, 1887, 1892
Kellum, Winford A. "Win" 1905
Kelly, Michael J. "King" 1892-93
Killen, Frank B. 1896-97
Kinslow, Thomas F. "Tom" 1892
Kittridge, Malachi J. 1890, 1899
Kitson, Frank R. 1902
Kling, John G. "Johnny" 1901
Knell, Philip H. "Phil" 1895
Knowles, James "Jimmy" 1892
Krieg, William F. "Bill" 1887
Leever, Samuel W. "Sam" 1900, 1904
Lindeman, Vivian A. "Vive" 1907
Lundgren, Carl L. 1905-06
Maloney, William A. "Billy" 1902
Manning, James H. "Jim" 1886
Mathews, Robert T. "Bobby" 1882
Mathewson, Christopher "Christy" 1901, 1907
McAleer, James R. "Jim" 1893
McAllister, Lewis W. "Sport" 1899
McCarthy, Thomas F. M. "Tommy" 1896
McCauley, Allen A. "Al" 1890
McCauley, Patrick M. "Pat" 1896
McCormick, James "Jim" 1885
McFarland, Edward W. "Ed" 1896
McGarr, James B. "Chippy" 1895
McGinnity, Joseph J. "Joe" 1900
McGuire, James T. "Deacon" 1886, 1894, 1896, 1901
McKinnon, Alexander J. "Alex" 1886
McMahon, John H. "Sadie" 1893
Meekin, Jouette 1895-96
Menefee, John "Jock" 1903
Mertes, Samuel B. "Sam" 1905
Miller, George F. "Doggie" 1893, 1896
Miller, Joseph H. 1884
Moran, Patrick J. "Pat" 1901
Mullane, Anthony J. "Tony" 1893

Mulvey, Joseph H. "Joe" 1895
Murphy, Morgan E. 1893, 1896, 1898
Murphy, William H. "Yale" 1895, 1897
Murray, Jeremiah J. "Miah" 1895
Myers, George D. 1886
Needham, Thomas J. "Tom" 1904, 1907
Newton, Eustace J. "Doc" 1902
Nichols, Charles A. "Kid" 1900-01
Nolan, Edward S. "The Only" 1881
Noonan, Peter J. "Pete" 1906-07
O'Brien, John F. "Darby" 1889
O'Connor, John J. "Jack" 1893, 1901
O'Day, Henry F. "Hank" 1888-89
O'Neill, Michael J. "Mike" 1904
O'Rourke, James H. "Jim" 1893
Orth, Albert L. "Al" 1901
Overall, Orval 1905, 1910
Peitz, Henry C. "Heinie" 1901, 1906
Phelps, Edward J. "Ed" 1912
Phillippe, Charles L. "Deacon" 1903
Quinn, Joseph J. "Joe" 1894, 1896
Reilly, Charles T. "Charlie" 1892, 1894-95
Reitz, Henry P. "Heinie" 1895
Rhines, William P. "Billy" 1891, 1896
Richardson, A. Harding "Hardie" 1892
Richmond, J. Lee 1883
Robinson, Wilbert 1898
Ryan, James E. "Jimmy" 1892
Sanders, A. Bennett "Ben" 1889
Schmidt, Henry M. 1903
Schriver, William F. "Pop" 1901
Serad, William T. "Billy" 1884
Smith, A. Edgar 1883
Smith, Charles M. "Pop" 1881
Smith, Edgar E. 1890
Smith, George H. "Heinie" 1901
Smith, Harry T. 1903
Smith, William E. "Bill" 1886
Sommers, Joseph A. "Joe" 1889
Staley, Harry E. 1892, 1895
Stearns, D. Eckford "Ecky" 1881
Stein, Edward F. "Ed" 1890, 1894, 1896
Stivetts, John C. "Jack" 1894
Stocksdale, Otis H. 1895
Stricker, John A. "Cub" 1892
Stricklett, Elmer E. 1907
Sugden, Joseph "Joe" 1897
Sullivan, James E. "Jim" 1896
Sullivan, Martin C. "Marty" 1889
Sullivan, Michael J. "Mike" 1897
Sullivan, Thomas J. "Sleeper" 1881
Sutcliffe, Elmer E. "Sy" 1889, 1892
Tannehill, Jesse N. 1897, 1901-02

Tate, Edward C. "Pop" 1888
Taylor, John B. "Jack" 1899
Taylor, John W. "Jack" 1901, 1905
Tener, John K. 1889
Terry, William H. "Adonis" 1892, 1895-96
Tiernan, Michael J. "Mike" 1895
Vaughn, Harry F. "Farmer" 1892, 1899
Viau, Leon "Lee" 1891
Vickery, Thomas G. "Tom" 1890
Walker, Thomas W. "Tom" 1905
Wall, Joseph F. "Joe" 1901
Wallace, Roderick J. "Bobby" 1895
Ward, John M. "Monte" 1888
Warner, John J. "Jack" 1896-97, 1901, 1903
Weaver, William B. "Farmer" 1893
Weimer, Jacob W. "Jake" 1905, 1907
Welch, Michael F. "Mickey" 1881-82, 1885-86, 1888
Weyhing, August "Gus" 1899-1900
Whistler, Lewis "Lew" 1891
White, Guy H. "Doc" 1901-02
White, James L. "Deacon" 1880
Whitney, James E. "Jim" 1884, 1886
Wilhelm, Irving K. "Kaiser" 1904-05
Williamson, Edward N. "Ned" 1878, 1880
Willis, Victor G. "Vic" 1903
Wilmot, Walter R. "Walt" 1897
Wilson, Frank A. "Zeke" 1896, 1899
Wilson, Parke A. 1894-96, 1899
Wilson, William G. "Bill" 1890
Wright, William H. "Harry" 1876-77
Yeager, George J. 1901
Young, Denton T. "Cy" 1896
Young, Irving M. "Irv" 1905, 1907
Zimmer, Charles L. "Chief" 1889, 1901

American Association (1882-91)

Baldwin, Clarence G. "Kid" 1887
Becannon, James M. "Buck" 1884
Bond, Thomas H. "Tommy" 1884
Booth, Amos S. 1882
Boyle, John A. "Jack" 1888
Brennan, John G. "Jack" 1888
Briody, Charles F. "Fatty" 1888
Burns, Thomas P. "Oyster" 1888
Bushong, Albert J. "Doc" 1888-89
Carlin, William J. "Billy" 1886
Carsey, Wilfred "Kid" 1891
Cassidy, John P. 1884
Chamberlain, Elton P. 1887, 1891
Cross, Lafayette N. "Lave" 1889
Crowell, William T. "Billy" 1888
Darling, Conrad "Dell" 1891
Donahue, James A. "Jim" 1888

Easton, John S. "Jack" 1891
Ehret, Philip S. "Phil" 1890
Ewing, John 1889
Fulmer, Charles J. "Chick" 1888
Galvin, James F. "Jim" 1886
Ganzel, Charles W. "Charlie" 1886
Goldsby, Walton H. "Walt" 1888
Greenwood, William F. "Bill" 1884
Griffith, Clark C. 1891
Gunning, Thomas F. "Tom" 1888-89
Healy, John J. 1890
Hecker, Guy J. 1888
Herr, Edward J. "Ed" 1888
Higgins, William E. "Bill" 1890
Holbert, William H. "Bill" 1888
Johnston, Richard F. "Dick" 1884
Keefe, Timothy J. "Tim" 1884
Keenan, James W. "Jim" 1887-88
Kilroy, Matthew A. "Matt" 1887
Kirby, John F. 1888
Knell, Philip L. "Phil" 1891
Latham, George W. "Juice" 1884
Lynch, John H. "Jack" 1884
Macullar, James F. "Jimmy" 1886
Mattimore, Michael J. "Mike" 1888
Mays, Albert C. "Al" 1887
McCarthy, Thomas F. M. "Tommy" 1889
McKelvy, Russell E. "Russ" 1882
McMahon, John J. "Sadie" 1890
McSorley, John B. "Trick" 1884
Merrill, Edward M. "Ed" 1884
Mountain, Frank H. 1884
Mullane, Anthony J. "Tony" 1888
Murphy, Joseph A. "Joe" 1887
O'Brien, William D. "Darby" 1887-88
O'Connor, John J. "Jack" 1889
O'Day, Henry F. "Hank" 1884
Peoples, James E. "Jimmy" 1888-89
Pierce, Grayson S. "Gracie" 1882
Sage, Harry 1890
Serad, William I. "Billy" 1888
Smith, Charles M. "Pop" 1882, 1886
Smith, Frederick C. "Fred" 1890
Smith, John F. "Phenomenal" 1888
Snyder, Charles N. "Pop" 1886
Sommer, Joseph J. "Joe" 1888
Sprague, Charles W. "Charlie" 1890
Stivetts, John C. "Jack" 1891
Sweeney, Charles J. "Charley" 1887
Sylvester, Louis J. "Lou" 1888
Terry, William H. "Adonis" 1884, 1888
Townsend, George H. 1890
Traffley, William F. "Bill" 1884

Vaughn, Harry F. "Farmer" 1891
Weyhing, August "Gus" 1891
Wheeler, Harry E. 1882
Wood, George A. 1891
Zimmer, Charles L. "Chief" 1888

Union Association (1884)

Bradley, George W. 1884
Callahan, Edward J. "Ed" 1884
Carroll, Patrick "Pat" 1884
Cuthbert, Edgar E. "Ned" 1884
Kelly, John F. 1884
McLaughlin, James C. "Jim" 1884
Oberbeck, Henry A. 1884
Wheeler, Harry E. 1884
Williams, Washington J. "Wash" 1884

Players League (1890)

Bakely, Edward E. "Ed" 1890
Carney, John J. 1890
Comiskey, Charles A. "Charlie" 1890
Daily, Cornelius F. "Con" 1890
Gumbert, Addison C. "Ad" 1890
Haddock, George S. 1890
Hallman, William W. "Bill" 1890
Keefe, Timothy J. "Tim" 1890
Kelly, Michael "King" 1890
Madden, Michael J. "Kid" 1890
Milligan, John "Jocko" 1890
O'Day, Henry "Hank" 1890
Tener, John K. 1890

American League (1901-)

Altrock, Nicholas "Nick" 1907
Bernhard, William H. "Bill" 1903
Beville, H. Monte 1903-04
Callahan, James J. "Nixey" 1901
Conlan, John B. "Jocko" 1935
Coughlin, William P. "Bill" 1904
Cronin, John J. "Jack" 1901
Davis, Harry H. 1903
Donahue, Francis R. "Red" 1903, 1906
Donovan, William E. "Bill" 1903, 1906
Drill, Lewis L. "Lew" 1903-04
Flaherty, Patrick J. "Patsy" 1903
Foreman, Francis I. "Frank" 1901
Grady, Michael W. "Mike" 1901
Griffith, Clark C. 1903
Howell, H. Harry 1904, 1906
Kittridge, Malachi J. 1905
Leahy, Thomas J. "Tom" 1901
Leppert, Donald G. "Don" 1978
Lowe, Robert L. "Bobby" 1905
McAllister, Lewis W. "Sport" 1901-02
McGuire, James T "Deacon" 1905

Moore, Earl A. 1903
O'Brien, Peter J. "Pete" 1907
Patten, Case L. 1903
Pelty, Barney 1906
Powers, Michael R. "Mike" 1902
Schreckengost, Ossee F. 1903
Siever, Edward T. "Ed" 1901
Warner, John J. "Jack" 1908
White, Guy H. "Doc" 1903
Winter, George L. 1903, 1905
Young, Denton T. "Cy" 1903
Zimmerman, Gerald R. "Jerry" 1978

UMPIRES DURING STRIKES

National League (1876-)

Anderson, Lewis E. "Andy" 1978-79
Andress, William J. "Bill" 1979
Baird, John 1979
Ballino, Frank 1991
Barston, Michael "Mike" 1979
Baswell, Jack S. 1979
Beck, Robert "Bob" 1979
Bendekovits, Joseph "Joe" 1979
Betcher, Ralph A. 1976
Blandford, Fred 1970
Bovey, Terry R. 1979, 1984
Bruns, Randy 1991
Campagna, Frank J. 1979, 1984
Cavenaugh, Richard P. "Dick" 1979, 1984
Cohen, Alfred A. "Al" 1976
Cote, Emilien 1979
Cuneo, James "Jim" 1978-79
Deniston, Shannon W. "Shan" 1978
Dierking, Roger A. 1978
Edwards, Larry 1978
Fick, Jerry D. 1978-79
Fisher, Frank 1979, 1984
Fleming, Thomas E. "Tom" 1979
Floras, John 1991
Fowler, A. Wheeler 1978
Freels, Robert L. "Bob" 1979
Gisondi, Tony 1991
Graham, Scott 1991
Grimsley, John 1970
Grinder, Scott 1976
Grooms, Roger C. 1979
Grygiel, George R. 1970
Guckert, Elmer 1976
Hadry, Merrill A. 1979
Hamil, Ray 1979
Hansen, Howard 1978-79
Hantak, H. Robert "Bob" 1979
Henry, William "Bill" 1979
Holoka, Mike 1991
Hutson, Ronald "Ron" 1979
January, Don 1991
Jeffers, Ronald L. "Ron" 1979
Jones, James "Jim" 1979
Jumper, Howard 1979
Lauzon, Jacques 1979
Lawson, William R. "Bill" 1979
Loeber, Gerald G. "Jerry" 1979
Lospitalier, Philip A. "Phil" 1979

Lupo, Charles "Charlie" 1978-79
Maher, Robert J. "Bob" 1979, 1984
Martine, Bruce 1991
Mauer, Boyd 1978-79
Melton, David "Dave" 1978
Miller, Marvin G. "Bud" 1979
Mills, Greg 1979
Morgenweck, Henry C. "Hank" 1970
Mrvos, Joseph S. "Joe" 1979
Myers, Joseph "Joe" 1979
Negri, Peter "Pete" 1979
Nelson, Robert "Bob" 1979, 1991
Norris, Edward E. "Ed" 1978-79
Oliger, Edward C. "Ed" 1979
Patch, Tony D. 1978-79
Perez, J. Ray 1979
Pomponi, Joseph L. "Joe" 1979, 1984
Rains, James "Jim" 1979
Riccio, Dennis R. 1979
Riccio, L. Leonard "Len" 1979
Roth, Roy 1978-79
Rountree, Henry J. "Hank" 1978-79
Schaller, Cliff 1978-79
Schleyer, John 1979
Schratz, Joseph "Joe" 1979
Schroeder, Robert L. "Bobby" 1978-79
Scott, James "Jim" 1978-79
Sharkey, Michael E. "Mick" 1978-79
Sharp, Robert C. "Bob" 1979
Siroka, Harold L. 1979
Slattery, Donald L. "Don" 1979
Slickenmeyer, David W. "Dave" 1979, 1984
Smail, Harry F. 1979
Spange, John 1991
Spinelli, Michel 1979
Stansell, B. Jack 1979
Stewart, John 1979, 1984
Strey, Murray W. 1978-79
Telford, Thomas "Tom" 1979
Tillman, Henry T. "Hank" 1978-79
Treitel, Leslie J. "Les" 1978-79
Tremblay, Richard H. "Dick" 1979
Urlage, Richard C. "Dick" 1979, 1991
Waller, James "Jim" 1979
Williams, Dale 1978-79
Willman, Bob 1991

American League (1901-)

Arata, Mark 1991
Berry, Charles F. "Charlie" 1970
Bible, Jonathan D. "Jon" 1984
Bishop, Homer L. 1979
Borga, Steven A. "Steve" 1979
Briscese, Michael L. "Mike" 1979
Brown, Buddy Lee "Bud" 1979
Brown, Douglas D. "Doug" 1979
Brown, Jeff 1978-79

Camp, John W. 1979
Campbell, Robert "Bob" 1979
Clegg, Richard "Dick" 1979
Clement, Robert F. "Bob" 1978-79
Contant, Alan 1978-79
Cossey, Douglas C. "Doug" 1978-79, 1984
Cuneo, James "Jim" 1979
Cristal, W. Randle "Randy" 1984
Davidson, Dale F. 1979
Deegan, William E. "Bill" 1970, 1984, 1991
DeFlesco, Pete 1991
Denny, Richard 1984
Dreke, Roy 1979
Driscoll, Joseph M. "Joe" 1978
Dunne, James "Jim" 1978-79
Easley, Harold L. 1979
Eshelman, George R. 1979
Evans, Jeff 1991
Farmer, Michael "Mike" 1979
Farnsworth, Harry 1979
Feaser, Richard L. "Dick" 1979
Fitzpatrick, Michael N. "Mike" 1979
Follmer, William A. "Bill" 1979
Forman, Allen S. "Al" 1978-79
Fuchs, Lester 1978-79
Gallagher, Lawrence E. "Larry" 1979
George, Edward "Ed" 1979
Giard, Robert "Bob" 1978
Gustafson, G. David "Dave" 1978
Hafner, William F. "Bill" 1979
Hadry, Merrill A. 1979
Harvey, Randy 1991
Heitzer, Richard "Dick" 1979
Henry, William E. "Bill" 1979
Higgins, John 1991
Ivory, William J. "Bill" 1979
Jackson, Charles L. 1979
James, John F. "Johnny" 1978-79
Jones, Robert G. "Bob" 1979, 1984
Jordan, Harold E. 1984
Kavulich, Joseph "Joe" 1978-79
Keister, R. Wayne 1978-79
Kelly, Eugene C. "Gene" 1979
Kimball, Shawn 1991
Kirby, Kenneth "Ken" 1979
Klein, Gus 1991
Knauss, Jim 1991
LaPierre, Richard 1979
Laude, William F. "Bill" 1978-79
Lazar, Richard R. "Richie" 1978-79
Levet, Jay 1979
Loeber, Gerald G. "Jerry" 1979
Lospitalier, Philip A. "Phil" 1979
Lupo, Charles "Charlie" 1979
Mabbot, Frederick J. "Fred" 1979
Mackin, John F. 1979
Marino, James H. "Jimmy" 1979
Mauer, Boyd 1979
McDougall, Scott 1991
McNally, James "Jim" 1979

Merritt, Clarence 1979
Miller, Gale 1979
Miller, John A. "Jack" 1979
Moyer, Robert "Bob" 1979
Mulcahy, James "Jim" 1979
Murray, Ed 1991
Nelson, Richard "Dick" 1979
Nothhnagel, Carl L. 1984
Novack, Lester A. "Les" 1979
O'Brien, James D. "Jim" 1979
O'Connor, James "Jim" 1978-79
O'Connor, Thomas M. "Tom" 1979
O'Dell, Mikel R. "Mike" 1984
Panas, Richard J. "Rich" 1978-79
Parks, Dallas 1991
Patch, Tony D. 1979
Perez, David A. "Dave" 1979
Phipps, George H. "Jerry" 1978-79
Pratt, Lester 1979
Purduski, Al J. 1979
Ravashiere, Thomas "Tom" 1979
Riccio, L. Leonard "Len" 1979
Rice, Robert W. "Bob" 1979
Robinson, William N. "Bill" 1978-79
Roesner, Robert A. "Bob" 1978-79
Roth, Roy 1979
Rountree, Hank 1991
Runchey, Richard D. "Dick" 1979, 1984
Satchell, Darold L. 1970
Sawchuk, Joseph W. "Joe" 1978-79
Scheel, Alfred M. "Al" 1979
Schirmer, Donald A. "Don" 1979
Schulte, Donald E. "Don" 1979
Shaw, A. Duane 1979
Shewmake, James B. "Jim" 1978
Siroka, Harold L. 1979
Slattery, Donald L. "Don" 1979
Slickenmeyer, David W. "Dave" 1979, 1991
Spenn, Fred 1991
Sprincz, William "Bill" 1978-79
Stevens, John W. "Johnny" 1970
Sweeney, George P. 1979
Swenson, Charles H. 1979
Taylor, Joe Bob 1979
Terlop, Russell F. "Russ" 1979
Theilander, Theodore "Ted" 1979
Thompson, Michael G. "Mike" 1978-79
Tillman, Henry "Hank" 1979
Trimmer, Harry 1979
Turner, Leo I. 1978
Urchak, Woody J. 1978-79
Uremovich, Jim 1991
Williams, Dale 1979
Zirbel, Lawrence A. "Larry" 1979, 1984
Zivic, Richard J. "Dick" 1984
Zuccaro, Amerigo J. "Rico" 1978-79

The Owners and Officials Roster

Major League Baseball dates its inception from 1876 with the formation of the National League, not 1871, the founding date of the National Association. Because the latter year marks the beginning of professional league play, *Total Baseball* includes NA player records with those of the MLB-recognized leagues; however, it is undeniable that something dramatic occurred in 1876 that altered forevermore the character of professional baseball: the division of the game into two classes, labor and management.

The National Association of Professional Base Ball Players was an outgrowth of the amateur association of the same name, in which baseball clubs were formed as organizations devoted to social intercourse and fraternal competition. Amateur clubs were organized along the same lines as today's Elks or Odd Fellows, with elected officials and dues-paying members. As players of special skill were invited into these clubs, their dues might be forgiven or "emoluments" offered—no-show jobs or under-the-table payments. The abuses of the amateur system of the mid-1860s led to the declaration by several clubs of their openly professional status; players would sometimes draw salaries and as often would share in gate receipts. By the end of the decade gambling and game-fixing were rife.

Despite the formation of the National Association, these evils continued largely unabated into the 1870s. A monopolization of talent, largely in Boston, rendered Western clubs uncompetitive, and spectator rowdyism spawned by gambling interest, and the open sale of hard liquor burdened the new league. Clubs were admitted into the NA for paltry fees and fulfilled their schedules half-heartedly. Some of the member clubs had active presidents who functioned much as owners later would; other clubs were "cooperative nines," managed by the players themselves; still others were hybrids, born of civic boosterism. By 1876, the odd amalgam of the NA, presided over by Brooklyn Atlantics star Bob Ferguson, was failing.

Thus in 1876 William Hulbert, president of the Chicago club, combined with seven other team representatives to form the National League, a circuit run entirely by owners. Since then, fan interest has focused on the players, of course, and to a lesser extent on the managers, coaches, and umpires. But it can be said with some justice that while the on-field personnel and personalities "are" the game, it is the club owners, presidents, and league officials who make the game possible and ensure its continuity.

The Owners and Officials Roster that follows represents a first attempt in a baseball encyclopedia to recognize these individuals. As we did with the Coach Roster in the first edition of *Total Baseball,* we offered this section in the second edition with full knowledge that there were gaps and probably gaffes in our research; we hope that our readers will continue to advise us of omissions so that we can improve the roster in future editions. (The names of National Association club presidents and officials are listed below despite our understanding that these individuals were, by and large, not owners in the sense used after 1876.)

For prose accounts of the history of owners and officials, see the articles by David Voigt and by Steve Mann and David Pietrusza.

Commissioners, Major League Baseball

1920–1944	Kenesaw M. Landis
1945–1951	Albert B. Chandler
1951–1965	Ford C. Frick
1965–1968	William D. Eckert
1969–1984	Bowie K. Kuhn
1984–1989	Peter Ueberroth
1989	A. Bartlett Giamatti
1989–1992	Francis T. Vincent, Jr.

National Association

Association President

1871	James W. Kerns
1872–1875	Robert W. Ferguson

Club Presidents and/or NA Convention Delegates

Baltimore Lord Baltimores

1872	—
1873	R. C. Hall
1874	C. A. Hadel

Baltimore Marylands

1873	W. J. Smith

Boston Red Stockings

1871	Ivers Whitney Adams
1872	Col. Charles H. Porter
1873–1875	Nathan Taylor Appolonio

Brooklyn Atlantics

1872–1873	Robert W. Ferguson
1874	—
1875	B. Van Delft

Brooklyn Eckfords

1872	William H. Ray

Chicago White Stockings

1871	J. M. Thatcher
1874	Mr. Gassette
	George W. Gage
1875	William A. Hulbert

Cleveland Forest City

1871	J. F. Evans
1872	H. C. Doolittle

Elizabeth Resolutes

1873	Charles N. Garrighan

Fort Wayne Kekiongas

1871	George J. E. Mayers

Hartford Dark Blues

1874	G. B. Hubbell
1875	Morgan G. Bulkeley

Keokuk Westerns

1875	W. Trimble

Middletown Mansfields

1872	B. Douglass, Jr.
	T. W. Ratcliff

New Haven Elm City

1875	W. S. Arnold

New York Mutuals

1871–1872	Alexander V. Davidson
1873	Robert Mathews
1874	Alexander V. Davidson
1875	William H. Cammeyer

Philadelphia Athletics

1871	James W. Kerns
1872–1873	E. H. Hayhurst
1874	D. F. Houston
1875	George W. Thompson
	C. Spering

Philadelphia White Stockings

1873	Frank McBride
1874	D. L. Reid
1875	George Concannon

Philadelphia Centennials

1875	E. H. Hayhurst

Rockford Forest City

1871	Hiram Waldo

St. Louis Brown Stockings

1875	C. O. Bishop

St. Louis Red Stockings

1875	A. Blong

Troy Haymakers

1871	J. W. Scofield
1872	C. C. Clark

Washington Nationals

1872	Mr. Millar
	R. Hough

Washington Olympics

1871	Nicholas E. Young
1872	Mr. Pike

Washington

1873	Nicholas E. Young
1875	D. W. Bruce
	A. F. Childs

National League

Presidents

1876	Morgan G. Bulkeley
1877–1882	William A. Hulbert
1882	Arthur H. Soden
1883–1884	Abraham G. Mills
1885–1902	Nicholas E. Young
1903–1909	Harry C. Pulliam
1909	John A. Heydler
1910–1913	Thomas J. Lynch
1913–1918	John K. Tener
1918–1934	John A. Heydler
1934–1951	Ford C. Frick
1951–1969	Warren C. Giles
1970–1986	Charles S. Feeney
1986–1989	A. Bartlett Giamatti
1989–1992	William White

Vice Presidents

1929–1932	Barney Dreyfuss
1933–1936	Charles A. Stoneham
1936–1947	Samuel Breadon
1947–1966	Philip K. Wrigley
1966–1969	Horace C. Stoneham
1970–1986	John J. McHale
1987–1992	Phyllis Collins

Club Presidents

Atlanta

1966	John J. McHale
1967–1972	William C. Bartholomay
1973–1975	Daniel J. Donahue
1976–1986	R. E. (Ted) Turner
1987–1992	William C. Bartholomay (Ch. of Bd.)

Baltimore

1892	Harry B. Von der Horst
1893–1899	Edward H. Hanlon

Boston (to Milwaukee)

1876	Nathan Taylor Appolonio
1907–1909	George B. Dovey
1909–1910	John S. Dovey
1911	W. Hepburn Russell
1912	John M. Ward
1913–1915	James E. Gaffney
1916–1918	Percy D. Haughton
1919–1922	George W. Grant
1923	Christopher Mathewson
1924	J. A. Robert Quinn
1925	Christopher Mathewson
1926	J. A. Robert Quinn
1927–1935	Emil E. Fuchs
1936–44	J. A. Robert Quinn
1945–1956	Louis R. Perini

Brooklyn (to L.A.)

1890–1897	Charles H. Byrne
1898–1925	Charles H. Ebbets
1925	Edward J. McKeever
1925–1929	Wilbert Robinson
1930–1932	Frank B. York
1933–1938	Stephen W. McKeever
1939–1942	Leland S. MacPhail, Sr.
1943–1950	W. Branch Rickey
1950–1957	Walter F. O'Malley

Buffalo

1879–1880	E. B. Smith
1880	John B. Sage

1881–1885	Josiah Jewett

Chicago

1876–1881	William A. Hulbert
1882–1891	Albert G. Spalding
1892–1905	James A. Hart
1906–1913	Charles W. Murphy
1914–1915	Charles H. Thomas
1916–1918	Charles H. Weeghman
1919	Fred F. Mitchell
1919–1933	William L. Veeck, Sr.
1934	William M. Walker
1934–1977	Philip K. Wrigley
1977–1981	William J. Hagenah, Jr.
1982–1983	Andrew J. McKenna (Ch. of Bd.)
1984	James E. Finks (Pres./CEO)
1985–1987	Dallas Green
1988	John W. Madigan (Ch. of Bd.)
1989–1991	Donald C. Grenesko (Pres./Ch. of Bd.)

Cincinnati

1876–1877	Josiah L. Keck
1878–1879	J. Wayne Neff
1880	Justus Thorner

Cincinnati

1890	Aaron A. Stern
1891–1902	John T. Brush
1902–1927	August Hermann
1928–1929	C. J. McDiarmid
1930–1933	Sidney Weil
1934–1946	Powel Crosley, Jr.
1946–1951	Warren C. Giles
1951–1961	Powel Crosley, Jr.
1961–1966	William O. DeWitt
1967–1973	Francis L. Dale
1973–1978	Robert L. Howsam
1979–1983	Richard Wagner
1984–1985	Robert L. Howsam (Pres./CEO)
1986–1992	Marge Schott

Cleveland

1879–1881	J. Ford Evans
1882–1884	C. H. Bulkley

Cleveland

1889–1898	Frank D. Robison
1899	M. Stanley Robison

Colorado

1992	Steve Ehrhardt

Detroit

1881–1884	William G. Thompson
1885–1886	Joseph H. Marsh
1887–1888	Fred K. Stearns
1888	Charles W. Smith

Florida

1992	Carl Barger

Hartford

1876–1877	Morgan G. Bulkeley

Houston

1962	Craig Cullinan, Jr.
1963–1971	Roy Hofheinz
1972–1973	Reuben W. Askanase
1974–1975	T. H. Neyland
1976	Sidney L. Shlenker
1976–1980	Talbot M. Smith
1981–1985	Albert L. Rosen
1986–1987	Dick Wagner
1988	Fred Stanley
1980–1992	Dr. John J. McMullen (Ch. of Bd.)
1992	Drayton McLane, Jr. (Ch. of Bd.)

Indianapolis

1878	William D. Perritt

Indianapolis

1887–1889	John T. Brush

Kansas City

1886	Joseph J. Heim

Los Angeles

1958–1969	Walter F. O'Malley
1970–1992	Peter O'Malley

Louisville

1876–1877	Walter N. Haldeman

Louisville

1892	T. Hunt Stucky
1893–1896	Fred Drexler
1897–1899	Harry C. Pulliam
1899	Barney Dreyfuss

Milwaukee

1878	J. R. Kaine

Milwaukee Braves (to Atlanta Braves)

1953–1956	Louis R. Perini
1957–1961	Joseph F. Cairnes
1962–1966	John J. McHale

Montreal Expos

1969–1986	John J. McHale
1987–1992	Claude R. Brochu (Pres./CEO)
1969–1991	Charles R. Bronfman (Ch. of Bd.)
1992	Jacques Menard

Mutual Club (N.Y.)

1876	William H. Cammeyer

New York Giants (to San Francisco)

1883–1892	John B. Day
1893–1894	C. C. Van Cott
1895–1902	Andrew Freedman
1903–1912	John T. Brush
1912–1918	Harry N. Hempstead
1919–1935	Charles A. Stoneham
1936–1957	Horace C. Stoneham

New York Mets

1962–1966	George M. Weiss
1967	Vaughan P. Devine
1968–1975	Mrs. Joan W. Payson
1976–1979	Mrs. Lorinda de Roulet
1980–1992	Fred Wilpon (Pres./CEO)

Philadelphia Athletics

1876	Thomas J. Smith

Philadelphia Phillies

1883–1902	Alfred J. Reach
1903–1904	James Potter
1905–1908	William J. Shettsline
1909	Israel W. Durham
1909–1912	Horace S. Fogel
1912	Alfred D. Wiler
1913	William H. Locke
1913–1930	William F. Baker
1931–1932	L. Charles Ruch
1933–1942	Gerald P. Nugent
1943	William D. Cox
1943–1972	Robert M. Carpenter, Jr.
1973–1981	Robert M. Carpenter III
1982–1992	Bill Giles (Pres./General Partner)

Pittsburgh

1887–1890	William A. Nimick
1891	J. Palmer O'Neill
1892	William C. Temple
1893	Albert C. Buckenberger
1894–1897	William W. Kerr
1898	William H. Watkins
1899	William W. Kerr
1900–1932	Barney Dreyfuss
1932–1946	William E. Benswanger
1946–1950	Frank E. McKinney
1951–1969	John W. Galbreath
1970–1985	Daniel M. Galbreath
1986–1987	Malcolm Prine
1988–1991	Carl Barger
1992	Mark Sauer (Pres.)
1988–1992	Douglas D. Danforth (Chairman/CEO)

Providence

1878	John D. Thurston
1879–1881	Henry J. Root
1882–1883	Henry B. Winship
1884–1885	Henry J. Root

St. Louis Brown Stockings

1876–1877	John R. Lucas

St. Louis Maroons

1885–1886	Henry V. Lucas

St. Louis Cardinals

1892–1897	Chris Von der Ahe
1898	Benjamin S. Muckenfuss
1899–1906	Frank D. Robison
1907–1910	M. Stanley Robison
1911–1912	E. A. Steininger
1912	James C. Jones
1913–1916	Schuyler P. Britton
1916	Mrs. Schuyler P. Britton
1917–1919	W. Branch Rickey
1920–1947	Samuel Breadon
1947–1949	Robert E. Hannegan
1949–1952	Fred M. Saigh, Jr.
1953–1989	August A. Busch, Jr.
1990–1991	Fred L. Kuhlmann (Pres./CEO)
1992	Stuart Meyer (Pres./CEO)
1991–1992	Dick Freeman

San Diego

1969–1977	Emil J. Bavasi
1977–1980	Ray A. Kroc
1981–1983	Ray A. Kroc (owner)
1980–1987	Ballard F. Smith, Jr.
1988	Chub Feeney
1990	Dick Freeman
1984–1990	Joan Kroc (owner)

San Francisco

1958–1975	Horace C. Stoneham
1976–1985	Robert A. Lurie
1976–1990	Robert A. Lurie (owner)
1986–1992	Al Rosen

Syracuse

1879	Hamilton S. White

Troy

1879–1880	Gardner Earl
1881–1882	A. L. Hotchkin
1882	Francis N. Mann

Washington

1886–1888	Robert C. Hewitt
1889	Walter F. Hewitt

Washington

1892–1899	George W. Wagner

Worcester

1880–1882	Elbert B. Pratt

American Association

League Presidents

1882–1885	H. D. McKnight
1886–1889	Wheeler C. Wyckoff
1890	Zach Phelps
1891	Louis Kramer
	Ed Renau
	Zach Phelps

Club Presidents

Baltimore

1882	H. C. Myers (?)
1883	William Barnie (?)
1884	H. T. Houck
1885–1887	William Barnie
1888	Harry Von der Horst
1889	William Barnie
1891	Harry Von der Horst

Boston

1891	Charles A. Prince

Brooklyn

1884–1889	Charles H. Byrne

Brooklyn–Baltimore

1890	James M. Kennedy
	Wm. Barnie (?)

Cincinnati

1882	Justus Thorner
1883–1884	Aaron S. Stern
1885	George L. Herancourt
1886	John Hauck
1887–1889	Aaron S. Stern

Cincinnati-Milwaukee

1891	Albert Johnson

Cleveland

1887–1888	Frank Robison

Columbus

1883–1884	H. T. Crittendon (?)
1889–1891	Conrad Born, Jr.

Indianapolis

1884	Joseph Schwabacher

Kansas City

1888	Joseph J. Heim

1889	John W. Speas

Louisville

1882–1883	J. H. Pank
1884	William L. Jackson, Jr.
1885–1887	Zach Phelps
1888	W. L. Lyons
1889	M. H. Davidson
1890	Lawrence S. Parsons
1891	Julian B. Hart

New York

1883–1884	John B. Day
1885	Frank Rhouer
1886–1887	Erastus Wiman

Philadelphia

1882	Lew Simmons (?)
1883–1886	William Sharsig
1887	Lew Simmons
1888–1890	H. C. Pennypacker
1891	J. Earle Wagner

Pittsburgh

1882–1883	H. D. McKnight
1884	E. E. Converse
1885–1886	William A. Nimick

Richmond

1884	W. C. Seddon

Rochester

1890	Henry Brinker

St. Louis

1882–1891	Chris Von der Ahe

Syracuse

1890	George K. Frazier

Toledo

1884	W. J. Colburn
1890	V. H. Ketcham

Washington

1884	L. Moxley
1891	H. B. Bennett

Union Association

League Presidents

1883	H. B. Bennett
	Henry V. Lucas
1883–1885	Henry V. Lucas

Club Presidents

Altoona

1884	W. W. Rich

Baltimore

1884	J. W. Lowe

Boston

1884	Frank E. Winslow

Chicago-Pittsburgh

1884	A. H. Henderson

Cincinnati

1884	Justus Thorner

Kansas City

1884	Americus V. McKim

Milwaukee

1884	Charles Kippen (?)

Philadelphia

1884	Thomas J. Pratt

St. Louis

1884	H. V. Lucas

St. Paul

1884	A. M. Thompson (?)

Washington

1884	H. B. Bennett

Wilmington

1884	John T. West

Players League

League President

1890	Col. Edward A. McAlpin

Club Presidents

Boston
1890	Col. Charles H. Porter

Brooklyn
1890	Wendell Goodwin

Buffalo
1890	Moses Shire

Chicago
1890	John Addison

Cleveland
1890	Albert L. Johnson

New York
1890	Cornelius Van Cott

Philadelphia
1890	H. M. Love

Pittsburgh
1890	William McCallin

American League

Presidents

1901–1927	B. Bancroft Johnson
1927–1931	Ernest S. Barnard
1931–1959	William Harridge
1959–1973	Joseph E. Cronin
1974–1984	Leland S. MacPhail, Jr.
1984–1992	Robert W. Brown, M.D.

Vice Presidents

1901–1916	Charles W. Somers
1917–1919	Charles A. Comiskey
1921–1935	Frank J. Navin
1935–1938	Jacob Ruppert
1939–1955	Clark C. Griffith
1955–1976	Thomas A. Yawkey
1976–1982	Calvin R. Griffith
1983–1984	Calvin R. Griffith
	John Fetzer
	Gene Autry
1985	John Fetzer and Gene Autry
1986–1989	Calvin R. Griffith
	John Fetzer
	Gene Autry
1990	John Fetzer and Gene Autry
1991	Jean Yawkey and Gene Autry
1992	Gene Autry

Club Presidents

Baltimore (to New York)
1901	Sidney W. Frank
1902	John J. Mahon

Baltimore
1954–1955	Clarence W. Miles
1956–1959	James Keelty, Jr.
1960–1965	Leland S. MacPhail, Jr.
1966–1979	Jerold C. Hoffberger (Ch. of Bd.)
1980–1982	Jerold C. Hoffberger (as Pres.)
1983–1988	Edward B. Williams (Ch. of Bd./Pres.)
1989–1992	Lawrence Lucchino

Boston
1901–1902	Charles W. Somers
1903–1904	Henry J. Killilea
1904–1911	John I. Taylor
1912–1913	James R. McAleer
1913–1916	Joseph J. Lannin
1917–1923	Harry H. Frazee
1923–1932	John A. Quinn
1933–1976	Thomas A. Yawkey
1977–1988	Jean R. Yawkey (majority owner)
1989–1992	John L. Harrington

California (includes Los Angeles, 1961–64)
1961–1974	Robert Reynolds
1975–1977	Arthur E. Patterson
1977–1990	Gene Autry (owner/president)
1990–1992	Richard M. Brown

Chicago
1901–1931	Charles A. Comiskey
1932–1939	J. Louis Comiskey
1940	Harry Grabiner (VP)
1941–1956	Mrs. Grace Comiskey
1957–1958	None
1959–1961	William L. Veeck, Jr.
1961–1969	Arthur C. Allyn, Jr.
1970–1975	John W. Allyn
1976–1980	William L. Veeck, Jr.
1981–1990	Eddie Einhorn
1981–1992	Jerry M. Reinsdorf (Chairman)

Cleveland
1901–1909	John F. Kilfoyl
1910–1915	Charles W. Somers
1916–1922	James C. Dunn
1922–1927	Ernest S. Barnard
1928–1946	Alva Bradley
1946–1949	William L. Veeck, Jr.
1950–1952	Ellis W. Ryan
1953–1962	Myron H. Wilson, Jr.
1963–1971	Gabriel H. Paul
1972–1975	Nick Mileti
1975–1977	Alva T. Bonda
1978–1983	F. J. (Steve) O'Neill
1983–1986	Patrick J. O'Neill (Chairman)
1978–1985	Gabriel H. Paul
1986	Peter Bavasi
1987–1990	Richard E. Jacobs (Ch. of Bd.)
1988–1991	Hank Peters
1992	Rick Bay (Pres./CEO)

Detroit
1901	James D. Burns
1902–1903	Samuel F. Angus
1904–1907	William H. Yawkey
1908–1935	Frank J. Navin
1936–1952	Walter O. Briggs, Sr.
1952–1956	Walter O. Briggs, Jr.
1957	Frederick A. Knorr
1957–1959	Harvey R. Hansen
1960	William O. DeWitt
1961–1989	John E. Fetzer (Chairman)
1978–1989	James Campbell
1984–1990	Thomas S. Monaghan
1990–1992	Glenn E. (Bo) Schembechler

Kansas City A's (to Oakland)
1955–1959	Arnold Johnson
1960	Parke Carroll (VP)
1961–1967	Charles O. Finley

Kansas City Royals
1969–1981	Ewing Kauffman
1982–1992	Joe Burke

Milwaukee (to St. Louis)
1901	Matthew Killilea

Milwaukee Brewers
1970–1992	Allan H. "Bud" Selig

Minnesota
1961–1984	Calvin R. Griffith (Chairman/Pres.)
1985–1986	Howard T. Fox, Jr.
1987–1989	Jerry Bell
1985–1990	Carl Pohlad (owner)

New York
1903–1906	Joseph W. Gordon
1903–1915	Frank J. Farrell and William S. Devery (owners)
1907–1914	Frank J. Farrell
1915–1938	Jacob Ruppert
1939–1944	Edward G. Barrow
1945–1947	Leland S. MacPhail, Sr.
1948–1966	Daniel R. Topping
1966–1973	Michael Burke
1973–1977	Gabriel H. Paul
1978–1980	Albert Rosen
1980–1990	George M. Steinbrenner (Ch. of Bd.)
1990	Robert Nederlander (Managing General Partner)

Oakland
1968–1980	Charles O. Finley
1981–1987	Roy Eisenhardt
1981–1992	Walter Haas (owner)
1990–1992	Walter J. Haas (Pres./CEO)

Philadelphia (to Kansas City)
1901–1921	Benjamin F. Shibe
1922–1935	Thomas S. Shibe
1936	John D. Shibe
1937–1954	Connie Mack

Seattle Pilots (to Milwaukee)
1969	Dewey Soriano

Seattle Mariners
1977–1979	Danny Kaye and Lester Smith
1980–1983	Daniel F. O'Brien
1981–1989	George L. Argyros (Ch. of Bd./CEO)
1984–1989	Charles G. Armstrong
1990–1992	Jeff Smulyan (Ch. of Bd.)
1992	John W. Ellis (Ch. of Bd.)

St. Louis (to Baltimore)
1902	Ralph T. Orthwein
1903–1915	Robert L. Hedges
1916–1933	Philip D. Ball
1934–1936	Louis B. Von Weise
1937–1945	Donald L. Barnes
1946–1948	Richard C. Muckerman
1949–1951	William O. DeWitt
1951–1953	William L. Veeck, Jr.

Texas
1972–1974	Robert E. Short
1974	Robert W. Brown, M.D.
1975–1980	Bradford G. Corbett
1980–1987	Eddie Chiles (Owner/Ch. of Bd./CEO)
1984–1990	Michael H. Stone
1991–1992	J. Thomas Schieffer

Toronto
1977–1981	Peter Bavasi
1977–1988	R. Howard Webster (Ch. of Bd.)
1989–1992	Paul Beeston

Washington (to Minnesota)
1901–1903	Frederick Postal
1904	Thomas J. Loftus
1904	Harry B. Lambert
1905–1912	Thomas C. Noyes
1920–1955	Clark C. Griffith
1956–1960	Calvin R. Griffith

Washington
1961–1962	Elwood R. Quesada
1963–1967	James M. Johnston (Ch. of Bd.)
1968	James H. Lemon (Ch. of Bd.)
1969–1971	Robert E. Short

Federal League

League Presidents

1914–1915	James A. Gilmore

Club Presidents

Baltimore
1914–1915	Carrol W. Rasin

Brooklyn
1914–1915	Robert B. Ward

Buffalo
1914	Walter F. Mullen
	William E. Robertson
1915	William E. Robertson

Chicago
1914–1915	Charles A. Weeghman

Indianapolis
1914	J. E. Krause

Kansas City
1914	C. C. Madison
1915	Charles Baird
	Conrad H. Mann

Newark
1915	P. T. Powers
	Harry Sinclair

Pittsburgh
1914	John R. Barbour
1915	Edward W. Gwinner

St. Louis
1914	E. A. Steininger
1915	Lloyd H. Rickart

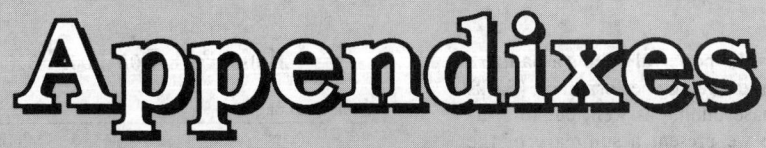

Park Factor Statistics

This section illustrates the powerful effects a ballpark can have on batting and pitching performance. (Parks affect fielding and baserunning as well, but to a far lesser degree.) Here we present a summary of the won-lost records and run-scoring characteristics of every park for all years of the four most significant major leagues—the American and National leagues and the American and National associations.

What is the definition of success at home and on the road? Every team is expected to win more games at home than it does on the road, to the extent that if it only breaks even on the road it is thought to have a shot at the pennant. No matter whether its home park favors hitters or pitchers, a home team should be able to take advantage of the park's peculiarities better than the visiting team can. The Houston Astros may score fewer (and the Boston Red Sox more) runs at home than they do on the road, but their *differential* between runs scored and runs allowed will be greater than their run differential on the road. Greater run differential means more wins.

Almost anybody, it seems, can play .500 ball at home (in the NL of 1983, for example, only one team had a losing record on its own turf). This is somewhat deceptive, for while .500 is the average of all games played, and a team that goes 81–81 is thus defined as average, .500 is not the average at home nor, for that matter, away. The table below, which gives the home park won-lost records of all major leagues since 1900, shows the home average to be .543. The inverse, .457, is the average road record in this century.

If the average home winning percentage is .543, then an average team (81–81) should be expected to go 44–37 at home and 37–44 on the road. Until 1987, only four teams with road records that were below average—that is, 37–44—ever won the pennant, and none went on to win the World Series. Then the Minnesota Twins took the American League flag with a regular-season road mark of 29–52, by far the worst ever for a pennant or division winner, and then proceeded to lose all three World Series road games while winning all four at home. We are not likely to see such a performance again.

Just as runs scored and runs allowed may predict won-lost records, as discussed in the Introduction to the Annual Record, so may we move backward from won-lost records (the actual home-park norm of 44–37, which is between 5 and 10 percent better than the theoretical norm of 41–40) to examine runs scored and runs allowed. Runs (and home runs) per inning at home are indeed accumulated at a rate per inning about 10 percent higher than on the road, but the totals presented in this section fall short of that mark. The reason: since the number of innings played at home is about 5 percent lower than on the road (leading home teams do not bat in the bottom half of final innings), total runs and homers are in actuality only about 5 percent higher.

Home Park Won-Lost Records

National League

Years	W	L	Pct.
1900–10 ('01 AL)	3489	2995	.538
1911–20	3189	2775	.537
1921–30	3360	2770	.548
1931–40	3353	2760	.549
1941–50	3319	2823	.540
1951–60 ('61 NL)	3681	3098	.543
1961–68 ('62 NL)	3075	2591	.543
1969–76	4088	3638	.529
1977–92	8274	6926	.544
	41,976	35,526	.542

American League

Years	W	L	Pct.
1900–10 ('01 AL)	3345	2530	.569
1911–20	3201	2754	.537
1921–30	3344	2787	.545
1931–40	3349	2753	.549
1941–50	3383	2754	.551
1951–60 ('61 NL)	3291	2863	.535
1961–68 ('62 NL)	3462	3003	.535
1969–76	4142	3568	.537
1977–92	9653	8110	.543
	52,799	44,212	.544

Federal League

Years	W	L	Pct.
1914–15	660	560	.541

Major League

Years	W	L	Pct.
1900–92	86,991	73,237	.543

Detailed technical information about the formulas and calculations behind Park Factor, as applied to teams as well as individuals, will be found in the Glossary.

For additional useful information about home-road differences, we refer the reader to the Annual Record and the Glossary. For a key to the team and league abbreviations used throughout this section, flip to the last pages of this volume.

Other abbreviations follow.

TM	Team
LG	League
W	Wins
L	Losses
T	Ties
R	Runs
OR	Opponents' Runs
HR	Home Runs
OHR	Opponents' Home Runs
HRF	Home Run Factor (A measure of the home runs hit in a given ballpark, with 100 representing the average home park and the highest figure above that representing the best home-run park.)
RF	Run Factor (A measure of the runs scored in a given ballpark compared to other ballparks, with 100 representing the average home park and the highest figure above that representing the best hitters' park.)

						HOME							ROAD						
PARK	TM	LG	YEARS	RF	HRF	W	L	T	R	OR	HR	OHR	W	L	T	R	OR	HR	OHR
AMERICAN LEAGUE																			
Oriole Park	BAL	A	1901–1902	115	120	72	56	2	821	736	27	29	46	97	3	654	862	30	22
Memorial Stadium	BAL	A	1954–1991	92	91	1687	1310	9	12262	11286	2490	2262	1515	1502	0	13015	12634	2804	2475
Oriole Park at Camden Yards	BAL	A	1992–1992	98	113	43	38	0	339	333	75	69	46	35	0	366	323	73	55
Huntington Avenue Grounds	BOS	A	1901–1911	102	172	464	357	10	3494	3075	219	173	386	424	14	3230	3201	106	120
Fenway Park (I)	BOS	A	1912–1933	96	52	834	821	15	6819	7273	180	359	679	983	16	6743	8007	476	557
Fenway Park (II)	BOS	A	1934–1992	114	112	2727	1898	16	24204	21373	4145	3687	2151	2478	12	19995	20279	3588	3423
Chavez Ravine	CAL	A	1965–1965	92	65	46	34	0	265	254	36	35	29	53	0	262	315	56	56
Anaheim Stadium	CAL	A	1966–1992	93	98	1109	1051	0	8514	8571	1584	1725	990	1161	2	8935	9423	1624	1726
South Side Park (II)	CHI	A	1901–1909	89	32	433	235	21	2811	1987	31	31	311	340	13	2598	2659	73	116
Comiskey/White Sox Park	CHI	A	1910–1990	97	86	3346	2917	32	26769	26375	2811	3464	2871	3416	34	26920	27825	3351	3992
Comiskey Park (II)	CHI	A	1991–1992	94	104	96	67	0	746	651	128	141	77	84	0	750	720	121	136
League Park (I)	CLE	A	1901–1909	96	64	384	281	14	2846	2379	65	60	313	351	8	2614	2763	107	86
League Park (II)	CLE	A	1910–1931	107	67	906	761	15	8159	7759	287	295	781	884	19	7368	7575	416	450
League/Municipal shared	CLE	A	1932–1946	95	73	667	495	7	5485	4939	558	418	532	598	12	5300	5495	710	592
League Park (II)				110	96	408	280	2	3706	3224	443	312							
Municipal Stadium				77	40	259	215	5	1779	1715	115	106							
Municipal/Cleveland Stadium	CLE	A	1947–1992	99	110	1929	1701	7	15519	15499	3185	3134	1681	1947	9	15545	15870	2894	2828
Bennett Park	DET	A	1901–1911	107	97	483	327	15	3727	3284	105	93	375	438	13	3199	3364	99	107
Navin Field	DET	A	1912–1937	102	93	1089	891	9	10250	9715	631	727	939	1031	22	9832	9783	751	709
Briggs/Tiger Stadium	DET	A	1938–1992	105	127	2423	1916	16	20229	18920	4253	4092	2062	2258	18	18699	18526	3375	3162
Municipal Stadium (I)	KC	A	1955–1967	106	108	452	575	2	4267	5067	767	1086	377	649	5	3837	4917	713	995
Municipal Stadium (II)	KC	A	1969–1972	100	65	159	159	1	1211	1227	137	175	136	185	0	1169	1277	216	268
Royals Stadium	KC	A	1973–1992	103	74	927	659	1	7338	6560	956	961	753	840	0	6776	6868	1297	1321
Wrigley Field	LA	A	1961–1961	127	199	46	36	0	447	421	122	126	24	55	1	297	363	67	54
Chavez Ravine	LA	A	1962–1964	86	52	124	119	0	851	900	106	125	114	128	0	1008	1017	228	213
Lloyd Street Grounds	MIL	A	1901–1901	92	97	32	37	1	342	373	15	14	16	52	1	299	455	11	18
County Stadium	MIL	A	1970–1992	96	89	966	862	1	7902	7778	1421	1422	825	1008	1	8067	8208	1578	1636
Metropolitan Stadium	MIN	A	1961–1981	108	110	910	759	5	7698	7026	1424	1443	809	853	2	6929	6680	1325	1270
Humphrey Metrodome	MIN	A	1982–1992	109	103	501	393	0	4297	4151	792	908	373	515	0	3662	4036	756	875
Hilltop Park	NY	A	1903–1912	116	166	400	344	8	3299	3270	134	124	334	415	19	2702	3082	58	101
Polo Grounds (IV)	NY	A	1913–1922	101	197	416	335	10	3312	2916	332	292	358	378	6	3054	2945	190	119
Yankee Stadium (I)	NY	A	1923–1973	91	103	2553	1410	16	19607	14741	3654	2408	2168	1790	26	20696	17497	3532	2427
Shea Stadium	NY	A	1974–1975	92	92	90	69	0	638	571	92	106	82	81	0	714	640	119	102
Yankee Stadium (II)	NY	A	1976–1992	97	100	789	554	0	6191	5526	1294	1108	665	684	0	6221	6025	1313	1120
Oakland Coliseum	OAK	A	1968–1992	88	89	1136	860	1	8249	7580	1677	1529	958	1033	0	8959	8937	1832	1769
Columbia Park	PHI	A	1901–1908	107	109	383	189	11	2758	2121	128	65	256	321	14	2228	2406	107	74
Shibe Park/Connie Mack Stadium	PHI	A	1909–1954	102	125	1762	1705	31	16080	16885	1809	1900	1485	2033	23	15447	17212	1458	1533
Sportsman's Park (III)	STL	A	1902–1908	93	104	275	243	12	1906	1793	61	73	215	300	10	1849	2087	56	71
Sportsman's Park (IV)	STL	A	1909–1953	108	137	1615	1796	40	15888	17694	1680	2004	1309	2126	34	13902	17170	1217	1459
Sicks Stadium	SEA	A	1969–1969	100	125	34	47	1	329	399	74	93	30	51	0	310	400	51	79
Kingdome	SEA	A	1977–1992	104	132	588	687	0	5504	6122	1210	1340	496	765	2	4948	6006	869	1032
Arlington Stadium	TEX	A	1972–1992	99	94	856	813	0	7114	7300	1233	1319	723	939	4	7018	7544	1354	1336
Exhibition Stadium	TOR	A	1977–1988	107	106	480	462	0	4243	4319	798	914	414	529	2	3890	4147	810	803
Skydome	TOR	A	1989–1992	101	112	189	135	0	1464	1327	311	264	173	151	0	1498	1289	294	223
American League Park (I)	WAS	A	1901–1903	104	214	100	103	4	1015	1065	67	98	65	138	6	811	1187	30	47
American League Park (II)	WAS	A	1904–1910	92	46	224	297	16	1709	2048	31	32	157	380	10	1671	2418	65	71
Griffith Stadium (I)	WAS	A	1911–1955	93	39	1842	1602	38	15224	14999	529	784	1524	1885	24	15531	16598	1410	1870
Griffith Stadium (II)	WAS	A	1956–1961	101	99	192	272	1	1858	2361	364	449	180	287	2	1859	2291	409	411
R.F.K. Stadium	WAS	A	1962–1971	96	96	363	441	0	2906	3356	616	715	316	491	1	2928	3580	652	735
NATIONAL LEAGUE																			
Atlanta/Fulton County Stadium	ATL	N	1966–1992	113	138	1083	1059	4	9450	9811	2046	2011	947	1210	3	8173	8934	1576	1364
Union Park	BAL	N	1892–1899	103	46	380	167	15	4107	2772	72	54	264	280	11	3391	3256	114	158
South End Grounds (I)	BOS	N	1876–1893	103	100	624	327	16	6241	4295	296	200	478	467	16	5090	5188	230	265
South End Grounds (II)	BOS	N	1894–1914	110	200	807	718	28	7845	7453	517	536	610	917	27	6382	7479	209	315
Braves Field	BOS	N	1915–1952	89	67	1411	1430	23	10995	11822	893	1002	1188	1739	27	12211	14098	1281	1632
Washington Park (II)	BRO	N	1890–1890	98	80	58	16	0	547	303	27	9	28	27	0	337	318	16	18
Eastern Park	BRO	N	1891–1897	89	88	293	182	11	3026	2567	117	117	188	281	6	2831	3282	114	145
Washington Park (III)	BRO	N	1898–1912	96	82	554	556	17	4460	4647	168	155	436	662	20	4314	5092	184	206
Ebbets Field	BRO	N	1913–1957	102	110	1974	1453	34	16259	14848	1957	1933	1683	1749	24	15470	15108	1753	1783
Riverside Park	BUF	N	1879–1883	104	35	123	87	3	1278	1068	12	12	89	125	2	997	1285	31	38
Olympic Park (I)	BUF	N	1884–1885	113	96	56	56	3	674	717	36	33	46	65	1	521	668	26	44
23rd Street Grounds	CHI	N	1876–1877	125	69	42	18	0	558	299	3	5	36	29	1	432	333	5	8
Lake Front Park (I)	CHI	N	1878–1882	109	78	150	56	2	1443	875	21	16	104	81	5	1056	916	16	28
Lake Front Park (II)	CHI	N	1882–1884	120	475	75	30	1	908	566	142	72	46	59	0	605	621	13	32
West Side Park (I)	CHI	N	1885–1890	121	300	267	123	6	2934	1994	318	230	209	162	10	2069	1916	92	86
South Side Park (I)	CHI	N	1891–1893	105	110	117	87	3	1297	1092	68	54	91	113	1	1000	1247	50	60
West Side Park (II)	CHI	N	1894–1915	101	90	1008	635	28	8152	6881	333	246	816	750	35	7404	6967	361	263
Wrigley Field	CHI	N	1916–1992	106	116	3231	2786	30	27311	26694	4456	4272	2660	3300	32	24536	25892	3748	3677
Avenue Grounds	CIN	N	1876–1879	86	147	64	65	2	681	766	18	11	40	93	1	666	1043	5	15
Bank Street Grounds	CIN	N	1880–1880	103	341	14	25	1	163	216	5	8	7	34	2	131	256	2	2
League Park (I)	CIN	N	1890–1893	99	126	158	123	5	1630	1378	86	84	122	144	6	1294	1590	54	74
League Park (II)	CIN	N	1894–1901	105	61	349	217	12	3532	3113	100	108	214	319	14	2778	3224	142	182
Palace of the Fans	CIN	N	1902–1911	108	58	410	355	14	3436	3108	84	61	326	412	14	2848	2993	121	120
Redland/Crosley Field	CIN	N	1912–1969	99	86	2441	2043	26	19346	18722	2315	2156	1961	2484	26	18426	19751	2475	2653
Riverfront Stadium	CIN	N	1970–1992	103	110	1040	788	2	8166	7484	1555	1474	949	883	1	7832	7410	1444	1330
Kennard Street Park	CLE	N	1879–1884	94	39	132	139	3	1226	1310	17	23	110	160	5	1209	1471	45	58
National League Park	CLE	N	1889–1890	95	53	63	72	3	710	696	21	20	42	88	4	570	855	25	49
League Park (I)	CLE	N	1891–1899	107	38	360	198	7	3818	2956	56	68	273	406	17	3570	4265	164	234
Recreation Park	DET	N	1881–1888	100	108	248	179	8	2602	2146	153	95	178	258	9	2245	2621	111	124
Hartford Ball Club Grounds	HAR	N	1876–1876	106	0	23	9	0	220	107	0	0	24	12	1	209	154	2	2
Union Grounds (Brooklyn)	HAR	N	1877–1877	71	107	19	8	2	167	92	2	1	12	19	0	174	219	2	1
Colt Stadium	HOU	N	1962–1964	86	64	117	125	2	750	898	98	119	79	163	0	801	1087	139	194
Astrodome	HOU	N	1965–1992	89	61	1248	989	0	8585	8132	1021	1078	944	1294	2	8930	9871	1612	1821
South Street Park	IND	N	1878–1878	68	62	10	17	1	106	115	1	1	14	19	2	187	213	2	2
Athletic Park (I)	IND	N	1887–1887	99	98	24	39	1	349	456	19	28	13	50	0	278	507	14	32
Athletic Park (II)	IND	N	1888–1889	111	275	63	71	1	823	780	77	94	46	89	1	595	842	19	43
Association Park	KC	N	1886–1886	124	40	19	42	1	301	456	9	4	11	49	4	193	420	10	23
Memorial Coliseum	LA	N	1958–1961	113	146	172	137	0	1474	1430	346	397	158	151	0	1296	1291	257	254
Chavez Ravine/Dodger Stadium	LA	N	1962–1992	89	86	1437	1045	0	9568	8275	1605	1486	1247	1233	6	10452	9760	1914	1699
Louisville Baseball Park	LOU	N	1876–1877	133	675	36	25	2	368	326	13	6	29	36	2	251	307	2	1
Eclipse Park (I)	LOU	N	1892–1892	82	35	37	31	2	309	286	7	3	26	58	0	340	518	11	23
Eclipse Park (II)	LOU	N	1893–1899	93	123	202	233	12	2422	2727	130	136	154	361	4	2604	3770	114	134
Milwaukee Base-ball Grounds	MIL	N	1878–1878	126	35	7	18	0	127	177	1	0	8	27	1	129	209	1	3
County Stadium	MIL	N	1953–1965	87	82	602	414	7	4408	3694	998	776	544	476	1	4977	4424	1232	951
Jarry Park	MON	N	1969–1976	106	119	285	356	0	2519	2927	461	519	269	378	1	2347	2792	382	442

						HOME							ROAD						
PARK	TM	LG	YEARS	RF	HRF	W	L	T	R	OR	HR	OHR	W	L	T	R	OR	HR	OHR
Olympic Stadium	MON	N	1977–1992	98	86	687	568	0	5101	4768	798	851	613	664	2	5162	5130	996	960
Union Grounds (Brooklyn)	NY	N	1876–1876	78	646	13	20	0	143	207	2	7	8	15	1	117	205	0	1
Polo Grounds (I)	NY	N	1883–1888	92	71	234	112	12	2111	1418	87	46	186	161	12	1973	1905	100	89
Polo Grounds (II)	NY	N	1889–1890	98	54	84	42	3	874	583	26	17	62	69	6	769	820	51	35
Polo Grounds (III)	NY	N	1891–1910	97	134	876	564	38	7664	6329	377	280	686	736	27	7029	7160	227	255
Polo Grounds (IV)	NY	N	1911–1957	97	170	2106	1465	24	16900	14430	3146	2524	1833	1749	29	16963	15533	1763	1603
Polo Grounds (IV)	NY	N	1962–1963	110	162	56	105	0	611	891	154	213	35	126	1	507	831	81	141
Shea Stadium	NY	N	1964–1992	94	98	1184	1131	5	8763	8763	1544	1648	1038	1275	2	9026	9548	1581	1647
Jefferson Street Grounds	PHI	N	1876–1876	114	55	10	24	1	259	309	4	0	4	21	0	119	225	3	2
Recreation Park	PHI	N	1883–1886	95	32	102	117	5	1115	1286	21	21	81	134	3	1013	1435	42	84
Philadelphia Baseball Grounds	PHI	N	1887–1894	102	96	353	200	6	3889	2735	185	117	230	276	13	2871	3201	136	157
Baker Bowl	PHI	N	1895–1937	114	159	1607	1577	25	16007	16788	1617	1393	1288	1913	35	13361	15590	905	997
Shibe Park/Connie Mack Stadium	PHI	N	1938–1970	96	89	1211	1350	13	10001	11185	1552	1731	1062	1516	7	10096	11829	1702	1971
Veteran's Stadium	PHI	N	1971–1992	105	109	970	784	3	7818	7315	1461	1293	777	970	1	6898	7469	1257	1256
Recreation Park	PIT	N	1887–1890	79	14	122	117	7	1229	1138	15	12	83	204	3	1249	2230	81	144
Exposition Park	PIT	N	1891–1908	99	65	813	503	9	7060	5718	226	103	641	603	32	6374	6192	245	245
Forbes Field	PIT	N	1909–1969	102	69	2593	2113	35	21368	20076	1849	1930	2162	2508	38	20019	20318	2533	2924
Three Rivers Stadium	PIT	N	1970–1992	99	93	1046	784	1	8031	7083	1305	1230	891	933	3	7752	7458	1422	1318
Messer Street Grounds	PRO	N	1878–1885	91	61	244	114	4	2027	1354	44	28	194	164	5	2010	1774	54	66
Grand Avenue Park	STL	N	1876–1877	77	65	44	16	0	327	182	1	2	29	35	0	344	365	2	3
Union Park	STL	N	1885–1886	87	58	50	67	4	503	575	19	14	29	84	3	435	731	19	35
Sportsman's Park (I)	STL	N	1892–1892	92	241	37	36	2	379	380	32	32	19	58	3	324	542	13	15
Robison Field	STL	N	1893–1919	97	110	885	1063	39	8223	9497	385	424	691	1268	25	7718	10289	275	450
Sportsman's Park (IV)	STL	N	1920–1965	106	103	2133	1429	28	18069	15545	2305	2266	1810	1730	24	16384	15239	2192	2222
Busch Stadium	STL	N	1966–1992	100	80	1170	989	5	8900	8478	1004	1225	1060	1086	1	8729	8516	1231	1539
Jack Murphy Stadium	SD	N	1969–1992	92	96	933	983	1	7050	7617	1204	1443	789	1119	1	7293	8576	1239	1502
Seals Stadium	SF	N	1958–1959	94	97	86	68	0	702	625	165	151	77	77	0	730	686	172	154
Candlestick Park	SF	N	1960–1992	96	97	1475	1160	0	11125	10289	2220	1917	1226	1411	5	11073	11287	2253	2029
Newell Park	SYR	N	1879–1879	80	53	11	22	1	115	200	1	2	11	26	0	160	257	4	2
Putnam Grounds	TRO	N	1879–1879	94	96	12	27	2	191	263	3	6	7	29	0	130	281	1	7
Haymakers' Grounds	TRO	N	1880–1881	113	479	44	39	1	426	453	9	15	36	48	0	365	413	1	4
Troy Ball Clubs Grounds	TRO	N	1882–1882	93	57	22	20	0	238	217	7	2	13	28	2	192	305	5	11
Swanpdoodle Grounds	WAS	N	1886–1889	90	91	96	141	13	1136	1362	71	66	67	196	1	1023	1865	54	102
Boundary Field	WAS	N	1892–1899	99	126	265	269	11	3416	3346	222	139	145	428	7	2802	4360	116	184
Worcester Driving Park Grounds	WOR	N	1880–1882	118	151	55	69	2	703	777	21	25	35	90	1	498	737	10	20
AMERICAN ASSOCIATION																			
Newington Park	BAL	A	1882–1882	94	98	9	25	1	138	225	2	7	10	29	0	134	287	2	8
Oriole Park	BAL	A	1883–1890	98	75	240	181	18	2689	2263	72	39	159	303	7	2168	3179	62	95
Union Park	BAL	A	1891–1891	102	49	44	24	2	481	354	13	8	27	40	2	367	442	17	25
Congress Street Grounds	BOS	A	1891–1891	93	170	51	17	2	520	295	37	22	42	25	2	507	379	15	20
Washington Park (I)	BRO	A	1884–1889	99	132	241	149	10	2555	1971	91	72	169	205	9	2045	2360	52	67
Ridgewood Park	BRO	A	1890–1890	100	41	15	22	1	220	252	4	3	11	51	0	272	481	9	18
Bank Street Grounds	CIN	A	1882–1883	100	273	69	24	0	651	294	29	18	47	38	0	495	387	10	6
League Park (I)	CIN	A	1884–1889	105	180	264	146	3	2838	1973	165	93	169	188	9	1970	2122	63	65
Pendleton Park	CIN	A	1891–1891	122	210	24	20	1	297	289	21	9	19	37	1	250	354	7	11
National League Park (II)	CLE	A	1887–1888	100	50	55	64	2	734	777	10	19	34	110	3	647	1162	16	53
Recreation Park (I)	COL	A	1883–1884	83	120	56	45	1	480	490	28	22	45	59	1	579	628	27	16
Recreation Park (II)	COL	A	1889–1891	83	56	117	84	2	1169	859	26	27	83	125	7	1144	1456	46	55
Seventh Street Park	IND	A	1884–1884	99	115	17	39	1	257	380	13	15	12	39	2	206	375	7	15
Association Park (I)	KC	A	1888–1888	124	124	23	34	0	330	392	15	10	20	55	0	249	502	4	22
Exposition Park	KC	A	1889–1889	121	55	35	35	0	523	518	8	17	20	47	2	329	512	10	34
Eclipse Park (I)	LOU	A	1882–1891	96	67	357	238	12	3704	2949	83	66	218	400	8	3074	4083	91	138
Athletic Field	MIL	A	1891–1891	140	383	16	5	0	172	82	11	5	5	10	0	56	74	2	1
Polo Grounds (I) West Diamond	NY	A	1883–1885	87	52	100	50	5	905	580	24	13	73	88	1	854	936	25	50
St. George Cricket Grounds	NY	A	1886–1887	89	72	55	67	5	658	750	20	19	42	104	2	715	1108	19	43
Oakdale Park	PHI	A	1882–1882	127	325	21	18	0	236	220	3	11	20	16	0	166	166	2	2
Jefferson Street Grounds	PHI	A	1883–1890	105	84	322	189	10	3699	2780	122	70	197	275	8	2559	3164	102	109
Athletic Park	PHI	A	1891–1891	105	72	43	26	3	465	366	29	9	30	40	1	354	427	26	26
Expositon Park (I)	PIT	A	1882–1883	95	110	35	49	0	477	493	22	6	35	57	1	470	646	9	19
Recreation Park	PIT	A	1884–1886	92	26	101	86	2	990	864	6	10	65	104	3	774	1043	17	39
Allen Pasture	RIC	A	1884–1884	101	117	5	15	2	96	142	3	8	7	15	2	98	153	4	6
Culver Field (I)	ROC	A	1890–1890	82	57	40	22	1	348	252	13	4	23	41	6	361	458	18	15
Sportsman's Park (I)	STL	A	1882–1891	116	202	460	177	6	4749	2924	214	145	322	256	14	3196	2999	91	75
Star Park (II)	SYR	A	1890–1890	81	19	30	30	0	321	320	2	4	25	42	1	378	511	12	24
League Park	TOL	A	1884–1884	107	33	28	25	2	270	267	3	2	18	33	4	193	305	5	10
Speranza Park	TOL	A	1890–1890	104	143	40	27	1	422	316	17	11	28	37	1	316	374	7	12
Athletic Park	WAS	A	1884–1884	82	37	10	20	0	137	181	3	4	2	31	0	111	300	3	17
Boundary Field	WAS	A	1891–1891	98	88	28	40	4	389	519	13	18	16	51	0	300	547	6	26
NATIONAL ASSOCIATION																			
Jefferson Street Grounds	ATH	N	1871–1875	109	102	104	28	5	1516	834	23	4	61	58	3	1013	930	10	14
Capitoline Grounds	ATL	N	1872–1872	147	205	6	12	0	153	265	0	4	3	16	0	84	208	0	2
Union Grounds	ATL	N	1873–1875	78	93	30	53	2	464	641	8	14	11	59	0	335	795	1	18
Newington Park	BAL	N	1872–1874	102	285	46	26	3	799	544	22	5	32	53	2	689	846	5	6
South End Grounds (I)	BOS	N	1871–1875	109	170	120	23	1	1714	806	36	4	105	37	6	1513	951	19	6
Centennial Grounds	CEN	N	1875–1875	93	0	0	7	0	25	77	0	0	2	5	0	45	61	0	0
Union Base-Ball Grounds	CHI	N	1871–1871	119	98	13	3	0	196	135	6	3	6	6	0	106	106	4	3
23rd Street Grounds	CHI	N	1874–1875	101	27	34	26	1	439	373	1	1	24	42	1	358	523	2	6
National Association Grounds	CLE	N	1871–1872	95	286	5	15	0	165	227	4	13	11	20	0	258	368	3	6
Union Grounds	ECK	N	1872–1872	77	21	3	11	0	75	167	0	1	0	15	0	77	246	0	5
Hartford Ball Club Grounds	HAR	N	1874–1875	116	25	39	28	2	533	397	1	1	31	37	2	395	417	3	5
Hamilton Field	KEK	N	1871–1871	110	0	5	4	0	78	112	0	0	2	8	0	59	131	2	5
Mansfield Club Grounds	MAN	N	1872–1872	99	23	4	7	0	130	133	1	0	1	12	0	90	215	0	5
Newington Park	MAR	N	1873–1873	85	0	0	1	0	3	24	0	0	0	5	0	23	128	0	4
Union Grounds (Brooklyn)	MUT	N	1871–1875	93	161	94	53	3	1213	837	21	9	57	69	2	864	1025	5	11
Nationals Grounds	NAT	N	1872–1872	154	0	0	7	0	65	135	0	0	0	4	0	15	55	0	2
Hamilton Park	NH	N	1875–1875	79	95	3	24	0	87	211	1	3	4	16	0	83	186	1	2
Olympics Grounds	OLY	N	1871–1872	111	244	9	11	0	197	218	5	2	8	11	2	167	225	1	2
Jefferson Street Grounds	PHI	N	1873–1875	106	48	54	30	1	760	527	8	0	48	47	1	712	673	6	13
Waverly Fairgrounds	RES	N	1873–1873	92	0	0	8	0	34	101	0	0	2	13	0	64	198	0	8
Agricultural Society Fair Gnds	ROK	N	1871–1871	91	0	3	4	0	72	66	0	0	1	17	0	159	221	3	3
Red Stocking Base Ball Park	RS	N	1875–1875	87	0	3	11	0	50	108	0	0	1	4	0	10	53	0	0
Grand Avenue Park	STL	N	1875–1875	78	53	21	12	1	183	135	0	1	18	17	1	203	234	0	2
Haymakers' Grounds	TRO	N	1871–1872	108	123	13	15	1	326	327	7	3	15	10	0	298	226	4	3
Olympics Grounds	WAS	N	1873–1873	102	45	6	12	0	157	208	3	1	2	19	0	126	277	0	10
Olympics Grounds	WAS	N	1875–1875	108	0	2	10	0	45	158	0	0	3	13	0	62	180	0	6
Perry Park	WES	N	1875–1875	113	0	1	7	0	30	57	0	0	0	5	0	15	31	0	0

Baseball, Computers, and New Statistics

Gary Gillette

With the coming of age of the personal computer, the sea of baseball statistics in recent years has become a veritable flood. With the baseball world seemingly inundated with numbers, there has been a backlash against statistics and the statisticians. Many fans—especially those of the "old school"—believe that baseball already had enough stats, and that the newer numbers served mostly to obscure the game they love, rather than to illuminate it.

Who is responsible for this flood of numbers? First, the fans, who have always looked for evidence to buttress their opinions. Second, the media, who have latched onto this trend and exploited it commercially. Third, Major League Baseball, which has aided and abetted the trend for publicity. Fourth, fantasy baseball players, many of whom were only casual fans before the advent of Rotisserie leagues. Fifth, authors and analysts, who use these new numbers to examine and explain the seemingly simple game of baseball.

Of all the new statistics, the type which has become most popular is the situational. In contrast to traditional baseball totals or averages like home runs and batting average, situational stats are an attempt to break baseball statistics into *how and when* they happened. The most important situational breakdowns are how batters perform versus lefthanded and righthanded pitchers (and pitchers vs. same and opposite handed batters) and how players perform in their home park as opposed to when they are on the road. In reality, these situational stats have been part of the game for decades, as generations of fans have argued about the effect of Yankee Stadium on sluggers like Ruth and Maris, while generations of managers have platooned their hitters. Aside from these two key categories, several other types of breakdowns have become prominent: "clutch" hitting measures, grass/turf splits, and individual pitcher-batter matchups.

At their best, these new statistics illuminate the various aspects of the game, making it easier to understand how and why players and teams win and lose. The fact that they describe performances in specific situations (hence their name) is both their strength and their weakness. At their worst, situational stats divide up the game into irrelevant categories which hinder understanding. The common parody of situational statistics—how a player hits "in Tuesday night games at home when facing a southpaw in July with the bases loaded"—is sometimes all too close to reality. In Game Seven of the 1992 World Series, for example, more than five hundred stats were bandied about by the network broadcasters or displayed on the screen during the game. With so many numbers coming fast and furious, the significant ones get lost in the trivial, and the currency of all analytical statistics is devalued.

The schizoid attitudes in baseball toward new statistics and analysis are shown by the fact that there isn't even general agreement on the use of the word *sabermetrics*: many fans have never heard of the term, and while some professionals in the field call themselves *sabermetricians*, others eschew the word and call themselves statistical analysts.

In the front offices of baseball teams, there have been two primary usages of these new statistics. Team Public Relations departments, aided by the computerized MLB–IBM Baseball Information System, have become increasingly more proficient and prolific at churning out special stats about their players. Most of these find their way to the fans via the media, who publicize these stats in print and on the air. The other way in which the new statistics have penetrated the business end of baseball is through salary arbitration, a quasilegal proceeding which directly sets salaries for a few dozen players each year. Indirectly, however, salary arbitration has a much broader impact on the game's salary structure. Newer statistical measures have been used by both management and labor in arbitration in recent years, although many analytical stats are still not admissible in arbitration proceedings by the mutual agreement of the disputing parties.

Outside the hearing room, new analytical measures have had a greater impact. Several major league teams have employed full-time professional statistical analysts in the past decade, and other teams have employed statistical analysts as consultants. Of these analysts, Eddie Epstein, now Director of Research and Statistics for the Baltimore Orioles, has risen the highest and had the most influence. Some other teams have employed computer systems to compile and analyze performance data, with the Oakland Athletics and manager Tony LaRussa getting the most credit for successfully using these tools.

In the publishing world, the main effect of the new statistics has been to create a new subgenre of baseball books. Celebrity biographies still sell the most sports books, but the number of statistically oriented titles released in recent years is astounding. Bill James, a Kansan who was not a sportswriter, made the bestseller lists year after year in the 1980s on the strength of his detailed statistical analysis as well as his witty and satirical prose. Pete Palmer, a computer programmer by trade, blazed the way for accurate historical comparisons of players and teams by combining his tireless research and top-notch computer skills to produce a comprehensive historical data base. Published for the first time in *Total Baseball*, a comprehensive reference work, Palmer brought sabermetrics and serious analytical measures to the general baseball public.

The Elias Sports Bureau, longtime official statisticians of the National League, made their mark by publishing their annual eponymous book of situational stats starting in 1985. These stats, previously available only to major-league teams, instantly became part of the baseball public's consciousness.

Just as James, Palmer, and Elias were preceded by the members of the Society for American Baseball Research, they were also followed by many others. Project Scoresheet, a nonprofit organization founded by James in 1984, coordinated the efforts of hundreds of volunteers and produced the first and only publicly available data base of contemporary baseball. Retrosheet, another volunteer group founded by David Smith (a longtime SABR member and professor at the University of Delaware), is now collecting scoresheets from pre-1984 games. Armed with copies of more than 60,000 scoresheets donated by teams, sports-

writers and fans, Retrosheet will soon make public its first computerized data (for the 1967 season). Stats, Inc., unites the sharp analytical minds of such sabermetricians as Dick Cramer, Bill James, Don Zminda, and John Dewan. The organization provides statistical services to television networks and periodicals like *Sports Illustrated* and *Baseball Weekly, and has an active publishing program with HarperCollins (as do Steve Mann and Ken Mallin, Pete Palmer and John Thorn, and myself).*

On the periodical side, media conglomerate Gannett founded a weekly newspaper in 1990 devoted solely to baseball—more specifically to baseball statistics, which take up a large portion of the paper. While the hundred-year-old Sporting News has deemphasized baseball, the hundred-week-old USA Today Baseball Weekly has found a market hundreds of thousands strong by focusing exclusively on the game. The regular publication by BBW in 1992 of OPS stats (On-Base Plus Slugging, an analytical measure developed by Pete Palmer) shows just how far the new statistics have come.

Probably the most high-profile and controversial element of the new statistics trend has been the explosion in popularity of fantasy baseball, a pastime that occupies several million players. An undeniable attraction of fantasy baseball is that it brings to baseball one element which football has had for decades: gambling. Gamblers, both fantasy players and others, make extensive use of the new stats. Fantasy baseball is firmly established and likely to increase in popularity.

Another area of great growth has been in baseball games. Baseball board games, using dice as the element of chance and statistics to recreate performance, have been played by a small but devoted group since the birth of APBA Baseball in the early 1950s. In the mid-1980s computer baseball games took hold and now appear to be the future of baseball gaming. While board games still have their audience, computer games are much more flexible and are able to provide fans with a variety of simulated experiences which board games cannot. Moreover, the virtues of a computer opponent, when a flesh-and-blood one is unavailable, are understandable.

The latest computer games simulate sophisticated opposing managers as well as recreating player performance. Moreover,

the era of almost real-time baseball games has already dawned. In 1991 the computer service Prodigy debuted a baseball game which used last night's real-life performances to play simulated games. The participants in "Big League Manager" send in their lineups by modem before they go to bed; the next morning, they dial up the Prodigy computer and see a boxscore for last night's game for *their* team displayed along with current league standings.

Yet another electronic milestone was reached in 1991–1992 with the debut of the electronic baseball encyclopedia, in two forms: *Total Baseball* became available in compact disc, read-only memory form (CD-ROM)—in a mini-disc for Sony's palmtop DataDiscman player and for the desktop computer, MS-DOS or Macintosh, in a conventional size disc published by CMC; also, *Big League Baseball*, a reference device published by Franklin Electronics which fit into a shirt pocket. The advantage of an electronic baseball encyclopedia like the Franklin or the CD-ROM *Total Baseball* is not simply its portability or its compact data storage and retrieval but its invitation to the user to manipulate the numbers, to make customized lists and complicated research requests.

Last, and least, is the negative reaction to the new statistics. There has been a backlash, and it's true that many fans believe the game has suffered from these stats and their purveyors, but the new statistics don't change the grand old game; they just provide new ways of looking at it. As with new strategies on the field, the old stats will persist while their replacements become established. During this time, the improvement in analysis will be obscured by the clash of stats and the arguments of the analysts. Inevitably, though, the best of the new stats will oust the worst of the old, and the game will look a little different in the future.

Not too long ago, you know, nobody bothered to count such silly things as runs batted in, batter strikeouts, times caught stealing, or saves. Players change, teams change, ballparks change, strategies change—even "the unchanging game" itself changes. Why shouldn't baseball statistics change along with them?

The First Great Pitcher

John Thorn

James Creighton (1841–1862) was famous principally for his exploits on behalf of the champion Excelsiors of Brooklyn in 1860–62. He possessed an unprecedented combination of speed, spin, and command that virtually defined pitching for all those who followed. Prior to Creighton, pitchers had been constrained by the rule that "the ball must be pitched, not thrown, for the bat." This meant that (a) the ball had to be delivered underhand, in the stiff-armed, stiff-wristed manner borrowed from cricket's early days and (b), in the absence of called strikes, an innovation of 1858, or called balls, which came into the game six years later, the ball had to be placed at the batter's pleasure. The infant game of baseball was designed to display and reward its most difficult skill, which was neither pitching nor batting, but fielding. Until Creighton added an illegal but imperceptible wrist snap to his swooping low release, the pioneer pitcher and batter were collaborators in putting the ball in play rather than the mortal adversaries they are today.

Born to James and Jane Creighton on April 15, 1841, in Manhattan, Jim grew up in Brooklyn. By the age of sixteen, his abilities in cricket and baseball were evident, particularly with the bat. In 1857, Jim joined the fledgling Niagara Base Ball Club of Brooklyn, for whom he claimed second base. At shortstop was George Flanley, another accomplished young player.

In 1859 the Niagaras challenged the Star Club, then the crack junior team. In the fifth inning of the game, with the Niagaras trailing badly, their regular pitcher, Shields, was replaced by Creighton. Peter O'Brien, captain of the mighty Atlantics, witnessed this game, and "when Creighton got to work," he observed, "something new was seen in base ball—a low, swift delivery, the ball rising from the ground past the shoulder to the catcher. The Stars soon saw that they would not be able to cope with such pitching. . . . [The Niagara Club afterwards broke up, and] Creighton and Flanley at once joined the Stars. The next year he with Flanley joined the Excelsior Club."

How to explain all this movement? That old snake in the garden, money. In the 1860s such restlessness came to be termed revolving; today it would be called free agency. According to the sporting press, Creighton was a high-principled, unassuming youth whose gentlemanly manner and temperate habits were ideal attributes for the amateur age of baseball; all the same, he became (at the same time as Flanley) baseball's first professional, through under-the-table "emoluments" from the Excelsiors, who were hungry to surpass the rival Atlantics. Just as he changed the game forever more by breaking the rule against the wrist snap, so did he assure that skilled baseball players could never again be content with field exercise followed by noble toasts and cornucopian banquets.

In 1860 in twenty match games, Creighton scored 47 runs while being retired only 56 times. Not once did he strike out. He also threw baseball's first recorded shutout, on November 8.

But the best was to be saved for last. After another championship campaign in 1861, Creighton went through the 1862 season as not only the game's peerless pitcher but also its top batsman, being retired only four times, either in plate appearances or on the basepaths (the statistics of the time do not permit us to differentiate between these kinds of out).

At the same time that Creighton was extending the frontier in baseball, cricket continued to be a source of pleasure and profit for him. English cricketer John Lillywhite, in the United States to play a series of exhibition matches, saw Creighton pitch a baseball and exclaimed, "Why, that man is not bowling, he is throwing underhand. It is the best disguised underhand throwing I ever saw, and might readily be taken for a fair delivery."

On October 14, 1862, in a match against the tough Unions of Morrisania, Creighton played the field while Asa Brainard (later to become famous as pitcher for the undefeated Cincinnati Red Stockings of 1869) pitched the first five innings. In four trips to the plate, he hit four doubles. In the sixth he came in to pitch, and then in the next inning something happened. John "Death to Flying Things" Chapman, star outfielder of the Atlantics, later wrote: "I was present at the game between the Excelsiors and the Unions of Morrisania at which Jim Creighton injured himself. He did it in hitting out a home run. When he had crossed the [plate] he turned to George Flanley and said, 'I must have snapped my belt,' and George said, 'I guess not.' It turned out that he had suffered a fatal injury. Nothing could be done for him, and baseball met with a severe loss."

Creighton had swung so mighty a blow—in the manner of the day, with hands separated on the bat, little or no turn of the wrists, and incredible torque applied by the twisting motion of the upper body—that he ruptured his bladder. After four days of hemorrhaging and agony at his Henry Street home, Jim Creighton passed away on October 18, at the age of twenty-one years and six months.

Creighton's last run home instantly ascended to the realm of myth, giving baseball its martyred saint. Obsequies included such syrupy statements as "He was very modest, and never severe in his criticisms of the play of others. He did not care to talk about his own playing, was gentlemanly in his deportment, and very correct in his habits, and to sum up all, was a model player in our National Games [understood here not as a typo, but signifying baseball *and* cricket]. His death was a loss not only to his club but to the whole base ball community, which needed such as he as a standard of honorable play and ability." Rule-breaking, revolving, *sub rosa* professionalism, all were now to be dismissed. Icon-making was in full production.

Creighton's Excelsior teammates subscribed toward a fine monument over his remains, in Brooklyn's Greenwood Cemetery. But the Excelsiors were not at all sure that it was a good thing for baseball to take the blame for Creighton's death; this might not promote the healthful properties of the new game. What if his injury had been sustained a day or two earlier, at a cricket match? Jim's talents had carried the game to new heights; in death he would prove even more useful.

According to a contemporary account, at the National Association convention of 1862, the Excelsior president, Dr. Jones, "briefly made allusion to the death of Creighton, and paid high tribute to his memory; in doing which he availed himself of the opportunity to correct a mis-statement that has found its way into print in reference to his death being caused by injuries

sustained in a baseball match. This, he said, was not so; the injury he received in a cricket match."

In death Creighton's real accomplishments rapidly took on an accretion of legend, much as his death itself may have. Baseball, today universally recognized as a vibrant anachronism, was not always a backward-looking game in which the plays and players of yore set unsurpassable standards of excellence. In the 1850s and '60s baseball was new, and strictly a "go ahead" business, in the watchword of the day. Creighton's death implanted the game with nostalgia. More than twenty years after his passing, veteran observers might say without fear of challenge that Keefe and Radbourn were fine pitchers, sure, but they "warn't no Creighton."

Rules and Scoring
Dennis Bingham and Thomas R. Heitz

The chronologies presented here trace the evolution of baseball's playing and scoring rules from those governing the first properly organized baseball club (1845) to the present major league clubs (through 1992).

Playing Rules

As a starting point, the rules of the 1845 Knickerbocker Base Ball Club of New York City are provided. During earlier decades, rules had been published for popular bat-and-ball and baserunning games played by eighteenth- and early nineteenth-century youths (indeed, some basic baseball principles can be traced back for centuries), but the codified Knickerbocker rules serve as a direct link to the rules of today. Their rules were the model for the hundreds of organized amateur clubs that sprang up in the 1850s. Following the 1845 rules is an outline listing the significant rule changes made in the next twelve years.

In 1858, several baseball clubs, including the old Knickerbockers, met to establish the National Association of Base-Ball Players and, in the process, greatly expanded, refined, and polished the rule book. Although the association was composed primarily of amateurs, this rule book became the core of every rule book for every baseball league that followed. These rules are set forth in their entirety and are followed by changes to the rules under annual headings through 1992.

The first major league, the National Association of Professional Base-Ball Players, was formed in 1871 and used essentially the same rule book as its predecessor. In 1876 the National League dethroned the professional players' association and adopted their rule book, with their amendments to the rules noted under that year's heading.

Rule differences for subsequent major leagues are also listed in the chronology and are noted under the annual heading in which they were introduced, e.g. Union Association (1884) and Players League (1890.)

In most cases, the actual text of a new rule or change has been taken verbatim from original sources. However, to reduce verbiage, the references to section numbering and headings, which have varied widely over the years, have been deleted along with other extraneous spacing and punctuation. In many cases, primarily in the early years, the wording has been slightly changed to convey the meaning of the rule more clearly. In a few cases the technical wording of complex rules has been summarized for ease of reading. Researchers requiring precise quotations of rules are advised to consult original sources, e.g., the *Spalding* and *Reach Baseball Guides*.

Headings have been added to each of the changes under the annual headings to assist the reader. By consulting the index and headings, readers may follow the evolution of any one particular rule through the years.

The chronology does not include *all* changes to the playing rules—only those of significance and substance. Numerous minor changes in wording not affecting meaning, or changes in punctuation and spelling which had no purpose other than gram-

matical correctness, have been ignored. Also, the chronology includes only those rules and regulations found in the official baseball rule book, not those found in other baseball documents such as league constitutions and the Basic Agreement. Thus rules and subject matter that may have been dropped from the early rule books, such as those concerning player eligibility and discipline, may still govern baseball for years later but had been inserted in the league's constitution.

In some instances, significant rule changes affecting umpires and little-used rules regarding suspended games or batting out of order have been summarized or simply alluded to in the interests of brevity. The scoring rules are presented in a separate section of this appendix because of their length and special interest.

Baseball's rules continue to evolve in the twentieth century despite the perception of many that "the game remains pretty much the same as it always has been." The most far-reaching revision of baseball's playing rules came in 1950 when the entire code was virtually rewritten. Additional changes and refinements were added throughout the 1950s, and it is the rules of 1950 for the most part that we use today.

The rules of baseball are commonly considered the means of keeping the game in that delicate balance between offense and defense with neither side enjoying a marked advantage. This balance is the dynamic force of competition, which drives the game and ultimately creates interest and motivation for players and spectators alike.

But changes to the playing rules can also be categorized in terms of response to various social, economic, and technological factors as well as to the need for competitive balance. For example, when the uncouth language of hard-bitten nineteenth-century players became offensive to female rooters, appropriate rules were adopted (in an attempt) to modify player behavior. Likewise, gloves were introduced gradually in the 1870s and 1880s to protect the players' catching hands from injury. However, when glove design clearly departed from the goal of protection and extended to aiding in the catching process, effectively making the glove an extension of the hand, it became necessary to invoke standards for gloves in the rules.

In terms of competitive balance, perhaps the most striking evolution is that of the pitching rules, which have undergone a remarkable transformation from the days of simple underhanded hurling from a boxlike enclosure to today's complex series of physical motions from which almost any deviation is likely to elicit a call of "balk."

In many cases, the introduction of a playing rule followed several years of development on the field of play. Like state and federal legislative bodies, baseball's rule-making authorities are often slow to respond to changing conditions or perhaps justifiably cautious about making such changes before the effects are fully understood. For example, there is no mention of pitching mounds in the playing rules until 1903, when the maximum elevation was fixed at 15 inches. However, pitching mounds were in general use many years prior to 1903 and may have come into vogue as early as the 1880s. The lifting of restrictions on the angle of pitching delivery in 1884 made overhanded throwing

legal, and it was not long before the hurlers realized the mechanical advantages of stepping off a short incline as they directed the ball toward the plate. Presumably, by 1903 the lack of uniformity in certain parks had become a problem, and so the rules set a standard.

Another point that should be kept in mind while reading this chronology is that just because a particular rule is "in the book" doesn't necessarily mean that it was (or is) always enforced.

The researcher is advised to scan the Index to Playing Rule Changes prior to consulting the chronology.

Scoring Rules

The chronology presented after that of the playing rules traces the evolution of professional baseball's scoring rules from 1877 through 1992.

Clubs, sportswriters, and fans had been keeping score and compiling statistics for decades, but the scoring rules of 1877 are presented as a starting point, in their entirety, because they are the first official scoring rules included in the rule book. Thereafter changes to the scoring rules are noted under annual headings.

In most cases, as with the playing rules, the actual text of a new scoring rule or change has been taken verbatim from original sources.

The scoring rules are at the heart of baseball's accountability to itself and to the millions of fans who follow the game day by day. Through the use of these rules the daily performance of players and teams is described and measured in a uniform and meaningful way. Baseball is unique in publishing the performance records of its key personnel, and in so doing it subjects the individual, the team, and its management to the scrutiny and judgment of anyone who has the price of a daily newspaper.

Like the playing rules, they have evolved from a rather primitive code to a complex, legalistic document. The scoring rules have been transformed over the decades from the simple recording of hits, outs, errors, and assists in the 1870s into a highly technical set of rules and guidelines used to record every significant offensive and defensive event that transpires on the field of play.

While the collection of such statistics as "caught stealing" did not commence until later years, still baseball's major performance records can be traced in an unbroken skein well back into the nineteenth century. As a result, no other professional sport can claim such a rich resource of historical statistics.

The researcher is advised to scan the Index to Scoring Rule Changes prior to consulting the chronology.

Playing Rules for 1845

1. Members must strictly observe the time agreed upon for exercise, and be punctual in their attendance.
2. When assembled for exercise, the President, or in his absence the Vice-President, shall appoint an Umpire, who shall keep the game in a book provided for that purpose, and note all violations of the By-Laws and Rules during the time of exercise.
3. The presiding officer shall designate two members as Captains, who shall retire and make the match to be played, observing at the same time that the players put opposite to each other should be as nearly equal as possible; the choice of sides to be then tossed for, and the first in hand to be decided in like manner.
4. The bases shall be from "home" to second base, forty-two paces; from first to third base, forty-two paces, equidistant.
5. No stump match shall be played on a regular day of exercise.
6. If there should not be a sufficient number of members of the Club present at the time agreed upon to commence exercise, gentlemen not members may be chosen in to make up the match, which shall not be broken up to take in members that may afterwards appear; but, in all cases, members shall have the

preference, when present, at the making of a match.
7. If members appear after the game is commenced they may be chosen in if mutually agreed upon.
8. The game to consist of twenty-one counts, or aces; but at the conclusion an equal number of hands must be played.
9. The ball must be pitched, and not thrown, for the bat.
10. A ball knocked out of the field, or outside the range of the first or third base, is foul.
11. Three balls being struck at and missed and the last one caught, is a hand out; if not caught is considered fair, and the striker bound to run.
12. If a ball be struck, or tipped, and caught, either flying or on the first bound, it is a hand out.
13. A player running the bases shall be out, if the ball is in the hands of an adversary on the base, or the runner is touched with it before he makes his base; it being understood, however, that in no instance is a ball to be thrown at him.
14. A player running who shall prevent an adversary from catching or getting the ball before making his base, is a hand out.
15. Three hands out, all out.
16. Players must take their strike in regular turn.
17. All disputes and differences relative to the game, to be decided by the Umpire, from which there is no appeal.
18. No ace or base can be made on a foul strike.
19. A runner cannot be put out in making one base, when a balk is made by the pitcher.
20. But one base allowed when a ball bounds out of the field when struck.

Rule Changes 1846–57

In 1848 a rule was amended declaring that the batter-runner was out if the ball was held on first base before he reached it; previously, the rule applied the situation to *all* bases. By 1852, the captains of each club had been given the authority to position each player in the field, which could not be changed without their consent, and that each club member would take turns as umpire.

The 1854 rule book included the following: "When a fair ball is struck and the striker not put out, the first base must be vacated as well as the next base or bases if similarly occupied; players may be put out, under these circumstances, in the same manner as when running to first base." In other words, the force out had been introduced.

The dimensions of the ball had also been established—from 5½ to 6 ounces in weight and from 2¾ to 3½ inches in diameter. A player was also now called out if he *intentionally* prevented an opponent from catching the ball.

A major rule change was made in 1857 when it was determined that nine complete innings would constitute a game rather than the first team to score 21 runs at the end of equal innings.

Playing Rules for 1858

Section 1. The ball. The ball must weigh not less than six nor more than six and one-quarter ounces avoirdupois. It must measure not less than ten nor more than ten and a quarter inches in circumference. It must be composed of India rubber and yarn, and covered with leather, and in all match games shall be furnished by the challenging club, and become the property of the winning club as a trophy of victory.
Section 2. The bat. The bat must be round and must not exceed two and a half inches in diameter in the thickest part. It must be made of wood and may be of any length to suit the striker.
Section 3. The bases. The bases must be four in number, placed at equal distances from each other, and securely fastened upon the four corners of a square whose sides are respectively thirty yards. They must be so constructed as to be distinctly seen by the

umpire, and must cover a space equal to one square foot of surface. The first, second, and third bases shall be canvas bags, painted white, and filled with sand or sawdust; the home base and pitcher's points to be each marked with a flat circular iron plate, painted or enameled white.

Section 4. Position of the bases. The base from which the ball is struck shall be designated the home base and must be directly opposite the second base; the first base must always be that upon the right hand, and the third base that upon the left hand side of the striker when occupying the position at the home base.

Section 5. The pitcher's position. The pitcher's position shall be designated by a line four yards in length, drawn at right angles to a line from home to the second base, having its center upon that line, at a fixed iron plate placed at a point fifteen yards from the home base. The pitcher must deliver the ball as near as possible over the center of said base, and for the striker.

Section 6. Delivering the ball. The ball must be pitched, not jerked or thrown, to the bat; and whenever the pitcher draws back his hand, or moves with the apparent purpose or pretension to deliver the ball, he shall so deliver it, and must have neither foot in advance of the line at the time of delivering the ball; and if he fails in either of these particulars, then it shall be declared a balk.

Section 7. Balking. When a balk is made by the pitcher, every player running the bases is entitled to one base without being put out.

Section 8. Foul and fair hit balls. If the ball, from a stroke of the bat, is caught behind the range of home and the first base or home and the third base, without having touched the ground, or first touches the ground behind those bases, it shall be termed foul and must be so declared by the umpire unasked. If the ball first touches the ground, either upon or in front of the range of those bases, it shall be considered fair.

Section 9. Scoring a run. A player making the home base shall be entitled to score one run.

Section 10. Running on third strike. If three balls are struck at and missed, and the last one is not caught flying or upon the first bound, it shall be considered fair and the striker must attempt to make his run.

How batsmen are put out.

Section 11. Caught foul ball. The striker is out if a foul ball is caught, either before touching the ground or upon the first bound;

Section 12. Three strikes. Or if three balls are struck at and missed, and the last is caught either before touching the ground or upon the first bound;

Section 13. Caught fair ball. Or if a fair ball is struck, and the ball is caught without having touched the ground or upon the first bound;

Section 14. At first base. Or if a fair ball is struck, and the ball is held by an adversary on the first base before the striker touches the base;

Section 15. Touched with ball. Or if, at any time, he is touched by the ball while in play in the hands of an adversary, without some part of his person being on a base.

Section 16. Running on fair and foul balls. No ace or base can be made upon a foul ball, nor when a fair ball has been caught without touching the ground; and the ball shall, in both instances, be considered dead and not in play until it shall first have been settled in the hands of the pitcher; in either case the players running the bases shall return to them, and shall not be put out in so running unless the ball has been first pitched to the striker.

Section 17. The batsman's position. The striker must stand on a line drawn through the center of the home base, not exceeding in length three feet from either side thereof, and parallel with the line occupied by the pitcher. He shall be considered the striker until he has made the first base. Players must strike in regular rotation and, after the first inning is played, the turn commences

with the player who stands on the list next to the one who lost the third hand.

Section 18. Forced off a base. Players must take their bases in the order of striking; and when a fair ball is struck, and not caught flying nor on the first bound, the first base must be vacated, as also the second and third bases if they are occupied at the same time. Players may be put out at any base, under these circumstances, in the same manner as the striker when running to the first base.

Section 19. Running out of line of bases. Players running the bases must, as far as possible, keep upon the direct line between the bases; and should any player run three feet out of this line, for the purpose of avoiding the ball in the hands of an adversary, he shall be declared out.

Section 20. Interfering with fielder. Any player who shall intentionally prevent an adversary from catching or fielding the ball, shall be declared out.

Section 21. Obstructing baserunners. If the player is prevented from making a base by the intentional obstruction of an adversary, he shall be entitled to that base and not be put out.

Section 22. Illegally stopping the ball. If an adversary stops the ball with his hat or cap, or takes it from the hands of a party not engaged in the game, no player can be put out unless the ball shall first have been settled in the hands of the pitcher.

Section 23. Caught fly balls. If a ball, from the strike of a bat, is held under any other circumstances than as enumerated in Section 22, and without having touched the ground more than once, the striker is out.

Section 24. No run scored. If two hands are already out, no player running home at the time a ball is struck can make an ace if the striker is put out.

Section 25. End of innings. An inning must be concluded at the time the third hand is put out.

Section 26. The game. The game shall consist of nine innings to each side, when, should the number of runs be equal, the play shall be continued until a majority of runs, upon an equal number of innings shall be declared, which shall conclude the game.

Section 27. Eligible players. In playing all matches, nine players from each club shall constitute a full field, and they must have been regular members of the club which they represent, and of no other club, for thirty days prior to the match. No change or substitution shall be made after the game has been commenced, unless for reason of illness or injury. Position of players and choice of innings shall be determined by captains previously appointed for that purpose by the respective clubs.

Section 28. Duties of the umpire. The umpire shall take care that the regulations respecting the ball, bats, bases, and the pitcher's and striker's positions are strictly observed. He shall keep a record of the game in a book prepared for the purpose; he shall be the judge of fair and unfair play, and shall determine all disputes and differences which may occur during the game; he shall take especial care to declare all foul balls and balks immediately upon their occurrence, unasked, and in a distinct and audible manner.

Section 29. Selection of umpire/scorers. In all matches, the umpire shall be selected by the captains of the respective sides, and shall perform all the duties enumerated in Section 28, except recording the game, which shall be done by two scorers, one of whom shall be appointed by each of the contending clubs.

Section 30. Betting prohibited. No person engaged in a match, either as umpire, scorer, or player, shall be directly or indirectly interested in any bet upon the game. Neither umpire, scorer, nor player shall be changed during a match, unless with the consent of both parties, except for a violation of this law and except as provided in Section 27, and then the umpire may dismiss any transgressor.

Section 31. Suspending and completing game. The umpire in any match shall determine when play shall be suspended; and if the game cannot be concluded, it shall be decided by the last even innings, provided five innings have been played, and the

party having the greatest number of runs shall be declared the winner.

Section 32. Special ground rules. Clubs may adopt such rules respecting balls knocked beyond or outside of the bounds of the field, as the circumstances of the ground may demand and these rules shall govern all matches played upon the ground, provided that they are distinctly made known to every player and umpire previous to the commencement of the game.

Section 33. Interfering with participants. No person shall be permitted to approach or to speak with the umpire, scorers, or players, or in any manner to interrupt or interfere during the progress of the game, unless by special request of the umpire.

Section 34. Eligible umpires and scorers. No person shall be permitted to act as umpire or scorer in any match, unless he shall be a member of a base ball club governed by these rules.

Section 35. Forfeited game. Whenever a match shall have been determined upon between two clubs, play shall be called at the exact hour appointed; and should either party fail to produce their players within fifteen minutes thereafter, the party so failing shall admit a defeat.

Section 36. Ineligible players. No person who may be in arrears to any club he may have belonged to previous to the one he is then a member of shall be competent to play in a match unless such arrears are paid.

Section 37. Calling strikes. Should a striker stand at the bat without striking at good balls repeatedly pitched to him, for the purpose of delaying the game or of giving advantage to a player, the umpire, after warning him, shall call one strike, and if he persists in such action, two and three strikes. When three strikes are called, he shall be subject to the same rules as if he had struck at the three balls.

Chronology of Rule Changes 1859–1992

1859

Ball The ball must weigh 5¾ to 6 ounces and measure 9¾ to 10 inches in circumference.

Player/Eligible No person who receives compensation for his services as a player shall be competent to play in any match.

Game/Number Every match shall be decided by a single game.

Note: In previous years, a series of games often determined the winner of a "match."

Runner/Advancing Caught fly balls which do not touch the ground are no longer considered dead balls.

Note: With this amendment it was understood that runners, following caught fly balls, could now advance after returning to their original base. This, however, was not as yet written into the rules.

1860

Game/Number Every match shall be decided by a single game unless otherwise mutually agreed upon by the contesting clubs.

Runner/Returning Runners, returning to their bases following foul balls and caught fly balls not touching the ground, may be put out in the same manner as the batter when running to first base.

Note: At the 1857 meeting of baseball clubs, the progressive Knickerbockers proposed that in order to retire the batter the ball must be caught on the fly and not on one bounce. It became a hotly debated topic during the next several conventions but, although it gained more support each year, the "fly rule" continued to be defeated when put to a vote. In 1860, however, the "fly game" was allowed if both contesting clubs agreed. This concession was not officially written into the rule book.

1861

Ball The ball must weigh 5½ to 5¾ ounces and measure 9½ to 9¾ inches in circumference.

Foul Ball If the ball, from the stroke of the bat, first touches the ground, the person of a player, or any object behind the range of home and first or home and third base, it shall be a foul ball.

Grounds A line connecting home and first base and home and third base shall be marked by chalk, or other suitable material, so as to be distinctly seen by the umpire.

Runner Players running the bases must make them in the following order: first, second, third, and home, and in returning must reverse this order.

Umpire The umpire, before leaving the grounds, must declare the winning club and record his decision in the scorebooks of the two clubs.

1862

There were no changes to the playing rules this year.

1863

Base on Balls When three "balls" have been called, the striker is entitled to first base, and each player occupying a base is entitled to one base without being put out.

Note: In actuality it took more than three balls to be awarded first base; see 1863, *Strike Zone.*

Pitcher/Delivery If the pitcher, at the time of delivery, has either foot off the ground or in advance of the front line of his position, it shall be declared a balk.

Pitcher/Position The pitcher's position shall be two lines, each twelve feet in length, with the front line forty-five feet and the back line forty-eight feet distant from home base.

Note: This introduces the pitcher's box, which replaces the single twelve-foot line.

Runner/Advancing Runners, after returning to their respective bases, may advance immediately after a fair fly ball has been settled in the hands of a fielder.

Note: This put into words what had been understood for the past four years; see 1859 rule.

Runner/Bases Each runner must touch each base in making the circuit.

Note: Runners were previously allowed to go around or near the bases.

Strike Zone Should the pitcher repeatedly fail to deliver "fair" balls, for the purpose of delaying the game or for any cause, the umpire, after warning him, shall call one "ball"; and if the pitcher persists, two and three balls.

1864

There were no changes to the playing rules this year.

1865

Batter/Caught Foul A batted ball in foul territory must be caught on the fly to be declared an out.

Note: The "fly game" has been adopted; fair balls caught on one bounce are no longer outs.

Interference/Spectator If a ball is stopped by any person not engaged in the game, no player may be put out unless the ball has first been settled in the hands of the pitcher.

Umpire The umpire is no longer responsible for keeping a record of the game in the scorebook.

Note: This amendment corrects a contradiction in earlier rule books in which one rule held the umpire responsible for keeping score and another rule instructed the umpire not to perform the duty.

1866

Bases First, second, and third bases shall be canvas bags, painted white and filled with some soft material.

Game/Legal Any game played in contravention of National Association rules shall be considered null and void and shall not be counted in the list of games won or lost; unless a game is delayed by rain beyond the appointed start. Any game may be put off by mutual consent of the two clubs. No game shall be commenced in the rain.

Game/Number Every game shall be decided by the best two games out of three, unless a single game is mutually agreed upon by the two clubs.

Pitcher/Position The back line of the pitcher's box is moved back one foot, increasing the length to 4 feet while remaining 12 feet in width.

1867

Batter/Position The batter, when in the act of striking, shall not step forward or backward but must stand on the three-foot line drawn through the center of home base.

Batter-Runner The batter shall be considered a baserunner as soon as he hits a fair ball.

Dead Ball Any pitch on which a "balk" or "ball" has been called is considered a dead ball, and the batter cannot be put out if he hits such a ball. Dead balls are returned to play when the ball has been settled in the hands of the pitcher while he stands within the pitcher's box.

Forfeited Game A club failing to produce their players within thirty minutes of the start of the game shall admit a defeat. The opposing club receives a win and is entitled to nine runs, and the game is counted in the list of games played. The game shall not be forfeited if the club fails to play because of the recent death of one of its members and there hasn't been sufficient time to notify the opposing club.

Pitcher/Delivery The pitcher must deliver the ball as near as possible over the center of home base and fairly for the striker.

The ball must be pitched, not jerked or thrown, to the bat. The ball shall be considered jerked if the pitcher's arm touches his person when the arm is swung forward to deliver the ball; and it is a throw if the arm is bent at the elbow at an angle from the body or horizontally from the shoulder when the arm is swung forward in delivery. A pitched ball is one delivered with arm straight and swinging perpendicularly and free from the body.

Note: The word *perpendicular* was used in the rule but the word *parallel* was intended. This error would be repeated for several years.

Pitcher/Position The pitcher's box is reduced in size to six feet in width and four feet in length.

Player/Eligible All players who play baseball for money, place, or emolument are regarded as professional players and shall not take part in any game. Any club giving compensation to a player or having knowledge that one of their players is playing for compensation shall be expelled from the National Association. Any club engaging in a game with an expelled club shall also forfeit membership.

Run Scored If there are two outs, no player can score a run if the batter is put out by a legal catch, forced between home and first base, or the ball is held by an adversary on first base before the batter reaches it.

Strikeout The batter is out if three balls are swung at and missed and the last one is caught either on the fly or on the first bound; provided the pitches are not those on which "balks" or "balls" have been called, or if the batter swings for the purpose of willfully striking out.

Strike Zone All pitches striking the ground in front of home base, over the head of the batter, or to the side opposite to that which the batter swings from, shall be considered unfair "balls."

Substitute An umpire, scorer, or player shall not be changed during a game except for reason of illness or injury and with the consent of both clubs; or when the umpire dismisses a transgressor for violation of the rules.

Umpire The umpire must declare when a player is out and in what position and manner.

Note: For example, if a batter is out on a caught fly to center, the umpire must yell, "Striker is out on the fly by the center fielder." This rule lasted only one year.

1868

Ball The ball must weigh from 5 to 5¼ ounces and measure from 9¼ to 9½ inches in circumference.

The challenging club must furnish a ball with the size, weight, and maker's name on it.

Bases The base-bag shall be considered the base and not the part to which it is or should be fastened.

Note: This rule was dropped in 1876.

The home plate and pitcher's points must be flat plates, painted white.

Bat The bat shall not exceed forty inches in length.

Batter/Position The batter, when about to strike the ball, must stand astride the three-foot line which is drawn through the center of home base and parallel with the front line of the pitcher's box.

The batter must not take any backward step when striking at the ball. The penalty is the calling of "foul strike," and when three such strikes are called, the batter is out. The batter is also out if he hits such a "strike" and the ball is caught, either fair or foul. No base may be run, but the baserunner is allowed to return to his base without being put out.

Catch If a fair ball is held by a fielder before touching the ground after it has rebounded from the hands or person of another player, it shall be considered a catch. A foul ball, if similarly held but touches the ground once, is also a catch.

Dead Ball No base may be run or player put out on a dead ball. If the batter hits a pitch on which a "balk" or "ball" has been called, no "strike" or foul ball shall be called, or a player put out; except bases may be taken on balks and calls of ball three.

Forfeited Game Any club failing to take their positions within five minutes after the umpire calls "play" shall forfeit the game.

Game/Rain No game shall be started when rain is falling and no game shall be continued when rain has fallen for five minutes.

Game/Scheduled When a challenge has been accepted for a series of games, each of the three games must be played at least within fifteen days of the previous game. The first game is played on the grounds of the challenger, the second game on the grounds of the challenged, and the third game, if necessary, on grounds mutually agreed upon. When a first-nine match is to be played, the clubs must play their recognized first nine, as far as practicable.

Note: This rule was dropped the next season.

Game/"Time" When the umpire calls "play," the game must begin at once. When the umpire calls "time," play shall be suspended until he calls "play" again. When the umpire "calls" a game, it shall end, but when he merely suspends play for any stated period, it may be resumed at the point at which it was suspended, provided it does not extend to the next day.

Obstruction If a runner is prevented from making a base by the intentional obstruction of an adversary, he shall be entitled to

that base and not be put out. Any obstruction that could readily have been avoided shall be considered intentional.

Pitcher/Delivery The pitcher is no longer required to keep both feet on the ground when delivering the ball.

Player Every player taking part in a regular match game, no matter how many innings have been played, shall be, in the meaning of these rules, considered a member of the club with which he plays.

Runner/Bases If a runner fails to touch each base, he shall be declared out unless he returns to the base before the ball is held on it.

Run Scored When there are two outs, no runner may score if the batter is put out.

Substitute No player may be substituted after the third inning except in cases of illness and injury.

Umpire/Decisions Only the captain of each club is allowed to appeal for the reversal of a decision by the umpire. No decision by the umpire shall be reversed by the testimony of any player; and no decision whatever shall be reversed except for a palpable infringement of the rules, and then only on an appeal by the captain.

Umpire/Scorer The umpire shall require that the game be recorded by a scorer for each of the contesting clubs.

Note: This rule was dropped from the rule book in 1874.

1869

Ball In the first and third games of a series the ball shall be furnished by the challenging club, and in the second game by the challenged club.

Base on Balls When the batter is awarded first base after three called balls, no other runner shall take a base unless he is obliged to vacate the base he occupies.

Bat The bat shall not exceed forty-two inches in length.

Batter/Fails to Bat Any player failing to take his turn at bat, unless for reason of illness or injury or by consent of the opposing captain, shall be declared out.

Note: In 1870, the rule was amended: Any player failing to bat "after the umpire has called for the striker . . . shall be declared out."

Catch It is not a catch if the ball is caught after touching any object [fence, building, tree] other than a player, even if the ball does not touch the ground.

Club/Eligible Any club willfully infringing any rule shall be suspended for a period not to exceed one year for the first offense, and expulsion from membership for the second offense, after trial by the judiciary committee.

Forfeited Game No game shall be forfeited because of the failure of the umpire to discharge his duties or for failing to declare the winning club of a match.

There must be at least a two-day notice for postponement of a game because of the death of a club member or the club is liable to forfeit.

Game/Drawn If the score is tied at the end of nine innings, the captains may mutually agree to consider the game a draw. In case of no such agreement, the club refusing to continue play shall forfeit the ball.

Game/Winner If the game cannot be continued, it shall be decided by the score of the last equal innings and the club having the greater number of runs is the winner; unless one club has completed their inning and the other club has exceeded their opponent's score in their uncompleted inning, in which case the club with the higher score is the winner. But no game shall be

considered as played unless five innings on each side have been completed.

Pitcher/Delivery When about to deliver the ball or at the actual time of delivery, the pitcher cannot have either foot outside the pitcher's box.

Pitcher/Position The pitcher's box is enlarged to a six-foot square.

Player/Eligible Players must not have been members of any other National Association club (college clubs excepted) for sixty days immediately prior to the game.

All players who play baseball for money or who at any time receive compensation for their services as players shall be considered professional players; and all others shall be regarded as amateur players.

Note: This rule officially recognized two distinct classes of players—professional and amateur—and permitted the participation of professional players.

Runner/Forced No baserunner shall be forced to vacate a base unless as provided in these rules.

Note: This amendment prevented a runner, not forced to vacate his own base, from forcing another to vacate his base. For example, if a runner attempts to steal third base, changes his mind before reaching third, and returns to second base to find the runner from first now standing on the bag, the original runner still has the right to the base.

Run Scored When there are two outs, no runner may score a run if the batter or player running the bases is put out before touching first base.

Strike Zone Balls and strikes may not be called unless there has first been issued a warning and they may not be called until the pitch has crossed the plate. All "balls" *must* be called by the umpire after the pitcher has been warned of the penalty. One warning for each batter shall suffice.

Substitute/Runner No player shall be allowed to have a substitute run the bases for him except in cases of illness or injury.

1870

Ball The challenged club must supply the means of ascertaining the size and weight of the ball furnished by the other club.

Note: This rule was dropped in 1871 and replaced with the previous rule requiring the challenging club to furnish a ball on which its size, weight, and the name of the manufacturer is stamped.

Base on Balls Any player awarded a base on balls is allowed to advance, at his own risk, beyond the base awarded him.

Note: This rule was inexplicably left out of the 1871 rule book but was back in 1872.

Dead Ball Called "balls" not hit by the batter are no longer dead balls, and any base can be run or player put out on such pitches.

Fair Ball If the ball, from the stroke of the bat, first touches the ground, the person of a player or any other object, either upon or in front of the foul lines, it shall be declared a fair ball.

Forfeited Game All games in which any rule is infringed shall be considered forfeited games and shall be recorded as games won by a score of 9 to 0 against the club infringing the rules.

No forfeit shall be declared if a club fails to play a game because of the recent death of one of its members.

Note: The requirement of two days notice has been dropped.

Grounds The lines of the batter's and pitcher's positions must be marked with chalk or other suitable material so as to be distinctly seen by the umpire.

Runner/Forced The moment the player running to first base is out, other baserunners previously forced to vacate their bases

shall cease to be forced and may return to their bases.

Note: In 1872 the rule was amended and clarified that runners could still be put out in returning to their base.

Strike Zone   The umpire no longer issues a warning before calling a pitch, but "balls" and "strikes" may not be called on the first pitch delivered.

All pitches which are not within the fair reach of the striker. such as pitches over the striker's head, on the ground in front of home base, to the side opposite to that the batsman strikes from, or which hit the striker while he is standing in his proper position, are considered unfair "balls" and must be called whenever delivered (except for the first pitch).

Umpire/Decisions   No decision given by the umpire shall be reversed by the testimony of any player, and the umpire shall not be guided in his decisions by any such testimony.

1871

The rule book is adopted by the National Association of Professional Base-Ball Players.

Ball   The ball must weigh from 5 to 5¼ ounces and must measure exactly 9¼ inches in circumference.

Batter/Position   The batter must stand at least one foot from home base and astride the three-foot line drawn through the center of home base. When striking at the ball, he may take a forward step but must keep one foot behind the line.

Dead Ball   It is a dead ball whenever a pitch touches the umpire, or is accidentally stopped by him.

Game/Legal   Under no circumstances shall a game be considered played unless five innings have been completed. Should darkness or rain prevent the continuing of the game before the end of the fifth inning, the umpire shall declare "no game."

Note: This made clearer what had long been understood by most.

Grounds   No fence may be erected within ninety feet of home base, unless the fence marks the boundary line of the field. Baserunners are entitled to one base whenever the ball passes the catcher and touches a fence located closer than ninety feet behind home base.

Pitcher/Delivery   The penalty for pitches thrown, jerked, or delivered other than with a straight arm swinging perpendicular [parallel] to the body shall be the calling of a "ball." If, after a warning by the umpire, three men are awarded first base in one inning on such called balls, the game shall be declared a forfeit.

Player/Eligible   Players who have been constitutionally expelled from another club for dishonorable conduct shall not be permitted to play in any game played during the year they were expelled.

Player/Position   The fielders may take any position in the field their captain may choose to assign them.

Note: This rule made it clear that the captains could position their players anywhere in the field they wished, including foul territory. The rule, with an obvious omission, was rectified in 1874 with the added phrase, "with the exception of the pitcher, who must occupy his appointed position."

Runner/Advancing   Baserunners, on caught fly balls, may advance after they return to their original base after the ball has been settled momentarily in the hands of the pitcher. Baserunners shall not be entitled to any base touched after a fair fly ball has been hit and prior to the catch being made.

Runner/Fielder   When a fielder, holding the ball, tags a runner who is off a base but the ball is knocked out of his hand by the runner, the runner is still out.

Runner/Overrunning First   A baserunner touching and overrunning first base shall be allowed to return at once to the base

without being put out, provided he does not attempt to make second base.

Strike Zone   The batter is allowed to call for either a "high" or "low" pitch, and the pitcher must deliver the ball as required. A "high" ball is one pitched between the waist and the shoulder of the batter; a "low" ball is one pitched between the knee and the waist. Should the batter refuse to swing at balls pitched over the home base and within the specified reach of the bat, it shall be a called "strike." All pitches over the home base that are between the batter's knee and shoulder are considered "fair" pitches.

No strike shall be called when the pitch is struck at for the purpose of willfully striking out.

Note: This sentence was deleted from the rules in 1874.

No strike shall be called on the first pitch delivered unless the batter swings at the pitch.

Note: This one was dropped in 1875.

Substitute/Runner   No player shall be allowed to have a substitute run the bases for him, except for illness or injury, unless by special consent of the opposing captain.

1872

Ball   The ball must weigh from 5 to 5¼ ounces and measure from 9 to 9¼ inches in circumference.

Note: These are the dimensions of today's ball.

The ball shall contain one ounce of vulcanized rubber in mold form.

If the ball becomes ripped, out of shape, or, in the umpire's opinion, unfit for play, the umpire shall call for a new ball at the end of a complete inning.

Bases   Home base shall be made of white marble or stone and fixed in the ground so as to be even with the surface.

Bat   A batter shall be privileged to use his own private bat exclusively. No player of the opposing club shall have any claim to the use of the bat except by consent of the owner.

Note: This rule was dropped in 1874.

Batter/Illegal Act   The batter is out if he willfully "balks" [interferes with] the catcher.

Batter/Position   When striking at the ball, the batter is allowed to make a backward step as well as a forward step as long as he keeps one foot on either side of the line.

Coach   The umpire shall require members of the side at bat to remain a reasonable distance (at least fifteen feet) from the foul lines while directing the movements of baserunners to prevent the interference of fielders. If a club persists in infringing this rule, the umpire shall declare a forfeit.

Dead Balls   Foul balls are dead and are not in play until the ball has been settled in the hands of the pitcher, no matter in what part of the field the pitcher may happen to be.

Forfeited Game   It is not a forfeit if a club fails to play because of the death of a club member or because of an unavoidable accident.

Note: This rule was dropped in 1876.

Game/Drawn   Clubs are no longer allowed to mutually agree to call a game a draw. Drawn games may only be declared if, after five or more innings, the game is prevented from being continued because of darkness, rain, or other cause, and the score is equal on the even innings played.

Game/Rain   Should rain begin to fall during a game, the umpire must promptly note the time and should the rain continue to fall for five minutes, the umpire shall suspend play and the game shall not continue until, in the umpire's opinion, the ground is fit for fair fielding.

Interference/Offensive   Any player who designedly [*willfully* and *intentionally* are used in subsequent years] lets the ball hit

him or kicks the ball while at bat or running the bases, thus preventing an opponent from holding or fielding the ball, shall be declared out. Any baserunner who, in any way, prevents a fielder from catching a batted fly ball, fair or foul, shall be called out.

Pitcher/Delivery   The pitcher must deliver the ball while within the lines of his position and must remain within them until the ball has left his hand. He shall not make any motion to deliver the ball while outside the box.

Whenever the pitcher delivers the pitch with an overhand or roundarm throw, the umpire shall call a "foul balk." Should the pitcher persist in such action, the umpire, after warning him of the penalty, shall declare the game forfeited. Baserunners are awarded one base on "foul balks" as on any other balk.

Note: This rule legalized the jerk, wrist snap, and bent-elbow deliveries and, thus, the curveball. It was now legal for the pitcher to snap his wrist as long as he kept his hand, while in the forward motion, below the hip.

Pitcher/Position   Iron plates must be placed at each end of the front line of the pitcher's box.

Player/Eligible   Any player who has willfully broken a written engagement to a club shall not be eligible to play in any game during the year the engagement was made. No engagement shall be considered binding unless made in writing and signed by at least two witnesses. This rule shall be binding unless rescinded by the judiciary committee.

Runner/Overrunning First   A runner may overrun first base without being put out if, after touching first, he runs straight down the line or to the right of the bag. Should he turn to the left or attempt to make second base, he shall be at risk of being put out.

Strike Zone   All pitches that come within one foot of the batter shall be called "balls."

All pitches that are sent in over home base at the height called for by the batter and are not delivered with an overhand throw or round-arm delivery as in cricket are "fair" pitches. Should the batter fail to call either a "high" or "low" pitch, no "ball" shall be called for "fair" pitches.

A "low" ball is a pitch between the waist of the batter and one foot from the ground.

Substitute/Runner   No player shall be allowed a substitute in running the bases, except for illness or injury, unless by special consent of the opposing captain; and in such case the captain shall select the player to run as substitute.

Umpire/Duties   The umpire is required to call all foul balls, while the ball is still in the air, as soon as he sees the ball is falling in foul territory.

Umpire/Replacing   The umpire shall not be changed during the game, unless with the consent of both captains, except for illness or injury or for violation of the rules.

1873

Interference/Spectator   If a ball is stopped in any way by a person not engaged in the game, no player can be put out until the ball has been first settled in the hands of the pitcher while he stands within the lines of his position.

Fielder/Illegal Act   If a fielder stops the ball with his hat or cap, no player can be put out and each baserunner shall be entitled to one base.

1874

Ball   The yarn used in the composition of the ball must be woolen.

The visiting club furnishes the ball for a series of games; the home team when only a single game is played.

Base   Home base must have one corner facing the pitcher's position.

Base on Balls   Note: In 1874 there were two classifications of base on balls. See explanation under *Strike Zone*.

Bat   The bat must be made wholly of wood.

Note: This made it clear that the bat must be made entirely of wood. Any metal or other material on it renders it illegal.

Batter/Fails to Bat   Any batter refusing to bat within three minutes after the umpire has called for him shall be declared out.

Batter/Position   The batter's position shall be a space on either side of home base, six feet long by three feet wide, which extends three feet in front and three feet behind the line drawn through the center of home base, and its nearest line one foot from home base. Batters must stand within this position when in the act of striking the ball.

Note: This introduces the batter's box.

Batter/Runner   When the batsman has fairly struck a fair ball, he shall vacate his position and is considered a baserunner until he is put out or scores his run.

Batting Order   The batsmen must take their positions in the order in which they are named on the scorebook.

Any batsman failing to take his position in the order of striking, unless by reason of illness or injury or by consent of the opposing captain, shall be declared out, unless the error is discovered before a fair ball has been hit or the batter is put out.

Catch   Should the umpire be unable to see whether a catch has been fairly made, he shall be privileged to appeal to the bystanders and render his decision according to the fairest testimony at command.

Coach/Offensive Team   The umpire shall require members of the batting side, who are not at bat or running the bases, to keep at a distance of at least fifty feet from the foul lines, or farther if the umpire desires. The captain and one assistant only are permitted to approach the foul lines, and not nearer than fifteen feet, to coach baserunners. If a club persists in infringing this rule, the umpire shall declare a forfeit.

Dead Ball   All pitches that touch the striker's bat without being swung at, or touch the batter while he is standing in his box, or which hit the umpire, shall be considered dead balls. No base shall be run or run scored on such balls. Pitches that strike the umpire are not dead balls unless the ball passes the catcher.

Should the batter swing at or hit any pitch on which a "ball" has been called, the umpire shall disregard his call and render his decision on the swing or hit made. It is not a dead ball.

Fielder/Illegal Act   Should any fielder stop the ball with his hat, cap, or any other part of his dress, the umpire shall call "dead ball" and the ball shall not be in play again until the umpire calls "ball in play." Baserunners are entitled to the base they were running for.

Forfeited Game   Any game in which the umpire declares any section of these rules to have been willfully violated, he shall at once declare the game a forfeit.

Gambling   Any player who shall, in any way, be interested in any bet or wager on the game in which he takes part, either as umpire, player, or scorer, or who purchases or has purchased for him any "pool" or chance, sold or given away, on the game in which he takes part, he shall be dishonorably expelled from both his club and the association [league in 1876]. Umpires, players, and scorers who have wagers on any other association [league] game shall be suspended for the season.

Ground Rules   Before calling "play," the umpire shall ask the home field captain whether there are any special ground rules and shall take note of such rules and see that they are enforced,

provided they do not conflict with any regular rules of the game. Should the umpire not be notified of any ground rules, the rules shall not be enforced.

Note: This last sentence was dropped from the 1876 rule book.

Grounds The foul ball lines shall be unlimited in length and shall run from the center of home base through the center of first and third bases to the foul ball posts, which shall be located at the boundary of the field and within the range of home and first base, and home and third base. Said lines shall be marked from base to base with chalk, or some other white substance, so as to be plainly seen by the umpire.

Interference/Spectator Should the ball be willfully stopped by any outside person not engaged in the game, the ball shall be dead until settled in the hands of the pitcher while standing in his box. Baserunners at the time shall be entitled to the base they were running for.

Pitcher/Delivery The ball must be delivered with the arm swinging nearly perpendicular [parallel] to the side of the body.

Should the pitcher deliver the ball by an overhand throw, outward swing of the arm, roundarm bowling, or any other swing other than nearly perpendicular to the body, it shall be a "foul balk." When a foul balk is called, the umpire shall warn the pitcher of the penalty and should three foul balks be called in one inning, the umpire shall declare a forfeit.

If the pitcher makes any motion to deliver the ball and fails to do so—except if the ball is accidentally dropped—the umpire shall call a balk.

Pitcher/Position Each corner of the pitcher's box must be marked by a flat six-inch square iron plate.

Player/Eligible Players must not have been members of any other club in the association for sixty days prior to the date of the game, unless their previous club has disbanded and their contract with such club has been canceled.

The rules of 1874 also include other rules concerning contracts including disciplinary actions for players who violate them.

Runner A player running the bases shall be considered holding a base—entitled to occupy it—until he has regularly touched the next base in order.

Note: This new rule is inaccurate because it neglects to mention the important exception of runners forced off their base. This correction would not be made until 1880.

Runner/Foul Ball In the case of a foul ball, the baserunner returning to touch the base must remain on it until the ball is held by the pitcher, no matter in what part of the field the pitcher happens to be.

Runner/Overrunning First The batter may overrun first base without risk of being put out provided he makes no attempt to run to second base and returns at once to first base.

Run Scored No run shall score unless the home base is touched before three players have been put out; and if the third player is put out before reaching first base, the run shall not be scored.

Spectators No person not engaged in the game shall be permitted to occupy any position within the lines of the field, or in any way interrupt the umpire during the game.

Strike Zone There are now two classifications of unfair pitches: "balls" and "wide balls."

"Balls" are pitches not at the height called for by the batter ("high" or "low") or are not exactly over home base. "Wide balls" are pitches that are out of the reach of the striker's bat, such as those that hit the ground or the batter, or are over the batter's head. The umpire shall call every third "ball." When three "balls" [actually nine pitches] have been called, the batter is awarded first base. With the exception of the first pitch, all

"wides" are called in the order of their delivery. When three "wides" have been called, the batter is awarded first base.

Note: When you consider that one type of base on balls required three (and sometimes four) pitches, while another required nine pitches—not to mention calling strikes—it's no wonder they started paying the unfortunate umpire of 1874. "Wide balls" as a special classification of unfair pitches lasted only one year and was dropped from the rule book in 1875.

Substitute No player not in position on the field or ready to bat after the close of the third inning and before the start of the fourth, shall be substituted for another player, except in running the bases.

Substitute/Runner A player serving as substitute for another in running the bases must cross the batter's position in front of home base, and must not start to run until the batter strikes at the ball.

Note: This clarified the position in which the substitute runner must stand. In previous years, substitute runners often ran behind the batter and interfered with the catcher.

Umpire/Decisions The umpire shall render no decision except when appealed to by a player, unless expressly required to do so by the rules of the game, as in calling "balls," etc.

No player shall be permitted to converse with the umpire during the game, except to make a legal appeal for his decision in giving a player out.

No decision by the umpire on any point of play in baserunning shall be reversed upon the testimony of any player. But if it is shown by the two captains that the umpire has misinterpreted the rules or has given an erroneous decision, the umpire shall be allowed to reverse his decision.

Umpire/Payment The umpire may receive compensation for his services as the clubs deem advisable, provided he receives the same amount from both clubs.

Note: This was dropped from the rule book in 1876.

Umpire/Replacing The umpire shall not be changed during the game, except for illness or injury, or by consent of both captains if the umpire has willfully violated the written rules of the game.

Should the umpire fail to enforce any section of the rules or should he interpret the rules other than the express letter of the rule, he shall cease to be eligible to act in the position and shall at once be dismissed.

Note: This last paragraph was dropped from the 1876 rule book.

1875

Ball When the ball becomes out of shape, cut or ripped to expose the yarn, or in any way injured to be unfit for fair use, the umpire, at the close of an even inning at the request of either captain, shall call for a new ball.

Base The corner of home base facing the pitcher's position must touch the intersection of the foul lines.

Note: This places home base entirely in foul territory.

Base on Balls See *Strike Zone*.

Batter/Position The batsman's position is six feet long by three feet wide, extending two feet in front of and four feet behind the center of home base. Its nearest line is one foot from home base.

Note: With the placement of home base in foul territory, the batter's box has also been moved back.

Should the batter step outside the batter's box while striking the ball, the umpire shall call "foul strike," and two such foul strikes shall put the batter out. All baserunners are allowed to return to their original base.

Game/Rain After rain has fallen for five minutes, the umpire shall suspend play at the request of either captain.

Strike Zone All pitches not over home base or at the height called for by the batter are considered unfair "balls." Every third consecutive "ball" must be called by the umpire. When three "balls" [nine pitches] have been called, the batter is awarded first base.

Note: The term *wide balls* has been dropped from the rule book. In 1876, the word *consecutive* was dropped.

Umpire The umpire shall not enter the infield while the ball is in play.

1876

The National League is founded and adopts the rule book.

Ball In all regular match games, the balls are furnished by the home club. Should any ball used in a game prove, on examination by the umpire, to be illegal in size, weight, or materials, balls of the same manufacture shall not be used thereafter in regular match games.

The rubber used in the composition of the ball must weigh not more than one ounce.

Should the ball be lost during a game, the umpire, at the expiration of five minutes, shall call for a new ball.

Batter/Position If the batter steps outside the batter's box when he strikes at the ball, the umpire shall call "foul balk and out" and baserunners shall return to their original base.

Fielder/Illegal Act Baserunners are entitled to two bases for any fair hit ball stopped or caught by a fielder with his hat, cap, or any part of his dress. The ball is dead.

Foul Ball See *Runner/Advancing.*

Game/Rain If a game cannot be concluded, it shall be decided by the score of the last equal innings played, unless one club has completed an inning and the other club has equalled or exceeded their opponent's score in an incomplete inning, in which case the game shall be decided by the total score.

Obstruction If a baserunner is prevented from making a base by the obstruction of an adversary, he shall be entitled to that base and shall not be put out.

Pitcher/Delivery It shall be a balk if the pitcher unnecessarily delays the game by not delivering the ball.

Player/Eligible Many rules and regulations concerning eligibility of players, contracts, and disciplinary actions are removed from the rule book.

Player/Illegal Act No manager, captain, or player shall address the audience except in case of necessary explanation. Any manager, captain, or player who uses abusive, threatening, or improper language to the audience shall be punished by suspension from play for twenty days and forfeiture of his salary for such period.

Rules No section of these rules shall be construed as conflicting with or affecting any article of the league's constitution.

Runner/Advancing Following caught fly balls, runners may advance after returning to their original base. On all other foul balls, including foul balls caught on one bounce, runners may not advance but may return to their original base without being put out.

Run Scored If the third out is forced out or is put out before reaching first base, no run shall be scored.

Strikeout Should the batter, with two strikes, not swing at the next "good ball," the umpire shall not call a "strike" but warn him by calling "good ball." But should the batter swing and miss or fail to swing at the next good ball, "three strikes" must be called and the batter must run to first as in the case of hitting a fair ball.

Strike Zone The batsman, on taking his position, must call for a "high," "low," or "fair" pitch, and the umpire shall notify the pitcher to deliver the ball as required; such call cannot be changed after the first pitch is delivered.

Substitute No player taking part in the game shall be replaced by another after the start of the fourth inning, except in running the bases.

Umpire No player shall be permitted to converse with the umpire during the game, except the two captains and then only to appeal a misinterpretation of the rules or an erroneous decision.

1877

Ball No ball is to be used except those furnished by the secretary of the league.

Bases First, second, and third bases must cover a space equal to 15 inches square.

Home base is to be placed entirely into fair territory with two of its sides forming part of the foul lines.

Batter/Fails to Bat Any batsman who fails to take his position at bat within one minute after the umpire has called for him shall be out.

Batter/Position The batter's box is six feet long by three feet wide with the line of home base running through its center.

Note: This arrangement permitted a batter to stand three feet in front of or three feet behind home base.

Coach See *Grounds.*

Foul/Fair Balls A batted ball striking in foul territory and then in fair is fair; a batted ball striking fair and then foul is foul.

Game The home club shall first take the bat.

Game/Rain Should rain continue to fall for 10 minutes (following suspension of play) the game shall terminate.

Grounds Lines parallel to the foul lines and 15 feet back are to be drawn to delineate a boundary for the captain and one assistant to coach baserunners. Lines parallel to the foul lines and 50 feet back are to be drawn to delineate a boundary for players on the batting side.

Note: In the rules of 1880, these lines are referred to as the "Captain's Lines" and the "Players' Lines" respectively.

Interference/Offensive When a fielder occupies the basepath in the act of fielding a ball, the baserunner shall run out of the path and behind the fielder to avoid interference.

A baserunner struck by a batted ball is out.

A baserunner, from home to first base, shall not run inside the foul line or more than three feet outside of it, or he shall be declared out.

Player/Expulsion Any player who shall, in any way, be interested in any bet or wager on any league game or who shall purchase or have purchased for him any "pool" or chance, sold or given away, shall be expelled.

The club is entitled to the best services of the player, and players who become indifferent or careless in play or who become unable to render satisfactory service to the club from any cause may have their salaries suspended or their contracts canceled.

Players conspiring against the interest of their clubs or who "manifest a disposition" to obstruct club management may be expelled.

Note: These three rules were removed from the rule book in 1878.

Runner/Fielder A baserunner who knocks the ball out of the hand of a fielder while in the act of running to a base is no longer out.

Strike Zone A "low" pitch is one thrown belt high or below the

belt and above the knee. A "high" pitch is one above the belt to the shoulder.

A ball pitched and called "dead" by reason of having struck the umpire shall be counted as one of nine called balls entitling the batter to a base if it is also an "unfair" ball.

Substitute   No substitution is to be made after the start of the second inning except in cases of illness or injury.

1878

Batting Order   The batsmen must take their positions in the order in which they are directed by their captain, and after each player has had one time at bat, the order established shall not be changed during the game.

Batter/Position   The batter must actually hit the ball while outside the batter's box to commit a "foul strike" and be called out.

Game   The club that bats first shall be determined by the two captains.

Grounds   The foul lines shall be continued to the limits of the field beyond and back of home base. This triangular area shall be for the exclusive use of the catcher, umpire, and batsman; and no offensive player (except the batsman) shall occupy it.

Note: In the rules of 1880, these lines are referred to as the "Catcher's Lines."

Pitcher/Delivery   The pitcher's hand must pass below the waist in delivering the ball.

Substitute/Runner   No player shall be allowed a substitute in running the bases except for illness or injury incurred in the game then being played, and then such substitute shall take the player's place only after the latter has reached first base.

1879

Ball   The "Spalding League Ball" is adopted as the official ball, which is indicated in the footnotes of some rule books.

Base on Balls   Note: The amount of unfair pitches is still the same for the awarding of a base on balls but, to everyone's delight, the terminology is finally changed from "every third ball must be called" to "every ball must be called." The result is the same, nine "balls" and the batter is awarded first base.

Batter/Caught Foul   A batted ball in foul territory must be caught on the fly to be declared an out.

Note: This rule was dropped in 1880 but was again added in 1883.

Batting Order   After the first inning, the first striker in each inning shall be the batsman whose name follows that of the last man who has completed his turn (time) at bat in the preceding inning.

Pitcher/Delivery   The pitcher, when taking his position to deliver the ball, must face the batter.

Pitcher/Illegal Act   If a pitcher delivers the ball to intentionally strike the batter, in the judgment of the umpire, the umpire shall fine the pitcher not less than $10 nor more than $50.

Pitcher/Position   The pitcher's box is now four feet wide and six feet long.

Strikeout   The batter is out after three strikes if the ball is caught before touching the ground.

1880

Appeal/Runner   A baserunner who fails to touch intervening bases when returning to a base shall not be declared out unless the opposing captain appeals to the umpire before the pitcher delivers the ball to the batter.

Base on Balls   A base on balls is awarded to the batter when eight balls have been called by the umpire.

Grounds   The ground must be an enclosed field sufficient in size to enable each player to play in his position as required by the rules.

Interference/Offensive   No run can be scored if a baserunner is declared out for being hit with a fair hit batted ball.

Runner/Returning   The baserunner is out if he fails to return to the base he occupied after a foul fly has been caught and the runner is touched with the ball or the ball is returned to the base the runner occupied before he returns.

Strikeout   The batter becomes a runner immediately when three strikes have been called by the umpire.

Umpire   No player except the captain or his assistant shall address the umpire concerning any point of play. Violators are subject to a fine.

1881

Base on Balls   A batter is awarded first base after seven balls are called by the umpire.

Forfeited Game   Every club shall furnish sufficient police force upon its own grounds to preserve order. In the event of a crowd entering the field during the progress of a game, and interfering with play in any manner, the visiting club may refuse to play further until the field is cleared; if the ground is not cleared within 15 minutes, the visiting club is entitled to a forfeit by a score of 9–0, regardless of the number of innings played.

Pitcher/Position   The pitcher's box is to be fifty feet from the center of home base.

Security   See *Forfeited Game*.

Spectators   No person shall be allowed upon any part of the field during the progress of the game, in addition to the nine players on each side and the umpire, except such officers of the law who are present in uniform to preserve the peace.

Strikeout   The batter, on a called third strike, is no longer given a warning of "good ball" by the umpire. (See 1876 *Strikeout*)

Substitute   A substitute is not permitted unless a player is disabled by injury or illness in the game being played.

Substitute/Runner   A player shall not have a substitute run the bases for him.

Umpire/Decisions   The umpire shall *not* reverse his decision on any point of play upon the testimony of any player or bystander.

1882

The American Association begins its first season and makes several modifications to the rule book to meet its own needs and wants. Among the rules not included in the AA rule book are the prohibition of liquor being sold on club grounds, and the fining of pitchers who, in the umpire's judgment, purposely hit batters with pitched balls. Other changes and amendments particular to the AA are noted below.

Ball   Should the ball become so injured as to be unfit for fair use in the opinion of the umpire, on being appealed to by either captain, a new ball shall be called for by the umpire at the end of an even inning.

Note: The AA's rule doesn't require an appeal by a captain.

Ball (American Association)   The ball must be stamped "American Association." Each ball shall be enclosed in a paper box and sealed by the manufacturer. The seal shall not be broken except by the umpire in the presence of the two captains after "play" has been called.

Note: The AA selected the Mahn Sporting Company's ball as its official ball.

Batter   The two players following the batsman, in the order in which they are named on the scorebook, must be ready with bat in hand to promptly take their position as batsmen.

Note: This rule was not adopted by the AA.

Game/"Time"   The umpire shall suspend play for an accident to himself or a player; but in case of an accident to a fielder, time shall not be called until the ball is returned and held by the pitcher standing in his position.

Note: The AA rule book does not include this important exception.

Grounds/Bench   The players' bench must be furnished by the home club and placed on a portion of the ground outside the players' lines. It must be twelve feet in length and fastened to the ground. Bat racks sufficient in size to hold twenty bats are to be adjacent to the players' bench.

Note: This is not in the AA rule book.

Grounds/Three-Foot Line   The three-foot line area, in which the batter-runner must run to avoid interference, must be marked on the field.

Note: The rules of the AA do not require the actual markings.

Interference/Offensive   A baserunner is out if he obstructs a fielder attempting to field a batted ball; provided that if two or more fielders attempt to field the ball and the runner comes in contact with one of them, the umpire shall determine which fielder is entitled to the benefit of the rule and shall not call the runner out for coming in contact with the other fielder.

Note: This provision isn't included in the AA rules.

The batter is out if he plainly attempts to hinder the catcher from catching the ball, without effort to make a fair hit.

Note: Not outlined in the AA rules.

Interference/Spectator   A "blocked ball" is a batted or thrown ball that is stopped or handled by any person not engaged in the game. Whenever a block is called, baserunners may run the bases without being put out until the ball is returned to and held by the pitcher standing in his position. Exception: When the person not engaged in the game retains possession of the ball or throws or kicks it beyond reach of fielders, the umpire should call time and require baserunners to stop at the last base touched by them.

Note: The AA does not use the term *blocked ball* and uses the following rule for spectator interference: "If a batted or thrown ball is stopped by any person not engaged in the game, the ball shall not be considered in play until it is held by the pitcher standing in his position. The baserunner shall be entitled to take one base."

Spectators   Spectators hissing or hooting at the umpire are to be promptly ejected from the grounds.

1883

Ball   In calling for a new ball, replacing one unfit for fair play, the umpire may call for one "at once" and does not have to wait until the end of the inning.

Note: The AA here still requires the umpire to wait until the close of an inning before calling for a new ball.

Ball (American Association)   The ball must be manufactured by A. J. Reach, according to the specifications, and stamped "American Association."

Note: The Mahn ball was found unsatisfactory.

Batter/Caught Foul   A batted ball in foul territory must be caught on the fly to be declared an out.

Note: Foul balls caught on one bounce are no longer outs. The AA refuses to go along with the rule and continues with the one-bound foul flyout.

Batting Order   The batter is out if he fails to take his position at bat in the order of batting, unless the error is discovered and the

proper batsman takes his position before a fair hit has been made. In such case, the "balls" and "strikes" called will be counted in the time at bat of the proper batsman.

Note: This last sentence is not included in the AA rule book.

Pitcher/Delivery   A fair ball is a ball delivered by the pitcher, while wholly within the lines of his position, and while facing the batsman and his hand, in delivering the ball, must not pass above the line of his shoulder.

When the umpire has called two "foul balks," the batter and all baserunners are awarded one base. Three foul balks in one inning no longer constitutes a forfeited game.

Note: The AA discards the term "foul balk."

Runner/Overrunning First   In the American Association a runner touching and overrunning first base is at risk of being put out while off the base if he turns to the left from the foul line while returning to the bag.

Runner/Returning   A baserunner who fails to return to his base at a run following a foul ball is liable to be put out by being touched by the ball while off his base.

Substitute/Runner   The American Association allows a substitute to run the bases for a player if the player is injured in the game being played and the opposing club consents to the use of a substitute runner.

Umpire   Umpires are to be salaried employees.

1884

In 1884 the Union Association became operational and adopted virtually the same rule book used by the American Association. The few exceptions include the additional rule requiring foul balls to be caught on the fly to record an out, and the Wright & Ditson ball as the league's official ball. The Union Association folded after one season.

Base on Balls   The batter is awarded a base on balls after six balls have been called by the umpire. Note: The AA and UA retain the seven-ball base on balls.

Bat Boy/Girl   The American Association allows "a person to take charge of the bats of each club" to be on the playing field.

Note: Not in the UA rule book.

Fair/Foul Balls   When a batted ball passes outside the grounds, the umpire shall declare it fair should it disappear within, or foul should it disappear outside of the range of the foul lines.

Note: This is not found in the AA and UA rule books.

Hit by Pitch   The American Association adds the following rule: If a batsman be solidly hit by a ball from the pitcher when he evidently cannot avoid the same, he shall be given his base by the umpire.

Note: The AA is the first league to award a batter first base for being hit with a pitch; not in the UA rule book.

Pitcher/Delivery   All restrictions on the delivery of the ball are lifted except that the pitcher must be entirely within the lines of his position and must face the batter.

Note: The overhanded delivery was thus permitted for the first time. The AA and UA kept the shoulder-high delivery.

1885

Bases   The home base may be made of white rubber or stone.

Note: In the AA, home base must be made of white rubber only.

Bat   The handle of the bat may be wound with twine not to exceed 18 inches from the end.

Note: No such rule in the AA rule book.

The bat must be round except that a portion of the surface on one side may be flat.

Note: The AA nixed this one also.

Batter/Caught Foul In a special midseason meeting held on June 7, 1885, the American Association adopts the rule that a foul ball must be caught on the fly to be declared an out.

Batter/Position The batter's box is now six feet long by four feet wide with its nearest line six inches from home base.

Note: The AA keeps the six by three foot box that is one foot from the plate.

Game The American Association gives the option of which club bats first to the home team captain.

Grounds/Fence A fair batted ball that goes over the fence at a distance less than 210 feet from home base shall entitle the batsman to two bases. A distinctive line shall be marked on the fence at this point.

Note: This is not in the AA rule book.

Grounds/Three-Foot Line The American Association requires the marking of the three-foot area in which the batsman must run to avoid interference.

Home Run/Double See *Grounds/Fence.*

Pitcher/Delivery The pitcher must have both feet touching the ground while making any one of the series of motions he is accustomed to make in the delivery of the ball. A violation of this rule shall be a "foul balk" and two foul balks shall entitle the batter and each runner to one base.

Note: At a special National League meeting held on June 7, 1885, this rule was dropped. The term "foul balk" was also dropped from the rules. However, in a special meeting of their own, also held on June 7, the AA adopted the rule allowing the overhand delivery, conforming with the NL rule.

A balk is made whenever the pitcher, when about to deliver the ball to the bat while standing in his position, makes any one of the series of actions he habitually makes in delivery, and he fails to deliver the ball to the bat.

Uniforms (American Association) Every club shall be required to adopt a neat and attractive uniform for its players, and shall at all times be required to present the same upon the field in a clean and attractive condition.

1886

Ball Should the ball be knocked outside of the enclosure or lost during the game, the umpire shall call at once for another ball.

Bat/Handle A granulated substance may be applied to the bat handle not to exceed 18 inches from the end.

Batter/Position The batter's box is returned to the six foot long by three foot wide area, one foot from home base.

Base on Balls The NL increases the number to seven balls for the awarding of a base on balls. The AA drops the number to six balls.

Pitcher/Delivery The pitcher is no longer required to keep both feet on the ground while delivering the ball.

Note: The term "foul balk" is dropped from the rules.

Pitcher/Position The pitcher's lines must be straight lines forming a box seven feet long by four feet wide.

1887

The National League and the American Association agree to be governed by the same rule book after several rules are rewritten.

Ball In all games, the ball or balls played with shall be furnished by the home club, and the last ball in play becomes the property of the winning club. Each ball to be used in championship games shall be examined, measured, and weighed by the Secretary of the Association, enclosed in a paper box, and sealed with the seal of the Secretary, which seal shall not be broken except by the umpire in the presence of the captains of the two

contesting nines after play has been called.

Note: The Spalding and Reach balls respectively remain the official balls of the National League and the American Association.

For each championship game, two balls shall be furnished by the home club to the umpire for use. When the ball in play is batted over the fence or stands, onto foul ground out of sight of the players, the other ball shall be immediately put into play by the umpire. As often as one of the two in use shall be lost, a new one must be substituted, so that the umpire may at all times, after the game begins, have two for use. The moment the umpire delivers the alternate ball to the catcher or pitcher, it comes into play, and shall not be exchanged until it, in turn, passes out of sight onto foul ground.

Base on Balls The batter is entitled to one base when five balls have been called by the umpire.

Bases Home base must be made of whitened rubber.

Second base shall be upon its corner of the infield, and the center of the first and third bases shall be on lines running to and from second base and 7½ inches from the foul lines, providing that each base shall be entirely within the foul lines.

Batter/Position The batter's box is again made four feet wide by six feet long.

Coach/Position The captain's or coacher's lines must be 15 feet from and parallel with the foul lines and should commence 75 feet distant from the catcher's line. Should the captain or coacher willfully fail to remain in said bounds, he shall be fined by the umpire $5 for each such offense, except upon an appeal by the captain from the umpire's decision upon a misinterpretation of the rules.

The captains and coachers are restricted in coaching to the baserunner only, and are not allowed to address any remarks except to the baserunner, and then only in words of necessary direction; no player shall use language which will, in any manner, refer to or reflect upon a player of the opposing club or the audience. To enforce the above, the captain of the opposing side may call the attention of the umpire to the offense and upon a repetition of the same the club shall be debarred from further coaching during the game.

Foul Ball See last paragraph under *Strike Zone.*

Game The choice of innings is given to the home team captain.

No game is to be begun later than two hours before sunset.

The players of each club in a match game shall be nine in number, and in no case shall less than nine men be allowed to play on each side.

Game/Rain The home club captain shall be the sole judge of the fitness of the ground for beginning a game after rain.

Game/"Time" The umpire may call "timeout" to enforce order in case of annoyance from spectators.

Grounds/Foul Lines The foul lines must be drawn in straight lines from the outer corner of home base along the outer edges of the first and third bases to the boundaries of the ground.

Note: Also see *Coach* for "Coacher's Lines."

Hit by Pitch The batter is entitled to take first base if his person or clothing is hit by a ball from the pitcher, unless in the umpire's opinion he intentionally permitted himself to be hit.

Interference/Offensive The baserunner is out if he intentionally interferes with a thrown ball.

Pitcher/Delivery The pitcher shall take his position facing the batsman, with both feet squarely on the ground, the right foot on the rear line of the "box," his left foot in advance of the right, and to the left of an imaginary line from his right foot to the center of the home base. He shall not raise his right foot, unless in the act of delivering the ball, nor make more than one step in such

delivery. He shall hold the ball, before delivery, fairly in front of his body, and in sight of the umpire. In the case of a lefthanded pitcher, the above words "left" and "right" are to be reversed. When the pitcher feigns to throw the ball to a base, he must resume the above position and pause momentarily before delivering the ball to the bat.

Any motion made by the pitcher to deliver the ball to the bat without delivering it is a balk, and shall be held to include any and every accustomed motion with the hands, arms, or feet, or position of the body assumed by the pitcher in his delivery of the ball, and any motion calculated to deceive a baserunner, except the ball be accidentally dropped.

It is a balk if the ball be held by the pitcher so long as to delay the game unnecessarily. It is a balk if the pitcher makes any motion to deliver the ball to the bat when any part of his person is upon grounds outside of the lines of his position, including all preliminary motions with the hands, arms, and feet. The batter becomes a baserunner after any illegal delivery of a ball by the pitcher.

Pitcher/Position   The pitcher's box is now 5½ feet long by four feet wide.

Player/Illegal Act   No umpire, manager, captain, or player shall address the audience during the progress of a game, except in case of necessary explanation.

Runner/Overrunning First   If the baserunner overruns first base and turns to his left from the foul line, he may be put out in returning to the base or in attempting to advance.

Runner/Returning   Baserunners need not return to their bags on the run following a foul ball etc., provided they do not unnecessarily delay the game.

Spectators   No person shall be allowed upon any part of the field during the progress of a game, in addition to the players in uniform, the manager on each side, and the umpire; except such officers of the law as may be present in uniform, and such officials of the home club as may be necessary to preserve the peace.

Strikeout   The batter is out after four strikes are declared by the umpire.

Strike Zone   The batter can no longer call for a "high" or "low" pitch.

A "fair" ball (strike) is defined as a legally pitched ball that passes over home base "not lower than the batsman's knee, nor higher than his shoulder."

A strike is called when the batter makes any obvious attempt to make a foul hit.

Umpire/Decisions   No one except the captains of the contending teams can question an umpire's decision; no player other than a captain can approach or address the umpire unless required to do so. Violators may be fined $10.

The umpire cannot reverse his decision by the testimony of a player or spectator. However, the umpire may consult a player on the question before rendering his decision.

Uniforms/Shoes   Every club shall be required to adopt uniforms for its players. Each player shall be required to present himself upon the field during the game in a neat and clean condition, but no player shall attach anything to the sole or heel of his shoes other than the ordinary baseball shoe plate.

1888

Interference/Offensive   If a fair hit ball strikes the baserunner before touching a fielder, the runner shall be declared out—however, in such case, no base shall be run unless forced by the batter becoming a baserunner, and no run shall be scored.

Note: In 1890, the rule was amended with the additional phrase, "and no other baserunner put out." This clarified that the

batter could not be thrown out nor any possible double play could be made on such a play.

Strikeout   The batter is out after three strikes are declared by the umpire.

The batter is out if, while making the third strike, the ball hits his person or clothing.

1889

Base on Balls   A batter is entitled to take first base when four balls have been called by the umpire.

Foul Tip   A foul tip is defined as a foul hit not rising above the batter's head and caught by the catcher playing within 10 feet of home base. In the case of a foul tip, the batter is not out and any baserunners may return to their bases without being put out.

Pitcher/Delivery   The pitcher shall take his position facing the batsman with both feet square on the ground, one foot on the rear line of the "box." He shall not raise either foot, unless in the act of delivering the ball, nor make more than one step in such delivery. He shall hold the ball, before the delivery fairly in front of his body, and in sight of the umpire. When the pitcher feigns to throw the ball to a base, he must resume the above position and pause momentarily before delivering the ball to the bat.

Substitute   One player, whose name shall be printed on the scorecard as an extra player, may be substituted at the end of any complete inning by either club, but the player retired shall not thereafter participate in the game. In addition thereto, a substitute may be allowed at any time in place of a player disabled in the game then being played, by reason of illness or injury, of the nature and extent of which the umpire shall be the sole judge.

Substitute/Runner   The baserunner shall not have a substitute run for him, except by consent of the captains of the contesting teams.

1890

In 1890, the Players League was in operation for its one and only season, for which they adopted the rule book and made several modifications.

Ball   The Players League used the "Keefe ball" as its official ball.

Ball/Defacing   At no time shall the ball be intentionally discolored by rubbing it with the soil or otherwise.

Note: This rule was not in the Players League rule book.

Forfeited Game (Players League)   If a club fails to begin play within one minute after the umpire calls "play" at the start of the game, unless such delay is unavoidable, the game shall be declared a forfeit.

If the club fails to resume play within five minutes after the umpire has called "play" (following suspension of play), the game shall be declared a forfeit.

Note: The NL and AA rule book allowed for just the opposite before declaring a forfeit—five minutes at the start of the game, one minute after suspended play.

Pitcher/Delivery   The Players League deleted the following line from its rule book: "He [the pitcher] shall not raise either foot, unless in the act of delivering the ball."

Note: See 1889 *Pitcher/Delivery.*

Pitcher/Position (Players League)   The pitcher's lines must be six feet long by four feet wide, its forward line distant fifty-one feet from the center of home base. Each corner of the "box" must be marked by a wooden peg.

Substitute   Two players, whose names shall be printed on the scorecard as extra players, may be substituted at any time by either club, but no player so retired shall thereafter participate in the game.

Note: The Players League applied this rule but required the substitution to be made at the end of a complete inning.

Umpire (Players League) There shall be two umpires at every championship game; one shall stand behind the bat and the other shall stand in the field.

Note: Leave it to the players to understand the importance of having at least two umpires on the field of play.

1891

Substitute Each team is required to have one or more substitutes available.

1892

Coach A team is permitted to have not more than two coaches who may be one player participating in the game and any other player under contract to the club.

Coachers are not to use language which in any manner refers to or reflects upon spectators.

Dead/Live Ball A legally delivered fair ball that touches the bat of the batter in his position shall be considered a batted ball and in play.

Forfeited Game A forfeit shall be declared if a team resorts to dilatory practices in order to gain time, for the purpose of having the game called on account of darkness or rain or for any reason whatsoever.

Game "No Game" shall be declared by the umpire if he shall terminate play on account of rain or darkness before five innings on each side are completed, except in a case when the game is called, the club second at bat shall have more runs at the end of its fourth inning than the club first at bat made in its five innings, then the umpire shall award the game to the club having made the greatest number of runs, and it shall be a game and be so counted in the championship record.

Grounds/Fence A fair batted ball that goes over the fence shall entitle the batter to a home run; except that should it go over the fence at a distance less than 235 feet from home base, the batter is entitled to only two bases. A distinctive line is to be marked on the fence showing the required point.

Hit by Pitch The batter becomes a baserunner if, while he be a batsman, his person—excepting hands or forearm, which makes it a dead ball—or clothing be hit by a ball from the pitcher, unless, in the opinion of the umpire, he intentionally permits himself to be so hit.

Home Run/Double See *Grounds/Fence.*

Interference/Offensive The batter is out if he attempts to hinder the catcher from fielding or throwing the ball by stepping outside the lines of his position or otherwise obstructing or interfering with the catcher.

Player/Bench Players' benches must be located at least 25 feet back of the players' lines.

1893

Bat The bat must be made wholly of hard wood except that the handle may be wound with twine, or a granulated substance applied, not to exceed 18 inches from the end. It must be round, not to exceed 2½ inches in diameter in the thickest part, and must not exceed 42 inches in length.

Note: Bats with a flat side are now illegal.

Batting Order The batsmen must take their positions within the batsmen's lines in the order in which they are named in the batting order, which batting order must be submitted by the captains of the opposing teams to the umpire before the game, and when approved by him this batting order must be followed except in the case of a substitute player, in which case the substitute must take the place of the original player in the bat-

ting order. After the first inning the first striker (batter) in each inning shall be the batsman whose name follows that of the last man who has completed his turn—time at bat—in the preceding inning.

Pitcher/Delivery The pitcher shall take his position facing the batter with both feet square on the ground, and in front of the pitcher's plate but in the act of delivering the ball one foot must be in contact with the pitcher's plate.

A balk is any motion in delivering the ball to the bat by the pitcher while not in the required position.

Pitcher/Position The pitcher's boundary shall be marked by a white rubber plate 12 inches long and 4 inches wide so fixed in the ground as to be even with the surface at the distance of *60 feet 6 inches* from the outer corner of the home plate, so that a line drawn from the center of the home base and the center of the second base shall give 6 inches on either side.

1894

Foul Ball See *Strike Zone.*

Grounds Detailed directions are included in the rules of 1894 for laying out a baseball diamond.

Strike Zone A strike is called when the batter makes a foul hit, other than a foul tip, while attempting a bunt hit that falls or rolls upon foul ground between home base and first or third bases.

1895

Bat The bat cannot exceed 2¾ inches in diameter.

Batting Order The batsman is out if he fails to take his position at the bat in his order of batting, unless the error be discovered and the proper batsman takes his position before a time "at bat" recorded; and in such case the balls and strikes called must be counted in the time "at bat" of the proper batsman, and only the proper batsman shall be declared out. This rule shall not take effect unless the out is declared before the ball is delivered to the succeeding batsman, and no runs shall be scored or bases run, and further, no outs shall be counted other than that of the proper batsman.

Foul Tip A strike is called when a ball is tipped by the batter and caught by the catcher within the 10-foot lines.

Glove The catcher and first baseman are permitted to wear a glove or mitt of any size, shape or weight. All other players are restricted to the use of a glove or mitt weighing not over 10 ounces, and measuring in circumference around the palm of the hand not over 14 inches.

Infield Fly The batter is out if he hits a fly ball that can be handled by an infielder while first and second bases are occupied, or first, second, and third, with only one out. If the third strike is called (on attempted bunt in foul territory) the umpire shall declare infield or outfield hit.

Pitcher/Position The pitcher's plate is enlarged to 24 by 6 inches.

Strike Zone See *Foul Tip.*

Umpire Umpires may assess fines of $25 to $100 for specified misconduct by players.

1896

Ball The home club shall have at least a dozen regulation balls on the field ready for use on the call of the umpire during each game.

Game/Rain The choice of innings shall be given to the captain of the home club, who shall also be the sole judge of the fitness of the ground for beginning a game after rain, but after play has been called by the umpire he alone shall be the judge as to the fitness of the ground for resuming play after the game has been

suspended on account of rain.

Pitcher/Delivery The pitcher is no longer required to hold the ball before the delivery fairly in front of his body and in the sight of the umpire.

Player/Bench No one is to occupy the players' bench under any circumstances except the club president, managers, and players in uniform.

Player/Illegal Act Players guilty of indecent or vulgar language or conduct shall be removed from the game and fined $25.

Umpire Umpires may assess fines of $5 to $10 for specified misconduct; repeat violators are to be fined $25.

1897

Ball/Defaced At no time shall the ball be intentionally discolored by rubbing it with the soil or otherwise. In the event of a new ball being intentionally discolored, or otherwise injured by a player, the umpire shall, upon appeal from the captain of the opposite side, forthwith demand the return of that ball and shall substitute another new ball and impose a fine of $5 upon the offending player.

Bunt A bunt hit is a ball delivered by the pitcher to the batsman who, while standing within the lines of his position, makes a deliberate attempt to hit the ball so slowly within the infield that it cannot be fielded in time to retire the batsman. If such a bunt hit goes to foul ground a strike shall be called by the umpire.

Defense/Illegal Act See *Ball/Defacing.*

Fair/Foul Ball A fair hit is a ball batted by the batsman—while he is standing within the lines of his position—that first touches "fair" ground, or the person of a player or the umpire while standing on fair ground, and then settles on fair ground before passing the line of first or third base.

A foul hit is a similarly batted ball that first touches "foul" ground or the person of a player or the umpire while standing on foul ground.

Should such "fair hit" ball bound or roll to foul ground before passing the line of first or third base and settle on foul ground, it shall be declared by the umpire a foul ball.

Should such "foul hit" ball bound or roll to fair ground and settle there before passing the line of first or third base, it shall be declared by the umpire a "fair ball."

Foul Tip A foul tip is a ball batted by the batsman while standing within the lines of his position that goes foul sharp from the bat to the catcher's hands.

Obstruction The baserunner shall be entitled, without being put out, to take a base in the following cases: (1) If he be prevented from making a base by the obstruction of an adversary, unless the latter be a fielder having the ball in his hand ready to meet the baserunner; (2) If the fielder stop or catch a batted ball with his hat or any part of his uniform except his gloved hand.

Runner/Bases The baserunner must touch each base in regular order, viz., first, second, third, and home bases, and when obliged to return (except on a foul hit) must retouch the base or bases in reverse order. He shall only be considered as holding a base after touching it, and shall then be entitled to hold such base until he has legally touched the next base in order or has been legally forced to vacate it for a succeeding baserunner. However, no baserunner shall score a run to count in the game until the baserunner preceding him in the batting list (provided there has been such a baserunner who has not been put out in that inning) shall have first touched home base without being put out.

Substitute In every championship game, each side shall be required to have present on the field, in uniform, a sufficient number of substitute players to carry out the provision which requires that not less than nine players shall occupy the field in any inning of a game.

Umpire The umpire shall not address the spectators at any time, except in case of necessary explanation of misunderstood decision or points of play.

Umpire/Decisions No decision, rendered by the umpire, shall be reversed by him in which the question of an error of judgment is alone involved.

Should the umpire render any decision based on an illegal interpretation of any rule of the game, the same shall be reversed on the appeal of either of the two captains, but not otherwise.

1898

Batting Order The batsman is out if he fails to take his position at the bat in his order of batting, unless the error be discovered and the proper batsman takes his position before a time "at bat" is recorded, and, in such case, the balls and strikes called must be counted in the time "at bat" of the proper batsman, and only the proper batsman shall be declared out, and no runs shall be scored or bases run because of any act of the improper batsman. Provided, this rule shall not take effect unless the out is declared before the ball is delivered to the succeeding batsman. Should the batsman declared out by this rule be sufficient to retire the side, the proper batsman the next inning is the player who would have come to bat had the players been out by ordinary play.

Pitcher/Delivery A balk shall be: (1) Any motion made by the pitcher to deliver the ball to the bat without delivering it; (2) Any delivery of the ball to the bat while his pivot foot is not in contact with the pitcher's plate; (3) Any motion in delivering the ball to the bat by the pitcher while not in the position required by the rules; (4) The holding of the ball by the pitcher so long as, in the opinion of the umpire, to delay the game unnecessarily; (5) Standing in position and making any motion to pitch without having the ball in his possession, except in the case of a "block ball"; (6) The making of any motion the pitcher habitually makes in his method of delivery, without his immediately delivering the ball to the bat; (7) If the pitcher feigns to throw the ball to a base and does not resume his legal position and pause momentarily before delivering the ball to the bat. When the pitcher feigns to throw the ball to a base he must resume the required position and pause momentarily before delivering the ball to the bat.

Player/Illegal Act Players in uniform shall not be permitted to occupy seats in the stands or to stand among the spectators.

Umpire The rules of 1898 describe in detail the responsibilities of each umpire in games where two umpires are assigned.

1899

Catcher/Position The catcher must stand within the lines of his position whenever the pitcher delivers the ball to the bat.

Foul Tip A foul tip by the batter, caught by the catcher while standing within the lines of his position is a strike.

Game If the umpire calls "Game" on account of darkness or rain at any time after five innings have been completed, the score shall be that of the last equal innings played, but if the side second at bat shall have scored in an unequal number of innings or before the completion of its unfinished inning one or more runs than the side first at bat, the score of the game shall be the total number of runs made.

Interference/Defensive The batter becomes a baserunner if the catcher interferes with him, preventing him from striking the ball.

Pitcher/Delivery In addition to the rules for "balk" promulgated in 1898, the rules of 1899 state: A balk shall be: (1) The throwing of the ball by the pitcher to any base to catch the

baserunner without first stepping directly towards said base immediately before throwing the ball; (2) Any delivery of the ball to the bat by the pitcher while his pivot foot is not in contact with the pitcher's plate, and he is not facing the batsman; (3) If the pitcher delivers the ball to the bat when the catcher is standing outside the lines of the catcher's position as defined by the rules.

The batter becomes a baserunner when a balk is called by the umpire.

Player/Bench The players' benches must be furnished by the home club and placed upon a portion of the ground not less than 25 feet outside of the players' lines. One such bench shall be for the exclusive use of the visiting club, and one for the exclusive use of the home club. The benches must be covered by a roof and closed at the back and each end; a space, however, not more than six inches wide may be left just under the roof for ventilation. All players of the side at bat must be seated on their bench, except such as are legally assigned to coach baserunners, and also the batsman, except when called to the bat by the umpire, and under no circumstances shall the umpire permit any person, except managers and players in uniform to occupy seats on the benches.

Strike Zone See *Foul Tip*.

Substitute In any championship game, each side shall be required to have present on the field, in uniform, conforming to the suits worn by their teammates, a sufficient number of substitute players to carry out the provision which requires that not less than nine players shall occupy the field in any innings of a game.

Uniforms Every club shall adopt uniforms for its players, and the suit of each team shall conform in color and style. No player who shall attach anything to the sole or heel of his shoes other than the ordinary baseball shoe plate, or who shall appear in a uniform not conforming to the suits of the other members of his team, shall be permitted to take part in the game.

1900

Bases The shape of home base is changed from a 12-inch square to a five-sided shape, 17 inches wide.

Pitcher/Delivery The batter does not become a runner when the pitcher balks in throwing to pick off a runner on the bases.

Any motion made by the pitcher to deliver the ball to the bat or to first base without delivering it is a balk.

Note: This rule previously specified "any base."

1901

The American League begins operation and adopts the rule book with only a few modifications.

Catcher/Position The catcher must stand within the lines of his position whenever the pitcher delivers the ball to the bat and within 10 feet of the home base.

Note: This rule was adopted by the National League in 1901. The American League adopted the rule in 1902.

Foul Ball A foul hit ball not caught on the fly is a strike unless two strikes have already been called.

Note: This rule was used by the National League in 1901 and 1902. The American League adopted the rule in 1903. See 1902 summary for further elaboration of this rule by the National League.

A "bunt hit" which sends the ball to foul ground either directly or by bounding or rolling from fair ground to foul ground and which settles on foul ground is a strike.

Infield Fly The batter is out if he hits a fly ball that can be handled by an infielder while first and second bases are occupied, or first, second, and third, unless two hands are out. In such case the umpire shall, as soon as the ball is hit, declare infield or outfield hit.

Pitcher/Delivery If the ball is thrown by the pitcher to any player other than the catcher (except to retire a baserunner) and the batsman is standing in his proper position ready to strike at a pitched ball, each ball so delivered shall be called a ball.

The umpire shall call a ball on the pitcher each time he delays the game by failing to deliver the ball to the batsman when in position for a longer period than 20 seconds.

Strike See *Foul Ball*.

1902

Foul Ball The batter is out if after two strikes have been called he obviously attempts to make a foul hit.

Hit by Pitch The batsman becomes a baserunner if while he be a batsman, without making any attempt to strike at the ball, his person or clothing be hit by a ball from the pitcher, unless in the opinion of the umpire he plainly avoids making any effort to get out of the way of the ball from the pitcher and thereby permits himself to be so hit.

Pitcher/Delivery The umpire shall call a ball on the pitcher each time he delays the game by failing to deliver the ball to the batsman when in position for a longer period than 20 seconds, excepting that in the case of the first batsman in each inning, the pitcher may occupy not more than one minute in delivering [warm-up pitches] not to exceed five balls to a baseman.

If the ball is thrown by the pitcher to any player other than the catcher (except to retire a baserunner) after the batter is standing in his position ready to strike at a pitched ball each ball so delivered will be called a ball.

Strike/Strikeout See *Foul Ball*.

1903

Pitcher/Position The pitcher's box shall be no more than 15 inches higher than the baselines and home plate. The baselines and home plate shall be on a perfect level, and the slope from the pitcher's box towards the baselines and home plate shall be gradual.

Note: In 1904, the phrase "pitcher's box" was deleted from this rule and replaced by the phrase "pitcher's plate."

Umpire The rules of 1903 contain an extensive reorganization and rewriting of the rules pertaining to umpires.

1904

Ball Two regulation balls of the make adopted by the league of which the contesting clubs are members shall be delivered by the home club to the umpire at or before the hour for the commencement of a championship game. If the ball first placed in play be batted or thrown out of the grounds or into one of the stands for spectators or, in the judgment of the umpire, become unfit for play from any cause, the umpire shall at once deliver the alternate ball to the pitcher and another legal ball shall be supplied to him, so that he shall at all times have in his control one or more alternate balls to substitute for the ball in play in any of the contingencies above set forth. Provided, however, that all balls batted or thrown out of the ground or into a stand, shall, when returned to the field, be given into the custody of the umpire immediately and become alternate balls, and so long as he has in his possession two or more alternate balls, he shall not call for a new ball to replace a ball that has gone out of play. The alternate balls shall become the ball in play in the order in which they were delivered to the umpire.

Bunt A bunt hit is a legally batted ball, not swung at, but met with the bat and tapped slowly within the infield by the batsman with the expectation of reaching first base before the ball can be fielded to that base. If the attempt to bunt result in a foul, a strike shall be called by the umpire.

Coach/Illegal Act The baserunner is out if, before two hands are out and while third base is occupied, the coacher stationed

near that base shall run in the direction of home base on or near the baseline while a fielder is making or trying to make a play on a batted ball not caught on the fly, or on a thrown ball, and thereby draws a throw to home base. The baserunner entitled to third base shall be declared out by the umpire for the coacher's interference with and prevention of the legitimate play.

Note: In 1914, the words "on a fly ball" were inserted in this rule.

Dead/Live Ball   Immediately upon the delivery to him of the alternate ball by the umpire, the pitcher shall take his position and on the call of "Play," by the umpire, it shall become the ball in play. Provided, however, that play shall not be resumed with the alternate ball when a fair batted ball or a ball thrown by a fielder goes out of the ground or into a stand for spectators until the baserunners have completed the circuit of the bases unless compelled to stop at second or third base in compliance with a ground rule.

Grounds/Fences   To obviate the necessity for ground rules, the shortest distance from a fence or stand on fair territory to home base should be 235 feet and from home base to the grandstand 90 feet.

Interference/Offensive   The baserunner is out if one or more members of the team at bat stand or collect at or around a base for which a baserunner is trying, thereby confusing the fielding side and adding to the difficulty of making such play. The baserunner shall be declared out for the interference of his teammate or teammates.

The players of the side at bat must speedily abandon their bench and hasten to another part of the field when by remaining upon or near it they or any of them would interfere with a fielder in an attempt to catch or handle a thrown ball.

Player   The players of each club, actively engaged in a game at one time, shall be nine in number, one of whom shall act as captain; and in no case shall more or less than nine men be allowed to play on a side in a game.

Note: The previous rule read, "in no case shall less than nine men be allowed to play."

Runner   The baserunner is out if he touch home base before a baserunner preceding him in the batting order, if there be such preceding baserunner, lose his right to third base.

Uniform   Every club shall adopt two uniforms for its players, one to be worn in games at home and the other in games abroad, and the suits of each of the uniforms of a team shall conform in color and style.

1905

There were no changes in the playing rules this year.

1906

Bunt   A bunt hit is a legally batted ball, not swung at, but met with the bat and tapped slowly within the infield by the batsman. If the attempt to bunt result in a foul not legally caught, a strike shall be called by the umpire.

Game/Rain   The choice of innings shall be given to the captain of the home club, who shall be the sole judge of the fitness of the ground for beginning a game after a rain; but, after play has been called by the umpire, he alone shall be the judge as to the fitness of the ground for resuming play after the game has been suspended on account of rain, and when time is so called the groundskeeper and sufficient assistants shall be under the control of the umpire for the purpose of putting the ground in proper shape for play, under penalty of forfeiture of the game by the home team.

Ground/Foul Lines   Foul lines are to be clearly visible from any part of the diamond, and no wood or other hard substance shall be used in the construction of such lines.

1907

Ball/Defaced   In the event of a ball being intentionally discolored by rubbing it with the soil or otherwise by any player except the pitcher, or otherwise damaged by any player, the umpire shall, upon appeal by the captain of the opposite side, forthwith demand the return of that ball and substitute for it another legal ball and impose a fine of $5 on the offending player.

Batter/Awarded Bases   The baserunner shall be entitled to advance one base without liability to be put out if, while the batsman, he becomes a baserunner by reason of "four balls" or for being hit by a pitched ball, or for being interfered with by the catcher in striking at a pitched ball.

Batter/Position   The batter is out if he steps from one batsman's box to the other after the pitcher has taken his position.

Batter/Runner   The batter becomes a baserunner if a fair hit ball strike the person or clothing of the umpire or a baserunner on fair ground.

Defense/Illegal Act   See *Ball/Defaced*.

Game/Legal   If the umpire calls a game at any time after five innings have been completed, the score shall be that of the last equal innings played, except that if the side second at bat shall have scored in an unequal number of innings, or before the completion of the unfinished inning, at least one run more than the side first at bat, the score of the game shall be the total number of runs each team has made.

Game/Rain   If the game be called by the umpire on account of darkness, rain, fire, panic, or for other cause which puts patrons or players in peril, the game shall terminate.

Interference/Offensive   The baserunner is out if with one or no one out and a baserunner on third base, the batsman interferes with a play being made at home plate.

See also *Batter/Runner*.

Interference/Umpire   See *Batter/Runner*.

Pitcher/Delivery   A fairly delivered ball is a ball pitched or thrown to the bat by the pitcher while standing in his position and facing the batsman that passes over any portion of the home base, before touching the ground, not lower than the batsman's knee, nor higher than his shoulder. For every such fairly delivered ball, the umpire shall call one strike.

An unfairly delivered ball is a ball delivered to the bat by the pitcher while standing in his position and facing the batsman that does not pass over any portion of the home base between the batsman's shoulder and knees, or that touches the ground before passing home base, unless struck at by the batsman. For every unfairly delivered ball the umpire shall call one ball.

Runner/Illegal Act   The baserunner is out if he passes a baserunner who is caught between two bases. He shall be declared out immediately upon passing the preceding baserunner.

1908

Ball/Defacing   The rule prohibiting the discoloring of the ball by rubbing it with the soil was amended to include the pitcher as well as all players.

1909

Dead/Live Ball   In case of a foul strike, foul hit ball not legally caught, dead ball, interference with the fielder or batsman, or a fair hit ball touching a baserunner, the ball shall not be considered in play until it be held by the pitcher standing in his position and the umpire shall have called "Play."

Fair/Foul Ball   A fair hit is a legally batted ball that settles on fair ground between home and first base or between home and third base or that is on fair ground when bounding to the outfield past first or third base or that first falls on fair territory beyond

first or third base or that, while on or over fair ground, touches the person of the umpire or a player.

A foul hit is a legally batted ball that settles on foul territory between home and first base or home and third base or that bounds past first or third base in foul territory or that falls on foul territory beyond first or third base or while on or over foul ground, touches the person of the umpire or a player.

Ground Rules Before the commencement of a game the umpire shall see that the rules governing all the materials of the game are strictly observed. He shall ask the captain of the home club whether there are any special ground rules, and if there be, he shall acquaint himself with them, advise the captain of the visiting team of their scope, and see that each is duly enforced, provided that it does not conflict with any of these rules, and are acceptable to the captain of the visiting team. If the latter object to a proposed ground rule, the umpire shall have authority to adopt or reject it.

Pitcher When the umpire announces the pitcher prior to commencement of the game, the player announced must pitch until the first batsman has either been put out or has reached first base.

Player/Ejected In the event of removal of player or manager by the umpire, he shall go direct to the club house and remain there during progress of the game, or leave the grounds; and a failure to do so will warrant a forfeiture of the game by the umpire.

Relief Pitcher In event of the pitcher being taken from the game by either manager or captain, the player substituted for him shall continue to pitch until the batsman then at bat has either been put out or has reached first base.

1910

Batter/Awarded Bases The baserunner shall be entitled, without liability to be put out, to advance a base if, while the batsman, he becomes a baserunner by reason of "four balls" or for being hit by a pitched ball, or if a fair hit ball strike the person or clothing of the umpire or a baserunner on fair ground.

Batter/Position The batter is out if he steps from one batsman's box to the other while the pitcher is in his position ready to pitch.

An illegally batted ball is a ball batted by the batsman when either or both of his feet are upon the ground outside the lines of the batsman's position.

Note: This rule replaced the term "foul strike."

Batting Order The batting order of each team must be on the scorecard and must be delivered before the game by its captain to the umpire at home plate, who shall submit it to the inspection of the captain of the other side. The batting order delivered to the umpire must be followed throughout the game unless a player be substituted for another, in which case the substitute must take the place in the batting order of the retired player.

Dead/Live Ball In case of an illegally batted ball, a balk, foul hit ball not legally caught, dead ball, interference with the fielder or batsman, or a fair hit ball striking a baserunner or umpire before touching a fielder, the ball shall not be considered in play until it be held by the pitcher standing in his position, and the umpire shall have called "Play."

Fielder/Illegal Act If the fielder stop or catch a batted ball with his cap, glove, or any part of his uniform, while detached from its proper place on his person, the runner or runners shall be entitled to three bases.

Ground Rules/Spectators In case of spectators overflowing on the playing field, the home captain shall make special ground rules to cover balls batted or thrown into the crowd, provided such rules be acceptable to the captain of the visiting club. If the

latter object, then the umpire shall have full authority to make and enforce such special rules, and he shall announce the scope of same to the spectators.

Interference/Offensive The baserunner shall return to his base without liability to be put out if the umpire declares the batsman or another baserunner out for interference.

Interference/Umpire If a thrown or pitched ball strike the person or clothing of an umpire on foul ground the ball shall be considered in play and the runner or runners shall be entitled to all the bases they can make.

The baserunner shall return to his base without liability to be put out if the umpire be struck by a fair hit ball before touching a fielder; in which case no base shall be run unless necessitated by the batsman becoming a baserunner, and no run shall be scored unless all the bases are occupied.

Pitcher/Delivery An unfairly delivered ball is a ball delivered to the bat by the pitcher while standing in his position and facing the batsman that does not pass over any portion of the home base between the batsman's shoulder and knees, or that touches the ground before passing home base, unless struck at by the batsman; or, with the bases unoccupied, any ball delivered by the pitcher while either foot is not in contact with the pitcher's plate. For every unfairly delivered ball the umpire shall call one ball.

Player/Position The players of the team not at bat may be stationed at any points of the field on fair ground their captain may elect, regardless of their respective positions, except that the pitcher, while in the act of delivering the ball to the bat must take his position as defined in the rules and the catcher likewise must be within the lines of his position and within 10 feet of home base whenever the pitcher delivers the ball to the bat.

Relief Pitcher In event of the pitcher being taken from his position by either manager or captain, the player substituted for him shall continue to pitch until the batsman then at bat has either been put out or has reached first base.

Runner/Awarded Bases In all cases where there are no spectators on the playing field, and where a thrown ball goes into a stand for spectators, or over or through any fence surrounding the playing field, into the players' bench (whether the ball rebounds into the field or not), the runner or runners shall be entitled to two bases. The umpire in awarding such bases shall be governed by the position of the runner or runners at the time the throw is made.

Substitute Whenever one player is substituted for another, whether as batsman, baserunner, or fielder, the captain of the side making the change must immediately notify the umpire, who in turn must announce the same to the spectators. A fine of $5 shall be assessed by the umpire against the captain for each violation of this rule, and the president of the League shall impose a similar fine against the umpire who, after having been notified of a change, fails to make proper announcement. Play shall be suspended while announcement is being made, and the player substituted shall become actively engaged in the game immediately upon his captain's notice of the change to the umpire.

Umpire The rules of 1910 contain new provisions for umpires and describe the respective duties of the Umpire-in-Chief and the Field Umpire.

1911

Ball Cork-center balls are used for the first time as regulation balls in all games.

1912-13

There were no changes in the playing rules in these years.

1914

The Federal League begins operation and adopts virtually the entire rule book. The Victor Sporting Goods Company provides the new league's official ball. The Federal League folded after the 1915 season.

Ball League presidents are no longer required to examine, measure, and weigh baseballs for use in championship games.

Coach A coach may address words of assistance and direction to the baserunners and to the batter.

Coach/Illegal Acts If, while third base is occupied, the coacher stationed near that base shall run in the direction of home base on or near the base line while a fielder is making or trying to make a play on a batted ball not caught on the fly or on a thrown ball or a fly ball [see note below], and thereby draws a throw to home base, the baserunner entitled to third base shall be declared out by the umpire for the coacher's interference with and prevention of the legitimate play.

Note: This rule was first adopted in 1904 but did not include the phrase "or a fly ball."

If a coach at third base touch or hold a baserunner at third base or a baserunner who is rounding third base for home plate, such baserunner is out.

Fielder/Illegal Acts The baserunner is entitled to advance a base without liability to be put out if the fielder stop or catch a batted ball or a thrown ball with his cap, glove, or any part of his uniform, while detached from its proper place on his person, the runner or runners shall be entitled to three bases if a batted ball or to two bases if a thrown ball.

Home Run/Double See *Runner/Bases.*

Interference/Offensive The batter is out if he obstructs or interferes with the catcher except when he does so with a runner on third base (with one out or no one out) in which case the baserunner is out.

Interference/Umpire The baserunner shall return to his base without liability to be put out if the person or clothing of the umpire, while stationed back of the bat, interfere with the catcher in an attempt to throw.

The baserunner is entitled to advance a base if a thrown or pitched ball strike the person or clothing of an umpire. The ball shall be considered in play and the baserunner or runners shall be entitled to all the bases they can make.

Note: Under the previous rule only balls striking the umpire in foul territory entitled the baserunner to advance.

Pitcher/Delivery The pitcher is permitted to have his feet on top of the pitcher's plate or in front of the plate preliminary to pitching.

Runner/Awarded Bases In all cases where there are no spectators on the playing field, and where a thrown ball goes into a stand for spectators or over or through any fence surrounding the playing field or into the players' bench (whether the ball rebounds into the field or not) or remains in the meshes of a wire screen protecting the spectators, the runner or runners shall be entitled to two bases. The umpire in awarding such bases shall be governed by the position of the runner or runners at the time the throw is made.

Runner/Bases A batter who hits a home run or a ground-rule double must touch all of the bases in regular order.

1915–19

There were no changes in the playing rules in these years.

1920

Ball The President of the League of which the contesting clubs are members shall specify the number of baseballs which the home club must deliver to the umpire prior to the hour set for the commencement of a championship game, and all of such baseballs shall be of the regulation make adopted by the league.

The seal on boxes of new balls is not to be broken by the umpire except prior to game time and for the purpose of inspecting the ball and removing the gloss therefrom.

Ball Defacing In event of the ball being intentionally discolored by any player, either by rubbing it with the soil, or by applying rosin, paraffin, licorice, or any other foreign substance to it, or otherwise intentionally damaging or roughening the same with sandpaper or emery paper, or other substance, the umpire shall forthwith demand the return of that ball and substitute for it another legal ball, and the offending player shall be disbarred from further participation in the game. If, however, the umpire cannot detect the violator of this rule, and the ball is delivered to the bat by the pitcher, then the latter shall be at once removed from the game, and as an additional penalty shall be automatically suspended for a period of 10 days.

At no time during the progress of the game shall the pitcher be allowed to: (1) Apply a foreign substance of any kind to the ball; (2) Expectorate either on the ball or his glove; (3) Rub the ball on his glove, person, or clothing; (4) Deface the ball in any manner; (5) or to deliver what is called the "shine" ball, "spit" ball, "mud" ball, or "emery" ball. For violation of any part of this rule the umpire shall at once order the pitcher from the game, and in addition he shall be automatically suspended for a period of 10 days, on notice from the president of the League.

Note: In adopting the foregoing rule against "freak" deliveries on February 9, 1920, it was understood and agreed that all bona fide spitball pitchers would be certified to the respective presidents of the National and American leagues at least 10 days prior to April 14, 1920, and that the pitchers so certified would be exempt from the operation of the rule, as far as it related to the spitball only.

Batter/Awarded Bases The baserunner shall be entitled to advance one base if, while the batsman, he becomes a baserunner by reason of "four balls" or for being hit by a pitched ball or for being interfered with by the catcher in striking at a pitched ball or if a fair hit ball strike the person or clothing of the umpire or a baserunner on fair ground before touching a fielder. Provided, that if a fair hit ball strike the umpire after having passed a fielder or having been touched by a fielder, the ball shall be considered in play. Also, if a fair hit ball strike the umpire on foul ground, the ball shall be in play.

Catcher/Position It shall be illegal for the catcher to leave his natural position immediately and directly back of the plate for the purpose of aiding the pitcher to intentionally give a base on balls to a batsman. If the catcher shall move out of position prior to the time of the ball leaving the pitcher's hand, all runners on bases shall be entitled to advance one base.

Also see *Interference/Defensive.*

Coach See *Interference/Offensive.*

Dead Ball The baserunner shall return to his base without liability to be put out if the umpire declares a dead ball, unless it also be the fourth unfair ball, and he be thereby forced to take the next base as provided in the rules. Provided, such fourth unfair ball shall not be called if the umpire declare the ball "dead" because of a pitched ball accidentally hitting the bat.

Fair/Foul Ball A fair or foul fly must be judged according to the relative position of the ball and the foul line, and not as to whether the fielder is on fair or foul ground at the time he touches the ball.

Fielder See *Runner Tagged.*

Force Out A force out can be made only when a baserunner legally loses the right to the base he occupies by reason of the batsman becoming a baserunner, and he is thereby obliged to advance.

Game/Doubleheader Whenever necessity demands that two games be played in one afternoon, the first game shall be the regularly scheduled game for that day.

Game/Drawn A drawn game shall be declared by the umpire if the score is equal on the last even inning played when he terminates play in accordance with the rules after five or more equal innings have been played by each team. But if the side that went second to bat is at bat when the game is terminated, and has scored the same number of runs as the other side, the umpire shall declare the game drawn without regard to the score of the last equal inning. Provided, that if the side last at bat shall, before the completion of the fifth inning, equal the score made by the opposing side in five complete innings then the game shall be declared as legally drawn, and the individual and team averages shall be incorporated in the Official Playing Records.

Game/Legal "No Game" shall be declared by the umpire if he terminates play in accordance with the rules before five innings are completed by each team. Provided, however, that if the club second at bat shall have made more runs at the end of its fourth inning, or before the completion of its fifth inning, than the club first at bat made in five completed innings of a game so terminated, the umpire shall award the game to the club having made the greater number of runs, and it shall count as a legal game in the championship record.

Game/"Time" The rules of 1920 contain several new provisions governing the calling of "Time" by the umpire, the most important of which is the following: That in case of an accident to a player or players in attempting to make a play on either a batted or a thrown ball, "Time" shall not be called until, in the judgment of the umpire, no further play is possible.

Hit by Pitch A "dead" ball is a ball delivered to the bat by the pitcher, not struck at by the batsman, that touches any part of the batsman's person or clothing while he is standing in his position or a wildly pitched ball which the batsman plainly makes an attempt to dodge to avoid being hit, but which ball accidentally hits his bat.

Home Run/Game-Ending If a batsman, in the last half of the final inning of any game, hit a home run over the fence or into a stand, all runners on the bases at the time, as well as the batsman, shall be entitled to score, and in such event all bases must be touched in order, and the final score of the game shall be the total number of runs made.

Infield Fly If, before two hands are out, while first and second or first, second, and third bases are occupied, he hit a fair fly ball, other than a line drive, that can be handled by an infielder, the batter is out. In such case, the umpire shall, as soon as the ball be hit, declare it an infield or outfield hit; but the runners may be off their bases or advance at the risk of the ball being caught, the same as on any other fly ball. Provided, that, with first and second bases occupied, with less than two out, any attempt to bunt which results in a fair fly ball shall not be regarded as an infield fly.

Interference/Defensive In the event a baserunner is trying to score from third base on a pitched ball or the "squeeze" play, a "balk" and also an "interference" should be called if the catcher runs out in front of the plate to catch the ball; the runner shall be allowed to score and the batsman entitled to first base. The same penalties must be imposed in case the catcher pushes the batsman out of the way or tips his bat.

Interference/Offensive The baserunner is out if, in the judgment of the umpire, the coacher at third base by touching or holding the runner physically assists him in returning to or leaving third base. The runner, however, should not be declared out if no play is being made.

The baserunner shall be entitled to advance one base if a thrown ball strike a coacher on foul ground and the ball shall be considered in play. Provided, that if in the opinion of the umpire the coacher intentionally interfere with such thrown ball, the runner or runners must return to the last bases touched, and the coacher penalized by removal from the playing field.

The baserunner is *not* out if a fair hit ball goes through an infielder, and hits a runner immediately back of him. The umpire must be convinced that the ball passed through the infield and that no other infielder had the chance to make a play on the ball. If, in the judgment of the umpire, the runner deliberately and intentionally kicks such a hit ball, on which the infielder has missed a play, then the runner must be called out for interference.

Interference/Umpire See *Batter/Awarded Bases.*

Pitcher/Delivery The following prohibitions were added to the previous balk rule in 1920:

A balk shall be: Making any motion to pitch while standing in his position without having the ball in his possession; or, regardless of whether he makes any motion to pitch or not, if the pitcher takes a legal position on the rubber without the ball in his possession, or if he takes a position off the rubber and feints to deliver the ball to the bat.

A balk shall be: After the pitcher has taken position, with both hands holding the ball in front of him, he cannot take either hand off the ball except in the act of delivering the ball to the batsman or in throwing to bases.

A balk shall be: If, with one or more runners on bases, the pitcher, in the act of delivering the ball to the batsman or in throwing to first base, drop the ball, either intentionally or accidentally, the umpire shall call it a "balk" and advance runner or runners. No penalty shall be imposed if, with no one on bases, the pitcher drop the ball while delivering it to the batsman.

If the pitcher steps off the rubber, after being in position, for the purpose either of drying his hands or rubbing his eyes, or for other reasons, and it is a legitimate action not understood or interpreted by the umpire to deceive the baserunner, then the umpire shall call "Time."

In case a balk is called, the ball shall be considered "dead" when announcement is made, and no play can be made until the runner or runners reach the base or bases to which they are entitled.

If, with no one on base, the pitcher deliver the ball while off the rubber, the umpire shall call a "ball" whether it goes over the plate fair or not. If, however, the batsman strikes at such illegally delivered ball it counts either for a strike or whatever play may follow.

Pitcher/Illegal Act See *Ball/Defacing.*

Player/Position The players of the team not at bat may be stationed at any points of the field on fair ground their captain may elect, regardless of their respective positions, except that the pitcher, while in the act of delivering the ball to the bat must take his position and the catcher must be within the lines of his position, and within 10 feet of home base, whenever the pitcher delivers the ball to the bat; nor shall the catcher leave his natural position immediately and directly back of the plate for the purpose of aiding the pitcher to intentionally give a base on balls to a batsman.

Runner/Advancing A baserunner who holds his base on a fly ball shall have the right to advance the moment such fly ball touches the hands of a fielder.

Runner/Bases The failure of a preceding runner to touch a base (and who is declared out therefore) shall not affect the status of a succeeding runner who touches each base in proper order.

Runner/Illegal Act A baserunner having acquired legal title to a base cannot run bases in reverse order for the purpose either of confusing the fielders or making a travesty of the game. A runner

violating this rule is out if touched with the ball, or the ball held on the base said runner was entitled to hold.

Runner/Returning   In case a runner is being run down between bases, and the following runner occupies the same base the first runner has left, the second man cannot be put out while holding said base. If the first runner, however, returns safely to the base he left, and both runners are then occupying the same base, the second runner is the man out, if touched with the ball.

Runner/Tagged   The baserunner is out if at any time while the ball is in play, he be touched by the ball in the hands of a fielder, unless some part of his person be touching the base he is entitled to occupy; provided, however, that the ball be held by the fielder after touching him, unless the baserunner deliberately knock it out of his hand. The ball must be firmly held by the fielder after touching the runner. The ball cannot be juggled, even though the fielder may retain possession of the ball and prevent same from dropping to the ground.

Substitute   When a substitution is made but no announcement of the substitution is made as required by the rules the substitute will nevertheless be considered in the game as follows: if a pitcher, when he takes his place on the rubber; if a batter, when he takes his place in the batsman's box; if a fielder, when he takes the place of the fielder substituted for; if a runner, when the substitute replaces him on the base he is holding, and any play made by such unannounced substitute shall be legal under the rules.

Umpire   The rules of 1920 contain various new provisions governing umpires and their respective duties.

1921

Pitcher   Note: By concurrent action of the National and American leagues taken at their respective annual meetings held in New York in December 1920, it was agreed that all bona fide spitball pitchers then remaining in the National and American leagues be exempt from the operation of the rule against the use of the spitball during the balance of their major league careers. The pitchers so exempted were: National League—William Doak, Phil Douglas, Dana Fillingim, Ray Fisher, Marvin Goodwin, Burleigh Grimes, Clarence Mitchell, and Richard Rudolph (8). American League—A. W. Ayers, Ray Caldwell, Stanley Coveleskie, Urban Faber, H. B. Leonard, Jack Quinn, Allan Russell, Urban Shocker, and Allan Sothoron (9).

1922–25

There were no changes to the playing rules in these years.

1926

Batter/Awarded Bases   A fair batted ball that goes over the fence or into a stand shall entitle the batsman to a home run, unless it should pass out of the ground or into a stand at a distance less than 250 feet from the home base, in which case the batsman shall be entitled to two bases only. In either event the batsman must touch the bases in regular order. The point at which a fence or stand is less than 250 feet from the home base shall be plainly indicated by a white or black sign or mark for the umpire's guidance.

Pitcher/Legal Act   Under the supervision and control of the umpire, the pitcher may use to dry his hands a small, finely meshed sealed bag containing powdered rosin, furnished by the League.

Note: This rule was first adopted by the National League only.

1927–30

There were no changes to the playing rules in these years.

1931

Batter   The rules of 1931 provide new wording for the rule governing when the batter is out without changing the substance of the rule.

Batter/Awarded Bases   A fair hit ball that bounds into a stand or over a fence shall be a two-base hit.

Note: There is no reference to distance in this rule and any fair hit ball bounding over the fence or into the stand is a two-base hit.

Coach   See *Interference/Offensive.*

Dead Ball   The rules of 1931 merge two previous rules governing dead balls in one differently worded rule without changing the substance of the old rules.

Fair/Foul Ball   When a batted ball passes outside the playing field the umpire shall decide it fair or foul according to where it leaves the playing field.

Game   The rules of 1931 merge four previous rules governing regulation games in one differently worded rule without changing the substance of the old rules.

Game/Legal   "No game" shall be declared by the umpire if he terminates play in accordance with the rules before five innings have been completed by each team; but if the team last at bat is at bat in the last half of the fifth inning and has equaled before the completion of that inning the score of the side first at bat, the umpire shall declare the game "legally drawn" in accordance with the rules. If the team second at bat shall have made more runs at the end of its fourth inning or before the completion of its fifth inning, than the team first at bat has made in five completed innings of a game so terminated, the umpire shall award the game to the team having made the greater number of runs, and it shall count as a legal game in the championship record.

Glove/Pitcher   The pitcher's glove must be uniform in color.

Interference/Offensive   The players or coachers of the side at bat must immediately vacate any space occupied by them if it is needed by a fielder attempting to handle a batted or thrown ball.

The baserunner is out if, in running the last half of the distance from home base to first base, while the ball is being fielded to first base, he run outside the three-foot lines, and, in the opinion of the umpire, interferes with the fielder taking the throw at first base; except that he may run outside the three-foot lines to avoid a fielder attempting to field a batted ball.

Obstruction   The baserunner shall advance one base if he be prevented from making a base by the obstruction of a fielder, except when a fielder is trying to field a batted ball unless the latter has the ball in his hand ready to touch the baserunner. The ball is still in play so far as other baserunners are concerned.

Pitcher/Delivery   Preliminary to pitching, the pitcher shall take his position facing the batsman, with both feet squarely on the ground and on top of the pitcher's plate, or one foot on top of the pitcher's plate and the other foot in contact with same, or one foot in front of the pitcher's plate and the other foot on top of same, and in the act of delivering the ball to the batsman he must keep one foot in contact with the pitcher's plate. He shall not raise either foot until in the act of delivering the ball to the batsman, or in throwing to a base; nor may he make more than one step in such delivery. With a runner on first base or on second base, the pitcher must face the batsman with both hands holding the ball in front of him. If he indulges in a preliminary stretch by raising his arms above his head or out in front, he must return to a natural pitcher's position and stop before starting his delivery of the ball to the batsman.

Runner/Awarded Bases   In all cases where there are no spectators on the playing field and where a thrown ball goes into a stand for spectators or over or through any fence surrounding the

playing field or into the players' bench (whether the ball rebounds into the field or not) or remains in the meshes of a wire screen protecting the spectators, the runner or runners shall be entitled to two bases. When the throw is made by an infielder, the umpire, in awarding such bases, shall be governed by the position of the runner or runners at the time the ball was pitched; when the throw is made by an outfielder, the award shall be governed by the position of the runner or runners at the time the throw was made.

The baserunner shall advance one base without liability to be put out if a ball delivered by the pitcher pass the catcher and touch any fence or building within 60 feet of the home base. The ball shall be dead in such case.

Runner/Bases The baserunner is out if, when advancing bases or obliged to return to a base while the ball is in play, he fail to touch the intervening base or bases, if any, in the regular or reverse order, as the case may be, he may be put out by the ball being held by a fielder on any base he failed to touch or by being touched by the ball in the hand of a fielder in the same manner as in running to first base; provided, that the baserunner shall not be out in such case if the ball be delivered to the bat by the pitcher before the fielder hold it on said base or touch the baserunner with it; however, after a fly ball other than a foul tip be legally caught by a fielder, the baserunner who complies with this rule can only be retired by the ball being held by a fielder on the base occupied by the runner when such ball was batted or by being touched by the ball in the hand of the fielder.

The failure of a preceding runner to touch a base (and who is declared out therefore) shall not affect the status of a succeeding runner who touches each base in proper order; except that, after two are out, a succeeding runner cannot score a run when a preceding runner is declared out for failing to touch a base as provided in the rules. This exception also applies to a batsman who hits the ball out of the playing field for an apparent home run.

Substitute Substitutions shall not be in effect until the manager or captain of the team making the change notifies the umpire.

Substitute/Runner The manager or the captain of the opposing team must consent before a runner can be substituted for another baserunner.

Note: Previously this rule referred only to the captain. Throughout the rules of 1931, wherever authority or decision-making authority is granted to the captain, the words "or manager" have been added.

Uniform Glass buttons or polished metal must not be used on a uniform.

1932–38

There were no changes to the playing rules in these years.

1939

Batter/Caught Fly The baserunner is out if, having made a fair hit while batsman, such fair hit ball be caught by a fielder before touching the ground or any object other than a fielder; provided, it be not caught in a fielder's hat, cap, protector, pocket, or other part of his uniform.

Fielder/Drops Fly Ball If, before two are out, while first and second or first, second, and third bases are occupied, an outfielder, in the judgment of the umpire, intentionally drops a fly ball or a line drive, he shall immediately rule the ball has been caught.

Note: Baserunners are obliged to "tag up" after the out has been declared before they can advance.

Gloves The catcher may wear a leather glove or mitt of any size, shape or weight.

The first baseman may wear a leather glove or mitt not more than 12 inches from top to bottom and not more than 8 inches wide across the palm, with thumb and palm connected by leather lacing of not more than 4 inches from thumb to palm, which lacing shall not be enlarged, extended or reinforced by any process or material whatever.

Every other player is restricted to the use of a leather glove weighing not over 10 ounces and measuring not over 14 inches around the palm. The pitcher's glove must be uniform in color.

Pitcher/Delivery Preliminary to pitching, the pitcher shall take his position facing the batsman with both feet squarely on the ground, but his pivot foot must be on or in front in contact with the pitcher's plate; his other foot may be directly behind or in front (not on the side) of the pitcher's plate, and in the act of delivering the ball to the batsman he must keep one foot in contact with the pitcher's plate. He shall not raise either foot until in the act of delivering the ball to the batsman or in throwing to a base; nor may he make more than one step in such delivery. With a runner on first base or second base, the pitcher must face the batsman with both hands holding the ball in front of him. If he indulges in a preliminary stretch by raising his arms above his head or out in front, he must return to a natural pitcher's position and stop before starting his delivery of the ball to the batsman.

Note: After pitcher takes legal position for delivery of ball to batsman, he can take but one step and that must be forward.

A balk will be called (entitling the runner or runners to advance one base) if the pitcher makes any delivery of the ball to the bat while his pivot foot is back of and not in contact with the pitcher's plate.

1940

Bat The bat must be made entirely of hardwood in one piece.

Coach No fines are to be assessed for violations of the coaching rules.

Dead Ball A batted or thrown ball touched, stopped, or handled by a person not engaged in the game is dead and not in play. If a fair hit, the batsman making the hit shall be entitled to two bases and each baserunner shall be entitled to advance two bases. If a thrown ball, each baserunner shall be entitled to advance in accordance with the rules governing a thrown ball.

Note: This rule replaces the rule regarding "blocked balls."

Fielder See *Runner/Tagged.*

Fielder/Drops Fly Ball See *Runner/Advancing.*

Foul Ball A foul hit is a legally batted ball that settles on foul territory between home and first base or home and third base or that bounds past first or third base on or over foul territory or that falls on foul territory beyond first or third base or, while on or over foul ground, touches the person of the umpire or a player or any object foreign to the natural ground. A foul fly must be judged according to the relative position of the ball and the foul line, and not as to whether the fielder is on foul or fair ground at the time he touches the ball.

Game/Doubleheader No club or clubs shall engage in more than two championship games within a period of one day.

Game/Start No inning of any night game shall be started after 11:50 P.M. standard time.

Grounds The ball ground must be enclosed. To obviate the necessity for ground rules, the shortest distance from a fence or stand on fair territory to the home base should be 250 feet and from home base to the grandstand 60 feet.

Grounds/Foul Lines The foul lines are to be continued until they reach the boundary lines of the ground and not less than 10 feet above the top of the fence or stand. The foul lines are to be made, on the playing field, of lime, chalk, or other powder or paint.

Infield Fly The batter is out if, before two are out, while first and second or first, second, and third bases are occupied, he hit a fair fly ball, other than a line drive, that can reasonably be caught by an infielder. In such case, the umpire shall declare it an infield fly. However, the runners may be off their bases or advance at the risk of the ball being caught, the same as on any other fly ball; but if hit by the ball while standing on base, that baserunner shall not be called out, but the ball is dead and the batsman shall be called out and if the baserunner be hit while off base, both that baserunner and the batsman shall be called out and the ball is dead. Provided, that, with first and second bases occupied or first, second, and third bases occupied, with less than two out, any attempt to bunt which results in a fair fly ball shall not be regarded as an infield fly.

Interference/Defensive The batter becomes a baserunner if the catcher interferes with him, unless he makes a safe hit.

The baserunner is entitled to advance one base if the catcher interferes with the batsman while a baserunner is attempting to steal a base.

Interference/Offensive If one or more members of the team at bat stand or collect at or around a base for which a baserunner is trying, thereby confusing the team in the field and adding to the difficulty of making such play or if a batsman or baserunner who has just been retired obstructs or interferes with any following play being made on a baserunner, the baserunner shall be declared out for the interference of his teammate or teammates.

The baserunner is out if, after having hit or bunted a ball to fair territory, his bat again hits the ball on or over fair territory and deflects its course. Other baserunners cannot advance.

Pitcher/Delivery Preliminary to pitching, the pitcher shall take his position facing the batsman with his pivot foot always on or in front of and in contact with the pitcher's plate. In the act of delivering the ball to the batsman, the pitcher's other foot is free, except that he cannot step to either side of the pitcher's plate. He shall not raise either foot until in the act of delivering the ball to the batsman or in throwing to a base. With a runner on first or second base, the pitcher must face the batsman with both hands holding the ball in front of him. If he raises his arms above his head or out in front he must return to a natural pitcher's position and stop before starting the delivery of the ball to the batsman.

Note: After pitcher takes legal position for delivery of ball to batsman, he may take one step backward and one step forward, but not to either side.

It is a balk if the pitcher, in the act of delivering the ball to the batsman or in throwing to first base, drop the ball, either intentionally or accidentally.

Note: With no one on base, it is not a balk if the pitcher drops the ball while delivering it to the batsman.

A balk (entitling the runner or runners to advance one base) shall be called for: (1) Throwing the ball by the pitcher to any base to catch the baserunner without first stepping directly toward such base in the act of making such throw; or throwing or feinting to throw to an unoccupied base; (2) Making any motion of the arm, shoulder, hip, knee, foot, or body the pitcher habitually makes in his method of delivery, without immediately delivering the ball to the bat.

Runner/Advancing A baserunner who holds his base on a fly ball shall have the right to advance the moment such fly ball touches the person or uniform of a fielder.

The baserunner may "tag up" and advance if, before two are out, while first, or first and second, or first, second, and third bases are occupied, any player, in the judgment of the umpire, intentionally drops a fly ball or a line drive, the umpire shall immediately rule the ball has been caught.

Runner/Awarded Bases In all cases where there are no spectators on the playing field, and where a thrown ball goes into a stand for spectators, or over or through any fence surrounding the playing field, or into the players' bench (whether the ball rebounds into the field or not), or remains in the meshes of a wire screen protecting the spectators, the runner or runners shall be entitled to two bases. When a first throw made by an infielder, the umpire, in awarding such bases, shall be governed by the position of the runner or runners at the time the ball was pitched; when the throw is made by an outfielder or is the result of any following plays or attempted plays, the award shall be governed by the position of the runner or runners at the time the last throw was made.

Runner/Overrunning First The baserunner is permitted to "overslide" as well as overrun first base without liability to be put out.

Runner/Tagged The baserunner is out if at any time while the ball is in play, he be touched by the ball in the hand of a fielder, unless some part of his person be touching the base he is entitled to occupy; provided, however, that the ball be held by the fielder after touching him, unless the baserunner deliberately knock it out of his hand. The ball must be firmly held by the fielder after touching the runner. The ball cannot be juggled, even though the fielder may regain possession of the ball and prevent same from dropping to the ground.

Note: The previous rule read: "even though the fielder may *retain* possession of the ball."

Trainer Trainers are permitted to occupy the players' bench.

Trainer/Umpire Umpires are given authority over trainers.

Umpire The rules of 1940 describe the procedures to be used when more than two umpires are assigned.

The Umpire-in-Chief is to make all decisions regarding batters.

1941

There were no changes to the playing rules this year.

1942

Game/Start No inning of any night game shall be started after 12:50 A.M. war time.

1943–48

There were no changes to the playing rules in these years.

1949

Catcher/Position The catcher must stand with both feet inside the catcher's lines until the ball leaves the pitcher's hand.

Coach First base coaches as well as third base coaches must refrain from touching or holding the runner physically or the runner is out.

Foul/Fair Ball A foul fly must be judged according to the relative position of the ball and the foul line, including the foul pole, and not as to whether the fielder is on foul or fair ground at the time he touches the ball.

Game/Start No inning of any night game shall be started after 12:50 A.M. local city time.

Pitcher/Delivery No balk can be committed with all bases empty.

Player/Illegal Act No manager, captain, coach, or player shall address the spectators before or during a game except in reply to a request for information about the progress or state of the game or to give the name of a player.

1950

Bases The home plate and the pitcher's plate shall be of whitened rubber, anchored in the ground, even with its surface. The home plate, with beveled edges, shall be level with the baselines.

The pitcher's plate shall be on a mound 15 inches higher than home plate. The slope from the pitcher's plate to the baselines shall be gradual.

First, second, and third bases shall be approved bags of white canvas, securely anchored in the ground. They shall be 15 inches square and not less than three, nor more than five inches thick and shall be filled with soft material.

Bat The bat shall be round, not over 2¾ inches in diameter at the thickest part, not more than 42 inches in length, and entirely of hard, solid wood in one piece. Twine may be wound around it or a granulated substance applied to it, for a distance of 18 inches from the end of the handle, but not elsewhere.

Batter/Awarded Bases Each runner including the batter-runner may, without liability of being put out, advance to home base, scoring a run, if a fair ball goes over the field fence in flight and he touch all bases legally; or if a fair ball which, in the umpire's judgment, would have cleared the field fence in flight, is deflected by the act of a defensive player in throwing his glove, cap, or any article of his apparel, the runner shall be awarded a home run.

The rules of 1950 include various new provisions for baserunners when balls are hit or thrown into the stands.

The batter becomes a baserunner when a fair ball, after touching the ground, bounds into the stands or passes through or under a fence or through or under a scoreboard or through or under shrubbery or vines on the fence, in which case the batter and the baserunners shall be entitled to advance two bases.

The batter becomes a baserunner when any fair ball which, either before or after striking the ground, passes through or under a fence or through or under a scoreboard or through any opening in the fence or scoreboard or through or under shrubbery or vines on the fence, in which case the batter and the baserunners shall be entitled to two bases.

The batter becomes a baserunner when any bounding fair ball is deflected by the fielder into the stands or over or under a fence on fair or foul ground, in which case the batter and all baserunners shall be entitled to advance two bases.

The batter becomes a baserunner when any fair fly ball is deflected by the fielder into the stands or over the fence into foul territory, in which case the batter shall be entitled to advance to second base; but if deflected into the stands or over the fence in fair territory, the batter shall be entitled to a home run.

Batter/Illegal Act The batter is out for illegal action when he fails to take his position in the batter's box promptly. If he persists in unwarranted delay in taking his position the umpire shall direct the pitcher to deliver the ball to the bat and every such pitch shall be called "strike" by the umpire. If he enters the batter's box in the interval between any such pitches, the ball and strike count shall continue regularly, but if he has not entered the batter's box when three strikes are called he shall be declared "out."

Catch A catch is the act of a defensive player in receiving, and holding firmly in his hand or glove, a batted or thrown ball. It is not a catch, however, if simultaneously or immediately following his contact with the ball, he collide with a player or with a wall or if he fall down, and as a result of such collision or falling, drops the ball. If the player has made the catch and drops the ball while in the act of making a throw following the catch, the ball shall be adjudged to have been caught. In establishing the validity of the catch, the player shall hold the ball long enough to prove that he has complete control of the ball and that his release of the ball is voluntary and intentional.

Dead/Live Ball See *Game/"Time."*

Definitions Rule Two of the rules of 1950 includes the definitions of 69 baseball terms as used in the rules. Several of the key definitions are quoted throughout this year's rule entries.

Fair Territory Fair territory is that part of the playing field within, and including the first and third baselines, from home base to the bottom of the playing field fence and perpendicularly upwards. All foul lines are in fair territory.

Foul Tip A foul tip is a ball batted by the batter that goes sharp and direct from the bat to the catcher's hands and is legally caught. It is not a foul tip unless caught and any foul tip that is caught is a strike, and the ball is in play. It is not a catch if it is a rebound from any part of the catcher's equipment other than the catcher's glove or hand.

Game Baseball is a game between two teams of nine players, each with adequate substitutes, coaches, and trainers, under direction of a manager, played in accordance with these rules, under jurisdiction of an umpire or umpires on an enclosed field.

The object of each team is to win by scoring the more runs.

A game consists of nine innings, except as otherwise provided, and an inning is that portion of the game during which each team shall play both offensively and defensively.

The winner of the game shall be that team which shall have scored, in accordance with these rules, the greater number of runs at the conclusion of a regulation game.

Game/Doubleheader The rules of 1950 include a series of new provisions governing the conduct of doubleheaders.

Game/Rain The manager of the home team shall be the sole judge of the fitness of the playing field for the beginning of any game other than the second game of a doubleheader. Exception: Any league may permanently authorize its president to suspend the application of this rule as to that league during the closing weeks of its championship season in order to ensure that the championship is decided each year on its merits. When the postponement of, and possible failure to play, a game in the final series of a championship season between any two teams might affect the final standing of any club in the league, the president, on appeal from any league member, may assume the authority granted the home team manager by this rule.

Game/Start The players of the home team shall take their defensive positions, the first batter of the visiting team shall take his position in the batter's box, the umpire shall call "Play," and the game shall proceed.

The rules of 1950 include a series of new provisions governing the preliminaries before championship games.

Game/"Time" The ball is dead when the umpire-in-chief suspends play by calling "Time" when a manager requests "Time" for a substitution or for conference with his player.

The ball is dead when the umpire-in-chief suspends play by calling "Time" when a fielder, after catching a fly ball, falls into a bench, dugout, or stand or falls across ropes into a crowd (when spectators are on the field), and baserunners may advance one base without liability to be put out.

Note: If player after making the catch steps into the dugout but does not fall, the ball is alive and in play and runners may advance at their own peril.

After the umpire calls "Play" the ball is alive and in play and remains alive and in play until for legal cause, or at the umpire's call of "Time" suspending play, the ball becomes dead. While the ball is dead no player may be put out, no bases may be run, and no runs may be scored, except that runners may advance as legally provided.

Glove/Fielder Each player, other than the first baseman and the catcher, is restricted to the use of a leather glove not more than twelve inches long nor more than eight inches wide, measured from the base of the thumb crotch to the outside edge of the glove. The space between the thumb and the forefinger shall not exceed 4½ inches at the top nor more than 3½ inches at the base of the thumb crotch. The webbing may be standard leather or lacing and shall not be enlarged, extended, or reinforced by

any process or materials whatever. The webbing cannot be constructed of wound or wrapped lacing to make a net type of trap. The glove may be of any weight.

Glove/First Baseman The first baseman may wear a leather glove or mitt not more than 12 inches long from top to bottom and not more than eight inches wide across the palm, measured from base of thumb crotch to outer edge of the mitt. The space between the thumb section and the finger section of the mitt shall not exceed four inches at the top of the mitt and 3½ inches at the base of the thumb crotch. The mitt shall be constructed so that this space is permanently fixed and cannot be enlarged, extended, widened, or deepened by the use of any materials or process whatever. The web of the mitt shall measure not more than five inches from its top to the base of the thumb crotch. The web may be either a lacing, lacing through leather tunnels, or a center piece of leather which may be an extension of the palm connected to the mitt with lacing and constructed so that it will not exceed the above-mentioned measurements. The webbing cannot be constructed of wound or wrapped lacing or deepened to make a net type of trap.

Glove/Pitcher The pitcher's glove shall be uniform in color and cannot be white or gray.

Home Run See *Batter/Awarded Bases.*

Infield Fly An infield fly is an out called by the umpire on the batter—if, before two are out, while first and second or first, second, and third bases are occupied, he hit a fair fly ball, other than a line drive, that in the judgment of the umpire can reasonably be caught by an infielder. Where a defensive player who normally plays in the outfield places himself in the infield, he shall for the purpose of the infield fly rule be considered an infielder. In such case, the umpire shall declare it an infield fly. However, the runners may be off their bases or advance at the risk of the ball being caught, the same as on any other fly ball. If a runner is hit by the ball while standing on base, he shall not be called out, but the ball is dead and the batter shall be called out; but if a baserunner is hit while off base, both he and the batter shall be called out and the ball is dead. Provided, that, with first and second bases occupied, or first, second, and third bases occupied, before two are out, any attempt to bunt which results in a fair fly ball shall not be regarded as an infield fly.

Interference/Offensive The rules of 1950 include several new provisions describing the circumstances under which a baserunner is out for interference.

The batter is out when a preceding runner shall, in the umpire's judgment, intentionally interfere with the play of a defensive player who is attempting to catch a thrown ball or to throw the ball in an attempt to complete any play.

The batter is out when with two out, a runner on third base, and two strikes on the batter, the runner attempts to steal home base on a legal pitch and the ball strikes the runner in the strike zone. The umpire shall call "strike three," the batter is out and the run shall not count; with less than two out the umpire shall call "strike three," the ball is dead, and the run counts.

The batter is out when after striking or bunting the ball he intentionally strikes the ball a second time, or strikes it with a thrown bat or deflects its course in any manner while running to first base. The ball is dead and no runners may advance. If the runner drops his bat and the ball rolls against the bat and, in the umpire's judgment, there was no intention to interfere with the course of the ball, the ball is alive and in play.

Obstruction A batter who has become a runner is entitled to unimpeded progress as he advances around the bases. Whenever a defensive player impedes the runner in any way, unless he is attempting to field a batted ball or has the ball in his possession, the umpire shall call "obstruction," the ball shall remain in play, and all runners shall be permitted to advance, without liability to be put out, to the bases which, in the judgment of the umpire, the

runners would have reached had obstruction not been called.

In a "run-down" play, if the runner's progress is impeded by any defensive player who does not have the ball in his possession, the umpire shall call "obstruction" and the runner shall be entitled to occupy the base he is attempting to reach when the obstruction occurred.

Pitcher/Delivery There are two legal pitching positions: The "Wind-up" position and the "Set" position. Either position may be used at any time.

Pivot Foot The pitcher's pivot foot is that foot which is in contact with the pitcher's plate as he delivers the pitch.

Set Position Set position is the pitcher's position when he stands facing the batter with his entire pivot foot on or in front of and in contact with, and not off the end of the pitcher's plate, and his other foot in front of the pitcher's plate, holding the ball in both hands in front of his body and coming to a complete stop of at least one second.

Wind-up Position Wind-up position is the pitcher's position when he stands facing the batter, his pivot foot on or in front of and touching the pitcher's plate, and the other foot free.

From the set position, the pitcher may deliver the ball to the batter, throw to a base, or step backward off the pitcher's plate with his pivot foot. Before assuming set position the pitcher may elect to make any natural preliminary motion such as that known as "the stretch." But if he so elects, he must come to set position before delivering the ball to the batter. After assuming set position, any natural motion associated with his delivery of the ball to the batter commits him to the pitch without alteration or interruption.

If there is a runner or runners it is a balk if the pitcher delivers the pitch from "set position" without coming to a stop of one full second.

Pitcher/Illegal Act The pitcher shall not be allowed to pitch at a batter's head, and if, in the umpire's opinion, such violation occurs, he shall call "Time" and warn the pitcher and the manager of the defensive team that another such pitch will mean the immediate expulsion of the pitcher from the game. If such pitch is repeated, the umpire shall inflict the penalty as follows: The pitcher shall be removed from the game and from the grounds. The president of the League shall impose such fine and suspension as his judgment warrants.

See also *Pitcher/Uniform.*

Pitcher/Illegal Pitches If the pitcher makes an illegal pitch with the bases unoccupied it shall be called a ball, unless the batter shall make a fair hit or reaches first base on an error or otherwise.

The pitcher shall not be allowed to pitch the "quick return ball." Whenever such pitch is attempted the umpire shall call "Time." If the offense is repeated the umpire shall call each such repeated offense a "ball," unless the batter reaches first base on a fair hit, an error, or otherwise, and no other runner is forced by his reaching first base, in which case the play proceeds.

Pitcher-Infielder If the pitcher removes his pivot foot from contact with the pitcher's plate by stepping backward with that foot, he thereby becomes an infielder and, if his subsequent throw to a base, when off the pitcher's plate, goes into a stand or over, through, or under a fence or into a bench or dugout (whether the ball rebounds or not) or remains in the meshes of a wire screen protecting the spectators, the ball is dead and all runners shall be entitled to advance two bases.

Pitcher/Pick-Off At any time during the pitcher's preliminary movements and until his natural pitching motion commits him to the pitch, he may throw to any base provided he step directly toward such base before making the throw.

Pitcher/Position See *Bases* for pitcher's plate.

Pitcher/Uniform The pitcher shall not be allowed to wear a

garment with ragged, frayed or slit sleeves, and shall not be permitted to attach tape or other material of a color different from his uniform or glove to his glove or clothing.

Pitcher/Warm-Ups When a pitcher takes his position at the beginning of each inning or when he relieves another pitcher, he shall be permitted to pitch not to exceed eight preparatory pitches to his catcher during which play shall be suspended. Such preparatory pitches shall not consume more than one minute of time.

Player/Illegal Acts Players in uniform shall not address nor mingle with spectators, nor sit in the stands before or during a game. No manager, captain, coacher, or player shall address any spectator before or during a game. Players of opposing teams shall not fraternize at any time while in uniform. Penalty: The president of the league shall impose fines for violation of this rule at his discretion.

No manager, player, substitute, coacher, trainer, or batboy shall at any time, whether from the bench, the coacher's box, or on the playing field, or elsewhere call "Time," or employ any other word or phrase while the ball is alive and in play for the obvious purpose of confusing an umpire or an opposing player.

Except the batter, or a runner attempting to score, no offensive player shall cross the catcher's lines when the ball is in play.

Runner/Out The baserunner is out if, after he has acquired legal possession of a base, he or that base is tagged while he is running the bases in reverse order for the purpose of confusing the defense or making a travesty of the game. No runner may advance in this situation in the event of an error on this play by the defensive team.

The baserunner is out if, in running or sliding for home base, he fails to touch home base and makes no attempt to return to the base, when a defensive player holds the ball in his hand while touching home base and appeals to the umpire for the decision.

Strike Zone The strike zone is that space over home plate which is between the batter's armpits and the top of his knees when he assumes his natural stance.

Substitute A player or players may be substituted during a game at any time the ball is dead. A substituted player shall bat in the replaced player's position in the team's batting order. A player once removed from a game shall not re-enter that game. If a substitute enters the game in place of a manager, the manager may thereafter go to the coaching lines at his discretion. When two or more substitute players of the defensive team enter the game at the same time, the manager, or his designated representative, shall, immediately before they take their position as defensive players, designate to the umpire-in-chief such players' positions in the team's batting order and the umpire-in-chief shall so notify the official scorer. If this information is not immediately given to the umpire-in-chief, he shall have authority to designate the substitutes' places in the batting order.

Substitute/Runner A player whose name is on his team's batting order may not become a substitute runner for another member of his team.

Umpire Each umpire is the representative of the president of the league, the president of the National Association and the Commissioner of Baseball.

The umpire-in-chief shall enforce the rules from the moment he receives the batting order from the manager of the home team until termination of the game. This shall include control of ground crews, newsmen, and photographers, and any other persons whose duties require their presence upon the field.

1951–53

There were no changes to the playing rules in these years.

1954

Bat The bat shall be a smooth, rounded stick not more than 2¾ inches in diameter at the thickest part and not more than 42 inches in length. The bat shall be one piece of solid wood or formed from a block of wood consisting of two or more pieces of wood bonded together with an adhesive in such a way that the grain direction of all pieces is essentially parallel to the length of the bat. Any such laminated bat shall contain only wood or adhesive, except for a clear finish.

For a distance of 18 inches from the end by which the bat is gripped, it may be roughened or wrapped with tape or twine.

Note: Approval of the laminated bat is experimental for the 1954 season, and no laminated bat shall be used in a professional game until the manufacturer has secured approval from the Rules Committee of his design and method of manufacture. In giving or withholding such approval, the Rules Committee will be guided by comparison of the laminated bat with one-piece solid wood bats. Laminated bats which are inferior to one-piece solid wood bats in safety or durability will not be approved. A design or method of manufacture which produces a "loaded" or "freak" type of bat or which produces a substantially greater reaction or distance factor than one-piece solid wood bats will not be approved.

Batter/Illegal Act See *Interference/Offensive.*

Catch A catch is the act of a fielder in getting secure possession in his hand or glove of a ball in flight and firmly holding it; providing he does not use his cap, protector, pocket, or any other part of his uniform in getting possession.

Dead/Live Ball See *Game/"Time."*

Definitions Rules Two and Three of the rules of 1954 contain several new definitions of baseball terms as used in the rules.

Fielder/Drops Fly Ball The batter is out when, with less than two out and first, first and second, first and third, or first, second, and third bases occupied, a fielder intentionally drops a fair fly ball or line drive. Runners need not re-touch and may advance at their own peril.

Fielder/Illegal Act No fielder shall take a position in the batter's line of vision, and with deliberate unsportsmanlike intent, act in a manner to distract the batter.

Game The rules of 1954 contain a series of new provisions governing suspended games.

Game/"Time" After the umpire calls "Play" the ball is alive and in play and remains alive and in play until for legal cause, or at the umpire's call of "Time" suspending play, the ball becomes dead. While the ball is dead no player may be put out, no bases may be run, and no runs may be scored, except that runners may advance one or more bases as the result of acts which occurred while the ball was alive (such as, but not limited to, a balk, an overthrow, interference, or a home run or other fair hit out of the playing field).

Gloves/Equipment Members of the offensive team shall carry all gloves and other equipment off the field and to the dugout while their team is at bat. No equipment shall be left lying on the field, either in fair or foul territory.

Interference/Defensive Defensive interference is an illegal act by a fielder which hinders or prevents a batter from hitting a pitch.

Interference/Offensive The batter is out after hitting or bunting a fair ball, when his bat hits the ball a second time in fair territory. The ball is dead and no runners may advance. If the batter-runner drops his bat and the ball rolls against the bat in fair territory and, in the umpire's judgment, there was no intention to interfere with the course of the ball, the ball is alive and in play.

The batter is out after hitting or bunting a foul ball, when he intentionally deflects the course of the ball in any manner while running to first base. The ball is dead and no runners may advance.

The batter is out when his fair ball touches him before touching a fielder.

It is interference by a batter or runner when he intentionally deflects the course of a foul ball in any manner.

Interference/Spectator   The batter is out when spectator interference clearly prevents a fielder from catching his fly ball.

Spectator interference occurs when a spectator reaches out of the stands, or goes on the playing field and touches a live ball. When there is spectator interference with any thrown ball, except a throw by the pitcher, the ball shall be dead at the moment of interference and the umpire shall impose such penalties as in his opinion will nullify the act of interference.

Pitcher/Delivery   In the event a balk is called, the ball is dead, and each runner shall advance one base without liability to be put out unless the batter hits the pitch on which the balk is made, in which case the manager of the offensive team may elect to accept either the balk penalty or the result of the batter's action.

Pitcher/Illegal Pitch   A quick return pitch is a pitch made with obvious intent to catch a batter off balance.

Pitcher/Starter   The pitcher named in the batting order handed the umpire-in-chief shall pitch to the first batter or any substitute batter until the batter is put out or reaches first base, unless the pitcher sustains injury or illness which, in the judgment of the umpire-in-chief, incapacitates him from pitching further.

If the pitcher is replaced, the substitute pitcher shall pitch to the batter then at bat, or any substitute batter, until such batter is retired or reaches first base, or until the offensive team is retired, unless the substitute pitcher sustains injury or illness which, in the umpire-in-chief's judgment, incapacitates him for further play as a pitcher.

Relief Pitcher   See above, *Pitcher/Starter.*

Runner   The rules of 1954 include several new provisions awarding baserunners additional bases in various circumstances.

Squeeze Play   Squeeze play is a term to designate a play when a team, with a runner on third base, attempts to score that runner by means of a bunt.

Triple Play   A triple play is a play by the defense in which three offensive players are legally put out as a result of continuous action, providing there is no error between the putouts.

Umpire   The umpire's authority to act in legal manner on all matters pertaining to a game shall not be questioned. The umpire shall have power to make decisions on any points not specifically covered in the rules.

Wild Pitch   A wild pitch is one so high, so low, or so wide of the plate that it cannot be handled with ordinary effort by the catcher.

1955

Ball   The ball shall be a sphere formed by yarn wound around a small core of cork, rubber or similar material, covered with two strips of white horsehide, tightly stitched together. It shall weigh not less than 5 nor more than 5¼ ounces avoirdupois and measure not less than 9 nor more than 9¼ inches in circumference.

Batter/Position (Illegal)   An illegally batted ball is one hit by the batter with one or both feet outside of the batter's box.

Batting Order   The umpire-in-chief shall make certain that the original and copies of the respective batting orders are identical, and then tender a copy of each batting order to the opposing manager. The copy retained by the umpire shall be the official

batting order. The tender of the batting order by the umpire shall establish the batting orders. Thereafter, no substitutions shall be made by either manager, except as provided in the rules.

Catcher/Position   The catcher shall stand with both feet within the lines of the catcher's box, directly back of the plate, until the ball leaves the pitcher's hand. The intent of this rule is to deter the giving of intentional bases on balls. If the catcher has either foot outside his box when the pitcher delivers the ball, it is a balk.

Dead/Live Ball   See *Game/"Time."*

Interference/Defensive   The batter becomes a runner and is entitled to first base when the catcher or any other fielder interferes with him, unless the batter reaches first base on a hit, an error, or otherwise, and all other runners advance at least one base, in which case the play proceeds without reference to the interference.

Interference/Offensive   It is interference by a batter or runner when any member or members of the offensive team stand or gather around any base to which a runner is advancing, to confuse, hinder, or add to the difficulty of the fielders. Such runner shall be declared out for the interference of his teammate or teammates.

It is interference by a batter or runner when any batter or runner who has just been retired hinders or impedes any following play being made on a runner. Such runner shall be declared out for the interference of his teammate.

Forfeited Game   A game shall be forfeited in favor of the opposing team when a team is unable or refuses to place nine players on the field.

Game   The rules of 1955 include new provisions for determining a suspended game and its resumption.

Game/Rain   The manager of the home team shall be the sole judge as to whether a game shall be started because of unsuitable weather conditions or the unfit condition of the playing field, except for the second game of a doubleheader.

Game/"Time"   The ball becomes dead when the umpire-in-chief suspends play by calling "Time" when an accident incapacitates a player or umpire, or if it is necessary to remove a player or spectator from the grounds. The umpire shall not call "Time" because of an accident to player or umpire during a play, until in his judgment, no further action is possible in that play, unless an accident to a runner is such as to prevent him from proceeding to a base to which he is legally entitled, as on a home run hit out of the playing field, or an award of one or more bases, in which case a substitute runner shall be permitted to complete the play.

Pitcher/Delivery   When the bases are unoccupied, the pitcher shall deliver the ball to the batter within 20 seconds after taking his pitching position. Each time the pitcher delays the game by violating this rule, the umpire shall call "Ball."

1956

There were no changes to the playing rules this year.

1957

The rules of 1957 contain new wording and explanation for the rules governing a batter who bats out of order.

Ball/Defacing   See *Pitcher/Illegal Act.*

Batter/Position   The batter shall take his position in the batter's box promptly when it is his time at bat.

The batter shall not leave his position in the batter's box after the pitcher comes to the Set Position, or starts his windup. Penalty: If the pitcher pitches, the umpire shall call "Ball" or "Strike," as the case may be.

Catcher/Position   When the ball is put in play at the start of or during a game, all fielders other than the catcher shall be on fair

territory. The catcher shall station himself directly back of the plate. He may leave his position at any time to catch a pitch or make a play except that when the batter is being given an intentional base on balls, the catcher must stand with both feet within the lines of the catcher's box until the ball leaves the pitcher's hand. Penalty: Balk.

Coach The offensive team shall station two coaches on the field during its term at bat, one near first base and one near third base. Failure to place two coaches on the field shall subject the manager to fine or suspension or both by the league president.

Coaches shall be limited to two in number and shall (1) be in team uniform; (2) remain within the coach's box at all times; and (3) address players of their own team only. Penalty: The offending coach shall be removed from the game, and shall leave the playing field.

Game When the winning run is scored in the last half-inning of a regulation game, or in the last half of an extra inning, as the result of a base on balls, hit batsman, or any other play with the bases full which forces the runner on third to advance, the umpire shall not declare the game ended until the runner forced to advance from third has touched home base and the batter-runner has touched first base. Penalty: If the runner on third refuses to advance to and touch home base in a reasonable time, the umpire shall disallow the run, call out the offending player, and order the game resumed. If, with less than two out, the batter-runner refuses to advance to and touch first base, the run shall count, but the offending player shall be called out.

The rules of 1957 include a rewording of the rules governing suspended games and the resumption of suspended games.

Game/Doubleheader A league may adopt a rule providing that one game of a doubleheader shall be seven innings in length. In such games, any of these rules applying to the ninth inning shall apply to the seventh inning.

The second game of a doubleheader shall start 20 minutes after the first game is completed, unless a longer interval (not to exceed 30 minutes) is declared by the umpire-in-chief and announced to the opposing managers at the end of the first game. Exception: If the league president has approved a request of the home club for a longer interval between games for some special event, the umpire-in-chief shall declare such longer interval and announce it to the opposing managers. The umpire-in-chief of the first game shall be the timekeeper controlling the interval between games.

Hit by Pitch The batter becomes a runner and is entitled to first base without liability to be put out (provided he advances to and touches first base) when he is touched by a pitched ball which he is not attempting to hit unless: (1) The ball is in the strike zone when it touches the batter, or (2) The batter makes no attempt to avoid being touched by the ball.

Note: If the ball is in the strike zone when it touches the batter, it shall be called a strike, whether or not the batter tries to avoid the ball. If the ball is outside the strike zone when it touches the batter, it shall be called a ball if he makes no attempt to avoid being touched.

Infield Fly An infield fly is a fair fly ball (not including a line drive nor an attempted bunt) which can be caught by an infielder with ordinary effort when first and second, or first, second, and third bases are occupied, before two are out. The pitcher, catcher, and any outfielder who stations himself in the infield on the play shall be considered infielders for the purpose of this rule.

When it seems apparent that a batted ball will be an infield fly, the umpire shall immediately declare "Infield Fly" for the benefit of the runners. If the ball is near the baselines, the umpire shall declare "Infield Fly, if Fair."

The ball is alive and runners may advance at the risk of the ball being caught, or re-touch and advance after the ball is touched, the same as on any fly ball. If the hit becomes a foul

ball, it is treated the same as any foul.

Note: If a declared infield fly is allowed to fall untouched to the ground, and bounces foul, it is a foul ball. If a declared infield fly falls untouched to the ground outside the baseline, and bounces fair, it is an infield fly.

Interference/Defensive If, with a runner on third base and trying to score by means of a squeeze play or a steal, the catcher or any other fielder steps on, or in front of home base without possession of the ball, or touches the batter or his bat, the pitcher shall be charged with a balk, the batter shall be awarded first base on the interference, and the ball is dead.

Each runner, other than the batter, may without liability to be put out, advance one base when he is attempting to steal a base, if the batter is interfered with by the catcher or any other fielder.

Note: When a runner is entitled to a base without liability to be put out, while the ball is in play, or under any rule in which the ball is in play after the runner reaches the base to which he is entitled, and the runner fails to touch the base to which he is entitled before attempting to advance to the next base, the runner shall forfeit his exemption from liability to be put out, and he may be put out by tagging the base or by tagging the runner before he returns to the missed base.

Obstruction In a rundown play, if the runner is obstructed by any fielder who does not have the ball in his possession (unless the fielder is in the act of fielding the ball), the umpire shall call "Obstruction" and the runner shall be entitled to occupy the base he is attempting to reach when the obstruction occurs. If such base is held by a following runner, any following runner forced to vacate his base by the obstructed runner's return shall be permitted to return to his last-held base without liability to be put out.

Pitcher/Delivery When the bases are unoccupied, the pitcher shall deliver the ball to the batter within 20 seconds after he receives the ball. Each time the pitcher delays the game by violating this rule, the umpire shall call "Ball."

Note: The intent of this rule is to avoid unnecessary delays. The umpire shall insist that the catcher return the ball promptly to the pitcher, and that the pitcher take his position on the rubber promptly. Obvious delay by the pitcher should instantly be penalized by the umpire.

If there is a runner or runners it is a balk if the pitcher, while giving an intentional base on balls, pitches when the catcher is not in the catcher's box.

If there is a runner or runners it is a balk if the pitcher makes an illegal pitch.

Pitcher/Illegal Act The pitcher shall not (1) apply a foreign substance of any kind to the ball; (2) expectorate either on the ball or his glove; (3) rub the ball on his glove, person, or clothing; (4) deface the ball in any manner; (5) deliver what is called the "shine" ball, "spit" ball, "mud" ball or "emery" ball. The pitcher, of course, is allowed to rub the ball between his bare hands. Penalty: For violation of any part of this rule, the umpire shall immediately disqualify the pitcher, and the league president shall suspend the pitcher for a period of 10 days. If a pitch is delivered in violation of this rule, it shall be treated as an illegal pitch.

Player/Illegal Act Players in uniform shall not address nor mingle with spectators, nor sit in the stands before, during, or after a game. No manager, captain, coach, or player shall address any spectator before or during a game.

Players of opposing teams shall not fraternize at any time while in uniform. Penalty: The league president shall impose fines for violation of this rule at his discretion.

Player/Position See *Catcher/Position*.

Relief Pitcher If an improper substitution is made for the pitcher, the umpire shall direct the proper pitcher to return to

the game until the provisions of this rule are fulfilled. If the improper pitcher is permitted to pitch, any play that results is legal. The improper pitcher becomes the proper pitcher as soon as he makes his first pitch to the batter, or as soon as any runner is retired.

Strike Zone   A strike is a legal pitch when so called by the umpire which (a) is struck at by the batter and is missed; (b) enters the strike zone in flight and is not struck at; (c) is fouled by the batter when he has less than two strikes; (d) is bunted foul; (e) touches the batter as he strikes at it; (f) touches the batter in flight in the strike zone; or (g) becomes a foul tip. Note: (f) was added to the former rule and definition.

Touch/Definition   To touch a player or umpire is to touch any part of his body, clothing, or his equipment.

Umpire   Each umpire has authority to disqualify any player, coach, manager, or substitute for objecting to decisions or for unsportsmanlike conduct or language, and to remove such disqualified person from the playing field. If an umpire disqualifies a player while a play is in progress, the disqualification shall not take effect until no further action is possible in that play.

Each umpire has authority at his discretion to remove from the playing field (1) any person whose duties permit his presence on the field, such as ground-crew members, ushers, photographers, newsmen, broadcasting-crew members, etc., or (2) any spectator or other person not authorized to be on the playing field.

Umpire/Decisions   If different decisions should be made on one play by different umpires, the umpire-in-chief shall call all the umpires into consultation, with no manager or player present. After consultation, the umpire-in-chief (unless another umpire may have been designated by the league president) shall determine which decision shall prevail, based on which umpire was in best position and which decision was most likely correct. Play shall proceed as if only the final decision had been made.

1958

Appeal/Runner   Any runner shall be called out, on appeal, when (a) after a fly ball is caught, he fails to re-touch his base before he or his base is tagged; (b) with the ball in play, while advancing or returning to a base, he fails to touch each base in order before he, or a missed base is tagged; (c) he overruns or overslides first base and fails to return to the base immediately, and he or the base is tagged; (d) he fails to touch home base and makes no attempt to return to that base, and home base is tagged. Any appeal under this rule must be made before the next legal pitch. If the violation occurs during a play which ends a half-inning, the appeal must be made before the defensive team leaves the field.

Note: Appeal plays may require an umpire to recognize an apparent "fourth out." If the third out is made during a play in which an appeal play is sustained on another runner, the appeal play decision takes precedence in determining the out. If there is more than one appeal during a play that ends a half-inning, the defense may elect to take the out that gives it the advantage. If the third out on appeal is a force play or failure of the batter-runner to touch first base, no runs can score on the play. Otherwise runs made before the appeal is sustained shall count. For the purposes of this rule, the defensive team has "left the field" when the pitchers and all infielders have left fair territory on their way to the bench or clubhouse.

1959

Grounds   Any playing field constructed by a professional club after June 1, 1958, shall provide a minimum distance of 325 feet from home base to the nearest fence, stand, or other obstruction on the right and left field foul lines, and a minimum distance of 400 feet to the center field fence. No existing playing fields shall be remodeled after June 1, 1958, in such manner as to reduce the

distance from home base to the foul poles and to the center field fence below the minimum distances.

Interference/Spectator   When there is spectator interference with any thrown ball, the ball shall be dead at the moment of interference, and the umpire shall impose such penalties as in his opinion will nullify the act of interference.

Runner/Awarded Bases   The runner is entitled to advance one base, if a ball, pitched to the batter, or thrown by the pitcher from his position on the pitcher's plate to a base to catch a runner, goes into a stand, or players' bench, or over or through a field fence or backstop. The ball is dead.

Note: If such a wild pitch is ball four, the batter-runner is entitled to first base only.

Each runner, including the batter-runner, may advance two bases, if a fair ball bounces or is deflected into the stands outside the first or third base foul lines; or if it goes through or under a field fence, or through or under a scoreboard, or through or under shrubbery or vines on the fence; or if it sticks in such fence, scoreboard, shrubbery, or vines.

1960–62

There were no changes to the playing rules in these years.

1963

Interference/Offensive   Offensive interference is an act by the team at bat which interferes with, obstructs, impedes, hinders, or confuses any fielder attempting to make a play. If the umpire declares the batter, batter-runner, or a runner out for interference, all other runners shall return to the last base that was, in the judgment of the umpire, legally touched at the time of the interference.

Pitcher/Delivery Wind-up Position   The pitcher shall stand facing the batter, his entire pivot foot on, or in front of and touching and not off the end of the pitcher's plate, and the other foot free. From this position any natural movement associated with his delivery of the ball to the batter commits him to the pitch without interruption or alteration. He shall not raise either foot from the ground, except that in his actual delivery of the ball to the batter, he may take one step backward, and one step forward with his free foot.

Note: When a pitcher holds the ball with both hands in front of his body, with his entire pivot foot on, or in front of and touching but not off the end of the pitcher's plate, and his other foot free, he will be considered in a Windup Position.

If there is a runner, or runners, it is a balk when the pitcher, after coming to a legal pitching position, removes one hand from the ball other than in an actual pitch, or in throwing to a base.

Pitcher/Warm-Up Pitches   When a pitcher takes his position at the beginning of each inning, or when he relieves another pitcher, he shall be permitted to pitch not to exceed eight preparatory pitches to his catcher during which play shall be suspended. A league by its own action may limit the number of preparatory pitches to less than eight preparatory pitches. Such preparatory pitches shall not consume more than one minute of time. If a sudden emergency causes a pitcher to be summoned into the game without any opportunity to warm up, the umpire-in-chief shall allow him as many pitches as the umpire deems necessary.

Runner   A runner acquires the right to an unoccupied base when he touches it before he is out. He is then entitled to it until he is put out, or forced to vacate it for another runner.

Unless two are out, the status of a following runner is not affected by a preceding runner's failure to touch or re-touch a base. If, upon appeal, the preceding runner is the third out, no runners following him shall score. If such third out is the result of a force play, neither preceding nor following runners shall score.

Strike Zone   The strike zone is that space over home plate which is between the top of the batter's shoulders and his

knees when he assumes his natural stance. The umpire shall determine the strike zone according to the batter's usual stance when he swings at a pitch.

1964

Bat No colored bat may be used in a professional game unless approved by the rules committee.

Interference/Defensive The batter becomes a runner and is entitled to first base when the catcher or any fielder interferes with him. If a play follows the interference, the manager of the offense may advise the plate umpire that he elects to decline the interference penalty and accept the play. Such election shall be made immediately at the end of the play. However, if the batter reaches first base on a hit, an error, a base on balls, a hit batsman, or otherwise, and all other runners advance at least one base, the play proceeds without reference to the interference.

Interference/Offensive It is interference by a batter or a runner when a batter-runner willfully and deliberately interferes with a batted ball or a fielder in the act of fielding a batted ball, with the obvious intent to break up a double play. The ball is dead. The umpire shall call the batter-runner out for interference and also call out the next preceding runner for the action of his teammate. In no event may bases be run or runs scored because of such action by a runner.

It is interference by a batter or a runner when, in the judgment of the umpire, a baserunner willfully and deliberately interferes with a batted ball or a fielder in the act of fielding a batted ball with the obvious intent to break up a double play. The ball is dead. The umpire shall call the runner out for interference and also call out the batter-runner because of the action of his teammate. In no event may bases be run or runs scored because of such action by a runner.

Pitcher/Delivery The Set Position Set Position shall be indicated by the pitcher when he stands facing the batter with his entire pivot foot on, or in front of, and in contact with, and not off the end of the pitcher's plate, and his other foot in front of the pitcher's plate, holding the ball in both hands in front of his body and coming to a complete stop. From such Set Position he may deliver the ball to the batter, throw to a base or step backward off the pitcher's plate with his pivot foot. Before assuming Set Position, the pitcher may elect to make any natural preliminary motion such as that known as "the stretch." But, if he so elects, he shall come to Set Position before delivering the ball to the batter. After assuming Set Position any natural motion associated with his delivery of the ball to the batter commits him to the pitch without alteration or interruption.

Uniforms Any part of an undershirt exposed to view shall be of a uniform solid color for all players on a team. Any player other than the pitcher may have numbers, letters, insignia attached to the sleeve of an undershirt.

1965

Glove/Catcher The catcher may wear a leather glove or mitt no more than 38 inches in circumference, nor more than 15½ inches from top to bottom. Such limits shall include all lacing and any leather band or facing attached to the outer edge of the mitt. The space between the thumb section and the finger section of the mitt shall not exceed six inches at the top of the mitt and four inches at the base of the thumb crotch. The web shall measure not more than seven inches across the top or more than six inches from its top to the base of the thumb crotch. The web may be either a lacing or lacing through leather tunnels, or a center piece of leather which may be an extension of the palm, connected to the mitt with lacing and constructed so that it will not exceed any of the above mentioned requirements. The glove may be of any weight.

Interference/Offensive It is interference by a batter or runner if a batter-runner willfully and deliberately interferes with a batted ball or a fielder in the act of fielding a batted ball.

Runner/Bases Any runner shall be called out, on appeal, when with the ball in play, while advancing or returning to a base, he fails to touch each base in order before he, or a missed base, is tagged. Approved Ruling: (1) No runner may return to touch a missed base after a following runner has scored. (2) When the ball is dead, no runner may return to touch a missed base or one he has left after he has advanced to and touched a base beyond the missed base.

1966

There were no changes to the playing rules this year.

1967

Catch A catch is the act of a fielder in getting secure possession in his hand or glove of a ball in flight and firmly holding it; providing he does not use his cap, protector, pocket, or any other part of his uniform in getting possession. It is not a catch, however, if simultaneously or immediately following his contact with the ball, he collides with a player, or with a wall, or if he falls down, and as a result of such collision or falling, drops the ball. It is not a catch if a fielder touches a fly ball which then hits a member of the offensive team or an umpire and then is caught by another defensive player. If the fielder has made the catch and drops the ball while in the act of making a throw following the catch, the ball shall be adjudged to have been caught. In establishing the validity of the catch, the fielder shall hold the ball long enough to prove that he has complete control of the ball and that his release of the ball is voluntary and intentional.

Coach/Manager See *Pitcher/Visits.*

Interference/Offensive It is interference by a batter or runner when, in the judgment of the umpire, a batter-runner willfully and deliberately interferes with a batted ball or a fielder in the act of fielding a batted ball, with the obvious intent to break up a double play. The ball is dead. The umpire shall call the batter-runner out for interference and shall also call out the runner who had advanced closest to the home plate regardless where the double play might have been possible. In no event shall bases be run because of such interference.

The players, coaches, or any member of an offensive team shall vacate any space (including both dugouts) needed by a fielder who is attempting to field a batted or thrown ball. Penalty: Interference shall be called and the batter or runner on whom the play is being made shall be declared out.

The batter becomes a runner when a fair ball, after having passed a fielder other than the pitcher, or after having been touched by a fielder, including the pitcher, shall touch an umpire or runner on fair territory.

Interference/Umpire See above, *Interference/Offensive.*

Pitcher/Delivery Pitchers shall take signs from the catcher while standing on the rubber.

The ball becomes dead and runners advance one base, or return to their bases, without liability to be put out when a balk is committed.

Pitcher/Visits A professional league shall adopt the following rule pertaining to the visit of the manager or coach to the pitcher: (a) This rule limits the number of trips a manager or coach may make to any one pitcher in any one inning; (b) A second trip to the same pitcher in the same inning will cause the pitcher's automatic removal; (c) The manager or coach is prohibited from making a second visit to the mound while the same batter is at bat; but (d) If a pinch-hitter is substituted for this batter, the manager or coach may make a second visit to the mound, but must remove the pitcher.

A manager or coach is considered to have concluded his visit

to the mound when he leaves the 18-foot circle surrounding the pitcher's rubber.

Runner   A runner acquires the right to an unoccupied base when he touches it before he is out. He is then entitled to it until he is put out, or forced to vacate it for another runner legally entitled to that base.

1968

Ball/Defaced   See *Pitcher/Illegal Act.*

Coach   See *Interference/Offensive.*

Interference/Offensive   The ball becomes dead and runners advance one base or return to their bases without liability to be put out when a base coach intentionally interferes with a thrown ball. Runners return to the base last legally touched.

Pitcher/Illegal Act   The pitcher shall not (1) bring his pitching hand in contact with his mouth or lips. Penalty: For violating this part of this rule the umpire shall warn the pitcher and if this action is repeated the umpire shall immediately disqualify the pitcher; (2) apply a foreign substance of any kind to the ball; (3) expectorate on the ball, his pitching hand, or his glove; (4) rub the ball on his glove, person, or clothing; (5) deface the ball in any manner; (6) deliver what is called the "shine" ball, "spit" ball, "mud" ball, or "emery" ball. The pitcher, of course, is allowed to rub the ball between his bare hands. Penalty: For violation of any part of this rule the umpire shall immediately disqualify the pitcher.

1969

Game   A game called at the end of a completed inning with the score tied after nine innings shall be a suspended game.

Pitcher/Position   The pitcher's plate shall be 10 inches above the level of home plate. The degree of slope from a point six inches in front of the pitcher's plate to a point six feet toward home plate shall be one inch to one foot, and such degree of slope shall be uniform.

Runner/Advancing   Any runner is out when he fails to re-touch his base after a fair or foul ball is legally caught before he or his base is tagged by a fielder. He shall not be called out for failure to re-touch his base after the first following pitch, or any play or attempted play. This is an appeal play.

Strike Zone   The strike zone is that space over home plate which is between the batter's armpits and the top of his knees when he assumes his natural stance. The umpire shall determine the strike zone according to the batter's usual stance when he swings at a pitch.

1970

There were no changes to the playing rules this year.

1971

Helmet   All players shall use some type of protective helmet while at bat.

1972

Appeal   An appeal is not to be interpreted as a play or an attempted play.

Successive appeals may not be made on a runner at the same base. If the defensive team on its first appeal errs, a request for a second appeal on the same runner at the same base shall not be allowed by the umpire.

Game/Suspended   A game may be suspended to be completed at a future date by reason of light failure or malfunction of a mechanical field device, e.g., automatic tarpaulin or water-removal equipment.

1973

Designated Hitter   Any league may elect to use the Designated Hitter (DH) rule as follows: (1) A hitter may be designated to bat for the starting pitcher and all subsequent pitchers in any game without otherwise affecting the status of the pitcher or pitcher in the game. A DH for the pitcher must be selected prior to the game and must be included in the lineup cards presented to the umpire-in-chief; (2) It is not mandatory that a club designate a hitter for the pitcher, but failure to do so prior to the game precludes the use of a DH for that game; (3) Pinch hitters for a DH may be used. Any substitute hitter for a DH becomes the DH. A replaced DH shall not re-enter the game in any capacity; (4) The DH may be used defensively, continuing to bat in the same position in the batting order, but the pitcher must then bat in the place of the substituted defensive player, unless more than one substitution is made, and the manager then must designate their spots in the batting order; (5) A runner may be substituted for the DH and the runner assumes the role of DH; (6) A DH is "locked" into the batting order. No multiple substitutions may be made that will alter the batting rotation of the DH; (7) Once the game-pitcher is switched from the mound to a defensive position this move shall terminate the DH role for the remainder of the game; (8) Once the game-pitcher bats for the DH this move shall terminate the DH's role for the remainder of the game. The game pitcher may only pinch-hit for the DH; (9) Once a DH assumes a defensive position this move shall terminate the DH role for the remainder of the game.

Note: The DH rule was adopted only by the American League.

Game   In all protested games, the decision of the league president shall be final.

1974

Ball/Defaced   See *Pitcher/Illegal Act.*

Helmet   All players are required to wear batting helmets with ear flaps.

Pitcher/Illegal Act   If, in his judgment, the umpire determines that a foreign substance has been applied to the ball, he shall (a) call the pitch a ball, warn the pitcher and have announced by the public address system the reason for the action; (b) in the case of a second offense by the same pitcher any time later in the game, the pitcher shall be disqualified from the game and may additionally be subject to such action as may be imposed by the league office; (c) if a play follows the violation called by the umpire, the manager of the offensive team may advise the plate umpire that he elects to decline the penalty and accept the play. Such election shall be made immediately at the end of the play. However, if a batter reaches first base on a hit, an error, a base on balls, a hit batsman, or otherwise, and no other runner is put out before advancing at least one base, the play shall proceed without reference to the violation; (d) even though the offense elects to take the play, the violation shall be recognized and the penalties in (a) and (b) will still be in effect; (e) the umpire shall be the sole judge on whether any portion of this rule has been violated.

1975

Ball   The ball can be covered with white cowhide as well as horsehide.

Bat   Cupped Bats   An indentation in the end of the bat up to one inch in depth is permitted and may be no wider than two inches and no less than one inch in diameter. The indentation must be curved with no foreign substance added.

Bat/Illegal   A batter is out for illegal action when he hits a fair ball with a filled, doctored, or flat-surfaced bat in which event he shall be immediately ejected from the game and suspended by his league president for three days.

Fielder/Drops Fly Ball   A batter is out when an infielder intentionally drops a fair fly ball or line drive, with first, first and second, first and third, or first, second, and third bases occupied

before two are out. The ball is dead and runner or runners shall return to their original base or bases. Approved Ruling: In this situation, the batter is not out if the infielder permits the ball to drop untouched to the ground, except when the infield fly rule applies.

Game A game may be suspended if local law prohibits the use of lights and it is too dark to continue.

Infield Fly See *Fielder/Drops Fly Ball.*

Pitcher/Illegal Act The pitcher shall not have on his person, or in his possession, any foreign substance. For such infraction of this section the penalty shall be immediate ejection from the game.

Runner/Advancing Any runner shall be called out, on appeal, when after a fly ball is caught, he fails to re-touch his original base before he or his original base is tagged.

Runner/Awarded Bases Each runner, including the batter-runner, may advance one base if a ball, pitched to the batter, or thrown by the pitcher from his position on the pitcher's plate to a base to catch a runner, goes into a stand or a bench, or over or through a field fence or backstop. The ball is dead. Approved Ruling: When a wild pitch or passed ball goes through or by the catcher, or deflects off the catcher, and goes directly into the dugout, stands, above the break, or any area where the ball is dead, the awarding of bases shall be one base. One base shall also be awarded if the pitcher, while in contact with the rubber, throws to a base, and the throw goes directly into the stands or into any area where the ball is dead.

If, however, the pitched or thrown ball goes through or by the catcher or through the fielder, and remains on the playing field, and is subsequently kicked or deflected into the dugout, stands or other area where the ball is dead, the awarding of bases shall be two bases from position of runners at the time of the pitch or throw.

1976

Bat The bat handle, for not more than 18 inches from the end, may be covered or treated with any material (including pine tar) to improve the grip. Any such material, including pine tar, which extends past the 18-inch limitation, in the umpire's judgment, shall cause the bat to be removed from the game. No such material shall improve the reaction or distance factor of the bat.

Bat/Illegal The batter is out for illegal action when he uses or attempts to use a bat that, in the umpire's judgment, has been altered or tampered with in such a way to improve the distance factor or cause an unusual reaction on the baseball. This includes, bats that are filled, flat-surfaced, nailed, hollowed, grooved, or covered with a substance such as paraffin, wax, etc. No advancement on the bases will be allowed and any out or outs made during a play shall stand. In addition to being called out, the player shall be ejected from the game and may be subject to additional penalties as determined by the league president.

Designated Hitter A Designated Hitter (DH) may not pinch run.

Once a pinch hitter bats for any player in the batting order and then enters the game to pitch, this move shall terminate the DH role for the remainder of the game.

A substitute for the DH need not be announced until it is the DH's turn to bat.

Player/Illegal Act No manager, player, substitute, coach, trainer, or batboy shall at any time, whether from the bench, the coach's box or on the playing field, or elsewhere make intentional contact with the umpire in any manner.

Umpire See *Player/Illegal Act.*

Uniform/Shoes No player shall attach anything to the heel or toe of his shoe other than the ordinary shoe plate or toe plate.

Shoes with pointed spikes similar to golf or track shoes shall not be worn.

1977

There were no changes to the playing rules this year.

1978

Designated Hitter In the event of interleague competition between clubs of leagues using the Designated Hitter rule and clubs of leagues not using the Designated Hitter rule, the rule will be used as follows: (1) In exhibition games, the rule will be used or not used as is the practice of the home team; (2) In All-Star Games, the rule will only be used if both teams and both leagues so agree; (3) In World Series play, the rule will be used every other year. It will not be used in 1977, but will be used in 1978, etc.

Pitcher/Illegal Act The pitcher shall not intentionally pitch at the batter. If, in the umpire's judgment, such a violation occurs, the umpire shall warn the pitcher and his manager that another such pitch will mean immediate expulsion of the pitcher. At the same time the umpire shall warn the opposing manager that such an infraction by his pitcher shall result in that pitcher's expulsion. If, in the umpire's judgment, there is another such pitch during the game by any pitcher, the umpire shall eject the pitcher from the game. If, in the umpire's judgment circumstances warrant, one or both teams may be officially "warned" prior to the game or an actual violation during the game in progress. League presidents may take additional action under the rules.

Note: To pitch at a batter's head is unsportsmanlike and highly dangerous. It should be—and is—condemned by everybody. Umpires should act without hesitation in enforcement of this rule.

1979

There were no changes to the playing rules this year.

1980

Game The rules of 1980 include several amendments to the rules governing suspended games and protested games.

Substitute/Fielder If no announcement of a substitution is made, the substitute shall be considered as having entered the game when, if a fielder, he reaches the position usually occupied by the fielder he has replaced and play commences.

1981

Designated Hitter The Designated Hitter (DH) named in the starting lineup must come to bat at least one time, unless the opposing club changes pitchers.

1982

Pitcher Under extreme cold weather conditions a pitcher may warm his throwing hand by blowing on it provided that both managers and umpires have agreed to this before the game begins.

1983

Helmet All players shall use some type of protective helmet while at bat. All players in National Association Leagues shall wear a double ear-flap helmet while at bat. All players entering the major leagues commencing with the 1983 championship season and every succeeding season thereafter must wear a single ear-flap helmet (or at the player's option, a double ear-flap helmet), except those players who were in the major leagues during the 1982 season, and who, as recorded in that season, objected to wearing a single ear-flap helmet. If the umpire observes any violation of these rules, he shall direct the violation to be corrected. If the violation is not corrected within a reasonable

time, in the umpire's judgment, the umpire shall eject the offender from the game.

1984

Bat   The bat handle, for not more than 18 inches from its end,
may be covered or treated with any material or substance to
improve the grip. Any such material or substance, which extends
past the 18-inch limitation, shall cause the bat to be removed
from the game.

1985

Uniform   No part of the uniform shall include patches or designs relating to commercial advertisements.

A league may provide that the uniforms of its member teams
include the names of its players on their backs. Any name other
than the last name of the player must be approved by the league
president. If adopted, all uniforms for a team must have the
names of its players.

1986

Designated Hitter   The Designated Hitter (DH) rule will be
used or not used in World Series or exhibition games according
to the practice of the home team.

1987

There were no changes to the playing rules this year.

1988

Bases   Home base shall be marked by a five-sided slab of whitened rubber. It shall be a 17-inch square with two of the corners
removed so that one edge is 17 inches long, two adjacent sides
are 8½ inches and the remaining two sides are 12 inches and set
at an angle to make a point. It shall be set in the ground with the
point at the intersection of the lines extending from home base to
first base and to third base; with the 17-inch edge facing the
pitcher's plate, and the two 12-inch edges coinciding with the
first and third baselines. The top edges of home base shall be
beveled and the base shall be fixed in the ground level with the
ground surface.

Helmet   All catchers shall wear a catcher's protective helmet,
while fielding their position.

All bat/ballboys or girls shall wear a protective helmet while
performing their duties.

Pitcher/Delivery   The Set Position   Preparatory to coming to
a set position, the pitcher shall have one hand by his side.

Set Position is assumed by the pitcher when he stands facing
the batter with his entire pivot foot on, and parallel to, the
pitcher's plate, or in front of, parallel to, and in contact with, the
pitcher's plate. The non-pivot foot must be on the ground in front
of the pitcher's plate. The pitcher must hold the ball in both
hands in front of his body and come to a single complete and
discernible stop before throwing the ball. A complete stop shall
not be construed as occurring because of a change in direction of
the hands and arms.

From such set position he must deliver the ball to the batter,
throw to a base, or step backward off the pitcher's plate with his
pivot foot.

Before assuming set position, the pitcher may elect to make
any natural preliminary motion such as that known as "the
stretch." But if he so elects, he shall come to a set position before
delivering the ball to the batter. After assuming set position, any
natural motion associated with his delivery of the ball to the
batter commits him to the pitch without alteration or
interruption.

The pitcher, following his stretch, must (a) hold the ball in
both hands in front of his body and (b) come to a complete and
discernible stop, with both feet on the ground. This must be
enforced. Umpires should watch this closely, and should immediately call a "balk" for any violation.

Pitcher/Illegal Act   The pitcher shall not intentionally pitch at
the batter. If, in the umpire's judgment, such a violation occurs,
the umpire may elect either to: (1) expel the pitcher, or the
manager and the pitcher, from the game, or; (2) may warn the
pitcher and the manager of both teams that another such pitch
will result in the immediate expulsion of that pitcher (or a replacement) and the manager. If, in the umpire's judgment, and
circumstances warrant, both teams may be officially "warned"
prior to the game or at any time during the game. League
presidents may take additional action under the rules.

1989

Bat   The bat shall be a smooth, *round* stick not more than 2¾
inches in diameter at the thickest part and not more than 42
inches in length. The bat shall be one piece of solid wood.

Note: No laminated or experimental bats shall be used in a
professional game (either championship or exhibition games)
until the manufacturer has secured approval from the Rules
Committee of his design and methods of manufacture.

Pitcher/Delivery   The Set Position   Set Position shall be indicated by the pitcher when he stands facing the batter with his
entire pivot foot on, or in front of, and in contact with, and not off
the end of the pitcher's plate, and his other foot in front of the
pitcher's plate, holding the ball in both hands in front of his body
and coming to a complete stop. From such Set Position he may
deliver the ball to the batter, throw to a base, or step backward
off the pitcher's plate with his pivot foot. Before assuming Set
Position, the pitcher may elect to make any natural preliminary
motion such as that known as "the stretch." But if he so elects, he
shall come to Set Position before delivering the ball to the batter.
After assuming Set Position, any natural motion associated with
his delivery of the ball to the batter commits him to the pitch
without alteration or interruption.

Preparatory to coming to a set position, the pitcher shall have
one hand on his side; from this position he shall go to his set
position as defined above without interruption and in one continuous motion.

The whole width of the foot in contact with the rubber must be
on the rubber. A pitcher cannot pitch from off the end of the
rubber with just the side of his foot touching the rubber.

The pitcher, following his stretch, must (a) hold the ball in
both hands in front of his body and (b) come to a complete stop.
This must be enforced. Umpires should watch this closely. Pitchers are constantly attempting to "beat the rule" in their efforts to
hold runners on bases and in cases where the pitcher fails to
make a complete "stop" called for in the rules, the umpire should
immediately call a "balk."

1990–1992

There were no changes to the playing rules in these years.

Index to Playing Rule Changes 1845–1992

Note: Dates shown following an entry refer to the year a rule
change or amendment was adopted. Rule changes and summaries of rules are to be found in the chronology.

1875; 1876; 1877; 1880; 1887; 1888; 1894; 1895; 1899; 1901; 1902; 1904; 1906; 1907; 1909; 1910; 1920; 1950; 1954; 1955; 1957; 1963; 1969

Substitution 1858; 1868; 1869; 1871; 1872; 1874; 1876; 1877; 1878; 1881; 1889; 1890; 1891; 1893; 1897; 1899; 1909; 1910; 1920; 1931; 1950; 1957; 1976; 1980

Substitution for batter 1893; 1910; 1954; 1955

Substitution for designated hitter (*See* Designated Hitter rule)

Substitution for fielder 1980

Substitution for pitcher (*See* Relief Pitcher)

Substitution for runner 1869; 1871; 1872; 1874; 1878; 1881; 1889; 1910; 1931; 1950; 1955; 1976

"Time" called during game (*See also* Dead Ball) 1868; 1882; 1887; 1920; 1950; 1954; 1955

Touch, definition of 1957

Trainers 1940

Tripleheaders prohibited 1940

Triple play, definition of 1954

Umpire, accident to 1867; 1872; 1874; 1882; 1955

Umpire addressing spectators 1874; 1881; 1887; 1897; 1910

Umpire, addressing the 1858; 1874; 1876; 1880; 1882; 1887

Umpire, appealing to (*See also* Appeal plays) 1868; 1874; 1875; 1876; 1880; 1882; 1887; 1897; 1907

Umpire, appealing to spectators for assistance by 1874; 1881

Umpire as judge of fitness of grounds 1872; 1887; 1896; 1906; 1950

Umpire as paid employee 1874; 1883; 1884

Umpire assessing fines 1879; 1880; 1887; 1895; 1896; 1910

Umpire, authority to accept or reject ground rules by 1874; 1909

Umpire, authority to disqualify and remove personnel from field 1867; 1882; 1909; 1957

Umpire, calling foul balls by (*See also* Fair and Foul Balls) 1858; 1872

Umpire, calling pitch too early by 1874

Umpire consulting player before decision 1887

Umpire hit by batted ball 1907; 1910; 1920; 1967

Umpire hit by pitched or thrown ball 1877; 1910; 1914

Umpire, intentional contact prohibited with 1976

Umpire interference (*See* Interference by umpire)

Umpire, keeping score of game by 1845; 1858; 1865; 1867

Umpire, position of 1875; 1878; 1890

Umpire, replacing of 1867; 1872; 1874

Umpire reversing decision 1868; 1870; 1874; 1881; 1887; 1897

Umpire, selection of 1845; 1846-57; 1858

Umpires, procedure when decisions are in conflict by 1957

Umpires, system using two (Umpire-in-Chief) 1890; 1940; 1950; 1958

Umpire, uniform of 1885

Umpire, various responsibilities of 1845; 1858; 1861; 1867; 1868; 1869; 1872; 1874; 1876; 1879

Wild pitch, definition of 1954

Windup position, definition of 1950; 1963

Winner of game (*See* Game winner defined)

Scoring Rules for 1877

Batting

Section 1. The first item in the tabulated score, after the player's name and position, shall be the number of times he has been at bat during the game. Any time or times where the player has been sent to base on called balls shall not be included in this column.

Section 2. In the second column should be set down the runs made by each player.

Section 3. In the third column should be placed the first-base hits made by each player. A base hit should be scored in the following cases:

When the ball from the bat strikes the ground between the foul lines and out of the reach of the fielders.

When a hit is partially or wholly stopped by a fielder in motion, but such player cannot recover himself in time to handle the ball before the striker reaches first base.

When the ball is hit so sharply to an infielder that he cannot handle it in time to put out a man. In case of doubt over this class of hits, score a base hit and exempt the fielder from the charge of an error.

When a ball is hit so slowly toward a fielder that he cannot reach it before the batsman is safe.

Section 4. In the fourth column should be placed to the credit of each player the total bases made off his hits. The unit, or base, consists in getting from any one base to any other base without being put out, and the striker is to be credited not only with the number of bases which he himself makes after a hit, but, in addition, with those safely made by every other player who is on base at the time he runs toward first. It should be understood that a base or bases made off an error of a fielder count toward the score of the player who ran from home base toward first base when the error was made. All the bases made off such error, whether by the striker or by some other player then on base, shall go to the credit of the striker. The striker shall be credited with a base when he is sent to base on called balls, and, in addition, with all the bases made by other players who may be advanced on the play under the rules.

A base or bases shall be given to the runner for a successful steal, whether made on an error of his opponents, or without error.

Bases shall not be given to a striker when any player, other than himself, shall be put out on his strike.

Fielding

Section 5. The number of opponents put out by each player shall be set down in the fifth column. Where a striker is given out by the umpire for a foul strike or because he struck out of his turn, the putout shall be scored to the catcher.

Section 6. The number of times a player assists shall be set down in the sixth column. An assist should be given to each player who handles the ball in a runout or other play of the kind.

An assist should be given to the pitcher when a batsman fails to hit the ball on the third strike.

An assist should be given to the pitcher in each case where the batsman is declared out for making a foul strike or striking out of turn.

An assist should be given to a player who makes a play in time to put a runner out, even if the player who should complete the play fails, through no fault of the player assisting.

An assist should not be given to a player who muffs the ball, or allows it to bound off his body toward a player who then assists or puts out a player.

And, generally, an assist should be given to each player who handles the ball from the time it leaves the bat until it reaches the player who makes the putout, or in case of a thrown ball, to each player who throws or handles it cleanly, and in such way that a putout results, or would result, if no error were made by the receiver.

Section 7. An error should be given for each misplay, which allows the striker or baserunner to make one or more bases, when perfect play would have insured his being put out. In scoring errors off batted balls, see Sec. 3 of this Article.

Chronology of Scoring Rules 1878-1992

1878

Assist An assist is no longer denied a player who has a ball bounce off him toward a player who then makes the play.

On-Base In the fourth column should be placed to the credit of each player the number of times he reaches first base during the game, whether upon hits, errors, called balls, or in any other way he is not put out.

Total Bases The statistic crediting players with total bases is dropped from the rule book (Section 4 in 1877).

1879

There were no changes to the scoring rules this year.

1880

Base Hit Score a base hit when a ball is hit so slowly toward a fielder that he cannot handle it in time to put out a man.

Total Bases In the fourth column should be placed to the credit of each player the total bases run during the game. In scoring "bases run" where a player has reached first base as the result of the putting out of another player, such first base shall not be credited to the striker as one of the bases run by him.

Total Chances In the seventh column should be placed the "total chances offered" to retire players, which should include each perfect play, as well as each misplay or failure to accept a chance to retire a batsman or baserunner. "Chances offered" should not include "passed balls," "called balls," or "wild pitches." In scoring "chances offered" off batted balls, see Sec. 3 of the Scoring Rules.
   Note: This rule does not appear in the scoring rules following 1880.

1881

Total Bases In the fourth column should be placed to the credit of each player the total bases made by him off his hits.

1882

In 1882 the American Association was founded, adopted the rule book, and made the following addition and deletion for their scoring rules:

Assist (American Association) An assist should be given to the pitcher on every chance offered to the catcher for a putout on a foul ball.

Total Bases (American Association) Total bases were not credited to the player's record.

1883

Assist The pitcher is no longer credited with an assist when the batsman fails to hit the ball on the third strike, or when the batsman is declared out for making a foul strike or for striking out of turn.

Assist (American Association) An assist should be given to the pitcher when a batsman fails to hit the ball on the third strike.
   An assist should be given to the pitcher in each case where the batsman is declared out for making a foul strike, or striking out of turn. Such assistance is to be placed in the summary of the score.
   Note: These two rules were dropped by the AA in 1884.

Error An error should be given to the pitcher when the batsman is given first base on "called balls."

Scoring Summary In the summary of the game should be credited to the pitcher the number of times a batsman fails to hit the ball on the third strike.

Scoring Summary (American Association) The summary shall contain: (1) The number of earned runs made by each side; (2) The number of two-base hits made by each player; (3) The number of three-base hits made by each player; (4) The number of home runs made by each player; (5) The number of men on

each side left on bases; (6) The number of double and triple plays made by each side; (7) The number of men struck out by each pitcher; (8) The number of men given base on balls by each pitcher; (9) The number of passed balls by each catcher; (10) The number of wild pitches by each pitcher; (11) The time of game; (12) The name of the umpire.

1884

In 1884 the Union Association was formed and adopted the same scoring rules used by the American Association, with the exception that the new league credited assists to the pitcher for strikeouts, batters called out for batting out of turn, and batters striking the ball while out of the batter's box. The Union Association existed for one season.

Scoring Summary (American Association) The number of men given bases from being hit by pitched balls is added to the summary.
   Note: The Union Association did not include this in their summary.

Strikeout (American Association) A strikeout should be given to the pitcher when a batsman fails to hit the ball on the third strike, and in each case where the batsman is declared out for making a foul strike, or striking out of turn.

1885

Assist An assist shall be given the pitcher when the batsman fails to hit the ball on the third strike, and the same shall also be entered in the summary under the head of "struck out."
   Note: This rule was dropped in 1889.

Error Wild pitches and passed balls shall be charged to the pitcher and catcher respectively in the error column, and shall also appear in the summary.
   Note: This rule was dropped in 1886.

Error (American Association) An error shall be given for each misplay which allows the striker or baserunner to make one or more bases, when perfect play would have insured his being put out; except that wild pitches, bases on called balls, bases on the batsman being struck by a pitched ball, balks, and passed balls shall not be included in said column.
   Note: The National League adopted this rule in 1887 and added the term "illegal pitched ball" to the exceptions. The phrase "bases on called balls" was deleted from the exceptions in 1888 only.

1886

Stolen Base Bases stolen by players shall appear to their credit in the summary of the game.

1887

In 1887 the National League and the American Association agreed to use the same scoring rules.

Assist An assist shall be given the pitcher when the batsman fails to hit the ball on the fourth [third in 1888] strike, and the same shall be entered in the summary under the head of "struck out."
   Note: This rule was dropped in 1889.

Base Hit A base hit is to be scored when the batsman is awarded a base on balls.
   Note: This rule was dropped in 1888.

Scoring Summary The summary shall contain: (1) The number of earned runs made by each side; (2) The number of two-base hits made by each player; (3) The number of three-base hits made by each player; (4) The number of home runs made by each player; (5) The number of double and triple plays made by each side, with the names of the players assisting in the same; (6) The number of men given bases on called balls by each pitcher;

(7) The number of men given bases from being hit by pitched balls; (8) The number of passed balls by each catcher; (9) The number of wild pitches by each pitcher; (10) The time of the game; (11) The name of the umpire.

Stolen Base In the fourth column shall be scored bases stolen, and shall include every base made after first base has been reached by a baserunner, except those made by reason of, or with the aid of, a "battery" error, or by batting, "balks" or by being forced off. In short, shall include all bases made by a "clean steal," or through a wild throw or muff of the ball by a fielder who is directly trying to put the baserunner out while attempting to steal a base.

Time at Bat The first item in the tabulated score, after the player's name and position, shall be the number of times he has been at bat during the game. Any time or times where the player has been sent to base by being hit by a pitched ball or by the pitcher's illegal delivery, shall not be included in this column.

1888

Base Hit In all cases where a baserunner is retired by being hit by a batted ball, the batsman should be credited with a base hit.

That when a player reaches first base through an error of judgment such as two fielders allowing the ball to drop between them, the batter shall not be credited with a base hit, nor the fielder charged with an error, but it shall be scored as an unaccepted chance, and the batter shall be charged with a time at the bat.

Note: This rule was dropped in 1889.

Earned Run An earned run shall be scored every time the player reaches the home base unaided by errors before chances have been offered to retire the side, but bases on balls, though summarized as errors, shall be credited as factors in earned runs.

Note: This rule was deleted in 1898 but reappears in 1917. Also see 1912.

Stolen Base In the fourth column shall be scored bases stolen, and shall be governed as follows: Any attempt to steal a base must go to the credit of the baserunner, but any manifest error is to be charged to the fielder making the same. If the baserunner advances another base he shall not be credited with a stolen base, and the fielder allowing the advancement is also to be charged with an error. If a baserunner makes a start and a battery error is made, the runner secures the credit of a stolen base, and the battery error is scored against the player making it. Should a baserunner overrun a base and then be put out, he should receive the credit for the stolen base.

Time at Bat The first item in the tabulated score, after the player's name and position, shall be the number of times he has been at bat during the game. At any time or times where the player has been sent to base by being hit by a pitched ball, by the pitcher's illegal delivery, or by a base on balls shall not be included in this column.

1889

Base Hit A base hit should be scored when a batted ball hits the person or clothing of the umpire as provided in the playing rules.

Earned Run An earned run shall be scored every time the player reaches the home base unaided by errors before chances have been offered to retire the side.

Note: See entries under 1888, 1912, and 1917.

Sacrifice In the fourth column shall be placed sacrifice hits, which shall be credited to the batsman, who when but one man is out advances a runner on base on a fly to the outfield or a ground hit, which results in putting out the batsman, or would so result if handled without error.

Scoring Summary The number of bases stolen is added to the scoring summary.

1890

Assist Assistances on strikes are not to be included in the record of fielding assistances.

Earned Run Earned runs should be charged against the pitcher only on the basis of base hits made off the pitching, and should not include stolen bases or bases scored in any other way.

1891

Scoring Summary The number of runs batted in by base hits by each batsman is added to the scoring summary.

1892

Stolen Base The following sentence is added to the 1888 rule for scoring stolen bases: If a baserunner advances a base on a fly out, or gains two bases on a single base hit, or an infield out, or attempted out, he shall be credited with a stolen base, provided there is a possible chance and a palpable attempt made to retire him.

Note: This sentence was dropped from the rule in 1897.

1893

There were no changes to the scoring rules this year.

1894

Sacrifice A sacrifice hit is to be credited to the batsman who advances a runner with no one out or one out by a bunt sacrifice which results in putting out the batsman.

Note: Previously the rule applied only with one out. See 1889.

Time at Bat The batter is not charged with a time at bat for a sacrifice hit purposely made to the infield which advances a runner without resulting in a putout except to the batsman.

1895–6

There were no changes to the scoring rules in these years.

1897

Earned Run An earned run shall be scored every time the player reaches the home base by the aid of base hits only before chances have been offered to retire the side.

Note: See entries under 1888, 1912 and 1917.

Sacrifice In the fourth column shall be placed the sacrifice hits, which shall be credited to the batsman who, when no one is out or when but one man is out, advances a runner a base by a bunt hit, which results in putting out the batsman, or would so result if the ball were handled without error.

Scoring Summary The summary shall contain: (1) The number of earned runs made off each pitcher; (2) The number of two-base hits made by each player; (3) The number of three-base hits made by each player; (4) The number of home runs made by each player; (5) The number of bases stolen by each player; (6) The number of double and triple plays made by each side and the names of the players assisting in the same; (7) The number of men given bases on called balls by each pitcher and the names of the players who were thus given bases; (8) The number of men given bases from being hit by pitched balls by each pitcher and the names of the players who are thus given bases; (9) The number of men struck out by each pitcher and the names of the players struck out; (10) The number of passed balls by each catcher; (11) The number of wild pitches by each pitcher; (12) The number of baserunners left on bases by each side; (13) The number of innings each pitcher played; (14) The number of base hits made off each pitcher; (15) The number of bases on balls given by each pitcher; (16) The number of batsmen hit by each pitcher; (17) The number of batsmen struck out by each pitcher [Note: This requirement apparently duplicates Sec. 9 above];

(18) The number of baserunners of each side who reached first base by fielding errors; (19) The time it took to play the game; (20) The condition of the weather; (21) The condition of the playing field; (22) The name of the umpire.

Stolen Base The rule regarding stolen bases is now the same as that used between 1888 through 1891. Additional language adopted in 1892 and included through 1896 has been deleted. See 1892.

Time at Bat The first item in the tabulated score, after the player's name and position, shall be the number of times he has been at bat during the game. The time or times when the player has been sent to base by being hit by a pitched ball, by the pitcher's illegal delivery, or by a base on balls, or has made a sacrifice hit which was manifestly intentional, shall not be included in this column.

1898

Assist Assists should be credited to every player who handles the ball in the play which results in a baserunner being called out for interference or for running out of line.

Base Hit A base hit should be scored when a ball is hit with such force to an infielder that he cannot handle it in time to put out the batsman. In case of doubt over this class of hits, score a base hit and exempt the fielder from the charge of an error.

In no case shall a base hit be scored when a baserunner has been forced out by the play.

Error An error shall be given in the seventh column for each misplay which allows the striker or baserunner to make one or more bases when perfect play would have insured his being put out, except that "wild pitches," "bases on balls," bases on the batsman being struck by a "pitched ball," or in case of illegal pitched balls, balks and passed balls, all of which comprise battery errors, shall not be included in said column. In scoring errors of batted balls see Sec. 3 of this rule.

An error shall not be scored against the catcher for a wild throw to prevent a stolen base, unless the baserunner advances an extra base because of the error.

No error shall be scored against an infielder who attempts to complete a double play, unless the throw is so wild that an additional base is gained.

Putout The number of opponents put out by each player shall be set down in the fifth column. Where a batsman is given out by the umpire for a foul strike, or where the batsman fails to bat in proper order, the putout shall be scored to the catcher. In all cases of "out" for interference, running out of line, or infield fly dropped, the "out" should be credited to the player who would have made the play but for the action of the baserunner or batsman.

Scoring Summary The summary shall contain: (1) The score made in each inning of the game; (2) The number of bases stolen by each player; (3) The number of two-base hits made by each player; (4) The number of three-base hits made by each player; (5) The number of home runs made by each player; (6) The number of double and triple plays made by each side and the names of the players assisting in the same; (7) The number of innings each pitcher pitched in; (8) The number of base hits made off each pitcher; (9) The number of times the pitcher strikes out the opposing batsmen; (10) The number of times the pitcher gives bases on balls; (11) The number of wild pitches charged to the pitcher; (12) The number of times the pitcher hits batsmen with pitched ball; (13) The number of passed balls by each catcher; (14) The time of the game; (15) The names and positions of each umpire.

Stolen Base A stolen base shall be credited to the baserunner whenever he reaches the base he attempts to steal unaided by a fielding or by a battery error or a hit by the batsman.

Time at Bat The first item in the tabulated score, after the player's name and position, shall be the number of times he has been at bat during the game. No time at bat shall be scored if the batsman be hit by a pitched ball while standing in his position, and after trying to avoid being so hit, or in case of the pitcher's illegal delivery of the ball to the bat which gives the batsman his base, or when he intentionally hits the ball to the field, purposely to be put out, or if he is given first base on called balls.

1899–1903

There were no changes to the scoring rules in these years.

1904

Assist The number of times, if any, each player assists in putting out an opponent shall be set down in the sixth column. An assist should be given to each player who handles the ball in aiding in a run-out or any other play of the kind, except the one who completes it.

Note: The rule remains unchanged except to clarify that the fielder completing a run-down play by making the putout is not to be credited with an assist even if he handled the ball prior to receiving it again to make the putout. But see the entry under 1910.

Base Hit A base hit should be scored when the ball is hit so slowly toward a fielder that he cannot handle it in time to put out the batsman or force out a baserunner.

Note: The phrase "or force out a baserunner" has been added to the original rule. See 1878.

Error An error shall be given in the seventh column for each misplay which prolongs the time at bat of the batsman or allows a baserunner to make one or more bases when perfect play would have insured his being put out. But a wild pitch, a base on balls, a base awarded to a batsman by being struck by a pitched ball, an illegal pitch, a balk and a passed ball, each of which is a battery and not a fielding error, shall not be included in the seventh column.

In case a baserunner advance a base through the failure of a baseman to stop or try to stop a ball accurately thrown to his base, he shall be charged with an error and not the player who made such throw, provided there were occasion for it. If such throw be made to second base, the scorer shall determine whether the second baseman or shortstop shall be charged with an error.

Putout The number of opponents, if any, put out by each player shall be set down in the fifth column. Where the batsman is given out by the umpire for a foul strike, or fails to bat in proper order, the putout shall be scored to the catcher. In cases of the baserunner being declared "out" for interference, running out of line, or on an infield fly, the "out" should be credited to the player who would have made the play but for the action of the baserunner or the announcement of the umpire.

Note: The phrase "or the announcement of the umpire" has been added in place of "or batsman." See 1898.

Sacrifice In the fourth column shall be placed the sacrifice hits. A sacrifice hit shall be credited to the batsman who, when no one is out or when but one man is out, advances a runner a base by a bunt hit, which results in the batsman being put out before reaching first, or would so result if it were handled without error.

Note: The phrase "before reaching first" has been added to the rule. See 1889.

Scoring Summary The scoring summary is to include the total runs by each side as well as the score made in each inning.

Stolen Base A stolen base shall be credited to the baserunner whenever he advances a base unaided by a base hit, a putout, a fielding or a battery error.

Time at Bat The first item in the tabulated score, after the player's name and position, shall be the number of times he has been at bat during the game, but the exceptions made in rule 82 must not be included.

Note: See rule 82 below.

"A Time at Bat" is the term at-bat of a batsman. It begins when he takes his position, and continues until he is put out or becomes a baserunner. But a time at bat shall not be charged against a batsman who is awarded first base by the umpire for being hit by a pitched ball or for the illegal delivery of the pitcher, or on called balls, or when he makes a sacrifice hit.

1905–06

There were no changes to the scoring rules in these years.

1907

Base Hit In all cases where a baserunner is retired by being hit by a batted ball, unless batted by himself, the batsman should be credited with a base hit.

Game Played All appearances by a player in a championship game count as a game played in the American League, which prior to 1907 had not so credited the appearances of pinch hitters, pinch runners, and defensive substitutes in most cases. See 1912 for National League.

1908

Sacrifice A sacrifice hit shall be credited to the batsman who, when no one is out or when but one man is out, advances a runner a base by a bunt hit, which results in the batsman being put out before reaching first, or would so result if it were handled without error. A sacrifice hit shall also be credited to a batsman who, when no one is out or when but one man is out, hits a fly ball that is caught but results in a run being scored.

1909

Double Play A double play shall mean any two continuous putouts that take place between the time the ball leaves the pitcher's hands until it is returned to him again standing in the pitcher's box.

Error In case a runner advances a base through the failure of a baseman to stop or try to stop a ball accurately thrown to his base, the latter shall be charged with an error and not the player who made such throw, provided there was occasion for it. If such throw be made to second base, the scorer shall determine whether the second baseman or shortstop shall be charged with an error.

An error shall be given in the sixth column for each misplay which prolongs the time at bat of the batsman or allows a baserunner to make one or more bases when perfect play would have insured his being put out. But a base on balls, a base awarded to a batsman by being struck by a pitched ball, an illegal pitch, a balk, a passed ball or wild pitch, unless such wild pitch or passed ball be on the third strike and allow the batter to reach first base, shall not be included in the sixth column. In case of a wild pitch or a passed ball allowing the batter to reach first base, the pitcher or the catcher, as the case may be, shall be charged with an error.

In event of a fielder dropping a fly but recovering the ball in time to force a batter at another base, he shall be exempted from an error, the play being scored as a "force-out."

Putout The number of opponents, if any, put out by each player shall be set down in the fourth column. Where the batsman is given out by the umpire for a foul strike, or fails to bat in proper order, or is declared out on third bunt strike, the putout shall be scored to the catcher. In cases of the baserunner being declared "out" for interference, running out of line, or on an infield fly, the "out" should be credited to the player who would

have made the play but for the action of the baserunner or the announcement of the umpire.

Sacrifice A sacrifice hit shall be credited to the batsman who, when no one is out or when but one man is out, advances a runner a base by a bunt hit, which results in the batsman being put out before reaching first, or would so result if it were handled without error. A sacrifice hit shall also be credited to a batsman who, when no one is out or when but one man is out, hits a fly ball that is caught but results in a run being scored, or would in the judgment of the scorer so result if caught.

Scoring Summary The summary shall contain: (1) The score made in each inning of the game and the total runs of each side in the game; (2) The number of stolen bases, if any, by each player; (3) The number of sacrifice hits, if any, made by each player; (4) The number of sacrifice flies, if any, made by each player; (5) The number of two-base hits, if any, made by each player; (6) The number of three-base hits, if any, made by each player; (7) The number of home runs, if any, made by each player; (8) The number of double and triple plays, if any, made by each club and the players participating in same; (9) The number of innings each pitcher pitched in; (10) The number of base hits, if any, made off each pitcher and the number of legal at-bats scored against each pitcher; (11) The number of times, if any, the pitcher strikes out the opposing batsmen; (12) The number of times, if any, the pitcher gives bases on balls; (13) The number of wild pitches, if any, charged against the pitcher; (14) The number of times, if any, the pitcher hits a batsman with a pitched ball, the name or names of the batsman or batsmen so hit to be given; (15) The number of passed balls by each catcher; (16) The time of the game; (17) The name of the umpires.

Stolen Base A stolen base shall be credited to the baserunner whenever he advances a base unaided by a base hit, a putout, a fielding or a battery error, subject to the following exceptions: (1) In event of a double steal being attempted from bases one and two to bases two and three, where either is thrown out, the other shall not be credited with a stolen base; (2) In event of a baserunner being touched out after sliding over a base, he shall not be regarded as having stolen the base in question; (3) In event of a baserunner making his start to steal a base prior to a battery error, he shall be credited with a stolen base; (4) In event of a palpable muff of a ball thrown by the catcher, when the baserunner is clearly blocked, the infielder making the muff shall be charged with an error and the baserunner shall not be credited with a stolen base.

1910

Assist The number of times, if any, each player assists in putting out an opponent shall be set down in the fifth column. An assist should be given to each player who handles the ball in aiding in a run-out or any other play of the kind, even though he complete the play by making the putout.

Note: Compare to the 1904 rule.

Error An error shall be given in the sixth column for each misplay which prolongs the time at bat of the batsman or allows a baserunner to make one or more bases when perfect play would have insured his being put out. But a base on balls, a base awarded to a batsman by being struck by a pitched ball, a balk, a passed ball, or wild pitch shall not be included in the sixth column.

Passed Ball A passed ball is a legally delivered ball that the catcher should hold or control with ordinary effort, but his failure to do so enables the batsman, who becomes a baserunner on such pitched ball, to reach first base or a baserunner to advance.

Stolen Base In event of a double or triple steal being attempted, where either runner is thrown out, the other or others shall not be credited with a stolen base.

Wild Pitch   A wild pitch is a legally delivered ball, so high, low or wide of the plate that the catcher cannot or does not stop and control it with ordinary effort, and as a result the batsman, who becomes a baserunner on such pitched ball, reaches first base or a baserunner advances.

1911

There were no changes to the scoring rules this year.

1912

Earned Run   An earned run is charged to the pitcher every time a player scores by the aid of safe hits, sacrifice hits, bases on balls, hit batters, wild pitches, and balks before fielding chances have been offered to retire the side.

Note: This rule is not included in the scoring rules for 1912 but earned runs were compiled in the official pitching records of the National League (1912) and American League (1913). The earned run scoring rule does not appear in the scoring rules until 1917.

Game Played   All appearances by a player in a championship game count as a game played in the National League, which prior to 1912 had not so credited the appearances of pinch hitters, pinch runners, and defensive substitutes, with certain exceptions.

1913

There were no changes to the scoring rules this year.

1914

Assist   The number of times, if any, each player assists in putting out an opponent shall be set down in the fifth column. One assist and no more shall be given to each player who handles the ball in aiding in a run-out or any other play of the kind even though he complete the play by making the putout.

Note: Compare to 1910 and 1904.

Base Hit   A base hit should be scored when the ball from the bat strikes the ground on or within the foul lines and out of reach of the fielders, provided the batter reaches first base safely.

When a fielder, after handling a batted ball, elects to try to retire a baserunner instead of the batter, the play is known as a "fielder's choice." In case the runner is retired, or would be retired but for an error, the batter shall be charged with a time at bat, but no hit. If the runner is not retired, and no error is made, the batter shall be charged with a time at bat, but no hit, provided he swung at the ball, and shall be credited with a sacrifice hit, provided he bunted the ball; if, however, in the judgment of the scorer, the batter could not have been retired at first base by perfect fielding, he shall be credited with a base hit.

Error   In event of a baserunner making his start to steal a base prior to a battery error, he shall be credited with a stolen base and the battery error shall also be charged.

An error shall not be scored against the catcher or an infielder who attempts to complete a double play, unless the throw be so wild that an additional base be gained. This, however, does not exempt from an error a player who drops a thrown ball when by holding it he would have completed a double play.

An error shall be given in the sixth column for each misplay which prolongs the time at bat of the batsman or prolongs the life of the baserunner or allows a baserunner to make one or more bases when perfect play would have insured his being put out. But a base on balls, a base awarded to a batsman by being struck with a pitched ball, a balk, a passed ball, or wild pitch shall not be included in the sixth column.

Note: The phrase "or prolongs the life of the baserunner" has been added to the existing rule.

Fielder's Choice   See *Base Hit.*

Sacrifice   A sacrifice hit shall also be credited to a batsman who, when no one is out or when but one man is out, hits a fly ball that is caught but results in a run being scored on the catch, or would in the judgment of the scorer so result if caught.

1915–16

There were no changes to the scoring rules in these years.

1917

Earned Run   A run earned off the pitcher shall be scored every time a player reaches home base by the aid of safe hits, sacrifice hits, stolen bases, bases on balls, hit batsmen, wild pitches, and balks, before fielding chances have been offered to retire the side.

The pitcher shall be given the benefit of doubt whenever fielding errors are made and in determining the base to which a runner should have been held with perfect support on part of fielders. A fielding error made by the pitcher shall be considered the same as any other fielding error. No run can be earned that scores as a result of the batsman having reached first base on a fielding error or passed ball; nor can any run be earned after the fielding side has failed to accept chances offered to retire the side.

Percentage   To determine the pitcher's percentage for the season, the total number of runs earned off his pitching shall be divided by the total number of innings he has pitched; then multiplied by nine, to find his average effectiveness for a complete game.

1918–19

There were no changes to the scoring rules in these years.

1920

Error   An error shall be charged to the first baseman if, on receiving a throw in ample time to retire the batsman, he fail to touch first base.

An error shall be charged to the catcher if he drop a third strike, allowing the runner to reach first base; except this rule is not to apply in case of a wild pitch.

Game Ending Hit   If, in the last half of the final inning, with the winning run on base, the batsman drives home that run, credit shall be given him for as many bases on his hit as the runner advances; except, however, that in case of the batsman driving a fair ball out of the playing field, he shall receive credit for a home run.

Percentage   To determine the percentage of games won and lost, divide the total number of games won and lost into the number won.

To determine batting averages, divide the total "Times at Bat" into the total number of base hits.

To determine fielding averages, divide the total of putouts, assists, and errors into the total of putouts and assists.

In all cases where the remaining fraction is one-half or over, a point is added to the average.

Sacrifice   A sacrifice hit shall also be credited to a batsman who, when no one is out or when but one man is out, hits a fly ball that is caught but results in a run being scored on the catch, or would in the judgment of the scorer so result if caught; but no distinction shall be made in the summary as between bunted or fly-ball sacrifices.

Scoring Summary   The scoring summary is to include sacrifice flies (within the category of sacrifice hits) and the number of runs batted in by each batsman.

Stolen Base   No stolen base shall be credited to a runner who is allowed to advance without any effort being made to stop him.

Wild Pitch   See *Error*, second paragraph.

1921–25

There were no changes to the scoring rules in these years.

1926

Error See *Wild Pitch*.

Passed Ball The catcher shall be charged with a passed ball when a baserunner is enabled to advance by the catcher's failure to hold or control a legally delivered ball that should have been held or controlled with ordinary effort.

Wild Pitch An error shall be charged to the pitcher if he make a wild pitch for the third strike, and the batsman reach first base; in such case the pitcher shall not have credit for a strikeout.

A wild pitch is a legally delivered ball, so high, low, or wide of the plate that the catcher cannot or does not stop and control it with ordinary effort, and as a result the batsman reaches first base or a baserunner advances.

Sacrifice Fly Awarded if any runner is advanced.

1927–30

There were no changes to the scoring rules in these years.

1931

Assist Credit an assist to a player who, by deflecting a batted ball with his glove or any part of his body, aids in retiring the batsman or another baserunner.

Credit an assist to each player who handles and throws the ball in such a way that a putout would have resulted except for the error of a teammate.

Do not credit an assist to a fielder who makes a bad throw, even when a runner trying to advance on it is subsequently retired. A play that follows an error is a new play and the player making an error is not entitled to an assist unless he takes part in the new play.

Do not credit an assist to the pitcher when, in legally delivering the ball to the batsman, he helps to retire a runner attempting to steal home.

Base Hit A base hit shall be scored in the following cases: (1) When a fair hit is made, as defined in the Playing Rules, and the batsman reaches first base safely; (2) When a fair hit ball is partially or wholly stopped by a fielder in motion, but such player cannot recover himself in time to field the ball to first before the batsman reaches that base, or to some other base in time to force out another runner; (3) When a ball is hit with such force to an infielder or pitcher that he cannot handle it in time to put out the batsman or force out a baserunner; except when the ball is recovered by another fielder in time to retire the batsman or force out a baserunner. In case of doubt over this kind of hit, a base hit should be scored and the fielder be exempted from the charge of an error.

Earned Run A run earned off the pitcher shall be scored every time a player reaches home base by the aid of safe hits, sacrifice hits, stolen bases, putouts, bases on balls, hit batsman, wild pitches, or balks, before fielding chances have been offered to retire the side.

The pitcher shall be given the benefit of doubt whenever fielding errors are made and in determining the base to which a runner should have been held with perfect support on part of fielders. A fielding error made by the pitcher shall be considered the same as any other fielding error. No run can be earned that scores as a result of the batsman having reached first base on a catcher's interference, a fielding error, or passed ball; nor can any run be earned after the fielding side has failed to accept chances offered to retire the side.

Note: The phrase "catcher's interference" has been added to the prior rule. See entry for 1917.

Error An error, but not a passed ball, shall be charged to the catcher if he drops or misses a third strike, allowing the batsman to reach first base. Credit the pitcher with a strikeout.

An error shall be charged to the first baseman (or the pitcher or second baseman when covering first base) if, on receiving a throw in ample time to retire the batsman, he does not touch first base as required by rule. The same rule shall be followed with respect to any fielder covering any other base on a force play.

Forfeited Game In a regulation game which the umpire shall declare forfeited after four and one-half innings have been played, all individual and team averages shall be incorporated in the official playing records.

Game-Ending Hit If, in the last half of the final inning, with the winning run on base, the batsman drives home that run, credit shall be given him for as many bases as, in the judgment of the official scorer, he would have made under normal conditions; the number, however, not to exceed the number of bases advanced by the runner; except when the batsman drives a fair ball out of the playing field, he shall receive credit for a home run, provided he legally touches each base in proper order.

Hit by Pitch When a batsman is hit by what would have been the fourth called ball, it shall be scored as a "hit by pitcher."

Passed Ball See *Error*.

Percentage In determining averages where the remaining fraction is one-half or over, a full point is to be added to the average.

Putout The number of opponents, if any, put out by each player shall be set down in the fourth column. When the batsman is called out by the umpire for an illegally batted ball, or for a foul third strike bunt, or for being hit by his own batted ball, or for interference with the catcher, or for failing to bat in proper turn, the putout shall be credited to the catcher. When a baserunner is declared out on an infield fly, the putout shall be credited to the player who would have made the play except for the action of the runner or the announcement of the umpire. When a baserunner is declared out because of being hit by a batted ball, the putout shall be credited to the fielder nearest to the ball at the time of the occurrence.

Run Batted In Runs batted in should include runs scored on safe hits (including home runs), sacrifice hits, infield outs, and when the run is forced over by reason of batsman becoming a baserunner. With less than two out, if an error is made on a play on which a runner from third would ordinarily score, credit the batsman with a run batted in.

Sacrifice Rule Awarding of sacrifice flies is abolished.

Stolen Base In the event of a palpable muff of a ball thrown by the catcher, when, in the judgment of the scorer, the baserunner would have been out if the ball had been held, the infielder making the muff shall be charged with an error and the baserunner shall not be credited with a stolen base.

When a wild pitch or a passed ball occurs after a runner has started to steal, do not credit the runner with a stolen base but charge the wild pitch or passed ball.

Do not give a stolen base to a runner who has started to steal and the pitcher balks.

Time at Bat A "Time at Bat" is the term at bat of a batsman. It begins when he takes his position, and continues until he is put out or becomes a baserunner. But a time at bat shall not be charged against a batsman who is awarded first base by the umpire for being hit by a pitched ball, or on called balls, or when he makes a sacrifice hit, or for interference by the catcher.

Note: This rule is Rule 69, Sec. 5, of the Playing Rules.

The first item in the tabulated score, after the player's name and position, shall be the number of times he has been at bat during the game, but the exceptions made in Rule 69, Sec. 5, must not be included.

Note: See above entry for Rule 69, Sec. 5.

Wild Pitch A wild pitch is a legally delivered ball, so high, low, or wide of the plate that the catcher cannot or does not stop and control it with ordinary effort, and as a result the batsman reaches first base or a baserunner advances. Any pitched ball that strikes the ground before reaching the home plate and passes the catcher, allowing runners to advance, shall be scored as a wild pitch.

1932–38

There were no changes to the scoring rules in these years.

1939

Base Hit/Value In event of a batsman oversliding second or third bases and being tagged by the opposing fielder when said batsman is attempting to stretch a single into a two-base hit or a two-base hit into a three-base hit, the play should be scored the same as when a baserunner attempts to steal, overslides the base and is tagged out. In other words, the batsman oversliding second base and is tagged out shall be credited only with a single, while one who overslides third base and is tagged out shall be credited only with a two-base hit.

Earned Run A wild pitch which is a third strike is to be used in determining earned runs charged to the pitcher.

Run Batted In The batsman shall not be credited with driving in a run when a runner scores as he hits into a force infield double play or a double play in which the first baseman picks up a fair hit ground ball, touches first base and then throws to second retiring the runner who had been on first, said runner not being forced, has to be tagged out.

Sacrifice A sacrifice hit also shall be credited to the batsman who, when no one is out or when but one man is out, hits a fly ball that is caught but which results in a baserunner scoring, or would have scored a runner if said fly ball had not been dropped for an error, in the judgment of the scorer; but no distinction shall be made in the summary as between bunted or fly ball sacrifices.

1940

Base Hit In all cases where a baserunner is retired by being hit by a batted ball, unless batted by himself, the batsman should be credited with a base hit, except if the runner is hit by an infield fly, the play should be scored as provided in the Playing Rules (Sec. 8 of Rule 44).

Earned Run A run earned off the pitcher shall be scored every time a player reaches home base by the aid of safe hits, sacrifice hits, stolen bases, putouts, bases on balls, hit batsman, wild pitches, or balks, even though the wild pitch be a third strike, before fielding chances have been offered to retire the team. The preceding pitcher, and not a relieving pitcher shall be charged with runs scored by any runners on base when such relief pitcher entered the game. The relieving pitcher shall not be charged with his first batsman reaching first base if such batsman had any advantage because of poor pitching by the preceding pitcher. With the count two or three balls and one or no strikes, or three balls and two strikes, charge preceding pitcher if batsman reaches first base, but credit relieving pitcher if batsman is retired. With count one or two balls and two strikes, charge relieving pitcher if batsman reaches first base and credit him if batsman is retired.

Forfeited Game In a regulation game which the umpire shall declare forfeited after four and one-half innings have been played, all individual and team averages shall be incorporated in the official playing records, except that no pitcher shall be credited with a victory or charged with a loss in said game.

1941–49

There were no changes to the scoring rules in these years.

1950

Assist An assist shall be credited to each player who throws or deflects a batted or thrown ball in such a way that a putout results, or would have resulted except for a subsequent error by a teammate, but only one assist and no more shall be credited to each player who throws or deflects the ball in a rundown play which results in a putout, or would have resulted in a putout, except for a subsequent error.

Credit an assist to each player who throws or deflects the ball during a play which results in a baserunner being called out for interference, or for running out of line.

Do not credit an assist to a pitcher when, in legally delivering the ball to a batter, he helps to retire a baserunner attempting to steal home.

Situations will arise in which a wild throw shall be scored as an assist and not as an error while on some plays a wild throw shall be scored both as an assist and as an error.

Note: The scoring rules for 1950 then present four detailed examples illustrating the application of the assist provisions.

Base Hit A base hit shall be scored under these circumstances: (1) When a batter reaches first base (or any succeeding base) safely on a legally batted ball which settles on fair ground or strikes a fence behind fair ground before being touched by a fielder, or which clears a fence behind fair territory; (2) When a batter reaches first base after hitting a ball with such force, or so slowly, that the pitcher or fielder attempting to make a play with it has no opportunity to do so; (3) When a batter reaches first base safely on a batted ball which strikes either first base, second, or third base before being touched by a fielder and bounces away from the reach of the fielder; (4) When a batter reaches first base safely on a legally batted ball which has not been touched by a fielder and which is in fair territory when it bounds into the outfield unless in the scorer's judgment it could have been handled with ordinary effort; (5) When a legally batted ball which has not been touched by a fielder becomes "dead" by reason of touching the person or clothing of a runner or umpire, except that when a runner is called out for having been struck by an "infield fly" the batter shall not be credited with a hit; (6) When, in the scorer's judgment, the batter could not have been retired at first base by perfect fielding, when the fielder fails in an attempt to retire a preceding baserunner; (7) Always give the batter the benefit of the doubt. A safe course to follow being to score a hit when exceptionally good fielding of a batted ball fails to result in a putout; (8) In no case shall a base hit be scored when a runner is forced out by a batted ball, or would have been forced out except for a fielding error. Nor shall a hit be scored when an infield batted ball results in another runner, who is attempting to advance one base, being retired, whether forced out or not; (9) Score the play as a "fielder's choice" when a fielder uses a batted ball to retire a preceding baserunner, or would have retired one with ordinary effort except for a fielding error, charging the batter with time at bat, but no hit.

Base Hit/Value Whether a safe hit shall be scored as a one-base hit, two-base hit or a three-base hit when no error or putout results shall be determined as follows:

It is a one-base hit if the batter stops at first base; it is a two-base hit if the batter stops at second base; it is a three-base hit if the batter stops at third base, but note this exception: the batter must, if attempting to take two or three bases on a safe hit by sliding, hold the last base to which he advances. If he overslides and is tagged out before getting back to the base safely he shall be given credit for only as many bases as he safely attained. If he overslides second base and is tagged out he shall be given a one-base hit; if he overslides third base and is tagged out, he shall be given a two-base hit. If he runs past second base after reaching that base on his feet, attempts to return and is tagged out, he shall be given credit for a two-base hit. If he runs past third base after reaching that base on his feet, attempts to return and is

tagged out, he shall be given credit for a three-base hit.

If a batter is awarded three bases on a batted or bunted ball because a fielder has touched the ball with his glove, cap, or any other part of his uniform while such article is detached from its proper place on his person, the scorer's judgment shall dictate whether the batter shall be given credit for a one-base hit, a two-base hit, a three-base hit, or a home run. If the scorer believes the fielder could have, by ordinary effort, kept the hit from being good for more than one, two, or three bases he shall score it as a one-base hit or as a two-base hit or as a three-base hit and charge the fielder with an error. If, however, the scorer believes the hit would have been a legitimate home run, despite illegal use of equipment, he shall so score it if the batter touches all bases in the proper order.

In no instance shall the batter be credited with a two-base hit or a three-base hit if he fail to advance a preceding runner whose advance is necessary to permit the batter to reach second or third base. Example: Runner on first, batter makes a long hit and reaches second but runner is thrown out at third. Score a one-base hit and credit batter with reaching second on the play.

Should a batter, after making a safe hit, be called out for having failed to touch a base, the last base he reached safely shall determine if his hit is scored as a one-base hit, a two-base hit, or a three-base hit. If he is called out for missing second base, the hit shall be scored as a one-base hit. If he is called out for missing third base, his hit shall be scored as a two-base hit. If he is tagged out after missing home base, his hit shall be scored as a three-base hit. If he is called out for missing first base, he shall be charged with a time at bat but no hit.

When a batter ends a game with a safe hit, other than a home run, which drives in as many runs as are necessary to put his team in the lead, he shall be credited with only as many bases on his hit as are advanced by the runner who scores the winning run, and then only if the batter runs out his hit for as many bases as are advanced by the runner who scores the winning run, touching each base in the proper order.

If a batter ends a game with a home run out of the playing field and touches all the bases in their proper order, his run, and also the runs of all other runners who were on base when the home run was hit, shall count in the final score even though this gives the team last at bat a winning margin in excess of one run.

Base on Balls   A base on balls shall be scored whenever a batter is awarded first base by the umpire because of four balls having been pitched outside the strike zone, but when the fourth such ball strike the batter it shall be scored as a "hit batter."

Championship   To be eligible for the individual batting championship of any minor league, a player must have appeared in at least two-thirds of the games played by his team. Thus, if a team plays 154 games, a player must appear in 102 games. If his team plays 150 games he must appear in 100. If his team plays 140 games he must appear in 93, etc.

To be eligible for the individual batting championship of a major league, a player must be credited with at least 400 official "times at bat."

Double Play   A double play is any two successive putouts which take place between the time a ball leaves a pitcher's hand and is returned to him while he is standing in the pitcher's box.

Earned Run   An earned run is a run for which the pitching is held accountable.

An earned run shall be scored every time a player reaches home base by the aid of safe hits, sacrifices, stolen bases, put-outs, bases on balls, hit batters, balks, or wild pitches (even though a wild pitch be a third strike which enables a batter to reach first base), before fielding chances have been offered to retire the offensive team.

Since a wild pitch on which a batter reaches first base is the pitcher's fault, solely, even though it is scored as a fielding error, it shall be disregarded as an error and considered as a wild pitch

in computing earned runs and is the only instance in which an error is so disregarded.

In computing earned runs, any type of fielding error made by a pitcher (other than the one mentioned in the preceding two paragraphs) shall be considered in the same light as an error by any other fielder.

Whenever a fielding error occurs the pitcher shall be given the benefit of the doubt in determining to which bases any baserunners would have advanced had the fielding by the defensive team been errorless.

No run can be earned which scores as a result of a batter having reached first base safely because of a catcher's interference, or because of any fielding error, except a wild pitch.

When pitchers are changed during an inning, the preceding pitcher, and not the relieving pitcher, shall be charged with any earned or unearned runs scored by any runners on base when such relief pitcher entered the game. There is, however, this exception: If the action of any batter to whom the relieving pitcher pitches results in the retirement of a runner left on base by the preceding pitcher, the batter whose action resulted in the retirement of that runner shall be considered as having been left on base by the preceding pitcher and any run scored by such runner shall be charged to the preceding pitcher.

A relieving pitcher shall not be held accountable for the first batter to whom he pitches reaching first base if that batter had a decided advantage because of ineffective pitching by the pitcher whom the relieving pitcher succeeded. Thus, if the count is two or three balls and one or no strikes, or if the count is three balls and two strikes when pitchers are changed, and the batter reaches first base safely, charge that batter to the pitcher who was replaced. If such a batter is retired, or would have been retired except for a fielding error, the batter shall be credited to the relieving pitcher. Likewise, if such a batter hits into a force-out or into a fielder's choice on which a runner is retired, or would have been retired except for a fielding error, credit the action of such a batter to the relieving pitcher. (The foregoing sentence is not to be construed as affecting or conflicting with the exception noted.) If pitchers are changed when the count is two balls and one or no strikes, or one ball and one or no strikes, the relieving pitcher shall be held accountable for whatever the batter does.

Error   An error shall be scored for each misplay (fumble, muff, or wild throw) which prolongs the time at bat of a batter, or which prolongs the life of a runner, or which permits a runner to advance one or more bases when perfect play would have resulted in the batter or the runner being retired.

Certain misplays by the catcher and pitcher known as "passed balls" and "wild pitches" are not errors but items for the summary and are defined elsewhere in these rules.

Errors are not charged when a batter is awarded first base because of a base on balls, or for being struck by a pitched ball, or if a runner, or runners, advance because of a passed ball or because of the pitcher making a balk or a wild pitch, except: If a batter swings at a wild pitch for his third strike and thereby is enabled to reach first base, it shall be scored as a strikeout and also as an error for the pitcher and not a wild pitch; when a catcher muffs a third strike, thereby permitting a batter to reach first base, it shall be scored as an error for the catcher, not a passed ball, and as a strikeout.

No error shall be charged against the catcher or any other player for making a wild throw in attempting to prevent a stolen base or any other advance by a runner, unless the scorer is convinced such wild throw permitted the runner to advance one or more bases. If the wild throw permits a runner to advance an extra base, or bases, one error shall be charged to the player making the wild throw.

When any player throws wildly in attempting to complete a double play, or a triple play, no error shall be scored unless the throw is so wild that at least one additional base be gained. However, if a fielder muff a thrown ball which, if held, would

have completed a double play or a triple play, score an error for the player who drops the ball.

An error shall be scored against any player who, on receiving a thrown ball in ample time to retire a batter or any other baserunner on a force play, does not touch the base as required by the rules.

When a runner advances because of the failure of a fielder to stop, or try to stop, an accurately thrown ball, the fielder failing to stop the ball shall be charged with an error and not the player making the throw, provided there was occasion for the throw. If such throw be made to second base the scorer shall determine whether it was the duty of the second baseman or the shortstop to stop the ball, and he shall charge the error to the negligent player.

No error shall be scored if any fielder, after dropping a fly ball, a line drive or a thrown ball recovers the ball in time to force out a runner at another base.

Accurately directed throws, especially from the outfield, which strike a baserunner or an umpire, or which take an unnatural bounce and permit a baserunner or baserunners to advance, shall be scored as errors for the player making the throw, even though it appears to be doing an injustice to the thrower. Every base advanced by a baserunner must be accounted for.

Game-Ending Hit   See last two paragraphs, *Base Hit/Value.*

Hit by Pitch   See *Base on Balls.*

Innings Pitched   In giving a pitcher credit for the number of innings pitched divide each inning into three parts. Thus, if a pitcher is replaced, with one opponent out, in the sixth inning the pitcher so replaced shall be credited with having pitched 5⅓ innings. If a pitcher is replaced with none out in the opposing team's sixth inning he shall be credited with having pitched 5 innings and a notation made to the effect that there were none out in the sixth inning.

Passed Ball   A catcher shall be charged with a passed ball when a runner, or runners, advance because of the catcher's failure to hold or to control a legally pitched ball which should have been held or controlled with ordinary effort.

Percentage   To determine a pitcher's earned run prevention average for a season, the total number of earned runs charged against his pitching shall be divided by the total number of innings he has pitched, then multiplied by nine to find his average effectiveness for a complete game.

(a) To determine the percentage of games won and lost divide the total number of games won and lost into the number won.

(b) To determine a batting average, divide the total "times at bat" into the total number of safe hits.

(c) To determine a slugging percentage, divide the total "times at bat" into the total bases of all safe hits.

(d) To determine a fielding average, divide the total of putouts, assists, and errors into the total of putouts and assists.

Putout   A putout shall be recorded each time a defensive player catches a fly ball, whether fair or foul, a line drive or a thrown ball which retires a batter or runner, or when a fielder tags a runner with the ball when the runner is off the base to which he legally is entitled.

Automatic putouts shall be credited to the catcher as follows: (1) When a batter is called out by the umpire for an illegally batted ball; when a batter is called out by the umpire for bunting foul for his third strike; when a batter is called out by an umpire for being struck by his own batted ball; when a batter is called out by an umpire for interfering with the catcher; when a batter is called out by an umpire for failing to bat in his proper turn. (Note exception in 10.14 (a).) (2) Other automatic putouts shall be credited as follows: (3) When a batter is called out on an infield fly which is not caught, the putout shall be credited to the fielder whom the scorer believes could have made the putout; (4) When a runner is called out for being struck by a fair ball

(including an infield fly) the putout shall be credited to the fielder nearest the ball; (5) When a runner is declared out by an umpire for running out of line to avoid being tagged by the ball in the hands of a fielder, the putout shall be credited to the fielder whom the runner avoided; (6) When a runner is declared out by the umpire for having interfered with a fielder, credit the putout to the fielder with whom the runner interfered, unless the fielder was in the act of throwing the ball when interfered with, in which case the putout shall be credited to the fielder for whom the throw was intended, and the fielder whose throw was interfered with shall be credited with an assist.

Relief Pitcher   See last two paragraphs, *Earned Run.*

Runs Batted In   A run batted in is a run which reaches home base safely because of a safe hit, sacrifice hit, infield putout or outfield putout, or which is forced over home plate by reason of the batter being struck by a pitched ball, or being awarded a base on balls, or being awarded first base because of interference by the catcher. If a batter hit a home run with the bases empty, score both a home run and a run batted in. If, with less than two out, an error is made on a play on which a runner from third base ordinarily would score and does score, credit the batter with a run batted in.

The batter shall not be credited with a run batted in if a run scores when he hits into a force double play, or into a double play in which the first baseman fields a fair hit ground ball, touches first base ahead of the batter for an out, then throws to second or third base, retiring a second runner who has to be tagged.

Sacrifice   Score a sacrifice if, with less than two out, the batter advances one or more runners with a bunt and is retired at first base, or would have been retired except for a fielding error. In case a runner is forced out at any base on a bunt, it shall be scored as a time at bat but no sacrifice.

Scorer   The scorer is an actual official of the game he is scoring, is an accredited representative of the league, is entitled to the respect and dignity of his office and shall be accorded full protection by the president of the league.

The scorer shall report to the President of the league any indignity expressed by manager, player, club employee or club official in the course of, or as the result of, the discharge of his duties.

To promote uniformity in keeping the records of championship games, scorers shall conform to the instructions of this scoring code.

Scoring Summary   In making a box score of a game, each player's name and the fielding position or positions he has played shall be listed in the order in which he batted, or would have batted if the game ends before he gets to bat, followed by a tabulated record of each player's batting and fielding. (a) The first column shall show the number of times each player batted during the game, but no time at bat shall be charged against a player when he is awarded first base on four called balls, for being hit by a pitched ball, or because of being interfered with by the catcher, or for being obstructed by the catcher or any other player, while en route to first base. A sacrifice also exempts a player from being charged with a time at bat. (b) The second column shall show the number of runs, if any, made by each player. (c) The third column shall show the number of safe hits, if any, made by each player. (d) The fourth column shall show the number of putouts, if any, made by each player. (e) The fifth column shall show the number of fielding assists, if any, made by each player. (f) The sixth column shall show the number of fielding errors, if any, made by each player. (g) All players inserted into each team's lineup as substitute batters or substitute runners shall be so designated by special symbols plus notations at the bottom of their team's tabulated record. The symbols a, b, c, d, etc., are recommended. It also is recommended that

the notations should describe what the extra batters did, such as—a-Singled for _____ in sixth inning; b-Flied out for _____ in third inning;c-Forced _____ for _____ in seventh inning; d-Grounded out for _____ in ninth inning. (h) The score by innings of each team follows the box score tabulations and precedes the summary in which should be listed the following items in this order: (1) Runs batted in; (2) Two-base hits; (3) Three-base hits; (4) Home runs, together with the names of the pitchers off whom hit; (5) Stolen bases; (6) Sacrifices; (7) Double plays; (8) Triple plays; (9) Number of runners left on base by each team; (10) Number of bases on balls issued by each pitcher; (11) Number of batters struck out by each pitcher. These shall be listed as "strikeouts"; (12) Number of hits and runs (also earned runs) allowed by each pitcher (if one or both teams use more than one pitcher), together with the number of innings pitched by each pitcher. If a team uses only one pitcher, list the number of earned runs he allowed; (13) The names of any hit batters together with the names of the pitchers who hit them, if a team uses more than one pitcher; (14) The number of wild pitches made; (15) The number of passed balls made by the catchers; (16) The name of the winning pitcher, if the winning team uses more than one pitcher; (17) The name of the losing pitcher, if the losing team uses more than one pitcher; (18) The names of the umpires, listed in this order: (a) plate umpire; (b) first base umpire; (c) second base umpire; (d) third base umpire; (19) The time of game with any delays for rain, fog, snow, light failure or violent wind storm deducted; (20) All individual and team records of any forfeited or tied game which has reached or exceeded legal length when ended shall become a part of the official averages except that no pitcher shall be credited with a victory or charged with a defeat; (21) A box score is in balance (or proved) when the total of a team's times at bat, bases on balls received, hit batters, sacrifices and batters awarded first base because of interference or obstruction equals the total of that team's runs, players left on base, and the other team's putouts.

Stolen Base A stolen base shall be credited to a runner whenever he advances one base unaided by a base hit, a putout, a forceout, a fielder's choice, a passed ball, a wild pitch or a balk, subject to the following exceptions:

If a double or triple steal is attempted and one runner is thrown out before reaching and holding the base he is attempting to steal, no other runner shall be credited with a stolen base;

A runner who is touched out after oversliding a base shall not be regarded as having stolen that base.

If it is the scorer's judgment that a palpable muff of a thrown ball prevents a runner who is attempting to steal from being retired, it shall be scored as an error for the player muffing the throw, an assist for the player throwing the ball, and not a stolen base.

No stolen base shall be scored when a runner advances solely because of the defensive team's indifference to his advancement.

If a runner advances while the defensive team, unsuccessfully, is attempting to retire another runner who, in attempting to steal, evades being put out in a rundown play and returns to the base he originally occupied, a stolen base shall be credited to the runner who so advances.

If a runner has started for a succeeding base before the pitcher delivers the ball and the pitch results in a wild pitch or a passed ball, credit the runner with a stolen base with this exception: If another runner also advances because of the pitch becoming a wild pitch or passed ball, the wild pitch or passed ball also shall be scored.

If a runner, attempting to steal, is well advanced toward the base he is attempting to steal and a balk is called on the pitcher, credit the runner with a stolen base and do not score the balk unless another runner who is not attempting to steal is advanced by the balk.

Note: This paragraph was dropped in 1951.

Squeeze Play "Squeeze play" is the term designating a play when a team, with a runner on third base, attempts to score that runner by means of a bunt. It also is a "squeeze play" if an attempt is made to score a runner from second base by means of a bunt.

Strikeout A strikeout shall be scored whenever a pitcher delivers three legal pitches at which the batter swings and misses, or which the umpire decrees are strikes even though the batter may reach first base safely after the third strike by reason of a wild pitch or the catcher's failure to hold the ball.

A strikeout shall be scored whenever a batter bunts foul when there are two strikes against him, except that should the bunt result in a foul fly caught by the catcher or any other player it shall not be scored as a strikeout but as a regular foul-fly putout.

When a batter goes out of the game with two strikes against him and the substitute batter completes a strikeout, score it as a strikeout for the first batter. If the substitute batter completes the turn at bat in any other manner, score the action as having been that of the substitute batter.

Substitute Batter See last paragraph, *Strikeout*.

Triple Play A triple play is any three successive putouts which take place between the time a ball leaves a pitcher's hand and is returned to him while he is standing in the pitcher's box.

Wild Pitch A wild pitch shall be scored when a legally delivered ball is so high, or so wide, or so low that the catcher does not stop and control the ball by ordinary effort and, as a result, a runner, or runners, advance.

Any legally pitched ball which strikes the ground before reaching home plate and passes the catcher, permitting a runner, or runners, to advance shall be scored as a wild pitch.

Winning and Losing Pitcher Determining the winning and losing pitcher of a game often calls for much careful consideration.

Do not give the starting pitcher credit for a game won, even if the score is in his favor, unless he has pitched at least five innings when replaced.

The five-inning rule to determine a winning pitcher shall be in effect for all games of six or more innings. When a game is called after five innings of play the starting pitcher must have pitched at least four innings to be credited with the victory. If the starting pitcher is replaced (except in a five-inning game) before he has pitched five complete innings when his team is ahead, remains ahead to win, and more than one relief pitcher is used by his team, the scorer shall credit the victory (as among all relieving pitchers) to the pitcher whom the scorer considers to have done the most effective pitching. If, in a five-inning game, the starting pitcher is replaced before pitching four complete innings when his team is ahead, remains ahead to win, and more than one relief pitcher is used by his team, the scorer shall credit the victory (as among all relieving pitchers) to the pitcher whom the scorer considers to have done the most effective pitching.

Regardless of how many innings the first pitcher has pitched, he shall be charged with the loss of the game if he is replaced when his team is behind in the score, and his team thereafter fails to either tie the score or gain the lead.

If a pitcher retires from the game for a substitute batter, or a substitute runner, after pitching five or more innings and his team scores enough runs in the inning in which he is replaced to take the lead, those runs shall be credited to his benefit. Thus, if a pitcher is removed for a substitute batter or a substitute baserunner in any inning after the pitcher has pitched at least five complete innings and during the inning in which he is removed his team assumes the lead, he shall be credited with the victory if his team remains ahead until the finish of the game.

Examples: If the pitcher of the team first at bat is removed in the first half of the sixth inning for a substitute batter, or a substitute runner, and his team gains the lead in that inning and

the relieving pitcher holds the lead through the last half of the ninth inning, the pitcher who was removed shall be credited with the victory; if the pitcher of the team last at bat is removed in the last half of the fifth inning for a substitute batter, or a substitute runner, and his team gains the lead in that inning with the relieving pitcher holding the lead through the ninth inning, the pitcher who was removed shall be credited with the victory.

1951

Base Hit When a batter apparently hits safely and a runner who is obliged to advance by reason of the batter becoming a baserunner misses touching the first base to which he is advancing and is called out on appeal, charge the batter with a time at bat but no hit.

Caught Stealing When records are kept of players caught stealing by catchers, credit the catcher with preventing a stolen base each time he traps a runner off any base with a thrown ball and, as a result of such throw, the runner is retired or would have been except for a subsequent error by any fielder, including the catcher. Runners who are retired in rundown plays started by the catcher trapping a runner off any base, or whose baserunning life is prolonged by an error after they have been trapped off base by the catcher, are to be included among those prevented from stealing by the catcher.

Championship To be designated as the leader of his league's pitchers in the minimum average number of earned runs allowed, a pitcher is required to pitch at least as many innings as the number of games scheduled for each team in his league. (This would be 154 innings in a major league.)

Error If a batter is awarded first base by an umpire because of interference by the catcher, charge the catcher with an error; if an umpire awards a runner or runners one or more bases because of interference or obstruction by any defensive player, charge the player who committed the interference or obstruction with one error, no matter how many bases the runner or runners are advanced.

An error is to be charged when a fielder, in violation of the playing rules, touches a thrown ball with his cap, glove, or uniform while such article is detached from its proper place.

Sacrifice Score a sacrifice if, with less than two out, the batter advances one or more runners with a bunt and is retired at first base, or would have been retired except for a fielding error. In case a runner is forced out at any base on a bunt, it shall be scored as a time at bat but no sacrifice. Also score a sacrifice if, with less than two out, the fielders handle a bunted ball without error in attempting to force a preceding runner but fail to do so. Exception: When such an attempt is made to turn a bunt into a force-out of a preceding runner and fails and it is the scorer's judgment that perfect play would not have retired the batter at first base, it shall be scored as a one-base hit and not as a sacrifice.

Shutout No pitcher shall be credited with pitching a shutout unless he pitches the complete game. When two or more pitchers combine to pitch a shutout, a notation to that effect should be included in the league's official pitching records.

Stolen Base See *Caught Stealing*; also see 1950 *Stolen Base* entry.

Time at Bat See *Base Hit*.

Winning and Losing Pitcher Determining the winning and losing pitcher of a game in which a team uses more than one pitcher often calls for careful consideration. Scorers can be guided by these rules: (1) Credit the starting pitcher with a game won only if he has pitched at least five complete innings and his team not only is in the lead when he is replaced but remains in the lead the remainder of the game; (2) They "must pitch five complete innings" rule in respect to the starting pitcher shall be in effect for all games of six or more innings. When a game is ended after five innings of play the starting pitcher must have pitched at least four complete innings to be credited with a victory. As stated in 10.16 (a), the starting pitcher in a five-inning game can be credited with a victory only if his team is in the lead when he is replaced (after pitching at least four complete innings) and his team remains in the lead to the finish of the game; (3) Except in a five-inning game (when they "must pitch at least four complete innings" rule applies) if the winning team uses more than two pitchers and the starting pitcher has not pitched at least five complete innings the victory shall be awarded one of the relieving pitchers on this basis: (a) Once the opposing team assumes the lead, all pitchers who have pitched for the winning team up to that point are excluded from being credited with the victory with the exception that if the pitcher against whose pitching the opposing team gained the lead continues to pitch until his team regains the lead which it holds to the finish of the game that pitcher would be the winning pitcher; (b) If, after the starting pitcher is replaced before pitching at least five complete innings, the opposing team does not tie the score or take the lead, credit the victory to the relief pitcher deemed by the scorer to have done the most effective pitching; (c) Whenever the score is tied, the game becomes a new contest insofar as determining the winning and losing pitchers are concerned; (d) With one exception, no pitcher can be credited with a victory unless he is the pitcher of record when his team assumes a lead and maintains the lead to the finish of the game; (e) The exception to the foregoing is: Do not credit a game won to a relief pitcher who pitches briefly and ineffectively and is the pitcher of record when his team assumes a lead which it maintains over a period of innings to the finish of the game. If a succeeding relief pitcher pitches effectively in helping to maintain his team in the lead credit such relief pitcher with the victory.

1952

Championship The individual batting champion of any league shall be the player with the highest batting average, if he is credited with as many or more times at bat as the number of games scheduled for one club in his league during the season, multiplied by 2.6. However, if there is any player in a league with fewer than the required number of times at bat whose average would be the highest if he were charged with this required at-bat total, then that player shall be awarded the batting championship.

Putout When a runner is declared out by an umpire for running out of line to avoid being tagged by the ball in the hands of a fielder, the putout shall be credited to the fielder whom the runner avoided; when a runner is called out for passing another runner, credit the putout to the fielder nearest the spot at which the violation took place.

1953

There were no changes to the scoring rules this year.

1954

Double Play A double play is a play by the defense in which two offensive players are legally put out as a result of continuous action, providing there is no error between putouts.

Sacrifice The following section was added to the rule regarding sacrifice bunts and flies: Also score a sacrifice if, with less than two out, the batter hits a fair fly ball which is caught, and a runner scores after the catch, or is dropped for an error, and a runner scores, if in the scorer's judgment, the runner could have scored after the catch had the fly been caught.

Scorer To promote uniformity in keeping the records of championship games, scorers shall conform to the instructions of this scoring code, but in no case shall the scorer's decisions conflict with the playing rules.

Scoring Summary Sacrifice flies and bunts are to be listed separately in the scoring summary.

1955

Assist Mere ineffective contact with the ball shall not be considered an assist. "Deflect" shall mean to slow down or change the direction of the ball and thereby effectively assist in retiring a batter or runner.

Do not credit an assist to the pitcher when, as the result of a legal pitch caught by the catcher, a runner is retired, as when the catcher picks a runner off base, throws out a runner trying to steal or tags a runner trying to steal home.

Do not credit an assist to a fielder whose wild throw permits a runner to advance, even though the runner subsequently is retired as a result of a continuous play. A play which follows an error is a new play, and the player making an error is not entitled to an assist unless he takes part in the new play.

Base Hit A base hit shall be scored when a batter reaches first base safely on a fair ball which takes an unnatural bounce so that a fielder cannot handle it with ordinary effort, or which strikes the pitcher's plate or any base (including home plate) before being touched by a fielder and bounces so that a fielder cannot handle it with ordinary effort.

A base hit shall be scored when the fielder throws to another base in an unsuccessful attempt to retire a preceding runner, and in the scorer's judgment the batter-runner would not have been retired at first base by perfect fielding.

A base hit shall not be scored when a fielder fails in an attempt to retire a preceding runner, and in the scorer's judgment the batter-runner could have been retired at first base.

A base hit shall not be scored when a fielder handles a batted ball and retires a preceding runner, or would have retired one with ordinary effort except for a fielding error. Charge the batter with a time at bat but no hit.

Note: This shall not apply if the fielder merely looks toward or feints toward another base before attempting to make the putout at first base.

Base Hit/Value Whether a safe hit shall be scored as a one-base hit, two-base hit, or three-base hit when no error or putout results, shall be determined as follows: When, with one or more runners on base, the batter advances more than one base on a safe hit and the defensive team makes an attempt to retire a preceding runner, the scorer shall determine whether the batter made a legitimate two-base hit or three-base hit, or whether he advanced beyond first base on the fielder's choice.

Note: The rules of 1955 include a series of examples to illustrate the application of this rule for the guidance of the scorer.

When the batter attempts to make a two-base hit or a three-base hit by sliding, he must hold the last base to which he advances. If he overslides and is tagged out before getting back to the base safely, he shall be credited with only as many bases as he attained safely. If he overslides second base and is tagged out, he shall be credited with a one-base hit; if he overslides third base and is tagged out he shall be credited with a two-base hit.

Note: If the batter overruns second or third base and is tagged out trying to return, he shall be credited with the last base he touched. If he runs past second base after reaching that base on his feet, attempts to return and is tagged out, he shall be credited with a two-base hit. If he runs past third base after reaching that base on his feet, attempts to return and is tagged out, he shall be credited with a three-base hit.

Subject to provisions of the playing rules, when the batter ends a game with a safe hit which drives in as many runs as are necessary to put his team in the lead, he shall be credited with only as many bases on his hit as are advanced by the runner who scores the winning run, and then only if the batter runs out his hit for as many bases as are advanced by the runner who scores the winning run, touching each base in proper order.

Note: Apply this rule even when the batter is theoretically entitled to more bases because of being awarded an "automatic" extra-base hit under various provisions of the playing rules.

Base on Balls A base on balls shall be scored whenever a batter is awarded first base because of four balls having been pitched outside the strike zone, but when the fourth such ball strikes the batter it shall be scored as a "hit batter."

Note: The scoring rules contain detailed instructions for charging runners who receive a base on balls when the pitcher is changed in mid-batter.

Batter/Out of Turn When a player bats out of turn, and is put out, and the proper batter is called out before the ball is pitched to the next batter, charge the proper batter with a time at bat and score the putout and any assists the same as if the correct batting order had been followed. If an improper batter becomes a runner by reason of a hit, error, fielder's choice, hit batter, base on balls, interference or obstruction, and the proper batter is called out for having missed his turn at bat, charge the proper batter with a time at bat, credit the putout to the catcher, and ignore everything entering into the improper batter's safe arrival on base. If more than one batter bats out of turn in succession, score all plays just as they occur, skipping the turn at bat of the player or players who first missed batting in the proper order.

Box Score A box score is in balance (or proved) when the total of the team's times at bat, bases on balls received, hit batters, sacrifice bunts, sacrifice flies, and batters awarded first base because of interference or obstruction, equals the total of that team's runs, players left on base, and the opposing team's putouts.

Caught Stealing Do not credit the catcher with a man "caught stealing" when he traps a runner off base after fielding a batted ball or on any play started by another fielder.

Championship The individual fielding champions shall be the fielders with the highest fielding average at each position, subject to the following: (1) A catcher must have participated as a catcher in at least 90 games (80 games in leagues playing schedules of 140 games or less); (2) An infielder or outfielder must have participated at his position in at least 100 games (90 games in leagues playing schedules of 140 games or less); (3) A pitcher must have pitched in at least as many innings as the number of games scheduled for each club in his league that season.

Earned Run The scoring rules of 1955 contain detailed provisions for charging runners and runs to starting pitchers and relief pitchers where pitching changes are made in mid-batter.

No run can be earned which scores as a result of the batter reaching first base (1) on a hit or otherwise after his time at bat is prolonged by a muffed foul fly; (2) because of interference or obstruction; or (3) because of any fielding error, except for a wild pitch charged as an error.

Error Slow handling of the ball which does not involve mechanical misplay shall not be construed as an error.

An error shall be charged against any fielder when he muffs a foul fly, to prolong the time at bat of the batter, whether the batter subsequently reaches first base or is retired.

If a runner advances on a throw by a fielder, and in the scorer's judgment there was no occasion for the throw, an error shall be charged to the fielder making the unnecessary throw.

An error shall be charged against any fielder whose throw takes an unnatural bounce, or strikes a base or the pitcher's plate, or strikes a runner, a fielder or an umpire, thereby permitting any runner to advance.

Note: Apply this rule even when it appears to be an injustice to a fielder whose throw was accurately directed. Every base advanced by a runner must be accounted for.

When an umpire awards the batter or any runner or runners one or more bases because of interference or obstruction, charge the fielder who committed the interference or obstruction with

one error, no matter how many bases the batter, or runner or runners, may be advanced.

No error shall be charged against the catcher when he makes a wild throw in attempting to prevent a stolen base, unless such wild throw permits the base stealer to advance one or more extra bases, or in the scorer's judgment permits another runner to advance one or more bases. Charge only one error on such a wild throw, regardless of the number of bases advanced by the runner or runners.

No error shall be charged against any fielder when he makes a wild throw in attempting to prevent a runner's advance, unless in the scorer's judgment such wild throw permits the runner to advance beyond the base he would have reached had the throw not been wild, or permits any other runner to advance one or more bases beyond the base he would have reached had the throw not been wild. Charge only one error on such wild throw, regardless of the number of bases advanced by the runner or runners.

See also *Wild Pitch.*

Fielder's choice　Fielder's choice is the act of a fielder who handles a fair grounder and, instead of throwing to first base to retire the batter-runner, throws to another base in an attempt to retire a preceding runner. The term is also used by scorers (1) to account for the advance of the batter-runner who takes one or more extra bases when the fielder who handles his safe hit attempts to retire a preceding runner; and (2) to account for the advance of a runner (other than by stolen base or error) while a fielder is attempting to retire another runner.

Note: This definition appears in the Playing Rules for 1955.

Game-Ending Hit　See last paragraph, *Base Hit/Value.*

Putout　When a runner is called out for running the bases in reverse order, credit the putout to the fielder covering the base he left in starting his reverse run. Do not credit any assist on such plays.

When the batter-runner is called out because of interference by a preceding runner, credit the putout to the first baseman. If the fielder interfered with was in the act of throwing the ball, credit him with an assist, but credit only one assist on any one play.

Run Batted In　A run batted in is a run which reaches home base safely because of a safe hit, a sacrifice bunt, a sacrifice fly, a putout via a foul fly, an infield putout, or a fielder's choice; or which is forced over home plate by reason of the batter being struck by a pitched ball, or being awarded a base on balls, or being awarded first base because of interference or obstruction. If a batter hits a home run always score the home run as a run batted in. Also count all other runs which score ahead of the batter who hit the home run as runs batted in. If, with less than two out, an error is made on a play on which a runner from third base ordinarily would score and does score, credit the batter with a run batted in.

Sacrifice　Score a sacrifice bunt when, with less than two outs, the fielders handle a bunted ball without error in an unsuccessful attempt to retire a preceding runner advancing one base. Exception: When an attempt to turn a bunt into a putout of a preceding runner fails, and in the scorer's judgment perfect play would not have retired the batter at first base, the batter shall be credited with a one-base hit and not a sacrifice.

Do not score a sacrifice bunt when a runner is retired attempting to advance one base on a bunt. Charge the batter with a time at bat.

Scorer　The Official Scorer shall keep records of each game as outlined in the scoring rules. He shall have sole authority to make all decisions involving judgment, such as whether a batter's advance to first base is the result of a hit or an error. In no event shall a scorer make a decision conflicting with the Official Playing Rules or with an umpire's decision.

Scoring Summary　The scoring summary shall contain: (1) Number of runners left on base by each team. This total shall include all runners who get on base by any means and who do not score and are not put out. Include in this total a batter-runner whose batted ball results in another runner being retired for the third out; (2) Total number of bases on balls issued by each pitcher and a separate listing of the number of intentional bases on balls issued by each pitcher.

The scoring rules of 1955 also include detailed instructions for notations to the tabulated game records. It is recommended that letters a, b, c, d, etc., be used in the notations as symbols for substitute batters and that numerals 1, 2, 3, 4, etc., be used as symbols for substitute runners. Also the instructions detail notations needed when a substitute is announced but removed for another substitute before he actually enters the game.

Stolen Base　A stolen base shall be credited to a runner whenever he advances one base unaided by a base hit, a putout, an error, a force-out, a fielder's choice, a passed ball, a wild pitch or a balk, subject to the following: When a runner, attempting to steal, evades being put out in a rundown play and advances to the next base without the aid of an error, credit the runner with a stolen base. If another runner also advances on the play, credit both runners with stolen bases. If a runner advances while another runner, attempting to steal, evades being put out in a rundown play and returns safely, without the aid of an error, to the base he originally occupied, credit a stolen base to the runner who advances.

Strikeout　A strikeout shall be scored whenever a pitcher delivers three legal pitches at which the batter swings and misses, or which the umpire decrees are strikes. A strikeout shall be scored even though the batter reaches first base safely after the third strike because of an error by the pitcher or catcher as defined in the scoring rules.

Wild Pitch　When the batter's fourth called ball is a wild pitch and as a result (1) the batter-runner advances to a base beyond first base; (2) any runner, forced to advance by reason of the batter becoming a runner, advances more than one base; or (3) any runner, not forced to advance by reason of the batter becoming a runner, advances one or more bases, score the base on balls and also an error for the pitcher and do not score a wild pitch.

When the batter swings at a wild pitch for his third strike and thereby is enabled to reach first base, score a strikeout and also an error for the pitcher, and do not score a wild pitch.

When the batter swings at a wild pitch for his third strike or when the catcher muffs a third strike, if the catcher recovers the ball and throws out the batter-runner trying to reach first base, but another runner or runners advance, score the strikeout and error the same as if the batter had reached first base. Credit an assist to the catcher, and a putout to the fielder taking the throw at first base.

Winning and Losing Pitcher　In some non-championship games (such as the Major League All-Star Game) it is provided in advance that each pitcher shall work a stated number of innings, usually two or three. In such games, it is customary to credit the victory to the pitcher of record, whether starter or reliever, when the winning team takes a lead which it maintains to the end of the game, unless such pitcher is knocked out after the winning team has a commanding lead, and the scorer believes a subsequent pitcher is entitled to credit for the victory.

1956

Base Hit　A base hit should be scored when the fielder unsuccessfully attempts to retire a preceding runner, and, in the scorer's judgment, the batter-runner would not have been retired at first base by perfect fielding.

Also see *Time at Bat.*

Run Batted In　The batter shall not be credited with a run

batted in if a run scores when he grounds into a force double play, or grounds into a double play in which the first out is made at first base and the second made by tagging a runner who was originally forced, attempting to advance one base.

Time at Bat When a fielder handles a batted ball and retires a preceding runner who is attempting to advance one base, or would have retired one with ordinary effort except for a fielding error, charge the batter with a time at bat but no hit.

1957

Base Hit A base hit shall be scored when a batter reaches first base safely on a fair ball hit with such force, or so slowly, that any fielder attempting to make a play with it has no opportunity to do so.

Note: A hit shall be scored if the fielder attempting to handle the ball cannot make a play, even if such fielder deflects the ball from or cuts off another fielder who could have retired a runner.

Also see *Time at Bat.*

Championship To assure uniformity in establishing the batting, pitching and fielding championship of professional leagues, such champions shall meet the following minimum performance standards: The individual batting champion shall be the player with the highest batting average, provided he is credited with as many or more total appearances at the plate in league championship games as the number of games scheduled for each club in the league that season, multiplied by 3.1. Total appearances at the plate shall include official times at bat, plus bases on balls, times hit by pitcher, sacrifice hits, sacrifice flies and times awarded first base because of interference or obstruction.

Earned Run An earned run shall be scored every time a runner reaches home base by the aid of safe hits, sacrifice bunts, a sacrifice fly, stolen bases, putouts, fielder's choices, bases on balls, hit batters, balks or wild pitches (including a wild pitch on third strike which permits a batter to reach first base) before fielding chances have been offered to retire the offensive team.

Note: A wild pitch is solely the pitcher's fault, and contributes to an earned run just as a base on balls or a balk.

No run can be earned which scores as a result of the batter reaching base (1) on a hit or otherwise after his time at bat is prolonged by a muffed foul fly; (2) because of interference or obstruction; or (3) because of any fielding error.

An error by the pitcher is treated exactly the same as an error by any other fielder in computing earned runs.

Error No error shall be charged to any fielder who permits a foul fly to fall safe with a runner on third base before two are out, if in the scorer's judgment the fielder deliberately refuses the catch in order that the runner on third shall not score after the catch.

Because the pitcher and catcher handle the ball much more than other fielders, certain misplays on pitched balls are called "wild pitches" and "passed balls," and are defined elsewhere in the scoring rules. No error shall be charged when a wild pitch or passed ball is scored. No error shall be charged when the batter is awarded first base on four called balls or because he was touched by a pitched ball, or when he reaches first base as the result of a wild pitch or passed ball. When the third strike is a wild pitch, permitting the batter to reach first base, score a strikeout and a wild pitch. When the third strike is a passed ball, permitting the batter to reach first base, score a strikeout and a passed ball.

Passed Ball See second paragraph, *Error.*

Run Batted In Scorer's judgment must determine whether a run batted in shall be credited for a run which scores when a fielder holds the ball, or throws to a wrong base. Ordinarily, if the runner keeps going, credit a run batted in; if the runner stops and takes off again when he notices the misplay, credit the run as scored on a fielder's choice.

Scorer The league president shall appoint an official scorer for each league championship game. The official scorer shall observe the game from a position in the press box. The scorer shall have sole authority to make all decisions involving judgment, such as whether a batter's advance to first base is the result of a hit or an error. He shall communicate such decisions to the press box and broadcasting booths by hand signals or over the press box loudspeaker system, and shall advise the public address announcer of such decisions if requested.

After each game, including drawn, forfeited and called games, the scorer shall prepare a report, on a form prescribed by the league president, listing the date of the game, where it was played, the names of the competing clubs and the umpires, the full score of the game, and all records of individual players compiled according to the system specified in these Official Scoring Rules. He shall forward this report to the league office within 36 hours after the game ends. He shall forward the report of any suspended game within 36 hours after the game has been completed, or after it becomes an official game because it cannot be completed, as provided by the Official Playing Rules.

To achieve uniformity in keeping the records of championship games, the scorer shall conform strictly to the Official Scoring Rules.

If the teams change sides before three men are put out, the scorer shall immediately inform the umpire of the mistake.

If the game is protested or suspended, the scorer shall make note of the exact situation at the time of the protest or suspension, including the score, the number of outs, the position of any runners, and the ball and strike count on the batter.

Note: It is important that a suspended game resume with exactly the same situation as existed at the time of suspension. If a protested game is ordered replayed from the point of protest, it must be resumed with exactly the situation that existed just before the protested play.

The scorer shall not make any decision conflicting with the Official Playing Rules or with an umpire's decision.

The scorer shall not call the attention of the umpire or of any member of either team to the fact that a player is batting out of turn.

The scorer is an official representative of the league, and is entitled to the respect and dignity of his office, and shall be accorded full protection by the league president. The scorer shall report to the president any indignity expressed by any manager, player, club employee or club officer in the course of, or as the result of, the discharge of his duties.

The umpire-in-chief shall inform the official scorer of the official batting order, and any changes in the lineups and batting order, on request.

Wild Pitch See second paragraph, *Error.*

Winning and Losing Pitcher Regardless of how many innings the first pitcher has pitched, he shall be charged with the loss of the game if he is replaced when his team is behind in the score, and his team thereafter fails either to tie the score or gain the lead.

1958

Championship The individual fielding champions shall be the fielders with the highest fielding average at each position, provided: (1) A catcher must have participated as a catcher in at least one-half the number of games scheduled for each club in his league that season; (2) An infielder or outfielder must have participated at his position in at least two-thirds of the number of games scheduled for each club in his league that season; (3) A pitcher must have pitched at least as many innings as the number of games scheduled for each club in his league that season.

Percentage To compute the pitcher's earned run average, multiply the total earned runs charged against his pitching by 9, and divide the result by the total number of innings he pitched.

Sacrifice Score a sacrifice fly when, before two are out, the batter hits a fair fly ball which: (1) is caught, and a runner scores after the catch, or (2) is dropped, and a runner scores, if, in the scorer's judgment, the runner could have scored after the catch had the fly been caught.

Note: Score a sacrifice fly in accordance with the scoring rules even though another runner is forced out by reason of the batter becoming a runner.

1959–64

There were no changes to the scoring rules in these years.

1965

Championship To qualify for the fielding championship at his position a pitcher must have pitched at least as many innings as the number of games scheduled for each club in his league that season. Exception: If another pitcher has a fielding average as high or higher, and has handled more total chances in a lesser number of innings, he shall be the fielding champion.

1966

There were no changes to the scoring rules this year.

1967

Championship The individual batting champion shall be the player with the highest batting average, provided he is credited with as many or more total appearances at the plate in league championship games as the number of games scheduled for each club in his league that season, multiplied by 3.1. Exception: However, if there is any player with fewer than the required number of plate appearances whose average would be highest if he were charged with the required number of plate appearances or official at-bats, then that player shall be awarded the batting championship.

Error Mental mistakes or misjudgments are not to be scored as errors unless specifically covered in the rules.

No error shall be charged against any fielder when, after fumbling a ground ball or dropping a fly ball, a line drive or a thrown ball, he recovers the ball in time to force out a runner at any base.

Sacrifice Do not score a sacrifice bunt when, in the judgment of the scorer, the batter is bunting for a base hit and not solely for the purpose of advancing a runner or runners. Charge the batter with a time at bat.

Note: In applying this rule always give the batter the benefit of the doubt.

Stolen Base When a runner, attempting to steal, or after being picked off base, evades being put out in a rundown play and advances to the next base without the aid of an error, credit the runner with a stolen base. If another runner also advances on the play, credit both runners with stolen bases. If a runner advances while another runner, attempting to steal, evades being put out in a rundown play and returns safely, without the aid of an error, to the base he originally occupied, credit a stolen base to the runner who advances.

1968

There were no changes to the scoring rules this year.

1969

Double Play/Triple Play Credit participation in the double play or triple play to each fielder who earns a putout or an assist when two or three players are put out between the time a pitch is delivered and the time the ball next becomes dead or is next in possession of the pitcher in pitching position, unless an error or misplay intervenes between putouts.

Note: Credit the double play or triple play also if an appeal play after the ball is in possession of the pitcher results in an additional putout.

Earned Run An earned run is a run for which the pitcher is held accountable. In determining earned runs, the inning should be reconstructed without the errors and passed balls, and the benefit of the doubt should always be given to the pitcher in determining which bases would have been reached by errorless play.

When pitchers are changed during an inning, the relief pitcher shall not have the benefit of previous chances for outs not accepted in determining earned runs.

Note: It is the intent of this rule to prevent relief pitchers from not being charged with earned runs for which they are solely responsible.

Error When an umpire awards the batter or any runner or runners one or more bases because of interference or obstruction, charge the fielder who committed the interference or obstruction with one error, no matter how many bases the batter, or runner or runners, may be advanced.

Note: Do not charge an error if obstruction does not change the play in the opinion of the scorer.

Relief Pitcher See *Earned Run*, second paragraph.

Sacrifice Do not score a sacrifice bunt when, in the judgment of the scorer, the batter is bunting *primarily* for a base hit and not for the purpose of advancing a runner or runners. Charge the batter with a time at bat.

Note: In applying this rule always give the batter the benefit of the doubt.

Note: The rule is the same as that appearing in the 1967 scoring rules with the addition of the word *primarily*.

Save Credit a save to a relief pitcher who enters a game with his team in the lead if he holds the lead the remainder of the game, provided he is not credited with the victory. A relief pitcher cannot be credited with a save if he does not finish the game unless he is removed for a pinch hitter or pinch runner. When more than one relief pitcher qualifies for a save under the provisions of this rule, credit the save to the relief pitcher judged by the scorer to have been the most effective. Only one save can be credited in any game.

1970–72

There were no changes to the scoring rules in these years.

1973

Save A pitcher shall be credited with a save when, in entering a game as a relief pitcher, he finds the potential tying or winning run either on base or at the plate or pitches at least three or more effective innings and, in either case, preserves the lead.

1974

Hitting/Playing Streaks A consecutive hitting streak shall not be terminated if the plate appearance results in a base on balls, hit batsman, defensive interference or a sacrifice bunt.

A sacrifice fly shall terminate the streak.

A consecutive-game hitting streak shall not be terminated if all the player's plate appearances (one or more) result in a base on balls, hit batsman, defensive interference or a sacrifice bunt. The streak shall terminate if the player has a sacrifice fly and no hit.

A consecutive-game playing streak shall be extended if the player plays one half-inning on defense, or if he completes a time at bat by reaching base or being put out. A pinch-running appearance only shall not extend the streak. If a player is ejected from a game by an umpire before he can comply with the requirements of this rule, his streak shall continue.

Suspended Game For the purpose of the scoring rules, all performances in the completion of a suspended game shall be considered as occurring on the original date of the game.

1975

Sacrifice Score a sacrifice fly when, before two are out, the batter hits a fly ball or a line drive handled by an outfielder or an infielder running in the outfield which: (1) is caught, and a runner scores after the catch, or (2) is dropped, and a runner scores, if in the scorer's judgment the runner could have scored after the catch had the fly been caught.

Note: Score a sacrifice fly in accordance with the scoring rules even though another runner is forced out by reason of the batter becoming a runner.

Save Credit a pitcher with a save when he meets all three of the following conditions: (1) He is the finishing pitcher in a game won by his club; and (2) He is not the winning pitcher; and (3) He qualifies under one of the following conditions: (a) He enters the game with a lead of no more than three runs and pitches for at least one inning; or (b) He enters the game with the potential tying run either on base, or at bat, or on deck (that is, the potential tying run is either already on base or is one of the first two batsmen he faces); or (c) He pitches effectively for at least three innings. No more than one save may be credited in each game.

1976

Base on Balls See *Strikeout*.

Earned Run An earned run is a run for which the pitcher is held accountable. In determining earned runs, the inning should be reconstructed without the errors (which includes catcher's interference) and passed balls, and the benefit of the doubt should always be given to the pitcher in determining which bases would have been reached by errorless play.

When pitchers are changed during an inning, the relief pitcher shall not be charged with any run (earned or unearned) scored by a runner who was on base at the time he entered the game, nor for runs scored by any runner who reaches base on a fielder's choice which puts out a runner left on base by the preceding pitcher.

Note: It is the intent of this rule to charge each pitcher with the number of runners he put on base, rather than with the individual runners. When a pitcher puts runners on base and is relieved, he shall be charged with all runs subsequently scored up to and including the number of runners he left on base when he left the game, unless such runners are put out without action by the batter, i.e., caught stealing, picked off base, or called out for interference when a batter-runner does not reach first base on the play. Exception: The pitcher walks batter A and is relieved. The relief pitcher allows B to single, but runner A is out trying for third. Runner B takes second on the throw. Batter C singles, scoring runner B. Charge the run to the relief pitcher rather than the preceding pitcher.

Game Played When a player listed in the starting lineup for the visiting club is substituted for before he plays defensively, he shall not receive credit in the defensive statistics (fielding), unless he actually plays that position during a game. All such players, however, shall be credited with one game played (in batting statistics) as long as they are announced into the game or listed on the official lineup card.

Percentage For purposes of earned run average calculations and innings pitched totals, innings pitched shall be rounded off to the nearest whole inning. Examples: 200⅓ innings becomes 200; 200⅔ becomes 201.

Note: This standard was changed in 1982 and fractions were no longer rounded off but counted for their full value. Also see rule addition under 1981.

Relief Pitcher See *Earned Run*, second paragraph.

Scoring Summary The name of a pitcher credited with a save is to be shown on the scoring summary.

Strikeout When the batter leaves the game with two strikes against him, and the substitute batter completes a strikeout, charge the strikeout and the time at bat to the first batter. If the substitute batter completes the turn at bat in any other manner, including a base on balls, score the action as having been that of the substitute batter.

Substitute Batter See *Strikeout*.

1977

Base on Balls Intentional base on balls shall be scored when the pitcher makes no attempt to throw the last pitch to the batter into the strike zone but purposely throws the ball wide to the catcher outside the catcher's box.

1978

There were no changes to the scoring rules this year.

1979

Caught Stealing A runner shall be charged as "caught stealing" if he is put out, or would have been put out by errorless play, when he (1) tries to steal; (2) is picked off a base and tries to advance (any move toward the next base shall be considered an attempt to advance); (3) overslides while stealing.

Note: In those instances where a pitched ball eludes the catcher and the runner is put out trying to advance, no caught stealing shall be charged.

Earned Run An earned run is a run for which the pitcher is held accountable. In determining earned runs, the inning should be reconstructed without the errors (which include catcher's interference) and passed balls, and the benefit of the doubt should always be given to the pitcher in determining which bases would have been reached by errorless play. For the purpose of determining earned runs, an intentional base on balls, regardless of the circumstances, shall be construed in exactly the same manner as any other base on balls.

Scorer The official scorer must make all decisions concerning judgment calls within twenty-four (24) hours after a game has been officially concluded. No judgment decision shall be changed thereafter except, upon immediate application to the league president, the scorer may request a change, citing the reasons for such. In all cases the official scorer is not permitted to make a scoring decision which is in conflict with the scoring rules.

1980

Run Batted In Game-winning RBI is credited for the RBI that gives a club the lead it never relinquishes.

Note: There does not have to be a game-winning RBI in every game and all game-winning RBIs must conform to the scoring rule governing RBIs.

1981

Percentage For purposes of earned run average calculations and innings pitched totals, do not round off the fraction where a pitcher has only ⅓ of an inning for the entire season. In such cases carry his total for innings pitched as ⅓.

1982

Percentage Earned run averages shall be calculated on the basis of total innings pitched, including fractional innings. Example: 9⅓ innings pitched and three earned runs is an earned run average of 2.89 (3 ER times 9 divided by 9⅓ equals 2.89).

1983

Championship The individual batting champion or slugging champion shall be the player with the highest batting average or slugging percentage, provided he is credited with as many or more total appearances at the plate in League championship games as the number of games scheduled for each club in his

League that season, multiplied by 3.1 in the case of a major league player. Exception: However, if there is any player with fewer than the required number of plate appearances or official at-bats, but who, when credited with an out for each of his deficient at-bats, still has the highest average, then that player shall be awarded the batting championship or slugging championship.

1984

Percentage To compute on-base percentage, divide the total of hits, all bases on balls, and hit by pitch, by the total of at-bats, all bases on balls, hit by pitch, and sacrifice flies.

Note: For the purpose of computing on-base percentage, ignore being awarded first base on interference or obstruction.

1985–88

There were no changes to the scoring rules this year.

1989

Run Batted In The game-winning RBI is dropped from the rule book.

1990–1992

There were no changes to the scoring rules this year.

Index to Scoring Rule Changes 1877–1992

Lifetime Fielding

In this edition of *Total Baseball,* we have eliminated the Fielding Register that occupied so many pages in the second edition. As indicated in the Introduction to Part 2 and the chapter on sabermetrics that followed, the editors are skeptical about the usefulness of raw fielding data. As a rule, putouts are the significant stat for outfielders and assists for infielders (even first basemen). Outfield assists are of enormous defensive value, but they are four times less prevalent today than at the dawn of big-league play—because the less resilient ball of the turn of the century permitted outfielders to play shallow and thus pile up assists. The top fifteen outfielders in lifetime assists, excepting Max Carey and Sam Rice, played all or most of their games before 1920; they did not all have better arms than Roberto Clemente. And again because of the dead ball and styles of play (little free-swinging and consequently few strikeouts) consistent with that reality, infield assist totals of the early years are also astronomical. Because of barehand play and then the use of small, unconstructed gloves, error totals were also much higher years ago than today, at all positions. Chances accepted (putouts plus assists, usually measured on a per-game basis) are more meaningful than the fielding percentage, with its well-known reward for immobility.

So what do the traditional fielding stats mean? Without historical context and manipulation, not a lot. But fielding itself is certainly important. A run saved in the field is the same as a run saved from the mound, or one gained at the bat or on the basepaths. That is why the editors advocate the use of Fielding Runs (FR), a stat supplied for every man in the Player Register and, as Pitcher Defense (PD), in the Pitcher Register.

The various formulas employed in calculating Fielding Runs normalize to the league average for chances accepted at each position (isolating left field, center field, and right field for more accurate comparisons); are calculated on a per-inning rather than a per-game basis; encompass within the formulas double plays and errors as well as putouts and assists; and for catchers, Fielding Runs give credit for handling a pitching staff—they are given one tenth of the total difference between the team's adjusted runs allowed and the league average. For more on this, see the Glossary.

Although Pitcher Defense is a column entry in the Pitcher Register, even those men who hurl the most innings handle so few chances per season as to render negligible their fielding contribution to the team. All the same, over the course of a career a pitcher may pile up some meaningful fielding totals, and his Fielding Runs may show that he saved (or cost) himself some extra wins. Look, for example, at the fine records of Carl Mays or Tommy John and the unimpressive totals of Nolan Ryan or Jim Bunning.

Recognizing, however, that most fans will continue to appreciate familiar statistics as well as sabermetric measures, in this third edition we provided traditional fielding averages throughout the Player Register, and here provide basic lifetime fielding data for position players. (For those interested in a similar presentation for pitchers, consult the second edition.) Those listed have played at least 700 games at the position. No attempt is made to combine totals from different positions, for such totals would be meaningless.

Note that outfielders have an additional column in this section—LCR, which indicates whether they played left, center, or right fields. An asterisk preceding the letter L, C, or R indicates at least 1000 games in that field. A capital letter (LCR) signifies at least 600 games in that field, and a lowercase letter (lcr) means at least 300 games in that field. Fewer than 300 games at an outfield position are not shown.

First Base	PCT	G	PO	A	E	DP	FR
Joe Adcock	.994	1501	13006	879	83	1228	-43
Dick Allen	.989	807	6747	418	82	640	-32
Cap Anson	.974	2058	20794	955	583	1189	51
Ernie Banks	.994	1259	12005	809	80	1005	5
Jake Beckley	.981	2377	23709	1315	481	1326	21
Dave Bergman	.992	866	5066	448	46	469	26
Lu Blue	.989	1571	15644	1016	191	1187	-1
Bruce Bochte	.992	1008	8355	614	76	833	-20
Zeke Bonura	.992	900	8808	595	72	815	27
Jim Bottomley	.988	1885	18337	814	223	1562	-119
Kitty Bransfield	.983	1291	12797	737	236	670	-16
Sid Bream	.991	854	6750	713	65	550	69
Greg Brock	.994	942	7578	684	51	680	30
Dan Brouthers	.971	1633	16365	654	512	890	-14
Bill Buckner	.992	1555	13901	1351	128	1200	121
George Burns	.987	1671	16892	1094	245	1117	0
Jack Burns	.992	879	8063	525	66	776	18
Dolph Camilli	.990	1476	13724	957	141	1189	2
Rod Carew	.991	1184	10930	774	106	1130	-25
Norm Cash	.992	1943	15157	1317	131	1347	51
Danny Cater	.994	731	5567	458	39	534	19
Phil Cavarretta	.990	1254	11375	796	123	1012	-5
Orlando Cepeda	.990	1683	14459	1012	162	1192	-37
Chris Chambliss	.993	1962	17771	1351	130	1687	22
Frank Chance	.987	997	9885	615	135	470	14
Hal Chase	.980	1815	18185	1049	402	934	-31

First Base	PCT	G	PO	A	E	DP	FR
Will Clark	.993	995	9136	724	72	812	2
Donn Clendenon	.988	1200	10913	819	146	1136	18
Nate Colbert	.991	890	7754	568	74	686	2
Ripper Collins	.992	894	7747	608	68	695	26
Joe Collins	.990	715	4555	376	49	580	11
Charlie Comiskey	.973	1363	13821	508	403	740	2
Roger Connor	.978	1758	17605	856	419	955	48
Cecil Cooper	.992	1475	13361	1000	121	1348	-14
Babe Dahlgren	.990	1030	9619	587	102	848	-20
Jake Daubert	.991	2002	19634	1128	181	1199	20
Alvin Davis	.992	887	7803	572	67	789	-26
Glenn Davis	.992	848	7241	605	67	565	8
Harry Davis	.980	1628	15666	950	343	682	8
Jiggs Donahue	.987	745	8151	556	112	336	43
Jack Doyle	.975	1043	10165	645	277	603	19
Dan Driessen	.995	1375	10863	732	58	979	-24
Walt Dropo	.992	1174	9173	672	84	968	1
Mike Epstein	.991	823	6957	477	70	681	-9
Nick Etten	.988	903	8030	545	107	797	-23
Darrell Evans	.992	856	6515	752	57	571	76
Ferris Fain	.987	1116	9530	927	138	1124	59
Ron Fairly	.991	1218	9294	704	92	854	2
Sid Farrar	.974	943	9550	358	262	431	8
Elbie Fletcher	.993	1380	13237	975	107	1086	32
Dee Fondy	.988	874	7434	641	98	690	6
Jack Fournier	.984	1313	12375	788	208	777	16

First Base	PCT	G	PO	A	E	DP	FR
Jimmie Foxx	.992	1919	17207	1222	155	1528	43
Andres Galarraga	.992	923	8041	595	68	622	-14
Chick Gandil	.992	1138	11118	754	99	630	36
John Ganzel	.987	726	7430	416	102	362	1
Steve Garvey	.996	2059	18844	1026	81	1498	-115
Lou Gehrig	.991	2137	19510	1087	193	1575	-59
Jim Gentile	.990	854	6725	564	73	671	11
Mark Grace	.994	745	6836	701	47	525	65
Hank Greenberg	.991	1138	10564	724	104	973	24
Charlie Grimm	.993	2131	20711	1214	162	1733	10
Mike Hargrove	.991	1378	11274	1022	115	1043	54
Buddy Hassett	.985	747	6630	649	108	642	54
Keith Hernandez	.994	2014	17909	1682	115	1654	150
Dick Hoblitzel	.987	1284	12584	661	180	641	-27
Gil Hodges	.992	1908	15344	1281	126	1614	39
Walter Holke	.993	1193	12158	665	96	859	8
Kent Hrbek	.994	1422	12219	927	80	1183	-23
Don Hurst	.987	863	7950	586	110	732	21
Deron Johnson	.993	880	6439	418	50	587	-28
Doc Johnston	.989	1023	9739	507	113	526	-37
Tom Jones	.984	1033	10872	698	183	456	24
Mike Jorgensen	.994	1052	6529	537	44	601	44
Wally Joyner	.994	985	8652	770	59	895	28
Joe Judge	.993	2084	19264	1301	142	1500	14
George Kelly	.992	1373	14232	861	121	1111	37
Harmon Killebrew	.992	969	7521	555	69	678	-15
Ted Kluszewski	.993	1481	12652	799	97	1269	-82
Ed Konetchy	.990	2073	21361	1292	224	1086	60
Ed Kranepool	.994	1304	10492	779	72	900	13
Joe Kuhel	.992	2057	19386	1163	173	1769	-50
Candy LaChance	.984	1176	12320	457	207	649	-69
Henry Larkin	.971	710	6804	250	209	388	-28
Whitey Lockman	.989	771	6716	510	80	672	-9
Dale Long	.988	819	6960	550	88	672	-6
Fred Luderus	.986	1326	13126	843	201	725	37
Don Mattingly	.996	1282	10977	870	52	1192	-15
Lee May	.994	1507	12885	894	88	1235	-21
John Mayberry	.994	1478	13169	827	88	1307	-48
Frank McCormick	.995	1448	13798	1001	78	1221	31
Willie McCovey	.987	2045	17170	1222	233	1405	-24
Tommy McCraw	.991	911	6581	513	68	552	22
Dan McGann	.989	1376	13682	798	168	701	30
Fred McGriff	.992	778	6750	536	56	621	-10
Mark McGwire	.995	885	7209	559	40	695	-18
Stuffy McInnis	.993	1995	19962	1238	160	1309	29
George McQuinn	.992	1529	13414	1074	113	1265	32
Fred Merkle	.985	1547	15419	847	252	839	-8
Dots Miller	.988	737	7433	407	97	423	0
Don Mincher	.990	1138	9181	696	95	796	2
Johnny Mize	.992	1667	14850	1032	133	1320	-11
Willie Montanez	.992	1164	10006	714	87	962	1
John Morrill	.971	916	9152	375	285	450	39
Eddie Murray	.993	2214	19523	1717	143	1878	63
Stan Musial	.992	1016	8709	688	78	935	3
Pete O'Brien	.994	1368	11575	1056	78	1076	55
Al Oliver	.990	733	5904	433	67	499	-16
Dave Orr	.973	787	7923	254	227	356	0
Wes Parker	.996	1108	9640	695	45	757	19
Joe Pepitone	.993	953	8172	627	61	781	11
Tony Perez	.992	1778	14481	936	117	1342	-41
Bill Phillips	.971	1032	10540	305	324	511	7
Wally Pipp	.992	1819	18779	1152	168	1290	8
Boog Powell	.991	1479	12130	859	116	1131	-21
Vic Power	.994	1304	10141	1078	66	1056	124
John Reilly	.972	1075	10875	286	316	655	-20
Eddie Robinson	.990	1126	9832	636	109	1018	-46
Pete Rose	.994	939	7881	665	51	649	24
Vic Saier	.986	838	8392	378	129	422	-33
George Scott	.990	1773	15405	1132	165	1480	-10
Earl Sheely	.991	1220	12067	744	113	890	-16
Norm Siebern	.992	827	6905	571	61	655	10
Dick Siebert	.990	949	8523	741	94	732	36
Roy Sievers	.991	888	7241	551	70	747	-8
George Sisler	.987	1971	18837	1529	269	1468	89
Bill Skowron	.992	1463	12043	903	102	1266	-1
Jim Spencer	.995	1221	9898	797	55	956	32
Jake Stahl	.983	839	8458	462	150	328	-19
Willie Stargell	.991	848	7293	384	67	701	-55
Joe Start	.968	797	8691	184	294	359	-7
George Stovall	.986	1217	12712	846	192	702	51
Dick Stuart	.982	1024	8294	758	169	837	15
Gus Suhr	.992	1406	13103	766	116	1086	-53
Fred Tenney	.983	1810	17903	1363	327	956	129
Bill Terry	.992	1579	15972	1108	138	1334	67
Jason Thompson	.992	1314	11818	819	97	1090	-28
Andy Thornton	.992	729	6223	501	51	558	17
Phil Todt	.992	904	9079	623	80	713	26
Earl Torgeson	.989	1416	11680	814	143	1097	-37
Joe Torre	.993	787	6342	478	49	607	11
Hal Trosky	.991	1321	12124	752	121	1146	-13
Tommy Tucker	.978	1669	16393	749	393	925	-7

First Base	PCT	G	PO	A	E	DP	FR
Willie Upshaw	.990	1094	8939	799	98	845	18
Mickey Vernon	.990	2237	19808	1448	211	2044	-31
Eddie Waitkus	.993	1049	9150	716	72	886	11
Bob Watson	.991	1088	8930	653	83	771	-3
Vic Wertz	.989	715	5098	447	63	537	7
Bill White	.992	1477	12735	960	105	1157	11
Carl Yastrzemski	.994	765	6459	512	41	610	9
Rudy York	.990	1263	11359	963	122	1072	44

Second Base	PCT	G	PO	A	E	DP	FR
Jerry Adair	.985	810	1860	2008	58	465	-9
Bernie Allen	.980	914	1960	2151	86	539	-42
Roberto Alomar	.979	747	1591	2147	81	397	-24
Sandy Alomar	.977	1156	2572	2988	128	729	10
Mike Andrews	.973	787	1838	1951	107	438	-44
Bobby Avila	.979	1168	2820	3126	130	785	-52
Wally Backman	.980	825	1405	1952	69	383	-100
Marty Barrett	.986	908	1827	2631	63	580	66
Glenn Beckert	.973	1242	2710	3712	179	758	-5
Tony Bernazard	.978	1000	2100	2901	114	623	-46
Lou Bierbauer	.935	1364	3724	4555	574	620	152
Max Bishop	.976	1230	2752	3850	163	639	-56
Don Blasingame	.979	1310	3065	3550	144	834	-1
Jimmy Bloodworth	.975	867	2257	2498	123	571	57
Frank Bolling	.982	1518	3423	4019	136	1003	-98
Jack Burdock	.912	956	2694	2968	543	389	10
Rod Carew	.973	1130	2573	2928	154	664	-58
Dave Cash	.984	1330	3185	3841	117	901	47
Cupid Childs	.930	1454	3859	4678	646	602	93
Horace Clarke	.983	1102	2682	3179	104	695	34
Eddie Collins	.970	2650	6526	7630	435	1215	52
Hughie Critz	.974	1453	3446	5138	231	960	110
Julio Cruz	.983	1123	2393	3435	103	780	97
Tony Cuccinello	.973	1205	2883	3891	190	812	1
George Cutshaw	.965	1486	3762	4473	299	635	64
Tom Daly	.931	1056	2646	3017	418	421	-72
Rich Dauer	.987	964	2004	2451	57	636	-106
Bobby Doerr	.980	1852	4928	5710	214	1507	180
Bill Doran	.983	1342	2591	3625	106	737	-101
Larry Doyle	.949	1728	3635	4655	443	694	-152
Denny Doyle	.977	912	1891	2409	101	547	-59
Fred Dunlap	.924	963	2909	3169	498	513	137
Jimmy Dykes	.958	722	1866	2343	183	376	99
Johnny Evers	.955	1735	3758	5124	423	688	63
Jack Farrell	.899	740	1778	2480	477	278	-35
Hobe Ferris	.954	1019	2503	3148	271	353	92
Doug Flynn	.986	961	1920	2415	61	532	44
Nellie Fox	.984	2295	6090	6373	209	1619	42
Lonny Frey	.973	966	2369	2986	151	642	31
Frankie Frisch	.974	1762	4348	6026	280	1064	140
Tito Fuentes	.974	1275	3046	3654	182	832	-16
Jim Gantner	.985	1449	3139	4347	115	1036	58
Damaso Garcia	.980	960	1928	2784	98	602	-56
Billy Gardner	.978	839	1923	2173	91	559	3
Phil Garner	.974	975	2124	2760	129	606	-14
Charlie Gehringer	.976	2206	5369	7068	309	1444	31
Joe Gerhardt	.913	880	2766	2941	543	477	160
Billy Gilbert	.942	715	1647	2200	237	253	74
Jim Gilliam	.979	1046	2279	2724	107	628	-43
Kid Gleason	.938	1583	3883	4768	571	584	20
Joe Gordon	.970	1519	3600	4706	260	1160	55
George Grantham	.949	848	1987	2712	250	483	-89
Dick Green	.983	1158	2518	3063	96	712	33
Bobby Grich	.984	1765	4217	5381	156	1302	101
Bill Hallman	.940	1135	2692	3386	385	479	-75
Bucky Harris	.965	1253	3412	3842	263	801	42
Jackie Hayes	.976	904	2189	2983	126	639	42
Tommy Helms	.983	1129	2688	3237	101	807	35
Billy Herman	.967	1813	4780	5681	354	1177	78
Tom Herr	.989	1416	2932	3999	77	991	-95
Rogers Hornsby	.965	1561	3206	5166	307	893	-112
Glenn Hubbard	.983	1332	2795	4444	127	975	229
Miller Huggins	.956	1530	3425	4697	376	597	76
Ron Hunt	.976	1260	2734	3512	156	685	-111
Julian Javier	.972	1552	3380	4113	219	907	-65
Davey Johnson	.980	1198	2837	3153	123	759	12
Otto Knabe	.957	1239	2743	3583	287	483	62
Bobby Knoop	.980	1116	2566	3218	119	779	150
Duane Kuiper	.983	920	2000	2466	76	551	-36
Nap Lajoie	.963	2035	5496	6262	451	1050	370
Frank LaPorte	.952	731	1468	2075	180	299	-12
Tony Lazzeri	.967	1456	3351	4445	263	808	-106
Jose Lind	.987	774	1685	2365	52	397	46
Davey Lopes	.977	1418	3142	3829	162	811	-176
Bobby Lowe	.950	1313	3326	4171	395	530	72
Jerry Lumpe	.984	1100	2469	2845	88	662	-40
Ray Mack	.966	788	1897	2236	144	597	2
Billy Martin	.980	767	1734	1840	74	532	-37
Bill Mazeroski	.983	2094	4974	6685	204	1706	363
Dick McAuliffe	.977	971	2155	2299	104	552	-39

Second Base	PCT	G	PO	A	E	DP	FR
Marty McManus	.965	927	2430	2853	194	557	8
Bid McPhee	.944	2126	6545	6905	791	1186	315
Ski Melillo	.973	1316	3437	4448	215	965	148
Cass Michaels	.973	800	2073	2343	124	633	-15
Felix Millan	.980	1450	3495	3846	151	855	-130
Joe Morgan	.981	2527	5742	6967	244	1505	-205
Danny Murphy	.953	839	1686	2320	199	210	-25
Buddy Myer	.974	1340	3487	4068	200	963	-87
Al Myers	.914	806	2029	2547	430	330	-41
Danny O'Connell	.980	713	1657	2049	74	508	27
Ron Oester	.980	1171	2591	3197	116	647	-16
Dick Padden	.950	780	1937	2291	224	269	-1
Fred Pfeffer	.920	1537	4713	5104	857	893	258
Del Pratt	.960	1688	4069	5075	381	825	87
Jerry Priddy	.973	1179	3226	3567	190	906	81
Joe Quinn	.946	1303	3315	3805	408	557	-72
Willie Randolph	.980	2152	4859	6336	234	1547	0
Johnny Rawlings	.968	709	1530	2233	123	362	-17
Johnny Ray	.982	1277	2682	3836	118	828	23
Jerry Remy	.981	1117	2292	3241	110	744	-66
Harold Reynolds	.978	1133	2327	3406	130	812	126
Bobby Richardson	.979	1339	3125	3445	143	963	-14
Claude Ritchey	.957	1478	3440	4474	355	560	51
Jackie Robinson	.983	748	1877	2047	68	607	33
Cookie Rojas	.984	1447	3100	3819	115	953	-48
Connie Ryan	.970	980	2447	2818	164	573	-10
Juan Samuel	.973	1100	2416	3018	153	590	-84
Ryne Sandberg	.990	1551	3071	5096	84	907	129
Steve Sax	.978	1672	3558	4782	187	995	-114
Red Schoendienst	.983	1834	4616	5243	170	1368	78
Ted Sizemore	.979	1288	2928	3761	143	835	33
Pop Smith	.904	711	2012	2354	466	303	43
Eddie Stanky	.975	1152	3030	3215	162	816	13
Rennie Stennett	.978	1049	2568	3100	129	687	44
Snuffy Stirnweiss	.980	787	1978	2224	84	572	17
Cub Stricker	.907	1145	3447	3387	701	513	26
Pete Suder	.982	805	1879	2292	75	613	-11
Gary Sutherland	.971	717	1445	1816	98	483	-9
Tony Taylor	.976	1498	3274	3818	178	950	-69
Johnny Temple	.974	1312	3172	3329	172	829	-172
Tim Teufel	.980	754	1304	1861	66	342	-86
Robby Thompson	.981	963	1966	2806	90	665	61
Manny Trillo	.981	1518	3403	4699	157	973	135
Emil Verban	.971	802	1994	2179	123	534	1
Bill Wambsganss	.958	1203	2981	3666	292	605	31
Aaron Ward	.970	809	1846	2546	134	378	-5
Lou Whitaker	.984	2052	4293	5923	162	1377	-66
Frank White	.984	2150	4740	6250	178	1382	20
Burgess Whitehead	.972	718	1847	2297	118	462	95
Rob Wilfong	.982	839	1554	2335	72	507	80
Jimmy Williams	.955	1176	2759	3509	292	426	53
Bump Wills	.979	800	1815	2582	94	495	42
Ralph Young	.959	993	2356	2954	228	354	-32

Third Base	PCT	G	PO	A	E	DP	FR
Max Alvis	.956	971	962	1693	123	144	-65
Bob Aspromonte	.960	1094	1025	1879	121	120	-51
Jimmy Austin	.933	1431	2042	2949	358	229	47
Bob Bailey	.946	1194	793	2262	175	203	-50
Frank Baker	.943	1548	2154	3155	322	259	38
Sal Bando	.959	1896	1647	3720	228	345	-104
Buddy Bell	.964	2183	1798	4925	254	430	199
Les Bell	.939	828	814	1412	144	161	-50
Ossie Bluege	.957	1487	1551	3040	208	266	19
Tony Boeckel	.941	755	912	1356	143	111	-55
Wade Boggs	.959	1520	1165	2956	177	299	18
Clete Boyer	.965	1439	1470	3218	168	315	201
Ken Boyer	.952	1785	1567	3652	264	355	79
Bill Bradley	.933	1390	1753	2943	336	182	44
George Brett	.951	1692	1372	3674	261	307	1
Tom Brookens	.943	1065	728	1833	155	171	11
Steve Buechele	.968	1000	728	1847	86	142	76
Tom Burns	.886	704	1043	1494	327	118	47
Bobby Byrne	.934	1147	1456	2221	258	133	7
Enos Cabell	.944	888	744	1527	134	105	-84
Andy Carey	.958	882	847	1692	111	194	47
Hick Carpenter	.853	1059	1450	1991	591	142	-79
Doc Casey	.915	1100	1312	2184	325	119	-75
Ron Cey	.961	1989	1500	4018	223	315	31
Ed Charles	.957	942	879	1833	122	165	-15
Harlond Clift	.948	1550	1777	3262	279	309	66
Jimmy Collins	.929	1683	2372	3702	465	225	139
Bill Coughlin	.931	983	1269	1859	231	93	-35
Billy Cox	.965	700	668	1273	71	154	0
Lave Cross	.938	1721	2306	3706	394	212	132
Jim Davenport	.964	1130	863	1816	100	155	3
Charlie Deal	.958	823	956	1705	117	126	49
Doug DeCinces	.958	1543	1256	3215	198	331	47
Jerry Denny	.882	1109	1777	2338	552	147	97
Art Devlin	.938	1192	1399	2481	257	132	89

Third Base	PCT	G	PO	A	E	DP	FR
Joe Dugan	.957	1048	1099	1932	137	165	-120
Jimmy Dykes	.952	1257	1361	2403	188	199	-7
Bob Elliott	.947	1365	1448	2744	236	252	-39
Darrell Evans	.946	1442	1273	3123	253	270	92
Eddie Foster	.930	1161	1289	2384	278	213	-18
Gene Freese	.934	781	589	1341	136	129	-62
Gary Gaetti	.963	1530	1256	3182	171	343	119
Larry Gardner	.948	1656	1788	3406	286	246	-40
Phil Garner	.944	839	593	1542	127	135	44
Wayne Garrett	.956	792	548	1515	95	148	34
Jim Gilliam	.952	761	533	1265	90	110	-4
Eddie Grant	.942	769	962	1423	148	105	-15
Heinie Groh	.967	1299	1456	2554	136	268	27
Wayne Gross	.941	903	717	1437	134	149	-91
Kelly Gruber	.955	829	601	1608	103	107	57
Stan Hack	.957	1836	1944	3494	246	255	-6
Sammy Hale	.939	704	686	1373	133	145	-32
Lee Handley	.949	713	703	1464	117	107	36
Frank Hankinson	.875	764	1029	1579	373	116	50
Toby Harrah	.963	1099	781	1942	106	177	-118
Grady Hatton	.956	956	979	1844	129	169	-20
Richie Hebner	.946	1262	839	2346	182	224	-77
Pinky Higgins	.935	1768	1848	3258	356	288	-131
Andy High	.956	790	725	1307	93	113	-73
Don Hoak	.959	1199	1219	2331	153	227	21
Roy Howell	.944	846	651	1666	137	160	-37
Charlie Irwin	.921	865	1228	1685	250	134	-23
Randy Jackson	.955	844	868	1725	123	157	19
Brook Jacoby	.958	1166	776	2058	123	168	-63
Howard Johnson	.928	930	499	1388	147	123	-94
Billy Johnson	.959	897	860	1728	111	163	19
Bob Jones	.953	774	917	1600	124	96	-2
Willie Jones	.963	1614	2045	2934	192	273	-55
Bill Joyce	.851	733	1041	1453	438	105	-42
Willie Kamm	.967	1674	2151	3345	185	299	65
George Kell	.969	1692	1825	3303	166	306	-17
Ken Keltner	.965	1500	1576	3070	171	306	36
Harmon Killebrew	.940	791	607	1388	127	88	-85
Ray Knight	.957	1021	694	1653	105	144	-48
Bill Kuehne	.876	798	932	1694	373	128	9
Whitey Kurowski	.957	868	1025	1569	116	137	-8
Carney Lansford	.966	1720	1382	2799	148	256	-225
Arlie Latham	.870	1571	1975	3545	822	253	67
Vance Law	.956	700	442	1115	71	102	-41
Tommy Leach	.909	955	1323	2127	344	113	74
Freddy Lindstrom	.959	809	835	1536	102	135	26
Hans Lobert	.944	1000	1292	1601	172	96	-99
Harry Lord	.924	907	1046	1583	217	95	-123
Denny Lyons	.882	1083	1672	2127	507	164	-25
Bill Madlock	.948	1440	949	2546	193	200	-143
Hank Majeski	.968	861	911	1750	89	192	46
Frank Malzone	.955	1370	1308	2884	196	289	50
Eddie Mathews	.956	2181	2049	4322	293	369	-15
John McGraw	.898	782	868	1600	280	104	-49
Marty McManus	.957	725	866	1450	103	132	38
Ken McMullen	.961	1318	1259	2731	162	258	62
Bill Melton	.949	901	700	2045	147	184	56
Paul Molitor	.950	791	642	1639	121	185	-1
Don Money	.968	1025	897	2061	97	224	-12
George Moriarty	.931	796	951	1727	199	84	23
Mike Mowrey	.944	1196	1363	2363	221	172	-9
Rance Mulliniks	.961	730	395	1009	57	95	-66
Joe Mulvey	.871	983	1235	1962	475	131	-46
Billy Nash	.897	1464	2219	3119	614	265	81
Graig Nettles	.961	2412	1898	5279	295	470	136
Ken Oberkfell	.965	1046	627	1996	96	180	20
Marv Owen	.953	921	1032	1695	135	168	-31
Mike Pagliarulo	.953	1004	582	1822	119	165	13
Larry Parrish	.941	1021	810	1918	171	160	-50
Terry Pendleton	.958	1214	958	2809	166	213	162
Tony Perez	.946	760	644	1496	123	141	-15
Rico Petrocelli	.970	727	581	1453	63	150	-36
Bubba Phillips	.960	762	808	1416	92	133	-6
George Pinkney	.897	1061	1343	2042	387	143	-86
Jim Presley	.949	911	633	1709	127	152	-5
Doug Rader	.956	1349	1138	2887	187	256	86
Ken Reitz	.970	1321	996	2477	109	219	-57
Brooks Robinson	.971	2870	2697	6205	263	618	152
Aurelio Rodriguez	.964	1983	1529	4150	215	408	185
Red Rolfe	.956	1084	1220	2128	155	184	-16
Rich Rollins	.947	830	716	1582	129	133	-23
Al Rosen	.961	932	970	1773	112	159	-58
Luis Salazar	.950	863	555	1562	112	119	19
Ron Santo	.954	2130	1955	4581	317	395	135
Paul Schaal	.943	1053	726	2038	166	152	-83
Mike Schmidt	.955	2212	1591	5045	313	450	265
Kevin Seitzer	.950	816	554	1524	109	150	-17
Billy Shindle	.892	1272	1815	2886	568	215	86
Red Smith	.932	1050	1210	2136	244	152	0
Eric Soderholm	.962	759	620	1589	88	113	28
Harry Steinfeldt	.926	1386	1774	2799	365	172	18

Third Base	PCT	G	PO	A	E	DP	FR
Milt Stock	.945	1349	1392	2508	228	198	-73
Joe Stripp	.961	914	956	1665	106	149	32
Jim Tabor	.933	980	1077	1979	220	178	-19
Pie Traynor	.947	1863	2289	3521	324	303	36
Ossie Vitt	.960	833	1026	1846	119	135	49
Tim Wallach	.959	1624	1355	3285	199	277	97
Billy Werber	.944	1143	1264	2415	220	214	63
Don Wert	.968	1043	914	1987	97	173	-22
Deacon White	.853	826	954	1618	444	118	-37
Pinky Whitney	.961	1358	1455	2640	164	219	65
Art Whitney	.888	802	1026	1691	344	112	22
Ned Williamson	.866	716	878	1719	401	119	102
Harry Wolverton	.909	756	989	1625	263	93	6
Eddie Yost	.957	2008	2356	3659	270	345	-167
Heinie Zimmerman	.928	957	1082	1956	236	118	10

Shortstop	PCT	G	PO	A	E	DP	FR
Gene Alley	.970	977	1609	3198	149	709	95
Ruben Amaro	.967	705	1146	1762	100	387	18
Luis Aparicio	.972	2581	4548	8016	366	1553	50
Luke Appling	.948	2218	4398	7218	643	1424	58
Dave Bancroft	.944	1873	4623	6561	660	1017	200
Ernie Banks	.969	1125	2087	3441	174	724	3
Jack Barry	.935	877	1599	2607	290	340	-79
Dick Bartell	.953	1679	3872	5590	471	1072	153
Mark Belanger	.977	1942	3005	5786	210	1054	166
Lou Boudreau	.973	1539	3132	4760	223	1180	136
Larry Bowa	.980	2222	3314	6857	211	1265	-77
Eddie Bressoud	.963	1002	1630	2633	164	515	-21
Al Bridwell	.939	1094	2267	3351	366	391	26
Ed Brinkman	.970	1795	2924	5466	259	1005	94
Larry Brown	.964	712	1131	1855	112	374	-35
Rick Burleson	.971	1192	2151	3871	179	827	88
Donie Bush	.936	1867	4038	6119	689	585	15
Bert Campaneris	.964	2097	3608	6160	365	1186	-93
Leo Cardenas	.971	1843	3218	5303	259	1036	-36
Chico Carrasquel	.969	1241	2131	3619	185	770	-42
Ray Chapman	.939	957	2204	2950	336	350	24
Dave Concepcion	.971	2178	3670	6594	311	1290	-35
Tommy Corcoran	.924	2073	4550	7106	956	798	108
Joe Cronin	.951	1843	3696	5814	485	1165	66
Frankie Crosetti	.949	1516	3061	4484	402	944	-16
Monte Cross	.920	1676	3975	5369	810	534	16
Bill Dahlen	.927	2132	4850	7500	975	881	302
Alvin Dark	.960	1404	2672	4168	286	933	-27
George Davis	.940	1372	3231	4787	511	589	187
Ivan DeJesus	.963	1303	1839	4036	228	700	35
Joe DeMaestri	.967	1029	1689	2852	156	612	-2
Bucky Dent	.976	1382	2116	4332	156	839	68
Mickey Doolan	.940	1625	3578	5290	570	637	166
Frank Duffy	.977	839	1292	2445	87	497	44
Shawon Dunston	.968	909	1638	2635	142	496	46
Leo Durocher	.961	1509	3097	4431	307	895	3
Kid Elberfeld	.920	944	2184	3080	458	343	46
Bones Ely	.923	1236	2581	4323	578	473	27
Woody English	.957	826	1693	2523	191	492	-33
Frank Fennelly	.860	769	1013	2615	590	259	-4
Chico Fernandez	.960	810	1403	2082	146	394	-81
Tony Fernandez	.980	1309	2270	3785	125	781	35
Art Fletcher	.939	1448	2836	5134	521	614	163
Scott Fletcher	.971	834	1191	2211	101	486	0
Tim Foli	.973	1524	2687	4804	210	1028	55
Hod Ford	.960	846	1821	2644	185	565	9
Julio Franco	.960	715	1161	2020	134	439	-59
Jim Fregosi	.963	1396	2397	4169	251	836	-26
Shorty Fuller	.891	924	1768	3047	592	333	27
Greg Gagne	.971	1112	1572	3005	137	580	12
Chick Galloway	.943	993	2058	2839	296	474	-28
Wally Gerber	.943	1447	2960	4319	439	741	44
Jack Glasscock	.910	1628	2821	5630	832	620	244
Bill Gleason	.860	796	920	2360	535	186	-105
Alfredo Griffin	.961	1841	3173	5149	337	1044	-18
Dick Groat	.961	1877	3505	5811	374	1237	25
Ozzie Guillen	.975	1087	1813	3350	133	694	97
Granny Hamner	.946	934	1572	2811	248	571	-61
Ron Hansen	.968	1143	2011	3503	185	722	86
Toby Harrah	.960	813	1331	2403	155	458	-14
Bud Harrelson	.969	1400	2387	3975	203	751	2
Charlie Hollocher	.954	751	1587	2569	202	360	-12
Arthur Irwin	.881	947	1301	3093	594	293	36
Travis Jackson	.952	1326	2877	4635	381	826	102
Hughie Jennings	.922	899	2390	3147	470	411	150
Eddie Joost	.958	1296	2755	3844	291	928	-34
Billy Jurges	.964	1540	3133	4959	305	929	125
Buddy Kerr	.967	1038	2045	3297	185	548	91
Don Kessinger	.966	1955	3151	6212	334	1170	75
Mark Koenig	.927	747	1457	2193	286	416	-24
Red Kress	.944	835	1761	2357	243	558	-20
Tony Kubek	.967	882	1544	2734	144	569	58
Harvey Kuenn	.964	748	1343	2116	129	431	-111

Shortstop	PCT	G	PO	A	E	DP	FR
Barry Larkin	.973	800	1301	2463	105	409	72
Lyn Lary	.956	1138	2373	3388	268	632	11
Doc Lavan	.930	1126	2451	3628	455	559	84
Johnnie LeMaster	.961	992	1545	2811	179	461	-14
Johnny Lipon	.961	717	1350	2143	140	481	14
Johnny Logan	.965	1380	2612	4397	256	894	103
Herman Long	.906	1794	4225	6136	1070	765	94
Rabbit Maranville	.952	2153	5139	7354	631	1183	177
Marty Marion	.969	1547	2986	4829	252	978	93
Dal Maxvill	.973	1207	1759	3405	145	649	128
George McBride	.948	1626	3585	5274	484	610	173
Ed McKean	.900	1564	2820	4853	855	497	-227
Roy McMillan	.972	2028	3705	6191	290	1304	64
Denis Menke	.961	841	1218	2355	144	419	-75
Roger Metzger	.976	1173	1845	3535	135	671	-37
Gene Michael	.962	844	1402	2576	155	489	53
Eddie Miller	.972	1395	2976	4500	217	946	111
Willie Miranda	.962	768	1117	1916	119	412	83
Billy Myers	.946	712	1397	2220	208	475	22
Skeeter Newsome	.959	902	1736	2713	190	548	58
Charley O'Leary	.935	737	1709	2241	273	200	-33
Ivy Olson	.932	1054	2389	3313	417	425	-68
Spike Owen	.978	1247	1944	3456	122	668	57
Freddy Parent	.927	1129	2253	3788	473	372	13
Freddie Patek	.962	1588	2690	4786	293	1004	-16
Roger Peckinpaugh	.949	1982	3919	6337	553	952	98
Rico Petrocelli	.969	774	1283	2283	113	433	19
Rafael Ramirez	.953	1386	2159	3978	301	842	-59
Pee Wee Reese	.962	2014	4040	5891	388	1246	-33
Craig Reynolds	.966	1240	1741	3484	182	658	-12
Cal Ripken	.978	1723	2858	5285	180	1183	37
Phil Rizzuto	.968	1647	3219	4666	263	1217	86
Billy Rogell	.956	1235	2362	3886	287	805	60
Bill Russell	.960	1746	2536	5546	339	909	-54
Heinie Sand	.943	772	1811	2443	258	495	-22
Dick Schofield	.977	1195	1913	3497	130	811	56
Everett Scott	.965	1643	3351	5053	306	710	115
Joe Sewell	.951	1216	2591	3933	333	665	84
Roy Smalley	.966	1069	1688	3274	174	702	26
Roy Smalley	.947	820	1435	2291	207	465	1
Germany Smith	.902	1665	2813	6154	971	587	157
Ozzie Smith	.979	2188	3713	7342	239	1361	218
Chris Speier	.970	1900	3057	5781	275	1043	-63
Vern Stephens	.960	1330	2385	4150	269	853	-30
Frank Taveras	.953	1113	1640	3099	236	555	-178
Garry Templeton	.961	1964	3393	6041	384	1164	8
Tommy Thevenow	.950	848	1751	2818	243	523	28
Dickie Thon	.965	1115	1580	3141	170	586	8
Joe Tinker	.938	1743	3758	5848	635	668	206
Alan Trammell	.977	1910	3057	5544	205	1190	-83
Cecil Travis	.955	710	1347	2128	162	512	-31
Terry Turner	.952	741	1379	2450	192	288	4
Jose Uribe	.970	974	1402	2770	131	545	56
Arky Vaughan	.951	1485	2995	4780	397	850	-40
Zoilo Versalles	.956	1265	2126	3645	268	727	-4
Tom Veryzer	.966	927	1372	2579	140	463	-17
Heinie Wagner	.928	824	1954	2634	356	260	22
Honus Wagner	.940	1887	4576	6041	676	766	114
Bobby Wallace	.938	1826	4142	6303	685	642	152
John Ward	.885	826	1422	2641	530	294	58
Rabbit Warstler	.942	705	1421	2267	225	429	17
U L Washington	.956	737	1005	2077	141	413	-88
Buck Weaver	.935	822	1878	2570	311	348	41
Maury Wills	.963	1555	2550	4804	284	859	28
Bobby Wine	.971	1067	1754	2974	141	698	129
Glenn Wright	.941	1051	2156	3473	351	695	-37
Robin Yount	.964	1479	2588	4794	272	941	14

Outfield	PCT	G	PO	A	E	DP	FR	LCR
Hank Aaron	.980	2760	5539	201	117	41	59	*Rc
Tommie Agee	.975	1073	2371	53	61	18	21	*C
Ethan Allen	.981	1123	2746	103	56	23	0	Cl
Bob Allison	.975	1320	2486	82	67	18	29	RI
Felipe Alou	.979	1531	2879	82	62	13	-29	Rcl
Jesus Alou	.968	1050	1691	63	58	15	-27	Lr
Matty Alou	.979	1312	2346	88	51	15	-32	C
George Altman	.977	783	1446	52	35	11	5	r
John Anderson	.939	1009	1852	111	127	27	-15	.l
Tony Armas	.981	1306	3091	78	60	17	39	RC
Richie Ashburn	.983	2104	6089	178	110	43	234	*C
Earl Averill	.970	1589	3969	115	126	29	-9	*C
Harold Baines	.978	1060	2031	69	47	17	5	*R
Dusty Baker	.985	1842	3663	110	56	21	-45	*LC
Jesse Barfield	.980	1387	2951	162	62	48	112	*R
Jimmy Barrett	.954	855	1814	143	95	38	44	C
Kevin Bass	.982	1103	2044	64	38	14	9	R
Johnny Bates	.955	1080	2078	162	106	37	8	C
Hank Bauer	.982	1449	2384	107	46	20	-65	*R
Frank Baumholtz	.980	843	1785	62	38	13	-17	rc
Don Baylor	.977	822	1575	27	38	0	-31	L

Outfield	PCT	G	PO	A	E	DP	FR	LCR
Ginger Beaumont	.956	1407	2845	167	139	52	-26	*C
Beals Becker	.955	758	1327	103	68	19	-15	r
Gus Bell	.985	1642	3500	133	54	28	2	CR
George Bell	.964	1227	2292	81	88	11	1	*L
Juan Beniquez	.977	1155	2535	69	60	12	-50	C
Wally Berger	.974	1296	3324	87	91	21	25	Cl
Ken Berry	.989	1311	2722	85	30	15	-6	*C
Bob Bescher	.960	1188	2493	137	109	28	11	*L
Carson Bigbee	.966	1031	2302	142	86	32	62	L
Joe Birmingham	.958	709	1476	130	70	38	44	C
Paul Blair	.988	1878	4343	111	54	26	49	*C
Ping Bodie	.965	995	1893	139	73	33	-28	C
Barry Bonds	.985	986	2236	74	34	9	100	L
Bobby Bonds	.977	1736	3659	128	89	40	88	*R
Barry Bonnell	.982	859	1643	58	32	8	-35	l
Daryl Boston	.976	752	1413	31	36	11	-45	c
Phil Bradley	.988	996	1931	60	24	7	-4	L
Jackie Brandt	.980	1100	2131	76	44	12	-27	Cl
Rube Bressler	.971	840	1712	61	53	12	-2	L
John Briggs	.973	1037	1971	57	56	6	0	L
Lou Brock	.959	2507	4394	142	196	29	-95	*L
Steve Brodie	.959	1420	3139	208	142	52	48	*C
Eddie Brown	.970	731	1867	38	59	9	14	cl
Ollie Brown	.977	992	1622	71	39	15	0	R
Tom Brown	.890	1783	3623	348	491	85	41	*Cr
George Browne	.927	1077	1619	129	137	34	-31	R
Pete Browning	.883	998	1892	143	269	36	-5	cl
Tom Brunansky	.983	1560	3272	112	57	28	75	*R
Bill Bruton	.981	1561	3905	105	77	32	69	*C
Al Bumbry	.986	1241	2975	68	44	10	-30	Cl
Eddie Burke	.921	789	1673	119	153	25	20	L
Jesse Burkett	.917	2053	3961	270	383	62	-19	*L
Ellis Burks	.986	701	1662	43	25	6	25	C
George Burns	.970	1844	3918	197	128	42	31	*Lr
Oyster Burns	.920	894	1271	139	123	34	-24	R
Jeff Burroughs	.974	1281	2144	84	59	19	-58	Rl
Jim Busby	.988	1280	3284	68	42	16	27	*C
Brett Butler	.992	1640	4148	97	36	27	103	*C
Ivan Calderon	.974	708	1442	42	39	12	18	lr
Johnny Callison	.984	1777	3349	175	57	34	102	*R
Bruce Campbell	.956	1194	2186	105	105	27	-18	*R
Jose Canseco	.974	820	1683	51	47	15	28	r
Bernie Carbo	.978	702	1234	63	29	12	-9	rl
Jose Cardenal	.976	1778	3565	143	90	27	51	CR
Max Carey	.966	2421	6363	339	235	86	202	*CL
Cliff Carroll	.905	991	1683	156	194	37	23	L
Joe Carter	.978	1108	2524	79	58	18	26	lcr
Rico Carty	.970	807	1338	33	43	6	-35	c
George Case	.970	1187	2805	88	90	15	28	lr
Cesar Cedeno	.985	1718	4131	102	64	23	29	*C
Sam Chapman	.972	1309	3579	115	107	25	51	*C
Ben Chapman	.967	1495	3476	156	125	31	60	crl
Gino Cimoli	.974	909	1547	61	43	12	-48	r
Jack Clark	.978	1039	2004	96	48	25	25	*R
Fred Clarke	.952	2189	4790	254	256	42	61	*L
Roberto Clemente	.973	2370	4696	266	140	42	162	*R
Gil Coan	.973	749	1741	53	49	12	25	L
Ty Cobb	.961	2935	6361	392	271	107	55	*CR
Rocky Colavito	.980	1774	3323	123	70	26	69	*Rl
Vince Coleman	.974	992	1904	82	53	12	34	L
Dave Collins	.986	1118	2275	50	34	17	-7	L
Shano Collins	.962	1343	2442	177	103	43	19	*R
Earle Combs	.974	1387	3449	69	95	23	-12	*C
Adam Comorosky	.972	718	1660	38	49	11	9	I
Tony Conigliaro	.979	839	1483	48	33	7	20	R
Duff Cooley	.945	1094	2388	96	145	28	1	lc
Johnny Cooney	.988	794	1791	56	22	12	-10	C
Pop Corkhill	.947	1041	2158	224	134	47	84	Cr
Wes Covington	.961	812	1054	41	45	10	-61	L
Al Cowens	.985	1477	2854	112	46	19	-3	*R
Doc Cramer	.979	2142	5412	172	118	37	19	*C
Gavvy Cravath	.944	1090	1675	176	109	28	-6	R
Sam Crawford	.965	2299	3626	268	143	59	-49	*Rc
Willie Crawford	.975	982	1659	54	44	11	-30	R
Warren Cromartie	.977	780	1615	74	39	13	41	l
Jose Cruz	.974	2156	4391	125	120	28	64	*Lrc
Roy Cullenbine	.969	843	1666	100	57	24	12	R
Kiki Cuyler	.972	1807	4034	191	121	44	10	RCl
Abner Dalrymple	.863	951	1655	146	285	26	-5	L
Vic Davalillo	.986	1066	2121	58	31	11	43	C
Chili Davis	.971	1182	2560	77	80	15	10	cr
Eric Davis	.984	879	2022	39	34	11	24	C
Tommy Davis	.970	1233	1900	63	61	13	-49	*L
Mike Davis	.968	819	1719	46	58	15	-8	R
Willie Davis	.978	2323	5449	143	127	23	53	*C
Andre Dawson	.984	2238	5037	154	84	28	83	*C
Rob Deer	.977	913	1948	69	48	18	52	R
Ed Delahanty	.951	1344	2951	243	166	45	98	*L
Frank Demaree	.978	1076	2124	97	51	21	-22	rc
Don Demeter	.990	802	1424	35	14	12	-16	c
Bob Dernier	.982	794	1596	25	30	6	5	C

Outfield	PCT	G	PO	A	E	DP	FR	LCR
Dom DiMaggio	.978	1373	3859	147	89	32	100	*C
Joe DiMaggio	.978	1721	4516	153	105	30	50	*C
Vince DiMaggio	.981	1081	2840	125	57	35	72	*C
Larry Doby	.983	1440	3616	88	63	26	4	*C
Cozy Dolan	.931	723	1144	98	92	15	-19	r
Mike Donlin	.924	867	1521	109	135	24	-31	c
Patsy Donovan	.941	1813	2924	264	201	69	11	*R
Patsy Dougherty	.935	1181	1775	117	132	20	-75	*L
Taylor Douthit	.972	1036	3109	70	91	21	69	C
Tommy Dowd	.933	960	1816	100	137	31	-30	rc
Brian Downing	.995	777	1491	39	7	2	-8	L
Hugh Duffy	.943	1681	3392	240	220	46	2	Clr
Pat Duncan	.970	707	1466	70	47	13	1	L
Lenny Dykstra	.989	879	2148	47	25	16	65	C
Del Ennis	.969	1840	3621	150	120	27	30	*Lr
Dwight Evans	.987	2146	4371	157	59	42	91	*R
Steve Evans	.955	902	1389	114	71	28	-29	R
Hoot Evers	.983	1051	2440	71	43	13	-3	lc
Ron Fairly	.981	1037	1475	69	30	13	-25	R
Bibb Falk	.967	1222	2520	136	92	38	-3	*L
Happy Felsch	.975	741	1921	116	53	41	67	C
Max Flack	.972	1336	2282	181	71	33	-9	*R
Ira Flagstead	.974	1036	2482	159	71	40	65	C
Elmer Flick	.947	1456	2370	197	145	50	24	*R
Curt Flood	.987	1697	4021	114	54	28	67	*C
Dan Ford	.974	1065	2206	49	60	11	-16	R
George Foster	.984	1880	3809	119	62	28	66	*L
Bob Fothergill	.961	832	1646	37	69	6	-53	l
Pete Fox	.977	1368	2793	96	68	16	-20	*R
Tito Francona	.984	911	1581	34	26	4	-36	lr
Johnny Frederick	.974	733	1813	60	50	12	9	c
Buck Freeman	.950	837	1167	76	66	17	-45	R
Carl Furillo	.979	1739	3322	151	74	34	21	*Rc
Augie Galan	.981	1359	2996	88	61	21	12	*Lc
Oscar Gamble	.977	818	1412	59	35	17	-20	rl
Ralph Garr	.968	1176	2237	77	76	17	-6	Lr
Cito Gaston	.970	773	1479	64	48	13	-12	c
Gary Geiger	.986	749	1464	58	21	8	32	c
Cesar Geronimo	.988	1376	2901	81	35	18	3	*C
Doc Gessler	.945	713	915	95	59	15	-25	R
Kirk Gibson	.975	1168	2371	38	61	12	-12	lr
Pete Gillespie	.903	714	1229	90	142	21	-6	L
Dan Gladden	.984	1051	2324	72	40	19	65	Lc
Tony Gonzalez	.987	1447	2783	73	39	15	-44	Cl
Ival Goodman	.975	1000	2061	78	55	14	12	R
Sid Gordon	.985	918	1788	69	29	5	4	L
George Gore	.876	1297	2359	243	368	47	-14	*C
Goose Goslin	.960	2188	4793	222	209	47	65	*L
Jack Graney	.953	1282	2488	151	130	34	-2	*L
Danny Green	.941	912	1578	107	105	46	3	R
Lenny Green	.984	883	1659	29	27	3	-94	Cl
Mike Greenwell	.980	752	1351	49	29	8	9	L
Ken Griffey	.981	1703	3258	106	66	22	-8	Rl
Mike Griffin	.956	1478	3535	243	173	75	99	*C
Tommy Griffith	.956	1333	2164	189	108	36	-18	*R
Greg Gross	.982	1204	1596	83	31	17	-47	rl
Johnny Groth	.987	1155	2566	82	36	23	-40	C
Johnny Grubb	.981	1042	1992	66	39	13	-44	lc
Tony Gwynn	.986	1449	3095	116	44	19	115	*R
Mule Haas	.984	1022	2486	68	42	21	5	C
Chick Hafey	.971	1195	2527	106	80	23	0	L
Jimmie Hall	.982	806	1507	48	29	10	-10	c
Mel Hall	.981	1037	2011	56	39	15	-16	L
Billy Hamilton	.926	1584	3444	182	288	55	-6	Cl
Ned Hanlon	.891	1251	2653	208	350	47	21	*C
Dick Harley	.918	738	1447	125	141	18	10	l
George Harper	.970	933	1925	96	62	24	-5	R
Tommy Harper	.986	1227	2168	51	31	11	-8	Lr
Topsy Hartsel	.956	1312	2115	108	102	21	-52	*L
Billy Hatcher	.985	925	1841	53	28	11	3	lc
Von Hayes	.983	1040	2247	56	41	12	7	rc
Jeff Heath	.972	1299	2705	85	80	21	-21	*L
Cliff Heathcote	.971	1157	2620	157	82	42	45	Rc
Emmett Heidrick	.946	748	1562	133	97	29	35	c
Harry Heilmann	.962	1594	2794	183	117	42	-33	*R
Charlie Hemphill	.944	1175	2033	139	130	29	-28	Cr
Dave Henderson	.984	1272	3057	88	50	24	37	*C
Ken Henderson	.977	1252	2552	68	61	15	13	Lc
Rickey Henderson	.980	1762	4496	96	95	16	158	*Lc
Steve Henderson	.968	898	1680	67	57	12	-15	L
George Hendrick	.985	1813	3751	114	57	25	-26	RC
Tommy Henrich	.981	1017	2008	96	40	27	9	R
Babe Herman	.961	1185	2270	106	96	21	-54	R
Larry Herndon	.972	1337	2675	76	80	17	-8	*L
Mike Hershberger	.980	1037	1763	84	38	17	-20	R
Jim Hickman	.976	871	1470	51	38	7	-41	C
Bill Hinchman	.954	750	1229	91	64	15	-4	rl
Paul Hines	.887	1251	2393	221	332	51	3	*C
Chuck Hinton	.979	928	1590	47	35	10	-42	l
Larry Hisle	.978	1017	2213	70	52	8	13	cl
Myril Hoag	.965	876	1673	78	63	20	-66	lcr

Outfield	PCT	G	PO	A	E	DP	FR	LCR
Danny Hoffman	.951	809	1564	99	85	30	16	C
Solly Hofman	.967	702	1478	113	55	33	28	c
Bug Holliday	.935	891	1690	125	127	31	-42	c
Ducky Holmes	.924	883	1605	137	143	30	8	l
Tommy Holmes	.989	1231	2823	115	33	37	54	Rc
Harry Hooper	.966	2284	3981	344	151	81	93	*R
Johnny Hopp	.985	717	1664	24	26	9	-27	c
Joe Hornung	.922	1054	1925	176	178	33	53	*L
Willie Horton	.972	1190	1921	58	58	8	-24	*L
Pete Hotaling	.869	825	1476	163	246	38	-8	C
Frank Howard	.975	1435	2114	82	57	12	-55	Lr
Dummy Hoy	.915	1795	3958	273	394	72	3	*C
Pete Incaviglia	.964	761	1342	57	52	9	-5	l
Joe Jackson	.962	1289	2362	183	100	36	24	lr
Reggie Jackson	.967	2102	4062	133	142	31	5	*R
Baby Doll Jacobson	.973	1378	3477	113	99	36	31	*C
Charlie Jamieson	.967	1638	3423	196	122	39	23	*L
Jackie Jensen	.977	1391	2739	124	68	20	26	*R
Alex Johnson	.953	1000	1641	61	84	9	-15	L
Bob Johnson	.968	1769	4003	208	141	35	82	*L
Roy Johnson	.938	1066	2231	128	156	22	22	lr
Dick Johnston	.903	743	1621	172	193	34	54	C
Jay Johnstone	.979	1308	2373	100	53	18	-15	Cr
Charley Jones	.882	872	1685	161	248	25	52	L
Cleon Jones	.978	1111	2007	64	47	10	-17	L
Davy Jones	.962	1006	1969	119	83	25	17	l
Fielder Jones	.964	1770	3580	225	144	70	26	*Cr
Mack Jones	.976	871	1529	27	38	5	-54	c
Ruppert Jones	.986	1205	3051	75	43	22	32	C
Al Kaline	.986	2488	5035	170	73	29	106	*Rc
Benny Kauff	.960	853	1881	136	85	29	23	C
Willie Keeler	.960	2039	3097	258	138	60	2	*R
Charlie Keller	.980	1019	2235	46	46	6	-3	L
Joe Kelley	.955	1465	2864	212	144	44	2	*Lc
Pat Kelly	.978	997	1770	61	42	15	-16	R
King Kelly	.820	750	892	285	259	26	36	R
Steve Kemp	.982	1004	1962	55	37	12	11	L
Bob Kennedy	.978	821	1400	63	33	14	-44	R
Ralph Kiner	.974	1382	2875	80	80	14	3	*L
Jim King	.984	851	1505	70	26	13	14	R
Willie Kirkland	.974	995	1740	83	48	19	-1	R
Chuck Klein	.962	1600	3250	194	135	39	15	*R
Mike Kreevich	.982	1177	3304	93	64	21	47	*C
Harvey Kuenn	.978	826	1396	43	32	8	-14	r
Chet Laabs	.977	820	1780	62	44	15	-21	l
Lee Lacy	.983	1006	1860	79	34	15	8	R
Jim Landis	.989	1265	2927	72	32	17	58	*C
Ken Landreaux	.981	1138	2206	57	44	11	-73	C
Bill Lange	.942	716	1732	136	116	39	53	C
Freddy Leach	.975	875	1940	76	51	23	-6	lc
Tommy Leach	.975	1079	2548	133	70	37	53	C
Hal Lee	.973	718	1696	40	49	8	19	L
Ron LeFlore	.968	1040	2521	89	86	18	33	C
Nemo Leibold	.961	1120	2318	176	101	39	36	cr
Chet Lemon	.984	1925	4993	115	81	25	119	*Cr
Jim Lemon	.961	901	1631	47	68	12	-6	rl
Jeffrey Leonard	.974	1147	2045	75	57	12	5	L
Duffy Lewis	.959	1432	2657	210	123	40	17	*L
Sixto Lezcano	.980	1196	2401	106	51	28	42	*R
Danny Litwhiler	.982	915	1927	57	37	9	5	L
Don Lock	.976	831	1789	59	45	16	41	C
Whitey Lockman	.976	752	1660	43	41	9	4	l
Bris Lord	.957	713	1226	97	60	27	8	l
John Lowenstein	.984	906	1391	55	23	10	-81	L
Peanuts Lowrey	.983	978	2113	81	38	18	0	lc
Mike Lum	.986	816	1450	36	21	6	17	rl
Harry Lumley	.946	700	1052	97	66	31	-4	R
Greg Luzinski	.972	1221	1845	67	55	8	-108	*L
Jerry Lynch	.964	706	955	44	37	12	-57	lr
Fred Lynn	.988	1825	4556	114	55	33	34	*C
Elliott Maddox	.989	719	1493	61	18	19	9	c
Garry Maddox	.983	1687	4449	94	78	21	67	*C
Sherry Magee	.970	1861	3800	176	123	39	11	*L
Candy Maldonado	.978	1074	1745	61	41	4	-45	Rl
Les Mann	.966	1368	2610	173	97	29	-33	Lc
Rick Manning	.985	1508	3831	71	58	13	38	*C
Mickey Mantle	.982	2019	4438	117	82	27	-5	*C
Heinie Manush	.979	1845	3841	105	83	26	-51	*Lc
Roger Maris	.982	1383	2649	76	49	15	-3	*R
Mike Marshall	.978	777	1219	39	28	5	-22	R
Willard Marshall	.979	1145	2184	125	50	28	18	R
Jerry Martin	.982	910	1530	44	29	11	-11	c
Dave Martinez	.982	766	1536	46	29	8	-33	c
Gary Matthews	.968	1876	3226	135	112	17	-42	*Lr
Charlie Maxwell	.988	834	1665	44	21	5	41	L
Dave May	.978	1021	2177	68	50	17	11	cr
Lee Maye	.970	1040	1793	47	57	7	-18	lr
Willie Mays	.981	2843	7095	195	141	60	136	*C
Lee Mazzilli	.986	868	1933	48	28	11	-1	c
Jimmy McAleer	.944	1015	2464	151	154	36	55	C
Bake McBride	.989	963	2163	59	25	12	26	Rc
Jack McCarthy	.946	1046	1960	128	120	29	-18	L
Tommy McCarthy	.897	1189	2019	268	263	60	62	Rl
Barney McCosky	.984	1036	2490	48	41	12	-2	cl
Willie McGee	.977	1406	3433	91	82	18	62	*C
Matty McIntyre	.964	1039	2037	133	81	31	55	L
Kevin McReynolds	.986	1318	2838	98	42	20	68	Lc
Jim McTamany	.913	813	1542	151	161	39	17	C
Joe Medwick	.980	1852	3994	139	84	27	52	*L
Sam Mele	.985	840	1480	67	23	9	-39	L
Sam Mertes	.938	974	1737	140	123	28	-2	L
Irish Meusel	.959	1216	2391	129	107	23	-23	*L
Bob Meusel	.958	1304	2426	157	114	36	-17	Lr
Clyde Milan	.953	1903	4095	294	216	58	59	*C
Bing Miller	.971	1601	3342	126	102	29	3	Rl
Rick Miller	.986	1248	2786	69	42	21	-10	C
Eddie Milner	.987	719	1690	44	23	8	42	C
Minnie Minoso	.974	1665	3276	139	91	22	65	*L
Dale Mitchell	.985	931	1906	41	30	8	-33	L
Mike Mitchell	.959	1107	2107	180	97	40	62	R
Rick Monday	.979	1688	3534	86	76	21	-46	*C
Wally Moon	.978	1141	1939	75	46	13	-49	lr
Gene Moore	.975	914	1892	109	52	13	32	R
Johnny Moore	.970	737	1522	78	49	16	-6	r
Jo-Jo Moore	.975	1294	2501	116	68	17	-15	*L
Terry Moore	.985	1189	3117	102	48	23	81	*C
Jerry Morales	.983	1256	2357	73	43	21	3	rl
Omar Moreno	.982	1323	3405	93	63	26	59	*C
Lloyd Moseby	.984	1529	3765	73	62	14	29	*C
Wally Moses	.973	1792	4000	147	113	35	50	*R
Johnny Mostil	.971	907	2561	101	79	25	73	C
Manny Mota	.979	1021	1459	57	33	12	-59	*L
Don Mueller	.982	1084	1816	69	35	20	-39	*R
Jerry Mumphrey	.981	1386	3057	74	60	13	-19	*C
Bobby Murcer	.981	1644	3269	125	65	19	-31	RC
Dale Murphy	.983	1840	4037	112	71	22	27	*CR
Dwayne Murphy	.987	1272	3579	80	47	11	101	*C
Red Murray	.950	1171	1962	176	113	28	-5	Rl
Stan Musial	.984	1890	3730	130	64	27	-60	LRc
Hy Myers	.972	1182	2898	151	87	36	41	*C
Greasy Neale	.972	736	1569	87	48	22	24	r
Bill Nicholson	.979	1471	2954	118	67	20	17	*R
Hugh Nicol	.912	823	1290	226	146	22	61	R
Bob Nieman	.975	926	1672	47	44	9	-7	L
Otis Nixon	.987	741	1371	33	18	4	-49	cl
Irv Noren	.984	801	1778	76	31	11	12	c
Billy North	.981	1066	2820	63	57	15	52	*C
Ron Northey	.972	820	1361	81	42	24	-40	R
Jim Northrup	.981	1267	2470	56	50	10	-55	Rcl
Rebel Oakes	.961	970	2154	119	93	25	1	C
Darby O'Brien	.934	703	1331	90	101	17	11	L
Lefty O'Doul	.964	804	1591	35	60	6	-33	L
Rowland Office	.985	771	1480	27	23	8	-30	C
Ben Oglivie	.978	1439	3030	102	70	17	48	*Lr
Rube Oldring	.966	1130	2116	95	78	29	-38	Cl
Tony Oliva	.975	1178	2332	71	61	19	77	*R
Al Oliver	.980	1376	3136	65	64	14	-1	Cl
Tip O'Neill	.917	1024	1794	81	169	16	-37	*L
Paul O'Neill	.988	711	1399	52	17	5	39	R
Jim O'Rourke	.898	1377	2152	216	268	25	-37	Lc
Joe Orsulak	.985	841	1711	76	27	14	21	r
Amos Otis	.991	1928	4936	126	47	35	95	*C
Mel Ott	.980	2313	4511	256	98	60	-5	*R
Tom Paciorek	.979	794	1223	34	27	4	-38	l
Andy Pafko	.984	1570	3199	130	54	24	-27	Crl
Dave Parker	.965	1867	3791	143	142	27	70	*R
Dode Paskert	.969	1633	3734	223	125	49	55	*C
Albie Pearson	.980	833	1725	40	36	10	1	c
Gary Pettis	.986	1128	2948	63	44	21	55	*C
Dave Philley	.981	1454	3242	137	64	33	7	Rc
Ollie Pickering	.949	859	1628	109	94	30	6	C
Jim Piersall	.990	1614	3851	95	39	21	84	*Cr
Lou Piniella	.981	1401	2529	105	52	16	20	*L
Vada Pinson	.981	2403	5097	172	101	29	46	*Cr
Wally Post	.970	1055	2002	103	64	15	39	R
Ray Powell	.959	826	2020	124	91	24	29	C
Kirby Puckett	.989	1353	3682	107	42	32	125	*C
Terry Puhl	.993	1300	2576	57	18	18	1	Rl
Blondie Purcell	.869	995	1465	147	243	20	-48	lr
Rip Radcliff	.967	887	1655	45	58	13	-60	l
Paul Radford	.901	902	1404	217	179	44	30	R
Tim Raines	.988	1580	3284	111	42	16	94	*L
Gary Redus	.974	709	1310	56	37	11	-3	l
Rick Reichardt	.982	882	1545	49	29	14	-1	l
Rip Repulski	.976	802	1555	28	39	4	-24	l
Merv Rettenmund	.985	747	1346	37	21	10	-33	r
Carl Reynolds	.970	1112	2539	88	81	22	15	rc
Sam Rice	.965	2270	4774	278	184	67	76	*RC
Harry Rice	.966	911	2160	114	80	24	44	cr
Jim Rice	.980	1543	3103	137	66	19	71	*L
Gene Richards	.972	806	1550	74	47	8	-15	L
Jim Rivera	.977	1038	2065	78	51	24	-32	rc

Outfield	PCT	G	PO	A	E	DP	FR	LCR
Mickey Rivers	.982	1253	3150	95	61	21	56	*C
Leon Roberts	.982	788	1574	40	30	9	-5	r
Dave Robertson	.955	726	1258	70	63	14	-17	r
Floyd Robinson	.981	886	1470	42	30	6	-51	R
Frank Robinson	.984	2132	3978	135	68	26	60	*RL
Bill Robinson	.979	1059	1783	66	40	9	-25	rl
Gary Roenicke	.988	918	1608	53	20	3	-92	L
Pete Rose	.991	1327	2579	99	24	15	46	LR
Braggo Roth	.944	727	1184	97	76	20	-28	r
Edd Roush	.972	1848	4537	222	137	41	23	*C
Joe Rudi	.991	1195	2294	60	22	12	25	*L
Jim Russell	.981	942	2255	67	45	18	30	lc
Babe Ruth	.968	2241	4444	204	155	48	2	*L
Jimmy Ryan	.918	1943	3698	375	365	71	34	CRI
Bill Sample	.987	711	1378	32	18	5	-19	l
Hank Sauer	.974	1228	2408	105	67	21	19	*L
Frank Schulte	.966	1737	2689	194	103	41	-70	*RI
Fred Schulte	.976	1060	2853	81	72	20	36	*C
Tony Scott	.986	853	1803	53	27	8	8	C
Emmett Seery	.896	914	1567	173	203	25	37	L
Kip Selbach	.944	1568	3392	197	214	49	75	*L
George Selkirk	.977	773	1559	55	38	18	-1	rl
Socks Seybold	.961	935	1398	91	60	29	1	R
Cy Seymour	.945	1333	2855	188	177	52	58	*C
Orator Shaffer	.865	832	1268	289	244	31	83	R
Howie Shanks	.971	702	1423	99	45	20	36	L
Jimmy Sheckard	.958	2071	4203	307	197	80	93	*L
John Shelby	.982	948	1949	55	36	15	-35	C
Pat Sheridan	.983	779	1448	33	26	5	-48	r
Burt Shotton	.942	1280	2816	173	184	51	26	Cl
Ruben Sierra	.973	1035	1966	76	57	16	13	R
Roy Sievers	.981	838	1790	56	35	8	29	L
Al Simmons	.982	2142	4988	169	94	37	53	*LC
Ken Singleton	.980	1538	2684	82	57	17	-59	*R
Bob Skinner	.969	950	1600	71	53	9	0	L
Jimmy Slagle	.950	1292	2692	168	150	57	21	Cl
Enos Slaughter	.980	2064	3925	152	82	35	1	*RI
Al Smith	.974	1118	2050	63	56	10	-22	RI
Reggie Smith	.976	1668	3676	127	94	25	78	RC
Elmer Smith	.921	1086	2202	143	200	35	2	L
Elmer Smith	.957	870	1429	95	69	31	-30	R
Jack Smith	.961	1219	2476	141	106	43	-33	cr
Lonnie Smith	.963	1290	2277	98	90	18	1	*L
Duke Snider	.985	1918	4099	123	66	18	-56	*Cr
Fred Snodgrass	.965	818	1757	134	69	27	24	C
Cory Snyder	.984	712	1445	74	25	12	36	R
Russ Snyder	.981	1099	1856	49	37	13	-94	lcr
Moose Solters	.960	825	1852	88	80	17	36	L
Joe Sommer	.901	713	1326	109	157	26	35	l
Billy Southworth	.965	1115	2442	127	92	33	24	R
Al Spangler	.973	714	1034	27	29	6	-45	L
Tris Speaker	.970	2698	6787	448	222	139	246	*C
Stan Spence	.984	990	2582	96	44	21	35	C
Chick Stahl	.961	1295	2435	162	105	38	-5	Cr
Mickey Stanley	.991	1290	2819	61	27	14	15	*C
Willie Stargell	.961	1293	1985	102	84	12	-61	*L
Rusty Staub	.969	1675	3018	165	103	35	48	*R
Casey Stengel	.964	1183	2171	147	87	35	-10	R
Jake Stenzel	.927	741	1569	93	131	25	-29	C
Gene Stephens	.973	772	1063	51	31	11	-88	l
Riggs Stephenson	.978	913	1759	68	42	18	-14	L
George Stone	.958	837	1490	76	68	22	-3	L
John Stone	.967	1131	2398	101	85	25	25	lr
Harry Stovey	.896	944	1801	165	229	33	45	l
Darryl Strawberry	.979	1263	2330	71	52	22	22	*R
Amos Strunk	.980	1327	2830	159	61	36	15	C
Homer Summa	.961	773	1368	75	58	20	-36	R
Ron Swoboda	.972	767	1218	53	37	8	-27	r
Frank Thomas	.978	1045	2116	96	50	14	15	Lc
Gorman Thomas	.984	1159	2905	53	49	12	3	C
Roy Thomas	.972	1434	3291	188	102	48	71	*C
Milt Thompson	.981	820	1820	36	35	7	19	c
Sam Thompson	.935	1405	2165	283	171	61	52	*R
Bobby Thomson	.980	1506	3563	111	74	24	29	Cl
Mike Tiernan	.924	1474	2100	159	187	32	-92	*R
John Titus	.959	1356	2139	201	101	40	5	*R
Jack Tobin	.957	1491	2614	202	127	43	-18	*R
Bobby Tolan	.976	1005	2131	50	54	10	6	c
Cesar Tovar	.980	945	2043	71	44	18	14	cl
Tom Tresh	.979	727	1380	50	31	6	-13	l
Bill Tuttle	.983	1191	2698	97	48	18	26	*C
Ted Uhlaender	.991	793	1588	36	15	8	0	C
Del Unser	.984	1407	3123	112	52	26	44	*C
Ellis Valentine	.972	856	1570	85	47	17	-2	R
Elmer Valo	.977	1329	2769	72	67	9	1	RI
George Van Haltren	.915	1827	3490	348	358	64	10	*Cl
Andy Van Slyke	.987	1249	2733	89	37	24	42	Cr
Bobby Veach	.964	1740	3754	211	150	42	37	*L
Bill Virdon	.982	1542	3777	100	73	18	42	*C
Joe Vosmik	.979	1370	2958	107	66	25	35	*L
Leon Wagner	.964	1140	1705	51	65	5	-44	*L

Outfield	PCT	G	PO	A	E	DP	FR	LCR
Tilly Walker	.949	1348	2904	221	167	46	42	Lc
Dixie Walker	.972	1736	3455	154	103	33	-18	*Rc
Gee Walker	.961	1613	3661	112	154	28	-5	Lcr
Curt Walker	.963	1310	2776	144	112	48	-1	*R
Lloyd Waner	.983	1818	4860	151	87	30	77	*C
Paul Waner	.975	2288	4872	241	132	53	46	*R
Gary Ward	.984	1094	2436	81	41	21	56	L
Claudell Washington	.973	1685	3198	104	91	22	-54	*Rcl
George Watkins	.954	817	1684	69	84	19	-20	r
Mitch Webster	.981	875	1795	32	36	3	-23	cr
Curt Welch	.933	1075	2366	210	185	50	103	*C
Vic Wertz	.973	889	1709	72	49	20	5	R
Sam West	.983	1573	4300	151	76	42	94	*C
Wally Westlake	.983	834	1840	58	33	15	-3	rc
Zack Wheat	.966	2337	4996	232	183	54	50	*L
Devon White	.984	903	2461	61	42	16	76	C
Roy White	.988	1625	3356	86	43	13	77	*L
Billy Williams	.973	2088	3562	143	101	24	-29	*Lr
Cy Williams	.973	1818	4180	226	123	40	13	*Cr
Ken Williams	.958	1298	2948	167	137	40	49	*L
Ted Williams	.974	2151	4158	140	113	30	-35	*L
Walt Wilmot	.903	956	1968	147	227	23	27	L
Glenn Wilson	.977	1126	2220	107	54	23	58	R
Chief Wilson	.968	1269	2430	181	85	48	42	*R
Hack Wilson	.965	1257	2810	98	105	28	-61	C
Mookie Wilson	.982	1273	3084	54	58	21	19	*C
Willie Wilson	.987	1939	4942	75	66	15	75	*CL
Dave Winfield	.982	2437	4910	164	95	35	37	*RI
Whitey Witt	.971	729	1601	59	50	10	-15	c
Jim Wohlford	.980	877	1550	46	33	8	-23	L
Jimmy Wolf	.918	1042	1642	229	168	42	56	*R
George Wood	.895	1232	2139	203	276	46	21	*L
Gene Woodling	.989	1566	2924	93	35	13	-30	*L
Taffy Wright	.972	898	1778	63	53	17	-20	R
Jim Wynn	.981	1810	3912	139	80	40	80	Cl
Marvell Wynne	.985	839	1629	38	26	12	-44	C
Johnny Wyrostek	.975	1105	2372	96	64	15	20	Rc
Carl Yastrzemski	.981	2076	3941	195	82	30	143	*L
Joel Youngblood	.981	745	1242	71	26	14	9	r
Ross Youngs	.953	1199	2160	192	116	46	-2	*R
Robin Yount	.990	1104	2903	48	31	13	53	*C
Al Zarilla	.974	978	1869	69	51	16	-53	R
Gus Zernial	.968	1007	2081	81	71	14	26	*L
Richie Zisk	.981	905	1680	68	33	20	3	rl

Catcher	PCT	G	PO	A	E	DP	FR
Eddie Ainsmith	.966	993	4399	1088	193	96	41
Jimmy Archer	.971	736	3293	979	127	76	8
Alan Ashby	.986	1299	7086	684	113	74	-40
Joe Azcue	.992	868	5329	452	44	67	26
Ed Bailey	.986	1064	5267	450	80	57	-54
Johnny Bassler	.980	756	2607	708	67	69	-2
John Bateman	.982	953	5686	491	113	81	-4
Earl Battey	.990	1087	6176	501	69	73	23
Johnny Bench	.990	1744	9260	850	97	127	-24
Bruce Benedict	.990	971	4651	577	53	50	46
Charlie Bennett	.942	954	5123	1048	379	114	78
Bill Bergen	.972	941	4233	1444	161	106	115
Yogi Berra	.989	1699	8738	798	110	175	57
Bob Boone	.986	2225	11260	1174	178	154	7
Frank Bowerman	.963	826	3659	1055	182	103	39
Bob Brenly	.984	705	3577	408	63	41	-10
Roger Bresnahan	.971	974	4309	1195	167	96	-53
Smoky Burgess	.988	1139	5214	441	71	63	-94
Roy Campanella	.988	1183	6520	550	85	82	31
Chris Cannizzaro	.983	714	3161	333	62	42	-29
Gary Carter	.991	2056	11785	1203	121	149	61
Paul Casanova	.985	811	4040	395	69	65	-38
Rick Cerone	.990	1279	6548	536	70	59	-18
Boileryard Clarke	.947	739	2587	806	190	66	-25
Jack Clements	.937	1073	4780	1079	392	93	-34
Mickey Cochrane	.985	1451	6414	840	111	104	15
Walker Cooper	.977	1223	5166	589	138	80	-63
Clint Courtney	.987	802	3556	379	50	63	-47
Del Crandall	.989	1479	7352	759	89	116	62
Lou Criger	.971	984	4354	1342	170	102	135
Clay Dalrymple	.987	1003	5557	566	78	79	27
Harry Danning	.985	801	3257	455	57	64	8
Jody Davis	.987	1039	5520	640	81	65	-15
Spud Davis	.984	1282	4374	684	84	97	-53
Rick Dempsey	.988	1633	7367	768	99	111	63
Bo Diaz	.986	965	5294	525	82	60	5
Bill Dickey	.988	1708	7965	954	108	137	22
Red Dooin	.957	1195	5480	1590	320	122	27
Dave Duncan	.984	885	4528	352	79	64	-34
Johnny Edwards	.992	1392	8925	703	82	105	97
Andy Etchebarren	.987	931	4884	365	68	45	33
Duke Farrell	.938	1003	4101	1417	365	102	93
Joe Ferguson	.987	766	3905	376	56	54	-32
Rick Ferrell	.984	1806	7248	1127	135	139	22

Catcher	PCT	G	PO	A	E	DP	FR
Carlton Fisk	.988	2204	11294	1043	155	147	-45
Mike Fitzgerald	.988	748	4184	304	54	44	-18
Silver Flint	.913	727	3520	1052	436	53	38
Ray Fosse	.985	889	4831	438	78	61	30
Bill Freehan	.993	1581	9941	721	72	98	-38
Rich Gedman	.984	979	5274	431	92	62	19
George Gibson	.977	1194	5214	1386	153	112	-16
Mike Gonzalez	.980	868	3050	838	79	95	43
Johnny Gooch	.973	758	2279	511	78	70	-1
Hank Gowdy	.975	893	3149	1000	105	93	7
Jerry Grote	.991	1348	8081	635	78	76	85
Tom Haller	.992	1199	7012	508	64	86	-18
Bubbles Hargrave	.983	747	2420	493	49	46	-50
Gabby Hartnett	.984	1793	7292	1254	139	163	76
Ron Hassey	.993	946	4828	364	39	54	12
Frankie Hayes	.977	1311	4938	661	129	106	-105
Mike Heath	.981	1083	4919	537	106	73	-25
Jim Hegan	.990	1629	7506	695	86	136	149
Rollie Hemsley	.978	1482	5868	897	154	141	89
Ed Herrmann	.987	817	4230	442	61	65	28
Shanty Hogan	.985	908	3190	493	56	73	-25
Elston Howard	.993	1138	6447	479	51	87	8
Randy Hundley	.990	1026	5765	493	61	65	2
Fred Kendall	.987	795	3733	336	54	51	-73
Terry Kennedy	.985	1378	6555	623	106	92	-99
Bill Killefer	.976	1005	4830	1319	148	129	137
Malachi Kittridge	.961	1196	5121	1363	264	99	50
Johnny Kling	.971	1168	5468	1552	210	126	8
Mike LaValliere	.992	709	3455	347	31	47	6
Sherm Lollar	.992	1571	7059	688	62	101	-17
Ernie Lombardi	.979	1544	5694	845	143	107	-112
Al Lopez	.985	1918	6644	1115	122	137	66
Gus Mancuso	.977	1360	5613	803	148	100	76
Buck Martinez	.984	1008	4038	396	70	59	19
Phil Masi	.983	1101	3690	495	72	59	-28
Milt May	.986	1034	5091	589	82	73	15
Tim McCarver	.990	1387	8206	588	91	73	0
Clyde McCullough	.984	989	3953	477	72	64	9
Ed McFarland	.967	830	3139	1024	144	73	22
Deacon McGuire	.938	1611	6852	1859	578	142	-12
Larry McLean	.973	761	3032	905	110	105	-21
Chief Meyers	.974	911	4537	996	146	99	-5
Otto Miller	.973	890	3870	917	135	85	12
George Mitterwald	.987	796	4289	434	64	54	39
Charlie Moore	.980	894	3723	435	86	45	8
Les Moss	.978	720	2612	279	64	52	-42
Ray Mueller	.988	917	3095	503	43	66	23
Thurman Munson	.982	1278	6253	742	127	82	2
Glenn Myatt	.974	734	2061	419	66	47	-76
Russ Nixon	.988	722	3708	238	47	31	-86
Jack O'Connor	.961	860	3435	984	177	59	0
Bob O'Farrell	.976	1338	4295	980	130	101	-8
Steve O'Neill	.972	1532	5967	1698	217	175	-10
Mickey Owen	.982	1175	4527	581	96	93	3
Jim Pagliaroni	.991	767	4139	302	41	50	-34
Lance Parrish	.991	1703	9029	914	88	121	7
Heinie Peitz	.963	960	3723	1094	187	112	23

Catcher	PCT	G	PO	A	E	DP	FR
Tony Pena	.990	1589	9270	898	102	131	69
Cy Perkins	.978	1111	3809	1037	109	100	65
Val Picinich	.970	935	3251	732	123	69	10
Darrell Porter	.982	1506	6756	754	134	104	-38
Dave Rader	.983	771	3391	285	63	41	-55
Bill Rariden	.973	948	4127	1231	150	82	11
Del Rice	.987	1249	5353	537	75	72	26
Wilbert Robinson	.941	1316	5174	1454	412	112	-32
Bob Rodgers	.988	895	4750	472	63	74	5
Ellie Rodriguez	.989	737	3713	360	45	37	-10
Johnny Romano	.990	810	4415	343	47	51	-36
Phil Roof	.986	835	4151	356	63	48	61
Buddy Rosar	.992	934	3845	511	36	92	34
Johnny Roseboro	.989	1476	9291	675	107	111	-23
Muddy Ruel	.982	1410	5347	1136	116	135	55
Manny Sanguillen	.986	1114	5996	540	94	74	-30
Benito Santiago	.980	778	4259	447	97	61	-39
Ray Schalk	.981	1727	7168	1811	175	226	56
Wally Schang	.967	1435	5202	1420	223	149	-69
Walter Schmidt	.980	734	2598	858	69	86	20
Ossee Schreck	.970	751	4321	969	166	58	97
Mike Scioscia	.988	1395	8335	737	114	97	65
Andy Seminick	.977	1213	5030	598	133	80	13
Hank Severeid	.978	1225	4657	1112	131	101	-51
Luke Sewell	.978	1562	5444	1084	150	138	46
Ted Simmons	.987	1772	8906	915	130	104	-75
Don Slaught	.985	948	4551	351	75	50	-61
Earl Smith	.971	720	2117	502	78	64	-19
Pop Snyder	.904	744	3676	1295	529	66	151
Frank Snyder	.981	1247	4308	1332	112	106	17
Al Spohrer	.972	731	2182	347	74	30	-38
Oscar Stanage	.961	1074	4276	1381	229	107	-104
Joe Sugden	.957	708	2822	860	165	84	37
Billy Sullivan	.976	1122	4776	1314	148	111	-5
Jim Sundberg	.993	1927	9767	1007	81	145	99
Bob Swift	.985	980	3601	477	64	75	-4
Zack Taylor	.977	856	2880	752	86	83	0
Birdie Tebbetts	.978	1108	4667	666	119	87	19
Gene Tenace	.986	892	3945	441	63	65	-67
Mickey Tettleton	.991	760	3468	306	36	34	-60
Bob Tillman	.988	725	4230	253	55	40	-32
Al Todd	.977	752	3006	411	81	59	2
Joe Torre	.990	903	4850	428	56	57	-50
Mike Tresh	.983	1019	3961	575	78	72	21
Alex Trevino	.979	742	3850	398	89	42	17
Gus Triandos	.987	992	5123	448	72	70	-9
John Warner	.966	1032	4498	1309	205	100	75
Wes Westrum	.985	902	3639	415	62	82	63
Sammy White	.984	1027	4738	506	84	83	30
Ernie Whitt	.991	1246	6091	497	59	67	34
Art Wilson	.972	738	2930	796	108	60	-16
Jimmie Wilson	.977	1351	4916	931	136	153	16
Ivey Wingo	.962	1233	4409	1487	234	141	16
Butch Wynegar	.989	1247	6281	583	75	88	-43
Steve Yeager	.987	1230	6110	674	88	75	91
Chief Zimmer	.952	1239	4883	1580	328	135	105

Forfeit and No-Decision Games

A forfeited game is one in which the umpire, having observed any one of a number of specified flagrant violations of the rules, declares the game over and awards the decision to the offended team by a score of 9–0. Such games are relatively rare in major league history, but they have provided scoring problems—whether to award wins and losses to the contending pitchers, whether to include batting, fielding, and pitching statistics in the player and team records, and whether to count such games as victories/defeats for the opposing manager.

Originally there was no rule that covered wins and losses for pitchers in forfeits. However, practices indicate that the present rule was followed, except that wins and losses were also awarded in tie games.

In 1904 forfeits were covered by Rule 26, which made no mention of whether player stats should be recorded or not. In 1931 the standard covering forfeits was changed to Rule 24; section 24-11 specified that all stats in a regulation forfeit should be counted. From 1931 through 1939 there were no instances of a losing team being ahead at the time of forfeit, so no decisions were awarded in a manner contrary to present rules. In 1940 Rule 24-11 was changed; now no win or loss would be accorded a pitcher in a forfeit, regardless of score. In 1950, a year of massive rules modification, rules were revised and the question of forfeited games was shifted to Section 10.03. In 1963 this rule was revised to give a win if the team was ahead at the time of the forfeit, but no decision was to be recorded for pitchers or managers if the score was tied. During the 1941–62 period, the only case in which the winning team was ahead at the time of the forfeit was the Giants-Phillies game in 1949.

This section details the conclusions the editors have reached regarding how the totals for these forfeit games should be recorded, if at all; in some cases reference is made to the Macmillan *Baseball Encyclopedia* to illustrate differences between how a game has been previously regarded and how it is counted in *Total Baseball*. We follow with an evaluation of no-decision games, that is, games that were terminated without a win or loss awarded to either club.

Forfeit Games

All forfeit games show the winner listed first. For games in which no win or loss was awarded, the appended comment "no game" means it was not a regulation game; otherwise, the loser was ahead at the time of forfeit. In those cases in which the team that was ahead at the time of forfeit won, and the game was a regulation game, the appended comment is "OK" followed by the score. In a game noted as

"OK," a win and loss should be awarded to individual pitchers. The research of Frank Williams into early scoring practices has shown that the rules of the day indicated that in some years tied forfeit games should also have wins and losses awarded to the pitchers.

In the lists below, the victorious team is presented first. If that team was the home team, it is followed by "vs" and the visiting team; if the visiting team was victorious, it is presented first, followed by "at" and the name of the home team. For a key to the abbreviations used in these tables, see the last page of the book. The official score of all these games is 9–0.

Year	Date	League	Teams	Notes
1871	May 11	NA	Chi at Cle	Game OK, Chi ahead 18–10
	May 17	NA	Oly at Rok	Later ruled a forfeit because Rok used ineligible player Scott Hastings
	May 23	NA	Kek vs Rok	Later ruled a forfeit because Rok used ineligible player Scott Hastings
	June 5	NA	Ath vs Rok	Later ruled a forfeit because Rok used ineligible player Scott Hastings
	June 15	NA	Ath vs Rok	Later ruled a forfeit because Rok used ineligible player Scott Hastings
	June 19	NA	Tro vs Kek	Kek ahead 6–3, no pitcher win/loss
1872	Aug. 31	NA	Ath vs Eck	Game OK, score tied 5–5
1874	Sept. 28	NA	Ath vs Chi	Game OK, Ath ahead 15–7
1875	May 29	NA	Was vs NH	Game OK, Was ahead 11–10
1876	Aug. 3	N	Chi at Lou	No game (Chicago was 4–1 in the fifth when Lou began to stall, hoping for rain; game was forfeited to Chi but later thrown out; researcher Jim Smith claims it should have been counted as a forfeit with stats included; the stats are not yet counted in this edition of *Total Baseball*.
	Aug. 21	N	StL vs Chi	Game OK, StL ahead 7–6
1877	May 15	N	Cin vs Lou	Lou ahead 8–5 (game later thrown out)
1880	Sept. 10	N	Buf vs Cin	Score tied 11–11 (game later thrown out, however Macmillan counted it as a tie; counted as a tie in *Total Baseball*, since Tattersall stats included it, and these do not have day-by-day breakdowns)
1882	June 29	A	StL vs Lou	No game (later thrown out; however, it was counted as a no-game forfeit by Macmillan, which did not count either the StL vs Lou tie (6–6) on Oct 3 or the StL vs Lou win (6–2) on Oct 5, which were treated as if they were exhibition games. They should have been counted, and *Total Baseball* does.)
	Aug. 16	N	Cle at Wor	No game (game later thrown out)
1883	July 4	N	Phi vs Pro	Game OK, Pro won 11–9 in AM game (Pro had to leave for PM game in NY after 7 innings), no pitcher win/loss
	July 27	AA	NY vs Phi	No game (game later thrown out)
	Aug. 1	N	Bos at Cle	Game OK, Bos ahead 10–3
1884	May 31	AA	Cin at Was	Game OK, Cin ahead 6–0
	July 5	U	Bal vs Cin	No game (umpire late, Cin refused to play)

Year	Date	League	Teams	Notes
	Aug. 11	N	Buf at Chi	No game (1st game; argument in first inning; the second game, a makeup, ended in a 6–6 tie)
	Aug. 22	U	StL at KC	Game OK, KC ahead 6–3, no pitcher win/loss
	Aug. 23	N	Bos vs Det	Game OK, Bos ahead 7–5 (Macmillan gave no win or loss in this game, should be Whitney-W, Meinke-L)
	Aug. 25	U	Bos vs Wil	No game (1st game; Wil arrived late)
	Aug. 30	AA	Tol at StL	Game OK, Tol ahead 2–1 (PM game)
	Sept. 8	U	Was vs Pit	No game (Pit failed to appear)
	Sept. 20	U	Was vs Cin	No game (Cin failed to appear) (This game not counted by Macmillan or *Total Baseball*)
	Sept. 24	AA	Tol vs Ric	No game (Ric failed to appear)
	Sept. 24	A	Bal at Pit	Game OK, Bal ahead 8–6
	Oct. 11	U	StL vs Was	No game (Was refused to continue)
	Oct. 11	U	Bos at Cin	No game
1885	Aug. 5	AA	Bal vs. Phi	Game OK, Bal ahead 8–7
1886	July 30	N	Det at Was	Game OK, Det ahead 13–9 (Macmillan gave no win or loss in this game. Win should go to Hardy Richardson in relief, loss to George Keefe; Getzien started for Det but left in the 5th behind 9–6. Det got 7 in 7th. There is some controversy on this game because a lot of runs were scored before the game was actually forfeited)
	Sept. 29	N	Was vs StL	Score tied 2–2
	Oct. 7	N	Was vs KC	No game (1st game, AM)
	Oct. 8	N	Was vs KC	No game (1st game, AM)
	Oct. 9	N	Was vs KC	No game (1st game, AM; KC refused to play morning games on these three dates)
1887	Apr. 30	AA	Lou vs Cin	No game (Cin arrived late)
	June 27	N	Det vs NY	No game (1st game; game thrown out on Aug. 14)
	July 3	AA	Lou at StL	No game
	July 22	AA	Phi vs Cle	Game OK, Cle ahead 6–4 (no pitcher win/loss)
	Aug. 12	AA	NY at Phi	Game OK, NY ahead 9–7
1888	May 31	N	NY vs Pit	No game (Pit did not appear)
	July 14	AA	KC vs Bro	Game OK, KC ahead 5–4
	Sept. 12	N	Chi vs NY	Game OK, Chi ahead 8–2 (Macmillan awarded no win or loss in this game, should be Krock-W, Keefe-L)
	Oct. 13	N	Phi vs Chi	No game (Chi did not appear; Macmillan has extra win for Phi, extra loss for Pit—they counted a Phi win over Pit May 5 which was later thrown out; Buffington should have one less win, Morris one less loss; *Total Baseball* counts stats for May 5th game except for wins and losses)
1889	May 5	AA	Phi at Bro	Game OK, Phi ahead 11–1
	June 24	AA	Bro vs Col	No game (1st game; Col refused to play with sub ump; second game was played)
	Sept. 7	AA	Bro vs StL	StL ahead 4–2 (this forfeit later overruled and given back to StL as normal game)
	Sept. 8	AA	Bro vs StL	No game (StL did not appear)
	Sept. 26	AA	Cle vs Was	No game (Washington's train delayed; game later thrown out, played on Sept 28)
1890	Apr. 20	AA	Lou vs StL	No game
	Apr. 24	N	Bos vs NY	Game OK, score tied 2–2
	June 17	N	Pit vs Cle	No game (train delay; game later thrown out)
	July 2	AA	Phi at Tol	Game OK; score tied 5–5
	July 27	AA	Col vs Bro	Game OK; Bro ahead 13–8 (no pitcher win/loss)
	Aug. 3	AA	Syr vs Lou	No game
	Aug. 5	AA	Tol vs Roc	Game OK, Tol ahead 7–3
	Sept. 2	N	Chi at Bos	No game (1st game; umpire late, game not started; later forfeited to Bos and then thrown out)
	Sept. 21	AA	Stl at Roc	Game OK (2nd game), StL ahead 10–3
1891	Apr. 8	AA	StL vs Cin	No game, tied 7–7 (overruled and replayed on Apr. 13; counted by Macmillan and *Total Baseball* as a tie)
	Sept. 12	AA	StL vs Bos	Game OK, StL ahead 4–2
	Sept. 20	AA	Lou vs Phi	No game; Phi refused to continue (2nd game)
	Sept. 25	N	Chi vs Pit	Game OK, score tied 4–4
	Sept. 25	AA	StL at Lou	
	Oct. 2	AA	StL vs Lou	(These two games were exhibitions but were counted by Macmillan and *Total Baseball 1* but should not have been. Meekin beat McGill, 7–4, in the first one, McGill beat Fitzgerald, 13–8, in the second)
	Oct. 5	AA	Was vs Bal	Game OK, Bal ahead 4–1, no pitcher win/loss (counted as a win for Bal in Macmillan; there should be win for Healy or loss for Foreman)
1892	Apr. 20	N	NY at Bal	Game OK, Balt ahead 6–5, no pitcher win/loss
	Apr. 23	N	Lou at Chi	Game OK, Chi ahead 4–2, no pitcher win/loss (Macmillan has extra loss for Chi, extra win for NY. They gave a loss to Luby on Apr. 23 and a win to King on Apr. 20, although the opposing team pitcher in each case had his decision removed)
	May 10	N	Pit vs NY	No game (NY refused to play in rain)
	May 21	N	Cle vs StL	No game (1st game; StL arrived late)
	Aug. 16	N	Pit vs Was	Game OK, score tied 2–2
	Sept. 22	N	Pit vs Chi	No game (Chi trying to delay for rain)
	Oct. 12	N	Pit vs Cle	No game (Cle did not appear)
1893	May 25	N	Lou vs Chi	No game (Chi did not appear)
	Sept. 16	N	Cle vs Bal	Game OK, Cle ahead 15–11
1894	May 1	N	Bro vs Was	Game OK, Was ahead 2–1; no pitcher win/loss (Macmillan gave a loss (and shutout!) to Stephens of Was in this game)
	May 26	N	Pit at Cle	Game OK, Pit ahead 12–3
	July 17	N	Phi vs Bos	Game OK, Phi ahead 12–2
	Aug. 3	N	Lou vs Chi	No game (Chi refused to play)
	Sept. 5	N	Was vs StL	Game OK, Washington ahead 7–4
1895	May 23	N	Bro at Lou	No game
	Aug. 28	N	Bal vs Pit	No game (1st game; Pit arrived late)
1896	May 13	N	Bos at Chi	Game OK, score tied 4–4
	July 24	N	Bal vs StL	Game OK, Bal ahead 13–8
1897	May 3	N	NY at Was	No game
	June 1	N	NY vs Pit	Game OK, Pit ahead 7–4, no pitcher win/loss
	June 4	N	Phi vs Pit	No game
	July 24	N	Cle vs Phi	Game OK, Phi ahead 4–3, no pitcher win/loss
	Aug. 1	N	StL vs Lou	Lou ahead 5–4 (2nd game, later thrown out)
	Aug. 4	N	Lou vs Cle	No game (1st game; Cle refused to continue)
	Sept. 8	N	Was vs Cle	No game (2nd game)
	Sept. 10	N	Bal vs Lou	Game OK, Bal ahead 6–5
1898	July 25	N	Bal vs NY	No game (NY refused to continue)
	Sept. 16	N	Phi vs Chi	(1st game) Chi ahead 2–1 (Macmillan gave Donahue, Phi a win in this game, but this was not a regulation game and should have no stats counted)
1899	May 19	N	StL vs NY	Game OK, NY ahead 10–9, no pitcher win/loss
	June 16	N	Bro at NY	No game
	Oct. 14	N	Bro vs Bal	No game (1st game)
1900	June 22	N	Bro at Phi	Game OK, Bro ahead 20–13
	Sept. 19	N	Bro vs StL	No game (StL refused to continue)
1901	May 2	A	Det at Chi	Game OK, Det ahead 7–5
	May 13	NL	NY vs Bro	Game OK, score tied 7–7
	May 31	AL	Det vs Bal	Game OK, score tied 5–5
	June 9	NL	NY at Cin	Game OK, NY ahead 25–13
	July 23	AL	Cle vs Was	Game OK, score tied 4–4 (This game ruled a tie by the league and so counted by *Total Baseball*, but counted as a forfeit by Macmillan/ICI)
	Aug. 21	AL	Det vs Bal	No game (crowd swarmed on field)
1902	June 16	NL	Pit at Bos	No game (Bos trying to delay for rain)
	June 28	AL	Bos vs Bal	Game OK, Bos ahead 9–4

Year	Date	League	Teams	Notes
	July 17	AL	StL at Bal	No game (Bal did not appear)
1903	Aug. 8	AL	Det at Cle	Game OK, Det ahead 6–5
1904	Oct. 4	NL	StL at NY	No game (2nd game; NY refused to continue)
1905	Aug. 5	NL	Pit vs NY	Game OK, score tied 5–5
	Aug. 22	AL	Was at Det	Game OK, Washington ahead 2–1
1906	June 9	NL	Pit vs Phi	Game OK, Pit ahead 7–1
	July 2	AL	NY at Phi	Game OK, NY ahead 5–1
	Aug. 7	NL	Chi at NY	No game (umpire not allowed into park)
	Sept. 3	AL	NY vs Phi	Game OK (2nd game, score tied 3–3)
1907	Apr. 11	NL	Phi at NY	Game OK, Phi ahead 3–0
	Oct. 5	NL	StL vs Chi	No game (1st game, Chi refused to continue)
1909	Oct. 4	NL	NY vs Phi	No game (2nd game, score tied 1–1 in 4th inning; this was not a regulation game but was included in the official stats)
1913	July 6	NL	StL at Chi	No game (2nd game, Chi tried to stall so that curfew would be invoked; this was not a regulation game but was included in the official stats)
1914	June 26	AL	Phi vs Was	No game (1st game, Washington refused to continue)
1916	July 18	NL	Bro at Chi	Game OK, score tied 4–4
1917	Sept. 9	AL	Chi vs Cle	Game OK, score tied 3–3
1918	July 20	AL	Cle at Phi	Game OK (2nd game, Cle ahead 9–1)
	Sept. 2	A	Cle at StL	No games (doubleheader; Cle did not show up for last games of war-shortened season, not wanting to bear expense of trip to StL; two losses for Cle were counted at time but later thrown out; no league umpires were present to forfeit games)
1920	Aug. 20	AL	Chi at Phi	Game OK (2nd game, Chi ahead 5–2)
1924	June 13	AL	NY at Det	Game OK, NY ahead 10–6
1925	Apr. 26	AL	Cle at Chi	Game OK, Cle ahead 7–2
1937	June 6	NL	StL vs Phi	No game (2nd game, Phi tried to stall so that curfew would be invoked)
1939	Sept. 3	A	NY at Bos	Game OK (2nd game, NY ahead 7–5 when curfew near, so Yanks tried to make outs to get game in; Bos fans littered field in protest, umpire forfeited game to NY, later overruled; game declared a tie and NY players fined)
1941	Aug. 15	AL	Bos at Was	Game OK, Washington ahead 6–3, no pitcher win/loss)
1942	Sept. 26	NL	Bos at NY	Game OK (2nd game, NY ahead 5–2, no pitcher win/loss)
1949	Aug. 21	NL	NY at Phi	Game OK (2nd game, NY ahead 4–2 in top of ninth; no win or loss given, per rules of day; Larry Jansen pitched for NY, Schoolboy Rowe for Phi)
1954	July 18	NL	Phi at StL	No game (2nd game, StL tried to stall for darkness)
1971	Sept. 30	AL	NY at Was	Game OK (Washington ahead 7–5, no pitcher win/loss; this was the last game in Washington and fans vandalized the field in the 9th)
1974	June 4	AL	Tex at Cle	Game OK, scored tied 5–5 (crowd invaded field)
1977	Sept. 15	AL	Tor vs Bal	Game OK, Tor ahead 4–0 (Bal refused to continue)
1979	July 12	AL	Det at Chi	No game (2nd game, crowd littered field between games)

No-Decision Games

In the National Association of 1871–75, no-decision games were counted in the records by researcher Michael Stagno and thus are adopted in *Total Baseball*. In the National League of 1876–1890, no-decision games were counted by researcher John Tattersall and thus were adopted by the Macmillan *Baseball Encyclopedia* and *Total Baseball*. In the ensuing period, covered by ICI

research and the computer printouts that ICI deposited at the Hall of Fame, protested games were not counted. Although they may have been included in the official averages, source data for these has been lost. In the 1910–19 period, protested games were not counted at all. From 1920–92, protested games were counted. Because of the effect these games had on the records of the teams' managers, the managers are listed. For more on this, see the Introduction to the Manager Roster, criterion number 7.

This list of no-decision games does not include protests that were upheld in which the game was resumed from the point of protest; it includes only those games that were thrown out entirely. These games did ultimately come to a decision.

Year	Date	League	Teams	Notes/Managers
This was counted by Michael Stagno:				
1872	May 20	NA	Ath at Bal	Game disallowed (McBride–Craver)
These were counted by Tattersall:				
1877	May 15	NL	Lou at Cin	Forfeit to Cin overruled (Chapman–Pike)
1880	Sept. 10	NL	Cin at Buf	Forfeit to Buf overruled; this game counted as a tie with all stats in by Macmillan (Clapp–Crane)
1887	Sept. 23	NL	Bos at Chi	Second game
1887	Sept. 24	NL	Bos at Chi	First and second games; these two games plus the one of the day before were ties replayed without proper consent; counted as no-decisions but included in averages by Tattersall and Macmillan (Morrill–Anson)
	July 4	NL	Bos at Det	2nd game was a 4½-inning, 7–7 tie; since it did not go five innings, it should not have counted in the records, but it was included by Tattersall and Macmillan. It was not protested (Kelly–Watkins)
1888	May 5	NL	Phi at Pit	Phi ahead 4–3; this game counted by Tattersall and Macmillan as a win for Phi (Wright–Phillips)
These were not counted by Macmillan:				
1888	June 10	AA	Bal at Phi	(Barnie–Sharsig)
1890	July 10, 11, 12	PL	Pit at Bos	Three games in which Bos used Gil Hatfield, on loan from NY, against league rules (Hanlon–Kelly)
1891	Apr. 8	AA	Cin at StL	Forfeit overruled (Kelly–Comiskey)
1894	Apr. 26	NL	Phi at Bro	(Irwin–Foutz)
	May 23	NL	Pit at Chi	Forfeit overruled (Buckenberger–Anson)
	Aug. 18	NL	Chi at NY	1st game (Anson–Ward)
	Aug. 25	NL	Lou at NY	1st game (Barnie–Ward)
	Aug. 27	NL	Cin at Phi	1st game (Comiskey–Irwin)
	Sept. 6	NL	Cin at Phi	1st game (Comiskey–Irwin) (Macmillan threw out the first game and counted the second game; four games above were transferred without league approval; Jim Smith claims that first game should count and second game be thrown out)
1895	June 1	NL	Pit at Bro	(Mack–Foutz)
	July 14	NL	Cle at StL	(Schmelz–Selee)
	Aug. 12	NL	Was at Bos	(Tebeau–Quinn)
1897	June 3	NL	Lou at NY	1st game (Rogers–Joyce)
	Aug. 1	NL	Lou at StL	2nd game (Clarke–Hallman)
1899	May 3	NL	Lou at Pit	(Clarke–Watkins)
	May 30	NL	NY at Cin	PM game (Ewing–Day)
1902	May 7	NL	NY at Chi	(Fogel–Selee)
	May 8	NL	NY at Chi	Pitching distance too short; this game and the one above may have been included in the official averages, but no record exists (Fogel–Selee)

Year	Date	League	Teams	Notes/Managers
These were not counted in the official averages or by Macmillan:				
1911	May 30	NL	Chi at Pit	Ist game (Chance–Clarke)
1912	Oct. 2	NL	Pit at Chi	(Clarke–Chance)
1914	May 14	FL	Chi at Buf	(Tinker–Schafly)
	June 19	FL	Chi at Bal	(Tinker–Knabe)
	Sept. 3	AL	Cle at Chi	2nd game (Fohl–Rowland)
	Aug. 17	NL	Chi at Pit	1st game; Benton pitched for Pit (Bresnahan–Clarke)
1917	Apr. 17	NL	Bos at Phi	(Stallings–Moran)
	Aug. 19	AL	Was vs Det	(Griffith–Jennings)
1918	Apr. 29	NL	StL at Cin	(Hendricks–Mathewson)
	June 3	NL	StL at Bro	(Hendricks–Robinson)
These were counted by both the offical averages and Macmillan:				
1890	May 23	N	Chi vs Phi	(Researcher Joe Wayman claims this is a protested game not counted in standings, per baseball guide for 1891; however, Tattersall and Macmillan have counted game as win for Chi)

Year	Date	League	Teams	Notes/Managers
1909	Apr. 23	NL	Cin at Pit	(Griffith–Clarke)
1924	July 15	NL	NY at Chi	(McGraw–Killefer)
1924	July 28	AL	Bos at StL	Individual data counted, team data not counted; Macmillan originally took out the individual records; later editions have added the batting records, but omitted the pitching records (Fohl–Sisler)
1932	Aug. 19	AL	NY at Det	All data counted except in the games-played column in official records; games played added by Macmillan (McCarthy–Harris)
1937	Aug. 6	AL	NY vs Cle	(McCarthy–O'Neill)
1938	May 14	NL	StL vs Cin	(7–6, this game later declared a tie)
1939	Sept. 12	AL	Chi at Was	(Dykes–Harris)
1940	June 20	AL	Chi vs NY	(Dykes–McCarthy)
1947	July 20	NL	Bro vs StL	(3–2, this game later declared a tie)

Phantom Ballplayers

Clifford S. Kachline

arbage in, garbage out is an expression that gained currency with the advent of the computer age. The logic behind the catch phrase, however, prevailed long before the electronic marvels came into being. Baseball, in fact, has had its own version of the maxim almost since the game's earliest days, largely as a consequence of recordkeepers who sometimes unwittingly entered erroneous data into the record books.

Numerous examples of the *garbage in, garbage out* principle have been discovered in baseball's statistical archives through the years. But statistics aren't the only area where the phenomenon has shown up. Another involves what researchers of the sport refer to as "phantoms"—players credited with having performed in the major leagues but who in reality never did appear in a big league game.

Phantoms are hardly a recent phenomenon. They have existed almost as long as boxscores have been published. Some were the product of misunderstandings by—or misinformation given to—official scorers or the parties who compiled the boxscores. A few of these crept into the leagues' official records. Others were created by mistakes on the part of telegraph operators or by typographical errors and appeared only in newspaper boxscores.

Little if any attention was paid to the situation until the 1950s. The original edition of *The Official Encyclopedia of Baseball*, published by A. S. Barnes and Co. in 1951, provided fans for the first time with a supposedly complete alphabetical tabulation of every man who ever played in the majors, together with his basic yearly big league stats. The publication stimulated the interest of the sport's researchers. When editors Hy Turkin and S. C. Thompson deleted the names of some players—most of whom were previously shown as having a one-game career—from subsequent revised editions, the matter of phantoms started to become a source of fascination.

Who really were the "impostors" that were listed in earlier editions? What had prompted the editors to include them in the first place? And what evidence had been found to prove conclusively that they never played in the big leagues?

The introduction of *The Baseball Encyclopedia* by the Macmillan Publishing Company in 1969 focused additional attention on the subject. In compiling data for that publication, David Neft and his crew of Information Concepts, Inc. researchers continued the process of purging phantoms from the records. Since then, further investigation by Neft, Pete Palmer, Bill Haber, Al Kermisch, and others has led to the expunging of several more players.

In many instances confirming the status of a phantom was a complicated chore. The task sometimes was made more difficult because the player's name was included in the official league statistics. In other cases, especially those involving nineteenth-century performers, the fact that official league records no longer exist compounded the problem because it made it impossible to determine who was credited by the official scorer and/or league statistician with appearing in the game or games in question. (The American League's official game-by-game player sheets of 1901–1904 reportedly were destroyed by fire decades

ago, while the official National League data also vanished for the pre-1902 period except for the 1899 season.)

An example of a phantom who appears in the league records is Albert W. Olsen. For thirty-five years he was carried in the *Encyclopedias* and shown as participating in one game—as a pinch hitter—for the Boston Red Sox in 1943. Olsen did train with the Red Sox that spring, but he was shipped to San Diego of the Pacific Coast League before opening day and spent the entire season in the minors. In addition, it was his exploits as a left-handed pitcher, not as a hitter, that originally attracted the Red Sox.

Nevertheless, American League records list Olsen as playing for Boston in a game in Chicago on May 16, 1943. Newspaper boxscores credited him with drawing a walk while batting for pitcher Dick Newsome and subsequently stealing a base. However, research has confirmed that the Red Sox pinch-hitter on that occasion definitely was not Olsen. Instead, it may have been outfielder Leon Culberson, who had just been called up from Louisville of the American Association, or possibly another Boston rookie outfielder, Johnny Lazor.

And why is there still uncertainty as to who the pinch-hitter really was? How could this mistake have occurred? First off, the exchange of roster data among major league teams during that period was quite limited. Consequently scorecards often contained the same player names and uniform numbers for the visiting team, especially early in the season, as the team listed in spring training. For example, the scorecard for a Red Sox–Senators game in Washington approximately a week before the incident in question showed Olsen on Boston's roster with uniform number 14, even though he was pitching for San Diego. Second, it's unlikely there were phone lines from the pressbox to the dugouts in those days, and in the absence of being able to call down to check on the identity of a player, the media and official scorers relied on outdated roster information.

Several years ago researchers felt they had cleared up the Olsen mystery upon discovering that one Boston newspaper identified the pinch-hitter as "Culbeson." This seemed to settle the matter. After all, Culberson had joined the team that day and was installed as the Red Sox' leadoff batter in the second half of the afternoon doubleheader, collecting a single and triple in five at-bats. But the mystery was revived when Ed Walton, a Red Sox historian, discussed the situation with Culberson at a Red Sox Old Timers affair in 1986. According to Walton, Culberson contended he did not pinch-hit in the twin-bill opener, but rather made his debut in the second game. He added that manager Joe Cronin said he wanted the young newcomer to sit beside him (Cronin) through the first game to get a feel of the big leagues. However, the records reveal Cronin played third base during the entire first game. All of which raises the questions: Was Culberson's memory playing tricks on him and was he indeed the pinch-hitter listed as Olsen? Or was it Lazor, who is shown as wearing uniform number 14 later in the year but who was batting a mere .136 (3 for 22) at the time? Because the passage of time makes memories hazy and also because the incident was of no particular significance, the mystery may never be solved.

A manager's pique led to a phantom known as J. A. Costello getting into the early *Encyclopedias*. Curiously, the incident also took place in Chicago and likewise involved a player's big league debut. It occurred in the morning half of a holiday bill between Cleveland and the White Sox on July 4, 1912. Late in the contest, Indians' Manager Harry Davis, still burning over an umpire's decision, sent the newcomer into the game to replace center fielder Joe Birmingham and instructed him to announce himself to umpire Gene Hart as "Costello."

In reality, the player was Kenneth Nash, who had only recently joined Cleveland from Boston University law school. He subsequently appeared in ten additional games with Cleveland that season under his correct surname, mostly as a shortstop, and then played with the St. Louis Cardinals for part of 1914. Nash later became a prominent state representative, state senator, and judge in his home state of Massachusetts.

The 1903 official National League records contain a phantom who long baffled researchers. Among the Pittsburgh player sheets is one headed "George Gray" with entries for two games as an outfielder—on May 28 and May 31. Four years earlier the Pirates had a pitcher named George "Chummy" Gray, and it's possible the scorer or league statistician remembered him while filling in the player's first name. When the first *Official Encyclopedia* appeared in 1951, the player was identified as William (rather than George) Gray, a native of Pittsburgh.

It turns out that the two George (or William) Gray entries properly belonged to not one, but two different players. The Pirates' left fielder in the May 28 game really was Romer Carl "Reddy" Grey, younger brother of novelist Zane Grey. He had been obtained on loan from the Worcester club of the Eastern League to fill in that afternoon in the final game of a series in Boston.

On the other hand, while boxscores in Cincinnati newspapers listed the Pittsburgh left fielder for the May 31 game in Cincinnati as "Gray," the player actually was Ernest Diehl, a Cincinnati sandlotter who had been recruited by the injury-riddled Pirates. The game represented Diehl's first appearance in the major leagues and his only game that season, but he played 12 more games with Pittsburgh the following year. It should be noted that ever since the original Turkin/Thompson tome, the *Encyclopedias* have credited Diehl with playing one game with Pittsburgh in 1903, but until recent years they also carried William Gray with two games.

A majority of baseball's phantoms were the product of typographical errors—instances where a linotypist or a typesetter mistakenly included one or more incorrect letters in a name, or where a printer inserted a correction line in the wrong place. In compiling data for the *Encyclopedias,* the authors/researchers relied not only on the so-called official league records but also combed boxscores published in *The Sporting News, Sporting Life, The New York Clipper,* and various local newspapers. In the process they occasionally came upon what appeared to be a previously unlisted "new" player who, in the final analysis, proved to be someone else. Even today, misspellings of this type in newspapers can cause great befuddlement.

A classic illustration of a phantom who was created by a typographical error is the player carried in the early *Encyclopedias* as John P. Morgan. He was listed as appearing in one game as a third baseman with the Philadelphia Athletics in 1916. A study of A's boxscores for the season disclosed the source of the mix-up: It was *The Sporting News*'s boxscore of the August 3 game at Cleveland. (*Sporting Life* had dropped boxscores by this time.) The Philadelphia half of *TSN*'s box has "Morgan, 2b," while on the same line in Cleveland's half is "Gandil, 1b."

Careful examination reveals the Morgan/Gandil type slug was a correction line that the printer inserted in the wrong place. It was intended for the Washington-at-Cleveland boxscore of the previous day (August 2) in which the Senators' second baseman, Harry Morgan, appeared on the same line as Chick Gandil and contained the identical AB-H-PO-A-E figures given for each player in the misaligned August 2 line.

This explanation may well leave you, the reader, with several questions, to wit: (1) Who did play third for the A's that day, and was he properly credited in the official records? (2) Why did the *Encyclopedia* compilers show Morgan as a third baseman instead of a second baseman? (3) How did they come up with "John P." for the impostor's name?

The answers are: (1) Lee McElwee and, yes, he was credited with this game; (2) because veteran Nap Lajoie played the entire game at his usual second base position for the A's, the researcher who made this "discovery" apparently assumed it should have read "Morgan, 3b" rather than "2b"; (3) an infielder named John P. Morgan was active in the minor leagues that season, and the *Encyclopedia* editors probably figured the A's had given him a trial. Numerous other phantoms were similarly tagged with the first names of then-current minor leaguers.

Typos involving misspelled names led to a number of one-game phantoms. Two examples will serve to demonstrate the point. They are John H. Carlock (1912, Cleveland) and a player listed simply as Deniens (no first name given) with the 1914 Chicago Federals. *Sporting Life* had "Carlock, ph" for Cleveland in an August 24, 1912, game at Boston, but Cleveland newspapers and *The Sporting News* reported the pinch-hitter was Fred Carisch, a reserve catcher with the Indians. Official AL records also credit Carisch with that appearance. "Deniens, c" turned out to be Clem Clemens, a catcher in 13 games with the 1914 ChiFeds. One can readily visualize how handwritten names "Carisch" and "Clemens" could have been misinterpreted by a telegrapher or linotypist for "Carlock" and "Deniens."

The origins of some other phantoms are more mysterious. Take the case of Lou Proctor. The *Encyclopedias* credited him with one appearance with the 1912 St. Louis Browns. *The Sporting News* and *Sporting Life,* which may have obtained their boxscores from the same source, show "Proctor, ph" and "Procter, pi," respectively, in a May 13 game at Boston. However, a Boston newspaper referred to the pinch hitter as Albert "Pete" Compton, a catcher with the Browns that season (whose real first name was, of all things, Anna). While AL records contain no reference to Proctor, they unfortunately also fail to include the May 13 appearance among Compton's 100 games. Rumor has it that Proctor was a prankish Western Union telegrapher who inserted his own name as a pinch hitter.

The presence on one team of two players with the same or an almost similar surname can lead to problems. The Washington Senators figured in three such mixups. Ironically, in one instance research by Kermisch has established that a player long labeled a phantom was, in fact, the real McCoy. The player in question was Charles C. Conway. In 1911 the Senators had both Conway, a rookie outfielder up from Youngstown (Ohio-Pennsylvania), and William "Wid" Conroy, veteran infielder-outfielder, on their spring roster. When the season began, Conroy was idled by a stone bruise of the foot. Meantime, Conway appeared in two games during opening week, finishing up in right field on April 15 and starting at that position three days later, before the Senators returned him to Youngstown. Unfortunately, *Sporting Life* and *The Sporting News* each showed "Conroy" as the replacement in the first contest, but both had "Conway, rf" in their April 18 boxscore. Although the early *Encyclopedias* listed Conway and credited him with playing two games, the Macmillan compilers dropped his name 20 years ago on the erroneous premise that it was the veteran Conroy who participated in the April 15-18 games. Actually, Conroy didn't make the first of his 106 appearances that year until April 27.

An equally confusing puzzle centered on a 1914 Washington pitcher known as Barron or Barton. The early *Encyclopedias* carried both John J. Barron (later changed to Frank John Barron) and Carroll R. "Buck" Barton and credited each with pitching in one game for the '14 Senators. Actually only one pitcher was involved (and just one appearance), but which pitcher was

it? Player contract data of the period reveal that Washington signed Carroll R. Barton in 1913 and retained rights to him while he pitched for Newport News (Virginia League) that season and again in 1914. During the same two years John J. Barron was pitching in the New England League. To complicate matters further, Washington signed Frank J. Barron in 1914 and shipped him to Newport News, where he became a teammate of Barton. While Barron posted a dismal 1-3 record, Barton was a 16-game winner that year.

So who was the 1914 Washington pitcher? The American League player records contain an entry headed "Barron" with data for an August 18 game, and boxscores of the contest likewise have "Barron" pitching one inning—the ninth—for the Senators against the visiting St. Louis Browns. The player's correct identity was confirmed when, shortly before his death in 1964, Frank Barron disclosed in an interview that while still studying for his law degree at West Virginia University he was signed by Clark Griffith in 1914, was assigned to Newport News and later pitched one inning for Washington before resuming his law studies.

The third Washington mix-up relates to a 1944 player identified in the *Encyclopedias* as Armando Viera Valdes. Official AL records contain a sheet for Armand (without the final "o") Valdes and note that he made a pinch-hitting appearance for the Senators in a May 3 game at Boston, but Richard Topp's research has disclosed that the pinch hitter was Rogelio "Roy" Valdes, a fellow Cuban but no relative of Armando.

With many major leaguers lost to military service in 1944, scout Joe Cambria lined up several Cubans to fill voids on the Senators' roster. Early in the year he signed an outfielder who was listed in the 1944 *American League Red Book* as Armand (without the "o") Valdes. Several weeks thereafter—too late for inclusion in the *Red Book*—Cambria signed Rogelio Valdes, a catcher. Both spent the early weeks of the season with Washington (each was later optioned to Williamsport of the Eastern League), and presumably the official scorer and/or league statistician picked up the incorrect first name from the Senator roster in the *AL Red Book*.

As in the case of Charles Conway, another player once regarded as a phantom has turned out to be a legitimate athlete after all. The Turkin-Thompson tomes listed him as William Krouse, a second baseman in one game with Cincinnati in 1901. Compilers of the Macmillan encyclopedia decided he was an imposter and dropped him, crediting his appearance to Bill Fox, the Reds' regular keystoner. However, research has revealed that the "Krouse, 2b" for Cincinnati in the July 27, 1901 game at Chicago was a recently-released minor leaguer whose correct name was Charles "Famous" Krause. Krause, who was on his way home to Detroit at the time, was given a chance with the Reds because Fox was sidelined with a split finger, but the newcomer performed so poorly that he was dumped after that one appearance.

Recent research has revealed that one player long listed as a phantom—Ivan Bigler, who was shown in one boxscore at first base with the 1917 St. Louis Browns when George Sisler actually played there that day—really did make an appearance with the Browns as a pinch runner on May 6 that season, and thus he's been restored to the all-time list of major leaguers.

The accompanying table lists the phantoms who have been eliminated from the all-time roster of major league players since the first Turkin/Thompson *Official Encyclopedia* of 1951. In the absence of an official clearinghouse for such data, no claim is made that the list is complete. Where it is available, brief information on the reason for the deletion of the player is given. Unfortunately, documentation by Turkin/Thompson and the ICI group that compiled the 1969 *Encyclopedia* disappeared years ago.

With today's sophisticated technology and record-keeping procedures, the margin for error in the identification of players—and in the official statistics—has been reduced considera-

bly. Still, a slipup that occurred in the 1984 official American League averages (Alvaro Espinoza was omitted completely, even though he appeared in one game with Minnesota) emphasizes that mistakes still are possible.

A factor that poses the potential for error is the frequency of teams having two players with the same—or nearly identical—surname. In 1987, for instance, the Atlanta Braves' pitching staff at one time or another included two Smiths (Zane and Pete) as well as a Cary (Chuck) and Clary (Marty), while the St. Louis Cardinals had two relief specialists named Dayley (Ken) and Dawley (Bill) and also a Perry (Pat) and a Terry (Scott), two pitchers who coincidentally were traded for each other during the season. Meanwhile, Seattle's lineup often included both Phil Bradley and Scott Bradley, while Craig Reynolds and Ronn Reynolds occasionally appeared in the same lineup for Houston, and Baltimore, of course, had the brothers Ripken. Other examples—such as Sandberg (Ryne) and Sundberg (Jim) of the Cubs and infielders Jeltz (Steve) and Jelks (Greg) of the Phillies—could be cited, but the duo that could cause the greatest difficulty for researchers circa 2000 consists of pitchers Don Robinson and Jeff Robinson, both of whom pitched for San Francisco and Pittsburgh in 1987.

Couple this with the typographical errors that still show up in newspaper boxscores, and you can see that the days of *garbage in, garbage out* are likely to continue.

Tabulation of Phantoms

Allen, Robert. 1919 Philadelphia AL, 9 games as OF. Pseudonym used by Alvah C. "Rowdy" Elliott, long-time minor leaguer.

Baldwin,——. 1907 Boston NL, 1 game as C. One of James C. Ball's 10 games.

Barton, Carroll R. 1914 Washington AL, 1 game as P. Same as game credited to Frank J. Barron.

Boylan,——. 1887 Philadelphia NL, 1 game as 2B. One of Charles J. Bastian's 60 games.

Carlock, John H. 1912 Cleveland AL, 1 game as PH. Typographical error; one of Frederick B. Carisch's 26 games.

Christman, H. B. 1888 Kansas City AA, 1 game as C. Documentation behind deletion no longer available.

Costello, J. A. 1912 Cleveland AL, 1 game as OF. One of 11 games played by Kenneth L. Nash, who used pseudonym in debut.

Davis, Thomas J. 1890 Cleveland NL, 1 game as OF. One of George Stacey Davis' 136 games.

Davis, ——. 1903 Chicago NL, 1 game as OF. Documentation behind deletion no longer available.

Deniens,——. 1914 Chicago FL, 1 game as C. Typographical error; one of Clement L. Clemens' 13 games.

Drennan, K. John. 1904 Detroit AL, 1 game as 1B. Typographical error; one of William "Wild Bill" Donovan's 46 games.

Dresser, Edward. 1898 Brooklyn NL, 1 game as SS. Typographical error; one of Jack Dunn's 51 games.

Dugan, E. 1884 Kansas City UA, 3 games as OF. Same player as William H. Dugan, who played 9 games with Richmond AA the same year.

Gray, William. 1903 Pittsburgh NL, 2 games as OF. One game belongs to Romer C. Grey; other game belongs to Ernest G. Diehl.

Kerns, Daniel P. 1920 Philadelphia AL, 1 game as PH. Pseudonym used by Edward "Ted" Kearns, later a 1B with 1924–25 Chicago NL.

King, Frederick. 1901 Milwaukee AL, 1 game as C. Game belongs to John A. Butler, later with St. Louis and Brooklyn NL, who used pseudonym in debut.

Lane,——. 1901 Boston NL, 1 game as 3B. Typographical error; one of Bobby Lowe's 129 games.

Mares,——. 1894 Louisville NL, 1 games as OF. Documentation behind deletion no longer available.

McCauley, William. 1884 St. Louis AA, 1 game as C. Game belongs to James A. McCauley, who also played in 1885–1886.

Meddlebrook,——. 1884 Baltimore UA, 1 game as OF. Documentation behind deletion no longer available.

Merson,——. 1914 Brooklyn FL, 1 game as PH. Typographical error; one of George J. Anderson's 98 games.

Miller, Bert. 1897 Philadelphia NL, 3 games as 2B. Games belong to Frank A. Miller, formerly listed as Frederick Miller, who also played one game each with Washington NL and St. Louis NL in 1892.

Miller, Henry D. 1892 Chicago NL, 4 games as P. Games belong to Harry DeMiller, who was erroneously listed for 1 game as 3B with 1892 St. Louis NL.

Moore, Guy W. 1922 St. Louis NL, 1 game as OF. Documentation behind deletion no longer available.

Morgan, John P. 1916 Philadelphia AL, 1 game as 3B. Typographical error; one of Leland S. McElwee's 54 games.

Olsen, Albert W. 1943 Boston AL, 1 game as PH. Appearance apparently belongs to either Leon Culberson or Johnny Lazor.

Pratt, Thomas J. 1884 Baltimore AA, 1 game as OF. Documentation behind deletion no longer available.

Proctor, Lou. 1912 St. Louis AL, 1 game as PH. Game belongs to Anna S. "Pete" Compton, who played in 101 games that season.

Ritchie,——. 1910 St. Louis NL, 1 game as PH. Documentation behind deletion no longer available.

Schauer,——. 1890 Columbus AA, 1 game as 1B. Documentation behind deletion no longer available.

Seymour, Thomas. 1882 Pittsburgh AA, 1 game as P. Player's correct name was Jacob Semer.

Sheehan, Timothy. 1884 Washington UA, 1 game as OF. One of John A. Ryan's seven games.

Smith, Charles H. "Pacer." 1877 Chicago/Cincinnati NL, 34 games as 2B-OF-C. Record belongs to Harry W. Smith, who also played 1 game with 1889 Louisville AA.

Smith, E. J. 1890 Buffalo PL, 1 game as 1B. One of John Irwin's 77 games.

Strands, Lewis. 1915 Chicago FL, 1 game as 2B. One of John J. Farrell's 70 games.

Thayer, Edward L. 1876 New York NL, 1 game as 2B. Player's correct name was George T. Fair.

Turbot,——. 1902 St. Louis NL, 1 game as OF. Documentation behind deletion no longer available.

Valdes, Armando V. 1944 Washington AL, 1 game as PH. Game belongs to a different player, Rogelio "Roy" Valdes.

Young, David. 1895 St. Louis NL, 1 game as 3B. Documentation behind deletion no longer available.

Fans and Concessions

Paul D. Adomites

Called "kranks" or "bugs" during the early days of professional baseball, the followers of the sport were allegedly given the name of "fans" by Ted Sullivan, manager of the St. Louis Browns in 1883. Although some say the word came from "fanatic," etymologist Peter Tamony has stated it probably derived from "fancier,"—i.e., one who fancies the sport.

Famous Fans

Along with heroic athletes and staunch umpires, baseball has had a large number of fans who also achieved celebrity status. In the first modern World Series in 1903, the Boston "Royal Rooters" were headed by the tall, bulky bartender Mike McGreevy, whose stature as ultimate authority on all baseball matters earned him the sobriquet of "'Nuf Ced." The Rooters sang parodies of popular songs with new lyrics uncomplimentary to Boston's opponents: "Tessie, why do I love you madly?" became "Honus [Wagner], why do you hit so badly?" for example. When Boston triumphed in the Series, at least one Pirate gave the Rooters credit. Tommy Leach noted, "It was that damn song."

'Nuf Ced and the Rooters also had an effect on the 1912 World Series, although an opposite one. When a 6–6 tie in the second game, called on account of darkness after 10 innings, sent the Series back to Boston for an additional game, the Rooters expected they would keep the rights to the seats they had for Games Two, Three, and Five. But a clerk wasn't thinking; he sold the Rooters' seats for Game Seven.

The game was nearly ready to begin when 'Nuf Ced and his gang (five hundred strong), including Boston Mayor John Fitzgerald (whose daughter would bear future President John Fitzgerald Kennedy) marched onto the field and toward their seats, only to discover other people sitting there. The Rooters took to the field in protest. Today it would have been called a riot. It took mounted police more than a half hour to clear the crowd from the field. Meanwhile, Boston starting pitcher Smokey Joe Wood, who had stopped his warmups while the police rounded up the Royal Rooters, cooled off, and was ineffective.

But before 'Nuf Ced and the Royal Rooters, many teams had fans who earned fame, usually through lung power. In the 1890s, Frank B. Wood of the grizzled countenance and loud voice became a minor celebrity at the Polo Grounds for his editorial "Well well well."

The 1940s and '50s were the era of three of the most famous female fans. One, Mary Ott of St. Louis, had a "neigh . . . known to cause stampedes in Kansas City stockyards"; Lollie Hopkins, a prim Bostonian, used a megaphone to cheer for both sides when they played well; the legendary Hilda Chester toted two large cowbells and displayed a banner saying "Hilda is here" to make her voice heard in Ebbets Field for years.

Ebbets Field featured another famous fan in the late 1930s who did more than just root. Jack Pierce used to buy ten seats, a bottle of Scotch, balloons and the gas to blow them up, all to salute Dodgers' shortstop Cookie Lavagetto. Pierce's dedication was so complete that he continued his gaseous act even in 1942, when Cookie was in the Army.

Legendary lungs could be found in nearly every big league town. In the 1930s, the Kessler Brothers, Bull and Eddie, of Philadelphia,

would sit "on opposite sides of the grandstand and conduct what practically amounted to a private conversation across the diamond." In Pittsburgh, Bruce McAllister's screeching could be heard at every game and over the radio, too. Detroit's Patsy O'Toole was hailed as the "All-American earache."

Then there were the fans of dedication, not just noise. Some fans received press mention because they routinely took road trips with their favorite team. Others made a point of never missing a World Series, spring training, or All-Star Game, thereby meriting recognition. Still others built extensive (and expensive) "museums" or libraries.

The Royal Rooters tradition of fan groups—sitting together, leading cheers, and heckling the opposition—also had counterparts in most towns. In St. Louis it was the Ice Wagon Boys, in Chicago the Stockyards Boys, and in Pittsburgh the Steel Puddlers. But group cheering was less popular during the thirties and forties until it reappeared in the form of Wrigley Field's Bleacher Bums, who have inspired their own literature, including an Off-Broadway play. Active in the 1960s, dormant in the '70s, and resuscitated in the '80s, the Bleacher Bums were described tongue-in-cheek as "almost on a par with the old Brooklyn Dodger fans, but with more taste."

Fandom once created an on-the-field star. In 1902, Bill Armour, manager of the pitching-short Cleveland team, was told by a Philadelphia ticket-taker that a talented young pitcher was in the stands. Given a quick tryout and just as quickly signed, Charlie Smith won the game and went on to a ten-year big league career.

Worthy of special mention are the Brooklyn Dodger fans of today who still cannot mention the name of Walter O'Malley without a curse, and the St. Louis Browns Fan Club, active today more than thirty years after their team's demise.

Many people who achieved celebrity status in other fields were famous fans, too. Poetess Marianne Moore's love of the game was legendary. Composer Charles Ives wrote a piano piece called "Some Southpaw Pitching." Broadway, music, and film stars, including De-Wolf Hopper, Harry Ruby, George M. Cohan, Jack White, and Pearl Bailey were avid fans, along with many politicians, especially Presidents Taft, Eisenhower, and Nixon, and Speaker of the House Uncle Joe Cannon. Of course, many pols used fandom to garner favor; it was never certain whether they attended because they truly loved the game or whether they simply loved being seen in public.

Being Rowdy

The color that fun-loving fans add to a game turns, however, when fans interfere with the on-the-field action. Baseball kranks were causing trouble from the beginning. As early as 1857, there were eight incidents of bad fan behavior altering a game's result.

In fact, in the game that many call the first great American professional game (the Cincinnati Red Stockings vs. the Brooklyn Atlantics, June 14, 1870), a Brooklyn fan is said to have jumped on the back of Red Stockings' outfielder Cal McVey as he tried to field a ball in the eleventh inning. Brooklyn won the game 8–7, ending Cincinnati's 84-game winning streak.

Through the 1890s, a fan attacking the umpire or an opposing player was considered a social gaffe, but hardly a criminal offense.

There are several instances cited of umpires being mobbed, seriously injured, or two-fistedly turning on their attackers. Pop bottles were the commonest weapons for umpire abuse, and a record of a woman serving time for tossing a bottle at an ump was not described in the outraged tone one might expect.

Fans could harm the game even without maiming the umpires or attacking opponents. In the 1880s, tossing straw hats on the field to acknowledge a good play was common. However, cleaning up the skimmers often delayed the proceedings. In 1892, a Chicago crowd "cheered madly as Anson's men thrashed the whey out of Louisville." The exuberant fans demonstrated their joy by tossing a deluge of seat cushions on the field. Manager Cap Anson pleaded with them to stop, but to no avail. Chicago lost in a forfeit.

In 1911, William Phelon described a different kind of fan behavior. "Out at Kansas City, the crowd had a custom, once, that was all its own. Whenever the multitude couldn't see the wisdom of a decision, they arose, marched down onto the field, and advanced upon the umpire. They never offered harm or discourtesy to that official, but simply asked him, with all courtesy, to tell them the rules governing that one decision. The umpire would tell them, and then with a chorus of thanks, they would turn, march back to their seats, and let the game go on."

But two major factors changed the sentiment about what made a baseball outing fun. The first was the gradual elimination of ballpark gambling, which altered behavior both off and on the field. Another was the increased presence of women at the parks.

Legend has it that Ladies Day began in 1889 in Cincinnati because the women wanted to see handsome Tony Mullane pitch. However, the New York Knickerbockers had established a regular Ladies Day by 1867. The Athletics and Orioles did the same in 1883, Brooklyn in 1885. *The Sporting News* pointed out in 1886 that when women are present, the men become less excited and exercise "more choice in their selection of adjectives."

By the turn of the century, baseball was less a rowdy afternoon for gamblers and toughs, and much more of a family enterprise. The newer parks of the century were larger, too, making it harder for the fans to interfere.

But they still managed. A rain of snowballs from the stands in April 1907 led to forfeiture of the Giants' Opening Day game to the Phillies. The same year, some thought the pop-bottle hit taken by umpire Billy Evans would be fatal. (Evans did survive, though, and his teenaged assailant was fined $100.) This kind of behavior was hardly unexpected; a popular song of the teens was "Let's Get the Umpire's Goat."

On May 15, 1912, Ty Cobb leaped into the stands to beat up a fan who was harassing him—a fan described in the press as a "helpless cripple." Cobb's suspension for this act led his teammates to walk out the following day, and the locally recruited "substitutes" took a 24–2 licking from the Athletics before Cobb's reinstatement.

After Yankee center fielder Whitey Witt was struck by a pop bottle in 1922, the leagues cracked down on bottle throwing, and seriously. Ban Johnson offered a $1,000 reward to find the culprit. However, he received so many versions of what happened that he finally settled on $100 cash, railroad fare, and a World Series ticket to someone who claimed that "Witt stepped on the neck of a bottle and caused it to jump up and hit him on the head." The stricter enforcement (and public relations efforts of paper cup manufacturers) did the trick.

Fan violence was minimal in the 1920s. By the '30s, things had resoured. In the seventh game of the 1934 World Series, Cardinal left fielder Joe Medwick slid hard into third baseman Marv Owen. When Medwick took his defensive position the next inning, the Tiger fans showered him with fruit. Four times he was forced off the field. (Allegedly the concessionaire was increasing the price of an apple each time.) Finally Commissioner Landis ordered both Medwick and Owen out of the game. Owen later admitted that he overreacted (the score was 7–0 at the time) and probably helped to incite the crowd.

In 1940 umpire George Magerkurth was attacked in Ebbets Field by a Frank Germano. The story goes that the attacker, looking

toward a sentence of six months at hard labor, commented, "I'll be out in time for Opening Day."

The Cleveland Indians of 1940 earned the nickname of "Cry Babies" for their public dissatisfaction with manager Ossie Vitt. Fans demonstrated their displeasure by hurling baby bottles. The changing tables were turned, however, when Cleveland fans pelted the Detroit Tigers' Hank Greenberg with fruit in a critical series at the end of that year.

In 1941, a sportswriter, reflecting on "Fifty Years of Being a Baseball Fan," said that night baseball and broadcasting had resulted in a "marked increase in the baseball intelligence of the fans ... Perhaps this increased knowledge is responsible for one marked change for the better I have noticed over these fifty years—the improvement in sportsmanship of the fans."

His perception held true throughout the 1950s and '60s. But the 1970s were the noisiest years of fan violence since the early days of professional baseball. Unlike the literal "Kill the umpire" cries of the 1870s and '80s, however, the violence of the 1970s was undirected and mindless. Fans turned on each other, on the players, on the fields themselves. "Celebrations" after winning playoff or World Series games became orgies of destruction that spilled out of the ballparks into city streets.

Several ballpark promotions to boost attendance resulted in hometeam forfeits when fans got out of hand, most memorably a riot during a "10-cent Beer Night" at Cleveland in 1974. At Chicago's Comiskey Park in 1979, a "Disco Demolition" record-burning event began rowdy and got worse. The second game scheduled for that night was canceled and forfeited to Detroit.

An incident in the 1973 National League Championship Series in New York's Shea Stadium paralleled the Medwick/Owen spat. Pete Rose slid hard into Mets' shortstop Bud Harrelson; ballplayer fisticuffs resulted; the fans got into the act when Rose took his place in left field the next inning. Their garbage and abuse actually drove the Reds from the field. It took a peace delegation—Yogi Berra, Tom Seaver, Cleon Jones, Rusty Staub and Willie Mays (a legend on his last legs)—to walk to the outfield and settle the crowd.

All in all, the 1970s had nearly forty "noteworthy" examples of bad fan behavior, with 1974 and 1979 being the worst years. The nation's sportswriters were unable to offer viable reasons. One national columnist interviewed a medical nutritionist who said additives in the ballpark food were the culprit, another lay the blame at the feet of the Watergate scandal ("Richard Nixon loves baseball and used to come out to the ballpark. No more. Wonder why?").

The situation stayed consistently grim for the first few years of the 1980s. Detroit owner Jim Campbell closed the bleachers after fourteen fans were arrested for fighting during a 1980 contest. On the day that Pittsburgh paid tribute to Willie Stargell, the noble heart of its "family" team, a battery nearly struck Pirate right fielder Dave Parker, and Parker and Pittsburgh were never on speaking terms again. During a 1981 playoff game, a Yankee fan jumped from the stands and attacked umpire Mike Reilly.

Since then, baseball teams have taken strong steps to prevent the ugliness that fan rowdiness can become. Tightening of alcohol sales—smaller cups, limited quantities per sale, closing of beer sales after a specified inning—have shown success. In every park, security is emphasized. The massive troubles of the 1970s have not recurred.

Curiously, more incidents occurred of ballplayers going after fans than fans attacking ballplayers. Twice in 1981 Reggie Smith felt the need to slug a heckler. In 1985 Rick Miller of the California Angels felt he had to leap into the Anaheim stands to protect his wife and son from harassment. Three stars showed thin skins in 1991: Albert Belle of the Indians, a recovering alcoholic, threw a ball at (and hit) a Cleveland fan who had loudly invited him to a beer party. Cincinnati reliever Rob Dibble hurled a ball into the stands after a game, injuring an unsuspecting fan. And Oakland's Jose Canseco charged the stands after a New York fan who had overzealously reminded him of his late exit the night before from Madonna's apartment. (We learned later that Jose was only giving Madonna batting tips for her upcoming role in *A League of Their Own*.)

Gambling

One of the major factors that changed baseball from crude entertainment to "the National Pastime" was the eradication of gambling from the game. In the early days, betting at ballparks was widespread, with a double effect. First, the atmosphere in the crowd was rowdy and vulgar; people with money at stake behave differently from people who are there merely for the pleasure of seeing a game well played.

The second effect was more damaging to the game's health. Ballplayers themselves were bettors, and "hippodroming," or throwing games, was common.

Despite fines and bans and the inclusion of antigambling statutes in the league bylaws, gambling remained a large part of the game. Along with the notorious Hal Chase, figures as "respectable" as John McGraw, Ty Cobb, and Tris Speaker had their names linked to game fixing. Every year the *Spalding Baseball Guide* railed against gambling evils in its introduction.

From the 1870s through the early 1900s, the baseball pools were the most popular form of gambling. Similar to today's football pools, a pool bettor simply picked the team that would win the most games or score the most or fewest runs in the week, rather than bet on a team to win a particular game. Although certainly less harmful than direct game betting, these pools still offered the gamblers great chances to win money by "involving" players or managers.

The betting was substantial. According to Professor Harold Seymour, one such pool in Pittsburgh ranged over the entire East Coast and Canada, offering prizes of $1,000 a week. (The average per capita income annually was less than $550.) Another pool earned its managers from $30,000 to $50,000 a week. A 1911 estimate said that in the city of New Haven alone, 40,000 factory workers and boys held pool tickets costing $10,000.

Baseball understood the danger and kept responding, in fits and starts, to the problem. On August 5, 1908, the *New York Evening Telegram* said, "Efforts to stamp out gambling in baseball will immediately be made by the American League." (Interestingly, this followed by two days a spurious announcement in the *New York American*: "Bookmaking on baseball games in Chicago has not been profitable, and bookmakers announced they are going out of the business . . . 'The baseball "fan" is too wise. He knows too much about the game,' said one disgusted bookmaker.")

The effort to eliminate betting continued throughout the 1910s. *New York Times,* 1913: "Gamblers ejected from game"; 1914, "Gambling pools barred"; 1915, "Arrests for gambling." By 1919, the *Times* could state "Gambling stopped at all ball parks."

But it wasn't until 1920, the year of the Black Sox Scandal, that the action to eradicate gambling took hold. That year six people were arrested for gambling in Boston, four at the Polo Grounds, forty-seven in Chicago, five more in New York, ten at a Pacific Coast League game. The uproar over a gambling-run World Series had finally been too much for baseball and its fans to take.

Today baseball is still heavily gambled; Las Vegas estimates of legal baseball gambling place it at around thirty million dollars a year, about a third of that wagered on pro football. But with major league baseball playing 2,000 games a year and pro football one-tenth as many, the difference per game is substantial. When less is wagered, less can be won, which means less incentive for someone to attempt to "swing the odds."

Attendance

Before the National League was founded in 1876, baseball already had recorded single-game attendances as high as 40,000. In 1876, the patent of Bright's self-registering turnstile helped keep baseball body counts, although formal data were not regularly available until the turn of the century.

1880s. According to baseball historian Bill James, "Systematic data [were] not available. [But] attendance grew rapidly during this period."

- 1884. The first "bargain bill" doubleheader was held by Cleveland.
- 1889. The White Stockings drew 216,802 at home.

1890s. The average per game according to Bill James, was 2,000–3,000. He described overall attendance during this period as "Awful, and declining," reporting that "In 1890 . . . the Players' League drew 981,000 fans, the National League 814,000."
- The first promotion and advertising occurred: streetcar billing, signboards, handbills, window hangers, posters, boys on streets giving out handbills. Cincinnati ran paid ads in local papers (including the German-language one).
- Baseball cards were introduced as advertisements.
- "Children's Days" with 10¢ admission were popular, and women were admitted free on Ladies Days.
- 1891. "Base Ball Day" in Chicago let all amateur teams in uniform in free.

1900s. Total attendance was about 50 million, or 4,100 per game.
- 1908. "Take Me Out to the Ball Game" was introduced.
- 1909. The first concrete and steel stadiums were built.
- Old Timers Days began, along with "days" to honor individual players.

1910s. Total attendance was about 56 million, or 4,500 per game. James: "Essentially a decade of no growth." Seymour: "A prodigious $100 billion increase in national wealth brightened the first two decades of the century." The effects included suburbs with trolley lines and stadiums as the population moved from the country to the city.

Sunday baseball, which had disappeared with the demise of the American Association in 1891, was finally permitted by state and local legislatures. By 1918 it was legal in Cleveland, Detroit, and Washington. New York voted it in the following year. (Boston didn't allow it till 1929; the state of Pennsylvania, the final holdout, did not until 1933.)
- 1912. "Foreign-born spectators from seventeen different countries were observed at a game in New York." (*Spalding Baseball Guide*). Blacks also were becoming avid fans.
- 1913. In Brooklyn, the first Honor Roll Day was held.
- 1917. Scorecard winning numbers become common.
- 1917. The first "Knothole Gang" was organized in St. Louis.
- Ladies Day, which had been abolished by the National League in 1909, resurfaced eight years later.

1920s. Total attendance, about 93 million, or 7,500 per game. The Yankees exceeded a million almost every year. Average club attendance rose 50 percent over what it had been the decade before. Seymour states that even though 1920–1930 showed the largest single-decade rise in American population ever (17 million), baseball attendance rose at an even faster rate.
- 1921. Pittsburgh, August 5. The first baseball broadcast occurred, over KDKA radio with Harold Arlin. The World Series (Giants vs. Yankees) was also broadcast that year.
- 1925. Philip K. Wrigley allowed all Cubs game to be aired every day.

1930s. Total attendance, about 81 million, or 6,600 per game. The first night baseball game was held in 1880, at Nantasket Beach, Massachusetts. Amateur players from two local department stores performed in a promotion for the light company; the event has since been celebrated in a General Electric television commercial. Described as having "innumerable" errors because of lights, the first effort was not successful. Three years later, a game in Fort Wayne, Indiana, was.

Night baseball was first embraced on the minor league level. By 1934, fifteen of nineteen minor leagues had at least one lighted park. On May 24, 1935, Cincinnati owner Larry MacPhail hosted the first major league night game, at Crosley Field. A total of 20,422 attended, President Franklin D. Roosevelt threw the switch from the

White House. Ford Frick, then the National League president, threw out the first ball, and the Reds defeated the Dodgers 2–1.

In 1938, when MacPhail moved to Brooklyn, so did lights. The first Brooklyn night game, on June 15, was Johnny Vander Meer's second successive no-hitter. The first American League team to play night games was Philadelphia, in 1939. By 1940, seventy major league night games were scheduled. The only parks without lights that year were Washington, which added them the next year; Yankee Stadium and Braves Field (which added them in 1946); Fenway Park (1947); Detroit (1948); and Chicago's Wrigley Field (1988). The first World Series game to be played at night happened on October 13, 1971, when the Pirates beat the Orioles at Three Rivers Stadium.

- 1930. Major league attendance in 1930 was 10,132,272—the highest of any season between 1901 and 1945.
- 1931. Players' numbers became official practice in the AL.
- 1935. Night baseball was introduced.
- 1939. All teams broadcast their games on radio.
- August 26, 1939. The first TV broadcast was made.

1940s. Total attendance, about 135 million, or 11,000 per game.

James describes 1946 as "the Great Leap Forward"—1946 attendance was 18.5 million, 71 percent above the previous high. He lists as reasons the advent of night baseball, a return to economic normalcy after World War II, and great pennant races.

1950s. Total attendance, about 165 million, or 13,500 per game.

- 1951. The first nationally televised World Series game occurred.

David Voigt says, "In the years after the war, baseball crowds became predominantly family gatherings, united by the ethic of 'togetherness' in their fun-seeking. Television pushed the trend by bombarding families with ball games in the summertime."

1960s. Total attendance, about 224 million, or 14,000 per game.

- Bill Veeck added players' names to their uniforms in 1960.
- Major League Baseball expanded (after changing only two locations in fifty-seven years previously), adding eight new teams.

1970s. Total attendance, about 330 million, or 16,500 per game.

- 1976. Free agency was instated by an arbitrator's decree.
- 1977. Cable television began to have an impact on viewing.
- 1978. Dodgers are first team with single-season attendance of more than 3 million.

1980s. Total attendance, about 512 million, or 24,300 per game.

- 1981. A strike by players eliminated as many as fifty-nine games of the season for some teams.
- 1982. Braves take name of "America's Team" for themselves.
- 1984. Cal Griffith sells the Twins.
- 1985. The Pittsburgh Drug Trials.
- 1985. Players' strike settled in two days by Commissioner Ueberroth.
- 1986. For the first time, all twenty-six teams pass 1 million mark in attendance.
- 1988. Night baseball comes to Wrigley Field.
- 1989. Toronto's new SkyDome opens.

1990–1992. Total attendance, about 167 million, or 26,500 per game.

- 1991. New Comiskey Park opens in Chicago.
- 1991. Toronto is first club to draw 4 million fans.
- 1992. Oriole Park at Camden Yards opens in Baltimore.
- 1992. Second overall attendance drop since 1989, attributed to bad teams in New York and Los Angeles.

Concessions

Food and beverages have been a big part of the fun at a baseball game from the beginning. In 1859, New Orleans ballclubs pitched

"commodious tents for the ladies . . . under the umbrageous branches of fine old live oaks" to shelter their delicate skin from the sun as they enjoyed refreshments as well as the local baseball rivalry.

In the first decade of professional baseball, you could find an array of food: peanuts, soft drinks, crackerjacks, ice cream, cherry pie, cheese, chocolates, planked onions, and even tripe. Vendors moved through the crowd hawking sandwiches, soda water, and chewing gum. By 1871 the Olympics of Washington, D.C., had anticipated the "stadium clubs" of today's parks when they opened a first-class restaurant at the park.

Ballpark concession stands as we have come to know them can be traced to 1875, from which time we have a photo of the Boston team posed in front of their grandstand clearly showing large painted signs saying SODA and REFRESHMENTS. During his tenure as owner of the Chicago team, Albert Spalding himself encouraged concession stands, rather than hawkers moving throughout the crowd. The ChiFeds of 1914 lay claim to the earliest permanent concession *stand* in Wrigley Field.

Along with various sorts of munchies, ballparks sold beer and hard liquor, too. In his *Baseball: The Early Years,* Harold Seymour lists how many beer and whiskey glasses the typical ballpark bar stocked. But in 1880, the always image-conscious National League tried to eliminate ballpark drinking, and the result was the second major professional league, the American Association.

The four-year-old National League was trying to civilize its image, fighting the coarsening effect of gambling and promoting the calming influence of female attendance. As part of this effort, in 1880 the league passed a law forbidding gambling and the sale of alcohol at the ballparks. Unfortunately the Cincinnati team had a long tradition of beer and whiskey sales; they were averaging $3,000 a season of concession income. Breweries and distilleries were two of the largest industries in the city. So rather than face the financial damage of a no-beer ballpark, Cincinnati quit the league and was the leader in starting the Association, which detractors unsurprisingly called "The Beer and Whiskey League." The *New York World,* with perfect big city parochialism, charged that Cincinnati was a place to "watch for flying mugs . . . cheap sports and toughs" gathered behind home plate. Meanwhile, the New York Giants had a bar in full view of the field.

Although the major league American Association folded after ten years, and the attempt to eliminate gambling continued for twenty more years, baseball and beer have always remained linked.

Ballpark food and drink and scorecards can be traced back to the 1850s and sixties, but it wasn't till the 1880s that one man turned these concepts into enterprise: the first professional concessionaire and the first concession empire. Harry M. Stevens, a British immigrant, went to a baseball game in Columbus, Ohio, one afternoon (so the story goes). Realizing that there was no way to identify the players, Stevens sought out the owner and for $500 obtained the right to publish and sell a program. (Scorecards predate this anecdote by twenty years, but they were usually very modest items, with little or no advertising. It took Stevens to see the potential for profits.) "Scorecard Harry" sold the programs himself, calling out the now famous slogan "You can't tell the players without a scorecard."

The scorecard idea had an intriguing spinoff. Although the ballplayers had no numbers on their uniforms, they were given numbers on the scorecards. Then, as each player came to bat, his number was placed on the scoreboard. A scandal occurred when people brought old scorecards into the park, or bought "counterfeit" ones from "illegal" scorecard vendors outside. The teams were forced to change the scorecard numbers often.

Harry M. Stevens didn't stop with scorecards. An ambitious promoter, he started selling food: hard-boiled eggs, sandwiches, even coconut custard pies. He expanded his business into Wheeling, Pittsburgh, Toledo, and Milwaukee. A conversation with New York Giants manager John Montgomery Ward in Pittsburgh in 1893 led to Harry's landing the Polo Grounds concession. Before long the Stevens empire used its New York connection to include contracts with Madison Square Garden, hotels, and racetracks.

Stevens was always the innovator. On a cold day in the Polo

Grounds in 1901, ice cream wasn't selling, but Harry had an idea. He sent an assistant out for frankfurters (locally called "dachshund sausages"), which were sold in the neighborhood German groceries, heated the sausages in hot water, and put them in long buns so the fans could hold and eat them. The vendors shouted out what made these inventions so special: "Get 'em while they're hot! Get your red hots here!"

Sports cartoonist Thomas A. "Tad" Dorgan, looking for an idea that day, drew a sketch of waiters serving talking frankfurters ("You're not so hot!" "Bologna!"). Some say Dorgan couldn't remember how to spell "dachshund"; others say his spelling problem was with "frankfurter." For whatever reason, he coined the term "hot dogs" instead. Baseball food has never been the same. To this day, hot dogs, soda pop, and beer are the three biggest-selling items in every major league park.

Stevens continued to bring new ideas to his business. Realizing that fans might not purchase soda pop because raising their heads to drink might make them miss some of the game action, Harry came up with the idea of selling the soda with a straw. Now even the most devoted fan could quench his or her thirst and never miss a single pitch.

Still largely family-owned and -operated, the Harry M. Stevens Company, one hundred years later, is one of the largest ballpark concessionaires in the nation, with sales close to $175 million overall.

During the early decades of the century, only scattered figures are available, but they mention profits of several thousand dollars a year for the average club. By 1929, *Baseball Magazine* was saying that concession "receipts at Wrigley Field soar far above $100,000 a year." The same article stated that money from gate sales created 87.6 percent of the major leagues' gross profit, and concessions 5.5 percent.

But the end of the Second World War brought a new popularity to baseball. America's return to normalcy was also a return to the ballpark. As historian David Voigt puts it, "In the years after the war, baseball crowds became predominantly family gatherings, united by the ethic of 'togetherness' in their fun-seeking . . . The new breed of fans demanded and won comforts and pleasures from promoters . . . including neatly packaged food, canned music and giveaways. Food and drink sales now rivaled ticket sales in revenue production."

Today selling food at the ballparks, stadiums, and racetracks of America is big business. Since Harry M. Stevens, many companies have entered the field. At the most basic level, professional concessionaires provide and prepare all the food for the ballgames, hire and train their employees, and then agree to pay the contractee a percentage of their gross. (The few absolute exceptions are those teams which act as their own concessionaire, subcontracting specialized stands for specific food items to outside companies—Kentucky Fried Chicken, Burger King, etc.)

By 1990 the average tab for the fan at a ballgame ran from $4 to $6 (that's up from 70¢ to 90¢ in the 1960s), so rough figures indicate that a ballclub with 2 million in attendance will generate as much as $12 million in concessions. How much the team gets, however, depends upon its contract with the ballpark's owners.

The contract to provide concession services may be with the baseball team, or it may be with the stadium authority, or it may be with the city or municipality that owns the stadium. Everyone gets a share; the main contractee gets the most. For example, some concessionaires pay as much as 52 percent of their receipts back to the contractee. If the baseball team signed the contract, it could receive 47 percent of that 52 percent, and give the rest to the other partners. Or the club could receive 24 or 25 percent (which is about average).

But few baseball teams own their ballparks; most share the facility with pro football or other teams. So the football team could receive a certain percentage of the gross, the baseball team another, the stadium authority another. In certain *categories* the percentage can vary; the baseball club may get a bigger percentage of soft drink sales than the football team, which might get more for hot drink sales; the city may take the lion's share of the concessionaire income and allot only a certain percentage to the teams, or vice versa.

With only a handful of major concessionaires (Harry M. Stevens, ARA Services, Ogden Allied, Sportservice, and a few others), and with contracts that typically run for fifteen to eighteen years (some for thirty), the competition is fierce.

The growth of fast food restaurants has changed the kinds of food available in ballparks, by making certain kinds of packaging acceptable. Because fans have become more demanding and the American palate is changing, concessionaires experiment, sometimes adding as many as twenty new menu items per year. For some reason soft ice cream is a hit in air-conditioned Houston, while windy Comiskey is selling a lot of cold deli sandwiches and funnel cakes. Cleveland is trying onion rings. Oriole Park at Camden Yards brags about its Maryland crab cakes ("made here fresh daily") and crab soup. Sausage varieties way past the humble hot dog (Italian, Polish, brat– and knockwursts) have proliferated. And in Toronto's SkyDome, the number two selling item in the park is the Big Mac, according to their chief concessionaire, McDonald's. But despite all the innovations, baseball fans remain traditionalists at heart.

In addition, the modern stadiums of today are echoing the earlier days, with their "cafes" and restaurants offering more serious fare before, during, and after the game. Homer Rose, longtime employee of the Harry M. Stevens Company, and grandson of Harry himself, said, "At first it was peanuts, ice cream cones, lemonade, and bottled soft drinks. Now in the dining rooms and private boxes we're serving shrimp salads and full-course dinners." The Stevens Company alone runs restaurants at dozens of racetracks and stadiums.

On the average, a typical ballpark hot dog costs $1.25 today, 87 years after its Polo Grounds introduction. A larger version sells for about $2.00. Hamburgers run close to $2.00, pizza $1.50 or so, french fries nearly $1.25, ice cream $1.00, and popcorn anywhere from $1.00 to twice that.

One more change is becoming apparent—beer, a ballpark staple since the beginning, is again less easy to obtain. Concern about drunk driving has resulted in every team selling beer in smaller servings, allowing fewer servings to be sold to one person at one time, having special no-alcohol sections, and stopping sales after a certain time in the game. So far, no one has raised a serious voice about banning all alcohol sales at the ballpark.

Bat, Ball, and Glove

Bill Felber

To promote uniformity and fair competition, rulesmakers have always felt the need to define how the ball should be made. That definition has changed very little over the course of more than a century. Notice how similar are the two definitions that follow, the first from an 1861 convention of the National Association of Base Ball Players, and the second taken from the Official Baseball Rules of 1992:

1861. "The ball must weigh not less than five and one-half, nor more than five and three-fourths ounces avoirdupois. It must measure not less than nine and one-half, nor more than nine and three-fourths inches in circumference. It must be composed of India rubber and yarn, covered with leather."

1992. "The ball shall be a sphere formed by yarn wound around a small core of cork, rubber or similar material, covered with two stripes of white horsehide or cowhide, tightly stitched together. It shall weigh not less than five nor more than five and one-quarter ounces avoirdupois and measure not less than nine nor more than nine and one-quarter inches in circumference."

How greatly has the ball changed in a century and a quarter? It is about five percent smaller, about nine percent lighter. Its core is different. The stitching is tighter. Still, the ball put in play in the amateur contests of 1861 would pass muster by modern rules.

That is not to say that the baseball of Civil War days and the official model of today are virtually identical. Today's ball is far more resilient and travels greater distances. The modern baseball also undergoes far less wear and tear. For many years it was customary for a game ball, even a mushy, discolored or lopsided one, to be kept in play until it was irretrievably lost. The idea of going through a few dozen boxes of balls per game—common today—would have seemed frivolously wasteful to great grandpa.

As was the case with the ball, the rulebook has licensed only minor adjustments with the bat, and then, generally, only by way of greater specificity. Again, compare the rules governing play in 1861 with the slightly more elaborate section from the modern rulebook:

1861. "The bat must be round, and must not exceed two and one-half inches in diameter in the thickest part. It must be made of wood, and may be of any length to suit the striker."

1992. "The bat shall be a smooth, rounded stick not more than two and three-quarter inches in diameter at the thickest part and not more than 42 inches in length. The bat shall be one piece of solid wood, or formed from a block of wood consisting of two or more pieces of wood bonded together with an adhesive in such way that the grain direction in all pieces is essentially parallel to the length of the bat. Any such laminated bat shall contain only wood or adhesive."

The modern rule also contains an allowance for a small "cupping" of up to one inch at the bat's end, and for use of a grip-improving substance on the bat handle. There is a length limit, but in today's major leagues it is virtually unheard-of for a bat to exceed thirty-six inches in length, much less forty-two. The modern bat has gained one-quarter of an inch in girth over its ancestor, but its biggest change—the trend toward ever lighter bats—was not mandated.

Place hitters of the years before 1920 coveted heavy "wagon tongue" models with thick barrels capable of driving the ball over the infield, even at the expense of bat speed. Cap Anson, legendary star of the Chicago White Stockings, used just such a bat, reputedly weighing in at a manly three pounds and then some. In the 1920s Babe Ruth menaced opposing pitchers with a 48 ounce model bat. But Ruth saw to it that the bat handle was tapered to accommodate his smaller than normal hands.

The modern bat has the skinny handle but seldom weighs more than thirty-three ounces. The reason is simple: batting instructors, who once looked upon mass as the key factor behind a mighty poke, now focus on bat speed instead. The faster a batter can move the bat through the strike zone, the greater force applied to the ball. And the greater force applied, the farther the ball travels.

As for gloves . . . in the game's early days players were expected to catch the ball barehanded. Until 1864 they were aided in that effort by a rule recording an out if a ball was caught on the first bounce. The earliest documented evidence of a fielding glove in big-league play was in 1875 by St. Louis first baseman Charlie Waitt. In his book *America's National Game* (1911), Albert Spalding reported that in a game that year Waitt donned a street-dress leather glove on his fielding hand. Waitt reportedly was ridiculed league-wide. But as more prominent players adopted Waitt's concept, the notion gradually came to be accepted. It was not until 1894, however, when third baseman Jerry Denny retired, that the era of the barehanded fielder passed.

The early gloves, lacking webbing and lacing, merely provided protection for the hands. Today larger, better-padded, webbed, laced, and pocketed gloves might more appropriately be described as "fielding devices," because it is they, not the fielder's hands, that do much of the actual fielding work. Also, and as verification of the first point, players of the previous century often wore gloves on both hands. For the throwing hand, they would simply snip the glove at the fingers for dexterity.

It was not until 1895 that stipulations concerning use of gloves were included in the rules: those limited the size of gloves to ten ounces and fourteen inches circumference for all players except catchers and first basemen, who were permitted to use any size glove. Today's rulebook, conversely, takes a page and a half to specify dimensions, materials, lacings, and webbings for gloves. Today there are thirteen different size limitations on the standard fielder's glove alone, ranging from palm width to the length of each separate finger.

Credit commonly is given to a pitcher, spitballer Bill Doak of the St. Louis Cardinals, for advancing glove technology from the primordial state. In 1920 Doak approached a glove manufacturer with a plan for a glove that included a square of reinforced webbing between the thumb and finger sections as an additional

aid to fielding. Previously the fingers simply had been laced together, or were left to flap independently. So advanced was Doak's model, by the way, that it remained popular for almost thirty years. And every subsequent advance in glove design, whether it be the hinged heel, short or long fingered design, or advanced webbing, can be traced to a concept originated by Doak.

Questions remained about enforcement of the 1950 size limits, however, as fielders' gloves and catchers' mitts seemed to grow with each passing year. So in 1972 the rules committee drafted the present thirteen-point measuring system. Fortunately, there is no record of a game ever being halted while a manager challenged the legality of a fielder's glove on all thirteen points.

Early Team Names

John Thorn

The Newark, New Jersey, team in the 1884 Eastern League had the most quotidian nickname of all time—the Domestics. Contrast that with its league rivals the Quicksteps of Wilmington, Delaware, and the Actives of Reading, Pennsylvania.

The famous Excelsior Club of Brooklyn was originally formed in the 1850s as the JYBBBC, standing for the Jolly Young Bachelors Base Ball Club.

Many clubs were named after volunteer fire companies, such as the Knickerbockers and Mutuals, both of New York, the Alerts of Philadelphia, the Americus of Newark, the Resolutes of Elizabeth, New Jersey, and countless more in this vigilant vein.

The Civil War supplied some grand names, such as the Antietam of Hagerstown, Maryland, the Monitor of Westport, Connecticut, and the McLellan of New Jersey.

Cosmological visions might have led to the naming of the Eons of Portland, Maine, the Constellations of Brooklyn, the Meteors of Addison, New York, the Mystics of New York, the Orions of Philadelphia, and the Harmony of Brooklyn.

Those of an exclamatory bent might have named the Eurekas of Newark, the Excelsiors of Brooklyn, and the Hunkidoris of Wheeling, West Virginia.

Literature may have given us the Pequods of New London, Connecticut, the Hiawathas of Kittanning, Pennsylvania, and the Mohicans of Hightstown, Maryland.

One is caught short by the Surprise Club of West Farms, New York, and the Black Joke of New York, and the Wide Awakes of Hartford and Monumentals of Baltimore.

On the major league level, besides the oft-remarked Cleveland Spiders and Brooklyn Bridegrooms, we have such marvels as the Molly Maguires of Cleveland (as the current Indians were known for a couple of years at the turn of the century), the New York Highlanders (so named not only because their ballpark, known as Hilltop Park, occupied the high ground now taken by Columbia Presbyterian, but also because their owner's name was Joseph Gordon . . . Gordon's Highlanders). We also have, as major league entrants, the Troy Haymakers; St. Louis Maroons, a.k.a. Black Diamonds; Boston Rustlers (later known as the Braves); Boston Pilgrims (today's Red Sox); Chicago Whales (Federal League, which also gave us the Newark Peps, Baltimore Terrapins, and Brooklyn Tip-Tops); Baltimore Canaries (National Association, 1872–74); Worcester Ruby Legs; Louisville Eclipse; Cincinnati Porkers; Toledo Maumees; and the Cleveland (again!) Infants.

Which last named brings to mind the neat little story of Adrian Anson and the White Stockings: as a young player, before he became the famous captain of the Chicago nine, thus the nickname "Cap," he was an umpire-baiter and complainer *par excellence* for the Rockford Forest City and Philadelphia Athletic clubs, at which time his universally accepted nickname was "Baby"—this for being a crybaby, principally, but also because he was the first white baby born in Marshalltown, Iowa, a tedious fact that became even more tiresome through repetition in the press. As Anson's playing career extended prodigiously into its third decade, his nickname became "Pop," and his inexperienced charges, the wretched White Stockings of 1893 and '94, became known as the Colts. This team nickname was also the basis of a starring vehicle that melodramatist Charles Hoyt wrote for Anson in 1895 called *The Runaway Colt.* When Chicago fired Anson as manager after the 1897 season, Pop's team became known in the press as the Orphans.

Famous Firsts

David Pietrusza

1845 Alexander Cartwright and the Knickerbocker Base Ball Club codify playing rules; also, first box score of baseball game, eight men to the side, is printed in New York *Morning News.*

1846 At Elysian Fields on June 19 in Hoboken, New Jersey, the N.Y. Knickerbockers lose to the New York Club in the first match game under Cartwright's rules.

1849 Knickerbockers develop first uniforms (colors: blue & white).

1853 First box score of Knick-style game is printed in New York *Clipper.*

1856 Henry Chadwick becomes the first regular baseball reporter.

1858 First admission (50 cents) charged, for game between All-Star teams representing New York and Brooklyn played at Long Island's Fashion Race Course on July 20.

1859 At Pittsfield, Massachusetts, on July 1, Amherst defeats Williams College 73–32 in first college game.

1860 The Excelsiors of Brooklyn make the first "road trip." Their first stop: Albany's Washington Parade Grounds on July 2.

1862 William Cammeyer's Union Grounds in Brooklyn is the first enclosed ballpark; it opens on May 15.

1863 First calling of balls and strikes.

1865 Ed Cuthbert of the Keystones steals the first base.

1866 Bob Addy of Rockford employs the first slide to steal a base; the Brooklyn Atlantics' Tom Barlow lays down the first bunt.

1867 First use of curveball, by William A. "Candy" Cummings.

1869 The Cincinnati Red Stockings are the first fully professional team; they are also the first team to wear knickers.

1871 First professional league is formed—the National Association; first game: Cleveland Forest Citys lose 2–0 at Fort Wayne on May 4.

1873 First doubleheader: Resolutes vs. Boston, July 4.

1874 Boston Red Stockings and Philadelphia Athletics conduct first foreign tour.

1875 Philadelphia's Joe Borden hurls first no-hitter in pro ranks, July 28.

1876 National League's first game: Boston at Philadelphia on April 22.

1877 International League becomes the first minor league; Tecumsehs and Maple Leafs are the first foreign professional teams; first professional gambling scandal—four Louisville players expelled from game.

1878 Turnstiles introduced; Paul Hines of Providence wins first triple crown and executes first unassisted triple play (May 8); Bud Fowler is first black in pro ball, for Lynn Live Oaks of International Association.

1879 Reserve clause first used.

1880 First night game—between two department store teams, at Nantasket Beach in Massachusetts; Worcester's Lee Richmond hurls first perfect game, against Cleveland on June 12.

1882 American Association introduces first salaried umpiring staff; first postseason playoff; first professional doubleheader, Providence vs. Worcester, September 25.

1884 First "third major league," the Union Association; first blacks in Major League Baseball—Moses and Weldy Walker of Toledo (AA).

1885 Umpires and catchers use first chest protectors.

1886 Players organize first union, "The Brotherhood of Ball Players"; first spring training camp (Chicago White Stockings) at Hot Springs, Arkansas.

1887 Charles Zimmer is first catcher to play consistently behind the batter; Baltimore's Mike Griffin of Baltimore and Cincinnati's George "White Wings" Tebeau are the first to homer in their first major league at-bat; both do it on the same day, April 16.

1888 First round-the-world baseball tour, by Chicago White Stockings and all-star squad; "Casey at the Bat" makes its debut in print and on the stage.

1892 National League allows Sunday baseball.

1894 Boston's Bobby Lowe is first major league player to smash four homers in one game.

1901 First American League game; Cleveland loses 8–7 at Chicago on April 24.

1903 First modern World Series—Boston defeats Pittsburgh five games to three.

1907 Giants catcher Roger Bresnahan introduces shin guards.

1909 First concrete-and-steel park opens—Philadelphia's Shibe Park; Cleveland's Neal Ball turns first modern unassisted triple play in majors, on July 19; William Howard Taft is first President to throw out "first ball".

1910 First cork-centered ball.

1911 First MVP Awards to the Cubs' Frank Schulte and the Tigers' Ty Cobb.

1917 First "knothole gang" organized in St. Louis.

1920 First Japanese pro team, the Nihon Undo Kyokai.

1921 First baseball commissioner, Kenesaw Mountain Landis; first radio broadcast of a game, by Harold Arlin of KDKA from Forbes Field on August 5; first World Series broadcast (Yankees vs. Giants).

1926 First amplifiers used (at Polo Grounds).

1930 First successful night ball in minors.

1933 First All-Star Game, at Chicago's Comiskey Park on July 6.

1935 First major league night game; Phils at Reds, May 24.

1936 First pro league in Japan; first players elected to Hall of Fame (Ty Cobb, Babe Ruth, Christy Mathewson, Honus Wagner, Walter Johnson).

1939 First AL night game, at Philadelphia Shibe Park on May 16; first televised game, from Ebbets Field on August 26.

1941 Dodgers are first club to wear batting helmets.

1946 Montreal's Jackie Robinson is the century's first black professional player.

1947 Robinson becomes first modern major league black player; Cleveland's Larry Doby is first black player in AL; first Rookie-of-the-Year Awards.

1951 Emmett Ashford is first black pro umpire (Southwestern International League); first game televised coast-to-coast (last game of NL Playoff); first nationally televised World Series (Yankees vs. Giants).

1956 Don Larsen hurls first World Series perfect game, on October 8.

1956 Frank Umont and Ed Rommel are first major league umps to wear eyeglasses on field.

1957 First Gold Glove Awards.

1959 Joe Cronin becomes first player to become league president when he assumes head of American League.

1962 Jackie Robinson becomes the first black elected to the Hall of Fame.

1965 First enclosed stadium, the Astrodome, opens on April 9.

1966 First major league black umpire, Emmett Ashford of AL.

1969 First major league game outside U.S., St. Louis at Montreal's Jarry Park on April 14.

1970 First strike by major league umpires—occurs during playoffs.

1972 First major league player strike; Bernice Gera is first female professional umpire.

1973 The Yankees' Ron Blomberg becomes the first designated hitter, on April 6.

1974 First major league Hispanic umpire: Armando Rodriguez in AL.

1975 Indians hire Frank Robinson as first black manager; first night World Series game—Baltimore at Pittsburgh on October 13; first players declared free-agents (on December 23), Andy Messersmith and Dave McNally.

1982 Joel Youngblood becomes first major league player to play for two different teams (Mets & Expos) in two different cities (Chicago & Philadelphia) on same day, August 4.

1989 Bill White becomes first black league president (NL).

1991 First modern teams to go from last to first (Twins and Braves) meet in World Series.

1992 First non-U.S. world champion, Toronto Blue Jays.

Notes on Contributors

Paul D. Adomites was born and raised in Pittsburgh, and lives there now. He was publications director for the Society for American Baseball Research from 1987–1990. He is the founding editor of *The SABR Review of Books* and its successor, *The Cooperstown Review,* which is published by his company, Sheraden Publishing.

Larry Amman was born and raised in the suburbs of Detroit. He graduated from Wayne State University with a B.A. in history and political science in 1967, then served in the U.S. Army Intelligence in Vietnam and Germany. Although he has lived in Washington, D.C., for the last ten years, the Detroit Tigers remain his favorite team. He has published several articles on the Tigers, and has compiled all their game-winning RBIs from 1901–1980. He is currently employed as a travel agent.

Dennis Bingham is editor of the Chicago Police Department's Publications Section, a freelance cartoonist, and an umpire for several adult and youth baseball leagues in the Chicago area. (His umpiring partner is often his father, Bill, who taught him the rules.) Bingham served as a historical adviser for the movie *Eight Men Out,* in which he also played a bit part as umpire Billy Evans. He was associate editor of the SABR publication *Baseball in Chicago* and has headed the rules section of SABR's Umpires and Rules Committee since its formation. A White Sox fan, Bingham lives with his wife, Diane, and sons Sean, Kevin and Dennis on Chicago's South Side.

Dick Clark, co-chairman of SABR's Negro Leagues Committee, was born and raised in Detroit and has been a lifelong Tiger fan. He has been active in Negro Leagues research for over ten years and has served as a consultant for numerous books on the subject. A resident of Ypsilanti, Michigan, he is the author of several articles on the Negro Leagues for *The Baseball Research Journal* and *The National Pastime.*

Merritt Clifton, an award-winning veteran environmental journalist, is news editor for *The Animals' Agenda,* an international magazine of animal rights and ecology. Clifton also is author of numerous works on "outlaw" baseball, especially as played in Quebec, Vermont, Japan, and Mexico, and *Relative Baseball,* a pioneering sabermetric study. Having recently relocated from Quebec to Connecticut, he would like to find a team that plays Saturdays or Sundays and could use an experienced righthander.

Eliot Cohen writes "Breaking Balls" for the Washington, D.C., weekly *City Paper,* edits *Who's Who In Baseball,* and has covered the Orioles, Mets, and Yankees as a wire service correspondent. Founder, editor and publisher of the pioneering newsletter *Major League Monthly* during its five-year printspan, Cohen is also the author of *The 1990 Baseball Annual* (with John Thorn and Pete Palmer) and *My Greatest Day In Baseball,* and has written for *Sports Illustrated, USA Today Baseball Weekly, The Sporting News,* and two editions of *The Elias Baseball Analyst.* Cohen is also a key pinch hitter for the Atlanta Braves as a newswriter for their CNN–Washington farm team.

Neil Cohen toiled for much of his professional career at *Sport* magazine, where he held positions of editor and managing editor. Following that, he was unlucky enough to be present at the demise of *The National Sports Daily,* where he served as senior editor. Lately Neil has turned his attention to explaining sports and its lessons to children as an associate editor at *Sports Illustrated for Kids* Books. He lives in Brooklyn, New York, with his wife and son.

L. Robert Davids, retired writer and historian, was born in rural Iowa in 1926. He graduated from the University of Missouri (BJ '49; MA '51) and received his Ph.D. from Georgetown University in 1961. He served in the Army Air Corps from 1944–1946 and worked for the U.S. Government in Washington, D.C., from 1951–1981. Davids organized SABR in 1971, served four years as president, and edited SABR publications from 1971–1983. He was a freelance writer for *The Sporting News* from 1951–1965, published *Baseball Briefs* from 1971–1975 and 1981–1990, and produced *Insider's Baseball* (Scribners) in 1983.

Bill Deane is senior research associate at the National Baseball Library in Cooperstown, New York. He has written for numerous baseball publications, including *Baseball Digest, Street & Smith's, The National Pastime,* and *The Bill James Baseball Abstract.* Born in Poughkeepsie, New York, in 1957, he now resides in Fly Creek, New York, with his wife, Pam, and daughter, Sarah.

Eddie Epstein is currently director of research and statistics for the Baltimore Orioles. In that capacity he evaluates professional talent, participates in the negotiation of major league player contracts, and provides information to the team's manager about upcoming opponents. His work has been published in Bill James' *The Baseball Book* and *Baseball Abstract, Sports Illustrated, USA Today Baseball Weekly,* and *The Sporting News.* A Baltimore native, Eddie earned a BA (1981) and an MA (1985) from the University of Delaware.

Bill Felber is executive editor of *The Manhattan Mercury* (Manhattan, Kansas). A native of Chicago, he has written articles on various aspects of baseball history that have appeared in journals such as *The National Pastime.* His treatment of the St. Louis Browns appeared in *The Encyclopedia of Major League Baseball Teams* (Meckler). He is a member of SABR.

Cappy Gagnon joined SABR in 1977 and has written articles for its *Baseball Research Journal* on Roger Bresnahan, Ed Reulbach, and the subject of "batting eye." Additionally, he has written for the Greenwood Press *Baseball Biographical Encyclopedia, The Ballplayers, The Chronological History of Baseball, Baseball Digest,* and *Baseball Quarterly Reviews,* and is in the midst of writing *Anson to Yaz,* a book about the sixty-five major leaguers who attended Notre Dame. Gagnon, who served two terms as SABR president, is currently serving as technical services manager of the Olympia (Washington) Police Department.

Larry R. Gerlach is professor of American sports history at the University of Utah. He is a member of the editorial board of *Nine,* the council of the North American Society of Sports History, the board of directors of SABR, and chair of SABR's Umpires and Rules Committee. He has published numerous

the Manager Roster as it appears in *Total Baseball*, and in 1992 won SABR's Bob Davids Award.

Richard Topp is an "accountant-turned-historian" from Chicago. A member of the Society for American Baseball Research since 1975, he served for many years as chairman of its biographical committee; from 1989 to 1991, he was SABR president. Topp has compiled the most extensive biographical data file on major league players since 1871, and his research has appeared in numerous books and newspapers across the nation. In 1988 he shared with Bob Tiemann of St. Louis an award given by SABR for his research on managers; this research informs the Manager Roster in *Total Baseball*.

Jules Tygiel is a professor of history at San Francisco State University. He is the author of *Baseball's Great Experiment: Jackie Robinson and his Legacy* (Oxford University Press, 1983; Vintage Paperback edition, 1984) and has contributed articles to many periodicals.

David Quentin Voigt is a baseball historian and a professor of sociology and anthropology at Albright College in Reading, Pennsylvania, where he teaches a popular course entitled "Baseball in American Culture." Over the years, he has written seven books and more than a hundred articles on the subject of baseball. His major works include *American Baseball*, a three-volume history (he is currently working on the fourth volume, as well as a volume on big league baseball in the 1890s); *Baseball: An Illustrated History*, a single volume published in 1987 by the Pennsylvania State University Press; and *America Through Baseball*. A past president of SABR, Voigt and his wife, Virginia, a teacher, reside in Shillington, Pennsylvania.

With appreciation to these readers of *Total Baseball 1* who sent in corrections or made suggestions on how to improve the second edition:

Larry Amman, Ray Andreotti, Mel Bailey, Craig Barbarino, Edgar K. Beatty, James M. Beck, Joseph R. Bender, Robert Beukelher, John Booth, Jim Bostain, Therese R. Brown, J. Paul Browne, Bob Cambris, Kevin A. Carleton, Bob Carroll, Anthony M. Chieco, Ken Coleman, Steve Cooper, Owen Curtis, Clay Davenport, L. Robert Davids, Bill Deane, Harold Dellinger, Ted D. DeVries, Don Dewey, Raymond A. DiSanto, Sam Elfand, Don Elliott, John Emerson, Eddie Epstein, Kenneth Fink, Robert L. Franz, Andrew Fussner, Cam Gibson, Steven Goldberg, Ray Gonzalez, Dan Greenia, Bill Haber, Rod Hay, Bob Hoie, Fred Ivor-Campbell, Tom Jennings, Bill Jensen, Warren Johnson, Cliff Kachline, James Kaufman, Dave Kemp, Larry Kempster, Randall Kleinman, Jack Lang, Ron Liebman, Jerry Malloy, James F. Maxfield, Bob McConnell, Joe M. McGowan, David Molnar, George S. Moskal, Frank J. Mueller, Neil Munro, Thomas L. Nester, Dave Nichols, Tom O'Brien, Yoshio Ohno, S. Mark Parker, Paul E. Pennebaker, Peretz Perl, Dave Pietrusza, Mike Post, Jorgen Rasmussen, Allan Rausch, Andrew Richardson, John Rickert, John M. Roca, Winslow Rogers, Tom Ruane, Bill Rubenstein, David Schermer, Leon Schmerhold, John Schwartz, Alfred Secondi, Sy Siegel, Richard Siegelman, Al Smith, David M. Snyder, David Stephan, Mike Sparks, Lyle Spatz, Dean Sullivan, Isaac Thorn, Richard Topp, Stephen Toth, T. Brook Treakle III, Jim Troisi, Jim Tuttle, Jim Vail, Cullen P. Vane, David Vincent, Joseph M. Wayman, Jim Weigand, Bernard Weisberger, Christopher Williams, Frank Williams, Joseph C. Williams, Ralph Winnie, Jim Wright, and Ed Yerha.

And to these readers of *Total Baseball II* who improved the third edition:

David Aceto, Robert Browning, Chuck Carey, Keith Carlson, Garrett M. Casey, Jim Conroy, Bob Davids, Bill Deane, Dennis DeValeria, Ted DiTullio, Robert Downer, Tom Dunken, Eddie Epstein, Ken Fetterman, Bob Franzosa, Gary Gillette, Jay Gregory, Charlie Harville, Jeffrey Hatt, Ralph Horton, Jeff James, Darlene Kadlecik, Jerry Kahn, John Kenyon, Patrick Kinas, Matthew Lesniewski, Morris Levin, Don Luce, Ed Luteran, Jeff Magalif, E.H. Marshall, Richard A. Marston, Ronald A. Mayer, John P. McBride, John McClaran, Randy Messel, Steve Moore, Neil Munro, John O'Malley, Ed Oswalt, Richard Pardoe, Danny Radakovich, Matt Rapacz, Louis Rauco, Matt Reese, Eric Reinholdt, Dennis Repp, John Richards, Bob Richardson, John M. Roca, Seth D. Rodgers, John Schwartz, John Scott, Jim Smith, Dave Smith, Lewis J. Snyder, Lyle Spatz, Alan Steinberg, David Stephan, James Swetnam, Robert Tiemann, Harry L. Turtledove, Bill Wallace, Patrick K. Walsh, Joe Wayman, Jim Weigand, Frank Williams, Walt Wilson, and Edgar M. Wyatt.

Glossary of Statistical Terms

This Glossary contains definitions of the statistical terms and measures carried in Part 2 of *Total Baseball* that may be unfamiliar to the average baseball fan or that represent what today might seem odd scoring practices. The Glossary will also be of value to the advanced fan who wishes to know more about the mathematical and theoretical foundations of certain statistics. Also included at the end of this section are the team and league abbreviations used in this book.

/A "Adjusted"; means that the statistic to the immediate left of this mark has been normalized to league average and adjusted for home park factor. Stats that are normalized in this book are Batting Runs, Production, Batting Average, On Base Percentage, Slugging Average, Earned Run Average, and Pitcher Runs.

Assist Although credited to pitchers on strikeouts in some of baseball's early years, not counted as such in this volume.

Assist Average Assists divided by games played. Stat created by Philadelphia baseball writer Al Wright in 1875.

At-Bats Charged to batters on sacrifice hits, 1889–1894; on sacrifice-fly situations, 1931–1938 and 1940–1953; bases on balls, 1876, 1887. However, we did not count at-bats for bases on balls.

Average and Over Early form of expressing averages for base hits, runs, and outs. The average of a batter with 23 hits in six games would be not 3.83 but 3–5 (an average of 3 with an overage, or remainder, of 5); borrowed from cricket.

Average Bases Allowed A pitcher's total bases allowed, divided by his innings pitched—what might be termed Opponents' Slugging Average. Created by Alfred P. Berry in 1951.

Average Batting (Pitching, Fielding) Skill The great philosophical as well as statistical puzzler: after one has normalized a player's performance to that of his league, how does one compare one season's league average with that of another far removed in time? Does a .266 batting average in the National League of 1902 mean the same thing as a .266 batting average in the American League of 1977?

Bases on Balls Counted as an out for batters in 1876 and as a hit for batters in 1887, but as neither throughout this book. Awarded for a varying number of errant pitches since 1876, from nine in that year to the current four (standardized in 1889). (After 1887, the batter was no longer allowed to specify strike zone as waist to shoulders or waist to shins.)

Bases on Balls Percentage Batters' stat: most walks per 100 at-bats.

Bases on Balls Per Game Game defined as nine innings; league-leading pitchers calculated on basis of lowest mark; computed as bases on balls times nine, divided by innings.

Base-Out Percentage Barry Codell's stat for measuring complete offensive performance, in which the elements of the numerator represent bases gained while the events in the denominator represent outs produced (sacrifices and sacrifice flies appear in both because they achieve both—gaining a base for the team while costing it an out). The formula:

$$\frac{\text{Total Bases} + \text{Walks} + \text{HBP} + \text{Steals} + \text{Sacrifices} + \text{Sacrifice Flies}}{\text{At-bats} - \text{Hits} + \text{Caught Stealing} + \text{GIDP} + \text{Sac.} + \text{Sac. Flies}}$$

(GIDP, in the equation above, stands for Grounded Into Double Play; HBP for Hit By Pitch.)

Batters Facing Pitcher Unavailable before 1909 in the National League and 1908 in the American; for earlier years, constructed from available data in this manner: subtract league base hits from league at-bats, divide by league innings pitched, multiply by the pitcher's innings, and add his hits allowed, walks, hit by pitch, and sacrifice hits, if available. Abbreviated as BFP.

Batter's Park Factor The Park Factor shown in the batters' section of the team statistics in the Annual Record, Player Register, and Home-Road Statistics. Above 100 means batters benefited from playing half their games in a good hitting park. Abbreviated as BPF or, in what are clearly batters' stats (as in the Player Register) simply as PF. See entry for *Park Factor* for an exhaustive explanation of the computation.

Battery Errors In baseball's early years, wild pitches, passed balls, and hit batsmen were lumped together in the statistical summary of a game as *battery errors* and were charged against the fielding percentage of the pitcher or catcher. Such battery errors have been removed from individual and team stats for this book.

Batting Average Calculated as base hits divided by at-bats ever since its first appearance in print in 1874. In 1876 walks were counted as at-bats, and in 1887 they were counted as at-bats and as hits. For this book, batting averages are computed in uniform fashion throughout baseball history. Abbreviated in Part 2 of this volume as AVG, although it is also commonly abbreviated BA.

Batting Runs The Linear Weights measure of runs contributed *beyond* those of a league-average batter or team, such league average defined as zero. The formula depends upon the run values for each offensive event that resulted from Pete Palmer's 1978 computer simulation of all major league games played since 1901. Run values change marginally with changing conditions of play (an out costs a team more in a hitters' year, such as 1930, than in a pitchers' year, such as 1908), and they differ slightly up and down the batting order (a homer is not worth as much to the leadoff hitter as it is to the fifth-place batter; a walk is worth more for the man batting second than for the man batting eighth); however, these differences have been averaged out historically in the figures below.

$$\text{Runs} = (.47)1B + (.78)2B + (1.09)3B + (1.40)HR + (.33)(BB + HB) - (.25)(AB - H) - (.50)OOB$$

(An out is considered to be a hitless at-bat and its value is set so that the sum of all events times their frequency is zero, thus establishing zero as the baseline, or norm, for performance.)

Some events one might expect to see included in this formula but that do not appear are sacrifices, sacrifice hits, grounded into double plays, and reached on error. The last is not known for most years and in the official statistics is indistinguishable from outs on base (OOB). The sacrifice has values that essentially cancel one another, trading an out for an advanced base which, often as not, leaves the team in a situation with poorer run potential than it had before the sacrifice. The sacrifice fly has dubious run value because it is entirely dependent on a situation not under the batter's control: while a single or a walk or a hit by pitch always has potential run value, a long fly does not unless a man happens to be poised at third base. Last, the grounded into double play is to a far greater extent a function of one's

2354

place in the batting order than it is of poor speed or failure in the clutch, and thus it does not find a home in a formula applicable to all batters. It is no accident that Hank Aaron, who ran well for most of his long career and wasn't too shabby in the clutch, hit into more DPs than anyone else, nor that Roberto Clemente, Al Kaline, and Frank Robinson, who fit the same description, are also among the ten "worst" in this department.

The Batting Runs formula can be condensed by eliminating the components for steals, caught stealing, and outs on base. Outs on base (calculated as *Hits + Walks + Hit Batsman − Left on Base − Runs − Caught Stealing*) is meaningful only for teams, not individuals. We eliminate steals from the formula in those years in which caught-stealing figures are not available, but the surviving data for the early years indicate that few of the men with high base-stealing totals exceeded the break-even point of 66.7 percent by a margin large enough to produce even one additional Batting Win. A further condensation that we have used for our historical data, as indicated in the formula above, involves setting the value of a single at .47 runs and each extra base at .31, making a double .78, a triple 1.09, and a homer 1.40. (This tends to even out the fluctuations in run values for base hits and extra bases over time: a double, for example, was in fact worth .82 runs from 1901–1920, .80 runs from 1941–1960, and .77 runs from 1961–1977.) Subtract the hits from the total bases and multiply the resulting extra bases by .31 and the hits by .47. This may introduce small variations from a more rigorous formula that includes differing run values for the differing periods or even for single years (generally amounting to a fraction of a run), but the calculation is much snappier for those without a complete computer database at the ready.

The Batting Runs formula may be long, even in its condensed form, but it calls for only addition, subtraction, and multiplication and thus is as simple as Slugging Average, whose incorrect weights (1, 2, 3, and 4) it revises and expands upon. Each event has a value and frequency, just as in Slugging Average, yet in Batting Runs outs are treated as offensive events with a run value of their own (albeit a negative one). Just as the run potential for a team in a given half-inning is boosted by a man reaching base, it is diminished by a man being retired; not only has he failed to brighten the situation on the bases but he has deprived his team of the services of a man further down the order who might have come up in this half-inning, either with men on base and/or with scores already in.

The Batting Runs stat treats every offensive event in terms of its impact upon the team—an *average* team, so that a man does not benefit in his individual record for having the good fortune to bat cleanup with the Red Sox or suffer for batting cleanup with the White Sox. The relationship of individual performance to team play is stated poorly or not at all in conventional baseball statistics. In Batting Runs it is crystal clear.

Recognizing that some readers will wish to keep track of batting performance by compiling Batting Runs themselves over the course of a season and that they may be frustrated by the difficulty of separating out pitcher batting or of calculating the (At-Bats − Hits) factor for the league, we advise that using the fixed value of −.25 for outs will tend to work quite well if you wish to include pitcher batting performance, and a fixed value of −.27 will serve if you wish to exclude it. Actually, any fixed value will suffice in midseason; it's only when all the numbers are in and you care to compare this year's results with last year's (or, e.g., with those of the 1927 Yankees) that more precision is desirable. At that point the value of the out may be calculated by the more ambitious among you, but, ideally, your newspaper or the sporting press will provide accurate Batting Runs figures. (Who, after all, calculates ERA for himself?) Batting Runs are abbreviated as BR.

Batting Wins Adjusted Batting Runs divided by the number of runs required to create an additional win beyond average (see *Runs Per Win*). That average is defined as a team record of .500 because a league won-lost average must be .500, or as an individual record of zero because the value of the out for a given year is calculated to establish a baseline of zero. Abbreviated as BW.

Calculated Stat One or more counting stats (see below) subjected to a mathematical process such as averaging.

Chances Accepted Total chances for putouts and assists, minus errors.

Clutch Hitting Index Calculated for individuals, actual RBIs over expected RBIs, adjusted for league average and slot in batting order; 100 is a league-average performance. The spot in the batting order is figured as

$$5 - (9 \times \text{BFPGP} - \text{BFPGT})$$

where BFPGP is the batters facing pitcher per game for the player, or plate appearances divided by games, and BFPGT is the batters facing pitcher per game of the entire team.

Expected RBIs are calculated as

$$(.25 \text{ singles} + .50 \text{ doubles} + .75 \text{ triples} + 1.75 \text{ homers}) \times \text{LGAV} \times \text{EXPSL}$$

where LGAV (league average) = league RBIs divided by (.25 singles + .50 doubles + .75 triples + 1.75 homers), and EXPSL (expected RBI by slot number) = .88 for the leadoff batter, and for the remaining slots, descending to ninth, .90, .98, 1.08, 1.08, 1.04, 1.04, 1.04, and 1.02.

Calculated for teams, Clutch Hitting Index is actual runs scored over Batting Runs. Abbreviated as CHI.

Clutch Pitching Index Expected runs allowed over actual runs allowed, with 100 being a league-average performance. Expected runs are figured on the basis of the pitcher's opposing at-bats, hits, walks, and hit batsmen (doubles and triples estimated at league average). Abbreviated as CPI.

Counting Stat A raw figure that tells how many of an item have been accumulated, as opposed to a calculated or derived figure such as an average.

Differential The difference between a team's actual won-lost record and that predicted by the total of its Pitching Wins, Batting Wins, Fielding Wins, and Stolen Base Wins; this measure indicates the extent to which a team outperformed or underperformed its talent. Abbreviated as DIF.

Earned Run Average Calculated as earned runs times nine, divided by innings pitched. For a few years after being introduced as an official stat in the National League in 1912 and the American League in 1913, runs aided by stolen bases were not counted as earned (see Chronology of Scoring Rules in Appendix 1, Rules and Scoring). For years before 1912, ERA has been constructed from raw data, but for some teams in some seasons, earned runs cannot be identified with perfect certainty. For those teams, we use the estimating procedure created by Information Concepts, Inc., of assigning to those runs whose earned/unearned status is unknown the percentage of earned runs to runs that characterize the team's known runs. In *Total Baseball*, we have created an Adjusted ERA by normalizing to the league average—which is done by dividing the league average ERA by the individual ERA—and then factoring in home park.

Expected Wins Calculated for the team based on its actual runs scored and allowed, not its predicted runs scored and allowed. A team that allows exactly as many runs as it scores is predicted to play .500 ball. The equation for expected wins is:

$$\frac{\text{Runs Scored} - \text{Runs Allowed} + 81}{\text{Runs Per Win}}$$

Abbreviated as W−EXP.

Fielding Average Defined as putouts and assists divided by the total of putouts, assists, and errors. The weakness of this stat is that it values a player with minimal range but good hands over another player who may accept many more chances but mishandle a few of these. Abbreviated as FA. See *Range Factor, Total Chances*.

Fielding Runs The Linear Weights measure of runs saved *beyond*

what a league-average player at that position might have saved, defined as zero; this stat is calculated to take account of the particular demands of the different positions.

For second basemen, shortstops, and third basemen, the formula begins by calculating the league average for the position, in this fashion:

$$\text{AVG} \begin{array}{c} \text{pos.} \\ \text{lg.} \end{array} = \left(\frac{.20\,(PO + 2A - E + DP)\ \text{league at position}}{PO\ \text{league total} - K\ \text{league total}} \right)$$

where A = assists, PO = putouts, E = errors, DP = double plays, and K = strikeouts. Then we estimate the number of innings for each player at each position based upon each player's entire fielding record and his number of plate appearances. So, if the team played 1,500 innings and one player was calculated to have played 1,000 of those innings at a given position, his Fielding Runs (FR) would be calculated as:

$$FR = .20\,(PO + 2A - E + DP)\ \text{player} - \text{avg. pos. lg.} \times \left(\frac{PO}{\text{team}} - \frac{K}{\text{team}} \right) \frac{\text{innings, player}}{\text{innings, team}}$$

Assists are doubly weighted because more fielding skill is generally required to get one than to record a putout.

For catchers, the above formula is modified by removing strikeouts from their formulas and subtracting not only errors but also passed balls divided by two. Also incorporated in the catcher's Fielding Runs is one tenth of the adjusted Pitching Runs for the team, times the percentage of games behind the plate by that catcher.

For pitchers, the above formula is modified to subtract individual pitcher strikeouts from the total number of potential outs (otherwise, exceptional strikeout pitchers like Nolan Ryan or Bob Feller would see their Fielding Runs artificially depressed). Also, pitchers' chances are weighted less than infielders' assists because a pitcher's style may produce fewer ground balls. Thus the formula for pitchers is $.10(PO + 2A - E + DP)$, whereas for second basemen, shortstops, and third basemen it is $.20(PO + 2A - E + DP)$.

For first basemen, because putouts and double plays require so little skill in all but the odd case, these plays are eliminated, leaving only $.20(2A - E)$ in the numerator.

For outfielders, the formula becomes $.20(PO + 4A - E + 2DP)$. The weighting for assists is boosted here because a good outfielder can prevent runs through the threat of assists that are never made; for them, unlike infielders, the assist is essentially an elective play, like the stolen base. Outfielders' Fielding Runs were subject to some degree of error because outfielders sometimes switch fields within a game or season (Babe Ruth, for example, was positioned in the field that required the lesser range—right field in Yankee Stadium, left field in most road parks). Also, short distances to left- or right-field walls in some parks tend to depress putout totals.

For this edition of *Total Baseball,* however, we have researched and obtained breakouts of all outfielders' games in left, center, and right fields. Previously, for example, center fielders were compared against the average of the regular center fielders each year, rather than against all men who played center, because it was relatively easy to pick out the regulars by looking at their putouts per game. The new data we gathered allowed an average to be calculated for *all* center fielders and this tended to be lower. Since the league average was thus lowered, center fielders now have higher ratings than they did in the first and second editions.

Fielding Runs are abbreviated as FR.

Fielding Wins Fielding Runs divided by the number of runs required to create an additional win beyond average. That average is defined as a team record of .500 because a league won-lost average must be .500. Abbreviated as FW. See *Runs Per Win.*

Games Behind Figured by adding the difference in wins between a trailing team and the leader to the difference in losses, and dividing by two. Thus a team that is three games behind may trail by three in the win column and three in the loss column, or four and two, or any other combination of wins and losses totaling six. Abbreviated as GB.

Game-Winning Run Batted In Credited to the batter who drives in a run that gives his club a lead that it never relinquishes, no matter

when that run is driven in nor what the final score is. Introduced in 1980 as an official stat and later disowned, the GWRBI has met with deserved scorn and is not recorded in this volume.

Grounded into Double Play Erratically recorded on an official basis, this stat tends to be overvalued by the general public as an indicator of rally-killing ineptitude. Instead, it is largely a function of high totals of at-bats, which tend to be accumulated by the game's best players, not its worst. Abbreviated as GIDP.

Hands Out The original 1840s scoring term for batters producing outs either at the plate or on the bases. On a force out, the runner retired on the bases would be charged with a hand out, not the batter. Also called Hands Lost, and abbreviated as HO or HL.

Hit by Pitch A batter struck by a pitched ball was not awarded first base until 1884 in the American Association and 1887 in the National League. Reconstruction of stats for batters and pitchers in the years 1897–1908 is in process. Abbreviated as HBP.

Hits Bases on balls originally counted as hits in 1887, but are recorded in this volume as neither hits nor at-bats.

Home Run Batter Rating A measure of a team's home-run ability, taking into account its Home Run Factor (see below) and its not having to face its own pitchers. The average mark is represented as 100 and the highest figure above that indicates the best. Abbreviated as HRB, it is computed by comparing homers scored and allowed per inning at home and on the road. Innings are estimated from the number of games and the number of games won (allowing for a leading home team not batting in the ninth). The team figure thus obtained is then compared to the league average.

Home Run Factor A measure of the home runs hit in a given ballpark, with 100 representing the average home park and the highest figure above that representing the best home-run park. Computed in the same manner as Home Run Batter Rating (see above). Abbreviated as HRF.

Home Run Percentage Home runs per 100 at-bats.

Home Run Pitcher Rating A measure of a team's ability to prevent home runs, taking into account the Home Run Factor (see above) of the park and the team's not having to face its own batters. The average mark is represented as 100, and the lowest figure beneath that indicates the best.

Home Runs When is a home run not a home run? Before 1920, not if it came with men on base in the ultimate inning and created a margin of victory greater than one run. A ruling of the Special Baseball Records Committee in 1969 reversed its earlier decision that had made home runs of 37 disputed final-inning, game-winning base hits. In accordance with the practice of the day, such a hit, even if it sailed out of the park, would be credited with only as many bases as necessary to plate the winning run. Thus Babe Ruth's "715th home run," hit on July 8, 1918, to win a game against Cleveland, remained a triple, and Jimmy Collins and Sherry Magee were each deprived of two home runs.

Innings Pitched Until 1976 official baseball practice was to lop off fractional innings for individuals; from that point until 1982, fractional innings were rounded off to the next highest inning. Since then fractional innings have been kept for individuals and teams. In this volume fractional innings are supplied for all individuals and all teams in all years. Those men who took a turn on the mound but failed to retire a batter are credited with no innings pitched and, if they allowed a runner or runners to score, an ERA of infinity.

Intentional Bases on Balls Recorded only since 1955.

Isolated Power Total bases minus hits, divided by at-bats; in other words, Slugging Average minus Batting Average. Appears to have been created by Allan Roth and Branch Rickey in the early 1950s.

League-Average Replacement Player That model player who performs at precisely the league average, creating a baseline against which to measure others.

Linear Weights A system created by Pete Palmer to measure all the events on a ballfield in terms of runs. At the root of this system, as with other sabermetric figures such as Runs Created, is the knowl-

edge that wins and losses are what the game of baseball is about, that wins and losses are proportional in some way to runs scored and runs allowed, and that runs in turn are proportional to the events that go into their making.

Normalizing Restating a figure as a ratio by comparing it to the league average, or norm.

On Base Percentage Created by Roth and Rickey in its current form—hits plus walks plus hit by pitch, divided by at-bats plus walks plus hit by pitch—in the early 1950s, although there were nineteenth-century forebears such as "Reached First Base." When OBP, as it is abbreviated, was adopted as an official stat in 1984, the denominator was expanded to include sacrifice flies. The effect is to penalize a batter in his on base percentage by giving him a plate appearance while at the same time crediting him in his batting average by deleting the plate appearance. In this book we calculate OBP without considering sacrifice flies, which in any event are calculable on a continuing basis only since 1954.

On Base plus Slugging See *Production.*

Opponents' Batting Average Hits allowed divided by at-bats allowed (or, if at-bats allowed is unknown, then at-bats equals hits plus inning times "K," where "K" is the league average of at-bats minus hits, all over innings). Abbreviated as OAV.

Opponents' On Base Percentage For years before 1908 in the American League and 1909 in the National League, the number of batters facing a pitcher has been constructed from the available raw data. We have subtracted league base hits from league at-bats, divided by league innings pitched, multiplied by the pitcher's innings, and added his hits and walks allowed and hit by pitch and sacrifices, if available. Abbreviated as OOB.

Outs Until 1883, included catching a ball on one bounce in foul ground. Not credited after three strikes in 1887, when the rule was "four strikes and yer out"—as it was, in fact, from 1871–1881, when batters commonly received "warning pitches" rather than called strikes.

Outs Per Game The 1860s successor to Hands Out (see above), it joined with Runs Per Game to form the batting record before the rise of professional league play.

Park Factor Calculated separately for batters and pitchers. Above 100 signifies a park favorable to hitters; below 100 signifies a park favorable to pitchers. The computation of PF is admittedly daunting, and what follows is probably of interest to the merest handful of readers, but we feel obliged to state the mathematical underpinnings for those few who may care. We use a three-year average Park Factor for players and teams unless they change home parks. Then a two-year average is used, unless the park existed for only one year. Then a one-year mark is used. If a team started up in Year 1, played two years in the first park, one in the next, and three in the park after that and then stopped play, the average would be as follows (where Fn is the one-year park factor for year n):

Year 1 and 2 = (F1 + F2)/2   Year 4 = (F4 + F5)/2
Year 3   = F3   Year 5 = (F4 + F5 + F6)/3
                              Year 6 = (F5 + F6)/2

Step 1. Find games, losses, and runs scored and allowed for each team at home and on the road. Take runs per game scored and allowed at home over runs per game scored and allowed on the road. This is the initial figure, but we must make two corrections to it.

Step 2. The first correction is for innings pitched at home and on the road. This is a bit complicated, so the mathematically faint of heart may want to head back at this point. First, find the team's home winning percentage (wins at home over games at home). Do the same for road games. Calculate the Innings Pitched Corrector (IPC) shown below. If it is greater than 1, this means the innings pitched on the road are higher because the other team is batting more often in the last of the ninth. This rating is divided by the Innings Pitched Corrector, like so:

$$IPC = \frac{(18.5 - \text{Wins at home} / \text{Games at home})}{(18.5 - \text{Losses on road} / \text{Games on road})}$$

Note: 18.5 is the average number of half-innings per game if the home team always bats in the ninth.

Step 3. Make corrections for the fact that the other road parks' total difference from the league average is offset by the park rating of the club that is being rated. Multiply rating by this Other Parks Corrector (OPC):

$$OPC = \frac{\text{No. of teams}}{\text{No. of teams} - 1 + \text{Run Factor, team}}$$

(Note that this OPC differs from that presented earlier in *The Hidden Game of Baseball*, for in preparing the pre-1900 data for *Total Baseball*, we discovered that for some parks with extreme characteristics, like Chicago's Lake Front Park of 1884, which had a Home Run Factor of nearly 5, the earlier formula produced wrong results. For parks with factors of 1.5 or less, either formula works well.)

Example. In 1982, Atlanta scored 388 runs and allowed 387 runs at home in 81 games, and scored 351 and allowed 315 on the road in 81 games. The initial factor is $(775/81) \div (666/81) = 1.164$. The Braves' home record was 42–39, or .519, and their road record was 47–34, or .580. Thus the IPC = $(18.5 - .519) \div (18.5 - .420) = .995$. The team rating is now $1.164/.995 = 1.170$. The OPC = $(12) \div (12 - 1 + 1.170) = .986$. The final runs-allowed rating is $1.170 \times .986$, or 1.154.

We warned you it wouldn't be easy!

The batter adjustment factor is composed of two parts, one the park factor and the other the fact that a batter does not have to face his own team's pitchers. The initial correction takes care of only the second factor. Start with the following (SF = Scoring Factor, previously determined [for Atlanta, 1.154], and SF1 = Scoring Factor of the other clubs [NT = number of teams]):

$$1 - \frac{SF - 1}{NT - 1}$$

Next is an iterative process in which the initial team pitching rating is assumed to be 1, and the following factors are employed:

RHT, RAT = Runs per game scored at home (H) and away (A), by team
OHT, OAT = Runs per game allowed at home, away, by team
RAL = Runs per game by both teams

Now, with the Team Pitching Rating (TPR) = 1, we proceed to calculate Team Batting Rating (TBR):

$$TBR = \left(\frac{RAT}{SF1} + \frac{RHT}{SF} \right) \left(1 + \frac{TPR - 1}{NT - 1} \right) \Big/ RAL$$

$$TPR = \left(\frac{OAT}{SF1} + \frac{OHT}{SF} \right) \left(1 + \frac{TBR - 1}{NT - 1} \right) \Big/ RAL$$

The last two steps are repeated three more times. The final Batting Corrector, or Batters' Park Factor (BPF) is

$$BPF = \frac{(SF + SF1)}{\left(2 \times \left[1 + \frac{TPR - 1}{NT - 1} \right] \right)}$$

Similarly, the final Pitching Corrector, or Pitchers' Park Factor (PPF) is

$$PPF = \frac{(SF + SF1)}{\left(2 \times \left[1 + \frac{TBR - 1}{NT - 1} \right] \right)}$$

Now an example, using the 1982 Atlanta Braves once again.

$$RHT = \frac{388}{81} = 4.79 \qquad RAT = \frac{351}{81} = 4.33$$

$$OHT = \frac{387}{81} = 4.78 \qquad OAT = \frac{315}{81} = 3.89$$

$$RAL = \frac{7947}{972} = 8.18 \qquad NT = 12$$

$$SF = 1.154 \qquad SF1 = 1 - \left(\frac{1.154 - 1}{11}\right) = .986$$

$$TBR = \left(\frac{4.33}{.986} + \frac{4.79}{1.154}\right)\left(1 + \frac{1-1}{11}\right)\bigg/ 8.18 = 1.044$$

$$TPR = \left(\frac{3.89}{.986} + \frac{4.78}{1.154}\right)\left(1 + \frac{1.044 - 1}{11}\right)\bigg/ 8.18 = .993$$

Repeating these steps gives a TBR of 1.04 and a TPR of .97. The Batters' Park Factor is

$$BPF = \frac{(1.170 + .986)}{\left(2 \times \left[1 + \frac{.99 - 1}{11}\right]\right)} = 1.07$$

This is not a great deal removed from taking the original ratio,

$$\frac{1.170 + 1}{2}, \text{ which is } 1.08.$$

The Pitchers' Park Factor may be calculated in analogous fashion.

To apply the Batters' Park Factor to Batting Runs, one must use this formula:

$$\frac{BR}{corr.} = \frac{BR}{uncorr.} - \frac{Runs\,(league)}{\underset{league}{(AB + BB + HBP)}} \times (BPF - 1) \times \underset{player\,or\,team}{(AB + BB + HBP)}$$

For example, if a player produces 20 runs above average in 700 plate appearances with a Batters' Park Factor of 1.10, and the league average of runs produced per plate appearance is .11, this means that the player's uncorrected Batting Runs is 20 over the zero point of 700 × .11 (77 runs). In other words, 77 runs is the average run contribution expected of this batter were he playing in an average home park. But because his Batters' Park Factor is 1.10, which means his home park was 10 percent kinder to hitters (than the average), you would really expect an average run production of 1.1 × 77, or 85 runs. Thus the player whose uncorrected Batting Runs is 97 with a BF of 1.1 is only +12 runs rather than +20, and 12 is his Park Adjusted Batting Runs (in the Player Register, BR/A):

$$12 = 20 - .11 \times (1.10 - 1) \times 700$$

Percentage of Team Wins A simple but deceiving measure of a good pitcher's contribution to a bad club; in this, it shares the virtues and flaws of Ted Oliver's Weighted Rating System and, to a lesser degree, our own Wins Above Team (both of which see). Steve Carlton had the highest single-season rating in this century when, in 1972, he went 27–10 for a Phillie club that won only 59 games. Yet his mark of 45.8 percent of his team's wins would not make the top 100 list of seasons since 1876, making this stat nearly useless for historical analysis.

Pitcher Defense Abbreviated as PD. See *Fielding Runs*.

Pitchers' Park Factor The same as the Park Factor shown in the pitchers' section of the team statistics portion of the Annual Record and in the Pitcher Register; above 100 means a pitcher was hurt by playing half his games in a good hitting park. See *Park Factor*.

Pitcher Strikeouts Made tougher or easier by cyclically varying rules and conditions. For instance, foul tips did not count as strikes for many years, even when deliberate, as with bunts; fouls caught on a bounce were outs until 1883; the ball-strike count underwent

much experimentation until settling at four balls and three strikes in 1889; not to mention the high-low strike zone, warning pitches, varying pitching distances, and restricted deliveries. It helps to know some history before rattling off stats to prove this or that, but normalizing a stat to its league helps, even with counting stats such as strikeouts.

Pitching Runs The Linear Weights measure of runs saved *beyond* what a league-average pitcher or team might have saved, defined as zero. The math is simple: *Pitching Runs = Innings Pitched × (League ERA/9) − Earned Runs Allowed.* An alternate version is: *Innings Pitched/9 × (Individual ERA − League ERA).* Abbreviated as PR.

Pitching Wins Park Adjusted Pitching Runs divided by the number of runs required to create an additional win beyond average. That average is defined as a team record of .500 because a league won-lost average must be .500. Abbreviated as PW. See *Pitching Runs,* above, and *Runs Per Win.*

Player Win Averages The title of a 1970 book issued by the Mills brothers, Harlan and Eldon, as well as the name of their overall method of determining not only the *what* of baseball statistics but also the *when,* or clutch element. Computerizing complete play-by-play data for a full season for their book, they assigned "Win Points"—reflective of that event's potential impact on the team's prospects of victory—to *every* event on a baseball field.

Positional Adjustment A key factor in the Total Player Rating that addresses the relative worth to a ball club of the defensive positions. A man who bats .270, hits 25 homers, and drives in 80 runs may be an average performer in left field, no matter how good his glove; but credit those batting stats to a shortstop or second baseman and you have a star, because the defensive demands of the position are so much greater. To balance the abundance of good-hitting outfielders or first basemen against the scarcity of such players at catcher or shortstop, we created a positional adjustment expressed in terms of the average batting skill needed to hold down a major league spot at that position.

To determine the average defensive skill required of a position, simply subtract the average batting skill at that position from his Total Player Rating. This may seem strange at first glance, but it does put, for example, shortstops, first basemen, and left fielders on the same footing. The explanation that follows represents a change from previous editions, in which players were measured against only those who played their position in their league in that year. We have now redefined the positional adjustment as an average over *both* leagues for a three-year period centered on the measured year. This raised the ratings for Lou Gehrig and Jimmie Foxx by a win or two, as they are now compared with sixteen first basemen over three years (a total of forty-eight) rather than just eight. In the 1950–1970 period, AL outfielders averaged a few more Batting Runs per season than their counterparts in the NL. When both leagues were counted, NL players dropped a few Wins and AL players gained. Hank Aaron lost 4 Wins for this reason.

In the years since 1977 the positional adjustment for, say a National League first baseman, will be in the context of the batting records of not merely twelve men, but twenty-six—times three, or seventy-eight—obviously, a much broader base of comparison. For this edition, which concludes with the 1992 season, positional adjustments for 1992 are based on an average of 1991 and 1992.

Let's say that last year all major league left fielders accounted for 198 batting runs. The positional adjustment, or factor for average defensive skill, for a left fielder who played in all 162 games would be 162 × 198/3,202 (which calculates to 10), where 3,202 is the number of games played in both leagues by all left fielders (or any other position, obviously). Thus a left fielder who played in all his team's games would have 10 runs subtracted from the sum of his Batting Runs, Stolen Base Runs, and Fielding Runs. If all major league shortstops last year accounted for 158 Batting Runs below average, the adjustment for a shortstop would be figured in the same way, multiplying his games played by −158/3,202, or −8 runs, meaning that 8 runs (minus a minus 8) would be *added* to his Total Player Rating.

Production On Base Percentage plus Slugging Average: a simple but elegant measure of batting prowess, in that the weaknesses of one-half of the formulation, On Base Percentage, are countered by the strengths of the other, Slugging Average, and vice versa. When PRO, as it is abbreviated, is adjusted for home park and normalized to league average to become PRO⁺, the calculation is modified slightly to create a baseline of 100 for a league-average performance. For PRO^+, the calculation is

$$\frac{\text{Player On Base Pct.}}{\text{League On Base Pct.}} + \frac{\text{Player Slugging Avg.}}{\text{League Slugging Avg.}} - 1$$

This produces a figure with a decimal point—an above-average figure, like 1.46, or a below-average figure, like 0.82. For ease of display, in this book we drop the decimal and express these as 146 and 82.

Putout Average Putouts divided by games played; a stat created by Philadelphia baseball writer Al Wright in 1875.

Quality Start A game started in which a pitcher lasts for six innings or more and allows three runs or less.

Ratio Hits allowed plus walks allowed plus bit batsmen, all per nine innings. Abbreviated as RAT.

RBI Opportunities An official American League stat for the first three weeks of 1918, until the league saw how much work it involved and scrapped it. Still a good idea, sort of, and the folks at the Elias Sports Bureau have tracked this type of "situational stat" since 1975.

Reached First Base A precursor of the On Base Percentage, this stat was introduced as an official National League measure in 1879, its one and only year of existence. It included times reached via hits, walks, and errors, but not hit by pitch because putting their bodies on the line did not yet, in 1879, send batters to first base. Trivia: the league leader in this stat's lone year of life was Paul Hines, with 193.

Relative Batting Average Pioneered by David Shoebotham in a *Baseball Research Journal* article in 1976, this was the first traditional stat normalized to league average so as to permit cross-era comparison. Most folks who have employed this measure simply divide individual batting average by league batting average. Shoebotham's original computation was more precise:

$$RBA = \frac{\text{player's hits}}{\text{player's AB}} \bigg/ \frac{\text{league hits} - \text{player's hits}}{\text{league AB} - \text{player's AB}}$$

In this manner a player's own performance would not be compared with itself.

Relief Points Relief wins plus saves minus losses was the original formula used as the basis for the Rolaids Company's annual award to the top reliever in each league. Recently the formula has been changed to include a debit for blown saves.

Relief Ranking Takes *Relief Runs* (which see), adjusts them for home park, then weights them by a factor (F in the formula below) reflecting the greater value of the innings pitched by a bullpen "closer." Relief Runs, which weights all innings identically, will tend to benefit long and middle relievers who are effective over many innings, while Relief Ranking—which is reserved for those men who pitch less than three innings per game over a season or career—will tend to benefit relievers who may have fewer innings but who have more saves and decisions. The formula is

$$(\text{Relief Runs}) \times F \text{ where the Factor} = \frac{9(\text{Wins} + \text{Losses} + \text{Saves}/4)}{IP}$$

Relief Runs Identical to Pitching Runs but confined to relief pitchers, defined as those who average less than three innings per appearance. Abbreviated as RR. See *Relief Ranking.*

Run Batted In Though widely regarded as a good measure of a batter's overall productivity and value to his team, the RBI is extremely situation-dependent, denying equal access to opportunity on the basis of a player's team, slot in the batting order, and particularly the men surrounding him in the batting order.

Run Factor A measure of the run scoring in a given ballpark compared to other ballparks, with 100 representing the average home park and the highest figure above that representing the best hitters' park. Abbreviated as RF, it is computed on the basis of comparing runs scored and allowed per inning at home and on the road. Innings are estimated from the number of games and games won, allowing for the home team not batting in the final inning of a game in which it leads. The resulting Run Factor is then compared to the league average.

Run Rating for Batters A measure of a team's run-scoring ability, taking into account the park's *Run Factor* (see above) and the team's batters not having to face its own pitchers, with 100 representing the average and the highest figure above that representing the best. Abbreviated as RB.

Run Rating for Pitchers A measure of a team's run-prevention ability, taking into account the *Run Factor* (see above) and the team's pitchers not having to face its own batters, with 100 representing the average and the lowest figure beneath that representing the best. Abbreviated as RP.

Runs Created Bill James's formulation for run contribution from a variety of batting and baserunning events. Many different formulas are used, depending upon data available. In its basic expression, the formula is:

$$\frac{(\text{Hits} + \text{Walks})\,(\text{Total Bases})}{\text{At-Bats} + \text{Walks}}$$

The essence of this formulation is that the ability to get on base and the ability to push baserunners around fairly describes offensive ability. James later refined the formula with a "stolen base version":

$$\frac{(\text{Hits} + \text{Walks} - \text{Caught Stealing})\,(\text{Total Bases} + .55 \times \text{Stolen Bases})}{\text{At-Bats} + \text{Walks}}$$

Next came the "technical version": a longer formulation, presented below using the standard abbreviations for the various offensive events (the two elements multiplied in the numerator are referred to below as "A" and "B," and the denominator is referred to as "C"):

$$\frac{(H + BB + HBP - CS - GIDP)\,(TB + .26[BB - IBB + HBP] + .52[SH + SF + SB])}{AB + BB + HBP + SH + SF}$$

From this technical version (Tech-1), James spun off 13 additional technical versions. "The reason that we have to do this," he wrote in *The Bill James Historical Baseball Abstract*, "is that the data set changes and evolves rapidly throughout the century, or at least up until about 1955, when the progress of evolution in statistical information came to a temporary halt (it stopped moving forward until Bill James and Pete Palmer came around, about twenty years later). In 1900 we have no data for how many times a player grounded into a double play, how many times he was hit by a pitch, how many of his walks might have been intentional, how many times he was caught stealing, or how many sacrifice flies he hit." Accordingly, James adjusted his Runs Created formula to fit the available data; some versions, such as Tech-3, cover as much as a decade in a given league, while others, such as Tech-4, are in force for only a single league season. In *Total Baseball*, we have computed Runs Created values for all players since 1876 using the version most applicable to the period, with the single exception of Tech-9, which James applied only to the American League of 1916 but which we use for 1914–1916 in the AL and 1915–1916 in the NL because we have discovered additional caught-stealing data. (For those players whose careers began before 1900, James used the Tech-11 formula "to estimate how many runs they had created," but appended a note saying that "these estimates were of indeterminate accuracy.")

Here are the formulas for Runs Created (RC) technical versions 2–14 (Tech-1 was used for both leagues in 1955–1988):

Tech-2 (1954)

Factors A and C of Tech-1 remain the same, while Part B simply drops Intentional Bases on Balls.

Tech-3 (AL 1940–1953; NL 1951–1953)
Factor A remains the same, while SF is dropped from Factor C; Factor B changes to: 1.025 TB + .26(BB + HBP) + .52(SH + SB).

Tech-4 (AL 1939)
Factors A and C remain the same, while B becomes: TB + .26(BB + HBP) + .52(SH + SB).

Tech-5 (AL 1931–1938)
Factors B and C remain the same, while A becomes: .96(H + BB + HBP − CS).

Tech-6 (AL 1928–1930, 1920–1926; NL 1920–1925)
Factors A and C remain the same, while B changes only in the value placed on the sacrifice hit and stolen base, which declines from .52 to .51.

Tech-7 (AL 1927; NL 1926–1930)
C remains the same, while A changes to: .93(H + BB + HBP), and B becomes: TB + .26(BB + HBP) + .46(SH).

Tech-8 (AL 1913, 1917–1919; NL 1913–1914, 1917–1919)
C remains the same, while A becomes: H + W + HBP − .02(AB), and B becomes: TB + .85(SH + SB).

Tech-9 (AL 1914–1916; NL 1915–1916)
B and C are the same, while A becomes: H + BB + HBP − CS.

Tech-10 (AL, NL 1908–1912)
A and C remain the same, while B becomes: 1.025(TB + SB) + .75(SH).

Tech-11 (AL, NL 1900–1907)
B and C remain the same, while A becomes: H + BB + HBP.

Tech-12 (NL 1939–1950)
A Factor: H + BB + HBP − GIDP
B Factor: TB + .26(BB +HBP) + .52(SH)

Tech-13 (NL 1933–1938)
A and C remain the same as above, while B becomes: 1.025(TB) + .26(BB + HBP) + .52(SH)

Tech-14 (NL 1931–1932)
B and C remain the same, but A becomes: .95(H + BB + HBP).

Runs Per Game With its mate *Outs Per Game* (which see), this was the precursor, in the 1860s, of the batting average; by the end of that decade it gave way to Hits Per Game.

Runs Per Win Branch Rickey and Allan Roth first stated the proportional nature of runs and wins in their 1954 article in *Life*. Since then the point has been expanded upon by George Lindsey, Pete Palmer, Bill James, and every sabermetrician worth his salt: the point being that just as runs scored and allowed are the key to victory in a given game, so are they the key to success over the course of a season and the predictors of won-lost record with a surprising degree of precision. In 1982, Palmer wrote in *The National Pastime*, "My work showed that as a rough rule of thumb, each additional ten runs scored (or ten less runs allowed) produced one extra win. . . . However, breaking the teams into groups showed that high-scoring teams needed more runs to produce a win. This runs-per-win factor I determined to be ten times the square root of the average number of runs scored per inning by both teams. Thus in normal play, when 4.5 runs per game are scored by each club, each team scores .5 runs per inning—totaling one run, the square root of which is one, times ten."

For *Total Baseball*, we have improved the Runs Per Win figure used in calculating the overall win figures in the Total Player Rating and the Total Pitcher Index. Rather than using 10 times the square root of the average number of runs scored per inning by both teams, we use adjusted runs per inning based on what the player or pitcher rating is. A hitter will increase the figure by adding in his rating over

the number of games played, while a pitcher will have his rating subtracted. Say the average number of runs scored per inning is 1, as in the model above; then Runs Per Win = 10. Take a pitcher who allows 45 runs less than average in 25 games. This lowers the runs per game by 1.8, or runs per inning by .2, so the new Runs Per Win figure is 10 times the square root of the average number of runs scored per inning by both teams, *minus the pitcher's rating*. So we take from the one run per inning the .2 run saved by the pitcher, giving a result of 0.8. Ten times the square root of 0.8 is 8.9, so the pitcher gets 45/8.9, or 5.1, wins instead of 4.5. A hitter with plus 45 runs in 150 games, or .3 runs per game, contributes .03 runs per inning. His Runs Per Win is now 10 times the square root of the average number of runs scored per inning *plus the batter's rating*. So we add to the 1 run per inning the .03 runs added by the batter, giving a result of 10.1. Ten times the square root of 10.1 gives the batter 4.4 wins. (This method makes makes more of a difference in pitching because the runs are contributed over fewer games. With the same run contribution—45 beyond average—the pitcher gains 0.7 wins over the batter. This is because when the total number of runs scored is lowered, the value of each run is greater).

Runs Produced Runs batted in plus runs scored minus home runs.

Sabermetrics Defined by Bill James, who coined the term in honor of the Society for American Baseball Research, as "the search for objective knowledge about baseball" and, earlier, as "the mathematical and statistical analysis of baseball records."

SABR Pronounced "saber," this is the acronym for the Society for American Baseball Research, the organization that has, since its founding by Bob Davids in 1971, steadily advanced the state of baseball knowledge.

Sacrifice Fly First recognized as an event in 1908 but indistinguishable in the official records from sacrifice hits until 1954. There has been much flip-flopping since 1930 on whether to credit the sacrifice flier with an at-bat or an RBI or whether a fly ball that advances a runner to a base other than home plate also should exempt a man from an at-bat.

Sacrifice Hits Invented in the 1860s, recorded since 1889; sacrificer charged with an at-bat until 1895. Sabermetricians frown on the strategy because all the studies show that the trading of an out for a base advanced is a losing strategy—lowering the run expectations of the team that attempts it—in all but the most unusual of cases . . . even if the sacrifice "succeeds."

Sacrifice Hits Allowed Computed officially in the NL in 1916, in the AL in 1922; what it signified is unclear.

Save Created by Jerry Holtzman of the Chicago *Sun-Times*, the save began to be reported by *The Sporting New* on a regular basis in 1960. The major leagues adopted the save in 1969, at which time it was credited to a reliever who finished a game that his team won. In 1973 the save was redefined so that a reliever had not only to finish the game but also to find the potential tying or winning run on base or at the plate, or, alternately, to pitch the final three innings of a victorious contest. In 1975 the rule was liberalized to include a reliever's appearance of one inning or more in which he protects a lead of three runs or less; or he enters the game with the tying or winning run on base, at bat, or on deck; or he pitches three innings to the game's conclusion. In this book, the 1969 definition is applied to all games before 1969; otherwise the rule in force at the time prevails. Abbreviated as SV.

Shutouts On an individual basis, credited only to pitchers of complete-game scoreless victories; former practice was to credit combined shutouts to the starting pitcher if he had pitched most of the way. Abbreviated as SH.

Situational Stats How does a batter perform with the bases loaded? At night? On artificial turf? With no one on base? After the seventh inning when his team is tied or trails? That kind of stuff, now the specialty of Stats, Inc., and the Elias Sports Bureau.

Slugging Average Total bases divided by at-bats; combines nicely with On Base Percentage to create *Production* (which see). Abbreviated as SLG.

Starter Runs Identical to *Pitching Runs* (which see) but confined

to starting pitchers, defined as those who average more than three innings per appearance. Abbreviated as SR.

Stolen Base Average Stolen bases divided by attempts; its computation is dependent upon the availability of caught-stealing numbers. Abbreviated as SBA.

Stolen Base Runs For teams, the Linear Weights measure of runs contributed *beyond* what a league-average basestealing team might have gained, defined as zero; for individuals, Stolen Base Runs are calculated on the basis of the 66.7 percent success rate that sabermetric studies have shown to be the break-even point for producing runs beyond the average. Availability dependent upon caught stealing data as with Stolen Base Average. The formula is simple: .30(Stolen Bases) − .60(Caught Stealing). A man who steals two bases in three attempts is merely spinning his wheels in terms of value to his team, and even a man who succeeds at an 80 percent clip will have to steal a lot of bases—about 65—to create just one win beyond average. Abbreviated as SBR.

Stolen Base Wins Stolen Base Runs divided by the number of runs required to create an additional win beyond average. Those runs are generally around around 10—historically in the range of 9–11. Abbreviated as SBW. See *Runs Per Win.*

Stolen Bases Recorded since 1886, but until 1898 steals are thought to have included a variety of daring baserunning exploits, such as going from first to third on a single or advancing an extra base on an out. Abbreviated as SB.

Strikeouts Varying rules concerning the strike zone, the foul strike, and the warning pitch—not to mention the fourth strike of 1887—all contribute to making the cross-era comparison of strikeout accomplishments a very sticky business. Abbreviated as SO.

Strikeout Percentage A batters' stat: fewest strikeouts per 100 at bats.

Total Average Tom Boswell's formulation for offensive contribution from a variety of batting and baserunning events; as with Runs Created, we have calculated Total Average to make use of the maximum available data in a given year. The concept of the numerator is bases gained, that of the denominator is outs made:

$$\frac{\text{Total Bases} + \text{Steals} + \text{Walks} + \text{HBP}}{\text{At-Bats} - \text{Hits} + \text{Caught Stealing} + \text{GIDP}}$$

Abbreviated as TA. See *Base-Out Percentage.*

Total Baseball Ranking The "MVP" of statistics, this ranks pitchers and position players by their total wins contributed in all their endeavors, revealing the most valuable performers in a given year. Abbreviated as TBR, it is not a computed stat but a sorting of players and pitchers by, respectively, their Total Batter Rating and Total Pitcher Index.

Total Bases Average Henry Chadwick's measure that divided total bases by games played; a forerunner of the Slugging Average.

Total Bases Run A silly stat of one year's duration, 1880, this was sort of an RBI in reverse, from the runner's perspective. Also called "Bases Touched," it was nothing more than that and signified nothing about individual talent. Trivia: the National League's leader in 1880 was Abner Dalrymple, with 501 bases touched.

Total Chances Putouts plus assists plus errors; in other words, total chances offered, not total chances accepted.

Total Pitcher Index The sum of a pitcher's Pitching Runs, Batting Runs (in the AL since 1973, 0), and Fielding Runs, all divided by the Runs Per Win factor for that year (generally around 10, historically in the 9–11 range); abbreviated as TPI. See *Runs Per Win.*

Total Player Rating The sum of a player's Adjusted Batting Runs, Fielding Runs, and Base Stealing Runs, minus his positional adjustment, all divided by the Runs Per Win factor for that year (generally around 10, historically in the 9–11 range). See *Runs Per Win.*

Triple Crown Long regarded as consisting of batting average, home runs, and RBIs, but was not always so. In the early years of this century, newspapers spoke of Ty Cobb shooting for the "triple crown" of batting average, runs, and hits.

Weighted Average The next step in statistical sophistication after first, counting and, next, averaging. Chadwick's Total Bases Average was probably the first weighted average, in that it assigned values of 1 to a single, 2 to a double, 3 to a triple, and 4 to a home run.

Weighted Rating System Ted Oliver's invention, promoted in a 1944 self-published booklet called *Kings of the Mound.* We have modified Oliver's pioneering effort to create *Wins Above Team* (see below), which entry presents a discussion of Oliver's effort.

Win Points See *Player Win Averages.*

Wins Above League A pitcher's won-lost record restated by adding his Pitching Wins above the league average to the record that a league-average pitcher would have had with his number of decisions. Example: Tom Seaver has a hard-luck season, going only 16–14 despite a 1.76 ERA and five Pitching Wins; applying the five wins to a league-average 15–15 mark in the same 30 decisions results in a WAL of 20-10.

Wins Above Team How many wins a pitcher garnered beyond those expected of an average pitcher for that team. As the editors of this volume, in their earlier *Hidden Game of Baseball*, modified Ted Oliver's *Weighted Rating System* (see above), they now improve this statistic thanks to Bill Deane's corrective for its tendency to overvalue the contributions of good pitchers on awful teams.

Oliver's Weighted Rating System for pitchers was motivated by the inadequacies of both the won-lost percentage and the ERA when it came to evaluating pitchers laboring for poor teams. The Oliver formula, ingenious if flawed, was: pitcher's won-lost percentage minus the team's won-lost percentage—after removing the pitcher's decisions from the team's record—then multiplying the difference by the pitcher's number of decisions. Here is an example of the Oliver method as applied to Bobby Castillo, who in 1982 pitched very well in going 13–11 for a very bad Minnesota club (60–102; without him, 47–91):

$$\left(\frac{13}{24} - \frac{47}{138}\right) \times 24$$

or

$$(.542 - .341) \times 24$$

or

$$.201 \times 24 = 4.824$$

The figure of 4.824 would have been represented by Ted Oliver as "4,824 points"; he did not seem to recognize that had he retained the decimal point, his rating would have been expressed directly in *wins.* Thus the number of wins Castillo accounted for in his 24 decisions that an average Minnesota pitcher would *not* have gained was 4.8.

Thanks to a key modification of our earlier formula for Wins Above Team, abbreviated as WAT, we now propose the following: calculate the pitcher's won-lost percentage and the team's winning percentage after his decisions have been set aside. If the pitcher's percentage is higher, then WAT is

$$\text{Pitcher decisions} \times \left(\frac{\text{Pitcher pct.} - \text{Team pct.}}{2 - 2 \times \text{Team pct.}}\right)$$

If the pitcher's percentage is lower, then WAT is

$$\text{Pitcher decisions} \times \left(\frac{\text{Pitcher pct.} - \text{Team pct.}}{2 \times \text{Team pct.}}\right)$$

Won-lost percentage Computed as wins over decisions.

Team and League Abbreviations

These are the 144 franchises, seven principal leagues, and their abbreviations as used throughout this book.

NATIONAL ASSOCIATION, 1871–1875 (shown as n or NA)

Abbrev.	First	Last	Team
ATH n	1871	1875	Philadelphia Athletics
ATL n	1872	1875	Brooklyn Atlantics
BAL n	1872	1874	Baltimore Lord Baltimores
BOS n	1871	1875	Boston Red Stockings
CEN n	1875	1875	Philadelphia Centennials
CHI n	1871	1871	Chicago White Stockings
CHI n	1874	1875	Chicago White Stockings
CLE n	1871	1872	Cleveland Forest City
ECK n	1872	1872	Brooklyn Eckfords
HAR n	1874	1875	Hartford Dark Blues
KEK n	1871	1871	Fort Wayne Kekiongas
MAN n	1872	1872	Middletown (Conn.) Mansfields
MAR n	1873	1873	Baltimore Marylands
MUT n	1871	1875	New York Mutuals
NAT n	1872	1872	Washington, D.C., Nationals
NH n	1875	1875	New Haven Elm City
OLY n	1871	1872	Washington, D.C., Olympics
PHI n	1873	1875	Philadelphia White Stockings
RES n	1873	1873	Elizabeth (N.J.) Resolutes
ROK n	1871	1871	Rockford (Ill.) Forest City
RS n	1875	1875	St. Louis Red Stockings
STL n	1875	1875	St. Louis Brown Stockings
TRO n	1871	1872	Troy Haymakers
WAS n	1873	1873	Washington Washingtons
WAS n	1875	1875	Washington Washingtons
WES n	1875	1875	Keokuk (Iowa) Westerns

NATIONAL LEAGUE, 1876– (shown as N or NL)

Abbrev.	First	Last	Team
ATL N	1966		Atlanta
BAL N	1892	1899	Baltimore
BOS N	1876	1952	Boston (transferred to Milwaukee)
BRO N	1890	1957	Brooklyn (transferred to Los Angeles)
BUF N	1879	1885	Buffalo
CHI N	1876		Chicago
CIN N	1876	1880	Cincinnati
CIN N	1890		Cincinnati
CLE N	1879	1884	Cleveland
CLE N	1889	1899	Cleveland
DET N	1881	1888	Detroit
HAR N	1876	1877	Hartford (played in Brooklyn in 1877)
HOU N	1962		Houston
IND N	1878	1878	Indianapolis
IND N	1887	1889	Indianapolis
KC N	1886	1886	Kansas City
LA N	1958		Los Angeles
LOU N	1876	1877	Louisville
LOU N	1892	1899	Louisville
MIL N	1878	1878	Milwaukee
MIL N	1953	1965	Milwaukee (transferred to Atlanta)
MON N	1969		Montreal
NY N	1876	1876	New York (played in Brooklyn)
NY N	1883	1957	New York (transferred to San Francisco)
NY N	1962		New York
PHI N	1876	1876	Philadelphia
PHI N	1883		Philadelphia
PIT N	1887		Pittsburgh
PRO N	1878	1885	Providence
STL N	1876	1877	St. Louis
STL N	1885	1886	St. Louis
STL N	1892		St. Louis
SD N	1969		San Diego
SF N	1958		San Francisco
SYR N	1879	1879	Syracuse
TRO N	1879	1882	Troy (N.Y.)
WAS N	1886	1889	Washington, D.C.
WAS N	1892	1899	Washington, D.C.
WOR N	1880	1882	Worcester (Mass.)

AMERICAN ASSOCIATION, 1882-1891 (shown as a or AA)

Abbrev.	First	Last	Team
BAL a	1882	1889	Baltimore
BAL a	1890	1890	Baltimore (combined with Brooklyn, shown as BB)
BAL a	1891	1891	Baltimore (transferred to National League)
BOS a	1891	1891	Boston
BRO a	1884	1889	Brooklyn (transferred to National League)
BRO a	1890	1890	Brooklyn (combined with Baltimore, shown as BB)
CIN a	1882	1889	Cincinnati (transferred to National League)
CIN a	1891	1891	Cincinnati
CLE a	1887	1888	Cleveland (transferred to National League)
COL a	1883	1884	Columbus (Ohio)
COL a	1889	1891	Columbus (Ohio)
IND a	1884	1884	Indianapolis
KC a	1888	1889	Kansas City
LOU a	1882	1891	Louisville (transferred to National League)
MIL a	1891	1891	Milwaukee
NY a	1883	1887	New York
PHI a	1882	1891	Philadelphia
PIT a	1882	1886	Pittsburgh (transferred to National League)
RIC a	1884	1884	Richmond
ROC a	1890	1890	Rochester
STL a	1882	1891	St. Louis (transferred to National League)
SYR a	1890	1890	Syracuse
TOL a	1884	1884	Toledo
TOL a	1890	1890	Toledo
WAS a	1884	1884	Washington, D.C.
WAS a	1891	1891	Washington, D.C. (transferred to National League)

UNION ASSOCIATION, 1884 (shown as U or UA)

Abbrev.	First	Last	Team
ALT U	1884	1884	Altoona (Pa.)
BAL U	1884	1884	Baltimore
BOS U	1884	1884	Boston
CHI U	1884	1884	Chicago (combined with Pittsburgh, shown as CP)
CIN U	1884	1884	Cincinnati
KC U	1884	1884	Kansas City
MIL U	1884	1884	Milwaukee
PHI U	1884	1884	Philadelphia
PIT U	1884	1884	Pittsburgh (combined with Chicago, shown as CP)
STL U	1884	1884	St. Louis
STP U	1884	1884	St. Paul (Minn.)
WAS U	1884	1884	Washington, D.C.
WIL U	1884	1884	Wilmington (Del.)

PLAYERS LEAGUE, 1890 (shown as P or PL)

Abbrev.	First	Last	Team
BOS P	1890	1890	Boston
BRO P	1890	1890	Brooklyn
BUF P	1890	1890	Buffalo
CHI P	1890	1890	Chicago
CLE P	1890	1890	Cleveland
NY P	1890	1890	New York
PHI P	1890	1890	Philadelphia
PIT P	1890	1890	Pittsburgh

AMERICAN LEAGUE, 1901– (shown as A or AL)

Abbrev.	First	Last	Team
BAL A	1901	1902	Baltimore (replaced by New York)
BAL A	1954		Baltimore
BOS A	1901		Boston
CAL A	1965		California
CHI A	1901		Chicago
CLE A	1901		Cleveland
DET A	1901		Detroit
KC A	1955	1967	Kansas City (transferred to Oakland)
KC A	1969		Kansas City
LA A	1961	1964	Los Angeles (transferred to California)
MIL A	1901	1901	Milwaukee (replaced by St. Louis)
MIL A	1970		Milwaukee
MIN A	1961		Minnesota
NY A	1903		New York
OAK A	1968		Oakland
PHI A	1901	1954	Philadelphia (transferred to Kansas City)
STL A	1902	1953	St. Louis (transferred to Baltimore)
SEA A	1969	1969	Seattle (transferred to Milwaukee)
SEA A	1977		Seattle
TEX A	1972		Texas
TOR A	1977		Toronto
WAS A	1901	1960	Washington, D.C. (transferred to Minnesota)
WAS A	1961	1971	Washington, D.C. (transferred to Texas)

FEDERAL LEAGUE, 1914-1915 (shown as F or FL)

Abbrev.	First	Last	Team
BAL F	1914	1915	Baltimore
BRO F	1914	1915	Brooklyn
BUF F	1914	1915	Buffalo
CHI F	1914	1915	Chicago
IND F	1914	1914	Indianapolis (transferred to Newark)
KC F	1914	1915	Kansas City
NEW F	1915	1915	Newark
PIT F	1914	1915	Pittsburgh
STL F	1914	1915	St. Louis